Who's Who in the West

Biographical Titles Currently Published by Marquis Who's Who

Who's Who in America

Who's Who in America derivatives:

- Who's Who in America Junior & Senior High School Version
- Geographic/Professional Index
- Supplement to Who's Who in America
- Who's Who in America Classroom Project Book

Who Was Who in America

- Historical Volume (1607-1896)
- Volume I (1897-1942)
- Volume II (1943-1950)
- Volume III (1951-1960)
- Volume IV (1961-1968)
- Volume V (1969-1973)
- Volume VI (1974-1976)
- Volume VII (1977-1981)
- Volume VIII (1982-1985)
- Volume IX (1985-1989)
- Index Volume (1607-1989)

Who's Who in the World

Who's Who in the East

Who's Who in the Midwest

Who's Who in the South and Southwest

Who's Who in the West

Who's Who in Advertising

Who's Who in American Law

Who's Who of American Women

Who's Who of Emerging Leaders in America

Who's Who in Entertainment

Who's Who in Finance and Industry

Index to Who's Who Books

Directory of Medical Specialists

Supplement to Directory of Medical Specialists

Who's Who in the West®

Including Alaska, Arizona, California, Colorado, Hawaii, Idaho, Montana, Nevada, New Mexico, Oregon, Utah, Washington, and Wyoming; and in Canada, the provinces of Alberta, British Columbia, and Saskatchewan.

22nd edition 1989-1990

MARQUIS
Who'sWho

Macmillan Directory Division
3002 Glenview Road
Wilmette, Illinois 60091 U.S.A.

Sandra S. Barnes—President
A. Robert Weicherding—Vice President, Publisher
Timothy J. Sullivan—Vice President, Finance
Dean A. Davis—Vice President, Operations
Jill E. Lazar—Product Manager
Paul S. Canning—Operations Manager
Frederick M. Marks—Manager, Biographical Research
Julia C. Forth—Publication Manager
Jean S. Donnelly—Researcher

James J. Pfister—Information Services Group Vice President, Macmillan, Inc.
Paul E. Rose—President, National Register Publishing Co.

Library of Congress Catalog Card Number 49–48186
International Standard Book Number 0–8379–0922–8
Product Code Number 030547

Distributed in Asia by
United Publishers Services Ltd.
Kenkyu-Sha Bldg.
9, Kanda Surugadai 2-Chome
Chiyoda-ku, Tokyo, Japan

Manufactured in the United States of America

Table of Contents

Preface

The twenty-second edition of *Who's Who in the West* is a current compilation of biographical information on men and women of distinction whose influence is concentrated in the western sector of North America. Such individuals are of decided reference interest locally and, in many instances, nationally.

The volume contains approximately 20,500 names from the western region of the United States including Alaska, Arizona, California, Colorado, Hawaii, Idaho, Montana, Nevada, New Mexico, Oregon, Utah, Washington, and Wyoming, and from the Canadian provinces of Alberta, British Columbia, and Saskatchewan. Reviewed, revised, and amended, the twenty-second edition offers up to date coverage of a broad range of Westerners based on position or individual achievement.

The persons sketched in this volume represent virtually every important field of endeavor. Included are executives and officials in government, business, education, religion, the press, civic affairs, the arts, cultural activities, law, and other fields. This edition also includes significant contributors in such areas as contemporary art, music, and science.

Each candidate for inclusion in *Who's Who in the West* is invited to submit biographical data about his or her life and career. This information is reviewed by the Marquis editorial staff before being written into sketch form. A prepublication proof of the sketch is sent to the biographee for verification. The verified sketch, when returned and accepted by Marquis Who's Who, is rechecked and put into final Who's Who format.

In the event that a reference-worthy individual fails to submit biographical data, the Marquis staff compiles the information through independent research. Such sketches are denoted by an asterisk. Brief key information is provided in the sketches of selected individuals who did not submit data.

The question is often asked, "How do people get into a Who's Who volume?" Name selection is based on one fundamental principle: reference value. Biographees of *Who's Who in the West* can be classified in two basic categories: (1) Persons who are of reference importance to colleagues, librarians, researchers, scholars, the press, historians, biographers, participants in business and civic affairs, and others with specific or general inquiry needs; (2) Individuals of national reference interest who are also of such regional or local importance that their inclusion in the book is essential.

In the editorial evaluation that resulted in the ultimate selection of the names in this directory, an individual's desire to be listed was not sufficient reason for inclusion. Only occupational stature or achievement in a field within the western region of North America influenced selection.

Marquis Who's Who editors exercise the utmost care in preparing each biographical sketch for publication. Occasionally, however, errors occur. Users of this directory are requested to draw to the attention of the publisher any errors found so that corrections can be made in a subsequent edition.

Board of Advisors

Marquis Who's Who gratefully acknowledges the following distinguished individuals who have made themselves available for review, evaluation, and general comment with regard to the publication of the twenty-second edition of *Who's Who in the West*. The advisors have enhanced the reference value of this edition by the nomination of outstanding individuals for inclusion. However, the Board of Advisors, either collectively or individually, is in no way responsible for the final selection of names appearing in this volume, nor does the Board of Advisors bear responsibility for the accuracy or comprehensiveness of the biographical information or other material contained herein.

Duncan Ferguson Cameron
Director Emeritus
Glenbow-Alberta Institute

Edward W. Carter
Chairman of the Board Emeritus
Carter Hawley Hale Stores, Inc.

Walter B. Gerken
Chairman of the Executive Committee
Pacific Mutual Life Insurance Company

Marion Irvine Lederer
Cultural Administrator
Los Angeles, California

James A. Mason
Dean
College of Fine Arts and Communications
Brigham Young University

Jerold D. Ottley
Music Director
Salt Lake Mormon Tabernacle Choir

Board of Nominators

Marquis Who's Who gratefully acknowledges the following distinguished nominators for their assistance with regard to the publication of the twenty-second edition of *Who's Who in the West*. They have enhanced the reference value of this edition by the recommendation of outstanding persons from their respective states or local areas. However, the Board of Nominators, either collectively or individually, is in no way responsible for the final selection of names appearing in this volume, nor does the Board of Nominators bear responsibility for the accuracy or comprehensiveness of the biographical information or other material contained herein.

Dickwin D. Armstrong
President
Bellevue Chamber of Commerce
Bellevue, Washington

John C. Bowers
President and General Manager
Jefferson County Chamber of Commerce
Lakewood, Colorado

David W. Graybill
President and Chief Executive Officer
Tacoma-Pierce County Chamber of Commerce
Tacoma, Washington

Lee Grissom
President
Greater San Diego Chamber of Commerce
San Diego, California

Jim Haynes
President and General Manager
Phoenix Chamber of Commerce
Phoenix, Arizona

Allan B. Hughes
Executive Director
Anaheim Chamber of Commerce
Anaheim, California

John H. Jacobs
Former Executive Director
San Francisco Chamber of Commerce
San Francisco, California

Terri L. Maisel
President
Greater Albuquerque Chamber of Commerce
Albuquerque, New Mexico

Donald S. McClave
President and Chief Executive Officer
Portland Chamber of Commerce
Portland, Oregon

Dorothy Perkins
Executive Vice President
Casper Area Chamber of Commerce
Casper, Wyoming

Art Pick
Executive Vice President
Greater Riverside Chambers of Commerce
Riverside, California

George Reitemeier
General Manager
Spokane Area Chamber of Commerce
Spokane, Washington

Ray Remy
President
Los Angeles Area Chamber of Commerce
Los Angeles, California

Robert B. Robinson
President
The Chamber of Commerce of Hawaii
Honolulu, Hawaii

Harry L. York
Executive Vice President
Concord Chamber of Commerce
Concord, California

Standards of Admission

The foremost consideration in selecting biographees for *Who's Who in the West* is the extent of an individual's reference interest. Such reference interest is judged on either of two factors: 1) the position of responsibility held, or 2) the level of achievement attained by the individual.

Admissions based on the factor of position include:

Members of the U.S. Congress

Federal judges

Governors of states covered by this volume

Premiers of Canadian provinces covered by this volume

State attorneys general

Judges of state and territorial courts of highest appellate jurisdiction

Mayors of major cities

Heads of major universities and colleges

Heads of leading philanthropic, educational, cultural, and scientific institutions and associations

Chief ecclesiastics of the principal religious denominations

Principal officers of national and international businesses

Others chosen because of incumbency or membership

Admission for individual achievement is based on objective qualitative criteria. To be selected, a person must have attained conspicuous achievement.

Key to Information

[1] **ASHTON, HARDY AMES,** [2] lawyer; [3] b. Topeka, Aug. 3, 1934; [4] s. Samuel Taylor and Barbara (Hanson) A.; [5] m. Nancy Richardson, June 20, 1955; [6] children: Marilyn Ashton Heim, Barbara Anne, William Marc. [7] BA, Pa. State U., 1955; JD, Syracuse U., 1960. [8] Bar: Calif. 1960, U.S. Supreme Ct. 1968. [9] Assoc. Prine, Belden & Coates, Sacramento, 1960-67; mem. Johnson, Randolph, Sikes and Bord, Sacramento, 1967—, ptnr., 1969-74, sr. ptnr., 1974—; legal cons. Sacramento Urban League. [10] Author: Urban Renewal and the Law, 1975, Changes in California Zoning Laws: A Perspective, 1987. [11] Commr. Sutter County Park Dist., 1971-78; mem. planning com. Arroyo Seco Redevel. Project, Sacramento, 1980; bd. dirs. Hargrave Inst., 1985—. [12] Served with U.S. Army, 1956-57. [13] Named Man of Yr., Sacramento C. of C., 1986. [14] Mem. ABA, Calif. Bar Assn., Sacramento Bar Assn., Am. Judicature Soc., Order of Coif. [15] Democrat. [16] Episcopalian. [17] Clubs: Twelve Trees Country, Tuesday Luncheon. [18] Lodge: Lions (Sacramento). [19] Home: 3080 Grant St Sacramento CA 95814 [20] Office: Johnson Randolph Sikes and Bord 10 Saint Paul Ave Sacramento CA 95822

KEY

[1]	Name
[2]	Occupation
[3]	Vital statistics
[4]	Parents
[5]	Marriage
[6]	Children
[7]	Education
[8]	Professional certifications
[9]	Career
[10]	Writings and creative works
[11]	Civic and political activities
[12]	Military
[13]	Awards and fellowships
[14]	Professional and association memberships
[15]	Political affiliation
[16]	Religion
[17]	Clubs
[18]	Lodges
[19]	Home address
[20]	Office address

Table of Abbreviations

The following abbreviations and symbols are frequently used in this book

*An asterisk following a sketch indicates that it was researched by the Marquis Who's Who editorial staff and has not been verified by the biographee.

AA, A.A. Associate in Arts, Associate of Arts
AAAL American Academy of Arts and Letters
AAAS American Association for the Advancement of Science
AAHPER Alliance for Health, Physical Education and Recreation
AAU Amateur Athletic Union
AAUP American Association of University Professors
AAUW American Association of University Women
AB, A.B. Arts, Bachelor of
AB Alberta
ABA American Bar Association
ABC American Broadcasting Company
AC Air Corps
acad. academy, academic
acct. accountant
acctg. accounting
ACDA Arms Control and Disarmament Agency
ACLU American Civil Liberties Union
ACP American College of Physicians
ACS American College of Surgeons
ADA American Dental Association
a.d.c. aide-de-camp
adj. adjunct, adjutant
adj. gen. adjutant general
adm. admiral
adminstr. administrator
adminstrn. administration
adminstrv. administrative
ADP Automatic Data Processing
adv. advocate, advisory
advt. advertising
AE, A.E. Agricultural Engineer
A.E. and P. Ambassador Extraordinary and Plenipotentiary
AEC Atomic Energy Commission
aero. aeronautical, aeronautic
aerodyn. aerodynamic
AFB Air Force Base
AFL-CIO American Federation of Labor and Congress of Industrial Organizations
AFTRA American Federation of TV and Radio Artists
AFSCME American Federation of State, County and Municipal Employees
agr. agriculture
agrl. agricultural
agt. agent
AGVA American Guild of Variety Artists
agy. agency
A&I Agricultural and Industrial
AIA American Institute of Architects
AIAA American Institute of Aeronautics and Astronautics
AICPA American Institute of Certified Public Accountants
AID Agency for International Development
AIDS Acquired Immune Deficiency Syndrome
AIEE American Institute of Electrical Engineers
AIM American Institute of Management
AIME American Institute of Mining, Metallurgy, and Petroleum Engineers
AK Alaska
AL Alabama
ALA American Library Association
Ala. Alabama
alt. alternate
Alta. Alberta
A&M Agricultural and Mechanical
AM, A.M. Arts, Master of
Am. American, America
AMA American Medical Association
amb. ambassador
A.M.E. African Methodist Episcopal
Amtrak National Railroad Passenger Corporation
AMVETS American Veterans of World War II, Korea, Vietnam
anat. anatomical
ann. annual
ANTA American National Theatre and Academy
anthrop. anthropological
AP Associated Press
APO Army Post Office
apptd. appointed
Apr. April
apt. apartment
AR Arkansas
ARC American Red Cross
archeol. archeological
archtl. architectural
Ariz. Arizona
Ark. Arkansas
ArtsD, ArtsD. Arts, Doctor of
arty. artillery
AS American Samoa
AS Associate in Science
AS Associate of Applied Science
ASCAP American Society of Composers, Authors and Publishers
ASCE American Society of Civil Engineers
ASHRAE American Society of Heating, Refrigeration, and Air Conditioning Engineers
ASME American Society of Mechanical Engineers
ASPCA American Society for the Prevention of Cruelty to Animals
assn. association
assoc. associate
asst. assistant
ASTM American Society for Testing and Materials
astron. astronomical
astrophys. astrophysical
ATSC Air Technical Service Command
AT&T American Telephone & Telegraph Company
atty. attorney
Aug. August
AUS Army of the United States
aux. auxiliary
Ave. Avenue
AVMA American Veterinary Medical Association
AZ Arizona

B. Bachelor
b. born
BA, B.A. Bachelor of Arts
BAgr, B.Agr. Bachelor of Agriculture
Balt. Baltimore
Bapt. Baptist
BArch, B.Arch. Bachelor of Architecture
BAS, B.A.S. Bachelor of Agricultural Science
BBA, B.B.A. Bachelor of Business Administration
BBC British Broadcasting Corporation
BC, B.C. British Columbia
BCE, B.C.E. Bachelor of Civil Engineering
BChir, B.Chir. Bachelor of Surgery
BCL, B.C.L. Bachelor of Civil Law
BCS, B.C.S. Bachelor of Commercial Science
BD, B.D. Bachelor of Divinity
bd. board
BE, B.E. Bachelor of Education
BEE, B.E.E. Bachelor of Electrical Engineering
BFA, B.F.A. Bachelor of Fine Arts
bibl. biblical
bibliog. bibliographical
biog. biographical
biol. biological
BJ, B.J. Bachelor of Journalism
Bklyn. Brooklyn
BL, B.L. Bachelor of Letters
bldg. building
BLS, B.L.S. Bachelor of Library Science
Blvd. Boulevard

BMW Bavarian Motor Works (Bayerische Motoren Werke)
bn. battalion
B.& O.R.R. Baltimore & Ohio Railroad
bot. botanical
BPE, B.P.E. Bachelor of Physical Education
BPhil, B.Phil. Bachelor of Philosophy
br. branch
BRE, B.R.E. Bachelor of Religious Education
brig. gen. brigadier general
Brit. British, Brittanica
Bros. Brothers
BS, B.S. Bachelor of Science
BSA, B.S.A. Bachelor of Agricultural Science
BSBA Bachelor of Science in Business Administration
BSChemE Bachelor of Science in Chemical Engineering
BSD, B.S.D. Bachelor of Didactic Science
BST, B.S.T. Bachelor of Sacred Theology
BTh, B.Th. Bachelor of Theology
bull. bulletin
bur. bureau
bus. business
B.W.I. British West Indies

CA California
CAA Civil Aeronautics Administration
CAB Civil Aeronautics Board
CAD-CAM Computer Aided Design-Computer Aided Model
Calif. California
C.Am. Central America
Can. Canada, Canadian
CAP Civil Air Patrol
capt. captain
CARE Cooperative American Relief Everywhere
Cath. Catholic
cav. cavalry
CBC Canadian Broadcasting Company
CBI China, Burma, India Theatre of Operations
CBS Columbia Broadcasting Company
CCC Commodity Credit Corporation
CCNY City College of New York
CCU Cardiac Care Unit
CD Civil Defense
CE, C.E. Corps of Engineers, Civil Engineer
cen. central
CENTO Central Treaty Organization
CERN European Organization of Nuclear Research
cert. certificate, certification, certified
CETA Comprehensive Employment Training Act
CFL Canadian Football League
ch. church
ChD, Ch.D. Doctor of Chemistry
chem. chemical
ChemE, Chem.E. Chemical Engineer
Chgo. Chicago
chirurg. chirurgical
chmn. chairman
chpt. chapter
CIA Central Intelligence Agency
Cin. Cincinnati
cir. circuit
Cleve. Cleveland
climatol. climatological
clin. clinical
clk. clerk
C.L.U. Chartered Life Underwriter
CM, C.M. Master in Surgery
CM Northern Mariana Islands
C.&N.W.Ry. Chicago & North Western Railway
CO Colorado
Co. Company
COF Catholic Order of Foresters
C. of C. Chamber of Commerce
col. colonel
coll. college
Colo. Colorado
com. committee
comd. commanded
comdg. commanding
comdr. commander
comdt. commandant
commd. commissioned
comml. commercial
commn. commission
commr. commissioner
compt. comptroller
condr. conductor
Conf. Conference
Congl. Congregational, Congressional
Conglist. Congregationalist
Conn. Connecticut
cons. consultant, consulting
consol. consolidated
constl. constitutional
constn. constitution
constrn. construction
contbd. contributed
contbg. contributing
contbn. contribution
contbr. contributor
contr. controller
Conv. Convention
coop. cooperative
coord. coordinator
CORDS Civil Operations and Revolutionary Development Support
CORE Congress of Racial Equality
corp. corporation, corporate
corr. correspondent, corresponding, correspondence
C.&O.Ry. Chesapeake & Ohio Railway
coun. council
C.P.A. Certified Public Accountant
C.P.C.U. Chartered Property and Casualty Underwriter
CPH, C.P.H. Certificate of Public Health
cpl. corporal
C.P.R. Cardio-Pulmonary Resuscitation
C.P.Ry. Canadian Pacific Railway
CRT Cathode Ray Terminal
C.S. Christian Science
CSB, C.S.B. Bachelor of Christian Science
C.S.C. Civil Service Commission
CT Connecticut
ct. court
ctr. center
CWS Chemical Warfare Service
C.Z. Canal Zone

D. Doctor
d. daughter
DAgr, D.Agr. Doctor of Agriculture
DAR Daughters of the American Revolution
dau. daughter
DAV Disabled American Veterans
DC, D.C. District of Columbia
DCL, D.C.L. Doctor of Civil Law
DCS, D.C.S. Doctor of Commercial Science
DD, D.D. Doctor of Divinity
DDS, D.D.S. Doctor of Dental Surgery
DE Delaware
Dec. December
dec. deceased
def. defense
Del. Delaware
del. delegate, delegation
Dem. Democrat, Democratic
DEng, D.Eng. Doctor of Engineering
denom. denomination, denominational
dep. deputy
dept. department
dermatol. dermatological
desc. descendant
devel. development, developmental
DFA, D.F.A. Doctor of Fine Arts
D.F.C. Distinguished Flying Cross
DHL, D.H.L. Doctor of Hebrew Literature
dir. director
dist. district
distbg. distributing
distbn. distribution
distbr. distributor
disting. distinguished
div. division, divinity, divorce
DLitt, D.Litt. Doctor of Literature
DMD, D.M.D. Doctor of Medical Dentistry
DMS, D.M.S. Doctor of Medical Science
DO, D.O. Doctor of Osteopathy
DPH, D.P.H. Diploma in Public Health

DPhil, D.Phil. Doctor of Philosophy
D.R. Daughters of the Revolution
Dr. Drive, Doctor
DRE, D.R.E. Doctor of Religious Education
DrPH, Dr.P.H. Doctor of Public Health, Doctor of Public Hygiene
D.S.C. Distinguished Service Cross
DSc, D.Sc. Doctor of Science
D.S.M. Distinguished Service Medal
DST, D.S.T. Doctor of Sacred Theology
DTM, D.T.M. Doctor of Tropical Medicine
DVM, D.V.M. Doctor of Veterinary Medicine
DVS, D.V.S. Doctor of Veterinary Surgery

E, E. East
ea. eastern
E. and P. Extraordinary and Plenipotentiary
Eccles. Ecclesiastical
ecol. ecological
econ. economic
ECOSOC Economic and Social Council (of the UN)
ED, E.D. Doctor of Engineering
ed. educated
EdB, Ed.B. Bachelor of Education
EdD, Ed.D. Doctor of Education
edit. edition
EdM, Ed.M. Master of Education
edn. education
ednl. educational
EDP Electronic Data Processing
EdS, Ed.S. Specialist in Education
EE, E.E. Electrical Engineer
E.E. and M.P. Envoy Extraordinary and Minister Plenipotentiary
EEC European Economic Community
EEG Electroencephalogram
EEO Equal Employment Opportunity
EEOC Equal Employment Opportunity Commission
E.Ger. German Democratic Republic
EKG Electrocardiogram
elec. electrical
electrochem. electrochemical
electrophys. electrophysical
elem. elementary
EM, E.M. Engineer of Mines
ency. encyclopedia
Eng. England
engr. engineer
engring. engineering
entomol. entomological
environ. environmental
EPA Environmental Protection Agency
epidemiol. epidemiological
Episc. Episcopalian
ERA Equal Rights Amendment
ERDA Energy Research and Development Administration
ESEA Elementary and Secondary Education Act
ESL English as Second Language
ESPN Entertainment and Sports Programming Network
ESSA Environmental Science Services Administration
ethnol. ethnological
ETO European Theatre of Operations
Evang. Evangelical
exam. examination, examining
Exch. Exchange
exec. executive
exhbn. exhibition
expdn. expedition
expn. exposition
expt. experiment
exptl. experimental
Expwy. Expressway

F.A. Field Artillery
FAA Federal Aviation Administration
FAO Food and Agriculture Organization (of the UN)
FBI Federal Bureau of Investigation
FCA Farm Credit Administration
FCC Federal Communications Commission
FCDA Federal Civil Defense Administration
FDA Food and Drug Administration
FDIA Federal Deposit Insurance Administration
FDIC Federal Deposit Insurance Corporation
FE, F.E. Forest Engineer
FEA Federal Energy Administration
Feb. February
fed. federal
fedn. federation
FERC Federal Energy Regulatory Commission
fgn. foreign
FHA Federal Housing Administration
fin. financial, finance
FL Florida
Fl. Floor
Fla. Florida
FMC Federal Maritime Commission
FOA Foreign Operations Administration
found. foundation
FPC Federal Power Commission
FPO Fleet Post Office
frat. fraternity
FRS Federal Reserve System
Frwy. Freeway
FSA Federal Security Agency
Ft. Fort
FTC Federal Trade Commission

G-1 (or other number) Division of General Staff
GA, Ga. Georgia
GAO General Accounting Office
gastroent. gastroenterological
GATT General Agreement of Tariff and Trades
GE General Electric Company
gen. general
geneal. genealogical
geod. geodetic
geog. geographic, geographical
geol. geological
geophys. geophysical
gerontol. gerontological
G.H.Q. General Headquarters
GM General Motors Corporation
GMAC General Motors Acceptance Corporation
G.N.Ry. Great Northern Railway
gov. governor
govt. government
govtl. governmental
GPO Government Printing Office
grad. graduate, graduated
GSA General Services Administration
Gt. Great
GTE General Telephone and Electric Company
GU Guam
gynecol. gynecological

HBO Home Box Office
hdqrs. headquarters
HEW Department of Health, Education and Welfare
HHD, H.H.D. Doctor of Humanities
HHFA Housing and Home Finance Agency
HHS Department of Health and Human Services
HI Hawaii
hist. historical, historic
HM, H.M. Master of Humanics
HMO Health Maintenance Organization
homeo. homeopathic
hon. honorary, honorable
Ho. of Dels. House of Delegates
Ho. of Reps. House of Representatives
hort. horticultural
hosp. hospital
HUD Department of Housing and Urban Development
Hwy. Highway
hydrog. hydrographic

IA Iowa
IAEA International Atomic Energy Agency
IBM International Business Machines Corporation
IBRD International Bank for Reconstruction and Development
ICA International Cooperation Administration

ICC Interstate Commerce Commission
ICU Intensive Care Unit
ID Idaho
IEEE Institute of Electrical and Electronics Engineers
IFC International Finance Corporation
IGY International Geophysical Year
IL Illinois
Ill. Illinois
illus. illustrated
ILO International Labor Organization
IMF International Monetary Fund
IN Indiana
Inc. Incorporated
Ind. Indiana
ind. independent
Indpls. Indianapolis
indsl. industrial
inf. infantry
info. information
ins. insurance
insp. inspector
insp. gen. inspector general
inst. institute
instl. institutional
instn. institution
instr. instructor
instrn. instruction
internat. international
intro. introduction
IRE Institute of Radio Engineers
IRS Internal Revenue Service
ITT International Telephone & Telegraph Corporation

JAG Judge Advocate General
JAGC Judge Advocate General Corps
Jan. January
Jaycees Junior Chamber of Commerce
JB, J.B. Jurum Baccalaureus
JCB, J.C.B. Juris Canoni Baccalaureus
JCD, J.C.D. Juris Canonici Doctor, Juris Civilis Doctor
JCL, J.C.L. Juris Canonici Licentiatus
JD, J.D. Juris Doctor
jg. junior grade
jour. journal
jr. junior
JSD, J.S.D. Juris Scientiae Doctor
JUD, J.U.D. Juris Utriusque Doctor
jud. judicial

Kans. Kansas
K.C. Knights of Columbus
K.P. Knights of Pythias
KS Kansas
K.T. Knight Templar
KY, Ky. Kentucky

LA, La. Louisiana
L.A. Los Angeles
lab. laboratory
lang. language
laryngol. laryngological
LB Labrador
LDS Church Church of Jesus Christ of Latter Day Saints
lectr. lecturer
legis. legislation, legislative
LHD, L.H.D. Doctor of Humane Letters
L.I. Long Island
libr. librarian, library
lic. licensed, license
L.I.R.R. Long Island Railroad
lit. literature
LittB, Litt.B. Bachelor of Letters
LittD, Litt.D. Doctor of Letters
LLB, LL.B. Bachelor of Laws
LLD, L.L.D. Doctor of Laws
LLM, L.L.M. Master of Laws
Ln. Lane
L.&N.R.R. Louisville & Nashville Railroad
LPGA Ladies Professional Golf Association
LS, L.S. Library Science (in degree)
lt. lieutenant
Ltd. Limited
Luth. Lutheran
LWV League of Women Voters

M. Master
m. married
MA, M.A. Master of Arts
MA Massachusetts
MADD Mothers Against Drunk Driving
mag. magazine
Man. Manitoba
Mar. March
MArch, M.Arch. Master in Architecture
Mass. Massachusetts
math. mathematics, mathematical
MATS Military Air Transport Service
MB, M.B. Bachelor of Medicine
MB Manitoba
MBA, M.B.A. Master of Business Administration
MBS Mutual Broadcasting System
M.C. Medical Corps
MCE, M.C.E. Master of Civil Engineering
mcht. merchant
mcpl. municipal
MCS, M.C.S. Master of Commercial Science
MD, M.D. Doctor of Medicine
MD, Md. Maryland
MDiv Master of Divinity
MDip, M.Dip. Master in Diplomacy
mdse. merchandise
MDV, M.D.V. Doctor of Veterinary Medicine
ME, M.E. Mechanical Engineer
ME Maine
M.E.Ch. Methodist Episcopal Church
mech. mechanical
MEd., M.Ed. Master of Education
med. medical
MEE, M.E.E. Master of Electrical Engineering
mem. member
meml. memorial
merc. mercantile
met. metropolitan
metall. metallurgical
MetE, Met.E. Metallurgical Engineer
meteorol. meteorological
Meth. Methodist
Mex. Mexico
MF, M.F. Master of Forestry
MFA, M.F.A. Master of Fine Arts
mfg. manufacturing
mfr. manufacturer
mgmt. management
mgr. manager
MHA, MH.A. Master of Hospital Administration
M.I. Military Intelligence
MI Michigan
Mich. Michigan
micros. microscopic, microscopical
mid. middle
mil. military
Milw. Milwaukee
Min. Minister
mineral. mineralogical
Minn. Minnesota
MIS Management Information Systems
Miss. Mississippi
MIT Massachusetts Institute of Technology
mktg. marketing
ML, M.L. Master of Laws
MLA Modern Language Association
M.L.D. Magister Legnum Diplomatic
MLitt, M.Litt. Master of Literature
MLS, M.L.S. Master of Library Science
MME, M.M.E. Master of Mechanical Engineering
MN Minnesota
mng. managing
MO, Mo. Missouri
moblzn. mobilization
Mont. Montana
MP Northern Mariana Islands
M.P. Member of Parliament
MPA Master of Public Administration
MPE, M.P.E. Master of Physical Education
MPH, M.P.H. Master of Public Health
MPhil, M.Phil. Master of Philosophy
MPL, M.P.L. Master of Patent Law
Mpls. Minneapolis
MRE, M.R.E. Master of Religious Education
MS, M.S. Master of Science
MS, Ms. Mississippi

MSc, M.Sc. Master of Science
MSChemE Master of Science in Chemical Engineering
MSF, M.S.F. Master of Science of Forestry
MST, M.S.T. Master of Sacred Theology
MSW, M.S.W. Master of Social Work
MT Montana
Mt. Mount
MTO Mediterranean Theatre of Operation
MTV Music Television
mus. museum, musical
MusB, Mus.B. Bachelor of Music
MusD, Mus.D. Doctor of Music
MusM, Mus.M. Master of Music
mut. mutual
mycol. mycological

N. North
NAACP National Association for the Advancement of Colored People
NACA National Advisory Committee for Aeronautics
NAD National Academy of Design
NAE National Academy of Engineering
NAFE National Association of Female Executives
N.Am. North America
NAM National Association of Manufacturers
NAPA National Association of Performing Artists
NARAS National Academy of Recording Arts and Sciences
NAREB National Association of Real Estate Boards
NARS National Archives and Record Service
NAS National Academy of Sciences
NASA National Aeronautics and Space Administration
nat. national
NATAS National Academy of Television Arts and Sciences
NATO North Atlantic Treaty Organization
NATOUSA North African Theatre of Operations
nav. navigation
NB, N.B. New Brunswick
NBA National Basketball Association
NBC National Broadcasting Company
NC, N.C. North Carolina
NCAA National College Athletic Association
NCCJ National Conference of Christians and Jews
ND, N.D. North Dakota
NDEA National Defense Education Act
NE Nebraska
NE, N.E. Northeast
NEA National Education Association
Nebr. Nebraska
NEH National Endowment for Humanities
neurol. neurological
Nev. Nevada
NF Newfoundland
NFL National Football League
Nfld. Newfoundland
NG National Guard
NH, N.H. New Hampshire
NHL National Hockey League
NIH National Institutes of Health
NIMH National Institute of Mental Health
NJ, N.J. New Jersey
NLRB National Labor Relations Board
NM New Mexico
N.Mex. New Mexico
No. Northern
NOAA National Oceanographic and Atmospheric Administration
NORAD North America Air Defense
Nov. November
NOW National Organization for Women
N.P.Ry. Northern Pacific Railway
nr. near
NRA National Rifle Association
NRC National Research Council
NS, N.S. Nova Scotia
NSC National Security Council
NSF National Science Foundation
NSW New South Wales
N.T. New Testament
NT Northwest Territories
numis. numismatic
NV Nevada
NW, N.W. Northwest
N.W.T. Northwest Territories
NY, N.Y. New York
N.Y.C. New York City
NYU New York University
N.Z. New Zealand

OAS Organization of American States
ob-gyn obstetrics-gynecology
obs. observatory
obstet. obstetrical
Oct. October
OD. O.D. Doctor of Optometry
OECD Organization of European Cooperation and Development
OEEC Organization of European Economic Cooperation
OEO Office of Economic Opportunity
ofcl. official
OH Ohio
OK Oklahoma
Okla. Oklahoma
ON Ontario
Ont. Ontario
oper. operating
ophthal. ophthalmological
ops. operations
OR Oregon
orch. orchestra
Oreg. Oregon
orgn. organization
ornithol. ornithological
OSHA Occupational Safety and Health Administration
OSRD Office of Scientific Research and Development
OSS Office of Strategic Services
osteo. osteopathic
otol. otological
otolaryn. otolaryngological

PA, Pa. Pennsylvania
P.A. Professional Association
paleontol. paleontological
path. pathological
PBS Public Broadcasting System
P.C. Professional Corporation
PE Prince Edward Island
P.E.I. Prince Edward Island
PEN Poets, Playwrights, Editors, Essayists and Novelists (international association)
penol. penological
P.E.O. women's organization (full name not disclosed)
pers. personnel
pfc. private first class
PGA Professional Golfers' Association of America
PHA Public Housing Administration
pharm. pharmaceutical
PharmD, Pharm.D. Doctor of Pharmacy
PharmM, Pharm.M. Master of Pharmacy
PhB, Ph.B. Bachelor of Philosophy
PhD, Ph.D. Doctor of Philosophy
PhDChemE Doctor of Science in Chemical Engineering
PhM, Ph.M. Master of Philosophy
Phila. Philadelphia
philharm. philharmonic
philol. philological
philos. philosophical
photog. photographic
phys. physical
physiol. physiological
Pitts. Pittsburgh
Pk. Park
Pkwy. Parkway
Pl. Place
Pla. Plaza
P.&L.E.R.R. Pittsburgh & Lake Erie Railroad
P.O. Post Office
PO Box Post Office Box
polit. political
poly. polytechnic, polytechnical
PQ Province of Quebec
PR. P.R. Puerto Rico

prep. preparatory
pres. president
Presbyn. Presbyterian
presdl. presidential
prin. principal
proc. proceedings
prod. produced (play production)
prodn. production
prof. professor
profl. professional
prog. progressive
propr. proprietor
pros. atty. prosecuting attorney
pro tem pro tempore
PSRO Professional Services Review Organization
psychiat. psychiatric
psychol. psychological
PTA Parent-Teachers Association
ptnr. partner
PTO Pacific Theatre of Operations, Parent Teacher Organization
pub. publisher, publishing, published
pub. public
publ. publication
pvt. private

quar. quarterly
qm. quartermaster
Q.M.C. Quartermaster Corps
Que. Quebec

radiol. radiological
RAF Royal Air Force
RCA Radio Corporation of America
RCAF Royal Canadian Air Force
RD Rural Delivery
Rd. Road
R&D Research & Development
REA Rural Electrification Administration
rec. recording
ref. reformed
regt. regiment
regtl. regimental
rehab. rehabilitation
rels. relations
Rep. Republican
rep. representative
Res. Reserve
ret. retired
Rev. Reverend
rev. review, revised
RFC Reconstruction Finance Corporation
RFD Rural Free Delivery
rhinol. rhinological
RI, R.I. Rhode Island
RISD Rhode Island School of Design
Rm. Room
RN, R.N. Registered Nurse
roentgenol. roentgenological
ROTC Reserve Officers Training Corps
RR Rural Route
R.R. Railroad
rsch. research
Rte. Route
Ry. Railway

S. South
s. son
SAC Strategic Air Command
SAG Screen Actors Guild
SALT Strategic Arms Limitation Talks
S.Am. South America
san. sanitary
SAR Sons of the American Revolution
Sask. Saskatchewan
savs. savings
SB, S.B. Bachelor of Science
SBA Small Business Administration
SC, S.C. South Carolina
SCAP Supreme Command Allies Pacific
ScB, Sc.B. Bachelor of Science
SCD, S.C.D. Doctor of Commercial Science
ScD, Sc.D. Doctor of Science
sch. school
sci. science, scientific
SCLC Southern Christian Leadership Conference
SCV Sons of Confederate Veterans
SD, S.D. South Dakota
SE, S.E. Southeast
SEATO Southeast Asia Treaty Organization
SEC Securities and Exchange Commission
sec. secretary
sect. section
seismol. seismological
sem. seminary
Sept. September
s.g. senior grade
sgt. sergeant
SHAEF Supreme Headquarters Allied Expeditionary Forces
SHAPE Supreme Headquarters Allied Powers in Europe
S.I. Staten Island
S.J. Society of Jesus (Jesuit)
SJD Scientiae Juridicae Doctor
SK Saskatchewan
SM, S.M. Master of Science
So. Southern
soc. society
sociol. sociological
S.P. Co. Southern Pacific Company
spl. special
splty. specialty
Sq. Square
S.R. Sons of the Revolution
sr. senior
SS Steamship
SSS Selective Service System
St. Saint, Street
sta. station
stats. statistics
statis. statistical
STB, S.T.B. Bachelor of Sacred Theology
stblzn. stabilization
STD, S.T.D. Doctor of Sacred Theology
Ste. Suite
subs. subsidiary
SUNY State University of New York
supr. supervisor
supt. superintendent
surg. surgical
svc. service
SW, S.W. Southwest

TAPPI Technical Association of the Pulp and Paper Industry
Tb. Tuberculosis
tchr. teacher
tech. technical, technology
technol. technological
Tel. & Tel. Telephone & Telegraph
temp. temporary
Tenn. Tennessee
Ter. Territory
Terr. Terrace
Tex. Texas
ThD, Th.D. Doctor of Theology
theol. theological
ThM, Th.M. Master of Theology
TN Tennessee
tng. training
topog. topographical
trans. transaction, transferred
transl. translation, translated
transp. transportation
treas. treasurer
TT Trust Territory
TV television
TVA Tennessee Valley Authority
TWA Trans World Airlines
twp. township
TX Texas
typog. typographical

U. University
UAW United Auto Workers
UCLA University of California at Los Angeles
UDC United Daughters of the Confederacy
U.K. United Kingdom
UN United Nations
UNESCO United Nations Educational, Scientific and Cultural Organization
UNICEF United Nations International Children's Emergency Fund
univ. university
UNRRA United Nations Relief and Rehabilitation Administration
UPI United Press International
U.P.R.R. United Pacific Railroad
urol. urological
U.S. United States

U.S.A. United States of America
USAAF United States Army Air Force
USAF United States Air Force
USAFR United States Air Force Reserve
USAR United States Army Reserve
USCG United States Coast Guard
USCGR United States Coast Guard Reserve
USES United States Employment Service
USIA United States Information Agency
USMC United States Marine Corps
USMCR United States Marine Corps Reserve
USN United States Navy
USNG United States National Guard
USNR United States Naval Reserve
USO United Service Organizations
USPHS United States Public Health Service
USS United States Ship
USSR Union of the Soviet Socialist Republics
USTA United States Tennis Association
USV United States Volunteers
UT Utah

VA Veterans' Administration
VA, Va. Virginia
vet. veteran, veterinary
VFW Veterans of Foreign Wars
VI, V.I. Virgin Islands
vice pres. vice president
vis. visiting
VISTA Volunteers in Service to America
VITA Volunteers in Technical Service
vocat. vocational
vol. volunteer, volume
v.p. vice president
vs. versus
VT, Vt. Vermont

W, W. West
WA Washington (state)
WAC Women's Army Corps
Wash. Washington (state)
WAVES Women's Reserve, US Naval Reserve
WCTU Women's Christian Temperance Union
we. western
W. Ger. Germany, Federal Republic of
WHO World Health Organization
WI Wisconsin
W.I. West Indies
Wis. Wisconsin
WSB Wage Stabilization Board
WV West Virginia
W.Va. West Virginia
WY Wyoming
Wyo. Wyoming

YK Yukon Territory
YMCA Young Men's Christian Association
YMHA Young Men's Hebrew Association
YM & YWHA Young Men's and Young Women's Hebrew Association
yr. year
YT, Y.T. Yukon Territory
YWCA Young Women's Christian Association

zool. zoological

Alphabetical Practices

Names are arranged alphabetically according to the surnames, and under identical surnames according to the first given name. If both surname and first given name are identical, names are arranged alphabetically according to the second given name. Where full names are identical, they are arranged in order of age—with the elder listed first.

Surnames beginning with De, Des, Du, however capitalized or spaced, are recorded with the prefix preceding the surname and arranged alphabetically under the letter D.

Surnames beginning with Mac and Mc are arranged alphabetically under M.

Surnames beginning with Saint or St. appear after names that begin Sains, and are arranged according to the second part of the name, e.g. St. Clair before Saint Dennis.

Surnames beginning with Van, Von or von are arranged alphabetically under letter V.

Compound hyphenated surnames are arranged according to the first member of the compound. Compound unhyphenated surnames are treated as hyphenated names.

Parentheses used in connection with a name indicate which part of the full name is usually deleted in common usage. Hence Abbott, W(illiam) Lewis indicates that the usual form of the given name is W. Lewis. In such a case, the parentheses are ignored in alphabetizing. However, if the name is recorded Abbott, (William) Lewis, signifying that the entire name William is not commonly used, the alphabetizing would be arranged as though the name were Abbott, Lewis.

Who's Who in the West

AADAHL, JORG, business executive; b. Trondheim, Norway, June 16, 1937; came to U.S., 1966; s. Ottar P. and Gurli (Lockra) A.; MS in Mech. Engring., Tech. U. Norway, 1961; MBA, U. San Francisco, 1973; m. Inger R. Holst, July 13, 1973; children: Erik, Nina. Research fellow Tech. U. Norway, Trondheim, 1961-62; mgr. arc welding devel. NAG, Oslo, 1964-66; mfg. engr. Varian Assocs., Palo Alto, Calif., 1966-67; bus. mgr. United Airlines, San Francisco, 1974-75, sr. systems analyst, 1977-81; strategic planning specialist Magnex Corp., San Jose, 1981-82; cons. in mgmt., 1982-84; founder, pres. Safeware, Inc., Santa Clara, Calif., 1984—. Developer Safechem Hazardous Chem. Mgmt. System. Recipient Certificate of Honor, San Francisco Bd. Suprs., 1973. Mem. Leif Erikson League (pres. 1973), Norwegian Soc. Profl. Engrs. Club: Young Scandinavians (v.p. 1971). Author: Strength Analysis, Welded Structures, 1967; contbr. articles in various fields to profl. jours.; editor Nordic Highlights, 1972. Office: Safeware Inc 4677 Old Ironsides Dr Santa Clara CA 95054

AAMODT, PAUL LEROY, geologist; b. San Francisco, Aug. 26, 1944; s. Rodney Lee and Barbara Helen (Quinn) A.; m. Barbara Lee Smith, Jan. 3, 1964; children: James Edward, Kristi Colleen. Student, N. Mex. State U., 1962-63, U. Ariz., 1970; BS in Geology, U. Nev., 1971; postgrad., U. Phoenix. Field geologist Fenix & Scisson, Inc., Las Vegas, 1971-73; staff geologist Fenix & Scisson, Inc., Tulsa, 1973-75; mem. staff Los Alamos (N. Mex.) Nat. Lab., 1975-77, asst. group leader, 1977-79, project leader, 1979-88. Home: Rte 5 Box 251 AA Santa Fe NM 87501 Office: Los Alamos Nat Lab Group ESS 1 MS D462 Po Box 1663 Los Alamos NM 87545

AARON, ROY HENRY, lawyer, entertainment company executive; b. Los Angeles, Apr. 8, 1929; s. Samuel Arthur and Natalie (Krakauer) A.; m. Theresa Gesas, Dec. 20, 1953; 1 child, Jill. B.A., U. Calif.-Berkeley, 1951; LL.B., U. So. Calif., 1956. Bar: Calif. 1957. Mem. Pacht, Ross, Warne, Bernhard & Sears, Inc., Los Angeles, 1957-79, of counsel, 1979-83; sr. v.p., gen. counsel Plitt Theatres, Inc. and Plitt Theatre Holdings, Inc., Los Angeles, 1978-80, pres., chief operating officer, 1980-85; pres. Plitt Entertainment Group, Inc., Los Angeles, 1985—; pres., chief exec. officer Showscan Film Corp., Los Angeles, 1985—; lectr. Calif. Continuing Edn. of Bar; lectr. continuing legal edn. Loyola U. Law Sch., Los Angeles. Mem. editorial bd. U. So. Calif. Law Rev., 1954-56. Trustee, mem. exec. com. Vista Del Mar Child-Care Service, 1968-80, Reiss-Davis Child Study Center, 1977-80; bd. dirs. Jewish Fedn. Council Greater Los Angeles, 1970-75; vice chmn. lawyers div. United Crusade Campaigns, 1971, 72; mem. adv. bd. dirs. Rape Treatment Center of Santa Monica Hosp.; mem. exec. com. Royce Two Seventy, pres. 1986-88; mem. exec. com. UCLA Performing Arts. Served with USAF, 1951-53. Fellow Am. Bar Found. (life), Los Angeles County Bar Found. (life); mem. ABA, State Bar Calif., Los Angeles County Bar Assn. (trustee 1977-83, v.p. 1979-80, pres. 1982-83), Beverly Hills Bar Assn., Women Lawyers Los Angeles, UCLA Found. (bd. dirs.), U. So. Calif. Law Alumni Assn., Legion Lex, Found. Motion Picture Pioneers (bd. dirs.), Order of Coif, Am. Judicature Soc., Chancery Club Los Angeles. Office: Plitt Entertainment Group Inc 1801 Century Pk E Ste 1225 Los Angeles CA 90067

AARON, SHIRLEY MAE, tax consultant; b. Covington, La., Feb. 28, 1935; d. Morgan and Pearl (Jenkins) King; m. Richard L. King, Feb. 16, 1952 (div. Feb. 1965); children: Deborah, Richard, Roberta, Keely; m. Michael A. Aaron, Nov. 27, 1976 (dec. July 1987). Adminstrv. asst. South Central Bell, Covington, La., 1954-62; acct. Brown & Root, Inc., Houston, 1962-75; timekeeper Alyeska Pipeline Co., Fairbanks, Alaska, 1975-77; adminstrv. asst. Boeing Co., Seattle, 1979—; pres. Aaron Enterprises, Seattle, 1977—. Bd. dirs. Burien 146 Homeowners Assn., Seattle, 1979—, pres., 1980-83. Mem. NAFE. Avocation: singing.

AASAND, KAREN LEA, financial analyst; b. Oakland, Calif., Jan. 11, 1955; d. Ian Marshall and Joyce (Croze) Watson; m. Henry Eugene Aasand, Dec. 20, 1980. BS in Fin., Golden Gate U., 1982. Acct. exec. Equitec Leasing Co., Oakland, 1983-84; fin. planner AIS Fin. Svcs., Oakland, 1984-86; fin. planner, prin. Aasand Fin. Planning, Oakland, 1986—. Vol. Adventure Unltd., 1978—. Mem. Internat. Assn. Fin. Planners (v.p. programs 1988-89). Republican. Christian Scientist. Office: Aasand Fin Planning 519 17th St Ste 700 Oakland CA 94612-1503

ABARBANEL, JUDITH EDNA, marketing executive; b. N.Y.C., Jan. 26, 1956; d. Albert Brandt and Dorothy Irene (Fennell) A.; m. Christopher George Lucas, June 17, 1984. BA, UCLA, 1977; MBA, MA, Ohio State U., 1980. Accredited pub. relations profl., 1988. Sales mgr. Columbus Magic, Ohio, 1979; account mgr. Mktg. Centre, St. Petersburg, Fla., 1980-82; asst. mktg. dir. MBI, Inc., Golden, Colo., 1983; dir. mktg. Colo. Outward Bound. Sch., Denver, 1983—; owner A Sporting Proposition, Boulder, Colo., 1984—. Adv. bd. Learning Unltd. Mem. Denver Advt. Fedn., Pub. Relations Soc. Am. Avocations: mountain biking, race organizing, teaching. Office: Colo Outward Bound Sch 945 Pennsylvania St Denver CO 80203

ABARQUEZ, JOSUE MARTINEZ, medical administrator; b. San Juan, Batangas, Philippines, Sept. 1, 1938; s. Victoriano Tapat and Constancia (Martinez) A.; m. Delia Hidalgo, Apr. 14, 1968. AA, Manila Cen. U., 1958, MD, 1966; postgrad., U. So. Calif., 1979. Med. resident San Sebastian Gen. Hosp., Philippines, 1967-70; med. dir. Nat. Investment Devel. Corp., Philippines, 1970-72; asst. adminstr. St. Therese Med. Clinic, L.A., 1983-85; med. examiner Equifax Svcs., Burbank, Calif., 1987-88, Am. Para Profl. System, Los Angeles, 1988; med. adminstr. Dept. Pub. Social Svcs., MIED-Sect., Los Angeles, 1989—. Pres. Batangas Assn. So. Calif., L.A., 1980-81, 83-85, bd. dirs. Cuenca Assn. So. Calif., L.A., 1984—, Californians of San Juan, L.A., 1984—, v.p. Filipino Am. Community, L.A., 1988—, bd. dirs. United Batanguenos So. Calif., L.A., 1988—. Mem. Manila Cen. Alumni Assn., Fgn. Med. Graduates, Dux Internat. (hon. 1986—). Home: 763 N Edgemont St Los Angeles CA 90029 Office: Dept Pub Social Svcs MIED-Sect 300 W 6th St Los Angeles CA 90020

ABBINANTE, JENNIFER ANN, nurse; b. Mariemont, Ohio, Aug. 9, 1961; d. Paul Charles and Barbara (Colling) A. BA in Psychology, U. Minn., 1983; Diploma Nursing, Fairview Deaconess Hosp., Mpls., 1986. RN, N.Y., Advanced Cardiac Life Support Cert., 1988. Staff nurse Nicollet Health Care Ctr., Mpls., 1986, Meml. Hosp. Sweetwater County, Rock Springs, Wyo., 1987—; instr. cert. nursing asst. program, Western Wyo. Coll., Rock-springs, 1988. Co-organizer fund ARC, 1985. Mem. Am. Nursing Assn., Wyo. Nurses Assn. Roman Catholic. Home: 385 Anvil Dr A Green River WY 82935 Office: Meml Hosp Sweetwater County 1200 College Dr Rock Springs WY 82901

ABBOTT, CARL JOHN, urban studies and planning educator; b. Knoxville, Tenn., Dec. 3, 1944; s. Lyndon Ewing and Mildred Naomi (Schaeffer) A.; m. Margery Post, Aug. 5, 1967. BA, Swarthmore Coll., 1966; MA, U. Chgo., 1967, PhD, 1971. Asst. prof. U. Denver, 1971-72; asst. prof., assoc. prof. Old Dominion U., Norfolk, Va., 1972-78; assoc. prof., prof. urban studies and planning Portland State U., 1978—, head Urban Studies and Planning dept., 1984—; Aspinall prof. Mesa Coll., Grand Junction, Colo., 1985; Banneker prof. George Washington U., Washington, 1987. Bd. dirs., treas. Historic Preservation League Oreg., Portland, 1980-84; bd. dirs. Ctr. Urban Edn., Portland, 1987-88. Club: City (Portland). Office: Portland State U Portland OR 97207

ABBOTT, CHARLES FAVOUR, JR., lawyer; b. Sedro-Woolley, Wash., Oct. 12, 1937; s. Charles Favour and Violette Doris (Boulter) A.; m. Oranee Harward Sept. 19, 1958; children: Patricia, Stephen, Nelson, Cynthia, Lisa, Alyson. BA in Econs., U. Wash., 1959, JD, 1962. Bar: Calif. 1962, Utah 1981. Law clk. Judge M. Oliver Koelsch, U.S. Ct. Appeals (9th cir.), San Francisco, 1963; assoc. Jones, Hatfield & Abbott, Escondido, Calif., 1964; sole practice, Escondido, 1964-77; of counsel Meuller & Abbott, Escondido, 1977—; ptnr. Abbott, Thorn & Hill, Provo, Utah, 1981-83; sole practice, Provo, Utah, 1983—. Mem. Utah Bar Assn., Calif. Bar Assn., Assn. Trial Lawyers Am. Mem. Ch. of Jesus Christ of Latter Day Saints. Editorial bd. Wash. Law Rev. and State Bar Assn. Jour., 1961-62; author: How to Do Your Own Legal Work, 1976, 2d edit., 1981, How to Win in Small Claims Court, 1981, How to be Free of Debt in 24 Hours, 1981, How to Hire the Best Lawyer at the Lowest Fee, 1981, The Lawyers' Inside Method of Making Money, 1979, The Millionaire Mindset, 1987, How to Make Big Money in the Next 30 Days, 1989; contbr. articles to profl. jours. Home: 3737 Foothill Dr Provo UT 84604

ABBOTT, JOHN RODGER, electrical engineer; b. Los Angeles, Aug. 2, 1933; s. Carl Raymond and Helen Catherine (Roche) A.; B.S. with honors, UCLA, 1955; M.S., U. So. Calif., 1957; m. Theresa Andrea McQuaide, Apr. 20, 1968. Advanced study engr. Lockheed Missile Systems, Los Angeles, 1955-56; radar systems engr. Hughes Aircraft Co., Los Angeles, 1956-59; devel. engr. Garrett Airesearch Co., Los Angeles, 1959-63, instr. plant tng. program, 1962-63; asst. project engr. Litton Industries, Los Angeles, 1963; space power systems engr. TRW Systems, Los Angeles, 1963-65; engr. specialist Los Angeles Dept. Water and Power, 1965—; frequency coordination chmn. Region X, Utilities Telecommunications Council, 1977-79, sec.-treas. Utilities Telecommunication Council, 1979-80; instr. electronics course Los Angeles City Schs., 1965-66, Birmingham High Sch., Van Nuys, Calif. Registered profl. engr., Calif. Mem. IEEE, Am. Radio Relay League (Pub. Service award 1971), Tau Beta Pi. Contbr. articles to profl. jours. Office: PO Box 71 Cambria CA 93428

ABBOTT, MARLENE LOUISE, nursing agency administrator; b. Hornell, N.Y., Aug. 11, 1935; d. George Wilfred and Eloise Lois (Simpson) Little; m. Robert Leroy, Mar. 16, 1953; children: Valarie, Kimberley, Steven, Tracey. AAS in Nursing, Corning Community Coll., 1968; BSN, Ariz. State U., 1984. Registered psychiatric community mental health nurse. R.N. ICU-CCU Arnot-Ogden Hosp., Elmira, N.Y., 1968-70, Good Samaritan Hosp., Phoenix, 1972-73; R.N. Scottsdale (Ariz.) Meml. Hosp., 1973-74; inservice dir. Mohave Gen. Hosp., Kingman, Ariz., 1974-75; school nurse Manzanita Elem. Sch., Kingman, 1975-77; R.N. staff surgical VA Med. Ctr., Phoenix, 1979-83; R.N. med., surgical Humana Hosp., Phoenix, 1983-84; R.N. psychiatric staff Camelback Hosp., Phoenix, 1984-86; owner, adminstr. Tri-Nursing, Inc., Phoenix, 1986—; bd. dirs. Career One/Ariz. Coll., Phoenix, 1987—. Precinct committee person Dem. Party, Phoenix, 1984—. Mem. Am. Nurses' Assn., Psychiatric Nurses' Assn., Nat. Nurses in Bus. Assn., Ariz. Assn. Health Care Agencies (pres. 1988-89). Office: Tri Nursing Inc 1901 W Earll Dr #1 Phoenix AZ 85015

ABBOTT, PATTI MARIE, teacher; b. Lewistown, Mont., Mar. 15, 1942; d. Vernal Hall and Marquerite (Cowen) A. BS, Eastern Mont. Coll., 1963, MS, 1968; postgrad. in adminstrn., Mont. State U., 1980. Tchr. Sch. Dist. No. 1, Glendive, Mont., 1964; tchr. Billings (Mont.) Pub. Schs., 1964—, pub. rels. rep., 1983-87. Contbr. articles to profl. jours. Resource person Girl Scouts U.S.A., Billings, 1973—, cadet leader, 1976-79; resource person Campfire Girls, Billings, 1978—; vol. Heart Fund, Am. Cancer Soc., Birth Defects Found., 1976—. Named Tchr. of Yr., Masonic Order, Billings, 1985, 86. Mem. NEA, Am. Bus. Womens Assn. (pres. Billings 1980-82, Woman of Yr. award 1980), AAUW (sec. Billings 1985-87, scholar 1987), Sweet Adlines (v.p. Billings 1981-83), Alpha Delta Kappa (internat. exec. bd., grand historian, grand v.p. 1983—), Harmony Club (pres. 1986-87), Rebeccas, Eagles. Home: 701 Torch Dr Billings MT 59102 Office: Sch Dist No 2 101 10th St W Billings MT 59102

ABBOTT, ROBERT CARL, management company executive; b. Riverside, Calif., Oct. 20, 1955; s. Orville Hancock and Erna Adella (Sparber) Whitney; m. Diane Alicia Sallstrom, Aug. 5, 1978; children: Ryan Christian, Aaron Matthew, Kalen James. Ordained to ministry Calvary Grace Christian, 1976; firefighter, Wash., Emergency Med. Tech., first aid instr. and survival instr. Affirmative action officer State of Wash., Spokane, Wash., 1976-77; personnel supr. Key Tronic Corp., Spokane, 1977-80; personnel mgr. ISC Systems Corp., Spokane, 1980-84; fire chief Millwood Fire Dept., Millwood, Wash., 1982-88; pres. and chief exec. officer Total Mgmt. Systems, Inc., Millwood, 1984-88; gen. mgr. Ptarmigan Village, Whitefish, Mont., 1988--; bd. dirs. Jans Touch, Hayden Lake, Idaho, Air Quality Labs, Spokane; pres. IEESA, Spokane; cons. Total Mgmt. Systems, Spokane. Mem. Gov's. Com. of Veteran Bus., Wash., 1983-84; bd. dirs. Life Outreach, Outdoor Youth Leadership, Spokane, 1976--. Named Most Influential for the Year, Millwood Fire Dept., 1984. Mem. Am. Soc. Personnel Adminstr., Am. Comp. Assn., Millwood Fire Assn., Inland Empire Emergency Svcs. Assn. (pres.). Christian. Home: PO Box 4092 Whitefish MT 59937 Office: Ptarmigan Village 3000 Big Mt Rd Whitefish MT 59937

ABBOTT, RUSSELL J., computer science educator; b. Bklyn., Mar. 1, 1942; s. Samuel and Lillian (Ginsberg) A.; m. Gail Ann Whitley, May 6, 1981; children: Michael Cole, Julian Carey, Danielle Lynn. BA, Columbia U., 1962; MA, Harvard U., 1963; PhD, U. So. Calif., 1973. Researcher The Aerospace Corp., El Segundo, Calif., 1978-84, 87—; prof. computer sci. Calif. State U.-Northridge, 1973-84, Calif. State U.-L.A., 1987—; chief scientist Silogic, Inc., L.A., 1984-87. Author: An Integrated Approach to Software Development, 1986; contbr. articles to profl. jours. Mem. ACM, IEEE, Assn. for Auto Reasoning, Cognitive Sci. Soc., Assn. for Computational Linguistics, Am. Assn. for Artificial Intelligence. Office: Calif State U Dept Math & Computer Sci 5151 State University Dr Los Angeles CA 90032

ABBOTT, SCOTT ROBERT, musician, music writer; b. Mpls., Sept. 30, 1961; s. Robert Franklin and Juanita Darlene (Debord) A. BA in Psychology, So. Calif. Coll., Costa Mesa, 1983. Pres. Periferal Vision Music Prodns., Orangevale, Calif., 1986—; profl. studio singer. Songwriter: (album) One Day, 1986. Named Teen Talent Nat. Vocal Winner, Assemblies of God Ch., 1979. Republican. Assemblies of God.

ABBOTT, WALTER FREDERICK, management consultant; b. Detroit, Aug. 11, 1937; s. Lawrence Frederick and Kathleen Margaret (Mulligan) A.; m. Susan Ann King, Nov. 10, 1979. BS, St. Joseph's Coll., Rensslaer, Ind., 1967. Sales rep. Am. Airlines, L.A., 1959-64; v.p. Careers, Inc., N.Y.C., 1964-71; dep. dir. Peace Corps, Washington, 1971-73; pres. Abbott-Bowe & Co., Inc., San Francisco, 1973-83; sr. v.p. Houze, Shourds & Montgomery, Inc., Rolling Hills, Calif., 1983-87; prin. W.F. Abbott & Co., San Diego, 1987—; bd. dirs. Computer Careers, Inc., Orange County, Calif.; guest lectr. U. Md., College Park, 1971-72. Fund raiser Am. Cancer Assn., San Diego, 1988. Mem. Am. Electronics Assn., San Francisco C. of C. Republican. Roman Catholic. Home: 2122 San Jose Ave Alameda CA 94501 Office: WF Abbott & Co 11545 W Bernardo Ct San Diego CA 92128

ABBREDERIS, DALE EDWARD, insurance company executive; b. Milw., May 5, 1957; s. Edward E. and Jeanette R. (Jach) A.; m. Lucille Andersen, Dec. 26, 1987. BBA, U. Wis., 1979. CPA, Wis. Staff acct. Touche Ross & Co., Milw., 1979-80, sr. acct., 1980-82; sr. auditor Armco Ins. Group, Milw., 1982, supervising auditor, 1982-84, mgr. internal auditing, 1984-85; mgr. corp. audit services Unigard Ins. Group, Bellevue, Wash., 1985-88; v.p. personal lines Unigard Ins. Group, Bellevue, 1988—. Mem. Ins. Acctg. Statis. Assn. (pres. elect 1987-88, pres. 1988-89, v.p. 1985-87), Wash. Soc. CPA (mem. ins. com. 1985-87, student rels. com. 1987-88), Wis. Inst. CPA (mem. svc. com. 1982-85), Am. Inst. CPAs, Bellevue Athletic Club, Downtown Club (Milw.). Office: Unigard Ins Group 15805 NE 24th St Bellevue WA 98008

ABBRUZZESE, CARLO ENRICO, physician, writer; b. Rome, Italy, May 28, 1923; s. Aurelio and Maria (Sbriccoli) A.; Liceo-Ginnasio Dante Alighieri, Roma, 1935-43; Facoltà di Medicina e Chirurgia, Università di Roma, 1943-49; m. Jovanka N. Vasin, Feb. 14, 1976; children by previous marriage—Marco A., Carlo M., Eric L., Christopher E. Came to U.S., 1951, naturalized, 1959. Resident in tropical subtropical diseases U. Rome, 1950-51; intern Woman's and Highland Park Gen. hosps., Detroit, 1951-53; resident in family practice Saratoga Gen. Hosp., Detroit, Columbus Hosp., Newark, 1953-57; gen. practice occupational and sport medicine, Rome, 1949-51, Oakland, Calif., 1958-75, Santa Ana, Calif., 1975-84; dir. emergency and outpatients depts. Drs. Hosp. of Santa Ana (Calif.), 1975-77. Founder, leader polit. youth movements, Rome, 1943-47. Co-founder, nat. chmn. divorce reforms orgns., 1975; UN rep. on domestic human rights, 1977. Decorated Commendatore di Merito, 1950. Fulbright fellow, 1951-53. Fellow Am. Acad. Family Physicians; mem. Am. Acad. Gen. Practice, Ordine dei Medici di Roma Società Italiana di Chirurgia, Am. Coll. Emergency Physicians, Union Am. Physicians. Author: Storia della Psicologia, 1949; L'ascoltazione stetoscopica, 1955, 56, 83, 86; Esercitazioni di diagnostica ascoltatoria, 1983, 86; founder, pub., editor-in-chief ESDNA, Rome, 1983, ESDI, Rome, 1986; pub. Med. Newsletter, 1987. Contbr. articles to profl. jours. Office: 316 N Bristol St Santa Ana CA 92703

ABDEEN, ADNAN MUHAMMAD, accounting educator, researcher, consultant; b. Damascus, Syria, July 20, 1935; came to U.S., 1960; s. Hamdi and Kother (Darcazallie) A.; m. Paulette Cox, Aug. 30, 1963 (div. 1967); 1 child, Eddie; m. Barkuzan Darcazallie, Feb. 25, 1968; children: Omaran, Hanan. BS in Acctg., U. So. Miss., 1963, MBA, 1965; DBA, Miss. State U., 1974. CPA, Tenn. Mem. jr. staff Peat Marwick, CPA's, Atlanta, 1962-63; asst. prof. acctg. U. Tenn., Chattanooga, 1965-72; assoc. prof. U. Tenn., 1974-75; asst. prof. acctg. West Ga. Coll., Carollton, 1972-74; assoc. prof. acctg. U. Petroleum and Minerals, Dhahran, Saudi Arabia, 1975-86, Calif. State U., L.A., 1986—; cons. Heritage Quilt, Inc., Rossville, Ga., 1970-72. Author: English Arabic Dictionary of Computer Terms, 1979, English-Arabic Dictionary of Accounting and Finance, 1981, (with Dale Shook) The Saudi Financial System, 1984, (with John Meredith) Payroll Accounting in Saudi Arabia, 1986, (with Muhammad AlBuraey) Management in the Islamic Heritage, Vol. 1, 1987; contbr. articles to profl. jours. Mem. Tenn. Soc. CPA's, Nat. Assn. Accts., Am. Acctg. Assn. Muslim. Home: 1515 S Gide Ct Diamond Bar CA 91765 Office: Calif State U 5151 State University Dr Los Angeles CA 90032

ABDULAZIZ, SAM K., lawyer; b. Bagdad, Iraq, Apr. 10, 1939; came to U.S., 1946; s. Joseph S. Abdulaziz and Rachel J. Hawa; m. Joyce Joan; children: Michael Joseph, Deborah Ann. BBA, UCLA, 1962; JD, Loyola U., Los Angeles, 1971. Calif. 1972, U.S. Supreme Ct. 1981. Author: Contractors Guide to the Contractors Board Citation Procedure, 1974, Construction Law, 1985; contbr. chpt. California Administrative Practice Guide Covering Constractors. Mem. Los Angeles County Bar Assn. (Lawyer of Yr. award Constl. Rights Found. 1977). Office: Abdulaziz & Grossbart 6454 Coldwater Canyon North Hollywood CA 91606

ABDUL-JABBAR, KAREEM (LEWIS FERDINAND ALCINDOR), former professional basketball player; b. N.Y.C., Apr. 16, 1947; s. Ferdinand Lewis and Cora Alcindor; m. Habiba (Janice Brown), 1971 (div. 1973); children: Habiba, Kareem, Sultana, Amir. B.A., UCLA, 1969. Basketball player with Milw. Bucks, 1969-75, Los Angeles Lakers, 1975-89. Became NBA all-time leading scorer, 1984; appeared on TV in episodes of Mannix, The Man from Atlantis, Diff'rent Strokes, Tales from the Darkside, Pryor's Place, The ABC Afterschool Spl.; appeared in movies: The Fish that Saved Pittsburgh, 1979, Airplane, 1980, Fletch, 1985; author: (with Peter Knobler) Giant Steps: An Autobiography of Kareem Abdul-Jabbar, 1983. Named Rookie of Year NBA, 1970; recipient Maurice Podoloff Cup; named Most Valuable Player NBA, 1971, 72, 74, 76, 77, 80; player NBA All-Star game, 1970-87, 89; named to NBA 35th Anniversary All-Time Team, 1980; NBA Playoff Most Valuable Player, 1971, 85; mem. NBA Championship Team, 1971, 80, 82, 85, 87, 88, NCAA Championship Team, 1967, 68, 69; named NCAA Tournament Most Outstanding Player, 1967, 68, 69. Muslim. Office: care Los Angeles Lakers The Forum PO Box 10 Inglewood CA 90306 *

ABEJO, SISTER MARIA ROSALINA, nun; b. Tagoloan, Philippines, July 13, 1922; came to U.S., 1977, 1985; d. Don Pedro Abejo y Villegas and Dona Beatriz Zamarro de Abejo. AA in Music, St. Scholastica's Coll., Manila, 1949; MusB, Philippine Womens U., 1956, MusM, 1958; postgrad., Cath. U. Am., 1962-64; postrad. studies in theory and composition, Eastman Sch. Music, 1962; studies with, Fritz Mahler, N.Y.C., summers 1964, 65, 68, Maestro Franco Ferrara, Rome, 1972-75. Dean Lourdes Coll., Manila, 1958-61, Immaculate Coll., Manila, 1961-62, St. Mary's Coll., Manila, 1964-76; music dir. Holy Spirit Ch., Fremont, Calif., 1978-82, St. Leonard's Ch., Fremont, 1982—; sec. Nat. Liturgical Commn. Sacred Music, Manila, 1964-76; rep. Cath. ch. Ecumenical Council Chs., Manila, 1966-76; founder, dir., conductor Nuns Concerts For Charities, 1967-76; lectr. music Kans. U., Lawrence, 1977-79, Consular Wives and All Nations Group, San Francisco, 1980-82; faculty dir. Schola Cantroum & Seminarians Glee Club St. Pius X Sem., Covington, Ky., 1978-79; founder, dir., conductor Ars Nova Symphony Orchestra and Ars Nova Concert Chorus, Fremont, 1979—; cultural officer U.N. Assn., Manila, 1967-77, Dr. J.P. Rizal Found., MacArthur Found.; del. music convs., assemblies to Russia, Poland, Hungary, Czechoslovakia, Europe, U.S.A. Composer: Why Should We Weep So, 1968, First Oratorio in Pilipino, 1969, Ode to the Statesmen, 1971, Guerilla Symphony, 1971, Onward Ye Women, 1975, Death and Victory, 1976, Loops Circles & Squares, 1979, Five Wedding Songs, 1983, Surge of the Fair Sex, 1984, Explosion of the Pyramids, 1985, Brotherhood Symphony and Muslim Diver, 1986, The Mutiny and The Woman: Bloodless Revolution, 1987, over 500 others; commd. works include: The Conversion of King Humabon, 1967, Panahon, 1969, Fanfare For 8 Instruments, 1970, Overture 1081, 1972, (ballet) The Ritual, 1976, Eternal Memory, 1978, Strings on the Dignity of Man, 1980, Jubilee Cantata, 1984, The Absent Baritone, 1985; various compositions recorded on discs and tapes; author: (textbooks) Learning To Read and Write Music, Music for Philippine High Schools, Kantahin Pilipino, Our

Own Choruses; commd compositions: Iberian Promenade, 1980, Hold High The Torch, 1981, Dithyrambic Strings for Gen. C.P. Romulo, 1982, Jubilee Symphoney, 1984, Symphony of Psalms, 1988, Genesis, 1986, World Premiere the Mutiny and the Woman, 1987, Symphony of Life, 1988, Dance of Adam and Eve, 1989, The Bridges of Fremont, 1989, Symphony of Fortitude and Sudden Spring, 1989; other works include Vespers in a Convent Garden, 1957, Advent Cantata, 1957, Thirteen Variations for Two Pianos, 1957, Three String Quartets, 1958, Piano Pieces, 1959-60, Bank Marches for World Pres., 1961-62, Pope VI Pontifical March, 1964, Lut Us Play The Piano, 1965, Recuerdos De Manila, Blood Compact, 1966, The Conversion of King Humabon, (Philippine Rep. Cultural Heritage award), 1967, Why Shouls We Weep, 1968, Filipiniana, 1969. Recipient numerous awards including: Republic Heritate award, Govt. of Manila, 1967, U.N. award, 1972, Pontifical Plaque of Recognition, 1972, Plaque of Recognition Zonta, 1973, Dr. J.P. Rizal-MacArthur award, 1974, Internat. Womens award In Womens Yr., 1975, Bay Area Recognition plaque, 1984, Philippine Consulate Gen. Recognition Plaque, 1984; Contbg.-Activities-Participating-Achievement Internat. award Philippine Women's Univ. Centennial Celebration, 1986. Mem. Conductors Assn. (v.p.), League of Filipino Composers (sec.-treas. 1966-77), Internat. Music Council (bd. dirs.), Internat. Soc. Music Edn., League of Asian Composers. Home and Office: 37950 #62 Fremont Blvd Fremont CA 94536

ABEL, ALLAN BERNARD, management consultant; b. Williams, Calif., Dec. 22, 1924; s. Allen and Consuelo (Benham) A.; student U. Calif., Berkeley, 1943-50, Golden Gate Coll., 1947, Instituto Cultural Mexicano-Americano, Guadalajara, Mexico, 1961; m. Maria Socorro; children—Allan Bernard, Allen Raymond, Sonya. Practice in Reno, 1954-69, Las Vegas, 1969—; investment adviser, tax cons., rare coinbroker, 1963-67; asso., bus. cons. Bus. Consultants, Inc., bus. and mgmt. cons. in 11 Western states and Mexico, 1967—; pres. SUMCO, Inc.; officer, dir. Centro de Vivienda para Retirados, S.A., Abel de Mexico., S.A.; sec.-treas. Magic Valley Enterprises, Inc.; sec.-treas. Central Devel. Co., Las Vegas, also dir.; sec. Gastrox Constrn. Co., Las Vegas. Agt., Nev. Gaming Control Bd., Nev. Gaming Commn., 1956; dir. So. Nev. conf. Pop Warner Jr. Football, 1st v.p., 1981—; mem. nat. com. Young Democrats Clubs Am., 1955-57, bd. dirs., 1957-59; mem. exec. bd. Clark County Dem. Central Com., 1970—; mem. Nev. State Dem. State Central Com., 1970—, vice chmn., 1957-58; gen. mgr. retirement housing project, Mexico, 1965-67; pres. chpt. 15 Mother Earth News; state chmn. com. select del. Humphrey; chmn. Lucy Branch Kidney Fund; counselor Family Abuse Center; pres. Flame Soccer Club; dir. Las. Las Vegas Under 23 Select Soccer Team; Lic. pub. accountant, Nev. Mem. Nat. Soc. Pub. Accountants, U. Calif. Alumni Assn. (life), Inst. Indsl. Relations Alumni Assn., Internat. Platform Assn., Am. Numis. Assn. Democrat. Spaceite. Clubs: Calif. 23 (Berkeley); Tower and Flame, Daily Californian, Am. Soc. Jalisco. Pub.: Nev. Report. Research on problems of aged living in fgn. country, 1963-64. Home: 900 Antonio Dr Las Vegas NV 89107 Office: 3540 W Sahara Ste 298 Las Vegas NV 89104

ABEL, RICHARD WAYNE, marketing communications consultant; b. San Luis Obispo, Calif., July 4, 1941; s. John William and Olive Mae (Bickmore) A. B.F.A., Cornell U., 1963; M.F.A., U. Hawaii, 1966. Advt. trainee Persons Advt., N.Y.C., 1963-64; campaign dir. Am. Cancer Soc., San Francisco, 1966-67; instr. theatre Occidental Coll., Los Angeles, 1967-69; pres., owner COMM/COORD, Los Angeles, 1969-72; dir. communications TRAN Corp., El Segundo, Calif., 1972-74; communications cons., Laguna Beach, Calif., 1974-84; founder Accomplishmence Systems & Cons., Inc., San Juan Capistrano, Calif., 1984—, also pres., Opera Pacific, also bd. dirs. and strategic planning com. Co-founder Nautical Heritage Mus.; founder Heritage Players; founder, capt. Californian, Ofcl. Tallship Ambassador State of Calif. Address: 3531 Calle La Quinta San Clemente CA 92672 Office: Accomplishmence Systems & Cons Inc 27292 Calle Arroyo San Juan Capistrano CA 92675

ABELL, LINDA JACOBS, accountant, oil and gas landman; b. Thermopolis, Wyo., July 20, 1946; d. Leonard T. and Isabel (Toth) Jacobs; m. Robert A. Wyss, Aug. 3, 1968 (div. Mar. 1980); children: Kenneth Franklin, Curtis Dean, Jon Cordell; m. Stanton Janney Abell, Jr., Dec. 31, 1984. Student, Ea. Mont. Coll., 1964-66, N.W. Community Coll., Powell, Wyo., 1967; student acctg.-bus. law, U. Wyo. Acct. Empire State Oil Co., Thermopolis, 1964-72; cons. Ashland (Ky.) Oil, Inc., 1972-73; prodn. acct. Husky Oil Co., Cody, Wyo., 1972-73; acct., adminstrv. mgr. Christler Flying Svc., Inc., Thermopolis, 1973-74; pub. acct. C.E. Hale, Pub. Acct., Thermopolis, 1975-76; asst. sec.-treas., adminstrv. mgr. Natural Gas Processing Co., Worland, Wyo., 1976-84; adminstrv. asst., oil and gas landman Washakie Oil Co., Worland, 1984-87; sec.-treas. Jacobs Energy Corp./Jedi Oil & Gas Co., Worland, 1987—. Mem. Am. Assn. Petroleum Landmen, Petroleum Accts. Soc., Desk and Derrick Clubs Am., NAFE, Nat. Arbor Day Found., Washakie Humane Soc., Jobs Daughters (life), Beta Sigma Phi. Democrat. Episcopalian. Home: 3012 Columbine Ln Worland WY 82401 Office: JEDI Oil and Gas Co PO Box 261 Worland WY 82401

ABELS, ROBERT FREDERICK, tax consultant; b. West Palm Beach, Fla., Nov. 18, 1926; s. John Frederick and Nelly (Bulfin) A.; m. Shirley Mae Larsen, May 31, 1953; children: Robert Frederick, Steven John, Richard Alan. BS, U.S. Naval Acad., 1965, postgrad., 1965; MBA in Finance, U. West Fla., 1971. Enlisted USN, 1944, commd. ensign, 1949, advanced through grades to comdr., 1963, aviator in Korea and Vietnam; dir. Naval Officer Candidate Sch. USN, Pensacola, Fla., 1966-68; ret. USN, 1969; tchr. math. and bus. Skyline High Sch., Lemon Grove, Calif., 1971-83; tax counselor, real estate salesman. Decorated Bronze Star, Air medal, Commendation medal; Vietnamese Cross Gallantry. Mem. Nat. Assn. Enrolled Agts., Inland Soc. Tax. Cons., Nat. Assn. Tax Consultors. Republican. Lutheran. Office: 10257 Caminito Covewood San Diego CA 92131

ABERBACH, JOEL DAVID, political science educator, author; b. New York City, June 19, 1940; s. Isidore and Miriam (Meltzer) A.; m. Joan F. Gross, June 17, 1962; Children: Ian Mark, Amy Joyce, Matthew Daniel, Rachel Ann. AB, Cornell U., 1961; MA, Ohio State U., 1963, Yale U., 1965; PhD, Yale U., 1967. Asst. prof. U. Mich., Ann Arbor, 1967-72; research scientist U. Mich., 1967-88, assoc. prof., 1972-78, prof., 1978-88; sr. fellow Brookings Inst., Washington, 1977-80; dir. Ctr. for Am. Politics and Pub. Policy, UCLA, 1988; prof. UCLA, 1986—; cons. Commn. on the Op. of the Senate, Washington, 1976, U.S. Office of Personnel Mgmt., Washington, 1983, Nat. Pub. Radio, Washington, 1983-84. Co-Author: Bureaucrats and Politicans in Western Democracies, 1981. Del. Mich. Dem. Conv., Detroit, 1972; editorial bd. Congress and the Presidency, Washington, 1981—, Governance, Oxford, Eng., 1987—. Research grantee Nat. Sci. Found., Washington, 1969-73, 1978-81, 1986-89. Fellow Brookings Inst., Ctr. for Advanced Study in the Behavioral Scis; mem. Am. Polit. Sci. Assn., Am. Sociol. Assn., Research Comm. on the Structure and Orgn. of Govt. Internat. Polit. Sci. Assn. (exec. bd., sec., treas. 1986—), Phi Beta Kappa . Jewish. Home: 10453 Colina Way Los Angeles CA 90077 Office: UCLA 4289 Buche Hall Los Angeles CA 90024

ABLES, ERNEST DAVID, wildlife educator; b. Hugo, Okla., Jan. 13, 1934; s. Ernest Elmer and Annie Mae (Cooper) A.; m. Juanita Covington, Aug. 21, 1960; children: Christopher David, Brian Allen. BS in Zoology, Okla. State U., 1961; MS in Wildlife Mgmt., U. Wis., 1964, PhD in Zoology and Wildlife, 1968. Asst. prof. Tex. A&M U., College Station, 1968-71, assoc. prof., 1971-73; prof. wildlife U. Idaho, Moscow, 1973—, assoc. dean coll. forestry, 1974-82, head dept. wildlife, 1982—, acting dean coll. forestry, 1984-85. Author/editor Axis Deer in Texas, 1977 (pub. award 1977). Served with U.S. Army, 1954-57. Recipient Outstanding Tchr. award Coll. Forestry U. Idaho, 1973, Disting. Faculty award U. Idaho, 1983, Alumni award for Excellence, U. Idaho, 1982. Mem. The Wildlife Soc. (cert.), The Wilderness Soc. Democrat. Baptist. Home: Rte 1 Box 101 Troy ID 83871 Office: U Idaho Coll Forestry Moscow ID 83843

ABOOD, RICHARD R., pharmacy educator; b. Kearney, Nebr., Nov. 26, 1948; s. Roy S. and Doris E. (George) A.; m. Jeri L. Bigbee, Jan. 2, 1983; children: Aaron, Meredith. BS in Pharmacy, U. Nebr., 1972, JD, 1976. Registered pharmacist; Bar: Nebr. Pharmacist OSCO Drug, Waterloo, Iowa, 1972-73, Bryan Meml. Hosp., Lincoln, Nebr., 1973-75, K-Ray Pharmacy, Lincoln, 1973-76; asst. prof. pharmacy U. Wyo., Laramie, 1976-82, assoc. prof. pharmacy, 1982-89, prof., 1989—; exec. dir. Wyo. Pharm. Assn., Laramie, Wyo., 1984—; cons. to state and nat. pharmacy orgns., 1979—. Contbr. articles to profl. jours. Pres. Neighborhood Tree Area Assn., Laramie, 1984—; mem. Trees for Laramie, 1986—. Named Nat. Council State Pharm. Assn. Execs. grantee, 1983, Wyo. Dept. Health and Social Services grantee, 1988. Mem. NARD, Am. Pharm. Assn., Nat. Health Lawyers Assn., Wyo. Pharm. Assn. Democrat. Home: 1115 E Custer Laramie WY 82070 Office: U Wyo Box 3375 University Station Laramie WY 82071

ABOUD, KATHY ELAINE, restaurant owner; b. Winnemucca, Nev., Feb. 22, 1959; d. Jay Woodruff and Anna Bell (Smith) A.; m. David Braheem Aboud, July 22, 1977; children: Rose Anna, Abraham Alexander. Grad. high sch., Winnemuca, Nev. Owner, cook The Griddle, Winnemucca, 1977—. Republican. Home: 1840 Mizpah St Winnemucca NV 89445 Office: The Griddle 460 W Winnemucca Blvd Winnemucca NV 89445

ABOWD, ANTHONY MICHAEL, data processing consultant, financial consultant, educator; b. Detroit, Mar. 12, 1953; s. Richard George and Sara Abowd. B.A. in Econs., U. Notre Dame, 1974, M.A. in Econs., 1975; M.B.A. in Fin., U. Chgo., 1977, Ph.D. in Bus. Econs., 1983. Tech. cons. U. Notre Dame, U. Chgo., also other businesses, 1973-77; exec. asst. to assoc. v.p. U. Ill., 1977-80; mgr. expense control Carter Hawley Hale Stores, Los Angeles 1980-81; co-founder, ptnr. Data Strategies, Irvine, Calif., 1981—; speaker in field. Contbr. articles to profl. jours. Mem. Data Processing Mgmt. Assn., Computer Measurement Group. Clubs: Notre Dame (Ind.); U. Chgo. Grad. Sch. Bus. Office: Data Strategies 9 Aberdeen St Irvine CA 92720

ABRAHAM, KENNETH L., dentist; b. Albuquerque, Oct. 3, 1953; s. Jake and Birdye-Bonnie (Hawkinson) A.; m. Nona Christine Gottlieb; children: Kami Ashley, Koby Lee. BS, Creighton U., 1975, DDS, 1980. Heavy equipment operator Hamilton Constrn. Co., Jackpile, N.Mex., 1976-80; gen. practice dentistry Grants, N.Mex., 1980—. Mem. Greater Grants Rodeo Assn. Mem. ADA, N.Mex. Dental Assn., Northwest Dist. Dental Soc., Ducks Unltd., Grants C. of C. Republican. Roman Catholic. Lodge: Rotary. Home: 901 E Roosevelt Grants NM 87020

ABRAHAMS, JOSEPH ISAAC, psychiatrist; b. Dallas, Sept. 27, 1916; s. Harry George and Sarah (Galperin) A.; m. Apr. 20, 1948 (div. Nov. 1976); 1 child, Lisa Ann. MD, Emory U., 1939. Diplomate Am. Bd. Psychiatry and Neurology. Intern City Hosp., N.Y.C., 1939-41; resident in psychiatry St. Elizabeths Hosp., Washington, 1946-47, dir. group psychotherapy, 1947-50, cons., 1952-70; pvt. practice Washington, 1950-70, San Diego, 1970—; cons. fed. Prison Svc. NIMH, Washington, 1952-70, Bethesda (Md.) Naval Med. Svc., 1952-70, Mesa Vista Hosp., 1970-74. Organizer Workshop on County Polit. Orgn., San Diego, 1985; bd. dirs. San Diego County Dem. Cen. Com., 1988—. Capt. M.C., AUS, 1941-46. Recipient Plaque, St. Elizabeths Hosp., 1970. Fellow Am. Psychoanalytic Assn. (life), Am. Psychiat. Assn. (life); mem. San Diego Psychoanalytic Soc. (sec. 1974-75), San Diego Psychoanalytic Inst. (sr. faculty), Wash. Pschoanalytic Soc. Jewish. Office: Box 2077 La Jolla CA 92038

ABRAHAMSON, LARK ANNE, teacher; b. Salem, Oreg., Mar. 15, 1952; d. Stanton Walter and Joan Myrtle (Larson) Zelmer; m. Melvin John Abrahamson, Oct. 6, 1972; children: Melanie Megan, Grant Matthew. BS, Western Oreg. State U., Monmouth, 1975. Recreation dir. City of Salem Parks and Recreation, 1975-76; tchr. Pratum Pub. Sch., Salem, 1976-83, N. Santiam Sch., Aumsville, Oreg., 1983-84; tchr. 2d grade Salem Pub. Schs., 1985—. Mem. LWV (v.p. 1986-88), Oreg. Edn. Assn., Salem Edn. Assn., Salem Jr. Women's Club (edn. chmn. 1982-84), Salem Home Bldrs. Aux. (edn. chmn. 1986-87), Middle Grove Sch. PTA.

ABRAMOVICE, BEN, hospital administrator; b. Chgo., Dec. 12, 1932; s. Norman Wolfe and Rose (Kushner) A. AB in Zoology, U. Calif.-Berkeley, 1954; MBA, U. Chgo., 1960; PhD, Coll. of the Pacific. Adminstrv. asst. Ohio State U. Med. Ctr., Columbus, 1959-61; asst. dir. Jewish Home for Aged, San Francisco, 1961-66; adminstr. Parkland Convalescent Hosp., San Leandro, Calif., 1966-69; dir. planning and devel. Jewish Welfare Fedn., Oakland, Calif., 1969-71; exec. dir. Home for Jewish Parents, Oakland, 1971-81; exec. adminstr. Laguna Honda Hosp., San Francisco, 1981-86; policy scholar Inst. Health & Aging, 1986—; mem. White House Conf. on Aging; instr. Golden Gate U.; lectr.; mem. Jewish Commn. on Aging., Bd. Examiners Nursing Home Adminstrs. State of Calif., numerous panels on long term care. Contbr. articles to profl. jours.; author video and films. Bd. dirs. Berkeley Law Found.; bd. dirs City Art Celebration, San Francisco. Served with U.S. Army, 1956-58. Mem. Am. Assn. Homes for Aging (ho. of dels.), Western Gerontol. Soc. (past chmn. pub. policy and legis. action com.), Calif. Assn. Homes for Aging (pres. 1975-77 Pres.'s award of merit), Am. Hosp. Assn., Gerontol. Soc., Nat. Assn. Jewish Homes for Aging (dir., chmn. seminar). Office: Laguna Honda Hosp 375 Laguna Honda Blvd San Francisco CA 94116

ABRAMS, LOIS M., psychotherapist; b. Chgo., May 20, 1936; d. Charles and Florence (Goldstein) Gould; m. Herbert I. Abrams, Aug. 21, 1955; children: Floree Lucas, Mark Alan. BA, Pepperdine U., 1956; MA, Calif. State U., Long Beach, 1969; PhD, U.S. Internat. U., 1974. Pres. Calif. Assn. Marriage and Family Therapists, San Diego, 1980-81, pres. edn. found., 1981-82, fellow, 1982—, chairperson honors com., 1984-86; chairperson elections com. Am. Assn. Marriage and Family Therapists, Washington, 1983-85; bd. dirs. So. Calif. chpt. Am. Assn. Marriage and Family Therapists, Los Angeles, 1986—; sec. Abrams Devel. Inc., Los Alamitos, Calif., 1985—; cons. Interval House, Seal Beach, Calif., 1981—, Casa de Bienvenidos, Los Alamitos, 1982—, Hospice, Los Alamitos, 1983—; sec., bd. dirs. Abrams Devel. Inc., 1983—. Author: Humanizing Student-Teacher Relationship, 1974, The ABC's of Marriage, 1985. Chairperson Long Beach Heart Assn., 1984-85, Am. Cancer Soc., 1984-85; bd. dirs. United Way, Garden Grove, Calif., 1985—. Club: Old Ranch Tennis (Seal Beach). Home: Box 306 Surfside CA 90743 Office: Los Alamitos Counseling Ctr 10861 Cherry St 202 Los Alamitos CA 90720

ABRAMS, RICHARD LEE, physicist; b. Cleve., Apr. 20, 1941; s. Morris S. and Corinne (Tobias) A.; m. Jane Shack, Aug. 12, 1962; children: Elizabeth, Laura. B. Engring. Physics, Cornell U., Ithaca, N.Y., 1964, Ph.D., 1968. Mem. tech. staff Bell Telephone Labs., Whippany, N.J., 1968-71; sect. head Hughes Research Labs., Malibu, Calif., 1971-75, dept. mgr., 1975-83; chief scientist Space and Communications group Hughes Aircraft Co., El Segundo, Calif., 1983-89; chief scientist Hughes Rsch. Labs., Malibu, Calif., 1989—; program co-chmn. Conf. on Laser Engring. and Applications, Washington, 1979; chmn. Conf. on Lasers and Electro-Optics, Phoenix, 1982. Assoc. editor: Optics Letters, 1979-82; patentee in field. Fellow IEEE (assoc. editor Jour. Quantum Electronics 1980-83, centennial medal 1989), Optical Soc. Am. (bd. dirs. 1982-85, v.p. 1988, pres.-elect 1989); mem. IEEE Quantum Electronics and Applications Soc. (adminstrve. com. 1980-83, v.p. 1982, pres. 1983, bd. editors 1987-89), Tau Beta Pi, Phi Kappa Phi. Club: Riviera Country (Pacific Palisades, Calif.). Home: 922 Enchanted Way Pacific Palisades CA 90272

ABRAMSON, MARK JOSEPH, county official, data processing executive, consultant; b. Torrance, Calif., July 13, 1949; s. Harvey Stanley and Gladys (Kaufman) A.; m. Ilene Marcia Simons, Aug. 5, 1977; children: Elizabeth Jane, Daniel Kevin. BS, Calif. Inst. Tech., 1971; MEng, UCLA, 1984. Programmer Jet Propulsion Labs, Pasadena, Calif., 1971-72; systems analyst Bio Sci Labs, Van Nuys, Calif., 1972-77; sr. programmer and analyst Meml. Med. Ctr., Long Beach, Calif., 1977-84, mgr. systems applications, 1984-86; applications specialist Health Data Scis., San Bernardino, Calif., 1986-87; data processing specialist Los Angeles County, Downey, Calif., 1987—; cons. Control Data Inst. Los Angeles, 1979-86, Tandem Computers, Cupertino, Calif. 1986, Sci Applications Internat., San Diego, 1987—. Mem. Mumps Users Group, Calif. Inst. Tech. Alumni Assn., Riviera Country Club (Los Angeles). Office: County of Los Angeles Data Processing Dept 9150 E Imperial Hwy Downey CA 90242

ABRAMSON, MASON HARRY, pediatrician; b. Portland, Oreg., May 31, 1916; s. Philip and Sara (Tobias) A.; m. Beatric Aronson, June 10, 1939 (dec. 1956); m. Yvonne E. Stowell, June 17, 1956; children: Gerry, Mason, Elesa, David, Donald, Christopher, Joni, Marc. BA with distinction, Stanford (Calif.) U., 1937, MD, 1942. Intern Stanford Hosps., 1941-42, asst. resident in pediatrics, 1942-43; resident in communicable diseases San Francisco, 1943-44; pvt. practice Redwood City, Calif., 1946—; chmn. utilization rev. com. Sequoia Hosp., 1978—. Contbr. articles to profl. jours. Mem. San Mateo County Med. Soc., Calif. Med. Assn., Am. Pediatrics, Am. Acad. Pediatrics, Phi Beta Kappa, Alpha Omega Alpha, Sigma Xi. Democrat. Home: 3765 Country Club Dr Redwood City CA 94061 Office: 155 Birch St Redwood City CA 94062

ABRAMSON, TREVA THOMASSON, teacher; b. Midland, Tex., Nov. 26, 1931; d. Wilford Winn and MayLarue (Harp) Thomasson; m. Walter Leroy Hulen, June 16, 1950 (div. Nov. 1960); children: Sandra Lee Kaufmann, Julie Kathleen Wheeler; m. Bernard G. Abramson, Aug. 10, 1963 (div. Aug. 1978); 1 child, David M. BS, U. Tex. (name formerly Tex. Western Coll.), El Paso, 1962; MA, Ariz. State U., 1969. Tchr. El Paso Pub. Schs., 1962-63, Scottsdale (Ariz.) Pub. Schs., 1966—. Bd. dirs. 1st Ch. Christ Scientist, Scottsdale, 1986—; tchr. Adventure Unltd. Ranches, Buena Vista, Colo., 1980, 84, 85, 87. Mem. Ariz. Assn. Tchrs Math., Ariz. Reading Tchrs., Ariz. Assn. for Learning about Environ. (com.), Scottsdale Edn. Assn. (sec., treas. 1987-88), Ariz. Sci. Tchrs. Assn., Phi Delta Kappa. Republican. Club: Principia (Phoenix) (treas. 1976-87, pres. 1974-75). Home: 8555 E Rose Ln Scottsdale AZ 85253

ABRAVANEL, ALLAN RAY, lawyer; b. N.Y.C., Mar. 11, 1947; s. Leon and Sydelle (Berenson) A.; m. Susan Ava Paikin, Dec. 28, 1971; children: Karen, David. BA magna cum laude, Yale U., 1968; JD cum laude, Harvard U., 1971. Bar: N.Y. 1972, Oreg. 1976. Assoc. Paul, Weiss, Rifkind, Wharton & Garrison, N.Y.C., 1971-72, 74-76; fellow Internat. Legal Ctr., Lima, Peru, 1972-74; from assoc. to ptnr. Stoel, Rives, Boley, Fraser & Wyse, Portland, Oreg., 1976-83; ptnr. Perkins Coie, Portland, 1983—. Mem. ABA, Inter-Am. Bar Assn., Phi Beta Kappa. Office: Perkins Coie 111 SW 5th Ave Portland OR 97204

ABRUMS, JOHN DENISE, internist; b. Trinidad, Colo., Sept. 20, 1923; s. Horatio Ely and Clara (Apfel) A.; m. Annie Louise Manning, June 15, 1947; children: Louanne C. Abrums Sargent, John Ely. BA, U. Colo., 1944; MD, U. Colo., Denver, 1947. Diplomate Am. Bd. Internal Medicine. Intern Wisc. Gen. Hosp., Madison, 1947-48; resident in internal medicine VA Hosp., Albuquerque, 1949-52, attending physician, 1956-80; mem. staff Presbyn. Hosp. Ctr., Albuquerque; cons. staff physician St. Joseph Hosp., Albuquerque, 1957—; attending physician U. N.Mex. Hosp. (formerly Bernalillo County Med. Ctr.), Albuquerque, 1954—; cons. physician A.T. & S.F. Meml. Hosp., Albuquerque, 1957-83; clin. assoc. in medicine U. N.Mex. Bd. dirs. Blue Cross/Blue Shield, 1962-76. Fellow ACP (life), AMA, Am. Soc. Internal Medicine (trustee 1976-82, pres. 1983-84), N.Mex. Soc. Internal Medicine (pres. 1962-64), N.Mex. Med. Soc. (pres. 1980-81), Nat. Acads. Practice (disting. practitioner), Albuquerque and Bernalillo County Med. Assn. (bd. govs. 1959-61, chmn. pub. rels. com. 1959-61), Am. Geriatric Soc. Brig. gen. M.C., U.S. Army, ret. Republican. Episcopalian. Office: N Mex Med Group PC 717 Encino Pl NE Encino Medical Pla Albuquerque NM 87102

ABRUNZO, VICTOR DANIEL, JR., finance company executive; b. Teaneck, N.J., Dec. 28, 1946; s. Victor Daniel and Jane Aline (Bates) A. BS, Fairfield U., 1970; MBA, Golden Gate U., 1972; postgrad., U. San Francisco, 1976; JD, Golden Gate U., 1980. Bar: Calif. 1982, U.S. Dist. Ct. (no. dist.) Calif. 1982. Sch. adminstr. Fairfield-Suisun U. San Diego, 1972-78; estate adminstr. bankruptcy U.S. Cts., Oakland, Calif., 1982-83; bankruptcy analyst Dept. of Justice State of N.Y., N.Y.C, 1983-85, asst. U.S. trustee Dept. of Justice, 1985-87; group v.p. Mfrs. Hanover Fin. Mgmt. Systems, Santa Ana, Calif., 1987—; lectr. Golden Gate U., San Francisco, 1976-79; speaker small bus. assn., N.Y.C., 1984-85; mem. Fed. Exec. Bd., N.Y.C., 1985-86; moot ct. judge Fordham U. Sch. of Law, N.Y.C., 1985-87. Pres. Assist A Grad. Scholarship Found., Fairfield, Calif., 1976. With USAF, 1968-72. Mem. ABA, Calif. Bar Assn., Nat. Assn. Bankruptcy Trustee (editor com. 1988), N.Y.C. Bankruptcy Bar, Santa Ana C. of C., Fairfield C. of C. Republican. Roman Catholic. Office: Plotkin & Rapoport 16633 Ventura Blvd 6th Fl Encino CA 91436

ABUL-HAJ, SULEIMAN KAHIL, pathologist; b. Jordan, Apr. 20, 1925; s. Sheik Khalil and S. Buteina (Oda) Abul-H.; B.S., U. Calif. at Berkeley, 1949; M.S., U. Calif. at San Francisco, 1951, M.D., 1955; m. Elizabeth Abood, Feb. 11, 1948; children—Charles, Alan, Cary; came to U.S., 1946, naturalized, 1955. Intern, Cook County Hosp., Chgo., 1955-56; resident U. Calif. Hosp., San Francisco, 1949, Brooke Gen. Hosp., 1957-59; chief clin. and anatomic pathology Walter Reed Army Hosp., Washington, 1959-62; assoc. prof. U. So. Calif. Sch. Medicine, Los Angeles, 1963—; sr. surg. pathologist Los Angeles County Gen. Hosp., 1963; dir. dept. pathology Community Meml. Hosp., Ventura, Calif., 1964-80, Gen. Hosp. Ventura County, 1966-74; dir. Pathology Service Med. Group, 1970—; cons. Calif. Tumor Tissue Registry, 1962—, Camarillo State Hosp., 1964-70, Tripler Gen. Hosp., Hawaii, 1963-67, Armed Forces Inst. Pathology, 1960—. Bd. dirs. Tri-Counties Blood Bank, Am. Cancer Soc. Served to maj., M.C., U.S. Army, 1956-62. Recipient Borden award Calif. Honor Soc., 1949; Achievement cert. Surgeon Gen. Army, 1962. Fellow Am. Soc. Clin. Pathologists, Coll. Am. Pathologists; mem. Internat. Coll. Surgeons, World Affairs Council, Jonathan Club. Contbr. articles to profl. jours. Research in cardiovascular disease, endocrine, renal, skin diseases, also cancer. Home and Office: 105 Encinal Way Ventura CA 93001

ABU ZAYYAD, RAY S., electronics executive. BS, U. Calif., Berkeley; MS, San Jose State U. With IBM Corp., 1962—, engr., 1962, asst. mgr. tech. mfg., 1980-81, gen. mgr., 1981-82; gen. mgr. gen. products div. IBM Corp., San Jose, Calif., 1982-83, div. v.p., 1983-85, asst. to infosystems tech. group exec., 1985, pres. gen. products div., from 1985, corp. v.p., 1986—; pres. Rolm Corp. subs. IBM Corp., Santa Clara, Calif., 1987—. Office: Rolm Corp 4900 Old Ironside Corp Santa Clara CA 95050 *

ACHESON, MURRAY JAMES, real estate corporation executive; b. Winnipeg, Manitoba, Canada, June 23, 1952; came to U.S., 1955; s. Charles E. and Yvonne Margaret (Ryckebosch) A.; m. Linda Elaine Eich, Apr. 2, 1983; children: Wendy, Mike, Steve. Student, Cypress (Calif.) Coll., 1970-72, Fullerton (Calif.) Coll., 1970-72, Calif. State U., Fullerton, 1972-74. Lic. real estate broker, Calif. Sales rep. Pacific Fin., Lallabra, Calif., 1974-75, Tiffany Realty, Cerritos, Calif., 1975-77; v.p. sales Realty World, Anaheim, Calif., 1977—. Republican. Roman Catholic. Office: Realty World 925 W Lincoln Anaheim CA 92805

ACHILLES, STEPHEN FIELD, management consultant; b. Boston, Feb. 4, 1962; s. Theodore Carter and Joan (Baker) A.; m. Lisa Yvette Milner, June 14, 1986. BA, Bowdoin Coll., 1984; MBA, U. Wash., 1989. Rsch. assoc. Greenwich (Conn.) Assocs., 1984-86; dir. mkt. rsch. People's Bank, Providence, R.I., 1986-87; cons. United Rsch. Co., Inc., Seattle, Wash., 1989—. Steward All Sts. Episcopal. Parish, Attleboro, Mass., 1986-87. Mem. Cons. Club (pres. 1986-88). Home and Office: United Rsch Co Inc 25 Airport Rd Morristown NJ 07960

ACHTEL, ROBERT ANDREW, pediatric cardiologist; b. Bklyn., May 5, 1941; s. Murray and Amelia (Ellian) A.; m. Erica Noel Woods, Mar. 10, 1963; children: Bergen Alison, Roland Hugh. BA, Adelphi U., 1963; MD, U. Cin., 1967. Diplomate Am. Bd. Pediatric Cardiology. Intern, Cin. Children's Hosp., 1967-68; resident in pediatrics Yale U., 1968-69, fellow in pediatric cardiology, 1969-71; clin. instr. pediatrics U. Calif.-Davis, 1972-73, clin. asst. prof., 1977-83; asst. prof. pediatrics, U. Ky., 1973-76; dir. pediatric ICU, Sutter Meml. Hosp., Sacramento, 1977-85, dir. pediatric Cardiology, 1982—, chmn. instl. rev. com., 1981-85; chmn. dept. pediatrics Mercy Hosp., Sacramento, 1981-83, vice chmn. pediatrics, 1983-85; dir. pediatric ICU, 1982-83; dir. Laurel Hills Devel. Ctr., 1985-89.; chmn. rsch com. Sutter Inst. for Med. Rsch., 1989—. Contbr. articles in cardiovascular research. Bd. dirs. Sutter Meml. Hosp. Found., 1986—; bd. dirs. Sutter Found., 1989, trustee, 1989—. Maj. M.C., USAF, 1971-73. Recipient grants from Heart Assn., U. Ky. Tobacco and Health Research Found. Mem. Am. Heart Assn. (dir. Sacramento chpt., mem. councils congenital heart disease and atherosclerosis and cardiovascular surgery), Am. Coll. Chest Physicians, Am. Acad Pediatrics, SW Pediatric Cardiology Soc., So. Soc. Pediatric Research. Office: Pediatric Cardiology Assocs 5609 J St Ste A Sacramento CA 95819

ACKERLEY, BARRY, professional basketball team executive. Chmn. bd. dirs. Seattle Supersonics; pres. Sta. KJR. Office: Seattle Supersonics 190 Queen Anne Ave N Box C-900911 Seattle WA 98109 *

ACKERMAN, DAVID JOHN, management consultant; b. Phila., Aug. 27, 1950; s. Adrian John and Madeline (Ruit) A.; m. Kay Louise Gebhardt, Sept. 5, 1975 (div. May 1986); m. Ann Elizabeth Stewart, Aug. 12, 1988; adopted children: Karin Louise, Jason Matthew Stewart. BA in Polit. Sci., Purdue U., 1971; MBA, No. Ill. U., 1976. Commd. ensign USCG, 1977, advanced through grades to lt., 1983, resigned, 1987; parole officer State of N.J., Jersey City, 1971-73; asst. dir. Pollack Rehab. Ctr., Pensacola, Fla., 1973-74; residential dir. Ctr. Human Devel., Sterling, Ill., 1974-75; advt. salesman Dixon (Ill.) Evening Telegraph, 1975-76; office adminstr. Rappleyea, Beck, Helterline, Spencer & Reskie, Portland, Oreg., 1987-88, Tooze Marshall Shenker Holloway & Duden, Portland, 1988; pres. Portland Office Systems, 1988—; systems mgr. Nendels/Pacific, Inc., Portland, 1989—. Mem. Assn. Legal Adminstrs., Oreg. Legal Mgmt. Assn., U.S. Naval Inst., Masons, Nat. Sojourners. Office: Portland Office Systems Inc 2235 NE Sandy Blvd Portland OR 97232 also: Nendels/Pacific Hospitality Inc 12323 SW 66th Ave Portland OR 97223

ACKERMAN, DOUGLAS JAMES, information systems specialist; b. Chgo., Sept. 28, 1960; s. James Leroy and Doris Ann (Immel) A. BS, Mt. Union Coll., 1982. Computer programmer analyst Hughes Aircraft, El Segundo, Calif., 1982-85; sr. programmer analyst Union Bank, L.A., 1985-87; project analyst Flying Tigers, L.A., 1987—. Republican. Roman Catholic. Home: 1200 E Imperial Ave El Segundo CA 90245

ACKLES, JANICE VOGEL, fundraising executive, writer; b. Pasadena, Calif.; d. Roy George August and Genevieve Irene (Hunter) Vogel; m. David Thomas Ackles, Dec. 9, 1972; 1 child, George Arthur Vogel. BA in Art History, Calif. State U., L.A., 1970; postgrad., U. So. Calif. Free-lance writer 1972—; asst. editor Am. Jour. Physiology, L.A., 1980-84; dir. devel. rsch. World Vision, Monrovia, 1985-88, Childrens Hosp., L.A., 1988—. Contbr. articles to nat. mags. and newspapers. Vol. researcher L.A. County Mus. Art, 1973-75; mem. assistance League So. Calif., L.A., East African Wildlife Soc., Mus. Contemporary Art, L.A., Greater L.A. Zoo Assn., Natural History Mus. Mem. Am. Prospect Rsch. Assn., Nat. Soc. Fund Raising Execs., NAFE, Ind. Writers So. Calif., Calif. Press Women, Inc. Democrat. Congregationalist.

ACKLEY, MARJORIE ROSE, health science facility administrator, educator; b. Shanghai, China, Nov. 15, 1922; came to U.S., 1926; d. Millard Charles Ackley and Luella Alice (Williams) Scharffenberg; m. Donald Wilton Oswald, Sept. 24, 1942 (div. 1955); children: Donald Theodore Oswald, Jaclyn Rae Seward. AS, Grossmont Coll., 1977; BS in Allied Health Professionsdean's award, Loma Linda U., 1987, MPH, 1988. Registered nurse, registered dietitian, fitness instr., ocean skipper operator. Adminstrv. grant sec. Palo Alto (Calif.) Med. Research Found., 1962-67; devel. dir. San Francisco Eye and Ear Hosp., 1967-70; fin. planner Robert W. P. Holstrom Co., San Francisco, 1971-74; registered nurse Groves Registry, San Francisco, 1977-88, Humana Hosp., Achorage, 1983-86, MedPro Nurses Registry, San Diego, 1986-88; health educator San Francisco, 1972-74, Anchorage, 1983-85; med. coordinator, Canvasback Mission, Inc., Benecia, Calif., 1987-88. Author of numerous articles in field. Health educator, Sch. of Pub. Health, Loma Linda, Calif., 1988, Seventh-Day Adventist Ch., San Francisco, 1973, Health Expo, Yucaipa, Calif., 1988. Mem. Am. Critical Care Nurses, Am. Dietetic Assn. (Eleanor Mitchell Meml. award, 1986), Seventh-Day Adventist Dietetic Assn., Am. Pub. Health Assn., Inst. for Advancement of Health, Creative Cooking Club (Anchorage). Republican. Seventh-Day Adventist. Home: 4279 Woodland Dr La Mesa CA 92041

ACKLEY, PEGGY JO, illustrator; b. Sacramento, Oct. 18, 1955; d. Harry Albright Ackley and Lois Irene Johnson; m. Fredrick Harold Mosher, Oct. 8, 1983. BA with honors, U. Calif.-Davis, 1977; postgrad., NYU, 1975-76. Patent illustrtor N.Y.C., 1979-80; staff artist Family Line, Inc., Westmont, Ill., 1980-85; freelance illustrator, designer San Francisco, 1985—; illustrator Renaissance Greeting Cards, Springvale, Maine, 1985—; designer Enesco Designed Giftware, Elk Grove Village, Ill., 1986-89, C.R. Gibson Co., Norwalk, Conn., 1988—. Illustrator (books) When Springtime Comes, 1984, If Christmas Were A Poem, 1983, Our Baby's First Seven Years, 1988. Democrat. Address: 3343 Folsom St San Francisco CA 94110-5210

ACQUILANO, DONNA MARIE, interior designer; b. Rochester, N.Y., Jan. 11, 1958; d. Dominick and Rose (DeMuzio) A.; m. Owen C. Leslie III, Sept. 20, 1981. BA in Environ. Design, U. Tenn., 1981; postgrad., U. Ga., 1981. Designer ISD Inc., Denver, 1981-83; sr. designer CRS Architects, Denver, 1983-85, Hellmuth Obata & Kassabaum Architects Inc., Dallas, 1985-86; prin. Acquilano Design, Denver, 1986—; pres. APS, Inc. Mem. Denver's Hist. Lower Downtown Dist. Assn. Mem. Greater Denver C. of C. Home: 111 Dreher Dr Evergreen CO 80439 Office: Acquilano Design 1529 Market St Denver CO 80202

ADA, JOSEPH FRANKLIN, territorial governor; b. Agana, Guam, Dec. 3, 1943; s. Jose Torres and Regina (Herrero) A.; m. Rosanne Jacqueline Santoes, 1967; children: Eric, Tricia, Esther, George, Anthony. BA, U. Portland, 1968. Dep. dir. Guam Dept. Pub. Works, 1970-72; senator Guam Legis., 1973-78, 83-86; lt. gov. Guam, 1979-82, elected gov., 1986. Republican. Office: Office of Gov Guam Territory Agana GU 96910 *

ADAIR, DIANNA LYNN, software engineer; b. Woodbury, N.J., Jan. 23, 1950; d. Marion Ezelle and Opal Jeanette (Keller) Braden; m. Vernon H. Adair, July 30, 1973. BS, Utah State U., 1972; postgrad., Stanford U., 1983-86. Sr. software engr. Unisys Corp., Santa Clara, Calif., 1982—; v.p. Volpar Inc., Santa Clara, Calif., 1984—. Editor book Parts By Application, 1985. Planning commr. Sunnyvale (Calif.) Planning Commn., 1988—; elections inspector Sunnyvale Voting Div., 1986-87; gymnastics coach Fla. Sch. for Deaf and Blind, St. Augustine, 1972-76; bd. dirs. Sunnyvale Sch. Dist. Edn. Found., 1988—; mem. mus. council Women in the Arts-Nat. Mus., 1988—; capt. Emergency Response Team. Fellow Smithsonian Instn.; mem. IEEE, Toastmasters (pres. 1983, area gov. 1983-84, named Able Toastmaster 1985), Decathlon Club. Home: 399 E Maude Ave Sunnyvale CA 94086 Office: Volpar Inc 941 Laurelwood Rd Santa Clara CA 95054-2717

ADAMICH, RICHARD JOHN, controller; b. Pueblo, Colo., Feb. 4, 1946; s. Ludwig Phillip and Grace Adeline (Masciotra) A.; m. Eleanor Mary Ellis, Aug. 24, 1974; children: Richard Gregory, Kelly Marie. BS in Acctg., U. So. Colo., 1968; MBA, U. Notre Dame, 1970. CPA, Colo. Jr. acct. Touche Ross & Co., Denver, 1970-71; auditor II State of Colo., Denver, 1971-74, budget analyst office of state planning and budgeting, 1974-75, sr. auditor office planning and budgeting, 1975-76, sr. auditor dept. adminstrn., 1976-77, field controller state controller's office, 1977-82, prin. auditor office state auditor, 1982-83, controller dept. natural resources, 1983—; chmn. steering com. Statewide Fin. Info. System, Denver, 1988—. Chmn. pack com. Boy Scouts Am., Littleton, Colo. 1987-88; fund raiser youth program YMCA, Denver, 1988. Mem. Am. Inst. CPA's, Colo. Fiscal Mgrs. Assn. (v.p. 1980-81, pres. 1981-82, Outstanding Employee 1987), Colo. State Mgrs. Assn., Colo. State Govt. Accting. Standards Bd., Notre Dame Club (bd. dirs. Denver chpt. 1978-79), Toastmasters (pres. Denver chpt. 1978-79). Democrat. Roman Catholic. Home: 5546 E Hinsdale Circle Littleton CO 80122 Office: Colo Dept Natural Resources 1313 Sherman St Rm 423 Denver CO 80122

ADAMS, ANDREW MARTIN, vineyard executive; b. Canastota, N.Y., May 20, 1943; s. Andrew Martin and Helen (Thurlow) A.; m. Maureen Burke, July 26, 1966; children: Katherine Grace, Andrew Burke. BA, Marquette U., 1965. With distbn. sales dept. Procter and Gamble, Ewing, N.J.; with prodn. and mktg. dept. Johnson and Johnson, New Brunswick, N.J.; with sales and mktg. support Baxter-Travenol, Deerfield, Ill.; sales mgr. Foremost KcKesson, Kansas City & Chgo., Federated Distbrs.; pres. Cray Wholesale, Kansas City, Mo., 1978-81, McCormick Distilling Co., Weston, Mo., 1981-86, Sebastiani Vineyards, Sonoma, Calif., 1986—. Mem. Young Pres. Orgn., Am. Mktg. Assn. Pres. Club, Distilled Spirits Council, Wine and Spirits Wholesalers Assn., Am. Beverage Alcohol Assn. Home: 20415 5th St E Sonoma CA 95476 Office: Kendall Jackson Winery 50 Francisco St San Francisco CA 94133

ADAMS, ANN LOUISE, publisher; b. Palestine, Tex., Nov. 17, 1934; d. Henry George and Ola Monteel (Goodin) Beard; m. J.G. Price, Mar. 15, 1956 (div. 1973); m. Mark Adams, May 12, 1979. BA, U. Tex., Austin, 1957. Proofreader Austin (Tex.) Am.-Statesman, 1960-67; typesetter Tulsa World, 1967-68, San Antonio Express-Light, 1970-73, Austin Am.-Statesman, 1973-77, Albuquerque Jour., 1977-78, Everett (Wash.) Herald, 1978-80; editor U. Okla. Press, Norman, Okla., 1968-70; freelance editor Everett and Oak Harbor, Wash., 1981—; pub. Packrat Press, Oak Harbor, 1981—; pub. cons. Wash. Pub. Utility Dists. Assn., Seattle, 1987-88. Editor: The Clay Pedestal (Wash. Gov.'s award), 1981, Public. and Private Letters of Franklin Jones, Sr. (4 vols.), 1982-89; author: Travels With A Donkey, 1982; contbr. articles to various publs. Mem. Com. of Corr., Pandorans. Home and Office: Packrat Press 4366 N Diana Ln Oak Harbor WA 98277

ADAMS, ARTHUR CLARK, insurance executive; b. New Haven, Jan. 17, 1948; s. John Howard and Dorothy (Wheeler) A.; m. Janet Jordano, Nov. 25, 1972; 1 child, Bradley Chapin. BA, U. Calif.-Santa Barbara, 1971; postgrad., U. Santa Clara, 1979-82, Am. Inst. Property & Liabil. Underwriters. Assoc. in Risk Mgmt. With agys. adminstrn. div. Occidental Life of Calif., 1971-74; gen. ins. broker Andreini & Co., San Mateo, Calif., 1974-76, Winn Ins. Co., Gilroy, Calif., 1976-79; v.p. Fin. Guardian Ins. Brokers, San Jose, Calif., 1979—; bd. dirs. Jantro Investments, Santa Barbara. Mem. Western Assn. Ins. Brokers, Risk and Ins. Mgmt. Soc., Ind. Ins. Agts. and Brokers Assn. (bd. dirs. 1983), Good Samaritan Hosp. Found. (charter), Univ. Club (bd. dirs. 1984), Rotary, Sigma Chi. Office: Fin Guardian Ins Brokers 950 S Bascom Ave Ste 3011 San Jose CA 95125

ADAMS, BERNARD SCHRODER, retired college president; b. Lancaster, Pa., July 20, 1928; s. Martin Ray and Charlotte (Schroder) A.; m. Natalie Virginia Stout, June 2, 1951; children: Deborah Rowland, David Schroder. B.A., Princeton, 1950; M.A., Yale, 1951; Ph.D., U. Pitts., 1964; LL.D. (hon.), Lawrence U., 1967. Asst. dir. admissions, instr. English Princeton, 1953-57; dir. admissions and student aid U. Pitts., 1957-60, spl. asst. to chancellor, 1960-64; dean students, lectr. English Oberlin (Ohio) Coll., 1964-66; pres. Ripon (Wis.) Coll., 1966-85, Ft. Lewis Coll., Colo., 1985-87; v.p. resources Goodwill Industries, Colorado Springs, Colo., 1988—; dir. Wis. Power & Light Co., Newton Funds, 1970-85; cons., examiner Commn. on Instns. Higher Edn., North Cen. Assn. Colls. and Secondary Schs., 1972-87, exec. commr., 1981-86; bd. dirs. Four Corners Opera Assn., 1985-87, pres., 1986-87. Author articles. Served to 1st lt. USAF, 1951-53. Woodrow Wilson fellow, 1951. Mem. Assoc. Colls. Midwest (bd. dirs. 1966-85, pres. 1973-75), Wis. Assn. Ind. Colls. and Univs. (dir. 1966-85, pres. 1969-71, 83-85). Home: 90 Ellsworth St Colorado Springs CO 80906

ADAMS, BROCK, senator; b. Atlanta, Jan. 13, 1927; s. Charles Leslie and Vera Eleanor (Beemer) A.; m. Mary Elizabeth Scott, Aug. 16, 1952; children: Scott Leslie, Lewis Dean, Katherine Elizabeth, Aleen Mundy. BA in Econs. summa cum laude, U. Wash., 1949; LLB, Harvard U., 1952. Bar: Wash. 1952. Ptnr. LeSourd, Patten & Adams (formerly Little, LeSourd, Palmer, Scott & Slemmons), Seattle, 1952-61; U.S. atty. U.S. Dist. Ct. (we. dist.) Wash., Seattle, 1961-64; mem. 89th-94th Congresses from 7th Wash. dist., 1965-77, mem. sci. and astronautics com., interstate and fgn. commerce com., chmn. budget com.; U.S. Sec. Transp. Washington, 1977-79; ptnr. Garvey, Schubert, Adams and Barer, 1979-86; U.S. Senator from Wash. 1987—; instr. Am. Inst. Banking, 1954-60. Chmn. Western Wash. dist. Kennedy for Pres. campaign, 1960; former pres. Neighborhood House, Seattle; exec. dir. Wash. dist. Carter for Pres. campaign; past trustee Civic Unity Com., Seattle. With USN, 1944-46. Recipient Disting. Svc. award Seattle Jr. C. of C., 1960. Mem. ABA, Fed. Bar Assn., Wash. Bar Assn., Seattle-King County Bar Assn., Puget Sound Assn. (pres. 1962-63), U. Wash. Alumni Assn. (past trustee), Phi Beta Kappa. Democrat. Episcopalian. Office: 513 Hart Senate Office Bldg Washington DC 20510

ADAMS, CHARLES FRANCIS, advertising and real estate executive; b. Detroit, Sept. 26, 1927; s. James R. and Bertha C. (DeChant) A.; m. Helen R. Harrell, Nov. 12, 1949; children: Charles Francis, Amy Ann, James Randolph, Patricia Duncan. BA, U. Mich., 1948; postgrad., U. Calif., Berkeley, 1949. With D'Arcy-MacManus & Masius, Inc., 1947-80, exec. v.p., dir., 1970-76, pres., chief operating officer, 1976-80; pres. Adams Enterprises, 1971—; exec. v.p., dir. Washington Office, Am. Assn. Advt. Agys., 1980-84; chmn., chief exec. officer Wajim Corp., Detroit; past mem. steering com. Nat. Advt. Rev. Bd.; mem. mktg. com. U.S. Info. Agy.; pres. Internat. Visitors Ctr. of the Bay Area, 1988-89. Author: Common Sense in Advertising, 1965, Heroes of the Golden Gate, 1987. Past chmn. exec. com. Oakland U. Mem. Am. Assn. Advt. Agys. (dir., mem. govt. relations com.), Advt. Fedn. Am. (past dir.), Nat. Outdoor Advt. Bur. (past chmn.), Theta Chi, Alpha Delta Sigma (hon.). Republican. Roman Catholic. Clubs: Bloomfield Hills Country; Carmel Valley Ranch (Calif.); Nat. Golf Links Am. (Southampton, L.I.); Olympic, The Family (San Francisco). Home: 2240 Hyde St San Francisco CA 94109 also: 25450 Loma Robles Carmel CA 93923 Office: 10 W Long Lake Rd Bloomfield Hills MI 48013

ADAMS, CLIFFORD E., service and light manufacturing company owner; b. Harper, Kans.; s. Walter Emerson and Lucy Alice (Coleman) A.; m. Mary Lois Lamont, aug. 14, 1940 (dec. Jan. 1982); children: Elizabeth Ann Cason, Barbara Jane jenkins, Judith Kathryn Craig; m. Eleanor Geneva Knight, Mar. 1, 1983. Student, Wichita Bus. Coll., 1937-38. Sales mgr. Stoody Co., Whittier, Calif., 1943-44; founder, mgr. Adams Hard Facing Co., Wakita, Okla., 1946-50; pres., founder Adams Alloy Co., Wakita, 1947-55; pres. Adams Hard Facing Co., Guymon, Okla., 1955-60, Shafter, Calif., 1960-67; pres., founder Adams Mfg. Co., Shafter, 1965-67, Casa Grande, Ariz., 1965-68; pres., founder Feed Builders, Inc., Shafter, Calif., 1967-70, Fil-T-Vac Corp., Tempe, Ariz., 1972-77, Re-Cy-Kleen, Inc., Riverside, Calif., 1977—; co-founder Farm Equipment Mfrs. Assn., St. Louis, 1947, Nat. Welding Supply Assn., Phila., 1948; speaker Am. Welding Supply, 1948. Bd. dirs. Oklahoma Devel. Coun., Oklahoma City, 1947, Guymon C. of C., 1956, Nat. Security Coun./Calif., Washington, 1985-88. With USN, 1944-45. Mem. Assn. Energy Engrs., Inst. Heating & Air Conditioning, Rotary (pres.-elect Shafter chpt. 1967), Lions (pres. Wakita chpt. 1946), Masons (32d degree, Scottish Rite), Shriners. Democrat. Methodist. Home: 3500 Buchanan 147 Riverside CA 92503 Office: Re-Cy-Kleen Inc 3136 12th St Riverside CA 92507

ADAMS, DAVID BENNION, psychologist; b. Salt Lake City, May 21, 1945; s. Ferrell Harrison and Maurine (Bennion) A. B.A., U. Utah, 1968, M.S. (Kappa Sigma fellow), 1972, Ph.D. in Psychology cum laude, 1976. Staff psychologist Granite Mental Health Center, 1972-74; dir. Juvenile Alcohol Program, 1974-75; clin. supr. Adolescent Residential Treatment Ctr., 1974-79; pvt. practice clin. psychology, Salt Lake City, 1976—, also clin. dir. Am. Community Youth Services, 1979-82, Intermountain Youth Care, 1982—; instr. U. Utah, Brigham Young U.; program coordinator Children's div. Charter Summit Hosp. Local dist. Dem. del., 1972. Served with USAR, 1963-71. Lic. and cert. psychologist, Utah; cert. marriage and family counselor, Utah. Mem. Am. Psychol. Assn., Utah Psychol. Assn., Utah Psychologists in Pvt. Practice, Zero Population Growth, Nat. Register for Health Service Providers in Psychology, Sierra Club, Utah Assn. Juvenile and Adult Corrections, Kappa Sigma. Contbr. articles to profl. jours. Home: 1036 E Countrylane Rd Holladay UT 84117 Office: 470 E 3900 S Ste 200 Salt Lake City UT 84107

ADAMS, DAVID JOHN, art history educator; b. Ft. Wayne, Ind., Feb. 8, 1949; s. Vernon John and Barbara Jean (Morton) A.; m. Jane Murrell Johnson, June 9, 1979 (div. 1983); m. Janet Olive, Dec. 4, 1987. BA, New Coll. Sarasota, 1971; postgrad., Met. State Coll., Denver, 1973, Waldorf Inst., Detroit, 1975-76; PhD, Union Grad. Sch., Cin., 1978. Cert. tchr., Colo. Utilization rsch. analyst Blue Cross & Blue Shield Mich., Detroit, 1977, 78-79; instr., exhbn. curator Found. Yr. Adult Edn. Program, Spring Valley, N.Y., 1980-81; gen. mgr. J & R Lamb Studios, Philmont, N.Y., 1980-83; indexer Art Index, Bronx, N.Y., 1985-86; instr., adminstr. Threefold Painting Sch., Spring Valley, N.Y., 1983-86; asst. prof. art history U. Minn., Morris, 1987-88, Calif. State U., Fresno, 1988—; instr. Interior Design Inst., Woodcliff Lake, N.J., 1985-86; vis. asst. prof. art history U. Mont., Missoula, 1986-87; bd. dirs. Ctr. for Archtl. & Design Rsch., Spring Valley, Fresno; bd. govs. The Census of Stained Glass Windows in Am.1840-1940, Worcester, Mass., 1980—. Contbr. articles to profl. jours. Mem. Coll. Art Assn., Mid-Am. Coll. Art Assn., Soc. Archtl. Historians, Decorative Arts Soc., Am. Assn. Museums, Anthrop. Soc. in Am. (Chgo.). Office: Calif State Univ Dept of Art Fresno CA 93740

ADAMS, DAVID LEE, acoustics and theater design consultant; b. Kansas City, Kans., Nov. 2, 1939; s. Donald D. and Opal A. (Ryan) A.; m. Margaret M. Schlonga, Feb. 9, 1964; children: Matthew, Nicole, Stephanie, Katrina. BSEE, U. Kans., 1964; MSEE, Wichita (Kans.) State U., 1969; postgrad., Inst. Logopedics, Wichita, 1968-69. Registered profl. engr., Colo., Calif., N.J. Engr. Boeing Aircraft Co., Wichita, 1964-67, rsch. engr., 1967-69; instr. engring. dept. Wichita State U., 1967-70; engr., head dept. acoustics and noise control Engring.-Sci., Inc., Arcadia, Calif., 1970-76; dir. Cedar Knolls (N.J.) Acoustical Lab., 1972-74; v.p., prin. cons. Jaffe Acoustics, Inc., Denver, 1976-79; owner, prin. cons. David L. Adams Assocs., Denver, 1979-83, pres., 1983—; tech. cons. on acoustics Sound & Video Contractors mag., 1985—. Mem. Nat. Coun. Acoustical Cons. (bd. dirs. 1984-86, v.p. 1986-88, pres.-elect 1988—), U.S. Inst. for Theatre Tech., Acoustical Soc. Am., Colo. Assn. Commerce and Industry, Cons. Engrs. Coun. Colo., Greater Denver C. of C. Home: 773 S Beech St Lakewood CO 80228 Office: 1701 Boulder St Denver CO 80211

ADAMS, ERNEST JOSEPH, realtor, oil and gas executive; b. Cleve., July 21, 1927; s. Joseph Stanley and Valeria (Iglar) A.; widowed; children: Kenneth, Paul, William, Richard, James; stepchildren: Edward, Dennis, Patricia, Theresa, Joseph, Michael, Loreen O'Brien. Student, Kent State U., 1948-50, Cleve. State U., 1951-56. Clk. acctg. USN, Cleve., 1947-48; acct. and IBM operator The East Ohio Gas Co., Cleve., 1950-66, land man, 1967-83; land agt. CNG Devel. Co., Pitts., 1983-86; pres. Teri Leasing Co., Inc., Newbury, Ohio, 1986—; realtor Pridemark Realtors, Huntington Beach, Calif., 1987—. Sgt. U.S. Army, 1945-47. Mem. Am. Assn. Petroleum Landmen, Ohio Oil and Gas Assn. (active landman), Huntington Beach Fountain Valley Bd. Realtors. Roman Catholic. Home: 13891 Lipkin Dr Westminster CA 92683 Office: Pridemark Realtors 7151 Warner Ave Huntington Beach CA 92647

ADAMS, GLEN CAMERON, publisher; b. Trent, Wash., June 19, 1912; s. Otto Ulysses and Mae (Cameron) A.; m. Nina Lenore Finch, Apr. 30, 1936 (div. June 1939); 1 child, Robert Glen; m. Jean Pierie Evers, June 29, 1946. BA, Eastern Wash. U., 1938. Prin. Burbank (Wash.) Sch. Dist., 1938-39; livestock breeder Fairfield, Wash., 1939-51; postmaster Fairfield Post Office, 1951-72; printer, pub. Ye Galleon Press, Fairfield, 1972—; hon. prof. history Eastern Wash. U., Cheney, 1983. Mayor Town of Fairfield, 1974-78. Named to Wash. State Hall of Honor, Washington State Hist. Soc., Tacoma, 1983. Democrat. Presbyterian. Home: 103 Brewster St Fairfield WA 99012 Office: 103 E Main St Fairfield WA 99012

ADAMS, JACK, film company executive, screenwriter, educator; b. Lakehurst, N.J., Sept. 15, 1952; s. John Carey and Dorothy Jeanne (Conover) A.; m. Shirley Janulewicz, June 28, 1975; children: Carey Miller, Chanine Angelina, Mikael Walter. MusB in Music Edn., U. Del., 1974. Pres. Koala Studio, Valencia, Calif., 1977—; v.p. Unifilms, Inc., North Hollywood, Calif., 1984—; tchr. film, TV writing Coll. of the Canyons, Valencia, 1988—, L.A. City Coll., 1989—. Composer (film) EAT, 1980 (Filmex award 1981, Best Short Film award Cinemagic mag. 1981); columnist Hollywood Scriptwriter, 1987—. Mem. Am. Film Inst., (alumni assn. writers workshop), Scriptwriters Network (bd. advisors), Film Artists Network (bd. dirs.), NBC Writers Workshop (pres.), Ind. Writers So. Calif. Scriptwriters Caucus, Assn. Info. Systems Profls. (dir. 1983), Larry Wilson Devel. Workshop (Paramount Studios), L.A. Filmmakers Workshop, Ind. Feature Project West, Santa Clarita Scriptwriters Workshop (founder). Home: 22931 Sycamore Creek Dr Valencia CA 91354-2050 Office: Unifilms Inc 6748 Clybourn Ave Ste 124 North Hollywood CA 91606

ADAMS, JAL GUSTAV, naval architect, engineer; b. Bombay, Aug. 6, 1914; came to U.S. 1969; m. Jean Adams, Jan. 22, 1959; 1 child, Tina. BME, Coll. Engring., Poona, India, 1941; BEE, Coll. Engring., 1941. Registered profl. engr., Calif. With various firms U.K. and India, 1941-69; rep. Morris Guralnick Global Marine-Santa Fe Internat., San Francisco, L.A., Orange, Tex., 1970-71; head naval architect Global Marine, Inc., L.A., 1971-77; asst. chief naval architect, chief hull sect., then project mgr. Morris Guralnick Assocs., Inc., San Francisco, 1977-80; ret. Morris Guralnick Assocs., Inc., 1980; cons. in field. Fellow Royal Instn. Naval Architects, NE Coast Inst. Engrs. and Shipbuilders, Engring. Coun. London; mem. Soc. Naval Architects and Marine Engrs., Am. Soc. Naval Engrs. Home: 750 Gonzalez Dr #M-D San Francisco CA 94132

ADAMS, JEFFREY KARL, insurance company executive; b. Greeley, Colo., Aug. 5, 1950; s. Karl L. Adams and Barbara J. Girnt; m. Susan G. Adams, Dec. 14, 1985; 1 child, Sean H. BA, MA, U. Colo., 1974, PhD, 1977. Asst. v.p. Capitol Life Ins. Co., Denver, 1982-85; v.p. ITT Life, Mpls., 1985-88, Am. Founders Life, Phoenix, 1988—. Contbr. numerous articles. Mem. Assn. Life Underwriters, Internat. Fin. Planning. Republican. Home: PO Box 1 Greeley CO 80632 Office: Am Founders Life 8400 E Prentice Ave Greeley CO 80111

ADAMS, JOAN MARIE, electrical engineer; b. Glendale, Calif., July 9, 1958; d. Walter Gerald and Gisele Rose (Allard) Olsen; m. Bryan Edward Adams, Mar. 11, 1978. BS with honors, Calif. State U., Sacramento, 1985. Mem. tech. staff Hughes Aircraft Co., El Segundo, Calif., 1985—. Hughes Microwave Masters fellow Calif. State U., Northridge, 1986-87. Mem. IEEE, Tau Beta Pi. Republican. Baptist. Office: Hughes Aircraft Co PO Box 92426 Bldg R2 M/S 9M20 160 Los Angeles CA 90009

ADAMS, JO-ANN MARIE, real estate executive; b. Los Angeles, May 27, 1949; d. Joseph John and Georgia S. (Wein) A.; A.A., Pasadena City Coll., 1968; B.A., Pomona Coll., 1970; M.A., Calif. State U., Los Angeles, 1971; M.B.A., Pacific Luth. U., 1983. Secondary tchr. South Pasadena (Calif.) Unified Schs., 1970-71; appraiser Riverside County (Calif.) Assessor's Office, 1972-74; systems and procedures analyst Riverside County Data Processing Dept., 1974-76, supervising systems analyst, 1976-79; systems analyst computer Boeing Computer Services Co., Seattle, 1979-81; sr. systems analyst Thurston County Central Services, Olympia, Wash., 1981-83, data processing systems mgr., 1983-84; data processing systems engr. IBM Corp., 1984-87; realtor-assoc., Dower Realty, 1987—; corp. sales rep. UniGlobe Met. Travel, 1988-89; asst. project mgr., Servco Pacific, 1989—; instr. Riverside City Coll., 1977-79. Chairperson legis. task force Riverside/San Bernardino chpt. NOW, 1975-76, chpt. co-chairperson, 1978; mem. ethics com. Calif. NOW Inc., 1978; alt. del. Calif Democratic Caucus, 1978. Mem. Nat. Abortion Rights Action League, Nat. Assn. Female Execs., Assn. Systems Mgrs., Nat. Assn. Computing Machinery, Pomona Coll. Alumni Assn. Home: 1031 Maunaihi Pl #502 Honolulu HI 96822 Office: Servco Pacific Honolulu HI 96813

ADAMS, JOHN PHILLIPS, JR., economics educator, forensic economics consultant; b. Dothan, Ala., June 29, 1920; s. John Phillips Sr. and Lucile (Brown) A.; m. Flavienne Marcelle David, Dec. 5, 1946; children—Gilles David, Sidney Michel. Student Ga. Sch. Tech., 1939-43, U. S.C., 1964-65; M.A., Claremont Grad. Sch., 1968, Ph.D., 1972. Commd. 2d lt. U.S. Army, 1943, advanced through grades to lt. col., 1963, ret., 1963; lectr. econs. Calif. State Poly. U., Pomona, 1968-70; prof. econs., Calif. Poly. State U., San Luis Obispo, 1970—; trustee Calif. Council on Econ. Edn., 1972-78; forensic econs. cons., San Luis Obispo, 1976—. Pres. Calif. Cen. Coast chpt. Mended Hearts, Inc., Arroyo Grande, 1983-84. Mem. Am. Econ. Assn., Western Econ. Assn. Internat., Atlantic Econ. Soc., Indsl. Relations Research Assn., Western Soc. Scis. Assn., Nat. Assn. Forensic Economists (charter mem., West regional dir. 1986-87, v.p. 1988—), Ret. Officers Assn. (life), White Sands Pioneer Group (life), Aircraft Owners and Pilots Assn., Omicron Delta Epsilon, Delta Sigma Pi, Alpha Tau Omega. Home: 2000 Wilding Ln San Luis Obispo CA 93401 Office: Calif Poly State U Dept Econs San Luis Obispo CA 93407

ADAMS, LARRY J., construction contracting company executive; b. Cedar City, Utah, Sept. 30, 1940; s. J.V. and Pharol (Slack) A.; m. Colleen Hutchings, Aug. 19, 1960; children: Don Larry, Tamara Lee. AS, Coll. South Utah, 1961; BS in Engring., Utah State U., 1963. Registered profl. engr., Calif., Utah, Colo., Nev. Project engr. AEC, Los Alamos, N.Mex., 1963-66, Albuquerque, 1966-67, Denver, 1967-70; constrn. engr. AEC, Washington, 1970-74; asst. mgr. Dept. Energy, Richland, Wash., 1974-80; project mgr. H.P. Foley Co., Richland, 1980-82; pres., chmn., bd. dirs. Skyline Constrn. Co., Richmond, Va., 1982-85; pres. Rodgers Constrn. Co., Albuquerque, 1985-87; chmn., v.p. Teton Constrn. Co., Cheyenne, Wyo., 1987—; also bd. dirs. Teton Constrn. Co., Cheyenne; ptnr. Adams Livestock, Cedar City, Utah, 1981—; owner, cons. LJA Investments, St. George, Utah, 1988—. Pres. Quince Orchard Civic Assn., Gaithersburg, Md., 1972; mem. nat. adv. coun. Utah State U., Logan, 1987—. Mem. Nat. Soc. Profl. Engrs., Utah Soc. Profl. Engrs. Republican. Mormon.

ADAMS, LAWRENCE CHARLES (LARRY ADAMS), auditor, financial controller; b. Johnson City, N.Y., Apr. 25, 1948; s. Charles Albert and Audrey Jane (Bennett) A. AAS, SUNY, Canton, 1968; BS, U. Nev., Las Vegas, 1970; MBA, U. Ariz., 1973; postgrad., Phoenix Coll. and Ariz. State U., 1988-89. CPA; cert. internal auditor, info. systems auditor, systems profl., quality analyst, fraud examiner. Auditor Treadway Inns, Nantucket Island, Mass., 1967-68; asst. to gen. mgr. Micronesia TraveLodge Internat. Inc., El Cajon, Calif., 1971-72, area mgr. S.E. U.S., 1972; supr. internal audit Del E. Webb Corp., Phoenix, 1974-78; div. controller L'Ermitage Hotel, Beverly Hills, Calif., 1978-80; auditing dir. The O'Malley Companies, Phoenix, 1980-88, controller, 1988—, adv. to bd. dirs.; advisor to bd. dirs. Ariz. Lumber and Bldg. Supply Assn., Phoenix; lectr. U. Las Vegas, Nev., 1975-77. Mem. Phoenix Little Theatre, 1980—, Ariz. Humane Soc.; chmn. Block Watch, Phoenix, 1987—; founding mem. Challenger Ctr. Space Edn., Washington, 1987—; bd. dirs. Desert Dance Theatre, Phoenix, 1982. Mem. Nat. Retail Merchants Assn., Inst. Internal Auditors, EDP Auditors Assn., Ariz. Soc. CPAs, Nat. Assn. Cert. Fraud Examiners, Inst. Fin. Crime Prevention, Am. Mgmt. Assn., Balloon Fedn. Am., ARC, Ariz. Balloon Club. Republican. Methodist. Home: 1820 W Northview Ave Phoenix AZ 85021 Office: The O'Malley Cos PO Box 10532 Phoenix AZ 85064

ADAMS, MARIANNE KATHRYN, management consultant; b. Albany, N.Y., Jan. 10, 1924; d. Harold James and Marion Stern (Schwartzman) A. BA, SUNY, Albany, 1945, MA, 1946. Sr. pers. technician N.Y. State Dept. Civil Svcs., Albany, 1959-62; sr. adminstrv. analyst N.Y. State Dept. Health, Albany, 1962-63; asst. dir. pers. N.Y. State Dept. Sch. Svcs., Albany, 1963-65; assoc. adminstrv. analyst N.Y. State Dept. Health, Albany, 1965-68, dir. health manpower resources, 1968-69, dir. adminstrv. analysis, 1969-74, cons. pub. health planning and grants, 1974-80; pvt. practice mgmt. cons., San Diego, 1980—; lectr. procedures and communications Russell Sage Coll. (evening div.), Albany, 1972-76. Editor: N.Y. State Preretirement Counseling Guide, 1962. Vice chmn., chmn. state agy. campaign United Fund, Albany, 1965, 73, 74; campaign worker Albany Symphony Orch.-Saratoga Performing Arts Ctr., 1970-80; v.p. membership San Diego Symphony Orch., 1986-87, 88—; vice chmn. Rancho Bernardo Aux., 1986—; chair, council on ministries, mem. adminstrv. bd. Hope United Meth. Ch., San Diego, 1984-89; mem. residential com., asst. sec. Rancho Bernardo Community Planning Bd., San Diego, 1985-86; co-chair membership Bernardo Home Owners Corp., 1988—. Recipient Cert. for Outstanding Contbn. SUNY-Albany Alumni Bd. Dirs., 1978, Citation Gov. Hugh L. Carey, State of N.Y., 1980. Mem. Am. Soc. for Pub. Adminstrn. (bd. dirs. Capital dist. chpt. 1972-74), Am. Pub. Health Assn., AAUW (treas. Rancho Bernardo chpt. 1981-83, v.p. program 1983-84, pres. 1984-85, chair legis. 1987-89, sec., treas. San Diego Imperial Interbranch chpt. 1985-87), NAFE, Bus. and Profl. Womens Club. Club: Cornell of N.Y. Home: 12417 Lomica Dr San Diego CA 92128

ADAMS, NORMAN JOSEPH, economist, corporate mergers broker; b. Los Angeles, Feb. 21, 1930; s. Joseph O'Neil and Florence Mary (Michalek) A.; B.S., U. So. Calif., 1951; diploma Oxford U., 1953; postgrad. Harvard U., 1956; Ph.D., U. Karachi (Pakistan), 1958; m. Julia Jewell, Oct. 16, 1960; children: Darlene, Janet. Pres., Adams & Co., mergers and aquisitions, Newport Beach, Calif.

ADAMS, PAULINE DEHAART, artist, consultant; b. Heerlen, Limburg, The Netherlands, July 20, 1926; d. Pieter and Adriana Cornelia (Zijp) DeHaart; children: Peter D., Diane L., Laurie J., Steven M. BA, U. Rochester, 1964, MA, 1966. Artist, tchr. The Harley Sch., Rochester, N.Y., 1958-64; registrar Mus. of Arts and Scis., Rochester, 1965-66, Seattle Art Mus., Seattle, 1966-76; workshop chmn. Northwest Watercolor Soc., Seattle, 1989—. Home hopitality hostess World Affairs Coun., Seattle, 1986—. Mem. Netherlands Bus. Assn. (bd. dirs. 1986—), Mountaineers. Republican. Home and Office: 928 E Allison Seattle WA 98102

ADAMS, PHILIP, lawyer; b. Los Angeles, July 18, 1905; s. Thaddeus Lafayette and Lena (Kelly) A.; m. Alice Rahman, 1933; children—Stephen, Judith, Deborah, Kate; m. Elaine Margaret Anderson, 1968. Student, Pomona Coll., 1924-27; J.D., Hastings Coll. Law, U. Calif., 1938; LL.D. (hon.), Ch. Div. Sch. of Pacific, Berkeley, Calif., 1965. Bar: Calif. bar 1938. Purser Panama Mail S.S. Line, 1928-29; profl. investigator 1930-38; individual practice law San Francisco, 1938—; atty. U.S. Govt., 1942-46; instr. domestic relations Golden Gate Law Sch., 1971-72. Author: Adoption Practice in California, 1956. Dir. Children's Protective Soc., 1939-44, United Cerebral Palsy Assn., San Francisco, 1952-72, Assn. for Mental Health, 1952—, United Bay Area Crusade, 1955-61, United Community Fund, San Francisco, 1957-62, San Francisco State Coll., 1964-69, Am. Democratic Action; trustee Ch. Div. Sch. of Pacific, 1951-76; nat. v.p. Episcopal Evang. Fellowship, 1952-61; chancellor Episcopal Diocese of Calif., 1960-67; dep. Episcopal Gen. Conv., 1946-70; pres. bd. trustees Grad. Theol. Union, Berkeley, 1963-66. Fellow Am. Acad. Matrimonial Lawyers (dir. No. Calif. chpt. 1968—;mem. ABA (chmn. com. on adoption, family law sect. 1959-60), Calif., San Francisco Bar Assn., Lawyers Club San Francisco (gov. 1956), Am. Acad. Polit. and Social Sci., San Francisco Symphony Assn., Chamber Soloists San Francisco (dir. 1985—), Soc. Genealogists (London). Clubs: Villa Taverna, Commonwealth. Home: 2170 Jackson St San Francisco CA 94115 Office: 220 Montgomery St San Francisco CA 94104

ADAMS, RICHARD MAXWELL, English professor; b. Merton Park, Surrey, United Kingdom, June 13, 1938; came to U.S., 1985; s. Ernest Maxwell and Beatrice Gladys (Barker) A. BA, U. Oxford, Eng., 1961, MA, 1965, M of Letters, 1965. Special diploma in Edn. Studies (with distinction). Asst. tutor (English) St. Catherine's Coll., Oxford U., Oxford, United Kingdom, 1962-70; tchr., administr. Lord William's Sch., Thame, Oxfordshire, United Kingdom, 1965-84; lectr. San Jose (Calif.) State U., 1986; asst. prof. Calif. State U., Sacramento, 1986—; examiner, awarder, Oxford U. delegacy of local examinations, 1962-88; U.S. affiliate, Shakespeare and Sch., U. Cambridge, 1985—. Author: Teaching Shakespeare, 1985, A Book of British Music Festivals, 1986; gen. editor: Longman Study Texts, 1983-89; editor: Shakespeare: Richard III, 1974, Shakespeare: Richard II, 1975, Shakespeare: Antony and Cleopatra, 1984. With Royal Air Force, 1956-58, United Kingdom. Recipient Meritorious Performance awards, Calif. State U., Sacramento, 1988-89, Classroom Excellence award, Calif. Assn. Tchrs. of English, 1989. Mem. Soc. of Authors, Calif. Faculty Assn., Nat. Council Tchrs. of English. Anglican/Episcopalian. Home: 2238 Gateway Oaks Dr 321 Sacramento CA 95833 Office: Calif State U Dept of English 6000 J St Sacramento CA 95819

ADAMS, ROBERT GRANVILLE, marketing professional; b. Indpls., July 2, 1927; s. Jack and Iris (Trippeer) A.; m. Marilyn Howe (div.); m. Ilona Molnar; children: Lynn, Victoria, Amy. BS, Ind. U., 1953. Capt. USAF, 1945-65; horse rancher Am. Quarter Horse Assn., Scottsdale, Ariz., 1965-88; wholesaler Nat. Home Furnishings Assn., Scottsdale, 1988—. Mem. Desert Caballeros, Wickenburg Ariz. Club, Rancheros Visitadores, Santa Barbara, Calif. Club., Sigma Chi. Home: 10444 N 69th St Scottsdale AZ 85253 Office: PO Box 1747 Scottsdale AZ 85252

ADAMS, RODNEY FRANKLIN, marketing executive; b. Charleston, S.C., June 30, 1936; s. Jewete Franklin and Dorothy (Beard) A.; m. Elizabeth Gail Dendy, Jan. 15, 1956; children: Richard Franklin, Randall Lane, Michael Andrew. Student, U. Ariz., 1954-55, No. Ariz. U., 1955-56, Ariz. State U., 1970-73. Sr. engring. asst. Motorola Inc., Phoenix, Ariz., 1959-66; mktg. mgr. Motorola Inc., Tempe, Ariz., 1969—. Served with U.S. Army, 1956-59. Mem. Assn. of U.S. Army, Am. Def. Preparedness Assn., Tech. Mktg. Soc. Am. Republican. Lodge: Elks.

ADAMS, ROMA LEE, real estate company executive; b. Belleville, Kans., Mar. 25, 1929; d. Jonathan Ervin and Mary Ellen Huckins; m. Robert Weary, 1946 (div. Oct. 1967); children: Anita Lee Weary Brubaker, Roberta Kay Weary McEvoy, Melody Sue Weary Morgan; m. Derwin Adams, Mar. 28, 1961. BA in Choral Music with distinction, Ariz. State U., 1971, MusM, 1978; student, Ariz. Sch. Real Estate, 1979, 83. Telephone operator Chester, Nebr., 1946; tchr. accordion United Tchrs. Music, York, Nebr., 1950-58; piano tchr. Tempe, Ariz., 1950-80; tchr. music Sierra Vista Sch., Phoenix, 1971-75; dir. children's groups numerous orgns., 1971-75; tchr. music Erie Sch., Chandler, Ariz., 1976-79; real estate assoc. Century 21 A.M. Realty, Tempe, 1979-83; owner, mgr., real estate broker Roma Realty, Tempe, 1968—; organist, pianist Seventh-day Adventist Ch., Tempe, 1968--, music planner, 1968--, Mountain View Seventh-day-Adventist Ch., Phoenix, 1987--, Brother Orley Sings program Sta. KASA, Phoenix, 1987--. Mem. Nat. Assn. Realtors, Mesa-Tempe-Chandler Bd. Realtors (Million Dollar Producer award 1984, 87), Ariz. State U. Alumni Assn. Office: Roma Realty 206 S Farmer Ave Tempe AZ 85281

ADAMS, RONALD JOHN, insurance company executive; b. Chgo., Nov. 17, 1943; s. Henry John and Lorraine Claire (Swetman) A.; m. Antoinette Kerber, June 24, 1978; children: Kristene, Jennifer, Eryn, Kylie. BA, U. Nebr., 1966; postgrad., Creighton U., 1966-68. CLU. Compliance officer Nebr. Dept. Revenue, Omaha, 1968-71; life ins. agt. Mass. Mutual Life, Las Vegas, Nev., 1971-74; unit supr. Conn. Mutual Life, Las Vegas, Nev., 1974-77; regional v.p. Lone Star Life Ins. Co., Mpls., 1977-82; founder, chief exec. officer Assn. Ins. Services Co., Sacramento, 1982--. Co author: Personal Dynamics, 1975, Leadership Dynamics, 1977. Mem. exec. council, sec., treas., Calif. Bus. League, Sacramento, 1987--. Mem. Nat. Assn. Life Underwriters, Am. Soc. CLU/Chartered Fin. Cons. (3d v.p. Sacramento chpt. 1987--), Leaders Club. Republican. Christian Evangelistic Alliance. Home: 3819 Country Haven Ct Sacramento CA 95821 Office: Assn Ins Svcs Co 775 Sunrise Blvd Ste 150 Roseville CA 95661

ADAMS, SARAH VIRGINIA, family counselor; b. San Francisco, Oct. 23, 1955; d. Marco Tulio and Helen (Jorge) Zea; m. Glenn Richard Adams, Mar 22, 1980; children: Mark Vincent, Elena Giselle, Johnathan Richard. BA, Calif. State U., Long Beach, 1978, MS, 1980. Lic. marriage, family, child counseling. Tutor math. and sci. Montebello, Calif., 1979-82; behavioral specialist Cross Cultural Psychol. Corp., L.A., 1979-80; psychol. asst. Legal Psychology, L.A., 1980-82, Eisner Psychol. Assocs., L.A., 1982-83; assoc. dir. Legal Psychodiagnosis and Forensic Psychology, L.A., 1982-83; adminstrv. dir. Diagnostic Clinic of West Covina, Calif., 1983-85, dir., 1985—; owner Adams Family Counseling Inc. (name formerly Diagnostic Clinic of West Covina), Calif., 1987—; exec. dir. John V. Gilmore Jr. Psychology Corp., 1988—; tchr. piano, Montebello, 1973-84; ins. agent Am. Mut. Life Ins., Des Moines, 1982-84. Fellow Am. Assn. Marriage and Family Therapists, Calif. Assn. Marriage and Family Therapists, Calif. State Psychol. Assn., Calif. Soc. Indsl. Medicine and Surgery, Los Angeles County Psychol. Assn., Nat. Assn. Female Execs., Psi Chi, Pi Delta Phi. Republican. Roman Catholic. Home: 3402 Sunset Hill Dr West Covina CA 91791 Office: Adams Family Counseling Inc 260 S Glendora #101 West Covina CA 91790

ADAMS, STEPHEN EUGENE, accountant; b. Wichita, Kans., May 5, 1953; s. Billy Dean and JoAnn (Grogan) A.; m. Joan Loretta Hammond, Dec. 1, 1972; children: Eric Christopher, Daniel Edward, Patrick Michael. Student, USAF Acad., 1971-72; BS in Acctg., Ariz. State U., 1974. Staff acct. Touche Ross & Co., Phoenix, 1974-79, supr., 1979-81, mgr., 1981-85, ptnr., 1985--. Vice pres. East Valley Boys and Girls Club, Tempe, Ariz.; mem. fin. com. Theodore Roosevelt council Boy Scouts Am.; treas. Phoenix Little Theatre, 1980. Mem. AICPA, Ariz. Soc. CPA's, Nat. Assn. Accts. (pres. 1984-85). Democrat. Roman Catholic. Office: Touche Ross & Co 2901 N Central Ste 1200 Phoenix AZ 85012

ADAMS, STEPHEN SHAWN, management consultant, hotel caterer; b. Chgo., Apr. 8, 1961; s. Leonard G. Mano and Rose Mary (Sharber) Bassett. Grad. high sch., Palmer, Alaska. Mgr. lounge The Pines Hotel, Anchorage, Alaska, 1979-81; dist. mgr. Pines Corp., Anchorage, 1985-86; mgr. Sheffield Hotels, Valdez, Alaska, 1981-85; project mgr. Global Svcs., Inc., Anchorage, 1986—; pres. Focus Enterprises, Inc., Anchorage, 1988—. Author: A Collection of Shawn, 1988, Uncommon Sense, 1989. Com. leader Valdez Jaycees, 1983; bd. dirs. Valdez Conv. and Visitors' Bur., 1983-84. Named King of Accommodations Mayor of Valdez, 1984. Republican. Home: 200 W 34th Ave Ste 346 Anchorage AK 99503

ADAMS, STEVEN ALVA, management consultant; b. Beemer, Nebr., July 7, 1946; s. Alan James and Lillian (Holden) A.; m. Cecilia Croce, Jan. 20, 1969; children: Xenon, Alaine, Carl. BS, U. Colo., 1968; MBA, Regis Coll., 1975; PhD, Harvard U., 1982. Systems analyst M.D.C. Corp., Denver, 1969-82; v.p. research Boettcher & Co., Denver, 1977-83; pres. Research Analysts, Denver, 1983—. Author: Correlation Analysis, 1985, Technical Investigating, 1986, Post-Crash Perspectives, 1988. Mem. Am. Mgmt. Assn. (Cons. of Yr. 1987), Denver C. of C. Office: Rsch Analysts PO Box 3695 Littleton CO 80161

ADAMSON, GEOFFREY DAVID, reproductive endocrinologist, surgeon; b. Ottawa, Ont., Can., Sept. 16, 1946; came to U.S., 1978, naturalized, 1986; s. Geoffrey Peter Adamson and Anne Marian Allan; m. Rosemary C. Oddie, Apr. 28, 1973; children: Stephanie, Rebecca, Eric. BSc with honors, Trinity Coll., Toronto, Can., 1969; MD, U. Toronto, 1973. Diplomate Am. Bd. Ob-Gyn; cert. Bd. Reproductive Endocrinology. Resident in ob-gyn Toronto Gen. Hosp., 1973-77, fellow in ob-gyn, 1977-78; fellow reproductive endocrinology Stanford (Calif.) U. Med. Ctr., 1978-80; practice medicine specializing in infertility Los Gatos, Calif., 1980-84, Palo Alto, Calif., 1984—; clin. asst. prof. sch. med. Stanford (Calif.) U., 1980—; dir. Fertility and Reproductive Health Inst. of No. Calif., San Jose, 1988—. Mem. editorial adv. bd. Can. Doctor mag., 1977-83; contbr. articles to sci. jours. Ontario Ministry of Health fellow, 1977-78. Fellow ACS, Royal Coll. Surgeons Can., Am. Coll. Ob-Gyns.; mem. AAAS, AMA, Soc. Reproductive Endocrinologists (charter), Soc. Reproductive Surgeons (charter), Fallopius Soc. (charter), Pacific Coast Fertility Soc., Am. Assn. Gynecol. Laparoscopists, Gynecologic Laser Soc., N.Y. Acad. Scis., Shufelt Gynecologic Soc., Peninsula Gynecol. Soc., Calif. Med. Assn., San Mateo County Med. Assn., Santa Clara County Med. Assn., No. Calif. Resolve (bd. dirs.), Am. Fedn. Clin. Rsch., Can. Assn. Internes and Residents (hon. life, pres. 1977-79, bd. dirs. 1974-79, rep. AMA resident physician sect. 1978-79, rep. Can. Med. Protective Assn. 1975-78, rep. Can. Med. Assn. 1975-78, Disting. Svc. award 1980), Profl. Assn. Internes and Residents Ont. (bd. dirs. 1973-74, v.p. 1974-75, pres. 1975-76), Royal Coll. Physician and Surgeons Can. (com. exams. 1977-80), Ont. Med. Assn. (sec. internes and residents sect. 1973-74), San Francisco Obstet. and Gynecol. Soc. Home: 16520 S Kennedy Rd Los Gatos CA 95032 Office: 540 University Ave #200 Palo Alto CA 94301

ADAMSON, GERALD EDWIN, physics technician; b. Glendive, Mont., Dec. 21, 1934; s. Ralph Lawton and Edamae (Jones) A.; m. Shirley May Carnes, Apr. 10, 1954; children: Ralph Edwin, Jeffrey Linn, Todd Evan, Tamera Gay. AS, Oreg. Inst. Tech., 1960. Mech. technician Lawrence Radiation Lab., Mercury, Nev., 1960-67; thin film technician Battelle N.W., Richland, Wash., 1967-70; physics and engring. technician Westinghouse Hanford Co., Richland, 1970—. Patentee high temperature ultrasonic transducer. Chmn. bd. Columbia Basin Concert Band, Pasco, Wash., 1986-87, bd. dirs., 1988—, also euphonium soloist. Sgt. U.S. Army, 1953-56, Korea; Sr. chief petty officer USNR, 1965-88. Republican. Home: 1103 Cottonwood Dr Richland WA 99352 Office: Westinghouse Hanford Co Box 1970 Mail Stop L6-38 Richland WA 99352

ADDAMS, ROBERT JEAN, business and financial consultant; b. Salt Lake City, Sept. 24, 1942; s. Harvey J. and Virginia (Dutson) A.; m. Mary A. Watkins, Feb. 10, 1973; children—Ryan, Kelley, Amy, Michael. B.S., U. Utah, 1968, M.B.A., 1969. Fin. analyst Western Airlines, Inc., Los Angeles, 1969-72, mgr. budgets and cost control, 1972-74, controller mktg. div., 1974-76, dir. budgets and cost control, 1976-80; v.p., gen. mgr. Ball Bros., Inc., Everette, Wash., and Anchorage, 1980-82; pres., cons. Addams & Assocs., Redmond, Wash., 1982—. Author: Care and Handling of Wetsalted Cod Fish, 1984; also articles on budgeting and business plans to monthly newsletter. Scoutmaster, Explorer advisor Gt. Salt Lake and Los Angeles councils Boy Scouts Am., 1973-75; served 2-yr. mission for Ch. Jesus Christ Latter-day Saints, 1962-64. Served with U.S. Army, 1961-62. Named Outstanding Grad., Coll. Bus., 1968, Beehive Honor Soc., 1969. Mem. U. Utah Alumni Assn. (pres. So. Calif. chpt. 1976-80), U. Utah Coll. of Bus. Alumni (pres. So. Calif. group 1978-79), Alpha Kappa Psi. Republican. Home and Office: Addams & Assocs 17003 NE 136th Pl Redmond WA 98052

ADDIE, HARVEY WOODWARD, teacher, music director; b. Birmingham, Ala., June 14, 1930; s. LeRoy and Frances (Driscoll) A.; m. Gwendolyn Marie Mendes, June 5, 1955; children: Cynthia Marie Marlow, Julie Ann Lorch, Mary Elizabeth. MusB, Coll. Pacific, 1959; MusM, U. Pacific, 1970. Cert. life music tchr., Calif. Mgr. dept. S.H. Kress and Co., Santa Monica and Stockton, Calif., 1953-55; head produce, mgr. area Safeway Stores Inc., Lodi, Stockton, Calif., 1955-61; tchr. music Manteca (Calif.) Elem. Sch. Dist., 1959-61, San Joaquin County Sch. Music Office, Stockton, 1961-71; mgr. store Bill's Music Sales, Stockton, 1971-73; dir. music El Dorado High Sch., Placerville, Calif., 1973, Stockton Unified Sch. Dist., 1973—; pres. San. Joaquin County Band Dirs. Assn., Stockton, 1984-86, Stagg High Sch. Faculty Assn., 1984-85. 1st. v.p. San Joaquin Concert Ballet Assn., Stockton, 1966; bd. dirs. Stockton opera Assn., 1968, Stockton Concert Band Assn., 1986-88. Served to cpl. U.S. Army, 1951-53, Korea. Mem. Nat. Assn. Jazz Educators, Calif. Music Educators Assn. (bd. dirs. 1983-87), Stockton Tchrs. Assn. (treas. 1986-87, 88-89), Am. Fed. Musicians (life), Calif. Tchrs. Assn. (state coun. 1986-89). Democrat. Methodist. Club: Lions. Home: 1426 W Euclid Ave Stockton CA 95204 Office: Amos Alonzo Stagg High Sch 1621 W Brookside Rd Stockton CA 95209

ADDIS, RICHARD BARTON, lawyer; b. Columbus, Ohio, Apr. 9, 1929; s. Wilbur Jennings and Leila Olive (Grant) A.; m. Marguerite C. Christjohn, Feb. 9, 1957; children—Jacqueline Carol, Barton David. BA, Ohio State U., 1954, JD, 1955. Bar: Ohio 1956, U.S. Dist. Ct. (no. dist.) Ohio 1957, N.Mex. 1963, U.S. Dist. Ct. N.Mex. 1963, Laguna Pueblo (N.Mex.) Tribal Ct. 1986. Pvt. practice, Canton, Ohio, 1956-63, Albuquerque, 1963—, Laguna Pueblo, Navajo Nation, 1986—. With USMC, 1946-48, 50-52. Mem. Ohio Bar Assn., N.Mex. Bar Assn., Am. Arbitration Assn. (arbitrator 1968—), Soc. Mining Engrs. Address: 5111 San Mateo Blvd NE Albuquerque NM 87109

ADDIS, THOMAS HOMER, III, professional golfer; b. San Diego, Nov. 30, 1945; s. Thomas H. and Martha J. (Edwards) A.; student Foothill Jr. Coll., 1963, Grossmont Jr. Coll., 1965; m. Susan Tera Buckley, June 13, 1966; children: Thomas Homer IV, Bryan Michael. Head golf profl., mgr. Sun Valley Golf Course, La Mesa, Calif., 1966-67; asst. golf profl. Singing Hills Golf Course, El Cajon, Calif., 1967-69, head golf profl., dir. golf ops., 1969—; area cons. Nat. Golf Found.; gen. chmn. Nat. Jr. Golf championship U.S. Golf Assn., 1973-89; mem. policy bd. Jr. World Golf Championships, rules chmn.; lectr. Bd. dirs. San Diego County Open, West Coast Golf Conf. and Mdse. Show, El Cajon Pony Baseball, 1981-82; trustee Calif. State Open, pres., 1980-84; chmn. Nat. Com. Liaison for Physically Challenged. Recipient Retailer award Golf Industry mag., 1985; named to Lady Aztec San Diego State U. Hall of Fame. Mem. Profl. Golfers Assn. (pres. San Diego chpt. 1978-79, v.p. chpt. 1980-81; sec. So. Calif. sect. 1978-79, pres. sect. 1980-82, bd. dirs. sect. 1974—, speaker, long-range planning com. 1983—, chmn. mem. service com. 1986-87, bd. dirs. San Diego sect. 1974—, assn. coordinator bus. schs. and seminars; named Profl. of Yr., So. Calif. sect. 1979, Nat. Golf Day Contbn. Leader, So. Calif. sect. 1973-76, 79; Horton Smith award So. Calif. sect. 1980-81, Nat. Horton Smith award 1981, Joe Graffis award Nat. Golf Found., 1988, Resort Merchandiser of Yr., So. Calif. sect. 1978, 83; ofcl. del. nat. PGA meeting, annually 1978-88, mem. nat. bd. control 1978-85, membership com. 1978, 89; nat. edn. com. 1980-85, 89, long-range planning com. 1983-85, PGA nat. bd. dirs., 1986-88, PGA rules com. 1986—, PGA championship com. 1986—, hon. life mem. So. Calif. sect., chmn. rev. com. assoc. devel. program), Nat. Amputee Golf Assn. (hon. mem.), San Diego Jr. Golf Assn. (dir.), Golf Collector's Soc., Singing Hills Tennis Club, Rotary. Author articles. Office: Singing Hills Golf Course 3007 Dehesa Rd El Cajon CA 92019

ADEGBOLA, SIKIRU KOLAWOLE, aerospace engineer, educator; b. Ibadan, Nigeria, Jan. 21, 1949; came to U.S., 1971; s. Lasisi and Moriamo Abeke (Akinyemi) A. BSME, Calif. State U., Fullerton, 1974; MBA, Calif. State U., Dominguez Hills, 1988; MSME, U. Ariz., 1975; MS in Applied Mechanics, U. So. Calif., 1977; PhD in Engring., Calif. Coast U., 1983. Registered profl. mech. engr., Calif., Ariz. Research engr. Jet Propulsion Lab., Pasadena, Calif., 1976-78; stress analyst Bechtel Power Corp., Norwalk, Calif., 1978-87; engring. mem. tech. staff Structural Analysis dept. Space Transp. Systems div. Rockwell Internat., Downey, Calif., 1987—; prof. engring. Calif. State U., Fullerton, 1984—. Leopold Schepp Found. fellowship, 1972-74. Mem. ASME (assoc.), NSPE, Calif. Soc. Profl. Engrs., Nat. Mgmt. Assn. Home: PO Box 345 Downey CA 90241 Office: Rockwell Internat Corp Space Transp Systems Div Structural Analysis Dept 12214 Lakewood Blvd Downey CA 90241

ADELIZZI, ROBERT FREDERICK, savings and loan executive; b. Phila., Feb. 9, 1935; s. Alfred Frederick and Natalie Marie (Vilotti) A.; m. Thomasine Starr Lane, Dec. 22, 1959; children: Mary Lee, Judith Anne, James Frederick. A.B., Dartmouth, 1957; J.D., U. San Diego, 1963. Bar: Calif. 1964. Pres., dir. Home Fed. Savs. & Loan Assn., San Diego, 1981—, also chief operating officer; bd. dirs. Pioneer Fed. Savs. & Loan Assn., Honolulu. Chmn. bd. trustees Children's Hosp. and Health Ctr.; gen. campaign chmn. United Way San Diego County. Served to capt. USMC, 1957-61. Mem. ABA, Calif. Bar Assn., San Diego County Bar Assn. Republican. Roman Catholic. Clubs: Kona Kai, San Diego Tennis and Racquet, San Diego Yacht. Office: Home Fed Savs & Loan Assn 625 Broadway Ste 1400 San Diego CA 92101

ADELMAN, JONATHAN REUBEN, political science educator, consultant; b. Washington, Oct. 30, 1948; s. Benjamin and Kitty (Sandler) A.; m. Dora Zhu, Aug. 12, 1988. BA, Columbia U., 1969, MA, 1972, M in Philosophy, 1974, PhD, 1976. Vis. asst. prof. Columbia U., N.Y.C., 1977; vis. asst. prof. U. Ala., Tuscaloosa, 1977-78; asst. prof. Grad. Sch. Internat. Studies, U. Denver, 1978-85, assoc. prof., 1985—; sr. research analyst Sci. Applications, Inc., Denver, 1981-87, cons. 1988—; Lady Davis vis. assoc. prof. Hebrew U. Jerusalem, 1986; vis. fellow Soviet Acad. Scis., 1989, Chinese Inst. Contemporary Internat. Rels., Beijing, 1988; vis. lectr. Japan, India, Hong Kong; vis. prof. Beijing U., 1989; with U.S. Info. Agy., 1989. Author: The Revolutionary Armies, 1980, Revolution, Armies and War, 1986, Prelude to the Cold War: Tsarist, Soviet and U.S. Armies in Two World Wars, 1988; co-author: The Dynamics of Soviet Foreign Policy, 1987; editor: Communist Armies in Politics, 1982, Terror and Communist Politics, 1984, Superpowers and Revolution, 1986; co-editor: Contemporary Soviet Military Affairs: The Legacy World War II, 1989; contbr. numerous articles in field to profl. jours. Charles Phelps Taft fellow U. Cin., 1976-77; Am. Philos. Soc. grantee, 1980. Mem. Am. Polit. Sci. Assn., Am. Assn. Advancement Slavic Studies, Inter-Univ. Sem. Armed Forces and Soc. Democrat. Jewish. Office: U Denver Grad Sch Internat Studies Denver CO 80210

ADELMAN, RICK, professional basketball coach; b. June 16, 1946; m. Mary Kay Adelman; children: Kathryn Mary, Laura, R.J., David. Master's, Loyola Marymount U. Profl. basketball player San Diego, 1968-70; profl. basketball player Portland (Oreg.) Trail Blazers, 1970-73, asst. coach, 1983-89, head coach, 1989—; basketball player Chgo., New Orleans, Kansas City, and Omaha, 1973-75; head coach Chemeketa Community Coll., Salem, Oreg., 1975-83. Office: Portland Trail Blazers 700 NE Multnomah St Lloyd Bldg Ste 950 Portland OR 97232 *

ADELSON, MAXINE, nurse; b. Paterson, N.J., Dec. 14, 1941; d. George and Rose (Schlifkowitz) Weisfeld; m. David Albert Adelson, Dec. 18, 1965; children: Steven Alan, Lewis Brian, Robert Howard. RN, Newark Beth Israel Hosp., 1962; BS health svc. adminstrn., U. Phoenix, 1982. Lic. RN, N.J., N.Y., Calif. Surgical nurse Beth Israel Hosp., Passaic, N.J., 1962-63; head nurse Mt. Sinai Hosp., Los Angeles, 1963-66; office mgr. B&W Heating & Cooling, Inc., Canoga Park, 1973-79; spl. perdiem float nurse St. Joseph Med. Ctr., Burbank, 1979-86; med. review audit analyst Blue Cross Southern Calif., Woodland Hills, Calif., 1983-85; utilization review mgr. SAVECARE

(Health West), Chatsworth, 1985-87; profl. svcs. mgr. Health Internat., Los Angeles, 1987--. Mem. Tri Valley Profls. Assn. (program chmn.), Calif. Assn. Quality Assurance Profls., Nat. Assn. Quality Assurance Profls., B'Nai B'Rith Women (pres. 1973-74).

ADELSON, MERVYN LEE, entertainment and communication industry executive; b. Los Angeles, Oct. 23, 1929; s. Nathan and Pearl (Schwarzman) A.; m. Barbara Walters, May 10, 1986; children from previous marriage: Ellen, Gary, Andrew. Student, Menlo Park Jr. Coll. Pres. Markettown Supermarket and Builders Emporium, Las Vegas, 1953-63; mng. ptnr. Paradise Devel., Las Vegas, 1958—; pres. Realty Holdings, 1962—, La Costa, Inc., 1963-87; chmn. bd. dirs. Lorimar Inc., Culver City, Calif., 1969-86; chmn. bd. dirs., chief exec. officer Lorimar Telepictures Corp., Culver City, 1986-89; vice chmn. Warren Communicaitons, 1989—; chmn. East-West Capital Assocs., Inc., 1989—. Co-founder Nathan Adelson Hospice Found. Recipient Sherill Corwin Human Relations award Am. Jewish Com., 1987. Mem. Am. Film Inst. (trustee), Am. Mus. of Moving Images (trustee), Entertainment Industries Council (trustee), Acad. Motion Pictures Arts and Scis., Acad. TV Arts and Sciences, Nat. Acad. Cable Programming, Alliance for Capital Access (bd. dirs.), Com. Publicly Owned Cos. (bd. dirs.).
•

ADELSTEIN, ROBERT MILTON, social worker; b. Sioux City, Iowa, Nov. 8, 1934; s. Morris and Bertha (Greenberg) A.; m. Joanie Greintz, Aug. 26, 1956 (div. Nov. 1972); children: Deborah Kay Adelstein-Morrison, Dana Jo, David Aaron; m. Sheila Greenberg, Sept. 18, 1986. BA, Met. State Coll., Denver, 1971; MSW, U. Denver, 1975. Lic. social worker II, Colo. Equipment mgr. Northwestern Engrng. Co., Denver, 1957-69, corp. sec., 1969—; pvt. practice psychiat. social work and family therapy Denver, 1975--. Trustee Allied Jewish Fedn., Denver, 1979—; bd. dirs. Coun. of Jewish Fedns., N.Y., 1988—, Jewish Telegraphic Agy., N.Y.C., 1981—; nat commr. B'nai B'rith Hillel, Washington, 1986—; pres. Hillel Coun., Colo., 1987—. Mem. Acad. Cert. Social Workers, Am. Assn. Marriage and Family Therapists, Nat. Assn. Social Workers (diplomate in clin. social work). Republican. Office: 3601 S Clarkson St Suite 540 Englewood CO 80220

ADELSTONE, JEFFREY ALAN, accountant, tax law specialist, educator; b. Los Angeles, Feb. 15, 1947; s. James and Joyce S. (Waldman) A.; m. E. Ruth Wilcox, Apr. 6, 1968; children: Kimberley, Stacey, Toni. BS, U. Ariz., 1969; M.Edn., 1971. Cert. Jr. Coll. Instr., Ariz; cert. instr. Ariz. Dept. Real Estate, accredited Accreditation Council for Accountancy, enrolled to practice, IRS; cert. fin. planner. Tchr., Tucson High Sch., 1969-72; instr. Pima Community Coll., Tucson, 1970-78; pres., owner Adelstone Assocs., Inc. Tucson, 1970—. Active Rep. Task Force. Named Nat. Acct. of Yr., 1985, Ariz. Acct. Advocate of the Year SBA, 1988. Mem. Nat. Soc. Pub. Accts. (mem. fed. taxation com., assoc. state dir. for Ariz. 1983-84, state dir. 1987—), Nat. Assn. Enrolled Agts., Ariz. Soc. Practicing Accountants (dir. credit union, pres. Tucson chpt., state v.p. 1983-84, state pres. 1984-86), Cen. Ariz. Soc. Enrolled Agents (dir.), Enrolled Agts. Practicing in Ariz. (state pres. 1987-88), U.S. C. of C., Ariz. C. of C., Tucson Better Bus. Bur., Nat. Fedn. Ind. Bus., Registry Fin. Planning Practioners, Inst. Cert. Fin. Planners, Internat. Assn. Fin. Planners. Contbr. articles to profl. jours. Office: Adelstone Assocs Inc 165 Sarnoff St Tucson AZ 85710

ADEN, GARY DEE, healthcare company executive; b. Beatrice, Nebr., June 30, 1942; s. Fred P. and Evelyn Marie (Whiteside) A.; m. Carol Louise Dumpert, June 25, 1966; children: Marcie Lynn, Jeremy Adam. BA, U. Nebr., 1964, JD, 1966; MS, U. Pitts., 1968. Bar: Nebr. 1966, N.Y. 1971. Adminstrv. asst. Montefiore Hosp. & Med. Ctr., Bronx, N.Y., 1968-69; asst. adminstr. Albert Einstein Coll. Hosp., Bronx, 1969-72; dir. div. health econs. Am. Hosp. Assn., Chgo., 1972-75; v.p. Pa. Hosp., Phila., 1975-82, sr. v.p., 1982-86; exec. v.p., chief operating officer Am. Healthcare Systems, La Jolla, Calif., 1986—; bd. dirs. Health Insights, Inc., Baton Rouge. Contbr. articles to profl. jours. Pres. Travelers Aid Soc., Phila., 1979-80; mem. Lead San Diego, 1986—. Fellow Am. Coll. Healthcare Execs.; mem. Health Execs. Group. Republican. Office: Am Healthcare Systems 1205 Prospect La Jolla CA 92037

ADENIRAN, DIXIE DARLENE, library administrator; b. L.A., May 26, 1943; d. Alfred and Madge (Clare) Harvey. BA, U. Calif., Santa Barbara, 1965; MA, Mich. State U., 1968; MLS, U. Mich., 1970. Libr. Free Libr. of Phila., 1970-72, Coll. Sci. and Tech., Port Harcourt, Nigeria, 1972-73; libr. Ventura (Calif.) County Libr. Svcs. Agy., 1974-79, libr. dir., 1979—. Pres. Ventura County Master Chorale and Opera Assn., 1985. Mem. ALA, Calif. Libr. Assn., Calif. County Librs'. Assn. (pres. 1988), Soroptimists (pres. Ventura club 1984). Home: 5548 Rainier St Ventura CA 93003 Office: Ventura County Libr Svcs 651 E Main St Ventura CA 93003

ADICKES, H. WAYNE, research administrator, chemical engineer; b. Cuero, Tex., Sept. 6, 1940; s. Aline A. (Reed) Patterson. BS in Chemistry, Stephen F. Austin Coll., 1962; PhD in Organic Chemistry, Tex. Christian U., 1968. Sr. rsch. chemist AM Internat., Cleve., 1971-74; dir. materials tech. St. Regis Corp., West Nyack, N.Y., 1974-83; v.p. engrng. and devel. Packaging Corp. Am., Evanston, Ill., 1983-86; dir. ops., dept. chemistry U. Ariz., Tucson, 1986—; cons. to paper industry; bd. dirs. Performance Paper Corp., Kalamazoo. Mem. Am. Chem. Soc., Soc. Rsch. Adminstrs., Alpha Chi Sigma. Lutheran. Office: U Ariz Dept Chemistry Tucson AZ 85721

ADKINS, BEN FRANK, management and engineering consultant; b. West Liberty, Ky., Mar. 6, 1938; s. Stuart Kendall Adkins and Dorothy Elizabeth (Shaver) Indes; m. Judith Ann Williams, Mar. 14, 1959; children: Michelle Rene, Lori Lee. BS in Indsl. Engrng., Ariz. State U., 1964; MBA, Western New Eng. Coll., Springfield, Mass., 1971; MS in Systems Mgmt., U. So. Calif., 1983. Registered profl. engr. Enlisted USAF, 1955, commd. 2d lt., 1964, advanced through grades to maj., 1975, ret., 1979; internal cons., mgr. State of Wash., Olympia, 1979-87; mgmt. and engrng. cons. Olympia, 1987-88; sr. rsch. sci. Battelle Pacific N.W. Labs., Richland, Wash., 1988-89; mgmt. and engrng. cons. N.W. Mgmt. Engrs., Olympia, 1989—. Decorated Bronze star USAF. Mem. Inst. Indsl. Engrs. (sr.; bd. dirs. Puget Sound chpt. 1984-86, asst. dir. and dir. govt. div. 1979-83, v.p. Washington chpt. 1969-76). Home: 6606 Miner Dr SW Tumwater WA 98502 Office: NW Mgmt Engrs PO Box 7613 Olympia WA 98507

ADLAI, RICHARD SALVATORE, financial and management executive; b. Los Angeles; s. Al and Hadia Salvatore. Student, U. So. Calif., 1966-67; BS, NYU, 1975; MBA, Pepperdine U., 1982. Writer, tech. dir. Paramount Pictures Corp., Hollywood, Calif., 1967-71; writer, film producer Hollywood Cinema Center Inc., 1971-78; bus. exec. IME, Inc., Beverly Hills, Calif., 1978—, The Hilton Group, Inc., Beverly Hills, 1980—; bd. dirs. Hilton Fin. Group, Hilton Mgmt. Group, CMA, M. Margani, Inc., Hollywood Cinema Ctr., Inc., Calif. Beverage Corp., Chateau Madeleine, Baron du Bordeaux, Hilton Creative Agy. Author: King Tarick, 1965, Winternude, 1980; plays 22 Miles To Bagdad, 1966, Hassan & Hanna, 1967, By Love Defiant, 1968. Mem. Pepperdine U. Assocs., Export Mgrs. Assn. (bd. dirs. 1978-83), Toluca Lake C. of C. (bd. dirs., exec. v.p. 1974-78, world affair coun. 1978-87). Republican. Lodge: Rotary (pres. Toluca Lake, Calif. 1982-83, bd. dirs., exec. v.p., chmn. internat. relations). Home and Office: Hilton Group Inc PO Box 2026 North Hollywood CA 91610-0026

ADLER, CARY MICHAEL, automobile agency official; b. Bronx, N.Y., Feb. 24, 1950; s. Milton and Florence (Wolfe) A.; m. Amy Louise Haner, Dec. 31, 1986; children: Sharon, Brian. BA in Polit. Sci., Calif. State U., Fullerton, 1972. V.p., gen. mgr. Holiday Pools, Garden Grove, Calif., 1974-81; asst. sales mgr. Crown Toyota, Ontario, Calif., 1981-83; fleet mgr. Crown Toyota, 1983-87, sales mgr., 1987—. Adminstrv. aide to congressman Richard Hanna, Cypress, Calif., 1968-72; organizer Orange County Dems., Santa Ana, Calif., 1972—. Mem. Toyota Sales Soc., Toyota Dealers Coun., Delta Sigma Phi. Jewish. Home: 6333 Napa Ave Alta Loma CA 91701 Office: Crown Toyota 1201 Kettering Dr Ontario CA 91761

ADLER, CHARLES SPENCER, psychiatrist; b. N.Y.C., Nov. 27, 1941; s. Benjamin H. and Anne (Greenfield) A.; m. Sheila Noel Morrissey, Oct. 8, 1966. B.A., Cornell U., 1962; M.D., Duke U., 1966. Diplomate Nat. Bd. Med. Examiners, Am. Bd. Psychiatry and Neurology. Intern Tucson Hosps. Med. Edn. Program, 1966-67; psychiat. resident U. Colo. Sch. Medicine, Denver, 1967-70; pvt. practice medicine specializing in psychiatry and psychosomatic medicine, Denver, 1970—; chief div. psychiatry Rose Med. Ctr., 1982-87; co-founder Applied Biofeedback Inst., Denver, 1972-75; prof. pro tempore Cleve. Clinic, 1977; clin. asst. prof. psychiatry U. Colo. Med. Ctr., 1987—, chief of psychiatry and psychophysiology Colo. Neurology and Headache Ctr., 1988—. Recipient Award of Recognition, Nat. Migraine Found., 1981; N.Y. State regents scholar, 1958-62. Fellow Am. Psychiat. Assn.; mem. AAAS (rep. med. sect. com.), AMA, Am. Assn. Study Headache, Internat. Headache Soc. (chmn. subcom. on classifying psychiatric headaches), Am. Acad. Psychoanalysis (sci. assoc.), Colo. Psychiatry Soc., Biofeedback Soc. Colo. (pres. 1977-78), Biofeedback Soc. Am. (chmn. ethics com. 1983-87). Jewish. Author: (with Gene Stanford and Sheila M. Adler) We Are But a Moment's Sunlight, 1976; editor: (with Sheila M. Adler and Russell Packard) Psychiatric Aspects of Headache, 1987; contbr. chpts. to books, articles to profl. jours.; mem. editorial bd. Cephalalgia: an Internat. Jour. of Headache. Office: 955 Eudora St Ste 1605 Denver CO 80220

ADLER, ERWIN ELLERY, lawyer; b. Flint, Mich., July 22, 1941; s. Ben and Helen M. (Schwartz) A.; m. Stephanie Ruskin, June 8, 1967; children—Lauren, Michael, Jonathan. B.A., U. Mich., 1963, LL.M., 1967; J.D., Harvard U., 1966. Bar: Mich. 1966, Calif. 1967. Assoc. Pillsbury, Madison & Sutro, San Francisco, 1967-73; assoc. Lawler, Felix & Hall, Los Angeles, 1973-76, ptnr., 1977-82; ptnr. Rogers & Wells, Los Angeles, 1982-84, Richards, Watson & Gershon, Los Angeles, 1984—. Bd. dirs. Hollywood Civic Opera Assn., 1975-76, Children's Scholarships Inc., 1979-80. Mem. ABA (vice chmn. appellate advocacy com. 1982-87), Calif. Bar Assn., Phi Beta Kappa, Phi Kappa Phi. Jewish. Office: Richards Watson & Gershon 333 S Hope St 38th Fl Los Angeles CA 90071

ADLER, LARRY R., manufacturing company executive; b. Monroe, Wis., Apr. 21, 1944; m. Mary Elizabeth Flanagan; children: Kimberley, Stephen. BBA, U. Wis.-Whitewater, 1966. CPA, Hawaii, Wis. Staff mem., mgr., acct. Arthur Young & Co., Milw., 1968-73; prin. Arthur Young & Co., Honolulu, 1973-82; controller Fin. Security Ins. Co., Honolulu, 1982-85; v.p. fin. Osteon, Inc., Wahiawa, Hawaii, 1985—. Sec.-treas., bd. dirs. Assn. Apt. Owners Sovereign, Honolulu, 1979-86; treas., bd. dirs. Assn. Apt. Owners Kuapa Isle, Honolulu, 1978—. Served with U.S. Army, 1966-68, Vietnam. Mem. Hawaii Soc. CPA's, Am. Inst. CPA's. Home: 274 Opihikao Way Honolulu HI 96825 Office: Osteon Inc 410 Kilani Ave Ste 202 Wahiawa HI 96786

ADLER, LAUREL ANN, educational administrator, consultant; b. Cleve., Sept. 6, 1948; d. Clarence Linsley and Margaret Ann (Roberts) Wheeler; m. Thomas Jay Johnson, June 6, 1981; children—David, Anthony, Jennifer. B.A., U. Calif.-Irvine, 1968; M.A., Calif. State U.-Los Angeles, 1972; Ed.D., U. La Verne, 1980. Audlt Edn. adminstr. Hacienda La Puente Unified Sch. Dist., 1972-79; dir. career and vocat. edn. El Monte Union High Sch. Dist., 1979-83; dir. East San Gabriel Valley Regional Occupational Ctr., West Covina, Calif., 1984—; instr. Calif. State U.-Los Angeles, 1979-81; instr. UCLA, 1989—; cons. Trust Ty. Pacific Islands, 1979—. Active El Monte Coordinating Council. Recipient Nat. Vol. Action award 1974; Calif. Consortium Ind. Study Recognition award of Outstanding Ednl. Program, 1983, Calif. Sch. Adminstrs. award, 1981; named Citizen of Yr., La Puente C. of C., 1977, Outstanding Vocat. Educator, Hoffman Ednl. Systems, 1983. Mem. Assn. Calif. Sch. Adminstrs., Internat. Reading Assn., Assn. Supervision and Curriculum Devel., Calif. Consortium Ind. Study, Phi Delta Kappa. Club: Soroptomist. Author: A Self Evaluation Model for Micronesian Education Programs, 1980, Poor Readers, What Do They Really See on the Page?, 1987; pub. Essential English for Micronesians, Beginning, 1980; Essential English for Micronesians, 1980; Reading Exercises for Micronesians, 1980; contbr. articles to profl. jours. Home: 3366 Garden Terr Hacienda Heights CA 91745 Office: East San Gabriel Valley Regional Occupational Ctr 1024 W Workman West Covina CA 91790

ADLER, PATRICIA ANN, sociologist, educator; b. N.Y.C., Sept. 7, 1951; d. Benjamin Theodore and Judith Ann (Goldhill) Heller; m. Peter Adler, Aug. 20, 1972; children: Jori Ann, Brye Jacob. AB in Sociology summa cum laude, Washington U., St. Louis, 1973; MA in Sociol. Sci., U. Chgo., 1974; PhD in Sociology, U. Calif., San Diego, 1984. Instr. Tulsa Jr. Coll., 1981-83; rsch. assoc. U. Tulsa, 1983-84; asst. prof., 1984-85; asst. prof. sociology Okla. State U., Stillwater, 1985-86; asst. prof. U. Colo., Boulder, 1987—; vis. asst. prof. sociology Washington U., St. Louis, 1986-87. Author: Wheeling and Dealing, 1985, (with others) The Social Dynamics of Financial Markets, 1984, The Sociologies of Everyday Life, 1980, Membership Roles in Field Research, 1987; editor Jour. Contemporary Ethnography, 1986—, (ann. series) Sociol. Studies of Child Devel., 1984—; assoc. editor Social Problems Jour., 1984—, Jour. Urban Life, 1982—; contbr. articles to profl. jours. Mem. Am. Sociol. Assn., Soc. for Study Social Problems, Am. Soc. Criminology, Sociologists for Women in Soc., Soc. for Study of Symbolic Interaction (publ. com. 1985-88, program chmn. 1984, 86), Phi Beta Kappa. Avocations: aerobics, travel, photography, skiing, travel. Office: U Colo Dept Sociology CB 327 Boulder CO 80309

ADOLPH, DALE DENNIS, agricultural executive; b. Roundup, Mont., Apr. 28, 1948; s. Albert Jake and Lillian (Schaefer) A.; m. Victoria Marie Clark, 1967; 1 child, Steven Daniel. BS in Agrl. Bus. and Econs., Mont. State U., 1968. Field dept. mgr. Lamb Weston, Inc., Connell, Wash., 1970-75; procurement mgr. R.T. French Co., Shelley, Idaho, 1975-79; gen. mgr. Dave Kingston Produce, Inc., Ucon, Idaho, 1979—. V.p. Connell (Wash.) C. of C., 1972-73. Mem. Exchange Club (v.p. 1979-80, pres. 1980-81), Idaho Leadership Agri. Republican. Lutheran. Home: 1836 Malibu Idaho Falls ID 83404 Office: Dave Kingston Produce Inc PO Box 158 Ucon ID 83454

ADOLPH, MARY ROSENQUIST, financial company executive; b. Springfield, Mass., Oct. 7, 1949; d. Jesse Woodson and Doris May (Marquette) Rosenquist; m. Earl Anthony Soares, Mar. 18, 1972 (div. 1982); m. Joseph Edward Adolph, Oct. 3, 1986. Student San Domenico Sch., 1966-68, Dominican Coll., San Rafael, 1967-69, Calif., San Francisco Conservatory of Music, 1968-70; A.A., Coll. of Marin, 1969. Asst. v.p. Western Travelers Life Ins. Co./Putnam Fin. Services, San Rafael, 1970-80; v.p. Unimarc, Ltd., Novato, Calif., 1980-83; v.p. mktg. Western States Monetary Planning Services, Inc., Newhall, Calif., 1983-88; asst. to pres. Fed. Inventory Wholesale, Inc., 1988—. Mem. exec. com. San Marin Valley Homeowners Assn., 1979-81. Mem. Internat. Assn. Fin. Planners, Life Underwriters Assn. Democrat. Roman Catholic. Home: 14710 Burbank Blvd #102 Van Nuys CA 91411 Office: Fed Inventory Wholesale Inc 4716 Vineland Ave North Hollywood CA 91602-1222

AEMMER, KURT ROBIN, social worker; b. Bellingham, Wash., Dec. 1, 1952; s. Elmer Reynold and Myrtle Francis (Lueken) A.; m. Stella Dall' Acqua, Feb. 4, 1981; stepchildren: Angela A. Bisson, Elizabeth A. Bisson. BA in Sociology, Wash. State U., 1976; MSW, U. Mich., 1980. Mem. crisis care team St. John's Hosp., Longview, Wash., 1976-79, supr. crisis care team, 1978-79; emergency svcs. coord. Lower Columbia Mental Health Ctr., Longview, 1981-84; social worker Care Unit, Monticello Med. Ctr., Longview, 1981-84; program cons. Comprehensive Care Corp, Irvine, Calif., 1984-87, quality assurance specialist, 1987—. Office: Comprehensive Care Corp 18551 Von Karman Irvine CA 92714

AFLATOONI, SANDY JOHNSON, nurse anesthetist; b. Wahoo, Nebr., May 20, 1957; d. Weldon Wilber and Edna Theresa (Schuessler) Johnson; m. Kian Aflatooni, May 23, 1981. Dip. in Nursing, Bryan Meml. Sch. Nursing, 1979; BS in Allied Health, Nebr. Wesleyan, 1983, BS in Anesthesia, 1986. Cert. registered nurse anesthetist. Staff float RN Bryan Meml. Hosp., Lincoln, Nebr., 1979-81, ICU/CCU critical care RN, 1981-86; home health care vis. medicare nurse Upjohn HHC, Lincoln, Nebr., 1981-86; ICU/CCU RN instr. Bryan Meml. Sch. Nursing, Lincoln, Nebr., 1983-86; cert. RN anesthetist U. Utah, Salt Lake City, 1986—, Tooele (Utah) Regional Ctr., 1987—, Jordan Valley Hosp., West Jordan, Utah, 1987—; pres. bd. dirs. Mountain West Anesthesia Inc., Midvale, Utah, 1987—, CPR instr., Am. Heart Assn., 1978—, advanced cardiac life support cert., 1981—. Church organist United Meth. Ch., Valparaiso, Nebr., 1971-75; mem. curriculum com. Bryan Meml. Sch. Nursing, 1983-84. Mem. Am. Assn. Nurse Anesthetists, Utah Cert. Registered Nurse Anesthetist Assn., Phi Mu. Office: Mountain West Anesthesia Inc 991 Floret Ln #33C Midvale UT 84047

AFZAL, SAYED MOHAMMAD JAVED, laboratory staff scientist; b. Saharanpur, India, Oct. 4, 1952; came to U.S., 1979; s. S.M. Afzal and Ahmer (Jehan) H.; m. Veena Afzal, Oct. 28, 1977; 1 child, Sarah Yasmeen. BS in Biology, Meerut U., India, 1969; MS in Botany, Aligarh Muslim U., India, 1971; MPhil in Radiobiology, Jawaharlal Nehru U., New Delhi, 1975, PhD in Radiobiology, 1978. Pool officer Scientist Pool, Council for Sci. and Indsl. Research, New Delhi, 1979; research scientist Cancer Research and Treatment Ctr., U. N.Mex., Albuquerque, 1979-80; staff scientist Lawrence Berkeley Lab., U. Calif., 1980—. contbr. articles to profl. jours. Mem. Am. Soc. Therapeutic Radiology and Oncology, N.Y. Acad. Scis., Soc. for Free Radical Research, Radiation Research Soc., Environ. Mutagen Soc., AAAS. Home: 3380 Chamberlain Ct Walnut Creek CA 94598 Office: U Calif Lawrence Berkeley Lab 1 Cyclotron Rd Bldg 74 Berkeley CA 94720

AGARWAL, AVADHESH KUMAR, import company executive; b. Bareilly, India, Feb. 25, 1945; came to U.S., 1976; s. Ram Saroop and Luxmidevi (Agarwal) A.; m. Uma Rani Sharma, June 15, 1975; children: Amit, Anisha. MSc, Lucknow U., India, 1964; LLB, Delhi U., India, 1974. Statistician Civil Aviation Dept., New Delhi, India, 1970-75; pres. Uma Enterprises Inc., Los Angeles, 1980—. Home: 1927 Upland St Rancho Palos Verdes CA 90732

AGEE, WILLIAM M., construction company executive; b. Boise, Idaho, Jan. 5, 1938; s. Harold J. and Suzanne (McReynolds) A.; m. Mary Cunningham, June 5, 1982; children: Mary Alana, William N. AA, Boise Jr. Coll., 1958; BS with high honors, U. Idaho, 1960; MBA with distinction, Harvard U., 1963; DSc in Indsl. Mgmt. (hon.), Lawrence Inst. Tech., 1977, Nathaniel Hawthorne Coll., 1977; D.C.S., Eastern Mich. U., 1978; LLD (hon.), U. Detroit, 1980; DBA (hon.), Bryant Coll., 1980, Cleary Coll., 1980. Various positions Boise Cascade Corp., 1963-69, sr. v.p., chief fin. officer, 1969-72; exec. v.p., chief fin. officer Bendix Corp., Southfield, Mich., 1972-76, pres., 1976-79, chief oper. officer, 1976-77, chmn. bd., 1977-83; chmn., chief exec. officer Semper Enterprises, Inc., Osterville, Mass., from 1983; chmn. bd., pres., chief exec. officer Morrison Knudsen Corp., Boise, 1988—; bd. dirs. Dow Jones & Co., Lo Jack Corp.; chmn. data processing and office automation Grace Commn., 1981-82; presdl. appointee U.S. Quadrennial Commn., 1988. Chmn. Gov.'s Higher Edn. Capital Investment Adv. Com., 1979; mem. adv. coun. Japan-U.S. Econ. Relations, 1982-84. Named Disting. Alumnus Boise State U. (formerly Boise Jr. Coll.), 1972; recipient Alumni Achievement Award Harvard U. Bus. Sch., 1977; named to U. Idaho Hall of Fame, 1978. Mem. Am. Inst. CPA's, Idaho Soc. CPA's, Mich. Assn. CPA's, Council on Fgn. Relations, Brit-N.Am. Com., Conf. Bd., Bus. Roundtable, Harvard Bus. Sch. Assocs., Phi Kappa Phi, Arid Club Boise, Economic Club, Hillcrest Country Club, Boise Oyster Harbors. Republican. Roman Catholic. Office: Morrison Knudsen Corp Morrison-Knudsen Pla PO Box 73 Boise ID 83707

AGERBEK, SVEN, mechanical engineer; b. Soerabaya, Dutch Indies, Aug. 2, 1926; came to U.S., 1958, naturalized, 1964; s. Niels Magnus and Else Heidam (Nielsen) Agerbek-Poulsen; m. Helen Hadsbjerg Gerup, May 30, 1963; 1 child, Jesper. MSME, Tech. U., Denmark, 1952; LLB, LaSalle Estension U., 1967; postgrad., UCLA, 1969. Registered profl. engr., Calif., Ohio, Fla. With Danish Refrigeration Research Inst., Copenhagen, 1952; engr. B.P. Oil Co., Copenhagen, 1952-54; refrigeration insp. J. Lauritzen, Copenhagen, 1954-56; engr. Danish-Am. Gulf Oil Co., Copenhagen, 1956-58; instr. Ohio U., Athens, 1958-60; asst. prof. Calif. State Poly. U., San Luis Obispo, 1960-62; prin. engr., environment dept. Ralph M. Parsons Co., Los Angeles, 1962-73; engrng. supr. Bechtel Power Co., Norwalk, Calif., 1973-85; pres., owner Woodcraft Cabinets, Inc., Rancho Cordova, Calif., 1985—. Past mem. Luth. Ch. council, pres. Luth. Sch. bd. Served with Danish underground movement, World War II. Mem. ASHRAE (mem. tech. com., author Guide on Air Conditioning of Nuclear Power Plants), Danish Engrng. Soc. Home: 5201 Vista del Oro Way Fair Oaks CA 95628 Office: Woodcraft Cabinets Inc 11386 Amalgam Way Rancho Cordova CA 95670

AGHABEGIANS, VAHE, data processing executive; b. Tehran, Iran, Nov. 26, 1952; came to U.S., 1973; s. George and Manoush (Minassian) A.; m. Veronic Aghayan, July 29, 1974 (div. 1982); m. Odette Markarian, July 4, 1986; 1 child, George. BSEE, Northeastern U., Boston, 1978. Pres. Universal Transport Services, Boston, 1978-79, Uniprint, Inc., Boston, 1979-80, The Romney Group, Inc., Boston, 1980-83, Microcomp, Inc., Boston, 1983-86, Microcomp Enterprises, Inc., Burbank, Calif., 1986—. Office: Microcomp Enterprises Inc 321 E Alameda #D Burbank CA 91502

AGNEW, HAROLD MELVIN, physicist; b. Denver, Mar. 28, 1921; s. Sam E. and Augusta (Jacobs) A.; m. Beverly Jackson, May 2, 1942; children: Nancy E. Agnew Owens, John S. A.B., U. Denver, 1942; M.S., U. Chgo., 1948, Ph.D., 1949. With Los Alamos Sci. Lab., 1943-46, alt. div. leader, 1949-61, leader weapons div., 1964-70, dir., 1970-79; pres. GA Techs. Inc., San Diego, 1979-85, dir., 1985—; dir. Blaws Corp., 1967-72; dir. DBA Systems, Inc.; sci. adviser Supreme Allied Comdr. in Europe, Paris, France, 1961-64; Chmn. Army Sci. Adv. Panel, 1965-70, mem., 1970-74; mem. aircraft panel Pres.'s Sci. Adv. Com., 1965-73; mem. USAF Sci. Adv. Bd., 1957-69, Def. Sci. Bd., 1965-70, Gov. N.Mex. Radiation Adv. Council, 1959-61; sec. N.Mex. Health and Social Services, 1971-73; chmn. gen. adv. com. ACDA, 1974-77, mem., 1977-81; mem. aerospace safety adv. panel NASA, 1964-70, 86—; mem. U.S. Army Sci. Bd., 1978-80, White House Sci. Council, 1982-89; adj. prof. U. Calif., San Diego, 1988—. Mem. council engrng. NRC, 1978-82; mem. Los Alamos Bd. Ednl. Trustees, 1950-55, pres., 1955; trustee San Diego Mus. Art, 1983-87; mem. Woodrow Wilson Nat. Fellowship Found., 1973-80; N.Mex. State senator, 1955-61; sec. N.Mex. Legis. Council, 1957-61; chmn. N.Mex. Senate Corp. Commn., 1957-61; mem. Fed. Emergency Agy., 1982-88; bd. dirs. Fedn. Rocky Mountain States, Inc., 1975-77. Recipient Ernest Orlando Lawrence award AEC, 1966; Enrico Fermi award Dept. Energy, 1978. Fellow Am. Phys. Soc., AAAS; mem. Nat. Acad. Scis., Nat. Acad. Engrng., Council on Fgn. Relations, Phi Beta Kappa, Sigma Xi, Omicron Delta Kappa. Home: 322 Punta Baja Solana Beach CA 92075

AGNEW, THOMAS EDWARD, communications executive; b. Spokane, Wash., Feb. 26, 1950; s. Edward John and Mary Ann (Schroeder) A.; m. Stephanie Stone, Sept. 3, 1977; children: Anna Maria, Julia Jean, Therese Alexandria. BA in Polit. Sci., U. Wash., 1972, postgrad., 1972-73. Asst. dir. Seattle Dept. Human Resources, 1972-74; mgmt. cons. Toner & Assocs., Seattle, 1974-76; sales mgr. Sta. KAOI Radio, Wailuku, Maui, Hawaii, 1976-81, Sta. KXLY News Radio, Spokane, Wash., 1981-82, Sta. KAYU TV, Spokane, 1982-86; gen. mgr. Sta. KXLY AM-FM, Spokane, 1986—; guest lectr. Maui Community Coll, 1979-80; mem. Spokane Community Coll. Radio Broadcasting Adv. Com., 1988. Pres. exec. bd. St. Mary's Sch., Spokane, 1987-88, bd. dirs. Maui Jr. Achievement, 1984-85, Kihei (Maui) Aloha Assn.; v.p. Liberty Lake (Wash.) Property Owners' Assn., 1988-89. Mem. Nat. Assn. Broadcasters, Radio Advt. Bur., Spokane Area Radio Broadcasters, Spokane Executive Assn. Roman Catholic. Office: KXLY AM-FM W 500 Boone Ave Spokane WA 99201

AGNOS, ARTHUR CHRIST, mayor; b. Springfield, Mass., Sept. 1, 1938; s. Christ and Mary A.; m. Cheryl Hankins, 1975; children: Christopher, Stephen. BS, Bates Coll., 1960; MSW, Fla. State U., 1966. With human relations dept. San Francisco Housing Authority, 1966-69; cons. Assemblyman Leo MacCarthy, Sacramento, Calif., 1969-76; mem. Calif. Legislature, Sacramento, 1976-87; mayor City of San Francisco, 1987—; chmn. joint audit com. Calif. State Legis., vice chmn. joint com. refugee settlement. Chmn. joint com. Welfare Reform, Sacramento, 1985-87. With U.S. Army, 1961-63. Named Assemblyman of the Year Network of Older Californians; recipient Jerry Sampson award Jewish Pub. Affairs com. of Calif., Homeless Youth award Advocates for Children and Youth, Outstanding Leadership award Calif. Nurses Assn. Mem. Am. Hellenic Ednl. Progressive Assn., Dynamis. Democrat. Greek Orthodox. Office: Office of Mayor City Hall Rm 200 San Francisco CA 94102

AGNOST, FRANK PETER, publishing executive, editor; b. Chgo., June 15, 1918; s. Peter and Effie (Kellar) A.; m. Mildred Corby, Aug. 31, 1940;

children—Frank Peter, Adrienne Verreos; m. 2d, Melissa Caravellas, Sept. 24, 1970. Student U. Calif.-Berkeley, 1940. Commr. dept. pub. welfare City and County of San Francisco, 1951-58; copy boy, reporter, asst. fgn. editor, then asst. to pub. San Francisco Chronicle, 1940-61; pres. Falcon Assocs. Inc., San Francisco, 1961—; editor, pub. Hellenic Jour., San Francisco, 1975—. Served to capt. USAAF, 1942-46. Decorated Gold Cross, Order of Phoenix (Greece), Meml. Medal 1971, Archon, Order of St. Andrew, Ecumenical Patriarchate (Constantinople), recipient Award of Honor, United Greek Orthodox Charities N.Y., 1971; Disting. Service Award, Greek Orthodox Archdiocese N.Y., 1976; Axion award Hellenic Am. Profl. Soc. of San Francisco, 1978; Extraordinary Community Service award Calif. Assembly, 1982; medal of St. Paul, Greek Orthodox Archdiocese, 1982. Mem. ASCAP, Am. Legion, Clubs: San Francisco Press, Bohemian, Masons, Ahepa. Home: 1170 Sacramento St San Francisco CA 94108 Office: Falcon Assocs 527 Commercial St San Francisco CA 94111

AGOGINO, GEORGE ALLEN, anthropologist, educator; b. West Palm Beach, Fla., Nov. 18, 1920; s. Andrew and Beulah Mae A.; m. Mercedes Merner, Dec. 1, 1952; children: Alice, Karen. BA, U. N.Mex., 1948, MA, 1951; PhD, Syracuse U., 1958; postgrad., Harvard U., 1962-63. Asst. prof. anthropology Syracuse U., N.Y., 1956-58; asst. prof. anthropology U. S.D., Vermillion, 1958-59, U. Wyo., Laramie, 1959-61; Wenner-Gren postdoctoral fellow Harvard U., Cambridge, Mass., 1961-62; assoc. prof. Baylor U., Waco, Tex., 1962-63; assoc. prof. anthropology Eastern N.Mex. U., Portales, 1963-68, prof., 1968-85, disting. research prof. in anthropology, 1985—, dir. Indian Inst., 1963—, founding dir. Anthropology Mus., Blackwater Draw Mus., Miles Mus., 1967-86, chmn. dept. anthropology, 1963-80, dir. spl. programs, 1972-73, dir. humanities div., 1973-74; appointed disting. research prof. in anthropology Eastern N.Mex. U., 1985; cons. forensic phys. anthropology, U.S. Bur. Reclamation. Author monographs in field; contbr. numerous articles on Mexican anthropology, primitive religion and folklore to profl. jours.; cons. to mags. American Antiquity, Plains Anthropologist, National Geographic, Pursuit, Chesopiean. Served with Signal Corps, U.S. Army, 1942-46. Recipient Pres.'s award Eastern N.Mex. U., 1971, numerous rsch. grants; proclaimed Ofcl. Eminent Scholar by State of N.Mex. Fellow Explorers Club Am., Am. Anthrop. Assn., AAAS, Instituto Interamericana. Republican. Home: 1600 S Main Portales NM 88130 Office: Ea NMex U Paleo-Indian Inst Box 2154 Portales NM 88130

AGONIA, BARBARA ANN, English educator; b. St. Louis, June 11, 1934; d. Robert Lewis and Suzanne (Carter) Klinefelter; m. Robert James Agonia, Mar. 25, 1972. Student, U. Exeter, Devon, Eng., 1954-55; BA, Hanover Coll., 1957; MA, U. Nev., Las Vegas, 1971; postgrad., U. Nev., Reno, 1983—. Tchr. Carrollton (Ill.) Community Unit High Sch., 1955-56, 59-61, White Hall (Ill.) Community Unit High Sch., 1957-59; tchr., chmn. dept. English ROVA Community Unit High Sch., Oneida, Ill., 1961-69; prof. English Clark County Community Coll., North Las Vegas, Nev., 1971—, chmn. dept., 1972-75, dir. re-entry ctr., 1980-83; speaker in field, Ind., Ill., Nev., Eng., 1952—. Author poems. Vol. Opportunity Village, Las Vegas, Nev., 1985—; bd. dirs. Friends of Nev. Wilderness, Las Vegas, 1985—. Mem. Western Lit. Assn. (Golden award 1984), Shakespeare Assn. Am., Coll. Conf. Composition and Communication (exec. com.), Nev. State Edn. Assn. (exec. bd. 1975-79), League of United Latin Am. Citizens (nat. parliamentarian 1978-82), Internat. Platform Assn. Methodist (various offices held). Lodge: Soroptimists (parliamentarian Las Vegas club 1984—, pres.-elect 1986-87, pres. 1987-88, Women Helping Women award 1983, named Woman of Distinction 1986), Order of Eastern Star (Worthy Matron 1960-61). Home: 3411 Frontier St Las Vegas NV 89102 Office: Clark County Community Coll 3200 Cheyenne Ave North Las Vegas NV 89030

AGRUSA, ROSALIE, business owner, accountant; b. Aguilar, Colo., Nov. 10, 1931; d. Guiseppe and Maria (Rinauro) Brocato; m. Joseph Anthony Agrusa, Apr. 30, 1955; children: Tina Marie, Lori Ann, James Joseph, Joseph James. Grad. high sch., L.A. Exec. officer Agrusa's, Inc., Escondido, Calif., 1970—; office mgr. Crown Real Estate, Escondido, 1985-86; computer operator Orange Glen (Calif.) High Sch., 1984. Republican. Roman Catholic. Home: 1927 Acorn Glen Escondido CA 92027 Office: Agrusa Inc 1606 E Valley Pkwy Escondido CA 92027

AGUA, KATHERINE STORY, accountant; b. Sacramento, Mar. 5, 1929; d. Harrison Hayward and Olive (Wilson) Story; m. Michael Agua, Dec. 26, 1948; children: Michael Jay, James Andrew, Joanne Kathleen, Marianne Frances. CPA, Calif. Bookkeeper Western Calif. Canners, Antioch, 1947-51; clk. Pacific Gas and Electric Co., Antioch, 1952-53; acctg. clk. Fibreboard Corp., Antioch, 1955-56; office mgr., v.p. Crane Bros., Pittsburg, Calif., 1959-67; bookkeeper John L. Willis CPA, Pittsburg, 1967-71; CPA, ptnr. Willis & Agua CPAs, Pittsburg, 1972-77; CPA, owner Katherine S. Agua CPA, Antioch, 1977—. Treas. Antioch Meals on Wheels, 1980-82. Mem. Calif. Soc. CPAs, Soc. Calif. Accts. (pres. Diablo chpt. 1976-77). Republican. Roman Catholic. Office: 3009 Delta Fair Blvd Antioch CA 94509

AGUILAR, DOLORES BRAVO, nurse; b. LaBarca, Mex., July 5, 1965; came to U.S. 1976; d. Magdaleno N. and Margarita (Bravo) A. BSN, San Jose State U., 1988. Tutor Hartnell Coll. Tutorial Ctr., Salinas, Calif., 1984-85; personnel clk. Alexian Bros. Hosp., San Jose, 1985-86; receptionist Alexian Bros. Hosp., 1986-87, obstetrical technician, 1987—; clk. Berryessa Med. Ctr., San Jose, 1985-86; surg. technician San Jose Hosp., 1988—. Santa Clara County Med. Soc. scholar, 1988. Mem. Chicana Latina Nurses Assn. (scholar 1987-88). Home: 2295 Orlando Dr San Jose CA 95122

AGUILAR, MARGARET HOPE, lawyer; b. Wilmette, Ill., Aug. 13, 1951; d. Gabriel and Nona May (Linton) A. BSBA in Fin., U. So. Calif., 1979; JD, Loyola U., L.A., 1985. Bar: L.A. 1986. Intern TRW Def. & Space Systems, Redondo Beach, Calif., 1978; trader fgn. exch. Citibank, N.Y.C., 1979-80; corp. banker Security Pacific Bank, L.A., 1980-85, Calif. Fed. Savs. & Loan, Santa Monica, Calif., 1985-86; pvt. practice corp. law Century City, Calif., 1986-87; bankruptcy, securities lawyer Petillon & Davidoff, L.A., 1987—. Vol. work for terminally ill. Mem. ABA, L.A. County Bar Assn., Century City Bar Assn., Beverly Hills Bar Assn., Women Lawyers of L.A. Office: Petillon & Davidoff 9841 Airport Blvd Ste 1500 Los Angeles CA 90045

AGUIRRE, GERARDO, electrical engineer; b. El Paso, Tex., Dec. 21, 1960; s. Santiago and Carmen (Silva) A. BS, U. Tex., El Paso, 1983; MS, U. Ariz., 1986. Elec. engr. Lawrence Livermore (Calif.) Labs., 1983, 84, Sandia Nat. Labs., Albuquerque, 1986—. Contbr. articles to profl. jours. Mem. Mexican Am. Engring. and Sci. Soc. Democrat. Home: 10204 San Luis Rey Pl Albuquerque NM 87111 Office: Sandia Nat Labs PO Box 5800 Albuquerque NM 87185

AGUZZI-BARBAGLI, DANILO LORENZO, language educator; b. Arezzo, Italy, Aug. 1, 1924; came to U.S., 1950; s. Guglielmo and Marianna (Barbagli) Aguzzi-B. Dottore in Lettere, U. Florence (Italy), 1949; Ph.D., Columbia U., 1959. Instr., asst. U. Chgo., 1959-64; assoc. prof. Tulane U., New Orleans, 1964-71; prof. U. B.C., Vancouver, 1971—; Mem. Fulbright-Hayes final scholarship com., 1970—; adviser on scholarship application Can. Council, 1972-75. Author: Critical Edition of Della Poetica of Francesco Patrizi, 3 vols, 1969, 70, 71, 72, Critical Edition of Francesco Patrizi's Lettere ed opuscoli inediti, 1975; contbr. articles in field to profl. jours. Newberry Library fellow Chgo., 1974; Folger Shakespeare Library fellow Washington, 1975. Fellow Am. Philos. Soc.; mem. Newberry Library Assn., Dante Soc. Am., Italian Honor Soc. (regional rep.), Accademia Petrarca, Medieval Soc. Am., Renaissance Soc. Am., Modern Lang. Assn., AAUP, Am. Assn. Tchrs. Italian. Office: U BC, Vancouver, BC Canada V6T 1W5

AHERN, ARLEEN FLEMING, librarian; b. Mt. Harris, Colo., Oct. 15, 1922; d. John R. and Josephine (Vidmar) Fleming; B.A., U. Utah, 1943; M.A., U. Denver, 1962; postgrad. U. Colo., 1967; m. George Irving Ahern, June 14, 1944; 1 son, George Irving. Library asst. Army Air Force Library, Salt Lake City, 1943-44; library asst. Colo. Women's Coll. Library (now U. Denver/CWC Campus), 1952-60, acquisitions librarian, 1960—, rep. Adult Edn. Council Denver, 1960—, reference librarian Penrose Library, WEC librarian, assoc. prof. librarianship. Committeewoman, Republican Com., Denver, 1958-59. Mem. ALA, Mountain Plains Library Assn., Colo. (1st v.p., pres. 1969-70, dir. 1971—), Library Assn., Altrusa Club of Denver (2d v.p. 1968-69, dir. 1971-74, 76, 78), Soc. Am. Archivists, Mountain Plains Adult Edn. Assn., AAUP. Home: 746 Monaco Pkwy Denver CO 80220 Office: U Denver Penrose Libr Denver CO 80208

AHERN, GEORGE IRVING, JR., realtor; b. Salt Lake City, Mar. 20, 1945; s. George I. and Arleen Russell (Fleming) A.; m. Margery L. Blanc, Mar. 11, 1968 (div. 1976); m. Jane Carole Osiek, July 23, 1977; children: John C., Steven J., Michael K., Anne F. BA, U. Colo., 1967, MBA, 1971. Rsch. assoc. Hammer Siler George Assoc., Denver, 1972-76; comml. broker Coldwell Banker, Denver, 1976-81, Iliff Thorn and Co., Denver, 1981-83; v.p. Oxford Properties, Denver, 1983-88; pres., chief exec. officer Ahern and Co., Denver, 1988—. Bd. trustees Denver Symphony Orch., 1986—; advisor to bd. Denver Performing Arts Ctr., 1987—; bd. dirs. 16th St. Mall Market Dist., Denver, 1986—, Denver Civil Ventures/DDI, 1984—. With USN, 1968-71, Spain. Mem. Urban Land Inst., Denver Rotary, Denver Athletic Club, Crestmoor Club. Home: 2909 East 7th Ave Denver CO 80206 Office: Ahern & Co 707 17th St Denver CO 80202

AHERN, JOHN FRANCIS, author, artist; b. Berthold, N.D., Jan. 27, 1924; s. William and Gladys Marie (Brown) A. (div.) five children. Grad. high sch., Berthold, N.D. Announcer and program dir. Radio Station KYJC, Medford, Oreg., 1947-54; owner Art Ctr., Medford, 1954-56; advt. dir. basement May Co., L.A., 1956-60; owner In & Out Advt., Redondo Beach, Calif., 1960-69; freelance journalist Pasadena, Calif., 1969-84; freelance author Pasadena, 1985—. Author: Brandywine, 1988. With U.S. Mcht. Marine, 1944-45. Democrat.

AHLBERG, GUS, aerospace company executive, electrical engineer; b. Reval, USSR, May 12, 1936; s. Kurt Paul and Else (Fiedler) A.; m. Rosa Palacios, May 1956; children: Jeffrey Paul, Jennifer Christine. BSEE, Healds Coll., San Francisco, 1965; BA, Calif. State U., San Mateo, 1970. Elec. draftsman United Airlines, San Francisco, 1955-62, elec. engr., 1962-74, elec. technician, 1974-81; regional mgr. aerospace Fenwal Inc., Burlingame, Calif., 1982-87, mgr. new aerospace prodn., 1984-87, mgr. aerospace, 1987—; mgr., owner Electric Drafting Svc., San Mateo, 1968-75. Contbr. articles to profl. jours. Treas. Boy Scouts Am., San Mateo, 1975-76, scout master, 1976-78. With U.S. Army, 1959-62. Office: Fenwal Aerospace 1633 Old Bayshore Hwy Burlingame CA 94010

AHLERS, JOHN PETER, lawyer; b. Salzburg, Austria, Nov. 29, 1951; came to U.S., 1953; s. John Gordon and Maria Magdalena (Wieser) A.; m. Lynn Ann Burleson, May 22, 1982; children: Julia Ann, John Gordon, Carl Heinz. BSCE, Wash. State U., 1975; MS in Constrn. Engring., Stanford U., 1976; JD summa cum laude, Gonzaga U., 1982. Bar: Wash. 1983, U.S. Dist. Ct. (ea. and we. dists.) Wash. 1983, U.S. Claims Ct. 1986, U.S. Supreme Ct. 1986. Project engr. Mullen Constrn., Kent, Wash., 1976-78; project mgr. Mullen Constrn., Yakima, Wash., 1978-80; ops. engr. Mullen Mining, Casper, Wyo., 1978; Law clk. to presiding judge U.S. Dist. Ct. (ea. dist.) Wash., Spokane, 1982; assoc. Barokas & Martin, Seattle, 1983-89, ptnr., 1989—. ALCOA scholar Wash. State U., 1974. Mem. Wash. State Bar Assn., Assn. Trial Lawyers Am., ASCE (mgmt. award 1976), Am. Arbitration Assn. Home: 6231 44th Ave NE Seattle WA 98115 Office: Barokas & Martin 1422 Bellevue Seattle WA 98122

AHLGREN, GIBSON-TAYLOR, real estate broker; b. Memphis, Sept. 7, 1940; s. Frank Richard and Nona Elizabeth (Alley) A. B.S., U. Md., 1967; J.D., Western State U., San Diego, 1978. Legis. clk. U.S. Senate, Washington, 1963-67, spl. asst., 1970-71; legis. rep. Associated Gen. Contractors, Washington, 1971-73, San Diego, 1973-74; campaign dir. Brown for Gov. Calif., 1974; mgmt. cons. Ahlgren, Peters & Assocs., La Jolla, Calif., 1975-77; v.p., dir. pub. affairs Gt. Am. First Savs. Bank, San Diego, 1977-84; polit. cons., 1984-85; real estate broker, 1986—. Served to lt. USN, 1967-70; Vietnam. Mem. Pi Kappa Alpha.

AHLSTROM, JOHN KEITH, computer infosystem engineer, educator; b. Jamestown, N.Y., July 1, 1942; s. Paul A. and Ruth M. (Conner) A.; m. Anne D. Pemberton, Dec. 15, 1964 (div. June 1976); m. Janice Tribe, June 17, 1982; 1 child, Michele. BA in Internat. Relations, Am. U., Washington, 1964, MA in Internat. Relations, 1968. Founder, systems mgr. Data Resources Inc., Lexington, Mass., 1969-74; operating systems programmer Burroughs Corp., Goleta, Calif., 1974-76; computer micro architect Data Gen. Corp., Mass. and Calif., 1976-78; mgr. software devel. Olivetti Corp., Cupertino, Calif., 1978-79; founder CompuShop Inc., Dallas, 1976-85; mgr. systems architecture Bell-No. Research, Mountain View, Calif., 1979-82; founder, dir. systems engring. DAVID Systems, Sunnyvale, Calif., 1982—; adj. prof. computer sci. San Francisco State U., 1976-86, assoc. prof. computer sci., 1986—. Inventor in field. Mem. Assn. Computing Machinery, Computer Soc. of IEEE (affiliate). Office: DAVID Systems 701 E Evelyn Sunnyvale CA 94086

AHLSTROM, PATRICK CARLTON, police officer; b. Boone, Iowa, Dec. 11, 1945; s. William DeWayne and Mary Elizabeth (Barrett) A.; m. Mary Lundgren, Nov. 6, 1965; children: Timothy Carlton, Jeffrey James. BS, Iowa State U., 1977; MBA, U. Colo., 1988. Police officer Ames (Iowa) Police Dept., 1968-70; from police agt. to capt. Lakewood (Colo.) Police Dept., 1970-77; chief of police Sioux City (Iowa) Police Dept., 1977-79; dir. pub. safety Broomfield (Colo.) Dept. of Pub. Safety, 1979-87; chief of police Arvada (Colo.) Police Dept., 1987—; bd. dirs. Peace Officers Standards & Tng. for State of Colo., 1985—; chmn. Police Pension Bd., City of Arvada, 1987—. Contbr. articles to profl. jours. Chmn. logistics and fundraising for Torch Run for Spl. Olympics, Prairie Gold Area Council, Boy Scouts Am., 1977. Cited for Spl. Recognition, Regional Law Enforcement Assn., Denver, 1983; recipient outstanding Community Service, Broomfield Area C. of C., 1987, disting. service award, Denver Area Council of Govt., 1983. Mem. Colo. Assn. Chiefs of Police, Internat. Assn. of Chiefs of Police, Police Mgmt. Assn., Police Exec. Research Forum Colo., Major Cities Chiefs of Police Assn., Jefferson County Prevention Task Force. Office: Arvada Police Dept 8101 Ralston Rd Arvada CO 80002

AHOY, CHRISTOPHER KEEN, architect, facilities planner/designer, consultant; b. Kalimpong, India, May 29, 1939; came to U.S., 1964; s. King Nam (Lai) and Chun Oi (Tham) A.; m. Breena E. D'Silva (div.); m. E. Ruth Lynn, Nov. 6, 1981; stepchildren: Gregorio, Deborah, Claudette Altomirono. Student, St. Xavier's Coll., Calcutta, India, 1959; BArch, Indian Inst. Tech., Kharaspur, India, 1964; MArch, U. Calif., Berkeley, 1965, U.C. Regents fellow; postgrad., U. So. Calif. Registered architect, Calif., Alaska. Architect Joseph Esherick & Assocs., San Francisco, 1965-73; project mgr. M. Arthur Gensler & Assocs., San Francisco, 1973; chief architect, mgr. Nrtkin and Weber, San Francisco, 1973-74; from assoc. architect to asst. dir. design svcs. U. Calif., Berkeley, 1974-77, campus architect, sr. mgr. tech. svcs. dept. facilities mgmt., 1977-81; dir. statewide office facilities planning and constrn. U. Alaska, 1981-87; pres., chief exec. officer Comprehensive Facilities Mgmt., Berkeley, 1987—; conductor seminars; speaker in field. Author: Manual for Selection Consultants, 1988. Commr. Urban Beautification Commn., Fairbanks, Alaska, 1982-85, chmn. 1983-85. Mem. AIA (Cert. of Appreciation, 1974), Assn. Univ. Architects (Resolution Appreciation award, 1987, bd. regents U. Alaska 1987), Soc. Coll. Univ. Planners, Am. Planning Assn., Assn. Phys. Plant Adminstrs., Nat. Assn. Coll. Univ. Bus. Officers, Internat. Facility Mgmt. Assn., MIT Office of Facilities Mgmt. Systems (mem. bd. tech. adv. group), Toastmasters, Rotary. Office: Comprehensive Facilities Mgmt 15 Poppy Ln Berkeley CA 94708-1407

AHRENS, ERICK KARL FREDERICK, computer software executive; b. Detroit, Feb. 22, 1949; s. Herman Frederick Ahrens and Evelyn (Metcalf) Finch; m. Dorothy Ann Swiercz, June 22, 1972. AA in Math., Coll. San Mateo, Calif., 1975; BS in Engring. Math., U. Calif., Berkeley, Calif., 1980; MBA in Bus. Anlysis, San Francisco State U., 1987. Applications analyst Victor Comptometer Corp., South San Francisco, Calif., 1975; research and devel. engr. Earl and Wright Consulting Engrs., San Francisco, 1976-83; dir. product engring. Molecular Design, Ltd., San Leandro, Calif., 1984—. Contbr.to profl. jours. With USN, 1969-73, Vietnam. Mem. Assn. Computing Machinery, Am. Chem. Soc., Marin Power Squadron (exec. officer), Corinthian Yacht Club (Tiburon, Calif.). Home: PO Box 20984 Castro Valley CA 94546 Office: Molecular Design Ltd 2132 Farallon Dr San Leandro CA 94577

AHRONI, JESSIE HELEN, nurse, researcher; b. Berlin, Oct. 31, 1948; came to U.S., 1948; d. William S. and Waultraudis (Stocker) Minnich; m. Kenneth E. Ahroni, May 10, 1979; 1 child, Benjamin Lee. AAS, Seattle Cen. Community Coll., 1979; BS in Nursing, U. Portland, 1983; M in Nursing, U. Wash., 1987. RN, Wash. Family nurse practitioner, researcher Seattle VA Med. Ctr., 1987—. Mem. Am. Nurses Assn. (registered advanced nurse practitioner, cert. med.-surg. nurse), Wash. Assn. Diabetes Educators, Sigma Theta Tau. Home: 3027 NW 74th Seattle WA 98117

AHUMADA, ANNA LUCINDA, course developer, technical writer; b. Santa Fe, Oct. 30, 1949; d. James Anthony and Eloisa (Ortiz) Montano; m. Eduardo Antonio Ahumada, Aug. 10, 1968. BA, U. N.Mex., 1975. Dir., tchr. Care Barrio El Rocio Sch., Bogota, Colombia, 1968-70; simultaneous translater Lape Coll. Edn. U. N.Mex., Albuquerque, 1970-74; engr. Mountain Bell, Albuquerque, 1974-78; course developer Mountain Bell, Lakewood, Colo., 1978-80, course developer U.S. West Learning Systems, 1983—; asst. mgr. Southern Bell, Miami, Fla., 1980-83. Active mem. Choices, Odyssey of the Mind. Mem. Success Oriented Mgrs. Offering Support, Phi Beta Kappa. Democrat. Office: US West Communications Inc Mktg and Planning 1801 California St Rm 1840 Denver CO 80202

AIKEN, WILLIAM DAVID, lawyer; b. Sunnyside, Wash., Aug. 28, 1923; s. William Jerome and Louisa Gertrude (Nichols) A.; student Wash. State U., 1941-43, 46-47; JD, George Washington U., 1949; m. Dorothy Louise Snyder, May 28, 1948; children: Katherine Aiken Schwartz, Mary L. Aiken Fishback, Sally S. Aiken Fetterer, Jerome Ross. Admitted to Wash. bar, 1951; asso. firm Chaffee & Aiken, Sunnyside, Wash., 1951-60; sole practice law, Sunnyside, 1960—; mcpl. judge City of Sunnyside, 1951-58; justice of peace Yakima County, Wash., 1951-58. Mem. Yakima County Civil Service Com., 1969—, chmn., 1975-77; mem. Yakima County Boundary Rev. Bd., 1985—, Selective Service Bd. 31 Yakima and Klickitat Counties, 1982—. Served to with U.S. Army, 1943-46, lt. col. JAG Wash. State Guard. Decorated Bronze Star. Mem. ABA, Wash. State Bar Assn. (exec. com. family law sect. 1974-76), Yakima County Bar Assn. (pres. 1985-86), Am. Judicature Soc., Am. Acad. Polit. and Social Sci. Episcopalian. Clubs: Masons (32 deg.), Shriners, Coll., Seattle. Home: 1241 Sunset Pl Sunnyside WA 98944 Office: 1001 E Edison Ave Sunnyside WA 98949

AIRALL, ANGELA MAUREEN, management consultant; b. Ft. Dix, N.J., Nov. 8, 1954; d. Guillermo Evers and Clara Airall. BS in Journalism, The Am. U., 1972; MS in Pub. Rels., Boston U., 1976; MBA, U. So. Calif., 1988. Cert. lobbyist. Asst. dir. pub. rels. South Jersey Hosp., Mt. Holly, N.J., 1978; regional specialist U.S. Census Bur., Phila., 1978-80; state coord. N.J. Assn. Counties, Trenton, 1980-82; assoc. program dir. Ednl. Testing Svc., Princeton, N.J., 1982-86; nat. dir. program devel. and external communication Grad. Mgmt. Admission Coun., L.A., 1986—; adj. faculty mem. Mercer County Coll., Princeton; cons. edn. and mgmt. Media del. Nat. Dem. Com., N.Y.C.; publicist Miss Black Am. Beauty Pageant, Phila., Harvard Community Health Plan, Boston; active Princeton Philharmonic Orch. Mem. Pub. Relations Soc. Am., Nat. Black MBA Assn., Alpha Kappa Alpha. Office: Grad Mgmt Admissions Coun 11601 Wilshire Blvd Ste 1060 Los Angeles CA 90025

AJAWARA, AUGUSTUS CHIEDOZIE, engineering company executive; b. Umuowa, Imo, Nigeria, Aug. 8, 1953; came to U.S., 1974; s. Innocent Onyemekara and Patricia Nwamgbede (Ekpeogu) A.; m. Lettie Louise Tolbert, May 1, 1977; children: Augdosha Ijeoma, Christiana Chinwendu, Serenity Nkechinyere, James Patrick Okechukwu. BS in Civil and Transp. Engring., Calif. Polytech. State U., 1982; MPA, Golden Gate U., 1983. Registered profl. engr. Traffic engring. asst. Calif. Dept. Transp., San Luis Obispo, 1977-79; jr. civil engr. Calif. Dept. Transp., San Francisco, 1979-80; staff engr. Dept. Pub. Works City of Austin, Tex., 1983-84, engr. assoc. Land Devel. Svcs., 1984-85, engr. assoc., program mgr. Transp. Systems Mgmt., 1985, engr. assoc., program mgr. traffic safety Dept. Pub. Service/Transp., 1985-86; project mgr. Oji Internat., Pomona, Calif., 1987; v.p. Oji Internat., Pomona, 1988—, also bd. dirs.; cons. transp. engr. Pub. Works/Redevelopment Agy. City of Compton, Calif., 1988—. Campaign worker Brown for Pres., San Francisco, 1979-80, Jackson for Pres., 1984, Barientos for Sen., Austin, 1984; campaign coordinator Jackson for Pres., Pomona, 1988. Mem. ASCE (assoc.), Inst. Transp. Engrs. (tech. council 1986, com. mem. 1986-88), Am. Soc. Pub. Adminstrn., Toastmasters (adminstrv. v.p.), Knight of Peter Claver (comdr. jr. knight 1986-88). Democrat. Roman Catholic. Home: 23295 Via Bahia Mission Viejo CA 92691 Office: Oji Internat Inc 300 S Park Ave Ste 630 Pomona CA 91766

AKAKA, DANIEL KAHIKINA, congressman; b. Honolulu, Sept. 11, 1924; s. Kahikina and Annie (Kahoa) A.; m. Mary Mildred Chong, May 22, 1948; children: Millannie, Daniel, Gerard, Alan, Nicholas. Grad., U. Hawaii, postgrad., 1966. Tchr. schs. in Hawaii, 1953-60; vice prin., then prin. Ewa Beach Elem. Sch., Honolulu, 1960-64; prin. Pohakea Elem. Sch., 1964-65, Kaneohe Elem. Sch., 1965-68; program specialist Hawaii Compensatory Edn., 1978-79, from 1985; dir. Hawaii OEO, 1971-74; spl. asst. human resources Office Gov. Hawaii, 1975-76; mem. 95th-100th Congresses from 2d Dist., Hawaii, 1977—; chmn. Hawaii Principals' Conf. Bd. dirs. Hanahauoli Sch.; mem. Act 4 Ednl. Adv. Council, Library Adv. Council.; Trustee Kawaiahao Congl. Ch. Served with U.S. Army, 1945-47. Mem. NEA, Musicians Assn. Hawaii. Democrat. Office: US Ho of Reps 2301 Rayburn Office Bldg Washington DC 20515

AKE, MARY KATHERINE, librarian; b. East Chicago, Ind., Mar. 2, 1930; d. William Henry and Elsbeth Marguerite (Lenehan) Weichsel; m. John W. Ake, May 22, 1955 (div. May, 1981); children: J. David, Katherine Mary. BA, Youngstown State U., 1952; MS, Carnegie Mellon U., 1953. Cert. tchr. Libr. Pub. Library Youngstown And Mahoning County, Ohio, 1953-55; libr., media specialist Littleton (Colo.) Pub. Schs., 1974—. Author: (with others) Touchstones, 1985, Writers for Children, 1987. Founder Friends of the Library/Mus., 1964; served on numerous county, city, recreational, Littleton, sch. coms., 1962-75. Mem. Am. Assn. Sch. Libraries, Children's Lit. Assn. (bd. dirs. 1979-83), Colo. Ednl. Media Assn., AAUW (founder local chpt. 1963), Dr. Watson's Neglected Patients Club (co-founder, chief surgeons, 1988—). Republican. Presbyterian. Home: 1300 Ridge Rd Littleton CO 80120 Office: Walt Whitman Elem Sch 6557 S Acoma Littleton CO 80120

AKER, CHARLES MONTE, marine maneuvering company executive; b. Everett, Mass., Jan. 18, 1925. BA in Physics, Boston U., 1951; postgrad. in ocean sci., UCLA, 1963, postgrad. exec. program, 1972; postgrad. ice mechanics, U. Wis., 1984, 87. Engr. Raytheon Co., 1951-53; sr. rsch. engr. Lockheed Aircraft Corp., 1953-57; dir. engring. indsl. products div. ITT Corp., 1957-60, v.p. engring. and product mgmt., 1960-66, v.p., gen. mgr., 1966-69, v.p., gen. mgr. aerospace unit aerospace-optical div., 1969-71; v.p., gen. mgr. Automated Marine Internat. subs. Intelcom Industries, 1972-73, pres. subs., v.p. parent co., 1973-74, pres. subs., 1974-78; pres. Omnithruster, Inc., Calif. Contbr. articles to profl. publs.; patentee electronic instrumentation, TV camera, anti-swirl vane, fluid valve actuated boat thruster, shipboard ice lubrication system and jet pump for its use. Mem. dean's coun. UCLA Grad. Sch. Mgmt. Recipient award OSRD, devel. award Naval Ordnance Dept. Mem. ASME, Soc. Naval Architects and Marine Engrs. Home: 24912 Winterwood Dr Lake Forest CA 92630

AKINS, GEORGE CHARLES, accountant; b. Willits, Calif., Feb. 22, 1917; s. Guy Brookins and Eugenie (Swan) A.; A.A., Sacramento City Coll., 1941; m. Jane Babcock, Mar. 27, 1945. Accountant, auditor Calif. Bd. Equalization, Dept. Finance, Sacramento, 1940-44; controller-treas. DeVons Jewelers, Sacramento, 1944-73, v.p., controller, 1973-80, v.p., chief fin. officer, dir., 1980-84; individual accounting and tax practice, Sacramento, 1944—. Accountant, cons. Mercy Children's Hosp. Guild, Sacramento, 1957-77. Served with USAAF, 1942. Mem. Soc. Calif. Pioneers, Nat. Soc. Pub. Accountants, U.S. Navy League, Calif. Hist. Soc., English Speaking Union, Drake Navigators Guild, Internat. Platform Assn., Mendocino County Hist. Soc., Sacramento County Hist. Soc. Republican. Roman Catholic. Clubs: Commonwealth of Calif., Comstock. Contbg. author: Portfolio of Accounting Systems for Small and Medium-Sized Business, 1968, rev., 1977. Home and Office: 96 S Humboldt St Willits CA 95490

AKITA, RICHARD MITSUO, electronics engineer; b. Honolulu, Nov. 13, 1939; s. Mitsuyoshi and Tomoyo (Sueoka) A.; BS in Math., Oreg. State U., 1961; MSEE, Naval Postgrad. Sch., Monterey, Calif., 1968; m. Gwen Harumi Tateno, June 14, 1964; children: Michael T., Andrea N. Electronics engr. command and control div. Naval Ocean Systems Ctr., San Diego, 1970-77; supervisory engr., br. head navigation systems, 1977—; instr. engring. Calif. community colls., 1977—. Mem. sch. site council Wangeheim Jr. High Sch., 1978-80. Served to lt. USN, 1961-70. Mem. IEEE, Am. Assn. for the Advancement of Sci., N.Y. Acad. Sci., Armed Forces Communications and Electronics Assn., Sigma Xi, Lions (2d v.p. La Jolla, Calif. chpt. 1988—). Republican. Home: 1738 Sorrel Ct Carlsbad CA 92008 Office: Naval Ocean Systems Ctr Code 434 San Diego CA 92152

AKIYAMA, CAROL LYNN, motion picture industry executive; b. Chgo., Dec. 5, 1946; d. Makio M. Akiyama and Mary (Uyeda) Maruyama; m. Peter Richard Bierstedt, Aug. 23, 1980. BA magna cum laude, U. So. Calif., 1968, JD, 1971. Bar: Calif. Atty. NLRB, Los Angeles, 1971-75, ABC-TV, Hollywood, Calif., 1975-79, So. Calif. Edison, Rosemead, 1980-81; asst. gen. atty. CBS Inc., Los Angeles, 1981-82; sr. v.p. Alliance of Motion Picture and TV Producers, Sherman Oaks, Calif., 1982-88; ind. producer TV and motion pictures, personal mgr. in field Sherman Oaks, 1988—. Mem. Los Angeles County Bar Assn. (chmn. labor law sect. 1981-82, exec. com. 1975-85), Phi Kappa Phi, Phi Beta Kappa.

ALAMEDA, RUSSELL RAYMOND, JR., radiologic technologist; b. San Jose, Calif., Oct. 13, 1945; s. Russell Raymond and Rose Margaret (Manzone) A.; m. Gayle Evileen Allison, Feb. 16, 1969 (div. 1975); children: Lynda Rae, Anthony David. Student San Jose City Coll., 1963-65. Served with U.S. Navy, 1966-75; x-ray technician VA Hosp., Palo Alto, Calif., 1975-78; office mgr., radiologic tech. orthopedic surgery Mountain View (Calif.), 1978—; owner, operator Ren-Tech, San Jose, 1982-87. Recipient Mallinckrodt Outstanding Achievement award Mallinckrodt Corp., 1971. Mem. Am. Registry of Radiologic Technologists, Calif. Radiologic Technologists, DAV. Republican. Lutheran. Home: 165 Blossom Hill Rd SP76 San Jose CA 95123 Office: Orthopedic Surgery 2500 Dr Ste 7 Mount View CA 94040

ALARID, ALBERT JOSEPH, judge; b. Albuquerque, Sept. 4, 1948; s. Albert Joseph and Evelyn Sylvia (Torres) A. BA, U. N.Mex., 1970; JD, Georgetown U., 1973. Bar: N.Mex. 1973, U.S. Dist. Ct. N.Mex. 1973, U.S. Supreme Ct. 1977. Civil rights atty. U.S. Dept. Justice, Washington, 1973-74; legis. counsel to U.S. Senator Joseph Montoya, Washington, 1974-77; asst. atty. gen. Office of N.Mex. Atty. Gen., Santa Fe, 1977-80; judge. Met. Ct., Albuquerque, 1980-81; 2d Jud. Dist., Albuquerque, 1981-83, N.Mex. Ct. Appeals, Santa Fe, 1984—; adj. prof. U. N.Mex. Sch. Pub. Adminstrn., Albuquerque, 1980-81. Mem. Gov.'s Com. on Disting. Svc., Santa Fe, 1984; bd. dirs. N.Mex. Coun. on Crime and Delinquency, Albuquerque, 1983-84; mem. adv. bd. M.Mex. Law Related Edn. Project. Mem. N.Mex. Jud. Conf. (chmn. 1983-84), U. N.Mex. Alumni (bd. dirs. 1981-84, mem. appellate and dist. ct. jud. nominating commns.)), Kiwanis, Delta Theta Phi. Democrat. Roman Catholic. Office: N Mex Ct of Appeals PO Box 2008 Santa Fe NM 87501

ALBANESE, JOHN PATRICK, consulting geologist; b. Newark, July 11, 1925; s. John Salvatore and Helen (Black) A.; m. Evelyn Gerda Jacobsen, June 11, 1946; children: Arlene, Richard. BA, U. Wyo., 1948, MA in Geology, 1949. Cert. profl. geologist. Geologist Atlantic Refining Co., Casper, Wyo., 1949-51; dist. geologist Seaboard Oil Co., Casper, Billings (Mont.), Denver, 1951-58; cons. geologist Denver, 1958-62; exploration mgr. Wolf Land Co., Casper, 1962-63; area geologist Champlin Petroleum Co., Casper, 1963-67; gen. ptnr. Mountain Minerals Co., Casper, 1968-79; cons. geologist Casper, 1979—; research assoc. Smithsonian Instn., Washington, 1975-87; vis. lectr. dept. anthropology U. Wyo., Laramie, 1976-84. Contbr. articles to profl. jours., sects. to books. Mem. Netrona County Library Bd., Casper, 1967-81; mem. Wyo. Cons. Com. to Nat. Register, Cheyenne, 1976; mem. Wyo. Council Humanities, Laramie, 1988—; mem. Natrona County Hist. Preservation Com., Casper, 1986—. Served with U.S. Army, 1943-45. Recipient Steege award Wyo. Archaeol. Soc., 1973. Mem. Geol. Soc. Am., Soc. Am. Archaelogy, Am. Assn. Petroleum Geologists, Wyo. Geol. Assn. (v.p. 1956), Wyo. Assn. Profl. Archaeologists (pres. 1986-87), Wyo. Archaeol. Soc. (pres. 1971-72), Masons (sr. warden 1955-56). Republican. Presbyterian. Home: 3511 Carmel Dr Casper WY 82604

ALBANO, ANDRES, JR., real estate developer, real estate broker, engineer; b. Honolulu, Apr. 16, 1941; s. Andres Pacis and Florence (Paglinawan) A.; m. Sandra Kam Mee Ymas, Nov. 29, 1961; children: Cheryl Ann, Denise Lynn. BEE, U. Hawaii, 1965, MBA, 1972. Elec. engr. U.S. Aviation Adminstrn., Honolulu, 1967-69, Honolulu Bd. Water Supply, 1969-79; exec. v.p. MidPac Devel. Ltd., Honolulu, 1979-84; pres. Albano & Assocs., Honolulu, 1984—. Served with USN, 1965-67. Mem. Nat. Soc. Profl. Engrs., Hawaii Soc. Profl. Engrs. (pres. 1979-80), Devel Assn. Hawaii (v.p. 1985—), Nat. Assn. Realtors. Roman Catholic. Lodge: Rotary (Waikiki chpt. 1985—). Home: 748 Kokomo Pl Honolulu HI 96825 Office: Albano & Assocs Inc 3322 Campbell Ave Honolulu HI 96815

ALBERTSON, ROBERT PAUL, pharmacist; b. Ashland, Wis., Jan. 8, 1952; s. Alfred Olan and Adele Hermaine (Gervais) A.; m. Mary Lou Albertson, 1982 (div.); 1 child, Leif Eirik; m. Charlene Amar Albertson, Jan. 12, 1985. BS in Chemistry, Northland Coll., Ashland, 1973; BS in Pharmacy, U. Wis., 1976; RPH in Pharmacy, U. Wis. Hosp., 1977. Registered pharmacist, Wis., Ak. With bone marrow transplant dept. U. Wis., Madison, 1981-83; staff pharmacist U. Wis., 1983-84, neonatal specialist and program developer, asst dir. and neonatal specialist, 1983-85; asst. dir. of clin. programs Providence Hosp., Anchorage, Ak., 1986-87, critical care decentralized pharmacist, 1987—; cons. Seward Gen. Hosp. Speaker for high sch. age kids on drug prevention Alaska Diabetic Assn., 1986; mem. Citizens Com. For the Right to Keep and Bear Arms, 2d Amendment Found. Mem. Am. Soc. Hosp. Pharmacist, Soc. Hosp. Planning of Am. Hosp., Nat. Rifle Assn. Am., Sons of Norway. Home: 4227 Charing Cross Cr Anchorage AK 99504

ALBIN, RANDY CLARK, record company executive; b. Pasadena, Calif., Sept. 25, 1957; s. Clark Eugene and Aileen Mary (Vrooman) A. AA, Foothill Coll., Los Altos Hills, Calif., 1983; BA, Menlo Coll., 1985. With Recreation Tennis, Inc., Stanford, Calif., 1986, Roberta's Personnel Agy., Palo Alto, Calif., 1988, Wollborg-Michelson Personnel, Palo Alto, Calif., 1988; pres., chief exec. officer Randall Record Co., Los Altos, 1988–. Mem. Foothill Coll. Alumni Assn. (bd. dirs. 1986–). Home and Office: PO Box 920 Los Altos CA 94022

ALBRECHT, MAUREEN ANN, coroner, funeral director; b. Neptune, N.J., Nov. 7, 1952; d. David Ring and Geraldine Ruth (Pritchard) A.; m. Richard David Johnson, Oct. 31, 1986; 1 stepchild, Michelle Dolan Johnson. AS, Mercer County Community Coll., 1982; student, Calif. State U., L.A., 1988—. Funeral dir., embalmer Turner Stevens Mortuary, Pasadena, Calif., 1983-85; forensic technician Orange County Sheriff Coroner, Santa Ana, Calif., 1985-88, dep. coroner, 1988—; rec. sec. Coast Guard Aux., Sierra Madre, Calif., 1985-86, Animal Hosp. Asst. Assn., Newark, 1972-74; animal technician Millar Animal Hosp., Deal, N.J., 1968-78; pharmacy technician Parkwarner Drugs, Neptune, 1971-76; apprientice emblamer Johnson Funeral Home, Wall, N.J., 1980-82. Block parent Block Watch, Arcadia, Calif., 1985; recorder election bd., Arcadia, 1988. Roman Catholic. Office: Orange County Sheriff Coroner 1070 Santa Ana Blvd Santa Ana CA 92703

ALBRECHT, SHERI ANN, insurance company executive, educator; b. Fort Dodge, Iowa, Dec. 19, 1957; d. Maurice Joseph and Betty Jean (Westrum) A. BA, Ariz. State U., 1982. Documentation analyst Security Pacific Automation Corp., Tempe, Ariz., 1982-88; methods and procedures analyst Am. Founders Life, Phoenix, 1988—; acad. tutor Dept. Intercollegiate Athletics, Ariz. State U., 1984-88; freelance editorial cons. 1985-88. Mem. Soc. Tech. Communication. Democrat. Office: Am Founders Life 2720 E Camelback Phoenix AZ 85016

ALBRECHT, THOMAS CARL, sales executive; b. Tuknila, Wash., Aug. 26, 1955; s. Vern Eugene and Patricia Mae (O'Driscoll) A.; m. Pamela Anne Godin, Sept. 11, 1982; children: Jeremiah David, Benjamin Carl. BA in Psychology, Rockhurst Coll., 1977; postgrad., U. Wis., Eau Claire, 1978. Asst. mgr. Richman Bros., St. Paul, 1980; salesman Novatran Corp., Sunnyvale, Calif., 1981; ops. mgr. Novatran Corp., Montclair, Calif., 1982-86; regional sales rep. Novatran Corp., Ontario, Calif., 1986—; V.p. Tract 12219 Homeowners Assn., Ontario, Calif., 1986, pres., 1988-89. Republican. Evangleical Christian. Home: 6434 Teton Peak Ct Alta Loma CA 91701 Office: Novatron 4435 E Airport Dr Ontario CA 91761-8157

ALCINDOR, LEWIS FERDINAND **See ABDUL-JABBAR, KAREEM**

ALDAPE, ALINA ALICIA CATALINA ELIZABETH, lawyer; b. Mexico City, Sept. 21, 1952. BA with honors, Stanford U., 1974, JD, 1977. Bar: Calif. 1977, U.S. Ct. Appeals (9th cir.) 1981. Assoc. McCutchen, Doyle, Brown and Enersen, San Francisco, 1977-80, Lasky, Haas, Cohler and Munter, San Francisco, 1980-82; investment exec. Paine Webber Jackson and Curtis, San Francisco, 1983-84; dist. mktg. mgr. U.S. C. of C., Campbell, 1984-85; v.p. planning and communications, co-founder State of the Art Computer Confs., San Francisco, 1985; pvt. practice exec. recruitment, San Francisco, 1985-86; of counsel other law firms, 1986-89; pvt. practice, San Francisco, 1989—; reporter Am. Soc. Internat. Law Annual Proceedings, 1977. Fundraiser San Francisco Edn. Fund, World Affairs Council, Am.-Irish Found., Stanford Telethons; info. officer Pope's Visit to San Francisco, 1987; del. U.S./Japan Bilateral Session, 1988; participant World Peace through Law confs., 1965, 67; mem. Jr. League of San Francisco, vol. SPCA Animal Assisted Therapy, 1986. Named Outstanding Young Woman in Am., 1978. Mem. ABA, (internat., antitrust and litigation sects.), San Francisco Bar Assn. (steering com., barristers litigation com., intellectual property and computer law coms.), Bay Area Profl. Women's Network (membership chair 1980-81), Peninsula Mktg. Assn., Mktg. Rsch. Roundtable (co-founder, co-treas.), San Francisco Bay Club, The City Club. Home: 2100 Bay St Ste 304 San Francisco CA 94123 Office: 425 California St 19th Fl San Francisco CA 94104 also: 220 Sansome St 14th Fl San Francisco CA 94104

ALDERMAN, MINNIS AMELIA, psychologist, educator, small business owner; b. Douglas, Ga., Oct. 14, 1928; d. Louis Cleveland Sr. and Minnis Amelia (Wooten) A. AB in Music, Speech and Drama, Ga. State Coll., Milledgeville, 1949; MA in Supervision and Counseling Psychology, Murray State U., 1960; postgrad. Columbia Pacific U., 1987—. Tchr. music Lake County Sch. Dist., Umatilla, Fla., 1949-50; instr. vocal and instrumental music, dir. band, orch. and choral Fulton County Sch. Dist., Atlanta, 1950-54; instr. English, speech, debate, vocal and instrumental music, dir. drama, band, choral and orch. Elko County Sch. Dist., Wells, Nev., 1954-59; tchr. English and social studies Christian County Sch. Dist., Hopkinsville, Ky., 1960; instr. psychology, guidance counselor Murray (Ky.) State U., 1961-63, U. Nev., Reno, 1963-67; owner Minisizer Exercising Salon, Ely, Nev., 1969-71, Knit Knook, Ely, 1969—, Minimimeo, Ely, 1969—, Gift Gamut, Ely, 1977—; prof. dept. fine arts Wassuk Coll., Ely, 1986—, assoc. dean, 1986-87, dean, 1987—; counselor White Pine County Sch. Dist., Ely, 1960-68; dir. Child and Family Ctr., Ely Indian Colony, 1988—; supr. testing Ednl. Testing Svc., Princeton, N.J., 1960-68, Am. Coll. Testing Program, Iowa, 1960-68, U. Nev., Reno, 1960-68; chmn. bd. White Pine Sch. Dist. Employees Fed. Credit Union, Ely, 1961-69; psychologist mental hygiene div. Nev. Pers., Ely, 1969-75, dept. employment security, 1975-80; sec.-treas. bd. dirs. Gt. Basin Enterprises, Ely, 1969-71; pvt. instr. piano, violin, voice and organ, Ely, 1981—; bd. dir. band Sacred Heart Sch., Ely, 1982—. Author various news articles, feature stories, pamphlets, handbooks and grants in field. Pres. White Pine County Mental Health Assn., 1960-63, 78—; mem. Gov.'s Mental Health State Commn., 1963-65; bd. dirs. White Pine County Sch. Employees Fed. Credit Union, 1961-68, pres., 1963-68; 2d v.p. White Pine Community Concert Assn., 1965-67, pres., 1967, 85—, treas., 1975-79, dr. chmn., 1981-85; chmn. of bd. , 1984; bd. dirs. White Pine chpt. ARC, 1978-82; mem. Nev. Hwy. Safety Leaders Bd., 1979-82; mem. Gov.'s Commn. on Status Women, 1968-74; sec.-treas. White Pine Rehab. Tng. Ctr. for Retarded Persons, 1973-75; mem. Gov.'s Commn. on Hwy. Safety, 1979-81; dir. Ret. Sr. Vol. Program, 1973-74; vice chmn. Gt. Basin Health Coun., 1973-75, Home Extension Adv. Bd., 1977-80; sec.-treas. Great Basin chpt. Nev. Employees Assn.; bd. dirs. United Way, 1970-76; vice chmn. White Pine Coun. on Alcoholism and Drug Abuse, 1975-76, chmn., 1976-77; grants author 3 yrs. Indian Child Welfare Act, originator Community Tng. Ctr. for Retarded People, 1972, Ret. Sr. Vol. Program, 1974, Nutrition Program for Sr. Citizens, 1974, Sr. Citizens Ctr., 1974, Home Repairs for Sr. Citizens, 1974, Sr. Citizens Home Assistance Program, 1977, Creative Crafters Assns., 1976, Inst. Current World Affairs, 1989—; bd. dirs. Sacred Heart Parochial Sch., 1982—, dir. band, 1982—; candidate for diaconal ministry, 1982—. Precinct reporter ABC News 1966. Fellow Am. Coll. Musicians, Nat. Guild Piano Tchrs.; mem. NEA (life), Nat. Fedn. Ind. Bus. (dist. chair 1971-85, nat. guardian coun. 1985—, state guardian coun. 1987—), AAUW (pres. Wells br. 1957-58, pres. White Pine br. 1965-66, 86-87, bd. dirs. 1965-87, rep. edn. 1965-67, implementation chair 1967-69, area advisor 1969-73), Nat. Fedn. Bus. and Profl. Women (1st v.p. Ely chpt. 1965-66, pres. Ely chpt. 1966-68, 74-76, 85—, bd. dirs. Nev. chpt. 1966—, 1st v.p. Nev. chpt. 1970-71, pres. Nev. chpt. 1972-73, nat. bd. dirs. 1972-73), Mensa (supr. testing 1965—), Delta Kappa Gamma (chpt. pres. 1968-72, state bd. 1967—, chpt. parliamentarian 1974-78, state 1st v.p. 1967-69, state pres. 1969-71, nat. bd. 1969-71, state parliamentarian 1971-73), White Pine Knife and Fork Club (1st v.p. 1969-70, pres. 1970-71, bd. dirs. 1979—). Home: 945 Ave H PO Box 457 East Ely NV 89315 Office: 16 Shoshone Circle Ely NV 89301

ALDERSON, GARY DEAN, biology educator; b. Pasadena, Calif., Sept. 20, 1950; s. Murry Dean Alderson and Dorothy Lorraine (Thomas) Carroll; children: Kristina Marie, Julie Marie; m. Pamela Ann Langguth, Jan. 22, 1983; stepchildren: Karen Lynn Wanzung, Lisa Ann Wanzung. BS, U. Redlands, 1972; MA in Biology, U. Calif., Santa Barbara, 1975, PhD in Biology, 1976. Instr. biology Palomar Coll., San Marcos, Calif., 1976—; faculty advisor Life Sci. Soc., Palomar Coll., 1976-83, 88—. Author: Microbiology: Experiments and Lab Techniques, 1986, (computer programs) QuikXam, 1985, Micro ID, 1985. Named one of Outstanding Young Men of Am., 1978. Democrat. Home: 860 Red Hill Ln San Marcos CA 92069 Office: Palomar Coll 1140 W Mission Rd San Marcos CA 92069

ALDERSON, RICHARD LYNN, professional baseball team executive; b. Seattle, Nov. 22, 1947; s. John Lester and Gwenny (Parry) A.; m. Linda Lee Huff, Dec. 20, 1969; children—Catrin Gwennan, Bryn Ganeth. B.A., Dartmouth Coll., 1969; J.D., Harvard U., 1976. Assoc. Farella, Braun & Martel, San Francisco, 1976-81; gen. counsel Oakland Athletics, Calif., 1981-83, v.p. baseball ops., 1983—; dir. Major League Scouting Bur., Newport Beach, Calif. Served to lt. USMC, 1969-73, Vietnam. Office: Oakland Athletics Oakland Coliseum Oakland CA 94621 *

ALDRICH, DAVID LAWRENCE, public relations executive; b. Lakehurst Naval Air Sta., N.J., Feb. 21, 1948; s. Clarence Edward and Sarah Stiles (Andrews) A.; m. Benita Susan Massler, Mar. 17, 1974. BA in Communications, Calif. State U.-Dominguez Hills, 1976. Pub. info. technician City of Carson (Calif.), 1973-77; pub. rels. dir./adminstrv. asst. Calif. Fed. Savs., L.A., 1977-78; v.p., group supr. Hill & Knowlton, L.A., 1978-81; v.p., mgr. Ayer Pub. Rels. western div. N.W. Ayer, L.A., 1981-84; pres. Aldrich and Assocs. Inc., L.A., 1984—. Active allocations com. S.E. United Way, chmn. pub. info. com.; chmn., mktg. adv. com. Drum Corps Internat. With USAF, 1968-72. Democrat. Club: L.A. Athletic. Home: 550 Orange Ave #125 Long Beach CA 90802 Office: Aldrich & Assocs 110 Pine Ave Ste 510 Long Beach CA 90802

ALDRICH, DELL STANLEY, orthodontist; b. Southgate, Calif., July 31, 1938; s. Adelbert Carl and Marian Grace (Carlson) A.; m. Joanne Emily VanderByl, June 30, 1962 (div. 1976); children: Cheryl Marlene, Michelle Renee. AA, Glendale Coll., 1959; DDS, U. So. Calif., 1963, MS in Orthodontics, 1970. Intern U.S.C. Med. Ctr., L.A.; resident U.S.C. Sch. Dentistry, L.A.; clin. instr. fixed prosthetic dept. U. So. Calif., Los Angeles, 1962-63, 66-68; pvt. practice instr. Swiss Dental Assn., Geneva and Zurich, Switzerland, 1970-71; pvt. practice Descanso Med. Ctr., La Canada, Calif., 1972—; cons. U. Okla., 1975, U. Ind., 1976. Author: Differential Response Incident to Tooth Movement, 1970; contbr. articles to profl. jours. Mem. Rep. Presdl. Task Force, 1984. Capt. U.S. Army, 1963-66, Fed. Republic Germany. Mem. Am. Assn. Orthodontists, Pacific Coast Soc. Orthodontics, Am. Dental Assn., Calif. Dental Soc., Kiwanis, Tournament of Roses Assn., Omicron Kappa Epsilon Alumni Assn., Phi Kappa Phi. Home: 4542 Loma Vista Dr La Canada-Flintridge CA 91011 Office: Descanso Med Ctr 1346 Foothill Blvd La Canada-Flintridge CA 91011

ALDRICH, MICHAEL RAY, organization executive; b. Vermillion, S.D., Feb. 7, 1942; s. Ray J. and Lucile W. (Hamm) A.; AB, Princeton, 1964; MA, U. S.D., 1965; PhD, SUNY, 1970; m. Michelle Cauble, Dec. 26, 1977. Fulbright tutor Govt. Arts and Commerce Coll., Indore, Madhya Pradesh, India, 1965-66; founder Lemar Internat., 1966-71; mem. faculty Sch. Critical Studies, Calif. Inst. Arts, Valencia, 1970-72; workshop leader Esalen Inst., San Francisco, 1972; co-founder AMORPHIA, Inc., The Cannabis Coop., Mill Valley, Calif., 1969-74; curator Fitz Hugh Ludlow Meml. Library, San Francisco, 1974—; project adminstr. YES Tng. Ctr., San Francisco, 1989—. Freelance writer, photographer, lectr., cons. on drug research, and sociolegal reform specializing in drug laws and history to various colls., drug confs., publishers, service groups; cons. Commn. of Inquiry into Non-Med. Use of Drugs, Ottawa, Ont., 1973; research aide, select com. on control marijuana Calif. Senate, 1974. Bd. dirs. Ethno-Pharmacology Soc., 1976-83. Calif. Marijuana Initiative, 1971-74; mem. nat. adv. bd. Nat. Orgn. for Reform of Marijuana Laws, 1976—; asst. dir. Nat. Inst. on Drug Abuse AIDS Project Menu Youth Environment Study, San Francisco, 1987-88. Author: The Dope Chronicles 1850-1950, 1979, Coricancha, The Golden Enclosure, 1983; co-author: High Times Ency. of Recreational Drugs, 1978, Fiscal Costs of California Marijuana Law Enforcement, 1986; editor: Marijuana Review, 1968-74, Ludlow Library Newsletter, 1974—; contbg. author Cocaine Handbook, 1981, 2d edit., 1987; mem. editorial rev. bd. Jour. Psychoactive Drugs, 1981—, marijuana theme issue editor, 1988; research photographer Life mag., 1984; contbg. editor High Times, 1979-85; contbr. articles to profl. pubis. Office: PO Box 640346 San Francisco CA 94164-0346

ALDRIDGE, NOEL HENRY, radiologist; b. Durban, S.Africa, Dec. 19, 1924; s. Percy Verey and Isaleine (Wilson) A.; came to U.S., 1955, naturalized, 1967; M.B., Ch.B., U. Cape Town (S.Africa), 1951; D.M.R.D., Roy Coll., London, 1955; L.M.C.C., Royal Coll. Can., 1958, m. Theresa Horton, Dec. 19, 1981; children by previous marriage—Anthony Mark, Andrea Marie. Intern, Groot Schuur Hosp., Cape Town, 1951-52; asst. govt. pathologist, Cape Town, 1952-53; sr. house officer Leeds (Eng.) Gen. Hosp., 1953-55; postgrad. tng. Karolinska Sjukhusset, Stockholm, 1955; fellow Johns Hopkins Hosp., 1955, instr. radiology, 1956; asso. radiologist, instr. Victoria Hosp.-U. Western Ont., 1956-59; clin. fellow in radiology Mass. Gen. Hosp. and Harvard Med. Sch., 1960-61, assoc. radiologist, 1961-62; radiologist with pvt. group, Seattle, 1962-63; dir. dept. radiology Stevens Meml. Hosp., Edmonds, Wash., 1963—; pres. Stevens Radiologists, Inc. Diplomate Am. Bd. Radiology. Fellow Royal Coll. Physicians Can., Am. Coll. Radiology; mem. AMA, Canadian, Brit., Wash. State med. assns., King County Med. Soc., Am. Coll. Radiology, Royal Coll. Radiologists (London), Brit. Inst. Radiology, Canadian Assn. Radiologists, Johns Hopkins Radiologic Alumni Assn., Wash. State Radiologic Assn., Coll. Physicians and Surgeons of B.C., Coll. Physicians and Surgeons of Ont., Aircraft Owners and Pilots Assn., Wash. Pilots Assn., Am. Forestry Assn., Wildlife Fedn., Les Amis du Vin. Episcopalian. Club: Elks. Contbr. articles to profl. jours. Office: Stevens Meml Hosp Dept Radiology Edmonds WA 98020

ALENIUS, JOHN TODD, insurance executive; b. Denver, Sept. 27, 1938; s. Robert and Elizabeth Frances (Todd) A.; m. Sandra Lee Mally, June 30, 1962; children: Constance, Mark, Patricia, William. BBA, Regis. Coll., 1961; postgrad., Havard U., 1971; MA in Mgmt., Webster Coll., 1979. Commd. USAF, 1962, advanced through grades to col.; personnel mgr. USAF, Vietnam, 1966-67, Colorado Springs, Colo., 1962-67; systems mgr. USAF, San Antonio, 1971-75; with exchange duty Canadian Armed Forces, Ottawa, Ont., Can., 1975-77; various system mgmt. positions USAF, San Antonio, 1977-83; dir. logistic mgmt. systems USAF, Sacramento, 1983-85; v.p. info. systems Vision Service Plan, Sacramento, 1985-88, sr. v.p. ops., 1988—. Mem. Soc. Info. Mgmt., Am. Mgmt. Assn. Republican. Roman Catholic. Office: Vision Service Plan 100 Howe Ave Ste 200S Sacramento CA 95825

ALESHIRE, GORDON LEE, municipal official; b. Salem, Oreg., June 17, 1947; s. Everett Gordon A. and Minni Frances (Cooter) Notdurft; m. Lora Ann Clapp, July 2, 1972; children: Christopher Gordon, Aaron Lee, Amber D'Ann. Student, Oreg. Poly. Inst., 1977. Bldg. inspector City of Westminster, Colo., 1977-79, chief bldg. ofcl., 1979-84; chief bldg. inspector Commerce City, Colo., 1979; supr. plan rev., permits City of Lakewood, Colo., 1984—; bd. dirs. Colo. chpt. Internat. Conf. Bldg. Ofcls. Served with U.S. Army, 1968-70, Vietnam. Decorated Bronze Star. Mem. Regional Inspectors Assn. (bd. dirs.), Internat. Assn. Plumbing and Mech. Ofcls. (bd. dirs. Colo. chpt.). Methodist. Home: 11139 Depew Ct Westminster CO 80020 Office: City of Lakewood 445 S Allison Pkwy Lakewood CO 80226-3105

ALEXANDER, BARTON, executive director; b. Toledo, Dec. 8, 1951; s. Barton and Marian (Gordon) A. BA magna cum laude, Harvard U., 1973; MSc, London Sch. Econs., 1975. Exec. dir. Toledo Coalition, 1970; policy analyst U.S. Dept. HEW, 1971-72; spl. asst. Mass. Dept. Mental Health, 1973-74; analyst/sr. policy budget analyst Colo. Gov. Office, 1975-77; acting dir. Adams Co. (Colo.) Dept Social Svcs., 1978-79, asst. dir., 1977-80, dir. program devel., 1980-83; dep. dir. to acting exec. dir. Colo. Dept. Labor and Employment, 1983-87; dep. dir. econ. devel. Colo. Dept. Local Affairs Govs. Econ. Devel. Offices, 1987-88, dep. dir., 1988; exec. dir. Jobs for Colorado's Future, Denver, 1988—; adj. faculty U. Colo. Grad. Sch. Pub. Affairs; cons. in field. Chmn. human svcs. com. St. Thomas Episcopal Ch.; bd. dirs. Capital Hill Community Svcs., Adv. Matls. Inst., Colo.-Taiwan Trade Tourism, and Investment Council, Ctr. for Disput Resolution; mem. Colo. Job Tng. Coordg. Coun., Industry Edn. Mobilization Coun. Gates Found. Pub. Leadership fellow, 1986, Rotary Internat. fellow. Mem. Econ. Developers Council Colo., Colo. Constrn. Industry Adv. Council, London Sch. Econs. Soc., Am. Soc. Pub. Adminstrn. Democrat. Home: 935 Pennsylvania St #8 Denver CO 80203

ALEXANDER, CATHARINE COLEMAN, college administrator; b. Memphis, June 23, 1934; d. John Breen and Janie Elizabeth (Cobb) Coleman; m. John David Alexander, Aug. 26, 1956; children: Catharine McKinnon, John David III, Julia Mary. BA with distinction, Rhodes Coll., 1955. Coordinator spl. events Pomona Coll., Claremont, Calif., 1969—. Mem. Foothill Philharmonic Com., Claremont, Calif., 1969—; bd. dirs. Planned parenthood L.A., 1986—. Mem. Curtain Raiser Claremont Colls., ARCS Found. (hon.), KCET Women's Coun., League Women Voters, Rembradnt Club (life), Town Club, Phi Beta Kappa. Democratic. Presbyterian. Home: 345 N College Ave Claremont CA 91711 Office: Pomona Coll Pres Office Sumner Hall 209 Claremont CA 91711

ALEXANDER, CLIFTON JACK, physician; b. N.Y.C.; s. Louie and Sally Ann (Antler) A. Student, U. Ala., Columbia U., U. So. Calif.; MD, U. Lausanne, Switzerland. Intern, resident Morrisana City Hosp., N.Y.C.; chief of staff WHO U.S. Army, U.S. and French Zones of Germany, 1948-52. Co-author: Herpes Handbook, 1987, Kick the Habit, The Basic Guide, 1989. Physician, U.S. State Dept. and AMA, Vietnam, 1968. Mem. AMA, Acad. Family Physicians (pres. Ariz. chpt. 1968-69), Ariz. Med. Assn., So. Med. Assn., Masons.

ALEXANDER, DAVID CLEON, III, lawyer; b. New Orleans, July 13, 1941; s. David Cleon Alexander Jr. and Joyce (Bragg) Crane. BBA, U. Ga., 1963, MBA, Ga. State U., 1969; JD, U. Va., 1973; LLM in Taxation, NYU, 1976. Bar: N.Y. 1974, U.S. Tax Ct. 1974, Ariz. 1975. Assoc. White & Case, N.Y.C., 1973-75, Murphy & Posner, Phoenix, 1975-78; ptnr. Lewis & Roca, Phoenix, 1978—. Served to 1st lt. U.S. Army, 1962-64. Fellow Ariz. Bar Found; mem. ABA, Ariz. Bar Assn. (lectr., cert. specialist in taxation), Sports Car Club Am., Phi Kappa Phi, Beta Gamma Sigma. Republican. Episcopalian. Home: 8520 N 52d St Paradise Valley AZ 85253 Office: Lewis & Roca 100 W Washington Ste 1800 Phoenix AZ 85003

ALEXANDER, FRED SHARPE, III, architect, general contractor; b. Houston, July 21, 1941; s. Fred Sharpe and Bessie Grace (Tauber) A.; m. Carolyn Ann Compton, Apr. 16, 1966; 1 child, Katherine Rene; m. Susan

Elinor Hjertman, June 11, 1977; children: Zachary Lee, Andrew Tauber. Student Tex. A&M U., 1960; BArch, Tex. Tech. Coll., 1967. Registered architect, Colo., N.Mex., Nebr., Ariz., Wyo., Kans. Draftsman archtl. firms, Denver, 1967-72; project architect W. C. Muchow Assocs., Denver, 1970-72; prin. Alexander Assocs. Architects, Denver, 1972-85; v.p. architecture and engring. Internat. design and Constrn. Corp., Denver, 1985-87; chmn. bd. Constrn. 4 Inc., Denver, 1976-86; pres. Comml. Design Assocs., Denver, 1981-87; pres. Alexander Industries; proj. mgr. Daniel, Mann, Johnson & Mendenhall, 1987; instr. U. Colo., Denver Grad. Sch., 1975-77. Active Boy Scouts Am., 1968-73. Mem. AIA (sec. Denver chpt. 1976, dir. 1974, membership chmn. 1974-76), Nat. Council Archtl. Registration Bds. (grader nat. exams. 1984-86), Eastern Rockies Rugby Football Union (sec. 1975-77, chmn. disciplinary com. 1988). Republican. Home: 1193 S Biscay St Aurora CO 80017 Office: 1193 S Biscay Aurora CO 80017

ALEXANDER, GEORGE JONATHON, legal educator, former dean; b. Berlin, Germany, Mar. 8, 1931; s. Walter and Sylvia (Grill) A.; m. Katharine Violet Sziklai, Sept. 6, 1958; children: Susan Katina, George Jonathon II. A.B. with maj. honors, U. Pa., 1953, J.D. cum laude, 1969; LL.M., Yale U., 1965, J.S.D., 1969. Bar: Ill. 1960, N.Y. 1961, Calif. 1974. Instr. law, Bigelow fellow U. Chgo., 1959-60; instr. internat. relations Naval Res. Officers Sch., Forrest Park, Ill., 1959-60; prof. law Syracuse U. Coll. Law, 1960-70, assoc. dean, 1968-69; vis. prof. law U. So. Calif., 1963; prof. law U. Santa Clara (Calif.) Law Sch., 1970—, dean, 1970-85; vis. scholar Stanford Law Sch., 1985-86; dir. Inst. Internat. and Comparative Law, 1986—; cons. in field. Author: Civil Rights, U.S.A., Public Schools, 1963, Honesty and Competition, 1967, Jury Instructing on Medical Issues, 1966, Cases and Materials on Space Law, 1971, The Aged and the Need for Surrogate Management, 1972, Commercial Torts, 1973, 2d edit. 1988, U.S. Antitrust Laws, 1980, Writing A Living Will: Using a Durable Power of Attorney, 1988; also articles, chpts. in books, one film. Dir. Domestic and Internat. Bus. Problems Honors Clinic, Syracuse U., 1966-69, Regulations in Space Project, 1968-70; ednl. cons. Comptroller Gen., U.S., 1977—; Nat. Sr. Citizens Law Center, 1983—, pres., 1986—; co-founder Am. Assn. Abolition Involuntary Mental Hospitalization, 1970, dir., 1970-83. Served with USN, 1953-56. U.S. Navy scholar U. Pa., 1949-52; Law Boards scholar, 1956-59; Sterling fellow Yale, 1964-65; recipient Ralph E. Kharas Civil Liberties award, 1970, Owens award as Alumnus of Yr., 1984. Mem. Calif. Bar Assn. (first chmn. com. legal problems of aging), Assn. Am. Law Schs., Soc. Am. Law Tchrs. (dir., pres. 1979), AAUP (chpt. pres. 1962), N.Y. Civil Liberties Union (chpt. pres. 1965, dir., v.p. 1966-70), Am. Acad. Polit. and Social Sci., Order of Coif, Justinian Honor Soc., Phi Alpha Delta (chpt. faculty adviser 1967-70). Home: 11600 Summit Wood Rd Los Altos Hills CA 94022 Office: U Santa Clara Santa Clara CA 95053

ALEXANDER, HAROLD EDWIN, JR., psychiatrist; b. Austin, Tex., Mar. 27, 1949; s. Harold Edwin and Elizabeth Ann (Rowe) A.; m. Doreene Mary Ward, Mar. 25, 1978; 1 child, Allyson Kendall. BS in Chemistry, U. Tex., El Paso, 1971; MD, U. Tex., San Antonio, 1977. Diplomate Am. Bd. Psychiatry and Neurology. Analytical chemist Phelps Dodge Refining Corp., El Paso, 1972-73; asst. prof. psychiatry U. Tex. Med. Sch., San Antonio, 1981-84; pvt. practice Las Cruces, N.Mex., 1984—; med. dir. S.W. Counseling Ctr., Las Cruces, 1984-87; clin. dir. Mesilla Valley Hosp., Las Cruces, 1987—. Contbr. articles to med. jours. Ohio State U. fellow, 1971. Mem. Am. Psychiat. Assn., Beta Beta Beta, Alpha Chi. Methodist. Office: Mesilla Valley MH Assn 3521-A Del Rey Blvd Las Cruces NM 88001

ALEXANDER, JOHN DAVID, JR., college president; b. Springfield, Tenn., Oct. 18, 1932; s. John David and Mary Agnes (McKinnon) A.; m. Catharine Coleman, Aug. 26, 1956; children: Catharine McKinnon, John David III, Julia Mary. BA, Southwestern at Memphis, 1953; student, Louisville Presbyn. Theol. Sem., 1953-54; DPhil (Rhodes Scholar), Oxford (Eng.) U., 1957; LLD, U. So. Calif., Occidental Coll., 1970, Centre Coll. of Ky., 1971; LHD, Loyola Marymount U., 1983; LittD, Rhodes Coll., 1986. Assoc. prof. San Francisco Theol. Sem., 1957-65; pres. Southwestern at Memphis, 1965-69, Pomona Coll., Claremont, Calif., 1969—; Am. sec. Rhodes Scholarship Trust, 1981—; mem. commn. liberal learning Assn. Am. Colls., 1966-69, Assn. Am. Colls. (commn. instl. affairs), 1971-74; mem. commn. colls. So. Assn. Colls. and Schs., 1966-69; mem. Nat. Commn. on Acad. Tenure, 1971-72; dir. Gt. Western Fin. Corp.; Bd. dirs. Community TV of So. Calif., 1973-89, Louisville Presbyn. Theol. Sem., 1966-69; trustee Tchrs. Ins. and Annuity Assn., 1970—, Woodrow Wilson Nat. Fellowship Found., 1978—, vice chmn., 1989—; bd. dirs. Am. Coun. on Edn., 1981-84, Nat. Assn. Ind. Colls. and Univs., 1984-87. Mem. Am. Oriental Soc., Soc. Bib. Lit., Soc. Religion in Higher Edn., Phi Beta Kappa Alumni in So. Calif. (pres. 1974-76), Univ. Club, Century Club, Calif. Club, Bohemian Club, Phi Beta Kappa, Omicron Delta Kappa, Sigma Nu. Office: Pomona Coll Office of Pres 333 College Way Claremont CA 91711

ALEXANDER, LAWRENCE HOWARD, writer; b. Bronx, July 21, 1939; s. Jess and Adele (Kamph) A.; m. July 31, 1966 (div. 1979); children: Jaqcqueline Samantha, Daniel Randy. BA, CCNY, 1961. Assoc. editor MacFadden Pub., N.Y.C., 1961-66, McGraw Hill, N.Y.C., 1966-67; free lance writer L.A., 1968—. Author novels: The Big Stick, 1986, Speak Softly, 1987, The Strenuous Life, 1989; writer various TV episodes, 1973-86. Mem. Writers Guild of Am., Dramatists Guild, Havergal Brian Soc. Office: Nicewords Ent Inc 9201 Wilshire Blvd #202 Beverly Hills CA 90210

ALEXANDER, VERA, marine science institute director; b. Budapest, Hungary, Oct. 26, 1932; came to U.S., 1950; d. Paul and Irene Alexander; divorced; children: Graham Alexander Dugdale, Elizabeth Dugdale Jackson. BA in Zoology, U. Wis., 1955, MS in Zoology, 1962; PhD in Marine Sci., U. Alaska, 1965. From asst. prof. to assoc. prof. marine sci. U. Alaska, Fairbanks, 1965-74, prof., 1974—, dean Coll. Environ. Scis., 1977-78, 80-81, dir. Inst. Marine Sci., 1979—, acting dean Sch. Fisheries and Ocean Scis., 1987—; mem. adv. com. Office of Health and Environ. Rsch. Dept. Energy, Washington, 1987—; vice chmn. Arctic Ocean Scis. Bd., 1988—. Editor: (W.L. Rey) Marine Biological System of the Far North. Sec. Fairbanks Light Opera Theatre Bd., 1987—; chairwoman Rhodes Scholar Selection Com., 1986—;. Research grantee U. Alaska. Fellow Arctic Inst. N.Am.; mem. Am. Assn. Advancement of Sci., Am. Soc. Limnology and Oceanography, Explorer's Club (sec., treas. local chpt. 1987—), Rotary (chairwoman internat. com. coll. club). Office: PO Box 80650 Fairbanks AK 99708 also: U Alaska Inst Marine Scis Fairbanks AK 99775

ALEXANDRE, JUDITH LEE, social services administrator; b. N.Y.C., Dec. 14, 1944; d. Jerome Jacob and Dorothy Dale (Locks) A. BA, U. Calif., Santa Barbara, 1966; MSW, U. Denver, 1970; PhD, U.S. Internat. U., 1983. Lic. clin. social worker, Calif.; diplomate clin. social work. Social worker II Aid to Families with Dependent Children, Ventura, Calif., 1968-70; social worker IV Protective Services and Intake, Ventura, 1970-72; social worker dir. New Life Homes, Ventura, 1972-79; supr. Foster Care Placement, Ventura, 1973-74; counselor Bible Fellowship Ch., Ventura, 1976-80; asst. prof. sociology Westmont Coll., Ventura, 1976-83, assoc. prof. sociology, 1983—; coordinator counseling and outreach Bible Fellowship Ch. Counseling Ctr., Ventura, 1980-86, dir., 1980—; instr. Calif. Luth. Coll. Grad. Program Clin. Psychology, Thousand Oaks, 1988—; instr. grad. sch. marriage and family counseling Azusa Pacific U., 1982—, human services Ventura Coll., 1974-77; social work supr. II Protective Services Placement, 1974-76; liaison Foster Parents Assn., 1973-76; cons. Coalition Agy. Household Violence, Ventura, 1985—, pub. health dept. Ventura Adolescent Parent Program, 1986—; bd. dirs. Child Abuse and Neglect, Ventura, 1985—, mem. program com. 1985-86, v.p., pres. elect, 1987-88, pres. 1988—; lectr. confs. and sems.; dir. Christian Therapy Program Vista Del Mar Hosp., Ventura, 1989—. Contbr. articles to profl. jours. and mags. Bd. trustees Ventura (Calif.) Unified Sch. Dist., 1986—; tchr., active leader Sunday sch. Bible Fellowship Ch., Ventura, 1970—; mem. allocations panel United Way; group leader in-patient Vista Del Mar, 1986—. Mem. Nat. Assn. Social Workers, Nat. Assn. Social Workers Referral Service (v.p. 1986-87), Bus. and Profl. Women (chmn. spl. program 1984, Channel Island Woman of Yr. award 1986 1st v.p. 1987-88), Nat. Assn. Christian Social Workers (so. Calif. chpt.), Nat. Council on Social Work Edn., Am. Humane Soc. (children's div.). Democrat. Office: Bible Fellowship Ch Counseling Ctr 1788 Johnson Dr Ventura CA 93003

ALEXIS, JODY RAE, real estate broker; b. Langdon, N.D., Mar. 2, 1940; d. Raymond and Ada (Widwick) Armstrong; student Stephens Coll., 1959-61; BA, U. Nebr., 1963; MA, U. Colo., 1968; JD, U. Denver, 1971; div.; 1 son, Clark Kendall. Bar: Colo. 1971. Asst. dir. USO, Colorado Springs, Colo., 1964-65; asst. to dir. adminstrn. Aircraft Mechanics, Inc., Colorado Springs, 1965-67; pub. relations dir. Red Ram of Am. Corp., Colorado Springs, 1967-70, The Woodmar Corp., 1971; exec. dir. Rocky Mountain Land Devel. Assn., Denver, 1970-74; pres. Alexis & Assocs., Denver, 1974—; sole practice, Denver, 1974—; broker assoc. Van Schaack Fine Homes; dir. Colo. Mgmt. Rocky Mountain Log Homes Inc., Designs Internat. Bd. dirs. Colo. Convs.and Reservations, 1974—; chmn. Denver Art Mus.; mem. Denver Ctr. for Performing Arts, Jr. Symphony Guild, Denver Ctr. Alliance, Hope for the Children. Republican. Roman Catholic. Home: 202 Adams St Denver CO 80206

ALF, MARTHA JOANNE, artist; b. Berkeley, Calif., Aug. 13, 1930; d. Foster Wise and Julia Vivian (Kane) Powell; m. Edward Franklin Alf, Mar. 17, 1951; 1 child, Richard Franklin. BA with distinction, San Diego State U., 1953, MA in Painting, 1963, jr. coll. teaching credential, 1969; MFA in Pictorial Arts, UCLA, 1970. Rsch. asst. Health and Welfare Assn., Seattle, 1956; teaching asst. in drawing, instr. design San Diego State U., 1963; instr. drawing L.A. Valley Coll., 1970-73, El Camino Coll., Hawthorne, Calif., 1971; instr. drawing and painting L.A. Harbor Coll., Wilmington, Calif., 1971-75; instr. art UCLA Extension, 1971-79; instr. contemporary art Brand Library Art Ctr., Glendale, Calif., 1973; vis. artist Calif. State Coll., Bakersfield, 1980; freelance art critic Artweek, Oakland, Calif., 1974-77; guest curator Lang Art Gallery, Scripps Coll., Claremont, Calif., 1974. Retrospective exhbn. Fellows Contemporary Art, L.A., San Francisco, 1984; represented in permanent collections L.A. County Mus. Art; one woman shows include John Berggruen Gallery, San Francisco, 1977, The Forth Worth Art Mus., 1988, Dorothy Rosenthal Gallery, Chgo., 1982, Eloise Pickard Smith Gallery Cowell Coll. U. Calif., Santa Cruz, 1983, Newspace Gallery, L.A., 1985, ann. 1976-84, 1990, Tortue Gallery, Santa Monica, 1986, Jan Baum Gallery, L.A., 1988; exhibited in group shows at San Diego Mus. of Art, 1964, 67, 68, 70, 71, 77, 78, 83, Whitney Mus. of Contemporary Art Biennial, 1975, Newport Harbor Art Mus., 1975, Marion Koogler McNay Art Inst., San Antonio, 1976, Long Beach Mus. of art, 1972, 82, 86, Henry Art Gallery U. Wash., Seattle, 1985, L.A. County Mus. of Art , 1979, 82; rep. in permanent collections Chem. Bank of N.Y., Ga. Mus. of Art, L.A. County Mus. of Art., McCrory Corp., N.Y., Metromedic Inc., L.A., N.Y., San Diego Mus. of Art, Santa Barbara Mus. of Art, Southland Corp., Dallas, Spencer Mus. of Art U. Kanas., Lawrence. Nat. Endowment for Arts grantee, 1979. Home and Studio: 5701 Waring Rd San Diego CA 92120

ALFARO, FELIX BENJAMIN, physician; b. Managua, Nicaragua, Oct. 22, 1939; came to U.S., 1945, naturalized, 1962; s. Agustin Jose and Amanda Julieta (Barillas) A.; student (State scholar) U. San Francisco, 1958-59, 61-62; M.D., Creighton U., 1967; m. Carmen Heide Meyer, Aug. 14, 1965; children—Felix Benjamin, Mark. Clk., Pacific Gas & Electric Co., San Francisco, 1960-61; intern St. Mary's Hosp., San Francisco, 1967; resident Scenic Gen. Hosp., Modesto, Calif., 1970; practice family medicine, Watsonville, Calif., 1971—; active staff Watsonville Community Hosp., 1971—. Served to capt., M.C., U.S. Army, 1968-69. Lic. physician, Nebr., La., Calif. Diplomate Am. Bd. Family Practice. Fellow Am. Acad. Family Practice; mem. AMA, Calif. Med. Assn., Santa Cruz County Med. Soc., 38th Parrallel Med. Soc. of Korea, Nat Rifle Assn., VFW. Republican. Roman Catholic. Office: 30 Brennan St Watsonville CA 95016

ALFING, NORMAN LEE, mechanical engineer; b. South Haven, Mich., May 31, 1933; s. William Edward and Geraldine S. (Brooks) A.; m. Nancy Mae Zook, Aug. 22, 1953 (div. May 1976); children Gwen Lee Yeaman, Brian David. Student, Western Mich. U., BS in Indsl Supervision and Bus., 1959. Tool and die maker Bohn Alum and Brass Corp., South Haven, Mich., 1952-59; fuel and electronics machinist Ordnance Stas., Aberdeen, Md., Ft. Carson, Colo., Orleans, France, 1955-57; engr. process and devel. St. Regis Panalyte div., Kalamazoo, Mich., 1953-61; indsl. engr. Borg Warner-Ingersoll div., Kalamazoo, 1961-62; engr. applications and sales Armstrong Machine Works, Three Rivers, Mich., 1974-77; asst. to chief engr. Armstrong Mach. Works, Three Rivers, Mich., 1962-69, mgr. European facility, 1969-71; with Sturgis (Mich.) Foundry, 1972-74; mgr. plant Packless Industries, Mt. Wolf, Pa. and Waco, Tex., 1977; pvt. practice constrn. Three Rivers, 1978; project mgr. Gen. Motors plan Miller Davis Constrn. Mgrs., Three Rivers, 1978; engr. and mgr. tech. service Dock Foundry, Three Rivers, 1979; manuf. engr. Hughes Aircraft Co., Tucson, 1979-83, mem. tech. staff, 1983-84, staff engr., 1984—. Patentee radio frequency antennas. Pres. PTA, Portage, Mich., 1967. Served with U.S. Army, 1955-57. Mem. Soc. Manuf. Engrs., Soc. Advancement Mgmt. Congregationalist. Lodges: Masons (Steward 1958-59), Elks. Home: 2750 Camino Iturbide Green Valley AZ 85614 Office: Hughes Aircraft Co PO Box 11337 Bldg 808 K6 Tucson AZ 85734

ALFRED, LINDBERGH DAVIS, government official, lawyer; b. Tuba City, Ariz., Jan. 20, 1948; s. Johnnie D. and Lucille (Davis) A.; m. Della Jim, Nov. 23, 1985; children: Michelle, Melissa, Derrick. AS in Police Sci., Contra Costa Coll., San Pablo, Calif., 1968; BS in Law Enforcement Adminstrn., U. Ariz., 1971; JD, Antioch Sch. Law, 1976. Officer Navajo Police Dept., Tuba City, Ariz., 1971-72; hwy. patrolman Ariz. Dept. Pub. Safety, Phoenix, 1972-77; criminal investigator Bur. Indian Affairs, Tuba City, 1977-78; supervisory criminal investigator Bur. Indian Affairs, Chinle, Ariz., 1978-80, Valentine, Ariz., 1980-82, Red Lake, Minn., 1982, Window Rock, Ariz., 1982—; acting dir. Indian Police Acad., Marana, Ariz., 1984. Recipient Disting. Expert award Ariz. Dept. Pub. Safety, 1972, Superior Performance award Bur. Indian Affairs, 1984. Mem. Internat. Assn. Chiefs Police, Ariz. Law Enforcement Assn., Four Corners Police Assn., Federal Law Enforcement Officers Assn. Republican. Roman Catholic. Home: PO Box 1720 Window Rock AZ 86515-1720 Office: Bur Indian Affairs Navajo Br Criminal investigation Area Office PO Box M Window Rock AZ 86515-0714

ALFREY, THOMAS NEVILLE, lawyer; b. New Braunfels, Tex., Oct. 30, 1944; s. Clarence Powhattan and Lilla Carlton (Beadel) A.; m. Rebecca Ann Fruland, June 22, 1979; children: Kimberly, Jessica. BA, Tex. Christian U., 1967; JD, U. Tex., Austin, 1970. Bar: Colo. 1970, U.S. Dist. Ct. Colo. 1970, U.S. Ct. Appeals (10th cir.) 1970. Dep. dist. atty. State of Colo., Denver, 1971-72; asst. dist. atty. 9th jud. dist. State of Colo., Aspen, 1973-74; dir. organized crime strike force Colo. Atty. Gen., Denver, 1974-75; asst. U.S. atty. Dept. Justice, Denver, 1975; assoc. Hall & Evans, Denver, 1975, ptnr., 1976—; cons. Tex. Organized Crime Strike Force, Austin, 1975; lectr. various profl. groups; mem. faculty, Nat. Inst. Trial Advocacy, Denver, 1987-88. 1st lt. U.S. Army, 1970. Mem. ABA, Colo. Bar Assn., Colo. Def. Lawyers Assn., Internat. Assn. Def. Counsel, Denver Partnership, Glenmoor Country Club (bd. govs.). Office: Hall & Evans Ste 1700 1200 17th St Denver CO 80202

ALFVÉN, HANNES OLOF GOSTA, physicist; b. May 30, 1908. Ph.D., U. Uppsala, 1934. Prof. theory of electricity Royal Inst. Tech., Stockholm, 1940-45, prof. electronics, 1945-63, prof. plasma physics, 1963-73; prof. dept. applied physics and info. sci. U. Calif., San Diego, 1967—; mem. Swedish Sci. Adv. Council, 1963-67; past mem. Swedish AEC; past gov. Swedish Def. Research Inst., Swedish Atomic Energy Co.; past sci. adv. Swedish Govt.; pres. Pugwash Confs. on Sci. and World Affairs, 1970-75; mem. panel on comets and asteroids NASA. Author: Cosmical Electrodynamics, 1950; On the Origin of the Solar System, 1954; Cosmical Electrodynamics: Fundamental Principles, 1963; Worlds-Antiworlds, 1966; The Tale of the Big Computer, 1968; Atom, Man and the Universe, 1969; Living on the Third Planet, 1972; Evolution of the Solar System, 1976; Cosmic Plasma, 1981. Recipient Nobel prize for physics, 1970; Lomonsov gold medal USSR Acad. Scis., 1971; Franklin medal, 1971, Bowie Gold medal Am. Geophysical Union, 1987. Fellow Royal Soc. (Eng.); mem. Swedish Acad. Scis., Akademia NAUK (USSR), NAS (fgn. assoc.), others. also: Royal Inst Tech, Dept Plasma Physics, S-100-44 Stockholm 70, Sweden

ALGRA, RONALD JAMES, dermatologist; b. Artesia, Calif., Feb. 23, 1949; s. Cornelius and Helena Joyce (De Boom) A.; m. Phyllis Ann Brandsma, July 31, 1970; children: Brian David, Stephanie Ann. BS in Chemistry, Calvin Coll., 1971; MD, Baylor Coll. Medicine, 1974. Diplomate Am. Bd. Dermatology. Intern Gen. Hosp. Ventura County, Ventura, Calif., 1974-75; resident in dermatology Baylor Coll. Medicine, Houston, 1975-78; pvt. practice Hathorne, Calif., 1978-88, Hawthorne, Calif., 1988—; asst. med. dir. FHP, Inc., Fountain Valley, 1988—. Fellow Am. Acad. Dermatology; mem. Am. Coll. Physician Executives, Alpha Omega Alpha. Republican. Mem. Christian Reformed Ch. Office: FHP Inc 9900 Talbert Ave Fountain Valley CA 92708

ALI, MOSTAFA ABDUL MUNEIM, architectural designer; b. Alexandria, Arab Republic of Egypt, Oct. 3, 1957; s. Abdul Muneim and Zahia Ali. BS in Fine Arts, Helwan U., Alexandria, 1981; BS in Architecture, Sch. Architecture, Alexandria, 1981. Registered architect, Arab Republic of Egypt. Archtl. designer Conceptual Design Group, Irvine, Calif., 1984-85; archtl. intern Clyde Carpenter & Assocs., Santa Ana, Calif., 1985-86; archtl. designer Manor Care Inc., Santa Ana, 1986-88; pvt. practice archtl. design Calif., 1988—; cons., architect Mena for Trading & Constrn., Alexandria, 1983-84; architect, designer Nat. Bank of Oman Ltd., Alexandria, 1983. Mem. Egyptian Am. Orgn., L.A., 1984—, Arab Am. Orgn., L.A. Office: Archtl Presentations 10264 La Hacienda Fountain Valley CA 92708

ALIBRANDI, JOSEPH FRANCIS, diversified industrial company executive; b. Boston, Nov. 9, 1928; s. Paul and Anna (Amendolia) A.; m. Lambertha A. Araskiewicz, May 12, 1957; children: Paul, Ann-Marie, Carolyn. B.S.M.E., MIT, 1952. With Fairchild Engring. & Airplane Corp., 1951; mgr. indsl. engring. dept. Raytheon Co., Lexington, Mass., 1952-56; asst. plant mgr. Raytheon Co., Lowell, Mass., 1956-58, plant mgr., 1958-62, ops. mgr., 1962-65, v.p., gen. mgr., 1965-68, sr. v.p., gen. mgr., 1968-70; exec. v.p., dir. Whittaker Corp., Los Angeles, 1970, pres., 1970-86, chief exec. officer, 1974—, chmn., 1986—; dir. Fed. Res. Bank of San Francisco, 1973-76, chmn., 1977-79; dir. Daniel, Mann, Johnson & Mendenhall, Los Angeles, from 1979; mem. Western region adv. bd. Arkwright-Boston Ins., San Francisco, from 1978. Mem. corp. vis. com. Sloan Sch. Mgmt., MIT, from 1972, corp. vis. com. dept. biology, from 1979, mem. corp. devel. com., from 1973, mem. nat. bus. com., from 1977; chmn. bus. adv. council UCLA, from 1976, exec. com. bd. visitors Grad. Sch. Mgmt., from 1979; bd. councilors Sch. Bus. Adminstrn., U. So. Calif., from 1977; bd. dirs. Los Angeles World Affairs Council, from 1980. Served with U.S. Army, 1946-48. Mem. U.S. C. of C. (internat. policy com. from 1978). Office: Whittaker Corp 10880 Wilshire Blvd Los Angeles CA 90024 *

ALISON, PAUL NORDELL, retail executive; b. Denver, Jan. 26, 1950; s. Robert Franklin and Mary Lou (Nordell) A.; m. Nancy Ann Haight (div. Sept. 1986); children: Seth Andrew, Lesa Ann; m. Gloria Ann Spears, 1988. Student, Nebr. Wesleyan U., Lincoln, 1968-70, Regis Coll., 1983-84. Oncological asst. Denver Children's Hosp., 1970-71; gen. handyman Bros. Redevel., Denver, 1971-72; carpenter Lillibridge Constrn., Denver, 1972; cabinet maker Austro Furniture, Denver, 1972-74; asst. territory operator Dairy Queen Denver, 1974-79, gen. mng. ptnr., 1979-85, gen. ptnr. sales, 1985—. Bd. dirs. Family Tree, treas., 1987-88, pres. elect, 1989—. Mem. Ch. Religious Sci. Office: Dairy Queen Denver and Suburbs 7220 W Jefferson Ave #420 Lakewood CO 80235

ALKONS, JAMES JOSEPH, fine art conservator; b. Phila., Nov. 19, 1946; s. Joseph George and Frances Hope (Moseley) A.; m. Karen Renne Littau, Mar. 22, 1986; 1 child, Marc. BA, U. Calif., Davis, 1973, postgrad., 1973-74. Conservation asst. lab. for research and museology U. Calif., Davis, 1973-75; prin. conservator Sacramento, 1975-78; chief painting conservator No. Calif. Art Conservators, Sacramento, 1978-88; cons. for art constrn. State of Calif., 1977-88. com. mem. Sacramento Old City Assn., 1987-88. Served with USCG, 1966-67. Fellow Am. Inst. for Conservation; mem. Internat. Inst. for Conservation, Wester Assn. for Art Conservation. Republican. Lutheran. Home: 1930 N St Sacramento CA 95814 Office: No Calif Art Conservators 1930 N St Sacramento CA 95814

ALLABASHI, VASIL WILLIAM, insurance company executive; b. Southbridge, Mass., Feb. 2, 1936; s. Christo and Mary Allabashi; m. Carolyn Allabashi (div. 1980); m. Donna R. Margritz, May 14, 1981; children: Lynn, Kimberly, Karol. BBA, Baylor, 1960. CLU. Gen. agt. Paul Revere Life Ins. Co., Cleve., 1969; agy. head Lincoln Nat. Life Ins. Co., Denver, 1969-86; gen. agt. Guardian Life Ins. Co., Denver, 1987—. Home: 6661 S Trailway Circle Parker CO 80134

ALLAN, JAMES FREDERICK, research geologist; b. Washington, Dec. 3, 1956; s. Richard Thomas and Betty (Elsen) A. BA in Environ. Sci., U. Va., 1978; PhD in Geology, U. Calif., 1984; postgrad., Smithsonian Inst., 1984-85. Post-doctoral scientist Washington U., St. Louis, 1985-86, Northwestern U., Evanston, Ill., 1986-87, U. Brit. Columbia, Vancouver, Can., 1987—. Contbr. 13 articles to profl. jours. Named fellow Smithsonian Inst., Washington, 1984; recipient U. Calif. Patent Fund award, 1982, research grant Sigma Xi, 1982, Penrose grants, 1982, 83. Mem. Geol. Soc. Am., Mineral. Soc. Am., Am. Geophysical Union. Democrat. Home: 4243 W 12th Ave, Vancouver, BC Canada V6R 2P8 Office: U BC, Dept Geol Scis, 6334 Stores Rd, Vancouver, BC Canada V6T 2B4

ALLAN, ROBERT MOFFAT, JR., educator; b. Detroit, Dec. 8, 1920; s. Robert M. and Jane (Christman) A.; m. Harriet Spicer, Nov. 28, 1942; children—Robert M. III, Scott, David, Marilee. B.S., Stanford U., 1941; postgrad. Stanford Grad. Sch., 1941-42; M.S., UCLA, 1943; postgrad. Loyola Law Sch., 1947-50. Economist research dept. Security First Nat. Bank, 1942; exec. Marine Ins., 1946-53; asst. to pres., work mgr. Zinsco Elec. Products, 1953-55, v.p., dir., 1956-59; asst. to pres. The Times-Mirror Corp., 1959-60, corp. v.p., 1961-64; pres., dir. Cyprus Mines Corp., 1964-67; pres. Litton Internat., 1967-69; pres. U.S. Naval Postgrad. Sch. Found., prof. internat. mgmt. 1969-85. Bd. dirs., advisor U.S. Naval Acad.; trustee Boys Republic, Pomona Grad. Sch., Claremont Grad. Sch., Del Monte Forest Homeowners. Served with USAF, 1942-45. Recipient award Helms Athletic Found., 1947, 49; named Outstanding Businessman of Yr., Los Angeles, Nat. Assn. Accts., 1966; elected to Sailing Hall of Fame, 1969; recipient Meritorious Service award U.S. Navy, 1976; named Monterey Inst. Fgn. Studies trustee and sr. fellow, 1976. Mem. Mchts. and Mfrs. Assn. (dir.), Intercollegiate Yachting Assn. (regional dir. 1940-55), Phi Gamma Delta, Phi Delta Phi. Clubs: Newport Harbor Yacht (commodore 1962), Trans-Pacific Yacht, Monterey Country, Carmel Valley Country. Home: 169 Del Mesa Carmel CA 93921

ALLARD, EDWARD TIERNAN, III, total quality management consultant; b. Moulton, Ala., Aug. 3, 1945; s. Edward T. and Mary Elizabeth (Terry) A.; m. Lucille Roybal, Apr. 4, 1981; children: Lisa, Ricardo, Angelia, Guy-Mark. MBA, U. Miami. Enlisted USMC, 1963, advanced through grades to capt., resigned, 1973; electronics engr. Analog/Digital Computers; air traffic control office; tng. officer H & HS; Intern, sr. cons., dir. mktg. United Way of Am., Los Angeles, 1973-83; v.p. mktg. Los Angeles C. of C., 1985-85; pres. Profl. Cons. Group and Cons. Services of Am., Pasadena, 1985—, Allard & Assocs., 1985—; v.p. Deming Method Cons. Group, North Miami Beach, Fla., 1986—; mem. relations com. Los Angeles C. of C.; cons. productivity and quality improvement to govt. and agys., 1970—. Emcee local weekly show, Sta. WQAD-TV. Mem. bd. dirs. Hospice of Pasadena. Decorated USN Commendation with Battle Valor, Vietnam. Mem. Am. Mktg. Assn., Am. Mgmt. Assn., Sales and Mktg. Execs. Baptist. Home: 449 S Virginia Ave Pasadena CA 91107

ALLARD, ROBERT WAYNE, geneticist, educator; b. L.A., Sept. 3, 1919; s. Glenn A. and Alma A. (Roose) A.; m. Ann Catherine Wilson, June 16, 1944; children: Susan, Thomas, Jane, Gillian, Stacie. B.S., U. Calif., Davis, 1941; Ph.D., U. Wis., 1946. From asst. to assoc. prof. U. Calif., Davis, 1946—, prof. genetics, 1955—. Author books; contbr. articles to profl. jours. Served to lt. USNR. Recipient Crop Sci. award Am. Soc. Agronomy, 1964, DeKalb Disting. Career award Crop Sci. Soc. Am., 1983; Guggenheim fellow, 1954, 60; Fulbright fellow, 1955. Mem. Nat. Acad. Scis., Am. Acad. Arts and Scis., Am. Soc. Naturalists (pres. 1974-75), Genetics Soc. Am. (pres. 1983-84), Am. Genetics Assn. (pres. 1989), Phi Beta Kappa, Sigma Xi, Alpha Gamma Rho, Alpha Zeta. Democrat. Unitarian. Home: 2515 Bombadil Ln Davis CA 95616 Office: U Calif Davis 112 Parsons Hall Davis CA 95616

ALLARD, THURMAN J., electrical engineer; b. U.S. Canal Zone, Nov. 15, 1959; s. George W. and Martha Cynthia (Rapp) A.; m. Heather Lorelei Ingham, Aug. 12, 1983; children: Chase Kehr, Duncan G. BSEE, U.

N.Mex., 1981; MSEE, Purdue U., 1982. With Sandia Nat. Labs., Albuquerque, 1977-80; mem. tech. staff Sandia Nat. Labs., 1980—. Mem. IEEE. Republican. Home: 1135 Stutz NE Albuquerque NM 87123 Office: Sandia Nat Labs PO Box 5800 Div 5127 Albuquerque NM 87185

ALLBEE, CARLYNNE MARIE, college professor; b. Dayton, Ohio, July 1, 1947; d. Robert Gordon and Mary Louise (Thompson) Harvey. AA in Acctg., Grossmont Coll., El Cajon, Calif., 1968; BS in Acctg., San Diego State U., 1971; MBA in Govt. Relations, Nat. U., San Diego, 1980. Owner, trainer championship miniature horses Calif., 1980—; mgmt. cons. Wells Family Ranch, Lakeside, Calif., 1982—; acctg. cons. Jessie Paxton, Inc., San Diego, 1988—. Editor (newsletter) ABCSD, 1986-87; contbr. articles to profl. sports publs. elected official, bd. dirs. Lakeside Fire Protection Dist., 1981, re-elected, 1986; parade equestrianne Parades throughout So. Calif. Recipient numerous scholarships, San Diego, 1965-70. Mem. Pinto Horse Assn. Am. (nat. com. mem. 1986—), Nat. Assn. Accts. (most valuable mem. award 1975). Club: Toastmasters (first woman officer 1976). Office: Middle Earth Acres PO Box 454 La Mesa CA 92041

ALLBEE, CHARLES EUGENE, college professor; b. Holly, Colo., Nov. 18, 1937; s. Claudius Evan and Cora Ellen (Gillispie) A.; m. Nancy Jo Aughenbaugh, Dec. 23, 1961; children: Brian Dean, Janet Lynn. BA, Adams State Coll., Alamosa, Colo., 1960, MA, 1961; ArtsD, U. N. Colo., Greeley, 1979. Instr. Adams State Coll., 1961-64, asst. prof., 1965-80, assoc. prof., 1980-84; prof. English Met. State Coll., Denver, 1984—; pres. Faculty Senate Met. State Coll., 1986-88. Mem. Nat. Council Tchrs. English, Conf. on Coll. Composition and Communication. Democrat. Home: 6824 Urban St Arvada CO 80004

ALLBEE, SANDRA MOLL, real estate agent; b. Reading, Pa., July 15, 1947; d. Charles Lewars and Isabel May (Ackerman) Frederici; m. Thomas J. Allbee, Oct. 18, 1975 (div. 1987). Exec. sec. Hamburg (Pa.) State Sch. and Hosp., 1965-73; regional mgr. Am. Bus. Service Corp., Newport Beach, Calif., 1973-78; v.p. T.A.S.A., Inc., Long Beach, Calif., 1978-86; sales agt. Very Important Properties, Inc., Rolling Hills Estates, Calif., 1986—. Bd. dirs. Nat. Council on Alcoholism, Torrance, Calif., 1987—; pres. Rollingwood Homeowners Assn., Rolling Hills Estates, Calif., 1985—. Office: Very Important Properties 609 Deep Valley Dr Rolling Hills Estates CA 90274

ALLDIS, STEVE ALLEN, marketing professional; b. San Diego, Apr. 21, 1953; s. Ralph James and Geraldine (Williams) A.; m. Tina Mahvash, July 4, 1982 (divorced); 1 child, Michael. BSBA, Walla Walla Coll., 1975. Lic. real estate broker, Calif. Chief exec. officer Wall Street Mortgage, Inc., Downey, Calif., 1985—, United Exec. Realty, Downey, 1985—. Mem. Calif. Assn. Realtors, United Assn. Brokers, Downey Bd. Realtors, Downey Multiple Listing Svc., Nat. Assn. Realtors. Office: Wall Street Mortgage Inc 12010 Paramount Blvd Downey CA 90242

ALLDREDGE, ROBERT LOUIS, manufacturing company executive; b. Johnston City, Ill., Feb. 11, 1922; s. Samuel and Mary Elizabeth (Kreie) A.; B.S. in Chem. Engring., U. Denver, 1942; m. Shirley Alice Harrod, Dec. 15, 1944; children—Alice Louise, Mark Harrod. Research assoc. E.I. DuPont de Nemours & Co., Eastern Lab., Gibbstown, N.J., 1942-44; engring. research assoc. Manhattan Project, Los Alamos (N.Mex.) Sci. Lab., 1944-46; chem. engr. Denver Research Inst., U. Denver, 1946-50; pres. Alldredge & McCabe, Denver, 1950-81, exec., 1981—; pres. Serpentix Conveyor Corp., Denver, 1969—, Serpentix, Inc., Denver, 1969—; dir. Beryl Ores Co., Broomfield, Colo. Served with C.E., U.S. Army, 1944-46. Mem. Nat. Soc. profl. Engrs. (founding mem. Colo. div.), U. Denver Alumni Assn. (dir. 1965-72), Am. Chem. Soc., Profl. Engrs. Colo., AAAS, Sigma Alpha Epsilon. Methodist. Contbr. articles to profl. jours. Home: 130 Pearl St 1108 Denver CO 80203 Office: Alldredge & McCabe 9085 Marshall Ct Westminster CO 80030

ALLEN, BONNIE LYNN, pension actuary; b. Los Angeles, Oct. 2, 1957; d. David and Lucille M. (Scott) A. B.A. summa cum laude, UCLA, 1979. Math. tutor, Los Angeles, 1971—; reader math. dept. UCLA, 1977-79; pension actuary Martin E. Segal Co., Los Angeles, 1980—. Author short stories and poetry. Active mentor program UCLA Alumni Assn., 1978-79. Mem. Math. Assn. Am., Am. Math. Soc., Acad. Sci. Fiction, Fantasy and Horror Films, UCLA Alumni Assn. (life), Los Angeles Actuarial Club, Phi Beta Kappa. Office: Martin E Segal Co 500 S Virgil Ave Los Angeles CA 90020

ALLEN, BYRON SEDRIC, JR., physician; b. Center, Tex., Mar. 23, 1923; s. Byron Sedric and Thelma (Daugherty) A.; student S.W. Mo. State Tchrs. Coll., 1942-43, U. Houston, 1944-47; M.D., Tulane U., 1951; m. Alice Harrison, Aug. 21, 1947; children—Kathryn, Byron John, Diane. Intern, Fresno County (Calif.) Gen. Hosp., 1951-52, resident in obstetrics, 1952-53; gen. practice medicine and surgery, Fresno, Calif., 1953-63, Apple Valley Calif., 1963—; pres. med. staff St. Mary Desert Valley Hosp., Apple Valley, 1982-83; med. staff Victor Valley Hosp., Victorville, Calif., 1966—; vis. attending staff dept. family practice San Bernardino (Calif.) County Med. Center, 1973-76; guest lectr. in hypnosis Fresno State Coll., 1960-63; asst. prof. family medicine La. State U., 1976-77, clin. asst. prof., 1978-85. Trustee St. Mary Hosp., 1987-88. Served with USAAF, 1941-43. Named Outstanding Family Physicians in San Bernardino County, 1981-82; recipient Gierman-McKee Meml. award San Bernardino County Med. Ctr., 1982. Diplomate Am. Bd. Family Practice. Fellow Am. Acad. Family Physicians; mem. AMA, Calif. Acad. Family Physicians (chpt. pres. 1961, 80-81, del. Congress of Dels. 1982—, bd. dirs. 1985—), Calif. Med. Assn., San Bernardino County Med. Soc. (sec. 1976—, dir. 1972-83), Calif. Med. Assn. (del. 1974-80). Club: Rotary (pres. 1972—, Man of Year 1973). Home: 19004 Munsee Rd Apple Valley CA 92307 Office: 18327 Hwy 18 Apple Valley CA 92307

ALLEN, CHARLES BRYAN, data processing executive; b. Sugarland, Tex., Feb. 21, 1941; s. Richard Noah and Alice Rosalee (Johnson) A.; m. Barbara Jones, Mar. 1, 1963; children: Elizabeth, Beverly, Robyn. BBA, U. Tex., El Paso, 1966; MA, U. N.Mex., 1974. Cost acct. Armco Steel, Houston, 1966-69; acct. AEC, Albuquerque, 1969-75; budget analyst ERDA, Albuquerque, 1975-80; indsl. specialist U.S. Dept. Energy, Albuquerque, 1980-83, program analyst, 1983-84, sr. program analyst, 1984—. Served with U.S. Army, 1962-64. Mem. N.Mex. Wildlife Fedn., NRA (life). Mem. Ch. of Christ. Home: 9 Park Lane Circle Los Lunas NM 87031 Office: US Dept Energy PO Box 5400 Albuquerque NM 87185

ALLEN, DAVID CHARLES, educator; b. Syracuse, N.Y., Jan. 15, 1944; s. Charles Robert and Jane Loretta (Doolittle) A.; m. Mary Ann Stanke, June 15, 1968; children: Meredith Rae, Amelia Kathrine, Carl James. B.Tech. Edn., Nat. U., San Diego, 1983, MA in Human Behavior, 1984. Dir. retail sales Nat. U. Alumni Assn., 1981-83; audiovisual technician Grossmont Union High Sch. Dist., La Mesa, Calif., 1983-84; spl. project instr. San Diego Community Coll., 1985—. Mem. Presdl. Task Force; mem. Congl. Adv. Com. on Vets. Benefits for congressmen 44th and 45th dists. With USN, 1961-81. Mem. Am. Vocat. Assn., Nat. Assn. Performance and Instrn., Calif. Assn. Vocat. Edn., DAV, Vietnam Vets. Am., Fleet Reservation Assn., Nat. U. Student and Alumni Assn., Am. Tech. Edn. Assn., Beta Sigma Phi (hon.), K.C. Republican. Roman Catholic. Home: 8318 Blossom Hill Dr Lemon Grove CA 92045 Office: San Diego Community Coll Dist Mil Tng Program 3375 Camino del Rio S San Diego CA 92108

ALLEN, DAVID D., software systems engineer; b. Ft. Wayne, Ind., Aug. 25, 1938; s. Arthur August and Mildred Bertha (Lovin) Dobberkau; m. Carol Szilagyi, Apr. 3, 1965 (div. 1978); children: Robert, Charles, Alison. BS in Indsl. Econs., Purdue U., 1962. Engring. mgr. Allen Control Systems, La Canada, Calif., 1977-88; lead engr. technology McDonnell-Douglas Astronautics, Monrovia, Calif., 1988—. Home: 4461 AltaCanyada Rd La Canada CA 91011 Office: McDonnell Douglas Astronautics 700 Royal Oaks Dr Monrovia CA 91016-7105

ALLEN, DAVID HARLOW, aircraft company official, consultant; b. Lynn, Mass., May 26, 1930; s. Donald H. and Miriam Ellsworth (Harlow) A.; m. Roberta Arlene Miller, July 15, 1952; children: Donald Bruce, Richard Leroy, William David. BS in Gen. Edn., U. Nebr., Omaha, 1967; MBA, N.Mex. Highlands U., 1978. Cert. profl. logistician, cert. cost analyst. Commd. 2d lt. USAF, 1955, advanced through grades to lt. col., 1970; aircraft maintenance, staff, prodn. control officer, squadron comdr., wing asst., dep. comdr. maintenance SAC, 1948-74; dir. aircraft maintenance, dir. materiel Air Force Inspection and Safety Ctr., San Bernardino, Calif., 1969-72; dep. dir. logistics Air Force Test and Evaluation Ctr., Albuquerque, 1974-78; ret. 1978; sr. systems analyst, project leader Arinc Rsch. Corp., Santa Ana, Calif., 1978-84; dep. program mgr. for logistics, mgr. logistics project Ventura div. Northrop Corp., Newbury Park, Calif., 1984—; cons., instr. configuration and data mgmt., asst. dean West Coast U. Coll. Bus. and Mgmt., L.A., 1988—. Contbr. articles to profl. publs. Mem. state and nat. Rep. orgns., 1978—. Decorated Bronze Star. Mem. Soc. Logistics Engrs. (chmn. chpt. 1988—), Inst. Cost Analysis, Configuration and Data Mgmt. Assn. (chmn. fin. com. 1989), Am. Mgmt. Assn., Air Force Assn., Phi Kappa Phi. Home: 428 Moondance St Thousand Oaks CA 91360 Office: Northrop Corp Ventura Div 1515 Rancho Conejo PO Box 2500 Newbury Park CA 91320

ALLEN, DAVID RATCLIFF, management consultant; b. Jonesboro, La., Dec. 28, 1945; s. Gordon Emmet Allen and Miriam (Foster) Allen Drummond. BA, New Coll., 1968. Gen. mgr. Natural Landscape Co., L.A., 1977-80; pres. Allen Assocs., L.A., 1980-83; v.p. Insight Consulting Group, Santa Monica, Calif., 1983—. Author cassette program on productivity mgmt. Home: 16641 Merivale Ln Pacific Palisades CA 90272 Office: Insight Cons Group 2103 Wilshire St Santa Monica CA 90403

ALLEN, DEBRA JANIECE, pharmacist; b. Hanford, Calif., June 22, 1953; d. Keith Eugene and Patricia Marie (Falchi) Howe; m. John Alan Allen, July 24, 1976; children: Sean Adrian, Tonya Danielle. Student, West Hills Jr. Coll., Coalinga, Calif., 1969-72; D of Pharmacy, U. of the Pacific, 1972-76. Registered pharmacist, Calif. Pharmacy clk. Svc. Pharmacy, Inc., Coalinga, 1972-73; hosp. pharmacy intern Dameron Hosp., Stockton, Calif., 1974-76; mgr. Kernville (Calif.) Rexall Drug, 1976-78; staff pharmacist Tulare (Calif.) County Gen. Hosp., 1978-80; founder full-time svc., designer floor plans, dir. pharmacy Corcoran (Calif.) Dist. Hosp., 1980-83; staff pharmacist Hillman Health Ctr.-Tulare County Health Svcs., Tulare, 1984-86, Rush Pharmacy, Fresno, Calif., 1987—. Vol. Election Com. Tulare County, 1980, Petition Com. for the Prevention of Hosp. Closure, Tulare, 1980. Mem. Am. Soc. Hosp. Pharmacists, Calif. Pharmacy Assn., The Video Club Am., Lambda Kappa Sigma. Home: 5240 N Vernal Ave Fresno CA 93722 Office: Rush Pharmacy 4191 W Swift Ave Ste 101 Fresno CA 93722

ALLEN, DENNIS LEE, ophthalmology-para-medic-surgical technician; b. Glendale, Calif., Mar. 27, 1948; s. Charles Wesley Allen and Adrienne (McDade) Hunter; m. Kathleen Petersen, July 3, 1973 (div. Jan. 1980); 1 child, Benjamin William. AA in Anatomy, Glendale Jr. Coll., 1980; cert., Riverdale Sch. Ophthalmic Medicine, 1986. Ambulance driver Schaffer's Ambulance, L.A., 1972-74, Sheppard Ambulance, Seattle, 1975-78; materials mgr. operating room Glendale Adventist Med. Ctr., 1978-80; ophthalmic technician Larry G. Leiske, M.D., Inc., Glendale, 1980-85; ophthalmologist technician Murad A. Sunalp, M.D., Inc., Tulare, Calif., 1985-87; ophthalmologist technologist specialist David M. Shultz, M.D., Inc., Northridge, Calif., 1988—; pvt. practice, Northridge, 1988—; seminar instr. ophthal. convs.; lectr. So. Calif. elem. schs., Glendale, L.A., 1988—. Composer songs. Coach Girls Little League Softball. Sgt. USAF, 1966-69, Vietnam. Republican. Mormon. Home: 10500 Sherman Grove Ste 114 Sunland CA 91040 Office: David M Shultz MD Inc 18350 Roscoe Blvd Ste 300 Northridge CA 91325

ALLEN, DONALD BRUCE, public relations consulting firm executive; b. Rochester, N.Y., Aug. 23, 1941; s. Robert Thomas and Helen (Rife) A.; m. Irene Macinski, July 12, 1964 (div. 1984); children: Leigh Anne, Leslie Jennifer; m. Debra L. DeVore, Nov. 17, 1984. BA, SUNY-Albany, 1963; postgrad. in bus. adminstrn. U. So. Calif. Bur. mgr. UPI, Rochester, 1962-65; pub. relations mgr. Xerox Corp., Rochester and N.Y.C., 1965-69; account mgr. Hutchins Young & Rubicam, Rochester, 1969-71; pub. relations dir. Digital Equipment Corp., Maynard, Mass., 1971-72, Gen. Automation, Anaheim, Calif., 1972-75; ptnr. DeSpain & Allen, North Hollywood, Calif., 1975-79; pres. The Allen Group, San Juan Capistrano, Calif., 1979-89; sr. v.p. pub. rels. Roberts, Mealer , Emerson, Inc., 1989—. Author: Buying Your First Computer, 1976. Contbr. articles to profl. jours. Mem. Pub. Relations Soc. Am. (Counselor's Acad.), Nat. Investor Relations Inst., Fedn. Fly Fishermen, Calif. Trout Assn., Trout Unltd., Hell's Anglers (pres., bd. dirs.). Republican. Office: Roberts Mealer Emerson 3186-C Airway Ave Costa Mesa CA 92626

ALLEN, DONALD VAIL, investment executive; b. South Bend, Ind., Aug. 1, 1928; s. Frank Eugene and Vera Irene (Vail) A.; m. Betty Dunn, Nov. 17, 1956. BA magna cum laude, UCLA, 1972, MA, 1973. Editor Times-Herald, Washington, 1947-56; adminstrv. engr. Bendix Corp., Detroit, 1956-58; exec. mgr. Englander Corp., Detroit, 1958-69; with City Products, L.A., 1969-72; v.p. real property devel., holding and syndication Cambridge Investments, Pasadena, Calif., 1972-75; pres. Cambridge Investments, Pasadena, 1975—, also chmn. bd. dirs., 1979—; guest lectr. George Washington and Am. Univs., Washington, Pasadena City Colls. Contbr. several hundred articles to various publs. including L.A. Times, N.Y. Herald Tribune, Washington, D.C. Times-Herald, others, 1947—; translated works of Ezra Pound from Italian into English; performing musician (pianist, organist) Steinway roster of artists, specialist in works of Chopin, Debussy, Beethoven and Liszt; first performance of works by Am. composers Paul Creston, Norman dello Joio, Ross Lee Finney, appearances in N.Y., Washington (Nat. Gallery of Arts, Phillips Art Gallery). Pres. Funds for Needy Children, 1974-76. Mem. Am. Mgmt. Assn., Calif. Assn. Realtors, Am. Guild of Organists, Chamber Music Soc. Republican. Episcopalian. Home: 3371 Celinda Dr Carlsbad CA 92008 Office: Cambridge Investments 2940 Sombrosa St Carlsbad CA 92009

ALLEN, EDGAR BURNS, records management professional; b. L.A., Sept. 1, 1929; s. Harry James and Hela Ruth (Graham) A.; m. Eleanor Angela Gregory, July 24, 1960; children: Linda Marie, Lisa Ann. AA, L.A. City Coll., 1958; student, Calif. State U., L.A., 1958, 81; BS, UCLA, 1985. Supr. records ctr. L.A. Dept. Water and Power, 1958-67, records mgr., 1967-76; records mgmt. officer City of L.A., 1976-85; records mgmt. cons. 1985—. Creator records mgmt. systems. Chmn. Leimert Pk. Community Assn., L.A., 1972-75. Mem. Assn. Records Mgrs. and Adminstrs. (bd. dirs. 1975-76), Soc. Calif. Archivists, All Yr. Figure Skating Club (bd. dirs. 1970-79). Democrat. Roman Catholic. also: Profl Bus Systems 11823 E Slauson Ave #1 Santa Fe Springs CA 90670

ALLEN, EDMUND WALTER, structural engineer, surveyor, civil engineer, consultant; b. Vernal, Utah, Nov. 18, 1927; s. A. Edgar and Edith (McCoy) A.; m. Barbara Seegmiller, Mar. 17, 1950; children: Gregory L., Patti K., Ted W. BSCE, U. Utah, 1952. Cert. land surveyor, Utah; registered profl. engr. Utah, Nev., Idaho, Wyo., Colo., N.Mex. Surveyor Roger W. Sheridan Co., Salt Lake City, 1951-52, Harsh Devel. Corp., Portland, Oreg., 1952-53, Bechtel Corp., Salt Lake City, 1953-54; struct. engr. H.C. Hughes Co., Salt Lake City, 1954-57; engr. Alfred Brown Co., Salt Lake City, 1957-60; pres. E.W. Allen & Assocs., Salt Lake City, 1960—; chmn. Salt Lake City Bd. Appeals for Housing and Constrn., 1979, 84; mem. Mayor's Task Force on Preservation and Devel., Salt Lake City, 1983; mem. Landmarks Com. Salt Lake City, 1984-88. Prin. works include: Met. Hall of Justice building, Salt Lake City; Chase Fine Arts ctr., the Spectrum, Utah State U., Logan; Skaggs Coll. of Pharmacy building, behavioral sci. building, art and architecture building, addition to hosp. med. ctr U. Utah, Salt Lake City; clock tower Weber State Coll, Ogden, Utah; Valley Fair Mall, West Valley City, Utah; Snowbird tram sta., comml. plaza, hotel and Mid Gad restaurant; Rampton sci. building, Utah Tech. Coll., Salt Lake City; bridge across Green River near Vernal, Utah; 15 high schs., 80 elem. schs., 50 ch. buildings, various locations; J.C. Penney office building, Salt Lake City; Eaton-Kenway office tower, Salt Lake City; Gov.'s Plaza offices and condominiums, Salt Lake City; conv. and exhibit hall for the Salt Palace, Salt Lake City; also, restoration of the Devereaux House, Salt Lake City, Salt Lake City and County building. Served with U.S. Army, 1946-48. Recipient Disting. Alumnus award U. Utah, 1975, Engring. Excellence Honor award Consulting Engrs. Council Utah, 1983, Merit award Am. Inst. Steel Constrn., 1985, Award for Excellence in Masonry Engring. Utah Masonry Promotion, 1983, Engring. Excellence award; named Outstanding Utah Engr. of Yr. Utah Engrs. Council, 1985. Mem. ASCE, Am. Concrete Inst., Am. Inst. Steel Constrn., Consulting Engrs. Council Utah (v.p. 1977-78, pres.-elect 1978-79, pres. 1979-80, nat. dir. 1984-85), Masonry Soc., Earthquake Engring. Research Inst. Struct. Engrs. Assn. So. Calif. (allied), Struct. Engrs. Assn. Utah (founding, pres. 1980-81), Internat. Cof. Building Officials. Mormon. Home: 2567 S 150 E Bountiful UT 84010 Office: EW Allen & Assocs 16 Exchange Pl Salt Lake City UT 84111

ALLEN, EDWARD RAYMOND, educator, accountant; b. Indpls., Sept. 30, 1913; s. Edward L. and Emmeline (Rice) A.; B.S. in Commerce, Drake U., 1950, M.A. in Accounting, 1951; m. Norma D. M. Brennan, May 10, 1941. Asst. prof. bus. adminstrn. Parsons Coll., Fairfield, Iowa, 1952-56; faculty Coll. of Idaho, Caldwell, 1956—, prof. bus. adminstrn., 1956-73, head dept., 1962-70, chmn. dept., 1970-73, emeritus, 1973—, vis. lectr., 1976—; practicing C.P.A., Caldwell, 1958—. Served to capt. AUS, 1942-46; lt. col. Res. ret. Decorated Bronze Star with 1 palm; C.P.A., Iowa, Idaho. Mem. Am. Inst. C.P.A.s, Idaho Soc. C.P.A.s (dir., regional v.p. 1958-61, mem. standards of practice com. 1974-83, chmn. com. 1980-83, chmn. relations with ednl. instns. com. 1984-86), AAUP (past pres. Coll. of Idaho chpt.), C. of C., Pi Kappa Phi. Clubs: Elks. Contbr. articles to profl. jours. Home: PO Box 336 Caldwell ID 83606

ALLEN, FRANCES MICHAEL, publisher; b. Charlotte, N.C., Apr. 7, 1939; d. Thomas Wilcox and Lola Frances (Horne) A.; m. Joseph Taylor Lisenbee, Feb. 24, 1955 (div. 1957); 1 child, Leslie Autice. Abilene (Tex.) Christian Coll., 1954-56, Chico (Calif.) State U., 1957-59. Art dir. B&E Publs., L.A., 1963-65; editor B&E Publs., 1969-70; art dir. Tiburon Corp., Chgo., 1970-75; founder, editor Boxers, Internat., L.A., 1970-76; editor The Hound's Tale, 1974, Saints, Incorp., 1974-76; founder, editor Setters, Incorp., Costa Mesa, Calif., 1975-85; founder, owner Michael Enterprises, Midway City, Calif., 1976—; editor Am. Cocker Rev., Midway City, 1980-81; editor, publisher, ptnr. Am. Cocker Rev., 1981—. Illustrator : The First Five Years, 1970, The Aftercare of the Ear, 1975, The Shenn Simplicity Collection, 1976, The Miniature Pinscher, 1967; prin. works include mag. and book covers for USA, and most widely published show dog artist world wide, past 15 yrs. Recipient Dog World Award Top Producer, 5 times, 1966-88, numerous 1st awards in art fairs. Mem. Dog Writers Assn. Am. Republican. Mem. Ch. of Christ. Home and Office: 14531 Jefferson St Midway City CA 92655

ALLEN, GERALD LEE, business economist, researcher, consultant; b. Mt. Vernon, Ind., Sept. 30, 1926; s. Lealon and Edna Victoria (Fisher) A.; m. Gloria Jean Weiss, Feb. 26, 1950; children: Sheryl Lee, Pamela Jean. BS, Ind. U., 1950; postgrad., U. Colo., Denver, 1969. Salesman, budget adminstr. Seyvel, Evansville, Ind., 1951-54; fin. analyst Gen. Foods Corp., Evansville, 1954-55; office mgr., cost acctg. supr. Internat. Steel Co., Evansville, 1955-62; sr. fin. analyst Martin-Marietta Corp., Denver, 1962-64; econ. and bus. researcher Gates Rubber Co., Denver, 1964-66; chief economist, dir. bus. rsch. div. U. Colo. Coll. Bus., Boulder, 1966-88, sr. adviser, 1988—. Author: Colorado Business and Economic Outlook, 1976-88, Emerging High Technology Companies in Colorado, 1984; editor: Directory of Colorado Manufacturers, 1966-88, Statistical Abstract of Colorado, 1987. With USNR, 1944-46. Recipient Disting. Svc. award Denver Regional Coun. Govts., 1980, Outstanding Svc. award bus. rsch. div. U. Colo. Coll. Bus., 1988. Mem. Nat. Assn. Bus. Economists, Econ. Developers Coun. Colo. (hon. life, pres. 1987-88), Denver Assn. Bus. Economists (pres. 1978-79). Presbyterian. Home: 5395 Kewanee Dr Boulder CO 80303 Office: U Colo Coll Bus Rsch Div Campus Box 420 Boulder CO 80309

ALLEN, HOWARD PFEIFFER, electric utility executive, lawyer; b. Upland, Calif., Oct. 7, 1925; s. Howard Clinton and Emma Maud (Pfeiffer) A.; m. Dixie Mae Illa, May 14, 1948; 1 child, Alisa Cary. AA, Chaffey Jr. Coll., 1946; BA in Econs. cum laude, Pomona Coll., 1948; JD, Stanford U., 1951. Bar: Calif. 1951, U.S. Supreme Ct. Asst. prof. law, asst. dean law sch. Stanford (Calif.) U., 1951-54; with So. Calif. Edison Co., Rosemead, Calif., 1954—; v.p. So. Calif. Edison Co., Rosemead, 1962-71, sr. v.p., 1971-73, exec. v.p., 1973-80, pres., dir., 1980-84; chmn., chief exec. officer So. Calif. Edison Co., Rosemead, Calif., 1984—, also bd. dirs.; chmn. bd., chief exec. officer SCEcorp, 1988—, also bd. dirs.; bd. dirs. Cal Fed Inc., Calif. Fed. Savs. and Loan, Computer Scis. Corp., MCA Inc., Northrop Corp., PS Group Inc., Trust Co. West; vice chmn. bd., founding bd. mem. mayor's select com. on 1984 Olympics. Mem. exec. com. Bus. Coun., exec. com., policy com. Bus. Roundtable, commdr. coun. Salvation Army, bd. overseers Rand/UCLA Ctr. for Study Soviet Internat. Behavior; trustee, mem. nominating com. Conf. Bd.; trustee Com. Econ. Devel.; trustee, mem. exec. com. L.A. County Mus. Art, Pomona Coll.; bd. dirs., mem. exec. com. Calif. Econ. Devel. Corp.; bd. dirs. Edison Electric Inst., L.A. County Fair Assn; bd. dirs. LAOC Amateur Athletic Found.; dir. Calif. Civic Light Opera Assn., 1980-84; fin. chmn. Watts Summer Games, 1982. Recipient Whitney M. Young, Jr. award L.A. Urban League, 1985, Outstanding Pub. Svc. Recognition awards State of Calif., County of L.A., City of L.A., Carrie Chapman Catt award LWV, 1985, Human Rels. award Am. Jewish Com., 1986, Am. Spirit award Coun. Energy Resource Tribes, 1987, Spl. award Improvment for Sci. Edn. Calif. State Dept. Edn., 1988. Mem. ABA, NCCJ (nat. Protestant co-chmn. 1983-87, Brotherhood award 1988), Am. Judicature Soc., Pacific Coast Elec. Assn. (pres. 1984-85, bd. dirs.), Inst. for Resource Mgmt. (chmn. bd.), Assn. Edison Illuminating Cos. (bd. dirs.), Electric Power Rsch. Inst. (bd. dirs.), Calif. C. of C. (Outstanding Community Svc. Merit award 1982, bd. dirs.), Calif. Club (L.A.), Pacific Union Club (San Francisco), Bohemian Club (San Francisco), L.A. Country Club, La Quinta Hotel Golf Club, PGA West Golf Club, Mission Hills Country Club, 100 Club (exec. com.). Office: So Calif Edison Co 2244 Walnut Grove Ave Rosemead CA 91770

ALLEN, JEFFREY BLYNNE, real estate developer, consultant; b. Abington, Pa., Mar. 26, 1948; s. Francis Blynne and Julia (Obuhanych) A.; m. Carol Ann Imrie, June 28, 1975; 1 child, Julia Jane. BS, Cornell U., 1970; MBA, Harvard U., 1974. Project engr. Dravo Corp., Pitts., 1970-71, Metcalf & Eddy, Boston, 1971-72; project mgr. Cabot Cabot & Forbes, Los Angeles and Boston, 1974-77; v.p. Cabot Cabot & Forbes, Los Angeles, 1979-81; devel. mgr. The Koll Co., Newport Beach, Calif., 1977-79; mng. ptnr. Paragon Group, Los Angeles, 1981—, also bd. dirs. Active Los Angeles Hdqrs. City Assn. (past bd. dirs.), Urban Land Inst.; bd. dirs. Calif. Comml. Coun.; commr. Calif. Senate Adv. Commn. Real Property; mem. exec. com. Calif. Comml. Council. Fellow Chrysler Corp., Harvard U. Sch. Bus., 1973; recipient scholarship Owens- Ill. Corp., Cornell U., 1966. Mem. Harvard Bus. Sch. Assn. (v.p. 1977-79), Los Angeles C. of C., Soc. Indl. Office Realtors. Republican. Clubs: Jonathan (Los Angeles), Chaparral. Home: 330 E Cordova Ave Pasadena CA 91101 Office: Paragon Group 523 W 6th St Ste 515 Los Angeles CA 90014

ALLEN, JOHN BARCLAY, real estate company executive; b. Toronto, Ont., Can., Aug. 30, 1929; s. Edwin Boswell and Jessie (Phinnemore) A.; m. Janet Marie Kutch, June 30, 1951; children: Kathleen, James, John, Kenneth. BS, U. So. Calif., 1960, MBA, 1962. Co-owner, br. mgr. Forest E. Olson Co., Van Nuys, Calif., 1959-69; v.p. Coldwell Banker Co., L.A., 1969-75; owner, mgr. Arthur Turner Co., Santa Ana, Calif., 1975-79; sr. v.p. Grubb & Ellis Co., San Francisco, 1979--. Author: Selling Income Property Successfully, 1974, newsletter Investor Outlook,1979--. Cpl. U.S. Army, 1943-45. Mem. Newport Harbor Bd. Realtors, Nat. Assn. Realtors (bd. dirs. L.A. chpt. 1968-75, Chgo. chpt. 1973-75), Calif. Assn. Realtors (regional v.p. 1975), East Orange County Bd. Realtors (pres. 1974). Republican. Roman Catholic. Office: Grubb & Ellis Co 18400 Von Karman St Irvine CA 92715

ALLEN, KEITH FAULKNER, printing company executive; b. Seattle, Sept. 16, 1941; s. Guy Lovelace and Anne (Shea) A.; m. Donna Ison, July 8, 1978; 1 child, Jesse. Student, We. Wash. U., 1959-60, U. Wash., 1963-64. Copy editor Seattle Times Co., 1966—; printing exec. Pelican Press, Seattle, 1972—. Office: Pelican Press 5201 15th Ave NW Seattle WA 98107

ALLEN, LEW, JR., laboratory executive, former air force officer; b. Miami, Fla., Sept. 30, 1925; s. Lew and Zella (Holman) A.; m. Barbara Frink Hatch, Aug. 19, 1949; children: Barbara Allen Miller, Lew III, Marjorie Allen Dauster, Christie Allen Jameson, James Allen. BS, U.S. Mil. Acad., 1946; MS, U. Ill., 1952, PhD in Physics, 1954. Commd. 2d lt. USAAF, 1946;

advanced through grades to gen. USAF, 1977, ret., 1982; physicist test div. AEC, Los Alamos, N.Mex., 1954-57; sci. advisor Air Force Spl. Weapons Lab., Kirkland, N.Mex., 1957-61; with office of spl. tech. Sec. of Def., Washington, 1961-65; from dir. spl. projects to dep. dir. adv. plans Air Force Space Program, 1965-72; dir. Nat. Security Agy., Ft. Meade, Md., 1973-77; comdr. Air Force Systems Command, 1977-78; vice chief of staff USAF, Washington, 1978, chief of staff, 1978-82; dir. Jet Propulsion Lab., Calif. Inst. Tech., Pasadena, Calif., 1982—; chmn. COSEPUP (Nat. Acad. Scis.) panel on impact of nat. security controls on internat. tech. transfer, 1985-87. Decorated D.S.M. with 3 oak leaf clusters, Legion of Merit with 2 oak leaf clusters, Joint Service Commendation medal. Mem. Am. Phys. Soc., Am. Geophys. Union, Nat. Acad. Engring., Council on Fgn. Relations, Sigma Xi. Republican. Episcopalian. Clubs: Sunset (Los Angeles); Alfalfa (Washington). Office: Jet Propulsion Lab Calif Inst Tech 4800 Oak Grove Dr Pasadena CA 91109

ALLEN, LOWELL RAYMOND, insurance executive; b. Menan, Idaho, Mar. 23, 1933; s. Willard Lowe and Almira (Raymond) A.; m. Janine Rae Haislip, Aug. 15, 1958; children: Cheri Lynn, R. Dean, David W., Denise A. Student, Idaho State U., 1957-61. With GEM State Mut. Life Ins. Co., Pocatello and Twin Falls, Idaho, 1961-63; v.p. GEM State Mut. Life Ins. Co., Pocatello, Idaho, 1966-74; pres. GEM State Mut. Life Ins. Co., Pocatello, 1988—; state mgr. GEM State Mut. of Utah, Salt Lake City, 1963-66, v.p., 1966-74; v.p., co-owner Carefree, Inc., Pocatello, 1974-83; v.p. Housework, Inc., Pocatello, 1984-87; bd. dirs. GEM State Mut. Life Ins. Co., Pocatello, chmn. bd., 1988—; bd. dirs. GEM Ins. Co., Salt Lake City, GEM Holding Co., Salt Lake City. Mem. campaign com. United Way Fund, Pocatello. With USN, 1951-55. Mem. Rotary. Mormon. Home: 440 Washington Pocatello ID 83201 Office: GEM State Mut Life Ins Co 355 S Arthur Pocatello ID 83204

ALLEN, MARCUS, professional football player; b. San Diego, Mar. 26, 1960. Student, U. So. Calif. Running back with Los Angeles Raiders, NFL, El Segundo, Calif., 1982—; established NFL season record for most combined yards, 1985; played in NFL championship game, 1984; Pro Bowl, 1983, 85, 86, 88; co-owner, Pro Ball Beverage Corp. Recipient Heisman Trophy Downtown Athletic Club of N.Y.C., 1981; named The Sporting News NFL Rookie of Yr., 1982, Player of Yr., 1985. Office: care Los Angeles Raiders 332 Center St El Segundo CA 90245 *

ALLEN, MICHAEL E., staff engineer, project manager; b. Laplata, Md., Sept. 3, 1958; s. Carter E. and Maria (Ridi) A.; m. Joanne Winter, Aug. 18, 1979. BS in Computer Sci., U. Ga., 1980. Programmer Shaw Industries, Dalton, Ga., 1980-81, programmer, analyst, 1981; systems rep. Honeywell Info. Systems, Ft. Wayne, Ind., 1981-83, sr. systems rep., 1983-85; system design specialist, Mfg. Systems div. Honeywell Info. Systems, Phoenix, 1985-86, staff engr., Mfg. Systems div., 1986—. Recipient Tech. Merit award East Cen. Region, 1984, Mfg. Systems Div. Honeywell Info. Systems Dirs. award, 1986; named Systems Rep. of Yr. East Cen. Region, 1983. Republican. Roman Catholic. Home: 6922 W Kerry Ln Glendale AZ 85308 Office: Honeywell Info Systems 5115 N 27th Ave Phoenix AZ 85017

ALLEN, MICHAEL GRAHAM, management consultant; b. Pitts., Jan. 4, 1950; s. Louis A. and Ruth Ellen (Graham) A.; m. Sharon Kerrin, Dec. 16, 1978; children: Nolan, Erika. AB, U. Calif., Berkeley, 1973; MBA, U. Pitts., 1981. Mgr. mktg. Readers Digest, Pleasantville, N.Y., 1974-80; gen. mgr. Majers Corp., Omaha, 1981-86; pres. Louis Allen Assocs., Palo Alto, Calif., 1986—. Office: Louis Allen Assocs 3600 W Bayshore Rd Palo Alto CA 94303

ALLEN, NEIL HUTCHINS, physician; b. San Antonio, June 8, 1950; s. Cornelius Hutchins and Virginia Ella (Thomas) A.; m. Jennifer Lee Stimson, Sept. 18, 1981; children: Patrick James, Janine Adele. BS in Zoology, Tex. A&M U., 1972; MD, U. Tex., San Antonio, 1979. Diplomate Am. Bd. Ob-Gyn. Resident and intern Mich. State U., Edward Sparrow Hosp., Lansing, Mich., 1979-83; cardiovascular rsch. technician Baylor Coll. of Medicine and Veterans Hosp., Houston, Tex., 1973-75; physician Women's Clinic of Greeley, Greeley, Colo., 1983—; clin. prof. sch. of nursing U. of No. Colo., Greeley, 1986—; physician cons. U. No. Colo. Health Ctr., Greeley, 1983—; chmn. Dept. of Ob-Gyn. No. Colo. Med. Ctr., Greeley, 1988—. Author (with others) research article and abstracts. Vol. United Way Weld County, Greeley, 1986-88; bd. mem. KUNC Pub. Radio, Greeley, 1983-88, Am. Lung Assn., Loveland, Colo., 1983-87. Fellow Am. Coll. Ob-Gyn. Unitarian. Office: Womens Clinic of Greeley 2410 16th St Greeley CO 80631

ALLEN, PAUL, computer executive, professional sports team owner. Student, Wash. State U. Co-founder Microsoft Corp., Redmond, Wash., 1975, exec. v.p., 1975-83; pres. Asymetrix Corp., Bellevue, Wash., 1985—; owner, chmn. bd. Portland (Oreg.) Trail Blazers, 1988—; bd. dirs. Egghead Discount Software, Layered, Inc. Office: care Portland Trail Blazers 700 NE Multnomah St Lloyd Bldg Ste 950 Portland OR 97232 *

ALLEN, RANDALL HARRIS, retail executive; b. Franklinton, N.C., June 6, 1953; s. Archie Brown and Lida Joyce (Harris) A. AA, N.C. State Tech. Coll., 1974. Mgr. jewelry dept. Best Products Co., Inc., various locations, 1974-79; asst. store mgr. Best Products Co., Inc., San Antonio, 1979-80; store gen. mgr. Best Products Co., Inc., Sacramento, 1980—; cons. mgmt. Ram. Corp., Sacramento, 1982-85. Recipient Cert. of Achievement, Touche Ross, 1981. Republican. Methodist. Office: Best Products Co Inc 6990 65th St Sacramento CA 95642

ALLEN, RICHARD, physician; b. Portland, Oreg., Feb. 16, 1937; s. Jack and Lois Florene (Mower) A.; m. Patricia Elaine MacDonald, Oct. 3, 1959; children: Mark C., Rebecca L., Scott M. BA, U. Oreg., 1958; MA, U. Calif., Los Angeles, 1961; MD, N.Y. Med. Coll., 1965. Diplomate Am. Bd. OB-Gyn. Intern. Emanual Hosp., Portland, Oreg., 1965; resident Emanual Hosp., Portland, 1966-69; physician Portland (Oreg.) Ob-Gyn. Clin., 1971-88; clin. assoc. prof. Oreg. Health Scis. Univ., Portland, 1979—; pvt. practice Portland, 1988—. Contbg. author: How To Choose A Medical Specialist, 1986; contbr. articles to profl. jours. Mem. Office of Health Policy, State of Oreg., Salem, 1989, Gov's. Commn. on Health Care, Salem, 1988; pres. Oreg. Club of Portland, 1980-81, Mt. Hood Ski Patrol, Portland, 1979-81. With USAR, 1959-60. Fellow Am. Coll. Ob-Gyn.; mem. AMA (residency review comm., 1989), Oreg. Med. Assn. (pres. 1988-89), Pacific N.W. Ob-Gyn. Assn. (pres. 1987-88), Pacific Coast Ob-Gyn. Assn., Oreg. Ob-Gyn. Soc. (pres. 1980-81), Multnomah County Med. Soc. (pres. 1984-85), Am. Coll. Obstetricians and Gynecologists; mem. Sigma Phi Epsilon, Cor Et Manus. Democrat. Office: 2525 NW Lovejoy #301 Portland OR 97210

ALLEN, ROY VERLE, life insurance company executive; b. Hyrum, Utah, Aug. 3, 1933; s. Winfrd A. and Sarah Ann (Nielsen) A.; m. Judith Green, Aug. 11, 1961; children: Ann Marie Allen Webb, Michael R., Blair J. BS, Utah State U., 1958. CLU, Chartered Fin. Cons. Mgr. employee benefits Thiokol Chem. Corp., Brigham City, Utah, 1959-61; employment interviewer Hercules, Salt Lake City, 1962-63; agy. mgr. Standard Ins. Co., Salt Lake City, 1963—. Maj. U.S. Army Res., 1962-79. Mem. CLUs (bd. mem. 1973-75), Estate Planning Coun. (bd. mem. 1979-81), Utah Gen. Agts. and Mgrs. (sec., v.p., pres. 1979-83), Utah Assn. Life Underwrtiers (pres. 1988-89), Exchange Club. Republican. Mormon. Home: 2526 Olympus Dr Salt Lake City UT 84124 Office: Standard Ins Co 525 E 3d St S Salt Lake City UT 84102

ALLEN, STEVE, airline sales representative; b. East Rockaway, N.Y., Dec. 2, 1946; s. Arthur A. and Agnes (Harrigan) A.; m. Marcia Ann Richards, Feb. 9, 1974. BA, Marist Coll., 1968. Customer service rep. United Airlines, N.Y.C., 1969-75; account exec. United Airlines, Honolulu, 1975—. Mem. Makani Kai Yacht Club. Roman Catholic. Home: 272 Kuupua St Kailua HI 96734 Office: United Airlines Sales Box 35 Honolulu HI 96819

ALLEN, SUSAN MACALL, librarian; b. Detroit, Nov. 4, 1944; d. Edward and Barbara E. (Johnson) M.; m. William Barclay Allen, Oct. 14, 1969; children: Danielle, B. Marc. BA, U. Wis., 1967, MALS, 1968; MA, St. John's Coll., Santa Fe, N.M., 1989. Lic. life jr. coll. tchr., Calif. Asst. dir., librarian Coll. Student Personnel Inst., Claremont, Calif., 1968-70; abstracter Higher Edn Abstracts, Claremont, Calif., 1972-73, assoc. editor, 1973-78; master Webb Sch. Calif., Claremont, Calif., 1979-81; reference librarian Libraries of Claremont Colls., Claremont, Calif., 1981-87; asst. to dir., acting head Spl. Coll. Libraries, Claremont, Calif., 1987--; founder Oldtown Press, Claremont, 1984--; mem. adv. bd. Am. Antiquarian Soc. Program in the History of the Book, Worcester, Mass., 1988--. Contbr. articles in field to profl. jours. Mem. Calif. Rep. Cen. Com., 1987—. Mem. ALA, Am. Coun. Rsch. Librarians (mem. security com. rare books and manuscripts sect. 1988—), Am. Printing History Assn., Calif. Assn. Rsch. Librarians, Soc. Calif. Archivists, Book Club Calif. Republican. Office: Honnold/Mudd Libr 800 N Dartmouth Ave Claremont CA 91711

ALLENBAUGH, G. ERIC, organization development consulting company owner; b. San Fernando, Calif., Aug. 8, 1944; s. Donald Hoyt and Wilhelmina (Jordan) A.; m. Kay M. (Studebaker), Nov. 7, 1987; children: Peter Shea, Timothy Eric. BA, U. Calif., Northridge, 1966; MPH, UCLA, 1968; PhD, U. Oreg., 1981. Asst. adminstr. Valley Presbyn. Hosp., Van Nuys, Calif., 1968-71, Sacred Heart Gen. Hosp., Eugene, Oreg., 1971-79; pres. Allenbaugh Assocs., Inc., Lake Oswego, Oreg., 1979--. Recipient Walter S. Hilborne Human Relations award, 1962; Hosp. Council of So. Calif. Performance award, 1971; Ky. Colonel 1988. Fellow Am. Coll. Hosp. Adminstrs. Home and Office: 17443 Canal Circle Lake Oswego OR 97035

ALLERHEILIGEN, ROBERT PAUL, marketing educator; b. Denver, Dec. 23, 1944; s. Paul William and Helen Idris (Hodges) A.; m. Sandra Jeanne Lee, June 17, 1967 (div. 1982); children: Laura, Brad. BA, Colo. State U., 1967, MBA, 1974; PhD, U. So. Calif., 1986. Asst. prof. U. No. Colo., Greeley, 1974-75; coordinator spl. programs Colo. State U., Ft. Collins, 1975-79, asst. prof. mktg., 1985—; instr. U. So. Calif., L.A., 1979-85; officer JMN Enterprises, Inc., L.A., 1980—; prof. Exec. Devel. Inst., Ft. Collins, 1985—; cons. in field. Contbr. articles to profl. jours. Capt. USMC, 1967-70. Mem. Internat. Trade Assn. Colo., Colo. Internat. Edn. Assn., Am. Mktg. Assn., Internat. Bus. Assn. Rockies (bd. dirs. no. Colo.-Wyo. chpt.), Sertoma (bd. dirs.). Republican. Home: 1201 Solstice Ln Fort Collins CO 80525 Office: Colo State U Mktg Dept Clark Bldg Fort Collins CO 80523

ALLERTON, MICHAEL JOHN, performing arts administrator; b. Torquay, Devon, Eng., Mar. 5, 1935; children: Julie Kathryn, David Graeme. Chartered acct., Can. With Harrods of London, Morgan's (now Hudson's Bay Co.); acct. Coopers & Lybrand; mng. dir. Vancouver (B.C., Can.) Symphony Soc.; exec. dir. San Jose (Calif.) Symphony Orch.; past pres. Assn. Can. Orchs.; mem. Assn. Calif. Symphony Orchs. (exec. bd.). Pres. San Jose Arts Round Table. With Royal Navy. Recipient award of merit Community Arts Council, 1978, Silver Jubilee medal Govt. of Can., 1977. Anglican. Lodge: Rotary.

ALLIES, VICTORIA ROSSINI, electronics plant/process design consultant, chemical engineer; b. Southington, Conn., May 27, 1950; d. Leon and Lillian (Wanagus) Rossini; m. James M. McCarron, June 18, 1980; stepchildren: James Roy, Dolores, Lynn. Student Middlebury Coll., 1968-70; BA with honors, U. Conn., 1972, MS, 1979; postgrad. U. Phoenix, 1980-81. Adhesive chemist Loctite Corp., Newington, Conn., 1972-76, adhesives engr., 1976-78; market devel. mgr. laminated materials dept. Gen. Electric, Coshocton, Ohio, 1978-79; process/p.c.b. start-up engr. ITT-Courier Terminal Systems, Inc., Tempe, Ariz., 1979-80; sr. chem. process engr., environ. engring. supr. Digital Equipment Corp., Tempe, 1980-82; pres., cons. Tng. 'n' Tech., Inc., Tempe, 1982—; bd. dirs. Enterprise Network; facility design, review and implementation cons. Digitran Co. div. Becton Dickinson, Kodak, Hewlett-Packard, Xebec, Bechtel, L.M. Ericson, Sweden, 1982—, Sino-CAD, Peoples Republic of China and Can.; sec.-treas. MCW Assocs., Inc., 1983-85; instr. chemistry Maricopa Community Coll., Phoenix 1981-83; instr. Ctr. for Innovation, 1988-89; tech. expert cons. to joint venture of SWC and People's Republic of China, 1986—. Chair Small Bus. Programs, 1989—. Mem. Am. Electronics Assn. exec. coun. Ariz. chpt.), Am. Chem. Soc., Ariz. Printed Circuit Bd. Assn., Soc. Women Engrs. Patentee temp. bonding adhesives, Ariz. C. of C. (internat. bus. com.). Home: 11455 S Half Moon Dr Phoenix AZ 85044 Office: 2121 W University Dr #123 Tempe AZ 85281

ALLIN, ROBERT CAMERON, obstetrician and gynecologist; b. Evanston, Ill., Sept. 29, 1938; s. Frank Cameron and June Barber A.; m. Joann Elaine Spencer, Sept. 20, 1969; children: Blake Cameron, Kimberly June. BA, Northwestern, 1960, MD, 1964. Diplomate Am. Bd. of Obstetrics and Gynecology. Intern Highland Gen. Hosp., Oakland, Calif., 1964-65; resident Santa Clara Valley Med. Ctr., San Jose, Calif., 1967-70; med. staff Hawaii Permanente Med. Group, Honolulu, 1970-82; pvt. practice Honolulu, 1982—. Capt. USMC, 1965-67, Vietnam. Mem. Am. Coll. Obstetrics and Gynecology, Hawaii Med. Assn., Hawaii County Med. Assn. Republican. Club: Outrigger Canoe. Home: 1452 Kamole St Honolulu HI 96821

ALLINGTON, ROGER WALTER, civil engineer, engineering executive; b. French Camp, Calif., July 12, 1933; s. Walter Morrill and Elsie Irene (Coleman) A.; m. Marolyn Louise Enlow, Aug. 30, 1952 (div. 1965); children: Laura, Ronald, Kathryn, Edith; m. Ruth Ilene Howell, Nov. 10, 1967; stepchildren: Brady (dec.), Randel, Richard, Terrie Winniford. Student, Fresno State Coll., 1951-52, Chapman Coll., 1952-53, Fresno City Coll., 1954-64. Registered profl. engr. Calif., Oreg., Wash., Alaska. Asst. hwy. engr. Calif. Div. Hwys., Fresno, 1953-65; asst. city traffic engr. City of Santa Barbara, Calif., 1965-66; rd. adminstr. div. engr. Ventura (Calif.) County Dept. Pub. Works, 1966-69; state traffic engr. Alaska Dept. Hwys., Juneau, 1969-73; land and engring. officer Sealaska Corp., Juneau, 1973-78; chief engr. Kramer, Chin & Mayo, Juneau, 1979-81; gen. mgr., chief exec. officer Shaan-Seet, Inc., Craig, Alaska, 1981-82; state design standards engr. Alaska Dept. Transp. and Pub. Facilities, Juneau, 1982-85; traffic engr. City of Beverly Hills, Calif., 1985-88; dep. dir. engring. El Dorado County Dept. Transp., Placerville, Calif., 1988—; prin., owner Allington and Assoc., Juneau, 1978-79. Editor, compiler traffic and design manuals; contbr. to profl. publs. Assemblyman, City and Borough of Juneau, 1976-79; co-chmn. Alaska Coastal Policy Coun., Juneau, 1977-79; vice-chmn. Environ. Rev. Bd., Beverly Hills, 1987-88. Fellow Inst. Transp. Engrs.; mem. ASCE, Am. Pub. Works Assn., Nat. Soc. Profl. Engrs., Illuminating Engrs. Soc., Internat. Right of Way Assn., Lions. Home: 6801 Bertie Ln Placerville CA 95667 Office: El Dorado County Dept Transp 2441 Headington Rd Placerville CA 95667

ALLISON, DELBURT E., architect, engineer; b. Enid, Okla., Feb. 3, 1924; m. M. Carol Erickson, Sept. 12, 1953; children: Cathy, Paul, Patricia, Mary Ann. BS in Archtl. Engring., U. Ill., 1950; postgrad., U. Alaska. Lic. architect, Ill., N.J., Pa., Ohio, Minn., Alaska; registered profl. engr., Pa., Minn., Alaska. Chief architect Arctic Slope Consulting Group, Fairbanks, Alaska; prin. D.E. Allison & Assocs., Fairbanks; mem. enforcement adv. com., Alaska Bd. Registration for Architects, Engrs. and Land Surveyors, 1988—; mem. legis. liaison com., Alaska Profl. Design Conf., Fairbanks, 1987—. Loaned exec., United Way Mpls., 1977-79; mem. exec. bd. Fairbanks area Boy Scouts Am., 1981—. Mem. AIA (chmn. 1986), Alaska Soc. Profl. Engrs., Internat. Bldg. Ofcls. Conf. (pres.), Coun. Ednl. Facility Planners Internat. Home: 100 Dunbar Ave Fairbanks AK 99701

ALLISON, HERBERT REGINALD, JR., sales executive; b. Albuquerque, July 25, 1947; s. Herbert Reginald Sr. and Lorena Marie (Giesen) A.; m. Judith Dianne Herbert, Apr. 29, 1967; children: Jeffrey Scott, Sabrina Rene. BBA, U. New Mex., 1969. Rep. mktg. Burroughs Corp., Albuquerque, 1971-75; product tng. mgr. Burroughs Corp., Pasadena, Calif., 1975-76; product mgr. Burroughs Corp., Englewood, Colo., 1976-78; br. mgr. Burroughs Corp., Salt Lake City, 1978-81; regional sales mgr. Burroughs Corp., Irvine, Calif., 1981-83, CMI Corp., Irvine, 1983-87, CIS Corp., Laguna Hills, Calif., 1987-89; br. sales mgr. Bell Atlantic Systems, Costa Mesa, Calif., 1989—. Republican. Roman Catholic. Home: 24741 Camino Villa Lake Forest CA 92630 Office: Bell Atlantic Systems Leasing Internat 3200 Park Center Dr Costa Mesa CA 92626

ALLISON, JOY ELAINE, special education educator; b. Seattle, July 2, 1953; d. Charles O. and Phyllis Elaine (Neal) Swartfager; m. Patrick C. Allison, Aug. 10, 1980. BA in English Lit., U. Wash., 1975; MEd, Seattle Pacific U., 1984. Tchr. spl. edn. Grandview Sch., Kent, Wash., 1978-84, Kentwood High Sch., Kent, 1984—. Dir. ann. spring play Renton (Wash.) Park Dept. Developmentally Disabled program, 1984—. Home: 608 SW 3d Pl Renton WA 98055 Office: 25800 164th SE Kentwood Kent WA 98042

ALLISON, LAIRD BURL, business educator; b. St. Marys, W.Va., Nov. 7, 1917; s. Joseph Alexander and Opal Marie (Robinson) A.; m. Katherine Louise Hunt, Nov. 25, 1943 (div. 1947); 1 child, William Lee; m. Genevieve Nora Elmore, Feb. 1, 1957. BS in Personnel and Indsl. Relations magna cum laude, U. So. Calif., 1956; MBA, UCLA, 1958. Chief petty officer USN, 1936-51, PTO; asst. prof. to prof. mgmt. Calif. State U., L.A., 1956-83; asst. dean Calif. State U. Sch. Bus. and Econs., L.A., 1971-72, assoc. dean, 1973-83, emeritus prof. mgmt., 1983—; vis. asst. prof. mgmt. Calif. State U., Fullerton, 1970. Co-authored the Bachelors degree program in mgmt. sci. at Calif. State U., 1963. Mem. U.S. Naval Inst., Navy League U.S. Ford Found. fellow, 1960. Mem. Acad. Mgmt., Inst. Mgmt. Sci., Western Econs. Assn. Internat., World Future Soc., Am. Acad. Polit. Social Sci., Calif. State U. Assn. Emeriti Profs., Calif. State U. L.A. Emeriti Assn. (v.p. programs 1986-87, v.p. administrn. 1987-88, pres. 1988-89), Am. Assn. Individual Investors, Am. Assn. Retired Persons, Alpha Kappa Psi. Club: Retired Pub. Employees Assn. of Calif. (sec. Calif. State U. L.A. 1984-88, v.p. 1989). Home: 1615 S El Molino Alhambra CA 91801 Office: Calif State U Dept Mgmt 5151 State University Dr Los Angeles CA 90032

ALLISON, STEPHEN GALENDER, radio station executive; b. Springfield, Mo., Dec. 11, 1952; s. Edgbert and Naomi Louise (Chamless) A.; m. Linda Katherine Lavelle, Apr. 6, 1978 (div. Dec. 1983); children: Julie Ann, Jennifer Erin; m. Tara Rae Foster, Aug. 20, 1986. Personality Sta. WSBB, New Smyrna, Fla., 1971-72, Sta. WMFJ-AM-FM, Daytona Beach, Fla., 1972-75, Sta. KADI-FM, St. Louis, 1975-76, Sta. KAUM-FM, Houston, 1976-79, Sta. WKYS-FM, Washington, 1979-81; gen mgr. Sta. KSTM-FM, Phoenix, 1981-85; pres. Allison Broadcasting Co., Inc. (merged with The Daytona Group), Phoenix, 1985-87, The Daytona Group, Phoenix, 1987—, Allison Broadcast Group, Inc., Dallas, Del Mar, Calif., 1987—; owner Stas. KGRX-FM/KIKO, Phoenix, 1987—, Sta. KDGE-FM, Dallas; mktg. cons. St. Louis Post-Dispatch, 1975-76, Houston Chronicle, 1976-79, Washington Star, 1980-81; advt. cons. Celebrity Theatre, Phoenix, 1985-86. Bd. dirs. Desert-Mountain Foothills Assn., Scottsdale, Ariz., 1981—, Alwun House Cultural Ctr., Phoenix, 1982—, Film in Ariz., Phoenix, 1985—, Ariz. Commn. on the Arts, Phoenix, 1986—; mem. Nat. Rep. Congl. Com., 1988—. Mem. Nat. Assn. Broadcasters, Ariz. Broadcasters Assn. Republican. Club: Phoenix Active 20-30. Home: 7507 Summitview Dr Irving TX 75063 Office: 700 Courtyard Tower 1320 Greenway Dr Irving TX 75038

ALLNUTT, ALVIN HOWARD, manufacturing executive; b. Okla. City, Aug. 19, 1932; s. Alvin Matthew and Loretta Janetta (Zimmerman) A.; m. Kathryn Ann Miller, Dec. 19, 1953; 1 child, Wesley Howard. BS in Econs., Okla. City U., 1955; MBA, U. Mich., 1965. Commd. ensign USN, 1956, advanced through grades to capt., 1978; ret. U.S. Army, 1987; logistics mgr. western region Systems Engring. Assocs. Corp., Bremerton, Wash., 1987—. Task force dir. Flagship 88, Bremerton, 1988. Mem. Soc. Logistics Engrs., Rotary (membership chmn. 1988), Navy League. Republican. Home: 6289 Gleneagle Ave SW Port Orchard WA 98366 Office: Systems Engring Assocs Corp 2817 Wheaton Way Suite 212 Bremerton WA 98310

ALLOWAY, ANNE MAUREEN SCHUBERT, industrial waste administrator; b. Martinez, Calif., Oct. 19, 1954; d. James Benjamin and Mariel Ann (Phillips) Schubert; children from previous marriage: Joseph Benjamin, Odinn Glenn, Aaron Dean. AS in Life Sci., Allan Hancock Coll., 1982, AA in Liberal Arts, 1982. Cert. indsl. waste insp., 1984. Indsl. waste insp. City of Santa Maria, Calif., 1982-86; mgr. indsl. pretreatment program, collection systems Simi Valley (Calif.) County Sanitation Dist., 1986—; sect. chmn. Tri-Counties Pub. Edn. Mem. State Pub. Edn. Com., Ventura County Hazardous Waste Mgmt.(adv. com. bd. supr), Tri Counties Voluntary Cert. Com (sec. chmn.), State Voluntary Cert. Com., Tri Counties Pub. Edn. (sec. chmn.), Calif. Water Pollution Control Assn. indsl./hazardous waste com., pub. edn. com.), Water Pollution Control Fedn., Ventura County Hazardous Waste Mgmt. (adv. com.), Hazardous Waste Assn. Calif. Recipient Merit award Industrial Waste Inspection Tech., 1986. Republican. Roman Catholic. Club: Coast and Valley Health. Lodge: Keepers of the Flame. Avocations: painting, writing, sports, reading. Home: 1839 Colleen St Simi Valley CA 93063 Office: Simi Valley County Sanitation Dist 500 W Los Angeles Ave Simi Valley CA 93065

ALLSWANG, JOHN MYERS, computer science educator, historian; b. Chgo., Jan. 16, 1937; s. Eugene Allen and Katherine (Myers) A.; m. Suzanne Menzel, Dec. 19, 1964; children: Eden, Yael. BA, U. Ill., 1959; MA, U. Iowa, 1960; PhD, U. Pitts., 1967. Instr. No. Ill. U., Dekalb, 1965-66; asst. prof. No. Mich. U., Marquette, 1966-68; prof. Calif. State U., Los Angeles, 1968—; vis. prof. Hebrew U., Jerusalem, 1971-72, U. Leiden, The Netherlands, 1977-78; prin. Computer Explanations, Los Angeles, 1982—. Author: Bosses, Machines and Urban Voters, 1986, Physician's Guide to Computers, 1985, New Deal and American Politics, 1978, House for All Peoples, 1972; columnist Rx Home Care mag., Los Angeles, 1985-87; contbg. editor Interface Age mag., Cerritos, Calif., 1982-84, IBM PC Update mag., Indpls., 1984-87. Adult vol. SafeRides program, Los Angeles, 1986—. IBM fellow, 1968; recipient Merit award Calif. State U., Los Angeles, 1985, 86, 87, 88. Mem. Orgn. Am. Historians, Computer Press Assn. Democrat. Jewish. Home: 2438 La Condesa Dr Los Angeles CA 90049 Office: Calif State U 5151 State University Dr Los Angeles CA 90049

ALLUMBAUGH, BYRON, grocery company executive. Chmn. Ralph's Grocery Co., Compton, Calif. Office: Ralph's Grocery Co 1100 W Artesia Blvd Compton CA 90220 *

ALLWINE, LAWRENCE DAVID, management consultant; b. Shelby, Ohio, Oct. 19, 1941; s. Ralph James Allwine and Emily Spangler; m. Joan Ilene Lysinger, Jan. 4, 1964; children: Eric, Kevin, Lisa. BSCE, Ohio U., 1971. Quality control engr. Adams County Pub. Works, Commerce City, Colo., 1979-80; tech. coordinator Regional Transp. Dist., Denver, 1980-83; sr. cons. Hill Internat., Denver, 1983-86; region mgr. Kellogg Corp., Los Angeles, 1987-88; pres. L.D. Allwine & Assocs., Los Angeles, 1988—. Served with C.E. U.S. Army, 1967—, lt. col. res. Home: 25408 Via Escovar Valencia CA 91355

ALMEIDA, IRENE MARY, law court attendant; b. San Pedro, Calif., Aug. 20, 1929; d. Manuel Gonsalves and Mary Florence (Garcia) Horta; m. Arthur Anthony Almeida, Apr. 27, 1952; children: Arthur A.J., Irene Majella Maas, Lourette Marie Manghera. AA in Bus. Adminstrn., L.A. Harbor Coll., Wilmington, Calif., 1973; BSBA cum laude, Calif. State U., Dominguez Hills, 1977. Salesperson J.J. Newberry, San Pedro, Calif.; bookkeeper, credit mgr. Hartfield Stores, Inc., San Pedro, 1946-52; asst. bookkeeper Howard Hartry, Inc., Wilmington, 1971; real estate salesperson Landmark Realty Ctr., San Pedro, 1978-87; grand juror L.A. Grand Jury, 1979-80; ct. attendant Superior Ct., Santa Monica, Calif., 1980—. Editor, co-writer: (book) San Pedro, A Pictorial History, 1984; designer, co-author: The Vincent Thomas Bridge: San Pedro's Golden Gate, 1988; editor newspaper, Fore 'N 'Aft, 1946-47. Mem. San Pedro Bay Hist. Soc. (chmn. publs., organizer, sec., treas., bd. dir., tours), 1974—, Las Angelenas, Mayor's Hostess Group (Harbor chmn., sec.) San Pedro and L.A., 1975—, Conf. Calif. Hist. Soc., Sacramento, 1984—, regional v.p.; bd. dirs. Assoc. Hist. Soc. of L.A. (bd. dirs.), 1984—, Holy Trinity Confraternity of Christian Doctrine (Principal and chmn. of secondary and elem. tchrs. 1957-67); commr. and protocol hostess, L.A. Olympics, 1980-84; Harbor chmn., Pro-Life Council. Democratic. Clubs: Holy Trinity Youth (co-moderator, 1967-71), Five Ring, (L.A.; rec. sec. 1986—), 30 Yr. (San Pedro; bd. dirs. 1982—), Town and Country Cath. Women's (San Pedro; sec. and hostess), Holy Trinity Married Couples (San Pedro; pres., treas., hist. sec., 1952—).

ALMEN, LOIS SCHALL, executive director; b. Mpls., Jan. 2, 1931; d. Richard Cannon and Ilyvon (Langley) Schall; m. John S. Almen, Dec. 30, 1950 (dec. Feb, 1988); children: Sandra, Eric. BA, U. Mo., 1957; MA, Temple U., 1967. Speech services dir. Crystal Springs Rehab. Ctr., San Mateo, Calif., 1968-77; instr. Coll. San Mateo, 1968—; exec. dir. Human Investment Project, Inc., San Mateo, 1979—; cons. in field; co-convener Calif. Shared Homes Assn., 1988. Co-author: Homesharing: Successful Strategies, 1987. Chair Human Resources Commn., San Mateo, 1986-88; mem. Congl. Adv. Council, Calif., 1987—. Named Woman Distinction

Soroptimist Club, 1988; recognized for Outtanding Svc. State Senator Morgan, assembly woman Jackie Speier, 1988; Arts Coun. grantee State of Calif., 1980. Mem. Peninsula Press Club, AAUW, Hillbarn Theater, Am. Soc. on Aging, San Mateo C. of C. (bd. dirs. 1986—). Democrat. Office: Human Investment Project Inc 364 Railroad Ave San Mateo CA 94401

AL-NASSER, FAROUK ABDUL RAZZAK, engineering executive; b. Anna, Iraq, Nov. 22, 1939; came to U.S., 1962; s. Abdul Wahab and Kamila (Omran) Al-N.; m. Joan Therese Paradowski, May 25, 1968; 1 child, Omar Farouk. BS, Bagdad U., 1961; MS, U. Colo., 1968; PhD, U. Denver, 1975. Registered profl. engr., Calif. Engr., research scientist Ampex Corp., Red Wood City, Calif., 1964-68; prin. scientist Honeywell Inc., Denver, 1968-73; program mgr. Doric Scientific, San Diego, 1973-78; dir. engring. StorageTek, Louisville, Colo., 1978-85; corp. v.p. engring. Cipher Data, San Diego, 1985-87; v.p. engring. SyQuest Tech., Fremont, Calif., 1987—; lectr. San Diego State U., 1977. Contbr. articles to profl. jours. Mem. ADC, Washington, 1984—. Scholar Iraqi Govt., 1961. Mem. IEEE, Home Owner Assn. Democrat. Muslim. Home: 15940 Grey Stone Rd Poway CA 92064 Office: SyQuest Technology 47923 Warm Springs Blvd Fremont CA 94539

ALOFS, JOHN WILLIAM, II, optician, optical company executive; b. Gloversville, N.Y., June 13, 1955; s. John William I and Marguerite Mary (Pierce) A. AA, Erie Tech. Coll., 1979. Optician Bay Area Vision Ctrs., San Francisco, 1979, ops. mgr., 1979-82; dir. sales and tng. Western States Optical Co., Tempe, Ariz., 1982-85; dir. corp. devel. Avant Grade Optics, Port Washington, N.Y., 1985-86; founder, pres. Return on Investment Frame Co., Phoenix, 1986—; speaker, cons. in field. Author: Modern Sales Techniques for Ophthalmic Dispensers, 1986; contbg. editor Optical Mgmt. mag., 1985-86; contbr. articles to profl. publs. Mem. Am. Bd. Opticianry, Gainey Ranch Country Club (Scottsdale). Republican. Roman Catholic. Home: 10571 E Mission Ln Scottsdale AZ 85258 Office: Return on Investment Frame Co 3702 E Roeser Rd Ste 16 Phoenix AZ 85040

ALOIA, ROLAND CRAIG, research scientist; b. Newark, Dec. 21, 1943; s. Roland S. and Edna M. (Mahan) A.; m. Kathyrn A. Platt, June 15, 1974. BS, St. Mary's Coll., 1965; PhD, U. Calif., Riverside, 1970. Postdoctoral fellow City of Hope, Duarte, Calif., 1971-75; research biologist U. Calif., Riverside, 1975-76; asst. prof. biology Loma Linda (Calif.) U., 1976-79, assoc. prof., 1979-89, prof., 1989—; chemist Vets. Hosp., Loma Linda, 1979—. Editor: Membrane Fluidity in Biology vols. 1-4, 1983, 85; sr. editor: (series) Advances in Membrane Fluidity vols. 1-5. Pres. Riverside chpt. Calif. Heart Assn., 1979-80, 1984-86, bd. dirs., exec. com. mem., 1973-86. Calif. Heart Assn. fellow, 1971-73. Mem. Am. Chem. Soc., N.Y. Acad. Scis., Soc. Cell Biology, Sigma Xi. Address: Jerry Pettis Vets Hosp Anesthesiology Svc Loma Linda CA 92357 Office: Loma Linda U Med Ctr Dept Anesthesiology Loma Linda CA 92354

ALOOT, MARIANO DANIEL, training service company executive; b. Covina, Calif., Dec. 2, 1947; s. Mariano DeVera and Louise Ruby (Rundle) A.; m. Laura Ellen Hulsey, Dec. 14, 1968; children: John Daniel, Michael David. BA, San Jose State U., 1969. Asst. exec. dir. Mental Health Assn., Santa Clara, Calif., 1968-71; project dir. Op. Share, San Jose, Calif., 1971-73; asst. to v.p. Calif. State U., Hayward, 1973-80; exec. dir. Merit Shop Tng. Ctr., Dublin, Calif., 1980-82; v.p. bus. devel. San Jose Devel. Corp., 1985-87; prin. Mariano Group, San Jose, 1982—; pres., chief exec. officer Profl. Tng. Ctr., Inc., San Jose, 1987—; bus. cons. Bittinger Industries, Concord, Calif., 1982-83; devel. cons. Ctr. for Employment Tng., San Jose, 1983-84, Ctr. for Employment and Econ. Devel., San Jose, 1984-85; bus. cons. Ctr. Tng. and Careers, San Jose, 1985—. Mem. Calif. Assn. Rehab. Profls., Filipino-Am. C. of C., Vietnamese C. of C., San Jose C. of C. Republican. Lutheran. Office: Profl Tng Ctr Inc 1543 Parkmoor Ave San Jose CA 95128

ALPERS, ROBERT CHRISTOPHER, engineer; b. Lansing, Mich., Mar. 14, 1949; s. Robert Joseph and Elizabeth (Carroll) A.; m. Barbara Colleen Porter, June 9, 1973; children: Rhiannon, Julia, Nicholas. BS in Engring., Ohio State U., 1972. Registered profl. engr., Colo. Sales engr. Nelson Div. TRW, Columbus, Ohio, 1973-74; sr. sales engr. MCC Powers Regulator, Denver, 1974-79; project adminstr. RMH Group Cons., Lakewood, Colo., 2979-83; gen. mgr. Staefa Control Systems Inc., Denver, 1983—; instr. Tech Sch., Denver Pub. Sch., Emily Griffith, Denver, 1976-79; guest speaker Climitization, Madrid, 1989. Pres. St. Vincent DePaul Parish Council, Denver, 1984-86. Capt. USAR, 1972-80. Mem. ASHRAE. Republican. Roman Catholic. Home: 1134 S Williams St Denver CO 80210 Office: Staefa Control System Inc 2770 W 5th Ave Denver CO 80204

ALPERT, SHIRLEY MARCIA, librarian; b. Pitts., Aug. 6, 1936; d. Arthur and Lillian (Goldberg) Forman; m. Norman Joseph Alpert, Dec. 25, 1956; children: Gary H., Andrea P. BA, Ariz. State U., 1958; MA, San Diego State U., 1980. Cert. elem. tchr., library media specialist, learning resources specialist. Librarian San Diego Unified Sch. Dist., 1973-84; learning resources specialist Northside Ind. Sch. Dist., San Antonio, Tex., 1985-87; librarian Hayward (Calif.) Unified Sch. Dist., 1988—. Mem. AAUW, Nat. Council Jewish Women, Women's Am. ORT, Tex. Library Assn., Calif. Media Library Edn. Assn. Republican. Lodge: Order Eastern Star. Home: 69 Jamaica Dr San Ramon CA 94583

ALSAKER, ROBERT JOHN, information systems specialist; b. Los Angeles, June 15, 1945; s. Lauris Ronald and Hazel Mildred (Danz) A.; m. Cynthia Ann Gillesvog, Feb. 25, 1984; children: Troy R., Erik G. AA, Fullerton (Calif.) Jr. Coll., 1966; BS, Moorhead (Minn.) State Coll., 1970. Project mgr. Jet Propulsion Lab., Pasadena, Calif., 1970-80; mgr. mgmt. info. systems Kroy Inc., Scottsdale, Ariz., 1980-85; adminstr. City of Pasadena, 1985-86; mgr. tech. cons. U.S. West Info. Systems, Phoenix, 1986-88; v.p., mgmt. info. systems ACB Cos. Inc., Phoenix, 1988—; bd. dirs. ACB Cos. Inc., Phoenix, 1988—. Served in U.S. Army, 1968-69, Vietnam. Republican. Lutheran. Office: 714 E Van Buren Phoenix AZ 85006

ALSCHULER, GEORGE ARTHUR, lawyer; b. Aurora, Ill., Apr. 17, 1935; s. Jacob Edward and Carolyn Amelia (Strauss) A.; m. Mary Ann Yuen, July 1, 1983; 1 child, Erik Benjamin. AA, Menlo Coll., 1955; BA in Polit. Sci., Stanford U., 1957, JD, 1961. Bar: Calif. 1967; cert. level I police res. officer, Calif. Assoc. Hardin Fletcher Cook & Hayes, Oakland, Calif., 1968, Schofield & Cunningham, Oakland, 1968-70; ptnr. Vendt, Johnson & Alschuler, Berkeley, Calif., 1970-72; pvt. practice Oakland, 1972-77; ptnr. Curran & Alschuler P.C., Oakland, 1977—; pro tem judge Berkeley Mcpl. Ct., Oakland Mcpl. Ct.; arbitrator Alameda County Superior Ct., Am. Arbitration Assn.; sec., trustee Legal Aide Soc. Alameda County, Oakland, 1983-88. Res. police officer Berkeley Police Dept., 1975—; sec., trustee East Bay Zool. Soc., Oakland, 1984—. Mem. Calif. State Bar, Alameda County Bar Assn., Acad. Model Aeros. Democrat. Jewish. Office: 166 Santa Clara Ave Oakland CA 94610

ALSPACH, PHILIP HALLIDAY, manufacturing company executive; b. Buffalo, Apr. 19, 1923; s. Walter L. and Jean E. (Halliday) A.; m. Jean Edwards, Dec. 20, 1947; children—Philip Clough, Bruce Edwards, David Christopher; m. Loretta M. Hildebrand, Aug. 1982. B.Engring. in Mech. Engring, Tulane U., 1944. Registered profl. engr., Mass., Wis., La. With Gen. Electric Co., 1945-64, mgr. indsl. electronics div. planning, 1961-64; v.p., gen. mgr. constrn. machinery div. Allis Chalmers Mfg. Co., Milw., 1964-68; exec. v.p., dir., mem. exec. com. Jeffrey Galion, Inc., 1968-69; v.p. I.T.E. Imperial Corp., Springhouse, Pa., 1969-75; pres. E.W. Bliss div. Gulf & Western Mfg. Co., Southfield, Mich., 1975-79; group v.p. Katy Industries, Inc., Elgin, Ill., 1979-85; pres. Intercon Inc., Irvine, Calif., 1985—; bd. dirs. Winnebago Industries, Inc., Coen Co., Inc., A.J. Gerrard & Co., Advanced Computer Communications, Jandy Industries, Inc., Data-Design Labs., Pansini Corp. Author papers in field. Mem. pres.'s council Tulane U. Mem. Soc. Automotive Engrs. (sr.), IEEE, Soc. Mfg. Engrs., Nat. Assn. Corp. Dirs., Inst. Dirs. (U.K.), Am. Mgmt. Assn. Clubs: Canadian (N.Y.C.), Met. (N.Y.C.). Home: 23 Alejo Irvine CA 92715 Office: Intercon Inc 2500 Michelson Dr Ste 410 Irvine CA 92715

ALSTON, LELA, state senator; b. Phoenix, June 26, 1942; d. Virgil Lee and Frances Mae Koonse Mulkey; B.S., U. Ariz., 1967; M.S., Ariz. State U., 1971; children—Brenda Susan, Charles William. Tchr. high sch., 1968—; mem. Ariz. State Senate, 1977—. Named Disting. Citizen, U. Ariz. Alumni Assn., 1978. Mem. NEA, Ariz. Edn. Assn., Am. Home Econs. Assn., Ariz. Home Econs. Assn., Am. Vocat. Assn. Methodist. Office: State Senate State Capitol Phoenix AZ 85007

ALTAMURA, MICHAEL VICTOR, physician; b. Bklyn., Sept. 28, 1923; s. Frank and Theresa (Inganamorte) A.; BS, L.I. U., 1949; MA, Columbia U., 1951; DO, Kirksville Coll., 1961; MD, Calif. Coll. Medicine, 1962; m. Emily Catherine Wandell, Sept. 21, 1948; children: Michael Victor, Robert Frank. Intern, Los Angeles County Gen. Hosp., 1961-62; practice medicine specializing in family practice, Sunnyvale, Calif., 1962—; staff El Camino Hosp., chief family practice dept., 1972-73; preceptor family practice Stanford Sch. Medicine, 1972-73, clin. asst. prof., 1974-81, clin. assoc. prof., 1982—; assoc. prof. family medicine Calif. Coll. Osteopathic Medicine, 1985—; preceptor family practice Davis (Calif.) Sch. Medicine, 1974-75. Served to 1st lt. AUS, 1942-45, 51-53; ETO. Recipient Order of Golden Sword, Am. Cancer Soc., 1973. Diplomate Am. Bd. Family Practice. Fellow Am. Acad. Family Physicians (pres. Santa Clara County chpt. 1972-73, bd. dirs.), Royal Soc. Health, Am. Geriatric Soc.; mem. AMA, Calif., Santa Clara County socs., Internat. Platform Assn. Republican. Lutheran. Author: (with Mary Falconer and Helen Behnke) Aging Patients: A Guide for Their Care. Office: 500 E Remington St Sunnyvale CA 94087

ALTER, EDWARD T., state treasurer; b. Glen Ridge, N.J., July 26, 1941; s. E. Irving and Norma (Fisher) A.; m. Patricia R. Olsen, 1975; children: Christina Lyn, Ashly Ann, Darci Lee. B.A., U. Utah., 1966; M.B.A., U. Utah, 1967. C.P.A., Calif., Utah. Sr. acct. Touche Ross & Co., Los Angeles, 1967-72; asst. treas. U. Utah, Salt Lake City, 1972-80; treas. State of Utah, Salt Lake City, 1981—; pres. Nat. Assn. State Treas., 1987-88. Bd. dirs. Utah Housing Fin. Agy.; bd. dirs. Utah State Retirement Bd.; mem. Utah State Republican Central Com., from 1981. Served to sgt. USAR, 1958-66. Mem. Am. Inst. CPAs, Nat. Assn. State Treas. (past sr. v.p., pres. 1987), Delta Sigma Pi, Delta Phi Kappa. Club: Utah Bond (pres. 1981-82). Office: State Capitol Rm 215 Salt Lake City UT 84114

ALTER, GERALD L., real estate executive; b. Rensselaer, Ind., Aug. 24, 1910; s. Leslie and Lettie (Willis) A.; m. Margaret A. Davis, Sept. 15, 1939; children: Judith Ann (dec.), John Edward. Student Bus. Coll., 1927-28. Clk. and office mgr., 1929-35; bldg. contractor, 1936-45; real estate broker and ins. agt., 1946—; pres. Alter Realty & Ins., Leads, Inc., investments, Alter Ins. Agy., Inc., REMCO Real Estate Mgmt. Co., Alter Devel. Co.; pres. Developers & Builders. Planning commr. City of Torrance, 1966-83, chmn. Torrance Planning Commn. 1982-83; water commr. City of Torrance, 1984—, chmn. 1987-88; former bd. dirs. Harbor Area United Way. Mem. Torrance-Lomita-Carson Bd. Realtors (pres. 1978, v.p. 1980-81), Calif. Assn. Realtors (dir. 1978-81), Nat. Assn. Realtors, Torrance C. of C. (past dir.), Am. Legion. Republican. Clubs: OX-5 (pioneer airman). Lodge: Rotary. Home: 1337 Engracia Ave Torrance CA 90501 Office: 2305 Torrance Blvd Torrance CA 90501

ALTERMAN, CLIFFORD BRUCE, lawyer; b. N.Y.C., Apr. 12, 1925; s. David Philip and Selma (Solomon) A.; m. Charlotte Horner, Apr. 11, 1958; children: Dean, Penelope, Amy, Julie. AB, Harvard U., 1947; LLB, Yale U., 1950. Bar: N.Y. 1950, Oreg. 1954. Ptnr. Kell, Alterman & Runstein, Portland, 1955—. With U.S. Army, 1943-46, ETO. Mem. ABA, Oreg. Bar Assn., Multnomah County Bar Assn., Maritime Law Assn. (vice chmn. subcom. on pilotage), Japan-Am. Soc. Oreg. (pres. 1985-87), chmn. bd. dirs. 1987—), Assoc. Japan-Am. Socs. U.S. (nat. exec. com. 1985-87), Japanese Garden Soc. Oreg. (bd. dirs. 1985—). Office: Kell Alterman & Runstein 707 SW Washington #1300 Portland OR 97205

ALTERMAN, DEAN N., real estate agent; b. Portland, Oreg., Mar. 15, 1960; s. Clifford B. and Charlotte E. (Horner) A. AB, Harvard U., 1981; JD, Lewis & Clark Coll., 1989. Assoc. Craig Cooley & Co., Portland, 1981-89; with Stan Wiley, Inc., Portland, 1989—; cons. in field, Portland, 1981—; corp. sec. Pinnell Engring., Inc., Portland, 1988—. Author: Friend Family of West Virginia, 1985; mng. editor Environ. Law, 1987-88. Mem. Multnomah County Planning Commn., Portland, 1983—, chmn., 1984-86; bd. dirs. Portland Opportunities Industrialization Ctr., Portland, 1986—; annual fund chmn. Catlin Gabel Sch., Portland, 1987—; pres., trustee Friend Family Assn. Am. Inc., 1988—. Mem. Nat. Assn. Realtors, Catlin Gabel Alumni Ass. (pres. 1989—), Harvard U. Club Oreg. (treas. 1984—, v.p. 1986—). Democrat. Home: 5614 SW Westdale Dr Portland OR 97221 Office: Stan Wiley Inc 9900 SW Greenburg Rd Ste 220 Portland OR 97223

ALTHERR, LAWANDA, educational consultant, realtor; b. Ajo, Ariz., Jan. 27, 1926; d. Jesse Hoyt and Mayme Ellen (Amerson) Smith; m. Robert Kenneth Altherr, Aug. 5, 1946 (div.); children—Gary, Larry, Gregory, Brenda, Bryan, Robert. Assoc. in Nursing, Phoenix Coll., 1970; B.S. in Nursing, Ariz. State U., 1975; M.A. in Vocat. Edn., U. No. Ariz., 1978. Staff nurse surg. intensive care unit Maricopa County Gen. Hosp./Maricopa Med. Center 1970-72, inservice instr. 1973-75, dir. tng. and devel. 1975-83, dir. bio-med. communication dept. 1980-83, ret., 1983; ednl. cons., asst. project dir. U. Ariz., 1983-86; part time realtor Broad Investment Co., 1983—. Mem. Ariz. Vocat. Assn., Ariz. Assn. Realtors, Phoenix Bd. Realtors. Home: 1307 W Thomas St Phoenix AZ 85013 Office: 812 N 3d St Phoenix AZ 85004

ALTMAN, ADELE ROSENHAIN, radiologist; b. Tel Aviv, Israel, June 4, 1924; came to U.S., 1933, naturalized, 1939; d. Bruno and Salla (Silberzweig) Rosenhain; m. Emmett Altman, Sept. 3, 1944; children: Brian R., Alan L., Karen D. Diplomate Am. Bd. Radiology. Intern Queens Gen. Hosp., N.Y.C., 1949-51; resident Hosp. for Joint Diseases, N.Y.C., 1951-52, Roosevelt Hosp., N.Y.C., 1955-57; clin. instr. radiology Downstate Med. Ctr., SUNY, Bklyn., 1957-61; asst. prof. radiology N.Y. Med. Coll., N.Y.C., 1961-65, assoc. prof., 1965-68; assoc. prof. radiology U. Okla. Health Sci. Ctr., Oklahoma City, 1968-78; assoc. prof. dept. radiology U. N.Mex. Sch. Medicine, Albuquerque, 1978-85. Author: Radiology of the Respiratory System: A Basic Review, 1978; contbr. articles to profl. jours. Fellow Am. Coll. Angiology, N.Y. Acad. Medicine; mem. Am. Coll. Radiology, Am. Roentgen Ray Soc., Assn. Univ. Radiologists, Radiol. Soc. N.Am. Clubs: Hadassah, B'nai B'rith Women.

ALTMAN, BARRY, manufacturing executive; b. N.Y.C., Oct. 7, 1945; s. Herman Bernard and Dorothy (Freilich) A.; m. Rita Diane Eisgrau, Dec. 16, 1967; children: Elisa, Heidi. BS in Engring., U. Conn., 1967; postgrad., U. Bridgeport, 1970-72. With Gen. Elec. Co., various locations, 1967-72, Dresser Ind., various locations, 1972-84; v.p., gen. mgr. Fairchild Ind., Temple City, Calif., 1984-87; pres. Pacific Fabrication, Inc., Rancho Cucamonga, Calif., 1987—. Dir. La Habre Community Theater, 1987—. Mem. Am. Prodn. and Inventory Control Soc., Soc. Mfg. Engrs. Jewish. Office: Pacific Fabrication PO Box 1179 Rancho Cucamonga CA 91730

ALTMAN, SHELDON, veterinarian; b. Denver, May 15, 1937; s. Sam Bernard and Bessie (Radetsky) A.; B.S. in Biol. Sci., Colo. State U., 1959, D.V.M., 1961; m. Arlene Barbara Heller, Aug. 23, 1959; children—Susan Wendy, Howard William, Eden Debra. With Newmark Animal Hosp., 1961-62, Lockhart Animal Hosp., 1964; founder, operator Universal City Pet Clinic, North Hollywood, Calif, 1965-70, merged with M.S. Animal Hosps., Inc., Burbank, 1970—, v.p., 1970—; dir. vet. research and cons. acupuncture research project, pain control unit UCLA, 1975-80; hon. prof. Chinese Medicine U. Oriental Studies, Sch. Chinese Medicine, Los Angeles; mem. faculty Internat. Vet. Acupuncture Soc. Ctr. for Chinese Medicine. Author: An Introduction to Acupuncture for Animals; mem. editorial adv. bd. Calif. Veterinarian, Internat. Jour. Chinese Medicine; contbr. articles on vet. acupuncture to vet. jours. Bd. dirs. Emek Hebrew Acad. Served with AUS, 1962-64. Mem. AVMA (conv. speaker 1982), So. Calif., Calif. (co-chmn. com. on alternative therapies) vet. med. assns., Am. Animal Hosp. Assn., Am. Veterinarians for Israel (chpt. pres. 1972-73), Assn. Orthodox Jewish Scientists, Internat. Vet. Acupuncture Soc. (dir.), Center for Chinese Medicine, Internat. Congress Chinese Medicine, Acupuncture Research Inst., Colo. State U. Alumni Assn., Nat. Assn. Vet. Acupuncture (dir. research), Phi Kappa Phi, Phi Zeta, Beta Beta Beta. Jewish (pres. congregation 70-71, dir. 1964—). Home: 5647 Wilkinson Ave North Hollywood CA 91607 Office: 2723 W Olive St Burbank CA 91505

ALTON, DIRK RICHARD, public relations consultant; b. Little Silver, N.J., July 7, 1962; s. Gary Howard and Renate (Phillip) A. BA in Communications, San Francisco State U., 1986. Pub. relations dir. U.S. Water Polo Inc., Boulder, Colo., 1985; publicist Euthanasia Music, San Francisco, 1985-86; acct. exec. No. Calif. Communications Inc., San Francisco, 1986; gen. mgr., head adminstr. Bartenders Unlimited, San Rafael, Calif., 1986—. Mem. Marin Water Polo. Office: Bartenders Unlimited 1560 4th St San Rafael CA 94901

ALTOUNIAN, DAVID ALLEN, software company executive; b. Alexandria, La., May 22, 1961; s. Arthur Stephen and Donna Joyce (Cole) A.; m. Vicki Rae Reppert, Sept. 28, 1986; 1 child, Jessica Rae. Student, Calif. Coast U.; cert. in program tng., C.C.T. Quartermaster USCG, San Francisco, 1979-81; pvt. practice cons. L.A., 1981-83; mgmt. consultant Ernst & Whinney, L.A., 1983-87; test engr. Ashton-Tate, L.A., 1987, product analyst, 1987-88, bus. devel. mgr., 1988—. Author: Financial Information Systems, 1987, PC Users Guide to the Macintosh, 1988. Mem. Assn. for Software Test and Evaluation, Internat. Soc. Elec. Engrs. (assoc.), L.A. Athletic Club. Home: 5376 Fairview Blvd Los Angeles CA 90056 Office: Ashton-Tate 20101 Hamilton Ave Torrance CA 90502-1319

ALVARADO, MARILYN DEL MAR, paralegal; b. Los Angeles, Dec. 5, 1960; d. Eliud Eric Del Mar; m. Vicente Rolando Alvarado, Jr., Nov. 1, 1984. ABA paralegal cert. in litigation U. West Los Angeles Sch. Paralegal Studies, 1983; student Calif. State U., Los Angeles, 1978-80; BA in Psychology, Calif. State U., Northridge, 1982. Litigation paralegal Overton, Lyman & Prince, Los Angeles, 1982; litigation and bankruptcy paralegal Loeb & Loeb, Los Angeles, 1983-85; creditors' rights litigation paralegal Graham & James, Los Angeles, 1985—; cosmetic rep. Avon Products, Inc., Los Angeles, 1985-86. Intern Los Angeles Mayor's Office, 1980-81. Recipient cert. appreciation Los Angeles Mayor's Office, 1981; Calif. Scholarship Bd. grantee Calif. State U.-Los Angeles, then Calif. State U.-Northridge, 1978-82. Mem. Los Angeles Paralegal Assn., Nat. Paralegal Assn., Am. Film Inst. Republican. Baptist. Avocations: photography; music; horses; art. Home: 10757 Lemon Ave Alta Loma CA 91701 Office: Graham & James Citicorp Pla 725 S Figueroa St 34th Fl Los Angeles CA 90017

ALVERNAZ, RODRIGO, insurance company executive; b. Faial, Azores, Dec. 28, 1936; came to U.S., 1954; ; s. Frank P. and Ana (Leal) A.; m. Jean Bettencourt, May 31, 1958; children: Roderick, Mario, Anina, Gina. Gen. edn., Liceu Passos Manuel, Lisbon, Portugal, 1954; BBA in Acctg., Heald Coll., 1958; cert. bus. mgmt., Calif. State U., Hayward, 1980. Acct. United Nat. Life Ins. Soc., Oakland, Calif., 1958-62, asst. sec., agy. supr., 1962-64, asst. sec., treas., 1964-81, asst. v.p., 1970-81, sec., treas., 1981-83, sec. Luso-Am. Fraternal Fedn., 1981-88, v.p., sec., 1983-88; exec. v.p., chief exec. officer, Luso-Am. Fraternal Fedn. United Nat. Life Ins. Soc., Oakland, 1988—; v.p. Luso-Am. Edn. Found., 1979—. Pres. League Portugese Fraternal Socs. of Calif., 1986; co-chmn. Portugese-Ams. for Statue of Liberty, 1985-86. Recipient Commendation Order of Merit, Portugal, 1987. Mem. No. Calif. Life Ins. Assn., No. Calif. Policyowners' Svc. Assn. Republican. Roman Catholic. Lodge: Lions (local pres. 1980-81, local treas. 1981-86).

ALVERSON, JOY FERGUSON, nurse; b. Long Beach, Calif., Apr. 28, 1954; d. Ferdie Lawrence and Joyce (Berggren) Ferguson; m. Franklin Gray Alverson II, June 1, 1974; children: Nicholas, Clint. BS, Calif. State U., Long Beach, 1977. RN, Nev., Calif. Staff nurse Los Altos Hosp., Long Beach, 1977-78, Washoe Med. Ctr., Reno, 1979—; nurse Washoe County Sch. Dist., Sparks, Nev., 1988; instr. prenatal Washoe Med. Ctr., 1985—. Instr. CPR, ARC, Reno, 1982; helper Jr. Ski Program Reno Recreation Dept., 1988. Mem. Beta Sigma Phi (sec. 1987-88), Alpha Tau (various positions 1982-85). Mem. Diciples of Christ.

AMADO, PATRICIA ANN, management and marketing professional; b. Tucson, Nov. 10, 1960; d. Hector Gustelum Jr. and Betty Louise (Stull) A. BFA, U. Ariz., 1982, postgrad., 1988—. Asst. mgr. US. Shoe Corp., Houston, 1982-83; asst. mgr. to mgr. Matthews, Inc. Accessory Lady, Houston, 1983-84; mgr. to regional mgr. Decor Corp., Houston, 1984-87; dir. mktg. lab. Tucson Med. Ctr. Health Enterprises, 1988; freelance tech. writer Tucson, 1987—. State del. Ariz. Dem. Conv., 1980; docent Reid Park Zoo, 1988. Mem. Sierra Club, Gamma Phi Beta (corp. bd.). Democrat. Roman Catholic. Club: Smithsonian (Washington). Home: 5530 Placita de la Promesa Tucson AZ 85745

AMATO, CAROL JOY, anthropologist, technical publications consulting company executive, writer; b. Portland, Oreg., Apr. 9, 1944; d. Sam Lawrence and Lena Dorothy (Dindia) A.; m. Neville Stanley Motts, Aug. 26, 1967 (div. 1978); children: Tracy, Damon. BA, U. Portland, 1966; MA, Calif. State U., 1986. Freelance writer, Westminster, Calif., 1969—; human factor cons. Design Sci. Corp., Los Angeles, 1979—; dir. software documentation Trans-Ed Communications, Westminster, 1980-84, pres. Advanced Profl. Software, Inc., Westminster, 1984-86, Systems Rsch. Analysis, Inc., Westminster, 1986—. Editor, Cultural Futuristics, 1975-80; author numerous articles and short stories, 1973—; participant in numerous radio and TV interviews. Sec. bd. dirs. Am. Space Meml. Found., L.A., 1986—; bd. dirs. Coalition Concerned for Adolescent Pregnancy, Santa Ana, Calif., 1986—; bd. dirs. Orange County Acad. Decathalon. Mem. Am. Anthrop. Assn., Orange County C. of C., Anthropology Assn., Ind. Writers of So. Calif., Human Factor Soc., Writers' Club of Whittier, Inc. Home: 10151 Heather Ct Westminster CA 92683

AMATORI, MICHAEL LOUIS, radio production manager, consultant, performer; b. San Francisco, Jan. 26, 1951; s. Fred and Ana Dolores (Espitia) A. BA, San Francisco State U., 1974. Cert. Community Coll. instr., Calif. Announcer Sta. KCSM-FM, KCSM-TV, San Mateo (Calif.), 1969-71, Sta. KFOG-FM Kaiser Broadcasting Co., San Francisco, 1972, Sta. KRON-FM Chronicle Broadcasting Co., San Francisco, 1972; engr., producer Sta. KSFO Golden West Broadcasters, San Francisco, 1973-83; sports producer, prodn. dir. for prodn. mgr. Sta. KSFO/KYA King Broadcasting Co., San Francisco, 1983—; instr. in broadcasting Coll. of San Mateo (Calif.), 1980-83; program cons. Coll. San Mateo, 1975, prodn. cons. Salem Communications, San Francisco, 1987; network comml. announcer Oakland Athletics Baseball, Calif., 1988; owner, founder Creative Matrix Prodns., San Mateo, 1988. Cons. Childrens Fund for Adoption of Black Children, San Francisco, 1987. Recipient Paul Romagna award Coll. of San Mateo, 1971, Best Radio Entry award Nat. Assn. Consumer Adminstrs., 1988. Democrat. Roman Catholic. Office: KSFO/KYA Radio 300 Broadway San Francisco CA 94133

AMBER, RICH, electronics company official, freelance writer; b. McMinnville, Oreg., Feb. 23, 1949; s. Delmer Frank Isakson and Elizabeth Ann (Lambert) Madding; m. Valerie Ann Martin, Mar. 29, 1971 (div. Dec. 1979); 1 child, Samantha Jane; m. Terresa Lee Tuttle, May 23, 1986; 1 stepchild, John Paul Anthony Chadwick. Student, Wash. State U., Portland (Oreg.) State U., La Salle U., Chgo., USAF Sch. Applied aerospace sci. sr. design draftsman, jr. engr. SEMCO Control Systems, Tigard, Oreg., 1974-76; numerical controlled driller, profiler operator PCB mech. and cen. mfg. Tektronix, Inc., Beaverton, Oreg., 1976-77, schematic draftsman III, tech. illustrator manuals dept. frequency domain instrumentation div., 1977-78; product support specialist II CAD-CAM devel. dept. Computer Sci. Ctr., Aloha, Oreg., 1978-80; tech. writer III, editor tech. communications Computer Sci. Ctr., Beaverton, 1980-83; tech. publs. mgr. communications network analyzers div. Redmond, Oreg., 1983-85; engring. svcs. mgr. Computer Sci. Ctr., Redmond, Oreg., 1985--; instr. Tektronix Edn. and Tng. Ctr., Portland Community Coll., Beaverton. Author: Dirt Bike Visions; contbr. articles to trade publs., newspapers and mags., also poetry, cartoons. Loaned exec. campaign United Way, 1986-87; res. police officer. Served with USAF, 1967-73. Mem. Nat. Assn. Desktop Publs., Cen. Oreg. Macintosh Users Group, Am. Mgmt. Assn., Eagles, Elks, Cen. Oreg. Shooting Sports Assn. (sec.). Republican. Home: 813 NW Ogden Ave Bend OR 98770

AMER, KENNETH BENJAMIN, helicopter engineer; b. Bklyn., Mar. 23, 1924; s. Harry and Rose (Wolkow) Am; m. Hedie Ankle, Dec. 25, 1946; children: Harold, Les. B Aero. Engring., NYU, 1944; MS in Aero. Engring., MIT, 1947. Rsch. engr. NACA, Langley Field, Va., 1947-53; rsch. engr. Hughes Helicopters, L.A., 1953-60, mgr. tech. dept., 1960-85; chief scientist

McDonnell Douglas Helicopter Co., L.A., 1985-86; helicopter cons. Rand Corp, Santa Monica, Calif., 1987—. Contbr. articles on helicopters to profl. jours.; patentee helicopter field. McDonnell Douglas Corp. engring. and rsch. fellow, 1986. Fellow Am. Helicopter Soc. (hon., Alexander Klemin award 1976). Home: 8025 Alverstone Ave Los Angeles CA 90045

AMERINE, ANNE FOLLETTE, aerospace engineer; b. San Francisco, Sept. 27, 1950; d. William T. and Wilma (Carlson) F.; m. Jorge Armando Verdi D'Eguia, July 4, 1970 (div.); m. Donald Amerine, Dec. 18, 1983. AA, Coll. Marin, 1977; BA in Math. with honors, Mills Coll., 1979. Sr. computer operator Bank of Am. Internat. Services, San Francisco, 1972-74; mathematician Pacific Missile Test Ctr., Pt. Mugu, Calif., 1979-80; engr. Grumman Aerospace Corp., Pt. Mugu, 1979-83; engr. Litton Guidance and Control Systems, 1984-86, product support and assurance dept. project mgr., 1986—. Chmn. Marina West Neighborhood Council, 1982-84; mem. NOW; chmn. subcom. Ventura County Community Coll. Dist. Citizen's Adv. Com. on Status of Women, 1983-84. Aurelia Henry Reinhart scholar, 1978-79; recipient Project Sterling award Grumman Aerospace Corp., 1982. Mem. Nat. Assn. Female Execs., Soc. Women Engrs. (chmn. career guidance com. and speaker Ventura County sect.), Litton Women's Enhancement Orgn. (founder, v.p. and chmn. info. and edn. com. 1985-86, editor newsletter 1986-87), Assn. Old Crows, Mills Coll. Alumni, Alpha Gamma Sigma (life). Office: Litton Guidance & Control Systems 5500 Canoga Ave MS 80 Woodland Hills CA 91367-6698

AMERINE, MAYNARD ANDREW, enologist, educator; b. San Jose, Calif., Oct. 30, 1911; s. Roy Reagan and Tennie (Davis) A. B.S., U. Calif.-Berkeley, 1932, Ph.D. in Plant Physiology, 1936. Mem. faculty U. Calif., Davis, 1935—, prof. enology, enologist Exptl. Sta., 1952-74, emeritus Exptl. Sta., 1974—, chmn. dept. viticulture and enology, 1957-62; cons. Wine Inst., 1974-85. Author: (with M. A. Joslyn) Table Wines: The Technology of Their Production in California, 1951, 2d edit., 1970, (with Louise Wheeler) A Check-List of Books and Pamphlets on Grapes and Wines and Related Subjects, 1951, A Short Check-List of Books and Pamphlets in English on Grapes, Wine and Related Subjects, 1949-1959, 1959, (with others) The Technology of Wine Making, 4th edit., 1980, (with G. L. Marsh) Wine Making at Home, 1962, (with M.A. Joslyn) Dessert, Appetizer and Related Flavored Wines: The Technology of Their Production, 1964, (with V.L. Singleton) Wine: An Introduction for Americans, 1965, 2d edit., 1977, (with Rose M. Pangborn and E. B. Roessler) Principles of Sensory Evaluation of Food, 1965, A Check List of Books on Grapes and Wines, 1960-68, (with supplement for), 1949-59, 1969, (with G.F. Stewart) Introduction to Food Science and Technology, 1973, 2d edit., 1982, (with C.S. Ough) Wine and Must Analyses, 1974, 80, 2d edit., 1988, (with E.B. Roessler) Wines: Their Sensory Evaluation, 1976, 2d edit., 1983; (with H. Phaff) Bibliography of Publications, 1876-1980, on Grapes, Wines, and Related Subjects, 1986; editor and contbr.: Wine Production Technology in the U.S, 1981; co-editor and contbr. (with D. Muscatine and B. Thompson) The University of California/Sotheby Book of California Wine, 1984. Served to maj. AUS, 1942-46. Decorated chevalier de Merite Agricole (France), 1947, officier Ordre National du Merite (France), 1976; recipient diplôme d'honneur Office Internat. du Vin, 1952, 65, 84, 2d prize Oberly award A.L.A., 1953, Merit award Am. Soc. Enologists, 1967, Am. Wine Soc., 1976, Man of Year award Les Amis du Vin, 1976, The Wine Spectator, 1985, Adams award Wine industry Tech. Seminar, 1989; Guggenheim fellow, 1954-55. Mem. Am. Soc. Enologists (pres. 1958-59), AAAS, Am. Chem. Soc., Inst. Food Technologists. Republican. Baptist. Club: Bohemian (San Francisco). Home: PO Box 208 Saint Helena CA 94574

AMERMAN, JOHN W., toy company executive; b. 1932; married. BA, Dartmouth Coll., 1953, MBA, 1954. With Colgate-Palmolive Co., 1958-64, Warner-Lambert Co., 1965-80; v.p. Du Barry Cosmetics, 1971-72, v.p. internat. group, 1972-77, v.p. Am. Chicle div., 1977-79, pres. Am. Chicle div., 1979-80; pres. Mattel Internat., from 1980, exec. v.p. worldwide ops., from 1985; exec. v.p. Mattel Inc., Hawthorne, Calif., until 1987, chmn., chief exec. officer, 1987—, also bd. dirs. Served with U.S. Army, 1954-57. Office: Mattel Inc 5150 Rosecrans Ave Hawthorne CA 90250

AMES, A. GARY, communications company executive; b. 1944. BA, Portland State U., 1967. Acct. supr. Pacific N.W. Bell, 1967-72, with, 1974-83, treas., 1981; dist. mgr. fin. AT&T, N.Y., 1972-74; v.p., treas. U.S. West, Englewood, Colo., from 1983, group v.p., from 1984; chief operating officer, exec. v.p. Mountain State Tel. & Tel. Co., 1986-87; pres. Mountain Bell, Denver, 1987—, also bd. dirs. Office: Mountain Bell 1801 California St Denver CO 80202 *

AMES, BRUCE N(ATHAN), biochemist, geneticist; b. N.Y.C., Dec. 16, 1928; s. Maurice U. and Dorothy (Andres) A.; m. Giovanna Ferro-Luzzi, Aug. 26, 1960; children: Sofia, Matteo. BA, Cornell U., 1950; PhD, Calif. Inst. Tech., 1953. Chief sect. microbial genetics NIH, Bethesda, Md., 1953-68; prof. biochemistry U. Calif., Berkeley, 1968—, chmn. biochemistry dept., 1983—; adv. bd. Nat. Cancer Inst., 1976-82. Research, publs. on bacterial molecular biology, histidine biosynthesis and its control, RNA and regulation, mutagenesis, detection of environ. mutagens and carcinogens, genetic toxicology, oxygen radicals and disease. Recipient Flemming award, 1966, Rosenstiel award, 1976, Fedn. Am. Soc. Exptl. Biology award, 1976, Felix Wankel award, 1978, John Scott medal, 1979, Corson medal, 1980, N.B. lectureship Am. Soc. Microbiology, 1980, Mott prize Gen. Motors Research Found., 1983, Gairdner award, 1983, Tyler prize Environ. Achievement, 1985. Mem. Am. Soc. Biol. Chemists, Am. Soc. Microbiology, Environ. Mutagen Soc. (award 1977), Genetics Soc., Am. Assn. Cancer Research, Soc. Toxicology, Am. Chem. Soc. (Eli Lilly award 1964), Am. Acad. Arts and Scis., Nat. Acad. Sci. Home: 1324 Spruce St Berkeley CA 94709 Office: U Calif Dept Biochemistry Berkeley CA 94720 *

AMES, PATRICIA YVONNE, aerospace engineer; b. Norfolk, Va., Aug. 31, 1946; d. George Spenser Ames and Olive Marvil (Carranay) Thompson; 1 child, Lara Ellen. BA, Va. Poly. inst., 1970; MS in Edn., U. Va., 1973. Sci. and math. instr. Commonwealth of Va., 1970-76; project dir. Dept. Health, Edn. and Welfare, 1976-79; mgr. project and systems engring. Dept. Health, Edn. and Welfare, Lockheed, Calif., 1979—.

AMES, WILLIAM CLARK, academic administrator; b. Macomb, Ill., July 11, 1950; s. Clark Earl and Betty Amelia (Hegstrom) A.; BA, Knox Coll., 1972; MS, Western Ill. U., 1974; postgrad., Ariz. State U. Asst. to dean students, instr. human interaction Knox Coll., Galesburg, Ill., 1971-75; instr. human interaction, counselor edn. Western Ill. U., Macomb, 1974-75; resident area coord. Western Carolina U., Cullowhee, N.C., 1975-77; dir. Sahuaro Complex, Ariz. State U., Tempe, 1977-78, dir. housing office vending programs, 1978-79, asst. dir. housing-adminstrn., 1979-80, grad. assoc. for student leadership programs, 1980-81, rsch. assoc., office of pres., 1981-82; asst. to chancellor Maricopa Community Coll., Phoenix, 1982-84, dir. mgmt. and budget, 1984—; Am. Coun. Edn. fellow, 1989—. Mem. funding panel Phoenix United Way, 1988, Western Carolina coun. on Alcohol and Use and Abuse, 1975-77. NSF grantee, 1970-72; recipient Leadership award Elks Ill., 1968; Robert Cunningham Taylor Jr. scholar, 1968-72. Mem. Nat. Assn. student Pers. Adminstrs., Am. Pers. and Guidance Assn., Am. Coll. Pers. Assn., Am. Coun. Univ. Housing Officers, Southeastern Assn. Housing Officers, Smithsonian Inst. (asso.), Knox Coll., Western Ill. U. Alumni Assn. Contbr. articles to profl. jours. Home: 1321 W Lynwood St Phoenix AZ 85007 Office: Maricopa Community Coll 3910 E Washington St Phoenix AZ 85034

AMICO, CHARLES WILLIAM, management consultant; b. Boston, May 6, 1942; s. William Charles and Marie Josephine (Nicholas) A. Assoc. in Engring., Franklin Inst., 1962; BS, Suffolk U., 1968. Jr. chem. technician Avco Corp., Lowell, Mass., 1963-64; advanced vacuum tech. technician Nat. Rsch. Corp., Newton, Mass., 1964-68; semicondr. engr. IBM, Essex Junction, Vt., 1968-72, semicondr. mfg. engring. mgr., 1972-76, mgmt. devel. cons., 1976-86; founder, pres., chief exec. officer Creative Directions, Inc., Charlotte, Vt., 1982—; bd. dirs. Holiday Project, 1987-88. State chmn. Vt. Hugh O'Brian Youth Leadership Seminar; bd. dirs. Vt. Hugh O'Brian Youth Seminars, Inc., chief exec officer, 1984-85; mem. Bay Area Orgn. Devel. Network. Recipient Hugh O'Brian Outstanding State Chmn. in Nation award, 1984, 85. Mem. San Francisco C. of C. Office: Creative Directions Inc 2932 Pierce St San Francisco CA 94123

AMIOKA, WALLACE SHUZO, retired petroleum company executive, public affairs consultant; b. Honolulu, June 28, 1914; s. Tsurumatsu and Reye (Yoshimura) A.; B.A., U. Hawaii, 1966, M.B.A., 1968; m. Ellen Misao Honda, Aug. 9, 1942; children—Carol L. Amioka Price, Joanne M. Amioka Chikuma. With Shell Oil Co., 1931-77, fin. svcs. mgr., Honolulu, 1973-77; pub. affairs cons., Honolulu, 1977-87; gen. ptnr. Pub. Affairs Cons. Hawaii, 1988—; lectr. econs. U. Hawaii, 1969-79. Mem. Honolulu Police Commn., 1965-73, vice chmn., 1966, 68, chmn., 1971; U.S. civil adm. Ryuku Islands, 1950-52. Mem. City and County of Honolulu Charter Commn., 1981-82; bd. dirs. Honolulu Symphony Soc., 1968. Served with M.I., AUS, 1944-48. Mem. M.I. Service Vets. (pres. 1981-82), Hawaii C. of C. (chmn. edn. com. 1963-64, chmn. pub. health com. 1966-67), Hui 31 Club, Hui Aikene Club, Honolulu Police Old Timers Club, Phi Beta Kappa, Phi Kappa Phi. Home: 4844 Matsonia Dr Honolulu HI 96816 Office: Pub Affairs Cons-Hawaii 711 Keeaumoku St Honolulu HI 96814

AMISTAD, GLENN REPIEDAD, bank executive; b. Tamuning, Guam, Mar. 22, 1955; s. Felino Borbon and Polly (Repiedad) A. BBA in Acctg., Chaminade U., 1977; MBA in Real Estate, Golden Gate U., 1987. CPA, Hawaii. Tax preparer Beneficial Fin. & Loan Co., Union City, Calif., 1978-79; gen. ptnr. Amistad Properties, Fremont, Calif., 1980—; staff acct. Maisel & Bohn, CPAs, Hayward, Calif., 1980-81, Donald H. Seiler & Co., CPAs, Redwood City, Calif., 1981-82; internal auditor Polly's House of Fabrics, Agana, Guam, 1983-84; exec. comml. and consumer loans dept. Bank of Guam, San Francisco, 1984—. Mem. AICPA, Nat. Assn. Accts. (bd. dirs. local chpt. 1983-84, bd. dirs. member rels. 1984-85), Alameda Owners Assn., Golden Gate U. Alumni Assn. (mem. steering com. 1987—), Chaminade U. Alumni Assn. (pres. Bay Area chpt. 1988—). Republican. Roman Catholic. Home: 44201 Arapaho Ave Fremont CA 94539 Office: Bank of Guam 404 Montgomery St San Francisco CA 94104

AMOROSO, ANN-MARIE JOYCE, handcrafter, nurse; b. Providence, May 15, 1940; d. Carmine and Vera Claire (Colozzi) Palumbo; m. Michele Amoroso Jr., June 28, 1960; children: Barbara Jean Ingram, Sandra Lynne. Student, JoAnn Sch. Beauty, Providence, 1958-59; cert. in vocat. nursing, Golden West Coll., Huntington Beach, Calif., 1971. Various positions, Warwick, R.I., 1956-58; hairdresser, Providence, 1959-65; staff nurse Hoag Meml. Hosp., Newport Beach, Calif., 1971-72; office nurse Dr. J. Y. Watt, Newport Beach, 1972-75; nurse ICU and critical care unit Med. Staffing, Costa Mesa, Calif., 1975-82; handcrafter dollhouse accessories, Costa Mesa, 1982—. Fellow Internat. Guild Miniature Artisans, Nat. Assn. Miniature Enthusiasts (state rep. so. Calif., tchr. 1983—). Home and Office: 3117 Yukon Ave Costa Mesa CA 92626

AMSBARY, HARLOW BRUCE, corporate professional; b. Champaign, Ill., May 17, 1956; s. Frank Clifford Amsbury and Mina Mae (McHie) Coy. Student, Ill. State U., Normal, 1974-78; BS in Psychology, U. Ore., Eugene, 1980; Student, Portland State U., Ore., 1987—. Forestry technician USDA Forest Service-Region 6, Ore., 1979-82, 85-86; comml. fisherman Kodiak Ketchikan, Ore., 1983-84; fire technician Pvt. Contractor/US Forest Service, La Grande, Ore., 1987; with Siski Nat. Park Campaign, Portland, Ore., 1987—; intern Portland Ore. Visitors Assn., 1988. Editor: Nat. Park Proposal, Siskiyou Nat. Park 1989; Author: Commentary,. Adminstrv. asst. Oreg. Natural Resources Coun., 1989—; Nat. Wildlife Fedn., Oreg. Natural Resources Coun. Mem. Ancient Forest Alliance, Wakai Tea Sch. Portland Ore. Democrat. Office: Siskiyou Nat Park Campaign 522 SW Fifth Ste 1050 Portland OR 97204

AMSEL, ELLEN, computer auditor, infosystems specialist; b. Long Beach, N.Y., Sept. 1, 1955; d. Stanley and Bernice (Steinfeld) A. BA in Math., William Paterson Coll., 1977; cert. telecommunications, Golden Gate U., 1985. Mem. audit staff Bradford, N.Y.C., 1977-79; infosytems auditor 1st Fed. of Broward, Ft. Lauderdale, Fla., 1979-80; EDP auditor Crum & Forster Corp., Morristown, N.J., 1980-81; sr. corp. auditor F.W. Woolworth Co., N.Y.C., 1981-83; sr. EDP auditor Amdahl Corp., Sunnyvale, Calif., 1983-85, corp. computer security officer, 1985-88; corp. computer auditor Nat. Semiconductor Corp., Santa Clara, Calif., 1988—. Advisor Nat. Conf. on Synagogue Youth, 1975—; youth advisor local synagogue, Palo Alto, Calif., 1987—; chmn. Network Access Spl. Interest Group, 1985-87. Named one of Outstanding Young Women in Am., 1987. Mem. EDP Auditor's Assn. (bd. dirs. Silicon Valley, Calif. chpt. 1983-88, rsch. editor 1987-88), Bay Area Computer Soc. Interest Group (officer 1985-87), Oceanic Soc., Acad. of Scis. of San Francisco). Jewish. Office: Nat Semiconductor Corp 2900 Semiconductor Dr #15-120 Santa Clara CA 95052

AMSTUTZ, GARY PAUL, software engineer; b. Tulsa, July 23, 1955; s. Ray Warren and Sara Mae (Vance) A.; m. Janice Patrice Negri, Sept. 12, 1977 (div. 1982); m. Terri Lynn Easter. BA, St. Mary's U., 1976. Pres., chief exec. officer Apts.-on-TV, Inc., Tulsa, 1979-82; software engr. TanData Corp., Tulsa, 1982-87; mem. software tech. staff Ashton-Tate, Glendale, Calif., 1987-89; sr. software engr. Peter Norton Computing Co., Santa Monica, Calif., 1989—; cons., Singles Sta., Tulsa, 1982—, Margaret Hudson Program, Tulsa, 1983-87, Pasadena (Calif.) Rep. Club, 1988—. Creator, translator software; dir. film: 50 Times, 1973 (Best Film, Edison Film Festival). Mem. Pasadena Rep. Club (bd. dirs. 1988-89), Pasadena Area Young Reps., Lambda Chi Alpha (pres. 1976). Home: 18765 Malden St Northridge CA 91324 Office: Peter Norton Computing 100 Wilshire Blvd Santa Monica CA 90401

AMUNDSON, EVA DONALDA, civic worker; b. Langdon, N.D., Apr. 23, 1911; d. Elmer Fritjof and Alma Julia (Nelson) Hultin; m. Leif Amundson, Mar. 1, 1929 (dec. 1974); children: Constance, Eleanor, Ardis, Priscilla. Bd. dirs. Opportunity Workshop, Missoula, Mont., 1950—, Rockmont Group Homes, Missoula, 1976—, Bethany L'Arche (group home for girls), 1976—; mem. Missoula Sr. Citizen's Ctr., 1980-82, pres., 1982-85; tchr. Norwegian cooking and baking, 1954-56, Norwegian Rosemaling, 1975-79; treas. Sacakawea Homemakers Club, 1979-81; mem. Am. Luth. Ch. Women St. Pauls' Lutheran Ch., 1951—; active Easter Seal Program, Heart Fund, March of Dimes, United Way, Campfire Girls; mem. adv. council Area Agy. on Aging, Missoula, 1984—. Recipient Outstanding Sr. award Missoula Jr. C. of C., 1984. Mem. Sons. of Norway, Orchard Homes Country Club (mem. art judging com.), Order of Eastern Star, Elks. Avocations: rosemaling, oil painting, poetry. Home: 324 Kensington Ave Missoula MT 59801

ANACKER, R. DAVID, environmental services company executive; b. 1935. BA, Wash. State U., 1958. With Am. Bldg. Maintenence Industries, 1959—, asst. to gen. mgr., 1965-67, exec. v.p., from 1967; now pres., chief exec officer, dir. San Francisco. Office: Am Bldg Maintenance Industries 333 Fell St San Francisco CA 94102 *

ANAND, SURESH CHANDRA, physician; b. Mathura, India, Sept. 13, 1931; s. Satchit and Sumaran (Bai) A.; came to U.S., 1957, naturalized, 1971; M.B., B.S., King George's Coll., U. Lucknow (India), 1954; M.S., U. Colo., 1962; m. Wiltrud, Jan. 29, 1966; children—Miriam, Michael. Fellow pulmonary diseases Nat. Jewish Hosp., Denver, 1957-58, resident in chest medicine, 1958-59, chief resident allergy-asthma, 1960-62; intern Mt. Sinai Hosp., Toronto, Ont., Can., 1962-63, resident in medicine, 1963-64, chief resident, 1964-65, demonstrator clin. technique, 1963-64, U. Toronto fellow in medicine, 1964-65; research assoc. asthma-allergy Nat. Jewish Hosp., Denver, 1967-69; clin. instr. medicine U. Colo., 1967-69; pres. Allergy Assocs. & Lab., Ltd., Phoenix, 1974—; mem. staff Phoenix Bapt. Hosp., chmn. med .records com., 1987; mem. staff St. Joseph's Hosp., St. Luke's Hosp., Humana Hosp., Phoenix Bapt., John C. Lincoln, Maryvale Meml., Good Samaritan, Phoenix Children's Hosp., Tempe St. Luke, Desert Samaritan, Mesa Luth., Scottsdale Meml. Mem. Camelback Hosp. Mental Health Center Citizens Adv. Bd., Scottsdale, Ariz., 1974-80; mem. council Phoenix Symphony; mem. Ariz. Opera Co., Boyce Thompson Southwestern Arboretum. Diplomate Am. Bd. Allergy and Immunology. Fellow ACP, Am. Coll. Chest Physicians (critical care com.), Am. Acad. Allergy, Am. Coll. Cert. Allergists, Am. Assn. Clin. Immunology and Allergy; mem. AAAS, AMA, Ariz. Med. Assn., Maricopa County Med. Soc., West Coast Soc. Allergy and Immunology, Ariz. Soc. Allergists (v.p. 1988—), Greater Phoenix Allergy Soc. (v.p. 1984-86, pres. 1986-88), AAAS, Phoenix Zoo, N.Y. Acad. Scis., World Med. Assn., Internat. Assn. Asthmology, Assn. Care of Asthma, Ariz. Thoracic Soc., Nat. Geog. Soc., Ariz. Hist. Soc., Smithsonian Instn., Phoenix Art Mus., Am. Mus. Natural History, Nat. Audobon Soc. Clubs: Village Tennis, Ariz. Club, Sertoma Internat. Contbr. articles in field to profl. jours. Office: 2200 W Bethany Home Rd Phoenix AZ 85015 also: 1006 E Guadalupe Rd Tempe AZ 85283

ANANE-SEFAH, JOHN CAMARA, surgeon; b. Bepong, Ghana, June 27, 1941; came to U.S., 1963, naturalized, 1979; s. Sam Kwabena Mireku and Akua (Gyafo) Mawu; BS, Yale U., 1967; MD, Harvard U., 1970; m. Patricia Anne Lawrence, June 2, 1973; children: Jason, John. Intern in surgery U. Colo., Denver, 1970-71, resident in surgery, fellow in trauma surgery, 1971-75; practice medicine specializing in gen. and vascular surgery; pres. Mid-County Surg./Med. Group, Inc., 1983—; mem. staffs Dominican Hosp., Community Hosp. Diplomate Am. Bd. Surgery. Fellow ACS, Royal Soc. Medicine (London), Internat. Coll. Surgeons, Internat. Acad. Proctology; mem. Santa Cruz C. of C. Contbr. articles to profl. jours. Office: 603 Capitola Ave Capitola CA 95010

ANAST, DAVID GEORGE, editor, publishing executive; b. Joliet, Ill., Oct. 9, 1955; s. George F. and Athey (Kusunis) A. Student, Ariz. State U., 1973-74; B. in Pub. Adminstrn., Calif. State Coll., Bakersfield, 1975-79, M. in Pub. Adminstrn., 1979. Corr. The Bakersfield Californian Daily Newspaper, 1975-79; mktg. and publs. mgr. U. So. Calif., Los Angeles, 1979; assoc. editor Calif. Good Life mag., Los Angeles, 1979-80, Worldwide Meetings and Incentives mag., Los Angeles, 1980-81; from assoc. editor to mng. editor Contemporary Dialysis and Nephrology mag., Los Angeles, 1980-85, editor, assoc. pub., 1985-86; exec. editor, pub. Nephrology News and Issues mag., Huntington Beach, Calif., 1986—. Author: (chpt.) Clinical Vascular Surgery, 1988; contbr. articles to profl. jours. Bd. dirs. NOW, San Fernando Valley, Calif., 1984, publs. advisor, 1984. Recipient Pub. Service award Nat. Kidney Found., 1984, 88. Mem. Western Publs. Assn. (Maggie awards judge 1983-85). Greek Orthodox. Club: Hellenic U. of So. Calif. (sec. 1985-87). Home: 6600 Warner Blvd #69 Huntington Beach CA 92647 Office: Nephrology News and Issues Mag 18582 Beach Blvd Ste 201 Huntington Beach CA 92648

ANAWATI, JOSEPH SOLIMAN, pharmaceutical company executive; b. Alexandria, Egypt, Dec. 25, 1941; came to U.S., 1979; s. Soliman Youssef and Rosine (Naif) A.; children: Kevin Joseph, Caroline Jo. Degree in Pharmacy, U. Alexandria, 1966, MPharm, 1968; MBA, City Exec. Coll., 1985. Med. rep. Eli Lilly Co. Indpls., Cairo and Libya, 1966-71; surp. sales and mktg., dist. mgr., then area mgr. Upjohn Co. Kalamazoo, Middle East and Africa, 1971-79; group area mgr. Allergan Pharm.-Irvine, Calif., Middle East, Africa and Europe, 1979-82; prodn. and plant mgr., dir. internat. export MD Pharm., Santa Ana, Calif., 1983—; pres., IMS Consulting, Fountain Valley, Calif., 1983—. Mem. Cairo Bd. Pharmacy, Los Caballeros Club Orange County. Home: PO Box 8871 Fountain Valley CA 92728 Office: MD Pharm Inc 3501 W Garry Ave Santa Ana CA 92704

ANDARY, THOMAS JOSEPH, biochemist; b. Sault Sainte Marie, Mich., Oct. 8, 1942; s. Joseph Boula and Marion (Schwifetti) A. B.S., No. Mich. U., 1966, M.A., 1968; Ph.D., Wayne State U., 1974. Instr. biology No. Mich. U., Marquette, 1967-69; research asso. physiology Wayne State U., Detroit, 1973-76; sr. research scientist, mgr. coagulation research Hyland Labs., Costa Mesa, Calif., 1976-83; dir. quality control Hyland Therapeutics, Glendale, Calif., 1983—; lectr. in field. Recipient Research award Sigma Xi, 1973; NDEA fellow, 1969-72. Mem. Am. Chem. Soc., N.Y. Acad. Sci., Sigma Xi. Roman Catholic. Contbr. over 25 articles to profl. publs. Home: 531 N Canyon Monrovia CA 91016 Office: 4501 Colorado Blvd Los Angeles CA 90039

ANDERBERG, ROY ANTHONY, journalist; b. Camden, N.J., Mar. 30, 1921; s. Arthur R. and Mary V. (McHugh) A.; m. Louise M. Brooks, Feb. 5, 1953; children: Roy, Mary. AA, Diablo Valley Coll., 1975. Enlisted USN, 1942, commd. officer, 1960, ret., 1970; waterfront columnist Pacific Daily News, Agana, Guam, 1966-67; pub. relations officer Naval Forces, Mariana Islands, 1967; travel editor Contra Costa (Calif.) Times, 1968-69; entertainment and restaurant editor Concord (Calif.) Transcript, 1971-75; entertainment editor Contra Costa Advertiser, 1975-76; free-lance non-fiction journalist, 1976—. Mem. U.S. Power Squadron, DAV, Ret. Officers Assn., Am. Legion, VFW, U.S. Submarine Vets. World War II Assn., Naval Submarine League. Democrat. Clubs: Martinez Yacht, Treasure Island Yacht. Home: 2720 Lyon Circle Concord CA 94518 Office: Box 52 Concord CA 94522

ANDERSEN, DONALD LEWIS, quality assurance professional, chemist; b. Tacoma, Nov. 19, 1938; s. Ferdinand Andrew and Lucile Elinor (Dixon) A.; m. Joan Christie Clyde, Sept. 9, 1961; children: Gene Russell, Sheri Gail, Eric Andrew. BA in Chemistry, Western Wash. U., 1961; postgrad., Georgetown U., 1965-66; AA in Mgmt., Edmonds Community Coll., Lynwood, Wash., 1973. Lab. asst. Western Wash. U., Bellingham, 1958-61; chemist U.S. FDA, Seattle, 1961-73; supr. investigations U.S. Consumer Products, Seattle, 1973-81; quality supr. Physio Control Corp., Redmond, Wash., 1981-84; quality mgr. Quinton Instrument Co., Seattle, 1984—. Contbr. articles to profl. jours. Pres. Phinney Ridge Community Council, Seattle, 1971, Shady Lake Community Council, Renton, 1983—; chmn. Cub Scouts Am. Pack 122 and Troop 120, Seattle, 1972-81; active Mayor's Citizens Zoo Adv. Com., Seattle, 1972-73. Mem. Am. Soc. for Quality Control, Electronics Mfg. Assn. Home: 17837 SE 192d Dr Renton WA 98058 Office: Quinton Instrument Co 2121 Terry Ave Seattle WA 98121

ANDERSEN, DORIS EVELYN, real estate broker; b. Christian County, Ky., Oct. 30, 1923; d. William Earl and Blanche Elma (Withers) Johnston; m. Roger Lewis Shirk, July 9, 1944 (div. 1946); 1 child, Vicki Lee Shirk Sanderson; m. DeLaire Andersen, July 6, 1946; children: Craig Bryant, Karen Rae, Kent DeLaire, Chris Jay, Mardi Lynn. Diploma, South Bend Coll. Commerce, 1942; diploma in banking Notre Dame U., 1946; student Ind. U., 1942-44. Tng. dir. First Nat. Bank, Portland, Oreg., 1963-69; assoc. broker Stan Wiley, Inc., Portland, 1969-79; prin. Doris Andersen & Assocs., Portland, 1979—; speaker at seminars; mem. Gov.'s Task Force Council on Housing, Salem, Oreg., 1985-86. Contbr. articles to profl. jours. Mem. task force Oreg. Dept. Energy, Salem, 1984-85. Mem. Nat. Assn. Realtors (dir. 1983—, regional v.p. Northwest region 1988), Oreg. Assn. Realtors (dir. 1979—, pres. 1986—), Portland Bd. Realtors (pres. 1982), Women's Council Realtors (local pres. 1977, state pres. 1978, gov. nat. orgn. 1979), Internat. Platform Assn., Internat. Biog. Assn. Avocations: reading, travel. Home and Office: PO Box 1169 Shady Cove OR 97539

ANDERSEN, ERNEST CHRISTOPHER, lawyer; b. Minden, Nebr., Sept. 10, 1909; s. Dines Peter and Marie (Jensen) A.; m. Audrey Etta Robertson, Sept. 10, 1954; 1 dau., Elaine Carolyn Andersen Smith; 1 stepson, Albert Henry Whitaker. J.D., U. Denver, 1952, B.S. in Bus. Adminstrn., 1956. Bar: Colo. 1954, U.S. Supreme Ct. 1960. With U.S. Treasury Dept., Denver, 1935-39; accountant, Denver, 1939-41; with Civilian Prodn. Adminstrn., Denver, 1946-49; dep. state auditor Colo., 1949-51; with U.S. Commerce Dept., Denver, 1951-52; mgmt. cons., Denver, 1953-54; sole practice law, Denver, 1955-56, 69-75; asst. dir. GAO, Los Angeles, 1957-58, Denver, 1959, Washington, 1960-69, cons., 1969-75; sole practice law, Cedaredge, Colo., 1975-86; owner Cedar Crest Farm, 1983—, Stand Sure Press (later Christopher Pub. Co.), 1977—; mem. faculty U. Denver, 1948-56; mcpl. judge Cedaredge, 1977-86; exec. in residence Tulane U., spring 1973. Bd. dirs. Delta Montrose Electric Assn., 1976-84, Colo.-Ute Electric Assn., 1980-84. Served to lt. col. U.S. Army, 1941-46. Recipient Meritorious Service award GAO, 1968. Republican. Presbyterian. Clubs: Masons, Shriners. Home: 1856 Road 2375 Cedaredge CO 81413 Office: PO Box 747 Cedaredge CO 30747

ANDERSEN, GARY HOWARD, communications company executive; b. Olympia, Wash., Jan. 23, 1938; s. Howard Frederick and Jean (Mullan) A.; children from previous marriage: Christopher Cody, Dale Gary, Amy Jean Marie; m. Carolyn Annette Perez, Apr. 23, 1977; 1 child, Metian Allana. Student, Whitman Coll., Walla Walla, Wash., 1956-57; BS, U. Wash., 1961. Salesman Wash. Transit Advt. Inc., Seattle, 1961-68, pres., 1968-73; pres. Ilium Assocs., Inc., Seattle, 1973-80; sec., treas. Ilium Assocs., Inc., Bellevue, Wash., 1981—; pres. Forum Communications, Inc., Bellevue, 1980—. Mem. Mayor's Adv. Council, Seattle, 1972-74. Mem. Internat. Council of Shopping Ctrs. Office: Forum Communications Inc 500 108th Ave NE Ste 2400 Bellevue WA 98004

ANDERSEN, JAMES A., justice; b. Auburn, Wash., Sept. 21, 1924; s. James A. and Margaret Cecilia (Norgaard) A.; divorced; children: James Blair, Tia Louise. BA, U. Wash., 1949, JD, 1951. Bar: Wash. 1952, U.S. Dist. Ct. (we. dist.) Wash. 1957, U.S. Ct. Appeals 1957. Dep. pros. atty. King County, Seattle, 1953-57; assoc. Lycette, Diamond & Sylvester, Seattle, 1957-61; ptnr. Clinton, Andersen, Fleck & Glein, Seattle, 1961-75; judge Wash. State Ct. of Appeals, Seattle, 1975-84; justice Wash. State Supreme Ct., Olympia, 1984—. Mem. Wash. State Ho. of Reps., 1958-67, Wash. State Senate, 1967-72. Served with U.S. Army, 1943-45, ETO. Decorated Purple Heart. Mem. ABA, Wash. State Bar Assn., Am. Judicature Soc. Office: Wash Supreme Ct Temple of Justice M S AV-11 Olympia WA 98504-0511

ANDERSON, ARTHUR ROLAND, engineering company executive, civil engineer; b. Tacoma, Mar. 11, 1910; s. Eivind and Aslaug (Axness) A.; BS, U. Wash., 1934; MS, MIT, 1935, DSc, 1938; LLD (hon.), Gonzaga U., 1983; m. Barbara Hinman Beck, June 5, 1938; children: Martha Anderson Nelson, Karl, Richard, Elisabeth Anderson Zerzan, Deborah Anderson Ray. Mem. staff MIT, Cambridge, 1936-38, 39-41; design engr. Klonne Steel Co., Dortmund, Germany, 1938-39; head tech. dept. Cramp Shipyard, USN Bur. Ships, Phila., 1941-46; pvt. practice cons. civil engr., Stamford, Conn., 1946-51; co-founder Concrete Tech. Corp., Tacoma, 1951, sr. v.p., 1956—; pres. Anderson Enterprises Corp., Tacoma, 1957—; vis. lectr. U. Wash., 1954-55; chmn. bd. Anderson, Birkeland, Anderson & Mast, Engrs., Inc. (now ABAM Engrs. Inc.), Tacoma, 1951-77. Pres. Puget Sound (Wash.) Sci. Fair, 1954-58; mem. Tacoma Pub. Utility Bd., 1954-69, chmn., 1968-69; mem. edn. council MIT, 1954—, vis. com., 1960-70; mem. Pacific Luth. U. Collegium, 1976—; mem. vis. com. U. Wash.; mem. Wash. State Coun. for Post-Secondary Edn., 1977-84. Registered profl. engr., Wash., Conn., B.C., Can.; named Alumnus Summa Laude Dignatus, U. Wash., 1980. Mem. Am. Concrete Inst. (hon. mem., dir. 1962-69, pres. 1966-67, Constrn. Practice award 1962, Alfred E. Lindau medal 1970, Roger Corbetta award 1974, Charles S. Whitney award 1975, Turner medal 1977, Arthur J. Boase award 1979), ASCE (hon., life mem., mem. tech. com. 1963-66, T.Y. Lin award 1971), Soc. Exptl. Stress Analysis (charter), ASTM, Nat. Soc. Profl. Engrs., Soc. Naval Architects and Marine Engrs., Internat. Assn. Bridge and Structural Engrs. (hon.), Prestressed Concrete Inst. (pres. 1970-71), N.E. Coast Shipbuilders and Engrs., Japan Concrete Inst. (hon.), Fedn. Internat. de la Precontrainte (F.I.P. medal 1974), Comité European de Beton, Nat. Acad. Engring., Sigma Xi, Chi Epsilon, Beta Gamma Sigma, Tau Beta Pi. Contbr. numerous articles in tech. of concrete and research on welded steel ships to profl. jours.; patentee in field. Home: 502 Tacoma Ave N Tacoma WA 98403 Office: 1123 Port of Tacoma Rd Tacoma WA 98421

ANDERSON, BARBARA LOUISE, library director; b. San Diego, Jan. 5, 1933; d. Lorenzo and Louise (Morgan) A.; 1 child, Sean Allen. BS, San Diego State U., 1954; MLS, Kans. State Teachers Coll., 1955. Br. librarian L.A. Pub. Library, 1956-59; br. librarian, reference, young adult librarian San Diego Pub. Library, 1959-64; librarian U.S. Army, Europe, 1964-69; coordinator Serra Reference Project, Serra Regional Library System, San Diego, 1969-71; head readers services Riverside (Calif.) City and County Pub. Library, 1972-74; county librarian San Bernardino County (Calif.) Library, 1974—; del. White House Conf. on Libraries and Info. Services, 1979. Bd. dirs. Inland Empire Symphony, 1982-84, Riverside Mental Health Assn., 1975-79; mem. citizens adv. bd. San Bernardino YWCA, 1988-89. Mem. ALA, Calif. Library Assn., Black Caucus of Calif. Library Assn., Congress of Pub. Library Systems (pres. 1984), Calif. County Librarians Assn., Calif. Soc. Librarians (pres. 1974-75, mem. OCLC Users Council 1984-88), AAUW (pres. Riverside Br. 1976-77), NAACP, Bus. and Profl. Women San Bernardino. Democrat. Baptist. Contbr. articles to publs. in field. Office: San Bernardino County Libr 104 W 4th St San Bernardino CA 92415

ANDERSON, BARRY STANLEY, health care executive; b. Atlanta, Sept. 6, 1942; s. Rex and Virginia A.; m. Katherine Krupp, Dec. 26, 1966 (div. 1973); 1 child, Jon Robert; m. Patricia Ann O'Neil, May 25, 1974; children: Russell Barry, Robert Bruce. AA, Foothill Coll., 1968; BA, San Francisco State U., 1976; MBA, U. N.D., 1984. V.p. Ventilation Assocs., Inc., Houston, 1971-74; program dir. Inst. Med. Studies, Berkeley, Calif., 1976-78; program dir. Sch. Respiratory Care, St. Alexius Med. Ctr., Bismarck, N.D., 1978-84, health care cons., dir. edn., 1984-87; mgr. respiratory care ops. Medisys Mgmt. System, 1988; program dir. Loma Vista Adult Ctr., Concord, Calif., 1988—; instr. Entrepreneurial Mgmt. Bus. Tng. Internat., Sacramento, 1988—. chmn. bd. dirs., pres. Creative Mktg., Inc., Bismarck (N.D.), Vacaville (Calif.), 1982—; v.p. Baby Products Ltd., 1987—; asst. prof. U. of Mary, 1982-85; instr. bus. edn. div. Solano Community Coll., Suisun, Calif., 1988—. Author: (with D. Quesinberry) Blood Gas Interpretations, 1974; mem. editorial adv. bd. Respiratory Mgmt.; contbr. articles to profl. jours. Nominee Am. Coll. Healthcare Execs. Mem. Am. Mktg. Assn., Am. Mgmt. Assn., Am. Hosp. Assn., Acad. for Health Svcs. Mktg., Assn. MBA Execs., Ctr. for Entrepreneurial Mgmt., U. N.D. Alumni Assn., Elks. Avocations: computer programming, writing, reading, lecturing, sailing. Office: Loma Vista Adult Ctr 1266 San Carlos Ave Concord CA 94518

ANDERSON, BENNETT WADE, computer infosystems engineer; b. Williston, N.D., Jan. 8, 1961; s. Alfred Kermit and Alice (Hegland) A. BS with honors, Brigham Young U., 1987. Software engr. Word Perfect Corp., Orem, Utah, 1987—; software engr./coop. IBM, San Jose, Calif., 1986. Contbr. articles to profl. jours., 1987-88. Missionary LDS Church, Japan, 1980-82, quorum pres., Provo, Utah, 1988—. Recipient saxaphone solo medal. Mem. Phi Kappa Phi. Mormon. Home: 1593 N Willow Ln Provo UT 84604 Office: Word Perfect Corp 1600 N 800 E Research Park Orem UT 84057

ANDERSON, BRADFORD WILLIAM, food company sales executive; b. Redlands, Calif., Feb. 17, 1956; s. B.W. and Helen Louise (Wisel) A.; m. Diane Elizabeth Hutt, Aug. 22, 1981. BS in Mgmt., U. Redlands, 1978; MBA in Mktg. Mgmt., Calif. State U., 1982. Cert. instr. in bus. edn., Calif. Store mgr. Fringer's Market, Redlands, Calif., 1978-80; ter. mgr. Carnation Co., Fullerton, Calif., 1980-82, sr. ter. mgr., trainer, 1982-84, dist. sales coordinator, 1984-85; nat. mgr. sales planning Carnation Co., Los Angeles, 1985—, implementation coordinator, 1984; instr. Chaffey Coll., Alta Loma, Calif., 1984-87. Mem. Muckenthaler Cultural Ctr. and Theater, 1987—, Friends of Santa Ana Zoo, 1988, Diamond Bar Improvement Assn., Diamond Bar Ranch Festival. Named one of Outstanding Young Men in Am., Jaycees, 1984; recipient P. Pat Patterson Meml. Award, Santa Fe Fed. Savs., 1978; Harris Meml. scholar Harris Dept. Stores, 1978. Mem. Food Industry Sales Club, Alumni Assn. San Bernardino, Calif., Young Alumni Com. U. Redlands, Alpha Gamma Nu. Republican. Methodist. Home: 24442 Rosegate Pl Diamond Bar CA 91765 Office: Carnation Co 5045 Wilshire Blvd Los Angeles CA 90036

ANDERSON, C. LEONARD, librarian; b. Spokane, Wash., Jan. 13, 1946; s. Charles Arthur and Elsa Alida (Ericsson) A.; m. Shirley Rae Bacon, June 16, 1967; children: Douglas Arthur, Eric Bror. BA in Edn., Ea. Wash. State Coll., 1968; MLS, U. Oreg., 1972. Library asst. Spokane Pub. Library, 1962-68; with Portland Pub. Schs., 1968—, mid. sch. librarian, 1978-80, high sch. librarian, 1986—; pres. Portland Assn. Tchrs., 1977-78, 82-86. Mem. Oreg. Rep. Tchrs. Adv. Commn., Beaverton, 1985—; appointee Oreg. Congl. Awards Coun., Salem, 1986—; alt. del. Rep. Nat. Conv., Dallas, 1984; mem., chmn. Beaverton Library Bd., 1983—; bd. dirs. Nat. Found. for Improvement of Edn., Washington, 1981-84. Mem. NEA (bd. dirs. 1987—), Oreg. Edn. Assn. (bd. dirs., v.p. Tigard chpt. 1975—), Am. Library Assn., Nat. Coun. Accreditation Tchr. Edn. (bd. examines 1987—), Oreg. Tchr. Standards and Practice Commn. (chmn. 1981-86), Nat. Bd. Profl. Teaching Standards. Presbyterian. Home: 5595 SW Chestnut Ave Beaverton OR 97005 Office: Grant High Sch 2245 NE 36th Ave Portland OR 97212

ANDERSON, CARL DAVID, scientist; b. N.Y.C., Sept. 3, 1905; s. Carl David and Emma Adolfina (Ajaxson) A.; m. Lorraine Elvira Bergman; children—Marshall David, David Andrew. B.S., Calif. Inst. of Tech., 1927, Ph.D. magna cum laude, 1930; hon. Sc.D., Colgate U., 1937, Gustavus Adolphus Coll., 1963; LL.D. (hon.), Temple U., 1948. Coffin research fellow Calif. Inst. Tech., 1927-28, teaching fellow in physics, 1928-30, research fellow in physics, 1930-33, asst. prof. physics, 1933-37, assoc. prof., 1937-39, prof., 1939-76, prof. emeritus, 1976—, chmn. div. physics, math. and astronomy, 1962-70; researcher on x-ray photoelectrons, 1927-30, on gamma rays and cosmic rays, 1930—. Awarded gold medal Am. Inst. of City of N.Y., 1935; Nobel prize in physics, 1936; Elliott Cresson medal of the Franklin Inst., 1937; John Ericsson medal Am. Soc. Swedish Engrs., 1960. Mem. Am. Phys. Soc., Am. Philos. Soc., Nat. Acad. Scis., Sigma Xi, Tau Beta Pi. Office: Calif Inst Tech Dept Physics Pasadena CA 91109 *

ANDERSON, CAROL RUTH, secondary teacher; b. Conewango, N.Y., Aug. 24, 1926; d. Maynard William and Hila Martha (Kent) Phillips; m. George Boyer, Mar. 27, 1948 (div. July 1967); children: Gregory, Gail, Martha; m. Donald Anderson, Jan. 13, 1978 (div. Jan. 1981). Assoc. BS, Jamestown (N.Y.) Community Coll., 1962; BEd, U. Buffalo, 1966; MS in Edn., SUNY, Fredonia, 1971; postgrad., Ariz. State U., 1980-81. Cert. secondary tchr., N.Y., Ariz. Sec. Jamestown Metal Corp., 1957-61; sec. to judge Cattaragus County Cattaragus County Justice, Little Valley, N.Y., 1961-66; bus. educator Jamestown High Sch., 1966-82, Phoenix Union High Sch. Dist., 1982-88; ret. 1988. Rep. committeewoman Cattaragus County, 1960-62. Mem. N.Y. State Ret. Tchr.'s Assn., U. of Buffalo Alumni Assn., NEA, Jamestown High Sch. Tchrs. Club (sec., treas. 1967-82), Eagles, Women of Moose, Vasa. Republican. Methodist.

ANDERSON, CARSON ANTHONY, historic preservation planner; b. L.A., Aug. 8, 1951; s. Fred Arthur and Julia Alicia (Washington) A. BA, U. Calif., Berkeley, 1974; MA, U. Va., 1983. Planning asst. L.A. County Reg. Planning Dept., 1974-77; archtl. historian Vt. State Div. for Hist. Preservation, Montpelier, 1979-81; asst. planner City Beverly Hills, Calif., 1981-84; pvt. practice as hist. preservation cons. L.A., 1985; community planner U.S. Army Corps Engrs., L.A., 1986-87; sr. city planner City Pasadena, 1987—; hist. preservation cons. W. Adams Heritage Assn., L.A., 1987—; archtl. annotator Da Camera Soc., L.A., 1987—. Citizens adv. panel Downtown L.A. Redevel. Plan, 1975-76; vol. Aids Project L.A., 1985—; docent L.A. Conservancy, 1987—, mem. cultural resources com., 1981—; active Amnesty Internat., N.Y.C., 1981—, Ctr. Def. Info., Washington, 1983—, ACLU, L.A., 1984—. Mem. Soc. Archtl. Historians, Calif. Preservation Found. (so. Calif. chpt.), Nat. Trust for Hist. Preservation, Ephebian Soc., Ghosts. Democrat. Episcopalian. Home: 2004 Apex Ave #8 Los Angeles CA 90039 Office: City of Pasadena 100 N Garfield Ave #111 Pasadena CA 91109

ANDERSON, CHARLES JORDAN, marketing engineer; b. Madison, Wis., Mar. 23, 1932; s. Peter and Caroline Emily (Johnson) A.; m. Annick Paule Goudin, Dec. 10, 1964; children: Alexis Charles Jordan, Ariane Pauline. BEE, U. Colo., Boulder, 1974. Elec. engr. Pub. Service Co. of Color., Denver, 1974-78, sr. mktg. engr., 1978—. Served in USN, 1951-55, Korea. Recipient Gov.'s citation, State of Colo., 1987, Energy Innovation award, U.S. Dept. of Energy, Washington, 1987. Mem. IEEE. Republican. Roman Catholic. Clubs: Alliance Francaise, Swiss Soc. (Denver). Home: 6937 E Berry Ave Englewood CO 80111 Office: Pub Svc Co Colo 5525 E 38th Ave Denver CO 80207

ANDERSON, CHARLES ROSS, civil engineer; b. N.Y.C., Oct. 4, 1937; s. Biard Eclare and Melva (Smith) A.; m. Susan Breinholt, Aug. 29, 1961; children: Loralee, Brian, Craig, Thomas, David. BSCE, U. Utah, 1961; MBA, Harvard U., 1963. Registered profl. engr.; cert. land surveyor. Owner, operator AAA Engring. and Drafting, Inc., Salt Lake City, 1960—. Mayoral appointee Housing Devel. com., Salt Lake City, 1981-86; bd. dirs., cons. Met. Water Dist., Salt Lake City, 1985—; bd. dirs., v.p., sec. bd. dirs. Utah Mus. Natural History, Salt Lake City, 1980—; asst. dist. commr. Sunrise Dist. Boy Scouts Am., Salt Lake City, 1985-86; fund raising coord. architects and engrs. United Fund; mem. Sunstone Nat. Adv. Bd., 1980—; bd. dirs. Provo River Water Users Assn., 1986—. Fellow Am. Gen. Contractors, Salt Lake City, 1960; recipient Hamilton Watch award, 1961. Mem. ASCE, Am. Congress on Surveying and Mapping, Harvard U. Bus. Sch. Club (pres. 1970-72), Pres. Club U. Utah, U. Utah Alumni Assn. (bd. dirs. 1989—), The Country Club, Bonneville Knife and Fork Club, Rotary (chmn. election com. 1980-81, vice chmn. membership com. 1988-89), Pi Kappa Alpha (internat. pres. 1972-74, trustee endowment fund 1974-80, Oustanding Alumnus 1967, 72), Phi Eta Sigma, Chi Epsilon, Tau Beta Pi. Home: 2689 Comanche Dr Salt Lake City UT 84108 Office: AAA Engring & Drafting Inc 1865 S Main St Salt Lake City UT 84115

ANDERSON, CLIFFORD WARREN, marketing executive; b. San Diego, Mar. 15, 1946; s. Eugene Neu and Ruth Elizabeth (Troch) A.; m. Allison Diane White, Sept., 17, 1973; children: Erin Emily, Briana Elizabeth. BS in Psychology, Aurora Coll., 1968; MA in Psychology, San Diego State U., 1973. Founder San Diego Research Assn., 1972-73; sr. researcher Jagger-Pueschel & Assocs., San Diego, 1973-74, GMA Research, Portland, Oreg., 1974-79; pres. Griggs-Anderson Research, Portland, 1979—. Editor: New Scholar, 1969-73. Mem. Happy Valley Planning Commn. (Oreg.), 1981-82. Mem. Am. Mktg. Assn., Am. Advt. Fedn. Office: Griggs-Anderson Rsch 308 SW 1st Ave Portland OR 97204

ANDERSON, DAVID EDMOND, telecommunications company executive; b. Sioux City, Iowa, Nov. 17, 1926; s. David E. and Ella S. (Geneva) A.; m. Marilyn G. Hoefer, May 28, 1949; children—Susan Sonye, Nancy J. Anderson. B.S.E.E., Iowa State U., 1948. Plant engr. Gen. Telephone Wis., Sun Prairie, 1948, div. mgr., Black River Falls, 1961, chief engr., Sun Prairie, 1965-67, Gen. Telephone Ohio, Marion, 1967-68; v.p. operations Gen. Telephone Ill., Bloomington, 1968-77, pres., 1978-79; v.p. network engring. & constrn. Gen. Telephone Calif., Santa Monica, 1977-78, pres., chief exec. officer, from 1979, now ret. Trustee Santa Monica Hosp., Calif., 1979—; bd. dirs. Barclays Bank Calif., San Francisco, 1983—, Calif. State U. Found., Long Beach, 1982—, Independent Colls. So. Calif., 1982—, Los Angeles United Way, Los Angeles Opera Theatre; chmn. 1982 Hispanic Women's Council awards dinner, Coro Found. awards dinner, 1983, Nat. Hispanic Scholarship Fund annual awards dinner, 1983. Served with USN, 1944-46. Mem. Calif. Roundtable, Nat. Soc. Profl. Engrs., Calif. C. of C. (bd. dirs.), Los Angeles Area C. of C. (bd. dirs., chmn. 1985). Methodist. Office: Gen Telephone Co Calif One GTE Pl Thousand Oaks CA 91362 *

ANDERSON, DAVID GRAHAM, defense company executive, naval engineer; b. Macomb, Ill., Feb. 26, 1943; s. Robert Graham Anderson and Irene Lucy (Hill) Drouin; m. Sharon Lynne Ridley, June 11, 1965; children: Michael, Patrick. BS in Indsl. Mgmt., U. Southern Calif., 1985; MS in Engring., U.S. Naval Postgrad. Sch. Commd. Ensign, USN June, 1965; Commdr. USN 1980. ret. 1986. Commd. officer USN, 1965; ops. officer USS Thomas J. Gary, 1967-69; naval liason to comdg. gen. Field Forces Vietnam, 1969-70; ops. officer USS truxtun, 1973-75; combat systems officer USS Norton Sound, Washington, 1978-80; dir. 3D surveillance systems Naval Sea Systems Command, Washington, 1980-83; dir. systems engring. naval ship weapons systems Engrg. Station, Port Hueneme, Calif., 1983-86. Soccer coach, Springfield (Va.) Youth Club, 1980-84; Am. Youth Soccer Org., Camarillo-Somis Youth Soccer Assn., 1984-86. Decorated Bronze Star medal (Army), Meritorious Svc. medal (USN). Mem. U.S. Naval Inst., Am. Soc. Naval Engrs. (sect. chmn. 1984–, Pres.'s Award,1986). Republican. Episcopalian. Home: 1733 Brentwood Ave Upland CA 91788 Office: Gen Dynamics Co 1675 W Mission Blvd MZ50-50 Pomona CA 91769

ANDERSON, DAVID LEROY, marketing executive; b. Jamestown, N.Y., June 24, 1939; s. Gustav Leroy and Ethel (Harford) A.; m. Delores Ann Hern, July 10, 1958 (div. 1978); children: Marc Wayne, Olivia Marie, Roxanne Marie, Christopher Lee, Clinton Kyle; m. Michele Yvonne Pressfield, June 13, 1981; 1 child, Dustin Andrew. AS in Math., San Jose City Coll, 1966; BA in Psychology, Chapman Coll, 1973; postgrad., U. So. Calif., 1973-75. Math. tech. Lockheed Missiles & Space, Sunnyvale, Calif., 1962-67; aerospace engr. Chrysler Corp., New Orleans, 1967-68, Univac Corp., Vandenberg AFB, Calif., 1968-74; tech. supr. Univac Corp., 1974-80; tech. dir. Sperry Univac Corp., Valencia, Calif., 1980-81; mktg. mgr. Sperry Univac Corp., 1981-84; dir. bus. devel. Infotec Devel., Inc., Costa Mesa, Calif., 1984-87; v.p. bus. devel. Fail-Safe Tech., L.A., 1987-88; pres. Key Group, Inc., Fillmore, Calif., 1988–; bd. dirs. Epsilon Automation, Inc., Sacramento. Mem. Nat. Contract Mgmt. Assn., Armed Forces Communications and Electronics Assn., So. Calif. Aerospace Profls., Profl. Aerospace Contractors Assn. Republican. home: 1947 Grand Ave Fillmore CA 93015 office: Key Group Inc 410 Orchard St Fillmore CA 93015

ANDERSON, DAVID MELVIN, mechanical engineer, educator; b. Berkeley, Calif., July 2, 1944; s. Oscar Melvin and Helen Odessa (Haaland) A.; m. Lin Marie Nelson, Mar. 24, 1973. BS, U. Calif., Berkeley, 1967, MS, 1969, DEng, 1972. Registered mech. and mfg. engr., Calif., mech. and indsl. engr., Oreg. Asst. research engr. U. Calif., Berkeley, 1968-74; design engr. MB Assocs., San Ramon, Calif., 1974; project engr. DiGiorgio Corp., Reno, 1974-77; pres. Anderson Automation, Inc., Pleasanton, Calif., 1977-84; mgr. flexible mfg. Intel Corp., Hillsboro, Oreg., 1984-89; cons. Competitive Mfg., Hillsboro, Oreg., 1989—; adj. prof. U. Portland, Oreg., 1988—; cons. Anderson Automation, Inc., 1977-84. Patentee universal wheelchair, 1973, peach-pitting machine, 1977; contbr. articles to profl. jours. Served to capt. U.S. Army, 1972-75. Mem. Soc. Mfg. Engrs. (sr.), Robotics Internat. (charter), ASME, Calif. Alumni. Republican. Home: PO Box 400 Hillsboro OR 97123 Office: Competitive Mfg PO Box 400 Hillsboro OR 97123

ANDERSON, DEAN HERBERT, publisher; b. L.A., Dec. 18, 1950; s. R. Vernon and Edna (Carter) A.; m. Alison Williams, June 11, 1977. BA, U. Calif., Berkeley, 1976; MPA, Calif. State U., Hayward, 1977. Mgr. Hosp. of Good Samaritan, L.A., 1978-79; adminstr. Torrance Meml. Hosp., 1979-81; pres. COR Rsch., Inc., Santa Barbara, Calif., 1982—. Editor, pub. Hosp. Mgmt. Rev., Santa Barbara, 1982—, Healthcare Mktg. Abstracts, Santa Barbara, 1986—. Mem. Newsletter Assn. Democrat. Office: COR Rsch Inc PO Box 40959 Santa Barbara CA 93140

ANDERSON, DEE, public administrator; b. Fresno, Calif., Dec. 23, 1953; d. Calvin Carroll Coolidge and Gonvella (Parrish) A.; divorced; 1 child, Shakibria Shauntae. BA, U. Wash., 1978, MPA, 1987. Cert. secondary tchr., 1978. Adminstrv. asst. Head Start Program, Seattle, 1981-82; bus. tchr. Renton (Wash.) High Sch., 1983-84; bus. edn. instr. Seattle Cen. Community Coll., 1984-86; grad. teaching asst. U. Wash., Seattle, 1985-87; program specialist Wash. State Office of Minority and Women's Bus. Enterprises, Olympia, 1987-89; exec. dir. Operational Emergency Ctr., Seattle; legis. asst. Seattle City Council, 1984; com. clk. Wash. State Senate. Dep. dir. Mondale-Ferraro Presdl. campaign, Seattle, 1984; mem. Seattle Mcpl. League, 1986; guest speaker, mem. conf. panel polit. action forums; mem. World Affairs Coun., Seattle; bd. dirs. Operational Emergency Ctr., Seattle, 1986, St. Therese Sch.; chmn. Jackson 88 Exploratory Com. Recipient Outstanding Sales Achievement award Northwest Window Service, 1981. Mem. Cen. Area Youth Assn. (bd. dirs. 1982-86, Outstanding Bd. Mem. 1984), Nat. Women's Politic Caucus, Alpha Kappa Alpha. Democrat. Baptist.

ANDERSON, DONALD BERNARD, oil company executive; b. Chgo., Apr. 6, 1919; s. Hugo August and Hilda (Nelson) A.; m. Patricia Gaylord, 1945 (dec. 1978); m. Sarah Midgette, 1980. BS in Mech. Engring, Purdue U., 1942. Vice pres. Hondo Oil & Gas Co. (formerly Malco Refineries, Inc.), Roswell, N.Mex., Hondo Oil & Gas Co. and subs. corps., 1946-63; pres. Anderson Oil Co., Roswell, 1963—; pres. Cotter Corp., 1966-70, chmn. bd., 1966-74; founder, pres. Anderson Drilling Co., Denver, 1974-77; chmn. bd. Anderson Drilling Co., 1977-85. Curator fine arts, mem. acquisitions com. Roswell Mus. and Art Center, 1949-56, trustee, 1956-85, pres. bd., 1960-85, 87—; bd. dirs. Sch. Am. Rsch., Santa Fe, chmn. bd., 1985-88; bd. dirs. Jargon Soc., Penland, N.C.; regent Ea. N.Mex. U., 1966-72; commr. Smithsonian Instn., Nat. Mus. Am. Art, 1980-88. Lt. USNR, 1942-46. Address: PO Box 1 Roswell NM 88201

ANDERSON, DONALD NORTON, JR., retired electrical engineer; b. Chgo., Aug. 15, 1928; s. Donald Norton and Helen Dorothy (Lehmann) A.; B.S., Purdue U., 1950, M.S., 1952. With Hughes Aircraft Co., Culver City and El Segundo, Calif., 1952-84, sect. head, sr. project engr., 1960-65, tech. mgr. Apollo program, 1965-66, mgr. visible systems dept., 1966-69, 70-73, project mgr., 1969-70, mgr. space sensors lab., 1973-79, mgr. space electro-optical systems labs., 1979-80, mgr. space electro-optical systems labs., 1980-84, ret., 1984. Recipient Apollo Achievement award, 1970; Robert J. Collier Landsat award, 1974. Mem. Research Soc. Am., Nat. Speleological Soc., Am. Theatre Organ Soc., Sigma XI (sec. Hughes Labs. br. 1974-75), Eta Kappa Nu, Sierra Club. Home: 2625 Topanga Skyline Dr Topanga CA 90290

ANDERSON, DONALD RAYMOND, computer software company executive; b. Siloam Springs, Ark., June 23, 1938; s. John R. and Margaret U. (Chesney) A.; m. Dixie L. Waxman, May 28, 1961 (div. Apr. 1985); m. Janice S. Witt, Dec. 12, 1987. BS, Okla. State U., 1961; MA, Roosevelt U., 1972; MDiv, McCormick Sem., 1965; postgrad., Met. State Coll., Denver, 1982. Dir. edn. United Presbyn. Ch., South Bend, Ind., 1965-68; health educator Ind. Alcoholism Div., Gary, Ind., 1968-72; minister United Presbyn. Ch., Dix, Bushnell, Nebr., 1976-80, Strasburg, Colo., 1980-82; programmer, analyst Industry Media, Inc., Denver, 1982-84; project leader Computer Data Systems, Inc., Lakewood, Colo., 1984-85, SASC Svcs., Lakewood, 1985-87; pres. Micro Computer Cons. Inc., Denver, 1986—. Mem. Data Processing Mgmt. Assn. (newsletter staff), Colo. Assn. Computer Cons. (editor jour. 1988—), Centennial C. of C., Toastmasters (v.p. 1988—). Home: 585 Troy St Aurora CO 80011 Office: Micro Computer Cons 2305 S Syracuse Way #212 Aurora CO 80231

ANDERSON, DOROTHY FISHER, social worker, psychotherapist; b. Funchal, Madeira, May 31, 1924; d. Lewis Mann Anker and Edna (Gilbert) Fisher (adoptive father David Henry Fisher); m. Theodore W. Anderson, July 8, 1950; children: Robert Lewis, Janet Anderson Yang, Jeanne Elizabeth. BA, Queens Coll., Flushing, N.Y., 1945; AM, U. Chgo., 1947. Diplomate Am. Bd. Examiners in Clin. Social Work; lic. clin. social worker, Calif.; registered cert. social worker, N.Y.;. Intern Cook County (Ill.) Bur. Pub. Welfare, Chgo., 1945-46, Ill. Neuropsychiat. Inst., Chgo., 1946; clin. caseworker, Neurol. Inst. Presbyn. Hosp., N.Y.C., 1947; therapist, Mental Hygiene Clinic VA, N.Y.C., 1947-50; therapist, Child Guidance Clinic Pub. Elem. Sch. 42, N.Y.C., 1950-53; social worker, counselor Cedarhurst (N.Y.) Family Service Agy., 1954-55; psychotherapist, counselor Family Service of the Midpeninsula, Palo Alto, Calif., 1971-73, 79-86, George Hexter, M.D., Inc., 1972-83; clin. social worker Tavistock Clinic, London, 1974-75, El Camino Hosp., Mountain View, Calif., 1979; pvt. practice clin. social work 1978—; cons. Human Resource Services, Sunnyvale, Calif., 1981-86. Hannah G. Solomon scholar U. Chgo., 1945-46; Commonwealth fellow U. Chgo., 1946-47. Fellow Soc. Clin. Social Work (Continuing Edn. Recognition award 1980-83); mem. Nat. Assn. Social Workers (diplomate in clin. social work).

ANDERSON, E(MILE) PHILIP, engineer; b. Denver, Mar. 6, 1953; s. Emile Philip and Betty June (Reynolds) A.; 1 child, Bryan. BA in Chemistry and Math., Met. State Coll., 1980; postgrad., U. Colo., 1984-86, City U., 1988—. Instr. physics and laser tech. Met. State Coll., Denver, 1983-84, Denver Inst. Tech., 1984-86; physics engr. Hughes Aircraft Co., Manhattan Beach, Calif., 1986—. Co. chmn. United Way, Denver, 1985. Mem. Alpha Beta Kappa. Office: 33118 1st Pl SW Federal Way WA 98023

ANDERSON, EMMETT RAYMOND, electronics executive; b. Tacoma, Wash., May 16, 1931; s. Frederick Alvin and Winifred Victoria (Knightlinger) A.; m. Patricia Ann Myers, Feb. 1, 1957 (div. Feb. 1973); children: Gale Ann, Rhonda Rae Anderson Benjamin; m. Theresa M. Bohannon, Nov. 10, 1985. BSEE, U. Wash., 1955. Registered profl. engr., Calif. Application engr. RCA, Harrison, N.J., 1955-57; field engr. Westinghouse Electric, Seattle, 1957-60; project engr. Temercal Metall., Berkeley, Calif., 1960-61; chief elec. engr. Temescal Metall., Berkeley, Calif., 1961-65; v.p. elec. products Temercal Metall., Berkeley, Calif., 1965-70; v.p. Applied Materials, Santa Clara, Calif., 1970-77; pres. Eratron, Inc., Campbell, Calif., 1977-87; v.p. Innotec Group, Inc., Campbell, 1987—. Patentee in field. With USAF, 1951-52, USNR. Mem. IEEE. Republican. Home: 26010 Highland Way Los Gatos CA 95030 Office: Innotec Group Inc 504 E Vandell Way Campbell CA 95030

ANDERSON, ERIC EDWARD, psychologist; b. Mpls., Jan. 24, 1951; s. Charles Eric and Elizabeth Blanche (Engstrand) A.; m. Florence Kaye Anderson, June 18, 1978; children: Cara Elizabeth, Evan Travis. BA summa cum laude, U. Minn., 1973; MA, Fuller Theol. Sem., 1977, PhD in Clin. Psychology, 1978. Lic. cons. psychologist, Minn.; lic. psychologist, Calif.; community coll. teaching credential in psychology and philosophy, Calif. Postdoctoral intern U. Minn., Mpls., 1978-79, asst. prof., coord. tng. in aging, 1979-83; group v.p. Kiel Profl. Svcs., Inc., St. Paul, 1983-84; pres. Primary Mental Health Care, Inc., Bloomington, Minn., 1984-86; sr. v.p. Treatment Ctrs. Am., Inc., Pasadena, Calif., 1986-88, LifeLink, Inc., Laguna Hills, Calif., 1988-89; chief operating officer LifeLink, Inc., Laguna Hills, 1989—; cons. Ebenezer Soc., Mpls., 1979-82, Wilder Found., St. Paul, 1981-84; rsch. advisor Walden U., Mpls., 1982—; assoc. prof. Sch. Psychology, Fuller Theol. Sem., Pasadena, 1989. Contbr. articles to profl. jours. Mem. Am. Psychol. Assn. (div. mktg. com., conf. participant 1981), Soc. Psychologists in Mgmt., Calif. Psychol. Assn. Home: 30491 Via Lindosa Laguna Niguel CA 92677 Office: LifeLine Inc Mill Creek Rd Laguna Hills CA 92045

ANDERSON, GEORGE EDWARD, financial services company executive; b. Denver, Nov. 24, 1938; s. George Francis and Bernice Rose (Tartaglio) A.; m. Patricia Maxine Martinez, Dec. 6, 1957; children: Gregory George, Annette Marie. Student, Southwestern Coll., Chula Vista, Calif., 1969-73. Area v.p. Transam. Fin. Svcs., L.A., 1958-77; gen. mgr. La Mesa Recreational Products, Westminster, Calif., 1977-81; v.p. O'Rielly Recreational Products, Tucson, 1981-84; pres., chief exec. officer 1st Interstate Fin. Svcs., San Diego, 1984—. Pres. Tempe Jaycees, 1971-76; mem. Nice Guys, Inc., San Diego, 1988. Mem. Am. Fin. Svcs. Assn. (bd. dirs. 1988—), Nat. Second Mortgage Assn., Calif. Fin. Svcs. Assn. (bd. dirs. 1985—), San Diego C. of C., Hon. Dep. Sheriffs Assn. (capt. San Diego), Jaycees Internat. Senate (life), Harbor Island Yacht Club. Republican. Lutheran. Office: 1st Interstate Fin Svcs 401 West A St Ste 1900 San Diego CA 92101

ANDERSON, GERALD VERNE, aerospace company executive; b. Long Beach, Calif., Oct. 25, 1931; s. Gordon Valentine and Aletha Marian (Parkins) A.; m. Helen Jean Harman, May 7, 1954; children: Lori Jean Anderson Fronk, Gregory Verne, David Harman, Lynn Elain Anderson Lee, Brian Earl, Michael Gordon. AA, Long Beach City Coll., 1952; BS, U. Calif., Berkeley, 1958. Registered profl. engr., Calif. Tech. specialist N. Am. Aviation Co., L.A., 1958-65; tech. specialist McDonnell Douglas Astronautics, Huntington Beach, Calif., 1965-84; mgr. McDonnell Douglas Astronautics, Huntington Beach, 1984-87; sr. mgr. Mcdonnell Douglas Space Systems Co., Huntington Beach, 1987—; cons. Mitsubishi Heavy Industries, Nagoya, Japan, 1972-73, Aeritalia, Turin, Italy, 1975-76. Patentee, portable vacuum chamber, electron beam welding device. Mem. Westminster (Calif.) Planning Com., 1974, Huntington Beach Citizens Adv. Com., 1975, Westminster Bicentennial Com, 1976. Master sgt. U.S. Army, 1952-58. Mem. Soc. Mfg. Engrs., Soc. Automotive Engrs., Aerospace Industries Assn., AIAA. Republican. Mormon. Home: 13401 Lee Dr Westminster CA 92683 Office: McDonnell Douglas Space Systems Co 5301 Bolsa Ave Huntington Beach CA 92647

ANDERSON, GERALD WILLIAM, educational business administrator, computer programmer; b. Lake Norden, S.D., Mar. 20, 1934; s. William Gustav and Evelyn S. (Engberg) A.; m. Laurel Allen Higinbotham, Nov. 26, 1960; children: Debra Lynn, Gerald William Jr., Mark Allen. AA, North Park Coll., 1955; BBA, U. Minn., 1957; MBA, U. Wash., 1959. Fin. supr. The Boeing Co., Seattle, 1957-69; controller Marvin Windows Co., Warroad, Minn., 1969-78; bus. mgr. Hot Springs County Sch. Dist. 1, Thermopolis, Wyo., 1978—. Republican. Mem. Covenant Ch. Home: Lucerne RT Box 45B Thermopolis WY 82443 Office: Hot Springs County Sch Dist 1 415 Springview Thermopolis WY 82443

ANDERSON, GLENN MALCOLM, congressman; b. Los Angeles; m. Lee Dutton; children: Melinda (Mrs. Michael Keenan), Evan, Glenn Michael. BA, UCLA. Mayor City of Hawthorne, Calif., 1940-43; mem. Calif. Assembly from South Bay Area, Los Angeles, 1943-51; lt. gov. State of Calif., 1958-67; mem. 91st-101st Congresses from 32d dist. Calif., 1969—; chmn. pub. works and transp. com., chmn. State Lands Commn. 1959-67; past mem. Commn. Califs., Calif. Council Urban Growth; past chmn. Calif. Interstate Cooperation Commn. Hon. life mem. PTA.; Regent U. Calif., 1959-67. Served with AUS, World War II. Mem. Secondary Sch. Adminstrs. Assn., Am. Legion, DAV, Amvets, Native Sons Golden West, Redmen, Hawthorne C. of C. Democrat. Clubs: Elks, Kiwanis. Office: 2329 Rayburn House Office Bldg Washington DC 20515

ANDERSON, GORDON MACKENZIE, petroleum service contractors executive; b. Los Angeles, Mar. 25, 1932; s. Kenneth C.M. and Edith (King) A.; m. Elizabeth Ann Pugh, Mar. 21, 1959; children: Michael James, Greg Mark, Jeffrey Stevens. AA, Glendale Coll., 1951; BSME, U. So. Calif., 1954; grad., Officers Candidate Sch., Newport, R.I., 1955; student, various Navy Schs. including CIC Sch. Mgr. Santa Fe Drilling Co., Chile, 1960-63, Libya, 1963-67; mgr. contracts adminstrn. Santa Fe Drilling Co., Calif., 1967-70; pres. Santa Fe Drilling Co., Orange, Calif., 1970-80, 87—; sr. v.p. Santa Fe Internat. Corp., Alhambra, Calif., 1974-80, pres., chief operating officer, 1980-87, exec. v.p., 1987—; also dir.; bd. dirs. Baker Internat., Orange. Mem. adv. bd. U. So. Calif. Sch. Engring.; bd. dirs. St. Jude Hosp., Fullerton, Calif. Served to lt. (j.g.) USN, 1955-58. Mem. Young Pres.'s Orgn. (chmn. 1978-79), Internat. Assn. Oilwell Drilling Contractors. Office: Santa Fe Drilling Co 100 S Fremont Ave Box 4000 Alhambra CA 91802 *

ANDERSON, GORDON SUTHERLAND, periodontist; b. Chgo., Dec. 19, 1934; s. Donald Sutherland and Elsie Florence (Ferguson) A.; m. Marilynn LaVance Holm, Sept. 26, 1964; children: Lindsey Paige, Tracey Elisabeth. Student, Wheaton Coll., Ill., 1952-55; DDS, Northwestern U., Chgo., 1959; MSD, U. Wash., 1964. Pvt. practice peridontics San Mateo, Calif., 1964-82, Grants Pass, Oreg., 1983—. Pres. Grants Pass City Council, 1988-89. Lt. USN, 1959-69. Mem. We. Soc. Peridontology (sec. 1975-77), Am. Dental Assn., Oreg. Dental Assn., Am. Acad. Peridontology, Oreg. Soc. Peridontists, Rogue Valley Dental Soc., Rotary. Republican. Office: 1201E NE 7th St Grants Pass OR 97526

ANDERSON, GREGORY STEPHEN, investment company executive; b. Evanston, Wyo., Sept. 9, 1956; s. M. Woodruff and Ethel (Cowley) A. BS, Ariz. State U., 1979. Asst. v.p. 1st Interstate Bank, Phoenix, 1979-83, v.p., 1983-85; gen. mgr., ptnr. El Dorado Investment Co., Phoenix, 1985—; spl. ltd. ptnr. El Dorado Ventures, Pasadena, Calif., 1984—; bd. dirs. Sun Ven Ptnrs. I & II, Phoenix, 1985—, Dominion Ventures, San Francisco, 1986—; v.p., bd. dirs. Sundance Capital Corp., Menlo Park, Calif., 1988—; gen. ptnr. Sundance Venture Ptnrs., Menlo Park, 1988—; bd. dirs. Personics Corp., Regency Med., Inc., HML Med. Inc., O.P. Club Inc., Phoenix Suns, Gateway Data Scis., D&D Farms, Inc., Spectrascan, Inc., NuclearAssurance Corp., Domestic Automation Co., Alan Weston Pub. Co. Pres., bd. dirs. Pi Kappa Alpha House Corp., Tempe, Ariz., 1983-86; treas., chief fin. officer John McCain for U.S. Senator Campaign, Phoenix, 1984-87; mem. alumni bd. Ariz. State U., 1985-86; bd. dirs. Stanford U., 1988—. Mem. Nat. Assn. Venture Capitalists, NBA Club. Republican. Office: El Dorado Investment Co 2828 N Capital Ave 1275 Phoenix AZ 85004

ANDERSON, HAROLD PAUL, historian, archivist, bank executive; b. Darby, Pa., Oct. 4, 1946; s. Harold P. and Mary Ann A.; B.A., Villanova U., 1968; M.A., Ohio State U., 1969, Ph.D., 1978. Teaching and research fellow Stanford U., 1973-75; archives and library specialist Hoover Instn., Stanford, Calif., 1975-77; asst. archivist dept. history Wells Fargo Bank, N.A., San Francisco, 1977-79, pub. relations officer and corp. archivist dept. history, 1979, asst. v.p. and corp. archivist dept. history, 1979—, v.p. dept. history, 1984—; lectr. Stanford U., 1981; bd. dirs. Nat. Council on Pub. History, 1981-83. Mem. Am. Hist. Assn., Orgn. Am. Historians, Soc. Am. Archivists. Office: Wells Fargo Bank 420 Montgomery St San Francisco CA 94163

ANDERSON, HERSCHEL VINCENT, librarian; b. Charlotte, N.C., Mar. 14, 1932; s. Paul Kemper and Lillian (Johnson) A. B.A., Duke U., 1954; M.S., Columbia U., 1959. Library asst. Bklyn. Public Library, 1954-59; asst. bookmobile librarian King County Public Library, Seattle, 1959-62; asst. librarian Longview (Wash.) Public Library, 1962-63; librarian N.C. Mus. Art, Raleigh, 1963-64; audio-visual cons. N.C. State Library, Raleigh, 1964-68; dir. Sandhill Regional Library, Rockingham, N.C., 1968-70; asso. state librarian Tenn. State Library and Archives, Nashville, 1970-72; unit dir. Colo. State Library, Denver, 1972-73; state librarian S.D. State Library, Pierre, 1973-80; dir. Mesa (Ariz.) Public Library, 1980—; dir. Bibliographical Center for Research, Denver, 1974-80, v.p., 1977; mem. Western Council State Libraries, 1975-80, v.p., 1978, pres., 1979; mem. Ariz. State Library Adv. Council, 1981-84, pres., 1982-83; mem. library technician tng. adv. com. Mesa Community Coll., 1982-85; chmn. Serials On-Line in Ariz. Consortia, 1985-86. Jr. warden St. Mark's Episcopal Ch., Mesa, 1985-87, vestryman 1987-90; mem. Maricopa County Libr. Coun., 1981—, treas. 1981—, pres. 1983; bd. dirs. East Valley Rep. Forum, 1989—. Served with AUS, 1955-57. Recipient Emeritus Honors Ariz. Library Friends, 1987. Mem. ALA, S.D. Libr. Assn. (Libr. of Yr. 1977, hon. life 1980), Mountain Plains Libr. Assn. (pres. 1974, dir. 1974-77, 86-87), Ariz. State Libr. Assn. (exec. com. 1986-87), Chief Officers of State Libr. Agys. (dir. 1974-76), Kiwanis (dir. Mesa Club 1981-86, v.p. 1983, pres. 1985-86), Phi Kappa Psi. Office: Mesa Pub Libr 64 E 1st St Mesa AZ 85201-0904

ANDERSON, JACK JOE, communications executive; b. Lipan, Tex., Oct. 22, 1928; s. William Amon and Tommie Lucille (Roberts) A.; B.A., San Jose State U., 1965, M.A., 1967; postgrad. in bus. adminstrn. Pepperdine U., Los Angeles; m. Maria I. Kamantauskas, Mar. 13, 1976; children—Mark, Douglas, Craig. Asst. mgr. edn. systems Lockheed Missiles & Space Co., Sunnyvale, Calif., 1966-69; v.p. Learning Achievement Corp., San Jose, Calif., 1969-74; mgr. instrnl. systems Ford Aerospace & Communications Corp., Pasadena, Calif., 1974-83; pres. Anderson & Assocs., Alta Loma, Calif., 1983—; cons. tng. programs and systems, 1969-74. Served with USAF, 1946-66. Recipient Nat. award for tng. program design Indsl. TV Assn., 1974. Mem. Am. Mgmt. Assn., Am. Soc. Tng. and Devel. Contbr. tech. and gen. instrnl. materials in field. Office: Anderson & Assocs 9155 Carrari Ct Alta Loma CA 91701

ANDERSON, JACK WAYNE, marine science researcher, administrator; b. San Diego, Mar. 15, 1938; s. Neil S. Anderson and Ethel (Wills) Archer; m. Marilyn Sue Wallace, Sept. 1964 (div. 1974); m. Mary Linda McLain, Feb. 19, 1978; children: Amanda Lynn, Jacquelyn Lindsey. AA, El Camino Coll., 1960; BA, Calif. State U., Long Beach, 1964, MA, 1966; PhD, U. Calif., Irvine, 1969. Asst. prof. Tex. A&M U., College Station, 1969-74, assoc. prof., 1974-76; sr. research scientist Battelle Northwest Lab., Sequim, Wash., 1976-83, assoc. mgr. Marine Research Lab., 1983-85; dir. So. Calif. Coastal Water Research Project, Long Beach, 1985—; cons. EXXON Prodn. Research Co., Houston, 1973-76; chmn. com. biol. effects program NSF/IDOE, 1974-75; mem. 5 man NOAA adv. com. on Amoco Cadiz oil spill, 1978-81; mem. sci. adv. com. U.S. Sec. of Interior, 1979-81. Author 5 books on marine science; founding co-editor Marine Environ. Research, 1978-80; contbr. over 80 articles to profl. jours. Grantee Am. Petroleum Inst., U.S. Dept. Energy, Sea Grant, NSF, 1974-76. Mem. Am. Soc. Zoologists, AAAS, Western Soc. Naturalists, So. Calif. Acad. Scis., Sigma Xi. Office: So Calif Coastal Water Rsch Project Authority 646 W Pacific Coast Hwy Long Beach CA 90806 *

ANDERSON, JAMES MARTIN, investment banker; b. Denver, May 15, 1947; s. Raymond Roy and Helen Fern (Martin) A.; m. Cynthia Louise Hamilton, Sept. 12, 1970; children: Thomas H., Joseph M. Student, U. Calif., San Francisco, 1965-67; BSBA, U. Denver, 1969. Sr. v.p. Hanifen Imhoff, Inc., Denver, 1971-79; pres. Anderson DeMonbrun, Inc., Denver, 1979-84; mng. dir. Prudential-Bache Capital, Denver, 1984—; allied mem. N.Y. Stock Exchange, 1976—. Author: Increasing Public Finance Market Share, 1985. Democratic candidate for Arapahoe County Treasurer, 1970; dist. capt. Arapahoe County Dem. Com., 1971-72. Mem. Nat. Assn. Securities Dealers (gen. securities and fin. operating prin.), Colo. Mcpl. Bond Dealers Assn. (bd. dirs. 1977-80), Village Club (bd. dirs. Cherry Hills, Colo. chpt. 1983-85). Office: Prudential-Bache Capital 370 17th St 39th Fl Denver CO 80202

ANDERSON, JAMES MICHAEL, editor; b. Milw., July 22, 1944; s. Arvid Walter and Valberg Lucille (Mickelson) A.; m. Marilyn Kay Alexander, Aug. 25, 1973; 1 child, David James. BA, U. Colo., 1976. Editor Petroleum Info. Corp., Littleton, Colo., 1976—. With U.S. Army, 1965-69. Office: Petroleum Info Corp 4100 E Dry Creek Rd Littleton CO 80122

ANDERSON, JANE SMITH, language professional; b. Dallas, May 12, 1941; d. Richard Elbert and Marie (Overton) Smith; m. William Walt Anderson, July 31, 1965; children: Carson Rebecca, Douglas Walt. BS, U. Tex., 1963. Home econ. Nat. Cotton Coun., Memphis, 1963-65; mgr. Shop of John Simmons, Memphis, 1965-68; mgr. silver, china and gifts Broadway Stores, Phoenix, 1968; tchr. Peoria (Ariz.) Pub. Schs., 1968-69; pvt. practice lang. Manila, 1975-80; pvt. practice acad. lang. therapist Honolulu, 1984—. Mem. Orton Dyslexia Soc. Home: 2658 Hillside Ave Honolulu HI 96822

ANDERSON, JANET ALM, librarian; b. Lafayette, Ind., Dec. 20, 1952; d. Charles Henry and Lenore Elaine Alm; m. Jay Allan Anderson, May 21, 1983. BS, Bemidji State U., 1975; MA, Western Ky. U., 1981, MLS, 1982. Cert. elem. tchr., sch. libr. and media specialist. Storyteller, puppeteer North Country Arts Coun., Bemidji, Minn., 1975-76; head children's libr. Bemidji State U., 1976-77; middle sch. libr. Custer County Sch. Dist., Miles City, Minn.; tchr. for gifted & talented Custer County Sch. Dist., Miles City, 1979-80; folklore archivist Western Ky. U., Bowling Green, 1981-83; head children's and young adults' svcs. Bowling Green Pub. Libr., 1983-85; head of serials Utah State U., Logan, 1986—; adj. instr. Miles (Mont.) Community Coll., 1978-80; cons. to variety of Am. outdoor mus.; speaker Utah Endowment for the Humanities Speakers' Bur., Salt Lake City, 1987—. Author: Old Fred, 1972, A Taste of Kentucky, 1986, Ky. State Book Fair award; author:(with others) Advances in Serials Management, Vol. 3, 1989; contbr. entries to Encyclopedia of Am. Popular Beliefs and Superstitions, articles on foklore to mags. and periodicals; delivered radio and tv presentations on folklore, one nat. network and various local stations. Co-founder and past pres. Rosebud chpt. Nat. Audubon Soc., Miles, Mont., 1978-80. Recipient Exhibit and Program Grant Nat. Endowment for the Arts, Bowling Green, Ky., 1984-85. Mem. Am. Libr. Assn., Utah Libr. Assn., North Am. Serials Interest Group, Mt.-Plains Libr. Assn., Consortium of Utah Women in Higher Edn., Bridgerland Bus. and Profl. Women (bd. dirs., pub. chmn. Logan Utah chpt. 1986—), Ky. Coun. on Archives, Am. Folklore Soc., Utah Folklore Soc., Assn. of Living Hist. Farms and Agr. Mus. Democrat. Lutheran. Home: 1090 S 400 E Providence UT 84332 Office: Merrill Libr Utah State U Logan UT 84322-3000

ANDERSON, JEAN ELLEN, illustrator, corporate executive; b. Long Beach, Calif., Mar. 23, 1945; d. Jacob John and Phyllis Fern (Tamborello) Montgomery; m. Robert A. Anderson, Dec. 17, 1971; children: Tiffany Rose, Alison Grace. Student, San Francisco State Coll., Calif. State U., Northridge; BA, Calif. State U., Long Beach, 1970. Sec., editor, co-owner Stretching, Inc., Palmer Lake, Colo., 1971—. Illustrator, editor: Stretching, 1975, (with Lloyd Kahn) rev., 1980. Home: PO Box 767 Palmer Lake CO 80133 Office: Stretching Inc PO Box 767 Palmer Lake CO 80133

ANDERSON, JONPATRICK SCHUYLER, minister, financial consultant; b. Chgo., July 20, 1951; s. Ralph Anderson and Helena Hilda (Robinson) Hardy; children: André, Mary, David. AA, L.A. Trade and Tech. Coll., 1978; BA, UCLA, 1979; postgrad., SUNY, Albany, 1983, Govs. State U., 1985; MRE, DMin., Internat. Bible Inst. and Sem., 1989. Clerical supr. U.S. VA, L.A., 1976-80; fin. adminstr. Antioch Primitive Bapt. Ch., L.A., 1979-80; pres., exec. dir. All-Around Prodns., L.A., 1980-83; assoc. minister St. Stephen Ch., San Diego, Calif., 1983-87; stadium mgr. San Diego Jack Murphy Stadium, 1985-87; exec. dir. Christ-Immanuel Ministerial Assn., San Diego, 1983—; pvt. practice mgmt. cons., cons. comptroller, San Diego, 1981-82; cons. writer All-Around Music div. Broadcast Music, Inc., San Diego, 1980—. Mem. Am. Freedom Coalition, Washington, 1988, Causa, USA, Washington, 1985-87. With USAR, 1979-80. Grammy nominee NARAS, 1980; recipient Personal award former Pres. Ronald Reagan, L.A., 1988. Mem. Assn. MBA Execs. (Bus. award 1980), UCLA Alumni Assn. (life), Res. Officers Assn. of the U.S. (life). Democrat. Mem. Ch. of God. Office: Christ-Immanuel Ministries PO Box 1202 San Diego CA 92112

ANDERSON, KARL RICHARD, aerospace engineer, consultant; b. Vinita, Okla., Sept. 27, 1917; s. Axel Richard and Hildred Audrey (Marshall) A.; B.S., Calif. Western U., 1964, M.A., 1966; Ph.D., U.S. Internat. U., 1970; m. Jane Shigeko Hiratsuka, June 20, 1953; 1 son, Karl Richard. Engr. personnel subsystems Atlas Missile Program, Gen. Dynamics, San Diego, 1960-63; design engr. Solar div. Internat. Harvester, San Diego, 1964-66, sr. design engr., 1967-69, project engr., 1970-74, product safety specialist, 1975-78; aerospace engring. cons., 1979-86; cons. engring., 1979—; lectr. Am. Indian Sci. and Engring. Soc. Served to maj. USAF, 1936-60. Recipient Spl. Commendation San Diego County Bd. Supervisors, 1985, Spl. Commendation San Diego City Council, 1985. Registered profl. engr., Calif. Republican. Episcopalian. Home: 5886 Scripps St San Diego CA 92122

ANDERSON, KATHLEEN G., paralegal, arbitrator, educator; b. Cin., July 27, 1950; d. Harold B. and Trudi L. (Chambers) Briggs; m. J.R. Carr, July 4, 1988; 1 child, Jesse J. Anderson. Student, U. Cin., 1971-72, Antioch Coll., 1973-74; cert., Nat. Jud. Coll., U. Nev., Reno, 1987; grad., Inst. Applied Law, 1987. Paralegal Lauer & Lauer, Santa Fe, 1976-79, Wilkinson, Cragun & Barker, Anchorage, 1981-82; employment law paralegal specialist Hughes, Thorsness, Gantz, Powell & Brundin, Anchorage, 1983—; mem. faculty, Nat. Jud. Coll., U. Nev., Reno, 1988—; adj. prof. U. Alaska, Anchorage, 1985—, Charter Coll., Anchorage, 1986—; arbitrator/mediator, The Arbitration Group, Anchorage, 1987—. Author, editor: Professional Responsibility Handbook for Legal Assistants and Paralegals, 1986; contbr. articles to profl. jours. Lectr. Boy Scouts Am., Anchorage council, 1985—, Alaska Bar Assn., 1989—, NLRB, Anchorage, 1986, Alaska Assn. Bus. and Profl. Women, 1988—. Mem. Alaska Assn. Legal Assts. (pres. 1988—, chmn. ethics com. 1985—), Nat. Fedn. Paralegal Assn. (edn. task force coord. 1988-89, adminstrn. v.p. 1984—), Am. Soc. Personnel Adminstrn., Anchorage Personnel Assn., Alternative Dispute Resolution Assn. of Alaska, Am. Assn. for Paralegal Edn., Legal Asst. Mgmt. Assn. Home: PO Box 100098 Anchorage AK 99510 Office: Hughes Thorsness Gantz Powell & Brundin 509 W 3d Ave Anchorage AK 99501

ANDERSON, KELLY ELIZABETH, marketing professional; b. Oakland, Calif., June 7, 1957; d. Frank Stoakes Anderson and Emily Elizabeth (Wright) Kimlinger. BA in Math., BA in Environ. Studies, U. Calif., Santa Cruz, 1979, BA in Sci. Communications, 1980. Staff writer Charlotte (N.C.) Observer, 1980; sci. writer, editor Frank Porter Graham Child Devel Ctr., U. N.C., Chapel Hill, 1980-81; coordinator communications Sea Grant Coll. Program, U. Calif., San Diego, 1981-84; mgr. tech. publs. Loral Instrumentation, San Diego, 1984-87, mgr. mktg. communications, 1987—; acting dir. tech. services, Loral Instrumentation, San Diego, 1986. Contbr. more than 200 articles to profl. jours. Mem. Desktop Pub. Adv. Com. Grossmont Coll., San Diego, 1986—. AAAS fellow, 1980; recipient Excellence in Writing award Internat. Assn. Bus. Communicators, 1981, Council for Advancement and Support of Edn., 1984. Mem. Nat. Mgmt. Assn. (v.p. 1986), Soc. for Tech. Communication (awards of Excellence and Achievement 1981-84), Computer and Electronics Mktg. Assn. (officer 1987—). Office: Loral Instrumentation 8401 Aero Dr San Diego CA 92123

ANDERSON, KENNETH CHARLES, data processing executive; b. San Francisco, July 17, 1947; s. Delbert Clarence and Vera Virginia (Asaro) A. BA, U. Calif., Berkeley, 1970. Programmer/analyst Glen Slaughter and Assocs., Oakland, Calif., 1976-85, 86—; systems analyst 1st Nationwide Bank, Daly City, Calif., 1985-86. Contbr. to American Poetry Anthology, Vol. VIII, No. 3, 1989, Best New Poets of 1988, 1989. Home: 58 Belcher St San Francisco CA 94114 Office: Glen Slaughter and Assocs 1999 Harrison St #500 Oakland CA 94612

ANDERSON, KEVIN BRUCE, public relations executive; b. San Francisco, Aug. 5, 1955; s. Ralph W. and Florence A. (Speaker) A.; 1 child, Kevin B. II. BA in Polit. Sci., San Francisco State U., 1979, postgrad., 1981. Legal researcher, analyst San Francisco Dist. Atty.'s Office, 1979; interim instr. San Francisco Unified Sch. Dist., 1979; student loan analyst HEW, San Francisco, 1979-80; equipment controller, customer relations coordinator Xerox, San Francisco, 1980-83, mgmt. trainee, 1983-84, customer svc./billing mgr., 1984-85; fin. and credit mgr. Xerox, Oakland, Calif., 1985-86, pub. relations and devel. mgr., 1986; govt. relations mgr., pub. relations Xerox, San Francisco, 1986-89; area dir. No. Calif. United Negro Coll. Fund, San Francisco, 1989—. Editor, producer, writer video prodns.; host TV ednl. program Educational Highlights, 1984. Bd. dirs. Directions, Jobs for Youth, 1987, Project Interface, 1986-87, Stepping Stones Growth Ctr., 1984-85, Save San Francisco High Sch. Sports, 1988; advisor Jr. Achievement, San Francisco, 1985-86; press coordinator San Francisco campaign Dukakis for Pres., 1988; bus. com. vol. Dem. Nat. Convention, San Francisco, 1984; mem. steering com. Bradley for Gov. campaign, Alameda County, 1982. Recipient Meritorious Svc. award United Negro Coll. Fund, 1987, Outstanding Svc. award Project Interface, 1987; named to Outstanding Young Men Am., 1985-87. Mem. Bay Area Black Profl. Employees Xerox (treas. 1985-87). Baptist. Home: 300 Vernon #34 Oakland CA 94610

ANDERSON, LOUISE STOUT, crime analyst; b. Wellsville, N.Y., Aug. 11, 1952; d. Carlton C. and Mary (Gasdik) Stout; m. Leonard M. Anderson, June 2, 1973. BA in German Lit., Polit. Sci., Mt. Holyoke Coll., 1974; MA in Polit. Sci., San Diego State U., 1977. Cert. community coll. tchr., Calif. Statistician Grossmont Coll., El Cajon, Calif., 1976-78; crime analyst San Diego Police Dept., 1978-80; crime analyst Career Criminal Apprehension Program, Marin County Sheriff's Office, San Rafael, Calif., 1980-83; crime analyst CCAP Unit, Sonoma County Sheriff's Office, Santa Rosa, Calif., 1983-85; mgr. mktg. svcs. Command Data Systems, Dublin, Calif., 1985-87, client svcs. mgr., 1988—; cons. Search Group Inc. for Automated Crime Analysis. Contbr. articles in field. Mem. Antioch Police Commn.; alumna recruiter Mt. Holyoke Club No. Calif., 1981—. Named Outstanding Young Woman of Am., 1986. Mem. Am. Polit. Sci. Assn., Assn. Police Planners Research Officers, Calif. Women in Govt., Nat. Assn. Criminal Justice Stats. Assn. Office: Command Data Systems 6250 Village Pkwy Dublin CA 94568

ANDERSON, MARILYN NELLE, teacher; b. Las Animas, Colo., May 5, 1942; d. Mason Hadley Moore and Alice Carrie (Dwyer) Coates; m. George Robert Anderson, Sept. 4, 1974; children: Lisa Lynn, Edward Alan, Justin Patrick. BEd magna cum laude, Adams State Coll., 1962, postgrad., 1965; MEd, Ariz. State U., 1967; postgrad., Idaho State U., 1971, 86. Cert. elem. tchr., K-12 sch. counselor. Tchr. Wendell (Idaho) Sch. Dist. 232, 1962-66; Union-Endicott (N.Y.) Sch. Dist., 1967-68; counselor, librarian West Yuma (Colo.) Sch. Dist., 1968-69; elem. sch. counselor Am. Falls (Idaho) Sch. Dist. 381, 1969-73; project dir. Gooding County (Idaho) Sr. Citizens Orgn., 1974-75; tchr. Castleford (Idaho) Sch. Dist. 417, 1982—; mem. Castleford Schs. Merit Pay Devel. program, 1983-84, Accreditation Evaluation com., 1984-85, Math. Curriculum Devel. com., 1985-86. Leader Brownie Scouts, Endicott, 1967-68; chmn. fundraising com. Am. Falls Kindergarten, 1971-73; leader Gooding County 4-H Council, Wendell, 1983—. Recipient Leader's award Nat. 4-H Conservation Natural Resources Program, 1984. Mem. NEA, Idaho Edn. Assn., Idaho Council Internat. Reading Assn., Magic Valley Reading Assn., Internat. Platform Assn., Castleford Parent-Tchr. Youth Orgn., Castleford Tchr.'s Orgn. (sec.-treas. 1984-86). Republican. Baptist. Home: Rte 1 Box 293 Wendell ID 83355 Office: Castleford Schs Castleford ID 83355

ANDERSON, MARK ROBERT, data processing executive, biochemist; b. Oak Park, Ill., Aug. 11, 1951; s. Robert Hugo and Marilyn Pettee (Johnson) A.; m. Mary Jane Helsell, June 6, 1980; 1 child, Berit Bracken. BS, Stanford U., 1972; MS, Stanford U., Hopkins Marine Sta., 1973; postgrad., U. Brit. Columbia, Vancouver, 1973. Publisher Potlatch Press, Friday Harbor, Wash., 1974-77; assoc. prof. Western Wash. U., Bellingham, 1977, Harvard U., Boston, 1978; chief scientist Ocean Research & End. Soc., Boston, 1978; v.p. Moclips Cetological Soc., Friday Harbor, 1979-81; founder, dir. The Whale Mus., Friday Harbor, 1979-81; pres. The Oikos Co., Friday Harbor, 1980-88, San Juan Software, Friday Harbor, 1983-84, Island Tech. Inc., Friday Harbor, 1984—; also bd. dirs. Island Tech. Inc. Author: Nineteen Fathers, 1971, (software) The Agent's Advantage, 1983; producer TV film Survivors, 1980; editor, founder Jour. Cetus, 1981; discoverer Resonance Theory, 1981. Founder San Juan Musicians Guild, 1974-78, Anti-Spray Coalition, 1977. Mem. Wash. Software Assn., Database Standards Com., Am. Electronics Assn. Club: Wash. Athletic. Home: PO Box 1304 Beresford Rd Friday Harbor WA 98250

ANDERSON, MELVIN KEITH, electrical engineer; b. Pine Bluffs, Wyo., Aug. 11, 1925; s. Reuben V. and Ruth (Lundberg) A.; m. Phyllis Wilkinson, June 9, 1950; children: Rodeny E., Becky Anderson Richardson, Ricky K. BS in Radio Engring., John Brown U., Siloam Springs, Ark., 1948; MSEE, U. Wyo., 1949; PhD in Engring., U. Ark., 1967. Registered profl. engr., Tex. Asst. prof. John Brown U., 1950-57; assoc. prof. U. Ark., Fayetteville, 1957-68, LaTourneau Coll., Longview, Tex., 1968-75, Southern Ill. U., Carbondale, 1975-80; sr. staff engr. Martin Marietta Astronautics,

Denver, 1980—. Contbr. articles to profl. publs. With USN, 1943-46. Mem. IEEE (sr. mem., chmn. Littleton chpt. 1985—). Republican. Home: 3290 W Santa Anita Dr Englewood CO 80110 Office: Martin Marietta Astronautic PO Box 179 Denver CO 80201

ANDERSON, MICHAEL GEORGE, quality assurance and advertising executive; b. Boulder, Colo., Aug. 3, 1951; s. George Martin and Annette Elizabeth (Girmann) A.; m. Susan Elliott, Mar. 19, 1977; children: Gregory Michael, Richard Charles. BS in Aero. Engring., U. Colo., 1973, MBA in Fin., 1978. Design engr. Beech Aircraft, Boulder, 1976-78, liaison engr., 1978-79; mech. engr. Dieterich Standard, Boulder, 1979-80, mgr. engring. design, 1980-84, quality assurance mgr., 1984-87, mgr. advt., mktg. strategic planning and quality assurance, 1987—. Author (computer software) Tektronix Header Program, 1982. V.p. Luth. Ch. Coun., 1988—. Recipient NPT Stamp and Cert., ASME, Boulder, 1986. Mem. ASTM, Am. mgmt. Assn., Am. Soc. Quality Control, Boulder Flycasters Club, U. Colo. Alumni Assn. (bd. dirs. 1985-87, v.p. bd. dirs. Boulder chpt. 1985-86), Buff Club (v.p., bd. dirs. 1985-87, pres. 1988—), Moose. Republican. Home: 7400 Mount Meeker Rd Longmont CO 80501 Office: Dieterich Standard PO Box 9000 Boulder CO 80301

ANDERSON, MICHAEL L(ITTLE), forestry service administrator; b. Oakland, Calif., Feb. 2, 1949; s. Hough L. and Virginia L. (Kerns) A.; m. Kimberly Anderson, Sept. 21, 1986; 1 child, Timothy L. AA, Shasta Jr. Coll., 1975; BS, Humbolt U., 1978. Cert. emergency technician instr., Alaska. Vet. counselor Human Resources Dept., Arcate, Calif., 1975-78; helicopter technician U.S. Forest Service, Petersberg, Alaska, 1978-82; aviation specialist U.S. Forest Service, Ketchikan, Alaska, 1982-85; forest aviation officer U.S. Forest Service, Ketchikan, 1985—. Vol. Ketchikan Fire Dept., 1983—; pres. Ketchikan Emergency Med. Service, 1985—; bd. dirs. SE Alaska Emergency Med. Service, Ketchikan, 1984—. Served with U.S. Army, 1968-71, Vietnam. Republican. Baptist. Office: US Forest Svc Federal Bldg Ketchikan AK 99901

ANDERSON, MICHAEL ROBERT, marketing representative; b. Mpls., Nov. 3, 1953; s. Arthur Robert Anderson and Patricia Roberta Carlson; m. Rebecca Ellan Pierce, June 6, 1981; children: Jenna Courtney, Evan Brendan. BSEE, U. Minn., 1976; MS in Systems Mgmt., U. So. Calif., 1981. Microelectronics engr. Hughes Aircraft Co., Fullerton, Calif., 1977; mktg. rep. Hewlett Packard, Orange County, Calif., 1977-81; regional mgr. Group III Elec., Orange County, 1981-85; mktg. rep. Lisp Machines Inc., Los Angeles, 1985-87, SUN Microsystems, Inc., Orange, Calif., 1987—. Big Brother, Big Bros. Inc., Orange, Calif., 1979-81. Fellow mem. AAAS, Am. Assn. Artificial Intelligence, Planetary Soc. Home: 28152 Bedford Dr Laguna Niguel CA 92677 Office: Sun Microsystems 765 City Dr Ste 100 Orange CA 92668

ANDERSON, MICHAEL THOMAS, controller; b. Lander, Wyo., Dec. 3, 1951; s. Alfred Thomas and Margaret (Detloff) A.; m. Saundra Lee Carlston, Jan. 5, 1980; 1 child, Matthew Thomas. BS, Bringham Young U., 1975. CPA, Wyo. Acct. Stotts & McKee, CPA's, Lander, Wyo., 1978, C.H. Moore & Co., CPA's, Riverton, Wyo., 1978-86; controller Health Trust Inc., Riverton Meml. Hosp., 1986—; mem. supervisory com. Atlantic City Credit Union, Lander, 1986—; inst. Cen. Wyo. Coll., Riverton, 1983-88. Scoutmaster troop 86 Wind River Dist. Boy Scouts Am., 1980-85, dist. exec., 1985, chmn. camping, 1987—; treas. Fremont County Homebuilders, 1986—. Mem. Am. Inst. CPA's, Wyo. Soc. CPA's (bd. dirs 1986—), Utha Assn. CPA's, Fremont County Assn. CPA's (pres. 1980-81), Healthcare Fin. Mgmt. Assn., Rotary (bd. dirs. Riverton 1985-88, sec. 1986). Morman. Home: 665 S Missouri St Hudson WY 82515 Office: Riverton Meml Hosp 2100 W Sunset St Riverton WY 84501

ANDERSON, N. CHRISTIAN, III, newspaper editor; b. Montpelier, Idaho, Aug. 4, 1950; s. Nelson C. and Esther Barbara (Yackley) A.; m. Sara Ann Coffenberry, Dec. 11, 1971 (div.); children—Ryan, Erica; m. Aletha Ann Yurewicz, May 3, 1986; 1 child, Paul. B.A. in Liberal Studies with honors, Oreg. State U., 1972. Asst. city editor, city editor Albany Democrat-Herald, Oreg., 1972-75; mng. editor Walla Walla Union-Bull., Wash., 1975-77; assoc. mng. editor Seattle Times, 1977-80; editor The Orange County (Calif.) Register, 1980—; instr. Calif. State U.-Fullerton, 1983, 87; Pulitzer prize juror, 1987, 88. Bd. dirs. Santa Ana Rotary Found., 1984. Named Nat. Newspaper Editor of Yr., 1989; recipient George D. Beveridge award Nat. Press Found. Mem. AP Mng. Editors, Soc. Profl. Journalists (Barney Kilgore Finalist award 1971), Am. Soc. Newspaper Editors, Calif. Soc. Newspaper Editors (bd. dirs. 1984—, v.p. 1985, pres. 1986-87), Soc. Newspaper Design (steering com. 1978), New Directions for News (bd. dirs. 1987—, vice-chmn. 1987-88, chmn. 1988—). Roman Catholic. Office: The Register 625 N Grand Ave Santa Ana CA 92711

ANDERSON, NED, SR., Apache tribal chairman; b. Bylas, Ariz., Jan. 18, 1943; s. Paul and Maggie (Rope) A.; m. Delphina Hinton; children—Therese Kay, Linette Mae, Magdalene Gail, Ned, Sean. AA, Ea. Ariz. Coll., 1964; BS, U. Ariz., 1967, JD, 1973. Field dir. Nat. Study Indian Edn., dept. anthropology U. Ariz., Tucson, 1968-70; tech. asst. Project Head Start, Ariz. State U., Tempe, 1970; ethnographer Smithsonian Instn., Washington, 1970-73; dir. Jojoba Project, Office of Arid Land Studies, U. Ariz. Tucson, 1973-76; with Jojoba devel. project San Carlos Apache Tribe, Ariz., 1976-78, tribal chmn., 1978-86; dir. Southwestern Indian Devel., Inc., 1971; mem. affirmative action com. City of Tucson, 1975-76; bd. dirs. Indian Enterprise Devel. Corp., 1976-78; mem. study panel Nat. Acad. Scis., 1975-77; pres. Inter-Tribal Coun. Ariz., 1979—; mem. supervisory bd. Ariz. Justice Planning Commn., 1978—, Indian adv. bd. Intergovtl. Personnel Program, 1978—; pres. bd. Ft. Thomas High Sch. Unified Dist., 1987—, clk. bd., 1989—; trustee Bacone Coll., 1986—; mem. adv. bd. Am. Indian Registry for Performing Arts, 1985—. Mem. San Carlos Fish and Game Commn., 1975—, chmn., 1976—; mem. exec. com. San Carlos Apache Tribal Coun., 1976-78, budget, fin. com., 1976—, constn. and ordinance com. 1976-78, chmn. law and order com., 1976-78; adv. bd. Gila Pueblo Community Coll. extension Ea. Ariz. Coll., 1979—; mem. sch. bd. Ft. Thomas High Sch. Unified Dist., 1977—, County Govt. Study Commn. State Ariz., 1981-84; adv. bd. Indian Edn., Ariz. State U., Tempe, 1978—, U. Ariz., Tucson, 1978—. Contbr. articles and papers to publs. Mem. Nat. Tribal Chmn.'s Assn. (bd. edn. 1978—, adv. bd. 1978—), Ariz. Acad., Globe C. of C.

ANDERSON, NORMAN ROBERT, manufacturing company executive; b. Alta, Iowa, Apr. 8, 1941; s. Robert Vernette and Lois Mildred (Dieterich) A.; m.Carolyn Jean Calhoun, June 11, 1966; children: Jeffrey, Deborah. BA, Buena Vista Coll., Storm Lake, Iowa, 1964; MBA, U. Oreg., 1966. Acctg. supr. Fibre Bd. Corp., Antioch, Calif., 1970-71; plant controller Fibre Bd. Corp., San Jose, Calif., 1971-73; region controller Fibre Bd. Corp., L.A., 1973-76; corp. controller Fluidmaster, Inc., Anaheim, Calif., 1976-82; v.p. fin. Fluidmaster, Inc., 1982-85, exec. v.p., chief operating officer, 1985--, also bd. dirs. Lt. (j.g.) USN, 1966-69, Vietnam. Republican. Presbyterian. Office: Fluidmaster Inc 1800 Via Burton Anaheim CA 92806

ANDERSON, PATRICK MICHAEL, economic development executive, lawyer; b. Mt. Edgecumbe, Alaska, Oct. 26, 1953; s. Clifford Stephen Anderson and Patricia May (Mallott) Ouellette; 1 child, Ashley Elena. AB, Princeton U., 1975; JD, U. Mich., 1978. Bar: Alaska, 1978. Atty. Hedland, Fleischer & Friedman, Anchorage, 1978-82; lobbyist Municipality of Anchorage, 1982-84; loan adminstr. Community Enterprise Devel. Corp. Alaska, Anchorage, 1984-85; dir. Alaska Econ. Devel. Ctr., Juneau, 1986—; chmn. bd. dirs. Alaska Native Found., Anchorage, 1984—. Bd. dirs. Juneau Econ. Devel. Council, 1987—. Democrat. Lodge: Rotary. Office: Alaska Econ Devel Ctr 1108 F St Juneau AK 99801

ANDERSON, PAUL NATHANIEL, oncologist; b. Omaha, May 30, 1937; s. Nels Paul E. and Doris Marie (Chesnut) A.; BA, U. Colo., 1959, MD, 1963; m. Dee Ann Hipps, June 27, 1965; children: Mary Kathleen, Anne Christen. Intern Johns Hopkins Hosp., 1963-64, resident in internal medicine, 1964-65; research asso., staff assoc. NIH, Bethesda, Md., 1965-70; fellow in oncology Johns Hopkins Hosp., 1970-72, asst. prof. medicine, oncology Johns Hopkins U. Sch. Medicine, 1972-76; attending physician Balt. City Hosps., Johns Hopkins Hosp., 1972-76; dir. dept. med. oncology Penrose Cancer Hosp., Colorado Springs, Colo., 1976-86; clin. asst. prof. dept. medicine U. Colo. Sch. Medicine, 1976—; dir. Penrose Cancer Hosp., 1979-86; founding dir. Cancer Ctr. of Colorado Springs, 1986—; med. dir. So. Colo. Cancer Program, 1979-86; mem., chmn. treatment com. Colo. Cancer Control and Research Panel, 1980-83; prin. investigator Cancer Info. Service of Colo., 1981-86. Mem. Colo. Gov.'s Rocky Flats Employee Health Assessment Group, 1983-84; mem. Gov.'s Breast Cancer Control Commn. Colo., 1984—; pres., founder Oncology Mgmt. Network, Inc., 1985—; founder, bd. dirs. Timberline Med. Assocs., 1986—; founder, dir. So. Colo. AIDS project 1986—; mem. adv. bd. Colo. State Bd. Health Tumor Registry, 1984—; chmn., bd. dirs. Preferred Physicians, Inc.; bd. dirs. Share Devel. Co. of Colo., Share Health Plan of Colo., Preferred Health Plan, Inc. Served with USPHS, 1965-70. Diplomate Am. Bd. Internal Medicine, Am. Bd. Med. Oncology. Mem. Am. Soc. Clin. Oncology, Am. Assn. Cancer Research, Am. Assn. Cancer Insts. (liaison mem. bd. trustees 1980—), Am. Acad. Med. Dirs., Nat. Cancer Inst. (com. for community hosp. oncology program evaluation 1982—), Assn. Community Cancer Centers (chmn. membership com. 1980—, chmn. clin. research com. 1983-85, sec. 1983-84, pres.-elect 1984-85, pres. 1986-87, trustee 1981—), AAAS, N.Y. Acad. Scis., Johns Hopkins Med. Soc., AMA, Colo. Med. Soc., Am. Mgmt. Assn., Am. Assn. Profl. Cons., El Paso County Med. Soc., Coalition for Cancer, Alpha Omega Alpha. Contbr. articles to med. jours. Office: Cancer Ctr Colorado Springs 320 E Fontanero St Ste 100 Colorado Springs CO 80907 Address: 32 Sanford Rd Colorado Springs CO 80906

ANDERSON, POLLY GORDON, insurance rehabilitation nurse; b. Quincy, Mass., Dec. 18, 1934; d. Manson Lewis and Jean Nourse (Morrison) Gordon; m. Brooke Hamilton Anderson, Nov. 5, 1955; children: Wendy, Kimberley, Scott, Peter; m. R. Trent Coleman, Sept. 15, 1984. Grad., Mass. Gen. Hosp. Sch. Nursing, Boston, 1955. RN Mass., Calif. Cert. ins. rehab. specialist by Workers Copmpensation Claims Adminstrn. Clin. teaching intern Mass. Gen. Hosp., 1955-56; staff nurse Bataan Meml. Hosp., Albuquerque, 1962-64; sr. indsl. nurse San Pedro (Calif.) Inds. Clinic, 1965-75; rehab nurse Argonaut Ins., L.A., 1975-77; regional rehab. coord. Chubb & Sons, L.A., 1977-84; v.p. RTC Cons. Svcs. Inc., Escondido, Calif., 1984—; vocat. rehab. cons. Calif. Workers' Compensation System. Campaign mgr. for city coun. candidate, San Marcos, Calif., 1987. Mem. Nat. Assn. Rehab. Profls. in Pvt. Sector (standards and compliance rev. bd. 1986—), Rehab Nurses Soc., Southern Calif. Rehab. Exch., Assn. Indsl. Rehab. Reps., Rehab. Nurses Coords. Network (bd. dirs.-at-large 1987, edn. and program chmn. 1987—). Home: 538 Glenheather Dr San Marcos CA 92069 Office: RTC Cons Svcs Inc 210 S Juniper St Ste 100 Escondido CA 92025

ANDERSON, RALPH JONATHAN, real estate developer; b. Roseburg, Oreg., Oct. 26, 1956; s. Ralph and Eleanor Alice (Abbott) A. BS, U. Oreg., 1980. Constrn. mgr. Trammell Crow Co., Menlo Park, Calif., 1981-84; devel. mgr. Kotansky Devel., San Jose, 1984—. Youth ldr. Westminster Presbyn. Ch., San Jose, 1988—. Democrat. Presbyterian. Office: 828 S Bascom #280 San Jose CA 95128

ANDERSON, RAYMOND FERDINAND, retired aeronautical engineer; b. San Francisco, July 6, 1905; s. Axel Ferdinand and Lilie Jannet (Hamilton) A.; m. Virginia Eloise Bramlitt, Apr. 22, 1931 (dec. 1975). BSME, U. Calif., Berkeley, 1929. Registered profl. engr., Calif. Aero. engr. Nat. Adv. Com. for Aeros., Langley Field, Va., 1929-42; aero. rsch. engr. Lockheed, Burbank, Calif., 1942-46; aerodynamicist Northrop, Hawthorne, Calif., 1946-50; aero. engr. Naval Ordnance Test Sta., Pasadena, 1950-53, Marquardt Aircraft Co., Van Nuys, Calif., 1953-54; aerodynamicist Radioplane Co., Van Nuys, 1954-56; rsch. engr. Lockheed Missiles & Space Co., Van Nuys, Calif., 1956-57, aero. engr., 1957-70; ret. Lockheed Missiles & Space Co., Van Nuys, 1970. Contbr. articles to profl. jours. Mem. Inst. Aero. Sci., Sigma Xi.

ANDERSON, RAYMOND HARTWELL, JR., metallurgical engineer; b. Staunton, Va., Feb. 25, 1932; s. Raymond Hartwell and Virginia Boatwright (Moseley) A.; m. Dana Bratton Wilson, Sept. 5, 1959; children: Kathryn, Margaret, Susan. BS in Ceramic and Metall. Engring., Va. Poly. Inst. and State U., 1957, MSMetE, 1959. Registered profl. engr. Asst. prof. metall. engring. Va. Poly. Inst. and State U., Blacksburg, 1957-59; metall. engr. Gen. Dynamics Corp., Ft. Worth, 1959-61; sr. engr. Babcock & Wilcox Co., Lynchburg, Va., 1961-65; tech. specialist McDonnell Douglas Astronautics Co., Huntington Beach, Calif., 1965-88, sr. engring. specialist space sta. div., 1988—; cons. in field Los Angeles Area, 1967-71. Author, patentee Roll Diffusion Bonding of Beryllium, 1970-71, Increased Ductility of Beryllium, 1971-72. Served to 1st lt. U.S. Army, 1954-56. Mem. Am. Soc. Metals (lectr. 1968-70), Nat. Soc. Corrosion Engrs., Bolting Tech. Council., Am. Ceramic Soc., Alpha Sigma Mu, Tau Beta Pi, Sigma Gamma Epsilon. Republican. Home: 1672 Kenneth Dr Santa Ana CA 92705 Office: McDonnell Douglas Astronautics Co 5301 Bolsa Ave Huntington Beach CA 92647

ANDERSON, RICHARD ERNEST, energy and chemical research and development company executive, rancher; b. North Little Rock, Ark., Mar. 8, 1926; s. Victor Ernest and Lillian Josephine (Griffin) A.; m. Mary Ann Fitch, July 18, 1953; children: Vicki Lynn, Lucia Anita. B.S.C.E., U. Ark., 1949; M.S.E., U. Mich., 1959; Registered profl. engr., Mich., Va., Tex., Mont. Commd. ensign U.S. Navy, 1952, advanced through grades to capt., 1968; ret., 1974; v.p. Ocean Resources, Inc., Houston, 1974-77; mgr. maintenance and ops. Holmes & Narver, Inc., Orange, Calif., 1977-78; pres. No. Resources, Inc., Billings, Mont., 1978-81; v.p. Holmes & Narver, Inc., Orange, Calif., 1981-82; owner, operator Anderson Ranches, registered Arabian horses and comml. Murray Grey cows, Pony, Mont., 1982—; pres., dir. Carbon Resources Inc., Butte, Mont., 1983—. Trustee Lake Barcroft-Virginia Watershed Improvement Dist., 1973-74; pres. Lake Barcroft-Virginia Recreation Center, Inc., 1972-73. Served with USAAF, 1944-45. Decorated Silver Star, Legion of Merit with Combat V (2), Navy Marine Corps medal, Bronze Star with Combat V, Meritorious Service medal, Purple Heart; Anderson Peninsula in Antarctica named in his honor. Mem. ASCE, Soc. Am. Mil. Engrs. (Morrell medal 1965). Republican. Methodist. Home: PO Box 266 Pony MT 59747 Office: Carbon Resources Inc 305 W Mercury St Butte MT 59701

ANDERSON, ROBERT, manufacturing company executive; b. Columbus, Nebr., Nov. 2, 1920; s. Robert and Lillian (Devlin) A.; m. Constance Dahlun Severy, Oct. 2, 1942 (div.); children: Robert, Kathleen D.; m. Diane Clark Lowe, Nov. 2, 1973. BS in Mech. Engring, Colo. State U., 1943, LLD (hon.), 1966; M Automotive Engring., Chrysler Inst. Engring., 1948; DHL (hon.), U. Neb., 1985; JD (hon.), Pepperdine U., 1986; D of Engring. (hon.), Milw. Sch. Engring., 1987. With Chrysler Corp., 1946-68, v.p. corp., gen. mgr. Chrysler-Plymouth div., 1965-67; with Rockwell International Corp., 1968—, pres. comml. products group, 1968-69, v.p. corp., 1968-69, exec. v.p., 1969-70, pres., chief operating officer, 1970-74, pres., 1974-79, chief exec. officer, 1974-88, chmn., 1979-88, dir., 1968—, chmn. exec. com., 1988—; bd. dirs. Security Pacific Corp. and subs. Security Pacific Nat. Bank, Los Angeles, Hosp. Corp. Am., Tinker Co., Canton, Ohio, Optical Data Systems, Doheny Eye Clinic, L.A. Trustee Calif. Inst. Tech., bd. of overseers Exec. Council Fgn. Diplomats; chmn. bus.-higher edn. forum Am. Council on Edn., 1982-84; chmn. Western Hwy. Inst., 1983-84; trustee John E. Anderson Grad. Sch. Mgmt. UCLA. Served to capt. F.A. AUS, 1943-46. Named Exec. of Yr. Nat. Mgmt. Assn., 1980. Mem. Soc. Automotive Engrs., Phi Kappa Phi, Tau Beta Pi, Sigma Nu. Office: Rockwell Internat Corp 2230 E Imperial Hwy El Segundo CA 90245-2899

ANDERSON, ROBERT ARTHUR, renal technologist; b. Waterloo, Iowa, Sept. 2, 1945; s. Albert and Willia Marie (Sallis) A. AAS, City Colls. Chgo., 1974. Dialysis tech. U. Ill. Hosp., Chgo., 1970-74, Cathedral Shelter Dialysis, Chgo., 1974-76, Doctors Dialysis, L.A., 1977-78, Mobile Dialysis Svc., Compton, Calif., 1978-81; Dialysis tech. Cedars Sinai Hosp., L.A., 1981-86, Home Intensive Care, Carson, Calif., 1987—; dialysis tech. Mobile Dialysis Svc., Compton, 1986—; chief technician Home Intensive Care, Burbank, Calif., 1987—. Mem. Am. Assn. Nephrologist Nurses and Technicians. Democrat. Methodist. Home: 3857 Cloverdale Ave Los Angeles CA 90008

ANDERSON, ROBERT ERNEST, sales executive; b. Heavener, Okla., July 30, 1926; s. Ernest L. and Dewey M. (Vaught) A., m. Eleanor Jeanne Mauzy, Sept. 15, 1948; children: Robert, Sarah, David, Hans. BS, Okla. State U., 1949, MS, 1950. Registered profl. engr., Calif.; cert. safety profl. Instr. Okla. State U. Agr. and Applied Sci., Stillwater, 1950-51, asst. prof., 1951-52; with Mine Safety Appliances Co., Beaumont, Tex., Gary, Ind., and Little Rock, 1952-63; mgr. safety products MSA Internat., Pitts., 1963-67; mgr. intermountain dist. MSA Internat., Salt Lake City, 1967-87; pvt. practice safety engring. cons. Salt Lake City, 1987—; adj. asst. prof. safety engring. U. Utah., 1988—; cons. Indsl. Health Inc. With USNR, 1944-46. Mem. AIME, Am. Indsl. Hygiene Assn., Am. Soc. Safety Engrs. (v.p. region II 1986-87), Masons. Democrat. Methodist. Home and Office: 3372 Pioneer St Salt Lake City UT 84109

ANDERSON, ROBERT LOYD, mechanical engineer, consultant; b. Phoenix, July 10, 1945; s. Loyd Everett and Lillian Pirtle A.; m. Diane Lilian Nidey, Jan. 20, 1966; children: Robert, Alissa, Leah, Rebecca, Russell. AA in Engring., Phoenix Coll., 1964, BS in Engring. Sci., 1966, MS in Mech. Engring., 1969; postgrad., Ariz. State U., 1966-70. Engr. Allison div. Gen. Motors Corp., Cleve., 1967, AC Elec. div. Gen. Motors Corp., Santa Barbara, Calif., 1968; dept. mgr. Dynamic Sci., Phoenix, 1970-77; lectr. engring. and tech. Northern Ariz. U., Flagstaff, 1977-84; owner, pres. Applied Research and Investigations, Scottsdale, Ariz., 1977—; expert witness in vehicle safety research and litigation. Contbr. articles on vehicle safety research to profl. jours. Recipient numerous fellowships and scholarships NSF, Nat. Def. Edn. Act at Ariz. State U. Grad. Sch., 1966-70, Fred Hayes scholar Phoenix Coll. Mem. Soc. Automation Engrs., Am. Soc. Engring. Edn. (life), Tau Beta Pi. Home and Office: 17030 N 57th St Scottsdale AZ 85254

ANDERSON, ROBERT ORVILLE, oil and gas company executive; b. Chgo., Apr. 13, 1917; s. Hugo A. and Hilda (Nelson) A.; m. Barbara Phelps, Aug. 25, 1939; children: Katherine, Julia, Maria, Robert Bruce, Barbara Burton, William Phelps, Beverley. B.A., U. Chgo., 1939. With Am. Mineral Spirits Co., Chgo., 1939-41; pres. Malco Refineries, Inc., Roswell, N.Mex., 1941-63; with Atlantic Richfield Co., Los Angeles, retired chmn. bd., chief exec. officer; pres. Hondo Oil and Gas Co., Roswell; chmn. Pauley Petroleum, Inc., L.A.; mem. Com. Econ. Devel., Washington. Hon. chmn. (hon.) Aspen Inst. for Humanistic Studies; chmn. emeritus Lovelace Found.; trustee Calif. Inst. Tech., U. Chgo. Mem. Nat. Petroleum Council, Am. Petroleum Inst. Clubs: Century (N.Y.C.); California (Los Angeles); Metropolitan (Washington); Pacific-Union (San Francisco).

ANDERSON, ROBERT STEWART, corporation executive; b. Detroit, July 25, 1956; s. Walter Stewart and Mary A. BS in Aero Engring. Tech., Calif. State Poly. U., 1982. Research and devel. engr. McDonnell Douglas, Long Beach, Calif., 1982-85; pres. K.S.D. Inc., Banning, Calif., 1985—. Mem. Soc. Advancement Materials and Process Engring. Republican. Office: KSD inc 1550 E Ramsey Banning CA 92220

ANDERSON, ROGER BANKS, retired surgeon; b. Albert Lea, Minn., June 13, 1918; s. Joseph Leonard and Exine Pearl (Robertson) A.; m. June Beverly Green, Sept. 1, 1939 (dec. 1986); 1 child, David Roger; m. Emily Agnes Sheldorf, Feb. 5, 1988. Student, Macalester Coll., 1936-38; D of Osteopathy, Des Moines Coll. Osteopathy, 1942. Diplomate Am. Osteopathic Bd. of Surgery, 1962. Founder Manning (Iowa) Gen. Hosp., 1945, chmn. dept. surgery, 1951-64; chmn. dept. surgery Gordon Meml. Hosp., Sioux City, Iowa, 1957-64, Davenport (Iowa) Osteo. Hosp., 1969-75; staff mem. dept. surgery Mercy Hosp., Davenport, 1974-81, ret., 1981; cons. surgeon Dickenson County Hosp., Spirit Lake, Iowa, 1958-64; clin. assoc. prof. surgery Kirksville Coll. Osteopathy, 1969-77. Contbr. articles to profl. jours. Fellow Am. Coll. Osteopathic Surgeons; mem. Iowa Osteopathic Med. Assn., Am. Osteopathic Assn., Masons, Psi Sigma Alpha. Address: 12442 Marble Dr PO Box 5048 Sun City West AZ 85375

ANDERSON, ROGER BURKE, dentist; b. N.Y.C., Oct. 20, 1950; s. Arthur Ludwig and June (MacFarlane) A.; m. Kathleen Mary Kirk, May 14, 1988. BS in Biology, Norwich U., 1972; DMD, U. Pa., 1976. Gen. practice dentistry Tucson, 1978—; cons. Cigna Health Plans, Tucson, 1983—, Health Am., Tucson, 1983—, U. Ariz. Student Health, 1983—. Contbr. articles to profl. jours. Bd. dirs. Tucson Symphony Soc., 1983-86; chmn. United Way, Tucson, 1985. Capt., U.S. Army, 1976-78. Mem. ADA, Ariz. Dental Assn., So. Ariz. Dental Assn., Pima Dental Study Club (cons. 1983—), Pima Dental Assn. (pres. 1983—), La Paloma Country Club (chmn. social com. 1985). Republican. Home: 6451 N Columbus Blvd Tucson AZ 85718 Office: 1640 N Country Club Rd Tucson AZ 85716

ANDERSON, ROGER STANLEY, marketing professional; b. Glendale, Calif., Dec. 8, 1942; s. Edward Stanley and Bonnie Florence (Rood) A.; m. Judith Ann Richardson, July 21, 1967; children: Kimberly Jean, Karin Leigh. BS, U. Southern Calif., 1966. CPA, Calif. Sr. acct. Ernst & Ernst (now Ernst & Whinney), L.A., 1966-69; treas., controller McCarthy Co., Anaheim, Calif., 1969-72; controller, dir. mktg. Avco Community Developers, Glendora, Calif., 1972-73; dir. mktg., sales Kaufman & Broad, Glendora, 1973-75; bus. mgr. Desert Sun Pub. Co., Palm Springs, Calif., 1975-78; v.p. mktg. Lewis Homes of Calif., Upland, 1978--; bd. dirs. Baldy View Bldg. Industry Assn., Upland. Chmn. bd. Community Bapt. Ch., Alta Loma, Calif., 1985, New Hope Community Ch., Rancho Cucamonga, Calif., 1986-88, Ch. Planting Internat., Rancho Cucamonga, 1986--, Artists in Christian Testimony, Rancho Cucamonga, 1986--. Mem. Sales Mktg. Council Riverside and San Bernadino Counties, Upland (pres., bd. dirs. 1987--, Mktg. Dir. Yr. 1987), Rotary (newsletter editor 1976, 85). Republican. Home: 338 Paxton Ct Upland CA 91786 Office: Lewis Homes 1156 N Mountain PO Box 670 Upland CA 91785

ANDERSON, ROSCOE ODELL DALE, retired personnel officer; b. Snowville, Utah, Aug. 15, 1913; s. Roscoe Joseph and Diantha Jane (Robbins) A.; m. Elizabeth Jeanne Neil, June 4, 1939; 1 child, Dale neil. BS, U. Utah, 1937, MS, 1943; postgrad., Cornell U., 1965, U. San Francisco, 1972. Cert. tchr. and adminstr. in secondary edn. Employee relations officer Utah Gen. Depot, Ogden, 1943-48; dir. civilian personnel Sharpe Army Depot, Lathrop, Calif., 1948-52, Aberdeen Proving Ground U.S. Army, Aberdeen, Md., 1952-55; field rep. Office Civilian Personnel Dep. Chief Staff Personnel, San Francisco, 1955-60; chief employee mgmt. div. Office Civilian Personnel Dep. Chief Staff Personnel, Washington, 1960-66; dir. civilian personnel 6th U.S. Army, Presidio, San Francisco, 1966-73; zone IV coord. U.S. Dept. Defense, San Francisco, 1973-76; cons. Defense Supply Agy., GSA, 1977-80; nat. v.p. Soc. for personnel Adminstrn., 1962, charter mem., pres. No. Calif., 1967, charter mem., pres., Hartford County Md., 1955; guest lectr. U. San Francisco, 1969; chmn. Fed. Personnel Coun./No. Calif., San Francisco, 1967-68. Mem. Marin Coun. ARC, Marin County, Calif., 1975-80; sec. Ogden City Svc. Baseball League, 1944-47; chair fed. employee div. Community Chest Drive, San Joaquin County, Calif., 1952; dep. chmn. Community Chest Drive, Aberdeen Proving Grounds, 1955. Mem. Army Civilian Personnel Alumni Assn., nat. assn. Retired Fed. Employees, Am. Assn. Retired Persons., Wilderness Soc., Utah Golf Assn., Sierra Club, Crimson Club U. Utah. Mormon.

ANDERSON, ROYAL J., advertising agency executive; b. Portland, Oreg., Sept. 12, 1914; s. John Alfred and Martha Marie (Jacobsen) A.; B.A., Albany Coll., 1939; postgrad. U. Oreg., summers 1939-41, Oreg. Inst. Tech., 1940-41; m. Leticia G. Anderson; children: Michael, Johnny, Dora Kay, Mark Roy, Stan Ray, Ruth Gay, Janelle A., Jennifer T., Joseph, Daisy, Dina; 1 adopted dau., Muoi-Muoi. Corp. cons. Dupont Corp., Beverly Hills, Calif., 1967-68; editor-pub. Nev. State Democrat, Carson City, Nev. State Pub. Observer, Nev. State Congl. Assn., Carson City, 1962-78; pres. Allied-Western Produce Co., Yuma, Ariz., Nev. Dem. Corp., 1966-78; pres. Western Restaurant Corp., 1978-81, Nev. State Sage Co., 1979—, Midway Advt. Co., Environ. Research Corp., 1983—, Mid-City Advt. Agy., 1983—, Nat. Newspaper Found., 1969, 71-76, The Gt. North Banks Seafood Co., 1984—, Food Services Corp., 1985—, Sterling Cruise Lines, 1986—, No-Tow Mfg. Inc.; dir. plant research safari cen. Amazon Gador Expdn., 1988-89; chmn. bd. Press/Register Daily Newspapers, Foster Mortgage Co., 1983—. Inventor No-Tow, 1988 worldwide. Bishop, Ch. of Palms, Mexico. Dep. registrar voters, Washoe County, Nev., 1966. Recipient Heroism award for rescue, 1933. Research fellow, Alaska, 1936. Mem. Am. Hort. Soc., Sparks (pres. 1970-81), Nev. chambers commerce, C. of C. of U.S., Chatso Farm Assn. (pres. 1962-88), Smithsonian Assos., N.Am. C. of C. Execs., Nat. Geog. Soc., Am. Newspaper Alliance (v.p. 1976), Club: Millionare. Lodges: Kiwanis, Elks, Lions. Designer prefabricated milk carton container, 1933, well water locating under-stream device, 1938. Home: PO Box 4349

North Las Vegas NV 89030 Home: 5600 E Sundance Ave Las Vegas NV 89110

ANDERSON, SALLY JANE, artist; b. Rockford, Ill., Feb. 5, 1942; d. James Edward and Jane (Purnell) Moriarty; m. Charles Edward Anderson, Aug. 28, 1964; children: Erika Elizabeth, Seth Charles. Student, Inst. Allende, San Miguel de Allende, Mex., 1963; BA in Art, Beloit Coll., 1964; postgrad. in art, U. Wis., Milw., 1966. One-woman shows, 1964--, including Roswell (N.Mex) Mus. and Art Ctr., 1970, Jane Haslem Gallery, Washington, 1970, Gallery One, Albuquerque, 1975, Mariposa Gallery, Albuquerque, 1978, Gargoyle Gallery, Aspen, Colo., 1978, Suzanne Brown Gallery, Scottsdale, Ariz., 1980, Putney Gallery, Aspen, Colo., 1981, C.G. Rein Gallery, Santa Fe, 1982, 84, C.G. Rein Gallery, Edina, Minn., 1984, Works II Gallery, Southampton, N.Y., 1985; exhibited in numerous group shows, 1967—, including N.Mex. State U., Las Cruces, 1974, Carnegie Inst., Pitts., 1976, Albuquerque Mus., 1977, 79, Phoenix Art Mus., 1979, Los Angeles Craft and Folk Art Mus., 1980, C.G. Rein Gallery, Scottsdale, Ariz., 1984, Salon des nations, Paris, 1985; represented in permanent collections Bundy Mus., Stowe, Vt., Numerous Cos., banks; represented by C.G. Rein Galleries, Windsors Gallery, Miamia, Fla., Works II. Recipient 1st prize N.Mex. Crafts Biennial; Nat. Endowment for Arts grantee, also purchase prize. Home: 7522 Bear Canyon Rd NE Albuquerque NM 87109

ANDERSON, SCOTTY PAUL, surgeon; b. Portland, Oreg., Dec. 25, 1947; s. Merwin Eugene and Mildred (Gibbs) A.; m. Phyllis Marie Mazzarella; children: Jordan, Tylor, Elliott. BS, Portland State U., Portland, 1972, BS (psychology), 1972; D.M.D., OHSU, Portland, 1977; Specialty cert., U. Penn, Philadelphia, 1980. Chief, div. oral & maxillofacial surgery Good Smaritan Hosp., Portland, Oreg., 1980--; mem. surgical services com. Good Smaritan Hosp., Portland, 1980-; chmn., Delaware Valley Oral Surgery Residents Assoc., Phila., Pa.,. Author: In The Journal of Oral Surgery, Oral Medicine, 1978. Organizer, Greg Wolfe for Mayor Campaign Rotary Club, Portland, 1972;. Fellow Am. Assn. Oral & Maxillofacial Surgery (diplomate, bd. examiner), Am. Dental Soc. Republican Latter Day Saints. Office: Good Samaritan Hosp 511 SW 10th Ste 1214 Portland OR 97205

ANDERSON, STEPHEN HALE, judge; b. 1932; m. Shirlee G. Anderson. Student, Eastern Oreg. Coll. Edn., Brigham Young U.; LLB, U. Utah, 1960. Tchr. South High Sch., Salt Lake City, 1956-57; trial atty. tax div. U.S. Dept. Justice, 1960-64; ptnr. Ray, Quinney & Nebeker, 1964-85; judge U.S. Ct. Appeals (10th cir.), Salt Lake City, 1985—; spl. counsel Salt Lake County Grand Jury, 1975. Editor-in-Chief Utah Law Rev. Bd. govs. Salt Lake Area C. of C., 1984. Served as cpl. U.S. Army, 1953-55. Mem. ABA, Utah State Bar (pres. 1983-84, various offices), Salt Lake County Bar Assn. (pres. 1977-78), Am. Bar Found., U. Utah Alumni Assn. (trustee 1979-83, pres. 1982-83), Order of Coif. Office: US Ct Appeals 4201 Fed Bldg 125 S State Salt Lake City UT 84138-1102

ANDERSON, THOMAS ROBERT, scientist, entrepreneur; b. Bloomington, Ind., Nov. 17, 1954; s. Robert George and Ruth Juliet (Keller) A.; m. Sarah McCarthy. BS in Biology, U. Fla., 1976; PhD in Physiology, U. Calif., Berkeley, 1983. Teaching asst. U. Calif., Berkeley, 1977-80, rsch. asst., 1978-81; postdoctoral fellow U. Calif., San Francisco, 1983-86; instr. biology Coll. Marin, Kentfield, Calif., 1981; dir. rsch. and co-founder Berkeley Antibody Co., Richmond, Calif., 1981—, pres., 1986—, chmn. bd., 1988—; instr. U. Calif., Berkeley, 1988—. Democrat. Home: 1208 Kelley Ct Pinole CA 94564 Office: Berkeley Antibody Co 4131 Lakeside Dr Richmond CA 94806-1965

ANDERSON, WAYNE CARL, corporate executive; b. Sheboygan, Wis., May 5, 1935; s. Chester Phillip and Mabel Mary (Edler) A.; BS in Bus. Adminstrn., Upsala Coll., 1977; m. Joan Dorothy Staranick, May 18, 1963; children: David Wayne, Steven Michael, Karen Colleen. Dir. state govt. relations Nabisco Brands Co., Parsippany, N.J., 1974-78, dir. fed. govt. relations, 1978-79, dir. govt. relations, 1979-81, v.p. govt. relations, 1981-84, v.p. govt. and community relations, 1984-87, v.p. pub. affairs, 1987; non-lawyer exec. Evans Kitchel & Jenckes, P.C., 1988—; cheif exec. officer The Polaris Group, 1987—; guest lectr. in field. Editorial adv. bd. Pub. Affairs in Rev., 1980; contbr. articles to profl. jours. Mem. Roseland (N.J.) Planning Bd., 1978-79; mem. Roseland Citizens Adv. Com., 1977-78; pres. Grace Lutheran Ch., Roseland, 1980-81, chmn. bd. elders, 1981-82; trustee State Govt. Research and Edn. Found., 1981-82. Served with U.S. Army, 1958-60. Mem. Internat. Jaycees (senator 1989—), U.S. Jaycees (nat. dir. 1964-65), Pub. Affairs Council (exec. com. 1986, bd. dirs. 1988—), Nat. Fgn. Trade Council (dir. 1986), State Govt. Affairs Council (past pres. 1978-79), Ford's Theatre (bd. govs.), Acad. Polit. Sci., Pub. Affairs Profls. Ariz. (founder 1987—)., World Bus. Adv. Council, Thunderbird Am. Grad. Sch. Mgmt. Clubs: University, Capitol Hill, Nat. Press.

ANDERSON, WILLIAM, retail company executive, business education educator; b. L.A., May 21, 1923; s. William Bert and Marie (Novotney) A.; m. Margaret Lillian Phillips, Aug. 16, 1951; children: Margaret Gwen, Deborah Kay, William Keven, Denise Marie. BA in Econs., UCLA, 1948, MEd, 1957. Cert. secondary tchr. (life), Calif. Tchr. bus. edn. Big Bear Lake (Calif.) High Sch., 1949-52, Ventura (Calif.) Unified Sch. Dist. Buena High Sch., 1952—; mgr. Day's Aircraft Co., Santa Paula, Calif., 1967—; cons. micro computers Calif. State Dept. Edn., 1983-85. Crew chief Olympic Games basketball stats., 1984, basketball stats. World Games for the Deaf, 1985. Served with USAAF, 1943-45, PTO. Mem. NEA (life), Calif. Bus. Edn. Assn. (pres. So. sect. 1959-60, state sec. 1960-61), Calif. Assn. Work Experience Educators, Internat. Soc. Bus. Edn. (voting del. to Soc. Internat. Pour l'Enseignemer Comml., Western rep. 1988-89), Am. Aviation Hist. Soc., Calif. Assn. Work Experience Educators (life), Air Force Assn. (life), So. Calif. Badminton Assn. (bd. dirs.), Inplant Printing Mgmt. Assn., Phi Delta Kappa, Delta Phi Epsilon. Democrat. Lutheran. Home: 334 Manzanita Ave Ventura CA 93001 Office: Buena High Sch 5670 Telegraph Rd Ventura CA 93003

ANDRADE, JAIME DAVID, data processing executive; b. Quito, Pichincha, Ecuador, Sept. 22, 1933; came to U.S., 1958; s. Luis Ulpiano and Guillermina (Neira) A.; m. Elene M. Habis, Apr. 1, 1967; children: David, Luis. Student, La Salle U., Quito, Ecuador, IBM Edn. Ctr. operator report distbn. Catalina Sportswear, City of Commerce, Calif., 1962-66; computer operator R.T.W., City of Commerce, 1966-72; computer operator Transcon Lines, Los Angeles, 1972-74, lead computer operator, 1974-76, supr. computer ops., 1976-81, chief computer ops., 1981-84, mgr. computer ops., 1984—. Asst. scoutmaster Boy Scouts Am., 1983—, Order Arrow Boy Scouts Am., 1985; soccer coach Jr. United Soccer Assn., Yorba Linda Orange County, 1975—. Mem. Assn. Computer Ops. Mgmt. Home: 2336 Underhill Ave Anaheim CA 92806 Office: Transcon LInes 5700 Eastern Ave Los Angeles CA 90040

ANDRADE, NANCY LEE (BALL ANDRADE), realtor, jeweler; b. Seattle, Nov. 17, 1937; d. Hans Peter Marcher and Hilda Dorothy (Baisch) Middleton; m. Allan L. Andrade, Mar. 15, 1971 (div. 1980). Cert. travel agt., Cannon Bus. Coll., Honolulu, 1965; cert., Erhardt Seminar Tng., Honolulu, 1980; cert. real estate broker, Stapleton Sch. Real Estate, Honolulu, 1985. Model Kathleen Peck Modeling Agy., Seattle, 1956-60; communications mgr. RCA Communicaions, Royal Hawaiian Hotel, Honolulu, 1960-62; TV and fashion specialist Careers Unltd., Honolulu, 1960-65; travel agt. Waters Travel, Kailua, Hawaii, 1965—; realtor assoc., propert mgr. various realty firms, Honolulu, 1967-74; property mgr. Nancy Andrade Property Mgmt., Honolulu, 1974-85; realtor, broker, property mgr. Nancy Andrade Realty, Honolulu and Kaneohe, 1985—; jeweler, goldsmith Nancy Andrade Jewelry Design, 1974—; mfg. Koala Prodns., Hawaii and Australia, 1987—, Nancy Andrade Enterprises, Honolulu and Kaneohe, 1987—. Foster parent Children Internat.; active Waikki Residence Assn., 1978—, Neighborhood Bd., Honolulu, 1980—. Mem. Nat. Assn. Realtors, Nat. Notary Assn. (cert.), Small Bus. Hawaii, Honolulu Bd. Realtors, Australian-Am. C. of C., Beta Sigma Phi (v.p. Oahu coun. 1987—, v.p. Preceptor Delta 1988—, Preceptor degree 1980, Ritual Jewels degree 1962, Xi Zeta Exemplar degree 1969, Internat. Order Rose degree 1976, 25 Yr. Silver Circle award 1987, Alpha Chpt. Woman of Yr. 1965, Wi Zeta Chpt. Woman of Yr. 1977), Lani-Kailua Outdoor Circle Club, Ala Wai Plaza Club, Makani Kai Marina Club. Republican. Office: Nancy Andrade Realty & Property Mgmt 970 N Kalaheo Ave A-306 Kailua HI 96734

ANDRADE, NANCY MARIE, commercial interior designer; b. Coronado, Calif., Oct. 7, 1953; d. B.A. and Eleanor Margaret (Bulger) A. AA, Southwestern Coll, San Diego, 1973; BA, San Diego State U., 1975. Draftsman R. Elliott Smith, Interiors, San Diego, 1975-76; draftsman, designer Fischer Office Interiors, San Diego, 1976-79; design mgr. Fischer Design Group, San Diego, 1979-84; project mgr. Maday Design Cons., San Diego, 1984-85; ter. mgr. Sunar Hauserman, L.A., 1985-87; dir. design svcs. Imperial Corp., San Diego, 1987--. Mem. Inst. Bus. Designers, Women in Interiors Network. Republican. Roman Catholic. Home: l618 Monroe Ave San Diego CA 92116 Office: Imperial Corp 9275 Sky Park Ct San Diego CA 92123

ANDRADE, RONALD PHILIP, management consultant; b. Los Angeles, May 14, 1947; s. Louis Bernardo and Annie (Vasquez) A.; m. Ellen Gale Lowry, Sept. 19, 1987; children: Ronda, Adrin, Gavin, Elizabeth, Stephanie. Student, U. Calif., San Diego, 1971-72, San Diego State U., 1975-76; BA in Psychology, 1987, MA in Psychology, 1988; postgrad., Nat. U. Sch. Law, 1988—. Nat. exec. dir. Nat. Congress Am. Indians, Washington, 1980-83; staff asst. U.S. Dept. Interior Office of Indian Affairs, Washington, 1983-84; Indian civil rights specialist USDA, Washington, 1984-86; sr. planner La Jolla Indian Tribe, Valley Center, Calif., 1986-88; prin. Andrade & Assocs., Valley Center, 1988—; resource cons. Nat. Indian Luth. Bd., 1988—. Presdl. appointee Nat. Adv. Council on Indian Edn., Washington, 1988; del. All-Indian Housing Authority, 1987—; bd. dirs. Sta. KGTV Minority Adv. Council, San Diego, 1979-80; mem. Regional Employment Tng. Consortium, San Diego, 1979, La Jolla Indian Tribal Coun.; fundraising cons. DQ Univ., Davis, Calif., 1986—. Served to cpl. USMCR, 1966-70. Named one of Outstanding Young Men of Am., 1981; Dept. Edn. fellow, 1987. Mem. Nat. Am. Indian Council (exec. bd.), Nat. Congress Am. Indians, Nat. Indian Edn. Assn. Home and Office: PO Box 244 Valley Center CA 92082

ANDRADE, THERESA JANE, construction company executive; b. Kahului, Hawaii, July 19, 1959; d. Gerald Allen and Theone Jane (Oliveira) A. Cert. with distinction in Airline Travel Ops., Travel Inst. of Pacific, 1979. V.p. G. A. Constrn., Inc., Kahului, 1978—; bus. mgr. The Noodle Kitchen, Kahului, 1986—; cons. Christine's Restaurant, Lahaina, Hawaii, 1983—; owner The Window Magician, Kahului, 1981—. Mem. The Network, Mediation Svcs. Maui (bd. dirs. 1984—, pres. bd. dirs. 1987-88, Outstanding Svc. award 1983-87), Maui Contractors Assn., Maui C. of C. Republican. Roman Catholic. Office: G A Constrn Inc 210 Papa Pl Kahului HI 96732

ANDRASIK, STEPHEN SAMUEL, marketing professional; b. Weirton, W.Va., Oct. 19, 1961; s. Ernest E. and Joretta (Urso) A. Student, Calif. Poly. U., 1980-83; cert., Chenchi U., Taipei, Republic of China, 1984; BS, U. So. Calif., 1985. Maintenance mechanic Hughes Aircraft, Fullerton, Calif., 1982, asst. electrician, 1983; market specialist E-Hsin Internat. Corp., Taipei, 1984-85; purchaser Gen. Felt Industries, Pico Rivera, Calif., 1983-85; v.p. sales, mktg. EJS Internat., Santa Ana, Calif., 1985—. Grantee Assn. Western Furniture Suppliers, Los Angeles, 1985. Mem. Dean's Adv. Bd. Bus. Sch. (chmn. lunch com. 1985), Alpha Kappa Psi (v.p. ops.). Republican. Home and Office: 515 Delaware St Huntington Beach CA 92648

ANDREOPOULOS, SPYROS GEORGE, writer; b. Athens, Greece, Feb. 12, 1929; s. George S. and Anne Levas) A.; came to U.S., 1953, naturalized, 1962; A.B., Wichita State U., 1957; m. Christiane Loesch Loriaux, June 6, 1958; 1 child, Sophie. Pub. info. specialist USIA, Salonica, Greece, 1951-53; asst. editorial page editor Wichita (Kans.) Beacon, 1955-59; asst. dir. info. services, editor The Menninger Quar., The Menninger Found., Topeka, 1959-63; info. officer Stanford U. Med. Ctr., 1963-83, dir. communications and editor Stanford Medicine, 1983—; editor Sun Valley Forum on Nat. Health, Inc. (Idaho), 1972-83, 85—. Served with Royal Hellenic Air Force, 1949-50. Mem. AAAS, Assn. Am. Med. Colls., Nat. Assn. Sci. Writers, Am. Med. Writers Assn., Am. Hosp. Assn., Am. Soc. Hosp. Mktg. and Pub. Relations, Council for Advancement and Support of Edn. Co-author, editor: Medical Cure and Medical Care, 1972; Primary Care: Where Medicine Fails, 1974; National Health Insurance: Can We Learn from Canada? 1975; Heart Beat, 1978, Health Care for an Aging Society, 1989. Contbr. articles to profl. jours. Home: 1012 Vernier Pl Stanford CA 94305

ANDRESS, VERN RANDOLPH, psychologist, marriage and family therapist; b. Boulder, Colo., Mar. 29, 1935; s. Victor William and Frances Willette (Boyer) A.; children: Vivian Monica, Kimberley Dawn; m. Linda Kathleen Delgardo, Nov. 29, 1986. A.A., Southwestern Coll., Chula Vista, Calif., 1967; B.A., San Diego State Coll., 1969; M.S., San Diego State U., 1971; Ph.D., U.S. Internat. U., 1976. Pres. Beauty Boutique, Inc., San Diego, 1961-67; counselor San Diego Acad., 1969-70; dir. adminstrn. of justice Loma Linda U., Riverside, Calif., 1970-80, asst. prof. psychology, 1972-76, assoc. prof., 1976-79, prof., 1979—, chmn. dept. psychology, 1977-80, dean Coll. Arts and Sci., 1980-84; psychologist Riverside County Coroner's Office, 1976—; ptnr. Andress and Assocs., Counseling and Cons., Grand Terrace, Calif., 1988—; ptnr. Andress and Assocs., Counseling and Cons., Grand Terrace, Calif.; cons. psychology to law enforcement and industry, 1970—. Contbr. numerous articles to profl. jours., popular publs.; editor: Jour. Adventist Behavioral Scientists, 1974-79. Mem. Grand Terrace Planning Commn., Calif., 1978-86. Served with U.S. Army, 1954-56, France. Named Disting. Researcher Inland Counties Psychol. Assn., 1980; recipient Disting. Service award Calif. Sex Crimes Investigators, 1983. Mem. Am. Assn. Suicidology, Am. Psychol. Assn., Calif. State Psychol. Assn., Calif. Assn. Marriage and Family Therapists, Am. Orchid Soc., John Steinbeck Soc., Sigma Xi. Adventist. Office: Loma Linda U 4700 Pierce St Riverside CA 92515

ANDREW, ROBERT LYNAL, Canadian provincial official; b. Eston, Sask., Can., Apr. 13, 1944; s. Robert Elvin and Elizabeth Ann (Ellis) A.; m. N. Lynne Tunall, Dec. 22, 1964; children—Quinn, Kalen, Sharmen, Dreeson. B.A., U. Sask., 1966, L.L.B., 1970. Bar: Sask. With supply and transp. dept. Pacific Petroleums, Calgary, Alta., Can., 1967-68; programmer IBM, Saskatoon, 1968; with personnel dept. Allan Potash Mine, 1969-70; mem. Andrew, Ritter, Chinn, Kindersley, Sask., 1970-80, sr. ptnr., 1973-80; minister of fin., chmn. Treasury Bd., Govt. of Sask., Regina, 1982-85; vice chmn. Crown Mgmt. Bd., 1983-86, mem., 1986—; atty. gen. Minister of Justice, 1986—; minister Econ. Devel. and Trade, 1985—, Trade and Investment, 1988—. Mem. Eston Town Council, 1972-74. Progressive Conservative. Contbr. articles to parliamentary jours. Office: Govt Sask, 355 Legislative Bldg, Regina, SK Canada S4S 0B3

ANDREWS, GARTH E., public relations executive; b. Bakersfield, Calif., Mar. 5, 1943; s. Milton Dale and F. Janice (Schermerhorn) A.; m. Lennie May Husen, Dec. 22, 1964; children: Corinna, Heather. BA in Radio-TV, East Wash. U., Cheney, 1967. Accreditated pub. rels. Reporter, photographer King Broadcasting, Seattle, Spokane, Wash., 1967-68; reporter, anchorman, exec. producer KBOI/KBCI Radio/TV, Boise, Idaho, 1968-75; adminstrn. pub. info. Idaho Pub. Utilities Commn., Boise, 1975-78; sr. pub. rels. assoc. P. R. Mallory & Co. Inc., Indpls., 1978-79; communications rep. S.W. Gas Corp., Las Vegas, Nev., 1979-81, dir. pub. info., 1981-83; dir. communications S.W. Gas Corp., Tucson, Ariz., 1983-87, Phoenix, 1987—. Mem. publicity steering com. Fiesta Bowl, Phoenix, 1987-88; chmn. Fiesta Bowl Hot Air Balloon Classic, Phoenix, 1988-89; trustee Ariz. Mus. Sci. and Tech., Phoenix, 1987—; mem. Pima County Energy Commn., Tucson, 1984-87. With USNR, 1962-64, PTO. Mem. Pub. Rels. Soc. Am. Republican. Presbyterian. Office: SW Gas Corp 10851 N Black Canyon Hwy Phoenix AZ 85029

ANDREWS, GLENDON LOUIS, chemical engineer, consultant; b. Meadowdale, Wash., Aug. 1, 1917; s. Louis and Johanna Charity (Bray) A.; m. Maxine Anna Buchanan, Dec. 25, 1941; children: John Louis (dec.), Bruce Buchanan. BSChemE, U. Wash., 1942. Div. mgr. mfg. Procter and Gamble Co., Cin., 1942-62; pres. Andrews and Sons, Molalla, Oreg., 1962-73; mng. ptnr. A.F.S.-Cons. to Engrs., La Grande, Oreg., 1973—; gen. mgr. Courtright Irrigation Co., La Grande, 1976-79; pres., bd. dirs. Fed. Land Bank Assocs., Oregon City, Oreg., 1968-72. Com. mem. N.Y.C. Bd. Higher Edn., 1956-58; chmn. com. United Fund, Cin., 1961; chmn. Molalla Union High Sch. Bd., 1968-72; mem. gov.'s commn. State of Oreg., 1978-81; elder, trustee Presbyn. Ch., La Grande. Mem. Am. Charolais Assn. (bd. dirs. 1964-68), Western Charolais Assn. (bd. dirs., pres. 1963-72), Oreg. State U. Whityycomb Club (hon.), Tau Beta Pi. Democrat. Home and Office: PO Box 1721 La Grande OR 97850

ANDREWS, JAMES WHITMORE, JR., theatrical producer, director; b. New Haven, Sept. 30, 1950; s. James Whitmore Andrews and Nancy Lee (Peery) Levin; m. Sharon Gray Mills, Nov. 6, 1971; 1 child, Jesse Leigh. Student, U. N.C., 1968-71. Mng. dir. Homestead Arts Inc., Colorado Springs, Colo., 1970-73; producing dir. Theatreworks, Colorado Springs, 1977—; bd. dirs. Shakespeare In The Park, Colorado Springs; founder, dir. Playwrights Forum awards, Colorado Springs, 1981—; mem. selection com. gov.'s Awards for the Arts, 1989. Mem. Pike's Peak Arts Coun., Colorado Springs, 1983—; mem. grant rev. panels Colo. Coun. on Arts and Humanities, 1987-88, gov.'s award nomination panel, 1989. Mem. Am. Arts Alliance, Colo. Found. for the Arts, Colo. Citizens for the Arts, Colo. Theatre Producer's Guild, Rocky Mountain Theatre Guild. Democrat. Home: 436 Franklin Colorado Springs CO 80903 Office: U Colo Austin Bluffs Pkwy Colorado Springs CO 80907

ANDREWS, JILL C., association executive; b. Clinton, Iowa, June 28, 1943; d. Jack Jackells and Priscilla DeMiller (Bell) A.; divorced; children: Karen, Michael, David, Laura, Lisa. Student, Parsons Coll., 1960-61, Marycrest Coll., 1962-63, Northwestern U., 1965, U. Phoenix, 1987, 89. Campaign mgr., dist. rep. U.S. Rep. Eldon Rudd, Phoenix, 1976-77; campaign mgr. Stan Akers Corp. Commn., Phoenix, 1978; exec. dir. Rep. Legis. Campaign Com., Phoenix, 1979-80; dir. pub. relations Circle K Corp., Phoenix, 1980-82; pres. Impact S.W. Inc., Phoenix, 1982-86; exec. dir. Rocky Mountain region Reagan-Bush campaign, Phoenix, 1983-84; dir. pub. affairs Ariz. chpt. Assoc. Gen. Contractors, Phoenix, 1986--; trustee Ariz. Laborers Teamsters, Cement Masons and Operating Engrs. Editor Views and News mag., 1986--, News Notes newsletter, 1986--, Supervision, 1986--. Active numerous polit. campaigns, Iowa, Ill., Ariz.; bd. dirs. Phoenix Behavioral Health Found., 1982-87, So. Mountain Salvation Army, 1982-86, Community Network for Youth, Phoenix, 1983--; mem. Pro Act, Phoenix, 1971--. Mem. Ariz. Assn. for Indsl. Devel., Ariz. Club (Phoenix). Office: Assoc Gen Contractors 1825 W Adams St Phoenix AZ 85005

ANDREWS, JOHN KNEELAND, youth worker; b. Winchester, Mass., May 29, 1920; s. George Angell and Frances (Kneeland) A.; m. Marianne Hutchinson, Mar. 21, 1943 (dec. July 1978); children: John. K. Jr., James H., Eleanor Andrews Keasey, Sally Andrews Griego; m. Mary Folds, Feb. 14, 1979. BA, Principia, Elsah, Ill., 1942. Mgr. Fennville (Mich.) Milling Co., 1945-48; asst. traffic mgr. Mich. Fruit Canners, Fennville, 1948-50; food broker Rosen Brokerage Co., St. Louis, 1950-53; alumni sec., asst. to treas. The Principia, St. Louis, 1953-55; exec. dir. Sky Valley Ranch, Inc., Buena Vista, Colo., 1955-60; chief exec. officer, chmn. bd. dirs. Adventure Unltd., Englewood, Colo., 1960-83; chmn. emeritus Adventure Unltd., Englewood, 1983—; sole practice youth worker Denver, 1983—. Lt. Submarine Svc., USNR, 1942-45, PTO. Decorated Silver Star. Mem. Cherry Hills Country Club (Englewood), Rotary (bd. dirs. Denver chpt. 1983-85). Republican. Christian Scientist. Home and Office: 8505 E Temple Dr Unit 464 Denver CO 80237

ANDREWS, LAURA LOUISE, computer specialist, sales executive; b. Memphis, June 7, 1962; d. Richard Lee Anderson and Phyllis Joyce (Watt) Ross; m. Bret William Andrews, Dec. 31, 1983. BS, Kans. State U., 1983. Sales rep. Am. Passage Corp., Seattle, 1981, Manhattan, Kans., 1981-84; computer analyst Chubb and Assoc., Middletown, Pa., 1984-86; adminstrv. asst. Tele-Digit Corp., Flagstaff, Ariz., 1986-87; computer specialist New England Bus. Svc., Flagstaff, 1987-88, computer support, sales rep., 1988—. Mem. Big Sisters of Northern Ariz., Flagstaff, 1986—. Recipient Scholarship, Bus. and Profl. Women's Soc., Dodge City, Kans., 1981, Heaton Scholarship, 1981. Mem. Golden Key (lifetime mem.), Phi Kappa Phi. Republican. Methodist. Home: 3613 E Raccoon Way Flagstaff AZ 86004

ANDREWS, MICHAEL, chief scientist; b. Clifton, N.J., Apr. 19, 1940; s. Emil Sr. and Anna (Birish) Moherek; m. Sandra Sue Hines, Feb. 20, 1965; children: Jennifer, Christopher, Ginger, Rebecca. BSEE, Rutgers U., 1963, BA, 1963; MSEE, U. Ariz., 1969, PhD, 1972. Mem. tech. staff Hughes Aircraft, Tucson, 1967-68, Electro Tech. Analysis Corp., Tucson, 1969-71; sr. scientist Spectral Dynamics Corp., San Diego, 1973-74; advisor to elec. div. Army Research Office, Research Triangle Park, N.C., 1980-81; prof. elec. engring. Colo. State U., Fort Collins, 1974-84; pres., chief scientist Space Tech. Corp., Fort Collins, 1969—; evluator U. Miami, 1987; invited speaker SDIO Conf., Washington, 1988; lectr. IEEE, ACM. Author: Principles of Firmware Engineering in Microprogramming, 1980, Programming Microprocessor Interfaces for Control, 1982, Self-Guided Tour Through the 68000, 1984, Computer Organization, 1986; contbr. articles to profl. jours. Ch. deacon, tchr., seminar presenter, ministry team Vineyard Christian Fellowship, Fort Collins, 1988. Served as capt. USAF, 1963-66. Mem. IEEE, ASEE (chmn. 1976). Republican. Home: 2324 Manchester Ct Fort Collins CO 80526 Office: Space Tech Corp 125 Crestridge Dr Fort Collins CO 80525

ANDREWS, NANCY BOERSMA, software company executive, technical writer; b. Louisville, Feb. 16, 1945; d. Donald and Marie (Van Soest) Boersma; m. Carl A. Andrews, Aug. 20, 1966; children: Kaaren, Kirsten. BA in English, Wheaton (Ill.) Coll., 1966; MA in English, Northwestern U., 1969; BS in Computer Sci., Seattle Pacific U., 1986. Tchr. McClureJr. High Sch., Western Springs, Ill., 1966-70; coord. women's programs South Seattle Community Coll., Seattle, 1972-78; coord. Columbia Basin Community Coll., Richland, Wash., 1978-79; cons. Ekkeson-Oncken Corp., Seattle, 1979-81; owner, mgr. Plain English, Seattle, 1981-86; mgr. tng. materials Microsoft Corp., Redmond, Wash., 1986-88, user, edn. mgr., 1988—. Author: File: Organize Your Small Business, 1985, Windows, 1985, Command Performance: Word, 1986, Organizing Your Hard Disk, 1986; contbr. articles to profl. jours. Bd. dirs. Planned Parenthood, Everett, Wash., 1981-84, Shohomish County Arts Coun., 1985-88. Mem. Nat. Soc. Performance Instruction, Soc. Tech. Communication. Home: 702 Campbell Ave Mukilteo WA 98275 Office: Microsoft Corp 16011 NE 36th Way Redmond WA 98073-9717

ANDREWS, RICHARD JEROME, controller; b. Toledo, July 1, 1941; s. John Striker and Dorothy Katharine (Hanselman) A.; m. Sybil Dell Forest, Feb. 20, 1973 (div. 1984); children: Richard Jr., Caron, John, Jeffrey; m. Kathleen West, Sept. 21, 1985. BA in Psychology, Colgate U., 1963. Plant controller Owens-Corning Fiberglas, various locations, 1964-76; mktg. controller Owens-Corning Fiberglas, Toledo, 1976-81; pres. Andrews Enterprises, Amarillo, Tex., 1981-83; ind. mgmt. cons. Albuquerque, 1984-87; corp. controller Trax Instrument Corp., Albuquerque, 1987—. Republican. Episcopalian. Home: 9613 San Rafael Ave NE Albuquerque NM 87109

ANDREWS, RICHARD JOHN, financial executive; b. West Palm Beach, Fla., Oct. 9, 1954; s. Carl Edwin and Jane (Place) A.; m. Christie Francis Hewit, Apr. 15, 1989. BSBA, U. Denver, 1976; BSEE, U. Colo., 1977. Cert. fin. planner. Wildlife researcher Colo. Div. Wildlife, Red Feather Lakes, Colo., 1972-74; marine mammal researcher USN, Key Largo, Fla., 1976-77; dir. acctg. Miller Internat., Denver, 1977-80; fin. mgr. Adolph Coors Co., Golden, Colo., 1980—; field rsch. cons. USN, San Diego, 1986—. Contbr. articles to profl. publs. Planning adviser City of Golden, 1985. Mem. Indsl. Rsch. Inst. Home: 8314 Pondarosa Dr Parker CO 80134 Office: Adolph Coors Co Rsch and Devel Engring Dept MS BC542 Golden CO 80401

ANDREWS, SIMON, graphic designer; b. Detroit, Mar. 12, 1943; s. John J. and Virginia (Baird) A.; m. Julie Cairns, Apr. 28, 1985; children: Rachelle Virginia, Phoenix Coverley. AB in Psychology, San Francisco State U., 1968. Freelance in design projectsand travel San Diego, 1968-76; v.p. Graphic Solutions, Ltd., San Diego, 1976—. Mem. La Jolla (Calif.) Town Coun., 1985—; trustee La Community Planning Assn., 1988—; mem. facilities com. San Diego Park and Recreation Bd., 1988—. Mem. Soc. for Mktg. Profl. Svcs. (bd. dirs. 1988—), Soc. Environ. Graphic Designers, Am. Inst. Graphic Artists, AIA, Am. Soc. Landscape Architects, Subud Internat. Brotherhood. Office: Graphic Solutions Ltd 1750 Kettner Blvd San Diego CA 92101

ANDREWS, TRAVIS SCOTT, real estate salesman, consultant, developer; b. Tucson, Ariz., Feb. 7, 1956; s. Leo Dean and Jacquiline Adel (Hornbacher) A.; m. Pamela Ann Munden, Apr. 10, 1988. Grad. high sch., Tucson. Owner Andrews Plastering Inc., Tucson, 1978-83; land salesman Tucson Realty & Trust, 1983—; gen. ptnr. ORO Ptnrs., Tucson, 1985-87, ABU Properties, Tucson, 1986-88. Mem. fin. com. Tucson St. Patrick's Day Parade, 1987. Mem. Ariz. Bd. Realtors (cert. comml. investment mem.). Republican. Episcopalian. Office: Tucson Realty & Trust 1890 E River Rd Tucson AZ 85718

ANDREWS, VICTORIA JOY, clothing executive; b. Columbus, Ohio, Aug. 28, 1954; d. Paul Edward and Norma Jeanne (Dempsey) A. Grad. high sch., West Anchorage. Buyer Nordstrom, Seattle, 1973-77; buyer/merchandise mgr. Millers Outpost, Ontario, Calif., 1978-86; merchandiser Ocean Pacific, Irvine, Calif., 1986-87, Michael Gerald, Compton, Calif., 1987-88; owner Kiyo, Corona del Mar, Calif., 1988—. Mem. Newport Area Profls. Republican.

ANDROS, STEPHEN JOHN, architect; b. Joliet, Ill., July 21, 1955; s. Stephen Benedict and Jacquelyn M. (Schoob) A.; m. Vicki Lee McCaffery, June 24, 1978; children: Jeffrey Kenneth, Christopher John. BArch cum laude, Ariz. State U., 1978. Registered architect, Ariz.; cert. constrn. specifier. Project architect, specifier, contract adminstr. Cornoyer-Hedrick Architect and Planners Inc., Phoenix, 1978-83; ptnr. Perrell-Andros Cons. Architects, Scottsdale, Ariz., 1983-85; dir. specifications Haver, Nunn and Collamer Inc., Phoenix, 1985-86; faculty assoc. coll. architecture Ariz. State U., 1988; dir. specifications and quality control Gilleland, Hunt, Rehse, Ltd. Architects, Phoenix, 1986—; instr. Phoenix Inst. Tech., 1983-84; guest lectr. materials Ariz. State U., Tempe, 1984-88; mem. ad hoc contracting com. City of Phoenix, 1982. Prin. works include Banking and Revenue Bldg. State of Ariz., Phoenix, F-16 Squadron Ops., Luke AFB, Ariz., Scottsdale (Ariz.) Horseman's Park, McDonnell-Douglas Helicopter Co. Mesa (Ariz.) Facility, Spl. Mgmt. Unit for Ariz. Dept. Corrections, By Design at Ghiradelli Sq., San Francisco, Desert Valley Med. Ctr., Phoenix, Anasazi Bus. Park, Phoenix, Papago High Sch. BIA, San Simeon, Ariz., Student Activities Ctr. No. Ariz. U., Flagstaff, Remodel of Terminal 2 Sky Harbor Internat. Airport, Phoenix, Tempe Minicomputer Maintenance Ops. Ctr., Cen. One Thomas High Rise, Phoenix, Valley Nat. Bank, Phoenix. Mem. Osborn Sch. Dist. bond program, Glendale Union High Sch. Dist. Bond Program, Page Mid. Sch. Recipient Cert. Recognition Copper Devel. Assn., 1977. Mem. AIA (profl. Cen. Ariz. chpt.), Constrn. Specifications Inst. (profl. Phoenix chpt., moderator Pres.'s forum, 1985, leader cert. workshop S.W. region, 1986, rep. to Constrn. Industry Council Ariz., 1981-84, chmn. Phoenix chpt. program, 1979-80, sec. Phoenix chpt., 1980-81, 1st v.p. Phoenix chpt., 1981-82, pres. Phoenix chpt., 1982-83, 83-84, treas. Phoenix chpt., 1987-88, program chmn. S.W. region conf., 1985, mem. inst. cert. com., 1984-87, chmn., 1986-87), Specifications Cons. in Ind. Practice (corr., nat. v.p., 1984-85, editor newsletter, 1983-85). Republican. Methodist. Home: 7321 N 19th Dr Phoenix AZ 85021

ANDROSS, NORMAN ELLSWORTH, electronics engineer; b. Portland, Oreg., Mar. 20, 1921; s. Claude Ellsworth and Olive Mae (Boyd) A.; m. Delma May Pyle, Oct. 10, 1943 (div. 1971); children: Norman E. II, Stephanie L. Andross Schmitz; m. Gertrude Sanders, Aug. 1973. AA in Computer Tech., Santa Monica (Calif.) City Coll., 1974. Sr. rsch. analyst Northrop Corp., Hawthorne, Calif., 1966-70, sr. instr. avionics, 1974-85; sr. rsch. analyst System Devel. Corp., Hawthorne, 1971-72; instr. avionics Rockwell Corp., Hawthorne, 1972-74; pres., sr. cons. A&N Tech., Santa Maria, Calif., 1985—. Lt. col. USAAF, 1942-45, USAF, 1949-60. Decorated Silver Star, D.F.C. with two oak leaf clusters, Bronze Star, Air medal. Mem. Am. Legion, Ret. Officers Assn., Inst. of Navigation, Wild Goose Assn., Santa Maria C. of C. Home: 821 Greenacre Dr Santa Maria CA 93455

ANDRUS, CECIL DALE, governor of Idaho; b. Hood River, Oreg., Aug. 25, 1931; s. Hal Stephen and Dorothy (Johnson) A.; m. Carol Mae May, Aug. 27, 1949; children: Tana Lee, Tracy Sue, Kelly Kay. Student, Oreg. State U., 1948-49; LLD (hon.), Gonzaga U., U. Idaho, U. N.Mex., Coll. Idaho. State gen. mgr. Paul Revere Life Ins. Co., 1969-70; gov. State of Idaho, 1971-77, 87—; sec. of interior 1977-81; dir. Albertson's, Inc., 1985-87; mem. Idaho Senate, 1961-66, 69-70; mem. exec. com. Nat. Gov.'s Conf., 1971-72, chmn., 1976; chmn. Fedn. Rocky Mountain States, 1971-72. Chmn. bd. trustees Coll. of Idaho, 1985—; bd. dirs. Sch. Forestry, Duke University. Served with USN, 1951-55. Recipient Disting. Citizen award Oreg. State U., 1980, Collier County Conservancy medal, 1979; named Conservationist of Yr., Nat. Wildlife Fedn., 1980, Idaho Wildlife Fedn., 1972, Man of Yr., VFW, 1959. Mem. VFW, Idaho Taxpayers Assn. (dir. 1964-66). Democrat. Office: State Capitol Office of Gov Boise ID 83720

ANDRUS, PAUL WILLIAM, dentist; b. Lexington, Ky., July 30, 1956; s. Buel J. and Flora Ann (McDougall) A. DDS, U. Colo., 1982. Gen. practice resident Denver Gen. Hosp., 1983; dentist Youth with a Mission, S. Pacific Islands, 1983-84; dentist, adj. faculty mem. Michael Cardone Sch. Dentistry, Tulsa, 1984-85; pvt. practice dentistry Tulsa, 1984-86, Lakewood, Colo., 1986—. Mem. Am. Dental Assn. Office: 2009 Wadsworth Blvd Suite 102 Lakewood CO 80215

ANEMA-GARTEN, DURLYNN CAROL, communications and education professor, columnist; b. San Diego, Dec. 23, 1935; d. Durlin L. Flagg and Carolyn L. (Janeck) Owen; m. Charles Jay Anema, May 6, 1955 (dec. Sept. 1986); children: Charlynn, Raimundi, Charles Jay Jr., Richard F.; m. Vernon Ray Garten, July 30, 1988. Student, Stanford U., 1953-55; BA, Calif. State U., Hayward, 1968, MS, 1977; EdD, U. of the Pacific, 1984. Cert. secondary edn. tchr., Calif. Columnist, reporter San Leandro (Calif.) Morning News, 1960-62; adult tchr. Hayward Unified Sch. Dist., 1969, tchr. secondary edn., 1972-75, vice prin., 1975-77; tchr. secondary edn. San Leandro Unified Sch. Dist., 1970-72; vice prin. Lodi (Calif.) Unified Sch. Dist., 1977-80; rsch. dir. Ctr. for Econ. Edn., U. of the Pacific, Stockton, Calif., 1980-81; dir. lifelong learning U. of the Pacific, Stockton, 1981-84, prof., 1984—; columnist Stockton Record, 1984—; cons. in field. Author: Don't Get Fired, 1978, Get Hired, 1979, Sharing an Apartment, 1981, Designing Effective Brochures and Newsletters, 1987, Career Experiment, 1988, Late Life, 1988, (with others) California Yesterday and Today, 1983. Pres., bd. dirs. Bd. of Library Trustees, San Leandro, 1970-75; elder Grace Presbyn. Ch., Lodi, 1985-87; pres., bd. dirs. Valley Community Counseling, Stockton, 1986—; mem. Commn. on Children, San Joaquin County, Calif., 1986—; hon. life mem. Monroe PTA, 1965. Recipient Susan B. Anthony award Commn. on Women, 1989. Mem. Western Speech Communication Assn., AAUW, Assn. Journalism Media Educators, Investigative Editors and Reporters, Stanford U. Alumni Assn., Phi Kappa Phi, Delta Kappa Gamma, Sigma Delta Chi. Home: 1728 W Vine St Lodi CA 95242

ANGEL, ARMANDO CARLOS, internist; b. Las Vegas, N.Mex., Mar. 25, 1940; s. Edmundo Clemente and Pauline Teresa (Flores) Sanchez A.; m. Judith Lee Weedin, Aug. 5, 1961; children—Stephanie, Renee. B.A., San Jose State U., 1963; M.S., U. Ariz., 1970, Ph.D., 1971, M.D., 1977. Chemist Tracerlab, Inc., Richmond, Calif., 1963-67; prof. chemistry Pima Coll., Tucson, Ariz., 1971-74; intern U. N.Mex., Albuquerque, 1977-78, resident, 1978-80; resident VA Hosp., Lovelace Med. Ctr., Albuquerque, 1978-80; practice medicine specializing in internal medicine, Las Cruces, N.Mex., 1980—; cons. minority biomed. sci. project NIH, Washington, 1970-74, Ednl. Assocs., Tucson, 1971-74. Author: Llevve Tlaloc No. 2, 1973. Treas. Nat. Chicano Health Orgn., Los Angeles, 1974-75; v.p. Mexican-Am. Educators, Tucson, 1973-74; pres. N.Mex. affiliate Am. Diabetes Assn., Albuquerque, 1983-85. Fellow U. Ariz., 1988—. Mem. AMA, Am. Diabetes Assn., ACP, Dona Ana County Med. Soc. (pres. 1983), Am. Coll. Rheumatology, Am. Assn. Internal Medicine, Alpha Chi Sigma.

ANGELE, ALFRED ROBERT, police labor union administrator; b. N.Y.C., Dec. 9, 1940; s. Alfred Otto and Alma Margarert (Branda) A.; m. Barbara Ann Chaves, Sept. 30, 1961; children: Cynthia Lynn, Lynda Renee. AA, L.A. Valley Coll., 1968. Cert. tchr. community coll. police sci. Patrolman Burbank (Calif.) Police Dept., 1963-67, detective, 1967-74, sgt., dept. self def. instr., 1974-78; gen. mgr. Calif. Orgn. Police and Sheriffs, Sacramento, 1978—; Govt. appt. commr. on Peace Officer Standards/Tng., Sacramento, 1979-84; mem. Police Adv. Coun. on Car Clubs, 1967-70. Contbr. articles to profl. jours. including USA Today. Mem. AFL-CIO, 1985—. With USNR, 1957-58; also USMC 1958-62. Recipient Mike Maggiora Meml. Humanitarian award Maggiora family, 1980, Commendations, Letters of Appreciation Burbank Bar Assn., Elks, Calif. Hwy. Patrol, Mayor's Drug and Alcohol Abuse Com., L.A. County Dist. Atty.'s Office, Houston Police Patrolmans Union, Calif. Dept. Corrections, Mayor of L.A., numerous others; named 1st Officer of the Month Jaycees, 1977. Mem. Burbank Police Officers Assn. (pres. 1976-81, named dir. of year 1972, commendation award), Internat. Union of Police Assns. (sec.-treas. 1985—, dir. 1981-85, named law enforcement editor of the year 1987), Calif. Narcotics Officers Assn., Calif. Orgn. Police/Sheriffs (sec. 1976-78, commendation award), Calif. Narcotics Info. Network. Democrat. Roman Catholic. Home: 7410 Security Ave Burbank CA 91504 Office: 175 E Olive Ave Ste 400 Burbank CA 91502

ANGELILLIS, FABIO, computer engineer; b. Caracas, Venezuela, Mar. 5, 1961; s. Michele and Giuliana (Salsilli) A.; m. Ivette Rodriguez, Dec. 4, 1984. BS in Engring. cum laude, U. Fla., 1985. Computer engr. Hewlett-Packard Corp., Colorado Springs, 1985-88, Teradyne Inc., Mt. View, Calif., 1988—; chmn. Electronic Design Interchange Format Schematic Tech. Com., Washington, 1986—. Mem. Assn. for Computing Machinery, Tau Beta Pi, Upsilon Pi Epsilon. Roman Catholic. Office: Teradyne Eda 5155 Old Ironsides Dr Santa Clara CA 95054

ANGELL-COLE, KAREN DORIS, publishing company executive; b. Warwick, R.I., Mar. 22, 1953; d. Charles Edward and Lucille Jeanine (Robert) Angell; m. Robert William Cole, Oct. 5, 1976 (div. Feb. 1982); 1 child, Michaela Leigh. BA in Polit. Sci., U. Colo., 1983; Cert. Paralegal, Am. U., 1974. Paralegal R.I. Protection and Advocacy, Providence, 1971-75, Pikes Peak Legal Svcs., Colorado Springs, 1975-77; circulation mgr. Gazette Telegraph, Colorado Springs, 1977-80, Miramar Pub., L.A., 1981-82; circulation dir. High Tech. Publs., Torrance, Calif., 1982-85; circulation dir. The Apparel News Group, L.A., 1985-88, pub. cons., 1988—; mem. Am. Airlines Corp. adv. coun. Mem. AIDS L.A., 1988—. Mem. Western Fulfillment Mgrs. (bd. dirs. 1988—), Western Pubs. Assn., Nat. Orgn. Women. Democrat. Episcopalian. Home: 1445 Oahu Dr West Covina CA 91792 Office: Miller Mktg Inc 881 Dover Dr Newport Beach CA 92663

ANGELO, GAYLE-JEAN, mathematics and physical science educator; b. Winchester, Mass., Nov. 27, 1951; d. John William and Josephine Marie (Tavano) A.; B.A. in Physics with honor, Northeastern U., 1975, M.Ed. in Curriculum and Instrn. of Sci. and Math., 1978; M.S. in Applied Statis., Columbia U., 1984, postgrad., 1984—. Cert. secondary tchr., Mass.; cert. community coll. tchr., Calif. Clin. chemist Boston Med. Lab., Inc., 1971-73; exptl. physicist Northeastern U., 1975-76; tchr. natural scis., head sci. dept. Girls Cath. High Sch., Malden, Mass., 1977-78; research and teaching asst. Columbia U., N.Y.C., 1979-80, research assoc., 1982-83; research scientist Air Force Rocket Propulsion Lab., Edwards AFB, Calif., 1980-82; research and devel. analyst, engr. Varian-Extrion Div., Gloucester, Mass., 1984-86; instr. math. Golden Gate U., Cerro Coso Community Coll., 1981-82, Columbia U., N.Y.C., 1982-83; instr. chemistry North Shore Community Coll., 1984-86; instr. math., physics Imperial Valley Coll., Imperial, Calif., 1986—. Served with USAF, 1980-82, Air N.G., 1982-85, USAFR, 1985-87. Mem. Am. Assn. Physics Tchrs., Am. Phys. Soc., Mathematical Assn. of Am., Nat. Council Tchrs. Math., Nat. Sci. Tchrs. Assn., Soc. Coll. Sci. Tchrs., Mensa, Sigma Xi, Phi Delta Kappa, Sigma Pi Sigma. Sigma Delta Epsilon, Kappa Delta Pi. Office: Imperial Valley Coll Math Sci Engring Dept 380 E Aten Rd Imperial CA 92251

ANGLE, LISA ALISON, forester; b. Fort Dix, N.J., June 6, 1953; d. Frank Lee and Helen E. (Bonney) Vito; m. James Marcus Angle, Oct. 1, 1988; 1 child, Scott M. Vito. BS in Forest Mgmt., No. Ariz. U., 1975. Forestry aide U.S. Forest Service, Williams, Ariz., 1973; forestry tech. U.S. Forest Service, Pagosa Springs, Colo., 1974, Hebo, Oreg., 1975-78; forester U.S. Forest Service, Sierra Vista, Ariz., 1978-81, Safford, Ariz., 1981—. Republican. Methodist. Office: USFS Safford Ranger Dist PO Box 709 504 5th Ave Safford AZ 85548

ANGUS, EDWARD LUVERNE, college dean; b. Fredericksburg, Va., Feb. 12, 1939; s. Rudolph Luverne and Jessie (Stamper) A.; m. Judith Louise Larson, July 17, 1971. A.B., U. Ky.-Lexington, 1961; M.A., Pa. State U., 1963, Ph.D., 1970. Asst. prof. polit. sci. Humboldt State Coll., Arcata, Calif., 1970-71; dir. exptl. edn. and instl. research Mars Hill Coll., N.C., 1971-75; asst. to chancellor Johnston Coll., U. Redlands, Calif., 1975-76; dir. pub. service adminstrn. masters degree program U. Wis.-Oshkosh, 1976-79; provost, dean acad. affairs Coll. Idaho, Caldwell, 1979-81; dean arts and scis. Fort Lewis Coll., Durango, Colo., 1981—. Co-editor: Urban Politics and Problems, 1969. Pres. Durango Fine Arts Council, 1984-86; mem., commr. City of Durango Commn. on the Arts, 1984-85; bd. dirs. Four Corners Opera Assn., Durango, 1983-86. NDEA fellow, 1961-64; Nat. Ctr. for Edn. in Politics fellow, Ford Found., 1964-65. Mem. Rocky Mountain Acad. Deans Assn., Internat. Council Fine Arts Deans, Council of Coll. of Arts and Sci. Democrat. Home: Seven Delwood Circle Durango CO 81301 Office: Ft Lewis Coll College Heights Durango CO 81301

ANJARD, RONALD P., business executive and technical consultant, educator, material specialist, banker. s. Auguste L. and Florence M. A.; m. Marie B. Sampler; children: Ronald P., Michale P., Michele M., John R. AS, Ind. U., 1973; BA in Humanities, T.A. Edison Coll., 1979; BSBA, U.S.N.Y., 1978; BS in Metall. Engring., Carnegie Mellon U., 1957; MS, MBA, Purdue U., 1968; PDE, U. Wis., 1979; PhD in Edn., Calif. Poly. U., 1981, PhD in Mettall. Engring., 1982. Metallurgist U.S. Steel, 1955-57; metall. engr. Crucible Steel Corp., 1957-58; process engr. Raython Mfg., 1958-59; gen. mgr. Delco Electronics div., 1959-81; div. quality mgr. AUX/JMI Electronic Matls. div., 1981-83; corp. dir. quality Kaypro Corp., 1983-86; sr. bank officer Mission Viejo Nat. Bank, 1986-87; dir. Absolute Solutions, 1987-88; pres. Anjard Imports, 1965-80; sr. exec. broker Futures Investment Firm, 1983; v.p. engring. AG Tech., 1983—; v.p. mktg. Alpha Cast Products, 1987—; v.p. adminstrn. Triage Network, 1988—; pres. Anjard Solder Paste Tech., San Diego, 1983—, Anjard Solder & Mfg. Tech., San Diego, 1987-88, Anjard Internat. Cons., San Diego, 1983, GD-Convair, 1987—; lectr. in field; guest faculty various colls. and univs.; conductor seminars in field. Mem. parish coun. San Diego, 1986—. With U.S. Army, 1957-66. Mem. Internat. Soc. Hybrid Microelectronics (chpt. newsletter chmn.), Am. Ceramics Soc., Internat. Electronic Packaging Soc., Am. Soc. Quality Control (editorial rev. com.), ASTM (mem. editorial rev. bd.), IEEE Cirs. & Devices (editorial rev. com.), AIME, Internat. Soc. for Investigation of Ancient Civilizations (founder, internat. dir.), Internat. Brick Collectors Assn. (founder, charter pres., bd. govs.), ACS, Sigma Xi. Office: Box 24369 San Diego CA 92124

ANNOS, JAMES ARTHUR, computer scientist; b. Phoenix, June 6, 1956; s. Margaret Alice Annos; m. Julie A. Sinnott, Oct. 14, 1978; children: Jessica A., James R. BS, Calif. Poly. State U., 1979. Computer scientist Naval Weapons Ctr., China Lake, Calif., 1977—, cons., 1983—. Contbr. articles to profl. jours. Mem. Applied Dynamics Internat. Users Soc., Digital Equipment Corp. Users Soc. Republican. Lutheran. Home: 121 Holly Canyon Ridgecrest CA 93555 Office: Naval Weapons Ctr Code 3914 China Lake CA 93555

ANSCHUTZ, PHILLIP F., diversified company executive; b. 1939. B.S., Univ. Kansas, 1961. Chmn., pres. Anschutz Corp., Denver, 1965—, also dir. Office: Anschutz Corp 2400 Anaconda Tower Denver CO 80202 *

ANSELL, GEORGE STEPHEN, metallurgical engineering educator; b. Akron, Ohio, Apr. 1, 1934; s. Frederick Jesse and Fanny (Soletsky) A.; m. Marjorie Boris, Dec. 18, 1960; children: Frederick Stuart, Laura Ruth, Benjamin Jesse. B. in Metall. Engring., Rensselaer Poly. Inst., 1954, M. in Metall. Engring., 1955, PhD, 1960. Physical metallurgist USN Research Lab., Washington, 1957-58; mem. faculty Rensselaer Poly. Inst., Troy, N.Y., 1960-84, Robert W. Hunt prof., 1965-84, chmn. materials div., 1969-74, dean engring., 1974-84; pres. Colo. Sch. Mines, Golden, 1984—; cons. in field; mem. adv. council to bd. dirs. Adolph Coors Co., Golden; bd. dirs. United Bank Denver. Editor books; patentee in field; contbr. over 100 articles to profl. jours. Served with USN, 1955-58. Recipient Hardy Gold Medal AIME, 1961, Curtis W. McGraw award Am. Soc. Engring. Edn., 1971, Souzandrade Gold Medal of Univ. Merit Fed. U. Maranhao, 1986. Fellow Metall. Soc. (pres. 1986-87), Am. Soc. Metals (Alfred H. Geisler award 1964, Bradley Stoughton award 1968); mem. NSPE, Am. Soc. Engring. Edn. (Curtis W. McGraw award 1971), Sigma Xi, Tau Beta Pi, Phi Lambda Upsilon. Club: Denver. Office: Colo Sch of Mines 1500 Illinois St Golden CO 80401

ANSELMI, RUDOLPH RUDY, construction company executive; b. Rock Springs, Wyo., May 1, 1904; s. Joseph A. and Mary (Menghini) A.; BS, U. Wyo., 1925, LLD (hon.), 1977; m. Shuster, July 10, 1929; children: Mary Lou Anselmi Unguren, Lynn Anselmi Lockhart, Jerl Anselmi Kirk. Sec.-treas. HMA Realty, KOA Kampgrounds, Rock Springs; dir. North Side State Bank, Wyo.; sec. Huntley Constrn. Co., Rock Springs. Mem. Sch. Bd., Rock Springs, 1936-65, pres., 1942-65; mem. Wyo. Senate, 1937-65; mem. Gov.'s Com. on Edn., 1963-64, Gov.'s Re-orgn. Com., 1967-68, 69-71; state committeeman Democratic party, 1944-66; mem. Legislative Interim Com., 1945-65; chmn. Wyo. Tax Commn. and State Bd. Equalization, 1975-87; mem. Wyo. state treas. investment adv. com., 1973-75. Named Distinguished Alumnus, U. Wyo. Coll. Commerce and Industry, 1961-62, Disting. Alumnus, U. Wyo., 1984; recipient Disting. Service award Nat. Govs. Assn., 1980. Mem. Elks, Eagles, K.C. (past grand knight, Vocations (pres.), Lions (past pres.), Sigma Chi, Phi Kappa Phi. Roman Catholic. Home: care Lynn Lockhart RT 2 Box 428C Portland OR 97231

ANSIN, PETER DAVID, film producer; b. Boston, June 12, 1957; s. John Roos Ehrenfeld and Miki (Goodman) Ansin. BA, Columbia U., 1980; MBA, Stanford U., 1985; cert. French fluency, Sorbonne U., 1978. Producer Merchant Ivory Prodns., N.Y.C., 1980-82; dir. programming TeleFrance USA, N.Y.C., 1982-83; analyst Home Box Office, N.Y.C., 1984; dir. Homevideo Twentieth Century Fox, L.A., 1985-88. Bd. dirs. Gay & Lesbian Media Coalition, L.A., 1988; founding sec. WAVES, Santa Monica, Calif., 1987-88; chpt. dir. The Names Project, L.A., 1988. Mem. Ind. Feature Project/West. Democrat. Home: 420 Raymond Ave 16 Santa Monica CA 90405

ANSLEY, DAVID GEORGE, newspaper editor; b. Seattle, Mar. 22, 1956; s. George Francis and Jane (Braham) A.; m. Jeanne Huber, July 27, 1985. BA in Communication, Stanford U., 1978. Reporter, editor Casper (Wyo.) Star-Tribune, 1979-81; copy editor San Jose (Calif.) Mercury News, 1981-84, sci. and medicine editor, 1984—. Vannevar Bush sci. writing fellow MIT, 1985-86. Mem. Nat. Assn. Sci. Writers, Coun. for Advancement Sci. Writing (bd. dirs. 1987--), New Eng. Historic Geneal. Soc. Office: San Jose Mercury News 750 Ridder Park Dr San Jose CA 95190

ANSON, FRED COLVIG, chemistry educator; b. Los Angeles, Feb. 17, 1933; m. Roxana Anson; children: Alison, Eric. BS, Calif. Inst. Tech., 1954; MS, Harvard U., 1955, PhD, 1957. Instr. chemistry Calif. Inst. Tech., Pasadena, 1957-58, asst. prof., 1958-62, assoc. prof., 1962-68, prof. chemistry, 1968—, chmn. div. chemistry and chem. engr., 1984—. Contbr. numerous articles to profl. jours. Fellow J.S. Guggenheim Found. U. Brussels, 1964, Alfred P. Sloan Found., 1965-69; scholar Fulbright-Hays Found. U. Florence, Italy, 1972, A. von Humboldt Found. Fritz Haber Inst., Berlin, 1984-86. Mem. AAAS,Nat. Acad. Sci., Am. Chem. Soc., Am. Electrochem. Soc., Internat. Soc. Electrochemistry, Soc. Electroanalytical Chemistry, Tau Beta Pi. Office: Calif Inst Tech Div Chemistry MS 127-72 Pasadena CA 91125

ANSORGE, RICHARD JAMES, journalist; b. Des Moines, Aug. 4, 1953; s. Edwin James and Iona Marie (Bohn) A.; m. Sarah Jane Rogers, June 11, 1977. B of Gen. Studies, U. Iowa, 1975; M in Journalism, Columbia U., N.Y.C., 1987. News editor Tri-County Press, Polo, Ill., 1975-77; editor/reporter Barrington (Ill.) Press Newspapers, 1977-83; entertainment editor-critic Omaha World-Herald, 1983-86; feature writer Colorado Springs Gazette Telegraph, 1987—. Roberts-Chamberlain fellow Columbia U., 1986. Democrat. Home: 1813 W Vermijo Ave Colorado Springs CO 80904 Office: Colorado Springs Gazette Telegraph 30 S Prospect St Colorado Springs CO 80903

ANTHONY, CANDACE LYNNE, traffic administrator; b. Roseville, Calif., June 30, 1964; d. Jackie Lee Anthony and Bettye Jane (Chaney) Stratbucker. Student, Calif. State U., Sacramento, 1982-84. Clk. Cert. Flexstaff, Sacramento, 1984-85; asst. traffic mgr. KRBK-TV div. Koplar Communications, Sacramento, 1985-88; traffic asst. KTXL-TV div. Camella City Telecasters, Sacramento, 1988—. Mem. Aircraft Owners and Pilots Assn., The 99's, Internat. Women Pilots. Republican. Baptist.

ANTHONY, ELAINE MARGARET, real estate executive; b. Mpls., Apr. 23, 1932; d. Jerome Pius and Adeline (Shea) Clarkin; m. Ronald Carl Anthony, Aug 28, 1954 (div. 1977); children: Richard, Lisa, Laura. Student, U. Minn., 1950-51; AA, Diablo Valley Coll., 1978; postgrad., San Jose (Calif.) State U., 1979, U. Calif., Berkeley, 1983—. Agt., broker Sycamore Realty, Danville, Calif., 1972-75; broker, project sales mgr. Crocker Homes, Dublin, Calif., 1975-80; exec. v.p. BlackHawk Properties, Danville, 1980-82; broker, project sales mgr. Harold W. Smith Co., Walnut Creek, Calif., 1982-86; pres. Elaine Anthony & Assocs., Inc., Oakland, Calif., 1986—. Mem. vol. coun. San Francisco Symphony, 1986. Mem. Bldg. Industry Assn. (Outstanding Sales Peron of Yr. 1983 No. Calif. chpt.), Nat. Assn. Home Builders, Inst. Residential Mktg., Oakland Bd. Realtors, Commonwealth Club Calif., Women's Athletic Club Alameda County. Republican. Roman Catholic. Home and Office: 1875 Grand View Dr Oakland CA 94618

ANTIPA, GREGORY ALEXIS, biology educator, researcher; b. San Francisco, Aug. 9, 1941; s. August Alexander and Amanda (Kockos) A.; m. Sharon Dianne Haughee, Dec. 18, 1966 (dec. 1984); children: Alexander Thomas, Christopher Alexis. AB in Zoology, U. Calif., Berkeley, 1963; MA in Biology, San Francisco State U., 1966; PhD in Zoology, U. Ill., 1970. Postdoctoral fellow U. Chgo., 1970-71, Argonne (Ill.) Nat. Lab., 1971-74; prof. biology Wayne State U., Detroit, 1974-78; prof. biology San Francisco State U., 1978—, dir. research, 1986-89, acting dir. rsch., 1989—. Contbr. numerous articles to profl. jours. NIH Fellow U. Chgo., 1970; Atomic Energy Commn. fellow Argonne Nat. Lab., 1971; NSF research grantee, 1978. Mem. Am. Soc. of Cell Biology, Soc. for Protozoologists, Electron Microscope Soc. Am., Am. Soc. Zoologists, San Francisco Microscopical Soc. (pres. 1986-88). Office: San Francisco State U Dept Biology San Francisco CA 94132

ANTOCH, ZDENEK VINCENT, electronic engineering educator; b. Prague, Czechoslovakia, Oct. 16, 1943; came to U.S., 1950; s. Zdenek Antoch and Marta (Smidova) Frank; m. Maureen O. Shaw, June 24, 1968; 1 child, Anna Marie. BS, Portland State U., 1971, postgrad. in Engring., 1971-73, postgrad. in Physics, 1973-75. Research asst. Portland (Oreg.) State U., 1972-75; electronics instr. Portland (Oreg.) Community Coll., 1975-80, 81—; design engr. Coast TV Terminals, Inc., Florence, Oreg., 1980-81; cons., Transat Microwave Systems, Los Angeles, 1984—, dir. research and devel., 1984-85. Inventor in field. NSF grantee. Mem. IEEE, Am. Soc. Engring. Edn. Democrat. Office: Portland Community Coll 12000 SW 49th Ave Portland OR 97219

ANTOCI, MARIO, financial services company executive; b. 1934; married. With Southern Calif. Savs. & Loan Assn., Los Angeles, 1964-66; with Home Savs. & Loan Assn. (now Home Savs. Am.), Irwindale, Calif., 1962-64, 67—, exec. v.p. fin., now pres., chief operating officer; pres., chief operating officer H.F. Ahmanson and Co., until 1988; chmn., chief exec. officer Am. Savs. Bank S.A., 1988—. Office: Am Savs Bank 18401 Von Karman Ave Irvine CA 92715 also: H F Ahmanson & Co 3731 Wilshire Blvd Los Angeles CA 90010 *

ANTONINI, MICHAEL JOSEPH, dentist; b. Livermore, Calif., Apr. 21, 1946; s. Joseph and Doris Carolyn (Grana) A.; m. Linda Mae Madigan, May 12, 1973; children: John Michael, Peter Patrick, Gina Marie. BA, Santa Clara U., 1968; DDS, U. Pacific, 1972. Gen. practice dentistry San Francisco, 1972—. Coach baseball St. Brendan Sch., San Francisco, 1988, coach basketball, 1987, 88; mem. St. Brendans Men's Club. Mem. ADA, Calif. Dental Assn. (Best Editorial Newsletter award 1983, 84), San Francisco Dental Soc. (editor newsletter, 1982-84, v.p. 1984-85, pres. 1986-

87), Olympic Club. Republican. Roman Catholic. Home: 110 Broadmoor Dr San Francisco CA 94132 Office: Michael J Antonini DDS Inc 2827 Franklin St San Francisco CA 94123

ANTONOFF, STEVEN SCOTT, human resources executive; b. N.Y.C., Aug. 3, 1952; s. James Martin and Joan Doris (Mintz) A.; m. Elizabeth Ann Cashin, June 18, 1982; children: Leonore Ann Anselmo, Diane Anselmo. Student, George Washington U., 1970-73; BS in Polit. Sci., Hofstra U., 1975; MBA, NYU, 1981. Prodn. mgr. Erica Shoes, N.Y.C., 1976-78; personnel mgr. Todd Logistics, Inc., Bayonne, N.J., 1978-80; mgr. personnel ops. Savin Corp., Stamford, Conn., 1980-83; mgr. personnel Materials Rsch. Corp., Orangeburg, N.Y., 1983-86; mgr. employment Hyundai Motor Am., Garden Grove, Calif., 1987—. Mem. West Milford (N.J.) Econ. Devel. Counc., 1987. Mem. Am. Soc. Personnel Adminstrs., Employment Mgmt. Assn. Jewish. Office: Hyundai Motor Am 7373 Hunt Ave Garden Grove CA 92642

ANTONOVICH, MICHAEL DENNIS, county government official; b. L.A., Aug. 12, 1939; s. Michael and Francis Ann (McColm) A. BA, Calif. State U., L.A., 1963, MA, 1967; postgrad., Stanford U., 1968-70, Harvard U., 1984, 87. Govt. and history instr. L.A. Unified Sch. Dist., 1966-72; assemblyman State of Calif., 1972-78; supr. County of L.A., 1980—, chmn. bd. suprs., 1983, 87; instr. Pepperdine U., 1979, Calif. State U., L.A., 1979, 85; Rep. whip Calif. State Assembly, 1976-78; active Pres. Commn. on Privatization, 1987-88, Atty. Gen.'s Missing Children's Adv. Bd., 1987-88, Pres.' U.S.-Japan Adv. Commn., 1984, Commn. of White House Fellowships Regional Panel, 1981-86, governing bd. South Coast Air Quality Mgmt. Dist., L.A. Coliseum Commn., mem., 1981, chmn. 1988; bd. dirs. Pacific Data Mgmt. Co.; chmn. County-wide Criminal Justice Coordinating Com., 1983, 87. Active Tournament of Roses Com., L.A. Zoo Assn., Good Shepherd Luth. Home for Retarded Children, South Pasadena Police Dept. Res.; bd. govs. Glendale (Calif.) Symphony. With USAR. Named Alumni of Yr. Calif. State U., 1977; recipient Good Scout award, 1987, Valley Shelter award, 1987, San Fernando Valley Interfaith Coun. award, 1983, Leadership award United Way, 1983, 87, Brotherhood Crusade award, 1983, 87, Didi Hirsch Community Mental Health award, 1984, Award for Caring Foster Parents Assn., 1987, Wildlife Way Sta. award, 1984, Nat. Taxpayers Union award, 1984, L.A. Taxpayers Assn. award, 1981, L.A. Dep. Sheriffs Victims of Violent Crimes Found. award, 1981. Mem. Native Sons of Golden West, Phila. Soc., Glendale C. of C., Elks, Shomrim Soc. of So. Calif. (hon.), Sigma Nu. Lutheran. Home: 3023 San Gabriel Ave Glendale CA 91208 Office: County of LA Hall of Adminstrn 500 W Temple Rm 869 Los Angeles CA 90012

ANTONSEN, CONRAD (ROBERT MICHAEL ANTONSEN), priest, educator; b. Vallejo, Calif., May 24, 1937; s. R. Wallace and Zaira (Castagnini) A. BS, U. San Francisco, 1959; BPh, St. Albert's Coll., Oakland, Calif., 1962, MA in Philosophy, 1963, MA in Theology, 1965. Joined Dominican Order, 1960, ordained priest Roman Cath. Ch., 1966. Campus minister, instr. Dominican Coll., San Rafael, Calif., 1974-78; pastor Blessed Sacrament Parish, Seattle, 1979-85, St. Mary Magdalen Parish, Berkeley, Calif., 1987—; instr. Dominican Sch. Philosophy and Theology, grad. Theold. Union, Berkeley, 1975—, St. Thomas U., Rome, 1986, St. Mary's Coll., Moraga, Calif., 1987; dir., preacher retreats for Dominican Sisters New Zealand, 1976; facilitator for group dynamics Religious Women in Phoenix, 1973. Mem. N.Am. Acad. Liturgy, Am. Dominican Liturgical Commn., Pastoral Coun. Archdiocese Seattle, Western Dominican Planning and Ministry Commn, Alcuin. Democrat. Home and Office: 2005 Berryman St Berkeley CA 94709

ANTONSON, JOAN MARGARET, historian; b. Mpls., Dec. 1, 1951; d. Lyman Theodore and Gladys (Korzan) A.; m. Donald Ernest Mohr Jr., Oct. 15, 1977 (div.); 1 child, Justin Thomas. BA in History and Secondary Edn., U. Minn., 1973; MA in History, U. Oregon, 1975. Cert. secondary tchr., Alaska. Historian, rsch. assoc. State of Alaska Div. Parks, Anchorage, 1975-79, state historian, 1986—; historian U.S. Bur. Land Mgmt., Anchorage, 1980-81, State of Alaska Hist. Commn., Anchorage, 1981-86; instr. U. Alaska, 1977—. Author: (with W.S. Hanable) Alaska's Heritage, 1987, Administratative History of Sitka National Park; editor: Heritage newsletter, 1986—. Bd. dirs. race com. Alaska Women's Run, 1986—; bd. dirs., sec. Friends of Indep. Mine, Anchorage, 1986-88; bd. dirs., sec., pres. Cook Inlet Hist. Soc., 1974-85. U. Minn. scholar, 1973. Mem. Alaska Hist. Soc. (bd. dirs. 1983-86, assoc. editor newsletter Alaska History 1984—, Beaver Log Pres.'s award 1985), Western History Assn., Am. Assn. for State and Local History (membership chmn. 1982-87, cert. commendation 1988), Totally Fit Running Team (capt. 1988—), Anchorage Running Club (bd. dirs. 1987—). Home: 1026 Barrow St Anchorage AK 99501 Office: Office of History and Arch PO Box 107001 Anchorage AK 99510

ANVARI, MORTEZA, computer science and mathmatics educator; b. Tehran, Iran, Jan. 29, 1931; came to U.S., 1956; s. Kazem and Fatemeh (Salimi) A.; m. Nancy Ann Hutchison, Jan. 26, 1958; children: Alexander, Lawrence. BS, U. Tehran, 1953; MS, U. Ill., 1959, PhD, 1962. Prof. math. U. B.C., Can., 1963-68; chmn. math. computer sci. U. Tech., Tehran, 1968-71; pres., founder Computer Coll., Tehran, 1972-79; prof. computer sci. Calif. State U., Northridge, 1980-83; prof., chmn. dept. computer sci. Calif. State U., Fullerton, 1983—; cons. BDM Internat. Inc., Va., 1985—, Ashton-Tate, 1987. Contbr. numerous articles to profl. jours. Smith-Mundt fellow U.S. State Dept., 1956-58. Mem. IEEE, Assn. Computing Machinery.

APGAR, FRANK ALAN, internist, educator; b. Charleston, W.Va., Dec. 1, 1949; s. Robert Raymond and Helen Elizabeth (Schonwald) A.; m. Elise Cheryl Davis, Nov. 2, 1974; children: Kevin W., Erin C. BS in Zoology, San Diego State U., 1972; MD, UCLA, 1976. Diplomate Am. Coll. Physicians. Intern UCLA Med. Ctr., 1976-77, internal medicine resident, 1977-79, gen. internal medicine fellow, 1979-80, adj. assoc. prof. medicine, 1980-87, assoc. clin. prof. medicine, 1987—; med. dir. HealthNet, 1988—, vice chief of med. staff, 1988—. Mem. ACP, Soc. Gen. Internal Medicine. Office: UCLA Dept Medicine 10833 Le Conte Ave Los Angeles CA 90024

APGAR, HENRY ELSTON, JR., cost analysis consultant, systems engineer; b. Plainfield, N.J., July 5, 1937; s. Henry Elston Sr. and Ruth Edith (Lawrence) A.; m. Dulcie M. Steinbeck; children: Henry, Jane. BSEE, Rutgers U., 1959; BA, U. Md., 1966; MBA, Northeastern U., Boston, 1970; AS in Computer Sci., Moorpark Coll., 1984. Cert. cost analyst. Design engr. IBM Corp., Poughkeepsie, N.Y., 1959-60; commd. USAF, 1960, advanced through grades to col., resigned, 1970; systems engr. Bunker Ramo Corp., Westlake Village, Calif., 1970-83; cost analysis mgr. The Aerospace Corp., Los Angeles, 1983-87; cost cons. Mgmt. Cons. & Rsch., Inc., Oxnard, Calif., 1987—; ind. cons., Thousand Oaks, Calif, 1984-86. Mem. Internat. Soc. Parametric Analysts (pres. 1979-83, Parametrician of Yr. award 1986). Home: 776 Silver Cloud St Thousand Oaks CA 91360 Office: Mgmt Cons & Rsch Inc 300 Esplanade Dr Ste 1660 Oxnard CA 93030

APODACA, RUDY SAMUEL, judge; b. Las Cruces, N.Mex., Aug. 8, 1939; s. Raymond and Elisa (Alvarez) A.; m. Bunny N. Gray, Nov. 1958 (div. 1963); m. Nancy R. Apodaca, Jan. 16, 1967; children: Cheryl Ann, Carla Renee, Cynthia Lynn, Rudy Samuel. BS, N.Mex. State U., 1961; JD, Georgetown U., 1964. Bar: N.Mex. 1964, U.S. Dist. Ct. N. Mex. 1965, U.S. Ct. Appeals (10th cir.) 1965, U.S. Supreme Ct. 1971. Pvt. practice Las Cruces, 1964-86; appellate judge N. Mex. Ct. Appeals, Santa Fe, 1987—; real estate broker, Las Cruces, 1984-86; gen. counsel Citizens Bank Las Cruces, 1976-86. Author: The Waxen Image, 1977; author screenplay: A Rare Thing, 1987. Bd. regents N. Mex. State U., 1975-83; active Coordinating Council for Higher Edn., Santa Fe, 1975-78; pres. assocs. N. Mex. State U., Las Cruces, 1982-84; bd. dirs. Am. S.W. Theatre Co., Las Cruces, 1984-86. Capt. U.S. Army, 1964-66. Mem. Inst. Jud. Adminstrn., N. Mex. Bar Assn., Poets and Writers, Phi Kappa Phi, American Mensa, Intertel. Democrat. Home: 2602 Via Caballero del Norte Santa Fe NM 87505 Office: N Mex Ct Appeals PO Box 2008 Santa Fe NM 87504-2008

APONTÉ, CHRISTOPHER BENNEDETTEY, artistic director, choreographer, educator; b. N.Y.C., May 4, 1950; s. German and Anna (Perez) A. Diploma, Nat. Acad. Ballet and Theatre Arts, 1978. Prin. dancer Harkness Ballet, N.Y.C., 1968-74, Alvin Ailey Co., N.Y.C., 1974-75, Am. Ballet Theatre, N.Y.C., 1975-76, Ballet de Marseille Rolland Petite, Marseille, France, 1976-77, Balleto Reggio Emillia, Italy, 1978-79, numerous European dance cos., France, Italy, Fed. Republic of Germany, 1978-80; with Cleve. Ballet, 1981-82, Boston Ballet, 1982-85; dir. Spokane (Wash.) Ballet Co., 1986—; instr., choreographer Spokane Ballet, 1986—; producer Tours to the Orient, 1980-86. Creator 33 ballets since 1986 including Stravinsky's Violen Concerto, Lady Macbeth, Eau de Koln, Song of the Earth, Rhapsody in Blue. Democrat. Catholic. Office: Spokane Ballet W 820 Sprague Spokane WA 99204

APPLE, DAINA DRAVNIEKS, management analyst; b. Kuldiga, Latvia, USSR, July 6, 1944; came to U.S., 1951; d. Albins Dravnieks and Alina A. (Bergs) Zelmenis; divorced; 1 child, Almira Moronne; m. Martin A. Apple, Sept. 2, 1986. BS, U. Calif., Berkeley, 1977, MA, 1980. Economist U.S. Forest Service, Berkeley, 1976-84; mgmt. analysis officer U.S. Forest Service, San Francisco, 1984—. Author: Public Involvement In the Forest Service-Methodologies, 1977, Public Involvement-Selected Abstracts for Natural Resources, 1979, The Management of Policy and Direction in the Forest Service, 1982, An Analysis of the Forest Service Human Resource Management Program, 1984, Organization Design-Abstracts for Natural Resources Users, 1985; sect. editor: Jour. of Women in Natural Resources. Mem. Am. Forestry Assn., Assn. of Women in Sci., Sigma Xi, Phi Beta Kappa Assocs. (nat. sec. 1985-88, pres. No. Calif. chpt. 1982-84, 1st v.p. 1981). Club: Commonwealth of Calif. (100 Leaders of Tomorrow). Home: PO Box 26155 San Francisco CA 94126 Office: US Forest Svc Engring Staff 630 Sansome St San Francisco CA 94111

APPLE, MARTIN ALLEN, high technology company executive; b. Duluth, Minn., Sept. 17, 1938; children: Deborah Dawn, Pamela Ruth, Nathan, Rebeccah Lynn. AB, ALA, U. Minn., 1959, MSci, 1962; PhD, U. Calif., 1968. Chmn. Multidisciplinary Drug Rsch. Group, U. Calif., San Francisco, 1974-78; pres., Internat. Plant Rsch. Inst., San Carlos, Calif., 1978-81; with EAN-Tech., Inc., Daly City, Calif., 1982-84, chmn. bd., 1983-84; with Adytum Internat., Mountain View, Calif., 1982—, chief exec. officer, 1983—; ptnr. ITR-France; adj. prof. computers in medicine U. Calif., San Francisco, 1982-84; bd. dirs. Holden-Day Pubs., 1987-88. Author: (with F. Myers) Review Medical Pharmacology, 1976; (with M. Fink) Immune RNA in Neoplasia, 1976; (with F. Becker et al) Cancer: A Comprehensive Treatise, 1977; (with M. Keenberg et al) Investing in Biotechnology, 1981; (with F. Ahmad et al) From Genes to Proteins: Horizons in Biotechnology, 1983; (with J. Kureczka) Status of Biotechnology, 1987; (with M. Baum) Business Advantage, 1987 (winner Excellence award Software Pubs. Assn. 1987); mem. editorial bd. Computers in Medicine. Recipient Citation East West Ctr. Bd. of Govs., 1988. Mem. Calif. Council Indsl. Innovation, 1982. Fellow Am. Coll. Clin. Pharmacology, Am. Inst. Chemists; mem. Assn. Venture Founders (bd. govs. 1982-83), East-West Center Assn. (bd. trustees 1982-88, vice chmn. 1983-85), Profl. Software Programmers Assn., Commonwealth Club of California, Leaders of Tomorrow (chmn. 1987-88), Phi Beta Kappa (mem. Phi Beta Kappa Assocs., Disting. Service award 1984, 85), Sigma Xi (bd. dirs., chmn. long-range strategic planning com. 1988—). Home: PO Box 391043 Mountain View CA 94039

APPLE, STEVEN ANTHONY, city official; b. Los Angeles, Dec. 27, 1954; s. Nick P. and Joanne (Wilkin) A.; m. Rebecca McCorkle, Aug. 9, 1980. BA in Anthropology, Ohio State U., 1977; M in City Planning, San Diego State U., 1983. Freelance environ. cons. San Diego, 1979-80; environ. planner MSA, Inc., San Diego, 1981-82; land use planner New Horizons Planning Cons., San Diego, 1982-84, County San Diego, 1984-86; planning dir. City of Solana Beach (Calif.), 1986--; guest lectr., San Diego State U. 1984. Environ. chmn., Torrey Pines Community Planning Group, Del Mar, Calif., 1985--. Univ. scholar, San Diego State U., 1983. Mem. Am. Planning Assn., San Diego County Archeol. Soc. (libr. 1979-80), Eagle Scout Alumni Assn. (exec. com. San Diego 1985), Mensa. Office: City of Solana Beach 380 Stevens Ave Ste 120 Solana Beach CA 92075

APPLETON, PETER ARTHUR, motion picture editor and cameraman; b. Denver, June 10, 1941; s. David Olaf and Dorothea Virginia (Smith) A.; m. Wanda Lou Hoskins, Apr. 10, 1964; 1 child, Claire Palmer Brown. BA in Journalism, U. Denver, 1963; MA in Communications, U. Pa., 1964. Freelance film and video, editor, cameraman Los Angeles, 1964—; instr. cinematography Columbia Coll., Hollywood, Calif., 1980. Film editor Buffalo Bill, 1975 (1st Pl. Berlin Film Festival), The Late Show, 1977, Rainy Day Friends, 1984, The Passage, 1987; editor, dir. photography When I Am King, 1981; dir. photography TV series The Optimist, 1982, also numerous others. Recipient award Indsl. Film Producers Assn., 1973, cert. Chgo. Internat. Film Festival, 1973, CINE Golden Eagle award Coun. on Non-Theatrical Events, 1978. Mem. Internat. Alliance Motion Picture and Theatrical Stage Employees, Internat. Underwater Explorers Soc. (life), Phi Beta Kappa. Democrat. Home: 525 N Sycamore Ave Los Angeles CA 90036 Office: Cally Curtis Co 1111 N Las Palmas Ave Los Angeles CA 90038

APURON, THE MOST REV. ANTHONY SABLAN, archbishop; b. Agana, Guam, Nov. 1, 1945; s. Manuel Taijito and Ana Santos (Sablan) P. BA, St. Anthony Coll., 1969; MDiv, Maryknoll Sem., 1972, M Theology, 1973; MA in Liturgy, Notre Dame U., 1974. Ordained priest Roman Catholic ch., 1972, ordained bishop, 1984, installed archbishop, 1986. Chmn. Diocesan Liturgical Commn., Agana, 1974-86; vice chmn. Chamorro Lang. Commn., Agana, 1984-86; aux. bishop Archdiocese of Agana, 1984-85, archbishop, 1986—; chmn. Interfaith Vols. Caregivers, Agana, 1984—; mem. Civilian Adv. com., Agana, 1986—. Author: A Structural Analysis of the Content of Myth in the Thought of Mircea Eliade, 1973. Named Most Outstanding Young Man, Jaycees of Guam, 1984. Office: Archbishop's Office Cuesta San Ramon Agana GU 96910

ARACE, MICHAEL J., financial advisor; b. Kingston, N.Y., Nov. 12, 1943; s. Michael and Evelyn M. (Heaney) A.; m. Adrienne Ruth Traut, Nov. 14, 1970 (div. 1977); children: John, David; m. Martha Jimenez, Aug. 12, 1988. Bank acctg. rep. Burroughs Corp., Albany, N.Y., 1967-72; govt. market specialist Xerox Corp., Tarrytown, N.Y., 1972-76; fin. advisor Cigna Cos., Tarrytown, 1976-82, Denver, 1983-88; owner Arace Internat. Enterprises, Parker, Colo., 1988—; founder Denfield Corp., Springfield, Mass. Contbr. articles to profl. jours. 1st lt. U.S. Army, 1964-71. Republican. Roman Catholic. Office: Arace Internat Enterprises 13088 S Stuart Way Parker CO 80134

ARAGON VIAMONTE, ANDRES, civil engineer; b. Havana, Cuba, July 30, 1946; came to U.S., 1961; s. Jose M. Aragon and Luz M. Viamonte; m. Lorren M. Torres, Feb. 4, 1972; 1 child, Carlo Andres. BCE, U. N.Mex., 1968, MCE, 1970. Cert. profl. engr., N.Mex. Prin. investigator N.Mex. Accident U.S. Dept. Transp., Albuquerque, 1968-71; assoc. traffic engr. City of Albuquerque, 1970-74, engr. hwy. programs, 1974-75, head transp. planning div., 1975-78; head. transp. dept. Bohannan-Huston, inc., Albuquerque, 1978-83; ptnr., v.p. Bohannan-Huston, Inc., Albuquerque, 1983—. Fellow Inst. Transp. Engrs. (N.Mex. chmn. 1975-76, membership com. 1975-80), Am. Pub. Works Assn., Cons. Engrs. Coun. (subcoms. transp. 2020, 1978—), Soc. Hispanic Profl. Engring. Bd., Soc. Am. Mil. Engr. Republican. Roman Catholic. Club: Tanoan Country (Albuquerque). Home: 746 Tramway Ln NE Albuquerque NM 87122 Office: Bohannan-Huston Inc Courtyard I 7500 Jefferson NE Albuquerque NM 87109

ARANT, DAVID EUGENE, real estate broker, educator; b. Southgate, Calif., Apr. 17, 1935; s. Francis Marian and May Laveigh (Morris) A.; BS, Pepperdine U., 1957; MS, U. So. Calif., 1960; children: Brenda, Bradford. Treas., Vet. Escrow Co., Inc., L.A., 1958-61; prof. accounting L.A. Met. Coll. of Bus., 1961-66; prof. real estate L.A. Harbor Coll., 1966—, prof. real estate, 1984—; owner, realtor, operator Dave Arant Realty, Rancho Palos Verdes, Calif., 1979—; also painter and musician. VA grantee, 1972, 74. Mem. Calif. Real Estate Assn., Delta Pi Epsilon, Pi Gamma Mu, Alpha Gamma Sigma. Democrat. Home: 1890 Peninsula Verde Dr Rancho Palos Verdes CA 90717

ARATA, SIL LOUIS, industrial engineer; b. Concord, Calif., Mar. 22, 1930; s. Silvo Valentino Arata and Jean (Lund) Peterson; m. Dixie Lee Si8mmons, May 1, 1954 (div. 1974); children: Sil Louis, Susan M. Arata Svendsen. BS in Indsl. Engring., Oreg. State U., 1959. Prodn. foreman Signet Controls, Portland, Oreg., 1959-60; inspector Hyster Corp., Portland, 1960-61; packaging engring. mgr. Tektronix, Beaverton, Oreg., 1961-78; packing engr. John Fluke Mfg. Co., Everett, Wash., 1979; packing engr. Hewlett-Packard, Boise, Idaho, 1979-81, Corvallis, Oreg., 1981—. Capt. East County Multnomah Rep. Central Commn., Portland, 1966; loaned exec. United Way, Portland, 1971; fund raising chmn. Jr. Achievement, Beaverton, 1976. Fellow Soc. Packaging and Handling Engrs. (judge 1973, 87, chmn. nat. honros awards com. 1976-78, v.p. western region 1977-79, chmn. recert. com. 1986—, mem. nat. packaging com. 1986-87). Republican. Home: 22530 Woods Creek Rd Philomath OR 97370 Office: Hewlett Packard Co 1000 NE Circle Blvd Corvallis OR 97330

ARBUTHNOT, G(UY) LANE, III, engineering executive; b. Anniston, Ala., Oct. 6, 1936; s. Guy L. Arbuthnot and Eleen Marie (Packard) Robertson; m. Jo Ann Arbuthot. BS in Physics, U. Miss., 1959. Physicist U.S. Navy Mine Def. Lab., Panama City, Fla., 1961-62; tech. staff TRW, Cape Canaveral, Fla., 1962-69; section head systems engring. TRW, Houston, 1969-75; mgr. system software lab. TRW, Ogden, Utah, 1975-82; mgr. digital avionics lab. TRW, Redondo Beach, Calif., 1982-85; dir. support systems TRW, San Diego, 1985—; Adv. Jr. Achievement, Ogden, Utah, 1979. Coach Little League Baseball, Houston, 1973. Mem. Air Force Assn., AFCEA, Old Crows, Am. Def. Preparedness Soc. Republican. Home: 13125 Bavarian Dr San Diego CA 92129 Office: TRW 1 Rancho Carmel San Diego CA 92128

ARCADI, JOHN ALBERT, urologist; b. Whittier, Calif., Oct. 23, 1924; s. Antonio and Josephine (Ramirez) A; m. Doris M. Bohanan, Apr. 11, 1951; children: Patrick, Michael, Judith, Timothy, Margaret, William, Catherine. BS cum laude, U. Notre Dame, 1947; MD, Johns Hopkins U., 1950. Diplomate Am. Bd. Urology. Intern The Johns Hopkins Hosp., Balt., 1950-51, resident, 1951-52, 53-55; instr. urology Johns Hopkins U., Balt., Md., 1953-55, U. So. Calif., Los Angeles, 1955-60; research assoc. Whittier (Calif.) Coll., 1957-70, research prof., 1970—; staff mem. urology sect. Presbyn. Hosp., Whittier, 1960—. Fellow AAAS, Am. Coll. Surgeons; mem. Endocrine Soc., Am. Urology Assn., Am. Soc. Cell Biology, Am. Micro Soc., Internat. Urol. Soc., Am. Assn. Clin. Anatomy, Am. Assn. Anatomists, Soc. for Basic Urologic Rsch. Republican. Roman Catholic. Home: 6202 S Washington Ave Whittier CA 90608 Office: PO Box 9220 Whittier CA 90608

ARCHDEACON, JOHN ROBERT, orthopedic surgeon; b. N.Y.C., Aug. 1, 1919; s. Thomas Francis and Mary (O'Connor) A.; m. Molly Taylor Sinclair, Sept. 18, 1948; children—Patricia Archdeacon Holland, Douglas, John, Richard, Moira, Kenneth. Student Fordham U., 1939-41; MD, NYU, 1950. Diplomate Am. Bd. Orthopedic Surgery Am. Bd. Preventive Medicine. Commd. 1st lt. USAF, 1952, advanced through grades to col., 1965; intern St. Lukes Hosp., N.Y.C., 1950-51; resident orthopedic surgery N.Y. U.-Bellevue Med. Ctr., 1955-59; chief orthopedic surgery Carswell AFB Hosp., Ft. Worth, 1959-61; dir. orthopedic pathology course Armed Forces Inst. Pathology, 1963-64; chief of surgery, cons. to surgeon gen. Maxwell Air Force Hosp., Ala., 1964-66; chief profl. svcs., sr. med. adviser Air Evacuation Squadron, USAF Hosp., Clark Hosp., Philippines, 1966-68, hosp. comdr., 1967-68; hosp. comdr. 78th USAF Hosp., Hamilton AFB, Calif., 1968-69; ret., 1969; pvt. practice medicine specializing in orthopedic surgery, Los Gatos-Saratoga, Calif., 1969—. Decorated D.F.C., Air medal with 3 oak leaf clusters, Air Force Commendation medal, Legion of Merit. Fellow ACS, Am. Acad. Orthopedic Surgeons, Am. Coll. Preventive Medicine; mem. AMA, Santa Clara County Med. Assn., Calif. Med. Assn., Brit. Assn. Aviation Med. Examiners. Office: 800 Pollard Rd Los Gatos CA 95030

ARCHIBALD, JAMES DAVID, biology educator, paleontologist; b. Lawrence, Kans., Mar. 23, 1950; s. James R. and Donna L. (Accord) A. B.S. in Geology, Kent State U., 1972; Ph.D. in Paleontology, U. Calif., Berkeley, 1977. Gibb's instr. dept. geology Yale U., New Haven, 1977-79, asst., then assoc. prof. dept. biology, 1979-83; curator of mammals Peabody Mus. Natural Hist., New Haven, 1979-83; assoc. prof., then prof. dept. biology San Diego State U., 1983—; extensive field expeditions in Mont., Colo., N.Mex., Pakistan, 1973—. Author: A Study of Mammalia and Geology Across the Cretaceous-Tertiary Boundary, 1982; contbr. articles to profl. jours. Scholar Yale U., San Diego State U.; fellow Alcoa Found., U. Calif.-Berkeley; grantee Sigma Xi, Nat. Geog. Soc., NSF, Petroleum Research Found., San Diego State U. Mem. Soc. Vertebrate Paleontology, Geol. Soc. Am., Paleontol. Soc., Soc. Systematic Zoologists, Am. Soc. Mammalogists, Willi Hennig Soc., Sigma Xi. Office: San Diego State U Dept Biology San Diego CA 92182

ARCURI, MARY ANNE, health association director; b. Dallas, Mar. 13, 1947; d. Patrick Charles and Minnie Morson (Hemphill) Moran; m. Edward Louis Arcuri III, Apr. 4, 1970; children: Edward L. IV, Cathleen Lorraine, Charles Andrew, Anthony Patrick. BS in Nursing, Loretto Heights Coll., Denver, 1969. Med. dir. Western Med. Svcs., Colorado Springs, Colo., 1976-77; office mgr. Callaway Senatorial Campaign, Colorado Springs, Colo., 1980, Kramer Congl. Campaign, Colorado Springs, Colo., 1982; dir. El Paso div. Am. Heart Assn., Colorado Springs, Colo., 1984-87; dir. of programs Am. Heart Assn., Denver, 1987—. Mem. Arts Bus. and Edn., 1983-84, Colorado Springs Health Edn. Council, 1986-87, Coloradans for Clean Indoor Air, Colorado Springs, 1985-87; v.p. The Downtoners, Colorado Springs, 1981-85; pres. El Paso Rep. Women, Colorado Springs, 1979-84; chmn. community svcs., Cherry Creek Rep. Women, 1989—; bd. dirs. Springspree, Colorado Springs, 1984-86. Named an Outstanding Young Woman of Am., 1979-80, Young Rep. Woman of Colo., 1977. Roman Catholic. Home: 9899 E Colorado Ave Apt 514 Denver CO 80231 Office: Am Heart Assn of Colo 1280 S Parker Rd Denver CO 80231

ARDLEY, HARRY MOUNTCASTLE (MIKE ARDLEY), mathematical statistician, operations research consultant; b. Oakland, Calif., Jan. 22, 1926; s. Harry Mountcastle and Anne Alvina (Meyer) A.; m. Jane Partridge, June 24, 1948; children: David Michael, Douglas Mountcastle, Mary Elizabeth. AB, U. Calif., Berkeley, 1950, postgrad., 1950-51, 58-59, 62-63. Econ. statistician U.S. Dept. Commerce, Washington, 1951-53; math. statistician Pacific Telephone Co., San Francisco, 1953-59; gen. statistician San Diego, 1959-63; supr. math. and statis. research San Francisco, 1963-83; pvt. practice cons. 1984—. Active citizens com. to establish Foothill Coll., 1957-58, San Francisco Symphony Assn.; exec. com. Santa Clara County Dem. Council, 1957-59; pres. Palo Alto-Stanford Dem. Club, 1965; pres. Greenmeadow Community Assn., 1969. Served with USAAF, 1943-46. Mem. Am. Statis. Assn. (pres. San Francisco Bay area chpt. 1981-82), Ops. Research Soc. Am., Inst. Mgmt. Sci., Sierra Club, Western Wheelers Club. Home and Office: 352 Parkside Dr Palo Alto CA 94306

ARDREY, ROSS JAMES, management consultant; b. N.Y.C., Jan. 4, 1943; s. Robert and Helen (Johnson) A.; m. Janet Kathleen Leslie, June 20, 1970; children: Robert Thornton, Janet Elizabeth. AB, U. Chgo., 1963; MA, U. Wash., 1966, JD, 1970. Mgmt. cons. Harry J. Prior/Martech Assocs., Bellevue, Wash., 1972—. Bd. trustees Villa Acad., 1986—, Friends of Seattle Pub. Libr., 1985—; v.p., bd. dirs. Pacific N.W. chpt. Inst. Mgmt. Cons., 1985—; mem. Mcpl. League of Seattle and King County, Wash., 1976—; mem. nat. fund bd. U. Chgo., Ill., 1979-81. Mem. Inst. Mgmt. Cons., Pacific Northwest Personnel Mgmt. Assn. Office: Prior/Martech Assocs 700 112th Ave NE Bellevue WA 98104

AREF, HASSAN, fluid mechanics educator; b. Alexandria, Egypt, Sept. 28, 1950; s. Moustapha and Jytte (Adolphsen) A.; m. Susanne Eriksen, Aug. 3, 1974; children: Michael, Thomas. Cand.Sci., U. Copenhagen, Denmark, 1975; PhD, Cornell U., 1980. Asst. prof. Brown U., Providence, 1980-85, assoc. prof., 1985; assoc. prof. fluid mechanics U. Calif., San Diego, 1985-88, prof. fluid mechanics, 1988—; coord. U. Calif.-San Diego Water Rsch. Project, 1988—; chief scientist San Diego Supercomputer Ctr., 1989—. Contbr. articles to profl. jours.; assoc. editor Jour. Fluid Mechanics, 1984—. Recipient Presdl. Young Investigator award, NSF 1985. Fellow Am. Physical Soc.; mem. Soc. Indsl. and Applied Math. Home: 1117 San Patricio Dr Solana Beach CA 92075 Office: U Calif Inst Geophysics and Planetary Physics San Diego CA 92093

ARENA, ALAN JOSEPH, manufacturing executive; b. Chgo., June 23, 1950; s. Joseph James and Madelyn Adele (Castrovillari) A.; m. Mary Ann Guglielmo, Nov. 26, 1972 (dec.); 1 child, Monica Kristen. BS in Mech. and Aerospace Engring., Ill. Inst. Tech., 1972; MME, Calif. State U., Los Angeles, 1984. Research and devel. engr. Fiat-Allis CMI, Deerfield, Ill.,

1973-80; sr. project engr. Signet Sci. Co., El Monte, Calif., 1980-83; project mgr. def. electronics ops. Autonetics Strategic Systems div. Rockwell Internat., Anaheim, Calif., 1983-87; dir. engring. Ride and Show Engring., Inc., San Dimas, Calif., 1987—; Instr. Calif. Poly. Inst., Pomona, 1983—. Patentee in field. Roman Catholic. Home: 12515 Sterling Pl Chino CA 91710 Office: Ride & Show Engring Inc 276 E Arrow Hwy San Dimas CA 91773

ARENA, J. SYLVESTER, real estate professional; b. Phoenix, Jan. 27, 1961; s. John R. and Mary (Fennemore) A. BFA, U. Ariz., 1984. Ptnr. The Arena Cos., Phoenix, 1984—, Kleber, Lefteroff & Arena, Phoenix, 1988—; fellow, Ctr. Rural Leadership, Tucson, 1986-87; co-founder, spokesman, West Maricopa Landowners Assn., Phoenix, 1986-88; chairmanship Palmwest, Phoenix, 1988—. Bd. dirs., 4th Ave. Mchts. Assn., Tucson, 1983-84; com. mem., Maricopa County Westside Landfill Citizens Adv. Com., 1986, City of El Mirage Gen. Plan Adv. Com., 1987, Maricopa Assn. Govts. Westside Land Use Com., 1987-88. Mem. Urban Land Inst., Internat. Real Estate Fedn., Ariz. World Trade Assn., Ariz. Assn. Indsl. Developers. Office: The Arena Cos 1500 E Bethany Home Rd Phoenix AZ 85014

ARENOWITZ, ALBERT HAROLD, psychiatrist; b. N.Y.C., Jan. 12, 1925; s. Louis Isaac and Lena Helen (Skovron) A.; m. Betty Jane Wiener, Oct. 11, 1953; children: Frederick Stuart, Diane Helen. BA with honors, U. Wis., 1948; MD, U. Va., 1951. Diplomate Am. Bd. Psychiatry, Am. Bd. Child Psychiatry. Intern Kings County Gen. Hosp., Bklyn., 1951-52; resident in psychiatry Bronx (N.Y.) VA Hosp., 1952-55; postdoctoral fellow Youth Guidance Ctr., Worcester, Mass., 1955-57; dir. Ctr. for Child Guidance, Phila., 1962-65, Hahnemann Med. Service Eastern State Sch. and Hosp., Trevose, Pa., 1965-68; dir., tng. dir. Child and Adolescent Psychiat. Clinic, Phila. Gen. Hosp., 1965-67; asst. clin. prof. psychiatry Jefferson Med. Coll., Phila., 1974-76; exec. dir. Child Guidance and Mental Health Clinics, Media, Pa., 1967-74, Intercommunity Child Guidance Ctr., Whittier, Calif., 1976—; clin. asst. prof. child psychiatry Hahnemann Med. Coll., Phila., 1966-74; asst. clin. prof. psychiatry U. Wis., Madison, 1960-62, clin. asst. prof. psychiatry, behavioral scis., and family medicine U. So. Calif., Los Angeles, 1976—; mem. med. staff Presbyn. Intercommunity Hosp., Whittier, 1976—. Pres. Whittier Area Coordinating Council, 1978-80. Flight officer USAF, 1943-45. Fellow Am. Psychiat. Assn., Am. Acad. Child Psychiatry; mem. AMA, AAAS, Los Angeles County Med. Assn., So. Calif. Psychiat. Soc., So. Calif. Soc. Child Psychiatry, Phila. Soc. Adolescent Psychiatry (pres. 1967-68). Office: Intercommunity Child Guidance Ctr 8106 S Broadway Whittier CA 90606

ARENSON, BARBARA LEVINE, teacher; b. N.Y.C., Apr. 22, 1947; d. Abraham and Rebecca Levine; m. Paul Arenson, June 6, 1971; children: Adam, Aliza. BA in Sociology, U. Calif.-Berkeley, 1969; MA, San Francisco State U., 1970. Cert. elem., learning handicapped, severely handicapped tchr., adminstr., Calif. Spl. edn. tchr. Contra Costa County Pub. Schs., Alamo, Calif., 1970-72; spl. edn. diagnostic tchr. Children's Hosp., Boston, 1972-73; spl. edn. tchr. San Diego City Schs., 1973-76, spl. project tchr., 1976-78, resource tchr., 1978-82, mainstream project resource tchr., 1982-84, spl. edn. infant tchr., 1984—. Co-author: Hand in Hand--A Teacher's Guide to Preschool Mainstreaming, 1983. Mem. Assn. for Retarded Citizens, Phi Beta Kappa. Office: Alcott School 4680 Hidalgo St San Diego CA 92117

ARENTZ, DICK, photographer; b. Detroit, May 19, 1935; s. Ewald and Hermina (Auner) A.; m. Joan Carol, Apr. 4 (div. 1989); children: Paul, James, Pamela. MS, U. Mich., 1959, DSc, 1964. One-man shows include G. Ray Hawkins Gallery, L.A., 1987, Etherton Galler, Tucson, 1987, U. Mo., St. Louis, 1988, Images Gallery, 1988, Kauffman Gallery, Houston, 1988; exhibited in group shows Mus. Photographi Arts, 1987, U. Louisville, 1988, Fergus Jean Gallery, 1988; represented in permanent collections Mus. Modern Art, George Eastman house, Corcoran Gallery, Can. Ctr. for architecture, Amon Carter Mus. Western Art, Oaklan Art Mus., Nat. Mus. Am. Art. Capt. USAF, 1959-61. Isaac W. Bernheim fellow, 1988. Mem. Soc. Photographic Edn. Home and Office: 1640 N Spyglass Way Flagstaff AZ 86004

ARENTZEM, CHARLES, metallurgist, consultant; b. Grand Forks, N.D., Oct. 12, 1919; s. Karl Albert and Caroline (Larsen) A.; m. Marguerite Elizabeth Kane, July 14, 1951. BS in Metallurgy, Mont. Sch. of Mines, 1950; MetE (hon.), Mont. Coll. of Mineral Sci., 1970. Metall. engr. Galigher Co., Salt Lake City, 1950-51; asst. research engr., research engr. Anaconda Co., Mont., 1951-68; various positions to mgr. processs evaluation Anaconda Co., Tucson, 1968-84; metall. cons. Arentzen & Assocs., Tucson, 1984—. Contbr. articles to profl. jours.; atentee in field. Chief petty officer USN, 1938-46. Mem. Metall. Soc., AIME, Toastmasters Club. Home and Office: 7811 E Camino Bavispe Tucson AZ 85715

ARGUELLES, JOHN A., state judge; b. Los Angeles, Aug. 22, 1927; s. Arturo and Eva (Powers) A.; m. Martha Rivas. BA in Econs., UCLA, 1950, JD, 1954. Bar: Calif. 1955. Pvt. practice law East Los Angeles and Montebello, Calif., 1955-63; judge East Los Angeles Mcpl. Ct., 1963-69; presiding criminal ct. judge Los Angeles County Superior Ct., Pomona and Long Beach, Calif., 1969-84; judge 2d Dist. Ct. Appeals, Los Angeles, 1984-87, Calif. Supreme Ct., San Francisco, 1987—; instr. law U. Calif., San Francisco, 1971. Served with USN, 1942-45, ETO, PTO. Office: Calif Supreme Ct 350 McAllister St Ste 4058 San Francisco CA 94102

ARGYROS, GEORGE L., development company executive, professional sports team owner; b. Detroit; m. Judie Argyros. Student, Mich. State U.; B.S. in Bus. and Econs., Chapman Coll., 1959. Pres. Arnel Devel. Co.; chmn. bd. Arnel Mgmt.; chmn., dir. Air Cal, 1981—; dir. comml. financing services Newport bancorp and Coast Thrift and Loan Co.; prin. owner Seattle Mariners Baseball Team, 1981—; mem. Baseball's Revenue sharing Com., Restructuring Com., Commr. Selection Com.; bd. dirs. Am. League. Chmn. Western Wash.'s United Cerebral Palsy Telethon; chmn. fundraising Nat. Multiple Sclerosis Soc., Puget Sound chpt.; active NCCJ, Boy Scouts Am., World Affairs Council, Young Pres.'s Orgn.; chmn. bd. trustees Chapman Coll. Office: Seattle Mariners Baseball Club PO Box 4100 Seattle WA 98104 also: ACI Holdings Inc 3636 Birch St Newport Beach CA 92660 *

ARIK, TALI, cardiologist; b. Pueblo, Colo., May 19, 1956; s. Mehmet and Sevim A.; divorced; children: Doran, Leore. BA, Dartmouth Coll., 1977; MD, U. Louisville, 1980. Diplomate Am. Bd. Internal Medicine, Am. Bd. Cardiology. Intern Good Samaritan Hosp., Phoenix, 1981-82; resident Good Samaritan Hosp., 1982-83, fellow in cardiology, 1983-85, chief med. resident, 1985-86; pvt. practice cardiology Phoenix, 1986—; staff Good Samaritan Hosp., 1986—. Fellow ACP, Am. Coll. Cardiology, Am. Coll. Chest Physicians. Republican. Jewish. Office: Cardiology Consultants PC 1144 E McDowell Rd #304 Phoenix AZ 85006

ARISS, DAVID WILLIAM, real estate developer; b. Toronto, Ont., Can., Nov. 29, 1939; s. William H. and Joyce Ethel (Oddy) A.; m. Lillie, Jan. 26, 1962 (div. 1989); children: Kathryne Joyce, David William, Jr. BA, Claremont Men's Coll., 1961. Lic. real estate broker. Real estate broker Coldwell Banker, Torrance, Calif., 1971-75; v.p. The Lusk Co., Irvine, Calif., 1975-77; pres. DAL Devel. Co., Corona, Calif., 1977-84; mng. dir. Calif. Commerce Ctr. at Ontario, Ontario, Calif., 1984—. Dir. Inland Empire Economic Coun., Ontario, Calif., 1987—; pres. comml./indsl. coun. Baldy View chpt., Bldg. Industry Assn., San Bernardino County, Calif., 1987-88; pres., adv. com., Chaffey Coll., Ontario, 1989—. Maj. USMC, 1961-70, Vietnam. Decorated Silver Star, Disting. Flying Cross, two Purple Hearts, numerous Air medals. Mem. Urban Land Inst., Nat. Assn. Fgn. Trade Zone, Nat. Assn. Indsl. and Office Parks. Republican. Office: Calif Commerce Ctr 1325 S Rockefeller Ave Ontario CA 91761

ARITA, GEORGE SHIRO, biology educator; b. Honolulu, Oct. 9, 1940; s. Ichimatsu and Natsu (Kimoto) A.; m. Harriet Yooko Ide, Dec. 26, 1964; children: Laurie Reiko, Daren Shizuo. BA, U. Hawaii, 1962, MS, 1964; MS, U. B.C., Vancouver, 1967; postgrad., U. Calif., Santa Barbara, 1967-71. Cert. community coll. tchr., Calif. Prof. biology Ventura (Calif.) Coll., 1971—, curator fish collection, 1976—, head dept. biology, 1989—. Author: (with others, lab. manual) Basic Concepts in Biology, 1981, Study Guide to Accompany Biology: Today and Tomorrow, 2d edit., 1984; contbr. articles on ichthyology to profl. jours. Fushiminomiya Meml. scholar U. Hawaii, 1961-62, Fisheries Assn. B.C. scholar U. B.C., 1964-65; NSF grad. trainee U. Calif. Santa Barbara, 1969-71. Mem. AAAS, Am. Soc. Ichthyologists and Herpetologists, Western Soc. Naturalists, Sigma Xi. Home: 94 Howard Ave Oak View CA 93022 Office: Ventura Coll Dept Biology Ventura CA 93003

ARIYOSHI, GEORGE RYOICHI, lawyer, business consultant, former governor Hawaii; b. Honolulu, Mar. 12, 1926; s. Ryozo and Mitsue (Yoshikawa) A.; m. Jean Miya Hayashi, Feb. 5, 1955; children: Lynn Miye, Todd Ryozo, Donn Ryoji. Student, U. Hawaii, 1944-45, 47; B.A., Mich. State U., 1949, LL.D. (hon.), 1979; J.D., U. Mich., 1952; LL.D. (hon.), U. Philippines, 1975, U. Guam, 1975; H.H.D. (hon.), U. Visayas, Philippines, 1977, U. Hawaii, 1986. Bar: Hawaii 1953. Sole practice Honolulu, 1953-70; mem. T.H. Ho. of Reps., 1954-58; mem. T.H. Senate, 1958-70, chmn. ways and means com., 1963-64, majority leader, 1965-66, majority floor leader, 1969-70; lt. gov. State of Hawaii, 1970-73, acting gov., 1973-74, gov., 1974-86; of counsel Kobayashi, Watanabe, Sugita, Kawashima & Goda, Honolulu, 1986—; chmn. Western Govs. Conf., 1977-78; chmn. Western Govs. Assn., 1984-85; dir. Hawaiian Ins. & Guaranty, Ltd., 1966-70, First Hawaiian Bank, 1962-70, Honolulu Gas Co., Ltd. (Pacific Resources, Inc.), 1964-70; bus. cons. Chmn. small bus. div. Community Chest, 1963; fund raiser pub. employees div. Aloha United Fund, 1971-72; exec. bd. Aloha council Boy Scouts Am., 1970-72; chmn. Citizenship Day Com., 1971; pres. Pacific Basin Devel. Council, 1980-81; bd. mgrs. YMCA, 1955-57. Served with M.I. Service AUS, 1945-46. Recipient Distinguished Alumni awards U. Hawaii, 1975, Distinguished Alumni awards Mich. State U., 1975. Mem. Am. Bar Assn. (ho. dels. 1969—), Hawaii Bar Assn. (pres. 1969), Hawaii Bar Found. (charter mem., pres. 1969—). Democrat. Club: Military Intelligence Service Vets (pres. 1968-69).

ARKINSTALL, LEONARD, graphics company executive; b. Regina, Sask., Can., June 2, 1924; came to U.S., 1952; s. Leonard Henry and Dorothy Elsie (Muddle) A.; m. Edith Ellen Wittall; 1 child, Lynne Ryan. Student, Coste House, Calgary, Alta., Can., 1946-47, Brigdens, Winnipeg, Man., Can., 1947-48. Salesman advt. Calgary Albertan, 1947-50; mgr. advt. Restmore-Madson Furniture, Vancouver, B.C., Can., 1950-57; dir. art Sta. KNDO-TV, Yakima, Wash., 1957-63; mgr. sales Community Advocate, Hawaiian Gardens, Calif., 1963-65; prin. Culver (Calif.) Chronicle, 1965-70; dir. art Apco Publ., Lakewood, Calif., 1970-75; mgr. advt. U-Disco Stores, Southgate, Calif., 1975-78, K-Mart Foods, Wicovina, Calif., 1978-80; pres. ESP Graphics, Inc., Carson, Calif., 1980—; art cons. Substance Abuse and Narcotics Edn., Carson, 1988—. Mem. Write Your Congressman, Los Angeles, 1981-88. Served with Royal Can. Navy, 1942-45. Mem. Carson C. of C. Republican. Episcopalian. Lodges: Moose, Masons. Office: ESP Graphics Inc 225 W Torrance Blvd Carson CA 90745

ARLE, STEVEN WAYNE, radiologist; b. Aurora, Ill., Oct. 1, 1947; s. Edward Charles and Stella (Hausmann) A.; m. Kathleen Brannan, Mar. 13, 1948. AA, Concordia Coll., Milw., 1967; BA, Concordia Sr. Coll., Ft. Wayne, Ind., 1969; MDiv, Concordia Sem., St. Louis, 1973; MD, Ludwig-Maximillians U., Munich, 1981. Resident in radiology Mt. Sinai Hosp., Chgo., 1981-82, Ochsner Clinic, New Orleans, 1982-85; staff radiologist Alaska Native Med. Ctr., Anchorage, 1985-87, Wausau (Wis.) Med. Ctr., 1987-88; radiologist Magnetic Resonance Diagnostic Ctr., Sun City, Ariz., 1988—. Lt. USPHS, 1985-87. Mem. Radiol. Soc. N.Am., Soc. for Preservation and Encouragement Barber Shop Quartet Singing in Am. Lutheran. Office: MR Diagnostic Ctr 10405 W Thunderbird Sun City AZ 85321

ARMBRUSTER, GARY ELVIN, regional manager, consultant; b. Ann Arbor, Mich., June 18, 1940; s. Elvin Leroy and Eunice Bena (Boettger) A.; m. Martha Elnora Faust, Aug. 27, 1960 (div. Mar. 1976); children: Brian G., Kristin; m. Nancy Joan Jackson, May 22, 1976 (div. Apr. 1984); 1 child, David W. BBA in Acctg., Cleary Coll., 1963; postgrad., Wayne State U., 1963. Cert. personnel cons. Controller, treas. Gelman Instrument Co., Ann Arbor, 1962-69; controller Ready Power Co., Detroit, 1969-70, Fireplace Corp. Am., Walledlake, Mich., 1970-72; fin. v.p., controller Robert Half Personnel Agy., Inc., Detroit, 1972-77; mfg. mgr., controller Poly Cast, Inc., Highland, Mich., 1977-85; mgr. Robert Half So. Calif. and Accountemps, San Diego, 1985--; mem. adv. bd. Grossmont Calif. Job Tng. Placement Assn. Acctg. Curr., San Diego, 1985--, San Diego Community Coll. Acctg. Curr., 1987--. Mem. Nat. Assn. Accts., Nat. Assn. Personnel Cons., NAR, Thunderboast Unltd. San Diego. Home: PO Box 9240 San Diego CA 92109 Office: Accountemps/Robert Half 409 Camino Del Rio S #305 San Diego CA 92108

ARMENTROUT, STEVEN ALEXANDER, oncologist; b. Morgantown, W.Va., Aug. 22, 1933; s. Walter W. and Dorothy (Gasch) A.; m. Johanna Ruszkay; children—Marc, Susan, Sandra, Nancy. A.B., U. Chgo., 1953, M.D., 1959. Intern U. Hosp., Cleve., 1959-60; resident in medicine, fellow Am. Cancer Soc. Western Res. U. Hosp., 1960-63; project dir. USPHS, 1963-65; asst. prof. Case Western Res. U. Med. Sch., 1965-71; mem. faculty U. Calif. Med. Sch., Irvine, 1971—; prof. medicine, chief div. hematology-oncology U. Calif. Med. Sch., 1978—, also dir. program in oncology.; pres. med. staff U. Calif.-Irvine Med. Ctr., 1983-85; researcher in multiple sclerosis. Mem. Am. Assn. Cancer Research, AAUP, A.C.P., Am. Cancer Soc. (chmn. bd. 1973, pres. Orange County chpt. 1985-86), AMA, Am. Soc. Clin. Oncology, Am. Soc. Hematology, Orange County Med. Assn., Am. Soc. Internal Medicine, Calif. Med. Assn., Cen. Soc. Clin. Research, Leukemia Soc. Am., Orange County Chief of Staff Council. Office: 101 City Dr Orange CA 92668

ARMIJO, JACQULYN DORIS, interior designer; b. Gilmer, Tex., July 2, 1938; d. Jack King and Iris Adele (Cook) Smith; children—John, Christy, Mike. Student North Tex. State Coll., U. N.Mex. Profl. model, 1961-75; sec. State Farm Ins., Albuquerque, 1965-71; life ins. agt. Mountain States, Albuquerque, 1980; owner Interiors by Jacqulyn, Albuquerque, 1961—; cons., lectr. in field. Mem. Alby Little Theatre, Friends of Little Theatre, Symphony Women; fund raiser for Old Town Hist. Com., Arthritis Fund. Mem. Am. Soc. Interior Design (chmn. historic restoration Albuquerque), Internat. Soc. Interior Design, Internat. Platform Assn., Civil War Club (pres. local chpt.) Republican. Roman Catholic. Clubs: Albuquerque Jr. Women's, Los Amapolas Garden. Home and Office: 509 Chamiso Ln NW Albuquerque NM 87107

ARMINANA, RUBEN, university administrator, educator; b. Santa Clara, Cuba, May 15, 1947; came to U.S., 1961; s. Aurelio Ruben and Olga Petrona (Nart) A.; m. Marne Olson, July 2, 1977; children: Cesar A. Martino, Maria G. Arminana. AA, Hill Jr. Coll., 1966; BA, U. Tex., 1968, MA, 1970; PhD, U. New Orleans, 1983; postgrad. Inst. of Applied Behavioral Scis., Nat. Tng. Labs., 1971. Nat. assoc. dir. Phi Theta Kappa, Canton, Miss., 1968-69; dir. ops. and tng. Inter-Am. Ctr., Loyola U., New Orleans, 1969-71; adminstrv. analyst City of New Orleans, 1972, adminstrv. analyst and organizational devel. and tng. cons., 1972-78; anchor and reporter part time STA. WWL-TV, New Orleans, 1973-81; v.p. Commerce Internat. Corp., New Orleans, 1978-83; exec. asst. to sr. v.p. Tulane U., New Orleans, 1983-85, assoc. exec. v.p., 1985-87, v.p., asst. to pres., 1987-88; v.p. fin. and devel. Calif. Poly Inst., Pomona, 1988—; TV news cons., New Orleans, 1981-88; lectr. Internat. Trade Mart, New Orleans, 1983-89, U.S. Dept. Commerce, New Orleans. Co-author: Hemisphere West-El Futuro, 1968; co-editor: Colloquium on Central America-A Time for Understanding, Background Readings, 1985. Bd. dirs. Com. on Alcoholism and Substance Abuse, 1978-79, SER, Jobs for Progress, Inc., 1974-82, Citizens United for Responsive Broadcasting, Latin Am. Festival Com; dir., bd. advisors Sta. WDSU-TV, 1974-77; mem. Bus. Govt. Rsch., 1987-88, Coun. Advancment of Support to Edn. State Polytech. U.; mem. League of United Latin Am. Citizens, Mayor's Latin Am. Adv. Com., Citizens to Preserve the Charter, Met. Area Com., Mayor's Com. on Crime. Kiwanis scholar, 1966, Books scholar, 1966. Mem. Assn. U. Related Rsch. Prks., L.A. Higher Edn. Roundtable,Soc. Coll. and U. Planning, Nat. Assn. Coll. and U. Bus. Officers Cou., Am. Econ. Assn., Assn. of Evolutionary Econs., Am. Polit. Sci. Assn., AAUP, Latin Am. C. of C. (founding dir. New Orleans and River Region 1976-83), Cuban Profl. Club, Phi Theta Kappa, Omicron Delta Epsilon, Sigma Delta Pi, Delta Sigma Pi. Democrat. Roman Catholic. Avocation: mask collecting. Office: Calif Polytechnic U 3801 W Temple Ave Pomona CA 91768-4021

ARMOUR, GORDON CHARLES, emerging technology specialist; b. Denver, June 1, 1929; s. Gordon Thomas and Doris Hilda (Stoker) A.; m. Margaret Christine Graney, Sept. 22, 1951; children: Doris C., Thomas S. BS, UCLA, 1953, MBA, 1957, PhD, 1961. Registered profl. engr., Calif. Sr. indsl. engr. Johns-Manville Co., Long Beach, Calif., 1957-59; asst. prof. Grad. Sch. Bus., Ind. U., Bloomington, 1961-64; mgmt. systems specialist N.Am. Aviation Co., Anaheim, Calif., 1964-68; chief mgmt. systems and planning N.Am. Rockwell, Anaheim, Calif., 1968-69; exec. advisor N.Am. Rockwell, Anaheim, 1969-73; indsl. planning specialist Rockwell Internat., Anaheim, 1973-79, exec. advisor for computers, 1979-81, mgr. telecommunications and computer tech., 1981-83, specialist for emerging tech., 1983--; vis. prof. UCLA, 1963; cons. Gen. Water Heater Co., Burbank, Calif., 1960. Contbr. articles to profl. publs. Mem. selection panel for data processing mgr. City of Anaheim, 1980. With USMC, 1953-55. Jo Downing scholar, 1953; Ford Found. fellow, 1959-61, 63-64, Ind. U. rsch. fellow, 1962. Home: 12812 Bubbling Well Rd Santa Ana CA 92705 Office: Rockwell Internat 3370 Mira Loma Ave AE12 Anaheim CA 92803

ARMOUR, REGINALD, film producer and distributor; b. Chgo., Nov. 28, 1905; s. Philip and Marie (Valentine) A.; m. Joyce Armour, Nov. 25, 1956; 1 child, Andrew Philip. PhD in Econs., Edinburgh U., 1932. With RCA Victor Co., 1932-33; successively Far East gen. mgr., European gen. mgr., exec. asst. to pres., asst. gen. mgr. RKO Radio Studios, 1933-42; European rep. Walt Disney Prodns., 1942-43; with fin. field Walt Disney Prodns., N.Y.C., 1943-44; exec. v.p. Richard Condon, Inc., 1944-45; fgn. rep. Columbia Internat. Corp., N.Y.C., 1945-49; appt. v.p. Republic Pictures Internat. Corp., 1950-52, supr. Europe and Near East, 1952-55; exec. v.p., mng. dir. Republic Pictures Internat. Corp., Eng., 1955-60; pres. The Dorsey Corp., 1960-64, vice chmn., 1964-65; pres. SOS Photo-Cine-Optics, Inc., 1965-67, FB/Ceco of Calif., Inc., 1967-71, Instant Protection Systems, Inc., 1971-73; exec. v.p., treas. The Quedo Corp. and Internat. Producers Services, Inc., 1973; v.p., treas. Dyna-Sonar, Inc., 1974, Two Feathers Prodns., 1977-81; pres. Armour Enterprises, Inc., 1981-85, Group Media Prodns., Inc, 1985—. Served to Col. AUS, 1943-45, ETO. Office: 1544 N Canyon Dr Hollywood CA 90028

ARMOUR, SONJA RUTH, teacher; b. Monista, N.Mex., May 4, 1947; d. Fay Franklin and Beulah (Dunn) Hawkins; m. Ray Riley Armour (dec.); 1 child, Roxana Park. AA, Solano Community Coll., Suisun, Calif., 1980; BA in Polit. Sci., U. Calif., Berkeley, 1982, MA in Edn., 1985. Tchr. Martinez (Calif.) Jr. High Sch., 1985—. Regent scholar, 1981. Mem. Nat. Coun. Tchrs. English, NAACP, AAUW, Tchrs. of Tomorrow. Democrat. Home: 2859 Sheldon Dr Richmond CA 94803 Office: Martinez Jr High Sch Court and Warren Sts Martinez CA 94553

ARMSTRONG, CHARLES G., professional baseball executive, lawyer; b. Louisville, Aug. 31, 1942; m. Susan; children—Dorrie, Katherine, Chuck. B.S., Purdue U., 1964; J.D., Stanford U., 1967. Bar: Calif. Practice law Hill Farrer & Burrill, Calif., 1971—; pres., chief operating officer Seattle Mariners Baseball Team, 1983—. Served with USN, 1967-70. Office: Seattle Mariners 100 S King St Ste 300 Seattle WA 98104 *

ARMSTRONG, CHERYL B(URTON), manufacturing company executive; b. Walla Walla, Wash., Dec. 10, 1956; d. John Louis and Mary Lucille (Delbuono) Batt; m. Ray Burton, Sept. 2, 979 (div. 1983); m. Gary Armstrong Jr., Oct. 4, 1986. BA, U. Oreg., 1979. Freelance model Portland, Oreg., 1972-75; asst. dir. Patricia Stevens Modeling Sch., Portland, 1974-75; modeling instr. John Robert Powers Sch., Portland, 1975-79; owner, operator, tchr. Springfield Acad. Dance and Modeling, Eugene and Springfield, Oreg., 1980-83; sales rep. Skeie's Jewelers, Eugene, 1982-84; recruiter Fran Low, Ltd., Portland, 1984-85; sales rep. Ricoh Corp., Seattle, 1985-86, major acct. rep., 1986-87, major acct. mgr., 1987—. Home: 10010 NE 115th Ln Kirkland WA 98034 Office: Ricoh Corp 1 Lake Bellevue Dr Bellevue WA 98005

ARMSTRONG, DICKWIN DILL, chamber of commerce executive; b. Muncie, Ind., Aug. 18, 1934; s. Colby Cooler and Elizabeth A. (Houck) A.; m. Janice A. Flora, June 2, 1957; children—Brent D., Stacey J. B.S. in Gen. Bus, Ind. U., 1956. Chief exec. officer Madison C. of C., Ind., 1959-61; chief exec. officer Frankfort C. of C., Ind., 1961-63, Marion C. of C., Ind., 1963-66, Lakeland C. of C., Fla., 1966-80; chief exec. officer Portland C. of C., Oreg., 1980-86, treas. polit. action com.; pres. Bellevue C. of C., Wash., 1987—. Served to capt. AUS, 1957-59. Mem. Am. C. of C. Execs. (cert. chamber exec., past officer), U.S. C. of C., Oreg. Chamber Execs. (dir., com. chmn.), Washington C. of C. Execs. (v.p.), Rotary, Masons, Shriners, Sigma Alpha Epsilon. Republican. Presbyterian. Home: 15821 NE 67th Pl Redmond WA 98052 Office: Bellevue C of C 110-110th Ave NE Ste 300 Bellevue WA 98004

ARMSTRONG, GENE LEE, retired aerospace company executive; b. Clinton, Ill., Mar. 9, 1922; s. George Dewey and Ruby Imald (Dickerson) A.; B.S. with high honors, U. Ill., Urbana, 1948, M.S., 1951; m. Lael Jeanne Baker, Apr. 3, 1946; children—Susan Lael, Roberta Lynn, Gene Lee. With Boeing Aircraft, 1948-50, 51-52; chief engr. astronautics div., corp. dir. Gen. Dynamics, 1954-65; chief engr. Def. Systems GroupTRW, Redondo Beach, Calif., 1956-86, pvt. cons. systems engring., 1986—. Mem. NASA Research Adv. Com. on Control, Guidance & Navigation, 1959-62. Served to 1st lt. USAAF, 1942-45. Decorated Air medal; recipient alumni awards U. Ill., 1965, 77; registered profl. engr., Calif. Mem. Am. Math. Soc., AIAA, Nat. Mgmt. Assn., Am. Def. Preparedness Assn. Club: Masons. Contbr. chpts. to books, articles to profl. publs. Home: 5242 Bryant Circle Westminster CA 92683 Office: Armstrong Systems Engring Co PO Box 86 Westminster CA 92684-0086

ARMSTRONG, JENNIFER TAYLOR, publisher; b. Perth Amboy, N.J., Jan. 19, 1954; d. Joan D. (Vorhauer) McCarthy. BA in Journalism and Psychology, Marquette U., 1975. Pvt. practice pub. relations Los Angeles and Phoenix, 1978-85; publisher, editor FootPrints Publs., Phoenix, 1985—; freelance journalist, editor, publs. cons. Phoenix, 1988—. Contbr. articles to popular mags. and publs. Home and Office: PO Box 41921 Phoenix AZ 85080

ARMSTRONG, JOANNA, educator; b. Vienna, Austria, Feb. 3, 1915; came to U.S., 1946; m. David B. Armstrong, Mar. 12, 1946. Diploma, Kindergarten Tchr. State Coll., Vienna, 1933, Sorbonne, 1935; MA, U. Utah, 1951; EdD, U. Houston, 1959. Caseworker, interpreter Czech Refugee Turst Fund, London, 1939-41; tchr. French Gt. Missenden, Bucks, 1941-43; sec., interpreter U.S. Army, England and France, 1943-46; instr. Coll. William and Mary, Williamsburg, Va., 1951-55, U. St. Thomas, Houston, 1957-59; chmn. langs. sect. South Tex. Coll., Houston, 1961-62; dir. NDEA Inst. Tex. So. U., Houston, 1964-65, assoc. prof. fgn. langs., 1962-68; assoc. prof. sch. edn. U. Tex., El Paso, 1968-71; cons. office Child Devel. HEW, Kansas City, Mo., 1973; cons. Tex. Edn. Agy., Austin, 1965; sec. U.S. Forest Svc., Ely, Nev., 1948. Contbr. articles to profl. publs. Vol. Long Beach (Calif.) Symphony, 1978, Long Beach Grand Opera, 1982—. Recipient Chevalier dans l'Ordre des Palmes Academiques, 1957, Head Start award, 1971, Pres.' Plaque Alliance Francaise d'El Paso, 1971. Mem. Women's Music Club (program chmn. 1986-88), U.S.-China People Friendship Assn. (sec. 1987—). Home: 120 Alamitos Ave #34 Long Beach CA 90802

ARMSTRONG, LINDA GIOVANNIELLI, art director, graphic designer; b. Hackensack, N.J., July 20, 1961; d. Michael Jr. and Anna Maria (Orsini) Giovannielli. Student, William Paterson Coll., 1979-82. Art dir. Image Concepts, Inc., Paramus, N.J., 1983-86, Knotts Berry Farm, Buena Park, Calif., 1986-87, Halan & Assocs., Anaheim, Calif., 1987-88; owner Surf City Sportswear, Rancho Cucamonga, Calif., 1989—. Art dir. calendar AT&T Internat., 1986 (Creativity award 1986, Jersey award 1986). Mem. Art Dirs. Club N.J. (Image award 1987).

ARMSTRONG, NELSON BRADBERRY, engineer; b. Seattle, Feb. 22, 1931; s. Nelson Bradford and Ruth Margaret (Young) A.; m. Barbara Irene Kroll; children: Bruce Allen, Sharon Ann, Mary Anne. AA, Phoenix Coll., 1967; BS, Grand Canyon Coll., Phoenix, 1977. With No. Lights Inc., Sand Point, Idaho, 1955, Fish Svc. and Mgmt., Spokane, 1956, The Boeing Co., Seattle, 1957-62; field engr. Gen. Elec., Phoenix, 1962-69; engr.-in-chg.

Honeywell Info. Sys., Inc., Phoenix, 1969-78; prog. mgr. Gen. Elec. Aircraft Svc., Cin., 1978-84; engring specialist Gen. Dynamics, Corvair div., San Diego, 1984—. With USAF, 1951-52. Mem. Instrument Soc. Am., Mensa. Home: 9941 Ave Magnifica San Diego CA 92131 Office: Gen Dynamics Convair Div PO Box 85357 MZ 57-4730 San Diego CA 92138

ARMSTRONG, ORVILLE A., lawyer; b. Austin, Tex., Jan. 21, 1929; s. Orville Alexander and Velma Lucille (Reed) A.; m. Mary Dean Macfarlane; children. B.B.A., U. Tex., Austin, 1953; LL.B., U. So. Calif., 1956. Bar: Calif., 1957, U.S. Ct. Appeals (9th cir.) 1958, U.S. Supreme Ct. 1980. Ptnr., Gray, Binkley & Pfaelzer, 1956-61, Pfaelzer, Robertson, Armstrong & Woodard, Los Angeles, 1961-66, Armstrong & Lloyd, Los Angeles, 1966-74, Macdonald, Halsted & Laybourne, Los Angeles, 1975-88, Baker & McKenzie, 1988—; lectr. Calif. Continuing Edn. of Bar. Served with USAF, 1946-49. Fellow ABA, Am. Coll. Trial Lawyers; mem. State Bar Calif. (gov. 1983-87, pres. 1986-87), Los Angeles County Bar Assn. (trustee 1971-72), Am. Judicature Soc., Chancery Club (pres. 1988), Assn. Bus. Trial Lawyers, Am. Arbitration Assn. Democrat. Baptist. Clubs: Calif. (Oakmont). Home: 2385 Coniston Pl San Marino CA 91108 Office: 725 S Figueroa St 36th Fl Los Angeles CA 90017

ARMSTRONG, RICHARD LEROY, business owner, executive; b. Normal, Ill., Feb. 24, 1940; s. Roy Kenner and Alice Ruth (Thompson) A.; m. Susan E. Buchwalter, Apr. 22, 1962 (div. Sept. 1968); m. Charlotte Ann Wolf, Nov. 10, 1968; children: Kimberly Ann, Michael Wolf. BS in Bus., U. Ariz., 1963. Asst. mgr., loan officer Bank of Calif., Los Angeles, 1963-70; asst. v.p. loans Valley Nat. Bank, Phoenix, 1970-73; sales mgr. Sahuaro Petroleum & Asphalt Co., Phoenix, 1973-82; pres. Daycor Inc., Yorba Linda, Calif., 1982—. Bd. dirs. Maricopa County chpt. ARC, Phoenix, 1971-73, local chpts. of U. Ariz., Los Angeles, Phoenix and Orange County, 1963—, U. Ariz. Nat. Alumni Bd., Tucson, 1983—. Mem. Am. Pub. Works Assn., Am. Assn. Airport Execs. (assoc.), Associated Gen. Contractors. Home: 4358 Mahogany Circle Yorba Linda CA 92686 Office: Daycor Inc PO Box 1156 Paramount CA 90723

ARMSTRONG, ROBERT DEAN, entertainer; b. Serena, Ill., July 2, 1923; s. Francis Robert and Viola D. (Thompson) A.; m. Ardith Roberta Taylor, Jan. 10, 1943; 1 child, Larry Dean. Grad. high sch., Serena, Ill.; student, Joliet (Ill.) Conservatory of Music, 1942. Host Dean Armstrong Show Sta. KOLD-TV, Tucson, 1953-75; leader, owner Arizona Dance Hands, Tucson, 1946—. Served with U.S. Mil., 1943-45, ETO, PTO. Recipient Mayor of Tucson's Recognition award, 1979, This Is Your Life, Desert Life Health Ctr., Tucson, 1987; named Entertainer of Yr. Tucson TV mag., 1954. Mem. Tucson Musicians Assn. (meritorious service award 1981), VFW. Democrat. Methodist. Lodges: Elks, Eagles. Home and Office: 4265 Avenida del Cazador Tucson AZ 85718

ARMSTRONG, SEAN FREDERICK, real estate broker; b. L.A., Apr. 3, 1962; s. Desmond Anthony and Ann Margaret (Fitchew) A. BS in Biomedical Engring., U. So. Calif., L.A., 1983; postgrad., U. Calif., San Francisco, 1983-85. Sales assoc. South Bay Comml. Real Estate, Torrance, Calif., 1985-87; v.p. sales South Bay Comml. Real Estate, 1987-88; pres. Armstrong Hudson, Inc., Torrance, 1988—. Tchr. St. John Fisher Catholic Ch., Rancho Palos Verdes, Calif., 1985—. Republican. Office: Armstrong Hudson Inc 25202 Crenshaw Blvd 200 Torrance CA 90505

ARMSTRONG, WALLACE DOWAN, JR., data processor; b. Los Angeles, Feb. 9, 1926; s. Wallace Dowan and Vina Edith (Kreinbring) A.; B.S. cum laude, U. So. Calif., 1951; postgrad. U. Oslo (Norway), 1955; 1 son, Erik Bentung. Supr. accounting Ramo Wooldridge Corp., 1955-60; mgr. programmers, systems analyst Aerospace Corp., El Segundo, Calif., 1960-80, mgr. bus. systems, 1980—. Served with USMCR, 1944-46, 51. Mem. Data Processing Mgmt. Assn. Home: 25713 Crest Rd Torrance CA 90505 Office: Aerospace Corp 2350 E El Segundo Blvd El Segundo CA 90245

ARMSTRONG, WILLIAM L., senator; b. Fremont, Nebr., Mar. 16, 1937; s. William L. and Dorothy (Steen) A.; m. Ellen M. Eaton, July 15, 1962; children: Anne Elizabeth, William. Student, Tulane U., 1954-55, U. Minn., 1956. Pres. Sta. KPV1-TV, Pocatello, Idaho; mem. 93d-95th Congresses from 5th Dist. Colo.; mem. U.S. Senate from Colo., 1979—, chmn. Republican Policy Com., 1984—. Mem. Colo. Senate, 1965-72, majority leader, 1969-72; mem. Colo. Ho. of Reps., 1963-64. Served with U.S. Army N.G., 1957-63. Mem. AP Broadcasters Assn. (dir. 1971-72, v.p. 1972). Office: US Senate 528 Hart Senate Office Bldg Washington DC 20510 *

ARNDT, MICHAEL PAUL, financial consulting executive; b. Mt. Vernon, N.Y., Aug. 30, 1930; s. Stanley Morris Arndt and Helen Lucille (Wood) Arndt. BA, Pomona Coll., 1952; MBA, Harvard U., 1954. Analyst investment dept. N.Y. Life, San Francisco, 1954-56; v.p. fin. control TRW, Inc., L.A., 1956-86; pres. TOWR Assocs., L.A., 1987—, also bd. dirs.; bd. dirs. EECO, Inc., Santa Ana, Calif. Pres. Pomona Coll. Assocs., Claremont, Calif., 1983-87; trustee Pomona Coll., Claremont, 1985-87. Am. Chem. Soc. scholar, 1947. Mem. Fin. Analyst Assn., Fin. Exec. Inst., Phi Beta Kappa, Phi Delta (pres. 1952, bd. dirs. 1960-75), Mar de Cortez (La Paz, Mex., bd. dirs. 1963-78). Republican. Home: 251 S Barrington Ave Los Angeles CA 90049 Office: TOWR Assocs 11444 W Olympic Blvd Los Angeles CA 90064

ARNDT, STEPHEN ALLEN, school system administrator; b. Everett, Wash., May 5, 1949; s. Otto Paul Arndt and Julia R. (Gunderson) Leavitt; m. Diane Louise Gillette, May 19, 1978; children: Robert William, Amanda Katherine. BA, Oreg. Coll. of Edn., 1971, MA, 1974; postgrad., U. Oreg. Cert. sch. supt. Tchr. Newby Sch., McMinnville, Oreg., 1971-75; prin. Carlton (Oreg.) Sch., 1975-79; prin., spl. edn. dir. Mt. Angel (Oreg.) Schs., 1979-82; prin. Nellie Muir Sch., Woodburn, Oreg., 1982-87, Washington Sch., Salem, Oreg., 1987—; cons. Oreg. Dept. Edn., Career Edn., Salem, 1974-75, Yamhill County ESD, Metric Edn., McMinnville, 1976-78; participant Project Leadership, Eugene, Oreg., 1977-78, 88. Editor: (newsletter) Western Region What's Happening, 1988-89. Chmn. Kiwanis-Mayors Prayer Breakfast, Woodburn, 1986-88; bd. dirs. Faith Christian Sch., Woodburn, 1986-88; task force chmn. Woodburn Schs. Constrn. Com., 1986-87. Recipient Spl. Edn. grant, U.S. Govt., Oreg. Coll. Edn., 1973-74. Mem. Oreg. Elem. Sch. Prin. Assn. (exec. officer, 1988-91), Western Region-Elem. Prin. (pres. 1987-88, pres. award 1988), Assn. Supervision and Curriculum Devel., Nat. Assn. Elem. Prin., Oreg. Confedn. of Sch. Assn., Lions, Kiwanis, Elks, Gamma Theta Upsilon. Republican. Methodist. Home: 856 Gatch St Woodburn OR 97071 Office: Washington Sch 3165 Lansing Ave NE Salem OR 97303

ARNELL, WALTER JAMES WILLIAM, engineering educator, consultant; b. Farnborough, Eng., Jan. 9, 1924; came to U.S., 1953, naturalized, 1960; s. James Albert and Daisy (Payne) A.; m. Patricia Catherine Cannon, Nov. 12, 1955; children—Sean Paul, Victoria Clare, Sarah Michele Arnell. Aero. Engr., Royal Aircraft Establishment, 1946; BSc, U. London, 1953, PhD, 1967; MA, Occidental Coll., Los Angeles, 1956; MS, U. So. Calif., 1958. Lectr. Poly. and Northampton Coll. Advance Tech., London, 1948-53; instr. U. So. Calif., Los Angeles, 1954-59; asst. prof. mech. engring. Calif. State U., Long Beach, 1959-62, assoc. prof., 1962-66, prof., 1966-71, chmn. dept. mech. engring., 1964-65, acting chmn. div. engring., 1964-66, dean engring., 1967-69, researcher Ctr. Engring. Research; affiliate faculty dept. ocean engring. U. Hawaii, 1970-74; adj. prof. systems and insdl. engring. U. Ariz., 1981—; pres. Lenra Assocs. Ltd., 1973—; chmn., project mgr. Hawaii Environ. Simulation Lab., 1971-72. Contbr. articles to profl. jours. Trustee, Rehab. Hosp. of the Pacific, 1975-79. Mem. Royal Aero. Soc., AIAA, IEEE Systems Man and Cybernetics Soc., AAUP, Am. Psychol. Assn., Soc. Engring., Psychology, Human Factors Soc., Ergonomics Soc., Psi Chi, Alpha Pi Mu, Tau Beta Pi, Phi Kappa Phi, Pi Tau Sigma. Home: 4491 E Fort Lowell Tucson AZ 85712

ARNETT, CARROLL D., chemistry educator; b. Rowlesburg, W.Va., Aug. 22, 1946; s. Jerome C. and V. Maye (Fike) A.; m. Susan P. Crafton, June 20, 1970; 1 child, Christopher S. AB in Chemistry, Duke U., 1968; postgrad., Med. Coll. Va., 1968-69; PhD in Med. Chemistry, U. Md., 1976; postgrad., Duke U., 1976-79. Teaching asst. Med. Coll. Va., Richmond, 1968-69; chemistry assoc. Johns Hopkins Hosp., Balt., 1969-71; grad. asst. U. Md., Balt., 1971-75; rsch. assoc. Duke U. Med. Ctr., Durham, N.C., 1976-79; chemist Brookhaven Nat. Lab., Upton, N.Y., 1979-87; assoc. prof. psychiatry and behavioral scis. U. Wash., Seattle, 1988—, adj. assoc. prof. radiology, 1988—; cons. in field. Contbr. articles to profl. jours.; patentee in field. Biomed. Research Support grantee, U. Wash., 1988. Mem. ACS, Soc. Neurosci., Sigma Xi, Rho Chi. Home: 555 145th Ave SE Bellevue WA 98007 Office: Dept Psychiatry & Behavioral Sci U Wash Sch Medicine RP10 Seattle WA 98195

ARNEY, WILLIAM RAY, sociologist, educator; b. Charlotte, N.C., Sept. 18, 1950; s. John Wilson and Grace (Kuhn) A.; m. Deborah Henderson, Jan. 2, 1972; 1 child: John Arthur. BA with distinction, U. Colo., 1971, MA, 1972; PhD, 1974. Asst. prof. then assoc. prof. Dartmouth Coll., Hanover, N.H., 1974-81; dir. edn. and evaluation Vt.-N.H. Regional Perinatal Program, Hanover, N.H., 1978-80; mem. of the faculty Evergreen State Coll., Olympia, Wash., 1981—. Author: Power and the Profession of Obstetrics, 1982, Medicine and the Management of Living (with others), 1984, Understanding Statistics in the Social Sciences, 1989. NEH fellow, 1986; Rockefeller Found. resident Bellagio (Italy) Study and Conf. Ctr., 1988. Mem. Am. Statis. Assn., Am. Sociol. Assn. Mem. Disciples of Christ Church. Home: 2353 Crestline St NW Olympia WA 98502 Office: Evergreen State Coll Lab II Olympia WA 98505

ARNOLD, ARTHUR JAMES, state official; b. Kenosha, Wis., July 6, 1950; s. William James and Frances Letha (Lewis) A.; m. Susan Lynn Faraca, Dec. 31, 1971. Student, U. Wis., Whitewater, 1968-70; BA, U. Wis., Eau Claire, 1974, postgrad., 1974-78; postgrad., Alaska Pacific U., 1985-86. Cert. elem. tchr., spl. edn. tchr., Kans., Wis. Primary tchr. Parsons (Kans.) State Hosp. and Tng. Ctr., 1974-75, Sunburst Youth Homes, Inc., Neillsville, Wis., 1975-79; curriculum developer Eau Claire Acad., 1980-82; program coord. Hope Cottages, Inc., Anchorage, 1982-87; program dir. Assn. for Retarded Citizens Alaska, Anchorage, 1987-88; no. regional program specialist Alaska Div. Mental Health and Devel. Disabilities, Fairbanks, 1988—. Author: (poetry) Momentary Art, 1980, Any Voice You See, 1980. Del. Alaska Dem. Conv., 1988. Recipient Human Svcs. Edn. award U. Alaska, Anchorage, 1988. Mem. Am. Assn. on Mental Deficiency, Alternative Living Mgrs. Assn., Assn. for Retarded Citizens Anchorage, Assn. for Retarded Citizens Saskatoon. Office: Alaska Dept Mental Health and Devel Disabilities 1423 Peger Rd Fairbanks AK 99709

ARNOLD, DALE EUGENE, wastewater management administrator; b. Spokane, Wash., July 4, 1953; s. Clarence Eugene and Ruth Selma (Broberg) A.; m. Julie Ann Cullen, Sept. 1, 1974; 1 child: Genevieve Jane. BA in Biology, Gonzaga U., 1975. Chemist Wastewater Lab., Spokane, 1976-79; supr. Wastewater Treatment Plant, Spokane, 1979-85, Wastewater Mgmt., Spokane, 1986—; internship advisor U. Wis., Stevens Point, 1986, Spokane Community Coll., 1986—. Rep. City of Spokane Inland Northwest Govt. Task Force, 1983-86; mem. budget com. Spokane Credit Union, 1986—. Mem. Inland Empire Pollution Control Assn. (pres. 1985—, dir. wastewater cert. tng. 1985—, bd. dirs. 1985—), Inland Empire Pacific Northwest Pollution Control Assn. (v.p. 1984-85), Nat. Mgmt. Assn. (pub. relations dir. 1983—), Spokane Bicycle Club, Missoula Bicycle Club. Home: W 457 15th Spokane WA 99203 Office: Wastewater Mgmt N 4401 Al White Pkwy Spokane WA 99205

ARNOLD, FREDRIC, inventor, actor; b. Chgo., Jan. 23, 1922; s. David Arnold and Idele Edith (Horwitz) Kohn; m. Natalie Barbara Merriam, July 2, 1946; children: Marcie Barkin, Dana Schwartz, Marc Arnold. Grad. high sch. Artist Hearst Newspapers, Chgo., 1939-42; mgr. advt. Food Trade Jours., N.Y.C., 1946-47; founder, pres. Arnold Blau Corp., Bklyn., 1947-49, Fredric Arnold Co., Bklyn., 1949-57, Photo Engring. Corp. Internat., Chatsworth, Calif., 1957-81; artist/actor motion pictures/film/TV, L.A., 1981—; cons. mktg. and prodn., 1981—. Author: Doorknob Five Two, 1984, Kohn's War, 1985; inventions include aircraft aileron boost, 1943, tube bender, 1946, food cutting and rolling device, 1947, automatic onion peeler, 1959, automatic photography systems, 1958, many others. Maj. USAAF, 1942-46. Decorated DFC, air medal with 9 oak leaf clusters. Mem. SAG, AFTRA.

ARNOLD, HARRY LOREN, JR., dermatologist, editor, author; b. Owosso, Mich., Aug. 7, 1912; s. Harry L. and Meda (Sheldon) A.; m. Blanche G. Wetherald, 1934 (div. 1941); children—Sara Joan, Charles R.; m. Jeanne M. Prevost, July 11, 1942 (dec. Jan. 1983); children: Harry Loren III, John P., Susan M.; m. Jeanne S. Herman, Dec. 16, 1983. A.B. cum laude, U. Mich., 1932, M.D. cum laude, 1935; M.S., 1939. Diplomate: Am. Bd. Dermatology (mem. bd. 1966-76, pres. 1972-73). Intern U. Mich. Hosp., 1935-36, resident, 1936-37, instr. dermatology, 1937-39; chief dermatology Straub Clinic, Honolulu, 1939-69; clin. prof. medicine U. Hawaii.; clin. prof. dermatology U. Calif., San Francisco; pres. Straub Med. Research Inst., 1961-63; Frederick G. Novy, Jr. vis. scholar in dermatology U. Calif. Med. Sch., Davis, 1975; cons. emeritus U.S. Army Health Services Command, 1980. Author: Modern Concepts of Leprosy, 1953, Raibyo Gentaiteki Gainen, 1956, (with P. Fasal) Leprosy, 1973, (with R.B. Odom and W.D. James) Andrews' Diseases of the Skin, 8th edit, 1989; also numerous articles, editorials, columns, and chpts. in textbooks.; editor Hawaii Med. Jour, 1941-83, founding editor, 1983—; editor Straub Clinic Procs., 1941-77, editor emeritus, 1978—; editor The Schoch Letter, 1975—, Internat. Jour. Dermatology, 1978—, Janssen Masters in Dermatology, 1987; corr. editor: Internat. Jour. of Leprosy, 1950-84; editorial bd. Cutis, 1965—, Group Practice, 1966-74, Jour. Internat. Med. Research, 1972—, Archives Dermatology, 1973-83, Jour. AMA, 1973-74. Named Practitioner of Yr. Dermatol. Found., 1983, Janssen Master in Dermatology, 1987. Fellow ACP, AAAS, Royal Soc. Medicine; mem. Hawaii Med. Assn. (past pres.), Honolulu County Med. Assn. (past pres.), Hawaiian Acad. Sci. (past pres.), Am. Acad. Dermatology (hon.; pres. 1975-76), Internat. Soc. Tropical Dermatology (past v.p.), Internat. Leprosy Assn., Hawaii Dermatol. Soc. (hon. 1986), Pacific Dermatol. Assn. (hon. mem., pres. 1968), AMA (past del., sect. chmn., del. sect. dermatology), Am. Dermatol. Assn. (bd. dirs. 1969-70, pres. 1971), Sociedad Argentina de Leprología (corr.), Sociedad Cubana de Dermatología y Sifilografía (corr.), Asociacion Argentina de Dermatología (corr.), Sociedad Venezolana de Dermatología, Venereología y Leprología (corr.), Sociedad Mexicana de Dermatología (hon.), Sociedad Brasileira de Dermatologia (hon.), S. African Dermatol. Assn. (hon.), N.Y. Dermatol. Assn. (hon.), Swedish Dermatol. Soc. (corr.), Honolulu chpt. Internat. Wine and Food Soc. (pres. 1977), Social Sci. Assn. Honolulu (pres. 1984, hon. mem.), Sigma Xi, Kappa Beta Phi, Alpha Omega Alpha, Nu Sigma Nu, Phi Kappa Psi, Zeta Psi. Home and Office: 250 Laurel St Apt 301 San Francisco CA 94118

ARNOLD, HILDA F., librarian; b. Ennis, Ky., July 26, 1935; d. R. Ovid and Nora (Mercer) A.; m. John C. Elkins, Apr. 23, 1960 (div. 1980); 1 child, Robert Edward; m. Gary L. Butterfield, Aug. 1, 1981. AB, Western Ky. U., 1956; MS in LS, U. Ky., 1959; EdD, North Tex. State U., 1967. Sch. librarian Ludlow (Ky.) Pub. Schs., 1956-58, Woodford County Schs., Versailles, Ky., 1958-59; librarian Carver Sch. Missions, Louisville, 1959-61, Youth Svcs. Ctr., St. Anthony, Idaho, 1985-86, Gt. Falls (Mont.) Pub. Library, 1986—; asst. librarian Mary Hardin-Baylor Coll., Belton, Tex., 1962-63; assoc. prof. Kutztown (Pa.) State Coll., 1967-69; prof. Edinboro U. Pa. 1969-80. Mem. editorial bd. reference Books Bull., 1983-. Mem. ALA, Mont. Library Assn. Office: Great Falls Pub Libr 2d Ave N at 3d St Great Falls MT 59401

ARNOLD, JAMES RICHARD, chemist, educator; b. New Brunswick, N.J., May 5, 1923; s. Abraham Samuel and Julia (Jacobs) A.; m. Louise Clark, Oct. 11, 1952; children: Robert C., Theodore J., Kenneth C. A.B., Princeton U., 1943, M.A., 1945, Ph.D., 1946. Postdoctoral fellow Inst. Nuclear Studies, U. Chgo., 1946-47, mem. faculty, 1948-55; NRC fellow Harvard U., 1947-48; mem. faculty chemistry Princeton U., 1955-58; assoc. prof. chemistry U. Calif., San Diego, 1958-60; prof. U. Calif., 1960—, Harold C. Urey prof., 1983—, chmn. dept. chemistry, 1960-63; asso. Manhattan Project, 1943-46; dir. Calif. Space Inst., 1980—; mem. various bds. NASA, 1959—; mem. space sci. bd. Nat. Acad. Sci., 1970-74, mem. com. on sci. and public policy, 1973-77. Mem. editorial bd.: Ann. Rev. Nuclear Chemistry, 1972; asso. editor: Revs. Geophysics and Space Physics, 1972-75, Moon, 1972—; contbr. articles to profl. jours. Pres. Torrey Pines Elem. Sch. PTA, 1964-65; pres. La Jolla Democratic Club, 1965-66; mem. nat. council World Federalists-U.S.A., 1970-72. Recipient E.O. Lawrence medal AEC, 1968; Leonard medal Meteoritical Soc., 1976; asteroid 2143 named Jimarnold in his honor, 1980; Guggenheim fellow India, 1972-73. Mem. Nat. Acad. Sci., Am. Acad. Arts and Scis., Internat. Acad. Astronautics, Am. Chem. Soc., AAAS, Fedn. Am. Scientists, World Federalist Assn. Office: U Calif San Diego Dept Chemistry Code B-017 La Jolla CA 92037

ARNOLD, JOHN EMERY, public administrator; b. Atchison, Kans., Jan. 4, 1940; s. George Harley and Iva Belle (Bailey) A.; m. Kaye Evelyn Monteiro, June 12, 1965; children: John E. Jr., Lynn Thompson. BA, U. Kans., 1962, MPA, 1967. Adminstrv. asst. City of Atchison, 1962; vol. U.S. Peace Corps, The Philippines, 1962-64; asst. city mgr. City of Titusville, Fla., 1967; dir. model city City of Texarkana, Tex., 1967-69; asst. city mgr. City of Little Rock, 1969-72; city mgr. City of Minot, N.D., 1972-77, City of Ft. Collins, Colo., 1977-85; exec. dir. E-470 Authority, Denver, 1985—. Author: You Can Fight City Hall, 1987; columnist Perspective, 1985-88; contbr. articles to profl. jours. Pres. adv. com. Pub. Tech. Inc., Washington, 1982; mem. adv. bd. Ctr. for Pub.-Pvt. Cooperation U. Colo., Denver, 1985-88; bd. dirs. Energy Extension, Ft. Collins, 1983-85, United Way, Ft. Collins, 1982-85. Recipient 4 Tech. Achievement awards Pub. Tech. Inc., 1984. Mem. Internat. City Mgmt. Assn. Found., Internat. Bridge, Tunnel & Turnpike Assn., Internat. City Mgmt. Assn. (Mgmt. Innovation award 1981, Ridley Tng. award 1981, Retirement Corp. Founders Com.), Colo. City Mgmt. Assn. (pres. 1984), Metro Denver C. of C. (com. mem. 1987-88), Rotary (bd. dirs. Minot club 1976-77), Elks. Methodist. Home: 10173 E Fair Circle Englewood CO 80111

ARNOLD, KELLY LYNNE, interior designer; b. San Diego, Sept. 7, 1965; d. James Edward Jr. and Penelope Elizabeth (Pearse) A. Student, Orange Coast Coll., 1983-85; BA, Calif. State U., Long Beach, 1988. Office clk./ data entry Curci-Turner Co., Newport Beach, Calif., 1984-86; office clk. Honeybaked, Lakewood, Calif., 1986-87; asst. interior design Shores Interiors, Newport Beach, 1987-88; interior designer Kennard, Herbage and Assocs., Santa Ana, Calif., 1988-89, Grau-Englander Design, Newport Beach, 1989—. Vol. Children's Eye Testing, Long Beach, 1987. Mem. Am. Soc. Interior Designers, Delta Gamma, Omicron Nu. Methodist. Home: 17371 Mira Loma Circle Huntington Beach CA 92647

ARNOLD, LANDIS STEVENS, small business owner, Olympic athlete; b. Boulder, Colo., Aug. 6, 1960; s. Andrew L. and Rebecca (Roe) A.; m. Ivana Valešova, June 27, 1987. BA in Geography, Dartmouth Coll., 1983. Mem. U.S. Ski Team, 1980-85, U.S. Winter Olympic Team, 1984; pres., founder Wildwasser Sport USA, Boulder, 1984—. Home: 2227 Canyon # 210 Boulder CO 80302 Office: Wildwasser Sport USA PO Box 4617 Boulder CO 80306

ARNOLD, LEONARD J., construction executive; b. San Diego, Mar. 17, 1947; s. William W. and Thelma C. (Cook) A.; m. Judy Lynn Keeton, Aug. 30, 1970; children: Alyssa Noelle, Lorienne Eve. BS in Constrn. Mgmt., Colo. State U., 1970. V.p. G. E. Johnson Constrn., Colorado Springs, Colo., 1970-76; pres. Wyoming Johnson Inc., Casper, 1976-79; v.p. Hensel Phelps Constrn. Co., Greeley, Colo., 1979—. Chmn. Weld County Econ. Devel., Greeley, 1986-88. Mem. Urban Land Inst., Associated Gen. Contractors Am., Soc. Am. Mil. Engrs., U.S. Space Found., Colo. Assn. Sch. Bds., Sigma Lambda Chi. Republican. Club: Greeley Country. Home: 1309 42d Ave Greeley CO 80634 Office: Hensel Phelps Constrn Co 420 6th Ave PO Box 0 Greeley CO 80632

ARNOLD, MARTHA ANNE, insurance company executive; b. Bridgeport, Conn., Aug. 22, 1950; d. John Herron and Martha Elizabeth (Frey) Arnold. AA in Fashion Mdse., U. Bridgeport, 1970. Dept. mgr. Allied Stores Corp., Bridgeport, 1970-78, May Corp., Ft. Collins, Colo., 1978-82; unit dir. Am. Cancer Soc., Ft. Collins, 1982-83; adminstrv. asst. Sigma Ent., Ft. Collins, 1984-85; office adminstr. The Prin. Fin. Group, Ft. Collins, 1985—. Bd. dirs. Hope Counseling Ctrs., Ft. Collins, 1985—; career adv. com. Poudre R1 Sch. Dist., Ft. Collins, 1983-86; facilitator Women's Group, Colo., 1985. Named Mgr. of the Yr., May Corp., 1980, Outstanding Young Women of Am., 1986. Mem. Nat. Assn. Ins. Women, Ft. Collins Camera Club (v.p., sec. 1983-86), Ins. Women Lermer County (treas.), H.P. Harmont Shutterbugs Camera Clug. Home: 3219 Wedgewood Ct Fort Collins CO 80525 Office: The Principal Fin Group 343 W Drake Rd Ste 250 Fort Collins CO 80526

ARNOLD, SHEILA, state legislator; b. N.Y.C., Jan. 15, 1929; d. Michael and Eileen (Lynch) Keddy; coll. courses; m. George Longan Arnold, Nov. 12, 1960; 1 son, Peter; 1 son by previous marriage, Michael C. Young; stepchildren: Drew, George Longan, Joe. Mem. Wyo. Ho. of Reps., 1978—, mem. com. on revenue, com. on rules and procedures; dir. First Interstate Bank of Laramie. Former mem., sec. Wyo. Land Use Adv. Coms.; past pres. Dem. Women's Club, Laramie; past vice-chmn. Albany County Dem. Cen. Com.; past mem. Dem. State Com.; mem. adv. bd. Wyo. Home Health Care; mem. State Com. on Long Term Health Care, Nat. Conf. State Legislatures Com. on Fiscal Affairs and Oversight Com. Recipient Spl. Recognition award from Developmentally Disabled Citizens of Wyo., 1985. Mem. Laramie Area C. of C. (pres. 1982; Top Hand award 1977), LWV, Internat. Platform Assn., Faculty Women's Club (past pres.), Zonta, Laramie Women's Club, Cowboy Joe Club. Office: Capitol Bldg Cheyenne WY 82002

ARNOLD, TERRENCE EUGENE, project engineer; b. Hiawatha, Kans., Dec. 27, 1955; s. Harold Eugene and Mary Elizabeth (Farrell) A.; m. Ruth Ann Ferguson, May 29, 1976; children: Ashleigh Marie, Andra Nicole, Chelsey Ann. BS, Kans. State U., 1977, MS, 1978. Staff engr. Woodward-Clyde Cons., Denver, 1978-84, project engr., 1984-87, sr. project engr., 1987—. Mem. ASCE (assoc., asst. to sec. 1982-83, asst. to pres. 1984-85, Outstanding Young Profl. for Achievement 1986), U.S. com. Large Dams, Assn. State Dam Safety Ofcls. (affiliate). Roman Catholic. Office: Woodward-Clyde Cons 4582 S Ulster St Pkwy Ste 1000 Stanford Pl 3 Denver CO 80237

ARNOTE, STANLEY DEAN, naval officer; b. Polo, Mo., Aug. 26, 1947; s. Francis Jr. and Betty Jean (Conyers) A.; m. June 13, 1980; children: Alexander Hamilton, Crystal Bermuda. BS in Math., U. Mo., 1969; MS in OST, Naval Postgrad. Sch., 1977. Commd. officer USN, 1969, advanced through grades to comdr., 1985; dept. head USS Brooke-PT Defiance USN, San Diego, 1977-81, tng. adminstr. Fleet Tng. Ctr., 1981-83, exec. officer USS Hoel, 1983-85; war planner Comdr.-in-chief Pacific Fleet USN, Pearl Harbor, Hawaii, 1985--. Contbr. articles to profl. jours. Fundraiser pub. TV sta., San Diego, 1981; fundraiser Navy Relief, 1981--; bd. dirs. Kailua (Hawaii)úPTA, 1986-88. U. Mo. Bd. Trustees scholar, 1965-69; Mo. PTA grantee, 1968-69. Mem. Naval Inst. Office: USN Comdr in Chief Pacific Fleet Pearl Harbor HI 96734

ARNST, ALBERT, editor, forester; b. Portland, Oreg., July 9, 1909; s. David and Alwina (Lorenz) A.; B.S. in Forestry, Oreg. State U., 1931; m. Della Coleen Irwin, May 1, 1939; children—Audrey Karen, Robert Craig, Rosemary. Forester, Forest Service, U.S. Dept. Agr., Portland, Oreg., 1931-35, Medford, Oreg., 1935-36, Lakeview, Oreg., 1937, public info. officer, Washington, 1962-75, with Soil Conservation Service, Dayton, Spokane and Sedro-Woolley, (all in Wash.), 1937-45, Corvallis and Portland, Oreg., 1941-43; sales rep Skagit Steel & Iron Works, Sedro-Woolley, 1945-46; public info. rep. Weyerhaeuser Co., Tacoma, 1946-52; editor Timberman mag., Portland, 1952-53; editor Miller Freeman Publs., Portland, 1954-62; mng. editor Western Conservation Jour., Portland, 1975-82. Fellow Soc. Am. Foresters; mem. Soil Conservation Soc. Am., Oreg. Logging Conf. (hon. life), Oreg. Soc. Am. Foresters (Lifetime Achievement award 1989), Internat. Assn. Bus. Communicators (Rodney Adair Merit award, pres. 1962, 71, 79, named Communicator of Yr. 1966 nat. Pres.'s award 1983). Democrat. Clubs: Foggy Bottom (pres. 1971) (Washington). Lodge: Lions. Contbr. articles on forestry to profl. jours. Address: 2430 NE Stanton Portland OR 97212

ARONI, SAMUEL, architecture and urban planning educator; b. Kishinew, Romania, May 26, 1927; came to U.S., 1963; s. David and Haia (Apoteker) Aharoni; m. Malca Corenfeld, Nov. 11, 1956; children: Ruth, Miriam. BS in Civil Engring., U. Melbourne, Victoria, Australia, 1954; MS, PhD, U. Calif., Berkeley, 1965. Lectr. in civl engring. U. Melbourne, Victoria, 1955-63; teaching fellow in structural engring. U. Calif., Berkeley, 1963-66; assoc.

prof. San Francisco State Coll., 1966-67; rsch. engr. Am. Cement Corp., Riverside, Calif., 1967-70; prof. architecture and urban planning Grad. Sch. Architecture and Urban Planning, UCLA, 1970—, acting dean, 1974-75, 83-85. Contbr. articles to profl. publs. Mem. adv. com. NSF, Washington, 1985—, mem. panel reviewers applied sci. and rsch., 1979—; v.p. Archtl. Rsch. Ctrs. Consortium, Washington, 1985-86; bd. dirs. Urban Innovations Group, Westwood, Calif., 1983-85; bd. of govs. Ben-Gurion U. of Negev, Beer-Sheva, Israel, 1983—. Recipient Inst. prize Australian Town Planning Inst., 1955, Hon. Founder award Ben-Gurion U., 1984. Mem. ASCE (sec. com. 1970-71, J. James R. Cross Gold medal 1981), Am. Concrete Inst. (chmn. subcom. 1967-70), RILEM (membership com.), Sigma Xi. Jewish. Office: GSAUP UCLA Los Angeles CA 90024

ARONOW, JERRY L., economics educator; b. Bklyn., Aug. 27, 1930; s. Maurice and Elsie (Small) A.; m. Cyma B. Goodman, Nov. 8, 1953; children: David S., Susan L. BA in Social Scis., Calif. State U., L.A., 1956, MA in Polit. Sci., 1962; DD, Universal Life Ch., Modesto, Calif., 1969. Cert. secondary and elem. tchr., Calif. Tchr. Burbank (Calif.) Sch. Dist., 1956-58; tchr. L.A. Unified Sch. Dist., San Fernando, Calif., 1958-62, Van Nuys, Calif., 1962-86, Hollywood, Calif., 1986—; econs. cons. U. Calif., Los Angeles, 1987-88. Author: The Other Umpires, 1979, poetry. Chmn. Young Dem. Club., L.A., 1959-60; instructional chmn. So. Calif. Umpire Assn., L.A., 1974-79; bd. dirs. Jewish Marriage Enhancement Movement, weekend speaker. With USN, 1950-51. Teaching fellow Calif. State U., 1965-66. Democrat. Jewish. Office: Hollywood High School 1521 N Highland Ave Los Angeles CA 90028

ARONSON, FREDERICK RUPP, physician; b. N.Y.C., Nov. 5, 1953; s. Morton Jerome Aronson and Margaret (Rupp); m. Jennifer Ann Goldfarb, . BA, Johns Hopkins U., Baltimore, 1975; MPH, Yale U., New Haven, 1980, MD, 1980. Resident R.I. Hosp., Providence, 1980-83; clinical fellow New Eng. Med. Ctr., Boston, 1983-84; research fellow New England Medical Ctr., Boston, 1984-86; asst. professor of medicine Tuffs U. Sch. Medicine, Boston, 1986-88; rsch. fellow The Med. Found., Inc., Boston, 1986-88; asst. clin. prof. U. Calif., San Francisco, 1988—; bd. dir. Biological Response Modifiers Program UCSF, San Francisco, 1988. Contbr. chapters to various books, articles to profl. jours. Scientist, Science-by-Mail, Boston, 1987-88; speaker, U. Calif, San Francisco. Recipient Nat. Rsch. Svc. award Nat. Cancer Inst. Mem. Am. Coll. Physicians, Am. Fedn. for Clin. Rsch., Am. Soc. Clin. Oncology. Democrat. Jewish. Office: U Calif Cancer Rsch Inst San Francisco CA 94143-0128

ARONSON, JONATHAN DAVID, international relations educator; b. St. Louis, Oct. 28, 1949; s. Adam and Judith (Spector) A.; m. Joan Abrahamson, May 28, 1984; 1 child, AdamBrody. BA, Harvard U., 1971; MA in Polit. Sci., Stanford U., 1973, MA in Applied Econs., 1975, PhD in Polit. Sci., 1977. Asst. prof. internat. relations U. So. Calif., Los Angeles, 1976-82; internat. economist rep. Office of U.S. Trade, Washington, 1982-83; assoc. prof. Sch. of Internat. Relations U. So. Calif., 1982-88, prof., 1988. Author: Money and Power, 1977; editor: Debt and the Less Developed Countries, 1979; author (with others): Trade Talks, 1986, When Countries Talk, 1988. Fellow Internat. Affairs Council on Fgn. Relations, 1982, Ctr. for Internat. Affairs, Harvard, 1976. Jewish. Office: U So Calif Sch Internat Rels Los Angeles CA 90089-0043

AROS, ARNOLD ROBERT, banker; b. Tucson, May 4, 1947; s. Arnold E. and Connie (Armenta) A.; m. Deborah Lynn Bidwell, June 12, 1972; children: Scott Andrew, Heather Lynn. BS, U. Ariz., 1970; postgrad., So. Meth. U., 1987. Loan svc. specialist Valley Nat. Bank, Tucson, 1970-71, installment lending officer, 1971-73, asst. br. mgr., 1973-76, br. mgr., 1976-81, v.p., mgr., 1981-89, regional v.p., 1989—. Chmn. bd. of mgrs. LOHSE Meml. YMCA, Tucson, 1988; vice chmn. Pima County Crime Victim Compensation Bd., Tucson, 1988; bd. dirs. United Way of Greater Tucson, 1988, Metro Tucson Conv. and Visitors Bur., Tucson, 1988. Named Vol. of Yr. The United Way of Greater Tucson, 1986. Mem. U. Ariz. Bus. Pub. Adminstrn. Alumni Coun., Tucson C. of C. (leadership participant 1986). Democrat. Lodge: Lion (pres. 1980). Office: Valley Nat Bank PO Box 311 Tucson AZ 85702

ARP, FRED ALLEN, football coach; b. Salt Lake City, Oct. 14, 1944; s. Fred George and Anna Mae (Hadsel) A.; m. Ellen Jane Wroblewski, Dec. 17, 1966; 1 child, Benjamin Fred. AB, U. Calif., Davis, 1967; MA, Sacramento State U., 1971. Cert. secondary tchr., Calif. Asst. football coach U. Calif., Davis, 1966-72, 73—, U. No. Colo., Greeley, 1972-73. Recipient Coll. Football Centennial award NCAA, 1969, commendation Calif. Aggie Alumni Assn., Davis, 1978, Meritorious Civic Svc. award Davis C. of C., 1982. Mem. Am. Football Coaches Assn., AAHPER and Dance, Calif. Coaches Assn. Democrat. Office: U Calif Football Office Davis CA 95616

ARRAJ, ALFRED ALBERT, U.S. district judge; b. Kansas City, Mo., Sept. 1, 1906; s. Elias and Mary (Dervis) A.; m. Madge L. Connors, Nov. 12, 1929; 1 dau., Sally Marie. J.D., U. Colo., 1928, LL.D., 1977. Bar: Colo. 1928. Gen. practice law Denver, Springfield, Colo., 1928-36; county atty. Baca County, Colo., 1936-42, 46-48; dep. dist. atty. Baca County, 1946-48; dist. judge 15th Jud. Dist. Colo., 1949-57; U.S. judge Dist. of Colo., 1957-59, chief judge, from 1959, now sr. judge. Bd. dirs. Fed. Jud. Center. Served from 1st lt. to maj. USAAF, 1942-46, CBI. Recipient Norlin Recognition award for distinguished achievement U. Colo., 1968, William Lee Knous award U. Colo. Sch. Law, 1970. Mem. Am. Judicature Soc., Am. Bar Assn., Colo. Bar Assn., S.E. Colo. Bar Assn. (pres. 1940), Fed. Bar Assn., Denver Bar Assn., Order of Coif (hon.), Jud. Conf. U.S., Phi Delta Phi. Episcopalian. Club: University. Home: 200 Ivy St Denver CO 80220 Office: US Dist Ct US Courthouse Rm C-540 1929 Stout St Denver CO 80294

ARREGUIN, ESTEBAN JOSE, aerospace company executive; b. Celaya, Mex., Aug. 31, 1958; came to U.S., 1964; s. Agustin Montoya and Juana (Cacique) A.; m. Catharine Ann Barnett, Dec. 19, 1981; children: Christopher, Rachael, Michael. BME, UCLA, 1981; MME, U. So. Calif., 1984; postgrad., U. So. Calif., Sacramento, 1984—. Mem. tech. staff Aerospace Corp., El Segundo, Calif., 1981-85; engr. Aerojet Techsystems Co., Sacramento, Calif., 1985-86, mem. mgmt. tng. program, 1986-88; program supr. Aerojet Techsystems Co., Sacramento, 1988—; community adv. bd. U. Calif. Med. Ctr. Mem. River City Rep. Assembly, Sacramento, 1987; field coord. Sacramento Adult Soccer Assn., 1987. Aerospace Corp. fellow, 1987. Mem. Soc. Hispanic Profl. Engrs. (chmn. com. 1988), Sacramento C. of C. (mem. leadership Sacramento program 1987), League of United Latin Am. Citizens Club. Republican. Baptist. Home: 3220 Doe Ct Cameron Park CA 95682 Office: Aerojet Techsystems PO Box 13222 Sacramento CA 95813

ARRIGHI, EDWARD VASCO, land developer; b. San Francisco, Dec. 8, 1951; s. Vasco Dominic and Catherine Margret (Filipelli) A.; m. Mary Ann Evans, Oct. 14, 1984; 1 child, Catherine Lynn. AA, City Coll. San Francisco, 1971. Owner, developer Clovis Lakes Recreational Pk., Fresno, Calif., 1978-83, Blue Lagoon Waterpark, Vacaville, Calif., 1981-83; owner, developer, chief exec. officer Creative Water Pks., Inc., Tucson, 1983—. Contbr. articles to profl. jours. Temporary foster parent House of Samuel, Tucson, 1988—. Mem. World Waterpark Assn. (v.p. 1981, pres. 1982-83, 84-85, treas. 1986-87, contbr. risk and loss com. Lenexa, Kans. chpt. 1984—). Republican. Evangelical. Home: PO 37094 Tucson AZ 85740 Office: The Breakers Waterpark 8555 W Tangerine Rd Tucson AZ 85741

ARRIGONI, LOUIS, cooperative food distributor; b. S. Cle Elum, Wash., Aug. 4, 1916; s. Joseph and Esther (Paganelli) A.; m. Evelyn I. Pierson, Apr. 26, 1944; children: Nancy, Evelyn, James. B.S., U. Wash., 1938, M.S., 1940, Ph.D., 1945. Asst. prof. chemistry U. Wash., Seattle, 1943-49; with Consol. Dairy Products Co. (now Darigold, Inc.), Seattle, 1949-67, v.p., 1962-67, dir., 1962—, pres., 1971—; pres. Assoc. Grocers Inc., Seattle, 1967-71, also dir., 1988—, chmn. exec. com.; dir. Dairy Export Co., Inc., Rainier Nat. Bank. Mem. Am. Pharm. Assn., Sigma Xi. Clubs: Wash. Athletic (Seattle), Rainier (Seattle). Lodge: Elks. Home: 4845 NE 85th St Seattle WA 98115 Office: Consol Dairy Products Co 635 Elliott Ave W Seattle WA 98119

ARRIOLA, DAVID BRUCE, resort, hotel marketing executive; b. Winnemucca, Nev., June 18, 1950; s. Mario M. and Barbara M. (Metcalf) A.; m. Elizabeth S. Peterson, Apr. 28, 1979; children: Brittany, Michael. BA, U. Nev., Reno, 1973; postgrad., Ariz. State U., 1983-84. Dir. pub. relations Mt. Rose Resort, Reno, Nev., 1971-73; dir. mktg. Heavenly Valley Ski Resort, Lake Tahoe, Calif., 1973-75; dir. mktg. Crested Butte (Colo.) Devel. Corp., 1975-77; gen. sales mgr. Best Western Internat., Inc., Phoenix, Ariz., 1977-84; v.p. mktg. Recreational Properties div. Del Webb Corp., 1984-89; v.p. mktg. ARA Leisure Svcs., Phoenix, 1989—. Mem. Fiesta Bowl Com., 1983—; bd. dirs. Scottsdale Arts Ctr. Assn., 1985-88. Mem. Phoenix Valley of the Sun Visitors and Conv. Bur. (chmn. mktg. com. 1981-85, planning com. 1983-84), Am. Bus. Assn. (travel adv. com. 1982-83), Nat. Tour Assn. (mktg. and communications com. 1985-86). Republican. Office: ARA Leisure Svcs PO Box 56909 Phoenix AZ 85079

ARROW, KENNETH JOSEPH, economist, educator; b. N.Y.C., Aug. 23, 1921; s. Harry I. and Lillian (Greenberg) A.; m. Selma Schweitzer, Aug. 31, 1947; children: David Michael, Andrew. B.S. in Social Sci., CCNY, 1940; M.A., Columbia U., 1941, Ph.D., 1951, D.Sc., 1973; LL.D. (hon.), U. Chgo., 1967, City U. N.Y., 1972, Hebrew U. Jerusalem, 1975, U. Pa., 1976; D.Social and Econ. Scis. (hon.), U. Vienna, Austria, 1971; D.Social Scis. (hon.), Yale, 1974; Doctor (hon.), Université René Descartes, Paris, 1974, U. Aix-Marseille III, 1985; Dr.Pol., U. Helsinki, 1976; M.A. (hon.), Harvard U., 1968; D.Litt., Cambridge U., 1985. Research assoc. Cowles Commn. for Research in Econs., 1947-49; asst. prof. econs. U. Chgo., 1948-49; acting asst. prof. econs. and stats. Stanford, 1949-50, assoc. prof., 1950-53, prof. econs., statistics and ops. research, 1953-68; prof. econs. Harvard, 1968-74, James Bryant Conant univ. prof., 1974-79; exec. head dept. econs. Stanford U., 1954-56, acting exec. head dept., 1962-63, Joan Kenney prof. econs. and prof. ops. research, 1979—; economist Council Econ. Advisers, U.S. Govt., 1962; cons. RAND Corp. Author: Social Choice and Individual Values, 1951, Essays in the Theory of Risk Bearing, 1971, The Limits of Organization, 1974, Collected Papers, Vols. I-VI, 1983-85; co-author: Mathematical Studies in Inventory and Production, 1958, Studies in Linear and Nonlinear Programming, 1958, Time Series Analysis of Inter-industry Demands, 1959, Public Investment, The Rate of Return and Optimal Fiscal Policy, 1971, General Competitive Analysis, 1971, Studies in Resource Allocation Processes, 1977, Social Choice and Multicriterion Decision Making, 1985. Served as capt. AUS, 1942-46. Social Sci. Research fellow, 1952; fellow Center for Advanced Study in the Behavioral Scis., 1956-57; fellow Churchill Coll., Cambridge, Eng., 1963-64, 70, 73, 86; Guggenheim fellow, 1972-73; Recipient John Bates Clark medal Am. Econ. Assn., 1957; Alfred Nobel Meml. prize in econ. scis., 1972, von Neumann prize, 1986. Fellow Am. Acad. Arts and Scis. (v.p. 1979-81), Econometric Soc. (v.p. 1955, pres. 1956), Am. Statis. Assn., Inst. Math. Stats., Am. Econ. Assn. (mem. exec. com. 1967-69, pres. 1973), AAAS (chmn. sect K 1983), Internat. Soc. for Inventory Research (pres. 1983—); mem. Internat. Econs. Assn. (pres. 1983-86), Nat. Acad. Scis., Am. Philos. Soc., Inst. Mgmt. Scis. (pres. 1963, chmn. council 1964), Finnish Acad. Scis. (fgn. hon.), Brit. Acad. (corr.), Western Econ. Assn. (pres. 1980-81). Office: Stanford U Dept Econs Stanford CA 94305

ARSHAM, GARY MARTIN, medical educator; b. Cleve., 1941; s. Sanford Ronald and Florence Gail A.; m. Diana Silver, 1971. AB cum laude, Harvard U., 1963; MD, Case-Western Res. U., 1967; PhD, U. Ill., 1971. Fellow in med. edn. U. Ill., Chgo., 1968-71; asst. then assoc. dean curriculum devel., asst. prof. medicine and health scis. communication SUNY, 1971-72; assoc. prof., prof. health professions edn. U. of Pacific, San Francisco, 1972-79; chmn. Council on Edn. Pacific Med. Ctr., San Francisco, 1976-81; v.p. Arsham Cons., Inc., San Francisco, 1981—; adminstr. Pacific Vision Found., 1977-84, dir. edn., 1983—; mem. nat. adv. bd. John Muir Hosp. Med. Film Festival, 1981—; mem. task force on interdisciplinary edn. Nat. Joint Practice Commn., 1973-74; bd. dirs. U.S.-China Edn1. Inst., 1980—, sec., 1986-88. Co-author: Diabetes: A Guide To Living Well, 1989; chief editor Family Medicine Reports, San Francisco, 1983. Fellow ACP; mem. Am. Ednl. Rsch. Assocs., Assn. Am. Med. Colls., Assn. Study Med. Edn., Assn. Hosp. Med. Edn. (exec. com. 1980-84, sec.-treas. 1982-84), Am. Diabetes Assn. (bd. dirs. San Francisco chpt. 1984—, No. Calif. affiliate 1986-87, Calif. affiliate 1987—), Am. Assn. Diabetes Educators (assoc. editor 1985—), Calif. Med. Assn., San Francisco Med. Soc., Harvard Club San Francisco (bd. dirs. 1981-88, pres. 1984-86), Lane Med. Soc. (Sommelier 1985—), Am. Assn. Individual Investors (bd. dirs. San Francisco chpt. 1984-88), Tech. Security Analysts Assn. San Francisco. Office: Arsham Cons Inc PO Box 15608 San Francisco CA 94115

ARTHUR, JENNIFER LYNN, computer engineer; b. Honolulu, Dec. 18, 1962; d. James Douglas Arthur and Jean Klein. BS in Engring., UCLA, 1986. Mem. tech. staff radar systems group Hughes Aircraft Co., L.A., 1986—. Republican.

ARTHUR, NAN KENE, small business owner; b. Inglewood, Calif., Aug. 18, 1954; d. Kenneth Dwayne Heath and Donna Darlene (Arrigi) Cahow; m. Joseph Michael Parlato, Apr. 3, 1970 (div. June 1983); m. Michael Ellis Arthur, Dec. 31, 1983; children: Sashie Marie, Tiffanie Kene. Mgr. Bert's Photo, Bullhead City, Ariz., 1982-83; floor mgr. De La Fuente Cadillac, El Cajon, Calif., 1983-85; owner, pres. U.S. Photographics, El Cajon, 1985—; cons. James Internat. Art, Alameda, Calif., 1987—. Editor: Oxman Publishing, Fountain Valley, Calif., 1986—, 1988 Sprint Car Calendar, 1987, 1989 Sprint Car Calendar, 1988, Collector Cards-World of Outlaws, 1987, (photographer) Collector Cards-World of Outlaws, 1988; contbg. editor Open Wheel Mag., Ipswich, Mass., 1980—, Stock Car Racing Mag., Ipswich, 1980—. Office: U S Photographics PO Box 2928 El Cajon CA 92021

ARTHUR, PAUL KEITH, electronic engineer; b. Kansas City, Mo., Jan. 14, 1931; s. Walter B. and Frieda J. (Burckhardt) A.; m. Joy N. Lim, Apr. 26, 1958; children: Gregory V., Lia F. Student Ohio No. U., 1947, Taylor U., Upland, Ind., 1948-49; BSEE, Purdue U., 1956; postgrad. N.Mex. State U., 1957-78; Registered profl. engr., N.Mex. With White Sands Missile Range, N.Mex., 1956—, electronic engr. field engring. group missile flight surveillance office, 1956-60, chief field engring. group, 1960-62, project engr. Pershing weapon system Army Missile Test and Evaluation Directorate, 1962-74, chief high altitude air def. projects br., 1974-82, chief air def. materiel test div., 1982—, mem. exec. devel. group, career program mgr. for engrs. and scientists, pres. missile range pioneer group. Chmn. global missions com. Meth. Ch. Served with USN, 1949-53, rear admiral, sr. engring. duty officer Res., 1954-87. Decorated Legion of Merit, Meritorious Svc. medal, Navy Achievement medal, Mil. Order St. Barbara, others. Mem. Am. Def. Preparedness Assn. (past pres.), AIAA (past vice chmn.), Assn. Old Crows (dir.), Naval Res. Assn., Res. Officers Assn. (pres. 1983-85), United Vets. Council (chmn. 1984-85), Am. Soc. Naval Engrs., Naval Inst., Navy League, Assn. U.S. Army, Purdue Alumni Assn. (past pres.), N.Mex. State U. Alumni Assn., Sierra Club, Mesilla Valley Track Club, Bujutsukan Acad. Martial Arts. Author numerous plans and reports on weapon systems test and evaluation and topics in naval engring. Home: 2050 San Acacio Las Cruces NM 88001 Office: STEWS-TE-M White Sands Missile Range NM 88002

ARTIGUE, RAY JOSEPH, public relations executive; b. Phoenix, Oct. 8, 1954; s. Ray Norman and Gloria Anne (Fusco) A.; m. Martha Reeves, Sept. 23, 1978; 1 child, Jessica Lynne. BS in Journalism, Ariz. State U., 1976. Sales rep. Becton-Dickinson Corp., Scottsdale, Ariz., 1976-78; dir. mktg. Rodel Products Corp., Scottsdale, 1978-80; pres. Comml. Relations Inc., Scottsdale, 1980-82; v.p. communications The Pointe Resorts, Phoenix, 1982-87; founder, pres. Artigue & Assocs. Inc., Phoenix, 1987—. Author: (poems) Love Knows No Limits, 1977. Dir. leadership tng. Sigma Alpha Epsilon, Chgo., 1981-86; congl. intern U.S. Congressman John T. Rhodes, Washington, 1975; participant Valley Leadership, Phoenix, 1988. Mem. Pub. Relations Soc. Am. (bd. dirs. Phoenix chpt. 1984, treas. 1986, v.p. communications 1987, pres. 1989). Republican. Presbyterian. Home: 6333 E Lafayette Blvd Scottsdale AZ 85251 Office: Artigue & Assocs 335 E Palm Ln Phoenix AZ 85004

ARTINGSTALL, THOMAS, electrical and mechanical engineer; b. Chgo., Oct. 28, 1920; s. William Thomas and Louise Mary (Hanson) A.; m. Laura Ann Swanson, June 23, 1946 (div. June 1955); m. Arloah Darlene Norelius, June 25, 1965. BME, Ill. Inst. Tech., 1944; postgrad., U. So. Calif., 1956. Registered profl. engr., Calif., Ill. Designer Solar Capacitator Co., Los Angeles, 1945-48; chief designer, developer Kollsman Instrument, Los Angeles, 1948-55; mem. radar/antenna/transmitter devel. staff Autonetics, Anaheim, Calif., 1956-70; tech. research staff Los Angeles Aircraft, 1970-71; chief engr. Space Div. So. Calif., Yorba Linda, 1980-86; engring. specialist Rockwell Internat., Downey, Calif., 1977-86; cons. engr. Pace-Arrow, Pomona, Calif., 1970-78; engring. developer and researcher Swanson Electronics, Arcadia, Calif., 1965-70. Patentee in field. Mem. Archtl. com. City of Yorba Linda, 1968; mem. com. Ad Hoc City Incorp., 1966; mem. bd. parks and recreation City of Yorba Linda, 1975. Mem. ASME, Nat. Mgmt. Assn., Profl. Engrs., Langlauflers Ski Club. Democrat. Roman Catholic. Home: 19622 Larkridge Dr Yorba Linda CA 92686

ARTIST, EVERETTE WARD, brokerage house executive; b. Greeley, Colo., Sept. 13, 1954; s. Elmer Jacob and Ava Justine (Sutton) A.; m. Lori Ann Slabozewski, Oct. 17, 1987. BA in Bus., U. No. Colo., 1977. Registered rep. I.D.S., Phoenix, 1978-80; account exec. Thomson McKinnon, Scottsdale, Ariz., 1980-82, E.F. Hutton, Tempe, Ariz., 1982-84; 2d v.p. Shearson Lehman Bros., Scottsdale, Ariz., 1984-87; v.p. The Miller Group, Phoenix, 1987—; cons. CenPac Securities, Phoenix, 1987—. Producer (TV Program) Wall St. Awareness Series FNN, 1987. Fund Raiser Ariz. Arthritis Found., Phoenix, 1988. Mem. Scottsdale Racquet Club, Elks. Republican. Home: 3645 E Lavender Ln Phoenix AZ 85044

ARUNDEL, IAN BRESSON, art dealer; b. Mitchell, S.D., Feb. 22, 1914; s. Charles Henry and Mary Porter (Bresson) A.; student U. Mich., 1934-37; m. Millie Lewis Waugh, Nov. 8, 1952; children—Ann Waugh, Colin Waugh. Restorer paintings and art objects, Detroit, 1937-43; dealer antique art, conservator, Los Angeles, 1945-52; art dealer, appraiser, Los Angeles, 1952—; expert primitive tribal art, appraiser U.S. govt.; exhibited tribal art in group shows at Santa Barbara (Calif.) Mus. Art, Los Angeles County Mus. Art, Miami U., Pomona Coll., U. Calif. at Fullerton, Otis Art Inst. Served with AUS, 1943-45. Fellow Am. Inst. for Conservation Historic and Artistic Works; mem. Smithsonian Instn., Brit. Mus. Soc., Archives Am. Art, Mus. Alliance Los Angeles County Mus., Victorian Soc. Office: 7152 SE 13th Ave Portland OR 97202

ARVAY, NANCY JOAN, insurance company executive; b. Pitts., Aug. 27, 1952; d. William John and Cornelia (Prince) A. BA in History, Duke U., 1974; postgrad., Columbia U., 1974-75. Polit. and internat. communications specialist U.S. Senate Fgn. Relations Com., Washington, 1975-77; broadcast media relations rep. Am. Petroleum Inst., Washington, 1977-79; broadcast media relations rep. Chevron U.S.A., San Francisco, 1979-82, coordinator electronic news media relations, 1982-85; sr. media relations rep. Chevron Corp., San Francisco, 1985-87; dir. pub. relations Fireman's Fund Corp., Novato, Calif., 1987—; lectr. Dept. Interior-Park Service, Beckley, W.Va., 1983; chmn. pub. relations Internat. Oil Spill Conf., Washington, 1984-85. Author, coordinator: Research Studies in Business and the Media, 1980-83; contbg. author This Is Public Relations, 1985. Founding mem. San Francisco chpt. Overseas Edn. Group; mem. pub. relations com. World Affairs Council San Francisco. Mem. Pub. Relations Soc., Radio/TV News Dirs. Assn. (assoc.), San Francisco Women in Bus. Office: Firemen's Fund Corp 777 Marin Dr Novato CA 94998

ARVESCHOUG, STEVEN NEIL, communications executive, state representative; b. Maui, Hawaii, Dec. 19, 1958; s. Neil Gary and Vera Mae (Helm) A.; m. Christine Janice Gutcheck, June 5, 1982. BS, Mont. Coll. Mineral Sci. and Tech., 1982. Sales rep. Sunbrook Broadcasting/KQUY, Butte, Mont., 1982-83; sales mgr. Sunbrook Broadcasting/KCEZ, Butte, Mont., 1984-85, Sunbrook Broadcasting/KCSJ, Pueblo, Colo., 1984-86; gen. sales mgr. Sunbrook Broadcasting/KCSJ/KUSN, Pueblo, Colo., 1986-87, gen. mgr., 1987-88; licenced agt. N.Y. Life Ins. Co., Butte, Mont., 1983-84; pres., gen. mgr. Martec Broadcasting, Pueblo, 1988—; lectr. and speaker in field. Senate intern U.S. Senator Max Baucus, Butte, 1981; treas. Bob Boyd for County Treas., Pueblo, 1986; del. State Rep. Conv., Colo., 1986, 88; State Rep. Dist. 44, Pueblo, 1988—. Mem. Colo. Broadcasters Assn., Pueblo C. of C. (bd. dirs. 1987, Leadership Pueblo award 1987), Kiwanis Club (bd. dirs. 1985-88), Pachyderms (bd. dirs. 1986-88). Baptist. Home: 4 Gunesmith Ct Pueblo CO 81008 Office: Martec Broadcasting Co 2600 Hwy 50 W Pueblo CO 81008

ARVIDSON, RANDALL ANTHONY, real estate company executive; b. Eugene, Oreg., June 15, 1960; s. Donald Carl Arvidson and Marlene Louise (Perkins) Torrey. Student, Occidental Coll., 1978, U. Oreg., 1979; BS with honors, Stanford U., 1983. Lic. real estate broker, Oreg. Real estate sales assoc. Devel. Group, Portland, Oreg., 1980; gen. ptnr. Powell Plaza Joint Venture, Portland, Oreg., 1980—; pres. Madara Ltd., Inc., Portland, 1985—. Mem. Phi Beta Kappa. Republican. Presbyterian. Office: 7400 SW Barnes Rd #532 Portland OR 97225

ARVONEN, FAITH LYNN, nurse; b. Chico, Calif., Nov. 24, 1956; d. George Cortez and Adele Bernice (Coon) Hackett; m. Charles Michael Arvonen, Aug. 10, 1974 (div.); children: James Silva, Michael Lee, Marcie Lynn. AS with honors, Butte Community Coll., Oroville, Calif., 1984; BS, Calif. State U., Chico, 1986. RN, Calif. Health researcher Calif. State Health Dept., Oroville, 1986; nurse Oroville Hosp., 1986—. Mem. Relief Soc., Chico, 1974-83. Mem. Calif. Nurses' Assn, Sigma Theta Tau. Democrat. Mormon. Home: 600-A Espey Way Fort Bragg CA 95437 Office: Mendocino Coast Dist Hosp 700 River Dr Fort Bragg CA 95437

ARZUBE, JUAN ALFREDO, bishop; b. Guayaquil, Ecuador, June 1, 1918; came to U.S., 1944, naturalized, 1961; s. Juan Bautista and Maria (Jaramillo) A. B.S. in Civil Engring, Rensselaer Poly. Inst., 1942; B.A., St. John's Sem., 1954. Ordained priest Roman Catholic Ch., 1954; asso. pastor St. Agnes Ch., Los Angeles, Resurrection Ch., Los Angeles, Ascension Ch., Los Angeles, Our Lady of Guadalupe Ch., El Monte, Calif.; aux. bishop of Los Angeles, 1971—, episcopal vicar for Spanish speaking, 1973—; mem. nat. bishops coms. Ad Hoc Com. for Spanish Speaking; chmn. Com. for Latin Am. Recipient Humanitarian award Mexican Am. Opportunity Found., 1978, John Anson Ford award Los Angeles County Commn. Human Relations, 1979. Address: 3149 Sunset Hill Dr West Covina CA 91791 *

ASBURY, CHRIS MERLIN, surveyor, consultant; b. Salt Lake City, Dec. 31, 1952; s. Norman Paul and Karolyn Joy (Jensen); m. Marsha Ellin Brekke, May 28, 1977; children: Rachel Erika, Sara Elizabeth. AS, Casper Coll., 1975. lic. land surveyor, Wyo. Surveyor Am. Nuclear Corp., Casper, Wyo., 1976-82; v.p., ptnr. Forysyth-Asbury Surveying, Inc., Casper, 1978-83; county surveyor Natrona County Surveyors Office, Casper, 1983—; cons. Horton Engring., Casper, 1985—, Am. Nuclear Corp., 1985-86. Bd. dirs. Community Action, Referral and Emergency Svc., 1972; pres. Especially for Children Manor Heights Sch., Casper, 1989—. Mem. Am. Congress of Surveying and Mapping, Nat. Soc. Profl. Surveyors. Republican. Methodist. Home: 3830 E 20th St Casper WY 82609 Office: Natrona County Surveyors Office Drawer 848 Mills WY 82644

ASCHENBRENNER, FRANK ALOYSIOUS, former diversified manufacturing company executive; b. Ellis, Kans., June 26, 1924; s. Philip A. and Rose E. Aschenbrenner; B.S. with high honors, Kans. State U., 1950; Ph.D. in Physics, M.I.T., 1954; m. Gertrude Wilhelmina DeBie, Nov. 15, 1946; children—Richard David, Robert Wayne, Mary Lynne. Mgr. physics and math. Gen. Electric, Cin., 1958-61; asst. dir. space div. Rockwell Internat., Downey, Calif., 1961-69, corp. dir. tech., Pitts., 1969-71, v.p., gen. mgr. div. yarn machinery, Charlotte, N.C., 1971-75; pres. COR, Inc., Charlotte, 1975-77; v.p. research and devel. and engring. Ball Corp., Muncie, Ind., 1977-86; bus. cons., Poway, Calif., 1986—; chmn. bd. Ball Packaging Products, Inc., RAMZ Corp., Dunkirk, Ind., 1985—; nat. bd. advisors Rose-Hulman Inst., Terre Haute, Ind., 1984—, U. Tenn. Space Inst., Tullahoma, 1982—. Served with USN, 1943-47. Mem. AIAA, Am. Phys. Soc., Naval Res. Assn. Club: Delaware Country. Home and Office: 14258 Palisades Dr Poway CA 92064

ASCHER, EVERETT S., music company executive; b. N.Y.C., Apr. 3, 1936; s. Morton and Ruth (Klein) A.; m. Ann Fine, June 25, 1958; 1 child, Allison. BA, U. Rochester, 1957. Pres., Regent Recorded Music, Emil Ascher, Inc., L.A., 1959-87; chief oper. officer Cancashier of Calif., L.A., 1988—; vice-chmn. Westwood Bancorp., L.A., 1982-84. Trustee U. Rochester, 1983; founder L.A. Music Ctr.; mem. Citizens Adv. Commn. for 1984 Olympics, Blue Ribbon CItizens Adv. Com., Increase Police Protection in City L.A.; bd. dirs. Holmby-Westwood Property Owners Assn., pres. 1976-77. Lt. (j.g.) USN, 1957-59. Mem. ASCAP, L.A West Regional C. of C. (v.p., chmn. bd. dirs. 1986-87), Leadership L.A. (chmn. adv. com., 1987-89. Mem. Regency Club. Republican.

ASH, CHRISTOPHER PATRICK, real estate developer, architect; b. Galveston, Tex., Nov. 12, 1951; s. Paul George and Ruth (Brown) A.; m. Karen Jeanne Wilder, Apr. 28, 1979; children: Emily Roben, Christopher Patrick, Meagan Brittany. BArch, U. Houston, 1977. Registered architect, Calif., Tex. Project mgr. Farr Constrn., Houston, 1977-79; v.p. ops. Farr Constrn., Dallas, 1985-86; project mgr. Southwestern Bell Architects Office, Houston, 1979, McLean and Schulte, Fullerton, Calif., 1986-87; dir. constrn. services Southmark Comml. Mgmt. Inc., Long Beach, Calif., 1987—; ind. archictect, planner, South Coast Metro, Calif., 1987—; prin. Architectural Service Co., Dallas, 1986-87. Author: The Tenant Improvement Specialist, 1989. Bd. dirs. Pride Devel. Council, Santa Ana, 1987-88. Served to lt. commdr. USN, 1980-85. Named Eagle Scout Boy Scouts Am., 1967. Mem. AIA, Internat. Conf. Bldg. Officials, Soc. Am. Mil. Engrs. Republican. Mormon. Office: Southmark Comml Mgmt Inc 401 E Ocean Blvd Ste 200 Long Beach CA 90802

ASHBROOK, TAMMY JANE, travel agency executive; b. Ft. Dodge, Iowa, Dec. 8, 1959; d. Dean Philip and Ila Jean (Holtapp) A. Diploma in travel mgmt., Spencer (Iowa) Sch. Bus., 1979. Cert. travel cons. Travel cons. Dayton's Travel Service, Rochester, Minn., 1980-82; travel cons. AAA Travel Agy., Des Moines, 1982-83, Ft. Dodge, Iowa, 1983-85; corp. travel specialist AIT Travel, Phoenix, 1985-86, travel mgr., 1986-88; night instr. AIT Travel Sch. Instr. City of Mesa (Ariz.) Slimnastics, 1988; team leader City of Scottsdale (Ariz.) Volleyball, 1985-87. Mem. Chandler (Ariz.) C. of C. Lutheran. Home: 8055 E Thomas M104 Scottsdale AZ 85257 Office: AIT Travel Inc 1984 N Alma School Rd Chandler AZ 85224

ASHBY, LAURA LEE, maintenance company executive; b. Santa Monica, Calif., Jan. 13, 1954; d. Gordon Bruce Ashby and Norma Mary (Withers) Devincenzi. Student, Los Angeles Valley Coll., Van Nuys, Calif., 1971-72; cert. bus. mgmt., UCLA, 1989; pediatric radiologic technologist cert., Children's Hosp., L.A., 1975. X-ray technician Univ. Hosp., San Diego, 1975-76; radiol. tech. X-Ray Assocs., San Diego, 1976-77, Kaiser Lahaina Clinic, Maui, Hawaii, 1977-79; ptnr., gen. mgr. Ashby's White Glove, L.A., 1980—. Sec.-treas. Catharsis, Sherman Oaks, Calif., 1986—; adminstrv. asst. non-profit program Children of the Night, 1981-83. Mem. Am. Soc. Radiologic Technology, Marina Del Rey C. of C. (chair 1984), Hawaiian Soc. Radiologic Technologists, Am. Registry Radiologic Technologists, Calif. Soc. Radiologic Technologists, Nat. Assn. of Women in Constrn., Cai Club. Republican.

ASHBY, LUCIUS ANTONE, certified public accountant; b. Des Moines, Feb. 1, 1944; s. Ruth Moore A.; m. Penny Ware (div.); children: Felecia, Wind; m. Victoria Lacy, Nov. 1, 1984; 1 child, Armand. BS, U. Colo., 1969; grad. owner/pres. mgmt. program, Harvard U., 1985. Sr. acct. Arthur Andersen & Co., Denver, 1969-72; managing ptnr. Ashby, Armstrong & Co., Denver, 1973—. Bd. dirs. Salvation Army, Denver, 1988—, Red Shield Community Ctr., Denver, 1988—; mem. Minority Bus. Adv. Council, Denver, 1988—. With U.S. Army, 1961-64. Recipient Barney Ford Award for Bus. Achievement Eastside Action Movement, Denver, 1975, Entrepreneur award United Negro Coll. Fund, Denver, 1980. Mem. Colo. Soc. CPA's, Colo. State Bd. of Accountancy (pres. 1984), Nat. Assn. Black Accts. (Achievement award 1979). Democrat. Baptist. Office: Ashby Jackson 1900 Grant St Ste 1050 Denver CO 80203

ASHDJIAN, VILMA, cytotechnologist; b. Bucharest, Romania, Jan. 14, 1954; came to U.S., 1963; d. Kegham and Zaruhi (Seferian) A. BA, UCLA, 1976; Cert. in Cytotechnology, Good Samaritan Hosp., 1977. Cytotechnologist Pasadena Clin. Lab., 1978-79; researcher City Of Hope Nat. Med. Ctr., Duarte, Calif., 1980-84; instr. Loma Linda (Calif.) U. Sch. Allied Health Profls., 1984-86; supr. CLMG, Inc., Los Angeles, 1986—. Contbr. articles to profl. jours. Calif. State scholar, 1972-76. Mem. Calif. Assn. Cytotechnologists, Am. Soc. Clin. Pathologists.

ASHDOWN, FRANKLIN DONALD, physician; b. Logan, Utah, May 2, 1942; s. Donald and Theresa Marie (Hill) A. BA, Tex. Tech. U., 1963; postgrad., U. Tex., 1967. Chief of med. Holloman Air Force Base, New Mexico, 1971-73; chief of staff Gerald Champion Mem. Hosp., Alamogordo, N.M., 1976; pres. Otero County Concerts Assn., Alamogordo, 1985-89, Otero County Med. Soc., Alamogordo, 1986; cons. New Mexico Sch. for Visually Handicapped, Alamogordo, 1973-76. Bd. dir. Otero County Mental Health Assn., Alamogordo, 1973-77,. Mem. Gerald Champion Mem. Hosp., N.M. Med. Soc., Am. Soc. Internal Med., ASCAP. Republican. Home: 1435 Rockwood Cir Alamogordo NM 88310 Office: 1301 Cuba Ave Alamogordo NM 88310

ASHER, ALVIN BERNARD, financial planner; b. N.Y.C., Mar. 19, 1920; s. Isadore and Florence (Glaser) A.; m. Bernice Lipkin, May 23, 1942 (div. 1958); 1 child, Joanne S. Asher Oberlander; m. Maxine Broslow, Oct. 9, 1963 (div. 1976); m. Genevieve Hurwitz, Aug. 11, 1979. BA, Bklyn. Coll., 1940; postgrad. bus. adminstrn., N.Y. U., 1946-48. Estimator, salesman Union Port Glass Co., N.Y.C., 1949-51, Thompson Glass & Paint Co., L.A., 1952-60; dist. sales mgr. Investors Diversified Svcs., L.A., 1960-68; v.p., co-owner Gardner, Asher & Co., Inc., Encino, Calif., 1968-70; v.p., br. mgr. Universal Heritage Investments Corp., Encino, 1970-75; v.p. sales Am. Pacific Securities Corp., Santa Monica, Calif., 1975—; treas., bd. dirs. Dirs. Capital Corp., L.A., 1970-75. Mem. Town Hall, L.A., 1979—. Capt. USAF, 1942-45, CBI, 1951-52, Korea. Decorated air medal with oak leaf cluster, DFC. Mem. Inst. Cert. Fin. Planners (cert., treas. L.A. Soc. 1985, bd. dirs.), Internat. Assn. Fin. Planning (pres. L.A. chpt. 1974), Sales and Mktg. Execs. Assn. of L.A. (bd. dirs. 1982-83, pres.'s award 1979). Jewish. Home: 14210 Mulholland Dr Los Angeles CA 90077 Office: Am Pacific Securities Corp Div Fin Network Investment Corp 2850 Ocean Park Blvd #292 Santa Monica CA 90405

ASHER, EUGENE LEON, historian, educator; b. Cleve., Nov. 23, 1929; s. Samuel H. and Dorothy Denise (LePon) A.; A.B., UCLA, 1952, M.A., 1955, Ph.D., 1958; postgrad. (Fulbright fellow) U. Paris, 1956-57, U. Toulouse, 1957; m. Bonnie Jane Anderson, June 9, 1956; children—Allyson Elizabeth, Christine Marie. Asst. prof. history U. Wichita (Kans.), 1957-59; mem. faculty history Calif. State U.-Long Beach, 1959-67, 71—, prof., chmn. dept. history, 1971-76, exec. asst. to pres., 1976-80, exec. officer, 1980—, dir. univ. relations, 1984—; exec. dir. KLON-FM public radio, 1981—; dir. Am. Hist. Assn. History Edn. Project, 1968-75; prof. history Ind. U., Bloomington, 1969-71. Pres., Casa Dorado Mng. Agt. Inc., Palm Springs, Calif., 1975. Vice chmn. Long Beach Am. Revolution Bicentennial Commn., 1973-76; co-chmn. history adv. panel, mem. Calif. State Social Scis. Commn., 1965-68; chmn. Joint Anglo-U.S. Commn. Confs. History, Dept. State, 1972-75; trustee Los Angeles Theater Ctr., 1983—, v.p. bd. trustees, 1985-86, pres. 1986-87, chmn. bd. 1987—. Trustee Sloan Found. Notre Dame U. Program; Am. Council Learned Socs. fellow, 1962-63, 66-67; Social Sci. Research Council grantee, 1962, 66-67; HEW grantee, 1969-75. Mem. Soc. History Edn. (chmn bd. 1972-78), Am. Hist. Assn., Nat. Council Social Studies, Orgn. Am. Historians, Societe d'Histoire Moderne et Contemporaine, Phi Beta Kappa Alumni Assn. (council Calif. 1979—, v.p. 1982-84, pres. 1984-86). Author: The Resistance to the Maritime Classes: the Survival of Feudalism in the France of Colbert, 1960: (with others) A Framework for the Social Sciences: Report of the Statewide Social Science Study Commission, 1968. Contbr. articles to profl. publs.; producer film: Oil: The Pioneering Years, 1978. Home: 38 58th Pl Long Beach CA 90803 Office: Calif State U Office of Pres 1250 Bellflower Blvd Long Beach CA 90840

ASHER, HOWARD RALPH, medical products executive; b. Long Beach, Calif., Sept. 29, 1947; s. Ralph Eugene Asher and Joyce Colleen (Johnson) Fry; m. Carol P. Yokota, Mar. 28, 1965; children: Stacey L., Randy M. BA in Bus. Adminstrn., UCLA, 1969. Sales rep. Howmedica, Inc., Rutherford, N.J., 1970-72; eastern area sales mgr. Am. Hosp. Supply, V. Mueller Innomed Orthopedics, Chgo., 1972-75; mktg. mgr. Cutter Biomed., San Diego, 1975-78; dir. sales and mktg. Hexcel Med., Dublin, Calif., 1978-79; pres. Advanced Biosearch Assocs., Danville, Calif., 1979—. Contbr. articles to profl. jours. Mem. Regulatory Affairs Profls. Soc. (internat. sect.), Med. Mktg. Assn., Food and Drug Law Inst., Assn. for Advancement Med. Instrumentation, Assn. for Advancement of Sci., Soc. for Biomaterials. Republican. Home: 30 Hidden Oak Ct Danville CA 94526 Office: Advanced Biosearch Assocs 3880 Blackhawk Rd Danville CA 94526-4617

ASHER, JAMES EDWARD, forestry consultant, engineer, arborist; b. L.A., July 22, 1931; s. John Edward and Dorothy (Ingraham) A.; student Pasadena City Coll., 1949-50; BS, Oreg. State U., 1954; m. Marilyn Lee Struebing, Dec. 28, 1953; children: Lynne Marie, Laure Ann. With U.S. Forest Svc., San Bernardino (Calif.) Nat. Forest, summers 1950-53, forester, 1956-57; prin. James E. Asher, ACF, Cons. Forester, 1957—; capt., bn. chief, asst. chief, fire prevention officer Crest Forest Fire Protection Dist., Crestline, Calif., 1960-69, chief, 1969-71; forester Big Bear div. Golden State Bldg. Products, Redlands, 1972, timber mgr., 1972-74; mem. profl. foresters exam. com. Calif. Bd. Forestry, 1978—, vice chmn., 1982—; mem. Calif. Integrated Hardwood, Calif. Forest Pest Control Action Council; chmn. Profl. Foresters Ad Hoc Task Force, 1983—. Vol. firewarden State of Calif., 1967—; mem. adv. com. Range Mgmt. Program, 1986—; chmn. Tree Conservation Subcom., Fire Dist. Suprs. Ad Hoc Com. on Soil Erosion and Sediment Control, County of San Bernardino, 1984—. With AUS, 1954-56. Recipient Certificate of Merit Nat. Fire Protection Assn., San Bernadino Mountains Assn.; Resolution of Commendation, County Bd. Suprs.; Forester of Year award So. Calif. sect. Soc. Am. Foresters, 1977; others. Registered profl. forester, registered profl. engr., Calif.; lic. pest control advisor, pest control operator, Calif. Mem. So. Calif. Assn. Foresters and Fire Wardens, Soc. Am. Foresters (cert., chmn. licensing and ethics com. So. Calif. sect., chmn. So. Calif. 1983), Assn. Cons. Foresters, Internat. Soc. Arboriculture, Sierra-Cascade Logging Conf., Calif. Urban Forests Coun., Am. Forestry Assn., Masons, Tau Kappa Epsilon. Presbyterian. Author: (with others) A Technical Guide for Community and Urban Forestry in Washington, Oregon and California. Contbr. articles to profl. Office: PO Box 2326 Lake Arrowhead CA 92352

ASHER, JEFFERSON WILLIAM, JR., venture capitalist; b. Los Angeles, Sept. 6, 1924; s. Jefferson William and Emily Gertrude (Pinter) A.; m. Mary Frances Neville, Sept. 1, 1944; children—Susan Emily, Catherine Louise, Jefferson William. A.B. in Polit. Sci., UCLA, 1946; M.B.A. with distinction, Harvard U., 1948. Sales mgr. Sweet Sue Candy Co., Los Angeles, 1948-49; staff analyst Am. Research & Devel. Corp., Boston, 1949-51; gen. mgr., treas. Colter Corp., Palacios, Tex., 1951-52; mgmt. cons. Robert Heller & Assocs., Cleve., 1952-57; div. mgr. fittings div. Parker Aircraft Co., Los Angeles, 1957-58; controller, bus. mgr. Kirk Douglas & Related Entities, Beverly Hills, Calif., 1959-61; v.p. West Coast ops. Boston Capital Corp., Los Angeles, 1961-69; venture capitalist, mgmt. cons., Los Angeles, 1969—; dir., chmn. audit com. Baldor Electric Co., Ft. Smith, Ark., 1973—; dir. Fluid Components, Inc., San Marcos, Calif., Trans Tech. Corp., Sherman Oaks, Calif. Mem. task force for adminstrv. reorgn. of U.S. Dept. State, Washington, 1953-54. Served to lt. USNR, 1942-46; PTO. Decorated Purple Heart. Mem. Am. Arbitration Assn. (arbitrator 1979—), Phi Beta Kappa. Republican. Episcopalian.

ASHFORD-HIRANO, MARGUERITE K., librarian; b. Honolulu, Feb. 4, 1953; d. Clinton R. and Joan Beverly (Stutte) Ashford; m. Ronald K. Hirano, Aug. 2, 1986; 1 child, Clinton Kanoelani Tatsumi Hirano. BA with honors, Stanford U., 1974; P.G.D., U. Otego, Dunedin, New Zealand, 1975; MLS, U. Hawaii, 1976. Reference libr. Bernice P. Bishop Mus., Honolulu, 1976-87; assoc. libr. Bernice P. Bishop Mus., 1983-87, head libr., 1987—; cons. various Hawaiiana projects, Honolulu, 1984—. Contbr. articles to profl. jours. Exec. bd., pres.-elect, chair various coms. Punahou Alumni Assn., Honolulu, 1985—; com. mem. Hawaii State Bd. on Geog. Names, Honolulu, 1988—; dancer Halau Hula o Maiki, Honolulu, 1977-84, Na Wahine No me Ka Haàhaàa mai Maiki, Kailua, Hawaii, 1984—. Recipient Rotary Found. Award for Internat. Fellowship, Rotary Internat., Dunedin, New Zealand, 1974-75. Mem. Hawaii Libr. Assn. (exec. bd. 1981-82, 85-86, chair various sects.), ALA, Am. Assn. Museums, Soc. Am. Archivists, Hawaiian hist. Soc., Beta Phi Mu. Home: 44 509 Kaneohe Bay Dr Kaneohe HI 96744 Office: Bernice P Bishop Museum PO Box 19000 A Honolulu HI 96877

ASHLEY, HOLT, aerospace scientist, educator; b. San Francisco, Jan. 10, 1923; s. Harold Harrison and Anne (Oates) A.; m. Frances M. Day, Feb. 1, 1947. Student, Calif. Inst. Tech., 1940-43; BS, U. Chgo., 1944; MS, MIT, 1948, ScD, 1951. Mem. faculty MIT, 1946-67, prof. aero., 1960-67; prof. aeros. and astronautics Stanford U., Palo Alto, Calif., 1967—; spl. rsch. aeroelasticity, aerodynamics; cons. govt. agys., rsch. orgns., indsl. corps.; dir. office of exploratory rsch. and problem assessment and div. advanced tech. applications NSF, 1972-74; mem. sci. adv. bd. USAF, 1958-80; rsch. adv. com. structural dynamics NASA, 1952-60, rsch. adv. com. on aircraft structures, 1962-70, chmn. rsch. adv. com. on materials and structures, 1974-77; mem. Kanpur Indo-American program Indian Inst. Tech., 1964-65; AIAA Wright Bros. lectr., 1981; bd. dirs. Hexcel Corp. Co-author: Aeroelasticity, 1955, Principles of Aeroelasticity, 1962, Aerodynamics of Wings and Bodies, 1969, Engineering Analysis of Flight Vehicles, 1974. Recipient Goodwin medal M.I.T., 1952; Exceptional Civilian Service award U.S. Air Force, 1972, 80; Public Service award NASA, 1981; named one of 10 outstanding young men of year Boston Jr. C. of C., 1956; recipient Ludwig-Prandtl Ring, West German DGLR, 1987. Fellow Am. Acad. Arts and Scis., AIAA (hon., assoc. editor jour., v.p. tech. 1971, pres. 1973, Structures, Structural Dynamics and Materials award 1969), Royal Aeronautical Soc. (hon.); mem. Am. Meterol. Soc. (profl., recipient 50th Anniversary medal 1971), AAAS, Nat. Acad. Engring. (aeros. and space engring. bd. 1977-79, mem. coun. 1985—), Nat. Rsch. Coun. (governing bd. 1987—),, Phi Beta Kappa, Sigma Xi, Tau Beta Pi. Home: 475 Woodside Dr Woodside CA 94062

ASHLEY, LEN ROBERT, systems engineer; b. Detroit, Nov. 1, 1952; s. Ralph Leonard and Bernice Ilene (Gray) A.; m. Sandra Joan Souza, Feb. 29, . Grad., high sch., Livonia, Mich., 1971. Enlisted as airman USN, 1971; aviation electrician USN, Jacksonville, Fla., 1971-81, Norfolk, Va., 1971-81, Lemoore, Calif., 1971-81; resigned USN, 1981; field engr. Lundy Electronics and Systems, Detroit, Palo Alto, Calif., 1981-82; asst. engr., sr. research and devel. engr. Ford Aerospace Corp., Palo Alto, 1982--; Pvt. practice as cons., Morgan Hill, Calif., 1986--. Named Father of Yr. Livonia Jaycees, 1981. Mem. Nat. Computer Graphics Assn., Nor-Cal BMX Club (Gilroy, Calif.). Democrat. Baptist. Office: Ford Aerospace Corp 3939 Fabian Way MS-N01 Palo Alto CA 94303

ASHLEY, PAULA CLAIRE, engineer; b. Pasadena, Calif., Oct. 23, 1939; d. Pierre Marcel and Mabel Claire (Brown) Honnell; m. Paul Edward Ashley, Dec. 27, 1962 (div. 1986); children: Steven Lane, Loren Kendell. BA, Vassar Coll., 1961; MS, Ariz. State U., 1979. Mathematician Lawrence Radiation Lab., Livermore, Calif., 1961-64; scientific programmer Goodyear Aerospace, Litchfield Park, Ariz., 1976-80; mem. tech. staff GTE Communications Systems, Phoenix, 1980-82; sr. software engr. Digital Equipment Corp., Phoenix, 1982-84; systems software engr. Sperry Comml. Flight Systems, Phoenix, 1984-86; prin. engr. Honeywell Comml. Flight Systems, Phoenix, 1986-88, head engring. sect., 1988—. Mem. IEEE. Methodist. Office: Honeywell Comml Flight Sys PO Box 21111 Phoenix AZ 85036

ASHLEY, ROSALIND MINOR, writer; b. Chgo., Oct. 10, 1923; d. Jack and Frances (Wasser) Minor; m. Charles Ashley, Mar. 1, 1941; children: Stephen David, Richard Arthur. Student, Moser Bus. Coll., Chgo., 1940; BS in Edn., Northwestern U., 1963; postgrad., Nat. Coll. Edn., 1968. Sec. Platt Luggage, Inc., 1944; Chgo. producer, performer Story Book Ladies WEAW, Evanston, Ill., 1954-55; elem. tchr. Sch. Dist. No. 65, Evanston, 1962-63, Sch. Dist. No. 39, Wilmette, Ill., 1964-70; assoc. editor Scott Foresman & Co., Inc., Glenview, Ill., 1970-74; weekly humor columnist Citizen, Del Mar Citizen and La Costan, Solana Beach, Calif., 1986-87; freelance writer San Diego edit. L.A. Times and Citizen, 1987—; cons. Carlsbad (Calif.) Unified Sch., 1986-87. Author: Successful Techniques for Teaching Elementary Language Arts, 1970, paperback edit., 1981, Activities for Motivating and Teaching Bright Children, 1973, Portfolio of Daily Classroom Acitvities with Model Lesson Plans, 1979; editor: Language and How to Use It, 1970; contbr. articles to profl. and popular publs. Vol. Recs. for Blind, Chgo.; publicity chmn. Rancho Santa Fe (Calif.) Community Concerts Assn., 1986—; play judge Associated Community Theatres. Recipient grand prize for poetry Sta. KFAC-FM, L.A., 1984. Mem. AAUW, Welcome Wagon. Democrat. Home: 250 Via Taviar Encinitas CA 92024

ASHMEAD, ALLEZ MORRILL, speech-hearing-language pathologist, orofacial myologist, consultant; b. Provo, Utah, Dec. 18, 1916; d. Laban Rupert and Zella May (Miller) M.; m. Harvey Harold Ashmead, Sept. 24, 1940; children: Harve DeWayne, Sheryl Mae Harames, Zeltha Janeel Henderson, Emma Allez Moss. BS, Utah State U., 1938; MS summa cum laude, U. Utah, 1952, PhD summa cum laude, 1970; postgrad., Idaho State U., Oreg. State Coll., U. Denver, U. Utah, Brigham Young U., Utah State U., U. Washington, U. No. Colo. Cert. secondary edn., remedial reading, spl. edn., learning disabilities; cert. clin. competence speech pathology and audiology; profl. cert. in orofacial myology. Tchr. pub. schs. Utah, Idaho, 1938-43; speech and hearing pathologist Bushnell Hosp., Brigham City, Utah, 1943-45; sr. speech correctionist Utah State Dept. Health, Salt Lake City, 1945-52; dir. speech and hearing dept. Davis County Sch. Dist., Farmington, Utah, 1952-65; clin., field supr. U. Utah, Salt Lake City, 1965-70, 75-78; speech pathologist Box Elder Sch. Dist., Brigham City, 1970-75, 78-84; teaching specialist Brigham Young U., Provo, 1970-73; speech pathologist Primary Children's Med. Ctr., Salt Lake City, 1975-77; pvt. practice speech pathology and orofacial myology, 1970-88; del. USSR Profl. Speech Pathology seminar, 1984, 86; participant numerous internat. seminars. Author: Physical Facilities for Handicapped Children, 1957, A Guide for Training Public School Speech and Hearing Clinicians, 1965, A Guide for Public School Speech Hearing Programs, 1959, Impact of Orofacial Myofunctional Treatment on Orthodontic Correction, 1982, Meeting Needs of Handicapped Children, 1975, Relationship of Trace Minerals to Disease, 1972, Macro and Trace Minerals in Human Metabolism, 1971, Electromotive Potential Differences Between Stutterers and Non-stutterers, 1970, Learning Disability, An Educational Adventure, 1969, New Horizons in Special Education, 1969, Developing Speech and Language in the Exceptional Child, 1961, Parent Teacher Guidance in Primary Stuttering, 1951, numerous others; contbr. research articles to profl. jours. Student Placement chair Am. Field Service, Kaysville, Utah, 1962-66; ednl. del. Women's State Legis. Council, Salt Lake City, 1958-70; chairwoman fund raising Utah Symphony Orch., Salt Lake City, 1970-71; sec., treas. Utah chpt. U.S. Council for Exceptional Children, 1958-62, membership com. chair, 1962-66, program com. chair, 1966-68. Recipient Scholarship award for Higher Edn. U. Utah, Salt Lake City, 1969; Delta Kappa Gamma scholar, 1968; rsch. grantee Utah Dept. Edn., 1962. Mem. NEA, Utah Ednl. Assn., Am. Speech, Lang. Hearing Assn. (life, continuing edn. com. 1985, Ace award for Continuing Edn.), Western Speech Assn., Internat. Assn. Orofacial Myology (life, bd. examiners, Sci. Contribution award 1982), Utah Speech, Hearing and Lang. Assn. (life, sec., treas. 1956-60), AAUW (Utah state bd. chair status of women 1959-62, Kaysville br. 1957-60), Delta Kappa Gamma (state scholarship award 1968, del. Woman's State Legis. Council 1958-70, profl. affairs chair 1963-67, tchr. of yr. award 1978), Sigma Alpha Eta, Theta Alpha Phi, Psi Chi, Zeta Phi Eta, Phi Kappa Phi. Republican. Mormon. Lodges: Daus. Utah Pioneers (parlimentarian Kaysville chpt. 1980—, historian 1975-80), Soroptimist Internat. (charter mem. 1954, bd. dirs. 1954-56, pres. Davis County chpt. 1965-69, treas. 1956-54, Rocky Mountain regional bd. dirs. 1965-70, community service award 1968, pub. service award 1970). Home: 719 E Center St Kaysville UT 84037 Office: Harrison Profl Ctr 3293 Harrison Blvd Ogden UT 84403

ASHTON, RICK JAMES, librarian; b. Middletown, Ohio, Sept. 18, 1945; s. Ralph James and Lydia Marie (Thornbery) A.; m. Marcia K. Zuroweste, Dec. 23, 1966; children: Jonathan Paul, David Andrew. A.B., Harvard U., 1967; M.A., Northwestern U., 1969, Ph.D., 1973; M.A., U. Chgo., 1976. Instr., asst. prof. history Northwestern U., Evanston, Ill., 1972-74; curator local and family history Newberry Library, Chgo., 1974-77; asst. dir. Allen County Pub. Library, Ft. Wayne, Ind., 1977-80, dir., 1980-85; city librarian Denver Pub. Library, 1985—; mem. Ind. Coop Library Services Authority, 1980-85, pres., 1984-85; mem. Ft. Wayne Cable TV Adv. Council, 1982-85; cons. Nat. Endowment Humanities, Nat. Ctr. Edn. Stats., Northwestern U. Office Estate Planning. Author: The Life of Henry Ruiter, 1742-1819, 1974, The Genealogy Beginner's Manual: A New Edition, 1977, Stuntz, Fuller, Kennard and Cheadle Ancestors, 1987. Bd. dirs. Community Coordinated Child Care, Evanston, 1972-74; bd. dirs. Three Rivers Montessori Sch., Ft. Wayne, 1977-80; bd. dirs., sec. Allen County-Ft. Wayne Hist. Soc., 1977-83; Denver Mcpl. Access Cable TV Policy Bd. Conscientious objector. Recipient Nat. Merit scholar, 1963-67, Old City Hall Hist. Service award, 1985; NDEA fellow, 1967-69; Woodrow Wilson fellow, 1971-72. Mem. ALA, Colo. Libr. Assn., Colo. Alliance Rsch. Librs. (pres. 1987-88), Irving Libr. Network. Club: City (Denver). Home: 2974 S Verbena Way Denver CO 80231 Office: Denver Pub Libr 1357 Broadway Denver CO 80203-2165

ASHURST, PAULA ANNE, nurse, educator; b. Port Huron, Mich., Feb. 21, 1958; d. Robert Carl and Florence May (Lounsberry) Goodrich; m. Kevan John Ashurst, May 12, 1976 (div. 1981); 1 child, Ryan Glen. Diploma in Nursing, Bapt. Sch. Nursing, Louisville, 1981. RN, Ariz.; cert. diabetes educator, Ariz. Diabetes educator Humana Hosp., Louisville, 1983-85, Mayo Clin., Scottsdale, Ariz., 1987—; pvt. practice nursing, Scottsdale, 1986-87. Bd. dirs. Juvenile Diabetes Found., 1988. Mem. Am. Assn. Diabetes Educators (pres. elect, Phoenix chpt.), Cen. Ariz. Assn. Diabetes Educators, (pres. elect). Office: 4501 N 40th St Ste 306 Phoenix AZ 85018 Office: Mayo Clinic 13400 E Shea Blvd Scottsdale AZ 85259

ASHWOOD, ANDREW MARK, radio station executive; b. Milw., Feb. 28, 1957; s. Loren Frisk and Helen Elizabeth (Passmore) A. Student, Albion (Mich.) Coll., 1975-79. Program, music dir. Sta. WGBF-AM, Evansville, Ind., 1980-81, Sta. WKTI-FM, Milw., 1981-82; asst. program dir. Sta. WABX-FM, Detroit, 1983; on-air personality Sta. KOPA-AM/FM, Phoenix, 1983-85; program dir. Sta. KOOL-AM/FM, Phoenix, 1985—; cons. Satellite Music Network, Dallas, 1986—. Named Outstanding Citizen, Kelly Svcs., Airz., 1985, Outstanding Young Men of Am., 1988. Methodist. Office: KOOL Radio 2196 E Camelback St Phoenix AZ 85016

ASHWORTH, JEFFREY TODD, bioanalyst; b. Oxnard, Calif., Apr. 10, 1964; s. Douglas Kent and Judith Ann (Todd) A. BS in Statistics, U. Calif., Davis, 1987. Bioanalyst Syntex Rsch., Palo Alto, Calif., 1987—. Mem. Golden Gate Lacrosse Club (San Francisco). Home: 1000 Escalon Ave Apt H1060 Sunnyvale CA 94086

ASKIN, RICHARD HENRY, JR., television syndication company executive; b. Flushing, N.Y., Feb. 11, 1947; s. Richard H. and Anne Margaret A.; children: Jennifer Leigh, Michael Richard. BA in Econs., Rutgers U., 1969; MA in Communications, U. Tex., 1971; MBA in Fin., Fordham U., 1976. Sales rep. Proctor & Gamble Distbg. Co., Jericho, N.Y., 1969; account exec. CableRep, Inc., N.Y.C., 1973-74, WNBC-TV Nat. Broadcasting Co., N.Y.C., 1974-75, NBC-TV, NBC, N.Y.C., 1975-76, sales mgr. KNBC-TV, Los Angeles, 1976-79, dir. sales, 1979-85; v.p. domestic sales Fries Distbn. Co., Los Angeles, 1985-86, sr. v.p. distbn., 1986-87; pres. TV distbn. The Samuel Goldwyn Co., Los Angeles; pres. The Breckford Group, Inc. Served to 1st lt. Adj. Gen. Corps, U.S. Army, 1971-73. Decorated Army Commendation medal; Alcoa fellow, 1969-70. Mem. Hollywood Radio and TV Soc., Advt. Industry Emergency Fund (pres., bd. dirs.), Acad. of TV, Arts and Scis., Alpha Rho Alumni Assn., Chi Psi. Republican. Home: 1520 Aldercreek Pl Westlake Village CA 91362 Office: The Samuel Goldwyn Co 10203 Santa Monica Blvd Los Angeles CA 90067

ASLAKSEN, NGUYEN THI BA, printed circuit board quality control technician; b. My Tho, Socialist Republic of South Vietnam, Mar. 3, 1952; came to U.S., 1975; d. Van Day Nguyen and Thi Loc Le; m. Frank J. Fernandez, Apr. 15, 1972 (div. Oct. 1981); m. Carl Edward Aslaksen, Aug. 13, 1982. Electronics assembler Anderson Jacobson Inc., San Jose, Calif., 1982-83; quality control inspector Racal Vadic, San Jose, 1983-84, Sprig Circuits Inc., Vacaville, Calif., 1984-85; film processor Sprig Circuits Inc., 1985-86, silk screener, 1986-88, quality control supr., 1988—. Republican. Buddhist. Office: Sprig Circuits Inc 765 B Eubanks Dr Vacaville CA 95688

ASMUNDSON, ROBERT MARK, lawyer; b. Bellingham, Wash., Dec. 30, 1950; s. T.B. and Esther L. (Davy) A.; m. Christine Carlson, June 23, 1973 (div. 1988); children: Ingrid Marie, Erika Lynn, Anna Lee. BA, Western Wash. U., 1976; JD, U. of Pacific, 1980. Bar: Wash. 1980, U.S. Dist. Ct. (we dist.) Wash. 1980. Ptnr. Asmundson, Atwood & Hager, Bellingham, 1980—; bd. dirs. Indsl. Hydro-Chem Services Inc., Bellingham. Mem. Bellingham City Council, 1984-88; pres. Mt. Baker Area Council Boy Scouts

Am., 1987-88, Current Industries Workshop, Bellingham, 1982-84. Mem. Order of Coif, Wash. State Bar Assn., Lions (pres. Bellingham Cen. br. 1984-85). Home: 1305 W Clearbrook Bellingham WA 98226 Office: Asmundson Atwood & Hager 805 Dupont St #5 Bellingham WA 98225

ASPELL, AMY SUZANNE ZEHR, arts administrator; b. Chgo., June 28, 1942; d. Anthony Peter and Florence Amy (McCullagh) Zehr; div.; children: Valerie Noel, Megan Colleen. BA in Art., Knox Coll., 1963; MA in Art Edn., U. South Fla., 1976. Founder, pres., newsletter editor Suncoast Fiber Guild, Tampa, Fla., 1975-78; coord., then dir. Tampa Community Design Ctr., Inc., 1979-81; exec. dir. Ark. Arts Coun., Little Rock, 1984-87; dir. Irvine (Calif.) Fine Arts Ctr., 1987—; tchr. art, pub. elem. schs., Wis., 1963-68, Fla., 1983; curriculum organizer, tchr. arts program, Ark. State Sch. for Blind, Little Rock, 1969-70; presenter courses in weaving, fiber arts for adults and children, numerous arts ctrs. and ednl. instns.; evaluator, panelist Nat. Endowment for Arts, Washington. Author, designer: Cookbook Weaving I. Grantee, Nat. Endowment for Arts. Mem. Am. Assn. Mus., Irvine Contemporary Arts Coun. Unitarian Universalist. Office: Irvine Fine Arts Ctr 14321 Yale Ave Irvine CA 92714

ASPERGER, DONALD PAUL, lawyer; b. Fresno, Calif., June 2, 1955; s. Paul and Esther Louise (Weakley) A.; m. Lisa Elinor Ohlmann, June 26, 1976; children: Mary, Julie. AB with honors, U. Calif., Davis, 1977; JD, U. Calif., Berkeley, 1980. Bar: Calif. 1980, U.S. Tax Ct. 1983. Ptnr. Thomas, Snell, Jamison, Russell & Asperger, Fresno, 1982--. Mem. ABA, State Bar Calif., Fresno County Bar Assn., Boalt Hall Alumni Assn.

ASSIRI, ABDUL-REDA ALI, political scientist; b. Kuwait, Kuwait, May 5, 1946; s. Ali A. and Fatemah A. A.; m. Zahra M. Ghareeb, July 28, 1971; children: Adel, Basel, Noor. BS, East Tenn. State U., 1974; MA, U. Calif., 1977, PhD, 1981. Chmn. dept. of polit. sci. Kuwait U., 1982-84, assoc. dean coll. commerce, 1983-87, asst. prof. coll. commerce, 1981—; vis. scholar U. Colo., Boulder, 1988. Author: (book) Kuwait Foreign Policy, 1988; contbr. articles to profl. jours. Cons. Royal Ct. Diwan Al-Amiri, Kuwait, 1983-84. Mem. Middle East Studies Assn. of N.Am., Internat. Studies Assn., Amnesty Internat., Internat. Polit. Sci. Assn. Home: 850 Willowbrook Rd Boulder CO 80302 Office: Kuwait U, PO Box 5486, Safat 13055, Kuwait

ASSISI, RITA FERNANDEZ, real estate company executive; b. Quilon, Kerala, India, Sept. 27, 1943; came to U.S., 1964; d. Joseph Manuel Fernandez and Roselyn Vazhamootil; m. Francis K. Assisi, Sept. 18, 1968; children: Shashi, Aruna. BS magna cum laude, Kerala U., 1963; MS, Marquette U., 1967. Jr. lectr. Kerala U., 1963-64; research assoc. Sch. Medicine Stanford (Calif.) U., 1977-87; pres. Tiara Investment Co., Los Altos, Calif., 1987—; faculty India Cultural Sch., Los Altos, 1979—. Pres. Malayalee Assn. North Calif., San Jose, 1978-80; v.p. South India Fine Arts, San Jose, Calif., 1984-85. Marquette U. scholar, 1967. Mem. Nat. Assn. Realtors, Internat. Real Estate Fedn. Office: Tiara Investment Co 175 S San Antonio Rd Ste 102B Los Altos CA 94022

ASTLEY, EUGENE ROY, seamless tube manufacturing executive; b. Alameda, Calif., Dec. 5, 1926; s. Frank Robert Astley and Mary Grace (Barr) Pease; m. Peggy Lund, June 27, 1948; children: Clifford Andrew, Michael J., William Lawrence. BS in Physics and Math., U. Oreg., 1948; MS in Physics and Math., Oreg. State U., 1950. Physicist GE, Schenectady, N.Y., 1950-65; physicist GE, Richland, Wash., 1950-65; dir., inventor Fast Flux Test Facility Battelle Northwest, Richland, 1965-69; dir. Systems Electronics & Econs. Battelle Northwest, Richland, 1969-71; v.p. New Projects & Products Exxon Nuclear Co., Bellevue, Wash., 1971-79; v.p., bd. dirs. Mfg. Facilities-U.S. & Germany, Exxon Nuclear Co., Richland, 1979-83; pres., chief exec. officer, bd. dirs. Sandvik Spl. Metals Corp., Kennewick, Wash., 1983—; bd. dirs. Wash. Coun. for Tech. Advancement, Seattle; mem. Wash. State Research Coun., Seattle, 1986—, internat. trade assistance adv. com. Wash. State Dept. Trad & Econ. Devel., Olympia, 1987—, Gov.'s Adv. Forum on Internat. Trade, Olympia, 1988—. Contbr. articles to profl. jours.; inventor, patentee in field. Bd. dirs. Tri-City Indsl. Devel. Coun., Kennewick, Wash., 1983—, Southeastern Wash. Devel. Assn., Kennewick, 1983—, Econ. Devel. Partnership for Wash., Seattle, 1986—; pres., chief exec. officer commerce and industry div. Tri-City Indsl. Devel. Coun., Kennewick, 1988—; pres. Blue Mountain coun. Boy Scouts Am., Kennewick, 1987—. With USN, 1944-46. Mem. Nat. Assn. Corp. Dirs., U.S. Coun. for Energy Awareness, Am. Nuclear Soc. (Appreciation award 1958). Republican. Unitarian. Home: 2414 Harris Richland WA 99352 Office: Sandvik Spl Metals Corp PO Box 6027 Kennewick WA 99336

ASTON, HERBERT CHARLES, human resource development executive; b. Jersey City, Apr. 24, 1945; s. Samuel Herbert and Anne Virginia (Holden) A.; m. Deanna Maria Mendoza, June 21, 1970 (div. 1981); children: Ian Andrew, Evan Jeremy; m. Ilson Kim, Oct. 20, 1983; 1 child, Robert Brooks. Student, Fairleigh Dickinson U., 1963-67; BA, William Patterson Coll., 1970; postgrad., Pepperdine U., 1975-79. Tchr. Ramsey (N.J.) High Schs., 1970-72; mgr. tng. Volvo of N. Am., Rockleigh, N.J., 1972-78; mgr. orgn. devel. and tng. Levi Strauss, San Francisco, 1978-81; dir. human resources Atari, Sunnyvale, Calif., 1981-84, PH & H, Hunt Valley, Md., 1984-87; v.p. devel. and tng. Coldwell Banker Residential Group, Newport Beach, Calif., 1987—; lectr. U. San Francisco, 1978, USN Postgrad. Sch., Monterey, Calif., 1980, Mt. St. Mary's Coll., Moraga, Calif., 1982; cons. Iomega Corp., Roy, Utah, 1984, Haggerty & O'Sullivan, Brisbane, Calif., 1984-86. Contbr. editor Working Together, 1978. Gabrielson/Larsen & Engalau scholar, Sweden, 1975. Mem. Orgn. Devel. Network (speaker 1980), Acad. Mgmt., Am. Soc. Tng. and Devel., Am. Compensation Assn., Orgn. Devel. Inst., Runners Club of Am., Austin Healy Club of Am., Orange County Track Club, Am. Motorcycle Assn. Office: Coldwell Banker Residential Group 23046 Ave de la Carlota Ste 560 Laguna Hills CA 92653

ATAIE, ATA JENNATI, oil products marketing executive; b. Mashad, Iran, Mar. 15, 1934; s. Hamid Jennati and Mohtaram (Momeni) A.; came to U.S., 1957, naturalized, 1969; B.S. in Agr., Fresno (Calif.) State U., 1964; B.A. in Econs., San Francisco State U., 1966; m. Judith Garrett Bush, Oct. 7, 1961; children—Ata Jennati, Andrew J. Mktg. exec. Shell Oil Co., Oakland, Calif., 1966-75; pres. A.J. Ataie & Cos., Danville, Calif., 1975—; Am. Value Inc., 1976—. Served as 2d lt. Iranian Army, 1953. Mem. Nat. Petroleum Retailers Assn. Democrat.

ATCHESON, SUE HART, business educator; b. Dubuque, Iowa, Apr. 12; d. Oscar Raymond and Anna (Cook) Hart; m. Walter Clark Atcheson (div.); children: Christine A. Hischar, Moffet Zoe, Claye Williams. BBA, Mich. State U.; MBA, Calif. State Poly. U., Pomona, 1973. Cert. tchr. and administr. Instr. Mt. San Antonio Coll., Walnut, Calif., 1968—; bd. dirs. faculty assn. Mt. San Antonio Coll.; mem. acad. senate Mt. San Antonio Coll.; originator vol. income tax assistance Mt. San Antonio Coll.; speaker in field. Author: Fractions and Equations on Your Own, 1975. Speaker Howard Ruff Nat. Conv., San Diego, 1983, Mike DeFalco Numismatics Seminar, Claremont, Calif., 1986; charter mem. Internat. Commn. on Monetary and Econ. Reform; panelist infrastructure funding reform, Freeport, Ill., 1989. Office: Mount San Antonio Coll 1100 N Grand Ave Walnut CA 91789

ATCHISON, CHARLES MARVIN, management systems consultant; b. Pasadena, Calif., Mar. 27, 1933; s. Clarence Murray Atchison and Louella May (Migendt) Key; m. Maxine Womack, Nov. 3, 1954; children: Kay Marie, Alexander Charles. Student, So. Calif. Bible Coll., Pasadena, 1949, Reed Coll., 1956-57; cert. in mgmt., U. Calif., Berkeley, 1969; MBA, Golden Gate U., 1979. Lab. technician, computer services coordinator Gen. Electric Co., Vallecitos Atomic Labs, San Jose, Calif., 1957-59; computer ops. mgr. Control Data Corp., Palo Alto, Calif., 1959-62; programmer, ops. cons. Lockheed Missles and Space Co., Sunnyvale, Calif., 1962-65; supr. jobsite computing Bechtel Corp., San Francisco, 1966-69; dir. systems and computing Esco Corp., Portland, Oreg., 1970-73; field procurement mgr. Bechtel Corp., 1973-78, mgr. systems and planning, 1978-79; mgr. decentralization Fairchild Semiconductor, Mt. View, Calif., 1979-83; pres., chief exec. officer Alcinous Internat. Ltd., Palo Alto, 1983—; instr. mgmt. Golden Gate U., Los Altos, Calif., 1984-86, City U., Bellevue, Wash., 1986-88, chair Calif. adv. bd., 1988. Bd. dirs. Calif. Youth Symphony, Palo Alto, 1977-78; referee, commr. Am. Youth Soccer Orgn., Palo Alto, 1978-85; mem. World Affairs Coun., 1987—. Served with USN, 1952-56. Mem. Assn. for Computing Machinery (chpt. chmn. 1968), Assn. for Systems Mgmt., Planning Execs. Inst. (chpt. pres. 1985-86), World Future Soc., Cert. Systems Profls., MENSA. Republican. Office: Alcinous Internat Ltd PO Box 10538 Stanford CA 94309-0538

ATCHISON, SANDRA DALLAS, correspondent, writer; b. Washington, June 11, 1939; d. Forrest Everett and Harriett (Mavity) Dallas; m. Robert Thomas Atchison, Apr. 20, 1963; children: Dana Dallas, Kendal Dallas. BA, U. Denver, 1960. Asst. editor U. Denver Mag., 1965-66; editorial asst. Bus. Week, Denver, 1961-63, 67-69, bur. chief, 1969-85, sr. corr., 1985—; book reviewer Denver Post, 1961—, regional book columnist, 1980—. Author: Gaslights and Gingerbread, 1965, rev. edit., 84, Gold and Gothic, 1967, No More Than 5 In A Bed, 1967, Vail, 1969, Cherry Creek Gothic, 1971, Yesterday's Denver, 1974, Sacred Paint, 1980, Colorado Ghost Towns and Mining Camps, 1985, Colorado Homes, 1986; contbr. articles to various mags. Bd. dirs. Vis. Nurse Assn., Denver, 1983-85, Hist. Denver, Inc., 1979-82, 84-87. Recipient Wrangler award Nat. Cowboy Hall of Fame, 1980; named Colo. Exceptional Chronicler of Western History by Women's Library Assn. and Denver Pub. Library Friends Found., 1986. Mem. Women's Forum Colo., Denver Women's Press Club, Western Writers of Am., Nat. Book Critics Circle. Democrat. Presbyterian. Home: 750 Marion St Denver CO 80218

ATCHLEY, BILL LEE, university president; b. Cape Girardeau, Mo., Feb. 16, 1932; s. William Cecil and Mary (Bicket) A.; m. Pat Limbaugh, Aug. 1954; 3 children. B.S. in Civil Engring, U. Mo., Rolla, 1957, M.S., 1959; Ph.D., Tex. A&M U., 1965. Registered profl. engr., Mo., W.Va., S.C. From asst. prof. to prof. engring. mechanics U. Mo., Rolla, 1957-75; prof., dean Coll. Engring., W.Va. U., Morgantown, 1975-79; pres. Clemson (S.C.) U., 1979-85; pres., chief exec. officer Nat. Sci. Ctr. for Communication and Electronics Found. Inc., 1985-87; pres. U. of the Pacific, Stockton, Calif., 1987—; cons. Systems Cons. Inc., Savannah River Lab.; chmn. Gov. W.Va. Commn. Energy, Economy and Environment, 1975; sci. and tech. adviser to Senate and Ho. of Dels. W.Va., 1976; mem. W.Va. Bd. Registration Profl. Engrs.; sci. and tech. adviser to Gov. Mo., 1972-75, to Gov. W.Va., 1975-79; W.Va. gov.'s rep. to U.S. Govs. Commn. on Energy, 1979; energy advisor to Gov. S.C., 1980; mem. Gov.'s Council on Alcohol Fuels; mem. fed. fossil energy adv. com. Dept. Energy; mem. Nat. Coal Council 1985—; bd. dirs. Criticare Technologies Corp., Reno. Author papers in field. Bd. dirs. Southeast Energy Rsch. Inst., S.C. Energy Forum, S.C. Rsch. Authority, S.C. Sea Grant Consortium, mem. sports com. USIA; chmn. leadership gift club Stockton Area United Way; active Boy Scouts Am., Meth. Ch. Served with AUS, 1952-54. Recipient alumni merit award Southeast Mo. State U.; Ford Found. fellow; recipient Distinguished Service award Rolla Bicentennial Com., 1975; named S.C. Engr. of Yr., 1985. Mem. Nat. Govs. Conf., Am. Soc. Engring. Edn., ASCE, Nat. Soc. Profl. Engrs., Newcomen Soc. N.Am., Greater Stockton C. of C. (bd. dirs.), Future Farmers Am. (hon.), Sigma Nu, Phi Kappa Phi (hon.), Beta Sigma Gamma (hon.). Methodist. Office: U of the Pacific 3601 Pacific Stockton CA 95211

ATENCIO, LINDA LOU, company official; b. Sheldon, Iowa, Apr. 17, 1950; d. Jerald Clifford and Ardith Lavonne (Wesselink) F.; m. Sophocles Peter Vendouris, Feb. 22, 1972 (div. 1975); m. Ramon Walter Atencio, Apr. 9, 1979; children: Ramon Anthony, Briana Marie. Grad. high sch., Des Moines. Word processor Union Carbide Co., Moorestown, N.J., 1978-79, Warren Goldberg & Berman, Princeton, N.J., 1980-82, Am. Savs., Stockton, Calif., 1982-83, Homeland Ins. Co., San Jose, 1983-84; sr. word processor Plaza Bank Commerce, San Jose, 1984-87; exec. sec. Sci. Games, Gilroy, Calif., 1987—. Democrat. Home: 9050 Kern Ave C-2 Gilroy CA 95020

ATHA, GEORGE CRAWFORD, petroleum geologist; b. Fairmont, W.Va., Nov. 25, 1902; s. William Hunter and Jessie Julia (Dougan) A.; student in geology Ohio State U., 1922, Muskingum Coll., 1927; m. Gladys R. Wray, Apr. 7, 1948. Civil engr., Sebring, Fla., 1927; salesman, mgr. real estate, Lorain, Ohio, 1927-28; staff Midwest Re '29 Co., Roswell, N.Mex., 1928-29; staff City of Palos Verdes Estates (Calif.), 1930-31; pres. Hiawatha Exploration Co., San Marino, Calif., 1943—; pvt. practice, San Marino, 1947—. Recipient hon. award Muskingum Coll., 1983. Mem. Internat. Oil Scouts, Long Beach Petroleum Club, Elks (life), L.A. Athletic Club. Address: 2221 California Blvd San Marino CA 91108

ATHERTON, ALEXANDER SIMPSON, newspaper executive; b. Honolulu, Mar. 29, 1913; s. Frank Cooke and Eleanore Alice (Simpson) A.; m. LeBurta Marie Gates, Oct. 8, 1941; children—Burta Lee, Frank Cooke II, Marjory Gates. Grad., Tabor Acad., Marion, Mass., 1931; B.A., Dartmouth, 1936. With Hawaiian Trust Co., Honolulu, 1954-66; asst. v.p. Hawaiian Trust Co., 1958-66; pres. Honolulu Star-Bull., 1963—. past campaign chmn. Honolulu Community Chest.; trustee Atherton Family Found.; bd. dirs. Africare, Inc., Bishop Mus. Pres. Mid-Pacific Inst., 1955—. Mem. Royal Philatelic Soc. London, Theta Delta Chi. Republican. Mem. United Ch. Christ. Clubs: Pacific (Honolulu), Adventurers (Honolulu), Waialae Country (Honolulu); Oahu Country; Collectors (N.Y.C.), Outrigger Canoe. Home: 2150 Puualii Pl Honolulu HI 96822

ATKINS, MICHELLE BLAINE, nurse educator, consultant; b. N.Y.C., Feb. 12, 1953; d. Stanley Murray and Gilda Lee (Grossman) A. BSN, Brockport (N.Y.) Coll., 1974; MS, U. Ariz., 1978. Staff nurse Mt. Sinai Hosp., N.Y.C., 1974-76; sr. nurse Kino Community Hosp., Tucson, Ariz., 1976-79; unit dir. St. Mary's Hosp., Tucson, 1979-83; head nurse New Hanover Meml. Hosp., Wilmington, N.C., 1983-84; staff nurse Cape Fear Meml. Hosp., Wilmington, 1984-85; nurse educator, cons. St. Joseph's Hosp., Phoenix, 1985—. Contbr. articles to profl. jours. Chairwoman community rels. sub. Congressman Udall's Hispanic Coalition for Diabetes. 1st lt. Nurse Corps USAR. Mem. Am. Nurses Assn., Am. Assn. Diabetes Educators (cert.), Ariz. Nurses Assn., Am. Diabetes Assn. (5-yr. planning council Ariz. chpt. 1988—), Phoenix Nurses Consortium. Office: Saint Josephs Hosp 350 W Thomas Rd Phoenix AZ 85013

ATKINSON, RICHARD CHATHAM, cognitive psychologist, educator, university chancellor; b. Oak Park, Ill., Mar. 19, 1929; s. Herbert and Margaret (Feuerbach) A.; m. Rita Loyd, Aug. 20, 1952; 1 dau., Lynn Loyd. Ph.B., U. Chgo., 1948; Ph.D., Ind. U., 1955. Lectr. applied math. and stats. Stanford (Calif.) U., 1956-57, assoc. prof. psychology, 1961-64, prof. psychology, 1964-80; asst. prof. psychology UCLA, 1957-61; dep. dir. NSF, 1975-76, acting dir., 1976-77; dir., 1977-80; chancellor U. Calif., San Diego, 1980—; Mem. Pres.'s Com. Nat. Medal Sci. Author: (with Atkinson, Smith and Hilgard) Introduction to Psychology, 9th edit, 1987, Computer Assisted Instruction, 1969, An Introduction to Mathematical Learning Theory, 1965, Studies in Mathematical Psychology, 1964, Contemporary Developments in Mathematical Psychology, 1974, Mind and Behavior, 1980, Stevens' Hanbook of Experimental Psychology, 1988. Served with AUS, 1954-56. Guggenheim fellow, 1967; fellow Ctr. for Advanced Study in Behavioral Scis., 1963; recipient Distinguished Research award Social Sci. Research Council, 1962. Fellow Am. Acad. Arts and Scis., Am. Psychol. Assn. (pres. exptl. div. 1974-75, Disting. Sci. Contbn. award 1977, Thorndike award 1980), AAAS (chmn. psychology sect. 1975-76, pres. 1989); mem. Soc. Exptl. Psychologists, Nat. Acad. Scis. (council 1982-85), Am. Philos. Soc., Nat. Acad. Edn., Inst. of Medicine, Psychonomic Soc. (chmn. 1973-74), Psychometric Soc., Cognitive Sci. Soc., Sigma Xi. Clubs: Cosmos (Washington); Explorers (N.Y.C.). Home: 9630 La Jolla Farms Rd La Jolla CA 92037 Office: Univ Calif San Diego Office of the Chancellor La Jolla CA 92093

ATKINSON, SHERIDAN EARLE, lawyer; b. Oakland, Calif., Feb. 14, 1945; s. Arthur Sheridan and Esther Louise (Johnson) A.; m. Margie Ann Lehtin, Aug. 13, 1966. 1 son, Ian Sheridan. BS, U. Calif.-Berkeley, 1966, MBA, 1971; JD, U. San Francisco, 1969. Bar: Calif. 1970. Prin. Atkinson & Assocs., fin. and mgmt. cons., corp. and bus. valuations, San Francisco, 1968—; assoc. Charles O. Morgan, Jr., San Francisco, 1972-76; pvt. practice, San Francisco Bay Area,1976—. With USAR, 1970-76. Mem. ABA, Calif. Bar Assn. Republican. Office: 1327A Solano Ave Albany CA 94706

ATKINSON, TOMASINE, government official; b. Phila., May 26, 1939; d. Arthur James Etheridge and Fannie Elizabeth (McGill) Peurifoy; m. James Edward Atkinson, Sept. 3, 1970. Student, U. Pa., 1955-56, Temple U., 1956-57, Duquesne U., 1971, Loretta Heights Coll., Denver, 1973. Asst. to asst. regional adminstr. HUD, San Francisco, 1970; program specialist HUD, Pitts., 1970-72; mortgage svc. specialist HUD, Sacramento, 1972-73, loan specialist, 1973-75, housing counselor, 1975-79, housing mgmt. specialist, 1975-80, community servicer advisor, 1979-80, pub. affairs liaison person, 1985-89, Minority Bus. Enterprise/Women Bus. Enterprise coord., multifamily loan specialist, 1989—; bd. dirs. Tri Con, Inc., Washington, D.C., London, Hong Kong. Producer, dir. film Pusher Man, 1988; contbg. writer Sacramento Connection. Bd. dirs. Save Our Children Coalition, Sacramento, 1988, Sacramento Christian Club Organizers, 1988-89, Met. Rehab. Group, N.Y.C., Chgo., 1988-89, Sacramento Arts Coun., 1988-89, Black Ams. Against Cancer, 1988-89, Sacramento Alcohol Ctr.; mem. Calif. Homemakers Bd., 1985-88. Recipient Excellence Performance award HUD, 1988, 89, Outstanding Profl. award Fed. Exec. Bd., 1988, Congl. recognition, 1988. Mem. Nat. Assn. Real Estate Brokers (hon., cons. 1987—), Asian Pacific C. of C., Sacramento Black C. of C. (bd. dirs. 1989—), Nat. Network Crack Cocaine, Atty. Gen. Minority Roundtable, Black Am. Polit. Action Com. Office: HUD 777 12th St Ste 200 Sacramento CA 95814

ATKINSON, WALTER EUGENE, management executive; b. Brush, Colo., Jan. 30, 1936; s. Carey Ray and Irena Belle (Raichart) A.; m. Barbara Jean Neal, Aug. 3, 1958 (dec. 1974); children: Dawn Janean, Walter Troy, Kelly Cerryce, Rhonda Lynn; m. Susan JoAnn Lenz-Hinrichs-Piper, July 3, 1978; 1 child, Carey Walter. BA, Colo. U., Denver; postgrad., Denver U., 1972-73. Gen. mgr. Atkinson Ranches, Brush, 1952-56, oil field derrickman various drilling units, 1956-60; gen. steel erection supt. Sterling Ind., Denver, 1960-63; owner Colo. Elec. Co., Denver, 1963-65; gen. supt. Bee Constrn. Co., Denver, 1965-68; mfg. mgr. Gates Rubber Co., Denver, 1968-81; v.p., gen. mgr. Engineered Data Products, Inc., Broomfield, Colo., 1981—; rancher Morgan County, Colo. Mem. all state football player high sch. & coll. Home: 13457 W 22d Pl Golden CO 80401 Office: Engineered Data Products Inc 2550 N Midway Broomfield CO 80020

ATKINSON, WILLIAM WILDER, JR., geology educator; b. Albuquerque, Dec. 16, 1935; s. William Wilder and Josephine Elizabeth (Foster) A.; m. Carol Ann Bambrook, June 9, 1957; children: William W. IV, Ellen Annalies. BS, U. N.Mex., 1957, MS, 1960; postgrad., Hamburg U., Fed. Republic Germany, 1960-61; PhD, Harvard U., 1973. Geologist Anaconda Co., Salt Lake City, 1967-78, cons., 1978—; prof. geology U. Colo., Boulder, 1978—. Contbr. articles to sci. jours. NSF scholar, 1961; Deutsche Acad. Austausch Dienst fellow, 1960. Mem. Soc. Econ. Geologists (com. mem.), Geol. Soc. Am., Geol. Soc. Chile, Sigma Xi. Home: 255 Cimmaron Way Boulder CO 80303 Office: U Colo Dept Geol Sci Campus Box 250 Boulder CO 80309

ATLAS, JAY DAVID, philosopher, consultant, linguist; b. Houston, Feb. 1, 1945; s. Jacob Henry and Babette Fancile (Friedman) A. AB summa cum laude, Amherst (Mass.) Coll., 1966; PhD, Princeton (N.J.) U., 1976. Mem. common rm. Wolfson Coll., Oxford, Eng., 1978, 80; vis. fellow Princeton U., 1979; rsch. assoc. Inst. for Advanced Study, Princeton, 1982-84; vis. lectr. U. Hong Kong, 1986; vis. assoc. prof. UCLA, 1988, vis. prof., 1989; prof. Pomona Coll., Claremont, Calif., 1989—; sr. assoc. Jurecon, Inc., L.A. Author: Philosophy Without Ambiguity, 1989; contbr. articles to profl. jours. Mem. Am. Philos. Assn., Linguistic Soc. Am. Home: 1360 Oxford Ave 8 Claremont CA 91711 Office: Pomona Coll Claremont CA 91711

ATWOOD, KELLY PALMER, insurance company executive; b. Portland, Oreg., Jan. 7, 1946; s. Baird Ewing and Lelia Claire (Donham) McNeese A.; m. Regina Louise Hamilton, July 30, 1983; children: Derek, Lynn, Jason, Beri, Courtney. Student, U. Oreg., 1964-66, Chemeketa Community Coll., 1976-78. Pres., chief exec. officer Group Ins. Mktg., Inc., Salem, Oreg., 1970—; pres., chief exec. officer Metro Ins. Agy., Inc., Lake Oswego, Oreg., 1985—, also bd. dirs. Contbr. articles on ins. to profl. jours. Former mem. Reagan Task Force, Washington, 1985-86, Denny Smith Task Force on Crime, Salem, 1988. Served with USN, 1967-69. Named Sr. Agt. of Yr. Salem Life Underwriters Assn., 1980, 81. Mem. Nat. Assn. Life Underwriters, Nat. Assn. Home Builders, Oreg. State Home Builders Assn., Home Builders Assn. Met. Portland (bd. dirs. 1985—). Republican. Club: Quarry (Salem) (bd. dirs. 1985-87). Office: Metro Ins Agy Inc PO Box 2267 Lake Oswego OR 97035

ATWOOD, MARILYN SUE, realtor; b. LaGRande, Oreg., July 22, 1943; d. Lawrence Ira Wilson and Claribel Ardis (Rhine) Uto; m. George A. Hanson, June 10, 1961 (div. June 1980); children: Lisa A. Jackson, Philip M.; m. Vernon D. Atwood, Feb. 14, 1981. Cert. real estate broker, Sch. Profl. Studies, Bend, Oreg., 1981; student, Cen. Oreg. Community Coll., Bend, 1988. Sales assoc. Louderback & Assocs., Prineville, Oreg., 1979-81; assoc. broker Bartlett Realty, Prineville, 1983-85; owner, broker Atwood & Atwood Realty Inc., Prineville, 1983-85; assoc. broker Prineville Sun Country Realty, 1986—. Mem. Crook County Planning Commn., Prineville, 1987—. Mem. Nat. Assn. Realtors, Oreg. Assn. Realtors, Crook County Multiple Listing Svc. (pres. 1985-86), Crook County Women's Network, Prineville Golf and Country Club. Republican. Baptist. Club: Prineville Golf and Country. Office: Prineville Sun Country Realty 750 W 3d St Prineville OR 97754

ATWOOD, MARY SANFORD, author; b. Mt. Pleasant, Mich., Jan. 27, 1935; d. Burton Jay and Lillian Belle (Sampson) Sanford; B.S., U. Miami, 1957; m. John C. Atwood, III, Mar. 23, 1957. Author: A Taste of India, 1969. Mem. San Francisco/N. Peninsula Opera Action, Hillsborough-Burlingame Newcomers, Suicide Prevention and Crisis Center, DeYoung Art Mus., Internat. Hospitality Center, Peninsula Symphony, San Francisco Art Mus., World Affairs Council, Mills Hosp. Assos. Mem. AAUW, Suicide Prevention Aux. Republican. Club: St. Francis Yacht. Office: 40 Knightwood Ln Hillsborough CA 94010

ATWOOD, ROBERT BRUCE, publisher; b. Chgo., Mar. 31, 1907; s. Burton H. and Mary Beach (Stevenson) A.; m. Evangeline Rasmuson, Apr. 2, 1932; children: Marilyn A. Odom, Sara Elaine. A.B., Clark U., 1929; Litt.D. (hon.), Alaska Meth. U., 1967; D.Journalism (hon.), U. Alaska, 1979. Reporter Worcester (Mass.) Telegram, 1926-29, 34-35, Ill. State Jour., Springfield, 1929-34; pres. and pub. Anchorage Times, 1935—. Author pamphlets, articles, editorials pub. in various jours. Chmn. Alaska Statehood Com., 1949-59; hon. Norwegian consul at Anchorage, 1960-86; mem. civilian affairs bd. Alaskan Air Command, 1962—, now chmn. emeritus; chmn. Chancellor's Circle U. Alaska. Decorated knight of first rank Order of St. Olaf, 1976; Alaska commr. to Expo '88, Australia. Mem. AP, Am. Newspaper Pubs. Assn., Pacific N.W. Newspaper Assn., Allied Daily Newspapers, Am. Soc. Newspaper Editors, Am. Polar Soc. (bd. govs.), C. of C. (pres. 1944, 48), Soc. Profl. Journalists. Republican. Presbyterian. Clubs: Explorers, Nat. Press. Lodges: Sons of Norway, Rotary, Elks, Masons, Pioneers of Norway. Office: Anchorage Times 820 4th Ave Anchorage AK 99501

ATWOOD, SHERRELL JEAN TOWNSEND, mortgage banking official, entertainer; b. Los Angeles, Apr. 18, 1944; d. Robert and Sireaner Gwendolyn (Smith) Townsend; m. Julius E. Brooks, Aug. 2, 1961 (div. 1964); children: Stephen Mario, Michelle Irene, Rozzell Jean. AA, Los Angeles Community Coll., 1969; cert. in computer tech., Associated Tech. Colls., Los Angeles, 1986. Mortgage banking official Muneris Co., Los Angeles, 1985—. Sang with Bob B. Soxx and the Blue Jeans, The Crystals for Phil Spector/Philles Records, 1961-62, on Gone Records, 1962-63, Double Shot Records, 1969, A&M, Ode, Columbia Records, 1969-70; performed with the Doodletown Pipers, the Young Americans, 1969-72; singer-writer with Caney Creek Reunion on Dunhill Records, 1969, on Westbound Records, 20th Century Records, 1972-76; co-composer numerous popular songs. Co-founder, sec. Los Angeles Magnet Schs. Assn., 1982-83; active Los Angeles World Affairs Council, 1981—. Mem. AFTRA, Screen Actors Guild. Seventh-Day Adventist. Office: Muneris 2841 12th Ave Los Angeles CA 90018

ATWOOD, TERESA MURPHY, professional society administrator; b. Ft. Worth, Sept. 16, 1949; d. John Malcolm and LaVern (Ray) Murphy; m. Dee James Atwood, July 31, 1970. BS in Edn., David Lipscomb Coll., 1972; postgrad., Tex. Christian U., 1980, 82, 84. Tchr. Nashville Met. Schs., 1972-75; med. asst. Dr. D.D. Martin, Ft. Worth, 1978-84; regional program dir. for U.S. and Can. United Ostomy Assn. Inc., Los Angeles, 1984—; nat. bd.

dirs. United Ostomy Assn., 1982-86, state rep., 1981-82, regional coordinator, 1982-84, dir. vol. devel., 1986—; cons. ednl. materials, Enterostomal Therapy Cons., Inc., Ft. Worth, 1986—; co-founder Info. Utilization Inst., 1988—. Mem. Nat. Found. for Ileitis and Colitis, Inc., Friends of Internat. Ostomy Assn., Inc. Democrat. Mem. Disciples of Christ Ch. Home: 6205 Monterrey Dr Fort Worth TX 76112

AU, ALICE MAN-JING, chemist; b. Canton, People's Republic of China; d. Ying-Tak and Yeuk-Suet Au. BS, U. Calif., Riverside, 1972, PhD, 1976. Postdoctoral scholar U. Calif., San Diego, 1976-78; postgrad. researcher U. Calif., San Francisco, 1978-80, research biochemist, 1980-81; pub. health chemist sanitation and radiation lab. Calif. State Dept. Health Svcs., Berkeley, 1981-84, pub. health chemist food and drug lab., 1984-88, environ. biochemist food and drug lab., 1988-89, acting chief food and drug lab., 1989—; cons. Sci. Innovations, San Francisco, 1983-89. Contbr. articles to profl. jours. dir. adv. com. Calif. State Dept. Health Services EEO Com., Sacramento, 1986. Fellow NSF, 1972; DAR scholar 1970; Disting. Acad. scholar U. Calif., Riverside, 1972-76. Mem. AAAS, Am. Chem. Soc., N.Y. Acad. Scis., Phi Beta Kappa.

AUCOIN, LES, congressman; b. Portland, Oreg., Oct. 21, 1942; s. Francis Edgar and Alice (Atkinson) AuC.; m. Susan Swearingen, June 11, 1963; children: Stacy, Kelly. B.A., Pacific U., 1969. Reporter, editor Redmond (Oreg.) Spokesman, 1964; with Portland Oregonian, 1965-66; dir. pub. info. and publs. Pacific U., 1966-73; adminstr. Skidmore, Owings & Merrill, Portland, 1973-74; mem. 94th-101st Congresses from 1st Oreg. Dist., Com. on Appropriations, Subcom. on Interior, Def. and D.C.; chmn. House Dem. Trade Caucus, 1983-84; Mem. Oreg. Ho. of Reps., 1971-74, majority leader, 1973-74; chmn. Oreg. Ho. of Reps. (Com. on State and Fed. Affairs), 1973, Oreg. Ho. of Reps. (Com. on Rules), 1974; mem. State Emergency Bd., 1973-74; leader Whip Task Force on Arms Control. Served with inf. U.S. Army, 1961-64. Recipient One of 10 Outstanding Young Men of Am. award U.S. Jaycees, 1977; Brotherhood award B'nai B'rith, 1978. Office: 2159 Rayburn House Office Bldg Washington DC 20515

AUDETT, THEOPHILUS BERNARD, lawyer; b. Giltedge, Mont., Feb. 12, 1905; s. Joseph Abraham and Katherine Amanda (Johnson) A.; m. Beverly Corinne Lowery, Sept. 21, 1939 (dec.); m. Barbara M. Terini, Nov. 6, 1976 (div. Mar. 1978); 1 dau., Katherine Ann Audett MacCluer. J.D., U. Wash., 1926. Bar: Wash. 1926, Calif. 1964. With U.S. Customs Svc., 1930-63, asst. dep. commr., hdqrs., Washington, 1951-63; of counsel Stein, Shostak, Shostak & O'Hara, L.A., 1965—; customs expert with U.S. del. GATT, Geneva, 1956, 61; U.S. rep. on panel of experts on antidumping and countervailing duties GATT, Geneva, 1959, 60; chmn. Interdepartmental Com. for Study Antidumping Legis., Washington, 1962. Capt. U.S. Army, 1942-45. Recipient Exceptional Svc. award Dept. Treasury, 1963. Mem. ABA, Calif. State Bar, Am. Judicature Soc., Assn. Customs Bar. Republican. Club: L.A. Athletic. Home: 4139 Via Marina #704 Marina del Rey CA 90292 Office: 3580 Wilshire Blvd Los Angeles CA 90010

AUDINO, JOSEPH VINCENT, construction industry executive; b. L.A., Mar. 20, 1949; s. Vincent Alan and Elizabeth F. (Kubik) A.; m. Amy Soboroff, My 26, 1979. BA, UCLA, 1971; JD, Southwestern U., L.A., 1974. V.p. Rode Bros, Inc., L.A., 1981-87; pres. Rode Bros Inc., L.A., 1987—, Rode Bros. P.S. Inc., San Diego, 1978—; v.p. Kahala Wood Flrs., Honolulu, 1985-88. Contbr., organizer AIDS Hospice Project, L.A., 1988. Mem. Nat. Wood Flrs. Assn. (panelist Kans. City 1988), Western Flr. Assn., Hawaii Flr. Assn., UCLA Alumni Assn. Democrat. Roman Catholic. Office: Rode Bros Inc 8280 Melrose Ave Los Angeles CA 90040

AUERBACH, ARTHUR MICHAEL, orthopedic surgeon; b. N.Y.C., Feb. 19, 1937; s. Samuel and Gertrude (Steinberg) A.; m. Judith Ann Bernstein, June 1963 (div. 1977); m. Odette Tara Rauch, June 23, 1985; children: Adam Mark, Amy Lynn, Stefan David, Danielle Stacey. BA, Cornell U., 1957; MD, U. Chgo., 1961. Intern N.Y. Hosp., N.Y.C., 1961-62, resident surgery, 1962-63; orthopedic resident Mayo Clinic, Rochester, Minn., 1965-68; orthopedic surgeon Oakland (Calif.) Orthopaedic Med. Group, Inc., 1968—; bd. dirs. Trans Pacific Nat. Bank, San Francisco ; mem. exec. bd. Trans Pacific Nat. Bank, San Francisco, 1986; gen. ptnr. Redwood Athletic Club, Oakland; founder Summit Bank, Oakland; staff mem. Oakland Hosp., Providence Hosp., Oakland, Merritt Hosp., Oakland, Peralta Hosp., Oakland, Children's Hosp. of East Bay. Served to lt. commdr. USNR, 1963-65. Fellow Am. Acad. Orthopedic Surgery, Am. Coll. Surgeons, Internat. Coll. Surgeons; mem. Western Orthopedic Assn., Am. Coll. Sports Medicine, Am. Occupational Med. Assn., Royal Soc. Medicine, Bay Area Knee Soc., Mem. Am. Running and Fitness Assn., Alpha Epsilon Delta, Phi Beta Kappa, Alpha Omega Alpha. Republican. Office: Oakland Orthopaedic Med Group 3300 Webster St Suite 803 Oakland CA 94609

AUERBACH, IRVING, chemist; b. Cleve., May 24, 1919; s. Jacob and Fannie (Rothmen) A.; m. Hertha Bienes, July 4, 1969. BS in Chemistry, Ohio State U., 1942, PhD in Chemistry, 1948. Research assoc. Case Western Res. U., Cleve., 1948-49, Cleve. Indsl. Research, 1949-51; mem. research staff Goodyr. Research, Akron, Ohio, 1951-57; mem. tech. staff Sandia Nat. Labs., Albuquerque, 1957—. Contbr. articles to profl. jours. Fellow AAAS (chmn. phys. scis. div. 1982-84), N.Mex. Acad. Scis. (pres. 1960-62), Am. Inst. Chemists; mem. Sigma Xi. Home: 3425 Tahoe NE Albuquerque NM 87111 Office: Sandia Nat Labs PO Box 5800 Albuquerque NM 87185

AUERBACK, SANDRA JEAN, social worker; b. San Francisco, Feb. 21, 1946; d. Alfred and Molly Loy (Friedman) A.; m. Joseph Gauthier, June 10, 1968 (div. Aug. 1978). BA, U. Calif., Berkeley, 1967; MSW, Hunter Sch. Social Work, 1972. Diplomate clin. social work. Case aide Spaulding Youth Ctr., Tilton, N.H., 1968-69; case worker Lakeside Sch., Spring Valley, N.Y., 1969-70; clin. social worker Jewish Family Services, Bklyn., 1972-73, Hackensack, N.J., 1973-78; pvt. practice psychotherapy San Francisco, 1978—; dir. intake adult day care Jewish Home for the Aged, San Francisco, 1979—. Bd. dirs. Demarest (N.J.) Little Theater, 1977-78. Mem. Nat. Assn. Social Workers (cert., bd. dirs. Bay Area Referral Service 1983-87, chmn. referral service 1984-87, state practice com. 1987—, rep. to Calif. Council Psychiatry, Psychology, Social Work and Nursing 1987—, chmn. 1989), Mental Health Assn. San Francisco (trustee 1987—), Am. Group Psychotherapy Assn., Am. Soc. Aging, Spouses of Gays (founder). Home: 1100 Gough St Apt 8C San Francisco CA 94109 Office: 450 Sutter San Francisco CA 94108

AUGARTEN, STAN, technical writer; b. N.Y.C., Nov. 25, 1952; s. Abraham and Clara (Herzberg) A. BA, SUNY, Stony Brook, 1975; MA in U.S. History, Columbia U., 1977. Staff writer Lowry, Russom & Leeper Pub. Rels., San Francisco, 1979-81; instr. dept. journalism San Francisco State U., 1981; news writer, producer KTVU-TV Oakland, KRON-TV San Francisco, Calif., 1981-82; reporter Peninsula Times Tribune, Palo Alto, Calif., 1983-85; columnist PC mag., N.Y.C., 1985-86; sr. tech. writer Next, Inc., Palo Alto, 1987—; lectr. computer sci., Stanford (Calif.) U., 1985; co-founder, Liquid Crystal Optics, Inc., Soquel, Calif., 1987. Author: State of the Art: A Photographic History of the Integrated Circuit, 1983, Bit by Bit: An Illustrated History of Computers, 1984. Office: Next Inc 3475 Deer Creek Rd Palo Alto CA 94304

AUGSBURGER, WILSON LEE, army officer; b. Salem, Oreg., Feb. 19, 1939; s. William Ray and Billie (Polstra) A.; m. Frieda Bleich, June 17, 1967; children: Gretchen, Nikola. MusB, Wheaton Coll., 1960; MS, Juilliard Sch. Music, 1963; MA in Health Adminstrn., Baylor U., 1979. Commd. 1st lt. U.S. Army, 1963, advanced through graded to lt. col., 1984; platoon leader comdr. 46th Med. Bn., Fed. Republic of Germany, 1963-66; asst. registrar U.S. Army Hosp., Ft. Gordon, Ga., 1966-67; chief patient adminstrn. div. Frankfurt, Fed. Republic of Germany, 1969-72; patient adminstr. Office of Surgeon Gen., Washington, 1973-77; chief patient adminstrn. div. Blanchfield Army Hosp., Ft. Campbell, Ky., 1979-83, Acad. Health Scis., Ft. Sam Houston, Tex., 1983-84; dir. patient adminstrn. Fitzsimons Army Med. Ctr., Aurora, Colo., 1984—. Decorated Meritorious Service medal with oak leaf cluster. Mem. Am. Coll. Healthcare Execs., Assn. Mil. Surgeons U.S., Julliard Alumni Assn. Baptist. Home: 16 Halloran Circle Aurora CO 80045 Office: Fitzsimons Army Med Ctr Aurora CO 80045

AUGUST, RICHARD BRUCE, electrical engineer, consultant; b. Miami, Fla., June 19, 1952; s. John Joseph and Patricia Adele (Beaton) A.; B.S.E.E., U. So. Calif. 1973; M.S.E.E., M.I.T., 1974; m. Kathleen Leslie Perez, May 15, 1977; children: Richard Bruce II, Lesley Brooke. Pres., chmn. bd. dirs. Paradigm Techs. Corp., 1984—. Developer imaging systems for Viking and Voyager Space probes; mem. Viking and Voyager imaging team NASA Jet Propulsion Lab.; developer instrumentation telemetry system USAF Global Positioning System; developer TACFIRE/CCS arty. fire direction system for U.S. Army, developer communications systems for all source analysis system/enemy situation correlation element for U.S. Army, USAF Intelligence System. Inventor paradigm sphere. Mem. exec. com. Internat. Boxing Hall of Fame, Las Vegas; trustee Rep. Presdl. Task Force. Served with USNR. Mem. Am. Soc. Engrs. and Architects (former pres.). Contbr. papers to profl. insts. Home: 2680 Monterey Rd San Marino CA 91108

AUGUSTINE, BRADFORD GORDON, restaurateur, real estate executive; b. Seattle, Mar. 10, 1959; s. Webster and Jean (Ross) A.; m. Linda Burner, Aug. 23, 1986. BA in Hotel, Restaurant Adminstrn., Wash. State U., 1984. Owner, operator Stereo-Wholesalers, Seattle, 1977-78, The Corner Deli, Pullman, Wash., 1978-83; ptnr. Augustine Properties, Seattle, 1978—; pres. Christopher-Pullman Corp., Seattle, 1979-85; ptnr. Puget Sound Properties, Seattle, 1979—; pres., chief exec. officer Rare Bird Restaurants, Inc., Seattle, 1982—; pres. Everett (Wash.) Marina tenants Assn., 1984—. Sponser Ann. Waterfront 10K Run Providence Found., 1984—, Children's Hosp. Hospices de Beaune Wine Dinner, 1985, Salty Sea Days, Everett, 1984—, Snohomish Co. Family Counseling Benefit Dinner, 1986-87. Named Eagle Scout Boy Scouts Am., 1973; recipient Partnership award Snohomish County Family Counseling, 1986, 87. Mem. Nat. Restaurant Assn., Restaurant Assn. Wash. State., Seattle Tennis (chmn. food and beverage com. 1987—). Republican. Congregational. Office: Rare Bird Restaurants Inc 1724 W Marine View Dr Everett WA 98122

AUGUSTINE, RODNEY EUGENE HOPE, financial executive; b. Mpls., Mar. 31, 1947; s. Eugene Frank Augustine; m. Janet Marie Reyer, June 14, 1969 (div. 1978); m. Susan Augustine Hope, Mar. 17, 1980. BA, Bemidji State Coll., 1969; MEd, U. Minn., 1971. Elem. tchr. Lincoln County Sch. Dist., Lincoln City, Oreg., 1971-73, 74-79, 80-83, City and Borough of Juneau (Alaska), 1973-74; mem. staff World Edn. Ctr., Berkeley, Calif., 1979-80; co-owner, head chef Augustine's Restaurant, Bellevue, Oreg., 1983-87; pres. Augustine Fin. Svcs., McMinnville, Oreg., 1986—. Office: Augustine Fin Svcs Inc 1340 Yamhill St McMinnville OR 97128

AUREL-SCHNEIDER, JEANNE, artist, educator; b. San Francisco, May 12, 1930; d. Fernand Eugene and Marie-Therese Rose (Raynal) Aurel; m. Donald Leo Schneider, July 21, 1951; children: Catherine Marie, John Frederick, Frederick Aurel, Martin Eugene. BA, Mills Coll., Oakland, Calif., 1951; MA, San Jose (Calif.) State U., 1973. founder, educator San Jose Mus. Art Sch., 1976-80; featured artist Oakland Mus. Collector's Gallery, 1987-88. One-man shows include San Jose Mus. of Art, 1980, San Jose Inst. of Contemporary Art, 1982; two-person show Whittier Coll., Calif., 1986; three-person show Gallery 30, San Mateo, Calif., 1985. Vol. chmn. Tapestry & Talent-Magic City, San Jose, 1982; curator San Jose Inst. Contemporary Art-Exchange Exhibit, Grenoble, France, 1982; fin. chmn. Cultural Council Com. Edn. Arts, San Jose, 1984-87; mem. visual arts com. San Jose Fine Arts Commn., 1987. Mem. San Jose Mus. Art, San Jose Inst. Contemporary Art, Arts Internat. Roman Catholic. Home: 1129 Via Mateo San Jose CA 95120

AURNESS, CRAIG MICHAEL, photographer; b. L.A., Nov. 20, 1946; s. James K. and Virginia (Chapman) A.; m. Daphne Bowen, Feb. 9, 1974; children: Brian, Holly. BA, Prescott Coll., 1970. Freelance photographer Sunset mag., Menlo Park, Calif., 1971-75, Atlantic Richfield, L.A., 1972-78, Nat. Geog., Washington, 1978-88; prin. owner West Light, L.A., 1978—. Photographer, author: (photo books) Iowa: Americas Heartland, 1982, California: the Golden State, 1986, Colorado, 1987. Mem. Picture Agy. Coun. Am., Am. Soc. Mag. Photographers, Nat. Press Photographers Assn. (v.p. local chpt. 1982, Picture of Yr. award 1982), Am. Soc. Travel Writers. Office: West Light 2223 S Carmelina Los Angeles CA 90064

AUSLANDER, STEVEN LAWRENCE, newspaper editor; b. Passaic, N.J., Oct. 30, 1959; s. Tibor and Myrna Natalie (Sorkin) A.; m. Nancy Mosow, June 20, 1982. BA, U. Ariz., 1983. Pub., editor Tucson Thymes, 1982-83; copywriter Advantage Publs., Tucson, 1982-83; mgr. Am. Multi-Cinema, Tucson, 1984-85; advt. agy. owner Ad Infinitum, Tucson, from 1985; now exec. editor Ariz. Daily Star, Tucson; producer pub. service announcements Pima County Atty's Office, Tucson, 1982. Republican. Jewish. Office: Arizona Daily Star PO Box 26807 Tucson AZ 85726 *

AUSTEN, HALLIE IGLEHART, author; b. N.Y.C., Nov. 4, 1947; d. Francis Nash and Harriet Austen (Stokes) Iglehart. AB, Brown U., 1969; student, Union Grad. Sch., Columbus, Ohio, 1983-86. instr. Nat. Women's Studies Assn. Rutgers U., Camden, N.J., 1984, Graduate Theol. Union, Berkeley, Calif., 1984; lectr. UN Non-Govtl. Orgns, Women's Conf., Copenhagen, 1980, U. Calif., Santa Cruz, Calif., 1978, Berkeley, Calif., 1975-76, 86, 88, Feminist Therapy Ctr. Conf., Malibu, Calif., 1980, Heartwood Coll., Santa Cruz. 1981, Ancient Ways Festival, Harbin, Calif. 1984, Welcome Home Conf., San Francisco State U., 1985, Long Beach Woman spirit, 1988, John F. Kennedy U., Orinda, Calif., 1988, The Spotted Fawn Gallery, Pt. Reyes, 1988. Mem. Museum of Modern Art, San Francisco, 1978, Glyptotek Museum, Copenhagen, 1980, Damon Studio, N.Y.C., 1980, Cerridwen Salon, N.Y.C., 1980, Esalen Inst., Big Sur, Calif., 1981, U. Calif., L.A., 1985; dir., instr. Women In Spiritual Edn., Berkeley, Point Reyes, Calif., 1975—; instr. Nat. Women's Studies Assn. Rutgers U., Camden, N.J., 1984; lectr. U. Calif., Berkeley, 1975-76, 86, 88, Santa Cruz, 1978, Feminist Therapy Ctr. Conf., Malibu, Calif., 1980, UN N.G.O. Women's Conf., Copenhagen, 1980, San Jose State U., 1980, Heartwood Coll., Santa Cruz, 1981, San Francisco State U., 1985, Women's Alliance, Nevada City, Calif., 1985-86, Long Beach Womanspirit, 1988, U. Calif., 1988, John F. Kennedy U., Orinda, Calif., 1988, Calif. Sch. of Herbal Studies, Guerneville, Calif., 1978-80, 83-84, 87-88. Appeared in Take Back The Night, 1978, Presence of the Goddess (Balcorman Films), 1985; Author: (with Harper and Row) Womanspirit: A Guide To Women's Wisdom, 1983, The Great Goddess: Visions of Birth, Death and Sexuality, 1989, (with Harper and Row) Daily Meditations For Women, 1990, Quest: A Feminist Quarterly, 1977; contbr. numerous articles to books, newspaper and mag. Counselor San Francisco Women's Switchboard, 1973-74; instr. Am. Friends Svcs. Com., San Francisco, 1974; workshop leader Nat. Conf. on Violence Against Women, San Francisco, 1977; mem. Nat. Caucus of Women and the Arts, San Francisco, 1982, San Francisco Art Inst., 1982, Nat. Film Bd. of Can., 1985. Mem. San Francisco Women's Found. (assoc. 1983—), Point Reyes Dzog Chen, San Francisco Sonar, Druid Heights Artists Retreat (v.p. 1988—). Democrat. Office: Women In Spiritual Edn PO Box 697 Point Reyes Station CA 94956

AUSTIN, CAROL ROBINSON, government official; b. L.A., Sept. 5, 1936; d. Walter Lee and Dorothy Amelia (Koontz) Robinson; m. Charles Ward Austin, June 10, 1955; children: Catherine Elaine, John McCaine, David Holmes, Thomas Anthony. BA in Geography, Calif. State U., Long Beach, 1971, MA in Geography, 1974. Asst. dir. St. Anselm Indochinese Refugee Ctr., Garden Grove, Calif., 1975-78; tax auditor IRS, Santa Ana, Calif., 1978—. Parish registrar St. Anselm Episcopal Ch., Garden Grove, 1975-78; genealogy counselor Boy Scouts Am., Garden Grove, 1975-85. Mem. Calif. State U.-Long Beach Women's League, Phi Kappa Phi. Democrat. Home: 9726 Mirage Circle Garden Grove CA 92644 Office: IRS 24000 Avila Rd Laguna Niguel CA 92677

AUSTIN, CHARLES RAY, business owner, entrepreneur, farmer; b. Boulder, Sept. 13, 1944; s. Everly Wolfer and Oneta Lucille (King) A.; m. Linda Kay Flynn, Apr. 15, 1967 (div. Sept. 1975); children: Monica Lynn, David Everly; m. Patricia Lora Sullivan, Dec. 5, 1977; stepchildren: Patrick Beasley, Dana Beasley, Jay Beasley. Grad. high sch., Longmont, Colo. With parts sales div. Hajek Chevrolet, Longmont, 1965-67, Russ Lyons Chevrolet, Boulder, 1967-68; with chem. sales div. Arapahoe Chems., Boulder, 1968-69, Dayton, Ohio, 1969-74; with ins. sales dept. Great West Life, Boulder, 1974-76; owner, pres. Liqui-Lawn, Inc., Hygiene, Colo., 1975—, Revegetation Exch., Inc., Louisville, Colo., 1985—. Mem. Colo. Assn. Lawn Care Profls., Internat. Erosion Control Assn., Associated Landscape Contractors Colo., High Altitude Revegetation Assn., Yellowstone Recreation Assn. (treas. Longmont chpt. 1985—). Home: 8941 Woodland Rd Longmont CO 80501 Office: Revegetation Exch Inc 760 S 104th Louisville CO 80027

AUSTIN, DANIEL LYNN, insurance association manager; b. Holyoke, Colo., Dec. 29, 1952; s. Frank and Delores (Fisbeck) A.; m. Deborah L. Ocken, Sept. 7, 1974; children: Jordan K., Lindsey L. Bachelor degree, Colo. State U., 1975. Loan officer Fed. Land Bank, Denver, 1975-76, Greeley, Colo., 1976-78; credit officer Fed. Land Bank, Wichita, Kans., 1978-79; br. mgr. Fed. Land Bank, Colorado Springs, Colo., 1979-82; chief exec. officer Fed. Land Bank, Denver, 1982-86; adminstr. and mgmt. Farm Credit Svcs., Greeley, 1986-87; dist. rep. Aid Assn. for Lutherans, Greeley, 1987--. Mem. pres. cabinet Aid Assn. Lutherans, 1988. Named Nat. 4-H Winner, 1972, Lion of the Yr., Lions Club, 1982. Mem. Centennial Rotary (sec. 1988). Republican. Lutheran. Home and Office: Aid Assn for Luths 1414 41st Ave Greeley CO 80634

AUSTIN, DARRELL GLEN, protective services official; b. Portales, N.Mex., May 3, 1936; s. Glen Oren and Birdie Mae (Lane) A.; m. Wiley Jean Smith, Oct. 30, 1954; children: Elizabeth Jean, James Robert Glen (dec.), Darrell Keith. Grad., High Sch. Salesman Meads Fine Bread, Portales, 1955-57; fireman Portales Fire Dept., 1957-59; patroman N.Mex. State Police, 1959-75; sgt. N.Mex. State Police, Las Cruces, Grants, N.Mex., 1975-83; lt. N.Mex. State Police, Grants, Las Vegas, Gallup, N.Mex., 1983-87; capt. N.Mex. State Police, Gallup, 1987-88; instr. N.Mex. pupil trans. Silver City, N.Mex., 1968—; state trustee Fraternal Order of Police Grants. Founder Dona Ana Search & Rescue Coun., Las Cruces, 1976; vol. cons. ARC, Albuquerque, 1972-73; mem. Mid-Rio Grande EMS Coun., 1977. Named Vol. of Yr., Albuquerque, 1981; recipient Citation of Merit, Civil Air Pastrol, 1981, Clara Barton award, ARC, 1981. Mem. N.Mex. Sheriff & Police Assn. (bd. dirs.), N.Mex. Emergency Med. Tech. Assn. (pres. 1972-73, bd dirs. 1975-81), N. Mex. Mounted Patrol (hon. life), Elks, Lions (chartered, all offices 1965-71). Democrat. Baptist. Home: PO Box 1908 600 Cedar Grants NM 87020

AUSTIN, EUGENE HOWARD, writer; b. Poughkeepsie, N.Y., Sept. 1, 1926; s. Eugene Hiram and Florence A.; ed. Coll. of Sequoias; m. Lucy Mary Ruggiero, Nov. 18, 1950; children—Lucyanne, Eugene John. Free lance writer, poet, 1972—. Mem. Kings County Grand Jury, 1979-80, Kings County Parole Commn., 1980—. Served with USN, 1943-46; served as master sgt. U.S. Army, 1951-57. Recipient Disting. Service citation Conn. dept. Am. Legion. Mem. Am. Security Council (nat. adv. bd.), Am. Def. Preparedness Assn., U.S. Naval Inst., DAV (life, charter mem. comdrs. club), VFW (past comdr. Nisei Liberty Post, 24th dist., sr. vice comdr. Dept. Calif.). Club: K.C. (4th deg.). Home: 8606 La Vaca Way Hanford CA 93230

AUSTIN, GRETCHEN BACH, educator; b. San Francisco, Aug. 14, 1936; m. William L.W. Austin, Aug. 22, 1959; children: John Whitney, Stephen Fuller, Carter Bach. BS, U. Oreg., Eugene, 1958. Cert. elem. and jr. high sch. tchr. Tchr. Punahou Sch., Honolulu, 1958-59; tchr. Monte Vista Sch., Monterey, Calif., 1959-60, Gallinas Sch., San Rafael, Calif., 1961-62; tchr. various elem. and mid. schs. Novato, Calif., 1964—. Mem. Novato Fedn. Tchrs. (staff rep.). Republican. Episcopalian. Home: 2166 St Augustine Circle Petaluma CA 94954

AUSTIN, JAMES ALBERT, healthcare executive, obstetrician-gynecologist; b. Phoenix, Sept. 23, 1931; s. Albert Morris and Martha Lupkin (Mercer) A.; m. Margaret Jeanne Arnold, July 26, 1952 (div. Dec. 1978); children: Cynthia Milee Ludgin, Lauri Jeanne Henson, Wendy Patrice Rea; m. Sandra Lee Marsh, Jan. 3, 1979; stepchildren: Kathleen Elizabeth Bush, Daniel Bush, Jeffrey Bush. BA, U. So. Calif., 1952; MD, George Wash. U., 1956; MBA, Pepperdine U., 1987. Diplomate Am. Bd. Ob-Gyn. Ob-gyn. Washington Gynecologists, Washington, 1966-69; pres. Ariz. Obstetrics and Gynecology Ltd., Phoenix, 1969-79; chmn. dept. ob-gyn. USN, Agana Hgts., Guam, 1979-81; ob.-gyn. Sanger Med. Group, Coronado, Calif., 1981-83; chmn. ob-gyn. FHP, Inc., Salt Lake City, 1983-84, assoc. med. dir., 1984-85; hosp. med. dir. FHP, Inc., Fountain Valley, Calif., 1985-86; assoc. v.p. med. affairs FHP, Inc., Fountain Valley, 1987—; clin. prof. ob-gyn. George Wash. U., Georgetown, Washington, 1966-69; asst. clin. prof. U. Calif. San Diego, 1981-83, U. Utah, Salt Lake City, 1983-85. Rear adm. USNR, 1956-88. Fellow Am. Coll. Ob-Gyn.; mem. AMA, Am. Acad. Med. Dir., Ariz. Med. Assn. (bd. dirs. 1978). Republican. Presbyterian. Home: 14230 Oakdale Dr Lake Mathews Perris CA 92370-8419 Office: FHP Inc 9900 Talbert Ave Fountain Valley CA 92708-5153

AUSTIN, PHILIP EDWARD, university chancellor; b. Fargo, N.D., 1942; s. William and Angelyn A.; m. Susan Gates. B.S., N.D. State U., 1964, M.S., 1966; M.A., Mich. State U., 1968, Ph.D., 1969. Economist U.S. Office of Mgmt. and Budget, Washington, 1971-74; dep. asst. sec. HEW, Washington, 1974-77; acting asst. sec. HEW, 1977; dir. doctoral program in pub. policy George Washington U., Washington, 1977-78; provost, v.p. for acad. affairs Bernard Baruch Coll., N.Y.C., 1978-84; pres. Colo. State U., Fort Collins, 1984-89; chancellor U. Ala. System, Tuscaloosa, 1989—. Served with U.S. Army, 1969-71. Decorated Bronze Star. Mem. Am. Econ. Assn., Am. Assn. Higher Edn., Beta Gamma Sigma. Address: 700 Breakwater Dr Fort Collins CO 80525 Office: U Ala System Office of Chancellor Tuscaloosa AL 35487-0102

AUTRY, GENE (ORVON GENE AUTRY), actor, radio entertainer, broadcasting executive, baseball team executive; b. Tioga, Tex., Sept. 29, 1907; s. Delbert and Elnora (Ozmont) A.; m. Ina Mae Spivey, Apr. 1, 1932; m. Jacqueline Ellam, 1981. Grad., Tioga (Tex.) High Sch., 1925. R.R. telegraph operator Sapulpa, Okla., 1925; owner, chmn. bd. Calif. Angels; pres. Flying A Prodns.; owner Sta. KMPC AM & KEDG FM, Hollywood, Calif., Stas. KVI & KPLZ Radio, Seattle, Golden West Broadcasters; pres. several music and publ. cos. Made first phonograph record of cowboy songs, 1929; radio artist Sta. WLS, Chgo., 1930-34; motion picture actor, 1934-53, including In Old Santa Fe; starred in 88 musical Western feature pictures, 91 half-hour TV pictures 1950-55; has written or co-written over 200 songs including That Silver-Haired Daddy of Mine, 1931, You're the Only Star in My Blue Heaven, 1938, Dust, 1938, Tears On My Pillow, 1941, Be Honest With Me, 1941, Tweedle O'Twill, 1942, Here Comes Santa Claus, 1948; host Melody Ranch Theater Nashville Network, 1987, 88. Served with USAAF, 1942-45. Mem. Internat. Footprinters. Clubs: Masons (33 degree), Shriners, Elks. Address: PO Box 710 Los Angeles CA 90078 Office: care Calif Angels PO Box 2000 Anaheim CA 92803

AU-YEUNG, HANG STEPHEN, software engineer, consultant; b. Hong Kong, Dec. 3, 1953; came to U.S., 1973; s. Yue and Yau Lan (Sit) A-Y. BS in Math., Coll. Notre Dame, 1974; MS in Computer Sci., Coll. William and Mary, 1976; MS in Indsl. Engring., U. Calif., Berkeley, 1981. Instr., systems analyst Norfolk State Coll., Norfolk, Va., 1976-78; programmer Datapoint Corp., Berkeley, Calif., 1978, Electronic Research Lab., U. Calif., Berkeley, Calif., 1978-81, Tera Corp., Berkeley, Calif., 1980-81; software engr. NCA Corp., Sunnyvale, Calif., 1981-82, Tolerant Systems, Inc., San Jose, Calif., 1982-88; sr. software designer Stratus Computer, Inc., Saratoga, Calif., 1988; sr. mem. tech. staff Object Scis. Corp., Menlo Park, Calif., 1988—; cons. BIT Software, Inc., Milpitas, Calif., 1987--. Mem. Assn. for Computing Machinery. Home: PO Box 360685 Milpitas CA 95035 Office: Object Scis Corp 4700 Bohannon Dr Ste 125 Menlo Park CA 94025

AUZAT, GEORGE DOUGLAS, insurance agency administrator; b. Crystal City, Mo., Feb. 8, 1943; s. Robert William and Myra O. (Bond) Z.; m. Linda Lee Chilton, Feb. 17, 1962 (div. 1983); children: Robert David, Holly G., William D.; m. Judy Lynn Hanes, Mar.13, 1988. BS in Edn., So. Ill. U., 1965. Tchr. Lindberge Schs., St. Louis, 1965-67; agt. State Farm Ins. Co., St. Louis, 1967-71, agy. mgr., 1971-74; dir. agy. State Farm Ins. Co., San Diego, 1975-79; agy. mgr. State Farm Ins. Co., Westlake Village, Calif., 1979-88, Glendale, Calif., 1989—. Mem. Am. Assn. CLUs (v.p. 1974-75). Republican. Roman Catholic. Office: 454 W Broadway Glendale CA 91204

AVAKOFF, JOSEPH CARNEGIE, plastic surgeon; b. Fairbanks, Alaska, July 15, 1936; s. Harry B. and Margaret (Adams) A.; m. Teddy I. Law, May 7, 1966; children: Caroline, Joey, John. AA, U. Calif., Berkeley, 1955, AB, 1957; MD, U. Calif., San Francisco, 1961; JD, Santa Clara U., 1985. Bar: Calif. 1987; diplomate Am. Bd. Surgery, Am. Bd. Plastic Surgery. Physicist U.S. Naval Radiol. Def. Lab., San Francisco, 1957, 59; intern So. Pacific Gen. Hosp., San Francisco, 1961-62; resident in surgery Kaiser Found. Hosp., San Francisco, 1962-66; resident in plastic surgery U. Tex. Sch. Medicine, San Antonio, 1970-72; pvt. practice specializing in surgery Sacramento, 1966-70; pvt. practice specializing in plastic surgery Los Gatos and San Jose, Calif., 1972—; clin. instr. surgery Sch. Medicine U. Calif., Davis, 1967-70; chief dept. surgery Mission Oaks Hosp., Los Gatos, 1988—, chief div. plastic surgery Good Samaritan Hosp., San Jose, 1989—; presenter numerous med. orgns. Contbr. numerous articles to med. jours. Mem. San Jose Adv. Commn. on Health, 1975-82; bd. govs. San Jose YMCA, 1977-80. Fellow Am. Coll. Legal Medicine; mem. AMA, Am. Soc. Plastic and Reconstructive Surgeons, Calif. Med. Assn., Santa Clara County Bar Assn., Santa Clara County Med. Soc., Union Am. Physicians and Dentists, Phi Beta Kappa, Phi Eta Sigma. Republican. Presbyterian. Home: 6832 Rockview Ct San Jose CA 95120 Office: 15899 Los Gatos-Almaden Rd Los Gatos CA 95032

AVALLE-ARCE, JUAN BAUTISTA, language educator; b. Buenos Aires, Argentina, May 13, 1927; came to U.S., 1948; s. Juan B. and Maria Avalle-Arce; m. Constance Marginot, Aug. 20, 1953 (dec. 1969); children: Juan Bautista, Maria Martina, Alejandro Alcantara; m. Diane Janet Pamp, Aug. 30, 1969; children: Maria la Real Alejandra, Fadrique Martín Manuel. A.B., Harvard U., 1951, M.A., 1952, Ph.D., 1955. Tutor, Harvard U., 1953-55; asst. prof., then assoc. prof. Spanish, Ohio State U., 1955-62; prof. Spanish, Smith Coll., 1962-66, Sophia Smith prof. Hispanic studies, 1966-69; William Rand Kenan, Jr. prof. Spanish, U. N.C., 1969-84; prof. Spanish above scale U. Calif.-Santa Barbara, 1984—; vis. scholar Univ. Center in Ga., 1972, lectr., 1961—, Univ. Center Va., 1976; vis. prof. U. Salamanca, 1982, 84, 86, 88, U. della Tuscia (Italy), 1988, Sophia U. (Japan), 1988, Kyoto U. Fgn. Affairs, 1988, U. Buenos Aires, 1989; Ph.D. program evaluator N.Y. State Bd. Regents; cons. Council Grad. Schs. in U.S.; reader Nat. Humanities Ctr., Govt. Found. for 5th Centennial of Discovery of Am., Spain; cultural corr. Radio Nacional de España; official guest Eucrentro Colour-biuo, Spain, 1988-89. Author: Conocimiento y vida en Cervantes, 1959, La novela pastoril española, 1959, 2d enlarged edit., 1974, La Galatea de Cervantes, 2 vols., 1961, 2d. rev. edit., 1987, Gonzalo Fernández de Oviedo, 1962, El Inca Garcilaso en sus Comentarios, 1961, Deslindes cervantinos, 1961, Three Exemplary Novels, 1964, Bernal Francés y su Romance, 1966, El Persiles de Cervantes, 1969, Los entremeses de Cervantes, 1969, Don Juan Valera y Morsamor, 1970, El cronista Pedro de Escavias Una vida del Siglo XV, 1972, Suma cervantina, 1973, Narradores hispanoamericanos de hoy, 1973, Las Memorias de Gonzalo Fernández de Oviedo, 2 vols., 1974, El Peregrino en su patria de Lope de Vega, 1973, Nuevos deslindes cervantinos, 1974, Temas hispánicos medievales, 1975, Don Quijote como forma de vida, 1976, Dintorno de una época dorada, 1978, Cervantes, Don Quixote, annotated critical edit., 2 vols., 1978, 3d rev. edit., 1988, Cervantes, Novelas ejemplares, annotated edit., 3 vols., 1982, Lope de Vega, Las hazañas del Segundo David, 1984; La Galatea de Cervantes: 400 Años Después, 1985, Garci Rodriguez de Montalvo: Amadís de Gaula, 2 vols., 1985, Amadís de Gaula: El primitivo y el de Montalvo, 1987, Lecturas, 1987. Trustee Marqués de la Lealtad. Recipient Bonsoms medal Spain, 1961; Guggenheim fellow, 1961; grantee Am. Council Learned Socs., 1965, 68; grantee NEH, 1968, 1978-80; grantee Am. Philos. Soc., 1961, 67; recipient Susan Anthony Potter Lit. prize, 1951; Centro Gallego Lit. prize, 1947; Diploma of Merit, Università delle Arti, Italy; named Grand Companion, Societé Internationale de la Noblesse Héréditaire. Sr. fellow Southeastern Inst. Medieval and Renaissance Studies; hon. fellow Soc. Spanish and Spanish Am. Studies; fellow Colegio Mayor Arzobispo D. Alonso de Fonseca of U. Salamanca; mem. Am. Acad. Research Historians Medieval Spain, Academia Argentina de Letras, Anglo Am. Basque Studies Soc., Cervantes Soc. Am. (pres. 1979—), Soc. de Bibliofilos Espanoles, Modern Humanities Research Assn., South Atlantic Modern Lang. Assn., Assn. Internac. de Hispanistas, Modern Lang. Assn., Renaissance Soc. Am. (nat. del. to exec. council 1971), Real Sociedad Vascongada de Amigos del País, Centro de Estudios Jacobeos, Inst. d'Etudes Medievales, Inst. de Lit. Iberoamericana, Hispanic Soc. Am., Acad. Lit. Studies (charter), Mediaeval Acad. Am., Anglo Am. Basque Studies Soc., Instituto Internacional de Literatura Iberoamericana, Sovereign Mil. Teutonic Order of the Levant (bailiff, knight grand cross, Grand Prior, Grand Priory of the U.S.). Clubs: Triangle Hunt (Durham) (gentleman Whipper-in); U. N.C. Polo, Combined Training Events Assn. Home: Etxeberria 4640 Oak View Rd Santa Ynez CA 93460 Office: U Calif 4323 Phelps Hall Santa Barbara CA 93106

AVARELL, KORY KARIS, small business owner; b. Lake Arrowhead, Calif., Aug. 5, 1952; s. William J. and Virginia (Karis) A.; m. Jean Elizabeth Baugh, Jan. 2, 1977; children: Karynn, Kurt, Kollin, Kyle, Kelly. Grad. high sch., Lake Arrowhead. Owner, pres. Jewel Magic Inc., Culver City, Calif., 1976-78, Hiland Mountain Homes, Inc., Crestline, Calif., 1984—; owner, mgr. Arrowhead Carpet Co., Lake Arrowhead, 1978-83, PCMG, Crestline, 1983-84; bd. dirs. San Bernardino (Calif.) Mountain Bldg. Contractors, Stuart Ranch Water Co., Crestline. Home: Box 6638 Crestline CA 92325 Office: Hiland Mountain Homes Inc Box 6090 Crestline CA 92325

AVERY, GLENN R., publisher; b. Spokane, Wash., Dec. 6, 1945; s. Oral and Genevieve E. (Maher) A.; m. Helen A. McArdle, May 18, 1985. BA, Seattle U., 1967; MA, Ohio State U., 1968. Staff public affairs Weyerhaeuser Co., Everett, Wash., 1971-72; writer Am. Plywood Assn., Tacoma, 1972-75, promotion mgr., 1975-77, advt. mgr., 1977-78; pres. Wood Products Publications, Tacoma, 1978-79, Commerce Pub Corp., Seattle, 1979—; adviser Econ. Devel. Ptnrship., Seattle, 1984—; cons. various publishers, Seattle and Bellevue, 1988. Contbr. articles to profl. jours. Speech writer Senator W. Magnuson's 1968 campaign, Seattle; mem. Mayor's Adv. Com., Everett, Wash., 1971, Community Crime Com., Seattle, 1986-88. Served with U.S. Army, 1969-71. Office: Commerce Pub Corp 2815 2d Ave Seattle WA 98121-1261

AVERY, RICHARD EUGENE, instrumentation engineer; b. Newcastle, Pa., Oct. 21, 1935; s. Francis William and Thelma Marie (Inman) A.; m. Diane Marie Carter, Dec. 3, 1954; children: Richard William, Cynthia Ann. Student, U. Minn., 1956; AS, Pierce-Moorpark Coll., 1964. Rocket engr. test leadman Rocketdyne div. Rockwell Internat., Canoga Park, Calif., 1957-60, reactor operator, 1961, engring. assoc. instrumentman, 1962-68; sr. instrument engr. Rockwell Internat., El Segundo, Calif., 1970-85, Canoga Park, 1985—; sr. mfg. engr. Zerox Corp., El Segundo, 1968-70. Tenor Simi Valley (Calif.) Chorale, 1964; scoutmaster Boy Scouts Am., Simi Valley, 1968-72. Sgt. USAF, 1953-57. Mem. Simi Valley Hist. Soc., U.S. Power Squadron. Republican. Lutheran. Home: 8469 Waters Rd Moorpark CA 93021 Office: Rockwell Rockeydyne Div 6633 Canoga Ave Canoga Park CA 91304

AVILA, EDWARD JOHN, artist; b. Los Angeles, Sept. 26, 1949; s. John C. and Theresa M. (Gonzales) A. BFA, Sonoma State U., 1979; postgrad., Pratt Inst., 1980. Free lance artist Santa Fe Springs, Calif., 1980—. With U.S. Army, 1969-71, Vietnam. Home and Office: 11503 Joslin St Santa Fe Springs CA 90670

AVINA, PHILIP INDALECIO, jewelry designer, business owner; b. Chgo., July 14, 1940; s. Filimon Cecilio and Maxine (Hein) A.; m. Janet Diete, May 12, 1976. Student, Chgo. Art Inst., 1959-60, Tallieseneast Architectral Design, Wis., 1960-61. Instr. arts and crafts Rich High Sch., Park Forest, Ill., 1962-63; co-owner advt. agy. Phoenix, 1962-64; owner Jewelry by Philip, Phoenix and Scottsdale, Ariz., 1975—; speaker in field; instr. gemology (nights) Phoenix Jr. Coll., 1974. Designer 1982 Fiesta Bowl Queens Crown Ariz. State Univ. Co-chair Scottsdale Men's Leagues Culinary Events, 1983—. Recipient Designer award Spectrum Awards Ann. Nat. Competition, 1982; designer "1982" Fiesta Bowl Queens Crown. Mem. Ariz. Jewelers Assn. (asst. bd. dirs. 1976-78). Republican. Roman Catholic. Office: Jewelry by Philip 7373 N Scottsdale Rd D100 Scottsdale AZ 85253

AVNER, SANFORD ELDON, pediatrician; b. Gallipolis, Ohio, Apr. 20, 1940; s. Max and Ruth (Burech) A.; m. Susan E. Messinger; children: David Bryan, Marc Thomas. BA, Yale U., 1962; MD, SUNY, Bklyn, 1966. Diplomate Am. Bd. of Pediatrics, Am. Bd. of Immunology; Am. Bd. Internal Med. and Pediatrics. Sr. staff Nat. Jewish Hosp., 1972—; pres. Colo. Allergy Soc., 1974-76; fellow Am. Bd. Pediatrics, 1974, Am. Acad. Allergy, 1976; assoc. clin. prof. pediatrics U. Colo. Med. Ctr., 1974—. Author (with others) : Allergic Disease Information-Adult, 1988. Served to capt. USAF, 1968-70. Recipient Air Force Commendation medal, 1970. Mem. Physicians for Social Responsibility, AMA, Colo. Med. Soc., Am. Thoracic Soc., Aurora-Adams County Med. Soc. Home: 13 Red Fox Ln Englewood CO 80111 Office: Colorado Allergy and Asthma Clinic 1450 S Havana #500 Aurora CO 80012

AVOLIO, WENDY FREEDMAN, speech-language pathologist; b. Phila., Feb. 24, 1953; s. Harold Stanley and Phyllis Maxine (Broodno) Freedman; m. Michael Howard Strauss, Aug. 31, 1975 (Nov. 1981); 1 child, Nicole Erin; m. Mark Richard Avolio, Mar. 24, 1985. BS, Bradley U., 1973; MA, No. Ill. U., 1975. Speech-lang. pathologist Bartlett (Ill.) Sch. Dist., 1975-76, Proviso Area for Exceptional Children, Maywood, Ill., 1976-77, Cen. Reading and Speech Clinic, Mt. Prospect, Ill., 1977-78, Tucson Unified Sch. Dist., 1978-79, Handmaker Jewish Geriatric Ctr., Tucson, 1981; mgr. speech-lang. therapy program Dept. Econ. Security/Div. Devel. Disabilities, Tucson, 1981-86, So. Ariz. Spl. Edn. Coop., Vail, 1986—; cons. speech-lang. Parent Support Group, Tucson, 1981-87, Ariz. Adv. Com. For Deaf-Blind, Tucson, 1983-87; lang. cons. Community Outreach Program for Deaf, Tucson, 1983. Com. mem. Jewish Community Ctr. Youth and Children Com., Tucson, 1986—. Mem. Am. Speech Lang. and Hearing Assn. (cert.), Ariz. Speech and Lang. Assn. Home: 3532 N Fiesta Del Sol E Tucson AZ 85715 Office: So Ariz Spl Edn Coop PO Drawer #8 Vail AZ 85641

AVRAMIS, VASSILIOS IOANNIS, pediatrics and pharmacology educator; b. Kalamata, Messinia, Greece, Aug. 17, 1950; came to U.S., 1975; s. Ioannis E. and Maria B. (Malama) A.; m. Susan A. Spence, July 17, 1977; children: Ioannis Alexander, Earl V. BS, U. Athens, 1974; MS, Duquesne U., 1977; PhD, U. Houston, 1981. Postdoctoral tng. U. Tex. M.D. Anderson Hosp. and Tumor Inst., Houston, 1980-83; asst. prof. pediatrics and pharmacology U. So. Calif. Schs. Medicine and Pharmacology, L.A., 1983--. Contbr. articles to profl. jours. Am. Cancer Soc. grantee, 1984-87, NIH-Nat. Cancer Inst. grantee, 1986—. Mem. AAAS, Am. Assn. for Cancer Rsch., Am. Soc. for Clin. Oncology, N.Y. Acad. Scis., M.D. Anderson Assocs., Rho Chi. Office: Children's Hosp of LA 4650 Sunset Blvd Los Angeles CA 90027

AWBREY, S. SCOTT, communications executive; b. Lubbock, Tex., Jan. 10, 1952; s. Marvin R. and Opal (Tomlinson) A.; m. Gloria Rae Plant, Jan. 6, 1962; 1 child, Jason Scott. B Journalism, U. Tex., 1978. Dir. communications Re/Max Am., Denver, 1980-83, United Ch. of Religious Sci., L.A., 1986—; dir. info. svcs. Mile Hi Ch. of Religious Sci., Denver, 1983-86. Author: Path of Discovery, 1987; editor numerous jours., newsletters, mags.; contbr. to Sci. of Mind mag. Pres. bd. trustees Mile Hi Ch., 1984-86. Granville-Price scholar, 1978. Mem. Internat. Assn. Bus. Communicators, Religious Pub. Relations Soc.

AWRAMIK, STANLEY MICHAEL, geology educator; b. Lynn, Mass., Aug. 11, 1946; s. Stanley M. and Helen (Leskiewicz) A.; m. Jacqueline Greenshields, July 6, 1985. AB, Boston U., 1968; PhD, Harvard U., 1973. Asst. prof. geol. scis. U. Calif., Santa Barbara, 1974-79, assoc. prof., 1979-85, prof., 1985—. Named to Collegium of Disting. Alumnae, Boston U., 1982. Fellow Am. Assn. for the Advancement of Sci.; mem. Paleontol. Soc., Soc. Econ. Paleontologists and Minerologists, Internat. Soc. for the Study of the Origin of Life. Office: U Calif Dept Geol Scis Santa Barbara CA 93106

AX, PETER, investment banker, lawyer; b. Bklyn., Apr. 23, 1959; s. Joseph and Silvia (Karl) A. BSBA, U. Ariz., 1981, JD, 1984. CPA, Ariz. Lectr. U. Ariz., Tucson, 1983-84; tax mgr. Arthur Andersen & Co., Tucson, 1984-88; v.p. corp. fin. Young Smith & Peacock, Phoenix, 1988—. Recipient Outstanding Lectr. award U. Ariz. Coll. Bus., 1984. Mem. Ariz. Soc. CPA's, 20-30 Club. Republican. Jewish. Home: 4102 N 78th St Apt 103 Scottsdale AZ 85251

AXELROD, STEPHEN LEE, physician; b. Detroit, June 23, 1951; s. Reuben and Selma Josia (Kazanoff) A.; m. Paula Evans, May 24, 1986. BS, U. Mich., 1972; MD, Wayne State U., 1977. Diplomate Am. Bd. Emergency Medicine. Intern Presbyn.-Denver Med. Ctr., 1977-78; emergency physician Emergency Cons. Inc., Petoskey, Mich., 1978-80, Colo. Emergency Med. Assocs., Thornton, 1980-87; physician, med. dir. Med. Ctrs. Colo., Denver, 1980—; clin. instr. Okla. Coll. Medicine and Surgery, Tulsa, 1982-87; chmn. credential com. Humana Hosp., Thornton, 1984—. editorial adv. bd. Medicenter Mgmt. jour., 1986—. Physician Family Builders by Adoption-Fun Run, Denver, 1985-86, Community Home Health Care-Greek Marathon, Seattle, 1984; physician advisor Broomfield (Colo.) Vol. Ambulance Svc., 1980-83; corp. sponsor fin. com. Allied Jewish Fedn., Denver, 1987. Fellow Am. Coll. Emergency Physicians; mem. Colo. Med. Soc., Nat. Assn. for Ambulatory Care (bd. dirs. 1984-86, Cert. of Recognition 1985). Avocations: skiing, travel, squash. Home: 45 S Dexter Denver CO 80222 Office: Med First Inc 1200 17th St Ste 1320 Denver CO 80202

AXELSON, JOSEPH ALLEN, professional athletics executive; b. Peoria, Dec. 25, 1927; s. Joseph Victor Axelson and Florence (Ealen) Massey; m. Malcolm Rae Smith, Oct. 7, 1950; children: David Allen, Mark Stephen, Linda Rae. B.S., Northwestern U., 1949. Sports info. dir. Ga. So. Coll., Statesboro, 1957-60, Nat. Assn. Intercollegiate Athletics, Kansas City, Mo., 1961-62; tournament dir. Bowling Props. Assn. Am., Park Ridge, Ill., 1963-64; asst. exec. sec. Nat. Assn. Intercollegiate Athletics, Kansas City, Mo., 1964-68; exec. v.p., gen. mgr. Cin. Royals Profl. Basketball Team, Cin., 1969-72; mgr. Cin. Gardens, 1970-72; pres., gen. mgr. Kansas City Kings Profl. Basketball Team, Kansas City, Mo., 1972-79, 82-85; pres., gen. mgr. Sacramento Kings Profl. Basketball Team, 1985-88, exec. v.p., 1988—; pres. Arco Arena, Sacramento, 1985-88; exec. v.p. Sacramento Sports Assn., Arco Sports Complex, 1988—; v.p. ops. NBA, N.Y.C., 1979-82, chmn. competition and rules com., 1975-79; trustee Naismith Basketball Hall of Fame. Author: Basketball Basics, 1987. Mem. Emil Verban Meml. Soc., Washington. Capt. Signal Corps. AUS, 1949-54. Named Nat. Basketball Exec. of Yr. The Sporting News, St. Louis, 1973; recipient Annual Dirs. award Downtown, Inc., Kansas City, Mo., 1979, Nat. Assn. Intercollegiate Athletics Frank Cramer Nat. Svc. award, 1983. Mem. Am. Philatelic Soc., Phi Kappa Psi. Republican. Presbyterian. Home: 2950 Pasatiempo Pl Sacramento CA 95833 also: 230 B Ave Coronado CA 92118 Office: Sacramento Kings 1 Sports Pkwy Sacramento CA 95834

AYA, RODERICK HONEYMAN, tax consultant; b. Portland, Oreg., Sept. 17, 1916; s. Alfred Anthony and Grace Myrtle (Honeyman) A.; student U. Oreg., 1935-36, Internat. Accts. Soc., 1937-39, LaSalle Extension U., 1940-42, Walton Sch. Commerce, 1942, U. Calif. Extension, 1945; m. Helen Marjorie Riddle, June 16, 1945 (dec. Dec. 1983); children: Roderick Riddle, Deborah Germaine Aya Reynolds, Ronald Honeyman; m. Kathryn Rehnstrom Chatalas, June 22, 1986; stepchildren: John Todd, Paul Seth, Elizabeth Kate. Chief statistician Hotel Employers Assn., San Francisco, 1939-42; acct. Pacific Tel. & Tel. Co., San Francisco, 1942-52, spl. acct., 1952-63; tax acct., 1963-65; spl. acct. AT&T, N.Y.C., 1965-68, mgr. tax studies, 1968-73, div. mgr. tax research and planning, 1973-80; public acct., San Francisco, 1940—; music tchr., 1959—; v.p., treas., dir. Snell Research Assos., Inc., 1974-79; guest lectr. on taxes Westchester County Adult Edn. Program. Committeeman, Marin County council Boy Scouts Am., 1959-60, com. chmn., 1959-61; mem. Marin County Sheriffs' Reserve, 1963-65; law enforcement liaison com. on Juvenile Control; sec. Am. Nat. Standards Inst. Com. on Protective Headgear, 1967-80. Vice pres., treas., bd. dirs. Snell Meml. Found., 1957-80; trustee Snell Meml. Found. (U.K.), Ltd., 1972-88; mem. chmn.'s com. U.S. Senatorial Bus. Adv. Bd.; mem. Republican Presdl. Task Force; fin. com. Seaside (Oreg.) United Meth. Ch.; dir., past pres. Stuart Highlanders Pipe Band of San Francisco. Recipient Wisdom award of honor Wisdom Soc., 1970; Pres.'s Medal of Merit, 1981. Mem. ASTM, Nat. Soc. Pub. Accts., St. Andrews Soc., Telephone Pioneers Am., Soc. for Ethnomusicology (contbr. to jour.), U.S. Naval Inst., Phi Chi, Sigma Nu. Clubs: Corinthian Yacht (Tiburon, Calif.); Astoria Golf & Country; Sports Car of Am. (San Francisco region treas. 1957-58, dir. 1957-59); U.S. Yacht Racing Union. Author: The Legacy of Pete Snell, 1965; Determination of Corporate Earnings and Profits for Federal Income Tax Purposes, 2 vols., 1966. Home: PO Box 668 Seaside OR 97138

AYAD, BOULOS AYAD, archaeology educator; b. Egypt, May 3, 1928; came to U.S., 1967; s. Ayad A.; m. Suzanne E., Feb. 14, 1970; children: Mary, Thereza, Boulos. B.A., U. Cairo, 1952, M.A., 1957, Ph.D. with honors, 1963; M.A., U. Ain Shams, 1953, Higher Inst. Coptic Studies, 1960. Asst. prof. U. Utah, 1967-68; asst. prof. U. Colo., Boulder, 1968-72, assoc. prof., 1972-77, prof. archaeology and ancient langs. of Middle East, 1977—, univ. fellow, 1974-75. Author: Coptic Grammar and Texts, 1971, The Jewish-Aramaean Communities in Ancient Egypt, 1975, The Aramaeans in Egypt, 1975, The Aramaeans in the Ancient Middle East, 1986, The Jewish-Aramaean Civilization and Its Relationship to the Ancient Egyptian Civilization, 1982, The Four Gospels, 1983; translator: Book of Job (from Syriac into Arabic), 1975; contbr. articles to profl jours. Mem. African Studies Assn., Societe d'Archeologie Copte, AAUP, Am. Assn. Tchrs. Arabic, Smithsonian Instn., Soc. Bible Friends. Coptic Orthodox. Home: 1332 Scrub Oak Circle Boulder CO 80303 Office: U Colo Dept Anthropology Boulder CO 80309

AYALA, JOHN, librarian, associates professor, educator; b. Long Beach, Calif., Aug. 28, 1943; s. Francisco and Angelina (Rodriguez) A.; m. Patricia Marie Dozier, July 11, 1987; children: Juan, Sara. BA in History, Calif. State U., Long Beach, 1970, MPA, 1981; MLS, Immaculate Heart Coll., L.A., 1971. Library paraprofl. Long Beach Pub. Library, 1963-70; librarian L.A. Pub. Library, 1971-72; librarian Long Beach City Coll., 1972--, assoc. prof., 1972--, pres. acad. senate, 1985-87; chmn. L.A. County Com. to Recruit Mexican-Am. Librarians, 1973-74; mem. acad. senate Calif. Community Colls., 1985. Editor Calif. Librarian, 1971. Served with USAF, 1966-68, Vietnam. U.S. Office Edn. fellow for library sci., 1970-71. Mem. ALA (com. mem. 1971-85), Calif. Library Assn., Nat. Assn. to Promote Spanish Speaking Library Svc. (v.p., pres. 1973-76), Nat. Assn. Spanish Speaking Librarians (pres. L.A. County chpt. 1974-76). Democrat. Roman Catholic. Office: Long Beach City Coll Libr 1305 E Pacific Coast Hwy Long Beach CA 90806

AYALA, MITZI HENDERSON, television producer, columnist, farmer; b. Concord, Mass., Mar. 27, 1941; d. Ernest Flagg and Mary (Stevens) Henderson; m. Francisco J. Ayala, May 26, 1968 (div. 1985); children: F. Jose, Carlos Alberto. BA, Harvard U., 1963; MPA, George Washington U., 1965. Mgmt. intern Treasury Dept., Washington, 1963-65; editorial coordinator Ency. Brit., N.Y.C., 1965-68; mgr. Ceres Farms, Sacramento, 1974—; hostess, producer Sta. KXTV, Sacramento, 1980—; columnist Capitol News Service, Sacramento, 1980—. Author: The Farmer's Cookbooks, 1981—; contbr. numerous articles to profl. publs. Bd. dirs., v.p. Sta. KVIE, ednl. TV, Sacramento, 1980; vice chmn. Calif. Expn. and State Fair, Sacramento, 1983-84; mem. citizens adv. com. OEO, USDA, 1985-87, Nat. Govs. Image of Agr. Steering Com., 1985-86, Def. Adv. Com. on Women in Services, 1988—. Recipient Women Helping Women award Soroptimists Internat., Citrus Heights, Calif., 1986. Mem. Am. Agri-Women (pres. 1987—). Republican. Episcopalian. Home: 744 Lake Terr Davis CA 95616 Office: KXTV 400 Broadway PO Box 10 Sacramento CA 95801

AYARS, ALBERT LEE, school administrator, retired; b. Kettle Falls, Wash., Sept. 17, 1917; s. Glen Garrison and Ama Belle (Jennings) A.; m. Frances Louise Schaaf, June 21, 1941; children: Cheron Marie Holman, Judith Louise Templeman, Albert Lee Jr., Danielle Jo Alexander, Garrison Hubert, Debora Ann Dillon, Theodora Ama Crotti, Virginia Darlene Dick. BA in English, Wash. State U., 1939, B Ed, 1940, MA in Edn., 1942, DEd in Edn., Administrn., 1956. Cert. elem. and secondary teaching and administrn., accredited pub. relations counselor. English dept. chmn. Davenport (Wash.) High Sch., 1940-42; prin. Colville (Wash.) HighSch., 1942-45; supt. Omak (Wash.) Pub. Sch., 1945-49, Sunnyside (Wash.) Pub. Sch., 1949-52; assoc. dir. Joint Council on Edn. Edn., N.Y.C., 1952-53; dir. edn. dept., v.p. John W. Hill Foundn., Hill and Knowlton, Inc., N.Y.C., 1953-65; supt. Spokane (Wash.) Pub. Sch., 1965-72; supt. Norfolk (Va.) Pub. Sch., 1972-83, supt. emeritus, 1983--; vis. prof., lectr. Wash. State U., Mich. State U., U. Del., and others; adj. full prof. Old Dominion U., 1984-85; exec. officer Southeastern Cooperative Ednl. Programs 1977-83; cons. in planning of U. tchr. workshops; adv. com. U.S. Mil. Acad., West Point, Nat. Training Lab., and others. Author: (with others) How to Plan a Community Resources Workshop, 1975, (with others) The Teenager and the Law, 1978; author: The Teenager and Alcohol, 1970, Administering the People's Schools, 1957, How to Plan Your Community Resources Workshop, 1954; contbr. articles to profl. jours. Bd. dirs. Inland Empire Boy Scout Council, Council of Spokane County, Spokane Lilac Festival Assn., March of Dimes, Inland Empire YMCA, Northwest Regional Edn. Lab, 1962-72, Eastern Washington Hist. Soc., 1968-72, Spokane Symphony Soc., 1965-72, Urban League of Tidewater, 1978--, Cultural Experiences Unlimited, 1976-85, Juv. Ct./Pub. Sch. State Task Force, 1976; Edn. adv. com. Am. Cancer Soc., N.Y., 1963-65; exec. com. mem. N.Y.C. Council on Econ. Edn., 1963-65, and others. Recipient Am. Assn. of Sch. Adminstr. Leadership for Learning award, 1983, disting. service award, Am. Assn. of Sch. Administr., 1984, U.S. Treasury service medal for war bond sales, 1945, Baha'I Community Human Rights award, Spokane, 1972, Va. 4-H Alumni award, 1977. Mem. Pub. Relations Soc. of Am., Internat. Inst. of Arts and Letters, Am. Assn. Sch. Adminstr. Large City Supt. Group, Horace Mann League (v.p. 1979-80, pres.-elect, 1980-81, pres. 1981-82), Phi Kappa Phi, Phi Delta Kappa, Kappa Delta Pi, Delta Chi, Rotary, Mason. Baptist. Home: 4827 102nd Ln NE Kirkland WA 98003

AYCOCK, JOEL, astronomical telescope technician; b. Seattle, June 30, 1950; s. Marcus Hillman and Shirley Elaine (Williams) A. BA in Physics, Reed Coll., 1972; postgrad., U. Hawaii, 1976-77. Fire fighter USDA Forest Service, Portland, Oreg., 1969-72; data processor Sta. KGW TV, Portland, 1972-73; chief of consumer services Data Internat., Honolulu, 1975-76; laser ranger LURE Obs., Kula, Hawaii, 1977-85, chief opto-mech. technician, 1983-85; telescope technician UK Infrared Telescope, Hilo, Hawaii, 1985—. Co-discoverer Supernova 1986G, 1986. Prodn. support Videololo II, Honolulu, 1976—; contract video technician Ohlmeyer Prodn., ABC Sports, NBC Sports, ESPN, Los Angeles, 1976—; co-producer (video) Lanikai Tennis Tournament, 1983. Home: PO Box 1659 Keaau HI 96749 Office: UKIRT 665 Komohana Hilo HI 96720

AYER, FORREST K., personnel director; b. St. Louis, Jan. 7, 1930; s. Charles Harris and Loretta Josephine (Kuhlman) A. BS, U. Mo., 1957. Adminstrv. trainee Miss. Valley Barge Line, St. Louis, 1957-58; personnel dir. Yuba Power Products, Inc., Cin., 1958-60; personnel analyst Calif. State Personnel Bd., San Francisco, 1961-63; indsl. relations asst. San Francisco Port Authority, 1963-69; dir. of personnel Office of Edn. San Mateo County, Redwood City, Calif., 1969—. Bd. dirs. Skyline County Water Dist., Woodside, Calif., 1973-80, Kings Mountain Assn., Woodside, 1974-76. Served with U.S. Army, Japan and Korea. Mem. Internat. Personnel Mgmt. Assn., Calif. Sch. Personnel Commrs. Assn. (treas., bd. dirs. 1972-88, treas. salary survey group com. 1985-87, Schuyler C. Joyner award 1987, One and Only award 1987), Sch. Personnel Commrs. Assn. of No. Calif. Democrat. Roman Catholic. Clubs: Afghan Hound, Scottish Deer Hound. Home: 12400 Skyline Blvd Woodside CA 94062 Office: San Mateo County Office of Edn 333 Main St Redwood City CA 94063

AYERS, EVERETTE LEE, highway patrol director; b. Bowling Green, Va., Dec. 20, 1940; s. Everette L. and Hauzie (Rouse) A.; m. Donna Rae Rose, Aug. 24, 1961; children: Jeff, Shelley. Student, Laramie County Community Coll., 1976-77. Patrolman Why. Hwy. Patrol, Wheatland, 1964-72; sgt. Why. Hwy. Patrol, Rawlins, 1972-76; sgt. Why. Hwy. Patrol, Laramie, 1976-78, lt., 1978-81; maj. Why. Hwy. Patrol, Cheyenne, 1982-85, col., 1985—. Served with USAF, 1959-63. Mem. Peace Officer's Standards Tng. Commn., Internat. Assn. Chiefs of Police, Am. Assn. Motor Vehicle Adminstrs., Wyo. Hwy. Patrol Assn. Methodist. Lodge: Odd Fellows. Office: Wyo Hwy Patrol 5300 Bishop Blvd PO Box 1708 Cheyenne WY 82002-9019

AYERS, JAMES LEE, consulting company executive; b. Fort Worth, May 28, 1919; s. I. Edwin and Anna May (Houck) A.; m. Rennie Kay, Dec. 20, 1943; 1 child, Avril Rennie. Higher B.Tech. Sc. with 1st class honors in Elec. Engring., Manchester U., Eng., 1950, also assoc. Manchester Coll. Tech., 1950; postgrad. Imperial Coll., London, 1951-52, UCLA, Westwood,

1960-61. With Lockheed Overseas Corp., Langford Lodge Base, No. Ireland, 1942-44, research labs. GEC Ltd., Stanmore, Middlesex, Eng., 1950-56; head advanced devel. electronic systems Convair, San Diego, 1956-59; chief engr. electronics Lear, Inc., Santa Monica, Calif., 1959-63; space systems design, planning and mgmt. positions Hughes Aircraft Co., Los Angeles, 1963-76, mgr. advanced program ops. Space and Communications Group, 1967-76, mgr. advanced proposals Electro Optical and Data Systems Group, 1976-84; dir. Laser Tech., Inc., North Hollywood, Calif., v.p., 1964; v.p. Total Bus. Cons., Oceanside, Calif., 1983-86; mgmt. and cost analysis cons. Patentee in field; predesign and proposal mgr. Early Bird (Intelsat I), 1964-65. Pres. Malibu Freeway Com., Calif., 1962-66; mem. Malibu Community Coordinating Com., 1970-79; dir. Eastern Malibu precinct Malibu Twp. Council, 1970-77, treas. council, 1973-75. Served with Signal Corps, USAAF, 1944-46. Registered chartered eng., U.K. Fellow Instn. Elec. Engrs., Eng.; mem. IEEE (life), AIAA, Manchester Tech. Assn. (life), North County Concert Assn., UCLA Alumni Assn. (life), Big Rock Assn. Malibu (pres. 1962-63, 70-72). Club: Ocean Hills Country (bd. dirs., v.p. 1984-86). Home and Office: 4535 Cordoba Way Oceanside CA 92056

AYERS, STEPHEN THOMAS, air force officer, architect; b. Roanoke, Va., Aug. 13, 1962; s. William Bennett and Jane Harrison (Proffitt) A.; m. Jennifer Anne McIntosh, Sept. 21, 1985; 1 child, Stephanie Alison. BArch, U. Md., 1985; MS in Systems Mgmt., U. So. Calif., 1988. Commd. 2d. lt. USAF, 1985, advanced through grades to 1st lt., 1987; intern architect USAF, Edwards AFB, Calif., 1985—. Mem. Handicapped Individuals Program, Edwards AFB, 1985—. Mem. Am. Mil. Engrs. (chmn. program com. 1987—), Acad. Mgmt., Nat. Trust Hist. Preservation, Officers Open Mess. Roman Catholic. Home: 9 Kellie Ct Edwards AFB CA 93523-5000 Office: USAF AFFTC/DEEE Edwards AFB CA 93523-5000

AYLEN, ROBERT JOHNSTON, dentist; b. Sumner, Wash., Nov. 21, 1921; s. Charles Herbert and Beatrice Harriet (Hopkinson) A.; m. Patricia Jeanne Howard, Nov. 6, 1942; children: Molly Jo Aylen Tekel, Marc Andrews. DDS, U. Wash., 1950. Gen. practice dentist Puyallup, Wash., 1950—; part-time clin. dental instr. Sch. Dentistry U. Wash., 1950-58. Served to 1st lt. USAAF, 1942-45. Fellow Internat. Coll. Dentists; mem. Acad. Operative Dentists, ADA, Pierce County Dental Assn. Club: Tacoma Yacht. Lodges: Elks, Kiwanis. Home: 1405 21st SW Puyallup WA 98371 Office: 11208 94th Ave E Puyallup WA 98373

AYOUB, GEORGE TANIOS, electro-optics engineer; b. Hammana, Lebanon, Jan. 24, 1951; came to U.S., 1974; s. Tanios Tannous and Helene J. Ayoub; m. Manuella Issa Hindi, Jan. 31, 1988. Ingenieur diploma, U. St. Joseph, Beirut, 1974; MBA, U. Nebr., 1977, PhD in Engring., 1976. Postdoctoral fellow U. Nebr., Lincoln, 1976-78; rsch. scientist Marathon Oil Co., Denver, 1978-82; cons. AREC, London and Abu Dhabi, 1982-87; dir. Internat. Robomation Intelligence, Carlsbad, Calif., 1987—; cons. OAPEC, Kuwait, 1982-86. Contbr. articles to profl. jours. Mem. Optical Soc. Am., Sigma Xi. Home: 3341 Tournament Dr Oceanside CA 92056

AYRES, JANICE RUTH, social service executive; b. Idaho Falls, Idaho, Jan. 23, 1930; d. Low Ray and Frances Mae (Salem) Mason; m. Thomas Woodrow Ayres, Nov. 27, 1953 (dec. 1966); 1 child, Thomas Woodrow Jr. MBA, U. So. Calif., 1952, M in Mass Communications, 1953. Asst. mktg. dir. Disneyland, Inc., Anaheim, Calif., 1954-59; gen. mgr. Tamasha Town & Country Club, Anaheim, Calif., 1959-65; dir. mktg. Am. Heart Assn., Santa Ana, Calif., 1966-69; state exec. dir. Nev. Assn. Mental Health, Las Vegas, 1969-71; exec. dir. Clark Co. Easter Seal Treatment Ctr., Las Vegas, 1971-73; mktg. dir., fin devel. officer So. Nev. Drug Abuse Coun., Las Vegas, 1973-74; exec. dir. Nev. Assn. Retarded Citizens, Las Vegas, 1974-75; assoc., cons. Don Luke & Assocs., Phoenix, 1976-77; program dir. Inter-Tribal Coun. Nev., Reno, 1977-79; exec. dir. Ret. Vol. Program, Carson City, Nev., 1979—; conductor workshops in field. Named Woman of Distinction Soroptimist, 1988, Outstanding Dir. Excellence Nev. Gov. Bryan, 1989. Mem. Nat. Pub. Rels. Soc. Am. (chpt. pres.), women in Radio & TV, AAUW, Am. Assn. Profl. Fund Raisers, Nev. Fair & Rodeo Assn. Home: 1624 Karin Dr Carson City NV 89701 Office: Ret Sr Vol Program 308 N Curry St Ste 209 Carson City NV 89703

AZAR, RICHARD YAFFAR, real estate developer; b. Montebello, Calif., Nov. 10, 1965; s. Fernando and Ofelia (Yaffar) A. AS, Don Bosco Tech. Inst., 1985; BArch, Calif. Poly. Pomona, 1985. Bldg. intern City of Montebello, 1984-88; real estate agt. Home Brokers, Whittier, Calif., 1988—. Active Southern Orthodox Youth Orgn. Republican. Christian Orthodox. Clubs: Demolays. Home: 11527 Scenic Dr Whittier CA 90601 Office: Home Brokers 15334 E Whittier Blvd Ste 3 Whittier CA 90603

AZARCON, GERARDO FRANCIS VIRAY, data process executive; b. Manila, Apr. 23, 1964; came to Can., 1965; came to U.S., 1970; s. Alejandro Olandez and Corazon (Viray) A. BA in Computer Sci. and Bus. Mgmt., Cen. Coll., 1986. Systems analyst, programmer Meredith Corp., Des Moines, Iowa, 1986-87; rep. acct. Personal Computer Ctr., Torrance, Calif., 1987; sr. rep. acct. Computerland Laguna Hills, Calif., 1987-88; prin., developer Heartbeat Software Solutions, Cerritos, Calif., 1988—. Mem. ARC. Mem. Assn. Computing Machinery, Boston Computer Soc., World Wildlife Fund, Smithsonain Institution. Roman Catholic. Office: Heartbeat Software Solutions PO Box 4497 Cerritos CA 90703-4497

AZAROW, CHARLES, retired sugar corporation executive; b. Jersey City, Dec. 12, 1918; s. Isaac and Ruth (Laurie) A.; m. Dolores Marie Willcockson. Student, Hudson Coll. With B.W. Dyer & Co., N.Y.C., 1937-52; v.p. sugar div. Pepsico, Purchase, N.Y., 1952-68; pres. sweetener div. Sucrest Corp., N.Y.C., 1968-77; pres. Revere Sugar Corp., N.Y.C., 1977-81; pres., chief exec. officer Nat. Sugar Refining, N.Y.C., 1981-82; vice chmn. Holly Sugar Corp., Colorado Springs, Colo., 1982-86; pres., chief exec. officer Holly Sugar Corp., Colorado Springs, 1986-88; cons. in sugar industry, 1988—. Counsilman Demarest, N.J., 1975-77. Served with U.S. Army, 1941-45. Mem. U.S. Beet Sugar Assn., Sugar Assn., Inc., Internat. Sugar Club (past pres.), Sugar Industry Technologists, N.Y. Coffee/Sugar Exchange (on spot com.). Office: Holly Sugar Corp 100 Chase Stone Ctr Colorado Springs CO 80903

AZPEITIA, ANTHONY GEORGE, engineering specialist; b. Los Angeles, June 6, 1937; s. Sebastian Duran and Florinda (Vaca) A.; m. Aida Fierro, July 28, 1962; children: Anna A., Armando A., Alisa E. AA, L.A. Trade Tech., 1971. Mgr. service Copease Corp., Los Angeles, 1952-64; repairman Pacific Telephone, San Pedro, Calif., 1955-59; tech. rep., specialist Xerox Corp., Los Angeles, 1964-82; engring. specialist Xerox Corp., City of Industry, Calif., 1982—; mem. adv. com. Trade Tech. Elec. Curriculum, Los Angeles, 1974-81. Gov. Ch. Guilds, Gardena, Calif., 1970-75; com. chmn. Boy Scouts Am., 1973-75. Mem. Hispanic Assn. Profl. Advancement (chmn., treas. Los Angeles chpt. 1976-80.). Democrat. Roman Catholic. Office: Xerox Corp 13240 E Amar Rd City of Industry CA 91746

AZUMANO, GEORGE ICHIRO, travel agent; b. Portland, Oreg., June 9, 1918; s. Hatsutaro and Satsuki (Kinouchi) A.; m. Ise, Nov. 18, 1943 (dec. 1974); children: Loen, Bette-Jo-Jim; m. Nobuko, Mar. 21, 1976. BS, U. Oreg., 1940. Owner grocery store, 1940-41, 42; owner Azumano Ins. Agy., Portland, 1946—, Azumano Travel Svc., Inc., Portland, 1949—, Overseas Courier Svc., Portland, 1976—. Mem. Oreg. Tourism Coun., Salem, 1983—; bd. trustees Willamette View Manor Retirement Home, Portland, 1983-88, Willamette U., Salem, 1988—. Recipient Fourth Class Order of the Rising Sun, Gov. Japan, Portland, 1982, Outstanding Contbn. award to travel and tourism industries, Portland, 1985. Mem. Am. Soc. Travel Agts., Rotary (bd. dirs. 1980-82). Republican. Methodist. Home: 2802 SE Moreland Ln Portland OR 97202 Office: Azumano Travel Svc Inc 320 SW Stark St #600 Portland OR 97204

BABAUTA, JUAN NEKAI, senator; b. Saipan, No. Mariana Islands, Sept. 7, 1953; s. Santiago Miyasaki and Carmen (Nekai) B. BS, Ea. N.Mex. U., 1976, MA, 1976; MS, U. Cin., 1979. Health planner TTPI Dept. Health Services, Saipan, 1977; dep. exec. dir. State Health Planning Agy., Saipan, 1979, exec. dir., 1980-86; senator No. Marianas Commonwealth Legislature, Saipan, 1986—; instr. No. Marianas Coll., Saipan, 1986. Chmn. bd. regents No. Marianas Coll., 1982-83, 84-86; chmn. Bd. Edn., Saipan, 1982-83, 84-86; mem. Med. Profession Licensing Bd., Saipan, 1983-86, Nat. State Bd. Edn., Saipan, 1982-86. Mem. Phi Kappa Phi. Republican. Roman Catholic. Home: PO Box 1004 Saipan MP 96950 Office: No Mariana Islands Legislature Capitol Bldg Saipan MP 96950

BABAYANS, EMIL, financial planner; b. Tehran, Iran, Nov. 9, 1951; came to U.S., 1969; s. Hacob and Jenik (Khatchatourian) B.; m. Annie Ashjian. B.S., U. So. Calif., 1974, M.S., 1976; m. Annie Ashjian. Cert. fin. planner; chartered life underwriter, fin. cons. Pres. Babtech Internat., Inc., Sherman Oaks, Calif., 1975-85; sr. ptnr. Emil Babayans & Assocs., Woodland Hills, Calif., 1985—. Mem. Am. Mgmt. Assn., Nat. Assn. Life Underwriters, Inst. Cert. Fin. Planners, Internat. Assn. Fin. Planners, Am. Soc. CLU and Chartered Fin. Cons. Armenian Orthodox. Office: 21041 Burbank Blvd Suite 200 Woodland Hills CA 91367

BABBITT, BRUCE EDWARD, former governor of Arizona; b. June 27, 1938; m. Hattie Babbitt; children—Christopher, T.J. BS magna cum laude, U. Notre Dame; MS, U. Newcastle, Eng., 1962; LL.B., Harvard U., 1965. Bar: Ariz. Assoc. Brown and Bain, Phoenix, 1965-74; atty. gen. State of Ariz., Phoenix, 1975-78; gov. State of Ariz., 1978-87; mem. President's Commn. on Accident at Three Mile Island, 1979-80; chmn. Nuclear Safety Oversight Com., 1980-81, Western Govs.' Policy Office, 1982; mem. Adv. Commn. on Intergovtl. Relations, 1980-84; chmn. task force on fed. budget deficit Roosevelt Ctr. for Am. Policy Studies, 1984; chmn. Nat. Groundwater Policy Forum, 1984—. Author: Color and Light: The Southwest Canvases of Louis Akin, 1973, Grand Canyon: An Anthology, 1978. Trustee Dougherty Found. Recipient Thomas Jefferson award Nat. Wildlife Fedn., 1981, spl. conservation award Nat. Wildlife Fedn., 1983. Mem. Nat. Govs. Assn. (chmn. subcom. on water resources), Democratic Govs. Assn. (chmn. 1985). Democrat. Office: 3300 N Central Ave Ste 1650 Phoenix AZ 85012 *

BABCOCK, MALIN MARIE, biologist; b. Juneau, Alaska, Oct. 31, 1939; d. Douglas P. and Lillian L. (Peterson) B.; children: Douglass Howard Murray, Gwendolyn Marie Murray. BS, Oreg. State U., 1962; MS, U. Alaska, 1969. Physiologist Arctic Health Rsch. Ctr, USPHS, Fairbanks, Alaska, 1966-69; fishery rsch. biologist Auke Bay (Alaska) Lab. Nat. Oceanic & Atmospheric Adminstrn., Nat. Marine Fisheries, 1969—; pres. Mendenhall chpt. Federally Employed Women, Inc., Juneau, 1986-88. Contbr. articles to profl. jours. Organizer, firefighter Lynn Canal Vol. Fire Dept., Juneau, 1974-80. NSF fellow, 1966; recipient Fed. Employee of Yr. award Juneau Fed. Exec. Assn., 1986. Mem. AAUW, Am. Fisheries Soc., Am. Inst. Fisheries Res. Biology, Nat. Shell Fisheries Assn., Pioneers of Alaska. Home: PO Box 211033 Auke Bay AK 99821 Office: NOAA/NMFS Auke Bay Lab PO Box 210155 Auke Bay AK 99821

BABCOCK, PETER H., professional sports executive; b. Bangor, Maine, May 12, 1949; s. Bernard Roland and Jeanne Sargent (Heartz) B.; m. Yolanda Marie Cava; children: Amy, Katherine. BA, Ariz. State U., 1971, MA, 1976. Tchr., coach Glendale Union High Sch. Dist., Phoenix, 1972-80; asst. coach San Diego Clippers, 1980-82, dir. player pers., 1982-83, v.p. basketball ops., 1983-84; dir. player pers. Denver Nuggets, 1984-85, dir. basketball ops., 1985-86, v.p. basketball ops., 1986-87, pres., gen. mgr., 1987—; mem. competition and rules com. and dir. Chgo. pre-draft camp, NBA, 1985—. Mem. bd. addiction rsch. and treatment svcs. U. Colo. Med. Sch., 1986—, vis. mem. dept. psychiatry, 1989—; mem. bd. Adopt-A-School, Denver Pub. Schs., 1985-89; adv. bd. Big Brothers, Denver, 1985—, Kops N Kids, 1987—; exec. com. Communities for Drug Free Colo., Denver, 1987—; pres. NET Found./Charitable Fundraising, 1987—; mem. Mayor's Coun. on Phys. Fitness, 1987—. Mem. NBA (competition and rules com. 1985—, dir. Chgo. pre-draft camp 1985—), Denver C. of C. (sports com. 1987—). Episcopalian. Office: Denver Nuggets 1635 Clay St PO Box 4658 Denver CO 80204

BABCOCK, WILLIS, mechanical engineer; b. Waukesha, Wis., May 31, 1922; s. Barney and Helen (Reuter) B.; student Northland Coll., 1941-42, M.I.T., 1945-48, Cornell U., 1948; M.S.M.E., Century U., 1982; m. Elizabeth Anne Zimmerman, Sept. 26, 1947; children—Rudolph, Kathryn, Willis W., Gregory, Janet, Deborah. Chief engr. Domestic Engine and Pump Co., Shippensburg, Pa., 1948-53; chief engr. research and devel. Aurora Pump Co. (Ill.), 1953-59; v.p. engring., exec. v.p., gen. mgr. Carver Pump Co., Muscatine, Iowa, 1959-63, cons., 1963-64; chief engr. Mission Valve & Pump Co., Houston, 1964-66; dir. research and devel. Mech. Equipment Co., New Orleans, 1966-68; program mgr. Battelle N.W. Labs., Richland, Wash., 1968-71; sr. project engr. Emco Wheaton Inc., Conneant, Ohio, 1971-72; chief engr. Sta-Rite Industries, Inc., Delavan, Wis., 1972-77; mgr. engring. Wayne Home Equipment Co., Ft. Wayne, Ind., 1977-80; with Rockwell Internat., Richland, Wash., 1980—. Served with AUS, 1942-45. Mem. ASME, Nat. Soc. Profl. Engrs. Baptist. Home & Office: 8032 Penway Indianapolis IN 46226-5964

BABEL, HENRY WOLFGANG, astronautics company manager; b. Chgo., Oct. 14, 1933; s. Willi Paul and Frieda Martha (Schultz) B.; m. Joyce Joan Smoda, Nov. 15, 1952(div. 1980); children: Lisa Leigh Babel Ruegg, Todd Henry, Kurt Allan, Karen Leigh, Paul Allen; m. Ryoko Nakagawa, Mar. 14, 1980; children: James Takashi, Michiko Lori. Student, Ill. Inst. Tech., 1951-52; BSME, U. Ill., 1955, MSME, 1957; PhD, Ohio State U., 1966. Asst. instr. U. Ill., Champaign-Urbana, 1955-57; metall. engr. Battelle Meml. Inst., Columbus, Ohio, 1957; instr. Ohio State U., Columbus, 1957-60; engring. mgr. McDonnell Douglas Astronautics, Huntington Beach, Calif., 1960—. Contbr. articles to profl. publs.; patentee in field. TV moderator, session organizer Major Econ. Issues Newport Found., Newport Beach, Calif., 1983—; pres. Home Owners Orgn., Huntington Beach, 1971-78, HomeownersWatch Program, Huntington Beach, 1977-78. Mem. Soc. Materials and Processes. Home: 6872 Loyola Dr Huntington Beach CA 92647

BABIKIAN, GEORGE H., petroleum products company executive. BS, Syracuse U., 1953. With Atlantic Refining Co., 1954-69, sales supr., 1957-67, regional mgr., 1967-69; with Atlantic Richfield Co. (now ARCO), 1969—, mgr. sales devel., 1969-70, gen. mgr. Rocky Mountain Plains area, 1970-72, retail mgr. East Coast, 1972-74, retail sales mgr., 1974-76, v.p. retail mktg., 1976-77, v.p. wholesale mktg., 1977-78, sr. v.p., 1978—; now pres. ARCO Products Co. with USN, 1946-48, 51-53. Office: ARCO Products Co 1055 W 7th St PO Box 2570 Los Angeles CA 90051 *

BABINCHAK, DONALD LEAVITT, mining company executive; b. Rock Springs, Wyo., Nov. 8, 1935; s. Andrew Edward and Maribelle (Leavitt) B.; m. Kae Geddes; children: Paige, Brion Troy, Stephanie, Trecia Kae. BS in Polit. Sci., Utah State U., 1969, MPA, 1970. Dir. project Kennecott, Salt Lake City, 1970-72, dir. compensation, 1972-84, dir. human resources, 1984-87, v.p. human resources, 1987—. Registered lobbyist Utah State Legislature, Salt Lake City, 1984—; bd. dirs. Jr. Achievement, Salt Lake City, 1987—. With U.S. Army, 1956-58, Korea. Mem. Am. Soc. for Personnel Adminstrn., Am. Compensation Assn. Republican. Reorganized Ch. of Jesus Christ of Latter-day Saints. Home: 3009 E 9800 S Sandy UT 84092 Office: Kennecott 10 E South Temple Salt Lake City UT 84147

BABINEC, GEORGE FREDERICK, savings and loan association auditor; b. Bridgeport, Conn., Apr. 29, 1957; s. George and Jean Lois (Williams) B.; m. Janice Lynn Carlson, Oct. 25, 1982; children: Kathryn Jean, Margaret Ann, Todd Alfred. BA in Acctg., U. Bridgeport, Conn., 1979; postgrad., Ariz. State U., Tempe, 1987—; grad. bank adminstrn., U. Wis., 1988. Chartered bank auditor, 1984; cert. internal auditor, 1986. Internal staff auditor Milton H. Friedberg, Smith and Co., CPA's, Bridgeport, 1978, People's Bank, Bridgeport, 1978-79; mgr. in audit dept. Union Trust Co., Stamford, Conn., 1980-83, Western Savs. and Loan Assn., Phoenix, 1983—; compliance officer bank secrecy Western Savs. and Loan Assn., Phoenix, 1987—. Mem., supporter Phoenix Zoo, 1984, Heard Mus., Phoenix, 1988—; vol. Ariz. Spl. Olympics, Tempe, 1987. Mem. Inst. Internal Auditors (bd. of govs. Phoenix chpt. 1987—), Bank Adminstrn. Inst. (v.p. Ariz. chpt. 1986-88, pres., bd. dirs. 1988—). Republican. Episcopalian. Home: 4051 E Jicarilla St Phoenix AZ 85044 Office: Western Savs & Loan Assn 3200 E Camelback Rd Ste 253 Phoenix AZ 85018

BABINGTON, RENNIE FREDERIC, real estate broker, educator; b. Oakland, Calif., May 21, 1938; s. Suren H. and Mary (Dieckmann) B.; m. Jerilynn Ann Ganiats, July 15, 1984; 1 child, Alexandria Jeanette. BA, St. Mary's Coll., Moraga, Calif., 1962; MA, Calif. State U., 1971. Tchr. Hawyard (Calif.) Unified Sch. Dist., 1968—; v.p., sec. Jerilynn Babington Inc., Real Estate, Piedmont, Calif., 1987—; real estate broker Oakland, Calif., 1968—; ptnr. J. Praditamas & Co., San Francisco, 1984—. Bd. dirs. Berkeley Med. Ctr., 1965-75; fundraiser Rep. Party, Alameda County, 1980—; bd. dirs. Havens Fathers Club, Piedmont, 1986—; mem. Piedmont Ednl. Found., 1986—; mem. Rep. Presdl. Task Force. Mem. Am. Fedn. Tchrs. (del. 1976-78), Hayward Fedn. Tchrs. (pres. 1977-80), Nat. Council for Social Studies, Calif. Council for Social Studies, Calif. PTA, Claremont Country Club, Berkeley Tennis Club, Phi Delta Kappa. Republican. Office: 2220 Mountain Blvd #207A Oakland CA 94611

BABISH, TIMOTHY JAMES, physiologist; b. Seweckly, Pa., Mar. 19, 1951; s. Frank Theodore and Ruth Elizabeth (Booth) B.; children: Jenifer, Lance, Kristi, Timothy James Jr., 1 adopted child, Nicholas. BS in Biol. Scis., U. Mont., 1972; AS, Mt. San Antonio Coll., 1975; MS in Biochemistry, U. Southern Calif., 1978, PhD in Physiology, 1980. Tech. dir. dept. physiology U. Calif. Med. Ctr., Irvine, 1975-77; sales mgr. Oxy Med Inc., Chatsworth, Calif., 1977-84; tech. rep. US Surgical Corp., Norwalk, Conn., 1984-86; mfrs. rep. Neurometrics Inc., San Diego, 1986-88, Puritan-Bennett Corp., Carlsbad, Calif., 1988—. Com. mem. Calif. State Bd. Licensure, Sacramento, 1981. Mem. Am. Lung Assn. (exec. com.). Republican. Baptist.

BACA, AUGUSTINE CHRISTOBAL, executive administrator, human services consultant; b. Albuquerque, Mar. 29, 1949; s. Pedro Griego Baca and Josefita (Gonzales) B.; m. Jeanette Elizabeth Temer, Sept. 19, 1975; children: Marcos Gabriel, Angelo Christobal. BS in Bus. Adminstrn., U. Albuquerque, 1972; MA in Pub. Adminstrn., U. N.M., 1973; postgrad., N.M. Highlands U., 1976. Intern Dept. Arch. U. N.M., Albuquerque, 1972; govt. intern Dept. Econ. Devel., Albuquerque, 1972-73; exec. dir. Youth Devel., Inc., Albuquerque, 1973—; cons. Nat. Assn. Counties, Washington, 1980-81, Coalition Spanish Speaking Mental Health Orgns., Washington, 1982-83, Clinch Powell, Tazewell, Tenn., 1989. Mem. President's Com. on Juvenile Justice, Washington, 1975; pres. Bd. of Albuquerque Family Health Ctr., 1977-79; trustee U.N.M. Mental Health, Albuquerque, 1986-87; advisor Capitol Cities ABC Inc. Youth Plus, Washington, 1989; fellow Western Interstate Commmn. on Higher Edn., 1972-73, Housing and Urban Devel., 1972-73; chmn. Gov.'s Commn. on Juvenile Justice, 1973-76. Recipient Thomas Jefferson award, Sta. KOAT-TV, Alburquerque, 1986, Service award, STA. KLUZ, Alburquerque, 1989; named Leader of Tomorrow, Alburquerque Magazine, 1988. Mem. Kiwanis, Optimist Internat. Office: Youth Devel Inc 1710 Centro Familiar SW Albuquerque NM 87105

BACA, JOSEPH FRANCIS, judge; b. Albuquerque, Oct. 1, 1936; s. Amado and Inez (Pino) B.; m. Dorothy Lee Burrow, June 28, 1969; children: Jolynn, Andrea, Anna Marie. BA in Edn., U. N.Mex., 1960; JD, George Washington U., 1964. Asst. dist. atty. 1st Jud. Dist., Santa Fe, 1965-66; pvt. practice Albuquerque, 1966-72; dist. judge 2d Jud. Dist., Albuquerque, 1972-88; justice N.Mex. Supreme Ct., Santa Fe, 1989—; spl. asst. to atty. gen. Office of N.Mex. Atty. Gen., Albuquerque, 1966-71. Dem. precinct chmn., Albuquerque, 1968; del. N.Mex. Constl. Conv., Santa Fe, 1969. Mem. ABA, N.Mex. Bar Assn., Albuquerque Bar Assn., U. N.Mex. Alumni Assn. (pres. 1980-81), Kiwanis (pres. Albuquerque chpt. 1984-85), KC (dep. grand knight 1968). Roman Catholic. Office: NMex Supreme Ct PO Box 848 Santa Fe NM 87504-0848

BACCIGALUPPI, ROGER JOHN, agricultural company executive; b. N.Y.C., Mar. 17, 1934; s. Harry and Ethel (Hutcheon) B.; m. Patricia Marie Wier, Feb. 6, 1960 (div. 1978); children: John, Elisabeth, Andrea, Jason; m. Iris Christine Walfridson, Feb. 3, 1979. B.S., U. Calif., Berkeley, 1956; M.S., Columbia U., 1957. Asst. sales promotion mgr. Maco Mag. Corp., N.Y.C., 1956-57; mdsg. asst. Honig, Cooper & Harrington, San Francisco and L.A., 1957-58, 1958-60; asst. dir. merchandising Honig, Cooper & Harrington, 1960-61; sales rep. Blue Diamond Growers (formerly Calif. Almond Growers Exch.), Sacramento, 1961-64, mgr. advt. and sales promotion, 1964-70; v.p. mktg. Blue Diamond Growers (formerly Calif. Almond Growers Exch.), 1970-73, sr. v.p. mktg., 1973-74, exec. v.p., 1974-75, pres., 1975—; bd. dirs. Almond Bd. Calif., Nat. Coun. Farmer Coops., Grocery Mfrs. Am., Inc.; vice chmn., bd. dirs. Agrl. Coun. Calif., mem. consumer-producer com., adminstrn. com.; mem. U.S. adv. com. TRADE Negotiations, 1983—, U.S. adv. bd. Rabobank Nederlands. Vice chmn. Calif. State R.R. Mus. Fedn.; active Los Rios Community Coll. Found. Dist.; bd. visitors U. Calif., Davis; vice chmn. Grad. Inst. of Cooperative Leadership, 1986—, chair, 1987—. With AUS, 1957. Mem. Calif. C. of C. (internat. trade com., bd. dirs. 1988—, statewide agrl. com.), Sacramento C. of C. (bd. dirs. host com. 1983), Calif. for Higher Edn., Grad. Inst. Coop. Leadership (chmn., trustee), Grocery Mfrs. Am., Inc. (mem., bd. dirs. 1988—), Sutter Club, Del Paso Country Club. Office: Calif Almond Growers Exch 1802 C St Sacramento CA 95814

BACH, MARTIN WAYNE, stockbroker, owner antique clock stores; b. Milw., Mar. 30, 1940; s. Jack Baer and Rose (Weiss) B.; m. Roberta Sklar, Aug. 19, 1962; children: David Louis, Emily Elizabeth. BA, U. Wis., 1963. Stockbroker J. Barth & Co., Oakland, Calif., 1966-72, v.p., 1970-72; sr. v.p., stockbroker Dean Witter & Co., Oakland, 1972—; founder The TimePeace, Carmel, Calif., 1972-83, San Francisco, 1975—, La Jolla, 1977—; instr. fin. San Leandro Lafayette and Hayward (Calif.) Adult Sch., 1970—. Chmn. bd. dirs. Diablo Light Opera Co., 1985—; bd. dirs. East Bay Hosp., 1985—. Served to 1st lt., U.S. Army, 1963-65. Mem. Calif. Thoroughbred Breeders Assn., Calif. Thoroughbred Assn., Nat. Assn. Clock & Watch Collectors, Am. Horse Council. Clubs: East Bay Brokers, Moraga Country, Dean Witter Chairmen's. Lodge: B'nai B'rith. Home: 180 Sandringham S Moraga CA 94556 Office: 1 Kaiser Plaza Suite 1950 Oakland CA 94556

BACH, MURIEL DUNKLEMAN, author, actress; b. Chgo., May 14, 1918; d. Gabriel and Deborah (Warshauer) Dunkleman; m. Joseph Wolfson, June 16, 1940 (div. Apr. 1962); 1 child, Susan; m. Ira J. Bach, Apr. 14, 1963 (dec. Mar. 6, 1985); stepchildren: Caroline Bach Marandos, John Lawrence; m. Josef Diamond, May 18, 1986. Student Carleton Coll., 1935-37; BS, Northwestern U., 1939. Researcher original manuscripts for One-Woman Theatre, also costume designer, writer, set designer; actress TV commls., indsl. films, radio commls.; photog. model; tchr. platform speaking techniques to corp. execs. Active sr. citizens groups, youth groups. Recipient Career Achievement award Chgo. Area Profl. Pan Hellenic Assn., 1971. Mem. Screen Actors Guild, AFTRA, Arts Club, Wash. Athletic Club, Seattle Tennis Club, Rainiers Club, Zeta Phi Eta. Author: (plays) Two Lives, 1958; ... because of Her!, 1963; Madame, Your Influence is Showing, 1969; MS ... Haven't We Met Before?, 1973; Lady, You're Rocking the Boat!, 1976; Freud Never Said It Was Easy, 1978; Of All the Nerve, 1982; vignettes for theatre.

BACHER, ROSALIE WRIDE, educational administrator; b. Los Angeles, May 25, 1925; d. Homer M. and Reine (Rogers) Wride; AB, Occidental Coll., 1947, MA, 1949; m. Archie O. Bacher, Jr., Mar. 30, 1963. Tchr., English, Latin, history David Starr Jordan High Sch., Long Beach, Calif., 1949-55, counselor, 1955-65, Lakewood (Calif.) Sr. High Sch., 1965-66; research asst., counselor Poly. High Sch., Long Beach, 1966-67; counselor, office occupational preparation, vocational guidance sect. Long Beach Unified Sch. Dist., Long Beach, 1967-68; vice prin. Washington Jr. High Sch., Long Beach, 1968-70; asst. prin. Lakewood Sr. High Sch., Long Beach, spring 1970; vice prin. Jefferson Jr. High Sch., Long Beach, 1970-81, Marshall Jr. High Sch., Long Beach, 1981-87; vice prin. Lindbergh Jr. High Sch., Long Beach, 1987—; counselor Millikan High Sch., 1988—, Hill Jr. High Sch., 1988—; chmn. vocat. guidance steering com. Long Beach Unified Sch. Dist., 1963—. Mem. Internat. Platform Assn., AAUW, Long Beach Personnel and Guidance Assn. (dir. 1958-60), Long Beach Sch. Counselors Assn. (sec. high sch. segment 1963-64), Phi Beta Kappa, Delta Kappa Gamma (pres. Delta Psi chpt., area dir.; Calif. profl. affairs com. chmn. 1972-74), Phi Delta Gamma (pres. chpt. 1977-78, 87—, nat. chmn. bylaws com. 1980-81, Nat. Conv. Com. 1987-88), Pi Lambda Theta (pres. chpt. 1974-76, v.p. So. Calif. council 1974-76), Phi Delta Kappa (sec. Long Beach chpt. 1977-80, pres. 1988—). Home: 265 Rocky Point Rd Palos Verdes

Estates CA 90274 also: 17721 Misty Ln Huntington Beach CA 92649 Office: Hill Jr High Sch 1100 Iroquois Ave Long Beach CA 90815

BACHMAN, BRIAN RICHARD, electronics executive; b. Aurora, Ill., Jan. 14, 1945. BS, U. Ill., 1967; MBA, U. Chgo., 1969. Mktg. mgr. Gen. Electric Semiconductor Products, Syracuse, N.Y., 1982-85; bus. dir. TRW Electronic Assemblies Div., Schaumburg, Ill., 1985-87; pres. Gen. Semiconductor Industries, Tempe, Ariz., 1987—. Bd. dirs., sec. Ariz. Assn. Industries, Phoenix, 1987—. Mem. Assn. Corp. Growth. Office: Gen Semiconductor Industry 2001 W 10th Pl Tempe AZ 85281

BACHSTEIN, HARRY SAMUEL, lawyer, educator; b. Oakland, Calif., Aug. 6, 1943; s. Elizabeth (Rodenhouse) B.; m. Kathy Ann Hill; children: Harry S. III, David Jason, Shane Thomas, Jacob William, Jesse Remington. BS in Bus. Adminstrn., No. Ariz. U., 1966; JD with honors, U. Ariz., 1969. Bar: Ariz. 1969, U.S. Supreme Ct. 1973, U.S. Ct. Customs and Patent Appeals, U.S. Dist. Ct. Ariz., U.S. Ct. Appeals (9th cir.), U.S. Bankruptcy Ct. Spl. investigator ethics com. Pinal County Bar Assn., 1971; juvenile ct. referee Ariz. Superior Ct., 1972-76; mem. Superior Ct. Med. Liability Rev. Panel, 1981, Domestic Relations Rules com., 1988; lawyer arbitrator Better Bus. Tucson. Mem. Devel. Authority for Tucson's Expansion, 1970-76; mem. U.S. Presdl. Task Force, 1981—; faculty Pima Coll., 1982-83. Mem. State Bar of Ariz. (sec., exec. council young lawyers' sect. 1972-73), ABA (Ariz. rep. com. on div. law and procedures 1976), Pima County Bar Assn. (grievance com. 1978-86, spl. investigator for ethics com. 1971), Profl. Assn. of Diving Instrs., Profl. Diving Instrs. Corp. (cert. open water scuba instr. 1988), Confdn. Mondiale des Activites Subaquatiques de Paris (instr.), Delta Chi (sec., pledgemaster 1961-65). Clubs: Optimist Internat. (state gov. Ariz. 1976, lt. gov. 1972-73, pres. 1971-72, Outstanding Gov. and Disting. Gov. 1976), Mason. Editor: Ariz. Law Rev., 1967-69. Avocations: hunting, deep sea diving. Office: PO Box 43188 Tucson AZ 85733-3188

BACHTEL NASH, ANN ELIZABETH, educational consultant, researcher, educator; b. Winnipeg, Man., Can., Dec. 12, 1928; d. John Wills and Margaret Agnes (Gray) Macleod; m. Richard Earl Bachtel, Dec. 19, 1947 (div.); children: Margaret Ann, John Macleod, Bradley Wills; m. Louis Philip Nash, June 30, 1978. AB, Occidental Coll., 1947; MA, Calif. State U.-Los Angeles, 1976; PhD, U. So. Calif., 1989. Cert. tchr., adminstr., Calif. Elem. tchr. pub. and pvt. schs. in Calif., 1947-50, 64-77; dir. Emergency Sch. Aid Act program, spl. projects, spl. arts State of Calif., 1977-80; leader, mem. program rev. team Calif. State Dept. Edn., 1981—; cons. Pasadena Unified Sch. Dist., 1981—; teaching asst., adj. prof. U. So. Calif.; cons. sch. dists., state depts. edn.; presenter workshops/seminars; mem. legis. task forces. Chmn. resource allocation com. City of Pasadena, Pasadena-Mishima (Japan) Sister Cities Internat. Com.; mem. Los Angeles World Affairs Council, docent council Pasadena Hist. Soc., Pasadena Philharm. Com., women's com. Pasadena Symphony Assn.; Emergency Sch. Aid Act grantee, 1977-81. Mem. World Council Gifted and Talented Children, Internat. Soc. Edn. Through Art, Council Exceptional Children, Am. Ednl. Research Assn., Assn. Supervision and Curriculum Devel., Nat. Art Educators Assn., Calif. Art Educators Assn., Calif. Humanities Edn. Assn., AAUW, Phi Delta Kappa, Kappa Delta Pi, Pi Lambda Theta, Assistance League of Pasadena. Contbr. articles to publs.; writer/editor: Arts for the Gifted and Talented, 1981; author Nat. Directory of Programs for Artistically Gifted and Talented Students, K-12. Office: 732 Pinehurst Dr Pasadena CA 91106

BACHUS, BENSON FLOYD, mechanical engineer, consultant; b. LeRoy, Kans., Sept. 19, 1917; s. Perry Claude and Eva Marie (Benson) B.; m. Ruth Elizabeth Beck, May 31, 1942; children: Carol Jean Schueler, Bruce Floyd, Linda Ruth Gadway. Degree, Hemphill Diesel Sch., Chgo., 1937; student, Sterling Coll., 1937-39; BSME, Kans. State U., 1942; MBA, Creighton U., 1967, Ohio State U., 1961; postgrad., Stevens Inst., 1964. Registered profl. engr., Ariz. Researcher, mech. engr. Naval Ordnance Rsch. Lab., Washington, 1942-43; jr. product engr. Western Electric Co., Inc., Chgo. and Eau Claire, Wis., 1944-46; sr. devel. engr. Western Electric Co., Inc., Chgo., 1946-56; devel. engr. Western Electric Co., Inc., Omaha, 1960-66; product engr. mgr. Century Electronics and Instruments, Inc., Tulsa, Okla., 1956-60; sr. staff engr. Western Electric Co. div. AT&T Technologies, Phoenix, 1966-85; cons. in field Phoenix, 1985—; chmn. energy conservation AT&T Technologies, Inc., 1973-85; engring. student advisor, Ariz. State U., 1967—. Patentee in field. Trustee, Village of Westchester (Ill.), 1949-53; sec., treas. Westchester Broadview Water Commn., 1949-53; Sunday Sch. supt. Westchester Meth. Community Ch.,1949-56; vol. campaign worker, Phoenix Rep. Party, 1986-88. Named Westchester Family of Year, Westchester Community Ch., 1952; recipient Centennial medallian, American Soc. Am., 1979. Mem. Nat. Soc. Profl. Engrs. (named Engr. of the Year 1979), ASME (fellow, state legis. coord. 1985-86, 88—, Ariz. sect. chmn. 1974-75, vice chmn. 1973-74, sec. 1972-75), Soc. Profl. Engrs. (editor Ariz. Profl. Engr. mag. 1972-76), Ariz. Council Engring. and Sci. Assn., Am. Security Coun., Order of Engrs., Telephone Pioneer of Am., TAPPI, Soc. Plastic Engrs., Weoma Sci. Club (pres. 1963-66), Elks. Home and Office: 5229 N 43d St Phoenix AZ 85018

BACKE, PAMELA RENEE, auditing administrator; b. Marinette, Wis., Dec. 25, 1955; d. Wilbur Milton and Eulalia Ellen (Johnson) Mandigo; m. Stephen Allen Backe, June 15, 1974. AA, Truckee Meadows Community Coll., 1981, AAS in Data Processing, 1982; BS in Infosystems, U. Nev., 1987. Proof operator Bank of Am., Watsonville, Calif., 1973-76; adminstrv. asst. Truckee Meadows Christian Ctr., Reno, 1976-82; mgr. info. systems Sierra Office Concepts, Reno, 1982-84; auditor electronic data processing Harrah's, Reno, 1984-86, sr. auditor electronic data processing, 1986-87, mgr. internal audit, 1987—. Mem. Data Processing Mgmt. Assn., Inst. Internal Auditors. Republican. Club: Silver State Striders. Home: 12980 Broili Dr Reno NV 89511 Office: Harrah's 300 E 2d St Reno NV 89502

BACKER, BRUCE EVERETT, trade show exhibit design, manufacturing executive; b. L.A., June 1, 1955; s. Thomas Griffin and Beverly Ann (Ulsh) B.; m. Vanessa Raffi Marootian, July 21, 1979. BS in Indsl. Design, San Jose State U., 1981. Constrn. inspector, various cities, Calif., 1974-77; designer Exhibits of Calif., Palo Alto, 1977-80; design cons. Giltspur Exhibits, San Francisco, 1980-81; sr. designer Dimensional Coordinates, Inc., San Diego, 1981-82; founder, chief exec. officer Exponents, Inc., San Diego, 1982—. Inventor and patentee in field; designer of numerous exhibits. Office: Exponents Inc 3290 Kurtz St San Diego CA 92110

BACKLUND, BRANDON HAZE, consulting engineer; b. Amarillo, Tex., June 13, 1918; s. Francis Victor and Nancy (Haze) B.; m. Emily Louise Hess, June 5, 1941; children: Nancy, Mark, Greg. Student, Nebr. U., 1937-40; BCE, Iowa State U., 1941. Registered profl. engr., Calif. Constrn. engr. Peter Kiewit Sons Co., Omaha, 1946-47; structural engr. Ceco Steel Products Corp., Omaha, 1947-48; dist. structural engr. Portland Cement Assn., Omaha, 1948-51; pres. World Wide Cons., Inc., Saigon, Vietnam, 1965-66, B.H. Backlund & Assocs., Inc., Omaha, 1951-69; v.p., gen. mgr. McGaughy, Marshall, McMillan & Backlund, Omaha, 1969-76; pres. Backlund Engring. Co., Inc., Omaha, 1976-86; cons. engr. Backlund Engring. Co., Arroyo Grande, Calif., 1987—; resident engr. City of San Luis Obispo, Calif., 1986-87; instr. Calif. Poly. State U., San Luis Obispo, 1986—; chmn. Arroyo Grande St. and Hwy. Commn., 1988. Fellow ASCE, Am. Consulting Engrs.; mem. Nat. Soc. Profl. Engrs. (pres. 1964-65), Calif. Soc. Profl. Engrs. (v.p. cen. coast chpt. 1988—), Nebr. Soc. Profl. Engrs. (pres. 1956-57), Consulting Engrs. Assn. Calif., Arroyo Grande C. of C., Shriners, Masons, Scottish Rite, Rotary, Elks. Republican. Office: Backlund Engring Co 219 Miller Way Arroyo Grande CA 93420

BACKMAN, LYNDA WALKER, hotel and motel broker; b. Oakland, Calif., July 27, 1942; d. Glenn Anton and Bettye Frances (Daunt) Heimsoth; m. Lawrence E. Walker, Jan. 30, 1959 (div. 1970); children: Sherri Lynn, Mark Emory, Colleen Lea; m. Ted. E. Backman, Sept. 4, 1988. BSChemE, San Jose State U., 1976. Rsch. fellow Hewlett Packard Co., Palo Alto, Calif., 1967-78; broker Nat. Hotel and Motel Brokers, San Mateo, Calif., 1978-83; pres., broker Nat. Hotel and Motel Brokers, San Mateo, 1987—; broker Am. Motel Brokers, Burlingame, Calif., 1983-86; v.p. Pacific Motel Investments, Burlingame, 1986-87; owner, pres., chmn. of bd. Nat. Hotel and Motel Brokers, San Mateo, Calif., 1986—. Fellow Hotel Motel Brokers Am. (bd. dirs. 1980-83). Office: Nat Hotel and Motel Brokers 337th Ave PO Box 5446 San Mateo CA 94402

BACKUS, ANNE, health educator, dentist; b. Goffstown, N.H., Apr. 6, 1944; d. Richard Allison and Harriet (Wright) B.; m. George Benjamin Hartzog III, Nov. 9, 1977; children: Barbara Ellen, Rebekah Anne. Cert. elem. tchr., Mass.; lic. dentist, Calif. Head biology dept. Milford (N.H.) Area Sch., 1966-67; tchr. Albuquerque Pub. Schs., 1968-69; mid. sch. coord. Sandia Prep. Sch., Albuquerque, 1969-77; sec. Office of Pres. Sch. Theology at Claremont, Calif., 1977-78; mem. clin. faculty U. Southern Calif. Sch. Dentistry, L.A., 1983-86; pvt. practice L.A., 1983-86; health dir. Navajo United Meth. Mission Sch., Farmington, N.Mex., 1986—; researcher Woods Hole (Mass.) Oceanographic Inst., 1974; cons. health svcs. Pacific Geriatric Edn. Ctr., L.A., 1984-85, Palomar, Centinela Nursing Homes, L.A., 1984-86; dir. health svcs. Navajo United Meth. Mission, Farmington, 1986—. Mem. health and welfare com. Glendale (Calif.) United Meth. Ch., 1979-83, La Tijera United Meth. Ch., Westchester, Calif., 1983-86; ranger U.S. Nat. Park Svc., Maine and Wyo., 1972-77; bd. dirs. San Juan Symphony, 1987—. Dentistry fellow U. Seattle, 1989; recipient Excellence in Journalism Leadership award Mosby Book Co., L.A., 1983. Mem. ADA, Am. Assn. Women Dentists (Calif. chairperson 1983-85, Outstanding Sr. Woman 1983, Outstanding Dist. Chairperson 1985), Am. Soc. Geriatric Dentistry, Acad. Gen. Dentistry, Physicians for Social Responsibility. Office: Navajo United Meth Mission 1200 W Apache St Farmington NM 87401

BACKUS, GEORGE EDWARD, theoretical geophysicist; b. Chgo., May 24, 1930; s. Milo Morlan and Dora Etta (Dare) B.; m. Elizabeth Evelyn Allen, Nov. 15, 1961 (div. 1971); children—Benjamin, Brian, Emily; m. Varda Esther Peller, Jan. 8, 1977. Ph.B., U. Chgo., 1947, B.S. in Math., 1948, M.S. in Math. and Physics, 1950, 53, Ph.D. in Physics, 1956. Jr. mathematician Inst. for Air Weapons, Chgo., 1951-53; physicist Project Matterhorn, Princeton, N.J., 1957-58; asst. prof. math. MIT, Cambridge, 1958-60; assoc. prof. geophysics U. Calif.-San Diego, La Jolla, 1960-62, prof. geophysics, 1962—; mem. vis. com. Institut de Physique du Globe de Paris, 1987—; co-chmn. Internat. Working Group on Magnetic Field Satellities, 1983—. Contbr. articles to profl. jours. Guggenheim Found. fellow, 1963, 71; Royal Soc. Arts fellow, London, 1970—. Fellow Royal Astron. Soc. (Gold medal 1986), Am. Geophys. Union (John Adam Fleming medal 1986); mem. Nat. Acad. Scis. (com. on grants and fellowships Day Fund 1974-79, Com. on Sci. and Pub. Policy 1971-74), Am. Acad. Arts and Scis., N.Y. Acad. Scis., Am. Phys. Soc., Am. Math. Soc., Soc. for Indsl. and Applied Math., Seismol. Soc. Am. Office: U Calif Inst of Geophysics & Planetary Physics A-025 La Jolla CA 92093 *

BACON, BETTY RUTH, real estate broker; b. Craig, Colo., May 8, 1944; d. Wayne Theodore and Virginia Wyoma (Simonson) Jones; m. Albert Edward Lay, June 17, 1967 (div. 1975); 1 child, William Bradley. Student, Ariz. State U., 1962-65. Assoc. real estate broker Century 21, Grand Junction, Colo., 1976-78; real estate broker, prin. Bacon Realty, Grand Junction, 1978-84; broker assoc. Realty World, Grand Junction, 1984-85; ptnr. The Real Estate Group, Grand Junction, 1985-87; real estate broker, prin. The Buyer Rep., Inc., Grand Junction, 1988—. Mem. Nat. Assn. Realtors, Grand Junction Bd. Realtors (editor, author newsletter 1985-87), Women's Council Realtors (pres. 1985), Colo. Assn. Realtors (bd. dirs. 1986-87), Grand Junction C. of C. Home: 1329 Pitkin St Apt 2 Glenwood Springs CO 81601 Office: The Buyer Rep Inc 826 1/2 Grand St Glenwood Springs CO 81601

BACON, LEONARD ANTHONY, accounting educator; b. Santa Fe, June 10, 1931; s. Manuel R. and Maria (Chavez) Baca; m. Patricia Balzaretti; children—Bernadine M., Jerry A., Tiffany A. B.E., U. Nebr.-Omaha, 1965; M.B.A., U. of the Americas, Mexico City, 1969; Ph.D., U. Miss., 1971. CPA; cert. mgmt. acct., internal auditor. Commd. 2d lt. U.S. Army, 1951, advanced through grades to maj., 1964, served fin. and acctg. officer mainly Korea, Vietnam; ret., 1966; asst. prof. Delta State U., Cleveland, Miss., 1971-76; assoc. prof. West Tex. State U., Canyon, 1976-79; prof. acctg. Calif. State U., Bakersfield, 1979—; cons. Kershen Co. (now Atlantic Richfield Oil Co.), Canyon, 1979-80. Contbr. articles to profl. jours. U.S., Mex., Can., papers to profl. confs. Leader Delta area Boy Scouts Am., Cleveland, 1971-76; dir. United Campus Ministry, Canyon, 1976-79; minister Kern Youth Facility, Bakersfield, 1983—. Paratrooper Brazilian Army, 1955. Mem. Am. Acctg. Assn., Am. Inst. CPA's, Am. Assn. Spanish Speaking CPA's, Nat. Assn. Accts. (pres. Bakersfield chpt. 1981-82, Most Valuable Mem. award 1981), Am. Mgmt. Assn., Inst. Mgmt. Acctg., Calif. Faculty Assn., Acad. Internat. Bus., Inst. Internal Auditors, Inst. Cost Analysts, Alpha Kappa Psi (Dedicated Service award 1979). Clubs: Jockey (Rio de Janeiro). Lodges: Lions (v.p. Cleveland 1971-73), Kiwanis (v.p. 1974-79, A Whale of a Guy award, Cleveland 1975). Office: Calif State U 9001 Stockdale Hwy Bakersfield CA 93309

BACON, MARTHA SCRIMSHIRE, elementary teacher; b. Perla, Ark., Nov. 3, 1942; d. Woodard Lewis and Zoie Lee (Lowry) Scrimshire; m. Bob Bacon; children: Dawn, Jo Lynn. BS in Edn., Coll. of Southwest, 1970; postgrad., E. N.Mex. U., 1971-86. Cert. elem. tchr., N.Mex. Freelance artist Albuquerque, 1972-85; pvt. practice in interior design San Diego, 1983-85; tchr. gifted students Carlsbad (N.Mex.) Mcpl. Schs., 1987—. Author: How to Paint South West Miniatures, 1980. Recipient Third Place award N.Mex. Area Art League Show, 1980, First Place award Tri-State Show Carlsbad Area Artists Assn., 1986. Republican. Baptist. Home: 2010 Patricia Dr Carlsbad NM 88220

BACON, PAUL CALDWELL, SR., training systems company executive, aviations consultant, engineering test pilot; b. Camp Lejeune, N.C., Oct. 8, 1945; s. Franklin Camp and Marjorie Edna (Caldwell) B.; m. Carol Wetherell, June 7, 1967 (div. Oct. 1974); 1 child, Paul Caldwell Jr.; m. Martha Jean Court, Feb. 2, 1986. BS in Aerospace Engring., U.S. Naval Acad., 1967; MS in Aerospace Engring., U.S. Air Force Test Pilot Sch., 1976; MS in Systems Mgmt., U. So. Calif., 1979. Commd. 2nd lt. USMC, 1967, advanced through grades to maj., 1978, ret., 1980; advanced through grades to lt. col. USMCR, 1980—; fighter pilot, maintenance mgr. USMC, Beaufort, S.C., 1969-70, Danang, Socialist Republic of Vietnam, 1970-71, Kaneohe, Hawaii, 1971-73; advanced flight instr. USMC, Meridian, Miss., 1973-75; exptl. test pilot 1st F18 USMC, Patuxent River, Md., 1977-80; engring. test pilot United Airlines, Denver, 1980-84; dir. systems implementation United Airlines Svcs. Corp., Lakewood, Colo., 1984-86; dir. product assurance, chief pilot United Airlines Svcs. Corp., Lakewood, 1986—; cons. Nat. Traffic Safety Bd., FAA, NASA, USAF, Australian Aviation Agy., aircraft simulator mfrs., 1980—; info. officer U.S. Naval Acad., Denver. Decorated Air medal. Mem. Soc. Exptl. Test Pilots, Tech. Mktg. Soc. Am., Hornet 100 Club, U. So. Calif. Alumni Assn., U.S. Naval Acad. Alumni Assn. Republican. Presbyterian. Home: 12582A E Evans Circle Aurora CO 80014 Office: 3609 S Wadsworth Blvd Lakewood CO 80235

BACON, VICKY LEE, lighting services executive; b. Oregon City, Oreg., Mar. 25, 1950; d. Herbert Kenneth and Lorean Betty (Boltz) Rushford; student Portland Community Coll., 1974-75, Mt. Hood Community Coll., 1976, Portland State Coll., 1979; m. Dennis M. Bacon, Aug. 7, 1971; 1 dau., Randene Tess. With All Electric Constrn., Milwaukie, Oreg., 1968-70; with Lighting Maintenance Co., Portland, Oreg., 1970-78; service mgr. GTE Sylvania Lighting Services, Portland, 1978-80, br. mgr., 1980-83; div. mgr. Christenson Electric Co. Inc., Portland, 1983—. Mem. Nat. Secs. Assn., Illuminating Engring. Soc., Nat. Assn. Lighting Maintenance Contractors. Office: Christenson Electric Co Inc 111 SW Columbia Ste 480 Portland OR 97201

BADGER, MICHAEL JAY, career planning counselor; b. Salem, Oreg., Jan. 31, 1946; s. Ralph R. and Ardyth L. (Shelton) B.; m. Pamela Kay Trask, Sept. 10, 1983; 1 child, Christopher Michael Brian. BS in Journalism, U. Oreg., 1968, PhD in Psychology, 1976; MA, Syracuse U., 1970. Lic. psychologist, Wash., Oreg. Psychologist crippled children div. U. Oreg. Med. Sch., Portland, 1976-78; pvt. practice Portland, 1978-79; cons., psychologist Rohrer, Hibler & Replogle, Portland, 1979-82; v.p., regional mgr. Ward Assocs., Kirkland, Wash., 1982-86; pres. Ward Assocs., 1986—. NIMH fellow, 1969-70. Mem. Am. Psychol. Assn., Wash. State Psychol. Assn., Outplacement Internat. (bd. dirs.), Seattle C. of C., Assn. Outplacement Cons. Firms (bd. dirs.) Rotary. Democrat. Office: Ward Assocs 10628 NE 38th Pl Ste 105 Kirkland WA 98033

BADGER, RODNEY SEYMOUR, cardiologist, consultant; b. San Francisco, July 13, 1952; s. Sidney V. and Frances (Rogers) B.; m. Shauna Louise Jones, Aug. 14, 1976; children: Brandon, Troy, Jennifer, Andrew. BA, Stanford U., 1976; MD, U. Calif.-San Diego, 1980. Diplomate Am. Bd. Internal Medicine, Am. Bd. Cardiovascular Disease. Resident in internal medicine U. Wash., Seattle, 1980-83, cardiology fellow, 1983-85; practice medicine specializing in cardiology Pinole, Calif., 1985--; cons. Advanced Cardiovascular Systems, Mountain View, Calif., 1986--. Contbr. articles to profl. jours., inventor cardiac catheter. Fellow Am. Coll. Cardiology; mem. Alameda-Contra Costa County Med. Assn., Phi Beta Kappa. Republican. Mormon. Home: 5 Lisa Ln Morage CA 94556 Office: Pinole Cardiology Group 1580 Mann Dr Pinole CA 94564

BADGLEY, EDMUND KIRK, JR., geologist, educator; b. Missoula, Mont., Aug. 8, 1923; s. Edmund Kirk and Nell (Shepard) B.; m. Carol E. Hanley, June 10, 1951 (div. 1961); children: Brenda Benoit, Sara Moody, Marlene; m. Marie E. (Minor) Curry, Aug. 12, 1967; stepchildren: Robert Curry, Warren Curry, Patricia Pope,. BA, U. Mont., 1948; MA, U. Wyo., 1953; postgrad., U. Wash., 1964, 66, U. Denver, 1973, U. No. Colo., 1986. Registered geologist, Calif.; cert. tchr., Colo., N.M. Ops. geologist Shell Oil Co., Billings, Mont., 1951-59; test engr. Inland Analytical Labs., Spokane, Wash. and Rapid City, S.D., 1960-61; sci. and math. tchr. Powell County (Mont.) High Sch., 1959-60, Bighorn County (Mont.) High Sch., 1961, Idaho Falls High Sch., 1962-63, Carmilla (Calif.) Mid Sch., 1964, Mt. San Antonio (Calif.) Coll., 1964, Coeur d'Alene (Idaho) High Sch., 1965-67, U. Ariz., Tucson, 1967-68; earth found. insp. various locations, 1969-71; seismologist Rockwell Internat., various locations, 1972-73; coal cons. Gillette, Wyo., 1974-78; oil cons. Billings, 1979-81; sr. geologist Asamera Oil Inc., Colo., 1982; sci. and math tchr. Woodlin (Colo.) Sch. Dist., 1985-87, Tohatchi High Sch., Gallup, N.Mex., 1987—; founder, dir. Embark Endeavors Co.; coal energy cons.; instr. mining tech., Sheridan (Wyo.) Community Coll. Contbr. articles to profl. jours. Tchr., advisor Navaho Indian Tribe. Served to lt. USNR, 1943-46, PTO. NSF grantee, 1963, 64, 66. Mem. NEA, Geol. Soc. Am., Geol. Soc. N.Mex., Soc. Earth Sci. Tchrs., Rocky Mtn. Assn. Geologists, Sigma Xi, Phi Delta Theta. Republican. Office: Gallup-McKinley Sch Dist Tohatchi High Sch Unit 700 Boardman Rd Gallup NM 87301

BADGLEY, JOHN ROY, architect; b. Huntington, W. Va., July 10, 1922; s. Roy Joseph and Fannie Myrtle (Limbaugh) B.; AB, Occidental Coll., 1943; MArch, Harvard, 1949; postgrad., Centro Internazionale, Vincenza, Italy, 1959; m. Janice Atwell, July 10, 1975; 1 son, Adam; children by previous marriage: Dan, Lisa, Holly, Marcus, Michael. Prin. architect own firm, San Luis Obispo, Calif., 1952-65; chief architect, also planner Crocker Land Co., San Francisco, 1965-80; v.p. Cushman & Wakefield Inc., San Francisco, 1980-84; pvt. practice architecture, San Rafael, Calif., 1984—; tchr. Calif. State U. at San Luis Obispo, 1952-65. Served with USCGR, 1942-46. Mem. AIA, Am. Arbitration Assn. Oceanic Soc. (trustee). Clubs: Golden Gate Wine Soc. Home and Office: 1356 Idylberry Rd San Rafael CA 94903

BADGLEY, MARIE CURRY, educator, counselor; b. Berlin, Wis., Dec. 18, 1926; d. Morris C. and Elizabeth (Klinkenberg) Minor; m. John C. Curry, Apr. 1944 (div. June 1956); children: Robert W., Patricia A., Warren H.; m. E. Kirk Badgley, Aug. 14, 1967. AA, Mesa Coll., 1952; BA, Ariz. State U., 1958, MA, 1962; postgrad., U. Colo., 1973, U. No. Colo., 1974, U. Wyo., 1977-78, U. N.Mex., 1984. Cert. tchr., counselor Colo., N. Mex. Tchr. elem. and jr. high schs. Colo., 1951-58; tchr. elem. and jr. high schs. Ariz., 1967-70, Marycrest High Sch., 1971-73; jr. and sr. high sch. counselor, coordinator, dean students Coeur d'Alene (Idaho) High Sch., 1966—, Milliken Jr. High Sch., Gillette, Wyo., 1975-79, Lincoln Jr. High Sch., Billings, Mont., 1979-82, Woodlin (Colo.) Sch. Dist., 1987; head girls' counselor J.F. Kennedy Middle Sch., Gallup, N. Mex., 1987—; sec.-treas. Embark Endeavors, Gallup. Home: PO Box 5006 Gallup NM 87301

BADHAM, ROBERT E., former congressman; b. Los Angeles, June 9, 1929; s. Byron J. and Bess (Kissinger) B.; m. Anne Carroll; children: Sharron, Robert, William, Phyllis, Jennifer. A.B., Stanford U., 1951. V.p., dir. Hoffman Hardware Co., L.A., 1955-69; mem. Calif. Assembly from 71st Dist., 1962-76, 95th-100th Congresses from 40th Calif. Dist., 1977-89. Author articles. Mem. Orange Empire Area coun. Boy Scouts Am.; del. So. Pacific Dist. conv. Am. Luth. Ch., 1967, Nat. conv., 1968; alt. del. Rep. Nat. Conv., 1964-68, del., 1980, 84, 88; mem. Calif. Rep. Central Com., 1962-88, Orange County Rep. Cen. Com., 1962-88. Lt. (j.g.) USNR, 1951-54. Mem. Am. Soc. Archtl. Hardware Cons., Orange Coast Assn., Orange County Asso. Chambers Commerce, Am. Legion, NRA, Phi Gamma Delta. Office: 881 Dover Dr Ste 14 Newport Beach CA 92660

BADISH, KENNETH MICHAEL, film executive; b. Baldwin, N.Y., Dec. 30, 1951; s. Alan W. and Adele Y. (Goodman) B.; m. Laurie Jean Halloway, May 1, 1985. BA in Psychology, U. Pa., 1973. Media dir. Benton & Bowles Inc., N.Y.C., 1973-77; dir. film acquisition Home Box Office, N.Y.C., 1978-81; pres., chief exec. officer Moviestore Entertainment, L.A., 1981—; educator UCLA, L.A., 1986-87. Office: Moviestore Entertainment 11111 Santa Monica Blvd Ste 1850 Los Angeles CA 90025

BAECKER, CHARLES LOUIS, data processing company executive; b. Long Beach, Calif., Sept. 8, 1951; s. Marvin Philip and Ann Charlotte (Preston) B.; m. Adele Daversa, May 27, 1978; 1 child, Kent Stephen. BA in Econs., U. So. Calif., 1973; MBA, Calif. State U., Pomona, 1988. Cert. in inventory control, prodn. mgmt. Inventory control coord. Hyland Labs., Costa Mesa, Calif., 1973-76; gen. mgr. Laguna Mfg., Irvine, Calif., 1976-79; mfg. specialist Beckman Inst., Fullerton, Calif., 1979-81; project leader Exxon Enterprises, L.A., 1981-82; mgr. cons. Ernst & Whinney, L.A., 1982-85; regional CAD/CAM mgr. Prime Computer, Irvine, 1985-88; pres. Assembly Tech. Corp., Santa Ana, Calif., 1988—; com. mem. Am. Electronics Assn., Irvine, 1988. Author articles, presentations in field. V.p. Windwood Maintenance and Mgmt. Assn., Irvine, 1986-88. Mem. Soc. Mfg. Engrs. (sr.), Am. Prodn. and Inventory Control Soc., Am. Electronics Soc., Nat. Computer Service Network. Office: Assembly Techs Corp 2921 W Central Santa Ana CA 92704

BAEHR, ROBERT E., electrical contractor; b. Deer Lodge, Mont., Jan. 19, 1919; s. Alexander Ernest and Bertha (McKy) B.; m. Kathryn E. Kendig, Mar. 14, 1953. Student, Mont. Sch. Mines, 1937-38, Mont. State U., 1938-40. V.p. Baehr Elec. Shop Inc., Deer Lodge, 1953-78, pres., 1978—. Active Mont. Radio Amateur Civil Emergency Svc., Deer Lodge, 1975-85, Navy-Marine Corps Mil. Affiliate Radio System, 1962—; emergency coord. Powell County, Deer Lodge, 1968—. Capt. U.S. Army, 1940-47, ETO, PTO. Mem. Vets. of Office of Strategic Svcs., Am. Radio Relay League, Masons, Blue Lodge, Royal Arch Lodge, Commandry Lodge, Shriners. Republican. Presbyterian. Home: 803 Mill St Deer Lodge MT 59722

BAENDER, MARGARET WOODRUFF, free-lance writer; b. Salt Lake City, Apr. 1, 1921; d. Russell Kimball and Margaret Angline (McIntyre) Woodruff; m. Phillip Albers Baender, Aug. 17, 1946 (dec.); children: Kristine Lynn, Charlene Anne, Michael Phillip, Russell Richard. B.A., U. Utah, 1944. In clerical, personnel work various firms, San Francisco Bay area, 1970-75; reporter, columnist Valley Pioneer, Danville, Calif., 1975-77; editor Diablo (Calif.) Inferno, 1971-76; author Shifting Sands, 1981, Tail Waggings of Maggie, 1982. Fellow Internat. Biog. Assn.; mem. Nat. Writers Club, AAUW, Soc. Children's Book Writers, Am. Biog. Inst. (life, Raleigh, N.C.), Internat. Women's Writers Guild, Alpha Delta Pi (pres.). Republican. Episcopalian.

BAER, WILLIAM BRUCE, ophthalmologist; b. Louisville, Sept. 30, 1938; s. Louis and Miriam (Wile) B.; m. Joan Anita Teckler, Apr. 26, 1966 (dec. Oct. 1968); m. Sydney Ann Anker, Dec. 26, 1976; children: Allison, Louis. BSEE, MIT, 1960; BA, U. Louisville, 1961, MS in Pathology, MD cum laude, 1965. Diplomate Am. Bd. Ophthalmology. Intern, then resident SUNY Upstate Med. Ctr., Syracuse, 1965-67; resident in ophthalmology U. Oreg., Portland, 1969-72; pvt. practice, Portland, 1972—. Capt. USAF, 1967-69. Fellow Am. Acad. Ophthalmology; mem. AMA, Oreg. Med. Assn., Oreg. Acad. Ophthalmology, Multnomah County Med. Soc. (trustee 1988—), Multnomah Athletic Club, Oswego Lake Country Club. Jewish. Office: 1130 NW 22d Ave Portland OR 97210

BAERWALD, JOHN EDWARD, traffic engineer, educator; b. Milw., Nov. 2, 1925; s. Albert J. and Margaret M. (Brandt) B.; m. Elaine S. Eichstaedt, Apr. 3, 1948 (dec.); children: Thomas J., James K., Barbara Baerwald Bowman; m. Donna D. Granger, May 24, 1975. BS in Civil Engring., Purdue U., 1949, MS in Civil Engring., 1950, PhD in Civil Engring., 1956. Registered profl. engr., Calif., Ill., Ind. Research asst. Purdue U., 1949-50, research assoc., instr. hwy. engring., 1950-52, research engr., instr. hwy. engring., 1952-55; asst. prof. traffic engring. U. Ill., Urbana, Champaign, 1955-57; assoc. prof. traffic engring. U. Ill., Urbana, 1957-60, prof. traffic engring., 1960-69, prof. transp. and traffic engring., 1969-83, univ. traffic engr., 1957-63, dir. Hwy. Traffic Safety Ctr., 1961-83, prof. emeritus, 1983—; staff assoc. Police Tng. Inst., 1969—; cons. traffic engr., 1952—; pres. John E. Baerwald P.C., Santa Fe, 1983—; chmn. Champaign Parking and Traffic Commn., Ill., 1960-69; liaison mem. staff subcom. Ill. Gov.'s Ofcl. Traffic Safety Coordination Com., 1962-69, mem. subcom. hwy. safety program deficiencies, 1970-72; mem. Champaign-Urbana Urbanized Area Transp. Study, 1963-83, tech. adviser to policy com., 1963-75, chmn. policy com., 1977-83; mem. Ill. Sec. State Adv. Com. Vehicle Registration and Titling Matters, 1973-74; trustee Champaign-Urbana Mass Transit Dist., 1973-83, chmn., 1975-83; mem. tech. adv. com. Ill. Transp. Study Commn., 1977-81. Served with AUS, 1943-46. Recipient Pub. Service award Ill. Sec. State, 1976, past. pres. award Ill. Sec. Inst. of Transp. Engrs., 1983. Fellow ASCE, Inst. Transp. Engrs. (internat. pres. 1970, dir. 1964-65, 67-71, internat. council 1977-83, dir. Ill. sect. 1963-64, other offices and coms., exec. com. expert witness council 1986—, vice-chmn. 1988, chmn. 1989—, Past Pres.' award 1953, Theodore M. Matson Meml. award 1988); mem. Nat. Safety Council (dir. 1975-80, other offices and coms.), Am. Rd. and Transp. Builders Assn. (safety and environ. com. 1975-78, mem. transp. safety adv. council 1976-83, 89—, pres. edn. div. 1979, dir. 1979-83, mem. exec. com. 1979-80), Transp. Research Bd. (div. B council 1974-83, other offices and coms.), Pan Am. Hwy. Congress (best tech. paper award 1963, 67), Lions, Masons, Sigma Xi, Chi Epsilon. Lutheran. Home: RR 2 PO Box 927 Santa Fe NM 87505

BAGDASARIAN, ANDRANIK, biochemist; b. Tehran, Iran, Dec. 5, 1935; s. Mamegon and Satenik (Gregorian) B.; m. Vilma T. Rincon, Mar. 15, 1979; children: Patrick, Armen, Levon. PhD in Biochemistry, U. Louisville, 1967; Doctorate in Pharmacy, U. Tehran, Iran, 1962. Rsch. asst. prof. U. Pa., Phila., 1975-78; sr. rsch. scientist Hyland Therapeutics, Costa Mesa, Calif., 1978-80, rsch. mgr., Costa Mesa, 1980-83, assoc. dir. rsch., Duarte, Calif., 1983-85, mgr. spl. projects, 1985-88; with family bus., 1989—. NIH grantee, 1975-78; Nat. Cancer Inst. grantee, 1975-78; Am. Cancer Soc. grantee, 1975-77. Mem. Am. Soc. Biol. Chemists, Sigma Xi. Republican. Mem. Armenian Apostolic Ch. Home: 1227 Calle Estrella San Dimas CA 91773

BAGDAZIAN, RICHARD WILLIAM, electrical engineer; b. Sacramento, Calif., Oct. 14, 1955; s. Soren William and Evamaye (Green) B.; m. Christina Louise Copelin, Aug. 23, 1980; children: Meredith Suzanne, Whitney Allison. BSEE, U. So. Calif., 1977, MEE, 1979, postgrad., 1982. Registered profl. engr., Calif. Staff engr. Hughes Aircraft Co., Los Angeles, 1977-82; prin. engr. Gen. Data Communications Industries, Inc., Middlebury, Conn., 1982-84; dir. engring. Paragon Networks Internat., San Diego, 1984-88; prin. engr. Hughes Network Systems, San Diego, 1988—; cons. Internat. Leadership Group, San Diego, 1988—. Contbr. articles to profl. jours. Fellow High Ground Assocs., San Diego, 1988. Mem. Inst. Electrical and Electronics Engrs. Republican. Home: 12214 Colony DR Poway CA 92064

BAGDIKIAN, BEN HAIG, journalist, university dean; b. Marash, Turkey, Jan. 30, 1920; came to U.S., 1920, naturalized, 1926; s. Aram Theodore and Daisy (Uvezian) B.; m. Elizabeth Ogasapian, Oct. 2, 1942 (div. 1972); children—Christopher Ben, Frederick Haig; m. Betty L. Medsger, 1973 (div.); m. Marlene Griffith, 1983. A.B., Clark U., 1941, D.Litt., 1963; L.H.D., Brown U., 1961. Reporter Springfield (Mass.) Morning Union, 1941-42; asso. editor Periodical House, Inc., N.Y.C., 1946; successively reporter, fgn. corr., chief Washington corr. Providence Jour., 1947-62; contbg. editor Sat. Eve. Post, 1963-67; project dir. study of future U.S. news media Rand Corp., 1967-69; asst. mng. editor for nat. news Washington Post, 1970-71, asst. mng. editor, 1971-72; nat. corr. Columbia Journalism Review, 1972-74; prof. Grad. Sch. Journalism, U. Calif., Berkeley, 1976—, dean, 1985-88; M. Lyle Spencer vis. prof. Syracuse U., 1973. Author: In The Midst of Plenty: The Poor in America, 1964, The Information Machines: Their Impact on Men and the Media, 1971, The Shame of the Prisons, 1972, The Effete Conspiracy, 1972, Caged: Eight Prisoners and their Keepers, 1976, The Media Monopoly, 1983, rev. edit., 1987; also pamphlets.; Contbr.: The Kennedy Circle, 1961; Editor: Man's Contracting World in an Expanding Universe, 1959; Bd. editors: Jour. Investigative Reporters and Editors, 1980—. Mem. steering com. Nat. Prison Project., 1974-82; Trustee Clark U., 1964-76; bd. dirs. Nat. Capital Area Civil Liberties Union, 1964-66, Com. to Protect Journalists, 1981—; pres. Lowell Mellett Fund for Free and Responsible Press, 1965-76; acad. adv. bd. Nat. Citizens Com. for Broadcasting., 1978—. Served with USAAF, 1942-45. Recipient George Foster Peabody award, 1951; Sidney Hillman Found. award, 1956; Most Perceptive Critic citation Am. Soc. Journalism Adminstrs., 1978; Ogden Reid Found. fellow, 1956; Guggenheim fellow, 1961-62. Mem. ACLU. Home: 25 Stonewall Rd Berkeley CA 94705 Office: U Calif North Gate Hall Berkeley CA 94720

BAGGERLY, LEO LON, physicist; b. Wichita, Kans., Mar. 13, 1928; s. Isaac Edison and Elna Matilda B; m. Jean Louise Bickford, June 8, 1951 (div., Jan. 1966); children: Philip, Jennifer; m. Carole Christine Applewhite, Apr. 2, 1966; children: Keith, Derek, Christine. BS in Sci., Calif. Inst. Tech., 1951, MS in Physics, 1952, PhD, 1956. Sr. rsch. engr. Jet Propulsion Lab., Pasadena, Calif., 1955-56; Fulbright lectr. U. Ceylon, Columbo, 1956-59; asst. prof., assoc. prof., prof. Physics Tex. Christian U., Ft. Worth, 1959-69; program mgr. NSF, Washington, 1969-71; vis. fellow Cornell U., Ithaca, N.Y., 1971-72; prof. Physics Calif. State Coll., Bakersfield, 1972-75; vis. prof. Pomona Coll., Claremont, Calif., 1975-76, Harvey Mudd Coll., Claremont, Calif., 1976-77; sr. staff scientist Ballistics Missiles Div TRW, San Bernardino, Calif., 1977—; cons. Tex. Nuclear Corp. Austin, 1960-61, Milco Internat., Huntington Beach, Calif., 1975-77; cons. scientist LTV Rsch. Ctr., Grand Prarie, Tex., 1962-67. Contbr. articles to profl. jours. V.p. So. Calif. chpt. ACLU, 1955-56; treas. Am. Field Svc., Claremont, 1984-. With USN, 1946-48. Mem. Am. Assn. Physics Tchrs. (pres. So. Calif. chpt. 1973-75), AAAS, UN Assn. (treas. Pomona Valley chpt. 1979-86), Sigma Xi. Mem. Soc. of Friends. Home: 2218 Grand Ave Claremont CA 91711 Office: TRW PO Box 1310 San Bernardino CA 92402

BAGGETT, KELSEA KINDRICK, nurse; b. Pine Bluff, Ark., Nov. 19, 1937; s. Joe Layton and Mildred (Franks) B.; m. Roxanna Veronica Dixon, Jan. 5, 1963; children: Daniel Kenneth, Sheryl Angela, Noel Alexander, Douglas Anthony. AS, Cypress (Calif.) Coll., 1975; BS, Calif. State U., Fullerton, 1980. RN, Calif. Staff nurse Los Angeles County Sheriff's Dept., 1964-69, supr. nurse, 1969-75, dir. nursing sheriff med. services, 1975-86, head mgmt. services, 1986—. Chmn. Gifted and Talented Assn., Garden Grove Sch. Dist., 1986. Served with USAF, 1956-60. Mem. Am. Correctional Health Services Assn. (pres. elect Calif. chpt. 1988—, bd. dirs. 1981-87). Home: 13231 Rainbow St Garden Grove CA 92643 Office: Los Angeles County Sheriffs Dept 441 Bauchet St Los Angeles CA 90012

BAGGOT, JAMES JOSEPH, retired educator and coach; b. Chgo., Mar. 23, 1912; s. James Patrick and Alice Mary (Moloney) B.; m. Aline Sadler, Aug. 21, 1936; children: Patrick, William, Thomas. AB, Western State Coll. Colo., 1935; postgrad., U. Colo., 1939-41; MA, U. No. Colo., 1946. Basketball coach, dir. athletics Fountain (Colo.) High Sch., 1937-39, Aurora (Colo.) high Sch., 1939-42, Greeley (Colo.) High Schs., 1942-64; dir. athletics Greeley Pub. Schs., 1964-72; salesman Lincoln Nat. Life Ins. Co., Greeley, 1964-72; dir. coachs' clin., Greeley, 1964. Author: Pressing Defense, 1959, Fast Break Basketball, 1959; contbr. numerous articles on basketball to profl. publs. Bd. dirs. Greeley Recreation Commn., 1945-48, Greeley Civic Recreation Com., 1945-72. Named Coach of the Yr., Colo. Activities Assn., 1956, 57, 59, 60, 62, Colo. Coaches Hall of Fame, 1980, All Time High Sch. Basketball Coach, Denver Post, 1985; recipient Outstanding Alumni award Western State Coll. Colo., 1981. Mem. Colo. Coaches Assn. (pres. 1953-54, coach of yr. award 1963), Kiwanis (dir. recreation 1945-60). Republican. Roman Catholic. Home: 2119 15th St Greeley CO 80631

BAGNAL, CHARLES WILSON, army officer; b. Mont Clare, S.C., Apr. 15, 1934; s. William Kenneth and Clara (Wilson) B.; m. Patricia Anne Smith, June 6, 1956; children—Charles, Joel. B.S. in Mil. Engring., U.S. Mil. Acad., 1956; M.S. in Aerospace Engring., Ga. Inst. Tech., 1966. Commd. 2d lt. U.S. Army, 1956, advanced through grades to lt. gen., 1983; mil. asst. to sec. of army Washington, 1969-71; comdr. 52d Aviation Battalion (Combat), 17th Aviation Group, 1st Aviation Brigade, Vietnam, 1971-72; aviation staff officer 1972; chief staff mgmt. div. Office of Chief of Staff, Washington, 1973-74, dep. dir. of Army staff, 1974-75; comdr. 101st Aviation Group, 101st Airborne Div. (Air Assault), Fort Campbell, Ky., 1975-76; asst. div. comdr. 101st Airborne Div. (Air Assault), 1976-77, comdg. gen., 1981-83; dep. supt. U.S. Mil. Acad., West Point, N.Y., 1977-80; dir. Officer Personnel Mgmt. Directorate, U.S. Army Mil. Personnel Ctr., Alexandria, Va., 1980-81; dep. comdg. gen. tng. and doctrine 1983-85; comdg. gen.western command U.S. Army, 1985—; dir. profl. devel. of officers study, 1985. Bd. dirs. Boy Scouts Am. of Hawaii. Decorated D.S.M. Silver Star, Legion of Merit with two oak leaf clusters, D.F.C., Bronze Star, Meritorious Service medal, Air medals, Army Commendation medal, Purple Heart, Master Army Aviation badge, Air Assault badge. Mem. Army Aviation Assn. Am., Assn. U.S. Army. Baptist. Home: Quarters 5 Palm Circle Honolulu HI 96819 Office: Comdg Gen US Army Western Command Fort Shafter HI 96858-5100

BAGUE, JEFFREY STEVEN, architect; b. Los Angeles, Sept. 17, 1957; s. Carl Edward and Eleanor Elain (Quan) B.; m. Mary Jean Beardsley, May 21, 1989; 1 child, Miranda Lynn. BS, Calif. Poly. U., 1980. Registered architect Calif. Draftsman Neil Stanton Palmer, Irvine, Calif., 1980-83; architect RRM Design Group, San Luis Obispo, Calif., 1983-88; v.p. architecture Sykes Group, San Luis Obispo, 1988—. Works include Rehab. Bldg. (recipent SLOBA award 1986), hotels and comml. retail. Mem. AIA. Democrat. Home: 1607 Lima Dr San Luis Obispo CA 93401 Office: Sykes Group 979 Osos St Ste F San Luis Obispo CA 93401

BAGWELL, ROBERT STEVEN, health care executive, consultant; b. Clifton Heights, Pa., Oct. 1, 1949; s. Samual Woodson and Nellie Ann (Romanski) B.; m. Darlene Diana Brown, June 21, 1968; children: Mary Ann, Apri Ann, Stefanie Alice. Diploma, Cabrillo Pacific U., 1971; AA, Southwestern Coll., 1974; BA, U. Redlands, Calif., 1984, MA, 1986. Cert. secondary edn. tchr., Calif. Ops. officer Bank of Am., San Diego, 1973-77; ops. mgr. United Calif. Bank, San Diego, 1977-81; dir. Eisenhower Med. Ctr., Rancho Mirage, Calif., 1981-87; owner LaserVideo, Moreno Valley, Calif., 1986—; cons. Mgmt. Svcs., Moreno Valley, 1987—; owner Ednl. Assistance Svc., Moreno Valley, 1988—; chmn. safety com. and cost containment com. Eisenhower Med. Ctr., Rancho Mirage, 1981-86, mem. ins. and contract rev. com., 1981-86. Sponsor Girl Scouts U.S., Palm Springs, Calif., 1986; cons., aide Sam Bagwell for U.S. Congress, San Diego. Mem. Video Software Dealers Assn., U. Redlands Alumni Assn. Republican. Roman Catholic. Office: LaserVideo 24592 Sunnymead Blvd Moreno Valley CA 92388

BAHA, DANIEL SCOTT, lawyer; b. N.Y.C., Nov. 30, 1955; s. Douglas Scott and Robin (Von Hefflin) Mont Bahatten Berke. BA, Oklahoma State U., 1976; MBA, U. So. Calif., 1980; JD, Northrop U., 1985. Bar: Calif. 1985. Sole practice Redondo Beach, Calif., 1986—. Mem. ABA, Los Angeles County Bar, South Bay Bar. Republican. Office: 1840 S Elena St Redondo Beach CA 90277

BAHLO, PETER, civil engineer; b. Bridgeport, Conn., Jan. 27, 1959; s. Klaus Wolfgang and Helga (Sahner) B. BSCE, U. Mass., 1983. Registered profl. engr., Calif. Staff sr. engr. L.A. County Bldg. and Safety Dept., 1983-86; staff engr. ICBO, Inc., Whittier, Calif., 1986—. Mem. Am. Concrete Inst., Structural Engrs. of So. Calif.

BAHN, IRENE ELIZA SCHUYLER, writer; b. Borodino, N.Y., June 19, 1895; d. William Scott and Carrie Eugene (Kennedy) Schuyler; A.B., Syracuse U., 1918; m. Chester Bert Bahn, June 25, 1921 (dec. 1962); children—Gilbert Schuyler, Chester Bert, Jerrold Philip. News reporter Syracuse (N.Y.) Jour., 1918-21; free lance poet and news corr. various newspapers, N.Y., Pa., 1921-32; publicity agt. Loew's Theatre, Syracuse, 1932-34, RKO Theatres, Syracuse, 1934-36; vol. publicity agt. various charitable orgns., Malverne, N.Y., 1936-60, Thousand Oaks, Calif., 1960-82. Vol., S. Nassau Communities Hosp. Malverne Aux., 1944-62, pres., 1956-57; organizer Save the Name referendum upon incorporation Thousand Oaks, 1964; founding pres. Conejo Valley Hosp. Aux., 1963-68; vol. Los Robles Hosp. Aux., 1968—; founding mem. Conejo Valley Debutantes Ball Com., 1968-81; bd. dirs. Conejo Valley Hist. Soc., 1968-80, named Dona Conejo, 1970. Recipient Community Service medal Thousand Oaks C. of C., 1963; life mem. Conejo Players, 1976. Mem. AAUW, Alpha Chi Omega. Republican. Presbyterian. Clubs: Conejo Valley Garden (hon. mem. 1975); Las Patronas. Home: 238 Encino Vista Dr Thousand Oaks CA 91362 Office: 615 Brandywine Dr Newport News VA 23602

BAIER, JOHN CHRISTOPHER, yacht broker; b. N.Y.C., June 21, 1959; s. Henry Louis and Margaret Mary (Lynch) B. Student, Villanova U., 1977-79, San Francisco State U., 1981-84. V.p., broker Rex Yacht Sales, Sausalito, Calif., 1984—. Mem. steering com. DeYoung Mus. Soc. Art Connection, San Francisco, 1987—. Mem. Sausalito Yacht Club. Republican. Roman Catholic. Home: 4A Cazneau Ave Sausalito CA 94965 Office: 308 Harbor Dr Sausalito CA 94965

BAIK, HYO WHI, automotive import company executive; b. Kae Sung, Republic of Korea, Sept. 6, 1942; came to U.S., 1987; s. Sun Kyung and Soo (Park) B.; m. Young Jin Chang, Dec. 9, 1969; children: Sung Hak, Ji Yun. BA, Korea U., Seoul, 1968. Mng. dir. Hyundai Engring. and Constrn. Co., Republic of Korea, throughout Asia, 1968-85, Hyundai Motor Co., 1985-87; pres., chief exec. officer Hyundai Motor Am., Garden Grove, Calif., 1987—. Office: Hyundai Motor Am 7373 Hunt Ave Garden Grove CA 92660

BAILEY, BARBARA JEAN, nurse; b. Spooner, Wis., Oct. 13, 1932; d. Edward Rydberg and Linda C. (Nystrom); m. Charles Swanson, July 3, 1953 (dec. May 1980); children: Jerri, Jan, Joan, Jill; m. James D. Bailey, Sept. 18, 1981; children: Dianne, Andrea. Diploma in nursing, Hamline U., St. Paul, Minn., 1953. Staff nurse Rush City (Minn.) Community Hosp., 1953-54; supr. Indianhead Med. Ctr., Shell Lake, Wis., 1962-86; staff nurse Terraceview Living Ctr., Shell Lake, 1986-87; staff charge nurse ARA Living Ctr., Sun City, Ariz., 1987-88, Sun Grove Care Ctr., Sun City, 1988—. Sec. Washburn County Rep. Party, Wis., 1986-87; county chmn. Kasten for Senator Com., Shell Lake, 1986. Mem. United Meth. Ch. Clubs: Shell Lake Lioness (sec. 1986-87), Mid-Week Lioness (Sun City). Home: 19622 Willowcreek Circle Sun City AZ 85373

BAILEY, BRIAN DENNIS, management consultant, author, publisher; b. Tacoma, June 10, 1952; s. Hugh Charles and Elsie Denise (Hinds) B.; BBA, Pacific Luth. U., Tacoma, 1975; MBA, City U. Seattle, 1982; PhD in Bus. Adminstrn., Century U., Beverly Hills, Calif., 1985. Prin. Brian D. Bailey, Mgmt. Cons., Tacoma, 1975—; pres. and chief exec. officer Baico Industries Inc., Tacoma, 1975—; adj. instr. City U., Seattle, 1986—. Mem. corp. bd., pres. Shekinah Ministries, Tacoma; pres. Young Democrats So. Pierce County, 1975-76. Served with USAF, 1971-73, with res. Mem. Full Gospel Businessmen's Fellowship Internat., World Bible Way Fellowship, Inc., Christian Writers Guild, Grange of Washington State. Home: PO Box 44757 Tacoma WA 98444 Office: Baico Industries Inc PO Box 44757 Tacoma WA 98444-0757

BAILEY, CHARLES SAWYER, manufacturing executive; b. L.A., Dec. 10, 1924; s. George S. and Katherine (Sawyer) B.; m. Gwen Lomison, Aug. 11, 1951; children: Cheryl, Patricia, Brad. BA, UCLA, 1947; MBA, Harvard U., 1949. V.p. Bailey Hat Co., L.A., 1961-66, pres., 1966—. Mem. Mens Apparel Guild Calif. (pres. 1973-75), Apparel Mfrs. (pres. 1971-72), UCLA Alumni Assn. (bd. dirs. 1972-77), Western Wear Mfrs. Assn. (pres. 1973-74), Young Pres.'s Orgn., Bel Air Bay Club (pres.). Republican. Home: 14915 Ramos Pl Pacific Palisades CA 90272 Office: Bailey Hat Co 13245 Riverside #350 Sherman Oaks CA 91413

BAILEY, DANA KAVANAGH, radiophysicist, botanist; b. Clarendon Hills, Ill., Nov. 22, 1916; s. Dana Clark and Dorothy (Kavanagh) B. B.S. with highest distinction, U. Ariz., 1937; postgrad., Harvard U., 1940; B.A. (Rhodes scholar) Queen's Coll., Oxford U., 1940, M.A., 1943, D.Sc., 1967. Astronomer expdn. to Peru for Hayden Planetarium, N.Y.C., 1937; physicist Antarctic expdn. U.S. Antarctic Service, 1940-41; project engr. Project RAND Douglas Aircraft Co., Santa Monica, Calif., 1946-48; physicist Nat. Bur. Standards, Washington, 1948-55; physicist, cons. Nat. Bur. Standards, Boulder, Colo., 1959-66; radiophysicist, research botanist Space Environment Lab., Environ. Research Labs., Nat. Oceanic and Atmospheric Adminstrn., Boulder, 1966-76; sci. dir. Page Communications Engrs., Inc., Washington, 1955-59; U.S. Exchange rep. Brit. Antarctic Survey Falkland Islands and Antarctica, 1967-68; research assoc. in physics Rhodes U., Grahamstown, Republic South Africa, 1970-71; assoc. in gymnosperms U. Colo. Mus., 1972—; internat. chmn. study group internat. radio consultative com. Internat. Telecommunication Union, Geneva, 1956-78. Contbr. articles to profl. jours. Served to maj., Signal Corps AUS, 1941-46. Decorated Legion of Merit; recipient Arthur S. Flemming govt. award Washington Jr. C. of C., 1951; Silver medal Dept. Commerce, 1952; Gold medal, 1956. Fellow AAAS, Am. Phys. Soc., Am. Geog. Soc., Royal Astron. Soc., Royal Geog. Soc.; mem. Sci. Research Soc. Am. (pres. Boulder br. 1967-68), Am. Geophys. Union, Am. Astron. Soc., Geog. Soc. Lima (hon.), Phi Beta Kappa., Sigma Xi. Clubs: Cosmos (Washington); Explorers (N.Y.C.). Home: 1441 Bluebell Ave Boulder CO 80302 Office: U Colo Mus Boulder CO 80309

BAILEY, DON MATTHEW, aerospace company executive; b. Pitts., Jan. 2, 1946; s. William and Vera (Mitchell) B.; m. Linda Reed, Sept. 15, 1967; children: Don Matthew Jr., Kirsten Paige, Terrance Reed. BSME, Drexel U., 1968; MS in Ops. Rsch., U. So. Calif., 1971; MBA, Pepperdine U., 1986. Programmer Naval Air Systems Command, Washington, 1963-69; engr. Rockwell Internat., Anaheim, Calif., 1969-71; program mgr. Logicon, Inc., San Pedro, Calif., 1971-80; sec., v.p. corp. devel. Comarco, Inc., Anaheim, 1980—; bd. dirs. Devel. Disabilities Ctr. Orange County, Anaheim, Calif., Perspective Instructional Communications, San Diego. Mem. Assn. for Corp. Growth. Office: Comarco Inc 160 S Old Springs Rd Anaheim CA 92647

BAILEY, DOUGLAS KENT, data processing executive; b. Pensacola, Fla., Mar. 16, 1949; s. Homer Dwight and Marjorie Louise (Shaw) B.; m. Wynette Lynn Kau, Apr. 26, 1986; 1 child, Luisa Michelle. BS cum laude, Wake Forest U., 1971; JD, Case Western Res. U., 1974. Bar: Ohio. Bus. analyst Union Carbide Corp., N.Y.C., 1974-76; legal analyst Fed. Jud. Ctr., Washington, 1976-81; court mgmt. analyst Jud. Council Calif., San Francisco, 1981-82, mgr. court mgmt. svcs. unit, 1982, mgr. data processing unit, 1982-87; gen. mgr. western regional office CMC Assocs., Inc., Alameda, Calif., 1987—. Home: 1434 Saint Charles St Alameda CA 94501 Office: CMC Assocs 1001 Marina Village Pkwy Ste 100 Alameda CA 94501

BAILEY, EDWARD HOPKINS, management consultant; b. Boston, Nov. 10, 1939; s. Edward Hopkins Bailey and Joyce Coburn (Haskell) Dickinson; m. Patricia Anne Wynne, May 21, 1964; children: Dorothy, John, Jacqueline, Nicholas, Edward. BA, Harvard U., 1962; M Aero. Engring., Cornell U., 1966; MBA, NYU, 1973. Sr. mfg. engr. GE, Schenectady, N.Y., 1967-69; cons. GE, N.Y.C., 1969-73; mfg. mgr. GE, Milw., 1973-78; program mgr. GE, Bridgeport, Conn., 1978-88; prin. Gabriel Group, Alta Loma, Calif., 1988—. Treas., Christ's Ch., 1980-86. Fellow Am. Prodn. and Inventory Control Soc. (chmn. edn. com., Fairfield, Conn. chpt. 1980-82); mem. Assn. Mfg. Excellence. Republican. Episcopalian. Home: 5917 N Archibald Ave Alta Loma CA 91701 Office: Gabriel Group 5917 N Archibald Ave Alta Loma CA 91701

BAILEY, EILEEN, editor, publisher; b. Elgin, Tex., May 6, 1940; d. Taylor Bell Bailey and Bernice Liebold (Smith) Morris; m. Gerald O. Brooks, Sept. 8, 1957 (div. 1968); children: Kelly Brooks Calzaretta, Shelly Brooks Duebler, Laurie. Student, Phoenix Coll., 1971-72, Ariz. State U., 1972-85. Prin. Eileen Bailey Pub. Rels., Phoenix, 1974-87; pub., editor V Mag., Phoenix, 1987—. Contbr. to Family Circle mag. Bd. dirs. Ariz. Kidney Found., 1974-83. Mem. Western Publs. Assn., Charter 100, Phoenix Art Mus. Democrat. Home: 938 W Campus Dr Phoenix AZ 85013 Office: V Mag PO Box 36355 Phoenix AZ 85067

BAILEY, GEORGE PAUL, infosystems specialist; b. Denver, June 17, 1961; s. George Edward and Mary Carolyn (Gaul) B. B in Environ. Design, U. Colo., 1983. Sales display rep. Tektronix, Inc., Wilsonville, Oreg., 1984; systems analyst assoc. Tektronix, Inc., Englewood, Colo., 1984-85, systems analyst, 1985-87, product systems analyst, 1987-89, specialist cartographic applications, 1989—; mem. strategic games, U. Colo., Engelwood, 1989—. Dir., producer cable program, Denver's Homeless, 1986. Mem. ARC Emergency Broadcasting, Jefferson County, Colo., 1987-88. Mem. Front Range Unix Users' Group, Jaycees, U.S. Chess Fedn., Scotch and Soda Club, Sports Cars of Am. Club. Home: 12954A W 64th St Arvada CO 80004-2271 Office: Tektronix Inc 393 Inverness Dr S Englewood CO 80112-5669

BAILEY, JANET ADALIND, computer scientist; b. La Jolla, Calif., Mar. 27, 1960; d: Gilbert Newton and Doris Irene (Price) B. BA in Math., Humboldt State U., 1983. Lectr. dept. math. Humboldt State U., Arcata, Calif., 1983-84; systems analyst Def. Systems Corp., Escondido, Calif., 1984-85; computer scientist Logicon Inc., San Diego, 1985-89; scientist Naval Ocean Systems Ctr., San Diego, 1989—.

BAILEY, JERRY WAYNE, municipal government official; b. Bellingham, Wash., Mar. 29, 1948; s. Loyd Herbert and Betty May (Blowers) B.; m. Nicki Lynn Husted, Sept. 18, 1982; children: Andrea Illona, Drew James. BA, Western Wash. U., 1973, MA, 1981. Capt. Bellingham Fire Dept., 1974—; co-owner Bailey & Assocs., Bellingham, 1983—; archaeol. field worker Western Wash. U., Bellingham; presenter in field. Mem. Soc. Am. Archaeology, Am. Acad. Forensic Scis., Internat. Assn. Arson Investigators. Presbyterian. Office: Bellingham Fire Dept 1200 Dupont St Bellingham WA 98225

BAILEY, JOHN TAYLOR, systems analyst, microcomputer consultant; b. Arcata, Calif., July 15, 1958; s. Melvin D. and Patricia A. (Larsen) B.; m. Judith Ann Bardella, July 16, 1983. AA, Coll. of Redwoods, 1983; BA, Humboldt State U., 1988. Microcomputer cons. Bailey, Olson, and Kosarich Software, Eureka, Calif., 1982—; computer products salesman WCI Computer Cen., Eureka, 1983-85; cons. Superior Alarm Co., Eureka, 1983—, Humbolt Steel Shelving, Eureka, 1985—. Creator computer programs on market share analysis, small ch. database, naval combat simulation. Vol. United Way, Eureka, 1983. With USAF, 1978-80. Humboldt Area Found. Bancroft scholar, 1986-87. Mem. Data Processing Mgmt. Assn., Am. Assn. for Artificial Intelligence, Navy League U.S. Democrat. Mem. Evang. Covenant Ch. Home: 2614 Patricia Dr Des Moines IA 50322 Office: Bailey Olson & Kosarich Software PO Box 85 Ferndale CA 95536

BAILEY, LEONARD LEE, surgeon; b. Takoma Park, Md., Aug. 28, 1942; s. Nelson Hulburt and Catherine Effie (Long) B.; m. Nancy Ann Schroeder, Aug. 21, 1966; children: Jonathan Brooks, Charles Connor. BS, Columbia Union Coll., 1960-64; postgrad., NIH, 1965; MD, Loma Linda U., 1969. Diplomate Am. Bd. Surgery, Am. Bd. Thoracic Surgery. Intern Loma Linda U. Med. Ctr., 1969-70, resident in surgery, 1970-73, resident in thoracic and cardiovascular surgery, 1973-74; resident in pediatric cardiovascular surgery Hosp. for Sick Children, Toronto, Ont., Can., 1974-75; resident in thoracic and cardiovascular surgery Loma Linda U. Med. Sch., 1975-76, asst. prof. surgery, 1976—, asst. prof. pediatrics, 1978—, dir. pediatric cardiac surgery, 1976—. Mem. Am. Coll. Cardiology, Soc. Thoracic Surgery, Am. Assn. Thoracic Surgery, Western Thoracic Surg. Assn., Western Soc. Pediatric Research, Walter E. McPherson Soc. (clin. investigator of year 1976, 85). Democrat. Seventh-day Adventist. Office: Loma Linda U Med Ctr Loma Linda CA 92350

BAILEY, MAJOR WINDSOR, II, asbestos abatement superintendent; b. Gettysburg, S.D., Apr. 14, 1961; s. Major Windsor and Doris Elaine (Marshall) B. Cert. OSHA worker, Calif., EPA supr., Calif. Helper Bailey Painting Contractors, Mardela Springs, Md., 1970-78; finish painter Bailey Painting Contractors, Mardela Springs, 1978-79; foreman painter Griffith

Painting Contractors, Ocean City, Md., 1979-81; painting contractor MWB Enterprises, Ocean City, 1981-82; taper, finisher Kevin Bray Constrn., San Francisco, 1982-83; gen. foreman Energy Conservation Unltd., San Francisco, 1983-86; gen. supt. North Bay Specialty Contracting, Petaluma, Calif., 1986—. Sr. patrol leader troop 262 Boy Scouts Am., Salisbury, Md., 1970-79. Mem. Am. Motorcycle Assn. Republican.

BAILEY, MICHAEL JOHN, engineering manager; b. Phila., Oct. 16, 1953; s. Theodore Warren and Anne (Pomeroy) B.; m. Cheryl Lee Meyer, Aug. 23, 1974. BS in Mech. Engring., Purdue U., 1975, MS in Mech. Engring., 1976, PhD, 1979. Mem. tech. staff Sandia Nat. Labs., Albuquerque, 1979-81; prof. mech. engring. Purdue U., West Lafayette, Ind., 1981-85; dir. advanced devel. Megatek Corp., San Diego, 1985-89; mgr. sci. visualization San Diego Supercomputer Ctr., 1989—; freelance cons. in field, 1981—. Recipient Ralph Teetor Teaching award Soc. Automotive Engrs., 1983. Mem. Assn. Computing Machinery, Spl. Interest Group on Computer Graphics (chmn. courses 1984-85, 87-88, exec. com. 1986—), Nat. Computer Graphics Assn., Am. Soc. Mech. Engrs. Office: San Diego Supercomputer Ctr PO Box 85608 San Diego CA 92138

BAILEY, ROBERT RAY, music educator; b. Enid, Okla., Nov. 23, 1938; s. Joseph Horace and Jessie Faye (Harman) B.; m. Virginia Anne Palencia, May 28, 1959 (div. June 1971); 1 child, Tamara Lynn; m. Dolores Roberta Hammond, Aug. 1, 1974; children: John Robert, Sharon Lynelle. BMEd., Phillips U., 1960; MMEd., Midwestern U., Wichita Falls, Tex., 1967. Dir. music Pond Creek (Okla.) Independent Sch. Dist., 1960-64; grad. asst. Midwestern U., Wichita Falls, Tex., 1964-66; dir. mus. Electra (Tex.) Independent Sch. Dist., 1966-67; dir. vocal music Washington Jr. High Sch., Albuquerque, 1967-68; dir. of bands McKinley Jr. High Sch., Albuquerque, 1968-71, Rio Grande High Sch., Albuquerque, 1971-85; chmn., performing arts West Mesa High Sch., Albuquerque, 1985—; festival dir., West Mesa Jazz Festival, Albuquerque, 1985-89. Mem. Music Educators Nat. Conf., N.Mex. Educators Assn. (dist. pres. 1971-72), Nat. Assn. Jazz Educators (v.p. N.Mex. State chpt. 1983-84), NEA, Am. Sch. Band Dirs. Assn., Internat. Council of Computer Users in Edn., Delta Kappa Gamma. Home: 9512 Villa Del Rey NE Albuquerque NM 87111 Office: West Mesa High Sch 6701 Fortuna Rd NW Albuquerque NM 87121

BAILEY, RODNEY LAWRENCE, business counselor, landscape services manager; b. Seattle, Dec. 12, 1937; s. William Carl and Joanne (Ballou) B.; m. Sue Ann Pullin Bailey, Mar. 19, 1960; children: Elizabeth Anne, Benjamin Edward, William Patrick. AB in Econs. and Indsl Engring., Stanford U., 1959, MBA, 1961. Engr. plant prodn. and inventory control Procter & Gamble Mfg. Co., Sacramento, 1963-65; mgmt. cons. Harry J. Prior & Assocs., Seattle, 1965-71; exec. v.p. Pacific SBG, Inc., Bellevue, Wash., 1971—; pres., treas., gen. mgr., co-owner Evergreen Svcs. Corp., Bellevue, 1971—; co-gen. ptnr. Evergreen Hill Ptnrship., Bellevue, 1973—; bd. dirs. The Bank of Northshore, Bothell, Wash. Lt. U.S. Army, 1981-83. Recipient Davis B. Gray Meml award, Nat. Purchasing Agts. Assn., 1961. Mem. Am. Inst. Indsl. Engrs. (pres. Seattle chpt. 1965), Wash. Assn. Landscape Profls. (bd. dirs. 1984-87, pres. 1987), Profl. Grounds Mgmt. Soc., Wash. State Nurserymen's Assn. (Outstanding Svc. award 1982), Associated Landscape Contractors of Am. (v.p. 1982, pres. elect 1983-84, pres. 1985), Bldg. Owners and Mgrs. Assn., Nat. Assn. Indsl. and Office Parks, Bellevue C. of C., Rotary Club. Republican. Presbyterian. Office: Evergreen Svcs Corp 12010 SE 32d St Bellevue WA 98005

BAILEY, THOMAS EVERETT, engineering company executive; b. Atlantic, Iowa, Mar. 30, 1936; s. Merritt E. and Clara May (Richardson) B.; m. Elizabeth Jane Taylor, Sept. 9, 1956; children: Thomas E., Douglas L., Steven W. BS, U. Iowa, 1959. Reg. profl. engr., environ. assessor. Engr. Calif. Dept. Water Resources, Sacramento, 1960-67; sr. engr. Calif. Water Quality Control Bd., San Luis Obispo, 1967-72; asst. div. chief, dir. water quality planning State Water Resources Control Bd., Sacramento, 1972-75, chief div. planning rsch., 1975-77, chief tech. support br., 1977-79; sr. tech. advisor Yemen Arab Republic, Sana'a, 1979-81; chief Calif. superfund program Calif. Dept. Health Svcs., Sacramento, 1982-86; prin., v.p. Kleinfelder Inc., Walnut Creek, Calif., 1986—; also bd. dirs. Kleinfelder Inc., Walnut Creek. Contbr. articles to profl. jours. Chmn. San Luis County Obispo Rep. Cen. Com., 1972; mem. State Rep. Cen. Com., 1970-72; vice-chmn. bd. trustees Meth. Ch., San Luis Obispo, 1970-72. With U.S. Army, 1959-60. Mem. ASCE, Water Pollution Control Fedn., Calif. Water Pollution Control Assn., Cons. Engrs. Assn. Calif. Home: 7064 Riverside Blvd Sacramento CA 95831 Office: Kleinfelder Inc 17100 Pioneer Blvd Artesia CA 90701

BAILIN, TOBY, public relations executive; b. Cleve., June 7, 1941; d. Hayman Edward and Annette (Shor) Bailin; m. John W. Gilje, Aug. 22, 1965 (div. 1970). B.A., U. Mich., 1963, M.A., 1964; now postgrad. U. Hawaii. Copywriter Sta. KGMB, CBS, Honolulu, 1969-72; mem. pub. relations dept. Milici Advt. affiliate Doyle, Dane Bernbach, Honolulu, 1972-73, First Hawaiian Bank, Honolulu, 1973-78; asst. to pub. relations dir. Amfac, Inc., Honolulu, 1978; asst. v.p., asst. to chmn. and pres., 1978-82; v.p., asst. to chmn., 1983—. Editor co. mag. Panako (Best Overall Publ. award 1977). Bd. dirs. Jewish Fedn. Hawaii, Honolulu, 1985, Coalition for a Drug Free Hawaii; gov. Pacific and Asian Affairs Council; chmn. Dem. for Reagan, Honolulu, 1984, publicity chmn. The Outdoor Circle, Honolulu, 1983—; mem. adv. bd. Hawaii State Dept. Human Services, Correction Industries. Mem. Pub. Relations Soc. Am., Honolulu C. of C. (bd. dirs. 1985—, pub. affairs com.), Japan Am. Soc. Honolulu, Honolulu Club, Plaza Club. Office: Amfac Inc 700 Bishop St 21st Fl PO Box 3230 Honolulu HI 96801

BAILY, DOUGLAS BOYD, state attorney general; b. Evanston, Ill., Jan. 27, 1937; divorced; 3 children. BS in Geology, Beloit Coll., 1959; JD, U. Ill., 1964. Bar: Alaska 1965. Field geologist, geophys. aid Pan Am. Petroleum Corp., United Geophys. Corp., Alaska, 1960-61; asst. atty. gen. Dept. Law, State of Alaska, Juneau and Fairbanks, 1964-69, state dist. atty. 3d jud. dist., 1968, 69; U.S. atty. State of Alaska, Juneau, 1969-71, state atty. gen., 1989—; ptnr. Baily & Mason, P.C., Anchorage, 1971-88; dir. Office External and Internat. Fisheries Affairs Alaska Dept. Fish and Game, 1988-89; comml. fishing deck hand, sport fishing, 1986-88; capt. charter fishing boat, Homer, Alaska, deckhand tour boat, Seward, Alaska, July-Sept. 1988. Vol., licensed for passenger vessels to 50 tons, U.S. Coast Guard; mem. ad hoc com. for creation of Chugach State Pk., Alaska, 1970-71. With U.S. Army, 1959-60, Res., 1960-66. Home: PO Box 21948 Juneau AK 99802 Office: State of Alaska Law Dept State Capitol PO Box K Juneau AK 99811-0300

BAILY, EVERETT MINNICH, electrical engineer; b. Twin Falls, Idaho, June 9, 1938; s. Charles Levi Baily and Helen Louise (Minnich) Wall; m. Donna Rae Larson, Sept. 8, 1961; children: Susan Gayle, Brian Charles. BSEE, U. Idaho, 1961, MSEE, 1964; PhD, Stanford U., 1968. Asst. prof. U. Idaho, Moscow, 1965-71; assoc. prof. U. Idaho, 1971-74, prof., 1974; prodn. engr. Hewlett Packard Co., Boise, Idaho, 1974-75; devel. engr. Hewlett Packard Co., 1975-81, reliability engr., 1981-83, reliability engring. mgr., 1983-86, prodn. engring. mgr., 1986—; cons. researcher U. Idaho Rsch. Found., Moscow, 1971-73. Patentee in field. Recipient Dow Outstanding Young Faculty award, Am. Assn. Engring. Edn. Pacific Northwest sect, 1970. Mem. IEEE (Boise sect. chmn. 1979, numerous com. offices), Model A Ford Club Am., Lions. Home: 12080 Chinden Blvd Boise ID 83714 Office: Hewlett Packard Co 11311 Chinden Blvd Boise ID 83714

BAIN, R(ALPH) BEN, JR., food service executive, business owner; b. Atascadero, Calif., Dec. 10, 1968; s. Ralph Benjamin Sr. Bain. Grad. high sch., Ogden, Utah, 1988. Owner Caspers Hotdogs, Ogden, 1987-88, Future Concept Carpet, Ogden, 1988—; sr. pres. Starr Industries. Democrat. Home: 1190 N 300 W Sunset UT 84015

BAIR, WILLIAM J., radiation biologist; b. Jackson, Mich., July 14, 1924; s. William J. and Mona J. (Gamble) B.; m. Barbara Joan Sites, Feb. 16, 1952; children: William J., Michael Braden, Andrew Emil. B.A. in chemistry, Ohio Wesleyan U., 1949; Ph.D. in Radiation Biology, U. Rochester, 1954. NRC-AEC fellow U. Rochester, 1949-50, research asso. radiation biology, 1950-54; biol. scientist Hanford Labs. of Gen. Electric Co., Richland, Wash., 1954-56, mgr. inhalation toxicology sect., biology dept., 1956-65; mgr. inhalation toxicology sect., biology dept. Battelle Meml. Inst., 1965-68; mgr. biology dept. Pacific Northwest Labs., Richland, Wash., 1968-74, dir. life scis. program, 1973-75, mgr. biomed. and environ. research program, 1975-76, mgr. environ. health and safety research program, 1976-86, mgr. life scis. ctr., 1986—; demonstrator toxicology of plutonium and carcinogenisis of radioactive particles in lung; lectr. radiation biology Joint Ctr. Grad. Study, Richland, 1955—; cons. to adv. com. on reactor safeguards Nuclear Regulatory Commn., 1971—; mem. several coms. on plutonium toxicology; mem. subcom. inhalation hazards, com. pathologic effects atomic radiation Nat. Acad. Sci., 1957-64; mem. ad hoc com. on hot particles of subcom. biol. effects of ionizing radiation Nat. Acad. Scis.-NRC, 1974-76, vice chmn. Com. on Biol. Effects of Ionizing Radiation IV Alpha Radiation, 1985-88; chmn. task force on biol. effects of inhaled particles Internat. Commn. on Radiol. Protection, 1970-79, mem. com. 2 on permissible dose for internal radiation, 1973—; chmn. Task Group on Respiratory Tract Models, 1984—; chmn. Hanford Symposium Inhaled Radioactive Particles and Gases, 1964; co-chmn. Hanford Symposium Biol. Implications of Transuranium Elements, 1971; chmn. Life Scis. Symposium on Radiation Protection: A Look to the Future, 1986; chmn. Am. Inst. Biol. Scis.-AEC-Energy Research and Devel. Adminstrn. Transuranium Tech. Group, 1972-75; mem. Nat. Council on Radiation Protection and Measurements, 1974—, bd. dirs., 1976-82, mem. com. of radionuclides on maximum permissible concentrations for occupational and non-occupational exposure, 1970-77, mem. com. basic radiation protection criteria, 1975—, chmn. ad hoc com. on hot particles, 1974, chmn. ad hoc com. internal emitter activities, 1976-77, mem. com. 57 on internal emitter standards, 1977—; U.S. participant and rep. numerous internat. confs., invited lectr. Japan AEC, Nat. Radiol. Health Inst., Chiba, 1969, South African Assn. Physicists in Medicine and Biology, Pretoria, 1980, North China Inst. Radiation Protection, 1984; mem. rev. com. Argonne Univs. Assn., 1977-80; chmn. Marshall Islands radiol. adv. group Dept. Energy, 1978-81; mem. staff Pres.'s Commn. on Accident at Three Mile Island, 1979-80; mem. regional steering com. on health effects from eruption of Mt. St. Helens, 1980-84; chmn. Dept. Energy task group on health and environ. consequences of Soviet nuclear accident, 1986-87; mem. U.S. delegation in meetings with USSR on Chernobyl accident Internat. Atomic Energy Agy.; guest of USSR at health consequences meeting of Chernobyl accident, 1988. Author 200 books, articles, reports, chpts. in books. Recipient E.O. Lawrence Meml. award, 1970; cert. of appreciation AEC, 1975; Alumni Disting. Achievement citation Ohio Wesleyan U., 1986. Fellow AAAS, Health Physics Soc. (dir. 1970-73, 83-86, pres.-elect 1983-84, pres. 1984-85); mem. Radiation Rsch. Soc., N.Y. Acad. Sci., Soc. Exptl. Biology and Medicine (vice chmn. N.W. sect. 1967-70, 74-75), Reticuloendothelial Soc., Soc. Occupational and Environ. Health, Sci. Soc. Pres. (coun. 1984-85), Sigma Xi. Club: Kiwanis (dir.). Home: 102 Somerset St Richland WA 99352 Office: Battelle Pacific NW Labs PO Box 999 Richland WA 99352

BAIRD, ALAN C., television producer, writer; b. Waterville, Maine, Jan. 5, 1951; s. Chester A. and Beverly E. (Gilbert) B. BA, Mich. State U., 1973. Pres. Souterrain Teeshirts, Nice, France, 1977-78; page NBC, N.Y.C., 1979-80; producer, dir. Random Prodns., Hollywood, Calif., 1981; writer, producer Preview STV, N.Y.C., 1982-83, Sta. KCOP-TV, Hollywood, 1983-84; writer Vidiom Prodns., Hollywood, 1985—. Author: ATS Operations, 1976; producer (TV script) Live at the Palomino, 1981; writer (TV scripts) Night Court, 1986, 20/60, 1986, Golden Girls, 1986, Family Ties, 1986, Max Headroom, 1987, (movie scripts) Trading Up, 1988, Merlinsky, 1989. Crisis counselor San Francisco Suicide Prevention, 1975; prodn. asst. March of Dimes Telethon, Hollywood, 1985. Recipient Harvard Book prize Harvard U., Cambridge, Mass., 1969.

BAIRD, DIANNE JESSOP, banker; b. Lodi, Calif., Mar. 10, 1947; d. Herbert Daunt and Peggy (Hundley) Jessop; m. Stanley Dale Baird, Sept. 23, 1967 (div. 1978); children: Christine, Kimberly. Student, Calif. State Poly. U., 1965-67. Co-owner Stan Baird, Realtor, Glendora, Calif., 1972-78; assoc. Colby Realtors, Glendora, 1978-79; v.p. Amenity Products, Inc., Calimesa, Calif., 1979-83; analyst Am. Diversified Savs. Bank, Costa Mesa, Calif., 1983-85; asst. v.p./loan officer Calmac Capital, Irvine, Calif., 1985; asst. v.p. Sanwa Bank Calif., Pasadena, 1985—, loan officer, 1985-87, dept. head, 1987—. Mem. Nat. Assn. Rev. Appraisers, Nat. Assn. Mortgage Underwriters, Bldg. Industry Assn., Nat. Assn. Female Execs. Republican. Office: Sanwa Bank Calif 171 S Lake Ave Pasadena CA 91101

BAIRD, JONI ELAINE, security professional; b. Denver, July 23, 1948; d. Walter Leslie and Jacqueline Mary (Bachelor) Soles; 1 child from previous marriage: Joel Elaine. BSBA, Regis Coll., 1989. Security mgr. Montgomery Ward, Thornton, Colo., 1969-75; security officer U.S. Postal Inspection Svc., Denver, 1975-76; investigator Jefferson County Sheriff's Dept., Golden, Colo., 1976-79; regional security mgr. Manville Corp., Denver, 1979-85, 86—; legis. project mgr. Manville Corp., Denver, 1985-86. Bd. dirs. Crimestoppers, Denver, 1986—; mem. selection com. Citizens Mil. Acad., Denver, 1987; security coord. Childrens Diabetes Found., Denver. Mem. Met. Law Enforcement Assn. (pres. 1976-77), Am. Soc. for Indsl. Security, Colo. Law Enforcement Officers Assn. Democrat. Roman Catholic. Office: Manville Corp PO Box 5108 Denver CO 80217

BAIRD, ROBERT ROY, real estate executive; b. Colorado Springs, Colo., Sept. 3, 1937; s. Eldred D. and Alice Eudora (Havens) B.; BS magna cum laude, Woodbury U., 1969; postgrad. Calif. State U., Northridge, 1970-71; m. Sally Ann Baird, Oct. 3, 1959; children: J. Brian, Sean Christopher, Robert Roy. Life agt. Manhattan Life Ins. Co., Encino, Calif., 1961-62; v.p. Red Top div. Am. Hosp. Supply Co., Los Angeles, 1962-73; pres. Baird Industries, Inc., Montrose, Calif., 1973-79; pres. Central Security Trust, Glendale, Calif., 1981-88, Pension Vest Inc., 1982—, Cluck-in-a-Bucket, Inc, 1984-88; chief fin. officer Baird-Frey, Inc., 1988—; TV talk show host Channel 22, Los Angeles, 1981-83; radio show host Sta. KIEV, Glendale, 1988-89. Lector, St. Bede's Catholic Ch., LaCanada, Calif., 1977-81; mem. Long Beach Redevel. Agy., 1976; chmn. bd. Local 117 Selective Service; dist. chmn. Am. Cancer Soc., 1962; v.p. Lakeview Terrace (Calif.) Little League, 1974; exec. mem. Town Hall of L.A. Served with U.S. Army, 1955-57; ETO. Decorated Letter of Commendation; recipient Outstanding State Vice Pres. award Jr. C. of C., 1962, Phi Gamma Kappa award Woodbury U., 1969, Dora E. Kirby award Woodbury Coll., 1969; named Outstanding Mktg. Dir., Red Top, Inc., 1971-73. Mem. Assn. Interior Environmentalists (charter), Calif. Assn. Realtors, U.S. Olympic Volleyball Assn. (charter), Crescenta Valley C. of C. (pres. 1985), Nat. Assn. Pvt. Placement Syndicators (pres. 1985). Author: The Checkerboard Theory of Life, 1985; contbg. author: Young Men Can Change the World, 1966. Pioneer Tele Tissue, roller ski poles. Home: 1040 S Orange Grove Pasadena CA 91105 Office: 18484 Hwy 18 Apple Valley CA 92307

BAKALY, CHARLES G., JR., lawyer; b. Long Beach, Calif., Nov. 15, 1927; s. Charles G. and Doris (Carpenter) B.; m. Patricia Murphey, Oct. 25, 1952; children: Charles G. III, John W., Thomas B. AB, Stanford U., 1949; JD, U. So. Calif., 1952. Bar: Calif., N.Y., U.S. Dist. Ct. (cen., no., ea. and so. dists.) Calif., U.S. Ct. Mil. Appeals, D.C., U.S. Ct. Appeals (9th, 2d, 10th and D.C. cirs.), U.S. Supreme Ct. Assoc. O'Melveny & Myers, L.A. and N.Y.C., 1956-63, ptnr., 1963—; lawyer del. 9th Cir. Jud. Conf., 1984-87, chmn., 1987-88; mem. dispute com. Ctr. for Pub. Resources; chmn. Dispute Resolution Adv. Coun., 1987-88; speaker to numerous employer indsl. rels. orgns. Contbr. articles to profl. jours., chpts. to books. Trustee, mem. exec. com. Scripps Coll., 1974-87; bd. fellows Claremont U. Ctr., 1974-87; bd. dirs., mem. exec. com. Childrens Hosp. L.A., 1985-88; bd. govs. Town Hall L.A., 1981-83; mem. edni. coun. and performing arts coun. Music Ctr. Los Angeles County; mem. exec. com. Calif. Rep. Com., 1970-81; bd. advisors Calif. Rep. League; trustee Rep. Assocs., 1983-84; chmn. Rose Inst. State and Local Govt., Claremont Men's Coll., 1975-83. 1st lt. JAGC, U.S. Army, 1952-56. Fellow Am. Bar Found.; mem. ABA (ho. of dels. 1984-87), Los Angeles County Bar Assn. (trustee 1963-64), D.C. Bar, N.Y. State Bar Assn., Am. Coll. Trial Lawyers, Mchts. and Mfrs. Assn. (bd. dirs., exec. com. 1965-87), NAM, C. of C. U.S., Internat. Soc. for Labor Law and Social Legis., L.A. World Affairs Coun., Am. Arbitration Assn. (bd. dirs.), Def. Rsch. Inst., L.A. Area C. of C., Law Soc., Chancery Club, Lincoln Club (bd. govs., v.p. 1987—), Valley Hunt Club, Calif. Club. Home: 521 Michigan Blvd Pasadena CA 91107 Office: O'Melveny & Myers 400 S Hope St Los Angeles CA 90071

BAKEMAN, CAROL ANN, administrative services manager, singer; b. San Francisco, Oct. 27, 1934; d. Lars Hartvig and Gwendolyne Beatrice (Zimmer) Bergh; student UCLA, 1954-62; m. Delbert Clifton Bakeman, May 16, 1959; children—Laurie Ann, Deborah Ann. Singer, Roger Wagner Chorale, 1954—, Los Angeles Master Chorale, 1964-86; librarian Hughes Aircraft Co., Culver City, Calif., 1954-61; head econs. library Planning Research Corp., Los Angeles, 1961-63; corporate librarian Econ. Cons., Inc., Los Angeles, 1963-68; head econs. library Daniel, Mann, Johnson & Mendenhall, architects and engrs., Los Angeles, 1969-71, corporate librarian, 1971-77, mgr. info. services, 1978-81, mgr. info. and office services, 1981-83, mgr. adminstrv. services, 1983—. Pres., Creative Library Systems, Los Angeles, 1974-83; library cons. ArchiSystems, div. SUMMA Corp., Los Angeles, 1972-81, Property Rehab. Corp., Bell Gardens, Calif., 1974-75, VTN Corp., Irvine, Calif., 1974, William Pereira & Assos., 1975. Mem. Assistance League, So. Calif., 1956-86, mem. nat. auxilaries com. 1968-72, 75-78, mem. nat. by laws com. 1970-75, mem. asso. bd. dirs., 1966-76. Mem. Am. Guild Musical Artists, AFTRA, Screen Actors Guild, Adminstrv. Mgmt. Soc. (v.p. Los Angeles chpt. 1984-86, pres. 1986-88, internat. conf. chmn. 1988-89, internat. bd. dirs. area 15 1988—), Los Angeles Master Chorale Assn. (bd. dirs. 1978-83), Roger Wagner Choral Inst. (com. planning and devel. 1988—). Office: Daniel Mann Johnson & Mendenhall 3250 Wilshire Blvd Los Angeles CA 90010-1599

BAKER, ALVIN BRADDOCK, corporate professional; b. Walnut Creek, Calif., Nov. 24, 1957; s. Alvin W. and Ethel (Richards) B. AA, Diablo Valley Coll., 1985, A in Computer Sci., 1983. Chief programmer Computime Computer Services, San Ramon, Calif., 1984-86; v.p. Optical Storage Solutions, Concord, Calif., 1986-88; cons. Fed. Gov., Washington, 1988-89; sr. mem. tech. staff level II Ashton-Tate, Walnut Creek, Calif., 1989—; cons. Pacific Gas & Electric, Diablo Canyon, 1986-87. Author: Technical Reference, 1988, Optical Storage A Study in System Integration, 1988. Mem. Soc. for Photo-Optical Instrumentation Engrs. Democrat. Mormon. Office: Ashton-Tate 2033 N Main St Ste 980 Walnut Creek CA 94596-3722

BAKER, ARNOLD BARRY, economist; b. N.Y.C., Feb. 3, 1946; s. Max Michael and Sue (Feingold) B. BA in History, Va. Poly. Inst., 1968; MA, in Econs., 1970, PhD, 1972. Spl. asst. to undersec. for monetary affairs U.S. Dept. Treasury, Washington, 1977-79; sr. cons. Atlantic Richfield Co., L.A., 1979-82; mgr. planning info. analysis Arco Exploration Co., Dallas, 1983; mgr. strategic planning Arco Oil & Gas Co., Dallas, 1983-85, dir. energy market analysis, L.A., 1986-89, dir. pub. issues, 1989—. Contbr. articles to profl. jours., chpt. to book. Mem. Am. Econ. Assn., Nat. Assn. Bus. Econs., Internat. Assn. Energy Econs. Avocation: jogging. Office: Arco 515 S Flower St Los Angeles CA 90071

BAKER, BRIAN REED, construction executive; b. Washington, Feb. 18, 1949; s. Charles Walter and Anna Hilda (Bethlehemian) B.; m. Kathleen Lorraine Kuni, 1979 (div. Aug. 1982); m. Stacy Lynn Selman, Dec. 5, 1984; 1 child, Nicole. Student, U. Md., 1967-69. Lic. building contractor. Actor, writer L.A., 1972—; sales mgr. Windsong Enterprises, Bellflower, Calif., 1975-82; territory mgr. Williams Furnace, Colton, Calif., 1982-86, Stonhard, Inc., Saugus, Calif., 1986—. Screenwriter: The 'Nam, 1980, Laney's Lancers, 1982; appeared in numerous TV shows. Vol. Spl. Olympics, Los Angeles, 1983. Served as sgt. U.S. Army, 1969-72, Vietnam. Mem. Screen Actors Guild, AFTRA, Nat. Rifle Assn., Aircraft Owners and Pilots Assn. Republican. Presbyterian. Home and Office: 27923 Milliken Dr Saugus CA 91350

BAKER, BRUCE FREDERICK, banker; b. Seattle, Sept. 23, 1930; s. Frederick Edward and Edel (Peterson) B.; m. Joyce Marie Norwick, Jan. 24, 1951; children: Jeffry, David, Bryan. BA, U. Wash., 1954. Assoc. Cappy Ricks and Assocs., Seattle, 1954-56; v.p. Ayer/Baker, Seattle, 1956-69; NW mgr. Boyden Assocs., Seattle, 1969-71; v.p. Pacific First Fed. Savs. Bank, Tacoma, 1971-74; sr. v.p. Wash. Mut. Savs. Bank, Seattle, 1974-81; pres. Donworth Taylor Assocs., Seattle, 1981-83; pres., chief exec. officer First Mut. Bank, Bellevue, Wash., 1983—, also bd. dirs., 1983—. Contbr. articles to profl. jours. Trustee Seattle Found., 1983—; pres. chief Seattle council Boy Scouts Am., 1981-82. Mem. Japan-Am. Soc. Wash. (v.p. 1988, dir. 1986—), Bellevue C. of C. (chmn. 1989—), Rotary, Rainier Club. Mem. Congregational Ch. Office: First Mut Savs Bank 400 108th NE Bellevue WA 98004

BAKER, BRYAN WILLIAM, marketing executive; b. Beloit, Wis., Oct. 15, 1948; s. Donald William and Blanche (Skarin) B.; m. Ioanna Jacqueline Cocolis, Dec. 27, 1970 (div. Dec. 1978); m. Sheila Marie Leins, May 29, 1988; one child, Bradley William. BA, Rockford Coll., 1970; MA, U. Americas, Cholula, Mex., 1974. Acct. mr. Burroughs Co., Cheyenne, Wyo., 1974-78; regional sales mgr. SDMI Corp., Prairie Valley, Kans., 1978-81; v.p. sales and mktg. PBL Assocs., Pt. Richmond, Calif., 1981—. Served with U.S. Army, 1970-72. Mem. Internat. Computer Programs Assn. Office: PBL Assocs 10 Cottage Ave Point Richmond CA 94801

BAKER, CHARLES DEWITT, medical manufacturing company executive; b. Dayton, Ohio, Jan. 5, 1932; s. Donald James and Lillian Mae (Pund) B.; m. June Thordis Tandberg, June 25, 1954; children: Charles, Robert, Thomas, Michael. AA in Electrical Engring., Long Beach City Coll., 1953; Boston U., 1954, Pacific Coast U., 1963, U. Utah, 1980. Registered profl. mfg. engr., Calif. Chemist Shell Oil, Torrance, Calif., 1957-60; materials and process engr. Northrop Corp., Hawthorne, Calif., 1960-63; packaging engr. Jet Propulsion Lab., Pasadena, Calif., 1963-71; med. design engr. Utah Biomed. Test Lab., Salt Lake City, 1971-78, sect. mgr., 1978-83; v.p. Tech. Research Assocs., Salt Lake City, 1983-88, pres., 1988—; pres. Thordis Corp., 1980—. Patentee in field. Pres. Utah Autistic Soc., 1984. Recipient Cost Reduction award NASA, 1969, New Tech. award, 1969, 71, 75. Republican. Mormon. Office: Tech Rsch Assocs 410 Chipeta Way Ste 222 Salt Lake City UT 84108

BAKER, CHERYL ANNE, community center executive; b. Utica, N.Y., Oct. 26, 1953; d. Lawrence James and Janet Lois (Bauman) Baker; m. John James Joseph Duffy, III. Lic. in real estate, Calif.; cert. housing specialist HUD. Housing paralegal Redwood Legal Assistance, Ukiah, Calif., 1980-81; property mgr. Rural Communities Housing Devel. Corp., Ukiah, 1981-87; exec. dir. Ukiah Community Ctr., 1987—. Mem. adv. com. Ukiah Redevel. Commn., 1987-89, Women's Econ. Devel. Project, Ukiah, 1988—. Recipient Good Hands award Ukiah Community Ctr., 1983. Mem. Nat. Assn. Female Execs. Democrat. Office: Ukiah Community Ctr 505 S State St Ukiah CA 95482

BAKER, DARRELL F., construction contract administrator; b. Boise, Idaho, Apr. 10, 1926; s. Francis Melton and Eunice Mabel (Yeck) B.; m. Zella McLombs, Mar. 10, 1952; children: Jann Lisa, Alan. BCE, U. N. Mex., 1947; MCE, Ill. Inst. Technology, 1949. Licensed profl. engr., Idaho, 1952. Engr. estimator Morrison-Knudson Co., Seattle, 1955-56; project mgr., engr. Morrison-Knudson Co., Anchorage, Alaska, 1956-59; div. chief estimator Morrison-Knudson Co., Seattle, Honolulu, 1959-61; research Boeing Co., Seattle, 1961-65; chief engr. S.S. Mullen Constrn., Seattle, 1965-68, bldg. div. mgr., 1968-71; constrn. sponsor Riedel Internat. Inc., Portland, Oreg., 1971-74; contract adminstr. Riedel Internat. Inc., Portland, 1975-86; constrn. cons. self-employed, Portland, 1987—. Lt. USNR, 1952-55. Republican. Mormon. Home and Office: 14784 NW Forestel Loop Beaverton OR 97006

BAKER, DAVID SCOTT, hospital administrator; b. Fresno, Calif., Jan. 19, 1946; s. Elton Murray and Letha (Mitts) B.; m. Carol Elise Rosenfeld, July 26, 1970; children: Scott, Emily. BA, U. Puget Sound, 1968; MBA, Oreg. State U., 1970. Project dir. Ernst & Whinney, Tacoma, 1970-71; contr. Quali-cast, Chehalis, Wash., 1971-73; instr. Centralia (Wash.) Community Coll., 1972; adminstr. fin. Met. Hosps., Portland, Oreg., 1973-80; accounts mgr. Emanuel Hosp., Portland, Oreg., 1976-77; adminstr. fin. Kerr Ctrs., Portland, 1980—. Active Hospice House, Inc; Cath. Youth Orgn.; treas. Portland Youth Philharm.; chmn. Opera Assn.; Country Classic Run. Recipient Service Commendation, Dept. Human Service, U. Oreg., 1988. Mem. Am. Soc. Pub. Adminstrs., Healthcare Fin. Mgmt. Assn., Alpha Kappa Psi. Club: 20/30 International (v.p. 1983-85). Office: Kerr Ctrs 424 NE 22d St Portland OR 97232

BAKER, DEBORAH ANN, business owner; b. Washington, May 12, 1956; d. Richard John and Shirley Ann (Jackson) Dunagan; m. Don Steven Baker, June 20, 1980; children: Adam Ross, Jason Richard, Natalie Rae. Grad.

High Sch., Novato, Calif. Buyer, dept. mgr. Carithers. Dept. Store, Novato, Calif., 1975-77; mgr. books Baker Installations, Denver, 1977-79; mgr. Fashion Carpets, Englewood, Colo., 1979-83; owner, operator Baker Interiors, Englewood, 1983—. Office: Baker Interiors 3535 S Platte Dr #L Englewood CO 80110

BAKER, DENYS MARIE, motel owner; b. Payson, Utah, Jan. 7, 1948; d. Grant William Koyle and Shirley Jayne (Garbett) Schena; m. Alexander Ray Perea, Apr. 28, 1968 (div. 1979); children: Gary A., Dennis A.; m. John Dean Baker, Oct. 21, 1981; step-children: Christina, David, Craig, Tom. BA magna cum laude, U. Utah, 1970; postgrad., U. Calif.-Long Beach, 1976-77. Cert. tchr., Utah. Owner, mgr. Border Inn, Baker, Nev., 1977-81, 85—. Mem. Nev. Democratic exec. com., 1984, mem. state central com.; sec. Baker Town Adv. Bd., 1985—. Recipient Gov.'s Tourism Devel. award, 1988. Mem. Nev. Cattlewomen's Assn. (officer local sect.). Office: Border Inn Hwy 50 at Hwy 6 Baker NV 89311

BAKER, DON ROBERT, chemist; b. Salt Lake City, Apr. 6, 1933; s. Ralph H. and Ruth Eve (Thalmann) B.; m. Shirley May Nelson, Nov. 20, 1954; children: Robert, David, George, Barbara. AA, Sacramento City Coll., 1953; AB, Calif. State U., Sacramento, 1955; PhD, U. Calif., Berkeley, 1959. Sr. rsch. chemist Stauffer Chem. Co., Richmond, Calif., 1958-72, rsch. assoc., 1970-74, supr., 1974-85, sr. rsch. assoc. ICI Ams., Inc. div., 1985—. Editor: California Chemists Alert, 1986—, Synthesis and Chemistry of Agrochemicals, 1987; contbr. articles to profl. jours.; patentee in field. Mem. Am. Chem. Soc. (chmn. Calif. sect. 1973, councilor Calif. sect. 1971—, chmn. nat. div. profl. relations 1980, coordinating com. Calif. sects. 1970—), Plant Growth Regulator Soc., Orchid Soc. Calif. (pres. 1979-80), Oakland Genealogy Library (librarian 1967—). Republican. Mormon. Home: 15 Muth Dr Orinda CA 94563 Office: ICI Americas Inc 1200 S 47th St Richmond CA 94804

BAKER, EDWIN MOODY, retired newspaper publisher; b. Cleve., Dec. 20, 1923; s. Alton Fletcher and Mildred Elizabeth (Moody) B.; m. Patricia Petersen, 1954 (dec. 1983); children: Bridget Baker Kincaid, Amanda Baker Barber, Jonathan; m. Marie Kottkamp Randall, 1984; children: Steven, Mark, Bruce Randall. B.S. in Bus. Adminstrn., U. Oreg., 1948. With Eugene (Oreg.) Register-Guard, 1948-88, successively advt. mgr., bus. mgr., gen. mgr., pub., pres., chmn. bd. Guard Pub. Co.; pres. Community Newspapers, Inc., Beaverton, Oreg., v.p. N.W. Web. Mem. exec. bd. Oreg. Trail Council, Boy Scouts Am., 1953—, pres. 1960-61, chmn. Region XI Area I (Northwest) 1971, pres., 1972, mem. nat. exec. bd., 1971-72, nat. adv. council, 1972—; trustee U. Oreg. Found., 1975—, Lane Community Coll.; bd. dirs. Oreg. Community Found., Oreg. Hist. Soc., Oreg. Youth Conservation Corp.; chmn., trustee Eugene Arts Found., 1980—; pres. Oreg. Pacific Econ. Devel. Corp., 1984-85; 2d v.p. Eugene Springfield Met. Ptnrship.; mem., chmn. Sister City com., 1986—. Served with AUS, World War II. Decorated Bronze Star, Purple Heart; recipient Silver Beaver award, Boy Scouts Am., 1962, Silver Antelope, 1965, Pioneer award U. Oreg., 1982, Awbrey Watzig award Lewis and Clark Coll., 1988; named Eugene First Citizen, 1983. Mem. Am. Newspaper Pubs. Assn. (research inst. lab. com. 1978-79), Oreg. Newspaper Pubs. Assn. (dir. 1982-83, pres. 1988-89), U. Oreg. Pres. Assocs. , Rotary, Eugene Country Club, Willow Creek Racquet Club. Home: 2121 Kimberly Circle Eugene OR 97405 Office: 1358 Oak Eugene OR 97401

BAKER, EDWIN STUART, computer consultant; b. Ottumwa, Iowa, Feb. 14, 1944; s. Edwin Moore and Geraldine Vivian (Irby) B; m. Wilma Jeanne Parker, 1968 (div. 1970). Student, Whitman Coll., 1962-64; BS, Oreg. State U., 1978. Programmer agrl. engring. dept. Oreg. State U., Corvallis, 1977-78, rsch. asst., 1979-83, sr. rsch. asst., 1984—; cons. in field. Mem. ACM, IEEE, DAV, Am. Legion, NRA, Nat. Intercollegiate Rodeo Assn. (faculty advisor 1986—), 59'ers Svc. Club. Home: PO Box 774 Philomath OR 97370 Office: Oreg State U Agrl Engring Dept Corvallis OR 97331

BAKER, ELAINE ROSE, internist, gastroenterologist; b. Portland, Oreg., Dec. 18, 1953; d. Robert John and Lydia (Zimmerman) Gossman; m. Laurence Hadley Baker, May 25, 1980; children: Aaron Jonathan, Madeline Ruth. BS, Portland State U., 1978; JD, Oreg. Health Scis. U., 1980. Diplomate Am. Bd. Internal Medicine and Gastroentology. Resident in medicine U. Conn. Health Ctr., Farmington, 1980-84, fellow in gastroenterology, 1984-86; pvt. practice Portland, 1986--. Mem. Oreg. Med. Assn., Multnomah County Med. Soc., Am. Gastroent. Assn. Democrat. Jewish. Office: U Conn Health Ctr 545 NE 47th Ste 206 Portland OR 97213

BAKER, ELIZABETH TATE, labor relations specialist; b. Boston, Dec. 5, 1949; d. Elwood Tate and Leonie (Vosburgh) B. BA, George Washington U., 1972, MEd, 1974. Cert. rehabilitation counselor. Br. chief U.S. Soldiers and Airmens' Home, Washington, 1974-76; labor relations specialist Social Security Adminstrn., Washington, 1976-78, U.S. Dept. Edn., Washington, 1978; labor relations officer San Francisco Mint, 1978—. Mem. Nat. Pub. Employers' Labor Relations Assn., Am. Congress Rehab. Medicine. Office: US Mint San Francisco 88 5th St San Francisco CA 94103

BAKER, FRED GREENTREE, hydrogeologist; b. Chgo., July 26, 1950; s. Con James and Ethel M. (Skowbo) B.; m. Judith Ann Krill, 1972 (div. 1974); m. Hannah F. Pavlik, Apr. 26, 1976. BS in Geology, U. Wis., 1972, MS in Soil Sci., 1975; MS in Civil Engring., U. Colo., Boulder, 1981, PhD in Geology, 1985. Registered geologist, Calif.; registered profl. engr., Colo. Rsch. specialist Wis. Geol. and Natural History Survey, Madison, 1973-76; rsch. assoc. dept. civil engring. Colo. State U., Fort Collins, 1977-78; hydrologist U.S. EPA, Denver, 1979-81; engring. geologist Charles C. Bowman Assocs., Inc., Boulder, Colo., 1982-85; sr. hydrogeologist Dames & Moore, Sacramento, 1985-88; dir. ops. On-Site Technologies, Inc., Sacramento, 1989; mgr. hydrogeologic svcs. Woodward-Clyde Cons., Denver, 1989—. Contbr. articles to profl. jours. Mem. ASCE, Am. Geophys. Union, Soil Sci. Soc. Am., Am. Assn. Petroleum Geologists, Assn. Ground Water Scientists and Engrs., Sigma Xi. Office: Woodward-Clyde Cons 4582 S Ulster St Pkwy Stanford Pl 3 Ste 1000 Denver CO 80237

BAKER, FREDERICK JOHN, university official, educator, consultant; b. Saginaw, Mich., Mar. 4, 1941; s. Benjamin George and Mary Louise (Ross) B.; m. Rosalie Giacchino, Aug. 26, 1968; children: John Benjamin, Michael Thomas, Sarah Beth. BA, Cen. Mich. U., 1964; MA, Antioch Coll., 1968; PhD, Mich. State U., 1973. Vol. Peace Corps, Thailand, 1964-66; jr. high sch. tchr. Wash. Pub. Schs., 1967-68; with USIS, Thailand, 1968-70; dir. Tchr. Corps Micronesia, Ponape, Trust Ter. Pacific, 1975-77; dir. field experiences Cen. Mich. U., Mt. Pleasant, 1972-82; dir. Cen. Mich. U., Belize, 1974-75; dir. Eng. student teaching Cen. Mich. U., Southampton, 1977-78; asst. dir. tchr. edn. U. Calif., Irvine, 1982-88; prof., coordinator of tchr. edn. Calif. State Polytechnic U., Pomona, 1988--; Fulbright prof., Bangkok, 1985-86. Author: Ponape Learning Resources, 1977; contbr. articles on tchr. and internat. edn. to profl. jours. Mem. Calif. Assn. Tchr. Edn. (v.p. 1984-85), Assn. of Tchr. Edn., Assn. for Supervision and Curriculum Devel., Tchr. Corps Far West Network (bd. dirs. 1975-77). Home: 1829 Shenandoah Dr Claremont CA 91711 Office: Calif State Poly U 3801 W Temple Ave Pomona CA 91768

BAKER, JEANETTE SLEDGE, educational administrator; b. Atlanta, June 24, 1947; d. Jesse Alexander and Carolyn (Chapman) Sledge; m. Donald Todd Baker, Sept. 6, 1969. B.Mus., Fla. STate U., 1970; MEd, U. Ariz., 1980, PhD, 1983; student, U. Fla., 1965-67. Asst. admissions and fin. aid officer Columbia U., N.Y.C., 1970-72; grad. admissions clk. U. Ariz., Tucson, 1972-73, degree certification officer, 1973-79; asst. to v.p. No. Ariz. U., Flagstaff, 1984-87, asst. v.p., 1987—. Contbr. to book: At The Crossroads: General Education in Community Colleges, 1983. Chmn. Coconino County Silent Witness Bd., Flagstaff, 1988-89 vice chmn. 1987. Mem. Flagstaff C. of C., Nat. Assn. Female Execs., We. States Govtl. Relations Network. Office: No Ariz U PO Box 4115 Flagstaff AZ 86011-4115

BAKER, JOHN ALBERT, JR., accountant; b. Port Angeles, Wash., July 2, 1919; s. John Albert and Rose (Anderson) B.; B.A., Wash. State U., 1943; m. P. Pasha Prossen, Nov. 25, 1978; children—Raymon Edward, Carlton Crawford, Cameron John, Peggy Melinda, Fred Albert. Sr. acct., audit supr., sr. tax cons. Cameron & Johnstone, Honolulu, 1946-50; partner Cameron, Tennent & Greaney, Honolulu, 1950-51, Baker & Gillette, Honolulu, 1951-65, Coopers & Lybrand, Honolulu, 1965-81; chmn. Pasha Pacific Properties, Inc., 1981—. Served with USMCR, 1943-46. Mem. Nat. Assn. Accountants, Hawaii Soc. C.P.A.s, Hawaii Estate Planning Council, Nat. Tax Assn., Hawaii Bd. of Accountancy (pres., disting. pub. service award 1984), Am. Inst. C.P.A.s (bd. examiners 1964-68), Nat. Assn. State Bds. Accountancy, Am. Acctg. Assn. Home: PO Box 3919 Honolulu HI 96812

BAKER, JOHN RICHARD, law enforcement official; b. Portland, Oreg., May 11, 1946; s. Arthur O. and Eleanore (Nietert) B.; m. Joan Elaine Foote, July 27, 1968. BS, Portland State U., 1971. Dep. sheriff County of Multnomah, Portland, 1971—. Bd. dirs., Sixth Man Found., Portland, 1984—, pres., 1986. Mem. McIntires Athletic Club. Republican. Baptist.

BAKER, JOSEPH RODERICK, III, parrot breeder; b. Middletown, Ohio, Sept. 26, 1947; s. Joseph Roderick and Lois Patricia (Barnhart) B. BS in Math., Rensselaer Poly. Tech., 1969. Systems rep. Burroughs Corp., Honolulu, 1973-80; mgr. data processing Kenault Inc., Honolulu, 1980-81; v.p. Software Solutions Inc., Honolulu, 1982-83; br. mgr. DataPhase Corp., Honolulu, 1983-88; pres. Birds of Paradise, Honolulu, 1987—. Lt. (j.g.) USN, 1969-73. Mem. Am. Fedn. Aviculture, Nat. Cockatoo Soc., Macaw Soc. Am., Eclectus Soc., Am. Contract Bridge League.

BAKER, KELLY SHANE, mechanical engineer; b. Salt Lake City, July 28, 1962; s. Quinton Hal and Marjorie (Tate) B. BS, U. Utah, 1986. Registered profl. engr., Utah. Design engr., space div. Morton Thiokol, Inc., Brigham City, Utah, 1987—. Republican. Mormon. Home: 2209 Far Down Ave Salt Lake City UT 84121

BAKER, KENT ALFRED, television news director; b. Sioux City, Iowa, Mar. 22, 1948; s. Carl Edmund Baker and Miriam M. (Hawthorn) Baker Nye. Student, Iowa State U., 1966-70. Mem. U.S. Peace Corps., 1971-72; editor The Glidden (Iowa) Graphic, 1973-75; bureau chief The Waterloo (Iowa) Courier, Iowa, 1975; state editor The Des Moines Register, 1976-77; news dir. Sta. WQAD-TV, Moline, Ill., 1978; Sunday editor The Des Moines Sunday Register, 1979; news dir. Sta. KHON-TV, Honolulu, 1980—. Mem. Hist. Hawaii Assn., Honolulu. Recipient numerous news writing awards Iowa Press Assn., 1973-74. Mem. Radio and TV News Dirs. Assn., Bishop Mus. Assn. (Honolulu chpt.), East-West Ctr. Assn. (Honolulu chpt.), Hoover Libr. Assn. (West br.). Lodge: Lions. Home: PO Box 23015 Honolulu HI 96822 Office: Sta KHON-TV 1170 Auahi St Honolulu HI 96814

BAKER, KENT RICHARD, pharmaceutical company executive; b. Decar, Utah, May 20, 1942; s. Paul James and Dorothy (Prince) C.; m. Mary Sander, June 10, 1961; children: Michael, K. Todd, Gregory, Danielle. BS in Mktg., U. Utah, 1970. Sales mgr I.T.T. Continental Baking, Salt Lake City, 1963-71; regional sales mgr Sandoz Pharmaceutical, East Hanover, N. J. 1971-72; v.p sales and mktg. Murdock Internat., Provo, Utah, 1982-84; pres. Puget Sound Fin. Group, Seattle, 1984-86; region dir. sales, western U.S. Connaught Labs., Inc., Seattle, Swiftwater,, Pa., 1986--; cons. Bread Garden, Seattle, 1983-84, Health Care-H.M.O., Seattle, 1982. Convention delegate, Republican Party, Utah, 1968, voting dist. chmn. Midvale, Utah, 1967-71; pres. Booster Club, Redmond High Sch., Redmond, Wash., 1986-87; leader, Boy Scouts Am., Utah, Wash. 1960-- (nat. pres. unit award, 1976). Mem. Brigham Young U. Mgmt. Soc., Bellevue C. of C., Rotary. Republican. Mormon. Office: Connaught Labs Inc 800 Koll Ctr Bellevue Ste 814 500-108th Ave Bellevue WA 98004-5560

BAKER, LARRY CURTIS, minister; b. L.A., Sept. 19, 1945; s. Charles Leonard and Genevee (Becker) B.; m. Mary Callicoat, Oct. 23, 1964; children: Christopher Daniel, Sarah Morgan. BA, Hardin-Simmons U., 1970; MDiv, Golden Gate U., 1975. Ordained to ministry, Bapt. Ch., 1969. Pastor First Bapt. Ch., Maryneal, Tex., 1968-69, Cen. Bapt. Ch., Stamford, Tex., 1969-71, DeAnza Bapt. Ch., Cupertino, Calif., 1971-73; pub. rels. assoc. Golden Gate Bapt. Sem., Mill Valley, Calif., 1973-75; pastor First So. Bapt. Ch., Lodi, Calif., 1975-77, Ventura, Calif., 1977-81; v.p. communications Golden Gate Sem., Mill Valley, 1981-83; pastor Bethel Bapt. Ch., Concord, Calif., 1983—. Editor newspaper the HSU Brand, 1968-70; asst. pubr. newspaper Stamford Am., 1970-71. With USAF, 1963-67. Republican. Baptist. Office: Bethel Bapt Ch 3578 Clayton Rd Concord CA 94519

BAKER, LEWIS NORMAN, legal adminstrator; b. Yuba City, Calif., Aug. 20, 1955; s. Friend Nathan and Ferne Irene (Hardy) B. BS in Bus. Adminstrn., Cal Poly, 1977; MBA, San Diego State U., 1988. Buyer, mgr. Bullock's Stores, Los Angeles, 1978-80; mktg. dir. Riviera Stores, Los Angeles, 1980-84; dir. ops. Brawn of Calif., San Diego, 1984-88; legal adminstr. Page, Tucker, Brooks & Busch, San Diego, 1989—. Mem. Cal Poly Alumni Assn., Phi Kappa Phi. Democrat. Episcopalian. Home: 3110 32nd St San Diego CA 92104 Office: Page Tucker Brooks & Busch 350 W Ash St Ste 900 San Diego CA 92101-3404

BAKER, LILLIAN, author, historian, artist, lecturer; b. Yonkers, N.Y., Dec. 12, 1921; student El Camino (Calif.) Coll., 1952, UCLA, 1968, 77; m. Roscoe A. Baker; children: Wanda Georgia, George Riley. Continuity writer Sta. WINS, N.Y.C., 1945-46; columnist, freelance writer, reviewer Gardena (Calif.) Valley News, 1964-76; freelance writer, editor, 1971—; lectr. in field.; founder/editor Internat. Club for Collectors of Hatpins and Hatpin Holders, monthly newsletter Points, ann. Pictorial Jour., 1977—, conv. and seminar coordinator, 1979—; co-founder Ams. for Hist. Accuracy, 1972, Com. for Equality for All Draftees, 1973; chair S. Bay primary campaign S.I. Hayakawa, for U.S. Senator from Calif., 1976; witness U.S. Commn. Wartime Relocation, 1981, U.S. Senate Judiciary Com., 1983, U.S. Ho. Reps. Judiciary Com., 1986. Recipient award Freedoms Found., 1971; Ann. award Conf. Calif. Hist. Socs., 1983; monetary award Hoover Instn. Stanford (Calif.) U., 1985; recipient award Pro-Am. Orgn., 1987. Fellow IBA (life); mem. Nat. League Am. Pen Women, Nat. Writers Club, Soc. Jewelry Historians USA, (charter), Art Students League N.Y. (life), Nat. Historic Soc. (founding), Nat. Trust Historic Preservation (founding), other orgns. Author: Collector's Encyclopedia of Hatpins and Hatpin Holders, 1976, second edit. 1988, 100 Years of Collectible Jewelry 1850-1950, 1978, rev. edit., 1986, 88, Jewelry: Art Nouveau and Art Deco, 1980, rev. edit. 1985, 87, 88, The Concentration Camp Conspiracy: A Second Pearl Harbor, 1981 (Scholarship Category award of Merit, Conf. of Calif. Hist. Socs. 1983), Hatpins and Hatpin Holders: An Illustrated Value Guide, 1983, rev. edit. 1988, Creative and Collectible Miniatures, 1984, Fifty Years of Collectible Fashion Jewelry: 1925-1975, 1986, rev. edit., 1988, Dishonoring America: The Collective Guilt of American Japanese, 1988; also articles; author poetry; editor: Insider; contbg. author Vol. VII Time-Life Encyclopedia of Collectibles, 1979; numerous radio and TV appearances. Home and Office: 15237 Chanera Ave Gardena CA 90249

BAKER, MARIAN IRENE ARBAUGH, retail company executive; b. Indpls., Apr. 1, 1935; d. Olin Thomas Warren Logan and Vivian Catherine (Wiley) Arbaugh; divorced; children: Beth Ann, Amy Lynn, Meg Eileen Vodjansky, Jo Nan English. BS in Edn., Ind. U., 1956; postgrad., U. No. Colo., 1975. Cert. tchr., Ind., Colo. Tchr. Indpls. Pub. Schs., 1956-58; tchr., tester St. Vrain Valley Pub. Schs., Longmont, Colo., 1978-80; lighting cons. Olde World Lighting, Boulder, Colo., 1980-82; mgr.-in-tng. K-Mart, Longmont, 1982-84; sports-auto mgr. K-Mart, Sterling, Colo., 1984—; lay adviser St. Vrain Valley Pub. Sch. Dist., 1969-79; tchr., tester pre-kindergarten screening, Longmont, 1975-78. Pres., chmn. bd. dirs. Santa Fe Jr. Women's Club, 1959-64; leader Camp Fire Girls, Albuquerque and Longmont, 1966-78. Recipient Comml. TV award Benton and Bowles Advt. Agy., 1962. Mem. AAUW (pres., mem. exec. bd. 1965—), Chi Omega Alumnae (pres. Santa Fe chpt. 1959—). Republican. Home: 416 S 3d Ave Sterling CO 80751

BAKER, RICHARD W., structural and architectural engineer; b. Glendale, Calif., Aug. 16, 1945; s. Elwood V. and Eleanor J. (Vickers) B.; m. Judith K. Fields, July 5, 1969; children: Carrie A., Brian R. AA, Pasadena City Coll., 1965; BS in Archtl. Engring., Calif. State Poly. Coll., San Luis Obispo, 1968. Naval architect Long Beach (Calif.) Naval Shipyard, 1965-69; stress engr. Lockheed Aero. Systems Co., Burbank, Calif., 1969-73, 75-87, group engr., 1987-89, project structures engr., 1989—; stress engr. Rockwell Internat., Downey, Calif., 1974; archtl. cons., Cerritos, Calif., 1972--. Editor: Aircraft Stress Analysis, 1987. Mgr. Frontier Little League, Cerritos, 1985--; coach City of Cerritos Parks & Recreation Dept., 1982-87. Mem. AIAA. Republican. Methodist. Home: 13518 La Jara St Cerritos CA 90701 Office: Lockheed Aero Systems Co Dept 72-37 Bldg B 90-4 A-1 PO Box 551 Burbank CA 91505

BAKER, RODNEY LEE, naval officer; b. Champaign, Ill., June 15, 1950; s. Claude William and Jean Madeline (Morrison) B.; m. Brenda Sue Siebert, Dec. 13, 1975; children: Deah, Jeffrey, Claire. BS in Edn., Southeast Mo. State U., 1975. Commd. ensign U.S. Navy, 197, advanced through grades to lt. comdr., 1986; Naval Aviation Trng. and Ops. Standardization officer VA-136 Electronic Warfare Squadron, U.S.S. Midway, 1979-82; administrv. officer VA-95 Attack Squadron, N Air Sta. Whidbey Island, Wash., 1985-88; student Armed Forces Staff Coll., Norfolk, Va., 1988--. Mem. Tail Hook Assn. Home: 521 E Sunrise Blvd Oak Harbor WA 98277

BAKER, ROLAND JERALD, association executive; b. Pendleton, Oreg., Feb. 27, 1938; s. Roland E. and Theresa Helen (Forest) B.; m. Judy Lynn Murphy, Nov. 24, 1973; children: Kristen L., Kurt F., Brian H. B.A., Western Wash. U., 1961; M.B.A., U. Mich., 1968. Cert. purchasing mgr. Asst. dir. purchasing and stores U. Wash., Seattle, 1970-75; mgr. purchasing and material control Foss Launch & Tug Co., Seattle, 1975-79; mem. faculty Shoreline Community Coll., 1972-79, Edmonds Community Coll., 1974-79; chmn. educators group Nat. Assn. Purchasing Mgmt., Tempe, Ariz., 1976-79; mem. faculty Pacific Luth. U., 1977-79; exec. v.p. Nat. Assn. Purchasing Mgmt., Tempe, Ariz., 1979-88, pres., 1988—; chmn. bd. trustees Ctr. for Advanced Purchasing Studies, 1986—. Author: Purchasing Factomatic, 1977, Inventory System Factomatic, 1978, Policies and Procedures for Purchasing and Material Control, 1980. Served with USN, 1961-70; comdr. Res. U.S. Navy postgrad. fellow, 1967. Mem. Purchasing Mgmt. Assn. Wash. (pres. 1978-79), Nat. Minority Supplier Devel. Council (bd. dirs.), Am. Prodn. and Inventory Control Soc., Nat. Assn. Purchasing Mgmt. (exec. v.p. 1979—), Nat. Contract Mgmt. Assn., Internat. Fedn. Purchasing and Materials Mgmt., Am. Soc. Assn. Execs. Office: Nat Assn Purchasing Mgmt PO Box 22160 Tempe AZ 85282

BAKER, RONALD JAY, SR., electrical engineer; b. Canton, Ohio, Feb. 6, 1936; s. Earl R. B. and Mary E. (Lehmiller) Davidson; m. Sharon L. Ostrom, Feb. 10, 1962; children: Ronald Jr., Donald I., Shirley A. Grad. high sch., Canton. Enlisted USN, Washington, 1956, advanced through grades to chief petty officer, 1962, ret., 1964; design engr. Tech. Materiel Corp., Mamaroneck, N.Y., 1964-67; sr. test, design engr. Applied Dynamics, Inc., Ann Arbor, Mich., 1967-73; sr. electronic engr. Applied Rsch. Labs., Inc., Valencia, Calif., 1973—. Author: (tng. manuals) Electronic Readout, 1976, Theory of Operation, 1978, Problem Solving, 1987. Democrat. Mormon. Office: Applied Rsch Labs 24911 Ave Stanford Valencia CA 91355

BAKER, SALLY, television writer, producer; b. Chgo., Sept. 22, 1932; d. Harry and Lillian (La Viet) S.; m. Walter P. Baker; children: Kathleen Lynda, Kolleen Lynn. Student, UCLA, 1949, Woodbury Coll., 1950, Bradley U., 1960, U. So. Calif., since 1970. Producer, TV host Sta. WESH-TV, Daytona Beach, Fla., 1958-59, Sta. WLOF-TV, Orlando, Fla., 1959-60; producer, writer, TV host Sta. WTVH-TV, Peoria, Ill., 1960-62, Sta. KCHU-TV, San Bernardino, Calif., 1962-64, Sta. KTTV-TV, Hollywood, Calif., 1964-66; producer, writer Hartwest Prodns., N.Y.C., 1966-67, Sta. KCOP-TV, Hollywood, 1967-74, Sta. KHJ-TV, Hollywood, 1975; TV devel. producer Hanna-Barbera, Hollywood, 1976; writer, producer Sta. KNBC-TV, Burbank, Calif., 1977, Sta. KHJ-TV, Hollywood, 1978—; co-producer Last Electric Knight ABC Network, 1985; co-producer Sidekicks Disney-Motown, ABC Network, Hollywood, 1985-87. Author: Color Me Love, 1978; producer: (TV show) Toyathon (nominated for Emmy, 1970), Hobo Kelly Show (nominated for Emmy, 1970, 71, 72), In Search of Reality (Emmy award, 1973); producer, writer: Salute to Hollywood, NBC Fall Preview, If I Should Die Before I Wake (nominated for Emmy, 1981), Our Small World, But Can She Type, A Whale of a Show (nominated for Emmy 1974), An Evening With Pat O'Brien, Sunday with Sally, Glamourama, The Magic Mirror, Knotts Berry Farm Spl., Election Show Central, Sidekicks, The Froozles (nominated for Emmy 1978); writer: (story) Highway to Heaven, "Another War Another Peace"; producer The Last Electric Knight. Recipient 8 Emmy award nominations, 1970, 71, 72, 73, 74, 78, 81. Mem. Women in Film (v.p. 1975-76, pres. 1976-77, Women in Govt. (Women of the Yr. 1981), YWCA Leadership Luncheon Search Com. (Silver Achievement Merit award, 1983), So. Calif. Motion Picture Council 1977 (Golden Halo award, Film Adv. bd. Salute to Hollywood, prodn. award, 1987), Am. Women in TV, (1970 Merit award). Mem. Religious Science.

BAKER, V. LILITH, laboratory administrative official; b. Zuni, N.Mex., July 12, 1935; d. Major V. and Virginia D. (Link) Bruton; m. Jack E. Baker, June 3, 1956 (div. Sept. 1971); children: Rhonda Gayle, David Randall. Student, U. N.Mex., 1953-54, N.Mex. State U., 1955-56. Clk. typist Bur. Indian Affairs, Window Rock, Ariz., 1954-55; credit card clk. Standard Oil of Tex., El Paso, 1956; teletype operator D&RG Railroad, Pueblo, Colo., 1957; clk. typist BIA, Shiprock, N.Mex., 1959-60; teletype operator to administrv. coord. Sandia Nat. Labs., Albuquerque, 1961—. Presbyterian.

BAKER, WARREN J(OSEPH), university president; b. Fitchburg, Mass., Sept. 5, 1938; s. Preston A. and Grace F. (Jarvis) B.; m. Carol Ann Fitzsimons, Apr. 28, 1962; children: Carrie Ann, Kristin Robin, Christopher, Brian. B.S., U. Notre Dame, 1960, M.S., 1962; Ph.D., U. N.Mex., 1966. Research assoc., lectr. E. H. Wang Civil Engring. Research Facility, U. N.Mex., 1962-66; assoc. prof. civil engring. U. Detroit, 1966-71, prof., 1972-79, Chrysler prof., dean engring., 1973-78, acad. v.p., 1976-79; NSF faculty fellow M.I.T., 1971-72; pres. Calif. Poly. State U., San Luis Obispo, 1979—; judge Internat. Sci. and Engring. Fair, 1974, 75, 77, 80; mem. adv. bd. Jr. Humanities and Sci. Symposium, 1976-78; mem. Bd. Internat. Food and Agr. Devel., 1983-86; mem. Nat. Sci. Bd., 1985—. Contbr. articles to profl. jours. Mem. Detroit Mayor's Mgmt. Adv. Com., 1975-76; mem. engring. adv. bd. U. Calif., Berkeley, 1984—; bd. dirs. Calif. Council for Environ. and Econ. Balance, 1980-85; trustee Nat. Coop. Edn. Assn. Fellow Engring. Soc. Detroit; mem. ASCE (chmn. geotech. div. com. on reliability 1976-78, civil engring. edn. and research policy com. 1985—), NSPE (pres. Detroit chpt. 1976-77), Am. Soc. Engring. Edn., Am. Assn. State Colls. and Univs. (bd. dirs. 1982-84). Office: Calif Poly State U Office of Pres San Luis Obispo CA 93407

BAKER-LIEVANOS, NINA GILLSON, jewelry store executive; b. Boston, Dec. 19, 1950; d. Rev. John Robert and Patricia (Gillson) Baker; m. Jorge Alberto Lievanos, June 6, 1981; children: Jeremy John Baker, Wendy Mara Baker, Raoul Salvador Baker-Lievanos. Student Mills Coll., 1969-70; grad. course in diamond grading Gemology Inst. Am., 1983; student in diamondtology designation Diamond Coun. Am., 1986—. Artist, tchr., Claremont, Calif., 1973-78; escrow officer Bank of Am., Claremont, 1978-81; retail salesman William Pitt Jewelers, Puente Hills, Montclair, Calif., 1981-83, asst. mgr., Montclair, 1983, mgr., Santa Maria, Calif., 1983—, corp. sales trainer, 1988—. Artist tapestry hanging Laguna Beach Mus. Art, 1974. Recipient Cert. Merit Art Bank Am., 1968. Mem. NAFE, Internat. Platform Assn., C. of C., Compassion Internat. Republican. Roman Catholic. Avocations: tapestry weaving, creative writing. Office: William Pitt Jewelers 158 Towne Ctr Santa Maria CA 93454

BAKES, ROBERT ELDON, state supreme court justice; b. Boise, Idaho, Jan. 11, 1932; s. Warren H. and Oral Bakes; m. Lurleen M. Fisher; children: Juliann, Colleen, Diane, Rachel. Bar: Idaho 1956, U.S. Ct. Appeals (9th cir.) 1963. Instr. U. Ill., 1956-57; legal counsel Idaho State Tax Commn., Boise, 1959-61; asst. U.S. atty. Boise, 1961-66; sr. ptnr. Bakes, Ward & Bates, Boise, 1969-71; justice Idaho Supreme Ct., Boise, 1971—, chief justice, 1981-82. Office: Idaho Supreme Ct Bldg 451 W State St Boise ID 83720

BAKKE, ERIC LARS, photojournalist; b. Denver, Feb. 7, 1951; s. Seymour Doss and Beverly Ann (Walters) B.; m. Karen Fitzgerald, July 14, 1979. BJ, U. No. Colo., 1973. Reporter, photographer Granby (Colo.) Sky Hi News, 1973; photographer Winter Park Ski Resort, Hideaway Park, Colo., 1973-74; reporter, photographer Golden (Colo.) Daily Transcript, 1974-76; photographer Boise (Idaho) Statesman, 1976-77, Sentinel Newspapers,

Denver, 1977-78; photographer Denver Post, 1978-81, chief photographer, 1984; chief Topeka Capital-Jour., 1981; co-owner Photostaff, Inc., Denver, 1985-87; pvt. practice Denver, 1987—. Contbr. photographs to Day in the Life of America, 1986, Day in the Life of Spain, 1987, Day in the Life of California, 1988, A Game for All America, 1988. Chmn. profl. photography div. Colo. State Bd. Occupational and Vocat. Edn. Recipient Best Feature Picture award The Sporting News, St. Louis, 1985, First Place Feature award, Suburban Newspapers of Am., 1977. Mem. Nat. Press Photographers Assn. (asst. dir., 1980), Am. Soc. Mag. Photographers. Lutheran.

BAKKEN, GARY MAYNARD, engineering educator, consultant; b. Westby, Wis., June 27, 1945; s. Maynard Joslyn and Evelyn (Carol) B.; m. Darlene Marie Gurney, June 7, 1969; children: Erik, Audreá. BSE, Ariz. State U., 1969; MS in Indsl. Safety, Cen. Mo. State U., 1974; PhD in Engring., Tex. Tech. U., 1983. Research asst. Cen. Mo. State U., Warrensburg, 1973-74; engr. 3M Co., St. Paul, 1974-76; research asst. Tex. Tech. U., Lubbock, 1976-78; asst. prof. U. Ariz., Tucson, 1978-81; cons. Tucson, 1981—. Contbr. articles to profl. jours. Asst. scoutmaster Troop 211 Boy Scouts Am., Tucson, 1984—. Capt. USAF, 1965-73. Mem. Human Factors Soc., Systems Safety Soc., Am. Acad. Forensic Scis., Am. Inst. Indsl. Engrs., Sigma Xi, Phi Kappa Phi, Alpha Pi Mu. Office: 1790 E River Rd #203 Tucson AZ 85718

BAKKER, MORRIS LEE, computer company executive; b. Renville, Minn., Jan. 20, 1943; s. Helmer W. and Jenny (Decknatel) B.; m. Vicki Ellen Royer, Dec. 2, 1966; children: Tanya Lynn, Tara Leigh, Aaron Lee. Student, Northwestern TV and Electronics Inst., Mpls., 1961-63. Customer engr. Control Data Corp., Mpls., 1963-64; sr. customer engr. Control Data Corp., Albuquerque, 1964-66, engr.-in-charge, 1966-69, sr. engr.-in-charge, 1969-78, service ctr. mgr., 1978-81, br. mgr., 1981—. Mem. Parent Adv. Com. Rio Grande High Sch., 1983—, Program Planning Com., Harrison (Md.) Sch., 1983-84; v.p. Full Gospel Businessmen Fellowship Internat., Albuquerque, 1971—. Republican. Home: 2515 Lakeview Rd SW Albuquerque NM 87105

BALBO, STEVEN THOMAS, realtor, developer; b. Chilicothe, Ohio, Aug. 1, 1955; s. Steven Anthony and Hazel (Harwood) B.; divorced; 1 child, Jennifer. AA in Gen. Edn., Essex Community Coll., Balt., 1974. Svc. rep. Cupentino Electric, Sunnyvale, Calif., 1980—; realtor Wagner Realty, Hollister, Calif., 1988—. Cubmaster Boy Scouts Am., San Jose, 1986-88; mem. Fremont Peak Observational Assn., San Juan Batista, Calif., 1986—. Mem. Internat. Brotherhood Elec. Workers (apprenticeship 1978), San Benito Bd. Realtors, Nat. Notary Assn., San Jose Bd. Realtors (affiliate). Democrat. Lutheran.

BALCH, GLENN MCCLAIN, JR., administrator, minister, former university president, author; b. Shattuck, Okla., Nov. 1, 1937; s. Glenn McClain and Marjorie (Daily) B.; student Panhandle State U., 1958-60, So. Meth. U., summers 1962-64; BA, S.W. State U. Okla., 1962; B.D., Phillips U., 1965; MA, Chapman Coll., 1973, MA in Edn., 1975, M.A. in Psychology, 1975; PhD, U.S. Internat. U., 1978; postgrad. Claremont Grad. Sch., 1968-70, U. Okla., 1965-66; m. Diana Gale Seeley, Oct. 15, 1970; children: Bryan, Gayle, Wesley, Johnny. Ordained to ministry Methodist Ch., 1962; sr. minister First Meth. Ch., Eakly, Okla., 1960-63, First Meth. Ch., Calumet, Okla., 1963-65, Goodrich Meml. Ch., Norman, Okla., 1965-66, First Meth. Ch., Barstow, Calif., 1966-70; asst. dean Chapman Coll., Orange, Calif., 1970-76; v.p. Pacific Christian Coll., Fullerton, Calif., 1976-79; pres. Newport U., Newport Beach, Calif., 1979-82; sr. pastor Brea United Meth. Ch., 1978-89; pres., chief exec. officer So. Calif. Inst., 1988—; edn. cons. USAF, 1974-75; mental health cons. U.S. Army, 1969. Mem. Community Adv. Bd. Minority Problems; Mayor's rep. to County Dependency Prevention Commn.; chmn. bd. For Kid's Sake; mem. Brea Econ. Devel. Com. With USMC, 1956-57. Recipient Eastern Star Religious Tng. award, 1963, 64; named Man of Year, Jr. C. of C., Barstow, 1969; Broadhurst fellow, 1963-65. Mem. Calif. Assn. Marriage and Family Therapists, Am. Assn. Marriage and Family Therapist, Rotary (pres. 1969-70, 83-84, dist. gov. 1987-88, 88-89), Masons, Shriners, Elks. Home: 1016 Steele Dr Brea CA 92621 Office: So Calif Inst 753 W Lambert Brea CA 92621

BALCOM, GLORIA DARLEEN, computer administrative and marketing consultant; b. Porterville, Calif., July 23, 1939; d. Orel A. and Eunice E. Stadtmiller; A.A., El Camino Coll., 1959; student computer sci. Harbor Coll., 1976-77; m. Orville R. Balcom, July 23, 1971; stepchildren—Cynthia Lou, Steven Raymond. Personnel trainee AiResearch div. Garrett Corp., Los Angeles, 1959-60, sales promotion adminstr., 1960-64; sales rep. Volt Temporary Services, El Segundo, Calif., 1965-69, mgr., Tarzana, Calif., 1969-71; co-owner, co-operator Brown Dog Engring., Lomita, Calif., 1972-77; pres., owner, cons. MicroSly Mktg., Lomita, 1977—. Mem. Ind. Computer Cons. Assn., Am. Soc. Profl. and Exec. Women, Nat. Assn. Female Execs. Club: Torrance Athletic. Home and Office: 24521 Walnut St Lomita CA 90717

BALCOM, ORVILLE, engineer; b. Inglewood, Calif., Apr. 20, 1937; s. Orville R. and Rose Mae (Argo) B.; B.S. in Math., Calif. State U., Long Beach, 1958, postgrad., 1958-59; postgrad. UCLA, 1959-62; m. Gloria Stadtmiller, July 23, 1971; children—Cynthia, Steven. Engr., AiResearch Mfg. Co., 1959-62, 64-65; chief engr. Meditron, El Monte, Calif., 1962-64; chief engr. Astro Metrics, Burbank, Calif., 1965-67; chief engr., gen. mgr. Varadyne Power Systems, Van Nuys, Calif., 1968-71; owner, chief engr. Brown Dog Engring., Lomita, Calif., 1971—. Mem. IEEE Computer Group, Independent Computer Cons. Assn. Patentee in field. Club: Torrance Athletic. Home: 24521 Walnut St Lomita CA 90717 Office: PO Box 427 Lomita CA 90717

BALDAUF, JOHN B., mechanical engineer; b. N.Y.C., Aug. 4, 1958; s. John and Frances Ann (Zaluk) B.; m. Robin Marie Link, Aug. 28, 1982. B in Engring., Cooper Union for the Advancement of Sci. and Art, 1980; MS in Engring. Mgmt., West Coast U., 1986—. Engr. McDonnell Aircraft Co., St. Louis, 1980-83; evaluation engr. Gen. Elec. AEBG, Cin., 1983-84; sr. evaluation engr. Gen. Elec. AEBG, Edwards AFB, Calif., 1985-86; prog. mgr. Gen. Elec. AEBG, 1986-87; sr. mfg. project engr. B-2 div. Northrop Corp., Palmdale, Calif., 1987-88; flight test project mgr. Douglas Aircraft Co., Long Beach, Calif., 1988—. Mem. AIAA, ASME, ASHRAE, Soc. Flight Test Engrs., Douglas Aircraft Mgmt. Club. Republican. Roman Catholic. Office: Douglas Aircraft Co 3855 Lakewood Blvd Long Beach CA 90846

BALDESCHWIELER, JOHN DICKSON, chemist, educator; b. Elizabeth, N.J., Nov. 14, 1933; s. Emile L. and Isobel (Dickson) B.; m. Marcia Ewing, June 20, 1959; children—John Eric, Karen Anne, David Russell. B. Chem. Engring., Cornell U., 1956; Ph.D., U. Calif. at Berkeley, 1959. From instr. to asso. prof. chemistry Harvard U., 1960-65; faculty Stanford (Calif.) U., 1965-71, prof. chemistry, 1967-71; chmn. adv. bd. Synchrotron Radiation Project, 1972-75; vis. scientist Synchrotron Radiation Lab., 1977; dep. dir. Office Sci. and Tech., Exec. Office Pres., Washington, 1971-73; prof. chemistry Calif. Inst. Tech., Pasadena, 1973—; chmn. div. chemistry and chem. engring. Calif. Inst. Tech., 1973-78; OAS vis. lectr. U. Chile, 1969; spl. lectr. in chemistry U. London, Queen Mary Coll., 1970; vis. scientist Bell Labs., 1978; mem. Pres.'s Sci. Adv. Com., 1969—, vice chmn., 1970-71; mem. Def. Sci. Bd., 1973-80, vice chmn., 1974-76; mem. carcinogenesis adv. panel Nat. Cancer Inst., 1973—; mem. com. planning and instl. affairs NSF, 1973-77; adv. com. Arms Control and Disarmament Agy., 1974-76; mem. Nat. Acad. Sci. Bd. Sci. and Tech. for Internat. Devel., 1974-76, ad hoc com. on fed. sci. policy, 1979, task force on synfuels, 1979; mem. Pres.'s Com. on Nat. Medal of Sci., 1974-76, ,pres., 1987—, Pres.'s Adv. Group on Sci. and Tech., 1975-76; mem. governing bd. Reza Shah Kabir U., 1975-79; mem. Sloan Commn. on Govt. and Higher Edn., 1977-79, U.S.-USSR Joint Commn. on Sci. and Tech. Coop., 1977-79; vice chmn. del. on pure and applied chemistry to People's Republic of China, 1978; mem. com. on scholarly communication with People's Republic of China, 1978-84; mem. research adv. council Ford Motor Co., 1979—, mem. chem. and engring. adv. bd., 1981-83. Mem. editorial adv. bd. Chem. Physics Letters, 1979-83. Served to 1st lt. AUS, 1959-60. Sloan Found. fellow, 1962-64, 64-65; recipient Fresenius award Phi Lambda Upsilon, 1968, Tolman award ACS, 1989. Mem. Nat. Acad. Scis., Am. Chem. Soc. (award in pure chemistry 1967), Council on Sci. and Tech. for Devel., Am. Acad. Arts and Scis., Am. Philos. Soc. Home: PO Box 5886 Pasadena CA 91106 Office: Calif Inst Tech Div Chemistry & Chem Engring #127-72 Pasadena CA 91125

BALDINGER, JAMES DAVID, test pilot, government official; b. Pitts., Nov. 18, 1928; s. Walter Allen and Bertha (Rockenstein) B.; m. Dolores Dorothy Demko, Aug. 13, 1955; children: Jeanne, Dianne, Brian, Richard, Gary, Cheryl. BSEE, U.S. Naval Acad., 1953. Commd. officer USMC, 1953, advanced through grades to capt., 1958; ret. 1966; test pilot Boeing Aircraft Co., Phila., 1966-75; air carrier ops. insp., test pilot FAA, Calif., 1975-88, ret., 1988. Mem. U.S. Naval Acad. Alumni Assn. Republican. Roman Catholic. Home: 3817 Howard Ave Los Alamitos CA 90720

BALDOCK, BOBBY RAY, federal judge; b. Rocky, Okla., Jan. 24, 1936; s. W. Jay and S. Golden (Farrell) B.; m. Mary Jane (Spunky) Holt, June 2, 1956; children—Robert Jennings, Christopher Guy. Grad., N.Mex. Mil. Inst., 1956; J.D., U. Ariz., 1960. Bar: Ariz. 1960, N.Mex. 1961, U.S. Dist. Ct. N.Mex., 1965. Ptnr. Sanders, Bruin & Baldock, Roswell, N.Mex., 1960-83; adj. prof. Eastern N.Mex. U., 1962-81; judge U.S. Dist. Ct. N.Mex., Albuquerque, 1983-86, U.S. Ct. Appeals (10th cir.), 1986—. Mem. ABA, N.Mex. Bar Assn., Chaves County Bar Assn., Ariz. Bar Assn., Phi Alpha Delta. Office: US Ct of Appeals PO Box 2388 Roswell NM 88202-2388

BALDOCK, MAX JOSEPH, realtor, business owner; b. Monroe, Mich., Sept. 9, 1948; s. Max Herschel and Frances Alice (Wahl) B. AA, Monroe Community Coll., 1968. Account exec. Theo H. Davies, Honolulu, 1971-76; real estate entrepreneur Honolulu, 1976-84; realtor assoc. Gretchen Duplanty, Ltd., Honolulu, 1984-88; owner, operator Complete Auto Prep. Corp., Honolulu, 1988—. Recipient Speak-Up award, Hawaii State Jaycees, Maui, 1974. Mem. Honolulu Bd. Realtors (dir. award com.). Office: Complete Auto Prep Corp 530 Paiea St # C Honolulu HI 96819

BALDON, CLEO, interior designer; b. Leavenworth, Wash., June 1, 1927; d. Ernest Elsworth and Esther Jane (Hannan) Chute; m. Lewis Smith Baldon, Nov. 20, 1948 (div. July 1961); 1 child, Dirk; m. Ib Jørgen Melchior, Jan. 18, 1964; 1 stepson, Leif Melchior. BS, Woodbury Coll., 1948. Ptnr. Interior Designs Ltd., Los Angeles, 1948-50; freelance illustrator Los Angeles, 1952-54; prin. Cleo Baldon & Assocs., Los Angeles and Venice, Calif., 1954—; ptnr. Galper/Baldon Assocs., Venice, 1970—. Author: Steps and Stairways; contbr. articles to profl. jours.; patentee in field. Recipient City Beautification awards Los Angeles 1974-77, 80, 83, 85-88, Beverly Hills 1982, Calif. Landscape Contractors, 1975, 79, Pacifica award Resources Council, Calif., 1979. Home: 8228 Marmont Ln Los Angeles CA 90069 Office: Galper/Baldon Assocs 723 Ocean Front Walk Venice CA 90291

BALDONI, LAUREN PATRICIA, computer automation consultant; b. Lynwood, Calif., July 12, 1958; d. Eugene Jr. Baldoni and Theresa Dolores (Harvey) Malone. BA with distiction, U. Calif., San Diego, 1981; MBA in Info. Systems, Calif. State U., San Diego, 1986. Mrg. trainee Safeway Stores, Del Mar, Calif., 1976-86; programmer analyst Centauraus Software, San Diego, 1981-83; tech. analyst mktg. rsch. Data Trek, Inc., Encinitas, Calif., 1986—. Home: 425 Stratford Ct #13 Del Mar CA 92014 Office: Data Trek Inc 167 Saxony Rd Encinitas CA 92024

BALDWIN, CARRIE MARIE, data processing executive; b. Covina, Calif., Apr. 16, 1965; d. Richard Darrell Baldwin and Donna Kay (Goodson) Hyatt. Student, El Camino Coll., 1987--. Computer specialist Hugh Gibbs & Donald Gibbs Architects, Long Beach, Calif., 1984-86, Hayakawa Associates, Los Angeles, 1986--. Mem. AIDS Project, Los Angeles, 1987. Democrat. Office: Hayakawa Assocs 1180 S Beverly Dr Los Angeles CA 90035 also: PO Box 2735 Palos Verdes CA 90274

BALDWIN, CHARLENE MARIE, librarian; b. San Francisco, Jan. 12, 1946; d. Gale Warren and Lois (Ward) Hudkins; children: Christopher Ward, Anne Haynes, Sarah Isabella. BA, Calif. State U., Sacramento, 1970; MA, U. Chgo., 1973. Tchr. Chgo. Bd. Edn., 1970-71; librarian Calif. Inst. Tech., Munger Library, Pasadena, 1974-75, Tetra Tech., Inc., Pasadena, 1976-81; chief reference librarian Lockheed-Calif. Co., Burbank, 1981-82; librarian Sci.-Engring. Library and adj. librarian Office of Arid Lands Studies U. Ariz., Tucson, 1984—; acting head map librarian U. Ariz., 1988—; tng. cons. Office of Arid Lands Studies U. Ariz., Tucson, 1986-87; free-lance info. specialist, Nigeria, 1975-76; field cons. sponsored devel. project U.S. Agy. Internat. Devel., Niamey, Niger, 1986; editorial cons. Santa Catalina Lab. Exptl. Research in Astromery, Tucson, 1985. Coauthor: Yoruba of Southwestern Nigeria, 1976. V.P., founding mem. Friends of Calif. Tech. Libraries; founding mem. Internat. Librarianship Round Table, 1988; vol. U.S. Peace Corps Govt. Nigeria, Western State, 1966-68. Mem. ALA, Ariz. State Library Assn., Spl. Libraries Assn. (pres. Ariz. chpt. 1988—), Ariz. Online User Group (chmn. 1985-86). Democrat. Office: U Ariz Libr Tucson AZ 85721

BALDWIN, GERALD ERWIN, airline pilot; b. Vandalia, Ill., Jan. 30, 1950; s. Hobart Erwin and Evelyn Violet (Wheatley) B.; m. Joan Beverly Koval, June 30, 1973. Student, Harris Community Coll., Houston, 1981, Prairie View A&M, 1981, U. Calif., San Diego, 1977-78; BS, U. Ill., 1972. Cert. naval aviator, airline transport pilot, flight engr. Houston dir. Corp. Campaign, Inc., 1980-81; pub. rels. spokesperson Continental Airlines master exec. coun. Air Line Pilots Assn., Houston, 1983-85; registered rep. 1st Am. Nat. Securities, Inc., Houston, 1983-88; div. mgr. A.L. Williams, Houston, 1983-88; pilot Tex. Internat. Airlines, Houston, 1979-81, Continental Airlines, Houston, 1981-85, United Airlines, Seattle, 1986—; . Del. Dem. State Conv., Dallas, 1984. Lt. USN, 1972-79. Mem. Air Line Pilots Assn. (del., com. chmn. 31st biennial bd. dirs. meeting 1988, sec.-treas. Coun. 27, 1987—). Office: Air Line Pilots Assn 15 S Grady Way Ste 526 Renton WA 98055

BALDWIN, GLADYS JANE, community services administrator; b. Conde, S.D., Jan. 6, 1924; d. Ransom H. and Edna Inez (Cunningham) W.; m. Theron Scott Knapp, Apr. 21, 1945 (div. Sept. 1969); children: Terry S. Knapp, Betty J. Baker, Lois A. Thurber, Donna J. Akins (dec.), Cheryl Smith; m. Gilbert Ralph Baldwin, Feb. 14, 1974. AA, Highline Community Coll., 1978; B cum laude, Eastern Wash. U., 1981, MSW cum laude, 1985. Adminstrv. sec. Social and Health Services, Ephrata, Wash., 1960-62, clerical supr. 2, 1962-70; fin. supr. Social and Health Services, Seattle, 1970-72, fin. mgr., 1972-77; adminstr. Social and Health Services, Colfax, Wash., 1977-82, Spokane, Wash., 1982—. Mem. Nat. Assn. Social Welfare, Wash. Assn. Social Work, Nat. Notaries Assn. Republican. Home: 13413 E 9th Spokane WA 99216 Office: Dept Social and Health Svcs 1313 N Maple Spokane WA 99201

BALDWIN, JIM D., supermarket chain executive. Pres. King Soopers Inc. div. Dillon Cos. Inc., Denver. Office: King Soopers Inc 65 Tejon St Denver CO 80223 *

BALDWIN, LARELL HARDISON, insurance company executive; b. Hanford, Calif., May 12, 1940; s. Leo H. and Bernice (Gash) B.; m. Kathleen L. Hardison, June 23, 1979; children: Jennifer Lin, Leslie Kari, Richard Allen, Michael Maxwell. Student Pasadena Coll., 1958-61; grad. Alexander Hamilton Inst. Bus., 1967. V.p. mortgage lending div. Standard Life & Accident Ins. Co. of Okla., Phoenix, 1961-64; sales mgr. Peterson Baby Products Inc., Burbank, Calif., 1964-67; v.p. sales Rotorway Aircraft Corp., Tempe, Ariz., 1967-69; pres. Trans World Arts Inc., San Jose, Calif., 1969-75, Baldwin Assocs. Devel. Corp., Santa Cruz, Calif., 1975-80; ptnr., v.p. Assurance Distbg. Co. Ltd., Santa Ana, Calif., 1979-82; pres. Baldwin Assurance Mktg. Corp., 1982—; nat. cons. ins. cos., author, lectr.; bd. dirs. Am. Acrylic Industries. Author in field. Office: Baldwin Assurance Mktg Corp PO Box 66972 Scotts Valley CA 95066

BALDWIN, RICHARD EUGENE, real estate executive; b. Sona Bota, Belgian Congo, July 25, 1940; came to U.S., 1942.; s. Russell Eugene and Jesse Adele Baldwin; m. Margaret Alice Kearns, Aug. 11, 1962; 1 child, Robert Lanoue. BA, Northwestern U., 1962; MA, U. Calif., Berkeley, 1964, PhD, 1967. Asst. prof. English U. Wash., Seattle, 1967-74; sales assoc. Windermere Real Estate, Seattle, 1974-77; broker, pres. Windermere Real Estate and Capitol Hill, Inc., 1977—; v.p. Windermere-Wall St., 1983—; pres. Windermere Condominiums, 1985—. Editor: Neighborhood Coun. Newsletter, Seattle, 1977-81; contbr. articles to profl. jours. Mem. Seattle-King County Bd. Realtors, Capitol Hill C. of C. (pres. 1985-87). Office: Windermere Real Estate 1112 19th Ave E Seattle WA 98112

BALDWIN, THOMAS JAMES, restaurant chain financial executive, accountant, educator; b. N.Y.C., May 31, 1955; s. Warren and Lillian Elizabeth (Oliveros) B.; m. Colleen Anne Dolan, Sept. 12, 1987. BBA in Acctg., Iona Coll., 1978, MBA in Fin. with honors, 1984. CPA, N.Y. Various sr. fin. mgmt. positions Gen. Foods Corp., N.Y.C. and Denver, 1976-85; v.p. strategic planning Citicorp-Citibank, N.Y.C., 1985-86; v.p. fin., chief fin. officer Le Peep Restaurants Inc., Denver and N.Y.C., 1986—; bd. dirs. PJL Restaurant Corp., N.Y.C.; adj. prof. Fordham U., 1985. Mem. Am. Inst. CPA's, N.Y. Soc. CPA's, Colo. Soc. CPA's, Calif. Soc. CPA's, Am. Mgmt. Assn., K.C. Republican. Roman Catholic. Office: Le Peep Restaurants Inc 1777 Harrison St Ste 802 Denver CO 80210 also: 6800 Jericho Turnpike Ste 113E Syosset NY 11791

BALICH, NICHOLAS SAMUEL, mining company executive; b. Bisbee, Ariz., Dec. 19, 1936; s. Samuel Steven and Noddie S. (Porobich) B.; m. Diana Houston Ragle, Sept. 11, 1969; children: Debra, Shannon, Barbara, Nicole, Sam, Stephanie. BSBA, U. Ariz., 1960. Grad. asst. football coach U. Ariz., Tucson, 1959-60; underground mine and carpenter shop Copper Queen br. Phelps Dodge Corp., Bisbee, Ariz., 1955-56, acct. Bisbee Daily Rev., 1961-63; internal auditor Western Hdqrs. Phelps Dodge Corp., Douglas, Ariz., 1963-68; constrn. acct. Tyrone (N.Mex.) br. Phelps Dodge Corp., 1968-70; chief acct. Copper Queen br. Phelps Dodge Corp., Bisbee, 1970-74; asst. controller Western Hdqrs. Phelps Dodge Corp., Douglas, 1974-79; controller Western Ops., Western Hdqrs. Phelps Dodge Corp., Douglas, Phoenix, 1979-89; v.p. Phelps Dodge Corp., Phoenix, 1987—; pres. Phelps Dodge Mercantile Co., Phoenix, 1987—. Co-chairperson Ariz. Kidney Found., Phoenix, 1986-87, pres. Region I, 1986-87, treas., 1985-86bd. dirs., 1982—; com. mem. Sunkist Fiesta Bowl, Phoenix, 1985—, co-chmn. Statewide Support, 1986-87, chmn. Statewide Support, 1987-88, chmn. Softball Com., 1988, coach fund raising, 1988, mem. exec. com., 1988-89, vice-chmn. Fiesta Bowl Com., 1989; campaign vice-chmn. Valley of the Sun United Way, 1984-85, audit com., 1985—; bd. dirs. Ariz. Theatre Co., 1987—, Boys/Girls Clubs, 1989-90; past pres. St. Stephen Nemanja Ch. Recipient Vol. of Yr. award Sunkist Fiesta Bowl, 1989, Rookie of Yr., 1986; named finalist Vol. of Yr. Sunkist Fiesta Bowl, 1987, finalist Valley Leadership Award, 1986. Mem. Ariz. C. of C. (tax com. 1989, bd. dirs. 1989-90), Ariz. Tax Res. Assn. (bd. dirs. 1979—, pres. 1988-89), Ariz. Mining Assn. (chmn. tax com. 1980—), Ariz. Acad., Phoenix Together, Valley Citizens League, Valley Contbn. Assn., U. Ariz. Wildcat Club, Masons, Shriners (pres. Cochise chpt. 1976), Jesters, Elks, Sigma Alpha Epsilon (pres. 1958). Republican. Mem. Serbian Orthodox Ch. Home: 5425 E Cholla St Scottsdale AZ 85254 Office: Phelps Dodge Corp 2600 N Central Ave Phoenix AZ 85004-3014

BALKO, GREGG BRIAN, convention manager; b. Detroit, June 29, 1951; s. Elmer Albert and A. Ruth (Esch) B. BS, Western Mich. U., 1973; MA, Ea. Mich. U., 1976. Tchr. Lapeer (Mich.) Pub. Schs., 1973-74, Novi (Mich.) Community Schs., 1974-79; meeting and conv. planner Soc. Mfg. Engrs., Dearborn, Mich., 1979-87; sales mgr. Photo and Sound Co., Costa Mesa, Calif., 1987-88; trade show coordinator Mktg./Assn. Services, Los Angeles, 1988; conv. mgr. Broadcast Promotion and Mktg. Execs., Los Angeles, 1988—. Mem. Novi Youth Assistance, 1975-77. Mem. Orange County Hotel Sales & Mktg. Assn. (bd. dirs. 1987-88), Nat. Assn. Catering Execs., Am. Soc. Assn. Execs., Grosse Pointe (Mich.) Sail Club (entertainment chmn. 1986-87), U. Mich. Mus. Soc. Office: BPME 6255 Sunset Blvd #624 Los Angeles CA 90028

BALL, DONALD EDMON, architect; b. Evansville, Ind., July 18, 1942; s. Harvey and Myrl (Norris) B. BA in Design, So. Ill. U., 1967. Registered architect, Ariz., Colo., Tex.; cert. Nat. Coun. Archtl. Registration Bd. With design dept. Leo A. Daly Co., Architects and Engrs., Omaha, 1968; project mgr. Buetow & Assocs., St. Paul, 1969-70; ptnr. Comprehensive Design, Mpls., 1971-73; with Caudill Assocs., Aspen, Colo., 1973-76, Hagman Yaw, Ltd., Aspen, 1977; project mgr. Hanter Assocs., Aspen, 1978; pres. Jacobs Ball & Assocs., Architects, Aspen and Denver, 1978-85; project mgr. Moshe Safdie & Assocs., Boston, 1985-87; dir. design Dwayne Lewis Architects, Inc., Phoenix, 1987-88; prin. Donald Ball and Assocs., Scottsdale, Ariz., 1988—. Mem. Aspen Bldg. Insp. Selection Com., 1982, Pitkin County Housing Authority Bd., Aspen, 1984. Mem. AIA (chmn. Colo. West chpt., documents com.), Ariz. Soc. Architects (profl. practice com.), Valley Ptnrship. Republican. Home: 7749 E Joshua Tree Ln Scottsdale AZ 85253 Office: 7201 E Camelback Rd Ste 255 Scottsdale AZ 85251

BALL, ERIC SAMUEL, insurance agent; b. Watsonville, Calif., Apr. 13, 1958; s. Ivan Jay and Ruth Helen (Jacoby) B. AA in History, U. Calif., Berkeley, 1978. CLU, chartered fin. cons. Sales rep. Ellis Brooks Chevrolet, San Francisco, 1978-81; sr. agent The Prin. Fin. Group, Porterville, Calif., 1981—. Finance chair Boy Scouts Am., Tule River Dist., 1987—. Named Paul Harris Fellow Rotary Internat., 1988; recipient Nat. Quality award Nat. Assn. Life Underwriters, 1984—, Nat. Sales Achievement award Nat. Assn. Life Underwriters, 1986—. Mem. Tulare-Kings County Assn. Life Underwriters (pres. 1987-88), Am. Soc. CLU's, Soc. Fin. Cons., Porterville C. of C., Porterville Rotary (pres. 1987-88). Democrat. Methodist. Home: The Ball Ranch 18629 Ave 169 Porterville CA 93257 Office: The Prin Fin Group 628 W Grand Ave Porterville CA 93257

BALL, FRED SHELTON, chamber of commerce executive; b. Ogden, Utah, Sept. 29, 1932; s. Fred S. and Gladys (Thornton) B.; m. Joyce Worsencroft, July 2, 1953; children: Kathryn, Kristine, Kimberly, Karalyn. AS, Weber State Coll., 1952; BS, U. Utah, 1955; MBA, Stanford U., 1966. Gen. sales mgr. IML Freight, San Francisco, 1954-71; pres., gen. mgr. Salt Lake Area C. of C., 1971—; pres. Creative Mgmt., Salt Lake City, 1970—; bd. dirs. Pierson Hosp., Salt Lake City, 1985—. Author: Ten Most Wanted Man, 1973, Authentic Achiever, 1975. Chmn. Cen. Bus. Improvement, Salt Lake City, 1986; mem. Gov.'s Law exec. com., Salt Lake City, 1986. Named Salesman of Yr., Sales Mktg. Execs., 1982, one of Top 10 Speakers in Am., Platform Speakers, 1983. Mem. Salt Lake Country Club, Toastmasters (named Speaker Yr. 1981), Rotary. Republican. Mormon. Home: 809 16th Ave Salt Lake City UT 84103 Office: Salt Lake Area C of C 175 E 400 S Salt Lake City UT 84111 .

BALL, GEOFFREY HADDON, management consultant; b. Bklyn., Dec. 10, 1933; s. Theodore Haddon Ball and Margot (Hudnut) Thompson; m. Camille Wrathall, Sept. 3, 1961; children: Jennifer C.L., Mark G. AB, Harvard U., 1955; MS, Stanford U., 1960, PhD, 1962. Mgr. artificial intelligence lab. ITT Fed. Labs., San Fernando, Calif., 1962-63; sr. research engr. Stanford U. Research Inst., Menlo Park, Calif., 1963-73; staff cons. Charles F. Kettering Found., Dayton, Ohio, 1973-74; mem. sr. staff Control Analysis Corp., Stanford, Calif., 1974-75; prin., cons. Geoff Ball & Assocs., Palo Alto, Calif., 1975-80, 86—; exec. dir. Forum on Community and Environment, Palo Alto, 1981-86. Author monographs: Using Graphics with Groups, 1977, Creative Problem Solving, 1982, When Controversy Comes to the City, 1986. Chmn. Met. Planning Br. Diocese of Calif., San Francisco, 1971-73; mem. adv. bd., policy council Nat. Conf. on Peace-Making and Conflict Resolution, 1983-86; bd. dirs. Peninsula Religious Drama Guild, Palo Alto, 1963-64; community advisor Palo Alto Jr. League, 1983-84. Served with USN , 1955-58, PTO. Named Eagle Scout Boy Scouts Am., Long Beach, Calif., 1948; NSF fellow, 1959-61. Democrat. Club: Aikido West (Redwood City, Calif.). Home: 315 Bryant St Palo Alto CA 94301 Office: Geoff Ball & Assocs 991 Commercial St Palo Alto CA 94301

BALL, JOHN CHARLES, military officer; b. Fairview Park, Ohio, Nov. 5, 1949; s. Charles Irvin and Sophie Mary (Maslanka) B.; m. Katherine Gay Bowell, Mar. 19, 1972; children: David Michael, Stephen Edward. BS in Aero. Engring., U.S. Naval Acad., 1971; MS in Aero. Engring., U.S. Naval Postgrad. Sch., 1977; grad. with distinction, U.S. Naval Test Pilot Sch., 1980. Commd. ensign USN, 1971, advanced through grades to comdr., 1985; asst. navigator USS Wichita USN, Long Beach, Calif., 1971; student pilot naval air tng. command USN, Pensacola, Fla., 1972-73; squadron pilot helicopter combat support squadron six USN, Norfolk, Va., 1973-76; officer-in-charge helicopter detachment USS Mt. Hood USN, San Diego, 1978-80;

test pilot naval air test ctr. USN, Patuxent River, Md., 1980-83; programs dir. naval plant rep.'s office USN, Stratford, Conn., 1983-85; dir. product support naval aviation depot USN, San Diego, 1986—. Contbr. articles to profl. jours. Coach South St. Mary's Youth Soccer League, Lexington Park, Md., 1981-82, Monroe Little League Baseball, 1986, Sweetwater Valley Little League, Bonita, Calif., 1988; bd. dirs. Newtowne S. Civic League, Norfolk, 1973. Mem. Soc. Exptl. Test Pilots, U.S. Naval Inst., Am. Helicopter Soc., Assn. Naval Aviation, Naval Helicopter Assn. (editor Rotor Rev. 1987—), Toastmasters. Republican. Roman Catholic.

BALL, JOSEPH EDWARD, pharmacist; b. Feb. 4, 1904; s. Edward Lewis and Nellie Francis (Cottrell) B.; m. Mable Marie Johnson, June 13, 1928 (dec. Apr. 1934); m. Violet Barbara Kaczmaryn, Aug. 25, 1934; children: Barbara Nell Evans Kavanaugh, Eugenia Marie Edwards. Degree in Pharm. Chem., Purdue U., 1931, BS, 1932, MS, 1933; PhD, Columbia Pacific U., 1987. Registered pharmacist, Ill., Ind., Calif. Profl. service rep. Abbott Labs., North Chicago, Ill., 1934-41; chief pharmacist St. Francis of Lynwood (Calif.), 1941-51; prin. Med. Ctr. Pharmacy, Inglewood, Calif., 1951-62; chief pharmacist City of Los Angeles, 1962-74, cons. contract pharmacist, 1974—. Mem. Calif. Employee Pharmacist Assn. Republican. Roman Catholic. Lodges: Elks, K.C.

BALL, TROY EUGENE, consultant; b. Gassville, Ark., Mar. 18, 1946; s. Troy Clifton and Lucy Victoria (Stanislawski) B.; m. Marilyn Elizabeth Brion, July 21, 1967 (div. 1987); m. Cathy Lynn Jones, Feb. 14, 1989; children: Tammy Ann, Troy Eugene III. AS, AA, physician's asst., Cuyahoga Community Coll., Parma, Ohio, 1971. Physician's asst. Marshfield (Wis.) Clinic, 1976-79; owner, operator Marshfield Air Svc., Inc., 1979-84; dir. med. dept. AOPA, Frederick, Md., 1984-87; cons. Norwood, Colo., 1987—; cons. med. certification Aircraft Owners and Pilots Assn., Frederick, 1987—; FAA designated pilot examiner, Salt Lake City, 1988—. With USN, 1967-71. Mem. Civil Aviation Med. Assn., Aerospace Med. Assn. Republican. Home: PO Box 531 Norwood CO 81423

BALL, WILLIAM PAUL, physicist, engineer; b. San Diego, Nov. 16, 1913; s. John and Mary (Kajla) B.; m. Edith Lucile March, June 28, 1941 (dec. 1976); children: Lura Irene Ball Raplee, Roy Ernest. AB, UCLA, 1940; PhD, U. Calif., Berkeley, 1952. Registered profl. engr. Calif. Projectionist, sound technician studios and theatres in Los Angeles, 1932-41; tchr. high sch. Montebello, Calif., 1941-42; instr. math. and physics Santa Ana (Calif.) Army Air Base, 1942-43; physicist U. Calif. Radiation Lab., Berkeley and Livermore, 1943-58; mem. tech. staff Ramo-Wooldridge Corp., Los Angeles, 1958-59; sr. scientist Hughes Aircraft Co., Culver City, Calif., 1959-64; sr. staff engr. TRW-Def. Systems Group, Redondo Beach, Calif., 1964-83, Hughes Aircraft Co., 1983-86; cons. Redondo Beach, 1986—. Contbr. articles to profl. jours.; patentee in field. Bd. dirs. So. Dist. Los Angeles chpt. ARC, 1979-86. Recipient Manhattan Project award for contbn. to 1st atomic bomb, 1945. Mem. Am. Phys. Soc., Am. Nuclear Soc., AAAS, AIAA, N.Y. Acad. Scis., Torrance (Calif.) Area C. of C. (bd. dirs. 1978-84), Sigma Xi. Home and Office: 209 Via El Toro Redondo Beach CA 90277

BALLANTINE, MORLEY COWLES (MRS. ARTHUR ATWOOD BALLANTINE), newspaper publisher; b. Des Moines, May 21, 1925; d. John and Elizabeth (Bates) Cowles; m. Arthur Atwood Ballantine, July 26, 1947 (dec. 1975); children—Richard, Elizabeth Ballantine Leavitt, William, Helen Ballantine Healy. A.B., Ft. Lewis Coll., 1975; L.H.D. (hon.), Simpson Coll., Indianola, Iowa, 1980. Pub. Durango (Colo.) Herald, 1952—, editor, pub., 1975-83, editor, chmn. bd., 1983—; dir. 1st Nat. Bank, Durango, 1976—, Des Moines Register & Tribune, 1977-85, Cowles Media Co., 1982-86. Mem. Colo. Land Use Commn., 1975-81, Supreme Ct. Nominating Commn., 1984—; mem. Colo. Forum, 1985—, Blueprint for Colo., 1985—; pres. S.W. Colo. Mental Health Ctr., 1964-65, Four Corners Opera Assn., 1983-86; mem. Colo. Forum, 1985—; bd. dirs. Colo. Nat. Hist. Preservation Act, 1968-78; trustee Choate/Rosemary Hall, Wallingford, Conn., 1973-81, Simpson Coll., Indianola, Iowa, 1981—, U. Denver, 1984—, Fountain Valley Sch., Colorado Springs, 1976-89. Recipient 1st place award for editorial writing Nat. Fedn. Press Women, 1955, Outstanding Alumna award Rosemary Hall, Greenwich, Conn., 1969, Outstanding Journalism award U. Colo. Sch. Journalism, 1967, Distinguished Service award Ft. Lewis Coll., Durango, 1970; named to Colo. Community Journalism Hall of Fame, 1987. Mem. Nat. Soc. Colonial Dames, Colo. Press Assn. (bd. dirs. 1978-79), Colo. AP Assn. (chmn. 1966-67), Federated Women's Club Durango. Episcopalian. Club: Mill Reef (Antigua, W.I.) (bd. govs. 1985—). Address: care Herald PO Drawer A Durango CO 81302

BALLARD, DAVID EUGENE, anesthesiologist; b. Carlsbad, N.Mex., July 30, 1949; s. Samuel Lafayette and Kathleen (Krebs) B.; m. Patricia Ann Lafferty, June 11, 1972; 1 child, Leslie Christine. BA, U. Kans., 1971; MD, U. N.Mex., 1975. Diplomate, Am. Bd. Anesthesiology. Intern and resident N.C. Meml. Hosp., U. N.C., Chapel Hill, 1975-78; pvt. practice Anesthesia Cons. Associated, El Paso, Tex., 1978-86; chief anesthesia sect. VA Med. Ctr., Albuquerque, 1986-88; chmn. dept. anesthesiology Lovelace Med. Ctr., Albuquerque, 1988—; asst. prof. anesthesiology, U. N.Mex., 1986-88, mem. resident selection com., 1986—. Mem. Am. Soc. Anesthesiologists (alt. del. 1988—), AMA, Internat. Anesthesia Rsch. Soc., Anesthesia Patient Safety Found., Soc. Ambulatory Anesthesia, Tex. Soc. Anesthesiologists (alt. del. dist. 5 1986), Greater Albuquerque Anesthesia Soc. (pres., v.p. 1987-89), N.Mex. Med. Sch. Alumni Assn. (bd. dirs. 1984-88, exec. com. 1988—). Office: Lovelace Med Ctr 5400 Gibson St SE Albuquerque NM 87108

BALLARD, DELBERT LEO, nuclear facility engineer; b. Billings, Mont., Jan. 24, 1930; s. Ross and Essie Francis (Perrine) B.; m. Margaret VIrginia Kelly, Aug. 15, 1953; children: Bruce E., Diane L. BSCE, Mont. State U., 1951; postgrad., U. Wash., 1955-61. Registered profl. civil engr., 1958; registered profl. mech. engr., 1962. Project engr. GE, Richland, Wash., 1951-65; mgr. devel. engrng. group Battelle N.W., Richland, 1965-70; mgr. test ops. and prin. engr. Westinghouse Hanford Co., Richland, 1970—. Bd. dirs. United Protestant Ch., Richland, 1973-76. Mem. ASCE (sect. pres. 1967-68, chmn. Pacific N.W. coun. 1984-85), Am. Nuclear Soc. Republican. Office: Westinghouse Hanford Co PO Box 1970 L4-71 Richland WA 99352

BALLARD, FLOYD LEON, manufacturing supervisor, engineer; b. Wendell, Idaho, June 2, 1950; s. Leo Arthur Ballard and Lois Mae (Anderson) Stoddard; children: Brandie Lyn, Casey Leon, Jodie Rhea. BSCE, U. Idaho, 1973, MSCE, 1975. Registered profl. engr., Mo., Idaho. Engr. Monsanto Co., St. Louis, 1975-78, sr. engr., 1978-79; process supr. Monsanto Co., Soda Spring, Idaho, 1979-81, engrng. supr., 1981-85, mfg. supr., 1985-88; pres., sr. indsl. cons. Thomas M. Laronge, Inc., Vancouver, Wash., 1988—; Patentee pollutant removal, 1978. Coach Little League Baseball, Soda Spring, 1986. Mem. ASCE. Home: 1512 NE 72d St #1 Vancouver WA 98665 Office: PO Box 4448 Vancouver WA 98662

BALLENGER, GREGORY BOYD, finance company executive; b. Concord, Calif., June 20, 1950; s. Willard Valores and Eleanore Katherine (Mahan) B. BA magna cum laude, Calif. State U., Hayward, 1972; MA, U. Calif., Berkeley, 1974. Adminstrv. aide City of Alameda, Calif., 1973-75; asst. to city mgr. City of National City, Calif., 1976-79; 1st v.p. Miller & Schroeder Financial Inc., Solana Beach, Calif., 1979—; owner Elite Racing Stables. Judge, instr. United Spirit Assn.; vice chmn. Pride of San Diego Week, 1985-88; vol. Muscular Dystrophy Telethon, Walnut Creek, Calif., 1974-77; chmn. Neighborhood Watch Golden Triangle, San Diego, 1986; precinct chmn. Reagan for Pres., San Diego, 1984; trustee Seaside Ch. of Religious Sci., Solana Beach, 1988; co-chmn. Alameda-Contra Costa County High Sch. All-Star Football, 1979—; panelist Calif. Southwest U.S. Recreation Conv., 1982; chmn. Concord Youth Council, 1974; vol. investigator Legal Aid Soc. Alameda County, Hayward, 1974-77; del. Concord Forum, 1975; pres. Villa Europa Homeowners' Assn. Mem. Nat. Assn. Securities Dealers, Pub. Securities Assn., Calif. State U. Alumni Assn., Alpha Phi Omega. Mem. Christian Church (Disciples of Christ). Home: 3962-102 Nobel Dr #102 San Diego CA 92122 Office: Miller & Schroeder 505 Lomas Santa Fe Dr Solana Beach CA 92075

BALLESTEROS, DANNEL RAMIREZ, contract administrator; b. San Fernando, Calif., May 10, 1929; s. Carlos E.B. and Julia (Ramirez) Garcia; children: Andrea Jo, Dannel Al, David William, Antoinette Lee, Deborah Ann, Kimberly Jo, Karole Ann, Todd Curtis. AA, E. L.A. Coll., 1952; BS, U. Redlands, 1981; MBA, U. Phoenix, 1983. Subcontract adminstr. Rockwell Internat. Corp., Downey, Calif., 1974-78; sr. buyer Northrop Corp., Hawthorne, Calif., 1978-79; procurement head Hughes Aircraft Co., El Segundo, Calif., 1979-83; subcontract mgr. Aerojet Ordnance Co., Downey, 1983-84; cons. mgr. Dannel Cons., L.A., 1984-85; contract adminstr. Hydro-Aire div. Crane Co., Burbank, Calif., 1985; sr. contract adminstr. Allied Aerospace Sys., Compton, Calif., 1985-87, Magnavox Advanced Systems, Torrance, Calif., 1987—; instr. adult edn. prog. L.A. and other sch. dists., 1960-66; adj. prof. Northrop U., Inglewood, Calif., 1982-85; cons. Dannel Cons., 1985--. Founder, sponsor Equestrian Scholarship Fund, Ballet Scholarship Fund, 1980-84; trustee Little Country Ch. of Belvedere, L.A., 1987--; charter mem. to Hist. Soc. of the United Meth. Ch. Mem. Nat. Contract Mgmt. Assn., Am. Soc. Tng. and Devel. Home: 321 Sunset Dr Channel Islands Mari CA 93035

BALLEW, ANTHONY ROBERT, nurse; b. Coffeyville, Kans., July 11, 1952; s. Thomas James Ballew and Sue Ann (Hicks) Faulkner; m. Susan Coleen Turley, Oct. 8, 1955; children: Christopher, Tamara, Sean. Diploma in nursing, Good Samaritan Hosp. Sch. Nsg., Phoenix, 1973; BSHSA, U. Phoenix, 1982; MBA, Calif. Coast U., 1989. RN, Ariz. Nurse practitioner LSAL, Jeddah, Saudi Arabia, 1984, health svc. adminstr., 1985, mgr. health svcs., 1986-87; E.D. mgr. Mesa (Ariz.) Luth. Hosp., 1988; ER nurse practitioner Maricopa Med. Ctr., Phoenix, 1989—; chief Nursing & Emergency Med. Svcs., Mesa, Ariz., 1989—; owner Holbrook (Ariz.) Emergency Med. Svcs., 1978-80; employee health nurse practitioner McDonnell Douglas Helicopters, 1989—; nurseS.W. Ambulance, 1989—; EMT instr. Ariz. Community Coll. Bd., 1989—. Diver, Maricopa County Sheriffs Office Diver's Posse, Phoenix, 1988—; instr. Rural/Metro Fire Dept. Dive Team, Scottsdale, Ariz., 1988—. Medictr. of Am. scholar, 1982. Mem. Ariz. Nurses Assn., Am. Nurses Assn., Assn. Ambulatory Health Care Adminstrs., Undersea Med. Soc., Profl. Assn. Diving Instrs. Republican. Mormon. Office: NAMES 1813 N Oracle Mesa AZ 85203

BALLHAUS, WILLIAM FRANCIS, JR., federal agency administrator, research scientist; b. L.A., Jan. 28, 1945; s. William Francis Sr. and Edna A. (Dooley) B.; m. Jane Kerber; children from previous marriage: William Louis, Michael Frederick; stepchildren: Benjamin Joel, Jennifer Angela. BSME with honors, U. Calif., Berkeley, 1967, MS in Mech. Engrng., 1968, PhD in Engrng., 1971. Rsch. scientist U.S. Army Aviation R & D, Ames Rsch. Ctr., Moffett Field, Calif., 1971-79; chief applied computation aeronautics br. NASA-Ames Rsch. Ctr., Moffett Field, 1979-80, dir. astronautics, 1980-84, dir., 1984—; acting assoc. adminstr. NASA Hdqrs., Washington, 1988-89. Contbr. articles on computational fluid dynamics to profl. jours. Mem. sci. and acad. adv. bd. U. Calif., 1987—; mem. engrng. adv. bd. U. Calif., Berkeley and Davis, San Jose State U.; chmn. govt. and edn. div. United Way of Santa Clara County, Calif., 1987. Capt. USAR. Decorated Presdl. Rank of Disting. Excellence, 1988, Disting. Exec., 1988; recipient H. Julian Allen award NASA-Ames Rsch. Ctr., 1977, Arthur S. Flemming award Jaycees, Washington, 1980, Disting. Profl. Engrng. Sci. and Tech. award NSPE, 1986, Disting. Exec. Svc. award Sr. Execs. Assn., 1989, Disting. Svc. medal NASA, 1989, Disting. Engrng. Alumnus award U. Calif., Berkeley, 1989. Fellow AIAA (pres. 1988-89, Lawrence Sperry award 1980), Royal Aero. Soc.; mem. NAE, Internat. Acad. Astronautics, Tau Beta Pi (named Eminent Engr. Berkeley chpt.). Roman Catholic. Office: NASA Ames Rsch Ctr Mail Stop 200-1 Moffett Field CA 94035

BALLIDIS, SHARON HOFMANN, fund raising consultant; b. Santa Monica, Calif., Dec. 21, 1956; d. Joseph A. and Lillian L. (Acrivos) Hofman; m. James E. Ballidis, May 24, 1980. AA, Cerritos Coll., 1976; BA, Calif. State U., Long Beach, 1979. Campaign assoc. United Way, Orange, Calif., 1979-80; dir. mktg. & devel. Providence Speech & Hearing Ctr., Orange, Calif., 1980-88; sr. cons. Robert B. Sharp Co., Santa Ana, Calif., 1988—. Mem. Nat. Soc. Fund Raising Execs. (pres., bd. dirs. Orange County chpt. 1988—). Republican. Home: 13191 Woodland Dr Tustin CA 92680 Office: Robert B Sharp Co Inc 1633 E 4th St Santa Ana CA 92701

BALLINGER, CHARLES KENNETH, information specialist; b. Johnstown, Pa., July 28, 1950; s. Delores Jean (Cool) B.; m. Deb C. Delger, Sept. 14, 1985. Programmer analyst Cowles Pub. Co., Spokane, Wash., 1975-78; systems analyst Old Nat. Bank, Spokane, 1978-82; software engr. ISC System, Spokane, 1982; micro computer analyst Acme Bus. Computers, Spokane, 1982-85; info. ctr. analyst Wash. Water Power Co., Spokane, 1985—; cons. IDP Co., Spokane, 1978—. Contbr. articles to profl. jours. Served with Signal Corps, U.S. Army, 1968-71. Mem. Assn. Computing Machinery, Spokane Heath Users Group (pres. 1979-83). Home: S 3810 Havana Spokane WA 99223 Office: Wash Water Power Co E 1411 Mission Spokane WA 99202

BALOGH, CONNIE LEE, technical educator; b. Hinsdale, Ill., Oct. 25, 1949; d. James Andrew Balogh and Kathryn Marceil (Allen) Balogh Buehler; m. Carroll Thurman Kane, May 21, 1988; 1 child, Tracy Kay Mercer. AA, Pima Community Coll., 1984; student, U. Phoenix, 1985; BBA, Nat. U., 1989. Instr. Hughes Missile Systems Group, Tucson, 1974-86; instr., supr. Hughes Ground Systems Group, Fullerton, Calif., 1986-87; tng. adminstr. Lear Astronics Corp., Santa Monica, Calif., 1987-88; instr. sr. tng. ops. electronics div. Northrop, Hawthorne, Calif., 1988—; cons. in field. Office: Northrop Electronics Div 2301 W 120th St Hawthorne CA 90250

BALSER, ELNORA MARIE, audiologist; b. Cleve., June 9, 1952; d. Charles Joseph and Lucy Ann (Englert) B. BA, Cleve. State U., 1974, MA, 1977; postgrad., Ariz. State U., 1982—. Cert. clin. audiologist. Clerk-cashier LACO Bookstore, Cleve., 1975-77; audiologist George Serbin, M.D., Phoenix, 1977-78; cons. audiologist Leon D. Zeitzer, M.D., Phoenix, 1977-88, Phoenix Meml. Hosp., 1978-88; pres. Sound Audiologics Inc., Tempe, Ariz., 1984—. Mem. IEEE (student), Am. Speech-Language-Hearing Assn. (com. on amplification for hearing impaired 1982-84), Am. Tinnitus Assn., Soc. Women Engrs. (student), Ariz. Speech-Language-Hearing Assn. Democrat. Roman Catholic. Office: 305 S McKemy Tempe AZ 85281

BALTUTIS, JOHN STANLEY, operations research analyst; b. Evergreen Park, Ill., Sept. 28, 1940; s. John S. Sr. and Helen M. (Kupetis) B. BA in Math., St. Mary's Coll., Winona, Minn., 1962; MS in Ops. Research, U.S. Naval Postgrad. Sch., 1972. Enlisted USN, 1962; Commd. ensign 1963, designated naval aviator, 1964, lt. comdr., 1970 ret. 1983; sr. engr./specialist Gen. Dynamics Convair, San Diego, 1983—. Mem. AIAA, Math. Assn. Am., Mil. Ops. Research Soc., Armed Forces Communications/Electronics Assn., Sigma Xi.

BALTZO, STANLEY ARTHUR, marketing executive; b. Seattle, Dec. 19, 1942; s. Charles Howard and Ann Parnelli (Hammer) B.; m. Joan Marie Robinson, Feb. 9, 1964 (div. 1988); 1 child, Kitsel; m. Michele Ann Fritts, Nov. 21, 1987; 1 child, Megan. Student, U. Wash., 1961-65. Sta. mgr. Std. Stas., Inc., Seattle, 1964-65; wholesale adminstr. Std. Oil Co. of Calif., Seattle, 1965-69; adminstrv. staff mkts. Chevron USA, Inc., Anchorage, 1969-73; pres. Island Chevron Svc., Inc., Kodiak, Alaska, 1973-83; lubricant sales staff Prudhoe Bay Supply, Anchorage, 1983-84; retail sales mgr. Tesoro Alaska Petroleum Co., Anchorage, 1984—. Bd. dirs., pres. Assn. of Alaska Sch. Bds., State of Alaska, 1975-83, Kodiak Island Borough Sch. Dist., 1974-83, Better Bus. Bur. of Alaska, Anchorage, 1985-88, Alaska Airmen's Assn., 1988—. With U.S. Army, 1966-68. Republican. Presbyterian. Home: 12631 Nautilus Ct Anchorage AK 99515 Office: Tesoro Alaska Petroleum Co PO Box 190272 Anchorage AK 99519

BALUNI, ALICE, electronics company executive; b. Cairo, Dec. 10, 1945; came to U.S., 1975; s. Arthur Z. and Angele Baluni. M Physics of Semicondrs., Moscow State U., 1969; M Engrng. Mgmt., Santa Clara U., 1981. Lectr. solid state physics Yerevan (Armenia) State U., 1969-75; engrng. supr. Intel Co., Santa Clara, Calif., 1975-81; sr. design engr. Synertek Co., Santa Clara, 1981-82; product engrng. mgr. Sygnetics Co., Sunnyvale, Calif., 1982-85; dir. reliability and quality assurance Zilog Co., Campbell, Calif., 1985—. Mem. IEEE, Am. Soc. for Quality Control. Republican. Office: Zilog Co 210 Hacienda Ave Campbell CA 95008

BALZER, CYNTHIA LOUISE, banker; b. Astoria, Oreg., Sept. 6, 1954; d. Robert Earl Thomson and Faye Marie (Bedortha) Vanvolkinburg; m. Ronald John Balzer, Feb. 14, 1981; 1 child, Rikki Lynn. Cert. in ops. mgmt. Bank Adminstrn. Inst. Teller Nat. Bank Alaska, Ketchikan, 1973; teller 1st Bank, Ketchikan, 1973-78, asst. cashier, 1980-88, asst. v.p., 1988—; teller U.S. Nat. Bank Oreg., Albany, 1978-79, note clk., Astoria, 1979-80. Republican. Roman Catholic. Home: 1028 Woodland Ave Ketchikan AK 99901 Office: 1st Bank 331 Dock St Ketchikan AK 99901

BAMBA, JOSEPH GEORGE, senator, insurance executive; b. Tamuning, Guam, July 19, 1951; s. George Mariano and Cecilia (Cruz) B.; m. Joyce Claire Charfauros, Jan. 17, 1970; children: Brian, Tanya, Tara, George II. Student, U. Guam, Mangilao, 1969-71, U. Guam, La Salle, 1972. Ins. underwriter Bamba's Ins., Agana, Guam, 1972-75; pres. Bamba's Ins., Agana, 1983—; staff asst. Office of Guam Del. to U.S. Congress, Agana, 1975-78; spl. asst. to gov. Office of Gov., Agana, 1979-81, exec. asst. to gov., 1981-82; pres. J. Bamba & Assocs., Agana, 1983—; senator Guam Legislature, Agana, 1984—; bd. dirs. GMP Assocs., Inc., Honolulu, 1983—, Guam Beauty Assn., Agana, 1986—; v.p., bd. dirs. Marianas Internat. Ins. Corp., Saipan, No. Marianas Islands, 1987—; mng. dir. MITA Travel (Guam), Inc., Agana, 1987—; minority leader, 1988—. Mem. cen. com. Rep. Party Guam, Agana, 1985—. Mem. Nat. Rep. Legis. Assn., Nat. Conf. State Legis., Paradise Jaycees (founder). Office: Guam Legislature Capitol Bldg 163 Chalan Santo Papa St Agana GU 96910

BAMBERGER, DAVID CHARLES, business owner, management consultant; b. Rockford, Ill., June 28, 1942; s. Jerome George and Lillian (Jensen) B.; m. Barbara Christine Franke, Jan. 23, 1965; children: Gina, Lucas. BBA, U. Tex., 1970, postgrad., 1971. Mgr. prodn. control Atlas Match Corp., Arlington, Tex., 1965-67; mgr. ops. rsch. Collins Radio Co., Richardson, Tex., 1967-71; asst. dir. PPACG, Colorado Springs, Colo., 1971-81; chief exec. officer, prin. Rsch. & Cons. Group, Inc., Colorado Springs, 1981—; cons. Citicorp, 1981—, Mobil Corp. Devel., 1981—, Aries Properties, 1981—, Ford Motor Co., 1981, Procter & Gamble, 1981—, Briargate Devel. Group, 1981—, Boettcher & Co., 1981—. Author: Climbers Guide to 11 Mile Canyon, 1978; contbr. articles to profl. jours. Mem. Econ. Devel. Council, Colorado Springs, 1981—, RCIS, Colorado Springs, 1981—, Clean Air Consortium, Colorado Springs, 1986—; bd. dirs. Palmer Found., Colorado Springs, 1981-87. Served with USAR, 1963-68. Mem. Urban Land Inst. (assoc.), Home Builders Assn., Bd. Realtors, Citizens Goals, Am. Alpine Club, Colorado Mountain Club (bd. dirs. Colorado Springs chpt. 1977-80), El Paso Club. Clubs: Am. Alpine (N.Y.C.); Colorado Mountain (Colorado Springs) (bd. dirs. 1977-80); El Paso. Home: 110 Old Broadmoor Rd Colorado Springs CO 80906 Office: Rsch & Cons Group Inc 20 Boulder Crescent Colorado Springs CO 80903

BANANAL, EDUARDO FLORENDO, lawyer, newspaper editor, writer; b. Naguilian, La Union, The Philippines, Sept. 17, 1911; came to U.S., 1977; s. Joaquin Perez and Artemia (Florendo) B.; m. Gorgonia Martinez, May 29, 1937; children: Lina, Eliseo, Arturo, Delia, Myrna, Oscar. BL, U. Philippines, 1935. Clk. Bur. Posts, Manila, 1931-36; pvt. practice La Union Province, 1936-52, 59-61, Manila, 1966-77; asst. sec.-treas., bd. sec., acting chief legal staff Cebu-Portland Cement Co., Manila, 1952-59; gen. mgr. Philippine Va. Tobacco Adminstrn., Quezon City, 1962-65; del. 1st Internat. Tobacco Trade Congress, Paris, 1963, 2d, Istanbul, Turkey, 1965; cons., contbg. editor Mabuhay Times, National City, Calif., 1986—. Author: Camilo Osias: Educator and Statesman, 1974, The Men at the Helm, 1980, The Presidents of the Philippines, 1986; contbr. articles to legal publs. Mcpl. councilor, Naguilian, 1938-40; pres. Naguilian Acad., 1947-49, Filipino-Am. Sr. Citizens Assn., San Diego, 1984-86, bd. dirs., 1986—; provincial coord. Macapagal-Pelaez Movement, La Union, 1961; vice chmn. Mira Mesa Sr. Ctr. Orgn., Inc., San Diego, 1986—. With U.S. Armed Forces, 1944-45. Named Citizen of Mo. San Diego County Bd. Suprs., 1986; recipient Disting. Svc. award Councilman Ed Struksma, San Diego, 1986. Office: Filipino-Am Sr Citizens Assn 8460 Mira Mesa Blvd San Diego CA 92126

BANAS, EMIL MIKE, physicist, educator; b. East Chicago, Ind., Dec. 5, 1921; s. John J. and Rose M. (Valcicak) B.; ed. Ill. Benedictine Coll., 1940-43; B.A. (U.S. Rubber fellow), U. Notre Dame, 1954, Ph.D., 1955; m. Margaret Fagyas, Oct. 9, 1948; children—Mary K., Barbara A. Instr. math. and physics Ill. Benedictine Coll., Lisle, 1946-48, adj. faculty mem., 1971-82, trustee, 1959-61; with Civil Service, State of Ind., Hammond, 1948-50; lectr. physics Purdue U., Hammond, 1955-60; staff research physicist Amoco Corp., Naperville, Ill., 1955-82; cons., 1983—. Served with USNR, 1943-46. Mem. Ill. Benedictine Coll. Alumni Assn. (dir. hon., named alumnus of yr., 1965, pres. 1959-60), Sigma Pi Sigma. Roman Catholic. Clubs: Soc. of Procopians. Contbr. articles to sci. jours. Home: SW 325 Clarkson Ct Apt 4 Pullman WA 99163

BANCHERO, JOSEPH JERRY, wine retailor; b. Seattle, Feb. 26, 1937; s. Christopher Mondo and Theresa Nellie (Greiner) B.; m. Mary Margaret Hoffman, Sept. 10, 1960 (div.); children: Theresa, Shari, J.J. Jr., Christopher. BS in Polit. Sci., U. Santa Clara, 1959. Owner Banchero Assocs./Mondo's World, Seattle, 1960—. Chairperson SE Seattle Effective Devel., Seattle, 1973; 1st v.p. SE Seattle Sr. Ctr., 1988. Lt. col. USAR, 1959-87. Mem. Enological Soc., Res. Officers' Assn., Knights of the Vine (master commdr. Wash. chpt. 1980). Office: Mondo's World 4223 Rainier Ave S Seattle WA 98118

BANDT, LAWRENCE EUGENE, electrical engineer; b. Reno, Nev., July 16, 1964; s. Perry Eugene and Emma Anne (Hunzlker) B. BSEE, U. Nev., 1987. Desk supr. Holiday Inn, Reno, 1982-87; elec. engr. Holiday Inn, 1987—. Mem. IEEE. Republican. Lutheran. Home: 1381 University Terr Reno NV 89503

BANEN, ALLEN, cabinet and furniture manufacturing company executive; b. Chgo., Jan. 2, 1933; s. Irving and Estell (Auslander) B.; m. Norm Feldman, May 2, 1954; children: Steven, Renee. Student, U. Ill., Chgo., 1952-53, Chgo. Musical Coll., 1952-54, De Paul U., 1954-56. Profl. musician Chgo., 1950-60; gen. mgr. Henry's Camera and Hi Fi, L.A., 1961-69; salesman BNA Div. Gillette Co., L.A., 1970-72, regional mgr., 1972-75; mgr. nat. sales BNA Div. Gillette Co., Boston, 1975-79; pres., chief exec. officer Noral Enterprises Ltd., Phoenix, 1980—. Served with USNR, 1950-52. Mem. Aircraft Owners and Pilots Assn., Am. Soc. Interior Designers. Home: 16208 E Trevino Dr Fountain Hills AZ 85268 Office: Noral Enterprises Ltd 2221 E Washington St Phoenix AZ 85034

BANGARU, BABU RAJENDRA PRASAD, engineer; b. Palakol, India, Oct. 24, 1947; came to U.S., 1972; s. Raghavaiah and Sarojini Devi (Segu) B.; m. Jagadamba Narayanam, June 15, 1974; children: Sarojkamal, Vijay R., Sridevi. BS in Engrng., Coll. Engrng., Kakinada, India, 1968; MS in Engrng., Coll. Engrng., Trivandrum, India, 1971; MS, SUNY, Stony Brook, 1978, PhD, 1981. Lectr. Regional Engrng. Coll., Calicut, India, 1971-72; research and tchng. asst. coll. engrng. SUNY, Stony Brook, 1972-75; programmer NASA, Greenbelt, N.Y., 1975-78; sr. computer applications engr. EBASCO Services, Inc., N.Y.C., 1979-83; mem. tech. staff AT&T Bell Labs., Holmdel, N.J., 1983-87; sr. telecommunications engr. Boeing Computer Support Services, Huntsville, Ala., 1987-88; mem. tech. staff U.S. West Advanced Techs., Englewood, Colo., 1988—. Mem. IEEE. Office: US West Advanced Techs 6200 S Quebec St Englewood CO 80111

BANGERTER, NORMAN HOWARD, governor of Utah, building contractor; b. Granger, Utah, Jan. 4, 1933; s. William Henry and Isabelle (Bawden) B.; m. Colleen Monson, Aug. 18, 1953; children: Garrett, Ann, Jordan, Blair, Alayne, Adam, Erdman (foster son). Student, U. Utah, 1956-57, Brigham Young U., 1951-55. Vice pres. B and H Real Estate Co., West Valley City, Utah, 1970—; sec. Dixie-Six Land Devel., West Valley City, Utah, 1980—; pres. Bangerter and Hendrickson Co., West Valley City, Utah, 1970—, NHB Construction Co., West Valley City, Utah, 1983—; gov. Utah 1985—. Mem. Utah Ho. of Reps., 1974-85, speaker, 1981-84, majority leader, 1977-78; chmn. task force for alternative forms of govt. West Valley City, 1982. Recipient Outstanding Legislator award VFW, 1981; recipient Disting. Service award Home Bldg. Industry; named Outstanding Businessman West Valley C. of C. Mormon. Office: Office of Gov 210 State Capitol Salt Lake City UT 84114

BANGERTER, WILLIAM GRANT, religious organization executive; b. Granger, Utah, June 8, 1918; s. William Henry and Isabelle (Bawden) B.; m. Mildred Lee Schwantes, Mar. 8, 1944 (dec. Aug. 1952); children: Lee Ann, Cory William, Glenda, Mildred Elizabeth; m. Geraldine Hamblin, Oct. 14, 1953; children: Julie, Grant Hamblin, Howard Kent, Peggy, Glenn, Layne, Duella. BA, U. Utah, 1948. Dairyman Granger, 1937-42, carpenter, 1942-74, bldg. contractor, 1948-74, real estate broker, 1966—; gen. authority LDS Ch., Salt Lake City, 1975—. Bd. dirs. LDS Hosp., Salt Lake City, U. Utah Alumni Bd.; pres. Magna (Utah) and Granger Sem. Bds.; councilman City of Alpine, Utah; mem. Salt Lake Council Boy Scouts Am. 1st lt. USAF. Office: LDS Ch 1st Quorum of the 70 50 E North Temple St Salt Lake City UT 84150

BANGHAM, ROBERT ARTHUR, orthotist; b. San Antonio, Sept. 12, 1942; s. Robert Dave and Marguerite C. (Wyckoff) B.; m. Yvonne Janice Parminter, Sept. 23, 1961. Grad. high sch., South Lyon, Mich. Cert. orthotist; ordained to ministry Jehovah's Witness Ch., 1957. Orthotic resident J. R. Reets, Ann Arbor, Mich., 1960-65; orthotist Dreher-Jouett, Inc., Chgo., 1965-68; cert. orthotist U. Mich., 1968-75, Wright & Filipis, Inc., Alpena, Mich., 1975-78; cert. orthotist Hittenbergers, Concord, Calif., 1978-81, Oakland, Calif., 1981-88; mgr., cert. orthotist Hittenbergers, Concord, Oakland, 1988—. Mem. Yosemite Park Assn., 1988. Mem. Am. Orthotics and Prosthetics, Calif. Coalition Allied Health Professions (pres. 1989), Am. Acad. Orthotists, Prosthetists (dir. 1989—, pres. northern Calif. chpt. 1987—), Nat. Sci. Chmn. of Acad., Nat. Park Assn., Wilderness Soc., Sierra Club. Home: 67 W Lake Dr Antioch CA 94509 Office: Hittenbergers 2930 Summit St Oakland CA 94609

BANGS, CATE (CATHRYN MARGARET BANGS), motion picture art director, interior designer; b. Tacoma, Mar. 16, 1951; d. Henry Horan and Belva Virginia (Grandstaff) B.; m. Steve Bangs, Nov. 1, 1986. Student, Hammersmith Coll Art and Bldg., London, 1971; BA cum laude, Pitzer Coll., 1973; MFA, NYU, 1978. Owner, interior designer Flying Pencil Design, Hollywood Hills, Calif., 1981—; art dir. Cobra, Stalone Prodns., 1985, Who Framed Roger Rabbit, 1986, A Year in the Life, Universal Studios, 1986, Beverly Hills Cop II, 1986-87, The Seventh Sign, 1987, Crime Story, 1987-88, Spies, Partners and Lovers, 1988, Far from Home, 1988, Hider in the House, 1988, Hard Time, 1988-89. Bd. dirs. Hollywood Heights Assn., 1982-87. Recipient Dramalogue Critics award, 1983. Mem. Soc. Motion Picture and TV Art Dirs., Soc. Set Designers and Model Makers (cert., exec. bd. 1985—), United Scenic Artists. Democrat. Buddhist. Home: 3180 Oakshire Dr Hollywood Hills CA 90068-1743

BANGS, JOHN WESLEY, III, law enforcement administrator; b. Phila., Dec. 26, 1941; s. John Wesley Jr. and Sarah Emily (Morcom) B.; m. Donna Louise McClanahan, June 1, 1963; children: Louis M., Terry M., John W. AA summa cum laude, E. Los Angeles Coll., 1976. Calif. Commn. on Peace Officer Standards and Training: Basic, Intermediate, Advanced, Supervisory, Mgmt. Police officer Los Angeles Police Dept., 1964-70, sgt., 1970-74, lt., 1974-84; chief spl. officer Los Angeles Dept. Airports Police, 1988—; lectr. U. So. Calif., 1978-79. Author: Narcotics Overview, 1983, Psychological Evaluation for Police Candidates, 1969. Cub master Cub Scouts Am., Ontario, Calif., 1968; scout master Boy Scouts Am., Ontario, 1971; explorer leader Explorer Scouts Am., Los Angeles, 1976; mem. Greater Los Angeles Scouting Council, 1976. Sgt. U.S. Army, 1959-62. Mem. Calif. Peace Officers Assn., Calif. Narcotics Officers, Los Angeles Police Protective League, Los Angeles Police Relief Assn., Lions Internat. Republican. Episcopalian. Office: Los Angeles Airport Police #1 World Way PO Box 92216 Los Angeles CA 90009-2216

BANGS, RICHARD JOHNSTON, business executive; b. New Haven, Aug. 24, 1950; s. Lawrence Cutler and Louise (Morton) B. BA, Northwestern U., 1972; MA, U. So. Calif., 1975. Pres. Angels Camp, Oakland Park, Calif., 1973--. Author: Rivergods 1985, Islands of Fire 1988, Race to the Yangtze. Home: 6267 Robinhood Way Oakland CA 94611 Office: Sober 535 Mira Vista Oakland CA 94610

BANGSUND, EDWARD LEE, aerospace company executive; b. Two Harbors, Minn., July 16, 1935; s. Ilo Henry and Hildur Margaret (Holter) B.; m. Caryl Ann Billingsley, Oct. 10, 1956; children: Julie Ann, Trina Lee, John Kirk, Edward Eric. BME, U. Wash., 1959. With Boeing Co., 1956-71; engr. Apollo program Boeing Co., Cape Kennedy, Fla., 1967-69, Houston, 1969-71; mgr. space vehicle design Space Systems div. Boeing Aerospace, Seattle, 1971-76, mgr. inertial upper stage futures, 1976-85, mgr. space transp., 1985-87, dir. strategic planning, 1987--. Contbr. articles to profl. publs.; patentee in field. Pres. Springbrook Parents Adv. Com., 1972-75; chmn. Citizens Budget Rev. Com., 1973-75, 76-78, Citizens Facility Planning Com., 1977-78, Citizens for Kent (Wash.) Schs. Levy, 1974, 76; bd. dirs. Kent Youth Ctr., 1980-83; pres. Kent Sch. Bd., 1978-84. Named to Apollo-Saturn Roll of Honor, NASA, 1969; recipient Golden Acorn award Wash. Congress PTA, 1977, Vol. of Yr. award Kent Sch. Dist., 1977, 78. Assoc. fellow AIAA (mem. space systems tech. com. 1985-87, dep. dir. region VI 1986--, chmn. space transp. tech. com. 1987--), Internat. Acad. Astronautics, Internat. Astronautical Fedn. (mem. space transp. exec. com. 1985--), Nat. Space Found., Aerospace Industries assn. (mem. space council 1987--), Space Bus. Roundtable (pres. Seattle chpt. 1988--, bd. dirs. 1988--). Republican. Lutheran. Home: 9441 S 202nd St Kent WA 98031 Office: Boeing Aerospace PO Box 3999 M/S 8C-22 Seattle WA 98124

BANKERT, JUDD CHARLES, data processing executive, consultant; b. Grand Rapids, Mich., Sept. 9, 1949; s. Charles Herbert and Dorothy (Cook) B.; m. Dabney Jo Anderson, Dec. 19, 1970; 1 child, Kelsey Kate. BA, Mich. State U., 1975. CPA, Washington, Mich. Sr. auditor Peat Martwick Mitchell, Detroit, 1975-76, Guam, 1981-82; mgr. mgmt. info. systems Atkins Kroll, Inc., Guam, 1982-85; pvt. practice as computer cons. Bellingham, Wash., 1985—; instr. U. Guam, 1985-86. Athlete Guam Nat. Olympic Com., Calgary, Can., 1988. Mem. Am. Inst. CPA's. Office: 119 N Commerial Bellingham Towers Ste 330 Bellingham WA 98225

BANKS, CARL L., pharmaceutical distribution executive; b. Oregon City, Oreg., Aug. 11, 1932; s. Otho John and Violet Elmira (Thomas) B.; m. Betty Ann Teller, Oct. 3, 1953 (div. Oct. 1978); children: Carlyn Marie, Connie Lee, Thomas John; m. Shirley Ann O'Brien, Mar. 17, 1979. BS, Seattle U., 1954, Portland State U., 1956. Sales mgr. Fruitland Wineries Inc., Portland, Oreg., 1954-60; sales rep. Endo Lab., N.Y.C., 1960-62; various positions E.R. Squibb & Sons, N.J., 1962-88; mgr. distbn. ctr. E.R. Squibb & Sons, Seattle, 1988—. Recpient Spoke award Jr. C. of C., Springfield, Oreg., 1968. Mem. CAP, NRA, Bellevue C. of C., Airplane Owner & Pilots Assn., Elks, Shriners. Republican. Lutheran. Home: 24247 NE 5th Pl Redmond WA 98053

BANKS, DAVID RUSSELL, health care executive; b. Arcadia, Wis., Feb. 15, 1937; s. J.R. and Cleone B.; married; children: Melissa, Michael. B.A., U. Ark., 1959. Vice pres. Dabbs, Sullivan, Trulock, Ark., 1963-74; chmn., chief exec. officer Leisure Lodges, Ft. Smith, Ark., 1974-77; registered rep. Stephens Inc., Little Rock, 1974-79; pres., chief operating officer Beverly Enterprises, Pasadena, Calif., 1979—; dir. Nat. Council Health Centers, Pulaski Bank, Little Rock. Served with U.S. Army. Office: Beverly Enterprises Inc 99 S Oakland Ave Pasadena CA 91101 *

BANKS, LISA JEAN, government official; b. Chelsea, Mass., Dec. 19, 1956; d. Bruce H. and Jean P. (Como) Banks. B.S. in Bus. Adminstrn., Northeastern U., 1979. Coop trainee IRS, Boston, 1975-79, revenue officer, Reno, 1979-81, spl. agt., Houston, 1981-84, Anchorage, 1984—, fed. womens program mgr., 1980-81. Recipient Superior Performance award IRS, 1981, 87, 89. Mem. Nat. Assn. Treasury Agts., Nat. Assn. Female Execs. Democrat. Roman Catholic Office: PO Box 1500 Anchorage AK 99510

BANKS, PETER MORGAN, electrical engineering educator; b. San Diego, May 21, 1937; s. George Willard and Mary Margaret (Morgan) B.; m. Paulett M. Behanna, May 21, 1983; children by previous marriage: Kevin, Michael, Steven, David. M.S. in E.E, Stanford U., 1960; Ph.D. in Physics, Pa. State U., 1965. Postdoctoral fellow Institut d'Aeronomie Spatiale de Belgique, Brussels, Belgium, 1965-66; prof. applied physics U. Calif., San Diego, 1966-76; prof. physics Utah State U., 1976-81, head dept. physics, 1976-81; prof. elec. engring. Stanford U., 1981—, dir. space, telecommunications and radiosci. lab., 1982—, dir. ctr. for aeronautics and space info. systems, 1983—, vis. assoc. prof., 1972-73; pres. Earth Data Corp., 1985-86; vis. scientist Max Planck Inst. for Aeronomie, Ger., 1975; pres. La Jolla Scis. Inc., 1973-77, Upper Atmosphere Research Corp., 1978-82; chmn. NASA adv. com on sci. uses of space sta., 1985-87; mem. Jason Group, 1983—. Author: (with G. Kockarts) Aeronomy, 1973, (with J.R. Doupnik) Introduction to Computer Science, 1976; assoc. editor: Jour. Geophys. Research, 1974-77; assoc. editor: Planetary and Space Sci, 1977-83, regional editor, 1983-86; contbr. numerous articles in field to profl. jours. Mem. space sci. adv. council NASA, 1976-80. Served with U.S. Navy, 1960-63. Recipient Appleton prize Royal Soc. London, 1978, Space Sci. award AIAA, 1981, NASA Disting. Service medal, 1986; Alumni fellow Pa. State U., 1982. Fellow Am. Geophys. Union; mem. Internat. Union Radio Sci. Episcopalian. Club: Cosmos. Home: 928 Casanueva Pl Stanford CA 94305 Office: Stanford U Elec Engring Dept Stanford CA 94305

BANNER, EARL J, human resources executive; b. Burley, Idaho, May 14, 1937; s. Clarence LeRoy and Olevia Leuanne (Hymas) B.; m. Nyla Wilcock, June 14, 1962; children: Brian, David, Denise, Nathan, Laurel, Rebecca, Kristin. BS in Econs., Brigham Young U., 1962; MS in Indsl. Relations, U. Utah, 1965. Employment interviewer Sperry Rand Co., Salt Lake City, 1962-64; mgr. personnel Ajax Presses, Salt Lake City, 1964-67, Marquardt Corp., Ogden, Utah, 1967-68; v.p. employee relations Macy's Calif., San Francisco, 1968-80; v.p. human resources U I Group Inc., Kennewick, Wash., 1980-87; exec. dir. dept. human resources mgmt. State Utah, Salt Lake City, 1988—. Bd. dirs. Bay Area Urban League, 1974-77; mem. exec. com. United for Wash., 1986-87. Mem. Am. Soc. Personnel Adminstrn. (pres. Utah chpt. 1968, sec. Columbia Basin chpt. 1984). Republican. Mormon. Lodge: Rotary, Kiwanis. Home: 698 E 650 N Centerville UT 84014 Office: 2229 State Office Bldg Salt Lake City UT 84114

BANNER, RUSSELL WILLIAM, engineering consulting company executive; b. London, Feb. 13, 1944; came to U.S., 1967; s. Thomas and Doris Emily (Oliver) B. Aero. engring. cert., Hatfield (Eng.) Coll. Tech., 1964. Aero. engr. Hawker Siddeley Aviation, Hatfield, 1964-67, Boeing Aircraft Co., Seattle, 1967-70, Israel Aircraft Industries, Tel Aviv, 1971-74, Messerschmitt-Bolkow Blum, Munich, 1974-75; cons. aero. engr. Hughes Helicopters, Inconen Corp., Culver City, Calif., 1975-81, at Northrop Aircraft, Hawthorne, Calif., 1981-86; v.p., mng. dir. co. Marina Del Rey, Calif., 1986--. Home: 1242 11th St Hermosa Beach CA 90254 Office: Inconen Corp 13160 Mindanao Way Ste 234 Marina Del Rey CA 90292

BANNISTER, WES, mayor, insurance company executive; b. Houston, Oct. 11, 1936; m. Betty Bannister, 1959; 3 children. BS in Polit. Sci., 1959. Ins. exec. Albuquerque, 1969, Huntington Beach, Calif., 1969-74; owner, pres. Bannister & Assocs. Ins., Huntington Beach, 1974—. Mayor City of Huntington Beach, mem. city coun., 1986—, active various community commns.; bd. dirs. Boys Club, YMCA; advisor Huntington Beach Search, Rescue Explorer Post, County 2001 Transp. Com. Capt. U.S. Army, 1959. Mem. Nat. Coalition for Marine Conservation (bd. dirs. Pacific Region), Huntington Beach C. of C., Rotary. Office: Office of Mayor 2000 Main St Huntington Beach CA 92648

BANNON, KEVIN J., printing company executive; b. N.Y.C., Dec. 19, 1956; s. Joseph Bannon and Rosalind (Cutler) Gerst; children: Robert, Cody. BS, Northeastern U., Boston, 1979. Customer service rep Bowne of N.Y., N.Y.C., 1979-82; plant supr. Pandick N.E., Boston, 1982-85; gen. mgr. Imperial Fin. Printing, Phoenix, 1985—; ptnr., cons. CVA Delivery Corp., Phoenix, 1987—. Bd. trustees Leukemia Soc. Am. Ariz. chpt. Mem. Enterprise Network, Phoenix Forum Breakfast Club (steering com.). Home: 6713 S Taylor Dr Tempe AZ 85283

BANTA, JOHN ERSKINE, hotel corporation executive; b. N.Y.C., Oct. 7, 1948; s. John Stuart and Maude (Erskine) B.; m. Karen Elaine Fogg, Jan. 12, 1980; children: Alicia Catherine, Nicholas Christopher. BS in Hotel Mgmt., Cornell U., 1972. Hotel mgr. New London (N.H.) Inn, 1973-74; food and beverage dir. Hyatt Hotels, Chgo., 1974-86; gen. mgr. Hyatt Hotels, Los Angeles, 1986-87; pres. hotel div. Rosewood-Stone Group, San Francisco, 1987-88; pres. Post Hotel Corp., San Francisco, 1988—. Vol. Hospitality House, San Francisco, 1988. Republican. Episcopalian. Lodge: Rotary (bd. dirs. Hollywood, Calif. club 1986—). Home: 1680 Indian Valley Rd Novato CA 94947 Office: Post Hotel Corp 85 5th St San Francisco CA 94103

BANVARD, KRIS, newspaper editor; b. L.A., Mar. 23, 1957; s. Roger Emil and Mary Elizabeth (Sturgeon) B.; m. Paula Vaadia Deming, June 10, 1978; children: Elaine, Honor. BA in Journalism, U. Oreg., 1978. Reporter, news editor Sun-Enterprise, Monmouth, Oreg., 1978-79; reporter Grants Pass (Oreg.) Daily Courier, 1979; reporter, asst. city editor Sacramento Union, 1979-87; asst. city editor Roanoke (Va.) Times & World-News, 1987—.

BAPTIST, OREN CECIL, petroleum engineer, genealogist; b. Uniontown, Kans., Oct. 17, 1912; s. John Oliver and Iva Marie (Jones) B.; m. Ellen Marie Bandy, Mar. 1, 1947; 1 child, Linda Marie Stockton. Grad., Ft. Scott Jr. Coll., 1937; BS, U. Kans., 1940, postgrad., 1941. Registered profl. engr., Wyo., Calif. Asst. engr. U.S.C.E., Albuquerque, 1942-43; geologist-engr. Socony Mobil Oil Co., Bogota, Columbia, 1943-45; petroleum engr. Mobil Oil Co., Casper, Wyo., 1945-47; supr. U.S. Dept. Interior, Laramie, Wyo., 1947-67; dir. San Francisco Energy Research Ctr. U.S. Dept. Energy, 1967-76; sr. petroleum specialist H.K. Van Poollen and Assocs., Littleton, Colo., 1976-81; cons. in petroleum engring. San Rafael, Calif., 1976—; author, pub. Oren C. Baptist & Assocs., 1980—. Author: Oil Production from Permafrost, Umiat, Alaska, The Baptist and Harden Families, The Baptista and Teixeira Families, Madeira and America, 1385-1986; co-author Enhanced Oil Recovery; contbr. 24 articles to sci. jours. Mem. Soc. Petroleum Engrs. (chmn. monograph com. 1969-71, mem. Anthony F. Lucas gold medal award com. 1980-84), NSPE, Am. Assn. Petroleum Geologists, Am. Petroleum Inst., Marin Geneal. Soc., Sigma Xi, Tau Beta Pi. Home and Office: 396 Monticello Rd San Rafael CA 94903

BAPTISTE, CLARENCE BOYSIE, minister; b. Scarborough, Tobago, Trinidad and Tobago, June 8, 1941; came to Can., 1969; s. George and Marjorie Enid (James) B.; m. Beryl Joan Durant, June 13, 1965; children: David J., Peter L., Philip P. AA, Kingsway Coll., Oshawa, Ont., Can., 1971; BA, Andrews U., 1973, MA, 1975, MDiv., 1977. Ordained to ministry Seventh-day Adventist Ch., 1981. Lit. evangelist South Caribbean Conf. Seventh-day Adventsits Ch., Port of Spain, Trinidad and Tobago, 1962-67; pub. dir. Port of Spain, Trinidad and Tobago, 1967-69; minister Man. and Sask. Conf. of Seventh-day Adventists Ch., Saskatoon, 1977-86; pastor, evangelist Yorkton (Sask.) Seventh-day Adventist Ch., 1983-86; pastor West Edmonton (Alta.) Seventh-day Adventist Ch., 1986—; lectr. Brandon (Man., Can.) U., 1979-80. Mem. Edmonton Coralwood Jr. Acad. Sch. Bd.; dir. human relations dept. Alta. Conf. Seventh-day Adventist Chs., chmn. human relations com. Mem. Yorkton Ministerial Assn., Dauphin Ministerial Assn., Saskatoon Ministerial Assn., Edmonton Chs. Ministeral Assn. (pres.), Can. Union Conf. of Seventh Day Adventist Ch. (human relations com.). Home: 11712-135 B St, Edmonton, AB Canada T5M 1L7 Office: W Edmonton Seventh-day Adventist Ch, Box 9049 Sta E, Edmonton, AB Canada T5P 4K1

BARAB, MARVIN, financial consultant; b. Wilmington, Del., July 16, 1927; s. Jacob and Minnie (Press) B.; m. Gertrude Klein, June 13, 1951; children: Jordan, Neal, Caryn. BS with distinction, Ind. U., 1947, MBA, 1951. Dir. mktg. Edward Weiss & Co., Chgo., 1951-56; dir. bus. rsch. Parker Pen Co., Janesville, Wis., 1956-59; dir. mktg. rsch. packaging and graphics Mattel Co. Inc., Hawthorne, Calif., 1959-65; pres. Barcam Pub. Co., Rolling Hills Estates, Calif., 1959-70, Rajo Publs., Rolling Hills Estates, 1967-70, So. Calif. Coll. Med. & Dental Careers, Anaheim, 1970-81, Barbrook, Inc., Rolling Hills Estates, 1981—; cons. Marvin Barab & Assocs., Rolling Hills Estates, Calif., 1981—. Editor: Rand McNally Camping Guide, 1967-70; contbr. articles to various publs., 1982-87. Mem. Nat. Assn. Trade & Tech. Schs. (sec. 1977-79, pres. 1979-81, life mem., bd. dirs.), Calif. Assn. Paramedical Schs. (pres. 1973-77), Inst. Bus. Counselors, Nat. Council Exchangers, Internat. Bus. Brokers Assn. Office: Barbrook Inc 655 Deep Valley Dr Ste 325 Rolling Hills Estates CA 90274

BARAD, JILL ELIKANN, toy company executive; b. N.Y.C., May 23, 1951; d. Lawrence Stanley and Corinne (Schuman) Elikann; m. Thomas Kenneth Barad, Jan., 28, 1979; children: Alexander David, Justin Harris. BA English and Psychology, Queens Coll., 1973. Asst. prod. mgr. mktg. Coty Cosmetics, N.Y.C., 1976-77, prod. mgr. mktg., 1977; account exec. Wells Rich Greene Advt. Agy., Los Angeles, 1978-79; product mgr. mktg. Mattel Toys, Inc., Los Angeles, 1981-82, dir. mktg., 1982-83, v.p. mktg., 1983-85, sr. v.p. mktg., 1985-86, sr. v.p. product devel., from 1986, exec. v.p. product design and devel., exec. v.p. mktg. and worldwide product devel., 1988—. Charter mem. Rainbow Guild/Amie Karen Cancer Fund, Los Angeles, 1983, Los Angeles County Mus., 1985. Mem. Am. Film Inst. (charter). Office: Mattel Inc 5150 Rosecrans Ave Hawthorne CA 90250

BARADAT, LEON P., political science professor; b. Tulare, Calif., June 27, 1940; s. Leon Pierre and Jeannette (Lasbareilles) B.; m. Elaine Louise Cote, Jan. 30, 1965; children: Leon Pierre, Rene Anicet. AA, Coll. Sequois, 1963; BA, Fresno State Univ., 1965, MA, 1969. Liftime spl. secondary teaching credential. Tchr. Tulare Western High Sch., 1965-70; prof. polit. sci. Mira Costa Coll., Oceanside, Calif., 1970—; cons. higher edn. Calif. State Legis., Sacramento, 1980; founder, dir. Ctr. for Internat. Understanding Mira Costa Coll., 1983—. Author: Political Ideologies: Their Origin and Impact, 1979, 84, 88, Soviet Political Society, 1986, 89; contbr. articles to profl. jours. and newspapers. Mem. Tulare County Dem. Cent. Com., 1966-70, San Diego County Dem. Cent. Com., San Diego, 1972; pres. Academic Senate for Calif. Community Colls., Sacramento, 1978-79; v.p. Faculty Assn. Calif. Community Colls., Sacramento, 1987-88; bd. trustees Palomar Coll., San Marcos, 1983-88; speaker various community and ednl. orgns., 1968—. With USMC Res., 1957-59. Recipient Commendtory Join Resolution Calif. State Legis., 1980. Mem. Textbook Authors Assn., Acad. Polit. Sci., NAACP, Am. Civil Liberties Union, League Women Voters, North Shores Dem. Club (pres. 1971-73). Home: 1125 Monte Vista Dr Vista CA 92084 Office: Mira Costa Coll 1 Barnard Dr Oceanside CA 92056

BARANEK, PAUL PETER, retired agriculturist; b. Wynn, Pa., Feb. 18, 1914; s. Joseph and Sophia (Koltas) B.; BS, U. Calif., Davis, 1936, cert. tchr., 1937, MEdn, 1946; m. Marie Agatha Herzog, Aug. 18, 1937 (dec. 1974); children: Jeanne Marie Baranek Olmstead, Robert Paul, Barbara May Baranek Plaskett, John Peter. Dir. inst. vocat. agr. Escalon (Calif.) High Sch., 1937-42; mgr., operator Delta Dairy, Courtland, Calif., 1942-45; land use specialist Delta dist., Bur. Reclamation, Sacramento, Stockton, Calif., 1946-50; regional weed specialist Bur. Reclamation, Sacramento 1950-53; farm adviser Agrl. Extension Svc. U. Calif., Madera, 1953-74, agriculturist emeritus, 1974—; cons. rsch. com. Calif. Raisin Adv. Bd., 1958—, grading com. Fed. Raisin Adv. Bd., 1965—; ofcl. judge vine judging contest Future Farmers of Am., Fresno, Calif., 1955-84. Advancement chmn. Sequoia council Boy Scouts Am., 1953-62, counselor, 1953-62. Mem. Am. Soc. Enologists, Young Men's Inst., Alpha Gamma Rho, Alpha Zeta, Commonwealth Club. Democrat. Roman Catholic. Contbr. articles to profl. jours. Address: 511 Barsotti Ave Madera CA 93637

BARATTA-LORTON, ROBERT, educator; b. Fresno, Calif., June 19, 1939; s. Paul Vernon and Jean (Steinbeck) Lorton; BA in Econs. with honors, Stanford U., 1961; MA in Edn., U. Calif., Berkeley, 1968; widower. Classroom tchr., tchr. educationally handicapped, Calif., 1966-73; instr. Miller Math. State Specialized Tchr. Improvement Program, also Center Improvement Math. Edn., San Diego, 1971-74; co-founder, 1975, since chmn. bd. dirs., dir. Center Innovation in Edn., Saratoga, Calif.; pres., bd. govs. Center Grad. Coll., Saratoga, 1980—. Lt. USNR, 1963-66; Vietnam. Mem. Internat. Reading Assn., Nat. Council Tchrs. Math., Assn. Supervision and Curriculum Devel., Nat. Assn. Edn. Young Children, Council Exceptional Children, Calif. Math. Council. Author: Mathematics. . .A Way of Thinking, 1977; Baratta-Lorton Reading Program, 1985. Office: 20665 4th St Saratoga CA 95070

BARAZONE, MOUNQUE, manufacturing company executive; b. Cleve., Dec. 9, 1948; s. Abraham and Helen (Leverstein) B.; m. Stephanie Evans, Aug. 30, 1986. BA, Cleve. State U. Gen. mgr. Chagrin Valley 66, Moreland Hills, Ohio, 1970-72; mgr. mktg., then v.p. Data Info. Systems, Chgo., 1972-78; field office mgr., then asst. to pres. W.J. Lazynski Constrn. Co., Milw., 1978-80; sales mgr. Am. Culvert Co., Redding, Calif., 1980-81; pres. Earth Fabrics, Inc., Redding, 1981-86; v.p. A.C.F. West, Inc., Richmond, Va., 1986—; also bd. dirs. A.C.F. West, Inc.; lectr. on geosynthetics. Patentee in field. Mem. Soc. Mil. Engrs., Internat. KenPo Karate Assn., Geotech. Fabrics Assn., Associated Gen. Contractors. Jewish. Home: PO Box 5217 Cottonwood CA 96022 Office: ACF West Inc 26250 Corporate Ave Hayward CA 94545

BARBEE, JOE ED, lawyer; b. Pharr, Tex., Feb. 27, 1934; s. Archie Allen and Concha (Leal) B.; m. Yolanda Margaret Atonna, Feb. 17, 1962; children—Cynthia M., Adam A., Walter J. BSEE, U. Ariz., 1961; JD, Western New Eng. Coll., 1973. Bar: Mass. 1973, U.S. Patent Office 1973, U.S. Ct. Appeals (fed. cir.) 1982. Engr. Gen. Electric Co., Pittsfield, Mass., 1961-73, patent atty., Fort Wayne, Ind., 1973-75; patent atty. Magnavox, Fort Wayne, 1975-76, Motorola, Inc., Phoenix, 1976—. Sgt. U.S. Army, 1953-56. Recipient Outstanding Performance award U.S. Civil Svc., 1960. Mem. ABA, Am. Patent Law Assn., Am. Intellectual Property Law Assn. Republican. Methodist. Avocations: tennis, hunting, fishing. Home: 7611 N Mockingbird Ln Paradise Valley AZ 85253 Office: Motorola Inc 4250 E Camelback Rd Phoenix AZ 85018

BARBER, ELTON DUDE, sales executive; b. Port Jervis, N.Y., June 27, 1926; s. Frank Edward and Marion Frieda (Weiss) B. BBA, Woodbury Coll., 1949; postgrad., U. So. Calif., L.A., 1951. Gen. mgr. Lamson & Gilbert Co., Inc., L.A., 1949-54; ptnr., gen. mgr. Carr Appliances, Hollywood, Calif., 1954-61; pres. T.C.B. Corp., L.A., 1957-58; appliance and television sales mgr. Barker Bros., L.A., 1961-63; western region sales rep. Clairtone Electronic Corp., Toronto, Ont., Can., 1963-68; v.p., gen. mgr. Telstar Electronics, L.A., 1968-71; sales mgr. western region Pfanstiehl Corp., Studio City, Calif., 1971—. Sgt. U.S. Army, 1944-47, ETO. Mem. Phi Theta Pi. Republican. Roman Catholic. Office: Pfanstiehl West 11652 Amanda Dr Studio City CA 91604

BARBER, HERBERT BRADFORD, medical physicist; b. Worcester, Mass., Nov. 30, 1943; s. Clarence Edward and Virginia (Amidon) B.; m. Kathleen Ann Starks, Nov. 17, 1985. BS, Worcester Polytech. Inst., 1965; MS, U. Ariz., 1971, PhD, 1976. Research engr. Morgan Constrn. Co., Worcester, Mass., 1965; grad. teaching asst. U. Ariz., Tucson, 1968-69; physicist U. Calif. at Livermore, 1969; grad. research assoc. U. Ariz., 1971-75; assoc. faculty mem. Pima Community Coll., Tucson, 1975-79; research assoc. U. Ariz. Health Sci. Ctr., Tucson, 1976-80, U. Minn., Mpls., 1980-82; research asst. prof. U. Ariz. Health Sci. Ctr., 1982—. Patentee imaging probe and method. Dem. committeeperson, Tucson, 1986; vol. Victim Witness, Pima County, 1987—. Mem. AAAS, Am. Phys. Soc., Soc. Nuclear Medicine, Am. Astronomical Soc., Profl. Ski Instrs. Am., Sigma Xi. Democrat. Club: Tucson Soaring. Office: U Ariz Health Scis Ctr Div Nuclear Medicine Tucson AZ 85724

BARBER, LINDA ANN, teacher; b. Clinton, Ill., Mar. 2, 1941; d. George Austin and Gladys Bell (Lighthall) Fosnaugh; m. John Ralph Barber, June 12, 1964; children: Amy Rebecca, Susan Jane. BA, Ill. Wesleyan U., 1963; MAT, Colo. Coll., 1980. Eng. tchr. Sch. Dist 11, Colorado Springs, Colo., 1963-68, 76—, Aims Community Coll., Greeley, Colo., 1971-72; yearbook adv. various high schs., Colorado Springs, 1965-68, 76-82, 84-85; relief tchr. So. Australia Edn. Dept., Adelaide, 1983; student tchr. prospects com. Colo. Coll. Edn. Dept., 1987. Author: Changing, 1879-1979, 1979. Singer Colorado Springs Chorale, 1987. Nominee Journalism Tchr. of Yr., Colo. High Sch. Journalism Soc. Mem. Colorado Springs Edn. Assn., Colo. Edn. Assn., NEA, Am. Music Soc. (v.p. 1986-88, pres. 1988—). Home: 3235 Montebello West Colorado Springs CO 80918

BARBER, MARK H., lawyer; b. Phila., Dec. 22, 1951; s. John Paul and Adelia (Huff) B.; m. Carolyn Sprogis, May 10, 1980 (div. 1985); m. Bonnie Russell, Sept. 6, 1986; children: Russell Prewitt, Brenna Leann. BA magna cum laude, Humboldt State U., 1975; JD, U. San Diego, 1978. Bar: Calif. 1978. Asst. mgr. Oaks Motel, Oakland, Calif., 1975; staff att. Gen. Atomic Co., San Diego, 1978-79; gen. counsel Digidyne Corp., San Diego, 1979-82;

assoc. Sedgwick, Detert, Moran and Arnold, San Francisco, 1982-85; ptnr. Laughlin, Falbo, Levy and Moresi, San Francisco, 1985—. Treas. Continuing Edn. Club, San Francisco, 1983-87; asst. campaign mgr. Sutlee for State Senate, Arcata, Calif., 1974. Mem. Calif. State Bar Assn. Democrat. Office: Laughlin Falbo Levy & Moresi 151 Union St 3d Fl San Francisco CA 94111-1221

BARBES, BENJAMIN, architect; b. Vladimirovac, Banat, Yugoslavia, May 30, 1957; s. Corneliu and Lucia (Cioban) B.; m. Georgina Zestrijan, May 28, 1983; 1 child, Nicole D. AA, Phoenix Coll., 1979, AA in Bus., 1980; BArch, Ariz. State U., Tempe, 1984. Registered architect, Ariz. Designer W.E. Meier and Assocs., Phoenix, 1977-81, Perlman-Niemiec and Assocs., Phoenix, 1981; capt. Design Lab., P.C., Phoenix, 1982-84; project mgr. Peter Lendrum and Assocs., Phoenix, 1984, assoc., 1984—; prin. Ariz. Design and Drafting Service, Phoenix, 1979—. Pres. Am. Romanian Orthodox Youth Assn., N.Y.C., 1973, St. John Bapt. Ch., Phoenix, 1988—; bd. dirs. strategic planning com. City of Glendale, Ariz., 1986—. Recipient City Beautification award City of Tempe, 1988. Mem. Nat. Geographic Soc. Republican. Eastern Orthodox. Home: 5504 W Redfield Rd Glendale AZ 85306 Office: Design Lab PC 6232 N 7th St #110 Phoenix AZ 85014

BARBEZAT, EUGENE LAVAR, software engineer, retired air force officer; b. St. Johns, Ariz., Sept. 28, 1936; s. Fred Eugene Barbezat and Madge (Gibbons) Kindall; m. Karen Elizabeth Leichner, Dec. 22, 1970; children: Michele Lynn, Sean Michael. BS in Sociology, Brigham Young U., 1963; MA in Internat. Rels., U. So. Calif., 1980. Probation officer Ada County Probate Ct., Boise, Idaho, 1963-65; state probation officer 9th Dist. Ct., Ogden, Utah, 1965-66; commd. 2d lt. U.S. Air Force, 1966, advanced through grades to lt. col., 1981; chief Intelligence Report Ctr., 497th Reconaissance Tech. Group, Wiesbaden, Fed. Republic Germany, 1968-73; staff officer Def. Intelligence Agy., Washington, 1973-77, 84-85, Hdqrs. U.S. European Command, Vaihaingen, Fed. Republic Germany, 1977-80; chief Indications and Warning Ctr., Hdqrs. Mil. Airlift Command, Scott AFB, Ill., 1980-84; ret. 1985; staff engr. Martin Marietta, Denver, 1985—; staff mem. com. on imagery and exploitation Dept. Def., 1975-77, mem. indications and warning study group, 1980-84. Commr., asst. scoutmaster Boy Scouts Am., Denver, 1986—; mem. Operation Santa Claus, Denver, 1987. Mem. Assn. Former Intelligence Officers, Air Force Assn., Denver Mus. Natural History, Denver Zool. Found., DAV (life), Order of Arrow. Republican. Mormon. Home: 7642 Sunshine Peak Littleton CO 80127 Office: Martin Marietta of Denver PO Box 1260 Denver CO 80201-1260

BARBOUR, MICHAEL G(EORGE), botany educator, ecological consultant; b. Jackson, Mich., Feb. 24, 1942; s. George Jerome and Mae (Dater) B.; m. Norma Jean Yourist, Sept. 30, 1963 (div. 1981); m. Valerie Ann Whitworth, Jan. 25, 1987; children: Julie Ann, Alan Benjamin, Steven Allan. B.S. in Botany, Mich. State U., 1963; Ph.D. in Botany, Duke U., 1967. Asst. prof. botany U. Calif., Davis, 1967-71; assoc. prof. U. Calif., 1971-76, prof., 1976—, chmn., 1982-85; ptnr. Ecolabs Cons., Davis, 1969—; vis. prof. botany dept. Hebrew U., Jerusalem, 1979-81; vis. prof. marine scis. dept. La. State U., Baton Rouge, 1984. Co-author: Coastal Ecology, Bodega Head, 1973, Botany, 6th edit., 1982, Terrestrial Vegetation of California, 1977, 2d edit., 1988, Terrestrial Plant Ecology, 1980, 2d edit., 1987, North American Terrestrial Vegetation, 1988. Fulbright Found. fellow Adelaide, Australia 1964; Guggenheim Found. fellow, 1978; NSF research grantee, 1968-78. Mem. Ecol. Soc. Am. (editorial bd.), Brit. Ecol. Soc., Sigma Xi. Democrat. Jewish. Office: U Calif Botany Dept Davis CA 95616

BARBOUR, ROBERT GORDON, manufacturing company executive; b. Buenos Aires, Feb. 8, 1947; s. Gordon and Mary (Calvo) B.; m. Monica Ann Schoppe, Mar. 21, 1982; children: Christopher, Katherine, Marissa. Student, UCLA, 1965-72; cert., Am. Entrepreneur Inst. Pres. Windline Marine, L.A., 1980-84, Seaway Indsl., L.A., 1984-87; pres., chief executive officer Windline Amanet, L.A., 1987—; cons. to Hughes Research Lab, L.A., 1976-80, Aerospace Corp., L.A., 1979-81. Contbr. articles to profl. jours.; patentee in field. Recipient Inc. 500 award, Inc. Mag., Boston, 1987, 88. Mem. Nat. Small Bus. Assn., Coun. on Growing Cos. Home: PO Box 25876 Los Angeles CA 90025 Office: Windline Amanet 4201 Redwood Ave Los Angeles CA 90066

BARCA, GEORGE GINO, winery executive; b. Sacramento, Jan. 28, 1937; s. Joseph and Annie (Muschetto) B.; m. Maria Sclafani, Nov. 19, 1960; children—Anna, Joseph, Gina and Nina (twins). A.A., Grant Jr. Coll.; student LaSalle U., 1963. With AeroJet Gen. Corp., Sacramento, 1958-65, United Vintners, Inc., San Francisco, 1960-73; pres., gen. mgr. Barcamerica Corp., Sacramento, 1963—; pres., gen. mgr. Barca Wine Cellars, Calif. Wine Cellars, Inc., Calif. Grape Growers, Inc., Calif. Vintage Wines, Inc., Am. Vintners, Inc.; cons. in field. Named Best Producer of Sales, United Vintners, Inc. Mem. Calif. Farm Bur., Met. C. of C., Better Bus. Bur., Roman Catholic. Club: KC. Developer wine trademarks.

BARCA, KATHLEEN, marketing executive; b. Burbank, Calif., July 26, 1946; d. Frank Allan and Blanch Irene (Griffith) Barnes; m. Gerald Albino Barca, Dec. 8, 1967; children; Patrick Gerald, Stacia Kathleen. Student, Pierce Coll., 1964; B in Bus., Hancock Coll., 1984. Teller Security Pacific Bank, Pasadena, Calif., 1968-69, Bank Am., Santa Maria, Calif., 1972-74; operator Gen. Telephone Co., Santa Maria, Calif., 1974-83, supr. operator, 1983-84; account exec. Sta. KRQK/KLLB Radio, Lompoc, Calif., 1984-85; owner Advt. Unltd., Orcutt, Calif., 1986-88; regional mgr. A.L. Williams Mktg. Co., Los Alamos, Calif., 1988—; supr. Matol Botanical Internat., 1989—. Author: numerous local TV and radio commercials, print advt. Activist Citizens Against Dumps in Residential Environments, Polit. Action Com., Orcutt and Santa Maria; chmn. Community advt. Com., Santa Maria, Workshop EPA, Calif. Div., Dept. Health Svcs. State of Calif.; vice coord. Toughlove, Santa Maria; parent coord., mem. steering com. ASAP and Friends. Mem. Nat. Assn. Female Exec., Womens Network-Santa Maria, Cen. Coast Ad (recipient numerous awards), Santa Maria Valley C. of C. Democrat. Home and Office: 509 Shaw St PO Box 676 Los Alamos CA 93440

BARCUS, BENJAMIN FRANKLIN, lawyer; b. Tacoma, June 24, 1960; s. George Eldon Barcus and Gwendolyn (Evans) Johnson. BBA, U. Wash., 1982; JD, U. Puget Sound, 1985. Bar. U.S. Ct. Appeals (9th cir.) 1986, U.S. Dist. Ct. (we. dist.) Wash. 1986, Wash. 1986. Customer svc. rep. Tacoma News Tribune, 1979-80; claims rep., investigator Office Atty. Gen. State of Wash., Seattle, 1980-81; ind. svc. contractor Am. Express Co. Inc., Seattle, 1981-85; assoc. Talbot, Orlandini, Waldron & Hemmen, Tacoma, 1986-88; pvt. practice Tacoma, 1989—. Precinct committeeman Wash. Dem. Com., Tacoma, 1982-88. Mem. Assn. Trial Lawyers Am., Wash. State Bar Assn. (young lawyers sect., criminal law sect.), Wash. State Trial Lawyers Assn., Wash. Assn. Criminal Def. Lawyers, Tacoma-Pierce County Bar Assn., Mopars Unltd. (treas. Tacoma chpt. 1982-88). Congregational. Home: 2223 E Day Island Blvd W Tacoma WA 98446 Office: 4041 Ruston Way Ste 1-B Tacoma WA 93402

BARD, RICHARD H., financial services company executive; b. Irvington, N.J., Nov. 30, 1947; s. Irving and Irene (Pearlman) B.; m. Diane Rose Gibson, Sept. 1984; children by previous marriage: Alison, Jonathan, Adam. B.S.C.E., Pa. State U., 1969; M.B.A., Baruch Coll., N.Y.C., 1973. Asst. v.p. Citibank, N.A., N.Y.C., 1970-74; mgr. Midwest region Citicorp Bus. Credit, Inc., Chgo., 1974-76; chief fin. officer LFV, Inc., Chgo., 1976-77; pres. FoxMeyer Corp., Aurora, Colo., 1977-86; chmn. and chief exec. officer Coast to Coast Stores, Inc., Denver, 1986-88; pres. Bard & Co., Denver, 1989—; dir. Capital Resource Mgmt., Inc., Denver, 1982—, Prime Home Improvement Ctrs., Inc., 1984—, Prudential Bancshares Inc., 1984—. Bd. dirs. The Denver Children's Mus., 1986—. Mem. Nat. Wholesale Hardware Assn. (chmn. 1982-83), Nat. Intergroup, Inc. (dir. 1986—). Home: 100 Vine St Denver CO 80206 Office: Bard & Co 3200 Cherry Creek S Dr Denver CO 80209 *

BARDACKE, PAUL GREGORY, lawyer, former attorney general; b. Oakland, Calif., Dec. 16, 1944; s. Theodore Joseph and Frances (Woodward) B.; m. Lauren Marble, June 21, 1980; children: Julie, Brynn, Francheska, Chloe. B.A. cum laude, U. Calif.-Santa Barbara, 1966; J.D., U. Calif.-Berkeley, 1969. Bar: Calif. 1969, N.Mex. 1970. Lawyer Legal Aid Soc., Albuquerque, 1969; assoc. firm Sutin, Thayer Browne, Albuquerque, 1970-82; atty. gen. State of N.Mex., Santa Fe, 1982-86; ptnr. Sutin, Thayer & Brown, 1987—; adj. prof. N.Mex. Law Sch., Albuquerque, 1973—; mem. faculty Nat. Inst. Trial Lawyers Advocacy, 1978—. Bd. dirs. All Faiths Receiving Home, Albuquerque; bd. dirs. Friends of Art, 1974, Artspace Mag., 1979-80, Legal Aid Soc., 1970-74. Reginald Heber Smith fellow, 1969. Mem. ABA, Calif. Bar Assn., N.Mex. Bar Assn. Democrat. Office: PO Box 1945 Albuquerque NM 87103-1945

BARDELL, ANNE MARIE, art director; b. Santa Monica, Calif., Sept. 27, 1953; d. Ernest George and Marjie Robin (Ellsworth) Emerson; m. Kevin Scott Bardell, Aug. 26, 1978. Frame finisher Saddleback Fine Arts, Orange, Calif., 1972-76; artist The Blue Shopper, Westminister, Calif., 1976-78, South Coast Shopper, Irvine, Calif., 1981-81, 83--. Democart. Office: Southcoast Shopper 17462 Armstrong Ave Irvine CA 92714

BARELA, ELIZABETH, real estate associate; b. Huntington Park, Calif., May 11, 1960; d. Clovis and Mary (Bardwell) B. BA, Calif. State U., Fullerton, 1986. Real estate assoc. Century 21 Inland Pacific, La Palma, Calif., 1986—; team leader Century 21 Inland Pacific, La Palma, 1987—. Mem. Calif. Assn. Realtors, Nat. Assn. Realtors, Buena Park (Calif.) Bd. Realtors. Roman Catholic. Office: Century 21 Inland Pacific 7002 Moody Ste 104 La Palma CA 90623

BARELA, ESMERLINDO JARAMILLO, infosystems specialist; b. Belen, N.Mex., Nov. 11, 1948; parents: Abelicio Baca and Beneranda (Jaramillo) B. AS in Electronics, Southeastern Signal Sch., Ft. Gordon, Ga., 1970. Asst. engr. GTE Lenkurt, Albuquerque, 1972-73, supr. quality control, 1973-75; successively computer technician, sr. computer technician, software specialist Pub. Service Co. N.Mex., Farmington, 1975-82, computer systems and process control data systems specialist III, 1982—; tech. cons. Pub. Service Co. N.Mex., 1982-84. Mem. Sportmen Concerned N.Mex., Albuquerque, 1974. Served with U.S. Army, 1968-72, Vietnam. Mem. VFW (life), Nat. Rifle Assn. (life), Vietnam Vets. N.Mex., Am. Legion, San Juan Fly Fishers. Democrat. Roman Catholic. Home: 5705 Plaza Dr Farmington NM 87401

BARENIS, PAT PEASTER, wholesale distribution company executive; b. Greenville, Miss., Sept. 7, 1951; d. Thomas Benjamin and Min (Young) Peaster; m. Uldis Atis Barenis, Nov. 13, 1975; children: Karl Alexander, Nicholas Benjamin. Mem. sales staff Nationwide Programming Co., Memphis, 1972-73; mktg. mgr. Nationwide Programming Co., Louisville, 1973-74; piano tchr. Deer Creek Acad., Arcola, Miss., 1977-80; pres., owner, chief exec. officer Barenis & Assocs., Vancouver, Wash., 1985—; cons., Security Products Group, Vancouver, 1987—. Tutor hosts program Felida Elem. Sch., Vancouver, 1985—; mem. bd. exec.. PTA, 1987—. Mem. Salmon Creek Soccer Club. Republican. Office: Barenis & Assocs 11703 NW 18th Ave Vancouver WA 98685

BARGER, STEPHEN RICHARD, plants company executive; b. Palo Alto, Calif., Feb. 26, 1950; s. Richard Hugh and Doris Jean (Murphy) B.; m. Mary Constance Steinfeld, July 20, 1974; children: Sarah Murphy, Benjamin David. BA, Williams Coll., 1972; MBA, Harvard U., Boston, 1974. Assoc. cons. Cresap, McCormick & Paget, N.Y.C., 1974-76; sr. assoc. cons. Cresap, McCormick & Paget, San Francisco, 1976-77; brand mgr. Olympia Brewing Co., Olympia, Wash., 1977-83; nat. mktg. mgr. Nursery Products div. Weyerhaeuser, Tacoma, 1983-86; v.p., gen. mgr. Weyerhaeuser Specialty Plants, Tacoma, 1986—. Treas. Great Schs. Tacoma, 1987—; advisor Outward Bound, Portland, Oreg., 1988—; activities council Tacoma Art Mus., 1988—; chmn. Olympia Recycling Com., 1984-85. Mem. Assn. Landscape Contractors Am., Am. Assn. Nurserymen, Williams Coll. Alumni Assn. Wash. (pres. 1988—), City Club Tacoma, Tacoma Lawn Tennis Club. Republican. Episcopalian. Home: 2704 Garfield Rd Tacoma WA 98403

BARHAM, ROBERT EDWARD, surgeon; b. Salt Lake City, Jan. 27, 1942; s. Tracy Robert and Margaret Ann (Rohrkemper) B.; children: Christopher, Kimberly; m. Lee Anne Zupan, June 14, 1989. BS, U. Utah, 1964, MD, 1969. Diplomate Am. Bd. Urology. Intern Providence Med. Ctr., Portland, Oreg., 1969-70; chmn. dept. surgery Providence Med. Ctr., Portland, 1984-87; resident in gen. surgery Ohio State U., Columbus, 1970-71; resident in urology U. Wash., Seattle, 1971-75, chief resident, instr., 1974-75; staff physician Urology Specialists, Portland, 1975—. Office: Urology Specialists 510 NE 49th #514 Portland OR 97213

BARHAM, STEVEN WALTER, executive director; b. Ogden, Utah, Apr. 18, 1953; s. Henry Garfield and Betty Jane (Chester) B.; m. Leona Ellen Shepherd, Nov. 19, 1982; 1 stepchild, Lisa Chappell. BS, Oreg. Coll. Edn., 1974; MBA, Portland (Oreg.) State U., 1981. Spl. projects aide Ea. Oreg. Hosp., Pendleton, 1975-77; asst. supr. adminstrv. services, bus. mgr. Callahan Ctr., Wilsonville, Oreg., 1978-80; bus. mgr. Bd. Nursing, Portland, 1981-85; exec. dir. Oreg. Racing Commn., Portland, 1985—; vice chmn. uniform rules com. Nat. Assn. State Racing Commrs., Lexington, Ky., 1986-87. Office: Oreg Racing Commn 1400 SW 5th Ave Rm 113 Portland OR 97201

BARKER, DEE H., chemical engineering educator; b. Salt Lake City, Mar. 28, 1921; s. John Henry and Christina Selina (Heaton) Barker; m. Catherine Thompson, Apr. 24, 1945; children: DeeAnn, Lynn, Craig, Gary, Pamela. BS, U. Utah, 1948, PhD, 1951. Research engr. E.I. DuPont de Nemours & Co., Inc., Wilmington, Del., 1951-54; reactor engr. E.I. DuPont de Nemours & Co., Inc., Baton, S.C., 1954-59; prof. chem. engring. Brigham Young U., Provo, Utah, 1959—; cons. Brila Inst. Tech. & Sci., Rajasthan, India, 1966-78; Chonnam Nat. U. fellow, 1980-81, 87; prof. emeritus Brigham Young U., Provo, 1986—. Active Boy Scouts Am., Salt Lake City. With USN, 1944-46. Fellow Am. Inst. Chem. Engrs.; mem. Am. Soc. Engring. Educators, Nat. Council Engring. Examinations, Kiwanis. Home: 1398 Cherry Ln Provo UT 84604

BARKER, GARY PAUL, teacher; b. Phila., Mar. 28, 1947; s. Charles Beverly and Terry Helene (Goldman) B.; m. Joanne Carole Jackson, Mar. 21, 1970; children: Karen Lynn, Philip Dorian. BEd, U. Miami, 1969; life teaching credential, U. Calif., Irvine, 1972; MA, Calif. State U., Long Beach, 1974. Tchr. Saddleback Valley Unified Sch. Dist., Mission Viejo, Calif., 1969-81, 83—, facilities planning specialist, 1981-83. Recipient Energy Conservation award San Diego Gas & Electric Co., 1983; track and cross-country scholarship U. Miami, 1965-69. Mem. NEA, Calif. Tchrs. Assn., Saddleback Valley Educators Assn. Democrat. Presbyterian. Home: 26352 Pacato Dr Mission Viejo CA 92691 Office: Saddleback Valley Sch Dist 25222 Pericia St Mission Viejo CA 92691

BARKER, LEROY N., agronomy educator, plant breeder; b. Brigham City, Utah, Oct. 18, 1928; s. Claude Rufus and Iva (Nelson) B.; m. Sara Ann Workman, Aug. 31, 1956; children—Michael, Dennis, LeAnn, Nanette, Amy. B.S., Utah State U., 1953, M.S., 1956; Ph.D., U. Wis., 1960. Plant breeder Asgrow Seed Co., Sun Prairie, Wis., 1960-65; asst. prof. agronomy Calif. State U.-Chico, 1965-68, assoc. prof., 1970-73, prof., 1973—; sr. lectr., plant breeder U. Ife, Ile-Ife, Nigeria, 1968-70; plant breeder U. Wis.-Madison, Rice Researchers, Inc., summers. Active Boy Scouts Am., 1966-68, 70-76; dist. leader, com. chmn. PTO, U. Ife. Served to 1st lt. U.S. Army, 1953-55. Cliff Poole fellow, 1956; U. Wis. research asst., 1956-60. Mem. Am. Soc. Agronomy, Crop Sci. Soc., Calif. Fertilizer Assn., Sigma Xi. Republican. Mormon. Assisted in devel. of three new rice varieties. Home: 2964 Alamo Ave Chico CA 95926 Office: Calif State U Plant & Soil Scis Chico CA 95929

BARKER, RICHARD ALEXANDER, industrial psychologist; b. San Diego, Aug. 11, 1947; s. Alexander Markewich and Donna Lee Barker; A.B. in Psychology, San Diego State U., 1974, M.S. in Indsl. and Organizational Psychology, 1976; m. Barbara Yvonne Schutt, Aug. 1, 1987; children—Jaime Lynn, Cory Richard. Statis. analyst U.S. Navy Personnel Research and Devel. Center, San Diego, 1974-75; personnel and testing analyst City of San Diego, 1976; cons. various orgns., 1976-78; employment mgr. Computer Scis. Corp., San Diego, 1978; indsl. psychologist Gen. Dynamics Corp., San Diego, 1978—; instr. music, San Diego City Coll., 1976—; lectr. psychology, mgmt. sci., stats., orgnl. behavior U. Redlands, 1978—. Bd. dirs. San Diego Youth Services, Inc., chmn. personnel com., 1978-81. Served with USNR, 1968-69. Mem. Am. Psychol. Assn. (asso.), Computer Automated Systems Assn./Soc. Mfg. Engrs., Nat. Mgmt. Assn., Internat. Assn. Applied Psychology (asso.), Am. Fedn. Musicians, Psi Chi. Home: 11082 Virgo Pl San Diego CA 92126-1843 Office: Gen Dynamics Electronics Div 5011 Kearny Villa Rd San Diego CA 92123

BARKER, ROBERT JEFFERY, financial executive; b. Glendale, Calif., Feb. 22, 1946; s. Albert and Margaret E. (Windle) B.; m. Ildiko Barker, Jan. 1, 1989. BSEE, UCLA, 1968, MBA, 1970. Cert. mgmt. acctg. Cost analyst Lockheed, Sunnyvale, Calif., 1976-78; from cost acctg. supr. to fin. systems mgr. Monolithic Memories Inc., Sunnyvale, 1976-84; dir. fin. Waferscale Integration, Inc., Fremont, Calif., 1984-88, v.p. fin., chief fin. officer, 1988—; bd. dirs., treas. Am. Electronics Assn. Credit Union, Santa Clara, Calif., 1988—; dir. Monolithic Memories Integration Fed. Credit Union, Sunnyvale, 1977-84, pres. 1983-84. Dir. Vets. Task Force, Palo Alto, Calif., 1980-87, pres. 1987. Capt. USAF, 1970-74. Mem. Nat. Assn. Accts., Toastmasters (pres. 1986-87). Republican. Methodist. Home: 1 Winchester Dr Atherton CA 91025

BARKETT, HENRY RICHARD FRANK, dentist; b. Oklahoma City, Nov. 12, 1958; s. Milton and Lucille (Ablah) B. BS in Biology, Pitts. State U., 1982; DDS, U. Mo., 1986. Gen. practice dentistry Tucson, 1986—. Mem. ADA, Acad. Gen. Dentistry.

BARKHOUDARIAN, SARKIS, aerospace executive, engineer; b. Tehran, Iran, Feb. 12, 1938; s. Aram and Loussik (Abrahamian) B.; m. Sophia Bap Kazarian, Jan. 12, 1978; children: Garni, Melita. BEE, U. Detroit, 1962; MEE, Carnegie Mellon U., 1963, postgrad. in elec. engring., 1964. Project engr. Gen. Motors Mfg. Devel., Warren, Mich., 1964-67, Atomic Power Devel. Assn., Detroit, 1967-70, Bendix Rsch. Ctr., Southfield, Mich., 1970-73; project engr. Automotive Tech. Ctr., Rockwell Internat., Troy, Mich., 1973-76, mgr. instrumentation, 1976-80; mem. tech. staff Rocketdyne div. Rockwell Internat., Canoga Park, Calif., 1980-82, project engr., 1982-84, mgr. advanced instrn., 1984—; tchr. indsl. electronics U. Detroit. Contbr. articles to profl. publs.; patentee in field. Fellow Instrument Soc. Am. (sr.). Home: 24415 Lemay St West Hills CA 91307

BARKLEY, PAUL C., airline holding company executive; b. 1929; married. BS, San Diego State Coll., 1958. With Arthur Young & Co., 1958-67, with Pacific Southwest Airlines, San Diego, 1967—, v.p. fin., 1968-73, sr. v.p. fin., chief operating officer, 1973-79, pres., chief operating officer, 1979-84, pres., chief exec. officer, 1984-89, now chmn. exec. com., also bd. dirs.; bd. dirs. Pancrete Inc. Served with USAF, 1951. Mem. Am. Inst. CPA's, Nat. Assn. Accts. Office: PS Group Inc PO Box 127405 San Diego CA 92112 *

BARKLEY, THIERRY VINCENT, lawyer; b. Paris, Mar. 21, 1955; s. Jacques and Michéline Marié (Rossi) B.; came to U.S., 1967, naturalized, 1974; m. Mary Ellen Gamble, June 18, 1983; children: Richard A., Robert V., Marriah E. B.A. in Polit. Sci., UCLA, 1976; J.D., Calif. Western Sch. Law, San Diego, 1979. Bar: Nev. 1980, U.S. Dist. Ct. Nev. 1982, U.S. Supreme Ct. 1986. Intern, Calif. Ct. Appeals 4th Circuit, San Diego, 1978-79; law clk. Nev. Dist. Ct., 7th Jud. Dist., Ely, 1979-81; assoc. firm C.E. Horton, Ely, 1982-83; asst. city atty. Ely, 1982-83; assoc. firm Barker, Gillock & Perry, Reno, 1983-87, Perry, Hebert & Spann, 1987—. Assoc. editor Internat. Law Jour., 1979. Mem. Internat. Moot Ct. Team, 1978; recipient Dean's award Calif. Western Sch. Law, 1979. Mem. ABA, Nev. Bar Assn., Washoe Bar Assn., U.S. Jaycees (past pres. White Pine, Nev.). Republican. Roman Catholic. Lodge: Elks (past treas. Ely club). Office: Perry Hebert & Spann 620 Humboldt St Reno NV 89509

BARKSDALE, RITA PHILLIPS, hotel-condomunium executive; b. Galesburg, Ill., Nov. 26, 1920; m. James Bailey Barksdale, Jr., May 10, 1947 (dec. May 1972); children: James Michael, Stephen Alan, Susan Marie Barksdale Jech. Edn. teaching degree, Western State U., Macomb, Ill., 1940. Tchr 1st grade Rio (Ill.) Pub. Schs., 1940-43; elem. tchr. Galesburg Pub. Sch. System, 1943-45, Roseland (N.J.) Sch., 1955-61; flight attendant United Airlines, Chgo., 1945-47; model, account exec. Mdse. Mart, Denver, 1961-69; mgr. Lincoln Property Co., San Jose, Calif., 1969-72, San Diego, 1972-76; mgr. Mana Kai-Maui, Kihei, Hawaii, 1976—. Pres. PTA, Roseland, 1956-57; bd. dirs. Vis. Industry Charity Walk, Maui, 1979-88, Maui Youth Theatre, 1988. Mem. Maui Hotel Assn., Maui Vis.' Bur., Maui C. of C. (bd. dirs. 1983-88, pres. 1988). Republican. Roman Catholic. Office: Mana Kai-Maui 2960 S Kihei Rd Kihei HI 96753

BARLOW, HAVEN J., state legislator, realtor; b. Clearfield, Utah, Jan. 4, 1922; s. Jesse and Asdora (Beck) B.; m. Bonnie Rae Ellison, Nov. 23, 1944; children: Jesselie Anderson, Heidi Harris, Rachel, Haven J., Stewart E., Duncan. BS, Utah State U., 1944, postgrad. U. Utah Law Sch., Harvard U. Sch. Bus. Sr. Senator State of Utah, 1957—, Utah Ho. of Reps., 1953-57; pres. Barlow Ins., Inc. 1950—; bd. dirs. Community 1st Bank (formerly Clearfield State Bank), Lockhart Corp. Past pres. Lake Bonniville council Boy Scouts Am.; bd. dirs. Utah State Symphony; trustee Humana Hosp. Davis North, Layton; mem. Davis County Pvt. Industry council, State Job Tng. Coordinating council. Served to lt. (j.g.) USN, 1942-44; PTO, ETO. Recipient Disting. Service award Utah State U., 1986, Humanitarian award Utah Vocat. Assn., Light of Learning award State Bd. Edn., Silver Beaver award Boy Scouts Am. Republican. Mormon. Home: 552 Elm St Layton UT 84041

BARLOW, HERMAN ZULCH, JR., academic administrator; b. Houston, Oct. 8, 1949; s. Herman Zulch Sr. and Billie (Hunter) B.; m. Rexene Treadwell, Aug. 29, 1981; 1 child, Meredith Arden. BA, Houston Bapt. Coll., 1972; MEd, U. Houston, 1975, EdD, 1985. Dir. admissions Houston Bapt. U., 1972-76, assoc. to the pres., 1976-77, dean of admissions, 1977-79, asst. v.p. devel., 1979-82, asst. to the pres., 1982-84, v.p. univ. affairs, 1984-87; prof. mgmt. and coll. pres. Coll. of the S.W., Hobbs, N.Mex., 1987—; vis. prof. mgmt. U. Houston, 1983—, So. Meth. U., 1982; adj. prof. U. St. Thomas, 1981-83, Houston Community Coll., 1979-81. Bd. dirs. Confederate Mus., Richmond, Tex., N.Mex. Symphony, Albuquerque, S.W. Symphony, Hobbs; past bd. dirs. Cultural Arts Coun., Houston Carriage Assn., Mus. of Fine Arts, United Way, Am. Heart Assn., others; tchr. Sunday Sch. Taylor Meml. Bapt. Ch. Mem. Am. Assn. of Higher Edn., AAAS, Am. Acad. Polit. and Social Sci., Am. Coun. on Edn., Am. Personnel and Guidance Assn., Am. Leadership Forum, Coun. for the Advancement and Support of Edn., NEA, Tex. State Tchrs. Assn., Assn. for Ednl. Communication and Tech., The Inst. of Mgmt. Sci., Soc. for the Advancement of Mgmt., Am. Symphony Orch. League, Am. Choral Dir. Assn., Music Educators Nat., Conf., Tex. Music Educators Assn., Chorister's Guild, Phi Delta Kappa, Kappa Delta Pi, Phi Mu Alpha Sinfonia, Omicron Delta Kappa, Kappa Alpha. Democrat. Home: 1420 W Kansas Hobbs NM 88240 Office: Coll of the SW 6610 Lovington Hwy Hobbs NM 88240

BARLOW, WILLIAM PUSEY, JR., accountant; b. Oakland, Calif., Feb. 11, 1934; s. William P. and Muriel (Block) B.; student Calif. Inst. Tech., 1952-54. AB in Econs., U. Calif.-Berkeley, 1956. CPA, Calif. Acct. Barlow, Davis & Wood, San Francisco, 1960-72, ptnr., 1964-72; ptnr., J.K. Lasser & Co., 1972-77, Touche Ross & Co., San Francisco, 1977-78; self employed acct., 1978—. Co-author: Collectible Books: Some New Paths, 1979, The Grolier Club, 1884-1984, 1984; editor: Book Catalogues: Their Varieties and Uses, 2d edit., 1986; contbr. articles to profl. jours. Fellow Gleeson Libr. Assocs., 1969, pres., 1971-74; mem. Coun. Friends Bancroft Libr., 1971—, chmn., 1974-79; bd. dirs. Oakland Ballet, 1982—, pres. 1986—. Recipient Sir Thomas More medal Gleeson Libr. Assocs., 1989. Mem. Am. Water Ski Assn. (bd. dirs., regional chmn. 1959-63, pres. 1963-66, chmn. bd. 1966-69, 77-79, hon. v.p. 1969—), World Water Ski Union (exec. bd. 1961-71, 75-78), Grolier Club (N.Y.C.), Roxburghe Club (San Francisco), Book of Calif. Club (bd. dirs. 1963-76, pres. 1968-69, treas. 1971-83). Home: 1474 Hampel St Oakland CA 94602 Office: 449 15th St Oakland CA 94612

BARNA, JOHN ROBERT, construction executive; b. Bismark, N.D., Mar. 13, 1949; s. John N. and Virginia Lee (Holbrook) B.; m. Cathy Louise Reid, Jan. 29, 1977; 1 child, Allison Paige. AA, McCook (Nebr.) Jr. Coll., 1969; BCE, U. Nebr., 1972. Structural engr. Rocky Mountain Prestressed Concrete, Sheridan, Colo., 1972-75, Front Range Erectors, Arvada, Colo., 1975-76; project engr. Rocky Mountain Prestressed Concrete, 1976-77; pres. Denver Comml. Builders, 1977—; chmn. adv. council Butler Mfg. Nat. Builders, Kansas City, Mo., 1984—; advisor Kelley Western, Wheatridge, Colo., 1985-87, Shoshoni Ranch, Boulder, Colo., 1985-87, Colo. Uplift, Denver, 1987—. Mem. Rocky Mountain Systems Builders Assn. (pres. 1986), Systems Builders Assn. (sec./treas. 1988), Associated Builders and Contractors (founding mem. state chpt., sec. 1988). Republican. Methodist. Lodges: Kiwanis, Elks. Home: 6003 W Iliff Dr Lakewood CO 80227 Office: Denver Comml Builders 909 E 62d Ave Denver CO 80216

BARNARD, CHARLOTTE D., nurse; b. Beverly, Mass., Apr. 27, 1936; d. Joseph Phillip and Alice Margaret (Fanning) Devarenne; m. Austin A. Barnard, Feb. 22, 1960; children: Michael, Kathleen. BS in Nursing, Mont. State U., 1971; MA in Edn., Chapman Coll., 1979. RN, Calif. Staff nurse Hunt Meml. Hosp., Danvers, Mass., 1950-57, USAF, Harlington AFB, Tex., 1958-60, Salem (Mass.) Hosp., 1966, Lompoc (Calif.) Unified Sch. Dist., 1973—, Lompoc Dist. Hosp., 1985—. Mem. sch. site coun. Los Padres Sch., Vandenberg AFB, Calif., 1974-79; family host Homestay Cultural Exch. Recipient Hon. Svc. award PTA, Vandenberg AFB, 1974. Mem. Lopoc Edn. Assn., Calif. Fedn. Tchrs., Calif. Sch. Nurse Orgn. Episcopalian.

BARNARD, KATHRYN ELAINE, nursing educator, researcher; b. Omaha, Apr. 16, 1938; d. Paul and Elsa Elizabeth (Anderson) B. B.S. in Nursing, U. Nebr.-Omaha, 1960; M.S. in Nursing, Boston U., 1962; Ph.D., U. Wash., Seattle, 1972. Acting instr. U. Nebr.-Omaha, 1960-61; acting instr. U. Wash., Seattle, 1963-65, asst. prof., 1965-69, prof. nursing, 1972—, now assoc. dean; bd. dirs. Nat. Ctr. for Clin. Infant Programs, Washington, 1980—. Chmn. research com. Bur. of Community Health Services, MCH, 1987—. Recipient Lucille Petry award Nat. League for Nursing, 1968, Martha Mae Eliot award Am. Assn. Pub. Health, 1983, Professorship award U. Wash., 1985. Fellow Am. Acad. Nursing (bd. dirs. 1980-82); mem. Inst. Medicine; mem. Am. Nurses Assn. (chmn. com. 1980-82, Jessie Scott award 1982, Nurse of Yr. award 1984), Soc. Research in Child Devel. (bd. dirs. 1981-87), Sigma Theta Tau (founders award in research 1987). Democrat. Presbyterian. Home: 11508 Durland Ave NE Seattle WA 98125 Office: U Wash Mailstop WJ-10 Seattle WA 98195 *

BARNARD, MICHAEL DANA, orthopedic surgeon; b. Denver, Nov. 14, 1946; s. Rollin Dwight and Patricia Reynolds (Bierkamp) B.; m. Susan Carole Bondo, Aug. 3, 1969; children—Alison, Melissa. B.A., Pomona Coll., 1968; M.D., U. Colo.-Denver, 1972. Diplomate Am. Bd. Orthopedic Surgery. Intern U. Oreg., Portland, 1972-73; resident U. Colo., Denver, 1973-77; practice medicine specializing in orthopedic surgery, Canon City, Colo., 1977—; chief of staff St. Thomas More Hosp., Canon City, 1982-84. Fellow Am. Acad. Orthopedic Surgeons; mem. Canon City C. of C. (pres. 1982-83, dir. 1979-82), Fremont County Med. Soc. (pres. 1986-88). Republican. Lutheran. Lodge: Rotary (pres. Canon City 1983-84). Home: 654 Van Loo Rd Canon City CO 81212 Office: 616 Yale Pl Canon City CO 81212

BARNARD, ROLLIN DWIGHT, financial executive, retired; b. Denver, Apr. 14, 1922; s. George Cooper and Emma (Riggs) B.; m. Patricia Reynolds Bierkamp, Sept. 15, 1943; children: Michael Dana, Rebecca Susan (Mrs. Paul C. Wulfestieg), Laurie Beth (Mrs. Kenneth J. Kostelecky). B.A., Pomona Coll., 1943. Clk. Morey Merc. Co., Denver, 1937-40; ptnr George C. Barnard & Co. (gen. real estate and ins.), Denver, 1946-47; v.p. Foster & Barnard, Inc., 1947-53; instr. Denver U., 1949-53; dir. real estate U.S. P.O. Dept., Washington, 1953-55; dep. asst. postmaster gen., bur. facilities U.S. P.O. Dept., 1955-59, asst. postmaster gen., 1959-61; pres., dir. Midland Fed. Savs. & Loan Assn., Denver, 1962-84; vice chmn. Bank Western Fed. Savs. Bank, 1984—; vice chmn. Western Capital Investment Corp., 1985—, pres., 1985-87; dir. Verex Assurance Inc., 1983-86. Pres. Denver Area council Boy Scouts Am., 1970-71, mem. exec. bd., 1962-73; adv. bd. Denver Area council Boy Scouts Am, 1973—; chmn. Planning and Zoning Commn. Greenwood Village, Colo., 1969-73; mem. Greenwood Village City Council, 1975-77; mem. nat. council Pomona Coll., 1963—; bd. dirs. Downtown Denver Improvement Assn., pres., 1965; bd. dirs. Bethesda Found., Inc., 1973-82; bd. dirs. Children's Hosp., 1979-84, treas., 1983-84; bd. dirs., Rocky Mountain Child Health Services, Inc., 1982—; trustee Mile High United Fund, 1969-72, Denver Symphony Assn., 1973-74; mem. bd. Colo. Council Econ. Edn., 1971-80, chmn., 1971-76; trustee, v.p., treas. Morris Animal Found., 1969-81, pres., chmn., 1974-78, trustee emeritus, 1981—. Served to capt. AUS, World War II. Nominated One of Ten Outstanding Young Men in Am. U.S. Jaycees, 1955, 57; recipient Distinguished Service award Postmaster Gen. U.S., 1960; Silver Beaver award Boy Scouts Am., 1969; Outstanding Citizen of Year Sertoma, 1982; Colo. Citizen of Year Colo. Assn. Realtors, 1982. Mem. Denver C. of C. (pres. 1966-67), U.S. League Savs. Instns. (bd. dirs. 1972-77, vice chmn. 1979-80, chmn. 1980-81, mem. nat. legis. com., exec. com. 1974-77), Savs. League Colo. (exec. com. 1969-73, pres. 1971-72), Colo. Assn. Commerce and Industry (dir. 1971-76), Fellowship Christian Athletes (Denver area dir. 1963-76), Western Stock Show Assn. (dir. 1971—, exec. com. 1982—, 1st v.p. 1985—), Nu Alpha Phi. Republican. Presbyn. Clubs: 26 (Denver) (pres. 1970), Rotary (Denver) (dir. 1979-81, 2d v.p. 1980); Mountain and Plains Appaloosa Horse (pres. 1970-71), Roundup Riders of the Rockies (dir. 1979—, treas. 1980-87, v.p. 1987—). Home: 3151 East Long Rd Littleton CO 80121

BARNBAUM, GEORGE DAVID, retired military officer; b. N.Y.C., Jan. 25, 1916; s. Sidney and Hannah (Wasch) B.; m. Louise Rocco, Feb. 1944 (div. 1976); m. Ellen Adan, May 10, 1977. BA, Cooper Union, N.Y.C., 1938; postgrad., NYU, 1938-39; MA, MS, Columbia U., 1961. Enlisted U.S. Army, 1940; advanced through grades to staff sgt. U.S. Army, Panama, 1940; served U.S. Army, Peoples Republica of Korea, 1952-54, Japan, 1954-55; ret. U.S. Army, 1964; coin dealer Albuquerque Coin & Stamp, 1964-76; coin and antique dealer Time and Money/Accent Antiques, Albuquerque, 1980-; v.p., bd. dirs. Adonis Enterprises, Albuquerque, 1980--. Mem. Am. Numis. Assn. (life), N.Mex. Coin Dealers Assn., DAV (life). Democrat. Office: Time & Money/Accent Antique 3413 Central NE Albuquerque NM 87106

BARNEA, URI N., music director, conductor, composer, violinist; b. Petah-Tikvah, Israel, May 29, 1943; came to U.S., 1971; s. Shimon and Miriam Burstein; m. Lizbeth A. Lund, Dec. 15, 1977; 1 child. Teaching cert., Oranim Music Inst., Israel, 1966; postgrad. Hebrew U., Israel, 1969-71; Mus.B., Rubin Acad. Music, Israel, 1971; M.A., U. Minn., 1974, Ph.D., 1977. Mus. dir. Jewish Community Ctr., Mpls. 1971-73; conductor Youval Chamber Orch., Mpls., 1971-73; asst. conductor U. Minn. Orchs., Mpls., 1972-77; music dir., conductor Unitarian Soc., Mpls., 1973-78, Kenwood Chamber Orch., Mpls., 1974-78, Knox-Galesburg Symphony, 1978-83, Billings Symphony Soc., Mont., 1984—; asst. prof. Knox Coll., Galesburg, Ill., 1978-83; violinist, violist Yellowstone Chamber players, Billings, 1984—; violist Tri-City Symphony, Quad-Cities, Ill., Iowa, 1983-84; conductor Cedar Arts Forum String Camp, Cedar Falls, Iowa, 1981, 82; European conducting debut, London, Neuchatel and Fribourg, Switzerland, 1986. Composer of numerous compositions including String Quartet (1st prize Aspen Composition Competition 1976), Sonata for Flute and Piano, 1975 (Diploma of Distinction 26th Viotti Internat. Competition, Italy 1975), Ruth A Ballet, 1974 (1st prize Oberhoffer Composition Contest 1976), Active in music adv. panel Ill. Arts Council, 1980-83; v.p. Community Concert Assn., Galesburg, 1980-83; bd. dirs. Knox Coll. Credit Union, Galesburg, 1982-83, Sta. KEMC Pub. Radio, Billings, 1984—, Fox Theater Corp., Billings, 1984-86. Recipient Friend of Arts title Sigma Alpha Iota, 1982; Ill. Arts Council grantee, 1979; Hebrew U. Jerusalem scholar, 1972-74, Hebrew U. and Rubin Acad. Mus. scholar, 1969, 70; Individual Artist fellow Mont. Arts Council, 1986. Mem. Minn. Composers Forum, Conductors Guild, ASCAP, Am. String Tchrs. Assn. Office: Billings Symphony Soc PO Box 602 Billings MT 59103

BARNES, AARON, physicist, researcher; b. Shenandoah, Iowa, May 9, 1939; s. Charles Raymond and Avis Irene (Ross) B.; m. Barbara JoAnne Dean, Sept. 17, 1962; children: Christopher, Stephen. SB, U. Chgo., 1961, SM, 1962, PhD, 1966. Nat. Acad. Scis.-NRC rsch. assoc. Ames Rsch. Ctr., NASA, Moffett Field, Calif., 1966-67, rsch. scientist, 1967—; vis.. scientist Max Planck Inst. for Extraterrestrial Physics, Garching and Munich, 1973; disting. lectr. Sackler Faculty Geophysics and Planetary Scis., Tel Aviv U., 1086. Contbr. numerous articles to sci. jours. Recipient medal Nat. Ctr. for Atmospheric Rsch., 1973, medal for exceptional sci. achievement NASA, 1982. Mem. Am. Phys. Soc., Am. Astron. Soc., Am. Geophys. Union, Internat. Astron. Union, AAAS. Office: NASA Ames Rsch Ctr Moffett Field CA 94035

BARNES, ALLAN RANDALL, educator, researcher; b. St. Louis, Aug. 10, 1946; s. Donald William and Lois Eileen (McDonough) B.; m. Mary Frances Schroeder, Aug. 4, 1984. BA, U. Mo., St. Louis, 1969; MA, U. Mo., 1975; PhD, Fla. State U., 1983. Police officer Hanley Hills (Mo.) Police Dept., 1971-73; asst. dir. First Step House, Lakeland, Fla., 1975-78; probation officer Fla. Dept. Corrections, Lakeland, 1978; prison psychologist Sumter Correctional Inst., Bushnell, Fla., 1978-79; sr. research asst. Fla. State U., Tallahassee, 1979-83; asst. prof. Fayetteville (N.C.) State U., 1983-84, U. Alaska, Anchorage, 1984—; cons. Fed. Bur. of Prisons, Tallahassee, 1981-83; dir. Alaska Statis. Analysis Unit, Anchorage. Contbr. articles to profl. jours. Bd. dirs. Parents United, Anchorage, 1988, Akeela House, Anchorage, 1988, Bapt. Student Union, St. Louis, 1968. Served with U.S. Army, 1969-71. Fellow USPHS, Columbia, 1971, 73; recipient Curator award U. Mo., 1965-69, Army Commendation award, 1971. Mem. AAUP, Acad. Criminal Justice Scis., Am. Soc. Criminology, Criminal Justice Stats. Assn., Soc. Police and Criminal Psychologists. Democrat. Baptist. Office: U Alaska Anchorage Sch of Justice 3211 Providence Dr Anchorage AK 99508

BARNES, AUDRA GUYTON, nursing educator; b. Galveston, Tex., July 16, 1921; d. Emmett Edward Guyton and Margaret Beatrice (Wright) Guyton-Carter; m. John Berrel Barnes Sr., Apr., 1950; children: Audra Yvonne, John Jr. Diploma in Nursing, Meharry Med. Coll., 1941; BS in Home Econs., Tenn. State U., 1949; BS in Nursing, Calif. State U., L.A., 1973, MS in Nursing, 1975. RN, Calif., Tenn. Staff nurse Dept. of Health, N.Y.C., 1942-44, St. Joseph's Hosp., Ft. Worth, 1944-46; pvt. duty nurse L.A., 1956-58; nurse L.A. City Schs., 1963-66; from instr. to assoc. prof. nursing Compton Community Coll., Calif., 1976—. Fellow Am. Nurses Assn.; mem. Am. Fedn. Tchrs., Black Nurses Assn. (pres. 1985—), Angel City Dental Soc. Aux. (pres. 1985-88), Alpha Kappa Alpha, Alpha Kappa Mu, Alpha Kappa. Democrat. Methodist. Home: 3751 Cherrywood Ave Los Angeles CA 90018 Office: Compton Community Coll 1111 E Artesia Blvd Compton CA 90221

BARNES, DAVID ROBERT, JR., sales executive; b. Yonkers, N.Y., Sept. 8, 1952; s. David Robert and Marion Cecilia (Boiling) B.; m. Deborah Fortado, June 15, 1981 (div. Aug., 1984); m. Paula Rose Wihongi, July 8, 1988. AA, Worcester Jr. Coll., 1972, BA, 1975; MEd, U. Mass., 1976. Sales merchandiser Menley & James Labs., Worcester, Mass., 1977-79; area sales rep. Menley & James Labs., Springfield, Mass., 1979-81; unit mgr. SmithKline Corp., Springfield, 1981-83; terr. mgr. SmithKline Corp., Huntington Beach, Calif., 1983—; basketball coach Worchester Jr. Coll., 1974-75; regional trainer Smith Kline Consumer Products, 1986-87. Democrat. Baptist. Office: SmithKline Consumer Products 129 28th St Upper Level Newport Beach CA 92663

BARNES, JOHN FAYETTE, research scientist, educator; b. Santa Cruz, Calif., Jan. 28, 1930; s. John Fayette and Bertha Henrietta (Youngman) B.; m. Joanne Cecily Lyle, Aug. 28, 1955; children—John Fayette, David Lyle. B.A., U. Calif., Berkeley, 1951; M.S., U. Denver, 1952; Ph.D., U. N.Mex., 1963, M. Mgmt., 1981. Asst. group leader Los Alamos Nat. Lab., N.Mex., 1968-71, dep. group leader, 1971, group leader, 1971-76, asst. theoretical div. leader, 1976-77, assoc. theoretical div. leader, 1977-80, dep. theoretical div. leader, 1980-81, dep. assoc. dir. for energy programs, 1981-82, dep. assoc. dir. for physics and math., 1982-83, applied theoretical physics div. leader, 1983-85, research scientist, group leader, 1985-87, cons., 1987—; mathematician Research Directorate, Air Force Spl. Weapons Ctr., Albuquerque, 1956-57; mem. research adv. bd. Lab. for Laser Energetics U. Rochester, N.Y., 1980—, chmn., 1981, 87; mem. core faculty U. N.Mex., Los Alamos, 1987—; coord. math. U. N.Mex., Los Alamos, 1988—. Contbr articles to profl. jours.; originator of SESAME equation of state libr. Active Boy Scouts Am., Los Alamos, 1967-79; precinct chmn. Republican Party, 1968-85; del. state conv. 1972. Mem. Am. Phys. Soc. Home: 2213 Calle Cacique Sante Fe NM 87505 Office: Los Alamos Nat Lab Theoretical Div Group T-1 MS B221 PO Box 1663 Los Alamos NM 87545

BARNES, JOSEPH CURTIS, aircraft development executive; b. Ashland, Oreg., Jan. 1, 1913; s. Joseph Curtis and Flora Ellis (Bushong) B.; m. Janet A. Eames, Nov. 1, 1942; children: Joseph Curtis III, Robin Bushong Spiegel, Bonnie McClean Arndt. AB, Stanford U., 1935, MA, 1938; student V-7 program, USN Acad., 1940. Artist Walt Disney Studio, Burbank, Calif., 1938-40; with Barnes Bros., Medford, Orgn., 1940-80; chief exec. officer Tipsy Bee Research, Medford, 1980-86. Patentee vertical lift by flettner rotor; inventor silent lift vehicle, vehicle for vertical flight and ground transport. Served to lt. comdr. USNR, 1940-46, PTO. Mem. Am. Helicopter Soc. Republican. Home and Office: 4455 Fern Valley Rd Medford OR 97504

BARNES, MARILYN, realtor; b. Oakland, Calif., Oct. 27, 1938; d. Robert Lee and Doris (Davidson) Sandstrom; m. Allan Marion Barnes, Apr. 29, 1962; children: Douglas Allan, Anne Elizabeth. AB, U. Calif., Berkeley, 1961. Cert. resdl. specialist. With ESO II State of Calif., Oakland and Berkeley, 1961-68; sales assoc. The Gwynn Co., Ft. Collins, Colo., 1980-83, Moore & Co., Ft. Collins, 1983; ptnr., sales assoc. The Group, Inc., Realtors, Ft. Collins, 1983—. Co-chmn. Ft. Collins Interfaith Council, 1987—; chmn. Dem. Forum, Ft. Collins, 1988—; mem. 8th Jud. Dist. Nominating Com., Larimer County, 1988—, Econ. Adv. Com., City of Ft. Collins, 1988—; mem. allocations com. United Way, 1982-87. Mem. Womens Council of Realtors, AAUW, Ft. Collins Symphony Guild. Democrat. Unitarian. Home: 1920 Osage St Fort Collins CO 80525 Office: The Group Inc 401 W Mulberry Fort Collins CO 80521

BARNES, RICHARD LEWIS, JR., military petty officer; b. Bellaire, Mich., Sept. 29, 1953; s. Richard Lewis Barnes and Elizabeth Ann (Converse) Grundel; m. Teddi Lynne Cordelius, Dec. 1, 1972; children: Jennifer, Susan, Richard III. AA, Chapman Coll., Orange, Calif., 1979. Enlisted USN, 1975, commd. ensign, 1975, advanced through grades to chief petty officer, 1988; 3d class petty officer USS Niagara Falls USN, San Francisco, 1976-81; 2d class petty officer USS Raleigh USN, Norfolk, Va., 1981-85; 1st class petty officer USS Missouri USN, Long Beach, Calif., 1985-88; chief petty officer Comnavsurfgru Long Beach USN, 1988—; pres. RT Promotions, San Pedro, Calif., 1988—. Decorated Navy Achievement medal. Mem. Surface Navy Assn. (treas. 1989—), Soc. for Am. Baseball Research. Home: 27421 S Samuel Dupont San Pedro CA 90732 Office: Comnavsurfgru Long Beach Bldg 1 Naval Sta Long Beach CA 90822

BARNES, ROGER PHILIP, electrical engineer, researcher; b. Aurora, Colo., Aug. 16, 1944; s. Philip H. and Sybil V. (Hohstadt) B.; m. Cherry Moore King, Jan. 25, 1964 (div. Jan. 1966); 1 child, Christopher Alan; m. Lavada A. Peters, Apr. 28, 1973; 1 child, Debbie Dee. BSEE, BS in Bus., U. Colo., Denver, 1980. Lab. technician Gates Rubber Co., Denver, 1964-66, supr. tire quality, 1969-73, tech. svc. auditor, 1973-74, tech. specialist, 1974-80, supr. tech. svcs., 1980-81, mgr. test methods gen. lab., 1981-82, supr. equipment engring., 1982-84, mgr. material processing equipment engring., 1984-88, sr. rsch. assoc. new products and processes, 1988—. With U.S. Army, 1966-69. Mem. IEEE, Am. Chem. Soc. (affiliate rubber div.), Canyon Wren Club (sec.-treas. 1986–), Gates Tech. Club (sec., v.p., pres. 1985-87), Masons (32 degree), Shriners. Ch. of Christ. Home: 5420 Garrison St Arvada CA 80002 Office: Gates Rubber Co AT&E PO Box 5887 Denver CO 80217

BARNES, RONALD ROGER, food company executive; b. Southampton, N.Y., Apr. 21, 1939; s. George Bertram and Esther (Rynalski) B.; m. Adelaide Louise Simermeyer, Nov. 28, 1970; children: Alison Jennifer, Meredith Sara. BA, Cornell U., 1961. Sales rep. Sealtest Foods Corp., N.Y.C., 1968-71, Wechsler Coffee Corp., N.Y.C., 1971-72; dist. mgr. Ralston Purina Co., N.Y.C., 1972-76; regional mgr. Stouffer Foods Corp., Tarrytown, N.Y., 1976-87; div. mgr. Stouffer Foods Corp., Santa Ana, Calif., 1987—. Capt. U.S. Army, 1961-67. Mem. Nat. Prepared Frozen Food Assn. (bd. dirs. 1979-81, v.p. 1981-82, pres. 1982-86). Democrat. Office: Stouffer Foods Corp 1920 E Warner Ave Santa Ana CA 92705

BARNES, RUSSELL HANLON, civil engineer; b. Valley Forge, Pa., May 16, 1959; s. Metullus Ard and Anne Wilshire (Meek) B. BA, Pomona Coll., 1982; BS, Calif. Inst. Tech., 1982; MSChemE, Stanford U., 1983. Registered profl. engr., Ariz. Engr. Spencer, White & Prentis, Inc., Rochelle Park, N.J., 1983-84; supt. Spencer, White & Prentis/Bauer, Boston, 1984-85, asst. project mgr., 1985-86; sales engr. Raymond Internat. Builders, Westville, N.J., 1986; asst. project mgr., project mgr. Raymond/Bauer Joint Venture, Boston, 1986-87; supt., asst. area mgr. Raymond Internat. Builders, Long Beach, Calif., 1987-88; project engr. Healy Tibbitts Constrn. Co., San Francisco, 1988—. Mem. ASCE, NSPE. Home: 8640 E Rancho Vista Dr Scottsdale AZ 85251 Office: Healy Tibbitts Constrn Co 411 Brannan St San Francisco CA 94107

BARNES, STANLEY NELSON, judge; b. Baraboo, Wis., May 1, 1900; s. Charles Luling and Janet (Rankin) B.; m. Anne Fisk, Oct. 18, 1929 (dec.); children: Janet Anne Hansen (dec.), Judith Fisk Melkesian, Joyce Rankin Robinson; m. Elizabeth MacDonald, Nov. 6, 1987. AB, U. Calif., 1922, JD, 1925, LLD, 1961; postgrad. in law, Harvard U., 1923-24. Bar: Cal. 1925. Sole practice San Francisco, 1925-28, Los Angeles, 1928-46; lectr. law U. So. Calif., 1947-52, lectr. forensic medicine, 1949-51; judge Superior Ct. of Los Angeles, 1947-53, presiding judge, 1952-53; asst. U.S. atty. gen; with anti-trust div. Dept. Justice, 1953-56; judge U.S. Ct. Appeals (9th cir.), 1956-70, sr. judge, 1970—; Mem. Pres.'s Conf. Adminstrv. Proc., 1953; co-chmn. Atty. Gen.'s Nat. Com. Study Antitrust Laws, 1953-55; adv. council appellate rules jud. Conf. U.S., 1963-68; adv. council Practising Law Inst. Bd. dirs. S.W. Mus., Los Angeles, Calif. Inst. for Cancer Research, UCLA Med. Sch., 1949-75; regent U. Calif., 1946-48; trustee Sigma Chi Found., 1955—. Named Alumnus of Year U. Calif., 1966; recipient award Boalt Hall Sch. Law, U. Calif., Berkeley, 1967, St. Thomas More award Loyola Law Sch., Los Angeles, 1973; named to Nat. Collegiate Football Hall Fame, 1954, Helms Athletic Found. Hall of Fame, San Diego Hall of Champions; Berkeley fellow, 1969. Fellow Am. Bar Found., Am. Coll. Trial Lawyers, Am. Acad. Forensic Sci.; mem. Fed. Bar Assn. (nat. pres. 1954-55), ABA (chmn. sect. jud. adminstrn. 1966-67, mem. judges adv. commn. to ABA com. on profl. ethics 1957-63), Calif. Bar Assn., San Francisco Bar Assn., Los Angeles Bar Assn. (Shattuck-Price distinguished service award 1971), N.Y.C. Bar Assn., Am. Judicature Soc., Inst. Jud. Adminstrn., Calif. Alumni Assn. (pres. 1946-48), Phi Delta Phi., Sigma Chi (nat. pres. 1952-55, nat. trustee 1950-52, trustee Found. 1955—). Episcopalian. Clubs: Rotary (hon.), Nat. Lawyers (hon.); Univ., Calif. (Los Angeles); Bohemian (San Francisco). Home: Smoke Tree Ranch Palm Springs CA 92264 Office: US Ct of Appeals 125 S Grand Ave PO Box 91510 Pasadena CA 91109-1510

BARNES, THOMAS AARON, SR., insurance broker; b. Toledo, June 4, 1928; s. Paul Nash and Thelma Morita (Williams) B.; m. Margaret Ellen Muth, Dec. 26, 1951; 1 child, Thomas Aaron Jr. Grad. high sch., Bellefontaine, Ohio. Licensed life and health ins. agent, Ariz. Enlisted U.S. Army Air Force, 1946; advanced to major USAF, 1968; ret. U.S. Air Force, 1968; intelligence staff officer Ohio Air N.G., Columbus, 1954-68; reporter Dun and Bradstreet, Inc., Dayton, Ohio, 1956-67; agent N.Y. Life Ins., Yuma, Ariz., 1968-73; owner Somerton (Ariz.) Trading Post, 1978-88; owner, mgr. Tom Barnes & Assocs., Yuma, Somerton, 1973—; sec. The Salvation Army Adv. Bd., Yuma, 1974—; chmn. Valley Health Ctr. Found., Somerton, 1987-88, Somerton Merchants Assn., 1978-86. Mayor Somerton City Council, 1981-84; mem. Western Ariz. Council Govts., Yuma, 1978-84, 87—; co-chmn. Rep. Cen. Com., Yuma County, 1983-84. Maj. USAFR 1968—. Recipient Montgomery Humanitarian award Ariz. State Council For Sr. Citizens, 1980, Citation For Outstanding Svc. Yuma Union High Sch. Dist., 1980; named to Life Membership Rep. Presdl. Task Force, 1988. Mem. Yuma County Pvt. Industry Coun., Ariz. Western Coll. Adv. Bd. (pres. 1988—), VFW (post commdr. 1976-77), Am. Legion (dist. comdr. 1987-88), Christian Businessmen's Com. (bd. dirs. 1986-87), Cocopah Indian Tribe (mem. personnel bd. 1986—), Rotary, Masons, Shriners. Republican. Methodist. Home: 1449 W Jennifer Ln Yuma AZ 85365-9310

BARNETT, DANIEL L., entrepreneur; b. Seattle, May 11, 1954; s. Donald L. and Barbara J. (Monroe) B.; m. Pamela J. Swanson, June 27, 1973; children: Robert L., Benton R. BS in Fin., Ariz. State U., 1981. Investment exec. Paine Webber, Bellevue, Wash., 1981-83; asst. v.p. E.F. Hutton, Bellevue, 1983-87; sr. account exec. Smith Barney, Bellevue, 1987-88; sr. v.p. corp. fin. PFG Securities, Inc., Bellevue, 1988; pres. Internat. Capital, Ltd., Bellevue, 1987—; ptnr. Oasis Capital Mgmt. Inc., Boston, 1988—, also bd. dirs. Home: 20724 NE 142d St Woodinville WA 98072 Office: Oasis Capital Mgmt Inc 10 Liberty Sq 6th Fl Boston MA 02109

BARNETT, DAVID IRA, dentist; b. Balt., Apr. 7, 1955; s. Donald Arthur and Leatrice Joy (Gordon) B.; m. Lynn Simon, Nov. 28, 1982; 1 child, Daniel. BA, Rutgers U., 1977; DMD, U. Pa., 1981. Pvt. practice dentistry Washington, 1981, Laurel, Md., 1982-83, Huntington Beach, Calif., 1984, Garden Grove, Calif., 1985—; on-call emergency dentist Western Med. Ctr., Santa Ana, 1986-87. Mem. ADA, Calif. Dental Assn., Orange Co. Dental Soc., Alpha Omega. Republican. Jewish. Office: 9872 Chapman Ave #110 Garden Grove CA 92641

BARNETT, MARIE, real estate executive; b. LaGrange, Ga., May 19; d. George and D. (Moore) B.; m. James Stephens Dick, Dec. 5, 1960 (div.); children: Karen MarieDick Vidal, Sonya Stephens Dick Tafolla. Student, Fla. State U., 1955, U. Ga., 1956-58, Perry Coll., 1959; grad., Century 21 Internat. Mgmt. Acad., 1988. Lic. Calif. Dept. of Real Estate. Staff Mastrose Devel. Co., Palm Beach, Fla., 1962-65; pres., owner Century 21 Calif. Hills, Orange, Calif., 1973-79; real estate exec. F.M. Tarbell, Orange, Calif., 1979-85; pres., owner Century 21 Assocs., Newport Beach, Calif., 1985-88; real estate exec. Century 21 Inland Pacific, Newport Beach, Calif., 1988—. Pres. Jr. Auxiliary, Pass Christian, Miss., 1965; VIP panel Easter Seals, L.A., 1989; active 552 Club, Cancer Unit Hoag Hosp., Newport Beach, 1989, Cen Pac, Washington, 1989. Mem. Nat. Assn. of Realtors (Grad. Realtors Inst.), Calif. Assn. of Realtors (state dir. 1976, 78-79, realtor-assoc. rels. com., publicity com., co-chmn. Pvt. Property Week, 99 Club), East Orange Bd. of Realtors (chmn. spl. activities 1974-75, chmn. real estate fin. 1976, chmn. realtor-assoc. rels. com. 1977, chmn. Pvt. Property Week 1978, Pres.'s award 1978, chmn. Pvt. Property Week Luncheon 1980-81, communications com. 1980-81, 83, Pvt. Property Week com. 1981), Newport Harbor/Costa Mesa Bd. of Realtors (communications com. 1986—, CANTREE reception 1986, multiple listings com. 1987-88, chmn. Ann. Awards and Installation 1987, chmn. Equal Opportunity com. 1988), Corona Del Mar C. of C., Newport Harbor C. of C. Democrat. Office: Century 21 Inland Pacific 2 Corporate Plaza Newport Beach CA 92660

BARNETT, MIKKY DEAN, chiropractor; b. Port Angeles, Wash., Dec. 2, 1947; s. Charles Glen and LaVerne Ellen (Wenner) B.; m. Christina Anne Armstrong, Nov. 14, 1969. AS, Skagit Valley Coll., 1966; A of Mortuary Sci. with highest honors, Calif. Coll. Mortuary Sci., 1969; D of Chiropractic cum laude, Palmer Coll. Chiropractic, 1981. Diplomate Nat. Bd. Chiropractic Examiners. Pvt. practice chiropractic medicine Stanwood, Wash., 1982—. Curator Blacksmith Mus., Stanwood-Camaro Fair, 1982—; scoutmaster troop 86 Boy Scouts Am., Stanwood, 1986—; active Nat Eagle Scouts Assn. Named Tyee Dist. Asst. Scoutmaster of Yr. Boy Scouts of Am., Stanwood, 1986—. Mem. Acad. Chiropractic Forensic Con's., Gonstead Clin. Studies Soc., Parker Chiropractic Rsch. Found., Lions (bd. dirs. Stanwood Club, past pres.). Home: 26919 78th Ave NW Stanwood WA 98292 Office: 8718 Nawoc Dr Stanwood WA 98292

BARNHART, CHRISTOPHER ENGLE, architecture company executive; b. Portland, Oreg., Feb. 18, 1942; s. Maurice Wendell and Mary (Dann) B.; m. Jo Ellen Cleaves, Dec. 26, 1970;. Student, Portland State Coll., Portland, 1961-64, Portland State U., 1969, 71, U. Oreg., 1964-66; BArch, U. Oreg., 1972. registered architect, Calif., Hawaii. Peace Corp vol. Somalia, Africa, 1966-68; draftsperson J & J Construction, Portland, 1969-72; architect S.T.R. Engrs., Portland, 1972-73, Fisher-Freedman, San Francisco, 1973-74, Roma Architects, San Francisco, 1974, Smart & Clabaugh, Redding, Calif., 1975-78, Humboldt Service Corp., Redding, 1978, Uwe H. H. Schulz, Lahaina, Hawaii, 1978-80, Woodward & Nichols, Redding, 1981-83; v.p. WKSB Architects, Redding, 1983-; cons. Trinity Co. Hist. Soc., Weaverville, Calif., 1980. Bd. dirs. chmn. Shasta Community Service Dist., Shasta, Calif. Recipient Beyond War Award to Peace Corp., Beyond War, Redding, 1987. Mem. CVCAIA, Kappa Sigma, Exchange Club. Democrat.

Episcopalian. Office: WKSB Architects 225 Locust St Ste 3 Redding CA 96001

BARNHART, STEVEN R., construction executive; b. Liberty, N.Y., Nov. 30, 1956; s. H. Robert and Irene Mary (O'Keefe) B.; m. Marsha Ann Izquerdo, July 31, 1980 (div. 1987); children: Clifton Richard, Laura Michelle; m. Terry Ann Fales, Feb. 14, 1988. Student, SUNY, Delhi, 1974-75, Brigham Young U., 1979-80. Contractor SRB Constrn., Lew Beach, N.Y., 1975-76, 77-78, Clearwater, Fla., 1976-77; missionary LDS Ch., Barcelona, Spain, 1978-79; contractor, developer SRB Constrn., Provo, Utah, 1980-85; speaker, dir. The Goodlife Experience, Mesa, Ariz., 1986-87; owner, mgr. C. C. & C. Constrn., Las Vegas, Nev., 1987—. Republican. Mem. Ch. Latter Day Saints. Home: 1640 Charles Las Ct Las Vegas NV 89102 Office: 3599 Polaris Ave Las Vegas NV 89103

BARNHILL, EDGAR WILLIAM, JR., retired special education instructor, realtor; b. Suffolk, Va., Apr. 5, 1926; s. Edgar William and Emma Jean (Harrell) B.; m. Susan Elizabeth Flemer, Sept. 9, 1950; children: Catherine Noelle, Susan, Edgar William III, Jacqueline Marie. BA, Coll. William and Mary, 1950; MA, Los Angeles State Coll., 1962; DEd, U. Oreg., 1970. Speech, drama tchr. Princess Anne County Sch., Virginia Beach, Va., 1951-53; social studies tchr. William S. Hart High Sch., Newhall, Calif., 1953-63; counselor William S. Hart High Sch., Newhall, 1964-68; instructional asst. spec. ed. U. Oreg., Eugene, 1969-70; prin. Bowman High Sch., Canyon Country, Calif., 1971-72, Wayside Adult Sch., Castaic, Calif., 1973-78; spl. edn. tchr. Saugus (Calif.) High Sch., 1978-88. Pres., v.p. Los Angeles County Rep. Assembly, 1985-86; del. Calif. Rep. Assembly, 1980-86; mem. Planning Adv. Com., Santa Clarita, Calif., 1983-87; com. mem. Calif. Rep. Assembly, 1982-85. Served as pfc. U.S. Army, ETO, 1944-45. Decorated Bronze Star, Purple Heart. Mem. Santa Clarita Valley Bd. Realtors Polit. Action Com. (chmn.), Bay Valley Calif. Tchrs. Assn. (dist. del., WHO award 1985-86), 1984-88. Republican. Roman Catholic. Lodge: KC (Grand Knight, Newhall, Calif., 1971-72). Home: 6822 Santa Barbara Ave Ventura CA 93001

BARNOSKI, RICHARD LEE, computer systems engineer; b. St. Joseph, Mo., June 4, 1936; s. Frank Paul and Helen Catherine B.; m. Nancy Louise Hames, Aug. 21, 1965; children: Kathryne L., Kristin L., Stephen A. BA in ME/EE, U. Mo., 1958; MS in Engring., U. So. Calif., 1959, PhD in Engring., 1964. Sr. engr. Hughes Aircraft Corp., El Segundo, Calif., 1959-65; sr. scientist, project mgr. Mgmt. Analysis Corp., Marina Del Rey, Calif., 1965-70; dir. SFO ops. Computer Scis. Corp., Mountain View, Calif., 1970-80; systems dir. The Aerospace Corp., El Segundo, Calif., 1980-83; sr. staff cons. ZeroOne Systems, Syscon Corp., Santa Clara, Calif., 1983-86; sr. staff/LMSC, v.p. programs and plans Sterling Software, Palo Alto, Calif., 1986—. Reviewer, contbr., adv. Jour. Applied Mechanics, 1966-77, Jour. Sound and Vibration, 1966-77. Sponsor Galileo Found., Moffett Field, Calif., 1975—; treas., bd. dirs. San Jose Community Concert Assn., 1975-79. Hughes fellow, Dodd fellow, 1955-64. Mem. AIAA, ASME, Pi Tau Sigma, Eta Kappa Nu, Tau Beta Pi, Omicron Delta Kappa, Sigma Xi. Home: 1524 Kathy Ln Los Altos CA 94022

BAROFF, LYNN ELLIOTT, management consultant; b. Oklahoma City, Feb. 22, 1949; s. Phillip Dee and Estelle Claire (Rass) B.; m. Beverly Ann Wolf, Mar. 21, 1970 (div. Dec. 1978); m. Janice Kazue Obita, Apr. 7, 1979; children: David Masanori, Steven Hideaki. BA in Mass Communications, Mundelein Coll., 1971. Producer, dir. Sta. WCIU-TV, Chgo., 1970-76; prodn. mgr. Sta. KWHY-TV, L.A., 1976-79; gen. mgr. Baroff Cons. Group, Inc., Santa Monica, Calif., 1979—; adj. prof. U. So. Calif. Internat. Tng. Trainers, L.A., 1985, 86, Antioch U. Grad. Sch., L.A., 1989—. Author poetry. Mem. adv. com. L.A. Valley Coll., 1977, Calif. State U., L.A., 1979-80, Antioch U., 1989—. Recipient Honor Resolution, L.A. City Coun., 1976. Mem. Am. Soc. for Tng. and Devel. (v.p. 1983, pres. 1984), L.A. Orgn. Devel. Network, Delta Kappa Epsilon. Jewish. Office: 1223 Wilshire Blvd Ste 335 Santa Monica CA 90403

BARON, JOSEPH, management consulting company executive; b. Passaic, N.J., Feb. 20, 1924; s. Harry and Edith (Zaentz) B.; m. Beatrice Caplan, Apr. 18, 1942; children: Marsha Lynn Baron Cooper, Rodney Jay. Engring. cert, MIT, 1944; BEngring., U. So. Calif., 1947, postgrad. bus. mgmt., 1958. Gen. mgr. Pacific Cast Iron Pipe & Fittings Co., South Gate, Calif., 1947-58; v.p. mfg. Price Pfister Brass Mfg. Co., Pacoima, Calif., 1958-75; v.p., gen. mgr. Gt. Am. Mfg. & Sales Co., Pacoima, 1975-82, Data Memory Corp., Woodland Hills, Calif., 1983-85; v.p. adminstrn. Com Systems Inc., Van Nuys, Calif., 1982-83; pres. Baron and Assocs., L.A., 1985—. Bd. dirs. City of Hope, Duarte, Calif., 1979—, Union Am. Hebrew Congregations, N.Y.C., 1983—; pres. Stephen S. Wise Temple, L.A., 1981-83. With AUS, 1943-46, ETO. Mem. Nat. Assn. Pipe Nipple Mfrs. (v.p. 1979-82), Am. Nat. Standards Inst. Office: Baron & Assocs PO Box 491160 Los Angeles CA 90049

BARON, JUDY KAPLAN, management consultant, career consultant, marriage, family and child counselor; b. Chgo., Dec. 5, 1952; d. Herman and Mignon (Damond) Kaplan; m. Fred Michael Baron, Mar. 22, 1981. BS, U. Tex., 1974; MS, Tex. A&I U., 1976; postgrad., U. San Diego, 1983-85. Lic. marriage, family and child counselor, Calif.; cert. career counselor. Employment counselor Snelling Personnel Cons., Corpus Christi, Tex., 1974; admissions counselor Tex. A&I U., Corpus Christi, 1975-76; vocational counselor Occupational Tng. Svcs., San Diego, 1977-79; pres. Judy Kaplan Baron Assocs., La Jolla, Calif., 1979—; cons., trainer in field. Author tng. guide: Selection Interviewing 1985. Named to Outstanding Young Women Am., 1983. Mem. Am. Assn. Counseling and Devel., Calif. Assn. Counseling and Devel., Calif. Career Devel. Assn. Democrat. Jewish. Office: Judy Kaplan Baron Assocs 737 Pearl Ste 208 B La Jolla CA 92037

BARON, NICHOLAS BRZOVIC, psychologist, educator, art appraiser; b. Braslewitz, Austria, Sept. 16, 1911; m. Katherine Baron, 1964; 1 child. BTh, Theological Coll., Srem Karlowitz, 1938; PhD, U. Marburg, Germany, 1947. Pvt. practice 1949—; founder Jan Hus U., Scottsdale, Ariz., 1969, pres., prof. psychology, counselor, 1972—; lectr. parapsychology, art and humanity; rebuilder destroyed churches and monasteries, 1949—. V.p., counselor Morning Star Found., 1975—, New Age Found., 1975—; supporter numerous charitable orgns. including Asian Relief Inc., Omaha Home for Boys and St. Labre Indian Sch. Named Serbian Ortodox Patriarch, Belgrade, 1976, Mitropolitan of Zagreb, 1976, Serbian Bishop, Karlovac, 1974. Mem. Am. Art Soc. (bd. dirs. 1972), Idaho Archaeologist, Congrl. Club.

BARR, DONALD ROY, statistics and operations research educator, statistician; b. Durango, Colo., Dec. 10, 1938; s. Russell Wesely and Elizabeth Joanette (Grommett) B.; m. Loudean Suttle, June 14, 1958; children: Mark Edward, Bryan Michael. B.A., Whittier Coll., 1960, Colo. State U., 1962; Ph.D., Colo. State U., 1965. Instr. Colo. State U., 1964-65; asst. prof. math. U. Wis.-Oshkosh, 1965-66; prof. stats. and ops. rsch. Naval Postgrad. Sch., Monterey, Calif., 1966-87; v.p. Evaluation Tech. Inc., 1987-88; pres. Evaluation Tech. Inc., Monterey, 1988—; v.p. VRC Corp., Monterey, 1989—; liaison scientist London br. Office Naval Rsch., 1982-83. Author: College and University Mathematics, 1968, Finite Statistics, 1968, Probability, 1971, Analytic Geometry: A Vector Approach, 1971, Probability: Modeling Uncertainty, 1981, Statistics by Calculator, 1983; contbr. articles to profl. jours. Mem. Am. Stat. Assn., Ops. Research Soc. Am., Internat. Test and Evaluation Assn., Sigma Xi. Home: 1495 Prescott Monterey CA 93940 Office: VRC Corp 2150 Garden Rd Monterey CA 93940-5327

BARR, KENNETH JOHN, mining company executive; b. Birmingham, Ala., Aug. 25, 1926; s. Archie and Mable Leona (Griffith) B.; m. Jeanne Bonner, Jan. 22, 1951; children: Marsha Jeanne, Kenneth John, Darren Clint. BS in Chem. Engring., Auburn U., 1947; grad., Advanced Mgmt. Inst. Northwestern U., 1964. Jr. petroleum engr. Stanolind Oil & Gas, Hobbs, N.Mex., 1948-49; chief engr. Amoco Prodn. Co., Tulsa, 1962-65; mgr. producing and v.p. producing dept. Amoco Can. Petroleum Co., Calgary, Alta, 1965-70; mgr. producing and v.p., div. mgr. Amoco Prodn. Co., New Orleans, 1970-73; mgr. supply dept. Standard Oil (Ind.), Chgo., 1973-75; exec. v.p. Amoco Internat., Chgo., 1975, Amoco Prodn. Co., Chgo., 1975-79; pres. Cyprus Mines (Std.), Los Angeles, 1979-80, Amoco Minerals Co., Denver, 1980-85; pres., chief exec. officer Cyprus Minerals Co., Denver, 1985—, also bd. dirs. Served with USAAF, 1945. Mem. Am. Mining Congress (bd. dirs. 1983—), AIME. Clubs: Snowmass (Aspen, Colo.); Longboat Key (Fla.). Office: Cyprus Minerals Co 9100 E Mineral Circle PO Box 3299 Englewood CO 80155

BARR, ROBERT DALE, university dean, educator; b. Fort Worth, Nov. 24, 1939; s. Robert Edward and Leota Oleta (Sanders) B.; m. Beryl Lucas, Aug. 26, 1956; children—Bonny, Brady. B.A., Tex. Christian U., 1961; M.S., North Tex. State U., 1965; Ph.D., Purdue U., 1969. Cert. sch. adminstr. and educator, Oreg. Tchr. social studies, dept. chmn. R.L. Paschal High Sch., Fort Worth, 1961-65; grad. instr. Purdue U., West Lafayette, Ind., 1965-67; asst. prof. edn. U. Tex.-Arlington, 1967-69; staff assoc. Nat. Council for Social Studies, Washington, 1969-70, asst. prof., assoc. prof. social studies edn. and secondary edn., dir. alternative schs. grad. program, 1970-77, prof. edn., dir. tchr. edn. and extended services, 1978; dir. Office Tchr. Edn. and Extended Services, Ind. U., Bloomington, 1980-81; dean Sch. Edn., Oreg. State U., Corvallis, 1982—; developer Ind. U. Weekender Inservice Program for Tchrs., 1978; asst. developer tchr. ctr. proposals Indpls. Pub. Schs., Bartholomew Pub. Schs., Columbus, Ind., 1977; vis. prof. Am. Summer Sch., U. Fla., U. New Orleans, U. Innsbruck, Austria, 1979; interim dir. Ctr. for Urban and Multicultural Edn.; co-dir. Nat. Consortium for Options in Pub. Edn., 1971-77; bd. advisors Fielding Inst., Santa Barbara, Calif., 1974—; chmn., mem. publs. bds. Nat. Council for Social Studies, 1970-74; mem. task force on compulsory edn. and transitions for youth, Phi Delta Kappa, 1976-77; mem. research team Project Alternative Edn., 1981; dir. project Nat. Inst. Profl. Devel., Santiago, Chile, 1980-81; co-dir. basic edn. project Lilly Endowment and Indpls. Pub. Schs., 1977-78; cons. and lectr. in field. Author: Optional Alternative Public Schools, 1971 (reprinted as School Violence and Vandalism: Model and Strategies for Change, 1975), Values and Youth, 1971, (with James L. Barth and S. Samuel Shermis) Defining the Social Studies, 1977, The Nature of the S Social Studies, 1978, (with Vernon H. Smith and Daniel J. Burke) Alternatives in Education: Freedom to Choose, 1976 (also Japanese transl.), co-editor: Changing Schools newsletter, Nat. Consortium for Options in Pub. Edn., 1971-77; producer, editor filmstrip To Lead a Profession, 1970; contbr. chpts. to books, reports, monographs, articles, revs., editorials to profl. jours. Recipient Disting. Achievement award Am. Assn. Colls. for Tchr. Edn., 1975; named to Internat. Invitational Colloquium on Adult Edn., U. Nottingham, 1981; Ford Found. Washington fellow, 1969-70. Office: Oreg State U Edn Hall Rm 215 Corvallis OR 97331

BARRACK, MARTIN, corporate executive; b. N.Y.C., July 26, 1948; s. David and Jean Barrack. MBA, City Coll. of N.Y., 1970. Key acct. nat. sales Sacha London, L.A., 1982-87; sales mgr. L.A. Gear, 1987; sales and mktg. dir. Terra Australis, L.A., 1987—.

BARRETO, KATHLEEN ANNE, technical writing consultant; b. New London, Conn., Sept. 5, 1954; d. Eugene Aloysius and Germaine Marie (Hangley) Coogan; m. Oscar Eduardo Barreto, May 28, 1972 (separated 1980); 1 child, Victoria Anne. AA in Tech. Writing, De Anza Coll., 1988. Banker 1974-80; tech. recruiter Menlo Svc. Corp., Sunnyvale, Calif., 1980-84; tech. writer Tectron-Singer-Dalmo Victor, Belmont and Fremont, Calif., 1984-87; tech. writing cons. Sunnyvale, 1987—; cons. Tech. for Communicators Internat., Fremont, 1987—, Ultra Systems, Sunnyvale, 1988. Author, co-producer High-Tech for Ind. Living, PBS-TV, 1988 (Waveform award 1988, Bay Area Cable Excellence award for best docudrama 1989); writer, producer, host On the Move, Able Cable TV, 1988—. Mem. Writer's Connection, Mensa. Libertarian. Roman Catholic. Office: 437-C Costa Mesa Terr Sunnyvale CA 94086

BARRETT, BARBARA MCCONNELL, lawyer; b. Indiana County, Pa., Dec. 26, 1950; d. Robert Harvey and Betty (Dornheim) McC.; m. Craig R. Barrett, Jan. 19, 1985. BA, Ariz. State U., 1972, MPA, 1975, JD, 1978. Bar: Ariz. 1978, U.S. Dist. Ct. Ariz. 1979, U.S. Supreme Ct. Ariz. 1979. Atty. The Greyhound Corp., Phoenix, 1976-80; assoc. gen. counsel, asst. sec. Southwest Forest Industries, Inc., Phoenix, 1980-82; exec. asst. to chmn. Civil Aeronautics Bd., Washington, 1982-83, mem., 1983-84, vice chmn., 1984-85; ptnr. Evans, Kitchel & Jenckes, P.C., Phoenix, 1985—; dep. adminstr. FAA, Washington, 1988—. Chmn. Ariz. Dist. Export Coun., 1985—, Ronald W. Reagan Scholarship Program, 1987—; bd. dirs. Nat. Air and Space Mus. Smithsonian Inst., 1988—. Named Woman of Yr. Ariz. State U., 1971; Dubois scholar, 1977; recipient Disting. Achievement award Ariz. State U., 1987, Woman Who Made A Difference award Internat. Women's Forum, 1988. Office: Evans Kitchel & Jenckes 2600 N Central Ave Phoenix AZ 85004-3099

BARRETT, DONALD JOHN, library administrator; b. St. Paul, Sept. 30, 1927; s. Lawrence John and Pauline Catherine (Huth) B.; m. June Lorraine Medalen, Jan. 27, 1962; 1 child, Barbara Sue. BS, Coll. St. Thomas, 1950; MA, U. Minn., 1954. Reference librarian Coll. St. Thomas Library, St. Paul, 1950-54; librarian Electronic Supply Office, Great Lakes, Ill., 1954-55; reference librarian USAF Acad. Library, Denver, 1955-58; chief pub. svcs. div. USAF Acad. Library, Colorado Springs, 1959-69, asst. dir. pub. svcs., 1969—; library bldg. cons., 1975—. Contbr. articles to profl. jours. With U.S. Army, 1946-47. Mem. ALA, Assn. Coll. and Rsch. Libraries, Colo. Library Assn., Library Adminstrn. and Mgmt. Assn., Air Force Assn. Roman Catholic. Home: 2624 Flintridge Dr Colorado Springs CO 80918 Office: USAF Acad Library USAF Academy CO 80840

BARRETT, EUGENE WADE, business broker; b. L.A., Sept. 2, 1929; s. Purl Wade and Helen Lou (Smith) B.; m. Anita Maxine Hartwick, June 8, 1963; children: Braden Hartwick, Barbara Lani. BS, U. So. Calif., 1956. Chief personnel ops. Holmes & Narver, Inc., Orange, Calif., 1956-73; owner, mgr. Irelands True Value Hardware Store, Hillsboro, Oreg., 1975-85; v.p. Truck Terminals, Inc., Beaverton, Oreg., 1975—; bus. broker Crader & Assocs., Inc., Lake Oswego, Calif., 1987—. Rep. precinct capt., Honolulu, 1970. Cpl. U.S. Army, 1950-52. Mem. Pacific NW Hardware Assn. (trustee 1980-85), Hillsboro C. of C. (bd. dirs. 1976-80), Hillsboro Downtown Bus. Assn. (pres. 1981), Rotary. Home: 1825 SW Pheasant Dr Beaverton OR 97006 Office: Crader & Assocs Inc 5285 SW Meadows Rd Lake Oswego OR 97035

BARRETT, IZADORE, fisheries research administrator; b. Vancouver, B.C., Can., Oct. 4, 1926; came to U.S., 1956; s. Samuel Barrett and Rose (Hyatt) Gordon; m. Fulvia Mercedes Quesada, July 5, 1958; children: Marcus, Byron, Norman, Dora. BA, U. B.C., 1947, MA, 1949; postgrad., U. Toronto, 1949-52; PhD, U. Wash., 1980. Chief hatchery biologist B.C. Game Commn., Vancouver, 1952-56; scientist Inter-Am. Tropical Tuna Commn., La Jolla, 1956-67; chief biologist UNDP Fisheries Devel. Project, Santiago, Chile, 1967-69; fisheries advisor FAO, Santiago, 1969-70; dep. dir. S.W. Fisheries Ctr., La Jolla, 1970-77, dir., 1977-88; sci. and research dir. S.W. region, Nat. Marine Fisheries Service, 1988—; research assoc. Scripps Inst. Oceanography, La Jolla, 1977—; mem. sci. and statis. com. Pacific Fisheries Mgmt. Council, Portland, Oreg., 1977—; chmn. sci. and statis. com. Western Pacific Fisheries Mgmt. Council, Honolulu, 1976-79. Contbr. articles to profl. jours. Bd. govs. San Diego Oceans Found., 1985—; chmn. Mayor's San Diego/La Jolla Underwater Park Comm., San Diego, 1978—; mem. adv. council Inst. Marine Resources U. Calif., La Jolla, 1979-85, bd. govs. San Diego Sci. Fair, 1984—. Fellow Am. Inst. Fisheries Research Biologists (v.p. 1973-76); mem. AAAS, Am. Soc. Ichthyologists and Herpetologists, Western Soc. Naturalists, Soc. Marine Mammals. Office: SW Fisheries Ctr PO Box 271 La Jolla CA 92038

BARRETT, JAMES E., judge; b. Lusk, Wyo., Apr. 8, 1922; s. Frank A. and Alice C. (Donoghue) B.; m. Carmel Ann Martinez, Oct. 8, 1949; children—Ann Catherine Barrett Sandahl, Richard James, John Donoghue. Student, U. Wyo., 1940-42, LL.B., 1949; student, St. Catherine's Coll., Oxford, Eng., 1945, Cath. U. Am., 1946. Bar: Wyo. 1949. Mem. firm Barrett and Barrett, Lusk, 1949-67; atty. gen. State of Wyo., 1967-71; judge U.S. Circuit Ct. Appeals, 10th Circuit, 1971—; county and pros. atty. Niobrara County, Wyo., 1951-62; atty. Town of Lusk, 1952-54, Niobrara Sch. Dist., 1950-64. Active Boy Scouts Am.; sec.-treas. Niobrara County Republican Central Com.; trustee St. Joseph's Children's Home, Torrington, Wyo., 1971-85. Served as cpl. AUS, 1942-45, ETO. Recipient Distinguished Alumni award U. Wyo., 1973. Mem. VFW, Am. Legion. Office: US Ct Appeals PO Box 1288 Cheyenne WY 82001

BARRETT, MARY PATRICIA, retail company executive; b. Detroit, Mar. 7, 1958; d. Raymond Joseph and Patricia Ann (Nelan) B. BA, U. Mich., 1980. Exec. trainee Saks Fifth Ave, Troy, Mich., 1980; dept. mgr. gifts, mens furnishings Saks Fifth Ave, Skokie, Ill., 1980-83; dept. mgr., mens accessories Saks Fifth Ave, San Diego, 1983-84; asst. gen. mgr., ops. and personnel dir. Saks Fifth Ave, La Jolla, Calif., 1984-85; asst. gen. mgr. ops. Saks Fifth Ave, San Diego, 1985—. Republican. Roman Catholic. Home: 2222 River Run Dr 129 San Diego CA 92108 Office: Saks Fifth Ave 1750 Camino del Rio N San Diego CA 92108

BARRETT, MICHAEL HENRY, civil engineer; b. Dove Creek, Colo., June 20, 1932; s. Frank Ace and Carrie Ethel (Snyder) B.; m. Barbara Jane Kreutz, Aug. 7, 1954; children: Robert, Mary, Bonnie, William. B.S. in Civil Engring, U. Colo., 1955, postgrad., 1955-64; M.B.A., U. Denver, 1979. Registered profl. engr., Colo., Calif., Fla., Wis., N.C., Minn., N.Mex., Utah. Design engr., then partner Ketchum & Konkel, Denver, 1955-69; pres. Ketchum, Konkel, Barrett, Nickel, Austin, Denver, 1969-79; chmn. bd. Ketchum, Konkel, Barrett, Nickel, Austin, 1979-85, pres., chmn., 1986-88; prin., cons. Martin/Martin, 1988—; prin. cons. Martin-Marietta, 1988—; dir. Testing Cons., Inc.; mem. faculty U. Colo., 1963-64, U. Denver, 1968-69; lectr. Civil Def., 1962-68. Patentee in field. Exec. bd. Denver Area council Boy Scouts Am., 1970—, pres., 1974-75, area v.p., 1976-82, area pres., 1982; mem. Westminster (Colo.) Planning Commn., 1971-72; chmn. bd. dirs. Denver Boys, Inc. Served with USNR, 1951-54. Recipient Lincoln Arc Welding award, 1966, 68, award Am. Inst. Steel Constrn., 1969, Disting. Engring. Alumnus award U. Colo., 1984. Mem. Nat. Soc. Profl. Engrs., ASCE, Am. Concrete Inst., Soc. Exptl. Stress Analysis, Profl. Engrs. Colo. (pres. 1970), Cons. Engrs. Council (1st pl. award 1973, pres. Colo. chpt. 1982), Structural Engrs. Assn. Colo., Am. Arbitration Assn., Harvard Bus. Sch. Club, Denver C. of C., Phi Kappa Tau, Chi Epsilon, Sigma Tau. Clubs: Rotary (Denver) (dir. 1976-78), Echo Hills Country (Perry Park, Colo.). Office: KKBNA Inc 4251 Kipling Wheat Ridge CO 80033

BARRETT, RICHARD HEWINS, oil company executive; b. Pitts., Dec. 5, 1949; s. Robert Hewins and Joan Lea (Mantler) B.; m. Virgini Kristine Arentzen, Apr. 14, 1973; children: Robert, Jeffrey, Douglas. BS, Pa. State U., 1971, MBA, 1973. Lic. soccer referee 1988. Ins./credit mgr. Perdue, Inc., Salisbury, Md., 1973-75, sales rep., 1975-76, dir. mgmt. analysis, 1976-77; sr. fin. analyst Gulf Oil Corp., Pitts., 1977-82, sr. cons., 1982-85; supr. sys. support Chevron Corp., San Francisco, 1985-86, sr. cash mgmt. analyst, 1986-87, mgr. banking ops., 1987—; instr. Golden Gate U., San Francisco, 1987—; adj. prof., Salisbury State Coll.,1975. Elder/trustee, Sharon Community Presbyn. Ch., Coraopolis, Pa., 1981-84; treas. bd. dirs., Moon Area Soccer Assn., Coraopolis, 1983-85; treas., bd. dirs., Mustang Soccer League, Danville, Calif., 1988—, youth soccer coach, 1980—. Mem. Nat. Corp. Cash Mgmt. Assn., Am. Petroleum Inst. (treasury issues com. 1988—). Republican. Presbyterian. Home: 244 Saint Christopher Dr Danville CA 94526 Office: Chevron Corp 225 Bush St San Francisco CA 94104

BARRETT, THOMAS JOSEPH, mental health center executive; b. Elmhurst, Ill., June 15, 1947; s. Francis J. and Hildegarde (Parr) B.; m. Dolores M. Heatherington, July 29, 1972; children: Gregory, Jennifer, Matthew. B.S. in Psychology, U. Ill., 1969; M.A. in Psychology, W.Va. U., 1971, Ph.D. in Clin. Psychology, 1973. Program evaluator Bethesda Community Mental Health Ctr., Denver, 1974-77, exec. dir., 1982—; dir. program evaluation Bethesda Hosp., Denver, 1977—; teaching affiliate U. Denver, 1980—; cons. VA, Denver, 1977-81, various fed. and state grants, Denver, 1974-81. Contbr. articles to profl. jours. Mem. Am. Psychology Assn., Colo. Assn. Community Mental Health Ctrs. & Clinics (pres. 1988—), Denver Mentl Health Consortium (v.p. 1986-88), Skyline Soccer Assn. (pres. 1986-88). Office: Bethesda PsyHealth System 4400 E Iliff Denver CO 80222

BARRETTE, JUDITH ANN, human resource executive, consultant; b. Aurora, Ill., June 5, 1950; d. Donald Quinton and Marion Teresa (Christoffel) B. AA, Waubonsee Jr. Coll., Sugar Grove, Ill., 1971; BS, George Williams Coll., 1973. Cert. community coll. tchr. Habilitation specialist Dept. Econ. Security, Phoenix, 1974-80, tng. specialist, 1980-81; tng. officer I Ariz. Dept. Transp., Phoenix, 1981-83, dir. employee devel., 1983—; assoc. Dyn-Excel, Inc., Phoenix, 1987—; instr. Rio Salado Community Coll., Phoenix, 1985—. Author tng. materials and books. Troop leader, Girl Souts U.S.A., Phoenix, 1986; v.p. Maricopa County Young Dems., Phoenix, 1982. Mem. Am. Soc. Tng. and Devel. (chmn. career devel. com. 1983-84), NAFE, Ariz. Bus. Industry Partnership (bd. dirs. 1986-88, Helping Hand award 1987), Ariz. Career Devel. Assn., Am. Fedn. State County and Mcpl. Employees, Ariz. Cert. Pub. Mgrs. (bd. dirs. 1988), Western Assn. Govt. Employees (sec. 1977-79), Ariz. Pub. Employees Assn. (v.p. 1978). Democrat. Roman Catholic. Office: Ariz Dept Transp 1739 W Jackson 100T Phoenix AZ 85007

BARRICELLI, JEAN-PIERRE, humanities and comparative literature educator, music critic; b. Cleve., June 5, 1924; s. Giovanni Alfonso and Orfea (Malpezzi) B.; m. Norma Gaeta, Oct. 19, 1957; children: Marco, Laura, Franca. BA, Harvard U., 1947, MA, 1948, PhD, 1953. Music dir. Radio Munich, 1945-46; teaching asst. Harvard U., Cambridge, Mass., 1948-50, 51-53; asst. prof. humanities and comparative lit. Brandeis U., Waltham, Mass., 1953-62, 63, dir. Vienna Internat. Sch. program, 1958-62, 63; prof. humanities and comparative lit. U. Calif., Riverside, 1963—; vis. prof. Norwegian Sch. Bus. Adminstrn., Bergen, 1962-63, NYU, N.Y.C., 1978; music critic Riverside Press, 1963—; disting. prof. humanities Coll. William and Mary, 1988. Author: Alessandro Manzoni, 1976, Giacomo Leopardi, 1986, Melopoiesis, 1988; editor: Interrelations of Literature, 1982. Sgt. AUS, 1943-46, PTO, lt. reserves, 1946-50. Fulbright fellow, 1950. Mem. Law and Humanities Inst. (bd. govs.), Internat. Comparative Lit. Assn., Am. Comparative Lit. Assn., MLA, Dante Soc. Am., Phi Beta Kappa. Roman Catholic. Home: 5984 Windmere Way Riverside CA 92506 Office: U Calif University Ave Riverside CA 92521

BARRON, CAROLINE JOAN, lawyer, editor; b. Orinda, Calif., Jan. 4, 1958; d. John Francis and Carolyn Patricia (Dunn) B.; m. Christopher Mead, Aug. 27, 1983. BA, Stanford U., 1978, JD, 1981. Bar: Calif. 1982, Ariz. 1983. Assoc. Brobeck, Phleger & Harrison, San Francisco, 1981-83, Beus, Gilbert, Wake & Morrill, Phoenix, 1983-88; editor Mead Ventures, Inc., Phoenix, 1983—; assoc. Law Offices of Gerald North, 1988-89; ptnr. North & Barron, 1989—; bd. dirs. 1st Cen. Bank, Phoenix, 1983-88. Vol. Phoenix Art Mus. Contemporary Forum, 1985—, Taliesin West/Frank Lloyd Wright Found., Phoenix, 1986—, Ariz. N.Am. Soc. Interior Designers, Phoenix, 1985-88, Valley Leadership, 1986-87, Valley Citizens League, 1988—, also speaker, arbitrator. Mem. ABA, Calif. Bar Assn., Ariz. Bar Assn., Maricopa County Bar Assn., Assn. Trial Lawyers Am. Office: North & Barron 505 N 2nd St Ste 420 Phoenix AZ 85004

BARRON, MARIETTA ELIZABETH, retired teacher, writer; b. Redding, Calif., May 3, 1921; d. Grover Cleveland and Alta (McQuirk) T.; m. Jose Isaac Barron, May 29, 1961. BA, Wash. State U., 1945. Cert. home economist; cert. tchr. Tchr. Battle Ground (Wash.) Jr. High Sch., 1945-47, Corbett (Oreg.) High Sch., 1947-50, Grant Union High Sch., Sacramento, 1951-52; home economist Pacific Gas & Electric Co., San Luis Obispo, Calif., 1952-53, Okla. Natural Gas Co., Tulsa, 1953-55, Sacramento Mcpl. Dist., 1955-61; tchr. Galileo High Sch., San Francisco, 1953-79, cons., 1979-84. Editor articles in Visitor and Valley, True West mags.; libr. Gerald Parsons Cassette of Afro-Am. folk songs, 1982. Mem. Calif. Writers' Club, Suburban Writers (v.p. 1986-87), Sacramento County Hist. Soc., Libr. of Congress Archive Folk Culture. Roman Catholic.

BARROW, ALAN EDWARD, JR., lawyer; b. Savannah, Ga., Dec. 14, 1944; s. Allen Edward and Dorothy (Dalton) B.; m. Luanne Ditez, Apr. 24, 1973; children: Christopher Allen, Allen Edward III. BBA, U. Okla., 1967; JD, U. Tulsa, 1969. Atty. Blackstock, Joyce & Pollard, Tulsa, 1972-73, Jarboe, Keefer & Barrow, Tulsa, 1973-76; ptnr. Barrow, Gaddis, Griffith & Grimm, Tulsa, 1976—. Mem. Interstate Oil Compact Commn., 1984—; v.p. Okla. Bd. Corrections, 1985—; dir. Nat. Council Christians and Jews, Tulsa, 1986—. Served to 1st lt. U.S. Army, 1970-71. Mem. ABA, Tulsa County Bar Assn., Am. Trial Lawyers Assn., Okla. Bar Assn., Okla. Bar Found., Metro. Tulsa C. of C. (mem. Com. 200, 1986—), Tulsa Club, Southern Hills Country Club, Empire Club, Sigma Chi (pres. Tulsa Alumni

1975). Democrat. Office: Barrow Gaddis Griffith & Grimm 610 S Main St Ste 300 Tulsa OK 74119

BARROWS, ROBERT GUY, scriptwriter; b. Ft. Collins, Colo., Feb. 9, 1926; s. Barney M. and Marian Louise (Walker) B.; divorced; children: Bret, Larry, David, Daniel, Josh, Grace. BA, U. Colo., 1950; MA, UCLA, 1954. Freelance writer NBC-TV, CBS-TV, ABC-TV, MGM, 20th Century Fox, Universal, Paramount, Columbia, Warner Bros., various ind. TV and film prodn. cos.; faculty mem., theater, TV and film NYU, 1957-62, Am. Acad., N.Y.C., 1960-62, UCLA, 1964-70, Art Ctr., Pasadena, Calif., 1980-82; mem. faculty, theater, TV and film Loyola Marymount U., Los Angeles, 1981-82. Writer: (TV episodes) Bonanza, Ben Casey, Combat, Destry, Daniel Boone, The Bold Ones, The Big Valley, Empire, The Fugitive, The Green Hornet, Felony Squad, Ironside, Kraft Suspense Theater, The Man Who Never Was, Mission: Impossible, Run for Your Life, Wild, Wild West, The Virginian. Served to master sgt. U.S. Army, 1943-46. Rockefeller Found. fellow. Mem. Writers Guild Am. (west). Democrat. Presbyterian. Lodge: Kiwanis.

BARRY, JAMES MICHAEL, property management company executive; b. Fontana, Calif., Dec. 22, 1956; s. Walter and Georgia Elizabeth (Spaeth) B. BA in Econs., U. Colo., 1979. Sales rep. Proctor & Gamble, Denver, 1979-81; sales rep. Becton Dickinson, Orangeburg, N.Y., 1981-84; dist. mgr., new dealer devel. Control-O-Fax, Denver, 1984-85; dist. br. mgr. Norrell Health Care, Denver, 1985-87; prin., owner Innovative Mgmt. Services, Inc., Denver, 1987—. Treas. Delta Upsilon Corp. Colo., Boulder, 1980-87; pres. Chestnut Homeowners Assn., Littlton, Colo., 1984-87; chmn. Rep. State Sen. Dist., Denver, 1987—, Rep. State Rep. Dist., Denver, 1987—; bd. dirs. Southwest Mental Health Services, Denver, 1988—. Mem. Community Assn. Inst. Republican. Roman Catholic. Home: 4899 S Dudley #A-18 Littleton CO 80123 Office: Innovative Mgmt Svc Inc 4899 S Dudley #A-18 Littleton CO 80123

BARRY, JOHN WILLARD, biologist; b. Columbus, Ohio, July 18, 1934; s. George Willard and Sylvia Evelyn (Ward) B.; m. Patricia Ann Arends Barry, Dec. 29, 1956 (div. 1986); children: Cynthia Shawn Wilkinson, Sandra Sue; m. Valerie Rubke Barry, May 30, 1987. BS, U. Cincinnati, 1956; postgrad., U. Utah, 1961-71, Brigham Young U., 1961-71. Test officer U.S. Army Dugway Proving Ground, Dugway, Utah, 1961-65; test dir. Deseret Test Ctr., Ft. Douglas, Utah, 1965-75; nat. aerial application specialist USDA Forest Svc., Davis, Calif., 1975—; mgr. Program WIND joint and USDA and DOD program, Davis, 1982-87. Author: American Indian Pottery, 1981; co-developer aerial spray models, 1985—. Leader and organizer Am. SW Ethnology Tours, 1985—; pres. and bd. dirs. Library Assocs. U. Calif., Davis, 1983-85, Davis Art Ctr., 1986—; mem. Mus. No. Ariz. and Nature Conservancy. Capt. U.S. Army, 1956-61. Mem. Am. Soc. Agr. Engring. Democrat. Lutheran. Office: USDA Foreste Svc 2121 C 2nd St Davis CA 95616

BARRY, SUSAN BROWN, writer, manufacturer; b. San Antonio, Tex., Sept. 14, 1944; d. Earl A. Jr. and Betty (Galt) Brown; m. Richard Hanley Barry, June 25, 1966 (div. 1973); children: Andrew Earl, Brice Galt. AB, Sweet Briar (Va.) Coll., 1966. Lic. real estate agt. Houston, 1983—; scriptwriter Stas. KHUT-TV, KDOG-TV, KEYT Radio, Houston, 1972-77; originator, adminstr., cons. publ. program Rice U., Houston, 1977-85; liaison book promotion Dell. Publs., Viking Publs., and others, Houston, 1979-85; pres. Savage Designs, Houston, 1985-88; coordinating cons. author programs U. Calif., Santa Barbara, 1985; rare book, manuscript cataloguer, writer Randall House Rare Books. Book critic, Houston Post, 1973-74; creator notecards, Neiman-Marcus Dept. Stores; writer Bicentennial play, 1976, Houston Pub. Schs. (now in Nat. Archives). Mem. Santa Barbara Com. on Fgn. Rels., 1986—; founder, coordinator Reach to Recovery Program, Am. Cancer Soc., Tarrant County, 1970-72. Mem. Jr. League, The Asia Soc. (adv. com., fin. chmn. Houston chpt., 1984-85). Republican. Unitarian. Home and Office: PO Box 5789 Santa Barbara CA 93150

BARRY, WILLIAM PATRICK, military officer; b. Boston, Aug. 1, 1957; s. John Joseph III and Esther Marie (Doherty) B.; m. Monica Marie Fournier. BS, U.S. Air Force Acad., 1979; MA in Polit. Sci., Stanford U., 1987. Commd. 2d lt. USAF, 1979, advanced through grades to capt., 1983; student pilot USAF, Williams AFB, Ariz., 1979-80; aircraft comdr. 42d Air Refueling Squadron USAF, Loring AFB, Maine, 1980-84; instr. pilot, exec. officer 509th Air Refueling Squadron USAF, Pease AFB, N.H., 1984-86; instr. dept. polit. sci. USAF Acad., Colorado Springs, Colo., 1987-89, asst. prof., 1989—. Named one of Outstanding Young Men of Am., Montgomery, Ala., 1986. Mem. Internat. Studies Assn. Office: USAF Acad Dept Polit Sci Colorado Springs CO 80918

BARSAN, RICHARD EMIL, oral surgeon; b. Selma, Ala., Dec. 18, 1945; s. Emil and Letitia (Dobrin) B.; m. Sandra Sherrick, June 22, 1974; children: Kelly Lynn, Robert Scott. BS in Chem. Engring., U. Cin., 1968; DDS, Ohio State U., 1979. Diplomate Am. Bd. Oral and Maxillofacial Surgery. Chem. engr. various cos., 1968-76; resident VA Hosp., Sepulveda, Calif., 1979-80; resident in oral and maxillofacial surgery La. State U., New Orleans, 1980-84; pvt. practice, La Jolla, Calif., 1984—. Pres. dental class, 1985—, mem. student council Ohio State U., 1978-79. Chrysler scholar U. Cin., 1964. Fellow Am. Assn. Oral and Maxillofacial Surgeons; mem. ADA, Calif. Dental Assn., San Diego County Dental Soc. (bd. dirs. 1988—), So. Calif. Soc. Oral and Maxillofacial Surgeons, Paul Revere Study Club (pres. 1988), Toastmasters (pres. La Jolla chpt. 1988), Omicron Kappa Upsilon. Republican. Office: 470 Nautilus St Ste 212 La Jolla CA 92037

BARSDATE, MARY KATHRYN, educator; b. Windber, Pa., Apr. 28, 1933; d. Stephen and Kathryn (Shuster) Haschak; m. Robert John Barsdate, June 9, 1959; children: Lory Ann, Kelly Joan. BA, Allegheny Coll., 1955, MA, 1960. Cert. tchr., Pa. Tchr. pub. schs., Pa., 1955-62; sec. dept. linguistics U. Alaska, Fairbanks, 1966; lectr. U. Alaska, 1966-67; instr. Am. ednl. complex Cen. Tex. Coll., Ft. Wainwright, Alaska, 1987--; critic tchr. U. Pitts.,1960-62; tutor, Fairbanks, 1968—; ind. editor, Fairbanks, 1977—. Vice chmn. Alaska Gov.'s State Adv. Coun. Libraries, 1989—; vice chmn. Fairbanks North Star Borough Library Commn., 1985-88, chmn., 1983-85; bd. dirs. Arts Alaska, Inc., Anchorage, 1983—, exec. com., 1985—; bd. dirs. adv. council KUAC TV-FM Pub. Broadcasting, Fairbanks, 1982-88, chmn., 1984-88; founder Fairbanks Montessori Assn., 1966-71; coord. Alaska State High Sch. Debate-Forensics Tournaments, 1984; trustee, sec.-treas.Library Found., Noel Wien Pub. Libr., Fairbanks, 1979—. Recipient Gov.'s Award for Arts, 1986. Mem. AAUW, Nat. Assn. Pub. TV Stas. (lay rep. bd. dels. 1984-88), Alaska State Coun. Arts (v.p. 1981-83), Assn. Alaska Sch. Bds. (v.p. 1977-78), Literacy Coun. Alaska, Fairbanks Arts Assn. (sec. 1970-79), Phi Beta Kappa. Republican. Carpatho-Russian Orthodox. Home and Office: PO Box 80174 Fairbanks AK 99708

BARSIS, EDWIN HOWARD, physicist; b. N.Y.C., June 28, 1940; s. Morris J. and Rose Barsis; children: James, Benjamin. BEP, Cornell U., 1963, MS, 1965, PhD, 1967. Mem. tech. staff Sandia Nat. Labs., Livermore, Calif., 1967-69; supr. applied physics Sandia Nat. Labs., Livermore, 1969-75, supr. advanced weapons div., 1975-77; mgr. electronic subsystems dept. Sandia Nat. Labs., Albuquerque, 1977-88, dir. computer sci. and math., 1986—; chmn. bd. dirs. Urologics, Inc., Albuquerque, 1984—. Contbr. articles to profl. jours. Capt. C.E., U.S. Army, 1967-69. Mem. Am. Phys. Soc. Home: 1538 Catron Ave SE Albuquerque NM 87123 Office: Sandia Nat Labs PO Box 5800 Albuquerque NM 87185

BARSKY, MARTIN, editor, publisher; b. Phila., Jan. 26, 1927; s. Philip and Mollie (Cohen) B.; children: Larry, Steve, Laura. Grad. high sch., Phila. Advt. mgr. Kiddie City Stores, Phila., 1954; sta. mgr., producer for various radio and TV stas. Pa., Mont., Calif., 1955-70; founder, editor, pub. So. Calif. Retailer, Los Angeles, 1971-81; owner, editor, pub. Retailer News, Anaheim, Calif., 1981-88; pres., pub. Video Software Dealer News, Los Angeles, 1984-86, Rental Dealer News, Orange, Calif., 1987—; ptnr. Am. Mktg. Assn., Orange. Producer Folk Music Theatre, 1967; contbr. articles to profl. jours. Bd. dirs. City of Hope Consumer Electronics, Los Angeles, 1987-88, pres., 1985-86. Served as sgt. USAAF, 1943-45. Recipient Cert. Appreciation Am. Legion, 1968, Outstanding Contributions award Associated Vol. Buyers, 1977, Outstanding Contributions award United Stores Inc., 1980. Mem. Soc. Profl. Journalists, Electronics Reps. Republican. Jewish. Home: 13490 Prospector Ct Victorville CA 92392 Office: Target Pub 249 E Emerson Ave #G Orange CA 92665

BARTEL, ARTHUR GABRIEL, educational administrator, city official; b. San Francisco, Oct. 20, 1934; s. Irving Peter and Elian Leah (Barker) B.; m. Dottie Lu Smith, Dec. 14, 1963 (dec. Apr. 1972); children: Brian Blake, Scott Michael. Student, San Jose State Coll., 1952-54; BS, U. Calif., Berkeley, 1957; postgrad., U. So. Calif., 1968-70; MA, Pepperdine U., 1973. Cert. FAA air traffic controller, 1957-77, naval flight officer, 1965; lic. standard tchr., life standard service, community coll. chief coll. adminstrv. officer, life community coll. supr., life community coll. instr., Calif. Commd. 2d lt. USMC, 1957, advanced through grades to maj., 1967; comdg. officer VMFA-314 Fighter-Attack Squadron USMC, El Toro, Calif., 1970-72; ret. USMC, 1977; gen. mgr. Nieuport 17 Restaurant, Santa Ana, Calif., 1977-78; pres., chief exec. officer High Flight Inc., Hanford, San Diego, Calif., 1978-81; teaching vice prin. Armona (Calif.) Union Elem. Sch., 1982-84, tchr. sci. and lang. arts., 1981-84; curriculum cons. Kings County Supt. Schs., Hanford, 1984-86, program specialist, 1986--; councilman City of Hanford, 1986--; area coordinator U. San Diego, 1987--; MayorCity of Hanford, 1988; mem. bd. San Joaquin Valley Writing Project, 1984-86. Vice chmn. Hanford Planning Commn., 1982-86. Decorated Air medal, Meritorious Service medal; Vietnam Cross of Galantry with Palm Combat Action Ribbon. Fellow U. Calif., Irvine, 1985; mem. Assn. Calif. Sch. Adminstrs., Calif. Soc. Program Specialists, DAV (life), Retired Officers Assn., Hanford C. of C., Delta Upsilon (life). Office: Kings County Supt Schs Kings Govt Ctr Hanford CA 93230

BARTEL, SHERYL JUNE, anesthesiologist; b. Portland, Oreg., Oct. 21, 1949; d. Walter Lawrence and Joan Vivian (Dick) B.; m. L.E. Christopher Mott, june 14, 1976; 1 child, Emily M. BA, Linfield Coll., 1971; postgrad., Wash. State U., 1971-72; BS in Med. Tech., U. Oreg., 1973, MD, 1977. Diplomate Am. Bd. Anesthesiology. Commd. 2d lt. U.S. Army, 1977; advanced through grades to maj., intern Brooke Army Med. Ctr., San Antonio, 1977-78; resident in anesthesia Letterman Army Med. Ctr., San Francisco, 1978-81; chief anesthesia service Gen. Leonard Wood Army Community Hosp., Ft. Leonard Wood, Mo., 1981-83; chief ast. chief anesthesia service Eisenhower Army Med. Ctr., Ft. Gordon, Ga., 1983-85; resigned 1985; staff anesthesiologist Skagit Valley Hosp., Mt. Vernon, Wash., 1985—, United Gen. Hosp., Sedro Woolley, Wash., 1986—. Mem. Am. Soc. Anesthesiology, Am. Soc. Regional Anesthesia, AMA, Wash. State Soc. Anesthesia, Wash. State Med. Assn. Office: Anesthesia Svc Inc 313 13th St Mount Vernon WA 98273

BARTELS, DONALD HOYT, design director; b. Kansas City, Mo., June 7, 1948; s. Rayburn Walker Bartels and Cleomae (Tennant) Howell; m. Nancy Ellen Smith, June 22, 1978; 1 child, Christopher Grant. BFA, Kansas City Art Inst., 1970. Designer Anspach Grossman Portugal, Inc., N.Y.C., 1976-80; sr. designer Saul Bass-Herb Yager Assocs., Los Angeles, 1981-82; project dir. Design West, Inc., Irvine, Calif., 1982-84; dir. design Landor Assocs., San Francisco, 1984—. Home: 608 Santa Rosa Ave Berkeley CA 94707 Office: Landor Assocs 1001 Front St San Francisco CA 94111

BARTELT, PAUL DOUGLAS, sports agent; b. L.A., Sept. 13, 1960; s. Kenneth Paul and Doris May (Reedy) B. BA in Communications, U. So. Calif., 1985. Asst. editor Rams Score mag., Laguna Beach, Calif., 1980-82; asst. dir. pub. rels. NFL L.A. Raiders, El Segundo, Calif., 1982-83; asst. editor CIF Sports mag., Laguna Beach, 1983-84; pres. Chain Trucking Co., Long Beach, Calif., 1984—; pres. Pro Sports Mgmt., Orange, Calif., 1989—. Sports editor Trojan Columns mag., 1980-82, Newport Ensign newspaper, 1986; corr. Daily Pilot newspaper, 1985-88; contbr. articles to L.A. Lakers Hoop mag., Dallas Cowboy Weekly. Active children's hosp. support group Admiralty Club, Newport Beach, 1983. Republican. Roman Catholic. Home: 15 Deerwood Ln Newport Beach CA 92660 Office: Pro Sports Mgmt 701 S Parker #7300 Orange CA 92668

BARTFIELD, WILLIAM, food products executive; b. Leeds, Eng., Mar. 6, 1932; came to U.S. 1978; s. Isaac and Emily (Goldstein) B.; m. Joyce Esme, Aug. 19, 1978; children: Andrea, Philip Daniel. Grad. high sch., Leeds. Ptnr. Bartfield & Co., Leeds, 1956-67; mng. dir. Allways Stores, Ltd., Preston Lances, Eng., 1967-76, Rave Stores, Ltd., Johannesburg, Republic of South Africa, 1978—; pres. Prize Frize, Inc., Palm Springs, Calif., 1981—. Patentee in field. Fellow Inst. Chartered Accts., Inst. Mktg. Assns. Jewish. Home: 3752B Bogert Tr Palm Springs CA 92264 Office: Prize Frize Inc 68350 Commercial Rd Cathedral City CA 92234

BARTH, DAVID VICTOR, technical supervisor; b. Tulsa, Sept. 23, 1942; s. Vincent David and Norma (Bell) B. BS summa cum laude, Met. State Coll., Denver, 1977; MS, U. No. Colo., 1982. Programming mgr. Am. Nat. Bank, Denver, 1967-72; cons. Colo. Farm Bur. Ins. Corp., Denver, 1972; systems analyst Mid-Continent Computer Services, Denver, 1972-73; programming mgr. Bayly Corp., Denver, 1973-75; project leader Cobe Labs. Inc., Denver, 1976-84; part-time tchr. Met. State Coll., 1982-83; systems analyst Affiliated Banks Service Co., Denver, 1985-87; broker Van Schaak & Co., Denver, 1985; tech. supr. Affiliated Banks Service Co., Denver, 1987—, 1987—; freelance flight inst., 1977—; real estate broker, Van Schaack and Co., Denver, 1985—. Vol. Am. Red Cross, 1987—; Served with USN, 1961-66. Mem. Soc. Info. Mgmt. (editor newsletter 1983), Boulder (Colo.) Area Radio Club, Aurora (Colo.) Repeater Assn., Flying Circus Skating Club. Republican. Home: 509 S Cody St Lakewood CO 80226 Office: Affiliated Banks Svc Co 445 E 124th Ave Thornton CO 80241

BARTH, THOMAS GLEN, rehabilitation educator; b. Lamar, Colo., May 24, 1949; s. Glen Leroy and Mary Maxine (Gebhardt) B.; m. Linda Kay Neumiller, May 7, 1976. BS in Rehabilitation, U. No. Colo., 1975; MS in Rehabilitation, U. Wis., Menomonie, 1977. Cert. learning disabilities, counseling, vocational evaluation. Vocational evaluator Northridge Hosp. Med. Ctr., Northridge, Calif., 1977-78; counselor Northridge Hosp. Med. Ctr., 1978-79, project dir., 1979-83; vocational evaluator Oxnard Coll., Oxnard, Calif., 1984—; assessment specialist Oxnard Coll., 1986-88, adaptive computer specialist, 1988—; cons. Calif. State Dept. Edn., Sacramento, 1986—. Mem. Calif. Assn. of Post-Secondary Educators of the Disabled. Office: Oxnard Coll High Tech Ctr 4000 S Rose Ave Oxnard CA 93033

BARTHOLOMAUS, VICKIE LEE, composer, researcher; b. Cumberland, Md., Mar. 19, 1947; d. Paul William Davidson and Evelyn Elizabeth (Wright) Davidson/Kelley; m. Michael G. Ruppenkamp, Feb. 13, 1966 (div. 1971); m. Richard Charles Bartholomaus, Aug. 24, 1973. AA in Arts and Scis., Frederick (Md.) Community Coll., 1979; BS in Mgmt., Rutgers U., 1980. Lab. tech. Sacred Heart Hosp., Cumberland, 1966-72; med. lab. tech. DADE div. Am. Hosp. Supply, Miami, Fla., 1973-74; clin. lab. tech. Gillette Med. Evaluation Labs., Rockville, Md., 1974-75; lab. tech. II Litton Bionetics, Frederick Cancer Research Ctr., 1975-76; med. lab. tech. BioDynamics, Inc., East Millstone, N.J., 1977-79; media buyer Mapes & Ross Advt. & Mktg. Research, Princeton, N.J., 1981-82; acct. coordinator Eisaman, Johns & Laws Advt. Inc., N.Y.C., Los Angeles, 1982-84; acctg. asst. Equity Advt., N.Y.C., 1984; composer, producer Victoria Prodns., Lambertville, N.J., 1984-86, Oceanside, Calif., 1986—. Composer 16 songs. Mem. Lambertville Hist. Soc., 1981-84, Rep. Nat. Com. (life). Mem. ASCAP (assoc.), Soc. Advancement Med. Tech. (charter), Songwriters' Guild, Am. PEN Women (assoc.), Smithsonian Assn. Home and Office: 2397 Carriage Circle Oceanside CA 92056

BARTHOLOMEW, HELEN MARIE, community health educator; b. Darlington, Pa., Apr. 8, 1937; d. William Emerson and Goldie Mae (Mankin) Forsythe. BS in Nursing, Ariz. State U., 1968; MS in Nursing, U. Ariz., 1976. RN, Pa. Office nurse Tom R. Miller II, Edinboro, Pa., 1958-60; operating rm. supr. NW Hosp., Glendale, Ariz., 1960-61; sch. nurse Glend Elem. Sch. Dist., Glendale, 1961-66; faculty assoc. Ariz. State U. Sch. Nursing, Tempe, 1968-70; dir. nursing in-svc. Boswell Meml. Hosp., Sun City, Ariz., 1970-72, dir. coordinated home health svcs., 1973-78, dir. nursing, 1978-79; dir. community edn. Sun Health, Sun City, 1979—, dir. coordinated home health svcs., 1981-87. Bd. dirs. Camelot Hospice, Peoria, Ariz., 1987—, Sun Cities Area Community Coun., 1980-85. Mem. Alzheimers Disease and Related Disorders Assn. (pres. 1984-87, founding dir. 1981-87), Sierra. Democrat. Office: Sun Health Community Edn 10503 Thunderbird Blvd #15 Sun City AZ 85351

BARTHOLOMEW, HENRY HOMER, surgeon; b. Fayette, Utah, Mar. 13, 1921; s. Henry L. and Ireta (Rallison) B.; m. Betty Ann Deakin, Mar. 6, 1953 (dec. 1973); children: Brent H., Susan, Diane, David S.; m. Ellen Nielsen, Apr. 18, 1977. BA, Brigham Young U., 1946; MD, U. Pa., 1949. Diplomate, Am. Bd. Ophthalmology, Am. Bd. Med. Examiners. Intern Latter-Saints Hosp., Salt Lake City, 1949-50; resident in ophthalmology Stanford U., San Francisco, 1953-56, instr. dept. ophthalmology, 1955-56; pvt. practice Salt Lake City, 1956-88, ret., 1988; chief dept. ophthalmology Salt Lake Clinic, 1961-88; cons. World-Wide Missionary Dept., Latter-Day Saints Ch., 1988—; mem. staff, Latter-day Saints Hosp., Primary Children's Med. Ctr.; clin. prof. ophthalmology, U. Utah, Salt Lake City, 1957—. Lt. USN, 1951-53, Korea. Fellow ACS, Am. Acad. Ophthalmology; mem. AMA, Pacific Coast Ophthalmology Soc. Mormon. Home: 1456 Roxbury Rd Salt Lake City UT 84108

BARTHOLOMEW, LEE HOUCK, lawyer; b. Evanston, Ill., Apr. 15, 1950; s. John Bryson and Dorothy Ellen (Houck) B.; m. Debra M. Creech, May 2, 1981; children: Kelly, Tracy. BA, U. Wis., 1972; JD, U. Colo., 1975. Bar: Colo., 1975. Pvt. practice Denver, 1976-80; ptnr. Bartholomew and Christiano, Denver, 1980—. Mem. Colo. Bar Assn., Denver Bar Assn. (corps. com. 1979—). Republican. Home: 389 Lafayette Denver CO 80218

BARTHOLOMEW, SHIRLEY KATHLEEN, county official; b. Marysville, Wash., Jan. 26, 1924; d. Clarence E. and Mary (Hall) B. Grad. high sch., Marysville. News dir. Sta. KRKO, Everett, Wash., 1943-80; sec., dir. Everett Broadcasting, Inc., 1955-76, First Pacific Broadcasting, Everett, 1976-80; county councilwoman Snohomish County, Wash., 1981—; chmn. Snohomish County Coun., 1987-88. Editor, reporter wire svc. reports (AP Mng. Editor award 1959, 78). Recipient Outstanding Contbn. award Wash. State Press Women, 1968; named to Edward R. Morrow-Wash. Hall of Fame, 1980. Mem. Nat. Assn. Elected Women, Wash. State Assn. Counties Republican. Home: 1525 5th St Marysville WA 98270 Office: Snohomish County Council Everett WA 98201

BARTICK, BARBARA JEAN, research company executive; b. N.Y.C., Apr. 18, 1943; d. Frederich Louis and Jeannette (Bradley) DeSanti; m. Brian A. Moore, May 7, 1966 (div. 1974); children: Brian, Brad; m. Gary A. Bartick, Dec. 10, 1978; 1 child, Beth. BS, Ohio State U., 1965; MS, UCLA, 1980. Cert. tchr., Mass., community coll. tchr., Calif. Dir. day treatment Orange County (Calif.) Dept. Mental Health, 1974-78; v.p. fin. Keep It Simple Software, Inc., Newport Beach, Calif., 1982-84; cons. Pacific Sanitary Co., Vallejo, Calif., 1985-87; pres., chief exec. officer Advanced Viral Rsch., Inc., Santa Ana, Calif., 1988-89, also dir.; pres. Elder Case Mgmt. Co., Inc., 1989—; bd. dirs. Jellico, Inc., Montecito, Calif. Bd. dirs. Orange County Chamber Orch., Yorba Linda, 1986-87. Mem. Am. Occupational Therapy Assn. Home: 175 Olive Mill Ln Montecito CA 93108 Office: Advanced Viral Rsch Inc 175 Olive Mill Ln Montecito CA 93108

BARTLETT, DUANE EDWARD, construction company executive; b. Marshalltown, Iowa, Nov. 8, 1947; s. Alva Allan and Viola (Slifer) B.; m. Beverly Jean Troutner, Dec. 5, 1970; 1 child, Kurt Edward. BSCE, Iowa State U., 1969. Resident constrn. engr. Iowa Dept. Transp., Ames, 1970-74; project mgr. Rohlin Industries, Des Moines, 1974-80; v.p. Terrain Inc., Glendale, Calif., 1980-84, Moulder Bros., Glendale, 1984-86; pres., bd. dirs. Earthmark Industries Inc., Glendale, 1986—; bd. dir. Terrain Inc., Glendale. Office: Earthmark Industries 1705 Lake St Glendale CA 91201

BARTLETT, ELIZABETH (ROBERTA), editor, writer; b. N.Y., July 20, 1921; d. Lewis Winters and Charlotte (Rose) Field; m. Paul A. Bartlett, Apr., 19, 1943. BS, Tchr. Coll., 1941; postgrad., Columbia U., 1941-43. Instr. Speech & Theatre Dept., Dallas, 1946-49; dir. Creative Writers Assn., New Sch. for Social Research, N.Y., 1955; asst. prof. San Jose State Univ., 1959-60; assoc. prof. Univ. Calif., 1960-64; poetry editor ETC Review of Gen. Semantics, San Francisco, 1963-76; lect. San Diego State Univ., 1979-81; Lect. Univ. San Diego English Dept., 1978-80. Author 17 books of poetry. Mem. Poetry Soc. Am., Internat. Soc. Gen. Semantics, Internat. Women Writers Guild, PEN, Authors Guild. Democrat. Home: 2875 Cowley Way #1302 San Diego CA 92110

BARTLETT, (HERBERT) HALL, motion picture producer, director; b. Kansas City, Mo., Nov. 27, 1929; s. Paul Dana and Alice (Hiestand) B.; m. Lupita Ferrer, Apr. 30, 1977 (div.); children: Cathy Bartlett Lynch, Laurie Bartlett Schrader. BA, Yale U., 1948. Owner, operator Hall Bartlett Prodn., Los Angeles, 1960—; pres. Jonathan Livingston Seagull Mcht. Co.; bd. dirs. James Doolittle Theatre, Hollywood, Calif., founder Music Ctr., Los Angeles. Producer, dir. (films) Navajo, 1953, Crazylegs, 1958, Unchained, 1957, All the Young Men, 1961, Durango, 1959, Zero Hour, 1961, The Caretakers, 1963, A Global Affair, 1968, Changes, 1968, Sandpit Generals, 1971, Jonathan Livingston Seagull, 1973, The Children of Sanchez, 1979, Catch Me If You Can, 1988, The Search of Zubin Mehta, 1975, The Cleo Laine Story, 1978, Comeback, 1983; author: The Rest of Our Lives, 1987. Mem. Friends of Library, Los Angeles, Cinema Circulus. Served to lt. USNR, 1949-51. Recipient 11 Acad. award nominations, Film Festival awards from Cannes 1961, 63, Venice 1959, 65, Edinburgh 1952, San Sebastian 1969, Moscow 1971, NCCJ 1955, Fgn. Press awards. Mem. Motion Picture Acad. Arts and Scis., Acad. TV Arts and Scis., Phi Beta Kappa. Republican. Presbyterian. Clubs: Bel-Air Country, Kansas City Country. Home: 861 Stone Canyon Rd Bel Air CA 90077 Office: 9200 Sunset Blvd Ste 908 Los Angeles CA 90069

BARTLETT, RICHARD WRELTON, manufacturing executive; b. San Diego, Mar. 25, 1939; s. Richard L. Bartlett and Bernice (Clarke) Boyer; m. Brenda Kaye Reagan, Apr. 16, 1965 (div. Jan 1987); children: Richard W. II, Bretley W. BSME, Calif. State Poltechnic U., 1960; MBA, SUNY, Buffalo, 1972. Test engr. Aerojet-Gen., Sacramento, Calif., 1960-65; engr. mgr. Bell Aerospace, Niagara Falls, N.Y., 1965-73; controller Xerox Corp., Rochester, N.Y., 1973-84; controller, dir of Mgmt.Info. Svcs. Bendix Corp., Dayton, Ohio, 1984-87; v.p. controller Transp. Mfg. Corp., Roswell, N.Mex., 1987—; vol. cost acct. Grandview Hosp., Dayton, 1987. Capt. United Fund drive, Xerox, Rochester, 1983; mem. fin. com. Unitarian Ch., Rochester, 1982-83; capt. U.S. Savs. Bonds, 1988—; bd. dirs. Roswell YMCA, 1989; corp. giving com. United Fund, Roswell, N.Mex., 1988. Mem. Am. Prodn. Inventory Control Soc., Roswell Running Club. Republican. Unitarian. Office: Transp Mfg Corp PO Box 5670 Roswell NM 88202-5670

BARTLETT, STEVEN THADE, aerospace engineer; b. Glendale, Calif., Sept. 13, 1962; s. Ronald Thade Bartlett and Frances Mae (Bailey) Arrington. BS in Physics, Calif. State U., Long Beach, 1985, postgrad., 1986-89. Retail salesman Tandy Corp., Beverly Hills, Calif., 1982-85; aerospace systems engr. McDonnell Douglas Corp., Huntington Beach, Calif., 1986—. Mem. Nat. Space Soc., Aircraft Owners and Pilots Assn., L.A. Sci. Fantasy Soc. Libertarian. Office: McDonnell Douglas Space Co 5301 Bolsa Huntington Beach CA 92647

BARTLETT, THOMAS ALVA, educational administrator; b. Salem, Oreg., Aug. 20, 1930; s. Cleave Wines and Alma (Hanson) B.; m. Mary Louise Bixby, Mar. 20, 1954; children: Thomas Glenn, Richard A., Paul H. Student, Willamette U., 1947-49, DCL (hon.), 1986; A.B., Stanford U., 1951, Ph.D., 1959; M.A. (Rhodes scholar), Oxford U., 1953; L.H.D. (hon.), Colgate U., 1977, Mich. State U., 1978, Union Coll., 1979; D.C.L. (hon.), Pusan Nat. U., Korea, 1985, U. Ala., 1986. Mem. U.S. Permanent Mission to UN, 1956-63; advisor Gen. Assembly Dels., 1956-63; pres. Am. U., Cairo, 1963-69, Colgate U., Hamilton, N.Y., 1969-77, Assn. Am. Univs., Washington, 1977-82; chancellor U. Ala. System, 1982-89, Oreg. State System of Higher Edn. Office, Eugene, 1989—; dir. Am. Cast Iron Pipe Co.; mem. UAR-U.S. Ednl. Exchange Commn., 1966-69; mem. Task Force on Financing Higher Edn. in N.Y. State (Keppel Commn.), 1972-73; chmn. Commn. Ind. Colls. and Univs. N.Y., 1974-76; bd. dirs. Nat. Assn. Ind. Colls. and Univs., 1975-76; trustee Univs. Field Staff Internat., 1985-87; mem. NASA Comml. Space Adv. Com., 1988. Mem. nat. bd. examining Chaplains Episcopal Ch.; trustee Gen. Theol. Sem., 1977-82, Am. U. in Cairo, 1978—, U.S.-Japan Found., 1988—. Mem. Council Fgn. Relations, Phi Beta Kappa. Clubs: Cosmos (Washington); Century Assn. (N.Y.C.). Home: 2237 Spring Blvd Eugene OR 97403 Office: Oreg State System Higher Edn/Office of Chancellor PO Box 3175 Eugene OR 97403-0175

BARTLETT, THOMAS HENRY, chemist; b. Great Falls, Mont., Jan. 1, 1931; s. Thomas Henry and Sophia (Stenseth) B.; m. Alice Kay Lee, Dec. 29, 1959 (div. Feb. 1962); one child, Brady; m. Iris Elaine Cooper, Aug. 25, 1967; children: Karleen, Elaine. BS, Coll. Great Falls, 1952; postgrad., U. Wash., 1953, LaSalle Extension U., 1958-63. Chemist Anaconda Co., Grest Falls, 1954-57, Am. Chrome Co., Nye, Mont., 1957-61; chief chemist Western Nuclear Inc., Jeffery City, Wyo., 1962-67; gen. mgr. Chem. and Geol. Labs., Casper, Wyo., 1967-76; pres., chief exec. officer WAMCO Lab. Inc., Casper, 1977—. Chmn., pres. Winter Meml. Presbyn. Ch., Casper, 1982—. Mem. ASTM. Lodge: Elks. Home: 3301 E 12th St Casper WY 82609 Office: WAMCO Lab Inc PO Box 2953 Casper WY 82602

BARTLETT, WILLIAM HOWARD, mortgage company executive; b. Huntington, W.Va., Aug. 9, 1950; s. William Howard and Ruby (Mae) B.; m. Frances Julie Leroy, Mar. 14, 1980; children: William Howard III, Rhonda Julie. AA, Fla. Jr. Coll., 1972. Program dir. Sta. WAIV-FM, Jacksonville, Fla., 1972-77, Sta. KISW-FM, Seattle, 1977-78; v.p. promotion Ariola Records, Beverly Hills, Calif., 1978-80; regional promotion dir. Capitol Records, Atlanta, 1980-83; nat. promotion dir. Capitol Records, Hollywood, Calif., 1983-87; cons. media various orgns., Northridge, Calif., 1989—; loan officer Uni Trust Mortage, Northridge, 1989—; cons. Global Satellite Network, L.A., 1987, Media Am., N.Y.C., 1987. Home: 19227-4 Index St Northridge CA 91326 Office: Uni Trust Mortgage 19524 Norohoff St #8A Northridge CA 91324

BARTOL, WALTER W., banker; b. Phoenix, June 24, 1931; s. Walter T. and Nora Mae (Trimble) B.; m. Betty Walker, Sept. 18, 1951; children: Thomas W., Nora Lisa, Walter Lynn. BS, U. Ariz., 1955. Mgr. Walker Feedyards, Glendale, Ariz., 1955-69; v.p. Valley Nat. Bank of Ariz., Phoenix, 1969-88; pres. Union Devel. Co., Inc., Phoenix, 1965—. Treas. Am. Nat. Livestock Show, Phoenix, 1988-89. Sgt. USAF, 1951-52. Mem. Elks. Republican. Office: Union Devel Co Inc 4546 N 17 Ave Phoenix AZ 85015

BARTON, ANN ELIZABETH, financial executive; b. Long Lake, Mich., Sept. 8, 1923; d. John and Inez Mabel (Morse) Seaton; student Mt. San Antonio Coll., 1969-71, Adrian Coll., 1943, Citrus Coll., 1967, Golden Gate U., 1976, Coll. Fin. Planning, 1980-82; m. H. Kenneth Barton, Apr. 3, 1948; children—Michael, John, Nancy. Tax cons., real estate broker, Claremont, Calif., 1967-72, Newport Beach, Calif., 1972-74; v.p., officer Putney, Barton, Assos., Inc., Walnut Creek, Calif., 1975—; bd. dirs., officer Century Fin. Enterprises, Inc., Century Adv. Corp., F.F.A., Inc., SKAIFE & Co. Cert. fin. planner. Mem. Internat. Assn. Fin. Planners, (registered investment advisor), Calif. Soc. Enrolled Agts., Nat. Assn. Enrolled Agts., Nat. Soc. Public Accts., Inst. Cert. Fin. Planners. Office: Putney Barton Assocs Inc 1705 N California Blvd Walnut Creek CA 94596

BARTON, CARRIE MAXEY, bassist; b. North Hollywood, Calif., July 19, 1954; d. George Harold and Maxine Elizabeth (Barker) B. Student, Calif. State U., Northridge. Bass player with numerous rock, pop and soul groups for albums, tours and telev ision presentations; performances on numerous albums. Presenter benefit concerts for AIDS, Am. Indians, world peace, other causes.

BARTON, GERALD GAYLORD, land development company executive; b. Oklahoma City, 1931. Student, U. Okla. Pres., chief exec. officer, dir. Landmark Land Co., Carmel, Calif.; also pres., dir. Barton Theatre Co.; bd. dirs. LSB Industries, Inc. Office: Landmark Land Co Inc 100 Clock Tower Place Ste 200 Carmel CA 93923 *

BARTON, PAUL DOUGLAS, group operations manager, photographer; b. Southampton, N.Y., Aug. 9, 1960. BA in Psychology, U. So. Calif., 1984. Night supr. U. So. Calif. Copy Ctr., L.A., 1980-83; reprographics dept. mgr. Pandick Press, Inc., L.A., 1983-85; sr. prodn. coord. Pandick Technologies, Inc., L.A., 1985, prodn. mgr., 1985-86, group ops. mgr., 1986—. Mem. Internat. Freelance Photographers Orgn., Summit. Democrat. Office: Pandick Technologies Inc 1901 S Flower St Los Angeles CA 90007

BARTON, WILLIAM CLYDE, JR., oil company executive; b. Cushing, Okla., Nov. 23, 1931; s. William Clyde and Hazel Jean (Morrow) B.; m. Doris Winnie Casey, Aug. 6, 1951; children: Deborah Sue, Richard Clyde, Charles Wayne. BS in Petroleum Engring., U. Okla, 1954. Div. reservoir engr. Pure Oil Co., Houston, 1963-66; with Union Oil Co. Calif., 1966—, regional engring. mgr., Los Angeles, 1968-75, dir. prodn. ops. internat. div., Los Angeles, 1975-83, v.p., Thailand, 1983-86, dir. Overseas Subs., 1986-87, v.p. internat., 1988—; mem. indsl. adv. com. Sch. Petroleum and Geol. Engring., U. Okla. Served as officer USAF, 1954-56. Decorated D.S.M.; registered profl. engr., Tex. Mem. Soc. Petroleum Engrs. (pres. 1982). Republican. Clubs: Toastmasters, Petroleum (Los Angeles). Office: 1201 W Fifth Los Angeles CA 90017

BARTON, WILLIAM HENRY, II, insurance executive; b. Portland, Oreg., May 24, 1921; s. William Henry and Louise Cardwell (Chalmers) B.; m. Mavis Fortier, Aug. 22, 1942; children: William Henry III, Steven John, Dana Barton Cress. BA, Oreg. State U., 1946. Broadcaster Sta. KBND, Bend, Oreg., 1942-42; broadcaster, mgr. sales Stas. KOIN-KALE Radio, Bend, Oreg., 1943-50; prin., agy. mgr. Barton & Assocs., Portland, 1950—. Active Rehab. Inst., Friends of Timberline, Oreg. Hist. Soc., Japanese Garden Soc., Oreg. Zool. Soc., Oreg. Estate Planning Council; mem. bldg. com. Trinity Episc. Ch., Portland, chmn. canvas com.; vestry mem. various Episc. chs., Bend, Oreg. and Yakima, Wash.; bd. dirs. DePaul Treatment Ctr. Named Outstanding Jr. Citizen, Jr. C. of C., Bend, 1950; recipient Nat. Quality award. Mem. Nat. Assn. Life Underwriters, Oreg. Assn. Life Underwriters, Lincoln Nat. Pres.'s Club (mem. pres.'s cabinet), Alano Club. Home: 3230 SW 48th Ave Portland OR 97221 Office: Barton & Assocs 1221 SW Yamhill #100 Portland OR 97205

BARTON, WILLIAM THOMAS, state senator; b. Salt Lake City, Feb. 18, 1933; s. Doran Warr and Beatrice (Orullian) B.; m. Karen Larson, May 26, 1958; children: Thomas Kim, Allison, Doran Lynn. Student, U. Utah, 1951-52, Utah Tech. Coll., 1955-56. Owner retail bldg. materials co. West Valley City, Utah; Utah state sen. Salt Lake City. Pres. Taxpayers for Accountable Govt., Salt Lake County, 1986—; chmn. Granger-Hunter Community Council, 1977. Mem. West Valley C. of C. (pres. 1978), Jaycees (pres. Granger chpt. 1965, Utah v.p. 1966, nat. dir. Utah 1967), Lions (pres. Granger club 1963-64). Republican. Mem. LDS Ch. Home and Office: 3940 W 4100 S West Valley City UT 84120

BARTSCH, RICHARD ALAN, school psychologist; b. Mpls., Dec. 31, 1950; s. Carl H. and Carol J. (Brusletten) B.; m. Nancy Rae Anderson, Aug. 26, 1972; children: Marcy, Jonathan, Jeffrey. BA, U. Minn., Duluth, 1973; MS in Edn., U. Wis., Superior, 1975. Cert. sch. psychologist, Mont.; nat. cert. sch. psychologist. Sch. psychologist Billings (Mont.) Pub. Schs., 1975—, supr. psychol. svcs., 1979—. Mem. Nat. Assn. Sch. Psychologists (elected del. 1989-91), Mont. Assn. Sch. Psychologists (treas. 1980-82,). Home: 1804 S Mariposa Ln Billings MT 59102 Office: Billings Pub Schs 101 10th St W Billings MT 59102

BARTZATT, RONALD LEE, research biochemist, consultant; b. Lincoln, Nebr., Dec. 18, 1953; s. Frank Wright and Lorretta (Warta) B.; m. Patricia Ann Dockham, July 30, 1979 (div. Oct. 1983). BS, U. Nebr., 1978, MS, 1980, PhD, 1982. Cert. med. lab. technician. Research biochemist U. Nebr., Lincoln, 1983-84, Eppley Cancer Ctr., Omaha, 1984-85, Theodor Gildore Ctr., San Diego, 1985, U. Calif., San Diego, 1985—; cons. IRCS Med. Sci., Lancaster, Eng., 1985—. Author: Proceedings of ACS Symposia on Computer Data Analysis and Optimization; contbr. articles to profl. jours. Deacon Luth. Ch., San Diego. Served with U.S. Army, 1973-76. Towle Scholar U. Nebr., 1973; NIH fellow, 1984; grantee Nebr. Water Co., 1981. Mem. Am. Soc. Clin. Pathologists, Am. Chem. Soc., AAAS, Planetary Soc., Phi Lambda Upsilon. Republican. Office: U Nebr Vet Basic Sci Lincoln NE 68583

BARVICH, BEVERLY JOYCE, graphologist; b. St. Paul, Sept. 26, 1940; d. Harry M. and Crystal Elizabeth (Bevan) Harrold; m. Larry L. Barvich; children: Michelle Marie, Timothy Lawrence. Grad. high sch., Puyallup, Wash. Cert. graphologist. Owner BJB Handwriting Analysis, Modesto, Calif., 1981—; lectr. on graphology, 1984—. Contbr. articles to profl. jours. Mem. Am. Handwriting Analysis Found. (bd. dirs., hospitality chmn. 1983-86, historian 1986-88), Council Graphol. Socs., Erika Karoh's Inner Circle. Roman Catholic. Home and Office: 3400 Sullivan Ct #269 Modesto CA 95356

BARVILLE, REBECCA PENELOPE, teacher; b. Tulare, Calif., Nov. 7, 1936; m. David Leopold Barville, June 8, 1958; children: Mark, Becky, Curtis. BA, Simpson Coll., San Francisco, 1958; MA summa cum laude, Fresno State U., 1974. Cert. reading specialist, edn. adminstr., elem. tchr., Calif. Social worker Tulare County Welfare Dept., Porterville, Calif., 1961-63, San Bernadino Welfare, Ontario, Calif., 1963-65; tchr., reading specialist Pleasant View Sch., Porterville, 1969—. Pres. PTA, Lindsay, Calif., 1966-67. Fellow Delta Kappa Gamma; mem. AAUW (bd. dirs. 1974-83), Calif. Reading Assn. (sec. 1974), Pleasant View Educators Assn. (past pres., sec. 1985—). Republican. Presbyterian. Club: P.E.O. (v.p. 1986-87).

BASDEN, BARBARA HOLZ, psychology educator; b. Coeur d'Alene, Idaho, Feb. 10, 1940; d. Albert R. and Carol (Utter) Holz; m.David R. Basden, May 25, 1962; children: Leslie H., Derin E. BA, Coll. Idaho, 1962; PhD, U. Calif., Santa Barbara, 1969. Prof. psychology Calif. State U., 1969. Author: Psychology, 2nd edit., 1987, Memory, Memory & Aging, Memory & Hypnosis, 1987-89. Mem. Psychonomic Soc., Am. Psychol. Assn., Western Psychol. Assn. Office: Calif State U Dept Psychology Fresno CA 93740

BASEY, GLEN ROBERT, college president, minister; b. Caldwell, Idaho, Dec. 9, 1942; s. Charles Howard and Lois Jean (Hutchison) B.; m. Judith Jo Mc Farland, Aug. 9, 1965; children: Michelle Carol, Sharon Lynn, Jenine Marie. Student, San Jose Bible Coll., 1961-65; BA, NW Nazarene Coll., 1967; M Religious Edn., Emmanuel Sch. Religion, 1970; D Ministry, San Francisco Theol. Sem., 1975. Ordained minister Christian Ch., 1967. Minister Ardmore Ch. of Christ, Winston-Salem, N.C., 1967-70; instr. Winston-Salem Bible Coll., 1967-70; prof. Christian edn. Puget Sound Coll. the Bible, Edmonds, Wash., 1971-85; dir. Christian Edn. Seminars, Edmonds, 1972—; pvt. practice counseling Edmonds, 1972-81; interim minister Everett Cen. Christian Ch., Everett, Wash., 1980-81; preaching minister Shoreline Christian Ch., Seattle, 1981-84; acting pres. Puget Sound Coll. the Bible, 1983-84; pres. Puget Sound Christian Coll., Edmonds, 1985—. Mem. Assn. Profs. and Researchers in Christian Edn., Coll. Pres. Assn. Ind. Christian Ch. Colls. (mem. exec. com. 1988), Pioneer Bible Translators (bd. dirs. 1985—). Republican. Home: 1109 3d Ave S Edmonds WA 98020 Office: Puget Sound Christian Coll 410 4th Ave N Edmonds WA 98020

BASHFORD, WILLIAM L., travel company executive; b. Pasadena, Calif., July 22, 1925; s. William L. and Marguerite (Teague) B.; m. Rebekah Ann Baumgarten, May 18, 1975; children: William Randall, Gregg. BS, U. So. Calif., 1949; MA, U. Geneva, 1950. Regional mgr. Pepsi-Cola, Internat., N.Y.C., 1950-55; pres. Bashford Travel Corp., Fresno, Calif., 1955—. Author: Tourist Guide to Mexico, 1954; patentee bottling machine. Capt. C.E., AUS, 1942-45, ETO. Mem. Bus. Travel Network (bd. dirs. 1988-89).

BASICHIS, GORDON ALLEN, author, screenwriter; b. Phila., Aug. 23, 1947; s. Martin and Ruth (Gordon) B.; m. Marcia Hammond; 1 child, Casey James. BS, Temple U., 1969. Reporter Phila. Bull., 1969; writer, reporter Santa Fe News, 1971-72; with advt., pub. relations Jay Bernstein Pub. Relations, Los Angeles, 1978-80; screenwriter various studios, networks, Los Angeles, 1978-83; producer, dir. Big Sky, Inc., Sherman Oaks, Calif., 1980; screenwriter Metro Goldwyn Mayer Feature Films, Culver City, Calif., 1982-83; ind. writer 1983—; pres. Moonlight, Inc., Los Angeles, 1982—; research cons. various pubs. Author: Beautiful Bad Girl: The Vicki Morgan Story, 1985, (novel) Constant Travelers, 1978; producer, dir. (video documentary) Jerry: One Man's Triumph, 1980; screenwriter (feature film) Return of the Jersey Devil, 1988, various other projects. Mem. Dem. Nat. Com. Mem. Writers Guild Am. West, Am. Film Inst., Simon Wiesenthal Inst., Nat. Rifle Assn., Statue of Liberty/Ellis Island Found. Jewish. Office: PO Box 1511 Beverly Hills CA 90210

BASILE, PAUL LOUIS, JR., lawyer; b. Oakland, Calif., Dec. 27, 1945; s. Paul Louis and Roma Florence (Paris) B.; m. Linda Lou Paige, June 20, 1970; m. 2d Diane Chierichetti, Sept. 2, 1977. BA, Occidental Coll., 1968; postgrad. U. Wash., 1969; JD, UCLA, 1971. Bar: Calif. Supreme Ct. 1972, U.S. Ct. Appeals (9th cir.) 1972, U.S. Dist. Ct. (cen. dist.) Calif. 1972, U.S. Dist. Ct. (no. dist.) Calif. 1985, U.S. Supreme Ct. 1977, U.S. Tax Ct. 1977, U.S. Ct. Clms. 1978, U.S. Customs Ct. 1979, U.S. Ct. Customs and Patent Appeals 1979, U.S. Ct. Internat. Trade 1981. Assoc., Parker, Milliken, Kohlmeier, Clark & O'Hara, Los Angeles, 1971-72; corporate counsel TFI Cos., Inc., Irvine, Calif., 1972-73; sole practice, Los Angeles, 1973-80; ptnr., Basile & Siener, Los Angeles, 1980-86; ptnr. Clark & Trevithick, Los Angeles, 1986—; gen. counsel J.W. Brown, Inc., Los Angeles, Calif., 1980—, asst. sec., 1984—; sec., gen. counsel Souriau, Inc., Valencia, Calif., 1981—; v.p., sec., dir., gen. counsel Pvt. Fin. Assocs., Los Angeles, 1983—. Trustee, sec. Nat. Repertory Theatre Found., 1975—, mem. exec. com. 1976—; mem. fin. com., bd. dirs. Calif. Music Theatre, 1988—; active Los Angeles Olympic Organizing Com.; dir. March Dimes Birth Defects Found., Los Angeles County, 1982-87, exec. com. 1983-86, sec. 1985-86; active Ketchum Downtown YMCA, Vols. Am. L.A.; bd. dirs. Canadian Soc. Los Angeles, 1980-83, sec., 1982-83; dist. fin. chmn. Los Angeles Area council Boy Scouts Am., 1982-83; active numerous other civic orgns. Mem. ABA, Can.-Am. Bar Assn., Los Angeles County Bar Assn., Italian-Am. Lawyers Assn., Asia Pacific Lawyers Assn., Fgn. Trade Assn. So. Calif., Can. Calif. C. of C. (dir. 1980-89, 2d v.p. 1983-84, 1st v.p. 1984-85, pres. 1985-87), French-Am. C. of C. (councilor 1979-84, v.p. 1980, 82-84), Los Angeles Area C. of C. (dir. 1980-81), Grand Peoples Co. (bd. dirs., 1985—, chmn. bd. 1986—), Japan-Am. Soc. So. Calif., L.A. World Affairs Council, Rotary, Jonathan Club. Democrat. Baptist. Home: 3937 Beverly Glen Blvd Sherman Oaks CA 91423 Office: Clark & Trevithick 800 Wilshire Blvd 13th Fl Los Angeles CA 90017

BASINGER, RICHARD LEE, lawyer; b. Canton, Ohio, Nov. 24, 1941; s. Eldon R. and Alice M. (Bartholomew) B.; m. Rita Evelyn Gover, May 14, 1965; children: David A., Darron M. BA in Edn., Ariz. State U., 1963; postgrad. Macalester Coll., 1968-69; JD, U. Ariz., 1973. Bar: Ariz. 1973, U.S. Dist. Ct. Ariz. 1973, U.S. Tax Ct. 1977, U.S. Ct. Appeals (6th cir.) 1975, U.S. Ct. Appeals (9th cir.) 1976, U.S. Supreme Ct. 1977. Assoc. law offices, Phoenix, 1973-74; sole practice, Scottsdale, Ariz. 1974-75; mem., pres. Basinger & Assocs., P.C., Scottsdale, 1975-88, dir., pres. Basinger & Morga PC, 1987— . Contbr. articles to profl. jours. Bd. dirs. Masters Trail Ventures, Scottsdale, 1984-85, Here's Life, Ariz., Scottsdale, 1976—; precinct committeeman Republican Party, Phoenix, 1983—. NSF grantee, 1968-69. Mem. ABA, Ariz. Bar Assn., Maricopa County Bar Assn., Ariz. State Horseman's Assn. (bd. dirs. 1984-86, 1st up 1986), Scottsdale Bar Assn. Baptist. Clubs: Western Saddle (Phoenix) (bd. dirs. 1983-86, pres. 1985-86); Scottsdale Saddle, Saguaro Saddle. Office: Basinger & Morga PC 4120 N 70th St Ste 211 Scottsdale AZ 85251

BASKERVILLE, TIM, communications executive; b. Burbank, Calif., July 31, 1949; s. David Ross and Roberta Mildred (Hollis) B.; m. Carol Kahler, Jan. 19, 1974 (div. June 1983); 1 child, Robin Ann. BA in Theatre Arts, TV, UCLA, 1971. Assoc. producer Sta. KNXT/CBS News, Hollywood, Calif., 1967-71; reporter Radio News West, Los Angeles, 1972; news producer Sta. KTVU Cox Broadcasting, Oakland, Calif., 1972-73; dep. bur. chief TV News, Inc., Los Angeles, 1973-74; pres. Media Service Corp., Hollywood, 1975-80, Video Mktg. (name now Vidmar Communications, Inc.), Hollywood, 1980—; cons. ABC, CBS, Metro-Goldwyn-Mayer/United Artists, Eastman Kodak, 20th Century Fox, IBM, Tribune Co., Young and Rubicam, J. Walter Thompson, Grey Advt., and others. Editor: (newsletters) Job Leads, 1977, Video Mktg., 1980— (also pub.); creator (TV documentary) Alien and Illegal, 1971 (Emmy award nomination 1972); contbr. articles to Los Angeles Times. Mem. Newsletter Assn. (founder, pres. So. Calif. chpt. 1981-82), Radio TV News Assn. So. Calif., Radio TV News Dirs. Assn., Writers Guild Am. West. Club: Overseas Press of Am.

BASKETT, BILLY WAYNE, systems engineer; b. Temple, Tex., Apr. 28, 1962; s. Charles Richter and Mary Jo (Robinson) B. BSE in Computer Systems, Ariz. State U., 1985. Customer svc. rep. Gold Mind Systems, Phoenix, 1979-80; programmer Collins Phoenix Corp., Tempe, Ariz., 1981; lead programmer Computerized Restaurant System, Santa Ana, Calif., 1981-82; data analyst Motorola, Scottsdale, Ariz., 1983-86; systems engr. Celerity, San Diego, 1986-88; engring. mgr. CE Systems, Tempe, 1988; systems engring. mgr. IM Systems, Scottsdale, 1988—; v.p. EuroRep Systems & Sales, Tempe, 1988—. Mem. Sierra Club. Republican. Home: 25 N Cottonwood St #58 Chandler AZ 85225 Office: EuroRep Systems and Sales 6202 S Maple #128 Tempe AZ 85283

BASKETT, DAVID ERNEST, transportation executive; b. Glendale, Calif., Feb. 3, 1943; s. William Ernest and Daisy Ruth (Bates) B.; m. Dorothy Perderson, May 1967 (div. 1968); m. Judy Marylon Hawkins, June 14, 1969; children: Christopher David, Scot Daniel, Katherine Laural. AS in Aviation Tech., Le Tourneau Coll., Longview, Tex., 1963; BS in Aerospace Mgmt., Metro State U., Denver, 1974. Cert. commercial pilot. Pilot Le Tourneau, Peru, 1963-64; enlisted U.S. Army, 1964, advanced through ranks to Chief Warrant Officer, commd. 2d lt., advanced through ranks to major, retired, 1984, ret., 1984; mktg. mgr. Armoflex Inc., Santa Maria, Calif., 1984-86; ops. officer Phrobis III Ltd., Carlsbad, Calif., 1986-88; dir. ops. Aviation Classics, Reno, Nev., 1987—; owner, chief exec. officer, IXOR, Santa Maria, 1986—; cons. Classics in Aviation, Reno, 1987—; bd. dirs. C3P, Dallas. Contbr. articles to profl. jours. Recipient DFC, Bronze Star, U.S. Army, Vietnam, 1968. Mem. Am. Defense Preparedness Assn., Experimental Aircraft Assn. (Designee). Republican. Mem. Christian and Missionary Alliance. Office: Aviation Classics 4825 Texas Ave Reno NV 89506

BASLER, JOHN MICHELL, communications executive; b. Los Angeles, Oct. 25, 1926; s. Louis Adair and Caroline Mary (Michell) B.; m. Mary Ann Mohlengraft, Nov. 15, 1947; children: David Sutherland, Jon Edward. BS in Elec. Engring., U. So. Calif., 1947, MBA, 1961. Div. mgr. Pacific Telephone & Telegraph, Glendale, Calif., 1966-68; from dir. gen. employment to gen. program engr. Pacific Telephone & Telegraph, San Francisco, 1968-72; successively chief engr., asst. v.p., gen. mgr. Pacific Telephone & Telegraph, Los Angeles, 1972-75; asst. treas. AT&T, N.Y.C., 1975-76; network v.p. Pacific Telephone & Telegraph, Pasadena, Calif., 1976-78; v.p. support serevices Pacific Bell, San Ramon, Calif., 1978—; bd. dirs. Archimede's Circle U. So. Calif.; mem. adv. bd. Constrn. Industry Inst. U. Tex., Austin, 1986-88; chmn. exec. com. Western Council Constrn. Consumers, Calif., 1980-88; mem. Nat. Bus. Roundtable Constrn. Com., N.Y.C., 1986-88. Com. chmn. Senate Adv. Commn. Cost Control State Govt., Sacramento, 1985-88; mem. Adv. Bd. Waste Mgmt., San Francisco, 1982-85; bd. dirs. San Francisco Opera Co., 1983-88. Served to sgt. USMC, 1952-54. Mem. Sigma Alpha Epsilon. Republican. Club: Engineer's (San Francisco), Commonwealth (San Francisco). Home: 46 Glenbrook Dr Hillsborough CA 94010

BASLER, RICHARD ALAN, biomedical instruments manufacturer; b. San Francisco, Sept. 12, 1939; s. Henry Edwin and Margaret Henrietta (Cooper) B.; m. Carol Audrey Foster, Aug. 4, 1962; children: Rodney Giles, Eric Richard. BA, U. Calif., Berkeley, 1960; MBA, U. Phoenix, Irvine, Calif., 1983. Indsl. engr., prodn. supr. Standard Register, Oakland and Corcoran, Calif., 1967-72; knitting supt. Duplan Knits West, Carson, Calif., 1972-75; prodn. supr. Am. Edwards Labs., Irvine, 1976-78, chief indsl. engr., 1978-80, supr. mfg. engring., 1980-86, with engring. systems devel., 1986-87; mgr. quality assurance/quality control Cardiovascular Devices Inc., 1987-88; dir. quality assurance/quality control Applied Vascular Devices Inc., 1988—; owner Internat. Numismatics, Irvine, 1974—. Editor Calif. Engr. mag., 1959; contbr. articles to mags. Bd. dirs. UNCAP, Inc., L.A., 1980-82. Lt. USN, 1960-67, Vietnam., with res. 1967-81. Recipient Kenneth Brainard Meml. Literary award, George Bennett Meml. Literary award. Mem. Am. Inst. Indsl. Engrs., Am. Soc. Quality Control, U.S. Kerry Blue Terrier Club (gov. 1983-85), Gt. Western Terrier (bd. dirs. 1979—). Republican. Office: Applied Vascular Devices Inc 2740 S Harbor Blvd Ste K Santa Ana CA 92705

BASS, DAVID JASON, manufacturing engineer; b. Denver, July 8, 1954; s. Grover Terril and Laura Ann (Whiting) B.; m. Debra Jean Meyer, Aug. 10, 1974; children: Jenell, Kevin, Kristyn, Staci. AS in Drafting Tech., Ea. Ariz. Coll., 1974; BS in Tech. Mgmt., Regis Coll., 1988. Electro-mech. designer electronics group Motorola, Inc., Scottsdale, Ariz., 1974-79; mech. designer Motorola, Inc., Tempe, Ariz., 1979-80; mech. and tooling engr. Kustom Electronics, Chanute, Kans., 1980-81, liaison engr., 1981-82, mgr. mfg. engring., 1982-84; sr. design engr. Martin Marietta Co., Denver, 1984-87, sr. mfg. engr., 1987; supr. mfg. engring. Global-Wulfsberg, Prescott, Ariz., 1987—. Mem. curriculum adv. com. Ea. Ariz. Coll., Thatcher, 1976-80. Mem. Soc. Mfg. Engrs. Republican. Home: 2090 Dineh Dr Prescott AZ 86301 Office: Global-Wulfsberg 6400 Wilkinson Dr Prescott AZ 86301

BASS, HAROLD NEAL, pediatrician, medical geneticist; b. Chgo., Apr. 14, 1939; s. Louis A. and Minnie (Schachter) B.; m. Phyllis Appell, June 25, 1961; children: Laura Renee, Alana Suzanne. Student, U. Ill., 1956-59; MS in Pharmacology, U. Chgo., 1963, MD, 1963. Diplomate Am. Bd. Pediatrics, Am. Bd. Med. Genetics. Intern Children's Meml. Hosp., Chgo., 1963-64; resident Children's Meml. Hosp., 1964-65, chief resident, 1965-66, fellow in med. genetics, 1965-66; attending pediatrician/med. geneticist Kaiser Permanente Med. Ctr., Panorama City, Calif., 1968—; dir. med. genetics prog. Kaiser Permanente Med. Care Program So. Calif., 1987—; clin. prof. pediatrics UCLA Med. Sch., 1970—; pres. med. staff Kaiser Permanente Med. Ctr., 1989. Contbr. articles to profl. jours. Mem. transp. commn. San Fernando Valley, City of L.A., 1973-78. Capt. M.C., USAF, 1966-68. Mem. Am. Soc. Human Genetics, Western Soc. Pediatric Rsch., L.A. Pediatrics Soc., Physicians for Nat. Health Ins. Democrat. Jewish. Home: 11922 Dunnicliffe Ct Northridge CA 91326-1324 Office: Kaiser Permanente Med Ctr 13652 Cantara St Panorama City CA 91402-5497

BASS, ROBERT RAYMOND, real estate executive; b. Artesia, Calif., Mar. 27, 1949; s. Willis J. and Robbie A. (Bone) B.; m. Mary P., Aug. 18, 1972 (div. July 1986); children: Jeffrey Paul, Kimberly Ann. BA in History, Calif. State U., Sacramento, 1972; MEd, Coll. Idaho, 1978. Tchr. Nampa (Idaho) South Jr. High Sch. Dist., 1974-79; agt. Boise (Idaho) Bd. Realtors, 1979—; prin. Park Pointe Realty, Inc., Boise, 1984—. Mem. Idaho Assn. Realtors, Southwestern Bldg. Constrn. Assn., Employee Relation Council, Boise Bd. Realtors, Million Dollar Club. Democrat. Home: 3011 Hillway Dr Boise ID 83702 Office: Park Pointe Realty Inc 733 Emerald Rd Boise ID 83704

BASSETT, CAROL ANN, news, magazines and radio documentary writer; b. Langley AFB, Va., Mar. 2, 1953; d. William Brainard and Genevieve (Rivaldo) B. BA summa cum laude in Humanities, Ariz. State U., 1977; MA in Journalism, U. Ariz., 1982. Freelance writer Tucson, 1980—; pntr. Desert West News, Tucson, 1985—. Contbr. numerous articles to nat. and internat. mags. and newspapers. Mem. Southwest Parks and Monuments Assn., Ariz.-Sonora Desert Mus. Recipient 2d Place Gen. Reporting award Ariz. Press Club, 1987; co-recipient Alfred I. duPont Columbia award, 1984-85, First Place award Investigative Reporting, 1986, 1st Place Polit. Reporting, 1989, First Amendment Journalism award, 1986; grantee Fund for Investigative Journalism, 1985, 87, Corp. for Pub. Broadcasting, 1988. Mem. Nat. Writer's Union, Investigative Reporters and Editors Inc., Ariz. Press Club.

BASSETT, EDWARD POWERS, university administrator; b. Boston, Feb. 27, 1929; s. Fraser W. and Fanny (Powers) B.; m. Karen Elizabeth Jack, Dec. 21, 1954; children: Sarah Jack Bassett Williams, Laura Powers, Lisa Wightman. AB, Washington and Lee U., 1951, LLD, 1984; MA, U. Mich., 1955; PhD, U. Iowa, 1967. Ct. reporter Louisville Courier-Jour., 1955-56; asst. editor Falmouth (Mass.) Enterprise, 1956-57; city editor Anderson (Ind.) Herald, 1957-58; editorial writer Longview (Wash.) Daily News, 1958-60; instr., pub. U. Iowa, 1960-67; asst. prof. journalism U. Mich., 1967-70, acting chmn. dept. journalism, 1969-70; dean Sch. Journalism U. Kans., 1970-74, assoc. vice chancellor acad. affairs, 1974-75; dir. Sch. Journalism U. So. Calif., 1975-80; editor Statesman-Jour., Salem, Oreg., 1980-84; dean Medill Sch. Journalism Northwestern U., Evanston, Ill., 1984-89; dir. Sch. Communications U. Wash., Seattle, 1989—; bd. dirs. Gannett Ctr. for Media Studies. Recipient citation for reporting Am. Polit. Sci. Assn., 1960. Mem. Assn. Edn. in Journalism and Mass Communication (pres. 1975-76), Am. Assn. Schs. and Depts. Journalism (pres. 1974-75), Quill and Scroll Soc. (bd. dirs.), Sigma Delta Chi, Kappa Tau Alpha., Delta Tau Delta. Office: U Wash Sch Communications DS-40 Seattle WA 98195

BASTON, VIRGIL FOREST, engineering consultant; b. Cowley, Wyo., June 9, 1938; s. V.C. And Mae (Titchenal) B.; m. J. Evelyn Ball, June 7, 1959; children: Patricia, Alan, Linda. BS in Gen. Engring., U. Wyo., 1960, PhD in Phys. Chemistry, 1965; postdoctoral, U. Tex., 1965-66. Cert. profl. engr., chem. engr., Colo., Idaho. Sr. scientist Idaho Nat. Engring. Lab., Idaho Falls, 1966-74; dir. R & D Energy Inc., Idaho Falls, 1974-79; pres. Phys. Scis. Inc., Sun Valley, Idaho, 1979—; cons. GPU Nuclear Corp. at TMI-2, Middletown, Pa., 1983-88. Contbr. articles to profl. jours. Sec.-treas. Larkspur Homeowners's Assn., Sun Valley, 1985—. Am. Petroleum Research Inst. fellow, 1962-66. Fellow Am. inst. Chemists (cert. profl. chemist & chem. engr.); mem. Am. Nuclear Soc., Am. Chem. Soc., Am. Inst. Chem. Engrs., Am. Soc. Testing Materials, Cons. Engrs. Idaho, Sigma Xi, Sigma Pi Sigma, Gamma Sigma Epsilon. Office: Physical Scis Inc PO Box 2120 Sun Valley ID 83353

BATARSE, ANTHONY ABRAHAM, JR., automobile executive; b. El Salvador, June 1, 1933; s. Antonio A. Sr. and Mirtha (Perla) B.; m. Esther Beltran, Nov. 27, 1953; children: Esther M., Rudy A., Mirtha C., Rocio L., Mark A., John A., James A. BS in Letters and Sci., Coll. Sci. and Letters, 1955; cert. in real estate fin. and law, Coll. San Mateo, 1969. Mgr. new car sales Hayward (Calif.) Ford, 1968-71; mgr. sales Lloyd A. Wise Oldsmobile, Oakland, Calif., 1971-75; pres., chief exec. officer Lloyd A. Wise, Inc., Oakland, 1975—. Recipient Commendation City of Miami, 1985, Commendation City of San Leandro, 1987, Retailer Yr. award Oakland C. of C., 1989. Mem. Calif. Hispanic C. of C. (Bus. Man of Yr. 1987). Republican. Office: Lloyd A Wise Co 10550 E 14th St Oakland CA 94603-3804

BATCHELOR, JAMES KENT, lawyer; b. Long Beach, Calif., Oct. 4, 1934; s. Jack Morrell and Edith Marie (Ottinger) B.; m. Jeanette Lou Dyer, Mar. 27, 1959; children: John, Suzanne; m. Susan Mary Leonard, Dec. 4, 1976. AA, Sacramento City Coll., 1954; BA, Long Beach State Coll., 1956; JD, Hastings Coll. Law, U. Calif., 1959. Bar: Calif. 1960, U.S. Dist. Ct. (cen. dist.) Calif. 1960, U.S. Supreme Ct. 1968; cert. family specialist, Calif. Dep. dist. atty., Orange County, Calif., 1960-62; assoc. Miller, Nisson, Kogler & Wenke, Santa Ana, Calif., 1962-64; ptnr. Batchelor, Cohen & Oster, Santa Ana, 1964-67, Kurilich, Ballard, Batchelor, Fullerton, Calif., 1967-72; pres. James K. Batchelor, Inc., Santa Ana, 1972—; tchr. paralegal sect. Santa Ana City Coll.; judge pro-tem Superior Ct., 1974—; lectr. family law Calif. Continuing Edn. of Bar, 1973—. Fellow Am. Acad. Matrimonial Lawyers; mem. ABA, Calif. Trial Lawyers Assn., Calif. State Bar (placque chmn. family law sect. 1975-76, advisor 1976-78), Orange County Barristers (founder, pres., placque 1963), Calif. State Barristers (placque 1965, v.p.), Orange County Bar Assn. (plaque sec. 1977, pres. family law sect. 1970-74). Republican. Methodist. Office: 820 N Parton Ste 1-A Santa Ana CA 92701

BATDORF, JAMES MICHAEL, bank loan officer; b. Dearborn, Mich., June 13, 1958; s. John Quimby and Vona Marie (Chapman) B.; m. Carol Elaine Stauffer, Dec. 30, 1981; children: Ryan James, Kristen Marie. BBA, U. Mich., 1980; MBA, Ariz. State U., 1982. Mgmt. trainee MBank of Houston (formerly Bank of the S.W.), 1983-84; A.V.P. comml. loan officer Citibank, Phoenix, 1984—. Vice chmn. Friendship Found., Inc., Glendale, Ariz., 1986—. Home: 7539 N 59th Ln Glendale AZ 85301

BATE, RICHARD HENRY, lawyer; b. Denver, Apr. 1, 1931; s. Harold Thomas and Eunice (Redmond) B.; m. Elaine Clara Schauer, Aug. 8, 1953; children: Thomas John II, David Harold. BS in Law, U. Denver, 1957, LLB, 1960. Bar: Colo. 1960. Ptnr. Barbary & Bate, Denver, 1960-68; exec. dir. Rocky Mountain Mineral Law Found., Denver, 1968-70; ptnr. Nelson & Harding, Denver, 1970-74, Schultz & Bate, Denver, 1974-80; sole practice Denver, 1980—; lectr. U. Denver Coll. Law, 1972; instr. Rocky Mountain Mineral Law Found., 1983—. Mem. editorial bd. Pub. Land and Resources Law Digest, 1984—, chmn. 1980-84; revision author title exam. Law of Fed. Oil and Gas Leases, 1984—. Mem. Colo. Bar Assn. (chmn. mineral law sect. 1973, mem. title standards com. 1986, title standards com. real estate sect. 1986), Denver Assn. Oil and Gas Title Lawyers (founder, pres. 1982). Home: 1777 Larimer St Apt 910 Denver CO 80202 Office: 600 17th St Denver CO 80202

BATEMAN, ANN CREIGHTON, minister; b. Blythe, Calif., June 7, 1943; d. William Stanley and Lucille Mildred (Beem) Creighton; m. Thomas Herbert Bateman, June 19, 1966; children: Mark Eric, Dale Kirk. BA, Whittier Coll., 1964; MAV, San Francisco Theol. Sem., 1981. Consecrated Diaconal Minister United Meth. Ch. Dir. Christian edn. Ch. of the Good Shepherd, Arcadia, Calif., 1965-67, Arlington United Meth. Ch., Riverside, Calif., 1970-74, First Unted Meth. Ch., Roseburg, Oreg., 1974-77; cons. Christian edn. Ch. Edn. Cons. Service, Salem, Oreg., 1977—; chairperson bd. diaconal ministry Oreg.-Idaho Ann. Conf., 1985-87; del. Western Jurisdictional Conf. United Meth. Ch., 1980, 84, 88; mem. gen. bd. higher edn. and ministry United Meth. Ch., Nashville, Tenn., 1988—. Author: Sermon Simulations, 1977, Doing the Bible, 1984; contbr. newsletter Teacher Training Topics, 1983-86. Project leader 4-H, Salem, 1979-88, mem. state recognition and awards com., Corvallis, Oreg., 1985. Mem. United Meth. Women (life), Oreg./ID Christian Educators Fellowship (life, treas. 1982, 84). Democrat. Office: Church Edn Cons Svc 595 Oregon Ave NE Salem OR 97301

BATES, CHARLES EMERSON, library administrator; b. Los Angeles, Dec. 1, 1946; s. Willard Emerson Bates and Erica (Schmidt) Bates Beckwith; m. Mary Joan Genz, Aug. 7, 1971; children—Christopher, Noah, Colin. B.A., Valparaiso U., 1968; M.Ed., Loyola U., Chgo., 1970; M.L.S., Rosary Coll., 1973. Head of reference Decatur Pub. Library, Ill., 1973-74; cons. Rolling Prairie Library System, Decatur, 1974-76; asst. dir. Fond du Lac Pub. Library, Wis., 1976-81; dir. Pueblo Library Dist., Colo., 1981—. Bd. dirs. Pueblo United Way, 1982-86 ; pres. bd. dirs. Rosemount Victorian House Mus., Pueblo, 1984—. Mem. ALA, Colo. Library Assn., Ark. Valley Library System (pres. 1984-85). Lutheran. Lodge: Rotary (pres. bd. dirs. 1981—). Office: Pueblo Libr Dist 100 E Abriendo Ave Pueblo CO 81004

BATES, CHARLES WALTER, human resources executive; b. Detroit, June 28, 1953; s. E. Frederick and Virginia Marion (Nunneley) B. BA in Psychology and Econs. cum laude, Mich. State U., 1975, M in Labor and Indsl. Relations, 1977; postgrad. DePaul U., 1979-80; JD William Mitchell Coll. Law, 1984. Vista vol., paralegal, Legal Aid Assn. Ventura County, Calif., 1975-76; substitute tchr. social studies and history, Lansing, Holt and Okemos, Mich. pub. sch. systems, 1976-77; job analyst Gen. Mills, Inc., Mpls., 1977-78, plant personnel asst. II, Chgo., 1978-80, asst. plant personnel mgr. , Chgo., 1980-81, personnel mgr. consumer foods mktg., Mpls., 1981-82; personnel mgr. consumer foods mktg. divs. Saluto Pizza, Mpls., 1982-84; human resource mgr. Western div., Godfather's Pizza, Costa Mesa, Calif., 1984-85, human resources mgr. Western region, Bellevue, Washington, 1985—. Candidate for lt. gov., 1982, Minn.; asst. scoutmaster Boy Scouts of Am., 1971—; candidate Sommanish Community Coun., Bellevue, 1989. Named Eagle Scout, Boy Scouts Am., 1969; recipient God and Country award Boy Scouts Am., 1967, Scouter's Tng. award Boy Scouts Am., 1979. Mem. Nat. Eagle Scout Assn., Pacific NW Personnel Mgmt. Assn. (Lake Washington chpt.), Am. Soc. Personnel Adminstrn., Mich. State U. Alumni Assn., William Mitchell Coll. Law Alumni Assn. Libertarian. Unitarian-Universalist. Home: 232 168th Ave NE Bellevue WA 98008-4522 Office: Godfather's Pizza Inc 11400 SE Sixth St Ste 100 Bellevue WA 98004

BATES, DAVID R., sales company executive; b. Oakland, Calif., Sept. 27, 1962; s. Carl M. and Ryoko (Niikura) B. BS in Fin., U. Fla. Dir. mktg. Taxan USA Corp., San Jose, Calif., 1985-87, dir. sales, 1987-89; dir. sales Genoa Systems, San Jose, 1989—; cons. various computer cos., San Jose, 1985—. U. Fla. scholar, 1980-82. Home: 34438 Alberta Terr Fremont CA 94538 Office: Genoa Systems 75 E Trimble Rd San Jose CA 95131

BATES, DWIGHT LEE, mechanical engineer; b. Miles City, Mont., Aug. 19, 1943; s. Edmond Russell and Verna Elizabeth (Johnson) B.; m. Diane Marie Seppi, Aug. 19, 1967. BSME, U. Wyo., 1966; MBA in Mktg., Seattle U., 1971. Registered profl. engr., Wash. Prin. engr. Heath Tecna, Kent, Wash., 1973-74; mech. design engr. Puget sound naval shipyard U.S. Dept. Def., Bremerton, Wash., 1974-78; supervisory indsl. engr. Supship Seattle, 1978-85; prin. engr. Comml. Airplane div. Boeing Co., Seattle, 1985—; cons. in field. Pres. Melrose E. Condo Assn., Seattle, 1978-81; mem. USCG Aux. Recipient letter of appreciation U.S. Dept. Def. Mem. AIAA (pres. Laramie, Wyo. chpt. 1966), Wash. State Profl. Engrs. Soc., Wash. State Power Squadron, NSPE, Seattle U. MBA Assn. Democrat. Lutheran. Home: 1912 E McGraw St Seattle WA 98112 Office: Boeing Co PO Box 707 Seattle WA 98124-2207

BATES, GEORGE EDMOND, Episcopal bishop; b. Binghampton, N.Y., Aug. 11, 1933; m. Sue Onstott; children: Richard Howard, Katherine Bates Schey. BA in Sociology and English, Dartmouth Coll., 1955; MDiv, Episcopal Theol. Sem., 1958. ordained deacon, The Episcopal Ch., 1958, priest, 1959. Parish priest Ithaca and Syracuse, N.Y.; rector Ch. of the Redeemer, Pendleton, Oreg., 1970-83, St. Mark's-on-the-Mesa, Albuquerque, 1983-86; consecrated bishop Diocese of Utah, 1986. Chmn. bd. dirs. St. Mark's Hosp.; bd. dirs. Westminster Coll., Rowland Hall-St. Mark's Sch.; mem. Gov.'s Task Force on Health Care Costs. Office: Diocese of Utah 231 E 1st St S Salt Lake City UT 84111 *

BATES, JACK ALFRED, service executive; b. Columbus, Ohio, Mar. 4, 1923; s. Merritt Allen and Bertha Helen (Lehman) B.; m. Marie Virginia Warriner, Nov. 2, 1946 (div. June 1971); children: Wesley, Daniel, Amy Marie Muccio; m. Betty Maxine Campbell, Nov. 3, 1972. Student, Ohio State U., 1941, Miami U., 1942-43, Franklin U., 1946-47. Pres. Jack Bates Carpet Cleaning, Columbus, 1947-72; pres. Stanley Steemer Internat. Inc., Columbus, 1972-85, chmn. bd., 1985—. Served as ensign USNR, 1943-46. Republican. Methodist. Home: 25306 Gallup Circle Laguna Hills CA 92653

BATES, JIM, congressman; b. Denver, July 21, 1941; s. Chester Owen and Asha (East) B.; m. Marilyn Brewer; 1 dau., Jennifer Leigh. BA, San Diego State U., 1975; LHD (hon.), Nat. U., San Diego, 1983. Loan officer Bank Am., San Diego, 1963-68; adminstr. Rohr, San Diego, 1968, Solar, San Diego, 1969; mktg. analyst Heavenly Donuts, San Diego, 1970; mem. San Diego City Council, 1971-74; supr. County of San Diego, 1975-82; mem. 98th-101th Congresses from 44th Dist. Calif. Mem. com. energy and commerce U.S. Congress, subcom.: telecommunication consumer protection, fin., heath, and environment, mem. ho. adminstrn. com., subcom.: personnel and police, services; chmn. gov. bd. Health Systems Agy.; chmn. mental health adv. bd. City of San Diego. Served with USMC, 1959-63. Recipient Diploma Magistrale and Decoration of Cavaliere nell'ordine al Merito della Repubblica Italiana, 1979, Outstanding Service award Mental Health Assn., cert. appreciation Census Bur., 1980, gavel and holder United Builders Am., 1979, Gary Dores Meml. award, Outstanding Young Citizen award Jaycees; cert. appreciation Mental Health Adv. Bd., Nat. Achievement award Urban League, 1982, Equal Rights award; named '84 San Diegans to Watch, San Diego Mag., 1984, Freshman to Watch, Congl. Insight mag., 1982. Democrat. Office: 1404 Longworth House Office Bldg Washington DC 20515 *

BATES, MAREL KENNETH, pension actuary; b. Lompoc, Calif., Nov. 16, 1943; s. Ernest Willard and Carrol Faye (Ehrke) B. BA, U. Calif., Berkeley, 1966; MA, UCLA, 1967, postgrad., 1967-71. Enrolled actuary. V.p. Martin E. Segal Co., L.A., 1971—. Chmn. Claridge Homeowners Assn., L.A., 1983, 85-86; mem. exec. com. Libertarian Party Calif., 1986. Fellow Soc. Actuaries (econs. exam. com. 1984-85); mem. Am. Acad. Actuaries, Am. Contract Bridge League (life master), Town Hall Calif. Congregationalist. Office: Martin E Segal Co 500 S Virgil St Los Angeles CA 90020

BATESON, MARION, entrepreneur, interior designer; b. Dallas, Aug. 6, 1935; d. Joseph Weldon and Marion (Monroe) B.; m. John Cilbert Rowe, May 24, 1955 (dec. 1967); children: Candy Ward, Cathy Rowe, Amy Folse. Student, Design Inst. of San Diego, 1978-79. Owner Marion Bateson Interior Design, La Jolla, Calif., 1980—. Bd. dirs. San Diego Opera, 1987-90, Salvation Army, 1987—, Door of Hope, 1987-89. Mem. La Jolla Beach and Tennis Club. Republican. Presbyterian.

BATEY, ANDREW WALTER, college dean, architect; b. Merced, Calif., Dec. 12, 1944; s. Carol Dean Loomis.; m. Hope Cobey, Aug. 31, 1968 (div. 1985). BA in History, Occidental Coll., 1966; diploma in art history, U. Oxford, Eng., 1968; MA in Architecture, U. Cambridge, Eng., 1971. Architect Norman Foster Assocs., London, 1972, Luis Barragan, Mexico City, 1973-78; prin. Batey & Mack, San Francisco, 1980-85; prof. Princeton (N.J.) U., 1984, U. Pa., Phila., 1985; dean Sch Architecture Calif. Coll. of Arts and Crafts, San Francisco, 1987—; lectr. in field. Founder, editor Archetype; exhibited in group shows at U. Calif., Berkeley, UCLA, U. Calif., San Diego, Mus. Modern Art, San Francisco, Venice Biennale, 1980, Presence of the Past, San Francisco, Young Ams., Rome, Nat. Acad. Art, N.Y.C., 1975, Castelli Gallery, L.A., Corcoran Gallery, L.A., Inst. for Architecture and Urban Studies. Mem. Assoc. of the Royal Inst. of Brit. Architects (cert.). Office: Calif Coll of Arts & Crafts Sch Archtl Studies 1700 17th St San Francisco CA 94103

BATHURST, REBECCA ELIZABETH, educator, writer; b. Bremerton, Wash., June 25, 1947; d. Norman Francis and Joan Marie (Tatham) Powers; m. Lauren Charles Bathurst, Feb. 11, 1967; children: Tobias, Adrian, Suzanne, Nate. AA, Olympic Coll., 1967; BA in Sociology and Anthropology, Western Wash. U., 1970; MFA in Creative Writing, Ea. Wash. U., 1988. Registrar Whatcom Mus. History and Art, Bellingham, Wash., 1971-73; rsch. and devel. assoc. Joy Martin Assocs., Davenport, Iowa, 1974-77; dir. elderly svcs. Project N.O.W., Rock Island, Ill., 1977-78; social svcs. planner Ea. Wash. Area Agy. on Aging, Spokane, Wash., 1980-81; freelance grant writer Spokane, Wash., 1980-81; tchr. parapsychology Spokane Community Coll., 1983-84; instr. English Eastern Wash. U., Cheney, 1985-88; instr. creative writing, composition and lit. North Idaho Coll., Coeur d' Alene, 1987-88; judge creative writing Cen. Valley Schs., Spokane, Wash., 1988, Coeur d' Alene Poets, 1988-89. Bus. mgr., bd. dirs. Pioneer Sch. for Gifted, Veradale, Wash., 1985-86; vestrywoman Ch. of Holy Spirit, Veradale, 1987-89; bd. dirs. Metaphys. Spiritual Ctr., Veradale, 1988. Democrat.

BATTAGLIA, ROBERT KENNETH, entrepreneur; b. Buffalo, Feb. 15, 1939; s. Russell and Jennie (Barreca) B.; m. Colette Marie Coury, Sept. 29, 1984. BS, Bowling Green U., 1960. Ea. region mgr. Libbey Div., Owens-Ill., Inc., N.Y.C., 1960-67; v.p. Saber Internat., Inc., N.Y.C., 1967-69; mng. dir. Deba & Shea, Ltd., Hong Kong, 1969-73, Deba Internat., Ltd., Manila, 1973-77; v.p. mktg. Koracorp. Industries, Inc., San Francisco, 1978-79; pres. Snow Lion Internat., Emeryville, Calif., 1979-80, Fettuccine Bros., Inc., San Francisco, 1981-88, Fax & File Legal Svcs. Inc., San Francisco, 1988—. Republican. Home: 199 Valley View Dr San Rafael CA 94901

BATTERSHELL, DANIEL CHESTER, real estate broker, consultant; b. Marion, Kans., June 26, 1943; s. Chester Everett and Berniece (Darling) B.; m. Angela Faye Waddell, Sept. 6, 1974; 1 child, Daniel Travis. AA in Electronics, San Diego State U., 1962; BBA, U. Tenn., 1965. Commd. ensign USN, 1960, advanced through grades to lt. comdr., resigned, 1972; owner The Gen. Store, Whitmire, S.C., 1973-75; foreman Ga. Pacific Plywood, Newberry, S.C., 1977-80; mgr. Kmart, Newberry, 1980-84; real estate broker Vet. Real Estate, Stockton, Calif., 1984-87; real estate assoc. Vet. Housing Ctr., Sacramento, 1987-88, U Sell Am., Sacramento, 1988—. Decorated Silver Star, Navy Cross. Mem. Sacramento Bd. Realtors. Republican. Baptist. Home: 4513 Oxbow Dr Sacramento CA 95864 Office: U Sell Am 9167 Kieter Blvd Sacramento CA 95826

BATTIN, JAMES FRANKLIN, judge, former congressman; b. Wichita, Kans., Feb. 13, 1925; m. Barbara Choate; children: Loyce Battin Peterson, Patricia Battin Pfeiffer, James Franklin. J.D., George Washington U., 1951. Bar: D.C., Mont. Practice in Washington, 1951-52; now in Billings; past dep. county atty.; past sec.-counsel City-County Planning Bd.; past asst. city atty. Billings; then city atty.; mem. Mont. Ho. of Reps., 1958-59; mem. 87th-91st congresses 2d Dist., Mont.; resigned when apptd. U.S. dist. judge Mont. Dist., 1969; chief judge 1978—. Served with USNR, World War II. Mem. Am. Legion, DeMolay Legion of Honor. Presbyterian. Club: Mason (Shriner). Office: US Dist Ct 5428 Fed Bldg 316 N 26th St PO Box 1476 Billings MT 59103

BATTISTI, PAUL ORESTE, county supervisor; b. Herkimer, N.Y., Mar. 16, 1922; s. Oreste and Ida (Fiore) B.; m. Constance Muth Drais, May 18, 1985; children—Paul J., Cathy (Mrs. D. Capage), Deborah, Thomas, Daniel, Melora, Stephen. Student, Cornell U., Ithaca, N.Y., 1947-48, U. Neb., 1951-52. With VA, 1946-75; dir. VA Hosp., Martinez, Calif., 1969-73; western region dir. VA Hosp., San Francisco, 1973-75; adminstr. State Vets. Home Calif., 1976-86; supr. County of Napa, 1989—; chmn., chief exec. officer Medam., Inc.; dir. Med. Am. Corp.; mem. Contra Costa County Comprehensive Health Planning, Health Facilities Task Force; chmn. adv. com. East Bay Med. Program.; bd. dirs. East Bay Hosp. Conf. Bd. dirs. Easter Seals Contra Costa County. With AUS, 1942-46. Fellow Am. Coll. Hosp. Adminstrs.; mem. Hosp. Conf. No. Calif. (pres.), Nat. Assn. State Vets. Homes (pres.), Rotary (Napa). Home: Silverado Country Club 877 Oak Leaf Way Napa CA 94558 Office: County Bd of Suprs County of Napa 1195 Third St Napa CA 94558

BATTJES, CARL ROBERT, electrical engineer; b. Grand Rapids, Mich., Dec. 30, 1929; s. Harold A. and Helen (Bolt) B.; m. Grace Lydia Battjes, Apr. 5, 1953 (div. 1979). BSEE, U. Mich., 1958; MSEE, Stanford U., 1960. Registered profl. engr., Oreg. Sr. engr. Sylvania Mt. View (Calif.) Labs., 1958-61; prin. engr. Tektronix, Inc., Beaverton, Oreg., 1961-83; pvt. practice Portland, Oreg., 1983—; vis. prof. U. Calif., Berkeley, 1974. Contbr. articles to profl. jours.; patentee in field. 1st lt. USAF, 1950-55. Home and Office: 8318 SW 41st Ave Portland OR 97219

BATTLE, EDWARD GENE, energy resources executive; b. Mont Belvieu, Tex., June 19, 1923; s. Paul E. and Annie-Mae B. B.S., Tex. A&M U., 1954. Pres., chief exec. officer, dir. Norcen Energy Resources Ltd., Calgary, Alta., Can., 1975—; with Continental Oil Co., Tex., from 1954; evaluation engr. Medallion Petroleums, Ltd., 1957, v.p prodn., 1965, exec. v.p., 1966, pres., from 1973; pres., chief operating officer No. and Central Gas Corp., 1974—; bd. dirs. Argus Corp. Ltd., Labrador Mining & Exploration Co. Ltd., Liquid Carbonic Inc., M.A. Hanna Co. Mem. Assn. Profl. Engrs., Geologists and Geophysicists Alta., Assn. Profl. Engrs. Ont., Soc. Petroleum Engrs., AIME. Clubs: Calgary Golf and Country, Rosedale Golf. Office: Norcen Energy Resources Ltd, 715 5th Ave SW, Calgary, AB Canada T2P 2X7

BATTY, JOHN CARL, controller; b. Providence, Jan. 13, 1955; s. W. Lawson and Eleanor (Trumpold) B.; m. Bonnie Reitnauer, July 3, 1982; children: Lauren, Michael. BA in Econs., U. N.H., 1977; MBA, U. Chgo., 1982. Sales engr. internat. sales Gleason Corp., Rochester, N.Y., 1977-80; fin. mgr. Intel Corp., Chandler, Ariz., 1982-86; controller VLSI Tech. Inc., Tempe, Ariz., 1986—. Named Loaned Exec. of Yr., United Way, Rochester, 1980. Mem. Nat. Contract Mgmt. Assn., Tempe C. of C. Republican. Presbyterian. Home: 211 E Dawn Dr Tempe AZ 85284 Office: VLSI Tech Inc 8375 S River Pkwy Tempe AZ 85284

BATZEL, ROGER ELWOOD, chemist; b. Weiser, Idaho, Dec. 1, 1921; s. Walter George and Inez Ruth (Klinefelter) B.; m. Edwina Lorraine Grindstaff, Aug. 18, 1946; children: Stella Lynne, Roger Edward, Stacy Lorraine. B.S., U. Idaho, 1947; Ph.D., U. Calif. at Berkeley, 1951. Mem. staff Lawrence Livermore (Calif.) Lab., 1953—, head chemistry dept., 1959-67, asso. dir. for chemistry, 1961-71, asso. dir. for testing, 1961-64, asso. dir. for space reactors, 1966-68, asso. dir. chem. and bio-med. research, 1969-71, dir. lab., 1971-88, assoc. dir. at large, 1988-89, dir. emeritus, 1989—. Served with USAAF, 1943-45. Named to Alumni Hall of Fame U. Idaho, 1972; recipient disting. assoc. award U.S. Dept. Energy, 1982. Fellow AAAS, Am. Phys. Soc.; mem. Sigma Xi. Office: Lawrence Livermore Lab PO Box 808 L-1 Livermore CA 94550

BAUCH, THOMAS JAY, lawyer, apparel company executive; b. Indpls., May 24, 1943; s. Thomas and Violet (Smith) B.; m. Ellen L. Burstein, Oct. 31, 1982; children: Chelsea Sara, Elizabeth Tree. B.S., U. Wis., 1964, J.D., 1966. Bar: Ill. 1966, Calif. 1978. Assoc. Lord, Bissell & Brook, Chgo., 1966-72; lawyer, asst. sec. Marcor-Montgomery Ward, Chgo., 1973-75; spl. asst. to solicitor Dept. Labor, Washington, 1975-77; dep. gen. counsel Levi Strauss & Co., San Francisco, 1977-81, sr. v.p., gen. counsel, 1981—; mem. U. Wis. Law Review, Madison, 1964-66. Bd. dirs. The Urban Sch., San Francisco, 1986. Mem. Am. Assn. Corp. Counsel (dir. 1982-87), Order of Coif. Democrat. Clubs: Univ. (San Francisco); Villa Taverna (San Francisco); Racquet (Chgo.). Office: Levi Strauss & Co Levi's Pla Box 7215 San Francisco CA 94120

BAUCUS, MAX S., senator; b. Helena, Mont., Dec. 11, 1941; s. John and Jean (Sheriff) B.; m. Wanda Minge, Apr. 23, 1983. BA, Stanford U., 1964, LLB, 1967. Bar: D.C. 1969, Mont. 1972. Staff atty. CAB, Washington, 1967-69; lawyer SEC, Washington, 1969-71; legal asst. to chmn. SEC, 1970-71; sole practice Missoula, Mont., 1971-74; mem. Mont. Ho. of Reps., 1973-74; mem. 94th-95th congresses from 1st Dist. Mont., 1975-79, mem. com. appropriations; U.S. senator from Mont. 1979—; acting exec. dir., com. coordinator Mont. Constl. Conv., 1972. Home: Missoula MT 59801 Office: US Senate 706 Hart Senate Bldg Washington DC 20510 *

BAUER, A(UGUST) ROBERT, JR., surgeon; b. Phila., Dec. 23, 1928; s. A(ugust) Robert and Jessie Martha-Maynard (Monie) B.; BS, U. Mich., 1949, MS, 1950, MD, 1954; M Med. Sci.-Surgery, Ohio State U., 1960; m. Charmaine Louise Studer, June 28, 1957; children: Robert, John, William, Anne, Charles, James. Intern Walter Reed Army Med. Ctr., 1954-55; resident in surgery Univ. Hosp., Ohio State U., Columbus, also instr., 1957-61; pvt. practice medicine, specializing in surgery, Mt. Pleasant, Mich., 1962-74; chief surgery Central Mich. Community Hosp., Mt. Pleasant, 1964-65, vice chief of staff, 1967, chief of staff, 1968; clin. faculty Mich. State Med. Sch., East Lansing, 1974; mem. staff St. Mark's Hosp., Salt Lake City, 1974—; individual practice surgery, Salt Lake City, 1974—; clin. instr. surgery U. Utah, 1975—. Trustee, Rowland Hall, St. Mark's Sch., Salt Lake City, 1978-84; mem. Utah Health Planning Coun., 1979-81. Served with M.C., U.S. Army, 1954-57. Diplomate Am. Bd. Surgery. Fellow ACS, Southwestern Surg. Congress; mem. AMA, Salt Lake County Med. Soc., Utah Med. Assn. (various coms.), Utah Soc. Certified Surgeons, Salt Lake Surg. Soc., Royal Soc. Medicine (affiliate), Pan Am. Med. Assn. (affiliate), AAAS (affiliate), Sigma Phi Epsilon, Phi Rho Sigma. Episcopalian. Club: Zollinger. Contbr. articles to profl. publs., researcher surg. immunology. Office: PO Box 17533 Salt Lake City UT 84117

BAUER, BRUCE F., aerospace engineer; b. Washington, Sept. 7, 1912; s. C. Max and Clara Z. Bauer; m. Myfanwy Rhys Bauer. Student, U. Colo., 1930-36; Aero. Engring. Degree, Curtiss-Wright Tech., 1937; Degree in Structural Engring., U. Calif., Long Beach, 1972. Design and devel. engr., flight test engr. Lockheed Aircraft Co., Burbank, Calif., 1937-48; flight test engr. Lark Missle and XD-92 Con-Vultee, San Diego and Downey, Calif., 1947-48; design and devel. engr. for C-74 and C-124 Douglas Aircraft Co., 1943-50; design and devel. and flight test engr. on C-125, F-89, F-5 Air Conditioner Northrop Aircraft Co., 1950-64, design and devel. engr. Snark Missle and Polaris Navy Submarine Datico Surveillance Computer System, 1950-64; Apollo space, reliability and acceptance engr. N.Am. Aviation, 1964; Saturn S-IVB design, reliability and acceptance engr. Douglas Spare Div., 1964-68; DC-10 air-conditioning system design and devel. engr. Douglas Aircraft Co., 1968-72; contract specifications, reliability, and acceptance engr. for landing assault ships Litton Ships, Pasagula, Mich., 1973; prin. engr. for final assembly and test facilities for Orbit Shuttle Rockwell Internat., 1973-78; cons. aerospace engr. 1978—; math and drafting instr. Curtiss-Wright Tech., Glendale, Calif., 1936-37; prefabricated housing engr., sales mgr. So. Calif. Homes., Inc. With USAAF, 1942-46, CBI, lt. col. USAFR, ret. Mem. AIAA (7 awards 1980-88), Air Force Assn. (3 meritorious awards, 3 state awards, 2 nat. meritorious awards). Home: 18882 Parkview Ter Santa Ana CA 92705

BAUER, CAROLINE FELLER, author; m. Peter A. Bauer; 1 child, Hilary A. BA, Sarah Lawrence Coll., 1957; MLS, Columbia U., 1958; PhD, U. Oreg., 1971. Children's and reference librarian N.Y. Pub. Library, N.Y.C., 1958-62; librarian Hewitt Sch., N.Y.C., 1960-61, Eron Prep. Sch., N.Y.C., 1962-63, Colo. Rocky Mountain Sch., Carbondale, 1963-65; art editor Pacific N.W. Library Assn. Quar., 1967-72; producer, instr. Oreg. Edn. Pub. Broadcasting System, 1973-74; assoc. prof. Sch. Librarianship U. Oreg., 1966-79; cons. Ednl. Cons. Assocs., Denver, 1979-81; vis. storyteller N.Y. Pub. Library, 1962-63; producer/performer Caroline's Corner Sta. KSNO, Aspen, Colo., 1964-66, Caroline: Folktales Around the World, NET affiliate, 1965-66, Caroline's Corner, Oreg. Ednl. Pub. Broadcasting System, 1972-80. Author: Children's Literature, 1973, Storytelling, 1974, Getting It Together

With Books, 1974, Caroline's Corner, 1974, What's So Funny? Humor in Children's Literature (cassette), 1977, Handbook for Storytellers, 1977, This Way To Books, 1981, My Mom Travels Alot, 1981, Too Many Books! 1984, Celebrations, 1985, Take a Poetry Break (video cassette) Creative Storytelling (video cassette), 1979, Presenting Reader's Theater, 1987, Rainy Day, Snowy Day, Windy Day, 1988, Halloween, 1989, others; contbr. articles to profl. jours. Recipient Ersted award for disting. teaching U. Oreg., 1968, Christopher award Jr. Literary Guild, award of excellence Chgo. Woman in Pub., 1978, Dorothy McKenzie award for disting. contbn. to children's lit. So. Calif. Coun. on Lit. for Young People, 1986. Mem. ALA (notable books com. 1977-79, chmn. 1980, chmn. Laura Ingalls Wilder com. 1973-75, mem. Newbery-Caldecott com. 1972-78, bd. dirs. children's div. 1987—), Pi Lambda Theta, Beta Phi Mu.

BAUER, CYNTHIA MARY, public affairs executive; b. Cleve., Oct. 14, 1955; s. Edward and Helen May (Hodus) B. BA, N.Mex. State U., 1978. Personnel specialist Naval Supply Ctr., Oakland, Calif., 1976-79; pub. info. officer Naval Supply Ctr., Oakland, 1979-80; asst. pub. info. officer Naval Air Sta., Alameda, Calif., 1981-82; media specialist Kirtland Air Force Base, Albuquerque, 1982-84; dir. pub. affairs Ho Air Force Office of Security Police, Albuquerque, 1984—; exercise media advisor Dept. of Energy-Albuquerque Office, 1986—. Pub. affairs com Law Enforcement Explorer Conf., 1984-88, mem. com. Boy Scouts Am. Arno Luehman scholar, 1986. Mem. Soc. Profl. Journalists, Am. Diabetes Assn., Air Force Assn., Phi Kappa Phi. Office: HQ AFOSP/PA Kirtland AFB NM 87117-6001

BAUER, HENRY LELAND, lawyer; b. Portland, Oreg., June 7, 1928; s. Henry and Emma L. (Peterson) B.; m. Doris Jane Philbrick, May 21; children—Henry Stephen, Thomas Leland. B.S. in Bus., Oreg. State U., 1950; J.D., U. Oreg., 1953. Bar: Oreg. 1953, U.S. Dist. Ct. Oreg., 1956; U.S. Ct. Appeals (9th cir.), 1960. Mem. Bauer & Bauer, Portland, Oreg., 1955-70, Bauer, Murphy, Bayless & Fundingsland, and successor firms, Portland, 1970-75; now sr. mem. Bauer, Hermann, Fountain & Rhoades P.C., Portland. Past mem. adv. council Oreg. State U. Coll. Bus.; past bd. dirs., vice chmn. St. Vincent Hosp. and Med. Ctr.; mem., pres. council of trustees St. Vincent Med. Found.; lifetime trustee Kappa Sigma Emdowment Fund; bd. dirs., pres. elect Nat. Interfrat. Conf.; past pres. Columbia Pacific council Boy Scouts Am., mem. nat. com.; past pres. Portland Civic Theatre; bd. visitors U. Oreg. Sch. Law, 1979-83. Served to 1st lt. USAF, 1953-55. Mem. ABA, Oreg. Bar Assn., Multnomah County Bar Assn., Am. Judicature Soc., Oreg. State U. Alumni Assn. (bd. dirs.), Delta Theta Phi, Kappa Sigma (past nat. pres.). Republican. Presbyterian. Clubs: Multnomah Athletic, Arlington, Masons, Rotary. Office: Commonwealth Bldg Ste 1100 Portland OR 97204

BAUER, JEROME LEO, JR., chemical engineer; b. Pitts., Oct. 12, 1938; s. Jerome L. and Anna Mae (Tucker) B.; m. Kim Kyung Sooky; children from previous marriage: children: Lori, Trish, Jeff. BSChemE, U. Dayton, 1960; MSChemE, Pa. State U., 1963; postgrad., Ohio State U., 1969. Registered profl. engr., Ohio. Asst. prof. chem. engring. U. Dayton, Ohio, 1963-67; mgr. advanced composites dept. Ferro Corp., Cleve., 1967-72; engring. material and process specifications mgr. Lockheed Missiles & Space Co., Inc., Sunnyvale, Calif., 1972-74; gen. dynamics design specialist Convair Div., San Diego, 1974-76, project devel. engr., 1976-77; dir. research Furane div. M&T Chems. Inc., Glendale, Calif., 1980-82; mem. tech. staff Jet Propulsion Lab., Calif. Inst. Tech., Pasadena, Calif., 1977-80, 82—. Editor: Materials Sciences for Future, 1986; contbr. articles to profl. jours. Jr. warden St. Luke Episcopal Ch., La Crescenta, Calif., 1980, sr. warden 1981. Mem. Am. Inst. Chem. Engrs. (founder, chmn. Dayton sect. 1964-66, spl. projects chmn. Cleve. sect. 1968-69), Soc. Advancement of Material Process Engring. (membership chmn. no. Calif. sect. 1973-74, sec. San Diego sect. 1974-75, vice chmn. 1975-76, chmn. 1976, chmn. Los Angeles sect. 1977, nat. treas. 1978-82, gen. chmn. 31st internat. symposium exhibition, Las Vegas, Nev., 1986, Meritorious Achievement award 1983, internat. v.p. 1987-89, internat. pres. 1989-90), Internat. Electronics Packaging Soc. (pres. Los Angeles chpt. 1982), Phi Lambda Upsilon, Delta Sigma Epsilon. Republican. Home: 1935 E Alpha 205 Glendale CA 91208 Office: Jet Propulsion Lab Calif Inst Tech 4800 Oak Grove Dr Pasadena CA 91109

BAUER, MAX WILLIAM, aerospace engineer; b. La Mesa, Calif., Nov. 12, 1957; s. Max Harnish and Ruby Nell (Daily) B.; m. Karen Dee Lepker, Jan. 5, 1985. BS, Colo. State U., 1985, MS, 1987. Engr. Rohr Industries, Inc., Chula Vista, Calif., 1981-83, rsch. engr., 1988—; asst. grad. teaching Colo. State U., Ft. Collins, Colo., 1986-87. Soc. of Mfg. Engrs. scholar, 1983. Mem. Am. Production and Inventory Control Soc., Golden Key Nat. Honor Soc., Phi Kappa Phi. Republican. Office: Rohr Industries Inc Foot of H St Chula Vista CA 92012

BAUER, PETER A., clothing executive; b. Vienna, Austria, Jan. 13, 1930; s. Ernest O. Bauer and Annie (Farchy) Elmer; m. Caroline Feller, Dec. 23, 1969; 1 child, Hilary. BA, Columbia U., N.Y.C., 1953. Sr. v.p. White Stag Mfg. Co., Portland, Oreg., 1963-78, pres. action sports div., 1978-83; pres., chief exec. officer Arena USA div. Adidas, Huntington Beach, Calif., 1983-87; v.p., dir. European ops. Hang Ten Internat., Chantilly, France, 1987-88; pres., chief exec. officer Young One Am., Seoul, People's Republic of Korea, 1988—, also bd. dirs.; bd. dirs. S.I.A., McLean, Va. 1st lt. USMC, 1953-56. Republican. Home: 6892 Seaway Circle Huntington Beach CA 92648 Office: Young One Am 6892 Seaway Circle Huntington Beach CA 92648

BAUER, PHILIP LANE, advertising executive; b. Holland, Mich., Jan. 11, 1941; s. George Louis Bauer and Gertrude Margaret (Seyler) Conley; m. Sharon Rose Schwab, May 5, 1962 (div. 1972); children: Michael Lane, Paul Edward; m. Marva Lynn Pearson, May 13, 1978. Student, Allan Hancock Coll., 1963, San Jose City Coll., 1964-66, Foothill Coll., 1968-70. Supr. graphic arts dept. Ampex Corp., Redwood City, Calif., 1969-74; sr. art dir. Tyler, Fultz, Bellack Advt., Palo Alto, Calif., 1974-80; exec. art dir. Sandeno-Simmons Advt., Seattle, 1980-81; creative dir. Imahara & Keep Advt., Santa Clara, Calif., 1981-83, Ogilvy & Mather, San Francisco, 1983-84; v.p., creative dir. Winston Advt., Santa Clara, 1984—. Writer, designer pub. service campaign Mothers Against Drunk Driving, 1988 (gold medal 1988, London Internat. Advt. awards). Served with USAF, 1960-64. Recipient 1st Place award Am. Adv. Fedn., 1972, Award of Excellence, N.Y. Art Dirs. Club, 1984, 1st Place award San Francisco Ad Club, 1987, Lulu Statue, Los Angeles Women in Advt., 1988, Gold statue London Internat. Advt. Awards, 1988. Mem. Wash. State Inventors Assn., Western Art Dirs. (officer 1976-77), Tech. Illustrators Mgmt. Assn. (officer 1966), Bus. Profl. Advt. Assn. (gold medal 1975). Office: Winston Advt 2350 Mission College Blvd Ste 700 Santa Clara CA 95054

BAUER, RANDY MARK, management training firm executive; b. Cleve., Sept. 2, 1946; s. Ralph I. and Gloria P. Bauer; B.S. summa cum laude, Ohio State U., 1968; M.B.A., Kent State U., 1971; m. Sue Dellva, July 4, 1975; children—Sherri, Kevin. Mgmt. auditor Peat Marwick Mitchell & Co., Cleve., 1971-72; mgmt. devel. specialist GAO, Denver, 1972-80; adj. prof. mgmt. Columbia Coll., Denver, 1979—; pres. Leadership Tng. Assos., Denver, 1979—; condr. exec. devel. workshops U. Colo., Denver, 1979—. Recipient Best in 1976 award GAO. Mem. Am. Soc. for Tng. and Devel., Beta Gamma Sigma. Address: 5767 S Laredo Ct Aurora CO 80015

BAUER, ROGER DUANE, university dean; b. Oxford, Nebr., Jan. 17, 1932; s. Albert Carl and Minnie (Lueking) B.; m. Jacquelyn True, Aug. 10, 1956; children—Lisa, Scott, Robert. BS, Beloit Coll., 1953; MS, Kans. State U., 1957, PhD, 1959. Asst. prof. chemistry Calif. State U., Long Beach, 1959-64; assoc. prof. Calif. State U., 1964-69, prof., 1969—; dean Calif. State U. (Sch. Natural Scis.), 1975-88. Served with U.S. Army, 1954-56. USPHS fellow, 1966; Am. Coun. on Edn. fellow, 1971. Mem. Am. Chem. Soc., Radiation Rsch. Soc., Sigma Xi, Phi Lambda Upsilon. Home: 6320 Colorado St Long Beach CA 90803 Office: Calif State U Coll Natural Sci Long Beach CA 90840

BAUER, STEVEN MICHAEL, nuclear engineer, consultant; b. Hemet, Calif., Nov. 8, 1949; s. Donald Richard and Jeanne Patricia (Lamont) B.; m. Myung-Hee Min, Sept. 10, 1983; children: Claudia Margaret, Monica Anne. BA in Physics, Calif. State U., San Bernardino, 1971, BS in Physics, 1984, cert. in acctg., 1980, cert. in computer programming, 1986; postgrad., U. Calif., 1974, post grad., 1982, 87—. Cons. mountain planning San Bernardino (Calif.) County, 1975-76; assoc. nuclear engr. Southern Calif. Edison Co., 1976—, with mail dept., 1989—; cons. rsch. svc. Jerry L. Pettis Meml. Hosp., 1978-79. Supporter Asian Relief Fund, 1985—, United Negro Coll. Fund, 1985—, vol., 1988—; friend Southern Poverty Law Ctr., 1986—; mem. Amnesty Internat., 1986—, Greenpeace, 1988—; vol., campaign worker Congressman George E. Brown, 1986—; mem. L.A. County Mus. Art; fellow Casa Colina Hosp. Mem. Am. Nuclear Soc., Calif. State U. San Bernardino Alumni Assn. (sec. bd. 1979-80, rep. food com. 1980-82), Nat. Assn. Accts., Astronomical Soc. of the Pacific, Assn. for Computing Machinery, Numismatic Assn. Southern Calif., The Wilderness Soc., KC (sec., recorder), Toastmasters. Home and Office: 2065 W College Ave Ste 2097 San Bernardino CA 92407-4654

BAUGH, L. DARRELL, financial executive; b. Prairie Grove, Ark., Oct. 7, 1930; s. Lacey D. and Mary Grace (Brown) B.; BBA, U. Ark., 1954; MBA, U. Colo., 1960; CLU, Am. Coll., 1967. Chartered fin. cons. m. Wileeta Claire Gray, June 15, 1958; children: Adrienne Leigh Calvo, John Grayson. With Penn Mut. Life Ins. Co., 1961-71, gen. agt., Sacramento, 1968-71; pres. Nat. Estate Planning Inst., Boulder, Colo., 1974—; bd. dirs. Sunshower Acres Ltd.; faculty estate planning seminars Colo. State U.; cons. U. Colo. Center for Confs. Mgmt./Tech. Programs, 1975-80; sponsor ednl. programs for profl. estate planners and estate owners. Bd. dirs. Stronghold Youth Found.; bd. dir. Boulder County Hospice, Boulder Men's Christian Fellowship. With U.S. Army, 1954-56. Mem. Boulder C. of C., Am. Soc. CLU's, Rocky Mountain CLU's (chmn. grad. studies programs), Boulder County Estate Planning Coun. (pres. 1972-73), Sacramento Estate Planning Coun., Nat. Registry Fin. Planners (interview com.), Am. Soc. Agrl. Cons. (cert.). Contbr. articles to profl. jours. Club: Flatirons Country. Home: 92 Caballo Ct Boulder CO 80303 Office: 75 Manhattan Dr Boulder CO 80303

BAUGHCUM, STEVEN LEE, physical chemist; b. Atlanta, Dec. 18, 1950; s. George Lee and Henrietta (Stevens) B.; BS, Emory U., 1972; MA, Harvard U., 1973, PhD, 1978. Teaching fellow Harvard U., Cambridge, Mass., 1973-76; NRC rsch. assoc. Joint Inst. Lab. Astrophysics, U. Colo., Nat. Bur. Standards, Boulder, Colo., 1978-80; mem. staff Los Alamos Nat. Lab., N.Mex., 1980-87; prin. rsch. scientist, mgr. chem. physics, Spectra Tech., Bellevue, Wash., 1987-88; resch. analyst atmospheric physics Boeing Aerospace, Seattle, 1988—. Contbr. articles to profl. jours. 1st lt. USAF, 1976. NSF grad. fellow, 1972-75. Mem. Am. Chem. Soc., Am. Phys. Soc., Inter-Am. Photochem. Soc., Phi Beta Kappa, Sigma Xi. Home: 2215 185th Pl NE Redmond WA 98052 Office: Boeing Aerospace PO Box 3999 MS 87-08 Seattle WA 98124

BAUGHMAN, DONALD LEROY, JR., engineer; b. Butler, Pa., May 4, 1958; s. Donald LeRoy Sr. and Pola Mae (Bandura) B.; m. Martha Valdez, June 20, 1981. BEE, U. Pitts., 1980. Mem. tech. staff Hughes Aircraft Co., El Segundo, Calif., 1980-82; engr. digital design Interstate Electronics Corp., Anaheim, Calif., 1982-85; cons. engring. Singer Librascope, Glendale, Calif., 1985; sr. engr. digital design Resdel Engring. Corp., Arcadia, Calif., 1985—; engr. project Resdel Engring. Corp., Arcadia, 1987-88. Republican. Office: Resdel Engring Corp 300 E Liveoak Ave Arcadia CA 91006

BAUGHN, ALFRED FAIRHURST, lawyer; b. Florence, Ariz., May 1, 1912; s. Otis James and Mary Holman (Fairhurst) B.; m. Barbara Hobbs, June 17, 1935; children—Brent F., Barbara Hendershot. AB, U. So. Calif., 1935, JD, 1938. Bar: Calif. 1938, U.S. Dist. Ct. (so. dist.) Calif. 1939, U.S. Ct. Appeals (9th cir.) 1945, U.S. Dist. Ct. Ariz. 1948, Ariz. 1959, U.S. Supreme Ct. 1967. With Title Guarantee & Trust, L.A., 1937-41; corp. counsel Pacific Western Oil Co., 1942-43; pvt. practice law, L.A. and Hollywood, Calif., 1943-56; Ariz. chief corp. counsel Garrett Corp., 1956-77, ret., 1977; pvt. practice law, Ariz. and Calif., 1989—; Ariz. Assn. Industries spl. counsel utility rate hearings Ariz. Corp. Commn., 1977-80; bd. dirs. EPI-HAB, Inc., 1974—. Adopted by Hopi Indian Chief Seletstewa and Squaw (2d Mesa), 1967; Pres. scholar U. So. Calif., 1931-35. Mem. Calif. Bar Assn., Ariz. Bar Assn., Maricopa County Bar Assn., L.A. Philanthropic Found. (life), Skull and Scales, Phi Alpha Delta (chpt. pres. 1938), Kappa Sigma (pres. L.A. alumni 1945, pres. Phoenix Alumni 1960), Phi Alpha Delta (pres. U. So. Calif. chpt. 1938). Republican. Mem. Christian Ch. Clubs: Hollywood Exch. (pres. 1947); Kiwanis (Phoenix pres. club 1965); Kachina Klub (organizer, charter v.p. 1974), Hon. Order Ky. Cols. (pres. Phoenix chpt. 1980—), Phoenix Teocali of Order Quetzalcoatl (pres. 1984), Ariz. Bola Tie Soc., Masons (Master 1953), Shriners (potentate 1971), Jesters (head Phoenix Ct. 1969), Internat. Gorillas (chief 1971—).

BAULER, JOHN JAY, metals company executive; b. Elmira, N.Y., Jan. 4, 1946; s. John Jay and Olive (Tilley) B.; m. Leslie Anne Tremonte (div. Feb. 1987); children: Christine Marie, Jeffrey David; m. Lynda Gail Turner, Apr. 1, 1989. Ceramic engr. degree, Alfred U., 1969. Sales engr. Norton Co., Worcester, Mass., 1969-71; quality control mgr. Electro Refractories, Ferro Corp., Buffalo, 1971-74; sales mgr. cal. R.A, Barnes, Seattle, 1974-78; sales trader Northbrook metals, Northbrook, Ill., 1978-81; pres. J & L Metals, Whittier, Calif., 1981-84; with sales Miller & Co., Chgo., 1984-86; dir. we. region Talco Metals, Phila., 1986—; lectr. Internat. Pack Electronics, 1986, AESF Northwestern Branches, 1988; instr., lectr. Am. Foundrymen's Soc., 1978. Referee Am. Youth Soccer Orgn., Orange County, Calif., 1977—, Calif. Interscholastic Fend., so. Calif., 1987—, Calif. Youth Soccer Assn., Calif., 1988; umpire Dist. 60, L.A. County, 1986. Mem. Airplane Owners & Pilots Assn., Exptl. Aircraft Assn., Dale Carnegie, Toastmasters (pres. Gavel Club II, Lakewood, Calif. chpt., membership chmn. dist. I, L.A. chpt. 1988). Republican. Home: 4110 Marsten Ave Belmont CA 94002

BAUM, CARL EDWARD, electromagnetic theorist; b. Binghampton, N.Y., Feb. 6, 1940; s. George Theodore and Evelyn Monica (Bliven) B.; BS with honors, Calif. Inst. Tech., 1962, MS, 1963, PhD, 1969. Commd. 2d lt. USAF, 1962, advanced through grades to capt., 1967, resigned, 1971, project officer Air Force Weapons Lab., Kirtland AFB, N.Mex., 1963-71, sr. scientist for electromagnetics, 1971—; U.S. del. to gen. assembly Internat. Union Radio Sci., Lima, Peru, 1975, Helsinki, Finland, 1978, Washington, 1981, Florence, Italy, 1984, Tel Aviv, 1987; mem. Commn. B U.S. Nat. Com., 1975—, Commn. E, 1982—. Commendation medal; recipient research and devel. award USAF, 1970, award Honeywell Corp., 1962. Fellow IEEE (Harry Diamond Meml. award, 1987, Richard R. Stoddart award, 1984); mem. Electromagnetics Soc. (pres. 1983-85), Sigma Xi, Tau Beta Pi. Roman Catholic. Author: (with others) Transient Electromagnetic Fields, 1976; Electromagnetic Scattering, 1978; Acoustic, Electromagnetic and Elastic Wave Scattering, 1980, Fast Electrical and Optical Measurements, 1986, EMP Interaction: Principles, Techniques and Reference Data, 1986; contbr. articles to profl. publs. Home: 5116 Eastern SE Unit D Albuquerque NM 87108 Office: Air Force Weapons Lab Kirtland AFB NM 87117

BAUM, DEREK MICHAEL, small business owner; b. London, Jan. 21, 1935; s. Abraham Bernard and Charlotte (Fisher) Tarl B.; m. Ruth (div. 1986); m. Magdalena, May 8, 1987; children: Joshua Bernard, Gregory David. AAS in Mgmt., NYU, 1966. Pres. Kandy Lou of Calif., L.A., 1968-84; quality control mgr. Stylecraft, L.A., 1985-87; v.p. Cuckoo's Nest Inc., L.A., 1974-78; prodn. mgr. M&R Internat., L.A., 1987-88; owner Room With A View, Sylmar, Calif., 1988—; bd. dirs. Garment Contractor Assn. So. Calif., 1975-82. Mem. Sylmar C. of C. Jewish. Home: 13442 Almetz St Sylmar CA 91342

BAUM, PHYLLIS GARDNER, travel management consultant; b. Ashtabula, Ohio, Dec. 13, 1930; d. Charles Edward Schneider and Stella Elizabeth (Schaefer) Gardner; m. Kenneth Walter Baum, Oct. 21, 1948 (div. July 1971); children: Deidre Adair, Cynthia Gail; m. Dennis Carl Marquardt, Sept. 22, 1979. Grad. high sch., Cleve. Am. Soc. Travel Agents. Travel cons. Fredo Travel Svc., Ashland, Ohio, 1960-66; sales mgr. Travelmart, Willoughby, Ohio, 1966-68; br. mgr. Travelmart, Mentor, Ohio, 1966-68, Diners Fugazy Travel, Sun City, Ariz., 1968-69; travel cons. Jarrett's Travel Svc., Phoenix, 1969-72; sr. cons. Loyal Travel, Phoenix, 1972-74; co-mgr. Phil Carr Travel, Sun City, 1974-77; tour ops. mgr. ASL Travel, Phoenix, 1978-79; owner, mgr. Travel Temporaries, Glendale, Ariz., 1979—; cons. and lectr. in field. Adv. bd. mem. Small Bus. Devel. Ctr., Phoenix, 1986—. Mem. Pacific Asia Travel Assn. (dir. 1986—), Ariz. Women in Travel, NAFE, Altrusa. Republican. Home and Office: Travel Temporaries 10249 N 45th Ave Glendale AZ 85302

BAUMAN, EARL WILLIAM, accountant, government official; b. Arcadia, Nebr., Jan. 30, 1916; s. William A. and Gracia M. (Jones) B.; B.S. with honors, U. Wyo., 1938; postgrad. Northwestern U., 1938-39; m. Margaret E. Blackman, Oct. 21, 1940 (dec. 1984); children—Carol Ann Bauman Ammerman. Earl William Jr. Acct., Haselmire, Cordle & Co., Casper, Wyo., 1939-42; asst. dir. fin. VA, Chgo., 1946-49, chief acctg. group VA, Washington, 1949-52, supr. systems acctg. GAO, Washington, 1952-55; supervising auditor GAO, Washington, 1955-58; dir. finance, asst. dir. Directorate Acctg. and Fin. Policy, Office Asst. Sec. Def., Washington, 1958-63; tech. asst. to comdr. AF Acctg. and Fin. Ctr., Denver, 1963-73; mem. investigations staff Ho. of Reps. Appropriations Com., 1953-54; prof. acctg. Benjamin Franklin U., 1960-63; mem. exec. council Army Finance, 1963-64; dir. Real Estate Investment Corp., 1962-64; sr. ptnr. EMB Enterprises, 1973—; chmn. Acctg. Careers Council Colo., 1969-71. Chmn. Aurora Citizens Adv. Budget Com., 1975-76; chmn. fin. and taxation com. Denver Met. Study, 1976-78. Served with AUS, 1942-46; col. Res., now ret. C.P.A. Mem. AICPA, Wyo. Assn. C.P.A.s, Fed. Govt. Accts. Assn. (nat. v.p. 1972-73, pres. Denver 1973-74), Army Finance Assn., Am. Soc. Mil. Comptrollers, Denver Am. Soc. Mil. Comptrollers (pres. 1968-69), Citizens Band Radio Assn. (pres. 1963), Nat. Assn. Ret. Fed. Employees (Aurora 1072 pres. 1986-87), Alpha Kappa Psi, Beta Alpha Psi, Phi Kappa Phi. Club: Columbine Sertoma (pres. 1975-76). Avocations: photography, tennis, collector cars. Home: 536 Newark Ct Aurora CO 80010

BAUMAN, RICHARD DUANE, postmaster; b. Great Falls, Mont., May 17, 1937; s. Joseph and Astrid (Johnson) B.; children: Valarie, Mitchal. Postmaster U.S. Postal Svc., Plains, Mont., 1971-75, Deer Lodge, Mont., 1976—; pres. Eddie's Corner Truck Stock, Moore, 1980—; pres. Powell Co. Mus. and Arts, Deer Lodge, 1985—. With USN, 1956-59. Mem. Rotary (pres. Deer Lodge chpt. 1981, sec. 1985—). Home: 720 Texas Ave Deer Lodge MT 59722-1642 Office: US Postal Svc 510 Main St Deer Lodge MT 59722-9998

BAUMAN, WILLIAM WINTER, portfolio sales manager; b. Washington, July 30, 1961; s. Walter Winter Bauman and Helen Charles (Murrell) Smith; m. Elizabeth Anne Bauman. BS in Fin., Ariz. State U., 1983, MBA, 1985. Treasury analyst Greyhound Capital Corp., Phoenix, 1983-84; investment analyst Greyhound Capital Mgmt. Corp., Phoenix, 1984-86; dir. investment analysis Venture Capital Mgmt. Corp., Phoenix, 1986-88; mgr. acquisitions Bell Atlantic Systems Leasing, Internat., Phoenix, 1988-89, portfolio sales manager, 1989—. Republican. Presbyterian. Home: 6737 Monte Vista Rd Scottsdale AZ 85257 Office: Bell Atlantic Systems 11811 N Tatum Blvd Ste 2050 Phoenix AZ 85028

BAUMANN, EUGENE HEINZ, pilot; b. San Francisco, Sept. 2, 1950; s. Eugene Paul and Liane Helga (Lautenschlager) B.; m. Vicki Susanne Nolan, Apr. 1, 1986; 1 child, Kyle Ryan. BS, U. Nev., 1976; cer. Cert. flight engr., flight instr., aircraft dispatcher, airline transport pilot. Pilot Swift Aire Lines, San Luis Obispo, Calif., 1979, Golden Gate Airlines, Monterey, Calif., 1979-81, Swift Aire Lines, San Luis Obispo, Calif., 1979, Commuter Airlines, Binghamton, N.Y., 1981-82; pilot and check airman Empire Airlines, Utica, N.Y., 1982-83; pilot Mid Pacific Airlines, Honolulu, 1983-84, Ryan Internat. Airlines, Wichita, Kans., 1984-85, Am. Airlines, L.A., 1985—; U.S. rep. Europa Cup Alpine Ski Circuit, 1974-75. Won U.S. Sr. Nat. Downhill Championships Silver medal Class I, 1977, Sr. Class I Champion Far West Competition, 1981, 1st place Regional Ski Club Championship, 1981, 2d place Nat. Ski Club Championship, 1981, Western States Masters Championship Class II, 1st Downhill, 2d Giant Slalom, 1st Combined, 1987, 1st place Internat. Masters Championship Gian Slalom, Squaw Valley, 1987, Final Standings N.Am. Airlines Ski Fedn. 2d Slalom, 3d Giant Slalom, 3d Overall, 1987, Internat. Airlines Ski Fedn., Söll, Austria 8th Combined, 9th Giant Slalom, 1987, U.S. Masters Nat. Alpine Championships, Class III, Silver medal Giant Slalom, Bronze medal Downhill, Silver medal Combined, 1988, Far West Ski Competition Masters Class 30 Champion and Overall Champion, 1988, Masters Western States Nat. Championships Class III, 1 Gold and 3 Silver medals, 1988, 3d place Internat. Masters Championships Class III Giant Slalom, Sun Valley, Idaho, 1988; named Outstanding Masters Ski Racer of the Yr., Far West Ski Competition, 1988; final standings N.Am. Airline Ski Fedn. 2d place Overall, 2d place Giant Slalom, 2d place Slalom, 1988. Mem. Allied Pilots Assn., Future Aviation Profls. Am., Am. Airlines Ski Team. Republican. Roman Catholic.

BAUMANN, RICHARD CHARLES, physician; b. Milw., June 10, 1935; s. Carl and Hazel (Shingen) B.; m. Barbara Guse, Jan. 25, 1958; children: Daniel, David, Mark, John, Jane, Alan, Mary, Ann. BSEE, Marquette U., 1957, MD, 1965. Intern. St. Joseph Hosp., Milw., 1965-66; resident Bernalillo County Med. Ctr., Albuquerque, 1968-70; fellow Med. Coll. Wis., Milw., 1970-71; pvt. practive specializing in allergies P & A Ltd., Albuquerque, 1971—; allergy cons. USAF, Kirtland AFB. Capt. USAF, 1966-68. Recipient Physicians Recognition award AMA, 1989. Fellow Am. Acad. Allergy, Am.Acad. Pediatrics; mem. N.Mex. Allergy Soc. (sec. 1987-88), N.Mex. Computer Soc. Office: P&A Ltd 2509 Virginia NE Albuquerque NM 87110

BAUMGARTNER, ALLAN RODNEY, computer company executive; b. N.Y.C., May 27, 1938; s. John Herbert and Claire Regina (Strobele) B.; B.S., Carnegie Inst. Tech., 1960; m. Dolores Zalewski, Dec. 4, 1975; children—Yvette Selena, Brendon Allan Hans. Product mgr. Westinghouse Electric Corp., Sunnyvale, Calif., 1966-67, data processing devel. mgr., 1967-71; data communications designer Pacific Telephone Co., San Francisco, 1971-74, internal cons., 1974-78; cons. to advanced communications system AT&T, Morristown, N.J., 1976-77; dir. tech. strategy Nat. Semicondr. Corp., San Diego, 1979-80, dir. software mktg. subs. Nat. Advanced Systems, Inc., Mountain View, Calif., 1980-83, pres. Gyrus Systems Corp., San Diego, 1983-84; v.p. sales and mktg. System Specialists and Cons., 1984-86; pres. Internat. Computer Contracting Corp., San Jose, Calif., 1986—; IBM analyst Dataquest, San Jose, 1987—; cons. mgmt. data processing, Data Quest Inc., 1987—. Capt. C.E., U.S. Army, 1960-65. Mem. Data Processing Mgmt. Assn., IEEE, Assn. Data Processing Service Orgns. Republican. Home: 4221 Quimby Rd San Jose CA 95148 Office: Internat Computer Contracting Corp 1758 G Junction Ave San Jose CA 95112

BAUMGARTNER, ANTON EDWARD, automotive sales professional; b. N.Y.C., May 18, 1948; s. Hans and Carmen Maria (Figueroa) B.; m. Brenda Lee lemmon, Aug. 24, 1969; 1 child, Anton Nichalous. BS, Woodbury U., 1970. Sales mgr. Maywood Bell Ford, Bell, Calif., 1966-69, O.R. Haan, Inc., Santa Ana, Calif., 1969-72; pres. Parkinson Volkswagen, Placentia, Calif., 1972-77; exec. v.p. United Moped, Fountain Valley, Calif., 1975-82; pres. Automobili Intermeccanica, Fountain Valley, 1975-82; gen. mgr. Bishop (Calif.) Volkswagen-Bishop Motors, 1982-85, Beach Imports-Irvine Imports, Newport Beach, Calif., 1985-88; exec. v.p. Credit Union Auto Hotline, Santa Ana, 1988—; mem. faculty, Automotive World Congress, Detroit, 1980. Mem. Coachbuilders Assn. N.Am. (sec. 1975-78). Office: Credit Union Auto Hotline 925 N Harbor St Santa Ana CA 92703

BAUMGARTNER, HAROLD FLOYD, farmer, contractor; b. Brush, Colo., Mar. 31, 1936; s. Henry K. and Mollie (Sprier) B.; m. Joyce Elain Beauprez, June 3, 1957 (div.); Lori, Russel, Kristi; m. Katherine Adelle Claasen, Dec. 13, 1988. Grad. high sch., Weldona, Colo. Oil producer Carmack Oil Co., Ft. Morgan, Colo., 1953-57; pres. Concrete Contractors, Inc., Brighton, Colo., 1957—, Adames Transit Mix, Brighton, 1962—, Plate Gravel Corp., Brighton, 1965—, Single Eagle Co.'s, Brighton, 1970—, Brighton East Devel. Co., Brighton, 1972—. Bd. dirs. 4-H Corp., Brighton, 1960—; chmn. Brighton Planning Commn., 1965-68. Mem. Colo. Ready Mixed Concrete Assn. (pres. Denver chpt. 1965-67), Elks, Rotary (bd. dirs. Commerce City, Colo. chpt.), Jaycees (bd. dirs. Brighton chpt., Outsanding Citizen award 1970, Outstanding Boss award 1972). Democrat. Methodist. Home: 9720 E 136th Brighton CO 80601 Office: Concrete Contractors Inc 975 Hwy 85 Brighton CO 80601

BAUMHOFF, WALTER HENRY, headmaster; b. N.Y.C., May 27, 1938; s. Joseph and Elli (Schillig) B. BA, Wagner Coll., 1959; MS, Ind. U., 1961; postgrad., Harvard U. Asst. dir. scholarship and fin. aid Ind. U., Bloomington, 1960-61; dean of freshmen St. Lawrence U., Canton, N.Y., 1961-65; dean of students St. Lawrence U., Canton, 1965-71; faculty, dept. of psychiatry and behavioral scis. Stanford U., Palo Alto, Calif., 1973-74; headmaster

The Buckley Sch., Sherman Oaks, Calif., 1978—. Mem. Valley Coun. L.A. County Museum of Natural History, 1987—. Mem. St. James Club. Republican. Office: The Buckley Sch 3900 Stansbury Ave Sherman Oaks CA 91423

BAUTISTA, NORMAN RONALD, printing salesman, recording engineer; b. North Borneo, East Indies, Aug. 17, 1952; came to U.S., 1954; s. Baltamaro Ronald Bautista and Evangeline (Tripplet) Assogna; m. Caprice Atterbury, June 19, 1976; 1 child, Norman Alexander. Student, Coll. of Marin, Kentfield, Calif., 1972-73. Print press operator 4th & D Copy Ctr. and Addresograph-Multigraph, San Rafael, Calif. and San Francisco, 1972-76; mgr. ops. Pacific Coast Tariff Bur., San Francisco, 1976-82; owner Offset Express Printing, San Rafael, 1982-87; printing salesman Krown Printing, Petaluma, Calif., 1988; founder, printing broker Calif. Graphics Group, 1988—; owner Caprice Recording, San Rafael, 1987—. Office: Caprice Graphics Group PO Box 4263 San Rafael CA 94913

BAWDEN, GARTH LAWRY, museum director; b. Truro, Eng., Dec. 31, 1939; s. Richard Thomas and Susan Elizabeth Olga (Lawry) B.; m. Margaret Ruth Greet, Dec. 21, 1963 (div. Mar. 1978); children: Michael Greet, Teona Mary, Kerenza Elizabeth; m. Elaine Louise Comack, Oct. 26, 1978; children: Jonathan Richard, Rebecca Lawry. Diploma in phys. medicine, West Middlesex Sch. Phys. Medicine, Isleworth, Eng., 1961; BA in Art History, U. Oreg., 1970; PhD in Anthropology, Harvard U., 1977. Assoc. in archaeology Harvard U., Cambridge, Mass., 1977-81, instr., 1980-85, asst., acting dir. Peabody Mus., 1980-85; assoc. prof. U. N.Mex., Albuquerque, 1985—; dir. Maxwell Mus., 1985—; dir. field research project Harvard U., Galindo, Peru, 1971-74, dir. field survey Peabody Mus., Saudi Arabian Archaeol. Survey, 1978-80; field supr. Cuntisuyu Project, Moquegua, Peru, 1983-86; dir. U. N.Mex. Acheol. Project, So. Peru, 1985—. Author: (with C. Conrad) The Andean Heritage, 1982; contbr. articles on archaeology to profl. jours. Fellow Woodrow Wilson, U. Oreg., 1970, Tinker, Harvard U., 1983. Mem. Soc. Am. Archaeology, Assn. Field Archaeology, Assn. Sci. Mus. Dirs., Current Anthropology (assoc.), Phi Beta Kappa, Sigma Xi. Home: 6 Applewood Ln NW Los Ranchos de Albuquerque NM 87107 Office: U NMex Maxwell Mus Anthropology Albuquerque NM 87131

BAXTER, CAROL CAIRNS, computer scientist; b. Oakland, Calif., Dec. 24, 1940; d. Walter V. and Helen Cairns; m. William F. Baxter, Mar. 27, 1987; 1 child, Bernard Treanor. AB, Stanford U., 1962; MA, U. Calif., 1966, EdD, 1969. Systems engr. Internat. Bus. Machines, Oakland, Calif., 1962-64; rsch. specialist U. Calif., Berkeley, 1969-71; rsch. dir. Ctr. for Advanced Study, Stanford, Calif., 1972-81, 83—; dir. computer rsch. Am. Enterprise Inst., Washington, 1981-83. Office: Ctr for Advanced Study 202 Junipero Serra Blvd Stanford CA 94305

BAXTER, DAVID RICHARD, dismantling company executive; b. Springfield, Mo., Dec. 25, 1946; s. Teddy and Ruth (Sloan) B.; m. Yolanda Fay Tucker, Nov. 28, 1985; 1 child, Brandon Richard. Grad. high sch., Greenfield, Mo. Master journeyman Hopper Inc., Bakersfield, Calif., 1977-84, Kern Rock Co., Bakersfield, 1984-87; owner, mgr. C Auto Wrecking, Bakersfield, 1987—. Mem. Nat. Assn. Ind. Businessmen, Bakersfield C. of C., L.A. Raiders Boosters. Home: 6ll Townsley Ave Bakersfield CA 93307

BAY, RICHARD ANTHONY, data processing professional; b. Erie, Pa., Sept. 19, 1948; s. Roy A. and M. Alice (Musser) B.; m. Linda L. Breaux, June 30, 1984; stepchildren: Daniel A. Breaux, Jasen A. Christian. BA in Philosophy, Vanderbilt U., 1970. With L.K. Lloyd & Assocs., San Francisco, 1979-81; systems analyst L.K. Lloyd & Assocs., 1986-87, asst. mgr. systems and programming, 1987, sr. mgr. systems and programming, 1987—; profl. musician, freelance graphic artist, Nashville, L.A. and San Francisco, 1970-79. Composer, lyricist over 80 songs. Vol. performer, Bread & Roses, Marin County, Calif., 1989. Grantee, Am. Film Inst., 1970. Mem. Computer Profls. for Social Responsibility, No. Calif. Pick Users Group, Amnesty Internat., Sierra Club. Democrat. Home: 21 Lorraine Ct Novato CA 94947 Office: LK Lloyd & Assocs 160 Spear St San Francisco CA 94105

BAYDA, EDWARD DMYTRO, judge; b. Alvena, Sask, Can., Sept. 9, 1931; s. Dmytro Andrew and Mary (Bilinski) B.; m. Marie-Thérèse Yvonne Gagné, May 28, 1953; children: Paula, Christopher, Margot, Marie-Thérèse, Sheila, Kathryn. B.A., U. Sask., 1951, LL.B. cum laude, 1953. Bar: Sask. 1954. Barrister, solicitor Regina, Sask., 1953-72; sr. ptnr. Bayda, Halvorson, Scheibel & Thompson, 1966-72; justice Ct. Queen's Bench for Sask., Regina, 1972-74, Ct. Appeal for Sask., Regina, 1974-81; chief justice Sask., Regina, 1981—. Mem. Law Soc. Sask. (past bencher), Can. Bar Assn. (past Sask. chmn. civil justice sect.), Regina Bar Assn. Roman Catholic. Club: Assiniboia (past. bd. dirs.). Home: 9 Turnbull Pl, Regina, SK Canada Office: Ct Appeal Sask/Courthouse, 2425 Victoria Ave, Regina, SK Canada S4P 3V7

BAYLEY, CHRISTOPHER T., real estate company executive; b. Seattle, May 25, 1938; s. Emery P. and Dorothy (Dunn) B.; m. Cynthia Conroy, May 31, 1972; children—Elizabeth, Kathryn. AB magna cum laude, Harvard U., 1960, JD, 1966. Bar: Wash. 1967. Dep. atty. gen., chief consumer protection and antitrust div. Atty. Gens. Office, Seattle, 1969-70; pros. atty. King County, Seattle, 1971-79; of counsel Perkins Coie, Seattle, 1979-80, ptnr., 1980-82; sr. v.p. law and corp. affairs Burlington No. Inc., Seattle, 1983-86, sr. v.p. corp. affairs, 1983—; sr. v.p. corp. affairs Burlington Resources, Inc., 1989—; pres., chief exec. officer Glacier Park Co., 1985—; bd. dirs. N.Mex. and Ariz. Land Co., Interpoint Corp., The Commerce Bank. Bd. dirs. The Nature Conservancy, Santa Fe Chamber Music Festival; bd. overseers Harvard Coll.; chmn. Seattle Found.; trustee Bush Sch., 1983-85. With USN, 1963-66, capt. Res., ret., 1985. Mem. University Club, Seattle Tennis Club, Knickerbocker Club (N.Y.C.). Home: 3702 E Prospect St Seattle WA 98112 Office: Glacier Park Co 1011 Western Ave Seattle WA 98104

BAYLIS, CHARLES MERRITT, electrical engineer; b. Cin., July 3, 1956; s. Richard Edwin and Marjory (Ackerman) B.; m. Cynthia Jean Staun, Sept. 3, 1984. AB in Engring. Sci., Dartmouth Coll., 1978; MS in Materials Sci., Stanford U., 1981; MEE, U. Calif.-Berkeley, 1981. Supr. semiconductor materials lab. Cin. Milacron, 1981-83; mktg. engr. Applied Materials, Santa Clara, Calif., 1983-84; pres. Baylis Automation, Inc., Scotts Valley, Calif., 1984--. Contbr. articles to profl. jours. Mem. IEEE, Assn. Computing Machinery. Roman Catholic. Office: Baylis Automation Inc 4340 Scotts Valley Dr Scotts Valley CA 95066

BAYLOR, DON EDWARD, professional baseball player; b. Austin, Tex., June 28, 1949; s. George Edward and Lillian Joyce B.; m. Rebecca Giles, Dec. 12, 1987; 1 child by previous marriage, Don Edward. Student, Miami-Dade Jr. Coll., Miami, Fla., Blinn Jr. Coll., Brenham, Tex. With Balt. Orioles, 1970-76, Oakland Athletics, 1976, 88, California Angels, 1976-82, N.Y. Yankees, 1983-86, Boston Red Sox, 1986-87, Minnesota Twins, 1987; mem. World Series Championship Team, 1987; Set new career record for hit by pitches; hit safely in 12 consecutive Am. League Championship Series games. Chmn. nat. sports Cystic Fibrosis Found.; bd. dirs. Austin (Tex.) Reportory. Named American League's Most Valuable Player, 1979, Sporting News Player of Yr., 1979; recipient Designated Hitter of Yr. award, 1985, 86; player, All-Star Game, 1979. Home: 733 Sapphire Ave Ventura CA 93004 Office: Major League Baseball Players Assn 805 3d Ave New York NY 10022

BAYLOR, ELGIN GAY, professional basketball executive; b. Washington, Sept. 16, 1934; m. Elaine; 1 dau., Krystle. Ed., Coll. Idaho, Seattle U. Professional basketball player Los Angeles (formerly Minneapolis) Lakers, 1958-72; asst. coach New Orleans Jazz, NBA, 1974-76, coach, 1976-79; exec. v.p., gen. mgr. Los Angeles Clippers, 1986—. Most Valuable Player, NCAA Tournament, 1958; mem. NBA All-Star Team, 1959-65, 67-70; Rookie of the Yr., NBA, 1959; co-Most Valuable Player, NBA All-Star Game, 1959; named to NBA 35th Anniversary All-Time Team, 1980. Office: care Los Angeles Clippers 3939 S Figueroa St Los Angeles CA 90037 *

BAYNE, WILLIAM, investment counselor; b. Boston, Feb. 10, 1929; s. William III and Margaret (MacGill) B.; m. Martha Gibb (div. 1971); children: Cynthia P., William Jr.; m. Elizabeth S. Grad. high sch., Newport, R.I., 1948; student, Yale U., 1950. Trainee F.S. Moseley, N.Y.C., 1950-51; govt. bond adv. Bankers Trust, N.Y.C., 1951-52, credit dept., 1954-57; v.p. sales C.A. Woolsey Paint and Color Co., N.Y.C., 1957-61; sales Dictaphone, Denver, 1961-62; sales Standard & Poor's Corp., Denver, 1962-63, mgr. investment counsel, 1963-67; pres. Performance Assocs., Denver, 1967-74; v.p. investments Albuquerque N/B, 1974-78; pres. Asset Mgmt., Inc., Albuquerque, 1978—. Fin. chmn. Mayor's Kitchen Cabinet, Albuquerque, 1984-89, gov.'s adv. coun., 1986—; chmn. ushers St. John's Cathedral, Albuquerque, 1987—. With USN, 1952-54. Mem. Investment Co. Inst., Nat. Fedn. Ind. Bus. (guardian), Hispanic C. of C., Assn. Commerce and Industry Conf. Bd., Petroleum Club. Republican. Episcopalian. Home: 4404 Kellia Ln NE Albuquerque NM 87111 Office: Asset Mgmt Inc 610 Gold SW Albuquerque NM 87102

BAYS, ERIC, bishop; b. Portage La Prairie, Manitoba, Can., Aug. 10, 1932; s. Percy Clarence and Hilda (Harper) B.; m. Patricia Ann Earle, Dec. 28, 1967; children: Jonathan Edmund, Rebecca Jane. BS, U. Man., Winnipeg, Can., 1955; BA, U. Sask., Saskatoon, Can., 1959; L in Theology, U. Emmanuel Coll., Saskatoon, Can., 1959, DD, 1987; M in Ministry, Christian Theol. Sem., Indpls., 1974; DD (hon.), U. of Emmanuel Coll., Saskatoon, 1987. Ordained to ministry Anglican Ch., 1959. Asst. curate All Saints' Anglican Ch., Winnipeg, 1959-61; lectr. Emmanuel Coll., Saskatoon, 1961-62; mission priest Diocese Caledonia, B.C., 1962-64; novice in religion Community of the Resurrection, Mirfield, Eng., 1964-65; vicar St. Saviour's with St. Catherine Parish, Winnipeg, 1965-67; rector All Saints' Parish, Winnipeg, 1968-76; prof. Coll. Emmanuel/St. Chad, Saskatoon, 1976-81; vice-prin. Coll. of Emmanuel/St. Chad, Saskatoon, 1981-86; bishop Diocese Qu'Appelle, Regina, Sask., 1986—; bd. dirs. Family Svc. Bur., Regina, 1987—. With RCAF, 1955-59. Office: Diocese of Qu'Appelle, 1501 College Ave, Regina, SK Canada S4P 1B8

BEACH, ARTHUR O'NEAL, lawyer; b. Albuquerque, Feb. 8, 1945; s. William Pearce and Vivian Lucille (Kronig) B.; B.B.A., U. N.Mex., 1967, J.D., 1970; m. Alex Clark Doyle, Sept. 12, 1970; 1 son, Eric Kronig. Admitted to N.Mex. bar, 1970; assoc. firm Smith & Ransom, Albuquerque, 1970-74; assoc. firm Keleher & McLeod, Albuquerque, 1974-75, ptnr., 1976-78, shareholder firm Keleher & McLeod, P.A., Albuquerque, 1978—; teaching asst. U. N. Mex., 1970. Bd. editors Natural Resources Jour., 1968-70. Mem. State Bar N.Mex. (unauthorized practice of law com., adv. opinions com., med.-legal panel, legal-dental-osteo.-podiatry com., jud. selection com.), Am., Albuquerque (dir. 1978-82) bar assns., State Bar Specialization Bd. Democrat. Mem. Christian Sci. Ch. Home: 2015 Dietz Pl NW Albuquerque NM 87107 Office: Keleher & McLeod PA PO Drawer AA Albuquerque NM 87103

BEACH, ROGER C., oil company executive; b. Lincoln, Nebr., Dec. 5, 1936; s. Melvin C. and L. Mayme (Hoham) B.; m. Elaine M. Wilson, Oct. 1954 (div. 1972); children: Kristi, Mark, Anne; m. Karen Lynn Ogden, July 27, 1974. BS, Colo. Sch. Mines, 1961. Registered profl. petroleum refining engr., Calif. Mgr. spl. projects UNOCAL Corp., Los Angeles, 1976-77, dir. planning, 1977-80, v.p. crude supply, 1980-86, pres. refining and mktg., 1986—. Mem. Am. Petroleum Inst., U.S.-Korea Soc., Nat. Petroleum Refiner's Assn., Pres.'s Interchange Exec. Alumni Assn. Office: UNOCAL Refining & Mktg Div 1201 W 57th St PO Box 7600 Los Angeles CA 90051 *

BEADLES, VERNON L., airline pilot, real estate investor, small business executive; b. Huron, S.D., June 24, 1933; s. Harry Ray and Hilda Johnson; m. Bernadine Schoof, Apr. 27, 1957; children—Bruce Allen, David Lawrence. Student pub. schs. Commd. 2d lt. U.S. Air Force, 1955, advanced through grades to lt. col., 1973; fighter pilot, 1955-65; mem. Mich. Air NG, 1965-74; pilot United Airlines, 1965—; pres. Nor Cal Auto-Vend, San Francisco, 1986—; pres. B&B Auto-Vend, Inc., Sacramento, 1987—; pvt. real estate investor, 1971—. Decorated Air Force Commendation medal. Mem. Air Force Assn., Airline Pilots Assn. Republican. Lutheran. Home: 15768 Hidden Hill Pl Los Gatos CA 95030 Office: United Airlines San Francisco Internat Airport San Francisco CA 94128

BEAGLE, JOHN GORDON, real estate broker; b. Spokane, Wash., Dec. 31, 1943; s. Gordon Avril and Sylvia Alberta (Dobbs) B.; m. Shihoko Ledo, Nov. 14, 1964; children: James, Steven, Kevin, Melanie. BS, Mont. State U., 1970; grad., Realtors Inst. Cert. real estate broker. Instr. Kalispell (Mont.) High Sch., 1970-71; gen. mgr. Equity Coop. Assn., Harlem, Mont., 1971-76; owner, operator Howards Pizza, Livingston, Mont., 1976-79; broker, owner ERA Beagle Properties, Sidney, Mont., 1979—. Mem. City Coun. City of Harlem, 1975. With USN, 1963-67. Mem. Mont. Assn. Realtors (v.p. ea. dist. 1982-84), Gateway Bd. Realtors (pres. 1987-88), Kiwanis, Lions. Republican. Mem. Ch. of Christ. Home: Holly and North Dr Sidney MT 59270 Office: ERA Beagle Properties 120 2d Ave SW Sidney MT 59270

BEAHM, SHEILA CATHERINE, airline pilot; b. Washington, May 20, 1962; d. Fred Eugene Beahm and Maxine Brandon (Brown) Watson. BS, San Jose State U., 1985. Flight instr. Aero Trends, Inc., San Jose, 1985, Flying Country Club, Palo Alto, Calif., 1985, Hawaii Country Club of the Air, Honolulu, 1985-86; cargo pilot Hutchinson Air, Honolulu, 1986; charter pilot Pearl Pacific Air, Honolulu, 1986; commuter pilot Princeville Airways, Honolulu, 1986-87; airline pilot Aloha Airlines, Honolulu, 1987--; pvt. practice, Honolulu, 1987--. Aviation scholarship Ninety-Nines, 1985, Pancho Barnes Meml. scholar Happy Bottom Riding Club, 1987. Mem. Internat. Soc. Women Airline Pilots, Gen. Aviation Coun. of Hawaii, NAFE, Kailua (Hawaii) Canoe Club. Democrat. Home: 1276 Mokula Dr Kailua HI 96734

BEAKE, JOHN, professional football team executive. m. Marcia Beake; children: Jerilyn, Chip, Christopher. Grad., Trenton (N.J.) State Coll.; M degree, Pa. State U. Asst. coach Pa. State U., 1961-62, Kansas City Chiefs, NFL, 1968-74, New Orleans Saints, NFL, 1976-77; offensive coordinator Colo. State U., 1974-76; dir. profl. personnel Denver Broncos, NFL, 1979-83, dir. football ops., 1983-84, asst. gen. mgr., 1984-85, gen. mgr., 1985—. Office: Denver Broncos 5700 Logan St Denver CO 80216 *

BEALE, STEPHEN BRUCE, editor, political activist; b. Phila., Aug. 9, 1958; s. Bruce Harrison Beale and Rosemary (Biddle) Lee. BA in journalism, Temple U., 1981. Editor Spice Mag., Phila., 1979-81; editor Vet. Computing, Santa Barbara, Calif., 1983-86; sr. editor Hispanic Bus. Mag., Santa Barbara, Calif., 1986-87, Micro Pub., Torrance, Calif., 1987--; corr. Vet. Econs., Lenexa, Kans., 1986--. Author (with James Caruoto): The Scanner Book, 1989. Chmn. Santa Barbara County Dem. Cen. Com., 1984-87; exec. bd. Calif. Dem. Party, Sacramento, 1984-87; chmn. 51st Assembly Dist. Dem. Com., L.A., 1988—. Recipient Journalism award Newsletter Assn., 1985. Clubs: Calif. Dem. Party Computer (Los Angeles) (bd. dirs. 1987--). Home: PO Box 14321 Torrance CA 90503 Office: Micro Publishing 21150 Hawthorne Blvd. #104 Torrance CA 90503

BEALL, DEWITT TALMADGE, interior designer; b. Ripley, W.Va., Apr. 10, 1940; s. DeWitt T.and Orpha Auline (Hartley) B.; m. Callista Marie Card, Sept. 15, 1973 (div. 1988); m. Elina Katsioula, Nov. 19, 1988; children: John Aaron, Olivia Simone. BA, Dartmouth Coll., 1965. Copywriter Leo Burnett, Chgo., 1965-66; freelance filmmaker Chgo., 1966-71, 73-75; producer, dir. WTTW, Chgo., 1971-73; assoc. producer Goldsholl Assocs., Northfield, Ill., 1975-78; freelance designer, writer L.A., 1979-87; pres. The Kitchen Architect, Pacific Palisades, Calif., 1988—. Author: Ravenswood, 1963; producer documentary and ednl. films. Founder, Found. Years., Chgo., 1968. Recipient Chgo. award Chgo. Internat. Film Festival, 1977, Cine Golden Eagle, 1969, 72, Silver medal Venice Film Festival, 1976; featured in cover story, Kitchen and Bath Design News, 1985, 88. Mem. Am. Soc. Interior Designers. Democrat. Methodist. Office: The Kitchen Architect 15207 Sunset Blvd Pacific Palisades CA 90272

BEALS, MARK GRADEN, educator; b. Irvona, Pa., Aug. 11, 1936; s. George Bylle and Leila Elzeda (Eidell) B. B.A., Lycoming Coll., 1956; M.A., U. Hawaii, 1958; Ph.D., U. Ariz., 1968. Psychologist Yakima, Wash., 1961-64; instr. psychology Yakima Valley Coll., 1961-64; asst. prof., coordinator program in spl. edn. No. Ariz. U., Flagstaff, 1966-69; prof., dir. undergrad. curricula, coordinator student teaching and programs for gifted U. Nev., Las Vegas, 1969-85, asst. dean Coll. Edn., 1985—; cons. State of Ariz. Dists. 15, 16, 22, 1970-79; founder cons. New Horizons Ctr. for Learning, Las Vegas, 1971—; cons. and lectr. in field. Author: Handbook for Teachers of the Culturally Deprived, 1966, Laughter of Children, 1968 (film); contbr. articles to profl. jours. Pres. So. Nev. Epilepsy Assn., Nev. Epilepsy Assn., 1972-75; mem. Com. on Rehab., 1969; mem. Gov.'s Com. on Gifted, 1975, Com. on Accreditation, 1981—, others. Served with U.S. Army, 1944-47. Recipient Gov.'s award State of Nev., 1968; Epilepsy Found. leadership award, 1975; award for leadership to children Ariz. Assn. Chronic Lung Disease, 1977. Fellow Menninger Found.; mem. Am. Psychol. Assn., Western Psychol. Assn., Council for Exceptional Children, AAAS, Ednl. Research Assn., Assn. for Retarded Citizens, Orton Soc. Humanistic Psychology Assn., Mensa. Republican. Office: Univ Nevada Coll of Edn Las Vegas NV 89154

BEALS, TERRENCE ROGER, banking consultant; b. Mendon, Ill., Oct. 3, 1941; s. Roy Washington and Mary (Gorman) B.; m. Wendy Jorgenson (div. Oct. 1985). BA, San Francisco State U., 1964, MA, 1968. Ednl. cons. United Airlines, San Francisco, 1968-70; mgr. tech. tng. div. Bechtel Corp., San Francisco, 1970-72; various positions Bank of Am., San Francisco, 1972-78; pres., founder Human Resources West Inc., San Francisco, 1978—. Author: Depository Institutions Today, 1987, (with others) Stanford Bank Game, 1988. Office: Human Resources Mgmt 604 Mission #802 San Francisco CA 94105

BEAMER, SCOTT, consulting electrical engineer, lecturer; b. Berkeley, Calif., Apr. 2, 1914; s. Joseph H. and Louise (Scott) B.; B.S. in Elec. Engring., U. Calif., 1936; m. Alpha Mae Rogers, Oct. 21, 1939; children—Joan Louise, Scott, Ronald Laurence, Alexander Rogers, Deborah. Jr. elec. engr. Pacific Electric Motor Co., 1938-40; asso. elec. engr. Farm Sect. Adminstrn., U.S. Dept. Agr., 1940-42; cons. engr. with Clyde E. Bentley, 1946-47, Beamer & Tilson, 1949-51; with Beamer/Wilkinson & Assos.; 1966-76, Scott Beamer & Assos., 1977—; mem. faculty U. Calif., 1948-63, teaching regular classes architecture and engring. and extension classes at Oakland and San Francisco, 1948-59, also univ. research projects; lighting cons. Bay Area Rapid Transit Dist. Joint Ventures. Former chmn. adv. council Salvation Army Hosp.; former chmn. troop com., mem. exec. council Boy Scouts Am., elected to Order of Arrow; former trustee Children's Hosp. Med. Center Found.; bd. dirs. Oakland Mus. Assn., Heart-Lung Inst. East Bay; mem. adv. bd. Ladies Home Soc., Oakland. Served as maj. AUS, Office Chief of Ordnance, 1942-46, in Washington, France and Germany on Proximity Fuse project; mem. O.R.C., 1937-63. Decorated Bronze Star medal, Distinguished Service Wreath, Army Commendation medal. Registered profl. engr., Calif., Nev., Oreg. Fellow Illuminating Engring. Soc.; mem. IEEE (life), Nat. Acad. Forensic Engrs. (diplomate grade), Nat. Soc. Profl. Engrs. Clubs: Rotary (past pres.), Claremont Country, 100 (past dir.). Contbr. articles to profl. jours. Patentee neon dimming transformer; co-author of patent luminous bodies. Home: 36 King Ave Piedmont CA 94611 Office: Scott Beamer & Assocs 618 Grand Ave Oakland CA 94610

BEAMER-PATTON, JUNE ELIZABETH, dermatologist; b. Martin's Ferry, Ohio, Mar. 9, 1944; d. Ralph Clark and Betty June (Sedgwick) Patton; m. Yancey Brintle, Aug. 20, 1967 (div. Dec. 1986). BS in Chemistry, Marshall U., 1965; MD, Med. Coll. Va., 1969. Diplomate Am. Bd. Dermatology; cert. Nat. Bd. Med. Examiners, Calif.; cert. Colo. Basic Sci., Colo., Utah; cert. X-ray Supr. and Operator, Calif. Intern Med. Coll. Va., Richmond, 1969-70, U. Calif., Irvine, 1970; resident in dermatology Long Beach (Calif.) Veteran's Hosp., 1970-73; with Placentia-Linda Community Hosp., Placentia, Calif., 1977, Children's Hosp. Orange County, Orange, Calif., 1974-79, We. Med. Ctr. (Calif.) Santa Ana, 1973-80, U. Calif. Med. Ctr., Irvine, 1970-82, Tustin (Calif.) Community Hosp., 1973-85, Healthcare Med. Ctr. Tustin, 1988; pvt. practice Tustin, 1988—; clin. assoc. medicine dermatology, U. Calif., Irvine, 1972, clin. instr. medicine dermatology, 1973, asst. clin. prof. 1976, clin. prof. 1977-82. Contbr. articles profl. jours. Mem. ABA, Am. Med. Women's Assn., Calif. Med. Assn., Pacific Dermatologic Assn., Orange County Med. Assn., Orange County Dermatological Soc., Am. Acad. Dermatology, Am. Coun. Hosp. Staffs, Internat. Acad. Cosmetic Surgery, Cooperative of Am. Physicians, Inc., Am. Soc. Dermatology Surgery, Audio Engring. Soc., Am. Mgmt. Assn., Nat. Assn. Women Bus. Owners, Am. Soc. Profl. and Exec. Women, Tustin C. of C., Wings Club, Alpha Epsilon Delta, Chi Beta Phi, Phi Alpha Theta. Republican. Methodist. Office: June E Beamer-Patton MD 13372 Newport Ave #A Tustin CA 92680

BEAMISH, JEROME JAMES, academic administrator; b. Montreal, Feb. 10, 1924; came to U.S., 1957, permanent resident, 1962; s. Gerald Gays and Vera Olivia (Crandell) B.; m. Alice Frances RossMcVeigh, Oct. 12, 1944; children: Christopher Carl, Kevin Keith, Maureen Davis. AA, Sir George Williams U., Montreal, 1956, BA, 1957; diploma in Bus. Adminstr., Mcgill U., Montreal, 1957; MA, Columbia U., N.Y.C., 1958, PhD, 1962. Adminstr. Royal Air Force. Royal Canadian Air Force, various locations, 1943-46; asst. personnel mgr. Springfield Ins. Group, Montreal, 1946-53; personnel dir. Adriatic Ins. Group, Montreal, 1953-57; teaching fellow Columbia U., N.Y.C., 1957-59; instr. in psychology Fairleigh Dickinson U., Hunter Coll., N.Y.C., 1960-61; counseling psycologist Stevens Inst. Tech., Hoboken, N.J., 1959-62; asst. prof., psychology U. Calif., Santa Barbara, 1962-64; assoc. dean, assoc. prof. Calif. State U. Stanislaus, Turlock, 1964-79, exec. dir., non traditional programs, prof., 1979—. Contbr. articles to profl. jours. Mem. exec. bd. Boy Scouts Am., Santa Barbara & Modesto, Calif., 1962—; bd. dirs. Community Concerts Assn., Modesto, 1988—; mem. chmn. adv. bd. Drug Programs, Stanislaus County, Calif. Recipient Wood Badge award Boys Scouts Am., 1963. Mem. Am. Psychol. Assn., Am. Personnel & Guidance Assn., Nat Assn. Fgn. Student Affairs, Calif. Assn. Post-Secondary Educators Disabled, Phi Delta Kappa, Kappa Delta Pi, Psi Chi. Democrat. Episcopalian. Home: 917 Woodrow Ave Modesto CA 95350 Office: Calif State U 801 W Monte Vista Ave Turlock CA 95380

BEAN, DAVID BALDWIN, executive director; b. Kentfield, Calif., May 3, 1946; s. David Ericson and Jean B.; m. Beatrice Lecocq, Nov. 22, 1975 (div. 1978). BA, U. Calif., Santa Cruz, 1978. Owner Wood Works- Custom Furniture, Greenbrae, Calif., 1978-81; sales rep. Books West, San Anselmo, Calif., 1981-83; dir. Pacific Way Books, San Anselmo, 1983-85, Pacific Way Internat., Portland, Oreg., 1985—. Mem. North-West China Coun., Portland Souzhou Sister City Com. Mem. Oreg. Assn. Acupuncturists Assocs. Democrat.

BEAR, JEFFREY WARREN, construction executive; b. Amittyville, N.Y., Mar. 18, 1945. BA, San Diego State U., 1972, MFA, 1975; postgrad., Harvard U., 1985; PhD with honors, Coll. of Edassea, Mararastra, India, 1978. Pres. Orion Fin. Fund, San Diego, 1972-83; bus. mgr. Matlines, Inc., San Diego, 1983-87; priest Good Samaritains, National City, Calif., 1978—; chief adminstrv. officer Phoenix Cos., San Diego, 1987—; chmn. Svc. Benefit Corp. of Am., San Diego, 1987—; cons. Arts Counsel, Reno, 1975—; bd. dirs. J. Christopher Enterprises, Reno. Author: American Contemporary Pottery, 1974; contbr. articles to profl. jours. Bd. dirs. Soc. St. Thomas, San Diego, 1978—; floor runner Dem. Conv., L.A., 1960. Mem. Am. Mgmt. Assn., Am. Bldg. Contractors, Assoc. Bldg. Contractor Assn., Internat. Assn. Concrete Repair Specialists (bd. dirs.), Nat. Restoration Contractors Assn. Eastern Catholic. Officer: Phoenix Cos 4901 Morena Blvd San Diego CA 92117

BEARDALL, JAMES C., lumber company executive; b. Springville, Utah, Sept. 6, 1939; s. W. Clyde and Florence (Lloyd) B.; m. LaRue Whiting, Sept. 9, 1960; children: Laurie Kae, Stacy Lyn, Michael James. BS in Acctg., Brigham Young U., 1962. C.P.A., Calif., Utah. With Haskins & Sells (C.P.A.s), Los Angeles, 1962-66; with Anderson Lumber Co., Ogden, Utah, 1966—; v.p. Anderson Lumber Co., 1977-79, pres., chief operating officer, 1979—, chief exec. officer, 1980—, chmn. bd., 1988—; pres., chmn. bd. dirs. Pioneer Wholesale Supply Co.; mem. adv. bd. Fist Security Bank; chmn. adv. coun. Sch. Bus. Weber State Coll.; dir. Indsl. Rels. Coun., 1985—; chmn. bd. dirs. Cen. Bldg. Supply; bd. dirs. First Security Corp. Mem. Am. Inst. C.P.A.s, Mountain States Lumber and Bldg. Material Assn. (pres. 1981-82), Utah Soc. C.P.A.'s, Ogden C. of C. (officer, dir. 1979—, chmn.-elect), Nat. Lumber and Bldg. Material Dealers Assn. (nat. bd. dirs. 1985-88). Republican. Mormon. Clubs: Golf and Country, Alta Lodge: Ogden Rotary (pres. 1983-84). Office: Anderson Lumber Co PO Box 9459 Ogden UT 84409

BEARDEN, THOMAS HOWARD, news program producer, correspondent; b. Washington, Feb. 14, 1948; s. Norman C. and Emma Dorothy (Jensen) B.; m. Ruth Ann Harrison, July 12, 1977; children: Jennifer Kate, Emily Jane. BS in Journalism, U. Miss., 1969, MA in Radio and TV, 1971. Reporter, anchorman Sta. WJTV-TV, Jackson, Miss., 1971-72; reporter, anchorman, assignment editor Sta. WHBQ-TV, Memphis, 1972-78; reporter, anchorman Sta. KMGH-TV, Denver, 1978-85; producer, correspondent MacNeil-Lehrer News Hour, Denver, 1985—. Producer/reporter TV news series documentary The Quicksilver Connection, 1984 (Emmy award 1984). Served to 1st lt. U.S. Army, 1971-72. Mem. Sigma Delta Chi. Club: Denver Press (news series award 1983). Office: MacNeil-Lehrer News Hour 2480 W 26th Suite 2B Denver CO 80211

BEARLEY, WILLIAM LEON, consulting company executive; b. Hays, Kans., June 6, 1938; s. William L. and Wilma M. (Sechrist) B.; B.S., U. Wyo., 1969, M.Ed., 1964; Ed.D., U. La Verne, 1983; M.H.R.D., Univ. Assos. Grad. Sch. Human Resource Devel., 1980; also grad. Lab. Edn. Intern Program; m. Diane Lee Kiser, Dec. 15, 1967. Tchr. math. Baldwin Park Unified Sch. Dist., Baldwin Park, Calif., 1961-64, chmn. dept. math, 1962-64; chmn. math. dept. Citrus Coll., Azusa, Calif., 1965-69, chmn. data processing dept., 1969-80, dir. computing and info. systems, 1972-80; pres. Computer Info. Assocs., Inc., Pasadena, Calif., 1980-82; prof. Edn. Mgmt., U. LaVerne, 1982—; v.p. Organizational Universe Systems, Valley Ctr., Calif., 1985—; cons., trainer info. resource mgmt., 1981—. Mem. Data Processing Mgmt. Assn. (cert.), Am. Soc. Tng. and Devel., Acad. Mgmt., Am. Mgmt. Assn., Orgn. Devel. Network, Am. Guild Organists, Assn. Computing Machinery, Assn. Systems Mgmt. (cert.), Phi Delta Kappa. Author/co-author computer software, books and articles in field. Home: 12665 Cumbres Rd Valley Center CA 92082 Office: U La Verne 1950 3d St La Verne CA 91750

BEARWALD, JEAN HAYNES, company executive; b. San Francisco, Aug. 31, 1924; d. Joseph Robert and Edna Haynes (Goudey) Bearwald; m. William Henry Sherburn, Apr. 12, 1969 (dec. 1970); 1 child by previous marriage, David Richard Cross. BA, Stephens Coll., Columbia, Mo., 1945. Adminstrv. asst. Bearwald & Assocs., Sacramento, 1966-78; acct. Truck Parts Co., Sand City, Calif., 1979-80; pres., chief exec. officer Bearwald & Assocs., Fresno, Calif., 1980—. Prog. dir. Alcoholics Anonymous, Sacramento, 1980-82. Republican. Episcopalian. Home: 1716 W Shaw Ave #F Fresno CA 93711

BEARY, ANICE CHRISTINE, speech therapist; b. Martinez, Calif., Mar. 17, 1947; d. George Joseph and Alice Louise (Martin) Larbaig; m. David Bradley Beary, Mar. 11, 1982. BS, Chico State Coll., 1970, postgrad., 1971. Speech and lang. therapist Stanislaus County Dept. Edn., Modesto, Calif., 1971—, Modesto, summer 1988; sec. Escalon M.A., Inc., 1987—; receptionist Weight Watchers, Inc., Modesto and Oakdale, Calif., 1988—. Mem. Calif. Tchrs. Assn. (lobbyist 1986), NEA, Aircraft Owners and Pilots Assn. Democrat.

BEASLEY, BRUCE MILLER, sculptor; b. Los Angeles, May 20, 1939; s. Robert Seth and Bernice (Palmer) B.; m. Laurence Leaute, May 21, 1973; children: Julian Bernard, Celia Beranice. Student, Dartmouth Coll., 1957-59; B.A., U. Calif. at Berkeley, 1962. Sculptor in metal and plastic, one man shows at, Everett Ellin Gallery, Los Angeles, Kornblee Gallery, N.Y.C., Hansen-Fuller Gallery, San Francisco, David Stuart Gallery, Los Angeles, Andre Emmerich Gallery, N.Y.C., De Young Mus., San Francisco, Santa Barbara Mus. Art, Fine Arts Gallery, San Diego; exhibited in group shows at, Mus. Modern Art, N.Y.C., Guggenheim Mus., N.Y.C., Albright Knox Gallery, Buffalo, LaJolla (Calif.) Art Mus., Musée d'Art Modern, Paris, San Francisco Mus. Art, Krannert Art Mus. at U. Ill., Jewish Mus., N.Y.C., Luxembourg Gardens, Paris, Calif. Palace of Legion of Honor, De Young Mus., Santa Barbara Art Mus., others; represented in permanent collections, Mus. Modern Art, Guggenheim Mus., Musée d'Art Modern, Paris, Los Angeles County Art Mus., Univ. Art Mus., Berkeley, Oakland (Calif.) Mus., Wichita (Kans.) Art Mus., San Francisco Art Commn., Santa Barbara Art Mus., Dartmouth Coll., others; major sculpture commns. include, State of Calif., 1967, Oakland Mus., 1972, City of San Francisco, 1976, U.S. govt., 1976, City of Eugene, Oreg., 1974, City of Salinas, Calif., 1977, Miami Internat. Airport, Fla., 1978, San Francisco Internat. Airport, 1981, Stanford U., 1982, City of Anchorage, Alaska, Los Angeles Olympic Stadium, 1984. Recipient Andre Malraux purchase award Biennale de Paris, 1961. Home: 322 Lewis St Oakland CA 94607

BEASLEY, KATHLEEN LINDA, state official, public relations consultant; b. Hayward, Aug. 23, 1951; d. Wilbur Allen and Anna Marie (Hopper) B.; 1 child, Melanie Marie. BS in Journalism, Calif. Poly. State U., San Luis Obispo, 1973; BA in Polit. Sci., U. Sheffield (Eng.), 1974. Reporter, editor San Luis Obispo Telegram Tribune, 1972-73, Riverside (Calif.) Press-Enterprise, 1978-79; reporter Redding (Calif.) Record Searchlight, 1974-76, A.P., L.A., 1976-77, Orange County Register, Santa Ana, Calif., 1977-78; pres. sec. to Assemblywoman Carol Hallett, Calif. Assembly, Sacramento, 1979-80; editor Sacramento Bee, 1980-86; press sec. to Assemblyman Stan Statham Calif. Assembly, Sacramento, 1988; project editor, press sec. Little Hoover Commn., Sacramento, 1988—; newsletter cons. Pacific Gas & Electric Co., Sacramento, 1989. Contbr. articles to newspapers and mags. Bd. dirs. Sierra Curtis Neighborhood Assn., Sacramento, 1986-88; newsletter editor Courtyard Pvt. Sch., Sacramento, 1988—. Mem. Pub. Rels. Soc. Am., Mensa, Sacramento Bridge Club (pres. 1985-89), Sigma Delta Chi, Phi Kappa Phi. Republican.

BEASON, JAMES DOUGLAS, air force officer, physicist, writer; b. Alexandria, La., Dec. 3, 1953; s. James Larry and Martha Grace (McCluney) B.; m. Cynthia Marie Olsen, Jan. 20, 1979; children: Amanda Grace, Tamara Jo. Student, La. Tech. U., 1972-73; BS in Physics and Math., U.S. Air Force Acad., 1977; MS in Physics, U. N.Mex., 1980, PhD in Physics, 1983. Commd. 2d lt. U.S. Air Force, 1977, advanced through grades to maj., 1988; computational physicist U.S. Air Force Weapons Lab., Kirtland AFB, N.Mex., 1977-79, sect. chief nuclear effects, 1979-80, chief plasma physics, 1986-88, chief advanced concepts, 1988—; asst. prof. physics U.S. Air Force Acad., Colorado Springs, Colo., 1983-86; cons. Lawrence Livermore (Calif.) Nat. Lab., 1985—, Ames Rsch. Ctr., NASA, Sunnyvale, Calif., 1985. Author: Return to Honor, 1989, Assault on Alpha Base, 1989; contbr. articles to profl. jours., short stories to sci.-fiction mags. Bd. dirs. Albuquerque Bible Coll., 1987-88. Decorated Meritorious Svc. medal. Mem. Am. Phys. Soc., Sci. Fiction Writers Am., Small Press Writers and Artists Orgn., Air Force Assn. Republican. Presbyterian. Office: Air Force Weapons Lab Advanced Concepts Kirtland AFB NM 87117

BEATON, DENNIS WAYNE, insurance executive; b. Quonset Point, R.I., June 1, 1949; s. Phillip John and Frieda Margaret (Donovan) B.; m. Susan Diane Babovêc, June 13, 1970; children: Jonathan, David, Kristina. BA, Los Angeles Bapt. Coll., 1973. Supr. claims Indsl Indemnity, Los Angeles, 1973-78; mgr. claims Redwood Fire & Casualty, Los Angeles, 1978-80; v.p. claims Ins. Co. the West, Woodland Hills, Calif., 1980-83; v.p. claims Pacific States Casualty Co., Los Angeles, 1983-87, v.p. policyholder services, 1987—. Mem. CWCI. Republican. Home: 20227 Cedarcreek St Canyon Country CA 91351 Office: Pacific States Casualty Co 5757 Wilshire Blvd #670 Los Angeles CA 90036

BEATON, JAMES DONALD, accountant; b. Lemars, Iowa, Aug. 18, 1940; s. Donald George and Marjorie Nan (McConnell) B.; m. Marjorie Ann Armstrong, Feb. 2, 1963; children: Shelley Marie, Jennifer Lynn. BS in Acctg., Ariz. State U., 1963. CPA, Ariz. Agt. IRS, Mesa, Ariz., 1963-70; supr. Peat, Marwick, Mitchell & Co., Phoenix, 1970-73; prin. Beaton, Horne & Gosney, P.C., Mesa, 1973-81; pres., owner Beaton & Debernardi, Ltd., Tempe, Ariz., 1981-85; tax prin. Peat Marwick Main & Co., Tempe, 1985-87; prin. James D. Beaton, P.C., Tempe, 1987--. Allocations com. Valley of Sun United Way, Tempe, 1983-88; bd. dirs. Friendship Village of Tempe, 1984-88; active Tempe Diplomats, 1985--. Mem. Ariz. Soc. CPAs (pres. 1982-83), Am. Inst. CPAs (mem. council 1984-87), Central Ariz. Estate Planning Council (bd. dirs. 1978-80), Sun Devil Sertoma (pres.1973-75), Ariz. Palomino Horse Exhibitors Assn. (pres. 1982-84). Republican. Methodist. Office: James D Beaton PC 1415 E Guadalupe St Suite 106 Tempe AZ 85283

BEATTIE, GEORGE CHAPIN, orthopaedic surgeon; b. Bowling Green, Ohio, Sept. 24, 1919; s. George Wilson and Mary Turner (Chapin) B.; m. Nancy U. Fant, Mar. 1, 1947; children: Michael, Suzanne, Eric. BA, Bowling Green U., 1939; MD, U. Chgo., 1943. Diplomate Am. Bd. Orthopaedic Surgery. Commd. lt MC USN, 1943, advanced through grades to lt. (j.g.), 1951; med. officer, intern U.S. Naval Hosp., Great Lakes, Ill., 1943-44; resident, fellow in orthopaedic surgery Lahey Clinic, Boston, 1944; ward med. officer orthopaedic services Naval Hosp., Guam, 1944-46; sr. med. officer USN, Manus Island, Papua New Guinea, 1946; resident tng. in orthopaedic surgery U.S. Naval Hosp. St. Albans, N.Y.C., 1947-48; resident in orthopaedic surgery Children's Hosp., Boston, 1949; asst. chief orthopaedic surgery U.S. Naval Hosp. Oak Knoll, Oakland, Calif., 1950-52; comdg. officer med. co. 1st Marine Div. Med. Bn., Republic of Korea, 1952-53; chief orthopaedic service Dept. Phys. Medicine and Navy Amputee Ctr. U.S. Naval Hosp., Phila., 1954; resigned USN, 1954; practice medicine specializing in orthopaedic surgery San Francisco, 1954—; co-chmn. handicapping conditions com. Health Action Study San Mateo County, 1965; 1st chmn. orthopaedic sect. surg. dept. Peninsula Hosp. and Med. Ctr., Burlingame, Calif., 1967, chmn. rehab. service, 1967-71, chmn. phys. therapy and rehab. com., 1956—, vice chmn. orthopaedic dept., 1973-76, chmn., 1977-79; med. dir. research and rehab. ctr. San Mateo (Calif.) County Soc. Crippled Children and Adults, 1958-63; mem. exec. com. Harold D. Chope Community Hosp., San Mateo, 1971-76, chief, co-chmn. orthopaedic sect., 1971-76; chief orthopaedic surg. sect. Mills Meml. Hosp., San Mateo, 1976-78; others. Contbr. articles to profl. jours. Active Indian Guides, 1972-77; pres. Calif. Easter Seal Soc., 1969-71. Decorated Bronze Star. Fellow Am. Acad. Orthopaedic Surgeons (exhibit com. 1979-86); mem. AMA (Billings Bronze medal 1954), Western Orthopaedic Assn. (pres., bd. dirs. 1986), Leroy Abbott Orthopaedic Soc. U. Calif. San Francisco (assoc. clin. prof.), Alpha Omega Alpha. Office: 1515 Trousdale Dr Burlingame CA 94010

BEATTY, HUGH TYRRELL, radiologist, naval officer; b. Wenatchee, Wash., Dec. 10, 1939; s. Donald Turner Beatty and Aileen Margurite (Tyrrell) Beatty Ramsey; m. Sara Ann Matthei, June 18, 1962 (div. Dec. 1968); children—Philip, Michael; m. Monty Lee Madsen, Dec. 21, 1968; children—D'Le Beatty Jackson, Todd, Terry, Michelle. B.S., U. Utah, 1965, M.D., 1968; postgrad. Sch. Submarine Medicine, Groton, Conn., 1969. Diplomate Nat. Bd. Med. Examiners. Commd. ensign USN, 1957, advanced through grades to comdr., 1975; intern Naval Hosp., Jacksonville, Fla., 1968-69; ship med. officer U.S.S. Patrick Henry, 1969-70; research med. officer, Naval Exptl. Diving Unit, Washington, 1970-72; resident in radiology Nat. Naval Med. Ctr., Bethesda, Md., 1972-75; chief radiology service Naval Hosp., Oak Harbor, Wash., 1975-81; med. officer Med. Clinic, Naval Submarine Base Bangor, Bremerton, Wash., 1981-82, sr. med. officer, 1984-85; ship's med. officer U.S.S. Ohio, 1982-84; radiol. cons. dysbaric osteonecrosis panel USN, Washington, 1972-85; pvt. practive cons., Oak Harbor, Wash., 1985—. Author monograph. Chmn. 4th of July Celebration Com., Oak Harbor, Wash., 1978; pres. Whidbey Playhouse, Oak Harbor, 1978-80. Mem. Undersea Med. Soc., Lions (3d v.p. Whidbey club). Republican. Mormon. Avocations: stamps, genealogy, backpacking. Home: 3135 Robin Ln Oak Harbor WA 98277 Office: 1214 Midway Blvd Oak Harbor WA 98277

BEATTY, MARTHA NELL, owner travel agency; b. San Francisco, Oct. 29, 1933; d. Harold Miles Tucker and Audrey Martha (Kirkbride) Pinney; m. Alden R. Crow, Feb. 9, 1956 (dec. Oct. 1984); children: Alana Sims, Tucker (dec. 1984); m. Denis Beatty, Sept. 19, 1986. BA, Stanford U., 1955. Cert. travel counselor. Sales cons. Thomas Cook, San Francisco, 1955-56, Am. Express, San Francisco, 1963-64, Gulliver's Travel, San Francisco, 1964-66; pres., owner Unravel Travel, Inc., San Francisco, 1969—. Author: (guide book) San Francisco at a Glance, 1971; contbr. articles to profl. jour. Mem. Carriage Trade Assn. (pres. 1987-88), Am. Soc. Travel Agents, Pacific Area Travel Assn., San Francisco Women in Travel, Francisca Club (sec. 1985-89). Republican. Episcopalian. Home: 2998 Jackson St San Francisco CA 94115 Office: Unravel Travel Inc 660 Market St San Francisco CA 94104

BEATY, LEWIS KENT, pharmacist; b. Waco, Tex., Oct. 23, 1943; s. Lewis Trent and Gwendolyn Eugene (Battaile) B.; m. Sarah Jane Moran, June 6, 1974; children: John Lewis, Eugene Patrick, Jacob Timothy. BS in Biology, Calif. State U., Fullerton, 1971; BS in Pharmacy, Wash. State U., 1976. Clin. staff pharmacist Group Health Coop. Puget Sound Pharmacy, Burien, Wash., 1976-77; dir. Group Health Coop. Puget Sound Pharmacy, Seattle, 1978—. With U.S. Army, 1967-69, Vietnam. Mem. Am. Pharm. Assn., Pharmacists Mgrs. Coun. (chmn. 1987). Republican. Roman Catholic. Home: 3510 SW 172nd St Seattle WA 98166 Office: Group Health Coop 509 Olive Way Ste 960 Seattle WA 98101

BEATY, PAUL RICHARD, aquatic biologist; b. Ames, Iowa, June 2, 1946; s. Harold Huxford and Judith Helen (Skromme) B.; m. Sue Ann Weber, Sept. 7, 1968; children: Joel R., Christopher P., Michael A. BS in Edn., Ea. Ill. U., 1969; MS, U. Ill., 1976, PhD, 1979. Tchr. Unit 7 Schs., Tolono, Ill., 1969-73; tech. asst. Ill. Nat. History Survey, Urbana, 1974-78, asst. profl. scientist, 1978-80; dir. aquatic rsch. Coachella (Calif.) Valley Water Dist., 1980-86; prin., pres. Beaty & Assocs. S.W. Aquatics, Palm Desert, Calif., 1985—. Contbr. articles to profl. jours. Bd. dirs. Family YMCA of Desert, Palm Desert, 1984-86, Desert Youth Sports Assn., 1984-85; player agt. Palm Desert Youth Sports Assn., 1984-85; pres. Riverside County Com. on Sch. Dist. Orgn., Palm Desert, 1986—. Mem. Aquatic Plant Mgmt. Soc., Western Aquatic Plant Mgmt. Soc. (program chmn. 1983), North Am. Lake Mgmt. Soc. (program co-chmn. 1986—), Calif. Lake Mgmt. Soc. (bd. dirs. 1987—), Am. Fisheries Soc., Optimists. Home: 73-605 Joshua Tree Ln Palm Desert CA 92260 Office: Paul R Beaty & Assocs PO Box 4441 Palm Desert CA 92261

BEAUDRY, JANIS STONIER, property manager; b. Sacramento, Calif., Feb. 8, 1956; d. William Henry and Vivian June (Terril) Stoner; m. John Joseph Beaudry, Sept. 17, 1978. BA in Social Sci. and Sociology, Calif. State U., 1978. Asst. head cashier Toys R Us, Sacramento, Calif., 1974-78; banking svcs. officer Wells Fargo Bank, Sacramento, 1979-82; loan mgr. Western Community Savs. and Loan, Walnut Creek, Calif., 1982-84; real estate loan officer Sunrise Bank, Sacramento, 1984-85; dir. property mgmt. Mark III Mgmt., Inc., Sacramento, 1985—; cons. self Resume writing and fin., 1986—. Co-producer The Show Below; exhibited in group shows, 1982—. Crisis counselor, speaker Rape Crisis Ctr., Sacramento, 1982-84 (counseling award 1984); com. worker for assemblyman compaign, Sacramento, 1984; mem. Sacto Area Literacy Coalition, Sacramento, 1989. Mem. Nat. Assn. Exec. Women, Sacramento Valley Apt. Assn., Sacto Women's Network, Backgammon Club, Lions (2d v.p. Sacramento chpt. 1988). Democrat. Baptist.

BEAUFORD, WILLIE, JR., retail executive; b. St. Stephen, S.C., Mar. 23, 1944; s. Willie and Sophie (Jones) B.; m. Bernice Mitchell, May 6, 1968; children: Willie, Courtney Dion. BS in Mgmt., Park Coll., Parkville, Mo., 1983. Field cons. The Southland Corp., Las Vegas, Nev., 1985-88; franchise coordinator The Southland Corp., 1988—. With USAF, 1965-85. Decorated Air Force Commendation medal. Mem. Air Force Assn., Toastmasters. Democrat. Episcopalian. Home: 6709 Reggie Cir Las Vegas NV 89107

BEAUMAN, JOHN GERALD, technical director; b. N.Y.C., July 28, 1936; S. Lorenz and Constance Minetti; m. Jane Houstan, Jan. 2, 1982 (div. 1987); children: Deborah Ann, Gerald, Brenda, John Jr. Student of Engring., SUNY, 1966-70; BSME, Calif. Coast U., 1976, MSME, 1983. Tech. mgr. Fairchild Republic Co., Farmingdale, N.Y., 1965-82, Northrop B-2 Div., Pico Rivera, Calif., 1982-88; group tech. dir. Parker Bertea Aerospace, Irvine, Calif., 1988—. Author: Flight Control Iron Birds, 1983; editor, pub.: (newsletter) Montefino Spotlight, 1982-86. Pres. Montefino Homeowners Assn., Diamond Bar, Calif., 1982-86. Mem. AIRA. Republican. Lutheran. Home: 23035 Paseo de Terrado Unit 1 Diamond Bar CA 91765

BEAUMONT, MONA, artist; b. Paris, Jan. 1, 1927; d. Jacques Hippolyte and Elsie M. (Didisheim) Marx; BA, U. Calif., Berkeley, 1945, M.A., 1946; postgrad. Harvard U., Fogg Mus., Cambridge, postgrad. spl. studies Hans Hoffman Studios, N.Y.C., 1946; m. William G. Beaumont; children—Garrett, Kevin. One-woman shows at Galeria Proteo, Mexico City, Gumps Gallery, San Francisco, Palace of Legion of Honor, San Francisco, L'Armitiere Gallery, Rouen, France, Hoover Gallery, San Francisco, San Francisco Mus. Modern Art, Galeria Van der Voort, San Francisco, William Sawyer Gallery, San Francisco, Palo Alto (Calif.) Cultural Ctr., Galerie Alexandre Monnet, Brussels, Honolulu Acad. Arts, exhibited in group shows at San Francisco Mus. Modern Art, San Francisco Art Inst., DeYoung Meml. Mus., San Francisco, Grey Found. Tour of Asia, Bell Telephone Invitational, Chgo., Richmond Art Ctr., Los Angeles County Mus. Art, Galerie Zodiaque, Geneva, others; represented in permanent collections: Oakland (Calif.) Mus. Art, City and County of San Francisco, Hoover Found., San Francisco, Grey Found., Washington, Bulart Found., San Francisco; also numerous pvt. collections. Recipient Jack London Sq. Ann. Painting award; Purchase award Grey Found.; Ann. awards San Francisco Women Artists (2); Purchase award San Francisco Art Festival; One-Man Show award San Francisco Art Festival; included in Printworld Internat., 1982-88, Internat. Art Diary, Am. Artists, N.Y. Art Review, Calif. Art Review, Art in the San Francisco Bay area. Mem. Soc. for Encouragement of Contemporary Art, Bay Area Graphic Arts Council, San Francisco Art Inst., San Francisco Mus. Modern Art, Capp Street Project, Langton Street Ctr., others. Address: 1087 Upper Happy Valley Rd Lafayette CA 94549

BEAUPEURT, JOSEPH EUGENE, design engineer; b. St. Joseph, Mo., Jan. 23, 1912; s. Joseph Eugene and Nora (Smith) B.; m. Helene Frances Alexander, Aug. 2, 1941; children: Sharon Lynn, Debra Jo Beau-Schantz, Edward Lee. Student aircraft design, Finlay Engring. Sch., Kansas City, Mo., 1940-41; student modern bus., Alexander Hamilton U., N.Y.C., 1947-48; cert. in mech. engring., I.C.S., Scranton, Pa., 1952; postgrad., Wichita U., 1953. Registered profl. engr., Kans. Display artist Plymouth Clothing Co., St. Joseph, 1935-37, Lee's Studio, St. Joseph, 1937-40; design engr., engring. supr. Boeing Co., Wichita, 1941-57, human factors chief, 1957-69, product devel. engr., 1969-72; chief engr. S.V. Tool Co., Newton, Kans., 1973-74; pvt. practice Manitou Springs, Colo., 1976-83; pvt. practice, Safford, Ariz., 1983—; prin. investigator, sponsor Office Naval Res., Washington, 1959-68. Election judge City of Manitou Springs, 1977-82; trustee Unity Ch., Wichita, 1956-59, pres. bd. trustees, 1959-60. Republican. Home and Office: 1312 Hopi Ln Safford AZ 85546

BECHER, EDMUND THEODORE, secondary teacher, administrator; b. Westgate, Iowa, Dec. 27, 1904; s. Thomas and Lena (Hartman) B.; m. Grace Marguerite Greenawalt, July 29, 1932; 1 child, Beverly Grace. BA, U. Idaho, 1927; MA, U. Wash., 1932. Cert. secondary tchr., Idaho. Secondary tchr. Malad (Idaho) High Schs., 1927-28, North Cen. High Sch., Spokane, Wash., 1928-31; teaching fellow U. Wash., Seattle, 1931-32; tchr. social studies John R. Rogers High Sch., Spokane, 1932-36, dept. head, 1936-65; social studies dir. Spokane Pub. Sch. Dist. # 81, 1965-70, ret., 1970. Author: History and Government of Spokane, 1950, Spokane Corona, 1974, Spokane Primer, 1984. Mem. NEA. Lt. ROTC, 1927-36. Mem. Spokane Edn. Assn., State of Wash. Edn. Assn., ASCD (pres. 1964), Lions, Masons, Shriner, Knife and Fork Internat. Club. Avocations: travel, carpentry, bridge, golf. Home: E 2419 S Altamont Blvd Spokane WA 99202

BECHLER, BRYAN DOUGLAS, import export executive, recreation specialist; b. Inglewood, Calif., Jan. 28, 1962; s. Melville Glenn and Marian (Tingley) B. AA, Santa Monica Coll., 1983; BS, Calif. State U., Northridge, 1988. Importer Direct West Imports, Culver City, Calif., 1983—; recreation specialist Holmes and Norves Inc., Honolulu, 1988—. Mem. Am. Mgmt. Assn., Nat. Employees Svc. and Recreation Assn., Resort and Comml. Recreation Assn., Calif. Park and Recreation Soc. (dist. IX), Alpha Mu Gamma, Alpha Kappa Psi. (profl. chair 1987-88). Home and Office: Direct West Imports 5117 Lindblade Dr Culver City CA 90230

BECHTEL, RILEY, engineering company executive. s. Stephen Davison Bechtel, Jr. Formerly exec. v.p. Bechtel Group Inc., San Francisco, pres., 1989—. Office: Bechtel Group Inc PO Box 3965 San Francisco CA 94119 *

BECHTEL, STEPHEN DAVISON, JR., engineering company executive; b. Oakland, Calif., May 10, 1925; s. Stephen Davison and Laura (Peart) B.; m. Elizabeth Mead Hogan, June 5, 1946; 5 children. Student, U. Colo., 1943-44; BS, Purdue U., 1946, D. in Engring. (hon.), 1972; MBA, Stanford U., 1948; DSc (hon.), U. Colo., 1981. Registered profl. engr., N.Y., Mich., Alaska, Calif., Md., Hawaii, Ohio, D.C., Va., Ill. Engring. and mgmt. positions Bechtel Corp., San Francisco, 1941-60; pres. Bechtel Corp., 1960-73, chmn. of cos. in Bechtel group, 1973-80; chmn. Bechtel Group, Inc., 1980—; bd. dirs. IBM; former chmn. Bus. Council; life councillor, past chmn. Conf. Bd.; mem. policy com. Bus. Roundtable; mem. Labor-Mgmt. Group, Nat. Action Council on Minorities in Engring., from 1974. Trustee, mem., past chmn. bldg. and grounds com. Calif. Inst. Tech.; mem. pres.'s council Purdue U.; mem. adv. council Stanford U. Grad. Sch. Bus. Served with USMC, 1943-46. Decorated officer French Legion of Honor; recipient Disting. Alumnus award Purdue U., 1964, Disting. Alumnus award U. Colo., 1978; Ernest C. Arbuckle Disting. Alumnus award Stanford U. Grad. Sch. Bus., 1974; Man of Yr. Engring. News-Record, 1974; Outstanding Achievement in Constrn. award Moles, 1977; Disting. Engring. Alumnus award U. Colo., 1979; Herbert Hoover medal, 1980; Washington award Western Soc. Engrs., 1985, Chmn.'s award Am. Assn. Engring. Socs., 1982. Fellow ASCE (Engring. Mgmt. award 1979, Pres. award 1985), Instn. Chem. Engrs. (U.K., hon.); mem. AIME, Nat. Acad. Engring. (past chmn., chmn. industry adv. bd.), Calif. Acad. Scis. (hon. trustee), Am. Soc. French Legion of Honor (bd. dirs.), Fellowship of Engring (U.K., fgn. mem.), Chi Epsilon, Tau Beta Pi. Clubs: Pacific Union, Bohemian, San Francisco Golf (San Francisco); Claremont Country (Berkeley, Calif.); Cypress Point (Monterey Peninsula, Calif.); Thunderbird Country (Palm Springs, Calif.); Vancouver (B.C.); Ramada (Houston); Links, Blind Brook (N.Y.C.); Met. (Washington); Augusta (Ga.) National Golf; York (Toronto); Mount Royal (Montreal). Office: Bechtel Group Inc 50 Beale St PO Box 3965 San Francisco CA 94119

BECK, GORDON EUGENE, art history educator, consultant; b. Goshen, Ind., Mar. 23, 1929; s. Ralph Lea and Lydia Elizabeth (Greenlee) B.; m. Elizabeth Alice Arnholt, Mar. 22, 1951; children: Anne Elizabeth, Susan Elizabeth, Stephen Lea, John Lyons. BA, Bowling Green State U., 1951; MA, Western Res. U., 1952; PhD, U. Ill., 1964; postdoctoral student, Cini Found., Venice, Italy, 1979. Asst. instr. U. Ill., Urbana, 1954-56; instr. Bowling Green (Ohio) State U., 1956-57; instr., dir. univ. theatre U. Kans., Lawrence, 1957-65; asst. prof., dir. univ. theatre Cornell U., Ithaca, N.Y., 1965-71; prof. art history Evergreen State Coll., Olympia, Wash., 1971—; cons. European travel, Euro-Files, Olympia; dir. U. Kans. Theatre, 1957-65, Cornell U. Cinema, 1965-70, Mus. and Monuments Program, Olympia, 1975—. Editor, Players Mag., 1961-67; contbr. articles to Theatre Ann., 1964-69, Ency. World Drama, 1969; producer feature film, Branches, 1970. Cpl. M.C., U.S. Army, 1952-54. Mem. Coll. Art Assn., Mediaeval Acad. Am., Am. Soc. Aesthetics. Democrat. Home: 2406 18th Ave NW Olympia WA 98502-4119 Office: Evergreen State Coll 1602 Library Bldg Olympia WA 98505

BECK, KEITH LINDELL, small business owner; b. Ranger, Tex., Sept. 21, 1946; s. Corvis Lavon and Alta Ileane (Carney) B.; m. Kathleen Moore, Dec. 1968 (div. 1973); m. Cheryl Lynn Holmoe, May 8, 1976; children: Heather Aileen, Chelsey Nicole, Cameron David. BA, U. Redlands, 1969; postgrad., Calif. State U., Long Beach, 1974-76. Cert. tchr., Calif. Vol. U.S. Peace Corps, Ponape Island, Micronesia, 1969-70; mgmt. trainee J.C. Penney Co., Palm Springs, Calif., 1970-71; regional mgr. Fidelity Union Life Ins. Co., Dallas, 1971-72; corp. personnel mgr. Mervyn's Dept. Stores, Hayward, Calif., 1972-87; pres., owner Proforma Pacific Systems, Pleasanton, Calif., 1987--. Named Western Regional adv. councilman Western Regional Franchise Owners, 1988. Mem. Bus. Forms Mgmt. Assn. Home: 2646 Calle Alegre Pleasanton CA 94566 Office: Proforma Pacific Systems 39 California Ave Ste 208 Pleasanton CA 94566

BECK, LEWIS MARTIN, air force officer; b. Hartford, Conn., Feb. 13, 1959; s. Thelton Daniel and Mary Ann Beck; m. Cynthia Murphy, May 11, 1985; 1 child, Whitney Greer. BA in Aviation Adminstrn., Embry-Riddle U., 1981. Commd. 2d lt. USAF, 1981, advanced through grades to capt., 1985; T-38 instr. pilot USAF, Williams AFB, Ariz., 1982-86; C-130 pilot USAF, Elmendorf AFB, Alaska, 1986--; corp. pilot A Bar V Ranch Corp., Prescott, Ariz., 1981--. Republican. Roman Catholic. Home: 10201 Lone

Tree Dr Anchorage AK 99516 Office: 17 TAS/DOP Elmendorf AFB Anchorage AK 99506

BECK, MAXINE LOUISE, teacher; b. Plainview, Tex., Feb. 1, 1917; d. Charles Lewis and Helen Louise (Thomas) Barrett; m. Paul Chris Beck, Oct. 13, 1940 (div.); children: Christine Louise, Thomas Paul. BA, Pomona Coll., 1938; MA, Claremont Grad. Sch., 1972. Cert. elem. tchr., counselor. Tchr. Calif. Pub. Schs., 1939-70, Foothill Country Day Sch., Claremont, Calif., 1956-64; headmistress Girls Collegiate Sch., Claremont, Calif., 1965-69; continuing edn. dir. counseling Claremont Grad. Sch., 1970-72; dir. Marlborough Lower Sch., L.A., 1972-74; ednl. cons. San Mateo Found., Menlo Park, Calif., 1980-81. Author: poetry 1988. Mem. Towne Hall, Yakima, Wash., 1982-87; publicity chmn. Yakima Community Concert Assn., 1985-87; mem. Yakima Symphpny Assn., 1983-88; coord., dir. Well-Elder program Peninsula Vols. Little House Sr. Ctr., Menlo Park, 1988—; mem. task force Spl. Com. on Shortage of RN's in Calif. Mem. AAUW (1st v.p. 1984-86), AARP (spokesperson women's initiative 1987, mem. leadership coun. Calif. 1989). Republican. Home: 2282 Eastridge Ave Menlo Park CA 94025

BECK, MICHAEL EUGENE, building engineering manager; b. Midland, Mich., Oct. 3, 1941; s. Donald Ellison and Harriet Dorothy (Brunkalla) B.; m. Frances Sharlene McDaniel (div. 1984); children: Terri Lynn, Suzette Jean. AA with honors, Phoenix Coll., 1968; BA with honors, Ariz. State U., 1975. With bldg. design & constrn. Mountain Bell, Phoenix, 1973-78; with mech. systems, energy systems, retrofit & redesign Mountain Bell, 1978-84; with mech. systems design AT&T, Pleasanton, Calif., 1984-86; with western region energy AT & T, 1986-87, with hazardous materials compliance, 1987—; tech. excellence com. Ariz. Consulting Engrs. Coun., Phoenix, 1981. Mem. energy efficiency in cities rep. Ariz. Dept. Energy, Phoenix, 1979. With USAF, 1961-65. Recipient Energy Innovation award U.S. Dept. Energy, 1984, Award of Merit, Retrofit awards So. Ariz. Electric League, Cen. Ariz. Electric League, 1982-84, Grand award Elec. League Ariz., 1980. Mem. ASHRAE, ICBO, AAII, Assn. Energy Engrs. (sr. mem., Outstanding Corp. Energy Mgmt. award 1982), Am. Radio Relay League (life), Ariz. State Alumni Assn. (life), Masons. Episcopalian. Office: AT&T Pleasanton CA 94568

BECK, ROBERT DONALD, engineer; b. L.I., N.Y., Aug. 25, 1953; s. Donald Edward and Roberta Evelyn (Winter) B.; m. Debra Jean Robertshaw, Aug. 18, 1984. BS in Math., Rensselaer Poly. Inst., 1975, MS in Math., 1975; MS in Computer Sci., U. Wis., 1977. Software engr. Intel Corp., Hillsboro, Oreg., 1977-83; prin. engr. Sequent Computer Systems, Beaverton, Oreg., 1983—. Contbr. articles to profl. publs. Mem. IEEE, Assn. for Computing Machinery. Home: 12160 NW Coleman St Portland OR 97229 Office: Sequent Computer Systems 15450 SW Koll Pkwy Beaverton OR 97006

BECK, ROD, senator, realtor; b. Rigby, Idaho, May 28, 1951; s. Wayne and Zara (Hendricks) B.; m. Rhonda Beck, July 25, 1974; children: Jeremy, Kirsten, Jolie, Tim, Mackenzie, Cade. Student, Ricks Coll., Brigham Young U. Senator State of Idaho. Republican. Reorganized Ch. of Jesus Christ of Latter-day Saints. Home: 4257 Tattenham Way Boise ID 83704

BECK, THOMAS EDWIN, furniture maker; b. Stockton, Calif., Dec. 31, 1946; s. Harold Marquis and Verna (Johnson) B.; m. Ellen Marie Hill, Apr. 15, 1973; 1 child, Alexander Hill. Student, San Francisco City Coll., 1964-66, U. Calif., Berkeley, 1966-67, Coll. of the Desert, 1984-85, Calif. Poly. State U., 1985. Carpenter U.C.B. of Am., Portland, Oreg., 1972-76, Palm Springs, Calif., 1977; carpenter apprentice Drago/Dimitri Furniture, Calgary, Alta., Can., 1976; owner, operator Thomas Beck Fine Furniture, Morongo Valley, Calif., 1981—; cons. San Bernardino County Regional Employment. Concientious objector, Vietnam War. Home: 52355 Altadena Dr Morongo Valley CA 92256

BECK, TIMOTHY DANIEL, risk management company executive; b. Santa Monica, Calif., Mar. 21, 1953; s. James Daniel and Bettye June (Cisler) B.; m. Marcia Ann Smith, Jan. 16, 1977; children: Tracy Beth and Erica Brandy (twins), Jenna Michelle. AA, El Camino Community Coll., 1974; BA, Calif. State U., Northridge, 1979. Registered health underwriter. Candidate cert. employee benefit specialist, group claims supr. Prudential Ins. Co. Am., L.A., 1973-79; employee benefits cons. Olanie, Hurst & Hemrich, L.A., 1979-81; v.p. policyholder svc. dept. Health Maintenance Life Ins. Co., Fountain Valley, Calif., 1981; v.p. Robert E. French Ins. Svcs., Inc., Huntington Beach, Calif., 1981-85; v.p., mng. cons. employee benefits Warren, McVeigh & Griffin, Inc., Newport Beach, Calif., 1985—; mem. Kaiser Permanente Orange County Consumer Coun., 1987—; mem. pub. edn. com. Calif. Health Decision, 1988—; mem. bus. and health adv. panel Am. Health Pub.; speaker to confs. and profl. socs. Creator, contbg. editor Employee Benefits Mgmt. Letter, 1985—; contbr. articles to profl. publs. Mem. Internat. Found. Employee Benefits, Nat. Assn. Health Underwriters, Calif. Assn. Health Underwriters, Employee Benefit Planning Assn. So. Calif., So. Calif. Assn. Benefit Plan Adminstrs., Orange County Assn. Health Underwriters (founder, 1st. v.p. 1987-88), Orange County Employee Benefit Coun., Calif. State U. Alumni Assn., U.S. Golf Assn. (assoc.).

BECKEN, GAROLD WALLACE, instrumentation engineer; b. Tacoma, July 4, 1953; s. Gerald Wallace and Marjorie Jean (Brumbach) B.; m. Majlis Marie Rhoads, Jan. 14, 1978; children: Gregory Ward, Amanda Elizabeth. BS in EE, Wash. State U., 1976. Engr. Westinghouse Hanford Co., Richland, Wash., 1980-81; sr. engr. Westinghouse Hanford Co., 1987—, Marine div. Westinghouse Co., Sunnyvale, Calif., 1982-85, UNC, Richland, 1985-87. Asst. coach Richland Soccer League, 1986-89; cub scout com. mem. Boy Scouts Am., Richland, 1987-88, asst cub master, 1989—. Capt. U.S. Army, 1976-80, with res. Mem. IEEE, Soc. Am. Mil. Engrs. (post v.p. 1974, 75). Office: Westinghouse Hanford Co PO Box 1970 MS L6-55 Richland WA 99352

BECKER, CHRIS J., insurance executive; b. Cleve., Apr. 18, 1952; s. Jay John and Ruth Elizabeth (Englert) B.; m. Rita Ann Steppe, Nov. 29, 1975; children: Bradley, Mathew. Student, Wright State U., 1971-72. Sales mgr. Schneider & Stanley, Dayton, Ohio, 1971-80; exec. v.p., chief ops. officer Nat. Deposit Ins. Group, Dublin, Ohio, 1980-87; pres. Internat. Credit Union Svcs., San Diego, Calif., 1987—; chmn. bd. Credit Union One, Columbus, Ohio. 1982-84, bd. dirs. Columbus Chpt. Ohio Credit Union League, 1982-84. Program dir. Dayton Airshow Dayton C. of C., 1974-75. With USANG, 1971-77. Named State Champion Pub. Speaking Sears Roebuck Found., 1970. Republican. Methodist. Home: 1510 St Andrews Shelbyville KY 40065 Office: Internat Credit Union Svcs 610 W Ash St San Diego CA 92101

BECKER, CURTIS MARSHAL, prosthodontist, educator; b. Jackson, Tenn., Dec. 7, 1943; s. Carryl Matthias and Doris Virginia (Craven) B.; m. Lois Elle Mary Spruit, May 29, 1970; children: Chad, Sydney, Brady, Jesse, Christopher. BS, Colo. State U., 1967; DDS, Marquette U., 1970; MSD, cert. in prosthodontics, U. Wash., 1974. Clin. prof. dentistry U. Wash., Seattle, 1973-74; clin. asst. prof. dentistry U. Colo., Denver, 1974-80, clin. assoc. prof. dentistry, 1980—. Contbr. articles to profl. jours. Asst. scoutmaster Boy Scouts Am., Greenwood Village, Colo., 1985—. Capt. USAF, 1970-72. Recipient Order of Arrow award Boy Scouts Am., 1987. Mem. ADA, Am. Coll. Prosthodontists, Colo. Prosthodontic Soc., Metro Denver Dental Soc. (bd. dirs. 1980-82, ethics com. 1985—, program chmn. 1987-88). Lutheran. Home: 6363 E Dorado Circle Greenwood Village CO 80111 Office: 5055 E Kentucky Ave Denver CO 80222

BECKER, DAVID STEPHEN, chiropractor; b. San Antonio, July 11, 1954; s. Jerrold Melvin and Rae (Brown) B. BA in Anthropology, Haverford (Pa.) Coll., 1977, BA in Sociology, 1977; BS in Human Anatomy, L.A. Coll. Chiropractic, 1984, DChiropractic, 1984. Cottage parent for abused children Pleasantville (N.Y.) Cottage Schs., 1977-78; pvt. practice Rialto, Calif., 1985-86, Inland Empire Chiropractic, San Bernardino, Calif., 1986—; mem. rsch./libr. consortia L.A. Coll. Chiropractic, Whittier, 1988—. Mem. young leadership group United Jewish Appeal. Mem. Calif. Chiropractic Assn., Am. Chiropractic Assn. Democrat. Office: Inland Empire Chiropractic 165 W Hospitality Ln Ste 12 San Bernardino CA 92408

BECKER, GORDON ALAN, insurance company executive; b. Washington, June 1, 1953; s. S. Victor Becker and Florence (Horowitz) Caruso; m. Sydna Wexler, Dec. 5, 1975 (div. June 1984); children: Matthew, Nicole; m. Karen R. Baum, Jan. 24, 1986; 1 child, Shaina. CLU; chartered fin. cons., registered fin. planner. Life ins. agt. Prudential Ins. Co., Bethesda, Md., 1976-78; pvt. practice Silver Spring, Md. and Encino, Calif., 1978-82; regional dir. N.Y. metro area Franklin Life, Springfield, Ill., 1982-85; sr. supt. agts. Franklin Life, Springfield, 1986, regional dir., Calif., Hawaii, Nev., 1987—. Mem. Republican Presidential Task Force, Washington, 1984. Mem. San Bernardino County Assn. Life Underwriters (pres. 1988-89), Am. Soc. CLU's, Nat. Assn. Life Underwriters (Nat. Sales Achievement award 1981), San Bernardino C. of C. Republican. Jewish. Office: Franklin Life 275 W Hospitality Ln Ste 310 San Bernardino CA 92408

BECKER, LARRY WAYNE, property and casualty insurance company official; b. Grand Rapids, Minn., Apr. 20, 1946; s. Carroll Robert and Evelyn Bernita (Schultz) B.; m. Katherine F. McFadden, Oct. 2, 1971; children: Heidi Katherine, Matthew Robert. BS in Fin., Portland State U., 1968. CPCU. Underwriter North Pacific Ins. Co., Portland, Oreg., 1969-72; personal lines mgr. North Pacific Ins. Co., Portland, 1972-77; br. mgr. North Pacific Ins. Co., Boise, Idaho, 1977-80; br. mgr. North Pacific Ins. Co., Portland, 1980-85, v.p. br. ops., 1985—, also bd. dirs.; bd. dirs. Idaho Survey and Rating Bur., Boise, 1988—; chmn. Oreg. Ins. Coun., Portland, 1988. Chmn. Oreg. Traffic Safety Now, Selam, 1988—. Soc. CPCU, Hon. Order Blue Goose (chmn. Portland 1985-87), Alpha Kappa Psi. Republican. Roman Catholic. Office: North Pacific Ins Co 1475 SW Marlow Ave Portland OR 97225

BECKER, MARK STEPHEN, military officer, pilot; b. Montreal, Que., Can., Feb. 16, 1960; came to U.S., 1962; s. Robert Edmund and Cecily Anne (Mader) B. BS, U. Conn., 1983; postgrad., U. West Fla., 1985. Officer candidate USMC, 1980-82, commd. 2d lt., 1983, advanced through grades to capt., 1986; inf. officer Basic Sch., Quantico, Va., 1983-84; fixed wing trainee Naval Air Tng. Command, Pensacola, Fla., 1984-85, rotary wing flight trainee, 1985-86; naval and marine aviator Marine Attack Squadron 169, Camp Pendleton, Calif., 1986—, adminstrv. officer, legal officer, ordnance officer, maintenance test pilot, 1988—; logistics officer Marine Attack Squadron 267, Camp Pendleton, 1986-87. Mem. Future Airline Profls. Am., El Toro Aero Club. Republican. Episcopalian. Office: HMLA 169 Marine Corps Air Sta Camp Pendleton CA 92009

BECKER, NANCY ANNE, judge; b. Las Vegas, May 23, 1955; d. Arthur William and Margaret Mary (McLoughlin) B. BA, U.S. Internat. U., 1976; JD, George Washington U., 1979. Bar: Nev. 1979, D.C. 1980, Md. 1982, U.S. Dist. Ct. Nev. 1987, U.S. Ct. Appeals (9th cir.) 1987. Legis. cons. D.C. Office on Aging, Washington, 1979-83; assoc. Goldstein & Ahalt, College Park, Md., 1980-82; pvt. practice Washington, 1982-83; dep. city atty., prosecutor criminal div. City of Las Vegas, 1983; judge Las Vegas Mcpl. Ct., 1987—; cons. MADD, Las Vegas, 1983-87. Contbr. articles to profl. publs. Pres. Clark County Pro Bono Project, Las Vegas, 1984-88. Mem. So. Nev. Assn. Women Attys. (past officer), Am. Businesswomen's Assn. (treas. Las Vegas chpt. 1985-86), NCCJ, Las Vegas and Latin C. of C., Vietnam Vets Am., Soroptimist Internat. Office: Las Vegas Mpcl Ct 400 E Stewart St Las Vegas NV 89101

BECKER, RICHARD EDWARD, small business owner; b. N.Y.C., Feb. 18, 1947; s. Stuart Malcolm and Barbara Ann (Ackerman) B.; m. Justine Witlox, Jan. 14, 1984. BS, Cornell U., 1968; MBA, Boston U., 1971; JD, U. So. Calif., 1974. Bar: Calif. 1974, N.Mex. 1978, U.S. Dist. Ct. (cen. dist.) Calif. 1974. Staff atty. SEC, Los Angeles, 1974-78, N.Mex. Atty. Gen.'s Office, Santa Fe, 1978-79; owner, mgr. Becker's Delicatessen, Santa Fe, 1979—. Mem. St. John's Search and Rescue Team, Santa Fe, 1987—. Served with USAR. Democrat. Jewish. Home: 525 1/2 Aqua Fria Santa Fe NM 87501 Office: Becker's Delicatessen Inc 403 Guadalupe Santa Fe NM 87501

BECKER, ROGER VERN, legal educator; b. Omaha, Apr. 12, 1947; s. LaVern Herman and Doris Bessie (Smith) B.; m. D'Lea Brauner; 1 child, Lindsey Vern. Student, U. Nebr., 1965-67, JD, 1970; LLM, U. Wash., 1971; cert. in Library and Info. Sci., Ind. U., 1981. Dir. info. svcs. U. Va. Sch. Law, Charlottesville, 1971-73; dir. legal rsch. U. N.D. Sch. Law, Grand Forks, 1973-80; rsch. and new systems devel. U. Ark. Sch. Law, Fayetteville, 1981-83; systems strategist U. Puget Sound Sch. Law, Tacoma, Wash., 1983—; bus. and mktg. advisor P.S. The Last Name in Personal Style, Mercer Island, Wash., 1984—. Producer various legal edn. video tapes; program designer various computer programs; author articles in field. Mem. Govs. Commn. on Libraries, N.D., 1974-76. Mem. Order of the Coif, Beta Phi Mu. Home: 2740 76th Ave SE #109 Mercer Island WA 98040 Office: U Puget Sound Sch Law 950 Broadway Pla Tacoma WA 98402

BECKETT, JOHN R., business executive; b. San Francisco, Feb. 26, 1918; s. Ernest J. and Hilda (Hansen) B.; m. Dian Calkin, Nov. 27, 1947 (dec. June 1968); children: Brenda Jean, Belinda Dian; m. Marjorie Abenheim, July 1969. AB, Stanford U., 1939, MA, 1940. Valuator Pacific Gas & Electric Co., 1941-42; utility fin. analyst Duff and Phelps, 1942-43; utility fin. expert SEC, 1943-44; asst. to pres. Seattle Gas Co., 1944-45; investment banker Blyth and Co., 1945-60, v.p., 1955-60; pres. Transam. Corp., 1960-79, chmn. bd. dirs., 1968-82, chief exec. officer, 1965-80, chmn. exec. com., 1982—, also bd. dirs.; bd. dirs. Kaiser Aluminum and Chem. Co., Tex. Eastern Corp., Bank Am., BankAm. Corp., Clorox Co. Clubs: San Francisco Golf, Pacific Union, Bohemian (San Francisco); Cypress Point (Pebble Beach, Calif.). Office: Transamerica Corp 600 Montgomery St San Francisco CA 94111

BECKETT, THOMAS ALLEN, facilities administrator, construction consultant, educator; b. Akron, Ohio, Jan. 29, 1949; s. James Deward and Margaret Ida (Widder) B.; m. Gloria Gaeton Bruccoleri, June 19, 1971; children: Lisa Louise, Ericka Ann. BS in Biology, Calif. State U., Northridge, 1972, MS in Environ. Health, 1976. Engr. Aeronutronic-Ford Corp., Newport Beach, Calif., 1973-76; corp. engr. Stauffer Chem. Corp., Westport, Conn., 1976-77; western regional engr. Stauffer Chem. Corp., San Francisco, 1977-78; western mgr. Allied Chem. Corp., Pittsburg, Calif., 1978-80; v.p. Vermillion Devel. Corp., Lafayette, Calif., 1980-82; dir. facilities maintenance Contra Costa Community Coll. Dist., Martinez, Calif., 1982—; instr. Diablo Valley Coll., Pleasant Hill, Calif., 1983-86, Calif. State U., Hayward, 1988—. Mem. Assn. Phys. Plant Adminstrs. Univs. and Colls. (instnl.), Rotary. Democrat. Roman Catholic. Office: Contra Costa Community Coll Dist 500 Court St Martinez CA 94553

BECKMAN, ARNOLD ORVILLE, chemist, instrument manufacturing company executive; b. Cullom, Ill., Apr. 10, 1900; s. George W. and Elizabeth E. (Jewkes) B.; m. Mabel S. Meinzer, June 10, 1925; children: Gloria Patricia, Arnold Stone. BS, U. Ill., 1922, MS, 1923; PhD, Calif. Inst. Tech., 1928; DSc (hon.), Chapman Coll., 1965; LLD (hon.), U. Calif., Riverside, 1966, Loyola U., L.A., 1969, Whittier Coll., 1971, U. Ill., 1982, Pepperdine U., 1977; DHL (hon.), Calif. State U., 1984. Rsch. assoc. Bell Tel. Labs., N.Y.C., 1924-26; chem. staff Calif. Inst. Tech., 1926-39; v.p. Nat. Tech. Lab., Pasadena, Calif., 1935-39; pres. Nat. Tech. Lab., 1939-40, Helipot Corp., 1944-58, Arnold O. Beckman, Inc., South Pasadena, Calif., 1946-58, Beckman Instruments, Inc., Fullerton, Calif., 1940-65; chmn. bd. Beckman Instruments, Inc. subs. SmithKline Beckman Corp.; vice chmn. SmithKline Beckman Corp., 1984-86; bd.dir. Security Pacific Nat. Bank, 1956-72, adv. dir., 1972-75; bd. dir. Continental Airlines, 1956-71, adv. dir., 1971-73. Author articles in field; inventor; patentee in field. Mem. Pres.'s Air Quality Bd., 1970-74; chmn. System Devel. Found., 1970-88; chmn. bd. trustees emeritus Calif. Inst. Tech.; hon. trustee Calif. Mus. Found.; bd. overseers House Ear Inst., 1981—; trustee Scripps Clinic and Rsch. Found., 1971—; bd. dirs. Hoag Meml. Hosp. With USMC, 1918-19. Benjamin Franklin fellow Royal Soc. Arts.; named to Nat. Inventors Hall of Fame, 1987. Fellow Assn. Clin. Scientists; mem. Am. Acad. Arts and Scis., L.A. C. of C. (bd. dir. 1954-58, pres. 1956), Calif. C. of C. (dir., pres. 1967-68), Nat. Acad. Engring. (Founders Award, 1987), NAM, Am. Inst. Chemists, Instrument Soc. Am. (pres. 1952), Am. Chem. Soc., AAAS, Social Sci. Rsch. Coun., Am. Assn. Clin. Chemistry (hon.), Newcomen Soc., Sigma Xi, Delta Upsilon, Alpha Chi Sigma, Phi Lambda Upsilon. Clubs: Newport Harbor Yacht, Pacific. Home: 107 Shorecliff Rd Corona del Mar CA 92625 Office: 100 Academy Dr Irvine CA 92715

BECKMAN, JAMES WALLACE BIM, economist, business executive; b. Mpls., May 2, 1936; s. Wallace Gerald and Mary Louise (Frissell) B. B.A., Princeton U., 1958; Ph.D., U. Calif., 1973. Pvt. practice econ. cons., Berkeley, Calif. 1962-67; cons. Calif. State Assembly, Sacramento, 1967-68; pvt. practice market research and econs. consulting, Laguna Beach, Calif., 1969-77; cons. Calif. State Gov.'s Office, Sacramento 1977-80; pvt. practice real estate cons., Los Angeles 1980-83; v.p. mktg. Gold-Well Investments, Inc., Los Angeles 1982-83; pres. Beckman Analytics Internat., econ. cons. to bus. and govt., Los Angeles and Lake Arrowhead, Calif., 1983—. Served to maj. USMC 1958-67. NIMH fellow 1971-72. Fellow Soc. Applied Anthropology; mem. Am. Econs. Assn., Am. Statis. Assn., Am. Mktg. Assn. (officer), Nat. Assn. Bus. Economists (officer). Democrat. Presbyterian. Contbr. articles to profl. jours. Home: Drawer 2350 Crestline CA 92325

BECKMAN, JOHN COYLE, management consultant; b. Portland, Oreg., Dec. 15, 1919; s. John Joseph Beckman and Lelah Mildred (Coyle) Halton; m. Elizabeth Hurlbut, 1947 (div. 1979); children: Barbara Elizabeth, Wendy Jean; m. Patricia Jane Huckins, 1980. Student, U. Portland, 1938-39. Various tech. positions Aircraft and Shipbuilding Cos., Oreg. and Wash., 1940-42; pres. Beckman & Whitley, Portland, 1942-48, San Mateo, Calif., 1948-64; cons. pvt. practice San Francisco, 1964-82, Portland, 1982—; pres. Collector's Press, San Francisco, 1967-72, First San Francisco Fin. Corp., 1970-72; livestock owner (Herefords) Etna. Calif., 1967-77; bd. dirs., treas. Hosts Corp., Vancouver, Wash., 1984—; bd. dirs. Multnomah Kennel, Fairview, Oreg. Inventor automatic film loader and phototimer. Trustee Oreg. Symphony Assn., Portland, 1983—; chmn., trustee San Francisco Conservatory Music, 1971-78; bd. dirs. Calif. Nev. Hereford Assn., Madera, Calif., 1971-77; pres. Siskiyou County Farm Bur., Yreka, Calif., 1976-77; regent U. Portland, 1971—. Mem. Am. Meteorol. Soc. (Charles Franklin Brooks award 1966, chmn. planning commn. 1959-64, councillor 1962-65), Univ. Club. Republican. Home: 2800 NW Linmere Dr Portland OR 97229

BECKMAN, RICHARD C., banker; b. Lock Haven, Pa., June 4, 1937; s. Howard Jerome and Ruth (Tyson) B.; m. Soni Smith, Oct. 30, 1970; 1 child, Richmond C. AA, Long Beach City Coll, 1959. Lic. private pilot. Oper. engr. Beckman Lumber Svc., Long Beach, Calif., 1955-59; sales mgr. Leo Rule Oldsmobile, Compton, Calif., 1959-60; agy. mgr. Transamerica Auto Leasing Owner/Operator, L.A., 1962-63; chief exec. officer, founder All Am. Auto Leasing, Cerritos, Calif., 1963-88; founder, dir. High Desert Nat. Bank, Hesperia, Calif., 1981—. With USAF, 1960-62. Mem. Long Beach Police Officers Assn. Republican. Roman Catholic. Office: All American Leasing 6330 Lincoln Ave #288 Cypress CA 90630

BECK-VON-PECCOZ, STEPHEN GEORGE WOLFGANG, artist; b. Munich, Oct. 18, 1933; came to U.S., 1937; s. Wolfgang Anna Marie and Martha Jeanette (Morse) Beck-von-P.; m. Dorothy Ann Freytag, June 16, 1956 (div. 1971); m. Michele Marie Perry, Feb. 8, 1972; children: Stephen Jr., David, Kenneth, Lisa. BEE, Cornell U., 1956; MA in Art, Calif. State U., San Diego, 1974. Electronic engr. Stromberg Carlson Co., San Diego, 1958-60; project mgr. Control Data Corp., San Diego, 1960-65, Digital Devel. Corp., San Diego, 1965-66; project engr. Stromberg Datagraphix, Inc., San Diego, 1966-69; project mgr. Digital Sci. Corp., San Diego, 1969-71; artist San Diego, 1974—; cons. elec. engring., San Diego, 1974-78. Designer Kinetic Sculptures, 1974-89, Kinetic Sculpture W252, 1980 (Architect's Choice award 1985). Served to 2d lt. USAF, 1956-58. Mem. Artists Equity Assn. (v.p. San Diego chpt. 1981-82), Internat. Sculpture Ctr., Kappa Alpha Soc. Home: 636 Nardito Ln Solana Beach CA 92075 Office: 11575 Sorrento Valley Rd Ste 201 San Diego CA 92121

BEDDOME, JOHN MACDONALD, oil company executive, engineer; b. Vernon, B.C., Can., Sept. 20, 1930; m. Barbara McCarthy; children—Maureen, David. BS in Chem. Engring., U. B.C., 1952. Various positions Gulf Oil Can., Calgary, Can., 1952-71; with Dome Petroleum Ltd., Calgary, Can., 1971-78, pres., chief operating officer, 1983-88, also bd. dirs.; bd. dirs., v.p. IPAC, Calgary, 1980-85; chmn., bd. dirs. TransCanada Pipeline Ltd., Calgary, 1979-83; bd. dirs. PanArctic Oil Ltd., Calgary, Dome Can. Ltd., Calgary, IPSCO Inc. Mem. Assn. Profl. Engrs., Geologists and Geophysicist Alta. Clubs: Ranchmen's, Calgary Petroleum. Office: John M Beddome, 125 9th Ave SE Ste 2410, Calgary, AB Canada T2G 0P6 *

BEDROSIAN, STEVE, professional baseball player; b. Methuen, Mass., Dec. 6, 1957; m. Tammy Blackwell, Oct. 20, 1984; children: Stephen, Cody. Student, U. New Haven. Player Atlanta Braves, 1981-85, Phila. Phillies, 1986-89, San Francisco Giants, 1989—; mem. Nat. League All-Star Team, 1987. Recipient Cy Young award Nat. League, 1987. Office: San Francisco Giants Candlestick Park San Francisco CA 94124 *

BEEBE, DALE DERMONT, electronics engineer; b. Cleve., July 15, 1950; s. Dermont Leroy and Marie Joan (Jankovich) B.; m. Lynne Louise Alessio, Dec. 31, 1977; children: Elizabeth Marie, Margaret Ann. BSEE, Purdue U., 1973. Sr. engr. McDonnell Douglas Co., Huntington Beach, Calif., 1975—. Contbr. articles to profl. jours. Home: 11441 Montclair Ct Garden Grove CA 92641 Office: McDonnell Douglas Co 5301 Bolsa MS 21-1 Huntington Beach CA 92647

BEEKER, MARVIN RAY, personnel executive; b. Washington, Ind., Oct. 1, 1941; s. Ora Louda and Rita (Ainscough) B. BA, Ind. U., 1967; MPA, Golden Gate U., 1981. Personnel staffing specialist U.S. CSC, Indpls., 1967-69; personnel mgmt. specialist U.S. CSC, Washington, 1969-77; placement officer U.S. Forest Svc., San Francisco, 1977-84; area mgr. U.S. Office Personnel Mgmt., Phoenix, 1984—. Mem. exec. com. Combined Fed. Campaign, Phoenix, 1985—. With USAF, 1961-65. Mem. Am. Soc. Pub. Adminstrn. (bd. dirs. Ariz. chpt. 1987-88), Internat. Personnel Mgmt. Assn. (bd. mem. Phoenix chpt. 1986-87), Phoenix Fed. Exec. Assn. (v.p. 1988-89), Acad. Polit. Sci. Republican. Methodist. Home: 5035 N 10th Pl Apt 213 Phoenix AZ 85014 Office: US Office Personnel Mgmt 522 N Central Ave Phoenix AZ 85004

BEELER, BARBARA LOUISE, auditor; b. Sterling, Ill., Sept. 24, 1963; d. Horace Walter and June (Norem) B. AA, Cottey Coll., Nevada, Mo., 1984; BBA in Acctg., U. San Diego, 1987. Auditor trainee Def. Contract and Audit Agy., San Diego, 1987-88; auditor Def. Contract Audit Agy., San Diego, 1988—. Mem. Assn. Govt. Accts., Beta Alpha Psi, Beta Gamma Sigma. Republican. Presbyterian. Office: Def Contract Audit Agy 5001 Kearny Villa Rd San Diego CA 92138

BEEMAN, BETTE JANE, elementary educator; b. Niobrara, Neb., Jan. 13, 1927; d. Burnice Wallace and Edith (Koenig) Percy; m. Frederick Alan Beeman, June 9, 1947; children: Linda Kay Beeman Shimp, Susan Jane Beeman Ahrens. BA in Elem. and Sec. Edn., Black Hills State Coll., Spearfish, S.D., 1969; M in Elem. Edn., Black Hills State Coll., 1975; MLS, No. Ariz. U., 1977, postgrad. Elem. tchr. Belle Fourche (S.D.) Sch., 1969-73; elem. tchr. La Senita Sch., Kingman, Ariz., 1974-76, elem. librarian, 1977-78; dist. librarian Lander County, Battle Mountain, Nev., 1980-82; elem. prin. Beowawe (Nev.) Sch., 1983, 85; debate coach Belle Fourche Hight Sch., 1969-70; speech coach for Lions Internat., Battle Mountain, 1980-82. Mem. Kingman Concert Bd., 1976-77; organizer Rep. Party, Battle Mountain, 1980-85. Mem. AAUW (sec.), Ariz. Library Bd., Ariz. Sci. Assn. (named Tchr. of Yr. 1975), Delta Kappa (v.p. 1977-78), Beta Sigma Phi. Lutheran. Home: 2551 Chicago St Kingman AZ 86401

BEEMAN, ROBERT DONALD, academic administrator; b. L.A., Dec. 18, 1926; s. Roy Leslie and Frances Marian (Troy) B.; m. Beverly Jean Phelps, Aug. 24, 1947; children: Julia Katherine, Robert Donald Jr., Jenelle Elaine, Jeffrey David, Margaret Frances. BA, Whittier Coll., 1951; postgrad., Ariz. State U., 1961-67. Dist. exec. Boy Scouts Am., L.A., and other locations, 1951-59; rsch. dir. Ariz. State Employment Svc., Phoenix, 1959-69; assoc. dir. Ariz. Office Planning and Devel., Phoenix, 1969-79; exec. coord. office of pres. Ariz. State U., Tempe, 1979-89, ret., 1989. Rsch. dir., editor various profl. publs.; contbr. articles on econs. to topical jours. With USN, 1944-46. Mem. Ariz. Statis. Assn., Planning Execs. Inst. Republican. Methodist. Home: 214 E Huntington Dr Tempe AZ 85282

BEER, JOSEPH ERNEST, telecommunications consultant; b. Pasadena, Calif., June 5, 1959; s. Joseph Andrew and Pauline Sylvia (Micciche) B.; m.

Amy Shun-Fong Wu, Oct. 13, 1984. BS in Internat. Bus., Calif. State U., L.A., 1982; MBA in Info. Tech. Mgmt., U. So. Calif., 1987. Asst. engr. ARCO-Electronics & Telecommunications, L.A., 1979-83, sr. coord., 1983-84, project engr., 1984-85, sr. project engr., 1985-87; sr. mgr. Arthur Young, L.A., 1987—. Recipient scholarship, Ebell Found., L.A., 1981, Bank Am. scholarship, Bank Am. Found., 1981. Mem. Soc. Telecommunications Consultants, Project Mgmt. Inst. Republican. Home: 530 S Sandy Hook St West Covina CA 91790 Office: Arthur Young 515 S Flower St Ste 2400 Los Angeles CA 90071

BEETS, RICHARD NATHANIEL, aerospace company executive; b. Beaver Falls, Pa., Jan. 17, 1956; s. Walter Douglas and Jane Ardith (Bittner) B. Student, Slippery Rock U., 1978-79, Loyola Marymount U., 1986-87. Spl. investigator Baden (Pa.) Police Dept., 1976-78; dept. head configuration mgmt. Hughes Aircraft Co., El Segundo, Calif., 1982—; disability substance abuse specialist. Served with USAF, 1975-76. Mem. Congress Chem. Dependency and Disability (bd. dirs. 1986—), So. Calif. Com. Chem. Dependency and Disability (chmn. 1986-87), Hands Across Hughes (chmn. 1986-87), Disabled Students for Action, Profl. Assn. Diving Instrs. (master scuba trainer 1988—), Soc. Preservation and Encouragement Barbershop Quartet Singing Am. (bd. dirs. 1984). Home: 6304 Vista Del Mar Playa Del Rey CA 90293 Office: Hughes Aircraft Co PO Box 92426 Los Angeles CA 90009

BEEZER, ROBERT RENAUT, judge; b. Seattle, July 21, 1928; s. Arnold Roswell and Josephine (May) B.; m. Hazlehurst Plant Smith, June 15, 1957; children—Robert Arnold, John Leighton, Mary Allison. Student, U. Wash., 1946-48, 51; B.A., U. Va., 1951, LL.B, 1956. Bar: Wash. 1956, U.S. Supreme Ct. 1968. Ptnr. Schweppe, Krug, Tausend & Beezer, P.S., Seattle, 1956-84; judge U.S. Ct. Appeals (9th cir.), Seattle, 1984—; alt. mem. Wash. Jud. Qualifications Commn., Olympia, 1981-84. Served to 1st lt. USMCR, 1951-53. Fellow Am. Coll. Probate Counsel, Am. Bar Found.; mem. ABA, Seattle-King County Bar Assn. (pres. 1975-76), Wash. Bar Assn. (bd. govs. 1980-83). Clubs: Rainier, Tennis (Seattle). Office: US Ct Appeals 802 US Courthouse 1010 5th Ave Seattle WA 98104

BEGAY, JEFFERSON LEE, general contracting company executive; b. Kayenta, Ariz., May 22, 1943; s. Harold Navajo and Stella Rose (Begay) Drake; m. Judith Ann Begay, Nov. 23, 1966 (div. Oct. 1983); children: Allison Marie, Tanabah Zahnie. AA in Engring. Scis., Phoenix Coll., 1971; BS in Constrn., Ariz. State U., 1974. Community planner and developer Navajo Tribe, 1974-76, 83-84; estimator, field engr. Kitchell Contractors, Inc., 1976-77; instr. constn. contracting and materialslab. No. Ariz. U., 1978; in charge tech. assistance and tng. programs Indian Devel. Dist. Ariz., 1978-79; field supr. structural steel design, constrn. and inspection M.M. Sundt Constrn. Co., 1979-80; with Hemley Lee Assocs., 1980; project engr. Terra Grande Constructors, Inc., 1980-82, Chanen Constrn. Co., 1982-83; project engr., estimator Fisher Contracting Co., 1981-82; pres. Amerind Devel., Inc., Tempe, Ariz., 1983-84, Amerind Constrn., Inc., Tempe, 1984—; spl. asst. to Navajo tribal chmn. Peterson Zah, Navajo-Hopi-Indian land dispute. Past bd. dirs. Utah Navajo Devel. Coun.; mem. Gov.'s Commn. on Ariz. Environ., 1974-76; mem. fin. com. Jenny Norton for State Rep., Tempe, 1986; bd. dirs. Urban Coalition West, Phoenix, 1987—, NCCJ, 1988—. Sgt. U.S. Army, 1966-68, Vietnam. Vinnell Found. scholar, 1972-73, Kitchell Corp. scholar, 1973-74. Mem. Am. Soc. Profl. Estimators, Am. Inst. Constructors, Tempe C. of C. Republican. Office: Amerind Constrn Inc 1820 W Drake St Tempe AZ 85283

BEGGS, HARRY MARK, lawyer; b. Los Angeles, Nov. 15, 1941; s. John Edgar and Agnes (Kentro) B.; m. Sandra Lynne Mikal, May 25, 1963; children—Brendan, Sean, Corey, Michael. Student, Ariz. State U., 1959-61, Phoenix Coll., 1961; LL.B., U. Ariz., 1964. Bar: Ariz. 1964, U.S. Dist. Ct. Ariz. 1964, U.S. Ct. Appeals (9th cir.) 1973. Assoc. Carson Messinger, Elliott, Laughlin & Ragan, Phoenix, 1964-69, ptnr., 1969—; mem. Civil Practice and Procedure Com., State Bar of Ariz., 1969-80, Fin. Insts. Counsels Com., 1980-83; founding fellow Ariz. Bar Found. Recipient award for highest grade on state bar exam. Atty. Gen. Ariz., 1964; Fegtly Moot Ct. award, 1963, 64; Abner S. Lipscomb scholar U. Ariz. Law Sch., 1963. Mem. State Bar of Ariz., Maricopa County Bar Assn., ABA. (litigation, antitrust sects.), Ariz. Acad. Clubs: Plaza, LaMancha Racquet. Mem. editorial bd. Ariz. Law Rev. 1963-64; contbr. articles to profl. jours. Address: PO Box 33907 Phoenix AZ 85067

BEGLEY, ED, JR., actor; b. Hollywood, Calif., Sept. 16, 1949; s. Edward James and Allene Jeanne (Sanders) B.; m. Ingrid Margaret Taylor (divorced); children: Amanda, Nicholas. Student, Los Angeles Valley Coll. Actor (films) including Cat People, The In-Laws, Goin' South, Citizen's Band, Blue Collar, Stay Hungry, Private Lessons, Buddy Buddy, The One and Only, Airport 79, Showdown, Transylvania 6-5000, Protocol, The Accidental Tourist, Meet The Applegates, Scenes from The Class Struggle in Beverly Hills, She Devil, (TV movies) A Shining Season, Elvis, Amateur Night at the Dixie, Dead of Night, Rascals & Robbers, Hot Rod, An American Love Affair, Spies, Lies and Naked Thighs, The Incredible Ida Early, Roman Holiday, Home, (TV series) Mary Hartman, Mary Hartman, Battlestar Galactica, Roll Out, Room 222, St. Elsewhere; also numerous TV guest appearances, commls., night club performances. Democrat. Roman Catholic.

BEGLEY, MAGGIE, public relations executive; b. Paterson, N.J., Oct. 5, 1953; d. Edward Peter and Agnes Marie (Moonan) B. BA, William Paterson Coll., Wayne, N.J., 1975. News researcher NBC, N.Y.C., 1975-77; mktg. analyst NBC, 1977-80; research adminstr. Sta. WMAQ-TV, Chgo., 1980-81; publicity dir. Sta. WMAQ-TV, 1981-84; dir. publicity, advt. and promotion Warner Bros. TV, Burbank, Calif., 1984-87; exec. v.p. Mahoney/Wasserman Pub. Rels., Beverly Hills, Calif., 1987—. Home: 345 N Maple Dr #185 Beverly Hills CA 90210

BEHLER, ANNE M., nurse; b. Pontiac, Mich., Aug. 25, 1959; d. John Frederick and Mary Jeanette (Haughexy) B. BS in Bus. Adminstrn., U. Ariz., 1981; BS in Nursing, Creighton U., 1984. RN, Wash. Nurse St. Joseph Hosp., Omaha, 1985, Harborview Med. Ctr., Seattle, 1986—. Mem. Nat. Union Health Care and Hosp. Employment, Signa Theaa Tau. Home: 6265 53d Ave NE Seattle WA 98115

BEHLMER, CURT RANDOLPH, recording engineer, consultant; b. Encino, Calif., Aug. 5, 1960; s. Rudolph Herman and Sandra Lee (Wightman) B.; m. Anna Gabellieri, July 22, 1984. Sound engr. Lion's Gate Films, Inc., Los Angeles, 1977-79; chief engr. Ryder Sound Services, Inc., Hollywood, Calif., 1979—; pres. Studio Systems, Inc., Studio City, Calif., 1988—; pres. Studio Systems, Inc., Studio City, Calif., 1988—. Mem. Acad. TV Arts and Scis. (gov. 1987—, Emmy awards 1981, 85, 87, 88), Acad. Motion Picture Arts and Scis., Soc. Motion Picture TV Engrs., Audio Engring. Soc., Internat. Alliance Theatrical Stage Employees. Home: 11500 Canton Dr Studio City CA 91604 Office: Ryder Sound Svcs Inc 1161 N Vine St Hollywood CA 90038

BEHLMER, RUDY H., JR., writer, film educator; b. San Francisco, Oct. 13, 1926; s. Rudy H. and Helen Mae (McDonough) B.; 1 child, Curt. Student, Pasadena Playhouse Coll., 1946-49, Los Angeles City Coll., 1949-50. Dir. Sta. KLAC-TV, Hollywood, Calif., 1952-56; network TV dir. ABC-TV, Hollywood, 1956-57; TV comml. producer-dir., exec. Grant Advt., Hollywood, 1957-60; exec. producer-dir. Sta. KCOP-TV, Hollywood, 1960-63; v.p., TV comml. producer-dir. Hollywood office Leo Burnett USA, 1963-84; lectr. film Art Ctr. Coll. of Design, Pasadena, Calif., 1967—, Calif. State U., Northridge, 1984—, UCLA, 1988—. Author: Memo From David O. Selznick, 1972; (with Tony Thomas) Hollywood's Hollywood, 1975; America's Favorite Movies-Behind the Scenes, 1982, Inside Warner Bros., 1985; co-author The Films of Errol Flynn, 1969; text on Warner Bros. Fifty Years of Film Music, 1973; editor: The Adventures of Robin Hood,1979, The Sea Hawk, 1982 (Wis./Warner Bros. screenplay series); various articles on aspects of film history; writer and narrator audio essays for Criterion Laserdiscs, 1988. Served with AC, USNR, 1944-46. Mem. Dirs. Guild Am.

BEHNEY, CHARLES AUGUSTUS, JR., veterinarian; b. Bryn Mawr, Pa., Nov. 30, 1929; s. Charles Augustus and Victoria Parks (Wythe) B.; B.S., U. Wyo., D.V.M., Colo. State U., 1961; m. Judith Ann Boggs, May 26, 1979; children—Charles Augustus III, Keenan F. Owner, Cochise Animal Hosp., Bisbee, Ariz., 1961—; veterinarian, dir. S.W. Traildust Zoo, Bisbee, 1966—; owner Kazam Arabians, Bisbee, 1969—; asso. prof. Cochise Coll. Chmn., Comprehensive Health Planning, Cochise County, Ariz., 1968. Mem. Am. Vet. Med. Assn., Soc. for Breeding Soundness, Internat. Platform Assn. Republican. Episcopalian. Rotarian, Elk. Patentee ultrasound device and eye cover for treating infections, apparatus to alter equine leg conformation, external vein clamp, equine sanitation instrument; developer ear implant instrumentation system. Home and Office: PO Box 4337 Bisbee AZ 85603

BEHRENBRUCH, WILLIAM DAVID, filmmaker, educator; b. South Bend, Ind., July 23, 1946; s. Willard Herman and Mildred Kathleen (Steele) B.; m. Ingrid M. Neuschwander, Aug. 16, 1969 (div. 1975). Student, Ind. U., 1970-71; BA, Brooks Inst., 1974. Editor Rex Fleming Prodns., Santa Barbara, Calif., 1974-76, Golden Coast Films, Santa Barbara, 1976; pres. Visual Systems, Santa Barbara, 1976—; adj. instr. Brooks Inst., Santa Barbara, 1978—. Graphic designer (motion picture) Sweat, 1986; designer optical effects and titles Death Spa, 1986, War, 1986, Private Road, 1987, Blue Movies, 1987, Prime Suspect, 1988, Never Cry Devil, 1988. Served to sgt. USAF, 1966-70. Mem. Soc. Motion Picture and TV Engrs., Assn. Ind. Video and Film Producers, Aircraft Owners and Pilots Assn. Club: Santa Barbara Flying. Office: Visual Systems 2050 Alameda Padre Serra Santa Barbara CA 93103

BEHRENDT, JOHN THOMAS, lawyer; b. Syracuse, Kans., Oct. 26, 1945; s. Thomas Franklin and Anna Iola (Carrithers) B. m. Martha Jean Montgomery, Dec. 28, 1967 (div.); children: Todd Thomas, Gretchen Jean; m. Theresa Ann Elmore, Oct. 27, 1985. BA, Sterling Coll.; J.D. cum laude, U. Minn. Bar: Calif. 1971, Tex. 1973. Assoc., then ptnr. Gibson, Dunn & Crutcher, Los Angeles, 1970-71, 1974—; lectr. Practicing Law Inst., Acctg. for Lawyers. Served to capt. JAGC, U.S. Army, 1971-74. Mem. ABA (law and acctg. com.), Los Angeles County Bar Assn, Order of Coif. Republican. Presbyterian. Clubs: Jonathan (Los Angeles); Union League (N.Y.); The Tuxedo (Tuxedo Park, N.Y.). Office: Gibson Dunn & Crutcher 333 S Grand Ste 5000 Los Angeles CA 90071 also: 200 Park Ave New York NY 10166

BEHRENS, JOHN JOSEPH, sales professional; b. San Gabriel, Calif., Feb. 14, 1951; s. James A. and Janice E. (Rosenga) B.; m. Kathleen Jane Morman, July 7, 1973; children: Michael J., Denise A. Student, Mt. San Antonio Jr. Coll., 1970-72, Park Coll., 1978-79; AS, USAF Community Coll., San Antonio, 1978-79. Enlisted USAF, 1974, advanced through grades to staff sgt., resigned, 1980; mgr. custom engring. Global Wulfsberg Systems, Irvine, Calif., 1982-88; sales mgr. Global Wulfsberg Systems, Irvine, 1988—. Republican. Office: Global Wulfsberg Systems 2144 Michelson Dr Irvine CA 92715

BEHRENS-NAGLE, ELIZABETH ANNE, nurse; b. Houston, May 17, 1951; d. Charles August and Mildred Dorothy (Garrett) Behrens; m. Barron Rogers Nagle, Oct. 6, 1979. BSN, Dominican Coll., 1973; postgrad., San Jose (Calif.) State U., 1986-89. Staff nurse St. Joseph's Hosp., Houston, summer 1973, Symmes Hosp., Arlington, Mass., 1973-75; emergency rm. charge nurse Meml. Hosp., Nacogdoches, Tex., 1975-76; staff nurse Community Hosp. of Monterey (Calif.) Peninsula, 1977-80; dir. nursing Cen. Coast Vis. Nurse Assn., Monterery and Salinas, Calif., 1980-86; patient care planner Hospice of Monterey Peninsula, 1986-89, dir. hospice home care, 1989—; educator HIV ARC Carmel (Calif.) chpt., 1988—. Mem. Oncology Nursing Soc. (treas. Monterey chpt. 1986—), Calif. Nurses Assn. (AIDS educator Sacramento chpt. 1986—). Home: 719 Mermaid Ave Pacific Grove CA 93950 Office: Hospice Monterey Peninsula 8900 Carmel Valley Rd Carmel Valley CA 93923

BEHRING, KEN, professional sports team owner. Calif. land developer; owner Seattle Seahawks, NFL, 1988—. Address: care Seattle Seahawks 11220 NE 53rd St Kirkland WA 98033 *

BEICHMAN, ARNOLD, political scientist instructor, writer; b. N.Y.C., May 17, 1913; s. Solomon and Mary Beichman; m. Carroll Aikins, Oct. 9, 1950; children: Charles, Janine, John. BA in Polit. Sci., Columbia U., MA in Polit. Sci., PhD in Polit. Sci. Assoc. prof., polit. scientist U. Mass.; instr. polit. scientist U. B.C., U. Calgary, Alta., Can.; adj. prof. polit. sci. Georgetown U.; mem. editorial adv. bd. Washington Times; vis. scholar Hoover Instn., 1982—, rsch. fellow, 1989—. Author: The "Other" State Department, Herman Wouk: The Novelist as Social Historian, Nine Lies About America, (with others) Yuri Andropov: New Challenge to the West; contbr. numerous articles to profl. jours. Founding mem. Consortium for the Study of Intelligence, Washington; v.p., trustee Phila. Soc. Home: PO Box 37, Naramata, AB Canada V0H 1N0 Office: Stanford U Hoover Instn Stanford CA 94305

BEIGEL, ALLAN, university administrator, psychiatry educator; b. Hamilton, Ohio, Apr. 4, 1940; s. Alfred and Mary (Schachter) B.; m. Joan Ellen Kaye, Dec. 24, 1962; children—Jennifer, Jill. A.B., Harvard U., Cambridge, Mass., 1961; M.D., Albert Einstein Coll., Bronx, 1965. Diplomate Am. Bd. Psychiatry and Neurology. Intern Mount Sinai Hosp., N.Y.C., 1965-66, resident in psychiatry, 1966-68; clin. assoc. Nat. Inst. Mental Health, Rockville, Md., 1968-70; dir. So. Ariz. Mental Health Ctr., Tucson, 1970-83; prof. psychiatry U. Ariz., Tucson, 1970—, v.p., 1983—; cons. in field; mem. Pres.'s Commn. on Mental Health, 1977. Author: Community Mental Health, 1972; Understanding Human Behavior for Effective Police Work, 1975, 82; Beneath the Badge, 1978. Contbr. chpts. to books, articles to profl. jours. Served as surgeon USPHS, 1968-70. Recipient Copper Letters, City of Tucson, 1973, 77, 89. Fellow Am. Psychiat. Assn. (v.p. 1987-89), Am. Coll. Psychiatrists (v.p. 1987-89, pres. elect. 1989—); mem. NAS, AMA (chmn. sec. coun. on psychiatry 1985-88), Group for Advancement of Psychiatry (sec. 1981-89, pres. elect 1989—), Nat. Coun. Community Mental Health (pres. 1976-77), Inst. Medicine. Home: 30 Camino Espanol Tucson AZ 85716 Office: U Ariz Tucson AZ 85721

BEILENSON, ANTHONY CHARLES, congressman; b. New Rochelle, N.Y., Oct. 26, 1932; s. Peter and Edna (Rudolph) B.; m. Dolores Martin, June 20, 1959; children: Peter, Dayna, Adam. B.A., Harvard Coll., 1954; LL.B., Harvard U., 1957. Bar: Calif. 1957. Mem. Calif. Assembly from 59th Dist., 1963-66, Calif. Senate from 22d Dist., 1967-76, 95th-101st Congresses from 23d Calif. Dist., 1977—. Democrat. Office: 1025 Longworth Bldg Washington DC 20515

BEISCH, HANS R., retired metal products manufacturing company executive; b. 1927; married. BS, Polytech. Inst., 1950. With SKG Mfg. Co., Ltd., 1951-62, then v.p., plant mgr.; gen. mgr. Rockwell Internat. Corp., 1962-70; gen. mgr. automotive div. Sargent Industries, 1970-73; pres. auto trim div. NI West Inc., 1973-78; sr. v.p. NI West Inc., Long Beach, Calif., 1978-84; pres., chief operating officer NI West Inc., 1984-89. Office: NI Industries Inc One Golden Shore Long Beach CA 90802 *

BEITER, JEANE MARIE, personnel executive; b. Akron, Ohio, Dec. 3, 1962; d. Karl Frederick and Virjeane Marie (Burns) B. BA in Communications, St. Mary Coll., Moraga, Calif., 1985. Adminstrv. asst. Levi Strauss and Co., San Francisco, 1985-86; regional rep. Carme Inc., Novato, Calif., 1986-87; exec. dir. Barbizon Schs., Internat., San Francisco, 1987-88; talent dir. Avalon Models, San Francisco, 1988—; account mgr. Bay Personnel Inc., Oakland, Calif., 1989—; owner Pub. Eye Promotions, San Francisco, 1986—. Republican. Roman Catholic. Home: 290 Moraga Way Orinda CA 94563 Office: Bay Personnel Inc 2030 Franklin St Fl 7 Oakland CA 94612

BEIZER, LANCE KURT, lawyer; b. Hartford, Conn., Sept. 8, 1938; s. Lawrence Sidney and Victoria Merriam (Kaplan) B.; m. Sandra Jenkins, Jan. 17, 1970 (div. Oct. 1974); m. Maribeth Scholze Frey, Nov. 23, 1984; 1 stepchild, Jessica. BA in Sociology, Brandeis U., 1960; MA in English, San Jose State U., 1967; JD, U. San Diego, 1975. Bar: Calif. 1975. Selective svc. affairs coord. U. Calif., La Jolla, 1969-73, vet. affairs coord., 1973-75; vet. outreach coord. San Diego Community Coll. Dist., 1975-76; dep. dist. atty. Santa Clara County, Calif., 1976—; judge pro-tem Santa Clara Mcpl. Ct., San Jose, 1984—. Bd. dirs. Santa Clara Valley YMCA, Saratoga, Calif., 1988—, The Lumen Found., San Francisco, 1985—; presiding bishop Ecclesia Gnostica Sacramentorum, San Jose. Lt. USNR, 1961-65. Mem. Calif. Dist. Attys. Assn., Santa Clara County Bar Assn., Palo Alto Area Bar Assn., Am. Weil Soc., Mensa, Commonwealth Club. Republican. Home: 1197 Capri Dr Campbell CA 95008 Office: Santa Clara County Dist Atty 70 W Hedding St San Jose CA 95110

BEKE, MARY ELIZABETH, legal secretary; b. L.A., Mar. 20, 1958; d. John C. and Jeanette L. (Pauley) B. BA in Physical Edn., U. Calif., Santa Barbara, 1981; postgrad., Calif. State U., Fullerton, 1984-85. Legal sec. Argue, Freston, Pearson, Harbison & Myers, L.A., 1981-85, Bonn & Pohlman Chartered, Phoenix, 1985-89, Pohlman & Sanders P.A., Phoenix, 1989—. Mem. Am. Coll. of Sports Medicine. Republican. Roman Catholic. Home: 900 W Grove Pkwy #1083 Tempe AZ 85283

BEKEY, GEORGE ALBERT, computer scientist, engineer, educator; b. Bratislava, Czechoslovakia, June 19, 1928; came to U.S., 1945, naturalized, 1956; s. Andrew and Elizabeth B.; m. Shirley White, June 10, 1951; children: Ronald Steven, Michelle Elaine. B.S. with honors, U. Calif., Berkeley, 1950; M.S., UCLA, 1952, Ph.D., 1962. Research engr. UCLA, 1950-54; mgr. computer center Beckman Instruments, Los Angeles and Berkeley, 1955-58; mem. sr. staff, dir. computer center TRW Systems Group, Redondo Beach, Calif., 1958-62; mem. faculty U. So. Calif., Los Angeles, 1962—, prof. elec. and biomed. engring. and computer sci., 1968-82, chmn. dept. elec. engring. systems, 1978-86, dir. Robotics Inst., chmn. computer sci. dept., 1984—, dir. Ctr. for Mfg. and Automation Research, 1987—; cons. to govt. agys. and indsl. orgns. Author: (with W.J. Karplus) Hybrid Computation, 1968; editor 3 books; mem. editorial bd. 3 profl. jours.; editor IEEE Jour. Robotics and Automation; contbr. over 120 articles to profl. jours.; patentee in field. Served with U.S. Army, 1954-56. Recipient Disting. Faculty award Sch. Engring. and Service award U. So. Calif., 1977. Fellow IEEE; mem. NAE, Am. Assn. for Artificial Intelligence, Assn. for Computing Machinery, Soc. for Computer Simulation, Biomed. Engring. Soc., AAAS, World Affairs Council, Sigma Xi, Tau Beta Pi, Eta Kappa Nu. Office: U So Calif Dept Computer Sci Los Angeles CA 90089-0782

BEKIR, NAGWA E., electrical engineer, educator, consultant; b. Cairo, Dec. 31, 1944; came to U.S., 1972; s. Mohammed Ragab Shalaby and Kamla (Abdel Megeed) Mahmood; m. Esmat Chibl, Sept. 23, 1971; children: Ahmad C., Badr E. BSEE, Cairo U., Egypt, 1966; MSEE, U. So. Calif., 1975, PhD in EE, 1978. Rsch. and hardware engr. Egyptian Indsl. Rsch. Inst., Cairo, 1966-69; quality control engr. Nat. Egyptian Co. for TV and Electronics, Cairo, 1969-72; mem. tech. staff Axiomatics, L.A., 1978, Hughes Aircraft Co., Canoga Park, Calif., 1978-80; assoc. prof. elec. and computer engring. dept. Calif. State U., Northridge, 1980-83, prof., 1984—; tech. staff ITT Gilfillan, Van Nuys, Calif., 1984; sr. staff engr. Hughes Aircraft Co., Canoga Park, Calif., 1985; cons. Aircraft div. Northrop Co., El Segundo, Calif., 1987. Contbr. articles to profl. jours. Mem. Calif. State U. Affirmative action com., 1986—. Mem. IEEE (sr.), Health and Tennis Corp. Am., Eta Kappa Nu, Tau Beta Pi. Office: Calif State U 18111 Nordhoff St Northridge CA 91330

BELCHER, WILLIAM WALTER, JR., electronics company executive; b. Sayre, Pa., Oct. 22, 1943; s. William Walter Sr. and Mildred Rae (Smith) B.; m. Carole Jean Drake, June 12, 1965; children: Jon Christian, Katryna Dora. BE, Mansfield (Pa.) State Coll., 1964. Cert. tchr., Pa. Tchr. Galeton (Pa.) Pub. Schs., 1964-65, Susquehanna Valley Cen. Schs., Conklin, N.Y., 1965-66; quality engr. GE, Binghamton, N.Y., 1966-74, mgr. quality engring., 1974-75; mgr. reliability and quality assurance GE, Erie, Pa., 1975-79; mgr. x-ray tube mfg. GE, Milw., 1979-85; mgr. mfg. GE, Syracuse, N.Y., 1985-87; v.p. ops. Naucom Def. Electronics, Inc., El Monte, Calif., 1988—. Mem. adv. coun. Calif. State Poly. Inst., Pomona, Calif., 1988—, ind. adv. coun. El Monte Adult Edn.; chmn. com. Boy Scouts Am., Erie, 1978, Waukesha, Wis., 1983-85; mem. adminstrv. coun. Salem Meth. Ch., Waukesha, 1981; elder First Presbyn. Ch., Waukesha, 1985. Mem. Armed Forces Communications and Electronics Assn. Republican. Home: 609 Calle Santa Barbara San Dimas CA 91773 Office: Naucom Def Electronics Inc 4323 Arden Dr El Monte CA 91731-1997

BELILLE, RONALD, security coordinator; b. Portland, Nov. 22, 1947; s. Frank and Geraldine (Kron) B. AA in Law Enforcement, Portland Community Coll., 1970; student, Fed. Law Enforcement Tng. Ctr., Glynco, Ga., 1978; BS in Adminstrn. Justice, Portland State U., 1979; AA in Occupational Safety and Health, Mt. Hood Community Coll., 1985; grad., Police Reserve Acad., Oregon City, Oreg., 1985; grad. Intermediate Security Acad., Clackamas Community Coll., 1987; AA in Mgmt. and Commerce, Portland Community Coll., 1988. Cert. emergency med. technician 1. Correctional officer State Penitentiary, Salem, Oreg., 1972; fed. protective officer Fed. Protective Services, Portland, 1978; safety/security officer Precision Castparts, Portland, 1979-83, security coordinator, 1983—; CPR instr., first aid instr., portable fire extinguishers instr. Precision Castparts, 1983-85; chmn. steering com. Intermediate Security Acad. Clackamas Community Coll., 1987. Vol. asst. counselor Multiple County Adult Probation/Parole, Portland, Oreg., 1975; vol. asst. recognizance Officer Multiple County Ct., Oreg., 1982; mem. Citizen's Crime Commn. With USAF, 1966-68. Mem. Am. Mgmt. Assn., Am. Soc. Indsl. Security (chmn. legis. subcom. 1989), Am. Soc. Safety Engrs., Nat. Assn. Chiefs, Internat. Assn. Quality Circles, Masons, Elks, Phi Theta Kappa. Home: 1238 SE 47th Ave Portland OR 97215

BELK, JOHN BLANTON, educational and cultural organization executive; b. Orlando, Fla., Feb. 4, 1925; s. John Blanton and Jennie (Wannamaker) B.; m. Elizabeth Jane Wilkes, Dec. 11, 1954; children: Virginia Elizabeth, Katherine Wilkes. Student, Davidson Coll., 1943, U. N.C., 1943-45. Congl. aide U.S. Congress, Washington, 1949-50; with Moral Re-Armament (numerous locations), 1950-68, exec. dir., 1966-68; founder, chmn. bd., pres. Up With People, Tucson, 1968—. Bd. dirs. Internat. Fund Sports Disabled, Arnhem, Netherlands; mem. adv. bd. U. Ariz. Coll. Nursing. Served to lt. (j.g.) USNR, 1943-45. Decorated letter of commendation; decorated Order Vasco Nunez de Balboa Panama. Mem. Zeta Psi. Clubs: Mountain Oyster; Guaymas Yacht (Mexico); VIP (Tucson). Home: 2920 Cerrado los Palitos Tucson AZ 85718 Office: Up With People 3103 N Campbell Ave Tucson AZ 85719

BELL, DANIEL CARROLL, rancher; b. Chgo., July 17, 1940; s. Daniel Gregory and Inez Margarite (Carroll) B.; m. Elaine Paula Rhody, Feb. 1, 1960; children: Tana Lou, Daniel Arden, Andrea Jane. Student, Colo. State U., 1958-62, Reisch Coll. Auctioneering, Mason City, Iowa, 1983. Mgr. ptnr. Three Bell Ranch, Ft. Collins, Colo., 1958-69; sales rep. Pacific Vegetable Oil Co., San Francisco, 1969-70; mng. dir. Paveocor A.G. subs. PVO Internat., Rotterdam, Netherlands, 1970-71; nat. sales mgr. PVO Internat., San Francisco, 1971-72; v.p. commodity trading San Pablo Mfg. Co. subs. PVO Internat., Manila, Philippines, 1972-74; v.p. Rothschild Brokerage Co., San Francisco, 1975-76; owner, prin. Feed, Etc., Harbor, Oreg., 1976-79; commodity specialist Shearson Loeb Rhodes, Medford, Oreg., 1979-80; exec. v.p., gen. mgr. Superior Credit Assocs., Inc., Medford, 1981-86; mng. ptnr. Three Bell Land Co., Pierce, Colo., 1986—. Mem. Medford Oreg. Planning Commn., 1981-84, Medford Sister Cities Commn., 1984, treas. Jackson County Rep. Central Com., Medford, 1982-84; arbitrator Better Bus. Bur., Medford and Ft. Collins, Colo., 1984—; candidate Oreg. Ho. Reps., 1984. With USAR, 1958-63, with Colo. Nat. Guard, 1963-65. Mem. Profl. Photographers Am., Photographic Soc. Am., Wildlife Photographers Assn., Am. Legion, Eaton Country Club, Heather Ridge Country Club, Elks. Republican. Presbyterian. Office: Three Bell Land Co 19255 Weld County Rd 88 Pierce CO 80650

BELL, DONALD ROBERT, engineer; b. Santa Barbara, Calif., Aug. 30, 1928; s. Stanley Garfield Vanderick and Ellen Agnes (Hart) B.; m. June Laverne Emge, Jan. 20, 1952 (div. Feb. 1962); children: Diane Elizabeth, Donna June; m. Dorothea Alice Searle, Oct. 13, 1962. Student, U.S. Naval Acad., 1948-49, West Coast U., 1953-54, Santa Monica (Calif.) City Coll., 1965-66. Registered quality engr., Calif., profl. engr., Calif. Asst. foreman Hughes Aircraft Co., Culver City, Calif., 1954-59; supr. Transvaal Electronics, El Segundo, Calif., 1959-60; sr. engring. aide Litton Systems, Inc., Woodland Hills, Calif., 1960-65; systems engring. asst. Hughes Aircraft Co.,

Culver City, 1965-67; test facilities engr. Hughes Aircraft Co., 1967-74, program quality engr., 1974-77, sr. project engr., 1977-78; sr. quality engr. Hughes Aircraft Co., El Segundo, 1978-83; staff engr. Hughes Aircraft Co., 1983-86, sr. staff engr., 1986—; sr. staff engr. Electro-Optical and Data Systems Group, El Segundo, 1983—. Served with USN, 1950-54, Korea. Mem. U.S. Naval Acad. Alumni Assn. (nat. chpt., Los Angeles chpt.), NRA (life), Am. Assn. Retired Persons, So. Calif. Past Masters Assn., Calif. Rifle and Pistol Assn. (life mem.), Golden State Mobile Home Owners League, Inc., Calif. Research Lodge, Hughes Aircraft Co. Mgmt. Club, Mut. Asst. Club. Democrat. Clubs: Marine's Meml. (San Francisco), West Los Angeles Builder's, Santa Monica Bay Staff (Pacific Palisades, Calif.). Lodges: Masons, Order Demolay, Independent Order Foresters, Order Eastern Star, Internat. Order Job's Daus. Home: 1065 Lomita Blvd # 276 Harbor City CA 90710

BELL, DONALD WILLIAM, experimental psychologist; b. Los Angeles, Apr. 28, 1936; s. Samuel Chamblis and Betty M. (Welz) B. BA, U. So. Calif., 1959, MA, 1963, PhD, 1966. Research assoc. Subcom. on Noise Research Ctr., Los Angeles, 1962-66; postdoctoral fellow Stanford (Calif.) U., 1966-68; research psychologist SRI Internat., Menlo Park, Calif., 1968-76, sr. research psychologist, 1976-82, program mgr., 1982-83, dir. speech research program, 1983—; pres. Digital Voice Corp., 1982—. Contbr. articles to profl. jours. Mem. planning commn. Town of Portola Valley, Calif. Mem. IEEE, Acoustical Soc. Am., Psychonomic Soc., Am. Voice I/O Soc. (dir.). Republican. Home: 15 Peak Ln Portola Valley CA 94025 Office: SRI Internat 333 Ravenswood Menlo Park CA 94025

BELL, DUANE HODGES, secondary school teacher; b. Wilmington, N.C., Oct. 1, 1945; s. Raymond and Maria Lee (Savage) B.; m. Kate Frohlich, Apr. 4, 1975; children: Maria, Karl H. BA in Spanish & French, U. N.C., Wilmington, 1967; MA in Spanish, U. Nev., Reno, 1973; MA in French, U. Calif., Santa Barbara, 1988. Cert. secondary school language tchr., Ariz.; cert. bilingual tchr. Jr. high Spanish/French tchr. Northwoods Pk. Jr. High Sch., Jacksonville, N.C., 1967-68; high sch. Spanish/French tchr. Summerville (S.C.) High Sch., 1968-70, Bishop Manogue High Sch., Reno, 1975-76, Nogales (Ariz.) High Sch., 1976—; cons. in field; instr. in field. Pres. Ariz. Right to Life Chpt., Nogales, Ariz., 1982-85; trustee Triumph Luth. Ch., Nogales, 1985-88. Recipient Foreign Language Fellowship Univ. Nev., 1971-73. Mem. Nogales Ind. Profl. Educators (pres. 1986—), Ariz. State Profl. Educators (state sec. 1987-88), Am. Assn. Tchrs. French, Am. Assn. Tchrs. Spanish & Portuguese, MLA. Republican. Lutheran.

BELL, JOHN CLINTON, manufacturing company executive; b. Van Buren, Ark., Apr. 26, 1935; s. Curtis Clinton and Geneva May (Rouw) B.; m. Wanda June Meadows, Aug. 28, 1954 (div. 1972); children: Pamela, Tina, Kellie; m. Mary Louise Stier, May 30, 1972; children: Steven, Michael. Student, Calif. State Polytech. Coll., 1954, Cerritos Jr. Coll., 1959, W. Coast U., 1961, U. Md., 1986. Guidance, navigation engr. Rockwell Internat., 1955-79; remote depot facility mgr. Rockwell Internat., RAF Lakenheath, U.K., 1979-87; logistics product support mgr. Rockwell Internat., Downey, Calif., 1987—, depot implementation cons., 1979-87; depot activation cons. Rockwell Internat., Cape Canaveral, Fla., 1987—. Mem. Nat. Mgmt. Assn. Republican. Roman Catholic. Office: Rockwell Internat Internat Space Transp System Astronaut Blvd Cape Canaveral FL 32920

BELL, KATRINA MARGARET, research analyst; b. Perrin Air Force Base, Tex., Nov. 5, 1961; d. Gladys M. Bell. BA in Written Communication, Mills Coll., Oakland, Calif., 1983; BA in Applied Communication Research, Stanford U., 1984; postgrad., U. Calif., 1988—. Mktg. research analyst Allstate Research and Planning, Menlo Park, Calif., 1984; research analyst San Francisco Newspaper Agy., 1984-85, Calif. State U., Hayward, 1985—; mng. ptnr. entertainment planning and promotion Bell and Assoc., Sacramento, Calif., 1985—. Dir. youth activities Faith Presby. Ch., Oakland, 1987—. Fellow U. Calif., Davis, 1988—. Mem. Sacramento Black Women's Network, Alpha Kappa Alpha (pres. local chpt. 1981-82). Democrat. Home: 3303 Holly Br Ct #465 Sacramento CA 95834 Office: Bell and Assocs 1008-10th St #396 Sacramento CA 95814

BELL, KRISTINE KAY, nurse; b. Kenosha, Wis., Apr. 22, 1965; d. Robert Lee and Anna Jane (Achenbach) Walker; m. Thomas Lawrence Bell, Sept. 2, 1966. Diploma, St. Luke's Hosp. Sch. Nursing, Racine, Wis., 1986. RN, Calif. Nurse St. Luke's Hosp., 1986-87, Loma Linda U. Med. Ctr., Calif., 1987—. Scholar, Bradford High Sch., 1983, 86, St. Luke's Hosp., 1986. Lutheran. Home: 33 Price St Redlands CA 92373 Office: Loma Linda U Med Ctr 11234 Anderson St Loma Linda CA 92350

BELL, LARRY STUART, artist; b. Chgo., Dec. 6, 1939; s. Hyman David and Rebecca Ann (Kriegmont) B.; 2 children. Student, Chouinard Art Inst., Los Angeles, 1957-59. instr. So. Calif. Inst. of Architecture, 1988. One man exhbns. include Stedelijk Mus., Amsterdam, 1967, Pasadena (Calif.) Art Mus., 1972, Oakland (Calif.) Mus., 1973, Ft. Worth Art Mus., 1975, Santa Barbara (Calif.) Mus. Art, 1976, Washington U., St. Louis, 1976, Art Mus. So. Tex., Corpus Christi, 1976, Hayden Gallery, M.I.T., 1977, Hudson River Mus., Yonkers, N.Y., 1981, Newport Harbor Art Mus., 1982, Marian Goodman Gallery, 1982, Ruth S. Schaffner Gallery, 1982, Cleve. Ctr. for Contemporary Art, Ohio, 1987, Erica Williams, Anne Johnson Gallery, 1982, Arco Ctr. Visual Arts, L.A., 1983, Unicorn Gallery, Aspen, Colo., 1983, Butler Inst. Am. Art, Youngstown, Ohio, 1984, Leigh Yawkey Woodson Art Mus., Santa Barbara, Calif., 1985, Colorado Springs Fine Arts Ctr., 1987, Mus. Contemporary Art, L.A., 1987, Am. Acad. and Inst. Arts and Letters, N.Y.C., 1987, Boise (Idaho) Gallery Art, 1987, Gilbert Brownstone Gallery, Paris, 1987, Braunstein/Quay Gallery, San Francisco, 1987, Fine Arts Gallery, N.Mex. State Fairgrounds, 1987, Kiyo Higashi Gallery, L.A., 1987, Laguna Art Mus., Laguna Beach, Calif., 1987; group exhbns. include Mus. Modern Art, N.Y.C., 1965, 79, Jewish Mus., N.Y.C., 1966, Whitney Mus. Am. Art, 1966, Guggenheim Mus., N.Y.C., 1967, Tate Gallery, London, 1970, Hayward Gallery, London, 1971, Detroit Inst. Arts, 1973, Nat. Collections Fine Arts, 1975, San Francisco Mus. Modern Art, 1976, Museo de Arte Contemporaneo de Caracas, Venezuela, 1978, Aspen Ctr. for Visual Arts, 1980, Fruit Market Gallery, Edinburgh, Scotland, 1980, Albuquerque Mus., 1980, Art Inst. Chgo., 1982, Santa Barbara Art Mus., 1984, The Rufino Tamayo Mus., Mexico City, 1985, Colorado Springs Fine Art Ctr., 1986, Mus. Comtemporary Art, 1986, Am. Acad. Arts and Letters, 1986, Ariz. State U., Tempe, 1987, Braunstein/Quay Gallery, 1987, The Works Gallery, Long Beach, 1987, Davis/McClain Gallery, Houston, 1987; represented in permanent collections including Nat. Collection Fine Arts, Mus. of Fine Arts, Santa Fe, N.Mex., 1989, Musee St. Pierre De L'Art Contemporaine, Lyon, France, 1989, Tucson Art Mus., 1989, San Antonio Art Inst., 1989, Albuquerque Mus., 1989, Mus. of Fine Arts, Santa Fe, N.Mex., 1989, Contemporary Art Ctr., Kansas City, 1989, Whitney Mus. Am. Art, Tate Gallery, Gallery New South Wales, Australia, Albright-Knox Gallery, Art Inst. Chgo., Denver Art Mus., Dallas Mus. Fine Arts, Guggenheim Mus., L.A. County Mus., Victoria and Albert Mus., London, San Antonio Mus. Art, others, Phoenix Art Mus., 1987, High Mus. Art, 1988; instr. sculpture, U. South Fla., Tampa, U. Calif., Berkeley, Irvine, 1970-73, Copley Found. grantee, 1962, Guggenheim Found. fellow, 1970, Nat. Endowment Arts grantee, 1975. Office: Box 4101 Taos NM 87571

BELL, LEO S., retired physician; b. Newark, Nov. 7, 1913; s. Alexander M. and Marie (Saxon) B.; AB, Syracuse U., 1934; MD, 1938; m. Edith Lewis, July 3, 1938; children: Jewyl Linn, David Alden. Intern, N.Y.C. Hosp., 1938, Bklyn. Hosp., 1939-40; resident in pediatrics Sea View Hosp., N.Y.C., 1940-41, N.Y.C. Hosp., 1941-42; practice medicine specializing in pediatrics, San Mateo, Calif., 1946-86; mem. staff Mills Meml. Hosp., San Mateo, Peninsula Hosp. & Med. Ctr., Burlingame, Children's Hosp., San Francisco; assoc. clin. prof. pediatrics U. Calif. Med Sch., San Francisco, Stanford Med. Sch. Palo Alto; mem. curriculum & ednl. affairs comm. U. San Francisco Med. Sch., adminstv. coun.; columnist San Mateo Times. Bd. dirs. Mills Hosp. Found., San Mateo, San Mateo County Heart Assn., Hillsborough Schs. Found. (Calif.), 1980-83. Capt. as flight surgeon USAAF, 1942-46. Recipient bronze and silver medals Am. Heart Assn.; diplomate Am. Bd. Pediatrics. Fellow Am. Acad. Pediatrics, Am. Pub. Health Assn.; mem. Calif. Fedn. Pediatric Socs. (pres.), Am. Fedn. Pediatric Socs. (pres.), Calif. Med. Assn., Am. Pub. Health Assn., Air Force Assn., AMA (alt. del. to ho. of dels.), Calif. Med. Assn. (ho. of dels.), San Mateo County Med. Assn. (sec.treas.), Internat. Med. Assn., Hong Kong Snuff Bottle Socs., World Affairs Coun. San Francisco, Peninsula Golf and Country Club, Commonwealth Club. Contbr. articles to profl. jours. Home: 220 Roblar Ave Hillsborough CA 94010 Office: PO Box 1877 San Mateo CA 94401

BELL, ROBERT CECIL, lawyer; b. San Francisco, June 1, 1951; s. Robert Elmer and Lillian Marie (Petrik) B. BJ, U. Nev., 1973; JD, U. Pacific, 1980. Bar: Nev. 1980, U.S. Dist. Ct. Nev. 1980, U.S. Bankruptcy Ct. 1981, U.S. Ct. Appeals (9th cir.) 1982, U.S. Supreme Ct., 1988. Investigator, legal asst. Washoe County Dist. Atty.'s Office, Reno, 1975-77; law clk. to presiding justice Washoe County Dist. Ct., Reno, 1980-81; sole practice Reno, 1981—; judge pro tem Reno Mcpl. Ct., 1985—, Sparks Mcpl. Ct. 1986—; bd. dirs. Washoe Legal Svcs., Reno. Bd. dirs. March of Dimes, Reno, 1985—; mem. Supreme Ct. Hist. Soc. Mem. ABA, Washoe County Bar Assn., Assn. Trial Lawyers Am., Nev. Trial Lawyers Assn., Reno Rodeo Assn., Reno Air Races, U. Pacific McGeorge Sch. Law Alumni Assn. (bd. dirs. 1986—). Democrat. Lutheran. Home: 1050 Cottonwood Rd Reno NV 89511 Office: 121 California Ave Reno NV 89509

BELL, WAYNE STEVEN, lawyer; b. L.A., June 24, 1954; s. Joseph and Jane Barbara (Barsook) B.; m. M. Susan Modzelewski, Apr. 1, 1989. BA magna cum laude, UCLA, 1976; JD, Loyola U., Los Angeles, 1979. Bar: Calif. 1980, U.S. Dist. Ct. (cen. dist.) 1981, U.S. Tax Ct. 1981, U.S. Ct. Appeals (9th cir.) 1981, U.S. Dist. Ct. (so. and no. dists.) Calif. 1983, U.S. Supreme Ct. 1984, D.C. 1986; lic. real estate broker, Calif. Intern office of gov. State of Calif., Sacramento, summer 1976; assoc. Levinson, Rowen, Miller, Jacobs & Kabrins, L.A., 1980-82; sr. assoc. Montgomery, Gascou, Gemmill & Thornton, L.A., 1982-84; counsel, project developer Thomas Safran & Assocs., L.A., 1984-85; of counsel Greenspan, Glasser & Medina, Santa Monica, Calif., 1984-86; assoc. gen. counsel Am. Diversified Cos., Costa Mesa, Calif., 1985-88; legal cons. Project Atty., L.A., 1988—; Judge pro tem Mcpl. Ct. South Bay Jud. Dist., 1987. Chief note and comment editor Loyola U. Law Rev., 1978-79; contbr. articles to profl. jours. Vol. atty. Westside Legal Services, Santa Monica, 1982-87; legal ombudsman Olympics Ombudsman program L.A. County Bar Assn., 1984; gov. appointed mem. Calif. adv. council Legal Services Corp., 1982-88, Autism Soc. Am., Amnesty Internat.; contbg. mem. Dem. Nat. Com., So. Poverty Law Ctr.; bd. dirs. Am. Theatre Arts, Hollywood, Calif., 1983-84; pres., mem. exec. com., bd. dirs. Programs for the Developmentally Handicapped, Inc., L.A., 1987—; chmn. bd. appeals handicapped accommodations City of Manhattan Beach, 1986-88. Mem. ABA, Calif. Bar (standing com. legal problems of aging 1983-86, chmn. legis. subcom. 1984-86 legal services sect., conf. dels. alternate 1987), UCLA Alumni Assn., Legal Assistance Assn. Calif. (bd. dirs., mem. exec. com., legis. strategy com. 1984-86), Loyola Law Sch. (assoc. adv.), Smithsonian Inst., Phi Beta Kappa, Pi Gamma Mu, Pi Sigma Alpha, Phi Alpha Delta. Democrat. Home and Office: 1761 N Beverly Glen Blvd Los Angeles CA 90077

BELLANDI, WILMA, export packing executive; b. Wellington, Ill., Aug. 11, 1914; d. William Henry and Rella (Clinard) Boyden; m. Raymond C. Hackett, Apr. 30, 1938 (div. 1959); children: Raymond Cornell, William Boyden; m. Mario Bellandi, May 5, 1968 (dec. 1973). Student, Lewis Inst., 1934, U. Calif., Berkeley, 1954-55, John F. Kennedy U., 1975, Contra Costa Jr. Coll., 1986-87. Enrolled agt. U.S. Dept. Treasury, lic. real estate agt., Calif. Office mgr. Linen Supply Co., Oakland, Calif., 1948-50; acct. various CPA firms, Oakland, 1950-60; pvt. practice Oakland, 1960-65; real estate developer Calif., 1965—; controller, mgr. Crown Industries, San Leandro, Calif., 1983--. Pres. Oakland Real Estate Toastmistress, 1950, Bus. and Profl. Lake Merrit, Oakland, 1978; candidate for Calif. State Assembly, 1958, 60; past. pres. 7th dist. Dem. Cen. Com. Mem. Am. Soc. Accts., Navy League U.S. (pres. eb. council 1974-75), HNC Symphony Assn. (pres. 1987--), Sons of Italy, Berkeley Club (pres., fin. sec.), Oakland Lodge. Roman Catholic. Home: 177 19th St Oakland CA 94612

BELLAVIA, CHARLES, accountant; b. Buffalo, Aug. 15, 1946; s. Charles W. and Helen Elizabeth (McCumber) B.; m. Sandra J. Flint. AA, Bryant and Stratton Bus. Inst., 1967; BBA, Ft. Lauderdale U., 1971. Auditor Diamond's Dept. Store, Phoneix, 1971-73, acctg. pay mgr., 1974-75; controller Starretts Fashion World, Phoneix, 1977-79, Profl. Retirement Svc., Mesa, Ariz., 1980-82; pres., owner The Auditor's Trail Inc., Phoenix, 1982—. Bd. dirs. Meml. Classic Girls Softball Tournament, Scottsdale, 1984-87. Mem. Ariz. Soc. Practical Acctg., Nat. Assn. Practical Acctg. Republican. Office: The Auditor's Trail Inc 532 E Maryland #F Phoenix AZ 85012

BELLER, GERALD STEPHEN, former insurance company executive; b. Phila., Aug. 6, 1935; s. Nathan and Adelaide B. (Goldfarb) B.; C.L.U., Am. Coll., Bryn Mawr, Pa., 1972; m. Nancy R. Nelson, June 8, 1968; children—Fay A., Mark S., Royce W., Merrilee A., Marie A., Frank A. Spl. agt. Prudential Ins. Co., San Bernardino, Calif., 1959-62, div. mgr., 1962-66; agy. supr. Aetna Life & Casualty Co., Los Angeles, 1966-69, gen. agt., 1969-77. Magician Magic Castle, Hollywood, Calif. Mem. adult correctional adv. coun. San Bernardino County, Calif. Served with USAF, 1953-57. Recipient Man of Year award, 1961; Manpower Builders award, 1966-69; Agy. Builders award, 1970-72; Pres.'s Trophy award, 1973-74; Nat. Mgmt. award, 1973-76. Mem. Los Angeles Life Underwriters Assn., Am. Soc. C.L.U.s, Golden Key Soc. of Am. Coll., Internat. Exec. Svc. Corps. (vol.), Calif. Assn. Life Underwriters, Los Angeles County C.L.U.s. Home: 20625 Tonawanda Rd Apple Valley CA 92307

BELLER, KATHLEEN JENNIFER, actress; b. Queens, N.Y., Feb. 10, 1956; d. Jesse and Barbara (Jackson) B.; m. Thomas Dolby, July 2, 1988. Recipient Golden Globe nomination, Golden Globe, Fgn. Press, 1979. Mem. Acad. Motion Picture Arts and Scis.

BELLINGER, JOHN DOOLEY, banker; b. Honolulu, May 13, 1923; s. Eustace L. and Lei (Williams) B.; m. Joan Simms, Apr. 7, 1945; children: Dona, Jan, Neil. Student, U. Hawaii, 1941-42, LL.D. (hon.), 1982; LHD (hon.), Hawaii Loa Coll., 1986. With First Hawaiian Bank (and predecessor), Honolulu, 1942—, chmn., chief exec. officer, 1969—; also bd. dirs. First Hawaiian Bank (and predecessor); chief exec. officer, chmn. bd. First Hawaiian, Inc., also bd. dirs.; chmn., chief exec. officer First Hawaiian Credit Corp.; chmn., chief exec. officer, dir. 1st Hawaiian Leasing, Inc.; dir. Alexander & Baldwin, Honolulu, Matson Nav. Co., Hawaiian Telephone Co., Restaurant Suntory, U.S.A., Halekulani Corp.; mem. Gov.'s adv. bd. Underwater Cable Transmission Project. Chmn. Japan-Hawaii Econ. Council; chmn., bd. dirs. Pacific Internat. Ctr. for High Tech.; bd. dirs. North Hawaii Community Hosp., Inc.; civilian aide to sec. Army for Hawaii; chmn. U.S. Army Civilian Adv. Steering Com.; trustee Francis H.I. Brown Found., Punahou Sch., Japan-Am. Inst. Mgmt. Sci. Fund; hon. trustee Bishop Mus.; bd. dirs. East-West Ctr. Found. Served with AUS, 1946-47; bd. govs. Japanese Cultural Ctr. Hawaii. Decorated Disting. Civilian Service Medal Sec. of Army, 1980; recipient Disting. Citizen award Congl. Medal of Honor Soc., 1981; decorated ProPatria award, 1984, Torch of Liberty award Anti-Defamation League of B'nai B'rith, 1984, Businessman of Yr. award Hawaiian Bus./Profl. Assn., 1984; Gen. Creighton W. Abrams medal, David Malo award Rotary Club Honolulu, 1986, Community Relations award of excellence Dept. Army, 1987; 3d Class Order Rising Sun, 1987; named Hawaii Disting. Citizen, Boy Scouts Am. Aloha council, 1987; named to Honolulu Dist. of Edn. Hall of Fame; numerous others. Mem. Hawaii C. of C. (bd. dirs.), Assn. U.S. Army, Navy League, Hawaii bankers assns. Clubs: Hawaiian Civic, Oahu Country, Waialae Country (Honolulu) (bd. dirs., past pres.); The 200 (treas., past pres.). Office: 1st Hawaiian Bank 165 S King St Honolulu HI 96813

BELLIS, CARROLL JOSEPH, surgeon; b. Shreveport, La.; s. Joseph and Rose (Bloome) B.; m. Mildred Darmody, Dec. 26, 1939; children—Joseph, David. BS, U. Minn., 1930, MS in Physiology, 1932, PhD in Physiology, 1934, MD, 1936, PhD in Surgery, 1941. Diplomate Am. Bd. Surgery. Resident surgery U. Minn. Hosps., 1937-41; pvt. practice surgery Long Beach, Calif., 1945—; mem. staff St. Mary's, Community hosps., Long Beach; cons. surgery Long Beach Gen. Hosp.; prof., chmn. dept. surgery Calif. Coll. Medicine, 1962—; surgical cons. to Surgeon-Gen., U.S. Army. Author: Fundamentals of Human Physiology, 1935, A Critique of Reason, 1938, Lectures in Medical Physiology; contbr. numerous articles in field of surgery, physiology to profl. jours. Served to col. M.C. AUS, 1941-46. Nat. Cancer Inst. fellow, 1934; recipient Charles Lyman Green prize in physiology, 1934; prize Mpls. Surg. Soc., 1938; ann. award Mississippi Valley Med. Soc., 1955. Fellow ACS, Internat. Coll. Surgeons, Am. Coll. Gastroenterology, Am. Med. Writers Assn., Internat. Coll. Angiology (sci. council), Gerontol. Soc., Am. Soc. Abdominal Surgeons, Nat. Cancer Inst., Phlebology Soc. Am., Internat. Acad. Proctology, Peripheral Vascular Soc. Am. (founding); mem. Am. Assn. Study Neoplastic Diseases, Mississippi Valley Med. Soc., N.Y. Acad. Scis., Hollywood Acad. Medicine, Am. Geriatrics Soc., Irish Med. Assn., AAAS, Am. Assn. History Medicine, Pan Pacific Surgical Assn., Indsl. Med. Assn., Los Angeles Musicians Union (hon.), Pan Am. Med. Assn. (diplomate), Internat. Bd. Surgery (cert.), Internat. Bd. Proctology (cert.), Wisdom Soc. (wisdom award of honor), Sigma Xi, Phi Beta Kappa, Alpha Omega Alpha. Office: 1045 Atlantic Ave Long Beach CA 90813

BELLMAN, WILLARD FRANKLIN, theater educator; b. Tacoma, May 4, 1920; s. William Franklin and Jennie Mae (Frost) B.; m. Kathleen Marion Hein, Aug. 22, 1949; children: Christopher, Deborah. BA, U. Puget Sound, 1946; MA, Northwestern U., 1947, PhD, 1949. Prof. theater Calif. State U., Northridge, 1958—. Author: Lighting the Stage, 1967, rev. edit., 1974, Scene Design, Stage Lighting, Sound, Costume and Make-Up, 1983. Acting v.p. Spl. Projects, 1989—. Fellow U.S. Inst. Theatre Tech. (bd. dirs. 1986—). Home: 20314 Haynes St Canoga Park CA 91306 Office: Calif State U Dept Theatre Northridge CA 91330

BELLONI, ROBERT CLINTON, judge; b. Riverton, Oreg., Apr. 4, 1919; s. John Edward and Della (Clinton) B.; children: James L., Susan K. BA, U. Oreg., 1941, LLB, 1951. Bar: Oreg. 1951. Practiced in Coquille, Oreg., 1951-52, Myrtle Point, Oreg., 1952-57; judge Oreg. Circuit Ct., Coos and Curry Counties, Coquille, 1957-67; U.S. dist. judge Dist. Oreg., 1967—, chief judge, 1971-76. Councilman, Myrtle Point, 1953-57, mayor, 1957; chmn. Coos County Democratic Central Com., 1957; Hon. trustee Boys and Girls Aid Soc. Oreg., 1960. Served to 1st lt. AUS, 1942-46. Robert C. Belloni Boys Forest Ranch dedicated in his honor Coos County Bd. Commrs., 1969. Mem. ABA, Oreg. Bar Assn., Am. Judicature Soc., Oreg. Juvenile Ct. Judges Assn. (pres. 1963), Circuit Ct. Judges Assn. Oreg. (pres. 1966), 9th Circuit Dist. Judges Assn. (pres. 1980-81), Sigma Alpha Epsilon, Delta Theta Phi. Episcopalian. Office: US Dist Ct 708 US Courthouse 620 SW Main St Portland OR 97205

BELL-PATTEN, KAREN, credit executive; b. Vallejo, Calif., Jan. 14, 1944; d. John Hardy and Thelma (Conlin) Bell; m. Bruce Patten, Aug. 17, 1943. Saleswoman Credit Data Corp. (div. Info. System Group), San Francisco, 1966-68, asst. to v.p. rsch. and devel., 1968-70, mgr. credit file ops., 1970-71, customer svc. rep., 1971-73, supr. customer svc., 1973-74, mgr. sales, 1974-85, br. mgr., 1985—. Recipient Charlie Benson award San Francisco Greater East Bay Internat. Credit Assn., 1987, Boss of Yr. award Credit Women of Marin, 1977. Mem. Soc. Certified Credit Exec., San Francisco Internat. Consumer Credit Assn. (dir. 1978—, pres. 1982-83, 1985-86), Consumer Credit Counselors (bd. dirs. San Francisco chpt. 1984—). Democrat. Presbyterian. Office: TRW Credit Data 770 Tamalpais Dr Ste 320 Corte Madera CA 94925

BELLUOMINI, FRANK STEPHEN, accountant; b. Healdsburg, Calif., May 19, 1934; s. Francesco and Rose (Giorgi) B.; m. Alta Anita Gifford, Sept. 16, 1967; 1 child, Wendy Ann. AA, Santa Rosa Jr. Coll., 1954; BA with honors, San Jose State U., 1956. CPA, Calif. Staff acct. Hood, Gire & Co., CPA's, San Jose, Calif., 1956-60, ptnr., 1960-66; ptnr. Touche Ross & Co., CPA's, San Jose, 1967—, ptnr.-in-charge San Jose office, 1971-85, sr. ptnr. San Jose office, 1985—. Mem. adv. bd. Salvation Army, San Jose, 1979-85, San Jose Children's Council, 1982—; trustee Santa Clara County (Calif.) United Way, 1979-83, v.p. planning and allocations, 1981-83, vice chmn., 1985-87, chmn. 1987-89; bd. dirs. San Jose Mus. Art, 1984-86. Named Disting. Alumnus, San Jose State U. Sch. Bus., 1978. Mem. Santa Clara County Estate Planning Council (pres. 1979-80), Calif. Soc. C.P.A.'s (pres. chpt. 1968-69, state v.p. 1976-77), Am. Inst. C.P.A.'s (chmn. state and local govt. com. 1976-79), San Jose State Alumni Assn. (treas. 1960-61, dir. 1961-62, exec. com. 1961-62), San Jose State Acctg. Round Table (bd. dirs., treas. 1982-87), Beta Alpha Psi (San Jose State U. Outstanding Alumnus award 1986). Roman Catholic. Club: San Jose Rotary (dir. 1979-81, trustee and treas. San Jose Rotary Endowment 1976-83).

BELLUS, RONALD JOSEPH, communications executive; b. Travis AFB, Calif., Feb. 25, 1951; s. Vincent Joseph and Katherine Veronica (Giudice) B.; m. Beth Ann Johnson, June 26, 1976; children: Veronica Lee, Joseph Vincent, Kenneth James. BA in Communications, Brigham Young U., 1977. Lic. FCC radio telephone operator, 1979. Sports dir. Sta. KGUY-AM Radio, Palm Desert, Calif., 1979; news, sports dir. Sta. KBLQ-AM/FM Radio, Logan, Utah, 1979-80; gen. sales mgr. Sta. KSTM-FM/KVVA-AM Radio, Phoenix, 1980-84, Sta. KLFF-AM/KMZK-FM Radio, Phoenix, 1984-85; media cons. Mediacorp Planning & Buying, Phoenix, 1985-86; press sec. Gov. of Ariz., Phoenix, 1986-87; asst. dir. Ariz. Office of Tourism, Phoenix, 1987-88; media cons. Bellus Media, Inc., Phoenix, 1988—; ptnr. Desertwest Media Group, Inc., Phoenix, 1988—; media cons. Mecham for Gov. com., Glendale, Ariz., 1986. Author: Mecham: Silence Cannot Be Misquoted, 1988, Tourism Travel Planner, 1988. Comm. mem. Phoenix Boys Choir, 1988; precinct committeeman Rep. State Com., Phoenix, 1987—, del., 1988; cand. for state senate, Phoenix, 1988. Named one of Outstanding Young Men Am., 1987. Mem. Phoenix Press Box Assn. (treas. 1984-85, exec. dir. 1985-86). Ch. of Latter Day Saints. Office: Bellus Media Inc 3636 N Central Ave Ste 120 One Columbus Pla Phoenix AZ 85012

BELLVILLE, RALPH EARL, banker; b. Lynn, Mass., June 15, 1925; s. Harold Eugene and Edith Floy (Simpson) B.; m. Crescentia Ranftl, Oct. 16, 1954. AB, Harvard U., 1950. Asst. mgr. No. Trust Co., Chgo., 1955-60; v.p. United Calif. Bank, L.A., 1960-69; exec. v.p. Security Pacific Nat. Bank, L.A., 1969-85; pres. REB Cons., Santa Monica, Calif., 1985—; bd. dirs. Security Pacific Overseas Corp., Security Pacific Overseas Investment Corp., Security Pacific Asian Bank, Hong Kong. Active L.A. Com. on Fgn. Rels. With inf. U.S. Army, 1943-46. Decorated Bronze Star with oak leaf cluster. Mem. Global Econ. Action Inst., Asia Soc., Jonathan Club, Internat. Club, Harvard Club So. Calif. Home: 211 24th St Santa Monica CA 90402 Office: REB Cons 211 24th St Santa Monica CA 90402

BELMONT, LARRY MILLER, health association executive; b. Reno, Apr. 13, 1936; s. Miller Lawrence and Madeline (Echante) B.; m. Laureen Metzger, Aug. 14, 1966; children: Miller Lawrence, Rebecca Madeline, Amie Echante, Bradley August. BA in Psychology, U. Nev., 1962; MPH, U. Mich., 1968; cert. in environ. mgmt., U. So. Calif., 1978; M in Pub. Adminstrn., U. Idaho, 1979. Rep. on loan to city health depts. USPHS, Los Angeles and Long Beach, 1962-63; advisor pub. health on loan to Alaska dept. health and welfare USPHS, Anchorage, 1963-64, Juneau and Anchorage, 1964-67; dep. dir. Wash./Alaska Regional Med. Program, Spokane, Wash., 1968-71; dir. Panhandle Health Dist., Coeur d'Alene, Idaho, 1971—; mem. adj. faculty Whitworth Coll., Spokane; presenter papers nat., region, state confs., 1981-82; testifier congl. coms., Washington, 1973, 76, state legis. com., Idaho, 1972-82. Chmn. nominating com. Kootenai Econ. Devel. Council, Idaho, 1985, bd. dirs. 1981-86; mem. adv. com. Kootenai County Council Alcoholism, 1979-80; regional coordinator Gov.'s Com. Vol. Services, Idaho, 1979-80; chmn. Montessori Adv. Bd., Idaho, 1975-79; chmn. personnel com. North Idaho Hospice, 1985-87, bd. dirs. 1985-88; bd. dirs. North Idaho Spl. Services Agy., 1972-76; active numerous other organizations. USPHS trainee U. Mich., 1967-68, EPA trainee U. So. Calif., 1978. Mem. Am. Pub. Health Assn., Nat. Assn. Home Health Agys. (chmn. legis. com. 1979-81, bd. dirs. 1978-81), Nat. Assn. County Health Officials (bd. dirs. 1986—), Idaho Pub. Health Assn. (bd. dirs., treas. 1973-77), Idaho Forest Owners Assn., Kootenai County Environ. Alliance, Idaho Conservation League, Ducks Ultd. Democrat.

BELOW, JOHN FREDERICK, mechanical engineer; b. Chgo., July 5, 1951; s. John Frederick Jr. and Genevieve Marie (Brons) B.; m. Holly Elizabeth Jenstad, Oct. 13, 1979; 1 child, Jennifer. BSME, U. Calif., Berkeley, 1973. Registered profl. mech. engr., Calif. Staff engr. Rix Industries, Emeryville, Calif., 1975-77, chief engr., 1977—; prin. John Below Engrig. Assocs., Oakland, Calif., 1987—; co-owner J & S Engring. Co., Pinole, Calif., 1981-86; co-owner Rescue Air Systems, Inc., Petaluma, Calif., 1988—. Recipient Pride in Pinole award City Council, 1987; named Athlete of Yr. Helms/Citizens Savs. Athletic Found., Los Angeles, 1977; U.S. Nat.

Skindiving Champion Underwater Soc. Am., 1977-78. Mem. NSPE, Calif. Soc. Profl. Engrs. (v.p. East Bay chpt. 1988), Soc. Automotive Engrs. Republican. Roman Catholic. Home: 1401 Mountain Blvd Oakland CA 94611 Office: Rix Industries 6560 Hollis St Emeryville CA 94608

BELT, AUDREY E., social worker, consultant; b. New Orleans, June 23, 1948. BS, Grambling (La.) State U., 1970; MSW, U. Mich., 1972. Adult probation officer City/County San Francisco Hall of Justice, 1973-74; child welfare worker dept. social svcs. City/County San Francisco, 1974-79; rsch. and planning spcialist City of Ann Arbor (Mich.) Model Cities Interdisciplinary Agy; cons. in field. Grambling State U. scholar, 1966-70, U. Mich. scholar, 1971-72. Mem. Nat. Assn. Social Workers (edn. task force) Am. Orthopsychiat. Assn., Am. Humane Soc., Child Welfare League Am., ABA, Black Am. Polit. Assn. Calif. (legis. com.). Democrat. Roman Catholic. Home: PO Box 5319 San Francisco CA 94101-5319

BELTRÁN, ANTHONY NATALICIO, military officer, deacon; b. Flagstaff, Ariz., Aug. 17, 1938; s. Natalicio Torres and Mary Mercedes (Sandoval) B.; m. Patricia Emily Cañez, Nov. 18, 1962; children: Geralyn P., Bernadette M., Albert A., Catherine M., Elizabeth R., Michael J., Theresa R., Christopher M. AA, Phoenix Jr. Coll., 1971. Ordained deacon Roman Cath. Ch., 1977. Gen. clk. Blue Cross Blue Shield, Phoenix, 1958-61; unit clk. Ariz. Air N.G., Phoenix, 1961, personnel technician, 1962-65, adminstrv. supr., 1965-81, support services supr., 1981-88, equal employment specialist, 1988—. Bd. dirs. Friendly House, Phoenix, 1982—; mem. Alma de la Gente, Phoenix, 1982—, Chiefs Police Community Adv. Group, Phoenix, 1984—, Mayor's Task Force on Juvenile Crime, Phoenix, 1979-81; pres. IMAGE de Phoenix, 1985-87. Served to staff sgt. USAF, 1961-62. Recipient Community Service award Phoenix C. of C., 1982. Mem. Fed. Exec. Assn. (sec., treas. Phoenix chpt. 1985-86, 1st v.p. 1987, pres. 1987-88, Community Svc. award 1986), Ariz. Hispanic Personnel Mgmt. Assn. (bd. dirs. 1983-86, sec. 1985), Ariz. Coun. Hispanic Employment Program Mgrs. (treas. 1980-81, v.p. 1981-82, pres. 1982-84, named Outstanding Mem. of Yr. 1981, 83), Enlisted Assn. N.G. Ariz. (pres. Copperhead chpt. 1987-88). Democrat. Home: 4109 W Monte Vista Rd Phoenix AZ 85009 Office: NG Ariz Hdqrs Support Personnel Mgmt Office 5636 E McDowell Rd Phoenix AZ 85008-3495

BELZBERG, SAMUEL, financial executive; b. Calgary, Alta., Can., June 26, 1928; s. Abraham and Hinda (Fishman) B.; m. Frances Cooper; children: Cheryl Rae, Marc David, Wendy Jay, Lisa. B.Comm., U. Alta., Edmonton, 1948. Chmn., chief exec. officer First City Fin. Corp. Ltd.; chmn. First City Trust Co.; bd. dirs. Enserv Corp., Am. Eagle Petroleums Ltd., First City Industries, Inc., Scovill, Inc., Pioneer Life Assurance Co.; hon. dir. Cantel Inc. Home: 3489 Osler St, Vancouver, BC Canada V6H 2W4 Office: First City Fin Corp Ltd, 777 Hornby St, Vancouver, BC Canada V6Z 1S4

BELZBERG, WILLIAM, financial company executive; b. 1932; married. Vice pres., dir. First City Fin. Corp. Ltd. Can.; pres., chief exec. officer Far West Fin. Corp., Newport Beach, Calif., 1976-80, chmn. bd., 1978—, dir.; chmn. bd., pres., chief exec. officer Far West Sav. and Loan Assn., Newport Beach. Office: Far W Fin Corp 4001 MacArthur Blvd Newport Beach CA 92660 *

BENACH, SHARON ANN, physician assistant; b. New Orleans, Aug. 28, 1944; d. Wilbur G. and Freda Helen (Klaas) Cherry; m. Richard Benach, Dec. 6, 1969 (div. Oct. 1976); children: Craig, Rachel. Degree, St. Louis U., 1978. Physician asst. VA Hosp., St. Louis, 1982-84, Maricopa County Health Services, Phoenix, 1984—. Served with USPHS, 1978-82. Recipient Outstanding Performance award Dept. Health and Human Services. Mem. Mensa. Jewish. Home: PO Box 1272 Mesa AZ 85211

BENALLY, RAYMOND A., civil engineer; b. Ft. Defiance, Ariz., Nov. 5, 1953; s. Robert A. and Grace (Frances) B.; m. Winnona Ann Brown, Aug. 22, 1972; children: Richard, Delbert, Wenona, Bryan. BS in Civil Engring., No. Ariz. U., 1976, MBA, 1978. Registered profl. engr., Ariz., land surveyor; cert. Emergency Med. Technician. Civil engr. Ariz. Pub. Service, Fruitland, N.Mex., 1976, Ariz. Dept. of Transportation, Flagstaff, Ariz., 1976-78; indsl. engr. Peabody Coal Co., St. Louis, 1978-80; civil engr. Peabody Coal Co., Kayenta, Ariz., 1980-84; indsl. engr. Peabody Coal Co., 1984—. Pres., treas. Kayenta Community Health Services, Inc., 1979; pres. Kayenta Sch. Dist. Parent Adv. Com., 1985; mem. Kayenta Planning and Zoning Bd.; offcl. high sch. sports Interscholastic Assn. Mem. Am. Soc. of Civil Engrs., Am. Inst. Indsl. Engrs., Lions Club, Kayenta Summer Recreation Club (coach 1985-88). Home: P O Box 23 Kayenta AZ 86033 Office: Peabody Coal Co P O Box 605 Kayenta AZ 86033

BEN-ASHER, M. DAVID, physician; b. Newark, June 18, 1931; s. Samuel Irving and Dora Ruth (Kagan)B.; m. Bryna S. Zeller, Nov. 22, 1956. BA, Syracuse U., 1952; postgrad., U. Buffalo Sch. Med., 1956. Intern E.J. Meyer Mem. Hosp., Buffalo, N.Y., 1956-57; resident Jersey City Mem. Ctr., 1957-58; asst. chief med. service U.S. Army Hosp., Ft. McPherson, Ga., 1958-60; resident Madigan Gen. Hosp., Tacoma, Wash., 1960-62; chief gen. med. service Walson Army Hosp., Ft. Dix, N.Y., 1962-64; attending staff St. Mary's Hosp., Tucson, Ariz., 1964—; private practice Self Employed, Tucson, 1964—; bd. trustees Pima County Med. Soc., 1964, v.p., 1974, pres., 1976. Mem. Tucson Symphony Bd. dirs., 1971-73, Ariz. State Bd. Med. Examiners,. Fellow Am. Coll. Physicians; mem. Am. Cu Med. Soc., Ariz. Med. Assn., Am. Med. Assn., Am. Coll. Democrat. Home: 5635 E 7th St Tucson AZ 85711 Office: So Ariz Med Specialists 4711 N 1st Ave Tucson AZ 85718

BENAVIDEZ, TOM R., state senator, realtor; b. Magdalena, N.Mex., Jan. 6, 1939; s. John Sanchez and Neph P. (Pino) B.; m. Kathleen Jacobsen, June 22, 1962; children: Tomas Rey, Michael Rey, David Rey. BSBA, U. Albuquerque, 1961; postgrad., U. N.Mex. State senator State of N.Mex., Albuquerque, 1966-70, 84—; owner, operator Tom Benavidez Realty Co.; pres. Salamanca Prodns. Ltd.; justice of the peace, Albuquerque, 1959-60; appraiser for Bernalillo County assessor, Albuquerque, 1961. Dem. candidate for gov. State of N.Mex., 1986; bd. dirs. Model Cities, Albuquerque, S.W. Area Council. Roman Catholic. Office: Tom Benavidez Realty Co 2821 Gun Club Rd SW Albuquerque NM 87105

BENBOW, RICHARD ADDISON, psychological counselor; b. Las Vegas, Dec. 27, 1949; s. Jules Coleman and Bonnie Ray B.; BBA, U. Nev. 1972, M.S. in Counseling, 1974; AAS in Bus. Mgmt. and Real Estate, Clark County Community Coll., 1980; PhD in Clin. Psychology, U. Humanistic Studies, 1986. Cert. tchr., Nev.; cert. clin. mental health counselor, substance abuse counselor, Nev., substance abuse program adminstr., Nev. Owner, mgr. Dick's Hardware, Las Vegas, 1981-82; jud. services officer Mcpl. Ct., City of Las Vegas, 1982—, inmate classification technician Detention and Correctional Services, 1982-83; stress mgmt. cons. Mem. Biofeedback Soc. Am., Assn. Humanistic Psychology, Nat. Assn. Psychotherapists, Am. Personnel and Guidance Assn., Am. Mental Health Counselors Assn., Am. Acad. Crisis Interveners, Am. Correctional Assn., U.S. Tai Kung Fu Assn. (black belt), Nev. Marshals Assn. (bd. dirs.), Nat. Assn. Underwater Instrs., So. Nev. Bluegrass Soc., Jr. C. of C., U.S. Jaycees (presdl. award of honor 1978-79), Delta Sigma Phi. Democrat. Christian Scientist. Home: 7131 Pleasant View Ave Las Vegas NV 89117 Office: Mcpl Ct Jud Svcs City of Las Vegas 400 E Stewart St Las Vegas NV 89101

BENCHENER, GAIL ZIROS, journalist; b. Chgo., Apr. 18, 1950; d. John and Lillian (Wetzelberger) Ziros; m. Paul George Benchener, Aug. 6, 1977; children: David Paul, Matthew John. BA in English, Calif. State U., Fullerton, 1972, MS in Edn., 1975. Life teaching credential, Calif. Tchr. Project Futureprint Calif. Demonstration Reading Program, Ontario, 1973-75; instr. readiing De Anza Coll., Cupertino, Calif., 1975-87; staff writer San Francisco Parent, Burlingame, Calif., 1985—; book reviewer, writer various coll. text pubs. Author: (book and software) Microspeedread, 1984 (Top 20 software award 1984), Supervocabulary Builder, 1986; contbr. articles to travel, edn. and govt. publs. Del. Democratic Nat. Conv., 1972. Apple Edn. Found. grantee, 1984, also various coll. grants. Home and Office: 2015 Broadway Burlingame CA 94010

BENCOE, MICHAEL KARL, systems analyst; b. N.Y.C., Nov. 13, 1950; s. Paul and Evelyn Louise (Davis) B.; m. Julie Patrice Martin, July 10, 1982; children: Brigette Jane, Sara Michelle. BS in Math/Spanish, U. N.Mex., 1971, MS in Computer Sci., 1980. Cert. in data processing. Computer programmer Bur. Bus. Rsch., Albuquerque, 1972-73; computer programmer, systems analyst, systems programmer Pub. Svc. Co. N.Mex., Albuquerque, 1973-83; systems analyst, systems programmer Sandia Nat. Labs., Albuquerque, 1984—; sci. fair judge U. N.Mex., Albuquerque, 1982-87, 89. Mem. Tech Support, Albuquerque System Programmers Users Group, Phi Beta Kappa, Phi Kappa Phi. Home: 3801 Tewa Dr NE Albuquerque NM 87111

BENDA, PETER HANS, aeronautical engineer; b. Wytheville, Va., July 17, 1960; s. Rudolf Anton Josef and Gertrude (Beer) B. BS, BA, Wash. and Lee U., 1981; MSAA, U. Wash., 1983. Aero. engr. E-Systems, Inc., Fairfax, Va., 1983-85; sr. engr. and program mgr. McDonnell Douglas Techs., Inc., San Diego, 1985—. Mem. AIAA, Am. Helicopter Soc., Phi Beta Kappa. Lodge: Order of Monocle (chmn. 1979-86). Home: PO Box 261052 San Diego CA 92126 Office: McDonnell Douglas Techs Inc 16761 Via Del Campo Ct San Diego CA 92127

BENDER, BETTY WION, librarian; b. Mt. Ayer, Iowa, Feb. 26, 1925; d. John F. and Sadie A. (Guess) Wion; m. Robert F. Bender, Aug. 24, 1946. B.S., N.Tex. State U., Denton, 1946; M.A., U. Denver, 1957. Asst. cataloger N. Tex. State U. Library, 1946-49; from cataloger to head acquisitions So. Meth. U., Dallas, 1949-56; reference asst. Ind. State Library, Indpls., 1951-52; librarian Ark. State Coll., 1958-59, Eastern Wash. Hist. Soc., Spokane, 1960-67; reference librarian, then head circulation dept. Spokane (Wash.) Public Library, 1968-73, library dir., 1973-88; vis. instr. U. Denver, summers 1957-60, 63, fall 1959; instr. Whitworth Coll., Spokane, 1962-64; mem. Gov. Wash. Regional Conf. Libraries, 1968, Wash. Statewide Library Devel. Council, 1970-71. Bd. dirs. N.W. Regional Found., 1973-75, Inland Empire Goodwill Industries, 1975-77, Wash. State Library Commn., 1979-87, Future Spokane, 1983—, vice chmn., 1986-87, pres., 1987-88. Recipient YWCA Outstanding Achievement award in Govt., 1985. Mem. ALA (mem. library adminstrn. and mgmt. assn. com. on orgn. 1982-83, chmn. nominating com. 1983-85, v.p./pres.-elect. 1985-86, pres. 1986-87), Pacific N.W. Library Assn. (chmn. circulation div. 1972-75, conv. chmn. 1977), Wash. Library Assn. (v.p./pres.-elect 1975-77, pres. 1977-78), AAUW (pres. Spokane br. 1969-71, rec. sec. Wash. br. 1971-73, fellowship named in honor 1972), Spokane and Inland Empire Librarians (dir. 1967-68), Am. Soc. Pub. Adminstrn. Republican. Lutheran. Club: Zonta (pres. Spokane chpt. 1976-77, dist. conf. treas. 1972). Home: 119 N 6th St Cheney WA 99004 Office: Spokane Pub Libr Comstock Bldg Libr W 906 Main Ave Spokane WA 99201

BENDER, BYRON WILBUR, linguistics educator; b. Roaring Spring, Pa., Aug. 14, 1929; s. Ezra Clay and Gertrude Magdalene (Kauffman) B.; m. Lois Marie Graber, Aug. 25, 1950; children: Susan Alice, Sarah Marie, Catherine Anne, Judith Lee, John Richard. BA, Goshen Coll., 1949; MA, Ind. U., 1950, PhD, 1963. Edn. specialist Trust Terr. of Pacific Islands, Majuro, Marshall Island, 1953-59, Saipan, Marianas Island, 1962-64; asst. prof. Goshen (Ind.) Coll., 1960-62; assoc. prof. linguistics U. Hawaii at Manoa, Honolulu, 1964-69, prof., chmn. dept., 1969—; bd. dirs. U. Hawaii Profl. Assembly, Honolulu, 1978-88, pres., 1982-88. Author: Spoken Marshallese, 1969, Linguistic Factors in Maori Education, 1971, (with others) Marshallese-English Dictionary, 1976; editor: Oceanic Linguistics Spl. Publs., 1965—, (with others) Studies in Micronesian Linguistics, 1984; mng. editor: Oceanic Linguistics, 1965-78. Bd. dirs. U. Hawaii State Pub. Employees Health Fund, 1987-91. Recipient Merit awards U. Hawaii 1971, 76, 86. Mem. NEA (standing com. higher edn. 1985-89), Linguistic Soc. Am. (bd. dir. Linguistic Inst. summer 1977, program com. 1987-89), The Polynesian Soc., U. Hawaii Profl. Assembly (pres. 1982-88). Mem. Soc. of Friends. Home: 7268 Kauhako St Honolulu HI 96825 Office: U Hawaii Dept Linguistics 1890 East-West Rd Honolulu HI 96822

BENDER, DORIS RAE, psychiatric nurse; b. Cedar Rapids, Iowa, Mar. 4, 1950; d. Raymond William and Jutta Waltraud (Otte) B.; m. Michael Owen Hodges, Mar. 30, 1974 (div. 1978); m. Matthew Karl Bender. BS in Nursing, U. Iowa, 1972; MA in Health Service Mgmt. and Computer Resource Mgmt., Webster U., Denver, 1987. Head nurse Prince George's Gen. Hosp., Cheverly, Md., 1978-79, McAuley Neuropsychiat. Inst., St. Mary's Hosp., San Francisco, 1979-81, Bethesda PsycHealth Hosp., Denver, 1985—; clin. mgr. Rocky Mountain Hosp., Denver, 1981-85. Capt. Nurse Corps, U.S. Army, 1970-78; mem. USAR. Mem. Nat. League Nurses, Colo. League Nurses. Presbyterian. Office: Bethesda PsycHealth Hosp 4400 E Iliff St Denver CO 80222

BENDURE, ALVA EARL, III, air force officer; b. N. Kansas City, Mo., Dec. 7, 1948; s. Alva Elmer Jr. and Rosaline Marie (Baker) B.; m. Katherine Mary Murphy, June 12, 1971; children: Matthew Stephen, Christopher Andrew. BS, USAF Acad., 1971; M Aero. Sci., Embry-Riddle Aero. U., 1987. Commd. 2d lt. USAF, 1971, advanced through grades to maj., 1984; flight commdr., instr. pilot USAF, Laughlin AFB, Tex., 1977-82; exec. officer, resource adviser NATO ops. support cell USAF, Kalka Air Sta., Fed. Republic Germany, 1982-85; chief of flight mgmt. USAF, Williams AFB, Ariz., 1986-87; chief academics, Embry-Riddle Aero. U. USAF, Williams AFB, 1987-88, spl. asst. dep. comdr. ops., 1988—. Chmn. supervisory com., Western Horizons Fed. Credit Union, Mesa, Ariz., 1987—. Mem. Order Daedalians (treas. 1989), Ariz. Macintosh Users Group. Republican. Lutheran. Office: USAF 82 Flying Tng Wing Williams AFB AZ 85240

BENEŠ, NORMAN STANLEY, meteorologist; b. Detroit, July 1, 1921; s. Stanley and Cecelia (Sereneck) B.; m. Elinor Simson, May 5, 1945 (div. Feb. 1972); children: Gregory, Heather, Michelle, Francine; m. Celia Sereneck, Mar. 3, 1972. BS, U. Wash., 1949; postgrad., U. Calif., Davis, 1963, U. Mich., 1966. Chief meteorologist Hawthorne Sch. of Aero., Moultrie, Ga., 1951-55; meteorologist U.S. Weather Bur., Phoenix, 1955-57, 59-60; meteorologist in charge NSF, Hallett, Antarctica, 1958; sta. sci. leader NSF, Byrd, Antarctica, 1960-61; meteorologist Nat. Weather Service, Sacramento, Calif., 1962-84; mem. exec. com. Benes Peak Range, Antarctica. Contbr. articles to profl. jours. Pres. local chpt. PTA, 1965. With USN, 1943-46, PTO. Mem. AAAS, Am. Meteorol. Soc., Am. Geophys. Union, Nat. Weather Assn., Masons. Home: 7612 Isles Ct Fair Oaks CA 95628 Office: PO Box 2184 Fair Oaks CA 95628

BENESCH, LISA ANN, construction manager; b. Walla Walla, Wash., Sept. 27, 1960; d. James Roger and Earlene Annette (Walker) Walston; m. Dudley Howard Benesch, June 9, 1984. BCE, U. Alaska, 1987. Legal asst. Robertson, Monagle & Eastaugh, Anchorage, 1979-82; engring. asst. Swalling Constrn. Co., Anchorage, 1985-86; project mgr. Lease Kissee Constrn. Co., Anchorage, 1987—. Republican. Methodist. Office: Lease Kissee Constrn Co 7801 E 36th Ave Anchorage AK 99504

BENET, LESLIE ZACHARY, pharmacokineticist; b. Cin., May 17, 1937; s. Jonas John and Esther Racie (Hirschfeld) B.; m. Carol Ann Levin, Sept. 8, 1960; children: Reed Michael, Gillian Vivia. AB in English, U. Mich., 1959, BS in Pharmacy, 1960, MS in Pharm. Chemistry, 1962; PhD in Pharm. Chemistry, U. Calif., San Francisco, 1965; PharmD (hon.), Uppsala U., Sweden, 1987. Asst. prof. pharmacy Wash. State U., Pullman, 1965-69; asst. prof. pharmacy and pharm. chemistry U. Calif., San Francisco, 1969-71, assoc. prof., 1971-76, prof., 1976—, vice chmn. dept. pharmacy, 1973-78, chmn. dept. pharmacy, 1978—, dir. drug studies unit, 1977—, dir. drug kinetics and dynamics ctr., 1979—; cons. to pharm. cos.; mem. pharmacology study sect. NIH, Washington, 1977-81, chmn. 1979-81, mem. pharmacol. scis. rev. com. 1984-88, chmn. 1986-88. Editor: Jour. Pharmacokinetics and Biopharmaceutics, 1976—; mem. editorial bd. Pharmacology, 1979—, Pharmacy Internat., 1979-82, Pharmaceutical Research, 1983—, ISI Atlas of Sci.: Pharmacology, 1988—; editor: The Effect of Disease States on Drug Pharmacokinetics, 1976, Pharmacokinetic Basis for Drug Treatment, 1984, Pharmacokinetics: A Modern View, 1984; contbr. articles to profl. jours. Appt. to Forum on Drug Devel. and Regulation, 1988. Fellow Acad. Pharm. Scis. (pres. 1985-86, chmn. basic pharmaceutics sect. 1976-77, mem.-at-large exec. com. 1979-83, Research Achievement award 1982), AAAS (mem.-at-large exec. com. pharm. scis. sect. 1978-81), Am. Assn. Pharm. Scientists (pres. 1986, treas. 1987, bd. dirs. 1988—); mem. Am. Found. for Pharm. Edn. (bd. dirs. 1987—), Internat. Soc. Immunopharmacology, Am. Coll. Clin. Pharmacology (Disting. Svc. award 1988), ISSX, Am. Pharm. Assn., Am. Soc. Clin. Pharmacology and Therapeutics, Am. Soc. for Pharmacology and Exptl. Therapeutics, AAUP, Inst. Medicine of Nat. Acad. Scis. (elected to Inst. of Med. 1987, mem. forum on drug devel. and regulation 1988), Internat. Pharm. Fedn. (bd. pharm. scis. 1988—), Drug Info. Assn., Sigma Xi, Rho Chi. Home: 53 Beach Rd Belvedere CA 94920 Office: U Calif San Francisco Dept Pharmacy San Francisco CA 94143

BENGFORT, SCOTT DEGARD, business development company executive; b. Ames, Iowa, Mar. 1, 1949; s. Jack Angelo and Marilyn Adele (Houser) Degard. BS, U. Iowa, 1971. Mgr. trainee Wilscam Enterprises, Denver, 1973-75; restaurant mgr. Emerson St. East, Denver, 1975-77, Mexican Foods Am., Denver, Mpls., Phoenix, 1977-79; stockbroker OTC Net, Inc., Denver, 1979-81, E.J. Pittock, Denver, 1981-84, Hamilton, Bohner & Van Vleck, Denver, 1984-85, J.W. Gant, Denver, 1985-87; pres. Equity Assoc., Inc., Aurora, Colo., 1987--; mem. Rockies Venture Group. Mem. Internat. Athletic Club (Denver). Republican. Methodist.

BENGTSON, VERN LEROY, sociologist, gerontologist, educator; b. Lindsborg, Kans., May 2, 1941; A.B., North Park Coll., 1963; M.A., U. Chgo., 1965, Ph.D., 1967. Asst. prof. sociology U. So. Calif., Los Angeles, 1967-70, assoc. prof., 1970-77, prof. sociology, 1977—, dir. gerontology research inst., 1982—; vis. assoc. in sociology Calif. Inst. Tech., 1975-76; vis. prof. sociology U. Stockholm (Sweden), 1979; vis. prof. Max Planck Inst., Berlin, 1988-89. Fellow Am. Psychol. Assn. (mem. coun. div. 20 adult devel. and aging, 1975-78), Gerontol. Assn. Am. (pres.-elect 1989—); mem. Nat. Coun. Family Rels., Soc. Study Social Problems, Internat. Assn. Gerontology . Assoc. editor Sociology of Education; series editor Brooks-Cole Series in Social Gerontology; mem. exec. bd. Sociology and Social Research; mem. editorial bd. Journal of Marriage and the Family, Journal of Gerontology, Sage Family Studies Abstracts, Research on Aging, NCFR Monographs; contbr. over 100 articles to profl. jours. and 6 books. Office: U So Calif Andrus Gerontology Ctr Los Angeles CA 90089

BENIGER, JAMES RALPH, university professor, writer; b. Sheboygan, Wis., Dec. 16, 1946; s. Ralph Joseph and Charlotte Emma (Nitsch) B.; m. Kay Diane Ferdinandsen, Dec. 7, 1984. BA magna cum laude, Harvard U., 1969; MA in Sociology, U. Calif., Berkeley, 1973, MS in Statistics, 1974, PhD in Sociology, 1978. Lectr. U. Calif., Berkeley, 1976-77; instr. Princeton U., N.J., 1977-79; asst. prof. Princeton U., 1979-85; assoc. prof. Annenberg Sch. of Communications U. So. Calif., L.A., 1985—; editorial bd. Pub. Opinion Quarterly, Ann Arbor, Mich., 1982-87; bd. overseers Gen. Social Survey, U. Chgo., 1984-87; assoc. editor Communication Rsch., L.A., 1988—. Author: Trafficking in Drug Users, 1983, The Control Revolution, 1986 (Assn. of Am. Pubs. award 1987). Named Samuel Lazero Mem. Lectr. Inst. for Sci. Info., Phila., 1988, Disting. Guest Contbr. Keio Univ., Tokyo, 1988. Mem. Am. Assn. Pub. Opinion (sec., treas. 1988-90), Am. Sociological Assn. (program chmn. 1987-88), Internat. Communication Assn., Am. Statistical Assn., AAAS. Home: 1204 Elm Ave Manhattan Beach CA 90266 Office: Sch Communications Univ So Calif Los Angeles CA 90089-0281

BENING, JEAN DIANNE, trauma administrator, nurse; b. Marshall, MInn., Nov. 20, 1952; d. Glen Alfred and Marguerite Edith (Finley) Borchard; m. James Bruce Bening, Aug. 11, 1984. Diploma, Good Samaritan Sch. Nursing, 1974. RN, Wash.; cert. neonatal nurse Nurses Assn. Am. Coll. Ob-Gyn.; advanced cardiac life support provider Am. Heart Assn. Labor and delivery nurse Scrips Meml. Hosp., LaJolla, Calif., 1974-78; intensive care nursery nurse Sacred Heart Med. Ctr., Spokane, Wash., 1978-85; neonatal flight nurse Sacred Heart Med. Ctr., Spokane, 1981-85, chief flight nurse, 1983-85, dir. flight ops., 1985—. Republican. Office: Heartflite Sacred Heart Med Ctr W 101 8th Ave TAF-C9 Spokane WA 99220

BENIRSCHKE, STEPHEN KURT, orthopaedic surgeon; b. Boston, Aug. 16, 1953; s. Kurt and Marion Elizabeth (Waldhausen) B.; m. Elizabeth Williamson Abu-Haydar, Aug. 25, 1984; 1 child, Leila Maria. BA in Biology, U. Calif., San Diego, 1975; MD, Case Western Res. U., 1979. Diplomate Am. Bd. Orthopaedic Surgery. Intern surgery Case Western Res. U., Cleve., 1979-81, resident in orthopaedics, 1984; A.O. fellow Chur, Switzerland, 1984; acting instr. U. Wash., Seattle, 1985-86, asst. prof. dept. orthopaedics, 1987—; assoc. chief orthopaedics Harborview Med. Ctr., U. Wash., Seattle, 1987—. Rsch. grantee A.O. Found., 1988. Democrat. Roman Catholic. Office: Harborview Med Ctr 325 9th Ave Seattle WA 98104

BENITEZ, JUAN ANTONIO, electronics company executive; b. Matanzas, Cuba, Apr. 9, 1949; came to U.S., 1965; s. Juan Francisco and Josefa (Guerra) B.; m. Darlene Marie Hoover, June 10, 1972; 1 child, Juan A. II. BS in Mech. Engring., U. Mo., Rolla, 1972. Tool process engr. assembly div. Gen. Motors, St. Louis, 1972-75; engr. mfg. Hitchner, St. Louis, 1975; sr. designer facilities/machines Ethicon-Johnson and Johnson, San Angelo, Tex., 1976-78; mgr. facility ops. Mostek, Dallas, 1978-80; mgr. facilities Micron Tech. Inc., Boise, Idaho, 1980-82, v.p. mfg., 1982-86, pres., chief operating officer, 1986-88. Bd. dirs. Boys Club Am., San Angelo, 1980. Mem. Boise C. of C. (bd. dirs. 1986-88). Episcopalian. Club: Arid (Boise). Office: Micron Tech Inc 2805 E Columbia Rd Boise ID 83706

BENITZ, MAX E., state legislator; b. Wathena, Kans., Oct. 9, 1916; s. Alto Richard and Nellie Beatrice (Willard) B.; m. Marie Benitz, June 9, 1940; children: Norma June, Eileen, Alvin, Max Jr., Ronnie. Grad. high school, Wathena. Mem. Wash. State Senate from 8th Dist.; agriculturist, Prosser, Wash.; past pres. Wash. State Farm Bur.; bd. dirs. Am. Farm Bur.; mem. Benton-Franklin County Fair Bd., Prosser Sch. Bd. Named Farmer of Yr. Future Farmers of Am. Republican. Lutheran. Avocation: growing wine grapes. Home: Rt 2 Box 2521 Prosser WA 99350 Office: Wash State Senate 103 Institutions Bldg Olympia WA 98504

BENJAMIN, ALICE IRENE, musician; b. Orange, N.J., Dec. 18, 1940; d. Harold Drake and Harriet (Whitmore) Tannar; m. William Henry Benjamin, Nov. 7, 1977; 1 child, David Arthur. BA, Montclair State Coll., 1962; MS, Juilliard Sch. Music, 1968. Cert. tchr., N.J. Vocal/instrumental music tchr. N.J. Pub. Schs., 1962-65; bassoonist N.J. Symphony, Newark, 1965-70, Lake George (N.Y.) Opera, 1965-70, Chautauqua (N.Y.) Symphony-Opera, 1971-74, Met. Opera Orch., N.Y.C., 1971-74; instr., bassoonist U. Victoria, B.C., Can., 1979-80; instr. San Jose (Calif.) State U., 1984; prin. bassoon San Jose Symphony, 1975—. Performances include solos, flute/bassoon duo recitals, recitals with N.Y. Bassoon Quartet and recs. of contemporary chamber music for Can. Broadcasting Corp. Vol. music tchr. Charquin-Markham Sch., Hayward, Calif., 1987-88; fund raiser San Jose Symphony, 1986-88. Office: San Jose Symphony 476 Park Ave San Jose CA 95110

BENJAMIN, BEVERLY PASCHKE, educator; b. Blue Earth, Minn., Nov. 6, 1928; d. Frank Alwin Paschke and Ola Beatrice (Lauren) Meierbachtol; m. Karl S. Benjamin, Jan. 29, 1949; children: Beth Marie, Kris Ellen, Bruce Lincoln. BA, U. Redlands, 1950; MA, Claremont Grad. Sch., 1968; PhD, Claremont U., 1980. Tchr. Bloomington (Calif.) Sch. Dist., 1950-52, Chino (Calif.) Unified Sch. Dist., 1952-53; owner, operator Playschool of Claremont, Calif., 1956-63; tchr., dir. Pomona (Calif.) Community Presch., 1967; tchr. Vista De Valle Sch. Claremont Unified Dist., 1967-73; instr., coordinator Chaffey Coll., Alta Loma, Calif., 1973—; owner, pres. Am. Nanny Plan Inc., Montclair, Calif., 1983—, Am. Nanny Coll., Claremont, 1985—, NannyPlan Agy., Montclair, 1986—; pres. Am. Family Coll. Seminars, 1987—; founder Calif. Community Coll. Early Childhood Educators, 1975—. Instr. Claremont chpt. ARC; v.p. Claremont Civic Assn., 1959-60. Mem. Am. Coun. of Nanny Schs. (founder, v.p. 1988—), Nat. Assn. Edn. Young Children-So. Calif. Assn. Edn. Young Children, Calif. Community Coll. Early Childhood Educators-Calif. Assn. Edn. Young Children, Claremont C. of C., Zonta Club, Pi Lambda Theta (chair interdisciplinary conf. on families). Home: 675 W 8th St Claremont CA 91711 Office: Am Nanny Plan Inc 4650 Arrow Hsy G-10 Montclair CA 91763

BENJAMIN, RICHARD VANCE, small business owner; b. Astoria, Oreg., Sept. 24, 1958; s. Richard Ludlow and Shirley May (McFarlane) B.; m.

Sharilyn Kay Newby. Grad. high sch., Portland, Oreg. Owner McCoy, Door & HardwoodCo., Portland. Mem. Oreg. Remodelers. With USN, 1976-79. Mem. U.S. C. of C., Small Bus. Assn., Home Builders Assn. Republic. Office: McCoy Door & Hardwood Co 323 NW 12th Portland OR 97209

BENJAMIN, ROBBA LEE, publisher; b. Glendale, Calif., Dec. 1, 1947; d. Gilbert Searle Benjamin and Vivian (Durr) Carpenter; m. Keshavan Nair. AB, Occidental Coll., 1969; MBA, Stanford U., 1978. Treas. Kirk Knight & Co., Inc., Menlo Park, Calif., 1970-74; transaction mgr. Itel Corp., San Francisco, 1975-76, 79-80; mgr. sales adminstrn. Shaklee Corp., San Francisco, 1978; founder, exec. v.p. Benjamin/Nair, Inc., San Francisco, 1981-84; exec. v.p., chief adminstrv. officer MeraBank, Phoenix, from 1984; pres. TransWestern Pub., San Diego. Bd. dirs., chmn. Jr. Achievement, Ariz., 1985-89; bd. dirs. Ariz. Clean and Beautiful, 1986-87; mem. adv. bd. Ariz. Theatre Co., 1986-88; mem. Phoenix Symphony Steering Com., 1987, Mayor's Commn. on Excellence in Edn., 1987-88. Mem. Am. Mgmt. Assn., Nat. Assn. Bank Women, Council Fin. Competition, (adv. bd.), Charter 100, Econ. Club Phoenix (bd. dirs. 1985-87). Office: TransWestern Pub 8328 Clairemont Mesa Blvd San Diego CA 92111

BENJAMIN, ROBERT CHARLES, service executive; b. Niles, Mich., Feb. 5, 1945; s. Charles Orlando and Dorothy Louise (Teeter) B.; m. Valerie Candace Sparks, Aug. 27, 1966; children: Brock Morgan, Brie Darby. BBA, Tulane U., 1967; MBA, Mich. State U., 1972; postgrad. cert., George Washington U., 1973. Asst. v.p. Lancaster (Pa.) Gen. Hosp., 1973-77; adminstr. Portage View Hosp., Hancock, Mich., 1977-80, Clinica Santa Maria, Santiago, Chile, 1980-82; pres. Casa Grande (Ariz.) Regional Med. Ctr., 1982-87; adminstr. Southeast Ariz. Med. Ctr., Douglas, 1987—. Co-author: Hosp. Adminstrs. Desk Reference, 1983. Served to capt. U.S. Army, 1968-71, Vietnam. Mem. Am. Coll. Health Execs., Ariz. Hosp. Assn. (bd. dirs. 1988—). Home: RR Box 260-N Douglas AZ 85607 Office: SE Ariz Med Ctr RR Box 30 Douglas AZ 85607

BENJAMIN, STEVEN JAMES, computer company executive; b. Kansas City, Mo., Sept. 25, 1953; s. James William Benjamin and Elizabeth Jocelyn (Horn) Sutoris; m. Deborah Ann Sprague, July 31, 1976; children: Lisa Michelle, Lindsay Leigh, Steven Reed. BA in Bus. Adminstrn., U. Kans., 1976. Assoc. systems analyst Honeywell Info. Systems, Omaha, 1977-78, systems analyst, 1978-79; sr. systems analyst Honeywell Info. Systems, Denver, 1979-81, tech. advisor, 1981-82, account mgr., 1982-85; br. sales mgr. Honeywell Info. Systems, Louisville, 1985-87; dist. mgr. Honeywell Bull Info. Systems, Phoenix, 1987-88; dist. dir. Bull Worldwide Info. System, Denver, 1988—. Office: Honeywell Bull 304 Inverness Way S Ste 400 Englewood CO 80112

BENNER, DOROTHY SPURLOCK, teacher; b. Greeley, Colo., Dec. 17, 1938; d. Lloyd Elsworth and Helen Rosalee (Pierce) Spurlock; m. Jerry Lee Benner, June 7, 1959; children: Shey Lee, Craig Lloyd. BA, Colo. State Coll., 1962, MA, 1968; EdS, U. No. Colo., 1978. Cert. tchr. elem. and bus. edn., spl. edn. and sch. psychology. Telephone operator Mountain Bell, Greeley, Colo., 1957; sec. Conn. Mut. Life, Greeley, Colo., 1960-61; substitute tchr. Sch. Dist. 6 and Outlying Dists., Greeley, Colo., 1962-67; tchr. Sch. Dist. 6, Greeley, Colo., 1968—; cons. Right to Read, Weld County, Colo., 1980—. Mem. Greeley Tchrs. Assn. (mem. negotiating team 1981-89, sec. 1985—), Nat. Edn. Assn. (life), Colo. Edn. Assn., Kappa Delta Pi, Delta Kappa Gamma (pres. 1980-81). Republican. Methodist. Home: 1839 26th St Greeley CO 80631

BENNETT, ALAN, magazine publishing executive. Student, Columbia U. Founder American Photographer, Savvy mags.; with California mag., 1983—, now pres. Office: Calif Mag 11601 Wilshire Blvd #1800 Los Angeles CA 90025 *

BENNETT, BRADFORD CARL, research scientist; b. Dayton, Ohio, May 27, 1953; s. Carl Vernon and Norma June (Linkinhoker) B. BSME, U. Wis., 1975; MSME, Stanford U., 1976, PhD in ME, 1982. Staff engr. Acurex Corp., Mt. View, Calif., 1988—. Mem. AIAA, Am. Soc. Engring. Edn., ASME, Trager Inst. Club: Cloud Hands West. Home: 270 Valley St San Francisco CA 94131 Office: MCAT Inst 3933 Bluegum Dr San Jose CA 95127

BENNETT, BRUCE DAVID, educational administrator; b. Putnam, Conn., Aug. 3, 1948; s. Wilfred H. and Rita A. (Orlowski) B.; m. Karson Joy Brazee, May 22, 1976. BS, E. Conn. State Coll., 1971; MA, U. Conn., 1980; postgrad, U. Washington, 1989. Asst. dir. community edn. Ea. Conn. State Coll., Willimantic, 1968-71; tchr. Thompson (Conn.) Pub. Sch. System, 1971-72; asst. dir. community edn. Mohegan Community Coll., Norwich, Conn., 1972-74; dir. student activities/alumni affairs Mohegan Community Coll., Norwich, 1975-81, adj. faculty, 1974-81, dir. fin. aid, 1981-83; asst. dir. student service/ fin. aid officer Seattle Opportunities Indsl. Ctr., 1983-86; coord. student svcs. Continuing Edn. Div. U. Wash., Seattle, 1986—; edn. cons. Bennett and Assocs., Seattle, 1986—. Bd. dirs. King County Council Vocat. Edn., Seattle, 1986—; mem. Burns Soc. Seattle. Mem. Am. Coll. Personnel Assn., Am. Assn. Counseling and Devel., Nat. Assn. Campus Activites (presentor/coordinator numerous conf.), Nat. Assn. Student Personnel Adminstrs., Nat. U. Continuing Edn. Assn. (conf. planner and presentor 1987-89), Nat. Assn. Student Fin. Aid Adminstrs. Home: 6511 23rd Ave NE Seattle WA 98115 Office: U Wash 5001 25th Ave NE GH-21 Seattle WA 98195

BENNETT, CARL MCGHIE, engineering company executive, consultant, national guard officer; b. Salt Lake City, Sept. 11, 1933; s. M. Woodruff and Sybil L. (McGhie) B.; m. Ardel Krantz, Aug. 10, 1954; children: Carlene, Matt, Brent, Dale, Hugh, Caren, Teri. BS, U. Utah, 1956; postgrad., U.S. Army Engr. Sch., 1964; M, Command and Gen. Staff Coll., 1974; postgrad., Indsl. Coll. Armed Forces, 1976. Commd. 2d. lt. ROTC U.S. Army, 1953; treas. and office mgr. Hercules Inc. and Data Source Corp., Salt Lake City and Los Angeles, 1963-70; controller Boise Cascade, Los Angeles, 1970-72; corp. controller Griffin Devel. Co., Los Angeles, 1972-75; controller Dart Industries, Dart Resorts, Los Angeles, 1975-78; chief fin. officer Ford, Bacon & Davis, Salt Lake City, 1978-87; pres. B&A Cons., 1987—; cons. Served to lt. col. U.S. Army Res., 1953-79, col. Utah N.G., 1985—. Recipient Meritorious Service medal Pres. of the U.S., 1979. Mem. Controllers Council, Nat. Assn. Accts. (v.p., bd. dirs. 1979-85). Republican. Office: Ford Bacon Davis 375 Chipeta Way Salt Lake City UT 84108

BENNETT, CHARLES ALAN, advertising agency executive; b. Spokane, Wash., Feb. 27, 1947; s. Charles Ehrenfeld and Ruth (Kealey) B.; m. Jo Ann Spaur, Apr. 13, 1987. BFA, Art Ctr. Coll. Design, Pasadena, 1972. Ptnr. Com. on Film, Hollywood, Calif., 1972-75; creative dir. The Committee, Los Angeles, 1975-78; pres. Committee Communications, Inc., Los Angeles, 1978—; dir. Under the Oaks Brewery, Ojai, Calif. Co-author: Make Your Own Greeting Card Book, 1977. Mem. Ventura (Calif.) Govt. Affairs Com., 1988—. 1st lt. U.S. Army, 1965-68. Decorated Purple Heart. Mem. So. Calif. Assn. Water Agys., Ventura C. of C. (bus. devel. com.), Soc. of Illustrators, Am. Soc. Advt. and Promotion, Advt. Club of Ventura Co., Advt. Club of Los Angeles, PICA of Ventura Co., Calif. Rare Fruit Growers, Studebaker Drivers, Ventura County Taxpayers Assn. (mem. com. on water). Republican. Roman Catholic. Home: 415 E Villanova Rd Ojai CA 93023 Office: Committee Communications 4741 Laurel Canyon Blvd Studio City CA 91607

BENNETT, CHARLES LEON, vocational and graphic arts educator; b. Salem, Oreg., Feb. 5, 1951; s. Theodore John and Cora Larena (Rowland) B.; m. Cynthia Alice Hostman, June 12, 1976 (div.); m. Lynn Marie Toland, Aug. 12, 1977 (div.); children: Mizzy Marie, Charles David; m. Christina M. Crawford, Dec. 19, 1987. AS in Vocat. Tchr. Edn., Clackamas Community Coll., 1977; AS in Gen. Studies, Linn Benton Community Coll., 1979; student SUNY, 1983—. Tchr. printing Tongue Point Job Corps, Astoria, Oreg., 1979-80; tchr., dept. chmn. Portland (Oreg.) pub. schs., 1980—; owner, mgr. printing and pub. co., Portland, 1981—. With AUS, 1970-72. Mem. Oreg. Vocat. Trade-Tech. Assn. (dept. chmn., pres. graphic arts div., Indsl. Educator of Year 1981-82), Oreg. Vocat. Assn. (Vocat. Tchr. of Yr. 1982-83), Graphic Arts Tech. Found., In-Plant Printing Mgmt. Assn., Internat. Graphic Arts Edn. Assn. (v.p. N.W. region VI), Oreg. Assn. Manpower Spl. Needs Personnel, Oreg. Indsl. Arts Assn., Nat. Rifle Assn., Internat. Platform Assn. Nat. Assn. Quick Printers, Am. Vocat. Assn., Portland Club Lithographers and Printing House Craftsmen. Republican. Home: 1838 SE Reedway Portland OR 97202 Office: 5040 SE Milwaukie Ave Portland OR 97202

BENNETT, CHARLES TURNER, social welfare administrator; b. Egypt, Ark., June 17, 1932; s. Charley Clower and Lois LaJoy (Turner) B.; m. Ella Jane Fye, July 6, 1962; children: Rebeca Joy, Lisa Anne. Grad., Moody Bible Inst., Chgo., 1953; student, UCLA, 1970; MA, Fuller Theol. Seminary, Pasadena, Calif., 1972, Claremont (Calif.) Grad. Sch., 1983. Bush pilot, missionary Mission Aviation Fellowship, Mexico, 1955-68; dir. research Mission Aviation Fellowship, Fullerton, Calif., 1968-72; pres., chief exec. officer Mission Aviation Fellowship, Redlands, Calif., 1973-85; exec. dir. Presby. Ctr. for Mission Studies, Fullerton, 1972-73; cons. various orgns., Redlands, 1985; exec. v.p. Food for the Hungry Internat., Geneva, Switzerland, 1985-88, Scottsdale, Ariz., 1988—; bd. dirs. Air Serv Internat., Redlands, Evangelical Fgn. Missions Assn., Washington, 1976-82; founder Redlands Aviation Corp., 1980; adv. bd. Presby. Ctr. for Mission Studies, 1973—. Author: Tinder in Tabasco, 1968, Pantano Ardiente, 1989, (with others) From Nairobi to Berkeley, 1967, God, Man and Church Growth, 1973. Chmn. world service Redlands Rotary Club., 1982-85. Named Alumnus of Yr. Fuller Theol. Seminary, 1985. Democrat. Home: 8414 E San Bernardo Scottsdale AZ 85258 Office: Food for Hungry Internat 7807 E Greenway Rd Scottsdale AZ 85260

BENNETT, CHARLES WILLIAM, sales executive; b. Atwater, Calif., Mar. 12, 1962; s. Charles William and Marion June (Hulsman) B.; 1 child, Austin Charles. Student, Ariz. State U., 1984. Mgr. trainee Walgreen's Drug Store, Phoenix, 1978-84; sales rep. Pameco-Aire, Phoenix, 1984—. Republican. Home: 8875 N 48th Dr Glendale AZ 85302 Office: Pameco-Aire 3156 W Lewis Ave Phoenix AZ 85009

BENNETT, CONNIE SUE, food product executive; b. Richland Center, Wis., Oct. 4, 1955; d. Robert Eugene And Lillian Theresa (Crusan) Cottrill; m. James A. Bennett III,Oct. 22, 1977 (div. 1989). Grad. high sch., Ithaca, Wis. Owner, chef A Taste Of Heaven Restaurant, Anchorage, 1978-80, Saucy Sisters Catering, Anchorage, 1980-86; pres. Good Taste Inc., Anchorage, 1986—. Mem. adv. bd. Hugh O'Brian Found., 1987-89. Named Small Bus. Person of Yr. State of Alaska, 1987, U.S. Western Region, 1987. Mem. Alaska St. C. of C., Anchorage C. of C., Internat. Assn. Cooking Profl., Am. Inst. Wine and Food, James Beard Found., Inflight Food Svc. Assn. Office: Good Taste Inc 2000 W Internat Airport #C Anchorage AK 99502

BENNETT, DARYL JOHN, retired oil company hazardous materials specialist; b. Cedar Rapids, Iowa; s. Orin Russell and Marlyse Katherine (Everhart) B.; widowed; 1 child, Kathleen Marie. BS in Agr., Calif. State Poly. Coll., 1948. With Atlantic Richfield Co., Carson, Calif., 1951-85; mem. quality control staff, then lab. computer info. service specialist, Atlantic Richfield Co., Carson. Vol., Doctors Hosp. Lakewood Aux., 1985, Meml. Med. Ctr. Aux., Long Beach, Calif., 1988. Served with U.S. Army, 1943-45, PTO. Democrat. Baptist. Home: 5847 Eckleson St Lakewood CA 90713

BENNETT, ELDEAN, mass communication educator, broadcaster; b. Provo, Utah, Feb. 11, 1928; s. C. Leslie and Leatha (Wright) B.; m. Maralin Payne, Mar. 21, 1947; children: Terri Anne, Randall Dean, Stephen Dean, Julia Anne, Barbara Anne, Allan Dean. BA, Brigham Young U., 1951; MA, Mich. State U., 1969, PhD, 1970. Broadcaster Sta. KSL-Radio-TV, Salt Lake City, 1950-65; dir. info. systems Sta. WEEI, Boston, 1965-66; instr. journalism, telecommunications , grad. asst. Mich. State U., East Lansing, 1966-70; asst. prof. Ariz. State U., Tempe, 1970-74, assoc. prof., 1974-79, prof., dir. sch. journalism and telecommunications, 1979-87; prof. mass communication U. Jos., Nigeria, 1977-78; Fulbright lectr. U. Jos NTV Stas., Nigeria; TV cons. Republican Party of Ariz., Phoenix, 1974-76; state dir. Ariz. Journalism and Telecommunications Endowment, 1982—; prof. devel. communication Acad. for Ednl. Devel., Lesotho and Swaziland, 1987-88, cons., Washington, 1987-88. Contbr. articles on mass communication to profl. jours.; narrator books for the blind, films for Cystic Fibrosis Found., also bus., indsl. films, video tapes. Mem. Ingham County Rep. Com., Lansing, Mich., 1966-67; with pub. rels. Cystic Fibrosis Found., Boston, 1965-66. NDEA fellow, 1966-68. Mem. Broadcast Promotion Assn., Broadcast Edn. Assn. (mem. com. 1970-83), Assn. for Edn. in Journalism (AEJ-APNA committee com. 1981-84). Mormon. Home: 3308 Mariana Circle Tempe AZ 85282 Office: Ariz State U Sch Journalism and Telecommunications Tempe AZ 85287

BENNETT, HAROLD EARL, physicist, optics researcher; b. Missoula, Mont., Feb. 25, 1929; s. Edward Earl and Linda Queen (McCoy) B.; m. Jean Louise McPherson, Aug. 17, 1952 (div. Nov. 1984); m. Dorothy Jean Searles, Nov. 17, 1984; children: Jeanie Nybo, Dorothy Ann Picking. BA, U. Mont., 1951; MS, Pa. State U., 1953, PhD, 1955. Grad. asst. Pa. State U., State College, 1951-55; physicist Wright Air Devel. Ctr., Dayton, Ohio, 1955-56; physicist Naval Ordnance Test Sta. (name Naval Weapons Ctr. 1964—), China Lake, Calif., 1956-62, rsch. physicist, 1962—, assoc. head rsch. dept. physics div., 1972—; co-chmn. Laser Induced Damage in Optical Materials Conf., Boulder, Colo., 1979—. Adv. editor Optics Communications, 1969-86; contbr. over 100 articles on optics to profl. jours., chpts. to books; patentee on optical instruments. Pres. Indian Wells Valley Community Concert Assn., Ridgecrest, Calif., 1974-75. Recipient LTE Thompson award Naval Weapons Ctr., 1974, Tech. Dir.'s award, 1983; Capt. Robert Dexter Conrad award Dept. Navy, 1979. Fellow Optical Soc. Am. (assoc. editor. Jour. 1968-79, bd. dirs. 1972-75), Internat. Soc. for Optical Engring. (bd. dirs. 1985-87, v.p. 1987, pres. 1988, Tech. Achievement award 1983), Maturango Mus. (life), Sierra Club (San Francisco). Republican. Home: 619 W Felspar Ave Ridgecrest CA 93555 Office: Naval Weapons Lab Michelson Lab Code 3810l China Lake CA 93555

BENNETT, HARRY DANIEL, aerospace engineer; b. Toms River, N.J., June 16, 1955; s. Harry Elmer and Joan Catherine (Sullivan) B.; m. Cynthia Ruth Hetrick, July 26, 1975 (div. 1983); children: David, Daniel; m. Donna Leigh Roth, Feb. 14, 1983; children: Andrea Rae, Harry Robert. AAS in Elec. Engring. Tech., Trident Tech. Coll., Charleston, S.C., 1978; diploma/ cert., Cleve. Inst. Electronics, 1984; BSEE, Columbia Pacific U., San Rafael, Calif., 1985. Jr. test tech. Collins div. Rockwell Internat., Cedar Rapids, Iowa, 1978-81; sr./lead electronics tech. Nimslo Corp., Atlanta, 1981-82; engring. specialist Bendix Aerospace, Teterboro, N.J., 1982-85; sr. design engr. advanced systems div. Northrop Corp., Pico Rivera, Calif., 1986-88; sr. engring. sci. specialist McDonnell Douglas Corp./Douglas Aircraft Co., Long Beach, Calif., 1988—; v.p. engring Aeroteck Co., Inc., Palmdale, Calif., 1986—. Author: Modern Filter Networks, 1985; patentee in field. With USN, 1973-77. Mem. Assn. Old Crows. Republican. Home: 3629 E 14th St Long Beach CA 90804 Office: McDonnell Douglas Corp 3855 Lakewood Blvd Long Beach CA 90846

BENNETT, JACQUELINE BEEKMAN, school psychologist; b. Santa Paula, Calif., Sept. 4, 1946; d. Jack Edward and Margaret Blanche (MacPherson) Beekman.; m. Thomas LeRoy Bennett Jr., Aug. 5, 1972; children: Shannon, Brian, Laurie. BA, U. Calif., Davis, 1968; MS, Colo. State U., 1975, PhD, 1984. Histologist Sch. Veterinary Medicine, Davis, 1969-71; sch. psychologist Poudre Sch. Dist. R-1, Ft. Collins, Colo., 1983—. Mem. Colo. State Grievance Bd. Augment Panel, 1988-89; nominating chmn. United Presbyn. Women, Timnath, Colo., 1982, pres., 1986; com. mem. Women and the Ch. Com., Boulder Presbytery, Colo., 1985-86; elder Timnath Presbyn. Ch., 1985—. Mem. NEA, Am. Psychol. Assn., Colo. Soc. Sch. Psychologists (cert.), Nat. Assn. Sch. Psychologists (cert.), Ft. Collins Parents of Twins (pres. 1977-78), Sigma Xi, Phi Kappa Phi. Democrat. Club: Squaredusters (Ft. Collins) (v.p. 1977-78). Home: 213 Camino Real Fort Collins CO 80524 Office: Poudre Sch Dist R-1 2407 Laporte Ave Fort Collins CO 80521

BENNETT, JEFFREY ALAN, teacher; b. Keokuk, Iowa, June 3, 1949; s. Donald L. and Myrtle L. (White) B.; m. Judy Ann Gannon, June 15, 1974; children: Don Dean, Christopher Lee, Alexander Jeffrey. BA, Morningside Coll., 1972. Cert. tchr., S.D., Wyo. Tchr. Wolsey (S.D.) Sch. Dist., 1974-75, Lake Central Sch. Dist., Madison, S.D., 1975-78, Uinta County Sch. Dist., Evanston, Wyo., 1978—. Del. Wyo. Democratic Conv., Casper, 1980, Sheridan, 1988; bd. dirs. Sagebrush Theatre Prodns., Evanston, 1983-85. Mem. Evanston Edn. Assn. (pres. 1980-81, v.p. 1985-86), Wyo. Edn. Assn., NEA, Purple Sage Golf Club, Elks. Methodist. Home: 1124 Summit St Evanston WY 82930

BENNETT, JIM, SR., insurance agent; b. Englewood, Colo., Aug. 20, 1952; s. D.L. and La Donna Jean (Pippitt) B.; m. Pam Sue Smiley, Nov. 24, 1973; children: LaAnne, Ja Nella, Jim Jr. Student, Belleville Jr. Coll., Belleville, Ill., 1970. Journeyman locksmith Henley's Key Svc., Colorado Springs, 1970-73; locksmith Quint City Security, Rock Island, Ill., 1973-74; mgr. Taco Bell, Colorado Springs, 1974-75; pres. Advanced Detection Systems, Colorado Springs, 1975-85; v.p. Bond's Burglar Alarm, Phoenix, 1985-86; agt. Am. Family Ins., Glendale, Ariz., 1986—. Mem. West Valley Assn. Life Underwriters. Republican. Office: Am Family Insurance 6033 W Bell Rd Ste K Glendale AZ 85308

BENNETT, JOHN A., judge; b. Chgo., Apr. 14, 1937; s. John William and Iren (Durnovich) Bocskovits; m. Jeanine Delores Boomgarden, July 23, 1960; children: Martin John, Renea Jean, Denise Lynn, Michelle Ann. AA, Univ. State of N.Y. Regents Coll. Degree, 1975, BS, 1981; AS in Law Enforcement, Blue Mountain Community Coll., Pendleton, Oreg., 1976; LLB, La Salle Extension U., Chgo., 1976; postgrad., Nat. Judicial Coll., Reno, Nev., 1979. Enlisted chief warrant officer U.S. Army, 1955-75; ret., 1975; served intelligence agy., U.S. Army Intelligence Command, 1966-75; judge Mcpl. Ct., Hermiston, Oreg., 1978—, Umatilla, Oreg., 1983—, Echo, Oreg., 1987—; discussion leader Nat. Jud. Coll., Reno, 1984; apptd. adv. and judicial coms. Oreg. Supreme Ct. Bd. dirs. People to People Handicapped Group, Hermiston, Oreg., 1980—; exec. dir. Hermiston Heritage Assn., 1982—; bd. dirs. Oreg. Trail Tourism Council, Hermiston, 1983—, Hist. Preservation League Oreg., 1985-87; active Umatilla County Hist. Soc., 1983—. Mem. Nat. Judges Assn. (pres. 1984-85, pub. quar. newspaper 1984, judicial career edn. achievement award, 1985, advanced achievement award in judicial edn., 1985), Oreg. Mcpl. Judges Assn. (bd. dirs. 1980—, v.p. 1987, pres. 1987—, editor quar. newspaper 1983-87, Meritorious Service award 1982), Assn. Former Intelligence Officers. Roman Catholic. Home: 820 W Highland St Hermiston OR 97838 Office: Mcpl Ct 330 S 1st St Hermiston OR 97838

BENNETT, JUNE NEWTON, interior designer; b. Windsor, Colo., June 17, 1926; d. Arthur Arnaud and Irma Mae (Wilkinson) Newton; m. Thomas Willard Bennett, Aug. 14, 1948; children: Polly Alison Bennett Wissing, Susan Jane Bennett Mallory. BA, U. Denver, 1948. Pvt. sec. to univ. dean Northwestern U., Evanston, Chgo., Ill., 1948-52; interior designer Bowling's Furniture, Ft. Collins, Colo., 1963-65; owner, designer Bennett-Raetzman Interior Design, Ft. Collins, 1965-67; owner, pres., designer June Newton Bennett Interior Design, Ft. Collins, 1967—. Sec., founder Ft. Collins Coun. Arts-Humanities, 1963; chairperson, founder Ft. Collins Hist. Landamrks Commn., 1968; project mgr. Avery House Restoration, 1974-79; mem. design com. Lincoln Ctr. for Performing Arts, Ft. Collins, 1982—; pres. bd. Ft. Collins Symphony, 1987-88. Mem. Interior Design Guild (sec. 1986-88). Republican. Episcopalian.

BENNETT, KEITH ERVIN, civil engineering consulting executive; b. Oklahoma City, Jan. 15, 1948; s. Jack I. and Wilma (Qualls) B.; m. Elizabeth J. Neylon, Nov. 15, 1975; children: Christopher, Rebecca, Matthew. BSCE, USAF Acad., 1970; MSCE, U. Ill., 1971; postgrad., U.S. Air Force Inst. Tech., 1974, U. Denver, 1981. Commd. 2d lt. USAF, 1970, advanced through grades to capt., 1973, civil engineer, 1971-75, resigned, 1975; project mgr. Benham Group, Oklahoma City, 1975-77, Engring. Enterprise, Norman, Okla., 1977-79, Greiner Engring., Denver, 1979-82; prin. Evans, Kuhn and Assocs., Denver, 1982—. Referee Columbine Soccer Assn., South Jefferson County, Colo., 1984-86; skit dir. YMCA Indian Guides, Chatfield, 1984-85; mem. com. Ken Caryl Ranch swim team, South Jefferson County, 1986. Decorated Bronze Star, 1973. Mem. ASCE, NSPE (student chpt. formation com. 1984-85), Colo. Cons. Engrs. Council (pub. relations com. 1985, 86, 87, scholarship com. 1983-85), USAF Acad. Alumni Assn. Office: Evans Kuhn and Assocs Inc 9034 E Easter Pl #202 Englewood CO 80112

BENNETT, MICHAEL WILLIAM, museum and historical society director; b. Springfield, Mass., Jan. 29, 1947; s. Leonard William and Betty Ann (Milloglav) B.; m. Tracy Lee Joy, Oct. 8, 1977. AA, Am. River Coll.; BS, Calif. State U., Sacramento. Curator San Joaquin County Hist. Mus., Lodi, Calif., 1977-80, dir., 1980-84, dir. hist. soc. and mus., 1984—. Designer Newcastle exhibit works. Chmn. San Joaquin County Historic Records Commn., 1987-88; bd. dirs. Lodi Area Crime Stoppers, 1986—. With U.S. Army, 1967-70. Mem. Lodi Dist. C. of C. (bd. dirs. 1985—), Rotary (pres. Lodi/Tokay club 1987-88). Office: San Joaquin County Hist Mus PO Box 21 Lodi CA 95241

BENNETT, PAUL LESTER, marketing promotions professional, producer; b. Jamaica, N.Y., Mar. 25, 1946; s. Frank and Frances (Katz) B. BA in Speech, Theater, L.I. U., 1970. Mgr. dir., producer New Artef Players, L.A., 1976-78, Actors Workshop & Repertory Co., West Palm Beach, Fla., 1982-83, Hippodrome State Theatre, Gainesville, Fla., 1983-84, East Coast Arts, New Rochelle, N.Y., 1986-87; mng. dir. Dupree Dance Acad., L.A., 1978-82; mng. dir., assoc. producer Two-Head Video Prodns., Gainesville, 1984-86; dir. mktg. Hesperia (Calif.) Incorporation Com., 1987-88; dir. promotions Comic Relief, L.A., 1988—; mng. cons., Fla. Theatre, Gainesville, 1985; mem. Gainesville Cultural Affairs Adv. Bd., 1985. Recipient Addy award, Golden Images award, Fla. Pub. Rels. Assn., 1984. Mem. C. of C., L.A. County Mus. Art. Democrat. Jewish.

BENNETT, POLLY CATHRYN, infosystems specialist; b. Dayton, Ohio, Jan. 29, 1938; d. Robert A. and Cathryn (Link) Franks; m. John Francis Bennett, Aug. 22, 1964; 1 child, Erica. BA in English Lit., Miami U., Oxford, Ohio, 1963; MLS, Drexel U., 1967. Librarian Los Lomitas Sch. Dist., Menlo Park, Calif., 1970-72; ednl. writer Sullivan Assocs., Menlo Park, 1972-75; computer specialist U.S. Geol. Survey, Menlo Park, 1985--. Active Fed. Women's Program Com., Washington, 1983-84. Office: US Geol Survey 345 Middlefield Rd Menlo Park CA 94025

BENNETT, ROBERT LOUIS, college administrator; b. Winnett, Mont., July 17, 1925; s. William and Florence B.; m. Jean Kathryn Pearson, Oct. 20, 1972; children—Mary, Jean, James, William, Stephen. B.A., Mont. State Coll., 1950; M.S., Eastern Mont. Coll., 1959; Ed.D., U. Calif.-Berkeley, 1967. Tchr., counselor, Billings, Mont., 1951-60; researcher in ednl. devel. San Mateo (Calif.) High Sch. Dist., 1961-67; coll. adminstr. in resource devel. San Mateo Community Coll. Dist.; project dir. Ford Found. Cooperative Edn. Program, Kellogg Found. Community Coll. Mgmt. by Objectives, U.S. Office Edn. Career Edn. Nat. Demonstration, High Tech. Bus. Tng. Ctr. Served with USN, 1945-46. Mem. Am. Soc. Tng. and Devel., Assn. Calif. Community Coll. Adminstrs. (charter), Internat. Platform Assn. Author: Identification of Curriculum Strengths and Weaknesses, 1967, An Improved Urban-Suburban Management Model for Community Colleges, 1977, Careers Through Cooperative Work Experience, 1978, Earning and Learning, 1980, Action Link Industrial Training Systems, 1986; Action Link automated prodn. system mgmt. quality control, team self-mgmt., 1989—. Address: 53 Condon Ct San Mateo CA 94403

BENNETT, RON STEPHAN, insurance broker; b. Portland, Oreg., Nov. 10, 1953; s. Joseph Floyd and Elaine Maxine (Rue) B.; m. Cynthia Marie Johnson, Feb. 4, 1984. BS in Bus. Adminstrn., Portland (Oreg.) State U., 1977. Sr. property underwriter Fireman's Fund Ins. Co., Portland, 1977-79, 79-81, mktg. rep., 1981-83; sr. mktg. rep. Fireman's Fund Ins. Co., Houston, 1983-85; asst. v.p. Fred S. James & Co., Portland, Oreg., 1986—. Bd. dirs. Portland Rose Festival Assn., Japan-Am. Soc. of Oreg. Mem. Risk Mgmt. and Ins. Soc., Nat. Assn. Surety Bond Producers, Constrn. Fin. Mgmt. Assn., Associated Gen. Contractors Am., Surety Assn. Oreg. Republican. Lutheran. Club: Multnomah Athletic (Portland). Office: Fred S James & Co of Oreg 111 SW Columbia #500 Portland OR 97201

BENNETT, STEVEN CARROLL, forester; b. Mankato, Minn., Feb. 19, 1952; s. Enoch Dale and Gail Louise (Laganeire) B.; m. Deborah Lynn Price, Sept. 9, 1978; children: Aaron Christopher, Sarah Elizabeth. BA, St. Thomas Coll., 1974; M of Forestry, U. Minn., 1980. Registered forester, S.C. Social worker Bridge for Runaway Youth, Mpls., 1974-78; research asst. Coll. Forestry, U. Minn., St. Paul, 1979-80; forest technician Stone Container Corp., Columbia, S.C., 1981-82; forester Stone Container Corp., Columbia, 1982-83; area mgr. Stone Container Corp., Orangeburg, S.C., 1983-85; regional mgr. Stone Container Corp., Orangeburg, 1985-87; regional procurement mgr. Stone Container Corp., Snowflake, Ariz., 1987—; tree farm inspector Am. Forest Inst., Orangeburg, 1984-86; mem. S.C. Tree Farm Productivity Project, Orangeburg, 1984-86. Mem. Ducks Unlimited, S.C., 1984—. Mem. Am. Forestry Assn., Soc. Am. Foresters, Am. Pulpwood Assn. Roman Catholic. Home: 2546 Broken Circle Flagstaff AZ 86004

BENNETT, WILLIAM RICHARD, utilities executive; b. Woodland, Calif., Nov. 5, 1948; m. Mary Louise Heflin, Aug. 7, 1979; children: Micaela Katherine, Heflin Charles. BS in Biology, Zoology, Botany, U. Nev., 1970, BA in Art, 1975, A in Mech. and Elec. Design, 1975. Supr. dist. office Sierra Pacific Power Co., South Lake Tahoe, Calif., 1979-83; supr. cen. credit Sierra Pacific Power Co., Reno, 1983—; v.p. Sierra Ice Unltd., 1985—, also bd. dirs. Commr. speed skating and floor hockey 1989 Internat. Winter Spl. Olympic Games, Reno; bd. dirs. Community Svcs. Agy., Reno, organizing com. Reno/Tahoe Winter Games 1987—. Mem. Credit Mgrs. of No. Nev. (pres., bd. dirs.), Kiwanis (treas. bd. dirs. Reno Sunrisers). Republican. Episcopalian. Home: 2445 Piping Rock Dr Reno NV 89502 Office: Sierra Pacific Power Co 6100 Neil Rd Reno NV 89502

BENNINGER, FRED, communications company executive; b. Germany, 1917. Grad., NYU, 1937, U. So. Calif., 1941. Pres., chmn. bd. MGM Grand Inc., Beverly Hills, Calif.; mem. bd. dirs., exec. com. MGM/UA Communications Co., Beverly Hills. Office: MGM Grand Inc 9744 Wilshire Blvd Beverly Hills CA 90212 *

BENNINGTON, LESLIE ORVILLE, JR., insurance agent; b. Sedalia, Mo., Dec. 29, 1946; s. Leslie Orville Sr. and Eunice May Marguerite (Cole) B.; m. Susan Frances Grotha, June 1, 1968; children: Leslie O. III, Jeremy Lawrence. BSME, U. Mo., Rolla, 1968; postgrad., U. Tenn. Space Inst., 1969; ChFC, Am. Coll., 1988. Registered profl. engr., Wash., Wyo.; CLU; chartered fin. cons. Design engr. Arnold Research Orgn., Tullahoma, Tenn., 1968-70; engr. Pacific Power & Light, Glenrock, Wyo., 1973-75; agt., asst. gen. agt. Am. Nat. Ins. Co., Casper, Wyo., 1975-85; gen. agt. Ins. Sales, Glenrock, 1985—. Pres. Cen. Wyo. Estate Planning Council, Casper, 1985-86; mem. Glenrock Vol. Fire Dept., 1973—, asst. chief, 1982; pres., v.p. Converse County Recreation Bd., Douglas, Wyo., 1980—; judge Dist. High Sch. Speech Contests, Glenrock; bd. dirs. Converse County Sch. Dist. #2, 1976. 1st lt. USAF, 1971-73. Mem. Nat. Assn. Life Underwriters (Nat. Quality award, Health Ins. Quality award, Nat. Sales Achievement award), Cen. Wyo. Life Underwriters (pres. 1978-80), Wyo. Life Underwriters Assn. (chmn. membership com. 1985-87, nat. com. 1982-87, v.p. 1986-87, bd. dirs. 1980—, Ins. Agt. of Yr., 1980, pres. 1988—), West Cen. Wyo. CLUs (pres. 1986-88), Million Dollar Round Table, Nat. Pony Express Assn. (pres. Ea. Wyo. div. 1985—), KC (grand knight, faithful navigator). Republican. Roman Catholic. Home: 6 Shannon Dr Glenrock WY 82637 Office: PO Box 2049 217 W Birch Glenrock WY 82637

BENNINGTON, WILLIAM LEWIS, biology educator; b. Portland, Oreg., Apr. 19, 1946; s. Elwin Everett Bennington and Marjory Catherine (Whorfield) Byrn; m. Joyce Elaine Hoshour, Mar. 1, 1966; children: Holli R., Shelly L. BS, Met. State Coll., 1970; MS, Eastern Wash. U., 1972; ArtsD, Idaho State U., 1982. Instr. biology Muskegon (Mich.) Community Coll., 1972-76, Coll. Ganado Navajo Reservation, Ariz., 1976-78; chmn. div. math. and sci. Coll. Ganado Navajo Reservation, 1976-78; instr. biology and chemistry Pike's Peak Community Coll., Colorado Springs, Colo., 1980—, pre-med. and math.-sci. advisor; state-wide biology chmn. Colo. Core-Curriculum Transfer Program, 1987-89. Capt. Ganado Vol. Fire Dept., 1976-78; bd. dirs. Muskegon Planned Parenthood, 1975-76. Fellow Ednl. Profl. Devel. Assistance Dept. Edn., Eastern Wash. U., 1970; named one of Outstanding Young Men. Am. Jaycees, 1978, Outstanding Arts and Scis. Instr. Pikes Peak Community Coll., 1985; grantee Natural Sci. Curriculum ImprovementDept. Edn., 1977. Mem. Colo.-Wyo. Acad. Scis. Democrat. Clubs: Muskegon Skydivers (safety officer 1974-76), Muskegon Community Coll. Ski (faculty advisor 1973-76). Office: Pikes Peak Community Coll 5675 S Academy Blvd Colorado Springs CO 80906

BENNION, JOHN W., school system administrator; b. Salt Lake City, Nov. 25; s. M. Lynn and Katherine Bennion; m. Sylvia Lustig; children: Philip, Stanford, David, Bryan, Grant, Andrew. BS in Philosophy, English, U. Utah, 1961, MA in Edn. Adminstrn., 1962; PhD in Edn. Adminstrn., Ohio State U., 1966. Tchr. Granite High Sch., Salt Lake City, 1961-63; asst. instr. Ohio State U., Columbus, 1963-64, adminstrv. asst., 1965-66; adminstrv. intern Parma (Ohio) Sch. Dist., 1964-65; asst. supt. Elgin (Ill.) Pub. Schs., 1966-68; asst. prof. edn. adminstrn. Ind. U., Bloomington, 1968-69; supt. Brighton Cen. Schs., Rochester, N.Y., 1969-79, Bloomington (Minn.) Pub. Schs., 1979-80, Provo (Utah) Sch. Dist., 1980-85, Salt Lake City Schs., 1985—. Mem. Assn. Supervision and Curriculum Devel., Assn. Early Childhood Edn., Am. Assn. Sch. Adminstrs., Sch. Mgmt. Study Group, Phi Delta Kappa. Home: 1837 Harvard Ave Salt Lake City UT 84108 Office: Salt Lake City Sch Dist Office of Supt of Schools 440 E 100 S Salt Lake City UT 84111 *

BENNIS, WARREN, business administration educator, author, consultant; b. N.Y.C., Mar. 8, 1925; s. Philip and Rachel (Landau) B.; m. Clurie Williams, Mar. 30, 1962 (div. 1983); children—Katharine, John Leslie, Will Martin; m. Mary Jane O'Donnell, Mar. 8, 1988. A.B., Antioch Coll., 1951; hon. cert. econs., London Sch. Econs., 1952; Ph.D., MIT, 1955; LL.D. (hon.), Xavier U., Cin., 1972, George Washington U., 1977; L.H.D. (hon.), Hebrew Union Coll., 1974, Kans. State U., 1979; D.Sc. (hon.), U. Louisville, 1977, Pacific Grad. Sch. Psychology, 1987. Diplomate Am. Bd. Profl. Psychology. Asst. prof. psychology MIT, Cambridge, 1953-56, prof., 1959-67; asst. prof. psychology and bus. Boston U., 1956-59; prof. Sloan Sch. Mgmt., 1959-67; provost SUNY-Buffalo, 1967-68, v.p. acad. devel., 1968-71; pres. U. Cin., 1971-77; U.S. prof. corps. and soc. Centre d'Etudes Industrielles, Geneva, Switzerland, 1978-79; exec.-in-residence Pepperdine U., 1978-79; George Miller Disting. prof.-in-residence U. Ill., Champaign-Urbana, 1978; Disting. prof. Bus. Adminstrn. Sch. Bus., U. So. Calif., 1980-88; univ. prof. U. So. Calif., 1988—; vis. lectr. Harvard U., 1958-59, Indian Mgmt. Inst., Calcutta; vis. prof. U. Lausanne (Switzerland), 1961-62, INSEAD, France, 1983; bd. dirs. First Exec. Corp., The Foothill Group. Author: Planning of Change, 4th edit., 1985, Interpersonal Dynamics, 1963, 3d edit., 1975, Personal and Organizational Change, 1965, Changing Organizations, 1966, repub. in paperback as Beyond Bureaucracy, 1974, The Temporary Society, 1968, Organization Development, 1969, American Bureaucracy, 1970, Management of Change and Conflict, 1972, The Leaning Ivory Tower, 1973, The Unconscious Conspiracy: Why Leaders Can't Lead, 1976, Essays in Interpersonal Dynamics, 1979; (with B. Nanus): Leaders, 1985, On Becoming a Leader, 1989, (with I. Mitroff) The Unreality Industry, 1989, Why Leaders Can't Lead, 1989; columnist, chmn. bd. editors New Mgmt.; assoc. editor Jour. Transpersonal Psychology, Community Psychology; cons. editor Jour. Creative Behavior, Jour. Higher Edn., Jour. Occupational Behavior, Ency. of Econs. and Bus., Jour. Humanistic Psychology. Mgmt. Series Jossey-Bass Pubs. Mem. Pres.' White House Task Force on Sci. Policy, 1969-70; mem. FAA study task force U.S. Dept. Transp., 1975; mem. adv. com. N.Y. State Joint Legis. Com. Higher Edn., 1970-71; mem. Ohio Gov.'s Bus. and Employment Council, 1972-74; mem. panel on alt. approaches to grad. edn. Council Grad. Schs. and Grad. Record-Exam Bd., 1971-73; chmn. Nat. Adv. Commn. on Higher Edn. for Police Officers, 1976-78; adv. bd. NIH, 1978-84; trustee Colo. Rocky Mountains Sch., 1978-82; bd. dirs. Am. Leadership Forum, 1984-89, Foothill Group, First Exec. Corp., Calif. Sch. Profl. Psychology; mem. vis. com. for humanities MIT, 1975-81. Served to capt. AUS, World War II. Decorated Bronze Star, Purple Heart; recipient Dow Jones award, 1987. Fellow Am. Psychol. Assn., AAAS, Am. Sociol. Assn.; mem. Am. Acad. Arts and Scis. (co-chmn. policy council 1969-71), Am. Soc. Pub. Adminstrn. (nat. council), Am. Mgmt. Assn. (dir. 1974-77), U.S. C. of C. (adv. group scholars). Office: U So Calif Sch Bus University Park Los Angeles CA 90089-1421

BENOIT-CHRISTIAN, PAULETTE THERESE, cosmetics executive, educator; b. Orleans, Vt., Jan. 9, 1947; d. Raymond Josephat and Gertrude (Poirier) Benoit; m. Robert Anthony Christian, June 10, 1981. AA, Scottsdale (Ariz.) Community Coll., 1976; postgrad., Westmore Acad. of Cosmetic Arts, 1987; diploma in beauty therapy, Aesthetics Unltd., Phoenix, 1988. Cosmetic sales exec. Colorful You, Phoenix, 1981—; curriculum developer, educator Glendale (Ariz.) Community Coll., 1985—; speaker various edni. orgns., 1985—. Author various works in field. Mem. NAFE, Ariz. Soc. Profl. Image Cons., Nat. Cosmetology Assn., Am. Inst. Esthetics, Robert Schuller's Eagle Club (Orange, Calif.), 500 Club (Phoenix). Republican. Roman Catholic. Office: Colorful You PO Box 26937 Phoenix AZ 85068

BENSCHEIDT, STEVEN EUGENE, veterinarian; b. La Junta, Colo., Sept. 19, 1954; s. George N. and Charlotte J. (Reams) B.; m. Beth Ann Bolton, July 15, 1976; 1 child, Nicole L. DVM, Colo. State U., 1980. Pvt. practice Modesto, Calif., 1980-81, Nelson Road Vet. Clinic, Longmont, Colo., 1983—; agrl. dir. Western Food Products, La Junta, 1891-83. Bd. dirs. Colo. Small Animal Commn., 1988--. Mem. AVMA (small animal commn. 1988—), Colo. Vet. Medicine Assn. (bd. dirs. 1988—, dist. rep.), Denver Vet. Med. Soc. (assoc.), Nat. Food Processors (nat. agrl. com. 1982-83), Rotary (bd. dirs. Longmont and Twin Peaks chpts. 1988—). Republican. Mennonite. Office: Nelson Road Vet Clinic 8875 Nelson Rd Longmont CO 80501

BENSON, ALFRED M., real estate appraiser, analyst; b. Jamaica, N.Y., Jan. 21, 1941; s. Peter Henry Benson and Susan (Maloney) Benson Alexander; m. Kathleen Mary Laffan, Feb. 8, 1964; children—Jonathan, Jennifer, Eileen. Student Brown U., 1958-62; B.Econs., C.W. Post Coll., 1963. Appraiser James Matthews, MAI, Mineola, N.Y., 1964-67; pres. Peter H. Benson, Inc., New Hyde Park, N.Y., 1967-76; asst. v.p. Seamen's Bank, N.Y.C., 1969-76; ptnr. Klafter and Benson, Tucson, 1976-81; prin. Burke, Hansen & Homan, Tucson, 1981-83, Alfred M. Benson, MAI, Tucson, 1983—; pres. Alfred M. Benson Co., real estate investment analysis, Tucson, 1984—. Mem. vestry Christ Episcopal Ch., Garden City, N.Y., 1973-76. Adv. bd. Appraisal Jour. Mem. Am. Inst. Real Estate Appraisers (pres. Ariz. chpt. 1984, mem. MAI examination subcom. 1986-89), Ariz. Assn. Realtors (bd. dirs. 1984), Tucson Bd. Realtors, Soc. Real Estate Appraisers (pres. Tucson chpt. 1983, mem. examinations sub com. 1987-88), Am. Soc. Appraisers (v.p. Tucson chpt. 1983), Omega Tau Rho. Republican. Home: 3232 N Placita Brazos Tucson AZ 85715 Office: Alfred M Benson Co 6115 E Grant Rd Tucson AZ 85712

BENSON, ALISON COLTON, university director; b. Boston, Apr. 13, 1951; d. David Marshall and Mary Jean Allerton (Dunsmore) Cox; m. James Darrell, July 4, 1981; children: James Scott, Robert Stuart. BA, U. Nev., 1975, MA, 1981. With U. Nev., Reno, 1976—, dir. student fin. svcs., 1985—. Bd. dirs. No. Nev. Reading Ctr., 1986—. Recipient Most Watchable Woman award Reno Toastmaster's Club, 1987. Mem. Nev. Assn. Fin. Aid Adminstrs. (pres. 1982-83), Western Assn. Student Fin. Aid Adminstrs. (sec. 1986-87, conf. chair 1989), Nat. Assn. Student Fin. Aid Adminstrs., Nat. Assn. Vet.'s Programs (adminstr.), Nat. Assn. Student Employment Adminstrs. Home: 3463 Skyline Blvd Reno NV 89509 Office: U Nev 200 TSS Reno NV 89557

BENSON, BRADLEY DUANE, banker; b. La Mesa, Calif., Apr. 10, 1959; s. Robert Omer and Margere Anne (Cain) B.; m. Jill Theresa Jaramillo, Mar. 3, 1984; 1 child, Ashley Laine. AA, Grossmont Coll., 1978; BSBA, Calif. State U., Sacramento, 1982; MS in Systems Mgmt., U. So. Calif., 1988. Credit authorizer Sears Roebuck & Co., Sacramento, 1980-82; auditor Inventory Auditors, Inc., Sacramento, 1982; personal banking officer Seafirst Nat. Bank, Spokane, Wash., 1988—. Capt. USAF, 1982-88. Mem. Am. Inst. Banking, Air Force Assn. Republican. Baptist. Home: N 8028 Pamela St Spokane WA 99208 Office: Seafirst Nat Bank W 601 Riverside St Spokane WA 99201

BENSON, EZRA TAFT, church executive, former secretary agriculture; b. Whitney, Idaho, Aug. 4, 1899; s. George Taft and Sarah (Dunkley) B.; m. Flora Smith Amussen, Sept. 10, 1926; children: Reed, Mark, Barbara, Beverly, Bonnie, Flora Beth. Student, Utah State Agrl. Coll., Logan, 1918-21; BS, Brigham Young U., 1926, Dr. Pub. Service (hon.), 1955; MS in Agrl. Econs., Iowa State Coll., 1927, D Agrl. (hon.), 1953; postgrad., U. Calif., 1937-38; HHD, Coll. Osteo. Physicians and Surgeons, 1951; LLD, U. Utah, 1953, Bowdoin Coll., 1955, U. Maine, 1956; D Agr. (hon.), Mich. State Coll., 1955; DSc (hon.), Rutgers U., 1955. Mission Ch. Jesus Christ Latter-day Saints, Brit. Isles and Europe; pres. Newcastle dist. Ch. Jesus Christ Latter-day Saints, 1921-23; farm operator 1923-30; county agrl. agt. U. Idaho Extension Service, Preston, 1929-30; extension economist and mktg. specialist in charge econ. and mktg. work State of Idaho, 1930-38; organizer, sec. Idaho Coop. Council, 1933-38; exec. sec. Nat. Council Farmer Coops., 1939-44; mem. exec. com., bd. trustees Am. Inst. Co-op, 1942-52, vice chmn. bd. trustees, 1942-49, chmn., 1952; sec. agr. U.S., Washington, 1953-61; dir. Olson Bros., Inc.; bd. dirs. Farm Found., 1946-50; mem. Nat. Agrl. Adv. Com., World War II; mem. Nat. Farm Credit Com., 1940-43; U.S. del. 1st Internat. Conf. of Farm Orgns., London, 1946. Contbr. to agrl., coop. and church jours. Mem. nat. exec. bd. Boy Scouts Am., 1948-66, awarded Silver Antelope, 1951, Silver Buffalo award, 1954; mem. Boise Stake Presidency, Ch. of Jesus Christ of Latter-day Saints, Idaho, 1935-39, pres. Boise Stake, 1938-39; pres. Wash. Dist. Council, Eastern States Mission, 1939-40, Washington Stake, 1940-44; ordained apostle of Ch., mem. Council of Twelve, 1943, pres. European Mission, 1946, 63-65, mem. Gen. Ch. Bd. Edn.; pres. Ch. Jesus Christ Latter-day Saints, Salt Lake City, 1985—; br. trustees Brigham Young U. Recipient testimonial for distinq. service to agr. U. Wis., 1952; scholarship Gamma Sigma Delta, hon. soc. agr. Iowa State Coll.; fellow U. Calif., Berkeley. Mem. Am. Mktg. Assn., Farm Econs. Assn., Delta Nu, Alpha Zeta. Office: Ch Jesus Christ Latter Day Sts 50 E N Temple St Salt Lake City UT 84150 *

BENSON, FRANCIS M., aerospace manufacturing engineer; b. Bklyn., Oct. 7, 1958; s. Francis Gerald Benson and Grace Angela (Superty) Brothers; m. Jerri. Student, Palmdale High Sch., Calif. Cert. Airframe & Powerplant Mechanic, Calif. Structure mechanic B Lockheed Aircraft Co., Palmdale, Calif., 1979-80, final assembly mechanic, 1980-83, structure mechanic B, 1985-86, mfg. supr., 1986-87; structure mechanic B Rockwell Internat., Palmdale, Calif., 1983-85, hydraulic checkout mechanic, 1985; structure mechanic A Northrop B-2 Division, Palmdale, Calif., 1987-88, mfg. supr., 1988, mfg. planner, 1988-89, mfg. engr., 1989—; union steward Internat. Assn. Machinists & Aerospace, Palmdale Calif. Republican. Roman Catholic. Home: 1761 West Ave K-11 Lancaster CA 93534 Office: Northrop B-2 Div 3520 East Ave M Palmdale CA 93550

BENSON, GORDON LARIS, college director; b. Ottumwa, Iowa, Apr. 4, 1936; s. Laris and Belva (Hannah) B.; m. Joanna M. Carcagno, Nov. 28, 1972. BSBA, NE Mo. State U., 1960, BEd, 1960; MS in Guidance and Sch. Adminstrn., So. Ill. U., 1965, postgrad., 1967; postgrad., St. Louis U., 1968, U. Nev., Las Vegas, 1982. Salesman, div. mgr. Sears, Roebuck & Co., Des Moines and Ottumwa, 1954-60; tchr., counselor St. Louis Pub. Schs., 1960-68, asst. prin., 1965-68; asst. registrar St. Louis Community Coll., Forest Park, Mo., 1968-70, asst. dean admissions, 1970-74, assoc. dean admissions, 1974-78, dir. admissions, 1978-82; dir. admissions Clark County Community Coll., North Las Vegas, Nev., 1982-84; asst. vice chancellor student svcs. U. Houston, 1984-86; vice provost enrollment and student svcs. Wayne County Community Coll., Detroit, 1986-89; with Mesa Community Coll., Chandler, Ariz., 1989—. Contbr. articles to profl. jours. Mem. White House Conf. on Edn., St. Louis, 1962-82, High Tech. Com. and Coll. Prep. Com. Clark County Pub. Schs., Las Vegas, 1983, Alternative Edn. Com. Clark County Pub. Schs., 1982; bd. dirs. Mo. Bot. Garden, 1979-80; sec. St. Louis Bd. Edn., 1977-78, pres., 1979-80, chmn. mgmt. com., 1980-82; chmn. St. Louis Nat. Coll. Fair, 1974-75; commr. Met. Youth Commn., St. Louis, 1970-73. With U.S. Army, 1960-66. Mem. Mich. Coll. Student Personnel Assn., Mich. Chief Acad. Officers Assn., Mich. Assn. Coll. Registrars and Admissions Officers, Nat. Assn. Coll. Admissions Counselors (coll. fair chmn. 1973-74), Midwest Soc. Individual Psychology, Phi Delta Kappa. Home: 2405 W Palomino Ct Chandler AZ 85224 Office: Mesa Community Coll 1833 W Southern Mesa AZ 85224

BENSON, JAMES BERNARD, JR., clinical hynotherapist; b. Phila., May 8, 1930; s. James Bernard Benson and Elizabeth (Smeaton) Caswell; m. Hiroko Nakamura, Apr. 14, 1955. LLD (hon.), Nat. Law Enforcement Acad., 1968; BA in Police Sci., Pacific Coll., 1976; PhD (hon.), St. John's U., Springfield, La., 1988. Cert. behavioral therapist, Calif. Chief criminal investigator U.S. Marine Corps, 1947-66; corp. officer Bank of Am., L.A., 1966-85; pvt. practice Anaheim, Calif., 1985--; mem. Nat. Bd. Hypnotic Anesthesiology. Editor: (poetry) Devotion in Blue, 1973, Lawman's Lament, 1974; contbr. articles to police mags. Fellow Am. Assn. Profl. Hypnotherapists; mem. Nat. Soc. Clin. Hypnotherapists. Republican. Home and Office: 1400 S Sunkist St Apt 199 Anaheim CA 92806

BENSON, JAMES CARL, accountant; b. Mpls., Aug. 24, 1935; s. Fritz L. and Annie C. (Nordstrom) B.; m. Ruth Ann Backlin, Sept. 10, 1960; 1 child, Emily Ruthann. BBS with distinction, U. Minn., 1960. CPA, Calif. Intern Greyhound Co., 1959, Haskins & Sells, 1960; with Arthur Andersen & Co., San Francisco, Brussels, San Jose, Calif., 1960—, ptnr., 1970—. Pres. Trinity Luth. Ch., Oakland, Calif., 1966, bd. dirs. West Valley Aquatic Team, 1978-80, pres., 1979-80; bd. dirs. Family Services Assn., 1980-81; Alexian Bros. Hosp. Found., 1977-82, pres., 1981-82; trustee Alexian Bros. Hosp., 1982—; mem. planning and allocations com. United Way of Santa Clara County, 1981-82; mem. council Prince of Peace Luth. Ch., 1977-79, 83-87, pres., 1986-87; bd. dirs. San Jose Opera Assn., 1985-87, San Jose Mus. of Art, 1987—. Sloan scholar U. Minn. Mem. Am. Inst. CPA's, Nat. Assn. Accts., Calif. CPA Soc., Alliance Francaise of Saratoga (treas.), Beta Alpha Psi, Beta Gamma Sigma. Club: Am. Men's (Brussels). Lodge: Kiwanis (bd. dirs. West Valley chpt.).

BENSON, JOHN ALEXANDER, JR., physician, educator; b. Manchester, Conn., July 23, 1921; s. John A. and Rachel (Patterson) B.; m. Irene Zucker, Sept. 29, 1947; children—Peter M., John Alexander III, Susan Leigh, Jeremy P. B.A., Wesleyan U., 1943; M.D., Harvard U., 1946. Diplomate: Am. Bd. Internal Medicine (mem. bd. 1969—, sec.-treas. 1972-75), and subsplty. bd. gastroenterology (mem. 1961-66, chmn. 1965-66). Intern Univ. Hosps., Cleve., 1946-47; resident Peter Bent Brigham Hosp., Boston, 1949-51; fellow Mass. Gen. Hosp., Boston, 1951-53; research asst. Mayo Clinic, Rochester, Minn., 1953-54; instr. medicine Harvard, 1956-59; prof. medicine U. Oreg., 1965—, head div. gastroenterology, 1959-75; pres. Am. Bd. Internal Medicine, 1975—; cons. VA Hosps., Madigan Gen. Army Hosp. Editorial bd.: Am. Jour. Digestive Diseases, 1966-73; Contbr. articles to profl. jours. Mem. Oreg. Drug Adv. Council, 1965-73; Dir. Oreg. Med. Ednl. Found., 1967-73, pres., 1969-72. Served with USNR, 1947-49. Mem. Am. Gastroenterol. Assn. (sec. 1970-73, v.p. 1975-76, pres.-elect 1976-77, pres. 1977-78), Am. Clin. and Climatol. Assn., ACP (master), AMA, Am. Soc. Internal Medicine, Western Assn. Physicians, North Pacific Soc. Internal Medicine, Am. Fedn. Clin. Research, Federated Council for Internal Medicine, Am. Assn. Study Liver Disease, Western Soc. Clin. Investigation, Soc. Health and Human Values, Phi Beta Kappa, Sigma Xi, Alpha Omega Alpha. Office: Am Bd Internal Medicine 200 SW Market St Portland OR 97201

BENSON, JOHN DAVID, civil engineer; b. Humacou, P.R., Dec. 2, 1943; s. John Edward and Dorthy O. (Springhorn) B.; m. Theresa Ann Dolan, June 17, 1971; children: Andrea Renee, Michael Jared. BSCE, Utah State U., 1970; MS in Engring. Mgmt., U. Alaska, 1974; MSCE, U. Wash., 1985. Registered profl. engr., Alaska, Wash., Oreg. Idaho, Mont., Wyo., Utah; registered profl. land surveyer, Alaska, Wash.; registered structural engr., Oreg., Wash. With State of Mont. Dept. Transp., Helena, 1970-72; project engr. Dept. Waters and Harbors, State of Alaska, Juneau, 1972-74; sr. engr. KPFF Cons., Inc., Anchorage, 1975-76; prin. structural engr. PEI Cons., Inc., Ketchikan, Alaska, 1976-84, Bellevue, Wash., 1984-88; capital improvements engr. Snohomish County, Everett, Wash., 1988—. With U.S. Army, 1966-68, Vietnam. Mem. Am. Concrete Inst., Strucutral Engrs. Assn. .Wash., ASCE (sec., v.p. local chpt. 1983-84), Am. Congress on Surveying and Mapping, Am. Soc. Testing Materials. Home: 19815 Yew Way Snohomish WA 98290 Office: Snohomish County Dept Water 5th Fl Adminstrv Bldg Everett WA 98201

BENSON, KENNETH PETER, forest industry executive; b. Vancouver, B.C., Can., Mar. 1, 1927; s. Lawrence and Clara (Peel) B.; m. Joyce Alice Heino, Nov. 4, 1949; children: David, Sally. Student, U. B.C., Vancouver, chartered acct., 1953. Asst. controller Powell River Co., Vancouver, 1955-62; with B.C. Forest Products Co., Vancouver, 1962, comptroller, 1962, v.p. fin., 1967, dir., 1970, exec. v.p. ops., 1972, sr. exec. v.p., 1974, pres., chief operating officer, 1976-79, pres., chief exec. officer, 1979-84, chmn., chief exec. officer, 1984—; bd. dirs. Pulp & Paper Indsl. Relations Bur., Council Forest Industries, Can. Pulp & Paper Assn., Forest Engring. Research Inst. Can. Office: BC Forest Products Ltd, 1050 W Pender St, Vancouver, BC Canada V6E 2X3 *

BENSON, PHILLIP STANLEY, small business owner, entrepreneur; b. Missoula, Mont., June 28, 1943; s. Stanley Orlando and Mary Emily (MacKenzie) B.; m. Sharon Lynn Vinal, May 22, 1967 (div. 1976); children: Bendi Lynn, Cale Stanley; m. Carla Marie Mathison, Aug. 16, 1980; children: Andrew Carl, Adam Phillip. Student, U. Mont. Various svc. positions Missoula, 1960-66; salesman Penn Mut. Life Ins., San Francisco, 1966-69; sales rep. various cos., Missoula, 1969-76; rte. supr., collector Mont. Music Rentals Inc., Missoula, 1977-80, v.p., owner, 1980—; ptnr. Century Amusement, Missoula, 1981-88, Big Sky Amusement Games, Missoula, 1984—; pres., owner Mont. Mining & Reclamation Inc., Missoula, 1987—; ptnr. Quick It Darts, Missoula, 1987—; boxing ring announcer, U.S., 1976-80. Pres. Missoula Athletic Coun., 1976-77, dir. horse race, 1984; commr. gambling City and County of Missoula, 1981-88; fund raiser YMCA, Missoula, 1981-84. Mem. Amusement and Music Operators Assn. (nat. bd. dirs. 1985-88, v.p. 1988-91), Mont. Coin Machine Operators Assn. (sec.-treas 1978-80, v.p. 1980-84, pres. 1984-88). Democrat. Lutheran. Office: Mont Music Rentals Inc 629 Woody St Missoula MT 58902

BENSON, SIDNEY WILLIAM, chemistry researcher; b. N.Y.C., Sept. 26, 1918; m. Anna Seldis, 1986; 2 children. A.B., Columbia Coll., 1938; A.M., Harvard U., 1941, Ph.D., 1941; Docteur Honoris Causa, U. Nancy, France, 1989. Research asst. Gen. Electric Co., 1940; research fellow Harvard U., 1941-42; instr. chemistry CCNY, 1942-43; group leader Manhattan Project Kellex Corp., 1943; asst. prof. U. So. Calif., 1943-48, assoc. prof., 1948-51, prof. chemistry, 1951-64, dir. chem. physics program, 1962-63; dir. dept. kinetics and thermochemistry Stanford Research Inst., 1963-76; sci. dir. Hydrocarbon Research Inst. U. So. Calif., 1977—; research assoc. dept. chemistry and chem. engring. Calif. Inst. Tech., 1957-58; vis. prof. UCLA, 1959, U. Ill., 1959; hon. Glidden lectr. Purdue U., 1961; vis. prof. chemistry Stanford U., 1966-70, 71, 73; mem. adv. panel phys. chemistry Nat. Bur. Standards, 1969-72, chmn., 1970-71; hon. vis. prof. U. Utah, 1971; vis. prof. U. Paris VII and XI, 1971-72, U. St. Andrews, Scotland, 1973, U. Lausanne, Switzerland, 1979; Frank Gucker lectr. U. Ind., 1984; Brotherton prof. in phys. chemistry U. Leeds, 1984; disting. prof. U. So. Calif., 1985; cons. G.N. Lewis; lectr. U. Calif. Berkeley, 1989. Author: Foundations of Chemical Kinetics, 1960, Thermochemical Kinetics, 1968, 2d edit., 1976, Critical Survey of the Data of the Kinetics of Gas Phase Unimolecular Reactions, 1970, Atoms, Molecules, and Chemical Reactions, 1970, Chemical Calculations, 3d edit., 1971; editor in chief Internat. Jour. Chem. Kinetics, 1967-83; mem. editorial adv. bd. Combustion Sci. and Tech., 1973—; mem. editorial bd. Oxidation Communications, 1978-88, Revs. of Chem. Intermediates, 1979-87; mem. Hydrocarbon Letters, 1980-81; mem. editorial bd. Jour. Phys. Chemistry, 1981-85. Recipient Polanyi medal Royal Soc. Eng., 1986, Faculty award U. So. Calif., 1984, Presdl. medal U. So. Calif., 1986; Guggenheim fellow, 1950-51; NSF fellow, 1957-58, 71-72. Fellow AAAS, Am. Phys. Soc.; mem. Am. Chem. Soc. (Tolman medal 1977, Hydrocarbon Chem. award 1977, Langmuir award 1986, Orange County award 1986), Faraday Soc., Nat. Acad. Scis., Sigma Xi, Phi Beta Kappa, Pi Mu Epsilon, Phi Lambda Upsilon, Phi Kappa Phi. Home: 1110 N Bundy Dr Los Angeles CA 90049 Office: U So Calif University Pk MC-1661 Los Angeles CA 90089

BENSON, SUSANNE ELIZABETH, financial analyst; b. Ventura, Calif., Apr. 9, 1964; d. William Joseph and Josephine Mary (Somma) B. BA, Calif. Lutheran U., 1987. Aide to the blind retired tchr., home, Camarillo, Calif., 1978-87; religious edn. tchr. St. Mary Magdalen Ch., Camarillo, 1981-86; sales clk. Paseo Stationers, Camarillo, 1984-85, lead, 1985-87, asst. mgr., 1987-88; ops. mgr. Paseo Stationers/Kerth Enterprises, Oxnard, Calif., 1988;

financial analyst Integrated Systems Analysts, Inc., Camarillo, 1988—; tutor, math, Camarillo, 1985—. Youth ministry leader, St. Mary Magdalen Youth Ministry, Camarillo, 1986-88. Recipient Pope Pius X award, St. Mary Magdalen Ch., Camarillo, 1983. Mem. Calif. Lutheran U. Alumni Club, Am. Diabetes Assn., Calif. Lutheran U. Acctg. Assn. Republican. Roman Catholic. Home: 220 Lantana St Camarillo CA 93010 Office: Integrated Systems Analysts 751 Daily Dr Ste 208 Camarillo CA 93010

BENSUASKI, FERNANDO, financial consultant; b. Sao Paulo, Brazil, Oct. 13, 1949; s. Fernando and Luzia Cruz (Oliveira) B.; m. Margaret E. Smith, Nov. 15, 1972; children—Max, Andrea K. B.A. in Physics, Northwest Nazarene Coll., 1972. Asst. v.p. comml. loans Idaho First Nat. Bank, Boise, 1973-80; pres. Bensuaski & Co., Boise, 1980—; pres. Kahala Devel. Corp., Las Vegas, Nev., 1986—. Mem. Am. Bankers Assn., Am. Inst. Banking. Mem. Ch. of Nazarene. Office: 2300 Paseo del Prado Ste B107 Las Vegas NV 89102

BENT, MICHAEL WILLIAM, realty company executive, consultant; b. Oakland, Calif., Mar. 7, 1951; s. William Camp and Lorene (Howson) B.; children: John D., Chelsea L.; m. Laurie Sue Nelson, Dec. 15, 1984. Student Rutgers U., 1969-72. Lic. real estate broker. V.p. Century 21 Kato & Co., Denver, 1979-80; broker, mgr. Century 21 Hasz & Assocs., Denver, 1980-81; sec. Metro Brokers, Inc., Denver, 1982-83, v.p., 1983-84; sec., dir. Metro Brokers Fin. Svcs., Inc., 1984-85, dir., 1984-86, Metro Brokers, Inc., 1982-85 ; broker, owner Metro Broker M. Bent Realty & Mgmt. Co., Aurora, Colo., 1981-88; pres., broker Piney Creek Realty, Inc., 1988—; bd. dir. Metro Brokers, Inc.; past pres. Country Club Real Estate, Inc. Com. chmn., Boy Scouts Am., 1987—. Mem. Denver Bd. Realtors, Aurora Bd. Realtors, Realtors Nat. Mktg. Inst., Internat. Assn. Fin. Planners (cert. comml. investment mem., cert. residential specialist, grad. realtors inst.). Republican. Roman Catholic. Club: Optimist (pres. 1982-84, Heather Ridge chpt.). Home: 17096 E Dorado Cir Aurora CO 80015 Office: Piney Creek Realty Inc 15434 E Orchard Rd Aurora CO 80015

BENTALL, SHIRLEY FRANKLYN, church organization administrator; b. Regina, Sask., Can., July 28, 1926; d. Frank and Viola Louise (Thom) May; m. Charles Howard Bentall, June 15, 1946; children: Edna Louise, Kathleen Margaret, Joan Elizabeth, Barnard Franklin. BA, McMaster U., Hamilton, Ont., 1946; PhD (hon.), McMaster U., 1989. Retreat leader The Bapt. Union Western Can., 1971—; lectr. Bapt. Leadership Tng. Sch., Calgary, Alta., 1975-85; pres. The Bapt. Union of Western Can., 1976-77, Can. Bapt. Fedn., 1985—; mem. The Bapt. World Alliance Coun., 1985-88; mem. The Human Rights Commn. of Bapt. World Alliance, 1985-90. Writer Musings column for The Can. Bapt., 1965-88; author: Buckboard to Brotherhood, 1975, Amusings, 1980, The Charles Bentall Story, 1986, Discovering the Deep Places, 1988. Recipient Merit award The Bapt. Union of Western Can., 1982. Home: 500 Eau Claire Ave SW, Apt H 202, Calgary, AB Canada T2P 3R8

BENTLEY, PETER JOHN GERALD, forest industry company executive; b. Vienna, Austria, Mar. 17, 1930; s. Leopold Lionel Garrick and Antoinette Ruth B.; m. Sheila Farrington McGiverin, May 23, 1953; children: Michael Peter, Barbara Ruth, Susan Patricia, Joan Katherine, Lisa Marie. Ed., U. B.C. Sch. Forestry, Banff Sch. Advanced Mgmt. Chmn., chief exec. officer, dir. Canfor Corp., Vancouver, B.C., Can. Forest Products Ltd., Vancouver, B.C.; co-chmn., dir. Howe Sound Pulp & Paper Ltd.; pres., dir. Canfor Investments Ltd., Vancouver, B.C., Canfor Capital Ltd., Vancouver, B.C.; bd. dirs. Bank Montreal, Shell Can. Ltd., Seaboard Lumber Sales Co., Ltd., Seaboard Shipping Co. Ltd., Forest Indsl. Relations Ltd., Canfor-Weldwood Distbn., Ltd., Soc. Bank of Montreal Pension Fund; bd. dirs., chmn. Pulp and Paper Indsl. Relations Bur.; gov. Olympic Trust Can.; bd. dirs., chmn. bd. Balfour Forest Products, Inc.; mem. internat. adv. bd. Chem. Bank, N.Y.C.; co-chmn. Howe Sound Pulp and Paper Ltd. Bd. dirs. Jr. Achievement of Can.; past chmn., trustee Vancouver Gen. Hosp. Found.; mem. Bus. Coun. on Nat. Issues, Ottawa; mem. adv. coun. to faculty commerce and bus. adminstrn., adv. coun. faculty of forestry U. B.C.; trustee B.C. Sports Hall of Fame and Mus.; hon. dir. Can. Profl. Golfers' Assn.; vice chmn. bus. coun. B.C. Decorated Officer, Order of Can. Mem. B.C. Forestry Assn. (past pres. hon. life). Clubs: Capilano Golf and Country, Marine Drive Golf, Vancouver, Vancouver Lawn Tennis and Badminton; Thunderbird Country (Palm Springs, Calif.); Morningside (Rancho Mirage, Calif.); Royal and Ancient Golf (St. Andrews, Scotland). Office: Canfor Corp, PO Box 49420, Bentall Postal Sta, Vancouver, BC Canada V7X 1B5

BENTLY, DONALD EMERY, electrical engineer; b. Cleve., Oct. 18, 1924; s. Oliver E. Bently and Mary Evelyn (Conway) B.; m. Susan Lorraine Pumphrey, Sept. 1961 (div. Sept. 1982); 1 child, Christopher Paul. BSEE with distinction, Iowa State U., 1949, MSEE, 1950; DS (hon.), U. Nev., 1987. Registered profl. engr., Calif., Nev. Pres. Bently Nev. Corp., Minden, 1961-85, chief exec. officer, 1985—; chief exec. officer Bently Rotor Dynamics and Research Corp., Minden, 1985—; also chmn. bd. dirs. Bently Nev. Corp., Minden; chmn. bd. dirs. Gibson Tool Co., Carson City, Nev., 1978—. Contbr. articles to profl. jours.; inventor in field. Served with USN, 1943-46, PTO. Named Inventor or Yr., State of Nev. Invention and Tech. Council, 1987. Mem. IEEE, Am. Petroleum Inst., Soc. Tribologists and Lubrication Engr., ASME, Sigma Xi, Tau Beta Pi, Eta Kappa Nu. Episcopalian. Home: Bently Buckeye Ranch Minden NV 89423 Office: Bently Nev Corp 1617 Water St Minden NV 89423

BENTON, BRADLEY KEITH, electrical engineer, computer executive; b. Yuma, Ariz., May 21, 1957; s. F. Keith and Margaret Ann (Yarwood) B. B in Engring., U. Ariz., 1975-83. Computer programmer, operator Yuma Proving Grounds, 1974-76; ops. mgr. Wood Bros., Tucson, 1977-80; field svcs. engr. Bus. Products Svcs., Tucson, 1980-81; prodn. mgr. Applied Micro Tech. Inc., Tucson, 1981-82; dir. engring. Tri-Tech. Systems, Inc., Tucson, 1982-83; elec. engr., mem. tech. staff Hughes Aircraft Co., Tucson, 1983-86; elec. engr. Hughes Aircraft Co., Carlsbad, Calif., 1986—; prin. Small Computer Systems, Tucson, 1983-86, Carlsbad, Calif., 1986—. Recipient Superior Performance Rating, Yuma Proving Grounds, 1976, Outstanding Achievement award Yuma Proving Grounds, 1976. Mem. IEEE. Republican. Baptist. Club: Hughes Mgmt. (Tucson, Carlsbad). Home: 144 Sequoia Ave #4 Carlsbad CA 92008 Office: Hughes Aircraft Co 6155 El Camino Real Carlsbad CA 92008

BENTON, DONALD MARK, national media consultant; b. Agua Dulce, Calif., Apr. 8, 1957; s. Arlis Redford and Dorothy Helen B.; m. Mary E. Enders, Nov. 6, 1982; children Jennifer Marie, Adam Carson. Founder, chief exec. officer S.C.V. Temporaries, Newhall, Calif., 1978-83; v.p., bd. dirs. S.C.V. Temporaries, Newhall, 1978—; dist. mgr. Farmers Ins. Group, L.A., 1981-89; nat. sales trainer, speaker Am. Consulting Svcs., Vancouver, Wash., 1989—. Author: How To Start a Temporary Service, 1981; inventor aerovane. Clk., trustee Santa Clarita Community Coll. Dist., Valencia, Calif., 1981-88, pres. bd. trustees, 1985; pres. Santa Clarita Valley Jaycees, 1981-82; chmn. bd. dirs. Santa Clarita Valley unit ARC, 1983-86. Recipient resolution Calif. Assembly, 1981, ofcl. resolution L.A. County Bd. Suprvs., 1982, spl. recognition U.S. Congress, 1982, Outstanding Young Man award Santa Clarita Valley Jaycees, 1982. Office: Am Consulting Svcs 11818 SE Millplain Blvd Ste 311 Vancouver WA 98684

BENTON, ELIZABETH LAQUETTA, real estate executive, consultant, educator; b. Ozark, Ala., Apr. 1, 1936; d. Horace and Dovie Lee (Gulledge) Pippin; m. Charles Wayne Benton, Dec. 17, 1954; children: Lisa Ann, Charles W. Jr. Diploma Napier Bus. Coll., 1955; student Minot State Coll., 1963-64, U. Md., 1965, 67; grad. Realtors Inst. Cert. residential broker residential specialist. Sec., Aeronca Aircraft Corp., Ft. Rucker, Ala., 1955, Strachan Shipping, Savannah, Ga., 1956, USAF, Savannah, 1956-58; supr. Internal Revenue, Denver, 1959-60; adminstrv. asst. Chrysler Corp., Izmir, Turkey, 1961-63; substitute tchr. Dept. Edn., Honolulu, 1968-71; agt. Naomi Grout Real Estate, Ewa Beach, Hawaii, 1971-77; v.p., ptnr. Benton & Large Realty, Honolulu, 1977; pres., owner Liz Benton, Inc., Aiea, Hawaii, 1977—; dir. Founders Title & Escrow Co., Honolulu, 1983—; resource person, study on agy. Nat. Assn. Real Estate Lic. Law Ofcls., Salt Lake City, 1984, 85; mem. adv. council Hawaii Real Estate Research and Edn. Ctr., 1985—. Contbr. articles to profl. jours. Mem. Small Bus. Council Am., Honolulu, 1977—; mem. Aloha United Way, Honolulu 1974—; bd. dirs. Big Bros., Big Sisters, Honolulu, 1982—; chmn. Easter Seals VIP Panel, Honolulu, 1981—; mem. Realtors Polit. Action Com., Honolulu, 1980—; bd. dirs. Am. Cancer Soc., 1985-86. Recipient Vol. of Yr. award ARC, 1965, Outstanding Service award Dept. of Air Force, 1966, Top Producer award Naomi Grout Real Estate, 1972, 73, 74, 75, 76, Cert. of Excellence award Nat. Research Co., 1980-87. Mem. Hawaii Assn. Realtors (chmn. convention com. 1984, chmn. edn. com. 1979, dir.-at-large 1979, 80, bd. dirs. 1979, chmn. fin. and audit com. 1980, 81, sec. 1981, judge parade of homes 1982, treas. 1982, v.p. 1983, pres. elect 1986, pres. 1987, mem. strategic planning com. 1984, chmn. strategic planning com. 1986, chmn. nominating com. 1986), Honolulu Bd. Realtors (bd. dirs. 1978, chmn. election com. 1979, sec. 1979, chmn. multiple listing service, 1980, 81, pres.-elect 1982, chmn. realtor of yr. selection com. 1983, pres. 1983, chmn. nominating com. 1984, Realtor of Month award June 1981, Realtor of Yr. award 1981, chair strategic planning com. 1986, chair nominating com. 1986, liaison to real estate commn. 1986), Nat. Assn. Realtors (chmn. convention activities subcom. 1984, nat. bd. dirs. 1984-86, prof. standards and arbitration com. 1986, 87, state leadership forum, 1986-87), The Investment Group Realtors, Leeward Regional Group, Realtors Nat. Mktg. Inst. (cert., Hawaii chpt., v.p. 1981, pres. 1982, treas. cert. residential brokers chpt. 1985), C. of C. Office: 98-211 Pali Momi St Suite 411 Aiea HI 96701

BENTON, GLADYS GAY, teacher, musician; b. Fayette, Mo., Nov. 17, 1906; d. Benjamin Franklin and Celoa Alice (Perry) Hill; m. Robert Withrow, 1929; m. Charles B. Howell, July 12, 1939; children: Frances, Alice; m. Chester Roland Benton, July 7, 1951 (dec. 1989). BA in Music and Psychology, San Francisco State U., 1937; MA in Reading, U. Calif.-Northridge, 1979. Cert. Ryan reading specialist; Laubach tutor trainer; life cert. kindergarten, primary and elem. tchr., Calif. Tchr. Malen Burnett Sch. Music, San Francisco, 1925-30, Mendocino County, Solano, Imperial, Ventura County Pub. Schs., Calif., 1929—; owner, tchr. Gladys Benton Music Studio and Reading Clinic, Ojai, Calif. Vol. ESL tchr., Ojai, Calif.; helper Little House, Ojai, 1978; docent Ojai Mus., 1984-85; tutor Topa Topa-Meiners Oaks Sch., Ojai, 1988-89; dir., organist Meth. Ch., Oak View, Calif., 1952; asst. leader Girl Scouts U.S.A.; choir dir. Shakespeare Club, Ojai; vol. Boy Scout Camp, Meals on Wheels. Mem. Calif. Retired Tchrs. Assn., Am. Assn. Retired Persons, Legion Aux. (past pres.), Rural Carriers Aux., Music Tchrs. Assn. Woman's Club, Order Eastern Star.

BENZ, ALLEN, foundation administrator; b. St. Louis, Aug. 12, 1945; s. Allen Jacob and Sally Beatrice (Thurman) B. BA, U. San Diego, 1967, postgrad., 1967-69; MLS, U. Mo., 1971; postgrad., Ashby Inst. Profl. Devel., 1987. Tchr. St. Andrews Sch., Tipton, Mo., 1969-70; tech. svcs. librarian Twin Falls (Idaho) Pub. Library, 1971-73; computer coord. Geauga County Library, Chardon, Ohio, 1973-74; serials supv. Cleve. Pub. Library, 1974-76; staff librarian Aerial Phenomena Rsch. Orgn., Tucson, 1977-81; pres. Found. for UFO Rsch., Tucson, 1982—; cons. Mutual UFO Network, Seguin, Tex., Columbia Pictures Corp., L.A., 1976, Broadcast Svcs. Inc., Clearwater, Fla., 1988. Editor mag. UFO Commentary, 1972-74; contbr. articles to profl. jours. Mem. Pub. Access Com. of Tucson, 1979-80, Tucson Community Cable Corp., 1981--. Mem. Soc. for Advancement of Mgmt., Tucson C. of C., Plaza Club, Tucson Computer Club, Beta Phi Mu. Roman Catholic. Office: care Assn Mgrs Inc Found for UFO Rsch 3900 E Timrod Box 182 Tucson AZ 85702-0182

BENZEEVI, BENNY SIMON, corporate executive; b. Tel Aviv, Nov. 9, 1962. BS, U. Calif., Irvine, 1985. Ptnr. CREI, Santa Ana, Calif., 1984-85; pres. Let's Do Lunch, Irvine, 1986-87, BPG, Irvine, 1988—. Graphics specialist Cancer Surveillance Program, Irvine, 1988—.

BENZER, SEYMOUR, neurosciences educator; b. N.Y.C., Oct. 15, 1921; s. Mayer and Eva (Naidorf) B.; m. Dorothy Vlosky, Jan. 10, 1942 (dec. 1978); children: Barbara Ann Benzer Freidin, Martha Jane Benzer Goldberg; m. Carol A. Miller, May 11, 1980; 1 child, Alexander Robin. B.A., Bklyn. Coll., 1942; M.S., Purdue U., 1943, Ph.D., 1947, D.Sc. (hon.), 1968; D.Sc., Columbia U., 1974, Yale U., 1977, Brandeis U., 1978, CUNY, 1978, U. Paris, 1983. Mem. faculty Purdue U., 1945-67, prof. biophysics, 1958-61, Stuart distinguished prof. biology, 1961-67; prof. biology Calif. Inst. Tech., 1967-75, Boswell prof. neurosci., 1975—; biophysicist Oak Ridge Nat. Lab., 1948-49; vis. asso. Calif. Inst. Tech., Pasadena, 1965-67. Contbr. articles to profl. jours. Research fellow Calif. Inst. Tech., 1949-51; Fulbright research fellow Pasteur Inst., Paris, 1951-52; sr. NSF postdoctoral fellow Cambridge, Eng., 1957-58; recipient Award of Honor Bklyn. Coll., 1956; Sigma Xi research award Purdue U., 1957; Ricketts award U. Chgo., 1961; Gold medal N.Y. City Coll. Chemistry Alumni Assn., 1962; Gairdner award of merit, 1964; McCoy award Purdue U., 1965; Lasker award, 1971; T. Duckett Jones award, 1975; Prix Leopold Mayer French Acad. Scis., 1975; Louisa Gross Horwitz award, 1976; Harvey award Israel, 1977; Warren Triennial prize Mass. Gen. Hosp., 1977; Dickson award, 1978; Rosenstiel award, 1986; T.H. Morgan medal Genetics Soc. Am., 1986, Karl Spencer Lashley award, 1988, Gerard award Soc. Neurosci., 1989. Fellow Indian Acad. Scis. (hon.); mem. Nat. Acad. Scis., Am. Acad. Arts and Scis., Am. Philos. Soc. (Lashley award 1988), Harvey Soc., N.Y. Acad. Scis., AAAS, Royal Soc. London (fgn. mem.), Indian Acad. Sci. (fgn. mem.). Home: 2075 Robin Rd San Marino CA 91108

BENZIE-YOUSSEF, ARTA LOUISE, librarian; b. Du Bois, Pa., Feb. 5, 1955; d. Arthur Stewart and Bonnie Isabel (Smith) Benzie; m. Mohammad S.R. Youssef, May 26, 1979; children: Dane, Brie. BA in English Lit., Edinboro State U., 1976; MSLS, Clarion State U., 1979. Asst. dir., children's coord. Clarion (Pa.) Free Libr., 1980-82; children's librarian Oakland (Calif.) Pub. Libr., 1984-85, librarian, dept. head, 1985—; bd. dirs. Info. and Referral Svc., Clarion, 1981-82. Contbr. book revs. to various publs. Fund raiser Salvation Army, Clarion, 1981; storyteller Romper Room, Oakland, 1987. Mem. Calif. Libr. Assn., LWV (bd. pub. rels. Clarion 1981-82), Beta Phi Mu. Democrat. Home: 1557 Jackson St Apt 112 Oakland CA 94612 Office: Oakland Pub Library-Youth 125 14th St Oakland CA 94612

BENZING, DAVID WARREN, semiconductor equipment company executive; b. Perth Amboy, N.J., Feb. 11, 1953; s. Walter Charles and Ruth E. (McBride) B.; m. Pamela Jean Drummond, Dec. 28, 1972 (div. 1982); 1 child, Thor A.; m. Cathleen Lynn Hays, Sept. 12, 1985 (div. 1988); 1 child, Allison G. BSChemE, U. Calif., Berkeley, 1974; PhD in Chem. Engring., Princeton U., 1978. Sr. engr. Signetics Corp., Sunnyvale, Calif., 1978-81, Applied Materials, Inc., Santa Clara, Calif., 1981-82; dir. research and devel. Anelva Corp., San Jose, Calif., 1982-84; pres., founder Benzing Techs., Inc., Santa Clara, 1984—; lectr. Sci. and Tech. Inst., Mt. View, Calif., 1981-83; cons. Ube Industries, Ltd., Tokyo, 1984-87. Contbr. articles to profl. jours.; patentee in field. Mem. Electrochem. Soc., Thin Film Soc., Semiconductor Equipment and Materials Inst. Republican. Office: Benzing Techs Inc 301 Laurelwood Rd Santa Clara CA 95054

BERAN, ANDREW NAST, financial executive; b. Boston, Aug. 12, 1958; s. Mark Jay and Barbara Nancy (Black) B.; m. Patricia Linda Nast, Aug. 25, 1980. AB, Dartmouth Coll., 1980; MBA, Northwestern U., 1984. Fin. analyst automotive div. Intel Corp., Phoenix, 1984-86, Jerusalem, 1986-87; fin. mgr. Intel Corp., Albuquerque, 1987—. Bd. dirs. Tri-City Jaycees, 1985-87, B'nai Israel, Albuquerque, 1989; mem. fin. com. Tanaon Assn., Albuquerque, 1988-89. Office: Intel Corp FB9-09 Rio Rancho NM 87124

BERCQ, ALEXIS CLAUDE, air force non-commissioned officer; b. Paris, Mar. 10, 1960; came to U.S., 1964; s. Jean Claude Bercq and Sandra Shahan; m. Laura Anne Moyer, Apr. 10, 1982 (div. 1982); m. Susan Gail Van Pelt, June 11, 1986 (div. 1989). Enlisted U.S. Air Force, 1979; aircraft maintenance specialist Nellis AFB, Nev., 1979-83; flight engr. Norton AFB, Calif., 1983-86; flight engr. Spl. Air Missions detachment 1 89th Mil. Airlift Wing, Hickam AFB, Hawaii, 1986—. Mem. Calif. Rifle and Pistol Assn. (life), NRA (life). Republican. Office: Detachment 1 89 Mil Airlift Wing Hickam AFB HI 96853-5000

BERDEL, RICHARD LEE, agricultural researcher; b. San Diego, Sept. 19, 1936; s. Richard Ralph and Grace Eulah (Brower) B.; m. Mable Barbie Kinzie, Dec. 22, 1984. Student, Woodbury U., 1955-56, San Diego City Coll., 1957, U. Ariz., 1984; A in Gen. Studies, Pima Community Coll., 1986. Research aid USDA, Tucson, 1970-72; research asst. Agrl. Research Service USDA, Tucson, 1972-73, research technician, 1973—; cons. statis., Tucson, 1984—. Co-producer documentary on water harvesting, U. Ariz., 1983; contbr. articles to profl. jours. Mem. Tucson Community Cable Corp., 1984—. Recipient Cert. of Merit, USDA, 1972, 78. Mem. Tucson Computer Soc. Democrat. Unitarian. Office: Interactive Systems Analyst 747 Madison Ave Charlottesville VA 22903

BERDROW, STANTON K., power company executive; b. Long Beach, Calif., Oct. 4, 1928; s. Earl Lester and Martha Ann B.; m. Rosa R. Rottger, Feb. 22, 1951; children: Nancy, John, Matthew. BS, Armstrong Coll., Berkeley, Calif., 1950; postgrad. Sch. Bus. Syracuse U., 1951-52. Dist. advt. and sales promotion mgr. The Pennzoil Co., Los Angeles, 1953-59; v.p., mgmt. supr. Batten, Barton, Durstine & Osborn, Inc., San Francisco, 1960-77; v.p., dir. acctg. services Commart Communications, Santa Clara, Calif., 1978-80; v.p. communications and pub. affairs Sierra Pacific Power Co., Reno, 1980—. Adminstr. Sierra Pacific Charitable Found., 1987—; bd. dirs. PBS-TV, Reno. Served with U.S. Army, 1946-48. Mem. Am. Advt. Fedn. (Best in the West award 1985), Pub. Utility Communicators Assn. (1st award complete campaign 1986, 88, 1st award employee communications 1984), Am Mktg. Assn. (recipient Silver Effie award N.Y. chpt., 1987, 88), Pub. Relations Soc. Am. (past pres. Sierra Nev. chpt.), Reno Advt. Club, Newcomen Soc. Republican. Clubs: Innisfree Beach (Lake Tahoe, Calif.); Rotary. Contbr. articles to profl. jours. Home: 3925 Skyline Blvd Reno NV 89509 Office: Sierra Pacific Power Co PO Box 10100 Reno NV 89520

BEREAN, GEORGE SIDNEY, architect; b. Ketchidan, Ala., Oct. 12, 1943; Garth Berean and Helen (Gardikis) Berg; m. Theresa Lynn, Nov. 27, 1970 (div. 1988); 1 child, Elayna Maria. AA, Lovver Columbia Coll., 1964; BArch, U. Wash., 1969. Designer Ashley, Myer, Smith Architects, Cambridge, Mass., 1970-71; designer Wimberly Whisenand et al, Honolulu, Hawaii, 1971-72; assoc. Wimberly Whisenand et al, Honolulu, 1972-79, prin., 1979—; lectr. Travel Industry Mgmt., Honolulu; devel. authority Pacific Asia Travel Assn., San Francisco. Recipient Aga Kahn award, Aga Kahn Found., Trengganu, Malaysia, 1983. Mem. Hawaii Soc. Am. Inst. of Architects (Waterfront Com., Honolulu, 1988, Energy Design Guidelines Com., Honolulu Honor award), Internat. Council of Shopping Ctrs., Sales and Mktg. Execs., Pacific Club. Office: Wimberly Whisenand et al 2222 Kalakaua Ave Penthouse Honolulu HI 96815

BERENTSEN, KURTIS GEORGE, music educator, choral conductor; b. North Hollywood, Calif., Apr. 22, 1953; s. George O. and Eleanor J. (Johnson) B.; m. Jeanette M. Sacco, Aug., 1975 (div. 1977); m. Floy I. Griffiths, March 17, 1984; 1 child, Kendra Irene. MusB, Utah State U., 1975; MA in Music, U. Calif., Santa Barbara, 1986. Cert. community coll. tchr., Calif., pub. tchr., Calif. Dir. music Hope Luth. Ch., Daly City, Calif., 1975-81; condr. U. Calif., Santa Barbara, 1981-86; dir., condr. Santa Barbara oratorio Chorale, 1983-85; dir. music 1st Presbyn. Ch., Santa Barbara, 1983-84, Goleta (Calif.) Presbyn. Ch., 1984-85; minister music Trinity Luth. Ch., Ventura, Calif., 1985—; instr. Ventura Coll., 1987-88; dir., condr. Gold Coast Community Chorus, Ventura, 1988—; choir dir. Temple Beth Torah Jewish Community, Ventura, 1982-87; adj. prof. Pepperdine U., Malibu, Calif., 1988; chorus master Ventura Symphony Orch., 1987. Condr. oratorios Chritus Am Oelberg, 1983, Elijah, 1984, Hymn of Praise, 1988, cantata Seven Last Words, 1979, 84, Paukenmesse, 1989; soloist 15 major oratorio and opera roles, 1971-88. First place winner baritone vocalist Idaho Fedn. Music Clubs, 1971, recital winner Utah Fedn. Music Clubs, 1974. Mem. Choral Condrs. Guild, Assn. Luth. Ch. Musicians, Am. Guild of English Handbell Ringers, Sigma Nu (sec., song leader 1973-75). Home: 450 Frances St Ventura CA 93003 Office: Trinity Luth Ch 196 N Ashwood Ave Ventura CA 93003

BERG, CAROLYN NOURSE, research analyst; b. Des Moines, July 17, 1938; d. Archie B. and Katie Matilda (Taylor) Nourse; divorced; children: Christina Carole, Anna Lorraine. BA in History, U. Idaho, 1971; MBA, Ariz. State U., 1983. Sr. sec. U. Idaho, Moscow, 1972-74; owner, mgr. Something Different, Moscow, 1974-79, Inner Space, Moscow, 1979-81; coord. Moscow Downtown Assn., 1981-82; rsch. asst. Ariz. State U., Tempe, 1982-84; mgr. Door Store, Mesa, Ariz., 1984-86; rsch. analyst O'Neil Assocs., Tempe, 1986—. Home: 1202 S Mandan St Phoenix AZ 85044 Office: O'Neil Assocs Inc 412 E Southern Ave Tempe AZ 85282

BERG, DENNIS RAY, air force officer; b. Des Moines, Iowa, Oct. 13, 1946; s. Robert Anton and Connie Marie (Ward) B.; m. Cheryl Lynn Squire, Dec. 23, 1972. BS, U. Wis., La Crosse, 1970; MA, Cen. Mich. U., 1979. Commd. 2d lt. USAF, 1970, advanced through grades to lt. col., 1986; br. chief B-52 standards-evaluation 319th Bomb Wing, Grand Forks, N.D., 1975-78; air staff tng. action officer Hdqrs. USAF, Arlington, Va., 1978-79; SR-71 aircraft comdr. 9th Strategic Reconnaissance Wing, Beale AFB, Calif., 1979-81; assigned to Air Command Staff Coll., Air U., Montgomery, Ala., 1981-82; B-52 and KC-135 div. chief 320th Bomb Wing, Sacramento, 1982-85; bomb br. chief requirements SAC Hdqrs., Omaha, 1985-86, reliability-maintainability div. chief, 1986-88; chief nuclear ops. Pacific Command Hdqrs., Honolulu, 1988—. Mem. Daedalians. Republican. Roman Catholic. Home: 98-2013 Pahido St Aiea HI 96701 Office: USCINC PAC Box 13 Honolulu HI 96861

BERG, EDNA BARROWCLOUGH, volunteer; b. Paterson, N.J., Mar. 17, 1915; d. Charles and Cornelia (Patmos) Barrowclough; m. Lloyd Berg; children: Sally, Charles, John, Ann. BA, Mont. State Coll., 1936; MS, Mont. State Coll., 1961. Tchr. Hampton (N.J.) Sch., 1936-37; libr. asst. Paterson Pub. Lib., 1937-39, Purdue U., West Lafayette, 1939-42; libr. Bozeman (Mont.) Sr. High, 1961-84; vis. prof. Ind. U., Bloomington, 1966-67; adj. inst. Mont. State U., Bozeman, 1986. Chmn. Bozeman Pub. Libr. Bd., 1986—; bd. dirs. Gallatin County Hist. Soc., Bozeman, 1987—; mem. Am. NOrdic Ski Team, 1986-87. Mem. Mont. Libr. Assn. (pres. 1979-80), Mont. Sch. Libr. Assn. (chmn. 1971-72), Mont. Libr. Assn., Am. Assn. Univ. Women, ALA.

BERG, JACQUELINE M., interior designer; b. N.Y.C., Feb. 12, 1954; d. Felk and Barbara (Amsberg) B. BA in Interior Design, Ohio U., 1976; grad., N.Y. Sch. Interior Design, 1981. Interior designer Globe Furniture, Cin., 1976-79, H.M. Keiser and Assocs., N.Y.C., 1980-82; owner, designer The Quilt Exchange, N.Y.C., 1982—; pvt. practice interior design cons. N.Y.C., 1982—, San Francisco, 1984—; lectr. in field. Exhibitions include Eastern L.I. Quilters' Guild Show, Southampton, N.Y., 1983, Manhattan Quilters' Guild Show, N.Y.C., 1984, 85, Addison/Ripley Galley, Washington, 1987; contbr. articles to N.Y. Times, Quilt Mag., Family Circle Mag. and others. Recipient 2d place Best Original Design award Am. Mus. Sci. and Energy, Oakridge, Tenn., 1982, 1st place award Magical Colors Contest, Washington, 1982, Most Striking Use of Color Am. Mus. Sci. Energy, Oakridge, 1983. Office: 1625 Chestnut St San Francisco CA 94123

BERG, MICHAEL ERIC, director of research; b. Omaha, Aug. 29, 1948; s. Nathan Norman and Ida (Lea). BS in Chemistry, Creighton U., 1970; PhD, U. Nebr., 1977. Teaching asst. U. Nebr., Lincoln, 1972-75, rsch. asst., 1975-77; rsch. assoc. U. Wash., Seattle, 1977-79; chemist Ferrous Corp., Bellevue, Wash., 1979-81, chief chemist, 1981-85, dir. of rsch., 1985—. Contbr. articles to profl. jours. Co-leader Lake Wash. PASG, Kirkland, 1987—. Mem. Am. Chem. Soc., Am. Soc. for Testing and Materials (sect. chmn.). Office: Ferrous Corp 12729 NE 20th St #15 Bellevue WA 98005

BERG, PAUL, biochemist, educator; b. N.Y.C., June 30, 1926; s. Harry and Sarah (Brodsky) B.; m. Mildred Levy, Sept. 13, 1947; 1 son, John. B.S., Pa. State U., 1948; Ph.D. (NIH fellow 1950-52), Western Res. U., 1952; D.Sc. (hon.), U. Rochester, 1978, Yale U., 1978, Wash. U., St. Louis, 1986. Postdoctoral fellow Copenhagen (Denmark) U., 1952-53; postdoctoral fellow Sch. Medicine, Washington U., St. Louis, 1953-54; Am. Cancer Soc. scholar cancer research dept. microbiology Sch. Medicine, Washington U., 1954-57, from asst. to assoc. prof. microbiology, 1955-59; prof. biochemistry Stanford Sch. Medicine, 1959—, Sam, Lula and Jack Willson prof. biochemistry, 1970, chmn. dept., 1969-74; dir. Stanford U. Beckman Ctr. for Molecular and Genetic Medicine, 1985; non-resident fellow Salk Inst., 1973; adv. bd. NIH, NSF, MIT; vis. com. dept. biochemistry and molecular biology Harvard U.; bd. sci. advisors Jane Coffin Childs Found. Med. Research, 1970-80; chmn. sci. adv. com. Whitehead Inst., 1984; internat. adv. bd. Basel Inst. Immunology. Contbr. profl. jours.; Editor: Biochem. and Biophys. Research Communications, 1959-68; editorial bd.: Molecular Biology, 1966-69. Served to lt. (j.g.) USNR, 1943-46. Recipient Eli Lilly prize biochemistry, 1959; V.D. Mattia award Roche Inst. Molecular Biology, 1972; Henry J. Kaiser award for excellence in teaching, 1972; Disting. Alumnus award Pa. State U., 1972; Sarasota Med. awards for achievement and excellence, 1979; Gairdner Found. annual award, 1980; Lasker Found. award, 1980; Nobel award in chemistry, 1980; N.Y. Acad. Sci. award, 1980; Sci. Freedom and Responsibility award AAAS, 1982; Nat. Medal of Sci., 1985; named Calif. Scientist of Yr. Calif. Museum Sci. and Industry, 1963; numerous spl. and disting. lectureships including Harvey lectr., 1972, Lynen lectr., 1977, Priestly lectrs. Pa. State U., 1978, Dreyfus Disting. lectrs. Northwestern U., 1979, Lawrence Livermore Dir.'s Disting. lectr., 1983, W.H. Stein Meml. lectr. Rockefeller U., 1984, Charles E. Dohme Meml. lectr. Johns Hopkins U., 1984, Weizmann Inst. Sci. Jubilee lectr., 1984, U. Houston Nobel Prize Winners Series, 1985. Mem. Inst. Medicine, Nat. Acad. Scis., Am. Acad. Arts and Scis., Am. Soc. Biol. Chemists (pres. 1974-75), Am. Soc. Microbiology, Am. Philos. Soc., Japan Biochem. Soc. (elected fgn. mem. 1978), French Acad. Sci. (elected fgn. mem. 1981). Office: Stanford Sch Medicine 838 Santa Fe Ave Stanford CA 94305

BERG, TERRY ALAN, office machine company executive; b. Wenatchee, Wash., Dec. 19, 1949; s. Jean Patterson and Anne Laurence (Jensen) B.; m. Carol Ruth Richardson, Oct. 19, 1977; children: Andrea Jean, Ryan Patterson, Jarred Ray. AA in Bus., Wenatchee Valley Coll., 1970; AA in Police Sci., Olympic Coll., 1974. Mgr. Western Auto Co., Cleelum, Wash., 1972-73; patrolman Wenatchee Police Dept., 1973-78; dep. supr. Douglas County Sheriff's Dept., East Wenatchee, 1978-85; area mktg. mgr. Cert. Labs., East Wenatchee, 1985-86; area mgr. Savin of Wash., East Wenatchee, 1986—. Coach Big River Soccer Club, East Wenatchee, 1985, 86, 87, 88. Served with U.S. Army, 1969-74. Recipient Coaching award U.S. Soccer Fedn., 1986, 87, 88. Office: Savin of Wash 111 S Mission Wenatchee WA 98801

BERGANDI, HÉCTOR LUIS, illustrator; b. Rafaela, Santa Fe, Argentina, Dec. 11, 1943; came to U.S., 1984; s. Renato Oreste and Lucrecia Antonia (Tomas) B.; m. Marta Raquel Mayorga Sanchez de Bustamante, May 30, 1970; children: Maria Cecilia, Luis Esteban, Juan Nicolas, Fiorella Lucia. Student, Academia Bolognini, Buenos Aires, 1962. Shop clk. El Politecnico, Buenos Aires, 1962; sales rep. Editorial Tebas, Buenos Aires, 1963; illustrator Ingenieros de Combate, Santo Tomé, Argentina, 1963-64; advt. chief exec. Barbieri & Cia, Mar Del Plata, Argentina, 1965-66; pvt. practice decoratin Mar Del Plata, 1967; illustrator, writer Corsa Mag., Buenos Aires, 1968-76; illustrator, pres. Little Snail S.A., Buenos Aires, 1976-84; illustrator, owner Little Snail Inc., La Verne, Calif., 1984—. Recipient Moto award Automotive Mag. Pub., 1985-87. Mem. Soc. Illustrators L.A. (Silver medal 1986). Roman Catholic. Home and Office: Little Snail Inc 4436 Bixby Dr La Verne CA 91750

BERGEN, CHRISTOPHER BROOKE, opera company administrator, translator, editor; b. L.A., Jan. 11, 1949; s. Edward Grinnell Bergen and Alvina Ellen (Temple) Stevens; m. Tessa Jennifer von Grunebaum, May 7, 1972. BA, UCLA, 1971; MA, Yale U., 1977. Conf. officer IAEA, Vienna, Austria, 1973-75, data analyst, 1979-81; import mgr. COBEC Trading Corp., N.Y.C., 1978-79; assoc. Geissler Engring. Co., Oakland, Calif., 1982-83; dir. Yale Cons. Assocs., San Francisco, 1983-84; editor INPUT, Mountain View, Calif., 1984; adminstr. surtitles San Francisco Opera, 1985—. Editor profl. jours; translator operatic texts for projection during performances. Democrat. Home: 1450 Greenwich St Apt 604 San Francisco CA 94109 Office: San Francisco Opera War Meml Opera House San Francisco CA 94102

BERGENDORFF, FREDERICK L., advertising executive, writer; b. Bremerton, Wash., Feb. 7, 1944; s. Fred R. and Lola M. (Young) B. BA, San Diego State U., 1965; MA, Columbia Pacific U., 1983, PhD, 1983. Publicity mgr. Time-Life Broadcast, San Diego, 1966-68; promotion dir. KABC Radio, Los Angeles, 1968-69; dir. advt., promotion KNX CBS Radio, Los Angeles, 1969—; prof. San Diego State U., 1985—, UCLA, 1989. Author: Broadcast Advertising and Promotion, 1983. Recipient Clio award 1982, Nat. Addy award Am. Advt. Fedn., 1982. Mem. ASCAP, Advt. Club Los Angeles, San Diego State Athletic Fedn. (bd. dirs.), San Diego State Alumni Assn., Columbia Pacific Alumni Assn., Nat. Speakers Assn., Broadcast Promotion Mktg. Execs. (pres. 1984). Home: PO Box 3235 Seal Beach CA 90740 Office: CBS Radio 6121 Sunset Blvd Los Angeles CA 90028

BERGER, DAN LEE, newspaper wine columnist; b. Bklyn., Aug. 28, 1941; s. Joseph and Frances (Sarver) B.; m. D. J. Freeman, Nov. 28, 1976; children: Marc, Adam, Joel. BA, Calif. State U., L.A., 1967. Reporter AP, L.A., 1967-77; reporter, editor NFL Properties, L.A., 1977; reporter, columnist San Diego Union, 1978-86; editor, columnist Santa Rosa (Calif.) Press-Dem., 1986-88; columnist, reporter L.A. Times, 1988—. Author: Basketball: The Sports Playbook, 1975, San Diego: Where Tomorrow Begins, 1985. Named Wine Writer of Yr. Wines and Vines mag., 1988. Jewish. Office: Los Angeles Times Times Mirror Sq Los Angeles CA 90053

BERGER, DIANE KLEIN, small business owner; b. Miami, Fla., Oct. 18, 1946; d. Bernard L. and Molly (Bear) Klein; m. Stephen E. Berger, Dec. 24, 1967; children: Michael Allen, Gary David. BE, U. Miami, 1968. Cert. elem. and early childhood tchr. Dir. Headstart Program Dade County Pub. Schs., Miami, 1968-69, tchr. 2d grade, 1970-71; dir. pre-kindergarten program Oxnard (Calif.) Sch. Dist., 1969-70; tchr. Green Valley Pre-Sch., San Pedro, Calif., 1973-76, Tuvia Pre-Sch., Redondo Beach, Calif., 1976-78; co-organizer Temple Eilat Pre-Sch., Mission Viejo, Calif., 1978; mgr. wallpaper dept. Frazee Paint and Wall Coverings, Mission Viejo, 1978—; owner Thing-a-majigs and Whatcha-ma-callits, El Toro, Calif., 1978—; mktg. rep. Discovery Toys, El Toro, 1980—, Initial's Plus, El Toro, 1987—. v.p. B'nai Brith Women, Torrance, Calif., 1971. Research grantee U. Miami, 1968. Mem. Jewish Orgn. for Rahb. and Tng. Home: 24392 Mockingbird Pl El Toro CA 92630

BERGER, GARY JOHN, human resource survey consultant; b. Toledo, May 15, 1944; s. John Ora and Mary Elizabeth (Bott) B.; m. Miriam Elizabeth Swartz; children: April E., Stephanie A., Christine T. Student, U. Dayton, 1962-63; BS, Defiance Coll., 1972; MEd, U. Toledo, 1975; PhD, Century U., 1985. Dir. human resources Pillsbury Corp., Mpls., 1975-78, Shaklee Corp., San Francisco, 1978-81; human resources div. mgr. Impell Corp., San Francisco, 1981-84; sr. v.p. Am. Savs., Stockton, Calif., 1984-85; dir. Internat. Survey Research, Walnut Creek, Calif., 1985—; cons. L.I. (N.Y.) Lighting Co., 1983-84, Gencola, 1987, Amex Life Assurance Co., 1987, Candle Corp., 1987, Meruyn's, 1987, Case Internat. Harvester, 1988, Vanguard Group, 1988, Indland Steel, 1988. Author: Customer Service Practices by California Savings and Loan Employees, 1984, Adult Education Practices in Industry, 1975. Historian Carondelet Parents Bd., Concord, Calif., 1985-86. Mem. Am. Soc. Tng. Devel., Am. Soc. Personnel Adminstrn., Am. Edn. Communications and Tech., Organizational Devel. Network, Tau Kappa Epsilon. Democrat. Roman Catholic.

BERGER, HOWARD MARTIN, industrial and service company executive; b. Jamestown, N.Y., Aug. 31, 1927; s. Frederick S. and Millicant (Petschau) B.; m. Barbara Diane Lubin, June 25, 1950; children: Teri Anne, Patricia Jeanne, Lisa Diane. BSE in Aeros. and Math., U. Mich., 1948; MS, Calif. Inst. Tech., 1949, PhD, 1954. Program dir. Inst. for Def. Analyses, Arlington, Va., 1961-66; dir. strategic forces div. Dept. Def., Arlington, 1966-69; mgr. strategic analysis Xerox Corp., Rochester, N.Y., 1969-75; sr. project mgr. Rand Corp., Santa Monica, Calif., 1975-76; asst. v.p. Sci. Applications Inc., El Segundo, Calif., 1976-77; pres. HMB Assocs., Palos Verdes, Calif., 1977-78; v.p. Analytical Assessments Corp., Marina del Rey, Calif., 1978-80, Logistics Tech. Internat., Torrance, Calif., 1980-81; pres., chmn. bd. Robotix Corp., Torrance, 1981—; bd. dirs., chief fin. officer Keats Manhattan, Inc., Torrance, 1980—, Justin-Time Svcs., Inc., Torrance, 1980—. Contbr. articles to profl. jours. With AUS, 1946-47. Recipient numerous scholarships and fellowships. Mem. Computer and Automated Systems Assn. of Soc. Mfg. Engrs. (sr., chmn. Greater L.A. chpt. 1987-88). Republican. Home: 2108 Via Fernandez Palos Verdes Estates CA 90274 Office: Robotix Corp 23326 Hawthorne Blvd Ste 300 Torrance CA 90505

BERGER, JAY VARI, executive recruiter, import company executive; b. San Francisco, Aug. 31, 1944; s. Jack Vari and Ruth (Wasserman) B.; m. Margareta Ahlberg, June 14, 1969; children: Karin Britta Margareta, John Vari Sten. BS, U. So. Calif., 1966, MS, 1967, PhD, 1971. Assoc. dean admissions U. So. Calif., L.A., 1969-76, dir. admissions, 1976-82, asst. v.p. devel., 1982-86; v.p., ptnr. Cowen, Morris, Berger, Pasadena, Calif., 1986—; chmn. bd. Berger & Berger Internat., Pasadena, 1976—. Author: (juvenile) Willie the Worm, 1986; columnist Venture Connections, 1988. Bd. dirs. The Sycamores, Pasadena, 1985—; pres., trustee Chandler Sch., Pasadena, 1987—. Mem. Calif. Exec. Recruiters Assn., Calif. Assn. Ind. Schs. (bd. trustees 1988—), Annandale Golf Club, Valley Hunt Club, Pasadena Athletic Club, Rotary (bd. dirs. Pasadena chpt. 1988—). Home: 412 Oaklawn Ave South Pasadena CA 91030 Office: Cowen Morris Berger 100 S Los Robles Ave Ste 420 Pasadena CA 91101

BERGER, KENNETH JAMES EDWARD, oceanographer, consultant; b. Astoria, N.Y., Mar. 14, 1951; s. Edward Berger and Helen Lucille (Roland) Manfredi. BS, Pace U., 1972; MS, NYU, 1974, postgrad., 1974-78; PhD in Environ. Sci. and Engring., UCLA, 1982; MA, U. San Diego, 1989. Cert. community coll. instr., ESL tchr. Rsch. asst. N.C. State U., Raleigh, 1972, Inst. for Marine and Atmospheric Sci., N.Y.C., 1973-74; oceanographer U.S. Dept. of Interior, N.Y.C., 1975-79; postgrad. reseacher II UCLA, 1979-82; sr. scientist IWG Corp., San Diego, 1980-81; prof. Chapman Coll., San Diego, 1982—; section mgr., systems scientist Computer Scis. Corp., San Diego, 1984-85; cons. in marine sci., San Diego, 1982—; adj. instr. Cen. Tex. Coll., Clark AFB, Philippines, 1983, U. LaVerne, San Diego, 1985—. Contbr. articles to profl. jours. Served with USCG aux., 1981. Recipient Unit Citation award U.S. Dept. Interior, 1978, first place San Diego Brit. Car Club Council, 1980, second place San Diego Brit. Car Club Council, 1981; N.Y. State scholar, 1972; Pace U. Sci. scholar, 1972, San Diego State U. scholar, 1988; UCLA fellow. Mem. AAAS, Internat. Oceanographic Found., N.Y. Acad. Scis., Assn. Asian Studies, Kappa Mu Epsilon. Clubs: San Diego, San Diego MG (sec. 1983), San Diego MGA's (v.p. 1982), New Eng. MG "T" Register, Ltd. Office: Chapman Coll REC Naval Tng Ctr Bldg 214 San Diego CA 92133

BERGER, LEV ISAAC, physicist, educator; b. Rostov, USSR, June 23, 1929; came to U.S., 1978; s. Isaac Mark and Sara (Poltevsker) B.; m. Ninelle Rossine, July 2, 1956; 1 child, Yuri. MS in Physics, State U., Moscow, 1955; PhD in Physics, State U., Minsk, USSR, 1959; PhD in Tech. Scis., U. Steel Alloys, Moscow, 1968. Lectr. physics U. Nonferrous Metlas, Moscow, 1956-60; docent Physics U. Metallurgy, Moscow, 1960-62; prof. Poly. Inst., Moscow, 1962-77; sr. scientist New Eng. Research Ctr., Sudbury, Mass., 1979-81; lectr. physics Calif. State U., San Diego, 1981—; dir. div. Inst. Spl. Pure Substances, Moscow, 1962-71, Introscopy Research Inst., Moscow, 1971-77. Author: Ternary Diamond-like Semiconductors, 1969; contbr. articles to profl. jours.; patentee in field. Bd. dirs. Inst. Electronics San Diego State U., 1983—. San Diego State U. grantee, 1983. Mem. AAAS, Am. Phys. Soc., Am. Assn. Crystal Growth, Materials Rsch. Soc., Calif. Inst. Electronics and Materials Sci. (pres. 1981—). Home: 2115 Flame Tree Way Hemet CA 92343 Office: San Diego State U Dept Physics San Diego CA 92182

BERGER, NEWELL JAMES, JR., security professional; b. Pitts., Oct. 26, 1926; s. Newell James and Marjorie Ikler (Herndon) B.; m. Grace Darlene Ingram, Oct. 8, 1950; 1 child, Nell Darlene. BS, Mich. State U., 1958; grad., U.S. Army Command and Gen. Staff Coll., 1963, U.S. Army War Coll., 1972. Commd. 2d lt. U.S. Army, 1948, advanced through grades to col., 1970; chief corrections Hdqrs. Dept. Army, Washington, 1970-72; dir. security Office Surgeon Gen. U.S. Army, Washington, 1972-73, U.S. Army Health Svcs. Command, Ft. Sam Houston, Tex., 1973-78; ret. 1978; security cons. Phoenix and San Diego, 1979-84; chief plant security Teledyne Ryan Aero. Co., San Diego, 1985-86; with security memt. electronics div. Gen. Dynamics Co., San Diego, 1986—. Decorated Legion of Merit with two oak leaf clusters. Mem. Internat. Assn. Chiefs Police, Am. Soc. for Indsl. Security (cert. protection profl.). Republican. Episcopalian. Home: 44029 Northgate Ave Rancho California CA 92390

BERGER, WILLIAM HAROLD, physical therapist; b. Chgo., June 11, 1930; s. Max and Sadie (Ickovitz) B.; m. Nancy Morse, Dec. 23, 1951; children: Jay Alan, Mitchell Lee. BA, Roosevelt U., 1951; MA, Claremont Grad. Sch., 1975; PhD, Western States U., 1985. Lic. phys. therapist, Ill., Calif., Ariz., Hawaii. V.p. Med Tek Corp., Northbrook, Ill., 1976-80; adminstr. Musculoskeletal Rehab. Ctr., L.A., 1980-82; pres. Kustomer Kinetics, Inc., Arcadia, Calif., 1980—; dir. rehab. Riverside (Calif.) Med. Clinic, 1982-88; cons. health care 1988—; cons. FDA, Washington, 1979-80. Author: (textbook) Physical Therapist Aid Training Manual, 1988; inventor rehabilitation device, 1958. Mem. Am. Phys. Therapy Assn., Inst. for Profl. Health Service Adminstrn. Home and Office: Kustomer Kinetics Inc 1145 Encanto Dr Arcadia CA 91006

BERGESEN, JOANN MARIE, nurse, consultant; b. Oakland, Calif., July 25, 1948; d. Joseph Paul and Ruth Maude (Emmer) Carpaneto; m. William Bradford Bergesen, Feb. 27, 1971; children: Erik Bradford, Karl Gregory. Diploma in Nursing, Merritt Hosp. Sch. Nursing, Oakland, 1969. Cert. lactation cons. Maternity nurse Merritt Hosp., Oakland, 1969—; pvt. practice lactation cons. Hayward, Calif., 1986—. Mem. Am. Nurses Assn., Internat. Lactation Cons. Assn. Republican. Roman Catholic. Home and Office: 2075 Nina Ct Hayward CA 94541

BERGH, DAVID MORGAN, entrepreneur; b. Boise, Idaho, Aug. 8, 1947; s. Rolfe Roald and Margaret Rose (Morgan) B.; m. Jan R. Seda, May 17, 1975; children: Hillary Lauren, Benjamin Morgan, Salle Alberta. BS in Mgmt., U. Idaho, 1972. Chpt. cons., then dir. expansion, asst. exec. dir. Kappa Sigma Internat. Fraternity, Charlottesville, Va., 1972-75; propr. Morgan's Exchange, Boise, 1975-79, Strato Lanes, Mountain Home, Idaho, 1979—; concessionaire, various recreational concerns, Alaska and Idaho. Bd. dirs. Cen. Dist. Health, Idaho, 1983—; mem. Mil. Affairs Com. of 50, Mountain Home, 1985—. Mem. Idaho State Bowling Proprs., Bowling Proprs. Assn. Am., Nat. Restaurant and Beverage Assn., Kappa Sigma (dist. prs. 1975—), Elks. Republican. Roman Catholic. Home: Drawer B Mountain Home ID 83647 Office: Drawer B Mountain Home ID 83647

BERGH, DONALD CHARLES, regional representative; b. Staten Island, N.Y., Mar. 10, 1945; s. Harold Carston and Violet Rose (Jakaboski) B.; m. Peggy E. White, Dec. 27, 1972 (div. July 1979); 1 child, Jason Charles; m. Diane G. Curtiss, Mar. 28, 1980. AA, Am. River Coll., 1980; BA, Calif. State U., Sacramento, 1982. Instr. commercial graphics Calif. State U., Sacramento, 1982-84; instr. Clover Park Vocat. Tech., Tacoma, Wash., 1984; cons. quality control Bergh & Assocs., Tumwater, Wash., 1984-87. Publicity dir. Capital City Marathon Assn., Olympia, Wash. Mem. Toastmasters (adminstrv. v.p.), Lions. Republican. Home: 6614B Littlerock Rd Tumwater WA 98502 Office: The Ind Order of Foresters 10107 S Tacoma Way Ste A-1 Tacoma WA 98499

BERGH, WILLIAM EDWARD, finance company executive, marketing professional; b. Eau Claire, Wis., Feb. 6, 1960; s. Gary Laverne and Lorraine Daisy (Lee) B.; m. Shelly Rae Ottinger, May 10, 1980; children: Nathan E., Joshua L., Brent E. Student, U. Wis., 1978-80. Sales rep. Met. Life Ins. Co., Eau Claire, 1980-81; owner Nat. Fin. Group, Eau Claire, 1981—; mgr. Prudential Fin. Svcs., Phoenix, 1984—. Recipient Presdl. Sports award Pres. U.S., 1976, Badger Boys State award State of Wis., 1977. Mem. Nat. Assn. Life Underwriters (bd. dirs. 1987—), Phoenix Assn. Life Underwriters (pub. rels. dir. 1987-88), Life Underwriters Tng. Coun. (chmn. 1988—). Republican. Lutheran. Home: 10023 N 64th Ave Glendale AZ 85302 Office: 1717 W Northern #116Q Phoenix AZ 85021

BERGHUIS, PETER LANGE, sales representative; b. Glendale, Calif., Feb. 1, 1951; s. Floyd P. and Jennie (De Lange) B.; m. Carole Branch, Aug. 26, 1977; children: James G. and Jennie Lynn. AA, Glendale (Calif.) Community Coll., 1971; BA, Calif. State U., Los Angeles, 1973; postgrad., Pierce Community Coll., 1974. Ptnr. Berghuis Bros., Glendale, 1967-74, Berghuis Landscape Co., Glendale, 1974-78; owner Berghuis Landscape Co., Sun Valley, Calif., 1978-82; accounts mgr. Leland Capitol Corp., Century City, Calif., 1982-84; sales mgr. Greater Pacific Securities, Canoga Park, Calif., 1984; fleet mgr. Holiday Buick Oldsmobile, Lancaster, Calif., 1984-87; sales, client rep. Environ. Care, Inc., Sacramento, 1987—; chmn. Calif. Landscape Mag. adv. com.; mem. Grounds Maintenance Mag. Quality Rev. Bd. Chmn. 1988 Sacramento Valley Chpt. Landscape Achievement awards; v.p. Calif. Landscape Contractor's Assn. (v.p. 1989); judge Antelope Valley Fair and Alfalfa Festival; vol. Assn. for Developmentally Disabled, Nev. County. Recipient CLCA First Place award Residential Irrigation, 1977, First Place Spl. Effect, 1977, First Place Resident award, 1977, Outstanding Achievement in Residential Estates award, 1978, First Place Custom Residential award, 1979, First Place Pub. Works award, 1979, First Place Pub. Works, 1980, First Place Comml. Living Facilities, 1980, Outstanding Achievement Small Comml. Indsl., Residential Estates Medium Landscape Maintenance, 1980. Mem. Calif. Landscape Contractor's Assn., Bldg. Owners and Mgrs. Assn. Republican. Protestant. Club: Rotary (rep. 1987-88, chmn. North Sacramento chpt. Opportunity for Handicapped Bus Stop Constrn. Project.). Home: 2312 Ruldat Circle Rancho Cordova CA 95670

BERGMAN, CHARLES CARROLL, mechanical engineer; b. Wheatland, Wyo., Apr. 6, 1932; s. Charles Edwin and Marjorie Elizabeth (Ankeny) B.; m. Dolores Ann Hermanson, July 6, 1968; children: Christopher C., Scott Carl. AA, N. Wyo. Community Coll., Sheridan, 1952; BSME, U. Wyo., 1955; MSME, U. Idaho, 1973. Registered profl. engr., Idaho. Mech. engr. various cos., Tex., Idaho and Oreg., 1955-82, Amalgamated Sugar Co., Twin Falls, Idaho, 1982—; instr. Frank Phillips Coll., Borger, Tex., 1958. Mem. ASME, NSPE. Home: Rte 2 Box 5220 Twin Falls ID 83301 Office: Amalgamated Sugar Co PO Box 127 Twin Falls ID 83303

BERGO, EDWARD ARTHUR, marketing research company executive; b. Evanston, Ill., Apr. 29, 1938; s. Arthur Conrad and Mary Margaret (Hunter) B.; m. Phyllis Elaine Dahlk, Aug. 29, 1959; children: Steven Edward, Mark Conrad. BA, St. Olaf Coll., Northfield, Minn., 1960; BS, U. Wis., Milw., 1966. With consumer rsch. dept. Johnson Wax Co., Racine, Wis., 1960-70; European market rsch. coord. Johnson Wax Co., Amsterdam, The Netherlands, 1970-72; with mktg. resch. dept. Johnson Wax Co., Racine, 1972-74; pres. Wis. Rsch. Co., Green Bay, 1974-84, Sandia Mktg. Svcs., Albuquerque, 1978—, Bergo & Assocs., Scottsdale, Ariz., 1984—. Mem. Mktg. Rsch. Assn. (bd. dirs. 1983-84, 88—, Southwest chpt. 1984-88), Am. Mktg. Assn. (treas. Phoenix chpt. 1988-89). Republican. Office: 6535 E Osborn Rd Ste 402 Scottsdale AZ 85251

BERGSTEIN, SCOTT DRYFUSS, record company executive; b. Midland, Mich., June 8, 1952; s. Stuart J. and Ruth Ann (Labowich) B. BA, Am. U., 1974. Mgr. Sunshine Records, Encino, Calif., 1974; head buyer Wherehouse Entertainment, Hawthorne, Calif., 1975-76, West Coast Music Sales, Los Angeles, 1976; mgr. internat. ops. Casablanca Records & Filmworks, Hollywood, Calif., 1976-79; co-owner Bergstein & Green Mgmt., Hollywood, 1979-83; dir. artist relations Allegiance Records, Hollywood, 1983-86; dir. mktg. Chameleon Music Group, Hawthorne, 1986-87; sr. v.p. Higher Octave Music, Los Angeles, 1987—; internat. cons. various recording cos., Los Angeles, 1983—. Mem. New Dem. Coalition, Midland, Mich., 1968-72; del. Dem. State Conv., Grand Rapids, Mich., 1972. Mem. Nat. Acad. Jazz, Nat. Assn. Record Merchandisers, Nat. Assn. Ind. Record Distbrs. Jewish.

BERGSTROM, LAVONNE BERNADENE, educator, surgeon; b. Erskine, Minn., Oct. 17, 1928; d. Harry Bernard Reuben and Clara Marie (Bjornson) B. BA in Journalism, U. Minn., 1952, Bs in Medicine, 1955, MD, 1957. Diplomate Am. Bd. Otolaryngology. Rotating intern Mpls. Gen. Hosp., 1957-58; gen. practitioner Bd. Nat. Missions United Presbyn. Ch., Embudo, N.M., 1958-61, San Luis, Colo., 1961-65; resident otolaryngology Sch. Medicine U. Colo., Denver, 1965-69, fellow NIH, 1969-70, instr., 1969-70, asst. prof., 1970-74, assoc. prof., 1974-75; assoc. prof. UCLA, 1975-79, prof., 1979—; mem. rev. com. NIH, Washington, 1984-86. Co-author: Congenital Deafness High Risk Register, 1971; asst. editor: Birth Defects Atlas and Compendium, 1973. Recipient cert. award Am. Acad. Otolaryngology, Washington, 1981. Fellow Am. Bronchoesophagological Assn. (v.p. 1988—), Am. Triological Assn. (Fowler award research 1977), Am. Otological Soc., ACLU, LWV. Democrat. Presbyterian. Office: UCLA Div Head & Neck Surgery 31-34 1000 Veteran Ave Los Angeles CA 90024-1794

BERK, KAREN M., marketing professional; b. Bklyn., Mar. 29, 1943; d. Harry and Minerva G. (Liptzin) Sternberg. BA, UCLA, 1964. Field office mgr. Employment Devel. Dept., Sacramento, 1970-73, asst. dep. dir., 1973-76, adminstr. evaluations div., 1976-84; v.p. Pvt. Industry Council, Los Angeles, 1984-88; dep. dir. mktg. services Employment Devel. Dept., Los Angeles, 1988—; ptnr. Ideas In Motion, Los Angeles, 1988—. Contbr. to profl. publs. Mem. The Bus. Network. Home: 10400 Ashton Ave #8 Los Angeles CA 90024 Office: Employment Devel Dept 1525 S Broadway Rm 334 Los Angeles CA 90015-3030

BERKE, JUDIE, publisher, editor; b. Mpls., Apr. 15, 1938; d. Maurice M. and Sue (Supak) Kleyman; student U. Minn., 1956-60, Mpls. Sch. Art, 1945-59. Free lance illustrator and designer, 1959—; pres. Berke-Wood, Inc., N.Y.C., 1971-80, Manhattan Rainbow & Lollipop Co. subs. Berke-Wood, Inc., 1971-80; pres. Get Your Act Together, club act staging, N.Y.C., 1971-80; pres. Coordinator Pubs.,Inc., 1982-87; pres., chief exec. officer, Health Market Communications, 1987—; pres. Pub. and Media Services, Burbank, 1987—; pub., editor Continuing Care Coordinator, Health Watch mags.; pres. Continuing Care Coordinator Convs. and Seminars; cons. to film and ednl. cos.; guest lectr. various colls. and univs. in Calif. and N.Y., 1973—; cons., designer Healthy Lifestyles mag.; writer, illustrator, dir. numerous ednl. filmstrips, 1972—, latest being Focus on Professions, 1974, Focus on the Performing Arts, 1974, Focus on the Creative Arts, 1974, Workstyles, 1976, Wonderworm, 1976, Supernut, 1977; author, illustrator film Fat Black Mack (San Francisco Ednl. Film Festival award, part of permanent collection Mus. Modern Art, N.Y.C.), 1970; designer posters and brochures for various entertainment groups, 1963—; composer numerous songs, latest being Time is Relative, 1976, Love Will Live On in My Mind, 1976, My Blue Walk, 1976, You Make Me a Baby, 1982, Let's Go Around Once More, 1983, Anytime Anyplace Anywhere, 1987, Bittersweet, 1987, Sometimes It Pays, 1987; composer/author off-Broadway musical Street Corner Time, 1978; producer: The Reals Estate TV Shows 1988—; contbr. children's short stories to various publs., also articles. Trustee The Happy Spot Sch., N.Y.C., 1972-75. Mem. Nat. Fedn. Bus. and Profl. Women, Nat. Assn. Female Execs., Am. Acad. Polit. and Social Sci. Home and Office: 958 N Vista St Los Angeles CA 90046

BERKES, LESLIE JOHN, psychologist; b. Simbach, Bavaria, Fed. Republic of Germany, Aug. 18, 1946; came to U.S., 1949; naturalized; s. Leslie Michael and Marie Gizella (Villanyi) B.; m. Cheryl Kaye Stelter, Dec. 28, 1968; children: Adrienne Villanyi, Andrew Stelter, Kathryn Fowlkes. BS, U. So. Calif., 1968; MS, U.S. Naval Portgrad. Sch., 1969; postgrad., Union coll., 1971, SUNY, 1971-72; PhD, U. Calif., 1976; postgrad., Wright State U., 1983. Lic. psychologist, Ohio, Calif. Mgmt. auditor U.S. Gen. Acctg. Office, L.A., 1972-73; asst. rsch. specialist Pub. Policy Rsch. Orgn. U. Calif., Irvine, 1974-76; faculty rsch. assoc. Program Study Crime and Delinquency Ohio State U., Columbus, 1980-82; asst. prof. mgmt. sci. Ohio State U., Columbus, 1976-82; clin. psychologist Psychol. Cons. Inc., Columbus, 1981-82; psychologist Mgmt. Health & Devel. Corp., Malibu, Calif., 1983-86; v.p., chief tech. officer Netmap Internat. Inc., San Francisco, 1986—; adj. faculty Grad. Sch. Mgmt. U. Calif., Irvine, 1985-86; cons., presenter in field. Contbr. articles to profl. jours. Chair St. Monica's Town Hall, Moraga, Calif., 1988-89; co-dir. 7th grade edn. St. Monic's, 1988-89. With USN, 1968-72, Vietnam. Mem. Acad. Mgmt., Am. Inst. Decision Scis., Am. Med. Joggers Assn., Am. Phychological Assn., Am. Soc. Pub. Adminstrn., Calif. State Psychol. Assn., Internat. Assn. Applied Psychology, Soc. Indsl. and Orgnl. Psychology, Soc. Psychol. Study Social Issues, Beta Gamma Sigma. Democrat. Roman Catholic. Home: 292 Calle La Montana Moraga CA 94556 Office: Netmap Internat 505 Samsome St Ste 1500 San Francisco CA 94111

BERKMAN, SUSAN C. J., educational administrator; b. L.A., Apr. 17, 1953; d. Fred and Alice Hodes Josephs; m. Donald W. Berkman Jr., Aug. 10, 1974; 1 child, Daniel. BA, U. Calif., Irvine, 1974; MA, UCLA, 1977, Calif. State U., Los Angeles, 1988. Cert. adult edn. tchr. Specialist personnel mgmt. U.S. Civil Svc. Commn., Washington, 1974-75; teaching asst. UCLA, 1976-77; rsch. editor Regensteiner Press, Sherman Oaks, Calif., 1977; dir. music Braille Inst., L.A., 1978-82, asst. dir. student tng., 1982-87, dir. spl. projects, 1987-89, dir. bus. svcs., 1989—. Author: Teaching Music to the Blind, 1980, Teaching Music to the Visually Handicapped, 1982; (ednl. program) Just Like Me, 1983. Mem. Hermosa Beach (Calif.) Coordinating Council, 1986; bd. dirs. Community Family Guidance Clinic, Cerritos, Calif.,

1987—. Travel grantee, UCLA, 1977; Calif. State scholar, 1970-73, William S. Schwartz Meml. scholar, 1974. Mem. AAUW, Assn. for Edn. and Rehab. of the Blind and Visually Impaired (v.p. so. Calif. region 1987-88, pres. 1988—), Calif. Transcribers and Educators of the Blind and Visually Impaired, Kappa Delta Pi, Phi Kappa Phi. Baha'i. Home: 13227 Volunteer Ave Norwalk CA 90650-3123 Office: Braille Inst 741 N Vermont Ave Los Angeles CA 90029

BERKOWITZ, ROBERT DENNIS, business executive; b. Phila., Feb. 24, 1945; s. Allan A. and Esther (Wolf) B.; m. Barbara Canavan, Aug. 1, 1971; children: Charles Alexander, Allison Page. BS, Princeton U., 1967; MBA, Stanford U., 1969. Asst. to v.p. planning Bell Aerosystems Co., Buffalo, 1966-68; systems cost analyst Inst. Def. Analysis, Arlington, Va., 1969-71; chief spl. projects br. U.S. EPA, Washington, 1971-73; dir. corp. planning Syntex Corp., Palo Alto, Calif., 1973-81; chmn., chief exec. officer Hana Biologics Inc., Alameda, Calif., 1981-87, Cyto Scis. Inc., Cupertino, Calif., 1987—; also bd. dirs. Cyto Scis. Inc., Cupertino; co-founder, bd. dirs. Mgmt. Ctr., San Francisco, 1971-81; bd. dirs. Hana Biologics Inc. Coord. Princeton Med-Peninsula Sch. Com.; bd. dirs. San Francisco Bay Area Juvenile Diabetes Found. Mem. Am. Inst. Astronautics and Aeronautics, Princeton Alumni Assn., Stanford U. Bus. Sch. Alumni Assn., Calif. Thoracic Soc., The Am. Pub. Health Assn., U. Club of Palo Alto, Dial Lodge. Office: Cyto Sciences Inc 1601 Saratoga Sunnyvale Rd Cupertino CA 95014

BERKUS, DAVID WILLIAM, computer company executive; b. Los Angeles, Mar. 23, 1941; s. Harry Jay and Clara S. (Widess) B.; m. Kathleen McGuire, Aug. 6, 1966; children: Eric, Matthew, Amy. BA, Occidental Coll., 1962. Pres. Custom Fidelity Inc., Hollywood, Calif., 1958-74, Berkus Compusystems Inc., Los Angeles, 1974-81; pres., chief exec. officer Computerized Lodging Systems Inc. and subs., Los Angeles, 1981—. Author: (software) Hotel Compusystem, 1979; creator 1st artificial intelligence-based yield mgmt. system, 1987. Council commr. Boy Scouts Am., San Gabriel Valley, 1986, mem. exec. council. Served to lt. USNR, 1963-72. Recipient Dist. award of merit Boy Scouts Am., 1986, INC. mag. 500 award, 1986, Silver Beaver award Boy Scouts Am., 1988. Mem. Am. Hotel-Motel Assn., Audio Engring. Soc. (chmn. Los Angeles sect. 1973-74). Office: Computerized Lodging Systems Inc 4800 Airport Plaza Dr #160 Long Beach CA 90815

BERLAD, ABRAHAM LEON, engineering educator, consultant; b. N.Y.C., Sept. 20, 1921; s. Harry and Celia B.; m. Alice Mae Halber, July 10, 1949; children—Glenda, Edward, Nancy. B.A., Bklyn. Coll., 1943; Ph.D., Ohio State U., 1950. Research scientist NASA, Cleve., 1951-56; sr. staff scientist Gen. Dynamics Corp., San Diego, 1956-64; research scientist Gen. Research Corp., Santa Barbara, Calif., 1964-66; chmn. dept. mech. engring. SUNY-Stony Brook, 1966-69, prof., 1966-84, prof. emeritus, 1984—; adj. prof. combustion sci. U. Calif.-San Diego, 1984—; chmn. combustion sci. working group NASA, 1980—; energy cons. U.S. Dept. Energy, 1973—, U.S. Nuclear Regulatory Commn., 1979—; vis. prof. U. Calif.-Berkeley, 1963, U. Calif.-San Diego, 1973, Hebrew U. Jerusalem, 1973. Author numerous tech. papers. Editorial adv. bd. Combustion and Flame, 1964—. Served with U.S. Army, 1943-46, PTO. Grantee NASA, U.S. Dept. Energy, NRC, U.S. Dept. Agr., Dept. Def., NSF, others. Mem. Internat. Combustion Inst. (bd. dirs. 1974-82), Am. Phys. Soc., Com. Space Research, Internat. Astronautical Fedn. Jewish. Avocations: tennis, gardening. Office: U Calif La Jolla CA 92093

BERLO, ROBERT CHRISTOPHER, publications executive; b. San Francisco, Mar. 29, 1941; s. Ernest and Victoria Louise (Schoenstein) B.; m. Juanita Maria Vogal, June 14, 1969; children: Mark Douglas, John Louis. BS, U. San Francisco, 1962; postgrad., MIT, 1962-65. Tech. journalist Am. Chem. Soc., Washington, 1966-68; tech. writer Lawrence Livermore (Calif.) Nat. Lab., 1968-78, editorial mgr., 1978-81, graphics mgr., 1981-85, prodn. mgr., 1985-87, dep. dept. head tech. info. dept., 1987—. Author: Ovulation (Billings) Method of Natural Family Planning 1976, (with others) The Scientific Report: A Guide for Authors. Nat. Merit scholar, 1958-62. Mem. Soc. Am. Baseball Rsch., BaseLine Club. Office: Lawrence Livermore Nat Lab PO Box 808 Livermore CA 94550

BERMAN, BARUCH, electrical engineer; b. Israel, Nov. 10, 1925; s. Joseph and Sonia (Leoff) B.; m. Rose S. Goodman, Sept. 22, 1952; children: Sharon J., Orrie A. B.S.E.E., Israel Inst. Tech., 1947, diploma Ingenieur, 1948; M.S.E.E., Columbia U., 1957, postgrad., 1958-60. Chief engr., mgr. engring. and sect. head aerospace and indsl. firms 1948-66; v.p., asst. gen. mgr. engineered magnetics div. Gulton Industries, Inc., Hawthorne, Calif., 1974-77; mgr. power systems and control advanced tech. div. and energy tech. div. TRW, Redondo Beach, Calif., 1966-74, 77-82; with Satellite and Space Electronics div. Rockwell Internat., Seal Beach, Calif., 1982—; pres. Berman Engring., Palos Verdes Peninsula, Calif., 1966—. Contbr. articles to profl. jours.; patentee transistorized regulators. Served with Brit. Coast Guard, 1944-45. Recipient Outstanding Engr. Merit award Inst. Advancement of Engring., 1987. Fellow IEEE (exec. com. region 6 1981, nat. ethics com.), Inst. for Advancement Engring.; mem. Nat. Soc. Profl. Engrs. (nat. state govs. com.), Calif. Soc. Profl. Engrs. (past state chmn. profl. engr. in industry practice div.), Industry Application Soc., Indsl. Electronics and Control Instrumentation Soc., Magnetic Soc. Home: 28739 Trailriders Dr Rancho Palos Verdes CA 90274 Office: Rockwell Internat 2600 Westminster Blvd Seal Beach CA 90740

BERMAN, HOWARD LAWRENCE, congressman; b. Los Angeles, Apr. 15, 1941; s. Joseph M. and Eleanor (Schapiro) B.; m. Janis Schwartz, 1979; children: Brinley Ann, Lindsey Rose. BA, UCLA, 1962, LLB, 1965. Bar: Calif. 1966. Vol. VISTA, Balt., San Francisco, 1966-67; assoc. Levy, Van Bourg & Hackler, Los Angeles, 1967-72; mem. Calif. State Assembly from 43d Dist., 1972-82 (majority leader), 98th-101st Congresses from 26th Calif. Dist.; freshman rep. steering & policy com. 1983, mem. judiciary com., courts, intellectual property & adminstrv. justice, immigration subcoms., mem. fgn. affairs com., internat. ops., arms control subcoms. Pres. Calif. Fedn. Young Democrats, 1967-69 (budget com.); mem. exec. bd. Ams. for Democratic Action, Anti-Defamation League B'nai B'rith. Office: Cannon House Office Bldg Rm 137 Washington DC 20515

BERMAN, MARK LAURENCE, clinical psychologist; b. Los Angeles, Sept. 13, 1940; s. Joseph Erwin and Bernice (Levin) B.; m. Teresa Rose Davich, July 3, 1966; children—Alisa Ruth, Joseph Daniel. B.A. in Anthropology, UCLA, 1962; M.A. in Cultural Anthropology, Ariz. State U., 1964, Ph.D. in Psychology, 1969. Lic. psychologist, Ariz. Asst. prof. Pa. State U., 1968-70; research coordinator U. Wash., 1970-72; pvt. practice psychology, Phoenix, 1973—; cons. in field. Author (with others): Essentials of Clothing Construction, 1971; editor, co-author: Motivation and Learning, 1971; contbr. articles to profl. jours., chpts. to books. Mem. Ariz. State Task on Elder Abuse; co-chmn. Hispanic-Jewish Coalition; mem. exec. com. Community Rels. Council, Phoenix chpt. Am. Jewish Com.; mem. vol. task force Phoenix Union High Sch. Dist. Recipient Profl. Achievement award County Bar Assn., Profl. Achievement award Ariz. State Bar Assn.; grad. scholar Ariz. State U., 1963-68; Systems Devel. Corp. fellow, 1965; grantee Pa. State U., U.S. Office Edn., 1970-72. Mem. Maricopa Psychol. Soc. (pres. 1982), Ariz. State Psychol. Assn. (polit. action com. 1983—, Profl. Achievement award, ins. com.), Am. Psychol. Assn., Am. Assn. Family and Conciliation Cts., Ariz. Assn. Family and Conciliation Cts. Democrat. Jewish. Avocations: fishing, camping, traveling, reading, music. Home: 5714 N 21st St Phoenix AZ 85016 Office: 1702 E Highland Ave Ste 211 Phoenix AZ 85016

BERMAN, STEVE WILLIAM, lawyer, author; b. Chgo., Nov. 13, 1954; s. Mert E. and Lois Ann (Eliot) B.; m. Janet S. Friend, June 18, 1979; 1 child, Eliot Michael. BS, U. Mich., 1976; JD, U. Chgo., 1980. Bar: Ill. 1980, Wash. 1982, U.S. Dist. Ct. Ill. 1980, U.S. Ct. Appeals (7th cir.) 1980, Wash. 1982, U.S. Dist. Ct. 1982, U.S. Ct. Appeals (3d and 9th cirs.), U.S. Supreme Ct. 1986. Assoc. Jenner & Block, Chgo., 1980-82, Shidler, McBroom & Gates, Seattle, 1982-85; resident ptnr. Bernstein, Litowitz, Berger & Grossman, Seattle, 1986-89; ptnr. Betts, Patterson & Mines, Seattle, 1989—; adj. prof. law U. Puget Sound, Tacoma, 1983-85; asst. coach Syracuse U., 1976. Author: A Tarnished Hero, 1988. Mem. com. Juvenile Conf., Seattle, 1984; apptd. spl. counsel Wash. State Bar, 1988. Mem. ABA (trial practice com., discovery com.), ACLU (bd. dirs. 1989—), Lake Washington Rowing Club, Mercer Island Rowing Club. Democrat. Jewish. Office: Betts Patterson & Mines 1215 Fourth Ave Seattle WA 98106

BERMINGHAM, RICHARD P., restaurant and food products company executive; b. Glen Ridge, N.J., Apr. 24, 1939. Student, U. Colo. With Arthur Andersen & Co., 1962-67; v.p., sec. fin. Collins Foods Internat., Los Angeles, 1967-73, v.p., sec., gen. mgr. Collins Food Service div., 1973-81, pres., chief operating officer, 1981—, chief exec. officer, 1987—. Office: Collins Foods Internat Inc PO Box 92092 Los Angeles CA 90009

BERNAL, HARRIET JEAN, real estate salesperson; b. Cin., Sept. 28, 1931; d. Ernest Richard and Amy Lillian (Jeffries) Daniels; m. Gil Bernal, July 9, 1950; children: Gil Jr., Lisa, Nicholas, Colette, Michelle. AA in Theatre Arts, Los Angeles City Coll., 1949-62; student, Kimballs Real Estate Sch., Burbank, Calif., 1974; AA in Humanities, Glendale Coll., 1982; BA in Polit. Sci. Pre-Law, Calif. State U., Los Angeles, 1987. Lic. real estate agt. Dancer, entertainer Greek Theatre, Los Angeles, 1949-50; travel, reservation agt. Iver's Dept. Store, Los Angeles, 1970-73, editor, dept. store news letters, 1972-73; sec. to area supt. and social chmn. Los Angeles Bd. Edn., 1973-74; exec. sec. CBS-TV City, Los Angeles, 1974; real estate salesperson, relocation mgr. Century 21 Realty, Los Angeles, Pasadena, Calif., San Marino, Calif., 1974-86; real estate salesperson Coldwell Banker Residential, Pasadena, Caiif., 1986-89, Glendale, Caiif., 1989—. Contbr. articles on sch. sci. ctrs., schs. in Russia, and schs. for the handicapped for local sch. paper, Ann. awards. Pres. San Pascual Elem. Sch. (PTA), Los Angeles, 1969-70, hon. life mem., 1970—; fundraiser various groups to elect Mayor Tom Bradley, Los Angeles; wedding hostess Pasadena Ch. of Angels, Calif., 1980-88. Mem. Pasadena Bd. Realty (local govt. com.), Pub. Relations Com., Met. Player Guild. Democrat. Episcopalian. Home: 1075 Rutland Ave Los Angeles CA 90042 Office: Coldwell Banker Real Estate 3901 E. Foothill Blvd Pasadena CA 91107

BERNAL, JOHN ORIS, III, information systems manager; b. Nashville, Oct. 2, 1951; s. John Oris Jr. and Betty Sue (Parman) B. Staff clk. Pacific Bell, San Francisco, 1978-79; adminstrv. staff asst. Pacific Bell, 1980-83, asst. staff mgr., 1983-85, database specialist, 1985-89, info. systems mgr., 1989—. Democrat. Home: 235 De Montford Ave San Francisco CA 94112

BERNARD, ALEXANDER, city official; b. L.A., Apr. 23, 1952; s. Louis and Hannah (Bergman) B.; m. Diana LoRee Winstead, Dec. 17, 1976; children: Michael Alexander, Andrew Alexander. AA magna cum laude, Los Angeles Valley Coll., 1976; BS, Calif. State U., L.A., 1989. Parking meter collector L.A. City Clk.'s Office, 1973-79; police officer L.A. Airport, 1979—. Contbr. articles to profl. jours. Mem. NRA, Internat. Police Assn., Indsl. Relations Rsch. Assn., Am. Arbitration Assn., Calif. Peace Officers Assn., L.A. County Peace Officers Assn., Peace Officers Rsch. Assn. Calif. (chpt. pres. 1982-84, 85-87, state bd. dirs. 1984-85, 88—), L.A. Airport Peace Officers Assn. (pres. 1981—), Calif. Rifle and Pistol Assn. (life), Golden Key (life), Phi Kappa Phi. Democrat. Mem. Assemblies of God Ch. Office: LA Airport Police div 16461 Sherman Way Van Nuys CA 91406

BERNARD, DIANNA MAE, childcare educator; b. Grand Island, Nebr., Sept. 24, 1934; d. Leo Otto William and Hilda Helen (Muller) Bartelt; m. Robert Henry Bernard, Aug. 28, 1960; children: Heidi, Eric. BS, Concordia Tchrs. Coll., Seword, Nebr., 1957. Cert. elem. tchr., Calif. Tchr. Grace Luth. Ch., Channelview, Tex., 1954-55, Key West, Fla., 1957-59; tchr. St. John's Luth. Sch., Orange, Calif., 1960-61; substitute tchr. Redondo Beach (Calif.) City Schs., 1962-75; tchr. Little Red Schoolhouse, Manhattan Beach, Calif., 1980-84, Christ Luth. Sch., Rolling Hills Estates, Calif., 1984-85; dir., tchr. Rainbow River, Inc., Manhattan Beach, Calif., 1985—; dir. accredited school-age childcare Nat. Acad. Edn. Young Children, Rainbow River-Meadows, 1987. Block capt. Neighborhood Watch, Manhattan Beach, 1984—. Mem. AAUW (publicity chmn. 1981-83), Nat. Assn. Edn. Young Children, Aid Assn. Luths. (pres. Silver Star 1987-88), So. Calif. Assn. Edn. Young Children (publicity com. 1981-83). Republican. Lutheran. Office: Rainbow River Inc 1401 John St Manhattan Beach CA 90266

BERNARD, JAMES WILLIAM, industry executive; b. Brainerd, Minn., June 25, 1937; s. Paul Raymond and Maybelle Gertrude (Fynskov) B.; m. Maureen Day, Sept. 6, 1958; children: David, Kenneth, Kathleen. BS, U. Oreg., 1960. Trainee Univar Corp., San Francisco, 1960-61; resident mgr. Univar Corp., Honolulu, 1961-65; sales mgr. Univar Corp., San Francisco, 1965-67; v.p. Univar Corp., Phoenix, 1967-71; v.p. Univar Corp., San Francisco, 1971-74, corp. v.p., 1974-82; sr. v.p. Univar Corp., Seattle, 1982-83, exec. v.p., 1983-86, pres., chief exec. officer, 1986—, also bd. dirs.; bd. dirs. U. Wash. Exec. MBA Program, Seattle, 1984—, VMR Corp., Bellevue, Wash. Mem. Am. Chem. Soc., Seattle C. of C., Columbia Tower Club, Rainier (Seattle) Club. Republican. Office: Univar Corp 801 2d Ave Ste 1600 Seattle WA 98104

BERNARD, THELMA RENE, construction company administrator; b. Phila.; d. Michael John and Louise Thelma (Hoffman) Campione; m. Gene Bernard. Grad. high sch. Sec. Penn. Mut. Life Ins. Co., Phila., Suffolk Franklin Savs. Bank, Boston, Holmes and Narver, Inc., Las Vegas; constrn. site office mgr. Miles R. Nay, Inc., Las Vegas; adminstrv. asst to pres. N.W.S. Constrn. Corp., Inc., Las Vegas, 1982-86, corp. sec., 1982-86; gen. mgr., corp. sec. D.A.P., Inc. Author: Blue Marsh, 1972, Winds of Wakefield, 1972, Moonshadow Mansion, 1973, 2d edit., 1976, Spanish transl., 1974, German transl., 1977; contbr. articles to Nat. Doll World, other mags.; also song lyrics; past editor: Cactus Courier; editor/pub. The Hoyer Enthusiastic Ladies Mail Assn. Mem. Nat. League Am. Pen Women (v.p. Red Rock Canyon br. 1986-88), Original Paper Doll Artists Guild, Nat. Orgn. Miniaturists and Dollers, United Fedn. Doll Clubs. Office: PO Box 14002 Las Vegas NV 89114

BERNARDI, MARIO, conductor; b. Kirkland Lake, Ont., Can., Aug. 20, 1930; s. Leone and Rina (Onisto) B.; m. Mona Kelly, May 12, 1962; 1 d., Julia. Ed., Coll. Piox, Treviso, Italy, Benedetto Marcello Conservatory, Venice, Italy, Mozarteum, Salzburg, Austria, Royal Conservatory, Toronto. Began career as pianist Italy; music dir. Sadler's Wells Opera Co., 1967-69; music dir., condr. Nat. Arts Centre, Ottawa, Ont., 1969-82; music dir. Calgary Philharm. Orch., 1984—; prin. condr. CBC Vancouver Orch., 1982—; guest condr. with San Francisco Opera Assn., Vancouver Opera, Canadian Opera Co., Met. Opera, Chgo. Symphony, Washington Opera, Houston Symphony Orch.; prin. condr. with CBC, Vancouver Orch. Decorated companion Order of Can. Club: Savage. Office: Calgary Philharm Orch, 205 8th Ave SE, Calgary, AB Canada T2G 0K9

BERNEE, ANDREA LOREL, editor, operator; b. Chgo., May 30, 1960; d. Lewis Joseph and Rose (Eisenberg) B.; m. Scott Alan Davidson, Oct. 14, 1988. BA, U. Ariz., 1981; MS, Bklyn. Coll., 1984. Tech. dir. KZAZ-TV, Tucson, 1982-83; camera operator Video Cen., Inc., N.Y.C., 1984-85; prodn. tech. Doyle, Dane, Advt., N.Y.C., 1985; editor Golden Gaters Prodns., Corte Madera, Calif., 1985-86; ops. supr. KSTS-TV, San Jose, 1986-87; master control operator KEYT-TV, Santa Barbara, Calif., 1987; video instr UniLex Coll., San Francisco, 1988; head tape operator West Coast Video Inc., Brisbane, Calif., 1987-88; editor Coastar Prodns., Monterey, Calif., 1988-89; asst. editor The Post Group, Hollywood, Calif., 1989—; freelance video installer One Pass Film & Video, San Francisco, 1989. Vol. Woman Inc., San Francisco, 1988—, Peace Corps, Fiji Islands, 1985. Mem. Broadcast Edn. Assn. Democrat. Jewish.

BERNHARD, JON CASPER, architect, property manager; b. St. Paul, Feb. 10, 1961; s. James Casper and Jean Marie (Stougaard) B.; m. Theresa Ann Betting, Sept. 21, 1985. BS, N.D. State U., 1984, BArch, 1985. Draftsman Trice, Elson Assocs., Scottsdale, Ariz., 1985-86; project mgr. Vernon Swaback Assocs., Scottsdale, 1986—; property mgr. Studio Garden Offices, Scottsdale, 1987—; co-owner, mgr. Style Hair Co., Phoenix, 1988—. Prin. works include pvt. residences and beauty salon. Mem. Multiple Sclerosis Pancake Feed, Fargo, N.D., 1983-85, Meals on Wheels, Fargo, 1985. Mem. AIA, Smithsonian Nat. Inst. (hon.), Alpha Tau Omega. Lutheran. Home: 4150 E Cannon Dr Phoenix AZ 85028 Office: Vernon Swaback Assocs 7550 E McDonald Dr Scottsdale AZ 85253

BERNHARDT, RICHARD BRUCE, electronic company executive; b. Bronx, N.Y., Apr. 18, 1961; s. Irwin and Norma B. BA, U. Calif., Davis, 1983; JD, Calif. Western Sch. Law, 1986. Coord. legal and govtl. affairs Atari Corp., Sunnyvale, Calif., 1986—. Coach, lectr. Speech and Debate Dept. Cupertino High Sch., Calif., 1986—; commr. planning commn. City of Sunnyvale, 1987—. Mem. Calif. Western Internat. Law Soc., Nat. Forensic League (degree of Distinction and Excellence, 1979), Hammerskkjold Internat. House (pres., dir. community services 1979-81, life), Sunnyvale C. of C. (bd. dirs. 1988—), Phi Alpha Delta. Home: 1157 Snowberry Ct Sunnyvale CA 94087 Office: Atari Corp 1196 Borregas Ave Sunnyvale CA 94086

BERNHEIMER, MARTIN, music critic; b. Munich, Germany, Sept. 28, 1936; came to U.S., 1940, naturalized, 1946; s. Paul Ernst and Louise (Nassauer) B.; m. Lucinda Pearson, Sept. 30, 1961; children: Mark Richard, Nora Nicoll, Marina and Erika (twins). MusB with honors, Brown U., 1958; student, Munich Conservatory, 1958-59; MA in Musicology, NYU, 1961. Free-lance music critic 1958—; mem. music faculty NYU, 1959-62; contbg. editor Mus. Courier, 1961-64; temporary music critic N.Y. Post, 1961-65; N.Y. corr. for Brit. publ. Opera 1962-65, Los Angeles corr., 1965—; contbg. critic N.Y. Herald-Tribune, 1959-62; asst. to music editor Saturday Rev., 1962-65; mng. editor Philharmonic Hall Program, N.Y.C., 1962-65; music editor, chief critic Los Angeles Times, 1965—; faculty U. So. Calif., 1966-71; mem. music faculty UCLA, 1969-75, Calif. Inst. for the Arts, 1975-82, Calif. State U., Northridge, 1978-81, Rockefeller Program for Tng. of Music Critics; mem. Pulitzer Prize Music Jury, 1984, 86. Contbg. author New Groves Dictionary; contbr. liner notes for recordings; appearances on radio and TV, Met. Broadcast Opera; contbr. articles to Vanity Fair, Music Quar., The Critic, Opera News, Mus. Am., others. Recipient Deems Taylor award ASCAP, 1974, 78, Headliners award, 1979, Pulitzer prize for disting. criticism, 1981. Mem. Nat. Opera Inst. (ind. selection com. 1980), Pi Kappa Lambda (hon.). Office: Los Angeles Times Times-Mirror Sq Los Angeles CA 90053

BERNIER, PAUL-EMILE, educator; b. St. Michel, Quebec, Can., Oct. 22, 1911; came to U.S., 1947; s. Phileas and Claire (Lagueux) B.; m. Isabelle Enrichetta Siracusa, June 20, 1940. BSc in Agr., Laval U., Quebec, 1932; student, McGill U., 1935-36; PhD, U. Calif., Berkeley, 1947. Lectr., asst. assoc. prof. Faculte d'Agriculture, La Pocatiere, Quebec, 1932-45; geneticist Can. Agr., Ottawa, Ontario, Can., 1945-47; assoc. prof. Oreg. State U., Corvallis, Oreg., 1947-55; prof. poultry genetics Oreg. State U., Corvallis, 1955-77, prof. emeritus, 1977—. Contbr. articles to profl. jours. Mem. Oreg. State Employees Assn. (pres., dist. cir., State Employee of Yr. award 1968), AAAS, Poultry Sci. Assn. (Poultry Sci. Rsch. prize 1951), World's Poultry Sci. Assn., Genetics Soc. Am., Teratology Club, Kiwanis (pres. Corvallis chpt. 1968-69). Democrat. Roman Catholic. Office: Oreg State U Poultry Sci Corvallis OR 97331-3402

BERNINGER, RONALD WILLIAM, biochemist; b. Bloomsburg, Pa., Apr. 3, 1945; William Jackson and Bethena (Peckne) B.; m. Virginia Wise, Aug. 3, 1968. BS in Chemistry, Drexel U., 1968; PhD, U. Pitts., 1972. Fellow in immunology Johns Hopkins U. Sch. Medicine, Balt., 1975-77, instr., 1977-79, asst. prof., 1979-80; asst. prof. Tufts U. Sch. Medicine, Boston, 1980-86; sr. scientist NeoRx Corp., Seattle, 1986—; mem. Biomedical Research Grant Support Com., Boston, 1982-86; site visit mem. Nat. Inst. Health, Washington, 1980, mem. spl. rev., 1985-86; reviewer profl. jours., 1977-86. Author: Alpha-1-Andtrypsin Laboratory Manual, 1978; contbr. articles to profl. jours. Served as capt. U.S. Army, 1972-75. Mem. AAAS, Am. Chem. Soc., N.Y. Acad. Sci. Lutheran. Home: 10018 64th Pl W Everett WA 98204 Office: NeoRx Corp 410 W Harrison Ave Seattle WA 98119

BERNS, ARNOLD, artist; b. Emporia, Kans., Feb. 18, 1943; s. Arnold Jr. and Mary (Slough) B. Freelance artist 1970–. With USAF, 1964-68. Mem. Internat. Alliance of Theatrical and Stage Employees Local 480, Screen Actors Guild, Albuquerque Woodworkers Assn. (sec.-treas. 1984). Democrat. Home: 615 Mission Ave NE Albuquerque NM 87107

BERNSTEIN, ARTHUR HAROLD, venture capital executive; b. N.Y.C., June 8, 1925; s. Charles and Eva (Aronson) B.; m. Barbara R. Ettinger, June 24, 1951; children: Jeffry R., Diane. B of Chem. Engring., Cornell U., 1947, LLB, 1950. Bar: N.Y. 1950, Fla. 1956, Calif. 1972, U.S. Supreme Ct. 1962, U.S. Dist. Ct. (so. dist.) N.Y. 1951, U.S. Dist. Ct. (ea. dist.) N.Y. 1952, U.S. Ct. Appeals (2d cir.) 1952. Staff atty. N.Y. Cen. R.R. Co., N.Y.C., 1950-55; gen. counsel Ryder System, Inc., Miami, 1955-58, v.p., treas., 1958-65; sr. assoc. Lazard Freres & Co., N.Y.C., 1966-68; v.p. Norton Simon, Inc., Los Angeles, 1968-70; sr. v.p. Max Factor & Co., Los Angeles, 1970-77; mgr. ptnr. Calif. Capital Investor, L.A., 1980—; pres. Bancorp Capital Group Inc., Bancorp Venture Capital Inc., L.A., 1988—, also bd. dirs.; bd. dirs. Ryder System, Inc., Canoga Park, Calif. Served with USN, 1943-46, PTO. Mem. ABA. Jewish. Office: Bancorp Venture Capital Inc 11812 San Vicente Blvd Los Angeles CA 90049

BERNSTEIN, DEBORAH ELLEN, retail company official; b. San Juan, P.R., Feb. 4, 1956; d. Abraham Myron and Joan Sandra (Schultz) B. BA, Ariz. State U., 1978. Mgr. trainee Macys Calif., San Francisco, 1978-79; asst. buyer Broadway Southwest, Mesa, Ariz., 1979-81; buyer women's apparel Broadway Southwest, Mesa, 1981-83, May Co. Calif., North Hollywood, Calif., 1983-88; division mdse. mgr. May Co. Calif., North Hollywood, 1988—. Mem. Am. Film Inst., Mus. Contemporary Art. Democrat. Jewish. Office: May Co Calif 6160 Laurel Canyon Blvd North Hollywood CA 91606

BERNSTEIN, ELMER, composer, conductor; b. N.Y.C., Apr. 4, 1922; s. Edward and Selma (Feinstein) B.; m. Pearl Glusman, Dec. 21, 1946; children: Peter Matthew, Gregory Eames; m. Eve Adamson, Oct. 25, 1965; children: Emily Adamson, Elizabeth Campbell. Student, NYU. Pres. Young Musicians Found., 1961—. Concert pianist, N.Y.C., Phila., Chgo., 1946-50; composer music for UN radio shows, 1949; composer mus. scores, 1950—, including: Man with the Golden Arm, The Ten Commandments, The Magnificent Seven, Summer and Smoke, Walk on the Wild Side, To Kill a Mockingbird (Golden Globe award Hollywood Fgn. Press 1962), The Great Escape, The Birdman of Alcatraz, Hud, Sudden Fear, God's Little Acre, Sweet Smell of Success, Desire Under the Elm, Some Came Running, From the Terrace, Love With the Proper Stranger, Baby the Rain Must Fall, The Caretakers, The Sons of Katie Elder, Cast a Giant Shadow, Hawaii, Seven Women, True Grit, Thoroughly Modern Millie, The Shootist, National Lampoon's Animal House, Bloodbrothers, Meatballs, Airplane!, Airplane II, Stripes, Heavy Metal, An American Werewolf in London, Honky Tonk Freeway, The Chosen, Genocide, Five Days One Summer, Class, Trading Places, Ghostbusters, The Black Cauldron, Spies Like Us, Legal Eagles, Three Amigos, Amazing Grace and Chuck, 1987, Leonard Part 6, 1987; scores for TV include: Serpico, Little Women, The Rookies, Guyana Tragedy: The Story of Jim Jones. Recipient Motion Picture Exhibitor Laurel awards 1956, 57, 62, Emmy award for best music written for TV, Making of a President 1964, Acad. award for best original music score for Thoroughly Modern Millie 1968. Mem. Acad. Motion Picture Arts and Scis. (1st v.p. 1963—), The Thalians (v.p. 1959-62), Screen Composers Assn. (dir.), Composers and Lyricists Guild Am. (pres. 1970—), Nat. Acad. Rec. Arts and Scis. (dir.). •

BERNSTEIN, GERALD WILLIAM, management consultant, researcher; b. Boston, Nov. 25, 1947; s. Alan Irwin and Anne (Fine) B.; m. Kathleen Ann Chaikin, Jan. 12, 1985. BS in Aero. Engring., Rensselaer Poly. Inst., 1969; MS in Engring., Stanford U., 1978. Transp. engr., dept. transp. State of N.Y., Albany, 1969-70; transp. planner Kennebec Regional Planning Com., Winslow, Me., 1974-77; mgr. aerospace industries practice SRI Internat., Menlo Park, Calif., 1979—; session chmn. aviation workshop NSF, 1985; profl. conf. chmn. Contbr. articles to profl. jours. Chmn. Transp. com. Glenn Park Neighborhood Assn., San Francisco, 1982-85; dir. Balboa Terrace Neighborhood Assn., San Francisco, 1986—. Served with U.S. Army, 1970-72. Recipient Cert. Appreciation City of Waterville, Maine, 1977. Mem. Transp. Research Bd. of Nat. Research Council. Democrat. Jewish. Club: Toastmasters (Menlo Park, pres. 1986). Office: SRI Internat Menlo Park CA 94025

BERNSTEIN, SOL, cardiologist, medical services administrator; b. West New York, N.J., Feb. 3, 1927; s. Morris Irving and Rose (Leibowitz) B.; m. Suzi Maris Sommer, Sept. 15, 1963; 1 son, Paul. A.B. in Bacteriology, U. Southern Calif., 1952, M.D., 1956. Diplomate: Am. Bd. Internal Medicine. Intern Los Angeles County Hosp., 1956-57, resident, 1957-60; practice medicine specializing in cardiology Los Angeles, 1960—; staff physician dept. medicine Los Angeles County Hosp. U. So. Calif. Med. Center, Los Angeles, 1960—; chief cardiology clinics Los Angeles County Hosp. U. So. Calif. Med. Center, 1964, asst. dir. dept. medicine, 1965-72; chief profl. services Gen. Hosp., 1972-74; med. dir. Los Angeles County-U So. Calif. Med. Center, 1974—; med. dir. central region Los Angeles County, 1974-78; dir. Dept. Health Services, Los Angeles County, 1978; assoc. dean Sch. Medicine U. So. Calif., Los Angeles, 1986—; asso. prof. medicine U. Southern Calif. Sch. Medicine, Los Angeles, 1968—; cons. crippled Childrens Ser. Calif., 1965—. Contbr. articles on cardiac surgery, cardiology, diabetes and health care planning to med. jours. Served with AUS, 1946-47, 52-53. Fellow A.C.P., Am. Coll. Cardiology; mem. Am. Acad. Phys. Execs., Am. Fedn. Clin. Research, N.Y. Acad. Sci., Los Angeles, Am. heart assns., Los Angeles Soc. Internal Medicine, Los Angeles Acad. Medicine, Sigma Xi, Phi Beta Phi, Phi Eta Sigma, Alpha Omega Alpha. Home: 4966 Ambrose Ave Los Angeles CA 90027 Office: 1200 State St N Los Angeles CA 90033

BERNTSON, ERIC, Canadian provincial official; b. Oxbow, Sask., Can., May 16, 1941; s. Arthur and Johanna B.; m. Jean Howell; children—Kira, Lee Anne, Roland, Ben. Student U. Calgary. Mem. Sask. Legis. Assembly, Regina, 1975—, former minister of agr., dep. premier, govt. house leader, minister econ. devel. and trade, provincial sec., now Dep. Premier and Provincial Sec. Served with RCAF, Royal Can. Navy. Progressive Conservative. Club: Royal Can. Legion. Office: Sask Legis Assembly, Legislative Bldg Rm 322, Regina, SK Canada S4S 0B3

BERRIER, DAVID JEWELL, aerospace executive; b. Murphysboro, Ill., Mar. 20, 1934; s. Jewell Hilbourne and Thelma Irene (Walker) B.; m. Mary Rose Butcher, Dec. 26, 1954; children: James, Michael, Daniel. BSEE, U. Ill., 1957. Elec. project engr. GE, Ontario, Calif., 1960-65; engrng. specialist McDonnell-Douglas Corp., Long Beach, Calif., 1965-67; test project engr. TRW Systems, Redondo Beach, Calif., 1967-70; program mgr. Hughes Aircraft Co., Fullerton, Calif., 1970-79; systems dir. Aerospace Corp., El Segundo, Calif., 1979—. Elder, Christian Ch., Upland, Calif., 1964-65, Huntington Beach, 1987—. Lt. USN, 1957-63. Mem. AIAA, IEEE, Tech. Mktg. Soc. Am., Nat. Security Indsl. Assn. Republican. Home: 7071 Valentine Dr Huntington Beach CA 92647 Office: Aerospace Corp Box 92957 Los Angeles CA 90009

BERRING, ROBERT CHARLES, JR., educator, law librarian, dean; b. Canton, Ohio, Nov. 20, 1949; s. Robert Charles and Rita Pauline (Franta) B.; m. Barbara Rust, June 20, 1975; children: Simon Robert, Daniel Fredrick. B.A. cum laude, Harvard U., 1971; J.D., U. Calif.-Berkeley, 1974, M.L.S., 1974. Asst. prof. and reference librarian U. Ill. Law Sch., Champaign, 1974-76; assoc. librarian U. Tex. Law Sch., Austin, 1976-78; dep. librarian Harvard Law Sch., Cambridge, Mass., 1978-81; prof. law, law librarian U. Wash. Law Sch., Seattle, 1981-82; prof. law, law librarian Boalt Hall Law Sch., Berkeley, Calif., 1982—, dean sch. library and info. scis., 1986—; mem. Westlaw Adv. Bd., St. Paul, 1984—; cons. various law firms, Com. on Legal Exchange with China, 1983. Author: How to Find the Law, 8th edit. 1984, 9th edit. 1989, Great American Law Reviews, 1985; co-author: Authors Guide, 1981; editor Legal Reference Service Quar., 1981—. Robinson Cox fellow, U. Western Australia, 1988. Mem. Am. Assn. Law Libraries (pres. 1985-86), Calif. Bar Assn., ABA, ALA. Home: 1969 Marin Ave Berkeley CA 94707 Office: U Calif Berkeley Sch of Libr & Info Studies Berkeley CA 94720

BERRY, EDWIN X., physicist; b. San Francisco, June 20, 1935; s. Edwin Flower and Frances Alice (Foley) B.; m. Carole Dianne Wallace, Sept. 4, 1957 (div. 1972); children: Kim Andrew, Jay Scott, Ingrid Minette. BSEE, Calif. Inst. Tech., 1957; MA in Physics, Dartmouth Coll., 1960; PhD in Physics, U. Nev., 1965. Rsch. assoc. Desert Rsch. Inst., Reno, Nev., 1965-72; program mgr. NSF, Washington, 1972-74, Burlingame, Calif., 1974-76; pres. Atmospheric Rsch. & Tech., Inc., Sacramento, 1976-86, Edwin X. Berry & Assocs., Sacramento, 1987—; cons. Naval Weapons Ctr., China Lake, Calif. 1965-72, Zond Systems, Tehachapi, Calif., 1981—, Calif. Energy Comn., 1979-84, Westinghouse, 1988—. Contbr. articles to profl. pubis.; patentee in field. Mem. Am. Meteorol. Soc., Am. Wind Energy Assn. Republican. Office: Edwin X Berry & Assoc 6040 Verner Ave Sacramento CA 95841

BERRY, GLENN, educator, artist; b. Glendale, Calif., Feb. 27, 1929; s. B. Franklin and Heloise (Sloan) B.; BA magna cum laude, Pomona Coll., 1951; BFA (Honnold fellow), MFA, Sch. Art Inst. Chgo., 1956. Faculty, Humboldt State U., Arcata, Calif., 1956-81, prof. art, 1969-81, emeritus, 1981—. Exhibited one-man shows Ingomar Gallery, Eureka, Calif., 1968, Ankrum Gallery, L.A., 1970, Esther Bear Gallery, Santa Barbara, Calif., 1971, Coll. Redwoods, Eureka, Calif., 1989; exhibited in group shows Palace of Legion of Honor, San Francisco, Pasadena (Calif.) Art Mus., Rockford (Ill.) Coll., Richmond (Calif.) Art Mus., Henry Gallery U. Wash., Seattle; represented in permanent collections at Storm King Art Center, Mountainville, N.Y., Kaiser Aluminum & Chem. Corp., Oakland, Calif., Palm Springs (Calif.) Desert Mus., Hirshhorn Mus., Washington, others; mural Griffith Hall, Humboldt State U., 1978. Mem. Phi Beta Kappa. Home: PO Box 2241 McKinleyville CA 95521

BERRY, JANICE RAE, printing company executive; b. Baker, Oreg., Dec. 6, 1937; d. Frank James and Lilly Fae (Kennedy) Colton; m. Larry Joe Berry, Aug. 25, 1956; children: Frank Joseph, Nancy Rae Clark, Ellen Marie McCowan, Jeffrey Allen. Typist Times Litho, Forest Grove, Oreg., 1970-72, prodn. coordinator, 1973-74, prodn. mgr., 1975-81, plant mgr., 1982-85, mfg. mgr., 1986, v.p. mfg., bd. dirs., 1987—. Mem. Graphic Arts Tech. Found. (cert.). Republican. Roman Catholic. Club: Portland Lithographers and Printing House Craftsmen. Office: Times Litho 2014 A St Forest Grove OR 97116

BERRY, JOHN CHARLES, clinical psychologist, educational administrator; b. Modesto, Calif., Nov. 29, 1938; s. John Wesley and Dorothy Evelyn (Harris) B.; A.B., Stanford, 1960; postgrad. Trinity Coll., Dublin, Ireland, 1960-61; Ph.D., Columbia, 1967; m. Arlene Ellen Sossin, Oct. 7, 1978; children—Elise, John Jordan, Kaitlyn. Research assoc. Judge Baker Guidance Center, Boston, 1965-66; psychology asso. Napa State Hosp., Imola, Calif., 1966-67, staff psychologist, 1967-75, program asst., 1975-76; program dir. Met. State Hosp., Norwalk, Calif., 1976-77; asst. supt. Empire (Calif.) Union Sch. Dist., 1977—. Mem. Am. Psychol. Assn., Assn. Calif. Sch. Adminstrs., Sigma Xi. Contbg. author: Life History Research in Psychopathology, 1970. Home: 920 Eastridge Dr Modesto CA 95355 Office: Empire Union Sch Dist 200 G St Empire CA 95319

BERRY, KATHLEEN ANN, foundation administrator; b. Anaheim, Calif., July 12, 1961; d. Bryan Kent and Darlene Louise (Waller) B. BJ in Pub. Rels., U. Nev., Reno, 1983. Communications asst. Nat. Judicial Coll., Reno, 1983; editorial asst. Nat. Coun. of Juvenile and Family Ct. Judges, Reno, 1983-84; coord. pub. rels. MS Soc., Reno, 1984-85, exec. dir., 1985-88; publicist Reno Conv. and Visitors Authority, 1988—. Active media com., spl. events com., Internat. Spl. Olympics, Reno, 1988—; chmn. edn. project com. Aid Abused Women, Sparks, Nev., 1983; image task force Biggest Little City Com., Reno, 1987. Mem. Pub. Rels. Soc. (treas. 1986-87, student liaision 1987—). Republican. Office: Reno Conv and Visitors Authority PO Box 837 Reno NV 89504-0837

BERRY, RANSFORD BRONSON, service executive; b. Seattle, June 6, 1943; s. Warren Hayden and gloria Jacquine (Bronson) B.; m. Nancy Corbin, Aug. 20, 1966; children: Jennifer Elaine, Elizabeth Anne. BA, Whitworth Coll., Spokane, Wash., 1966. Asst. dir. fed. programs San Diego Unified Sch. Dist., 1967-71; regional dir. Behavioral Rsch. Labs., Inc., Atlanta, 1971-73; dir. agy. devel. Allied Van Lines, Inc., Chgo., 1973-76; v.p. sales & mktg. Graebel Mowers, Inc., Wausau, Wis., 1977-86; chief oper. officer All Methods Moving Systems, Phoenix, 1988-89, Scottsdale Jaguar/Range Rover, 1989—; pres. Jr. Achievement Ctr. Ariz., Inc., Phoenix. Bd. dirs. Am. Humanics, Performing Arts Found., 1980-84, Valley Leadership, JuvenileJustice State Adv. Coun. Mem. Pres's. Roundtable, Rotary (bd. dirs.). Republican. Presbyterian. Home: 301-E Country Gables Dr Phoenix AZ 85022 Office: Scottsdale Jaguar/Range Rover Scottsdale AZ 85257

BERRY, ROBERT BRUCE, electrical engineer; b. Albuquerque, Aug. 19, 1957; s. Robert Earl and Anita Jo (Cantrell) B.; m. Mary Alice Arnold, Oct. 15, 1983. BS in Chemistry/Biology, N.Mex. State U., 1979; MSEE, U. N.Mex., 1982. Device engr. Signetics Corp., Albuquerque, 1982-85; failure analyst Allied-Signal Aerospace, Albuquerque, 1985—. Pres., search and rescue, N.Mex. Bloodhound Assn., Albuquerque, 1985-87; v.p. Cibola Search and Rescue, Albuquerque, 1987-89. Mem. Harmony Lodge #75. Republican. Episcopalian. Office: Allied-Signal 1515 Eubank SE Albuquerque NM 87123

BERRY, ROBERT EDWARD FRASER, retired bishop; b. Ottawa, Ont., Can., Jan. 21, 1926; s. Samuel and Clara (Hartley) B.; m. Margaret Joan Trevorrow, May 12, 1951; children: Christopher Fraser, Elisabeth Joan. B.A., Sir George Williams Coll., 1950; B.D., McGill U., 1953; D.D. (hon.), Montreal Diocesan Theol. Coll., 1972. Ordained deacon Anglican Ch. Can., 1953, ordained priest, 1954. Asst. curate Christ Ch. Cathedral, Victoria, B.C., Can., 1953-55; Priest St. Margaret's Ch., Hamilton, Ont., 1955-61; priest St. Mark's Ch., Orangeville, Ont., 1961-63, St. Luke's Ch., Winnipeg, Man., Can., 1963-67, St. Michael and All Angels Ch., Kelowna, B.C., 1967; supr. pastor Central Okanagan Region Diocese of Kootenay, Kelowna, 1967-71, bishop, 1971-89. Served with RCAF, 1943-45. Home: 1857 Maple St, Kelowna, BC Canada V1Y 1H4

BERRY, THOMAS CLAYTON, securities broker, brokerage owner, energy company owner; b. Roswell, N.Mex., May 23, 1948; s. Homer C. and Betty J. (Cronic) B.; m. Bonnie L. Shamas, May 30, 1969; children: Lisa C., Joshua E. AA, N.Mex. Mil. Inst., 1969; Assoc. course in real estate, 1984, NASD DPP rep. and prin. courses, 1983. Farmer Berry Farms, Dexter, N.Mex., 1969-72; sec., dir. Victor & Assoc., Phoenix, 1972-74; dir., foreman Berry Land & Cattle, Dexter, 1974-82; v.p., dir. Trinity Investment Corp., Roswell, 1982-83; pres., dir. Jordache Investments, Roswell, 1982-83; v.p., dir. Diamond Braich Realtors, Roswell, 1982-83; v.p., dir. Tierra Fin. Group, Roswell, 1985-86, pres., dir., 1986—; v.p., dir. Tierra Capital Corp., Roswell, 1984-86, pres., dir., 1986—; pres., dir. Tierra Energy Corp., Roswell, 1987—. Deacon North Phoenix Bapt. Ch., Phoenix, 1973-74; bd. dirs. First Assembly of God Ch., Roswell, youth group sponsor, 1978—; coach Roswell Youth Soccer, 1978—. Named one of Outstanding Men of Am., 1982. Mem. Nat. Assn. Securities Dealers, Roswell Realtor Assn., N.Mex. Realtor Assn.,. Republican. Mem. Nazarene Ch. Home: 2010 Brazos Roswell NM 88201 Office: Tierra Fin Group Inc 400 N Pennsylvania Roswell NM 88201

BERRY, WILLIAM BENJAMIN NEWELL, geologist, museum administrator; b. Boston, Sept. 1, 1931; s. John King and Margaret Elizabeth (Newell) B.; m. Suzanne Foster Spaulding, June 10, 1961; 1 child, Bradford Brown. A.B., Harvard U., 1953, A.M., 1955; Ph.D., Yale U., 1957. Asst. prof. geology U. Houston, 1957-58; asst. prof. to prof. paleontology U. Calif., Berkeley, 1958—; curator Mus. of Paleontology U. Calif., Berkeley, 1960-75; dir. Mus. of Paleontology U. Calif., 1975-87, chmn. dept. paleontology, 1975-87; cons. U.S. Geol. Survey. Author: Growth of a Prehistoric Time Scale, 1968, revised ed., 1987; assoc. editor Paleoceanography; contbr. numerous articles on stratigraphic and paleontol. subjects to profl. jours.; editor publs. in geol. scis. Guggenheim Found. fellow, 1966-67. Fellow Calif. Acad. Scis.; mem. Paleontol. Soc., Geol. Soc. Norway, Internat. Platform Assn., Explorers Club, Commonwealth Club Calif. Home: 1366 Summit Rd Berkeley CA 94708 Office: U Calif Mus Paleontology Earth Scis Bldg Berkeley CA 94720

BERRYESSA, RICHARD GREAVES, cardiovascular perfusion educator; b. Ogden, Utah, Feb. 9, 1947; s. Max Joseph and Janet Marion (Greaves) B.; m. Susan Reeder, Aug. 9, 1969; children: Shannon, Adrien, Lauren. Student, Brigham Young U., 1966, 70, U. Utah, 1971; BS, U. Tex., Houston, 1986. Surg. asst. Western Cardiovascular Assocs., Salt Lake City, 1973-74; chief perfusionist Western Cardiovascular Assocs., 1980-83; perfusionist Rumel Chest Clinic, 1974-79; assoc. dir. clin. perfusion tech. Tex. Heart Inst., Houston, 1983-84; regional mgr. PSICOR, Inc., San Diego, 1984-88; cons. continuing edn. PSICOR, Inc., 1988—; examiner Am. Bd. Cardiovascular Perfusion, 1978-86; clin. instr. Sch. Medicine, U. Colo., Denver, 1986-88; instr. perfusion tech. prog. Grossmont Coll., San Diego, 1988; presenter in field. Manuscript editor Jour. Extracorporeal Tech., 1980-88; contbr. articles to profl. jours.; patentee in field. Fellow Am. Soc. Extracorporeal Tech.; mem. Am. Acad. Cardiovascular Perfusion. Mormon. Office: PSICOR Inc 16818 Via del Campo Ct San Diego CA 92127

BERTAIN, G(EORGE) JOSEPH, JR., lawyer; b. Scotia, Calif., Mar. 9, 1929; s. George J. and Ellen Veronica (Canty) B.; m. Bernardine Joy Galli, May 11, 1957; 1 son, Joseph F. A.B., St. Mary's Coll. of Calif., 1951; J.D., Cath. U. Am., 1955. Bar: Calif. Assoc. Joseph L. Alioto, San Francisco, 1955-57, 59-65; asst. U.S. Atty. No. Dist. Calif., 1957-59; pvt. practice of law San Francisco, 1966—. Editor-in-chief, Law Rev. Cath. U. Am. (vol. 5), 1954-55. Chmn. San Francisco Lawyers Com. for Elections of Gov./Pres. Ronald Reagan, 1966, 70, 80, 84; spl. confidential adviser to Gov. Reagan for jud. selection, San Francisco, 1967-74; chmn. San Francisco Lawyers for Better Govt., 1978—; confidential adv. on jud. selection to Senator Hayakawa, 1981-82, to Gov. Deukmejian, 1983—; bd. regents St. Mary's Coll. of Calif., 1980—; mem. civilian adv. com. U.S. 6th Army, Presidio, San Francisco. Recipient De La Salle medal St. Mary's Coll. of Calif., 1951, Signum Fidei award St. Mary's Coll. of Calif., 1976. Mem. ABA, Calif. Bar Assn., Fed. Bar Assn. (del. 9th Circuit Jud. Conf. 1967-76), Am. Judicature Soc., St. Thomas More Soc. San Francisco, Calif. Acad. Scis., Mus. Soc., Assn. Former U.S. Attys. and Asst. U.S. Attys. of No. Calif. (past pres.), Supreme Ct. Hist. Soc., Commonwealth Club, Commercial Club, Western Assn., K.C., Order of Knights of Malta. Republican. Roman Catholic. Office: Alcoa Bldg Ste 1600 One Maritime Pla San Francisco CA 94111

BERTHELSDORF, SIEGFRIED, psychiatrist; b. Shannon County, Mo., June 16, 1911; s. Richard and Amalia (Morschenko) von Berthelsdorf; m. Mildred Friederich, May 13, 1945; children: Richard, Victor, Dianne. BA, U. Oreg., 1934, MA, MD, 1939. Lic. psychiatrist, psychoanalyst. Intern U.S. Marine Hosp., Staten Island, N.Y., 1939-40; psychiat. intern Bellevue Hosp., N.Y.C., 1940-41; psychiat. resident N.Y. State Psychiat. Hosp., N.Y.C., 1941-42; research assoc. Columbia U. Coll. Physicians and Surgeons, N.Y.C., 1942-43; asst. physician Presbyn. Hosp. and Vanderbilt Clinic, N.Y.C., 1942-51; supervising psychiatrist Manhattan (N.Y.) State Hosp., 1946-50; assoc. adolescent psychiatrist Mt. Zion Hosp., N.Y.C., 1950-52; psychiat. cons. MacLaren Sch. for Boys, Woodburn, Oreg., 1952-84, Portland (Oreg.) Pub. Schs., 1952-67; clin. prof. U. Oreg. Health Scis. Ctr., 1956—. Author: Treatment of Drug Addiction in Psychoanalytic Study of the Child, Vol. 31, 1976, Ambivalence Towards Women in Chinese Charactores and Its Implication For Feminism; American Imago, 1988. Bd. dirs., v.p., Portland Opera Assn., 1960-64, Portland Musical Theatre, 1987—; bd. dirs., pres., Portland Chamber Orch., 1964-70. Served to major USAF, 1943-46. Recipient Henry Waldo Coe award U. Oreg. Med. Sch., Portland, 1939, citation Parry Ctr. for Children, Portland, 1970. Fellow Am. Psychiat. Assn. (life), Am. Geriatrics Soc. (founding fellow); mem. Am. Psychoanalytic Assn. (life), Portland Psychiatrists in Pvt. Practice (charter, pres. 1958), Mental Health Assn. (bd. dirs., chmn. med. adv. com. 1952-60), Multnomah County Med. Soc. (pres.'s citation 1979), Oreg. Psychoanalytic Found. (founding mem.), Am. Rhododendron Soc. (bd. dirs., v.p. Portland chpt. 1956—, Bronze medal and citation 1974), Am. Rhododendron Species Found. (bd. dirs. 1960—), Phi Beta Kappa, Sigma Xi, Phi Sigma. Home and Office: 1125 SW Saint Clair Ave Portland OR 97205

BERTINO, FRANK CHRISTEN, superintendent of schools; b. Culbertson, Mont., June 11, 1938; s. Frank Louis and Belvina (Williamson) B.; m. Memory Lee Robertson, Feb. 16, 1963; children: Shawna Estill, Lani Bertino. BS in Secondary Edn., Mont. State U., 1961, postgrad., 1976-84; ME in Sch. Adminstrn., U. Mont., 1965. Cert. tchr., Idaho; cert. adminstr. Band dir. Hinsdale (Mont.) Pub. Schs., 1961-62, Medicine Lake (Mont.) Pub. Schs., 1962-63; prin. Arlee (Mont.) Elem. Schs., 1963-67, Belgrade (Mont.) Elem. Schs., 1967-69; supt. Harrison (Mont.) Pub. Schs., 1969-72, Heart Butte (Mont.) Sch. Dist. #1, 1972-76; grad. asst. Mont. State U., Bozeman, 1976-78; asst. supt. Wallace (Idaho) Sch. Dist. #393, 1978-79, supt., 1979—; adj. instr. Lewis and Clark Coll., Lewiston, Idaho, 1962-84. Author poetry; contbr. articles to profl. jours. Chief organizer Heart Butte TV Translator Project, 1973; comptroller Water Users Assn., Heart Butte, 1974; mem. consol. task force State Dept. Edn., Boise, Idaho, 1988; mem. county census com., Wallace, 1982. Mem. Am. Assn. Sch. Adminstrs., Idaho Sch. Supts. Assn. (region I pres. 1983-85, bd. dirs. 1983-85), Phi Delta Kappa, Rotary (pres. 1985-88), Elks. Home: 207 W Oak Box 768 Osburn ID 83849 Office: Wallace Sch Dist #393 401 River St Wallace ID 83873

BERTRAM, JACK RENARD, infosytems specialist; b. Lincoln, Nebr., Nov. 20, 1943; s. John Lewis and Emma Louise (Doerr) B.; m. Ingrid Frieda Reschke, Feb. 14, 1975; children: Deborah Geniene, Kenneth Brian. BS, Stanford U., 1966, MA, 1971; MS, Santa Clara U., 1988; cert. mgr., James Madison U., 1988. Scientific programming specialist Lockheed Missles & Space Co., Sunnyvale, Calif., 1980—. Mem. Am. Assn. for Artifical Intelligence, Am. Astronautical Soc., AIAA, Assn. for Computing Machinery, Computer Soc. IEEE, ACLU, Nat. Mgmt. Assn., People for the Am. Way. Democrat. Home: 1580 Alameda de las Pulgas Redwood City CA 94061-2404 Office: Lockheed Missles & Space Co Bldg 590 S Orgn 62-82 PO Box 3504 Sunnyvale CA 94088-3504

BESS, JAMES EARNEST, television executive; b. Albuquerque, July 2, 1950; s. Earnest Murell and Barbara (Pollock) B. Student, U. N.Mex., 1969-72, 89—. News dir. N.Mex. Broadcasting, KGGM-TV, Albuquerque, 1969-76, dir., 1988—; spl. project dir. Pulitzer Broadcasting-KOAT-TV, Albuquerque, 1976-78; news producer Hubbard Broadcasting-KOB-TV, Albuquerque, 1978-80, KVOA-TV 4, Tucson, 1980-81; owner, prin. Directline Video, Albuquerque, 1981—; asst. prodn. mgr. Pullitzer Broadcasting, Albuquerque, 1981-86. Contbr. photographs to book. Recipient award of merit Assn. Trial Lawyers Am., 1983, N.A.T.A.S., N.Mex. Broadcasters Assn., 1986. Mem. Nat. Assn. TV Arts and Scis., Albuquerque Press Club (1st Place award 1985), Rio Grande Valley Golden Retriever Club. Episcopalian. Home: 3111 Aliso NE Albuquerque NM 87110 Office: Sta KGGM-TV 13 Broadcast Plaza SW Albuquerque NM 87104

BESSE, ROBERT GALE, food technologist; b. Calgary, Alta., Can., Feb. 11, 1923 (parents Am. citizens); s. Rene A. and Doria (Bray) B.; student N.Mex. State Tchrs. Coll., 1941-42; B.S., Oreg. State Coll., 1948; m. Mary A. McKay, Sept. 11, 1948; children—Rene A., Madeleine E., Leon J., Alan G., Michele M., Marc P., Angelique C. Supt., also in quality control Alderman Farms Frozen Foods, Dayton, Oreg., 1948-50, plant supt., 1950-54; chief food technologist Kuner Empson Co., Brighton, Colo., 1954-60; food technologist Northwest Packing Co., Portland, Oreg., 1960-62; food technologist research and devel. Nat. Can Corp., San Francisco, 1962-67, mgr. Pacific Area tech. research service, 1967-70; mgr. tech. services Western Can Co., 1970-86 ; customer tech. services Continental Can Co., 1986-88; cons. to food and can industries, RGB Cons., 1988—; dir. Material Metrics. Pres. St. Gregory's Theatre Guild; vol. hunting safety instr. Calif. Fish and Game Dept., 1972—. Served with Signal Corps, AUS, 1942-45. Mem. Soc. Plastic Engrs., Pacific Fish Tech. (pres.), Inst. Food Technologists (sec.-treas. Rocky Mountain sect.; exec. com. Oreg. sect.), Confraternity of Christian Doctrine Cath. (pres.), N.W. Canners and Packers, Packaging Inst. (profl. mem.), Nat. Canners Assn. (mem. Western lab. adv. com.), No. Calif. Metal Decorating Assn. (pres.), Western Packaging Assn.; Soc. Mfg. Engrs. Club: Elks. Home and Office: 264 Portola Dr San Mateo CA 94403

BEST, ALAN JOHNSTON, businessman; b. Winnipeg, Can., Mar. 15, 1922; s. James Samuel and Margaret Elizabeth (McCombe) B.; divorced; children: Linda Best Adams, Susan, Grace Best Taylor. BS, U. Manitoba, 1944; postgrad., El Camino Coll., 1957-58. Chief chemist rsch. dept. Continental Can Co., Montreal, Que., 1946-47; cons. Brit. West Indies Pvt. Food Plant, Barbados, 1947-49; with various food mfg. plants Calif., 1950-71; v.p., owner Indsl. Protective Coatings, Inc., L.A., 1971-81, Best Protective Coatings, Inc., L.A., 1981—; cons. in field. Sunday sch. tchr. St. Andrews Presbyn. Ch., Redondo Beach, Calif., 1980-86, Rolling Hills (Calif.) Covenant, 1983-85; v.p. Am. Cancer Soc., Torrance, Calif., 1981-82. Mem. Food Technologists Am. Home: 4426 Green Meadows Torrance CA 90505 Office: Best Protective Coatings Inc 1834 E 42d St Los Angeles CA 90058

BEST, BARBARA, personal manager; b. San Diego, Dec. 2, 1921; d. Charles Lewis and Leila Harrison (Sanders) B. BA in Journalism, U. So. Calif., Los Angeles, 1943. Unit publicist 20th Century Fox Co., Los Angeles, 1943-50; reporter San Diego Jour., 1950; asst. to publicity dir. Stanley Kramer Co., Los Angeles, 1950-53; Owner, mgr. Barbara Best & Assocs., Los Angeles, 1953-66; v.p. Jay Bernstein Pub. Relations, Los Angeles, 1967-75; owner, pres. Barbara Best, Inc., Pub. Relations, Los Angeles, 1975-87; personal mgr. Barbara Best Mgmt., Los Angeles, 1987--; exec. v.p. Maribar Prodns., Hollywood, Calif., 1986-. Co-founder, exec. dir. Vikki Carr Scholarship Found., Hollywood, 1971-82; pres. Publicists Fed. Credit Union, Hollywood, 1976-85. Mem. Hollywood Womens Press Club (past pres., bd. dirs.), Women in Film. Democrat. Episcopalian. Office: Barbara Best Mgmt 14159 Riverside Dr Sherman Oaks CA 91243

BEST, HOLLIS GARBER, judge; b. Currie County, N.Mex., July 10, 1926; s. Ernest and Neely Civil (Stratton) B.; m. Kathryn Jean LaFollette, Aug. 4, 1947; children: David S., Daniel E., Laura J. Best Marks, Kathryn A. AB, Fresno State U., 1948; JD, Stanford U., 1951. Bar: Calif. 1951. Dep. dist. atty. County of Fresno, Fresno, Calif., 1951-53; ptnr. Manfred, Best & Forbes, Fresno, 1953-63, McCormick, Barstow, Sheppard, Coyle & Best, Fresno, 1963-72; judge Calif. Superior Ct., Fresno, 1972-84; assoc. justice Calif. 5th dist. Ct. Appeals, Fresno, 1984—; mem. exec. com., Conf. State Bar Dels., Calif., 1969-71; adj. prof. law, San Joaquin Coll. Law, Fresno, 1984-84. Lt. (j.g.) USNR, 1944-46, PTO. Mem. Calif. Judges Assn. (sec.-treas. 1979-80), Calif. Judges Found. (bd. dirs. 1987-90), Fresno County Bar Assn. (pres. 1963), Rotary. Republican. Office: 5th dist Ct Appeals 2550 Mariposa Mall Fresno CA 93721

BEST, JOY MORGAN, home economist; b. Portales, N.Mex., Oct. 21, 1934; d. R.C. Ike and Nell (Bruton) Morgan; m. Wendell Best, Dec. 29, 1952; children: Barbara Best Rogers, Monte, Kent, Kyle. BS, Ea. N.Mex. U., 1970, MEd, 1971. Cert. home economist, N.Mex. Substitute tchr. Floyd (N.Mex.) Mcpl. Sch., 1957-64; bus driver Nash Sch. Transp., Floyd, 1964-67; instr. home econs. Ea. N.Mex. U., Portales, 1969-74; home economist Coop. Extension Svc., Portales, 1977-84, county dir., 1984—. Named Outstanding Agr. Family, Portales Bus. and Profl. Women, 1973; recipient Disting. Svc. award Coll. Agr. and Home Econs., N.Mex. State U., 1987, Outstanding N.Mex. Women award Gov. of N.Mex., 1988. Mem. Am. Home Econs. Assn., N.Mex. Home Econs. Assn. (treas. 1986-87), N.Mex. Assn. Extension Home Economists (pres. 1981), Roosevelt County C. of C., Floyd Sch. Alumni Assn. (pres. 1982-87), P.E.O., Phi Kappa, Epsilon Sigma Phi, Beta Sigma Phi (Woman of Yr. award), Federated Women's Club. Democrat. Baptist. Office: Coop Extension Svc Courthouse B-6 Portales NM 88130

BEST, RICHARD ALLEN, JR., architect; b. Somers Point, N.J., Apr. 26, 1957; s. Richard Allen Sr. and E. Jeanne (Cunningham).B. BA, U. N.C., 1979, BArch, 1980; MArch, UCLA, 1982. Registered architect, Calif. Intern architect Urban Innovations Group, Los Angeles, 1981; designer, draftsman Charles Moore, Inc., Los Angeles, 1982-84; sr. draftsman WZMH Group, Inc., Los Angeles, 1984-85, project cpt., designer, 1985-87; with Elbasani & Logan Architects, Berkeley, Calif., 1987; owner Richard A. Best, Jr. Architect, Beverly Hills, Calif., 1988—; teaching asst. UCLA Sch. Archtecture, 1981-82. Co-author: Un Storico Aldente, 1981; co-designer Mercatale e Albergo, 1981; designer Beverly Hills Civic Ctr., 1982 (1st place 1982); capt., designer Mission Inn, Riverside, Calif., 1986. Fellow UCLA, 1980; scholar UCLA, 1981, Bell Telephone Co., N.J., 1977; named one of Outstanding Young Men Am., Nat. Jaycees, 1982. Mem. AIA, NCARB (cert.). Democrat. Methodist. Home: 9364 Beverlycrest Dr Beverly Hills CA 90210 Office: 9364 Beverlycrest Dr Beverly Hills CA 90210

BEST, ROBERTA LOUISE, export company executive; b. Mpls., Apr. 8, 1941; d. Irving Wolfe and Beatrice Theresa (Marcus) Lichterman; m. Charles Patrick Best, Sept. 25, 1963 (div. Nov. 1966); 1 child, Bennett Thomas; m. Masaharu Ichino, May 29, 1977. AA, L.A. City Coll., 1962; paralegal cert., UCLA, 1974, postgrad. Internat. Bus., 1986—. Exec. legal sec. Litton Industries, Inc., Beverly Hills, Calif., 1967-73; life underwriter Conn. Mut. Life Ins. Co., L.A., 1976-80, Mut. Benefit Life Ins. Co., L.A., 1977—; v.p.

Romac Export Mgmt. Corp., L.A., 1978—; owner, mgr. Canyon Gallery Two, L.A., 1978-82. Mem. steering com. Beverly Hills Democratic Clu, 1972; bd. dirs. West Adams Hist. Assn., L.A., 1985, Ctr. for Creative Change, Newberry Park, Calif. 1987—; pres. West Adams Heights Neighborhood Assn., 1986—. Mem. Profl. Referral Orgn. (pres. 1980-81), Export Mgrs. Assn., Greater L.A. Trade Ctr. Assn., Nat. Assn. Women Bus. Owners, L.A. C. of C., Nat. Assn. Life Underwriters (women's leaders roundtable 1978), L.A. Natural History Mus., Tree People, World Wildlife Fund, Alpha Pi Epsilon. Home and Office: Romac Export Mgmt Corp 2242 S Hobart Blvd Los Angeles CA 90018-2149

BEST, ROBIN LATTA, nurse; b. Vancouver, B.C., Can., Mar. 31, 1946; came to U.S., 1952; d. Gordon Eric and Irene (Thompson) Latta; m. Robert Eugene Best, May 3, 1975; children: Carrie, Michael, Nicole, Brett. AA, AS, Cuesta Coll., 1974. RN, Calif. Psychiat. technicial, nurse II, Atascadero (Calif.) State Hosp. for Criminally Insane, 1971-80, 84-89, unit supr., 1988-89; staff nurse, instr. Plumas Dist. Hosp. and Unified Sch. Dist., Quincy, Calif., 1980-84; staff RN psychiat. svcs. Good Samaritan Hosp., San Jose, Calif., 1989—; chmn. Plumas County Mental Health Adv. Bd., 1982-84, patient rights adv., 1984. Bd. dirs. CETA Child Care Ctr., Quincy, 1983-84, Atascadero State Hosp. Bldg. Blocks, 1987-88; com. mem. adv. bd. Monterey Road Sch., Atascadero, 1987. Mem. ANA (cert. psychiat. RN III), Calif. Nursing Assn., Nat. League Nurses, Calif. League Nurses, Profl. Nursing Assn. Atascadero State Hosp., Calif. Tchrs. Assn., Calif. State Employees Assn. Democrat. Episcopalian. Office: Good Samaritan Hosp 2425 Samaritan Way San Jose CA 95120

BEST, ROGER NORMAN, real estate investment manager; b. Los Angeles, Apr. 16, 1949; s. Norman Frank and Muriel Noreen (Atkinson) B.; m. Sheri Lyn Kruyer, Oct. 16, 1982. BA, U. Wash., 1971. Lic. Real Esate Broker, Calif., 1985. Musician, entertainer L.A., 1963-69; pres. Best Enterprises, Los Angeles, 1969—, Tazio Prodns., Los Angeles, 1973-76; v.p. DSL Constrn. Corp., Los Angeles, 1977-85; v.p., chief operating officer Scott Properties, Inc., Los Angeles, 1978-85; pres., chief exec. Tazio Properties, Inc., Los Angeles, 1980—. Inventor correctable typewriter ribbon, visual music. Mem. Van Nuys Airport Adv. Council, 1987. Office: Tazio Properties, Inc. 3580 Wilshire Blvd 17th fl #1918 Los Angeles CA 90010

BESTALL, ALAN S., realtor; b. Oklahoma City, Dec. 14, 1942; s. John Bolton and Joyce Elizabeth (Williamson) B. BA, U. Redlands, 1964; post-grad., Claremont Grad. Sch., 1964-65; MPH, UCLA, 1966. Lic. real estate salesman, Ariz. Health advisor HEW, San Francisco, Washington, and Kansas City, Mo., 1966-75; exec. dir. Compcare Health Plan, Milw., 1975-77; grants and contracts adminstr. Fla. Dept. Health and Human Svcs., St. Petersburg, 1977-78; assoc. adminstr. group health plan Mo. Pacific Hosp., St. Louis, 1978-80; pres. Mo. Pacific Employees Health Plan, St. Louis, 1980-86; realtor Tom Jackson & Assocs. Inc., Scottsdale, Ariz., 1986-87, residential mgr., 1987—; health care cons. Oblinger-Smith Corp., Wichita, Kans. and Kansas City, Mo., 1975, Prime Health, Little Rock, 1986; chmn. Ariz. Relocation, 1989; mem. urban health svcs. task force USPHS, Washington, 1968. Mem. funding com. United Way, St. Petersburg, 1977-78; mem. exec. com. S.E. Area Regional Commerce and Growth Assn., St. Louis, 1984-85; bd. dirs. Valley Citizens League, Govt. Reorgn. Task Force, 1988-89. Mem. Ariz. Assn. Realtors, Scottsdale Assn. Realtors, Kiwanis (pres. North scottsdale 1988). Democrat. Office: Tom Jackson & Assocs Inc 6808 E Camelback Rd Scottsdale AZ 85251

BETTER, WILLIAM JOEL, utilities executive; b. Phoenix, Jan. 24, 1951; s. Julius Frank and Eleanor M. (Morgan) B.; m. Dona Bascom, Mar. 30, 1972; children: Rhonda, Jason Andrew, Joseph Earl, Elizabeth, Matthew John, Rebecca Anne. AA, Victor Valley Coll., 1971. Cert. pub. utilities operation and mgmt. Dist. storekeeper Contel Calif., Ridgecrest, 1973-74; employment ctr. rep. Contel Calif., 1974-75; state supply mgr. Contel NW, Silverton, Oreg., 1975-78; div. supply coord. Contel of the West, Phoenix, 1978-81; state supply mgr. Contel of the West, Lakeside, Ariz., 1981-83; engr. Contel of the West, Homedale, Idaho, 1983-84; material svcs. mgr. Citizens Utilities Co., Kingman, Ariz., 1984—. Cubmaster Boy Scouts Am., Show Low, Ariz., 1981-83, dist. scout leader., trainer, Caldwell, Idaho, 1983-84, fundraiser, Kingman, 1984—. Mem. Purchasing Mgmt. Assn. Ariz., Nat. Assn. Purchasing Mgmt., Ariz. Altos Users Group, Nat. Eagle Scout Assn. Office: Citizens Utilities Co 3405 Northern Ave Kingman AZ 86401

BETTINGER, MICHAEL JOHN, lawyer; b. Youngstown, Ohio, Aug. 31, 1958; s. John Arthur and Barbara Marion (Bowen) B. BS summa cum laude, St. Joseph's Coll., Rensselaer, Ind., 1976-1980; JD, U. Notre Dame, 1980-83. Bar: Ill. 1983, U.S. Dist. Ct. (no. dist.) Ill. 1983, U.S. Ct. Appeals (7th cir.) 1983, Calif. 1985, U.S. Dist. Ct. (no. dist.) Calif. 1985. Law clk. to presiding justice U.S. Ct. Appeals (7th cir.), Chgo., 1983-85; assoc. Pillsbury, Madison & Sutro, San Francisco, 1985—. Contbr. articles to profl. jours. Vol. Thomas J. Campbell for U.S. Congress campaign, 1987—. Mem. ABA, State Bar of Calif., State Bar of Ill., San Francisco Bar Assn, Chgo. Bar Assn., Woodrow Wilson Internat. Ctr. for Scholars. Republican. Roman Catholic. Home: 3484 Scott St San Francisco CA 94123 Office: Pillsbury Madison & Sutro 225 Bush St PO Box 7880 San Francisco CA 94120

BETTS, BARBARA LANG (MRS. BERT A. BETTS), lawyer; b. Anaheim, Calif., Apr. 28, 1926; d. W. Harold and Helen (Thompson) Lang; B.A. magna cum laude, Stanford U., 1948; LL.B., Balboa U., 1951; m. Roby F. Hayes, July 22, 1948 (dec.); children—John Chauncey IV, Frederick Prescott, Roby Francis II; m. Bert A. Betts, July 11, 1962; 1 son, Bruce Harold; stepchildren: Bert Alan, Randy W., Sally Betts Joynt, Terry Betts Marsteller, Linda Betts Hansen, LeAnn Betts Wilson. Bar: Calif. 1952, U.S. Supreme Ct. 1978; pvt. practice law, Oceanside, Calif., 1952-68, San Diego, 1960—, Sacramento, 1962—; partner firm Roby F. Hayes & Barbara Lang Hayes, 1952-60; city atty., Carlsbad, Calif., 1959-63; v.p. Isle & Oceans Marinas, Inc., 1970-80, W. H. Lang Corp., 1964-69; sec. Internat. Prodn. Assos., 1968—, Margaret M. McCabe, M.D., Inc., 1977-88 . Chmn., Traveler's Aid, 1952-53; pres. Oceanside-Carlsbad Jr. Chambrettes, 1955-56; vice chmn. Carlsbad Planning Commn., 1959; mem. San Diego Planning Congress, 1959; v.p. Oceanside Diamond Jubilee Com., 1958; dir. No. San Diego County Chpt. for Retarded Children, 1957-58. Candidate Calif. State Legislature, 77th Dist., 1954; mem. Calif. Dem. State Central Com., 1958-66 ; co-chmn. 28th Congl. Dist., Dem. State Central Com., 1960-62; alt. del. Dem. Nat. Conv., 1960. Named to Fullerton Union High Sch. Wall of Fame, 1986. Mem. Am. Judicature Soc., Nat. Inst. Mcpl. Officers, ABA, Calif. Bar Assn.,, San Diego County Bar Assn., Oceanside C. of C. (sec. 1957, v.p. 1958, dir. 1953-54, 57-59), AAUW (legis. com. 1958-59; local pres. 1959-60; asst. state legis. chmn. 1958-59), No. San Diego County Assn. Chambers of Commerce (sec.-treas.), Bus. and Profl. Women's Club (So. dist. legislation chmn. 1958-59), DAR (regent Oceanside chpt. 1960-61), San Diego C. of C., San Diego Hist. Soc., Fullerton Jr. Assistance League, U.S. Supreme Ct. Hist. Soc., Calif. Scholarship Fedn., Loyola Guild of Jesuit High Sch., Phi Beta Kappa. Clubs: Soroptimist Internat. (pres. Oceanside-Carlsbad 1958-59, sec. pub. affairs San Diego, Imperial Counties 1954; pres. of pres.'s council San Diego and Imperial counties and Mexico 1958-59), Barristers, Stanford (Sacramento), Stanford Mothers. Author: (with Bert A. Betts) A Citizen Answers. Office: Betts Ranch PO Box 306 Elverta CA 95626 also: 3119-A Howard Ave San Diego CA 92104

BETTS, JAMES WILLIAM, JR., financial analyst, consultant; b. Montclair, N.J., Oct. 11, 1923; s. James William and Cora Anna (Banta) B.; m. Barbara Stoke, July 28, 1951; 1 dau., Barbara Susan (dec.). B.A., Rutgers U., 1946; M.A., U. Hawaii, 1957. With Dun & Bradstreet, Inc., 1946-86, service cons., 1963-64, reporting and service mgr., 1964-65, sr. fin. analyst, Honolulu, 1965—; owner, operator Portfolio Cons. of Hawaii, 1979—. Served with AUS, 1942-43. Mem. Am. Econ. Assn., Western Econ. Assn., Atlantic Econ. Soc. Republican. Episcopalian.

BETTS, WILBUR WARD, mechanical engineer, author, historian; b. Rockford, Ill., Aug. 28, 1904; s. Fred Grant and Edith Belle (Beach) B.; BS with honors in Mech. Engring., U. Ill., 1935; m. Sarah Elizabeth Farrey, June 2, 1928 (div.); children: Mary Edith, Sharon Ann; m. Mary Roberta Van DeWalker, Oct. 19, 1970. Design engr. Ingersoll Milling Machine Co., Rockford, 1922-32; asst. sales mgr. Barnes Drill Co., Rockford, 1935-37; sales engr. English & Miller Machinery Co., Detroit, 1937-38; design engr. Farrel Birmingham Gear Corp., Buffalo, 1938-40; group leader Bell Aircraft Corp., Buffalo, 1940-42, W. Coast Engring. rep. B-29 Com., 1942-44; product analyst Webster-Brinkley Co., Seattle, 1944-46; chief engr. Kirsten Pipe Co., Seattle, 1946-48; adminstrn. engr. B47 and Bomarc Functional tests Boeing Co., Seattle, 1948-61; test devel. engr. DynaSoar Gliders, Seattle, 1962, charge test verification saturn booster, New Orleans, 1963-65, adminstrn. engr. 747 airplane, 1965-69; test procedures cons., Seattle, 1969—. Chmn. adv. com. Office of Price Adminstrn., State of Wash., 1944-46. Recipient Bronze Tablet award U. Ill., 1935. Mem. Soc. Automotive Engrs. (25-Yr. Membership award 1969), Am. Indian Profl. Assocs., Mayflower Soc., Sons of Union Vets. of Civil War, SAR, Gen. James A. Longstreet Meml. Assn., James Willard Schultz Soc., Jet Pioneers Assn. U.S.A., Phi Eta Sigma, Pi Tau Sigma, Theta Tau, Tau Beta Pi, Horseless Carriage Club (pres. 1958), N.W. Intertribal Club. Methodist. Author: (with Schultz) Bear Chief's War Shirt, 1983. Contbr. articles to profl. jours., also short story. Home: 1317 44th Ave SW Seattle WA 98116 Office: PO Box 3707 13 59 Seattle WA 98124

BEVAN, DONALD EDWARD, marine scientist, university dean; b. Seattle, Feb. 23, 1921; s. Arther and Violette B.; m. Tanya L. Potapova, Sept. 8, 1971. B.S., U. Wash., 1948, Ph.D., 1959; postdoctoral student, Moscow U., 1959-60. Sr. fisheries biologist U. Wash., Seattle, 1955-59; lectr., rsch. asst. prof. U. Wash., 1959-61, rsch. assoc. prof, 1961-64, assoc. prof., 1964-66, prof., 1966-86, prof. emeritus, 1986—, assoc. dean Coll. Fisheries, 1965-69, dean, 1980-85, dir. Univ. Computer Ctr., 1968-69, asst. v.p. research, 1969-77, adj. prof. Inst. Marine Studies, 1973—, assoc. dean Coll. Ocean and Fishery Scis., 1984-86; pres., dir. Univ. Book Stores, 1977—, ptnr. emeritus, 1986—; mem. US-USSR Pacific Fisheries Negotiations. Author articles and pamphlets in field. Served to capt., arty. U.S. Army, World War II. Decorated Purple Heart, Bronze Star. Mem. Pacific Region Fisheries Council (chmn. sci. and statis. com.), N. Pacific Fisheries Council, Marine Tech. Soc., Am. Inst. Fishery Research Biologists, Pacific Fisheries Biologists, Sigma Xi, Phi Sigma. Home: 29801 NE Cherry Valley Rd Duvall WA 98019 Office: U Wash Henderson Hall HN15 Seattle WA 98195

BEVERETT, ANDREW JACKSON, merchandising executive; b. Midland City, Ala., Feb. 21, 1917; s. Andrew J. and Ella Levonie (Adams) B.; B.S., Samford U., 1940; M.B.A., Harvard U., 1942; m. Martha Sophia Landgrabe, May 26, 1951; children—Andrew Jackson III, James Edmund, Faye A. Various exec. positions in corporate planning and mgmt. United Air Lines, Chgo., 1946-66; dir. aviation econs., sr. mktg. and econ. cons. Mgmt. and Econs. Research, Inc., Palo Alto, Calif., 1966-71; sr. economist Stanford Research Inst., Menlo Park, 1971-72; pres. Edy's on the Peninsula stores, 1973-78; real estate broker, fin. and tax cons., Saratoga, Calif., 1979—. Served from ensign to lt. USNR, 1942-46. Mem. Nat. Assn. Enrolled Agts., Nat. Assn. Realtors, Pi Gamma Mu, Phi Kappa Phi. Home: 19597 Via Monte Dr Saratoga CA 95070 Office: 12175 Saratoga Sunnyvale Rd Ste A Saratoga CA 95070

BEYDLER, JON MICHAEL, technology company executive, consultant; b. Springfield, Mo., July 3, 1951; s. Stanley Joseph and Jeanne (Wiley) B.; m. Polly Rae Crawford, May 28, 1971 (div. 1977); Donna Marie Warren, May 21, 1977; 1 stepchild, Douglas Basil Dubrosky. BA, Evangel. Coll., 1973; MPA, Am. U., 1975. Sales rep. Kroy Industries, Denver, 1978-80; br. mgr., regional mgr. Kroy Industries, Phoenix, 1980-81; account exec. Compugraphic Corp., Phoenix, 1981-82; br. mgr. Savin Corp., Phoenix, 1982; mktg. exec. Prime Computer, Inc., Phoenix, 1982-84; v.p. B.C. Computing, Phoenix, 1984-85; pres. IMS-Div. Castillo Co., Phoenix, 1985-87; pres., chief exec. officer The Beydler Co., Phoenix, 1987—. Author: Community Needs and Resources Assessment Review, 1974. Pres. Fairfax (Va.) County Vol. Action Ctr., 1975, Greater Paradise Valley Community Council, Phoenix, 1985; candidate Phoenix City Council, 1983. Republican. Lodge: Lions. Home: 5437 E Sandra Terr Scottsdale AZ 85254 Office: The Beydler Co/IMS 9850 N 32d St Ste 1 Phoenix AZ 85028

BEYERLEIN, DOUGLAS CRAIG, hydrologic engineer; b. Portland, Oreg., Sept. 23, 1950; s. R.W. and Marjorie Mae (Hovenden) B.; m. Marie Joan Cockrell, Apr. 26, 1975. BSCE, U. Wash., 1972, MSCE, 1973. Registered profl. engr., Wash. Hydrologist Hydrocomp, Inc., Palo Alto, Calif., 1973-79; sr. hydrologist Anderson-Nichols & Co., Inc., Palo Alto, 1979-85; v.p. Aqua Terra Cons., Mountain View, Calif., 1985-86; sr. hydrologic engr. Snohomish County Dept. Pub. Works, Everett, Wash., 1987—. Author: Beyerlein Beginnings, 1989. Me. Am. Inst. Hydrology, Am. Water Resources Assn., San Jose Bicycle Club. Office: Snohomish County Pub Works 5th Floor County Adminstrn Everett WA 98201

BEZANSON, RONALD SCOTT, JR., clergyman, army chaplain; b. Laconia, N.H., Oct. 28, 1936; s. Ronald Scott and Avis Maria (Preble) B.; m. Mary Joan Arthur, June 28, 1958; children: Deborah K. Rebecca K., Timothy S., Angela L. BA, Aurora (Ill.) Coll., 1958, BTh, 1959; MDiv, Evangel. Theol. Sem., Naperville, Ill., 1962; MBA, U. Tex., Austin, 1975. Ordained to ministry, Advent Christian Ch., 1962. Commd. 1d lt. U.S. Army, 1962, advanced through grades to col., 1982; chaplain, chief adminstrn. and mgmt. U.S. Army, Vietnam, 1970; staff chaplain Army Air Def. Command U.S. Army, Colorado Springs, Colo., 1971-73; instr. Chaplain Sch. U.S. Army, Ft. Wadsworth, N.Y., 1974-77; dep. chaplain materiel command U.S. Army, Alexandria, Va., 1977-81; chaplain 2d inf. div. U.S. Army, Camp Casey, Korea, 1981-82; dir. adminstrn., office chief chaplain, Pentagon U.S. Army, Washington, 1982-85; command chaplain hdqrs. Western command U.S. Army, Ft. Shafter, Hawaii, 1985-89; chief dept. of ministry and pastoral care Tripler Army Med. Ctr., Ft. Shafter, Hawaii, 1989—; treas., First United Presbyn. Ch., Woodbridge, Va., 1982-85; bd. dirs. Dept. Army Coun. Chaplain Cols., Washington, 1982-89; pastor, Ft. deRussy Chapel, Honolulu, 1985-89. Pub., Westcom Chaplain newsletter, 1985-89; columnist, Hawaii Army Weekly, 1988-89. Mem. steering com., Gov.'s and Mayor's Prayer Breakfast, Honolulu, 1986-89. Decorated Legion of Merit, 3 Bronze Star medals, 9 Air Medals. Mem. Mil Chaplains Assn., Officers Club, Army Golf Assn. Republican. Home: 46-381 Kumoo Loop Kaneohe HI 96744-3532 Office: US Army Western Command Attn APCH Fort Shafter HI 96858-5100

BEZER, DAVID LEON, real estate appraiser; b. Phila., Nov. 25, 1943; s. Samuel and Frances (Rees) B.; m. Ellen Berkowitz, July 2, 1967; children: Daniel, Adam, Samara, John. Student, NYU, 1962-63, Temple U., 1969-70. Real estate salesman Magnus Internat. Inc., Camden, N.J., 1964-65; right of way agt. St. Davids, Pa., 1965-66; chief real estate appraiser Mfrs. Appraisal Co., Phila., 1966-70; exec. v.p. Enterprise Appraisal, Devon, Pa., 1971-75; pres. David L. Bezer & Co. Inc., Phila., 1975-86; v.p., treas. Valuation Network, Inc., N.Y.C., 1982-83, pres., 1983-84; pres. Valuation Network Inc. of So. Calif., San Diego, 1985-86; owner VNI Rainbow Appraisal Service, San Diego, 1986—. Mem. Am. Inst. Real Estate Appraisers, Am. Soc. Appraisers. Democrat. Jewish. Home: 2144 Belloc Ct San Diego CA 92109 Office: VNI Rainbow Appraisal Service 11650 Iberia Pl Suite N San Diego CA 92128

BHADRIRAJU, NATARAJ, telecommunications engineer; b. Visakhapatnam, Pradesh, India, Sept. 26, 1957; s. Krishnamurti and Syamala (Baptala) B.; m. Padmini Bhadriraju, Jan. 28, 1982; children: Raenuka, Ravi Prakash. BSEE, U. Calif., Berkeley, 1979; MSEE, Ariz. State U., 1986. Design engr. Teltone Corp., Kirkland, Wash., 1979-82; mgr. GTE/Siemens Transmission System, Phoenix, 1982-87; dir. engring., co-founder Poynting Corp., Scottsdale, Ariz., 1987—. Patentee in field. Pres. Phoenix Telugu Assn., 1986-87. Mem. IEEE. Home: 3301 W Angela Dr Phoenix AZ 85023 Office: Poynting Corp 7721 E Gray Rd Scottsdale AZ 85260

BHANDARI, ANIL KUMAR, cardiology educator; b. New Delhi, India, Jan. 26, 1953; came to U.S., 1977; s. Mukand Lal and Pushpa (Vij) B.; m. Eve-Marie Brindak, Mar. 29, 1980. Student, Panjab U., India, 1967-69; MB, BS, All India Inst. Med. Scis., New Delhi, 1975. Lic. physician, N.Y., Calif.; diplomate Am. Bd. Internal Medicine, Am. Bd. Cardiovascular Disease. Intern All India Inst. Med. Scis., New Delhi, 1975, resident in cardiology, 1976; intern in straight internal medicine SUNY, Stony Brook, 1977-78, resident in straight internal medicine, 1978-80; fellow in cardiology U. Rochester Med. Ctr., N.Y., 1980-82; fellow in clin. electrophysiology U. Calif. Med. Ctr., San Francisco, 1982-83; asst. prof. medicine U. So. Calif., 1983-87, assoc. prof., 1987—; staff physician Los Angeles County Med. Ctr. U. So. Calif., 1983—, dir. Electrophysiology Lab., 1985—; presenter numerous seminars, studies to univs., hosps. and agys., 1981—. Assoc. editor Jour. of Electrocardiology, 1988—; contbr. articles and revs. to profl. jours., chpts. to books. Grantee Am. Heart Assn., 1982-83, Sandoz Labs., 1983-84, 84—, Riker Labs. 1985—; fellow NIH, 1981-82, Am. Heart Assn., 1982. Mem. AAAS, Am. Heart Assn. (Los Angeles chpt.), Am. Coll. Cardiology, N. Am. Soc. Pacing and Electrophysiology, Assn. Physicians of Los Angeles County Hosps., Greater Los Angeles Electrophysiology Soc. Home: 2231 Pelham Ave Los Angeles CA 90064 Office: U So Calif Los Angeles County 2025 Zonal Ave Los Angeles CA 90033

BHATIA, TARUN KUMAR, market analyst; b. New Delhi, India; came to U.S., 1986; s. Saina Pati and Dharam Davi Bhatia; m. Neeru Kambos, June 22, 1985; children: Monica, Sean. BA in Chem. Engring., U. Toronto, Ont., Can., 1984, MS in Chem. Engring., 1986. Project engr. Ensotech, Inc., North Hollywood, Calif., 1986-87; market analyst U.S. Borax Rsch., Anaheim, Calif., 1987-88, U.S. Borax, L.A., 1988—. Home: 19202 Newhouse St Canyon Country CA 90010 Office: US Borax 3075 Wilshire Blvd Los Angeles CA 90010

BHATT, MUKESH BALVANTRAY, pharmacist; b. Ahmedabad, India, Jan. 10, 1958; came to U.S., 1984; s. Balvntray M. and Ramaben B. (Thaker) B.; m. Kalyani M. Joshi, July 4, 1983. MPhar, L.M.C.P., Ahmedabad, 1980; BS in Pharmacy, Temple U., 1985. Registered pharmacist, Calif., N.J., Pa. Pharmacist Cadila Lab., Gujarat, India, 1980-82, mgr. mfg., 1982-85; staff pharmacist Rite Aid Pharmacy, Phila., 1985-86; dir. pharmacy Calexico (Calif.) Hosp., 1986—; ptnr., pharmacist Calexico Pharmacy, 1986—. Mem. Calif. Pharmacists Assn. Hare Kirshna. Home: 2095 Cottonwood Circle Apt 119 El Centro CA 92243 Office: Celexico Pharmacy 325 Imperial Ave Calexico CA 92231

BHAYANI, KIRAN LILACHAND, environmental engineer; b. Bhavnagar, Gujarat, India, Dec. 2, 1944; came to U.S., 1968, naturalized; s. Lilachand Premchand and Rasila (Chhotalal Shah) B.; m. Chandra Vasantlal Gandhi, June 24, 1971; children: Nikhil K., Mihir K. B.Engring. with honors, U. Bombay, India, 1965, M.Engring., 1968; MS, U. R.I., 1970. Diplomate Am. Acad. Environ. Engrs.; registered profl. engr., Va., Ga., Utah. San. engr. Greeley & Hansen, N.Y.C., 1971-72, Hayes, Seay, Mattern & Mattern, Roanoke, Va., 1972-77; environ. engr. Hussey, Gay & Bell, Inc., Savannah, Ga., 1977-80; sr./prin. environ. engr., Utah Bur. Water Pollution Control, Salt Lake City, 1980—; innovative/alternative tech. coordinator State of Utah, Salt Lake City, 1983—. Reviewer (practice manual) Financing Sewer Projects, 1984. Fellow ASCE (profl. coordination com. 1981—); mem. Am. Water Works Assn., Water Pollution Control Fedn. (internat. com. 1984), NSPE. Jain. Office: Utah Bur Water Pollution Control PO Box 16690 Salt Lake City UT 84116

BIA, NELSON, management consultant firm executive; b. Shiprock, N.Mex., Dec. 19, 1955; s. Paul Sr. and Sadie B.; m. Karri Huges, Aug. 23, 1979 (div. 1986); children: Shone Lee, Kelli Gene. BS, Brigham Young U., 1982. Econ. devel. specialist Navajo Div. Econ. Devel., Window Rock, Ariz., 1983-84; dir. fin. and acctg. Navajo Housing Authority, Window Rock, 1984-86, dep. dir., 1986; regional v.p. United Indian Devel. Assn., Tempe, Ariz., 1986—; mgmt. cons. Navajo Bus. Assn., Window Rock, 1986-87; mem. steering com. Turner Constrn. Co., Phoenix. 1987—. Mem. Tempe C. of C., Tribe Many Feathers, Profl. Fin. Assn. Democrat. Mormon. Office: United Indian Devel Assn 2111 E Baseline Rd Ste F8 Tempe AZ 85283

BIALOSKY, BRUCE LAWRENCE, accountant; b. Detroit, Oct. 7, 1953; s. Franklin A. and Jacqueline (Stone) B.; m. Teri Michaels, Aug. 31, 1986. BS, San Diego State U., 1976. CPA, Calif. Staff acct. Peat Marwick Main, Newport Beach, Calif., 1976-78; sr. acct. Ronald Lederman & Assocs., Beverly Hills, Calif., 1978-79; chief fin. officer Parts World, Reno, 1979-83; owner, mgr. Bruce L. Bialosky, CPA, Sherman Oaks, Calif., 1983—. Author: Bialosky's Tax Facts and More, newsletter, 1985—. Bd. dirs. New Dem. Channel, L.A., 1983-86; chmn. New Leadership for McCarthy, L.A., 1988—, Super Sunday United Jewish Fund, L.A., 1988—, mem. Nat. Young Leadership Cabinet. Mem. AICPA, Young Execs. Group (fin. chmn. 1986-87), L.A. Bus. Coun. Home: 4120 Laurelgrove Ave Studio City CA 91604 Office: 13412 Ventura Blvd Sherman Oaks CA 91423

BIANCO, MICHAEL FABIUS PATRICK, financial executive; b. West Pittston, Pa., Dec. 27, 1940; s. Joseph Paul and Mary (Compitello) B., m. Marcia Ellen Schroeder, Apr. 27, 1968: children: Suzanne, Francesca, Michael Joseph. Student, Wilkes Coll., 1962, Georgetown U. Law Sch., 1963, U. Mich, 1968. Banking officer Chase Manhattan Bank, N.Y.C., 1968-72; pres., chief exec. officer Loeb Rhoades Securities Corp., N.Y.C., 1972-77; mng. dir. Security Pacific Leasing Corp., San Francisco, 1977-80, Internat. Bank, Washington, 1980-81; with Bank of Calif., San Francisco, 1981-82; v.p. Barclay's Bank, San Francisco, 1982-84; v.p., mgr. The Hibernia Bank, San Francisco, 1984-88; pres. Asia Pacific Capital Corp., San Francisco, 1988—. Bd. dirs. San Francisco Library Assn., 1986-88; speaker Bus. Week Exec. Programs, N.Y., 1987, The Planning Forum, San Francisco, 1988. James A. Finnegan Found. fellowship, 1960-61. Mem. The Foreign Correspondents Club of Japan, Calif. Council on Internat. Trade (dir., treas. 1987-88), Assn. MBA Execs., Japan Soc. of No. Calif., World Trade Assn., U. Mich. Alumni Assn., Stanford U. Alumni Assn. Roman Catholic. Clubs: Peninsula Golf and Country (San Mateo) San Francisco Tennis. Home: 1420 Oak Rim Dr Hillsborough CA 94010 Office: Asia Pacific Capital Corp One Sansome St Ste 2000 San Francisco CA 94104

BIANCO, NICOLE ANN, data processing executive; b. Allentown, Pa., Sept. 30, 1949; d. Welch Collerige and Ruth Ellen (Sacher) Everman; m. William Joseph Bianco, Aug. 19, 1971. Cert., Pa. State U., 1967. Programmer RCA, Moorestown, N.J., 1967-69, Trenton (N.J.) Trust Co, 1969-71, Food Fair, Inc., Phila., 1971-73; data processing officer Provident Nat. Bank, Phila., 1973-77; grant coordinator Burlington County Coll., Pemberton, N.J., 1977-79; asst. v.p. Valley Nat. Bank, Phoenix, 1979-85; cons. in field Phoenix, 1985-87; dir. tech. services Trak-Tech, Inc., Phoenix, 1987—; educator/tchr. Computer Systems Devel., Phoenix, 1985-87; adv. editor John Wiley & Sons, Inc., 1986-87. Author: (textbooks) Introduction to Data Base, 1985, Data Communications, 1985, Advanced Project Management, 1986; author and devel.: (software) Parolee Tracking System, 1987. Mem. Profl. Software Programmers Assn. Home: 9209 N 63d Dr Glendale AZ 85302 Office: Trak-Tech Inc 7310 N 16 St Phoenix AZ 85020

BIBLE, LAVERNE JO (COOKIE BIBLE), nurse practitioner; b. San Francisco, July 30, 1945; d. Arthur Nelson and Miriam (McManus) Pacheco; m. William Alan Bible, Nov. 25, 1965. BS in Nursing, U. Nev., 1971. Lic ob-gyn nurse practitioner, Nev. Obsetrics floor and staff nurse, head nurse Carson-Tahoe Hosp., Carson City, Nev., 1971-73; nurse practitioner med. office, Carson City, 1973-83; sr. nurse practitioner Planned Parenthood, Reno, 1983—; bd. dirs., pres. Nev. Bd. Nursing, Reno, 1983—. Pres. Zephur Cove (Nev.) Gen. Improvement Dist., 1978—; bd. dirs. Nev. Women's Fund, Reno, 1983—; mem. bd. Girl Scouts Am., Reno, Nev., 1989—. Mem. Am. Nurses Assn., Nat. Assn Ob-Gyn Nurses, Nat. Nurse Practitioners in Family Planning, Sigma Theta Tau. Democrat. Episcopalian.

BICK, RODGER LEE, physician, medical researcher, author; b. San Francisco, May 21, 1942; s. Jack A. and Pauline E. Bick; student U. Calif., Berkeley; MD, U. Calif., Irvine, 1970; m. Marcella, Oct., 1979; 1 child, Shauna Nicole; children by previous marriage: Michelle, Le Anne Bick. Intern in straight medicine Kern County Gen. Hosp., Bakersfield, Calif., 1970-71, resident in internal medicine, 1971-72; fellow in hematology and med. oncology dept. of medicine UCLA Ctr. for Health Scis., 1972-73, assoc. prof. medicine, mem. med. staff, 1974—; hematology fellow Hyland Labs., Costa Mesa, Calif., 1966-67; practice medicine specializing in hematology/oncology and thrombosis, Santa Monica, Calif., 1974-77; dir. hemostasis and thrombosis research lab. Kern County Gen. Hosp., 1973-74, dir. med. edn., 1973-74, chief med. oncology, 1973-74; attending physician Wadsworth VA Hosp., L.A., 1974—; mem. med. staff St. John's Hosp. and Health Center, Santa Monica, 1974-78, Santa Monica Hosp. and Med. Center, 1974-78, mem. rsch. com., 1975-77; prof. Calif. State U., Bakersfield, 1977—, assoc. prof. physiology Wayne State U. Sch. Medicine, Detroit; cons. to Nigeria Hematology Center, Lagos, Nigeria, 1973-75; med. dir. San Joaquin Hematology and Oncology Med. Group, Bakersfield, 1977—; med. dir. Regional Cancer and Blood Dir. Disease Ctr. of Kern; dir. hematology/oncology San Joaquin Community Hosp., Bakersfield. Fellow Am. Coll. Physicians, Am. Soc. Clin. Pathologists (dir. coagulation workshop 1974—), Am. Coll. Angiology, Internat. Coll. Angiology; mem. A.C.P., Am. Soc. Hematology, Internat. Soc. Hematology, Am. Assn. for Clin. Rsch., AAAS, Am. Soc. of Mammalolgists, Fedn. of Am. Scientists, Internat. Assn. for Study of Lung Cancer (founding mem. 1974), Am. Geriatrics Soc., N.Y. Acad. Scis., Am. Heart Assn., Nigerian Hematology Soc., Internat. Soc. on Thrombosis and Haemostasis, Am. Cancer Soc., Calif. Coll. Honor Soc. Author: (with others) Modern Concepts and Evaluations of Hemostasis and Thrombosis, 1975, Difficult Diagnosis Problems in Hemostasis and Thrombosis, 1976, Recent Concepts and Developments in Evaluating Disorders of Hemostasis and Thrombosis, 1976, Current Concepts of Hemostasis and Thrombosis, 1976, Basic Concepts of Hemostasis and Thrombosis, 1980; contbr. chpts. in field to books in medicine; contbr. numerous articles on hematology and angiology to med. jours. Home and Office: 3550 Q St #105 Bakersfield CA 93301

BICKAL, ROBERT RICHY, university administrator; b. Ft. Dodge, Iowa, Feb. 2, 1927; s. S.L. and France Fay (Ristine) B.; m. Janet Marie Regottaz, June 14, 1952 (div. 1981); children: Jean Marie, Ellen Jane, James Ristine. Student, State U. of Iowa, 1944-45; BA, Grinnell Coll., 1949; MA, Columbia U., 1954. Instr. in English Eastman Sch. Music, Rochester, N.Y., 1954-57; dir. sales promotion Midland Specialty Co., El Paso, Tex., 1957-59; prof. of English Rochester (N.Y.) Inst. Tech., 1959-64, dir. contract adminstrn., 1964-68; dir. state and fed. relations Alfred (N.Y.) U., 1968-69; spcl. asst. to chancellor N.J. Dept. Higher Edn., Trenton, 1969-71; dir. manpower resources Coll. of Med. & Dentistry, N.J., Newark, 1971-73; dir. employee relations Rutgers U., New Brunswick, N.J., 1973-81; dir. labor relations U. Calif., Santa Cruz, 1981—; mediator, fact-finder N.Y. Pub. Employment Relations Bd., Albany, 1968-81; cons. labor relations, U.S. Colls. and Univs., 1971—, Academic Collective Bargaining Info. Svcs., 1975-80; adjunct prof. Calif. State U. Consortium, San Jose, 1984-87. Mem. Rochester Bd. Edn., N.Y., 1961-68; bd. dirs. Rochester Lib. System, 1963-64, Santa Cruz (Calif.) Metro Transit Dist., 1987-89; vice chmn., govn. body Midcoast Health Systems Agcy., Santa Cruz, 1983-86. With U.S. Navy, 1945-46. Mem. Nat. Pub. Employment Labor Relations Assn., Acad. of Academic Personnel Adminstrs. Democrat. Home: PO Box 612815 South Lake Tahoe CA 95761 Office: Univ Calif Office Labor Relations Santa Cruz CA 95064

BICKAR, BETTY ARLENE, business systems executive; b. Plattville, Colo., Nov. 14, 1931; d. Leslie William and Kathryn Mabel (Rutherford) Clawson; children—Patricia J., Andrew L. Bookkeeper, office mgr. Manes Logging Co., Clallam Bay, Wash., 1958-70; lic. ins. agt. life and disability, Wash.; stenographer, prodn. acct. Crown Zellerbach Corp., Sekiu, Wash., 1970-73; bookkeeper, acct., office mgr., A. W. Logging Inc., Corner Bay, Alaska, 1973-79; owner, operator Spectra Northwest, specializing in photo identification and lamination, Bellevue, Wash., 1979—; northwest regional mgr. Am. Pub. Life Ins. Co., 1988—; dir. Nat. Safety Assocs. Inc., 1989—. Mem. Faith, Hope and Love Christian Ctr., Issaquah, Wash.; vol. counselor 700 Club. Mem. Nat. Fedn. Ind. Bus. Office: Spectra Northwest 1840 130th Ave NE Ste 6 Bellevue WA 98005

BICKEL, NANCY KRAMER, writer; b. Phoenix, Feb. 23, 1941; d. Sidney David and Miriam (Zales) Kramer; m. Peter John Bickel, Mar. 2, 1964; children: Amanda Sidney, Stephen Eliezer. BA with high honors, Swarthmore Coll., 1962; MA, U. Calif., Berkeley, 1965. Acting instr. English dept. U. Calif., Berkeley, 1974; bd. dirs., v.p. writer League of Women Voters, Berkeley, 1977-84; TV producer League of Women Voters, Oakland, Calif., 1978-86; writer, producer League of Women Voters, Calif., 1985—; organizer, mgr. Israel Statistical Assn., 1981-82. Author and co-producer TV documentary Can I Drink the Water, 1986 (Silver Apple award 1987), Toxic Chemicals: Information is the Best Defense, 1 & 2, 1984 (Blue Ribbon award 1985). Chair person Citizens Adv. Com. Negotiations, Berkeley; v.p., trustee Berkeley Pub. Lib., 1983-85; chair Cable TV Task Force, Berkeley, 1988—. Woodrow Wilson fellow. Mem. Bay Area Video Coalition, Assn. Ind. Video & Filmmakers, Inc., Internat. TV Assn., Phi Beta Kappa. Home: 1522 Summit Rd Berkeley CA 94708 Office: 926 J St Ste 1000 Sacramento CA 95814

BICKELL, ROY A., wood products company executive. Pres., chief operating officer Canfor Corp., Vancouver, B.C., Can. Office: Canfor Corp, 1055 Dunsmuir St, Vancouver, BC Canada V6C 1N5 *

BICKER, DANIEL WAYNE, travel agency executive; b. Pasadena, Jan. 17, 1953; s. Robert Paul and Beverly June (Wessel) B.; m. Susan Lowell Ilsley, Mar. 20, 1976; children: Kimberly, Elizabeth, Jonathan, Phillip. BA in Polit. Sci., Calif. State Poly. U., 1976. With United Airlines, Chgo., Denver, 1974-84; v.p. mktg. Destination Travel, Inc., Denver, 1984-87; pres. Assn. World Travel, Inc., Denver, 1988—; ptnr. Trinity Group Cons., Denver, 1987—. Mem. Am. Soc. Assn. Execs., Profl. Conv. Mgmt. Assn. (adv. bd. Convene mag. 1986--). Republican. Presbyterian. Home: 5566 E Davies Pl Littleton CO 80122-2516 office: Assn World Travel Inc 5420 S Quebec St #100 Englewood CO 80155-4015

BICKERSTAFF, BERNIE LAVELLE, professional basketball coach; b. Benham, Ky., Feb. 11, 1944; m. Eugenia Bickerstaff; children: Tim, Robin, Cyndi, Bernard, John. Student, U. San Diego. Formerly asst. coach U. San Diego; then asst. coach Washington Bullets, Nat. Basketball Assn., Landover, Md.; head coach Seattle SuperSonics, 1985—. Office: care Seattle Supersonics 1980 Queen Anne Ave N Box 900911 Seattle WA 98109 *

BICKFORD, WADE ELSON, research engineer; b. Tacoma, Wash., May 12, 1951; s. Earl and Thelma Louise (Gerspacher) B.; m. R. Linnea Burr, May 16, 1981. BA in Math., Wash. State U., 1973; MS in Nuclear Engring., U. Wash., 1977, PE in Mech. Engring., 1987. Sr. research engr. Battelle Meml. Inst. div. Pacific N.W., Richland, Wash., 1974—. Writer numerous patent disclosures dealing with passively safe nuclear plants, 1986-88. Mem. ASME, Nat. Rifle Assn., Phi Beta Kappa. Republican. Club: Porsche of Am. (Richland). Office: Battelle Meml Inst PO Box 999 Battelle Blvd Richland WA 99352

BICKNELL, ARTHUR DWAYNE, insurance company executive; b. Alameda, Calif., Mar. 12, 1933; s. Arthur Henry and Kathleen (Williams) B.; m. Margaret Ann McPhee, Sept. 11, 1954; children: Kathleen Ana, Arthur K., Brian P. Gen. mgr. Trader Bicknell's, Alameda, Calif., 1954-63; dist. mgr. Equitable Life, Oakland, Calif., 1963-66; exec. v.p. San Francisco Fidelity Corp., Menlo Park, Calif., 1966-69; store mgr. Hadley Furniture, Hayward, Calif., 1964-72; gen. mgr. Russells Fine Furniture, Santa Clara, Calif., 1972-76; pvt. practice Brookdale, Calif., 1976-81; account exec. Sta. KOTI-TV, Klamath Falls, Oreg., 1981-86; dist. agt. Prudential Fin. Svc., Klamath Falls, 1986—. Author: 5 of ME, 1976. bd. dirs. ARC, Klamath Falls, 1988-89; pres., bd. mem. Wednesday's Child Sexual Abuse Agy., Klamath Falls, 1985-87. Sgt. USMC, 1950-54, Korea. Mem. Nat. Assn. Life Underwriters (publicity chmn. 1987, Nat. Quality award 1988, Nat. Sales Achievement award 1988), CLU/CHFC Soc. Office: Prudential Fin Svc 520 Klamath Ave Klamath Falls OR 97601

BIDDLE, DONALD RAY, aerospace company executive; b. Alton, Mo., June 30, 1936; s. Ernest Everet and Dortha Marie (McGuire) B.; student El Dorado (Kans.) Jr. Coll., 1953-55, Pratt (Kans.) Jr. Coll., 1955-56; B.S. in Mech. Engring., Washington U., St. Louis, 1961; postgrad. computer sci. Pa. State U. Extension, 1963; certificate bus. mgmt. Alexander Hamilton Inst., 1958; m. Nancy Ann Dunham, Mar. 13, 1955; children—Jeanne Kay Biddle Bednash, Mitchell Lee, Charles Alan. Design group engr. Emerson Elec. Mfg., St. Louis, 1957-61; design specialist Boeing Vertol, Springfield, Pa., 1962; cons. engr. Ewing Tech. Design, Phila., 1962-66; chief engr. rotary wing Gates Learjet, Wichita, Kans., 1967-70; dir. engring. Parsons of Calif. div. HITCO, Stockton, Calif., 1971—. Cons. engr. Scoutmaster, counselor, instl. rep. Boy Scouts Am., St. Ann, Mo., 1958-61; mem. Springfield Sch. Bd., 1964. Mem. Am. Helicopter Soc. (sec.-treas. Wichita chpt. 1969), ASME, Am. Mgmt. Assn., ASTM, Am. Inst. Aeros. and Astronautics, Exptl. Pilots Assn. Republican. Methodist (trustee, chmn. 1974-76, 84-86, 87-89, staff parish 1987-88). Patentee landing gear designs, inflatable rescue system, glass retention systems, adjustable jack system, cold weather start fluorescent lamp, paper honeycomb core post-process systems. Home: 1140 Stanton Way Stockton CA 95207 Office: HITCO 3437 Airport Way Stockton CA 95206

BIDDLE, WAYNE THOMAS, oil and gas exploration company executive; b. Miller, S.D., May 13, 1924; s. Clifford Henry and Neva Berniece (Rhodes) B.; m. LaFawn H. Hall, Mar. 20, 1952; children—Belinda G., Barbara G. B.S. in Petroleum Engring., U. Okla., 1948. Engr., Stanolind Oil & Gas Co., Ardmore, Okla., 1948-50; sales engr. Dunigan Tool & Supply Co., Abilene, Tex., 1950-53; dir. mgr. Am. Iron & Machine Works, Denver, 1953-56; vice chmn. Exeter Drilling Co., Denver, 1956-83; owner Triple B Co., 1983—; also dir.; dir. Union Bank and Trust, N.J. Nat. Resources, Natural Gas Assocs. Named Man of Month, Western Oil Reporter, 1971. Mem. Internat. Assn. Drilling Contractors (dir.), Ind. Petroleum Assn. Am., Am. Petroleum Inst. Republican. Congregationalist. Clubs: Denver Petroleum (Man of Year 1978), Cherry Hills Country (Englewood); Castle Pine (Castle Rock); Old Baldy (Saratoga, Wyo.); Fairbanks Ranch Country (Rancho Santa Fe, Calif.). Home: 4001 Nassau Circle Englewood CO 80110 Office: 1801 Broadway Ste 1204 Denver CO 80202

BIDWELL, ROY W., title insurance company executive, real estate developer and investor. came to U.S., 1958; m. Eileen Bidwell; children: Paul, Mark. Student, Enfield Tech. Coll., Ohio State U.; MA in Comml. Banking, Rutgers U. V.p. First Nat. Bank, Albuquerque, 1958-70; chmn., chief exec. officer Rio Grande Title Co., Inc., Albuquerque, 1970—; vice chmn. N.Mex. Internat. Trade and Investment Council; chmn. N.Mex. Bus. and Investment Conv., London, 1984-85. Chmn. Exec. Liaison Com. Albuquerque Bd. Realtors; mem. Mayor's Community Econ. Devel. Action Grant com.; pres. St. Joseph Hosp. and Health Care Found; trustee St. Joseph Health Care Corp.; chmn. strategic planning St. Joseph Healthcare Corp.; bd. dirs. Albuquerque Econ. Devel./Indsl., Ballet West N.Mex.; bd. dirs., chmn. Capital Campaign. Recipient Disting. Community Service award Anti-Defamation League B'nai Brith, 1984, Economic Devel. Achievement award Bus. Expo, 1987. Mem. Am. Inst. Banking (pres. Albuquerque chpt.), Am. Bankers Assn. (ednl. sect.), Greater Albuquerque C. of C. (chmn. perceptions Albuquerque task force, pres. 1983), New Mex. First Econ. Forum. Clubs: Albuquerque Country, Albuquerque Petroleum. Home: 9919 Tanoan Dr NE Albuquerque NM 87111 Office: Rio Grande Title Co Inc PO Box 3565 Albuquerque NM 87190-3565

BIDWELL, SONDRA LEE MARIE, psychotherapist; b. Portland, Nov. 22, 1939; d. Homer Gerald and Orba Ammonica (Kropp) B.; children: Brett Gerald Lubahn, Kevin Michael Lubahn, Kristin Melinda Whittaker, Pamela Lynn Boury. AA, Edmonds Community Coll., Wash., 1981; BA in Psychology, Seattle U., 1983, MA in Psychology, 1985. Mental health therapist Mental Health North, Seattle, 1983-85, Eastside Mental Health, Bellevue, Wash., 1985-87; mental health, alcohol, drug therapist, counselor First Step, Seattle, 1987--. Democrat. Roman Catholic.

BIDWILL, WILLIAM V., professional football executive. s. Charles W. and Violet Bidwill; m. Nancy; children: William Jr., Michael, Patrick, Timothy, Nicole. Grad., Georgetown U. Co-owner St. Louis Cardinals Football Team (now known as Phoenix Cardinals), 1962-72, owner, 1972—, also chmn., 1972—. Office: Phoenix Cardinals 51 W 3d St 5th Fl Tempe AZ 85281 *

BIE, JAMES EDWARD, nutritional research company executive, writer; b. Racine, Wis., Dec. 26, 1927; s. William Howard and Margaret Mary (Hanish) B.; m. Victoria Elizabeth Betts, Sept. 13, 1979; children: James Patrick, Garry Edward. BS in Journalism, U. Wis., 1950. Asst. exec. v.p. Assn. of Commerce, Milw., 1950-58; adminstrv. sec. U. Wis. Found., Madison, 1958-63; v.p. Marquette U., Milw., 1963-66; account exec. Hayden-Stone, Inc., La Jolla, Calif., 1966-69; v.p. San Diego Securities, Inc., 1969-78; pres. Nutrition 21, San Diego, 1978—. Editor: (fin.) La Jolla mag.; contbr. articles on health, nutrition and travel to numerous pubs. Chmn. La Jolla chpt. Am. Cancer Soc., 1969-71. Served to cpl. U.S. Army, 1946-48. Mem. (charter) Internat. Assn. Fin. Planners, Nat. Nutritional Foods Assn., (charter) Mutual Fund Council of Million Dollar Producers, Stock and Bond Club (pres. 1976), Wis. Indsl. Editors Assn. (pres. 1954), Mensa Soc. (pres. 1973), Wis. Alumni Club of San Diego (pres. 1974), Alpha Tau Omega. Republican. Home: 5930 La Jolla Hermosa Ave La Jolla CA 92037 Office: Nutrition 21 1010 Turquoise St San Diego CA 92109

BIEBER, DANIEL DARREL, technical institute official; b. Tucson, Dec. 27, 1951; s. William L. and Virginia Marie (Jones) B.; m. Charlene Marie Koth, June 13, 1973; children: Angella Mary, Scott David, Andrew Joseph. BA in Edn., Eastern Wash. U., 1974, MS in Math. and Computer, 1980. High sch. tchr. math. Wilbur (Wash.) Sch. Dist., 1974-76; programmer, analyst Boeing Computer Services, Kent, Wash., 1977-79, Eastern Wash. U., Cheney, Wash., 1979-82; dir. computer instrn. Spokane (Wash.) Tech. Inst., 1982-88, owner, v.p., dir. edn., 1988—. Mem. Data Processing Mgmt. Assn. (bull. chmn. 1986-87, v.p. 1987-88, pres. 1989-90). Office: Spokane Tech Inst N 1101 Fancher Rd Spokane WA 99212

BIEBERBACH, WILLIAM HUNT, management consultant; b. Detroit, Jan. 17, 1944; s. George Bieberbach and Agnes Emily (Hunt) Goss. BA in Physics, Rollins Coll., 1970, MBA, 1971. Mktg. mgr., research mgr. Walt Disney World Co., Lake Buena Vista, Fla., 1971-76; dir. group ops. Taft Broadcasting Co., Cin., 1976-80; mgmt. cons. W.H. Bieberbach and Assocs., Santa Ana, Calif., 1980—; co. rep. Regional Planning Council, Orlando, Fla., 1972-76; recreational council, Urban Land Inst., Washington, 1981-88. Author: (research study) Tourist Transportation Study, 1986, Attendance Analysis, 1983, Field Ion Microscope, 1967. Mem. Discover Am., Washington, 1978-83. Recipient Sullivan Medallion, Rollins Coll., Winter Park, Fla., 1970. Mem. Tourist Research Assn., Internat. Assn. Amusement Parks and Attractions, Traveland Tourist Research Assn., Isleworth, Pacific Golf Club, Racquetball Club, Bay Hill Club. Presbyterian. Home: 1404 N Tustin X-1 Santa Ana CA 92701-3026

BIEDERMAN, DONALD ELLIS, lawyer; b. N.Y.C., Aug. 23, 1934; s. William and Sophye (Groll) B.; m. Marna M. Leerburger, Dec. 22, 1962; children: Charles Jefferson, Melissa Anne. AB, Cornell U., 1955; JD, Harvard U., 1958; LLM in Taxation, NYU, 1970. Bar: N.Y. 1959, Calif. 1977, U.S. Dist. Ct. (so. dist.) N.Y. 1967. Assoc. Hale, Russell & Stentzel, N.Y.C., 1962-66; asst. corp. counsel City of N.Y., 1966-68; assoc. Delson & Gordon, N.Y.C., 1968-69; ptnr. Roe, Carman, Clerke, Berkman & Berkman, Jamaica, N.Y., 1969-72; gen. atty. CBS Records, N.Y.C., 1972-76; sr. v.p. legal affairs and adminstrn. ABC Records, L.A., 1977-79; ptnr. Mitchell, Silberberg & Knupp, L.A., 1979-83; sr. v.p. legal and bus. affairs Warner Bros. Music (now Warner/Chappell Music Inc.), L.A., 1983—; adj. prof. law Southwestern U. Sch. Law, L.A., 1982—, Pepperdine U., Malibu, Calif., 1985-87. Editor: Legal and Business Problems of the Music Industry, 1980; co-author: Law and Business of the Entertainment Industries, 1987. Bd. dirs. Calif. Chamber Symphony Soc., L.A., 1981—. 1st lt. U.S. Army, 1959. Recipient Hon. Gold Record Recording Industry Assn. Am., 1974, Trendsetter award Billboard Mag., 1976. Mem. N.Y. State Bar, State Bar Calif., Riviera Country Club (Pacivic Palisades, Calif.). Democrat. Jewish. Home: 2406 Pesquera Dr Los Angeles CA 90049 Office: Warner Bros Music 9000 Sunset Blvd Los Angeles CA 90069

BIENENSTOCK, ARTHUR IRWIN, physicist; b. N.Y.C., Mar. 20, 1935; s. Leo and Lena (Senator) B.; m. Roslyn Doris Goldberg, Apr. 14, 1957; children—Eric Lawrence, Amy Elizabeth (dec.), Adam Paul. B.S., Poly. Inst. Bklyn., 1955, M.S., 1957; Ph.D., Harvard U., 1962. Asst. prof. Harvard U., Cambridge, Mass., 1963-67; mem. faculty Stanford (Calif.) U., 1967—, prof. applied physics, 1972—, vice provost faculty affairs, 1972-77, dir. synchrotron radiation lab., 1978—; mem. U.S. Nat. Com. for Crystallography, 1983-88; lectr., cons. in field. Author papers in field. Bd. dirs. No. Calif. chpt. Cystic Fibrosis Research Found., 1970-73, mem. pres.'s adv. council, 1980-82; trustee Cystic Fibrosis Found., 1982-88. Recipient Sidhu award Pitts. Diffraction Soc., 1968, Disting. Alumnus award Poly. Inst. N.Y., 1977; NSF fellow, 1962-63. Fellow Am. Phys. Soc., AAAS; mem. Am. Crystallographic Assn., N.Y. Acad. Scis. Jewish. Home: 967 Mears Ct Stanford CA 94305 Office: Synchrotron Radiation Lab Bin 69 Box 4349 Stanford CA 94309

BIENVENU, ROBERT CHARLES, lawyer; b. Milw., Dec. 3, 1922; s. Harold John and Nellie (Davidson) B.; AB, U. Calif., Berkeley, 1947; JD, U. Pacific, 1953. Bar: Calif. 1954. m. Martha Beard, Mar. 28, 1945 (dec. 1969); children: Susan Krestan, Nancy Simas, John; m. Joyce Marlene Holley, Aug. 13, 1971. State parole officer Dept. Corrections, Sacramento, 1947-54; mem. Hoover, Lacy & Bienvenu, Modesto, Calif., 1954-66; pvt. practice, 1966—. Pres., Stanislaus County Sch. Bds. Assn., 1968-69; mem. Modesto City Schs. Bd. Edn., 1961-81; mem. Calif. Rep. Cen.Com. 1960-70; bd. dirs. Modesto Symphony Orch., 1966-72, Retarded Children's Soc. Stanislaus County, 1965-70, Am. Cancer Soc., 1955-60. With AUS, 1942-45. Mem. ABA, State Bar Calif., Stanislaus County Bar Assn., Am. Trial Lawyers Assn., Modesto Racquet Club. Home: 218 Brook Way Modesto CA 95354 Office: 726 10th St Modesto CA 95354

BIERBAUM, PAUL MARTIN, JR., lawyer; b. Alton, Ill., Oct. 31, 1946; s. Paul Martin and Maryella (Godwin) B.; m. Kay Sheldon Edmunds, June 23, 1973; 1 child, Kim Elizabeth. BA, DePauw U., 1968; JD, U. Ill., 1972. Bar: Ill. 1972, Colo. 1973, U.S. Dist. Ct. Colo. 1973. Asst. prof. bus. and labor law Western Ill. U., Macomb, 1972-73; legal staff asst. II, 20th Jud. Dist., Boulder, Colo., 1974-76; assoc. Johnson, Doty & Johnson, Boulder, 1976-78; ptnr. Doty, Johnson & Bierbaum, Boulder, 1978-85, Doty, Johnson, Bierbaum & Shapiro, Boulder, 1985-88; pvt. practice law Boulder, 1988—; instr. bus. law U. Colo., Boulder, 1977-78; vol. atty. Boulder County Legal Svcs., 1978—. Bd. dirs. Boulder County Humane Soc., 1977-78; bd. dirs. Counseling Ctr., Inc., Boulder, 1977—, pres., 1978-87. Rector scholar, 1964-68. Mem. Ill. Bar Assn., Colo. Bar Assn., Boulder County Bar Assn. (chmn. corp., banking and bus. sect. 1986-88). Democrat. Office: 2010 14th St Boulder CO 80302

BIERBAUM-BREWER, TERESA ANN, judicial administrator; b. Chicapee Falls, Mass., Nov. 26, 1951; d. Henry George Sr. and Mariann Victoria (Foster) Bierbaum; m. Richard Allan Hartman, Sept. 28, 1971 (div. 1976); 1 adopted child, Michael Christopher; m. Michael David Brewer, Mar. 16, 1985. Student, Seattle City Coll., 1980. Legal sec. various law firms, Tacoma, 1974-76; Wash. campaign mgr. J. Bruce Burns for State Atty. Gen., Tacoma, 1976; sec. to legis. com. Wash. Ho. of Reps., Olympia, 1977; legal sec. Davies, Pearson, Inc., P.S., Tacoma, 1977-80; real estate agt. Spartus Real Estate Co., Tacoma, 1977-81; jud. adminstr. Pierce County Superior Ct., Tacoma, 1981—. Pierce County Democratic precinct committeeperson, Tacoma, 1980-83; bd. dirs. Tacoma Community Mental Health Ctr., 1987—. Mem. Consumers Union, People for Ethical Treatment of Animals, Greenpeace, Humane Soc. of U.S., Humane Soc. Tacoma/Pierce County. Home: PO Box 98003 Tacoma WA 98498 Office: Pierce County Superior Ct 930 Tacoma Ave S Tacoma WA 98402

BIERI, SCOTT ANDREW, logistic support warehouse foreman; b. Montgomery, Ala., Sept. 23, 1964; s. Albert Paul and Lois (Stewart) B.; m. Martha Macias parra, Jan. 18, 1986; 1 child, Bryce Andrew. Student, Community Coll. Air Force, Edwards AFB, Calif., 1984—, Cerro Coso Community Coll., Edwards AFB, Calif., 1985. Logistic support warehouse foreman Quad-S Inc., NASA Ames-Dryden, Edwards AFB, 1987—. With USAF, 1983-87. Republican. Home: 43312 N Gadsden Ave #123 Lancaster CA 93534 Office: Quad S Inc NASA Ames Dryden 4832 Lilly Dr Warehouse Edwards AFB CA 93523-5000

BIERMAN, LAURENCE WILLIAM, science administrator; b. Aberdeen, Wash., Apr. 28, 1933; s. Laurence William and Clara Romana (Kuchnick) B.; m. Rosemarie Moore, Aug. 22, 1958; children: Karl Patrick, David William, Margaret Louise. BSChemE, U. Wash., 1955; BBA in Bus., Idaho State U., 1969. Jr. engr. Boeing Aircraft Co., Seattle, 1956-57; sr. process engr. Am. Potash & Chem. Co., Trona, Calif., 1959-65; dir. rsch. and devel. J.R. Simplot Co., Pocatello, Idaho, 1965—; technology com. mem. The Fertilizer Inst., Washington, 1978—. Patentee in field. Advisor Jr. Achievement, Pocatello, 1970-72; scoutmaster Boy Scouts Am., Pocatello, 1972-76. Recipient Kirkpatrick award Am. Inst. Chem. Engr., 1965. Mem. Am. Chem. Soc. (div. sec.-treas. 1982, div. chmn. elect 1983, chmn. 1984), Pocatello C. of C., KC (trustee 1988—). Republican. Roman Catholic. Home: 121 Foothill Blvd Pocatello ID 83204 Office: JR Simplot Co PO Box 912 Pocatello ID 83201

BIERWAG, GERALD O., economics and finance educator; b. Rupert, Idaho, Feb. 4, 1936; s. Frederick R. and Ida R. (Mehrer) B.; m. Mildred A. Kroetch, Aug. 14, 1959; children: Morella, Alexander. BA, U. Idaho, 1958; PhD, Northwestern U., 1962. Asst. prof. econs. U. Oreg., Eugene, 1962-65, assoc. prof., 1965-69, prof., 1969-81; prof. econs. and fin. U. Ariz., Tucson, 1981—; reviewer NSF, Washington, 1978—. Author: Duration Analysis: Interest Rate Risk, 1987; contbr. numerous articles to fin. jours. Grantee NSF, 1966-67, Inst. Chartered Fin. Analysts, 1987, Prochnow Found., 1988, Fed. Home Loan Bank Bd., 1988-89. Mem. Am. Econ. Assn. (bd. editors 1981-83), Western Fin. Assn. (pres. 1986-87), Am. Fin. Assn., Soc. for Fin. Studies, Fin. Mgmt. Assn., Inst. Chartered Fin. Analysts (bd. dirs. Rsch. Found. 1987—). Office: U Ariz Coll Bus Dept Fin and Real Estate Tucson AZ 85721

BIESECKER, LYNOIS W., legal administrator, paralegal; b. Klamath Fall, Orgn., May 16, 1949; d. Daniel Terrance and N. Pearl (Payne) Wiley; m. Robert G. Biesecker, May 2, 1974. Student, Bethany Bible Coll., 1967-71; paralegal cert., St. Mary's Coll., Moraga, Calif., 1978; student, Day Spring Counceling,Inc., 1987. Cert. paralegal, Calif. Sales mgr. The Trader's Hut, Inc., Danville, Calif., 1974-78; office mgr. Legal Clin. of Charles M. Worrell, Antioch, Calif., 1977-78; legal research asst. Pacific Gas and Electric Co., San Francisco, 1979-80; unit mgr. Maloney, Chase, Fisher & Hunt, San Francisco, 1980-81; pvt. practice legal adminstr. Concord, Calif., 1982-87; paralegal adminstr. Real Property Services Corp., Carlsbad, Calif., 1988—; tchr. St. Mary's Coll., 1986-87; paralegal Oceanside Sr. Citizen Ctr., Calif., 1988. Counselor I'm a Woman, Inc., Concord, 1987. Del Norte County Scholarship Found., Calif., 1967. Mem. Nat. Fedn. and Paralegal Assns., San Francisco Assn. Legal Assts., San Diego Assn. Legal Assts. (co-chmn. 1988), Legal Adminstrs. Assn., St. Mary's Alumni Assn. (dir. 1985-86). Republican. Home: PO Box 6432 Oceanside CA 92056 Office: Real Property Svcs Corp 1935 Camino Vida Roble Carlsbad CA 92008

BIESEL, HEINER DETLEF PETER, computer scientist, consultant; b. Klosterheide, Germany, Feb. 20, 1944; came to U.S., 1959; s. Heinz F. Kurz and Ursula Kathe (Biesel) Schlesier; m. Karen Marie Rapp, May 17, 1980; children: Michael Kenneth, Stephan Richard. BA in Philosophy, U. Ark., 1971, MS in Computer Sci., 1973; PhD in Computer Sci., Rutgers U., 1985. Mem. tech. staff TI, Huntsville, Ala., 1973-74; rsch. asst. Rutgers U., New Brunswick, N.J., 1974-80; instr. U. Ark., Fayetteville, 1980-83; project engr. Evans & Sutherland, Salt Lake City, 1983-88, project mgr., 1988—; pres. Intelligent Systems, Sandy, Utah, 1985—. Pres. Utah Hang Gliding Assn., Draper, 1988. With USAF, 1961-65. Mem. Utah Soc. Photo-Optical Engrs., Am. Def. Preparedness Assn. Home: PO Box 510122 Salt Lake City UT 84151 Office: Evans & Sutherland 580 Arapeen Dr Salt Lake City UT 84108

BIEVER, KEITH JAMES, planning consultant; b. Hot Springs, S.D., Apr. 16, 1936; s. Joseph Nemecious and Violet S. (Williams)B.; m. Shelley Kathern Sundet, June 14, 1959. BS, S.D. State U., 1958; MS, U. Nebr., 1961; postgrad., Seattle Pacific U., 1961-62, U. Wash., 1965-66. Cert. secondary sci. tchr., Wash. Sci. tchr. Shoreline Pub. Schs., Seattle, 1962-64; biology tchr. Everett (Wash.) Pub. Schs., 1964-65; prof. chemistry, chmn. scis., math. and engring. Bellevue (Wash.) Community Coll., 1965-79; owner, founder Kathy's Klaythings, Lake Stevens, Wash., 1972-81; gen. contractor comml. and multiple design and constrn. Biever Bldg., Lake Stevens, 1977-82; owner, mgr. Travel Designers, Everett, 1980-87; tech. planning cons. for bus. and edn. Keith Assocs., Clinton, Wash., 1988—; grants writer NSF, NIH, NDEA, 1966-74. Patentee ceramics mfg. process. Bd. dir. Snohomish County Pvt. Industry Coun., Everett, 1982-86; mem. Snohomish County Com. for Improved Transp.; mem., planner Everett Sister City Assn. 1st lt. U.S. Army, 1958-66. Fellow U. Nebr., 1959, NSF, 1965; recipient Community Svc. award Snohomish County Econ. Devel. Coun., 1981. Mem. Am. Chem. Soc. (nat. curriculum com. 1972-78), Internat. Caribbean Tourism Bd. (rep. western states chpts. 1983-84), Caribbean Tourism Assn. (northwest chpt. 1983-85), Am. Soc. Travel Agts. (nat. membership com. 1986-87), Rotary (chmn. internat. group exchange 1986). Home and Office: 7576 S Maxwelton Rd Clinton WA 98936

BIFFLE, RICHARD LEE, III, teacher, researcher; b. Denver, Nov. 23, 1949; s. Richard Lee Jr. and Louise Sally (Hill) B.; m. Ana L. Cardenas, Dec. 31, 1977; 1 child, Maria L. BA, U. Calif., Riverside, 1971; MA, Ea. Mich. U., 1974; PhD in Edn., U. N.Mex., 1989. Youth counselor Calif. Youth Authority, Chino, 1971; mid-Atlantic regional youth dir. NAACP, Phila., 1971-72; youth ctr. dir. Holman Youth Ctr., Los Angeles, 1972-73; fellow, intern C.S. Mott Found. Nat. Ctr., Flint, Mich., 1973-74; elem. tchr. Val Verde Sch. Dist., Perris, Calif., 1974-76; assoc. prof., dir. community edn. ctr. U. of Redlands, Calif., 1976-80; supr., instr., reseach asst. U. N.Mex., Albuquerque, 1980-83; Pace instr. USN, San Diego, 1983-85; elem. resource tchr. San Diego Unified Sch. Dist., 1985—; commr., sec. Riverside (Calif.) County Juvenile Justice Delinquency Prevention Commn., 1977-80; pres. Nat. Alliance Black Community Educators, St. Louis, 1980; cons. U.S. Office Edn., Washington, 1977-81. Author: Intern Program Ethnic Studies, 1971, Comm Ed and School Desegregation, 1979. Bd. dirs. Calif. Community Edn. Assn., San Diego, 1977-80; v.p. Calif. Fedn. Black Leadership, Anaheim, 1977-80. Recipient Mary McLeod Bethune award Nat. Council of Negro Women, San Diego, 1987, Spl. Recognition award Excel Tchr. Program, San Diego, 1988; nominated Tchr. of Yr. San Diego City Schs., 1986-87; Mott Found. fellow. Mem. Nat. Community Edn. Assn., NEA, Calif. Tchrs. Assn., Am. Assn. Polit. Sci., Am. School Curriculum Devel., Phi Kappa Phi (hon.), Alpha Phi Alpha, Phi Delta Kappa. Democrat. Office: San Diego City Schs Staff Devel 4100 Normal Ave San Diego CA 92103

BIGANDO, CHARLES ROBERT, JR., county official; b. Globe, Ariz., June 7, 1948; s. Charles Robert Bigando and Marjorie Ann Perry; m. Jo Nell Brantley,. Postgrad., U. Ariz., 1966, Ariz. State U., 1967; AA, Phoenix, 1971. Asst. mgr. Beneficial Fin. Co., Phoenix, 1968-71; metall. acct. Inspiration (Ariz.) Copper Co., 1971-76; pres. Hacienda del Sol Constrn., Globe, 1978-85; dir. Gila County Devel. Office, Globe, 1982—; bd. dirs. Ariz. Enterprise Devel. Corp., 1985—. Author: The Catholic Church in Globe, Ariz. 1886-1986, 1988, Besh-Ba Gowah Archaeological Park Interpretive Guide, 1987, The Gold Miner's Pocket. Dir. Gila County Bd. Suprs., Globe, 1977-81; chmn. bd. dirs. Cobre Valley Ctr. for the Arts, Globe; chief canyon vol. F.D. Mem. Am. Planning Assn. Dem. Roman Catholic. Office: Gila County Devel Office 1400 E Ash St Globe AZ 85501

BIGAY, RHU ARANILLA, artist; b. Manila, Philippines, Dec. 13, 1953; s. Telesforo Bigay and Cresencia (Aranilla) Luz; children: Kristeena A., Jhanelle A. Student, Hartnell Coll., 1981-83; student, Dominican Coll., San Rafael, Calif., 1984-85. Lic. vocat. nurse. Clin. specialist ISR Burn Unit BAMC, Ft. Sam Houston, Tex., 1979-81; med. technician 102nd Med. Group CSMR, San Francisco, 1984-89; vocat. nurse VA Hosp., Martinez, Calif., 1986, CPC Walnut Creek Psychol. Hosp., Walnut Creek, Calif., 1986-89; artist Bigay Stipplegraphic Art Ltd., Concord, Calif., 1989—. Artist (stipple art) Pope Paul II, 1987, represented in Vatican collection, (pencil drawing), Am. Folk Hero, 1986, represented in collection of Philippine Pres. Aquino, (stipple art) John Steinbeck, 1982, represented in J. Steinbeck Soc. With U.S. Army, 1972-81. Decorated Navy/Marine Unit commendation; recipient 1st place 1975 Kung Fu-Karate Championship, Furth, Fed. Republic Germany, 1975, 2nd place D'assaro Fencing competition, San Jose, 1985. Roman Catholic. Home: 613 Countryside Dr Salinas CA 93905 Office: Bigay Stipplegraphic Arts PO box 31107 Walnut Creek CA 94598

BIGGS, DOROTHY ELNORA, librarian; b. Weed, N. Mex., Oct. 17, 1941; d. Stephen E. and Mable Wesley (Lewis) Winters; m. Clinton A. Biggs III, . BA, Met. State U., Denver, 1979; MLS, U. Denver, 1981. Research analyst Morris Animal Found., Englewood, Colo., 1981-86; librarian EPA, Denver, 1986--. Editor: Nat. Enforcement Investigations Ctr. newsletter, 1986—. Founder, pres. Wash. Park Early Learning Ctr., Denver, 1974; fundraiser. Mem. Spl. Libraries Assn., Colo. Assn. Law Libraries. Democrat. Episcopalian. Office: EPA/NEIC Libr PO Box 25227 DFC Denver CO 80225

BIGGS, THOMAS WYLIE, chemical executive; b. Seattle, Oct. 28, 1950; s. Ray Wylie and Mildred Virginia (Ramsey) B.; m. Marcia Jean Holts, Aug. 4, 1973; children: Jennifer Tamar, Jordan Wylie. BA, U. Wash., 1972. Chemisty tchr. Samammish High Sch, Bellevue, Wash., 1972-74; sales rep. Litton Industries, Seattle, Wash., 1974-75; sales rep. Van Waters & Rogers (subs. Univar), Kent, Wash., 1975-80, area chem. mgr., 1988—, field sales mgr., 1980-85; sales mgr. Van Waters & Rogers (subs. Univar), South Bend, Ind., 1985-86; mgr. chem. dept. Van Waters & Rogers (subs. Univar), Indpls., 1986-88. 1st lt. USAR, 1973-80. Mem. Chgo. Drug and Chem. Assn., N.W. Paint and Coating Assn. Office: Van Waters and Rogers 8201 S 212th Kent WA 98032

BIGLER, PAMELA ANN, orthopaedic technologist; b. Waupaca, Wis., Sept. 5, 1963; d. Gary Charles Minton and Judith Ann (Bowker) Lick; m. Michael Robert Bigler, Jan. 13, 1984. Student, Thomas Nelson Community Coll., Hampton, Va., 1984, Cosumnes River Coll., Sacramento, 1986-87. Typesetter, proofreader Waupaca Pub. Co., 1979-81; orthopaedic technologist Med. Clinic Sacramento, 1985-86, Michael R. Shapiro, M.D., 1986-88, Norman K. Poppen, M.D., Sacramento, 1988—. With USAF, 1981-85. Fellow Nat. Assn. Orthopaedic Technologists (cert.); mem. NAFE, Nat. Honor Soc., Quill and Scroll. Lutheran. Home: 1722 Urbana Way Sacramento CA 95833 Office: Norman K Poppen MD 2801 K St Ste 440 Sacramento CA 95816

BIGLEY, GEORGE KIM, JR., neurologist; b. Brawley, Calif., Oct. 28, 1951; s. George Kim and Carolyn (Goree) B. BA, U. Calif., San Diego, 1973; MD, U. Chgo., 1977. Diplomate Am. Bd. Psychiatry and Neurology. Intern U. Calif., San Diego, 1977-81, resident in neurology, 1978-81; asst. prof. U. Nev. Sch. Medicine, Reno, 1981-86, assoc. clin. prof., 1986—; practice medicine specializing in neurology Reno, 1986—; mem. bd. med. advisors Multiple Sclerosis Soc., N.Y.C., 1986—, vice-chmn. council profl. adv. com. chmn., 1988—. Bd. trustees No. Nat. Multiple Sclerosis Soc., Reno, 1987—. Mem. Am. Acad. Neurology. Office: G Kim Bigley MD Ltd 50 Kirman Suite 201 Reno NV 89502

BILBERRY, DEBRA SUE, accountant; b. Clovis, N.Mex., June 20, 1954; d. Edwin Lee Baldridge and Bettie Gene (Gerber) Miller; m. Monty John Bilberry, Aug. 18, 1973; children: John Stewart, Sean David. BBA, Ea. N.Mex. U., 1978, MBA, 1981. Bookkeeper Gary L. Bender CPA, Portales, N.Mex., 1978-79; accounts payable clk. Ea. N.Mex. U., Portales, 1979-80, student internal auditor, 1981, instr. acctg. Clovis br., 1982; acct., internal auditor City of Clovis, 1982-84; controller Borden Peanut Co. Inc., Portales, 1984-85; acct. Los Alamos (N.Mex.) Schs., 1985-88, Los Alamos Nat. Lab., 1988—. Mem. Nat. Assn. Female Execs., Phi Gamma Nu. Democrat. Baptist. Home: PO Box 252 Los Alamos NM 87544-0252 Office: Los Alamos Lab PO Box 1663 Mail Stop P240 Los Alamos NM 87545

BILBRAY, JAMES HUBERT, congressman, lawyer; b. Las Vegas, May 19, 1938; s. James A. and Ann E. (Miller) B.; m. Michaelene Mercer, Jan. 1960; children: Bridget, Kevin, Erin, Shannon. Student, Brigham Young U., 1957-58, U. Nev., Las Vegas, 1958-60; B.A., Am. U., 1962; J.D., Wash. U., 1964. Bar: Nev. 1965. Staff mem. Senator Howard Cannon U.S. Senate, 1960-64; dep. dist. atty. Clark County, Nev., 1965-68; mem. firm Lovell, Bilbray & Potter, Las Vegas, 1969—; mem. Nev. Senate, 1980-86, chmn. taxation com., 1983-84, chmn. interim com. on pub. broadcasting, 1983; mem. 100th Congress from 1st Nev. dist., 1987-89, 101st Congress, 1989—; mem. Com. on Armed Svcs., Sub Com. Mil. Constrn., Sub Com. Readiness, Com. on Small Bus., Fgn. Affairs Com. Small Bus. Com., Select Com. on Hunger, 1987—, Select Com. on Aging, 1988, subcoms. Africa, trade, exports and tourism, energy and agr.; alt. mcpl. judge City of Las Vegas, 1978-80; del. N. Atlantic Alliance, 1989—. Bd. regents U. Nev. System, 1968-72; mem. Nat. Council State Govts. Commn. on Arts and Historic Preservation. Named Outstanding Alumni, U. Nev., Las Vegas, 1979, Humanitarian of the Year, 1984. Mem. Nev. State Bar Assn., Clark County Bar Assn., Phi Alpha Delta, Sigma Chi. Democrat. Roman Catholic. Lodges: Elks, Rotary. Office: Longworth House Office Bldg Rm 1431 Washington DC 20515 also: 4836 Kingston Dr Annandale VA 22023-6147

BILBY, RICHARD MANSFIELD, federal judge; b. Tucson, May 29, 1931; s. Ralph Willard and Marguerite (Mansfield) B.; m. Ann Louise Borchert, July 6, 1957; children: Claire Louise, Ellen M. Moore. B.S., U. Ariz., 1955; J.D., U. Mich., 1958. Bar: Ariz. bar 1959. Since practiced in Tucson; law clk. to Chief Judge Chambers, 9th Circuit Ct. Appeals, San Francisco, 1958-59; mem. firm Bilby, Thompson, Shoenhair & Warnock, 1959-79, partner, 1967-79; judge U.S. Dist. Ct., Dist. Ariz., Tucson, 1979—; chief judge U.S. Dist. Ct., Dist. Ariz., 1985—; conscientious objector hearing officer Dept. Justice, 1959-62; chmn. (Pima County Med.-Legal panel), 1968-70; Mem. Tucson Charter Revision Com., 1965-70. Chmn. United Fund Profl. Div., 1968; chmn. Spl. Gift Div., 1970, St. Joseph Hosp. Devel. Fund Drive, 1970; Republican state chmn. Vols. for Eisenhower, 1956; Rep. county chmn., Pima County, Ariz., 1972-74; Past pres. Tucson Conquistadores; bd. dirs. St. Josephs Hosp., 1969-77, chmn., 1972-75. Served with AUS, 1952-54. Fellow Am. Coll. Trial Lawyers; mem. Ariz. Acad., Town Hall (dir. 1976-79). Office: US Dist Ct Rm 426 US Courthouse 55 E Broadway Tucson AZ 85701

BILDERBACK, DIANE ELIZABETH, garden writer; b. Medford, Ore., Apr. 13, 1951; d. Richard Middleton and Mary Lou (Harris) Letsom; m. David Earl Bilderback, June 27, 1970; children: Eric Leland, Christopher Brian. BS in Botany with honors, U. Mont., 1974. Freelance writer for various mags. including Nat. Gardening and Family Circle, 1974--; calender columnist Rodale's Organic Gardening, Emmaus, Pa., 1984-87, regional advisor, 1987--88; instrnl. aide Mt. Jumbo Elem. Sch., Missoula, Mont., 1987-88. Co-author: Garden Secrets, 1982, Backyard Fruits and Berries, 1984. Home: 5520 Larch Ln Missoula MT 59802

BILEZIKJIAN, EDWARD ANDREW, architect; b. Los Angeles, Mar. 29, 1950; s. Andrew and Alice (Dardarian) B. BSArch, U. So. Calif., 1973, MArch, 1977. Registered architect, Calif. Project mgr. RMA Archtl. Group, Inc., Costa Mesa, Calif., 1977-78; dir. architecture Donald De Mars Assocs., Inc., Van Nuys, Calif., 1978-85; prin. architect EAB Architects, Sepulveda, Calif., 1985-87, Laguna Hills, Calif., 1988—; architect, planner III Trammell Crow Co., Irvine, Calif., 1986-88. Chmn. parish council Armenian Apostolic Ch. Newport Beach, 1988—. Mem. AIA, Archtl. Guild U. So. Calif., Triple-X Fraternity of Calif. (corresponding sec. 1984-85), Nat. Council Archtl. Registration Bds. (cert.). Democrat. Mem. Armenia Apostolic Ch.

BILL, GREGORY STUART, marketing specialist; b. Easton, Pa., Jan. 27, 1946; s. John Llewellyn and Florence Virginia (Schmickle) B.; m. Ann Marie Castele, Oct. 12, 1985. Grad. high sch., Nazareth, Pa. Comml. artist Am. Can Co./Dixie Cup, Easton, 1963-65; guitar maker C.F. Martin & Co., Nazareth, 1965-68; sales mgr. A.L. French Co., Anchorage, 1968-84; exec. dir. Iditarod Trail Sled Dog Race, Wasilla, Alaska, 1984-86, devel. dir., 1986-87; owner Alaskan Events Mktg., Palmer, Alaska, 1987—; mem. adv. coun. Iditarod Nat. Hist., Washington, 1986—. Vice pres. bd. Iditarod Trail Com., Inc., Wasilla, 1982-84; bd. dirs. Greater Anchorage, Inc., 1976-85, pres. bd., 1982; bd. dirs. Alaska Spl. Olympics, Anchorage, 1982-84. Sgt. U.S. Army, 1965-67. Lutheran. Home and Office: Alaskan Events Mktg HC01 Box 6058 Palmer AK 99645

BILLINGS, CHARLES EDGAR, physician; b. Boston, June 15, 1929; s. Charles Edgar and Elizabeth (Sanborn) B.; m. Lillian Elizabeth Wilson, Apr. 16, 1955; 1 dau., Lee Ellen Billings Kreinbihl. Student, Wesleyan U., 1947-49; M.D., N.Y. U., 1953; M.Sc. (Link Found. fellow), Ohio State U., 1960. Diplomate: Am. Bd. Preventive Medicine. Instr. to prof. depts. preventive medicine and aviation Ohio State U. Sch. Medicine, 1960-73, dir. div. environ. health, 1970-73, clin. prof., 1973-83, prof. emeritus, 1983—; med. officer NASA Ames Research Center, Moffett Field, Calif., 1973-76; chief Aviation Safety Research Office, 1976-80, asst. chief for research Man-Vehicle Systems research div., 1980-83, sr. scientist, 1983—; cons. Beckett Aviation Corp., 1962-73; surgeon gen. U.S. Army, 1965-77, FAA, 1967-70, 75, 83; assoc. adviser USAF Sci. Adv. Bd., 1978—; mem. NATO-AGARD Aerospace Med. Panel, 1980-86. Contbr. chpts. to books, numerous articles in field to med. jours. Served to maj. USAF, 1955-57. Recipient Air Traffic Service award FAA, 1969; Walter M. Boothby research award, 1972; PATCO Air Safety award, 1979; Disting. Service award Flight Safety Found., 1979; John A. Tamisea award, 1980; Laura Taber Barbour Air Safety medal, 1981; NASA outstanding leadership medal, 1981; AIAA Jeffries Aerospace Med. Research medal, 1986. Fellow Am. Coll. Preventive Medicine, Aerospace Med. Assn. (pres. 1979-80), Am. Acad. Occupational Medicine; mem. AMA. Clubs: Atlantic Whippet Assn, Am. Whippet; Midland Whippet, Royal Air Force (Gt. Britain). Home: 10460 Albertsworth Ln Los Altos Hills CA 94022 Office: NASA-Ames Rsch Ctr Moffett Field CA 94035

BILLINGS, DONALD LAWRENCE, marketing executive; b. Jamaica Plains, Mass., Mar. 25, 1946; s. William Ricker and Marjorie (Gaffney) B.; m. Marilyn Smith, Jan. 16, 1970; children: Heather Nicole, Adam Lawrence. Student, Orange Coast Coll., 1964-66, Calif. State U., Long Beach, 1966-68. Lic. in travel by Mass. Dept. Edn. Various mgmt. positions 1968-76; travel industry specialist Integral Bus. Computing, Los Angeles, 1976-78; v.p. sales. Automated Travel Acctg. Systems, Los Angeles, 1976-78; travel exec. Maritz Travel Co., St. Louis, 1978-81; v.p. mktg. Corp. Resort and Travel, Irvine, Calif., 1981-83, Joint Venture Travel, Orange, Calif., 1983-84; account mgr. Maritz Motivation Co., St. Louis, 1984-89; exec. v.p., chief fin. officer Image Design Assocs., Inc., St. Louis, 1989—. Editorial cons. Fin. Communications in the Travel Industry, 1982-83. Mem. Am. Mktg. Assn., Soc. Incentive Travel Execs., Inst. Cert. Travel. Agts. (cert. travel cons.). Republican. Home and Office: 7620 Cortina Ct Rancho La Costa CA 92009

BILLINGS, THOMAS NEAL, computer and publishing executive, consultant; b. Milw., Mar. 2, 1931; s. Neal and Gladys Victoria (Lockard) B.; A.B. with honors, Harvard U., 1952, M.B.A., 1954; m. Barta Hope Chipman, June 12, 1954 (div. 1967); children—Bridget Ann, Bruce Neal; m. Marie Louise Farrell, Mar. 27, 1982. Vice pres. fin. and adminstrn. Copley Newspapers Inc., La Jolla, Calif., 1957-70; group v.p. Harte-Hanks Communications Inc., San Antonio, 1970-73; exec. v.p. United Media, Inc., Phoenix, 1973-75; asst. to pres. Ramada Inns, Inc., Phoenix, 1975-76; exec. dir. Nat. Rifle Assn., Washington, 1976-77; pres. Ideation Inc., Washington, 1977-81; chmn. Bergen-Billings Inc., N.Y.C., 1977-80, Franchise Mgmt. Corp., Reno, 1988—; pres. The Assn. Service Corp., San Francisco, 1978-88, Accuprint Inc., Carlsbad, Calif., 1989—; pres. Recorder Printing and Pub. Co. Inc., San Francisco, 1980-82; v.p. adminstrn. Victor Techs. Inc., Scotts Valley, Calif., 1982-84; mng. dir. Saga-Wilcox Computers Ltd., Wrexham, Wales, 1984-85; chmn. Thomas Billings & Assocs., Inc., Reno, 1978—, Intercontinental Travel Svc. Inc., Reno, 1983—, Oberon Internat. Ltd., 1985-86; dir., chief exec. officer Insignia Solutions group, High Wycombe, England, Cupertino, Calif., 1986-89; bd. dirs. Lenny's Restaurants Inc., Wichita, Kans., Tymyndr Corp., Dover Del., Zzyzzyx Corp., Reno; guest lectr. in field. Bd. dirs. Nat. Allergy Found., 1973—, The Wilderness Fund, 1978—, San Diego Civic Light Opera Assn., 1965-69; chief exec. San Diego 200th Anniversary Expn., 1969. Served with U.S. Army, 1955-57. Recipient Walter F. Carley Meml. award, 1966, 69. Fellow U.K. Inst. Dirs.; mem. Am. Newspaper Pubs. Assn., Inst. Execs. Inc. (dir.), Inst. Newspaper Controllers, Am. Assn. V.P.s (dir.), Sigma Delta Chi. Republican. Clubs: West Side Tennis, LaJolla Country; Washington Athletic; San Francisco Press; Harvard (N.Y.C.); Elks. Author: Creative Controllership, 1978; editor The Vice Presidents' Letter, 1978—, Intercontinental News Service, London, England, 1985—; pub. The Microcomputer Letter, 1982—, Synthetic Hardware Update, 1987—. also: 100 W Grove St #360 Reno NV 89509 Office: 100 W Grove St Ste 360 Reno NV 89509 also: 1255 Post St Ste 625 San Francisco CA 94109

BILLINGS-HARRIS, LENORA, management consultant; b. Newark, Aug. 9, 1950; d. Wendell Kenneth and Lois (Perkinson) Billings; m. Charles Sommerville Harris, Aug. 10, 1974. BS, Hampton U., 1972; MA, U. Mich., 1977. Tchr. Hampton (Va.) High Sch., 1972-74; program dir. U. Mich. Grad. Sch. of Bus., 1974-79; project adminstr. Gen. Motors Corp., Flint, Mich., 1977-79; mgr. human resource planning CIGNA Corp., Phila., 1979-81, dir. human resources, 1979-85; personnel and training dir. Culiver Pontiac, Nissan, GMC, Phoenix, 1985-86; pres. Excel Devel. Systems, Inc., Chandler, Ariz., 1986—; faculty assoc., Ariz. State U., Tempe, 1985--; guest speaker, Am. Soc. of Training and Devel., 1984. Author: Effective Automotive Sales, 1987. Bd. dirs. Phoenix Urban League, 1986--, KAET (pub. tv), Tempe, 1986--, Big Bros. Big Sisters, Maricopa City, Ariz., 1985-86. Mem. Am. Soc. of Training and Devel., Am. Soc. of Personnel Adminstrs., Nat. Speakers Assn. Office: Excel Devel Systems PO Box 1002 Tempe AZ 85281

BILLS, RONALD J., dentist; b. Santa Monica, Calif., June 29, 1945. Student, U. Calif., Berkeley, 1963-65, Calif. State Poly. Coll., 1965-66; DDS, Marquette U., 1970. Resident dept. pediatric dentistry Ctr. Health Scis. U. Calif. L.A. Sch. Dentistry, 1970-72; mem. faculty UCLA Dental Sch., 1971-72, UCLA Tokyo Extension Ctr., 1973; pvt. practice Oceanside, Calif., 1974—; asst. clin. instr. pediatrics U. Calif. San Diego Sch. Medicine, 1974—; mem. faculty dental hygiene curriculum Mesa Jr. Coll., 1975-77; attending pediatrics U. Calif. San Diego Med. Sch. Children's Hosp., 1974-77; mem. staff Tri-City Hosp., 1974-78. Bd. dirs. Santa Mareita YMCA; dentist, edn. council U.S. Ski Team; active Boy Scouts Am. With Dental Corps, USNR, 1967-73. Mem. ADA, Calif. Soc. Pediatric Dentistry, San Diego County Dental Soc., Phi Kappa Psi, Delta Sigma Delta. Home: 2719 Bayside Walk San Diego CA 92109 Office: 3230 Waring Ct Ste Q Oceanside CA 92054

BILOW, STEVEN CRAIG, computer graphics specialist; b. L.A., July 10, 1960; s. Norman and Selma (Rifkin) B. BFA in Music Composition, Calif. Inst. of the Arts, 1982; cert. logic design/theory, U. So. Calif., 1983. Cert. tchr. of movement expression, L.A., 1985. Mfg. engr. Hughes Aircraft EDSG, El Segundo, Calif., 1981-85; project engr. electro-optical test systems Hughes Aircraft EDSG, El Segundo, 1985-86; sr. systems analyst Tektronix, Info Display Group, Woodland Hills, Calif., 1986-88; software engr., math. surface representation Tektronix, Interactive Technologies Div., Wilsonville, Oreg., 1989—; cons. in graphics, Numerical Simulations Group, L.A., 1987—; cons. in music composition and ethnomusicology, Structured Perceptions Music, L.A., 1980—; mem. ACM Spl. Interest Group in Computer Graphics, 1988—. Composer various compositions, electro-acoustic instrumental and choral, 1978-83; author: (theater piece) Indra's Net, 1987; author/editor: (book) Designing For Productibility, 1980; contbr. articles and technical papers to jours. Mem. Human/Dolphin Found., Malibu, Calif., 1977, Self-Realization Fellowship, L.A., 1985. Recipient Technical Excellence award, Tektronix, Inc., Wilsonville, 1988. Mem. Am. Musicological Soc., Assn. of Computing Machinery, IEEE (tech. com. on computer graphics, 1985—, tech. com. on super computer applications, 1988). Democrat. Office: Tektronix Interactive Tech PO Box 1000 61/028 Wilsonville OR 97070

BILSON, JEFFREY HARRIS, employment executive; b. L.A., Aug. 28, 1959; s. Wesley and Barbara Jean (Trattner) B. BS with honors, Sociology, U. Calif., Davis, 1981. Counselor U. Calif., Davis, 1979-81; pres. Druthers Agy., Inc., Santa Monica, Calif., 1981—; pres., founder Take Note Prodns., Pacific Palisades, 1987—. Mem. cabinet, health div. United Jewish Fund, Beverly Hills, Calif., 1984-87. Mem. United Hosp. Assn. (bd. advisors 1988—), Calif. Assn. Health Facilities, Calif. Assn. Homes for Aged. Democrat. Jewish. Office: Druthers Agy Inc 119 Colorado Ave #8 Santa Monica CA 90401

BILYEU, CHARLES PIERCE (CHIP BILYEU), electronic technician; b. Fairbanks, Alaska, Feb. 8, 1954; s. Hiram Pierce and Patricia (Downing) B.; m. Nancy Ann Hill, Jan. 4, 1974 (div. May 1987); children: Sarah Ann, Robert Pierce; m. Pamela Jean Higbee, July 29, 1988. AS in Tech., Idaho State U., 1983. Electronics technician Gould Semiconductor Corp., Pocatello, Idaho, 1979-84, supr. I, 1984-87, supr. II, 1987—. Home: 256 Roscoe PO Box 88 Inkom ID 83245 Office: Gould Semiconductor Corp 2300 Buckskin Rd Pocatello ID 83201

BINDER, JAMES KAUFFMAN, computing consultant; b. Reading, Pa., Nov. 20, 1920; s. Paul Burdette and Edna (Kauffman) B.; B.A., Lehigh U., 1941; M.A., Johns Hopkins U., 1952; profl. cert. in systems mgmt. U. Calif.-San Diego, 1976; A.S. in Data Processing, San Diego Evening Coll., 1979, A.A. in Fgn. Lang., 1979; A.A. in Spanish, Mira Costa Coll., Oceanside, Calif., 1981. Instr. English, Notre Dame U., South Bend, Ind., 1948-49; prof. English, Athens (Greece) Coll., 1950-51; CARE rep., Greece, 1951-52; reporter, staff writer Athens News, 1952-53; dir. lang. tng. World Council Chs. Refugee Service, Athens, 1953-54; co-editor Am. Overseas Guide, N.Y., West Berlin, 1957-58; lectr. English, U. Md. Overseas Program, European and Far East divs., 1958-66; successively supr. Cen. Info. Ctr., supt. documents, sr. systems analyst GA Techs., Inc., La Jolla, Calif., 1968-85. Recipient Williams Prize, Lehigh U., 1939, 41; Johns Hopkins U. Grad. Sch. Pres. scholar, 1945-48. Mem. San Diego Opera Assn., Friends of U. Calif.-San Diego Library, IEEE Computer Soc., Assn. Computing Machinery. Roman Catholic. Clubs: Tudor and Stuart, Automobile of So. Calif. Author: The Correct Comedy, 1951; contbg. translator Modern Scandinavian Poetry, 1948; editor: (with Erwin H. Tiebe) American Overseas Guide, 1958.

BINDRA, JEET SINGH, oil company executive, chemical engineer; b. Varanasi, India, Sept. 18, 1947; came to U.S., 1969; s. Gian Singh and Daya Kaur (Johar) B.; m. Janice Elaine Cooper, May 23, 1971; children: Amby Jeet, Shammi Jeet. BTech. in Chem. Engring. with distinction, Indian Inst. Tech., 1969; MSChemE, U. Wash., 1970; MBA with honors, St. Mary's Coll., Calif., 1979. Process engr. Western Processing Co., Kent, Wash., 1971-72, Fiberglass Pilkington Ltd., Bombay, 1972-74; gen. mgr. ops. Snowhite Engrs. (Pvt.) Ltd., New Delhi, 1974-77; rsch. environ. engr. Chevron, Richmond, Calif., 1977-79, sr. environ. and refinery engr., 1979-80; supervising engr. Richmond lube oil project Chevron, 1980-82, asst. constrn. mgr., 1982-84; asst. constrn. mgr. Sudan petroleum devel. project Chevron, Khartoum, 1984; design mgr. phosphate fertilizer project Chevron, Tampa, Fla., 1984-85; constrn. mgr. Chevron, Rock Springs, Wyo., 1985-86; chief engr. desings El Segundo (Calif.) refinery Chevron U.S.A. Inc., 1986-88; supt. ops. Chevron U.S.A. Inc., El Segundo, 1988—; mem. program evaluation com. Western Wyo. Coll., Rock Springs, 1985-86, mem. pres.'s adv. council, 1985-86; mem. peer tech. rev. group, EPA. Contbr. articles to profl. jours. Advisor Southwest Wyo. Rehab. Ctr., Rock Springs, 1985-86. Home: 4411 Clubhouse Dr Lakewood CA 90712 Office: Chevron USA Inc 324 W El Segundo Blvd El Segundo CA 90245

BINEGAR, GWENDOLYN ANN, social worker; b. Phoenix, Sept. 23, 1924; d. Glenn Marvin and Mary Lenore (Cartwright) Redington; B.S. in Sociology, Iowa State U., 1948; M. Social Svc., Bryn Mawr Coll., 1967; m. Lewis Albert Binegar, Nov. 2, 1951; children—Glen Albert, Birne Thomas, William Lewis, Alan Martin. Coord. vols. Santa Barbara Mental Health Svc., Lompoc, Calif., 1964; psychiat. social worker Child Study Inst., Bryn Mawr (Pa.) Coll., 1967-71; supervising counselor San Gabriel Valley Regional Ctr., Pomona, 1975-78, program mgr. six L.A. County Regional Ctrs' High Risk Infant Projects, 1978-79; chief case mgmt. svcs. San Diego Regional Ctr., 1981—, assoc. dir., 1988—; v.p. Golden Years, Inc., Valley Ctr., Calif., 1987—. Lic. clin. social worker. Fellow Soc. Cert. Social Workers; mem. Am. Acad. Certified Social Workers, Am. Assn. on Mental Deficiency , Nat. Assn. Social Workers. Republican. Presbyterian. Home: 28809 Lilac Rd Valley Center CA 92082 Office: San Diego Regional Ctr 4355 Ruffin Rd San Diego CA 92123

BING, RALPH SOL, advertising executive; b. Cleve., May 21, 1917; s. Sol Ralph and Helen (Einstein) B.; m. Barbara Cohen, Nov. 8, 1953; children: Aleta, Ralph Sam. Student, U. Ill., 1936-37; cert., John Huntington Poly., Cleve., 1939, Kent State U., 1966. Advt. copywriter The May Co., Cleve., 1938-41; advt. mgr. The Heights Press (now named Sun Newspapers), Cleve., 1941-42; ptnr. Bing and Haas Advt., Cleve., 1946-51; pres. Ralph Bing Advt. Co., Cleve., 1951—, Mktg. Assocs., Beachwood, Ohio, 1975-79; owner Ralph Bing Advt. Cons., San Diego, 1980-87. Author: SMOKE DREAMS, 1950, History of the Temple, 1950; contbr. numerous articles to profl. jours., also radio and TV commls. Councilman City of Beachwood, 1965-79; pres. grouping of municipalities Council of Cleve., 1978-79; mem. Pub. Utilities Commn., Rancho Bernardo, Calif., 1983-85; chmn. Community Alert Program Rancho Bernardo, 1986. Served with U.S. Army, 1942-45, ETO. Recipient Outstanding Citizen award Beachwood Civi League, 1980, Outstanding Service award United Appeal, 1950, 51, Appreciation plaque Ohio Bar Assn., 1975; Ralph S. Bing Day named in his honor Beachwood City Council, 1979, 80. Mem. Family Service Assn. (hon. life). Republican. Clubs: Oakwood (Cleve.) (pub. newsletter 1946-80); Rancho Bernardo News; Woodcrafts. Lodges: Masons, Kiwanis (pres. 1976). Home and Office: 16109 Selva Dr San Diego CA 92128

BINGAMAN, JEFF, senator; b. Silver City, N.Mex., Oct. 3, 1943; s. Jesse and Beth (Ball) B.; m. Anne Kovacovich, Sept. 13, 1968. Ed., Harvard U., 1965; J.D., Stanford U., 1968. Bar: N.Mex. 1968. Partner firm Campbell, Bingaman & Black, Santa Fe, 1972-78; atty. gen. State of N.Mex., from 1979; now U.S. senator from N.Mex. Democrat. Methodist. Home: PO Box 5775 Santa Fe NM 87501 Office: US Senate 502 Hart Senate Bldg Washington DC 20510

BINI, DANTE NATALE, architect; b. Castelfranco Emilia, Modena, Italy, Apr. 22, 1932; came to U.S., 1981; s. Giovanni and Maria (Cavallini) B.; m. Adria Vittoria Moretti, June 27, 1963; children: Stefano Alec, Nicolo Guiseppe. Grad., L.S.A. Righi, Bologna, Italy, 1952; PhD in Architecture, U. Florence, 1962. Chmn. Societa' Anonima Immobiliare Castelfranco Emilia, Castelfranco Emilia, 1960-64, Vedova Bini, Castelfranco Emilia, 1960-64; founder, chmn. Unipack, Old Home, Bologna, 1961-65; founder, exec. v.p. Binishell Spa, Bologna, 1966-69; cons. Dept. Pub. Works New South Wales, Sydney, Australia, 1972-74, Jennings Industries Ltd., Melbourne, Australia, 1975-80; founder, pres., chmn. Binistar, Inc., San Francisco, 1981—; external cons. Bechtel Nat., Inc., San Francisco, 1985-86; founder, pres., chmn. Pak-Home, Inc., San Francisco, 1986—; spl. cons. to UN, Rome, 1968, Shimizu Technology Ctr. Am., 1989; lectr. Moscow Expocentre, 1986. Contbr. articles to profl. jours.; patentee self-shaping structures for low-cost, sport and industrial/commercial buildings. Recipient Eurostar award European Inst. Packaging, 1964, Excellence in Engring. Design award Design News Mag., 1968, Best Idea of Yr. award European Design News Mag., 1968, Excellence in Indsl. Design award I.E.S. Australia, 1976. Mem. Bd. Architects Emilia e Romagna, Assn. Architects Bologna (co-founder 1963), Italian Assn. Indsl. Design, Italian Inst. Packaging Design (Oscar award 1961-63), Royal Australian Inst. Architects New South Wales, Am. Assn. Mil. Engrs. Roman Catholic.

BINNIE, NANCY CATHERINE, nurse, educator; b. Sioux Falls, S.D., Jan. 28, 1937; d. Edward Grant and Jessie May (Martini) Larkin; m. Charles H. Binnie. Diploma, St. Joseph's Hosp. Sch. Nursing, Phoenix, 1965; BS in Nursing, Ariz. State U., 1970, MA, 1974. Intensive care charge nurse Scottsdale (Ariz.) Meml. Hosp., 1968-70, coordinator critical care, 1970-71; coordinator critical care John C. Lincoln Hosp., Phoenix, 1971-73; prof. nursing GateWay Community Coll., Phoenix, 1974—; coord. part-time evening nursing programs Gateway Community Coll., 1984—. Mem. Orgn. Advancement of Assoc. Degree Nursing (interim dir. 1989). Office: Gateway Community Coll 104 N 40th St Phoenix AZ 85034

BINNING, BYRON DEE, corporate professional; b. Atwood, Kans., Dec. 1, 1935; s. Thomas LaVelle and Ruth Marie (Cox) B. BS, Century U., 1988, postgrad., 1988—. Cert. x-ray tech. surgical tech. Administrator Atomic Energy Commn., Christmas Island, 1962, Johnston Island, 1962-64; asst. mgr. Normandie Inn, Carmel, Calif., 1964-69; chief med. tech. Cardinal Med. Enterprises, L.A., 1970-73; mgr. West Covina (Calif.) Indsl. Med. Group, 1973-78; adminstr. Community Med. Enterprises, Alhambra, Calif., 1979-83, Alpha Med. Group, Santa Fe Springs, Calif., 1983-86; pres. Genesis Med. Mgmt., Inc., Baldwin Park, Calif., 1986—; cons. JTM Mgmt., Downey, Calif., 1988; administrv. cons., Park Med. Clinic, Baldwin Park, Calif., 1987—. Author: (analysis) Economic Impact of Chiro. Hospital Privileges, 1988. With USN, 1955-60. Recipient cert. merit SBA, Calif. Polytech. U., 1979. Mem. Am. Acad. Med. Adminstrs., Am. Mgmt. Assn. Republican. Roman Catholic. Home: 14228 MacDevitt St Baldwin Park CA 91706 Office: Genesis Med Mgmt Inc 14600 E Ramona Blvd Baldwin Park CA 91706

BIONDO, MARSHA LINDA, insurance executive; b. Denver, Nov. 3, 1948; d. Ralph Leroy and Enid Louise (Adams) Whitney; m. Franklyn B. Biondo, Aug. 6, 1982; 1 child, Chad Andrew Johnson. BS, Colo. State U., 1970; MS, Western Wash. U., 1972. Mktg. rep. Safeco Ins., Seattle, 1980-83; sr. mktg. rep. Home Ins. Cos., Seattle, 1983-85; risk mgr. Oil Heat Inst., Portland, Oreg., 1985—. Alumni ambassador Colo. State U., 1984—. Mem. Oregon Assn. CPCU's (sec. 1987—).

BIONDO, SARAH FRANCES, artist, educator; b. Baton Rouge, La., Aug. 19, 1941; d. John Toto and Virginia Anna (Termini) B.; m. Phillip Edward O'Neill, Oct. 15, 1968 (div. 1969); children: Damian Marcus Biondo O'Neill. BFA in Sculpture and Painting, Kans. City Art Inst., 1967; MFA Sculpture and Ceramics, La. State U., 1969. Instr. La. State U., Baton Rouge, 1967-69, U. Ala., Montevallo, 1969-70, Russell Sage Coll., Troy, N.Y., 1970-76; mem. curatorial staff Contemporary Arts Mus., Houston, 1976-79; freelance graphic artist, drafter Houston, 1979-87; instr. Houston Community Coll., 1982-86; freelance artist Sequim, Wash., 1987—. One-woman show include Fine Arts Ctr., Houston, Houston Community Coll., Blvd. Gallery, Houston, Jewish Community Ctr., Houston and Schnenectady, N.Y., Nassau (N.Y.) Show, Bienville Gallery, New Orleans, Saratoga (N.Y.) Arts Wkshp., Jr. Coll. of Albany, N.Y., numerous others; represented in permantent collections Russell Sage Coll., Superior Oil Co., Houston, W. Houston Med. Ctr., Houston Community Coll., Art Collector Gallery, San Diego, and others; nat. exhibits include Downtown Houston Library, 1984, Nat. Arts Exhibit, Cooperstown, N.Y., 1974, Juried Nat. Arts Exhibit, Tyler, Tex., 1965, Nat. Invitational Show Madison Sq. Garden, N.Y.C., 1976. Exhibiting mem. San Francisco Women Artist Gallery, 1988-89. Recipient Cert. Excellence in Sculpture award Art Horizon, 1988, Best Craftsman award N.Y. State Craftsman Assn., 1975, and others; Adolph and Esther Gottlieb Found grantee, 1989, Russell Sage Coll. grantee, 1973, 75; Kans. Art Inst. sr. scholar, 1966, La. State U. Bd. Suprs. scholar, 1968-69. Mem. Women's Caucus on Art (regional v.p. Olympic Peninsula 1989—), Nat. Assn. Artists Orgn., Nat. Artist Equity Assn. Home and Office: 102A Riverside Sequim WA 98382

BIRBECK, STEPHEN ANTHONY, city official; b. Washington, Sept. 14, 1947; s. Richard Wellington and Louise (Keebler) B.; m. Sharon Langmaid, July 28, 1979; children: Stephen Anthony, Walter Alexander, Amanda Rose. BA, U. Calif., Riverside, 1974; MA, U. Redlands, 1987. Adminstrv. asst. Coachella Valley Assn. Govts., Palm Desert, Calif., 1974-78; asst. city mgr. City of Rancho Mirage, Calif., 1978-83, 88—, 1984-85; exec. dir. Rancho Mirage Redevel. Agy., 1985-86; mng. dir. Riverside County Redevel. Agy., 1986-88. Mem. Eastside Adv. Coun., Riverside, 1973; bd. dirs. One-way Outreach Ctr., Coachella, 1979; mem. fin. com. Calvary Chapel, Cathedral City, Calif., 1987. Recipient Resolution of Appreciation Palm Desert City Coun., 1982, Rancho Mirage Parks Commn., 1985, Cove Communities Fire Commn., 1985. Democrat. Home: 78430 Discovery Bay Bermuda Dunes CA 92201 Office: City of Rancho Mirage 69-825 Highway 111 Rancho Mirage CA 92201

BIRD, CHARLES ALBERT, lawyer; b. Stockton, Calif., July 1, 1947; s. Donald Gladstone and Elizabeth Clara (Jongeneel) B.; m. Charlotte Laura Soeters, June 28, 1969. BA, U. Calif.-Davis, 1969, JD, 1973. Bar: Calif. 1973, U.S. Dist. Ct. (so. dist.) 1975, U.S. Ct. Appeals (9th cir.) 1975, U.S. Supreme Ct. 1980, U.S. Dist. Ct. (cen. dist.) Calif. 1981. Tchr. Woodland Unified Sch. Dist. (Calif.), 1969-70; law clk. justice Supreme Ct. Alaska, Juneau, 1973-74; assoc. Luce, Forward, Hamilton & Scripps, San Diego, 1975-79, ptnr., 1980—. Contbr. articles to profl. publs. Bd. dirs. Defenders Orgn., San Diego, 1982-84; founding dir. San Diego Vol. Lawyer Program, 1982—. Mem. San Diego County Bar Assn. (legis chmn. 1980-81, bd. dirs. 1982-85, sec. 1984, v.p. 1985), State Bar Assn. Calif. (exec. com. real property sect. 1982-86, chmn. exec. com. 1985-86). Democrat. Episcopalian. Home: 4182 Ingalls San Diego CA 92103 Office: Luce Forward Hamilton & Scripps 110 W A St Ste 1700 San Diego CA 92101

BIRD, ROBERT KENTON, journalist, newspaper editor; b. Kellogg, Idaho, Feb. 10, 1954; s. Robert Leizear and Amy Nell (Legg) B. BA in Journalism, U. Idaho, 1976; MS in Journalism Studies, Univ. Coll., Cardiff, Wales, 1980. Reporter Idahonian, Moscow, Idaho, 1975-77, acting mng. editor, 1979-80, asst. mng. editor, 1981-82, mng. editor, 1982-85, editor editorial page, 1985--; editing intern Washington Post, 1977; news editor Lewiston (Idaho) Morning Tribune, 1980-81; asst. mng. editor Daily News, Pullman, Wash., 1981-82, mng. editor, 1982-85, editor editorial page, 1985--; lectr. U. Idaho, Moscow, 1979, 81, Wash. State U., Pullman, 1980; cons. Cen. Idaho Star-News, McCall, 1981; commentator N.W. Pub. TV, Pullman, 1986-88. Mem. Moscow Community Theatre, 1976--, officer, 1982-86; mem. Moscow Community Band, 1984--, Malcolm Kerr Scholarship Com., Moscow, 1986--, Moscow Centennial Commn., 1987; vestryman St. Mark's Episcopal Ch., Moscow, 1988. Rotary Found. journalism fellow, 1978, Am. Polit. Sci. Assn. Congl. fellow, 1988—. Office: Idahonian 409 S Jackson St Moscow ID 83843

BIRD, ROGER, financial broker; b. Long Beach, Calif., Sept. 26, 1953; s. R.B. and Joyce Lorraine (Drake) B.; m. Kim Schultz, Jan. 27, 1973 (div. Oct. 1978); m. Vicki Sue Andrews, July 21, 1979; children: Brandon, Jocelyn, Brooke. AA, Centralia (Wash.) Community Coll., 1976. Bus. banking officer Seattle 1st Nat. Bank, 1976-83; comml. loan officer Idaho Bank & Trust Co., Boise, 1983-84; fin. div. mgr. Trebar, Inc., Boise, 1984-86; pres. Fin. Resources, Inc., Boise, 1985—. Group coordinator Parents with Diabetic Children, Boise, 1988—; pres. Stanwood (Wash.) Jaycees, 1980-81; v.p. Stanwood C. of C., 1981. Republican. Methodist. Office: Fin Resources Inc 1555 Shoreline Dr Ste 110 Boise ID 83702

BIRD, ROSE ELIZABETH, former state chief justice; b. Tucson, Nov. 2, 1936. B.A. magna cum laude, L.I. U., 1958; J.D., U. Calif., Berkeley, 1965. Bar: Calif. 1966. Clk. to chief justice Nev. Supreme Ct., 1965-66; successively dep. public defender, sr. trial dep., chief appellate div. Santa Clara County (Calif.) Pub. Defenders Office, 1966-74; tchr. Stanford U. Law Sch., 1972-74; sec. Calif. Agr. and Services Agy., also mem. governor's cabinet, 1975-77; chief justice Calif. Supreme Ct., 1977-86; chairperson Calif. Jud. Council, Commn. Jud. Appointments; pres. bd. dirs. Hastings Coll. Law, U. Calif.; bd. councilors U. So. Calif. Law Center, 1975-77; past mem. Western regional selection panel President's Commn. White House Fellowships; bd. assos. San Fernando Valley Youth Found; TV commentator, 1988. Named Most Outstanding Sr. L.I. U., 1958; Ford Found. fellow, 1960. Democrat. Address: PO Box 51376 Palo Alto CA 94306

BIRDLEBOUGH, HAROLD, dentist; b. Yakima, Wash., May 4, 1928; s. Otis Theodore and Elizabeth (Brown) B.; D.D.S., U. Wash., 1959; m. Donna Mae Vensel, June 18, 1977; children: John Michael, Elizabeth, William Powers, Marcia; stepchildren: Steve Hassenfratz, Nancy Hassenfratz, Keith Fontel. Practice dentistry, Seattle, 1959-61, King County, Wash., 1961—; mem. dental adv. com. Blue Cross Ins. Co. Served with USNR, 1948-52. Mem. ADA, Wash. Dental Assn., Snohomish County Dental Soc., Gen. Acad. Dentistry, U. Wash. Dental Alumni, Soc. Preservation and Encouragement Barbershop Quartet Singing in Am., Delta Sigma Delta, Alpha Delta Phi (1st v.p. local alumni assn., del. nat. constl. conv. 1968). Republican. Episcopalian (sr. warden). Lodge: Kiwanis (v.p. Shoreline chpt.). Home: 16929 Inglewood Rd NE C-105 Bothell WA 98011 Office: 332 NW Richmond Beach Rd Seattle WA 98177

BIRDWELL, EDWARD R., symphony executive; b. Houston, Mar. 20, 1936; children: Edward Jr., Allen; m. Nancy Jamison. MusB, Houston Conservatory, 1957; postgrad., U. Tex., Austin, 1957-58, Berkshire Sch. Music, Lenox, Mass., 1961; M. of Music Edn., U. Houston, 1963. 2d French horn player N.Y.C. Ballet Orch., 1964-76; mng. ptnr. Am. Brass Quintet, N.Y.C., 1965-76; French horn player Am. Symphony Orch., N.Y.C., 1969-76; asst. to the dean Aspen Music Sch. and Festival, N.Y.C., 1971-76; dep. dir., mgr. concert ops. Carnegie Hall, N.Y.C., 1976-78; exec. dir. L.A. Chamber Orch., Pasadena, Calif., 1978-81; orch. mgr. Boston Symphony Orch., 1981-83; dir. music program Nat. Endowment for the Arts, Washington, 1984-87; exec. v.p., mgr. dir. Seattle Symphony Orch., 1987—; cons. Cedarpoint Co., Boston, 1983-84, JDC, Inc., Dorchester, Mass., Festival Casals, San Juan, Puerto Rico, Charles Ives Ctr. for the Arts, Danbury, Conn. With U.S. Army, 1958-61. Mem. Chamber Music Am. (bd. dirs. 1976-84), Am. Symphony Orch. (bd. dirs., treas. 1972-76), Am. Brass Chamber Music Assn. (pres. 1974-84), The Bohemians Club, Ranier Club, Rotary, Kappa Kappa Psi, Phi Mu Alpha. Office: Seattle Symphony Orch 305 Harrison St Seattle WA 98109

BIRKBY, WALTER HUDSON, physical anthropologist, curator; b. Gordon, Nebr., Feb. 28, 1931; s. Walter Levy and Margery Hazel (Moss) B.; m. Carmen Sue Gates, Aug. 18, 1955; children: Jeffrey Moss, Julianne. BA, U. Kans., 1961, MA, 1963; PhD, U. Ariz., 1973. Diplomate Am. Bd. Forensic Anthropology. Med. and X-ray technician Graham County (Kans.) Hosp., Hill City, 1955-58; phys. anthropologist Ariz. State Mus., Tucson, 1968-85; lectr. anthropology U. Ariz., Tucson, 1981—; curator phys. anthropology Ariz. State Mus., Tucson, 1985—; forensic anthropologist Pima County Med. Examiner, Tucson, 1981—; dental cons. USAF Hosp., Davis Monthan AFB, Tucson, 1984—; human osteologist, U. Ariz./Republic of Cyprus Archaeol. Expedition, 1985-87; dir. dept. Anthropology Masters Program in Forensic Anthropology, 1984—. Co-author video tng. film Identification of Human Remains, 1980; contbr. articles to profl. jours. Served as sgt. USMCR, 1951-52, Korea. NIH fellow, U. Ariz., 1966-68. Fellow Am. Acad. Forensic Scis. (exec. com. 1978-81); mem. Am. Assn. Phys. Anthropologists, Calif. Assn. Criminalists, Internat. Assn. Human Biologists Ariz. Div., Internat. Assn. for Identification, Am. Bd. Forensic Anthropology (pres. 1985-87, exec. com. 1980-87), Sigma Xi (pres. local chpt. 1984-85). Democrat. Home: 7349 E 18th St Tucson AZ 85710 Office: U Ariz Ariz State Mus Human Identification Lab Tucson AZ 85721

BIRKHOLM, MICHAEL PETER, advertising executive; b. St. Paul, Minn., Mar. 4, 1952; s. Harold Eugene and Janet Cecilia (Roy) B.; m. Karen Ilene Thompson, Nov. 22, 1977; children: Jennifer Lynn, Andrea Denise. Student, Los Angeles Harbor Coll., 1970-72, Calif. State U., Los Angeles, 1972-75, U. Redlands, 1975-77. Pub. health officer Calif. State Health Dept., Los Angeles, 1973-77; account supr. Smith & Hemmings, Los Angeles, 1978-80; account supr. Smith-Hemmings-Gosden, Los Angeles, 1980-82, v.p., 1982-84; pres. Hemmings, Birkholm & Grizzard, Los Angeles, 1985—; bd. dirs. Grizzard Advt. Inc., Atlanta, Tabulating Systems and Services, Houston. Bd. dirs. adv. bd. Salvation Army Booth Home, Los Angeles, 1985—; bd. dirs. and vice-chmn. adv. bd. Salvation Army Corps, 1979—; chmn. City Huntington Park, Calif. Planning com., 1983-86. Mem. Nat. Soc. F.R. Execs., Am. Mgmt. Assn., Kiwanis (v.p. 1985-86), Rotary. Republican. Roman Catholic. Home: 958 N Barcelona Pl Walnut CA 91789 Office: Hemmings Birkholm & Grizzard 1480 Colorado Blvd Los Angeles CA 90041

BIRKINBINE, JOHN, II, philatelist; b. Chestnut Hill, Pa., Mar. 29, 1930; s. Olaf Weimer and Gertrude Marie (Tyson) B.; m. Ausencia Barrera Elen, Dec. 19, 1969; children: John III, Bayani Royd. Chmn., chief exec. officer Am. Philatelic Brokerages, Tucson, 1946—; chmn. bd. Ariz. Philatelic Rangers, Tucson, 1987—. Chmn. bd. 1869 Pictorial Research Assn., 1969, bd. dirs. 1970-76; sheriff, chmn. Santa Catalina Corral of Westerners Internat., Tucson, 1986. Recipient Gold and Spl. award Spanish Soc. Internat., San Juan, P.R., 1982, Large Internat. Gold award Australian Soc. Internat., Melbourne. 1984, Swedish Soc. Internat., Stockholm, 1986. Mem. Am. Philatelic Soc. (U.S. Champion of Champions 1985), U.S. Philatelic Classics Soc., Collectors Club of N.Y., Western Cover Soc., Canal Zone Study Group,. Office: Am Philatelic Brokerages 7225 N Oracle Rd Tucson AZ 85704

BIRLEY, CINDY SUE, financial consultant; b. Waterloo, Iowa, May 5, 1959; d. Stuart M. and Liselotte (Lohmeyer) B. BBA summa cum laude, U. Iowa, 1981; JD, U. Mich., 1984. Bar: Colo. 1984; CPA, Iowa. Instr. acctg. U. Mich. Bus. Sch., Ann Arbor, 1982-84; assoc. Calkins Kramer Grimshaw & Harring, Denver, 1984-85, Davis, Graham & Stubbs, Denver, 1985-88; cons. Mercer Meidinger Hansen, Inc., Denver, 1988—. Presdl. Scholar U. Iowa, 1977-81. Mem. ABA, Western Pension Conf., Colo. Soc. Personnel Adminstrn., Iowa Soc. CPA's, Denver Bar Assn., Beta Apha Psi. Office: William M Mercer Meidinger Hansen 1700 Lincoln St Ste 3300 Denver CO 80203

BIRN, RAYMOND FRANCIS, historian, educator; b. N.Y.C., May 10, 1935; s. Saul Albert and Celia (Markman) B.; m. Randi Ingebrigtsen, July 18, 1960 (div. 1987); children—Eric Stephen, Laila Marie. B.A., NYU, 1956; M.A., U. Ill., 1957, Ph.D., 1961. Mem. faculty U. Oreg., Eugene, 1961—; assoc. prof. U. Oreg., 1966-72, prof. history, 1972—, head dept., 1971-78. Author: Pierre Rousseau and the Philosophes of Bouillon, 1964, Crisis, Absolutism, Revolution: Europe, 1648-1789/91, 1977; adv. editor Eighteenth-Century Studies, 1974-85, French Hist. Studies, 1977-80; editor: The Printed Word in the Eighteenth Century, 1984; contbr. articles to profl. jours. Mem. adv. screening com. Council for Internat. Exchange of Persons (Fulbright program), 1974-76. Served with AUS, 1959-60. Fulbright research fellow to France, 1968-69; Nat. Endowment for Humanities sr. fellow, 1976-77, 87-88. Mem. Am. Hist. Assn., Soc. French Hist. Studies, Am. Soc. 18th Century Studies. Office: U Oreg Dept History Eugene OR 97403

BIRNBACH, MARK JOSEPH, dentist; b. N.Y.C., Dec. 13, 1946; s. Sol and Minnie (Ortner) B.; m. Carolyn Eve Neustadter, Dec. 1, 1946; childre n: Samantha, Rebecca. BA, CUNY, 1968; DMD, Tufts U., 1973, Boston U., 1973. Pvt. practice Boulder, 1974—. Mem. ADA, Colo. Dental Assn., Boulder County Dental Assn., Boulder County Dental Forum (Clinician of the Yr. 1982-83, 87-88), Am. Equilibration Soc., Soc. Occlusal Studies. Home and Office: 1636 16th St Boulder CO 80302

BIRNBAUM, DENISE BARBARA, librarian; b. New Rochelle, N.Y., Aug. 18, 1951; d. Irving and Edith Dorothy Frank; m. Gary Lee Birnbaum, July 15, 1973. BA in Chemistry, SUNY, Binghamton, 1973; MLS, Ind. U., 1975. Rsch. asst. Ind. U., Bloomington, 1973-76; tech. librarian AiResearch Mfg. Co., Phoenix, 1976-87; supr. engring. library Garrett Engine Div., Phoenix, 1987--. Office: Garrett Engine Div 111 S 34th St Phoenix AZ 85034

BIRNBAUM, PHILIP HARVEY, business administration educator; b. San Diego, Jan. 21, 1944; s. Louis and Ruth Laureen (Bay) B.; m. Marlin Sue Van Every, Dec. 26, 1964; 1 child, Brian Philip. BA, U. Calif., Berkeley, 1965; PhD, U. Wash., 1975. Analyst Los Angeles County Civil Service Commn., 1965-67; teaching assoc. U. Wash., Seattle, 1972-74; asst. prof. bus. adminstrn. Ind. U., Bloomington, 1975-80, assoc. prof., 1980-85; prof. Ind. U., Bloomington, 1986, U. So. Calif., 1986—; resident dir. J.F.K. Inst., Tiburg U., The Netherlands; vis. scholar Polish Acad. Scis. Co-author: Organization Theory: A Structural and Behavioral Analysis, Modern Management Techniques for Engineers and Scientists; assoc. editor IEEE Transaction on Engring. Mgmt. jour.; contbr. articles to profl. jours., book revs., sects. to books, invited papers Germany, Poland, Eng., Can., Thailand, Hong Kong. Served with USAF, 1967-71. Recipient DBA Assn. Teaching award Ind. U., 1978; NSF fellow, 1974-75, N.Y. Acad. Scis. fellow, 1981; U. Hong Kong Sr. Fulbright scholar, 1981-82. Mem. Acad. of Mgmt., AAAS, Am. Inst. for Decision Scis., Soc. for Social Study of Sci., Engring. Mgmt. Soc., Inst. of Mgmt. Sci., Inter Inst. of Mgmt. Sci., Internat. Assn. for Study of Interdisciplinary Research, Beta Gamma Sigma, Beta Alpha Psi, Sigma Iota Epsilon. Methodist. Office: U So Calif Grad Sch Bus Admistrn Los Angeles CA 90089-1421

BIRNBAUM, STEVAN ALLEN, investment company executive; b. Los Angeles, Apr. 21, 1943; s. Eugene David and Bessie (Holtzman) B.; m. Barbara Patricia Ostroff, June 29, 1971; children: Marc, Jill. BS in Engring., UCLA, 1965; MBA, Harvard U., 1967. Dir. advanced programming Whittaker Corp., Los Angeles, 1967-69; v.p. Hohenberg & Assocs., Beverly Hills, Calif., 1969-74; dir. adminstrv. mgmt. Dames & Moore, Los Angeles, 1974-77; prin. Xerox Venture Capital, Los Angeles, 1977-81; venture capitalist Los Angeles, 1981-83; ptnr. Oxford Ptnrs., Santa Monica, Calif., 1983—; pres. Oxcal Venture Corp., Santa Monica, 1981—; bd. dirs. Micro Gen. Corp., Irvine, Calif., 1982—, Interactive Machines, Inc., Calabassa, Calif., 1986—, Cogensys, La Jolla, Calif., 1986—. Republican. Jewish. Office: Oxford Ptnrs 233 Wilshire Blvd #830 Santa Monica CA 90401

BIRREN, JAMES EMMETT, emeritus dean and professor, psychologist; b. Chgo., Apr. 4, 1918; m. Elizabeth S., 1942; children: Barbara Ann, Jeffrey Emmett, Bruce William. Student, Wright Jr. Coll., 1938; B.Ed., Chgo. State U., 1941; M.A., Northwestern U., 1942, Ph.D., 1947, DSc (hon.), 1986; postgrad., U. Chgo., 1950-51; Ph.D. (hon.), U. Gothenberg, Sweden, 1983. Tutorial fellow Northwestern U., 1941-42; research asst. project for study of fatigue Office Sci. Research and Devel., 1942; research fellow NIH, USPHS, 1946-47; research psychologist gerontology unit NIH, 1947-51; research psychologist NIMH, 1951-53, chief sect. on aging, 1953-64; dir. aging program Nat. Inst. Child Health and Human Devel., Bethesda, Md., 1964-65; dir. Gerontology Center; prof. psychology U. So. Calif., 1965—; dean Davis Sch. Gerontology, 1975-86; Brookdale disting. scholar 1986—; dir. Inst. Advanced Study in Gerontology and Geriatrics, 1981—; fellow Center for Advanced Study in Behavioral Scis., Stanford, Calif., 1978-79; Green vis. prof. U. B.C., 1979; vis. scientist Cambridge (Eng.) U., 1960-61; Harold E. Jones meml. lectr. U. Calif., Berkeley, 1965; mem. Los Angeles County Bd. Suprs.' Com. on Aging, 1967—; sr. fellow U. So. Calif. Urban Ecology Inst., 1968-70; mem. Dean's Council, U. So. Calif., 1970-86 ; chmn. aging rev. com. Nat. Inst. Aging, 1974-75; program dir. Integration of Info. on Aging: Handbook Project, 1973-76; mem. steering com. Care of Elderly, Inst. of Medicine, 1976-77; bd. dirs. Sears Roebuck Found., 1977-80; chmn. life course prevention research rev. com. NIMH, 1985-87; cons. Roche Seminars on Aging Series, 1980—. Author: Psychology of Aging, 1964; editor: Handbook of Aging and the Individual, 1959, (with K.W. Schaie) Handbook of the Psychology of Aging, 1977, (with R.B. Sloane) Handbook of Mental Health and Aging; contbr. articles to books, profl. publs.; bd. collaborators: Gerontologia, 1956—; asst. editor: Jour. Gerontology, 1956-61, assoc. editor 1961-63, editor-in-chief 1968-74, chmn. publs. com., 1975—, adv. editorial bd., 1956-69; bd. adv. editors: Devel. Psychobiology, 1967—; adv. editor: Jour. Human Devel, 1957-58. Served with USNR, 1943-46; to scientist dir. USPHS Scientist Corps, 1947-65. Recipient award for research on problems of aging CIBA Found., 1956, Stratton award Am. Psychopathol. Assn., 1960, Sr. 65er award Dist. 65 Retail Workers and Dept. Store Union, Sr. 65er award AFL-CIO, 1962, medal for meritorious service USPHS, 1965, citation Am. Assn. Ret. Persons, 1970, Am. Pioneers in Aging award U. Mich., 1972, commendation for disting. contbns. to field of gerontology Mayor of Los Angeles, 1968, 74, Merit award Northwestern U. Alumni Assn., 1976, Creative Scholarship and Research award U. So. Calif., 1979, Disting. Educator award Assn. Gerontology in Higher Edn., 1983, Eminent Service award Stovall Found., 1984, Award of Distinction Am. Fedn. for Aging Research, 1986; USPHS research fellow, 1946-47. Fellow AAAS, Am. Geriatrics Soc. (founding fellow Western div.), Am. Psychol. Assn. (Disting. Sci. Contbn. award 1968, chmn. membership com. 1969, Disting. Contbn. award Div. Adult Devel. and Aging 1978, pres. div. 1955-56, editor newsletter 1951-55), Gerontol. Soc. (pres. 1961-62, chmn. publs. com. 1974-77, award for meritorious research 1966, Brookdale award 1980); mem. Am. Physiol. Soc., Internat. Assn. Gerontology (chmn. exec. com. 1966-69, chmn. program com. 1968-69), Psychonomic Soc., Western Gerontol. Soc. (dir. 1965—, pres. 1968-69), Sigma Xi, Phi Kappa Phi. Office: Andrus Gerontology Center U So Calif Univ Park MC 0191 Los Angeles CA 90089

BISGARD, JULIE, marketing professional; b. Kansas City, Mo., Aug. 29, 1960; d. Richard Lowell and Juanita Jean (Bowes) B. BA, U. Denver, 1982, postgrad., 1986--. Mgr. new accounts Citicorp Retail Svcs., Englewood, Colo., 1981-85; dir. mktg. Tracom Corp., Denver, 1985—; cons. Cen. City Opera Co., Denver, 1982-83. Mem. Soc. Ins. Trainers and Educators, Am. Soc. Tng. and Devel. Roman Catholic. Office: 3773 Cherry Creek N Dr Ste 950 Denver CO 80209

BISHOP, BETTY J., financial advisor; b. Seattle, Wash., Feb. 27, 1947; d. Arthur Joseph and Julia Teresa (Azzolina) Lovett; m. Donald D. Bishop, Nov. 28, 1969 (div. 1976); children: Deborah, Scott. BS, Wash. State U., 1969; postgrad., Ohio State U., 1983. Tchr. Seattle Sch. Dist., 1973-75; appraiser Pacific First Fed., Tacoma, 1977-78, asst. v.p., mgr., secondary market ops., 1978-82; regional exec. United Guaranty, Westlake Village, Calif., 1982-83; sr. v.p. comml. secondary mktg. FCA Am. Mortgage Corp./Am. Savs., Santa Monica, Calif., 1983-85; v.p., mgr. secondary market ops. County Savs. Bank, Santa Barbara, Calif., 1985-88; pres. SMC Corp., Montecito, Calif., 1988—; mem. conf. subcom., sec. mktg. com. Calif. Savs. and Loan League, L.A., 1985-88; document subcom., sec. mktg. subcom. U.S. Savs. and Loan League, Chgo., 1987-88. Contbr. articles to profl. jours. Fund drive chmn. Easter Seal Soc., Seattle, 1972. Mem. Univ. Club, S.B. Assocs., Conejo Ski Club, Auslich Ski Club. Republican. Roman Catholic. Home and Office: 2696 Sycamore Canyon Rd Montecito CA 93108

BISHOP, C. DIANE, state agency administrator, educator; b. Elmhurst, Ill., Nov. 23, 1943; d. Louis William and Constance Oleta (Mears) B.; m. Richard Lee Morse, Oct. 20, 1984. BS in Maths., U. Ariz., 1965, MS in Maths., MEd in Secondary Edn., 1972. Lic. secondary educator. Tchr. math. Tucson Unified Sch. Dist., 1966-86, mem. curriculum council, 1985-86, mem. maths. curriculum task teams, 1983-86; state supt. of pub. instrn. State of Ariz., 1987—; assoc. faculty Pima Community Coll., Tucson, 1974-84; adj. lectr. U. Ariz., 1983, 85. Mem. Ariz. State Bd. Edn., 1984—, chmn. quality edn. commn., 1986-87, chmn. tchr. cert. subcom. 1984—, outcomes based edn. adv. com. 1986-87, liaison bd. dirs. essential skills subcom. 1985-87, gifted edn. com. liaison 1985—; mem. high sch. task force Ariz. Bd. Regents, 1984-85, com. on preparing for U. Ariz., 1983; mem. Ariz. Stat. Bd. Regents, 1987—, Ariz. State Community Coll. Bd., 1987—, Ariz. Joint Legis. Com. on Revenues and Expenditures, 1989—, Ariz. Joint Legis. Com. on Goals for Ednl. Excellence, 1987—. Woodrow Wilson fellow Princeton U., summer 1984; recipient Presdl. Award for Excellence in Teaching of Maths., 1983, Ariz. Citation of Merit, 1984, Maths. Teaching award Nat. Sci. Research Soc., 1984, Distinction in Edn. award Flinn Found., 1986; named Maths. Tchr. of Yr. Ariz. Council of Engring. and Sci. Assns., 1984. Mem. Nat. Council of Tchrs. of Maths. Council of Chief State Sch. Officers, NEA, Ariz. Edn. Assn., Tucson Edn. Assn., Ariz. Assn. Tchrs. of Maths., Women in Maths. Edn., Math. Assn. of Am., NRC (math. scis. edn. bd. 1987—), Ednl. Commn. of the States, Nat. Endowment for Arts (adv. bd. for arts edn.), Nat. Forum on Excellence in Edn., Nat. Honors Workshop, Pi Mu Epsilon, Pi Lambda Theta. Democrat. Episcopalian. Office: Ariz State Dept Edn 1535 W Jefferson Phoenix AZ 85007

BISHOP, EARLE CARL, electrical engineer; b. Toledo, Dec. 11, 1938; children: Carlynne M., E. Carl Jr. Student, Calif. State U., Sacramento, 1976; BSEE, U. Cen. Calif., 1982, MSME, 1984. Electronics engr. Radio Shack Service, Sacramento, 1975-77; prin. E. Bishop Gen. Contractors, Sacramento, 1977-80; cons. Albuquerque, 1980-84; contract engr. Intel, AT&T, IBM, Boeing, 1984—; pres. All Cities Engr. Services, Inc., Wilmington, Del., 1985—. Home: 3131 Candelaria NE Apt 215 Albuquerque NM 87107

BISHOP, EDWIN BURNETT, real estate executive; b. Haines, Oreg., Mar. 8, 1921; s. Jasper Newton and Vera Leta (Burnett) B.; m. Mary Ellen Mills, Feb. 25, 1953; children: Jeff, Nancy, Kim, Robert. BS, Oreg. State U., 1946. Cert. real estate broker, bldg. contractor. Mgr. Eugene (Oreg.) Sand and Gravel Co., 1954-59; owner Ed Bishop Contractor, Santa Barbara, Calif., 1959-64, Kailua, Hawaii, 1964-65, Lafayette, Calif., 1965-73; prin. Santana Properties, Santa Barbara, 1973—. Served as sgt. AC, U.S. Army, 1943-45. Mem. Calif. Assn. Realtors (bd. dirs. 1983—), Santa Barbara Bd. Realtors (pres. 1985, bd. dirs. 1981—, Realtor of Yr. 1984), Phi Delta Theta. Republican. Home and Office: 1936 D N Jameson Ln Santa Barbara CA 93108

BISHOP, ERNEST MERRILL, physical scientist; b. Soquel, Calif., Mar. 6, 1927; s. Ernest S. and Ruth (Merrill) B.; m. Barbara Maggio, June 20, 1948 (div. 1985); children: Ruth, Kathy, Mark, Gail, Chris, Matt, Amy; m. Roberta Henley, Dec. 5, 1985. BS, U. Calif., Berkeley, 1950. Chemist Pabco Products, Emeryville, Calif., 1950-56, Stanford Research Inst., Menlo Park, Calif., 1956-59, Carad Chem., Palo Alto, Calif., 1959-63; materials engr. Sandia Corp., Livermore, Calif., 1963-66; research assoc. Hexcel Corp., Dublin, Calif., 1967—. Patentee in field. Scoutmaster Boy Scouts Am., 1956-67. Served to sgt. U.S. Army, 1945-47. Mem. AAAS, Materials Rsch. Soc. Democrat. Roman Catholic. Office: Hexcel Corp 11711 Dublin Blvd Dublin CA 94568

BISHOP, JAY LYMAN, environmental chemist; b. Salt Lake City, July 7, 1932; s. Marvin James and Klar (Lyman) B.; m. Geneil True Walton, June 9, 1958; children: Peggy (dec.), Lynn, Janet, Nancy, Deanna, Linda, Michael, Stanley, Michelle. BS with honors, U. Utah, 1953, PhD, 1962. Lectr. U. Utah, Salt Lake City, 1960-62; rsch. assoc. Ariz. State U., Tempe, 1962-67, instr., 1964-67; sr. chemist Ciby-Geigy Corp., Summit, N.J., 1967-71; cons. Bishop Mfg. Co. and Western Cons., Bountiful, Utah, 1971—; chem. engr. civil svd. Tooele (Utah) Army Depot, 1982—; chemist Kennecott Copper Corp., Salt Lake City, 1972; chief chemist and metallurgist Assoc. Smelters Internat., 1973, United Refinery, 1973-75, Nat. Metals Inc., Salt Lake City, 1975-76; vis. lectr. Traveling Sci. Inst., Ariz. Acad. Sci., Tempe, 1962-66; historian, genealogist Western Cons., Bountiful, 1971—. Contbr. articles to profl. jours.; composer musical works; patentee in field. Missionary Ch. of Jesus Christ of Latter-Day Saints, German Dem. Republic, 1953-56, East German Mission, 1953-56; mem. Salt Lake Mormon Tabernacle Choir, 1976-78, ch. organist, 1945—, other civic and religious activities. With U.S. Army, 1956-57. Mem. Sigma Xi. Republican. Office: 11 W 900 North Bountiful UT 84010

BISHOP, LEROY HOWARD, corporate tax manager; b. Chgo., Mar. 9, 1941; s. Norman Leon and Dorothy (Brown) B.; m. Laura Helen Shaw, Aug. 9, 1963; children: Lisa Diane, David Louis, Michael Alan. AA, Prarie State Jr. Coll., 1971; BS, Ariz. State U., 1975. CPA, Ariz. Cost acct. Allan & Garcia Co., Chgo., 1965-67; corp. tax mgr. Bell Atlantic Systems Leasing Internat., Phoenix, 1967—. Chmn. finance Mt. View Baptist Ch., Phoenix, 1985—; chmn. deacons Mt. View Baptist Ch., Phoenix, 1987; trustee Mt. View Baptist Ch., 1983—. Sgt. U.S. Army, 1960-63. Mem. Tax Execs. Inst. (pres. Ariz. chpt. 1985-86), Am. Inst. CPA's, Ariz. Soc. CPA's, Inst. Property Taxation. Republican. Southern Baptist. Home: 4430 N 35th St Phoenix AZ 85018 Office: Bell Systems Leasing 11811 N Tatum Blvd Suite 2000 Phoenix AZ 85028-1601

BISHOP, MICHAEL MASON, sales engineer; b. Cleve., July 4, 1960; s. Lester M. and Elizabeth (Teagle) B.; m. Karen Elizabeth Twyford, Aug. 22, 1982. BS in Aviation Maintenance Mgmt., Embry-Riddle Aero. U., Daytona Beach, Fla., 1982. Crew chief Embry-Riddle Aero. U., Daytona, Fla., 1979-82; maintenance supr. Nat. Fla. Airlines, Daytona, 1983; head technician Stanley Aviation Corp., Aurora, Colo., 1984-85, sales engr., 1986—. Republican. Office: Stanley Aviation Corp 2501 Dallas St Aurora CO 80010

BISHOP, ROBERT CHARLES, metals and minerals company executive; b. Butte, Mont., June 6, 1929; s. Lester Farragut and Helen Katherine (Bauman) B.; m. B. Jean Rausch, June 29, 1957; children: Desta Fawn, Valerie Dawn. BS in Gen. Engring., Mont. State U., 1958, BArch., 1960. Assoc. architect various firms, Mont., 1960-64; owner, architect R.C. Bishop & Assocs., Butte, Great Falls and Missoula, Mont., 1965-69; owner, chief exec. officer Val-Desta 4M, Butte, 1980—, Val-Desta Mines and Minerals, Louisville, Ky., 1985—; prin. Archtl. Assocs., 1969—; chief exec. officer, pres. Cove-Lock Log Home Mfrs., Inc., Butte, 1968-72, Busy Beaver Enterprises, Great Falls, 1968-72, New Horizon Homes, Missoula, 1968-72; asst. contracts adminstr. Davy-McKee Constrn. Engrs., Butte, 1982-83. Patentee. Advisor, Kiwanis, Jaycees, Nat. Res., 1960-72, Am. Legion, 1976. With U.S. Army, 1953-55. Named One of 2,000 Men of Achievement Melrose Press, 1970, 73. Mem. Internat. Platform Assn., Nat. Hist. Soc. (founding assoc. 1971), Elk Bow Hunting Club (bugle tchr. 1970-84), Butte Mulitlist Club (real estate tchr. 1978-84). Presbyterian.

BISHOP, WILLIAM PAUL, insurance company executive; b. Denver, Aug. 15, 1956; s. Robert Paul and Elaine (Payne) B.; m. Cheryl Cowan, June 28, 1980; 1 child, William P. BSBA, U. Denver, 1978. CLU, chartered fin. cons. Am. Coll. Rep. group Union Mutual Cos., Denver, 1978-80, State Mutual Cos., Denver, 1980-82; group mgr. dist. State Mutual Cos., Dallas, 1982-86, asst. v.p. regional sales, 1986-87; v.p. regional sales State Mutual Cos., Denver and Dallas, 1987—. Mem. Am. CLU Soc., SE Denver Exchange (pres. 1982), Kiwanis, Los Charros Club. Republican. Roman Catholic. Office: State Mut Cos 6312 S Fiddler's Green Circle Englewood CO 80111

BISSELL, GEORGE ARTHUR, architect; b. L.A., Jan. 31, 1927; s. George Arthur and Ruby Zoe (Moore) B.; m. Laurene Conlon, Nov. 21, 1947; children: Teresa Ann, Thomas Conlon, William George, Robert Anthony, Mary Catherine. BArch, U. So. Calif., 1953. Registered architect, Calif. Ptnr. Bissell Co., Covina, Calif., 1953-57, Bissell & Durquette, A.I.A., Pasadena, Calif., 1957-72, Riley & Bissell, A.I.A., Newport Beach, Calif., 1967-72; owner, prin. Bissell Architects, Laguna Beach, Calif., 1961-67, Newport Beach, 1983—; pres. Bissell/August, Inc., Newport Beach, 1972-83. Bd. dirs. Newport Ctr. Assn., 1973-78, Lido Isle Community Assn., Newport Beach, 1985-87. With U.S. Mcht. Marine, 1944-46, PTO. Recipient Honor award Progressive Architecture mag., 1974. Fellow AIA (pres. Orange County chpt. 1975, Calif. coun. 1978, nat. bd. dirs. 1980-84, Nat. Honor award 1978, Honor award 1988); mem. Newport Harbor Yacht Club, Lido Isle Yacht Club. Home: 108 Via Havre Newport Beach CA 92663 Office: Bissel Architects 446 Old Newport Blvd Newport Beach CA 92663

BISTLINE, STEPHEN, justice; b. Pocatello, Idaho, Mar. 12, 1921; s. Ray D. and Martha (Faber) B.; m. Sharon Mooney; children: Patrick, Paul, Arthur, Claire, Susan, Shelley, Diana, Leslie. LL.B., U. Idaho, 1949. Bar: Idaho bar 1949. Individual practice law Sandpoint, Idaho, 1950-76; justice Idaho Supreme Ct., Boise, 1976—. Served with USN, 1941-45. Office: Idaho Supreme Ct 451 W State St Boise ID 83720

BITTENBENDER, BRAD JAMES, environmental and industrial hygiene manager; b. Kalamazoo, Dec. 4, 1948; s. Don J. and Thelma Lu (Bacon) B.; m. Susan Elizabeth Kastley, Aug., 1976 (div. 1986). BS, Western Mich. U., 1972; cert. in hazardous material mgmt., U. Calif., Irvine, 1987. Supr. mfg. Am. Cyanamid, Kalamazoo, 1973-77; supr. mfg. Productol Chem. div. Ferro Corp., Santa Fe Springs, Calif., 1977-79, environ. adminstr., 1979-80; sr. environ. engr. Ferro Corp., Los Angeles, 1980-87, mgr. environ. dept. composites div., 1988—; bd. dirs., mem. adv. bd. safety and health extension program U. Calif. Irvine, 1985—. Bd. dirs. adv. com. hazardous materials Culver City, Calif., 1987—; mem. Calif. Mus. Found., L.A., 1985—, Mus. Contemporary Art, L.A., 1985—. Mem. Am. Inst. Chem. Engrs., Am. Indsl. Hygiene Assn., Am. Film Inst., Nat. Fire Protection Assn., Beta Beta Beta. Republican. Presbyterian. Office: Ferro Corp Composites Div 5915 Rodeo Rd Los Angeles CA 90016

BITTERS, CONRAD LEE, biological sciences educator; b. Waco, Tex., Jan. 2, 1946; s. E. Conrad and Margaret Lee (Miles) B.; m. Karen Kay, May 1, 1970; children: Rebecca, Brian. BA, Calif. State U., Fresno, 1969. Life Credential, Biol./Phys. Sciences, Calif. Biology/zoology tchr. Clovis (Calif.) High Sch., 1970—, science dept. chmn., 1973-80, biology coordinator, 1980—; founder, sponsor Clovis (Calif.) High Ecology club, 1970—, Clovis High Foreign Studies Club, 1978-87; jr. div. judge Cen. Valley Sci. Fair, Fresno, Calif., 1975—; vertebrate advisory com. Cen. Valley Sci. Fair, 1978—; coach-sr. div. Cen. Valley Sci. Fair, Freno, 1972—; dist. rep. Jr. Sci. and Humanities Symposium, Berkeley, Calif., 1974—; Calif. Ednl. Initiatives Fund Grant Dir., 1986. Recipient Faculty award Eastman Kodak Co., 1980, Nat. Jr. Sci. and Humanities Symposium, 1985, Merit award Rotary Club of Fresno, 1985, 88, Faculty Commendation Lawrence Hall of Sci., 1985, 87, John D. Isaacs Scholarship Com., 1985, Outstanding Sci. Techr. Fresno County Dow Chem. Co., 1986, Presdl. Award in Sci. Teaching, Calif. State Dept. Edn., 1986, Faculty Commendation Calif. State Sci. Fair, 1988. Mem. Nat. Sci. Teachers' Assn. Republican. Church of Jesus Christ of Latter Day Saints. Home: 1330 Filbert Clovis CA 93612 Office: Clovis High Sch 1055 N Fowler Clovis CA 93612

BITTS, TODD MICHAEL, broadcasting executive; b. Seattle, Mar. 20, 1946; s. Max Krause and Joye (Kugler) B.; m. Cheryl Whiteman, Dec. 20, 1969 (div. Nov. 1983); children: Kimberly, Craig, Shaun; m. Marcia K. Dion, May 3, 1985. Student, Green River Coll., 1965. Account exec. Sta. KAYO, Seattle, 1967-73; account exec. Golden West Broadcasters Sta. KVI, Seattle, 1973-76; gen. mgr. Sta. KETO, 1974-75; v.p., gen. mgr. Sta. KPLZ, Seattle, 1976-83; pub. Monthly, Seattle, 1984—; Mem. exec. com. Seafair, Inc.; bd. affiliates Sta. RKO Radio Network, N.Y.C., 1981-83; bd. dirs. Media Credit Union, Seattle. Mem. Puget Sound Radio Broadcasters Assn. (past pres.). Republican. Lutheran. Clubs: Sahalee Golf & Country (Redmond, Wash.); Washington Athletic (Seattle). Home: 25128 SE 28th St Issaquah WA 98027 Office: Monthly 603 Stewart St Ste 1020 Seattle WA 98027

BIVENS, COURTLAND CLOUIS, aerospace engineer; b. El Paso, Tex., Aug. 11, 1951; s. Courtland Clouis Bivens II and Norine Arie (Roseborough) Bradford; m. Rhonda Marcet (div. Feb. 1989); 1 child, Courtland Clouis B. IV. BS in Aero Engring., U.S. Mil. Acad., 1973; MS in Aero Engring., U.S. Naval Postgrad. Sch., Monterey, Calif., 1986. Commd. 2d lt. U.S. Army, 1973, advance through grades to capt., 1977; aerospace engr. NASA Ames Rsch. Ctr., Moffett Field, Calif., 1981—. Maj. USNG. Mem. Graduates Assn., Am. Helicopter Soc. Protestant. Home: 951 Willowleaf Dr #1404 San Jose CA 95128 Office: Aero Flight Dynamics Directorate MS 210-7 Ames Research Ctr Moffett Field CA 94305

BIVINS, GAIL MARIE, computer software engineer; b. Seattle, Nov. 4, 1957; d. Richard Douglas and Esther Margaret (Wicklund) B. BS, U. Wash., 1980; postgrad., Seattle Pacific U. Software engineer, project leader The Boeing Co., Seattle. Mem. Phi Beta Kappa. Presbyterian. Office: The Boeing Co Seattle WA 98124

BIVINS, SUSAN STEINBACH, systems engineer; b. Chgo., June 5, 1941; d. Joseph Bernard and Eleanor Celeste (Mathes) S.; BS, Northwestern U., 1963; postgrad. U. Colo., 1964, U. Ill., 1965, UCLA, 1971; m. James Herbert Bivins, June 7, 1980. With IBM, 1967—, support mgr. East, White Plains, N.Y., 1977-78, systems support mgr., western region, L.A., 1978-81, br. market support mgr., 1981-84, mgr. IBM ops. and support L.A. Summer Olympics, 1984; mgr. IBM office supporting devel. FAA air traffic control system for 1990's, 1984-88, mgr. complex systems mktg., 1988—; pres. Jastech, 1986—. Vol. tchr. computer sci. Calif. Mentally Gifted Minor Programs; vol. L.A. Youth Motivation Task Force. Recipient Kranz award Northwestern U., 1963; various engring. and mgmt. awards IBM, 1969—. Mem. Systems Engring. Symposium, Pi Lambda Theta. Developed program to retrieve data via terminal and direct it to any appropriate hardcopy device, 1973. Office: 12501 E Imperial Hwy Norwalk CA 90650

BIXEL, DARLENE ROSE, small business owner; b. Walla Walla, Wash., Apr. 13, 1948; d. Daniel Lee Davidson and Leila June (Hibbs) Davidson; m. Wayne Ray Bixel, Nov. 10, 1974; children: David Wayne, Angela Rose, Michael Ray, Stephanie Darlene. Cert. in sec. tng., Walla Walla Coll., 1968. Med. sec. Lyle Johnson, D.O., Selah, Wash., 1972-73; legal sec. Gavin-Robinson, et al, Yakima, Wash., 1973-74; sec. Am. Hosp. Supply, Portland, Oreg., 1974-76; property mgr. Rowa Co., Portland, 1976-80; co-owner, co-operator X-L Donuts, Portland, 1979-80; sec. Perine Machine Tool Corp., Kent, Wash., 1980-82; sec., treas. Bixel Machine Tool Corp., Clackamas, Oreg., 1982-85; owner, operator The In Basket, Troutdale, Oreg., 1985—; editor, pub. Home Bus. Directory, Troutdale, 1988—. Mem. NAFE. Republican. Adventist. Home and Office: The In Basket 2734 SE Evans Troutdale OR 97060-2428

BJELLAND, HARLEY LEROY, writer; b. Erskine, Minn., Sept. 12, 1926; s. Even and Gina Emelie (Rud) B.; m. Delores Gabriel, Sept. 26, 1951 (div. 1977); children: Carol, David, Harley Jr., Darlene, Sandra; m. Doris Tokiko Onishi, Dec. 20, 1982. BSEE, Milw. Sch. Engring., 1951; postgrad., U. Okla., 1973-74. Sr. staff specialist various aerospace cos., L.A., 1951-82; sr. tech. writer IBM, Hughes Aircraft Co., TRW, Motorola, Northrop Co., various locations, 1982-86; freelance writer Springfield, Oreg., 1974—; owner, pres. Norway Books, Springfield, 1982—. Author: How to Sell Your Home, 1975, How to Buy the Right Home, 1980, How to Write Technical Articles, 1989, numerous short stories, articles; patentee advanced displays. Staff sgt. U.S. Army, 1944-46. Republican. Lutheran. Home and Office: 2305 N 6th PO Box 676 Springfield OR 97477

BJORKLUND, HAROLD PAUL, cable company executive; b. Hollywood, Calif., Apr. 10, 1940; s. Harold Eskil and Linnea Marie (Gowey) B.; divorce, 1976; 1 child, Sloan Kristine; m. Esther Eileen Lacy, July 4, 1981; 1 child, Adam Paul. Field engr. LTV Aerospace, 1962-64, Bendix Corp., Hawaii, 1964-65, Jet Propulsion Labs NASA, Calif., 1965-68; systems engr. Sylvania/GTE Internat., N.Y.C. and Boston, 1968-72; sales mgr. Am. Data Corp., Huntsville, Ala., 1972-75; dir. internat. ops. ADC div. No. Am. Philips, Huntsville, 1975-79; sales mgr. West Jerrold Div. Gen. Inst., Denver, 1979-81; chief exec. officer, pres., chmn. Cable Exchange, Inc., Denver, 1981—. 1st lt. AUS, 1959-62. Mem. Arapahoe C. of C., Kiwanis (pres. 1966-67). Republican. Lutheran. Office: Cable Exchange Inc 5730 E Otero Ave 700 Englewood CO 80112

BJORKLUND, JANET VINSEN, speech pathologist; b. Seattle, July 31, 1947; d. Vernon Edward and Virginia Lea (Rogers) B.; m. Dan Robert Young, Dec. 04, 1971; children: Emery Allen, Alanna Vinsen, Marisa Rogers. Student, U. Vienna, Austria, 1966-67; BA, Pacific U., 1969; student, U. Wash., 1970-71; MA, San Francisco State U., 1977. Cert. clin. speech pathologist, audiologist. Speech pathologist, audiological cons. USN Hosp., Rota, Spain, 1972-75; traineeship in audiology VA Hosp., San Francisco, 1976; speech pathologist San Lorenzo (Calif.) Unified Schs., 1975-77, 78-81; dir. speech pathology St. Lukes Speech and Hearing Clinic, San Francisco, 1977-78; audiologist X.O. Barrios, M.D., San Francisco, 1977-81; cons. Visually Impaired Infant Program, Seattle, 1981-82; speech pathologist Everett (Wash.) Schs., 1982—; cons. Madison House, Kirkland, Wash., 1983-88, NW Devel. Therapists, Everett, 1985-87, Providence Hosp. Childrens Ctr., Everett, 1985—, Pacific Hearing and Speech, 1988—. Author: (with others) Screening for Bilingual Preschoolers, 1977, (TV script), Clinical Services in San Francisco, 1978, Developing Better Communication Skills, 1982. Coordinator pre-sch. Christian edn. Kirkland Congl. Ch., Wash., 1983-85; organizer Residents Against Speeding Drivers, Madison Park, Seattle, 1985-87; chair staff devel. com. Everett Schs., 1988-89; rep. Barrier Resolution Project, 1988—. Mem. Am. Speech and Hearing Assn., Am. Speech and Hearing Found., Wash. Speech and Hearing Assn. (regional rep. 1985-86, chair licensure task force 1986-88, rep. Birth to Six Project 1988—), Phi Lambda Omicron (pres. Pacific U. chpt. 1968). Congregational. Office: Everett Sch Dist 2 202 Alder Everett WA 98203

BJORKLUND, KATHARINE BROWNE, librarian; b. Los Alamos, N.Mex., Feb. 17, 1952; d. Philip Lincoln and Margaret (Powell) Browne; m. Eric Alan Bjorkland, June 30, 1973. BA, U. N.Mex., 1974; MLS, U. Wis., 1978. Info. desk staffer Meml. Library, U. Wis., Madison, 1976-78; circulation desk clk. Mesa Pub. Library, Los Alamos, 1978-79, circulation chief, 1979-80, head adult services div., 1980-86, head adult services sect., 1986-88, head reference and info. div., 1988—. Mem. ALA, N.Mex. Library Assn. Presbyterian. Office: Mesa Pub Libr 1742 Central Ave Los Alamos NM 87544

BJORKLUND, LILA B., social services administrator; b. Ogden, Utah, Oct. 28, 1914; d. Michael and Harriet Serepta (Campbell) Burton; m. Russell Eric Bjorklund, Oct. 9, 1936 (dec. May 1977); children: Peter Burton, Jay Russell, Josef Robert, Anne B., Eric Wayne. Student, Weber Coll. Rep. Scholastic Mag. and Book Services, 1962-76; founder, dir. Utah Girls' Village, Salt Lake City, 1969—. Author monthly mags. Monthly Issues, 1962-65 (Nat. award 1965), Community Sch., 1972, Caring, 1986; author article series Critical Issues, 1962-72 (Cup award 1967). Adv. mem. Detention Ctr., Salt Lake City, 1961-68, Juvenile Ct., Salt Lake County, 1969-71, Utah Vocat. Edn. Com., Salt Lake County, 1969-71; pres. Utah State PTA, Salt Lake City, 1970-72; chmn. Utah State Bd. Edn., Salt Lake City, 1973-83; mem. Salt Lake City Commn. on Youth, COY Com. on Child Abuse, Utah Fedn. for Drug Free Youth. Recipient Disting. Service award Utah State Bd. Edn., 1969, Disting. Presdl. Citation Brigham Young U., 1988; named Outstanding Community Leader Eagles, 1984, Outstanding Community Leader St. Citizens chpt. 135, 1986. Mem. Sch. Counselors Assn. (adv. 1969-71), Altrusa (Woman of Yr. 1975), Nat. Assn. Homes for Children (bd. dirs. 1980—), Utah Teaching Family Assn. of Homes (officer, bd. dirs. 1982—), Utah Assn. for Care and Treatment Children and Youth (pres. 1979—), Nat. Teaching Family Assn., Salt Lake Council of Women (pres. 1961-62, Hall of Fame 1978), Alpha Delta Kappa, Delta Kappa Gamma. Republican. Mormon. Club: Aurora (Salt Lake City). Home: 791 9th Ave Salt Lake City UT 84103 Office: Utah Girls Village 3808 S W Temple Ste 1D Salt Lake City UT 84115

BJORKMAN, DONALD CARL, design educator, consultant; b. Norway, Mich., July 27, 1929; s. Carl Levine and Anna Marie (Herman) J.; m. Gloria Ann Gonser, Oct. 5, 1957; children: Kurt Donald, Karinn Ann. BA, U. Wash., 1963; MFA, Rochester Inst. Tech., 1965. Asst. prof. design Calif. Coll. Art and Design, Oakland, 1965-70; assoc. prof. U. Wis., Menomonie, 1970-73; project coordinator Agostruct Internat., Yakima, Wash., 1973-77; assoc. prof. Calif. Poly. State U., San Luis Obispo, 1977-81, No. Ariz. U., Flagstaff, 1981-87; cons. Dependable Furniture, San Francisco, 1967-70, Shell Lake (Wis.) Boat Co., 1972; cooperative furniture mfr. Kirkland, Wash., 1972. One-man shows include Bavier Gallery Rochester Inst. Tech., 1965, Crown Zellerback Bldg., San Francisco, 1966, Art Ctr. Gallery, San Luis Obispo, Calif., 1980, others; group exhbns. include Interiors Pavillion, Seattle World Fair, 1962, 65-66, Mus. Contemporary Crafts, N.Y.C., 1963, 66, Mus. West, San Francisco, 1967, First World Craft Congress, N.Y.C., 1964, No. Ariz. U. Art Gallery, Flagstaff, 1982, Coconino Ctr. for Arts, 1983, others; contbr. chpts. to books and articles on design to profl. jours. Served with USMC, 1947-54. Recipient 3rd prize Fine Hardwood Nat. Design Competition, 1963, 1st, 2d hon. mention, 1964, Best Design of Yr. awards Indsl. Design Annual Rev., 1964-65.

BJURMAN, GEORGE DAVID, investment counselor; b. Pa., Mar. 11, 1906; s. Andrew and Augusta (Bert) B.; BS, U. Calif., Berkeley, 1930; m. Dorothy Kuhlmeyer, Oct. 10, 1936; children: Susan A., George A. With Wells Fargo Bank, 1930-36; sr. trust investment officer Bank of America, L.A., 1936-46; dir., exec. v.p. fin. Occidental Life Calif., L.A., 1946-70; chmn. bd., chief investment officer George D. Bjurman & Assocs., L.A., 1970—. Fellow Fin. Analyst Fedn.; mem. L.A. Soc. Fin. Analysts, N.Y. Soc. Fin. Analysts, L.A. Country Club., Calif. Club, Mens Garden Club of L.A. Republican. Office: 10100 Santa Monica Blvd Ste 2300 Los Angeles CA 90067

BLACHER, JOAN HELEN, psychotherapist, educator; b. L.A., Aug. 10, 1928; d. Albert Scribner and Isabel (Marriott) Oakholt; m. Norman Blacher, July 27, 1973; stepchildren: Eric, Steven, Mark. BA, U. Calif., Berkeley, 1950; MEd, U. So. Calif., 1971, PhD, 1981. Lic. ednl. psychologist, marriage, family and child counselor, Calif. Elem. tchr. L.A. Unified Sch. Dist., 1962-71, sch. psychologist, 1971-72, 73-74; sch. psychologist Pasadena (Calif.) Unified Sch. Dist., 1972-73; sch. psychologist Ventura (Calif.) County Supt. Schs., 1974-79, prin., 1979-86; asst. prof. dept. edn., head counseling and guidance program Calif. Luth. U., Thousand Oaks, Calif., 1987—; pvt. practice, Ventura, 1984—. Bd. dirs. Coalition Against Household Violence, Ventura, 1984-85. Mem. Am. Ednl. Rsch. Assn., Am. Soc. Tng. and Devel. (v.p. membership Los Padres chpt. 1987), Calif. Assn. Counseling Devel., Phi Delta Kappa, Delta Kappa Gamma (pres. Phi Epsilon chpt. 1982-84). Republican.

BLACK, HUGH LAWRANCE, banker, lawyer; b. Cleve., Ohio, Mar. 8, 1942; s. Marion Eckert and Margaret Esther (Blaser) B. BA, Coll. Wooster, Ohio, 1964; JD, Case-Western Res. U., 1967. Bar: Ohio 1968, Fla. 1968, D.C. 1970, U.S. Supreme Ct. 1970. Asst. trust officer Cleve. Trust Co., 1968-70; trust officer, asst. v.p. Coconut Grove Bank, Miami, Fla., 1972-73; pvt. practice Miami and Palm Beach, Fla., 1973-76; mktg. specialist Wells Fargo Bank, Beverly Hills, Calif., 1976-80; asst. v.p., mgr. Lloyds Bank Calif., Newport Beach, 1980-84; v.p., regional mgr. personal capital mgmt. div. Union Bank, Irvine, Calif., 1984—; lectr. Orange County Coll., Costa Mesa, Calif., 1980-85; adj. prof. law Pepperdine U., Malibu, Calif., 1977-84. Mem. endowment adv. com. Orange County Performing Arts Ctr., Costa Mesa, 1980-85. Mem. ABA, Ohio Bar Assn., Fla. Bar Assn., D.C. Bar Assn., Orange County Trust Officers' Assn. (sec.-treas. 1986-87, pres. 1987-88), World Trade Ctr. Orange County, Am. Arbitration Assn., Newport Harbor C. of C. (chmn. bus. assistance and devel. com. 1980-83), Coconut Grove C. of C. (Disting. Citizen award 1972), Univ. Athletic Club, Breakers Beach Club. Presbyterian. Home: 900 Sea Ln Corona del Mar CA 92625 Office: Union Bank 18300 Von Karmen Ave Irvine CA 92715

BLACK, JOHN ARTHUR, JR., electrical engineer, computer scientist; b. Mexico, Mo., Feb. 9, 1949; s. John Arthur and Pauline (Cearley) B.; m. Beverly Marie Zimmerman, Aug. 5, 1947. BSEE, Ariz. State U., 1972, MS in Elec., 1985. Engr. Motorola Inc., Tempe, Ariz., 1972-75, engring mgr., 1977-85; engr. Sperry, Phoenix, 1975-77; editor, pub. VMEbus Systems Mag., Tempe, 1985—; cons. Micrology PBT, Tempe, 1985—. Author: The VMEbus Specification, 1985. Capt. USAR, 1972-79. Mem. IEEE, Upsilon Pi Epsilon. Republican. Office: Micrology PBT 2618 S Shannon Dr Tempe AZ 85282

BLACK, JOSEPH WAYNE, private investigator; b. Oakland, Calif., Aug. 12, 1953; s. Joseph Norrie and Mary Ann (Whitehurst) B.; m. Patricia Anne Jackson, Jan. 25, 1974. AA, Tyler (Tex.) Jr. Coll., 1977. Owner, photographer Latent Image Studios, Tyler, 1976-78; editorial staff writer, photographer Alamogordo (N.Mex) Daily News, 1978-79; installer, technician SOO Cable TV, Sioux City, Nebr., 1979-81; tech. supr. Global Communications, Inc., Houston, 1981-82; contract investigator, owner, photographer B & D Photography, Albuquerque, N. Mex., 1984-85; cable tv contract mgr. San Juan Cable TV Contractors, Albuquerque, 1982-85; computer technician operator Total Bus. Systems, Albuquerque, 1985-86; chief owner, investigator Aspen (Colo.) Agy. of Investigation, 1986—; vol. investigator Search Seven, N.Y.C., 1988; investigative rep. Milliken & Michaels, Inc., N.Y.C., Aspen, 1988—. Staff writer, photographer News and Features Alamogordo Daily News, 1978-79. Vol. Ford election campaign, 1977, Glenwood Fire Dept., Ambulance Svc. Mem. Am. Fedn. Police, Global Internat. Detective Assn., Nat. Assn. Investigative Specialist, Tyler Jr. Coll. Alumni Assn. Republican. Office: Aspen Agy of Investigation 926 1/2 Grand Ave Ste 26 PO Box 3004 Glenwood Springs CO 81602

BLACK, LYDIA T., anthropologist, educator; b. Kiev, USSR, Dec. 16, 1925; came to U.S., 1950; m. Igor A. Black, Jan. 12, 1947 (wid. 1969); children: Anna Black Treiber, Maria Black McEvoy, Elena, Zoe M. BS in History, Northeastern U., 1969; MA in Social Anthropology, Brandeis U., 1971; PhD in Social Anthropology, U. Mass., 1973. Asst. prof. to prof. anthropology Providence Coll., 1973-85; prof. anthropology U. Alaska, Fairbanks, 1985—; instr. anthropology U. Mass., 1972; vis. lectr. Am. Anthrop. Assn., 1974-76; cons. various orgns. Author: The Journals of Iakov Netsvetov—The Atkha Years, 1980, Aleut Art, 1982, Atkha—Ethnohistory of the Western Aleutians, 1983, The Yukon Years 1845-1863, 1984, Hieromonk Gideon: An Early Orthodox Missionary in Alaska, 1988; translator: Notes on the Islands of Unalaska District (by Ioann Veniaminov), 1984; contbr. numerous articles to profl. jours. Mem. Icon Preservation Task Force, Anchorage, 1986—. Eastern Orthodox. Office: U Alaska-Fairbanks Dept Anthropology Fairbanks AK 99775

BLACK, MARI KAMATA, computer specialist; b. Ohta-ku, Tokyo, Sept. 8, 1950; came to U.S., 1973; d. Hoju Kishi and Umeko Kamata; m. Richard Eugene Black, Feb. 9, 1973; 1 child, Richard Justyn. BA in English Lang., Dokkyo U., 1973. Office services asst. Office Services Controller's Office, Sacramento, Calif., 1977-80; computer programmer Sacramento Mcpl. Utility District, 1980-87; staff engr. Ultrasystems Def. and Space, Inc., Sunnyvale, Calif., 1987—. Republican. Baptist. Home: 10821 Johnson Ave Cupertino CA 95014 Office: Ultrasystems Def & Space 1327 Orleans Dr Sunnyvale CA 94089

BLACK, MIRIAM REBECCA, investment broker; b. N.Y.C., July 17, 1944; d. Milton Hyman and Bella (Gardyn) Miller; m. Sidney Y. Black, Mar. 25, 1967 (div. Jan. 1973); children: Michelle Paulette, Allison Hope. BA, U. Miami, Coral Gables, Fla., 1965; MA, Columbia U., 1966; MPA, U. Denver, 1979. Cert. secondary edn. and lang. arts tchr., N.Y., Colo. Rsch. analyst State of Colo., Denver, 1978-79; adminstrv. analyst Denver Water Dept., 1979-80; rsch. analyst. City of Thornton, Colo., 1980-83; investment broker Paine Webber, Inc., Denver, 1985—. Mem. utilities budget com. City of Aurora, Colo., 1984-87. Mem. AAUW, Am. Bus. and Profl. Women (fin. chmn. 1985-86), LWV. Home: 1354 S Zeno St Aurora CO 80017

BLACK, NOEL ANTHONY, television, film director; b. Chgo., June 30, 1937; s. Samuel Abraham and Susan (Quan) B.; m. Catherine Elizabeth Cownie, June 1, 1988; children: Marco Eugene, Nicole Alexandra, Carmen Elizabeth, Catherine Ellen. BA, UCLA, 1959, MA, 1964. Ind. fil, TV dir. 1966—. Dir.: (TV films) Trilogy: The American Boy, 1967 (Outstanding Young Dir. award Monte Carlo Internat. Festival of TV, Silver Dove award Internat. Cath. Soc. for Radio and TV), I'm a Fool, 1977, Mulligan's Stew, 1977, The Golden Honeymoon, 1979, The Electric Grandmother, 1981 (George Foster Peabody award 1982), The Other Victim, 1981, Prime Suspect, 1981, Happy Endings, 1982, Quarterback Princess, 1983, Deadly Intentions, 1985, Promises to Keep, 1985, A Time to Triumph, 1985, My Two Loves, 1986, Conspiracy of Love, 1987, The Town Bully, 1988, (short films) Skaterdater, 1966 (Grand Prix award Cannes XX Film Festival, Grand Prix Tech. Cannes XX Internat. Film Festival, awards Cork Film Festival, Silver medal Moscow Internat. Film Festival, others), Riverboy, 1967 (Lion of St. Mark award Venice Internat. Film Festival, 1st prize Vancouver Internat. Film Festival), (feature films) Pretty Poison, 1968, Mirrors, 1974, A Man, a Woman and a Bank, 1978; screenwriter Mischief, 1984.. Mem. Writers Guild Am., Dirs. Guild Am., Acad. Motion Picture Arts and Scis., Acad. TV Arts and Scis.

BLACK, REBECCA JANE, social services representative; b. Mt. Lookout, W.Va., Oct. 22, 1946; d. William Judson and Lola Virginia (Legg) Greaser; m. Paul Erickson, Aug. 14, 1964 (div. 1976); children: Angela Dawn, Anthony Paul, Joshua Allan; m. Ron Black, Dec. 12, 1980; adopted children: Jonathan Richard, Nicole Erana. Student, Idaho State U., 1976-79, 81-82. Counselor Ft. Hall (Idaho) Youth Home, 1975-79, South Idaho Girls Home, Pocatello, 1979-84; asst. dir. All About Children Services, Pocatello, 1984-85; rep. Job Corps, Nero & Assocs., Pocatello, 1985—; v.p. Synthesis, Inc., Pocatello, 1987—; pvt. contractor Nero & Assocs. Inc., Portland, Oreg. Cons. Stepping Stones Ministries Half-Way House, Boise, South Park Group Home, 1983-85; job developer Project Turnaround, 1987—; facilitator Sons and Daughters United, 1987—; chairperson Bannock County (Idaho) Planning and Zoning bd., 1985—, Salvation Army adv. bd., 1987—, Aid for Friends Shelter, 1984-85, Dist. Health Dept. Family Planning adv. bd., 1985-87, Families Through Adoption, Pocatello, 1979-81; adv. bd. Sch. Counselors, Pocatello, 1984-86, Idaho State U. Vocat. Edn., Pocatello, 1987-88; mem. Pocatello Community Services Council, 1983-84, Pocatello Ctr. for Peace and Justice, 1983-84, U. Idaho Expanded Food and Nutrition Program Bd., 1985; vol. Community Task Force on Child Sexual Abuse, Pocatello, 1983-85; active Youth Gang Task Force, Portland, Youth Employment Task Force. March of Dimes scholar, 1984, Children's Def. Fund scholar, 1985, North Am. Council on Adoptable Children scholar, 1982; grantee Menninger Found., 1984. Mem. Idaho Planners Assn., Nat. Assn. Female Execs., SE Idaho Job Developers, Portland Urban League. Democrat. Office: 4815 NE 7th Portland OR 97211

BLACK, RICHARD JAMES, state agency administrator; b. L.A., Jan. 11, 1944; s. Richard J. Henry II and Mary I. (Woods) B.; m. Kim S. Kienholz, Oct. 14, 1967; children: Kelly, Tad, Eric, Heather. BS, U. San Francisco, 1983. Account exec. Burroughs Corp., El Monte, Calif., 1969-71, TAC Inc., L.A., 1972-77; owner, mgr. Sierra Precast, Auburn, Calif., 1977-79; account exec., ops. mgr. AAA Filter Svc., West Sacramento, Calif., 1979-84; exec. officer cert. shorthand reporters bd. Dept. Comsumer Affairs State of Calif., Sacramento, 1984—. Chmn. Grass Valley Sch. Bd., 1980-87. Lt. U.S. Army, 1965-69, Vietnam. Decorated Bronze Star. Republican. Roman Catholic. Office: Calif Dept Consumer Affairs Cert Shorthand Reporters Bd 1021 O St Rm A-153 Sacramento CA 95814

BLACK, ROBERT JAMES, owner cabinet shop, licensed vocational nurse; b. Erie, Pa., Apr. 13, 1955; s. Charles Henry and Freida Drozdo (Stoneham) B.; m. Irene Drucilla Hagemaster, Apr. 20, 1975 (div. May 1983); m. Alma Marie Solomon, Dec. 19, 1987; 1 child, Heather Louise. BS in math, U. Akron, 1975; MBA, U. Calif., Berkeley, 1986. Lic. vocat. nurse Calif.; shop foreman Wooden Nickel Furniture, Meadville, Pa., 1978-81; bus. office mgr. Bayview Villa Hosp., Oakland, Calif., 1983-86; pres., owner Thoughts Wood, Inc., San Diego, Calif., 1986--; bus. cons. Profl. Bus. Services, San Diego and Oakland, Calif., 1986--. Author: Wives and Other Friends, 1978, Murphy, They're Doing It Again, 1986, (with others) The Refrigerator Commited Suicide, 1983. Leader 4-H Club Sunshine Riders, Akron, Ohio, 1975, Rep. canvasser, 1974. Served with USN, 1981-83. Assoc. mem. Assn. Surg. Technologists. Episcopalian. Office: Thoughts Wood Inc 125 Imperial Beach Blvd #41 Imperial Beach CA 92032

BLACK, VIOLA INEX, nurse; b. Chickasha, Okla., Mar. 8, 1941; d. Joseph Napolean and Viola Mae (Roberts) Willmon; m. Alfred Delbert Balck, Dec. 5, 1959; children: Jason, Carl, Andrew, Laurie. Grad., Am. Vocat. Nursing, Long Beach, Calif., 1975. Lic. vocat. nurse, Calif. Vocat. nurse Dr.'s Office, Yuba City, Calif., 1979-80, Fremont (Calif.) Med. Ctr., 1976-79, Biggs-Gridley (Calif.) Meml. Hosp., 1980-87; hospice worker Yuba City, 1986—. Democrat. Home: 5681 B Madden Ave Live Oak CA 95953

BLACK, WILFORD REX, JR., state senator; b. Salt Lake City, Jan. 31, 1920; s. Wilford Rex and Elsie Isabell (King) B.; m. Helen Shirley Frazer; children—Susan, Janet, Cindy, Joy, Peggy, Vanna, Gayle, Rex. Student schools in Utah. Locomotive engr. Rio Grande R.R., 1941-81; mem. Utah Senate, 1972—, speaker Third House, 1975-76, majority whip, 1977-78, minority leader, 1981—; chmn., vice chmn. United Transp. Union, 1972-78; sec. Utah State Legis. Bd., United Transp. Chmn. bd. Rail Operators Credit Union, 1958—; mission pres. Rose Park Stake Mormon Ch., high priest group leader Rose Park 9th Ward, 1980-83, mem. Rose Park Stake High Council, 1957-63. Served with U.S. Army, 1942-45. Recipient various awards r.r and legis. activities. Democrat. Office: 826 N 13th W Salt Lake City UT 84116

BLACK, WILLIAM ARTHUR (QUAL-LEE'-LAH), federal agency administrator; b. Omak, Wash., Feb. 17, 1948; s. Harry and Catherine Leone (Collar) B.; m. Jackie Marie Smith, Nov. 25, 1965 (div. 1988); children: William Arthur Jr., James Wyston, Megan Michelle; m. Patricia Ann Greenslitt, Oct. 2, 1988; children: Bruce Lloyd, Bradley Douglas. Student, U. Wash., Eastern Wash. U., Wenatchee Valley Coll. Enrollment officer Colville Confederated Tribes, Nespelem, Wash., 1969-74, Western Wash. Agy., Everett, 1974-76; tribal operation officer Puget Sound Agy., Everett, 1976-81; mgmt. trainee Dept. Interior, Washington, 1981-82; supt. Spokane Aty., Bur. Indian Affairs, Wellpinit, Wash., 1982-83; tribal ops. officer Juneau (Alaska) Bur. Indian Affairs, 1983; supt. Puget Sound Agy. Bur. Indian Affairs, Everett, 1983—; nat. coord. Goodwill Games, Bur. Indian Affairs, Washington, 1988—; mem. Am. Indian Trade/Devel. Coun., Everett, 1986—. Trustee Everett Community Coll., 1987—; scoutmaster Evergreen coun. Boy Scouts Am., com. mem.; asst. Congressman Al Swift, Washington; ex-officio mem. Puget Sound Child Protection Team, Am. Indian Goodwill Games Commn. Named Gentleman of Yr., Everett Community Coll. Women's Ctr., 1989. Mem. Assn. Community Coll. Trustees, Colville Confederated Tribes, Elks. Democrat. Office: Puget Sound Agy Bur Indian Affairs 3006 Colby Ave Everett WA 98201

BLACKBIRD, MIKE, state senator, sales representative; b. Kellogg, Idaho, Mar. 10, 1942; s. George Clifford and Joy Leatrice (Daniels) B.; m. Courtney Rae Harrison, Aug. 29, 1964; children: Michael Brian, Lynn René. BA in History and Polit. Sci., U. Calif., Long Beach, 1969. Salesman Upjohn Co., San Diego, 1970-79, Metpath Labs., Spokane, 1979-80; factory position Bunkerhill Co., Kellogg, 1980-81; salesman Far Western Hosp. Supply, Inc., Seattle, 1981-83, Biddle & Crowther Co., Spokane, 1983—; Idaho state senator Boise, 1986—. Mem. exec. com. Idaho Dem. Party, 1982-86, Cen. Com., 1980—, precinct com. Shoshone County Dem. Orgn., 1980—. With USN, 1960-64. Democrat. Roman Catholic. Home: 1606 Fairmont Loop Coeur d'Alene ID 83814 Office: Office of State Senate State Capitol Boise ID 83720 also: Biddle & Crowther Co E 715 Sprague Ave Spokane WA 99202

BLACKBURN, DANIEL M., correspondent; b. Xenia, Ohio, Nov. 6, 1938; s. A. D. and Helen M. B.; m. Sue Ellen Heiny, June 20, 1959 (div. 1972); children: Laura Jeanne, Lynne Danielle; m. Mariko Fukuda, Sept. 6, 1986; children: Dylan Daniel, Fukuda Blackburn. BA, Purdue U., 1961. Reporter Sta. WBBM-TV, Chgo., 1963-64; reporter, writer Sta. WNEW, N.Y.C., 1964-65; bur. chief, corr. Metromedia News, Washington, 1965-70; dep. dir. pub. affairs The Peace Corps, Washington, 1970-71; reporter, news anchor Sta. KNX-TV, L.A., 1971-75; corr. NBC News, Burbank, Calif., 1975-88, Cable News Network, L.A., 1988—; chmn. The Friday Group, L.A., 1974—; mem. Nat. Adv. Com. on High Sch. Journalism, Washington, 1975; co-chmn. Robert F. Kennedy Journalism Awards, Washington, 1968-71; guest lectr. Western Journalism Conf., L.A., 1976. Author: Zen and the Cross Country Skier, 1975; contbr. articles to profl. jours. Recipient Golden Mike award So. Calif. Broadcasters, 1975, Grand award Los Angeles Press Club, 1975, Calif. State award Calif. Exposition, Sacramento, 1974. Mem. AFTRA, Writers Guild, Sierra Club. Home: 3611 Lowry Rd Los Angeles CA 90027

BLACKBURN, JOHN LEWIS, consulting engineer; b. Kansas City, Mo., Oct. 2, 1913; s. John Ealy and Lela (Garnett) B.; m. Margaret Bailey, Sept. 12, 1943; children—Susan T., Joan Blackburn Krist, Margot A. Blackburn Jahns. BSEE with high honors, U. Ill., 1935. With Westinghouse Electric Corp., Newark, 1936-78, cons. engr., 1969-78; pvt. practice cons., Bothell, Wash., 1979—; adj. prof. Poly. Inst. N.Y., 1949-65, Poly. Inst. N.J., Newark, 1958-71; spl. lectr. IEEE Ednl. Activities, 1952—; affiliate prof. U. Wash., 1988; instr. North Seattle Community Coll., 1988. Author, editor: Applied Protective Relaying, 1978; author: Protective Relaying Principles and Application, 1987. Trustee, treas. Millington Bapt. Ch., N.J., 1952-69. Recipient Order of Merit award Westinghouse Electric Corp., 1971, Attwood Assocs. award U.S. Nat. Com. Internat. Conf. for Large High Voltage Electric Systems, 1986. Fellow IEEE (chmn. publ. dept. Power Engring. Soc. 1972-76, sec., 1977-79, chmn. power system relaying com. 1969-70, Disting. Service award 1978, Outstanding Service award IEEE ednl. bd. 1979, Centennial medal 1984); mem. China Stamp Soc. Inc. (pres. 1979—), Am. Soc. Polar Philatelists (bd. dirs., treas. 1967—), Sigma Xi, Tau Beta Pi, Eta Kappa Nu, Phi Kappa Phi. Home: 21816 8th Pl W Bothell WA 98021

BLACKBURN, LINDA KAYE, corporate executive; b. Bidwell, Ohio, Sept. 27, 1949; d. Randolph and Lena (Gaultney) B. Student, Ohio U., 1967-69. Sec. Turner & Shepard Inc., Columbus, Ohio, 1969-75; adminstrv. asst. Bancorp Svcs., Irvine, Calif., 1977-79; office mgr. Far West Data Svcs., 1979-81; mgr. warranty adminstrn. Global Wulfsberg Systems, 1981—. Mem. Nat. Assn. Female Execs. Democrat. Home: 2656D Orange Ave Costa Mesa CA 92627 Office: Global Wulfsberg Systems 2144 Michelson Irvine CA 92715

BLACK-BURRIS, UANITA EVELYN, sales professional; b. Mannheim, Fed. Republic of Germany, Dec. 21, 1959; came to U.S., 1968; d. Willard Jr. and Ilse Black; m. Londell Forté Burris, Aug. 22, 1987. AA, El Camino Coll., 1979; student in mktg., Calif. State U., Long Beach, 1979-82. Mgr. dept. The Broadway, Westchester, Calif., 1978-82; mgr. counter Clinique Cosmetics, Hawthorne, Calif., 1982-86; sales rep. ITT Tech. Inst., Carson, Calif., 1986—. Editor: (newspaper) The Broadview, 1985. Mem. NAFE, Calif. Scholarship Fedn. (cert. of merit), Summit Inc., Humane Soc. of U.S. Democrat.

BLACKFIELD, CECILIA MALIK, teacher, civic volunteer; b. Oakland, Calif., Jan. 18, 1915; d. Benjamin Malik and Mollie Saak; m. William Blackfield, Dec. 25, 1941; children: Leland Gregory, Pamela Esther, Karen Ann. BA, U. Calif., Berkeley, 1936; MEdn., San Francisco State Tchrs Coll, 1937. cert. elem. tchr. Calif. (lifetime). Tchr. Albany (Calif.) Sch. Dist., 1938-43; rep. NEA, Alameda County, Calif., 1938-43. Pres. Calif. Tchrs. Assn., Alameda County, Calif., 1939; mem. (charter) Territorial Hosp. Aux., Kauikeolani Children's Hosp. (bd. dirs.); bd. dirs. Hastings Law Sch. Found., San Francisco, Calif., McCoy Pavilion Park, Honolulu, Hi., Daughters of the Nile, Honolulu, Temple Emmanuel; mem. Mayor's Citizen Advisory Com. for Diamond Head, Wakiki, Honolulu, Mayor's Adv. Com. for Community & Urban Renewal, Beautification Com., League of Women Voters; chmn. Hawaii Cancer Fund Crusade and many more. Named Woman of the Year for Nat. Brotherhood Week, Honolulu, 1972. Mem. Hawaii Chpt. Women's Aux. Nat. Assn. Home Builders (pres.), Outdoor Circle (pres.), Friends of Foster Gardens, Washington Palace State Capitol, Hadassah (past pres. Oakland chpt.), Women's Com. Brandeis Univ. Home: 901 Kealaolu Ave Honolulu HI 96816

BLACKFORD, SHERYL LYNNE, infosystems specialist; b. Everett, Wash., Mar. 6, 1958; d. Paul Wesley and Judith Lee (Fuqua) B.; 1 child, April Lynne. Degree in Data Processing, Everett Community Coll., 1979. Programmer Bank of Everett, 1979-80; programmer/analyst Olympic Bank, Everett, 1980-84; sr. programmer John Fluke Mfg. Inc., Everett, 1984-87; systems analyst Eddie Bauer Inc., Redmond, Wash., 1987—; contract programmer Everett Terminal, 1979-81, Everett Ski Shop, 1986; contract operator Scott Paper Co., Everett, 1988. Pres. Salty Sea Pirates, Everett, 1983; sec. Salty Sea Days Com., Everett, 1983, parade chmn., 1984. Home: 14421 45th Ave W Lynnwood WA 98036 Office: Eddie Bauer Inc 15010 NE 36th St Redmond WA 98052

BLACKKETTER, BRUCE LLOYD, production engineer; b. Yuma, Ariz., Sept. 5, 1957; s. Dennis Oren and Sue Ellen (Locknane) B.; m. Dorean Inez Best, Apr. 21, 1978; children: Shyla Ruth, Alyson Marie. BSME, Mont. State U., 1985. Owner, pres. Blackketter Constrn. Co., Bozeman, Mont., 1978-85; design engr. FMC, Pocatello, Idaho, 1985-86; shift supr. FMC, Pocatello, 1986-87, prodn. engr., 1987—. Campaigner, Pocatello City Council, 1985. Mem. Tau Beta Pi, Pi Tau Sigma. Republican. Mem. Ch. of Christ. Home: 1930 Jean Pocatello ID 83201 Office: FMC PO Box 4111 Pocatello ID 83201

BLACKLEY, TERRY JOHN, college dean, consultant; b. Ottawa, Ill., Nov. 22, 1942; s. Russell John and Catherine Irene (Gulbronson) B.; m. Karen Sue Ray, July 24, 1965; children: Daniel John, Sarah Ray. BMus, Millikin U., 1964; MMus, U. Mich., 1969. Asst. dir. bands Prospect High Sch., Mt. Prospect, Ill., 1964-66; dir. bands Elk Grove (Ill.) High Sch., 1966-68, Fullerton (Calif.) High Sch., 1969-72; dir. bands Fullerton Coll., 1971-85, chmn. music dept., 1977-80, dean fine arts, 1980—, founder, dir. 17th ann. jazz festival, 1972—; clinician, adjudicator jazz festivals, western U.S., 1975—; guest condr. honor bands in so. Calif., 1980—; assoc. dir. All Am. Coll. Marching Band, Summer Olympics, L.A., 1984; bd. dirs. Reno Internat. Jazz Festival, 1988—. Contbr. articles to trade mags.; composer 12 chorale works. Recipient Outstanding Coll. Jazz Band Record of Yr. award Downbeat Mag., 1984; winner college jazz competition Disneyworld, Epcot, 1985; exptl. tchr. fellow U. Mich., 1968. Mem. Nat. Assn. Jazz Educators (editor newsletter 1984-86, bd. dirs. music performance trust fund 1986—), ASCAP, Music Assn. Calif. Community Colls. (sec. 1988), Assn. Calif. Community Coll. Adminstrs., So. Calif. Sch. Band and Orch. Assn. (hon. bd. dirs. 1984). Office: Fullertol Coll 321 E Chapman Ave Fullerton CA 92634

BLACKMAN, DAVID IRA, health science administrator; b. Los Angeles, Mar. 12, 1951; s. Soli and Erika Louise (Ullmann) B. BS, U. So. Calif., 1975; MS, U. LaVerne, 1986. Cert. tchr., Calif. Fin. specialist U. Calif. Med. Ctr., San Francisco, 1975-79; adminstrn. specialist U. Calif. Med. Ctr., Irvine, 1979-80; adminstr. Kaiser Found. Health Plan, Los Angeles, 1980—; cons. health care DIB Group, Glendale, Calif., 1980—. Recipient Gold Achievement award United Way Campaigns, Los Angeles, 1984. Mem. Am. Guild Patient Acct. Mgrs., Health Care Fin. Mgmt. Assocs., Am. Mgmt. Assn., Nat. Right to Work Found., Assn. Western Hosps., Lake Mirage Country Club. Republican. Home: 1203 Viola Ave Glendale CA 91202-1803

BLACKSHAW, GEORGE EDWARD, management executive; b. Bakersfield, Calif., Mar. 15, 1935; s. Joseph Turner and Clara Viola (Morris) B.; children: Jennifer, Michael, Brian, Lori, David. AA, Pasadena City Coll., 1954; BS, Calif. State Poly. U., 1958. Tech. dir. USAF Armament Lab.; dir. tacticle missiles, dir. air warfare Office of Undersecretary Dept. of Def., Washington; v.p. rsch. and engring., v.p. bus. devel. Convair Div. Gen. Dynamics Corp., San Diego, 1978-83; v.p., gen. mgr. United Techs. Advanced Systems, San Diego, 1983—. Office: United Techs Advanced Systems 10180 Telesis Ct San Diego CA 92121

BLACKSTOCK, JAMES FIELDING, lawyer; b. L.A., Sept. 19, 1947; s. James Carne and Justine Fielding (Gibson) B.; m. Kathleen Ann Weigand, Dec. 12, 1969; children: Kristin Marie, James Fielding. AB, U. So. Calif., 1969; JD, 1976. Bar: Calif. 1976, U.S. Dist. Ct. (cen. dist.) Calif. 1977, U.S. Supreme Ct. 1980. Law clk. Hill Farrer Burrill, L.A., 1975-76, assoc., 1976-80; assoc. Zobrist, Garner, Garrett, L.A., 1980-83; ptnr. Zobrist & Vienna, L.A., 1983; v.p., gen. counsel Tatum Petroleum, La Habra, Calif., 1983; atty. Thorpe, Sullivan, Workman & Thorpe, 1984; ptnr. Sullivan, Workman & Dee, 1985—. Mem. Town Hall, L.A., 1980—. Served to lt. USN, 1969-73, PTO; comdr. USNR. Mem. ABA, L.A. County Bar Assn. Saddle and Sirloin Club, Elks. Republican. Roman Catholic. Home: 5150 Solliden Ln La Canada CA 91011 Office: Sullivan Workman & Dee 800 S Figueroa St Ste 1200 Los Angeles CA 90017-2521

BLACKWELDER, KENT GENE, entertainment managment consultant; b. Alexandria, Minn., Dec. 3, 1955; s. Gene and Greta (Wick) B. BS in Indsl. Mgmt., Purdue U., 1977; MBA, Pepperdine U., 1982; postgrad., UCLA, 1983. Cons. Triad Microsystems, El Segundo, Calif., 1982-83; dir. plans and programs Mattel Elec., Hawthorne, Calif., 1983-84; cons. Tecolote Research, El Segundo, 1984-85, Blackbell, Redondo Beach, Calif., 1985-86, Blake Edwards Entertainment Mgmt., Redondo Beach, 1986-87, Scotti-McCleary Mgmt., Santa Monica, Calif., 1987—. Liaison officer explorer scouts Boy Scouts Am., Los Angeles, 1977-79; chmn. USAF Space Heritage Program, Los Angeles, 1980-81. Served to capt. USAF, 1977-82. Named one of Outstanding Young Men of Am., U.S. Jaycees, 1983. Mem. Planning Exec. Inst. (Los Angeles chpt.), Project Mgmt. Inst., (Los Angeles chpt.), Air Force Soc. (Los Angeles), Am. Soc. Mil. Comptrollers (Los Angeles chpt.), Kappa Sigma (grand procurator Purdue U. chpt. 1975-76). Baptist. Club: Arnold Air Soc. (West Lafayette, Ind.) (comptroller 1976-77). Office: Scotti Bros Entertainment 2114 Pico Blvd Santa Monica CA 90405

BLACKWELL, DAN P., physical education instructor; b. Amarillo, Tex., Jan. 20, 1952; s. Oliver Page Jr. and Lucille Elizabeth (Britten) B.; m. Debra Gay Goodin, Dec. 27, 1974; 1 child, Oliver Page III. BS, W. Tex. State U., 1974; MEd, Tex. Tech U., 1977. Cert. phys. and driver's edn. tchr., Tex., Wyo. Instr. phys. edn. Brownfield (Tex.) High Sch., 1974-78, Sch. Dist. 25, Riverton, Wyo., 1978—; instr. U. Wyo. Extension, Riverton, 1985. Author: So You Want to Jump Rope, 1982; contbr. articles to profl. jours. Lic. lay reader Wyo. Order of Lay Readers, Riverton, 1987— vestry mem. St. James Episc. Ch., Riverton, 1987—, lay eucharistic minister, 1987—. Named one of Outstanding Young Men in Am., Jaycees, 1983; named Vol. of the Yr., Am. Heart Assn., 1985, Wyo. Tchr. of the Yr., State of Wyo., 1984, 87. Mem. Wyo. Alliance for Health, Phys. Edn., Recreation and Dance (Phys. Edn. of the Yr. 1986), Am. Alliance for Health, Phys. Edn., Recreation and Dance. Republican. Office: Sch Dist 25 121 N SW Riverton WY 82501

BLACKWELL, FREDERICK WAYNE, computer science educator; b. Rensselaer, Ind., Mar. 10, 1937; s. Paul Francis and Ardis Caroline (Maines) B.; m. Iona Ruth Roberts, June 19, 1966 (div. Aug. 1975); children: Robert Howard, David Stuart; m. Linda Raeburn Montie, Nov. 28, 1981; 1 stepchild, Megan Elaine McCreary. AB, Ind. U., 1957; MS, Stanford U., 1962; grad. student, Rand Grad. Inst., Santa Monica, Calif., 1970-77; PhD, U. So. Calif., L.A., 1975. Mem. tech. staff TRW Systems, Redondo Beach, Calif., 1962-67; info. scientist The Rand Corp., Santa Monica, Calif., 1967-78; asst. prof. Calif. State U., Sacramento, 1978-80, computing acad. coord., 1981, assoc. prof., 1981-84, prof. computer sci., 1984—, acting dept. chair, 1985; vis. prof. Boston U. Overseas Program, Seckenheim, Fed. Republic Germany, 1987; cons. Shearson Loeb Rhoades, N.Y.C., 1980-81, Control Data Corp., Mpls., 1981-85, Adaptive Technologies, Sacramento, 1984-85, Lawrence Livermore Nat. Lab., Livermore, Calif., 1984. Author: (with others) The Emerging Technology, 1972, Introduction to Robotics, 1985. Conf. attendance grantee NRC, Stockholm, Sweden, 1974; Neural Net Research grantee Calif. State U., Sacramento, 1989. Mem. Assn. for Computing Machinery, Computer Soc. of IEEE, Pattern Recognition Soc., Internat. Neural Network Soc., Mensa. Office: Calif State Univ Computer Science Dept 6000 J St Sacramento CA 95819

BLADES, PHILIP DYSON, social worker administrator; b. Carroll, Iowa, Mar. 10, 1934; s. C. Stewart and Ethel G. (Dyson) B. BA, Mich. State U., 1956; MS in Social Work, U. Wis., Milw., 1965. Supr. Ky. Dept. Mental Health, Lexington, 1963-66; sr. caseworker Calif. Dept. Mental Health, Modesto, 1966-68, Assistance League, Hollywood, Calif, 1968-72; exec. dir. Family Svc. Agy. Burbank (Calif.), 1972—; Mem. Burbank Sch. Attendance Rev. Bd., 1976—; pres. Burbank Coordinating Coun., 1986-87; chmn. region IV, Calif. Coun. on Children and Youth, Glendale, 1989—. Bd. dirs. Burbank chpt. ARC, 1984—. Mem. Rotary (bd. dirs. Burbank 1983-85, 88-89). Democrat. Office: Family Svc Agy of Burbank 2013 W Magnolia Blvd Burbank CA 91506

BLADES, STEVEN PAUL, land and development corporation executive; b. Santa Barbara, Calif., July 15, 1951; s. William Jr. and Flora Jeanette (Johnson) B.; m. Deborah Ann Dean, May 11, 1974; children: Melissa, Robert, Kristen, Kerrie. AA, Santa Barbara City Coll., 1972; student, U. Calif., Santa Barbara, 1972-74. Supr. maintenance B.V. Hosps., Santa Barbara, 1974-76; mgr. data processing Bergen Brunswig Corp., Santa Barbara, 1976-79; dir. delivery svcs. U.S. Postal Service, Santa Barbara, 1979-86; v.p. Inland West Devel., Rancho Cucamonga, Calif., 1986—; pres. Santa Barbara Sports Assn., 1971-74; bd. dirs. Direct Link, Santa Barbara, 1986, ARC, Santa Barbara, 1984, instr. CPR, 1983; bd. of elders Community Bible Ch., San Bernardino, Calif., 1988. Mem. Awana Youth Clubs (chmn. 1986—).

Republican. Office: Inland West Devel 7365 Hellman Ave Rancho Cucamonga CA 91730

BLADINE, PHILIP NEWELL, newspaper and commercial printing executive; b. Cedar Falls, Iowa, Nov. 19, 1918; s. Lars Eric and Inez D. (Waterman) B.; m. Margaret Eleanor Greene, Feb. 19, 1943; children: Pamela Jane, Jon Eric. Student, Linfield Coll., 1936-37; BA in Journalism, U. Oreg., 1940. Editor Telephone-Register (named changed to News-Register 1953), McMinnville, Oreg., 1941-42, 45-57; pub. Telephone-Register (named changed to News-Register 1953), 1957—; co-owner Sta. KMCM, 1949-59; chmn. Bridgetown Printing Co., Portland, oreg., 1983—, Oreg. Lithoprint, Inc., McMinnville; bd. dirs. Gen. Telephone Co. Northwest, Everett, Wash., The Embarcadero, Newport, Oreg. Bd. dirs. Am. Advt. Mus., Portland; chmn. Oreg. adv. SBA; bd. dirs., past v.p. McMinnville Indsl. promotions; past chmn. fin. com. Oreg. Econ. Devel. Dept.; past mem., chmn. Oreg. Econ. Devel. Commn.; chmn. Oreg. 4-H Found., 1981-82; past chmn. Yamhill dist. Boy Scouts Am., Yamhill County Willamette Basin Project com.; past mem. exec. com. Oreg. Rep. Central Com.; mem. McMinnville Comporehensive Plan Com.; past capot. Yamhill County Sheriff's Mounted Possee, others. With USNR, 1942-45; PTO. Recipient editorial award Oreg. Farm Bur., 1963, Sr. 1st Citizen award City of McMinnville, 1976, Roger Williams award, 1987. Mem. Oreg. Newspaper Pubs. Assn. (pres. 1959, former legis. chmn., Pres.'s award 1971, 73, Amos Voorhies award 1976), McMinnville C. of C. (pres. 1955), Western Environ. Trade Assn. (pres. 1971-72), Assoc. Oreg. Industries (pres. 1969-71, Org. Bus. Leader of Yr. award 1984), Masters Printers Oreg. (past pres.), Sigma Delta Chi, Phi Gamma Delta, Alpha Delta Sigma. Home: 2110 Saint Andrews Dr McMinnville OR 97128 Office: News Register 611 3d St McMinnville OR 97128

BLAGG, CHRISTOPHER ROBIN, nephrologist; b. Retford, Eng., June 12, 1931; s. Albert Edgar and Emma Alice (Chambers) B.; m. Jean Winifred Thomas, Dec. 18, 1953; children: Alison Christine, Elizabeth Jane, Christopher James, Simon Francis. MB, U. Leeds Sch. Medicine, Leeds, England, 1954, MD, 1964. Mem. Royal Coll. Physicians, London. Research fellow U. Leeds, England, 1958-60; lectr. in medicine U. Leeds, 1961-65; research fellow U. Wash., Seattle, 1963-64; sr. lectr. in medicine U. Leeds, 1965-66; asst. prof. U. Wash., Seattle, 1966-72, assoc. prof., 1972-78; MD N.W. Kidney Ctr., Seattle, 1971-73, exec. dir., 1973—; prof. medicine U. Wash., Seattle, 1978—; com. mem. NIH, Washington, 1974—; chmn. sci. adv. com. U.S. Renal Data System, Washington, 1988—. Contbr. numerous articles to profl. jours. Capt. Royal Am. Mil. Corps, 1956-58, England. Fellow Royal Coll. Physicians; mem. Renal Physicians Assn. (pres. 1976-78), Am. Soc. Nephrologist, Am. Soc. Artificial Internal Organs, European Dialysis and Transplant Assn., Internat. Soc. Nephrology. Episcopalian. Home: 2427 84th SE Mercer Island WA 98040 Office: NW Kidney Ctr 700 Broadway Seattle WA 98122

BLAHETKA, RUSSELL ERNEST, data communications specialist; b. Chgo., Aug. 6, 1952; s. Ernest Anthony and Regina Helen (Weil) B.; m. Nancy Marie Aul, Sept. 18, 1971 (div. 1986); children: Russell Ernest, Kenneth James, Gregory Alan. Student, Ill. Inst. Tech., 1970-73. Design engr. Goldberg Emmerman Co., Elk Grove Village, Ill., 1973-74; field engr. Varian Data Machines Co., Des Plaines, Ill., 1974-77; tech. support specialist Auto-Trol Tech., Schaumburg, Ill., 1977-82; sr. system sales exec. Racal-Milgo Co., Des Plaines, 1982-85; product specialist, data communications Tandem Computers, Cupertino, Calif., 1985—. Mem. Mensa.

BLAINE, DOROTHEA CONSTANCE RAGETTÉ, lawyer, b. N.Y.C., Sept. 23, 1930; d. Robert Raymond and Dorothea Ottilie Ragetté; BA, Barnard Coll., 1952; MA, Calif. State U., 1968; EdD, UCLA, 1978; JD, Western State U., 1981; postgrad. in taxation Golden Gate U. Bar: U.S. Dist. Ct. (ea., so. and cen. dists.) Calif., 1982. Mem. tech. staff Planning Rsch. Corp., L.A., 1964-67; assoc. scientist Holy Cross Hosp., Mission Hills, Calif., 1967-70; career devel. officer and affirmative action officer County of Orange, Santa Ana, Calif., 1970-74, sr. adminstrv. analyst, budget and program coord., 1974-78; spl. projects asst. CAO/Spl. Programs Office, 1978-80, sr. adminstrv. analyst, 1980-83; sole practice, 1982—; instr. Am. Coll. Law, Brea, Calif., 1987; judge pro tem Orange County Mcpl. Ct., 1988; bd. dirs. Orange County Lawyers Referral, del. to state bar conv., 1985-88. Bd. dirs. Deerfield Community Assn., 1975-78, Orange YMCA, 1975-77. Mem. ABA, ACLU, Trial Lawyers Am., Calif. Trial Lawyers Assn., Orange County Trial Lawyers Assn., Calif. Women Lawyers, Nat. Women's Polit. Caucus, Calif. Bar Assn., Orange County Bar Assn. (Orange County del. to Calif. State Bar Conv. 1985-88, bd. dirs. Orange County Lawyers Referral Svc. 1988), Delta Theta Phi, Phi Delta Kappa. Office: 2130 E 4th St #115 Santa Ana CA 92705

BLAIR, FREDERICK DAVID, interior designer; b. Denver, June 15, 1946; s. Frederick Edward and Margaret (Whitely) B. BA, U. Colo., 1969; postgrad. in French, U. Denver, 1981-82. Interior designer The Denver, 1969-76, store mgr., 1976-80; v.p. Hartley House Interiors, Ltd., Denver, 1980-83; pvt. practice interior design Denver, 1983—; com. mem. Ice House Design Ctr., Denver, 1985-86, Design Directory Western Region, Denver, 1986. Designs shown in various mags. Mem. Rep. Nat. Com. Mem. Am. Soc. Interior Designers (co-chmn. com. profl. registration 1986), Denver Art Mus., Nat. Trust for Hist. Preservation, Hist. Denver, Inc. Christian Scientist.

BLAIR, GLORIA CHRISTINE, pathology secretary; b. South Gate, Calif., Sept. 5, 1946; d. Arthur Chester and Gloria Magdalen (Neilson) B.; 1 child, Christopher Arthur. BA, Chaminade U., 1984. Long distance operator Pacific Telephone, Huntington Park, Calif., 1965-66; phone operator Tel-Page Answering Service, Compton, Calif., 1966-76; supr. Rowe Service Co., Compton, Calif., 1972-79; receptionist Hacker Clinic, Lynwood, Calif., 1980-81; library asst. Chaminade U., Honolulu, 1982-84; secretary Spring Anesthesia Group, Inc., Norwalk, Calif., 1985—. Democrat. Roman Catholic. Office: Spring Anesthesia Group Inc 12440 Firestone Blvd Ste 101 Norwalk CA 90650

BLAIR, JUDITH ANN, marketing executive; b. Milw., Mar. 6, 1952; d. Eugene Alan Macsurak and Frances Jenni (Turko) Senak; m. Howard Leroy Monty, Aug. 17, 1973 (div. Jan. 1981); 1 child, James Leroy.; m. Frederick Quintin Blair, Aug. 25, 1985; 1 child, Quintin Theodore. Student, U. Wis., 1973-78. Cert. tour profl. Internat. mkt. dir. Med. Engring. Corp., Racine, Wis., 1973-78; cons. internat. sales/mktg. Ideal Mgmt. Inc., Racine, 1978-79; office mgr. Cody (Wyo.) Paint and Body, 1980-83; adminstrv. asst. Cody County C. of C., 1983-85; mktg. dir. Quin Blair Enterprises, Cody, 1985—; participant internat. trade mission Foremost/West-TWA Airlines, Salt Lake City, 1986, United Airlines/United Express, Colo., Wyo., 1987-88. Bd. dirs. Cody Main St. Council, 1988—. Recipient Presdl. award for Excellence in Exporting U.S. Dept. Commerce, Racine, 1979. Mem. Am. Bus. Assn., Nat. Tour Assn., Meeting Planners Internat., Wyo. Meeting/Conv. Council (bd. dirs. 1984, 86, pres. 1987, 88), S.E. Wis. World Trade Bd. (pres. 1977-79), Soroptimist Club (bd. dirs. 1987—), Venture Club (chmn. 1977). Republican. Mormon. Office: Blair Hotels of Wyo 1701 Sheridan Ave Cody WY 82414

BLAIR, KERRIE JANE, secretary, teacher; b. Pauline, Kans., Dec. 12, 1956; d. Duane Charles and Jane (Heubner) B. BA in Bus. Edn., U. No. Colo., 1978, postgrad., 1988--. Cert. tchr., vocat. tchr., secondary bus. tchr., post-secondary adult tchr., Colo. Instr. Aims Community Coll., Greeley, Colo., 1978; exec. sec. Colo. div. Kodak Co., Windsor, 1978-81, Chorney Oil Co., Denver, 1981, Transcontinental Drilling Co., 1982; sec. to chmn., loan processor, new account rep. Estes Park (Colo.) Bank, 1983-88; substitute tchr. Park R-3 Sch. Dist., Estes Park, 1988--. Mem. Bus. and Profl. Women (pres. 1986-87, dist. sec.-treas. 1987-88, mem. state strategic long range com. 1988--), AAUW, PEO, Quota Club (growth and devel. com., Heart Fund drive), Epsilon Sigma Alpha, Pi Omega Pi. Republican. Home: 922 Peakview St PO Box 423 Estes Park CO 80517

BLAIR, ROBERT PARK, real estate broker; b. Idaho Falls, Idaho, June 21, 1950; s. Park Riley and Eunice Jeanine (McCarty) B.; m. Marilyn Jones (div. Feb. 1985); children: Shiloh, Arianne, Timothy. Degree in computer programming, LaSalle U., 1971. Realtor Century 21, Ventura, Calif., 1985, real estate assoc., 1985-88; owner Blair & Assocs. Real Estate, Ventura, 1988—. Mem. Nat. Assn. Realtors, Calif. Assn. Realtors, Ventura Bd. Realtors, Ventura Jaycees. Republican.

BLAIR, SIDNEY ROBERT, petroleum company executive; b. Port of Spain, Trinidad, Aug. 13, 1929; s. Sidney Martin and Janet (Gentleman) B.; m. Lois Wedderburn, June 13, 1953; children: Megan, James, Robert, Martin, Charlotte. BS, Queens U., 1951. Field engr., mgr. constrn. of gas and oil pipe lines and refineries 1951-58; dir. gas ops. and purchasing Alta. (Can.) and So. Gas Co. Ltd. and affiliates, 1959-69; exec. v.p. The Alta. Gas Trunk Line Co. Ltd., 1969-70, pres., chief exec. officer, from 1970; past chmn., chief exec. officer Nova, an Alta. (Can.) Corp., Calgary; former pres., chmn. bd. dirs. Husky Oil Ltd. subs. Calgary; chmn., chief exec. officer, dir. Nova Corp. Alta., Calgary, 1988—. Office: Nova Corp of Alta, 801 Seventh Ave SW, Calgary, AB Canada T2P 2N6 *

BLAIR, STEPHEN ALEXANDER, software engineer; b. Toledo, Ohio, Dec. 23, 1947; s. James Wright and Kathryn Ross (Crow) B.; m. Barbara-Ann Reich, Nov. 26, 1971; 1 child, Paul Ives. BA in Psychology, Lake Forest (Ill.) Coll., 1969; BS in Nursing, Berea (Ky.) Coll., 1976. Asst. controller FAA, Aurora, Ill., 1969-70; asst. adminstrs. Dine Bitsiis Baa Aha Yaa div. Navajo Corp., Chinle, Ariz., 1971-72; staff nurse Kenrich Nursing Home, Richmond, Ky., 1975-76, Garrard County Meml. Hosp., Lancaster, Ky., 1976-77; tuberculosis control officer Madison County Health Dept., Richmond, 1977-78; system tech. support engr. Lycor Corp. (name now Pallm), Indpls., 1978-82; adminstrv. analyst Servio Logic Corp., Portland, Oreg., 1982-84; software engr. Tektronix Corp., Portland, Oreg., 1984-88, Mentor Graphics Corp., Portland, Oreg., 1988—. Asst. scoutmaster Boy Scouts Am., Milwaukie, Oreg., 1986—. Mem. Baha'i Faith. Office: Mentor Graphics Corp 8500 SW Creekside Pl Beaverton OR 97005

BLAIR, STEWART D., communications company executive; b. Scotland, 1950. MA in Econs. and Polit. Sci., U. Glasgow, Scotland. With Chase Manhattan Bank, London; with Chase Manhattan Bank, Denver, from 1972, v.p.; dir. fin., later v.p. fin. Tele-Communications Inc.; now pres., chief exec. officer United Artists Communications Inc., Denver. Office: UA Communications Inc 2930 E 3d Ave Denver CO 80206 *

BLAIS, BETTY ANN, software company executive; b. Columbus, Ga., Nov. 27, 1948; d. Max Ray Whittington and Golda Faye (Hammell) Fabian; m. Gregory MacDonald Blais, Sept. 28, 1968. Grad. high sh., Portland, Oreg. Payroll clk. Consol. Freightways, Portland, 1966-74; various positions to sr. dir. systems and programming Dealer Svcs. div. ADP, Portland, 1975-85; owner, v.p. programming, corp. sec., treas. SofTac Corp., Lake Oswego, Oreg., 1987--. Republican. Roman Catholic. Office: SofTac Corp 4000 Kruse Way Pl Bldg 2 Ste 285 Lake Oswego OR 97035

BLAISE, MARGARET LYNETTE, insurance company executive; b. Los Angeles, Jan. 22; d. Duane M. and Esther H. (Ruddock) Free; m. Roy E. Sowers, Sept. 1965 (div. 1972); Children: Eric E., Robb D. Cert. in Gen. Ins., Ins. Inst., Malvern, Pa., 1981; Cert. Bus. Law, Hancock Coll., Santa Maria, Calif., 1987; Ins. Solicitor Lic., Celina Ins. Sch., Celina, Ohio, 1981; Assoc. in Claims, Ins. Inst., Malvern, 1984. CPIW. Ins. Claims Asst. Ins. Co. of No. Am., St. Charles, Ill., 1959-61; ins. mgr. Nelson Chevrolet, Seattle, 1961-63; ins.mgr. Superior Underwrtiers, Seattle, 1963-66; bus. owner Mar-Win Constrn. Co., Seattle, 1966-74; ins. adjuster Westfield Ins. Co., Aurora, Ill., 1976-84; mktg. and underwriter asst. Pollard & Cossa Ins., Santa Maria, Calif., 1984-85; ind. claims adj. & adminstrn. Carl Warren & Co., Sanluis Obispo, Calif., 1985-88; mgr. Carl Warren & Co., Santa Barbara, Calif., 1988—; del. Nat. Covn. Aurora Assn. of Ins. Women, Ill. 1981, del. State Conv. Cen. Coast Ins. Women, Santa Maria, Calif. 1986; Host Calif. Assn. of Ins. Ins. Adj. Mid-term Conv. Avila Beach, Calif. 1989. Author: ins. articles Nat. Publications, 1983/1984; training materials, Metropolitan Ins. Col., 1983; editor: Aurora Borelis (Assn. Newsletter) 1983-84, Ins. Claims Field Manual, 1982. Com. mem. Santa Barbara Traditions Com. 1989—, Cen. Coast J.P.A. Safety Com. San Luis Obispo, 1986—. Mem. Nat. Assn. of Ins. Women, Mid. Coast Adj. Assn. (pres. 1988), Cen. Coast Ins. Women (v.p. 1985, pres. 1986, past pres. 1987), Aurora Assn. of Ins. Women (numerous chmns. 1978-84), Nat. Notary Assn.; assoc. mem. Profl. Ins. Agents Assn. Republican. Christian. Office: Carl Warren & Co 330 E Gutierrez Santa Barbara CA 93101

BLAKE, DAVID JOSEPH, air force officer; b. Albany, N.Y., Nov. 30, 1963; s. Albert Leon Blake and Patricia Maria (Blanch) Warrington; m. Dawn Alison. Grad. with distinction, Non-commd. Officers Leadership Sch. Electronic technician USAF, Lajes Field Azores, Portugal, 1984-86, Holloman AFB, N.M., 1986--. Mem. Holloman AFB Non-com. Officers Club. Home: PO Box 572 Holloman AFB NM 88330 Office: 4th Satellite Comm Squadron Holloman AFB NM 88330

BLAKE, LAURA, architect; b. Berkeley, Calif., Dec. 26, 1959; d. Igor Robert and Elizabeth (Denton) B. BA in Art History, Brown U., 1982; MArch, UCLA, 1985. Cons. designer, draftsperson IDG Architects, Oakland, Calif., 1985-86; architect The Ratcliff Architects, Berkeley, 1986—. Organizer charity ball The Spinsters of San Francisco, 1988, sec., 1988-89. Recipient Alpha Rho Chi bronze medal, 1985. Republican. Episcopalian. Office: The Ratcliff Architects PO Box 1022 Berkeley CA 94701

BLAKELEY, GARY, marketing consultant; b. New Orleans, Sept. 2, 1948; s. Jess C. amd Dorothy L. (Brown) B. BS, Ea. N.Mex. U., 1972. Commr. N.Mex. Pub. Service Commn., Santa Fe, 1975-79; fed. co-chmn. Four Corners Regional Commn., Washington, 1979-81; pvt. practice mktg. and govt. relations Santa Fe, 1981—; chmn. bd. N.Mex. Boys & Girls Ranch Found.; bd. dirs. N.Mex. Boys & Girls Ranch, Ea. N.Mex. U. Found., 1980—; mem. adv. bd. N.Mex. Fed, Savs. & Loan, 1982-88; mem. bd. regents Ea. N.Mex. U., 1985—, pres. 1987. Mem. N.Mex. Bd. Ednl. Fin., 1971-72, N.Mex. Organized Crime Prevention Commn., 1985. Mem. Order of DeMolay (chevalier 1970, legion of honor 1978), N.Mex. Amigos (sec.-treas. 1985—). Democrat. Baptist. Office: PO Box 4475 Santa Fe NM 87502

BLAKEY, SCOTT CHALONER, journalist, writer; b. Nashua, N.H., Nov. 19, 1936; s. Elmer F. and Mildred Livingstone (Chaloner) B.; m. Lone Erting, July 18, 1970 (div.); 1 child, Nicholas Scott; m. Caroline M. Scarborough, June 28, 1985; children: Alexandra Scarborough; Susannah Chaloner. BA, U. N.H., 1960. Reporter, photographer Nashua (N.H.) Telegraph, 1960-62, polit. reporter, 1963-64; legis. asst. Congressman James C. Cleveland, Washington, 1963; mng. editor Concord (N.H.) Monitor, 1964-68; urban affairs corr. San Francisco Chronicle, 1968-70, reporter, asst. city editor, 1979-84, TV corr., 1985-87; corr., asst. news dir. KQED-TV, San Francisco, 1970-74; free-lance writer San Francisco, 1974-79; news editor KRON-TV (NBC), San Francisco, 1987—. Writer, field producer TV documentary 2251 Days, 1973 (2 Emmy awards 1974); author (books) San Francisco, 1976, Prisoner at War, 1978; contbr. articles to profl. jours. Recipient Best Polit. Writing award New Eng. AP News Editors Assn., 1965, Dupont Columbia award, 1974. Mem. The Authors Guild, Am. Air Mail Assn., Nat. Acad. TV Arts and Scis., The Audubon Soc. Democrat. Home: 2626 Sutter St San Francisco CA 94115 Office: KRON-TV 1001 Van Ness Ave San Francisco CA 94109

BLAMA, ROBERT JAMES, communications equipment manufacturer company official; b. Youngstown, Ohio, Oct. 28, 1937; s. Andrew and Ann (Yavorsky) B.; B.S., Youngstown, U., 1961; postgrad. Case Western Res. U. Statistician, U.S. Navy Fin. Ctr., 1962-63; sales rep. IBM, 1963-65; systems analyst/sales rep. Gen. Electric Co., 1965-69; account mgr. Honeywell, Inc., 1969-77; sr. sales rep. Data Gen. Co., 1977-80; dir. Western region Halcyon Communications, Inc., San Jose, Calif., 1980-84, v.p. sales, 1984-86, mgr. west region Precision Image, Redwood City, Calif., 1986-87; mgr. west region Verilink, mfrs. high speed communications equipment, 1987— Office: Precision Image 501 Chesapeake Dr Redwood City CA 94062

BLANCHARD, DAVID MICHAEL, aerospace engineer, consultant; b. Tulsa, June 13, 1961; s. Ronnie Joseph and Linda Ann (LeBlanc) B. BS in Aerospace Engring., U. Ariz., 1983. Mem. tech. staff Hughes Aircraft Co., Tucson, 1983—; cons. Two Star Techs., Tucson, 1985—. Mem. AIAA (treas. 1986-88, vice-chmn. 1988—). Democrat. Office: Hughes Aircraft Co Tucson AZ 85712

BLANCHARD, SYM WILLIAM, mechanical engineer; b. L.A., Oct. 6, 1952; s. Gale Boyd and Arlene Ethyl (Koehler) B.; m. Kristi Jo Kennelly, July 9, 1983; 1 child, Tym Douglas. BA in Math., Calif. State U., Fullerton, 1976; BSME, Calif. Poly. State U., 1981. Registered profl. engr., Calif. Asst. mech. engr. IBM, San Jose, Calif., 1979; with Pacific Gas and Electric Co., 1981—; sr. gas distbn. engr. Pacific Gas and Electric Co., San Jose, 1984-87; supt. gas ops. Pacific Gas and Electric Co., Santa Rosa, Calif., 1987--. Mem. ASME, Pacific Coast Gas Assn. Home: 2527 Sea Biscuit Ct Santa Rosa CA 95401 Office: Pacific Gas & Electric Co 111 Stony Circle Santa Rosa CA 95401

BLANCHARD, WILLIAM HENRY, psychologist; b. St. Paul, Mar. 25, 1922; s. Charles Edgar and Ethel Rachael (Gurney) B.; m. Martha Ida Lang, Aug. 11, 1947; children: Gregory Marcus, Mary Lisa. Diploma in Sci. Mason City Jr. Coll., 1942; BS in Chemistry, Iowa State U., 1944; PhD in Psychology, U. So. Calif., 1954. Lic. clin. psychologist, Calif. Shift chemist B.F. Goodrich Chem. Co., Port Neches, Tex., 1946-47; court psychologist L.A. County Gen. Hosp., 1954-55; psychologist, dir. rsch. So. Reception Ctr. and Clinic, Calif. Youth Authority, Norwalk, 1955-58; social scientist Rand Corp., 1958-60, System Devel. Corp., 1960-70; mem. faculty Calif. State U.-Northridge, L.A., 1970; assoc. prof. UCLA, 1971; faculty group leader urban semester U. So. Calif., L.A., 1971-75; sr. rsch. assoc. Office of Chancellor, Calif. State U., L.A., 1975-76; sr. rsch. fellow Planning Analysis and Rsch. Inst., Santa Monica, Calif., 1976—; psychologist Chatsworth Health and Rehab., Calif., 1976—; clin. assoc. dept. psychology U. So. Calif., 1956-58. Author: Rousseau and the Spirit of Revolt, 1967; Aggression American Style, 1978; Revolutionary Morality, 1984. Contbr. articles to profl. jours. Mem. com. on mental health West Area Welfare Planning Council, L.A., 1960-61; bd. dirs. L.A. County Psychol. Assn., 1969; commr. Bd. Med. Examiners, Psychology Exam. Com., State of Calif., 1969; v.p. Parents and Friends of Mentally Ill Children, 1968—, pres., 1966-68, trustee, 1968—. Mem. Am. Psychol. Assn., Internat. Soc. Polit. Psychology, AAAS, Brit. Psychol. Assn. Home: 4307 Rosario Rd Woodland Hills CA 91364 Office: Planning Analysis and Rsch Inst 3166 Sapulveda Blvd #29 West Los Angeles CA 90403

BLANCHARD, WILLIAM STRONG, television producer; b. Seattle, Feb. 11, 1953; s. William Livingston and Barbara (Strong) B.; m. Joan Marie Dempsey, Sept. 22, 1977; children: Ben, Casey, Taylor. BA in Communications, U. Wash., 1980. Producer Sta. KOMO TV, Seattle, 1980-82, Sta. KING TV, Seattle, 1982-83; ind. producer TV show, Gardening In America, Seattle, 1983-84; producer Kaye-Smith Prodns., Seattle, 1984-87; ind. writer, producer Seattle, 1987-88; exec. producer Paul Hopkins Prodns., Seattle, 1988—. Office: Paul Hopkins Prodns 215 Second Ave S #6 Seattle WA 98104

BLANCHETTE, JAMES EDWARD, psychiatrist; b. Syracuse, N.Y., Aug. 28, 1924; s. Joseph M. and Margaret (Vincent) B.; m. Shirley Ruth Brisco, Sept. 1, 1948 (dec. May 1981). BA, Syracuse U., 1950; MD, SUNY-Syracuse Sch. Med., 1953. Intern, St. Vincent's Hosp., N.Y.C., 1953-54; resident Patton (Calif.) State Hosp., 1954-55, Met. State Hosp., Norwalk, Calif., 1957-59; pvt. practice psychiatry, Redlands, Calif., 1959—; chief profl. edn. Patton State Hosp., 1960-64, tchg. cons., 1964-69; asst. clin. prof. psychiatry Loma Linda Med. Sch.; mem. staffs San Bernardino Community Hosp., St. Bernadine Hosp. (both San Bernardino), Charter Hosp. Redlands, Calif.; cons. psychiatry Redlands Community Hosp. Served with USAAF, 1945-47. Diplomate Am. Bd. Med. Examiners, Am. Bd. Psychiatry and Neurology. Fellow Am. Psychiat. Assn., AAAS, Pan-Am. Med. Assn.; mem. AMA, Calif. Med. Assn., San Bernardino Med. Soc., Internat. Platform Assn., So. Calif. Psychiat. Soc. (pres. Inland chpt. 1963-64, pres. 1983-84), Royal Soc. Health, Am. Med. Soc. Vienna, Phi Mu Alpha Symphonia, Nu Sigma Nu. Home: 972 W Marshall Blvd San Bernardino CA 92405 Office: 236 Cajon St Redlands CA 92373

BLAND, LAUREL LE MIEUX, human resources executive, consultant; b. Spokane, Wash., Feb. 23, 1926; d. Alfred Theodore Le Mieux and Bernice Catherine (Lawrence) Alburty; m. Curtis Allen Bland, July 22, 1944 (div. June 1972); children: Laurel Kathleen Bland Eisinger, Daniel Matthew; m. Frank Hubert Schricker, Mar. 30, 1976. AA, Anchorage Community Coll., 1966; vis. student, Hebrew U., Jerusalem, 1968; BE cum laude, U. Alaska, 1968, MA, 1969. Tech. asst. Alaska Human Rights Commn., Anchorage, 1967; liaison 2d jud. dist. Alaska Legal Svcs., Nome, 1968; instr. edn. Alaska Meth. Univ., Anchorage, 1969-73; asst. prof. U. Alaska, Fairbanks, 1974; prof. cross cultural edn. Sheldon Jackson Coll., Sitka, Ak., 1975; chief exec. officer Human Environ. Resources Svcs., Inc., Kennewick, Wash., 1976—; project dir. spl. hist. and cultural inventory Imuruk Basin, Ak., 1969-73; cons.cons. manpower devel. and cultural heritage documentation and preservation various state and fed. agys., others. Author: Northern Eskimos of Alaska, 1972, (with William Oquilluk) People of Kauwerak, 1973, 2d edit., 1980, Alaska Native Population and Manpower, 1978, Careless Boy, 1980; contbr. articles on edn. and anthropology to profl. jours., 1969—. Appointee gov. adv. com. Office Minority and Women's Bus. Enterprises, Olympia, Wash., 1985--; mem. apportionment panel United Way, Benton and Franklin Counties, Wash., 1988; participant seminar Future of Alaska, Brookings Inst., 1969. Teaching fellow Alaska Dept. Edn., 1968, 69. Roman Catholic. Home and Office: 1921 W 17th Ave Kennewick WA 99337

BLAND, WILLIAM CHARLES, retail executive; b. Rochester, Minn., July 12, 1943; s. William Merideth and Evelyn (Lunneborg) B.; m. Deanna Mary Diebner, Dec. 24, 1977; children: Abram Benjamin, Ilya Justine, Avram BenAdam. Student, U. Wis., 1960-64. Pres. Archtl. Graphic Systems, San Francisco, 1965-70; owner Mingus Guitars, Tucson, 1970-75; pres. Workshop Music & Sound, Tucson, 1975--. Pres. Unitarian Universalist Ch. of Tucson, 1986-87. Mem. Exec. Assn. Tucson. Democrat. Office: Workshop Music & Sound 4408 E Speedway Tucson AZ 85712

BLANDY, JOHN FREDERIC, emergency lighting company executive, consultant; b. Woodbury, N.J., Sept. 9, 1936; s. John Chase and Josephine S. (Black) B.; m. Alice Clayton (div. 1965); 1 child, Jacqueline Josephine; m. Karen Lea Feick, Aug. 10, 1970. BS in Indsl. Mgmt., Armstrong Coll., Berkeley, Calif., 1963. Lic. elec. contractor, Calif. Foreman, supt. Gen. Cable Co., Emeryville, Calif., 1964-67; plant mgr. Fiberboard Corp., Antioch, Calif., 1967-71; gen. mgr. Heitz Winery, St. Helena, Calif., 1972; mgr. CIS, Colorado Springs, Colo., 1973-78; pres. ELSAR, Inc., Hayward, Calif., 1979—; sec., bd. dirs. NEB Electric, Inc., Hayward, 1988—. Pres. Oakland Young Reps., 1967; chmn. Alameda County Young Reps., 1968; conv. chmn. Calif. Young Reps., 1969; campaign mgr. Rep. 8th Congl. Dist., 1978. With USAF, 1954-58. Recipient Guardian award Nat. Fedn. Ind. Bus., 1985. Mem. Hayward C. of C., Armstrong Coll. Alumni Assn. (pres. 1986-88, Gavel award 1988), Am. Legion, Exchange Club (bd. dirs. Alameda, Calif. 1988—, nat. cert. of accomplishment 1988). Episcopalian. Home: 23 Evirel Pl Oakland CA 94611 Office: ELSAR Inc 27343 Industrial Blvd Unit B Hayward CA 94545

BLANK, LAWRENCE FRANCIS, computer consultant; b. Detroit, Oct. 4, 1932; s. Frank A. and Marcella A. (Pieper) B.; m. Carol Louise Mann, Oct. 12, 1963; children: Ann, Steven, Susan, Lori. BS, Xavier U., 1954. Asst. engr. Gen. Electric Co., Evendale, Ohio, 1956-60; research engr. Gen. Dynamics Corp., San Diego, 1960-62; mem. tech. staff Computer Scis. Corp., El Segundo, Calif., 1962-64; programming mgr. IBM, Los Angeles, 1964-69, Xerox Corp., El Segundo, 1969-74; ind. computer cons., 1974—. Mem. Assn. Computing Machinery, Ind. Computer Cons. Assn. Home and Office: 212 Via Eboli Newport Beach CA 92663

BLANK, WILLIAM, physician, andrologist; b. Bklyn., May 21, 1950; s. Kermit Carl and Lorraine (Kitman) B.; m. Pamela Sherwood, Oct. 19, 1982; children: Adam, Eric. BA in Biology, SUNY, Buffalo, 1972; MD, U. Okla., 1977. Diplomate Nat. Bd. Med. Examiners. Intern, then resident; fellow in residence Med. Coll. Cornell U., N.Y.C., 1984-86; head div. urologic microsurgery SUNY, Bklyn., 1986-87; head div. urology VA Med. Ctr., 1986-87; pvt. practice Newport Beach, Calif., 1987-89; male infertility cons. Huntington Meml. Hosp., Pasadena, Calif., 1988—. Author: Male Infertility, 1987. Awarded 1st place in lab. rsch. N.Y. Acad. of Medicine, 1983; recipient Best Overall Movie award Am. Fertility Soc., 1986, Scholars award Am. Urological Assn., 1983; F.C. Valentine fellow, 1983. Mem. AMA, Internat. Microsurg. Soc., Am. Fertility Soc., Am. Soc. Urology, Am. Paralysis Assn. Home: 4838 Bluebell Ave North Hollywood CA 91607 Office: Huntington Reproductive Ctr 39 Congress St Pasadena CA 91105

BLANKENSHIP, EDWARD G., architect; b. Martin, Tenn., June 22, 1943; s. Edward G. and Martha Lucille (Baldridge) B. B.Arch., Columbia U., 1966, M.Sc. in Architecture, 1967; M. Litt. Arch., Cambridge U., 1971. Registered architect, N.Y., Calif. Sr. v.p. Thompson Cons. Internat., Los Angeles. Author: The Airport-Architecture, Urban Integration, Ecological Problems, 1974. William Kinne fellow, 1966; alt. Fulbright fellow to Eng., 1967. Mem. AIA. Episcopalian. Clubs: United Oxford and Cambridge U.; Meadow (Southhampton), Am. Friends of Cambridge U. (sec. Los Angeles chpt.). Lodge: Rotary Internat. Home: 4260 Via Arbolada #207 Monterey Hills CA 90042 Office: 8929 S Sepulveda Blvd Los Angeles CA 90045

BLANKENSHIP, ROBERT EUGENE, chemistry professor; b. Auburn, Nebr., Aug. 25, 1948; s. George Robert and Jane (Kehoe) Leech; m. Elizabeth Marie Dorland, June 26, 1971; children: Larissa Dorland, Samuel Robert. BS, Wesleyan U., Nebr., 1970; PhD, U. Calif., Berkeley, 1975. Postdoctoral fellow Lawrence Berkeley Lab., Berkeley, 1975-76, U. Washington, Seattle, 1976-79; asst. prof. Amherst (Mass.) Coll., 1979-85; assoc. prof. Ariz. State U., Tempe, 1985-88, prof., 1988—, dir. Ctr. Study of Early Events in Photosynthesis, 1988—. Editor-in-chief Photosynthesis Research; contbr. numerous sci. research articles. Mem. Biophysical Soc., Am. Soc. of Photobiology, Am. Chem. Soc., Am. Assn. for the Advancement of Sci. Democrat. Home: 1806 S Paseo Loma Circle Mesa AZ 85202 Office: Ariz State U Dept Chemistry Tempe AZ 85287

BLANKS, HERBERT BEVERLY, pest control company executive; b. Cleve., Oct. 27, 1915; s. Anthony Faulkner and Dorothy McGee (Welch) B.; B.S. in Forestry, U. Calif.-Berkeley, 1937; postgrad. Civil Affairs Tng. Sch., U. Chgo., 1944; m. Roxana Caroline Holmes, May 26, 1937; children—George Anthony, Herbert Elliot, Donald Allen. With U.S. Forest Service, Tahoe Nat. Forest, 1936-38; park ranger Sequoia Nat. Park, Calif., 1938-42; co-partner Ailing House Pest Control, Carmel, Calif., 1946-73, pres., 1974-80, chmn. bd., 1980—. Scoutmaster Boy Scouts Am., Carmel, 1949-55. Charter mem. City of Carmel Forestry Commn., 1955; planning commr., Carmel, 1955-62, chmn., 1960-61; councilman, Carmel, 1962-70, mayor, 1964-66; mem. Monterey County (Calif.) Local Agy. Formation Commn., 1967-70, chmn., 1967-68. Bd. dirs. Assn. Monterey Bay Area Govts., 1966-70; trustee Harrison Meml. Library, 1971-77. Served with AUS, 1942-46; lt. col. Res. ret. Decorated Bronze Star, Army Commendation medal. Mem. PTA (hon., life), Pest Control Operators Calif. (dir. 1963-64, sec.-treas. Monterey Bay Area dist. 1974-80), Nat. Pest Control Assn. (committeeman 1962-64), Res. Officers Assn. (life), Ret. Officers Assn. (life). Mem. Community Ch. (pres. bd. govs. 1972, 76). Clubs: Commonwealth, Masons (past master Carmel; knight comdr. Ct. of Honor 1975; 33 deg. 1981; treas. Monterey County Scottish Rite club 1972—); Hi-12. Home: PO Box 241 Carmel CA 93921 Office: PO Box 4977 Carmel CA 93921

BLANTON, JOHN ARTHUR, architect; b. Houston, Jan. 1, 1928; s. Arthur Alva and Caroline (Jeter) B.; BA, Rice U., 1948, BS in Architecture, 1949; m. Marietta Louise Newton, Apr. 10, 1953 (dec. 1976); children: Jill Blanton Lewis, Lynette Blanton Rowe, Elena Diane. With Richard J. Neutra, Los Angeles, 1950-64; pvt. practice architecture, Manhattan Beach, Calif., 1964—; lectr. UCLA Extension, 1967-76, 85, Harbor Coll., Los Angeles, 1970-72. Mem. Capital Improvements Com., Manhattan Beach, 1966, city commr. Bd. of Bldg. Code Appeals; mem. Bd. Zoning Adjustment. Served with Signal Corps, U.S. Army, 1951-53. Recipient Best House of Year award C. of C., 1969, 70, 71, 83, Preservation of Natural Site award, 1974, design award, 1975, 84. Mem. AIA (contbr. book revs. to jour. 1972—, recipient Red Cedar Shingle/nat. merit award 1979), Soc. Archtl. Historians. Club: Rotary. Six bldgs. included in A Guide to the Architecture of Los Angeles and Southern California; works featured in L'architettura mag., 1988. Office: 2100 Sepulveda Blvd Ste 14 Manhattan Beach CA 90266

BLANTON, KATHRYN ANN, educator; b. Corcoran, Calif., Sept. 13, 1950; d. Richard Harley and Lorraine (Dunning) B.; m. Gary Wayne Maxwell, Dec. 16, 1949; children: Andrew Dunning, Caitlin Elizabeth. BA, San Diego State U., 1972; MA, San Francisco State U., 1978. Tchr. Arcadia (Calif.) Sch. Dist., 1973-74; flight attendant TWA, 1974-78; tchr. spl. edn. Calif. Sch. for Blind, Fremont, Calif., 1978-84; infant specialist educator Santa Barbara (Calif.) County Schs., 1984—; tchr., interpreter Gorilla Found., Koko Woodside, Calif., 1981-84. Contbr. articles to profl. jours. Mem. Calif. Transcribers and Educators for the Visually Handicapped, Internat. Assn. for Edn. Deaf and Blind. Democrat.

BLATT, MORTON BERNARD, medical illustrator; b. Chgo., Jan. 9, 1923; s. Arthur E. and Hazel B. Student Central YMCA Coll., 1940-42, U. Ill., 1943-46. Tchr., Ray-Vogue Art Schs., Chgo., 1946-51; med. illustrator VA Center, Wood, Wis., 1951-57, Swedish Covenant Hosp., Chgo., 1957-76; med. illustrator Laidlaw Bros., River Forest, Ill., 1956-59; cons., artist health textbooks, 1956-59; illustrator Standard Edn. Soc., Chgo., 1960; art editor Covenant Home Altar, 1972-83, Covenant Companion, 1958-82. Served with USAAF, 1943-44. Mem. Art Inst. Chgo. Club: Chgo. Press. Illustrator: Atlas and Demonstration Technique of the Central Nervous System, also numerous med. jours.; illustrator, designer Covenant Hymnal, books, record jackets. Address: PO Box 489 Mill Valley CA 94942

BLATTNER, ERNEST WILLI, mechanical engineering educator; b. Aarau, Switzerland, Apr. 14, 1929; came to U.S., 1957; naturalized, 1970; s. Ludwig and Martha Blattner; m. Anneke Geurds, May 24, 1958; children: Mark Hermann, Flora Grazia, Elisabeth Rose, Paul Johann. MSME, Swiss Fed. Inst., Zurich, 1953; postgrad., Drexel Inst., 1959-60. Design engr. Brown Boveri Ltd., Baden, Switzerland, 1954-57; engr.-in-charge De Laval Turbine, Inc., Trenton, 1957-65; chief engr. Chicago Pneumatic Tool Co., Franklin, Pa., 1965-73; mgr. advanced design EIMCO div. Envirotech Corp., Salt Lake City, 1973-79; mgr. engring. and mfg. Biphase Energy Systems div. Transam.-De Laval, Santa Monica, Calif., 1979-81; dir. engring. Mafi-Trench Corp., Santa Maria, Calif., 1981-83; prof. mech. engring. Calif. Poly. State U., San Luis Obispo, 1983—; cons. mech. engring. Inventor turbines, compressors. Mem. Franklin Waste and Water Authority, 1963-65. Fellow ASME (chmn. Utah sect. 1976-77, mem. regional policy bd. 1977-79); mem. Am. Soc. for Metals, Am. Soc. Engring. Edn. Home: 490 Miles Ave Santa Maria CA 93455 Office: Calif Poly State U Dept Mech Engring San Luis Obispo CA 93407

BLATTNER, MEERA MCCUAIG, educator; b. Chgo., Aug. 14, 1930; d. William D. McCuaig and Nina (Spertus) Klevs; m. Minao Kamegai, June 22 1985; children: Douglas, Robert, William. B.A., U. Chgo., 1952; M.S., U. So. Calif., 1966; Ph.D., UCLA, 1973 . Research fellow in computer sci. Harvard U., 1973-74; asst. prof. Rice U., 1974-80; asso. prof. applied sci. U. Calif. at Davis, Livermore, 1980—; adj. prof. U. Tex., Houston, 1977—; vis. prof. U. Paris, 1980; program dir. theoretical computer sci. NSF, Washington, 1979-80. NSF grantee, 1977-81. Mem. Soc. Women Engrs., Assn. Computing Machinery, IEEE Computer Soc. Contbr. articles to profl. jours. Office: U Calif Davis/Livermore Dept Applied Sci Livermore CA 94550

BLAUTH, EUGENE KARL, architect; b. Queens, N.Y., Aug. 30, 1945; m. Patricia Maryanne Maron, Jan. 27, 1968; children: Jennifer Alyssa, Kimberly Erin. BArch, U. Okla., 1970. Registered architect, Colo. Draftsman H.D.R. Corp., Denver, 1971, Tech. Service Co., Denver, 1972; asst. project mgr. RNL, Inc., Denver, 1973; project architect Fisher, Reece & Johnson Architects, Denver, 1974-76, Bourn & Dulaney Architects, Englewood, Colo., 1976, Walter's C.M., Inc., Englewood, 1977, U. Colo. Health Scis. Ctr., Englewood, 1977-82; prin. Archtl. Workshop, Englewood, 1982—. Traveling fellowship Nat. Endowment for the Arts, 1970. Mem. Nat. Fire Protection Assn., Internat. Conf. of Bldg. Ofcls. Lutheran. Home and Office: 820 Milwaukee St Denver CO 80206

BLAZ, BEN, government official; b. Agana, Guam, Feb. 14, 1928; m. Ann Evers; children: Mike, Tom. BS, U. Notre Dame, 1951; MA, George Washington U., 1963; grad., U.S. Naval War Coll., 1971; LLD (hon.), U. Guam, 1974. Commd. 2d lt. USMC, 1951, advanced through grades to brig. gen., ret., 1980; prof. U. Guam, Mangilao, 1983-84; del. from Guam to U.S. Congress, 1985—. Decorated Legion of Merit, Bronze medal with Combat V, Vietnamese Cross of Gallantry; recipient Freedoms Found. Medal of Freedom, 1969. Mem. Guam C. of C., Marine Corps Assn., Young Mens League of Guam. Republican. Lodge: KC. Office: 1130 Longworth Bldg Washington DC 20515

BLAZEK, JOHN WILLIAM, JR., manufacturing executive; b. Ft. Eustis, Va., Oct. 31, 1952; s. John William and Mary Jane (Kabur) B.; m. Mary Jo Van Brocklin, June 12, 1982; children: Dawn, Amber. AAS, Prairie State Jr. Coll., Chicago Heights, Ill., 1972; BS, No. Ill. U., 1974. Sr. research tech. Searle Radiographics, Des Plaines, Ill., 1974-78; field svc. engr. Searle Ultrasound, Santa Clara, Calif., 1978-80, Siemens Ultrasound, Des Plaines, 1980-82; quality assurance mgr. Diasonics, Milpitas, Calif., 1982-83; sustaining engr. mgr. Diasonics, Milpitas, 1983-84, prodn. planning mgr., 1984-87, prodn. mgr., 1987-88, plant mgr., 1988—. Home: 1640 Isabel Dr San Jose CA 95125 Office: Diasonics MRI Div 280 Utah Ave San Francisco CA 94080

BLECH, ELIZABETH GAY, teacher; b. Albuquerque, Mar. 3, 1956; d. Alec Paul and Virginia Lee (Taylor) Grossetete; m. Douglas Lee Blech, Apr. 3, 1979; children: Elisabeth Briana, Kessick Paul Arnold. BS, U. N.Mex., 1980. Tchr. Arroyo Del Oso Elem. Sch., Albuquerque, 1981, Dolores Gonzales Elem. Sch., Albuquerque, 1981-84, Eugene Field Elem. Sch., Albuquerque, 1984-87, Hubert Humphrey Elem. Sch., Albuquerque, 1987—; mem. Sch. Improvement Team, Albuquerque, 1984-87, computer key person, 1985-87; cooperating tchr. U. N.Mex., Albuquerque, 1984-87. Vol. coordinator composition contest A Sr. Citizen I Know, Albuquerque, 1982—. Mem. Nat. Council Tchrs. Math. Republican. Presbyterian. Home: 12337 Claremont NE Albuquerque NM 87112 Office: Hubert Humphrey Elem Sch 9801 Academy Hills NE Albuquerque NM 87111

BLEIBERG, LEON WILLIAM, surgical podiatrist; b. Bklyn., June 9, 1932; s. Paul Pincus and Helen (Epstein) B.; m. Beth Daigle, June 7, 1970; children: Kristina Noel, Kelley Lynn, Kimberly Ann, Paul Joseph. Student, L.A. City Coll., 1950-51, U. So. Calif., 1951, Case Western Res. U., 1951-53; DSc with honors, Temple U., 1955; PhD, U. Beverly Hills, 1970. Served rotating internship various hosps., Phila., 1954-55; resident various hosps., Montebello, L.A., 1956-58; surg. podiatrist So. Calif. Podiatry Group, Westchester (Calif.), L.A., 1956-75; health care economist, researcher Drs. Home Health Care Svcs., 1976—; podiatric cons. U. So. Calif. Athletic Dept., Morningside and Inglewood (Calif.) High Schs., Internet Corp., Royal Naval Assn., Long Beach, Calif. Naval Sta.; lectr. in field; healthcare affiliate Internat. div. CARE/ASIA, 1987; pres. Medica, Totalcare, Cine-Medics Corp., and World-Wide Health Care Svcs. Producer (films) The Gun Hawk, 1963, Terrified, Day of the Nightmare; contbr. articles to profl. jours. Hon. Sheriff Westchester 1962-64; commd. mem. Rep. Senatorial Inner Circle, 1984-86; lt. comdr. med. svcs. corps Brit.-Am. Cadet Corps, 1984—. With USN, 1955-56. Recipient Medal of Merit, U.S. Presdl. Task Force. Mem. Philippine Hosp. Assn. (Cert. of Appreciation 1964, trophy for Outstanding Svc. 1979), Calif. Podiatry Assn. (hon.), Am. Podiatric Med. Assn. (hon.), Acad. TV Arts and Scis., Royal Soc. Health (Eng.), Western Foot Surgery Assn., Am. Coll. Foot Surgeons, Am. Coll. Podiatric Sports Medicine, Internat. Coll. Preventive Medicine, Hollywood Comedy Club, Sts. and Sinners Club, Hall Und Beinbruch Ski Club, Beach Cities Ski Club, Orange County Stamp Club, Las Virgenes Track Club, Masons, Shriners. Home: 15622 E Tierra Rejada Rd Moorpark CA 93021

BLEIWEISS, MAX PHILLIP, physicist; b. Nogales, Ariz., June 23, 1944; s. Max Bleiweiss and Mildred (Fisher) Christensen; m. Gail Annette Siebenthal, Dec. 27, 1963; children: David Brian, Mark Daniel. BS, Calif. State Polytech. Coll., 1966; MS, Calif. State Coll., L.A., 1969. Physicist Naval Weapons Ctr. Corona Labs., Corona, Calif., 1966-70, Naval Ocean Systems Ctr., San Diego, Calif., 1970-77; v.p. Deseret Dental Supply, Salt Lake City, 1977-85; physicist U.S. Army Dugway (Utah) Proving Grounds, Utah, 1985-89; withMeasurements & Analysis div. White Sands Missile Range, N.Mex., 1989—. Scoutmaster Troop 13, 1st Bapt. Ch., Salt Lake City, 1982-85. Mem. Am. Astron. Soc. (pres. 1977), Am. Geophys. Union (pres. 1971), Sigma Pi Sigma. Home: 2046 Kane Circle Salt Lake City UT 84121 Office: US Army Dugway Proving Grd Dugway UT 84022

BLEMEL, KENNETH GERALD, management sciences company executive; b. Springville, N.Y., Apr. 12, 1938; s. Gerald Francis and Erma Bertha (Aldrow) B.; m. Marlene Kay Kihnke, July 2, 1960; children: Kenneth D., Maria G., Peter A., Edward G., Michelle A., Marlene M. BS in Applied Math., U. Cin., 1966; MS in Applied Math., U. Rochester, 1970. Engring. technician dept. air pollution U.S. Dept. Pub. Health, Cin., 1961-66; engr. Gen. Dynamics, Inc., Rochester, N.Y., 1966-68; founder, engr., v.p. Panalogic, Inc., Henrietta, N.Y., 1968-73; rsch. engr. Calspan, Inc., Buffalo, 1973; founder, v.p. R/M Systems, Inc., Albuquerque, 1973-76, Mgmt. Scis., Inc., Albuquerque, 1976–. With U.S. Army, 1955-58. Mem. IEEE, Am. Soc. Quality Control (adviser sec. 14 1984–), Elks. Home: 12412 Sierra Grande NE Albuquerque NM 87112 Office: Mgmt Scis Inc 6022 Constitution Ave NE Albuquerque NM 87110

BLEMKER, MARGARET RUTH, educator, world mission executive; b. New Bremen, Ohio, Apr. 2, 1915; d. Rudolf William and Lillian (Kohl) B. BA, Heidelberg Coll., Tiffin, Ohio, 1936, LHD (hon.), 1958; MEd, Syracuse U., 1942. Tchr. North Canton (Ohio) High Sch., 1936-39, Timken Voc. High Sch., Canton, 1939-40, Amerikan Kiz Koleji, Izmir, Turkey, 1945-48; dir. residences Univ. Hosps., Cleve., 1942-45; Near East exec. United Ch. Bd. for World Ministries, Boston, N.Y.C., 1949-80. Mem. AAUW, LWV. Democrat. Mem. United Church of Christ.

BLESSINGER, MICHAEL ANTHONY, physicist; b. New Albany, Ind., Sept. 14, 1956; s. Claude Martin and Mary Elaine (Henderzahs) B. BS, Purdue U., 1978; MS, Calif. Ins. Tech., 1980; postgrad., Calif. State U., 1984. With tech. staff Jet Propulsion Lab., Pasadena, Calif., 1980-84; sr. rsch. specialist Rockwell Internat. Sci. Ctr., Thousand Oaks, Calif., 1984—. Contbr. articles to profl. jours. Calif. Inst. Tech. fellow, 1978. Mem. APS, IEEE, Phi Beta Kappa, Sigma Pi sigma, Conejo Valley Cyclists. Home: 1642 E Hillcrest Dr Apt 105 Thousand Oaks CA 91362 Office: Rockwell Internat Sci Ctr 1049 Camino Des Rios Thousand Oaks CA 91360

BLETHEN, HAROLD DAVID, entrepreneur; b. Bristol, Conn., June 26, 1939; s. Kenneth Albion and Margaret Janet (Bickford) B.; m. Sandra May Loux, Nov. 16, 1960 (div. 1965); 1 child, Harold David II; m. Linda Lee Wall, Sept. 30, 1967; 1 child, Scott David. AA, Contra Costa Coll., 1960. Cons. plant security Ford Motor Co., Richmond, Calif., 1959-61; plantman Atlantic Richfield Corp., Richmond, 1963-67; field clk. Pacific Gas & Electric, San Francisco, 1967—; entrepreneur Lindave Bus. Services, San Jose, Calif., 1968—; assoc. agt. NCC Investment Banking, San Jose; corr. cons. Muirie & Assocs., Switzerland; innovator, designer Harold the Hairman, San Jose, 1973—; v.p. Orbitron Cons. Services, San Francisco, 1983-84; pres. Halstan Cons. Services, San Jose, 1985—, Pacific Service Employees Assn.; chmn. gen. constrn. com. Pacific Gas & Electric, San Francisco, 1979-80. Mem., trustee Rep. Presdl. task force, Washington, 1984. Recipient Presdl. Commn. Rep. Presdl. Task Force, 1986. Mem. Pacific Service Employees Assn. (gen. com. chmn. credit union 1981—, named Mem. of Yr. 1982), Smithsonian Assocs., Travelers Protective Assn. Office: 4960 Almaden Expwy Ste 136 San Jose CA 95118 also: PO Box 6175 San Jose CA 95150

BLEVINS, BRUCE ALLYN, electrical engineer; b. Los Alamos, N.Mex., Jan. 7, 1951; s. David Jesse and Janice (Hazard) B.; m. Geri T. Murphy, Jan. 20, 1978; children: Joanie, Jessi. BS in Mathematics, N.Mex. Inst. Mining & Tech., 1972, MS in Physics, 1975; PhD. in Elec. Engring., N.Mex. State U., 1978. Rsch. assoc. N.Mex. Solar Energy Inst., Las Cruces, 1978-79; sr. engr. Physical Sci. Lab., Las Cruces, 1980-83, 85-88; adj. prof. N.Mex. State U., Las Cruces, 1980-83; instrumentation engr. N.Mex. Inst. Mining & Tech., Socorro, 1983-85; dir. rsch. and devel. Xytec Group, US Enertek, Farmington, N.Mex., 1983-88; owner Tesota Products, 1989—; sr. scientist Amparo Corp., Las Cruces, 1989—. Contbr. articles to profl. jours. Mem. IEEE. Democrat. Home: 4110 Tesota Dr Las Cruces NM 88001 Office: Amparo Corp Genesis Ctr Bldg D Rm #103 Arrowhead Rsch Park Las Cruces NM 88003

BLEYL, KATHERINE LORRAINE, biotechnology company executive; b. Gloversville, N.Y., Aug. 29, 1949; d. Robert Charles and Anna Lorraine (Brooks) B.; m. Francis Noon, Jan. 6, 1979 (div. 1982). Cert. in Radiol. Tech., BS in Biology, U. Rochester, 1978; MBA, Russell Sage Coll., 1984. Radiographer St. Mary's Hosp., London, 1969; vascular x-ray technologist U. Rochester, N.Y., 1970-75; rsch. technologist U. Rochester, 1975-77, 77-79; clin. rsch. assoc. Sterling-Winthrop Rsch. Inst., Rensselaer, N.Y., 1979-84; sr. clin. rsch. assoc. Cetus Corp., Emeryville, Calif., 1984-87; mgr. clin. trials Cetus Corp., Emeryville, 1988-89, assoc. dir. clin. rsch. and devel., 1989—; speaker in field. Contbr. articles to profl. publs. Vol., Bethlehem Community Ch., Delmar, N.Y., 1980-84, Orinda (Calif.) Community Ctr., 1987-88. Mem. Am. Soc. Radiol. Technologists, Drug Info. Assn., Encinal Yacht Club. Methodist. Home: 73 Brookwood Rd Orinda CA 94563 Office: Cetus Corp 1400 53d St Emeryville CA 94608

BLIGHT, MICHAEL ANDREW, design engineer; b. Durban, Natal, Republic of South Africa, May 23, 1963. BS, Brigham Young U., 1985. Plant mgr. SPUDNIK Equipment Co., Blackfoot, Idaho, 1985—; also bd. dirs. SPUDNIK Equipment Co., Blackfoot; v.p. sales Computer Specialists Co., Blackfoot, 1986—. Mormon. Home: 775 Lakeside Dr Blackfoot ID 03221 Office: Spudnik Equipment Co 1250 W Bridge PO Box 1045 Blackfoot ID 83221

BLINDER, MARTIN S., publishing company executive; b. Bklyn., Nov. 18, 1946; s. Meyer and Lillian (Stein) B.; m. Janet Weiss, Dec. 10, 1983. BBA, Adelphi U., 1968. Account exec. Bruns, Nordeman & Co., N.Y.C., 1968-69; v.p. Blinder, Robinson & Co., Westbury, N.Y., 1969-73; treas. BHB Prodns., L.A., 1973-76; pres. Martin Lawrence Ltd. Edits., Van Nuys, Calif., 1976—, also chmn. bd. dirs.; pres., dir. Corp. Art Inc., Visual Artists Mgmt. Corp., Art Consultants Inc.; lectr. bus. symposia. Contbr. articles to mags. and newspapers; appeared on TV and radio. Mem. Dem. Nat. Com.; mem. benefit com. AIDS project, L.A., 1988; bd. dirs. Very Spl. Arts, 1989, chmn. visual arts Internat. Very Spl. Arts Festival, 1989; patron Guggenheim Mus., N.Y.C., Mus. Modern Art, N.Y.C., L.A. County Mus. Art, L.A. Mus. Contemporary Art (hon. founder), Whitney Mus. Am. Art, Palm Springs Mus. Art, Hirschhorn Mus., Washington, Skirball Mus., L.A., Diabetes Found. of City of Hope, B'nai B'rith Anti-Defamation League, Very Spl. Arts; mem. Citizens for Common Sense; bd. dirs., pres. Rsch. Found. for Crohns Disease. Read into Congl. Record, 1981, 83, 86, 88; recipient resolution of commendation L.A. City Coun., 1983, State of Calif. resolution for contbn. to arts in Calif., 1983, Merit award Repubic Haiti for contbn. to arts, 1985, U.S. Senate commendation, 1983, County of L.A. Bd. Suprs. resolution for Contbn. to arts in So. Calif., 1983, Gov. of R.I. resolution for contbns. to arts, 1985. Nov. 18, 1985 declared Martin S. Blinder Day in L.A. in his honor by Mayor Tom Bradley. Office: Martin Lawrence Ltd Edits 16250 Stagg St Van Nuys CA 91406

BLINN, JOHNA See DORSEY, HELEN DANNER

BLISH, EUGENE SYLVESTER, trade association administrator; b. Denver, Oct. 9, 1912; s. George Joseph and Lillian Lenox (O'Neill) B.; m. Susan M. Monti, Feb. 21, 1950; children—Eugene A., Mary, Susan Blish Clarke, Julia. B.S.C., U. Notre Dame, 1934. Advt. dir. Colo. Milling and Elevator Co., Denver, 1934-45; advt. and mktg. cons., Denver, 1945-57; asst. exec. dir. Am. Sheep Producers Council, Denver, 1957-74; merchandising rep. Nat. Potato Bd., Denver, 1974—. Mem. alumni bd. dirs. U. Notre Dame, 1947-49. Mem. Soc. Mayflower Desc., Barnstable Hist. Soc. (Mass.). Clubs: Denver Athletic, Mt. Vernon Country, Denver Notre Dame. Home and Office: 1370 Madison St Denver CO 80206

BLISS, DONALD ALLAN, telecommunications executive; b. Mpls., Aug. 24, 1932. BSEE, U. Minn., 1963. Splicers helper Northwestern Bell, St. Paul, 1951-52, lineman, frameman, switchman, service foreman, 1952-63; dist. mgr., toll area mgr., installation repair Northwestern Bell, Omaha, 1963-70, gen. customer svcs., supr., gen. supr. switching, 1970-76; facilities mgr. S.D. customer svcs. Northwestern Bell, Sioux Falls, 1976-78; asst. v.p. customer svcs./residence Northwestern Bell, Omaha, 1978-83; v.p., chief executive officer, N.D. Northwestern Bell, Fargo, 1983-84; v.p. regulatory and ext. affairs, chief executive officer Northwestern Bell, Omaha, 1984-87; v.p., chief executive officer U.S. West Communications, Phoenix, 1987—; dir. Continental Gen., Omaha, 1988—, Phoenix Community Alliance, 1987—, Inroads/Phoenix, Inc., 1988—, COMPAS, Phoenix, 1988—. Dir. United for Ariz., Phoenix, 1987—, Phoenix Economic Growth Corp., 1987—; chmn. bd. River City Roundup, Omaha, 1986; chmn. United Way Corp. Div. Camp, Omaha, 1985, U.S. Savings Bonds Campaign, Phoenix, 1989. With USN, 1952-54. Office: US West Communications 3033 N 3d St Rm 1001 Phoenix AZ 85012

BLISS, EDWIN CROSBY, business executive, consultant; b. Salt Lake City, Feb. 15, 1923; s. Edwin S. and Naomi (Crosby) B.; m. Mary Elizabeth Miller, Jan. 21, 1956; children: Rebecca, William, Roger, Kevin. BS, U. Utah, 1949, MS, 1958. Cert. speaking profl. Reporter Salt Lake Tribune, Salt Lake City, 1947-48; Sunday mag. editor Deseret News, Salt Lake City, 1948-52; asst. dir. pub. relations U. Utah, Salt Lake City, 1952-54; Sunday mag. editor Columbus (Ohio) Dispatch, 1954-55; exec. asst. Senator Wallace F. Bennett, Washington, 1955-63; pub. affairs dir. Nat. Assn. Mfrs., Washington, 1963-77; cons. Edwin C. Bliss and Assocs., Mountain Ranch, Calif., 1973—. Author: Getting Things Done, 1976, Doing It Now, 1983. Contbr. articles to profl. jours. Served to lt. col. U.S. Army, 1944-46. Mem. Nat. Assn. Parliamentarians, Am. Inst. Parliamentarians (adv. council 1984—). Home and Office: Edwin C Bliss & Assocs 5776 Hangmans Tree Rd Mountain Ranch CA 95246

BLISS, JEFFREY ROSS, marketing consultant; b. Needham, Mass., Jan. 25, 1953; s. Willard Robinson and Faith Ada (Ross) B. BA, Colgate U., 1975; MBA, Boston U., 1988; postgrad., UCLA. Sr. mktg. rep. Xerox Corp., Lexington, Mass., 1976-78; asst. product mgr. H.P. Hood, Boston, 1978-80; sr. assoc., product mgr. The Gillette Co., Boston, 1980-82; internat. product mgr. New Balance Athletic Shoe Co., Boston, 1982-83; dir. corp. sponsorship Los Angeles Olympic Com., 1983-84; pres. Creative Corp. Mktg., Santa Monica, Calif., 1984—; cons. City Gardens, Inc., Boston, 1979, Internat. Spl. Olympics Games, South Bend, Ind., 1985—, End Hunger Network, Los Angeles, 1985—, Viet Vets Benefit Concert, Los Angeles, 1986, McLuhan Found., Malibu, Calif., 1986, City of Los Angeles, 1986, World Cup Soccer Com., L.A. C. of C., 1988. Speaker Nat. Jaycees Conv., Newport, R.I., 1975; vol. Navajo Indian Reservation, Delba Sekai Sch., Ariz., 1972, Migrant Workers Assn., 1973. Named one of Outstanding Young Men of Am. Mem. Alpha Tau Omega (pres. 1974-75), Konosioni Honor Soc. (pres. 1974-75). Methodist. Office: Creative Corp Mktg 2941 Main St #300A Santa Monica CA 90405

BLITS, HENRI JACQUES, project leader trainer; b. Amsterdam, The Netherlands, Mar. 4, 1950; came to U.S., 1950; s. Jacques and Flora (Pezarro) B.; m. Audrey Joy Spector, Dec. 28, 1975 (div. Feb. 1982); m. Judy Eileen Puls, June 12, 1983. BA in Psychology, Calif. State U., Northridge, 1973. Cert. secondary sch. tchr., Calif. Tchr. Los Angeles and Ventura County (Calif.) Schs., 1974-77; dist. exec. Boy Scouts Am., Van Nuys, Calif., 1977-80; prodn. and material planner Superior Industries, Van Nuys, 1980-81; project leader for user tng. Hughes Aircraft Co., El Segundo, Calif., 1981—. Voice-over numerous, radio commercials and indsl. films. CPR instr. ARC, Van Nuys, 1980—. Served with Calif. Air N.G., 1968—. Recipient Community Service award City of Santa Monica, Calif., 1972, Canoga Park (Calif.) C. of C., 1979. Lodge: Kiwanis (exec. bd. Canoga Park club 1977-80). Office: Hughes Aircraft Co 2000 E Imperial Blvd El Segundo CA 90245

BLITZ-WEISZ, SALLY, speech pathologist; b. Buffalo, Nov. 9, 1954; d. Isaac and Paula (Goldstein) Blitz; m. Andrew Weisz, Dec. 16, 1984. BA in Speech Pathology, Audiology, SUNY, Buffalo, 1976, MA in Speech Pathology, 1978. Lic. speech/lang. pathologist, Calif. Speech, lang. pathologist Lang. Devel. Program, Tonawanda, N.Y., 1978-82, Bailey and Drown Assocs., La Habra, Calif., 1982-83; speech, lang. specialist, cons.

Pasadena (Calif.) Unified Schs., 1983—. Active Anti-Defamation League, San Fernando Valley, 1985-86; mem. 2d Generation Holocaust Survivors, Los Angeles, 1986—. Recipient Excellence in Studies award Temple Shaarey Zedek, Buffalo, 1968. Mem. Am. Speech-Lang.-Hearing Assn. Democrat. Club: Jewish Young Adults. Lodge: B'nai Brith. Home: 11671 Amigo Ave Northridge CA 91326 Office: Pasadena Unified Sch Dist 351 S Hudson Ave Pasadena CA 91101

BLOCH, CLIFFORD ALAN, pediatric endoctrinologist; b. Johannesburg, Republic of South Africa, May 13, 1953; came to U.S., 1984; s. Leonard E. and Audrey (Silver) B.; m. Natalie Cohen, Dec. 5, 1976; children: Tracy L., Jennifer K. B Medicine and Surgery, Witwatersrand U., 1976. Diplomate Am. Bd. Pediatrics. Med. and surg. intern U. Witwatersrand, Johannesburg, Rep. S. Africa, 1977; med. officer S.A. Med. Corps, Johannesburg, 1978-79; pediatric resident U. Witwatersrand, 1980-83, cons. pediatrician, 1984; pediatric endocrine fellow U. Cin., 1984-87; asst. prof. Childrens Hosp. of Denver, 1987—. Contbr. articles to profl. jours. Served to capt. SAMC, 1983. Grantee U. Colo. (BRS), 1988, Childrens Hosp. Denver (kempe research ctr.), 1987. Fellow Am. Acad. Pediatrics; mem. Am. Diabetes Assn., Endocrine Soc., Pediatric Endocrine Soc., Western Soc. for Pediatric Research, Colo. Soc. for Endocrinology and Metabolism. Jewish. Home: 5791 S Havana Ct Englewood CO 80111 Office: Childrens Hosp 1056 E 19th Ave Denver CO 80218

BLOCH, PHILIP ALAN, digital music consultant; b. Rochester, N.Y., May 18, 1953; s. A. Leonard and Marilyn June (Melen) B.; m. Denise Gerolimatos, Aug. 24, 1985. Drummer Rochester, 1969-80; drummer L.A., 1980—, digital music equipment cons., 1985—; cons. Yamaha Corp. of Am., Buena Park, Calif., 1985—. Mem. Am. Fedn. Musicians, Apple Developer's Assn., Prospect Digital (cert. developer). Democrat. Home and Office: 11248 Blix St North Hollywood CA 91602

BLOCK, ALVIN LEE, physician, lawyer; b. Orlando, Fla., Sept. 23, 1929; s. Milton Herbert and Dorothy (Kottelman) B.; children: Kevin, Gregory, William. AB, Emory U., 1950, MD, 1954; LLB, La Salle U., 1974. Bar: Calif. 1976. Practice medicine specializing in gen. medicine Napa, Calif., 1960—; med. coordinator, dir. Queen of the Valley Hosp., Napa, 1974-82; chmn. bd. dirs. Napa Valley Wine Train, Inc.; bd. dirs. Napa Nat. Bank. Served to capt. USMC, 1955-57. Mem. Phi Beta Kappa, Alpha Omega Alpha. Office: 3230 Beard Rd Napa CA 94558

BLOCK, ROBERT JACKSON, investment banker; b. Seattle, Oct. 20, 1922; s. Max Harry and Esther Ida (Parker) B.; m. Dorothy Wolens, Aug. 11, 1946 (dec.); children: Jonathan, Adam, Daniel, Kenan, Susanna, Mary Judith; m. Mary Lou Moats, Dec. 26, 1972; children: Melinda Mulvaney, Newton Moats, Christina Moats, Tamara Ingle. Student Stanford U., 1940-43, U. Wash., 1943-44. Asst. to pres. Block Shoe Stores, Inc., Seattle, 1946-56, pres., 1956-58; pres. Columbia-Cascade Securities Corp., Seattle, 1958-77; pres. Nat. Securities Corp., Seattle, 1977-80, chmn., chief exec. officer, 1980-85, founding dir., chmn. bd., 1985—; founding dir. North West Bank (merged with Old Nat. Bank); cons. Area Redevel. Adminstrn., 1961-62; exec. reservist policy secretariat Nat. Def. Exec. Res.; GSA, 1968—. Named to Seattle Ctr. Legion of Honor Seattle Ctr. Adv. Commn. & Seattle Ctr. Found., 1987. Pres. Block Found., Inc., Allied Arts Found.; former chmn. Puget Sound chpt. Nat. Found. March of Dimes; mem. nat. exec. council Am. Jewish Com.; former mem. Seattle Bd. Park Commrs.; chmn., dir. Cornish Inst., 1980-82; trustee Pilchuck Sch., Stanwood, Wash.; bd. dirs. Seattle Pub. Library Found.; chmn. King County (Wash.) USO Com., 1950-52; chmn. Civic Ctr. Com., Seattle, 1954; co-chmn. Metro Campaign Com., Seattle, 1958; alt. del. Democratic Nat. Conv., 1956; King County co-chmn. Vols. for Stevenson, 1956; elected King County Freeholder, 1967. Mem. Wash. Bar Assn. (fee arbitration panel, vis. cons.), Wash. Athletic Club, College Club (Seattle), Rainier Club. Home: 1617 E Boston Terr Seattle WA 98112 Office: 500 Union St Seattle WA 98101

BLODGETT, ELSIE GRACE, association executive; b. Eldorado Springs, Mo., Aug. 2, 1921; d. Charles Ishmal and Naoma Florence (Worthington) Robison; m. Charles Davis Blodgett, Nov. 8, 1940; children: Carolyn Doyel, Charleen Bier, Lyndon Blodgett. Student Warrensburg (Mo.) State Tchrs. Coll., 1939-40; BA, Fresno (Calif.) State Coll., 1953. Tchr. schs. in Mo. and Calif., 1940-42, 47-72; owner, mgr. rental units, 1965—; exec. dir. San Joaquin County (Calif.) Rental Property Assn., Stockton, 1970-81; prin. Delta Rental Property Owners and Assocs., 1981-82; propr. Crystal Springs Health World, Inc., Stockton, 1980-86; bd. dirs. Stockton Better Bus. Bur. Active local PTA, Girl Scouts U.S., Boy Scouts Am.; bd. dirs. Stockton Goodwill Industries. Named (with husband) Mr. and Mrs. Apt. Owner of San Joaquin County, 1977. Mem. Nat. Apt. Assn. (state treas. women's div. 1977-79), Calif. Ret. Tchrs. Assn. Republican. Methodist. Lodge: Stockton Zonta. Home and Office: 2285 W Mendocino Ave Stockton CA 95204

BLODGETT, FORREST CLINTON, economics educator; b. Oregon City, Oreg., Oct. 6, 1927; s. Clinton Alexander and Mabel (Wells) B.; B.S., U. Omaha, 1961; M.A., U. Mo., 1969; Ph.D., Portland State U., 1979; m. Beverley Janice Buchholz, Dec. 21, 1946; children—Cherine (Mrs. Jon R. Klein), Candis Melis, Clinton George. Joined C.E., U.S. Army, 1946, commd. 2d lt., 1946, advanced through grades to lt. col., 1965; ret. 1968; engring. assignments Japan, 1947-49, U.K., 1950-53, Korea, 1955-56, Alaska, 1958-60, Vietnam, 1963; staff engr. 2d Army Air Def. Region, Richards-Gebaur AFB, Mo., 1964-66; base engr. Def. Atomic Support Agy., Sandia Base, N.Mex., 1966-68; bus. mgr., trustee, asst. prof. econs. Linfield Coll., McMinnville, Oreg., 1968-73, assoc. prof., 1973-83, prof., 1983—; pres. Blodgett Enterprises, Inc., 1983-85; founder, dir. Valley Community Bank, 1980-86, vice chmn. bd. dirs., 1985-86. Commr., Housing Authority of Yamhill County (Oreg.), chmn., 1980-83; mem. Yamhill County Econ. Devel. Com., 1978-83; bd. dirs. Yamhill County Found., 1983—. Decorated Army Commendation medal with oak leaf cluster; recipient Joint Service Commendation medal Dept. of Def. Mem. Soc. Am. Mil. Engrs. (pres. Albuquerque post 1968), Am. Econ. Assn., Western Econ. Assn. Internat., Nat. Retired Officers Assn., Res. Officers Assn. (pres. Marion chpt. 1976), SAR (pres. Oreg. soc. 1985-86), Urban Affairs Assn., Pi Sigma Epsilon, Pi Gamma Mu, Omicron Delta Epsilon (Pacific NW regional dir. 1978—). Republican. Episcopalian. Lodge: Rotary (pres. McMinnville club 1983-84). Office: Linfield Coll McMinnville OR 97128

BLODGETT, JAY ALAN, savings and loan executive; b. Ogden, Utah, Nov. 7, 1933; s. Orvil W. Blodgett and Leona (Staley) Wade; m. Eleanor Call Blodgett, July 25, 1956; children: Jeffery A., Michele Blodgett Cockayne, Linda Blodgett Fotheringham, Mark C. BS, Brigham Young U., 1955, MS, 1962. CPA, Utah. Auditor Brigham Young U., Provo, Utah, 1953-60; acct. Deloitte, Haskins, Sells, Portland, Oreg., 1960-61; auditor, acct. Ch. of Latter Day Saints, Salt Lake City, 1962-69, fin. officer, 1969-85; pres., chief exec. officer Am. Savs., Salt Lake City, 1985—, also bd. dirs. Bd. dirs. Salt Lake Airport Authority, 1976—, Utah Symphony, Salt Lake City, 1983-86, Utah State Retirement Bd., Salt Lake City, 1983-85. Served as cpl. U.S. Army, 1956-57. Mormon. Office: Am Savings & Loan Assn 77 W 2nd South Salt Lake City UT 84101 *

BLOEDE, VICTOR CARL, lawyer, university executive; b. Woodwardville, Md., July 17, 1917; s. Carl Schon and Eleanor (Eck) B.; m. Ellen Louise Miller, May 9, 1947; children—Karl Abbott, Pamela Elena. A.B., Dartmouth Coll., 1940; J.D. cum laude, U. Balt., 1950; LL.M. in Pub. Law, Georgetown U., 1967. Bar: Md. 1950, Fed. Hawaii 1958, U.S. Supreme Ct. 1971. Sole practice Balt., 1950-64; mem. Goldman & Bloede, Balt., 1959-64; Md. counsel Seven-Up Bottling Co., Balt., 1958-64; dep. atty. gen. Pacific Trust Ter., Honolulu, 1952-53; asst. solicitor for ters. Office of Solicitor, U.S. Dept. Interior, Washington, 1953-54; atty. U.S. Justice, Honolulu, 1955-58; asst. gen. counsel Dept. Navy, Washington, 1960-61, 63-64; spl. legal cons. Md. Legislature, Legis. Council, 1963-64, 66-67; assoc. prof. U. Hawaii, 1961-63, dir. property mgmt., 1964-67; house counsel, dir. contracts and grants U. Hawaii System, 1967-82; house counsel U. Hawaii Research Corp., 1970-82; legal counsel Law of Sea Inst., 1978-82; legal cons. Research Corp. and research div., U. Hawaii, 1982—; spl. counsel to Holifield Congl. Commn. on Govt. Procurement, 1970-73. Author: Hawaii Legislative Manual, 1962, Maori Affairs, New Zealand, 1964, Oceanographic Research Vessel Operations, and Liabilities, 1972, Hawaiian Archipelago, Legal Effects of a 200 Mile Territorial Sea, 1973, Copyright-Guidelines to the 1976 Act, 1977, Forms Manual, Inventions: Policy, Law and Procedure, 1982; writer, contbr. Coll. Law Digest and other publs. on legislation and pub. law. Mem. Gov.'s Task Force Hawaii and The Sea, 1969, Citizens Housing Com. Balt., 1952-64; bd. govs. Balt. Community YMCA, 1954-64; bd. dirs. U. Hawaii Press, 1964-66, Coll. Housing Found., 1968-80; internat. rev. commn. Canada-France Hawaii Telescope Corp., 1973-82, chmn., 1973, 82; co-founder, incorporator First Unitarian Ch. Honolulu. Served to lt. comdr. USNR, 1942-45, PTO. Grantee ocean law studies NSF and NOAA, 1970-80. Mem. ABA, Balt. Bar Assn., Fed. Bar Assn., Am. Soc. Internat. Law, Nat. Assn. Univ. Attys. (chmn. patents and copyrights sect. 1974-76). Home: 635 Onaha St Honolulu HI 96816

BLOESSER, REX WILLIAM, general manager, underwriter, financial consultant; b. Witcha, Kans., Aug. 13, 1952; s. William James and Glennis (Benjamin) B. Cert. flight instr., underwriter, fin. cons. Cpt. Horizon Airlines (formerly Air Oreg.), Portland, 1978-80; gen. mgr. N.Y. life Ins. Co. and N.Y. Life Securities, Inc., Stockton, Calif., 1980—; assoc. gen. mgr. N.Y. life Ins. Co. and N.Y. Life Securities, Inc., Anchorage, 1982-86. Co-chmn. Multiple Sclerosis Young Profl. Group, Stockton, Calif. Mem. Am. Soc. CLU and Chartered Fin. Cons., San Joaquin Bus. Coun., Stockton C. of C., Nat. Assn. Life Underwriters, Stockton Visitors and Conv. Bur. (bd. dirs.). Republican. Home: 8529 Helen Ln Stockton CA 95212 Office: NY Life Ins Co and NY Life Securities Inc 501 W Weber Ste 500 Stockton CA 95203

BLOME, ROBERT ARTHUR, physician; b. Iowa City, June 13, 1931; s. Glenn C. and Laura (Bolle) B.; m. Louann M. Nochtels, Mar. 25, 1958 (div. 1982); children: Elizabeth Ann, Jennifer Lynn, Lori Lynn; m. Dixie V. Kyoush, Apr. 26, 1984. BA, Grinnel Coll., 1952; MD, State U. Iowa, 1955. Diplomate Am. Bd. Surgeons. Intern Emanuel Hosp., Portland, Oreg., 1955-56; resident U. Iowa Hosp., Iowa City, 1956-60, staff physician, 1960-61; practice medicine specializing in general and thoracic surgery Nampa, Idaho, 1963—; pres. med. staff, chief surgery Mercy Hosp., Nampa. Contbr. articles to profl. jours. Chmn. Nampa chpt. ARC; bd. dirs. United Way, Nampa. Capt. USAF 1961-63. Mem. Idaho State Med. Soc., SW Dist. Med. Soc. (sec., pres.), Nampa Aquatic Club (pres.), Kiwanis (bd. dirs. Nampa club). Republican. Methodist. Office: Med Ctr Physicians 215 E Hawaii Nampa ID 83686

BLOMKER, DALE LYNN, customer service agent; b. Humboldt, Iowa, Aug. 13, 1942; s. Myrl Richard and Bessie Evelyn (Mattoon) B.; m. Donna Jeanne Terwische, Sept. 9, 1967 (div. Nov. 1981); children: Daniel, Melissa; m. Marcia Kay Gross, Dec. 7, 1981. Grad. high sch., Humboldt. Supr. airport services Am. Airlines, Portland, Oreg.; Indpls.; Des Moines; Chgo., 1966-83; owner, operator River City Bowl and Lounge, Mason City, Iowa, 1983-84; correctional services officer Ariz. Dept. Corrections, Goodyear, 1984-87; customer service rep. Am. West Airlines, 1987, L.A., 1988, Indpls., 1987—; appointed agt. Farmers Ins. Group, 1986—; sta. tng. instr., Fishers, Ind., 1988. Asst. cubscout master Boy Scouts Am., Des Moines, 1972-73. Served with U.S. Army, 1963-66, Vietnam. Lodge: Moose. Home: 11585 Maple Dr Fishers IN 46038 Office: USAIR Indpls Internat Airport Indianapolis IN 46241

BLOMSTEDT, HERBERT THORSON, symphony director, conductor; b. Springfield, Mass., July 11, 1927; s. Adolphe and Alida Armintha (Thorson) B.; m. Waltraud Regina Petersen, May 29, 1955; children: Cecilia, Maria, Elisabet Vivianne, Kristina Ulrika. Diploma in music edn., Royal Acad. Music, Stockholm, 1948, diploma: organist, 1950, diploma: orch. condr., 1950; fil. kand., U. Uppsala, Sweden, 1952; MusD (hon.), Andrews U., Mich., 1978. Music dir. Norrköping Symphony, Sweden, 1954-61; prof. conducting Royal Acad. Music, Sweden, 1961-70; permanent condr. Oslo Philharm., Norway, 1962-68; music dir. Danish Radio Symphony, Copenhagen, 1967-77, Dresden Staatskapelle, German Dem. Republic, 1975-85, Swedish Radio Symphony, Stockholm, 1977-82, San Francisco Symphony, 1985—; condr. (hon.) NHK Symphony, Tokyo, 1986—. Author: Till Kännedomen om J.C. Bach's Symfonier, 1951; Lars Erik Larsson och hans Concertinor, 1957; contbr. articles to profl. jours.; editor: (mus. score) Franz Berwald: Sinfonie Singulière, 1965; 120 recordings. Jenny Lind scholar Royal Acad. Music, Stockholm, 1950; recipient Expressen Music prize, 1964, numerous rec. prizes; decorated Knight Royal Order North Star, King of Sweden, 1971; Knight Royal Order Dannebrogen, Queen of Denmark, 1978; Litteris et Artibus, Gold medal, King of Sweden, 1979. Seventh Day Adventist. Office: Interartists, Frans van Mierisstraat 43, 1071 RK Amsterdam Netherlands also: San Francisco Symphony Davies Symphony Hall San Francisco CA 94102

BLOODGOOD, PATRICIA ANNETTE, marketing executive; b. New Brunswick, N.J., Dec. 7, 1947; d. Robert and Jessie (Van Liew) Amrein; m. David L. Bloodgood, Nov. 27, 1976. Student, Juliet Gibson Coll., Phila., 1967, Middlesex County Coll., Edison, N.J., 1981. Licensed cemeterian, N.J., Calif.; cert. cemetery exec. Customer svc. rep. Chicopee Mfg. Co. div. J. and J., Milltown, N.J., 1967-72; credit rep. Texaco, Inc., East Brunswick, N.J., 1972-74; purchasing agt. Aero Filter Devel. Corp., South Plainfield, N.J., 1974-78; sales and mktg. Eastern Steel Barrel Corp., Piscataway, N.J., 1978-81; v.p. pub. relations Franklin Meml. Park, North Brunswick, N.J., 1982-88; regional trainer Svc. Corp. Internat., San Diego, 1988, mktg. coordinator, 1989—; panelist Bio-Ethics-Right to Die, St. Peter's Hosp., New Brunswick, N.J., 1987; moderator Coping with Grief seminars, North Brunswick, 1982-88, pub. relations seasonal programs Franklin Meml. Park, 1982-88. Contbr. articles to profl. jours. Named Outstanding Cemetery Women Am. Cemetery Mag., 1987. Mem. Am. Cemetery Assn. (bd. dirs., speaker in nat. programs, Cert. Cemetery Exec. award 1989, recipient numerous sales and mktg. awards), Cremation Assn. N.Am., Chinese Shar-Pei Club of Am., N.Am. Hot Air Balloon Team. Roman Catholic. Office: Svc Corp Internat 9830 Willow Creek Rd PO Box X-1010 Bldg 1 San Diego CA 92112

BLOOM, DAVID ARTHUR, retail executive; b. Tucson, Sept. 19, 1916; s. David Walter and Clara (Ferrin) B.; m. Leona Sylvia Goldberg, Sept. 19, 1943; children: Alan David, Richard Joseph. BSBA, U. Ariz., 1938. Advt. mgr. Dave Bloom & Sons, Tucson, 1938-85, exec. v.p., co-owner, 1938-89. Bd. dirs. Menswear Retailers Am., Tucson, 1953-66, pres. and founder; pres., co-founder So. Ariz. chpt. Jewish Hist. Soc., 1982; bd. dirs. BPA Alumni Coun., U. Ariz., 1982-87; founder 1953 Man and Woman of Yr. award sponsored by Tucson Met. C. of C., Levna G. and David Arthur Bloom Jewish Archives U. Ariz., Tucson, 1989. Recipient Silver medal Am. Advt. Fedn., 1956, City of Hope Nat. Spirit of Life award, 1988. Mem. Tucson Advt. Club (pres. 1953), Tucson Metro C. of C. (bus. devel. com. 1987-88, Founders award 1987), El Con Mchts. Assn. (promotion com.), DeMolay (jr. deacon 1933), Kiwanis (pres. 1953, lt. gov. 1978), Masons (32 degree), Epes Randolph (sec., Sunday sch. dir. Temple Evian 1938-41), Shriners. Home: 4210 E 4th Pl Tucson AZ 85711 Office: Dave Bloom & Sons El Con Mall Tucson AZ 85716

BLOOM, FLOYD ELLIOTT, physician, research scientist; b. Mpls., Oct. 8, 1936; s. Jack Aaron and Frieda (Shochman) B.; m. D'Nell Bingham, Aug. 30, 1956 (dec. May 1973); children: Fl'Nell, Evan Russell; m. Jody Patricia Corey, Aug. 9, 1980. A.B. cum laude, So. Meth. U., 1956; M.D. cum laude, Washington U., St. Louis, 1960; D.Sc. (hon.), So. Meth. U., 1983, Hahnemann U., 1985, U. Rochester, 1985. Intern Barnes Hosp., St. Louis, 1960-61; resident internal medicine Barnes Hosp., 1961-62; research asso. NIMH, Washington, 1962-64; fellow depts. pharmacology, psychiatry and anatomy Yale Sch. Medicine, 1964-66, asst. prof., 1966-67, asso. prof., 1968; chief lab. neuropharmacology NIMH, Washington, 1968-75; acting dir. div. spl. mental health NIMH, 1973-75; commd. officer USPHS, 1974-75; dir. Arthur Vining Davis Center for Behavorial Neurobiology; prof. Salk Inst., La Jolla, Calif., 1975-83; dir. div. preclin. neurosci. and endocrinology Research Inst. of Scripps Clinic, La Jolla, 1983—; mem. Commn. on Alcoholism, 1980-81, Nat. Adv. Mental Health Council, 1976-80. Author: (with J.R. Cooper and R.H. Roth) Biochemical Basis of Neuropharmacology, 1971, 5th edit., 1987; (with Lazerson and Hofstadter) Brain, Mind, and Behavior, 1984, (with Lazerson) 2d edit., 1988; editor: Peptides: Integrators of Cell and Tissue Function, 1980; co-editor: Regulatory Peptides. Recipient A. Cressy Morrison award N.Y. Acad. Scis., 1971, A.E. Bennett award for basic research Soc. Biol. Psychiatry, 1971, Arthur A. Fleming award Science mag., 1973, Mathilde Solowey award, 1973, Biol. Sci. award Washington Acad. Scis., 1975, Alumni Achievement citation Washington U., 1980, McAlpin Research Achievement award Mental Health Assn., 1980, Lectr.'s medal College de France, 1979, Steven Beering medal, 1985, Disting. fellow Am. Psychiatric Assn., 1986. Fellow AAAS (bd. dirs 1986—), Am. Coll. Neuropsychopharmacology (mem. council 1976-78, chmn. program com. 1987, pres. 1988—); mem. Am. Philos. Soc., Nat. Acad. Sci. (chmn. sect. neurobiology 1979-83), Inst. Medicine (mem. council 1986—), Am. Acad. Arts and Scis., Soc. Neurosci. (sec. 1973-74, pres. 1976), Am. Soc. Pharmacology and Exptl. Therapeutics, Am. Soc. Cell Biology, Am. Physiol. Soc., Am. Assn. Anatomists, Research Soc. Alcoholism (chmn. program com. 1985-87). Home: 1145 Pacific Beach Dr Apt B405 San Diego CA 92109 Office: Research Inst of Scripps Clinic La Jolla CA 92037

BLOOM, MARY CATHERINE, civil engineer; b. Binghamton, N.Y., Aug. 25, 1957; d. Edwin John and Mary Concetta (Caciola) B. BS in Civil Engring., Rensselaer Poly. Inst., 1979; ME in Civil Engring., 1980; MBA, Harvard U., 1985. Registered profl. engr., Tex. Calif. Engr. Exxon Prodn. Research Co., Houston, 1980-81; constrn. engr. Esso Japan, Wakamatsu, 1981-83; project engr Exxon USA, Thousand Oaks, Calif., 1985-87; staff engr. Exxon USA, Leiden, Netherlands, 1988—. Mem. ASCE, Tau Beta Pi, Chi Epsilon. Roman Catholic. Office: Exxon USA PO Box 5025 Thousand Oaks CA 91359

BLOOM, MICHAEL EUGENE, communications executive; b. Pittsburg, Calif., Jan. 16, 1947; s. Benjamin Bernard and Mildred (Haims) B.; m. Deborah Ann Bresler, Aug. 6, 1977; children: Benjamin Solomon Bresler, Miriam Hannah Bresler. BA in Sociology, U. Calif.-Santa Barbara, 1969, postgrad. elec. engring., 1969-71; MBA, Stanford U., 1979. Broadcaster, Sta. KCSB-FM, Santa Barbara, 1964-68, gen. mgr., 1968-69; broadcaster KKIS-AM, Pittsburg, Calif., 1965, KMUZ-FM, Santa Barbara, 1965-67, KTMS-AM-FM, Santa Barbara, 1967-69; mem. tech. staff Gen. Rsch. Corp., Santa Barbara, 1970-72; mgmt. scientist, cons. Sci. Applications, Inc., LaJolla, Calif., 1973-74, Planning and Mgmt. Cons. Corp., Cleve., 1974, Bloom Enterprises, Santa Monica, Calif., 1975-77; project team leader, sr. programmer Bendix Field Engring. Corp., Sunnyvale, Calif., 1977; retail product planner Crocker Nat. Bank, San Francisco, 1978; dir. corp. devel. Am. TV & Communications Corp., Englewood, Colo., 1979-82, dir. new bus. devel., 1983-84, dir. bus. and tech. devel., 1984-85; dir. video svcs. devel. Pacific Bell, San Francisco, 1985-86, dir. product strategy and devel., San Ramon, Calif., 1986-87, dir. market strategy group, 1987-88, dir. customer premises Broadband Mktg. div., 1988—, Japan task force, 1988—; chmn. communications bd. U. Calif.-Santa Barbara; v.p., bd. dir. Intercollegiate Broadcasting System, Inc., 1967-70; founder, dir. U. Calif. Radio Network, 1967-69; chmn. systems standards task force on teletext Nat. Cable TV Assn., 1980-81. Adv. coun. Coll. Info. Studies, U. Denver, 1982-85. Recipient Pres.'s Merit award U. Calif., 1965. Mem. IEEE, Am. Mktg. Assn. (exec.), Soc. Cable TV Engrs., Nat. Cable TV Assn., U. Calif.-Santa Barbara Alumni Assn. (life), Stanford U. Bus. Sch. Alumni Assn. (program chmn. Rocky Mountain chpt. 1982-85), Stanford U. Alumni Assn. (life). Author: (with L.A. Sibley) Carrier Current System Design, 1967. Office: Pacific Bell 2600 Camino Ramon Rm 1 South 953 San Ramon CA 94583

BLOOMBERG, ROBERT JOSEPH, internist; b. Montreal, Que., Can., Dec. 2, 1947; came to U.S., 1980; s. William and Clara (Sederoff) B.; m. Kerri M. Zalasin, July 2, 1978; children: Joshua Z., Micah M., Leah R. BS in Biochemistry, Sir George Williams U., 1969; PhD in Biochemistry, U. Wyo., 1973; MD, McMaster U., Hamilton, Ont., 1976. Diplomate Am. Bd. Internal Medicine. Intern Georgetown U. Hosp., Washington, 1976-77, resident, 1977-79, chief med. resident, 1979-80; research asst. McGill U., Montreal, 1969-70; postdoctoral fellow Purdue U., Lafayette, Ind., 1973; practice medicine specializing in internal medicine Tempe, Ariz., 1980—; mem. Desert Samaritan Hosp, Mesa, Ariz., Mesa Luth. Hosp., Valley Luth. Hosp., Mesa, Tempe St. Lukes Hosp.; cons. Drug Utilization Data Corp., Tempe, 1979—. Bd. dirs. East Valley Hospice, Mesa Christian Found. of Mesa-Tempe, Ariz., 1986-88. Fellow Royal Coll. Physicians and Surgeons (Can.); mem. Am. Coll. Physicians, Southern Med. Assn., N.Y. Acad. Scis., Maricopa County Med. Soc. Home: 8527 S Willow Dr Tempe AZ 85284 Office: 2501 E Southern Ave Tempe AZ 85282

BLOOMFIELD, ARTHUR JOHN, music critic; b. San Francisco, Jan. 3, 1931; s. Arthur L. and Julia (Mayer) B.; m. Anne Buenger, July 14, 1956; children: John, Cecily, Alison. AB, Stanford U., 1951. Music and art critic San Francisco Call-Bull., 1958-59, San Francisco News Call-Bull., 1962-65; co-music and art critic San Francisco Examiner, 1965-79; corr. Musical America mag., 1958-61, 63-64, Opera mag., 1964—; restaurant critic Focus mag., San Francisco, 1979-83. Author: The San Francisco Opera, 1923-61, 61, Fifty Years of the San Francisco Opera, 1972, Restaurants of San Francisco, 1975, Guide to San Francisco Restaurants, 1977, The San Francisco Opera 1922-78, 1978, Arthur Bloomfield's Restaurant Book, 1987. Served with AUS, 1953-55. Home: 2229 Webster St San Francisco CA 94115

BLOOMFIELD, JORDAN JAY, chemist, researcher; b. South Bend, Ind., Feb. 25, 1930; s. John Jacob and Edith (Gilman) B.; m. Elizabeth Helen Curtis, June 11, 1960 (div. Nov. 1982); children: Jaclyn Louise, Linda Joyce, Janet Lorene; m. Doris Joan Jameson, May 19, 1984. BS with highest honors, UCLA, 1952; PhD, MIT, 1958. Chemist E.I. DuPont, Waynesboro, Va., 1953; inst. U. Tex., Austin, 1957-60; post doctoral U. Ill., Urbana, 1960-61, U. Ariz., Tucson, 1961-62; asst. prof. to assoc. prof. U. Okla., Norman, 1962-66; sr. group leader, vis. prof. Monsanto Co., St. Louis, 1966-67, sr. research spl., 1967-81, fellow, 1981-85; v.p., research Organic Cons., Inc., Eugene, Oreg., 1987—; adj. assoc. prof., U. Mo., St. Louis, 1975-78, adj. prof., 1978-87; cons., vis. prof. U. Mich., Ann Arbor, 1985-86; presenter papers at numerous nat. and internat. meetings in field; mem. numerous profl. coms. and councils in field. Co-author: The Dieckmann Reaction, 1967, The Acyloin Reaction, 1976; contbr. articles to profl. jours.; patentee in field. With U.S. Army, 1953-55. Mem. Am. Chem. Soc. (chmn. St. Louis section, 1976, councilor, 1972-87, recipient St. Louis award, 1980), Royal Soc. Chem., AAAS, Am. Soc. Photobiology. Office: Organic Cons Inc 132 E Broadway Ste 107 Eugene OR 97401

BLOOMFIELD, JULIA MARY, publishing executive, editor; b. London, June 24, 1944; came to U.S., 1969; d. Victor Kenneth and Diana Mary (Wallace) B. Asst. Alison & Peter Smithson, Architects, London, 1963-65; with M. Glickman Assocs., London, 1966; trainee architect D. Stephen and Ptnrs., London, 1963-70; exec. asst. Richard Meier, Architect, N.Y.C., 1970-71; fellow Inst. for Architecture, N.Y.C., 1971-83; assoc. dir. Buell Ctr. Columbia U., N.Y.C., 1983-86; vis. scholar Harvard U. Grad. Sch. Design, Cambridge, Mass., 1986-87; head dept. publs. J.P. Getty Ctr. for the History of Art, Santa Monica, Calif., 1987—; cons. editor The Archtl. Rev., London, 1987—. Editor (book) The History of Harvard's Graduate School of Design, 1986; (journal) Oppositions, 1971-83 (recipient AIA medal 1981). Home: 1020 19th St Santa Monica CA 90403 Office: The Getty Ctr for the History of Art and Humanities 401 Wilshire Blvd Santa Monica CA 90401

BLOTZER, TIMOTHY ROBERT, food products executive; b. Vallejo, Calif., July 9, 1952; s. Robert Stephen and Mary Josephine (Broderick) B.; children: Brian Timothy, Kevin Matthew. BS in personnel and indsl. relations, San Francisco StateU., 1981; cert. of achievement, U. So. Calif., 1983, cert. in Mgmt. Devel. Program, 1988. Various positions Safeway Stores, Fremont, Calif., 1972-83, store mgr., 1983-85, dist. mgr., 1986—; speaker U. So. Calif. Food Industry Mgmt. Western Assn. Food Chains Conv., Hawaii, 1983; cons. Time and Attendance Group, Oakland, Calif., 1984-85. Mem. Smithsonian Instn., Commonwealth Club Calif., U. So. Calif. Alumni Assn.

BLOUNT, HARRY NEIL, heavy equipment executive, marketing consultant; b. Blount, W.Va., Nov. 22, 1944; s. Harry and Stella Mae (Branard) B.; m. Dorothy Ann McDaniel, Oct. 1, 1965 (div. June 1977); children: Harry Neil II, Patricia Suzzette; m. Dolores Ruiz, Aug. 13, 1977. Student, W.Va. U., 1963-65; in bus. mgmt., Hartnell Coll., 1974-77. Warranty adminstr. C.I. Walker Equipment Co., Charleston, W.Va., 1965-70; lt. Belle W.Va. Fire Dept., 1970-73; svc. advisor Quinn Co., Salinas, Calif., 1973-86; region sales mgr. Northwest Motor Welding, San Leandro, Calif., 1986-87; founder, pres. Parts World, Salinas, 1987—; ptnr. West World Mktg., Salinas, 1988—; account exec. Empire Tractor Co., Newark, Calif., 1988—; group advisor Equipment Explorers, Belle, 1970-73; cons. Indsl. Safety Club,

Salinas, 1977-84. Author: Back Roads & Home, 1980; contbr. articles to publs. Mem. Big Buddy Program, Monterey County, Calif., 1981, Citizen's Traffic Com., Salinas, 1987, Friend's Outside, Monterey, 1988; asst. mgr. Community Recycle Program, Salinas, 1986. Recipient Outstanding Svc. award State of W.Va., 1970, Vol. Achievement award Vol. Bur., Monterey County, 1984; named Bay Area Booster, KDON Radio, Salinas, 1981. Mem. Salinas C. of C., Lions (bd. dirs. Salinas Club 1984-86 spl. svc. award 1986). Republican. Methodist. Home: 1605 Siskiyou Dr Salinas CA 93906 Office: Empire Tractor Co 28600 Cedar Blvd Newark CA 94560

BLOW, JOHN NEEDHAM, social services educator; b. Whitby, Ont., Can., Nov. 30, 1905; came to U.S., 1952; s. Ezekiel Richard and Edith May (Correll) B.; m. Emma Jane White, June 6, 1942; children: Carol Anne, Brenda Jane, Mary Roberta, Elizabeth Diane. BA, McMaster U., 1939; MSW, U. Toronto, Ont., 1948. Cert. elem. tchr., Toronto, community colls. instr., Calif. Exec. sec. Community Welfare Planning Council Ont., Toronto, 1948-52; exec. v.p. Motel Corp., Las Vegas, Nev., 1952-54; exec. dir. Nev. div. Am. Cancer Soc., 1954-56, assoc. exec. dir. Los Angeles County br., 1956-70; program assoc. Am. Heart Assn., Los Angeles, 1970-74; project dir., coordinator sr. community service employment program Orange County, Calif., 1974-75; instr. community service programs for adults North Orange County Community Coll. Dist. and Coastline Coll., 1976-79, Mira Costa and Palomar Community Colls., 1979-85. Author: (poems) New Frontiers, 1984. Vol. Arthritis Found.; asst. commr. tng. Boy Scouts Can., Ottawa, 1934-41; Chaplain Tri-City Coun. Navy League. Wing comdr. RCAF, 1941-46. Recipient Commendation for Outstanding Service to Srs., Orange County Sr. Citizens Council, 1977, Gold award Orange County United Way, 1977. Mem. Nat. Assn. Social Workers, Acad. Cert. Social Workers, San Luis Rey Officers Club, Valley Sr. Ctr., North County Concert Assn., So. Calif. McMaster U. Alumni Assn. (past pres., inducted Alumni Gallery 1986), Can. Soc. Los Angeles (charter, past pres.), U. Toronto Alumni Assn. (exec. com., past pres. So. Calif. br.), Internat. Platform Assn. Presbyterian. Lodge: Elks. Home: 3725 Sesame Way Oceanside CA 92056

BLUECHEL, ALAN, state senator, wood structural components manufacturing company executive; b. Edmonton, Alta., Can., Aug. 28, 1924; s. Joseph Harold and Edith (Daly) B.; m. Aylene Loughnan, Nov. 2, 1958; children: Gordon, Turner; m. Jeanne Ehrlichman, Aug. 8, 1981. BSc in Elec. Engring., BA, U. B.C.; postgrad. U. Wash.; diploma Harvard U., 1988. Vice pres. Loctwall Corp., Kirkland, Wash., 1948-64, pres., 1964—; pres. Crystal Mtn. Inn Co., developer condominiums, restaurants, hotels, swimming pools, 1968-80; mem. Wash. State Ho. of Reps., 1966-74; mem. Wash. Senate, 1974—, pres. pro tem, 1988-89, vice-chmn. rules com. 1988-89, Rep. whip, 1979-81, 83—, majority whip, 1981-83, mem. ways and means, energy and utilities vice chmn., 1988-89, bd. dirs. Wash. State Inst. Pub. Policy, 1988; mem. exec. com. Western Legis. Conf., 1988-89, speaker various confs., convs., orgns. Mem. Wash. State Land Planning Commn., 1969-73, Wash. State Women's Council, 1976, Spl. Com. on Office State Actuary, 1983; chmn. Wash. State Winter Recreation Commn., 1983, Wash. State Commn. on Environ. Policy, 1983; mem. arts, tourism and cultural affairs com. Nat. Conf. of State Legis., 1976-897; mem. Juanita Citizens Devel. Council, 1975-79, King County Conservation Com., 1967-69, King County Flood Control Adv. Bd., 1968-70, Com. To Save Sch. Trust Lands, 1975—, Edwards Park Adv. Bd., 1977-79, Seattle Symphony Phonathon Fundraisers, 1980, 81, Gov.'s Council on Child Abuse and Neglect, 1983, Wash. State Expo '86 Commn., 1985-87; mem. conservation com. King County Environ. Devel. Commn., 1969-74, numerous other civic orgns. Recipient Outstanding Service award Lake Washington PTSA Council, 1982, Mountaineers Club, Sun Valley Ski Club, Forelaufer Ski Club.

BLUEMLE, PAUL EDWARD, college administrator; b. Springfield, Ohio, Sept. 9, 1926; s. Carl Henry and Mary Ann (Wolbert) B.; m. Helen Jean Smain, Sept. 13, 1958; children: Joy, Christine, Jude, Laura, Peter. BBA magna cum laude, Xavier U., 1951; MA, U. Oreg., 1953; postgrad., Mich. State U., 1957-63. Reporter Springfield Daily News, 1943-51; exec. sec. Young Christian Students, Chgo., 1952-54; dir. pub. relations Thomas More Coll., Covington, Ky., 1954-55; bus. mgr. Today mag., Chgo., 1955-56; instr. Mich. State U., East Lansing, 1956-59; editor univ. publs. Bowling Green (Ohio) State U., 1959-60; asst. prof., assoc. prof., exec. sec., asst. dean Monteith Coll., Wayne State U., Detroit, 1960-76; admissions dir., asst. dean U. Detroit, 1976-80; city clk. Pleasant Ridge, Mich., 1980-82; asst. to v.p. academics Northwood Inst., Midland, Mich., 1983; dir. admissions, rsch. and planning Holy Names Coll., Oakland, CA, 1983—; bd. dirs. Chgo. Research Group Corp., 1956-73. Pres. sch. bd. St. Mary's Parish, Royal Oak, Mich., 1966; mem. Citizen's Adv. Commn., Ferndale (Mich.) Sch. Dist., 1972; chmn. com. on community Archdiocese of Detroit, 1972-74. Served with U.S. Army, 1945-46. Mem. Soc. Profl. Journalists, Am. Newspaper Guild (v.p. Springfield 1945), AAUP (sec. Wayne State U. chpt. 1971-72), Nat. Assn. Coll. Admission Counselors, Kappa Tau Alpha. Roman Catholic. Home: 2235 Lincoln #207 Alameda CA 94501 Office: 3500 Mountain Blvd Oakland CA 94619

BLUE-SPRUCE, GEORGE, JR., dentist; b. Jan. 16, 1931; s. George and Juanita (Cruz) Blue-S.; m. Sylvia Ann Hamblin; children: Sharon, Reni, Duane. DDS, Creighton U., 1956; MPH, U. Calif., Berkeley, 1967. Chief D.A.U. sect. NIH, Bethesda, Md., 1970; spl. asst. to dir. Bur. Health Manpower Edn., Bethesda, 1971; dir. Office Health Manpower Opportunities, Bethesda, 1971-73; liaison officer Health Resource Adminstrn., Bethesda, 1973-74; dir. Office Native Am. Programs, Washington, 1974-76; chmn. Intra Departmental Council Indian Affairs, Washington, 1976-78; dir. Indian Health Manpower Devel., Rockville, Md., 1978-79, Phoenix Area Indian Health Svcs., 1979-86; cons. Assn. Am. Indian Physicians, Oklahoma City, 1986—; bd. dirs. Phoenix Indian Ctr., St. Josephs Hosp., bd. dirs. minority affairs, 1987—; bd. youth programs Phoenix Indian Ctr., 1987—. Contbr. articles to profl. jours. Active dental alumni adv. bd. Creighton U., 1984—; mem. adv. com. Mesa Community Coll., 1985—; bd. dirs. Sr. Citizens Program, 1987—; chmn. Am. Indian Sr. Citizens, Phoenix, 1987—. Mem. Assn. of Am. Indian Physicians (recipient Merit award 1985), North American Indian Tennis Assn. Office: 5050 N 8th Pl Ste 3 Phoenix AZ 85014

BLUM, BARRY, orthopedic surgeon; b. Bklyn., Nov. 21, 1940; s. Joseph and Jeanne (Masef) B.; m. Gloria Jeanne Itman, July 14, 1966; 1 child, Michelle Katie. AB, Columbia Coll., 1961; MD, U. Rochester, 1965. Intern U. Minn. Hosps., Mpls., 1966; resident in orthopedics Stanford (Calif.) Med. Ctr., 1971; asst. to prof. Nuffield Orthopedic Ctr. Oxford U., 1972; pvt. practice Greenbrae, Calif., 1973-74, Larkspur, Calif., 1974-86, Kealakekua, Hawaii, 1986—; asst. chief orthopedics Stanford/V.A. Hosp., Palo Alto, Calif., 1973; edn. dir. Arthritis Found., Kailua-Kona, Hawaii, 1988—. Musical director: (music album) The Golden Gate Gypsy Orchestra of America and California Otherwise Known as the Travelling Jewish Wedding, 1988; editor, pub.: The Doctor's Directory. Surgeon USPHS, 1966-68. Fellow Am. Acad. Orthopedic Surgeons; mem. Am. Bd. Orthopedic Surgery, Union of Am. Physicians and Dentists, Western Orthopedic Assn., Hawaii Med. Assn. Office: PO Box S Kealakekua HI 96750

BLUM, FRED ANDREW, electronics company executive; b. Austin, Tex., Nov. 30, 1939; s. Freddie A. and Margaret E. (Stark) B.; children: Craig Houston, Karisa Laine; m. Diane F. Harbert, June 11, 1988. BS in Physics, U. Tex., 1962; MS in Physics, Calif. Inst. Tech., 1963, PhD, 1968. Rsch. scientist Gen. Dynamics, Ft. Worth, 1963-64; mem. tech. staff Hughes Rsch. Labs., Malibu, Calif., 1966-68, Lincoln Lab., MIT, Lexington, 1968-73; program mgr. Cen. Rsch. Labs., Tex. Instruments, Dallas, 1973-75; dir. solid state electronics Rockwell Internat., Thousand Oaks, Calif., 1975-79; v.p. Microelectronics R&D Ctr. Rockwell Internat., Anaheim, Calif., 1979-81; pres. GigaBit Logic, Newbury Park, Calif., 1981-86; chief exec. officer Sequel, Westlake Village, Calif., 1986—. Mem. editorial bd. Fiber Optics and Integrated Optics, 1977-83; contbr. numerous articles on solid state electronics to sci. jours. Chmn. local adv. coun. Am. Cancer Soc., 1980-81. NSF fellow, Howard Hughes fellow. Fellow IEEE; mem. AAAS, Am. Phys. Soc., Am. Mgmt. Assn., Phi Beta Kappa, Sigma Xi. Office: Sequel 2899 Agoura Rd Ste 347 Westlake Village CA 91361

BLUM, JOHN ALAN, urologist, educator; b. Bklyn., Feb. 2, 1933; s. Louis J. and Pauline (Kushner) B.; A.B., Dartmouth, 1954; M.D., N.Y. U., 1958; M.S., U. Minn., 1965; m. Debra Merlin Ackerman, June 30, 1957; children—Louis Jeffrey, Alfred Merlin, Jacqueline. Intern, U. Minn. Hosp., Mpls., 1958-59, resident, 1959-64; practice medicine, specializing in urology, Chgo., 1964-66, Mpls., 1966-67, San Diego, 1969—; chmn. dept. urology Mt. Sinai Hosp., Chgo., 1965-66; asst. prof. urology U. Minn., Mpls., 1967; assoc. clin. prof. urology U. Calif., San Diego, 1969—; mem. staff Mercy, Donald Sharp, Children's hosps., San Diego, 1969—, Scripps Hosp., La Jolla, Calif., 1969—. Bd. dirs. Vietnam Vet. Leadership Program. Served to capt. USNR, 1967—; Vietnam. Diplomate Am. Bd. Urology. Fellow A.C.S.; mem. Am., Calif. med. assns., Am. Urol. Assn., San Diego Urol. Soc., San Diego Surg. Soc. (pres. 1977—), Phi Beta Kappa, Sigma Xi, Alpha Omega Alpha. Club: San Diego Yacht. Research in devel. of silicone rubber for urinary tract. Home: 890 Cornish Dr San Diego CA 92107 Office: 3415 6th Ave San Diego CA 92103

BLUM, ROSLYN, interior designer; b. N.Y.C., Feb. 4, 1926; d. Samuel and Anna (Ravitz) Silver; m. Albert Alexander Blum, Jan. 16, 1949; children: Steven Ephraim, David Joshua. BS, Hunter Coll., 1950. Editor of pubs. Mich. State U., Coll. Edn., E. Lansing, 1961-65; editorial cons. Mich. State U., Coll. Human Medicine, E. Lansing, 1969-73; design cons. Abacus Antiques, Portland, Oreg., 1982-87, Art Design & Interiors, Portland, 1987—; art cons. Contbr. articles to profl. jours.; editor numerous books. Precinct capt. Dem. Party, E. Lansing, 1968-73. Democrat. Address: care of Whiting 2621 SW Brixton Gresham OR 97030

BLUM, WILLIAM HENRY, writer, filmmaker; b. Bklyn., Mar. 6, 1933; s. Isadore and Ruth (Katz) B.; m. Adelheid Zöfel, Feb. 8, 1979; 1 child, Alexander. BBA, CUNY, 1955. Acct. various CPA firms, N.Y.C.; computer systems analyst, programmer IBM, N.Y.C., 1960-64, Dept. State, Washington, 1964-67; founder, editor Washington Free Press, 1967-69; freelance journalist 1970-76; bus. mgr., news writer Sta. KPFA, Berkeley, Calif., 1976-80; gen. mgr., writer The Daily Calif., Berkeley, 1981-82; freelance writer 1982-86, ind. filmmaker, 1988—. Author: The CIA, A Forgotten History, 1986; contbr. articles to newspapers and popular mags. Mem. Internat. Documentary Assn. Home: 1531 N Fuller Ave #12 Los Angeles CA 90046

BLUMENTHAL, MARTIN A(ARON), small business owner; b. L.A., Aug. 13, 1951; m. Debra Ann Flores, May 24, 1980; 1 child, Mark David. BSBA, Calif. State U., Northridge, 1975. Salesperson Moore Bus. Forms, Van Nuys, Calif., 1975-87; owner Dataform, Chatsworth, Calif., 1987—. Sgt. Calif. Air N.G., 1971-77. Mem. Western Bus. Forms Assn. Jewish. Home and Office: 21957 Merridy St Chatsworth CA 91311

BLUMENTHAL, RICHARD CARY, construction executive, consultant; b. Bklyn., Dec. 18, 1951; s. Mervin Harold and Barbara June (Engelson) B.; m. Ginnilyn Hawkins; children: Aaron Joseph, Meredith Taylor. BS, U. N.H., 1974. Planner RECON Assocs., Hamilton, Mont., 1976-77; project mgr. Grizzly Mfg., Hamilton, 1977-78; profl. carpenter Ed Brown Constrn., Bainbridge Island, Wash., 1978-79; gen. contractor, profl. builder, project mgr. Richard Blumenthal Constrn., Bainbridge Island, 1979—. Democrat. Jewish. Home: 330 Nicholson Pl NW Bainbridge Island WA 98110 Office: 330 Nicholson Pl NW Bainbridge Island WA 98110

BLUMMER, KATHLEEN ANN, counselor; b. Iowa Falls, Iowa, Apr. 17, 1945; d. Arthur G. and Julia C. (Ericson) Thorsbakken; m. Terry L. Blummer, Feb. 13, 1971 (dec. 1980); 1 child, Emily Erica. AA, Ellsworth Coll., Iowa Falls, 1965; BA, U. Iowa, 1967; postgrad., Northeastern Ill. U., 1969-70, U. N.Mex., 1980—; MA, Western N.Mex. U., 1973. Asst. buyer Marshall Field & Co., Chgo., 1967-68; social worker Cook County Dept. Pub. Aid, Chgo., 1968-69; tchr. Chgo. Pub. Schs., 1968-69; student fin. aid counselor Western N.Mex. U., Silver City, 1971-72; family social worker, counselor Southwestern N.Mex. Svcs. to Handicapped Children and Adults, Silver City, 1972-74; career edn. program specialist Galluo McKinley County (N.Mex.) Schs., 1974-76; dir. summer sch. Loving (N.Mex.) Mcpl. Schs., 1977; counselor, dept. chmn. Carlsbad (N.Mex.) Pub. Schs., 1977-82; counselor Albuquerque Pub. Schs., 1982—. Mem. AAUW (topic chmn. Carlsbad chpt., v.p. Albuquerque chpt.), N.Mex. Personnel and Guidance Assn., Theos Club, Highpoint Swim and Racquet Club (Albuquerque), Elks. Democrat. Lutheran.

BLUNT, ROBERT MATTESON, pyrotechnics and ordnance researcher emeritus; b. Denver, Oct. 21, 1916; s. Laurence Calvin and Ruth Esther (Howe) B.; m. June Correan Romelle Buros, Sept. 9, 1939; children: Tona Louise, Robert Matteson, Peter Howe, Stephen Thomas, John Eric. Student, MIT, 1935-39; BSc, U. Denver, 1947, MSc, 1958. Registered profl. engr., Colo. Rsch. engr. Douglas Leigh Inc., N.Y.C., 1939; sr. ballistic engr. Denver Ordnance Plant, 1941-43; rsch. physicist Remington Arms Co., Bridgeport, Conn., 1943-46; rsch. physicist U. Denver Rsch. Inst. Labs. for Applied Mechanics, 1948-80, sr. rsch. fellow, 1980-87, sr. rsch. fellow emeritus, 1987—; founder Internat. Pyro, Denver, 1980, pres., 1980-84, gen. chmn. emeritus, 1980—. Mem. Internat. Pyrotechnics Soc. (founder, pres. 1980-82), Masons, Sigma Xi (pres. 1975), Pi Delta Theta, Sigma Pi Sigma. Home: 692 S High St Denver CO 80209

BLUTH, GEORGE JOSEPH, psychotherapist; b. Aurora, Ill., Nov. 8, 1953; s. George Joseph Bluth and Blanche Marie (Erickson) Rydquist. BS, U. Calif., Riverside, 1975; MA, Calif. State U., San Bernardino, 1978. Cert. addiction counselor, Ariz. Psychology assoc. II State of Ariz., Coolidge, 1979-83; psychotherapist Park Cen. Counseling and Rehab. Svcs., Phoenix, 1983—; cons. St. Luke's Hosp., Phoenix, 1983—, Ariz. Dept. Econ. Security, Phoenix, 1984—; presenter in field. Mem. Ariz. Psychol. Assn., Maricopa Psychol. Soc., Nat. Rehab. Assn., Nat. Rehab. Counseling Assn., Camelback bus. and Profl. Assn. (program bd. dirs. 1986-87), Phi Beta Kappa, Psi Chi. Home: 373 E Coronado Phoenix AZ 85004 Office: Park Cen Counseling and Rehab Svcs 550 W Thomas C-225 Phoenix AZ 85013

BLY, DAVID ALAN, computer services company executive; b. Kansas City, Mo., Nov. 9, 1953; s. Chauncey Goodrich and Ruth Madeline (Henion) B; m. Christine Elizabeth Bidle, Mar. 10, 1973; children: Sarah Christine, Adam David. Student, Boise State U., 1974-76; BA in Bus. Adminstrn., U. Wash., 1978; MBA, Pacific Luth. U., 1982. Fin. analyst Boeing Comml. Airplanes, Seattle, 1978-80; systems analyst and cons. Boeing Computer Svcs., Seattle, 1980-83; mgr. publs. and quality assurance Boeing Computer Svcs., 1983-85, mgr. strategic planning, 1985-86, mgr. customer support, 1986—; lectr. in field. Bd. dirs. Wash. Future Bus. Leaders of Am., 1986—. With USAF, 1972-76. Mem. Puget Sound PCjr User Group (sec. 1985-86), Beta Gamma Sigma. Home: 25712 119th Ave SE Kent WA 98031

BO, NING, badminton coach; b. Nanjing, Jiangsu, People's Rep. China, Feb. 10, 1960; came to U.S., 1985; s. Gong-bao Pee and Zuo-xi (PingDi) Wang; m. Stephanie H. Xiao-Wan, Feb. 28, 1984; children: Roland Ji-er, Oliver Le-er. Grad. high sch., Nanjing; grad., Nanjing Phys. Edn. Inst., 1973. Asst. gen. mgr. Shenzhen Internat. Econ. Info. Co., Shenzhen City, People's Rep. China, 1984-85; head coach U.S.A. Badminton Team, Lawndale, Calif., 1987—. Winner Badminton Championship men's single Nanjing City Athletic Games, 1981, men's double Shenzhen City Athletic Games, 1984; recipient Second place Badminton men's double Calif. State Games, 1988, men's double Northern Calif. Indoor Badminton Games, 1988. Mem. U.S. Badminton Assn., Am. Sports Found., Manhattan Beach Badminton Club (life). Home: 4029 W 160th St Lawndale CA 90260 Office: USA Badminton Team 4166 W 160th St Lawndale CA 90260

BOARDMAN, ROSANNE VIRGINIA, military science executive; b. Twin Falls, Idaho, Oct. 4, 1946; d. Gordon Ross and Garnet Othalia (Peterson) Tobin; m. Lowell Jay Boardman, May 12, 1973; 1 child, Christina Garnet. BA cum laude, Occidental Coll., 1968; MA with honors, Columbia U., 1969; postgrad., U. Calif., Irvine, 1971-72, U. Calif., Los Angles and Santa Barbara, 1969, 73-74. Cert. jr. coll. tchr., Calif., cert. secondary tchg., Calif. Instr. U. Calif., Irvine, 1971-72, Ventura (Calif.) Community Coll., 1973-77; tech. writer Raytheon Service Co., Ventura, 1977-78; engring. analyst John J. McMullen Co., Ventura, 1978-80; sr. logistics specialist Raytheon Co., Ventura, 1977-78, 80-83; civilian tech. writer, editor USN, Port Hueneme, Calif., 1983-84, civilian logistics mgr., 1984-88; cons. Support Mgmt. Systems, Oxnard, Calif., 1988—. Author numerous manuals and logistics guides. Internat. fellow Occidental Coll., 1967; recipient Outstanding Performance award Naval Ship Weapon Systems Engring. Sta., 1985, 86. Mem. Soc. Logistics Engrs., Phi Beta Kappa.

BOARDMAN, WILLIAM TYLER, III, air force officer; b. Mobile, Ala., June 26, 1941; s. William T. Jr. and Elizabeth Sue (Burns) B. BS in Aero. Engring., Auburn U., 1963, MS in Aero. Engring, 1964; Aero. and Astro. Engring., Stanford U., 1968. Registered profl. engr., Calif. Commd. lieut USAF, 1968, advanced to maj., retired 1988; project officer Air Force Avionics Lab., Wright Patterson AFB, Ohio, 1968-72, Advanced Ballistics Reentry Systems, L.A. AFB, 1972-76; chief Space-Craft Guidance Div., Sec. of Air Force L.A., 1976-81, Inertial Measurement Unit Br. Ballistics Missile Office, Norton AFB, Calif., 1981-86, Adaptive Optics Br. Space Def. Expts., L.A. AFB, 1986-88; sr. engr. scientist Astronautics Div. McDonnell-Douglas, Huntington Beach, Calif, 1988—. Mem. AIAA, IEEE, Inst. Navigation. Baptist. Home: 1707 Pacific Coast Hwy Hermosa Beach CA 90254

BOATWRIGHT, DANIEL E., state legislator; m. Margaret Shedd; children—Dan, David, Donald. Student Vallejo Jr. Coll., Calif.; A.B., J.D., U. Calif.-Berkeley. Former mayor City of Concord, Calif., mem. city council, 1966-72; city atty. City of Brentwood, Calif., 1965-72; former dist. atty. Contra Costa County, Calif.; sole practice, Concord, from 1970; former mem. Calif. State Assembly; state senator 7th Dist. State of Calif., 1980—, chmn. Revenue and Taxation com., Select com. on State Procurement and Expenditure Practices. mem. coms. on fin., banking and commerce, elections and reapportionment, joint com. on prison constrn. and ops., joint com. on campaign and election reform, select com. on Auburn Dam project. Active community sporting and charitable orgns. Served with U.S. Army, Korea. Address: 3086 State Capitol Sacramento CA 95814 *

BOBER, HAROLD LEWIS, publishing executive, educator; b. Winnipeg, Man., Can., Sept. 18, 1936; came to U.S., 1968; s. Max and Eva (Zelman) B.; divorced; children: Simone Robin, Melanie Lisa. BS in Pharmacy, U. of Man., 1960; MS in Pharmacy, U. Colo., 1967; PhD in Ednl. Adminstrn. and Bus. Adminstrn., U. N.MeX., 1977. Pharmacy mgr. Gurveys Pharmacies Ltd., Winnipeg, 1960-65; mgr. market research Eli Lilly & co., Toronto, Can., 1967-68; asst. prof. U. N.Mex., Albuquerque, 1968-74, asst. dean, 1974-75; v.p. Pharmaco-Nuclear, Inc., Kansas City, Mo., 1975-76; asst. prof. N.D. State U., Fargo, 1976-79; pres. Pro-Scan, Inc., Denver, 1979-82; pres., chief exec. officer Paul de Haen Internat., Inc., Englewood, Colo., 1982—; adj. asst. prof. U. Colo., 1987—. Bd. dirs. Community Assns. Inst., Denver, 1986. Recipient Spl. Pharmacy award N.Mex. Pharm. Assn., Albuquerque, 1975. Fellow Am. Coll. Apothecaries; mem. Am. Assn. Colls. of Pharmacy, Drug Info. Assn., Rho Chi. Home: 6391 Hudson St Littleton CO 80121 Office: 2750 S Shoshone St Englewood CO 80110

BOCK, JEFFREY WILLIAM, lawyer; b. Mpls., Mar. 26, 1950; s. Frederick Garland Bock and Vera (Lewer) Randall; m. Elaine Drinkwater, Dec. 5, 1976 (div. 1981). BA, Dartmouth Coll., 1972; JD, U. Chgo., 1975. Bar: Oreg. 1975. Assoc. Tonkon, Torp & Galen, Portland, Oreg., 1975-78, McEwen, Hanna & Gisvold, Portland, 1978-81; corp. counsel Thermo Electron, Waltham, Mass., 1981-83; assoc. Perkins Coie, Portland, 1983—. Mem. Univ. Club, Founders Club. Office: Perkins Coie 111 SW 5th Ave Ste 2500 Portland OR 97204

BOCKSCH, ROBERT DONALD, chemistry educator; b. Detroit, May 5, 1931; s. Paul R. and Frieda M. (Schmidt) B.; m. Mary June Fish, July 5, 1958; children: Brian, Linda, Karen, Donald, Kenneth. BS in Chemistry, Wayne State U., 1954; PhD in Organic Chemistry, U. Wis., 1960. Asst. prof. chemistry Whitworth Coll., Spokane, Wash., 1958-61; assoc. prof. chemistry Whitworth Coll., Spokane, 1961-68, chmn. dept. chemistry, 1963-70, 75—, chmn. health scis., 1971-75, prof. chemistry, 1968—. Mem. Spokane Solid Waste Adv. Com., 1988—. Mem. Am. Chem. Soc., Phi Lambda Upsilon, Sigma Xi. Mem. Disciples of Christ Ch. Office: Whitworth College W Hawthorne Rd Spokane WA 99251

BODDIE, LEWIS FRANKLIN, SR., obstetrics-gynecology educator; b. Forsyth, Ga., Apr. 4, 1913; s. William F. and Luetta T. (Sams) B.; m. Marian Bernice Claytor, Dec. 27, 1941; children: Roberta Boddie Miles, Lewis Jr., Bernice B. Jackson, Pamela, Kenneth, Fredda, Margaret. BA, Morehouse Coll., 1933; MD, Meharry Med. Sch., 1938. Diplomate Am. Bd. Ob-Gyn (proctor parti exam Los Angeles area 1955-63). Intern Homer-Phillips Hosp., St. Louis, 1938-39, resident in ob-gyn, 1939-42; mem. attending staff Grace Hosp., Detroit, 1944048, Parkside Hosp., Detroit, 1944-48, Los Angeles County Gen. Hosp., 1952-79; sr. mem. attending staff Queen of Angels Hosp., Los Angeles, 1964-86, chmn. dept. ob-gyn, 1968-70; asst. prof. U. So. Calif. Sch. Medicine, Los Angeles, 1953-79, asst. prof. emeritus, 1979—; assoc. prof. U. Calif., Irvine, 1956-81. vice chmn. bd. mgrs. 28th St. YMCA, Los Angeles 1960-75; steward African Meth. Episc. Ch., Los Angeles, 1949—. Fellow ACS (life), Am. Coll. Ob-Gyn (life), Los Angeles Ob-Gyn Soc. (life): mem. Los Angeles United Way (priorities and allocations coms., 1985—), Children's Home Soc. (bd. dirs. 1952-89, , trustee 1989—, v.p. 1963-68, pres. 1968-70), Child Welfare League Am. (bd. dirs. 1969-76). Republican. Office: 231 W Vernon Ave Los Angeles CA 90037

BODE, FRANCES LOUISE MAINO (MRS. WILLIAM THEODORE BODE), author, lecturer; b. San Luis Obispo, Calif., Mar. 1, 1920; d. Theodore Michael and Eleanor Elizabeth (Hazard) Maino; B.A., Mills Coll., 1940; postgrad. U. Calif. at Berkeley, 1941; M.A., Sacramento State U., 1958; m. William Theodore Bode, Dec. 25, 1942; children—Eleanor Bode Cauldwell, Catherine Bode Appel, William T. II. Tchr., Ceres Union High Sch., 1941-43, Sacramento State Coll., 1957; free-lance tchr. flower arrangement, 1946—; lectr. on flower arrangements to various orgns. throughout U.S. Teaching specialist Ala. Judges Council, 1971, Ohio Judges Council, 1971, Ga. Judges Council, 1978, Judges Council So. Calif., 1978; dir. Sacramento Garden and Art Center, 1958-68, v.p., 1977-79; floriculture coordinator Calif. State Fair, 1981-84, chmn. Garden Club Day, 1983-85. Recipient Exec. Com. award Calif. Expn., 1969, 82; Community Service award Sacramento Soc. for the Blind, 1976; Design award Calif. State Fair, 1978. Mem. Profl. Arrangers No. Calif. (pres. 1968-69), Am. Horticultural Soc., Calif. Writers Club, Garden Writers Assn. Am., Carmichael Arrangers Guild, Sacramento Arrangers Guild, Kingsley Art Club, Nat. Council State Garden Clubs (Flower Arranger of Yr. 1987), Am. Guild Flower Arrangers, Calif. State Garden Clubs, Inc. (life), Mignonette Garden Club. Author: Creativity in Flower Arrangement, 1967; New Structures in Flower Arrangement, 1968; Dried Flower Designs, 1975; Designing with Flowers, 1976; contbr. author: Brooklyn Botanic Gardens Handbooks. Contbr. pictures of arrangements to various mags, articles on design and color to garden mags. Home: 2800 Huntington Rd Sacramento CA 95864

BODE, KRIS ANN, nurse; b. Denver, Apr. 14, 1958; d. Rockford Julius Johnson and Jeanne Ann Sadler. BS in Nursing, Creighton U., 1981. Cert. advanced burn life support instr., Colo. Evening supr. Long Term Care Facility, Denver, 1981-82; staff nurse ICU and burn ctr. Children's Hosp., Denver, 1981-84, pediatric burn nurse clinician, 1984—; speaker on TV and radio shows about burn prevention and first aid; speaker nat. burn confs. Author articles on burn prevention. Mem. N.Am. Burn Soc. (charter), Am. Burn Assn. Office: The Children's Hosp Denver CO 80218

BODE, LORI MONNEY, nurse; b. Buffalo, Dec. 28, 1950; d. Elwood John and Dorothy Isabel (Reid) Monney; m. David Arthur Bode, Aug. 28, 1981. BS, U. Utah, 1973; BS in Nursing, Mont. State U., 1980. Psychiatric nurse Sacred Heart Med. Ctr., Spokane, Wash., 1980-84; drug and alcohol treatment nurse Deaconess Med. Ctr., Spokane, 1983-84; home health and hospice nurse, diabetic educator Mercy Med. Ctr., Durango, Colo., 1984—. Mem. Nat. Assn. Diabetes Educators (cert.).

BODENSIECK, ERNEST JUSTUS, mechanical engineer; b. Dubuque, Iowa, June 1, 1923; s. Julius Henry and Alma Freida (Sommer) B.; BS in ME, Iowa State U., 1943; m. Margery Elenore Sande, Sept. 9, 1943; children: Elizabeth Bodensieck Eley, Stephen. Project engr. TRW Inc., Cleve., 1943-57; supr. rocket turbomachinery Rocketydyne div. Rockwell Internat., Canoga Park, Calif., 1957-60, supr. nuclear turbomachinery Rocketydyne div., 1964-70; advance gear engr. Gen. Electric Co., Lynn, 1960-64; asst. mgr. engine components Aerojet Nuclear Systems Co., Sacramento, 1970-71; gear and bearing cons. AiResearch div. Garrett Corp., Phoenix, 1971-81; transmission cons. Bodensieck Engring. Co., Scottsdale, Ariz., 1981—. Registered profl. engr., Ariz. Mem. ASME, AIAA, Soc. Automotive Engrs. (various coms.), Aircraft Industries Assn. (various coms.), Am. Gear Mfrs. Assn. (mem. aerospace, gear rating and enclosed epicyclic coms.), Nat. Soc. Profl. Engrs., Pi Tau Sigma. Lutheran. Patentee in field. Home: 7133 N Via De Alegria Scottsdale AZ 85258

BODETT, THOMAS EDWARD, writer, radio personality; b. Champaign, Ill., Feb. 23, 1955; s. Peter C. and Florence E. (De Paun) B.; m. Debi J. Hochstetler, Dec. 26, 1978; 1 child, Courtney H. Student, Mich. State U., 1973-75. Bldg. contractor Petersburg and Homer, Alaska, 1976-84; commentator All Things Considered Nat. Pub. Radio, Washington, 1984-87; author Addison-Wesley Pub., Boston, 1984—; radio spokesman Motel 6, Dallas, 1986—, The End of the Road, Dallas, 1988—; chmn. Kachemak Bay Broadcasting Inc., Pub. Radio Sta. KBBI, Homer, 1985—. Author: As Far As You Can Go Without A Passport, 1985, Small Comforts, 1987, The End of the Road, 1989. Recipient Best Radio Commentary and Best Radio Feature awards Alaska Press Club, Anchorage, 1985, 86, 3 Motel 6 Clio awards, 1988. Mem. AFTRA, Authors Guild. Home and Office: PO Box 2858 Homer AK 99603

BODINE, RALPH E., food products company executive; b. 1942. AB, Princeton U., 1966. With Sunkist Growers Inc., Calif., 1977—; chmn. Sunkist Growers Inc., 1986—, also bd. dirs. With USNR, 1961-63. Office: Sunkist Growers Inc PO Box 7888 Van Nuys CA 91409-7888 *

BODINSON, HOLT, conservationist; b. East Orange, N.J., Nov. 14, 1941; s. Earl Herdien and Hermoine (Holt) B.; B.A., Harvard, 1963; m. Ilse Marie Maier, Feb. 29, 1970. Sr. asso. Am. Conservation Assn., Inc., N.Y.C., 1966-70; dir. Office of Policy Analysis, N.Y. State Dept. Environ. Conservation, Albany, 1970-71, dir. div. ednl. services, 1971-77; dir. Ariz.-Sonora Desert Mus., 1977-78; exec. dir. Safari Club Internat./Safari Club Internat. Conservation Fund, Tucson, 1980-1989; Committeeman, Montgomery Twp. Conservation Commn., 1967-70; sec. N.Am. del. Conseil Internat. de la Chasse et de la Conservation du Gibier, 1988—; gen. sec. World Hunting and Conservation Congress, 1988. Served with arty. AUS, 1964-66. Mem. Stony Brook-Millstone Watershed Assn. (dir.), Safari Club Internat. (dir. Ariz. chpt.), N.Y. Outdoor Edn. Assn. (dir.), Outdoor Writers Assn. of Am., N.Y. State Rifle and Pistol Assn. (dir.). Episcopalian. Club: Harvard of So. Ariz. (pres.). Author: (with Clepper and others) Leaders in American Conservation, 1971. Contbg. editor Jour. Environmental Edn., 1968—; dir. Conservationist mag. 1971-77, N.Y. State Environment newspaper, 1971-74. Home: 4525 Hacienda del Sol Rd Tucson AZ 85718 Office: 1730 E River Rd Ste 200 Tucson AZ 85718

BODWAY, JOANN OLSON, teacher, home economist; b. Painesville, Ohio, July 16, 1953; d. Elmer John and Clara May (Schupp) Olson; m. David Robert Bodway, Mar. 7, 1981; children: Justina, Holly. AA, Phoenix Coll., 1973; BA, Ariz. State U., 1975, MA, 1981. Cert. secondary home econs., basic vocat. educator, Ariz. Aquatics mgr. WSI, Phoenix, 1972-73; tchr., coach South Mountain, Phoenix, 1977-78, West, Phoenix, 1978-79; tchr. Maryville High Sch., Phoenix, 1979-83, Metro Tech VIP, Phoenix, 1985—. Vol. ARC, 1972—; troop leader Girl Scouts U.S.A., 1978-80; mo. Mem. Fashion Group, Sewing Guild, Nat. Vocat. Assn., Ariz. Vocat. Assn. Office: Metro Tech VIP 1900 W Thomas Rd Phoenix AZ 85015

BOE, CATHY MARIE, therapist; b. Sandwich, Ill., Sept. 29, 1949; d. Carl Edward and Evelyn Marie (Skeldon) B. BS, Western Ill. U., 1971; MS, Calif. State U., San Jose, 1982. Social worker Elgin (Ill.) State Hosp., 1971-73; child care worker Ming Quong Children's Ctrs. Homemakers, Los Gatos, Calif., 1974-75; with social svcs. Remedy Homemakers, San Jose, Calif., 1976-78; therapist, program dir. Rehab. Mental Health Svcs., San Jose, 1979-84; program dir. Miramonte Mental Health, Palo Alto, Calif., 1984-85; clin. therapist pub. rels. Clara County Mental Health, San Jose, 1985—; pvt. practice, Palo Alto, 1985—. Mem. Calif. Assn. Marriage and Family Therapists, Nat. Assn. Adult Children of Alcoholics, Bay Area Career Women. Democrat. Office: 825 San Antonio Rd #100 Palo Alto CA 94303

BOEDER, THOMAS L., lawyer; b. St. Cloud, Minn., Jan. 10, 1944; s. Oscar Morris and Eleanor (Gile) B.; m. Carol-Leigh Coombs, Apr. 6, 1968. BA, Yale U., 1965, LLB, 1968. Bar: Wash. 1970, U.S. Dist. Ct. (we. dist.) Wash. 1970, U.S. Dist. Ct. (ea. dist.) Wash. 1972, U.S. Ct. Appeals (9th cir.) 1970, U.S. Supreme Ct. 1974, U.S. Ct. Appeals (D.C. cir.) 1975. Litigation atty. Wash. State Atty. Gen., Seattle, 1970-72, antitrust div. head, 1972-76, chief, consumer protection and antitrust, 1976-78, also sr. asst. atty. gen. and criminal enforcement, 1979-81; ptnr. Perkins Coie, Seattle, 1981—. Served with U.S. Army, 1968-70, Vietnam. Mem. ABA (antitrust sect.), Wash. State Bar Assn. (antitrust sect.). Lutheran. Office: Perkins Coie 1201 3d Ave Bldg Seattle WA 98101

BOEHMER, RONALD GLENN, financial executive; b. Detroit, Apr. 12, 1947; s. Harry Byron and Ollie Violet (Kumka) B.; m. Linda Dershow, July 10, 1977 (div. Nov. 1981); m. Valerie Jean Adams, Sept. 1, 1984; 1 child, Cathryn Megan. BS, Xavier U., Cin., 1969. Worker's compensation adjuster Liberty Mut. Ins. Co., Southfield, Mich., 1971-73; area mgr. Reed, Roberts Assocs., Southfield, 1973-79, Frick Co., Southfield, 1979-81; div. svc. mgr. Frick Co., Chgo., 1981-86; div. mgr. Frick Co., Thousand Oaks, Calif., 1986—; mem. labor adv. com. Mich. C. of C., 1979-81, Minn. Assn. Commerce and Industry, 1981-86, Ill. C. of C., 1981-86, Calif. C. of C., 1986—, Assn. Wash. Bus., 1986—. Mem. Young Friends of Art, Chgo., 1981-84. Capt. U.S. Army, 1969-71, Vietnam. Republican. Roman Catholic. Home: 30957 Minuteman Way Westlake Village CA 91361

BOELE, MICHAEL EDWARD, insurance company executive; b. Fresno, Calif., Nov. 2, 1950; s. Edward A. and A. Faye (Horstmeier) B.; m. Nancy L. Rudden, Nov. 18, 1977 (div. 1984); m. Mary Lenore Lacorazza, Sept. 27, 1986. BS, St. Mary's Coll., Moraga, Calif., 1972. CPCU. Premium auditor Indsl. Indemnity, Walnut Creek, Calif., 1974-76, underwriter, 1976-80; analyst Indsl. Indemnity, San Francisco, 1980-81; sr. underwriter Indsl. Indemnity, Walnut Creek, 1981-88, chief underwriter, 1988—. Mem. Soc. CPCU (pres. Mt. Diablo chpt. 1988-89, v.p. No. Calif. 1984-87). Democrat. Roman Catholic. Office: Indsl Indemnity 225 Lennon Ln Ste 200 Walnut Creek CA 94596

BOESCH, BRICE E., agricultural engineer; b. Sebewaing, Mich., Apr. 28, 1937; s. Edgar Stephen Rudolph and Agnes Alfreda (Sting) B.; m. Patricia Anne Lawrence, Mar. 22, 1958; children: Cynthia J. Boesch Hyman, Linda D. Boesch King, Heidi M. BS in Agrl. Engrin.g, Mich. State U., 1959. Registered profl. engr., Mich., Colo., Wyo. Area engr. Soil Conservation Service USDA, Wellton, Ariz., 1957-75; project engr. Soil Conservation Service USDA, Denver, 1977-82; sr. irrigation engr. Bishop Assocs., Denver, 1982-83; pres. Boesch-Fisher Engring., Inc., Littleton, Colo., 1983—. Contbr. articles to profl. jours. Coach Littleton Soccer Assn., 1979-85, South Suburban Softball Assn., Littleton, 1979-87. Mem. Irrigation Assn., Soil Conservation Soc. Am. (pres. Colo. chpt. 1986-87, nat. chmn. soil-water div. 1987-88), Am. Soc. Agrl. Cons. Methodist. Home and Office: 7363 S Franklin St Littleton CO 80122

BOETTGER, WILLIAM F., data processing executive; b. Ravenna, Ohio, Oct. 18, 1945; s. William Henry and Annabelle (Myers) B.; m. Patricia Ann Mackey, Aug. 25, 1972; children: Rebecca, Micki, Ella. BS in Math., U. Wash., 1971; BA, Ind. U., 1966. Tech. aide, propulsion staff Boeing Comml. Airplane Co., Everett, Wash., 1974-77, graphics operator, 1977-81, CAD-CAM systems analyst, 1977-83; prin. cons. Control Data Corp., Mpls., 1983-86; exec. cons. CAE and CIM implementations Control Data, Bellevue, Wash., 1986—. With USAF, 1965-68. Office: PO Box 628 Freeland WA 98249

BOGAARD, WILLIAM JOSEPH, lawyer; b. Sioux City, Iowa, Jan. 18, 1938; s. Joseph and Irene Mary (Hensing) B.; B.S., Loyola Marymount U., Los Angeles, 1959; J.D. with honors, U. Mich., 1965; m. Claire Marie Whalen, Jan. 28, 1961; children—Michele, Jeannine, Joseph, Matthew. Bar: Calif. 1966. Ptnr. firm Hufstedler, Miller, Kaus & Beardsley, Los Angeles, 1971-82; exec. v.p., gen. counsel First Interstate Bancorp, Los Angeles, 1982—. Mem. Pasadena (Calif.) City Council, 1978-86; mayor City of Pasadena, 1984-86. Served to capt. USAF, 1959-62. Mem. Am. Bar Assn., Los Angeles County Bar Assn. (Outstanding Corp. Counsel award 1987). Office: 1st Interstate Bancorp 707 Wilshire Blvd Los Angeles CA 90017

BOGANI, TINA MARIE, systems engineer; b. Colorado Springs, Colo., Feb. 10, 1962; d. Arthur P. and Mary Ann Elizabeth (Flynn) B. BS in Aerospace Engring., U. Colo., 1984. Commd. contr. Lab. Atmospheric and Space Physics, Boulder, Colo., 1982-85; project engr. gamma ray observatory TRW, Redondo Beach, Calif., 1985-87; systems engr. classified program TRW, Denver, 1987—. Vol. tchr. Lennox (Calif.) Elem. Sch., 1986. Mem. Lowry Ski Team. Home: 13711-A Lehigh Ave Aurora CO 80014

BOGARD, DAVID KENNETH, service executive; b. Peoria, Ill., Mar. 6, 1953; s. Dallas Kenneth and Emma Sue (Baker) B.; m. Candietta Ann Dominguez, May 7, 1976; children: Brittney Ann, Preston David. BA, So. Ill. U., 1974. Treas., v.p. Ken Bogard Remodeling, East Peoria, Ill., 1977-82; zone supr. Allright Houston, Inc., 1982-83; ops. auditor western div. Allright Auto Parks, Inc., Houston, 1983-84; city mgr. Allright San Francisco, 1984-86, Bay Park/Oakland, Calif., 1985-86; asst. regional mgr. no. Calif. and Nev. Allright Calif., Inc., 1986; regional mgr. no. Calif. Allright Sierra/ Nev., 1986—. Republican. Home: 34857 Skylark Dr Union City CA 94587 Office: Allright Calif Inc 1624 Franklin St #722 Oakland CA 94612

BOGARD-REYNOLDS, CHRISTINE ELIZABETH, financial services executive; b. Aberdeen, Md., Apr. 15, 1954; d. Charles Francis and Donna June (Mosbaugh) Bogard; divorced; 1 child, Zachary Kagan. Student, U. Colo., 1972-73. Adminstrv. asst. Lange Co., Broomfield, Colo., 1973-74; field sales and service rep. Bowman Products Div., Denver, 1974-75; cashier Regency Inn, Denver, 1975-76; gen. mgr., sec.-treas., Edison Agy. Inc., Denver, 1976-81; gen. mgr. Edison Press, Inc., Englewood, Colo., 1979-80, 81; advt. dir. Blinder, Robinson & Co., Englewood, 1981-89; ptnr., v.p. Market Svcs., 1989—. Active fundraising Passages, Inc., Contacts for Kids Sake, Denver, 1987—, Rocky Mountain Multiple Sclerosis Ctr. Mem. Direct Mktg. Assn., Denver Advt. Fedn., Am. Mgmt. Assn. Home: 6860 S Bannock #H Littleton CO 80120 Office: Blinder Robinson & Co 4643 S Ulster St Ste 1360 Denver CO 80237

BOGART, WANDA LEE, interior designer; b. Ashville, N.C., Feb. 26, 1939; d. Bob West and Virginia Elizabeth (Worley) McLemore-Snyder; m. Sterling X. Bogart, Feb. 12, 1962; children: Kevin Sterling, Kathleen Elisabeth. BA, San Jose (Calif.) State U., 1961. Tchr. Redondo Beach (Calif.) Sch. Dist., 1962-65; free-lance interior designer Ladera, Calif., 1970-75; head designer MG Interior Design, Orange, Calif., 1975-80; prin., pres. Wanda Bogart Interior Design Inc., Orange, 1980—. Contbr. articles to profl. jours. Named on of Top 20 Interior Designers in So. Calif. Ranch and Coast Mag., 1987. Mem. Internat. Soc. Interior Design, Orange C. of C. Office: Wanda Bogart Interior Design Inc 1440 E Chapman Ave Orange CA 92666

BOGDAN, LIVIUS SILVIU, real estate developer; b. Bucharest, Romania, Nov. 28, 1932; s. Silviu and Margaret (Laurentzy) B.; m. Florina Tanasescu, Feb. 22, 1955 (div. 1957); m. Margareta Batsu, July 2, 1962. MA, Archtl. Inst., Romania, 1955; BArch, Met. Collegiate, London, 1966. Am. Reg. Architect; lic. personal property broker, Calif.; cert. registered appraiser, Ariz. Dir. architecture and engring. Govt. Agy., Romania, 1957-66; v.p., sr. project dir. Welton/Becket, N.Y.C., 1967-78; pres. 1st Regency Devel. Corp., N.Y., Fla., London, 1978-84; v.p. E&E Devel. Corp., L.A., 1985-87; pres. Regal Regency Devel. Corp, North Hollywood, Calif., 1988—; mortgage underwriter, Ariz., 1983. Mem. Condo Developers Council of Am., Am. Land Devel. Assn., Am. Hotel and Motel Assn., Merchants-Brokers Exchange, Audobon, Masons. Republican.

BOGGAN, DANIEL, JR., city administrator; b. Albion, Mich., Dec. 9, 1945; s. Daniel and Ruthie Jean (Crum) B.; m. Jacqueline (Boggan,) Oct. 4, 1977 (div.); children: DeVone, Daniel, Dhanthan, Alike. BA, Albion Coll., 1967; MSW, U. Mich., 1968. Clin. supr. West Campus, Starr Commonwealth for Boys, 1968-70; asst. city mgr., Jackson, Mich., 1970-72; dep. city mgr., then city mgr., Flint, Mich.; dir. mgmt. services City of Portland, Oreg., 1976-78; asst. chief adminstrv. officer San Diego County, Calif., 1978-79; adminstr. Essex County, N.J., 1979-81; city mgr., Berkeley, Calif., 1982-86; former mem. faculty Jackson Community Coll., Portland State U., Upsala Coll.; assoc. vice chancellor Bus. Adminstrv. Services, U. Calif., Berkeley, 1986, acting vice chancellor, 1986-87, vice chancellor, 1987—. Bd. dirs. local United Way 1971-72. Recipient Soc. Afro Am. Police award, 1974; named an Outstanding Young Man Am., U.S. Jaycees, 1974, Outstanding Black Pub. Adminstr., 1987. Mem. Internat. City Mgrs. Assn., Am. Mgmt. Assn., NAACP (Outstanding Youth Services award 1965). Democrat. Baptist. Office: 2180 Milvia Berkeley CA 94708

BOGGIO, DENNIS RAY, architect; b. Detroit, Jan. 28, 1953; s. Michael Anthony and Esther Theresa Boggio; m. Meredith Coleen Ream, June 25, 1983. BArch, Ohio State U., 1975; MArch, U. Colo., 1977. Lic. architect, Colo., Wyo., Utah, N.M., Ga., Ariz., Nev. Ptnr. Lantz-Boggio Architects, Denver, 1980—; visiting critic Sch. Architecture, U. Colo., Denver, 1981—. Recipient Design Excellence award USAF Acad., 1985. Mem. AIA, Denver C. of C., Centennial C. of C. Lodge: Rotary. Home: 8101 E Dartmouth #53 Denver CO 80231 Office: Lantz-Boggio Architects 5200 DTC Pkwy #500 Denver CO 80111

BOGNAR, CHARLES RALPH, marketing manager; b. Phila., Feb. 2, 1926; s. Charles S. and Anna Bognar. Student Pa. State U., 1957-67; m. Bernadine L. Schantz, Oct. 2, 1948. Tool and model maker in machine shop Franklin Inst. Research Labs., Phila., 1949-55, sr. tech. assoc. friction lubrication div., 1955-70, sr. test engr. utilities services group, 1970-73; mgr. test ops. and cofounder turbo exptl. div. Turbo Research, West Chester, Pa., 1973-75; cofounder Energy Tech., Inc., West Chester, 1975, v.p., dir. mktg., 1975-79; new bus. devel. mktg. spl. services div. Ebasco Services, Inc., N.Y.C., 1979-80, mgr. project devel./mktg. for process indsl. div., Los Angeles, 1980-83, mgr. project devel./mktg. for indsl. bus. devel. for Pacific S.W. and Hawaii, 1983-86; regional sales mgr. Pall Well Tech. Corp. (subs. Pall Micro Trinity Corp.), 1986—. Mem. ASME, Research Engrs. Soc. Am., Sigma Xi. Mem. Christian Ch. Home: 817 Quailridge Dr #30 Bakersfield CA 93309 Office: 920 Wible Rd Ste 2A Bakersfield CA 93304 also: 2200 Northern Blvd East Hills NY 11548

BOGRAKOS, WILLIAM LOUIS, osteopathic physician, air force officer; b. Dover, N.H., Aug. 31, 1954; s. Louis and Evangeline (Pierrochakow) B.; m. Iris Michelle Monteith, May 25, 1985. BA, U. N.H., 1977; DO, New Eng. Coll. Osteo. Medicine, 1985. Rsch. asst. in psychopharmacology Lenox Hill Hosp., N.Y.C., 1978-79; intern Bapt. Med. Ctr., N.Y.C., 1985-86; commd. capt. USAF, 1986; emergency room physician 92d Strategic Hosp., Fairchild AFB, Wash., 1986—. Recipient physician recognition award AMA, 1988; Am. Heart Assn. fellow, 1984. Mem. Am. Osteo. Assn., N.W. Ki Soc. Republican. Greek Orthodox. Office: SGH/GE 92 Strategic Hosp Fairchild AFB WA 99011

BOGUMILL, MICHAEL THOMAS, federal agency executive; b. Owen, Wis., Dec. 20, 1938; s. Edward Leonard and Clara Emma (Pierce) B. BS, U. Wis., Eau Claire, 1961; MA in Teaching, U. N.C., 1970. Cert. tchr. Wis., Calif., specialized law enforcement officer Calif. Tchr. Auburndale (Wis.) Pub. Sch., 1961-63, Neillsville (Wis.) Pub. Sch., 1963-69, Hilmar (Calif.) Unified Sch. Dist., 1969-70; food and drug inspector Bur. Food and Drugs, Berkeley, Calif., 1971-73; food and drug supervising inspector Bur. Food and Drugs, Los Angeles, 1973-78; food and drug program coordinator Bur. Food and Drugs, Sacramento, 1978-88; compliance officer U.S. Consumer Product Safety Commn., L.A., 1989—. Contbr. articles to profl. jours. Recipient Cert. Appreciation U.S. Consumer Product Safety Commn., 1982, 87. Mem. AAAS, The Cousteau Soc., The Nature Conservancy, Assn. Food and Drug Ofcls., Western Assn. Food and Drug Officials, Nat. Council Against Health Fraud, Sacramento Bowling Assn. (bd. dirs. 1984-89), River City Bowlers (sec., treas. 1983-88), Nat. Wildlife Found., Smithsonian Assocs., Nat. Apple Works Users Group, Kiwanis (pres. Neillsville 1968-69). Democrat. Roman Catholic. Home: 1820 N La Brea Ave #10 Los Angeles CA 90046-3014 Office: US Consumer Product Safety Commn 4221 Wilshire Blvd Ste 220 Los Angeles CA 90010

BOHANNAN, PAUL JAMES, anthropologist, writer, former university administrator; b. Lincoln, Nebr., Mar. 5, 1920; s. Hillory and Hazel (Truex) B.; m. Laura Marie Smith, Mar. 15, 1943 (div. 1975); 1 son, Denis Michael; m. Adelyse D'Arcy, Feb. 28, 1981. B.A., U. Ariz., 1947; B.Sc., Oxford U., Eng., 1949, Ph.D., 1951. Lectr. social anthropology Oxford (Eng.) U., 1951-56; asst. prof. anthropology Princeton (N.J.) U., 1956-59; prof. Northwestern U., Evanston, Ill., 1959-75, U. Calif., Santa Barbara, 1976-82; prof., dean social scis. and communications U. So. Calif., Los Angeles, 1982-87, prof. emeritus, 1987—. Author: Justice and Judgement, 1957, Africa and Africans, 1964, Divorce and After, 1970, All the Happy Families, 1985. Served to capt. U.S. Army, 1941-45. Decorated Legion of Merit. Mem. Am. Anthrop. Assn. (pres. 1979-80), Am. Ethnol. Soc. (dir. 1963-66), African Studies Assn. (pres. 1963-64), Social Sci. Research Council (dir. 1962-64).

BOHLMANN, DANIEL ROBERT, financial planner, lawyer; b. Portland, Oreg., Apr. 28, 1948; s. Walter Richard and Nora Laticia (DeCandido) B.; m. Sylvia Maria Martha Bachand, June 20, 1981. AA with honors, Multnomah Jr. Coll., 1969; BSBA in Polit. Sci., Lewis & Clark Coll., 1970; J.D., Northwestern Sch. Law, 1974. Bar: Oreg. 1976, U.S. Dist. Ct. Oreg., U.S. Ct. Appeals (9th cir.), U.S. Supreme Ct. Supr., Bohlmann & Bohlmann Investment Trust, 1970—; sole practice, Oreg., 1976—; chief exec. Atlas Internat. Investments, Ltd., 1981—; officer, co-owner, investor Investors Gen. Computer Software, Inc., 1981—; investor, founder Rangefinder Petroleum, Ltd., Black Giant Mining & Petroleum; founder, owner Sun West Energy, Inc.; owner Gem-Con, Inc., 1979-81, Hopps Body and Paint Shop, Inc., 1976-80; owner Racquet Club Cove Hotel/Apts. of Palm Springs; bd. dirs. Shakey's Pizza, Palm Springs. Internat. fin. advisor U.S. Presdl. Task Force, 1981-84; mem. subcom. Oreg. Bd. Edn., 1973-75; bd. dirs. Willamette Democratic Soc., 1979-81; precinct committeeman, Oreg., 1976, 78, 80; mem. U.S. Senatorial Bus. Adv. Bd., 1981-83; active Oreg. Arts Found.; mem. Palm Srinngs Desert Mus., L.A. Bicentennial Coordinating Com., 1975-76. With USAR, 1967. Named one of Outstanding Young Men of Am. U.S. Jaycees, 1978-85. Mem. Assn. M.B.A. Execs., Assn. Trial Lawyers Am., Oreg. Trial Lawyers Assn., Am. Judicature Soc., Am. Soc. Agrl. Engrs., Oreg.-U.S. and Palm Springs C. of C., Internat. Assn. Fin. Planners, U.S. Hist. Soc., Smithsonian Assocs., Am. Mgmt. Assn., Nat. Fedn. Ind. Businessmen, Nat. Life Underwriters Assn., Oreg. Environ. Council, U.S. Antique and Collectors Automobile Assn., Am. Legion, Calif. Apt. Owners Assn., U.S. Restaurant Owners Assn., Phi Alpha Delta, Phi Theta Kappa. Republican. Lutheran. Clubs: Variety (Palm Springs) , Columbia River Yacht, Desert Mus., Living Desert Reserve, Oreg. Auto Body Craftsmen Assn. Lodges: Rotary, Elks (nat. found. outstanding benefactor 1980). Contbr. articles to fin. jours. Address: Vista Las Palmas 1022 Friar Ct Palm Springs CA 92262

BOHMFALK, GERALD THOMAS, entomologist; b. Douglas, Ariz., Apr. 25, 1950; s. Dell Louis and Madelyn Ann (Dugan) B.; m. Cynthia Ann Taylor, Dec. 31, 1976; children: Holly Ann, Maddie Dell. BS, Tex. A&M U., 1972, MS, 1974, PhD, 1980. Teaching asst. Tex. A&M U., College Station, 1972-74; field inspector State of Tex., Austin, 1974-76; research assoc. Tex. A&M U., College Station, 1976; extension entomologist Tex. A&M U., San Angelo, 1976-80; field mgr. Sandoz, Inc., San Antonio, 1980-81; product mgr. Sandoz, Inc., San Diego, 1981-83; mktg. dir. Zoecon Corp., Dallas, 1983-84, research mgr., 1984-86; owner InterMountain Agy. Inc., Douglas, Ariz., 1986—; owner, pres. Growers AG Suppply, Willcox, Ariz., 1986—, Marlin's Saddle Shop, Douglas, 1986—. Author: Control of Cotton Insects, 1982; editor Use of Biocontrol, 1982. Pres. Entomology Graduates, College Station, 1980, San Angelo (Tex.) Council of Presidents, 1977; bd. dirs. Cochise County (Ariz.) Fair Bd., 1986-88. Named Outstanding Entomologist Cen. TEx. ARPE, 1979, Chmn. Honorary Two Flags Art Festival, 1986. Mem. Entomol. Soc. Am., Soc. Vector Ecologist, Biol. Research Inst., Am. Registry Profl. Entomologists, S.E. Ariz. Food and Fiber Coun., Assn. Invertebrate Pathologists, Rotary, Lions, Douglas C. of C. (pres.). Democrat. Roman Catholic. Office: InterMountain Ag Inc 930 G Ave Douglas AZ 85607

BOHN, CHERYL METCALFE, electronics company executive; b. Salem, Oreg., Jan. 4, 1955; d. Lee Floyd Metcalfe and Delores Irene (Ostrem) Bensor; m. John Scott Spencer, Aug. 7, 1974 (div. 1984); m. William Steven Bohn, Oct. 6, 1985. BA in Bus. Adminstrn., San Diego State U., 1984. Mgr. Exclusively Woman's Spa, San Diego, 1981-83; office mgr. Grantree Furniture, San Diego, 1983-84; lead saleswoman Grantree Furniture, 1984-85; sales mgr. Dir. Mktg. & Printing Co., San Diego, 1985-86; v.p. sales San Diego Micro Techs., 1986—. With USAF, 1974-78. Recipient spl. commendation City of San Diego, 1987, cert. of appreciation San Diego Mayor's Adv. Bd., 1987. Fellow Le Tip Mission Valley (sec. 1984-86, v.p. 1986-87, pres. 1987--), Internat. Dance Exercise Assn. Democrat. Office: San Diego Micro Techs 6725 Mesa Ridge Rd Ste 210 San Diego CA 92121

BOHN, DENNIS ALLEN, electrical engineer, consultant, writer; b. San Fernando, Calif., Oct. 5, 1942; s. Raymond Virgil and Iris Elouise (Johnson) B.; 1 dau., Kira Michelle; m. Patricia Tolle, Aug. 12, 1986. B.S.E.E. with honors, U. Calif.-Berkeley, 1972, M.S.E.E. with honors, 1974. Engring. technician Gen. Electric Co., San Leandro, Calif., 1964-72; research and devel. engr. Hewlett-Packard Co., Santa Clara, Calif., 1973; application engr. Nat. Semicondr. Corp., Santa Clara, 1974-76; engring. mgr. Phase Linear Corp., Lynnwood, Wash., 1976-82; v.p. research and devel., ptnr. RANE Corp., Everett, Wash., 1982—; founder TOLECO Systems, Kingston, Wash., 1980. Suicide and crisis ctr. vol., Berkeley, 1972-74, Santa Clara, 1974-76. Served with USAF, 1960-64. Recipient Am. Spirit Honor medal U.S. Air Force, 1961; Math. Achievement award Chem. Rubber Co., 1962-63. Mem. IEEE, Audio Engring. Soc., Tau Beta Pi. Libertarian. Editor: We Are Not Just Daffodils, 1975; contbr. poetry to Reason mag.; tech. editor Audio Handbook, 1976; contbr. articles to tech. jours.; columnist Polyphony mag., 1981-83. Patentee in field. Office: Rane Corp 10802 47th Ave W Everett WA 98204

BOHN, ROBERT F., university dean, management educator; b. L.A., Feb. 10, 1942; s. james Andrew and Madge (Hutchings) B.; m. Peggy Ann Pettit, June 3, 1965; children: Jeffrey, David, Matthew, Michael, Mark. BA, Brigham Young U., 1965, MBA, 1969, PhD, 1975. Cert. fin. planner. Banker Bank of Am., L.A., 1965-67, Zions 1st Nat. Bank, Salt Lake City, 1968; internat. banker Citicorp., N.Y.C. and Frankfurt, Fed. Republic Germany, 1969-71; fin. aid adminstr. Brigham Young U., Provo, Utah, 1971-72, prof., 1972-82; MBA dir. Golden Gate U., San Francisco, 1982-84, assoc. dean, 1984-86, dean, 1986-89; dean Sch. Fin. Golden Gate U., San Francisco, 1989—; fin. cons., Danville, Calif. Author (book) A Budge Book and Much More, 1980; columnist Salt Lake Tribune; contbr. articles to profl. jours. Trustee San Ramon Valley U. Sch. Dist., Danville, 1983-88, pres. sch. bd., 1987; mem. Calif. State Senate Subcom., Sacramento, 1987-88. Capt. U.S. Army, 1966-72. Mem. Acad. Fin. Svcs. (pres. 1986-87), Fin. Mgmt. Assn. (deans roundtable), Assn. Mormon Counselors and Psychotherapists, Western Acad. Mgmt. Republican. Office: Golden Gate U Sch Fin Services 536 Mission St San Francisco CA 94526

BOHOSKEY, BERNICE FLEMING, rancher, mineral-land owner, writer; b. Seattle, Feb. 9, 1918; d. Katherine Elizabeth Emmeluth; m. Woodward Bohoskey, Aug. 6, 1942 (dec.); children: Charles W., Katherine A., Michael J., Constance E. Student, Mills Coll., Oakland, Calif., 1935-36, Cornish Sch. Arts, Seattle, 1936-38. Model various newspapers. mags., 1936-38; mem. Earl Carroll's Vanities; actress various movies, choreographer Hollywood, Calif.; ptnr. Yakima Ranches Ltd. Composer: (hymn) Blessed Trinity, 1948, (song) Just Give Me the Merry-Go-Round, 1949; contbr. articles to profl. jours. Republican. Episcopalian.

BOHRER, RUTH DAVIS, educator; b. Riverside, Utah, Nov. 25, 1930; d. Jesse and Vesta (Bigler) Davis; m. Leroy P. Bohrer, Jan. 24, 1950 (dec. Mar. 1967); children: Carson, Lorraine Bohrer Waterhouse, Jacqueline Bohrer Barth, Susan Bohrer Allen, Betty. BS in Elem. Edn., Weber State Coll., 1969, BS in Secondary Edn., 1975, MEd, 1980; MEd, Utah State U., 1980. Elem. tchr. Ogden (Utah) City Schs., 1969-81, mid. sch. tchr., 1981—. Vol. local polit. candidate, 1988. Democrat. Mormon. Home: 6109 South 2175 East Ogden UT 84403

BOILANGER, MITZI LU, nurse; b. Cleve., Dec. 14, 1953; d. Herbert Merl and Ruby Louise (Parrott) B. BS in Nursing, U. Evansville, 1977; MS in Nursing, U. Calif., San Francisco, 1983. RN, cert. in Inpatient Obstetrics. Clin. nurse I U. Hosps. Cleve., 1977-78; clin. nurse II U. Calif. Davis Med. Ctr., Sacramento, 1978-81; perdiem nurse U. Calif., San Francisco, 1981-83; staff nurse, nursing instr. U. Va. Hosp., Charlottesville, 1983-86; clin. nurse specialist obstetrics Sutter Meml. Hosp. Perinatal Ctr., Sacramento, 1986—. Contbr. papers and articlea to profl. jours. Active Keeping Kids Healthy, Charlottesville, 1986. 1st lt. USAFR, 1987—. Mem. Nurses Assn. of the Am. Coll. Obstetricians & Gynecologists (chpt. coord. 1988—), Orgn. Obstetric, Gynecologic & Neonatal Nurses (coord. Jefferson chpt. 1985-86, conf. chmn. No. Calif. sect. 1988), Calif. Perinatal Assn., Sigma Theta Tau, Phi Kappa Phi. Democrat. Office: Sutter Meml Hosp 5275 F St Sacramento CA 95819

BOISSE, JOSEPH ADONIAS, library administrator; b. Marlboro, Mass., June 20, 1937; s. Anthony J. and Blanch Marie (Demers) B. BA, Stonehill Coll., 1963; MA, Brown U., 1965; MLS, Simmons Coll., 1967; EdD, Temple U., 1986. Regional librarian Va. Dept. Libraries, Montpelier, 1967-68, dep. state librarian, 1971-73; asst. library dir. Lawrence U., Appleton, Wis., 1968-71; dir. libraries U. Wis.-Parkside, Kenosha, 1973-79, Temple U., Phila., 1979-83; univ. librarian U. Calif., Santa Barbara, 1983—; bd. govs. Research Libraries Group, Stanford, Calif., 1981—; dir. Ctr. for Research Libraries, Chgo., 1983—. Contbr. numerous articles to profl jours. Recipient Disting. Service award Wis. Library Assn., 1978. Mem. ALA, Assn. Coll. & Research Libraries (v.p. 1987-88, pres. 1988-89). Home: 911 W Campus Ln Goleta CA 93117 Office: Univ of Calif Univ Library Santa Barbara CA 93106

BOISSONEAU, ROBERT ALLEN, educator; b. Detroit, Sept. 23, 1937; s. Sylvester Napoleon Boissoneau and Dorothea Verjean (DeLamarter) Ball; m. Jo Ellen Marie Fitzgerald, Oct. 15, 1960; children: Mark N., Deborah Jean, Keith Allen. BA, Eastern Mich. U., 1960; MHA, Va. Commonwealth U., 1965; PhD, Ohio State U., 1974; DS (hon.), Ind. No. Grad. Sch. Profl. Mgmt., 1979. Asst. adminstrn. Detroit Meml. Hosp., 1965-67; adminstr. of Means Hall Ohio State U., Columbus, 1967-69, instr., 1969-72; asst. prof. U. Mo., Columbia, 1972-75; dean coll. human services Eastern Mich. U., Ypsilanti, 1975-80; prof. coll. bus. Ariz. State U., Tempe, Ariz., 1980—; cons. Mich. Dept. Mental Health, Lansing, 1978, G.E. Dantona and Assocs., Inc., Phoenix, 1982—, The Health Cen. System, Mpls., 1984—. Author: Continuing Education in the Health Professions, 1980, Health Care Organization and Development, 1986; contbr. articles to profl. jours. Active Planning Com. Community Adv. Bd., St. Joseph Mercy Hosp., Ann Arbor, Mich. 1976-77; chmn. Legis. Com. Adv. Bd., Desert Samaritan Hosp., Mesa, Ariz., 1982-83; judge Profl. Secs. Internat., Phoenix, 1983. Served to 1st lt. U.S. Army, 1960-62. Mem. The Acad. Mgmt., Am. Hosp. Assn., Am. Soc. Allied Health Professions (editorial bd. 1983—). Office: Ariz State U Coll Bus Tempe AZ 85287

BOKELMANN, STANLEY OTTO, construction consultant; b. Roselle, Ill., Feb. 3, 1923; s. Henry August and Louise Ann (Poppe) B.; married, May 24, 1946; children: Beth, Jean, Bill and John (twins). BS, U. Wis., 1949; MBA, U. Nev., Las Vegas, 1971. Project mgr. Erdman Constrn., Madison, Wis., 1949-51; asst. chief expeditor Liberty Power Co., Baraboo, Wis., 1951-53; gen. contractor Bokelmann and Assocs., Madison, 1953-60; archtl. inspector Weiler and Strang, Madison, 1960-63; dir. sch. constrn. Clark County Sch. Dist., Las Vegas, 1963-79; cons. constrn. Las Vegas, 1979—. Served to staff sgt. USAF, 1942-45, PTO. Mem. Am. Soc. Test Materials, Urethane Foam Contractor's Assn., Am. Arbitration Assn., Constrn. Specifications Inst. Republican. Home and Office: 4604 Carriage Ln Las Vegas NV 89119

BOLAK, WILLIAM MICHAEL, dentist; b. Nyack, N.Y., Mar. 29, 1951; s. William J. and Dorothy M. (Rose) B.; m. Diane Robinson, Aug. 14, 1971; children—Kimberly Ann, Lauren Marie, Jason Matthew, Mark Andrew. B.A. in Chemistry, Cornell U., 1972; D.M.D., Fairleigh Dickinson U., 1976. Pvt. practice dentistry, Alamogordo, N.Mex. Served to capt. USAF, 1976-79. Mem. ADA, Acad. Gen. Dentistry. Office: 3400 High Sierra Ave Alamogordo NM 88310 Office: 880 Telshor Blvd Las Cruces NM 88001

BOLAND-ROBILLARD, VIRGINIA ANNE, dentist; b. New Brunswick, N.J., Dec. 8, 1958; d. Martin Stephen and Ruth Virginia (Larney) Boland; m. David Charles Robillard, May 30, 1987; 1 child. BS in Biology, Loyola U., Chgo., 1981, DDS, 1985. Pvt. practice Cleve., 1985-87, Tucson, 1988--. Mem. ADA, Acad. Gen. Dentistry, Am. Soc. Dentistry for Children, Am. Assn. Women Dentists, Chgo. Dental Soc. (assoc.), Delta Sigma Delta. Roman Catholic. Home: 4669 W Lessing Ln Tucson AZ 85741 Office: 4640 E Sunrise Tucson AZ 85718

BOLDEN, EDWARD LEWIS, JR., civil engineer, surveyor; b. El Paso, Tex., May 26, 1926; s. Edward Lewis and Paulethis Elizabeth (Clark) B.; m. Anna Rose Bolden, Aug. 14, 1949; children: Norman Edward, Michael Dwuane. BS, U. Ill., 1949. Registered profl. engr., surveyor. Civil designer, survey party chief Ill. Hwy. Dept., Ottawa, 1949-55; civil designer Calif. Div. Hwys., L.A., 1956-57; civil engr. Lovett and Assocs., Pico Rivera, Calif., 1957-59, Nerenbaum and Assocs., L.A., 1959-60, McIntire and Quiros, Monterey Park, Calif., 1961-63; chief engr. Andel Engring. Co., Newhall, Calif., 1964—; engr. in charge, cons. various engring. projects. pres. Boys Club (pres. 1970-71), Girls Club, Newhall, 1970; chmn. bldg. com. Henry Mayo Newhall Meml. Hosp., Valencia, Calif., 1971-76; moderator San Fernando Presbytery, San Fernando Valley, Calif., 1989. Recipient Excellence in Alley Design award Portland Cement Co., Venice, Calif., 1975; named Citizen of Yr. Santa Clarita Valley C. of C., Newhall, 1970. Mem. Calif. Coun. Civil Engrs. and Land Surveyors, Rotary (pres. Newhall chpt. 1970-71, gov. dist. 526 1984-85.). Democrat. Home and Office: 24707 San Fernando Rd PO Box 428 Newhall CA 91322

BOLDEN, MARK ALLEN, infosystem specialist, consultant; b. San Antonio, Oct. 9, 1952; s. Charles A. and Alice Louise (Krause) B.; divorced; 1 child, Patrick Matthew. BS in Math., N.Mex. Inst. Mining and Tech., 1974. Systems programmer IBM Corp., Kingston, N.Y., 1974-78; systems programmer IBM Corp., Tuscon, Ariz., 1978-85, human factors engr., 1985—. Chmn. platform com. Ariz. Libertarians, 1981, chmn. 1980 ballots status com., Pima County Libertarians, 1980; pres. Ridge 22 Condominium Assn., Tucson. Mem. Human Factors Soc. (assoc.), IEEE, Soc. for Tech. Communication. Republican. Home: 7662 56 E 22d St Tucson AZ 85710

BOLDEN, MICHAEL GERONIA, finance company executive; b. Sumter, S.C., Nov. 26, 1953; s. Vermell Bolden. AA, Am. River Coll., Sacramento, Calif., 1978. Enlisted USAF, 1974; air traffic controller 1982d Communications Squadron, Travis AFB, Calif., 1974-82; resigned USAF, 1984; securities broker Robert Thomas Securities, Laguna Hills, Calif., 1980—; tax preparer Bolden Fin. Services Group Inc., Sacramento, Calif., 1980—; ins. agt. First Capital Life Ins., La Jolla, Calif., 1980-88; gen. ptnr. Bell & Assocs., Sacramento, 1986—, Entertainer Network Services, Sacramento, 1987—, Chanteclair Realty and Investments, Sacramento, 1987—. Bd. dirs. Celebration Arts Dance, Sacramento, 1986-88, LaSalle Thompson Kings for Kids, 1986-88, Brotherhood Crusade, 1988—; active Urban League, Concerned Black Men of Sacramento; mentor Grant Union High Sch., Sacramento, 1987-88. Named one of Outstanding Young Men of Am. U.S. Jaycees, 1985. Mem. NAACP, Sacramento C. of C., Sacramento Black C. of C., Sacramento Hispanic C. of C. Clubs: International Fitness, Price, Thunderbird; Tahoe Beach and Ski. Office: BFSG Inc 9837 Folsom Blvd Ste 1 Sacramento CA 95827

BOLENDER, DAVID FRANCIS, utility company executive. Grad. Colo. Sch. of Mines, 1954. Pres. Pacific Power & Light Co., Denver. Office: Pacific Power & Light Co 920 SW 6th Ave Portland OR 97204 •

BOLF, RON B., quality assurance manager; b. Lebanon, Oreg., Oct. 7, 1954; s. Bernard R. and Lillie M. (Urubek) B.; m. Corinne S. Sanders, July 21, 1984. BS in Microbiology, Oreg. State U., 1977, MS in Microbiology, 1979. Microbiologist Miller Brewing Co., Irwindale, Calif., 1979-81; engr. Allergan Med. Optics, Irvine, Calif., 1981-83, staff engr., 1983, quality assurance mgr., 1983-85, quality assurance ops. mgr., 1985—. Contbr. author: Point and Non Point Pollution, 1979. Mem. Am. Soc. Microbiology, Am. Soc. Quality Control, Regulatory Affairs Profl. Soc. Club: Allergan Med. Optics Mgmt. (pres. 1987). Home: 26181 Camino Adelanto Mission Viejo CA 92691 Office: Allergan Med Optics 9701 Jeronimo Rd Irvine CA 92718

BOLIN, RICHARD LUDDINGTON, industrial development consultant; b. Burlington, Vt., May 13, 1923; s. Axel Birger and Eva Madora (Luddington) B.; m. Jeanne Marie Brown, Dec. 18, 1948; children: Richard Luddington, Jr., Douglas, Judith, Barbara, Elizabeth. BS in Chem. Engring., Tex. A&M U., 1947; MS in Chem. Engring., MIT, 1950. Jr. rsch. engr. Humble Oil & Refining Co., Baytown, Tex., 1947-49; staff mem. Arthur D. Little, Inc., Cambridge, Mass., 1950-56, Caribbean office mgr. San Juan, 1957-61, gen. mgr., Mex., 1961-72; pres. Internat. Parks, Inc., Flagstaff, Ariz., 1973—; dir. The Flagstaff Inst., 1976—; dir. Parque Indsl. de Nogales, Nogales, Sonora, Mex. With U.S. Army, 1942-46. Mem. World Export Processing Zones Assn. (dir., secretariat 1985—), Univ. Club (Mex.). Office: PO Box 986 Flagstaff AZ 86002

BOLIN, VERNON SPENCER, microbiologist, consultant; b. Parma, Idaho, July 9, 1913; s. Thadeus Howard Bolin and Jennie Bell Harm; m. Helen Epling, Jan. 5, 1948 (div. 1964); children—Rex, Janet, Mark; m. Barbara Sue Chase, Aug. 1965; children—Vladimir, Erik. B.S., U. Wash., 1942; M.S., U. Minn. 1949. Teaching asst. U. Minn.-Mpls., 1943-45; research assoc. U. Utah, Salt Lake City, 1945-50, fellow in surgery, 1950-52; research virologist Jensen-Salsbery Labs., Inc., Kansas City, Mo., 1952-57; research assoc. Wistar Inst. U. Pa., 1957-58; research virologist USPHS, 1958-61; founder Bolin Lab., 1959; dir. Bolin Labs., Inc., Phoenix. Contbr. articles to profl. jours. Served with U.S. Army, 1931-33. Mem. N.Y. Acad. Scis., Phi Mu Chi. Home: 4812 W Greenway Rd Glendale AZ 85036

BOLLER, JOHN HALL, JR., minister; b. N.Y.C., Sept. 4, 1949; s. John Hall Sr. and Claudia (Pinza) B.; m. Lillian Wong, June 1, 1974; children: Alisha Carole, Jenna Kaitlin. BS, Calif. State U., Long Beach, 1970; M of Christian Theology, San Francisco Theol. Sem., San Anselmo, Calif., 1972, M of Divinity, 1973; MS, Calif. State U., San Diego, 1978. Youth minister Chinese Congl. Ch., San Francisco, 1970-73; campus pastor U. Calif., Irvine, 1973-74; asst. pastor St. Mark's Presbyn. Ch., Newport Beach, Calif., 1973-74; assoc. pastor Coll. Park Presbyn. Ch., San Diego, 1974-79; pastor Northminster Presbyn. Ch., San Diego, 1979—; marriage, family and child counselor, San Diego, 1986—. Chairperson Dropout Prevention Roundtable, San Diego, 1987—; moderator Presbytery of San Diego, 1988. Mem. Calif. Assn. Marriage and Family Therapists, Assn. Presbyn. Ch. Educators, Witherspoon Soc. Democrat. Club: San Diego Train. Office: Northminster Presbyn Ch 4324 Clairemont Mesa Blvd San Diego CA 92117-1945

BOLLES, RONALD KENT, music educator; b. El Paso, Dec. 29, 1948; s. Robert Benjamin and Audrey Nadine (Hawkins) B.; m. Terri Sue Alburger Aka Reina Marie, Apr. 7, 1979; children: Gina Marie, Heather Michelle. BA in Music, San Diego State Coll., 1971, MEd, 1975. Cert. secondary life tchr. Tchr. Castle Pk. Jr. High Sch., Chula Vista, Calif., 1972-74; dir. choir Pacific Beach United Meth., San Diego, 1973-75, All Hallows Cath. Ch., La Jolla, Calif., 1978-79, First Christian Ch., Chula Vista, 1980-87; tchr. Bonita Vista Jr. High Sch., Chula Vista, 1985—, Bonita Vista Sr. High Sch., Chula Vista, 1974—; dist. vocal music chmn. Sweetwater Union High Sch. Dist., Chula Vista, 1980-86; site div. chmn. Bonita Vista High Sch., 1975-77. Dir. high sch. show choir "The Music Machine", 1976-88; author (with Terri Sue Bolles) Preparing an Awesome Musical Theater Audition, 1983. Mem. PTA, Chula Vista, 1984-88. named Tchr. Yr. San Diego County, 1987, Bonita Vista High Sch., Chula Vista, 1983. Mem. San Diego City/County Music Educators (pres. 1983-88), Music Educators Nat. Conf. Assn., Calif. Music Educators Assn., Am. Choral Dirs. Assn., So. Calif. Vocal Assn. Office: Bonita Vista High Sch 751 Otay Lakes Rd Chula Vista CA 92013

BOLNICK, DAVID ALAN, physiologist, researcher; b. Long Beach, Calif., Oct. 25, 1955; s. Leonard L. and Elaine I. (Applebaum) B.; m. Jennifer A. Hoffman, Sept. 23, 1984; 1 child, Reuven S. BS, U. Calif., Davis, 1978, MS, 1982, PhD, 1984. Postgrad. researcher U. Calif., Davis, 1978-84; postdocoral researcher U. Calif., San Francisco, 1984—, computer programmer, 1988—; computer programmer Photographic Software, San Francisco, 1986—. Contbr. articles to profl. jours. Recipient Individual Nat. Research Service award NIH, 1985-88. Democrat. Jewish.

BOLTE, KEITH ALAN, manufacturing company executive; b. Huron, S.D., Jan. 9, 1944; s. Irven Harold and Mildred Emma (Langbehn) B.; m. Connie Beth Castleman, Oct. 1, 1965; children: Timothy Alan, Chad Anthony. BA in Polit. Sci., Huron Coll., 1969; MEd in Guidance and Counseling, S.D. State U., 1974. Social worker S.D. Dept. of Social Svcs., Rapid City, 1970-73; quality assurance specialist S.D. Dept. of Social Svcs., Huron, 1973-75; asst. state dir. S.D. Dept. of Social Svcs., Pierre, S.D., 1975-78; prin. ptnr. Arthur Young & Co., Seattle, 1978-80; corp. dir. productivity Intel Corp., Santa Clara, Calif., 1981-84; pres. N.W. Counsel to Mgmt., Portland, Oreg., 1985-86; chief exec. officer Pacificrane Internat. Inc., Portland, 1987—; corp. advisor Seattle Pacific Industries, 1986—, Nike, Inc., Portland, 1985—. Contbr. articles to profl. publs. Named Profl. Analyst Yr. Sci. Mgmt. Corp., 1979. Fellow Nat. Truck Equipment Assn.; mem. Def. Preparedness Assn., Am. Inst. Indsl. Engrs., Christian Businessman, Phi Kappa Phi, Pi Sigma Alpha. Republican. Baptist. Home: 11565 SW Walnut St Tigard OR 97223 Office: Pacificrane Internat Inc 4243 SE International Way Portland OR 97222

BOLTON, EARL CLINTON, lawyer, consultant; b. Los Angeles, Aug. 22, 1919; s. John R. and Hazel A. (Van Order) B.; m. Jean Studley, June 27, 1942; children—Barbara Bolton Poley, Elizabeth Ann Bolton Newell, William Earl. A.B. magna cum laude, U. So. Calif., 1941, J.D., 1948; LL.D. (hon.), U. San Diego, 1963. Bar: Calif. 1949, U.S. Supreme Ct. 1958. Staff, Coordinator Inter-Am. Affairs, N.Y.C., also Washington, 1941; v.p., treas. Nat. Public Discussions, Inc., N.Y.C., 1942; lectr. polit. sci. dept. U. So. Calif., 1946-48; asst. prof. U. So. Calif. (Coll. Liberal Arts and Sch. Commerce), 1948-50, assoc. prof. law and v.p. planning, 1952-60; spl. asst. to pres. U. Calif., Berkeley, 1960-61; v.p. univ. relations U. Calif., 1962-64, v.p. adminstrn., 1964-66, v.p. govtl. relations, 1966-68, v.p. adminstrn., 1968-70; v.p. Booz, Allen & Hamilton, Inc., Chgo., 1970-79; of counsel firm Willis Butler & Scheifly, Los Angeles, 1979-81, Pepper, Hamilton & Scheetz, 1981-84, Earl C. Bolton & Assocs., 1984—. Editorial bd.: Law Rev., U. So. Calif., 1947-48. Mem. Calif. Gov.'s Mental Health Adv. Com., Citizens' Legis. Adv. Com.; past chmn., founding mem. Calif. Scholarship Com. Served to capt. USNR, 1942-46, 50-52. Mem. State Bar Calif., Order of Coif, Phi Beta Kappa, Phi Kappa Phi. Home: 630 S Orange Grove Pasadena CA 91105 Office: 1143 Leeward Ln Alameda CA 94501

BOLTON, MARTHA O., writer; b. Searcy, Ark., Sept. 1, 1951; d. Lonnie Leon and Eunice Dolores (Stevens) Ferren; m. Russell Norman Bolton, Apr. 17, 1970; children: Russell Norman II, Matthew David, Anthony Shane. Grad. high sch., Reseda, Calif. Freelance writer for various artists including Phyllis Diller, Joan Rivers, 1975-86; newspaper columnist Simi Valley Enterprise, Simi, Calif., 1979-87; staff writer Bob Hope, 1986—. Author: A Funny Thing Happened to Me on my Way Through the Bible, 1985, A View from the Pew, 1986, What's Growing Under Your Bed?, 1986, Tangled in the Tinsel, 1987, 'So, How'd I Get to be in Charge of the Program?' Help Book, 1988, Humorous Monologues, 1989. Pres. Vista Elem. Sch. PTA, Simi, 1980-81. Recipient Emmy award nomination for outstanding achievement in music and lyrics Nat. Acad. TV Arts and Scis., 1988. Mem. Nat. League of Am. Pen Women (br. pres. 1984-86, state letters chmn. 1986-88, Woman of Achievement award Simi Valley br. 1984), Writers Guild Am. West, ASCAP, Soc. Children's Book Writers.

BOLTON, ROBERT FLOYD, construction executive; b. Dunlap, Iowa, Oct. 18, 1942; s. Russel J. And Mary Jane (Lacey) B.; m. Mary Louise Hartman, May 15, 1988. Lic. contractor. Sole practice farming Dunlap, Iowa, 1967-72; supr. Phillips Constrn. Co., Cottonwood, Ariz., 1972-84; contracto Bolton Bldg. and Devel. Co., Sedona, Ariz., 1984—; cons. in field. With U.S. Army, 1964-66. Mem. Nat. Assn. Realtors, Nat. Assn. Home Builders, Am. Soc. Home Inspectors, C. of C., VFW, Meth. Mens Fellowship Club. Republican. Methodist. Home: 90 Evening Glow Pl Sedona AZ 86336 Office: Bolton Bldg & Devel Co PO Box 754 Sedona AZ 86336

BOMZE, F(ERN) BARBARA, clinical social worker; b. N.Y.C., May 12, 1934; d. Philip and Estelle Mildred (Rothnagel) Stein; m. Marc Raymond Bomze, Feb. 12, 1956 (div. Jan. 1985); children: Rhonda Jarema, Jay Bomze, Michelle Bomze. BA, U. Miami, Coral Gables, Fla., 1954; MSW, Wayne State U., 1976. Cert. social worker, marriage counselor, Mich.; lic. social worker, marriage and family counselor, Calif. Psychiat. social worker Henry Ford Hosp., West Bloomfield, Mich., 1976-83; clin. social worker, ptnr. Saddleback Counseling and Psychotherapy Assocs., Laguna Hills, Calif., 1984—; cons. Saddleback Women's Ctr., Laguna Hills, 1985—, Saddleback Hosp. Cardiac Rehab., 1986—; mem. faculty eating disorder program U. Calif.-Irvine. Mem. Nat. Assn. Social Workers (cert., diplomate, bd. dirs. referral svc. 1985—), Calif. Assn. Marriage and Family Therapists, Am. Group Psychotherapy Assn., Saddleback C. of C., Lions Club (charter mem. of Mission Viejo, newsletter editor). Democrat. Jewish. Office: Saddleback Counseling Assocs 23521 Paseo de Valencia #302A Laguna Hills CA 92653

BONACINA, JOSEPH ANDREW, retired lawyer, writer; b. Gravedona, Italy, Oct. 30, 1903; s. Antonio and Annunciata (Riella) B.; PhB, U. Santa Clara, 1927, JD, 1931; student Humboldt State Coll., 1926; m. Clare M. Valle, Nov. 28, 1928 (dec. May 1981); m. Eileen S. Stark, Dec. 5, 1981. Newspaper reporter San Jose (Calif.) Mercury Herald, San Jose News, San Francisco Examiner, 1923-36; dep. county clk., ct. clk. Santa Clara County, 1935-41; city atty. City of Sunnyvale (Calif.), 1942-48; practice, San Jose, 1951—; city atty. City of Campbell (Calif.), 1952-71, emeritus, 1971—; now writer. Active numerous civic orgns. Clubs: KC (4 deg.), St. Thomas More, others. Home: 3482 N Country Club Vista Circle Tucson AZ 85715

BONAPARTE, JOSEPH LINCOLN, cost engineer; b. Charleston, S.C., Dec. 31, 1947; s. Charles Sr. and Henrietta Marie (Spann) B. BS, Tuskegee (Ala.) Inst., 1971. Cost estimator B.G. Daxis Corp., Dayton, Ohio, 1977-81; mgr. Fling Constrn. Mgmt., Columbus, Ohio, 1981-82; cost engr. USN C.E. Corps, San Bruno, Calif., 1982--. Chmn. inter alumni coun. United Negro Coll. Fund, Oakland, Calif., 1986; supporter Omega Boys Club, Vallejo, Calif. Served with U.S. Army, 1971-75. Recipient ARCOM award Ohio Army N.G., 1982, Meritorious Svc. State award Calif. Army N.G., 1983. Mem. Tuskegee Alumni Club (reporter L.A. chpt. 1985-86). Democrat. Methodist. Home: 189 Crestwood Dr #10 Daly City CA 94015-3252

BONAR, ROLAND BIRT, educational administrator; b. El Paso, Tex., Jan. 24, 1934; s. Bernard E. and Dorothy L. (Birt) B.; student Calif. Inst. Tech., 1951-54, U. Tex. at El Paso, 1957-62; L.H.D., Lincoln Meml. U., 1968; Ph.D., Columbia U., 1972; children: Robert James, Marla Lynn, Michael G. Vice-pres., gen. mgr. Western GMC Truck Co., El Paso, 1955-60; tchr. Dale Carnegie courses N.Mex. and W. Tex., 1960-66; prin. Roland B. Bonar & Assos., presenting Dale Carnegie courses, Balt., 1966-73, Denver, 1973—; past pres. Dale Carnegie Internat. Sponsors Assn.; guest lectr. U. Md., 1968-74; chmn. bd. Explorex Oil Co., Houston, 1975—; past chmn. First Savs. & Loan of Orland Park, Chgo.; dir. Transportes de Ref de Mex. S.A., Bombas Turbinas de Mex. S.A., B & M Oil Co., N.Mex. Vice pres. Denver area Boy Scouts Am., 1973—; past chmn. fin. Denver area council; fin. dir., 1974-75; mem. Pres. Johnson's Council on Mental Retardation, 1965-68; mem. cabinet Mile Hi United Way, 1978—; bd. dirs. Balt. Cystic Fibrosis Found., 1966-70, U. Colo. Health Scis.; trustee Lincoln Meml. U., 1969-85. Served with USAF, 1950-54; Korea. Decorated D.F.C., Air medal; named outstanding citizen Albuquerque, 1972; Group Pres.'s awardee Dale Carnegie & Assos., 1974-76. Mem. Am. Soc. Tng. Dirs., Am. Mgmt. Assn., U. Tex., Columbia, Lincoln Meml. U. alumni assns., Denver C. of C., Colo. Assn. Commerce and Industry (chmn. fin.), Civil War Round Table. Republican. Lutheran. Clubs: Rolling Hills Country; Denver Rotary, Masons. Office: 210 University Blvd Ste 820 Denver CO 80206

BOND, ENNIE ANGEL, gaming industry executive; b. Windsor, Ont., Can., July 22, 1950; d. Joseph and Magdalena (Schlosser) Pocantos; m. Joesph Bond, Jan. 12, 1984 (div. Aug. 1986); 1 child, Cortney. BA, Oakland U., 1976; MA in Clin. Psychology, U. Houston, 1978; postgrad., U. Humanistic Studies, 1981-84. Blackjack dealer Caesars Palace, Las Vegas, 1979-87; blackjack/roulette dealer caesars Palace, Las Vegas, 1987—. Columnist Wheeling and Dealing, 1984—. Mem. NAFE, Am. Psychol. Assn., Am. Assn. Advancement Tension Control. Democrat. Home: 4323 Del Santos Dr Las Vegas NV 89121 Office: Caesars Palace 3570 Las Vegas Blvd Las Vegas NV 89109

BOND, RICHARD RANDOLPH, biology educator, legislator; b. Lost Creek, W.Va., Dec. 1, 1927; s. Harley Donovan and Marcella Randolph B.; m. Reva Stearns, Apr. 20, 1946; children: David, Philip, Josette, Michael. BS, Salem Coll., 1948, LHD (hon.), 1979; MS, W.Va. U., 1949; PhD, U. Wis., 1955; postdoctoral studies, U. Mich., 1958-95. Various teaching and fellowship positions 1949-59; dean of faculty Elmira (N.Y.) Coll., 1959-63; dean coll. of Liberal Arts U. Liberia, Monrovia, 1963-64; chief of party Cornell U. Project in Liberia, Monrovia, 1964-66; v.p. acad. affairs Ill. State U., Normal, 1966-71; pres. U. No. Colo., Greeley, 1971-81, pres. emeritus, prof. zoology, 1981-89; state rep. Colo. Gen. Assembly, Denver, 1984—; founder Nat. Student Exchange; cons., examiner North Cen. Accrediting Assn., 1969-82; bd. dirs. Greeley Nat. Bank; founder, bd. dirs. First. No. Savs. and Loan. Contbr. articles to profl. jours. Dir., chmn. Sunrise Community Health Ctr.; commr. Greeley Urban Renewal Assn.; founding mem. Dream Team on Dropout Prevention. Served with U.S. Army, 1945-47. NSF fellow, 1953-54; Am. Physiol. Soc. fellow, 1958; Carnegie Found. fellow in Coll. Adminstrn., 1958-59; recipient Legislator of Yr. award Disabled Am. Vets., Denver, 1988, Legislator of Yr. award Colo. Acad. Pediatrics, 1989. Mem. Am. Ornithologists Union, Am. Assn. Colls. and Univs. (bd. dirs. 1979-81), Colo. Assn. Colls. and Univs. (chmn. 1979-81), Rotary (bd. dirs. local chpt.), Sigma Xi. Democrat. Presbyterian. Home: 1954 25th Ave Greeley CO 80631

BOND, THOMAS MOORE, JR., labor mediation and arbitration executive; b. Louisville, Dec. 17, 1930; s. Thomas Moore and Louise Elleanor (Jones) B.; m. Kathryn Keith, Apr. 10, 1950 (dec.); children: Gilbert, Louise, Lela; m. Ethel Ayako Kuramitsu, Aug. 15, 1965; children: Richard, Jane, Julian Horace. BS in Econs., Ind. U., 1953. Bus. agt. organizer Hosp. Workers, San Francisco, 1961-65; internat. rep. organizer Svc. Employees' AFL-CIO, Louisville, 1965-70; exec. dir. Union Am. Physicians, San Francisco, 1973-78; owner Thomas Moore Bond & Assocs., Berkeley, Calif., 1979—; pvt. practice labor mediator and arbitrator, mgmt., labor cons., Berkeley, 1981—. Editor: The Negro Conservative, 1981. Bd. dirs. adv. com. for paralegal tng. Merritt Coll., Oakland, Calif., 1983; mem. labor commn. City of Berkeley, 1986-88. 1st lt. inf., U.S. Army, 1946-50. Mem Indsl. Rels. Rsch. Assn., Soc. Fed. Labor Rels. Profls., Inst. Advanced Law Study. Republican. Congregationalist. Office: Thomas Moore Bond & Assocs 2123 1/2 5th St Berkeley CA 94710

BONDAREFF, WILLIAM, psychiatry educator; b. Washington, Apr. 29, 1930; s. Leon and Gertrude Bondareff; children by previous marriage: Hyla, Sarah; m. Rita Kassoy, Jan. 2, 1988. BS in Zoology, George Washington U., 1951, MS in Zoology, 1952; PhD in Anatomy, U. Chgo., 1954; MD, Georgetown U., 1962. Lic. physician, Calif., Ill., Md. Rsch. assoc., instr. anatomy U. Chgo., 1955; rotating intern USPHS Hosp., Balt., 1962-63; resident in psychiatry Northwestern Meml. Hosp. Inst. Psychiatry, Chgo., 1978-80; asst. prof. anatomy Northwestern U., Evanston, Ill., 1963-65, assoc. prof., 1965-69, prof., 1969-78, chmn. dept. anatomy, 1970-78; prof. psychiatry and gerontology U. So. Calif., L.A., 1981—; mem. staff Hosp. Good Samaritan, L.A., 1981—, St. John's Hosp. and Health Ctr., L.A., 1981—, Norris Cancer Hosp., 1987—; physician/cons. VA Hosp., Downey, Ill., 1969-80, Jewish Home for Aged, Reseda, Calif., 1981—; vis. staff mem. medicine Passavant Pavilion Northwestern Meml. Hosp., 1972-80; dir. div. geriat. psychiatry U. So. Calif., 1981—; dir. U. So. Calif.-St. Barnabas Alzheimer Disease Ctr., 1985—; acting dir. dept. Gerontology Research Inst. Andrus Gerontology Ctr.-U. So. Calif., 1982; staff psychiatrist Los Angeles County Hosp., 1981—; past holder various com. offices Northwestern U. Editor Mechanisms of Aging and Devel., 1970—; assoc. editor Am. Jour. Anatomy, 1970-76; mem. editorial Bd. Alzheimer Disease and Associated Disorders-An Internat. Jour., 1985—, Neurobiology of Aging, 1980—; The Jour. of Gerontology, 1981-84; contbr. articles to profl. jours. Served with USPHS, 1955-63. USPHS fellow, 1955, U. Cambridge Clare Hall vis. fellow, 1980, Hughes Hall vis. fellow, 1988; scholar Allergy Found., 1960, U. Chgo.,

1953; recipient Career Devel. award Nat. Inst. Neurol. Disease and Blindness, 1966-69, Sesquicentennial award Hobart and William Smith Colls., 1972, Sandoz prize Internat. Assn. Gerontology, 1983, Alzheimer Disease and Related Disorders Assn. award, 1984; Fulbright Lectr., U. Goteborg, Sweden, 1967-68. Fellow AAAS (councilor 1970-74), Gerontol. Soc.; mem. Am. Assn. Anatomists (chmn. local com. ann. meeting 1969), Electron Microscope Soc. Am., Am. Soc. Cell Biology, Am. Acad. Neurology (chmn. neuroanatomical scis. sect. 1971-77), Soc. Neurosci., Assn. Anatomy Chmn. (councilor 1975-77), Am. Psychiat. Assn. (geriatrics task force 1981), Am. Geriat. Soc., Am. Assn. Geriat. Psychiatry (program com. 1984—, bd. dirs. 1985—), So. Calif. Psychiat. Soc., Internat. Psychogeriat. Assn., Cajal Club, Sigma Xi. Office: U So Calif Sch Medicine Mudd Bldg Rm 620 Dept Psychiatry 1333 San Pablo St Los Angeles CA 90033

BONDI, BERT ROGER, accountant, financial planner; b. Portland, Oreg., Oct. 2, 1945; s. Gene L. and Elizabeth (Poynter) B. BBA, U. Notre Dame, 1967. CPA, Colo., Calif., Wyo. Sr. tax acct. Price Waterhouse, Los Angeles, 1970-73; ptnr. Valentine Adducci & Bondi, Denver, 1973-76; sr. ptnr. Bondi & Co., Englewood, Colo., 1977—; dir. Citizens Bank. Bd. govs. Met. State Coll. Found. Served with U.S. Army, 1968-70. Mem. C. of C., Community Assns. Inst., Govt. Fin. Officers Assn., Home Builders Assn., Am. Inst. CPAs, Colo. Soc. CPAs, Wyo. Soc. CPAs. Roman Catholic. Clubs: Notre Dame, Metropolitan (Denver); Castle Pines Country. Home: 49 Glenalla Way Castle Rock CO 80104 Office: Bondi & Co 44 Inverness Dr E Bldg B Englewood CO 80112

BOND-UPSON, DEBORAH GWENDOLYN, educational administrator; b. Plainfield, N.J., July 1, 1949; d. Paterson and Gwendolyn Avis (Stenehjem) Bond; m. Leland Upson, Dec. 31, 1976; children: Gwendolyn, Alexandra, Max Carlos, Valery Blake. BA, Swarthmore Coll., 1971; postgrad., Inst. Allende, Guanajuato, Mex., 1972, 74; MDiv, Starr King Sch. for Ministry, Berkeley, Calif., 1976. Adminstr. No. Calif. region Stanley H. Kaplan Ednl. Ctr. Ltd., Larkspur, 1973—. Trustee Starr King Sch. for Ministry, 1978-85, chair search coms. for pres. and endowed professorship for woman theologian, 1985, 83; mem. Kentfield (Calif.) Schs. Found., 1986—. St. Lawrence Found. fellow, 1974. Mem. No. Calif. Ednl. Cons., Western Assn. Coll. Admissions Counselors. Democrat. Office: Stanley H Kaplan Ednl Ctr 20 Magnolia Ave Larkspur CA 94939

BONDURANT, DAVID WILLIAM, marketing professional; b. Kirksville, Mo., June 8, 1948; s. William George and Leila Ruth (Mulford) B.; m. Judy Helen Rindahl, Mar. 17, 1983; children: Matthew David, Erik William. BSEE, U. Mo., Rolla, 1971; BS in Physics, Northeast Mo. State Coll., 1971. Registered profl. engr., Minn. Assoc. design engr. Control Data Corp., Arden Hills, Minn., 1971-72; sr. design engr. Sperry-Univac, Eagan, Minn., 1972-75; project engr. Robertshaw Controls Co., Richmond, Va., 1975-76; prin. design engr. Sperry-Univac, Eagan, 1976-80; mgr., systems applications Honywell Solid State, Electronics Div., Plymouth, Minn., 1980-84; com. bus. devel. mgr. Honywell Solid State, Electronics Div., Colorado Springs, Colo., 1984-88; dir. mktg. Ramtron Corp., Colorado Springs, 1988—; ind. cons. Technomics Cons., Chgo., 1987. Contbr. articles to profl. jours. Mem. IEEE (pres., v.p., sec. 1977-79), Twin Cities Computer Soc., Country Club of Colo., Tau Beta Pi, Eta Kappa Nu, Phi Kappa Phi. Republican. Lutheran. Home: 4025 Becket Dr Colorado Springs CO 80906 Office: Ramtron Corp 1873 Austin Bluffs Pkwy Colorado Springs CO 80918

BONDY, LINDA LORENE, real estate executive; b. Spokane, Wash., June 30, 1946; d. Roy B. and Hazel I. (Underdahl) F.; m. Dwight C. Bondy, May 2, 1961 (div., 1988); children: Gregory R., Jason S.. Cert. in Real Estate, Peninsula Coll., 1986. Sales agt. United Olympic Realty, Inc., Port Angeles, Wash., 1977-79, assoc. broker, 1979–; cons. Wash. Bd. Health, On-Site Regulations, 1988. Mem. Diversion Juvenile Ct., Clallam County, Wash., 1979–; pres. Port Angeles Food Bank, 1987=88. Mem. Wash. Assn. Realtors (bd. dirs. 1980-87, 88, task force Puget Sound Water Quality Authority, 1986-88, state chmn. Make Am. Better campaign 1985-87),Port Angeles Bd. Realtors, (bd. dirs., pres. 1987), Women's Council Realtors (pres. 1979-80), Alpha Zeta, Beta Sigma Phi, Sons of Norway, Lady Lions, YMCA Century. Baptist. Office: United Olympic Realty Inc 701 E Front St Port Angeles WA 98362

BONÊ, HARRY, aeronautical engineer; b. Edmonton, Alberta, Canada, June 26, 1939; came to U.S., 1958; s. Howard and Leona (LeBlanc) B.; m. Renate Maria Dietl, Nov. 4, 1987. MCIT (MSc), Cranfield Inst Tech., Bedford, U.K., 1978. Registered profl. engr., Eng., Fed. Republic Germany. Tech. rep. Gen. Elec. Co., Cin., 1963-66; flight data engr. McDonnell Douglas, St Louis, 1967-71; chmn. Panavia Group Multiple Launch Rocket System, Munich, 1971-77; test engr. Messerschmitt-Bölkow Blohm Co., Madrid, 1979-81; test engr. tanker cargo project Dornier A/C Co., Munich, 1981-82, project engr., 1983-85; owner Joey Sports, Trier/Munich, 1982-83; test mgr. MLRS - EPG, Munich, 1985—; chmn. BOD Tierra Linda Corp., Las Cruces, N.Mex., 1988—. Cons. German Hockey Fedn. Internat.-Ice Hockey Fedn., Munich, 1983-85, organizer hockey tournaments. 1st lt. CAF, 1962-66. Mem. Canadian Old Timers Hockey Assn. Home: 3000 Majestic Ridge #87 Las Cruces NM 88001 Office: MLRS-EPG PO Box 250 White Sands Missile Range NM 88002

BONE, ROBERT WILLIAM, writer, photojournalist; b. Gary, Ind., Sept. 15, 1932; s. Robert Ordway and Georgia Juanita (Clapp) B.; m. Sara Ann Cameron, Aug. 14, 1965; children: Christina Ann, David Robert. BS in Journalism, Bowling Green State U., 1954. Editor, tng. literature The Armor Sch., Ft. Knox, Ky., 1954-56; reporter, photographer Middletown (N.Y.) Daily Record, 1956-59, San Juan (Puerto Rico) Star, 1959-60; news editor Popular Photography Mag., N.Y.C., 1960-62; editor-in-chief Brazilian Bus. Mag., Rio de Janeiro, 1962-63; picture editor Time-Life Books, N.Y.C., 1963-68; sr. writer Fielding's Travel Guide to Europe, Mallorca, Spain, 1968-71; staff writer Honolulu Advertiser, 1971-84; free-lancer Honolulu, 1984—. Author: Maverick Guide to Hawaii, 1977, Maverick Guide to Australia, 1979, Maverick Guide to New Zealand, 1981, Fielding's Alaska and the Yukon, 1989; stringer Time-Life News Svc., 1981-86; travel editor Honolulu mag., 1985-88, R.S.V.P. mag., 1988—; contbg. editor Recommend mag., 1986. 1st lt., U.S. Army, 1954-56. Mem. Soc. of Am. Travel Writers, Am. Soc. Magazine Photographers, Hawaii Profl. Writers, Small Bus. Hawaii. Democrat. Home and Office: 1053 Luna'ai St Kailua HI 96734

BONFIELD, ANDREW JOSEPH, tax practitioner; b. London, Jan. 26, 1924; s. George William and Elizabeth Agnes B.; came to U.S., 1946, naturalized, 1954; m. Eleanor Ackerman, Oct. 16, 1955; children—Bruce Ian, Sandra Karen. Gen. mgr. Am. Cushion Co., Los Angeles, 1948-50, Monson Calif. Co., Redwood City, 1951-58; mfrs. mktg. rep., San Francisco, 1958-62; tax practitioner, bus. cons., Redwood City, San Jose, Los Gatos, Calif., 1963—. Past treas., dir. Northwood Park Improvement Assn.; mem. exec. bd. Santa Clara County council Boy Scouts Am., 1971—, past council pres., mem. Nat. council; mem. Santa Clara County Parks and Recreation Commn., 1975-81, 82-86; mem. County Assessment Appeals Bd., 1978-86. Served with Brit. Royal Navy, 1940-46. Decorated King George VI Silver Badge; recipient Silver Beaver award, Vigil honor award Boy Scouts Am.; enrolled to practice before IRS. Mem. Nat. Soc. Public Accts., Nat. Assn. Enrolled Agts., Calif. Soc. Enrolled Agts., Hawaii Assn. Pub. Accts., Hawaii Soc. Enrolled Agrs., Royal Can. Legion (past state parliamentarian, past state 1st vice comdr.). Club: Rotary (pres. San Jose E. 1977-78). Home: 760 S Kihei Rd #215 Kihei HI 96753

BONHAM, TERRENCE JAMES, lawyer, hearing officer; b. Richmond, Calif., June 8, 1938; s. Harry L. and Helen G. (Gately) B.; m. Joyce E. Trout, July 28, 1968; 1 dau., Teresa J. BA in Econs., St. Mary's Coll., 1960; JD, U. Calif., Hastings Coll. Law, San Francisco, 1963. Bar: Calif. 1964, U.S. Dist. Ct. (no. dist.) Calif. 1964, U.S. Ct. Mil. Appeals 1964, U.S. Ct. Appeals (9th cir.) 1964, U.S. Supreme Ct. 1983. Assoc. Halde, Battin, Barrymore & Stevens, Santa Barbara, Calif., 1968-73; ptnr. Barrymore, Stevens & Bonham, Santa Barbara, 1973-74; mem. Riley, Holzhauer, Denver & McClain, Santa Barbara, 1974-80; ptnr. Lawler & Ellis, Ventura, Calif., 1980-85, ptnr. Lawler, Bonham & Walsh, 1985—; judge protem Santa Barbara-Goleta Mcpl. Ct., Ventura County Superior Ct.; hearing officer County of Santa Barbara Civil Service Com., Santa Barbara Bd. Retirement; lectr. Bridging the Gap, Ventura County; lectr. to assns. Mem. Civil Arbitration Panel Ventura County, 1979—; mem. Republican Presdl. Task Force, Nat. Rep. Senatorial Com. Served to capt. U.S. Army, 1964-68. Decorated Bronze Star. Mem. Assn. So. Calif. Def. Counsel, Am. Bd. Trial Advs. (pres. 1984-85), Ventura County Bar Assn. (formerly exec. com., co-chmn. atty./client com., now mem. cts.-bar com.), ABA. Roman Catholic. Clubs: KC (past faithful navigator) (Santa Barbara); Elks (Ventura). Home: 2851 Seahorse Ave Ventura CA 93001 Office: PO Box 1269 Ventura CA 93002

BONICELLI, JOANNE, professional model; b. Columbus, Ga., Oct. 26, 1951; d. Joseph Carl Tucker and Helga Erika (Hachnel) McClow; m. Silvio Joseph Bonicelli, Jr.; Mar. 21, 1971; children: Jennifer, Christine, Julie Elizabeth. Student, U. So. Colo., 1969-71. Asst. mgr. Gibson Girl, Inc., Colorado Springs, Colo., 1972-76; model Vannoy Talent Agy., Denver, 1983-87, Spring Talent, Inc., Colorado Springs, 1987—. Editor (newsletter) Heartstrings, 1987-88. Vice-pres. bd. dirs. The Pikes Peak Hospice, Inc., Colorado Springs, 1985-89; bd. dirs. Southern Colo. Accent on Kids, Inc., Colorado Springs, 1988-89; chmn. bd. dirs. Jr. League Colorado Springs, 1989—; bd. dirs. Broadmoor Christian Women's Club, Colorado Springs, 1988. Mem. Country Club Colo. Republican. Roman Catholic. Home: 130 Sierra Vista Dr Colorado Springs CO 80906

BONKER, DON L., former congressman; b. Denver, Mar. 7, 1937; m. Carolyn Jo Ekern, 1971. A.A., Clark Coll., Vancouver, Wash., 1962; B.A., Lewis and Clark Coll, 1964; postgrad., Am. U., Washington, 1964-66. Research asst. to Senator Maurine B. Neuberger of Oreg., 1964-66; auditor Clark County, Wash., 1966-74; mem. 94th-100th Congresses from 3d Wash. Dist., 1975-89, mem. fgn. affairs com., chmn. internat. econ. policy and trade subcom., mem. select com. on aging, chmn. subcom. housing and consumer interest, mem. merchant marine com., chmn. house export task force, chmn. house dem. task force. Office: 434 Cannon House Office Bldg Washington DC 20515 *

BONNEY, DONALD ERNEST, physician; b. Escondido, Calif., Sept. 21, 1952; s. Frederick Augustus and Eloise Blair (Duke) B.; m. Deborah Lynn Parries, Apr. 7, 1984. AA, Palomar Jr. Coll., 1973; BA in Social Work, San Diego State U., 1975; D in Chiropractic, Western State Coll., Portland, Oreg., 1985. Legis. asst. Calif. State Assembly, San Diego, 1975-76; adminstrv. asst. Calif. State Assembly, Sacramento, 1976, County of San Diego, 1976-77; carpenter numerous constrn. cos., Oreg., 1977-78; contractor Donald E. Bonney Constrn., Oreg., 1978-85; chiropractor Albuquerque Health Ctr., 1986, Accident & Pain Ctr., Corrales, N.Mex., 1986—. With USN, 1971-72, Vietnam. Recipient Declaration, San Diego County, 1977; Western States Chiropractic scholar, 1984, W.A. Budden scholar Western States Chiropractic, 1985. Mem. N.Mex. Chiropractic Assn., Ariz. Chiropractic Assn., Rio Rancho TIPS Club, Rio Rancho C. of C. Office: Accident & Pain Ctr 10200 PO Box 5 Corrales NM 87048

BONO, SONNY SALVATORE, singer, composer, mayor; b. Detroit, Feb. 16, 1935; m. Donna Rankin; children: Christy, Santo, Jean; m. Cher LaPiere, Oct. 27, 1964 (div.); 1 child, Chastity; m. Susie Coehlo (div.); m. Mary Whitaker, Mar. 1986; 1 child, Chesare Elan. Songwriter, later artist and repertoire man for Speciality Records; singer with Cher as team Sonny and Cher, 1964-74, co-star The Sonny and Cher Show, 1976-77; now solo night club act; numerous recs., TV, concert and benefit appearances; has appeared on TV series The Love Boat; composer, lyricist, appearance in Good Times, 1966; films include: Escape to Athena, 1979, Airplane II-The Sequel, 1982, Hairspray, 1988; producer film: Chastity, 1969; composer: A Cowboy's Work is Never Done, I Got You, Babe, others. Restaurateur; mayor Palm Springs, Calif., 1988—. Office: care John LaRocca & Assocs 3907 W Alameda Ave Ste 101 Burbank CA 91505 also: PO Box 1786 Palm Springs CA 92263 *

BONOWSKI, STEPHEN JOHN, state social services official; b. Indpls., Sept. 12, 1949; s. John Louis and Oscal Elizabeth (Patrick) B. B.A., St. Joseph's Coll., 1971; M.A., Butler U., 1975. Successively disability examiner, vocat. specialist, tng. officer, quality assurance specialist Ind. Rehab. Services, Indpls., 1973-81; disability examiner, tng. officer, policy analyst, hearing officer, div. rehab. Colo. Dept. Social Services, Denver, 1981—. Author, editor various newsletters. Bd. dirs. Colo. Environ. Coalition, Denver, 1982-84, 86—, chmn. lobby support com., 1983-84, pres. 1988; mem. Denver Audubon Soc., 1984-87, sec., 1984-86; Polit. Action for Conservation, 1984—; mem. Denver Mayor's Task Force on Environ. Affairs, 1984—, chmn. 1985; mem. Govs. Colo. Environ. Zoo Project, 1988—. Mem. Nat. Assn. Disability Examiners (bd. dirs. 1977-83, pres. 1979-80, Charles O. Blalock Service award 1982, Lewis Buckingham Ten Yr. Svc. Award, 1987), Colo. Assn. Disability Examiners (chmn. bd. dirs. 1983-84). Democrat. C-lub: Colo. Mountain. Home: PO Box 24281 Denver CO 80224

BONSER, QUENTIN, surgeon; b. Sedro Wooley, Wash., Nov. 1, 1920; s. George Wayne and Kathleen Imogene (Lynch) B.; BA in Zoology, UCLA, 1943; MD, U. Calif., San Francisco, 1947; m. Loellen Rocca, Oct. 20, 1945; children: Wayne, Gordon, Carol, Patricia (Mrs. Martin Sanford). Intern U. Calif. Hosp., San Francisco, 1947-49, resident gen. surgery, 1949-56; practice gen. surgery, Placerville, Calif., 1956—; surgeon King Faisal Splty. Hosp., Saudi Arabia, Sept.-Oct., 1984; vis. prof. surgery U. Calif., San Francisco, 1968. Capt. M.C., USAF, 1950-51. Vol. physician, tchr. surgery Vietnam, 1971, 72, 73. Diplomate Am. Bd. Surgery. Fellow A.C.S.; mem. H.C. Naffziger Surg. Soc. (pres. 1974-75). Home: 2590 Northridge Dr Placerville CA 95667 Office: 1108 Corker Dr Placerville CA 95667

BONUTTI, ALEXANDER CARL, architect, urban designer; b. Cleve., June 25, 1951; s. Karl Borromeo and Hermina (Rijavec) B. BArch, Ill. Inst. Tech., 1974; MSArch in Urban Design, Columbia U., 1978. Registered architect Ohio, W.Va. With William B. Morris, AIA, Shaker Heights, Ohio, 1973; designer Stouffer's Hotels, Cleve., 1974, Ellerbe, Dalton, Dalton and Newport, Bethesda, Md., 1975-76; designer, asst. project mgr. Dalton, Dalton and Newport, Shaker Heights, 1976-79; prin. ACB Design, Cleve., 1980; studio dir. Kaplan, McLaughlin and Diaz, San Francisco, 1981—. Contbr. articles to profl. jours. Recipient Honor award Architects Soc. Ohio, Bay Village, 1979. Mem. AIA (steering com. 1989 Monterey Design Conf., Hon. awards U.S. Univ. Health Sci., Naval Facilities Command, Honor award for Pacific Presbyn. Profl. Bldg. 1987, Citation for Excellence, Urban Design Embarcadero Corridor Study, bd. dirs. Calif. coun. 1986—, chmn. urban design com. San Francisco chpt. 1986—, v.p., pres.-elect 1988, v.p./pres. elect 1988), Urban Land Inst. (assoc.), Nat. Trust Hist. Preservation, Inst. Urban Design, Phi Kappa Sigma (sec. 1970-71). Democrat. Office: Kaplan McLaughlin and Diaz 222 Vallejo St San Francisco CA 94111

BOOBYER, DON J., computer operator, bookkeeper; b. Phoenix, Dec. 1, 1953; s. Gordon Boobyer and Lois Eileen (Martz) Evans. AA, Pasadena City Coll., 1973. Computer operator Aireloom Bedding, El Monte, Calif., 1973-79, Miller Dial Corp., El Monte, 1981—; bookkeeper Franklin Computer Systems, South Pasadena, 1980.

BOOCHEVER, ROBERT, federal judge; b. N.Y.C., Oct. 2, 1917; s. Louis C. and Miriam (Cohen) B.; m. Lois Colleen Maddox, Apr. 22, 1943; children: Barbara K., Linda Lou, Ann Paula, Miriam Deon. AB, Cornell U., 1939, LLB, 1941; HD (hon.), U. Alaska, 1981. Bar: N.Y. 1944, Alaska 1947. Asst. U.S. atty. Juneau, 1946-47; partner firm Faulkner, Banfield, Boochever & Doogan, Juneau, 1947-72; asso. justice Alaska Supreme Ct., 1972-75, 78-80, chief justice, 1975-78; judge U.S. Ct. Appeals for 9th Circuit, 1980—; chmn. Alaska Jud. Council, 1975-78; mem. appellate judges seminar N.Y.U. Sch. Law, 1975; mem. Conf. Chief Justices, 1975-79, vice chmn., 1978-79; mem. adv. bd. Nat. Bank of Alaska, 1968-72. Chmn. Juneau chpt. ARC, 1949-51, Juneau Planning Commn., 1956-61; mem. Alaska Devel. Bd., 1949-52, Alaska Jud. Qualification Commn., 1972-75; mem. adv. bd. Juneau-Douglas Community Coll. Served to capt. inf. AUS, 1941-45. Named Juneau Man of Year, 1974. Fellow Am. Coll. Trial Attys.; mem. ABA, Alaska Bar Assn. (pres. 1961-62), Juneau Bar Assn. (pres. 1971-72), Am. Judicature Soc. (dir. 1970-74), Am. Law Inst., Juneau C. of C. (pres. 1952, 55), Alaskans United (chmn. 1962). Clubs: Marine Meml, Wash. Athletic, Juneau Racket, Altadena Town and Country. Home: 336 S Orange Grove Blvd Pasadena CA 91105 Office: US Ct of Appeals 125 S Grand Ave PO Box 91510 Pasadena CA 91109-1510

BOOHER, CAROL MERRICK, nurse; b. Los Banos, Calif., June 16, 1935; d. Frank Albert and Rose Margaret (Cavalla) Merrick; divorced 1975; children: John, Glen Michael, Susann, Denise. AA, San Jose State, Calif., 1955; BS, Stanford U., 1958. Staff nurse Los Banos Community Hosp., 1962-71—; head sch. nurse Los Banos Unified Sch. Dist., 1989—; operating room staff (part-time) Los Banos Community Hosp., 1971—. Mem. Westside Child Abuse Prevention Com., Los Banos, Salvation Army Com., Los Banos. Mem. Calif. Sch. Nurses Orgn., Order Ea. Star, Delta Kappa Gamma.

BOOHER, JOHN ARTHUR, clergyman; b. Feb. 26, 1942; s. Virgil and Lenora Booher; m. Patricia Eylene McClaflin, Aug. 1, 1964; children: Craig, Shana, Rachel. Student, N.W. Jr. Coll., 1960-62, U. Wyo., 1962, Cen. Bible Coll., Springfield, Mo., 1963-65. Ordained to ministry Assemblies of God Ch. Pastor Assemblies of God Ch., Stoneham, Colo., 1965-66, Tribune, Kans., 1966-67, Wichita, Kans., 1967-76; sr. pastor Fairlane Assembly of God, Dearborn Heights, Mich., 1976-88, Willamette Christian Ctr., Eugene, Oreg., 1988—; sectional youth leader Assemblies of God, Stoneham, 1965-66, Wichita, 1970-74, exec. presbyter Mich. dist., 1986-88; assoc. Internat. Corr. Inst., Ft. Worth, 1985—. Author: Catechism for Charismatics, 1980, I'm A New Creation, 1980, Catechism No. 2, 1989. Bd. dirs. Wichita Mental Health Assn., 1975-76, Women Aglow, Detroit, 1983-87. Mem. Studebaker Club, Lincoln Club, Chrysler 300 Club. Home: 1259 Courtney Pl Eugene OR 97405 Office: Willamette Christian Ctr 2500 W 18th St Eugene OR 97402

BOOKMAN, PHILIP, newspaper editor; b. N.Y.C., July 11, 1936; s. Henry and Anne (Mandel) B.; children: Jonathan, Charles; m. H. Mary (Bookman,) Oct. 25, 1975. BA in English Lit., U. Buffalo, 1957. Assoc. editor Lebhar-Friedman Publs., N.Y.C., 1959-63; regional editor Evening Press, Binghamton, N.Y., 1964-71; asst. mng. editor Sun-Bull., Binghamton, 1971-74; mng. editor Camden (N.J.) Courier-Post, 1975-80; exec. editor The Record, Stockton, Calif., 1980—. Served with USANG, 1959, 1959-61. Mem. Calif. Freedom of Info. Com. (former chmn., exec. com.), Am. Soc. Newspaper Editors, Sigma Delta Chi. Office: Stockton Record 530 E Market St Stockton CA 95202

BOOLOOTIAN, RICHARD ANDREW, communications executive; b. Fresno, Calif., Oct. 17, 1927; s. Vanig and Vivian (Ohannesian) B.; m. Mary Jo Blue, Oct. 20, 1945 (div. 1980); children: Mark, Alan, Craig; m. Yvonne Morse Daniels. BA, Calif. State U., Fresno, 1951, MA, 1953; PhD, Stanford U., 1957. Cert. tchr. (life) Calif. Assoc. prof. UCLA, 1957-67; cons. U. Colo., Boulder, 1967-68; pres. Sci. Software Systems Inc., Sherman Oaks, Calif., 1969—; cons. Morler Internat. Inc., Burbank, Calif., 1985—; dir. sci. curriculum Mirman Sch. Gifted, Los Angeles, 1974—. Author over 19 textbooks; contbr. articles to profl. jours. Fellow Lalor Found., 1963-64, NIH, 1965. Fellow AAAS; mem. Challenger Soc. Office: Sci Software Systems Inc 3576 Woodcliff Rd Sherman Oaks CA 91403

BOON, WILLIAM CLIFFORD, biotechnology company executive, civil engineer; b. Downers Grove, Ill., Sept. 9, 1932; s. William Clifford Sr. and Dorothy Virginia (Easley) B.; m. Mary Virginia Bennett, Feb. 1, 1953 (div. 1969); children: William Bennett, Rebecca Ann, Timothy Shaw, Kimberly Kay, Susan Virginia, Dina Maryka; m. Betty Ann Spore, May 29, 1970; stepchildren: Robert Allen, Angela Jo. BS in Civil Engring., U. Ill., 1955, postgrad. in math., 1958-59; postgrad. in math., U. Va., Hampton, 1956-58. Registered profl. engr., Ill., Iowa, Wis., Tex.; registered land surveyor, Ill., Iowa. Design engr. Heil Co., Milw., 1955-56, Clark, Daily & Dietz, Urbana, Ill., 1958-60; project mgr. Goodell Engring., Champaign, Ill., 1960-65; mgr. br. office Goodell Engring., East Moline, Ill., 1965-68; owner, chief exec. officer Boon Engring., East Moline, 1968-76; pres., chief exec. officer Impro, Inc., Rock Island, Ill., 1976-79; mgr. br. office Williams, Stackhouse Engring., San Antonio, 1979-81; v.p. mktg. URS Engrs., Denver, 1981-83; founder, chief exec. officer WaCon Corp. (subs. Ridgeview), Denver, 1983-87, v.p., chief exec. officer, 1987–. Mgr. primary campaign 10th dist. Ill. McGovern Presdl. campaign, 1972; bd. dis. ACLU, Rock Island, 1973-75; coord. Cisneros Mayoral campaign, San Antonio, 1980. 1st lt. Signal Corps, U.S. Army, 1956-58. Mem. Union Concerned Scientists. Home: 3367 E Geddes Dr Littleton CO 80122 Office: WaCon Corp 2250 S Raritan St Englewood CO 80110

BOONE, CLIFFORD SCOTT, banker; b. Toledo, Oreg., Oct. 31, 1948; s. Francis and June Aldyn (McMillan) B.; m. Veronica Eileen Teebay, Jan. 21, 1984; 1 child, Alexander Francis. BBA, U. Oreg., 1970, MBA, 1972. Trust officer Wells Fargo Bank, San Francisco, 1972-74; v.p., mgr. Lloyds Bank Calif., San Francisco, 1984-86; v.p. dept. head Sanwa Bank Calif., Pasadena, 1986—. Bd. dirs., chief fin. officer Sr. Help & Info & Networking for the Elderly, Glendale, Calif., 1986—, Support Svc. for Elders, San Francisco, 1982—; bd. dirs. Pasadena Humane Soc., 1987—. Served to 1st lt. U.S. Army, 1970-72. Mem. Life Ins. and Trust Coun. L.A., Calif. Bankers Assn., Univ. Club. Republican. Episcopalian. Office: Sanwa Bank Calif 595 E Colorado Blvd Ste 200 Pasadena CA 91101

BOONE, DAVID DOUGLAS, product management executive; b. Los Angeles, Mar. 31, 1950; s. Jacquelyn June (Allegar) B.; m. Teresa Bitton, Aug. 21, 1974; children: Parker, Adam, Brandon. Grad. high sch., Brea, Calif. Golf profl. Imperial, Brea, Altavista, Brea, 1970-78; sales rep. Wilson Sporting Goods, Commerce, Calif., 1978-81, Daiwa Golf Co., Garden Grove, Calif., 1981-85; product mgr. Lynx Golf, Inc., City of Industry, Calif., 1986—. Inventor improved golf equipment. Republican. Mormon. Office: Lynx Golf Inc 16017 E Valley Blvd City of Industry CA 91744

BOONE, JAMES VIRGIL, engineering executive; b. Little Rock, Sept. 1, 1933; s. Virgil Bennett and Dorothy Bliss (Dorough) B.; m. Gloria Marjorie Gieseler, June 5, 1955; children—Clifford B., Sandra J. Smyser, Steven B. B.S. in Elec. Engring., Tulane U., 1955; M.S.E.E., Air Force Inst. Tech., Ohio, 1959. Assoc. elec. engr. Martin Co., Balt., 1955; research and develop. engr. U.S. Air Force, 1955-62; electronics engr. Nat. Security Agy., Ft. Meade, Md., 1962-77, dep. dir. for research and engring., 1978-81; spl. asst. to gen. mgr. Mil. Electronics div. TRW, Inc., San Diego, 1981-83, asst. gen. mgr., 1983-85, dir. program mgmt. and group devel. TRW Electronic Systems Group, 1985-86, v.p., dir. program mgmt. and group devel, 1986-87; v.p., gen. mgr. Defense Communications div. TRW Electronic Systems Group, 1987; Served to capt. USAF, 1955-62. Recipient Nat. Security Agy. Exceptional Civilian Service award, 1975. Mem. IEEE (sr.), AIAA. Republican. Presbyterian (elder). Contbr. articles to profl. jours. Home: 3030 Deluna Dr Rancho Palos Verdes CA 90274 Office: One Space Park Redondo Beach CA 90278

BOONE, LARRY MURPHY, economist; b. Eureka, Kans., Dec. 10, 1937; s. Rollin Murphy and Inez (Gilbert) B.; m. Dorothy Arlene Minear, June 1, 1958; children: Dennis Reed, David Matthew. BS, Kans. State U., 1959, MS, 1960; PhD, Wash. State U., 1966. Asst. prof. U. Tenn., Knoxville, 1965-68; agrl. economist U.S. Dept. Agrl., Washington, 1968-87; assoc. exec. dir. Consortium for Internat. Devel., Tucson, Ariz., 1987—; devel. economist Ministry of Agrl., Bogota, Columbia, 1968-71, Interam. Inst. of Agrl. Sci., San Jose, Costa Rica, 1976-79; chief-of-party Ministry of Agrl., Riyadh, Saudi Arabia, 1981-86 (recipient internat. honor award 1985). Mem. com. Boy Scouts, San Jose, 1976-79, Riyadh, 1981-86. Mem. Am. Agr. Econ. Assn., Assn. U.S. Univ. Dirs., Soc. Internat. Devel. Office: Consortium for Internat Devel 5151 E Broadway Ste 1500 Tucson AZ 85711-3766

BOONE, REBECCA A., university administrator; b. Springfield, Ohio, Mar. 7, 1946; d. Roger S. and Elizabeth Lupton (Walker) Boone; m. Dennis David Ash, Aug. 7, 1967 (div. 1975); m. Frederick Kellogg, July 11, 1979 (div. 1988). Student, Earlham Coll., 1964-67; BA, Case Western Res. U., 1968; MLS, U. N.C., 1970. Asst. reference librarian Princeton (N.J) U., 1970-76; head cen. reference dept. U. Ariz., Tucson, 1976-84, assoc. dean Coll. Arts and Scis.., 1984—; adminstrv. staff Ariz. Bd. Regents, 1988-89. Mem. ALA (div. pres. 1985-86), Nat. Assn. for Female Execs., Exec. Women's Council So. Ariz. Mem. Soc. of Friends. Office: Ariz Bd Regents 3030 N Central Ste 1400 Phoenix AZ 85012

BOOTH, DONALD RICHARD, economist, educator; b. Marble, Minn., June 1, 1931; s. Floyd James and Maude (Marquart) B.; m. Louise Hitt, Aug. 22, 1953; 1 child, David. BA, Whittier Coll., 1955; MA, Claremont Coll., 1956; PhD, UCLA, 1970. Grad. dean Chapman Coll., Orange, Calif.,

1973-77, acad. dean, 1977-78, exec. v.p., 1978-79, dean, sch. of bus., 1979-81, prof. econs., 1959—, v.p. fin., 1988—; cons. Am. Inst. Banking, Orange; bd. dirs. United Am. Bank, Westminster, Calif. Recipient Eliot Jones award, We. Econs. Assn., 1958; Danforth Teaching fellow, Danforth Found., 1962, NSF fellow, 1970. Office: Chapman Coll 333 N Glassell Orange CA 92666

BOOTH, JOHN LOUIS, service executive; b. Danville, Va., May 15, 1933; s. William Irvine and Melba (Harvey) B.; m. Ann Fennell, May 23, 1959; children: Mark, Robin. BA, U. Richmond, 1958; ThM, Dallas Theol. Sem., 1962, ThD, 1965; postgrad., Ariz. State U., 1972, 79. Pastor Skyway Bible Ch., Seattle, 1964-66, Mount Prospect (Ill.) Bible Ch., 1966-71, Camelback Bible Ch., Paradise Valley, Ariz., 1971-78; counselor Camelback Counseling Ctr., Phoenix, 1978-79; dir. Paradise Valley Counseling, Inc., Phoenix, 1980—; chmn. bd. Paradise Valley Counseling, Inc., 1980—; chmn. bd. Paradise Valley Counseling Found., Inc., Phoenix, 1982—; adj. prof. Grand Canyon U., 1981—, Southwestern Coll., Phoenix, 1979—, Talbott Theol. Sem. Phoenix Ext., 1983-85; seminar speaker frequent engagements, 1965—. Author: Understanding Today's Problems, 1980, Marriage by the Master Plan, 1980, Equipping for Effective Marriage, 1983, (tape series) Starting Over, 1982, Enjoying All God Intended, 1988. Precinct committeeman Rep. Party, Phoenix, 1983-84, 87-88; chaplain Arizona State Senate, Phoenix, 1973. Mem. Christian Assn. for Psychol. Studies, Internat. Assn. Biblical Counselors. Baptist. Club: Pinewood Country (Munds Park, Ariz.). Office: Paradise Valley Counseling Inc 10210 N 32d St Ste 211 Phoenix AZ 85028

BOOTH, WALLACE WRAY, retired electronics and aerospace executive; b. Nashville, Sept. 30, 1922; s. Wallace Wray Booth and Josephine England; m. Donna Cameron Voss, Mar. 22, 1947; children: Ann Conley (Mrs. F. Brian Cox), John England. BA, U. Chgo., 1948, MBA, 1948. Various positions Ford Motor Co., Dearborn, Mich., 1948-59; v.p. fin., treas. dir. Ford Motor Co., Toronto, Ont., 1959-63; mng. dir., chief exec. officer Ford Motor Co. Australia, Melbourne, 1963-67; v.p. corp. staffs, indsl. products Philco-Ford Corp., Phila., 1967-68; sr. v.p. corp. staffs, mem. exec. com. Rockwell Internat. Corp., El Segundo, Calif., 1968-75; pres., chief exec. officer United Brands Co., Boston, 1975-77, also dir.; chmn. Ducommon, Inc., L.A., 1977-88, pres., chief exec. officer, 1978-88; bd. dirs. Rohr Industries, Litton Industries, Inc., Navistar Internat. Corp., Chgo., 1st Interstate Bank, L.A. Past chmn. United Way, L.A.; pres. Children's Bur. Los Angeles. Served to 1st lt. USAAF, 1943-46.

BOOZE, THOMAS FRANKLIN, toxicologist; b. Denver, Mar. 4, 1955; s. Ralph Walker and Ann (McNatt) B.; m. Patricia Jude Bullock, Aug. 8, 1981; 1 child, Heather N. BS, U. Calif., Davis, 1978; MS, Kans. State U., 1981, PhD, 1985. Asst. instr. Kans. State U., Manhattan, 1979-85; toxicologist Chevron Environ. Health Ctr., Richmond, Calif., 1985—; cons. in field, Manhattan, Kans., 1981-83. contbr. articles to profl. jours. Vol. Amigos de las Americas, Marin County, Calif., 1973, Hospice Care, Manhattan, 1985. Mem. AAAS, N.Y. Acad. Sci., Soc. of Toxicology, Sigma Xi. Home: 233 Oriole Ct Hercules CA 94547 Office: Chevron Environ Health Ctr PO Box 4054 Richmond CA 94804

BORAWICK, JOAN SUSAN, lawyer; b. Seattle, Feb. 5, 1957; d. Myron Louis and Carolyn Susan (Shay) B. BBA, U. Wash., 1979; JD, U. So. Calif., 1982. Assoc. O'Melveny & Myers, L.A., 1983-85; counsel Orion Pictures, L.A., 1985-86; assoc. Sheppard, Mullin, Richter & Hampton, L.A., 1986-87; sr. counsel MGm/UA Communications Co., L.A., 1987-88; assoc. Law Offices Sam Pearlmutter, L.A., 1988—. Mem. ABA, Calif. Bar Assn., L.A. Spinsters. Office: Law Offices Sam Perlmutter 5757 Wilshire Blvd Ste 636 Los Angeles CA 90036

BORCHERS, ROBERT REECE, physicist, laboratory administrator; b. Chgo., Apr. 4, 1936; s. Robert Harley and Rena Josephine (Reece) B.; m. Mary Bridget Hennessy, Nov. 26, 1960; children: Patrick Joseph, Anne Marie, Robert Edward. BS in Physics, U. Notre Dame, 1958; MS in Physics, Math., U. Wis., 1959, PhD in Nuclear Physics, 1961. Prof. physics U. Wis., Madison, 1961-76, vice chancellor, 1976-77; vice chancellor U. Colo., Boulder, 1977-79; dep. assoc. dir. MFE Program Lawrence Livermore Nat. Lab., Livermore, Calif., 1979-83, assoc. dir. computation, 1983—, cons. laser fusion program, 1972-79; mem. com. NSF, Washington, 1973—, Nat. Acad. Sci., Washington, 1983—. Editor Computers in Physics Jour., 1987—; assoc. editor Scientific Instrument and Methods, 1988—; contbr. numerous chpts. in books, articles on physics and computing. Mem. San Francisco Symphony Assn., 1984—. NSF postdoctoral fellow, 1964; A.J. Schmidt Found. fellow and scholar, 1954-60; Sloan Found. fellow, 1964-68; Guggenheim Found. fellow, 1970; recipient W.H. Kiekhofer Disting. Teaching award U. Wis., Madison, 1966; Centennial of Sci. Alumnus award U. Notre Dame, 1966. Fellow Am. Phys. Soc. Home: 2594 Chateau Way Livermore CA 94550 Office: Lawrence Livermore Nat Lab 7000 East Ave Livermore CA 94550

BORDENAVE, MARY ELIZABETH, pharmacist; b. Geneva, Ill., May 1, 1957; d. George John and Rose Barbara (Honisch) B.; m. George William Estes, June 8, 1985. BS in Microbiology, Ariz. State U., 1978; BS in Pharmacy, U. Ariz., 1988, PharmD, 1989. Med. technologist St. Louis U. Hosp., 1979-80; microbiologist Barnes Hosp., St. Louis, 1980, St. Louis County Hosp., St. Louis, 1980-81; med. technologist St. Joseph's Hosp., Phoenix, 1981-82, U. Med. Ctr., Tucson, 1982—. Mem. Am. Soc. Microbiology, Am. Soc. Hosp. Pharmacy. Republican. Roman Catholic.

BORDNER, GREGORY WILSON, air force officer; b. Buffalo, Aug. 16, 1959; s. Raymond Gordon and Nancy Lee (Immegart) B.; m. Margaret Patricia Toon, June 14, 1981; children: Eric Lawrence, Heather Rae. BS in Chem. Engring., Calif. State Poly. U., 1982; MS in Systems Mgmt., U. So. Calif., 1987. Commd. 2nd lt. USAF, 1983, advanced through grades to capt., 1987; engr., mgr. various air launched missile, anti-satellite and strategic def. initiative projects Air Force Rocket Propulsion Lab., Edwards AFB, Calif., 1983-86; asst. mgr. space transp. Air Force Astronautics Lab., Edwards AFB, 1986-87; plans and bus. mgr. small intercontinental ballistic missiles Hdqrs. Ballistic Missiles Office, San Bernardino, Calif., 1987—. Author: (manual) Pyrotechnic Transfer Line Evaluation, 1984, (with others) Rocket Motor Heat Transfer, 1984. MEm. Am. Inst. Chem. Engrs., Soc. Am. Military Engrs., Soc. for the Advancement of Processing Engring. Home: 1694 Rhone Ave Highland CA 92346

BORDOW, ROBERT ALEXANDER, electrical engineer; b. N.Y.C., Nov. 7, 1954; s. Burton William and Norma Marta (DiBenedetto) B.; m. Joan M. Kernis, Sept. 28, 1972; children: Daisy Doe, Dandelion Kellie, Alissa Devi. AS in Electronic Technology, Santa Rosa (Calif.) Jr. Coll., 1979; BSEE, U. Calif., Berkeley, 1982, MSEE, 1983. Chief engr. Sta. KZST-FM, Santa Rosa, 1975-80; engring. tech. Datapoint Corp., Berkeley, Calif., 1981; head teaching asst. U. Calif., Berkeley, 1982-83; research assoc. Lawrence Berkeley Lab., 1981; design engr. Hewlett Packard Corp., Rohnert Park, Calif., 1983—; physics lectr. Sonoma State U., Rohnert Park, 1985—; cons. Ice House Studio, San Rafael, 1982-83. Active World Runners, Santa Rosa, 1980—. Regents of U. Calif. Fellow, Berkeley, 1982, 83. Mem. Phi Beta Kappa. Democrat. Office: Hewlett Packard 1212 Valley House Dr Rohnert Park CA 94928

BOREL, JAMES DAVID, anesthesiologist; b. Chgo., Nov. 15, 1951; s. James Albert and Nancy Ann (Sieverson) B. BS, U. Wis., 1973; MD, Med. Coll. of Wis., 1977. Diplomate Am. Bd. Anesthesiology, Nat. Bd. Med. Examiners, Am. Coll. Anesthesiologists. Research asst. McArdle Lab. for Cancer Research, Madison, Wis., 1972-73, Stanford U. and VA Hosp., Palo Alto, 1976-77; intern. The Cambridge (Mass.) Hosp., 1977-78; clin. fellow in medicine Harvard Med. Sch., Boston, 1977-78, clin. fellow in anaesthesia, 1978-80, clin. instr. in anaesthesia, 1980; resident in anesthesiology Peter Bent Brigham Hosp., Boston, 1978-80; anesthesiologist Mt. Auburn Hosp., Cambridge, 1980; fellow in anesthesiology Ariz. Health Scis. Ctr., Tucson, 1980-81; research assoc. U. Ariz. Coll. Medicine, Tucson, 1980-81, assoc. in anesthesiology, 1981—; active staff Mesa (Ariz.) Luth. Hosp., 1981—; courtesy staff Scottsdale (Ariz.) Meml. Hosp., 1982—; vis. anaesthetist St. Joseph's Hosp., Kingston, Jamaica, 1980. Contbr. numerous articles to profl. jours. Mem. AMA, AAAS, Mass. Anesthesia Council on Edn., Ariz. Anesthesia Alumni Assn., Ariz. Soc. Anesthesiologists, Am. Soc. Regional Anesthesia, Can. Anesthetists' Soc., Internat. Anesthesia Research Soc., Am. Soc. Anesthesiologists. Office: Valley Anesthesia Cons 2950 N 7th St Phoenix AZ 85014

BORGATTA, MARIE LENTINI, sociologist; b. N.Y.C., Apr. 17, 1925; d. Paul and Linda (Marco) Lentini; m. Edgar F. Borgatta, Oct. 5, 1946; children:Lynn, Kim, Lee. BS, Queens Coll., 1945; MA, NYU, 1961; PhD, CUNY, 1980. Biochemist Continental Baking Co., Jamaica, N.Y., 1945-47; rsch. asst. Sloan-Kettering Inst. Cancer Rsch., N.Y.C., 1947-50; instr. U. Wis., Madison, 1969; adj. lectr. Bklyn. Coll., 1972-74; rsch. asst. Grad. Ctr., CUNY, 1974-75, tng. fellow, 1976-79; project dir. Am. Found. for Blind, N.Y.C., 1979-80; lectr., rsch. assoc. U. Wash., Seattle, 1981—. Mng. editor Ency. of Sociology, 1987—; co-editor: Marriage and the Family, 1969; contbr. articles to profl. jours. Mem. Am. Sociol. Assn., Am. Pub. Health Assn., Pacific Sociol. Assn., Internat. Inst. Sociology (congress coordinator 1984). Office: U Wash Mail Stop DK40 Seattle WA 98195

BORGER, EDWARD M., JR., farm managing partner; b. Easton, Pa., Aug. 11, 1947; s. Edward and Dorothy (Davis) B.; m. Edee Correa, Jan. 20, 1989. B.S.C.E., U. Pitts., Johnstown, Pa., 1976; MBA, Purdue U., 1977. Gen. mgr. Red Mountain Farming Co., Dateland, Ariz., 1983-85; mng. ptnr. Red Mountain Farms Mgmt. Co., Dateland, 1985—; bd. dirs. Calcot, Ltd., Bakersfield, Calif. Staff sgt. U.S. Army, 1970-71, Vietnam. Mem. Jojoba Growers Assn. (bd. dirs. 1989—). Republican. Office: Red Mountain Farms Mgmt Co 6405 North Ave Dateland AZ 85333

BORGES, WILLIAM, III, environmental analyst; b. Long Beach, Calif., Nov. 21, 1948; s. William Jr. Borges and Dorothy Mae (Raymond) Morris; m. Rosalind Denise Marye, Nov. 23, 1968; children: William IV, Blake Austin. BA in Geography, Calif. State U., Sonoma, 1973. Environ. planner Mendocino County Planning Dept., Ukiah, Calif., 1976; project mgr. Engring. Sci., Inc., Berkeley, Calif., 1976-79, Santa Clara County Planning Dept., San Jose, Calif., 1979-8l, Internat. Tech. Corp., San Jose, 1985-88; mgr. sales ops. Adac Labs., Milpitas, Calif., 1983-85; mgr. bus. devel. Western Techs., Inc., Phoenix, 1988—. Contbr. photographs to various mags. Coord. pub. rels. Stellar Acad. for Dyslexics, Hayward, Calif., 1988. With U.S. Army, 1967-70. Mem. Ariz. Hazardous Waste Soc. Democrat. Office: Western Techs Inc 3737 E Broadway Rd Phoenix AZ 85036

BORING, CHARLES MARION, credit manager; b. Ft. Knox, Ky., Jan. 14, 1943; s. William Lewis and Hilda Ethel (Crites) B.; m. Iris Marie Sauer-essig, June 3, 1967; children: Jennifer Lynn, Charles Darold. BS, U. Colo., 1972; MS, U. La Verne, 1981. Enlisted USAF, 1962, commd. 2d lt., 1972, advanced through grades to capt., 1982, ret., 1982, personnel officer, 1972-82; realtor Gallery of Homes, Anchorage, 1982-84, sales mgr., 1984-85; credit mgr. Anchorage Cold Storage, Anchorage, 1985—. Mem. Nat. Assn. Credit Mgmt. (Anchorage Group vice-chmn. 1987—). Lutheran. Office: Anchorage Cold Storage 240 W 1st Ave PO Box 100039 Anchorage AK 99501

BORJA, DALE RAYMOND PARAS, engineer; b. Tarlac, Philippines, Nov. 5, 1959; came to U.S., 1959; s. Domingo R.S. and Nympha (Paras) B.; m. Mariles Javier, Sept. 5, 1981; children: Ivan-Marc, Katerina-Marie. BS in Elec. Engring., Computer Sci., U. Calif., Berkeley, 1980. Sr. engr. Northrop Corp., Hawthorne, Calif., 1980-88, Arinc Rsch. Corp., Fountain Valley, CA, 1988—; computer cons. Applied Concepts, Gardena, Calif., 1982—. Republican. Roman Catholic. Home: 1103 Magnolia Ave #1 Gardena CA 90247

BORKOWSKI, MARK STEPHEN, air force officer; b. Killeen, Tex., Sept. 16, 1958; s. Julian Thomas and Marie Ellen (Reinbold) B. BS, SUNY, Albany, 1980; BS in Aeronaut. Engring., Air Force Inst. Tech., 1983, MS in Astronaut. Engring., 1984. Commd. 2d lt. USAF, 1981, advanced through grades to capt., 1985; strategic air launched missile propulsion engr. Rocket Propulsion Lab. USAF, Edwards AFB, 1984-85, chief air launched missile propulsion sect., 1985-86, chief aerospace launched missile br. Astronautics Lab., 1986—; part-time instr. in mech. engring. Calif. State U., Fresno, 1986. Mem. Math. Assn. Am., Am. Math. Soc., Air Force Assn. Republican. Home: Desert Vill 27-1 Edwards CA 93523 Office: USAF Astronautics Lab AFAL/RKA Edwards AFB CA 93523

BORNMANN, LEWIS JOSEPH, computer engineer; b. Atlantic City, Oct. 12, 1936; s. Lewis Joseph and Sue (Berish) B.; m. Helen Patricia O'Brien, Aug. 20, 1966 (div. Mar. 1974); children: Siobhan Kathleen, Lewis Joseph, Christopher Brendon; m. Barbara Nelle Long, Feb. 14, 1975. BS in Math. and Physics, Ind. Inst. Tech., Ft. Wayne, 1965; MS in Computer Sci., U. Wis., 1969; PhD in Computer Sci, Columbia Pacific U., 1986. Analyst, programmer Boeing Co., Renton, Wash., 1965-66; project mgr. Control Data Corp., Sunnyvale, Calif., 1969-72, 73-75; tech. staff Calma Co., Sunnyvale, Calif., 1972-73; sr. analyst Stanford U., Palo Alto, Calif., 1975-76; sect. mgr. EG&G Idaho Inc., Idaho Falls, 1976-78; mgr. info. processing STD Rsch. Crop., Arcadia, Calif., 1978-80; systems engr. space systems div. Gen. Electric, San Jose, 1980—; instr. Calif. State U., San Jose, 1981. With USAF, 1958-61. Mem. IEEE, Assn. Computing Machinery (Pacific regional rep., coun., standards com., chair chpt. com. 1965—), Sigma Phi Epsilon. Home: 760 Valencia Dr Milpitas CA 95035 Office: General Electric 1441 N First St San Jose CA 95134

BORNY, WALTER MICHAEL, real estate investment consultant, lawyer; b. Bklyn., June 23, 1948; s. Walter S. and Dolores (Kaplon) B.; m. Roseanne Hennion Borny, Aug. 25, 1984. AA, County Coll. Morris, Randolph, N.J., 1973; BA, Rutgers U., 1975, JD, 1979. Lic. real estate agt., Calif. Asst. counsel Chase Manhattan Bank, Englewood Cliffs, N.J., 1981-83; counsel CIS Leasing, San Francisco, 1983-84; pvt. practice law San Francisco, 1984-85; real estate investment cons. Montrose Barber Investments, San Mateo, Calif., 1985—. Sgt. U.S. Army, 1967-71, Vietnam. Mem. N.J. State Bar Assn., Phi Beta Kappa, Phi Alpha Theta. Home: 505 Barbados Ln Foster City CA 94404 Office: Montross Barber Investments 2050 Pioneer G #204 San Mateo CA 94403

BOROVANSKY, VLADIMIR THEODORE, librarian; b. Prague, Czechoslovakia, May 25, 1931; came to U.S., 1968; s. Ladislav and Karla (Uttlova) B.; m. Dagmar Korbelova, July 12, 1961; children: Dominika, Herbert. Cert., Czechoslavic Acad., Prague, 1946-49, 56-57; Grad. Libr., Charles U., Prague, 1965. Mgr. Rsch. Inst. Ferrous Metal, Prague, 1955-65, asst. dir. info. ctr., 1965-67; sci. reference head Ariz. State U., Tempe, 1968-78; reference dept. head U. Petroleum and Minerals, Dhahran, Saudi Arabia, 1978-79; reference dept. head Ariz. State U., Tempe, 1979-82, Noble sci. library head, 1982—. Contbr. articles to profl. jours.; editor Meteritics, 1971-87. Mem. Am. Soc. Eng. Edn. (Engring. Library div.), Am. Soc. for Metals, Czechoslovakia Soc. Arts and Sci., Internat. Assn. of Tech. U. Libraries. Republican. Roman Catholic. Home: 7026 N 14th St Phoenix AZ 85020 Office: Ariz State U Tempe AZ 85287

BORRUP, RONALD JAMES, manufacturer's representative; b. New Brunswick, N.J., Apr. 19, 1920; s. John Jensen and Margaret Elizabeth Addison (Jack) B.; B.S., Worcester Poly. Inst., 1942; m. Margo Vivian Peterson, Aug. 25, 1979; children by previous marriage—David Hollister, Carol Elizabeth, Beth Tracy, John William. Test engr. Hamilton Standard div. United Aircraft Corp., 1946-48; chief design, devel. engr. Safeway Heat Elements Co., 1948-54; founder, pres., chmn. bd. Electro-Flex Heat Inc., 1954-63; founder, dir. Electro-Flex Calif., 1958-61; market devel. engr. Pratt & Whitney Aircraft div. United Aircraft Corp., 1963-67; project engr. Hamilton Standard div., Windsor Locks, Conn., 1967-70; sales mgr. Kaman Automation div. Kaman Aerospace Corp., Bloomfield, Conn., 1970-73; chief engr. Thermal Systems div. Sierracin Corp. (formerly Electroflex Corp. Calif.), Los Angeles, 1974-81; founder Rongo Co., South Pasadena, Calif., 1981—. Pres. congregation Congregational Ch., South Glastonbury, Conn., 1959-60. Served from ensign to lt. USNR, 1942-46. Mem. Lambda Chi Alpha. Republican. Patentee in field. Home: 1311 Lyndon St South Pasadena CA 91030 Office: Rongo Co PO Box 1472 South Pasadena CA 91030

BORSCH, FREDERICK HOUK, bishop; b. Chgo., Sept. 13, 1935; s. Reuben A. and Pearl Irene (Houk) B.; m. Barbara Edgeley Sampson, June 25, 1960; children: Benjamin, Matthew, Stuart. AB, Princeton U., 1957; MA, Oxford U., 1959; STB, Gen. Theol. Sem., 1960; PhD, U. Birmingham, 1966; DD (hon.), Seabury Western Theol. Sem., 1978, Gen. Theol. Sem., 1988; STD (hon.), Ch. Div. Sch. of Pacific, 1981, Yale U., 1983. Ordained priest Episcopal Ch., 1960; curate Grace Episcopal Ch., Oak Park, Ill., 1960-63; tutor Queen's Coll., Birmingham, Eng., 1963-66; asst. prof. N.T. Seabury Western Theol. Sem., Evanston, Ill., 1966-69, assoc. prof. N.T., 1969-71; prof. N.T. Gen. Theol. Sem., N.Y.C., 1971-72; pres., dean The Ch. Div. Sch. of Pacific, Berkeley, Calif., 1972-81; dean of chapel, prof. religion Princeton U., 1981-88; bishop Episc. Diocese, L.A., 1988—; rep. Faith and Order Commn., Nat. Coun. Chs., 1975-81; mem. exec. coun. Episc. Ch., 1981-88, Anglican Cons. Coun., 1984-88; chair bd. of govs. Trendy Press Internat., 1989—. Author: The Son of Man in Myth and History, 1967, The Christian and Gnostic Son of Man, 1970, God's Parable, 1976, Introducing the Lessons of the Church Years, 1978, Coming Together in the Spirit, 1980, Power in Weakness, 1983, Anglicanism and the Bible, 1984, Jesus: The Human Life of God, 1987, Many Things in Parables, 1988. Keasbey scholar, 1957-59. Fellow Soc. Arts, Religion and Contemporary Culture; mem. Am. Acad. Religion, Soc. Bibl. Lit., Studiorum Novi Testamenti Societas, Phi Beta Kappa. Home: 2930 Corda Ln Los Angeles CA 90049 Office: Episcopal Diocese of Los Angeles PO Box 2164 Los Angeles CA 90051-2145

BORSON, ROBERT OLIVER, communication executive, consultant; b. Tyler, Minn., Oct. 5, 1938; s. Albert Oliver and Hazel Inga (Esping) B.; m. Elizabeth Jean Erickson, June 26, 1960 (div. Dec. 1976); children: Nathan Scott, Niklas Erik; m. Susan Arlene Haynes, June 15, 1984. BA, Concordia Coll., Moorhead, Minn., 1960. Writer, editor of employee publications Kemper Ins., Chgo., 1960-64; assoc. editor of VIP mag. HMH Publishing Co., Chgo., 1964-65; asst. editor of Sweden Now mag. Industria Press, Stockholm, 1965-68; foreign corr. Madrid, 1968-70; editor Pacific Bus. mag. Calif. C. of C., Sacramento, 1970-72; sr. communications officer BankAmerica Corp., San Francisco, 1972-79, chief speechwriter, 1979-82; prin. Robert Borson Communications, Palo Alto, Calif., 1982—. Contbr. articles profl. jours. Club: Commonwealth Club of Calif. Office: 865 Oregon Ave Palo Alto CA 94303

BORTON, GEORGE ROBERT, airline captain; b. Wichita Falls, Tex., Mar. 22, 1922; s. George Neat and Travis Lee (Jones) B.; m. Anne Louise Bowling, Feb. 5, 1944; children: Trudie T., Robert B., Bruce M. AA, Hardin Coll., Wichita Falls, 1940. Cert. airline transport pilot, FAA flight examiner. Flight sch. operator Vallejo (Calif.) Sky Harbor, 1947-48; capt. S.W. Airways, San Francisco, 1948-55; check capt. Pacific Airlines, San Francisco, 1955-68, Hughes Air West, San Francisco, 1968-71; capt. N.W. Airlines, Mpls., 1971-82, ret., 1982. Col. USAFR, 1943-73. Decorated Air medal. Mem. Airline Pilots Assn., Res. Officers Assn., Air Force Assn., Horseless Carriage Club, Model T of Am. Club (Phoenix). Repubilcan. Congregationalist. Home: 4612 W Monte Cristo Ave Glendale AZ 85306

BORTON, WILLIAM MONROE, management consultant; b. Cambridge, Ohio, Nov. 26, 1914; s. Grover Cleveland and Estella Corinne (Monroe) B.; BSc with honors in Mktg., Ohio State U., Columbus, 1938, MBA, 1944; PhD (grantee Sales Execs. Club L.A.), U. So. Calif., 1956. Advt. mgr., gen. mgr. J.G. Bair Co., Cambridge, 1939-44; market analyst, sales mgr. Van Tuyl Engring. Corp., L.A., 1944-45; market analyst Lane-Wells Co., L.A., 1945-46; market, product research mgr. Weber Showcase & Fixture Co., L.A., 1946-47; mgmt. cons., L.A., 1947—; instr. bus. Ohio State U., 1944, U. So. Calif., 1946-49, Calif. State U. at L.A., 1949-51, UCLA, 1957-59, 77. Lic. psychologist, Calif. Mem. Am. Psychol. Assn., Am. Mktg. Assn., AAAS, Phi Delta Theta, Phi Eta Sigma, Beta Gamma Sigma, Sports Connection Club. Contbg. editor So. Calif. Yachting News, 1968-69; contbr. articles on bus., social sci. to profl. jours. Address: 8400 De Longpre Ave Suite 411 Los Angeles CA 90069

BOSBOOM, JEFFREY, marketing executive; b. N.Y.C., Apr. 3, 1958; s. Herman D. and Barbara E. (Roth) B. BSBA, U. Denver, 1980, MBA, 1982. Mktg. mgr. H. Roth & Son, N.Y.C., 1983-85; v.p. computer discount div. Progressive Peripherals & Software, Inc., Denver, 1986—; v.p. Computer Discount Ariz., Phoenix, 1987—. Home: 1777 Larimer St #1903 Denver CO 80202 Office: Progressive Peripherals & Software Inc 464 Kalamath St Denver CO 80204

BOSCO, DOUGLAS H., congressman; b. N.Y.C., July 28, 1946. B.A. in English, Willamette U., 1968, J.D., 1971. Bar: Calif. Practiced la; mem. 98th-101st Congresses from 1st Dist. Calif.; chmn. pub. works subcom. on pub. bldgs. and grounds, also mem. mcht. marine and fisheries com. and fgn. affairs com. Bd. dirs. Marin County Housing Authority; bd. dirs. Marin County Consumer Protection Agy., Sonoma County Fair; fundraiser hosp. ship S.S. Hope; co-founder No. Calif. Emeritus Coll. for Sr. Citizens; mem. Calif. Wildlife Conservation Bd.; mem. Calif. State Assembly, 1978-81, Democratic caucus chmn., 1981. Office: US Ho of Reps 225 Cannon House Office Bldg Washington DC 20515

BOSEKER, EDWARD HERBERT, orthopedic surgeon; b. Fort Wayne, Ind., Feb. 16, 1936; s. Herbert W. and Helen M. (Mueller) B.; B.S. with honors, U. Mich., 1958; M.D., Ind. U., 1962; M.S. in Orthopedic Surgery, 1967; m. Yvonne Jean Park, June 9, 1962; children—Andrea, Susan, Resa. Intern, Lutheran Hosp., Ft. Wayne, Ind., 1962-63; resident Mayo Clinic, Rochester, Minn., 1963-67; practice medicine, specializing in orthopedic surgery, Santa Ana, Calif., 1967—; asst. clin. prof. U. Calif., Irvine, 1970—. Pres. Tustin (Calif.) Unified Sch. Dist., 1980-81, 83-84. Diplomate Am. Bd. Orthopedic Surgeons. Fellow ACS; mem. Am. Acad. Orthopedic Surgeons. Office: 801 N Tustin Santa Ana CA 92705

BOSLEY, GARY OSCAR, civic organization administrator; b. Oakland, Calif., Apr. 11, 1944; s. Allen Eugene and Eva Marie Bosley; AB in Econs., U. Calif., Berkeley, 1966. Agrl. specialist, analyst Merrill Lynch, Pierce, Fenner & Smith, Winnipeg, Man., Can., 1971-72, stockbroker, commodity broker, Houston, 1972-74; stockbroker, commodity broker Dean Witter & Co., Hayward, Calif., 1975-84; pvt. investor, 1984-85; exec. v.p. Hawthorne (Calif.) C. of C., 1986-87, Laguna Beach (Calif.) C. of C., 1988-89, Found. for Study of Cycles, Irvine, Calif., 1989—. Rep. candidate for Calif. Assembly, 1976; mem. Alameda County Rep. Cen. Com., 1977-78; mem. Calif. State Rep. Cen. Com., 1977-78; past bd. dirs. Regional Citizens Forum, San Francisco Bay Area; past deacon, past mem. council, past moderator Broadmoor Congregational Ch., San Leandro, Calif. Served to capt. USAF, 1967-71. Decorated Commendation medal. Mem. Rep. Bus. and Profl. Club of Hayward (past pres.), Delta Tau Delta, Commonwealth (San Francisco), Rotary (past dir. Castro Valley, Calif. club, Lawndale, Calif. club). Address: 17887 Trenton Dr Castro Valley CA 94546

BOSMAN, PAUL WRAY, wildlife artist; b. Glen, Republic of South Africa, Aug. 2, 1929; s. Ferdinand Hugo and Edith Cecilia Mary (Townshend) B.; m. Valerie Elaine Roos, July 7, 1956; children: Christopher Paul, Simon Villiers, Elizabeth Kate. Diploma, Johannesburg Art Sch., Republic of South Africa, 1950; postgrad., Cen. Sch. Art, London, 1951. Artist S.A. Litho Ltd., Johannesburg, 1952-53; visualiser Colman, Prentis & Varley Ltd., London, 1954-55; artist Bomac Ltd., Montreal, Que., Can., 1956-57, Afamal Advt. Ltd., Durban, Republic of South Africa, 1957-58; from art dir. to creative dir. Lindsay Smithers Advt. Ltd., Durban and Johannesburg, 1959-68; wildlife artist, owner Malapati Game Lodge, Rhodesia, 1969-75; wildlife artist Johannesburg, 1976-81, Phoenix, 1982—. Fellow Endangered Wildlife Trust So. Africa, Johannesburg, 1978—; advisor Rhino and Elephant Found., Johannesburg, 1986—. Mem. Soc. Wildlife Artists. Home and Office: 4426 N 85th St Scottsdale AZ 85251

BOSS, KATHLEEN ALICE, art director, graphic designer; b. Burbank, Calif., July 9, 1957; d. Kenneth Howard and Narlene Wallace (Barr) B. Student, Coastline Coll., 1976-79, Glendale Coll., 1976-77; AA, Orange Coast Coll., 1982; BFA, Art Ctr. Coll., Pasadena, Calif., 1985. Photographer Figge Photography, Newport Beach, Calif., 1975-80; designer Ocean Pacific Sportswear, Anaheim, Calif., 1983, Marliss-Seeff Prodns., L.A., 1987; designer, cons., owner, mgr. Kathleen Boss Design, Beverly Hills, Calif., 1985—; art dir. Ogilvy & Mather Advt., L.A., 1986, Eisaman, Johns & Laws, Inc., L.A., 1987—; cons. Andresen Typographics, L.A., 1985—. design theme cons. Pasadena Centennial Celebration, 1985; design cons. Children's Hosp., L.A., 1987—, Dorothy Goldeen Gallery, Santa Monica, Calif., 1987-88, ARC, L.A., 1988—. Vol. Concern II, cancer rsch., L.A., 1986—, Mus. Contemporary Art, L.A., 1987—. Recipient awards of merit Art Dirs. Club L.A., 1986, Western Art Dirs. Club, 1986, cert. of excellence Advt. Club

Orange County, 1986, award of excellence L.A. Advt. Women, 1987, merit awards Photo Design, 1987. Democrat. Home: 404 Shirley Pl Beverly Hills CA 90212 Office: Eisaman Johns & Laws Inc 6255 Sunset Blvd Ste 1400 Los Angeles CA 90028

BOSSAERT, SABINE MARIE, marketing executive; b. San Francisco, Nov. 7, 1958; d. Pierre Marie and Marie Claire (Lagae) B. AA in Econs., De Anza Coll., 1978; BS in Fin., Mktg., Econs., Santa Clara U., 1980. Acct. IBM, San Jose, Calif., 1978-80; acct., supr. Hewlett-Packard, Cupertino, Calif., 1980-83; fin. mgr. Hewlett-Packard, Cupertino, 1983-86, mktg. mgr., 1986—. Mem. Beta Gamma Sigma. Republican. Roman Catholic.

BOSSERT, PHILIP JOSEPH, information systems executive; b. Indpls., Feb. 23, 1944; s. Alfred Joseph and Phyllis Jean (Cashen) B.; m. Jane Elisabeth Shade, June 29, 1968. BA in Econs., Rockhurst coll., 1968; cert. in Philosophy, U. Freiburg, Fed. Republic Ger., 1970; MA in Philosophy, Washington U., St. Louis, 1972, PhD in Philosophy, 1973. Asst. prof. philosophy Hawaii Loa Coll., Honolulu, 1973-76, pres., 1978-86; dir. Hawaii com. for the humanities Nat. Endowment for the Humanities, Honolulu, 1976-77; dir. long range planning Chaminade U., Honolulu, 1977-78; pres. Strategic Info. Solutions, Honolulu, 1986—; mgr. strategic info. systems GTE Hawaiian Telephone, Honolulu, 1987—; cons. Ssangyong Bus. Group, Seoul, Korea, 1987—, Nat. Assn. Colls. Univs. and Bus. Officers, Washington, 1980—. Author: Strategic Planning and Budgeting, 1989; author, editor numerous books on philosophy; contbr. articles to profl. jours. Sgt. U.S. Army, 1962-65. Fulbright-Hays fellow, 1968-70, Woodrow Wilson fellow, 1972-73, Nat. Endowment for Humanities fellow, 1976. Mem. Data Processing Mgmt. Assn., Soc. Corp. Planners, Rotary Club. Office: Strategic Info Solutions Inc PO Box 37849 Honolulu HI 96837

BOST, THOMAS GLEN, lawyer; b. Oklahoma City, July 13, 1942; s. Burl John and Lorene Belle (Croka) B.; m. Sheila K. Pettigrew, Aug. 27, 1966; children: Amy Elizabeth, Stephen Luke, Emily Anne, Paul Alexander. BS in Acctg. summa cum laude, Abilene Christian U., 1964; JD, Vanderbilt U., 1967. Bar: Tenn. 1967, Calif. 1969. Instr. David Lipscomb Coll., Nashville, 1967; asst. prof. law Vanderbilt U., Nashville, 1967-68; ptnr. Latham & Watkins, Los Angeles, 1968—; lectr. on taxation subjects. Chmn. bd. regents, law sch. bd. visitors Pepperdine U., Malibu, Calif., 1980—. Mem. ABA (chmn. standards of tax practice com., sec. taxation 1988—), Calif. Bar Assn., Los Angeles County Bar Assn. (chmn. taxation sect. 1981-82). Republican. Mem. Ch. of Christ. Club: Calif. (Los Angeles). Office: Latham & Watkins 555 S Flower St Los Angeles CA 90071

BOSTICK, VIRGINIA HALTON LORD, writer, librarian; b. West Somerville, Mass., July 15, 1912; d. John Bertram and Mildred Mabel (Godden) Lord; m. Winston Harper Bostick, June 16, 1942; children: Joel Lord, Verity Jo Reed, Kent Anthony. BA magna cum laude, Tufts U., 1933, MA in English, 1934; MLS, Rutgers State U., 1968. Cert. profl. librarian, N.J., N.Y., N.Mex. Editor-in-chief climatology div. Weather Directorate, Army Air Forces, Washington, 1942-43; scriptwriter, editor radiation lab. MIT, Cambridge, 1943-46; head libr. reference dept. Pub. Libr. of Morristown (N.J.) and Twp. Free Pub. Libr., 1968-70; head libr. acquisitions dept. Morris County Libr., Morristown, 1971-75, libr., archivist N.J. Room, 1975-79; libr. U.S. Geol. Survey Libr., Albuquerque, 1981-84; freelance writer 1942—; dir. various drama groups, Tyngsboro, Mass., 1945-47. Author: (books) History of the Public Monuments of Morristown, N.J., 1978, History of the Public Monuments and Sculpture of Morris County, N.J., 1978, (book for mus.) Jim White's Addiction, 1982 (also dir.), (movie script) Autobiography, 1939 (Allied Artists award 1948); contbr. articles to tech. jours., also scripts and films on radar systems to Joint Chiefs of Staff, style manuals for Weather Directorate, Army Air Forces and Tech. Services, MIT. Active N.J. Hist. Society, Corrales (N.Mex.) Hist. Society (cert. appreciation 1982). Scholar Tufts U., 1933, 34, Rutgers State U., 1968; Nat. Endowment for the Arts grantee, 1978. Mem. Phi Beta Kappa. Home: PO Box 1652 Corrales NM 87048

BOSTON, BETTY ROACH, realtor; b. Linton, Ind., May 16, 1926; d. Raleigh Owen and Pearl C. (Chaney) Roach; m. O.E. Boston, Oct. 11, 1952; children: Brian R., Kerry A. BS, Ind. State U., 1948. Cert. residential brokerage. Placement, employee relations adv. USAF, Dayton, Ohio, 1948-52; mgr. placement services CSC, Cin., 1953-56; substitue tchr. Pasco (Wash.) Sch. Dist., 1970-73; office and property mgr. Keith Adams & Assocs., Richland, Wash., 1973-81; assoc. broker, co-owner Boston Real Estate Assocs., Richland, 1981—. Civil Service commr. Franklin County, 1986—; precinct com. person Franklin County, 1972-76; active Franklin County Rep. Cen. Com., 1970-76. Mem. Wash. Assn. Realtors (bd. dirs. 1983-86), Columbia Basin Apt. Assn. (pres., bd. dirs. 1985—), Tri-City Bd. Realtors (v.p., sec.-treas., bd. dirs. 1982—), Realtors Inst. (grad.), Altrusa Club (sec.), Franklin County Rep. Women's Club (pres.), Women of Rotary (pres. Richland chpt.). Home: 420 Road 39 Pasco WA 99301 Office: Boston Real Estate Assocs 511 Lee Blvd Richland WA 99352

BOSTWICK, RICHARD RAYMOND, lawyer; b. Billings, Mont., Mar. 17, 1918; s. Leslie H. and Maude (Worthington) B.; m. Margaret Florence Brooks, Jan. 17, 1944; children: Michael, Patricia, Ed, Dick. Student, U. Colo., 1937-38; A.B., U. Wyo., 1943, J.D., 1947. Bar: Wyo. 1947. Claim atty. Hawkeye Casualty Co., Casper, Wyo., 1948-49; ptnr. Murane & Bostwick, Casper, 1949—; lectr. U. Wyo. Coll. Law. Contbr. articles profl. jours. Past trustee Casper YMCA; dep. dir. Civil Def., 1954-58; chmn. local SSS, 1952-70; mem. curriculum coordinating com. Natrona Co. Sch. Dist. 2, High Sch. Dist.; Wyom. rep. adv. com. U.S. Tenth Circuit Ct. Appeals, 1985-87; mem. U. Wyo. Coll. Law Adv. Com., 1987—. Capt. AUS, 1943-46. Decorated Bronze Star medal; recipient Silver Merit awards Am. Legion. Mem. ABA, Wyo. Bar Assn. (pres. 1964-65, 1st Pro Bono award 1987), Natrona County Bar Assn. (pres. 1956), Am. Judicature Soc. (exec. com. 1973-75, sec. 1975-77 Herbert Harley award), Internat. Assn. Def. Counsel, Fedn. Ins. and Corp. Counsel, Nat. Conf. Bar Pres. (exec. council 1970-72), Internat. Soc. of Barristers (dir. 1971-76, pres. 1975), Am. Legion (dir. 1951-58, post comdr. 1953-54), Wyo. Alumni Assn. (trustee 1955-57), Casper C. of C. (chmn. legis. com. 1955-57, dir. 1959-62, v.p.). Presbyn. Club: Mason (Shriner, KT). Home: 1137 Granada Ave Casper WY 82601

BOSUSTOW, NICK ONSLOW, film producer; b. Los Angeles, Mar. 28, 1940; s, Stephen Reginald and Audrey Mildred (Stevenson) B.; m. Julienne Bosustow, Apr. 17, 1971; children: Nichole, Jeniffer. BS, Menlo (Calif.) Sch. of Bus. Adminstr., 1963. Pres. Bosustow Entertainment, Los Angeles, 1968—. Producer numerous TV spls. including Always Right To Be Right? (Acad. award 1971), Legend of John Henry (Acad. award nomination 1972), Incredible Book Escape (Emmy nomination 1981), Misunderstood Monsters, Tale of Four Wishes, Wrong Way Kid (Emmy award 1984), Haley Mills Story Book Series (Best Children's Series award Parents Mag. 1987). Served with U.S. Army. Mem. Acad. Motion Pictures Arts and Scis. (mem. short film exec. com.), Internat. Animated Film Assn. (bd. dirs., past pres.).

BOSWORTH, BRUCE LEIGHTON, teacher, consultant; b. Buffalo, Mar. 22, 1942; s. John Wayman and Alice Elizabeth Rodgers; children—David, Timothy, Paul, Reuben, Sheri, Roy, Quincy, Terry, Skyler. BA, U. Denver, 1964; MA, U. No. Colo., 1970; EdD, Walden U., 1984. Elem. tchr. Littleton (Colo.) Pub. Schs., 1964-67, 70-81; bldg. prin. East Smoky Sch. Div. 54, Valleyview, Alta., Can., 1967-70; pres., tchr. Chatfield Sch., Littleton, 1981—; mem. research bd. advisors Am. Biog. Inst.; adoption cons. hard-to-place children; ednl. cons. spl. needs children. Dir. Christian Edn.; mem. adminstrn. bd., mem. fin. com. Warren United Meth. Ch.;. Mem. Council Exceptional Children, Assn. Supervision and Curriculum Devel., Englewood C. of C. Republican. Methodist. Clubs: Masons, Shriners, York Rite. Home: 6170 S Bemis St Littleton CO 80120 Office: Chatfield Sch PO Box 1039 Littleton CO 80160

BOTIMER, ALLEN RAY, surgeon; b. Columbus, Miss., Jan. 30, 1930; s. Clare E. and Christel J. (Kalar) B.; m. Dorris LaJean, Aug. 17, 1950; children: Larry Alan, Gary David. BS, Walla Walla Coll., 1951; MD, Loma Linda U., 1955; FACS, Am. Coll. Surgeons, 1966. Diplomate Am. Bd. Surgery. Surgical resident U.S. Naval Hosp., San Diego, 1955-60; asst. chief surgery U.S. Naval Hosp., Guam, 1960-62, Bremerton, Wash., 1962-64; chief surgery Ballard Community Hosp., Seattle, 1970, chief of staff, 1972-87, chief surgery, 1986-87; practice medicine specializing in surgery Seattle, 1964-87; ret. 1987. Served to lt. comdr. USN, 1955-64. Fellow Am. Coll. Surgeons, Seattle Surgical Soc.; mem. King County Med., Wash. State Med. Soc. Home: 18419 17th St NW Seattle WA 98177

BOTT, RICHARD WARNER, aerospace engineer; b. Monterey, Calif., July 18, 1959; s. Alan Richard and Jean (Hemore) B. BS in Aero Engring., San Diego State U., 1986. Aerospace engr. Naval Aviation Depot North Island, San Diego, 1987—. Historian Navy League of U.S., San Diego, 1987. Mem. (charter) Nat. Air and Space Mus., (life) San Diego Aerospace Mus., Am. Inst. Aeros. and Astronautics (pres. 1988—), U.S. Naval Inst. Republican. Home: 1509 Meade Ave San Diego CA 92116

BOTTI, RICHARD CHARLES, association executive; b. Brockton, Mass., May 1, 1939; s. Alfred Benecchi and Elizabeth Savini; stepson Ernest Botti; student Pierce Jr. Coll., 1959, Orange Coast Coll., 1964; m. Gwen Botti; children—Randolph K., Douglas S., Richard II. Pres., Legis. Info. Services Hawaii, Inc., Honolulu, 1971—; exec. dir., profl. lobbyist Hawaii Food Industry Assn., Honolulu, Hawaii Automotive & Retail Gasoline Dealers Assn., Inc., Honolulu, Hawaii Bus. League, Retail Liquor Dealers Assn. Hawaii, Liquor Dispensers of Hawaii, Honolulu. Mem. Food Industry Assn. Execs., Am. Soc. Assn. Execs., Aloha Soc. Assn. Execs., Hawaii Pubs. Assn., Automotive Body & Painting Assn., Hawaii Pubs. Assn. Address: Legis Info Services 677 Ala Moana Blvd Suite 815 Honolulu HI 96813

BOTTJER, DAVID JOHN, geological sciences educator; b. N.Y.C., Oct. 3, 1951; s. John Henry and Marilyn (Winter) B.; m. Sarah Ranney Wright, July 26, 1973. BS, Haverford Coll., 1973; MA, SUNY, Binghamton, 1976; PhD, Ind. U., 1978. NRC postdoctoral rsch. assoc. U.S. Geol. Survey, Washington, 1978-79; asst. prof. dept. geol. scis. U. So. Calif., L.A., 1979-85, assoc. prof. dept. geol. scis., 1985—; rsch. assoc. L.A. County Mus. Natural History, 1979—; vis. scientist Field Mus. Natural History, Chgo., 1986. Editor Palaios, 1989—; assoc. editor Cretaceous Rsch., 1988—; mem. editorial bd. Geology, 1984—, Hist. Biology, 1988—. Fellow Geol. Soc. Am.; mem. Paleontol. Soc., Soc. Econ. Paleontology and Mineralogy, AAAS, Internat. Paleontology Assn. Office: U So Calif Dept Geol Sci Los Angeles CA 90089-0740

BOTTOMS, WILLIAM CLAY, JR., aviation company executive; b. Atlanta, June 13, 1946; s. William Clay and Alice Elizabeth (Walker) B.; m. Nancy Lou Snodgrass, Mar. 16, 1968; children: Janet Elizabeth, Sharon Suzanne. B in Aerospace Engring., Ga. Inst. Tech., 1969. Aerodyn. engr. McDonnell Aircraft Co., St. Louis, 1969-73; dir. engring. and quality control Southern Airways, Atlanta, 1973-78; staff v.p. maintenance Tex. Internat. Airlines, Houston, 1978-80; v.p. tech. services N.Y. Air, N.Y.C., 1980-83; sr. v.p. ops. Rocky Mountain Airways, Denver, 1983-85; exec. dir. Colo. Aero Tech., Broomfield, 1985—; regional cons. Robert Jameson Assocs., Denver, 1985;. Pres. Golden Meadows Homeowners Assn., Morrison, Colo., 1983-87; del. Regional Homeowners Assn., Aspen Park, Colo., 1985-86; bd. dirs. Colo. Pvt. Sch. Assn., 1987—, pres.-elect, 1989—; bd. dirs. Broomfield (Colo.) Econs. Devel. Corp., 1988—. Mem. Colo. Tng. Assurance Found. (bd. dirs. 1987—), Aviation Tech. Edn. Council (bd. dirs. 1988—). Republican. Baptist. Home: 8244 Wagon Wheel Rd Morrison CO 80465 Office: Colo Aero Tech 10851 120th Ave Broomfield CO 80020

BOTTS, WILLIAM VENN, JR., software company executive; b. San Bernardino, Calif., Sept. 17, 1935; s. William Venn and June Louise (Strout) B.; m. Barbara Anne Brock, June 8, 1955 (div. 1959); 1 child, Leslie Karen; m. Margaret Anne Laituri, July 10, 1962. BSEE, BS in Math., Calif. Poly. U., San Luis Obispo, 1959; postgrad., UCLA, 1960-61. Rsch. engr. N.Am. Aviation Co., L.A., 1959-61, project engr., 1962-63; program mgr. Rockwell Internat., L.A., 1964-68, dir., 1969-72, v.p., 1972-78; pres., chief exec. officer Energy Inc., Idaho Falls, Idaho, 1978-80; pres., chief exec. officer, chmn. EI Internat., Idaho Falls, 1981-88; pres., chief exec. officer Vertex Inc., San Francisco, 1988—, also bd. dirs.; lectr. on nuclear power mgmt. and quality assurance, 1980-88; chmn. bd. dirs. Energy Products of Idaho, 1980-85, Agrodyne Inc., 1978-80, EI Technology Inc., 1980-85, Wast Tech. Sewcer Inc., 1984-85. Patentee thermopac. Active United Way, Jr. Achievement, also other civic orgns., Idaho Falls, 1978-88; founder, pres. CHC Found., Idaho Falls, 1984-88. Mem. Am. Nuclear Soc., Am. Mgmt. Assn. Republican. Baptist. Home: 2362 Pine St San Francisco CA 94115 Office: Vertex Inc 140 2d St Ste 500 San Francisco CA 94105

BOUCHER, BILL ANTONIO, telecommunications consulting company executive; b. Nome, Alaska, Mar. 28, 1934; s. Wilfred Amade and Emily Pasqualina (Polet) B.; m. Brenda Joyce Agsten, July 22, 1984. Student in Engring., U. Va., 1952-54; student in Liberal Arts, U. Alaska, 1957-59. Installer, repairman Alaska Telephone & Telegraph, Nome, 1950-52; pvt. practice elec. contracting Nome, 1952-59; installer, asst. mgr. Fairbanks (Alaska) Mcpl. Utilities Svcs., 1959-73; contractor, cons. Digital Switching Assoc., Fairbanks, 1973-82; cons. Fairbanks and San Diego, 1985-; v.p. ops. Starnet, San Diego, 1982-85; mem. customer adv. panel ITT, Caracas, Venezuela, 1973. Sr. mem. CAP, Alaska, 1951--. With USAF, 1954-56. Mem. Soc. Mining Engrs., Aircraft Owners and Pilots Assn., Mooney Aircraft Pilots Assn. Home: PO Box 60174 Fairbanks AK 99706

BOUCHER, MAYO TERRY, lawyer, judge; b. Stephenville, Tex., July 15, 1918; s. Terry S. and Henryetta (Turley) B.; m. Mary Catherine Lake, July 31, 1942; children: Phillip Larry, Terri Sue. Student, Tex. Tech, 1937-41; LLB, U. N.Mex., 1952, JD, 1969. Bar: N.Mex.; ordained deacon Bapt. Ch. With Atchison, Topeka & Santa Fe Ry., Belen, N.Mex., 1946-52; sole practice Belen, 1952-80; dist. judge 13th Jud. Dist. 1980—; mem. ho. of reps. State of N.Mex., 1957-64; v.p. Belen Broadcasting Co., 1963-64; city atty. City of Belen, 1956-57; sec.-treas. First Belen Escrow Co., 1986—. Served with USNR, 1942-45. Mem. C. of C. (dir. 1954-57, pres. 1955), Pi Sigma Alpha. Lodges: Masons (past master), Order Eastern Star (past patron Jessamine chpt., 1954, 78, 89—, past grand patron, grand jurisdiction N.Mex., 1984-85), Rotary (pres. 1961-62). Home: 1620 Velta Dr Belen NM 87002 Office: 13th Jud Dist PO Box 1089 Los Lunas NM 87031

BOUDART, MICHEL, chemist, chemical engineer; b. Belgium, June 18, 1924; came to U.S., 1947, naturalized, 1957; s. Francois and Marguerite (Swolfs) B.; m. Marina D'Haese, Dec. 27, 1948; children: Mark, Baudouin, Iris, Philip. BS, U. Louvain, Belgium, 1944, MS, 1947; PhD, Princeton U., 1950; D honoris causa, U. Liège, U. Notre Dame, U. Nancy, U. Ghent, Belgium. Research asso. James Forrestal Research Ctr., Princeton, 1950-54; mem. faculty Princeton U., 1954-61; prof. chem. engring. U. Calif., Berkeley, 1961-64; prof. chem. engring. and chemistry Stanford U., 1964-80, William M. Keck prof. chem. engring., 1980—; cons. to industry, 1955—; co-founder Catalytica, Inc.; Humble Oil Co. lectr., 1958, Am. Inst. Chem. Engrs. lectr., 1961, Sigma Xi nat. lectr., 1965; chmn. Gordon Research Conf. Catalysis, 1962. Author: Kinetics of Chemical Processes, 1968, (with G. Djéga-Mariadassou) Kinetics of Heterogeneous Catalytic Reactions, 1983; editor: (with J.R. Anderson) Catalysis: Science and Technology, 1981; adv. editorial bd. Jour. Internat. Chem. Engring., 1964—, Advances in Catalysis, 1968—, Catalysis Rev., 1968—, Accounts Chem. Research, 1978—. Belgium-Am. Ednl. Found. fellow, 1948; Procter fellow, 1949; recipient Curtis-McGraw research award Am. Soc. Engring. Edn., 1962, R.H. Wilhelm award in chem. reaction engring., 1974. Fellow AAAS; mem. Am. Chem. Soc. (Kendall award 1977, E.V. Murphee award in Indsl. & Engring. Chemistry 1985), Catalysis Soc., Am. Inst. Chem. Engrs., Chem. Soc., Nat. Acad. Sci., Nat. Acad. Engring.; fgn. assoc. Académie Royale de Belgique. Home: 512 Gerona Rd Stanford CA 94305 Office: Stanford Univ Dept Chem Engring Stanford CA 94305

BOUDREAU, KEVIN PAUL, accountant; b. Kankakee, Ill., Oct. 7, 1964; s. Wayne Vincent and Brenda Joyce (Johnson) B.; m. Eileen Antoinette Brennan, Nov. 11, 1989. BS in Acctg., Marquette U., 1986. C.P.A., Ariz.; Cert. Managerial Acct. Fin. cons. sr. Arthur Andersen & Co., Phoenix, 1986—; cons. Phoenix Econ. Growth Corp., 1986—. Sports corr. Mesa Tribune, 1986—. Mem. Nat. Assn. Accts., Am. Inst. CPAs, Ariz. Soc. CPAs, Marquette U. Club (Phoenix, prs. 1988, bd. dirs. 1987—). Republican. Roman Catholic. Home: 1424 S Doran Mesa AZ 85204 Office: 2 N Central Ste 1000 Phoenix AZ 85004

BOUGHTON, JAMES WALTER, resort development executive; b. Atlantic City, N.J., Dec. 16, 1946; s. Walter Lennie and Janet Caroline (Mossman) B.; m. Sharon Carter, Mar. 10, 1980; children: Jennifer Christine, Matthew James. Student, U. Colo., 1967-68, U. Md., 1968-70, Met. State Coll., 1972-73. Salesman Woodmoor Corp., Denver, 1971-73; regional sales dir. Del E. Webb, Colo., Inc., Denver, 1973-76; pres. J. Broughton, Inc., Miami, Fla., 1976-83, Spectrum Mktg. Group, Inc., Vail, Colo., 1983-84; sr. v.p. Fairfield Communities, Inc. New York Stock Exchange, Atlanta, 1984-85; chmn. of the bd., pres. and chief exec. officer LEXES Enterprises, Inc., Las Vegas, 1985—; gov. bd. mem. Nat. Timesharing Council, Washington, 1983—; adv. bd. mem. Interval Internat., Miami, Fla., 1982—; bd. dirs. Resort Computer Corp., Denver. Editor/Pub.: (10 vol. compendium) Time Sharing Ency., 1980-82, (trade newspaper) Time Sharing Industry Review, 1981-82; contbr. articles to profl. jours. Scout leader Boy Scouts Am., Las Vegas, 1988. Svc. award Nat. Timesharing Council, 1987. Mem. Am. Resort and Residential Devel. Assn. (bd. dirs. 1985—, meetings com. chmn. 1983—, exec. com. mem. 1987—, Closer of Yr. award 1985-86, Pres.'s award 1988). Republican. Office: LEXES Enterprises Inc 1500 E Tropicana Ave Ste 215 Las Vegas NV 89119

BOUKIDIS, CONSTANTINE MICHAEL, lawyer; b. Burbank, Calif., Nov. 16, 1959; s. Michael A. and Frances (Mavros) B.; m. Eugenia Demetra Rodinos, May 17, 1987. BA in Econs., Northwestern U., 1981; JD, Loyola Law Sch., L.A., 1984. Bar: Calif. 1985, U.S. Dist. Ct. (cen. dist.) Calif. 1985, U.S. Ct. Appeals (9th cir.), 1985. Investigator Harney & Moore, L.A., 1980-82; assoc. Harney & Packer, L.A., 1985—. Treas., chmn. cathedral planning com. St. Sophia Cathedral Orthodox Community, L.A., 1989. Mem. ABA, Assn. Trial Lawyers Am., Calif. Trial Lawyers Assn., L.A. County Bar Assn., Glendale (Calif.) Bar Assn., Phi Kappa Sigma (trea. 1980-81). Democrat. Home: 1641 Country Club Dr Glendale CA 91208 Office: Harney & Packer 201 N Figueroa St #1300 Los Angeles CA 90012

BOULDIN, DANNY LEE, electrical engineer; b. Fyffe, Ala., Oct. 31, 1953; s. Virgil Dee and Johnnie Mag (Gibson) B.; m. Brenda Gale Wooten, Apr. 13, 1974; children: Kelly, Stacey. BSEE, Auburn U., 1978; MSEE, Fla. Inst. Tech., 1983. Sr. engr. Harris Corp., Ft. Walton Beach, Fla., 1978-80, Martin Marietta Aerospace Div., Orlando, Fla., 1980-83, ITT Corp., Roanoke, Va., 1983-85; devel. engr. Hewlett Packard Corp., Palo Alto, Calif., 1985—. Republican. Home: PO Box 51477 Palo Alto CA 94303 Office: Hewlett Packard Corp 370 W Trimble Rd San Jose CA 95131

BOULET, TAMI LEE, social worker; b. Lawton, Okla., Sept. 12, 1958; d. Aristide Ferdinand and Sharon Ann (Adeline) B.; m. Gary Wade Verboon, May 17, 1980 (div. Nov. 1985). BA in Religion, B in Social Work, Azusa Pacific U., 1980; MSW, UCLA, 1984. Licensed clin. social worker, Calif. Social work intern East Los Angeles Regional Ctr. for Developmentally Disabled, Alhambra, Calif., 1979-80; social worker United Cerebral Palsy, Sylmar, Calif., 1980-82; social work intern St. John's Hosp., Santa Monica, Calif., 1982-83, Didi Hirsch Community Mental Health Ctr., Culver City, Calif., 1983-84; social worker Hollygrove Residential Treatment Ctr. for Children, Hollywood, Calif., 1984—; dir. clin. services Hollygrove Residential Treatment Ctr. for Children, Hollywood, 1987—. Participant South American Mission, Columbia, 1978, Latin American Mission, Mexico City, 1979, travel seminar on world religions, Inter-Religious Found., 1985; Amnesty Internat. group 96, Santa Monica, 1982—; mem. vestry St. Augustine's Episcopal Ch., Santa Monica, 1987—. Mem. Nat. Assn. Social Workers, UCLA Sch. Social Welfare Alumni Assn. Democrat. Episcopalian. Home: 1626 Armacost #5 West Los Angeles CA 90025 Office: Hollygrove 815 N El Centro Ave Los Angeles CA 90038

BOULWARE, RICHARD STARK, airport administrator; b. Chgo., Aug. 28, 1935; s. John Stark and Ellen Bradley (Bowlin) B.; m. Sylvia Grace Panaro, Sept. 17, 1960 (div. Jan. 1980); children: Susan Bradley, Robert Stark. BFA, Art Ctr. Coll., 1967. Photographer Hughes Aircraft, Los Angeles, 1960-61; chief photographer U. Iowa, Iowa City, 1962-67; dir. audio/visual media TransWorld Airlines, N.Y.C., 1968-70; owner, mgr. RBA Prodns., Denver, 1970-80; dir. photography Colo. Inst. Art, Denver, 1980-84; dep. dir. aviation Stapleton Internat. Airport, Denver, 1984—. Served with USN, 1954-58. Recipient Golden Eagle award CINE, 1976, award Bus. and Profl. Advt. Assn., Alfie award Denver Advt. Fedn., Christensen Meml. award Iowa Press Photographers Assn., award Art Dirs. Club Denver; named Nat. Photographer of Yr. U. Profl. Photographers Assn. Am., 1967. Mem. Pub. Relations Soc. Am. (award Colo. chpt.), Colo. Broadcasters Assn., Colo. Press Assn. Club: Art Dirs. (Denver) (v.p.). Home: 9112-E E Amherst Dr Denver CO 80231 Office: Stapleton Internat Airport Terminal Bldg 3232 Denver CO 80207

BOUMANN, ROBERT LYLE, lawyer; b. Holdrege, Nebr., June 9, 1946; s. John G. and Loretta M. (Eckhardt) B. BS, U. Nebr., 1968, JD, 1974. CPA, Nebr.; bar: Nebr., 1974, Colo. 1987. Sr. acct. Peat, Marwick, Main and Co., Denver, 1968-71; atty., asst. sec. K N Energy, Inc., Lakewood, Colo., 1974—; bd. dirs. Consolidated Motor Freight, Inc., Hastings, Nebr. Treas. YMCA, Hastings, 1979-80. Mem. Nebr. Soc. CPAs, Nebr. State Bar Assn., Colo. State Bar Assn., ABA, Def. Rsch. Inst., Jaycees (treas. Hastings chpt. 1977-78), Phi Eta Sigma, Beta Gamma Sigma. Republican. Roman Catholic. Office: K N Energy Inc 12055 W 2d Pl Lakewood CO 80228

BOURDETTE, JACQUELINE CAROL, dentist, educator; b. West Covina, Calif., Dec. 11, 1951; d. Stanley Gail and Virginia Jean (Phillips) Trujillo; m. Dennis Neil Bourdette, June 12, 1981. BA in Behavioral Sci., San Jose State U., Calif., 1975; DMD, Oreg. Health Scis. U., Portland, 1986. Asst., prof. pub. health Oreg. Health Scis. U., Portland, 1986—. Mem. Acad. Gen. Dentistry, Oreg. Soc. Dentistry for Children. Office: Oreg Health Scis U Dept Pub Health Dentistry Sch Dentistry Portland OR 97201

BOUREKIS, JAMES GEORGE, dentist; b. Warren, Ohio, Mar. 30, 1930; s. George and Maria (Kontos) B.; m. Katherine Barbas, Sept. 2, 1956; children: Maria Theresa, George James. DDS, Northwestern U., 1954. Pvt. practice, Warren, 1957-59, Spokane, Wash., 1960—; bd. dirs. Modern Electric Water Co., Spokane. Capt. USAF, 1954-56. Mem. ADA, Wash. State Dental Assn., Spokane Dist. Dental Soc., Rotary. Office: 20 Pines Rd S Spokane WA 99206

BOUSFIELD, KENNETH HAROLD, civil engineer; b. L.A., Nov. 14, 1946; s. William Harold and Shirley (Burgess) B.; m. Gail Natall, Sept. 2, 1970; children: Tara Lee, Julie, Timothy Kenneth, Kelly Jean. BSCE, Brigham Young U., 1971; postgrad., U. Utah, 1976-80. Registered profl. engr., Utah. Engr. Utah Dept. Health, Salt Lake City, 1971-72; assoc. engr. Nielsen Maxwell & Wangsgard, Salt Lake City, 1973-76; compliance mgr. Utah Dept. Health, Salt Lake City, 1976—. Contbr. articles to profl. jours. Fellow EPA; mem. Am. Water Works Assn. Republican. Mormon. Office: Utah Dept Health 288 N 1460 W Salt Lake City UT 84116-0690

BOUVET, PIERRE, food products executive; b. Bombay, Jan. 6, 1921; came to U.S., 1965; s. Pierre and Marie F. (Yernel) B.; m. Josee de Marigny, Dec. 16, 1948; children: Jacques, Bernadette Lang, Dominique, Didier, Marie Woolard; m. Nancy S. Snively, Nov. 28, 1980. Diploma, Mauritius Coll. of Agr., 1942; BS, U. Witwatersrand, 1947. Factory supt. St. Antoine Sugar Estate, Mapou, Mauritius, 1956-57; mgr. Rose Belle Sugar Estate, New Grove, Mauritius, 1957-65; factory supt. Laupahoehoe Sugar Co., PaPaaloa, Hawaii, 1965-68; asst. mgr. Honokaa Sugar Co., Haina, Hawaii, 1968-69; plantation mgr. Theo. H. Davies Co., Ltd., Honolulu, 1969-72; v.p., gen. mgr. Theo. Davies Hamakua Sugar Co., Paauilo, Hawaii, 1979-83; pres., chief exec. officer Syner-Tech, Inc., Richardson, Tex., 1985-87; cons. Bouvet & Assocs., Inc., Kamuela, Hawaii, 1987—; cons. ABA Internat., Inc., Honolulu, 1983-88, P.T. Agriconsult Internat., Jakarta, Indonesia, 1988—. Patentee in field; contbr. articles to profl. jours. Lt. Republic of South Africa Air Force, 1943-45. Recipient cert. of recognition State of Hawaii Legislature, 1983, cert. of recognition Hawaii County Council, 1983, cert. of recognition Mayor of Hawaii County, 1983; named Boss of Yr. Hamakua Jaycees, 1981. Mem. Hawaii Island Profl. Engrs., Hawaii Sugar Tech. Assn. Republican. Roman Catholic. Home: 33 Wai Aka Pl Kamuela HI 96743 Office: Bouvet & Assocs Inc PO Box 2439 Kamuela HI 96743

BOVAL, LAWRENCE STEVEN, water resource engineer; b. Dayton, Ohio, May 9, 1948; s. Norman Frederick and Edna Paulene (Ison) B. BSEE, Cornell U., 1970. Registered profl. engr., Tex. Elec. engr. Engring. Cons. Inc., Denver, 1970-75; sr. elec. engr. Bechtel Inc., Houston, 1975-76; asst. v.p. PRC Engring. Cons., Englewood, Colo., 1977-79, exec. v.p., 1980-83; v.p., chief fin. officer PRC Consoer Townsend Inc., Chgo., 1983-85; pres. ATC Engring. Cons., Englewood, 1986—. Mem. Colo. Cons. Engr. Council (membership com. 1987-88). Republican. Methodist. Club: Glenmoor Country (Cherry Hills, Colo.). Office: ATC Engring Cons Inc 7935 E Prentice Ave 2d Fl Englewood CO 80111

BOVE, TONI MICHELLE, retail executive; b. West Chester, Pa., July 13, 1952; d. Anthony and Barbara (Shirey) B. AA, Golden West Coll., 1985; student, Calif. State U.-Fullerton, 1985-86. Asst. mgr. Bustle Stop, Kennett Square, Pa., 1970; mgr. Bove Fashions, Kennett Square, 1970-75; sales rep. Uniroyal, Inc., N.Y.C., 1976-78, Brown Shoe Co., St. Louis, 1978-79; asst. mgr. J. Herbert Hall Jewelers, Westminster, Calif., 1980-81, Apropos, Orange, Calif., 1981; mgr. Slavicks Jewelers, Santa Monica, Calif., 1982-86; buyer, mgr. Bayly OP Apparel Group, Santa Ana, Calif., 1987-88; mgr. jewelery gallery Geoffrey Roth, Ltd. Tlaquepaque, Sedona, Ariz., 1988—. Mem. Himalayan Inst. Yoga and Sci., Planetary Soc., Am. Film Inst. Home: 75 Box Canyon Rd Sedona AZ 86336 Office: Geoffrey Roth Ltd Sedona AZ 86336

BOVERO, ALDO, restaurateur; b. Turin, Italy, Sept. 11, 1928; came to U.S., 1960; s. Pietro and Maria (Gallenca) B.; children by previous marriage: Graziella, Ricardo, Gina; m. Sydney Marie Smith, Dec. 25, 1980; children: Adriane and Claudia (twins). Ed. pub. schs., Turin. Waiter, bus person various restaurants, Italy, Switzerland and France, 1940-53; capt., maître d' hotel Restaurant Le Bistro, Rio de Janeiro, 1953-54; maître d' hotel Victoria Plaza Hotel, Montevideo, Uruguay, 1954-60, Palace Hotel, San Francisco, 1960-62; owner, pres. Aldo's Restaurant, Sacramento, 1965—. Mem. exec. com. March of Dimes, Sacramento, 1986-87. Named Restauranteur of Yr., Sacramento, 1986; Aldo's Restaurant rated 5 stars Holiday Awards, 1965—. Mem. Calif. Restaurant Assn. Office: Aldo's Inc 2914 Pasatiempo Ln Sacramento CA 95821

BOVEY, TERRY ROBINSON, insurance executive; b. Oregon, Ill., May 13, 1948; s. John Franklin and Frances (Robinson) B.; m. Diana Carmen Rodriguez, Aug. 29, 1970 (div. July 1980); 1 child, Joshua; m. Kathy Jo Johnston, Sept. 14, 1985: stepchildren: Lara, Mickey, Keri; 1 child, Courtney. Student, Ariz. Western Coll., 1966-68, Grand Canyon Coll., 1968-69; BBA, U. Ariz., 1972. Salesman All-Am. Dist. Co., Yuma, Ariz., 1972-76; dist. asst. mgr. Equitable Life Ins., Yuma, 1976-81; gen. sales mgr. Ins. Counselors, Yuma, 1981-83; mng. gen. agt. First Capital Life Ins. Co., Ariz., N.Mex., So. Calif. and N.C., 1983—; regional commnr. Ariz. Interscholastic Assn., Yuma, 1972-88. mem. Century Club, Boy's Club of Yuma. Mem. Nat. Assn. Life Underwriters (nat. sales achievement award 1979, 82, 84, 86, 87, Nat. Quality award 1984-88), Life Underwriters Polit. Action Com., Tucson City Assn. Republican. Presbyterian.

BOWDOIN, LESLEY, administrative assistant; b. L.A., Sept. 14, 1962; d. Rodney S. Bowdoin and Mary Ann (Chatman) Smith. BA, Calif. State U.-Northridge, 1985. Mem. temporary staff Valley Temps, Woodland Hills, 1987—, Manpower, Woodland Hills, Calif., 1988—. Mem. Maranatha Community Ch.; sec. Dorsey outreach program Marantha Community Ch., L.A., 1988. Democrat.

BOWE, THOMAS EDWARD, III, architect; b. Stockton, Calif., Apr. 26, 1954; s. Thomas Edward Jr. and Joan (Hunter) B.; m. DiAnne Lynn Rodriquez, May 14, 1983; children: Courtney Hunter, Zachary Robert. BA, U. Calif., 1976; MArch, U. Mich., 1978. Lic. architect, Calif. Assoc. architect Morris and Wenell, Lodi, Calif., 1978—. Commr. cultural heritage bd. City of Stockton, 1989—; bd. dirs. Easter Seals Soc., San Joaquin County, Calif., 1979-81, Hospice San Joaquin, Stockton, 1983— (sec., pres. elect). Recipient Home of Yr. award Met. Home Mag., 1983. Republican. Roman Catholic. Home: 837 W Harding Way Stockton CA 95203 Office: Morris & Wenell 222 W Lockeford Ste 9 Lodi CA 95240

BOWEN, ASTA, author; b. Chgo., Aug. 12, 1955. BA, St. Olaf Coll., 1977. Dir. pub. rels. Flathead Valley Community Coll., Kalispell, Mont., 1980-84; dir. campaign U. Mont., Missoula, 1984-85; columnist Seattle Post-Intelligencer, 1988—; founder Mother Lode comedy group, 1988. Author: The Huckleberry Book, 1988; contbr. articles to mags. Founder Flathead Women's Network, 1986. Mem. Phi Beta Kappa. Address: 234 Old Hwy 93 Somers MT 59932

BOWEN, CHARLES HUGH, JR., lawyer, electronics engineer, retired naval officer; b. Belle Ellen, Ala., Jan. 8, 1923; s. Charles Hugh and Lavada (Lawley) B.; m. Nina Gwen Stevens, July 29, 1945 (div.); children: David Hugh, Charles Hugh III; m. Joan H. Steffens, Mar. 18, 1978. Student, U. Ariz., 1939-40, 46, U. So. Calif., 1946-47; B.S. in Engring. Electronics, Naval Postgrad. Sch., 1953, M.S., 1954; grad., Naval War Coll., 1961; J.D., U. Santa Clara, 1977. Bar: Calif. Commd. ensign U.S. Navy, 1943, advanced through grades to capt., 1965; flight tng. 1942-43; pilot and flight officer PTO, 1944-45; flight instr. Aviation Tng. Unit 5, 1947-49; radar projects supr. VX-1 Key West, Fla., 1949-51; operations officer Attack Squadron 55, 1954-55; aviation electronics engring. officer, staff Comdr. Naval Air Force Pacific Fleet, 1956-58; assigned spl. studies sect. Spl. Projects Office, Bur. Weapons, 1958-60; student replace air tng. group Attack Squadron 122, 1961; comdg. officer Attack Squadron 115, 1962-63; navigator U.S.S. Kitty Hawk, 1963-64, exec. officer, 1964; tchr. elec. sci. U.S. Naval Acad., also head sci. dept., 1965-67; command U.S.S. Vesuvius, 1967-68; advanced devel. engr. Sylvania Electronics Systems, Mountain View, Calif., 1968-72, mktg. mgr., 1972-74; jud. extern with Justice Calif. Supreme Ct., 1976; individual practice law Campbell, Calif., 1978-81, 88—; ptnr. Finch & Bowen, Campbell, Calif., 1981-87. Decorated D.F.C. with gold star, Air medal with silver star. Mem. IEEE, Naval Inst., Internat. Platform Assn. Democrat. Home: 5941 Drytown Pl San Jose CA 95120

BOWEN, CLOTILDE DENT, retired army officer, psychiatrist; b. Chgo., Mar. 20, 1923; d. William Marion Dent and Clotilde (Tynes) D.; m. William N. Bowen, Dec. 29, 1945 (dec.). B.A., Ohio State U., 1943, M.D., 1947. Intern, Harlem Hosp., N.Y.C., 1947-48, resident and fellow in pulmonary resident in psychiatry VA Hosp., Albany, N.Y., 1959-62; private practice, N.Y.C. 1950-55; chief pulmonary disease clinic, N.Y.C. 1950-55; chief psychiatry VA Hosp., Roseburg, Oreg., 1962-66, acting chief of staff, 1964-66; commd. capt. U.S. Army, 1955, advanced through ranks to col., 1968; neuropsychiat. cons. U.S. Army Vietnam, 1970-71; chief dept. psychiatry Fitzsimmons Army Med. Ctr., 1971-74; chief dept. psychiatry. Tripler Army Med. Center, 1974-75, chief dept. primary care and community medicine, 1978-83, chief psychiat. consultation service, 1983-85; chief psychiatry svc. med./regional office ctr. VA, Cheyenne, Wyo., 1987—; assoc. prof. psychiatry U. Colo. Med. Center, Denver, 1970-83. Decorated Legion of Merit, several other medals. Fellow Menniger Found. Fellow Am. Psychiat. Assn., Acad. Psychosomatic Medicine; mem. AMA. Home: 1020 Tari Dr Colorado Springs CO 80921

BOWEN, DAVID ALLEN, film producer; b. Cambridge, Mass., Feb. 28, 1963; s. Henry Ervin and Estelle Mildred (Dill) B. Student, Pima Coll. V.p. GCO Pictures, Inc., Sherman Oak, Calif., 1986-88; pres. Cinecraft Pictures, Inc., Burbank, Calif., 1988—; mgr. Show-Biz softball league, Reseda, Calif., 1988—. Assoc. producer: (movie) An American Murder, 1987; exec. producer (movies) The Haunted, 1988, Outside, 1989; writer/producer: (movie) Vendetta, 1989. Mem. Am. Film Inst., Ind. Feature Project/West. Office: Cinecraft Pictures Inc 150 East Olve 211 Burbank CA 91502

BOWEN, DENVER GERRY, school system administrator; b. Clarkesville, Ga., Oct. 12, 1945; s. Luther Graves and Blanche Hautense (Truelove) B.; m. Alva Ruth Haynes, Dec. 19, 1966 (div. May 1975); 1 child, Linka Ruth; m. Pamela Ann Patten, July 16, 1976. BS in Agronomy, U. Ga., 1966, MS in Sch. Administrn., 1973, EdS in Sch. Leadership, 1975. Sci. tchr., dept. chmn. North Hall High Sch., Gainesville, Ga., 1967-71; asst. prin. North Hall High Sch., Gainesville, 1971-72; prin. White Sulphur Springs Elem., Gainesville, 1972-76; prin./tchr. St. George Island Sch., St. George, Alaska, 1976-78; prin. St. Paul (Alaska) Sch. and Pribilof Dist., 1978-81; adminstrv. asst. Pribilof Sch. Dist., St. Paul, 1981-82, asst. supt., 1982-85, supt., 1985—. Mem. Am. Assn. Sch. Adminstrs., Alaska Council Sch. Adminstrs., Alaska Assn. Sch. Bus. Officials, Am. Assn. for Supervision and Curriculum Devel., Am. Assn. Ednl. Communications and Technology, Mason. Home: 133 Oceanview Dr PO Box 126 Saint Paul Island AK 99660 Office: Pribilof Sch Dist Dist Office Bldg Saint Paul Island AK 99660

BOWEN, FRANCIS LEE, electrical engineer; b. Lincoln, Nebr., Jan. 17, 1932; s. Earl and Besse B.; B.E.E., U. Nebr., 1958; M.B.A., Calif. Luth. Coll., 1977; m. Bonnie Jean Yentes, June 5, 1951; children—Sandra Fern, Scott LeMar. With Pacific Missile Test Center, Point Mugu, Calif., 1958—, head communications engring. br., from 1970, now head inservice engring. div. Design and Fabrication Dept. Mem. Camarillo (Calif.) Planning Commn., 1970-82, chmn., 1971-75, 78-79; mem. Camarillo City Council, 1982-86, vice mayor, 1983-84, mayor, 1984-85; trustee Camarillo Meth. Ch., 1976-79, chmn., 1977. Served in USN, 1952-54. Republican. Clubs: Masons, Shriners, Order of DeMolay. Office: Code 3510 Point Mugu CA 93042

BOWEN, JAMES ROSS, weapons design engineer; b. Wooster, Ohio, Feb. 20, 1935; s. James W.R. and Gayle L. (Altland) B.; m. Glada Roberts, Sept. 2, 1958; children: Michael D. Oliver (stepson), James R., Jason M. Project engr. guidance system for air-to-air missiles system Naval Weapons Ctr., China Lake, Calif., 1958-59, program mgr. weapons system, 1969-72, line supr. design groups, mgr. weapon systems, div. head, 1972-78, mgr. spl. facilities and equipment study, 1978-81, dep. support dir., 1981-88; acting head dept. moral, welfare and recreation Naval Weapons Ctr., China Lake, 1987-88, head div. moral, welfare and recreation, 1988—. Safety dir. Ridgecrest (Calif.) Little League, 1975—; bldg. com. Calvary Assembly of God Ch., Ridgecrest, 1975—; pres. Indian Wells Valley chpt. Full Gospel Bus. Men's Fellowship Internat., 1978-81, field rep., 1980-85, internat. dir., 1985—; v.p. Sierra Breeze Mobil Home Estates, 1980, pres., 1981. Recipient Michelson Lab. award Naval Weapons Ctr., 1985. Mem. Nat. Contract Mgmt. Assn., Internat. Footprinters Assn. (chpt. bd. dirs. 1986-88), Tech. Mktg. Soc. Am., Am. Def. Preparedness Assn., Soc. Am. Mil. Engrs. Republican. Home: 5233 Ocotillo Ave Ridgecrest CA 93555 Office: Naval Weapons Ctr Comdr Code 229 China Lake CA 93555

BOWEN, JAMES THOMAS, military officer; b. Mason City, Iowa, May 4, 1948; s. Stanley Thomas and Marilyn Louise (Ott) B.; m. Joyce Anne Kermabon, Sept. 10, 1977; 1 child, Steven James. BBA, U. Iowa, 1969; MS, U. So. Calif., Los Angeles, 1974. Commd. 2nd lt. USAF, 1969, advance through grades to lt. col., 1986; student pilot 3575th Pilot Tng. Wing, Vance AFB, Okla., 1969-70; co-pilot 773rd Tactical Airlift Squadron, Clark AFB, Phillipines, 1971; pilot 6594th Test Group, Hickam AFB, Hawaii, 1971-75; acquisition program mgr. Aeronautical Systems Div., Wright-Patterson AFB, Ohio, 1976-82; chief, standoff surveillance and attack systems HQ USAF, Rsch. Devel. and Acquistion, Pentagon, Va., 1984-87; chief, acquistion plans and programs br. Air Force Inspection and Safety Ctr., Norton AFB, Calif., 1988—. Decorated Air medal USAF, 1972. Mem. Air Force Assn., Def. Systems Mgmt. Coll. Alumni Assn., Nat. Def. U. Alumni Assn. Methodist. Office: HQ AFISC/IGY Norton AFB CA 92409

BOWEN, MYRON L., school system official; b. Burley, Idaho, Feb. 3, 1929; s. Daniel and Ida (Tueller) B.; m. Jeanine Johnson, Feb. 14, 1951; children: Scott L., Todd M., Jason B. AA, E. L.A. Jr. Coll., 1959; BA, Calif. State U., L.A., 1969. Cert. purchasing mgr. Purchasing agt. Pasadena (Calif.) City Schs., 1957-70; dir. purchasing svcs. Fresno (Calif.) Unified Sch. Dist., 1970—; cons. L.A. County Supt. Schs., 1969-70. Editor: Sch. Purchasing Handbook for State of Calif., 1976. Sgt. U.S. Army, 1951-53. Recipient Art Baker award, Purchasing Mgmt. Assn. L.A., 1982. Mem. Nat. Assn. Purchasing Mgmt., Calif. Assn. Sch. Bus. Officials (state chmn. purchasing research and devel. com. 1970-74), Calif. Assn. Pub. Purchasing Officers (pres. 1979-80, officer, bd. dirs. 1974-79). Republican. Mormon. Home: 6262 N Sharon Ave Fresno CA 93710 Office: Fresno Unified Sch Dist Tulare and M Sts Fresno CA 93721

BOWEN, NANCY LYNN, electrical engineer; b. Las Vegas, Nev., July 15, 1955; d. Edward Robert and Shirley Jean (Krug) Johnston; m. Bruce Keefe Bowen, June 3, 1978. BS magna cum laude, U. Mo., 1977; MS in Elec. Engring., MIT, 1979. Design engr. Analog Devices, Inc., Wilmington, Mass., 1979-82, Palo Alto, Calif., 1983-84; sr. design engr. Advanced Micro Devices, Sunnyvale, Calif., 1982-83; staff design engr. Micro Linear Co., San Jose, Calif., 1984—. Contbg. mem. Sempervirens Fund, Los Altos, Calif., 1986-88. Mem. Ice Skating Inst. Am., Underwater Photography Soc. Democrat. Home: 1484 Chukar Ct Sunnyvale CA 94087 Office: Micro Linear Co 2092 Concourse Dr San Jose CA 95131

BOWEN, PETER GEOFFREY, real estate investment advisor; b. Iowa City, Iowa, July 10, 1939; s. Howard Rothmann and Lois Berntine (Schilling) B.; m. Shirley Johns Carlson, Sept. 14, 1968; children—Douglas Howard, Leslie Johns. B.A. in Govt. and Econs., Lawrence Coll., 1960; postgrad. U. Wis., 1960-61, U. Denver, 1965. cert. expert real estate witness, Denver Dist. Ct., 1987. Dir. devel. Mobile Home Communities, Denver, 1969-71; v.p. Perry & Butler, Denver, 1972-73; exec. v.p., dir. Little & Co., Denver, 1973; pres. Builders Agy. Ltd., Denver, 1974-75; pres. The Investment Mgmt. Group Ltd., Denver, 1975—; gen. ptnr. 8 real estate ltd. ptnrships.; lectr. on real estate syndications. Contbr. articles to profl. pubs. Vice-chmn. Greenwood Village (Colo.) Planning and Zoning Commn., 1983-85; elected mem. City Council Greenwood Village, 1985-86, also mayor pro tem, 1985-86; trustee Vail Mountain Sch. Found., 1987—; bd. dirs. Colo. Plan for Apportionment, 1966; speaker Forward Metro Denver, 1966-67. Mem. Lawrence U. Alumni Assn. (bd. dirs. 1966-72, 82-86). Home: 5047 Main Gore Dr Vail CO 81657 Office: PO Box 1355 Vail CO 81658

BOWEN, RICHARD L., academic administrator; b. Avoca, Iowa, Aug. 31, 1933; s. Howard L. and Donna (Milburn) B.; m. Connie Smith Bowen, 1976; children: James, Robert, Elizabeth, Christopher; children by previous marriage—Catherine, David, Thomas. B.A., Augustana Coll., 1957; M.A., Harvard, 1959, Ph.D., 1967. Fgn. service officer State Dept., 1959-60; research asst. to U.S. Senator Francis Case, 1960-62; legis. asst. to U.S. Senator Karl Mundt, 1962-65; minority cons. sub-com. exec. reorgn. U.S. Senate, 1966-67; asst. to pres., assoc. prof. polit. sci. U. S.D., Vermillion, 1967-69, pres., 1969-76, disting. prof., 1980-85; commr. higher edn. Bd. Regents State S.D., Pierre, 1976-80; disting. prof. polit. sci. Idaho State U., Pocatello, 1980-85, pres., 1986—. Served with USN, 1951-54. Recipient Outstanding Alumnus award Augustana Coll., 1970; Woodrow Wilson fellow, 1957, Congl. Staff fellow, 1965; Fulbright scholar, 1957. Office: Idaho State U Office of Pres Campus Box 8310 Pocatello ID 83209-0009

BOWEN, ROBIN DIANE, nurse; b. Fallon, Nev., Dec. 21, 1955; d. James Richard and Gail Evia (McBride) Smith; m. David M. Bowen, Aug. 11, 1984; 1 child, Janice. Student, Idaho State U., 1976. Lic. practical nurse, Alaska. Pvt. practice nursing Boise, Idaho, 1976-85; owner, mgr. Anchorage Med. Cons., 1986—; instr. Healthwise, 1978-80. Author: Night Thoughts, 1976, Spilled Milk, 1986. Mem. Child Adv. Network, Child Care Connection, ARC Nursing Team, Anchorage. Golden Cross Nursing scholar, 1976. Democrat. Baptist.

BOWEN, TIMOTHY DANA, geologist; b. The Hague, Netherlands, June 1, 1956; came to U.S., 1960.; s. Paul Joseph and Patricia Lee (Conrad) B; m. Anne Curley, Dec. 10, 1988. BA, Amherst (Mass.) Coll., 1978; MS, U. Mich., 1982. Exploration geologist Oxoco Internat., Newport Beach, Calif., 1978; staff geologist Woodward-Clyde Cons., Clifton, N.J., 1978-80; field engr. Aguirre Engrs., Denver, 1983; project geologist Colo. Dept. Hwys., Glenwood Springs, Colo., 1983-84; sr. engring. geologist Colo. Geological Survey, Glenwood Springs, 1984--; instr. Houston Community Coll., 1983. Coach Youth Soccer, Glenwood Springs, 1985-87; bd. dirs. Frontier Hist. Mus., Glenwood Springs, 1987. Mem. Geological Soc. Am., Trans. Research Bd. (com. soil and rock properties), Colo. State Mgrs. Assn., Internat. Soc. Rock Mechanics, Am. Assn. State Hwy. and Transp. Ofcls., Associated Gen. Contractors Am., Am. Road and Transp. Builders' Assn. (task force 27 on ground improvement techniques). Democrat. Home: 1104 Parkwood Ln Glenwood Springs CO 81601 Office: Colo Geol Survey 201 Centennial #304 Glenwood Springs CO 81601

BOWER, CHRISTOPHER JAMES, investment banker; b. Sterling, Ill., Mar. 5, 1957; s. William Joseph and Elsie Sandra (Sopko) B.; m. MaryLynne Perry, June 23, 1984. BS in Acctg. and Fin., U. Colo., 1978; JD, U. San Diego, 1983. CPA, Calif. Mem. profl. staff Arthur Young and Co. Internat., Denver, 1978-79; founder, mng. dir. Pacific Corp. Group Inc., L.A., La Jolla, Calif., Chgo. and London, 1979—; bd. dirs. Pacific Corp. Internat., L.A., Pacific Corp. Fin. Inc., La Jolla; chmn. Pacific Corp. Valuation Inc., La Jolla, 1979—. Contbr. articles to profl. jours. Mem. AICPA, Calif. State Soc. CPAs. Home: 1576 Law St San Diego CA 92109 Office: Pacific Corp Group Inc 1200 Prospect St 2d Fl La Jolla CA 92037

BOWER, DONALD EDWARD, author; b. Lockport, N.Y., July 19, 1920; B.A., U. Nebr., 1942. Pres., D.E. Bower & Co., Inc., Denver, 1945-60; editor, pub. Arapahoe Tribune, 1960-62; editor Adams County Almanac, Adams County Dispatch, Jefferson County Herald, 1962-65; editor, pub. Buyer's Showcase mag. and FURN Club News 1965-66; exec. editor Colo. mag., 1966-69; editor-in-chief, v.p., dir. Am. West Pub. Co., editor Am. West mag., 1970-74; pres. Colo. Authors League, 1975-76; dir. Nat. Writers Club, Denver, 1974-86; dir. Assoc. Bus. Writers Am., 1978-86, also pres. Assn. Hdqrs., 1978-86; editorial dir. Nat. Writers Press, 1982-86; freelance staff Writer Fawcett Publs., 1962-64; lit. cons., 1962-67. Mem. Soc. Authors and Journalists, Authors Guild Am., Denver Posse, The Westerners (dir. 1976), Outdoor Writers Assn. Am., Western Writers Assn. Am., Friends of Denver Pub. Libr., Denver Press Club, Sigma Delta Chi. Author: Roaming the American West, 1970; Ghost Towns and Back Roads, 1972; intro. to The Magnificent Rockies, 1972; Fred Rosenstock: A Legend in Books and Art, 1976; The Professional Writers' Guide, 1984;Ten Keys to Writing Success, 1987, Sex and Spies, 1989; also 4 paperback detective novels, 1960-64; editor: Living Water, Living Earth, 1971; Anasazi: Ancient People of the Rock, 1973; The Great Southwest, 1972; Edge of a Continent, 1970; The Mighty Sierra, 1972; The Magnificent Rockies, 1972; The Great Northwest, 1973; Gold and Silver in the West, 1973; Steinbeck Country, 1973; contbr. articles to mags. Address: 15087 E Radcliff Dr Aurora CO 80015

BOWER, FAY LOUISE, nurse; b. San Francisco, Sept. 10, 1929; d. James Joseph and Emily Clare (Andrews) Saitta; BS with honors, San Jose State Coll., 1965; MSN, U. Calif., 1966, DNSc, 1978; children: R. David, Carol Bower Tomei, Dennis James, Thomas John. Office nurse Dr. William Grannis, Palo Alto, Calif., 1950-55; staff nurse Stanford Hosp., 1964-72; asst. prof. San Jose State U., 1966-70, asso. prof., 1970-74, prof., 1974-82, coord. grad. program in nursing, 1977-78, chairperson dept. nursing, 1978-82; dean U. San Francisco, 1982-89, v.p. acad. affairs, 1988-89, exec. v.p, 1989—, speaker; cons. univs.; vis. prof. Harding Coll., 1977, U. Miss., 1976; lectr. U. Calif., San Francisco, 1975. Cert. pub. health nurse, sch. nurse, Calif. Fellow Am. Acad. Nursing; mem. Calif. Nurses Assn., Nurses Assn. Coll. Ob-Gyn, Calif. Tchrs. Assn., AAUP, Pub. Health Assn. Calif., Nat. League Nursing (bd. dirs.), Calif. League for Nursing (pres.), Western Gerontol. Assn., Sigma Theta Tau (pres. Beta Gamma chpt.), Jesuit Deans in Nursing (chair). Democrat. Roman Catholic. Club: Commonwealth (San Francisco). Author: (with Em O. Bevis) Fundamentals of Nursing Practice: Concepts, Roles and Functions, 1978; (with Margaret Jacobson) Community Health Nursing, 1978; The Process of Planning Nursing Care, 3d edit., 1982; Theoretical Foundations of Nursing I, II, and III, 1972; editor: Normal Development of Body Image, 1977; Distortions in Body Image in Illness and Disability, 1977; Foundations of Pharmacologic Therapy, 1977; Nursing Assessment, 1977. Home: 1820 Portola Rd Woodside CA 94062 Office: U San Francisco Sch Nursing San Francisco CA

BOWER, JEAN HELEN, civic volunteer; b. Seattle, June 12, 1933; d. Harold Elmer and Alice Josephine (Shiach) Lokken; m. Gene Alden Bower, Apr. 12, 1957; children: Gordon, Jeff, Sheryl. BA in Chemistry, U. Wash., 1956. Standard gen. cert. in edn. Vol. treas., Northshore Sch. Dist., Bothell, Wash., 1963-66, game chmn., 1969-70, health chmn., 1971-72, picture lady, 1973-74, hostess chmn., 1975-76, sr. party chmn., 1976, high sch. treas., 1977-79; treas. Northshore PTSA, Bothell, 1979-80, parent edn. chmn., 1980-81; sec. pastor seeking com., Inglewood Presbyn. Ch., Bothell, 1969, Sunday sch. tchr., 1970-75, 77, mem. adult edn. staff, 1986-88, deacon, 1985-88, elder, 1989; family interviewer, Kenmore (Wash.) C. of C., 1969; leader, Camp Fire Girls of Am., Seattle, 1970-75. Mem. AAUW (v.p. 1983-85, internat. rels. chmn. 1987-89), Christian Women's Club (treas. 1982-85).

BOWERS, ALBERT, pharmaceutical company executive; b. Manchester, Eng., July 16, 1930; came to U.S., 1954; s. Albert and Mary (Munn) B.; m. Eileen Easthope, Sept. 26, 1953 (div. May 1985); children—Anita, Karen, Deborah; m. Gwynn C. Akin, Dec. 23, 1985. BS in Chemistry, U. London, 1951; PhD in Organic Chemistry, U. Manchester, 1954. Group leader research Syntex S.A., Mexico City, 1956, v.p., dir. research, 1963; v.p. internat. Syntex, 1964; dir. Syntex Corp., Palo Alto, Calif., 1968; pres. Syntex Corp., 1976-82, 86, also bd. dirs., chief exec. officer, 1980-89, chmn., 1981-89; pres. Syntex Labs., 1967-73, Syntex USA, 1967-82; dir. U.S. Leasing Internat.; former mem. adv. com. N.Y. Stock Exchange. Contbr. articles to profl. jours.; patentee in selective fluorination of steroids, corticoid compounds synthesis, norethindrone synthesis. Active Calif. Bus. Roundtable, Bus. Higher Edn. Forum, Rockefeller U. Council, U. Calif.-San Francisco Found.; external adv. bd. U. Calif.-San Francisco Cancer Research Inst.; adv. bd. Ctr. for History of Chemistry. Recipient Sci. prize Mex. Acad. Sci., 1964; Fulbright fellow Wayne State U., 1954-55. Mem. Pharm. Mfrs. Assn. (bd. dirs., former chmn.). Office: Syntex Corp 3401 Hillview Ave Palo Alto CA 94304 *

BOWERS, DEANNA LOUISE, nurse; b. Madison, Wis., Jan. 18, 1938; d. Howard Duane and Martha Eva (Niesen) DeBower; m. Warren Duane Bowers, June 11, 1960; children: Mark Warren, Christopher Clarke, Wendi Carole. BS, U. Wis., 1960. Staff nurse Bapt. Hosp., Pensacola, Fla., 1960; psychiat. staff nurse Long Beach (Calif.) Meml. Hosp., 1961-62; obstetrics staff nurse Hartland Hosp., Baldwin Park, Calif., 1962-68; sch. dist. nurse Rancho Cucamonga, Calif., 1973—; substance abuse coordinator Cen. Sch. Dist., Rancho Cucamonga, 1987—; mem. San Antonio Hosp. Child Abuse Treatment Team, Upland, Calif., 1978—, Citizens Against Substance Abuse, 1987—. Bd. dirs. Bilingual Family Counseling Ctr., Ontario, Calif., 1978—; clinic coordinator West End Child Devel. Ctr., Ontario, 1986-88; sec. Rancho Cucamonga Citizens Against Substance Abuse, 1987-88; pres. St. Anthony's Parish Council, Upland, 1987-88. Mem. NEA, Calif. Tchrs. Assn., Calif. Orgn. Sch. Nurses (chmn. spl. edn. 1988—, pub. rels. sec. 1986-88), San Bernardino-Riverside Sch. Nurses, Nat. Assn. Sch. Nurses. Democrat. Roman Catholic. Home: 858 Dublin Ct Upland CA 91786 Office: Cen Sch Dist 9457 Foothill Blvd Rancho Cucamonga CA 91730

BOWERS, JACK (JOHN BURTON BOWERS, JR.), artist, real estate broker; b. Big Spring, Tex., Feb. 4, 1947; s. John Burton Bowers and Nola Mae Penny (Cuthberson) Reynolds; m. Victoria Barret Fuller, July 2, 1977 (div. 1982); m. Carol Ann Carbone, Oct. 11, 1985; 1 child, Carly Elizabeth. Student, N. Tex. State U., 1965-66; MFA, San Francisco Art Inst., 1984. Lic. real estate agt., Tex. Agy. sales mgr. The Penn Mutual Life Ins. Co., Dallas, 1967-74; mng. gen. ptnr. Bowers Enterprises, San Francisco, 1975—; nat. mgr. corp. real estate Werner Erhard & Assocs., San Francisco, 1986—; Artist in residency, Moffet County High Sch., Craig, Colo., 1981. Represented in shows at Vallauris, France, 1988, N.Y.U., 1988, Boulder (Colo.) Art Ctr., 1987, Chgo. Internat. Art. Expo, Navy Pier, 1987, Dorothy Weiss Gallery, San Francisco, 1987, Berkeley (Calif.) Exhibition '87, 1st Internat. Ceramics Show, Aichi-ken Chusho Kigyo Ctr., Mino, Japan, 1986, Pro Arts Annual Exhibition, Pro Arts Galleries, Oakland, Calif., 1985, San Francisco Fine Arts Show, 1983, Aspen (Colo.) Mus. Art, Arvada Ctr. for the Arts, 1980, El Paso (Tex.) Mus. Fine Art, 1977, and numerous others; works include Space Case, Black Box, First Blond, Red and Black Box, Sally Cenotaph, 2 Dozen Roaring Valleys, and numerous others; works reviewed in numerous mags. including The San Francisco Mag., 1988, San Francisco Chronicle, 1987, Oakland Tribune, 1987, Rocky Mtn. News, 1981, Westword, 1981, Art Space, 1981. Named Best of Show, Redding (Calif.) Mus., 1987, U. Ark., 1987, Aspen Mus. Art, 1980; recipient Honorable Mention, Mino, Japan, 1986, Purchase award, State of Colo., 1980, 81, Aspen Mall Competition, 1978, Juror's award, Aspen Mus. Art, 1979. Office: First Union Investment Co 100 Spear St Ste 200 San Francisco CA 94105

BOWERS, JEFFREY LYNN, programmer; b. Defiance, Ohio, July 11, 1952; s. Clifford Lee and Geneva (Lucas) B. BS in Edn., Bowling Green (Ohio) State U., 1974; postgrad., U. Mich., 1975-77. With Chief Supermarket, Defiance, 1967-70; computer operator State Bank and Trust Co., Defiance, 1974-75, data processing supr., 1975-78; data processing mgr. Treu House of Munch, Toledo, 1975-82; systems analyst The Crocker Bank, San Francisco, 1982-86; quality assurance analyst Wells Fargo Bank, San Francisco, 1986-88; tech. programmer 1st Nationwide Bank, San Francisco, 1988—. Mem. Data Processing Mgmt. Assn. (chartered), Internat. Tandem User's Group, Tandem User's of the Bay Area. Home: 1970 15th St San Francisco CA 94114 Office: 1st Nationwide Bank 355 Gellert Blvd Daly City CA 94015

BOWERS, JOHN C., association executive; b. Plattsburg, Mo., Dec. 18, 1939; s. Raymond and Ruth Charlotte (Anderson) B.; m. Shirley Kathleen Tucker, Feb. 16, 1962; children: John Bradford, Craig Andrew, Beth Anne. BS, S.W. Mo. State U., 1961. Mgr. Augusta C. of C., Kans., 1964-66; exec. v.p. Newton C. of C., Kans., 1966-70; pres., gen. mgr. Jefferson County C. of C. (formerly Lakewood-South Jeffco C. of C.), Lakewood, Colo., 1970—; dir. Jefferson Econ. Council, Golden, Colo., 1976—. Bd. dirs. Lakewood on Parade, 1977—. Served to 1st lt. U.S. Army, 1962-64. Mem. Colo. C. of C. Execs. (pres. 1976-77), Kansas Jaycees (v.p. 1966, Outstanding State Vice-pres. award 1966), Colo. Assn. Commerce and Industry (dir. 1976-77), Mountain States Assn. (pres. 1983-84), Am. C. of C. Execs. (com. chmn. 1973-74, cert. chamber exec. 1985), C. of C. of U.S. Republican. Home: 918 S Swadley St Lakewood CO 80228 Office: Jefferson County C of C 12600 W Colfax Ave #B-440 Lakewood CO 80215

BOWERSOX, GLEN, Episcopal priest, foundation executive; b. York, Pa., Mar. 20, 1920; s. George Edward and Anna May (Hankey) Bowersox. BA, Gettysburg Coll., 1942; MS, Northeastern U., 1942-44; postgrad., Purdue U., 1944-45, U. Chgo., 1950-54; LHD, Gettysburg Coll., 1973. Ordained priest ch. Pakistan, 1973. Civilian specialist U.S. Army, Philippines, 1945-48; instr. Muhlenberg (Pa.) Coll., Allentown, 1948-50; field rep. Inst. Internat. Edn., Chgo., 1951-54, asst. dir., 1954-59; asst. rep. The Asia Found., N.Y.C., 1959-60; program officer The Asia Found., San Francisco, 1960-62; asst. rep. The Asia Found., Tokyo, Japan, 1962-66; program officer The Asia Found., San Francisco, 1966-68; rep. The Asia Found., Kabul, Afghanistan, 1968-73; priest assoc. Ch. of the Advent, San Francisco, 1973—; fgn. study advisor U. Chgo., 1950-53; program officer The Asia Found., San Francisco, 1973-77; Luce Scholars coordinator The Asia Found., San Francisco, 1977-86. Home: 2484 Bush St San Francisco CA 94115 Office: Ch of the Advent of Christ the King 162 Hickory St San Francisco CA 94102

BOWES, DAVID DWIGHT, ballet company director; b. Sanford, Fla., Aug. 16, 1951; s. Charles Roderick and Elizabeth Fanning (Thurmond) B. BA in Theater with honors, Tulane U., 1973. Dir. N.Y.C. Opera Theater, 1975-79; dir. prodn. Mich. Opera Theater, Detroit, 1979-81, stage dir., 1986; gen. mgr. Orlando (Fla.) Opera Co., 1981-83; gen. dir. Ft. Worth Opera Assn., 1983-85; cons., co-mgr. Tex. Opera Theater, Houston, 1985-86; exec. dir. Sacramento Ballet Assn., 1986-88; v.p. San Jose (Calif.) Cleve. Ballet, 1988—; stage dir. U. Ill. Opera, Champaign, 1987—; cons. Thomas Deans & Co., Tallahasse, 1984-87. Trans. (opera libretto) The Impressario, 1979. Mem. Mayor's Spl. Task Force on Meml. Auditorium, Sacramento, 1987. Mem. Dance Calif. (bd. dirs. 1986—), Sacramento Area Dance Alliance (bd. dirs. 1986—). Democrat. Episcopalian. Club: Nat. Arts (N.Y.C.). Office: Sacramento Ballet 4052 Manzanita Ave Carmichael CA 95608 also: San Jose Cleve Ballet PO Box 1666 San Jose CA 95109

BOWES, FLORENCE (MRS. WILLIAM DAVID BOWES), writer; b. Salt Lake City, Nov. 19, 1925; d. John Albreckt Elias and Alma Wilhelmina (Jonasson) Norborg; student U. Utah, 1941-42, Columbia, 1945-46, N.Y. U., 1954-55; grad. N.Y. TV Workshop, 1950; m. Samuel Ellis Levine, July 15, 1944 (dec. July 1953); m. 2d, William David Bowes, Mar. 15, 1958 (dec. 1976); 1 son, Alan Richard. Actress, writer Hearst Radio Network, WINS, N.Y.C., 1944-45; personnel and adminstrv. exec. Mut. Broadcasting System, N.Y.C., 1946-49, free-lance editor, writer, 1948-49; freelance writer NBC and ABC, 1949-53; script editor, writer Robert A. Monroe Prodns., N.Y.C., Hollywood, Calif., 1953-56; script and comml. dir. KUTV-TV, Salt Lake City, 1956-58; spl. editor, writer pub. relations dept. U. Utah, Salt Lake City, 1966-68, editor, writer U. Utah Rev., 1968-75; author: Web of Solitude, 1979; The MacOrvan Curse, 1980; Interlude in Venice, 1981; Beauchamp, 1983. Mem. Beta Sigma Phi. Home: 338 K St Salt Lake City UT 84103

BOWIE, CELESTINE, government official; b. Gene Autry, Okla., July 4, 1943; d. Hollie B. Denson and Exzetta Mae (Pickens) Denson-Parker; children: Tonia Mechelle, Darren Ronnell. BA, Calif. State U., Fresno, 1975; MPA, Calif. State U., Hayward, 1988. Supr. IRS, Fresno, 1977-80, employment devel specialist, 1979; budget analyst IRS, San Francisco, 1980-85, mgmt. analyst, 1985—; program coord. fed. women's program IRS, 1975-76, mem. black adv. com., 1976-79. Mem. Fresno Commn. on Status of Women, 1977; chmn. polit. action com. South Alameda Black Leadership Forum, 1986; tutor Am. Literacy Council, Fremont, Calif., 1987. Recipient spl. achievement award IRS, 1973, 76, 81, outstanding female employee award, 1978; letter of commendation Fresno Commn. on Status of Women, 1977, Minds of Community Conf., Fresno, 1978. Mem. Blacks in Govt. (charter), Alpha Kappa Alpha (grad. advisor Fresno 1977-80). Democrat. Baptist. Home: 4513 Capwood Terr Fremont CA 94538 Office: IRS 1650 Mission St San Francisco CA 94105

BOWLEN, PATRICK DENNIS, holding company executive, lawyer; b. Prairie du Chien, Wis., Feb. 18, 1944; s. Paul Dennis and Arvella (Woods) B. B.B.A., U. Okla., 1966, J.D., 1968. Bar: Alta. 1969. Read law Saucier, Jones, Calgary, Alta., Can., assoc., 1969-70; asst. to pres. Regent Drilling Ltd., 1970-71; pres. Batoni-Bowlen Enterprises Ltd., 1971-79, Bowlen Holdings Ltd., Edmonton, Alta., Can., 1979—; pres., chief exec. officer, owner Denver Broncos, 1984—. Mem. Law Soc. Alta., Can. Bar Assn., Young Presidents Orgn. Roman Catholic. Clubs: Mayfair Golf and Country; Edmonton Petroleum; Outrigger Canoe (Honolulu). Office: Denver Broncos 5700 Logan St Denver CO 80216 *

BOWLER, BRIAN, automobile company executive. Formerly exec. v.p., pres. DDB Needham Detroit (formerly Doyle Dane Bernbach Inc.), Troy, Mich.; pres. Porsche Cars N.Am. Inc., Reno, 1988—. Office: Porsche Cars N Am Inc 200 S Virginia Reno NV 89501 *

BOWLER, JOHN PATRICK, radio executive, air personality; b. Evanston, Ill., Nov. 18, 1959; s. John Patrick Bowler Sr. and Mary Joan (Mohr) Sanders. B in Broadcasting, Spring Hill Coll., 1981. Air personality Sta. WABB, Mobile, Ala., 1978-83, program dir., 1982-83; promotion dir., air personality Sta. WMJI-FM, Cleve., 1983-84; ops. mgr. Sta. WABB-AM-FM, Mobile, 1984—; prof. radio broadcasting Spring Hill Coll. Upward Bound, Mobile, summers 1980—; asst. sports dir. Sta. WABB-AM-FM, Mobile, 1984—; sports rap host BAY-TV, Comcast Cablevision, Mobile, 1985-89, talking baseball host, 1989—. Republican. Roman Catholic.

BOWLER, MICHAEL LEE, lawyer; b. San Diego, Aug. 3, 1949; s. Leo Francis and Elizabeth Anne (Shepperd) B.; m. Julie Ann St. Jacques, Mar. 8, 1969; children: Shawna, Lee Matthew, Ryan. BA, San Diego State U., 1976; JD, U. San Diego, 1983. Bar: Calif. 1983, U.S. Dist. Ct. (so. dist.) Calif. 1983. Literary agt. Waterside Prodns., Camino Del Mar; assoc. editor, media columnist San Diego mag., 1977-83; assoc. Miller & Gibbs, San Diego, 1983-84, Higgs, Fletcher & Mack, San Diego, 1984-86; sole practice San Diego, 1986—; exec. dir. Inst. Quality Constrn., San Diego, 1986, 88; cons. mktg., San Diego, 1983—. Mem. editorial bd.: Attorneys Marketing Report, 1987-88; contbr. articles to profl. jours. including California Lawyer, San Diego mag. and California mag. Served as sgt. USAF, 1968-72. Recipient 7 San Diego Press Club awards. Mem. ABA, San Diego Bar Assn., Calif. State Bar Assn., San Diego Trial Lawyers Assn., Soc. Profl. Journalists, Phi Beta Kappa, Phi Kappa Phi. Democrat. Roman Catholic. Club: San Diego Press. Office: 530 B St Suite 910 San Diego CA 92101

BOWLES, CEPHAS, communications executive; b. Newark, Apr. 20, 1952; s. Carey Cornish and Sarah Rosa (Wilson) B. BS, Syracuse U., 1974. Lic. FCC. Desk asst. CBS Radio News, N.Y.C., 1974-76, asst. producer, 1976-78; program asst. Sta. KUAT-AM-FM, Tucson, 1980-83, program mgr., 1980-83, sta. mgr., 1983-89, acting gen. mgr., 1989—. Producer: (radio documentaries) Juneteenth, 1979 (Ariz. Press Club award), Cowboy Humor, 1982 (Best of West award), The Unknown West (Ohio State award 1989). Mem. Planned Parenthood Tucson, 1986—; bd. dirs. Community Orgn. Against Drug Abuse, Tucson, 1978-80, Sun Sounds Radio Reading Service, Tucson, 1985—. Mem. NAACP (bd. dirs. 1983), Blacks in Pub. Radio (sec. 1988—), Rocky Mountain Pub. Radio (mem. exec. com.), Syracuse U. Alumni Assn. Democrat. Home: 3104 Corte de la Raqueta Tucson AZ 85716 Office: Sta KUAT-AM-FM U Ariz Modern Langs Bldg Tucson AZ 85721

BOWLING, DANNY WOLF, landscape contractor; b. Prosser, Wash., June 30, 1952; s. Eugene Pearl and Virginia Ann (Wolf) B.; m. Ann Marie Pearson, Apr. 8, 1978; children: Nathan Charles, Hannah Jeanne. BS, Wash. State U., 1977. Cert. landscaper, Wash. With Blue Sky Landscape Svcs., Inc., Puyallup, Wash. With U.S. Army, 1970. Mem. Wash. State Nursery & Landscape Assn. (treas. 1988, named Young Nurseryperson of the Yr. 1987), Assoc. Sub-Contrs. of Wash. (trustee 1986-88), Kiwanis. Office: Blue Sky Landscape Svcs 8719 42nd St Ct E Puyallup WA 98371

BOWLING, NINA RICHARDSON, dentist; b. Tokyo, Jan. 23, 1956; d. Donald McCuaig and Patricia Ann (Johnson) Richardson; m. Franklin L. Bowling Jr., Aug. 14, 1982; children: Patricia Ruth, Christopher Franklin. BS in Psychology, Coll. of William and Mary, 1976; DMD, Washington U., St. Louis, 1981. Assoc. dentist Dr. James Crandall, St. Louis, 1981-83; dentist, co-owner Broomfield (Colo.) Plaza Family Dentistry, 1983—. Am. Assn. Bus. Women grantee, 1978. Mem. ADA, Colo. Dental Assn., Boulder County Dental Soc., Delta Sigma Delta. Home: 1026 E 6th Ave Circle Broomfield CO 80020 Office: Broomfield Plaza Family Dentistry 5015 W 120th Ave Broomfield CO 80020

BOWMAN, BRUCE, writer, artist, educator; b. Dayton, Ohio, Nov. 23, 1938; s. Murray Edgar Bowman and Mildred May (Moler) Elleman; m. Julie Ann Gosselin, 1970 (div. 1980); 1 child, Carrie Lynn. AA, San Diego City Coll., 1962; BA, Calif. State U.-Los Angeles, 1964, MA, 1968. Tchr. art North Hollywood Adult Sch., Calif., 1966-68; instr. art Cypress Coll., Calif., 1976-78, West Los Angeles Coll., 1969—; tchr. art Los Angeles City Schs., 1966—; seminar leader So. Calif., 1986—. Author: Shaped Canvas, 1976; Toothpick Sculpture and Ice Cream Stick Art, 1976; Ideas: How to Get Them, 1985, (cassette tape) Develop Winning Willpower, 1986, Waikiki, 1988. Contbr. articles to profl. jours. One-man shows include Calif. State U.-Los Angeles, 1968, Pepperdine U., Malibu, Calif., 1978; exhibited in group shows McKenzie Gallery, Los Angeles, 1968, Trebor Gallery, Los Angeles, 1970, Cypress Coll., Calif., 1977, Design Recycled Gallery, Fullerton, Calif., 1977, Pierce Coll., Woodland Hills, Calif., 1978, Leopold/Gold Gallery, Santa Monica, Calif., 1980. Served with USN, 1957-61. Home: 28322 Rey De Copas Malibu CA 90265

BOWMAN, GARY MARTIN, social worker; b. Chatham, Ont., Can., July 13, 1943; came to U.S., 1960; s. John Martin and Hilda Ruth (Shaw) B.; m. Gwendolyn Yit-Wah Lee, July 3, 1970 (div. Dec. 1982); m. Jacqueline Custis Miller Lien, Mar. 17, 1984; 1 child, Alexander Stewart Bauman-Bowman. BA, Graceland Coll., 1965; MSW, U. Hawaii, 1972. Diplomate Clin. Social Work Am. Bd. Examiners. Pub. social service worker Linn County Dept. Social Services, Cedar Rapids, Iowa, 1965-67; dir. Joint Services Recreation Assn. for Handicapped, Honolulu, 1967-69, 71-72; social group worker Adolescent Unit Hawaii State Hosp., Kaneohe, 1970-73, 81-83; coordinator adolescent mental health services St. Joseph's Hosp. Health Ctr., Syracuse, N.Y., 1973-74; community services coordinator Elmcrest Children's Services, Syracuse, 1974-75; psychiat. social worker Santa Rosa County Mental Health ctr., Milton, Fla., 1975-80, St. Francis Hosp. Health Care, Honolulu, 1980-81, Los Angeles County Coastal Community Mental Health Ctr., Carson, Calif., 1984-86, West-Cen. Family Mental Health Services, Los Angeles, 1986—; pvt. practice cons., therapy and tng. Burbank, 1986—; adj. faculty mem. U. Syracuse, Western Fla. U. at Pensacola, U. Hawaii, 1976-83; trainer crisis mgmt. Syracuse Police Dept., 1974; presentor Hawaii-Pacific Gerontology Conf., 1981, Happy Valley Singles Camp, Santa Cruz, Calif., 1984, Stas. KRLA-AM, KBZT-FM Separation/Divorce Trauma, Pasadena, Calif., 1986, Parenting By Men Cable TV, 1988, Buckhorn Women's Camp on Grief and Reconnection, Idlewild, Calif., 1988, Erie Beach Camp Families, Ont., Can., 1989, Norturing Adolescent Nonconformists to Help Group, Van Nuys, Calif., 1989. Author: Joys, Fears, Tears, 1968; editor (newsletter) The Javelin, 1967-69. Bd. dirs., program chmn. Summer Action Vol. Youth Program, Honolulu, 1972-73, 80-83; pres. Friends of Library Santa Rosa County, Milton, 1979-80; founder singles separated divorced support group Reorganized Ch. Jesus Christ Latter-day Saints, Burbank, Calif., 1985—; founder Camp In Search Of, 1978-80. Named Citizen for Day Sta. KGU, Honolulu, 1972; recipient Unheralded Humanitarianism, Dist. 1 Mental Health Bd., 1980. Mem. Nat. Assn. Social Workers (cert., steering com. region H&I Calif., 1983—, alt. dir. region H, Calif., 1984-85, chmn. licensing com. 1979-80, mem. program and continuing edn. coms. 1980-83, Loyal and Dedicated Leadership award 1980), Assn. Labor Mgmt. Adminstrs. and Cons. on Alcoholism, Inc. Lodges: Kiwanis, Optimist (youth ctr. dir. Hiawatha, Iowa club 1966-67). Home: 4433 E Sinova St Los Angeles CA 90032 also: 4444 Riverside Dr #206 Toluca Lake Burbank CA 91505 also: Family Svcs LA San Fernando Valley Unit 17400 Victory Blvd Van Nuys CA 91406

BOWMAN, JAMES ANDREW, pharmaceutical sales representative; b. Denver, Sept. 21, 1961; s. James Anthony and Joan Virginia (Murray) B. BA in Polit. Sci., U. Denver, 1984. Asst. to dean U. Denver-New Coll., 1982-83; asst. golf profl. Rupert Country Club, Rupert, Idaho, 1983; mktg. mgr. Landmark Nat. Bank, Denver, 1984-86; dir. chpt. svcs. Bacchus of the U.S., Inc., Denver, 1986-88; sales rep. Merrell Dow Pharmaceuticals, Inc., Denver, 1988—; pres., chmn. Alpha-Pi Zeta Ednl. Found., Denver, 1988-89. Author, editor: Alcohol Awareness Guide, The G.A.M.M.A. Guide, 1988. Vol. Denver Boys, Inc., 1988, Excelsior Youth Ctr., Denver, 1988-89; advisor, U. Denver Freshman Class, 1987. Mem. Denver Active 20/30, Denver U. Young Alumni Club (pres. 1986-87), Phi Beta Kappa. Democrat. Roman Catholic. Office: Merrell Dow Pharmaceuticals 1073 S Downing St Denver CO 80209

BOWMAN, JEAN LOUISE, lawyer, civic worker; b. Albuquerque, Apr. 3, 1938; d. David Livingstone and Charlotte Louise (Smith) McArthur; student U. N.Mex., 1956-57, U. Pa., 1957-58, Rocky Mountain Coll., 1972-74; B.A. in Polit. Sci. with high honors, U. Mont., 1982, J.D., 1985; children—Carolyn Louise, Joan Emily, Amy Elizabeth, Eric Daniel. Dir. Christian edn. St. Luke's Episcopal Ch., 1979-80; law clk. to assoc. justice Mont. Supreme Ct., 1985-87; exec. v.p. St. Peter's Community Hospital Found., 1987—; dir. 1st Bank West. Bd. trustees Rocky Mountain Coll., 1972-80; bd. dirs. Billings (Mont.) Area C. of C., 1977-80; mem. City-County Air Pollution Control Bd., 1969-74, chmn., 1970-71; del. Mont. State Constnl. Conv., 1971-72, sec. conv., 1971-72; chmn. County Local Govt. Study Commn., 1973-76; mem. Billings Sch. Dist. Long Range Planning Com., 1978-79; former pres. Billings LWV, dir., 1987—, pres. Helena LWV, 2d v.p. Mont. LWV; former pres. Silver Run Ski Club. Named one of Billings' most influential citizens, Billings Gazette, 1977; Bertha Morton Scholar, 1982. Rotary. Republican. Home: 481 S Park Ave Helena MT 59601

BOWMAN, LINDA SPEIER, college president; b. Bridgeton, N.J., Dec. 25, 1951; d. John H. and Rosemary (Ivory) Speier; m. Roger L. Bowman, July 22, 1987; children: Robert, Rachel, Tony. BA, U. South Ala., 1973; MA, U. New Orleans, 1981. Retail buyer Merc. Stores, Mobile, Ala., 1972-75; tchr. Ridgewood Prep. Sch., Metairie, La., 1977-80; instr. Phillips Colls., Inc., New Orleans, 1980-81, dept. chmn., 1981-82, assoc. dean, 1982-83, acad. dean, 1983-84, campus dir., 1984-86; pres. Parks Jr. Coll. Phillips Colls., Inc., Denver, 1986—. Mem. Assn. Ind. Colls. and Schs., Colo. Assn. for Commerce and Industry (edn. coun. 1988—), Denver C. of C., Metro North C. of C. Office: Parks Jr Coll 9065 Grant St Denver CO 80229

BOWMAN, RICHARD WILLIAM, publications executive; b. Cleve., June 17, 1941; s. William Byron and June Adelle (Pickard) B.; m. Jackie Carmichael, Sept. 16, 1967 (div. Dec. 1971). AA, Orange Coast Coll., 1973; BA, San Jose State U., 1984. Tech. writer ISS Sperry Univac, Cupertino, Calif., 1976-78, Rolm Corp., Santa Clara, Calif., 1978-81, Zilog, Campbell, Calif., 1981-83; specialist No. Telecom, Santa Clara, Calif., 1983-84; mgr. Fujitsu Am. Inc., San Jose, Calif., 1984-86, NEC Electronics Inc., Mountain View, Calif., 1986—. Served as cpl. USMC, 1960-65. Mem. Peninsula Mktg. Assn., Soc. Tech. Communication. Republican. Home: 600-236 E Weddell Dr Sunnyvale CA 94089

BOWYER, JANE BAKER, educator; b. Dayton, Ohio, Mar. 16, 1934; d. Homer Kenneth and Helen Elizabeth (Brown) Baker; m. Charles Stuart Bowyer, Feb. 27, 1957; children: William Stuart, Robert Baker, Elizabeth Ann. BA, Miami U., Oxford, Ohio, 1956; MA, U. Calif., Berkeley, 1972; PhD, U. Calif., 1974. Prof. Mills Coll., Oakland, Calif., 1975—, head dept. edn., 1986—; cons. Lawrence Hall Sci., U. Calif., Berkeley, 1975—, Nat. Assn. Ednl. Progress, 1975-78, Utah State Bd. Edn., 1985-86; mem. Calif. Round Table's Math/Sci. Task Force, 1983-85; dir. ednl. research Industry Initiatives in Sci. and Math Edn., 1985-86, bd. dirs., 1985—. Author: Science and Society, 1984, Science and Societies Activity Book, 1984; contbr. articles to profl. jours. Bd. dirs. Oakland Sci. and Art Sch., 1979-82, Eric Erickson Sch., San Francisco, 1983-85; prin. investigator Projects in Sci. Edn. Fullbright Research fellow, 1982-83. Mem. Nat. Assn. Research in Sci. Teaching (mem. editorial bd. 1980-82, bd. dirs. 1985—, Outstanding Paper award, 1979, 81), Am. Ednl. Research Orgn. Home: 147 Overhill Rd Orinda CA 94563

BOXER, ALAN LEE, certified public accountant; b. Denver, Sept. 9, 1935; s. Ben B. and Minnette (Goldman) B.; m. Gayle, Dec. 21, 1958; children: Michael E., Jodi S., Richard S. BSBA in Acctg., U. Denver, 1956. Cert. Pub. Acct. Audit mgr. Touche, Ross & Co. CPAs, Denver, 1956-60, Ballin, Milstein & Feinstein CPAs, Denver, 1960-61; prin. Alan L. Boxer, CPA, Denver, 1961-69; v.p and treas. The Pawley Co., Denver, 1969-78; pres. Sci-Pro Inc., Denver, 1978-82; regional mgr. ATV Systems, Inc., Denver, 1982-83; prin. The Enterprise Group, Denver, 1983-86; shareholder, pres. Alderdice, Baroch, Boxer & Co., CPAs, Denver, 1986-87; prin. Alan L. Boxer, CPA, Denver, 1987—. Bd. dirs. Anti Defamation League, Denver, 1986—, BMH Congregation, Denver, 1986—. Mem. Am. Inst. CPAs, Colo. Soc. CPAs, Bnai Brith #171 (pres. 1982, trustee 1983—). Republican. Jewish. Office: Alan L Boxer CPA 4155 E Jewell Ave Ste 904 Denver CO 80222

BOXER, BARBARA, congresswoman; b. Bklyn., Nov. 11, 1940; d. Ira and Sophie (Silvershein) Levy; m. Stewart Boxer, 1962; children: Doug, Nicole. B.A., Bklyn. Coll., 1962. Journalist, assoc. editor Pacific Sun, 1972-74; congl. aide to rep. 5th Congl. Dist. San Francisco, 1974-76; mem. Marin County Bd. Suprs., San Rafael, Calif., 1976-82; mem. 98th-101st Congresses from 6th dist. Calif., 1983—, mem. budget com., armed services com., select com. children, youth and families; chairwoman budget com. task force on AIDS 98th-100th Congresses from 6th dist. Calif., majority whip at large. Pres. Marin County Bd. Suprs., 1980-81; mem. Bay Area Air Quality Mgmt. Bd., San Francisco, 1977-82, pres., 1979-81; bd. dirs. Golden Gate Bridge Hwy. and Transport Dist., San Francisco, 1978-82; founding mem. Marin Nat. Women's Polit. Caucus, Marin Community Video; pres. Dem. New Mems. Caucus, 1983. Recipient Open Govt. award Common Cause, 1980. Jewish. Office: 307 Cannon House Office Bldg Washington DC 20515

BOXER, HARRY, employment services executive; b. Munich, Germany, Dec. 10, 1946; came to U.S., 1949; s. Ben and Reneé (Nussenbaum) B. BS in Fin., Fairleigh Dickinson U., 1969. Stockbroker, tech. analyst Weis, Voisin, Cannon, N.Y.C., 1969-72, Philips, Appel and Walden, N.Y.C., 1969-74; western regional mgr. The Foster-McKay Group, Livingston (N.J.), L.A., 1974-83; co-owner, sr. v.p. Harris-Klein & Co., Encino, Calif., 1983-86; sr. v.p. Intersearch subs. Appleone Employment Svcs., Inglewood, Calif., 1986—, investments and stockmarket analyst. Republican. Jewish. Office: Intersearch Div Appleone 9920 S LaCienega Ste 710 Inglewood CA 90301

BOXER, JEROME HARVEY, accountant; b. Chgo., Nov. 27, 1930; s. Ben Avrum and Edith (Lyman) B.; A.A. magna cum laude, East Los Angeles Coll., 1952; m. Sandra Schaffner, June 17, 1980; children by previous marriage: Michael, Jodi. AB with honors, Calif. State U., Los Angeles, 1954. Lab. instr. Calif. State U., Los Angeles, 1953-54; staff accountant Dolman, Freeman & Buchalter, Los Angeles, 1955-57; sr. accountant Neiman, Sanger, Miller & Beress, Los Angeles, 1957-63; partner firm Glynn and Boxer, CPAs, Los Angeles, 1964-68; v.p., sec. Glynn, Boxer & Phillips Inc., CPA's, Los Angeles and Glendale, 1968—; pres. Echo Data Services, Inc., 1978—; instr. data processing Los Angeles City Adult Schs.; tchr. lectr., cons. wines and wine-tasting; instr. photography. Mem. ops. bd. Everywoman's Village; bd. dirs., v.p. So. Calif. Jewish Hist. Soc.; co-founder Open Space Theatre; former officer Ethel Josephine Scantland Found.; past post adviser Explorer Scouts, Boy Scouts Am., also Eagle Scout. Recipient Youth Service award Mid-Valley YMCA, 1972-73; CPA, Calif., cert. systems profl. Mem. Am. Inst. CPAs, Calif. Soc. CPAs, Assn. for Systems Mgmt., Data Processing Mgmt. Assn., Am. Fedn. Musicians, Am. Jewish Hist. Soc., Friends of Photography, Los Angeles Photog. Ctr., Acad. Model Aeros., Nat. Model Railroad Assn., Maltese Falcons Home Brewing Soc., San Fernando Valley Silent Flyers, San Fernando Valley Radio Control Flyers, Associated Students Calif. State U., Los Angeles (hon. life), Acad. Magical Arts, Internal Brotherhood of Magicians, Soc. Preservation of Variety Arts, Les Amis du Vin, Knights of the Vine, Soc. Wine Educators, Soc. Bacchus Am., German Shepherd Dog Club Am., German Shepherd Dog Club Los Angeles County, Blue Key, Alpha Phi Omega. Clubs: Verdugo, Kiwanis (pres. Sunset-Echo Park 1968), Braemar Country, Pacific Mariners Yacht, S.Coast Corinthian Yacht (Former dir., officer), B'nai B'rith. Cons., contbr. Wine World Mag., 1974-82. Home: 15534 Morrison St Sherman Oaks CA 91403 Office: Glynn Boxer & Phillips Inc CPAs 1000 N Central Ave Glendale CA 91202

BOYCE, ROBERT ABBOTT, service executive; b. Gallup, N.Mex., Apr. 10, 1942; s. George A. and Elizabeth (Coleman) B.; m. Shirley Cole, June 26, 1966 (div. 1987); children: Robert A. Jr., Jeffry H. LLB, LaSalle U., Chgo., 1974. Hotel credit mgr. Flamingo Hotel, Las Vegas, 1970-72; credit exec. Desert Inn Hotel, Las Vegas, 1972-75, 78-80, Aladdin Hotel, Las Vegas, 1975-78; exec. casino host Landmark Hotel, Las Vegas, 1980-85, Maxim Hotel, Las Vegas, 1985-86, Sahara Hotel, Las Vegas, 1986-89, Peppermill Hotel, Reno, 1989—. Contbr. articles to popular mags. Cub scout exec. com. Boulder dam area Boy Scouts Am., Las Vegas, 1976-86; bd. dirs. Clark County Optimist Boys Home, Las Vegas, 1976-88. With USAF, 1960-65. Recipient Award of Merit Boulder dam area Boy Scouts Am., 1985. Mem. Optimists Club (pres. Las Vegas chpt. 1976, 84, outstanding service award 1988), Masons. Republican. Office: Peppermill Hotel & Casino 2707 S Virginia Reno NV 89502

BOYD, BRENT ROGER, respiratory therapist; b. Twin Falls, Idaho, Mar. 3, 1960; s. Roger Bert and Doris Leona (French) B. AS in Respiratory Therapy, Boise State U., 1982, BS in Mgmt., 1983. Cert. and registered respiratory therapist. I.C. respiratory therapist St. Luke's Regional Med. Ctr., Boise, 1981-83, supr. respiratory therapist, 1983-87; mgr. Interwest Med., Boise, 1987-. Coord. family asthma program Idaho Lung Assn., Boise, 1987; league dir. Babe Ruth Baseball, Boise, 1987; del. Am. Legion Boys State, Twin Falls, Idaho, 1977. Mem. Idaho Assn. Respiratory Care, Idaho Thoracic soc., Am. Assn. Respiratory Care, Nat. Assn. Med. Equipment Suppliers, Idaho Assn. Med. Equipment Supplies. Republican. Mem. Christian Ch. Office: Interwest Med 514 N Curtis Boise ID 83706

BOYD, DANIEL JAMES, security company executive; b. Granada Hills, Calif., Sept. 13, 1964; s. Raymond George and Barbara (Kelly) B. BBA, Loyola U., L.A., 1986; cert., L.A. Inst. Polygraph. Mrg. investigations Boyd & Assocs., North Hollywood, Calif., 1986--. Contbr. Rep. Nat. Com., Washington, 1986--. Mem. Am. Polygraph Assn., Calif. Assn. Polygraph Examiners, So. Calif. Businessmen's Assn., Delta Sigma Phi. Roman Catholic. Office: Boyd & Assocs 6319 Colfax Ave North Hollywood CA 91606

BOYD, EDWARD HASCAL, retired military officer; b. Kevil, Ky., Sept. 4, 1934; s. Lloyd E. and D. Irene (Steinbeck) B.; m. D. Ann Creecy, Jan. 13, 1956 (dec. Mar. 1970); children: Lawrence H., Debra A.; m. Margaret Lorene Hogan, Nov. 7, 1970; 1 child, Laura Irene. AA, Phoenix Coll., 1954; BS, Ariz. State U., 1956, MBA, 1972. Cert. secondary tchr., Ariz. Commd. 2d lt. USMC, 1956, advanced through ranks to col., 1980, exec. officer Marine Detachment USS Helena, 1959-60; mem. staff MCRD USMC, San

Diego, 1961-63; instr. ops. and intelligence Landing Force Tng. Command USMC, 1963-65, mem. 1st Bn. 4th Marines, 1966-67, instr. Amphibious Warfare Sch., 1967-70, spl. asst. for joint matters Hdqrs., 1973-76, various positions 3d Marine Div., 1972-80; comdr. Hdqrs. Bn. USMC, Camp Pendleton, Calif., 1981-84; ret. USMC, 1984; substitute tchr. Mesa (Ariz.) Unified Sch. Dist., 1984—. Mem. Marine Corps Assn., Ret. Officers Assn., Williams AFB Officers Club, Alta Mesa Country Club, Delta Pi Epsilon, Alpha Tau Omega. Home: 5851 E Elmwood St Mesa AZ 85205

BOYD, JAMES PAUL, dentist; b. New Castle, Ind., Apr. 23, 1957; s. Dan Rader Boyd and Susan Elizabeth (Pope) Simeon; m. Marianne Sodaro, Apr. 19, 1986. AS in Biology, West Valley Coll., 1978; BS in Biology, U. Calif., Irvine, 1980; DDS, U. of Pacific, 1984. Pvt. practice gen. dentistry Tustin, Calif., 1984—. Vol. dentist Flying Samaritans, Orange, Calif., 1986—. Mem. ADA, Calif. Dental Assn., Orange County Dental Assn. Republican. Roman Catholic. Club: Westmed Gold (Santa Ana). Office: 17400 Irvine Blvd Ste D Tustin CA 92680

BOYD, JOHN GARTH, manufacturing production and operations consultant; b. Greeley, Colo., Sept. 17, 1942; s. Jack Gardner and Madelyn Ilene (Bucher) B.; m. Cherie Kay Graves, Mar. 16, 1962 (div. June 1982); children: Jeffrey G., Daryl I., Peggy N.; m. Ellen Lea Meyers, Aug. 8, 1987; 1 child, Ian T. BA, U. No. Colo., 1963; MA, Colo. State U., 1965; MS, U. Colo., 1972. Teaching asst. Colo. State U., Ft. Collins, 1964-65; instr. No. Ariz. U., Flagstaff, 1965-67; teaching asst. U. Colo., Boulder, 1967-72; systems rep. Burroughs Corp., Englewood, Colo., 1972-76; mgr. Touche Ross & Co., Denver, 1977-84; chief fin. officer, chief operating officer Catalina Controls Corp., Longmont, Colo., 1984-86; ptnr. High Plains Ptnrship., Boulder, 1987—; adminstr. technology tng. Martin Marietta Astronautics Group, Denver, 1988—. Scoutmaster Boy Scouts Am., Boulder, 1969-72, troop scoutmaster, Denver, 1972-75; loaned exec. Colo. Gov.'s Mgmt. and Efficiency Study, 1982. NASA fellow, 1968. Mem. Am. Prodn. and Inventory Control Soc. (treas. Denver 1983-84, pres. 1984-85, Gold award 1985). Avocations: hiking, mountain climbing, fishing, cross-country skiing. Office: High Plains Ptnrship 3360 34th St Suite D Boulder CO 80301

BOYD, LEONA POTTER, former social worker; b. Creekside, Pa., Aug. 31, 1907; d. Joseph M. and Belle (McHenry) Johnston; grad. Ind. Normal Sch., 1927; student Las Vegas Normal U., N.Mex., summer 1933; postgrad. Carnegie Inst. Tech. Sch. Social Work, summer 1945, U. Pitts. Sch. Social Work, 1956-57; m. Edgar D. Potter, July 16, 1932 (div.); m. Harold Lee Boyd, Oct. 1972. Tchr., Creekside (Pa.) pub. schs., 1927-30, Papago Indian Reservation, Sells, Ariz., 1931-33; caseworker, supr. Indiana County (Pa.) Bd. Assistance, 1934-54, exec. dir., 1954-68, ret. Bd. dirs. Indiana County Tourist Promotion; former bd. dirs. Indiana County United Fund, Salvation Army, Indiana County Guidance Ctr., Armstrong-Indiana Mental Health Bd.; cons. asso. Community Research Assos., Inc.; mem. Counseling Center Aux., Lake Havasu City, Ariz., 1978-80; former mem. W.stern Welcome Club, Lake Havasu City, Sierra Vista Hosp. Aux., Truth or Consequences, N.Mex. Recipient Jr. C. of C. Disting. Service award, Indiana, Pa., 1966, Business and Profl. Women's Club award, Indiana, 1965. Mem. Am. Assn. Ret. Persons, Daus. Am. Colonists, Internat. Platform Assn., Sierra County hist. socs. Lutheran. Home: 507 N Foch St Truth or Consequences NM 87901

BOYD, STEPHEN CURTIS, business owner, educator; b. L.A., Mar. 21, 1949; s. Edwin Forrest Jr. and Francis (Ross) B.; m. Sally Kathleen Cornyn, May 4, 1986. Student, Montclair Coll. Prep, 1966, U. Denver, 1966-67. Real estate assoc. Century 21 Action!, Long Beach, Calif., 1982-85; logistics mgr. Quantum Mgmt. Systems, Long Beach, 1985-87; owner Otter Discovery Tours, Long Beach, 1987—; co-owner, co-founder Interactional Perspectives, Newport Beach, Calif., 1988—; cons. Quantum Mgmt. Systems, Long Beach, 1983—, Fusionary Techs., Newport Beach, 1986—, Boy Scouts Am., La Canada, Calif., 1987—. Vol. counselor Nat. Coun. on alcoholism, Long Beach, 1985-87. Staff sgt. USAF, 1968-72. Mem. Am. Mountain Guides Assn., Masons. Republican. Presbyterian. Office: Otter Discovery Tours 5555 Sterns Ave Long Beach CA 90815

BOYD, WILLIAM ELKINS, lawyer; b. San Mateo, Calif., Oct. 13, 1947; s. William Sprott and Katherine (Elkins) Boyd; m. Elizabeth Johnston Kroeber, May 19, 1984. BA, Stanford U., 1969; JD, Hastings Coll. of Law, 1974. Admitted to Calif. bar, 1975; ptnr. firm Boyd and McKay, San Francisco, 1980—; v.p. Boyd Bros., investments, San Francisco, 1980—; pres. Trio I Assocs. Investments, San Francisco, 1985—. Spl. asst. to chmn. Calif. Republican Com., 1968; bd. dirs. San Mateo County Planned Parenthood, 1971-73, Hastings Child Care Center, 1974-76. Mem. Am. Bar Assn., State Bar Calif. Assn. (bus. law sect.), Stanford U. Alumni Assn., Hastings Alumni Assn. Episcopalian. Clubs: Burlingame Country, Hastings 1066 Club. Home: 590 Remillard Dr Hillsborough CA 94010 Office: 101 California St Ste 4040 San Francisco CA 94111

BOYD, WILLIAM HARLAND, historian; b. Boise, Idaho, Jan. 7, 1912; s. Harland D. and Cordelia (Crumley) B.; A.B., U. Calif.-Berkeley, 1935, M.A., 1936, Ph.D., 1942; m. Mary Kathryn Drake, June 25, 1939; children—Barbara A. Boyd Voltmer, William Harland, Kathryn L. Tchr. Fall River High Sch., McArthur, Calif., 1937-38, Watsonville (Calif.) High Sch., 1941-42, San Mateo (Calif.) High Sch., 1942-44; prof. history Bakersfield Coll., 1946-73, chmn. social sci. dept., 1967-73. Pres., Kern County Hist. Soc., 1950-52; adv. com. Kern County Mus., 1955-60; chmn. Fort Tejon Restoration Com. Bakersfield, 1952-55, sec., 1955-60; mem. Kern County Hist. Records Commn., 1977—, Bakersfield Hist. Preservation Commn., 1984-87. Recipient Merit award Kern County Bd. Trade, 1960; commendation Kern County Bd. Suprs., 1952, 76, 78. Mem. Calif. Tchrs. Assn., Am. Hist. Assn., Phi Alpha Theta. Republican. Baptist. Author: Land of Havilah, 1952, (with G.J. Rogers) San Joaquin Vignettes, 1955, (with others) Spanish Trailblazers in the South San Joaquin, 1957; A Centennial Bibliography on the History Kern County, California, 1966; A California Middle Border, 1972; A Climb Through History, 1973; Bakersfield's First Bapt. Church, 1975; Kern Country Wayfarers, 1977; Kern County Tall Tales, 1980; The Shasta Route, 1981; Stagecoach Heyday in the San Joaquin Valley, 1983. Contbr. to Ency. Brit. Home: 339 Cypress St Bakersfield CA 93304

BOYER, CARL, III, teacher; b. Phila., Pa., Sept. 22, 1937; s. Carl Boyer Jr. and Elizabeth Campbell Timm; m. Ada Christine Kruse, July 28, 1962. Student, U. Edinburgh, Scotland, 1956-57; BA, Trinity U., 1959; MEd in Secondary Edn., U. Cin., 1959; postgrad., Calif. Luth. U., Brigham Young U., Calif. State U., Northbridge. Tchr. Edgewood High Sch., San Antonio, Tex., 1959-60; librarian U. Cinn., Cincinnati, Ohio, 1960-61; tchr. Eight Ave. Elem. Sch., Dayton, Ky., 1961-62, Amelia High Sch., Amelia, Ohio, 1962-63; instr. Kennedy San Fernando Comm. Adult Sch., San Fernando, Calif., 1964-74, Mission Coll., San Fernando, 1971; tchr. San Fernando High Sch., San Fernando, Calif., 1963; faculty chmn. San Fernando High Sch.; dept. chmn. San Fernando High Sch. Author, compiler 10 books on genealogy and family history; contbr. articles to profl. jours. Councilman City of Santa Clarita, Calif., 1987—, mayor pro-tem, 1989—; bd. trustees Santa Clarita Community Coll. Dist., 1973-81; dir. Castaic Lake Water Agy., 1982-84; pres. Del Prado (Condominium) Assn., Inc., Newhall, Calif. Mem. United Tchrs. Los Angeles, New Eng. Hist. Geneal. Soc. Rep. Methodist. Home: PO Box 333 Santa Clarita CA 91322 Office: City of Santa Clarita 23920 Valencia Blvd #300 Santa Clarita CA 91355

BOYER, DANIEL JEFFREY, aerospace engineer; b. Portland, Oreg., July 29, 1964; s. Norbert Daniel and Marietta Louise (Rigert) B. BS in Mech. Engring., Loyola Marymount U., 1986; M in Systems Engring., Va. Poly. Inst. and State U., 1988. Research asst. Va. Poly. Inst. and State U., Blacksburg, Va., 1986088; engr., scientist McDonnel Douglas Space Systems Co., Huntington Beach, Calif., 1988—. Letter writer, fin. supporter Amnesty Internat., N.Y.C., 1987—. Mem. AIAA, Tau Beta Pi. Roman Catholic. Home: 97 Greenmoor Irvine CA 97124 Office: McDonnell Douglas Systems 5301 Bolsa Ave MS 11-3 Huntington Beach CA 92647

BOYER, FORD SYLVESTER, therapist; b. Cadet, Mo., Jan. 12, 1934; s. Wilford Robert and Mary Elizabeth (DeClue) B.; m. Juelle-Ann Rupkalvis, May 2, 1970. BA in Psychology, U.S. Air Force Inst., 1957; DD, Am. Bible Inst., Kansas City, Mo., 1977; postgrad., John F. Kennedy U.; apprenticed, Spurling Chem. Hypnosis Lab., L.A., 1958-61. Adminstr. Getz Bros., San Francisco, 1969-73; supr. word processing U.S. Leasing Corp., San Francisco, 1977-82, dir. tng. and applications-word processing, 1982-84; computer cons Petaluma, Calif., 1984-87; massage therapist Petaluma, 1985-87; pvt. practice hypnotherapy Alameda, Calif., 1987—; cons. for chem. dependency Alameda, 1987—. Contbr. articles to profl. publs.; writer, pub.: (newsletter) Starfire, 1988—. With USAF, 1953-57, Korea. Mem. Am. Council Hypnotist Examiners, Nat. Assn. Alcohol and Drug Abuse Counselors, Calif. Assn. Alcohol and Drug Abuse Counselors, Alameda C. of C. Home and Office: 3327 Cook Ln Alameda CA 94501

BOYER, HERBERT WAYNE, biochemist; b. Pitts., July 10, 1936; m. Grace B., 1959; 2 children. BA, St. Vincent Coll., Latrobe, Pa., 1958, DSc (hon.), 1981; MS, U. Pitts., 1960, PhD, 1963. Mem. faculty U. Calif., San Francisco, 1966—; prof. biochemistry U. Calif., 1976—; investigator Howard Hughes Med. Inst., 1976—; co-founder, dir. Genentech, Inc., South San Francisco, Calif., now cons. Mem. editorial bd.: Biochemistry. Recipient V.D. Mattai award Roche Inst., 1977; Albert and Mary Lasker award for basic med. research, 1980; USPHS postdoctoral fellow, 1963-66. Fellow AAAS; mem. Am. Soc. Microbiology, Am. Acad. Arts and Scis., Nat. Acad. Scis. Office: U Calif Dept Biochemistry HSE 1506 San Francisco CA 94143 *

BOYER, JACOB TWYMAN, dentist, public health service officer; b. Louisville, Feb. 26, 1945; s. Paul Evans and Mary Helen (Orem) B.; m. Peggy Ann Ferriel, Mar. 14, 1969 (div. May 1980); children: Jason Paul, Aaron Robert; m. Michelle Rae Eagle, Aug. 16, 1985. BA in Chemistry, U. Ky., 1967; DMD, U. Louisville, 1975. Comd. lt. USPHS, 1975; advanced through grades to comdr. 1983; student intern USPHS, Norfolk, Va., 1974; resident in gen. practice Indian Health Svc., Anchorage, 1975-76; staff dental officer Indian Health Svc., Shiprock, N.Mex., 1976-77; asst. chief dental officer Indian Health Svc., Shiprock, 1977-78; facility dental officer Indian Health Svc., Towaoc, Colo., 1978-87; chief So. Colo. Ute svc. unit Indian Health Svc., Towaoc, 1987-89; chief svc. unit dental unit program Indian Health Svc., Chinle, Ariz., 1989—; mem. hosp. staff Indian Health Svc., Anchorage, 1975-76, Shiprock, 1976-78, Chinle, 1989—; mem. staff Southwest Meml. Hosp., Cortez, Colo., 1980--; cons. Vista Grande Nursing Home, Cortez, 1980--; clin. instr. Sch. Dentistry, U. Colo., Denver, 1984--. Fellow Am. Acad. Dentistry; mem. Omicron Kappa Upsilon, Phi Delta, Beta Delta. Democrat. Presbyterian. Home: 1800 E Empire Cortez CO 81321

BOYER, LAURA MERCEDES, librarian; b. Madison, Ind., Aug. 3, 1934; d. Clyde C. and Dorcas H. (Willyard) Boyer. A.B., George Washington U., 1956; A.M., U. Denver, 1959; M.L.S., George Peabody U., 1961. Pub. sch. tchr., Kankakee, Ill., 1957-58; asst. circulation librarian U. Kans., Lawrence, 1961-63; asst. reference librarian U. of Pacific Library, Stockton, Calif., 1963-65, head reference dept., 1965-84, coordinator reference services, 1984-86; reference librarian Calif. State U.-Stanislaus, Turlock, 1987—. Compiler of Play Anthologies Union List, 1976. Author article in profl. jour. Mem. Am. Soc. Info. Sci., ALA, Calif. Library Assn., AAUP, Nat. Assn. Female Execs., Nat. Assn. Vietnamese Am. Educators, DAR, Daughters of the Am. Colonists, Phi Beta Kappa, Kappa Delta Pi, Beta Phi Mu. Republican. Episcopalian. Home: 825 Muir Rd Modesto CA 95350

BOYER, ROBERT JAY, civil engineer, surveyor, land use planner; b. Fargo, N.D., Apr. 23, 1951; s. Kenneth Ward and Lucille Agnes (Kruse) B. BSCE, U. N.D., 1973. Profl. engr., Alaska, Oreg., Wash.; lic. land surveyor, Alaska, Oreg. Constrn. engr. Santa Fe Internat., Orange, Calif., 1981; structural engr., sales mgr. HP Marine, Gothenburg, Sweden, 1981; player, instr., coach of basketball Travelodge All Stars, Nat. Basketball League, Bucks, Eng., 1981-82; engr. Boyer Engring., Portland, Oreg., 1982-83, Advance Engring., Wasilla, 1983; constrn. engr. State of Alaska, Anchorage, 1983-84; sanitation engr. City of Galena (Alaska), 1984-85; bldg. mgmt. specialist II State of Alaska, Anchorage, 1985-86; project engr. Engineered Concepts, Inc., Portland, Oreg., 1986-88; profl. engr., land surveyor, prin. Global Engring., Land Surveying, Planning Co., Portland, 1988—. V.p. Young Adult Ministry, Portland, 1980. Named Most Valuable Basketball Player Sioux Booster Club, Grand Forks, 1972. Mem. ASCE (Outstanding Sophomore Engring. Student Ladies Aux. 1971), Profl. Land Surveyors of Oreg., Nat. Soc. Profl. Engrs., Portland Skyliners, Chancellor Club. Roman Catholic. Home: 4046 SE Boise St Portland OR 97202 Office: Global Engring/Land Survey 7315 SE Clay St Portland OR 97215

BOYER, RUSSELL DEAN, food company executive; b. Painesville, Ohio, Dec. 13, 1938; s. Bernard Ardell and Hattie (Roerdanz) Neibauer; m. Harue Yamada, Nov. 25, 1964. Student, Case Inst., Cleve., 1956-57, Kent State U., 1958, 62. Detailman Ames Co., div. Miles Labs., Elkhart, Ind., 1964-65; mktg. devel. mgr. Dome Labs., div. Miles Labs., N.Y.C., 1965-67; mktg. mgr. Vicks Japan, Inc., Osaka, 1967-75; mktg. devel. mgr. Vicks Internat., Wilton, Conn., 1975-82; mktg. dir. Richardson-Vicks Inc., Manila, Philippines, 1982-84; pres., dir. P.T. Richardson-Vicks Indonesia, Jakarta, 1984-87; pres. Nippon Vicks KK, Osaka, 1987, Homebest, Inc., Alameda, Calif., 1988—. With U.S. Army, 1958-62. Libertarian. Office: Homebest Inc 2200 Central Ave Alameda CA 94501

BOYKIN, JAMES LESTER, aerospace engineer, consultant; b. Clarendon, Tex., Jan. 6, 1928; s. Garland Lester and Lucy Edna (Matthews) B.; m. Dulcie Mildred Ligon, Sept. 2, 1958; children: Tracy Lynette, Leslie Dee, James Russell, Robin Elisa. BSME, N.Mex. State U., 1951, BSEE, 1959. Comml. pilot rating. With Hughes Aircraft Co., 1951-54; fighter pilot U. S. Air Force, 1954-58; flight test engr., test ops. supr. N.Am. Aviation div. Rockwell Internat., L.A., 1959-63, Las Cruces, N.Mex., 1963-69; test ops. supr. LTV (Ling Temco Vaught), Las Cruces, 1969-71, Dynalectron Corp., Las Cruces, 1971-74; with Rockwell Internat., Las Cruces, 1974-85, ops. supr., 1978-85, project engr., 1981, sr. project engr., 1981-85; cons.; charter flying, instr., 1985—. Capt. USAF, 1946-48, 54-58; with USAFR, 1969. (ret.). Mem. Nat. Rifle Assn. (life), Air Force Assn., Res. Officers Assn., Lions (pres. 1975-76). Republican. Methodist. Home: 2390 Rosedale Dr Las Cruces NM 88005

BOYKIN, RAYMOND FRANCIS, management science professor, consultant; b. Santa Monica, Calif., Nov. 18, 1953; s. Francis Raymond and Doris Elaine (Davis) B.; m. Shelley Lynne Ladd, July 30, 1977; children: Jennifer Lynne, Whitney Michele. BA in Quantitative Method, Calif. State U., Fullerton, 1975; MS in Mgmt. Sci., San Diego State U., 1976; PhD in Mgmt. Sci., St. Louis U., 1986. Indsl. engr. Rockwell Internat., L.A., 1976-77; sr. scientist Rockwell Internat., Richland, Wash., 1977-80; sr. mgmt. scientist Monsanto Co., St. Louis, 1980-86; prof. mgmt. sci. Calif. State U., Chico, 1986—; assoc. sr. cons. Pickard, Lowe and Garrick, Inc., Newport Beach, Calif., 1986—; mem. tech. adv. com. State of Calif., Sacramento, 1988—. Author, editor: Risk Analysis in the Chemical Industry, 1985; contbr. articles to profl. jours. Advisor Butte County Health Dept., Oroville, Calif., 1987—. Mem. Soc. for Risk Analysis (chartered, ann. meeting chair 1984, 89), Inst. Mgmt. Sci. (Achievement award 1984). Republican. Home: 862 Westmont Dr Chico CA 95926 Office: Calif State U Coll of Bus Chico CA 95929-0011

BOYKIN, SUSAN MICHELLE, sales professional; b. Oxnard, Calif., Mar. 9, 1958; d. Isaac June and Rosemary Michelle (Wuich) B. AA, Moorpark Coll., 1978; BA, Calif. State U., Northridge, 1983. Nat. sales mgr. Brinsdon Corp., Newbury Park, Calif., 1985-86; asst. to v.p. mktg. Brady Mktg. Co., Newbury Park, 1985-87; sales rep. Robert Valentine & Assocs., Thousand Oaks, Calif., 1987--. Mem. Tole Assn. Republican. Roman Catholic. Home and Office: 1290 White Cliff Rd Thousand Oaks CA 91360

BOYKO, EDWARD JOHN, internist, medical researcher; b. Bethlehem, Pa., Feb. 19, 1953; s. Edward and Mary (Levan) B.; m. Beth Welcome Alderman, Sept. 27, 1980; 1 child, Bryan Martin. BA, Columbia U., 1975; MD, U. Pitts., 1979; MPH, U. Wash., 1984. Resident in internal medicine U. Chgo., 1979-82; fellow Robert Wood Johnson Found., Seattle, 1982-84; attending physician U. Colo., Denver, 1984—; asst. prof. medicine and preventive medicine U. Colo., 1984—; cons., Alaska Native Health Svc., Anchorage, 1985—; spl. mem. NIH study sect., Washington, 1988—. Contbr. articles to med. jours. Recipient Career Devel. award, Nat. Found. Ileitis and Colitis, 1986, First award, NIH, 1988. Mem. Soc. Gen. Internal Medicine (Rocky Mountain region coord. 1988), Soc. Epidemiologic Rsch., Am. Fedn. Clin. Rsch., Denver Athletic Club, Colo. Mountain Club, Alpha Omega Alpha. Home: 2324 Bellaire St Denver CO 80207 Office: U Colo Health Scis Ctr Box B180 4200 E 9th Ave Denver CO 80262

BOYLAN, RICHARD JOHN, psychologist, educator; b. Hollywood, Calif., Oct. 15, 1939; s. John Alfred and Rowena Margaret (Devine) B.; m. Charnette Marie Blackburn, Oct. 26, 1968 (div. June 1983); children: Christopher J., Jennifer April, Stephanie August; m. Judith Lee Keast, Nov. 21, 1987; stepchildren: Darren Andrew Keast, Matthew Grant Keast. BA, St. John's Coll., 1961; MEd, Fordham U., 1966; MSW, U. Calif., Berkeley, 1971; PhD in Psychology, U. Calif., Davis, 1984. Lic. psychologist, clin. social worker, marriage, family and child counselor. Asst. dir. Berkeley (Calif.) Free Ch., 1970-71; psychiat. social worker Marin Mental Health Dept., San Rafael, Calif., 1971-77; dir. Calaveras Mental Health Dept., San Andreas, Calif., 1977-85; prof., coord. Nat. U., Sacramento, 1985-86; instr. Calif. State U., Sacramento, 1985—, U. Calif., Davis, 1984-88; dir. U.S. Behavioral Health, Sacramento; pvt. practice psychotherapy, Sacramento, 1974—. Cons. Calif. State Legis., Sacramento, 1979-80; chmn. Calaveras County Bd. Edn., Angels Camp, Calif., 1981-84. Recipient Geriatric Medicine Acad. award NIH, 1984, Experiment Station grant USDA, Calif., 1983. Mem. Am. Psychol. Assn., Sacramento Soc. of Profl. Psychologists (pres.-elect), Nat. Assn. Social Workers, AAUP, Sierra Club. Democrat. Taoist. Home: 6724 Trudy Way Sacramento CA 95831 Office: 3455 American River Dr Ste A Sacramento CA 95864

BOYLE, BARBARA DORMAN, motion picture company executive; b. N.Y.C., Aug. 11, 1935; d. William and Edith (Kleiman) Dorman; m. Kevin Boyle, Nov. 26, 1960; children: David Eric, Paul Coleman. BA in English with honors, U. Calif., Berkeley, 1957; JD, UCLA, 1960. Bar: Calif. 1961, N.Y. 1964, U.S. Supreme Ct. 1964. Atty. bus. affairs dept, corp. asst. sec. Am. Internat. Pictures, L.A., 1960-65; ptnr. Cohen & Boyle, L.A., 1967-74; exec. v.p., gen. counsel, chief op. officer New World Pictures, L.A., 1974-82; sr. v.p. prodn. Orion Pictures Corp., L.A., 1982-85; exec. v.p. prodn. RKO Pictures, L.A., 1986-87; pres. Sovereign Pictures, Inc., L.A., 1988—; lectr. in field. Exec. producer (Film) Eight Men Out, 1987; contbr. articles to profl. jours. Bd. dirs. UCLA Law Fund Com., Ind. Feature Project/West, L.A. Women's Campaign Fund; founding mem. entertainment adv. coun. sch. law UCLA, co-chmn. 1979-80; mem. adv. bd. Am. Film Inst., Womens Directing Workshop. Mem. Acad. Motion Picture Arts and Scis., Women in Film (pres. 1977-78), Hollywood Women's Polit. Com., Women Entertainment Lawyers Assn., Calif. Bar Assn., N.Y. State Bar Assn., Hollywood Women's Polit. Com., Am. Film. Inst. (bd. dirs. Women dir.'s workshop). Office: Sovereign Pictures Inc 11845 W Olympic Blvd Los Angeles CA 90064

BOYLE, CAROLYN MOORE, public relations executive, marketing communications manager; b. Los Angeles, Jan. 29, 1937; d. Cory Orlando Moore and Violet (Brennan) Baldock; m. Robert J. Ruppelt, Oct. 8, 1954 (div. Aug. 1964); children: Cory Robert, Traci Lynn; m. Jerry Ray Boyle, June 1, 1970 (div. 1975). AA, Orange Coast Coll., 1966; BA, Calif. State U., Fullerton, 1970; student, U. Calif., Irvine, 1970-71. Program coordinator Newport Beach (Calif.) Cablevision, 1968-70; dir. pub. relations Fish Communications Co., Newport Beach, 1970-74; mktg. rep. Dow Pharm. div. Dow Chem. Co., Orange County, Calif., 1974-77, Las Vegas, Nev., 1980-81; mgr. product publicity Dow Agrl. Products div. Dow Chem. Co., Midland, Mich., 1977-80; mgr. mktg. communications Dowell Fluid Services Region div. Dow Chem. Co. Houston, 1981-84; adminstr. mktg. communications Swedlow, Inc., Garden Grove, Calif., 1984-85; cons. mktg. communications, 1985-86; mgr. mktg. communications Am. Convertors div. Am. Hosp. Supply, 1986-87; mgr. sales support Surgidev Corp., Santa Barbara, Calif., 1987-88; owner Barrel House, Victorville, Calif., 1988—; guest lectr. Calif. State U., Long Beach, 1970; seminar coordinator U. Calif., Irvine, 1972; mem. Western White House Press Corps, 1972; pub. relations cons. BASF Wyandotte, Phila., 1981-82. Author: Agricultural Public Relations/Publicity, 1981; editor Big Mean AG Machine (internal mag.), 1977; contbr. numerous articles to trade publs.; contbg. editor Dowell Mktg. Newsletter, 1983; creator, designer Novahistine DMX Trial Size nat. mktg. program, 1977. Com. mem. Dow Employees for Polit. Action, Midland, 1978-80; bd. dirs. Dowell Employees for Polit. Action Com., Houston, 1983-84. World Campus Afloat scholar, U. Seven Seas, 1966-67; recipient PROTOS award, 1985. Mem. Pub. Relations Soc. Am. (cert.), Soc. Petroleum Engrs., Internat. Assn. Bus. Communicators. Episcopalian. Recipient first rights to televise President Nixon in Western White House. Office: 16805 D St Victorville CA 92392

BOYLE, THERESA ANN, marketing executive; b. Port Jefferson, N.Y., June 14, 1962; d. Francis and Dorothy Ann (Nutz) B. BS, Stanford U., 1984. Mech. engr. Integrated Handling Systems, Menlo Park, Calif., 1984-85; communications asst. Campus Crusade for Christ, Muelheim, Fed. Republic of Germany, 1985-86; purchasing coord. for devel. Oracle Corp., Belmont, Calif., 1986-87; event planner Amazing Events, Palo Alto, Calif., 1987-88; with sales and mktg. Oracle Corp., Belmont, 1988—; career counselor, recruiter, Calif., 1986—. Recipient Svc. award athletic dept. Stanford U., 1988. Mem. Stanford Athletic Alumni Club (nat. chmn. 1986—), Stanford Buck/Cardinal Club (bd. dirs. 1988). Home: 825 Live Oak Ave Apt E Menlo Park CA 84025

BOYLES, GARY EDWARD, protective services official; b. San Diego, Apr. 18, 1951; s. Calvin Ray Boyles and Alice Irene (Lane) Bilbrey; m. Jolene Young, July 17, 1971; children: Jeffrey, Gregory. AS in Police Sci., Chaffey Coll., 1971, AS in Fire Sci., 1975; BA in Mgmt., U. Redlands, 1984; postgrad., Calif. State U., San Bernardino, 1989—. Cert. state fire officer, Calif. Firefighter Central Valley Fire Dist., Fontana, Calif., 1972-77; engr. Central Valley Fire Dist., Fontana, 1977, capt., 1977-84, fire prevention supr., 1984-85, battalion comdr., 1985-88; div. chief, fire prevention San Bernardino County Fire Agy., Fontana, 1988—. Mayor pro tem, City of Fontana, 1986—, councilman, 1984—, chmn. redevelopment agy., 1987—, mem. redevelopment agy., 1984—, bd. dirs., 1984—; v.p. Cen. Valley Firefighters, 1984-88; sec. Internat. Assn. Firefighters Local 935, 1977-79; bd. dirs. Omnitrans, 1986—. Completed L.A. Marathon, 1987, 88. Mem. So. Calif. Assn. Govts. (energy and environment com. 1988—), San Bernardino Associated Govts., Elks, Toastmasters. Home: 9616 Kempster Fontana CA 92335 Office: San Bernardino County Fire 11611 Industry Ave Fontana CA 92335

BOYLE-SULLIVAN, KATHLEEN MARIE, service organization administrator; b. Tulsa, Feb. 9, 1958; d. Thomas Anthony and Jeanne Lee (Agnew) Sullivan; m. Thomas C. Boyle. BS in Polit. Sci., Ariz. State U., 1980; MA in Govt., Coll. William and Mary, 1982. Sec. Ariz. Rep. Party, Phoenix, 1980-81; rsch. asst. Pete Dunn for U.S. Senate Campaign, Phoenix, 1982; adminstra. sec Ariz. Corp. Commn., Phoenix, 1983-84; pub. relations dir. Epoch Univs. Publ., Phoenix, 1984-86; membership dir. Tempe (Ariz.) C. of C., 1986—. Sec. community chmn., publicity Cactus Wren Rep. Women, Phoenix, 1983—; sec. women's com. Fiesta Bowl. Mem. Soroptimist (past pres.), Pub. Rels. Soc. Am., Alpha Phi. (chmn. conv.). Republican. Office: Tempe C of C 60 E 5th St #3 Tempe AZ 85281

BOYNTON, BUCK WILLIAM, physician; b. Houston, Feb. 27, 1920; s. George Wesley and Mabel (Palmer) B.; B.A., U. Tex., 1950, M.D., 1954; m. Maryanna Craig, Sept. 3, 1947 (div. Jan., 1965); children—Buck William, Suzanne; m. 2d, Donna Carlisle, Apr. 22, 1978. Intern, Riverside County Gen. Hosp., 1954-55, resident, 1955-56; gen. practice of medicine, Riverside, Calif., 1954-82; physician Riverside County Jail, 1971-83; staff physician and surgeon Folsom State Prison, Represa, Calif., 1983-86; cons. joint legis. com. on prison constrn. and operation Calif. Legis.. Served with USNR, 1942-45. Lodges: Masons, Shriners. Home: PO Box 699 Gualala CA 95445

BOYNTON, ROBERT GRANVILLE, computer systems analyst; b. North Bend, Oreg., Aug. 11, 1951; s. Granville Clarence Jr. and Leatrice Anne (Yoder) B. Student, Central Oreg. Community Coll., 1969-70. cert. career data processing Heald Coll. Bus., 1972. Computer operator Coca-Cola Bottling Co. Calif., San Francisco, 1973-76, data processing mgr., 1977-78; computer operator Warn Industries, Milwaukie, Oreg., 1979-81, computer programmer, 1981-85, analyst, 1983-85, computer systems analyst, 1985--. Vol. Oreg. Spl. Olympics, 1985-86. Democrat. Home: 8126 SE Lake Rd Apt 122 Milwaukie OR 97222 Office: Warn Industries 13270 SE Pheasant Ct Milwaukie OR 97222

BOYNTON, ROBERT MERRILL, psychology educator; b. Evanston, Ill., Oct. 28, 1924; s. Merrill Holmes and Eleanor (Matthews) B.; m. Alice Neiley, Apr. 9, 1947; children: Sherry, Michael, Neiley, Geoffrey. Student, Antioch Coll., 1942-43, U. Ill., 1943-45; A.B., Amherst Coll., 1948; Ph.D., Brown U., 1952. Asst. prof. psychology and optics U. Rochester, N.Y., 1952-57; asso. prof. U. Rochester, 1957-61, prof., 1961-74, dir. Center for Visual Sci., 1963-71, chmn. dept. psychology, 1971-74; prof. psychology U. Calif., San Diego, 1974—, assoc. dean grad. studies and research, 1987—; guest researcher Nat. Phys. Lab., Teddington, Eng., 1960-61; vis. prof. physiology U. Calif. Med. Center, San Francisco, 1969-70. Author: Human Color Vision, 1979; chmn. bd. editors Vision Research, 1982-86; contbr. articles to profl. jours. Served with USNR, 1943-45. Fellow AAAS, Optical Soc. Am. dir.-at-large 1966-69), Am. Psychol. Assn., Nat. Acad. Scis., Assn. for Research in Vision and Ophthalmology (trustee 1984—). Home: 376 Bellaire St Del Mar CA 92014

BOYNTON, WILLIAM LEWIS, electronic manufacturing company official; b. Kalamazoo, May 31, 1928; s. James Woodbury and Cyretta (Gunther) B.; ed. pub. schs.; m. Kei Ouchi, Oct. 8, 1953. Asst. mgr. Speigel J & R, Kalamazoo, 1947-48; served with U.S. Army, 1948-74, ret., 1974; with Rockwell/Collins div., Newport Beach, Calif., 1974-78, supr. material, 1978-81, coord., 1981-88; supr. coord. Rockwell/CDC, Santa Ana, Calif., 1981—, coord. investment recovery, 1982-86, shipping and material coordinator, 1987-88, material coordinator, 1988, environ. coordinator Rockwell/SPD, Newport Beach, 1988—; mem. faculty Western Mich. U., 1955-58. Trustee Orange County Vector Control Dist., 1980—; mem. adv. panel for bus./econ. devel. Calif. State Legislature, 1979-86. Decorated Bronze Star. Mem. Assn. U.S. Army, Assn. U.S. Army, Non-Commd. Officers Assn., Nat. Mgmt. Assn., Nat. Geog. Soc. Republican. Roman Catholic. Home: 5314 Lucky Way Santa Ana CA 92704 Office: 4311 Jamboree Rd Newport Beach CA 92660

BOZARTH, PAUL JONATHAN, architect; b. L.A., May 22, 1956; s. David Harmon and Flora Annarose (Black) B.; m. Rhonda Annette Gisler, June 17, 1978; 1 child, Brandon Scott. BArch, Calif. Poly. State U., 1981. Registered architect, Calif. Project mgr. The Warkentin Archtl. Group, Irvine, Calif., 1981-83; project architect Architects Orange, Orange, Calif., 1983-84; prin. Paul Bozarth Architect, Costa Mesa, Calif., 1984—. Mem. Rotary (community service dir. and club service dir. Newport Beach chpt. 1988-89, pres.-elect 1989-90). Home and Office: 557 Sturgeon Dr Costa Mesa CA 92626

BRAASCH, WILLIAM MICHAEL, computer software company executive; b. Chicago, Aug. 10, 1947; s. Robert John and Mary Rita (Burke) B.; m. Vera Lou Louie, June 23, 1979; children: Kristen, Andrea Mei, Lanceolot Joseph. BA in Math., Lewis U., 1969. Programmer, analyst Chgo. and Northwestern Rwy., 1969-73; project mgr. Indsl. Indemnity, San Francisco, 1973-76, Pacific Fareast Lines, San Francisco, 1976-78; pres. Braasch and Assocs., Oakland, Calif., 1978-81, Network Data Base Systems, Mountain View, Calif., 1981-83, Data Base Architects, Alameda, Calif., 1983—. Contbr. articles in field to profl. jours. With U.S. Army, 1969-75. Mem. Assn. Data Processing Svc. Orgns., Tau Kappa Epsilon. Roman Catholic. Office: Data Base Architects Inc 980 Atlantic Ave Alameda CA 94501

BRACHER, GEORGE, radiologist; b. Portland, Oreg., Mar. 20, 1909; s. George Michael and Anna (Ris) B.; m. Helen Arndt, Oct. 6, 1936; children: Randall W., Ann Louise. BS, U. Oreg., 1932, MD, 1934. Diplomate Am. Bd. Radiology. Intern St. Vincent's Hosp., Portland, 1935; resident fellow U. Chgo., 1936-38; asst. prof. radiology U. Oreg. Med. Sch., Portland, 1938-39; radiologist King County Hosp. System, Seattle, 1939-41, Hilo (Hawaii) Hosp., 1960-85, Lucy Henriques Med. Ctr., Kamuela, Hawaii, 1985—; pvt. practice Seattle and Spokane (Wash.), 1941-60; cons. radiologist Honokaa (Hawaii) Hosp., 1960—, Kohala (Hawaii) Hosp., 1960—, Kau Hosp., Pahala, Hawaii, 1960—. Pres. Hawaii County unit Am. Cancer Soc., Hilo, 1970, Hawaii Pacific div. Honolulu, 1972, chmn. Pacific and related islands com. 1975. Mem. ABA, Hawaii Med. Assn., Hawaii County Med. Soc. (pres. 1969), Am. Coll. Radiology, Hawaii Radiologic Soc., Wash. Athletic Club, Hilo Yacht Club. Home: 134 Puako Beach Dr Kamuela HI 96743 Office: Lucy Henriques Med Ctr PO Box 1108 Kamuela HI 96743

BRACHTENBACH, ROBERT F., state justice; b. Sidney, Nebr., Jan. 28, 1931; s. Henry W. and Elizabeth A. (Morfeld) B.; m. Marilyn; children: Rick, Jeff, Randal, Curtis, David. BS, U. Wash., 1953, LLB, 1954. Bar: Wash. 1954. Instr. sch. law U. Calif., Berkeley, 1954-55; practiced in Selah, Wash., 1955-72; justice Wash. Supreme Ct., 1972-81, chief justice, 1981-83. Contbr. articles to law revs. Mem. Selah Sch. Bd., 1960-72; mem. Wash. State Ho. of Reps., 1963-67; trustee Eastern Wash. State Coll. Office: Wash Supreme Ct Temple of Justice Olympia WA 98504

BRADEN, VERLON PATRICK, author, automotive writer, producer, photographer; b. Flint, Mich., July 8, 1934; s. Verlon Lee and Mary Virginia (Presson) B.; m. Marie Elsie Kobrehel, June 30, 1956 (dec.); children: Mark Patrick, Leslie Marie; m. 2d, Cheryl Marie Olson, Oct. 5, 1980; children: Mary Kathryn, Lee Patrick. BA, Western Mich. U., 1956; MA, U. Mich., 1957; postgrad. U. Iowa, 1959. Cert. secondary tchr., Mich. Tchr., prison social worker, probation officer State of Mich., 1959-67; writer Bill Sandy Co., Communico, and Maritz Communications, Bob Thomas & Assocs., Saatchi & Saatchi, Torrance, Calif., 1969—; editor The Alfa Owner. Mem. Am. Alfa Romeo Owners Club, Am. Abarth Register. Author: The 365 GTB/4 Daytona Ferrari, 1982, Abarth, 1983, Weber Carburetors, 1988 (Best Tech. Content award Moto, 1988, Best Cover award Moto 1988), Toyota, 1990, Alfa Romeo Giulia, 1991, Alfa Romeo Bible, 1990.

BRADFIELD, STEPHANIE ALISON, communications company executive; b. Pasadena, Calif., June 24, 1950; d. Theodore C. and Karen (Coene) B.; m. John R. Balzar, Mar. 18, 1978. BA in Mass Communications, Calif. State U., Chico, 1972. Pub. info. officer Calif. Gov.'s Office Emergency Services, Sacramento, 1972-76; chief pub. info. Calif. Energy Commn., Sacramento, 1976-78, asst. exec. dir., 1978-80; chief office legis. and pub. affairs Calif. State Water Resouces Control Bd., Sacramento, 1980-85; pub. info. mgr. Gen. Telephone Calif., Santa Monica, 1985-87; pub. info. dir. GTE Calif., Thousand Oaks, 1987—. Bd. dirs. Coro Found. So. Calif., Los Angeles, 1987—. Mem. Pub. Relations Soc. Am., Women in Communications. Office: GTE Calif 1 GTE Pl RC 3130 Thousand Oaks CA 91362-3811

BRADFORD, DAVID ALLAN, broadcast executive; b. Dyersburg, Tenn., Dec. 8, 1947; s. Jessie Herman Bradford and Clarice Imogene (Bell) Hill; m. Evelyn Louise Philpott, May 29, 1977; children: Christopher, Molly, Katie. Student, Ind. U., Gary, 1973-77, U. N.Mex., 1977-86. Gen. mgr. Albuquerque Cable TV, 1979-86; chmn., chief exec. officer Bradford Communications, Inc., Albuquerque, 1986—; pres. Empire Communications, Inc., Albuquerque, 1987—; pres. N.Mex. Cable TV Assn., Santa Fe, 1984-86; bd. dirs. Rocky Mountain Cable Assn., Denver, 1985-86; pres., bd. dirs. Albuquerque Utilities Coun., 1981-84. Precinct chm. Bernalillo County Dem. Com., Albuquerque, 1985. Cpt. USMC, 1966-71, SE Asia. Mem. Nat. Cable TV Assn., Soc. Cable TV Engrs. Lodge: Rotary (Albuquerque). Office: Bradford Communications Inc PO Box 3057 Albuquerque NM 87190

BRADFORD, DAVID GALEN, air force officer; b. Graham, Tex., July 20, 1948; s. Leo Galen and Elizabeth Arline (Younger) B.; m. Irene Carol Boehning, June 2, 1972; children: Emily Neumann, Scott Galen. AA, Howard Coll., 1968; BA, S.W. Tex. State U., 1970; MA, U. No. Colo., 1974; diploma, U.S. Army Comdr. and Gen. Staff Coll., 1985, USAF Air War Coll., 1987. Commd. 2d lt. USAF, 1972, advanced through grades to lt. col., 1988; logistics plans officer USAF, Vandenberg AFB, Calif., 1980-82; exec. officer dep. chief of staff logisitics Strategic Air Command, 1982-83, exec. officer dep. chief of staff plans, 1983; staff officer long range planning staff Strategic Air Command, Omaha, 1983-84; plans officer N.E. Asia div. Comdr.-in-Chief U.S Comdr.-in-Chief Pacific Command, Hawaii, 1985-89, strategist, dep. fgn. policy adv. to Comdr-in-Chief, 1987-89; mem. adj. faculty English, History and Bus., Wayland Bapt. U., Honolulu, 1986-89. Mem. USAF Assn., World Future Soc., Japan-Am. Soc. Honolulu., Internat. Churchill Soc. Republican. Baptist. Home: 302-A Travis Ave Honolulu HI 96818 Office: USCINCPAC/FPA Camp Smith HI 96861

BRADFORD, JOHN WESLEY, JR., cardiopulmonary technologist; b. N.Y.C., June 8, 1928; s. John Wesley and Agatha Johanna (Kern) B.; children: Roger David, Dianne Mary, Lisa Maureen. BS in Sci., USN Postgrad. Sch., Monterey, Calif., 1962; BS in Health Sci., SUNY, 1974. Commd. ensign USN, 1950, advanced through grades to comdr., ret., 1972; shift coordinator U. Calif. San Diego Med. Ctr., 1974-79; chief cardiopulmonary technologist Coronado (Calif.) Hosp., 1979-86; pulmonary function technologist Scripps Research Found., La Jolla, Calif., 1987-88; pulmonary function respiratory therapist Respiratory Temporary Services, San Diego, 1986—; technologist USAF Research, La Jolla, 1987-88. Contbr. aviation articles to profl. jours. Bd. dirs. Vista (Calif.) Community Clinic, 1978-86. Recipient 2nd Place Custom award Exptl. Aircraft Assn., San Diego, 1987. Mem. DAV, Am. Assn. Respiratory Care, Nat. Soc. Cardiopulmonary Technologists, Calif. Thoracic Soc. (assoc. mem.). Republican. Club: Caterpillar (N.J.). Home: 309 Via Nancita Encinitas CA 92024

BRADFORD, RICHARD BARTHOLOMEW, industrial relations professional; b. Lancaster, Ohio, Apr. 8, 1939; s. LeeRoy and Mary Elizabeth (Jadwin) B.; m. Judith Marie Madsen, Oct. 10, 1987; children: Laure, Chris, Brent, Stephanie, Lynn, Dina, Eric. BS, Ind. U., 1961, MBA, 1963. With Hotppint, Chgo., 1963-64; with appliance park div. Gen. Electric Co., Louisville, 1964-65, mgr. union rels., 1966-70; mgr. employee rels. transformer div. Gen. Electric Co., Pittsfield, Mass., 1970-72; mgr. labor rels. aircraft engine group Gen. Electric Co., Evendale, Ohio, 1972-77, mgr. relation planning, 1977-83, mgr. salaried resources, 1983-85; mgr. orgn., human resources med. systems mfg. div. Gen. Electric Co., Milw., 1985-87; mgr. indsl. relations Pacific Gas & ElectricCo., San Francisco, 1987—. Contbr. articles to profl. jours. Pres. Touchdown Club, Fairfield, Ohio, 1980-81; active Fairfield and Joint Vocat. Sch. Bd., 1981-85. Recipient Exemplary Svc. to Edn. award Ohio Sch. Bd., Columbus, 1985. Republican. Home: 1000 Springfield Dr Walnut Creek CA 94598

BRADLEY, CHARLES WILLIAM, podiatrist; b. Fife, Tex., July 23, 1923; s. Tom and Mary Ada (Cheatham) B.; student Tex. Tech., 1940-42; D. Podiatric Medicine, 1949, Calif. Coll. Podiatric Medicine U. San Francisco, MPA, 1987; D.Sc. (hon.), Calif. Coll. Podiatric Medicine; m. Marilyn A. Brown, Apr. 3, 1948 (dec. Mar. 1973); children—Steven, Gregory, Jeffrey, Elizabeth, Gerald. Practice podiatry, Beaumont, Tex., 1950-51, Brownwood, Tex., 1951-52, San Francisco, San Bruno, Calif., 1952—; chief of staff Calif. Podiatry Hosp., San Francisco; mem. surg. staff Sequoia Hosp., Redwood City, Calif.; mem. med. staff Peninsula Hosp., Burlingame, Calif.; chief podiatry staff St. Luke's Hosp., San Francisco; pres. Podiatry Ins. Co. Am.; cons. VA. Mem. San Francisco Symphony Found.; mem. adv. com. Health Policy Agenda for the Am. People, AMA. Chmn. trustees Calif. Coll. Podiatric Medicine, Calif. Podiatry Coll., Calif. Podiatry Hosp. Mem. Am. Podiatric Med. Assn. (trustee, pres. 1983-84), Calif. Podiatry Assn. (pres. No. div. 1964-66, state bd. dirs., pres. 1975-76, Podiatrist of Yr. award 1983), Nat. Council Edn. (vice chmn.), Nat. Acads. Practice, Am. Legion, San Bruno C. of C. (dir. 1978—). Clubs: Elks, Lions, Commonwealth of Calif., Olympic (San Francisco). Served with USNR, 1942-45. Home: 2965 Trousdale Dr Burlingame CA 94010 also: 560 Jenevein Ave San Bruno CA 94066 Office: 2469 Mission St San Francisco CA 94110

BRADLEY, DONALD EDWARD, lawyer; b. Santa Rosa, Calif., Sept. 26, 1943; s. Edward Aloysius and Mildred Louise (Kelley) B.; m. Barbara Phelps Hood, June 17, 1967 (div. Aug. 1988); children: Evan Patrick, Matthew Jordan, Andrea Phelps. AB, Dartmouth Coll., 1965; JD, U. Calif., San Francisco, 1968; LLM, N.Y.U., 1972. Bar: Calif. 1968, U.S. Dist. Ct. (no. dist.) Calif. 1968, U.S. Ct. Appeals (9 cir.) 1968, U.S. Tax Ct. 1972, U.S. Ct. Claims 1973, U.S. Supreme Ct. 1981. Assoc. Pillsbury, Madison & Sutro, San Francisco, 1972-77, ptnr., 1978-84; ptnr. Wilson, Sonsini, Goodrich & Rosati, Palo Alto, Calif., 1984—; adj. prof. Golden State U., San Francisco, 1973-82; pres., chmn. bd. dirs. Attorney's Insurance Mutual, Bridgetown, Barbados, 1986—. Capt. U.S. Army, 1969-70. Recipient Charles M. Ruddick award N.Y.U., 1972, award Bureau of Nat. Affairs, Washington, 1968. Mem. ABA, Internat. Bar Assn., Santa Clara Bar Assn., San Francisco Bar Assn., Internat. Tax Club. Office: Wilson Sonsini Goodrich & Rosati 2 Palo Alto Sq Ste 900 Palo Alto CA 94306

BRADLEY, HUGH EDWARD, information systems executive; b. Olean, N.Y., Nov. 4, 1934; s. Hugh Edward and Gladys Pearl (Lampe) B.; m. Mary Ann Hahl, Jan. 31, 1959 (div. 1973); 1 child, Mary Josita; m. Carolyn Ann Hoag, Sept. 26, 1973; 1 child, Emily Elizabeth. BS, MIT, 1957, MS, 1957; PhD, Johns Hopkins U., 1963. Research engr. Sperry Gyroscope Co., Great Neck, N.Y., 1957-60; asst. prof. indsl. engring. U. Mich., Ann Arbor, 1963-67; group mgr. mgmt. info. systems Upjohn Co., Kalamazoo, Mich., 1967-79; dir. mgmt. info. systems Syntex Corp., Palo Alto, Calif., 1979-81, Kaiser Aluminum Corp., Oakland, Calif., 1981-84; dir. info. systems Shaklee Corp., San Francisco, 1984—. NSF fellow, 1962. Mem. Ops. Research Soc. Am. (pres. 1985-86), Inst. Mgmt. Scis. (v.p. 1977-80), Pharm. Mgmt. Sci. Assn. (bd. dirs. 1977-80), Internat. Fedn. Operational Research Socs. (editor 1968-79, 88—). Republican. Roman Catholic. Office: Shaklee Corp 444 Market St San Francisco CA 94111

BRADLEY, KAREN LOUISE, insurance underwriter; b. Hollywood, Calif., June 2, 1947; d. William John Jr. and Patricia Dorothy (White) B.; divorced; children: Maya L. Verdun, Matthew A. Verdun, Jon M. Verdun, Jason William Verdun. Student, U. Calif., Santa Barbara, 1965-66, Calif. State U., Northridge, 1966-67, U. Calif., San Diego, 1975-76; BS, Boise State U., 1987. Owner, mgr. Interiors by Karen, San Diego, Twin Falls (Idaho), 1978-88; sales rep. KEEP-KEZJ, Twin Falls, 1981-85; sales mgr. John Alden Life Ins. Co., Boise, Idaho, 1987-88; agt. The Equitable, Boise, 1988—. Presbyterian. Office: The Equitable 1199 Shoreline Dr Ste 300 Boise ID 83702

BRADLEY, KENNETH DANIEL, insurance company executive; b. Ft. Clayton, Panama Canal Zone, Feb. 13, 1949; s. William Perry and Dorothy Marie (Gill) B.; m. Millajean Miller, Nov. 21, 1987. BSBA, Seton Hall U., 1971. CPCU. Rating analyst Nat. Council on Compensation Ins., Lyndhurst, N.J., 1971-73; underwriter Cen. Mut. Ins. Co., N.Y.C., 1973-75; v.p. dept. casualty Am. Home Assurance Co., N.Y.C., 1975-85; v.p. Western region, Los Angeles, 1985-87; resident v.p. Alliance Ins. Services, Inc., Los Angeles, 1987—. Scoutmaster Boy Scouts Am., Clifton, N.J., 1975-76; umpire Lyndhurst Little League, 1966-67; coach Clifton Little League, 1976; soccer coach St. John Kanty Sch., Clifton, 1980-81. Mem. N.A.P.S.L.O., Underwriters Assn. Home: 8302 Summertime Ln Culver City CA 90230 Office: Alliance Ins Svcs Inc 3435 Wilshire Blvd Ste 2024 Los Angeles CA 90010

BRADLEY, MARION ZIMMER, novelist, educator; b. Albany, N.Y., June 3, 1930; d. Leslie Raymond and Evelyn Parkhurst (Conklin) Zimmer; m. Robert Alden Bradley, Oct. 26,1949; 1 son, David Robert; m. Walter H. Breen, Feb. 14, 1964; children: Patrick Russell Donald, Moira Evelyn Dorothy. B.A., Hardin Simmons U., 1964; postgrad., U. Calif.-Berkeley, 1965-67. Author: (Darkover novels) Planet Savers, 1962, The Sword of Aldones, 1962, The Bloody Sun, 1964, The Winds of Darkover, 1970, The World Wreckers, 1971, Darkover Landfall, 1972, The Spell Sword, 1972, The Heritage of Hastur, 1975, The Shattered Chain, 1976, The Forbidden Tower, 1977, Stormqueen, 1978, The Bloody Sun (rewritten) 1979, Two to Conquer, 1980, The Keeper's Price, 1980, Sharra's Exile, 1981, Sword of Chaos, 1982, Hawkmistress, 1982, Thendara House, 1983, City of Sorcery, 1984, other sci. fiction, anthologies, gothics, mainstream novels, The Catch Trap, 1979, The Mists of Avalon, 1983, The Firebrand, 1987. Home and Office: PO Box 352 Berkeley CA 94701

BRADLEY, SISTER MYRA JAMES, health science facility executive; b. Cin., Feb. 1, 1924; d. John Joseph and Mary (McMannus) B. BS in Edn., Atheneum Ohio, 1950; BS in Nursing, Mt. St. Joseph Hosp., 1954; MHA, St. Louis U., 1959. RN, Ohio. Mem. faculty U. Dayton, Ohio, 1955-57, Good Samaritan Hosp., Dayton, 1955-57; asst. adminstr. St. Mary-Corwin Hosp., Pueblo, Colo., 1960; adminstr. St. Joseph Hosp., Mt. Clemens, Mich., 1960-65; pres., chief exec. officer Penrose Hosp., Colorado Springs, Colo., 1965—, Penrose-St. Francis Cath. Healthcare, Colorado Springs, Colo., 1987—. Recipient Disting. Service award U. Colo., 1983, Civis Princeps award Regis Colle., Colorado Springs, 1984, Elizabeth Ann Seton nursing award for excellence dept. nursing Penrose Hosp. and Penrose Community Hosp., 1987, Sword of Hope Am. Cancer Soc., 1988; named Woman of Distinction Soroptimist Internat., 1988. Mem. Cath. Hosp. Assn., Am. Hosp. Assn., Colo. Hosp. Assn. (trustee), Nat. Coun. Community Hosps. (trustee), Am. Coll. Hosp. Adminstrs., Healthcare Forum (trustee), Downtown Rotary Club. Office: Penrose-St Francis Healthcare 2215 N Cascade Ave PO Box 7021 Colorado Springs CO 80933

BRADLEY, RANDALL REED, computer analyst; b. L.A., Apr. 29, 1957; s. Stanley Wayne and Laura Lorena (Rhoten) B. BS in Stats., U. Calif., Riverside, 1981. Jr. programmer World Vision Internat., Monrovia, Calif., 1982, lead operator, 1982-84, system programmer, 1984-85; contract programmer Infocentre, Anaheim, Calif., 1985-86; v.p., programmer E-Mail, Inc., L.A., 1987-88; vol., tchr's aide Helping Hands Sch., Fullerton, Calif., 1988—; cons. Bradley & Assocs., Fullerton, Calif., 1985-87. Republican. Home: 2911 Ruby Dr #C Fullerton CA 92631

BRADLEY, SHARON JOHNSON, designer; b. Seattle, Mar. 30, 1943; d. Ralph Leonard and Hazel (Brickson) Johnson; m. James Alan Bradley, Feb. 22, 1986; children: David Hallett, Lisa C. Van Brunt, Hannah Hallett. Student, Merritt Coll., Oakland, Calif., 1961-62, Boise State U., 1978-80. Lic. real estate broker. Broker, prin. Mountain Mut. Ins. Co., McCall and Boise, Idaho, 1976-82, RBS Brokerage, Anchorage, 1982—; owner Sunburst Inc., Honolulu, 1980—; v.p. Bradley Pacific Ltd., Honolulu, 1983—; chmn. bd. dirs. Hale Walina, Honolulu. Author monthly real estate column, 1984-86; contbr. stories, poetry, profl. and tech. articles to jours., mags. and newspapers. Bd. dirs. Anchorage Mcpl. Child Abuse Task Force, 1985-86; pres. Anchoragate Rape and Assault Ctr., 1975-76; chmn. bd. dirs. Children's Support Council, Anchorage, 1983-86; treas., counselor Parents Support Network, 1986-88. Recipient Membership award Women's Leaders Roundtable, 1979-80, Pub. Svc. award Mayor of Anchorage, 1985. Mem. AIA (assoc.), Hawaii Soc. Architects. Republican. Mem. Science of the Mind Ch. Home: Rte 1 Box 885 Bandon OR 97411 also: 424 Walina #34 Honolulu HI 96814 Office: Bradley Pacific Ltd 1257 S Beretania St Honolulu HI 96814

BRADLEY, THOMAS (TOM BRADLEY), mayor of Los Angeles; b. Calvert, Tex., Dec. 29, 1917; s. Lee Thomas and Crenner (Hawkins) B.; m. Ethel Mae Arnold, May 4, 1941; children: Lorraine, Phyllis. Student, UCLA, 1937-40; LL.B., Southwestern U., 1956, LL.D., 1980; LL.D., Brandeis U., 1974, Oral Roberts U., 1974, Pepperdine U., 1974, Loyola Marymount U., 1974, Calif. Lutheran U., 1974, Wilberforce U., 1974, Whittier Coll., 1976, Yale U., 1979, U. So. Calif., 1979, Princeton U., 1979, Bus Nat. U., Korea, 1979, Antioch U., 1983, N.C. Central U., 1983; Ph.D. (hon.), Humanity Research Ctr. Beverly Hills, 1976. Bar: Calif. 1956. Police officer Los Angeles, 1940-62; practiced in Los Angeles, 1956-73; mem. Los Angeles City Council, 1963-73; mayor of Los Angeles, 1973—; founder, dir. Bank of Fin., Nat. Urban Coalition; pres. Nat. League Cities, 1974, also mem. nat. bd. dirs.; pres. League of Calif. Cities, 1979, So. Calif. Assn. Govts., 1968-69, Nat. Assn. Regional Councils, 1969-71; mem. Nat. Energy Adv. Council, Nat. Commn. on Productivity and Work Quality; mem. advisory bd., vice chmn. transp. com. U.S. Conf. Mayors; former mem. Council Intergovt. Relations; chmn. State, County and Fed. Affairs Com.; former chmn. Pub. Works Priority Com., Com. for Proposed Legis. bd. dirs. Nat. Urban Fellows. Mem. Calif. Democratic Central Com.; del. Dem. Nat. Mid-Term Conf., 1974; co-chmn. Dem. Nat. Conv., 1976; former mem. bd. dirs. Joint Com. Mental Health for Children; former mem. adv. council Peace Corps. Named African Methodist Episcopal Man of Yr., 1974; recipient Dr. Martin L. King, Jr. award, 1974, Pub. Ofcl. of Yr. award Los Angeles Trial Lawyers Assn., 1974, award CORO Found., 1978, award of merit Nat. Council Negro Women, 1978, John F. Kennedy Fellowship award Govt. of N.Z., 1978, Internat. Humanitarian award M.E.D.I.C., 1978, City Employee of Yr. award All City Employees Benefits Service Assn., 1983, Magnin award, 1984. Mem. Los Angeles Urban League, NAACP (Spingarn medal 1985), So. Calif. Conf. on Community Relations, Los Angeles Conf. Negro Elected Ofcls., UN Assn. Los Angeles (bd. dirs.), Kappa Alpha Psi. Democrat. Mem. African Methodist Episcopal Ch. (trustee). Office: Office of Mayor City Hall Los Angeles CA 90012 *

BRADLEY, WILLIAM J., English language educator; b. Fremont, Nebr., Oct. 7, 1948; s. J.G. and Lois Helen (Henvy) B.; m. Elizabeth Ann Gordon, June 5, 1970 (div. Mar. 1983); children: Blue Emily, Blair Julie, Blake Laura; m. Meg. Ann Lemon, De. 20, 1986; 1 child, Jack Dawson. BA in Psychology, Amherst Coll., 1970; MA in Edn., SUNY, Albany, 1973; MA in English Lit., Colo. U., 1981, MA in Journalism, 1988. Chewy kitchen cook Russell Stover Candies, Denver, 1970-71; English educator Mont Pleasant High Sch., Schenectady, N.Y., 1971-73; reporter UPI, Denver, 1982-87; English educator Cherry Creek High Sch., Englewood, Colo., 1973—; co-dir. Sch.-within-a-ch., Englwood, 1974-81; coach baseball Cherry Creek High Sch., 1973-75; advisor Union St. Jour., Englewood, 1986-87. Contbr. articles to profl. jours. Pres. Cherry Creek Townhouse Assn., Denver, 1973-76; v.p. Liberty Hill Assn., Littleton, Colo., 1978-80. Recipient Gold Crown, Columbia U., N.Y.C., 1987. Mem. Cherry Creek Fedn. Tchrs., Cherry Creek Edn. Assn. (area dir. 1983-84). Democrat. Presbyterian. Club: Mens Sr. Baseball (Denver). Home: 6719 E Costilla Circle Englewood CO 80112 Office: Cherry Creek High Sch 9300 E Union Ave Englewood CO 80111

BRADO, MICHAEL WAYNE, infosystems specialist; b. Aberdeen, Wash., Oct. 26, 1958; s. Clarence Wayne and Karen (Copeland) B.; m. Rosela Bernabe Ventura, Aug. 23, 1987. BS, Wash. State U., 1982. Systems operator I Computing Svc. Ctr. Wash. State U., Pullman, 1980-82; firmware/diagnostics software engr. Altos Computer Systems, Inc., San Jose, Calif., 1982-84; corp. acct. mgr. Advanced Micro Devices, Sunnyvale, Calif., 1984-87, sr. prodn. control planner, bus. systems analyst, 1987—, info. ctr. cons., 1988—. Mem. working com. ASPEN, Sunnyvale, 1987—; registrar Campbell (Calif.) Reps., 1987. Mem. Am. Electronics Assn., San Jose Seahawks Rugby Club, Football Club, Elks. Home: 10660 Carver Dr Cupertino CA 95014 Office: Advanced Micro Devices 901 Thompson Pl M/S 199 Sunnyvale CA 94088

BRADSHAW, KENNETH D., social services administrator; b. Oakland, Calif., Sept. 13, 1946; s. Robert D. and Beulah (Tanner) B.; m. Penn McKeithan, Nov. 18, 1967; children: Brandy Nicole, Canada Laurel. BS, East Tenn. State U., 1971, MCM, 1973. Cert. health facilities adminstr. City adminstr. Erwin, Tenn., 1973; exec. dir. Salt Lake City County div. of Aging, 1973-75; city mgr. Clifton Forge, Va., 1975-77; exec. dir. dept. of aging, vol. svcs. Weber County, Ogden, UT, 1977—. Author: Ednl. needs Campbell, Clairborne, Hancock and Union Counties, 1972. Dem. candidate for State Legislature, 1984; bd. dirs. United Way No. Utah, 1987-88, Bonneville Chpt. Red Cross, 1986-87. With USN, 1965-68. Named Outstanding Young Men in Am. U.S. Jaycees, 1981, Boss of Yr. Am. Bus. Womens Assn., 1980. Democrat. Mormon. Office: Weber County Aging 2650 Lincoln Ave Ogden UT 84401

BRADSHAW, ROBERT V. (BRAD BRADSHAW), police chief, educator; b. Upland, Calif., Apr. 17, 1938; s. Charles B. and Alys P. (Dickinson) B.; m. Dixie L. Bradshaw, Aug. 16, 1960; children—Deborah A., Kelly L., Kimberly D. A.A. in Bus., Pasadena City Coll., 1959; B.A. in Criminal Justice, San Jose State Coll., 1964; M.P.A., Golden Gate U., 1980. Cert. secondary tchr., Calif. Successively police officer, sgt., lt., capt., dep. chief, asst. chief of police San Jose (Calif.) Police Dept., 1960-80; police chief Reno (Nev.) Police Dept., 1981—; instr. police adminstrn. Truckee Meadows Community Coll., Reno. Served with USAR. Mem. Internat. Assn. Chiefs of Police, Police Exec. Research Forum. Republican. Club: Rotary (Reno). Office: PO Box 1900 Reno NV 89505 *

BRADY, BARBARA C., psychologist; b. Burbank, Calif., May 29, 1946; d. Roger Ralph and Lespith (Albright) Crist; 1 son, Scott Thomas Bauer. B.A. in Psychology, San Jose State U., 1969; M.S. in Home Ecns., Calif. Poly. State U., 1974, M.A. in Counseling, 1976; Ph.D. in Ednl. Psychology, Brigham Young U., 1981. Instr. psychology Cuesta Coll., San Luis Obispo, Calif., 1974-76, counselor, 1976-80; counselor Brigham Young U., Provo, Utah, 1980-81, lectr., 1981; psychol. asst. Pacific Profl. Assocs., San Luis Obispo, 1981-83; pvt. practice psychology, San Luis Obispo, 1983—; lectr. in field, 1976—; cons. San Luis Obispo County Mental Health Services. Author: Reducing Anxiety in 30 Days: A Daily Activities Guide Toward Healthy Living. Bd. dirs. Family Services, San Luis Obispo, 1984-86, San Luis Obispo County Symphony; active Boy Scouts Am., San Luis Obispo,

1976-78. Mem. San Luis Obispo County Psychol. Assn. (pres. 1984-85), Rotary (pres.-elect), San Luis Obispo C. of C. (bd. dirs. 1986—, chmn. profl. devel. com., mem. exec. assn.), Toastmasters (pres. 1984), Phi Kappa Phi, Psi Chi, Phi Upsilon Omicron, Kappa Alpha Theta. Office: 1461 Higuera San Luis Obispo CA 93401

BRADY, C. JEAN, vocational education administrator; b. Lula, Okla., Sept. 22, 1935; d. Lewis J. and J. Mozella (Glover) Echols; 1 child, Connie Jo Brady. BS, East Cen. Okla. State U., 1957; MA, Western State Coll. Colo., 1963; postgrad., Colo. State U., 1979-82. Tchr. Belmont Elem. Sch., Pueblo, Colo., 1957-61, South High Sch., Pueblo, 1961-63; div. chairwoman East High Sch., Pueblo, 1965-72; state supr. Colo. Community Coll., Denver, 1972-83; dean bus. and commerce Seattle Cen. Community Coll., 1983-86; assoc. dir. Colo. Community Coll., Denver, 1986—. Co-author: Secondary Vocational Board of Education Policy and Procedure, 1979; editor various newspapers and newsletters. Mem. Am. Vocat. Assn., Colo. Vocat. Assn., Colo. Assn. Vocat. Adminstrs., Colo. Assn. Sch. Bds., Future Bus. Leaders Am.-Phi Beta Lambda (chairwoman Colo. chpt. 1957-83). Home: 358-B Hillview Dr Grand Junction CO 81503 Office: Colo Community Coll and Occupational Edn 1391 N Speer Blvd #600 Denver CO 81503

BRADY, COLLEEN ANNE, communications consulting company executive; b. Springfield, Ill., July 17, 1951; d. Robert Hatten and Eleanor (Lonergan) B. BA, So. Ill. U., 1973; MS, Humboldt State U., 1978. Instr. various adaptice Outward Bound programs 1975-78; mgr. tech. publs. Wood/Harbinger Engring. Inc., Kirkland, Wash., 1980-82; pres. Tech. Communications Cons. Inc., Seattle, 1978—. Editor: Softball Tune-Up Guide, 1988, Softball Practice Guide, 1988. Active Am. Cancer Soc., Seattle, 1987. Mem. Soc. Tech. Communications (tech. recognition award 1987, 88), Demonstrative Evidence Specialist Assn. (founding fellow), Wash. Tech. Assn. (sec. bd. dirs. 1987—), Emerald City Softball Assn. (rep. 1988—). Office: Tech Communication Cons 3043 California Ave SW Seattle WA 98116

BRADY, JANE MARIETTE, cleaning company and ceramics executive; b. Ft. Meade, Md., May 31, 1955; d. Allison Purvis and Monique Jeannine (Hutteau) B.; m. Jose Luis Millan Velazquez, Aug. 29, 1975 (div. Oct. 1982); 1 child, Jovan Jay Millan. AS, Cochise Coll., 1975. Aircraft mechanic Hawthorne Aviation Co., Ft. Huachuca, Ariz., 1975-77; owner, mgr. Sincerely Ceramics, Tucson, 1984—, Constantly Cleaning, Tucson, 1984—. Served with U.S. Army, 1979-84, Korea. Morris Udall grantee, 1974-75. Mem. Royal Order Roadrunners. Roman Catholic. Home and Office: 4402 E Sylvane St Tucson AZ 85711

BRADY, JOHN PATRICK, JR., electronics educator, consultant; b. Newark, Mar. 20, 1929; s. John Patrick and Madeleine Mary (Atno) B.; m. Mary Coop, May 1, 1954; children: Peter, John P., Madeleine, Dennis, Mary G. BSEE, MIT, 1952, MSEE, 1953. Registered profl. engr., Mass. Sect. mgr. Hewlett-Packard Co., Waltham, Mass., 1956-67; v.p. engring. John Fluke Mfg. Co., Inc., Mountlake Terrace, Wash., 1967-73; v.p. engring. Dana Labs., Irvine, Calif., 1973-77; engring. mgr., tech. advisor to gen. mgr. Metron Corp., Upland, Calif., 1977-78; ptnr. Resource Assocs., Newport Beach, Calif., 1978-86; prof. electronics Orange Coast Coll., Costa Mesa, Calif., 1977—, dean technology, 1983-84; instr. computers and electrinc engring. Calif. State U., Long Beach, 1982-84. Mem. evaluation team Accrediting Commn. for Community and Jr. Colls., 1982—. With USN, 1946-48. Mem. Measurement Sci. Conf. (dir. 1982-83), MIT (L.A.). Contbr. articles in field to profl. jours. Office: Orange Coast Coll Costa Mesa CA 92626

BRADY, MARGARET ANNE, health science educator; b. Memphis, Jan. 5, 1946; d. Bernard Joseph and Dorothy Anne (Brennan) B. BS in Nursing, Marquette U., 1968; MS, U. Colo., 1973. Staff nurse Hinsdale (Ill.) Hosp. and Sanitarium, 1968-69; staff nurse Loyola Med. Ctr., Maywood, Ill., 1969-70, coordinator pediatric patient care, 1970-72; asst. prof. Rush U. Coll. Nursing, Chgo., 1973-75; prof. Calif. State U., Long Beach, 1976—; bd. dirs. Isabel Patterson Child Devel. Ctr., Long Beach. Contbr. articles to profl. jours.; editor-reviewer Journal of Pediatric Health Care, 1986—. Fellow Nat. Assn. Pediatric Nurse Practitioners and Assoc.; mem. Assn. Care Children's Health, Assn. Faculties Pediatric Nurse Practitioner Programs, Nat. Assn. Pediatric Nurse Assoc./Practioners. Democrat. Roman Catholic. Home: 31 Madrona Irvine CA 92715 Office: Calif State U 1250 Bell Flower Long Beach CA 90840

BRADY, THOMAS DENIS, controller; b. Prescott, Ariz., June 2, 1955; s. Ormond Denis and Mary (Mei) B.; m. Kimberley Jo Huber, Apr. 21, 1978. BSBA, Ariz. State U., 1977, BS in Fin., 1983. Lic. real estate agt., Ariz., ins. agt. Ariz. Controller Twin Knolls Market, Inc., Mesa, Ariz., 1977-81; ins. agt. William Kirkendale & Assocs., Phoenix, Ariz., 1981; supr. accounts receivable dept. Associated Grocers Ariz., Phoenix, 1981-84; asst. controller SW Restaurant Systems, Inc., Tempe, Ariz., 1984-86; controller, treas. SW Restaurant Systems, Inc., Tempe, 1986—; bd. dirs., treas. Dobbins Enterprises, Durable Products Inc., United Comml. Realty, Inc.; controller, treas., Canyon Provisions, Inc., Tempe, 1986—, also bd. dirs. Active Dennis DeConcini for U.S. Senate campaign, 1976. Mem. Nat. Restaurant Assn., Ariz. Restaurant Assn., Mesa-Tempe-Chandler Bd. Realtors, Scottsdale Bd. Realtors. Democrat. Roman Catholic. Home: 3440 E Edgewood Ave Mesa AZ 85204 Office: SW Restaurant Systems 1979 E Broadway Rd Suite 3 Tempe AZ 85282

BRADY, THOMAS EDWARD, medical rehabilation specialist; b. Cin., Oct. 21, 1947; s. James William and Florence (McQuate) B.; m. Barbara Lynn Horwitz, Mar. 18, 1977; 1 child, Daniel. BA, Pa. State U., 1970; MSW, San Diego State U., 1976. Dir. Mountain Health Ctr., Boulevard, Calif., 1976-86; exec. dir. So. Health Svcs., San Diego, 1987-88; program dir. inpatient med. rehab. Rehab. Hosp. Svcs. Corp., Portland, Oreg., 1988—; pres. bd. dirs. San Diego Coun. Community Clinics, 1985-88. Chmn. Rural Providers Coun., San Diego, 1982-85; mem. San Diego Area Health Edn. Com., 1984-85; photographer slide presentation Cancer Soc. presentation for children's summer camp, 1984. County of San Diego grantee State of Calif., 1986, Robert Wood Johnson Found. grantee, 1987. Mem. NW Assn. Rehab. Facilities, City Club of Portland. Democrat. Home: 18825 Parkwood Pl West Linn OR 97068 Office: Eastmoreland Hosp 2900 SE Steele St Portland OR 97202

BRADY, WILLIAM KIM, obstetrician-gynecologist; b. Havre, Mont., Oct. 4, 1951; s. William C. Brady and Edna Ramona (Lidstone) Brownson; m. Millie M. Correa, Jan. 11, 1975; children: Kelly, Kendra, Kyle. BS, U.S. Mil. Acad., 1973; MD, Baylor U., 1980. Diplomate Am. Bd. Ob-Gyn. Commd. 1st lt. U.S. Army, 1973-76; major Med. Corps, U.S. Army, 1980—; intern ob-gyn. Fitzsimmons Army Med. Ctr., Aurora, Colo., 1980-81; resident ob-gyn. Fitzsimmons Army Med. Ctr., Aurora, 1981-84; asst. chief ob-gyn. svc. and dept. surgery 5th Gen. Hosp., Bad Cannstatt, Fed. Republic Germany, 1984-86; maternal fetal medicine fellow Madigan Army Med. Ctr., Tacoma, 1986-88, asst. chief obstetrics svc., 1988—; speaker at various presentations to several organizations. Contbr. articles to profl. jours.; jour. referee Am. Jour. Obstetrics and Gynecology. Mont. Boys state del., 1968. Decorated Army Commendation medal with first oak leaf cluster, Meritorious Svc. medal, Armed Forces Reserve medal, Army Achievement medal, Overseas Svc. medal, Army Svc. Ribbon, Army Reserve Components Achievement medal, Armed Forces Expeditionary medal, nat. Defense Svc. medal; Elks Nat. Found. scholar, 1969; NSF scholar U. Iowa, 1967, U.S. Army Health Professions' scholar, 1976-80. Fellow Am. Coll. Obstetricians and Gynecologists; mem. Soc. Perinatal Obstetricians (assoc.), Am. Coll. Surgeons (candidate). Roman Catholic. Office: Madigan Army Med Ctr Attn HSHJ OG Tacoma WA 98431-5418

BRAESTRUP, JOHN COSMUS, manufacturing executive; b. Copenhagen, May 30, 1933; came to U.S., 1934; s. Johan Cosmus B. and Else Gertrude (Jørgsholm) Neale; m. Ann Allen, May 5, 1963 (div. Jan. 1978); m. Justin Rae Clancey, May 14, 1983; children: Paul Cosmus, Carl Eric. AB, Dartmouth Coll., 1955; MBA, U. Chgo., 1969. Sales rep. Internat. Paper Co., N.Y.C., Chgo., 1958-67; sales rep. Boise Cascade, Oakbrook, Ill., 1967-68, dist. sales mgr., 1968-70; mgr. sales containerboard Boise Cascade, Portland, Oreg., 1970-82; pres. Am. Fibre Supplies, Inc., Portland, 1982—. Served to lt. U.S. Army, 1956. Republican. Office: Am Fibre Supplies Inc PO Box 4345 Portland OR 97208

BRAGDON, PAUL ERROL, state government official, former college president; b. Portland, Maine, Apr. 19, 1927; s. Errol Freemont and Edith Lillian (Somerville) B.; m. Nancy Ellen Horton, Aug. 14, 1954; children: David Lincoln, Susan Horton, Peter Jefferson. BA magna cum laude, Amherst Coll., 1950, DHL (hon.), 1980; JD, Yale U., 1953; LLD (hon.), Whitman Coll., 1985; DLitt. (hon.), Pacific U., 1988. Bar: N.Y. 1954. With firm Dewey, Ballantine, Bushby, Palmer & Wood, N.Y.C., 1953-58, Javits, Trubin, Sillcocks, Edelman & Purcell, N.Y.C., 1961-64; counsel Tchrs. Ins. and Annuity Assn. Coll. Retirement Equities Fund, N.Y.C., 1958-61; asst. to mayor City of N.Y., 1964-65, exec. sec. to mayor, 1965, exec. asst. to pres. City Council, 1966-67; v.p. NYU, 1967-71; pres. Reed Coll., Portland, Oreg., 1971-88; asst. for edn. to gov. State of Oreg., 1988—; bd. dirs. Tektronix, Inc.; chmn. bd. Portland br. Fed. Res. Bank San Francisco. Trustee Amherst Coll., 1972-78 Served with USMCR, 1945-46. Mem. Phi Beta Kappa, Phi Beta Kappa Assocs., Beta Theta Pi. Clubs: Century (N.Y.C.), Univ. (N.Y.C.); City (Portland, Oreg.), Univ. (Portland, Oreg.). Office: State Capitol Office of Gov Salem OR 97310-1347

BRAHINSKY, DAVID NORMAN, sales executive, metals purchaser; b. Concordia, Kans., May 25, 1927; s. Nathan and Dasha (Shapiro) B.; divorced, May 1967; 1 child, Benard; m. Joan Ellen Beldock, Nov. 25, 1984; stepchildren: Devra, John, Rachel. BBA, So. Meth. U., 1950. Sales and mfr. rep. Denver, 1965-67; sales mgr. Colo. Metals Co., Denver, 1967-75, Atlas Metal Sales, Denver, 1975—. Home: 1561 S Krameria Denver CO 80224

BRAKEBILL, JEAN NEWTON, nurse, naval officer; b. Mobile, Ala., Sept. 4, 1953; d. James Harold and Eleanor (Mrotek) Newton; m. James Arden Brakebill, Dec. 15, 1985. BS in Nursing, West Tex. State U., 1975; MS, Corpus Christi U., 1982; MBA in Health Adminstrn., Nat. U., 1984. R.N., Tex., Calif. Staff nurse Southwestern Gen. Hosp., El Paso, Tex., 1975-76; commd. ensign U.S. Navy, 1976, advanced through grades to lt. comdr., 1984; staff nurse Naval Hosp. U.S. Navy, Charleston, S.C., 1976-78, Okinawa, Japan, 1978-80; head nurse ICU U.S. Navy, Corpus Christi, Tex., 1980-83; head nurse, clin. cons., program adminstr. Naval Hosp. U.S. Navy, San Diego, 1983-89; div. head med. surgical ward Naval Hosp., Long Beach, Calif., 1989—; basic life support instr., trainer, Am. Heart Assn., various locations, 1985—; advanced trauma life support educator, ACS, San Diego, 1987—;. Mem. Oncology Nursing Soc., Kappa Delta. Roman Catholic. Office: US Navy Hosp Carson St Long Beach CA 92134-5000

BRAKEMAN, FRED ELLIS, sound systems designer; b. Culver City, Calif., July 7, 1950; s. Roy and Lynn (Goodale) B.; m. Cynthia L. Brinker, June 17, 1972; children: Christopher D., Amie M. Student, Fresno State Coll., 1970-71, Chabot Jr. Coll., 1976. Gen. mgr. Sta. KERI, Bakersfield, Calif., 1979-87, Sta. KKCM, Mnpls., 1987-88; sound systems designer Serban Sound Systems, Bakersfield, 1988—; dir. devel.-fundraising, OMS Internat., Greenwood, Ind., 1988—; pres. Aunt Cheries Home for Unwed Mothers, Bakersfield, 1987—. Active, Bethany Service Ctr., Bakersfield, 1987—; bd. dirs. agenda chmn. nat. gospel radio seminar, Gospel Music Assn., Nashville, 1979-87; local chmn. Marine Corp Reserve Toys for Tots Campaign, Bakersfield, 1981-85. With Calif. Air NG, 1969-78. Mem. Nat. Christian Radio Assn. (bd. dirs. 1987). Republican. Baptist. Office: Serban Sound Systems 312 Kentucky Bakersfield CA 93305

BRAMBILA, ROBERT LUIS, controller; b. L.A., Dec. 1, 1949; s. Raul Peralta and Rachel (Camerena) B.; m. Susan Rita Rincon Brambila, Feb. 13, 1971; children: Melissa Elise, Robert Andrew, Andrew Martin. AA, East L.A. Coll., 1973; BS in Mgmt. & Acctg., Calif. State U., Fullerton, 1976. Asst. to contr. Ford Motor Corp., Pico Rivera, Calif., 1968-80; contr. Max Factor & Co., Hollywood, Calif., 1980-84; pres. Cosmetic Depot, Puente Hills, Calif., 1984-86; contr. Vargas Furniture Mfg. Co., L.A., 1986—. Sgt. U.S. Army, 1969-71, Vietnam. Mem. Am. Prodn. & Inventory Control Soc., Am. Mgmt. Assn., Calif. Furniture Mfg. Assn. Democrat. Roman Catholic. Home: 1851 Paseo Azul Rowland Heights CA 91748 Office: Vargas Furniture Mfg Co 8255 Beach St Los Angeles CA 90001

BRAMBLE, JOHN MYLES, city manager; b. Vancouver, Wash., May 3, 1946; s. Paul Eugene and Beulah Elizabeth (Henderson) B.; m. JoAnn Tolle, May 2, 1980; children: Scott Byron, Steven Tolle. BS, Oreg. State U., 1969; MPA, U. Nev., Las Vegas, 1978. Adminstrv. asst. City of Salem (Oreg.), 1969-73; research analyst Abt Assocs., Inc., Cambridge, Mass., 1973-74; dir. budget and mgmt. City of Las Vegas (Nev.), 1975-79; asst. city mgr., fin. dir. City of Belmont (Calif.), 1979-81; city mgr. City of Commerce City (Colo.), 1981-84, City of Pueblo (Colo.), 1984-87; city adminstr., City of Bell, Calif., 1988—. Mem. exec. bd. Colo. Mcpl. League, 1982-83. Mem. Internat. City Mgmt. Assn., Denver Met. Mgrs. Assn. (chmn. 1983), Colo. City Mgmt. Assn. (pres-elect 1986-87), Kiwanis. Home: 9047 Chaney Ave Downey CA 90241 Office: 6330 Pine Ave Bell CA 90201

BRAME, ARDEN HOWELL, II, herpetologist, genealogist; b. Los Angeles, Mar. 19, 1934; s. Arden Howe and Marguerite Lucile (Adams) B.; m. Susan Diane Bronn, Aug. 23, 1964 (div. June 1969); m. Patricia Louise Verret Reinholtz, Apr. 19, 1970. BA, U. So. Calif., 1957, MS, 1967; student, UCLA, 1956-57. Grad. teaching asst. U. So. Calif., Los Angeles, 1959-65; also student profl. worker in ichthyology-herpetology and vertebrate paleontology Los Angeles County Mus., 1959-65, later research asst. in herpetology; supr. Eaton Canyon Nature Ctr., 1965-68, 70-78; asst. curator sect. herpetology Los Angeles County Mus. of Natural History, 1968-70; instr. genealogy Pasadena (Calif.) City Coll. and Calif. State U., Northridge, 1977—; mem. citizen nongame adv. com. Calif. Dept. Fish and Game, 1975-79; herpetol. group advisor Survival Service Commn., Internat. Union for Conservation Nature and Natural Resources, Morges, Switzerland, 1974-82. Author: (with Dr. D.B. Wake) The Salamanders of South America, 1963; Systematics and Evolution of the Mesoamerican Salamander Genus Oedipina, 1968; contbr. articles to scholarly and profl. jours.; assoc. pub. TV Facts of Pasadena and Altadena, 1978-79. Served with AUS, 1958. Fellow Herpetologists' League, Augustan Soc. (registered genealogist, pres. 1980-81); mem. Soc. Study Amphibians and Reptiles (bd. dirs. 1967-70, chmn. 1973), Southwestern Herpetologists Soc. (pres. 1971-74), Am. Soc. Ichthyologists and Herpetologists, Brit. Herpetol. Soc., Phila. Herpetol. Soc., N.Y. Herpetol. Soc., Ariz. Herpetol. Soc., N.Mex. Herpetol. Soc., Conn. Herpetol. Soc., Chgo. Herpetol. Soc., Soc. Study of Evolution, Soc. Systematic Zoologists, Ecol. Soc. Am., Western Soc. Naturalists, Biol. Soc. Wash., So. Calif. Acad. Scis., Soc. Tropical Biologists, Pasadena Audubon Soc. (pres. 1971-76), SAR (pres. Pasadena chpt. 1977-83, genealogist Calif. Soc.), S.R., SCV (camp comdr. 1979-83), Gen. Soc. War of 1812, Descendants of the Illegitimate Sons and Daus. of the Kings of Britain, Plantagenet Soc., Sovereign Colonial Soc. Ams. Royal Descent, Soc. Descendanta Knights of the Garter, Colonial Order of Crown, Magna Charta Barons, Order of Washington, Sons of Union Vets. of Civil War, Mil. Order Loyal Legion of U.S., Mil. Order of Stars and Bars (comdr. Calif. chpt.), Dames of Guild of St. Margaret of Scotland (protector), Order of Augustan Eagle, Descents From Antiquity, Order of Armigerous Augustans, Hospitaller Order of St. John of Jerusalem (companion of honor), Noble Co. of Rose, Jamestowne Soc., St. John's Vol. Corps, Sigma Xi, Phi Sigma. Home: 9545 E Guess St Rosemead CA 91770

BRAME, MARILLYN A., technical communications executive; b. Indpls., Sept. 17, 1928; d. David Schwalb and Hilda (Riley) Curtin. Student, Meinzinger Art Sch., Detroit, 1946-47, Orlando (Fla.) Jr. Coll., 1964-65, El Camino Coll., Torrance, Calif., 1974-75, U. New Mexico, 1963. Cert. and registered hypnotherapist. Color cons. Pitts. Plate Glass Co., Albuquerque, 1951-52; owner Signs by Marillyn, Albuquerque, 1952-53; design draftsman Sandia Corp., Albuquerque, 1953-56; designer The Martin Co., Orlando, 1957-65; pres. The Arts, Winter Park, Fla., 1964-66; supr. tech. publs. Gen. Instrument Corp., Hawthorne, Calif., 1967-76; pres. Camart Design, Westminster, Calif., 1977-86, Visual Arts, El Toro, Calif., 1978—; mgr. tech. publs. Archive Corp., Costa Mesa, Calif., 1986—; adj. instr. Orange Coast Coll., Costa Mesa, 1985—; hynotherapist, El Toro, 1986—. Author: (textbook) Folkdancing is for Everybody; prodn. editor: (newsletter) Technicribe, 1986; editor: (newsletter) Techniscribe, 1987; illustrator (tech. manual) AST-2000 User's Manual, 1986; inventor, designer dance notation system MS Method. Mem. bd. govs. Lake Forest II Showboaters Theater Group, 1985-88. Mem. Soc. Tech. Communication (v.p. programs, 1987—, newsletter editor 1986-87, newsletter prodn. editor 1985-86). Club: Hofshalom Internat. Folkdancers (sec. 1982-83) (Seal Beach, Calif.). Office: Visual Arts 25422 Trabuco Rd 105 El Toro CA 92630

BRAMMER, NORMAN DEAN, data processing educator; b. Leon, Iowa, Sept. 11, 1929; s. Ruby Evelyn (Foland) B.; m. Sylvia Carol Millerd, Sept. 8, 1951; children: Cynthia, Paul, Linda, Melanie. AB, Grinnell Coll., 1954; MBA, Northwestern U., 1959; PhD, U. Iowa, 1971. Credit analyst U.S. Steel Co., Chgo., 1954-65; instr. Western Ill. U., Macomb, 1965; asst. prof. computer infosystems Colo. State U., Ft. Collins, 1968-74, assoc. prof., 1974-; cons. systems analyst U.S. Forest Service, Ft. kCollins, 1976-84; faculty intern IBM, Boulder, Colo., summer 1981, Sandia Corp., Albuquerque, summers 1982, 84. Mem. Inst. for Cert. Comuter Profls. (cert. data processing). Episcopalian. Home: 1712 S Whitcomb St Fort Collins CO 80526 Office: Colo State U Dept Computer Info Systems Fort Collins CO 80523

BRAMWELL, MARVEL LYNNETTE, nurse; b. Durango, Colo., Aug. 13, 1947; d. Floyd Lewis and Virginia Jenny (Amyx) B. Diploma in lic. practical nursing, Durango Sch. Practical Nursing, 1968; AD in Nursing, Mt. Hood Community Coll., 1972; BS in Nursing, BS in Gen. Studies cum laude, So. Oreg. State Coll., 1980; cert. edn. grad. sch. social work, U. Utah, 1987. RN, LPN, cert. counselor alcohol, drug abuse. Staff nurse Monument Valley (Utah) Seventh Day Adventist Mission Hosp., 1973-74, La Plata Community Hosp., 1974-75; health coordinator Tri County Head Start Program, 1974-75; nurse therapist, team leader Portland Adventist Med. Ctr., 1975-78; staff nurse Indian Health Service Hosp., 1980-81; coordinator village health services North Slope Borough Health and Social Service Agy., 1981-83; nurse, supr. aides Bonneville Health Care Agy., 1984-85; staff nurse Latter Day Saints Adolescent Psychiat. Unit, 1985-86; coordinator adolescent nursing CPC Olympus View Hosp., 1986-87; charge and staff nurse adult psychiatry U. Utah, 1987-88; assisted with design and constrn. 6 high tech. health clinics in Ala. Arctic, 1982-83; creator after care program Greatest Love, 1986-87. Contbr. articles to profl. jours. Active Mothers Against Drunk Driving; mem. acad. rev. com. Community Health Assn. Program U. Alaska Rural Edn., 1981-83. Recipient Cert. Appreciation Barrow (Alaska) Lion's Club, 1983, U.S. Census Bur., Colo., 1970. Mem. Nat. League Nurses, Assn. Women Sci., Nat. Assn. Female Execs., Am. Soc. Circumpolar Health, NOW, Casandra. Home: PO Box 511282 Salt Lake City UT 84151

BRANCA, JOHN GREGORY, lawyer, consultant; b. Bronxville, N.Y., Dec. 11, 1950; s. John Ralph and Barbara (Werle) B. AB in Polit. Sci. cum laude, Occidental Coll., 1972; JD, UCLA, 1975. Bar: Calif. 1975. Assoc. Kindel & Anderson, Los Angeles, 1975-77, Hardee, Barovick, Konecky & Braun, Beverly Hills, Calif., 1977-81; ptnr. Ziffren, Brittenham & Branca, Los Angeles, 1981—; cons. N.Y. State Assembly, Mt. Vernon, 1978-82, various music industry orgns., Los Angeles, 1981—; bd. dirs. Michael Jackson Prodns., Los Angeles. Editor-in-Chief UCLA-Alaska Law Rev., 1974-75; contbr. articles to profl. jours. Cons. United Negro Coll. Fund; bd. dirs. Michael Jackson Burn Ctr., UCLA Law Sch. Com. Recipient Bancroft-Whitney award; named Entertainment Lawyer of Yr. Am. Lawyer mag., 1981. Mem. ABA (patent trademark and copyright law sect.), Calif. Bar Assn., Beverly Hills Bar Assn. (entertainment law sect.), Phi Alpha Delta, Sigma Tau Sigma. Office: 2121 Ave of Stars 32d Fl Los Angeles CA 90067

BRANCH, ALAN HENRY (SKIP BRANCH), advertising executive, consultant, educator; b. L.A., Aug. 28, 1942; s. C.H. Hardin Branch and Erma M. Smith; m. Judith Lovinger (div.); children: Scott Alan, Brooks Charles, Alison Wendy; m. Julie A. Holbrook, Sept. 3, 1983. BA in English, U. Utah, 1968. Sales svc. mgr. ABC Radio Network, L.A., 1963-66; sales mgr. KUTV Inc., Salt Lake City, 1966-73; pres., ptnr. Branch & Bell Inc., Salt Lake City, 1974-81; v.p., ptnr. Branch, Jones Inc., Salt Lake City, 1981—; adj. prof. Westminster Coll., Salt Lake City, 1974—. Author: The Grand Beehive, 1980; editor, contbr.: (mags.) Network, 1978-88, Utah Holiday, 1987; writer, producer video Golden Spike Empire, 1988. Co-chair affiliate pres. council, Planned Parenthood Fedn. Am., 1988-89, pres. Planned Parenthood Utah, 1987-89; founder, chmn. Utah Arts Festival, 1978; state rep. Unicef, 1988; mem. exec. com. Alta (Utah) Def. Fund, 1984—. Recipient Gold awards (16) Am. Advt. Fedn., 1974-88. Mem. Salt Lake Art Dirs. (recipient 4 Gold awards 1984-88), Salt Lake Tennis Club, Sitzmark Club. Democrat. Home: 1475 E 7200 South Salt Lake City UT 84121 Office: Branch Jones Inc 2632 E 3300 South Salt Lake City UT 84109

BRANCH, ROB HARDIN, communications executive; b. L.A., Oct. 12, 1939; s. Charles Henry Hardin and Erma Mae (Smith) B.; children: Kirsten Lynn, Kelley Robert Hardin; m. Luba Carlton, Dec. 12, 1986 (div. Jan. 1987). Grad. high sch., Salt Lake City. Announcer Sta. KALL-AM, Salt Lake City, 1968-72; asst. news dir. Sta. KOGO-AM, San Diego, 1973-80; asst. assignment editor Sta. KGTV, San Diego, 1980-81; host, reporter Sta. KSDO-AM, San Diego, 1981-85; program dir. Sta. KTMS-AM, Santa Barbara, 1985-86; news dir. Sta. KVSD-AM, Carlsbad, Calif., 1986-87, program dir., 1987-89; with Super Communications, San Diego, 1989—; instr. Grossmont Community Coll., El Cajon, Calif., 1983—, Santa Barbara City Coll., 1985-86. Facilitator Child Abuse Coodinating Com., San Diego, 1974. Recipient Golden Mike Award Am. Legion, 1965. Mem. A.M. Broadcaster's Assn., AFTRA (bd. dirs. 1980-82), San Diego Press Club (bd. dirs. 1975-77). Home: 7942 Topaz Lake Ave San Diego CA 92119 Office: Super Communications 7942 Topaz Lake Ave San Diego CA 92119

BRAND, MYLES, academic administrator; b. N.Y.C., May 17, 1942; s. Irving Philip and Shirley (Berger) B.; m. Wendy Hoffman (div. 1976); 1 child: Joshua; m. Margaret Zeglin, 1978. BS, Rensselaer Poly. Inst., Troy, N.Y., 1964; PhD, U. Rochester, 1967. Asst. prof. philosophy U. Pitts., 1967-72; from assoc. prof. to prof., dept. chmn. U. Ill., Chgo., 1972-81; prof., dept. head U. Ariz., Tucson, 981-83, dean, social & behavioral scis., 1983-86; provost, v.p. acad. affairs Ohio State U., Columbus, 1986-89; pres. U. Oreg., Eugene, 1989—. Author: Intending and Acting, 1984; editor: The Nature of Human Action, 1970, The Nature of Causation, 1976, Action Theory, 1976. bd. dirs. Ariz. Humanities Council, 1984-85. Recipient research award NEH, 1974, 79. Mem. Phi Kappa Phi, Am. Philos. Assn., Soc. for Philosophy & Psychology (exec. com.), Philosophy of Sci. Assn.. Office: U Oreg Office of Pres Eugene OR 97403-1226

BRANDAU, EUGENE CLINTON, real estate executive; b. Balt., Sept. 20, 1934; s. John Raymond and Elizabeth (Cassidy) B.; m. Bertha A. Densmore, Nov. 1955 (div. 1975); children: Daniel Eugene, Nancy Carol, Susan Elizabeth. AS, Southwestern Coll., Chula Vista, Calif., 1966; BA, San Diego State Coll., 1969; MBA, Nat. U., San Diego, 1977; PhD, Columbia Pacific U., 1985; LLB (hon.), La Salle Ext. U., Chgo., 1975. Commd. ensign USCGR, 1961, advanced through grades to lt. comdr., 1988; claims mgr. Century Nat. Ins., San Diego; port capt., mgr. U. So. Calif., L.A.; ships mgr. U.S. Mcht. Marine, Oakland, Calif.; corp. pres. Bano Corp., Reno, 1980—. Author ADP and the Administrator, 1969, Corporate Tax Advantages, 1985. With USCGR. Mem. Res. Officers Assn., Toastmasters (Internat. Speakers Bur., pres., dist. treas., Outstanding Club Pres. award 1987), Masons. Office: Bano Corp PO Box 21447 Reno NV 89515

BRANDENBURG, GLEN RAY, marine education administrator; b. Long Beach, Calif., July 28, 1950; s. Richard Stanley and Julia Amelia (Sudeiris) B. B in Indsl. Arts, San Diego State U., 1974. Dir. Mission Bay Aquatic Ctr., San Diego, 1970—; cons. in field. Producer movies in field. Chmn. San Diego City Lakes Master Plan, 1975; asst. regatta dir. Olympic Rowing Venue, L.A., 1984; bd. dirs Boating Safety Ctr. Calif. Dept Boating and Waterwasys, 1976—. Mem. Calif. Boating Ctr. Dirs. (chmn. 1980—), U.S. Yacht Racing Union, Nat. Boating Fedn., San Diego Assn. Yacht Clubs, Mission Bay Rowing Assn. (bd. dirs. 1975—), Boat/U.S. Democrat. Office: Mission Bay Aquatic Ctr 1001 Santa Clara Point San Diego CA 92109

BRANDENBURGH, DONALD CARTER, literary agent; b. Stuart, Iowa, July 4, 1931; s. Wilbur Hager and Esther Hadley (Carter) B.; m. Mary Isabelle Moore, June 5, 1953; children: Gregory, Curtis, Brenda. BA, William Penn Coll., 1953; MA, Whittier Coll., 1960; MDiv, Talbot Sch. Theology, La Mirada, Calif., 1970. Ordained minister Soc. of Friends, 1956; Pastor Paton (Iowa) Friends Ch., 1955-57; clk. So. Calif. Gas Co., L.A., 1958-59; ministry Christian edn. Alamitos Friends Ch., Garden Grove, Calif., 1959-68; bus. adminstr. Calif. Yearly Meeting Friends Ch., Whittier, Calif., 1968-73; exec. dir. Nat. Sunday Sch. Assn., Whittier, 1973-74, Evang.

Christian Publs. Assn., La Habra, Calif., 1974-80; assoc. pub., owner Home & Land mag., La Habra, 1981-85; lit. agt., owner, mgr. Brandenburgh & Assocs., La Habra, 1986—. Bd. dirs. Friends Ctr., Azusa, Calif., 1986-87. Mem. La Habra Area C. of C. (chmn. trade fair com. 1987-88, 2nd v.p. 1987-88, chmn. ambassador com. 1988—), greater L.A. Sunday Sch. Assn. (bd. dirs. 1962-82). Republican. Home: 72-706 Pitahaya St Palm Desert CA 92260 Office: PO Box 4073 Palm Desert CA 92261-4073

BRANDIS, PAMELA, evaluation sociologist; b. Chgo., Oct. 14, 1946; d. Theodore and Esther Ruth (Doege) B. BA, U. Wash., 1972, MA, 1977; MS, U. Oreg., 1982, PhD, 1989. Cert. secondary tchr., Wash. Instr. Edmonds Community Coll., Wash., 1977-79; teaching asst. U. Oreg., Portland, 1979-83; research analyst Columbia Info. Systems, Portland, 1984-86; evaluation sociologist Bonneville Power Adminstrn., Eugene, 1986—; cons., free-lance researcher, Portland, 1986—. Author: Energy Conservation Program Evaluation, 1988, The Persistence of Energy Savings, 1989, The Christian Science Periodicals; contbr. articles to newspapers. Swimming coach U.S.A. Paraplegic Assn., Seattle, 1969. Recipient cash award for outstanding work Bonneville Power Adminstrn., 1988. Mem. Soc. for Applied Sociology, Pacific Sociol. Soc., Pi Gamma Mu. Republican. Christian Scientist. Home: 4211 SW Woodside Circle Lake Oswego OR 97035

BRANDMEYER, MILO WARREN, JR., construction executive; b. Santa Monica, Calif., Dec. 3, 1930; s. Milo Warren Sr., and Norma (Smith) B.; m. Patricia Gayner, Apr. 16, 1955; children: Catherine, Laurie. Grad. high sch., West Los Angeles, Calif.; student, Santa Monica City Coll., 1949-51. Registered gen. contractor, Calif. V.p. Republic Homes, Costa Mesa, Calif., 1961-69; project mgr. Boise Cascade Residential, Washington, 1969-71; exec. v.p. Sining River Properties, Ocean Springs, Miss., 1971-75; dir. constr., owners rep. San Juan (P.R.) Racing Assn., 1975-80; dir. engring. Watt Industries, Santa Monica, 1980-81, Houston Sports Assn., 1981-83; v.p. constrn. Sunset Devel., Malibu, Calif., 1983-85, Regal Homes, Irvine, Calif., 1985-86, Pelican Properties, Santa Ana, Calif., 1987—. Mem. local govt. affairs com. Monitoring Program Subcom. Orange County, Calif., 1988. Served to PN3 USNR, 1951-53. Mem. Bldg. Industry Assn. (mem. local govt. affairs com. 1987-88). Republican. Home: 22704 Woodlake Ln El Toro CA 92630

BRANDNER, MARGARET ANNE SHAW, polygraph examiner; b. Denver, Sept. 4, 1937; d. Bertram James and Bessie (Syme) Shaw; m. Kenneth LeRoy Brandner, Dec. 26, 1970. BA in Elem. Edn., Loretto Heights Coll., 1959; polygraph examiner Rocky Mountain Security Inst., 1978; grad. Famous Writers' Sch., 1964, Inst. Forensic and Investigative Hypnosis, 1980; A.A.S. in Polygraph Tech., Pikes Peak Community Coll., 1982. Lic. polygraphist, Nebr., Utah.Acct., Denver Children's Home, 1970; acct.Keny's Equip., Inc., Green River, Wyo., 1971-78; polygraph examiner, sec.-treas. The Brandner Corp., Green River, Wyo., 1978—; founder KNM Enterprises, Inc., 1987—. Mem. Green River Planning Commn., 1971-79; bd. dirs. Green River Co-op Pre-Sch., Inc., 1977-79; trustee Sweetwater County Sch. Dist. #2, 1986—; vol. chmn. Arthritis Found., Sweetwater County, 1986-87, Sweet Water County United Way, 1984—. Mem. Am. Acad. Forensic Hypnotists, Am. Polygraph Assn., Utah Polygraph Assn., Wyo. Polygraph Assn. (charter, editor newsletter). Roman Catholic. Office: 78 W Railroad Ave PO Box 1147 Green River WY 82935

BRANDON, KATHRYN ELIZABETH BECK, pediatrician; b. Salt Lake City, Sept. 10, 1916; d. Clarence M. and Hazel A. (Cutler) Beck; MD, U. Chgo., 1941; BA, U. Utah, 1937; MPH, U. Calif., Berkeley, 1957; children: John William, Kathleen Brandon McEnulty, Karen. Intern, Grace Hosp., Detroit, 1941-42; resident Children's Hosp. Med. Center No. Calif., Oakland, 1953-55, Children's Hosp., L.A., 1951-53; pvt. practice, La Crescentia, Calif., 1946-51, Salt Lake City, 1960-65, 86—; med. dir. Salt Lake City public schs., 1957-60; dir. Ogden City-Weber County (Utah) Health Dept., 1965-67; pediatrician Fitzsimmons Army Hosp., 1967-68; coll. health physician U. Colo., Boulder, 1968-71; student health physician U. Utah, Salt Lake City, 1971-81; occupational health physician Hill AFB, Utah, 1981-85; ; child health physician Salt Lake City-County Health Dept., 1971—; cons. in field; clin. asst. U. Utah Coll. Medicine, Salt Lake City, 1958-64; clin. asst. pediatrics U. Colo. Coll. Medicine, Denver, 1958-72; active staff Primary Children's Hosp., LDS Hosp., and Cottonwood Hosp., 1960-67. Diplomate Am. Bd. Pediatrics. Fellow Am. Pediatric Acad., Am. Pub. Health Assn., Am. Sch. Health Assn.; mem. Utah Coll. Health Assn. (pres. 1978-80), Pacific Coast Coll. Health Assn., AMA, Utah Med. Assn., Salt Lake County Med. Soc., Utah Public Health Assn. (sec.-treas. 1960-66), Intermountain Pediatric Soc. Home: PO Box 58482 Salt Lake City UT 84156-0482 Office: 3236 E 3300 S Salt Lake City UT 84109

BRANDT, EDWIN RALPH, transportation director; b. N.Y.C., July 3, 1951; s. Ralph B. and Agnes (Haemmerle) B.; m. Kathryn Ann Deneui, Aug. 5, 1974. BS, U. Colo., 1973, MBA, 1976. Market analyst Norfolk So. Corp., Roanoke, Va., 1976-78; market mgr. So. Pacific R.R., San Francisco, 1976-81; mktg. dir. Pacific Intermountain Express, Walnut Creek, Calif., 1981-82; transp. dir. J. R. Simplot Co., Boise, Idaho, 1982--. Staff officer USCG, 1987--. N.W. Food Processor Assn., Am. Frozen Food Inst. (mem. distbn. com.), Nat. Indsl. Transp. League, The Fertilization Inst. (mem. distbn. com.), Assn. Transp. Practitioners, Am. Soc. Transp. and Logistics, Council of Logistics Mgmt., Calif. Fertilizer Assn. (mem. distbn. com. 1985--), Idaho Assn. Commerce and Industry (chmn. 1986--).

BRANDT, SUSAN LORAE, social worker; b. Washington, June 26, 1950; d. Lloyd Adrian and Rachel DeSpang (Miller) N.; m. James S. Brandt, May 31, 1986. Student, W.Va. Wesleyan, Buckhannon, 1968-69, Montgomery Coll., 1970, U. Md., 1971, Art Inst. Miami, 1971-72; BA, U. Mont., 1976. Layout, paste-up artist LithoComp, Bethesda, Md., 1973-74; receptionist Real Log Homes, Inc., Missoula, Mont., 1976-77, sec., bookkeeper, 1978, mktg. sec., 1978-79; gen. office clk. State of Montana, Missoula, 1979-80; social worker Mont. Social and Rehab. Services, Shelby, 1980-87, Toole County Hosp. and Nursing Home, Shelby, 1987—; dir. 9th Jud. Dist. Youth Guidance Home, Shelby, 1988—; rep. social and rehab. services 9th Jud. Foster Care Rev. Com., Choteau, Mont. 1982-86. Active Big Sister Big Bros. and Sisters Program, Shelby, 1980-84, Missoula, 1977-80; mem. Mental Health Adv. Bd., Shelby, 1980—, chairperson, 1981-83, 86, 87; bd. dirs. Triangle Transition, Shelby, 1981-83; vol. advisor Joint Action in Community Svc. Mem. Nat. Assn. Social Workers. Home: 649 N Teton Ave Shelby MT 59474 Office: 9th Judicia Dist Youth Guidance Home Shelby MT 59474

BRANIGAN, DONALD WILLIAM, mayor; b. Louerna, Sask., Can., Apr. 23, 1933; s. Philip Henry and Mary Irene (Code) B.; divorced; children: Philip, Karen, David, Warren. BSc, U. Alta., Edmonton, Can., 1958, MD, 1963. Cer. LMCC. Mayor City of Manning, Alta., Can., 1968-70, City of Whitehorse, Yukon, Can., 1978-80, 82—; dir. Fedn. Can. Municipalities, 1988—. Mem. Sci. Council of Can.; pres. Assn. Yukon Communities, 1988—. Mem. Holistic Health Med. Assn. (founder), Am. Holistic Med. Assn. (founding mem. 1977), Can. Coll. Physicians (cert.). Mem. Liberal Party. Anglican. Home: 33 Highland Ct, Whitehorse, YK Canada Y1A 4R6 Office: Office of Mayor, 2121 2d Ave, Whitehorse, YK Canada Y1A 1C2 also: Branigan Clinic, 106 Lambert St, Whitehorse, YK Canada Y1A 1Z2

BRANKOVICH, MARK J., restaurateur; b. Riteka, Yugoslavia, Mar. 4, 1922; came to U.S., 1951; s. Joseph M. and Rose (Haydin) B.; m. Marilyn J. Severin, Jan. 4, 1957; children: Mark, Laura. BA in Philosophy, U. Zurich, 1944; student, U. Geneva, 1945, U. Padua, Italy, 1947. Owner The Golden Deer, Chgo., 1953-55; mgr. Gaslight Club, N.Y.C., 1955-57; gen. mgr., exec. v.p., dir. Gaslight Club, Chgo., 1959-63; owner, mgr. Franchise Gaslight Club, L.A., 1963-66; owner Monte Carlo Italian Deli, Burbank, Calif., 1969—, Pinocchio Restaurant, Burbank, 1970—, Pinocchio Westwood (Calif.), 1979, Italia Foods Wholesale, Burbank. Mem. Presdl. Task Force, Washington, 1980—, Rep. Senatorial Inner Circle, 1986. Mem. Internat. Platform Assn. Serbian Orthodox. Home: 1250 N Hilldale Ave Los Angeles CA 90069 Office: Monte Carlo Italia Foods Inc 3103 W Magnolia Blvd Burbank CA 91505

BRANNAN, EVELYN SELLARS, retired school counselor, writer; b. Clovis, N.Mex., Jan. 12, 1930; d. William Jackson and Muriel Evelyn (Rodgers) Sellars; m. Joe Allen Brannan, Dec. 16, 1947; 1 child, Daniel Keith. BS in Bus. Edn., N.Mex. U., 1957; postgrad., So. U., 1964; MBA, Eastern N.Mex. U., 1967; MA, N.Mex. U., 1977. Tchr. bus. Belen (N.Mex.) Consol. Schs., 1958-78, head dept. bus. edn., 1970-76, high sch. counselor, 1979-84; ret. 1984, writer, 1985—. Author: The Great Siberian Adventure, 1988. Vice pres. Belen Histo. Soc., 1987, bd. dirs., 1988—. NSF grantee, 1964. Mem. N.Mex. Edn. Assn. (pres. central dist. 1972, Belen 1974), AAUW (treas., sec., v.p., pres. Belen 1958-68), Albuquerque Civic Chorus, Valencia County Art Guild, Pilot Club, Desert Stars Club (Belen), Phi Lambda Theta. Republican. Mem. Ch. of Christ. Home: 5555 Brannan Ln Belen NM 87002

BRANNON, LORI ANNETTE, agricultural specialist; b. Bakersfield, Calif., Dec. 30, 1959; d. Cleo Paul and Lura Jo (Wilson) B. AA, Bakersfield (Calif.) Coll., 1985; postgrad., Calif. State U. Ptnr. Brannons Picking Service, Bakersfield, 1980—; rehab. asst. Ctr. for Neuro Skills, Bakersfield, 1984-1988. Active People for the Ethical Treatment of Animals. Mem. Nat. Wildlife Fedn., Cheverolet Ltd. Club. Home: 3604 Amherst St Bakersfield CA 93305-1210

BRANSFORD, JAMES CHRISTIAN, petroleum geologist; b. Galveston, Tex., Aug. 7, 1900; s. Charles Dean and Carrie Martie (Whiteside) B.; m. Martie Elizabeth Wilkes, Aug. 20, 1975. Student Colo. Sch. Mines, 1918-19, U. Tex., El Paso, 1921. With Calif. Petroleum Corp. and Texas Co., L.A., 1923-29; petroleum geologist, L.A., 1929-50, Palm Springs, Calif., 1950—. Author oil maps. Mem. Am. Assn. Petroleum Geologists, Soc. Petroleum Engrs. Republican. Presbyterian. Address: 360 Monte Vista Dr Palm Springs CA 92262

BRANTINGHAM, CHARLES ROSS, podiatrist; b. Long Beach, Calif., Feb. 14, 1917; m. Lila Carolyn Price; children: Paul Jeffery, John Price, Charles Ross, James William. Student, Long Beach City Coll., 1935; D in Podiatric Medicine, Calif. Coll. Podiatric Medicine, 1939, cert. foot surgery, 1947. Resident in podiatry San Francisco, 1939-40; pvt. practice podiatry Long Beach, 1946-56; podiatrist, dir. Podiatric Group, Long Beach, 1956-71, Los Alamitos (Calif.) Podiatric Group, 1971-86; chief podiatry sect., dept. orthopedics Los Alamitos Med. Ctr., 1983—; clin. asst. prof. medicine U. So. Calif., Los Angeles, 1965—; adj. prof. Calif. State U., Long Beach, 1972—; cons. Specified Products Co., El Monte, Calif., 1968—, Armstrong World Industries, Lancaster, Pa., 1983—. Contbr. articles to profl. jours., chpts. to books. Bd. dirs. Diabetes Assn. of So. Calif., Los Angeles, 1964-67; cons., bd. dirs. Comprehensive Health Planning Assn., Los Angeles, 1969-72; pub. improvement and adv. cons. Long Beach City Council and Office of Mayor, 1957-67; co-chair Podiatric Med. Sect., 1985. Served to lt. comdr. USN, 1941-46. Named Disting. Practitioner of Podiatric Medicine Nat. Acad. Practice, 1982. Fellow Am. Assn. Hosp. Podiatrists (pres. 1958-60), Am. Pub. Health Assn. (council 1986—, Steven Toth award 1982), Am. Soc. Podiatric Medicine, Internat. Acad. for Standing and Walking Fitness (pres. 1963—); mem. Am. Podiatric Med. Assn. (exec. council 1957-59, Hall of Sci. award 1973), Assn. Mil. Surgeons of U.S. (life), Res. Officers Assn. of U.S. Republican. Mormon. Clubs: Exchange (Long Beach) (pres. 1948-49), Ind. Bus. (pres. 1958). Home: 11386 Holder St Cypress CA 90630 Office: 3791 Katella Ave Ste 207 Los Alamitos CA 90720

BRASCH, JOHN MICHAEL, management specialist; b. York, Pa., Nov. 21, 1955; s. John George and Mildred Ann (Braun) B.; m. Barbara Ann Smeltzer, Dec. 6, 1980; children: Joseph, Jordan. BS in Mgmt., York Coll. of Pa., York, Pa., 1986. Test Tech. Westinghouse Defense Ilso, Balt., 1979-82, test and repair mgr., 1982-85, ops. support mgr., 1985-87, repair program mgr., 1985-87; plant mgr. Elect. Svcs. Div., LASC Westinghouse Defense, Compton, Calif., 1988—. With USN, 1974-78, Calif. Republican. Roman Catholic. Home: 2546 Turquoise Cir Chino Hills CA 91709 Office: Westinghouse LASC 18020 S Santa Fe Ave Compton CA 90221

BRASDA, BERNARD WILLIAM, trust company owner; b. La Crosse, Wis., May 3, 1938; s. George John and Olga Mary Olive (Hanson) B.; m. Carol June Welch, June, 1962 (div. 1979); children: George Allen, Norma Jean. BA, LaSalle Extension U., 1958; PhD (hon.), Juan Hauz U., 1979. Abstractor's asst. Las Cruces (N.M.) Abstract & Title Co., 1963-66; owner Grant County Abstract Co., Silver City, N.M., 1966-69; chief title officer Transam. Title Ins. co., Casa Grande, Ariz., 1969-72; title officer Title Ins. Co., Minn. and Phoenix, 1972-75; owner Brasda Title Service, Phoenix, 1975-76, 1979—; unit mgr. First Am. Title Ins. Co., Phoenix, 1976-79; instr. searching techniques, pvt. practice, 1975—. With U.S. Army, 1959-63. Mem. Northwest Mining Assn. Republican. Office: Brasda Title Svc PO Box 1430 Black Canyon City AZ 85324

BRASEL, JO ANNE, physician; b. Salem, Ill., Feb. 15, 1934; d. Gerald Nolan and Ruby Rachel (Rich) B. B.A., U. Colo., 1956; M.D., U. Colo., 1959. Diplomate Am. Bd. Pediatrics, Am. Bd. Pediatric-Endocrinology. Pediatric intern, resident Cornell Med. Coll.-N.Y. Hosp., N.Y.C., 1959-62; pediatric endocrine fellow Johns Hopkins U. Sch. Medicine, Balt., 1962-65, asst. prof. pediatrics, 1965-68; asst. prof. then assoc. prof. pediatrics Cornell U. Med. Coll., N.Y.C., 1969-72; assoc. prof. then prof. pediatrics Columbia U. Coll. Physicians and Surgeons, N.Y.C., 1972-79, asst. dir. Inst. Human Nutrition, 1972-79; prof. pediatrics Harbor-UCLA Med. Ctr., UCLA Sch. Medicine, 1979—, program dir. Gen. Clin. Research Ctr., 1979—, prof. medicine, 1980—; mem. adv. com. FDA, Rockville, Md., 1971-75; mem. nutrition study sect. NIH, Bethesda, Md., 1974-78; mem. select panel for promotion of child health HEW, Washington, 1979-80; mem. life scis. D adv. screening com. Fulbright-Hays program, Washington, 1981-84, digestive disease and nutrition grant review group NIADDK, 1985—, U.S. Govt. Task Force on Women, Minorities and the Handicapped in Sci. and Tech., 1987—. Recipient Research Career Devel. award NIH, 1973-77, Irma T. Hirschl Trust Career Scientist award, 1974-79, Sr. Fulbright Sabbatical Research award, 1980. Mem. Soc. Pediatric Research (pres. 1978-79), Am. Fed. Clin. Research, Endocrine Soc., Am. Soc. Clin. Nutrition, Am. Inst. Nutrition, Lawson Wilkins Pediatric Endocrine Soc. (dir., mem. bd. 1972-74), Am. Pediatric Soc., Assn. Program Dirs. for Gen. Clin. Research Ctrs. (pres. 1982-83), N.Am. Assn. for Study Obesity, Internat. Orgn. for Study Human Devel., Western Soc. Pediatric Research, Phi Beta Kappa, Alpha Omega Alpha. Office: Harbor-UCLA Med Ctr 1000 W Carson St Torrance CA 90509

BRASELTON, JAMES TODD, lawyer; b. Harvey, Ill., Apr. 2, 1952; s. Verlon Wesley and Shirley (Budwash) B.; m. Bonnie Joan Aurelius. BS in Civil Engring., U. Ill., 1976; JD, Arz. State U., 1986. Civil engr. R. W. Rubinson & Assoc. Co., So. Holland, Ill., 1976-81, Ariz. Dept. Water Resources, Phoenix, 1982-83; of counsel Mariscal, Weeks, McIntyre & Friedlander, Phoenix, 1985—. Mem. Maricopa County Bar Assn., Ariz. State Bar Assn., Ill. State Bar Assn. Republican. Office: Mariscal Weeks McIntyre & Friedlander 201 W Coolidge St Phoenix AZ 85013

BRASMER, RANDALL DANE, revenue officer, consultant; b. Moline, Ill., July 20, 1952; s. Maurice Emanual and Marjorie Elaine (Prickrell) B.; m. Janet Dee Haynes (div.); 1 child, Amanda; m. Esther Nagel, Apr. 18, 1978; children: Craig, Christine. BSBA, U. Phoenix, 1988. Sr. asst. mgr. Household Fin. Corp., Sierra Vista, Ariz., 1979-81; loan mgr. Huachuca Fed. Credit Union, Ft. Huachuca, Ariz., 11981-83; revenue officer IRS, Phoenix, 1983—. With U.S. Army, 1972-78. Home: 18416 N 29th Ave Phoenix AZ 85023 Office: IRS 2400 W Dunlop #315 Phoenix AZ 85021

BRASS, ERIC PAUL, internal medicine and pharmacology educator; b. Bklyn., Sept. 3, 1952; s. Edward A. and Barbara (Rosen) B.; m. Debra A. Rudy, May 23, 1974; children: Carl, Courtney. BS in Chem. Engring., Case Western Res. U., 1974, MS in Chem. Engring., 1975, PhD in Pharmacology, 1979, MD, 1980. Diplomate Am. Bd. Internal Medicine. Resident in internal medicine U. Wash., Seattle, 1980-82, fellow in clin. pharmacology, 1982-83; asoc. prof. medicine and pharmacology U. Colo., Denver, 1983--. Contbr. articles to sci. jours. Recipient Faculty Devel. award Pharm. Mfrs. Assn. Found., 1985; NIH rsch. grantee, 1985. Mem. Am. Diabetes Assn. (rsch. grantee 1984), Am. Fedn. Clin. Rsch., Am. Soc. Pharmacology and Exptl. Therapeutics, Am. Soc. Clin. Pharmacology and Therapeutics (Young Investigator award 1987). Office: U Colo Health Scis Ctr 4200 E 9th Ave Denver CO 80262

BRASSARD, DENNIS JOSEPH, nuclear power consultant; b. Fitchburg, Mass., May 22, 1948; s. Bernard Joseph and Verna Beatrice (Gray) B.; m. Kathleen Ann Hoisington, June 14, 1969; children: Jeffrey Joseph, Tara Lynn. BS in Nuclear Engring., Lowell Tech. Inst., 1970. Test engr. Newport News (Va.) Shipbuilding Co., 1970-72, United Engrs. & Constrn., Middleton, Pa., 1972-76; sr. engr. United Engrs. & Constrn., Richland, Wash., 1979-84; adv. engr. Stone & Webster Engr. Corp., Boston, 1976-79; cons. nuclear power Mgmt. Analysis Co., Oswego (N.Y.) and Rancho Seco (Calif.), 1984-88, Sierra Tech., Rancho Seco, 1988; dir. plant ops. Meth. Hosp., Sacramento, 1988—. Author poetry; contbr. articles to profl. jours. Named Outstanding Brownfield Entry Paxton Area Jaycees Pa., 1975. Republican. Mormon. Office: Meth Hosp 7500 Timberlake Way Sacramento CA 95823

BRASSELL, ROSELYN STRAUSS, lawyer; b. Shreveport, La., Feb. 19, 1930; d. Herman Carl and Etelka (McMullan) Strauss. BA, La. State U., 1949; JD, UCLA, 1962. Bar: Calif. 1963. Legal sec. Welton P. Mouton, Lafayette, La., 1949-50; office sec. Leake, Henry, Golden & Burrow, Dallas, 1950-57; atty. CBS, Los Angeles, 1962-68, sr. atty., 1968-76, asst. gen. atty., 1976-83, broadcast counsel, 1983—. Co-writer: Life After Death for the California Celebrity, 1985; bd. editors U. Calif. Law Rev., 1960-62. Named Angel of Distinction Los Angeles Cen. City Assn., 1975. Mem. Calif. Bar Assn., Los Angeles County Bar Assn. (exec. com. 1970—, sect. chmn. 1980-81), Beverly Hills Bar Assn., Los Angeles Copyright Soc. (treas. 1977-78, sec. 1978-79, pres. 1981-82), Am. Women in Radio and TV (nat. dir.-at-large 1971-73, nat. pub. affairs chmn. 1977-78), Nat. Acad. TV Arts and Scis., Women in Film, Los Angeles World Affairs Council, U. Calif. Law Alumni Assn. (dir. 1971-74), Order of Coif, Alpha Xi Delta, Phi Alpha Delta. Republican. Home: 631 N Wilcox Ave Los Angeles CA 90004 Office: 7800 Beverly Blvd Los Angeles CA 90036

BRASSINGTON, JACQUELINE FOODY, special events executive; b. Belfast, Ireland, Apr. 26, 1961; came to U.S., 1962; d. James Joseph and Clare Bernadette (Barr) Foody; m. Andrew Stuart Brassington, Dec. 26, 1985. BA, U. Wash., 1983. Stock broker Shearson Lehman, Yakima, Wash., 1983-85; investment rep. Peoples Bank, Yakima, 1985-87; exec. dir. Wash. State Internat. Agrl. Symposium 1989, Yakima, 1987—; dir. The Maven Co., Yakima. Mem. Jr. League Yakima, Kappa Kappa Gamma. Republican. Roman Catholic. Home: 8 S 28th Ave Yakima WA 98902 Office: Internat Agrl Symposium 307 Larson Bldg Yakima WA 98902

BRASSWEL, KERRY, accountant, horsewoman. d. J.D. Jr. and Kathryn Elizabeth (Rimmer) Braswell. Student, Occidental Coll., L.A., 1964-66. Bus. mgr. to entertainers Segal, Skaff and Co., L.A., 1968, Cary Harwin and Assocs., Beverly Hills, Calif., 1968-72, Bisgeier, Breslauer and Co., L.A., 1972-74, M. Klaiman Accountancy Corp., Beverly Hills, 1974-75, Michael L. Laney, CPA, Beverly Hills, 1975-77; pvt. practice Tucson, Ariz., 1977—; owner Brasswel Arabians, L.A. 1966-76, KaBeArabie, Tucson, 1977—; appraiser St. Paul's Ins. Co., St. Paul, Minn.; equine, also accounting expert witness. Author: Herbal Horse Handbook, 1989. Judge, leader 4-H Club, Tucson, 1981-84; travel del. Calif. Horsemans People to People Goodwill Tour, 1970. Mem. Arabian Horse Registry Am., Internat. Arabian Horse Assn. (judge 1977-83), Am. Horse Show Assn. (judge 1976-83), Desert Show Horse Assn. (bd. dirs. 1980-83), So. Ariz. Arabian Horse Assn. (cert. appreciation 1978). Republican. Home and Office: 10151 W Picture Rocks Tucson AZ 85743

BRATTSTROM, BAYARD HOLMES, biology educator; b. Chgo., July 3, 1929; s. Wilber LeRoy and Violet (Holmes) B.; m. Cecile D. Funk, June 15, 1952 (div. May 1975); children: Theodore Allen, David Arthur.; m. Martha Isaacs Marsh, July 8, 1982. B.S., San Diego State Coll., 1951; M.A., UCLA, 1953, Ph.D., 1959. Dir. edn. Natural History Mus., San Diego, 1949-51; asst. curator herpetology Natural History Mus., 1949-51; assoc. zoology UCLA, 1954-56; research fellow paleoecology Calif. Inst. Tech., Pasadena, 1955; instr. biology Adelphi U., Garden City, N.Y., 1956-60; asst. prof. Calif. State U., Fullerton, 1960-61; assoc. prof. Calif. State U., 1961-66, prof., 1966—; assoc. prof. zoology UCLA, summers 1962-63; researcher and author of publs. in osteology, ecology, zoogeography of vertebrates, social behavior; hon. research assoc. herpetology, vertebrate paleontology Los Angeles County Mus., Los Angeles, 1961—; pres. Fullerton Youth Mus. and Natural Sci. Center, 1962-64, dir., 1962-66; vis. prof. zoology Sydney U., Australia, 1978, U. Queensland, Brisbane, Australia, 1984. Author: poetry The Talon Digs Deeply into My Heart, 1974; Contbr. chpts. to books. Research grantee Am. Philos. Soc., Mex., 1958; Research grantee Am. Philos. Soc., Panama, 1959; NSF, 1964-66; NSF Sr. Postdoctoral fellow Monash U., Australia, 1966-67; recipient Distinguished Teaching award Calif. State U., Fullerton, 1968. Fellow AAAS (mem. council 1965—), Herpetological League; mem. Am. Soc. Ichthyologists and Herpetologists (bd. govs. 1962-66, v.p. western div. 1965), Orange County Zool. Soc. (mem. bd. 1962-65, pres. 1962-64), So. Calif. Acad. Sci. (dir. 1964-67), Ecol. Soc. Am., Soc. for Study Evolution, Soc. Systematic Zoology, San Diego Soc. Natural History, Soc. Vertebrate Paleontology, Am. Soc. Mammalogists, Cooper, Am. ornithol. socs., Am. Soc. Zoologists, Sigma Xi. Office: Calif State U Dept Biology Fullerton CA 92634

BRAUER, MICHAEL DON, aerospace and defense consulting company executive; b. Denver, July 26, 1949. Student, U. Am., Mexico City, 1968-69; BA, Johns Hopkins U., 1971; JD, U. Colo., 1974. Bar: Colo. 1975, U.S. Supreme Ct. 1978. Owner, mgr. Box P Farm & Ranch, Harrisburg, Nebr., 1973—; asst. atty. City of Aurora, Colo., 1977-79; assoc. Sims & Richtsmeier, Denver, 1979; sole practice, Denver, 1979-80; pvt. practice in futures trading, Littleton, Colo., 1979—; owner Michael Brauer Commodities, Denver, 1980-83; dir. MB Group, Littleton; advisor to various countries, 1983—. Staff mem. Colo. Atty Gen. Campaign, Denver, 1974. Mem. U.S. Space Found., Am. Austronautical Soc., U.S. Naval Inst., USN League. Republican.

BRAUKUS, ROBERT MICHAEL, utilities executive; b. Wallace, Idaho, May 8, 1941; s. Joseph John and Anna Francis (Matusavage) B.; m. H. Jane Kennaugh, June 8, 1968; children: Susan, Greg. BSEE, Seattle U., 1965. Registered profl. engr., Calif., Wash., Idaho, Mont., Oreg., Alaska. Asst. engr. Puget Sound, Power & Light Co., Bellevue, Wash., 1968-71, communication engr., 1971-72, relay engr., 1972-75, asst. supt. substas., 1975-77, supt. T&D, 1977-80, dir. communication and system protection, 1982—; mgr. operation div. Chugach Electric, Anchorage, 1980-82. Co. co-chmn. United Way Fund, King County, Wash., 1986; mem. Engring. Advancement Council Seattle U., 1987-88; committeeman Mcpl. League, Bellevue, 1987; coord. capital campaign Salvation Army, Seattle, 1987; fund raiser Am. Cancer Soc., Bellevue, 1988; co. rep. 1990 Goodwill Games, Wash., 1988; bd. dirs. Bellevue Arts Assn. Lt. USNR, 1965-68, Vietnam. Recipient Citizen Community award Bellevue Downtown Park Com., 1987, Engr. Yr. award Puget Sound Engring. Council, 1989. Mem. IEEE (Seattle sect.), NSPE, Am. Soc. Quality Control, Electric Power Rsch. Inst. (adv. bd. integrated utility communication systems), Rotary. Republican. Roman Catholic. Office: Puget Sound & Light Co 13635 NE 80th St Redmond WA 98052

BRAULT, G(AYLE) LORAIN, health care executive; b. Chgo., Jan. 3, 1944; d. Theodore Frank and Victoria Jean (Pribyl) Hahn; m. Donald R. Brault, Apr. 29, 1971; 1 child, Kevin David. AA, Long Beach City Coll., 1963; BS, Calif. State U.-Long Beach, 1973, MS, 1977. RN, Calif. Dir. nursing Canyon Gen. Hosp., Anaheim, Calif., 1973-76; dir. faculty critical care masters degree program Calif. State U., Long Beach, 1976-79; regional dir. nursing and support services Western region Am. Med. Internat., Anaheim, Calif., 1979-83; v.p. Hosp. Home Care Corp., Santa Ana, Calif., 1983-85; pres. Hosp. Home Health Care Agy. Calif., Torrance, 1986--; invited lectr. China Nurses Assn., 1983; cons. AMI, Inc., Saudi Arabia, 1983; advisor dept. grad. nursing Calif. State U., L.A., 1988; guest lectr. Dept. Pub. Health UCLA, 1986-87; assoc. clin. prof. U. So. Calif., 1988-89. Contbr. articles to profl. jours., chpts. to books. Commr. U.S. Dept. Health and Human Svcs., Washington, 1988. HEW advanced nurse tng. grantee, 1978. Mem. Women in Health Adminstrn. (sec. 1989), Nat. Assn. Home Care, Am. Orgn. Nursing Execs., Calif. Assn. Health Services at Home (task force chmn. 1988, bd. dirs. 1989), Calif. League Nursing (bd. sec. 1983, program chmn. 1981-82), Am. Coll. Health Care Execs., Phi Kappa Phi. Republican. Methodist.

BRAULT-TERRIO, MARIE LOUISE, interior designer, art and design consultant; b. Saskatoon, Sask., Can., Sept. 4, 1928; came to U.S., 1965; d. Joseph Elphege and Marie Louise (Loiselle) Brault; m. Frank Edward Terrio, Oct. 24, 1984; stepchildren: Karen, Janet, Jack, James Chrissy. B Interior Design, U. Man., 1952; diploma, Ecole Beaux Arts, Montreal, Que., Can., 1960. Interior designer Ross, Fish, Duschenese, Barrett, Montreal, 1958-62, Arcop Architects, Montreal, 1962-65, Campbell, Aldrich Nulty, Architects, Boston, 1966-68, Knoll Internat., N.Y.C., 1968-70, Edward Durell Stone, Architect, N.Y.C., 1970-73, Harry, Oppenheimer & Ross Architects, Miami, Fla., 1973-75, Tenneco Inc., Houston, 1978-84; art and design cons. Interiors of Interest, L.A., 1986--. U. Sask. scholar, 1947. Mem. Am. Soc. Interior Designers, Inst. Bus. Designers, AAUW. Republican. Roman Catholic. Home and Office: 23428 W Magic Mountain Pkwy Valencia CA 91355

BRAUMAN, JOHN I., chemist, educator; b. Pitts., Sept. 7, 1937; s. Milton and Freda E. (Schlitt) B.; m. Sharon Lea Kruse, Aug. 22, 1964; 1 dau., Kate Andrea. B.S., Mass. Inst. Tech., 1959; Ph.D. (NSF fellow), U. Calif., Berkeley, 1963. NSF postdoctoral fellow U. Calif., Los Angeles, 1962-63; asst. prof. chemistry Stanford (Calif.) U., 1963-69, asso. prof., 1969-72, prof., 1972-80, J.G. Jackson-C.J. Wood prof. chemistry, 1980—, chmn. dept., 1979-83; cons. in phys. organic chemistry; adv. panel chemistry div. NSF, 1974-78; adv. panel NASA, AEC, ERDA, Research Corp., Office Chemistry and Chem. Tech., NRC. Mem. editorial adv. bd. Jour. Am. Chem. Soc, 1976-83, Jour. Organic Chemistry, 1974-78, Nouveau Jour. de Chimie, 1977-85, Chem. Revs, 1978-80, Chem. Physics Letters, 1982-85, Jour. Phys. Chemistry, 1985-87, Internat. Jour. Chem. Kinetics, 1987—; dep. editor for phys. scis. Science, 1985—. Fellow Alfred P. Sloan, 1968-70, Guggenheim, 1978-79; Christensen, Oxford U., 1983-84. Fellow AAAS; mem. Nat. Acad. Scis., Am. Acad. Arts Scis., Am. Chem. Soc. (award in pure chemistry 1973, Harrison Howe award 1976, James Flack Norris award 1986, Arthur C. Cope scholar award 1986, exec. com. phys. chemistry div.), Brit. Chem. Soc., Sigma Xi, Phi Lambda Upsilon. Home: 849 Tolman Dr Stanford CA 94305 Office: Stanford U Dept Chemistry Stanford CA 94305-5080

BRAUN, STEPHEN B., academic administrator; b. Cleve., Nov. 3, 1942; s. William B. and Louise M. (Baker) B.; m. Retta F. Kriefall, June 16, 1974; children: Elizabeth Rachel, Christopher Baker. BS, Xavier U., 1964; MBA, Fairleigh Dickinson U., 1976. Regional mgr. Northwest Airlines, Inc., St. Paul, Minn., 1967-72; v.p. Inflight Motion Pictures, Inc., N.Y.C., 1972-78; v.p., gen. mgr. Columbia Pipe & Supply, Inc., Portland, Oreg., 1978-79; exec. v.p. Golby Mfg. Co., Portland, 1979-80; v.p. fin. Timberline Systems, Inc., Portland, 1980-82; pres., founder Systems Supplyware, Inc., Portland, 1982-87; chmn., dir. The Bus. Mgmt. Programs Concordia Coll., Portland, 1987—; vice chmn., dir. CCNW Found., Portland, 1985—; bd. Regents, Concordia Coll., 1986-87; bd. dirs. Pacific Packaging Corp., 1986, Microlinear Systems, Inc., Hillsbro, Oreg., 1984-87, Almeda Resources Co., Tigard, Oreg., 1979—; lectr. in field.. Com. chmn., United Way, Boston, 1966. Served with USN, 1964-67. Mem. Oreg. Ctr. for Entrepreneurship (pres., founder, 1986), Am. Mktg. Assn. (panelist 1985-88), Assn. Data Processing Systems Orgn., Rotary. Republican. Lutheran. Office: Concordia Coll 2811 NE Holman St Portland OR 97211

BRAUN, STEPHEN HUGHES, psychologist; b. St. Louis, Nov. 20, 1942; s. William Lafon and Jane Louise B.; BA, Washington U., St. Louis, 1964, MA, 1965; PhD (USPHS fellow in Clin. Psychology), U. Mo., Columbia, 1970; m. Penny Lee Prada, Aug. 28, 1965; 1 son, Damian Hughes. Asst. prof. psychology Calif. State U., Chico, 1970-71; dir. social learning div. Ariz. State Hosp., Phoenix, 1971-74; chief bur. planning and evaluation Ariz. Dept. Health Svcs., Phoenix, 1974-79; pres. Braun and Assocs., human svc. program cons.'s, Scottsdale, Ariz., 1979—; also pvt. clin. practice; asst. prof. psychology Ariz. State U., 1971-79, vis. asst. prof. Ctr. of Criminal Justice, 1974-79, Ctr. for Pub. Affairs, 1979-81; cons. Law Enforcement Assistance Adminstrn., NIMH, Alcohol, Drug Abuse, and Mental Health Adminstrn., Ariz. Dept. Health Svcs., Ariz. Dept. Corrections, Ariz. Dept. Econ. Security, local and regional human svc. agys. NIMH rsch. grantee, 1971-74; State of Calif. rsch. grantee, 1971; cert. clin. psychologist, Ariz. Mem. Am. Psychol. Assn., Sigma Xi. Editorial cons.; contbr. articles to profl. publs. Office: 6122 E Calle Tuberia Scottsdale AZ 85251

BRAUNLICH, PETER FRITZ, physicist, college professor; b. Cretzschwitz, Fed. Republic Germany, Feb. 25, 1937; s. Richard Otto and Hildegard (Hilbert) B.; m. Elke Luise Rumpf, Oct. 4, 1963; children: Andreas, Kristina. Pre-diploma in physics, U. Marburg, Fed. Republic German, 1958; diploma in physics, U. Giessen, Fed. Republic German, 1961, Dr. rer. nat., 1963. Research assoc. Pa. State U., State College, 1965-66; from sr. physicist to sr. scientist Bendix Research Labs., Southfield, Mich., 1966-76; assoc. prof. physics Wash. State U., Pullman, 1977-79, prof. physics, 1979—; adj. prof. Wayne State U., Detroit, 1974-76; pres. Internat. Sensor Tech., Inc., Pullman, 1982—. Contbr. articles to profl. jours.; patentee in field; editor, co-author: Thermally Stimulated Relaxation in Solids, 1979. Research grants Nat. Sci. Found., Wash., 1981, Dept. Energy, Wash., 1984, Nat. Inst. Health, Wash., 1987, 88. Mem. Am. Physical Soc. Home: SW 730 City View St Pullman WA 99163 Office: Wash State Univ Dept Physics Pullman WA 99164-2814

BRAUNMULLER, A. R., English educator; b. Plainfield, N.J., Nov. 25, 1945; s. A.R. and Eleanor W. (Smart) B. BA, Stanford U., 1967; MPhil, Yale U., 1970, PhD, 1971. Asst. prof. dept. English UCLA, 1971-76, assoc. prof., 1976-82, prof. English and comparative lit., 1982—. Author: George Peele, 1983, A Seventeenth-Century Letter Book, 1983; editor: Shakespeare's King John, 1989; contbr. articles on Renaissance, modern lit. and drama to various publs. Fellow NDEA, 1967, NEH Folger Library, 1973, 88-89, Am. Coun. Learned Socs., Brit. Libr., 1985. Mem. Renaissance English Text Soc. (mem. coun. 1983—), Malone Soc., Renaissance Soc. Am., MLA. Office: Dept English UCLA 405 Hilgard Ave Los Angeles CA 90024-1530

BRAUNSTEIN, HERBERT, pathologist, educator; b. N.Y.C., Jan. 10, 1926; s. Max and Ida (Meyerson) B.; m. Frances Toomey, Aug. 1, 1954; children: Sheila, Mary, John, Anne. BS, CCNY and CUNY, 1944; MD, Hahnemann Med. Coll., 1950. Intern Montefiore Hosp., N.Y.C., 1950-51; resident in pathology U. Mich., Ann Arbor, 1951-52; resident in pathology U. Cin., 1952-55, from asst. prof. to assoc. prof. pathology, 1956-64; chmn. dept. pathology Michael Reese Hosp., Chgo.; also prof. pathology Chgo. Med. Sch., 1964-65; from assoc. prof. to prof. pathology U. Ky., Lexington, 1965-70; chmn. dept. labs. San Bernardino (Calif.) County Med. Ctr., 1970—, also dir. sch. med. tech.; clin. prof. pathology Loma Linda (Calif.) U., 1970—, UCLA, 1980-83; prof. in residence biomed. scis. U. Calif., Riverside, 1979-83. Mem. editorial bd. Modern Pathology; contbr. articles to sci. jours., chpts. to books. Served with USNR, 1944-46, PTO. Recipient numerous research grants, Career devel. award USPHS, 1958-64. Mem. AMA, Calif. Med. Assn., San Bernardino County Med. Soc., Am. Soc. Clin. Pathologists, Coll. Am. Pathologists, U.S.-Can. Acad. Pathology, Am. Assn. Pathologists, Histochem. Soc., Phi Beta Kappa, Sigma Xi, Alpha Omega Alpha. Republican. Home: 30524 Los Altos Dr Redlands CA 92373 Office: 780 E Gilbert St San Bernardino CA 92404

BRAUTBAR, NACHMAN, physician, educator; b. Haifa, Israel, Oct. 22, 1943; came to U.S., 1975; s. Pinhas and Sabine (Lohite) B.; m. Ronit Aboutboul, Mar. 25, 1968; children—Sigalit, Shirley, Jaques. M.D., Med. Sch. Jerusalem, 1968. Diplomate Am. Bd. Internal Medicine, Am. Bd. Nephrology. Intern, Rambam Hosp., Haifa, 1968-69; resident in internal medicine Hadassah Med. Center, Jerusalem, 1972-75; fellow in nephrology UCLA Med. Sch., 1975-77, asst. prof. medicine, 1977-78; asst. prof. medicine U. So. Calif., Los Angeles, 1978-80, assoc. prof. medicine, pharmacology and nutrition, 1980—, dir. Ctr. for Toxicology and Chem. Exposure; chmn. nephrology sect. Hollywood Presbyn. Med. Center, 1980—. Author: Cellular Bioenergetics, 1985. Contbr. numerous articles, papers to scientific publs. Chmn. research com., pub. relations com. Kidney Foundation Los Angeles, 1980—. Named Hon. Citizen, Los Angeles City Council, 1984; Grantee Am. Heart Assn., 1980—, NIH, 1983. Mem. Am. Soc. Nephrology, Am. Soc. Bone and Mineral Research, Am. Physiol. Soc., Am. Chem. Soc., Am. Soc. Parenteral Nutrition, Am. Coll. Nutrition, Israeli Soc. Nephrology (hon.). Office: U So Calif 2025 Zonal Ave Los Angeles CA 90023

BRAVENER, LEE CARIN, quality engineer; b. Tampa, Fla., Mar. 7, 1950; s. Robert LaVerne and Kathaleen Margaret (Carin) B.; m. Irwannah Jo Click, Mar. 15, 1980; children: Trevis Maran, Sean William, Tabatha Jo, Kelly Carin. AA, Allen Hancock Coll., 1974; BS, SUNY, Albany, 1981; MBA, West Coast U., 1989. Cert. quality auditor, quality engr. Supr. Dynalectron Corp., Norco, Calif., 1974-76; reliability analyst Dynalectron Corp., Corona, Calif., 1976-78; quality engr. Dynalectron Corp., Pueblo, Colo., 1978-80; sr. quality engr. Otis Elevator, Denver, 1980-81; quality auditor McDonnell Douglas, Riyadh, Saudi Arabia, 1981-84; sr. quality specialist McDonnell Douglas, Tiaf, Saudi Arabia, 1984-87; asst. project mgr. McDonnell Douglas, Long Beach, Calif., 1987-89; technical specialist, quality assurance McDonnell Douglas Space Sta. Div., Huntington Beach, Calif., 1989—. Mem. Point Roberts (Wash.) Voters Asn., 1988—, Homeowners Assn., Point Roberts, 1988—; pack leader Boy Scouts Am., Aurora Colo., 1980; Weblo leader, Riyadh, 1982. Served to sgt. USAF, 1970-74. Mem. Am. Soc. Quality Control (cert.), Am. Nat. Standards Com. (voting). Republican. Home: 1984 Johnson Rd Point Roberts WA 98281 Office: McDonnell Douglas Corp 5301 Bolsa Ave Huntington Beach CA 92647

BRAVERMAN, DONNA CARYN, fiber artist; b. Chgo., Apr. 4, 1947; d. Samuel and Pearl (Leen) B. Student, U. Mo., 1965-68; BFA in Interior Design, Chgo. Acad. Fine Arts, 1970. Interior designer Ascher Dental Supply-Healthco., Chgo., 1970-72, Clarence Krusinski & Assocs. Ltd., Chgo., 1972-74, Perkins & Will Architects, Chgo., 1974-77; fiber artist Fiber Co-op Fibrecations, Chgo., 1977, Scottsdale, Ariz., 1977—. Exhibited in group shows at Mus. Contemporary Crafts, N.Y.C., 1977, James Prendergast Library Art Gallery, Jamestown, N.Y., 1981, Grover M. Herman Fine Arts Ctr., Marietta, Ohio, 1982, Okla. Art Ctr., 1982, Middle Tenn. State U., Murfreesboro, 1982, Redding (Calif.) Mus., 1983, Tucson Mus. Art, 1984, 86, The Arts Ctr., Iowa City, 1985, The Wichita Nat., 1986; in traveling exhibitions Ariz. Archtl. Crafts, 1983, Clouds, Mountains, Fibers, 1983; represented in permanent collections Phillips Petroleum, Houston, Metro. Life, Tulsa, Directory Hotel, Tulsa, Keys Estate Ariz. Biltmore Estates, Phoenix, Sohio Petroleum, Dallas, Reichold Chem., White Plains, N.Y., Rolm Telecommunications, Colorado Springs, Mesirow & Co., Chgo., Exec. House Hotel, Chgo., Cambell Estate, Ariz.; contbr. articles to profl. jours. Home and Office: 7920 E Camelback Rd #511 Scottsdale AZ 85251

BRAWLEY, BILLY FRANK, oil company executive; b. Erick, Okla., Oct. 24, 1929; s. Samuel Franklin and Ida Mae (Moore) B.; m. Maxine M. Ellis, Nov. 25, 1949; children: Phyllis Lea Tidwell, William Wade. BS in Petroleum Engring., U. Okla., 1956. Sr. engr. Sunray DX Oil Co., Wichita, Kans., 1960-62; div. methods engr. Sunray DX Oil Co., Houston, 1962-64; dist. engr. Sunray DX Oil Co., Roswell, N.Mex., 1964-69; regional mgr. engring. Sun Exploration & Prodn. Co., Ventura, Calif., 1969-73; mgr. Calif. offshore Sun Exploration & Prodn. Co., Ventura, 1973-76; ops. mgr. Sun Exploration & Prodn. Co., Houston, 1976-80; dist. mgr. Sun Exploration & Prodn. Co., Valencia, Calif., 1980-84; gen. dist. mgr. Sun Exploration & Prodn. Co., Denver, 1984-88; exec. v.p. H&W Drilling Fluids Inc., Denver, 1988—. Chmn. Santa Clarita Valley United Way, Valencia, 1982; exec. com. Los Angeles United Way, Region 1, 1982, bd. dirs., 1982; bd. dirs. Boys & Girls Club Am., Valencia, 1983. Served as sgt. U.S. Army, 1950-52. Named Vol. of Yr., United Way, Valencia, 1984. Mem. Rocky Mountain Oil and Gas Assn. (bd. dirs. 1987—), Soc. Petroleum Engrs. (chpt. chmn. 1968-69), Am. Petroleum Inst., Internat. Assn. Drilling Contractors. Republican. Mem. Disciples of Christ Ch. Home: 3008 E Nichols Cir Littleton CO 80122 Office: H&W Drilling Fluids Inc 5524 S Prince St Littleton CO 80120

BRAY, ABSALOM FRANCIS, JR., lawyer; b. San Francisco, Nov. 24, 1918; s. Absalom Francis and Leila Elizabeth (Veale) B.; m. Lorraine Cerena Paule, June 25, 1949; children: Oliver, Brian, Margot. BA, Stanford U., 1940; JD, U. So. Calif., 1949. Bar: Calif. 1949, U.S. Supreme Ct. 1960. Sr. ptnr. Bray & Baldwin and successive firms to Bray, Breitwieser, Costanza & Bray, Martinez, Calif., 1949—, now pres.; founder, bd. dirs. John Muir Nat. Bank, Martinez. Chmn. Martinez Recreation Commn., 1949-54; chmn. nat. bd. dirs. Camp Fire Girls, 1959-61, 1969-71; pres. Contra Costa County (Calif.) Devel. Assn., 1959-60. Served tl lt. USNR, 1942-46. Mem. State Bar Calif. (chmn. adoption com. 1955-56), Martinez Hist. Soc. (pres. 1894), Navy League U.S. (pres. Contra Costa Council 1981-83), Martinez High Twelve Club (pres. 1987). Republican. Episcopalian. Lodges: Masons, Rotary (pres. Martinez chpt. 1970-71). Home: 600 Flora St Martinez CA 94553 Office: Ward & Ferry Sts Martinez CA 94553

BRAY, ALLEN ANTHONY, manufacturing executive; b. Milw., Apr. 30, 1949. BS, U. Wis.-Stout, 1971. Indsl. engr. Waukesha Mtr. Co., Wis., 1971-73; sr. process engr. Allis-Chalmers Corp., Milw., 1973-77; mgr. mfg. engring. Warner-Electric, Marengo, Ill., 1977-81; prodn. mgr. Energy Adaptive Grinding, Rockford, Ill., 1981-83; mgr. mfg. engring. Schlage Lock Co., Colorado Spgs., Colo., 1983--. Office: Schlage Lock Co 3899 Hancock Security CO 80911

BRAY, GEORGE AUGUST, physician, scientist, educator; b. Evanston, Ill., July 25, 1931; s. George A. and Mary H. B.; m. Martha, Aug. 8, 1959 (div. July 1981); children: George, Thomas, Susan, Nancy; m. Marilyn Rice, Jan. 1, 1983. BA summa cum laude, Brown U., 1953; MD magna cum laude, Harvard U., 1957. Diplomate Am. Bd. Internal Medicine; cert. Nat. Bd. Med. Examiners, Mass. Bd. Registration Medicine, Calif. Bd. Med. Examiners. Intern Johns Hopkins Hosp., Baltimore, Md., 1957-58; research assoc. NIH, Bethesda, Md., 1958-60; resident U. Rochester, N.Y., 1960-61; research assoc. Mill Hill Med. Research Ctr., London, 1961-62; asst. prof. Medicine Tufts U., Boston, 1964-69, assoc. prof., 1969-70; assoc. prof. UCLA, 1970-72, prof., 1972-81; prof. U. So. Calif., Los Angeles, 1981—, prof. medicine and physiology, 1983—, chief of Diabetes and Nutrition Los Angeles County USC Med. Ctr., 1983—; Alpha Omega Alpha vis. prof. U. Ill., 1981; cons. FDA, 1971, Can. Dept. of Health and Welfare, Ottawa, 1974, Nat. Inst. on Aging, 1982, Swedish Dept. of Health and Social Services, Stockholm, 1982, Nat. Diabetes Adv. Bd., Reston, Va., 1983, BBC, 1985, Wis. Regional Primate Ctr., 1983—; nutrition coordinator HEW office asst. sec., Washington, 1978-79. Author: Obese Patient, 1976; editor: Obesity in America, 1979, Obesity in Perspective, 1976, Treatment of Obesity, 1985, 89, profl. jours. Recipient Travel award Am. Thyroid Assn., 1970, Sam E. Roberts award Kans. Nutrition Soc., 1977; Wellcome Vis. Prof. award Mich. State U., 1978, U. Chgo., 1985, Alumni Day speaker Harvard Medical Sch., Boston, 1982, Osborne and Mendel award, AIN, 1988, E.V. McCollum award ASCN, 1989; grantee NIH, 1965-70, 1970-81, 1973-77, 1981-86, 1981-89, 1989-94. Weight Watchers Found., 1979-81, Kroc Found., 1980-81; fellow NSF, 1961-62, NIH, 1962-64. Fellow ACP (chmn.-elect council med. specialties 1987-88, bd. regents 1987—, chmn. 1988—), AAAS (council del. for med. scis. 1985-88); mem. Am. Soc. for Clin. Nutrition (councillor 1982-84, v.p. 1985-86, pres.-elect 1986-87, pres. 1987-88, McCollum award 1989), Assn. of Am. Physicians (hon.), The Endocrine Soc., Am. Diabetes Assn. (bd. dirs. So. Calif. 1984-87, 88—), Am. Fedn. for Clin. Research, Peripatetic Club (hon.), Am. Soc. Clin. Investigation (hon.), Am. Inst. of Nutrition (Osborne-Mendal award 1988), N.Am. Assn. for the Study of Obesity (pres. 1982-84, councillor 1984-88, pres.-elect 1988-89, editor Intern Jour. Obesity, 1974—), Nat. Inst. Arthritis Diabetes and Digestive and Kidney Diseases (adv. council 1985-89), Nat. Rsch. Counci (diet and health com. 1985-89), Phi Beta Kappa, Sigma Xi, Alpha Omega Alpha. Office: Sect Diabetes Nutrition 2025 Zonal Ave Los Angeles CA 90033

BRAY, MARILYN MCCLANAHAN, management consultant; b. Berne, Switzerland, Dec. 12, 1931; came to U.S., 1932; d. Carl O. and Lili (Gronna) Rice; m. William McClanahan, Dec. 28, 1955 (div. 1972); children: Timothy, Bradley, Clinton, Sally, William; m. George Bray, Dec. 31, 1982. BA, Brown U., 1953; MA, Calif. State U., Sacramento, 1974; MPH, Calif. State U., Northridge, 1978. Dir. High Blood Pressure Control, L.A., 1977-85; pres. Diet Way Products Inc., Van Nuys, Calif., 1980--; coordinator Good Samaritan, L.A., 1984--; cons. Valley Presbyterian Hosp., Van Nuys. Vol. L.A. Childrens Bur., Van Nuys, 1988--. Recipient Merit award UCLA Ctr. for Students' Programs, 1985, Field Tng. award Calif. State U., Northridge, 1981. Democrat. Congregational.

BRAY, MAUREEN ELIZABETH, clergywoman; b. Medford, Oreg., Nov. 23, 1946; d. Jouett Philip and Edith Pearl (Cape) Bray. B.A., Trinity Bible Inst., Jamestown, N.D., 1970; B.A., Northwest Coll., Kirkland, Wash., 1971. Ordained to ministry Assemblies of God, 1972; assoc. pastor Lake City Tabernacle, Seattle, 1970—, youth dir., 1972—, Christian edn. dir., 1972—, asst. dir., 1970—, trustee, 1970—. Mem. Alumni Assn. Northwest Coll., Alumni Assn. Trinity Bible Inst. Democrat. Home: 529 Taylor Pl NW Renton WA 98055 Office: Lake City Tabernacle 3001 NE 127th St Seattle WA 98125

BRAY, RONALD LAWRENCE, sales executive; b. New Haven, May 17, 1956; s. Lawrence William and Abby Christine (Willadsen) B.; m. Joanne Hanako. BA, U. Va., 1978; MA, Syracse U., N.Y., 1980. Direct mail coordinator G. Fox & Co., Hartford, Conn., 1980-81; advt. mgr. Coompumart Corp., Cambridge, Mass., 1981-82; asst. account exec. BBDO/West, Los Angeles, 1982-85; account supr. Smith-Hemmings-Gosten, El Monte, Calif., 1985-87; v.p., mktg. McClellan Corp. Internat., Woodland Hills, Calif., 1987-88; direct mktg. mgr. Ashton-Tate Corp., Torrance, Calif., 1988--. Mem. Direct Mktg. Club So. Calif. Los Angeles. Democratic. Home: 2045 Pullman Ave Simi Valley CA 93063 Office: Ashton Tate Corp 20101 Hamilton Ave Torrance CA 90502

BRAY, WILLIAM ALAN, life insurance agency executive; b. Chgo., Sept. 22, 1956; s. William Allen and Patricia Ann (Maxa) B.; m. Melodie Rae Klock, Sept. 26, 1983. BBA, U. Okla., 1980. Mud engr. N.L. Baroid, Oklahoma City, 1978-79; drilling engr. Neyrfor Turbodrilling, Elk City and L.A., 1979-81; supr. William T. Daniel Agy. of New Eng. Mut. Life, Oklahoma City, 1981-85; gen. agt. in tng. Mut. Trust Life Ins. Co., Oakbrook, Ill., 1985-86; gen. agt. William A. Bray & Assocs., San Diego and Huntington, Calif., 1986—; dir. Mut. Trust Life's Gen. Agts. and Mgrs. Assn., San Diego, 1987—. Contbr. articles profl. jours. Recipient scholarship, U. Okla., Norman, 1974-76. Mem. Nat. Assn. Life Underwriters, Gen. Agts. and Mgrs. Assn. (dir. 1987—), C. of C., Kiwanis (San Diego). Republican. Roman Catholic. Home: 11808 Via Hacienda Rancho San Diego CA 92019 Office: William A Bray and Assocs 2230 W Chapman Ste 109 Orange CA 92668

BRAZER, WYNONA MARIE, accountant; b. Seattle, Mar. 6, 1937; d. Perry Henry and Katherine Emma (Bjordal) Moler; m. Henry Brazer, Dec. 1, 1955 (div.); children—Ronald, Kenneth, Gregory, Jeffory, Samuel, Nancy. A.A., Olympic Community Coll., 1971. Gen. clk. GN and NP Laureland, Billings, Mont., 1955-63; office mgr. Denny's Music Co., Portland, Oreg., 1971-72; bookkeeper GAM Distbg. Co., Portland, 1972; Acme Signs Inc., Portland, 1972-73; acct. Old Spaghetti Factory Inc., Portland, 1973-74; close-down mgr., lead acct. Portland Met. Steering Com., 1973-78; asst. controller Harsh Investment Inc., Portland, 1979; acctg. mgr. United Cerebral Palsy Assn., Portland, 1980-83; acct. San Francisco Housing Authority, 1983—. Mem. Am. Bus. Women Assn., Nat. Assn. Female Execs., Nat. C. of C. for Women. Democrat. Roman Catholic. Home: 240 Dolores St Apt 236 San Francisco CA 94103

BRAZIER, ROBERT G., transportation executive. Student, Stanford U. With Airbone Aircraft Service Inc., 1953-63; v.p. ops. Pacific Air Freight Inc., 1963-68; sr. v.p. ops. Airbone Freight Corp., Seattle, 1968-73, exec. v.p., chief operating officer, 1973-78, pres., chief operating officer, dir., 1978—. Office: Airborne Freight Corp PO Box 662 Seattle WA 98111 *

BREAKER, RICHARD CARROLL, construction company executive; b. Cambridge, Nebr., Nov. 19, 1926; s. William C. and Clara (Ogorzolka) B.; m. Virginia C. Driscoll, Jan. 30, 1954; children: Kathryn, John, William, Michael. BS in Civil Engring., U. Colo., 1951. Registered profl. engr., Colo. Draftsman U.S. Geological Survey, Denver, 1946-47; engr. Colo. State Hwy. Dept., Denver, 1948-52; engr., estimator Peter Kiewit Sons Co., Denver, 1952-55; project mgr. Webb & Knapp Construction Corp., Denver, 1955-61; estimator Gerald H. Phipps Inc., Denver, 1961-64, chief estimator, 1964-67, v.p., 1967-84, pres., chief executive officer, 1984—; dir. Gerald H. Phipps, Inc., Denver, 1967—. With USAF, 1944-46. Mem. Am. Arbitration Assn., Associated Gen. Contractors of Colo. (sec. 1986-87, treas. 1987-88), Rolling Hills Country Club, Denver Athletic Club. Roman Catholic.

BREAKEY, LISA KATHERINE, speech pathologist; b. Los Angeles, Oct. 21, 1945; d. Melvin Harvey and Inez (Rey) Smith. BA in Speech Pathology and Audiology, U. Calif., Santa Barbara, 1967; MA in Speech Pathology, San Jose State U., 1975. Cert. community coll. spl. edn. tchr., Calif. Speech pathologist Manitoba (Can.) Rehab. Hosp., 1968-69; speech pathologist Kingston (Ont.) Health Unit, Can., 1969-70, dir. speech therapy, 1970-73; pvt. practice San Jose, Calif., 1975—; cons. Atari Inc., Sunnyvale, Calif., 1977-79, Evergreen Valley Community Coll., San Jose, 1977-80, Los Gatos (Calif.) Rehab. Hosp., 1977—, VA Med. Ctr., Livermore, Calif., 1979-83, Irwin Lehrhoff and Assocs., Beverly Hills, Calif., 1985-86; profl. staff priviledges Santa Teresa Hosp., San Jose, 1981—, Mission Oaks Hosp., San Jose, 1982—, Good Samaritan Hosp., San Jose, 1983—; presenter numerous seminars, workshops in adult communication disorders, 1979—; guest lectr. San Jose State U., 1975-88. Contbr. articles to profl. jours. Mem. Am. Speech Lang. and Hearing Assn. (legis. counselor 1986—, congl. action contact 1985, cert. appreciation 1983, 84), Calif. Speech Lang. Hearing Assn. (chmn. printing com. 1977, mem. conf. commn. 1982-84, task force on occupational therapy, 1983-84, hospitality com. 1984, legis. handbook com. 1985, state nominating com. 1986-88, editor newsletter 1985, dist. dir. elect 1988—, Outstanding Achievement award 1986), Calif. Speech Pathologists and Audiologists in Pvt. Practice (v.p. 1979-81, pres. 1983-85, chmn. speakers bur. 1981, 82, current trends workshop 1980, pvt. practice workship 1978-80, rev. course in preparation com. 1978-81, 83, 85-86, govt. affairs com. 1983—, nomination com. 1985—, cert. appreciation 1982), Santa Clara County Speech-Lang.-Hearing Assn. (bd. dirs. 1987—), Calif. Assn. Post Secondary Educators of Disabled, Profl. Group for Adult Communication Disorders (1st pres. 1977), Bay Area Group for Non-Oral, Bay Area Neurolinguistic Group, Bay Area Pvt. Practitioners Speech Pathology and Audiology (1st pres. 1977), Washington Sq. Soc.-San Jose State U., Phi Kappa Phi. Democrat. Roman Catholic. Office: 2444 Moorpark Ave Suite 300 San Jose CA 95128

BREAKFIELD, HEDY THERESIA, financial executive; b. Vienna, Austria, Apr. 21, 1939; came to U.S., 1956; d. Ernst J. and Herma (Kalser) Schubert; m. Joseph Walter Breakfield, Oct. 7, 1960 (dec. Oct. 1976); children: Ernest, Cynthia, Theresia Breakfield Johnston; m. Joseph Louis Pittfield, Oct. 31, 1987. Student, Balt. Jr. Coll., 1956-58, Temple U., 1958-60; BA in Bus. Adminstrn., Calif. State U., Fullerton, 1976. Acctg. mgr. Am. Hosp. Supply Co., Irving, Calif., 1971-80; asst. contr. Soule Steel Co., Carson, Calif., 1980-83; contr. Charlton Assocs. (acquired by Xidex Corp. 1976), Irvine, 1983-87, Data Tech. Corp. (name now QUME), Santa Clara, Calif., 1987-88; v.p. fin., chief fin. officer Sunward Techs., San Diego, 1988—. Treas. Mt. of Olives Luth. Ch., Mission Viejo, Calif., 1982-86, sec., 1987. Mem. Fin. Exec. Inst., Nat. Assn. Accts. Republican. Office: Sunward Techs 10070 Barnes Canyon Rd San Diego CA 92121

BREASHER, PHILIP M., telecommunications executive; b. Patterson, Calif., July 14, 1941; s. James Franklin and Roselyn (Anderson) B.; m. Tillie Avila, Dec. 26, 1964; children: Galen, Gregory, Gail. AA, BA, Modesto (Calif.) Jr. Coll., 1975. With Evans Telephone Co., Patterson, 1964-77, bus supr., 1978-81; sales mgr. Evans Telecommunications, Modesto, 1982-84; gen. mgr. Evans Telecommunications, Turlock, Calif., 1985—. Chmn. Evang. Covenant Ch., Patterson Recreational Commn., Patterson Planning Commn.; vice-mayor Patterson City Council; gen. chmn. Apricot Festival; bd. dirs. Turlock Econ. Devel. Com., Legis. Commn. Modesto C. of C. Served with USN, 1959-63. Mem. Modesto-Stan Trade Club (bd. dirs. 1986-88), No. Calif. Ofcl. Assn. (exec. bd. referee football team 1965-88), Sacramento Assn. Coll. Ofcls. (judge 1985-88). Republican. Lodge: Lions (3d v.p. 1987, 2d v.p. 1988). Home: 300 N 5th St Patterson CA 95363 Office: Evans Telecommunications 4918 Taylor Ct Turlock CA 95380

BRECHBILL, SUSAN REYNOLDS, lawyer, educator; b. Washington, Aug. 22, 1943; d. Irving and Isabell Doyle (Reynolds) Levine; B.A., Coll. William and Mary, 1965; J.D., Marshall-Wythe Sch. Law, 1968; m. Raymond A. Brechbill, June 29, 1973; children—Jennifer Rae, Heather Lea. Admitted to Va. bar, 1969, Fed. bar, 1970; atty. AEC, Berkeley, Calif., 1968-73, indsl. relations specialist AEC, Las Vegas, 1974-75; atty. ERDA, Oakland, Calif., 1976-77; atty. Dept. Energy, Oakland, 1977-78, dir. procurement div. San Francisco Ops. Office, 1978-85, asst. chief counsel, 1985—; mem. faculty U. Calif. Extension; speaker Nat. Contract Mgmt. Assn. Ann. Symposiums, 1980, 81, 83, 84; speaker on doing bus. with govt. Leader Girl

Scouts U.S.A., San Francisco area. Named Outstanding Young Woman Nev., 1974. Mem. Va. State Bar Assn., Fed. Bar Assn., Nat. Contract Mgmt. Assn. (pres. Golden Gate chpt. 1983-84, N.W. regional v.p. 1984-86), Nat. Assn. Female Execs. Republican. Contbr. articles to profl. jours. Home: 67 Scenic Dr Orinda CA 94563

BRECHT, GREG GLEN, agricultural company executive, farmer; b. Sterling, Colo., Apr. 23, 1952; s. Harold Glen and Gayle G. (Yount) B.; married, Aug. 25, 1973; children: Shawn, Megan. BS, Western State Coll., Gunnison, Colo., 1974. Ind. farmer Fleming, Colo., 1973—; acct. Fred Sneath, Sterling, 1974-87; owner N.E. Agrl. Svc., Sterling, 1987—. Mem. Nat. Soc. Pub. Accts. Democrat. Lutheran. Home: Rte 1 Sterling CO 80751 Office: NE Agrl Svc PO Box 1795 Sterling CO 80751

BRECK, ALLEN DU PONT, historian, educator; b. Denver, May 21, 1914; s. Chesney Yales and Isabelle Estelle (Lee) B.; m. Alice Rose Wolfe, Sept. 7, 1944 (dec. June 1973); 1 dau., Anne Rose Breck Peterson; m. Salome Ripley Hansen, Dec. 19, 1974. B.A., U. Denver, 1936, L.H.D. (hon.), 1973; M.A., U. Colo., 1939, Ph.D., 1950; D.Litt. (hon.), Regis Coll., 1974. Tchr. public schs. Denver, 1936-42; prof. history U. Denver, 1946-82, emeritus, 1982, univ. historian, 1982—; mem. commn. on coll. student Am. Council on Edn., 1958-61; mem. Colo. Commn. on Ednl. Standards, 1962-65; v.p. Colo. Commn. on Social Studies, 1964-68; regional program chmn. Danforth Found., 1960-63; mem. U. Denver Bd. Govs., 1987—; Danforth lectr., 1949-61. Author: A Centennial History of the Jews of Colorado, 1960, Johannis Wyclyf Tractatus de Trinitate, 1962, Episcopal Church in Colorado, 1860-1963, 1963, William Gray Evans, Western Business Executive, 1964, John Evans of Denver, 1971, Episcopal Church in Colorado, 1960-78, 1978, Johannis Wyclyf, Tractatus de Tempore, 1981, (with Salome J. Breck) The Episcopal Church in Colorado since 1963, 1989, From the Rockies to the World, A History of the University of Denver, 1864-89, 1989; editor: (with Wolfgang Yourgrau) Internat. Colloquium I: Physical Science, History, Philosophy, 1968, II: Biological Science, History, Natural Philosophy, 1971, III: Cosmology, History Theology, 1975, The West in America series, 1960—, Colorado Ethnic History series, 1977—; contbr. articles to profl. jours. With field arty. U.S. Army, 1942-46. Fellow Royal Hist. Soc. Gt. Britain; mem. Am. Hist. Assn., Medieval Acad. Am., Rocky Mountain Renaissance and Medieval Assn. (pres. 1968-76), Far Western Slavic Conv., Western Social Sci. Assn., Western History Assn., Phi Beta Kappa, Lambda Chi Alpha, Phi Alpha Theta, Omicron Delta Kappa. Republican. Episcopalian. Home: 2060 S Saint Paul St Denver CO 80210 Office: U Denver Dept History Denver CO 80208

BREDDAN, JOE, systems engineer; b. N.Y.C., Sept. 18, 1950; s. Hyman and Sylvia (Hauser) B. BA in Math. and Psychology, SUNY, Binghamton, 1972; MS in Ops. Research, U. Calif., Berkeley, 1975; PhD in Systems Engring., U. Ariz., 1978. Teaching and research assoc. Dept. Systems and Indsl. Engring. U. Ariz., Tucson, 1975-79; project engr. B.D.M. Services Co., Tucson, 1979-80; mem. tech. staff Bell Labs., Am. Bell, AT&T Info. Systems, Denver, 1980-86; staff mgr. AT&T, Denver, 1986—. Patentee in field. Regents scholar N.Y. State Bd. Regents, 1968. Home: 3455 Table Mesa Dr #158F Boulder CO 80303 Office: AT&T 11900 N Pecos St Denver CO 80234

BREDEMEIER, CHET LYNDON, corporate secretary-treasurer; b. Hermiston, Oreg., Nov. 15, 1955; s. Richard B. and Joyce R. (Hardt) B.; m. Cindy S. Brose, July 23, 1976; 1 child, Crista Lynne. BS in Math., Walla Walla Coll., 1978. Acct. DSU Peterbilt and GMC, Inc., Portland, Oreg., 1978-83; sec.-treas. Northside Ford Trk. Sales, Inc., Portland, 1983—; owner CCB & Assocs., Portland, 1978—. Mem. Nat. Assn. Credit Mgmt. Republican. Adventist. Home: 8417 SE Clatsop Ct Portland OR 97266 Office: Northside Ford Truck Sales 6221 NE Columbia Blvd Portland OR 97218

BREEDEN, KENNETH RAY, comptroller, military officer; b. Charleston, W.Va., Aug. 25, 1938; s. Earl Fry and Louise (Songer) B.; m. Virginia Florence Wilkes, Apr. 22, 1960; children: Kenra Ford, John, Susan Rapavi, Alex. BS, Cameron U., 1973; M. in Pub. Svc., We. Ky. U., 1978. Enlisted U.S. Army, 1958; platoon sgt. U.S. Army, Korea and Fed. Republic Germany; ret. U.S. Army, 1982, commd. 2d lt., 1966, advanced through grades to lt. col.; commdr. D Troop, 1st Calvalry Regiment, 11th Infantry Brigade, Am. div. U.S. Army, Vietnam; regimental advisor 116th Armored Calvalry Regiment U.S. Army, Boise, Idaho; dep. comtroller U.S. Army, Ft. Sill, Okla.; asst. inspector gen. U.S. Army, Ft. Knox, Ky.; instr. Armor Sch. U.S. Army, Ft. Knox; instr. Artillery Sch. U.S. Army, Ft. Sill; comptroller Cuban Refugee Resettlement Task Force U.S. Army, Ft. Chafee, Ark.; ops. officer 11th Armored Calvalry Regiment, 1st Squadron, 11th Armored Cavalry Regiment U.S. Army, Fulda, Fed. Republic Germany; ret. U.S. Army, 1987; chief resource mgmt. div. Tng. and Doctrine Commd. Analysis Commd., White Sands Missile Range, N.Mex., 1987—. Decorated Silver Star medal, Legion of Merit, Bronze Star medal with oak leaf cluster, Purple Heart with two oak leaf clusters, Joint Svc. Commendation medal, Army Commendation medal with two oak leaf clusters, Humanitarian Svc. medal, Vietnam Cross of Gallantry with palm. Mem. Shriners, Masons. Republican. Methodist. Home and Office: Bldg 504 Apt 33 White Sands Missile Range NM 88002

BREEN, JOHN, government official; b. Glasgow, Scotland, June 10, 1931; came to U.S., 1949; s. Edward E. and Elizebeth (Campbell) B.; m. Jane Breen, June 21, 1930 (dec. June 1974); children: Kevin, Ann Marie. BA in Econs., Calif. State U., Long Beach, 1960, BA in Bus., 1960. Investigator U.S. Dept. Labor, Wage-Hour Div., L.A., 1960-63, San Francisco, 1963-66; field office supr. U.S. Dept. Labor, Wage-Hour Div., Phoenix, 1966-70, area dir., 1970-88, dist. dir., 1988—. Cpl. U.S. Army, 1952-54. Recipient Office of Yr. award U.S. Dept. Labor, 1984, 86, 88, Excellence award Sunbelt Employers Assn., Phoenix, 1988. Mem. Field Labor Dirs. Assn. (v.p. 1970-76). Roman Catholic. Office: US Dept Labor Wage-Hour Div 3221 N 16th St Ste 301 Phoenix AZ 85106

BREEN, PETER A., human services consultant; b. San Francisco, Feb. 23, 1937; s. John Raymond and Aileen (Donohoe) B.; children: Katherine, Matthew. BS in English, U. Santa Clara, 1958; MSW, U. So. Calif., 1967. Lic. Clin. Social Worker. With social services program dept. Los Angeles County, 1963-72; asst. dir. Health and Human Services Marin County, San Rafael, Calif., 1972-79, county welfare dir., 1979-88; pres. Breen & Assocs., Human Svcs. Cons., San Rafael, 1988—. V.p. Marin Community Clinic, Fairfax, Calif., 1985—. Served with USAF, 1959-63. Recipient Braun Mental Health award Marin Mental Health Assn., 1988. Mem. Am. Pub. Welfare Assn. (pres. 1987-88). Democrat.

BREEN, WALTER HENRY, numismatic writer; b. San Antonio, Sept. 5, 1928; m. Marion Zimmer Bradley, Feb. 14, 1964; children: Patrick Russell Donald, Moira Evelyn Dorothy. AB, Johns Hopkins, 1952; MA, U. Calif., Berkeley, 1966. Researcher Wayte Raymond, Inc., N.Y.C, 1951-52; cataloguer New Netherlands Coin Co., Inc., N.Y.C, 1952-60, Lester Merkin, Inc., N.Y.C, 1968-72; mng. editor Twin Worlds Publs., N.Y.C, 1970-71; sr. v.p. research First Coinvestors, Inc., Albertson, N.Y., 1973-87; contbg. editor Guidebook of U.S. Coins, 1953—; cons. Smithsonian Inst., U.S. Secret Service, U.S. Treasury, 1961—; trustee New Eng. Jour. Numis. Author: A Coiner's Caviar: Walter Breen's Encyclopedia of U.S. and Colonial Proof Coins, 1722-1977, 1977, The Darkover Concordance: A Reader's Guide, 1979; (with Anthony Swiatek) Encyclopedia of U.S. Gold and Silver Commemorative Coins, 1981 (Book of Yr. award Numis. Lit. Guild 1982); (with Ron Gillio) California Pioneer Fractional Gold, 1983, Walter Breen's Encyclopedia of United States Half Cents, 1793-1857, 1984 (Book of Yr. award Numis. Lit. Guild, 1985), Walter Breen's Comprehensive Encyclopedia of United States Coins, 1988 (Book of Yr. award Numis. Lit. Guild, 1988, Friedberg Meml. award Profl. Numis. Guild, 1988); also articles, essays, monographs and revs. Recipient Silver Medal of Honor Roosevelt U., 1966, Order of the Laurel Soc. for Creative Anachronism, 1969. Mem. Am. Numis. Assn. (life, mem., Heath award 1952), Am. Numis. Soc., AAAS, Numis. Lit. Guild (Clemy award 1985). Democrat. Home: Box 245A Berkeley CA 94701

BREER, LAWRENCE LEE, writer, educator; b. Salina, Kans., Feb. 5, 1936; s. George Joseph Breer and Lila Iona (Armbruster) Fierro; m. Ardith Mary Grimmett, June 6, 1959 (div. Sept. 1975); children: Melinda, Cassandra, Laura, Michael; m. Carmen Eileen Fenn Barton, Sept. 18, 1977. BA in Journalism & English, Cen. Wash. U., 1980. Enlisted USAF, 1956, advanced through grades to sgt., ret., 1976; editor Selah (Wash.) Valley Optimist, 1980-81; corr. The Packer Newspaper, Shawnee Mission, Kans., 1982-86; freelance writer Cen. Wash. Agr. News, Yakima, 1981—; prof. English/journalism Heritage Coll., Toppenish, Wash., 1986-87. Editor: BMS Pub., 1988—; contbr. poetry various anthologies, 1978. Photographic contbr. Yakima (Wash.) River Greenway Assn., 1985-86. Democrat. Home and Office: 2911 Shelton Yakima WA 98902-4072

BREKHUS, ROBIN SUE, hotel manager; b. Minot, N.D., Aug. 28, 1960; d. Dave Vern and Joanne Joyce (Jellum) Webster; m. Henry Hartman, Dec. 9, 1988. Grad. high sch., Minot, N.D. Salesperson, asst. mgr. Kinney Shoe Corp., Minot, N.D., 1980-84; clubhouse mgr. Meml. Pk. Country Club, LaMoure, N.D., 1984-87; hotel mgr. Gadsden Hotel, Douglas, Ariz., 1987—; com. mem. Douglas Tourism Com., 1988-89. Home and Office: Gadsden Hotel 1046 G Ave Douglas AZ 85607

BREMER, DONALD DUANE, school administrator; b. Sioux City, Iowa, June 19, 1934; s. Donald Forbes and Irma Marjorie (Schaller) B.; m. Carol Louise Rankin, May 3, 1955; children—Douglas Duane, Robert Alan, Kevin Ray. B.A., Nebr. State U., 1958; M.A. sch. adminstr., Los Angeles State U., 1962; postgrad., U. Iowa, 1966, U. Calif., Riverside, 1967. Cert. tchr., Calif. Math. tchr. Chino Unified Sch. Dist., Calif., 1958-66; tchr. Chaffey Jr. Coll., Alta Loma, Calif., 1961-63; prin. summer sch., Chino Schs., 1966-67; vice prin. Ramona Jr. High Sch., Chino, 1967-77; prin. Boys Republic High Sch., Chino, 1978—, chmn. accreditation com., 1981-82. Com. chmn., asst. cubmaster Mt. Baldy council Boy Scouts Am., 1966-68. Grantee NSF, 1964. Served with U.S. Army, 1954-56. Mem. NEA, Calif. Tchrs. Assn., Assn. Calif. Sch. Adminstrs., Chino Adminstrs. Assn. (treas. 1971-73, pres. 1973-74, Am. Legion, Chino C. of C., Republican Senatorial Com. Club: Toastmasters. Lodges: Rotary Internat., Masons, Elks. Home: 12183 Dunlap Pl Chino CA 91710 Office: Boys Republic High Sch Chino CA 91709

BREMER, RONALD ALLAN, genealogist, editor; b. South Gate, Calif., May 2, 1937; s. Carl Leonard and Lena Evelyn (Jury) B.; m. Dorothy Louise Pinegar, May 12, 1958 (div.); Joan Ellen Brenner, Apr. 30, 1967 (div.); children—Ron, Trina, Rebecca, Serena, Lorrie, Jennie, Elizabeth, Hans, Adam, Rachel. Student Los Angeles Trade Tech., Cerritos Coll., Am. U., Brigham Young U. Research specialist Geneal. Soc., Salt Lake City, 1969-72; profl. lectr. on genealogy, Salt Lake City, 1973—; editor Genealogy Digest mag., Salt Lake City, 1983—, Roots Digest, 1984—; lectr. in field. Mem. German Harmony Choir. Mem. Fedn. Geneal. Socs. (founder), Wholistic Soc. (founder), Assn. Geneal. Editors (founder). Republican. Mormon. Author: World's Funniest Epitaphs, 1983; Compendium of Historical Sources, 1983. Office: PO Box 16422 Salt Lake City UT 84116

BREMNER, JAMES DOUGLAS, psychiatrist; b. Lynden, Wash., Aug. 9, 1932; s. George Adelbert and Marian Alica (Bay) B.; m. Linnea Marie Leonardson, June 4, 1966; children: Steven, Lynn, Anne, James Douglas. Student, U. Puget Sound, 1949-52; MD, U. Wash., 1956. Intern USPHS Hosp., N.Y.C., 1956-57; resident Menninger Sch. Psychiatry and Topeka VA Hosp., 1959-62; practice medicine specializing in psychiatry Olympia, Wash., 1962—; clin. assoc. prof. psychiatry U. Wash., 1968—; pharm. research Hoechst-Roussel Pharms., Hoffman-LaRoche Pharms., Eli Lilly and Co., Sandoz Pharms., Shering Plough, Beecham Labs., Glaxo Labs., Organon, Inc.; staff mem. St. Peter Hosp.; cons. Madigan Army Hosp. Chmn. bd. dirs. Thurston County Guidance Assn., 1965-66; bd. dirs. Wash. Capital Hist. Assn., 1963-64. Served with USPHS, 1956-59. Fellow Am. Psychiat. Assn. (pres. Tacoma chpt. 1968-69, pres. North Pacific br. 1972-73); mem. AMA, Wash. Med. Assn., Fellows Assn. Menninger Sch. Psychiatry (past pres.), Am. Acad. Psychiatry and Law (membership com.), Thurston-Mason Med. Soc. (pres. 1972), PSRO (mem. state bd.), Thurston County Med. Bur. (v.p. 1981—). Home: 3422 Country Club Dr NW Olympia WA 98502 Office: 1021 W 4th St Olympia WA 98502

BREMNER, STEVEN SCOTT, accountant; b. Chgo., July 16, 1950; s. James Vincent and Louise (Scott) B.; m. Kathleen Kucera, Sept. 3, 1977; children: David Paul, Alice Carol. BS in Forestry, U. Calif., Berkeley, 1973; MBA, U. Oreg., 1977. CPA, Wash. Forester J.E. Greig, Inc., Soquel, Calif., 1973-75; cons. Arthur Andersen & Co., Seattle, 1977-83; dir. fin. Marine Resources Co. Internat., Seattle, 1983—. Author: (monograph) Business Planning, 1983. Pres. Alzheimer's Disease and Related Disorders Assn.-Puget Sound, Seattle, 1986-87. Mem. AICPA, Wash. Soc. CPAs, Blue Ridge Club. Republican. Roman Catholic.

BREMS, DAVID PAUL, architect; b. Lehi, Utah, Aug. 10, 1950; s. D. Orlo and Geraldine (Hitchcock) B. B.S., U. Utah, 1973, M.Arch., 1975. Registered architect, Utah, Calif., Colo., Ariz., Wyo., N.Mex., Idaho, Mont. Draftsman, Environ. Assoc., Salt Lake City, 1971-73; draftsman/architect Environ. Design Group, Salt Lake City, 1973-76; architect Frank Fuller AIA, Salt Lake City, 1976-77; prin. Edwards & Daniels, Salt Lake City, 1978-83; pres. David Brems & Assocs., Salt Lake City, 1983-86; prin. Gillies, Stransky & Brems, Salt Lake City, 1986—; mem. urban design com. Assist, Inc., Salt Lake City, 1982—. Prin. works include solar twinhomes Utah Holiday, (Best Solar Design award), Sun Builder, Daily Jour., Brian Head Day Lodge, Easton Aluminum, Four Seasons Hotel, Gore Coll. Bus., CMF Tooele, Utah Regional Corrections Facility, St. Vincents De Paul Ctr., residences; mem. Leadership Utah. Mem. AIA (pres. Salt Lake chpt. 1983-84, pres. Utah Soc. 1987, chmn. Western Mountain Region conf., 1986, Honor awards 1983, 88, Merit awards 1983,85, 88, chmn. Western Mountain Region honor awards 1988. PCI award 1988. IFRAA award 1988). Home: 161 Young Oak Dr Salt Lake City UT 84108

BRENGLE, THOMAS ALAN, computer scientist; b. San Diego, Sept. 22, 1952; s. Alan Seymour and Nadeene Marie (Clark) B.; m. Anita Anne Jones, June 22, 1974; children: Adam Thomas, Evan John. BS in Physics, Harvey Mudd Coll., 1974; MS in Physics, So. Ill. U., 1976. Research asst. So. Ill. U., Edwardsville, 1975-76; physicist Lawrence Livermore (Calif.) Nat. Lab., 1976-77, computer scientist, 1977-79, group leader, 1979-86, mgr. user service ctr., 1983-86, assoc. div. leader, 1986—. Contbr. numerous articles to profl. jours. Mem. ARRAY (sec./treas. nat. chpt. 1982-83, v.p. 1983-84, pres. 1984-85). Home: 16312 W Diablo Ct Tracy CA 95376 Office: Lawrence Livermore Nat Lab PO Box 808 L-308 Livermore CA 94550

BRENKERT, DENNIS RICHARD, orthodontist; b. San Mateo, Calif., Dec. 26, 1945; s. George Elwyn and Barbara Lynn (Lininger) B.; m. Becky Ann Green, July 29, 1967; children: Kirsten Nicole, Jason Kristopher. BS, U. Colo., 1968; DDS, U. Mo., Kansas City, 1971, MS in Orthodontics, 1974. Speciality practice dentistry Fort Collins, Colo., 1978—; pres. Brenkert Devel. Corp., Fort Collins, 1986—. Served to maj. U.S. Army, 1974-78. Mem. ADA, Colo. Dental Assn., Larimer County Dental Assn., Am. Assn. Orthodontists, Am. Acad. and Bd. of Head, Facial and Neck Pain and Temporomandibular Joint Orthopaedics. Methodist. Lodge: Rotary. Office: 2001 S Shields Fort Collins CO 80526

BRENNAN, BARBARA JANE, rehabilitation center administrator; b. Oklahoma City, Mar. 22, 1936; d. Chanc T. and Mary E. (Parker) Roos; m. Donald H. Brennan, Sept. 13, 1958; children: Bridget, Brian, Joe (dec.), Kerry, Patrick. Student, U. Okla., 1954-58. Dir. pub. relations The Rehab. Ctr., Albuquerque, 1972-76, coord. community svcs., 1976-81; gen. mgr. RC Ink, Albuquerque, 1981-88; pres. Stride, Incorporated, Albuquerque, 1988—; bd. dirs. Presentation, Inc., Albuquerque. Ward chmn. Springfield (Va.) Dem. party, 1964; pres. Albuquerque High Sch. PTA, 1976-77; chmn. St. Patrick's Day Benefit Dinner, Albuquerque, 1981-83; pres. Little Bros. Good Shepherd Aux., Albuquerque, 1981-83. Democrat. Roman Catholic. Office: Stride Inc 607 4th St NW Albuquerque NM 87102

BRENNAN, CIARAN BRENDAN, accountant, independent oil producer, real estate developer; b. Dublin, Ireland, Jan. 28, 1944; s. Sean and Mary (Stone) B. BA with honors, Univ. Coll., Dublin, 1966; MBA, Harvard U., 1973; MS in Acctg., U. Houston, 1976. Lic. real estate broker, Calif. Auditor Coopers & Lybrand, London, 1967-70; sr. auditor Price Waterhouse & Co., Toronto, Ont., Can., 1970-71; project acctg. specialist Kerr-McGee Corp., Oklahoma City, 1976-80; contr. Cummings Oil Co., Oklahoma City, 1980-82; chief fin. officer Red Stone Energies, Ltd., 1982, Hibernia Oil Inc., 1980—; treas., chief fin. officer Leonoco, Inc., 1982-87, JKJ Supply Co., 1983-87, Saturn Investments Inc., 1983-87, JFL Co., 1984-87, Little Chief Drilling & Energy Inc., 1984-85; chief fin. officer St. Regis Resources Corp., Culver City, Calif., 1988; pres. Ciaran Brennan Corp., 1980, Rathgar Securities, Inc., 1989—; bd. dirs., cons. small oil cos.; adj. faculty Okla. City U., 1977-86; vis. faculty Cen. State U., 1977-86. Contbr. articles to profl. jours. Mem. Inst. Chartered Accts. England and Wales, Inst. Chartered Accts. Can., Inst. Chartered Accts. in Ireland, AICPA, Tex. Soc. CPAs, Okla. Soc. CPAs, Calif. Soc. CPAs. Republican. Roman Catholic.

BRENNAN, JERRY MICHAEL, economics educator, statistician, reseacher, clinical psychologist; b. Grosse Pointe, Mich., July 17, 1944; s. Walter X. and Aretta May (Gempler) B. Student Kalamazoo (Mich.) Coll., 1962-64, Pasadena (Calif.) City Coll., 1966-67; B.A., UCLA, 1969; M.A., U. Hawaii, 1973, Ph.D., 1978. Researcher, UCLA, 1968-69; researcher U. Hawaii, 1972, 74-78, cons., 1975, 77, 78, data analyst and statis. cons., 1979-80, lectr., 1976-80, asst. prof. econs., 1980—; pres. Sugar Mill Software, 1986—; cons. WHO; v.p. Forest Inst. Profl. Psychology. Light scholar, 1964-66. Mem. Am. Psychol. Assn., Soc. Multivariate Exptl. Psychology, Psychometric Soc., Western Psychol. Assn., AAUP, Hawaii Ednl. Research Assn. Contbr. psychol. articles to profl. jours. Address: U Hawaii 2424 Maile Way Porteus 247 Honolulu HI 96822

BRENNAN, JOHN PAUL, civil engineer, management consultant; b. N.Y.C., Sept. 19, 1938; s. John Edward and Ann Louise (Huss) B.; m. Janet Ann Wallace, Jan. 1, 1984; children: John Edward II, Karen, Patrick, Greta, Samantha, Kirsten. BCE, U. Calif., 1961; MBA in Mgmt., Calif. Luth. Coll., 1974; MBA in Mktg., U. Santa Clara, 1981. Registered profl. engr. Wash. Engr. Shell Oil Co., Ventura, Calif., 1961, Guy F. Atkinson Co., South San Francisco, 1965; naval officer Civil Engrs. Corp, Pacific Ocean, 1961-81; asst. prof. U.S. Naval Postgrad. Sch., Monterey, Calif., 1974-81; v.p. Arroyo Devel. Corp., Gilroy, Calif., 1981-85; pres. Brennan Assocs., Pacific Grove, 1985—; cons. Jan Bush Assocs., Ventura, 1986-87. Decorated Bronze Star. Mem. Sierra Club. Democrat. Office: Brennan Assocs Box 726 Pacific Grove CA 93950

BRENNAN, RICHARD ROBERT, JR., army officer; b. N.Y.C., Aug. 17, 1954; s. Richard Robert and Kathleen (Catto) B.; m. Carol Beth McClaskey, Nov. 13, 1956; children: Richard Robert III, Michelle Elizabeth. BS, Ariz. State U., 1979; MA in Internat. Rels., U. Calif.-L.A., 1989, postgrad., 1989—. Commd. U.S. Army, advanced through grades to capt.; platoon leader Co. C, 1st Bn., 327th Inf., Fort Campbell, Ky., 1980-81, exec. officer, 1981-82; personnel officer 1st Bn., 327th Inf., Fort Campbell, Ky., 1982-83; asst. personnel officer 7th Inf. Div., Fort Ord, Calif., 1983-84; co. comdr. Co. C, 3d Bn., 9th Inf. Regiment, Fort Ord, 1984-86; ops. officer 3d Bn., 9th Inf. Regiment, Fort Ord, 1986-87; asst. prof. internat. rels. U.S. Mil. Acad., West Point, N.Y., 1989—. Mem. Phi Kappa Phi. Republican. Baptist. Home: 18342 Jovan St Reseda CA 91335 Office: UCLA Dept Polit Sci Bunche Hall 405 Hilgard Ave Los Angeles CA 90024

BRENNAN, ROBERT EMMET, television writer; b. L.A., Apr. 19, 1957; s. Roger Edward and Helen Ruth (Taylor) B.; m. Melissa Ann Hayes, Mar. 15, 1987. Grad., Notre Dame High Sch., Sherman Oaks, Calif., 1975. Prodn. asst. Michael Fisher Prodns./Universal, Universal City, Calif., 1982; arbitrator Writers Guild of Am.-West, L.A., 1984—. Writer (Fantasy Island), Columbia Pictures Corp., L.A., 1979-81, (Matt Houston), Aaron Spelling Prodns., Hollywood, 1983-85, Pigelu Prodns., Ltd., Australia, 1986, (Mission Impossible) Paramount Pictures, L.A., 1988—, Lorimar TV Prodns., L.A. (Paradise), 1988—. Mem. World Affairs Council, L.A., 1987-89, 90. Mem. Writers Guild of Am.-West. Roman Catholic.

BRENNAN, SIDNEY MIJUL, real estate broker; b. San Pedro, Calif., Nov. 7, 1942; s. Philip Sidney Brennan and Emma (Widner) Bourque. Student, UCLA, 1960-62, U. Sao Paulo, Brazil, 1963-67. Real estate agent Angel Fire (N.Mex.) Corp., 1976-80, Sun Valle Realty, Angel Fire, 1980-82; real estate broker Polson-Mercer, Inc., Taos, N.Mex., 1983—. pres. Mountain Pines Homeowners Assn., Angel Fire, 1979-82, mng. agt., 1982—. Mem. Realtor's Assn. N.Mex. Home: Box 4584 Placitas Taos NM 87571 Office: Polson-Mercer Inc 627 Santa Fe Hwy Taos NM 87571

BRENNEMAN, JOHN, design and graphic arts marketing executive; b. Phoenix, June 22, 1945; s. Leroy John and Euta (Adams) B. BFA, Ariz. State U., 1968, MFA, 1971. Prin. John Brenneman Studios, Tempe, Ariz., 1972-78; mgr. Durst, U.S., Phoenix, 1978-79; pres. John Brenneman & Assocs., Tempe, 1979—; bd. dirs. GrafTek, Phoenix. Author: Documents, 1975. Served to sgt. U.S. Air N.G., 1968-73. Mem. Photo Mktg. Assn., Assn. Multi-Image, Assn. Profl. Color Labs., Soc. Motion Picture and TV Engrs. Republican. Episcopalian.

BRENNEMAN, MARY LOUISE, psychiatrist; b. Sewickley, Pa., Oct. 14, 1923; d. George Edward and Laura Marjory (Dryden) Black; m. Richard Henry Brenneman (div. 1971); children: Gayne Slay, James, Donna, Heidi. MD, U. Toronto, Ont., Can., 1947; MA in Pub. Health, U. Pitts., 1958; student, C.G. Jung Inst., 1975-78. Rotating intern Western Pa. Hosp., Pitts., 1947-48, resident I in pediatrics, 1948-49; resident II in pediatrics Children's Hosp., Pitts., 1949-50; pediatrician Pitts. Pub. Health Dept. and B.C.G. Vaccine Program, 1950-57, Kaiser Hosp., Hollywood, Calif., 1957-58, Santa Monica (Calif.) Hosp., 1961-62; resident I, 2, 3 in psychiatry Camarillo (Calif.) State Hosp., 1968-71, psychiatrist, 1968-73; day-care psychiatrist St. John's Hosp., Santa Monica, 1973-75; psychiatric cons. St. John of God Nursing Hosp., Los Angeles, 1975—; staff psychiat. Met. St. Hosp., Norwalk, 1987—; clin. instr. U. Pitts. Pediatrics, 1950-57, UCLA, 1957-68; cons. staff Rancho Los Amigos Hosp., 1963-65; founder Prolixin Clinic St. John's Hosp., 1974-75; sch. physician L.A. Bd. Edn., 1962-68; psychiatric dir. Penny Ln. Inst. for Teenage Emotionally Handicapped, Sepulveda, Calif., 1975-80. Mem. Am. Psychiatric Assn., So. Calif. Psychiatric Soc., L.A. Soc. for Adolescent Psychiatry, Am. Med. Women's Assn., L.A. County Med. Women's Assn., West Soc. for Scientific Study of Sex, YMCA, Sierra Club. Club: Sierra. Office: 10477 Santa Monica Blvd Westwood CA 90025

BRENT, PAUL LESLIE, educator; b. Douglass, Okla., July 3, 1916; s. Paul Leslie and Ruth (McKee) B.; m. Aledo Render, May 29, 1938; children: Carolyn J., Paul Richard; m. E. Ferne McCoy, Nov. 19, 1984. BS, Central State U., 1938; MEd, U. Okla., 1949, EdD, 1959. Tchr. math. and sci. public schs. Adair, Okla., 1938-40; prin. Alden Public Schs., Carnegie, Okla., 1940-43; supt. Alden Public Schs., 1950-58; tchr. public schs. Cooperton, Okla., 1946-47; prin. high sch., public schs. Washita, Okla., 1947-48; supt. 1948-50; asst. prof. Calif. State U., Long Beach, 1959-63, assoc. prof. edn., 1963-72, asst. to chmn. div. edn., 1961-67, prof. instructional media, 1972-86, coordinator graphics support sect. dept. mech. engring., 1981-86; mem. Baptist Edn. Study Task, 1966-67; trustee Calif. Bapt. Coll., 1969-74. Co-Author: Point, Line, Plane and Solid, 1984. Served with USNR, 1943-46. Mem. Calif. Faculty Assn. (pres. elect), NEA, Calif. Media and Library Educators Assn., Am. Assn. Sch. Adminstrs., Congress of Faculty Assns., Phi Delta Kappa, Kappa Delta Pi, Phi Kappa Phi, Phi Beta Delta. Democrat. Baptist. Home: 11112 Bos Pl Cerritos CA 90701 Office: 1250 Bellflower Blvd Long Beach CA 90840

BRES, PHILIP WAYNE, automotive executive; b. Beaumont, Tex., Mar. 6, 1950; s. Roland Defrance Bres and Edna Gene (Griffith) Rodemacher; m. Janet. BA, Lamar U., Beaumont, Tex., 1972; MBA, Stephen F. Austin State U., 1973. Distbn. mgr., bus. mgmt. mgr. Mazda Motors of Am., Houston, 1973-75; analyst, cons. C.H. McCormack and Assocs., Houston, 1975-76; assoc. Frank Gillman Pontiac/GMC/Honda, Houston, 1976-79, David Taylor Cadillac Co., Houston, 1979-80; pres. Braintrust Inc., Houston, 1980-83; sales mgr. Mossy Oldsmobile, Inc., Houston, 1983-84; gen. mgr. Mossy Nissan/Ford, Bellevue, Wash., 1984-86; dir. ops. Mossy Co., Encinitas, Calif., 1986—; seminar lectr. Rice U., Houston, 1980-83. Author: The Entrepreneurs Guide for Starting a Successful Business., 1982; contbr. (book) Business Planning for the Entrepreneur, 1983. Mem. Small Bus. Council Houston C. of C., U. Club, Phi. Eta Sigma, Phi. Republican. Home: 3141 Camino Del Arco Carlsbad CA 92009 Office: Mossy Co 2235 Encinitas Blvd #207 Encinitas CA 92024

BRESCIA, ANTHONY JOSEPH, federal agency administrator; b. Jersey City, Sept. 26, 1950; s. Anthony Joseph and Josephine (Russo) B.; m. Donna Mae Kremers, Apr. 5, 1974; children: Anthony Joseph, Brandon Michael. AA, Coll. of Sequoias, 1972; student, Calif. State U., Fresno, 1975-78; cert. in mgmt. devel., Ariz. State U., 1982. Supr. U.S. Postal Service, Hanford, Calif., 1973-78; sta. mgr. U.S. Postal Service, Bakersfield, Calif., 1978-80; mgr. stations and brs. U.S. Postal Service, Phoenix, 1980-83; dir. customer services U.S. Postal Service, Fresno, Calif., 1983-88, dir. city ops., 1988-89; mktg. and communications adminstr. U.S. Postal Service, Fresno, 1989—. Bd. dirs. Woodward Park Homeowner Assn., Fresno, 1985—. Served with USN, 1968-72. Mem. Fed. Exec. Assn., Am. Legion, U.S. Jaycees (external dir. 1975-76). Republican. Roman Catholic. Office: 205 Lake Vista Dr Mandeville LA 70448

BRESSLER, RICHARD MAIN, railroad executive; b. Wayne, Nebr., Oct. 8, 1930; s. John T. and Helen (Main) B.; m. Dianne G. Pearson, Apr. 17, 1981; children: Kristin M., Alan L. B.A., Dartmouth Coll., 1952. With Gen. Electric Co., 1952-68; v.p., treas. Am. Airlines Inc., 1968-72, sr. v.p., 1972-73; v.p. finance Atlantic Richfield Co., Los Angeles, 1973-75, sr. v.p. fin., 1975-77; pres. Arco Chem. Co., 1977-78, exec. v.p., 1978-80; pres., dir. Burlington No., Inc., St. Paul, 1980—, chief exec. officer, 1980-88; chmn. Burlington No., Inc., Seattle, 1982—; dir. Baker Internat., El Paso Co., Seafirst Corp., Honeywell Inc., Gen. Mills, Inc.; trustee Penn Mut. Life Ins. Co. Office: Burlington No Inc 999 3rd Ave Seattle WA 98104 *

BREUER, STEPHEN ERNEST, temple executive; b. Vienna, Austria, July 14, 1936; s. John Howard and Olga Marion (Haar) B.; came to U.S., 1938, naturalized, 1945; BA cum laude, UCLA, 1959, gen. secondary credential, 1960; m. Gail Fern Breitbart, Sept. 4, 1960 (div. 1986); children: Jared Noah, Rachel Elise; m. Nadine Bendit, Sept. 25, 1988. prin. Beverly Hills Schs., Los Angeles, 1960-62; dir. Wilshire Blvd. Temple Camps, Los Angeles, 1962-88; exec. dir. Wilshire Blvd. Temple, 1980—; dir. Edgar F. Magnin Religious Sch., Los Angeles, 1970-80. Instr. edn. Hebrew Union Coll., Los Angeles, 1965-76; field instr. San Francisco State U., 1970-80, Calif. State U., San Diego, Hebrew Union Coll., 1977-81. Vice pres. Los Angeles Youth Programs Inc., 1967-77; youth adviser Los Angeles County Comm. Human Relations, 1969-72. Bd. dirs. Community Relations Conf. So. Calif., 1965-85; regional bd. mem. Union Am. Hebrew Congregations, 1986-88; bd. dirs. Alzheimer's Disease and Related Disorders Assn., 1984—, v.p. L.A. County chpt., 1984-86, pres., 1986-88, nat. exec. com., 1987—, Calif. state coun. pres. 1987—, gov.'s adv. com. on Alzheimer's Disease, 1988—; mem. goals program City of Beverly Hills, Calif., 1985-86; bd. dirs. Echo Found., 1986-88, Wilshire Stakeholders, exec. com., treas. Wilshire Community Prayer Alliance, 1986-88; active United Way. Recipient Service awards Los Angeles YWCA, 1974, Los Angeles County Bd. Suprs., 1982, 87, Ventura County Bd. Suprs., 1982, 87, Weinberg Chai Achievement award Jewish Fed. Council Los Angeles, 1986. Mem. So. Calif. Camping Assn. (dir. 1964-82), Nat. Assn. Temple Adminstrs., Nat. Assn. Temple Educators (nat. bd. mem. 1987—), Los Angeles Assn. Jewish Edn. (dir.), Profl. Assn. Temple Adminstrs. (pres. 1985-88), Assn. Supervision and Curriculum Devel., Am. Mgmt. Assn., So. Calif. Conf. Jewish Communal Workers, Jewish Profl. Network, Amnesty Internat., Jewish Resident Camping Assn. (pres. 1976-82), UCLA Alumni Assn., Wilderness Soc., Center for Environ. Edn., Wildlife Fedn., Los Angeles Countyt Mus. Contemporary Art, People for the Am. Way, Assn. Reform Zionists Am., Union of Am. Hebrew Congregations (bd. dirs. Pacific SW region 1985-88). Office: Wilshire Blvd Temple 3663 Wilshire Blvd Los Angeles CA 90010

BREWER, DAVID AUGUSTINE, project manager, civil engineer; b. Portland, Oreg., Apr. 29, 1940; s. Myron L. and Ellen (Shade) B. BCE, Ga. Inst. Tech., 1964; MCE, Stanford U., 1976. Registered civil engr., Calif.; lic. gen. engring. contractor, Calif. Asst. project mgr., chief engr. McGuire & Hester, Oakland, Calif., 1971-74, 81-82; cons. D.A. Brewer, Santa Cruz, Calif., 1974-76; asst. project mgr. Huber Hunt & Nichols, Indpls., 1976-81; chief estimator Rosewall & Son, Watsonville, Calif., 1982-83; project mgr. Rudolph & Sletten, Foster City, Calif., 1983-88; sr. project mgr. Koll Constrn. Co., Pleasanton, Calif., 1988—; Instr. civil engring. Sacramento State U., 1977-80. Served to lt. USNR, 1963-68. Mem. Am. Arbitration Assn. (arbiter 1981—), Assn. Gen. Contractors (edn. com. 1976-77). Democrat. Roman Catholic. Home: 241 Bonita Rd Portola Valley CA 94025

BREWER, FRANCES HOLBROOK, English educator; b. Tacoma, July 26, 1931; d. Richard Clifford and Lucile (McMillan) Holbrook; m. Richard E. Ellingwood, Jr., Mar. 19, 1955 (div. 1983); children: Katherine, R. Holbrook, John Ross; m. John Wilmot Brewer II, Dec. 23, 1983. BA in English, U. Wash., 1954; MA in English, Eastern Wash. U., 1968. Prof. English Spokane Falls (Wash.) Community Coll., 1968—; dept. chmn. 1982—, staff developer, 1978-82; exchange tchr. Evergreen State Coll., Olympia, Wash., 1988. Bd. dirs., Friends of Wash. Commn. for Humanities, 1988; active in Wash. State HHist. Soc., Spokane, 1980—. Mem. Wash. Copmmunity Coll. Humanities Assn. (treas. 1983—), Nat. Council Tchrs. English, Am. Film Inst., AAUW, U. Wash. Alumni Assn., Spokane Club, Pi Lambda Theta, Chi Omega. Episcopalian. Home: S 5441 Quail Ridge Circle Spokane WA 99223 Office: Spokane Falls Community Coll W 3410 Ft Wright Dr Spokane WA 99204

BREWER, G(EORGE) WARNER, JR., steel fabrication company executive; b. Denver, Nov. 8, 1925; s. G. Warner and Elizabeth (Gibson) B.; m. Wanda Eastwood, July 9, 1950; children: Shelly Brewer Reese, Lind. Student, Colo. U., 1947-49; BS, U. Denver, 1950. Co-owner Arnold-Brewer Ford Motor Co., Estes Park, Colo., 1950-51; owner and pres. Brewer Steel Co., Greeley, Colo., 1951--. With U.S. Army, 1944-46. Decorated Bronze Star. Mem. Rotary (bd. dirs. Greeley Chpt. 1987--), Beta Theta Pi. Republican. Episcopalian. Office: Brewer Steel Co 527 6th Ave Greeley CO 80631

BREWER, JESSE ABRAHAM, III, dentist; b. Dallas, May 29, 1945; s. Jesse Abraham Jr. and Odessa (Amond) B.; m. Willette Files, Dec. 27, 1969 (div. 1971); m. Linda Monteiro, July 26, 1980; children: Justin Adam, Brandon Christopher. BA, UCLA, 1973; DDS, Howard U., 1981. Physician's asst. U. So. Calif. County Med. Ctr., L.A., 1970-73; engring. inspector Air Pollution Control Dist., L.A., 1973-77; pvt. practice Sierra Vista, Ariz., 1985--. With USN, 1966-70. Capt. U.S. Army, 1981-85. Decorated Silver Star, Purple Heart. Fellow Sierra Vista Exec. Assn.; mem. Optimist Club. Democrat. Roman Catholic. Home: 2046 Piccadilly Dr Sierra Vista AZ 85635 Office: 999 E Fry Blvd #108 Sierra Vista AZ 85635

BREWER, LEO, physical chemist, educator; b. St. Louis, June 13, 1919; s. Abraham and Hanna (Resnik) B.; m. Rose Strugo, Aug. 22, 1945; children: Beth A., Roger M., Gail L. BS, Calif. Inst. Tech., 1940; PhD, U. Calif., Berkeley, 1943. Mem. faculty U. Calif., Berkeley, 1946—; prof. phys. chemistry U. Calif., 1955—; research assoc. Lawrence Berkeley Lab. (formerly Radiation Lab.), 1943-61, head inorganic materials div., 1961-75, prin. investigator, 1961—, assoc. dir. lab., 1967-75; Huffman Meml. lectr. Calorimetry Conf., 1966; Coover lectr. Am. Chem. Soc., 1967; Robert W. Williams lectr. MIT, 1963; Henry Werner lectr. U. Kans., 1963; O.M. Smith lectr. Okla State U., 1964; G.N. Lewis lectr. U. Calif., 1964, faculty lectr., 1966; Corn Products lectr. Pa. State U., 1970; W.D. Harkins lectr. U. Chgo., 1974; Frontiers in Chem. Research lectr. Texas A & M U., 1981; research scholar lectr., Drew U., 1983; 10th Louis J. Bircher lectr., Vanderbilt U., 1985; Frontiers in chemistry lectr., Ariz. State U., 1989; mem. rev. com. reactor chem. div. Oak Ridge Nat. Lab.; research assoc. Manhattan Dist. U. Calif., Berkeley, 1943-45; sec. gas subcom. high temperature commn. Internat. Union Pure and Applied Chemistry, 1957-60; assoc. mem. commn. on thermodynamics and thermochemistry, 1973—; chmn. materials adv. bd. Com. Investigation Application Plasma Phenomena, 1959-60. Author: (with others) Thermodynamics, 1961; assoc. editor: Jour. Chem. Physics, 1959-63; mem. editorial adv. bd.: Jour. Physics and Chemistry Solids, Progress Inorganic Chemistry, Jour. Chem. Thermodynamics, 1968-77, Jour. High Temperature Sci., Leo Brewer Special Festschrift Volume, 1984, Jour. Solid State Chemistry, Jour. Chem. Engring. Data, 1977-83, Jour. Phys. Chemistry Reference Data, 1978-81, 89—; divisional editor high temperature sci and tech. div.: Jour. Electrochem. Soc., 1977-84. Fellow Great Western Dow, 1942, Guggenheim, 1950; recipient Ernest Orlando Lawrence Meml. award, 1961; Disting. Alumni award Calif. Inst. Tech., 1974. Mem. Nat. Acad. Scis. (exec. com. Office Critical Tables 1961-66, com. on Data Needs, 1975-78, com. on High Temperatures, 1975-85), AAUP, AAAS, Am. Acad. Arts and Scis., Am. Chem. Soc. (Leo H. Baekeland award 1953), Electrochem. Soc. (lectr. 1970, Palladium Medalist 1971, Linford award for disting. teaching 1988), Am. Plant Life Soc., ACLU, Cobletz Soc., Combustion Inst., Royal Soc. Chemistry, Fedn. Am. Scientist, Calif. Assn. Chemistry Tchrs., Internat. Plansee Soc. Powder Metallurgy, Am. Optical Soc., Materials Rsch. Soc., Metall. Soc. (William Hume-Rothery award 1983), Am. Phys. Soc., Am. Soc. for Metals Internat. council on Alloy Phase Diagrams, Calif. Acad. Sci., Calif. Native Plant Soc., Calif. Botanic Soc., Lawrence Hall of Sci., Nature Conservancy, Save Redwoods League, Sierra Club, Sigma Xi, Alpha Chi Sigma, Tau Beta Pi. Home: 15 Vista del Orinda Orinda CA 94563 Office: U Calif Dept Chemistry Berkeley CA 94720

BREWER, MARION ALYCE, lawyer; b. Brownfield, Tex., Dec. 28, 1949; d. Deral Henry and Marion Thomas (Magee) B. BA, Stanford U., 1972; JD, Georgetown U., 1980. Bar: Colo. 1982, U.S. Dist. Ct. Colo. 1982, D.C. 1983, 1982, U.S. Ct. Appeals (10th cir.), U.S. Tax Ct., 1984. Reporter, anchor woman Sta. KMGH-TV CBS, Denver, 1972-76; TV corr. Ind. TV News Assn., Washington, 1976-78; asst. dir. Law Sch. Admission Coun., Washington, 1978-79; asst. dean admissions law ctr. Georgetown U., Washington, 1979-80; law clk. to presiding justice U.S. Dist. Ct., Denver, 1981-83; assoc. Ireland, Stapleton, Pryor & Pascoe, Denver, 1983-87; gen. counsel Colo. Counties, Inc., Denver, 1987—; mem. coms. Women in Communications, Inc., Denver, 1972-76. Mem. fin. com. Schoettler for Treas., Denver, 1986; co-chmn. Lawyers for Wirth Com., Denver, 1986. Recipient Outstanding Svc. award United Vets. Coun. Colo., 1976, Outstanding Svc. award Optimists, Aurora, Colo., 1975. Mem. ABA, Denver Law Club (pres. 1988-89), Colo. Women's Bar Assn. (bd. dirs. 1984-86), Colo. Bar Assn. (bd. govs. 1985-87), Denver Bar Assn. (mem. coms. 1980—), Stanford Alumni Assn., Georgetown Law Alumni Assn. (inaugural nat. bd. dirs. and exec. com. 1986—), Denver Press Club, Rocky Mtn. Stanford Club (pres., chmn. bd. dirs. 1973-75, treas. 1983-88, v.p. 1988—), Nat. Press. Club. Episcopalian. Office: Colo Counties Inc 1177 Grant Denver CO 80202

BREWER, ROY EDWARD, lawyer; b. Atlanta, Dec. 22, 1949; s. Roy Mullin and Martha Joann (Still)) B.; m. Catherine Elizabeth Schindler, May 5, 1979. BA in Polit. Sci., U. Fla., 1971, MA in Polit. Sci., 1973; JD, U. Pacific, 1982. Bar: Calif., 1984, U.S. Dist. Ct. (ea. dist.) Calif. 1984. Regional planner North Cen. Fla. Regional Planning Council, Gainesville, Fla., 1975-78; dir. met. affairs Sacramento Met. C. of C., 1978-79; dir. land planning Raymond Vail and Assocs., Sacramento, 1979-84; pvt. practice Sacramento, 1984—. Bd. dirs. Sacramento Symphony, Am. Lung Assn., No. Calif. Rugby Football Union; chmn. Sacramento Ad-Hoc Charter Commn., 1988—, Healthcare, Sacramento, 1988—; pres. Am. River Natural History Assn., Sacramento, 1988—. Named one of Best and Brightest Sacramento Mag., 1985. Mem. Calif. State Bar Assn., AICP, Sacramento Rugby Club, (pres. 1985), Sacramento Met. C. of C. Office: 1700 Alhambra Blvd #150 Sacramento CA 95816

BREWSTER, RUDI MILTON, judge; b. Sioux Falls, S.D., May 18, 1932; s. Charles Edwin and Wilhemina Therese (Rud) B.; m. Gloria Jane Nanson, June 27, 1954; children: Scot Alan, Lauri Diane (Alan Lee), Julie Lynn Yahnke. AB in Pub. Affairs, Princeton U., 1954; JD, Stanford U., 1960. Bar: Calif. 1960. From assoc. to ptnr. Gray, Cary, Ames & Frye, San Diego, 1960-84; judge U.S. Dist. Ct. (so. dist.) Calif., San Diego, 1984—. Served to capt. USNR, 1954-82. Fellow Am. Coll. Trial Lawyers; mem. Am. Bd. Trial Advs., Internat. Assn. Ins. Counsel. Republican. Lutheran. Lodge: Rotary (pres. San Diego club 1980-81). Office: US Dist Ct 940 Front St San Diego CA 92189

BRICE, JANETTE RAE, savings and loan executive; b. Wheatland, Wyo., July 29, 1939; d. Ernie Bascum and Hattie Billie (Thomas) Creel; m. Thomas Brice, May 13, 1972. AA, San Luis Obispo Jr. Coll., 1959. Asst. sec., asst. v.p. Gt. Western Bank, San Luis Obispo, Calif., 1956-66; asst. treas. Gt. Western Bank, L.A., 1966-74; asst. treas., cons. Gt. Western Bank, Beverly Hills, Calif., 1974-87, asst. treas., cash mgr., 1987—. Bd. dirs. Yes on Malibu (Calif.), 1976; vol. Child Advocates Office, L.A., 1985—. Republican. Office: Gt Western Bank 8484 Wilshire Beverly Hills CA 90211

BRICKER, RUTH, national foundation administrator, real estate developer; b. Oak Park, Ill., Mar. 23, 1930; m. Neal S. Bricker; children: Daniel Baker, Cary, Dusty, Suzanne. MA in Urban Planning, postgrad. in pub. adminstrn. 1987—. Antioch U. Staff writer Artforum Mag., Los Angeles, 1966-69; western dir. Expts. in Art and Tech., Los Angeles, 1969-75; owner Empire Real Estate and Devel., Los Angeles, 1975-86; designer Trade-Off, a computer simulation for use in urban planning; developed programs in art and technology for Calif. State Coll.-Long Beach, U. So. Calif., UCLA; designer laser light wall Calif. Inst. Tech.; lectr. and cons. in field. Mem. Mayor's Housing Task Force, Los Angeles; bd. dirs. Redland Symphony, Wignall Art Mus.; councilor Loma Linda U. & Med. Sch. Internat. Inst. Kidney Diseases; mem. exec. com. Savings and Preserving Archtl. and Cultural Environ.; mem. Am. Found. for Pompidou Mus., Paris. Author: Getting Rich in Real Estate Partnerships, 1983; editor, contbg. author: Experiments in Art and Technology/Los Angeles jour., 1974-79.

BRICKNER, RALPH GREGG, physicist; b. Cin., Nov. 28, 1951; s. Ralph Harold and Heloise Janet (Fagedes) B. BS in Physics, U. Cin., 1974; MS in Physics, U. Conn., 1975, PhD in Physics, 1981. Mem. staff Los Alamos (N.Mex.) Nat. Lab., 1981—. Contbr. articles to profl. jours., mags. Sec., rescue dir., v.p., then pres. Los Alamos Mountaineers, Inc., 1981—; mem. Los Alamos Ski Patrol, 1985-86. Mem. Am. Phys. Soc., Sigma Pi Sigma. Home: 1914 San Ildefonso Rd Santa Fe NM 87501 Office: Los Alamos Nat Lab C-3 MS-B265 Los Alamos NM 87545

BRIDGE, JOE ANNE PITTMAN, psychologist; b. Kenly, N.C., Feb. 2, 1939; d. Jesse Carl and Piety Ophelia (Barns) Pittman; m. Ferdinand Leo Bridge, Mar. 21, 1975; children: Kenneth Dean Pergola, Kendall Rhea Pergola, Karl Garnett Pergola. BA, Va. Wesleyan Coll., 1972; MA, Norfolk State U., 1980; PhD, Calif. Coast U., 1989. Cert. tchr., Va.; cert. counselor-probation officer, Va. Probation officer State of Va., Norfolk, 1972-79; neuropsychology technician VA Hosp., Hampton, Va., 1979-82; guidance counselor U.S. Dept. Def., Ft. Belvoir, Va., 1982-85; armed forced vocat. aptitude battery test specialist U.S. Dept. Def., Albuquerque, 1985—. Mem. Am. Assn. for Counseling and Devel., N.Mex. Assn. for Counseling and Devel., N.Mex. Sch. Counselors Assn., Nat. Assn. for Secondary Prins., Am. Soc. for Tng. and Devel. Home: 13 Eagle Nest Dr NE Albuquerque NM 87122

BRIDGES, ROBERT MCSTEEN, mechanical engineer; b. Oakland, Calif., Apr. 17, 1914; s. Robert and Josephine (Hite) B.; BS cum laude in Mech. Engring., U. So. Calif., 1940; postgrad. UCLA; m. Edith Brownwood, Oct. 26, 1945; children: Ann, Lawrence, Robert. Engr. Nat. Supply Co., Torrance, Calif., 1940-41; design engr. landing gear and hydraulics Lockheed Aircraft Corp., Burbank, Calif., 1941-46; missile hydraulic controls design engr. Convair, San Diego, 1946-48; sr. staff engr. oceanic systems mech. design Bendix Corp., Sylmar, Calif., 1948—; adv. ocean engring. U.S. Congress. Com. chmn. Boy Scouts Am., 1961. Recipient award of Service Am. Inst. Aero. Engrs., 1965. Mem. Marine Tech. Soc. (charter; com. cables, connectors 1969), Tau Beta Pi. Republican. Patentee in field of undersea devices (53 internat., 14 U.S.), including deep ocean rubber band moor; inventor U.S. Navy sonobuoy rotochute; contbr. articles to profl. jours. and confs. Home: 10314 Vanalden Ave Northridge CA 91326 Office: Allied Bendix Aerospace Corp Oceanics Div 15825 Roxford St Sylmar CA 91342

BRIDGES, THOMAS WESTCOTT, electronics technician; b. Milw., Feb. 1, 1938; s. Charles Leroy and Mary Jane (Anderson) B.; children: Cynthia, Andrew, Rebecca, Abigail, Susannah, Tobias, Percival. AA, Riverside (Calif.) City Coll., 1960; BA, San Diego State U., 1962; MS in Edn., U. Utah, 1969. Cert. tchr., Utah, Calif. Tchr. Riverside Unified Sch. Dist., 1962-70, Uintah Sch. Dist., Vernal, Utah, 1970-77; electronic tech. Indsl. Communications, Vernal and Salt Lake City, 1977-79; sr. electronic tech. Ch. of Jesus Christ of Latter-day Saints, Salt Lake City, 1980—. Active earthquake relief Mormon Ch., Mexico City, 1985, San Salvador, El Salvador, 1986. Participated in acad. yr. inst. NSF, 1968-69. Mem. Nat. Assn. Radio and Telecommunication Engrs. (sr.). Republican. Home: 1054 S 400 E Salt Lake City UT 84111

BRIDGES, WILLIAM BRUCE, research electrical engineer, educator; b. Inglewood, Calif., Nov. 29, 1934; s. Newman K. and Doris L. (Brown) B.; m. Carol Ann French, Aug. 24, 1957 (div. 1986); children: Ann Marjorie, Bruce Kendall, Michael Alan; m. Linda Josephine McManus, Nov. 15, 1986. B.E.E., U. Calif. at Berkeley, 1956, M.E.E. (Gen. Electric Rice fellow), 1957, Ph.D. in Elec. Engring. (NSF fellow), 1962. Assoc. elec. engring. U. Calif., Berkeley, 1957-59, grad. research engr., 1959-61; mem. tech. staff Hughes Research Labs. div. Hughes Aircraft Co., Malibu, Calif., 1960-77; sr. scientist Hughes Research Labs. div. Hughes Aircraft Co., 1968-77, mgr. laser dept., 1969-70; prof. elec. engring. and applied physics Calif. Inst. Tech., Pasadena, 1977—, Carl F. Braun prof. engring., 1983—; exec. officer elec. engring. Calif. Inst. Tech., 1978-81; lectr. elec. engring. U. So. Calif., Los Angeles, 1962-64; Sherman Fairchild Disting. scholar Calif. Inst. Tech., 1974-75; chmn. Conf. on Laser Engring. and Applications, Washington, 1971. Author: (with C.K. Birdsall) Electron Dynamics of Diode Regions, 1966; contbr. articles on gas lasers, optical systems and microwave tube to profl. jours.; asso. editor: IEEE Jour. Quantum Electronics, 1977-82, Jour. Optical Soc. Am, 1978-83; inventor noble gas ion laser; patentee in field. Active Boy Scouts Am., 1968-82; bd. dirs. Ventura County Campfire Girls, 1973-76; mem. Air Force Sci. Adv. Bd., 1985-89. Recipient L.A. Hyland Patent award, 1969, Arthur L. Schawlow award Laser Inst. Am., 1986. Fellow IEEE (chmn. Los Angeles chpt. Quantum Electronics and Applications Soc. 1979-81, Quantum Electronics award 1988), Optical Soc. Am. (chmn. lasers and electro-optics tech. group 1974-75, objectives and policies com. 1981-86, 89—, bd. dirs. 1982-84, v.p. 1986, pres.-elect 1987, pres. 1988, past pres. 1989), Laser Inst. Am.; mem. Nat. Acad. Engring., Nat. Acad. Scis., Am. Radio Relay League, Phi Beta Kappa, Sigma Xi, Tau Beta Pi, Eta Kappa Nu (One of Outstanding Young Elec. Engrs. for 1966). Lutheran. Home: 413 W Walnut St Pasadena CA 91103 Office: Calif Inst Tech 128-95 Pasadena CA 91125

BRIDGFORTH, ROBERT MOORE, JR., aerospace engineer; b. Lexington, Miss., Oct. 21, 1918; s. Robert Moore and Theresa (Holder) B.; student Miss. State Coll., 1935-37; BS, Iowa State Coll., 1940; MS, MIT, 1948; postgrad. Harvard U., 1949; m. Florence Jarnberg, November 7, 1943; children: Robert Moore, Alice Theresa. Asst. engr. Standard Oil Co., of Ohio, 1940; teaching fellow M.I.T., 1940-41, instr. chemistry, 1941-43, research asst., 1943-44, mem. staff div. indsl. cooperation, 1944-47; asso. prof. physics and chemistry Emory and Henry Coll., 1949-51; rsch. engr. Boeing Airplane Co., Seattle, 1951-54, rsch. specialist 1954-55, sr. group engr., 1955-58, chief propulsion systems sect. Systems Mgmt. Office, 1958-59, chief propulsion rsch. unit, 1959-60; chmn. bd. Rocket Rsch. Corp. (name now Rockcor, Inc.), 1960-69, Explosives Corp. Am., 1966-69. Fellow AIAA (assoc.), Brit. Interplanetary Soc., Am. Inst. Chemists; mem. AAAS, Am. Astronautical Soc. (dir.), Am. Chem. Soc., Am. Rocket Soc. (pres. Pacific NW 1955), Am. Ordnance Assn., Am. Inst. Physics, Am. Assn. Physics Tchrs., Tissue Culture Assn., Soc. for Leukocyte Biology, N.Y. Acad. Scis., Combustion Inst., Sigma Xi. Home: 4325 87th Ave SE Mercer Island WA 98040

BRIDWELL, CHARMAINE CLAUDETTE, financial officer; b. Chula Vista, Calif., June 25, 1953; d. Charles Mike and Louise Julia (Flegal) Erreca; m. Dennis Wayne Bridwell, July 7, 1971 (div. 1976); 1 child, Joshua Wayne. Student, Southwestern Coll., Chula Vista, 1971. Bookkeeper Erreca's, Inc., Spring Valley, Calif., 1973-81, chief fin. officer, 1981—. Home: 1507 Sunrise Shadow Ct El Cajon CA 92019 Office: Erreca's Inc 8555 Paradise Valley Rd Spring Valley CA 92077

BRIDWELL, WILBURN FOWLER, food company executive; b. Atlanta, July 16, 1933; s. Floyd McRae and Marion (Fowler) B.; m. Naidyne Brown, June 21, 1958; children: Marion Mitchell, Laura Naidyne. BA, Vanderbilt U., 1955. Chemist Coca-Cola Co., Atlanta, 1955-59, Land O' Lakes Co., Mpls., 1956-61; food technologist Kroger Co., Cin., 1961-64; group leader Kraft Foods, Glenview, Ill., 1964-83; v.p. Hudson Industries, Troy, Ala., 1983-84; tech. dir. Rustco Products, Denver, 1984-86; prin. Bridwell Group, Denver, 1986—. Mem. Inst. Food Technologists, Am. Assn. Cereal Chemists (chmn. chem. levening 1984—). Baptist.

BRIEGER, STEPHEN GUSTAVE, management consultant; b. Marburg, Ger., Sept. 7, 1935; came to U.S., naturalized, 1945; s. Heinrich and Kate L. (Steitz) B.; B.Sc., Springfield (Mass.) Coll., 1955; M.S., Fla. State U., 1970, Ph.D., 1972; m. Karen L. Jentes, Nov. 27, 1968; children—Jennifer B., Benjamin A. Tchr., Calif. schs., 1954-69; indsl. cons. mgmt. tng., 1960-70; mgmt. cons. Nebr. Criminal Justice System, 1972; research criminologist Stanford Research Inst., 1972-74; evaluation cons. Office Gov. Calif., 1974-76; mgmt. devel. assoc. Am. Electronics Assn., 1976-80; mgr. employee and mgmt. devel. ISS Sperry Univac, Santa Clara, Calif., 1980-83; mgr. tng. recruiting and devel. Lawrence Livermore Nat. Lab., U. Calif., 1983—; mem. faculty U.S. Internat. U., St. Mary's Coll., U. San Francisco. Mem. Am. Soc. Tng. and Devel., Am. Mgmt. Assn., Am. Electronics Assn. Author studies, reports in field. Home: 1665 Fairorchard Ave San Jose CA 95125 Office: PO Box 5508 L-490 Livermore CA 94550

BRIER, CHARLES JAMES, finance company executive; b. Toledo, Jan. 31, 1937; s. Charles Ignatius and Thelma Generosa (Blaschko) B.; m. Ingeborg C.M. Ciesla, June 13, 1964; children: Karl R., Helene I., Dirk K. AB, UCLA, 1959; MS, U. So. Calif., 1971. Broker Quadrant (Weyerhaeuser), Federal Way, Wash., 1977-79; pres., chief exec. officer Beilex Corp., Renton, Wash., 1979—; trustee Green Hills Meml. Park, Kelso, Wash., 1980—; bd. dirs. Campbell Ranches, Wingate, Wash. Contbr. articles to profl. jours. Lt. U.S. Navy, 1959-62. Fellow Pakistan Project U. So. Calif., Los Angeles, 1963. Mem. Am. Bus. Cons., Continental Club, KC (Grand Knight 1985-86). Republican. Roman Catholic.

BRIERLEY, RICHARD GREER, business consultant; b. Kearney, N.J., July 1, 1915; s. Josiah Richards and Castella Sophia (Parker) B.; m. Margaret Jean LaLone, Aug. 24, 1940; children: Linda, Sandra, Martha, Ann. AB, Dartmouth Coll., 1936; MBA, Tuck Sch., 1937; AMP, Harvard U., 1952. Salesman Armstrong Cork Co., Lancaster, Pa., 1937-40; with Archer-Daniels-Midland Co., Mpls., 1940-64; exec. v.p. Arcaer-Daniels-Midland Co., Mpls., 1964-66, Drackett Co., Cin., 1961-66; pres., chief exec. officer Bristol Myers Can., Toronto, Ont., 1966-68; v.p. corp. planning Bristol Myers Co., N.Y.C., 1968-70; pres., chief exec. officer Stearns & Foster, Cin., 1970-75, chmn. bd. dirs., 1975-76; pres., chmn. bd. dirs. Brierley Assocs., Carefree, Ariz., 1976—; bd. dirs. Transcapital Fin. Corp., Cleve., Galleon Beach Club, Antiqua, W.I. Office: Brierley Assocs 34 Easy St PO Box 2659 Carefree AZ 85377

BRIERLY, KEPPEL, investment executive; b. Denver, Mar. 9, 1909; s. Justin Keppel and Pearl A. (Walters) B.; Engr. Mines, Colo. Sch. Mines, 1934; student, Denver U., 1936-37, U. Colo., 1939-41; m. Ruth E. Davis, Nov. 4, 1934; 1 child, Barbara Brierly Brann. Engr., Pub. Service Co. of Colo., Denver, 1930-38; coordinator, tchr. Denver pub. schs., 1938-41; pres. J & K Constrn. Co., Denver, 1945-68; investment exec.; v.p. Disputes Settlement Inc. Trustee, mayor pro tem Town of Bow Mar.; pres. Denver Lions Found., 1967-68; bd. dirs. Colo. Leukemia Soc. Served to lt. col. AUS, 1941-45; lt. col. Res. ret. Decorated Bronze Star Medal; also VI Haakon (Norway); award (France). Registered profl. engr., Colo.; real estate license, Colo. Mem. Denver Assn. Home Builders (pres. 1949, hon. life mem.), Asso. Bldg. Contractors Colo. (pres. 1956-57, Asso. Gen. Contractors Am. (dir. 1956-65), hon. life mem.), Am. Arbitration Assn., Theta Tau, Kappa Sigma, Blue Key. Presbyterian. Clubs: Denver Press (life), Denver Athletic (life), Pinehurst Country (life), Lions (pres. 1963-64), Masons, Shriners, Royal Order Jesters. Home: 5151 Juniper Rd Bow Mar Littleton CO 80123 Office: 601 Broadway Suite 206 Denver CO 80203

BRIGGS, ALBERT D., manufacturing engineer; b. Summit, N.J., Aug. 23, 1935; s. Albert D. and Anne Virginia (Lewis) B.; m. Andrea Malcolm, June 15, 1963; children: Marylin, Heather. BS in Mech. Engring., Pratt Inst., 1957; postgrad., U. Hartford, 1971, Union Coll., 1979-80, 1981-83. Owner, operator Briggs Movers, Springfield, N.J., 1955-64; mfg. engr. Pratt and Whitney Aircraft, East Hartford, Conn., 1964-73; start-up engr. Worthington Compressor, West Holyoke, Mass., 1973-74; cost engr. Worthington Pump, Harrison, N.J., 1974-80; mfg. supr. Fairchild Space and Electronics, Germantown, Md., 1980-82; mfg. estimator Williams Internat., Walled Lake, Mich., 1982-86; sr. cost engr. Garrett Engine Div., Phoenix, 1986—.

Contbr. articles to profl. jours. Pres. Rep. Cen. Com., Springfield, N.J., 1978-80. Sgt. USAR, 1958-63. Mem. Soc. Mfg. Engrs. (sr., chpt. chmn. 1986), Met. Phoenix Antique Auto Club (pres. 1989), Ariz. Auto Hobbyist Council (v.p. 1989), Horseless Carriage Club, Moose, Masons. Methodist. Home: 4230 E Western Star Phoenix AZ 85044 Office: Garrett Engine Div 111 S 34 St PO Box 5217 Phoenix AZ 85010

BRIGGS, DEAN WINFIELD, engineering consulting company executive; b. Boise, Idaho, Sept. 27, 1953; s. William Winfield and Shirley Anne (Churchill) B. BSCE, U. Idaho, 1975, MSCE, 1978. Registered profl. engr., Alaska, Ariz., Calif., Colo., Fla., Hawaii, Idaho, Nev., Oreg., Tex. Wash. Design engr. J-U-B Engrs. Inc., Boise, 1975-79, structural projects engr., 1980-83, mgr. structural dept., 1984-86; pres. Briggs Engring. Inc., Boise, 1986—. Mem. Boise City Bldg. Code Com., 1988—. Mem. Nat. Soc. Engrs., Constrn. Specifications Inst. (edn. chmn. 1988—), Prestressed Concrete Inst., Am. Concrete Inst., Structural Engrs. Assn. Idaho (bd. dirs. 1988—), Tau Beta Pi, Pi Delta Theta. Home: PO Box 6504 Boise ID 83707 Office: 4619 Emerald St Ste 2D Boise ID 83706

BRIGGS, DINUS MARSHALL, agriculturist; b. Stillwater, Okla., Mar. 5, 1940; s. Hilton Marshall and Lillian (Dinusson) B.; m. June Elaine Wolf, Sept. 2, 1962; children: Denise, Deborah. BS, S.D. State U., 1962; MS, Iowa State U., 1969, PhD, 1971. Asst. pastor Stroudsburg (Pa.) Meth. Ch., 1962-64; grad. asst. Iowa State U., Ames, 1964-66, research assoc., 1966-70; asst. prof. N.C. State U., Raleigh, 1970-75; asst. dir. Ark. Agrl. Expt. Sta., Fayetteville, 1976-82; assoc. dir. N.Mex. Agrl. Expt. Sta., Las Cruces, 1982—. Co-author: Modern Breeds of Livestock, 1980. Mem. Poultry Sci. Assn. (resolutions com. 1972-73), Am. Assn. Animal Sci., World's Poultry Sci., Sigma Xi. Lodge: Rotary. Home: 1927 Francine Ct Las Cruces NM 88005 Office: NMex Agrl Experiment Sta PO Box 3BF Las Cruces NM 88003

BRIGGS, LARRY RAY, management consultant; b. Olympia, Wash., Oct. 4, 1949; s. Vernon Ray and Evelyn Jane (Wick) B.; m. Janice Kay Kominski, June 23, 1973; children: Thomas, Lance. AAS, Centralia (Wash.) Coll., 1969; BA, U. Puget Sound, 1971. Mgr. Inst. Data, Agana, Guam, 1974-78; v.p. Timberline Software, Beaverton, Oreg., 1978-89; assoc. Werder & Assocs., Portland, Oreg., 1989—; mktg. mgr. Medallion Collection, 1983. With USNR, 1972-73. Office: Werder & Assocs 5440 SW Westgate Dr Ste 340 Portland OR 97221

BRIGGS, PETER STROMME, museum director, curator; b. Oak Park, Ill., Nov. 6, 1946; s. Robert M. and Alice (Neville) B. BA, No. Ill. U., 1972; MA, U. Ky., 1975; cert., U. de Bellas Artes, Tegucigalpa, Honduras, 1983; PhD, U. N.Mex., 1986. Curatorial asst. Maxwell Mus. of Anthropology, Albuquerque, 1975-76, asst. curator of collections, 1976-78; research fellow Orgn. of Am. States, Panama and Costa Rica, 1978-79; registrar art mus. U. N.Mex., Albuquerque, 1979-81, teaching assoc., 1981, curator of collections art mus., 1982-84; dir., chief curator Harrison Mus. of Art, Logan, Utah, 1984-89; chief curator Tucson Mus. Art, 1989—; adj. prof. Utah State U., Logan, 1987-89, U. Ariz., 1989—. Author: (exhbn. catalog) 4x4: Sixteen Contemporary Printmakers, 1987; editor (book) The Maya Image in the Western World, 1986; contbr. articles to profl. jours. Research grantee Tinker Found., 1980; Bainbridge Bunting fellow U. N.Mex., 1980-81, Nat. Endowment for the Arts, 1983. Mem. Internat. Council of Mus., Soc. for Am. Archaeology, Am. Mus. Assn., Coll. Art Assn., Utah Mus. Assn. Office: Tucson Mus Art 140 N Main Tucson AZ 85701

BRIGGS, WILLIAM MORSE, ski instructor; b. Augusta, Maine, Dec. 21, 1931; s. Henry Adie and Mary (Morse) B.; m. Julie Griffin, Nov. 25, 1963 (div. July 1968); m. Sabra Jean Palmer, Sept. 7, 1969 (div. Dec. 1979); 1 child, Berg Shanessa. Student, Dartmouth Coll., 1951-53. Ski instr. Cannon Mountain Ski Area, Franconia, N.H., 1955-56; dir. ski sch. Sugarloaf Mountain Ski Area, Kingfield, Maine, 1957; prin., dir. Suicide Six Ski Sch., Woodstock, Vt., 1958-60; ski instr. Sugar Bowl Ski Area, Norden, Calif., 1961-65, Jackson Hole Ski Area, Teton Village, Wyo., 1966; prin., dir. Snow King Ski Sch., Jackson, Wyo., 1967—; Exum mountain guide Sch. Am. Mountaineering, Moose, Wyo., 1958-80; founder Great Am. Ski Sch., Jackson, 1971—; ski area mgr. Snow King Mountain, Jackson, 1981. Author/pub. The Skier's Manual I & II, 1976, 79, The Ski Dictionary, 1978; editor/pub. Crud and Corruption, 1961; contbr. articles to profl. jours. Originator Teton Tea Party, Grand Teton Nat. Park, 1958; co-originator Climber's Campground, 1959, Episcople Horizons Folk Festival, Jackson, 1966-69; co-founder Stagecoach Band, 1969—, Jackson Hole Alliance Hoe Down, 1983—. Mem. Profl. Ski Instrs. Am. (founding), Internat. Assn. Scientologists (founding), Flag Artists Assn. (founding), Am. Mountain Guide Assn. (chmn. 1974-75). Mem. Profl. Ski Instrs. Am. (founding), Internat. Assn. Scientologists (founding), Am. Mountain Guide Assn. (chmn. 1974-75). Republican. Mem. Ch. Scientology (founding). Clubs: Dartmouth Mountaineering (Bugaboos, B.C., Can.) (explorer/surveyor 1951-54); Alpine Skiing (Jackson Hole) (founder/ expedition leader 1955-61); Am. Alpine (N.Y.C.) (guide cert. 1974-75). Home: 295 E Snow King Ave Mail Box 427 Jackson WY 83001 Office: Great Am Ski Sch 350 E Snow King Box SKI Jackson WY 83001

BRIGGS, WINSLOW RUSSELL, plant biologist, educator; b. St. Paul, Apr. 29, 1928; s. John DeQuedville and Marjorie (Winslow) B.; m. Ann Morrill, June 30, 1955; children: Caroline, Lucia, Marion. B.A., Harvard U., 1951, M.A., 1952, Ph.D., 1956. Instr. biol. scis. Stanford (Calif.) U., 1955-57, asst. prof., 1957-62, asso. prof., 1962-66, prof., 1966-67; prof. biology Harvard U., 1967-73; dir. dept. plant biology Carnegie Instn. of Washington, Stanford, 1973—. Author: (with others) Life on Earth, 1973; Asso. editor: (with others) Annual Review of Plant Physiology, 1961-72; editor (with others), 1972—; Contbr. (with others) articles on plant growth and devel. and photobiology to profl. jours. Recipient Alexander von Humboldt U.S. sr. scientist award, 1984-85; John Simon Guggenheim fellow, 1973-74, Deutsche Akademie der Naturforscher Leopoldina, 1986. Fellow AAAS; mem. Am. Soc. Plant Physiologists (pres. 1975-76), Calif. Bot. Soc. (pres. 1976-77), Nat. Acad. Scis., Am. Acad. Arts and Scis., Am. Inst. Biol. Scis. (pres. 1980-81), Am. Soc. Photbiology, Bot. Soc. Am., Nature Conservancy, Deutsche Akademie der Naturforscher Leopoldina, Sigma Xi. Home: 480 Hale St Palo Alto CA 94301 Office: Carnegie Inst Washington Dept Plant Biology 290 Panama St Stanford CA 94305

BRIGHAM, BRUCE JAMES, interior designer; b. Sona Bata, Belgian Congo, Feb. 4, 1951; came to U.S., 1951; s. Georges and Martha (Mason) B.; m. Jan Elizabeth Ambrose, Oct. 11, 1986. Student, Northwestern U., 1968; BA, Williams Coll., 1973. Owner The Brig Co., Seattle, 1976-86; interior designer Forma, Seattle, 1986-87; interior designer, project mgr. The Callison Partnership, Seattle, 1987—. Mem. Am. Soc. Interior Designers (legis. com. 1988), Inst. Store Planners (Seattle), Nat. Council Interior Design Qualification (cert.). Democrat. Episcopalian. Home: 3521 S Leschi Pl #1 Seattle WA 98144 Office: The Callison Partnership 1423 3d Ave Seattle WA 98101

BRIGHAM, JOHN ALLEN, JR., financial executive; b. San Francisco, June 17, 1942; s. John Allen, Sr. and Susan (Endberg) B.; m. Patricia Katherine Carney, Feb. 4, 1968; 1 child, Jennifer. BS in Acctg., San Jose State U., 1967. Acct. Shell Oil Co. Data Ctr., Palo Alto, Calif., 1963-66; asst. plant controller Brown Co., Santa Clara, Calif., 1966-68; budget mgr. Varian Assocs., Palo Alto, 1968-80; cost acctg. mgr. Adac Labs., San Jose, Calif., 1980-86; controller Crystal Tech., Palo Alto, 1986—. Del. League Calif. Cities, 1974-78; mem. Saratoga (Calif.) City Council, 1974-78; vice-chmn. Santa Clara County Polity Planning Use Commn., 1975-78; chmn. Santa Clara Com. on Mass Transit, 1976-78. Mem. Am. Entomol. Soc., Archeol. Inst. Am., Nat. Acctg. Assn., Sierra Club (treas. Loma chpt. 1985—), Delta Sigma Phi. Republican. Roman Catholic. Home: 18591 Perego Way Saratoga CA 95070 Office: Crystal Tech Inc 1060 E Meadow Circle Palo Alto CA 94303

BRIGHT, DONALD BOLTON, environmental consultant; b. Ventura, Calif., Nov. 28, 1930; s. Claude Wilson and Ruby Thelma (Bolton) B.; m. Patricia Jean McLaughlin, Nov. 25, 1955; children: Debra Ann, Steven Allan. BA in Zoology, U. So. Calif., 1952, MS in Biology, 1957, PhD in Biology, 1967; postdoctoral studies, Ariz. State U., 1974. Instr. Fullerton (Calif.) Coll., 1960-67; prof., chmn. dept. biol. scis. Calif. State U., Fullerton, 1967-77; dir. commerce Port of Long Beach, Calif., 1977-78, dir. environ. affairs, 1975-78; exec. v.p. EFS, Inc., Los Angeles, 1978-79; pres. Bright & Assocs., Anaheim, Calif., 1979—; chief exec. officer Environ. Audit Inc., Placentia, Calif., 1987—; Mem. Marine Sci. Coast Guard Adv. Com., Washington, 1977-80. Editor: Proc. National Magazine Science Edmc., 1970, Proc. Southern California Coastal Zone Supervisor, 1972; sci. advisor Am. Scientist mag., 1975-77; contbr. articles to profl. jours. Chmn. Calif. Regulatory Coastal Commn., Long Beach, 1973-75. Served to 1st lt. U.S. Army, 1952-55. Grantee NSF, 1969-75. Mem. Am. Inst. Planners, So. Calif. Acad. Sci. (v.p. 1975-78, fellow 1975), Western Soc. Naturalists, Sierra Club, Sigma Xi, Phi Sigma. Democrat. Presbyterian. Home: 921 Finnell Way Placentia CA 92670 Office: Bright & Assocs 1200 N Jefferson Ste B Anaheim CA 92807

BRIGHTMAN, MICHAEL JOHN, architect; b. Richland, Wash., Nov. 26, 1947; s. Howard Leston and Gladys (Rains) R.; m. Bette J. Bailey, Apr. 8, 1972; children: Matthew, Mark. BArch, Wash. State U., 1971. Registered architect, Calif., Wash. Archtl. group mgr. SCM Cons., Kennewick, Wash., 1988; planning commr. SCM Cons., Kennewick, 1988--. Mem. AIA. Republican. Home: 1800 S Ione Kennewick WA 99337 Office: SCM Cons 7601 W Clearwater Kennewick WA 99336

BRILHART, ARNOLD ROSS, product designer; b. Southington, Conn., Sept. 30, 1904; s. Charles Wesley Brilhart and Grace Belle Puffer; m. Verlye Mills Davis, July 10, 1933 (div. 1968); children: Robert, Arnold, William; m. Virginia E. Lowe, June 18, 1969. Grad. high sch., Yonkers, N.Y., 1921. Owner, pres. Arnold Brilhart Ltd., Great Neck, N.Y., 1940-50; pres. Brilhart Plastics Corp., Mineola, N.Y., 1950-54, Brilhart Mus. Instruments Corp., Carlsbad, Calif., 1954-66, Fibercane Corp., Carlsbad, Calif., 1954-66, U.S. Fiberwood Corp., Carlsbad, Calif., 1966-75, ARB Mus. Instruments Corp., Reseda, Calif., 1978-82; engr., research Roy J. Maier Corp., Sun Valley, Calif., 1982—. Musician to numerous performers including Bing Crosby, Bob Hope, Benny Goodman, also coast to coast radio shows, recordings and movies, N.Y.C., 1921-1940; patentee in field. Mem. Carlsbad Water Bd., 1954-60. Mem. Am. Fedn. Musicians (hon.), Musicians Union Local 47 (hon.). Republican. Lodges: Shriners, Rotary. Home: PO Box 366 Reseda CA 91335 Office: Roy J Maier Corp 8484 San Fernando Rd Sun Valley CA 91352

BRILL, JOEL VICTOR, gastroenterologist; b. Phila., Jan. 28, 1956; s. Earl Burton and Lois Elaine (Werner) B.; m. Laurie Ann Lissner, May 17, 1980. BA, UCLA, 1976; MD, Chgo. Med. Sch., 1976. Diplomate Am. Bd. Internal Medicine, Gastroenterology. Intern Sepulveda (Calif.) VA Hosp., 1980-81, resident internal medicine, 1981-83; fellow gastroenterology U. So. Calif. Med. Ctr., Los Angeles, 1983-85; pvt. practice gastroenterology Covington, Menz, Brill, Ventura, Calif., 1985—; instr. in field. Fellow Am. Coll Gastroenterology; mem. Am. Gastroent. Assn., Am. Soc. Gastrointestinal Endoscopy, Am. Coll. Physicians. Democrat. Jewish. Office: Covington Menz & Brill 2755 Loma Vista Rd Ventura CA 93003

BRILL, ROBERT WILKENS, electrical engineer; b. San Francisco, Dec. 30, 1930; s. Ralph Wilkens Brill and Vera Ann Sax; m. Marilyn Sheila Plant, Sept. 2, 1961; 1 child, Gerri Roanne. BA, U. Calif.-Berkeley, 1954, BSEE, 1958. Sr. engr. The Boeing Co., Seattle, 1958-70; devel. engr. Western Electric Co., Naperville, Ill., 1970-73; project mgr. Gen. Electric Co., San Jose, Calif., 1973-84; engring. mgr. electronic systems FMC Corp., San Jose, 1984—. Pres. Heatherwood Elem. Sch., Boulder, Colo., 1972; bd. dirs. Shadowbrook II Homeowners' Assn., San Jose, 1988—. With USAF, 1951-55. Mem. IEEE, U. Calif. Engrs., U. Calif. Alumni Assn. Jewish. Home: 951 Woodthrush Ct San Jose CA 95120 Office: FMC Corp 881 Martin Ave Box 58123 Santa Clara CA 95050

BRIMHALL, JOHN CLARK, editor, composer, arranger; b. Huntington Park, Calif., Nov. 22, 1928; s. John Clark and Nora Louise (Baffa) B.; m. Virgin Mae Ravain, Apr. 1, 1951; children—James, Mary, Anthony. Mus.B. cum laude, Loyola U., 1950; M.A., Calif. State U.-San Francisco, 1952. Tchr., Corcoran (Calif.) High Sch., 1953-55; supr. music Corcoran Union Sch. Dists., 1955-56; instr. Porterville (Calif.) Coll., 1956-59, Orange Coast Coll., Costa Mesa, Calif., 1959-61; chief editor Hansen Publs., Inc., Miami Beach, Fla., 1962-78; pres. Brimhall Publs., Inc., Las Vegas, 1978—; composer, arranger, numerous books, sheet music; composer primary series John Brimhall Piano Method, John Brimhall Organ Method; author: (theory notebook) Young Adult Piano Course. Recipient La Croix de Commandeur, Merite et Devouement Francais (France), 1973. Mem. ASCAP, Am. Coll. Musicians (faculty mem.), Nat. Assn. of Music Merchants, Am. Fedn. Musicians, Music Educators Nat. Conf. Home: 106 Matterhorn Way Mount Charleston NV 89124

BRIMMER, CLARENCE ADDISON, judge; b. Rawlins, Wyo., July 11, 1922; s. Clarence Addison and Geraldine (Zingsheim) B.; m. Emily O. Docken, Aug. 2, 1953; children: Geraldine Ann, Philip Andrew, Andrew Howard, Elizabeth Ann. B.A., U. Mich., 1944, J.D., 1947. Bar: Wyo. 1948. Pvt. practice law Rawlins, 1948-71, mcpl. judge, 1948-54; U.S. commr., magistrate 1963-71; atty. gen. Wyo. Cheyenne, 1971-74; U.S. atty. 1975; chief U.S. dist. judge Wyo. Dist. Cheyenne, 1975—. Sec. Rawlins Bd. Pub. Utilities, 1954-66, Gov.'s Com. on Wyo. Water, 1963-65; del. Rep. Nat. Conv., 1956; chmn. Wyo. Rep. Platform Com., 1966; sec. Wyo. Rep. Com., 1966, chmn., 1967-71, Rep. gubernatorial candidate, 1974; Trustee Rocky Mountain Mineral Law Found., 1963-75. Served with USAAF, 1945-46. Mem. ABA, Wyo. Bar Assn., Am. Judicature Soc., Laramie County Bar Assn., Carbon County Bar Assn. Episcopalian. Clubs: Masons, Shriners. Office: US Dist Ct PO Box 985 Cheyenne WY 82001 *

BRINEGAR, CLAUDE STOUT, oil company executive; b. Rockport, Calif., Dec. 16, 1926; s. Claude Leroy Stout and Lyle (Rawles) B.; m. Elva Jackson, July 1, 1950 (div. 1983); children: Claudia, Meredith, Thomas; m. Katharine (Schellenger) Potter, May 14, 1983. BA, Stanford U., 1950, MS, 1951, PhD, 1954. V.p. econs. and planning Union Oil (now Unocal), L.A., 1965; pres. pure oil div. Union Oil (now Unocal), Palatine, Ill., 1965-69; sr. v.p., pres. refining and mktg. Union Oil (now Unocal), L.A., 1969-73; U.S. sec. of transp. Washington, 1973-75; sr. v.p. adminstr. Unocal Corp., L.A., 1975-85, exec. v.p., chief fin. officer, 1985—; bd. dirs. AmTrack, Washington; founding dir. Consol. Rail Corp., Washington, 1974-75. Author: monograph on econs. and price behavior, 1970; contbr. articles to profl. jours. on statistics and econs. Sgt. U.S. Air Corp, 1945-47, Korea. Mem. Am. Petroleum Inst. (bd. dirs. 1976-85), Calif. Club, Georgetown Club, Internat. Club, Phi Beta Kappa. Republican. Office: Unocal Corp Unocal Ctr 1201 W 5th St Los Angeles CA 90017

BRINK, RANDALL WILSON, writer; b. Lewiston, Idaho, Feb. 22, 1955; s. Max Extein Brink and Joyce Elaine (Campbell) Bradbury; m. Shelly Stejer, Feb. 18, 1978 (div. 1985). BA, SUNY, 1978; postgrad., Gonzaga U., 1978. Captian ATA Airlines, Seattle, 1975-80, Empire Airlines, Coer d'Alene, Idaho, 1983-86; v.p. ops. Empire Airlines, Coer d'Alene, 1984-86; editor Air Progress Mag., L.A., 1980-85; contbg. editor Aviation Internat. News, Midland Park, N.J., 1980-88, Plane & Pilot Mag., L.A., 1983-88; dir. ops. Eagle Airways, San Luis Obispo, Calif., 1986-88; pres. Pantedhnicon Internat. Corp., Spokane, Wash., 1985-88. Author: Lost Star, 1988. Chmn. Kootenai County Republican Cen., 1974-76; candidate Idaho State House of Reps., 2nd dist., 1976. Mem. Writer's Guild of Am., Spokane. Republicn. Presbyterian. Home: Twin Lakes Village ID 83858

BRINK, ROBERT CHARLES, lawyer; b. Elmira, N.Y., Dec. 24, 1944; s. Harold Clifford and Virginia Belle (Rice) B. BA cum laude, U. Nebr., 1969; JD, Gonzaga U., 1979; LLM, U. Miami, 1980. Bar: Alaska 1979. Game warden Alaska Dept. Fish and Game, Homer, 1970; bush tchr. Alaska State Operated Schs., Anchorage, 1970-71; recruiter RCA Alascom, Anchorage, 1972-73, legal asst., 1973-75; pvt. practice as contractor 1975-78; assoc. Hartig, Rhodes, Normal et al., Anchorage, 1980-84; pvt. practice Anchorage, 1985--. Contbr. articles to legal and sports publs. Bd. dirs. Anchorage Sr. Ctr. Endowment Trust, 1985—, gov. body for judo, U.S. Olympic Com., 1980—; past mem. bd. dirs. Alaska USA Fed. Credit Union, Arctic Winter Games Corp., numerous other civic orgns. With USN, 1962-65, Vietnam. Recipient numerous awards Boy Scouts Am., local youth activity orgns., and community orgns., 1962--. Mem. Alaska Bar Assn. (officer tax sec. 1982--), Anchorage Estate Planning Council (officer 1986--), U.S. Judo Fedn. (1st v.p., bd. dirs.), several other sports orgns. Home: 2211 Sunburst Cir Anchorage AK 99503 Office: 1525 E Tudor Rd Anchorage AK 99507

BRINKER, CONNIE JUGE, graphoanalyst, document examiner; b. New Orleans, July 15, 1928; d. Edward Joseph and Faustine Madeline (Aleman) Juge; m. Robert William Brinker, Jan. 4, 1948; children: Richard, Susan, John, Craig, Randy. Student, Fullerton Coll., Calif., 1974-76. Master cert. graphoanalyst. Cosmetologist various salons, Fullerton, Calif., 1967-79; owner/operator cosmetology salon Fullerton, 1979—; graphoanalyst and document examiner Brinker & Assocs., Fullerton, 1980—; lectr. in field. Author: Reflections, 1984; contbr. articles to profl. jours. Active Boy Scouts Am., Girl Scouts U.S.A. Recipient Sharon Topper Humanitarian award, Fullerton Coll., 1976. Mem. Internat. Graphoanalysis Soc. (chpt. pres. 1978-79, cooperator of the yr. 1977, graphoanalyst of yr. 1977), World Assn. of Document Examiners, Amvets Aux. Democrat. Roman Catholic. Office: Brinker and Assocs 107 North Woods Ave Fullerton CA 92632

BRINKERHOFF, PHILIP RICHARD, financial institution executive; b. Wilmington, N.C., Apr. 2, 1943; s. James Marcus and Billie Lou (Benson) B.; m. Janice Swenson, June 11, 1968; children: Kimberly, Adam, Jennica, Allison, Mark. Student, U. So. Calif., 1960-61, San Fernando Valley State Coll., 1961-62; B.S., Brigham Young U., 1966; J.D., Harvard U., 1969. Bar: Ariz. 1970, U.S. Supreme Ct. 1977. Asso. firm Streich, Lang, Weeks, Cardon and French, Phoenix, 1969-73; v.p., gen. counsel Fed. Home Loan Mortgage Corp., Washington, 1973-75, exec. v.p., chief adminstrv. officer, 1975-77, pres., chief exec. officer, 1977-82; pres., chief operating officer 1st Charter Fin. Corp., Beverly Hills, Calif., 1982-83; pres. FCA Mortgage Securities, 1983-84; chmn., pres., chief exec. officer, dir. Fin. Corp. of Santa Barbara, Calif., 1984—; dir., mem. exec. com. AMMINET, Inc., 1974-78. Mem. Phi Kappa Phi. Mormon. Office: Fin Corp Santa Barbara PO Box 1109 Santa Barbara CA 93102 *

BRINKS, KENNETH JOHN HENRY, milling company executive; b. Quincy, Ill., May 18, 1935; s. William Michael and Grace Marie (Bergman) B.; m. Sharon Lee DeWitt, Dec. 27, 1957 (div. 1972); m. Darlene Mary Ann Ghelfi, Apr. 7, 1973; children—Vonnie, Danney, Sheri, Bradley. Student U. Ill., 1953-55; B.A., Quincy Coll., 1958. Purchasing agt. Electric Wheel div. Firestone Tire, Quincy, 1959-60; credit corr. Moorman Mfg. Co., Quincy, 1959-63; office mgr. Bell Grain & Milling Inc. Subs. Moorman Mfg. Co., Perris, Calif., 1963-64, sec., 1964-65, dir., 1965—; treas., sec., 1965-73, v.p. and treas., 1973-83, exec. v.p. and treas., 1983-87, chief fin. officer, gen. mgr., 1987—; sec. Bellmilling Corp. (subs.), Escondido, Calif., 1964-65, treas., sec., 1965-73, pres., chief exec. officer, 1973—; div., chmn. Marshall's Pullets Inc.. Bd. dirs., former treas. Nehi-Kai Villas Homeowners Assn., pres. 1986—. Served to sgt. 1st class U.S. Army. Mem. Toastmasters (treas., v.p., pres.). Lodge: Lions (treas., div.). Office: Bell Grain & Milling 17971 Hwy 215 Perris CA 92370

BRINLEY, LEONARD DEAN, lawyer; b. Palmdale, Calif., Nov. 5, 1943; s. Odis Leonard and Charlsie Marie (Mailey) B.; m. Janis Elaine Newman, July 30, 1966; children: Nancy Louise, Julie Denise. BSEE, U. So. Calif., 1966, MBA, 1968, JD, 1971. Bar: Calif. 1972, U.S. Dist. Ct. (cen. dist.) Calif. 1972, U.S. Ct. Appeals (9th cir.) 1976, U.S. Supreme Ct. 1975. Tech. staff Hughes Aircraft Co., Culver City, Calif., 1966-70; sr. auditor N.Am. Rockwell, El Segundo, Calif., 1971-72; dep. counsel Office of County Counsel, San Bernardino, Calif., 1972-81; jsr. atty. Orange County Supt. Schs., Costa Mesa, Calif., 1981-84; assoc. Buchalter, Nemer, Fields & Younger, Newport Beach, Calif., 1984-87; pvt. practice Newport Beach, 1987—. Editor, contbr. Sch. Law Newsletter, 1983-84. Mem. adv. coun. Orange County Constl. Rights Found., 1984-88; pres. Rocky Point Community Homeowners Assn., Anaheim, Calif., 1975-84; mem. Democratic Found. Orange County, 1986-88. Mem. ABA, Orange County Bar Assn., Nat. Assn. Sch. Attys., Kiwanis. Presbyterian. Office: Ste 1400 660 Newport Center Dr Newport Beach CA 92660

BRINTON, CHRISTINE LOUISE, financial planner, consultant; b. Snohomish, Wash., Nov. 18, 1948; d. Roy E. and Mary M. (Timmerman) Fritch; m. Michael L. Brinton, Sept. 4, 1971; children: Kyle, Conor. BS, Wash. St. U., 1971, postgrad., 1971-72; postgrad., U. of Wash., 1973-75; Certified Fin. Planner, Coll. for Fin. Planning, Denver, 1985. Tchr. Kern County High Schs., Ridgecrest, Calif., 1972-74; tchr. S.K. Sch. Dist., Pt. Orchard, Wash., 1974-76; instr. Olympic Coll., Bremerton, Wash., 1976-80; investment counselor Great Northwest Fed., Bremerton, 1982; fin. svcs. admin. N. Sound Bank, Poulsbo, Wash., 1983-85; fin. cons. Shearson Lehman Hutton, Bremerton, Wash., 1986—. Mem. Inst. Cert. Fin. Planners, C. of C. Poulsbo (dir. 1985-86), C. of C. Bremerton, Olympic Fin. Planners Assn. (co-founder, pres. 1985, v.p. 1989). Republican. Roman Catholic. Office: Shearson Lehman Hutton 645-4th St Bremerton WA 98370

BRINTON, DILWORTH CARLOS, underwriter; b. Victor, Idaho, Nov. 2, 1917; s. Van B. and Vida D. (Driggs) B.; m. Pearl Randall, May 2, 1946; children: Dilworth Carlos Jr., Barbara Nelson, Robert W., Richard R., Ann Despain. BSBA, U. Ariz., 1940; postgrad., U. Calif., Berkeley, 1943. CLU. Life underwriter N.Y. Life Ins. Co., Mesa, Ariz., 1946—. Contbr. articles to profl. jours. Pres., bd. dirs. Ariz. State Hosp. Bd., 1952-57. Staff sgt. U.S. Army, 1943-46. Mem. Nat. Assn. Life Underwriters (officer), Million Dollar Round Table, Ariz. Assn. Life Underwriters (pres., bd. dirs. 1967, Outstanding Life Underwriter 1982), Tri-City Life Underwriters (founding pres. Mesa chpt. 1972). Republian. Ch. of Jesus Christ Latter-day Saints.

BRINTON, RICHARD KIRK, marketing executive; b. Hanover, Pa., Apr. 21, 1946; s. James Henry and Mabel (Adelung) B.; m. Joan Marita Ayo, Mar. 21, 1970; children: Katherine, Mark, Michael. BA in Liberal Arts, BS in Indsl. Engring., Pa. State U., 1968. Registered profl. engr., Ohio. From systems engr. to dir. mktg. AccuRay/Combustion Engring., Columbus, Ohio, 1968-82; group mktg. dir. AccuRay/Combustion Engring., London, 1982-84; internat. sales mgr. Flow Systems, Seattle, 1984, v.p. mktg., 1985-87; dir. mktg., bus. devel. FlowMole Corp., Seattle, 1987—. Home: 18137 149th Ave SE Renton WA 98058 Office: FlowMole 21409 72d Ave S Kent WA 98032

BRISBIN, ROBERT EDWARD, insurance agency executive; b. Bklyn., Feb. 13, 1946; m. Sally Ann Tobler-Norton. BSBA, San Francisco State U., 1968. Cert. safety exec. Field rep. Index Research, San Mateo, Calif., 1969-82; mgr. loss control Homeland Ins. Co., San Jose, Calif., 1982-87; ins. exec. Morris and Dee Ins. Agy., San Luis Obispo, Calif., 1987—; prin., cons. Robert E. Brisbin & Assocs., Pismo Beach, Calif., 1972—, San Francisco, 1975—; mgt. cons.; pres. Profl. Formulas Amino Acid Food Supplements, 1987—. Author: Amino Acids, Vitamins and Fitness, 1986, Loss Control for the Small- to Medium-Sized Business, 1989; composer: Country Songs and Broken Dreams, 1978, America the Land of Liberty, 1986. Mem. Am. Soc. Safety Engrs., World Safety Orgn. (cert. safety exec.), United Nations Roster Safety Cons., Internat. Platform Soc. Republican. Office: PO Box 341 Pismo Beach CA 93449

BRISBOIS, RAPHAEL HUBERT, wine maker; b. Bouxwiller, France, May 21, 1951; came to U.S., 1987; s. Hubert and Emmy Ida (Schmidt) B.; m. Sylvie Therese Chaillou, July 15, 1972; children: Ludovic, Benoît. Diploma, INA PG, Paris, 1974. Winemaker Henri Maire, Arbois, France, 1976-81, Champagnes Piper Heidsieck, Reims, France, 1981-85; gen. mgr. Champagne India Ltd., Bombay, 1985-87; winemaker sparkling wines Iron Horse Vineyards, Sebastopol, Calif., 1987—; cons. Champagne Technologie, Reims, 1982-85. Mem. Union des Oenologues de France, Am. Soc. Viticulture and Enology. Office: Iron Horse Vineyards 9786 Ross Station Rd Sebastopol CA 95472

BRISCOE, JOHN FREDERICK, JR., food products executive; b. Altadena, Calif., Nov. 4, 1952; s. John Frederick and Guntrud Mardel (Hilmers) B.; m. Debra Fae Burns, July 12, 1975. BA in Psychology, BA in Speech Communication, Calif. State U., Long Beach, 1975, MPA, 1979. Sales mgr. Gen. Foods Inc., White Plains, N.Y., 1975-82; nat. trade devel. sales mgr. Kal Kan Inc., Vernon, Calif., 1982—. Dist. commr. Boy Scouts Am. Kenilworth, Ill., 1979-82; Boy Scouts Am. San Marino, Calif., 1982-84. Mem. Am. Logistics Assn., Phi Kappa Phi. Lutheran. Office: Kal Kan Inc 3250 E 44th St Vernon CA 90058-2499

BRISTOW, SANDRA SUE, data processing executive; b. Portland, Oct. 15, 1940; d. Thomas Herman and Helyne (Michael) Fruiht; m. Charles Manewal, Aug. 3, 1968 (div. 1978); m. John Blair Bristow, May 28, 1983; children: Michael, Denisa, Michelle, Gretchen, Kristina. Student, Linfield Coll., McMinnville, Oreg. Office mgr. Delta Sand & Gravel, Eugene, Oreg., 1972-76, Liberty Communications, Eugene, 1976-82; MIS dir. Chambers Communications, Eugene, 1982—. Mem. Eugene Arts Found., 1985-88; bd. dirs. Eugene Ballet, 1986-87. Mem. Data Processing Mgmt. Assn. (assoc. dir. 1982—, pres. 1981), Lane Postal Customer Council (pres. 1987-88), Eugene C. of C., Interex Hewlett Packard Users Groups, Women in Cable (officer 1982-88), Epsilon Sigma Delta (state pres. 1987-88), Tahoe Waterfront Club (dir. 1982— Home: 85007 Kensington Dr Pleasant Hill OR 97455 Office: Chambers Communications 2225 Coburg Rd Eugene OR 97401

BRITT, EUGENE LESLIE, business educator; b. Salt Lake City, Apr. 9, 1941; s. Eugene Leslie Sr. and Betty Verona (Burbank) B.; children: Lori Lee, Gena Lynn. BS, Weber State Coll., 1966; MBA, Ariz. State U., 1970. Mgmt. analyst USAF, Ogden, Utah, 1962-66; mgr. Mountain Bell Telephone, Salt Lake City, 1966-69; controller San Diego Prestressed Concrete Co., 1970-74; bus. instr. Grossmont Coll., El Cajon, Calif., 1974-85; dept. chair, mktg. mgmt. and internat. bus. Grossmont Coll., El Cajon, 1985—; vis. lectr. Beijing Inst. Fgn. Trade, 1982, Finnish Businessman's Comml. Coll., Helsinki, Finland, 1983; bd. dirs. San Diego Dist. Export Coun. Publisher, San Diego Internat. Bus. Calendar. Chmn. United Fund Drive, American Fork, Utah, 1968; bd. dirs. American Fork C. of C., mem. Rotary Club, American Fork, 1966-69. Named Outstanding Community Mem., Jaycees, American Fork, 1968. Mem. World Trade Assn. San Diego, Internat. Soc. for Bus. Edn. (del 1980, 83), Calif. Bus.-Edn. Assn. Republican. Office: Grossmont Coll 8800 Grossmont Coll Dr El Cajon CA 92020

BRITTAIN, DONALD LEE, software company executive, educator; b. Salisbury, Md., Mar. 9, 1959; s. Robert Leroy and Mary Louise (Cronin) B.; m. Skona Sari Libowitz, June 30, 1985. SB, MIT, 1980; PhD, U. Pa., 1984. Mem. Inst. for Advanced Study, Princeton, N.J., 1984-85; asst. prof. SUNY, Stony Brook, 1985-86; sr. programmer Wavefront Techs., Inc., Santa Barbara, Calif., 1986-87, sr. software mgr., 1987-88, dir. rsch., 1988--; lectr. U. Calif. Extension, Santa Barbara, 1987--. RCA telecommunications scholar, 1977; J. Clarence Karcher fellow U. Pa., 1980. Mem. Assn. for Computing Machinery, Computer Soc. IEEE, Nat. Computer Graphics Assn., USENIX, Sigma Xi. Home: 165 Santa Ana Ave Santa Barbara CA 93111 Office: Wavefront Techs 530 E Montecito St Santa Barbara CA 93103

BRITTAIN, JERRY LEE, clinical psychologist, naval officer; b. Bossier City, La., Aug. 4, 1947; s. Melvin Houston and Reba Cleo (Eaves) B.; BA in Psychology, Villanova U., 1972; BS in Biology, Centenary Meth. Coll., 1974; MA in Counseling Psychology, La. Tech., 1975; PhD in Clin. Psychology, Calif. Sch. Profl. Psychology, 1978; lic. clin. psychologist, Calif. Psychologist, medic U.S. Army, Valley Forge, Pa., 1969-72; med. intern Mental Health Ctr., Shreveport, La., 1975; pre-doctoral intern Calif. Mens Colony, San Luis Obispo, 1975-76; doctoral intern Visalia (Calif.) Community Counseling Ctr., 1976-77, Fresno County (Calif.) Mental Health Ctr., 1977-78; commd. lt. U.S. Navy, 1979; chief psychologist Naval Drug Rehab. Ctr., San Diego, 1979-83, Naval Hosp., Naples, Italy, 1983—; instr., pvt. practice psychology, San Diego. Postdoctoral fellow U. Ala. Mem. Am. Psychol. Assn. Republican. Mem. Ch. of Nazarene. Contbr. articles to profl. jours.

BRITTEN, ROY JOHN, biophysicist; b. Washington, Oct. 1, 1919; s. Rollo Herbert and Marion (Hale) B.; m. Jacqueline Reid, 1986; children: Gregory, Kenneth. BS, U. Va., 1941; PhD, Princeton U., 1951. Staff mem. dept. terrestrial magnetism Carnegie Instn., Washington, 1951—; sr. research assoc. Calif. Inst. Tech., Corona del Mar, 1973-81; discoverer repeated DNA sequences in genomes of higher organisms. Inventor in field. Named Disting. Carnegie Sr. Research Assoc. in Biology, 1981—. Fellow Am. Acad. Arts and Scis., AAAS; mem. Nat. Acad. Scis. Office: Calif Inst of Tech Kerchkhoff Marine Lab 101 Dahlia Ave Corona Del Mar CA 92625

BRITTO, GAIL LESLIE, investment manager; b. Pittsfield, Mass., Nov. 11, 1942; d. Charles Franklin and Eleanor Frances (Spall) Smith; m. Ronald Britto, July 5, 1965 (div. 1973); 1 child, Elvira Marion. BA, Smith Coll., 1964; MBA, UCLA, 1981. Chartered fin. analyst. 2d v.p. George D. Bjurman & Assocs., Los Angeles, 1974-82; mgr. investments Automobile Club So. Calif., Los Angeles, 1983—. Fellow Fin. Analysts Fedn.; mem. Los Angeles Soc. Fin. Analysts, Los Angeles Assn. Investment Women, Beta Gamma Sigma. Republican. Congregationalist. Home: 3602 Estates Ln #315 Palos Verdes Peninsula CA 90274

BRITTON, JOANNE MARIE, accountant, university official; b. Albany, N.Y., June 6, 1950; d. Herman Jesse and Emily Marie (Griffin) B. BA, SUNY, Buffalo, 1972, MLS, 1974, MBA in Acctg., 1982. Fund mgr. Arista Funding, Escondido, Calif., 1982-83; acctg. dir. John Fowler Resorts, Solana Beach, Calif., 1983-85; contr. Calif. Western Sch. Law, San Diego, 1985—. Office: Calif Western Sch Law 350 Cedar St San Diego CA 92101

BRITTON, MARY KAY, manufacturing executive; b. Great Falls, Mont., Sept. 27, 1939; d. Gerald Glen and Martha (Spitler) Emerson; m. Kent E. Gunnison, Sept. 7, 1963; (div. Jan., 1974); children: Mark E., Katie E.; m. James A. Britton, Dec. 10, 1977. BS, Lewis & Clark Coll., 1962. Elec. drafter Columbia Engrs. Svcs., Inc., Richland, Wash., 1975-76; drafter Westinghouse Hanford Co., Richland, 1976-77, supr. drawing and procedure control, 1977-79, supr. proj. Dalis (data base svc.), 1979-84, staff mgr. control & computer systems, 1984-87, mgr. data systems, 1987, mgr. data standards & adminstrn., 1987—. Guardian Ad Litem Ct. Jurisdiction, Benton-Franklin Counties, Wash., 1986-89; mem. Bus. Adv. Com., Tri-City Area Vocat. Ctr., Richland, Wash., 1984-86. Mem. Assn. for Systems Mgmt., Nat. Mgmt. Assn. Office: Westinghouse Hanford Co PO Box 1970 Richland WA 99352

BRITTON, STEVEN MICHAEL, teacher; b. Merced, Calif., Aug. 24, 1955; s. Richard Wayne and Patricia Ann (Moraine) B.; m. Debra Susan Rosander, June 22, 1985; 1 child, Joshua Clark. AS, Merced Coll., 1979; BA, Humboldt State U., 1982; teaching cert., Calif. State U., 1983. Educator Hemet (Calif.) Jr. High Sch., 1983-84; electronics educator Roosevelt High Sch., Fresno, Calif., 1984—; recorder Electronics Curriculum, Fresno, 1986-87, chmn., 1987-88. Active Boy Scouts Am., 1963—. With USN, 1973-77. Mem. Calif. Indsl. Edn. Assn., Viking Cycle Club (pres. 1986-87), Indsl. Arts Club (pres. 1981-82). Democrat. Methodist. Home: 1549 21st Ave Kingsburg CA 93631 Office: Roosevelt High Tech Edn 4250 E Tulare Fresno CA 93702

BRITTON, THOMAS WARREN, JR., management consultant; b. Pawhuska, Okla., June 16, 1944; s. Thomas Warren and Helen Viola (Haynes) B.; B.S. in Mech. Engring., Okla. State U., 1966, M.S. in Indsl. Engring. and Mgmt., 1968; m. Deborah Ann Mansour, Oct. 20, 1973; children—Natalie Dawn, Kimberly Ann. Cons., Arthur Young & Co., Los Angeles, 1968-72, mgr., 1972-76, prin., 1976-79, partner, 1979—, office dir. mgmt. services dept., Orange County, Calif., 1980-87; ptnr. West Region Mfg., 1987-88, Price Waterhouse; ptnr.-in-charge west coast mfg. cons. practice, Nat. Aerospace and Def. Industry, 1988—; lectr. in field. Mem. City of San Dimas Creative Growth Bd., 1976-77, chmn. planning commn., 1977-83; trustee World Affairs Council of Orange County, 1980; benefactor, founders com., trustee South Coast Repertory Theater; trustee Providence Speech and Hearing Ctr.; mem. devel. com. U. Calif.-Irvine Med. Sch.; chmn. Costa Mesa Arts Council. Served to capt. USAR, 1971-86. Cert. mgmt. cons. Mem. Los Angeles Inst. C.P.A.s, Mgmt. Adv. Services Com., Am. Inst. Indsl. Engrs., Greater Irvine Indsl. League, Okla. State Alumni Assn. Clubs: Jonathan, Ridgeline Country, Santa Ana Country. Home: 18982 Wildwood Circle Villa Park CA 92667

BROAD, ELI, financial services and home construction company executive; b. N.Y.C., June 6, 1933; s. Leon and Rebecca (Jacobson) B.; m. Edythe Lois Lawson, Dec. 19, 1954; children: Jeffrey Alan, Gary Steven. B.A. cum laude in Bus. Adminstrn, Mich. State U., 1954. Acct. 1954-56; asst. prof. Detroit Inst. Tech., 1956-57; co-founder Broad, Inc. (formerly Kaufman & Broad, Inc.), L.A., 1957, pres., chmn., 1957-72, part-time chmn., 1973-75, chmn., chief exec. officer, 1976—; chmn., chief exec. officer Sun Life Ins. Co. Am., Balt., 1976-79, SunAm. Corp. (merged with Sun Life Group of Am.), 1978—; bd. dirs. Fed. Nat. Mortgage Assn., Sun Life Ins. Co. Am., Balt., Anchor Nat. Life Ins. Co., 1986—, The Advest Group; real estate adv. bd. Citibank, N.Y.C.; chmn. Kaufman & Broad Home Corp., 1986—. Dir. devel. bd. Mich. State U., 1969-72; mem. Nat. Indsl. Pollution Control Council, 1970-73; co-founder Council Housing Producers; chmn. Los Angeles Mayor's Housing Policy Com., 1974-75; del. Democratic Nat. Conv., 1968; pres. Calif. Non-Partisan Voter Registration Found., 1971; bd. dirs. Nat. Energy Found., 1979—, NCCJ, YMCA, Los Angeles United Way, Haifa U.; bd. dirs., trustee Windward Sch.; mem. acquisition com. Los Angeles County Mus. Art, 1979-81; exec. com. Internat. Forum for Los Angeles World Affairs Council; exec. com., bd. fellows Claremont Colls.; adv. bd. Inst. Internat. Edn.; chmn. founding bd. trustees Mus. Contemporary Art, Los Angeles, 1980—; vis. com. U. Calif. at Los Angeles Grad. Sch. Mgmt.; trustee City of Hope, Calif. State Univs. and Colls.; trustee Pitzer Coll., 1979—, chmn. bd. trustees, 1972-79. Recipient Man of Year award City of Hope, 1965; Golden Plate award Am. Acad. Achievement, 1971; Humanitarian award NCCJ, 1977; Housing Man of Yr. Nat. Housing Conf., 1979; Am. Heritage award Anti-Defamation League, 1984. Mem. Beta Alpha Psi. Clubs: Regency, Hillcrest Country (Los Angeles). Home: 1 Oakmont Dr Los Angeles CA 90049 Office: Broad Inc 11601 Wilshire Blvd Los Angeles CA 90025

BROADHEAD, RONALD FRIGON, petroleum geologist, geology educator; b. Racine, Wis., July 22, 1955; s. Ronald Leslie and Therese (Frigon) B. BS, N.Mex. Tech. U., 1977; MS, U. Cin., 1979. Geologist, Cities Svc. Oil Co., Oklahoma City, 1979-81; head petroleum geologist N.Mex. Bur. Mines data section, Socorro, 1981—. adj. asst. prof. geology N.Mex. Tech. Coll., 1983—. Union Oil Co. summer fellow Duke U. Marine Lab., 1977. Mem. Am. Assn. Petroleum Geologists (Ho. of Dels., membership com.), Soc. Econ. Paleontologists and Mineralogists, N.Mex. Geol. Soc., Roswell Geol. Soc., Four Corners Geol. Soc., Sigma Xi. Roman Catholic. Office: N Mex Bur Mines Campus Sta Socorro NM 87801

BROADHURST, NORMAN NEIL, foods company executive; b. Chico, Calif., Dec. 17, 1946; s. Frank Spencer and Dorothy Mae (Conrad) B.; BS, Calif. State U., 1969; MBA, Golden Gate U., 1975; m. Victoria Rose Thomson, Aug. 7, 1976; 1 child, Scott Andrew. With Del Monte Corp., San Francisco, 1969-76, product mgr., 1973-76; product mgr. Riviana Foods, Inc., div. Colgate Palmolive, Houston, 1976-78; new products brand devel. mgr. foods div. Coca Cola Co., Houston, 1978-79, brand mgr., 1979-82, mktg. dir., 1982-83; v.p. mktg. Beatrice Foods Co., Chgo., 1983-86; pres., chief operating officer Famous Amos Chocolate Chip Cookie Co., Torrance, Calif., 1986-88; corp. sr. v.p., gen. mgr. Kerr Glass Mfg., L.A., 1988—. Chmn. youth soccer program Cystic Fibrosis; pres., chmn. South Coast Symphony, 1985-88. Recipient Cystic Fibrosis Community Svcs. award, 1982; bd. dirs. Literacy Vols. Am., Inc., 1987—. Mem. Am. Mgmt. Assn., Am. Mktg. Assn., Toastmasters Internat. (past chpt. pres.). Home: 5009 Queen Victoria Woodland Hills CA 91364 Office: Kerr Glass Mfg 1840 Century Park E Los Angeles CA 90067

BROADSTON, DONALD ANDREW, real estate broker; b. L.A., Oct. 25, 1940; s. James Andrew and Elizabeth Jeanette (Herrnstein) B.; m. Linda Merle Dority, June 24, 1972 (div. Dec. 1987); 1 child, Kerry; m. Shelley Brewer, Dec. 30, 1987; children: Sherrie, Daphne. BSEE, UCLA, 1963; postgrad., U. Calif., Santa Barbara, 1965-67. Lic. real estate broker. Rsch. engr. Rocketdyne div. N.A.A., Canoga Park, Calif., 1963-65; design engr. Electrokinetics div. Varo, Santa Barbara, 1965-68, mgr. quality assurance, 1968-75; quality assurance and prodn. mgr. Info. Magnetics Corp., Goleta, Calif., 1975-77; real estate broker, developer Century 21, Prescott, Ariz., 1977-80; broker, owner Realty Execs. of Prescott, 1980—. Author: (with others) Control of Surface Quality, 1977. Mem. Prescott Bd. Realtors (bd. dirs., Realtor of Yr. 1984), Rotary (bd. Prescott club 1983-84). Republican. Home: PO Box 1912 Prescott AZ 86302 Office: Realty Execs 125 E Gurley St Prescott AZ 86301

BROADSTREET, LYDIA SMITH, interior designer; b. Colo., Apr. 30, 1932; d. Hobart A. and Margaret (Townsend) Smith; m. James Anderson Broadstreet, 1955 (div. 1975); children: Margaret Anne, James Townsend. Student, Hastings Coll., Friends U., Wichita, Kans., 1949-75. Graphic artist McCormick-Armstrong, Wichita, Kans., 1955-57; design study Finland, 1957-58; graphic designer 1958-64; owner, chief exec. officer, interior designer Broadstreets, Inc., Springfield, Mo., 1964-86; pvt. practice Santa Cruz, Calif., 1987—. Pres. Springfield (Mo.) Network, Springfield Downtown Assn., Planned Parenthood; active in other charitable orgns. Mem. Springfield Design Assn. (founding mem.), Am. Soc. Interior Designers. Home and Office: 3326 Fairway Dr Soquel CA 95073

BROBERG, DAVID KENNETH, electronic design engineer; b. Mpls., July 23, 1956; s. Warren Keith Broberg and Marilyn Jean (Krause) Totushek; m. Linda Louise Acker, Dec. 31, 1975 (div. July 1986); 1 child, Jana. AA in Applied Scis., Mountain View Coll., 1980. Service ctr. supr. Sony Video Products Co., Dallas, 1977-80; v.p., co-owner New Tech. and Service Co., Dallas, 1980-81; dir. engring. Precision Electronics, Oklahoma City, 1981-83; software quality engr. RCA Videodisc Ops., Indpls., 1983; dir. research and devel. ICM Video div. Internat. Crystal, Oklahoma City, 1983-87; research and devel. engr. Laird Telemedia, Salt Lake City, 1987-88, dir. engring., 1988—. Patentee in field. Sgt. USAF, 1975-80. Mem. Soc. Motion Picture and TV Engrs., Soc. Broadcast Engrs., Internat. TV Assn. Republican. Home: 11361 S Windy Peak Ridge Sandy UT 84094

BROCCOLI, ALBERT ROMOLO, motion picture producer; b. N.Y.C., Apr. 5, 1909; s. Giovanni and Cristina (Vence) B.; m. Dana Natol Wilson, June 21, 1959; children: Michael Wilson, Anthony, Christina, Barbara. Student pub. schs., N.Y.C. Asst. dir. 20th Century Fox, 1941-42; RKO under Howard Hughes, 1947-48; theatrical agt. Charles Feldman, 1948-51; producer Warwick Films, 1951-60, Eon Prodns., Inc., from 1960. Producer: Red Beret, 1952, Hell Below Zero, 1953, Black Knight, 1954, Prize of Gold, 1955, Cockleshell Heroes, 1956, Safari, 1956, April in Portugal, 1956, Fire Down Below, 1956, Odongo, 1956, Pickup Alley, 1957, Arrivederci Roma, 1957, Interpol, 1957, How to Murder a Rich Uncle, 1957, High Flight, 1958, No Time to Die, 1958, The Man Inside, 1958, Killers of Kilimanjaro, 1958, Bandit of Zhobe, 1958, In The Nick, 1959, Jazz Boat, 1960, Let's Get Married, 1960, The Trials of Oscar Wilde, 1960, Idol on Parade, 1960, Johnny Nobody, 1961, Call Me Bwana, 1963, Chitty Chitty Bang Bang, 1967 (Family Film award So. Calif. Motion Picture Council 1968); James Bond films Dr. No, 1962, From Russia With Love, 1963 (Screen Producers Guild certificate of nomination as best picture 1964), Goldfinger, 1963 (Screen Producers Guild cert. of nomination as best picture 1964), Thunderball, 1964 (Mkkin Kogyo Tsushin cert. of award 1966), You Only Live Twice, 1966 (Mkkin Kogyo Tsushin cert. of award 1967), On Her Majesty's Secret Service, 1969, Diamonds Are Forever, 1971, Live and Let Die, 1972, The Man With the Golden Gun, 1974, The Spy Who Loved Me, 1977, Moonraker, 1979, For Your Eyes Only, 1981, Octopussy, 1983, A View to a Kill, 1985, The Living Daylights, 1987. Bd. Dirs. Boys Club of Queens, Inc., 1968, recipient Man of the Yr. award. Served to lt. (j.g.) USN, 1942-47, PTO. Decorated grand officer Order of Crown (Italy), Order St. Constantine (Italy), Caballero De Merito 1970 Order of Constantinana de St. Jorge of Spain, 1970, Commandatore Order of the Crown Grand Officer of Italy, Order of Brit. Empire HRH Queen Elizabeth II, 1987, Commandeur des Arts et Des Lettres Le Ministre de la Culture et de France la Communication, 1987; recipient Irving G. Thalberg Meml. award 54th ann. Acad. Awards, 1982. Mem. Producers Guild, Am. Film Inst. Roman Catholic. Club: Metropolitan (N.Y.C.). Office: care Gregory Davis & Co 1875 Century Pk E Ste 1160 Los Angeles CA 90067 *

BROCK, LARRY RAYMOND, senior programmer, analyst; b. Louisville, Sept. 24, 1946; s. Leon C. and LaVerne Elizabeth (Brand) B. Student, Calif. State U., L.A., 1975-78. Ops. mgr. United Silver and Cutlery, L.A., 1972-78; programmer, analyst Sav-On Drugs, Anaheim, Calif., 1978-79, Caesar's Palace, Las Vegas, Nev., 1979-82; sr. programmer, analyst S.W. Gas Corp., Las Vegas, 1982—. Singer S.W.G. Gashouse Singers, Las Vegas, 1986-88. With U.S. Army, Germany. Mem. Mensa (chmn. 1986). Democrat. Roman Catholic. Clubs: St. Francis Singles, B.A.S.S. Masters (Las Vegas). Home: 5917 Auborn Ave Las Vegas NV 89108 Office: SW Gas Corp 5241 Spring Mountain Rd Las Vegas NV 89114

BROCK, LONNIE REX, manufacturing executive; b. Mattoon, Ill., Nov. 13, 1950; s. Lyman Dale and Margaret Mary (Barnett) B.; m. Mary Kathryn Greider, May 24, 1975; 1 child, Lonnie Rex II. BSBA in Acctg., Ea. Ill. U., 1977. CPA, Wis., Colo. Mem. audit staff Price Waterhouse, Milw., 1978-80; audit sr. Price Waterhouse, Denver, 1980-82, audit mgr., 1982-85; contr. Western Gas Processors, Ltd., Denver, 1985—, v.p., 1988—; bd. dirs. TKE Enterprises, Denver. With USAF, 1971-74. Mem. Ranch Club. Republican. Home: 11200 Raritan St Denver CO 80234 Office: Western Gas Processors Ltd 10701 Melody Dr Denver CO 80234

BROCKISH, ROBERT FRANCIS, software systems consultant; b. Denver, July 14, 1931; s. Maruice Alexander and Clara Elizabeth (Gwartney) B.; m. Carol Marie Scott, Feb. 23, 1952; children: Timothy, Theodore, Mary, Thomas, Margaret, Madeline, Milissa, Amy. BS in Math., Regis Coll., 1956; postgrad., Denver U., 1957-59. Computer programmer The Martin Co., Denver, 1956-59; data processing mgr. Thiokol Chem. Co., Brigham City, Utah, 1959-66; sr. programmer IBM Corp., Boulder, Colo., 1966—; mem. exec. bd. Share, Chgo., 1963-64. lt. col. USMCR, 1949-52, Korea, ret. Res. 1974. Mem. Marine Corps Reserve Officers Assn., Boulder Assn. Computing Machines, Rocky Mountain Assn. Computing Machines, The Retired Officers Assn. Democrat. Roman Catholic. Lodges: KC, Elks. Home: 4095 Darley Ave Boulder CO 80303

BRODERICK, EDWARD MICHAEL, III, lawyer; b. Stamford, Conn., Nov. 4, 1947; s. Edward Michael Broderick and Lois Caroline (Brown) Contaras. BA, St. Anselm's Coll., Manchester, N.H., 1969; JD, St. John's U., N.Y.C., 1973. Bar: N.Y. 1974, Conn. 1974. Adminstrv. asst. of legis. affairs Royal Globe Ins. Cos., N.Y.C., 1970-74, atty., 1974-75; asst. gen. counsel and sec. Puritan Ins. Group, Stamford, 1975-79; sr. counsel Gen. Electric Credit Corp., Stamford, 1975-79; asst. gen. counsel ITT Fin. Corp., St. Louis, 1983-86; gen. counsel and sec. ITT Lyndon Ins. Group, St. Louis, 1979-86; v.p., gen. counsel Calfarm Ins. Group, Sacramento, 1986—. Mem. various Rep. campaigns, N.Y.C., Stamford and St. Louis, St. Louis Squires,, 1984-86. Mem. ABA, Conn. Bar Assn., N.Y. State Bar Assn. Republican. Roman Catholic. Office: Calfarm Ins Group 1601 Exposition Blvd Sacramento CA 95815

BRODERICK, HAROLD CHRISTIAN, interior designer; b. Oakland, Calif., Apr. 8, 1925; s. Harold Christian and Laura Jane (Lloyd) B. BA, U. Tex., 1947. A founder Arthur Elrod Assos., Inc., Palm Springs, Calif., 1954, now pres. Mem. Planning Commn., City of Palm Springs, 1972-74; trust Palm Springs Desert Mus.; mem. devel. com. Barbara Sinatra Children's Ctr. Mem. Am. Soc. Interior Designers. Republican. Office: Arthur Elrod Associates Inc 850 N Palm Canyon Dr Palm Springs CA 92262

BRODIAN, LAURA, broadcasting executive; b. Newark, Oct. 16, 1947; d. Sol and Jean Dolores (Posner) B.; m. Frank Kelly Freas, June 30, 1988. BA, Kean Coll., 1972; M in Music Edn., Ind. U., 1974, D in Mus. Edn., 1982. Lic. radio and TV operator. Tchr. various schs., N.J., 1967-72; assoc. instr. Ind. U., Bloomington, 1973-74; edn. dir. Ind. Arts Commn., Indpls., 1975-76; announcer, engr. Sta. WFIU-FM, Bloomington, 1979-80; announcer, producer Sta. KQED-FM, San Francisco, 1982-87; exec. producer, announcer Sta. KUSC-FM, L.A., 1987-88; exec. dir. fin., mktg., pub. rels. Kelly Freas Studios, 1988—. Host (syndicated classical music show) Music Through the Night, classical music in-flight program Delta Airlines, 1989—. Mem. Am. Women in Radio and TV, Bay Area English Regency Soc. (founder), So. Calif. Early Music Soc. (pres.). Jewish.

BRODIE, HOWARD, artist; b. Oakland, Calif., Nov. 28, 1915; s. Edward and Anna (Zeller) B. Student, Art Inst. San Francisco, Art Student's League, N.Y.C., U. Ghana, Accra; LHD (hon.), Acad. Art Coll., San Francisco, 1984. Mem. staff Life mag., Yank: the Army Weekly, Collier's, AP, CBS News, 1969—. Author: (book) Howard Brodie War Drawings, 1963; art journalist: (major wars) World War II, Korea, French Indo-China, Vietnam, (trials) Jack Ruby, Ray, Sirhan, My Lai, Chicago Seven, Watergate, John Hinckly, Klaus Barbie of France, (famous people) John Wayne, Pres. Kennedy, James Jones, Charles Manson; represented in pub. collections Calif. Palace of the Legion Hon., San Francisco, Soc. Illustrators, N.Y., Libr. Congress, Washington; guest on Merv Griffin Show, Charles Karalt Sunday Morning program. Sgt., U.S. Army. Decorated Bronze Star.

BRODNAX-WATSON, SHIRLEY JEAN, microbiologist; b. Norfolk, Va.; d. John B. and Louise (Booker) Holloway; m. Jack Leon Brodnax, July 31, 1976; children: Melodie, Tracey, Maisha. AA, Contra Costa Coll., 1978; BS in Cell and Molecular Biology, San Francisco State U., 1985. Jr. accountant Philco Corp., Phila.; sec., supr. U.S. Govt., Phila. and San Francisco, 1968-76; research asst., microbiologist Kelly Tech. Services, Oakland, Calif., 1986; microbiologist Nabisco Brands, Inc., Oakland, 1986—. Kennedy King scholar Contra Costa Coll., 1978-80. Mem. Internat. Platform Assn. Roman Catholic. Home: 1537 Hellings Ave Richmond CA 94801 Office: Nabisco Brands Inc 98th Ave Oakland CA 94630

BRODY, ADAM RANDALL, aerospace engineer; b. Aug. 1, 1963; s. Gary Robert and Sheila Claire (Weitzman) B. SB, MIT, 1985, SM, 1987; diploma, Internat. Space U., 1987. Research asst. MIT Space Systems Lab., Cambridge, Mass., 1985-87; aerospace engr. Sterling Software, Palo Alto, Calif., 1987—. Contbr. computer manuals in field. Mem. AIAA, Aerospace Med. Assn., Planetary Soc., Air and Space Smithsonian Instn. (assoc.). Club: Mountain View (Calif.) Tennis. Home: 333 Escuela Ave #117 Mountain View CA 94040 Office: Sterling Software NASA Ames Rsch Ctr MS239-15 Moffett Field CA 94035

BRODY, ROBERT ALAN, service executive; b. Bklyn., Dec. 24, 1945; s. Harold I. and Lillian (Albert) B.; m. Cynthia Dean Black, Sept. 29, 1984. BA, State U. Col., Cortland, N.Y., 1969; MS in Edn., SUNY, Albany, 1972; Le Grande Diplome d'Etudes Culinares, La Varenne Ecole de Cuisine, Paris, 1977. Chef Obadiah's Restaurant, Nantucket, Mass., 1979, Apley's Restaurant, Sheraton Hotel, Boston, 1980-83; exec. chef Sheraton Grand on Harbor Island, San Diego, 1983-85, Sheraton Hotels on Harbor Island, San Diego, 1985—; Bd. dirs. San Diego Chefs de Cuisine. Vol. Vista In Service to Am., W.Va., 1968. Included in Honor Roll of Am. Chefs, Food & Wine Mag., 1983; named Alumni of Distinction SUNY, Cortland, 1985, Alumni of Yr. SUNY Cortland, 1989; recipient Pres.'s award Sheraton Corp., 1989. Mem. San Diego Chefs de Cuisine, Sheraton Corp. N.Am. Culinary Team. Home: 4516 Lucille Dr San Diego CA 92115

BRODY-WATTS, STELLA, nurse; b. Athens, Greece, Oct. 15, 1939; came to U.S., 1965; d. Isaac Leon and Alice (Levy) Leontsini; m. William Brody, June 11, 1963 (div. 1977); children: Suzanne, David, Alexia; m. Dan Pike Watts III, Nov. 19, 1977. AA in Nursing, El Camino Coll., Torrance, Calif., 1974. RN, Calif. Operating room nurse Bay Harbor Hosp., Lomita, Calif., 1974-76, Kaiser Hosp., Harbor City, Calif., 1976-78, Dr. Sheldon Thorrens, Torrance, 1978-79, Long Beach (Calif.) Meml. Hosp., 1979-85; recreational nurse Am. Travel Cons., Redondo Beach, Calif., 1985—; part time nurse South Bay Hosp., Redondo Beach, 1989—. Editor newsletter South Bay Women in Travel, 1988—. Mem. Assn. Operating Room Nurses (editor newsletter South Bay chpt., pres., 1982-83), Opera Guild So. Calif. Democrat. Jewish. Home: 513 Via La Selva Redondo Beach CA 90177 Office: Am Travel Cons 114 S Catalina Ave Redondo Beach CA 90277

BROGLIATTI, BARBARA SPENCER, television and motion picture executive; b. Los Angeles, Jan. 8, 1946; d. Robert and Lottie (Goldstein) Spencer; m. Raymond Haley Brogliatti, Sept. 19, 1970. BA in Social Scis. and English, UCLA, 1968. Asst. press. info. dept. CBS TV, L.A., 1968-69, sr. publicist, 1969-74; dir. publicity Tandem Prodns. and T.A.T. Communications (Embassy Communications), L.A., 1974-77, corp. v.p., 1977-82, sr. v.p. worldwide publicity, promotion and advt. Embassy Communications, Los Angeles, 1982-85; sr. v.p. worldwide corp. communications Lorimar Telepictures Corp., Culver City, Calif., 1985-89; chmn. Brogliatti Co., Burbank, Calif., 1989—; bd. govs. TV Acad., L.A., 1984-86. Bd. dirs. KIDSNET, Washington, 1987—. Recipient Gold medallion Broadcast Promotion and Mktg. Execs., 1984. Mem. Dirs. Guild Am., Publicists Guild, Acad. TV

Arts and Scis. Office: Brogliatti Co 3601 W Olive Ave Ste 430 Burbank CA 91505

BROIDO, DEBRA ANN, real estate manager; b. Winston-Salem, N.C., Nov. 26, 1954; d. Billy Clay Foster and Edna Cleo (Wyatt) Radford; m. Edgar Alan Proido, Feb. 14, 1981 (div. 1986). AA in Bus. Adminstrn., Long Beach City Coll., 1985; student, Calif. State U., Long Beach, 1986—. Asst. v.p., maj. bldgs. mgr. Crocker Bank, L.A., 1979-80, asst. v.p., project mgr., 1980-84, asst. v.p., design mgr., 1984-85, asst. v.p., real estate negotiator, 1985-86; v.p., asst. real estate mgr. Wells Fargo Bank, L.A., 1986—; mem. curriculum rev. bd., Woodbury U., L.A., 1982-84. Mem. Assn. Corp. Real Estate. Office: Wells Fargo Bank Ste 840 333 S Grand Ave Los Angeles CA 90071

BROM, LIBOR, political science educator, journalist; b. Ostrava, Czechoslovakia, Dec. 17, 1923; came to U.S., 1958, naturalized, 1964; s. Ladislav and Bozena (Bromova) B.; m. Gloria S. Mena, Aug. 31, 1961; 1 son, Rafael Brom. Ing., Czech Inst. Tech., 1948; J.U.C., Charles U. Prague, 1951; postgrad., San Francisco State Coll.; M.A., U. Colo., 1962, Ph.D., 1970. V.p. Brom, Inc., Ostrava, 1942-48; economist Slovak Magnesite Works, Prague, Czechoslovakia, 1948-49; economist, chief planner Vodostavba, Navika, Prague, 1951-56; tchr. Jefferson County Schs., Colo., 1958-67; prof., dir. Russian area studies program U. Denver, 1967—; journalist, mem. editorial staff Denni Hlasatel-Daily Herald, Chgo., 1978—; Pres. Colo. Nationalities Council, 1970-72; comptroller Exec. Bd. Nat. Heritage Groups Council, 1970-72; mem. adv. bd. Nat. Security Council, 1980-85; acad. bank participant Heritage Found; adv. bd. Independence Inst. Author: Ivan Bunin's Proteges, Leonid Zurov, 1973, in Czech, In the Windstorms of Anger, 1976, On Restoring the Moral Order, 1980, Time and Duty, 1981, Teacher of Nations and Our Times, 1983, The Way of Light, 1983, On the Attack, 1983, Between the Currents, 1985; translator: Problems of Geography, 1955. V.p. Colo. Citizenship Day, 1968-69; pres. Comenius World Coun., 1976-85, World Representation of Czechoslovak Exiles, 1976-85; pres. Czeck World Union, 1985—; acting gen. sec. Czechoslovak Republican Movement. Recipient Americanism medal DAR, 1969, Disting. Service award Am. by Choice, 1968, Kynewisbov Pioneer award Denver U., 1989; named Tchr. with Superlative Performance MLA, 1961, Outstanding Faculty mem. Omicron Delta Kappa, 1972, The Order of M.R. Stefanik Provisional Czechoslovak Govt. in Exile. Mem. Econ. Inst. Rsch. and Edn., Am. Assn. Tchrs. Slavic and Eastern European Langs. (v.p. 1973-75), Am. Assn. Advancement Slavic Studies, Intercollegiate Studies Inst., Western Social Sci. Assn., Rocky Mountain Assn. Slavic Studies (sec. treas. 1975-78, v.p. 1978-81, pres. 1982-83), Rocky Mountain Modern Lang. Assn., Czechoslovak Christian Democratic Movement in Exile (central com. 1970-79), Dobro Slovo (hon.), Slava (hon.), Aleksandr Solzhenitsyn Soc., Shavano Inst. Nat. Leadership, Nat. Rep. Nationalities Coun. (co-chmn. human rights com. 1979-81), Lincoln Ednl. Found., Phi Beta Kappa (hon.). Republican. Roman Catholic. Home: 39 Hillside Dr Lakewood CO 80215 Office: Univ Denver Denver CO 80208-0293

BROM, ROBERT H., bishop; b. Arcadia, Wis., Sept. 18, 1938. Ed., St. Mary's Coll., Winona, Minn., Gregorian U., Rome. Ordained priest Roman Catholic Ch., 1963, consecrated bishop, 1983. Bishop of Duluth Minn., 1983-89; coadjutor bishop Diocese of San Diego, 1989—. Home and Office: Chancery Office 2031 Sunset Blvd San Diego CA 92103 *

BROMM, ROBERT DALE, nuclear engineer; b. San Pedro, Calif., Nov. 13, 1950; s. Robert and Olive Genevive (Hart) B.; m. Linda Suzanne Owens, June 30, 1973 (div. June 1986); children: Christina Ann, Ryan David; m. Margaret Rose Meusborn, Jan., 14, 1989; 1 adopted child, Mindy Christine. BSME, Calif. State Poly. U., 1973; MBA, Idaho State U., 1985. Registered profl. engr., Calif. Engr. Bechtel Power Corp., Norwalk, Calif., 1973-76; engring. specialist EG&G Idaho Inc., Idaho Falls, 1977-85; remote systems and robotics engr. Flour Daniel, Irvine, Calif., 1985—. Mem. Idaho Am. Nuclear Soc. (pub. info. chair, 1983-85), L.A. Am. Nuclear Soc. (pub. info. chmn. and bd. dirs. 1985—), Toastmasters (Irvine) (pres. 1988), Mensa (local sec. SE Idaho chpt. 1985). Office: Flour Daniel 3333 Michelson Dr Irvine CA 92730

BRONDOS, GREGORY ALAN, pathologist; b. West Frankfort, Ill., Jan. 7, 1938; s. Stephen and Margaret (Palic) B.; m. Sharon Elaine Hardy, May 7, 1966; children: Gregory A. Jr., Thomas Edward, Pamala Margaret. Student, U. Ill., 1958; BA, Milligan Coll., 1960; MD, Bowman Gray, 1964. Diplomate Am. Bd. Pathology, Anatomic Pathology, Clin. Pathology. Intern, resident N.C. Bapt. Hosp., Winston-Salem, 1964-66; resident New England Deaconess, Boston, 1966-69; pathologist Meml. Hosp. Natrona County, Wyo. Med. Ctr., Casper, Wyo., 1971—; cons. Converse County Meml. Hosp., Douglas, Wyo., 1981—; adj. prof. U. Wyo., Casper, 1976—; clin. faculty mem. family practice, pathology U. Wyo., 1988. Contbr. articles to profl. jours. Pres., bd. dirs. YMCA, Casper, 1978-81; pres. Grace Luth. Ch. Council, Casper, 1982-85; mem. Ft. Caspar Adv. Commn., 1981-88; mem. Natrona County Sch. Bd., Casper, 1982—, chmn., 1985-86. Served to maj. USAF, 1969-71. Fellow Am. Cancer Soc., Boston, 1967-68, Harvard Med. Sch., Boston, 1967-69. Fellow Am. Soc. Clin. Pathologists, Coll. Am. Pathologists; mem. Wyo. Soc. Pathologists (sec. treas. 1976-82), Colo. Soc. Clin. Pathologists. Republican. Lodge: Lions. Home: Box 9057 Casper WY 82609 Office: Wyo Med Ctr 1233 E 2d St Casper WY 82601

BRONNIMANN, DANETTA ANDREA, physician, researcher; b. Visalia, Calif., June 29, 1953; d. O. James and Ludmilla B.; m. Mark Bernard Mecikalski, June 13, 1983; 2 children. BA, U. Ariz., 1976, MD, 1981. Diplomate Am. Bd. Internal Medicine. Intern U. Utah Affiliated Hosps., Salt Lake City, 1981-82; resident U. Ariz. Health Sci. Ctr., Tucson, 1982-84; pulmonary fellowhip Div. Respiratory Sci., U. Ariz., Tucson, 1984-86, research assoc., 1986—. Contbr. articles to profl. jours. Grantee Charles A. Lindbergh Fund, 1988, Ariz. Lung Assn., 1988. Fellow Am. Coll. Chest Physicians; mem. AMA, Am. Coll. Physicians, Am. Thoracic Soc., AAAS. Office: U Med Ctr Div Respiratory Scis 1501 N Campbell Tucson AZ 85724

BRONSKI, EUGENE WILLIAM, corporate executive; b. Detroit, Apr. 12, 1936; s. Eugene and Frances (Maehler) B.; children: Donna, Karen, Michael; m. Frances P. Sweenie, July 26, 1986. B.A., Wayne State U., 1958, J.D., 1961. Bar: Mich. 1962. Staff atty. Detroit Edison Co., 1963-68; gen. counsel Greyhound Food Mgmt., Inc., Detroit, 1968-74; v.p. indsl. relations Greyhound Food Mgmt., Inc., 1974-76, v.p., corp. counsel, 1976-81; sr. v.p. adminstrn. The Greyhound Corp., Phoenix, 1981-87, sr. v.p. mfg. and services, 1988—; mem. panel arbitrators Am. Arbitration Assn., 1972—; dir. Foodservice & Lodging Inst., Washington, 1975—, pres., 1980—; dir. Restaura, S.A., Restauration Roger Lorent, S.A., Southcoast Systems, Dallas Smith Engring., Greyhound Exposition Service, Motor Coach Industries, Transp. Mfg. Corp., Universal Coach Parts. Bd. dirs. Nat. Com. Prevention fo Child Abuse, 1986, Ariz. Lung Assn. Mem. State Bar Mich. Address: 1933 Greyhound Tower Phoenix AZ 85077

BRONSTEIN, GERALD MORTON, holding company executive; b. N.Y.C., Jan. 16, 1927; s. Jay and Dorothy (Meyers) B.; m. Carolyn Zena Falitz, July 12, 1953; children: Nancy, John, William, Robert. BS, UCLA, 1947. C.P.A., Calif. Acct. Rashba, Pokart & Greene (C.P.A.s), Los Angeles and San Francisco, 1947-52; ptnr. Bronley Bldg. Co., Los Angeles, 1952-67, United Continental Devel. Corp., Los Angeles, 1967-69; pres. Bomaine Corp., Los Angeles, 1969—. Served with USNR, 1945-46. Home: 7102 Crest Rd Rancho Palos Verde CA 90274 Office: Bomaine Corp 2716 Ocean Park Blvd #1030 Santa Monica CA 90405

BROOK, WINSTON ROLLINS, audio-video design consultant; b. Cameron, Tex., Aug. 20, 1931; s. Winston Marshall and Maude Katherine (Woody) B. BA, U. Denver, 1955. Lic. radiotelephone operator, FCC. Engr. Sta. WKNO-TV, Memphis, 1965-67; instr. Memphis State U., 1967-69; audio-visual dir. So. Coll. Optometry, Memphis, 1968-73; sr. cons. Bolt Beranek and Newman, Chgo. and Los Angeles, 1973-87; owner, operator RB Systems, Los Angeles, 1987—; instr. various seminars and workshops; assoc. editor Theater Design & Tech. mag., N.Y.C., 1981-87; tech. cons. Sound & Video Contractor mag., Overland, Kans., 1987—. Contbr. articles to profl. jours., 1978-87; co-author: Handbook for Sound Engineers, 1987. Bd. dirs. Back Alley Theatre, Los Angeles, 1988. Mem. Audio Engring. Soc., Acoustical Soc. Am., U.S. Inst. for Theatre Tech. Democrat. Mormon. Home and Office: 5715 Calvin Tarzana CA 91356

BROOKBANK, JOHN W(ARREN), retired microbiology educator; b. Seattle, Apr. 3, 1927; s. Earl Bruce and Louise Sophia (Stoecker) B.; m. Marcia Ireland, Sept. 16, 1950 (div. 1978); children: Ursula Ireland, John W. Jr., Phoebe Bruce; m. Sally Satterberg Cahill, Aug. 6, 1983. BA, U. Wash., 1950, MS, 1953; PhD, Calif. Inst. Tech., 1955. Asst. prof. U. Fla., Gainesville, 1955-58, assoc. prof., 1958-68, prof. microbiology and cell sci., 1968-85, prof. emeritus, 1985—; vis. assoc. prof. U. Fla. Coll. Medicine, Gainesville, 1961-63, U. Wash., Seattle, 1965; cons. in field, Friday Harbor, Wash. 1986—. Author: Developmental Biology, 1978; (with W. Cunningham) Gerontology, 1988; editor: Improving Quality of Health Care for the Elderly, 1977; contbr. articles to profl. jours. Pres. Griffin Bay Preservation Com., Friday Harbor, 1985—, Bridge Council on Narcotics Addiction, Gainesville, 1974, Marine Environ. Consortium, 1986—; founding pres. Gainesville Regional Council on Alcoholism, 1976. Research grantee NIH, 1957-80, NSF, 1972-73. Mem. Am. Soc. Zoologists, Soc. Devel. Biology, The Gerontol. Soc. Am., Sigma Xi. Republican. Episcopalian. Club: Seattle Tennis. Home: PO Box 2688 Friday Harbor WA 98250

BROOKE, EDNA MAE, business educator; b. Las Vegas, Nev., Feb. 10, 1923; d. Alma Lyman and Leah Mae (Ketcham) Shurtliff; m. Bill T. Brooke, Dec. 22, 1949; 1 child, John C. BS in Acctg., Ariz. State U., 1965, MA in Edn., 1967, EdD, 1975. Grad. teaching asst. Ariz. State U., Tempe, 1968-69; prof. bus. Maricopa Tech. Coll., Phoenix, 1967-72, assoc. dean instl. services, 1972-74; prof. bus. and acctg. Scottsdale (Ariz.) Community Coll., 1974—; cons. in field. Author: The Effectiveness of Three Techniques Used in Teaching First Semester Accounting Principles to Tech. Jr. College Students, 1974. Mem. Nat. Bus. Edn. Assn., Western Bus. Edn. Assn., Ariz. Bus. Edn. Assn., Am. Acctg. Assn., Delta Pi Epsilon. Home: 2139 E Solano Dr Phoenix AZ 85016 Office: Scottsdale Community Coll 9000 E Chaparral Scottsdale AZ 85252

BROOKE, PENNY SIMPSON, lawyer, nurse; b. Salt Lake City, Sept. 25, 1945; d. Robert Dawson and Charlene (Lohman) Simpson; m. Wallace Sands Brooke Jr.; children: Amie Elizabeth, Benjamin Sands. BS in Nursing, U. Utah, 1969, MS in Psychiat. Nursing Children, 1974, JD, 1984. Bar: Utah 1984, U.S. Dist. Ct. Utah. Staff nurse Health Dept. Salt Lake City County, 1969-70; sch. nurse Anchorage Borough Sch. Dist., 1970-72; assoc. prof. Coll. Nursing U. Utah, Salt Lake City, 1974-88, asst. dean Coll. Nursing, 1985—; assoc., of counsel Winder & Haslam Law Firm, Salt Lake City, 1984—; exec. bd. U.S. West Communications, Salt Lake City, 1985—; trustee Intermountain Health Care, Salt Lake City, 1987—; mem. bd/ gov's. LDS Hosp., 1989—. Contbr. articles to profl. jours. Bd. dirs. Pioneer Theater Co., Salt Lake City, 1987—; mem. Govenors Com. on officer, dir. liability criminal justice systems. 1987-88. Mem. Am. Nurses Assn., Am. Assn. Nurse Atty's., Utah State Bar Edn. Law Sect. (chmn. 1988—, vice chmn. 1987-88, sec. 1986-87), Utah State Bar Assn., Nat. Assn. Coll. U. Attys., Utah Nurses Assn. (task force govt. rels. 1986-87), Attys., Jr. League (pub. issues, advocacy chmn. 1979-80, area IV dir. 1980-81), Sigma Theta Tau. Home: 2879 Jennie Ln Salt Lake City UT 84117 Office: U Utah Coll Nursing 25 So Medical Dr Salt Lake City UT 84112

BROOKES, VALENTINE, lawyer; b. Red Bluff, Calif., May 30, 1913; s. Langley and Ethel (Valentine) B.; m. Virginia Stovall Cunningham, Feb. 11, 1939; children—Langley (Mrs. Jerrold B. Brandt), Lawrence Valentine, Alan Cunningham. A.B., U. Calif., Berkeley, 1934, J.D., 1937. Bar: Calif. bar 1937, U.S. Supreme Ct. bar 1942. Asst. franchise tax counsel State of Calif., 1937-40; dep. atty. gen. Calif., 1940-42; spl. asst. to U.S. atty. gen., asst. to solicitor gen. U.S., 1942-44; partner firm Kent & Brookes, San Francisco, 1944-70, Alvord & Alvord, Washington, 1944-50, Lee, Toomey & Kent, Washington, 1950-79; partner firm Brookes and Brookes, San Francisco, 1971-88, of counsel, 1988—; lectr. Hastings Coll. Law, U. Calif., 1941-48, U. Calif. Law Sch., Berkeley, 1948-70. Author: The Continuity of Interest Test in Reorganizations, 1946, The Partnership Under the Income Tax Laws, 1949, The Tax Consequences of Widows Elections in Community Property States, 1951, Corporate Trasactions Involving Its Own Stock, 1954, Litigation Expenses and the Income Tax, 1957. Bd. dirs. Children's Hosp. Med. Center of N. Calif., 1963-74, v.p., 1968-70; trustee Oakes Found., 1957-70; regent St. Mary's Coll., Calif., 1968-88, pres. bd., 1970-72, emeritus mem., 1988—. Fellow Am. Bar Found. (life); mem. Am. Law Inst., ABA (chmn. com. on statute of limitations 1954-57, mem. council, tax sect. 1960-63), Calif. Bar Assn. (chmn. com. on taxation 1950-52, 60-61), Soc. Calif. Pioneers (v.p. 1964, 1975-86), Am. Coll. Tax Counsel, Phi Kappa Sigma, Phi Delta Phi. Republican. Clubs: Pacific Union, Orinda Country, Bankers, World Trade. Home and Office: 7 Sycamore Rd Orinda CA 94563

BROOKMAN, ANTHONY RAYMOND, lawyer; b. Chgo., Mar. 23, 1922; s. Raymond Charles and Marie Clara (Alberg) B.; m. Marilyn Joyce Brookman, June 5, 1982; children: Meribeth Brookman Farmer, Anthony Raymond, Lindsay Logan Christienson. Student Ripon Coll., 1940-41; BS, Northwestern U., 1947; JD, U. Calif.-San Francisco, 1953. Bar: Calif. 1954. Law clk. to presiding justice Calif. Supreme Ct., 1953-54; ptnr. Nichols, Williams, Morgan, Digardi & Brookman, 1954-68; sr. ptnr. Brookman & Hoffman, Inc., Walnut Creek, Calif., 1968—. Pres., Young Republicans Calif., San Mateo County, 1953-54. Served to 1st lt. USAF. Mem. ABA, Alameda County Bar Assn., State Bar Calif., Lawyers Club Alameda County, Alameda-Contra Costa County Trial Lawyers Assn., Assn. Trial Lawyers Am., Calif. Trial Lawyers Assn. Republican. Clubs: Masons, Athenian Nile, Crow Canyon Country, Shriners. Pub. Contra Costa New Register. Office: Brookman & Hoffman 901 H St Ste 200 Sacramento CA 95814 also: 1990 N California Blvd Walnut Creek CA 94596 also: 2119 W March Ln Ste A Stockton CA 95207

BROOKRESON, WILLIAM EDWARD, SR., state agency administrator; b. Las Cruces, N.Mex., Sept. 1, 1946; s. John William and Francis (Snyman) B.; m. Myra Lucretia Dodd; children: Leesa L., Elizabeth L., William Edward Jr., Nathaniel B. AA, Lower Columbia Coll., 1966; BA, Western Wash. U., 1968; MA, U. Ill., 1972. With Wash. State Dept. Agr., 1972—, chief dep., 1980-84; program mgr. Wash. State Dept. Agr., Olympia, Wash., 1985—. Del. Dem. State Convs., Longview, 1976, 80; precinct committeeman Dem. Party, Longview, 1980-82; del. to bd. dirs. United Ministries in Higher Edn., Seattle, 1988—; bd. dirs. Community Action Planning Coun., Longview, 1980-82, treas. bd., 1981, v.p. bd., 1982; bd. dirs. Cowlitz-Waikaikum Fedn. State Employees, Longview, 1980-82, Associated Ministries of Thurston County, Olympia, 1985-87, Thurston County Ministries in Higher Edn., Olympia, 1986—; outreach chair United Chs. of Olympia, 1986-87. NDEA Title IV fellow U. Ill., 1968-71; recipient Disting. Mgmt. award Gov. State of Wash., 1988. Mem. Am. Assn. Grain Inspection and Weighing Agys. (treas. 1986-88, v.p. 1988—), No. Grain Insps. Orgn., Wash. Dry Pea and Lentil Assn. (assoc.), Gov.'s Disting. Mgr.'s Assn., Wash. Fedn. State Employees (pres. Longview chpt. 1976-82). Presbyterian. Home: 4907 25th Ave SE Lacey WA 98503 Office: Wash State Dept Agr 2728 Westmoor Ct Ste B Olympia WA 98502

BROOKS, EDWARD HOWARD, college administrator; b. Salt Lake City, Mar. 2, 1921; s. Charles Campbell and Margery (Howard) B.; m. Courtaney June Perren, May 18, 1946; children: Merrillee Brooks Runyan, Robin Anne (Mrs. R. Bruce Pollock). B.A., Stanford U., 1942, M.A., 1947, Ph.D., 1950. Mem. faculty, adminstrn. Stanford U., 1949-71; provost Claremont (Calif.) Colls., 1971-81; v.p. Claremont U. Center, 1979-81; sr. v.p. Claremont McKenna Coll., 1981-84; provost Scripps Coll., 1987-89, acting pres., 1989—. Trustee EDUCOM, 1978-80, Webb Sch. of Calif., 1979—, Menlo Sch. and Coll., 1985-88; bd. overseers Hoover Instn., 1972-78; bd. dirs. Student Loan Mktg. Assn., 1973-77; mem. Calif. Student Aid Commn., 1984-88, chmn., 1986-88. Served with AUS, 1942-45. Clubs: University (Los Angeles); Bohemian (San Francisco). Home: PO Box 132S Claremont CA 91711 Office: Scripps Coll Balch 5 Claremont CA 91711

BROOKS, FOREST CLYDE, civil engineer; b. Seattle, Sept. 13, 1947; s. Clyde N. and Angela Teresa (Kennedy) B.; m. Catherine Susan Burns, Oct. 15, 1977. BSCE, Seattle U., 1970; water resources planner cert., Bd. Engrs. for Rivers and Harbors, Ft. Belvoir, Va., 1980. Survey crew mem. C.E., U.S. Army, Eureka, Mont., 1969; engr. trainee C.E., U.S. Army, Seattle, 1969-71, hydraulic engr., 1971-72, study mgr. asst., 1972-73, study mgr., 1973-84, project mgr., 1984—. Co-editor, author: (monthly newsletter) Unltd. News Jour., 1981—. basketball statistician Seattle U., 1965—; asst. cross country coach Seattle Prep High Sch., 1966—, asst. swimming coach, 1987—; asst. coach Tigers Masters Swim Team, 1984—; youth sport coach Cath. Youth Orgn., Seattle, 1967-79; survey and pit tour Seattle Seafair Hydroplane Race, 1972—. Recipient Commendation award Wash. Second. Sch. Athletic Adminstrs. Assn., 1982, Outstanding Achievement and Contbn. award, Seattle U., 1985. Mem. Soc. Am. Mil. Engrs., Steamship Hist. Soc. Am., Nat. Bldg. Mus., Wash. Environ. Council., Sierra Club, The Nature Conservancy, Am. Forestry Assn., Pacific N.W. Masters Swimming, Pacific NW Writers Conf., Am. Swimming Coaches Assn. (level 2 cert.), Masters Aquatics Coaches Assn., Tau Beta Pi, Pi Mu Epsilon, Alpha Sigma Nu. Republican. Roman Catholic. Clubs: Unltds. Unanimous (Seattle); Unlmtds. (Detroit). Home: 6917 S 131 St Seattle WA 98178 Office: Seattle Dist CE US Army 4735 E Marginal Way S Seattle WA 98124

BROOKS, GLENN ALLEN, telecommunications engineer; b. Pasadena, Calif., Mar. 23, 1960; s. Robert Allen and Sarah Eloise (Merritt) B.; m. Tracy Jo Williams, June 11, 1983; children: Joshua Allen Ray, Ashleigh Nicole, Jonathan Lincoln. AA, Golden West Coll., Huntington Beach, Calif., 1983; BS, San Diego State U., 1985. Owner Moriah Recording Svcs., San Diego, 1983-84; asst. account exec. Cox Cable, San Diego, 1985; 2d engr. Studio West, San Diego, 1983-84; audio engr. KPBS-TV, San Diego, 1984-85, Group W., Santa Monica, Calif., 1985-86; owner Small World Prodns., Huntington Beach, Calif., 1986—; freelance engr. Video General, Long Beach, Calif., 1988—; audio engr. KSCI-TV, Los Angeles, 1986-88; syncronist, audio engr. Chace Prodns., Hollywood, Calif., 1988; cons. in field; patentee in field. Mem. Internat. Alliance TV Sound Engrs. Republican. Home and Office: 5522 Harold Pl Huntington Beach CA 92647

BROOKS, JOHN ALLAN, petroleum engineer; b. Houston, June 8, 1961; s. Orban Charles and Georgia Ruth (Pitt) B. BS in Petroleum Engring., U. Tex., 1984. Summer intern engr. Union Tex. Petroleum Corp., Houston, 1982-84; directional drilling svc. engr. N.L. Sperry/ Sun, Houston, 1984; prodn. engr. Ranger Oil Co., Houston, 1985-87; petroleum engr. Ampol Exploration (U.S.A.) Inc., Denver, 1987—. Mem. Soc. Petroleum Engrs. (jr. mem., microcumpters study group steering com. Denver sect., newsletter editor 1989—, chpt. program chmn., v.p. 1983-84), U. Tex. Ex-Students Assn. Home: 1811 S Quebec Way 233 Denver CO 80231 Office: Ampol Exploration USA Inc 1225 17th St Ste 3000 Denver CO 80202

BROOKS, MARK DAVID, accountant; b. N.Y.C., May 20, 1962; s. Elmer and Frances Earlen (Thompson) B. BS in Acctg., U. Ariz., 1985. Sales rep. Sears & Roebuck, Tucson, 1984-85; procurement acct. The Ariz. Bank, Phoenix, 1985; deposit acct. The Ariz. Bank, 1985-86, acctg. officer, 1986—. Bd. dirs. Ariz. Supreme Ct., Foster Care Rev. Bd., Phoenix, 1988. Mem. Ariz. Assn. urban Bankers, Ariz. Alliance of Bus. Democrat. Baptist. Home: 347 W Carmen St Tempe AZ 85283

BROOKS, PATTON MARTIN, food products merchandiser; b. Comanche, Okla., Dec. 24, 1939; s. Cecil Bryant and Murrel (Bounds) B.; m. Patricia McMahan, June 1, 1963; children: Gary, Lynn. Student, Draughns Bus. Sch., 1958-59, Modesto Jr. Coll., 1961, Delta Jr. Coll., 1979-80. From clk. to asst. mgr. Safeway Stores, various locations, 1956-61, Save Mart Stores, Modesto, Calif., 1962-67; buyer, merchandiser Save Mart Stores, Modesto, 1981—; store mgr. Save Mart Stores, Manteca, Calif., 1967-80. Bd. dirs. Manteca C. of C., 1970-71, 77-78. Served with USAR, 1963-66. Mem. Frozen Food Council No. Calif. (charter, treas. 1985, sec. 1986, chmn. mem. 1987, 1st v.p. 1988, pres. 1989—). Democrat. Lodge: Kiwanis. Home: 136 Hintze Ave Modesto CA 95354 Office: Save Mart Supermarkets 1800 Standiford Ave PO Box 4278 Modesto CA 95352-4278

BROOKS, SHEILA JEANNE, librarian; b. San Francisco, May 13, 1944; d. John W. Brooks and Flora A. (Adams) Farnbach. BA, U. Calif., Davis, 1966. Cert. secondary teaching, adminstr., librarian. Tchr. Ukiah (Calif.) Unified Schs., 1967-75, librarian, 1975—; instr. Santa Rosa Jr. Coll. Extension, Ukiah, 1969-71; mem. Instructional Media Ctr. Adv. Bd., Ukiah, 1987—; adv. Calif. Scholarship Fedn., Ukiah, 1974-87. Mem. Mendocino County Public Library Adv. Bd., Ukiah, 1972-88. Mem. Calif. Media and Library Educators Assn., Calif. Tchrs. Assn., Am. Fedn. Tchrs., Ukiah High Sch. Faculty Assn. (sec. 1986-87, treas. 1987-88), AAUW Women (v.p. membership Ukiah br. 1985-87). Democrat. Club: Oak Hill Pool (Ukiah) (pres. 1982, treas. 1983). Office: Ukiah High Sch 1000 Low Gap Rd Ukiah CA 95482

BROOKS, SUSAN MARIE, editor in chief; b. Davenport, IA, Sept. 2, 1960; d. Alexander Adam and Marlys Ruth Teel; m. James Michael Brooks, April 1980; (div.) June 1982; m. Anthony Mario Assenza, Oct. 13, 1987; 1 child: Jenna Marie. Student, Los Angeles Valley Coll., N. Hollywood, 1979-80. Editorial ass. Larry Flynt Pub., Los Angeles, Calif., 1982-83, Petersen Pub., 1984-85; assoc. editor Weider Pub., Woodland Hills, Calif., 1985-86; freelance writer Los Angeles, Calif., 1986-87; mng. editor Liberation Pub., Los Angeles, Calif, 1987--. Author article 1988. Mem. PTA Canoga Park, Calif., 1988-89. Salesperson Calif. Dept real estate, 1987. Rep. Catholic. Home: 7501 Quakertown Ave Canoga Park CA 91306 Office: LP Inc 6922 Hollywood Blvd Los Angeles CA 91306

BROOKSHAW, SANDRA KAY, elementary school teacher; b. Joplin, Mo., Nov. 30, 1943; d. LeRoy Max and Helen Frances (Beach) Wade; m. James Theodore Lyle, Jan. 30, 1965 (div. May 1970); children: Troy James, Todd Lee; m. Terry Weldon Brookshaw, Feb. 10, 1979; 1 child, Ryan Wade. BS, U. So. Calif., 1965; MS, Calif. State U., Fullerton, 1979. Tchr. Inglewood (Calif.) Unified Sch. Dist., 1965-79, 85-86, Las Virgenes Unified Sch. Dist., West Lake Village, Calif., 1986—; tchr., mentor English-as-second lang., Las Virgenes Unified Sch. Dist., 1987-88; master tchr. Nat. Charity League U. So. Calif. Tchr. Tng. Ctr., 1987-88. Author: (with others) Fairy Tales, 1971, Continuous Progress Mathematics, vol. 1, 1973, vol. 2, 1974. Mem. Greater. Covington (La.) Jr. Service League, 1984-85, Parish Pres. Commn. on Women; pres. Tammany Parish, La., 1982-84; fund raising counselor Helen Grace Chocolates, Los Angeles, 1979-82; founder, dir. St. Timothy Mother's Day Out, Mandeville, La., 1981-83. Recipient Favorite Tchr. Apple award Daily News, San Fernando Valley, 1987, Am. Assn. Univ. Women scholar, 1984; recognised by Pres. Regan as Outstanding Community leader, New Orleans, 1984. Mem. PTA (hon. life mem. 1979), Las Virgenes Tchrs. Assn., Calif. Tchrs. Assn. NEA, AAUW (pres. Mandeville, La. 1982-84). Republican. Methodist. Office: Willow Elem Sch 29026 Lara Dr Agoura CA 91301

BROOMFIELD, ANN LOUISE, heavy construction company executive; b. Portland, Oreg., June 2, 1943; d. Harold Eugene and Betty Anne (Applegate) Sanders; m. Robert William Broomfield, July 1, 1978; 1 child, Mary Louise. AA, Pima Coll., Tucson, 1978, postgrad., 1978—. Cert. constrn. assoc. Civil engring. technician, maintenance analyst Ariz. Dept. Transp., 1975-82; office mgr., adminstrn. asst., comptroller Borderland Constrn. Co., Inc., 1982-86; office adminstr. Prodn. Concrete Constrn. Inc., Tucson, 1986—. Bd. dirs. Big Bros./Big Sisters; life mem. Girl Scouts US; active United Way. Mem. Nat. Assn. Women in Constrn. (chpt. pres. 1983-85, cert. constrn. assoc. coordinator for edn. found., 1986-88, nat. occupation rsch. and referral com. chmn., 1985-86, nat. nominating com. 1985-86, coordinator nat. com. 1987-88, regional dir. 1988—), NRA, Nat. Wildlife Fedn. (life), Am. Biog. Inst. (hon.), Nat. C. of C. for Women, NAFE, Nat. Fedn. Bus. and Profl. Women's Club, ACLU, NOW, Phi Theta Kappa. Democrat. Episcopalian.

BROOMFIELD, ROBERT CAMERON, judge; b. Detroit, June 18, 1933; s. David Campbell and Mabel Margaret (Van Deventer) B.; m. Cuma Lorena Cecil, Aug. 3, 1958; children: Robert Cameron Jr., Alyson Paige, Scott McKinley. BS, Pa. State U., 1955; LLB, U. Ariz., 1961. Bar: Ariz. 1961, U.S. Dist. Ct. Ariz. 1961. Assoc. Carson, Messinger, Elliot, Laughlin & Ragan, Phoenix, 1962-65, ptnr., 1966-71; judge Ariz. Superior Ct., Phoenix, 1971-85, U.S. Dist. Ct. Ariz., Phoenix, 1985—; faculty Nat. Jud. Coll., Reno, 1975-82. Contbr. articles to profl. jours. Avd. bd. Boy Scouts Am., Phoenix, 1968-75; training com. Ariz. Acad., Phoenix, 1980—; pres. Paradise Valley Sch. Bd., Phoenix, 1969-70; bd. dirs. Phoenix Together, 1982—, Crisis Nursery, Phoenix, 1976-81. Served to capt. USAF, 1955-58. Recipient Faculty award Nat. Jud. Coll., 1979, Disting. Jurist award Miss. State U., 1986. Mem. ABA (chmn. Nat. Conf. State Trial Judges 1983-84, pres. Nat.

Conf. Met. Cts. 1978-79, chmn. bd. dirs. 1980-82, Justice Tom Clark award 1980, bd. dirs. Nat. Ctr. for State Cts. 1980-85, Disting. Service award 1986), Ariz. Bar Assn., Maricopa County Bar Assn. (Disting. Pub. Service award 1980), Ariz. Judges Assn. (pres. 1981-82), Am. Judicature Soc. (spl. citation 1985), Maricopa County Med. Soc. (Disting. Service medal 1979). Lodge: Rotary. Office: US Dist Ct US Courthouse and Fed Bldg 230 N 1st Ave Rm 3077 Phoenix AZ 85025

BROPHY, TODD RANDALL, property management executive, rancher; b. Wray, Colo., Sept. 21, 1954; s. Desmond Daniel amd Delpha Jean (Bowman) B.; m. Caroline Brooks Lerew. BS in Agrl. Econs., Colo. State U., 1977; postgrad., U. Colo., Denver, 1980. Pres. A.S.L. Denver Inc., 1978—; ptnr. Brophy Bros. Ranch, Wray, Colo., 1983—; bd. dirs., sec., treas. A & H Inc., Denver, 1986—, Marina Devel. Inc., Denver, 1987—; bd. dirs., pres. Marina Assocs. Inc., Denver, 1987—; bd. dirs., sec. Mesa Azul Ltd., Gunnison, Colo., 1988. Dir. The Tiny Town Found. Inc., 1989—. Mem. Inst. Real Estate Mgmt. (v.p. communication 1987-88, v.p. Tiny Town 1988-89), Leadership Centennial, Chief Exec. Officers Mgmt. Cos. Com., Home Builders Assn. (affiliate), Community Assns. Inst. Republican. Office: ASL Denver Inc 359 Inverness Dr S Englewood CO 80112

BROSELOW, STANLEY DAVID, electrical engineer; b. Phila., Aug. 3, 1925; s. Herman George and Dorothy Edyth B.; m. Bernyce Helene Shulman, Mar. 27, 1949; children: Stephen Mark, Hope Gail. BSEE, Drexel U., 1946. Construction mgmt. engr. U.S. Army Engr. Dist., Balt., 1946-61; chief, contract adminstrn. Corps of Engrs. Ballistic Missile Construction Office, Norton AFB, Calif., 1961-66; chmn. Western Regional Renegotiation Bd., L.A., 1966-79; procurement mgr. Hughes Aircraft Co., El Segundo, Calif., 1979—. Mem. IEEE, Soc. Am. Mil. Engrs., ASCE, Nat. Contract Mgmt. Assn., Sigma Alpha Mu. Democrat. Jewish. Home: 2643 W 232d St Torrance CA 90505 Office: Hughes Aircraft Co 1700 Walnut St El Segundo CA 90245

BROSSARD, IRIS ALICIA, neurologist; b. N.Y.C., Nov. 27, 1950; d. Chandler Parkinson and Sally Joan (Ciccarelli) B.; m. William E. Mulligan, Apr. 5, 1986. Student, Old Westbury Coll., 1968-71; BA, Hunter Coll., 1978; postgrad., U. Monterrey, Mex., 1980-82; MD, Albany Med. Coll., 1985. Diplomate Nat. Bd. Med. Examiners. Intern Albany (N.Y.) Med. Ctr., 1985-86; resident in neurology U. Colo., Denver, 1986—. Contbr. articles to profl. jours. Mem. Am. Acad. Neurology. Home: 4950 E 9th Ave Denver CO 80220 Office: U Colo Health Sci Ctr 4200 E 9th Ave Denver CO 80262

BROSY, PAUL ROBERT, dentist; b. Portland, Oreg., Dec. 20, 1955; s. John Florin and Geraldine (Wachob) B.; m. Lynn Ann Park, July 10, 1982; children: Mara Catherine, Erin Aleksandra. BA in Biology, U. Oreg., 1979; DMD, Oreg. Health Scis. U., 1983. Asst. golf profl. Salishan Resort, Glenden Beach, Oreg., 1980-82; commd. USNR, 1983, advanced through grades to lt., 1989; dentist USNR, Jacksonville, N.C., 1983-85, Honolulu, 1985—; dir. br. clinic Naval Communications Sta. Eastern Pacific, Wahiawia, Hawaii, 1987—, Naval Mag. Lulualae, Wainae, Hawaii, 1987—. Pres. ch. coun. Gloria Dei Luth. Ch., Pearl City, Hawaii, 1987. Mem. Acad. Gen. Dentistry (command liaison), Nat. Dental Coun., ADA. Republican. Home: 1953 Union St Sparks NV 89431 Office: 555 Holcomb Ave Reno NV 89502

BROTMAN, RICHARD DENNIS, counselor; Detroit, Nov. 2, 1952; s. Alfred David and Dorothy G. (Mansfield) B.; m. Debra Louise Hobold, Sept. 9, 1979. AA, E. L.A. Jr. Coll., 1972; AB, U. So. Calif., 1974, MS, 1976. Instructional media coord. Audio-Visual Div., Pub. Library, City of Alhambra, Calif., 1971-78; clin. supr. Hollywood-Sunset Community Clinic, L.A., 1976—; client program coord. N. L.A. County Regional Ctr. for Developmentally Disabled, 1978-81; sr. counselor Eastern L.A. Regional Ctr. for Developmentally Disabled, 1981-85; dir. community svcs. Almansor Edn. Ctr., 1985-87; tng. and resource devel. Children's Home Soc. Calif., 1987—; intern student affairs div., U. So. Calif., 1976. Corp. dir. San Gabriel Mission Players, 1973-75. Lic. marriage, family and child counselor, Calif.; cert. counselor Calif. Community Coll. Bd. Mem. Calif. Personnel and Guidance Assn. (conv. participant, 1976, 77, 79), Calif. Rehab. Counselors Assn. (officer), San Fernando Valley Consortium of Agys. Serving Developmentally Disabled Citizens (chmn. recreation subcom.), L.A. Aquarium Soc. Democrat. Home: 3515 Brandon St Pasadena CA 91107 Office: Childrens Home Soc Calif 159 E Huntington Dr Ste 7 Arcadia CA 91006

BROUGH, KAREN TANASSY, accountant; b. Plainfield, N.J., May 13, 1946; d. Louis Julius and Katharyn (Drake) Tanassy; m. Thomas Miller Kaufmann, July 5, 1965 (div. Feb. 1968); m. Charles Nelson Brough, Aug. 29, 1970; children: John Tanassy, Christine Katharyn, Jessica Marie. Student, C.Z. Coll., 1964-67; BA in Anthropology, Calif. State U., Fresno, 1971, postgrad., 1982-83. CPA, Calif. Sec. hdqrs. South Command U.S. Army, Ft. Amador, C.Z., 1965-67, Quarry Heights, C.Z., 1967-68; real estate saleswoman Fresno and Clovis, Calif., 1976-78; loan agt. Wells Fargo Mortgage Co., Fresno, 1978-80; co-owner Applied Real Estate Seminars, Clovis, 1980-82; acct. KMG Main Hurdman, CPA, Fresno, 1983; internal auditor office auditor-contr.-treas. County of Fresno, 1983-87, sr. acct. computer svcs., 1987—. Contbr. articles to real estate publs. Chmn. Ft. Washington SheArea Rsch. Team, 1978-80; pres. scheduling com. Clovis Jr. Soccer League, 1980-83, sec., 1983-84, registrar, 1984-85, treas., 1985-87. C.Z. Soc. CPA's scholar, 1965. Mem. Phi Kappa Phi, Beta Alpha Psi. Democrat. Episcopalian. Home: 481 McArthur Ave Clovis CA 93612

BROUGH, THEODORE GORDON, statistician; b. Congress Park, Ill., Mar. 4, 1924; s. John Capen and Helen Merle (McFadden) B.; student Lyons Town Jr. Coll., 1945-46; A.B., UCLA, 1953; M.A., N.Mex. State U., 1966, Ph.D., 1974; m. Martha W. Johnson, July 4, 1964. Asst. to curator reptiles and invertebrates Brookfield Zoo, Chgo., 1947-48; lit. editor Inland Journalist, Congress Park, 1949-51; editor Sears Catalog, Chgo., 1950-52; sci. editor U.S. Naval Radiol. Def. Lab., San Francisco, 1953-59, publ. br. head, 1955-59, research physicist, 1959-61, sr. physicist, 1961-65; teaching asst. English dept. N.Mex. State U., Las Cruces, 1966, ednl. research tng. fellow Office of Edn., 1966-69; research specialist Western Nev. Regional Edn. Center, Lovelock, 1969-71; project supr. Pupil Personnel Center, Fallon, Nev., 1971-72; dir. Western Research and Evaluation Center, Las Cruces, 1972—; environ. scientist in radiation N.Mex. Environ. Improvement Div., Milan, 1977-86; cons. Bi-Lingual Migrant Student Project, Pasco, Wash., 1975-76. Co-dir., co-founder Mt. Taylor Wilderness Forum, Grants, N.Mex., 1978. Served with USNR, 1942-46. Recipient award for outstanding research in Nev., Office of Edn., 1970, HEW award for outstanding bilingual project, 1976. Mem. Am. Phys. Soc., Health Physics Soc., AAAS, Sigma Xi, Phi Delta Kappa, Beta Beta Beta, Sigma Pi Sigma, Psi Chi. Methodist. Club: Lions. Editor: Principles of Radiation Contamination and Control, 3 vols., 1959; contbr. chpt. to book, Effects of Nuclear Weapons, 1962, articles to sci. and edn. publs. Home: 1513 Andrews Dr Las Cruces NM 88001 Office: 1513 Andrews Dr Las Cruces NM 88001

BROUGHTON, RAY MONROE, economic consultant; b. Seattle, Mar. 2, 1922; s. Arthur Charles and Elizabeth C. (Young) B.; BA, U. Wash., 1947, MBA, 1960; m. Margret Ellen Ryno, July 10, 1944 (dec.); children: Linda Rae Broughton Hellenthal, Mary Catherine Broughton Boutin; m. 2d, Carole Jean Packer, 1980. Mgr. communications and managerial devel. Gen. Electric Co., Hanford Atomic Products Ops., Richland, Wash., 1948-59; mktg. mgr., asst. to pres. Smyth Enterprises, Seattle, 1960-62; dir. research Seattle Area Indsl. Council, 1962-65; v.p., economist (mgr. econ. research dept.) First Interstate Bank of Oreg., N.A., Portland, 1965-87; ind. economic cons., 1987—; mem. econ. adv. com. to Am. Bankers Assn., 1980-83; mem. Gov.'s Econ. Adv. Council, 1981-88; dir. Oregonians for Cost Effective Govt., 1989—; instr. bus. communications U. Wash., Richland, 1956-57. Treas., dir. Oreg. affiliate Am. Heart Assn., 1972-78, chmn., 1980-81, dir., 1980-84. Served to 1st lt. U.S. Army, 1943-46; ETO. Mem. Western Econ. Assn., Pacific N.W. Regional Econ. Conf. (dir. 1967—), Nat. Assn. Bus. Economists (co-founder chpt. 1971), Am. Mktg. Assn. (pres. chpt. 1971-72), Alpha Delta Sigma. Episcopalian. Author: Trends and Forces of Change in the Payments System and the Impact on Commercial Banking, 1972; contbg. editor Pacific Banker and Bus. mag., 1974-80.

BROVETTO, GARY, military officer; b. N.Y.C., June 5, 1946; children: Matthew, Luke. BS in Engring. Sci., Hofstra U., 1969; MA in Bus. Adminstrn., Webster Coll., St. Louis, 1977; grad. flying safety, U. So. Calif., L.A., 1977; postgrad., Am. Grad. U., Covina, Calif., 1988. Commd. 2d lt. USAF, 1970, advanced through grades to lt. col., various pos., 1970-76; wing flying safety officer USAF, Little Rock, 1976-77; asst. prof. aerospace studies USAF, W.Va., 1977-80; chief of safety, career advisor, aircraft comdr. sr. pilot USAF, Little Rock, 1980-82, wing exercise and plans officer, 1982-83; mission dir. for spl. satellite research and devel. programs USAF, Sunnyvale, Calif., 1983-86; chief AF scientific & tech. liaison office NASA Res. Ctr. USAF, Moffett Field, Calif., 1986—; USAF liaison Calif. Aerospace Profl. Rep., Sunnyvale, 1989—. Scoutmaster troop 52 Stanford area council Boy Scouts Am., Palo Alto, Calif., 1985-87, dist. advancement chmn. Santa Clara council Polaris, San Jose, Calif., 1989—; bd. advisors Santa Clara County Childrens Shelter Assn., San Jose, 1985-87. Decorated Meritorious Service medal, Air Force Commendation medal with four oak leaf clusters, Air Force Achievement medal; named one of Outstanding Young Men Am. Jaycees, 1973. Mem. AIAA, Sierra Club. Republican. Home: 6094 Elmbridge Dr San Jose CA 95129 Office: NASA-Ames Res Ctr MS 206-3 Moffett Field CA 94035

BROWER, MYRON RIGGS, architect, interior designer, educator; b. Muscatine, Iowa, Dec. 8, 1949; s. Myron Orson and Marcene P. (Shafnett) B. BArch, Ariz. State U., 1973, BA in Edn., 1977. Registered architect, Ariz., Calif. Architect in tng. Fenlason Assocs., Architects, Tempe, Ariz., 1975-77; pres. Myron Riggs Brower, Architect, Inc., Scottsdale, Ariz., 1977—; prof. Scottsdale Community Coll., 1982—. Mem. AIA, Am. Soc. Interior Designers. Republican.

BROWN, ALAN CHARLTON, aeronautical engineer; b. Whitley Bay, Eng., Dec. 5, 1929; came to U.S., 1956; s. Stanley and Dorothy (Charlton) B.; m. Gweneth Evelyn Bowler, July 26, 1952; children: Yvonne, Christine, Diane, Maureen. Diploma aeronautics, Hull (Eng.) Tech. Coll., 1950; MS, Cranfield (Eng.) Inst Tech., 1952, Stanford U., 1964. Apprentice Blackburn Aircraft Ltd., Brough, Eng., 1945-50; aerodynamicist Bristol (Eng.) Aeroplane Co., 1952-56; rsch. scientist U. So. Calif., L.A., 1956-58, Wiancko Engring. Co., Pasadena, Calif., 1958-60, Lockheed Missiles & Space Co., Palo Alto, Calif., 1960-66; group leader Lockheed Aerospace Systems Co., Burbank, Calif., 1966-69, dept. mgr., 1969-78, chief engr. F-117A, 1978-82, dir. spl. tech., 1982-89; dir. engring. Lockheed Corp., Calabasas, Calif., 1989—. Fellow Royal Aero. Soc., AIAA. Democrat. Home: 11853 Jellico Ave Granada Hills CA 91344 Office: Lockheed Corp 4500 Park Granada Blvd Calabasas CA 91389

BROWN, ALBERT CLARENCE, mayor; b. Los Angeles, Oct. 25, 1918; s. Albert C. and Wanda (Albright) B.; m. Virginia Little, 1941; children—Cheryl Kinsman, Susan Baltagi, Becky Westerdahl. A.A., Riverside City Coll., 1939. Owner, mgr. Brown's Engine, Riverside, Calif., 1948-84; mayor City of Riverside, 1978—. Trustee Riverside City Coll., 1964-78. Served with USN, 1940-45, PTO. Recipient Alumnus of Yr. award Riverside City Coll., 1977, Outstanding Service award Catholic Athletic League, Riverside. Republican. Lodges: Elks, Masons, Shriners, Lions (past pres.). Home: 2330 Prince Albert Dr Riverside CA 92507 Office: Office of Mayor 3900 Main St Riverside CA 92522

BROWN, ALBERTA MAE, respiratory clinician; b. Columbus, Ohio, Nov. 11, 1932; d. Sylvester Clarence and Malinda (Mason) Angel; grad. Antelope Valley Coll., 1961; A.A., Los Angeles Valley Coll., 1975; B.S., Calif. State U., Dominguez Hills, 1981; m. Norman Brown, Dec. 29, 1967; children—Charon, Charles, Stevan, Carole. Nurses aid, vocat. nurse, respiratory therapist St. Bernardines Hosp., 1965-69, Good Samaritan Hosp., Los Angeles, 1969-70, Midway Hosp., Los Angeles, 1973-81; allergy nurse, instr. respiratory therapy VA Hosp., Los Angeles, 1970—, also acting dept. head; nurse, respiratory splty. unit Jerry L. Pettis Meml. Hosp., Loma Linda, Calif., 1984—; instr. Los Angeles Valley Med. Technologists Sch., Compton Coll. seminar instr., 1979. Active Arrowhead Allied Arts Council of San Bernardino; CPR instr. Am. Heart Assn. Lic. vocat. nurse; R.N. Mem. Am. Assn. Respiratory Therapy, Nat. Honor Soc., Eta Phi Beta. Democrat. Baptist. Clubs: Social-Lites, Inc. of San Bernardino, (pres.) Order Eastern Star. Patentee disposable/replaceable tubing for stethoscope. Home: 1545 N Hancock St Orangewood Estates San Bernardino CA 92411 Office: Jerry L Pettis JA Hosp Loma Linda CA 92357

BROWN, ALFRED, social worker; b. Boston, June 1, 1931; s. Abraham and Ida (Winer) B.; m. Diane Carl, Sept. 6, 1959; children: Kara Suzanne, David Eli. BS in BA, Boston U., 1955, MS in Social Sci., 1959. Youth dir. Elizabeth Peabody House, Somerville, Mass., 1959-60; youth dir. Jewish Community Ctr., Tucson, 1960-62, San Francisco, 1962-63; div. dir. Dept. Social Svcs., San Francisco, 1963-74; prog. specialist U.S. Dept. Health & Human Svcs., Region IX, San Francisco, 1974—; field supr. B'nai B'rith Youth Orgn., San Mateo, Calif., 1968-72; cons. New Careers Fedn. Project, San Francisco, 1967-68; assoc. dir. Child Abuse Research Project, San Francisco, 1965-66; conductor workshops in field. Pres. United Homeowners Assn. of San Matedo, 1986-87; bd. dirs. Conflict Resolution Orgn., San Mateo, 1985-88; chmn. Human Resources Commn., San Mateo, 1977-78. With USN, 1950-51. Mem. Am. Orthopsychiatric Assn., Masons. Office: US Dept Health & Human Svcs 50 United Nations Plaza San Francisco CA 94403

BROWN, ALLEN ALFRED, dentist; b. Afton, Wyo., Mar. 26, 1950; s. Allen Keith and Ruth M. (Walton) B.; m. Paula Rae Hall, Aug. 3, 1973; children: Janae, Amy, Jeffrey, Ryan, Jenilyn. AA, Long Beach City Coll., 1972; BS, Brigham Young U., 1974; DDS, U. Pacific, 1977. Scout leader Boy Scouts Am., Orange County, Calif., 1985--. Mem. Harbor Dental Soc. Mormon. Office: 10952 Reagan Los Alamitos CA 90720

BROWN, ANTHONY B., aerospace executive; b. Mpls., Apr. 5, 1922; s. Wayland Hoyt and Adele (Birdsall) B.; m. Mary Alice Ann Anderson, July 28, 1956. BS, Rutgers U., 1949; postgrad. U. So. Calif., 1968-69; PhD, U. Beverly Hills, 1986. Cert. data processor, systems profl. Sr. system analyst Thrifty Corp., L.A., 1957-69; system engr. Informatics Gen., Inc., L.A., 1969-73; contract instr. computer software York U., 1970, McGill U., U. Victoria, 1971, USMC, Boston U., W.Va. U., U. Guelph, 1972; sr. system engr. Jet Propulsion Lab., La Canada, Calif., 1974-76; sr. system engr. Informatics Gen., Inc., Anchorage, L.A., Washington, 1976-78; supr. project control Hughes Aircraft Co., L.A., 1978-81; mgr. fin. Contel Corp., Redondo Beach, Calif., 1981-88. Author: A Century of Blunders--America's China Policy 1844-1949. Rep. precinct capt., presdl. election, 1964; chmn. bd. govs. La Brea Vista Townhouses, 1967-68; active numerous animal welfare orgns. Served with Finance Corps, U.S. Army, 1951-57. Decorated Bronze Star. Fellow Brit. Interplanetary Soc.; mem. AAAS, The Planetary Soc., Nature Conservancy, Town Hall of Calif., Assn. Computer Machinery (chpt. sec. 1973-74), Assn. Systems Mgmt., Mensa, Intertel, Armed Forces Communications and Electronics Assn., Assn. Inst. Cert. Computer Profls., Am. Assn. Fin. Profls., Am. Def. Preparedness Assn., Washington Legal Found., Am. Security Council (mem. nat. adv. bd.), Calif. Soc., SAR, Mil. Order World Wars, Aircraft Owners and Pilots Assn., Internat. Platform Assn., Theodore Roosevelt Assn., Res. Officers Assn., Delta Phi Epsilon. Republican. Club: Los Angeles Athletic. Lodges: Masons, Shriners, Nat. Sojourners. Home: 4333 Redwood Ave Marina Del Rey CA 90292

BROWN, ARCHIBALD MANNING, JR., magazine publisher; b. Burlington, Vt., Sept. 2, 1942; s. Archibald Manning and Mary Marshall (Canfield) B.; m. Laura Havemeyer Webb, July 12, 1969; children: Brewster, Hope, Alexander. BA, Boston U., 1965; MBA, U. Ariz., 1967. Account exec. Merrill Lynch, Tucson, 1972-79; advt. dir. Am. West Mag., Tucson, 1980-83, pub., 1983—; pres. Monterey (Calif.) Life Mags. Inc., 1984-85. Devel. dir. Green Fields Sch., Tucson, 1984-85; bd. dirs. Tucson Mus. Art., 1984-85, Ariz. Sonora Desert Mus., Tucson, 1976-78, nominating chmn., 1978; pres. Big Bros. of Tucson, 1978-79. Served to capt. USAF, 1967-72. Rebublican. Episcopalian. Home: 6161 E Miramar Dr Tucson AZ 85715 Office: Am West Mag 7000 E Tanque Verde Rd #30 Tucson AZ 85715 *

BROWN, ARTHUR, mining executive; b. Germiston, S.Africa, Oct. 27, 1940; s. Harry and Elsie (vandenBerg) B.; m. Tiia Haab, Oct. 7, 1961; children: Lisa Anne, Hayley Elaine, Laura Kathleen. Mining Engr., Witwatersrand Tech. Coll. (S.Africa), 1960. Supr. foreman Va. Gold Mining Co., S.Africa, 1958-60; supt., project mgr. Cementation Co., S.Africa and Can., 1960-67; engr. Hecla Mining Co., Wallace, Idaho, 1967-72, mgr. mines, 1972-80, v.p. ops., 1980-83, sr. v.p. ops., 1983-85, exec. v.p., 1985-86, pres., 1986-87, chief exec. officer, chmn., 1987—, dir., 1983—; pres. Consol. Silver Corp.; dir. Nine Corp. (all Wallace). Author articles on mining. Mayor, City of Pinehurst (Idaho), 1983-86. Mem. AIME, Can. Inst. Metall. and Mining Engrs., Idaho Mining Assn. (bd. dirs.), Idaho Assn. Commerce and Industry (bd. dirs.), Am. Mining Congress (bd. dirs.), The Silver Inst. (bd. dirs.), World Gold Council (bd. dirs.). Republican. Club: Wallace Gyro (pres. 1983-85). Home: PO Box 4566 Coeur d'Alene ID 83814 Office: Hecla Mining Co 6500 Mineral Dr Box C-8000 Coeur d'Alene ID 83814-1931

BROWN, ARTHUR CARL, retired minister; b. Stockton, Calif., Dec. 16, 1915; s. Arthur Carl and Maud (Twitchings) B.; m. Inez Lundquist, May 10, 1940 (dec. Aug. 1982); 1 child; Arthur Carl II; m. Alice Degerman, July 9, 1983. BA, Coll. of the Pacific, 1937; MA, San Francisco Theol. Sem., 1939, BD with honors, 1940; postgrad., Stanford U.,, 1949-50. Ordained to ministry Presbyn. Ch., 1940. Pastor Presbyn. Ch., Sedro Woolley, Wash., 1940-44, Community Ch., Santa Clara, Calif., 1944-46; assoc. pastor First Presbyn. Ch., San. Jose, Calif., 1946-49; minister edn. First Presbyn. Ch., Palo Alto, Calif., 1949-51; organizing pastor Covenant Presbyn. Ch., Palo Alto, 1951-74; pastor Trinity Presbyn. Ch., Santa Cruz, Calif., 1974-78; outreach assoc. Los Gatos (Calif.) Presbyn. Ch., 1978-81; commr. to gen. assembly United Presbyn. Ch., 1947, 52, 59; moderator San Jose Presbytery, 1950, chmn. various coms., 1950-78; mem. Synod Golden Gate and Synod of Pacific coms. Synod of Calif., 1947-88. Treas., chmn. fin. com., bd. dirs. Internat. House, Davis, Calif., 1984—. Mem. Rotary (sec. local chpt. 1941-44). Republican. Home: 4414 San Ramon Dr Davis CA 95616

BROWN, BILL, architect; b. Pitts., June 2, 1950; s. Vincent J. and Rose C. (Schillinger) B.; m. Dawn Ellen Gardner, June 23, 1973; children: Krista Ann, Lori Catherine. BArch with high honors, U. Notre Dame, 1973. Lic. architect, Ind., Colo., Minn.; cert. Nat. Council Archtl. Registration Bds. Archtl. grad. Leroy Troyer and Assocs., Mishawaka, Ind., 1973-76, architect, 1976—, ptnr., 1979-85; pres. Bill Brown AIA Profl. Corp., Colorado Springs, Colo., 1986—. Editor: (newsletter) Environment and Art, The Environment and Art Letter; contbg. author: Building and Renovation Kit for Places of Catholic Worship; contbg. author books on places of worship. Nat. adv. bd. Form/Reform Conf., 1987—. Recipient Reynolds Aluminum Prize for Design, 1972, Notre Dame Dept. of Architecture thesis prize, 1973, Bene award Modern Liturgy mag., 1982. Mem. AIA (pres. No. Ind. chpt., 1980), Ind. Soc. Architects (pres. 1984). Roman Catholic. Office: 102 S Tejon St Ste 1100 Colorado Springs CO 80903

BROWN, BILL E., accountant; b. Kearney, Nebr., Oct. 12, 1946; s. Herbert L. and Rosella M. (Sloan) B.; m. Pamela K. Schuman, Mar. 25, 1967; children: Tyler E., Carrie L. AS, Met. State Coll., Denver, 1970; BS, Bowling Green (Ohio) State U., 1978; MS in Bus., U. No. Colo., 1979. CPA, Fin. Planning Specialist. Acct. Great Western Sugar Co., Denver, 1968-74; acctg. mgr. Great Western Sugar Co., Eaton, Colo., 1974-76; regional acctg. mgr. No. Ohio Sugar Co., Fremont, 1976-78; acct. Stolberg, Wiley & Co., Durango, Colo., 1979-84; shareholder, acct. Stolberg, Brown & Wheeldon, P.C., Durango, Colo., 1984—. Mem. Colo. Soc. CPAs (recorder 1983, v.p. 1984, pres. 1985, 4 corners chpt.), Am. Inst. CPAs. Lodge: Kiwanis (pres. Durango club 1988—). Office: Stolberg Brown & Wheeldon PC PO Box 907 Durango CO 81302

BROWN, BRICE NORMAN, surgeon, educator; b. Chariton, Iowa, July 25, 1945; s. Brice Davis and Wilma (Bebout) B.; m. Barbara Lynn Barthel, July 26, 1969; children: Cherin Lynn, Peter Brice. BS in Chemistry, U. Iowa, 1967; MD, Stanford U., 1972. Diplomate Am. Bd. Surgery. Resident in surgery U. Calif., San Diego, 1972-78; pvt. practice Las Vegas, Nev., 1980—; mem. clin. faculty U. Nev. Sch. Medicine, Las Vegas, 1988—; mem. med. adv. bd. Las Vegas Surg. Ctr., 1983—. Maj. M.C., U.S. Armyy, 1978-80. Fellow ACS (sec.-treas. Nev. chpt. 1988—), Southwestern Surg. Congress; mem. AMA, Nev. Med. Assn., Clark County Med. Soc. (trustee 1983—), Spanish Trail Country Club. Home: 1708 Rambla Ct Las Vegas NV 89102 Office: Palomino Surg Group 2020 Palomino Ln Ste 220 Las Vegas NV 89106

BROWN, BYRON LESLIE, lawyer; b. Clarksburg, W.Va., Aug. 31, 1946; s. W. Glen and JoClaire (Cunningham) B. BA in Zoology, W. Va. U., 1969, BSBA, 1973; JD, U. Pugen Sound, 1976. Bar: Wash. 1976, U.S. Dist. Ct. (we. dist.) Wash. 1976, U.S. Dist. Ct. (ea. dist.) Wash. 1986, U.S. Ct. Appeals (9th cir.) 1977, U.S. Supreme Ct. 1980. Assoc. Law Firm Joseph Kane, Seattle, 1976-77; asst. atty. gen. Office Wash. State Atty. Gen., Olympia, 1977—; mem. Speaker's Bur., 1987—; presenter continuing legal edn. field. Bd. dirs. Sound Sound chpt. Dorian Group, Tacoma, 1981-85; bd. dirs. Met. Elections Com. South Sound, 1982-85, Pierce County AIDS Found., Tacoma, 1987—; vestryman Christ Episcopal Ch., Tacoma, 1986—. With U.S. Army, 1969-73m Vietnam. Mem. Wash. state Bar Assn. Democrat. Home: 1355 Highland Pkwy Tacoma WA 98406

BROWN, CAROLYN SMITH, communications educator, consultant; b. Salt Lake City, Aug. 12, 1946; d. Andrew Delbert and Olive (Crane) Smith; m. David Scott Brown, Sept. 10, 1982. BA magna cum laude, U. Utah, 1968, MA, 1972, PhD, 1974. Instr. Salt Lake Ctr., Brigham Young U., Salt Lake City, 1976-78; vis. asst. prof. Brigham Young U., Provo, 1978; asst. prof. Am. Inst. Banking, Salt Lake City, 1977—; prof., chmn. English, communication and gen. edn. depts. Latter Day Saints Bus. Coll., Salt Lake City, 1973—, acad. dean, 1986—; founder, pres. Career Devel. Tng., Salt Lake City, 1979—; field mktg. dir. Systems Internat./Performas Inc., Mpls., 1978—; cons. inhouse seminars First Security Realty Services, USDA Soil Conservation Service, Utah Power & Light, Utah State Social Services, HUD, Intermountain Health Care, Continental Bank; chmn. centennial coordination com. Latter Day Saints Bus. Coll., 1986-87, N.W. accreditation self-study com. 1980-82, 87, Title IX self-evaluation com., 1977, 79, grievance com., 1979—. Author: Writing Letters & Reports That Communicate, 6 ed., 1985; contbr. articles to profl. jours. Demi-soloist Utah Civic Ballet (now Ballet West), Salt Lake City, 1964-68; active Mormon Ch. Named Tchr. of Month, Salt Lake City Kiwanis, 1981; NDEA fellow, U. Utah, 1972. Mem. Am. Bus. Communications Assn. (lectr. West/N.W. regional chpt. 1987), Delta Kappa Gamma (2d v.p. 1977-79), Lambda Delta Sigma (Outstanding Woman of Yr. 1983), Kappa Kappa Gamma (Outstanding Alumnus in Lit. 1974). Republican. Clubs: Alice Louise Reynolds Literary (Salt Lake City) (v.p. 1978-79, sec. 1985-86). Office: LDS Bus Coll 411 E South Temple Salt Lake City UT 84111

BROWN, CHARLES IRVING, financial consultant; b. Bombay, India, Jan. 14, 1932; s. Charles Irving and Frances Belcher (Woods) B. (parents Am. citizens); BA in Geology, Williams Coll., 1954; MBA with distinction, Harvard U., 1959; m. Kathleen Mae Shrum, July 2, 1960; children: Dana Scott, Tracy Ann, Kelly Mae. Asst. mgr. credit dept. First Nat. City Bank of N.Y., Rio de Janeiro, Brazil, 1954-57; v.p. fin. Western Nuclear Inc., Denver, 1959-73, also dir.; v.p. fin. and mktg. Energy Fuels Corp., Denver, 1974-82, also dir.; fin. cons., 1982—; chmn. bd. Rawlins Nat. Bank (Wyo.), Am. Nat. Bank, Laramie, Wyo., Original Sixteen-to-One Mine, Allegheny, Calif., Clinical/Basis Inc., Olson Industries Inc., Colo.; Trustee Colo. Outward Bound, Colo. State U. Research Found. Mem. Am. Inst. Mining Engrs., Fin. Execs. Inst. Clubs: Univ., Denver Athletic, Am. Alpine. Home: 2691 Pinehurst Dr Evergreen CO 80439 Office: One Tabor Ctr 1200 17th St Ste 2450 Denver CO 80202

BROWN, CHET, JR. (CHESTER ARTHUR BROWN), sales executive; b. Boston, Oct. 14, 1938; s. Chester Arthur and Anna Hilda (Smith) B.; m. Marcie K. Brown; children—Patricia, Linda, Stephen, Christopher, Laura, Edward, Beth Ann. B.A. in Chemistry, Boston U., 1960; M.B.A. in Mktg., Northeastern U., 1962. Vice pres., sales and mktg. High Voltage Engring. Corp., Burlington, Calif., 1961-72; founder/ptnr. Ferro Fluidics Corp., Burlington, 1972-75; mgr. West Coast Office, Alpha Industries, San Jose, Calif., 1976-78; internat. mktg. mgr. Network Products Operation, Beckman Instruments, Fullerton, Calif., 78-80; group v.p. communications and subsystems Western Digital Corp., Irvine, Calif., 1980; chmn. bd., pres., chief exec. officer Western Digital Imaging, Mtn. View, Calif., pres. Paradise Systems, Inc.; bd. dirs. Dual Systems Corp. Paradise Systems, Inc. Mem.

IEEE, Am. Mgmt. Assn., Assn. Old Crows. Republican. Recipient Assn. Indsl. Advertisers award, 1967; Bus. Press Assn. awards; patentee in field. Office: Imaging 800 E Middlefield Rd Mountain View CA 94043

BROWN, CINDY ANNETTE, marketing professional; b. Spokane, Wash., Mar. 31, 1957; d. J. Clark Brown and Evelyn (Mackey) Nickel. Student, Scottsdale (Ariz.) Coll., 1978-81, Western Internat. U., 1984, Time Systems, 1988. Advt. salesperson Ariz. Silver Belt Newspaper, Globe, 1980, Times Newspaper, Fountain Hills, Ariz., 1981; asst. mgr. Ore House Restaurant, Phoenix, 1981-85; asst. sales dir. L'Auberge de Sedona, Scottsdale, 1986, dir. sales, 1986--. Mem. Scottsdale C. of C., Sedona C. of C. Home: 3216 W Belmont Phoenix AZ 85051 Office: L'Auberge de Sedona 14605 N Airport Dr #335 Scottsdale AZ 85260

BROWN, DALE FRANCIS, small business owner; b. Buffalo, Nov. 2, 1956; s. Francis D. and Lois A. B.; m. Jean R. Moses, Feb. 25, 1978. BA, Pa. State U., 1978. Commd. 2d lt. USAF, 1979, advanced through grades to capt., 1983, resigned, 1986; prin. Dale F. Brown, Inc., Sacramento, Calif., 1987—. Author: Flight of the Old Dog, 1987, Silver Tower, 1988, Day of the Cheetah, 1989. Mem. Air Force Assn. (life), Aircraft Owners and Pilots Assn., Literary Guild, Calif. Writer's Club. Republican. Roman Catholic. Office: Dale F Brown Inc 10665 Folsom Blvd Ste 246 Rancho Cordova CA 95670

BROWN, DANIEL R. See CURZON, DANIEL

BROWN, DANIEL WARREN, public relations executive; b. Portchester, N.Y., Oct. 26, 1930; s. Malcolm Doughty and Helen Ann (Warren) B.; m. Helen June Sproule, Mar. 15, 1953 (div. 1958); 1 child, Peter; m. Jean Frances High, Aug. 2, 1958; 1 child, Daniel Warren; stepchildren: Carole Hoppe, Fredric Hoppe, Catherine Hoppe. BA, Columbia U., 1952; MA in Journalism, U. Wis., 1971. Reporter Sun-Tattler, Hollywood, Fla., 1956-57, Miami Herald, Fla., 1957-61; dir. Combined Fed. Campaign, San Diego, 1980-82; dir. pub. affairs Aerojet, Sacramento, 1982—. Lt. Col. USMC, 1952-55, 61-80. Decorated Legion of Merit, Navy Commendation medal. Mem. Pub. Relations Soc. Am. (chpt. pres. 1988), Sutter Club. Republican. Office: Aerojet PO Box 13618 Sacramento CA 95628

BROWN, DAVID CLIFFORD, clergyman; b. Plainwell, Mich., Jan. 12, 1938; s. Maynard Fred and Geraldine Louise (Fish) B.; m. Kathleen Dianne Thomas, Aug. 25, 1979 (div. 1989); children: Lisa, Gordon, Mason, Stuart, David. BA, Kalamazoo Coll., 1960; BD, Colgate Rochester U., 1964; D Religion, Chgo. Theol. Sem., 1970. Assoc. minister Grace United Meth. Ch., Rochester, N.Y., 1961-64; minister Wesley United Meth. Ch., Niagara Falls, N.Y., 1964-67, Geneseo (N.Y.) United Meth. Ch., 1967-69; campus minister, dir. Wesley Found. SUNY, Geneseo, 1967-69; acting clin. dir. Chgo. Inst. Pastoral Care, 1970-71; sr. minister The Community Ch., East Williston, N.Y., 1971-78; v.p. Religion in Am. Life, Inc., N.Y.C., 1978-83; sr. minister The Congl. Ch., San Mateo, Calif., 1984—. Editor: Morality: Whose Responsibility?, 1983; editor The Pastor's Jour., 1978-83; contbr. articles and book revs. to various publs. Instr. English, So. Mich. State Prison, Jackson, 1971; interim dir., Interfaith Hunger Appeal, N.Y.C., 1983-84; mem. housing task force, San Mateo County Organizing Project, 1988—. Woodrow Wilson fellow (hon.), 1960. Mem. No. Calif. Conf. United Ch. Christ (mem. ministerial standing com. 1984—), Interreligious Task Force Soviet Jews (vice-chmn. 1987—), Clergy Fellowship San Mateo (pres. 1985—), Faith and Life Com., Nat. Coun. Community Churches (bd. dirs. 1973-79), Nat. Coun. Churches of Christ in U.S.A. (governing bd. 1975-77), World Coun. Churches (stewardship coun. U.S. coun. 1976-82), Kiwanis (Clergyman of Yr. 1988), Masons. Democrat. Mem. United Church of Christ. Office: Congl Ch 225 Tilton Ave San Mateo CA 94401

BROWN, DONALD DEAN, artist, educator; b. Keithsburg, Ill., Sept. 18, 1931; s. Daniel Lawrence and Ona Fay (Frazee); m. Phyllis Margeurite Jordan, Nov. 24, 1955; 1 child, Paul Martin. BS, So. Ill. U., 1953, MFA, 1954. Prof. art Idaho State U., Pocatello, Idaho, 1956—. Prin. works include numerous group and one person exhibitions and commns. Mem. Internat. Sculpture Assn., Nat. Audubon Soc., Nat. Wildlife Fedn., Nature Conservancy, World Wildlife Fund. Home: 4285 Bannock Hwy Pocatello ID 83204 Office: Idaho State U Box 8178 Pocatello ID 83209

BROWN, DONALD DOUGLAS, retired air force officer, transportation company executive, consultant; b. Montreal, Que., Can., Aug. 1, 1931; came to U.S., 1938; s. Donald Bannerman and Hilda Taylor (Noel) B.; m. Joan Teresa McAndrews, Aug. 7, 1954; children—Cathy J. Brown Peinhardt, James D., Nancy J. Brown. B.A., Columbia U., 1954; M.B.A., Syracuse U., 1965. Commd. officer U.S. Air Force, 1955, advanced through grades to maj. gen., 1979, ret., 1987; instr. transport tng. unit 1707th Air Transport Wing U.S. Air Force, Tinker AFB, Okla., 1962-64; supplies mgmt. officer SAC, U.S. Air Force, March AFB, Calif., 1964-66; asst. base supply officer, then base supply officer U.S. Air Force, Andersen AFB, Guam, 1966-68; squadron chief, then wing chief aircrew standardization 315th Spl. Ops. Wing, U.S. Air Force, Phan Rang Air Base, Vietnam, 1968-69; chief Weapon System Support div. in Directorate of Supply, then dir. logistics plans U.S. Air Force, Scott AFB, Ill., 1973-75, asst. dep. chief of staff for logistics, 1975-76; vice comdr. 62d Mil. Airlift Wing, U.S. Air Force, McChord AFB, Wash., 1976-77, comdr. 62d Mil. Airlift Wing,, 1977-79; asst. dep. chief of staff for ops. Mil. Airlift Command U.S. Air Force, Scott AFB, Ill., 1979-80, dep. chief of staff for plans, 1980-83, dep. chief staff for ops. Mil. Airlift Command, 1983-84; comdr. 22d Air Force, Mil. Airlift Command U.S. Air Force, Travis AFB, Calif., 1984-87; ret. U.S. Air Force, 1987; chmn. bd. Evergreen Air Ctr. Inc.; cons. in aviation/logistics mgmt. Decorated Disting. Service medal with oak leaf cluster, Legion of Merit with oak leaf cluster, D.F.C. with oak leaf cluster, Bronze Star, Air medal with 4 oak leaf clusters, Republic of Vietnam Cross of Gallantry with palm. Mem. Air Force Assn., Nat. Def. Transp. Assn., Beta Gamma Sigma.

BROWN, EVIE ANNE, nurse, legal consultant; b. Bentley, Alta., Can., Oct. 7, 1950; came to U.S., 1962; d. Jan and Elizabeth (Nieuwstraten) Appel; m. Kenneth Edward Brown, Dec. 5, 1981; children: Jonathan, Nathaniel. Student, Portland State U., 1968-71; diploma, Emanuel Hosp. Sch. Nursing, Portland, Oreg., 1971. RN, Oreg. Asst. head nurse Providence Hosp., Portland, 1971-72; various nursing positions Oreg. and Idaho, 1972-84; pvt. practice legal cons. Dayton, Wash., 1984—. Mem. Am. Nurses Assn., Oreg. Nurses Assn. Mem. Assembly of God Ch. Home and Office: Rte 3 Box 66A Dayton WA 99328

BROWN, GEORGE EDWARD, JR., congressman; b. Holtville, Calif., Mar. 6, 1920; s. George Edward and Bird Alma (Kilgore) B.; m. Rowena Somerindyke (dec. Feb. 1987); 4 children. B.A., UCLA, 1946; grad. fellow, Fund Adult Edn., 1954. Mgmt. cons. Calif., 1957-61; v.p. Monarch Savs. & Loan Assn., Los Angeles, 1960-68; mem. Calif. Assembly from 45th Dist., 1959-62, 88th-91st congresses from 29th Dist. Calif., 93d Congress from 38th Dist. Calif.; mem. 94th-101st Congresses from 36th Dist. Calif., mem. standing com. on agr., sci. space and tech. com., 1987, chmn. dept. ops., research and fgn. agriculture; apptd. to Office of Tech. Assessment; coll. lectr., radio commentator, 1971. Mem. Calif. Gov.'s Adv. Com. on Housing Problems, 1961-62; mem. Mayor Los Angeles Labor-Mgmt. Com., 1961-62, Councilman, Monterey Park, Calif., 1954-58, mayor, 1955-56; candidate for U.S. Senate, 1970. Served to 2d lt., inf. AUS, World War II. Mem. Am. Legion, Colton C. of C., Urban League, Internat. Brotherhood Elec. Workers, AFL-CIO, Friends Com. Legislation, Ams. for Dem. Action. Democrat. Methodist. Lodge: Kiwanis. Home: Riverside CA 92507 Office: US Ho of Reps 2188 Rayburn House Office Bldg Washington DC 20515

BROWN, GEORGE STEPHEN, physicist; b. Santa Monica, Calif., June 28, 1945; s. Paul Gordon and Frances Ruth (Moore) B.; m. Nohema Fernandez, Aug. 8, 1981; 1 child, Sonya. BS, Calif. Inst. Tech., 1967; MS, Cornell U., 1968, PhD, 1973. Mem. tech. staff Bell Labs., Murray Hill, N.J., 1973-77; sr. research assoc. Stanford (Calif.) U., 1977-82, research prof. applied physics, 1982—; assoc. dir. Stanford Synchrotron Radiation Lab., Stanford, 1980—. Mem. editorial bd. Rev. Sci. Instruments, 1983-86; contbr. articles to profl. jours. Fellow Am. Phys. Soc. Home: 740 Alameda Redwood City CA 94061 Office: SSRL Bin 69 PO Box 4349 Stanford CA 94305

BROWN, GILES TYLER, educator, lecturer; b. Marshall, Mich., Apr. 21, 1916; s. A. Watson and Ettroile (Kent) B.; m. Crysta Beth Cosner, Nov. 21, 1951. AB, San Diego State Coll., 1937; MA, U. Calif.-Berkeley, 1941; PhD, Claremont Grad. Sch., 1948; post-doctoral seminar, U. Edinburgh, Scotland, 1949. Tchr., counselor, Binet intelligence tester San Diego City Schs., 1937-46; chmn. social sci. div. Orange Coast Coll., Newport Beach, Calif., 1948-60; prof. history, chmn. social sci. div. Calif. State U., Fullerton, 1961-66; also chmn. history dept., dean grad. studies Calif. State U., 1967-83, assoc. v.p. acad. programs, 1979-83; pub. lectr. nat., internat. affairs, 1951—; also cons. gerontology; participant Wilton Park Conf., Eng., 1976; mem. instl. research bd. So. Calif. Coll. Optometry, 1980—; cons. Current Wisdom, 1988—; moderator Behind the Headlines Forum, Orange Coast Coll.; lectr. Laguna Hills Leisure World Forum; past chmn. Hist. Landmarks Com. Orange County; mem. nat. task force Assement Quality Masters' Degree, Council Grad. Schs., 1981-83. Author: Ships That Sail No More, 1966; Contbr. to: Help in Troubled Times, 1962; contbr. articles, book reviews to profl. jours. Trustee, past pres. and chmn. bd. World Affairs Council Orange County; past pres. U. Calif.-Irvine Friends Library; nat. bd. dirs., past nat. pres. Travelers Century Club; mem. grad. fellowship adv. com., State of Calif., 1980, Orange County Bd. NCCJ, 1984—; bd. dirs. Pacific Symphony Orch. Served to lt. USNR, 1942-46. Recipient Pacific History award Pacific Coast br. Am. Hist. Assn., 1950; hon. medal DAR, 1977; named Outstanding Prof. Calif. State U., 1966, Hon. Citizen of Orange County, 1969; hon. medal Nat. Soc. Daus. Colonial Wars, 1984. Mem. AAAS, Am. Hist. Assn., Western Assn. Grad. Schs. (exec. com. 1981-83), SAR, Phi Beta Kappa, Phi Delta Kappa, Phi Alpha Theta, Phi Beta Delta (hon. internat. scholar), Kappa Delta Pi. Baptist. Clubs: Explorers, Masons. Home: 413 Catalina Dr Newport Beach CA 92663

BROWN, GORDON WHITTIER, petroleum refining consultant; b. San Diego, Dec. 15, 1926; s. Harry Hunter and Ruth Ann (Wiggins) B.; m. June Alice Olson, Sept. 6, 1952; children: Cynthia J. Brown Wick, Stewart Whittier, Bonnie J. Brown Bird, Pamela L. Brown Glanville. BD in Naval Sci., U. So. Calif., 1947, BEngring.in ChemE, 1948, postgrad. in ChemE, 1951-56. Registered profl. engr., Colo. Chemist amd engr. Union Oil Co. Calif., Wilmington, 1948-58; product mgr. B.F. Goodrich Co., Rialto, Calif., 1958-60; foreman, supr. Gulf Oil Corp., Santa Fe Springs, Calif., 1960-70; dir. Gulf Oil Corp., Santa Fe Springs, 1970-77, Gulf Mineral Resources Co., Denver, 1977-81; mgr. Stone & Webster Engring. Co., 1981-88; cons. Refining Consulting Svcs., 1988—; rep. for Gulf Oil (Wilshire Oil) on tech. subcommittee Western Oil & Gas Assn., L.A., 1962-64; mem. question and answer panel Nat. Petroleum Refiner's Assn., Washington, 1977. Contbr. articles to profl. jours. Founder Brea (Calif.) Friends of Library, 1975; chmn. Parks and Recreation commn., Brea, 1976; capt. Rep. Precinct, Long Beach, Calif., 1951; program chmn. Realto (Calif.) Jr. C. of C., 1959. With ROTC, USN, 1944-46. Recipient resolution of appreciation City Coun. Brea, 1976. Mem. Am. Inst. Chem. Engrs. (profl. devel. recognition cert. 1985). Methodist. Office: Refining Cons Svcs 5261 So Quebec Ste 100 Englewood CO 80111

BROWN, H. DENNIS, information specialist; b. May 4, 1944; m. Mary Anne Winkelman. BA in Journalism, U. Iowa, 1966, MA in Print Journalism, 1968. News intern WMT Radio and TV, Cedar Rapids, Iowa, 1966-67; gen. assignment reporter Sioux City (Iowa) Jour., 1971-72; city govt. reporter Fort Dodge (Iowa) Messenger and Chronicle, 1972; asst. pub. rels. mgr. Brunswick div. Brunswick Corp., Skokie, Ill., 1972-76; news writer Nat. Assn. Realtors, Chgo., 1976-79; extn. info. specialist Wash. State U., Pullman, 1979—; extn. info. specialist U. Ariz., Tucson, 1983-84; mem. ACE nat. critique and awards com. 1988, regional program planning com. 1980, 85, program com. for nat. meeting 1980-81. Contbr. articles to profl. jours.; editor pamphlets for teenage parents, Alumni News, Coll. of Agr. and Home Econs. Wash. State U. Mem. Wash. State U. Bd. of Student Pubs. Com. 1985-89, Parking Appeals Com. 1982-83, Nat. 4-H Congress Press Com. 1980. With U.S. Army, 1968-71. Mem. Agrl. Communicators in Edn. (state rep. 1982-83), Soc. to Preserve and Encourage Radio Drama, Variety and Comedy, U. Iowa Alumni Assn., Wash. State U. Alumni Assn. (assoc.). Home: NW 1625 Deane Pullman WA 99163

BROWN, HANK, congressman; b. Denver, Feb. 12, 1940; s. Harry W. and Anna M. (Hanks) B.; m. Nana Morrison, Aug. 27, 1967; children: Harry, Christy, Lori. BS, U. Colo., 1961, JD, 1969; LLM, George Washington U., 1986, M in Tax Law, 1986. Bar: Colo. 1969; CPA, Colo. Tax acct. Arthur Andersen, 1967-68; asst. pres. Monfort of Colo., Inc., Greeley, 1969-70; corp. counsel Monfort of Colo., Inc., 1970-71; v.p. Monfort Food Distbg., 1971-72, v.p. corp. devel., 1973-75, v.p. internat. ops., 1975-78, v.p. lamb div., 1978-80; mem. 97th-101st Congresses from Colo. 4th dist., 1981—; mem. Colo. State Senate, 1972-76, asst. majority leader, 1974-76. With USN, 1962-66. Decorated Air medal. Mem. Colo. Bar Assn. Republican. Congregationalist. Office: US Ho of Reps 1424 Longworth House Office Bldg Washington DC 20515

BROWN, JACK H., supermarkets company executive; b. San Bernardino, Calif., June 14, 1939. Student, San Jose State U., UCLA. V.p. Sages Complete Markets, San Bernardino, 1960-71, Marsh Supermarkets, Yorktown, Ind., 1971-77; pres. Pantry Supermarkets, Pasadena, Calif., 1977-79; pres. mid-west div. Cullum Cos., Dallas, 1979-81; pres., chief exec. officer Stater Bros. Markets, Colton, Calif., 1981—; chmn. bd. dirs. Stater Bros. Inc., 1986—; dir. Life Savs. & Loan Assn., San Bernardino. Trustee, U. Redlands, Calif.; bd. dirs. Goodwill Industries of Inland Empire, San Bernardino; bd. councillors Calif. State U., San Bernardino. Served with USNR, 1958-60. Named Sagamore of the Wabash, Gov. Ind., 1978. Mem. Western Assn. Food Chains (v.p., bd. dirs., pres. 1987-88), Calif. Retailers Assn. (bd. dirs.), Food Mktg. Inst. (vice chmn.), So. Calif. Grocers Assn., Food Employers Council (bd. govs.). Republican. Presbyterian. Lodge: Elks. Office: Stater Bros Markets 21700 Barton Rd Colton CA 92324

BROWN, JAMES CARRINGTON, III (BING BROWN), utilities executive; b. Wilmington, Del., May 17, 1939; s. James Carrington Jr. and Virginia Helen (Miller); m. Carol Osman, Nov. 3, 1961. Grad. security mgmt. group, Indsl. Coll. of the Armed Forces; BBA, Ariz. State U., 1984. Newsman, disc jockey, program dir. various radio stas., Ariz., 1955-60; morning news editor Sta. KOY, Phoenix, 1960-61; staff writer, photographer Prescott (Ariz.) Evening Courier, 1961; bus. editor, staff writer, photographer Phoenix Gazette, 1961-65; various communications positions Salt River Project, Phoenix, 1965—; cons. communications The Browns, Phoenix, 1965—; guest lectr. various colls. and univs., 1975—. Bd. dirs. Theodore Roosevelt Coun. Boy Scouts, 1985—; deacon Meml. Prebyn. Ch., 1980-82, elder, 1985-87; spl. gifts com. United Way, Phoenix, 1986—. Mem. Western Systems Coordinating Coun. (chmn. pub. info. com. 1985-88), Ariz. Newspapers Assn. (Billy Goat award, Allied Mem. of Yr. 1985), Ariz. Broadcasters Assn., Western Energy Supply and Transmission Assocs. (mem. pub. info. com.), Phoenix Press Club (pres. 1982-83). Republican. Home: 3734 E Campbell Ave Phoenix AZ 85018 Office: Salt River Project PO Box 52025 Phoenix AZ 85072-2025

BROWN, JAMES EVAN, hospital official; b. Pocahontas, Ark., Feb. 7, 1947; s. Raymond U. and Eva Marie (Murdock) B.; m. Lynn Marie Kinman, Sept. 26, 1970; children: Matthew K., Bekka M., Benjamin M. BSBA, Harding U., 1970. Acctg. mgr. Gym-Dandy Inc., Bossier City, La., 1974-78; ter. mgr. Am. McGaw Co., Irvine, Calif., 1978-84; dir. material mgmt. United Gen. Hosp., Sedro Wooley, Wash., 1984—. Bd. dirs. Sauk River Christian Camp, Darrington, Wash., 1987. With USAF, 1970-74. Named Employee of Yr., United Gen. Hosp., 1987. Mem. Am. Soc. Healthcare Materials Mgmt., We. State Healthcare Materials Mgmt. Republican. Mem. Ch. of Christ. Home: 10537 105th St NW Oak Harbor WA 98277 Office: United Gen Hosp Hwy 20 at Sterling Rd Sedro Woolley WA 98284

BROWN, JAMES MARSTON, lawyer; b. Aberdeen, Wash., Feb. 5, 1950; s. Donald Matthew and Jeanette Marie (Phillips) B.; m. Coleen Tina Chin, July 6, 1974; children: William Lester, Peter James. Student U. Wash., 1968-72, Calif. State U.-Fullerton, 1975-76; BS in Laws, Western State U., Fullerton, 1977, JD, 1978. Bar: Calif. 1979, U.S. Dist. Ct. (no. dist.) Calif. 1979, Wash. 1981, U.S. Dist. Ct. (we. dist.) Wash. 1982. Law clk. Orange County Superior Ct., Santa Ana, Calif., 1977-78; assoc. Gladys & Phillips, Aberdeen, 1979-81; ptnr. Phillips & Brown, Aberdeen, 1981—; lectr. Grays Harbor Coll., Aberdeen, 1983—. Bd. dirs. Channel 10 Ministries, Aberdeen, 1980-83; trustee Aberdeen Pub. Library Bd., 1979—. Mem. ABA, Wash. Bar Assn. (bar examiner 1982-83, law sch. liason com.), Wash. State Trial Lawyers Assn. (chmn. Grays Harbor round table 1984-85), Assn. Trial Lawyers Am., Christian Legal Soc., Delta Theta Phi. Republican. Baptist. Home: 527 W 6th St Aberdeen WA 98520 Office: Phillips & Brown 525 Seattle First Nat Bank Bldg Aberdeen WA 98520

BROWN, JANICE, senior research analyst; b. Reno, July 22, 1935; d. Charles Emmett Brown and Sarah Margaret (Harrison) Selin. BS, U. Nev., 1957. Sec. to pres. Bonanza Air Lines, Las Vegas, Nev., 1957-58; sec. to comdg. officer U.S. Naval Supply Depot, Guam, Marianas Islands, 1958-61; sales promotion agt. Air France, Los Angeles, 1961-62, asst. cargo sales mgr., 1962-67; sec. Pangborn, Douglass & Morgan, Reno, 1968-74; sec. to assoc. dean of students U. Nev., Reno, 1974-80, mgt. analyst, 1980-84, research analyst, 1984—. Mem. Rocky Mountain Assn. for Instl. Research (Nev. corr. 1987—), Assn. Instl. Research, Univ. (Reno), Delta Delta Delta. Republican. Home: 3080 Achilles Dr Reno NV 89512 Office: U Nev Office Planning Budget Analysis Reno NV 89557

BROWN, JOHN WILBUR, secondary school teacher; b. Los Angeles, Oct. 7, 1929; s. Wilbur Edward and Bess (Wright) B.; m. Sally Marilyn McCubbin, Aug. 5, 1956 (div. 1980); children: John Michael, Catherine Anne, Linda Sue; m. Grace Evelyn Griffith, Mar. 22, 1986. BA, Occidental Coll., 1951; MA, Calif. State U., Long Beach, 1962; postgrad., U. Hawaii, 1967. Gen. secondary sch. tchr. life credential, Calif. Tchr. Los Angeles City Schs., 1954-55, Centinela Union High Sch. Dist., Hawthorne, Calif., 1955-88; evening tchr. El Camino Community Coll., Gardena, Calif., 1970-74, Centinela Adult Sch., Lawndale, Calif., 1976-88; substitute tchr. Mingus Union High Sch. Dist., Cottonwood, Ariz., 1988—; dept. head Hawthorne High Sch., 1961-88. Co-author: Contemporary International Problems, 1961. activist and P.A.C. mem. S. Bay United Tchrs., Redondo Beach, Calif., 1977-87; campaigner Pacific Palisades (Calif.) Dem. Club, 1978-81. Sgt. U.S. Army, 1952-54. Recipient Advanced Study Grant U.S. State Dept., 1966-67. Democrat. Congregationalist. Home: 1141 Sunrise Dr Clarkdale AZ 86324

BROWN, JUDITH ELLEN, community relations executive; b. Newark, Jan. 10, 1950; d. Richard Warren and Miriam (Laskowitz) B.; m. Terence Randolph Pitts, Oct. 21, 1979; children: Jacob, Rebecca. BA, Boston U., 1972, MA, 1975. Coord. program Boston Community Music Sch., 1975-76; coord. conf. U. Ariz., Tucson, 1976-83; dir. community relations City of Tucson, 1983—. Host and producer TV and radio show Topic of Tucson, 1983—. City liaison Tucson Conv. Ctr. Commn., 1983—; mem. Tucson Tomorrow, 1985—, Tucson/Pima Art Coun. Pub. Art Com., 1986—. Mem. Internat. Assn. Bus. Communicators, Pub. Relations Soc. Am. (treas. 1985—, pres.-elect 1989), Nat. Assn. Telecommunications Ops. and Advisors. Office: Community Rels Office 255 W Alameda Tucson AZ 85701

BROWN, JURUTHA DORIS, city official; b. San Diego, Apr. 11, 1950; d. Fred and Bertha (Stewart) B. BA, Occidental Coll., L.A., 1972. Various personnel positions City of L.A., 1972-84, chief of police and fire selection div., 1984-87, chief worker's compensation div., 1987—. Mem. Internat. Personnel Mgmt. Assn. (assessment coun. dir. 1984-87), Nat. Forum for Black Pub. Adminstrs. Democrat. Baptist. Office: City of LA Personnel Dept 111 E 1st St Rm G-1 Los Angeles CA 90012

BROWN, KENNETH A., physician; b. Portland, Oreg.; m. Kay Brown; children: Erin, Kevin. BA with honors, Linfield Coll., McMinnville, Oreg., 1973; MD, U. Oreg., 1977. Lic. MD, Ill., Ariz. Commd 2d lt. USAF, flight surgeon, 1978-82; chief aerospace medicine WAFB, 1980-82; from resident in emergency medicine to chief resident Christ Hosp., Oak Lawn, Ill., 1982-84; staff physician emergency medicine Mesa (Ariz.) Hosp., 1984-85; dir. emergency svcs. Chandler (Ariz.) Region Hosp., 1985—; chmn. quality assurance/utilization rev. com., Chandler Hosp., 1989; chief staff elect Chandler Regional Hosp., 1989. Pres., Community Emergency Specialists., Ltd., 1984—. Mem. AMA, Nat. Bd. Med. Examiners (cert.), Am. Bd. Emergency Medicine (cert.), Am. Coll. Emergency Physicians. Home: PO Box 748 Chandler AZ 85224

BROWN, LES, insurance counselor, business planner; b. Bklyn., Apr. 25, 1926; s. Robert and Rose (Solomon) B.; m. Doris Goldstein, Nov. 15, 1929; children: Sandy E., Joanie S., Gil W. Student, U. N.C., 1946-47, Columbia Sch. Broadcasting, 1947. Radio announcer various stas., 1945-49; sales mgr. Armour and Co., Bklyn., 1949-51; pres. Brown Bros., Rockville Ctr., N.Y., 1951-63; sales rep. Conn. Gen. Life, Queens, N.Y., 1963-76; sales rep. Lincoln Nat. Life, Albuquerque, 1976-79, Phoenix, 1979--; cons. in field. Bd. dirs. Anytown Am., Phoenix, 1985—, Consumer Credit Cons., Phoenix, 1981-85; founder Fairview Jewish Meml. Cemetery, Albuquerque, 1978. With Merchant Marine, 1943-45, USAF, 1945-46. Mem. KP (chancellor commander). Office: Lincoln Nat Life 2602 N 44th St Ste 104 Phoenix AZ 85008

BROWN, LEWIS FRANK, lawyer; b. Cleve., Aug. 4, 1929; s. Frank C. and Lula Y. (Armstrong) B.; m. Dorothy Jean Fitzgerald, Mar. 29, 1956; children: Lewis G., Orville Frank. AA, Vallejo (Calif.) Coll., 1955; BA, Calif. State U., San Francisco, 1957; JD, Lincoln U., 1965. Bar: Calif. 1970. Tchr. Vallejo Unified Sch. Dist., 1957-64; cons. Greenleigh Assocs., N.Y.C., 1964-66, Contra Costa County Office Econ. Opportunity, Martinez, Calif., 1966-70; assoc. Solano Legal Assistance, Vallejo, 1970-71; ptnr. Beeman, Bradley, Brown & Beeman, Vallejo, 1977—; cons. Exec. Office of Pres. Lyndon B. Johnson. Committeeman Solano County Dems., 1959-67; mem. planning commn. City of Vallejo, 1963-65, city councilman, 1965-69, vice mayor, 1967-69. Recipient Commendation award Solano County Dist. Atty., 1982, Jones County, Miss. Bd. Suprs., 1988, Laurel, Miss. Mayor and City Coun., 1988, Resolution awards Sen. Barry Keene and Thomas H. Hannigan, 1982; park named in his honor, Vallejo, 1969. Mem. NAACP (Golden Heritage award, Citizen of Yr. 1985), Calif. Bar Assn, Solano County Bar Assn. (sec.-treas. 1971), Charles Houston Bar Assn., Nat. Bar Assn. (life). Home: 400 Lakeside Dr Vallejo CA 94589 Office: Brown & Bradley 538 Georgia St Vallejo CA 94590-6096

BROWN, LORRAINE ANN, administrative services coordinator; b. Providence, Mar. 15, 1947; d. Leonard Francis and Elaine Frances (Pettis) Millen; m. Jeffrey Schofield Brown, May 22, 1976 (div. 1983); 1 child, Kaneeta Sage; m. Dieter Paul Wuennenberg, July 14, 1965; 1 child, Desiree Jacqueline Wuennenberg. Student, Manhattan Sch. Printing, 1972, Los Angeles Trade Tech Coll., 1981-83. Communications rep. TransAmerica Occidental, Los Angeles, 1973-77; owner, designer The Lorraine Brown Co., El Segundo, Calif., 1979-83; mgr. Silk Lingerie Outlet, Sherman Oaks, Calif., 1982-83; office mgr. Am. Silk Label, Los Angeles, 1984; asst. prodn. coordinator Pacific Coast Mills, Los Angeles, 1984-85; asst. designer Judy Knapp Inc., Los Angeles, 1986-87; sales exec. Integrated Aquatic Systems, Marina Del Rey, Calif., 1987-88; adminstrv. svcs. coord. Contel Fed. Systems, Marina Del Rey, Calif., 1988—; sales exec. Integrated Aquatic Systems, 1987—. Designer jewelry. Asst. leader Girl Scouts U.S., El Segundo, 1985-87. Mem. Young Exec. Singles, Advanced Degrees, Sierra Singles. Home: 133 1/2 Virginia St El Segundo CA 90245

BROWN, MARGARET DEBEERS, lawyer; b. Washington, Sept. 24, 1943; d. John Sterling and Marianna Hurd (Hill) deBeers; m. Timothy Nils, Aug. 28, 1965; children—Emeline Susan, Eric Franklin. B.A. magna cum laude, Radcliffe Coll., 1965; postgrad. Harvard U. Law Sch., 1965-67; J.D., U. Calif.-Berkeley, 1968. Bar: Calif. 1969, U.S. Ct. Appeals (9th cir.) 1971, U.S. Supreme Ct. 1972, U.S. Ct. Appeals (D.C. cir.) 1986, U.S. Ct. Appeals (2d cir.) 1987. Assoc. White, Hamilton, Wyche, Shell & Pollard, Petersburg, Va., 1969-70, Heller, Ehrman, White & McAuliffe, San Francisco, 1970-73; sole practice, San Francisco, 1973-77; atty. Pacific Telephone (name changed to Pacific Bell 1984), San Francisco, 1977-83, sr. atty., 1983-85; sr. atty. Pacific Telesis Group, 1985—; speaker McGeorge Law Sch., Sacramento, 1983. Mem. ABA, San Francisco Bar Assn., Phi Beta Kappa. Office: Pacific Telesis Group 130 Kearny St Rm 3659 San Francisco CA 94108

BROWN, MARY ELLEN, physical therapist; b. Sacramento, June 21, 1936; d. Hoyle Link and Corrie Elizabeth (Evans) Maloney; m. Robert William Brown Jr., June 24, 1962; children: Karen Ann, Robert Hoyle. BS, U.

Calif., San Francisco, 1958. Registered phys. therapist, Calf. Staff phys. therapist Fairmont Hosp., San Leandro, Calif., 1958-63, chief phys. therapist, 1963-64; on-call phys. therapist various hosps., clinics, San Francisco area, 1967-74; staff phys. therapist Ygnacio Valley Phys. Therapy, Walnut Creek, Calif., 1974-78; chief phys. therapist Ygnacio Valley Phys. Therapy, Danville, Calif., 1978—; part-time staff phys. therapist, instr. TMJ Clinic U. Calif., San Francisco, 1983—. Charter mem. Eugene O'Neill Found., Danville; mem. Danville Arts Council Alliance, 1982—, Contra Costa Musical Theater, Walnut Creek, 1984—, Internat. Polio Network. Mem. Am. Phys. Therapy Assn. (orthopedic sect. Calif. chpt.), Found. for Phys. Therapy, San Ramon Valley Hist. Soc., San Ramon Valley Geneal. Soc. Democrat. Methodist. Home: 24 Sorrel Ct Danville CA 94526 Office: Ygnacio Valley Phys Therapy 530 La Gonda Way Danville CA 94526

BROWN, MICHAEL PAUL, manufacturing company executive; b. Riverside, Calif., Oct. 31, 1952; s. Wayne Clyde Brown and Leatrice (De Groff) Kirtland. BS in Indsl. Engring., GM Inst., 1975. Maintenance foreman assembly div. GM, South Gate, Calif., 1974-77; owner, pres. Falcon Express Co., Irvine, Calif., 1977-78; mgr. customer svc., prodn. control Vard-Newport, Santa Ana, Calif., 1978-79; project mgr. Martin Marietta Aluminum Corp., Torrance, Calif., 1979-80, mgr. prodn. control, 1980-81; field sales rep. Martin Marietta Aluminum Corp., Atlanta and Cleve., 1981-85; bus. mgr. Internat. Light Metals, Torrance, Calif., 1985-87, gen. mgr., 1987—. Mem. Am. Soc. Metallurgists, Forging Industry Assn., Aluminum Assn., Phi Gamma Delta. Republican. Home: 2601 Vanderbilt Ln Unit E Redondo Beach CA 90278 Office: Internat Light Metals 19200 S Western Ave Torrance CA 90509

BROWN, NEAL BOYD, geophysics educator; b. Moscow, Idaho, Dec. 13, 1938; s. Kenneth Wayne and Ruth Alvina (Boyd)B.; m. Frances Claire Tannian, Aug. 23, 1980; children: Steven Ross Sweet, Kris David, Melody Jo, Michael Scott Sweet, Nathhaniel Scott. BS, Wash. State U., 1961; MS, U. Alaska, 1966. Rsch. engr. NASA Ames Rsch. Ctr., Moffett Field, Calif., 1961-62; rsch. scientist Am. Geophys. Soc., Thule, Greenland, 1962-63; asst. engr. Geophys. Inst. U. Alaska, Fairbanks, 1968-69; asst. prof. Poker Flat Rsch. Range U. Alaska, 1971--. Mem. Alaskaland Commn., City of Fairbanks, 1981. Mem. Am. Assn. Physics Tchrs., Am. Geophys. Union, AIAA, Air Force Assn., AAAS (pres. Arctic div. 1987-88), Alaska Assn. Computers in Edn., Sigma Xi. Home: 1569 La Rue Ln Fairbanks AK 99709 Office: U Alaska Geophys Inst Fairbanks AK 99775-0800

BROWN, OGDEN, JR., psychologist, educator; b. Evanston, Ill., Apr. 1, 1927; s. Ogden and Frances Louise (Falck) B.; AB in Psychology, Am. U., 1950, MA in Psychology, 1951; PhD in Indsl./Orgnl. Psychology, Purdue U., 1965; m. Alyce Marie Whitesides, May 1, 1953; children: Marsha Marie Brown Akse, Lynda Lou Brown Dunne, Ogden III, Tarleton II. Psychometrician, U.S. Employment Service, Washington, 1950-51; commd. 2d lt. USAF, 1951, advanced through grades to col., 1971; from instr. to assoc. prof. U.S. Air Force Acad., 1961-68; asst. for edn. and tng. Office of Sec. of Air Force, Washington, 1968-71; comdr. 3415 Spl. Tng. Group, Lowry AFB, Colo., 1971-73; ret., 1973; exec. v.p. Am. West Enterprises, Colorado Springs, Colo., 1973-78; from asst. prof. to prof. human factors, dir. systems mgmt. program Inst. Safety and Systems Mgmt., U. So. Calif., Los Angeles, 1978-87; pres. Mgmt. Devel. Assocs., Colorado Springs, 1973—; prof., dir. systems mgmt. program Coll. Systems Sci. U. Denver, 1988—. Decorated Legion of Merit, Meritorious Service medal, Commendation medal. Mem. Acad. of Mgmt., Am. Evaluation Assn., Am. Psychol. Assn., Assn. Human Resources Mgmt. and Organizational Behavior, Human Factors Soc., Internat. Ergonomics Assn., Rocky Mountain Psychol. Assn., Sigma Xi, Psi Chi, Omicron Delta Kappa, Delta Phi Alpha. Republican. Episcopalian. Club: Elks, Contbr. articles to profl. jours. Home: 2 Belle Aire Rd Colorado Springs CO 80906 Office: U Denver Coll Systems Sci Denver CO 80208

BROWN, PATRICIA CRETE, social worker, mediator; b. Yakima, Wash., Oct. 7, 1947; d. Walter Joseph and Anita Kathleen (Marquis) B. AA, Yakima Valley Coll., 1974; BA cum laude, Western Wash. U., 1976; MSW, Eastern Wash. U., 1986. Cert. social worker, Idaho. Civil rights mediator Idaho Human Rights Commn., Boise, 1979-86; ombudswoman Eastern Wash. U., Cheney, 1984-85; social work intern VA Mental Health Ctr., Boise, 1985-86; sr. social worker Idaho State Vets. Home, Boise, 1986-87; dir. Boise Mediation Ctr., 1982-87; family therapist Family and Children's Svcs., Pocatello, Idaho, 1987—. Co-founder Ada County 4th Jud Dist. Friends of Ct., 1985. Mem. Nat. Assn. Social Workers (acad. scholar 1984), Idaho Mediation Assn. (founder eastern chpt. 1988, pres. emeritus). Democrat. Unitarian. Home and Office: 422 N Buchanan Pocatello ID 83204

BROWN, PAUL FREMONT, aerospace engineer, educator; b. Osage, Iowa, Mar. 10, 1921; s. Charles Fremont and Florence Alma (Olson) B.; m. Alice Marie Culver, Dec. 5, 1943; children—Diane, Darrell, Judith, Jana. BA in Edn. and Natural Sci., Dickinson State Coll., 1942; BS in Mech. Engring., U. Wash., 1948; MS in Cybernetic Systems, San Jose State U., 1971. Profl. quality engr., Calif., 1978; cert. reliability engr., Am. Soc. Quality Control, 1976. Test engr., supr. Boeing Aircraft Corp., Seattle, 1948-56; design specialist, propulsion systems, Lockheed Missiles and Space Co., Sunnyvale, Calif., 1956-59; supr. system effectiveness, 1959-66, staff engr., 1966-76, mgr. product assurance, 1976-83; v.p. research, devel. Gen. Agriponics Inc. of Hawaii, 1971-76; owner Diversatek Engring. and Product Assurance Conss., 1983—; coll. instr., lectr., San Jose State U. Active in United Presbyn. Ch., 1965—; scoutmaster, Boy Scouts Am., 1963-65. Served to 1st lt., USAF, 1943-46. Recipient awards for tech. papers, Lockheed Missiles and Space Co., 1973-75. Mem. Am. Soc. Quality Control, AIAA. Clubs: Toastmasters (Sunnyvale, Calif.). Author: From Here to Retirement, 1988; contbr. articles to profl. jours. Home and Office: 19608 Braemar Dr Saratoga CA 95070

BROWN, PETER HARRISON, architect, construction consultant; b. N.Y.C., Apr. 25, 1943; s. William Seltzer and Sara (Ervin) B.; m. Anne Clark, 1970 (div. 1978); m. Barbara Elaine Allbut, Feb. 14, 1986. BArch, Cornell U., 1967; MArch, Columbia U., 1968. Registered architect N.Y. Architect/planner Gruzen Ptnrship., N.Y.C., 1968-70, 75-78, Norval White Assocs., Brooklyn Heights, N.Y., 1970-74; assoc. ptnr., mgr. project Skidmore, Owings & Merrill, N.Y.C., 1978-85, L.A., 1985-86; ptnr. Teubner and Brown, Santa Barbara, L.A. and Costa Mesa, Calif., 1988—. Mem. AIA. Club: U. (N.Y.C.). Home and Office: Teubner and Brown 1601 Mira Vista Ave Santa Barbara CA 93103

BROWN, PETER MANSON, administrative manager, musician; b. Troy, N.Y., Feb. 3, 1933; s. Alfred Marcus Malloy and Marguerite May (Lowrie) Brown; adopted son Udo Manson Brown; m. Joyce Katherine Connelly, Feb. 5, 1955 (div. July 1978); children: Pamela Sue, Peter Jeffrey; m. Connie Sue Carlson, Mar. 18, 1983. BMus, U. Rochester, 1955. Solo tubaist Rochester (N.Y.) Philharm. Orch., 1955-56, San Antonio Symphony Orch., 1959-60, Columbus (Ohio) Symphony Orch., 1960-64; news supr. McGraw-Hill, Inc., Columbus, 1960-64; asst. dist. mgr. McGraw-Hill, Inc., Cleve., 1964-65; zone news mgr. McGraw-Hill, Inc., L.A., 1965-70, regional mgr., 1970-80; adminstrv. mgr. Sage Publs., Inc., Beverly Hills, Calif., 1980-83; mgr. adminstrv. svcs. Avery Label Group, Azusa, Calif., 1983—. Mem. exec. bd. L.A. Postal Customer Council, 1970-75'; alumni admissions counselor U. Rochester, 1987—. U.S. Army, 1956-59. Mem. Nat. Assn. Fleet Adminstrs., Assn. Info. Systems Profls. Democrat. Episcopalian. Office: Avery Label Group 777 E Foothill Blvd Azusa CA 91702

BROWN, ROBERT ALAN, science educator; b. L.A., June 11, 1934; s. Carl Clayton and Olive (Hirst) B.; m. Marcia Louise Jobe, Dec. 12, 1957; children: Vanessa, Morgan, Tristin. BS, U. Calif., Berkeley, 1957, MS, 1963; PhD, U. Wash., 1969. Postdoctoral fellow U. Wash., Seattle, 1969-70; fellow Nat. Ctr. Atmospheric Sci., Boulder, Colo., 1970-71; rsch. P.I. U. Wash. Polar Sci. Ctr., Seattle, 1971-73; prof. atmospheric sci. U. Wash., Seattle, 1983—. Author: Analytic Methods in Planetary Boundary Layer Models, 1973, Fluid Dynamics for the Atmosphere, 1989; contbr. articles to profl. publs. 1st lt. U.S. Army, 1957-59. Fellow Am. Meteorol. Soc.; mem. Am. Geophys. Union, Am. Oceanographic Soc., Sigma Xi, Phi Kappa Psi. Democrat. Office: U Wash AK 40 Dept Atmospheric Sci Seattle WA 98195

BROWN, ROBERT ALLEN, military officer; b. Elmhurst, Ill., Dec. 20, 1954; s. Robert Otto and Phyllis (Kuffner) B. BS, Ariz. State U., 1977; MPA, Golden Gate U., 1988. Commd. 2d lt. U.S. Army, 1977, advanced through grades to maj., 1989; forward observer B battery 1-14 FA 2AD U.S. Army, Ft. Hood, Tex., 1978-79; battery exec. officer U.S. Army, Garlstedt, West Germany, 1979-80, adjutant, 1980-81; asst. ops. officer 7ID DivArty U.S. Army, Ft. Ord, Calif., 1981-82; fire support officer 6-8th FA 7ID U.S. Army, Ft. Ord, 1982-83, battery comdr. B battery 6-8th FA 7ID, 1983-85; instr., writer mil. intelligence ctr. U.S. Army, Ft. Huachuca, Ariz., 1985—. Fulbright scholar, 1974, Pillsbury scholar, 1988. Mem. Field Artillery Assn., Mil. Intelligence Assn., Thunder Mountain Running Club, Bowhunters Club, Phi Delta Theta. Roman Catholic. Home: 49 Terra Dr E Sierra Vista AZ 85635

BROWN, ROBIN LYNN, counseling administrator; b. Columbus, Ohio, Aug. 14, 1961; d. Robert Allen and Betty Jean (Brown) Smith; m. Terry Brown, July 25, 1987; 1 child, Christina Robyn. BSBA, Ohio State U., 1983. Market rsch. analyst Dow Chem. Co. Student Coop., Midland, Mich., 1980-82; asst. br. mgr. BankOne, Dayton (Ohio), N.A., 1984-86, br. mgr., 1986-87; co-dir. Pregnancy Counseling Ctr., San Bernardino, Calif., 1989—. Loaned exec., Dayton United Way, 1984; bd. dirs., San Bernardino (Calif.) chpt. Right to Life League, 1988—. Mem. Norton AFB Officers' Wives' Club, Mothers of Pre-schoolers. Republican. Office: Pregnancy Counseling Ctr 748 E Baseline St San Bernardino CA 92410

BROWN, RONALD MALCOLM, engineering corporation executive; b. Hot Springs, S.D., Feb. 21, 1938; s. George Malcolm and Cleo Lavonne (Plumb) B.; m. Sharon Ida Brown, Nov. 14, 1964 (div. Apr. 1974); children: Michael, Troy, George, Curtis, Lisa, Brittney. AA, Southwestern Coll., 1970; BA, Chapman Coll., 1978. Commd. USN, 1956, advanced through grades to master chief, 1973, ret., 1978; engring. mgr. Beckman Inst., Fullerton, Calif., 1978-82; mech. engring. br. mgr. Northrop Corp., Hawthorne, Calif., 1982-83; dir. of ops. Transco, Marina Del Rey, Calif., 1983-85; v.p. ops. Decor Concepts, Arcadia, Calif., 1985-87; design dir. Lockheed Aircraft Corp., Ontario, Calif., 1987—. Mem. Soc. Mfg. Engrs., Inst. Indsl. Engrs., Nat. Trust for Hist. Preservation, Fleet Res. Assn., Am. Film Inst., Nat. Mgmt. Assn.

BROWN, SHIRLEY ANNE, nurse; b. San Diego, Jan. 8, 1955; d. Martin Laurel and Beverly Jean (Eacock) B. BS in Nursing, Seattle Pacific U., 1979; M Nursing, U. Wash., 1984. RN, Wash. Staff nurse Swedish Hosp. Med. Ctr., Seattle, 1979-80, Ballard (Wash.) Community Hosp., 1980-83; nurse clinician Community Home Health Care, Seattle, 1983—; cons. in field. Vol. ARC, 1988. 1st lt. USAFR, 1985—. Mem. Am. Assn. Occupational Health Nurses (edn. chmn. 1984-85), USAF Assn., Reserve Officers Assn. (historian dept. Wash, 1988—, jr. v. p. 1989—, Seattle chpt. USAF committeeman, 1987—), Assn. Mil. Surgeons U.S., Order of Eastern Star, Sigma Theta Tau. Methodist. Office: Community Home Health Care 100 W Harrison St South Tower Seattle WA 98119

BROWN, STEPHEN LAMAR, savings and loan official, graphic design artist; b. Columbus, Ga., Nov. 9, 1949; s. James Lamar and Gwendolyn M. Brown; m. Linda Ann Jordan, July 4, 1986; 1 child, Abram. Student, Ventura Jr. Coll., 1968-71, U. Fresno, 1976-81. Postman U.S. Postal Svc., Port Hueneme, Calif., 1968-71, 73-76; mgr. apt. complex Fresno, Calif., 1976-79; promotions, pub. and community rels. officer Guarantee Savs. & Loan, Fresno, Calif., 1979—; computer graphic design artist Graphic Tech. Co., Fresno, 1979--. With U.S. Army, 1971-73. Home: 4929 N Winery Circle Apt 124 Fresno CA 93726 Office: Guarantee Savs & Loan 2540 W Shaw Ln Ste 101 Fresno CA 93700

BROWN, TODD HAMILTON, naval officer; b. Bedford, Ind., June 13, 1960; s. Thomas Richard Brown and Nancy Lee (Kier) Graham. BS in Aerospace Engring., U.S. Naval Acad., 1982. Commd. ensign USN, 1982, advanced through grades to lt.; elec. officer U.S.S. Hewitt, San Diego, 1983-84, main propulsion asst., 1984-85, towed array surveillance system officer, 1985-86; naval gunfire liaison officer 1st Marine Div. USMC, Camp Pendleton, Calif., 1986—. Contbg. author: Marine Corps Gazette. Mem. U.S. Naval Inst. Home: 1422 13th St Imperial Beach CA 92032 Office: 1st Marine Div (Rein) FMF 3d Bn 11th Marines Camp Pendleton CA 92055

BROWN, TONI C., teacher; b. Billings, Mont., Apr. 22, 1950; d. Alec Wilbert and Ruth Isabel (Uline) Brown; m. Mark A. Higdon; children: Marykitt, Elizabeth. BA, U. Wyo., 1972; MA, 1979, BS in Elem. Edn., 1988, postgrad., 1979-80. Tchr. Billings (Mont.) Sch. Dist. #2, 1973-77; admissions counselor Rocky Mt. Coll., Billings, 1977-78; tchr. Gillette Campus Sheridan Coll., 1979-80, dir. Region III Developmentally Delayed Presch. Prog., 1980; tchr. various grades Campbell County Sch. Dist., Gillette, Wyo., 1980-88; tchr. gifted resource rm. Campbell County Sch. Dist., Gillette, 1988—; cons. in field; lectr. in aerospace edn. Named Campbell County Am. Legion Educator of the Yr., 1988; Space Acad. grantee, Internat. Ninety-Nines, 1987. Mem. Campbell County Reading Assn., Wyo. Assn. Gifted Edn., Wyo. Coun. Tchrs. Math., Wyo. Reading Assn., Wyo. Sci. Tchrs. Assn. (Elem. Sc. Tchr. Yr. 1988), Am. Owners and Pilots Assn., Civil Air Patrol, Exptl. Aircraft Assn., Nat. Space Soc. (NW region phone tree coord.), Ninety Nines, Inc., Planetary Soc., Soc. Children's Book Writers, U. Wyo. Alumni Assn., Women's Sports Found., Wyo. Writers/ Poets, Young Astronauts of Am., Who. Aerospace Assn. (chmn.). Home: PO Box 222 Gillette WY 82717-0222

BROWN, VERLE H., mechanical engineer; b. Ogden, Utah, June 13, 1923; s. James Bertam and Lillian (Tomlinson) B.; m. Cornelia Visalia Wilson, Oct. 17, 1947; children: Robyn, Lauri, Adrian, Traci, Marla, Sheli, Harlan, Kymberle, Kevin. BS, U. Utah, 1943, MS, 1947; ASC OC (hon.), Oxford (Eng.) U. Registered profl. engr., Utah, Wash., Oreg. Architect Herzog & Barnes, Portland, Oreg., 1946-48; chief engr. The Lang Co., Inc., Salt Lake City, 1948-56; pres. Engring. Cons., Seattle, 1956-61; exec. v.p. E. Sam Dick Co., Inc., Seattle, 1961-74; pres. Internat. Gas Systems, Inc., Seattle, 1974—. Inventor gas processing devices. Sgt. 1st class U.S. Army, 1943-46, ETO. Mem. ASME, ASHRAE, NSPE, Instrument Soc. Am., Nat. Fire Protection Assn., Nat. LP Gas Assn. (chmn. indsl. com., tech. and standards com. 1969—). Home: 17769 Palatine Ave N Seattle WA 98133 Office: Internat Gas Systems Inc 7116 220th SW Mountlake Terrace WA 98043

BROWN, WADE H., publishing company executive; b. Glen Ridge, N.J., Sept. 22, 1940; s. John Henry and Kathryn A. (Nofsinger) Frankenbach B.; m. Kirsten Jacobsen, June 17, 1969 (div. 1985). BA in Chemistry, U. Ky., 1964. Rsch. chemist Geigy Rsch. Labs, Ardsley, N.Y., 1965-69; project mgr. Geigy Indsl. Chemicals, Ardsley, 1969-71; sr. salesman Ciba-Geigy Corp., Ardsley, 1971-74, product mgr., 1974-76, advt. dir., 1976-80; strategic planner Ciba-Geigy Corp., Basel, Switzerland, 1981-83; bus. mgr. Ciba-Geigy Corp., Fountain Valley, Calif., 1983-86; pres. ABB Composites Inc., Irvine, Calif., 1986-88, Rand Am. Corp., Irvine, 1988—; dir. Polysil Inc., Chatsworth, Calif., 1985—. Patentee in field. County committeeman Conservative Party, N.Y.C., 1968-69. Sgt. U.S. Army, 1964-65. Fellow Am. Inst. Chemists; mem. Soc. for the Advancement Materials & Processes, Am. Soc. Metals, Am. Inst. Aero. & Astronautics, Sierra, U.S. Recreational Ski Assn. Republican. Episcopalian. Home: 130 Oxford Irvine CA 92715 Office: Rand America Corp 2102 Business Center Dr Irvine CA 92715

BROWN, WALTER FRANKLIN, information systems executive; b. Phila., Apr. 3, 1952; s. Benjamin Franklin and Fidele Adeste (Van Beverhoudt) B.; m. Marie Magdalena Guerra, Aug. 8, 1971; 1 child, Angelique. AA in Acctg. and Data Processing, Chaffey Coll., Alta Loma, Calif., 1980; BSBA, Calif. State Poly. U., 1984. From mfg. cons. to nat. mgr. tech. services Xerox Computer Services, Los Angeles, 1978-85, mgr., major account support, 1985—. Dir. Cen. Assembly of God Ch., Ontario, Calif., 1985-88. Mem. Am. Mgmt. Assn., Data Processing Mgmt. Assn., Am. Prodn. and Inventory Control Soc. Democrat. Home: 11887 Roswell Ave Chino CA 91710-1547 Office: Xerox Computer Svcs 5310 Beethoven St Los Angeles CA 90066

BROWN, WALTER FREDERICK, lawyer; b. Los Angeles, July 28, 1926; s. Walter Andrew and Emily Anna (Weber) B.; m. Barbara Mae Porter Stahmann, Aug. 6, 1950; children: Jeffrey David, Kendall Paul, David Walter. BA, U. So. Calif., 1949, JD, 1952; MA, Boston U., 1961; MLS, U. Oreg., 1975. Bar: Calif. 1952, Oreg. 1981, U.S. Tax Ct. 1974, U.S. Supreme Ct. 1975; cert. Am. Assn. Law Librarians. Assoc. prof. and law librarian Northwestern Sch. Law Lewis and Clark Coll., Portland, Oreg., 1970-80; senator Oreg. Legis. Assembly, Salem, 1975-87; gen. counsel Oreg. Consumer League, Portland, 1987-89; counsel, dep. dist. atty. County of Malheur, Vale, Oreg., 1989—; chmn. Senate Agrl. and Forestry Com., 1985, Senate Task Force Vet.'s Home Loans, 1985-87; chmn. capitol constrn. subcom. Joint Ways and Means Com., 1983; chmn. Senate Bus. and Consumer Affairs Com., 1981; senate co-chmn. Joint Legis. Counsel Com., 1979-87; mem. Legis. Emergency Bd., 1983-84; senate co-vice chmn. Joint Trade and Econ. Devel. Com., 1985-87; commr. Gov.'s Commn. Sr. Services, 1985-87; vice chmn. Judiciary Com., 1975, 79, 81, 83, 85, Labor Com., 1983, Elections, 1981. Contbr. articles to law jours. Pres. Clackamas County Citizens Assn., Oreg., 1971-74; mem. Oreg. Environ. Council, Oreg. Natural Resources Council, N.W. Coalition for Alternatives to Pesticides, Nat. Pro-Life Democrats, Citizens Utility Bd. Comdr. JAGC, USN, 1944-70. Recipient Oreg. Civil Liberties Union award, 1983, Oreg. Environ. Council award, 1975, 79, 81, 83, 85, Trout Unltd. award Oregon City, 1975, Liberty award Oreg. Conf. Seventh-day Adventists, 1985. Mem. Oreg. State Bar Assn., Oreg. Dist. Attys. Assn., Malheur County Bar Assn., Nat. Officers Assn., Nat. Eagle Scout Assn., Oreg. Meml. Assn., Am. Legion (award 1981, 82), VFW, Sierra Club, Mazamas, Nat. Farmers Union, Masons, Phi Beta Kappa, Phi Kappa Phi, Kappa Sigma. Democrat. Unitarian Universalist. Home: 782 NW 16th St Ontario OR 97914 Office: Malheur County Courthouse 251 B St W Rm 105 Box 5 Vale OR 97918

BROWN, WANDA MARIE, financial consultant, educator; b. Birmingham, Ala., July 18, 1945; d. Earlie and Vivian Lee (Doby) Suttles. BS, Calif. State U., Long Beach, 1969; MBA, UCLA, 1973. Acct. various acctg. firms, 1968-75; sr. systems analyst Security Pacific Bank Corp., L.A., 1975-76; asst. prof. Calif. State U., L.A., 1975—; city treas. City of Inglewood (Calif.), 1981—; mng. dir. Mgmt. Control Systems, Inglewood, 1979—; cons. SBA, L.A., 1978-81. Vol. coord. Inglewood Police Dept., 1982; bd. dirs. Inglewood Philharmonic Assn., 1988—; mentor-advisor Inglewood Unified Sch. Dist., 1985. Mem. NAFE, Nat. Assn. of Accts., Nat. Assn. of Black Accts., Calif. Mcpl. Treas. Assn., Am. Acctg. Assn., Beta Gamma Sigma, Top Ladies of Dist., Inc. Home: 2611 W 78th Pl Inglewood CA 90305 Office: Mgmt Control Systems 8443 S Crenshaw #206 PO Box 2302 Inglewood CA 90305

BROWN, WILLIAM DONALD, aerospace engineer; b. Preston, Eng., Dec. 5, 1934; came to U.S., 1967; s. Joseph and Lily (Monk) B.; m. Sheila Margaret Walsh, Jan. 7, 1956. Higher nat. diploma, Tech. Coll., Blackpool, Eng., 1954. Registered profl. engr., Calif. Quality assurance apprentice Hawker Aircraft Co., Blackpool, Eng., 1951-54; engr. Brit. Aircraft Corp., Preston, 1954-67; tech. mgr. Rohr Industries, Inc., Riverside, Calif., 1967-87; dir. quality Hysol Aerospace & Indsl. Products div. Dexter Crop., Pitts., Calif., 1987—. Patentee in field. Mem. Soc. Advancement Materials and Process Engring., Soc. Mfg. Engring. (sr), Am. Soc. Quality Control, Toastmasters. Home: 4501 Fawn Hill Way Antioch CA 94509-7125 Office: Dexter Corp Hysol Div 2850 Willow Pass Rd Pittsburg CA 94565-0031

BROWN, WILLIAM EDWIN, construction executive, educator; b. Belknap, Ill., Jan. 11, 1934; s. Samual Edwin and Sarah Elizabeth (Kean) B. BS, So. Ill. U., 1956, MS, 1957; PhD, Ohio State U., 1964. Asst. instr. So. Ill. U., Carbondale, 1955-56; instr. U. Tenn., Knoxville, 1956-57; asst. prof. Ohio State U., Columbus, 1957-64, asst. to dean, 1964-67; prof. Trenton State Coll., N.J., 1967-76; regional dir. State of Calif., Sacramento, 1976-80; owner Dial One Bear Tavern Construction, Inc., Sacramento, 1979—; seminar dir. Dial One of No. Calif., 1985—; part-time prof. Calif State U., Sacramento, 1986—. Adv. Phi Alpha Delta, Trenton State Coll. Served with USAR, 1955-62. Mem. Am. Soc. Engring. Educators, Optimist (v.p. 1965-67), Phi Delta Kappa, Epsilon Phi Tau. Republican. Methodist. Home: 1110 Sierra Dr Sacramento CA 95864

BROWN, WILLIAM OSCAR, retired railroad executive; b. El Paso, Tex., May 16, 1915; s. Benjamin McCulloch and Alice Lillian (Drisdale) B.; m. Phyllis Ann Disano, July 6, 1940; children: William Drisdale, Marcia Jean. BSME, Rice U., 1937; postgrad., Stanford U., 1958, MIT, 1964. Registered profl. engr. With So. Pacific Transp. Co., 1937—; asst. supt. motive power So. Pacific Transp. Co., Sacramento, 1955-58, supt. mech. dept., 1959-67; asst. chief mech. officer So. Pacific Transp. Co., San Francisco, 1968-69, chief mech. officer, 1970-78, ret., 1978; mech. adv. mem. Trailer Train Corp., Chgo., 1970-78, Assn. Am. R.R. mech. div., Washingotn, 1970-78. Mem. ASME, So. Pacific Ret. Execs. Club (pres. 1987-88), Green Hills Country Club, Engrs. Club San Francisco. Republican. Baptist. Address: 1130 Murchison Dr Millbrae CA 94030

BROWN, WILLIAM PATRICK, manufacturing company executive; b. Denver, Mar. 25, 1945; s. William Emmett and Marie (Sullivan) B.; m. Karin Sue Anderson, Feb. 10, 1973; children: Matthew Todd, Jennifer Nicole. BBA, U. Ariz., 1967. Asst. mgr. Kmart, Inc., 1967-71, ops. mgr., 1971-74; mgr. Tertronix, Inc., Beaverton, Oreg., 1974-83, materials mgr., 1983-84, ops. mgr., 1984-85, dir. mktg. and sales, 1985-88; bus. devel. mgr. Nelco Tech. Inc., Tempe, Ariz., 1988—. Mem. Am. Mktg Assn., Am. Mgmt. Assn., Soc. Mfg. Engrs., Am. Prodn. Inventory Control Soc. Republican. Home: Rte 4 PO Box 707 Hillsboro OR 97123

BROWN, WILLIE LEWIS, JR., state legislator, lawyer; b. Mineola, Tex., Mar. 20, 1934; s. Willie Lewis and Minnie (Boyd) B.; children: Susan, Robin, Michael. B.A., San Francisco State Coll., 1955; LL.D., Hastings Coll. Law, 1958; postgrad. fellow, Crown Coll., 1970, U. Calif.-Santa Cruz, 1970. Bar: Calif. 1959. Mem. Calif. State Assembly, Sacramento, 1965—; speaker Calif. State Assembly, 1980—, chmn. Ways and Means Com., 1971-74; chmn. revenue and taxation com. 1976-79; Democratic Whip Calif. State Assembly, 1969-70, majority floor leader, 1979-80, chmn. legis. black caucus, 1980, chmn. govtl. efficiency and economy com., 1968-84. Mem. U. Calif. bd. regents, 1972, Dem. Nat. Com., 1989-90; co-chmn. Calif. del. to Nat. Black Polit. Conv., 1972, Calif. del. to Nat. Dem. Conv., 1980; nat. campaign chmn. Jesse Jackson for Pres., 1988. Mem. State Legis. Leaders Found. (dir.), Nat. Conf. State Legislatures, NAACP, Black Am. Polit. Assn. Calif. (co-founder, past chmn.), Calif. Bar Assn., Alpha Phi Alpha, Phi Alpha Delta. Democrat. Methodist. Office: Calif Assembly Office of Speaker State Capitol Sacramento CA 95814

BROWNE, ANTHONY LOUIS, corporate professional; b. Chgo., Feb. 1, 1942; m. Marguerite Thompson, Nov. 25, 1967; children: Anthony Abner, Allison Abner, Maya Browne. Mgr. bus. planning and devel. Ea. Airlines, 1962-68; dir. planning and devel. Singer Internat., 1968-70; v.p. planning and devel. Bendix Corp., 1970-74; asst. vice chancellor U. Calif., Berkeley, 1974-79; asst. sec. for bus. State of Calif., 1979; chmn., chief exec. officer Gingerbread Ltd., San Francisco, 1979—; mng. ptnr., sr. fin. officer Sacramento St. Properties, 1983—. Office: Gingerbread Ltd 3652 Sacramento St San Francisco CA 94118

BROWNE, JOSEPH PETER, librarian; b. Detroit, June 12, 1929; s. George and Mary Bridget (Fahy) B.; A.B., U. Notre Dame, 1951; S.T.L., Pontificium Athenaeum Angelicum, Rome, 1957, S.T.D., 1960; M.S. in L.S., Cath. U. Am., 1965. Joined Congregation of Holy Cross, Roman Cath. Ch., 1947, ordained priest, 1955; asst. pastor Holy Cross Ch., South Bend, Ind., 1955-56; librarian, prof. moral theology Holy Cross Coll., Washington, 1959-64; mem. faculty U. Portland (Oreg.), 1964-73, 75—, dir. library, 1966-70, 76—, dean Coll. Arts and Scis., 1970-73, asso. prof. library sci. 1967—, regent, 1969-70, 77-81, chmn. acad. senate, 1968-70, 1987-88; prof., head dept. library sci. Our Lady of Lake Coll., San Antonio, 1973-75; chmn. Interstate Library Planning Council, 1977-79. Mem. Columbia River chpt. Huntington's Disease Soc. Am., 1975—, pres., 1979-82. Recipient Culligan award U. Portland, 1979. Mem. Cath. Library Assn. (pres. 1971-73), ALA, Cath. Theol. Soc. Am., Pacific N.W. Library Assn. (pres. 1985-86), Oreg. Library Assn. (pres. 1967-68), Nat. Assn. Parliamentarians, Oreg. Assn. Parliamentarians (pres. 1985-87), Archdiocesan Hist. Commn. (pres. 1985—), Mensa Internat., All-Ireland Cultural Soc. Oreg. (pres. 1984-85). Democrat. Club: KC. Home: 5410 N Strong St Apt 8 Portland OR 97203 Office: U Portland 5000 N Willamette Blvd Portland OR 97203

BROWNE, ROBERT MCCORMICK, psychiatrist; b. Bklyn., Apr. 12, 1926; s. Robert Davis and Kathryn Cecelia (McCormick) B.; m. Mieko Gayle Morimoto, Aug. 8, 1952; children: Kevin, Sean, Kathleen, Sharon. BA, U. Rochester, 1946; MD, Johns Hopkins U., 1950. Intern, then psychiat. resident Queen's Med. Ctr., 1952-55; founding dir. Territorial Convalescent Ctr., Honolulu, 1957-59, Child Devel. Ctr., Honolulu, 1968-76; dir. psychiat. clinic St. Francis Hosp., Honolulu, 1959-81; psychiat. cons. Kamehameha Schs., 1959-82. Art works exhibited: Honolulu Acad. Arts, 1967, Art Inst. Chgo., 1967, 71, Mus. Primitive Art, New York, 1968, Dallas Mus. Fine Arts, 1970, U. Hawaii Art Gallery, 1976, Nat. Gallery Art, 1979-80. Founding bd. dirs. ACLU Hawaii, Honolulu, 1965-71; participant Civil Rights March, Selma, Ala., 1965, Martin Luther King rally, Montgomery, Ala., 1965. Served with USNR, 1944-46; capt. M.C., U.S. Army, 1955-57, Korea. Recipient citation Hawaii State Senate, 1965, Honolulu City Council, 1965, United Pub. Workers, 1965. Mem. Am. Psychiat. Assn. Hawaii Psychiat. Soc., Honolulu Acad. Arts (life), Contemporary Bishop Mus. Assn., Hawaii Opera Theatre, Monoa Valley Theatre, Arts Council Hawaii. Democrat. Home: 3625 Anela Pl Honolulu HI 96822

BROWNE, STEVEN EMERY, video editor; b. New Haven, Dec. 23, 1950; s. Robert Walter and Sara Elizabeth Brown; m. Michele Catherine Osterhout, June 16, 1979; children: Nikole, Kristopher. BS in TV/Radio, Ithaca Coll., 1973; postgrad., U. So. Calif., 1973-74. Page NBC, Burbank, Calif., 1975; apprentice editor Sta. KNBC-TV, Burbank, 1975; prodn. asst. Komack Co., Los Angeles, 1975-77; asst. editor Bob Best's Producers TV Services, Los Angeles, 1977; freelance editor Los Angeles, 1977-79; staff editor Video Transitions, Hollywood, Calif., 1979-86, sr. staff editor, 1986-87; staff editor Encore Video, Inc., Hollywood, 1987-88, Modern Videofilm, Hollywood, 1988—; cons. EECO Video Systems, 1984-86. Author: Video Tape Post Production Primer, 1982, Getting That Job In Hollywood, 1983, Video Editing, 1988. Mem. Internat. Alliance of Theatrical Stage Employees, Film and Video Tape Editors Guild. Office: Modern Videofilm 7165 Sunset Blvd Hollywood CA 90028

BROWNELL, DARREL DAVID, health services executive, accountant; b. Long Beach, Calif., Sept. 7, 1935; s. Robert Keith and Isabel Helen (Edmunds) B.; m. Marcea Lynn Gibson, Oct. 15, 1960 (div. 1978); children—Bradley, Marina, Randel. B.S., Calif. State U., 1964. C.P.A., Calif. Clerk State Calif., 1959-61; acct. Gibson Furniture, 1961-64; staff acct., Windes, McClaughry Inc., 1964-66; sr. v.p. Meml. Health Services, Long Beach, 1966—; dir. Multihosp. Mutual Ins. Ltd., Georgetown, Grand Cayman, Brit. W.I., 1981—. Served with USAF, 1955-59. Mem. Am. Inst. C.P.A.s, Calif. Soc. C.P.A.s, Hosp. Fin. Mgmt. Assn. (dir.), Beta Alpha Psi. Lodge: Rotary. Office: Meml Med Ctr 2801 Atlantic Ave Box 1428 Long Beach CA 90801

BROWNELL, JOHN HOWARD, physicist; b. Oneonta, N.Y., Oct. 4, 1942; s. Carl Leonard and Winifred Florence (Williams) B.; m. Sandra Marie Craig, June 26, 1965; children: Robert C., Laura A. BS, MIT, 1964; MS, Stanford U., 1970, PhD, 1971. Research asst. Radioactivity Ctr. MIT, Cambridge, 1964; staff Controlled Thermonuclear Fusion div. Los Alamos (N.Mex.) Nat. Lab., 1972-75; staff, asst. group leader Theoretical Design div. Los Alamos (New Mex.) Nat. Lab., 1975-80, assoc. group leader Applied Theoretical Physics div., 1980-86, group leader, 1986—; vis. scientist Stichting voor Fundamenteel Onderzoek der Materie, Inst. for Atomic and Molecular Physics, Amsterdam, The Netherlands, 1971-72; laser cons. Quantum Physics, Sunnyvale, Calif., 1969-70. Contbr. articles to sci. jours. Trustee United Ch. of Christ, Los Alamos, 1980-82; mem. troop com. Gt. Southwest Council Boy Scouts Am., Los Alamos, 1980-83; bd. dirs. Los Alamos Retirement Ctr., 1988—. Mem. Plasma Physics div. Am. Phys. Soc., Sigma Xi. Republican. Presbyterian. Office: X-10 Los Alamos Nat Lab MS-B259 Los Alamos NM 87545

BROWNING, HOWARD BEAL, civil engineer; b. Kansas City, Mo., May 15, 1934; s. Howard Beal Browning and Margaret Shepherd (Broach) Kirk; m. Jane Ann Williamson, July 14, 1958 (div. 1975); children: Kristen Kay, Eric Carter; m. Mary Louise Hammond, Feb. 14, 1975. BS, U. Kans., 1957; postgrad., Command & Gen. Staff Coll., Leavenworth, Kans., 1977, Nat. Def. U., Ft. Myer, Va., 1979. Reg. profl. engr. Chief planning City of Tulsa (Okla.), 1959-66, chief engring., 1966-67; dir. pub. works City of Westminster, Colo., 1967-75; assoc. Ketchum, Konkel, Barrett, Nickle, Austin, Lakewood, Colo., 1975-79; prin., v.p. KKBNA, Inc., Wheat Ridge, Colo., 1979-86; ret. 1986. Served as col. USAR, 1957—. Recipient Outstanding Community Service award Westminster C. of C., 1974. Fellow Am. Soc. Civil Engrs. (chpt. v.p. 1966); mem. Am. Pub. Works Assn. (chpt. pres. 1974, pres. award 1975), Am. Inst. Cert. Planners (charter), Nat. Soc. Profl. Engrs., Soc. Am. Mil. Engrs., Sigma Nu. Republican. Methodist.

BROWNING, JAMES OREN, lawyer; b. Levelland, Tex., Apr. 6, 1956; s. James Weldon and Shirley (Goodpasture) B.; m. Jan Ramey, Aug. 5, 1978; children: Eli Goodpasture, Jacob Ramey, Elizabeth Heatherly. BA, Yale U., 1978; JD, U. Va., 1981. Bar: N.Mex. 1983, U.S. Dist. Ct. N.Mex. 1983, U.S. Ct. Appeals (10th cir.) 1983, U.S. Ct. Appeals (fed. cir.) 1987, U.S. Supreme Ct. 1987. Law clk. to presiding judge U.S. Ct. Appeals 3d Cir., Wilmington, Del., 1981-82; law clk. to Justice Lewis F. Powell Jr. U.S. Supreme Ct., Washington, 1982-83; assoc. Rodey, Dickason, Sloan, Akin & Robb, P.S., Albuquerque, 1983-87, 88—, dir., 1988—; dep. atty. gen. Office Atty. Gen., Santa Fe, 1987-88; mem. litigation team Post-Conviction Assistance Program, Charlottesville, Va., 1979. Editor-in-chief Va. Law Rev., 1980-81, mem. editorial staff, 1979-80; contbr. articles to profl. jours. Deacon Montgomery Blvd. Ch. Christ, Albuquerque, 1985-86; del. Bernalillo County Rep. Conv. and N.Mex. Rep. Convs., Albuquerque, 1984-86; treas. Marshall for State Senate, 1984-86. Recipient Margaret G. Hyde award U. Va. Law Sch., Charlottesville, 1983. Mem. ABA, N.Mex. Bar Assn., Federalist Soc., Nat. Rep. Lawyers Assn., Albuquerque Bar Assn., Albuquerque Lawyers Club, Order Coif, Yale Club. Home: 8412 Cherry Hills Rd NE Albuquerque NM 87110 Office: Rodey Dickason Sloan Akin & Robb PA PO Box 1888 Albuquerque NM 87103

BROWNING, JAMES ROBERT, U.S. judge; b. Great Falls, Mont., Oct. 1, 1918; s. Nicholas Henry and Minnie Sally (Foley) B.; m. Marie Rose Chapell. BA, Mont. State U., Missoula, 1938; LLB with honors, U. Mont., 1941, LLD (hon.), 1961. Bar: Mont. 1941, D.C. 1950, U.S. Supreme Ct. 1952. Spl. atty. antitrust div. Dept. Justice, 1941-46; chief Dept. Justice (N.W. regional office), 1948-49, asst. chief gen. litigation sect. antitrust div., 1949-51, 1st asst. civil div., 1951-52; exec. asst. to atty. gen. U.S., 1952-53; chief U.S. (Exec. Office for U.S. Attys.), 1953; pvt. practice Washington, 1953-58; lectr. N.Y.U. Sch. Law, 1953, Georgetown U. Law Center, 1957-58; clk. Supreme Ct. U.S., 1958-61; judge U.S. Ct. Appeals 9th Circuit, 1961—, chief judge, from 1976; mem. Jud. Conf. of U.S., 1976—, exec. com. of conf., 1978-87, com. on internat. conf. of appellate judges, 1987—, com. on ct. adminstrn., 1969-71, chmn. subcom. on jud. stats., 1969-71, com. on the budget, 1971—; David T. Lewis Disting. Judge-in-residence, U. Utah, 1987; lectr. numerous univs. Editor-in-chief, Mont. Law Rev. Named to Order of the Grizzly, U. Mont., 1973. Mem. ABA (judge adv. com. to standing com. on Ethics and Profl. Responsibility 1973-75), D.C. Bar Assn., Mont. Bar Assn., Am. Law Inst., Fed. Bar Assn. (bd. dirs 1945-61, Nat. council 1958-62), Inst. Jud. Adminstrn., Am. Judicature Soc. (chmn. com. on fed. judiciary 1973-74, bd. dirs. 1972-75), Herbert Harley award 1984), Am. Soc. Legal History (adv. bd. jour.), Nat Lawyers Club (bd. govs. 1959-63). Office: US Ct of Appeals PO Box 547 San Francisco CA 94101 *

BROWNING, JESSE HARRISON, entrepreneur; b. Kingsville, Mo., July 27, 1935; s. Jesse Harrison and Anna Love (Swank) B.; m. Vicki Carol Thompson, Dec. 21, 1957; children: Caroline Kaye, Marcia Lynn, Nanci Ann, Susan Louise. Student, U. Wash., 1955-61; MPA, U. So. Calif., 1988. Cert. mfg. engr. Field engr. The Boeing Co., Los Angeles, 1961-64; gen. mgr. SPI, Los Angeles, 1964-70; chmn. Browning Inc., Los Angeles, 1970—, Indsl. Systems, Los Angeles, 1979-87, Vapor Engring., Los Angeles, 1979-87. Patentee in field. Mem. Palos Verdes Breakfast Club, Los Angeles C. of C., Am. Helicopter Soc., Am. Electroplaters Soc., Soc. Mfg. Engrs. Lutheran. Home and Office: 21 Oak Tree Ln Rolling Hills Estates CA 90274

BROWNING, MARK DEWITT, internist, hematologist, oncologist, naval officer; b. Evansville, Ind., May 16, 1951; s. Charles Herbert and Dolores (DeWitt) B.; m. Jennifer Miller, Sept. 28, 1985. BS, Loyola U., New Orleans, 1973; MD, Ind. U., 1977. Diplomate Am. Bd. Internal Medicine, Diplomate Am. Bd. Hematology. Commd. officer USN, 1973-87, advanced through grades to comdr., 1986; intern Nat. Naval Med. Ctr., Bethesda, Md., 1977-78, resident internal medicine, 1979-82; fellow in hematology and oncology Nat. Naval Med. Ctr., Bethesda, 1982-85; gen. med. officer USN, Okinawa, Japan, 1978-79; head hematology and oncology div. Oakland (Calif.) Naval Hosp., Oakland, Calif., 1985—; teaching fellow Uniformed Svcs. U. Health Scis., Bethesda, 1979-85. Contr. articles to med. jours. Mem. AMA, FACP, Am. Soc. Tropical Medicine and Hygiene, Am. Acad. Scis., N.Y. Acad. Scis., Tibet Soc., Beta Beta Beta, Alpha Sigma Nu, Delta Epsilon Sigma. Buddhist. Home: 4167 Eastlake St Oakland CA 94602 Office: Naval Hospital Oakland CA 94627

BROWNING, ROBERT MARK, lawyer; b. Corpus Christi, Tex., May 15, 1955; s. Edmond Lee and Patricia (Sparks) B.; m. Ella Marie Gifford, June 8, 1986; 1 child, Zachary Edmond. BA magna cum laude, U. of South, 1978; JD, Lewis and Clark U., 1983. Bar: Hawaii. Felony trial lawyer, team capt. Honolulu Prosecuting Atty., 1983-88; assoc. Shim, Tam, Kirimitsu, Kitamura & Chang, Honolulu, 1988—; mem. jud. adminstrn. com. Hawaii State Bar. Vol., Hawaii Suicide and Crisis Ctr., Honolulu, 1978-83, Aloha Homeless, Inc., Honolulu, 1988—; coord. Aloha United Way, Honolulu, 1988—; bd. dirs., Hawaii Child Birth Assn., Honolulu, 1988—. Mem. Hawaii Bar Assn., Fed. Bar Assn. (bd. dirs., v.p. 1988—), Assn. Trial Lawyers Am., Am. Inns of Ct. Episcopalian. Office: Shim Tam Kirimitsu et al Ste 900 333 Queen St Honolulu HI 96813

BROWNING, WILLIAM DOCKER, judge; b. Tucson, May 19, 1931; s. Horace Benjamin and Mary Louise (Docker) B.; m. Courteny Browning (div.); children: Christopher, Logan, Courtenay; m. Zerilda Sinclair, Dec. 17, 1974; 1 child, Benjamin. BBA, U. Ariz., 1954, LLB, 1960. Bar: Ariz., U.S. Dist. Ct. Ariz., U.S. Ct. Appeals (9th cir.), U.S. Supreme Ct. Sole practice Tucson, 1960-84; judge U.S. Dist. Ct., Tucson, 1984—; mem. jud. nominating comm. appellate ct. appointments, 1975-79. Del. 9th Cir. Jud. Conf., 1968-77, 79-82. Served to 1st lt. USAF, 1954-57, capt. USNG, 1958-61. Fellow Am. Coll. Trial Lawyers, Am. Bar Found.; mem. ABA (spl. com. housing andurban devel. law 1973-78, com. urban problems and human affairs 1978-80), State Bar Ariz. (securities regulation com. 1964-66, chmn. uniform jury instructions com. 1962-66, chmn. merit selection of judges com. 1973-76, bd. govs., 1968-74, pres.-elect 1971-72, pres. 1972-73, named Outstanding Mem. 1980), Pima County Bar Assn. (exec. com. 1964-68, med.-legal screening panel 1965-75, pres. 1967-68), Am. Bd. Trial Advocates, Am. Judicature Soc. (bd. dirs. 1975-77, Herbert Lincoln Harley award 1978), Inst. Ct. Mgmt. (trustee 1978—). Office: US Dist Ct US Courthouse Rm 301 55 E Broadway Tucson AZ 85701

BROWNLEE, ROBERT REX, astronomer; b. Zenith, Kans., Mar. 4, 1924; s. Clarence Wilson and Francis Elizabeth (McComb) B.; m. Addie Leah Wise, Oct. 23, 1943; children: Jeanne Downing, Nancy Bonnema, Wayne R., Wenda, Wendell R. BS, Sterling Coll., 1947, DSc (hon.), 1966; MS, U. Kans., 1951; PhD, Ind. U., 1955. Staff mem. Los Alamos (N.Mex.) Sci. Lab., 1955-68, test dir., 1968-70, group leader, 1971-74, div. leader, 1974-81; program mgr. Los Alamos Nat. Lab., 1981—. Contbr. articles to profl. jours; creator stained glass windows. Served to lt. U.S. Army, 1942-46, PTO. Mem. Am. Astron. Soc., Royal Astron. Soc., Internat. Astron. Union. Republican. Home: 3007 Villa St Los Alamos NM 87544 Office: Los Alamos Nat Lab MS 670 Los Alamos NM 87545

BROWNLEE, WILSON ELLIOT, JR., history educator; b. Lacrosse, Wis., May 10, 1941; s. Wilson Elliot Sr. and Pearl (Woodings) B.; m. Mary Margaret Cochran, June 25, 1966; children: Charlotte Louise, Martin Elliot. BA, Harvard U., 1963; MA, U. Wis., 1965, PhD, 1969. Asst. prof. U. Calif., Santa Barbara, 1967-74, assoc. prof., 1974-80, prof. history, 1980—; vis. prof. Princeton U., Princeton, N.J., 1980-81; chair dept. history U. Calif., Santa Barbara, 1984-87, acad. senate, 1983-84, 88—; chair, exec. com. dels. Am. Coun. Learned Societies, N.Y.C., 1988-89, bd. dirs.; bd. dirs. Nat. Coun. on Pub. History, Boston. Author: Dynamics of Ascent, 1974, 79, Progressivism and Economic Growth, 1974, co-author: Women in the American Economy, 1976, Essentials of American history, 1976, 80, 86, America's History, 1987. Chair schs. com. Harvard Club, Santa Barbara, 1971-80, 85, 86; pres. Assn. for Retarded Citizens, Santa Barbara, 1982-84; 1st v.p. Assn. for Retarded Citizens Calif., Sacramento, 1983-84; pres. Santa Barbara Trust for Hist. Preservation, Santa Barbara, 1986-87. Charles Warren fellow Harvard U., 1978-79, fellow Woodrow Wilson Ctr., Washington, 1987-88; recipient Spl. Commendation, Calif. Dept. Parks and Recreation, 1988. Mem. Am. Hist. Assn., Orgn. Am. Historians, Econ. History Assn. Office: U Calif Dept History Santa Barbara CA 93106

BRUBAKER, RUTH, charitable organization fund raiser; b. Bradford, Pa., Mar. 4, 1959; d. Robert Earl and Josephine (Mahaffey) B. BS in Speech Pathology, U. Ariz., 1981. Producer, talent coord. Ninos Contentos show Sta. KTSP-TV, CBS, Phoenix, 1983-87; sales rep. Princeton Industries, Phoenix, 1984-85; pres., owner Sweetshirts of Scottsdale (Ariz.), 1987—; v.p. resource devel. Valley of Sun United Way, Phoenix, 1987—; instr. Nat. Acad. Voluntarism, United Way Am., 1987-89, mem. nat. profl. adv. coun., 1988-89. Treas., bd. dirs. MADD, Phoenix, 1985-89; vol. Fiesta Bowl, Phoenix, 1989. Mem. Friends Vol. Ctr., Soc. Am. Ventriloquists. Republican. Methodist. Office: Valley of Sun United Way 1515 E Osborn St Phoenix AZ 85014

BRUCE, JOHN ANTHONY, artist; b. L.A., Apr. 8, 1931; s. Merle VanDyke and Katherine Mary (Butler) B.; m. Barbara Jean Kennedy, May 29, 1967 (div. June 1988); children: Marsha Lee, Margaret Lorren, James Cole, Glenn Allen, Mark Corwin, Leslie Ann. BA in Psychology and Art, Calif. State U., L.A., 1965. Design engr. N.Am. Aviation Corp., Downey, Calif., 1952-57; comml. artist Aerojet Gen. Corp., Sacramento, 1957-59; advt. mgr. Flow Equipment Co., Santa Fe Springs, Calif., 1959-63; art dir. Barnes-Champ Advt., Santa Ana, Calif., 1963-66, Long Beach (Calif.) Ind. Press Telegram News, 1970-73; freelance art cons. Epcot project Walt E. Disney Enterprises, Glendale, Calif., 1976-77. Permanent collections Smithsonian Inst., Washington, D.C.; one man shows Ghormley Gallery, L.A., 1966, Les Li Art Gallery, L.A., 1970, Upstairs Gallery, Long Beach, Calif., 1973, El Prado Gallery, Sedona, Ariz., 1987; group shows Newport Beach Invitational, Newport Beach, Calif., 1964, Laguna Beach Art Festival, Laguna Beach, Calif., 1962, 63, 64, 65, Butler Inst. Am. Art, Youngstown, Ohio, 1970, Allied Artists, N.Y.C., 1988; currently exhibiting with Bartfield Gallery, N.Y.C., El Prado Gallery, Sedona, Ariz., Trails West Gallery, Laguna Beach, Calif. With U.S. Army, 1949-52, Korea. Recipient John B. Grayback award Am. Profl. Artists League, 1988, numerous others. Mem. Knickerbocker Artists (Philip Isinberg award 1988), Am. Indian and Cowboy Artists (Eagle Feather award 1988). Republican. Home and Studio: 5394 Tip Top Rd Mariposa CA 95338

BRUCE, NADINE CECILE, internist; b. Oak Park, Ill., Apr. 6, 1942; d. Roy Alford and Henrietta Hedwige (Denk) B. BS in Chemistry, Coll. St. Francis, 1964; MD, U. Ill., 1970. Diplomate Nat. Bd. Internal Medicine, Nat. Bd. Med. Examiners. Resident in internal medicine St. Francis Intergrated Med. Program, Honolulu, 1970-74; pvt. practice Honolulu, 1974-77; assoc. program dir. Med. Residency Program U. Hawaii, Honolulu, 1974-87, dep. program dir., 1987—; staff Queens Med. Ctr., 1974—. V.p. bd. trustees Hawaii Bound Sch., 1977-80; bd. govs. Hawaii Med. Library, 1980-85, Hawaii Heart Assn., 1983-88; bd. dirs. Hawaii Blood Bank, 1983; chmn. drug products selection bd. State of Hawaii, 1984—. Fellow Am. Coll. Physicians (gov. 1989—); mem. AMA, Hawaii Med. Assn. (councillor 1979-82), Honolulu County Med. Soc. (prs. 1983-84), Am. Soc. Internal Medicine program dir.), Am. Assn. U. Profs., N.Y. Acad. Sci., Soc. Gen. Internal Medicine. Republican. Roman Catholic. Office: U Hawaii Dept Medicine 1356 Lusitana St Honolulu HI 96813

BRUCE, ROBERT CECIL, landscape architect; b. Washington, Nov. 21, 1950; s. Clarence Cecil and Ellen (Gaiennie) B.; m. Molly Louise O'Neil, . BS, Texas Tech., 1974, BA, 1976. Landscape architect Masters and Uzzle, Lubbock, Tex., 1975-76, Sabells, Denver, 1976-79, Colo. State Parks, Denver, 1979—; instr. Nat. Fedn. of Garden Clubs, Denver, 1986-88. Vol. case asst. atty. Guardian Advt. Litem, Jefferson County, Colo. Mem. Am. Soc. Landscape Architects. Roman Catholic. Home: 6659 W Roxbury Littleton CO 80123 Office: Colo State Parks 1313 Sherman Denver CO 80203

BRUEMMER, BARBARA ANN, nutritionist; b. Seattle, Aug. 10, 1950; d. George Arthur and Mary Louise (Broderick) Flajole; m. John Joseph Bruemmer, Aug. 26, 1972; children: Angela Lynn, Michael Ryan. BA, Calif. State U.-Long Beach, 1973; MS, U. Wash., 1983. Registered dietitian, Wash. Clin. dietitian Harborview Med. Ctr., Seattle, 1984; exec. sec. Wash. State Dietetic Assn., Seattle, 1984-85; rsch. dietitian Pacific Med. Ctr., Seattle, 1985-88; teaching asst. U. Wash., Seattle, 1988—. Mem. Am. Dietetic Assn., Wash. State Dietetic Assn. (treas. 1988—), Am. Coll. Sports Medicine, Soc. Epidemiologic Rsch., AAUW, Omicron Nu. Democrat. Roman Catholic. Home: 13207 233d Ave SE Issaquah WA 98027

BRUENING, REIMAR CASPAR, chemistry educator, marine bio-organic chemistry researcher; b. Munich, Dec. 31, 1948; came to U.S., 1981; s. Hans and Elizabeth (Gerlach) B. BS, U. Munich, 1970, MS, 1973, PhD, 1979. Research asst. U. Munich, 1978-79; research fellow U. Nagoya, Japan, 1979-81; research assoc. Columbia U., N.Y.C., 1981-85; asst. prof. U. Hawaii, Honolulu, 1985—. Co-author: Centrifugal Partition Chromatography, 1987. Recipient Eisai award NAITO Found, Japan. Mem. Gesellschaft Deutscher Chemiker, Am. Chem. Soc., Am. Assn. Adv. Sci. Office: U Hawaii Dept Chemistry 2545 The Mall Honolulu HI 96822

BRUGADA, TONI MARIE, real estate broker; b. Oklahoma City, June 14, 1946; d. Edward Bruce and Dorothy Ester (Bennett) Donnelly; m. Daniel Brugada, Oct. 4, 1967 (div. Mar. 1987); children: Rachelle, Danee, Christopher Michael; m. Dennis M. Naylor, Aug. 1989. Cert. in real estate, Colo. Real Estate Sch., 1974, Ariz. Sch. Real Estate, 1984; student, Mesa (Ariz.) Community Coll., 1982. Reception Anderson-Anderson, Wellington, Kans., 1967-71; supr. Am. Fabric and Foam, Kansas City, Mo., 1971-74; salesperson Taylor-Taylor Real Estate Investors, Denver, 1974-77; med. technician Moore Clinic, Kansas City, 1977-80; area supr. Micro Rel, Tempe, Ariz., 1981-84; salesperson Century 21 AWARE, Mesa, 1984-88; mgr. project sales and mktg. S.W. Properties Inc., Mesa, 1988—. Mem. Mesa Tempe Chandler Bd. Realtors (agt.). Home: 5909 E Nance Mesa AZ 85205 Office: SW Properties Inc 1855 E Southern Ave Ste 205 Mesa AZ 85204

BRUGGE, DAVID MARTIN, retired anthropologist, curator; b. Jamestown, N.Y., Sept. 3, 1927; s. Oswald Adolph and Frances Margaret (Jones) B.; m. Ruth Virginia Sherlog, Feb. 22, 1959; children: Douglas Martin, Steven Paul, Janet Esther. BA, U. N.Mex., 1950. Mem. staff Unitarian Service Com., Gallup, N.Mex., 1955-57; archeologist Four Corners Pipeline Co., Houston, 1957-58; anthropologist The Navajo Tribe, Window Rock, Ariz., 1958-68; curator Nat. Park Service, Ganado, Ariz., 1968-73; anthropologist Nat. Park Service, Albuquerque, 1973-77; regional curator Nat. Park Service, Santa Fe, 1977-88; seminar participant Sch. Am. Research, Santa Fe, 1979, 85; chmn. Navajo Studies Conf., Albuquerque, 1985-86. Author: Navajos in the Catholic Church 1694-1875, 1968, 2d rev. edit., 1986, Navajo Pottery and Ethnohistory, 1963, 2d rev. edit., 1981, A History of the Chaco Navajos, 1980, Tsegai: An Archeological Ethnohistory, 1986; co-editor: Navajo Religion and Culture, 1982. Bd. dirs. Navajo Nation Health Found., Ganado, 1972-73, Title I Ganado Pub. Sch.Bd., 1972-73. Served with U.S. Army, 1945-47. Recipient Cert. Recognition Project Hope, Ganado, 1973, Unit award Dept. Interior, Santa Fe, 1982. Mem. AAAS, Am. Anthrop. Assn., Soc. Am Archaelogy, Am. Soc. Ethnohistory (sec.-treas. 1966-67, nominating com. 1986), N.Mex. Assn. Mus. (treas. 1977-79). Democrat. Home: 1024 Indiana SE Albuquerque NM 87108

BRUGGEMAN, LEWIS LEROY, radiologist; b. N.Y.C., Sept. 9, 1941; s. Louis LeRoy and Edwina Jane (Mickel) B.; m. Ann Margaret Kayajan, May 28, 1966; children: Gretchen Ann, Kurt LeRoy. AB, Dartmouth Coll., 1963, B in Med. Sci., 1965; MD, Harvard U., 1968. Intern Los Angeles County Harbor Gen. Hosp., Torrence, Calif., 1968-69; resident in diagnostic radiology Columbia Presbyn. Med. Ctr., N.Y.C., 1969-72; chief dept. radiology Bremerton (Wash.) Naval Regional Med. Ctr., 1972-74; pvt. practice diagnostic radiology South Coast Med. Ctr., South Laguna, Calif., 1974—, dir. dept. radiology, 1983—, hosp. bd. trustees, 1985-87; pvt. practice diagnostic radiology Saddleback Community Hosp., Laguna Hills, Calif., 1974—; pres., chmn. bd. dirs. South Coast Med. Group Inc., South Laguna, Calif., 1983—; pres. So. Coast Radiol. Med. Group Inc., South Laguna, 1986—. Lt. comdr. Med. Corps USN, 1972-74. Mem. AMA, Radiol. Soc. N.Am., Am. Coll. Radiology, Calif. Med. Assn., Calif. Radiol. Soc., Dartmouth Club Orange County. Office: S Coast Radiol Med Group 28 Monarch Bay Pla Ste J South Laguna CA 92677

BRUGGER, PAUL RAYMOND, marketing professional; b. Glendale, Calif., July 31, 1942; s. Paul Joseph and Rita Marie (Wirth) B.; m. Carol Ann Tarleton, May 12, 1965; children: John-Paul, Eric, Joel, Beth, Dann, Elyn, KayCee. Student, Glendale Coll., 1960-64, L.A. City Coll., 1961, Western Nev. Community Coll., 1978-79, U. Nev., Las Vegas, 1981. Engring. asst. Nev. Controls, Inc., Minden, 1968; prodn. test technician Raven Electronics, Reno, 1968-69; electronics specialist Nev. Gaming Control Bd., Carson City, 1969-81; mgr. field support Summit Systems, Inc., Las Vegas, 1981-82; dist. mgr. Cal-Omega, Inc., Las Vegas, 1982-83; project engr. Sierra Control Systems, Carson City, 1983-85; electronics engr. Bally Systems, Reno, 1985—; owner, gaming cons. Paul R. Brugger Cons. Svcs., Carson City, 1979--. Adult leader Nev. Area coun. Boy Scouts Am., 1971--. With USN, 1964-68. Mem. IEEE (sect. chmn. 1988--). Republican. Mormon. Office: Bally Systems 255 Bell St Reno NV 89503

BRUHN, JOHN AUDOLPH, JR., finance executive, writer; b. Indpls., Oct. 13, 1935; s. John Audolph Bruhn and Rachell (Hull) Bruhn Ruddell; m. Joene Marie Cline, Dec. 28, 1957; children: John Allan III, Jeffrey Cline. BA in Econs. and Math., DePauw U., 1957; MBA in Mgmt., San Diego State U., 1961; postgrad., U. So. Calif., 1963-64; PhD in Communications, U.S. Internat. U., 1971. Cert. assessment evaluator. Asst. bus. mgr. U. Calif., San Diego, 1961-66; chief dep. assessor County San Diego, 1966-72, dir. fin., 1972-75, asst. county mgr., 1975-79; gen. mgr. Marine Corps Credit Union, San Diego, 1979-80; pres. and chief exec. officer Fin. Fed. Credit Union, San Diego, 1980—; instr. U. Calif., San Diego, 1963-75; trustee Consumer Credit Counselors, San Diego, 1983—; pres. chpt. Calif. Credit Unions League, 1983-84; chmn. bd. WesCorp, Pomona, Calif., 1984—. Author-editor: CUNA Management, 1981; editor and contbr. to numerous profl. and sci. jours. Bd. dirs. San Diego YMCA, 1967-71, Disabled Am. Vets. Served to maj. USMC, 1957-60. Recipient Internat. award in Govtl. Adminstrn., Internat. Assn. Assessing Officers, 1971; named Nat. Exec. of Yr., Credit Union Exec. Soc., 1983; nominated Outstanding Young Man, City of San Diego, 1973. Mem. Credit Union Mgrs. Assn. (pres. 1982-84), Am. Soc. Pub. Adminstrs. (pres. 1969-72), Credit Union Exec. Soc. (awards judge 1983-84), Calif. Credit Union League Coop. (founding trustee 1980-82), San Diego State U. Sch. Bus. (bd. dirs.), San Diego Jr. C. of C. (bd. dirs. 1971-73), Eagle Scout Alumni Assn. (founding chmn. 1971-81), DePauw U. Alumni Assn. (pres. 1966). Republican. Home: 4102 Point Loma Ave San Diego CA 92107 Office: Fin Fed Credit Union 440 Beech St San Diego CA 92101-3281

BRUKETTA, TERRILL JOSEPH, electronics engineer; b. Spokane, Wash., Dec. 26, 1940; s. Thomas Joseph and Donna Teresa (Dameskey) B. AS in Indsl. Arts, Santa Barbara City Coll., 1972; BS in Electronics Engring., Calif. Poly. State U., 1986. Mechanic Texaco Sta., Santa Barbara, 1971-72; clk. Alpha Beta, Santa Barbara, 1969-72; microwave and elec. insp. Electro Magnetic System div. Raytheon Co., Santa Barbara, 1979-82, sr. project test engr., 1983; engr. Missile System div. Raytheon Co., Oxnard, Calif., 1986—. With USN, 1972-78. Mem. Cousteau Soc. Office: Raytheon Co Missile System Div 4347 Raytheon Rd Oxnard CA 93033

BRUMAN, HENRY JOHN, university chairman, geography educator; b. Berlin, Mar. 25, 1913; came to U.S., 1922; Student, Calif. Inst. Tech., 1930-31, U. Mex., 1934; BA in Chemistry, UCLA, 1935, postgrad., 1936; PhD. in Geography, U. Calif., Berkeley, 1940. Asst. prof. geography Pa. State Coll., 1940-43; cultural geographer Inst. Social Anthropology Smithsonian Instn., Washington, 1943; mem. staff M Project Confidential Agy., Washington, 1943-44; from asst. prof. to prof. UCLA, 1945-82, chmn. dept. geography, 1957-61; mem. creating staff UCLA Map Libr., 1960-61 (renamed the Henry

J. Bruman Map Libr., 1987); assoc. dir. Latin Am. Ctr., UCLA, 1961-64; dir. NDEA Ctr. in Latin Am. Studies UCLA, 1961-65, Colombian Student Leader Seminars, UCLA, 1960-63, Brazil Student Leader Seminars, UCLA, 1964-66; vis. prof. U. Goettingen, Fed. Republic Germany, 1966-68, dir. Edn. Abroad Program, 1966-68. Contbr. articles to profl. jours.; discoverer only known copy Fries-Grieninger Carta Marina of 1531. Founder Henry J. Bruman Ednl. Found., 1980, pres. 1980—. Endowed grad. fellow in Cultural and Hist. Geography UCLA, 1977, Fulbright fellow to Portugal, 1963; recipient Alexander von Humboldt Gold medal, Fed. Republic Germany, 1971, Univ. medal U. Goettingen, 1978, 250th Anniversary medal U. Goettingen, 1987, Edn. Abroad Program 20th Anniversary medal, U. Calif., 1982, Excellence in Univ. Svc. award UCLA Alumni Assn., 1989. Office: UCLA Dept Geography Bunche Hall 1255 Los Angeles CA 90024

BRUMLEY, JEANNE MARIA, nurse; b. Hamilton, Ohio, Oct. 31, 1955; d. Eugene and Shirley Jean (Lattuga) Hacker Lewis; 1 child, Melinda Renee Wood, from previous marriage; m. Michael Allen Brumley, Feb. 18, 1989. AS in Nursing, Miami U., Oxford, Ohio, 1976. Cert. gerontol. nurse. Staff nurse Bethesda North Hosp., Cin., 1976-78; dir. staff Mt. Pleasant Retirement Village, Monroe, Ohio, 1980-83; shift supr. Adventist Convalescent Hosp., Glendora, Calif., 1983-86; dir. nursing svcs. Colonial Manor, West Covina, Calif., 1986-88, Brethren Hillcrest Homes, La Verne, Calif., 1988—; Contbr. articles to mags. Named Woman of Yr. Trenton Ch. of God, 1983. Mem. Calif. Coun. Long Term Care Nurses (sec. 1986—), Calif. Nurses Assn., Am. Soc. Aging, Calif. Assn. Health Facilities, West Covina C. of C. (mem. com.), Covina Women's Club. Republican. Home: 2931 Heller Dr Riverside CA 92509 Office: Brethren Hillcrest Homes 2600 A St La Verne CA 91750

BRUMLEY, STEVEN DONALD, lawyer; b. Aurora, Nebr., Dec. 29, 1941; s. Milburn M. and Helen Margaret (Strong) B.; m. Nancy Molly Schneller, Jan. 28, 1960 (div. 1980); children: Justine Leigh Brumley Fluharty, Steven Thomas; m. Vernetta Clark Wilson, Jan. 28, 1988. BS, U. Nebr., 1966, JD with distinction, 1968. Bar: Nebr. 1968, Colo. 1982, U.S. Supreme Ct. 1977. Staff atty. U.S. Dept. Energy, Idaho Falls, Idaho, 1968-78; asst. gen. counsel Western Area Power Adminstrn., Golden, Colo., 1978-84; counsel Rockwell Internat., Golden, Colo., 1984--; sec.-treas., bd. dirs. Applied Resource Mgmt., Inc., Golden, 1987--. Contbr. articles to profl. publs. Active Republican Nat. Com., 1985--. Mem. Nebr. Bar Assn., Colo. Bar Assn., Am. Corp. Counsel Assn., NRA (life), Order of Coif. Home: 14541 Archer Ave Golden CO 80401 Office: Rockwell Internat PO Box 464 Golden CO 80401

BRUMMEL, STEVEN WILLIAM, foundation administrator; b. L.A., Feb. 17, 1946; s. Henry William and Claudia (Borja) B.; m. Shari Marie Reville; children: Michael, Christopher, John William; stepson Netha Olive (Barlow) B.; BA in Govt. and Journalism with honors, Calif. State U., Sacramento, 1972, MA in Govt., 1975. Newsman, Sta. KNTV-TV, San Jose, Calif., 1969-71, Sta. KCRA-TV, Sacramento, 1971-73; cons. Calif. Assembly, 1973; dist. rep. U.S. Congressman Leo J. Ryan, 1973-75; pres. Pacific Cons., San Francisco, 1975, ELS, Inc., Santa Cruz, Calif., 1975-82; tchr., counselor Operation SHARE, 1970-71; pres., Elvirita Lewis Found. Geriatric Health and Nutrition, Palm Springs, Calif., 1976—; v.p. San Jose Ecology Action, 1970-71; pres., chmn. bd. dirs. Verde-Mar, Ltd., La Quinta, Calif., 1978—. Publicity chmn. Santa Clara County Easter Seals, 1970-71; bd. dirs. La Qunita Classic Jazz Festival, 1987—; mem. Rep. Nat. Com., Senatorial Inner Circle, Calif. Rep. Golden Circle; mem. Gov.'s Adv. Task Force on Long Term Care; mem. Santa Cruz County Housing Adv. Commn., 1976-81. With USN, 1964-67, Vietnam. Mem. Am. Acad. Polit. and Social Scientists, La Quinta C. of C. (bd. dirs. 1989—), Nat. Council on Aging, Am. Soc. Aging (chmn. communications com., editorial bd. 1984-86, bd. dirs. 1986-88), World Affairs Council San Francisco, Calif. Council on Internat. Trade, Calif. Farm Bur., Export Mgrs. Assn., Nat. Rifle Assn., Am. Assn. Internat. Aging (bd. dirs., sec. 1983—), Acad. Polit. Sci., Coachella Valley Mex.-Am. C. of C. (bd. dirs., treas. 1988-89), Smithsonian Instn., Am. Mus. Natural History, Gerontol. Soc., Internat. Council Nat. Founds. on Aging (bd. dirs.), Nat. Hispanic Council on Aging (bd. dirs. 1986—), Sigma Delta Chi (Journalism award 1972, 73), Pi Sigma Alpha, Commonwealth Club, La Quinta Tennis Club. Office: Elvirita Lewis Found 255 N El Cielo Rd Ste 144 Palm Springs CA 92262 also: PO Box 1508 La Quint CA 92253

BRUMMETT, ROBERT EDDIE, pharmacology educator; b. Concordia, Kans., Feb. 11, 1934; s. Gordon Legonia and Gladys Leona (Anderson) B.; m. Naomi Deen Weaver, Dec. 19, 1955; children: Randall, Wendy, Robin, Philip. BS, Oreg. State U., 1959, MS, 1960; PhD, U. Oreg., 1964. Registered pharmacist, Oreg. Asst. prof. pharmacology Oreg. State U., Corvallis, 1961-62; asst. prof. otolaryngology Oreg. Health Scis. U., Portland, 1964-70, assoc. prof. otolaryngology and pharmacology, 1970-80, prof. otolaryngology and Pharmacology, 1981—; mem. Oreg. Council on Alcohol and Drug Problems, Salem, 1979-85; instr. Am. Acad. Otolaryngology, Washington, 1964—; cons. in field, 1969—;. Patentee in field; contbr. 100 articles to profl. jours. Comdr. U.S. Power Squadron, Portland, 1982-86, adminstrv. officer 1986—. Grantee NIH, 1969—, Deafness Research Found., 1970, Med. Research Found., 1979, 83. Mem. AAAS, Am. Acad. Otolaryngology (instr. 1964—), Head and Neck Surgery, Associated Researchers in Otolaryngology, Sigma Xi. Republican. Club: Hayden Island Yacht (Portland) Lodge: Elks. Home: 545 N Hayden Bay Dr Portland OR 97217 Office: Oreg Health Scis U 3181 SW Sam Jackson Park Rd Portland OR 97201

BRUN, CHRISTIAN MAGNUS FROM, university librarian; b. Trondheim, Norway, Oct. 3, 1920; came to U.S., 1923; s. Aage and Petra Christine (From) B.; m. Jane Carey Fristoe, June 1, 1958; 1 child, Erik From. BA in Econs. and Bus., U. Wash., 1948; BLS, U. N.C., 1950; AM in L.S., U. Mich., 1952, MA in History, 1956. Asst. curator U. Pa. Library, Phila., 1950-51; bibliog. asst. U. Mich., Ann Arbor, 1951-52, asst. curator, 1952-55, resident advisor, 1955-63; head spl. coll. library U. Calif., Santa Barbara, 1963—; archivist U. Calif., 1963—, preservation officer, 1988—; curator William Wyles Coll., U. Calif., 1963—. Author: Guide to the MSS Maps, 1959, Wm. L. Clements Lib. Maps and Charts Pub. in Am. before 1800, 1969; author (with others): new edition, 1978. Decorated Bronze Star, 1945; recipient Acorn Found. award, Acorn Found., 1969, Bicentennial Citation City of Santa Barbara, 1982. Mem. Am. Scandinavian Found., Santa Barbara Hist. Soc., Map Soc. Calif., Soc. Calif. Archivists, Am. Printing Hist. Assn., Soc. History Discoveries, Friends UCBS Library. Democrat. Home: 5663 Via Trento Goleta CA 93117 Office: U Calif Libr Dept Spl Collections Santa Barbara CA 93106

BRUN, KIM ERIC, photographer; b. San Diego, Jan. 31, 1947; s. Henry Milton and Laurel Elizabeth (Von Heeringen) B.; m. Christine Helen Cuseo, June 21, 1975. BA, Humboldt State U., 1973; MBA, San Diego State U., 1976. Asst. rsch. physyologist Naval Personal Rsch. and Devel. Ctr., San Diego, 1973-76; sales rep. Sparkletts Water Co., San Diego, 1977-78; photographer Kim Brun Photography, San Diego, 1978-84, Kim Brun Studios, Inc., San Diego, 1984—. Co-author: Computer-Based Management Info Systems and Organizatio Behavior, 1980; contbr. photographs to numerous books, mag. covers and mags. Sgt. U.S. Army, 1968-70, Vietnam. Decorated Bronze star for valor with two oak leaf clusters. Mem. Am. Soc. Mag. Photographers (treas. 1985-87, bd. dirs. 1987-88), San Diego Fly Fishers, Sierra Club. Home: 1329 Calle Scott Encinitas CA 92024

BRUN, MARGARET ANN CHARLENE, buyer; b. Toledo, June 19, 1945; d. John Joseph and Maude Elizabeth (Harrell) Bartos; m. Paul Joseph Brun, June 17, 1967. Student, Phoenix Coll., 1964-67. Controller material inventory Digital Equipment Corp., Phoenix, 1975-76, controller prodn. inventory, 1976-77, prodn. control planner, 1977-79, inventory control planner, 1979, buyer, 1979—. Named Buyer of Yr., Purchasing World mag., 1987. Democrat. Methodist. Office: Digital Equipment Corp 2500 W Union Hills Dr Phoenix AZ 85027

BRUNACINI, ALAN VINCENT, fire chief; b. Jamestown, N.Y., Apr. 18, 1937; s. John N. and Mary T. Brunacini; B.S., Ariz. State U., 1970, M.P.A., 1975; m. Rita McDaugh, Feb. 14, 1959; children—Robert Nicholas, John Nicholas, Mary Candice. Mem. Phoenix Fire Dept., 1959—, bn. chief, then asst. fire chief, 1971-78, fire chief, 1978—; condr. nat. seminar on fire dept. mgmt., 1970—. Redford scholar, 1968. Mem. Am. Soc. Public Adminstrn. (Superior Service award 1980), Nat. Fire Protection Assn. (chmn. fire service sect. 1974-78, dir. 1978), Internat. Assn. Fire Chiefs, Soc. Fire Service Instrs. Author: Fireground Command; also articles in field. Office: Office of Fire Chief 520 W Van Buren Phoenix AZ 85003 *

BRUNEAU, BILL, architect; b. Phila., May 29, 1948; s. William Francis and Mabel Frances (Quiroli) B.; m. Carol Ann Cahoon, Aug. 29, 1982; children: Nicole Domenique, Mercedes Angelina, William Robert. BArch., Pa. State U., 1970; MArch., U. Colo., 1971; M. of Urban Design, Harvard U., 1974; Cert. in City Planning, U. Florence, Italy, 1969; Cert. in Urban Econs., MIT, 1970. Registered architect Colo., Calif., Mo., Mass., Wyo., Minn. Urban designer planning dept. City of Aurora, Colo., 1977-80; project interior architect Cannell & Chaffin, Denver, 1980-82; dir. architecture URS Co., Denver, 1982-84; mgr. facilities Frontier Airlines, Denver, 1984-86, United Airlines, Chgo., 1986-87; sr. aviation planner Burns & McDonnell, Denver, 1987—; instr. U. Colo., Denver, 1972, Community Coll. Denver, Red Rocks, Colo., 1975-80; prin. Bruneau Urban Design and Architecture Assocs., Denver, 1980-87; pres. Rocky Mountain Constrn. Mgmt. Inc., Aurora, 1982. Contbr. articles to profl. jours. Vol. YMCA, Colo.; lectr. Career Days, Colo. Harvard U. fellow, 1973; recipient award of Merit City and County of Denver, 1972; named Outstanding Young Man of Am., 1976. Mem. AIA, Am. Soc. Interior Designers, Am. Inst. Certified Planners, Illuminating Engring. Soc. Presbyterian. Home: 5440 E Vale Dr Denver CO 80222-2337 Office: Burns & McDonnell 8055 E Tufts Ave Ste 330 Denver CO 80237

BRUNELLO, ROSANNE, sales executive; b. Cleve., Aug. 26, 1960; d. Carl Carmello and Vivian Lucille (Caranna) B.; m. Bruce Jordan, Feb. 12, 1983 (div. Mar. 1986). Student, U. Cin., 1978-80, Cleve. State U., 1981. Indusl. Sales Engr. Alta Machine Tool, Denver, 1982; sales/purchasing Ford Tool & Machine, Denver, 1982-84; sales/ptnr. Mt. Rep. Enterprises, Denver, 1984-86; sales/pres. Mt. Rep. of Ariz., Phoenix, 1986—. Active mem. Republican Party, 1985—, Tempe C. of C., 1987—. Mem. NAFE, Soc. of Mfg. Engrs. (pres. award 1988), Computer Automated Assn. (chmn. elect 1988, chmn. 1989, Vocat. Ednal. Clubs of Am. (exec. bd., pres. 1987—), Italian Cultural Soc. Roman Catholic. Home and Office: Mt Rep of Ariz 255 S Kyrene Rd #207 Chandler AZ 85226

BRUNER, JEFFREY ALAN, medical diagnostics company executive; b. Berkeley, Calif., Jan. 21, 1952; s. Ruth (Rasmussen) French. BS in Indsl. Engring., San Jose State U., 1975. Mfg. engr. airline equipment div. FMC, San Jose, Calif., 1975-82; mfg. engr., mgr. Syva/Syntex, Mountain View, Calif., 1982-85; mgr. instrument ops. Syva/Syntex, Mountain View, 1985—. Mem. Am. Prodn. and Inventory Control Soc. (cert.), Soc. Mfg. Engrs. (sr. mem.), Am. Mgmt. Assn., Soc. Advancement Mgmt., Alpha Eta Rho, Decathlon Club (Santa Clara, Calif.), Toastmasters. Republican. Home: 524 Concho Dr Fremont CA 94539 Office: Syva Instruments 1375 Shorebird Way Mountain View CA 94043

BRUNGARDT, HELEN RUTH, minister; b. Littlefield, Tex., Sept. 2, 1931; d. Isaac Henry and Helen Irene (Hanna) Pelt; m. Guido Milton Brungardt, July 22, 1950 (div.); children: Karla Kay, Linda Gail, Mark Douglas, Celeste Dawn. Student, Tex. Christian U., 1948-49, U. N.Mex., 1969, Divine Sci. Ednl. Ctr., 1976-80. Tchr. Napoleon Hill Acad., Albuquerque, 1964-66; practitioner First Ch. Religious Sci., Albuquerque, 1969-72, tchr., 1971-72; founder, minister Symphony of Life Ch., Albuquerque, 1972-81; founder, dir., pres. Inst. for the Emerging Self, Albuquerque, 1981—; cons. ministers, individuals, 1977—; lectr. various orgns., radio, tv, 1975—; instr. Profl. Leadership Tng., Albuquerque, 1965-82; bd. dirs., co-founder Grand Teton Retreat. Author: Contemplation, 1975, Mystical Meaning of Jesus, 1980, Beyond Liberation, 1985; contbr. articles to profl. jours. Mem. Divine Sci. Fedn., Internat. New Thought Alliance. Republican. Mem. Ch. Divine Sci. Home: PO Box 567 Columbus NM 88029 Office: Inst for Emerging Self PO Box 75159 Sta 14 Albuquerque NM 87194

BRUNI, JOHN RICHARD, news journalist; b. Bklyn., Apr. 24, 1951; s. Albert P. and Doris L. (Burke) B.; m. Cynthia C. Bruni, Aug. 20, 1988. Electronic journalist NBC Network News, N.Y.C., 1973—; studio engr. Top NY DJ's, N.Y.C., 1973-76; soundman, cameraman Today Show and Nightly News NBC Network News, N.Y.C., 1976-78; soundman, electronic journalist for San Francisco Bur., Today Show and Nightly News with Tom Brokaw NBC Network News, San Francisco, 1978—. Recipient Emmy award Nat. Acad. TV Arts & Sciences, 1983-84. Presbyterian. Office: NBC News 1001 Van Ness Ave Ste 430 San Francisco CA 94109

BRUNN, ROBERT JAMES, educational administrator; b. San Francisco, Sept. 23, 1934; s. Charles A. and Rose Ann (Kennedy) B.; m. Margaret Brunn; children: Charles Laurence, Elizabeth Ann. BS, U. Chgo., 1959. Cert. tchr., N. Mex. Tchr. Santa Fe (N. Mex.) Prep. Sch., 1971-75; founder, headmaster Sun Mountain Sch., Santa Fe, 1975-80, Brunn Sch., Santa Fe, 1980--. With U.S. Army, 1951-54. Democrat. Office: Brunn Sch Botulph Rd Box 9 Santa Fe NM 87501

BRUNNER, EARL CHESTER, JR., school administrator; b. Los Angeles, Dec. 13, 1924; s. Earl Chester and Louise Esther (Jones) B.; m. Laurine Adams, July 28, 1948; children—Earl Claude, David Arnold, Michael Bruce, Karl Martin, Kurt Lafi, Laurine Louise. B.S., Brigham Young U., 1950, M.Ed., 1957. Tchr., Las Vegas Sch. Dist., Nev., 1950-52, biology Las Vegas High Sch., 1953-57, sci. and math. Ch. Coll. W. Samoa, Apia, Western Samoa, 1958-60; tchr. Las Vegas pub. schs., 1960-63, elementary prin., 1963-82; chief librarian Branch Genealogical Library, Las Vegas, Nev., 1980—, dir. Las Vegas Family History Ctr., 1988. Committeeman, Republican Central Com., Las Vegas, 1974-82; scoutmaster, dist. commr. Boy Scouts Am., Las Vegas, 1960-82. Recipient Scout award Boy Scouts Am. 1975. Republican. Mormon. Home: 330 N 9th St Las Vegas NV 89101 Office: Las Vegas Family History Ctr 509 S Ninth St Las Vegas NV 89101

BRUNNER, HOWARD WILLIAM, land surveyor; b. Mobile, Ala., July 24, 1946; s. Joseph Edward and Beaulah (Howard) B.; m. Linda Marie Parker, Dec. 20, 1963 (div. June 1978); children: Leah Marie, Anne Marie; m. Catherine Cecilia Byrnes, June 27, 1981. Grad. high sch., Santa Rosa, Calif. Registered profl. land surveyor. Survey technician Roemer & Estes, Mill Valley, Calif., 1964-65, Ken Frost & Assocs., Mill Valley, 1965-66; engring. aide County of Marin, San Rafael, Calif., 1966-75; pres. Engring. Field Svcs., San Rafael, 1975-77, Brunner, Phelps & Assocs., Inc., Cotati, Calif., 1977-80; v.p. Ray Carlson & Assocs., Inc., Santa Rosa, Calif., 1980—; expert examiner Bd. Registration for Profl. Engrs. and Land Surveyors, Sacramento, 1985-89. Mem. Geysers Geothermal Assn. (bd. dirs. 1985-88), Calif. Land Surveyors Assn. (pres. elect 1989—, sec. 1988-89). Roman Catholic. Home: 220 Chiquita Rd Healdsburg CA 95448 Office: Ray Carlson & Assocs Inc 807 St Helena Ave Santa Rosa CA 95404

BRUNNGRABER, LEE, psychiatric nurse; b. Dumont, N.J., June 8, 1954; d. Harold and Florence (Bieth) Stroessner; m. Rodric F. Brunngraber, June 19, 1976. BS in Nursing, U. Del., 1976; MS in Nursing, U. Colo., Denver, 1983. Psychiat. staff nurse VA Med. Ctr., San Diego, 1976-77, psychiat. rsch. staff nurse, 1979; psychiat. staff nurse, team leader VA Med. Ctr., Palo Alto, Calif., 1977-79, psychiat. clin. nurse specialist, 1983—, instr. nursing, 1983-84, psychotherapist psychiat. evaluation unit, 1984—; psychiat. nurse clinician partial hospitalization program Grossmont Hosp., La Mesa, Calif., 1979-80, acting coord., 1980-81. Mem. Nat. Assn. VA Nurses, Am. Assn. Psychiat. Clin. Nurse Specialists, Am. Nurses Assn. (cert. adult psychiat.-mental health clin. nurse specialist), No. Calif. Assn. Clin. Nurse Specialists (v.p. 1987—), Am. Assn. Psychiat. Nursing, Calif. Nurses Assn., Sigma Theta Tau, Phi Kappa Phi. Home: 19680 Brook Ln Saratoga CA 95070 Office: Piera Health Group 949 Sherwood Ave Ste 100 Palo Alto CA 94309

BRUNO, ARTHUR DOMINIC, electrical engineer; b. Price, Utah, June 27, 1951; s. Dominic and Marva Rae (Drolc) B.; m. Tonya Scorzato, Mar. 18, 1972; children: Scott Michael, Cori Dawn. AS in Engring., Coll. Ea. Utah, 1971; BSEE, U. Utah, 1974. Registered profl. engr., Utah. Dist. elec. engr. U.S. Steel Corp., East Carbon, Utah, 1974-76; chief electrician, elec. engr. Swisher Coal Co., Price, Utah, 1976-77; maintenance supt. Swisher Coal Co., Price, 1977-79; dir. maintenance Emery Mining Corp., Huntington, Utah, 1979-85; mine supt. Emery Mining Corp., Huntington, 1985-86; maintenance supt. Castle Gate Coal Co., Helper, Utah, 1986—; ptnr., Power Tech, Price, 1986—; elec. engring. cons., Price, 1987—. Patentee, power ctr. output tester; author tech. papers. Pres., Price Cen. League, Western Boys' Baseball Assn., 1986; chmn. program adv. com., dept. mining, Coll. Ea. Utah, Price, 1988—. Mem. Am. Soc. Mining Engrs., Elks, Carbon Country Club. Home: 985 N Drexel St Price UT 84501 Office: Castle Gate Coal Co PO Box 449 Helper UT 84526

BRUNO, JUDYTH ANN, chiropractor; b. Eureka, Calif., Feb. 16, 1944; d. Harold Oscar and Shirley Alma (Farnsworth) Nelson; m. Thomas Glenn Bruno, June 1, 1968; 1 child, Christina Elizabeth. AS, Sierra Coll., 1982; D of Chiropractic, Palmer Coll. of Chiropractic West, Sunnyvale, Calif., 1986. Diplomate Nat. Bd. Chiropractic Examiners. Sec. Bank Am., San Jose, Calif., 1965-67; marketer Memorex, Santa Clara, Calif., 1967-74; order entry clk. John Deere, Milan, Ill., 1977; system analyst Four Phase, Cupertino, Calif., 1977-78; chiropractic asst. Dr. Thomas Bruno, Nevada City, Calif., 1978-81; chiropractor Chiropractic Health Care Ctr., Nevada City, 1987—. Area dir. Cultural Awareness Coun., Grass Valley, Calif., 1977—; vol. Nevada County Library, Nevada City, 1987-88, Decide Team III, Nevada County, 1987—. Mem. Am. Chiropractic Assn., Calif. Chiropractic Assn., Toastmasters (sec. 1988), Soroptimists. Republican.

BRUNO, LOUIS BYRON, lawyer; b. Denver, June 26, 1944; s. Frank A. and Jennie L. (Grace) B.; m. Marilee I. Ferdinand, June 18, 1966; children: Andrea Ann, Christopher Frank. BA, U. Colo., 1965, JD, 1968. Bar: Colo. 1968, U.S. Dist. Ct. Colo. 1968, U.S. Ct. Appeals (10th cir.) 1971, U.S. Supreme Ct. 1978. Ptnr. Bruno & Bruno, Denver, 1968-79; pres. Bruno, Bruno & Bruno P.C., Denver, 1979-82, Bruno, Bruno & Colin, Denver, 1982—. Pres. Jefferson County Assn. for Retarded, Lakewood, Colo., 1978-79, Jefferson County Community Ctr. for Devel. Disabilities, Lakewood, 1973—; bd. dirs. Colo. Diversified Industries, Lakewood, 1978-85. Mem. Colo. Bar Assn., Jefferson County Bar Assn., Assn. Trial Lawyers Am., Colo. Trial Lawyers Assn. Republican. Office: Bruno Bruno & Colin PC 143 Union Blvd Lakewood CO 80228

BRUNO, SALVATORE THOMAS, engineer; b. Monterey, Calif., Nov. 3, 1961; s. Thomas Salvatore Bruno and Martha Scott (Martin) Thompson; m. Rebecca Grace Isaacs, Nov. 9, 1985. BSME, Calif. Polytechnic, 1985. Tech. asst. Lockheed Missiles & Space, Sunnyvale, Calif., 1984; structural designer Lockheed Missiles & Space, Sunnyvale, 1985-86, analyst, 1986-87, conceptual designer, 1987-88, analyst, 1988—; cons. Eaton, Calif. Polytechnic, 1984. Inventor in field. Recipient acad. scholarships, San Joaquin Delta Coll., Stockton, Calif., 1980, 81, 82. Mem. ASME, Soc. Automotive Engrs. (tech. com. 1988-89). Republican. Office: Lockheed Missiles & Space 0/81-34 B/157 1111 Lockheed Way Sunnyvale CA 94089-3504

BRUSCA, JANET RITA, teacher; b. Chgo., Mar. 27, 1950; d. Orlando Joseph and Gabriella Laura (Cammisa) B.; m. Lawrence Emil Bleikli, Feb. 11, 1984. BA, DePaul U., 1972; MEd, U. Ill., 1975; postgrad., Nat. Coll. Edn., 1976-83. Cert. spl. edn. tchr., Ill., Ariz. Tchr., supr. U. Ill., Champaign, 1975; tchr. West Suburban Spl. Edn. Assn., Oak Park, Ill., 1975-81, West Chgo. (Ill.) Sch. Dist., 1981-82; early childhood coord. Lockport (Ill.) Assn. Spl. Edn., 1982-84; tchr. Cartwright Sch. Dist., Phoenix, 1984—; workshop presenter Cartwright Sch. Dist., Phoenix, 1987-88, parent group facilitator, 1984—. Mem. Nat. Assn. for Young Children, NEA, Ill. Edn. Assn. (chief negotiator 1977-81), Ill. Edn. Assn. (leadership award 1980), Ariz. Occupational Therapy Assn. (recognition award 1988). Democrat. Roman Catholic. Home: 4918 E Redfield Rd Scottsdale AZ 85254

BRUSCA, RICHARD C., zoologist, museum curator, researcher; b. Los Angeles, Jan. 25, 1945; s. Finny John and Ellenora C. (McDonald) B.; m. Caren Irene Spencer, 1964 (div. 1971); children: Alec Matthew, Carlene Anne. BS, Calif. Poly. State U., 1967; MS, Calif. State U., 1970; PhD, U. Ariz., 1975. Curator and researcher Aquatic Insects Lab., Calif. State U., Los Angeles, 1969-70; resident dir. U. Ariz. and U. Sonora (Mex.) Cooperative Marine Lab., Sonora, 1970-72; prof. biology U. So. Calif., Los Angeles, 1975-86; head Invertebrate Zoology sect. Los Angeles County Mus. Natural Hist., 1984-87; Joshua L. Baily curator, chmn. dept. marine invertebrates San Diego Natural History Mus., 1987—, dep. dir. sci. div., 1989—; dir. acad. programs, Catalina Marine Sci. Ctr. U. So. Calif.; field researcher North, Central and South Americas, Antarctica, New Zealand, Europe; bd. dirs. Orgn. for Tropical Studies. Author: Common Intertidal Invertebrates of the Gulf of California, 1980; co-author: A Naturalist's Seashore Guide, 1978; contbr. over 50 sci. articles to profl. jours. Recipient Presdl. Medal Service U.S. Govt., 1965, numerous rsch. awards and grants NSF, Nat. Geog. Soc., others. Mem. Crustacean Soc., Soc. Systematic Zoology, Willi Hennig Soc., AAAS, U. Edinburgh Biog. Study Group, S.Am. Explorer's Club, Sigma Xi. Office: San Diego Natural History Mus PO Box 1390 San Diego CA 92112

BRUSH, DAVID ELDEN, broadcast executive; b. Albany, Oreg., Oct. 24, 1950; s. Leonard Gilmore and Helen Elizabeth (Kirkpatrick) B.; m. Donella J. Urban, Aug. 24, 1974 (div. 1987). Student, Oreg. State U., 1968-69, Chemeketa Community Coll., 1976; AS, Linn-Benton Community Coll., 1980. Lic. FCC 1st class radiotelephone operator. Electronics technician Toad Hall Hi-Fi, Corvallis, Oreg., 1974-76, Corvallis Audio-Video Systems, 1976-78, Albany TV, Oreg., 1978; programmer Forrest Industries Ins. Exchange, Albany, 1980-81; owner/operator Tangent TV Cable Co., Oreg., 1984—; programmer analyst Summit Info. Systems, Inc., Corvallis, 1981-85, tech. support rep., 1985-87, sr. tech. document writer, 1987—. Author: Tangent City Charter, 1981. Photographer Tangent Rural Fire Protection Dist., 1979-85 (named Rookie of Yr. 1980) councilman, City of Tangent, 1980-81, 1st elected mayor City of Tangent, 1981-83; instrumental in obtaining City of Tangent's 1st state-approved land-use plan, 1985, city's 1st sewer system, 1981-85. Served with USCG, 1970-74. Mem. Electronics Technicians Assn. 1979—, Internat. Soc. Cert. Electronics Technicians. Republican. Methodist. Lodge: Fairmount Grange #252. Office: Tangent TV Cable Co PO Box 201 Tangent OR 97389

BRUST, DAVID, physicist; b. Chgo., Aug. 24, 1935; s. Clifford and Ruth (Klapman) B.; BS, Calif. Inst. Tech., 1957; MS, U. Chgo., 1958, PhD, 1964. Rsch. assoc. Purdue U., Lafayette, Ind., 1963-64; rsch. assoc. Northwestern U., Evanston, Ill., 1964-65, asst. prof. physics, 1965-68; theoretical rsch. physicist U. Calif., Lawrence Radiation Lab., Livermore, Calif., 1968-73; cons. Bell Telephone Lab., Murray Hill, N.J., 1966. Campaign co-ordinator No. Calif. Scientists and Engrs. for McGovern, 1972. NSF travel grantee, 1964; NSF rsch. grantee, 1966-68. Mem. Am. Phys. Soc., Am. Assn. Coll. Profs., Internat. Solar Energy Soc., Pacific Assn. of AAU, Sierra Club, Sigma Xi. Office: PO Box 13130 Oakland CA 94661

BRUTLAG, DOUGLAS LEE, biochemistry educator, consultant; b. Alexandria, Minn., Dec. 19, 1946; s. Minehart and Cora (Lee) B.; m. Simone C. Manteuil, Oct. 11, 1975; children: Pauline, Benjamin. BS, Calif. Inst. Tech., 1968; PhD, Stanford U., 1972. ScientistCommonwealth Sci. & Indsl. Rsch. Orgn., Canberra, Australia, 1972-74; asst. prof. dept. biochemistry Stanford U., Palo Alto, Calif., 1974-80, assoc. prof., 1980—; biochemist Pasteur Inst., Paris, 1981-82; founder, dir. IntelliGenetics Inc., Palo Alto, 1981—, Intellicorp; mem. NIH Genetic Study Sect., 1982-86. Recipient Young Investigator award Basil O'Connor Nat. Found., 1975-78; fellow Andrew W. Mellon Found., 1974-76, Sr. Fogarty Internat. fellow NIH, 1981-82; Henry and Camille Dreyfus tchr.-scholar grantee, 1979-84. Fellow AAAS; mem. Fedn. Am. Socs. Exptl. Biology, Am. Soc. Biol. Chemists., Am. Assn. Artificial Intelligence, Nat. Libr. Medicine. Democrat. Office: Stanford U Dept Biochemistry Stanford CA 94305

BRUYN, HENRY BICKER, physician; b. Bklyn., Jan. 24, 1918; s. Henry Bicker and Mary Janet (Retter) B.; m. Marion Helen Burkhardt, Sept. 19, 1942; children—Martha Elizabeth, Barbara Jane, Charles DeWitt, Jonathan Henry; m. Harriet Hall Brainerd, Apr. 22, 1973. B.A., Amherst Coll., 1940; M.D., Yale, 1943. Intern pediatrics New Haven Hosp., 1943-44; resident Buffalo Children's Hosp., 1944-45; fellow infectious disease U. Calif. Med. Sch., San Francisco, 1946-47; mem. faculty U. Calif. Med. Sch., 1948—, asso. prof. medicine, pediatrics, 1956-69, clin. prof. medicine, pediatrics, 1969—; chief isolation service San Francisco Gen. Hosp., 1950-59, chief pediatrics, 1954-59; lectr. Sch. Pub. Health U. Calif. at Berkeley, 1960—, dir. student health service, 1959-72; cons. City of San Francisco, 1974-86, U.S. Naval Hosp., U.S. Army Hosp., Children's Hosp. East Bay, Calif. viral and rickettsial disease lab., City and County San Francisco; mem. med. service com. Alameda County Council Social Planning, 1962-64; med. cons. Morrison Center Rehab., 1954-58, Medic-Alert Found., Elizabeth Kenney Found., San Francisco, 1950-52; med. dir. Drug Abuse Rehab., New Bridge Inc.; pres. Berkeley Med. Instrument Co., 1960-68. Co-author: Handbook of Pediatrics, 1st-15th edit, 1979-86, Handbook of Medical Treatment, 1972, Current Diagnosis and Therapy, 1972, Practice of Pediatrics, 1963, Drinking Among Collegians, 1970, Parents Guide to Child Raising, 1978, Parents Medical Manual, 1978; contbr. articles to profl. jours. Bd. dirs. Alameda County Council Alcoholism, 1960-70, Alameda County Suicide Prevention, 1962-70, Ronoh Sch., 1966-70, New Bridge Found., 1968—, Carmel Valley Manor, 1969—, Goodwill Industries, 1972—, Com. Children's TV, 1977-79, Jack B. Goldberg Found., 1978—; trustee, mem. ch. council Arlington Community Ch., 1954-72. Served to lt. comdr. M.C. USNR, 1945-46, 53-54. Mem. A.M.A., Royal Soc. Health, Am. Pub. Health Assn., Am. Coll. Health Assn. (pres. 1965-66), Pacific Coast Coll. Health Assn. (pres. 1968-69), Am. Fedn. Clin. Research, Western Soc. Clin. Research, Am. Acad. Pediatrics (chmn. community health com., No. Calif. sect. 1962-88), Calif. Fedn. Pediatric Socs., Cal. Acad. Medicine, Order Golden Bear, Delta Tau Delta, Nu Sigma Nu. Home: 432 Woodland Rd Kentfield CA 94904

BRUZDA, LINDA SUE, printing company eexecutive; b. Mansfield, Ohio, Nov. 16, 1950; d. Steve John and Eva May (Welsh) B. Student, Ohio State U., 1969, Franklin U., 1974-78; Student, Mesa Community Coll., Mesa, Ariz., 1981-83. Press operator Shoe Corp. Am., Columbus, Ohio, 1973-75; press supr. Cardinal Foods, Columbus, 1975-79; mgr. print shop Price Club, Mesa, Ariz., 1979-83; owner, gen. mgr. Print Shop, Columbus, 1975-79, Price-Less Printing, Inc., Mesa, 1983—. Home: 2609 N Pleasant Dr Chandler AZ 85224 Office: Print-Less Printing Inc 1826 W Broadway Ste 25 Mesa AZ 85202

BRUZZONE, EDWARD JOSEPH, credit manager; b. San Francisco, Dec. 20, 1946; s. Frank Anthony and Erma Mary (Marsigli) B.; m. Linda Alda Montalto, Jan. 2, 1972; 1 child, Jennifer. AA, Coll. San Mateo (Calif.), 1966; BA in Psychology, U. San Francisco, 1968; MBA in Fin. and Mgmt., Pepperdine U., 1982. Editor, tng. officer DUN & Bradstreet Inc., San Francisco, 1972-75; asst. credit mgr. Dalgety, Inc., San Mateo, 1975-80; credit mgr. Ferrostaal Metals Corp., San Mateo, 1980-88; regional credit mgr. Hajoca Corp., Ardmore, Pa., 1988—. Sgt. U.S. Army, 1969-71, Vietnam. Mem. Assn. MBA Execs., Nat. Assn. Credit Mgrs., VFW, Young Men's Inst. (San Francisco, treas. 1987-88, 2nd v.p. 1988—). Republican. Roman Catholic. Home: 124 Windsor Ct San Carols CA 94070

BRYAN, ALICE RICCA, corporate risk manager; b. Kingman, Ariz., Sept. 17, 1940; d. Frank Alfred and Alice (Waters) Ricca; m. R.L. Bryan, July 26, 1956 (div. July 1969); children: Jesse Aaron II, Eleanore Alisa Gildersleeve. Grad. high sch., Lake Charles, La., 1959. CPCU; accredited residential mgr. Underwriting asst. Gen Conf. of Seventh Day Adventist Risk Mgmt., Riverside, Calif., 1964-72; risk mgmt. cons. Gen Conf. of Seventh Day Adventist Risk Mgmt., Washington, 1974-75, dir. ins. services, 1975-77; mgr. office Quinlan Ins., Newport Beach, Calif., 1972-73; comml. ins. underwriter CIMA, Washington, 1973-74; asst. dir. risk mgmt. Smithsonian Instn., Washington, 1977-82; ins. officer The World Bank, Washington, 1982-86; dir. risk mgmt. Adventist Health System West, Roseville, Calif., 1986—; dir. CHAIS workers compensation adv. bd., Sacramento, 1986-88; seminar developer Met. Mus. Edn. Program. Author, editor: Insurance and Risk Management for Museums and Historical Societies, 1985. Risk and Insurance Mgmt. Soc. (dep. San Francisco chpt., v.p. Washington chpt. 1978-84, pres. 1984-86), Soc. of CPCU, Internat. Found. Employee Benefits. Republican. Adventist. Home: 118 Silverado Circle Roseville CA 95678

BRYAN, A(LONZO) J(AY), service club official; b. Washington, N.J., Sept. 17, 1917; s. Alonzo J. and Anna Belle (Babcock) B.; student pub. schs.; m. Elizabeth Elfreida Koehler, June 25, 1941 (div. 1961); children: Donna Elizabeth, Alonzo Jay, Nadine; m. Janet Dorothy Onstad, Mar. 15, 1962 (div. 1977); children: Brenda Joyce, Marlowe Francis, Marilyn Janet. Engaged as retail florist, Washington, N.J., 1941-64. Fund drive chmn. ARC, 1952; bd. dirs. Washington YMCA, 1945-55, N.J. Taxpayers Assn., 1947-52; mem. Washington Bd. Edn., 1948-55. Mem. Washington Grange, Sons and Daus. of Liberty, Soc. Am. Florists, Nat. Fedn. Ind. Businessmen, Florists Telegraph Delivery Assn., C. of C. Methodist. Clubs: Masons, Tall Cedars of Lebanon, Jr. Order United Am. Mechanics, Kiwanis (pres. Washington (N.J.) 1952, lt. gov. internat. 1953-54, gov. N.J. dist. 1955, sec. N.J. dist. 1957-64, sec. S.E. area Chgo. 1965-74; editor The Jersey Kiwanian 1958-64, interview staff 1964-85); Breakfast (pres. 1981-82) (Chgo.); sec., treas. Rocky Mtn. Kiwanis Dist., 1989—; Breakfast (pres. 1981-82) (Chgo.). Home: Fox Ridge Apts #203 8115 S Poplar Way Englewood CO 80112-3137 Office: 11005 Ralston Rd #204-G Arvada CO 80004

BRYAN, DARRELL ERNEST, transportation executive; b. Long Beach, Calif., Aug. 25, 1948; m. Cathleen Patricia Beaumont, July 10, 1971; children: Patrick, Matthew. BA in History, Wash. State U., 1971; MBA, St. Mary's Coll., 1978. Various mgmt. positions AMTRAK, Seattle and San Francisco, 1972-78; mgr. on-bd. ops. AMTRAK, L.A., 1978-80; asst. regional dir. passenger service AMTRAK, Chgo., 1980-82; regional dir. passenger service AMTRAK, Albany, N.Y., 1982, Chgo., 1982-84; dir. sta. ops. Nat. Railroad Passenger Corp., Washington, 1984-86; v.p., gen. mgr. Clipper Navigation, Inc., Seattle, 1986—. Bd. dirs. Tourism Victoria, Victoria, B.C., Can., 1987; mem. Seattle King County Convention and Visitors Bur. Mem. Soc. Port Engrs., Seattle C. of C., Victoria C. of C., Propeller Club, Skal Club. Democrat. Home: 4009 97th Ave SE Mercer Island WA 98040 Office: Clipper Navigation Inc 2701 Alaskan Way Seattle WA 98121

BRYAN, JOYCE BEVERLY, gerontologist; b. Los Angeles, Jan. 12, 1938; d. David Chasen and Belle (Greenberg) Davis; m. David Marvin Galfond, June 23, 1957 (div. Oct. 1964); m. Edgar Coleman Bryan Jr., Nov. 15, 1968; children: Lauren Cherry, Adam Bryan. BA in Hebrew summa cum laude, UCLA, 1979; MSW, MS in Gerontology, U. So. Calif., 1981. Instr. Mt. St. Mary's Coll., Los Angeles, 1981-82; site dir. Long Beach (Calif.) Sr. Day Treatment Ctr., 1981-84; instr. Saddleback Community Coll., Mission Viejo, Calif., 1984; dir. vols. Everhealth Hospice, La Mirada, Calif., 1983-84; social worker Meml. Home Health, Long Beach, 1984-86; project dir. Sr. Connection div. St. Francis Med. Ctr., Lynwood, Calif., 1986—; lectr. Calif. State U., Long Beach, 1987-88; cons. Sr. Care Network, Huntington Meml. Hosp., Pasadena, Calif., 1987—; mem. exec. com. Los Angeles Community Long Term Care Task Force, 1987-88. Vol. vis. to shut-ins Jewish Family Svc., L.A., 1972-77; bd. advisors Rancho Los Amigos Family Resource and Alzheimer's Day Care Ctr., 1988, Sr. Care Options Program U. Calif at Irvine Med. Ctr, 1988; dir. Orange Regional Resource Ctr. for Brain-Impaired Adults, Fullerton, Calif., 1988; bd. dirs. Dayle McIntosh Ctr. for the Disabled; mem profl. adv. bd. Alzheimer's Assn. Orange County, Calif. Mem. Am. Soc. on Aging., Nat. Assn. Social Workers, Gerontol. Soc. of Am. Democrat. Jewish. Office: St Francis Med Ctr Sr Connection 3630 E Imperial Hwy Lynwood CA 90262

BRYAN, RICHARD H., U.S. senator; b. Washington, July 16, 1937; married; 3 children. B.A., U. Nev., 1959; LL.B., U. Calif.-San Francisco, 1963. Bar: Nev. 1963, U.S. Supreme Ct. 1967. Dep. dist. atty. Clark County, Nev., 1964-66; public defender Clark County, 1966-68; counsel Clark County Juvenile Ct., 1968-69; mem. Nev. Assembly, 1969-71, Nev. Senate, 1973-77; atty. gen. State of Nev. 1979-82, gov. Nev., 1982-89, U.S. Senator from Nevada, 1989—; mem. U.S. Senate coms. on commerce, sci. and transp., banking, joint econ.; mem. Dem. Policy Com.; chmn. western region Dem. Senate Campaign Com.; chmn. Senate Consumer Com. Bd. dirs. March of Dimes; former v.p. Nev. Easter Seal Soc.; former pres. Clark County Legal Aid Soc. Served with U.S. Army. Mem. ABA, Clark County Bar Assn., Am. Judicature Soc., Nat. Gov.'s Assn. (com. econ. devel. and technol. innovation, com. internat. trade and fgn. relations, task force on adult literacy, task force on jobs growth and competitiveness, chmn. subcom. tourism), Council of State Govts. (past pres.), Phi Alpha Delta, Phi Alpha Theta. Democrat. Clubs: Masons, Lions, Elks. Office: US Senate 364 Russell Senate Bldg Washington DC 20510

BRYAN, ROBERT J., judge; b. Bremerton, Wash., Oct. 29, 1934; s. James W. and Vena Gladys (Jensen) B.; m. Cathy Ann Welander, June 14, 1958; children: Robert James, Ted Lorin, Ronald Terence. BA, U. Wash., 1956, JD, 1958. Bar: Wash. 1959, U.S. Dist. Ct. (we. dist.) Wash. 1959, U.S. Tax Ct. 1965, U.S. Ct. Appeals (9th cir.) 1985. Assoc., then ptnr. Bryan & Bryan, Bremerton, 1959-67; judge Superior Ct., Port Orchard, Wash., 1967-84; ptnr. Riddell, Williams, Bullitt & Walkinshaw, Seattle, 1984-86; judge U.S. Dist. Ct. (we. dist.) Wash., Tacoma, 1986—; mem. State Jail Comm., Olympia, Wash., 1974-76, Criminal Justice Tng. Com., Olympia, 1978-81, State Bd. on Continuing Legal Edn., Seattle, 1984-86; mem., sec. Jud. Qualifications Commn., Olympia, 1982-83. Author: (with others) Washington Pattern Jury Instructions (civil and criminal vols. and supplements), 1970-85. Served to maj. USAR. Office: US Dist Ct 1102 S A St Rm 314 PO Box 1494 Tacoma WA 98401

BRYANT, ALAN WILLARD, JR., human resources executive; b. Glen Ridge, N.J., Aug. 17, 1940; s. Alan Willard and Clara Sherman (Clark) B.; m. Beverley Brown, Dec. 28, 1963; children: Hilary Ann, Christopher Bowman. AB, Dartmouth Coll., 1962, MBA, 1963; postgrad., St. Mary's U., San Antonio, 1964-65. Specialist profl. placement spacecraft dept. Gen. Electric Co., King of Prussia, Pa., 1965-66; foreman, methods analyst TV dept. Gen. Electric Co., Syracuse, N.Y., 1966-67; specialist salaried employment armament dept. Gen. Electric Co., Springfield, Mass., 1967-68; specialist profl. and salaried compensation info. systems equipment div. Gen. Electric Co., Phoenix, 1968-70; mgr. personnel relations nuclear energy dept. Gen. Electric Co., Wilmington, N.C., 1970-72; mgr. relations practices TV receiver products dept. Gen. Electric Co., Portsmouth, Va., 1972-76; mgr. employee and community relations meter bus. dept. Gen. Electric Co., Somersworth, N.H., 1976-85; mgr. relations ops. nuclear energy dept. Gen. Electric Co., San Jose, Calif., 1985—; mem. sr. staff positive mgmt. leadership course GE, Fairfield, Conn., 1981—, mem. adj. staff exec. assessment and devel., 1987—; speaker Am. Mgmt. Assn. Nat. Conf., 1986. Pres., campaign chair United Way of Strafford County, Dover, N.H., 1980-81; founding pres. Strafford Hospice Care, Somersworth, 1982-85; trustee Wentworth Douglass Hosp., Dover, 1982-85. Served to capt. U.S. Army, 1963-65. Recipient Pub. Svc. award Gov. Ariz., 1970, Pub. Svc. award Gov. N.H., 1982, 84. Mem. South Bay-Am. Soc. Personnel Adminstrn., No. Calif. Human Resources Council, Santa Clara County Mfg. Group Working Council, Dover C. of C. (pres. 1984-85), Rotary (Disting. Svc. award 1985). Republican. Home: 17325 Parkside Ct Monte Sereno CA 95030 Office: GE Nuclear Energy 175 Curtner Ave MC 820 San Jose CA 95125

BRYANT, ARCHER GOODNEY, director of photography; b. Springfield, Mass., Oct. 12, 1949; s. Carroll and Ruth (Carlson) B.; m. Katherine J. Horton, June 7, 1976; 1 child, Austin Brooks. Student, Bucknell U., 1969-71; BA, U. Minn., 1973. Dir. photography numerous films including A Whisperer Kills, The Case of the Avenging Ace, The Case of the Lady in the Lake, The Case of the Scandalous Scoundrel, The Case of the Married Madam, The Case of the Sinister Spirit, The Case of the Lost Love, A Prison of Children, Red Fury, Solo, commls. Godfathers Pizza, Ponderosa Steak House, McDonald's Hamburgers, Donimo's Pizza, Diet Coke, Glidden Paint, 7/11 Corp.; contbr. to numerous TV, theatrical and comml. prodns. Home and Office: PO Box 116 Elbert CO 80106

BRYANT, DEMETRIUS EDWARD, minister, actor; b. Mobile, Ala., June 30, 1956; s. James Edward Bryant and Thelma (Kennedy) Gibbons. BA in Psychology, U. So. Calif., 1985, BA in History, 1985; DD in Religion (hon.), Ministry of Salvation Ch., Chula Vista, Calif., 1988. Ordained minister, Calif., 1986. 2nd initiate Ministry of Abundant Life, L.A., 1978-79, 1st initiate, 1979-80, pastoral clinician univ. student, 1980-85; minister, actor Ministry of Salvation Ch., Chula Vista and L.A., 1982-86, minister, actor, consultant-at-large, 1986—. Cadet Civil Air Patrol, Otis AFB, Mass., 1971-76. Mem. Am. Film Inst., Smithsonian Inst., AFTRA, Screen Extras Guild, Assembly of the Holy Cross (initiate 1983—), Gnostic Group. Democrat. Orthodox Gnostic. Home: 4391 Sunset Blvd #282 Los Angeles CA 90029

BRYANT, DON ESTES, economist, scientist; b. Truman, Ark., May 18, 1917; s. James Monroe and Olivia (Mayfield) B.; m. Jess Ann Chailer, Jan. 27, 1956; children: Stephen Williamson (dec.), Patrice Ann. Student, Cass Tech. Trade Coll., 1938-41. Pres., founder Consol. Aircraft Products, El Segundo, Calif., 1949-57, Trilan Corp., El Segundo, 1957-62, The Am. Inventor, Palos Verdes Estates, Calif., 1962-68; chmn., founder Message Control Crop., Palos Verdes Estates, 1968-70; scientist Econ. Research, Palos Verdes Estates and Lake Arrowhead, Calif., 1970—; cons. Service Corps Ret. Execs. Assn.-SBA, Los Angeles, 1965-67. Inventor missle and satellite count-down systems for USAF, 1958; formulator sci. of human econs.; host TV talk show World Peace Through Free Enterprise, 1985; author: 10-book children's series The 1, 2, 3's of Freedom and Economics, 1988. Served with USN, 1935-37. Republican. Roman Catholic. Home: 282 S Sunset Lake Arrowhead CA 92352 Office: Econ Rsch PO Box 1023 Lake Arrowhead CA 92352

BRYANT, STEVEN HARRY, design engineer; b. Des Moines, Nov. 28, 1946; s. Harry Kenneth and Hannah Levey B. AA in Engring., Fullerton Coll., 1968; BA in History, Calif. State U., Long Beach, 1970. Practice design engr. So. Calif., 1966—; pres. Hawkeye Enterprises, Cathedral City, Calif., 1986—. Contbr. polit. commentary to local newspapers, 1979-82. Commr. San Bernardino County, Calif.; mem. Calif. Dem. State Cen. Com., 1979-85, county sec. 1985; alt. del. Dem. Nat. Conv., 1984; 39th Congl. dist. campaign coordinator Jimmy Carter Dem. Presdl. campaign, 1976; 35th Congl. dist. campaign coordinator Gary Hart Dem. Presdl. campaign, 1984; fin. contbr. Calif. Dems., Dem. Nat. Com., World Vision, Pasadena, Calif., 1985—, Cystic Fibrosis Found., Bethesda, Md., 1987—; charter mem. Statue of Liberty Ellis Island Found., 1984—; service area com. for area 19, Chino Hills, 1979-82; Cathedral City Citizens for Progress, 1989. Mem. Am. Soc. Engrs. and Architects (Pasadena chpt.).

BRYCHEL, RUDOLPH MYRON, engineer; b. Milw., Dec. 4, 1934; s. Stanley Charles and Jean Ann (Weiland) B.; m. Rose Mary Simmons, Sept. 3, 1955; children: Denise, Rita, Rudolph Myron Jr., Patrick, Bradford, Matthew. Student, U. Wis., Stevens Point, 1953, U.S. Naval Acad., 1954-55, U. Del., 1957, Colo. State U., 1969, North Park Coll., Chgo., 1973. Lab. and quality tech. Thiokol Chem. Co., Elkton, Md., 1956; final test insp. Martin Aircraft Co., Middle River, Md., 1956-57; system final insp. Delco Electronics Co., Oak Creek, Wis., 1957-58; test equipment design engr. Martin Marietta Co., Littleton, Colo., 1958-64; prodn. supr. Gates Rubber Co., Denver, Colo., 1964-65; freelance mfr., quality and project engr. Denver and Boulder, Colo., Raton, N.Mex., 1965-67; quality engr. IBM, Gaithersburg (Md.), Boulder (Colo.), 1967-73; sr. quality engr. Abbott Labs., North Chicago, Ill., 1973-74; instrumentation and control engr. Stearns Roger Co., Glendale, Colo., 1974-81; staff quality engr. Storage Tech., Louisville, Colo., 1981-83; sr. quality engr. Johnson & Johnson Co., Englewood, Colo., 1983-84; quality engr., cons. Staodynamics Co., Longmont, Colo., 1984-85; sr. engr. for configuration and data mgmt. Martin Marietta Astronautics Group, Denver, 1985—. With USN, 1953-56. Mem. Am. Soc. Quality Control (cert. quality engr.), Regulatory Affairs Profl. Soc., Soc. for Tech. Communications (regional chpt. chmn. 1970), KC. Democrat. Roman Catholic. Home: 203 W Rafferty Gardens Littleton CO 80120 Office: Martin Marietta Astronautics Group PO Box 179 Denver CO 80201

BRYDEN, MARY-EVELYN, government relations executive; b. Oxnard, Calif., Sept. 11, 1923; d. Albert L. and Mary Diana (Mizner) Estus; m. John Heilner Bryden, June 23, 1945; children: Linda Diane, David Campbell. BA, Calif. State U., Fullerton, 1971. Exec. asst. bd. suprs. Orange County, 1971-73; mgr. govt. rels. Orange County Transit Dist., 1973—. mem., officer, bd. dirs. Orange Co. Assn. Mental Health, Santa Ana, 1985-89; chmn. City of Fullerton energy and resources mgmt. com., 1980-88; vol. United Way. Mem. Orange County C. of C. (bd. dirs. 1979—), Am. Soc. Pub. Adminstrn. (dir. 1973-75), Town Hall Calif. (Orange County forum), LWV (local, county, state officer 1960-71). Republican. Presbyterian. Office: Orange County Transit Dist 11222 Acacia Pkwy Garden Grove CA 92642

BRYDON, HAROLD WESLEY, entomologist, writer; b. Hayward, Calif., Dec. 6, 1923; s. Thomas Wesley and Hermione (McHenry) B.; m. Ruth Bacon Vickery, Mar. 28, 1951 (div.); children: Carol Ruth, Marilyn Jeanette, Kenneth Wesley. AB, San Jose State Coll., 1948; MA, Stanford U., 1950. Insecticide sales Calif. Spray Chem. Corp., San Jose, 1951-52; entomologist, fieldman, buyer Beech-Nut Packing Co., 1952-53; mgr., entomologist Lake County Mosquito Abatement Dist., Lakeport, Calif., 1954-58; entomologist, adviser Malaria Eradication Programs ICA (name changed to AID), Kathmandu, Nepal, 1958-61, Washington, 1961-62, Port-au-Prince, Haiti, 1962-63; dir. fly control research Orange County Health Dept. Santa Ana, Calif., 1963-66; free-lance writer in field, 1966—; research entomologist U. N.D. Sch. Medicine, 1968; developer, owner Casierra Resort, Lake Almanor, Calif., 1975-79; owner Westwood (Calif.) Sport Shop, 1979-84; instr. Lassen Community Coll., Susanville, Calif., 1975—; mem. entomology and plant pathology del. People to People Citizen Ambassador Program, China, 1986. Research and publs. on insecticides, mech. methods for dispersing insecticides, biol. control parasites of houseflies. Served with USNR, 1943-46. Recipient Meritorious Honor award for work in Nepal, AID, U.S. Dept. State, 1972. Mem. Entomol. Soc. Am., Am. Mosquito Control Assn., Pacific Coast Entomol. Soc., Am. Legion. Republican. Methodist. Club: Commonwealth of California. Lodges: Masons, Rotary. Home: PO Box 312 Westwood CA 96137

BRYNGELSON, JIM, educational administrator; b. Billings, Mont., Mar. 8, 1941; s. Ivan Carl and Clarie (Ellingwood) B.; m. Judy Bryngelson, June 29, 1969; children—Joy, Nick. BS, U. Mont., 1959; MS, Purdue U., 1967; EdS, U. No. Colo., 1974, EdD, 1976. Tchr. sci. Littleton Pub. Schs., Colo., 1964-66, sch. counselor, 1967-73, sch. psychologist, 1974-75; spl. edn. cons., Steamboat Springs, Colo., 1975-78; asst. prin. pub. sch., Steamboat Springs, 1977-78; dir. edn. Yellowstone Boys and Girls Ranch, Billings, Mont., 1978—; pres. Self Esteem Assocs., Billings, 1980—. Bd. dirs. Tumbleweed Foster Homes, Billings, 1980-84, Rocky Mountain Little League, Billings, 1982, Mental Health Assn., Billings, v.p., 1986-87, pres. 1987-88. Recipient Disting. Educator award Charles Kettering Found., 1983; named U.S. Cultural Exchange Delegate to Republic of China, 1986. Fellow Assn. Supervision and Curriculum Devel., Sch. Adminstrs. Mont., Council Exceptional Children, Council for Children with Behavior Disorders, Mont. Assn. Supervision and Curriculum Devel. (bd. dirs. 1987-89), Council for Adminstrs. Spl. Edn., Albert Schweitzer Soc., John Dewey Soc., Phi Delta Kappa (v.p. 1984-85, pres 1985-86); mem. Mont. Educators Emotionally Disturbed (charter). Democrat. Roman Catholic. Home: 1144 Henry Rd Billings MT 59102 Office: Sch Dist 58 Rte 1 Box 212 Billings MT 59106

BRYSON, ELSA LOUISE, teacher; b. Yakima, Wash., May 28, 1934; d. Donald Griffin and Lydia Peggy (Blum) Slack; m. Carlton Wesley Bryson, June 5, 1954; children: Jana Sue Bryson Young, Philip Mark. BS in Edn., Oreg. State U., 1966; MEd, U. Oreg., 1973. Cert. elem. and physically handicapped tchr., Oreg. Kindergarten tchr. Portland (Oreg.) Pub. Schs., 1967, first grade tchr., 1967-71, 1983—; ungraded primary tchr. Holladay Ctr. Physically Handicapped Children, Portland, 1971-83; Mem. math text adoption com. Portand Pub. Schs.; involved in mainstreaming physically handicapped students, Portland Pub. Schs.; mem. dist. staff adv. com. Portland Pub. Schs. Sunday sch. tchr. Cen. Ch. of Nazarene, Portland, 1959—. State of Oreg. Grad. Study grantee, 1971. Mem. NEA, Oreg. Edn. Assn., Portland Assn. Tchrs., Kappa Delta Pi. Home: 2735 NE 38th Ave Portland OR 97212 Office: Boise-Eliot Elem Sch 620 N Fremont St Portland OR 97227

BRYSON, JOHN E., utilities company executive; b. N.Y.C., July 24, 1943; m. Louise Henry. B.A. with great distinction, Stanford U., 1965; student, Freie U. Berlin, Federal Republic Germany, 1965-66; J.D., Yale U., 1969. Bar: Calif., Oreg., D.C. Asst. in instrn. Law Sch., Yale U., New Haven, Conn., 1968-69; law clk. U.S. Dist. Ct., San Francisco, 1969-70; co-founder, atty. Natural Resources Def. Council, 1970-74; vice chmn. Oreg. Energy Facility Siting Council, 1975-76; assoc. Davies, Biggs, Strayer, Stoel & Boley, Portland, Oreg., 1975-76; chmn. Calif. State Water Resources Control Bd., 1976-79; vis. faculty Stanford U. Law Sch., Calif., 1977-79; pres. Calif. Pub. Utilities Commn., 1979-82; ptnr. Morrison & Foerster, San Francisco, 1983-84; sr. v.p. law and fin. Calif. Edison Co., Rosemead, 1984; exec. v.p., chief fin. officer SCEcorp. and So. Calif. Edison Co., 1985—; lectr. on pub. utility, energy, communications law.; former mem. exec. com. Nat. Assn. Regulatory Utility Commrs., Calif. Water Rights Law Rev. Commn., Calif. Pollution Control Financing Authority; former mem. adv. bd. Solar Energy Research Inst., Electric Power Research Inst., Stanford Law Sch.; bd. dirs. Pacific Am. Income Shares Inc. Mem. bd. editors, assoc. editor: Yale U. Law Jour. dir. or trustee World Resources Inst., Washington, Calif. Environ. Trust, Claremont U. Ctr., Grad. Sch., Stanford U. Alumni Assn. Woodrow Wilson fellow. Mem. Calif. Bar Assn., Oreg. Bar Assn., D.C. Bar Assn., Nat. Assn. Regulatory Utility Commrs. (exec. com. 1980-82), Stanford U. Alumni Assn. (bd. dirs. 1983-86), Phi Beta Kappa. Office: So Calif Edison Co 2244 Walnut Grove Rosemead CA 91770

BRZUSKIEWICZ, JOHN EDWARD, materials scientist; b. Evergreen Park, Ill., May 8, 1955; s. John and Dorothy (Stienz) B.; m. Ann Elizabeth Jarboe, Sept. 12, 1981; children: Jessica Marie, Jaime Lynn. BS in Chemistry, U. Ill., Chgo., 1977. Asst. chemist Ill. Inst. Tech. Rsch. Inst., Chgo., 1973-78; dir. materials rsch. Uresil Co., Inc., Morton Grove, Ill., 1978-81; project engr. Goodyear Aerospace Corp, Litchfield Park, Ariz., 1981-86; sr. rsch. projects engr. DSET Labs., Inc., New River, Ariz., 1986—. Co-author: Handbook of Materials for Solar Energy Utilization, 1980. Mem. ASTM, Soc. Plastics Engr., Soc. for Advancement of Material and Process Engring., Inst. Environ. Scis. Home: 7026 W North Ln Peoria AZ 85345 Office: DSET Labs Inc Box 1850 Black Canyon Stage Phoenix AZ 85029

BUBB, HARRY GEIPLE, insurance company executive; b. Trinidad, Colo., Dec. 16, 1924; s. Harry H. and Grace Alleine (Geiple) B.; m. Berdel Edrie Letcher, June 9, 1951; children—Melinda, Howard, Susan, John, Mary. BA in Econs, Stanford U., 1946, MBA, 1949; grad., Advanced Mgmt. Program, Harvard U., 1973. With Pacific Mut. Life Ins. Co., 1949—, asst. v.p., 1966-68, then v.p., 1968-72, sr. v.p. group ins., 1972-75, pres., 1975—, chief exec. officer, 1986—, chmn. bd., 1987—. Bd. dirs. Orange County Bus. Com. for Arts, Calif. Econ. Devel. Corp., Com. Econ. Devel.; trustee Newport Harbor Art Mus. Served as pilot USNR, World War II. Mem. Calif. C. of C. (bd. dirs.), L.A. C. of C. (bd. dirs.), Lincoln Club of Orange County, Balboa Yacht Club, California Club, Center Club, Lincoln Club. Clubs: Lincoln of Orange County, Balboa Yacht, California, Center. Home: 27 Beacon Bay Newport Beach CA 92660 Office: Pacific Mut Life Ins Co 700 Newport Center Dr Newport Beach CA 92663

BUBECK, ROBERT CLAYTON, hydrologist; b. Wilkes-Barre, Pa., Mar. 20, 1937; s. Leon Clayton and Helen (Bailey) B.; m. Phyllis Elaine Bubeck, Aug. 7, 1965; children: Janet Elaine Schuresko, Susan Louise Dawson. BA, U. Rochester, 1960, PhD, 1972; MS, Pa. State U., 1965. Cert. profl. hydrologist. Rsch. asst. Woods Hole Oceanography Inst., 1965-67; asst. prof. U.S. Naval Acad., 1965-67; chem. oceanographer Chesapeake Tech. Support Lab., Annapolis, Md., 1967-69; NOAA post doctoral rsch. assoc. dept. geoscis. U. Rochester, N.Y., 1972-73; hydrologist U.S. Geol. Survey, Menlo Park, Calif. and Harrisburg, Pa., 1973-76; chief inorganic chemistry and biol. analysis unit, staff hydrologist U.S. EPA, Annapolis, 1976-81; chief hydrologic studies sect., water quality specialist U.S. Geol. Survey, Albany, N.Y., 1981-85; regional water quality specialist U.S. Geol. Survey, Menlo Park, 1985—. Contbr. 25 articles, papers, chpts. to profl. jours. and books. Participant local high sch. Sci. in the Classroom program. With USN, 1960-63, capt. USNR, 1965—. Mem. Geol. Soc. Am., Am. Geophys. Union, Am. Soc. of Limnology and Oceanography, AAAS, Internat. Assn. for Great Lakes Rsch., Am. Water Resources Assn., Am. Radio Relay League, Naval Res. Assn., Sigma Xi. Home: 3940 Bibbits Dr Palo Alto CA 94303 Office: US Geol Survey Water Resources Div MS 470 345 Middlefield Rd Menlo Park CA 94025

BUBNIC, ANNE MARIE, nonprofit organization administrator; b. Springfield, Mass., Jan. 17, 1949; d. Stephen Borowiec and Marcelle (Denis) Weitzel; m. Brian J. Bubnic, May 23, 1979. BS in Biology and Chemistry, Coll. of Our Lady of the Elms, Chicopee, Mass., 1970; MPA, U. San Francisco, 1987. Cert. fund raising exec. Med. tech. Monson State Hosp., Palmer, Mass., 1970; biochemist Purdue U., West Lafayette, Ind., 1970-73; indsl. microbiologist Hazleton Labs., Vienna, Va., 1974-75; med. tech. No. Va. Tng. Ctr., Fairfax, 1975-76; research physiologist Cutter Labs., Berkeley, Calif., 1977-82; exec. dir. Nat. Found. Ileitis and Colitis, San Francisco, 1982-87; dir. sustaining gifts U. San Francisco, 1987-88; exec. dir. Marine World Found., Vallejo, Calif., 1988—. Contbr. articles to profl. jours. Pres.

Nat. Found. for Ileitis and Colitis, 1982; mem. adv. bd. Community Edn. Found., Novato Unified Sch. Dist., 1989—, Vol. Ctr. Solano County, 1989—; bd. dirs. Self-Help Clearing House of the Bay Area, San Francisco, 1982-86. Recipient Grad. Student Research award 1988, Founder's award Nat. Found. Ileitis and Colitis, 1988. Mem. AAUW, Nat. Soc. Fund Raising Execs. (bd. dirs. 1987—, treas. 1989—, Abel Hanson award 1986, 87, Pres.'s award 1988, Founder's award 1988), Am. Soc. Assn. Execs., NAFE, Soc. Nonprofit Orgns., Women in Computing, Community Entrepreneurs Orgn., Nat. Assn. Desk Top Pubs., Rotary. Democrat. Lodge: Zonta. Home: 3 Oak Forest Rd Novato CA 94949 Office: Marine World Found Marine World Pkwy Vallejo CA 94589

BUCCIGROSSI, DAVID ERIC, physician; b. Riverside, Calif., Sept. 12, 1956; s. Sam Anthony and Geraldine (Ligman) B.; m. Debbie Lee Winkelbauer, Sept. 7, 1985. BA, U. Calif., San Diego, 1979; MD, U. Calif., 1984. Chemistry researcher San Diego, 1978-80, guitar instr., 1973-78, chemistry instr., 1978-81; practice medicine specializing in internal medicine Seattle. Family Practice Preceptorship grantee U. Calif., San Diego, 1981. Mem. AAAS, Internat. Physicians for Prevention Nuclear War, Physcians Soc. Responsibility Speakers Bur., A. Baird Hasting Soc. Democrat. Roman Catholic. Home: 4436 Sirius Ave Lompoc CA 93436 Office: Northridge Med Group 8540 Reseda Blvd Northridge CA 91324

BUCHANAN, BEVERLY ANNE, pharmaceutical company official; b. Chgo., Aug. 29, 1946; d. Jack Warren and Florence A. (Krey) Rexroat; m. Kenneth W. Stinnett, June 6, 1965 (div. June 1978); children: Debra A., Kenneth W. Jr.; m. Ronald Cyril Buchanan, Oct. 27, 1979. Student, Orange Coast Coll., Costa Mesa, Calif., 1976-78. Drug buyer Westfield Med. Co., Orange, Calif., 1980-82; pharm. exempte Park Lido Med. Co., Costa Mesa, 1982-86; pharm. exempte, head buyer Deckert Med. Co., Santa Ana, Calif., 1987—. Com. mem. Tustin (Calif.) Sch. Bd., 1979. Republican. Home: 12802 Dean St Santa Ana CA 92705

BUCHANAN, BUCK, radio personality, singer; b. L.A., Apr. 18, 1946; s. Edgar and Mildred (Spence) B.; m. Darlene Celia, Aug. 22, 1981; children: Sheila, Rhonda, Amanda. AA in Journalism, Los Angeles Valley Coll., Van Nuys, Calif., 1968; BA in Radio, TV and Film, Calif. State U., Northridge, 1971. Newsman Stas. KBLA and KBBQ, L.A., 1965-68, Sta. KGIL, L.A., 1968-71; morning drive announcer Sta. KNUI, Kahului, Maui, Hawaii, 1971-72; announcer, program dir. Sta. KORL-ABC, Honolulu, 1972-76; announcer, program dir. Stas. WFBG and WEIR, Altoona, Pa., 1976-78, Weirton, W.Va., 1976-78; announcer Sta. KLAC, L.A., 1978-81; owner, mgr. Sta. KZHI, Honolulu, 1981-85; announcer, music dir. Sta. KRLA, L.A., 1985-86; announcer Sta. KRTH-AM, L.A., 1986—; singer Safari's. Bd. dirs. Big Bros., Maui, 1971-72, Pa. Assn. Retarded Citizens, Pitts., 1976-78, Adam Walsh Found., 1989—; goodwill amb. Waimanu Home for Retarded, Honolulu, 1972-76; lectr. Habilitat, Honolulu, 1972-84; dir. entertainment Doi for Gov., Howaii, 1974; advisor Fasi for Gov., Honolulu, 1984; vol. Adam Walsh Soc., L.A., 1986—. With U.S. Army, 1963-65, Vietnam. Recipient achievement award Waimanu Home, 1976. Mem. AFTRA, SAG, Beta Phi Bamma. Home: 3228 Tahoe Pl Hollywood CA 90068

BUCHANAN, JACK EVON, real estate appraiser; b. L.A., May 23, 1934; s. George Evon and Byrdie Bell (Harbour) B.; m. Phyllis Buchanan, Aug. 22, 1974 (div. Mar. 1987); m. Lynn D. LaPerriere, Oct. 20, 1987. AA, L.A. City Coll., 1953. Air cargo mgr. Ellis Airlines, Ketchikan, Alaska, 1956-66; asst. mgr., adminstrv. officer Anchorage Internat. Airport, 1967-72; broker, gen. mgr. Area Realtors Inc., Anchorage, 1972-79; pres., broker Pyramid Realtors Inc., Anchorage, 1979-81; appraiser Appraisal Assocs., Anchorage, 1981-84, ptnr., 1984—. With USCG, 1952-56. Mem. Am. Inst. Real Estate Appraisers (residential mem.), Nat. Assn. Realtors (Grad. Realtors Inst., pres. 1974—, mktg. coun. 1975), Lahaina Yacht Club, Associated Clubs Am., Elks. Home: 2965 Madison Way Anchorage AK 99508 Office: Appraisal Assocs of Alaska 2102 Cleveland Ave Anchorage AK 99517

BUCHANAN, JERRY MAJOR, advertising executive; b. Seattle, Dec. 10, 1923; s. Herbert H. and Doris Kathryn (DeNully) B. Airplane mechanic Boeing Airplane Co., Seattle, 1946-50; salesman various cos., Seattle, 1950-74; prin. J.B. Advt. Agy., Vancouver, Wash., 1974—; prin., editor, pub. TOWERS Club USA, Vancouver, 1974—; prin., chief exec. officer Jerry Buchanan Advt. Agy., Vancouver, 1976—; mktg. cons., ad copywriter, direct response adv. agy. owner. Author: Writer's Utopia Formula Report, 1974; editor TOWERS Club Newsletter, 1974—. With USMC, 1943-46, PTO. Democrat. Avocations: travel, music, philosophy. Home: 9107 NW 11th Ave Vancouver WA 98665 Office: TOWERS Club USA PO Box 2038 Vancouver WA 98668-2038

BUCHBINDER, GEORGEDA, physician, educator; b. N.Y.C., Feb. 2, 1939; d. Jacob H. and Gertrude (Rose) B. BA, Sarah Lawrence Coll., 1960; MA, Columbia U., 1966, PhD, 1973; MD, U. Chgo., 1981; MPH, Johns Hopkins U., 1984. Diplomate Am. Bd. Med. Examiners, Am. Bd. Preventive Medicine. Teaching asst. anthropology Columbia U., N.Y.C., 1962; lectr. White Plains (N.Y.) Adult Edn. Ctr., 1962, CUNY, 1963-65, Bklyn. Coll., 1965-70; asst. prof. Queens (N.Y.) Coll., 1970-77; cons. nutritional anthropology So. Highlands Devel. Project World Bank, Papua, New Guinea, 1977-79; vis. lectr. dept. psychiatry Chgo. Med. Sch., 1979-80; resident in ob-gyn. Columbia Presbyn. Med. Ctr., N.Y.C., 1981-83; resident in gen. preventative medicine Johns Hopkins, Balt., 1983-85, adj. instr. internat. health, 1984; assoc. prof. internat. health Sch. Pub. Health U. Hawaii, Honolulu, 1985—, assoc. prof. epidmiology, 1986; cons. many health care project in Hawaii, Asia and the Pacific, 1985—. Contbr. articles to profl. jours. Recipient numerous rsch. scholarships, fellowships and grants, 1956—. Mem. AMA, Hawaii Med. Assn., Nat. Council for Internat. Health, Am. Pub. Health Assn., AAAS, Am. Anthrop. Assn., Am. Assn. Phys. Anthropologists, Med. Anthropology Assn., Assn., Social Anthrolopogists in Oceania, Sigma Xi. Office: U Hawaii Sch Pub Health Honolulu HI 96822

BUCHMEIER, MICHAEL JOSEPH, virologist; b. Sedro-Wooley, Wash., Mar. 19, 1948; s. Joseph Anthony and Geraldine E. (Miller) B.; m. Nancy Ann Niederkorn, Jan. 25, 1972; children: Joshua Michael, Michelle Ann. BS in Bacteriology, Wash. State U., 1970, MS in Bacteriology, 1973; PhD in Virology, McMaster U., Hamilton, Ont., Can., 1976. NIH postdoctoral fellow Scripps Clinic & Rsch. Found., La Jolla, Calif., 1976-78, rsch. assoc., 1978-79, asst. mem., 1979-82, assoc. mem., 1982—; mem. sci. adv. bd. Synbiotics Corp., San Diego, 1986—, Terrapin Diagnostics, San Francisco, 1987—; cons. NIH, Bethesda, Md., 1983-89. Contbr. articles to sci. publs. Grantee Am. Heart Assn., 1979-84. Mem. Am. Soc. Virology, Am. Assn. Immunologists, Soc. Gen. Microbiology, Soc. Exptl. Biology and Medicine. Am. Assn. Pathologists, Pluto Club. Democrat. Office: Scripps Clinic & Rsch Found 10666 N Torrey Pines La Jolla CA 92037

BUCK, CHRISTIAN BREVOORT ZABRISKIE, independent oil operator; b. San Francisco, Oct. 18, 1914; s. Frank Henry and Zayda Justine (Zabriskie) B.; student U. Calif., Berkeley, 1931-33; m. Natalie Leontine Smith, Sept. 12, 1948; children—Warren Zabriskie, Barbara Anne. Mem. engring. dept. U.S. Potash Co., Carlsbad, N.Mex., 1933-39; ind. oil operator, producer, Calif., 1939-79, N.Mex., 1939—; owner, operator farm, ranch, Eddy County, N.Mex., 1951-79; dir. Belridge Oil Co. until 1979; dir. Buck Ranch Co. (Calif.). Served with RAF, 1942-45. Democrat. Episcopalian. Club: Riverside Country (Carlsbad). Home: 108 W Alicante Rd Santa Fe NM 87501 Office: PO Box 2183 Santa Fe NM 87504

BUCK, JOHN HARRISON, organization executive; b. Greenville, Maine, Aug. 7, 1942; s. Eli Harrison and Alta (Hatch) B.; m. Bobbyjean Rose Hamm, June 13, 1964; children: John Harrison Jr., Karen Elizabeth. BS in Acctg., Husson Coll., 1964. Auditor N.F. Bigelow, Jr. & Co., CPA's, Manchester, N.H., 1965-68; city fin. officer City of Nashua (N.H.), 1968-70; div. contr. Sanders Assocs., Nashua, 1970-75; exec. dir. mem. devel. U.S. Jaycees, Tulsa, 1975-79; asst. dir. fund raising U.S. Olympic Com., Colorado Springs, Colo., 1979-85, dir. fund raising, 1985-87, dir. planning and svcs., 1987—. Mem. exec. bd. Wagon Wheel coun. Girl Scouts U.S.A., 1987; mem. adv. bd. Colo. Amateur Sports Corp., 1988. Mem. Colorado Springs Racquet Club. Republican. Home: 4708 Vista View Ln Colorado Springs CO 80915 Office: US Olympic Com 1750 E Boulder St Colorado Springs CO 80909

BUCK, LINDA DEE, executive recruiting company executive; b. San Francisco, Nov. 8, 1946; d. Sol and Shirley D. (Setterberg) Press; student Coll. San Mateo (Calif.), 1969-70; divorced. Head hearing and appeals br. Dept. Navy Employee Relations Service, Philippines, 1974-75; dir. personnel Homestead Savs. & Loan Assn., Burlingame, Calif., 1976-77; mgr. fin. placement VIP Agy., Inc., Palo Alto, Calif., 1977-78; exec. v.p., dir. Sequent Personnel Services, Inc., Mountain View, Calif., 1978-83; Founder, pres. Buck & Co., San Mateo, 1983—. Publicity mgr. for No. Calif., Osteogenesis Imperfecta Found. Inc., 1970-72; cons. Am. Brittle Bone Soc., 1979-88. Mem. Nat. Assn. Personnel Cons. Jewish. Office: Buck & Co 100 S Ellsworth Ave 9th Fl San Mateo CA 94401

BUCK, NATALIE SMITH, former state official; b. Carlsbad, N.Mex., Jan. 10, 1923; d. Milton R. and Rosa Adele (Binford) Smith; student Coll. William and Mary, 1940-41; BBS, U. Colo., 1943; postgrad. U. Tex., 1945-46; m. C. B. Buck, Sept. 12, 1948; children: Warren Z., Barbara Anne. Chief clk., State Senate, N.Mex., 1951-53; sec. of state, N.Mex., 1955-59; chief personnel adminstr. N.Mex. Health and Social Services Dept., 1959-73. Democrat. Home: 108 W Alicante Rd Santa Fe NM 87501

BUCK, WILLIAM FRASER, II, sales executive; b. Salt Lake City, May 6, 1944; s. William Fraser and Ada (Dabling) B.; m. Lynette Riding, Jan. 27, 1967; children: Kimberly, Arienne, Tamara, Joshua Fraser, Zackary Erne, Gabriel Robert, Bethany, Emily, Cassandra. BS, Brigham Young U., 1977, MBA, 1988. Clk. Clark Drugs Inc., Hawthorne, Calif., 1962-63; gen. mdse. clk. Albertson's Inc., Orem, Utah, 1967-68, grocery mgr., Utah div., 1976-81; asst. mgr. Allen's Markets, Orem, 1968-72; mgr. Quality Market, Delta, Utah, 1972-76; gen. mdse. mgr. BYU Bookstore, Brigham Young U., Provo, Utah, 1981—. Troop leader Boy Scouts Am., Provo, 1969-85, dist. pub. chmn., Delta, 1973-76; mem. Delta Planning and Zoning Bd., 1974-76; sec.-treas. West Millard Golf Com., Delta, 1973-76; pres. Sunset ward elders quorum Ch. Jesus Christ of Latter-day Saints, Provo, 1971-72, ward exec. sec., 1976-77, pres. Orem (Utah) 25th ward elders quorum, 1988—. Mem. Nat. Assn. Coll. Stores (cert.), Western Coll. Bookstore Assn., Mountain States Coll. Store Assn. (instr. seminars 1983-85), Provo C. of C. (com. chmn. 1981-83). Office: Brigham Young U BYU Bookstore Provo UT 84602

BUCK, WILLIAM GERALD (JERRY BUCK), columnist; b. Lake Charles, La., June 4, 1931; s. Harold Campbell and Dorothy Melville (Chambers) B.; m. Carol Ann Boese, Mar. 29, 1953; children: Nancy, Doug, Susan, Scott, Robin. Student, McNeese U., 1950-53. Reporter Am. Press, Lake Charles, 1952-60; newsman AP, Richmond, Va., 1960-65, N.Y.C., 1965-71; columnist AP, L.A., 1972—. Author: (pen name Jerry Buck) novel Wheeler's Choice, 1989, Murder in Prime Time, 1989; contbr. articles to nat. jours. 1st lt. U.S. Army, 1953-55. Democrat. Methodist. Office: AP 1111 S Hill St Los Angeles CA 90015

BUCKELS, MARVIN WAYNE, savings and loan executive; b. Sterling, Colo., Feb. 11, 1929; s. Harvey and Myrl (Tarr) B.; m. Doris Torrance, Aug. 1, 1959; children: Lisa K., Devon Carol. BA, U. Denver, 1951; MS, U. Wis., 1952. Trainee Beatrice Foods, Denver, 1952-53, mgr. sales devel., 1953-54, sales mgr., 1954-55; loan counselor Midland Fed. Savs. and Loan Assn., Denver, 1955-56, asst. treas., 1956-58, treas., 1958-60, v.p., treas., 1960-62, exec. v.p., 1962-85; exec. v.p. Western Capital Investment Corp., Denver, 1985—. Vice chmn. Colo. Bd. for Community Colls. and Occupational Edn., 1967-75, chmn., 1975-78; vice chmn. Colo. Bd. Vocat. Edn., 1967; chmn. task force on employment Met. Denver Urban Coalition, 1970; pres. Adult Edn. Met. Denver, 1970; bd. dirs. Denver Opportunity, 1965-68, Downtown Denver, Inc., 1979—; bd. dirs. Auraria Higher Edn. Ctr., 1975-77, vice chmn. bd., 1977-78; bd. dirs. Rocky Mountain Hosp., 1979—, pres., 1980; chmn. Colo. Postsecondary Edn. Facilities Authority, 1981—; treas. Denver Civic Ventures Inc., chmn., 1987—; treas. Colo. Pub. Affairs Council. Served with U.S. Army, 1946-48. Mem. U.S. Savs. and Loan League, Colo. Savs. and Loan League (legis. com.), Am. Savs. and Loan Inst. (past pres. Denver chpt.), Controllers Soc. (past pres. Denver chpt., nat. gov.), Systems and Procedures Assn. (past pres. Denver chpt.), Adminstrv. Mgmt. Soc. (past pres. Denver chpt.), Denver C. of C. (past chmn. spl. task force studying sch. bond issue, loaned exec. Nat Alliance Businessmen's Program), Phi Beta Kappa. Democrat. Office: Western Capital Investments Corp 1675 Broadway #1700 Denver CO 80202

BUCKLEY, FRANCIS JOSEPH, priest, educator; b. Los Angeles, Aug. 31, 1928; s. Francis Joseph and Elizabeth Agnes (Haiss) B. Student, U. Notre Dame, 1944-45, U. Santa Clara, 1945-49; MST, U. Santa Clara, 1959; BA, Gonzaga U., 1951, MA in Philosophy, 1952; Licentiate in Sacred Theology, Alma Coll., 1959; STD, Gregorian U., Rome, 1964; DHL (hon.), Pacific Grad. Sch. Psychology, 1988. Joined S.J., 1945, ordained priest Roman Cath. Ch., 1958. Instr. classics, religion Bellarmine Coll. Prepatory Sch., San Jose, Calif., 1952-55; instr. theology U. San Francisco, 1960-61, asst. prof. theology, 1963-68, assoc. prof. theology, 1968-72, prof. theology, 1972—, acting chmn. dept. theology, 1971-73, chmn. dept. theology, 1978-79, 88—, dir. grad. programs in religious edn., 1974-75, 79-82, 86-87; chaplain St. Elizabeth Infant Hosp., San Francisco, 1963—; trustee Loyola Marymount U., Los Angeles, 1974—, Jesuit Community U. San Francisco, 1969-76, 78-82; theol. advisor to U.S. Bishops Synod of Bishops, Rome, 1977; del. to Asian Catechetical and Liturgical Conf., Manila, 1967, Latin Am. Catechetical Conf., Medellin, Colombia, 1968, Internat. Catechetical Congress, Rome, 1971; vis. scholar Ctr. for Research in Learning and Teaching U. Mich., Ann Arbor, 1973-74; bd. dirs. Paul Wattson Ecumenical Lecture Series, San Francisco; mem. Nat. Council Nat. Christian Leadership Conf. for Israel, 1979—. Author: Christ and the Church according to Gregory of Elvira, 1964, Children and God: Communion, Confession, Confirmation, 1970, I Confess: The Sacrament of Penance Today, 1972, Reconciling, 1981, Come Worship with US, 1987, (with Johannes Hofinger) The Good News and Its Proclamation, 1968; (with Sister Maria de la Cruz Aymes) (series) With Christ to the Father, 1966, Christ's Life in Us, 1967, Jesus, 1968, Spirit, 1968, Jesus in the Gospels and the Eucharist, 1969, In the Spirit of Jesus, 1969, One in Christ, 1970, God's People, 1970; (series) Our Father, 1971, Christ Our Life, 1971, Jesus Our Lord, 1971, Spirit of God, 1972, One in the Lord, 1973, God Among Us, 1973, Jesus Forgives, 1974, (series) Jesus Gives Joy, 1978, Jesus is with Us, 1978, Jesus and His Friends, 1978, Living God's Word, 1979, Celebrating God's Life, 1979, Sharing God's Promises, 1979, God Loves Me, 1980, We Share Forgiveness, 1980, We Share Reconciliation, 1980, Compartimos el Perdon, 1981, Fe Y Cultura, 1985; (with Sister Maria de la Cruz Aymes and Thomas H. Groome) (series) Growing with God, 1982, Growing with Jesus, 1982, Growing with the Church, 1982, Growing with God's Love, 1983, Growing with God's Life, 1983, Growing with God's Word, 1984, (with Donald Sharp) Deepening Christian Life: Integrating Faith and Maturity, 1987; contbr. articles to numerous jours. Trustee Pacific Grad. Sch. Psychology, Menlo Park, Calif., 1984-86, pres. bd. trustees, 1986. Mem. Coll. Theology Soc. (pres. 1972-74, bd. dirs. 1969-76, regional chmn. 1966-72), Cath. Theological Soc. Am., Cath. Bibl. Assn., Assn. Profs. and Researchers in Religious Edn., Religious Edn. Assn., Assn. Dirs. Grad. Religious Edn. Programs, Internat. Assn. Jesuit Ecumenists, Am. Soc. Ch. History, U. San Francisco Faculty Assn. (sec. 1980-88).

BUCKLEY, JAMES W., librarian; b. Los Angeles, Aug. 16, 1933; s. George W. and Alta L. (Hale) B.; m. Margaret Ann Wall, Aug. 7, 1965; children: Kathleen Ann, James William, John Whitney. AA, Los Angeles Harbor Coll., 1953; BA, Calif. State U., Long Beach, 1960; MLS, U. So. Calif., 1961, M in Pub. Adminstrn., 1974. Cert. tchr., Calif. Librarian West Gardena br. Los Angeles County Pub. Library, 1961-62, librarian Carson br., 1962-63; librarian Montebello (Calif.) Regional Library, 1963-68; regional librarian Orange County (Calif.) Pub. Library, 1968, dir. pub. services, 1969-74; county librarian San Mateo County (Calif.) Library, 1974-77, Marin County (Calif.) Library, 1978; city librarian Torrance (Calif.) Pub. Library, 1979—; exec. dir. Calif. Nat. Library Week, 1970; tchr. pub. service Coll. San Mateo, 1975. Served with U.S. Army, 1955-57. Mem. ALA, Am. Soc. Pub. Adminstrn., Calif. Library Assn., Pub. Library Execs. of So. Calif. Lodge: Rotary. Office: Torrance Pub Libr 3301 Torrance Blvd Torrance CA 90503

BUCKLEY, WILLIAM JOHN, electrical engineer; b. San Francisco, Sept. 29, 1940; s. William Francis and Margaret (Reid) B.; m. Loyola Antoinette Montana, Jan. 7, 1961; children: Margaret, Laura, William. AA, Coll. San Mateo, 1969; BS in Elec. Engring., Calif. State U., San Jose, 1971; MBA, U. Santa Clara, 1974. Sr. sales engr. GTE Lenkurt, San Carlos, Calif., 1975-76, Albuquerque, 1976-77; dir. engring. Cablewave Systems, North Haven, Conn., 1977-79; mfg. mgr. GTE Spl. Products, Aurora, Colo., 1979-82; mktg. mgr. GTE Spl. Products, Aurora, 1982-84; dir. mktg. Verilink Corp., Sunnyvale, Calif., 1984-85; dir. tech. devel. Verilink Corp., San Jose, Calif., 1985-87; asst. v.p. tech. devel. Verilink Corp., San Jose, 1987-88, v.p. tech. devel., 1988—. With USAF, 1958-63. Mem. Am. Assn. MBAs, IEEE, Am. Soc. Quality Control, Sierra Club, Sperdvac Club. Republican. Home: 10 Scenic Way #3R San Mateo CA 94403 Office: Verilink Corp 145 Baytech Dr San Jose CA 95134

BUCKLIN, DENNIS ARTHUR, social services administrator; b. Rockland, Maine, Jan. 28, 1949; s. Arthur Rodney and Gladys Ella (Pauquette) B.; m. Charlene Marie Jones; children: Keli R., Cori M. AA, U. So. Maine, 1977, BA, 1981, MS, 1984; MSW, U. Conn., West Hartford, 1984. Registered social worker, Oreg. Home/sch. coord. Maine Sch. Adminstrv. Dist. 57, Alfred, Maine, 1981-83; mental retardation case worker Community Support Svcs., Kennebunk, Maine, 1981-84; mental retardation/devel. disabled human svcs. case worker Maine Dept. Human Svcs./Mental Health, Portland, 1983-84; parent trainer Oreg. Children's Svcs. Div., Coos Bay, 1984-85; sexual abuse treatment dir. Oreg. Children's Svcs. Div., Salem, 1985—; instr. human svcs., Chemeketa Community Coll., Salem, Oreg., 1988—. With USN, 1967-69, Vietnam. Democrat. Office: Childrens Svcs Div 2450 Strong Rd Salem OR 97310

BUCKNER, FILLMORE, lawyer, physician; b. Tacoma, Nov. 8, 1926; s. Joseph Jay and Fannie (Marylander) B.; m. Chickie Lawson, June 15, 1952; children: Bruce Jay, Marcie Jo Rowe. BS, U. Wash., 1948, MD, 1952; JD, U. Puget Sound, 1984. Diplomate Am. Bd. Ob-gyn.; bar: Wash. Intern USPHS, San Francisco, 1952-53; sr. surgeon USPHS, 1953-55; resident and fellow Yale U. Med. Ctr., New Haven, 1955-58; pvt. practice ob-gyn., Seattle, 1958-82, pvt. practice med. and legal cons.,, 1985—; adj. prof. law U. Puget Sound, Tacoma, 1987—. Contbr. articles to profl. jours. Fellow Am. Coll. Ob-gyn., Am. Coll. Legal Medicine; mem. ABA, AMA, Am. Soc. Law and Medicine, Am. Soc. for the Right to Die, Seattle Gynecol. Soc. (pres. 1977-78, Outstanding Leadership award 1978), Seattle King County Bar Assn., King County Med. Assn., Wash. Athletic Club. Office: Skellenger & Bender 1111 3rd Ave #1500 Seattle WA 98101

BUCKNER, PHILIP FRANKLIN, newspaper publisher; b. Worcester, Mass., Aug. 25, 1930; s. Orello Simmons and Emily Virginia (Siler) B.; m. Ann Haswell Smith, Dec. 21, 1956; children: John C., Frederick F., Catherine A. AB, Harvard U., 1952; MA, Columbia U., 1954. Reporter Lowell (Mass.) Sun, 1959-60; pub. East Providence (R.I.) Post, 1960-62; from asst. to treas. Scripps League Newspapers, Seattle, 1964-66, div. mgr., 1966-71; pres. Buckner News Alliance, 8 newspapers, Seattle, 1971—. Office: Buckner News Alliance 221 1st Ave W Seattle WA 98119

BUCZYNSKI, WALTER EMRICK, manufacturing consultant, art consultant; b. Garfield, N.J., Sept. 7, 1946; s. Walter Joseph and Catherine (Polongi) B.; m. Sally Beth Kerberick, Sept. 1969 (div. 1973); 1 child, Erik Wade. BA in Art History, Rutgers U., 1968; MPA, U. Okla., 1974; postgrad., Golden Gate U., 1981—. Commd. 2d lt. USAF, advanced through ranks to capt., resigned, 1977; instr. Nat. Coll. Bus., Rapid City, S.D., 1977-78; subcontract adminstr. Lockheed Corp., Sunnyvale, 1978-79; subcontract supr. GTE Sylvania, Mountain View, Calif., 1979-82; materials mgr. Cadtrack Corp., Sunnyvale, 1982-84, Counterpoint Computer, San Jose, Calif., 1984-85, Diasonics MRI, South San Francisco, Calif., 1985-87; dir. ops. Micronics Computers, Sunnyvale, 1987-88; mfg. cons. Mountain View, 1988—; instr. Golden Gate U., San Francisco, 1985-89, dir. procurement, 1985-86. Contbg. editor art Silouette mag., San Jose, 1988-89; pub. Art-Smart, Mountain View, 1988; contbr. articles to profl. jours. Recipient Svc. award Jr. Achievement, 1982. Mem. Am. Prodn. Inventory Control Soc. (instr 1988-89.), Silicon Valley Purchasing Mgmt. Assn. (instr. 1988-89), Nat. Assn. Purchasing Mgmt. (cert. purchasing mgr.), Nat. Contract Mgmt. Assn., Rotary, Elks. Home and Office: 1940 Mt Vernon Ct #9 Mountain View CA 94040

BUDAGHER, JOHN ADALBERTO, lawyer, state senator; b. Albuquerque, June 13, 1946; s. John and Frances Dolores (Ramirez-Rodriguez) B.; m. Sandra K. C'DeBaca, July 28, 1979; children—John A., Joseph C. B.U.S., U. N.Mex., 1969; J.D., U. Tulsa, 1973; LL.M. in Estate Planning, U. Miami, 1976. Bar: N.Mex. 1974, U.S. Dist. Ct. N.Mex. 1974, U.S. Tax Ct. 1981. Assoc. Johnson Paulantis & Lanphere, Albuquerque, 1974-75; asst. dist. atty. Dist. Atty.'s Office, Santa Fe, 1975-76; sole practice John Budagher Law Offices, Albuquerque, 1976—; instr. bar revs. Bay Area Rev., Albuquerque, 1976-78; mem. N.Mex. Senate, 1980—; mem. Commn. Uniform State Laws, 1983—. Served with USAF, 1969-71, Vietnam. Mem. Am. Legion, VFW, DAV. Republican. Roman Catholic. Lodge: Elks. Home: 5804 Pauline Rd NW Albuquerque NM 87107 Office: 707 Broadway NE Ste 101 Albuquerque NM 87102

BUDD, ROBERT WESLEY, trade association executive; b. Laramie, Wyo., Apr. 22, 1956; s. William H. and Carolyn (Mockler) B.; m. Lynn Maree Bourn, Aug. 3, 1985. BS in Animal Sci. and Agrl. Bus., U. Wyo., 1979. Ranch hand Budd Ranches, Inc., Big Piney, Wyo., 1973-79; exec. sec. Wyo. Stock Growers Assn., Cheyenne, 1979-85, exec. v.p., 1985—; mgr. Wyo. Beef Coun., Cheyenne, 1979-85; profl. guide Diamond Tail Outfitters, Greybull, Wyo., 1981—. Author: Send Fresh Horse, 1987; contbr. articles to various publs. Mem. Wyo. Hist. Trails Adv. Bd., 1984—, Wyo. Coun. for Humanities, 1985—; mem. pub. relations com. Cheyenne Frontier Days, 1988—. Mem. Nat. Cattlemen's Assn., Soc. for Range Mgmt., Am. Animal Soc., Wyo. Assn. Trade Execs., Cheyenne C. of C. (pres. 1988). Republican. Episcopalian. Home: 6551 Moreland St Cheyenne WY 82009 Office: Wyo Stock Growers Assn 113 E 20th St Cheyenne WY 82003

BUDDENBOHM, HAROLD WILLIAM, aerospace project engineer; b. Wellington, Kans., Aug. 8, 1959; s. Harold William Buddenbohm (dec.) and Dorothy Ruth (Webber) B. BSMechE, U Ill, 1981; MBA, Pepperdine U., 1984; postgrad., West Coast U., 1986. Registered engr. in tng. Design engr. Rockwell Internat., Canoga Park, Calif., 1981-84, devel. engr., 1984-85, project engr., 1985—. Patentee turbine tip sealing. Recipient Achievement awards, Tech. Utilization award. Mem. ASME. Republican. Presbyterian. Home: 18419 Delano St Reseda CA 91335 Office: Rockwell Internat 6633 Canoga Ave Canoga Park CA 91304

BUDDINGH, JAMES LEROY, publications manager; b. Paris Twp., Mich., Mar. 24, 1934; s. Fredrick Rudolph and Carol Evelyn (VanZee) B.; m. Dahlia Contraras, Sept. 17, 1955 (div. Jan. 1984); children: Carla Jean, Dahlia Ann, Mark Wade, Pamila Lynn, James Mathew; m. Jean McCombs. Graduated, Acme Sch. of Tool and Die Engring., 1962; AA, Orange Coast Coll., 1972. Engring. illustrator Volt Tech. Corp., San Diego, 1957-60; tech. art dir. Volt Tech. Corp., Anaheim, Calif., 1961-65, cons., 1960-65; engring. illustrator Jules Fielding & Assocs., San Diego, 1960-61; staff illustrator McDonnel Douglas Corp., Huntington Beach, Calif., 1965-78; publs. adminstr. Argosystems Inc., Los Angeles, 1978-82; publs. mgr. Ultrasystems Def. and Space Systems Inc., Irvine, Calif., 1982—; freelance artist, Calif., 1953—; proprietor, artist Buddingh Enterprises, Westminster, Calif., 1980-82. Pub./author Yahweh's News, 1985. Served as cpl. U.S. Army, 1953-55. Republican. Roman Catholic. Home: PO Box 6359 Crestline CA 92325 Office: A Hadson Co Inc 16775 Von Karman Ave Irvine CA 92714

BUDELOV, PETER ROY, information services director, small business owner; b. Providence, R.I., July 13, 1947; s. William D. and Stella Budelov; m. Marilyn J. Coley, Aug. 14, 1982; children: Scott M. Browning, David M. Browning. BS in Physics, Pratt Inst., Bklyn., 1970. Sales engr. Sci. Systems Sales Corp., Little Neck, N.Y., 1970-71; programmer, analyst Bechtel Corp., San Francisco, 1972-75, Morrison-Knudson Co. (M-K), Boise, Idaho, 1975-77; mgr. computer ops. Morrison-Knudson Saudi Arabia Consortium, Al Khobar, 1977-79, King Khalid Mil. City, Saudi Arabia; mgr. data processing M-K Co., Columbia (Md.), Vancouver (B.C.), Boise, 1979-86; dir. info. systems Dillingham Constrn. Co., Pleasanton, Calif., 1986—; v.p., owner Calif. Data Systems, San Ramon, 1988—. Composer: Tomorrow Never Comes, 1968; patentee in field. Mem. 181st St. Civic Assn., Jamaica, N.Y., 1971; treas. Daybreak Homeowners Assn., San Ramon, 1989. Mem. Constrn. Info. Execs., U.S. Navy League. Democrat. Office: Dillingham Constrn 5960 Inglewood Dr Pleasanton CA 94566

BUDGE, NANCY ANN, paper mill executive; b. San Francisco, Oct. 4, 1955; d. Hamilton Whited and Elaine (Walton) B. BS, Yale U., 1977; MBA, Stanford U., 1983. Foreman Potlatch Co., Lewiston, Idaho, 1978-80, Weyerhaeuser Co., Klamath Falls, Oreg., 1980-81; adminstrv. asst. Boise Cascade Corp., Emmett, Idaho, 1982-87; mill supt. Boise Cascade Co., La Grande, Oreg., 1987-89; sr. analyst corp. planning and devel. Boise (Idaho) Cascade Co., 1989—. Troop leader Girl Scouts U.S.A., La Grande, 1987-88. Home: 138 N Bruce St Boise ID 83712 Office: Boise Cascade Corp One Jefferson Square Boise ID 83728

BUDLONG, DUDLEY WEBSTER, engineering company executive; b. Mount Prospect, Ill., May 9, 1922; s. Dudley W. and Louise B. (Schiller) B.; children from previous marriage: Gerald M., Steven C., Bruce E., Roger D.; m. Gladys M. Lacerda, Dec. 15, 1979. BS, Ill. Inst. Tech., 1948, postgrad., 1951-53; postgrad., U. So. Calif., 1953-54. Registered profl. engr., Calif., N.J., N.Y., Nev., Va., Fla., Mich., Minn., Alaska, Utah. Asst. staff engr. Standard Oil Co. of Ind. (now AMOCO), Whiting, 1948-51; plant engr. Argonne (Ill.) Nat. Lab., 1951-53; sr. job engr. Bechtel Corp., Los Angeles, 1953-54; chief engr. May Engring. Co., Van Nuys, Calif., 1954-58; pres., chief engr. Budlong & Assocs., Sherman Oaks, Calif., 1958-69; exec. v.p. Quinton-Budlong Architects, Engrs. & Planners, Los Angeles, 1969-73; pvt. practice cons. Northridge, Calif., 1973; pres. Killian Assocs. West Inc., Northridge, 1973-78; v.p. facilities systems group Boyle Engring. Corp., Northridge, 1974-81; pres. Dudley W. Budlong Cons., Woodland Hills, Calif., 1981-86; pres. Budlong & Moore Assocs., Woodland Hills, 1986-89, chmn. bd., 1989—; mem. planning cabinet Am. Cons. Engrs. Council U.S., 1970-76, chmn., 1975; mem. engring. profl. adv. council Sch. Engring. Calif. State U., Northridge, 1976—. 2d lt. USAF, 1943-45. Recipient Disting. Achievement award Los Angeles Council Engrs. and Scientists, 1986, Disting. Internat. Engring. Achievements award Calif. Council Indsl. and Bus. Assocs., Los Angeles, 1986. Fellow Inst. Advancement Engring. (charter); mem. Am. Inst. Plant Engrs. (cert.), Assn. Energy Engrs. (charter), Am. Cons. Engrs. Coun., Cons. Engrs. Assn. Calif. (past bd. dirs. 1960—, sec. 1965-66), Calif. Soc. Profl. Engrs. (past pres., state dir.), Cons. Elec. Engrs. So. Calif. (past pres., bd. dirs.), Illuminating Engring. Soc., Mech.-Elec. Engrs. Council Calif. (past state chmn.), Indsl. Assn. San Fernando Valley, Tau Beta Pi, Eta Kappa Nu, Alpha Phi Omega. Presbyterian. Club: Pres.'s of Calif. State U. (Northridge). Office: Budlong & Moore Assocs Inc 21241 Ventura Blvd #169 Woodland Hills CA 91364

BUDZINSKI, JAMES EDWARD, interior designer; b. Gary, Ind., Jan. 4, 1953; s. Edward Michael and Virginia (Caliman) B.; student U. Cin., 1971-76. Mem. design staff Perkins & Wills Architects, Inc., Chgo., 1973-75, Med. Architectonics, Inc., Chgo., 1975-76; v.p. interior design Interior Environs., Inc., Chgo., 1976-78; pres. Jim Budzinski Design, Inc., Chgo., 1978-80; dir. interior design Robinson, Mills & Williams, San Francisco, 1980-87, dir. design, interior architecture Whisler Patri, San Francisco, 1987— ; instr. design Harrington Inst. Design, Chgo.; cons. Chgo. Art Inst., Storwal Internat., Inc.; speaker at profl. confs. Designs include 1st Chgo. Corp. Pvt. Banking Ctr., 1st Nat. Bank Chgo. Monroe and Wabash Banking Ctr., 1978, IBM Corp., San Jose, Deutsch Bank, Frankfort, Crowley Maritime Corp., San Francisco, offices for Brobeck, Phleger and Harrison, offices for chmn. bd. Fireman's Fund Ins. Cos., Nob Hill Club, Fairmont Hotel, San Francisco, offices for Cooley, Godword, Castro, Huddleson, and Tatum, Palo Alto, Calif, offices for Pacific Bell Acctg. div., San Francisco, showroom for Knoll Internat., San Francisco, lobby, lounge TransAm. Corp. Hdqrts, San Fransisco, offices for EDAW, San Francisco, showroom for Steelcase Inc., Bally of Switzerland, N.Am. Flagship store, San Francisco; corp. Hqrs. Next Inc., Redwood City, Calif.; Schafer Furniture Design. Pres. No. Calif. chpt. Design Industries Found. for AIDS. Office: Whistler Patri 2 Bryant San Francisco CA 94108

BUEHLER, SALLY SALMEN, clinical social worker; b. Newton, Mass., July 31, 1938; d. Stanley and Margaret (Green) Salmen; m. John A. Buehler, Aug. 24, 1971; 1 child, Daniel. AB, U. N.H., 1960; MSW, U. Calif., 1963. Lic. clin. social worker, Calif. Social worker psychiat. Child Guidance Clinic Children Hosp., San Francisco, 1965-69, supt. social worker psychiat., 1968-69; social worker psychiat. Family Service Agy., Pittsfield, Mass., 1970-71; social worker clin. Kentfield, Calif., 1971—; cons. Pacific Recovery Ctr., Larkspur, Calif., 1983—. Fellow Soc. Clin. Social Work (cert. social worker). Home: 18 Turnagain Rd San Rafael CA 94904

BUEL, JAMES WES, food service executive, consultant; b. Long Beach, Calif., May 21, 1937; s. James Buel and June von Opperman; m. Renee J. Ellis; children: Frank Roddy, Tammy, Ty, Wesley, Elise. BS, Calif. Poly. State U., 1963. Food service mgr. Dole Philippines, 1964-69; dir. food and beverage Hyatt Hotels Asia, Philippines, 1969-79; food service dir. Western Innkeepers, Los Angeles, 1979-83, Service America, Long Beach, Calif., 1983-88; food service mgr. Lucky Food Stores, Redlands, Calif., 1988—; cons. in field. Author: Food Service in the Philippines, 1977, Food Service in Asia, 1978. Bd. dirs. Boy Scout Council, 1987—; v.p. Am. Assn., Manila, 1977. Served to 1st lt. U.S. Army, 1956-60. Recipient Cert. Leadership Cornell U., 1979. Republican.

BUFFALO, VICTOR S., financial institution executive. Student, So. Alta. Inst. Tech., Calgary. Former councillor, chief Samson Indian Bd.; oil and gas advisor Four Nations of Hubbema; bd. dirs. Peace Hills Trust Co., Samson Reserve, Alta., 1980—; chmn. bd. Peace Hills Trust Co., Samson Reserve, 1987—. Mem. Indian Assn. Alta., KC. Office: Peace Hills Trust Co, 10011 109th St, Edmonton, AB Canada T5J 3S8 *

BUFFALOW, OSCAR THOMAS, JR., oil company executive; b. Chatanooga, May 15, 1924; s. Oscar Thomas and Mamie (Van Dusen) B.; m. Jean Carolyn Hart, Feb. 2, 1946 (div. June, 1979); children: Victor Thomas, Edward Hart; m. Marie Antoinette Briggs, Jan. 9, 1988. BSChemE, Cornell U., 1948. Registered chem. engr., Calif. Engr., supr. engr. Standard Oil Calif., San Francisco, 1948-57, '60-63; asst. chief engr. Standard Oil Calif. Western Ops., Richmond, Calif., 1964-68; supr. Standard Oil Calif. Western Ops., Richmond, 1968-69, El Segundo, Calif., 1969-70; chief engr. Standard Oil Calif. Western Ops., El Segundo, 1970-71; mgr. ops. Standard Oil Ky., Pascagoula, Miss., 1971-72; chmn. bd. of engrs. and asst. v.p. Standard Oil of Calif., San Francisco, 1973-76; rsch. engr. Chevron Rsch. Co., Richmond, Calif., 1958-59; gen. mgr., mfg. dept. Chevron U.S.A., San Francisco, Calif., 1977—. Bd. dirs. San Francisco Grove Homeowners' Assn. (v.p. 6 yrs., pres. 2 yrs.), 1981-89. 1st lt. U.S. Army Air Corps, 1943-46. Mem. Mfg. Nat. Petroleum Refiners Assn., Engrs. Club San Francisco (bd. dirs. 1977-85), The Olympic Club. Republican. Methodist. Home: 54 Stern Grove Ct San Francisco CA 94132 Office: Chevron USA 575 Market St San Francisco CA 94105

BUFFINGTON, LINDA BRICE, interior designer; b. Long Beach, Calif., June 21, 1936; d. Harry Bryce and Marguerite Leonora (Tucciarone) Van Bellehem; student El Camino Jr. Coll., 1955-58, U. Calif., Irvine, 1973—; children: Lisa Ann, Phillip Lynn. with Pub. Fin., Torrance, Calif., 1954-55, Beneficial Fin., Torrance and Hollywood, Calif., 1955-61; interior designer Vee Nisley Interiors, Newport Beach, Calif., 1964-65, Leon's Interiors, Newport Beach, 1965-69; ptnr. Marlind Interiors, Tustin, Calif., 1969-70; owner, designer Linda Buffington Interiors, Villa Park, Calif., 1970—; cons. builders, housing developments. Mem. Bldg. Industry Assn., Internat. Soc. Interior Designers (sec. Orange County chpt.), Sales and Mktg. Council, Home Builders Council, Nat. Assn. Home Builders. Republican. Office: 17767 Santiago Blvd Villa Park CA 92667

BUFFORD, SAMUEL L., federal judge; b. Phoenix, Ariz., Nov. 19, 1943; s. John Samuel and Evelyn Amelia (Rude) B.; m. Julia Marie Metzger, May 13, 1978. BA, Wheaton (Ill.) Coll., 1964; PhD, U. Tex., 1969; JD, U. Mich., 1973. Bar: Calif. Instr. philosophy La. State U., Baton Rouge, 1967-68; asst. prof. Ea. Mich. U., Ypsilanti, 1968-74; asst. prof. law Ohio State U., Columbus, 1975-77; assoc. Gendel, Raskoff, Shapiro & Quittner, L.A., 1982-85; judge U.S. Bankruptcy Ct., L.A., 1985—; adj. prof. U. So. Calif., 1989; bd. dirs. Fin. Lawyers Conf., L.A., Bankruptcy Forum, L.A. Contbr. articles to profl. jours. Mem. ABA, L.A. County Bar Assn. (chmn. ethics com.). Office: US Bankruptcy Ct 300 N Los Angeles St Los Angeles CA 90012

BUHR, GARY ALAN, preventive medicine physician; b. Everett, Wash., Nov. 30, 1945; s. Glenn Elvin and Margaret Alea (Markham) B. BA, We. Wash. U., Bellingham, 1969; ND, Nat. Coll. Naturopathic Med., Portland, Ore., 1976. Owner, pres. N.W. Clinic Naturopathic Medicine, P.S. Inc., Bellingham, Wash., 1976-80; owner, physician Wholeperson Co., Mt. Vernon, Wash., 1980—; assoc. prof. Bastyr Coll. Nat. Sci., Seattle, 1984—; student adv. Bastyr Coll., Seattle 1984-87. Recipient Eagle Scout award Boy Scouts Am., Everett Wash. 1960, Dod &. Mem. Wash. Assn. Naturopathic Physicians, Am. Assn. Naturopathic. Home: 101 Claremont Pl Mount Vernon WA 98273

BUHR, KENNETH STEPHEN, marriage and family therapist; b. L.A., July 14, 1937; s. Edwin Charles and Emma Ann (Mannlein) B.; m. Deanna Joyce Mleynek, June 6, 1971; children: Gabriel John, Justin, Michael. BA, St. John's Coll., Camarillo, Calif., 1959; STB, Pontifical Gregorian U., Rome, 1963; MA, U. So. Calif., L.A., 1973, PhD, 1975. Asst. pastor Roman Cath. Parishes, L.A., 1965-71; teaching asst. U. So. Calif., 1972-74; pvt. practice San Diego, 1975—. Scout master Troop 634 Boy Scouts Am., Poway, Calif., 1986-88. Fellow Am. Assn. for Marriage and Family Therapy (clin., chmn. continuing edn. com. 1986-87, pres. So. Calif. chpt. 1982-84, sec., treas. 1978-80), Calif. Assn. Marriage and Family Therapists (clin., pres. San Diego chpt. 1975-77). Democrat. Home: 16314 Summer Sage Rd Poway CA 92064 Office: 11848 Bernardo Pla Ct #230B San Diego CA 92128

BUI, PHONG HUY, data processing executive; b. Saigon, Vietnam, May 23, 1960; came to U.S., 1980; s. Thong Huy and Vinh Thi Bui. AS in Computer Sci., Santa Ana Coll., 1984; BS in Computer Sci., U. Calif., Irvine, 1987. Semiconductor operator Tex. Instruments, Inc., Houston, 1980-81; semiconductor lead operator Western Digital Corp., Irvine, Calif., 1981-83, with prodn. control, 1983-88; programmer analyst Western Digital Corp., Irvine, 1988—. Mem. IEEE, ACM, Am. Film Inst., Alpha Gamma Sigma.

BUKEY, WARREN PAUL, communications specialist; b. Long Beach, Calif., July 2, 1948; s. Henry Clark and Mary Beth (Sattler) B.; m. Kristy Moore, Dec. 9, 1973; children: Jennifer Lisa, Jeffrey Neil. AA, El Camino Coll., 1970. Mail carrier U.S. Postal Service, Redondo Beach, Calif., 1973-84; researcher U.S. Postal Service, Temecula, Calif., 1984—. With U.S. Army, 1968-70. Recipient Outstanding Achievement award U.S. Postal Service, Temecula, 1987. Mem. Squatters Rights. Office: US Postal Svc 28360 Front St Temecula CA 92390

BULAND, RAYMOND PETER, seismologist; b. Bell, Calif., Sept. 5, 1948; s. Robert Noel and Marjorie Ruth (Fredriksen) B.; m. Lynne Maureen Rabiner, Feb. 24, 1974; 1 child, Michael Benjamin. BS in Physics, Calif. Inst. Tech., 1970; PhD in Earth Sci., U. Calif., San Diego, 1976. Rsch. asst. U. Calif., San Diego, 1976-78; geophysicist U.S. Geol. Survey, Golden, Colo., 1978—; software developer Golden Nat. Earthquake Info. Svc., 1979-81; cons. Nat. Acad. Sci.-Internat. Assn. Seismology and Physics of Earth Interior-Internat. Seismol. Ctr., 1983—, automation of Italian Nat. Seismic Network, Rome, 1984-87; project mgr. U.S. Nat. Seismograph Network, Golden, 1986—. author numerous rsch. reports. Mem. Seismol. Soc. Am., Am. Geophys. Union. Democrat. Office: US Geol Survey Stop 967 Box 25046 Denver Fed Ctr Denver CO 80225

BULEY, JOSEPH ROLAND, construction company executive; b. Burlington, Vt., Nov. 19, 1939; s. Roland J. and Mary (Dohney) B.; m. Geraldine Ann Greenwood, Sept. 1, 1962; children: Joe R., Will, Mike, Mary Ellen, Ann. BS in Civil Engring., U. Vt., 1961; MS in Civil Engring., Stanford U., 1962; postgrad., Western State U., 1985. Registered civil engr. Constrn. engr. Pickands Mather and Co., Cleve., 1965-68; supt. Nalews, Inc. Constrn. Engrs., Laconia, N.H., 1968-70; v.p. Carpenter Rigging and Contracting, Syracuse, N.Y., 1970-79, Dorcon Industries, Houston, 1979-81; mgr. S.W. region Centrig Industries, Houston, 1981-84; v.p. Summit Constrn. and Maintenance Co., Wilmington, Calif., 1984—. Served to capt. USAF, 1962-65. Mem. Associated Bldrs. and Contractors (chmn. indsl. tng. 1987—), Nat. Acad. Scis., Constrn. Inst., ASCE, Theta Chi (pres. 1960-61). Roman Catholic. Office: Summit Constrn & Maintenance Co 828 East G St Wilmington CA 90744

BULLA, LYNDA MARIE, real estate broker; b. Los Angeles, Feb. 27, 1943; d. Forrest Merle and Alice Doris (Lee) Garrett; m. Stanley David Bulla, Feb. 16, 1962; children: Cynthia Marie Bulla Paolercio, Stanley David IV, Denise Renee. BA, Calif. State U., Fresno, 1983. Lic. realtor, Calif. Libr. Fresno County Free Libr., 1972-83; sales assoc. Valley West Properties, Kerman, Calif., 1978-85, sales mgr., 1985-88; pres. Kerman Land Co., Inc., Kerman, 1987—; real estate broker Valley West Properties, Kerman, 1988—. Mem. Tranquillity Booster Club, Parent-Tchrs. Club, Tranquility. Mem. Fresno Bd. Realtors, Calif. Assn. Realtors, Nat. Assn. Realtors, Fresno Multiple Listing Service, DAR, Panoche Guild (pres. 1982-83, 86-88), San Joaquin C. of C. (pres. 1989). Democrat. Roman Catholic. Office: Valley West Properties 681 S Madera Ave Kerman CA 93630

BULLARD, GILDA, state official; b. Chicago Heights, Ill., Dec. 12, 1927; d. Pietro Antonio and Philomena D'Antonoli; BS, Calif. State U., Sacramento, 1967, MBA, 1973; 1 son, David L. Gard. With Pacific Telephone Co., 1945-61; with State of Calif., 1961—, fiscal specialist in state welfare programs, 1966-74, staff mgr. licensing div., Sacramento, 1974-76, San Jose, 1975, citation hearing officer on appeals by nursing homes Dept. Health, Berkeley, 1976-78, mgr., fed. audits specialist audits and investigations div. Dept. Health Svcs., 1978-84, appeals unit, 1984-86, mgr. audits, 1986-87, acctg. adminstr. State Dept. Indsl. Rels., 1987—; part-time instr. Am. River Coll., 1976-77, Cosumnes River Coll., 1980-86, Sacramento City Coll., 1985-86 . Mem. Nat. Assn. Accts. (asst. treas. 1971, editor 1971), AAUW, Calif. State Employees Assn. (editor 1971, 72, chpt. pres. 1977, 81-86). Presbyterian. Home: 2833 Danube Ave Davis CA 95616 Office: 525 Golden Gate Ave San Francisco CA 94102

BULLER, PATRICK EMMETT, electrical engineer; b. Salt Lake City, Mar. 10, 1936; s. Patrick Michael and Justine (Pruss) B.; m. Delia Ann Richards, June 29, 1963 (div. Sept. 23, 1977); children: Patrick Emmett Jr., Michael Lloyd; m. Ruth Eileen Schoenfeld, Sept. 23, 1977; children from previous marriage: Clint Sloan, Cheri Sloan, Shelly Sloan. Student, Weber State Coll., Ogden, Utah, 1954-55; BEE, Utah State U., 1964. Journeyman electrician Chase Electric, Ogden, 1959-63; asst. research engr. Utah State U., Logan, 1963-67; sr. project engr. Utah Power & Light Co., Salt Lake City, 1967-78; staff engr. Rockwell Internat., Richland, Wash., 1978-83; sr. design engr. Wash. State Patrol, Bellevue, 1983—; prin. P.E. Buller Cons. Engr., Salt Lake City, 1968-83. Co-author: (book) IEEE Tutorial, 1976; patentee in field. Chmn. Franklin County Mental Health Sub Com., Benton, Wash., 1980-82; del. State Dem. conv., Spokane, 1980. With USN, 1955-59. Mem. Assn. Pub. Safety communications Officers (tech. advisor NW chpt., Washington, 1986—), Nat. Assn. Radio and Telecommunication Engrs. Democrat. Roman Catholic. Clubs: Issaquah (Wash.) Amateur Radio (pres. 1986-87); Mercedes Benz of North Am. (Seattle). Home: 4539 191st Ave SE Issaquah WA 98027 Office: Wash State Patrol 2803 156th Ave SE Bellevue WA 98007

BULLIN, CHRISTINE NEVA, arts administrator; b. New Plymouth, N.Z., Apr. 13, 1948; d. Kenneth and Hazel Iris B. B.A., Wellesley Coll., 1969; M.L.A., Simmons Coll., 1973. Dir., Opera New England, Boston, 1974-78; with San Francisco Opera, 1978-81; mgr. San Francisco Opera Ctr., 1981—. *

BULLIS, JAMES RODNEY, automobile executive; b. Spokane, Wash., July 22, 1946; s. Stanley David and Sally Irene (Blankenhorn) B.; m. Judith Ann Lynn, May 29, 1977; children: Elizabeth Marie, Matthew James. V.p. J & J Restaurants, Spokane, Wash., 1972-75; gen. mgr. Stiles Imported Group, Spokane, 1975-78, Jaremko Motors, Spokane, 1978-80, Auto Martin, Ltd., Grants Pass, Oreg., 1980-85; v.p. Columbia Motors, Kennewick, Wash., 1985—. With USN, 1966-70; PTO. Mem. Wash. Auto Dealers Assn. (dir. 1986-88), Nat. Auto. Dealers Assn. (vice chmn. 1985-88), Tri-Cities Auto. Delaers Assn. (pres. 1986-88), Kennewick C. of C. (charter dir. 1986), TC Country Club, Rotary. Republican. Episcopalian. Home: 8400 W Falls Pl Kennewick WA 99336 Office: McCurley Imports PO Box 2698 Pasco WA 99302

BULLOCK, DONALD WAYNE, educator, educational computing consultant; b. Tacoma Park, Md., Mar. 24, 1947; s. B.W. and Margaret (Harris) B.; m. Pamela Louise Hatch, Aug. 7, 1971. AA in Music, L.A. Pierce Coll., Woodland Hills, Calif., 1969; BA in Geography, San Fernando Valley State Coll., 1971; Cert. Computer Edn., Calif. Luth. U., 1985, MA in Curriculum-Instrn., 1987. Tchr. music Calvary Luth. Sch., Pacoima, Calif., 1970-71; elem. tchr. 1st Luth. Sch., Northridge, Calif., 1971-73; elem. tchr. Simi Valley (Calif.) Unified Sch. Dist., 1973—, computer insvc. instr., 1982-85, computer mentor tchr., 1985-87; lectr. Calif. Luth. U., Thousand Oaks, 1985—; ednl. computer cons. DISC Ednl. Svcs., Simi Valley, 1985—. Contbr. articles to profl. publs. Pres. Amen Choir, Van Nuys, Calif., 1981-83. Recipient Computer Learning Month grand prize Tom Snyder Prodns., 1988; Tandy-Radio Shack, Inc. grantee, 1985, Calif. Dept. Edn. grantee, 1985. Mem. NEA, Assn. for Supervision and Curriculum Devel., Internat. Coun. for Computers in Edn., Computer Using Educators, Calif., Gold Coast Computer Using Educators (bd. dirs. 1988-89). Home: 2805 N Wanda Ave Simi Valley CA 93065 Office: Knolls Elem Sch 6334 Katherine Rd Simi Valley CA 93063

BULLOUGH, ROBERT VERNON, JR., education educator; b. Salt Lake City, Feb. 12, 1949; s. Robert Vernon and Dolores Elaine (Clarke) B.; m. Dawn Ann Mortensen, June 18, 1977; children: Joshua Benjamin, Seth Thomas, Adam Neve, Rachel Elizabeth. BS in History, U. Utah, 1971, MEd, 1973; PhD, Ohio State U., 1976. Tchr. East High Sch., Salt Lake City, 1971-73; teaching assoc., then fellow Ohio State U., Columbus, 1973-76; asst. prof., then assoc. prof. U. Utah, Salt Lake City, 1976-89, prof. ednl. studies, 1989—; mem. editorial bd., Jour. Curriculum Theorizing, 1979—, adv. bd., Teaching Edn., 1986—; mem. Holmes Group Writing Com., 1984-86. Author: Democracy in Education: Boyd H. Bode, 1981, Human Interests in the Curriculum: Teaching and Learning in a Technological Society (with others), 1984, The Forgotten Dream of American Education, 1988, First Year Teacher: A Case Study, 1989; contbr. articles to profl. publs. Mem. Assn. Tchr. Educators, Am. Assn. Colls. of Tchr. edn., Soc. for Study Curriculum History, Profs. of Curriculum, Phi Beta Kappa, Phi Eta Sigma, Phi Kappa Phi, Phi Delta Kappa. Mormon. Office: Grad Sch Edn U Utah 307 MBH Salt Lake City UT 84112

BULMER, CONNIE J., film librarian; b. Seattle, Jan. 22, 1931; d. George Arthur and Helen Harriet (Braman) Bulmer. Librarian Republic Studios, Studio City, Calif., 1950-54; head librarian Revue Prodns.-Universal Studios, Studio City, 1954-61, Twentieth Century Fox, Beverly Hills, Calif., 1961-62, Selmur Prodns., Culver City, Calif., 1963-68, Hope Enterprises, Burbank, Calif., 1968-71, Paramount Studios, Hollywood, 1972—. Mem. Acad. TV Acad. TV Arts and Scis., Motion Picture-Videotape Editors, Am. Film Inst. Office: Paramount Pictures 5555 Melrose Ave Los Angeles CA 90038

BULTMANN, WILLIAM ARNOLD, historian; b. Monrovia, Calif., Apr. 10, 1922; s. Paul Gerhardt and Elsa (Johnson) B.; AB, UCLA, 1943, PhD, 1950; m. Phyllis Jane Wetherell, Dec. 28, 1949; 1 child, Janice Jane. Assoc. prof. history Central Ark. U., Conway, 1949-52, prof., 1954-57; assoc. prof. Ohio Wesleyan U., Delaware, 1957-61, prof., 1961-65; prof. Western Wash. U., Bellingham, 1965-87, chmn. dept., 1968-70, dean arts and scis., 1970-72, provost, 1971-73; vis. assoc. prof. U. Tex., Austin, 1952-53; vis. prof. U. N.H., summers 1965, 66; acad. cons. Wash. Commn. for Humanities, 1973-87, Nat. Endowment for Humanities, 1976-87; reader Ednl. Testing Service Princeton, 1973-85. Bd. dirs. Bellingham Maritime Heritage Found., 1980-85; adminstrv. officer Bellingham Power Squadron, 1981-82, comdr., 1982-84. Fulbight sr. lectr. Dacca (Bangladesh) U., 1960-61; Ohio Wesleyan U. research fellow, 1964; Fund for Advancement Edn. fellow for fgn. study, 1953-54; recipient research award Social Sci. Research Council, 1957. Mem. Am. Hist. Assn., Ch. Hist. Soc., Conf. Brit. Studies, Pacific, Pacific N.W. confs. Brit. studies, AAUP, Mystery Writers of Am., Nat. Boating Fedn., Interclub Boating Assn. Washington, Seattle Power Squadron, Phi Beta Kappa, Phi Delta Kappa, Pi Gamma Mu. Episcopalian. Clubs: Park Athletic Recreation, Bellingham Yacht (chmn. public relations com. 1981-86), Squalicum Yacht (trustee 1979-82), Birch Bay Yacht; Wash. Athletic. Coauthor: Border Boating, 1978; co-founder, mem. editorial bd. Albion, 1968-84; mng. editor Brit. Studies Intelligencer, 1973-80; co-editor Current Research in British Studies, 1975; editor Jib Sheet, 1981-86; feature writer, columnist Sea mag., 1974—; feature writer Venture mag., 1981-85, Poole Publs., 1988—. Home: 1600 43d Ave E Ste 101 Seattle WA 98112

BUMANGLAG, ALEJANDRO GUIRA, sales executive, accountant; b. San Miguel, Philippines, Nov. 26, 1950; came to U.S., 1981; s. Martin Asuncion and Micaela Mamuad (Guira) B.; m. Divina Paguirigan Ulep, Apr. 12, 1980; children: Geraldine Joyce, Allen Mar, Beatriz Brittany. BS in Commerce, Divine Word Coll of Laoag, Laoag City, Philippines, 1974, MBA, 1977. CPA, Philippines. Staff auditor I Sycip, Gorres, Velayo & Co., CPAs, Makati, Philippines, 1975; clerical aide Philippine Nat. Bank, Laoag City, 1976-77, masagana clk., 1977-78, savs. bookkeeper, 1977-81; acctg. instr. Divine Word Coll. of Laoag, 1977-81; night auditor Hilton Hawaiian Village Hotel, Honolulu, 1981-83; controller asst. People's Savs., Honolulu, 1981-83; field underwriter N.Y. Life Ins. Co., Honolulu, 1983-86, sales mgr., 1986—; auditor Philippine Inst. CPAs, Ilocos Norte chpt., Laoag City, 1977. Assoc. editor: The Filipinian, 1969-70. Sr. counilman San Miguel Barrio Coun., San Nicolas, 1972-81; pres. Samahang Nayon ng San Miguel, San Nicolas, 1974-81. Republican. Roman Catholic. Home: 4489 Luapele Pl Honolulu HI 96818 Office: NY Life Ins Co 841 Bishop St Ste 1410 Honolulu HI 96813

BUMGARDNER, LARRY G., academic administrator; b. Chattanooga, June 10, 1957; s. Walter G. and Kathryn (Hamrick) B. BA, David Lipscomb Coll., 1977; JD, Vanderbilt U., 1981. Bar: Tenn. 1981, U.S. Dist. Ct. (cen. dist.) Tenn. 1982, Calif. 1984, U.S. Dist. Ct. (cen. dist.) Calif. 1985. From reporter to copy editor Nashville (Tenn.) Banner, 1975-79; editor Tenn. Attorneys Memo, Tenn. Jour., Nashville, 1979-83; dir. founds. Pepperdine U., Malibu, Calif., 1983-85, asst. v.p. for communications and grants, asst. prof. communications, 1986—. Contbr. numerous articles to various pubs. Mem. ABA, Calif. Bar Assn. Home: 24343 Baxter Dr Malibu CA 90265 Office: Pepperdine U 24255 Pacific Coast Hwy Malibu CA 90265

BUNCH, K. ALAN, insurance company executive; b. Bloomfield, Iowa, Jan. 28, 1961; s. John Wendall and Linda Lou (Gooden) B.; m. Dawn Lee Thompson, Apr. 20, 1985; children: Christopher A., Stephanie M. BS in Agr., Agrl. Econs., U. Mo., 1984. Purchasing agt. Cypress Mfg. Co., St. Louis, 1984; trainee The Hartford Ins. Group, St. Louis, 1984-85; from underwriter to supr. The Hartford Ins. Group, Atlanta, 1985-88; div. mgr. The Hartford Ins. Group, Sacramento, 1988—. Chmn. young families Ch. of Christ, Roseville, Calif., 1989. John Brown scholar U. Mo., Columbia, 1983. Mem. Nat. Agrl. Mktg. Assn., Buckmasters Club (Ala.), U. Mo. Alumni Assn. (Calif.), Alpha Gamma Rho (v.p. 1981-83). Republican. Home: 7975 Wapiti Pl Citrus Heights CA 95610 Office: The Hartford Ins Group 9300 Tech Center Dr Sacramento CA 95851

BUNDESEN, FAYE STIMERS, teacher, investment/management company owner; b. Cedarville, Calif., Sept. 16, 1932; d. Floyd Walker and Ermina Elizabeth (Roberts) Stimers; m. Allen Eugene Bundesen, Dec. 27, 1972; children—William, David, Edward Silvius; Ted, Eric Bundesen. B.A., Calif. State U.-Sacramento, 1955; M.A., Calif. State U.-San Jose, 1972. Licensed real estate broker, Calif. Elem. sch. tchr. San Francisco Pub. Schs., 1955-60; elem. and jr. high sch. tchr., lang. arts specialist Sunnyvale (Calif.) Schs., 1978-83; cons. Santa Clara County Office of Edn. and Sunnyvale Sch. Dist., 1983-86; v.p. Bundesen Enterprises, Elk Grove, Calif., 1975-81, pres., 1981—. Bd. dirs. Sunnyvale Sch. Employees' Credit Union, 1983-86, v.p., 1984-86; mem. City of San Jose Tenant/Landlord Hearing Com., 1983-86, v.p., 1984-85. Mem. Assn. Supervision and Curriculum Devel., Calif. Scholarship Fedn. (life), AAUW, Tri-County Apartment Assn., Calif. Apartment Assn., Nat. Apartment Assn., Santa Clara County Real Estate Bd., Calif. Assn. Realtors, Nat. Assn. Realtors, Sacramento Assn. Realtors. Presbyterian. Office: PO Box 2006 Elk Grove CA 95759-2006

BUNDSCHUH, MARJORIE LU, clinical laboratory technologist, chemist; b. Columbus, Ohio, July 27, 1952; d. Norman and Norma Jean (Stetelman)

Gurevitz; m. David Alan Clayman, June 5, 1977 (div. June 1981); m. John Phillip Bundschuh, May 25, 1986. Student, Ohio U., 1970-72; BS, U. Cin., 1976; postgrad., Cen. Mich. U., 1978, Calif. Coll. Arts and Crafts, 1981-82. Registered med. technologist Am. Soc. Clin. Pathologists; lic. clin. lab. technologist, Calif. Cell biology and immunology rsch. asst. Shriner's Burn Inst., Cin., 1974-75; spl chemistry lab. technician Doctor's Hosp. North, Columbus, Ohio, 1975, hematology med. technologist, 1977; chemistry and microbiology med. technologist Children's Med. Ctr., Dayton, Ohio, 1977-81; microbiology and chemistry clin. lab. asst. U. Calif. San Francisco Gen. Hosp., 1982-86, chemistry clin. lab. technologist, 1987—; sales cons. computer software packages Amron Systems, Columbus and San Francisco, 1981-82. Co-chmn. fundraising Women's Twig of Children's Med. Ctr., Dayton, 1980; vol. youth at risk program Breakthrough Found., San Francisco, 1983, fin. sponsor 1986—, Holiday Project, San Francisco, 1983-84; chpt. pres. Women's Am. ORT, Dayton, 1979-80; fin. family sponsor The Hunger Project, San Francisco, 1983—; active San Francisco Mus. Modern Art. Mem. Am. Assn. Clin. Chemistry, Am. Assn. for Med. Tech., Am. Assn. for Clin. Pathology (assoc.), Iota Sigma Pi. Jewish. Home: 730 Bay Rd Mill Valley CA 94941 Office: San Francisco Gen Hosp U Calif Clin Labs 1001 Potrero St Rm 2M San Francisco CA 94110

BUNKER, JOHN BIRKBECK, sugar company executive; b. Yonkers, N.Y., Mar. 28, 1926; s. Ellsworth and Harriet (Butler) B.; m. Emma Cadwalader, Feb. 27, 1954; children: Emma, Jeanie, Harriet, John C., Lambert C. BA, Yale U., 1950. With Nat. Sugar Refining Co., 1953-62; pres. Gt. Western Sugar Co., Denver, 1966; pres. Holly Sugar Co., Colorado Springs, Colo., 1967-81, chmn., 1971-81, chief exec. officer, 1971-81; pres., chief exec. officer Calif. and Hawaiian Sugar Co., San Francisco, 1981-86; bd. dirs., mem. exec. com., past chmn. The Sugar Assn., Inc., Washington; bd. dirs., mem. exec. com. World Sugar Research Orgn., London. Bd. dirs. Bay Area Council, San Francisco, World Affairs Council, San Francisco, Japan Soc. of No. Calif., World Affairs Council of Calif.; adv. bd. Leavey Sch. Bus. and Adminstrn., Santa Clara U.; trustee, mem. exec. com. Colo. Coll.; trustee Asia Found. Served to 1st lt. inf., AUS, 1951-52. Office: Calif & Hawaiian Sugar Co PO Box 4126 Concord CA 94524-4126

BUNN, CHARLES NIXON, strategic business planning consultant; b. Springfield, Ill., Feb. 8, 1926; s. Joseph Forman and Helen Anna Frieda (Link) B.; student U. Ill., 1943-44; BS in Engring., U.S. Mil. Acad., 1949; MBA, Xavier U., Cin., 1958; m. Cecine Cole, Dec. 26, 1951 (div. 1987); children: Sisene, Charles; m. Marjorie Fitzmaurice, Apr. 5, 1988. Flight test engr. Gen. Electric Co., Cin., also Edwards AFB, Calif., 1953-59; sr. missile test engr., space systems div. Lockheed Aircraft Corp., USAF Satellite Test Center, Sunnyvale, Calif., 1959-60, 63-70, economist, advanced planning dept., 1961-63; economic and long-range planning cons., Los Altos, Calif., 1970-73; head systems planning, economist, strategic bus. planning, Western Regional hdqrs. U.S. Postal Service, San Bruno, Calif., 1973-78; strategic bus. planning cons., investment analysis cons., 1978-79; strategic bus. planning Advanced Reactor Systems dept. Gen. Electric Co., Sunnyvale, Calif., 1979-84; strategic planning cons., 1984—. Served with inf. paratroops U.S. Army, 1944-45, with inf. and rangers, 1949-53; Korea. Decorated Battle Star (5). Mem. Nat. Assn. Bus. Economists, World Future Soc., Sigma Nu. Episcopalian. Home and Office: 222 Incline Way San Jose CA 95139

BUNN, DOROTHY IRONS, court reporter; b. Trinidad, Colo., Apr. 30, 1948; d. Russell and Pauline Anna (Langowski) Irons; m. Peter Lynn Bunn; children: Kristy Lynn, Wade Allen, Russell Ahearn. Student No. Va. Community Coll., 1970-71, U. Va., Fairfax, 1971-72. Registered profl. reporter; cert. shorthand reporter. Pres., chief exec. officer Ahearn Ltd., Springfield, Va., 1970-81, Bunn & Assocs., Glenrock, Wyo., 1981— ; asst. mgr. Bixby Hereford Co., Glenrock, 1981—. Del., White House Conf. on Small Bus., Washington, 1986. Mem. NAFE, Am. Indian Soc., Nat. Shorthand Reporters Assn., Wyo. Shorthand Reporters Assn. (chmn. com. 1984—), Nat. Fedn. Ind. Businesses, Nat. Assn. Legal Secs., Nat. Fedn. Bus. and Profl. Women, Nat. Assn. Legal Secs. Internat. Avocations: art, music. Home: PO Box 1602 Bixby Hereford Co Glenrock WY 82637 Office: Bunn & Assocs 81 Bisby Rd Glenrock WY 82637

BUNN, JAMES LEE, state senator; b. McMinnville, Oreg., Dec. 12, 1956; s. Benjamin Adam and Viola Mae (Fulgham) B.; m. Cindy Lou Mishler, Sept. 9, 1978; children: James Jr., Matthew, Phillip, Malachi. AA, Chemeketa Community Coll., Salem, Oreg., 1977; BA in Biology, N.W. Nazarene Coll., Nampa, Idaho, 1979. Farmer Oreg.; senator from dist. 15 Oreg. State Senate, 1987—; exec. dir. Oreg. Rep. Party. With Oreg. N.G. Res. Mem. Nazarene Ch. Home: 8157 SW Riverbend Rd McMinnville OR 97128 Office: Office of State Senate State Capitol Salem OR 97310

BUNN, WILLIAM BERNICE, III, physician, lawyer, epidemiologist; b. Raleigh, N.C., June 28, 1952; s. William Bernice Jr. and Clara Eva (Ray) B.; m. Shirley Welch, July 31, 1982; 1 child, Asheley Howell. AB, Duke U., 1974, MD, JD, 1979; MPH, U. N.C., 1983. Diplomate Am. Bd. Internal Medicine. Intern, then resident in internal medicine Duke U. Med. Ctr., 1981-83, fellow in occupational medicine dept. community medicine, 1983; asst. prof. Sch. of Medicine Duke U., Durham, N.C., 1984-86, dir. rsch. in occupational medicine Sch. of Medicine, 1985-86; dir. environ. affairs and occupational health Bristol Myers Co., Wallingford, Conn., 1986-87, sr. dir. occupational health and environ. affairs, 1987-88; asst. clin. prof. Yale U., New Haven, 1986—; corp. med. dir. Manville Sales Corp., Denver, 1988, v.p., corp. med. dir., 1988-89, sr. dir. for health safety and environ., v.p., 1989—; cons., author, co-editor Pfizor Corp., N.Y.C., 1984-87. Author: (with others) Effects of Exposure to Toxic Cases, 1986; author, editor: Poisoning, 1986. Bd. dirs. Colo. Safety Assn., Denver, 1988—, Gaylord Hosp., Wallingford, 1987-88, Meriden-Wallingford Hosp., 1986-88. NIOSH scholar, 1980; NIH fellow, 1982-83, Nat. Inst. Occupational Safety and Health fellow, 1983-84. Fellow Am. Occupational Medicine Assn. (co-chmn. acad. affairs com. and pubs. com. Chgo. chpt. 1985-88, nat. affairs com. 1985-86), Am. Acad. Occupational Medicine; mem. AMA, Am. Pub. Health Assn., ACP, Occupationa Medicine Assn. of Conn. (sec., pres.-elect Conn. chpt. 1986-88), Nat. Inst. Environ. Health (com. mem.), Phi Beta Kappa, Phi Eta Sigma. Home: 72 N Ranch Rd Littleton CO 80127 Office: Manville Corp 717 17th St Denver CO 80202

BUNNELL, RON DALE, personnel executive; b. Ft. Collins, Colo., July 25, 1945; s. Delbert Ashbey Bunnell and Wanda M. (Rank) Palmer; m. Donna Mae Schulze, June 25, 1966; children: Dale, Carl. AA, Aims Community Coll., 1970; BA, U. No. Colo., 1972, MBA, 1978. Tchr., coach Sch. Dist. RE-5J, Johnstown, Colo., 1972-77; mgr. employee relations ARCO Coal Co., Wright, Wyo., 1978-84; mgr. employee relations and safety Wycon Chem. Co., Cheyenne, Wyo., 1984-85; v.p. human resources First Wyo. Bancorp., Cheyenne, 1985-86; pres. Dunhill Personnel Cheyenne, Inc., 1986—. Author: To the Point - A View of Proactive Supervision, 1986. Chmn. bd. adjustments Town of Johnstown, 1975-78; pres. Johnstown/Milliken Edn. Assn., 1975-76; chmn. Wright Day Com., 1983; chmn. Rep. precinct, Johnstown, 1974-78; dir. Wyo. Safety Council, Cheyenne, 1984-86. Served as sgt. USAF, 1964-68. Mem. Wyo. Hist. Soc., Cheyenne Leads (v.p. 1987-88). Methodist. Lodge: Lions (v.p. 1982-84). Office: Dunhill Pers Cheyenne Inc 6106 Yellowstone Rd Ste B Cheyenne WY 82009

BURAS, NATHAN, hydrology and water resources educator; b. Barlad, Romania, Aug. 23, 1921; came to U.S., 1947; s. Boris and Ethel (Weiser) B.; m. Netty Stivel, Apr. 13, 1951; 1 child, Nir H. BS with highest honors, U. Calif., Berkeley, 1949; MS, Technion, Haifa, Israel, 1957; PhD, UCLA, 1962. Registered profl. engr., Israel. Prof. hydrology and water resources Technion, 1962-80, dean, 1966-68; vis. prof. Stanford (Calif.) U., 1976-81; prof., head of dept. hydrology and water resources U. Ariz., Tucson, 1981—; cons. Tahal, Ltd., Tel Aviv, 1963-73, World Bank, Washington, 1972-76, 79-81. Author: Scientific Allocation of Water Resources, 1972; editor: Control of Water Resources Systems, 1976. Mem. Israel-Mex. Mixed Commn. on Sci. Cooperation, 1976, So. Ariz. Water Resource Assn., 1982—. Named Laureat du Congres, Internat. Assn. Agrl. Engring., 1964; recipient Cert. of Appreciation, USDA., 1970. Fellow Ariz.-Nev. Acad. Sci; mem. ASCE (life), Am. Geophys. Union, Am. Water Resources Assn. (charter). Jewish. Home: 5541 Circulo Terra Tucson AZ 85715 Office: U Ariz Dept Hydrology and Water Resources Tucson AZ 85721

BURBANK, RANDY LEE, petroleum company executive; b. Idaho Falls, Idaho, Apr. 18, 1951; s. Chester Austin and Norma (Nielsen) B.; m. Kris L. Ladson, Apr. 25, 1974; children: Nathan Z., Erin Rose. BS in Biology, Idaho State U., 1973. Lab. technician water pollution control City of Idaho Falls, 1974; water quality supr. City of Boise Water Pollution Control, Idaho, 1974-76; outside sales rep. V.W.R. Sci. div. Univar, Salt Lake City, 1977, Paul Roberts Co., Twin Falls, Idaho, 1977-80; store mgr. Paul Roberts Co., Pocatello, Idaho, 1980-82; indsl. div. mgr. Leonard Petroleum Equipment, Twin Falls, Idaho, 1982—. Author computer program Flexnote, 1988. Home: 3192 N 3500 East Kimberly ID 83341 Office: Leonard Petroleum Equipment PO Box 818 Twin Falls ID 83301

BURBIDGE, GEOFFREY, astrophysicist, educator; b. Chipping Norton, Oxon, Eng., Sept. 24, 1925; s. Leslie and Eveline Burbidge; m. Margaret Peachey, 1948; 1 dau. B.Sc. with spl. honors in Physics, Bristol U., 1946; Ph.D., U. Coll., London, 1951. Asst. lectr. U. Coll., London, 1950-51; Agassiz fellow Harvard, 1951-52; research fellow U. Chgo., 1952-53, Cavendish Lab., Cambridge, Eng., 1953-55; Carnegie fellow Mt. Wilson and Palomar Obs., Calif. Inst. Tech., 1955-57; asst. prof. dept. astronomy U. Chgo., 1957-58, assoc. prof., 1958-62; assoc. prof. U. Calif. San Diego, La Jolla, 1962-63; prof. physics U. Calif. San Diego, 1963-83, 88—; dir. Kitt Peak Nat. Obs., Tucson, 1978-84; Phillips vis. prof. Harvard U., 1968; bd. dirs. Associated Univs. Research in Astronomy, 1971-74; trustee Associated Univs., Inc., 1973-82. Author: (with Margaret Burbidge) Quasi-Stellar Objects, 1967; editor Ann. Rev. Astronomy and Astrophysics, 1973—; contbr. articles to sci. jours. Fellow Royal Soc. London, Am. Acad. Arts and Scis., Royal Astron. Soc., Am. Phys. Soc.; mem. Am. Astron. Soc., Internat. Astron. Union, Astron. Soc. of Pacific (pres. 1974-76). Office: U Calif-San Diego Ctr for Astrophysics Space Scis C-011 La Jolla CA 92093

BURCH, MARY LOU, housing advocate, executive; b. Billings, Mont., Apr. 4, 1930; d. Forrest Scott Sr. and Mary Edna (Hinshaw) Chilcott; m. J. Sheldon Robinson, June 18, 1949 (div. 1956); m. G. Howard Burch, Nov. 27, 1957 (div. 1984); children: Julie Lynne Scully, Donna Eileen Burch, Carol Marie Kimball, Alan Robert Burch. AA, Grant TEch. Coll., Sacremento, 1949; AB, Sacremento State Coll., 1955; student, U. Alaska, 1976-78, Santa Rosa (Calif.) Jr. Coll., 1987. Diagnostic tchr. Calif. Youth Authority, Perkins, 1955-57; com. chmn. on pub. info. Sequoia Union High Sch. Dist., So. San Mateo County, Calif., 1970-72; exec. dir. Presbyn. Hospitality House, Fairbanks, Alaska, 1979-80; realtor Century 21 Smith/Ring, Renton, Wash., 1980-81; cons. Fairbanks, Alaska, 1981-84; exec. dir. Habitat for Humanity of Sonoma County, Santa Rosa, Calif., 1986-89, Affordable Housing Assoc., Santa Rosa, Calif., 1989—; bd. dirs. Hosp. Chaplainey Svcs, Santa Rosa, Villa Los Alamos Homeowners Assn.; cons. Access Alaska, Anchorage, 1983; contractor Alaka Siding, Fairbanks, 1982-83. Named vol. of the year, Hosp. Chaplaincy Svcs., 1987. Democrat. United Ch. of Christ. Home: 238 Los Alamos Rd Santa Rosa CA 95409 Office: 3430 Mendocino Ave Santa Rosa CA 95401

BURCHAM, JAY MARTIN, military officer; b. Boulder, Colo., Dec. 7, 1953; s. Jay Filmore and Shirley Louise (Martin) B.; m. Judith Gale Duncan, Oct. 10, 1984. BA, U. Santa Clara, 1976. Commd. U.S. Army, 1976, advanced through grades to major; armor platoon leader U.S. Army, Republic of Korea, 1976-78; bn. motor officer U.S. Army, Fort Carson, Colo., 1978-79, bn. S-3 air, 1979-80, G-3 tng. officer, 1980-81; asst. S-3, tng. U.S. Army, Nuremberg, Fed. Republic of Germany, 1981-83; co. comdr. U.S. Army, Amberg, Fed. Republic of Germany, 1983-85; dir. plans, tng., security U.S. Army, Yakima, Wash., 1985-87; bn. S-3 U.S. Army, Fort Lewis, Wash., 1987-88, bn. exec. officer, 1988-89, chief G-3 tng., 1989—. Decorated Ehrennadel, West German Army, Meritorious Svc. medal. Mem. U.S. Armor Assn., Assn. U.S. Army, 2d Cavalry Assn., Octofoil Assn., Pacific NW Airedale Club. Republican. Roman Catholic. Home: 9608 166 St East Puyallup WA 98373-2063

BURCHESS, ARNOLD A., artist, sculptor, educator; b. Chgo., June 7, 1912; s. Herman Burchess and Annetta Rossiny; m. Aline Thistlethwaite; 1 child, Robert. B.S.S., CCNY, 1934; student George W. Eggers, Robert Garrison. Asst. 3 stone bas-reliefs walls of Radio City, N.Y.C, 1935; lectr./demonstrator Shapes in Clay, Met. Mus. Art, N.Y.C., 1936; chmn. dept. fine art Fashion Inst. Tech., N.Y.C., 1963-73; instr. art Saddleback Coll. (Calif.), 1980-83; vis. prof. sculpture Bowdoin Coll., Maine, 1977. One-man shows include: Van Dimant Gallery, Southampton, N.Y., 1957, Mus. Modern Art, N.Y.C., 1959, Maine Art Gallery, Wiscasset, 1975, Walker Art Mus., Brunswick, Maine, 1978; exhibited in group shows: Riverside Mus., 1955, G.W.V. Smith Mus., Springfield, Mass., 1955, Contemporary Art Gallery, 1955, Birmingham Mus. Art, 1955, Calif. Watercolor Soc., 1955, Delgrado Mus. Art, 1957, Westchester Art Ctr., 1958, U.S. Nat. Mus., 1958, N.Y. City Ctr., 1958, Long Beach Mcpl. Art Ctr. (Calif.), 1957, Ala. Poly. Coll., 1957, Jacksonville Mus. Art (Fla.), 1957, Lauren Rogers Mus. Art, Laurel, Miss., 1957, Challis Gallery, Laguna Beach, Calif., 1983; executed portrait bust in bronze of Edmund Muskie, State Capitol, Augusta, Maine, 1972. Author: Understanding the Human Form, 1981. Featured water colorist Am.-Artist, 1959, 100 Watercolor Techniques, Watson-Guptill, 1968. Mem. Am. Watercolor Soc., Audubon Artists, Ala. Watercolor Soc., Springfield Art League, Calif. Watercolor Soc., New Orleans. Address: 5299 Cantante Laguna Hills CA 92653

BURDETT, JOSEPH WILLIAM, lawyer; b. Peoria, Ill., Oct. 23, 1936; s. Joseph L. and Elizabeth (Williams) B.; m. Mary Jean Pasco, June 15, 1958; children: Eric William, Jennifer Lynn. BS in Acctg., Bradley U., Peoria, 1957; MS in Fin., U. Utah, 1962; JD, Stanford U., 1965. Bar: Calif.; CPA, Calif. Acct. Price Waterhouse, Chgo. and Peoria, 1957-59; ptnr. Kindel & Anderson, L.A., 1965—; bd. dirs. Sunset Post, Inc., L.A., 1981—, Sunset Teleprodn. Ctr., L.A., 1984—; lectr. in field. Contbr. articles to profl. jours. Bd. dirs. Jonathan Art Found., L.A., 1986—; past bd. dirs. Easter Seal Soc., Nat. Assn. People with Disabilities. Capt. USAF, 1959-62. Recipient Jonathan Trumbull award, Jonathan Club, 1987. Mem. ABA, Calif. Bar Assn., L.A. Bar Assn., Beverly Hills Bar Assn., AICPA's, Calif. Soc. CPA's, Jonathan Club (pres. 1981-82, bd. dirs. 1979-82). Office: Kindel & Anderson 555 S Flower St 29th Fl Los Angeles CA 90071

BURDI, GIANFRANCO, psychiatrist; b. Sora, Italy, Oct. 11, 1949; came to U.S., 1981; s. Giovanni and Maria (Vettraino) B. BS, Liceo Scientifico G. Carducci, Cassino, Italy, 1967; postgrad., Universita Degli, Siena, Italy, 1967-73; MD, Universita Deli, Milano, Italy, 1974; cert. orthopaedic surg., Milano U., 1979. Diplomate Am. Bd. Psychiatry. Pvt. practice Milan, Italy, 1975-81; clin. pathologist R.I. Hosp., Providence, 1982-83; psychiatrist Norwich (Conn.) Hosp., 1983-85, New Eng. Med. Ctr., Tufts U., Boston, 1985-86; clin. psychiatrist Bedford (N.H.) Counseling, 1986-88, Ctr. for Life Mgmt., Salem, N.H., 1986-88; pvt. practice Cerritos and Costa Mesa, Calif., 1988—. Mem. Am. Psychiatric Assn., AMA, Nat. Alliance Mentally Ill, Ordine dei Medici di Milano. Office: 2723 W Coast Hwy Newport Beach CA 92663

BURDICK, JOHN RICHARD, computer company executive; b. Mt. Vernon, Ohio, July 16, 1957; s. Paul Burnell and Bille Louise (Kelly) B.; m. Sheryl Marie Little, Nov. 29, 1981; 1 child, Johnna Marie. Student, So. Coll., Collegedale, Tenn., 1977. Gen. mgr. Bus. Micro Products, Glenwood Springs, Colo., 1980-82; mgr. Mountain Data Systems, Aspen, Colo., 1982-83; owner, founder Burdick Computer, Aspen, Colo., 1983--. Republican. Adventist. Home: PO Box 2934 Aspen CO 81612 Office: Burdick Computer 315 E Hyman Ave Aspen CO 81611-1946

BUREAU, ANGELA MARY, publishing executive; b. Rochester, Minn., Dec. 3, 1939; d. Frank Theodore and Angela Maria (Stachowiak) Kubista; m. John Frederick Bureau, Dec. 26, 1964; children: Angela Mary, John Frederick, Julie Ann, David Joseph, Ann Louise, Theresa Marie. BA, Coll. St. Catherine, 1960; postgrad., Cath. U. Am., 1962, U. Minn., 1964. Pres. Theo's Books, St. Paul, 1982—; gen. comdr. God's Army, St. Paul, 1981—; guest nat. cable TV, Birmingham, Ala., 1987-88; instr. seminars on holiness, Minn., Wis. Author: Nine Keys to Sanctity, 1976; editor God's Army News, 1981—. Home and Office: 21 Red Fox Rd Saint Paul MN 55127-0632

BURG, GARY G., vocational expert; b. L.A., Aug. 24, 1956; s. George J. and Kathleen A. (Doheny) B.; m. Diane Teresa Giliotti, Aug. 5, 1978; children: Sean Douglas, Anthony Christian. BA in Psychology, Calif. State U., Los Angeles, MS in Rehab. Counseling. Diplomate Am. Bd. Vocat. Experts; cert. ins. rehab. specialist. Counselor East Valley Community Health Ctr., West Covina, Calif.; evaluation and tng. counselor Goodwill Industries So. Calif., L.A.; vocat. counselor, evaluator PAR Services, Santa Fe Spring, Calif.; exec. dir. West Mountain Community Services, Crestline, Calif.; vocat. evaluator, mgr. Anfuso Work Evaluation Ctr. Inc., Pasadena, Calif.; owner, dir. Testing, Evaluation and Mgmt., El Monte, Upland and Riverside, Calif.; forensic vocat. expert Associated Vocat. Experts, Inc., L.A., Riverside, Las Vegas and Anchorage; lectr. in field. bd. dirs. Crestline Area Preschool, Contact the Helpline, San Bernardino, Calif., East Valley Community Health Ctr., South Hills Little League, West Covina, Assn. Retarded Citizens, San Gabriel Valley, Calif.; active West End Industry Edn. Coordination Counsel, San Bernardino County. Mem. Calif. Assn. Rehab. Profl., Inland Empire Rehab. Group, Nat. Rehab. Assn., Nat. Assn. Rehab. Profl. Pvt. Sector, Vocat. Evaluators and Work Adjustment Assn. (bd. dirs. 1987-88, pres. 1989). Office: Testing Evaluation and Mgmt 11100 Valley Blvd Ste 218 El Monte CA 91731

BURG, GERALD WILLIAM, religious organization administrator; b. Pitts., Oct. 16, 1923; s. Julius Samuel and Anna (Shapiro) B.; student Walsh Inst., 1940-43; m. Flavia Kafton, Aug. 12, 1945; children—Cindy, Melinda, Andrew. Engring. rep. U.S. Rubber Co., 1943-45; adminstr. Beverly Hills (Calif.) B'nai B'rith, 1945-52, Univ. Synagogue, Brentwood, 1952-55; exec. dir. Wilshire Blvd. Temple, Los Angeles, 1956-80; mgmt. and fin. cons., 1980-85; adminstr. Sinai Temple, 1985—. Mem. Jewish relations com. Los Angeles council Boy Scouts Am., 1959-85; mem. Mayor's Adv. Com. on Community Activities, Los Angeles, 1963-73; chmn. Crime Prevention Fifth Councilmanic Dist., Los Angeles, 1968-73. Bd. dirs. McCobb Home for Boys, Los Angeles Psychiat. Service, Maple Ctr. for Crises Intervention, Save a Heart Found., Didi Hirsch Community Mental Health Services, pres., 1975-77; bd. dirs., chmn. finances, chmn. adminstrv. com. Community Care and Devel. Services, 1975—. Mem. Nat. (bd. dir., pres. 1975-77), Western (pres. 1969-71, bd. dirs.), So. Calif. (pres. 1958-60) assns. temple adminstrs., NCCJ (bd. dirs. brotherhood anytown 1966-82), Los Angeles Jewish Communal Execs. (dir.). Mem. B'nai B'rith (youth dir. 1945-82, Akiba award 1950, Beverly Hills pres. 1953-54). Club: Sertoma (v.p. 1973-82). Home: 5115 Kester Ave #202 Sherman Oaks CA 91403 Office: Sinai Temple 10400 Wilshire Blvd Los Angeles CA 90024

BURGESON, NICHOLAS RUDOLPH, healthcare facility executive; b. Portland, Oreg., July 4, 1943; s. Rudolph Benjamin and Grace Ruth (Nimlos) B.; m. Donna Irene MacGlashan, Oct. 18, 1964; children: Tina Lynn, Robert Gene. AS in Nursing Sci., Pacific Union Coll., 1964; BS in Commerce, Golden Gate U., 1977; MBA in Mgmt., U. Beverly Hills, 1981. RN, Calif.; lic. nursing home adminstr. Staff nurse Napa (Calif.) State Hosp., 1964-68, nursing coord., 1968-70, assist to med. dir., 1970-71; asst. chief hosp. svc. sect. Calif. Dept. of Health, Sacramento, 1971-77; adminstr. Met. State Hosp., Norwalk, Calif., 1977-81; assoc. adminstr. Loma Linda (Calif.) Community Hosp., 1981-82; mgr., psychiat. hosp. devel. Am. Med. Internat., Inc., Beverly Hills, Calif., 1983-84; pres. NRB & Assocs., San Luis Obispo, Calif., 1982—; dir. info. resources Atascadero (Calif.) State Hosp., 1984—. Appeared in TV Documentary Cry Help, 1970. With U.S. Army, 1966-68. Mem. Calif. Assn. Mgmt. (sec. 1975, pres. 1976-77), Calif. Health Review (editorial bd. dirs. 1981-83), Am. Coll. of Healthcare Execs., Forensic Mental Health Assn. Calif. (bd. dirs. 1988—), U.S. Judo Assn. (Gold life mem.). Republican. Home: PO Box 6236 Los Osos CA 93412 Office: Atascadero State Hosp PO Box 7001 Atascadero CA 93423-7001

BURGESS, JASON MCKINLEY, engineering company executive; b. Pendleton, Oreg., July 21, 1941; s. Lloyd Albert and Dorothy Charolette (Sellars) B.; m. Janet Ann Bower, June 14, 1964; children: Blake Christopher, Erica Ann. BSCE, U. Denver, 1965. Registered profl. engr., Ariz., Kans.; lic. land surveyor, Ariz. Jr. engr. Howard, Needles, Tammen and Bergendoff, Overland Park, Kans., 1965-68; office engr. Burgess Constrn. Co., Fairbanks, Alaska, 1968-69; project engr. Bucher & Willis, Kansas City, Mo., 1969-71; project engr., asst. v.p., nat. dir. land devel. Henningson Durham & Richardson, Phoenix, 1971-87; pres. Burgess & Robson Engring., Inc., Sun Lakes, Ariz., 1987—; bd. dirs. Burgess & Robson, Sun Lakes, Ariz. Cubmaster Boy Scouts Am., Phoenix, 1980-82. Named 1986 Engr. of Yr., HDR Infrastructure. Mem. ASCE, Am. Cons. Engrs. Assn. Republican. Presbyterian. Office: B & R Engring Inc 25612 E J Robson Blvd Sun Lakes AZ 85248

BURGESS, JOSEPH WESLEY, metallurgical engineer, photographer; b. St. Louis, Nov. 27, 1910; s. Joseph Francis and Amanda (Woodrome) B.; BS in Civil Engring., Washington U., 1932; m. Dorothea Ines Nelson, Mar. 5, 1941; children: Joseph Wesley, Sarah Jane. Trainee, Shell Pipe Line Corp., Kilgore, Tex., 1933-35, asst. div. supt., Tex., N.Mex., St. Louis, 1935-39; mgr. products pipe line dept. Shell Oil Co., N.Y.C., 1939-41; chief engr., gen. supt. Am. Zinc Co. of Ill., Dumas, Tex., 1941-59; gen. mgr. constrn. Uranium Reduction Co., Salt Lake City, Moab, Utah, 1955-59; chief engr. Am. Zinc Co., St. Louis, 1959-71; mgr. project engring. Fluor Utah, Inc., San Mateo, Calif. 1971-73, v.p. engring., 1973, v.p. project mgmt., 1974-76; ret., 1976; cons., 1976—, photographer, 1977—; photographs exhibited in one-man shows including: San Jose (Calif.) Mus. Art, 1980, Stanford U. Faculty Club, Palo Alto, Calif., 1981; group shows include: Olive Hyde Art Gallery, Fremont, Calif., 1977, Atkinson Art Gallery, Santa Barbara, Calif., 1978, Tower Art Gallery, Berkeley, Calif., 1979, Internat. Exhbn. of Photography, Adelaide, Australia, 1980, Westwood Arts Nat. Photog. Exhbn., L.A., 1980, others. Registered profl. engr., Tex. Mem. Am. Inst. Mining, Metall. and Petroleum Engrs., Nat., Calif. socs. profl. engrs., Mo. Hist. Soc., Calif. Hist. Soc., Am. Rose Soc., Sigma Xi, Tau Beta Pi. Coauthor: European Zinc Smelters, 1964; contbr. articles to profl. jours. Home: 1178 Hamilton Ave Palo Alto CA 94301

BURGESS, MICHAEL, library science educator, publisher; b. Fukuoka, Kyushu, Japan, Feb. 11, 1948; came to U.S., 1949; s. Roy Walter and Betty Jane (Kapel) B.; m. Mary Alice Wickizer, Oct. 15, 1976; stepchildren: Richard Albert Rogers, Mary Louise Reynells. AB with honors, Gonzaga U., 1969; MS In Library Sci., U. So. Calif., 1970. Periodicals librarian Calif. State U.-San Bernardino, 1970-81, chief cataloger, 1981—, prof., 1986—; editor Newcastle Pub. Co., North Hollywood, Calif., 1971—, publisher Borgo Press, San Bernardino, 1975—; adv. editor Arno Press, N.Y.C., 1975-78. Author 50 books, including: Cumulative Paperback Index, 1973, Things to Come, 1977, Science Fiction and Fantasy Literature, 1979, Tempest in a Teapot, 1984, Lords Temporal & Lords Spiritual, 1985, Futurevisions, 1985, Contemporary Science Fiction & Fantasy Authors III, 1988, Dictionary of Arms Control Disarmament and Military Security, 1989; editor 15 scholarly series, including Milford Series: Popular Writers of Today (40 vols.), Science Fiction (63 vols.), Stokvis Studies in Historical Chronology and Thought (10 vols.), editor 6 reprint series, 2 jours.; author over 100 articles. Recipient MPPP award, 1987; named Title II fellow U. So. Calif., 1969-70. Mem. NEA, AAUP, Calif. Tchrs. Assn., Kent Hist. Soc., Sci. Fiction Writers Am., Calif. Faculty Assn. (mem. state-wide librarians task force 1986—, editor newsletter 1987—), Sci. Fiction Research Assn., Horror Writers Am. Office: Borgo Press PO Box 2845 San Bernardino CA 92406 Mailing: Calif State U Libr 5500 University Pkwy San Bernardino CA 92406

BURGESS, MICHAEL ROBERT, mechanical engineer; b. Lansing, Mich., Oct. 27, 1959; s. Robert D. and Darlene J. (Dempsey) B. BS in Engring., Mich. State U., 1982; postgrad., U. Colo., Colo. Springs, 1988—. Design enr. Vemeer Sales and Svcs., Castleton-on-the-Hudson, N.Y., 1982-83; draftsman, engr. Skyline Products, Colorado Springs, Colo., 1983-84; ops. mgr. Skyline Electronics, Colorado Springs, 1984—. Recipient Evans Scholarsip Western Golf Assn. Am., 1977. Mem. Am. Soc. Agr. Engrs., Surface Mount Tech. Assn. (pres. local chpt. 1989). Soc. Mfg. Engrs., YMCA. Republican. Roman Catholic. Office: Skyline Electronics Inc 2865 Delta Dr Colorado Springs CO 80910

BURGESS, ROBERT CHARLES, mechanical engineer; b. Ann Arbor, Mich., Apr. 8, 1959; s. Charles Harry and Mary Ann (Titus) B. BS in Mech. Engring., U. Mich., 1981. Field engr. Bechtel Power Corp., Midland, Mich., 1981-84; mech. designer Di Clemente-Siegel Engring, Southfield, Mich., 1984; design engr. Hoyem-Basso Assocs., Inc., Troy, Mich., 1984-85; asst. project mgr. Hale Engring. Corp., Livonia, Mich., 1985-86; mech. engr. Brown and Caldwell Cons. Engrs., Pleasant Hill, Calif., 1986—, specifications writer, 1987—. Named Key Man Chelsea Area Jaycees, 1985. Mem. ASME (assoc.), U. Mich. Alumni Assn., Nat. Eagle Scout Assn., KC. Home: 1525 E Cheryl Dr Apt 2144 Phoenix AZ 85020 Office: Brown & Caldwell Cons Engrs 3480 Buskirk Ave Pleasant Hill CA 94523

BURGESS, SHERWOOD DENN, academic administrator, writer; b. Hartford, Conn., June 28, 1918; s. Denn Maltby and Ethel Irene (Bragg) B.; m. Constance Rose Sousa, Nov. 28, 1944; children: Dennise Constance, Pamela Marie. AB, U. Calif., Berkeley, 1940, MA, 1948; postgrad., Pan Am. Fellow, 1948-52. Cert. jr. coll. tchr., Calif. Mdse. trainee Capwell's Dept. Store, Oakland, Calif., 1946; proprietor Apparel Shop, Oakland, 1947-49; instr. history Lincoln U., Oakland and San Francisco, 1948-50, Reedley Jr. Coll., Reedley, Calif., 1952-55; tchr. Oakland Pub. Schs., Oakland, 1956-57; asst.dir., instr. Heald Bus. Coll., Oakland, 1958-65, dir., 1966-68, v.p., 1968-84; writer, history Calif., 1948—; mgmt. tng. cons. Heald Bus. Coll., San Francisco, 1984-85. Author: Anthony Chabot, 1988; contbr. articles profl. jours. Bd. mem. Walnut Creek Historical Soc., 1985—; archivist Shadelands Ranch Museum, Walnut Creek, 1985—; mem. Contra Costa County Historical Soc., Pleasant Hill, Calif., 1980—, Calif. Historical Soc., 1970—. Capt. USAAF, 1941-46, PTO; Maj. AUS, 1950-52. Mem. U. Calif. Alumni Assn., Rotary (Oakland and Walnut Creek). Republican. Roman Catholic.

BURGESS, WILLIAM VANDER, education educator; b. Brownfield, Ill., June 5, 1934; s. Felix Siegfried and Verna Gertrude (Stockdale) B.; m. Mary Etta Layman, Aug. 20, 1961; children: Eric, Sara, Brian. BS, U. Ill., 1955; MS, So. Ill. U., 1962; PhD, U. Calif., Berkeley, 1970. Cert. nurseryman, Calif. Tchr. agr. Rosiclare (Ill.) High Sch., 1955-56, St. Francisville (Ill.) High Sch., 1960-63, Mt. Auburn (Ill.) High Sch., 1963-64; supt. schs. Mt. Auburn Unit Dist., 1964-65; prof. edn. U. San Francisco, 1968—, dir. secondary tchr. internship, 1971-73, dean summer session and spl. programs, 1973-75, chmn. dept. orgn. and leadership, 1984-86, chmn. faculty council Sch. Edn., 1978-80, 84-86; pres. William V. Burgess & Assocs., San Ramon, Calif., 1983—. Editor: Current Issues in Organizational Leadership, 1983; co-editor: Handbook of High Speed Machining Technology, 1985. Arbitrator Better Bus. Bur., San Francisco, 1983—; docent Strybing Arboretum, San Francisco, 1982—. Served with U.S. Army, 1956-59. Grantee NSF, Washington, 1978, Calif. Community Colls., Sacramento, 1979. Mem. Phi Delta Kappa (pres. 1985-86, Service award 1986). Democrat. Home: 9593 Davona Dr San Ramon CA 94583 Office: U San Francisco Sch Edn Ignatian Heights San Francisco CA 94117

BURGETT, DAVID A., project engineer; b. Orange, Calif., Dec. 20, 1953; s. Clifford and Marion (Anderson) B.; m. Alicia S. Edwards, Apr. 14, 1984; 1 child, Sean Alexander. ASME, Casper (Wyo.) Coll., 1980; BSME, Colo. State U., 1982. Mech. engr. Hercules Aeropspace Div., Magna, Utah, 1982-85; project engr. Teledyne McCormick Selph, Hollister, Calif., 1985--. Served with USN, 1971-75. Mem. Pi Tau Sigma, Tau Beta Pi, Phi Theta Kappa, Teledyne Mgmt. Club (pres. 1988-89). Office: Teledyne McCormick Selph PO Box 6 Hollister CA 95024-0006

BURGIN, LINDA JEAN, state agency administrator; b. Yakima, Wash., Feb. 19, 1949; d. Paul J. and Blanche Lois (Keep) Fortier; m. Alexander H. Burgin, May 31, 1969; children: Heather J., Brian H., Meredith A. BSBA with honors, Oreg. State U., 1984; postgrad., Lewis and Clark Coll., 1987, Portland State U., 1987. Sr. office clk. Bur. Census, U.S. Dept. Commerce, Salem, Oreg., 1980; survey supr. CH2M Hill, Corvallis, Oreg., 1981, City of Salem, 1981; mktg. cons. Survey Rsch. Ctr., Oreg. State U., Corvallis, 1982-84; quality control rsch. analyst Adult and Family Svcs., Oreg. Dept. Human Resources, Salem, 1984-88; program coord. Occupational Employment State Employment Div., 1986—. Loaned exec. United Way, Salem, 1988. Mem. Am. Mktg. Assn., AAUW (treas. Salem chpt. 1987-88, budget com. 1988—), Alpha Mu Alpha, Beta Gamma Sigma. Home: 5161 Zosel Ave S Salem OR 97306

BURK, JACK ANDREW, investment company executive; b. Springfield, Tenn., Mar. 19, 1935; s. Andrew Jackson and Elizabeth Ethelyne (Revels) B.; student Central Bible Inst., Springfield, Mo., 1953-54, So. Calif. Coll., Costa Mesa, 1955; student San Fernando Valley Coll., 1956; m. Alice Jean Jackson, Apr. 24, 1965; children—Teresa Lynn, Cheryl Ninette, Loren Dwayne. With Rocketdyne div. N. Am. Aviation Santa Susana Rocket Test sect., 1959-65; with Equity Funding Corp., 1965-73, area. v.p. So. Calif., Century City, 1970-71, v.p., resident mgr., Tarzana, Calif., 1972-73; founder, pres. Preferred Exec. Programs Inc., Woodland Hills, Calif., 1973-76; mem. adv. com. Am. Pacific Life Ins. Co., San Rafael, Calif., 1973-77; dir. bus. affairs Peoples Found., Fresno, Calif., 1977-84; gen. mgr. PF Communications Inc., Fresno, 1979-84; mgmt. cons. TV stas. and prodn. facilities, 1984-85; dist. sales mgr., Omega Video, Inc., Lawndale, Calif., 1985-86; major account rep. U.S. Sprint, 1987—. Mem. Nat. Assn. Securities Dealers, Nat. Assn. Life Underwriters, Internat. Assn. Fin. Planners. Republican. Home: 9391 E Ellery Clovis CA 93612

BURKDOLL, FRANCIS BURCH, aircraft design engineer, consultant; b. Monson, Calif., July 31, 1923; s. Benjamin Harrison and Betty Mae (Burch) B.; m. Barbara Langdon, June 1947 (dec. Oct. 1974); children: Wayne, Karen, Diana; m. Joan Ellen Williams. BSME, U. Calif., Berkeley, 1955. Research engr. Caterpillar Tractor Co., Peoria, Ill., 1955-56, FMC Corp., San Jose, Calif., 1956-57; research engr. Stanford Research Inst., Menlo Park, Calif., 1957-59, test mgr., 1959-61; engr. mgr. Explosive Tech. Inc., Fairfield, Calif., 1961-67, pres., 1967-86; pres. Burkdoll Design, Vacaville, Calif., 1986—. Inventor aircraft escape systems and devices. Mem. Am. Defense Preparedness Soc. (bd. dirs. 1982—). Republican. Home: 130 Wykoff Dr Vacaville CA 95088

BURKE, ARTHUR THOMAS, engineering consultant; b. Pueblo, Colo., Nov. 26, 1919; s. Daniel Michael and Naomi Edith (Brashear) B.; BS, U.S. Naval Acad., 1941; postgrad. UCLA; m. Regina Ahlgren Malone, June 15, 1972; children: Arthur Thomas, Craig Timothy, Laura Ahlgren, Scott Ahlgren. With USN Electronics Lab. Center, San Diego, 1947-72, sr. satellite communications cons., 1964-72, satellite communications engrng. cons., 1974—. Judge, San Diego Sci. Fair, 1960—. With USN, 1938-46; comdr. Res., ret. Recipient Superior Performance award USN Electronics Lab. Center, 1967. Mem. IEEE (mem. San Diego membership com. 1958-68), AAAS, San Diego Astronomy Assn., San Diego Computer Assn., Am. Radio Relay League. Patentee electronic bathythermograph. Home and Office: 4011 College Ave San Diego CA 92115

BURKE, CHRISTINE ELEANOR, nurse-midwife; b. Washington, Nov. 12, 1948; d. Paul Joseph and Cynthia R. (Yates) B.; m. John M. Durrence, May 27 (dec. 1982); 1 child, Aubrey Burke Durrence. BS, Xavier Coll., Chgo., 1972; MS, Yale U., 1976. Nurse-midwife Georgetown U. HMO, Washington, 1976; mem. faculty Yale U., New Haven, 1977-83; pvt. practice nurse-midwifery County OB, P.C., New Haven, 1977-81; nurse-midwife Conn. Health Care Plan, New Haven, 1981-83; asst. prof. George Mason U. 1983-85; nurse-midwife, instr. Georgetown U., Washington, 1985-87; clin. dir., mem. faculty U. Colo., Denver, 1987—; cons. Joseph P. Kennedy Jr. Found., Washington, 1985—. Contbr. articles to profl. jours. Docent, speaker Nat. Mus. Women in the Arts. Mem. Am. Coll. Nurse-Midwife (site visitor accreditation div. 1984—, sec. found. 1985—), AAUP, NOW, Cherry Creek Sporting Club, Sigma Theta Tau. Roman Catholic. Office: U Colo Sch Nursing Box C0288 4200 E 9th Ave Denver CO 80266

BURKE, DAN EUGENE, art center director; b. Logan, Utah, Jan. 11, 1944; s. Vern LeRoy and Elsie LaPreal (Hall) B. BA in English, Utah State U., 1970; MA in English, U. Utah, 1976, MA in Art History, 1986. Registrar Utah Mus. Fine Arts, Salt Lake City, 1976-79; coord. visual arts Utah Arts Council, Salt Lake City, 1976-86; dir. Salt Lake Art Ctr., Salt Lake City, 1986—; grants reader Inst. Mus. Svcs., Washington, 1980-84; cons. Am. Assn. Mus., Washington, 1985—. Author: (catalogues) Utah Art of the Depression, 1986, Chase Home, 1984; (with others) Utah, A Guide to the State, 1983, Art in Action, 1984. Cutural chair Sister Cities Com., Salt Lake City, 1982-86. With USAR, 1962-70. Mem. Am. Assn Mus., Utah Mus. Assn. (bd. dirs., pres. 1979-80), Contemporary Arts Group (bd. dirs., pres. 1985-86), Rotary. Office: Salt Lake Art Ctr 20 SW Temple Salt Lake City UT 84101

BURKE, DANN GENE, corporate treasurer; b. Tulelake, Calif., July 27, 1957; s. John Francis and Lorraine Marie (Tanner) B.; m. Jane Narimatsu, Oct. 18, 1986. AA in Liberal Arts, San Jose State U., 1978, BS in Acctg., 1980; MBA, Calif. State U., Hayward, 1984. CPA, Calif.; lic. real estate agent, Calif. Tutor acctg. San Jose (Calif.) State U., 1979-80; acctg. intern Hewlett-Packard, San Jose, 1980; contr. Arch Billmire Co., Inc., Sparks, Nev., 1984-87, treas., 1987—. Mem. Thomas Creek Home Assn., Reno, 1987. Mem. Calif. Soc. CPA's, Beta Alpha Psi, Phi Kappa Phi. Home: 13145 Welcome Way Reno NV 89511 Office: Arch Billmire Co Inc 545 Coney Island Dr Sparks NV 89431

BURKE, JEAN TAIT, anthropologist, educator; b. Oil City, Pa., Sept. 11, 1921; d. Zachary R. and Mildred H. (Crouch) T.; m. Harold W. Burke, July 1, 1949 (dec. 1985). BS in Edn., Clarion State U., 1943; MEd, Stanford U., 1948, MA in Anthropology, 1953. Cert. jr. coll. tchr., gen. secondary credentials, Calif. Chief counselor Women Trinity U., San Antonio, 1948-49; elem. tchr. USN Sch., Saipan, Marianas Islands, 1949-50; rsch. asst. Anthropology dept. Stanford (Calif.) U., 1951-53, asst. dir. placement, 1953-54; rsch. assoc. Am. U. Beirut, Lebanon, 1955-57; sociology instr. U. Md., Taipei, Taiwan, 1958; dir. social survey Chinese Am. Com. for Rural Reconstruction, Taipei, Taiwan, 1961-62; instr. anthropology DeAnza Community Coll., Cupertino, Calif., 1968—. Author: Human Relations in Arab States of Middle East, 1956, Bibliography: Human Relations, 1956, Social Conditions in Shihmen Reservoir Area, Taiwan, 1962. Lt. Waves, U.S. Navy, 1943-47. Democrat. Home: PO Box 178 Los Altos CA 94023

BURKE, JOHN JAMES, utility executive; b. Butte, Mont., July 25, 1928; m. Nancy M. Calvert, July 12, 1952; children: Cheryl Burke Harris, Mary Burke Orizotti, Kathleen, John James, III, Elisabeth Prizotti. BS in Bus., BA in Law, U. Mont., 1950, J.D., 1952. Bar: Mont. 1952, U.S. Supreme Ct. 1957. Ptnr. Weir, Gough, Booth and Burke, Helena, 1954-59; atty. Mont. Power Co., Butte, 1959-67, v.p., 1967-78, exec. v.p., 1979-84, vice chmn. bd. dirs., 1984—; bd. dirs. Blue Cross/Blue Shield Mont. Trustee U. Mont. Found., Carroll Coll. Mont., Mont. Hist. Soc., 1988—; pres. City-County Planning Bd., 1966-78; past dir. Vigilante council Boy Scouts Am., Shining Mountains coun. Girl Scouts U.S.; bd. dirs. Lazard Freres Spl. Equity Fund). Capt. JAGC, USAF, 1952-54, with Res. 1954-61. Mem. ABA (mem. council pub. utility law sect.), State Bar of Mont., Silver Bow County Bar Assn., Mountain States Legal Found. (bd. dirs), Lazard Freres Spl. Equity Fund (bd. dirs.), Nat. Assn. Mfrs. (bd. dirs.), Edison Electric Inst. (exec. adv. com. on planning), Butte C. of C. (v.p. 1965-72), U. Mont. Alumni Assn. (past bd. dirs.), Phi Delta Phi. Roman Catholic. Clubs: Montana, Butte Country, Elks, Rotary (sec. Helena 1955-58); 116 (Washington). Home: 50 Burning Tree Ln Butte MT 59701 Office: Mont Power Co 40 E Broadway Butte MT 59701

BURKE, JOHN LESLIE, medical technologist; b. Chgo., Jan. 31, 1949; s. Kenneth Duane and Mary Margaret (McNerney) B.; m. Ida B. Ramos, Aug. 12, 1972; children: Justin Patrick, Erin Marie. BSc, U. Ill., Chgo., 1977. Med. technician S.E. Bapt. Hosp., San Antonio, 1972-74, Rush-Presbyn.-St. Luke's Hosp., Chgo., 1974-80, San Francisco Gen. Hosp., 1980-81; night mgr. SmithKline Biosci. Lab., Burlingame, Calif., 1981-83; SMAC operator, weekend mgr. SmithKline Biosci. Lab., Dublin, Calif., 1987—; hematology supr. ICL Western, Dublin, 1983-86, lab. mgr., 1986-87. Fund raiser Operation PUSH, Chgo., 1970; vol.local aldermanic campaign, Chgo., 1970. With USAF, 1970-74. Mem. Clin. Lab. Mgrs. Assn. Democrat. Home: 73 Fountainhead Ct Martinez CA 94553 Office: SmithKline Biosci Lab 65ll Golden Gate Dr Dublin CA 94568

BURKE, LEE STEPHEN, lawyer; b. Anchorage, Alaska, Oct. 23, 1951; s. Paul Fergus and Marilyn Jane (Murphy) B. BA, W. Wash. U., 1972; JD, Gonzaga U., 1976; postgrad., St. Martins Coll. Bar: Mont. 1977, Wash. 1978. Atty. Dept. Social and Health Services-Office Support Enforcement, Everett, Wash., 1979; adminstr. contract A&MS Kaki Group Cos., Dammam, Saudi Arabia, 1980-83; atty. Burke Electric, Bellevue, Wash., 1983; treas. Burke Electric, Bellevue, 1987—, bd. dirs.; atty. Wash. Pub. Power Supply System, Elma, 1984-86; sole practice Seattle, 1987—; bd. dirs. NW Merit Co. Inc., Auburn., Wash.; house counsel Sheralon Rice and Assocs., Seattle, 1986—, Spic N' Span Home and Office Cleaning Inc.; speaker Lions Clubs and Rotary Clubs, various locations throughout Wash., 1984-86. Active Cystic Fibrosis Auction, Seattle, 1987; caucus del. Wash. Reps., Seattle, 1988. Roman Catholic. Club: Wash. Athletic (Seattle). Home and Office: 511 Prospect St Seattle WA 98109-3820

BURKE, RAY A., oil company executive; b. 1921; married. BS, U. Tex., 1947. With Union Oil Co. Calif., Los Angeles, 1947—; now exec. v.p. Unocal Corp. Office: Unocal Corp Unocal Ctr Los Angeles CA 90017

BURKE, YVONNE WATSON BRATHWAITE (MRS. WILLIAM A. BURKE), lawyer; b. Los Angeles, Oct. 5, 1932; d. James A. and Lola (Moore) Watson; m. William A. Burke, June 14, 1972; 1 dau., Autumn Roxanne. A.A., U. Calif., 1951; B.A., UCLA, 1953; J.D., U. So. Calif., 1956. Bar: Calif. bar 1956. Mem. Calif. Assembly, 1966-72, chmn. urban devel. and housing com., 1971, 72; mem. 93d Congress from 37th Dist. Calif., 94th-95th Congresses from 28th Dist. Calif., House Appropriations Com.; chmn. Congl. Black Caucus, 1976; ptnr. Jones, Day, Reavis & Pogue, Los Angeles; dep. corp. commr., hearing officer Police Commn., 1964-66; atty., staff McCone Commn. (investigation Watts riot), 1965; bd. dirs. Ednl. Testing Service, L.A. br. Fed. Res. Bank. Vice chmn. 1984 U.S. Olympics Organizing Com.; bd. dirs. or bd. advisers numerous orgns.; regent U. Calif., Bd. Ednl. Testing Svc., Amateur Athletic Found.; bd. dirs. Ford Found., Brookings Inst.; chmn. Founders Savs. & Loan Assn. Recipient Profl. Achievement award UCLA, 1974, 84; named one of 200 Future Leaders Time mag., 1974; recipient Achievement awards C.M.E. Chs.; numerous other awards, citations.; fellow Inst. Politics John F. Kennedy Sch. Govt. Harvard, 1971-72; Chubb fellow Yale, 1972. Office: Jones Day Reavis & Pogue 355 S Grand Ave Ste 3000 Los Angeles CA 90071 also: Jones Day Reavis & Pogue 901 Lakeside Ave Cleveland OH 44114

BURKEE, IRVIN, artist; b. Kenosha, Wis., Feb. 6, 1918; s. Omar Lars and Emily (Quardokas) B.; diploma Sch. of Art Inst. Chgo., 1945; m. Bonnie May Ness, Apr. 12, 1945; children—Brynn, Jill, Peter (dec.), Ian. Owner, silversmith, goldsmith Burkee Jewelry, Blackhawk, Colo., 1950-57; painter, sculptor, Aspen, Colo., 1957-78, Cottonwood, Ariz., Pietrasanta, Italy, 1978—; instr. art U. Colo., 1946, 50-53, Stephens Coll., Columbia, Mo., 1947-49. John Quincy Adams travel fellow, Mex., 1945. Executed copper mural of human history of Colo. for First Nat. Bank, Englewood, Colo., 1970, copper mural of wild birds of Kans. for Ranchmart State Bank, Overland Park, Kans., 1974; exhibited Art Inst. Chgo., Smithsonian Instn. (award 1957), Milw. Art Inst., Krannert Mus., William Rockhill Nelson Gallery, St. Louis Art Mus., Denver Art Mus.; represented in permanent collections several southwestern galleries, also pvt. collections throughout U.S.; work illustrated in books Design and Creation of Jewelry, Design through Discovery, Walls. Address: Box 2071 Rio Verde Acres Cottonwood AZ 86326

BURKETT, ALBERT LEROY, environmental consultant; b. Rye, Colo., Sept. 12, 1897; s. Frederick Marion and Cora Ann (Ryan) B.; m. Cleta Martha Sterrett, June 20, 1920 (dec. Oct. 1978); children: Barbara L., Yvonne Carroll, Kathryn B. Correa. Student, Colo. Sch. of Agriculture, 1915-17, Am. Bus. Coll., 1919-20, U. Nebr., 1925-26, Calif. Tech., 1943-44. Salesman, div. mgr. Skelly Oil Co., Lincoln, Nebr., 1920-25; asst. pres. Mid-Continent Petroleum, Tulsa, 1925-32; v.p. sales Globe Oil Co., Wichita, Kans., 1932-35; dist. mgr. Hamilton Fund, Pueblo, Colo., 1935-37; gen. mgr. Bay Petroleum Co., McPherson, Kans., 1937-39; pres. Western Mines & Plymouth Mill, Colorado Springs, Colo., 1939-43, Western Mines & Combined Minerals, Denver, 1956-63; pres., dir. Vital Earth Products, Florence, Colo., 1963-69; inventor, manufacturer Centrifugal Waste Machine, Los Angeles, 1969-73; cons. environment and waste Los Angeles, 1973—; lobbyist Colo. Senate, Denver, 1942-52, U.S. Senate, Washington, 1946-52. Patentee in field. Originator Newcomers Club, Pueblo, 1934; del. Rep. Nat. Conv., 1988. Episcopalian. Lodge: Mason (32d degree), Shriners. Home and Office: 3984 N Roger Ln Tucson AZ 85719

BURKS, EVAN BRUCE, accountant; b. Clinton, Ind., Sept. 30, 1958; s. Samuel Edward and Velma Lucille (Davis) B.; m. Terry Lynn McAnally, Aug. 7, 1982. BS in Acctg., Ariz. State U., 1986. CPA, Ariz. Controller Gen. Cassette Corp., Phoenix, 1977-81, Valley Seed Co., Phoenix, 1981-86; treas., controller H.S. Pickrell Co., Phoenix, 1986—. Mem. Nat. Assn. Accts., Controllers' Coun., Ariz. State U. Alumni Assn. Republican. Office: HS Pickrell Co 24th Floor 3300 N Central St Phoenix AZ 85012

BURLEIGH, DOUGLAS GLEN, religious organization executive; b. Norman, Okla., Mar. 31, 1945; s. Gilbert Emmett and Grace Lorene (Cochran) B.; m. Deborah Jan Coe, Nov. 30, 1974; children: John Douglas, James David, Katherine Elizabeth, Peter Gilbert. BA in Polit. Sci., Willamette U., 1966; MA in Polit. Sci., U. Wash., 1967; M of Divinity, Fuller Theol. Sem., 1979. Ordained to ministry Presbyn. Ch. Area dir. Young Life Internat., Bellevue, Wash., 1967-72, Tacoma, 1972-74; regional dir., Seattle, 1974-78, Western states field dir.,, 1978-84; Ea. states field dir., Washington, 1984-87; pres., Colorado Springs, Colo., 1987—; cons. Nat. Student Movement, Washington, 1985—. Contbr. articles to ministry jours. Eagle scout Boy Scouts Am., Seattle, 1958; student body officer Willamette U., Salem, 1965-66. Recipient God and Country award Boy Scouts Am., 1957; Nat. Defense fellow U.S. Dept Health, Edn. and Welfare, 1965; Guy F. Atkinson scholar Willamette U., 1965-66. Mem. Phi Eta Sigma, Phi Delta Theta (pledge trainer 1965). Republican. Lodge: Rotary (boys work chmn. Tacoma club 1973-74). Home: 1630 Pinnacle Ridge Ln Colorado Springs CO 80919 Office: Youth Life Internat 720 W Monument St Colorado Springs CO 80919

BURLES, KENNETH THOMAS, publishing executive; b. Long Beach, Calif., July 9, 1946; s. George Kenneth and Elizabeth Marion (Thomas) B. BA, Brigham Young U., 1970. Grant adminstr. Inst. Internat. Edn., Chgo., 1976-77; foreign student adviser Univ. Chgo., Chgo., 1977-78; exec. v.p. Salem Press, Inc., Pasadena, Calif., 1978—. Home: 1115 E Cordova #123 Pasadena CA 91106 Office: Salem Press Inc 150 S Los Robles Ave Pasadena CA 91101

BURLET, RENE ROBERT, airline pilot; b. Santa Monica, Calif., Feb. 11, 1960; s. Marcel Josef and Margrith (Seiler) B.; m. Karen Marie Shaker, May 25, 1985. Cert. Airframe and Power Plant, Northrop U., 1980; BS, SUNY, Albany, 1984. Flight instr. Piper Air Ctr., Van Nuys, Calif., 1983-84; pilot Imperial Airlines, San Diego, 1984-85, Simmons Airlines, Chgo., 1985-86, United Express, Fresno, Calif., 1986-87; flight engr. Continental Airlines, Denver, 1987—. Mem. Air Safety Coun. Home: 11248 E Baltic Dr Aurora CO 80014 Office: Continental Airlines PO Box 4607 Houston TX 77210-4607

BURLINGAME, CATHERINE ANNE PATTE, metallurgist; b. San Rafael, Calif., Feb. 18, 1959; d. Ernest Glenn and Rosalie (Massingil) Patterson; m. Donald Robert Burlingame, June 28, 1980. BS, U. Calif, Berkeley, 1982. Electronics assembler and tester Nady Systems, Oakland, Calif., 1978-79; summer trainee U.S. Steel Corp., Pittsburg, Calif., 1981; supr. quality assurance U.S. Steel Corp., Pittsburg, 1982-86, USS-Posco Industries (renamed), Pittsburg, 1986—. Advisor Jr. Achievment, Antioch, Calif., 1983. Recipient Scholarship, Soc. for Women Engrs., 1977. Mem. Am. Soc. for Metals, Aikido of Berkeley (svcs. com. 1987—), Bay Area Orienteering Club (co-chmn. registration 1988—). Home: 1610 San Benito St Richmond CA 94804 Office: USS-Posco Industries 900 Loveridge Rd Pittsburg CA 94565

BURMAN, ALDEN HAYWARD, health facility executive; b. Bellingham, Wash., Nov. 18, 1919; s. John A. and Winifred C. (Larson) B.; student health care adminstrn. U. Wash., 1967-68; m. Miriam Rodriguez, July 10, 1983; children from previous marriage: Ronald Alden, Richard, James David, Shirley Ann. Pres., Federal Way Convalescent Center, Inc., 1968—; pres., Parklane Convalescent Center, Inc., Aberdeen, Wash., 1969—; owner The Gallery gift and antique store, Ocean Shores, Wash., 1962—; owner AFCO Personnel Services, Buffalo and Seattle, 1973—; v.p. Western Farms, Inc., Moses Lake, Wash., 1974—; Fellow Am. Coll. Health Care Adminstrs., Internat. Biog. Assn. (life); mem. Wash. Health Facilities Assn. (state pres. 1962, bd. govs. 1961-65), Am. Health Care Assn. (bd. govs. 1962), Nat. Employment Assn. Office: PO Box 3260 Federal Way WA 98063

BURMAN, DAVID JOHN, lawyer; b. Burlington, Iowa, Apr. 29, 1952; s. Keith Roland and Janet Black (Thomason) B.; m. DeeAnn Schaumberg, Aug. 10, 1974; children: Kendall, Blaire. BA, U. Wyo., 1974; JD, Georgetown U., 1977. Bar: Va. 1977, D.C. 1979, U.S. Ct. Appeals (D.C. cir.) 1979, Wash. 1980, U.S. Dist. Ct. (we. dist.) Wash. 1980, U.S. Ct. Appeals (9th cir.) 1980, U.S. Dist. Ct. (ea. dist.) Wash. 1982, U.S. Ct. Appeals (fed. cir.) 1982, U.S. Supreme Ct. 1982, U.S. Ct. Appeals (8th cir.) 1985. Law clk. to judge U.S. Ct. Appeals (D.C. cir.), Washington, 1977-78; law clk. to assoc. justice Byron R. White U.S. Supreme Ct., Washington, 1978-79; ptnr. Perkins Coie, Seattle, 1979—. Editor Georgetown Law Jour., 1976-77. Mem. legal, freedom of expression, privacy and tech. coms. ACLU, Wash., 1979—, exec. bd. Today's Constn. and You Project, Seattle, 1983-85; sec., counsel Ptnrs. in Pub. Edn. Mem. ABA (litigation, antitrust, criminal law, communications law sects., chmn. pro bono subcommn.), Wash. State Bar Assn. (exec. bd. antitrust sect.), Seattle-King County Bar Assn., N.W. Communications Law Group, Wash. Council Sch. Attys. Democrat. Office: Perkins Coie 1201 3d Ave Bldg Seattle WA 98101-3099

BURMAN, DEEANN SCHAUMBERG, public relations executive; b. Lincoln, Nebr., Nov. 11, 1949; d. William E. and Patricia A. (Ward) Schaumberg; m. David J. Burman, Aug. 10, 1974; children: Kendall Claire, Blaire Elizabeth. BA, Oreg. State U., 1971; postgrad., U. Wyo., 1971-72. Rsch. and teaching assoc. U. Wyo., Laramie, 1971-72; acting dir. of forensics Lewis & Clark Col., Portland, Oreg., 1972-73; mgr. C.B. Homes, Inc., Denver, 1973-74; sales asst. Sony, Washington, 1974-77; in pub. rels., lobbyist AARP, Washington, 1977-78; publicity dir. Olympic Ballet Theatre, Seattle, 1986—; cons. fund raising for non-profit orgns., Seattle, 1984—. Fund raiser Woodland Park Zoo, Seattle, 1984-87, mem. Savannah Club, 1987—. Mem. Columbia Tower Club. Home: 18238 Ridgefield Rd NW Seattle WA 98177

BURNASH, ROBERT JOHN CHARLES, hydrologist; b. Bklyn., Aug. 17, 1931; s. James Francis and Marion Josephine (Olifiers) B.; BS, Bucknell U., 1953; postgrad. Naval Postgrad. Sch., 1954; m. Jeanne Carolyn Mack, July 11, 1953; children: Charles, Kathleen, Mary, Elizabeth, David, Daniel. Hydrologist, Nat. Weather Svc. River Forecast Ctr., Cin., 1957-62, prin. asst., Sacramento River Forecast Ctr., 1963-71, hydrologist in charge Calif.-Nev. River Forecast Ctr., 1972-87, retired 1987—; guest lectr. hydrologic systems Australian Water Resources Council, Melbourne, Perth, Brisbane, Sydney, 1984; World Meteorological Orgn. lectr. U. Calif., Davis, 1983-86; prin. organizer Internat. Tech. Conf. on Mitigation of Natural Hazards through Real-Time Data Collection and Hydrological Forecasting, World Meteorol. Orgn., Sacramento, 1983; cons. Hydrologic Svcs., 1987—. With USNR, 1953-56. Recipient Bronze medal Dept. Commerce, 1970, Silver medal, 1975, Gold medal, 1980; Outstanding Pub. Svc. award NOAA, 1978. Fellow Am. Meteorol. Soc. (Outstanding Forecaster award 1979, Robert E. Horton meml. lectr. 1983); mem. Am. Geophys. Union, AAAS, N.Y. Acad. Scis., Western Snow Conf., Assn. State Flood Plain Mgrs., Delta Mu Delta, Phi Lambda Theta. Author: (with others) The Sacramento Model. Contbr. articles to profl. jours. Originator real time event reporting telemetering systems and ALERT flood warning system. Home: 3539 Ridgeview Dr El Dorado Hills CA 95630

BURNELL, GEORGE MARCEL, psychiatrist; b. Belfort, France, Mar. 17, 1930; came to U.S., 1949; s. Joryah Meyer; m. Dec. 22, 1957 (div. 1966); children: Cynthia, David; m. Mar.17, 1967. BA, U. Paris, 1949; BS, Columbia U., 1953, MD, 1957. Chief resident psychiatry U. Calif., San Francisco, 1963-65, staff psychiatrist, 1965-68; chief dept. health Leeward Mental Health Clinic, Honolulu, 1968-69; psychiatrist Kaiser Med. Ctr., Santa Clara, Calif., 1969-74, chief psychiatry dept., 1974-84; chief psychiatry dept. Kaiser Med. Ctr., Honolulu, 1984—. Author: Clinical Management of Bereavement, 1989. Capt. USAF, 1958-60. Recipient Physicians award AMA, 1980, 84. Fellow Am. Psychiatric Assn.; mem. World Psychiatric Assn., Hawaii Psychiatric Soc. Office: Kaiser Med Ctr 3288 Moanalua Rd Honolulu HI 96819

BURNETT, ERIC STEPHEN, environmental engineer; b. Manchester, Eng., Apr. 5, 1924; s. William Louis and Edith Winifred (Gates) B.; came to U.S., 1963; naturalized, 1974; BSc in Physics (with honors), London U., 1954; MS in Environ. Studies, Calif. State, Dominguez Hills, 1976; PhD in Environ. Engring., Calif. Coast U., 1982; children: Diana, Ian, Brenda, Keith. Program mgr. Brit. Aircraft Corp., Stevenage, Eng., 1953-63; sr. systems engr. RCA, Princeton, N.J., 1963-66; project mgr. Gen. Electric Co., Valley Forge, Pa., 1966-67; dept. head TRW systems Group, Redondo Beach, Calif., 1967-72; dir. energy and pollution control ARATEX Svcs., Inc., Calif., 1974-81, dir. tech. devel., 1981-83, staff cons., 1983—; cons., lectr. in energy conservation, environ. and contamination controls. With Royal Air Force, 1942-47. Assoc. fellow AIAA; mem. Water Pollution Control Fedn., Air Pollution Control Assn., AAAS, Inst. Environ. Scis. (sr.). Contbr. articles in field to profl. jours. Home: 22901 Leadwell St West Hills Encino CA 91416 Office: PO Box 3000 Encino CA 91316

BURNETT, JAMES ROBERT, aerospace company executive; b. Eldorado, Ill., Nov. 27, 1925; s. James Lawrence and Edith Lillian (Bramlett) B.; m. Betty Anne Knox, Aug. 18, 1949; children—James William, Karen Jean, Susan Anne, Janice Leigh. B.S. in Elec. Engring., Purdue U., 1946, M.S. in Elec. Engring., 1947, Ph.D., 1949, D.Engring. (hon.), 1969. Assoc. prof. elec. engring. Purdue U., Lafayette, Ind., 1946-56; dir. electromech. lab. TRW Systems Group, Redondo Beach, Calif., 1956-61; minuteman program mgr. TRW Systems Group, San Bernardino, Calif., 1961-66, mgr. ops., 1966-69; v.p., asst. gen. mgr. TRW Systems Group, Redondo Beach, 1969-70, v.p., gen. mgr. systems engring. and integration div., 1970-74, sr. v.p., 1974-77, asst. gen. mgr., 1977-82, v.p., gen. mgr. Def. Systems group, 1982-86; exec.v.p., dep. gen. mgr. S&D sector TRW Inc. Group, 1986—; dir. OEA, Inc., Denver. Served to 1st lt. USMC, 1943-50. Recipient Air Force Systems Command award; Charles A. Coffin fellow. Fellow AIAA; mem. IEEE, Nat. Acad. Engring. Republican. Office: TRW S&D Sector 1 Space Park Redondo Beach CA 92078

BURNETT, LYNN BARKLEY, health science educator; b. Reedley, Calif., Oct. 20, 1948; s. Charles Erbin and Ruth Clarice (Erickson) B. B.S., Columbia Pacific U., 1979, M.Sc., 1980; diploma in nat. security mgmt. Nat. Def. U. of U.S., 1988; postgrad. Columbia Pacific U., Nova U. Ctr. Higher Edn. Cert. community coll. tchr., Calif., instr. in advanced first aid, emergency care, basic CPR, Advanced Cardiac Life Support, Pediatric Basic Life Support. Med. advisor Fresno County Sheriff's Depart., 1972—, assoc. dir. Cen. Valley Emergency Med. Svcs. System, Fresno, Calif., 1974-75; faculty Calif. Fresno City Coll., 1978—, prof. health sci., 1981-87, dir. continuing edn. in health, 1981—, adj. faculty West Coast Christian Coll., 1989—, med. and health commentator Sta. KVPR-FM Valley Pub. Radio, 1989—; lectr., cons. in field; co-dir. conjoint research program of Stanford U. Sch. Medicine and Dept. Health Sci. Calif. State U., Fresno, 1986; established pilot paramedic programs Fresno County, 1974-75; dir. Cent. Valley's Inaugural Paramedic Tng. Program, 1975; established CPR tng. Programs Fresno Fire Dept., 1968, Fresno Police Dept., 1972, Fresno County Sheriff's Dept., 1973. Chmn. Fresno County steering com. The Chem. People, 1983-86, Generation at Risk, 1987; mem. Emergency Med. Care Com. Fresno County, 1979-85, vice chmn., 1984-85; mem. Calif. State Commn. Emergency Med. Services, 1974-75; mem. Fresno County Adv. Bd. on Drug Abuse, 1984—, chmn. drug adv. bd., 1985-88; bd. dirs., chmn. pub. edn. Fresno County unit Am. Cancer Soc., 1984—, v.p., 1985-87, pres. elect 1987-88, pres. 1988—, bd. dirs. 1984—, chmn. pub. edn. com. 1984-87; pres. Fresno County Safety Council, 1985—; mem. steering com. Fresno Health Promotion Coalition, chmn. com. on crime, violence and safety, 1987—; co-chmn. Drug and Alcohol Prevention Coalition Fresno County, 1987—; mem. med. staff, steering com. All-Star Football Game. 1965—; emergency med. cons. Dept. Intercollegiate Atheltics Calif. State U., Fresno, 1982—; mem. core com. Student Assistance Program for Substance Abuse and Other Problems Fresno City Coll., 1989—; faculty advanced trauma life support trauma nurse tactics Valley Med. Ctr., 1982—. Recipient State Service medal Calif. Mil. Dept., 1980; Bronze medal Am. Heart Assn., 1974, Appreciation award Am. Cancer Soc., 1985. Mem. Am. Coll. Preventive Medicine, Am. Acad. Forensic Scis. (alt. del. People's Republic of China, citizen ambassador program People to People Internat. 1986), Am. Assn. Suicidology, N.Y. Acad. Scis., AAAS, Internat. Platform Assn. Democrat. Baptist. Avocations: reading, musical conducting. Home: PO Box 4512 Fresno CA 93744 Office: Calif State U Fresno CA 93740-0026

BURNETTE, MICHAEL JACKSON, broadcasting executive; b. Fresno, Calif., Aug. 31, 1951; s. Woodrow Jackson and Ruth Marjorie (Loeffel) B.; m. Sarah Marx, June 10, 1977. Grad., U. N.H., 1984. Announcer Sta. KFIG Radio, Fresno, 1969-70; announcer and prodn. dir. Sta. KMAK Radio, Fresno, 1970-77; program dir. Sta. KJQY Radio, San Diego, 1977-82; group ops. mgr. Group W Radio, N.Y.C., 1982-86; v.p., gen. mgr. Sta. KMEO Radio, Phoenix, 1986—; bd. dirs. Walter Cronkite Sch. Journalism. Bd. dirs. Phoenix Symphony Orch., 1986—, Hope: Ctr. for Head Injury, Phoenix, 1986—. Mem. Met. Phoenix Broadcasters (bd. dirs. 1986—). Mem. Zen Baptist Ch. Club: Magic Castle (Los Angeles).

BURNEY, VICTORIA KALGAARD, business consultant, civic worker; b. Los Angeles, Apr. 12, 1943; d. Oscar Albert and Dorothy Elizabeth (Peterson) Kalgaard; children: Kim Elizabeth, J. Hewett. BA with honors, U. Mont., 1965; MA, U. No. Colo., 1980; postgrad. Webster U., St. Louis, 1983-84. Exec. dir. Hill County Community Action, Havre, Mont., 1966-67; community orgn. specialist ACCESS, Escondido, Calif., 1967-68; program devel. and community orgn. specialist Community Action Programs, Inc., Pensacola, Fla., 1968-69; cons. Escambia County Sch. Bd., Fla., 1969-71; pres. Kal Kreations, Kailua, Hawaii, 1974-77; instr., dir. office human resources devel. Palomar Coll., San Marcos, Calif., 1978-81; chief exec. officer IDET Corp., San Marcos, 1981-87; cons. County of Riverside, Calif., 1983. Mem. San Diego County Com. on Handicapped, San Diego, 1979; cons. tribal resource devel., Escondido, Calif., 1979; mem. exec. com. Social Services Coordinating Council, San Diego, 1982-83; mem. pvt. sector com. and planning and rev. com. Calif. Employment and Tng. Adv. Council, Sacramento, 1982-83; bd. mgrs. Santa Margarita Family YMCA, Vista, Calif., 1984-86; bd. dirs. North County Community Action Program, Escondido, 1978, Casa de Amparo, San Luis Rey, Calif., 1980-83; mem. San Diego County Pub. Welfare Adv. Bd., 1979-83, chairperson, 1981; assoc. mem. Calif. Republican Central Com., Sacramento, 1984-85, 89—; ofcl. San Diego County Rep. Central Com., 1985, exec. com., 1987—; chmn. 74th Assembly Dist. Rep. Caucus, 1989—; chmn. Working Ptnrs., 1987—. Mem. Nat. Assn. County Employment and Tng. Adminstrs. (chairperson econ. resources com. 1982-85), Calif. Assn. Local Econ. Devel., San Diego Econ. Devel. Corp., Oceanside Econ. devel. Council (bd. dirs. 1983-87), Oceanside C. of C., San Marcos C. of C. (bd. dirs. 1982-85), Carlsbad C. of C. (indsl. council 1982-85), Escondido C. of C. (comml. and indsl. devel. council 1982-87), Vista C. of C. (vice chairperson econ. devel. com. 1982-83), Vista Econ. Devel. Assn., Nat. Mgmt. Assn. (charter mem. North County chpt.), Nat. Job Tng. Partnership, Job Tng. Assn. San Diego, Am. Mgmt. Assns., San Diego County Golden Eagle Club, Oceanside Rep. Women's Club Federated.

BURNHAM, WILLIAM A., wildlife protection society administrator; b. Pueblo, Colo., Oct. 5, 1947; s. William H. and Bertha (Nemier) B.; m. Patricia Ann Wood, July 9, 1966; 1 child, Kurt Kristopher. BS, U. So. Colo., 1973; MS, Brigham Young U., 1975; PhD, Colo. State U., 1984. Tech. assoc. Cornell U., Colo. and Idaho, 1974-88; dir. World Ctr. for Birds of Prey, Boise, Idaho, 1984—; pres. The Peregrine Fund Inc., Boise, Idaho, 1986—; adj. faculty Boise State U., 1986—, trustee, 1985—; bd. dirs. The Raptor Fund Inc., Chgo. Contbr. articles to profl. jours. Mem. Cooper Ornithological Soc., Am. Ornighologists' Union, Wilson Ornithological Soc., Raptor Research Found., The Avicultural Soc., Internat. Council for Bird Preservation, Arctic Inst. of N. Am., The Ottawa Field-Naturalists' Club, The Wildlife Soc., Sigma Xi. Office: Peregrine Fund Inc 5666 W Flying Hawk Ln Boise ID 83709

BURNISON, BOYD EDWARD, lawyer; b. Arnolds Park, Iowa, Dec. 12, 1934; s. Boyd William and Lucile (Harnden) B.; m. Mari Amaral; children: Erica Lafore, Alison Katherine. BS, Iowa State U., 1957; JD, U. Calif., Berkeley, 1961. Bar: Calif. 1962, U.S. Supreme Ct. 1971, U.S. Dist. Ct. (no. dist.) Calif. 1962, U.S. Ct. Appeals (9th cir.) 1962, U.S. Dist. Ct. (ea. dist.) Calif. 1970. Dep. counsel Yolo County, Calif., 1962-65; of counsel Davis and Woodland (Calif.) Unified Sch. Dists., 1962-65; assoc. Steel & Arostegui, Marysville, Calif., 1965-66, St. Sure, Moore & Hoyt, Oakland, 1966-70; ptnr. St. Sure, Moore, Hoyt & Sizoo, Oakland and San Francisco, 1970-75; v.p. Crosby, Heafey, Roach & May, P.C., Oakland, 1975—, also bd. dirs. Adviser Berkeley YMCA, 1971—; adviser Yolo County YMCA, 1962-65, bd. dirs. 1965; bd. dirs. Easter Seal Soc. Crippled Children and Adults of Alameda County, Calif., 1972-75, Moot Ct. Bd., U. Calif., 1960-61; trustee, sec., legal counsel Easter Seal Found., Alameda County, 1974-79, hon. trustee, 1979—. Paul Harris fellow. Fellow ABA Found.; mem. ABA (labor rels. and employment law sect., equal employment law com. 1972—), Nat. Conf. Bar Pres.'s, State Bar Calif. (spl. labor counsel 1981-84, labor and employment law sect. 1982—), Alameda County Bar Assn. (chmn. memberships and directory com. 1973-74, 80, chmn. law office econs. com. 1975-77, assn. dir. 1981-85, pres., 1984, vice chmn. bench bar liaison com. 1983, chmn. 1984, Disting. Svc. award 1987), Yolo County Bar Assn. (sec. 1965), Yuba Sutter Bar Assn., Bar Assn. San Francisco (labor law sect.), Indsl. Rels. Rsch. Assn., Sproul Assoc. Boalt Hall Law Sch. U. Calif. Berkeley, Iowa State Alumni Assn., Order Knoll, Round Hill Country Club, Rotary, Pi Kappa Alpha, Phi Delta Phi. Democrat. Home: 2500 Caballo Ranchero Dr PO Box 743 Diablo CA 94528 Office: Crosby Heafey Roach & May 2300 Lake Merritt Pla Bldg 1999 Harrison St Oakland CA 94612

BURNS, ALEXANDRA DARROW (SANDRA BURNS), health program administrator; b. West Point, Ky., Mar. 28, 1946; d. Eugene Alexander and Phyllis Anna (Kedroski) Darrow; m. Maurice Edward Burns Jr., Sept. 8, 1966 (div. May 1985); 1 child, Megan Alexandra. BS in Journalism, U. Colo., 1967, MA in Guidance and Counseling, 1974. Cert. ins. rehab. specialist, rehab. counselor. Probation and parole officer Office of Probation and Parole, Olympia, Wash., 1969-70; employment counselor Div. Employment, Denver, 1971-73; rehab. counselor Colo. Div. Rehab.-Blind Svcs., Denver, 1973-77; rehab. supr. Colo. Div. Rehab., Denver, 1978-81, program supr. rehab. ins. svcs. for employment, 1981—. vice chmn. Juvenile Parole Bd., Denver, 1982—, acting chmn. 1987, chmn. 1988; del. Dem. County Caucus, Aurora, Colo., 1986, Girl Scout Coun., 1988—; mem. adv. bd. Indsl. Commn., 1983-86; mem. Jr. Symphony Guild, 1986—; co-leader Brownies Girl Scouts U.S., 1988—, brownie leader, 1988—, del. to coun., 1988-89, area svc. team mem., 1989—; sec., bd. dirs. Mission Viejo Homerowner Assn., 1989—. Mem. Nat. Rehab. Assoc., Nat. Rehab. Adminstrn. Assn., Colo. Rehab. Adminstrn. Assn. (bd. dirs. 1988—, pvt. sector div. pres. elect 1989), Zonta (corr. sec. 1984-86). Episcopalian. Home: 16299 E Nassau Dr Aurora CO 80013 Office: RISE Colo Div Rehab 6000 E Evans # 3-201 Denver CO 80222

BURNS, CONRAD RAY, senator; b. Gallatin, Mo., Jan. 25, 1935; s. Russell and Mary Frances (Knight) B.; m. Phyllis Jean Kuhlmann; children: Keely Lynn, Garrett Russell. Field rep. Polled Hereford World Mag., Kansas City, Mo., 1963-69; pub. rels. Billings (Mont.) Livestock Com., 1969-73; farm dir. KULR TV, Billings, 1974; pres., founder No. Ag-Network, Billings, 1975-87; commissioner Yellowstone County, Billings, 1987-89; U.S. Senator from Montana 1989—. With USMC, 1955-58. Mem. Nat. Assn. Farm Broadcasters, Rotary, Masons, Shriners. Republican. Lutheran. Home: 1330 Naples Billings MT 59105 Office: US Senate Senate Office Bldg Washington DC 20510

BURNS, DAN W., manufacturing company executive; b. Auburn, Calif., Sept. 10, 1925; s. William and Edith Lynn (Johnston) B.; 1 child, Dan Jr. Dir. materials Menasco Mfg. Co., 1951-56; v.p., gen. mgr. Hufford Corp., 1956-58; pres. Hufford div. Siegler Corp., 1958-61; v.p. Siegler Corp., 1961-62, Lear Siegler, Inc., 1962-64; pres., dir. Electrada Corp., Culver City, Calif., 1964-85; chief exec. officer Sargent Industries, Inc., L.A., 1985-88, now chmn. bd. dirs.; chmn. bd. dirs., chief exec. officer Arlington Industries, Inc.; dir. Gen. Automotive Corp., Dover Tech. Internat., Inc. Bd. dirs. San Diego Aerospace Mus., Smithsonian Inst. Served to capt. U.S. Army, 1941-47; prisoner of war Japan; asst. mil. attache 1946, China; a.d.c. to Gen. George C. Marshall 1946-47. Mem. Orgn. Am. States Sports Com. (dir.). Clubs: Los Angeles Country, St. Francis Yacht, Calif., Conquistadores del Cielo, Garden of the Gods. Home: 10851 Chalon Rd Bel Air Los Angeles CA 90077 Office: 833 Moraga Dr Ste 4 Bel Air Los Angeles CA 90049

BURNS, JAMES ALVIN, pharmacist; b. East Chicago, Ind., Sept. 24, 1935; s. Mallin Christie and Mary Jeannette (Sholes) B.; m. Suzanne Kay Sherk, Aug. 19, 1967 (div. Dec. 1978); children: Anthony J., Ellen K. BS, Purdue U., 1957. Lic. pharmacist Calif., Ind., Va. Pharmacist Haney's Prescription Ctrs., Hammond, Ind., 1957-58, 60-61, Moore's Arville Pharmacy, Arlington, Va., 1958-60, various pharmacies, So. Calif., 1981-83, L.M. Caldwell Pharmacist, Santa Barbara, Calif., 1983—; sales rep. Eli Lilly & Co., Calif., 1961-80; sales mgr. Rossin Corp., Goleta, Calif., 1980-81. With U.S. Army, 1958-60. Mem. Calif. Pharmacists Assn., Santa Barbara Pharmacists Assn. (bd. dirs.), Masons (past master 1976). Republican. Methodist. Home: 5096-D Rhoads Ave Santa Barbara CA 93111

BURNS, JAMES FRANCIS, JR., banker; b. N.Y.C., July 9, 1937; s. James Francis and Sarah (Mulligan) B.; children: Kimberly, Karen, Karla. B.B.A., Loyola U., Los Angeles, 1959. Audit mgr. Arthur Andersen & Co., Los Angeles, 1959-66; controller St. Joseph Hosp., Burbank, Calif., 1966-68; with First Interstate Bank, Los Angeles, 1970-82, v.p., chief fin. officer, 1972-75, sr. v.p., chief fin. officer, 1975-78, exec. v.p., chief fin. officer, 1978-82; exec. v.p. fin. First Interstate Bancorp, Los Angeles, 1982—; mem. bus. adv. coun. Loyola U., L.A., 1981—. Mem. Am. Inst. CPAs. Republican. Roman Catholic. Office: 1st Interstate Bancorp 707 Wilshire Blvd Los Angeles CA 90017

BURNS, JAN MARIE, computer engineer; b. Dallas, Sept. 25, 1943; d. Clifford Ferdinand and Barta Mae (Rayl) Deininger; divorced; children: Derek Erwin, Dustin Farrell. BS in Info. and Computer Sci., U. Calif.-Irvine, 1987. Software engr. UNISYS, Irvine, 1987. Mem. Nat. Mgmt. Assn. (mem. booster), Mensa. Republican. Office: UNISYS 25725 Jeronimo Rd Mission Viejo CA 92691

BURNS, JOHN MICHAEL, marketing and sales executive, consultant; b. Roswell, N.Mex., Oct. 25, 1946; s. John A. and Minnie R. (Harris) B.; m. Annette Lindsey, Oct. 13, 1986; 1 child, Jackie. BS in Bus., U. Ariz., 1976. With Mountain Bell, 1969-84; asst. v.p. sales dept. Mountain Bell, Denver, 1980-81, market mgr., 1981-84; nat. account mgr. U.S. West Info. Systems, Denver, 1984-85; dir. ops. U.S. West, Inc., Denver, 1985-86; prin., pres. CommServ, Denver, 1986-88; pres. Tienet Computer Systems, Boulder, Colo., 1988—. Author: Market Information Resource Guide, 1984. Exec. United Way, Tucson, 1972; pres. Arapahoe Ridge Assn., Denver, 1984-86. Sgt. USAF, 1966-69. Republican. Office: Tienet Inc 1832 55th St Boulder CO 80301

BURNS, REX SEHLER, English professor, writer; b. San Diego, June 13, 1935; s. Cecil Thomas Sehler and Janice Hazel (Heinrich) Burns; m. Emily Anne Sweitzer, Jan. 30, 1959 (div. Mar. 1984); children: Christopher, Erik, Andrew; m. Terry Deane Fostvedt, Apr. 10, 1987; children: Michael, Eric, Anakija, Kari Lea. BA, Stanford (Calif.) U., 1958; MA, U. Minn., 1963, PhD, 1965. Asst. prof. English Cen. Mo. State U., Warrensburg, Mo., 1965-68; assoc. prof. English U. Colo., Denver, 1968-75, prof. English, 1975—. Author: novel The Alvarez Journal, 1975 (Edgar award 1976), The Farnsworth Score, 1977 (Top Hand 1978), Speak for the Dead, 1978 (Top Hand 1979), Angle of Attack, 1979 (Top Hand 1980), The Avenging Angel, 1983, Strip Search, 1984, Ground Money, 1986, Suicide Season, 1987, The Killing Zone, 1988, Parts Known, 1990: non-fiction Success in America, 1976. Pres. Colo. Authors League, Denver, 1980-81. 1st lt. USMCR, 1958-61. Fulbright scholar Thessaloniki, Greece, 1969-70, Buenos Aires, 1976; recipient Chancellors award U. Colo., 1982. Mem. Bouchercon, Mystery Writers Am. (regional v.p. 1978-81, Edgar award 1976), Torch Club. Democrat. Episcopalian. Home: 1017 Vivian Circle Boulder CO 80303 Office: U Colo English Dept 1400 Larimer St Denver CO 80204

BURNSIDE, WALDO HOWARD, department store executive; b. Washington, Nov. 5, 1928; s. Waldo and Eleanor B.; m. Jean Mae Culbert, June 24, 1950; children: Diane Louise, Leslie Ann, Arlene Kay, William Howard. B.S., U. Md., 1949. With Woodward & Lothrop, Washington, 1949-80; divisional mdse. mgr. Woodward & Lothrop, 1957-65, v.p., gen. mdse. mgr., 1965-74, exec. v.p., 1974-78, pres., 1978-80; also dir.; vice chmn., chief operating officer Carter Hawley Hale Stores, Inc., Los Angeles, 1980-83, pres., chief operating officer, 1983—; dir. Security Pacific Corp. Trustee Md. Ednl. Found.; trustee St. John's Hosp. and Health Ctr. Found.; trustee, past chmn. U. Md. Alumni Internat. Mem. Ind. Colls. So. Calif. (bd. dirs.), Los Angeles Area C. of C. (bd. dirs.), Automobile Club So. Calif. (bd. dirs.), Phi Kappa Phi, Sigma Chi. Episcopalian. Clubs: California, Los Angeles Country, N.Y. Athletic. Office: Carter Hawley Hale Stores Inc 550 S Flower St Los Angeles CA 90071

BURRI, BETTY JANE, research chemist; b. San Francisco, Jan. 23, 1955; d. Paul Gene and Carleen Georgette (Meyers) B.; m. Kurt Randall Annweiler, Dec. 1, 1984. BA, San Francisco State U., 1976; MS, Calif. State U., Long Beach, 1978; PhD, U. Calif. San Diego, La Jolla, 1982. Research asst. Scripps Clinic, La Jolla, 1982-83, research assoc., 1983-85; research chemist Western Human Nutrition Research Ctr., USDA, San Francisco, 1985—. Contbr. articles to profl. jours. Affiliate fellow Am. Heart Assn., 1983, 84; grantee NIH, 1982, 85, U.S. Dept. Agr., 1986-89. Mem. Assn. Women in Sci. (founding dir. San Diego chpt.), N.Y. Acad. Sci., Union Concerned Scientists. Office: Western Human Nutrition Rsch Ctr PO Box 29997 Presidio CA 94129

BURROUGH, LARRY, newspaper editor. City editor Los Angeles Herald Examiner. Office: Los Angeles Herald Examiner City Desk 1111 S Broadway Los Angeles CA 90015 *

BURROUGHS, WALTER LAUGHLIN, publisher; b. Bridgewater, S.D., Aug. 21, 1901; s. William S. and Bertha (Laughlin) B.; m. Hazel Georgia Sexsmith, June 1, 1925 (dec. Oct. 1970); 1 child, Toni (Mrs. Philip Schuyler Doane); m. Lucy Bell, Feb. 28, 1972. BA, U. Wash., 1924; postgrad., U. Calif., Berkeley, 1925-28. Dir. publs. U. Calif., Berkeley, 1925-28; gen. mgr. North Pacific Gravure Co., Seattle, 1928-30; gen. mgr. Crocker Union Lithograph and Pub. Co., L.A., 1930-41; co-founder Bantam Books, L.A., 1938; ind. book pub. with Merle Armitage, 1938-42; Pacific coast rep. H.W. Kaster & Sons, L.A., 1941-42; exec. v.p. Eldon Industries Los Angeles, 1946-62; corp. pres., pub. Orange Coast Daily Pilot, Newport Beach, Costa Mesa, Huntington Beach, Calif., 1948-65, chmn. bd., 1965-68; pres. Orion Mgmt. Corp. Chmn. bd. dirs. emeritus Children's Hosp. Orange County; trustee Jefferson Trust, Western World Med. Found., Irvine, Calif.; active Ctr. for the Performing Arts. Col. U.S. Army, 1942-45. Honored (with late E.J. Power) for role in bringing U. Calif. to Irvine with dedication of Founders Ct. on campus, 1978. Mem. Soc. Profl. Journalists, Bohemian Club, Jonathan Club, Newport Harbor Yacht Club, Newport Beach Country Club, Center Club (Costa Mesa), Nat. Press Club, Rotary, Sigma Delta Chi (nat. pres.) Home: 260 Cagney Ln Apt 313 Newport Beach CA 92663 Office: 1670 Westminster Ave Costa Mesa CA 92627

BURROW, HAROLD, gas company executive; b. Navasota, Tex., Dec. 1, 1914; s. Benjamin Donald and Minnie (Weaver) B.; m. Vassa Woodley; children: Larry W., Harry W., Janice K. Grad., Harvard U. With Tenneco, Inc., Houston, 1943-66, pres., mem. exec. com., 1960-66; chmn. bd., chief exec. officer Colo. Interstate Gas Co., Colorado Springs, 1974—, also bd. dirs.; vice chmn. bd. Coastal Corp. (formerly Coastal States Gas Corp.), Houston, 1974, also mem. exec. com.; chmn. bd. Colo. Interstate Corp., Colorado Springs, 1982—, also bd. dirs.; vice chmn. bd., bd. dirs. Am. Natural Resources Co., Detroit. Mem. Petroleum Club (Houston), Ramada Club (Houston). Methodist. Club: Ramada (Houston). Office: 9 Greenway Pl Coastal Tower Houston TX 77046

BURROWS, ELIZABETH MACDONALD, religious organization executive; b. Portland, Oreg., Jan. 30, 1930; d. Leland R. and Ruth M. (Frew) MacDonald. Certificate, Chinmaya Trust Sandeepany, Bombay; PhD (hon.), Internat. U. Philosophy and Sci., 1975. Ordained to ministry First Christian Ch., 1976. Mgr. credit Home Utilities, Seattle, 1958, Montgomery Ward, Crescent City, Calif., 1963; supr. Oreg. Dist. Tng. West Coast Telephone, Beaverton, 1965; pres. Christian Ch. Universal Philosophy, Seattle, 1971—, Archives Internat., St. Louis, 1971—; v.p. James Tyler Kent Inst., 1984—, Internat. Inst. Complimentary Psychology, 1986—. Author: Crystal Planet, 1979, Pathway of the Immortal, 1980, Glory of Revelation, 1981, Maya Sangh, 1981, Harp of Destiny, 1984, Commentary for Gospel of Peace of Jesus Christ according to John, 1986, American Poetry Anthology, 1989. Mem. Internat. Speakers Platform, Internat. New Thought Alliance. Home: 10529 Ashworth Ave N Seattle WA 98133 Office: Christian Ch Universal Philosophy 10529 Ashworth Ave N Seattle WA 98133

BURSON, SCOTT FOSTER, labor lawyer; b. N.Y.C., May 28, 1952; s. Harold and Bette Anne (Foster) B.; m. Wendy Faith Liebow, Aug. 12, 1979; children: Allison Liebow, Esther Miriam Liebow. BA, Wesleyan U., Middletown, Conn., 1974; JD, U. Chgo., 1977; M. Law Libr., U. Wash., 1981. Bar: Mass. 1977, U.S. Dist Ct. Mass. 1978, U.S. Supreme Ct. (1st cir.) 1978, U.S. Dist Ct. R.I. 1980, Wash. 1981. Assoc. Palmer & Dodge, Boston, 1977-80; law clk. to judge U.S. Dist. Ct., Providence, 1980; document librarian law libr. U. Wash., Seattle, 1982-84; head reference librarian law libr. U. Wash., 1984-87; field atty. NLRB, Seattle, 1987—; adj. prof. law U. Wash., Seattle, 1987. Contbr. articles to Legal Reference Svcs. Quar., 1984, Law Libr. Jour., 1987. Mem. Solid Waste Adv. Com., Seattle, 1988. Mem. Seattle King County Bar Assn., Wash. State Bar Assn., Am. Assn. Law Librs., Beta Phi Mu, Phi Beta Kappa. Democrat. Jewish. Office: NLRB 2948 915 2nd Ave Seattle WA 98174

BURSTEIN, DAVID, astronomy educator; b. Englewood, N.J., May 19, 1947; s. Bernard and Mildred (Mindlin) B.; m. Gail Kelly, June 19, 1971; children: Jonathan, Elizabeth. BS in Physics with honors, Wesleyan U., Middletown, Conn., 1969; PhD in Astronomy, U. Calif., Santa Cruz, 1978. Research fellow dept. terrestrial magnetism Carnegie Instn., Washington, 1977-79; research assoc. Nat. Radio Astronomy Obs., Charlottesville, Va., 1979-82; asst. prof. dept. physics Ariz. State U., Tempe, 1982-88, assoc. prof., 1988--. Contbr. over 50 articles to astronomy and astrophysics jours. Mem. Am. Astron. Soc., Internat. Astron. Union, Sigma Xi. Office: Ariz State U Dept Physics Tempe AZ 85283

BURT, DAVID ANTHONY, health association administrator; b. Hawthorne, Calif., Feb. 22, 1960; s. David and Purita Faye B. BS in Mktg., Ariz. State U., 1982. Assoc. realtor Point Investment & Realty, Scottsdale, Ariz.; regional mgr. Nat. Med. Fin. Svcs., Inc., Burban, Calif.; v.p. Physician's Home Care Mgmt., Dallas; pres. Preferred Home Therapy, Inc., Tempe, Ariz., 1986—; v.p. mktg. Ring Fin., Inc., Santa Monica, Calif., 1989—. Vol. Rep., Malibu, Calif., 1984. Roman Catholic. Home: 1432-47 W Emerald Mesa AZ 85202 also: 1604 South Catalina #1 Redondo Beach CA 90277 Office: Preferred Home Therapy Inc 925 S 52d St Ste 4 Tempe AZ 85281 also: Ring Fin Inc 501 Santa Monica Blvd Ste 700 Santa Monica CA 90401

BURTCH, THOMAS DARROLD, transportation executive; b. Milw., Sept. 10, 1949; s. Ernest. Darrold Burtch and Mildred Margaret Ehrlichman. BS, Wis. State U., 1971, postgrad., 1971-72. Tchr. English Sun Prairie (Wis.) Sr. High Sch., 1972-73; transportation agt. NW Airlines, Washington, 1973-85, San Francisco, 1985—; supr. NW Airlines, 1978-80. Author: 1984 Directory of the Greater Washington Business and Professional Council. Soloist Gay Men's Chorus of Washington, 1983-85, San Francisco Gay Men's Chorus, 1985—; founder B.O.D. Golden Gate Choral Found., San Francisco, 1986—. Democrat. Lutheran.

BURTON, AL, producer, director, writer; b. Chgo., Apr. 9, 1928; s. D. Chester and Isabelle (Olenick) G.; m. Sally Lou Lewis, Jan. 8, 1956; 1 dau., Jennifer. B.S. cum laude, Northwestern U., 1948. Exec. v.p. creative affairs Norman Lear-Embassy Communications, Inc., 1973-83; exec. producer-cons. Universal TV, 1983—; bd. dirs. Pilgrim Group Funds; mem. Second Decade council Am. Film Inst., adv. bd. Samantha Smith Found. Producer various youth-oriented TV series, 1949-52; producer Johnny Mercer's Mus. Chairs, 1952-55, Oscar Levant Show, 1955-61; creative producer Teen-Age Fair, 1962-72; exec. producer Charles in Charge, CBS-TV, 1984-85, Tribune Entertainment, 1986—, Together We Stand, CBS-TV, 1986-87, Nothing Is Easy, 1987-88, Lassie, 1989—; creative supr. Mary Hartman, Mary Hartman; prodn. supr. One Day At a Time, Facts of Life, Silver Spoons, The Jeffersons, Square Pegs, Diff'rent Strokes. Composer-lyricist theme songs for

Facts of Life, Diff'rent Strokes, Charles in Charge, Lassie, Together We Stand, Nothing Is Easy; Cons. Domestic Life, CBS-TV, 1983-84, Alan King Show, 1986. Recipient Emmy award for outstanding comedy series All in the Family, 1978-79, Producers award Nat. Council for Families and TV, 1984; honored for Diff'rent Strokes, NCCJ, 1979-80, honored for Facts of Life, Calif. Gov's. Com. for the Employment of the Handicapped, 1981-82. Mem. Caucus for Producers, Writers and Dirs., Dirs. Guild Am., Writers Guild Am., AFTRA, Acad. of TV Arts and Scis., Acad. Magical Arts. Office: Universal Studio Universal City CA 91608

BURTON, CLIFTON ALLEN, manufacturing company executive; b. Elwood, Ind., July 29, 1933; s. Joseph Melvin and Florence P. (Knotts) B.; m. Joyce Lorraine Emerson, Sept. 22, 1957; children: Keith Allen, Phillip Glenn, Catherine Lorraine, Michael Scott. Student, Purdue U., 1956-59. Registered profl. engr., Calif.; cert. mfg. engr. Tool design engr. Delco Remy div. Gen. Motors Corp., Anderson, Ind., 1959-61; mfg. engr. ACF Industries, Albuquerque, 1961-64, Automation Industries, Abilene, Tex., 1964-66, 69-71, Hughes Aircraft, Tucson, Ariz., 1966-69; mgr. prodn. engring. Hughes Tool Co., Houston, 1971-77; v.p. mfg. Eastman Whipstock, Houston, 1977-86; dir. mfg. Eastman Christensen, Salt Lake City, 1986—; lectr., tchr. Coll. Tech., U. Houston, 1976-85; mem. bd. indsl. advisors U. Houston, 1981-87, chmn., 1984-85. Patentee in field. With USAF, 1952-56. Recipient Teaching Excellence award Coll. Tech., U. Houston, 1977. Mem. Soc. Mfg. Engrs. (chpt. chmn. 1984-85, Chmn.'s award 1985). Presbyterian. Home: 1536 Edgecliff Dr Sandy UT 84092 Office: Eastman Christensen 1937 S 300 W Salt Lake City UT 84115

BURTON, DONALD GENE, insurance company executive; b. Van Nuys, Calif., May 24, 1953; s. Gene and Ruth Betty (Cable) B.; m. Sandi Catherine Kohnen, Mar. 4, 1979; children: Tera Jean, Kevin Anthony. BA, UCLA, 1975; MBA, U. So. Calif., 1977. Br. mgr. Met. Life, Los Angeles, 1977-83; v.p. Eichberg Assocs., Reseda, Calif., 1983—. Mem. Profl. Ins. Agts., Ind. Ins. Agts., Photog. Soc. Republican. Club: Los Angeles Underwater. Home: 16601 Osborne St Sepulveda CA 91343 Office: Eichberg Assocs 17750 Sherman Way #200 Reseda CA 91335

BURTON, EDWARD LEWIS, utility company executive; b. Coltax, Iowa, Dec. 8, 1935; s. Lewis Harrison and Mary (Turner/Paine) B.; m. Janet Jean Allan, July 29, 1956; children: Mary, Cynthia, Katherine, Daniel. BA in Indsl. Edn., U. No. Iowa, 1958; MS in Indsl. Edn., U. Wis.-Stout, 1969; postgrad., Ariz. State U., 1971-76. Tchr. apprentice program S.E. Iowa Community Coll., Burlington, 1965-68; tchr. indsl. edn. Keokuc (Iowa) Sr. High Sch., 1965-68, Oak Park (Ill.)-River Forest High Sch., 1968-70; tchr. Rio Salado Community Coll., Phoenix, 1972-82; tchr. indsl. edn. Buckeye (Ariz.) Union High Sch., 1970-72; cons. curriculum Westside Area Career Opportunities Program - Ariz. Dept. Edn.; owner A-1 Alignment and Repair, Buckeye, 1977-81; instr. vocat. automotive Dysart High Sch., Peoria, Ariz., 1979-81; tng. adminstr. Ariz. Pub. Service Co., Phoenix, 1981—; mem. Western Systems Coordinating Council, Salt Lake City, 1986—, dispatching tng. com. Editor: Bright Ideas for Career Education, 1974, More Bright Ideas for Career Education, 1975. Mem. Citizens Planning Com., Buckeye, 1987—. NDEA grantee, 1967. Mem. NEA (life), Ariz. Indsl. Edn. Assn. (life), Personnel Testing Council of Ariz., NRA (life, endowment), Cactus Combat League, Mensa (test proctor 1987—), Masons. Republican. Methodist. Home: 19845 W Van Buren St Buckeye AZ 85326 Office: 502 S 2d Ave Phoenix AZ 85003

BURTON, JOHN ANTHONY, JR., employment consultant; b. Portland, Oreg., June 18, 1965; s. John T. and Meri (Pozzi) B.; m. Mary Louise Kern, Dec. 17, 1988. Grad. high sch., Eugene, Oreg.; student, Portland State U., 1989—. bd. dirs. Bravo Advt. Inc. Employment cons. Emerald Employment, Lake Oswego, Oreg., 1985—; speaker local high schs., 1985—. With USAR, 1983—. Mem. Nat. Assn. Personnel Cons., Oreg. Assn. Cert. Personnel Cons. (bd. dirs. 1989—, v.p.), Lake Oswego C. of C. (vol. 1985—), Lake Oswego Leadership (steering com. 1987-88, 89). Republican. Roman Catholic. Office: Emerald Employment 5285 SW Meadows Rd Ste 281 Lake Oswego OR 97035

BURTON, JOHN LANE, mortgage company executive; b. Phoenix, Oct. 14, 1952; s. John Lane Burton and Marion Maitland Pool; m. Melanie Lynn Morgan. AA, Phoenix Community Coll., 1972; BA, Ariz. State U., 1974. Loan officer First Fed. Savs., Phoenix, 1971-76; prin. Burton Enterprises, Phoenix, 1976—; mgr. Del E. Webb Employees Fed. Credit Union, Las Vegas, Nev., 1977-78; asst. v.p., mgr. Security Savs. Svc. Corp., Phoenix, 1978-80; v.p., mgr. First Security Realty Svcs., Phoenix, 1980-86; sr. v.p. John Hancock Real Estate Fin., Phoenix, 1986—; founder, mem. Comml. Mortgage Banker Roundtable, Phoenix, 1980—. Pres. bd. The New Found., Phoenix. Republican. Methodist. Office: John Hancock Real Estate Fin 11801 N Tatum Blvd #240 Phoenix AZ 85028

BURTON, JOHN PAUL, lawyer; b. New Orleans, Feb. 26, 1943; s. John Paul and Nancy (Key) B.; children: Jennifer, Susanna, Derek, Catherine. BBA magna cum laude, La. Tech. U., 1965; LLB, Harvard U., 1968. Bar: N.Mex. 1968, U.S. Dist. Ct. N.Mex. 1968, U.S. Ct. Appeals (10th cir.) 1973, U.S. Supreme Ct. 1979. Assoc., Rodey, Dickason, Sloan, Akin & Robb, Albuquerque, 1968-74, dir., 1974—, chmn. comml. dept., 1980-81, mng. dir. Santa Fe, N.Mex., 1986—; lectr. workshops, seminars. Contbr. articles to legal publs. Packleader, Greater Southwest council Boy Scouts Am., 1976-77; fellow State Bar Found.; chmn. St. Simeon's Found., 1988-89; chmn. com. N.Mex. Harvard Law Sch. Fund; pres. Brunn Sch., 1987-89. Fellow Am. Coll. Real Estate Lawyers; mem. ABA (pvt. litigation com. antitrust sect.), N.Mex. State Bar Assn. (dir., budget officer 1983, chmn. uniform comml. code study and legis. com., sect. corp. bus. and banking 1984; chmn. litigation and antitrust sect. 1985-86; mem. com. to revise antitrust laws 1985-87), Albuquerque Bar Assn., Santa Fe Bar Assn., Am. Law Inst. (cons. group for complex litigation project), Am. Coll. Mortgage Attys., Am. Arbitration Assn. (panel arbitrators, regional adv. com.). Republican. Episcopalian (vestry 1977-80; lay reader 1982-87, chmn. evaluation commn. 1986-87, mem. constn. and canons com. Diocese of Rio Grande). Club: Harvard-Radcliffe of N.Mex. (dir. 1981-84). Office: Rodey Dickason Sloan Akin & Robb PA PO Box 1357 Santa Fe NM 87504 Office: PO Box 1357 Santa Fe NM 87504

BURTON, MARGARET ANN, educational professional, consultant; b. Washington, Pa., Mar. 23, 1926; d. Lawrence George and Blanche Lulu (Van Kirk) Gideon; m. Foster Job, Margaret Jean, Elizabeth Lee. BFA, Ariz. State U., 1972, MFA, 1980, postgrad., 1981-86. Founding dir. hist. mus. Tempe (Ariz.) Hist. Soc., 1972-78; dir. children summer program Phoenix Zoo, 1979-80; art. dir., tchr. ceremics Scottsdale (Ariz.) Parks and Recreation Dept., 1981; dir. Stevens House Heritage Sq. Project Ariz. State U., Tempe, 1981-87, asst. to exec. dir., 1987—; cons. Guadalupe (Ariz.) Hist. Soc., 1977-79, Winslow (Ariz.) Hist. Soc., 1986-87, pilot program Arts for the Spl. Edn. Children, Tempe, 1979-80; mem. steering com. Heritage Sq. Matsuri Festival, Phoenix, 1985-88. Coordinator documentary Sta. KAET-TV, 1978; dir. video documentary Southwest Heritage, 1988. Chairperson heritage com. Tempe Bi-Centennial Commn., Tempe, 1976; vol. Sta. KAET, Tempe, 1974—; vol., del. Mike Dukakis for Pres., Tempe, 1988; mem. Citizens Bond Com., Tempe, 1976; apptd. cadre program Ariz. Dept. Edn., Phoenix, 1974. Recipient Al Merito award Ariz. Hist. Soc., 1974, merit award Ariz. State U., 1986; named Citizen of Yr. Meyer Elem. Sch., 1976. Mem. Cen. Ariz. Mus. Assn. (founder, v.p. 1978-79), Adult Continuing Edn. Assn. (charter, pres. 1983-84), Women Interest Now (charter), Faculty Women, Women in Higher Edn. (adv. council). Democrat. Presbyterian. Office: Ariz State U Pub Events Gammage 105 Tempe AZ 85287-0105

BURTON, PAUL FLOYD, social worker; b. Seattle, May 24, 1939; s. Floyd James and Mary Teresa (Chovanak) B.; BA, U. Wash., 1961, MSW, 1967; m. Roxanne Maude Johnson, July 21, 1961; children: Russell Floyd, Joan Teresa. Juvenile parole counselor Div. Juvenile Rehab. State of Wash., 1961-66; social worker VA, Seattle, 1967-72, social worker, cons. Work Release program King County, Wash., 1967-72; supr., chief psychiatry sect. Social Work Svc. VA, Topeka, Kans., 1972-73; pvt. practice, Topeka and L.A., 1972—; chief social work svc. VA, Sepulveda, Calif., 1974—, EEO coord. Med. ctr., 1974-77. Mem. Nat. Assn. Social Workers (newsletter editor Puget Sound chpt. 1970-71), Acad. Cert. Social Workers, Ctr. for Studies in Social Functioning, Am. Sociol. Assn., Am. Public Health Assn., Am. Hosp. Assn., Soc. Hosp. Social Work Dirs., Assn. VA Social Work Chiefs (founder 1979, charter mem. and pres. 1980-81, newsletter editor 1982-83). Home: 14063 Remington St Arleta CA 91331 Office: 16111 Plummer St Sepulveda CA 91343

BURTON, RICHARD CLERKE, art gallery chairman, publisher; b. Exeter, Devon, Eng., Nov. 20, 1938; s. Robert Clerke and Mary (Dixon) B.; m. Dolores Ortiz Echague, June 1978, (div. 1986); m. Hanna Pavliskovska, 1988. Student, Wellington Coll., Berkshire, Eng., 1957. Race car driver Frank Williams, Eng., 1964-68; chmn. Burton's Pub., Switzerland, 1980-87, Richard Burton Gallery, L.A., 1987—. Lt. Royal Navy Res., 1958-60. Mem. Turf Club, London. Home: 215 S Mansfield Ave Los Angeles CA 90036 Office: Richard Burton Gallery 806 N La Cienega Blvd Los Angeles CA 90069

BURTZLAFF, RICHARD JOSEPH, electrical engineer; b. Cleve., Apr. 25, 1940; s. Robert Albert and Mary Ellen (Bartley) B. BSEE, U. Notre Dame, 1963; MSEE, U. Denver, 1973, MBA, 1978. Mgr. space launch systems Martin-Marietta Corp., Denver, 1963--. Republican. Roman Catholic. Home: 8144 E Mineral Dr Englewood CO 80112 Office: Martin-Marietta Corp PO Box 179 Denver CO 80201

BURWASH, PETER FRANCIS, tennis management company executive; b. Brockville, Ont., Can., Feb. 10, 1945; s. Stanley Ernest and Barbara Hilda (Wright) B.; m. Lynn Harvey, June 1, 1984. BPE, U. Toronto, 1967. Profl. tennis player 1967-74; pres. Peter Burwash Internat., Honolulu, 1974—. Author: (books) Tennis for Life, 1981, Vegetarian Primer, 1983, Aerobics for Men, 1984; instrn. editor Tennis Mag., Trumbull, Conn., 1986—. Mem. Young Pres.'s Orgn., U.S. Profl. Tennis Assn., U.S. Tennis Assn., Honolulu Club. Office: Peter Burwash Internat 1909 Ala Wai Blvd Ste 1010 Honolulu HI 96815

BUSBY, WILLIAM CARL, computer programmer and analyst, educator; b. Aurora, Ill., Oct. 21, 1925; s. William Lewis and Lena Linton (Hahn) B.; m. Virginia Gail Pinkston, Dec. 21, 1947; children: Linda Claire, Marilyn Gail, Sharon Marie. BA with honors, Ottawa U., 1949; MPA, U. Kansas, 1951. Staff mem. Internat. City Mgrs. Assn., Chgo., 1951-53; adminstrv. staff Oakridge (Tenn.) Assn. U., 1953-57; staff mem., project leader Sandia Nat. Labs, Albuquerque, 1957-82; instr. Albuquerque Tech. and Vocat. Inst., 1982—; ptnr. Programmed Serendipity, Ltd., Los Lunas, N.Mex., 1984—. Editor Jour. Pub. Mgmt., 1951-53; asst. editor Mcpl. Yearbook, 1951-53. Vol. cons. Transitional Living Svcs., Albuquerque, 1988—; spokesman, bd. dirs. Community Neighborhood Orgn., Albuquerque, 1969. With C.E., USAR, 1944-46, MTO. Mem. Pi Kappa Delta, Pi Sigma Alpha. Republican. Office: Albuquerque Tech-Vocat Inst 4700 Morris NE Albuquerque NM 87111

BUSCH, JOYCE IDA, small business owner; b. Madera, Calif., Jan. 24, 1934; d. Bruno Harry and Ella Fae (Absher) Toschi; m. Fred O. Busch, Dec. 14, 1956; children: Karen, Kathryn, Kurt. Student, Calif. State U., Fresno, 1982—. Stewardess United Air Lines, San Francisco, 1955-57; prin. Art Coordinates, Fresno, 1982—; art cons. Fresno Community Hosp., 1981-83; docent Fresno Met. Mus., 1981-84. Treas. Valley Children's Hosp. Guidance Clinic, 1975-79, Lone Star PTA, 1965-84,; mem. Mothers Guild Jan Joaquin Mem. Hosp., 1984-88. Mem. Am. Soc. Interior Designers (student), Illuminating Engring. Soc. N.Am. Republican. Roman Catholic. Club: Sunnyside Garden (pres. 1987-88).

BUSCH, ROBERT DOUGLAS, nuclear engineer; b. Denver, Sept. 24, 1949; s. Edwin John Jr. and Eleanor (Edison) B.; m. Judith Wilde, May 27, 1972 (div. 1985); 1 child, Michelle Marie. BS in Physics, Harvey Mudd Coll., Claremont, Calif., 1971; MS, U. N.Mex., 1972, PhD, 1976. Lic. profl. engr., N.Mex. Research engr. N.Mex. Energy Inst., Albuquerque, 1977-79; tech. dir. Bickle Group/CRS Group Inc, Albuquerque, 1979-82; v.p. Area, Inc., Albuquerque, 1982-85; pres. R.D. Busch & Assocs., Albuquerque, 1985—; vis. asst. prof. chem. and nuclear engring. U. N.Mex., 1984—. Author: (with others) Design of Energy Responsive Commercial Buildings, 1985, New Mexico Conservation Code Applications Manual. Chmn. stewardship unit Presbytery of Santa Fe, Albuquerque, 1988—; elder Presbyn. Ch., Albuquerque, 1985—. Mem. Am. Soc. Heating, Refrigerating, and Air-Conditioning Engrs., Am. Solar Energy Soc., Am. Nuclear Soc. Republican. Office: RD Busch & Assocs 8209 Sprenger NE Albuquerque NM 87109

BUSCH, TYRONE GLEN, educational services administrator; b. Longview, Wash., Feb. 14, 1948; s. Carl J. and Ann L. (Sier) B.; m. Joan Busch, June 15, 1972 (dec. June 1980); m. Donna L. Busch, Aug. 15, 1980; children: Jessica, Don. BS, Portland (Oreg.) State U., 1970; MBA, Pacific Coll., 1975; ABD, Ohio U.; MA, U. Las Vegas, Nev., 1988. Cert. spl. edn. tchr., Nev. Dist. mgr. Burroughs Corp., Detroit, 1970-77; dir., chief exec. officer Bell Systems Inc., Gig Harbor, Wash., 1975-82; dir. Family Fitness, Portland, 1983-86, AFM Enterprises, Las Vegas, 1983-86; chief exec. officer Busch Edn. Svcs., Ltd., Las Vegas, 1985—; substitute tchr. Clark County Schs., Las Vegas, 1986—, Las Vegas Day Sch., 1988—, Bishop Gorman High Sch., Las Vegas, 1988—; pvt. practice hosp. cons., 1965-69; tchr. Tacoma Community Coll., 1980-83, Ft. Steilacoom Community Coll., Puyallup, Wash., 1980-83, Portland State U., 1985. Exec. dir. S.W. Area Health Planning Commn., Helena, Mont., 1969-70; state rep. Oreg. State House, Salem, Oreg., 1972-74; del. Dem. Nat. Conv., Chgo., 1976. Mem. Am. Fedn. Tchrs., NEA, Am. Pub. Health Assn. Mormon. Home and Office: 6211 Bullion Las Vegas NV 89103

BUSE, MARGARET LYNN, history educator, lumber company executive; b. Kirkland, Wash., Mar. 1, 1948; d. James William and Margaret Ann (Woodland) Hutchison; m. Michael Norman Buse, June 20, 1970; 1 child, Michael James. BA in English, U. Wash., 1970; postgrad., Western Wash. U., 1976. Cert. standard tchr., Wash. Tchr. English secondary schs. Stanwood (Wash.) Sch. Dist., 1970-76, 88—, home sch. tchr., 1987—; instr. adult edn. Everett (Wash.) Community Coll., 1979—; co-owner Liberty Lumber Co., Arlington, Wash., 1984—. Contbr. articles on history to newspapers. Vice pres. Kayak Point Citizens Group, Warm Beach, Wash., 1980—; mem. centennial com. Snohomish County, 1985—; trustee Stanwood-Camano Found., 1986—; bd. dirs. Stanwood-Camano Library, 1987—, Snohomish County Mus., 1987—; chmn. local celebrations Wash. Centennial, 1985—. AAUW Ednl. Found. grantee, 1977-78. Mem. Am. Assn. State and Local History, Wash. Hist. Soc., King County Hist. Soc., Stanwood Area Hist. Soc. (trustee 1976—), League Snohomish County Hist. Orgns. (bd. dirs. 1979-84), Oral History Assn., Wash. Coun. Social Studies, U. Wash. Alumni Assn., Warm Beach Community Club, Grange Club. Lutheran. Home: 19024 Sound View Dr Warm Beach WA 98292 Office: Liberty Lumber Co 19521 Ave NE Arlington WA 98292

BUSH, DAVID VICTOR, small business owner; b. Laramie, Wyo., Dec. 4, 1948; s. Gilbert Francis and Eunice (Olsen) B.; m. Cynthia Diane Wright, May 23, 1971; children: Trevor, Alissa. BS in Metallurgy, Colo. Sch. Mines, 1972. Engr. AMAX, Georgetown, Colo., 1974-79, project mgr., 1980-81, chief metallurgist, 1981-84, gen. foreman, 1984-85; pres. Innovation Systems Design, Englewood, Colo., 1985—; Bd. dirs., v.p. tech. svcs. Yukon Tanana Mining Corp.; cons in field. Rep. precinct committeeman Clear Creek County, Georgetown, 1976-87; bd. dirs. Georgetown Community Ctr., 1985-88; design rev. com. Town of Georgetown, 1983-85. Maj. USAR, 1972—. Mem. Am. Inst. Mining Engrs., MENSA, Masons. Presbyterian. Home: 4301 S Broadway Ste 102 Englewood CO 80110 Office: Innovative Systems Design 4301 S Broadway Ste 102 Englewood CO 80110

BUSH, JUNE LEE, real estate executive; b. Philippi, W.Va., Sept. 20, 1942; d. Leland C. and Dolly Mary (Costello) Robinson; m. Jerry Lee Coffman, June 15, 1963 (div. 1970); 1 child, Jason Lance; m. Richard Alfred Bush, May 20, 1972. Grad., Fairmont State Coll., 1962, Dale Carnegie, Anaheim, Calif., 1988. Exec. sec. McDonnell Douglas, Huntington Beach, Calif., 1965-72; adminstrv. asst. Mgmt. Resources, Inc., Fullerton, Calif., 1978-80; bldg. mgr. Alfred Gobar Assocs., Brea, Calif., 1980—; treas. Craig Park E., Fullerton, 1982, bd. dirs. 1982—. Author instrn. manual Quality Assurance Secretarial Manual, 1971. Sec. PTA, La Palma, 1974. Mem. Gamma Chi Chi. Home: 2517 Biscayne Pl Fullerton CA 92633 Office: Alfred Gobar Assocs Inc 201 S Brea Blvd Brea CA 92633

BUSH, SARAH LILLIAN, historian; b. Kansas City, Mo., Sept. 17, 1920; d. William Adam and Lettie Evelyn (Burrill) Lewis; m. Walter Nelson Bush, June 7, 1946; children: William Read, Robert Nelson. AB, U. Kans., 1941; BS, U. Ill., 1943. Clk. circulation dept. Kansas City Pub. Library, 1941-42, asst. librarian Paseo br., 1943-44; librarian Kansas City Jr. Coll., 1944-46; substitute librarian San Mateo County Library, Woodside and Portola Valley, Calif., 1975-77; various temporary positions 1979-87; owner Metriguide, Palo Alto, Calif., 1975-78. Author: Atherton Lands, 1979, rev. edition 1987. Editor: Atherton Recollections, 1973. Pres., v.p. Jr. Librarians, Kansas City, 1944-46; courtesy, yearbook & historian AAUW, Menlo and Atherton (Calif.); asst. Sunday sch. tchr., vol. Holy Trinity Ch., Menlo Park, 1955-78; v.p., membership com. Menlo Atherton High Sch. PTA, 1964-73; founder, bd. dirs. Friends of Atherton Community Library, 1967—, oral historian, 1968—, chair Bicentennial event, 1976; bd. dirs. Menlo Park Hist. Assn., 1973-80, oral historian, 1973—; bd. dirs. Civic Interest League, Atherton, 1978-81; mem. hist. county commn. Town of Atherton, 1987—; vol. Allied Arts Palo Alto Aux. Children's Hosp. at Stanford, 1967—, oral historian, 1980—, United Crusade, Garfield Sch., Redwood City, 1974-88; historian, awards chairperson Cub Scouts Boy Scouts Am. Episcopalian.

BUSHEHRI, ALI, engineering company executive; b. Santa Cruz, Calif., May 28, 1957; s. S. Reza and S. Catherine (Ghahremani) B.; m. Nassrin Barabi, Feb. 9, 1985. BS in Mech. Engring., U. Mo., Rolla, 1981. Engring. planning Bechtel Nat. Inc., San Francisco, 1981-86, sr. planner, 1986-87, asst. to mgr. of engring., 1987—; pres. UniQuest Internat. Inc., San Francisco, 1988—; bd. dirs. Oz Techs. Inc., Hayward, Calif.; cons. Xerxes Group Inc., Oakland, Calif., 1986-88. Bd. dir. Iranian-Am. Rep. Coun., San Francisco, 1988, pres. Contra Costa County, 1989. Mem. Am. Mgmt. Assn., Entrepreneur Inst. Home: 142 Del Monte Dr Walnut Creek CA 94595

BUSHEY, MARLINE RAY RIESE, retired elementary teacher; b. Highland Park, Mich., Oct. 24, 1926; d. Casper Aaron Raymond and Leona Clara (Krueger) Riese; m. Ralph Leo Bushey, Jr., July 10, 1948; children: Raymond Ralph, Bradford Aaron, Laura Lee. Student, Mich. State U., 1944-45; BA, U. Mich., 1948; postgrad., Long Beach State U., 1958, Dominguez State U., 1967, Pepperdine U., 1968, UCLA, 1968, San Jose State Coll., 1970-72. Cert. secondary tchr., 1948, elem. tchr., 1970, Mich. Tutor, reader for blind U. Fla., 1949-51; substitute tchr. L.A. Sch. Dist., 1959-61; sec. treas. Micro Miniature Mfg. Co., Gardenia, Calif., 1962-69; tchr. Chadwick Sch., Palos Verdes Penn, Calif., 1969-70; substitute tchr. San Jose and Los Gatos-Saratoga Sch. Dists., Calif., 1970-76; bilingual migrant tchr. Pajaro Sch. Dist., 1976-83, ret., 1983. V.p. PTA, Rolling Hills Estates, Calif., 1963-66; mem. library bd. Resurrection Luth. Sch., Torrance, Calif., 1963-68; pres., founder Alliance of Mentally Ill, Santa Cruz, 1977-82; leader Girl Scouts, Palos Verdes, 1964-67, Cub Scouts Boy Scouts Am., Palos Verdes, 1965; co-leader little league, 1963-66. Mem. Retired Tchrs. Assn., AAUW (pres. 1985-87), Affiliates U. Santa Cruz. Republican. Lutheran. Home: 315 Laguna St Santa Cruz CA 95060

BUSHMAN, EDWIN FRANCIS ARTHUR, engineer, plastics consultant, rancher; b. Aurora, Ill., Mar. 16, 1919; s. George J. and Emma (Gengler) B.; B.S., U. Ill., 1941, postgrad., 1941-42, Calif. Inst. Tech., 1941; m. Louise Kathryn Peterson, Jan. 3, 1946; children—Bruce Edwin, Gary Robert, Joan Louise, Karen Rose, Mary Elisabeth, Paul George. Jr. engr, Gulf Refining Co. Gulf Oil Corp., Mattoon, Ill., 1940-41; engr. radio and sound lab. war research, div. U. Calif. at Navy Electronics Lab., Pt. Loma, San Diego, 1942-45; project engr. Bell and Howell Co., Lincolnwood, Ill., 1945-46; research cons., Scholl Mfg. Co., Inc., Chgo., 1946-48; project engr. deepfreeze div. Motor Products Corp., North Chicago, Ill., 1948-50; research and product design engr. Bushman Co., Aurora, Ill. also Mundelein, Ill., 1946-55; with Plastics div. Gen. Am. Transp. Corp., Chgo., 1950-68, tech. dir., 1950-55, mgr. sales and sales engring. Western states, Compton, Calif., 1955-68, sales and sales engring. research and devel. div., 1962-64; with USS Chems., 1968-70; plastics cons. E.F. Bushman Co., 1970—, Tech. Conf. Assocs., 1974-80. Program mgr. Agriplastics Symposium Nat. Agrl. Plastics Conf., 1966; program mgr. Plastics in Hydrospace, 1967; originator Huisman Plastics awards, 1970, Un-Carbon Polymer prize and Polymer Pool Preserve Plan, 1975, Polymer Independence award, 1977, 78. Bd. dirs. Coastal Area Protective League, 1958-66, Lagunita Community Assn., 1959-66 (pres. 1964-65), Calif. Marine Parks and Harbors Assn., 1959-69. Sr. editor Plastic Trends mag., 1985—. Recipient Western Plastics Man of Yr. award, 1972. Mem. Soc. Plastics Industry Inc. (chpt. pres. 1971-72), Soc. Plastic Engrs. (Lundberg award 1981), Western Plastics Engrs., Western Plastics Mus. and Pioneers, Plastics Pioneers Assn., ASTM, Sunkist Growers, Calif. Avocado Soc., Cal. Citrus Nurserymen's Soc., Calif. Farm Bur. Fedn. U. Ill. Alumni Assn., Lemon Men's Club, Soc. for Advancement Materials and Process Engring., Geopolymers Inst. Roman Catholic. Moose. Author various profl. and strategic resource papers. Patentee in field of plastics, carbon and colored glass fibers, process, and applications. Home: 19 Lagunita Laguna Beach CA 92651 Office: PO Box 581 Laguna Beach CA 92652

BUSHNELL, RODERICK PAUL, lawyer; b. Buffalo, Mar. 6, 1944; s. Paul Hazen and Martha Atlee B.; m. Suzann Yvonne Kaiser, Aug. 27, 1966; 1 child, Arlo Phillip. BA, Rutgers U., 1966; JD, Georgetown U., 1969. Bar: Calif. 1970, U.S. Supreme Ct. 1980. Atty. dept. water resources Sacramento, 1969-71; ptnr. Bushnell, Caplan & Fielding, San Francisco, 1971—; bd. dirs. Bread & Roses, Inc., Mill Valley, Calif. Bd. dirs. Calif. Lawyers for the Arts, Pt. Mason, San Francisco, 1985—. Mem. San Francisco Bar Assn. (arbitrator), San Francisco Superior Ct. (arbitrator), Calif. Bar Assn., Trial Lawyers Assn. Am., Lawyers Club of San Francisco, Calif. Trial Lawyers Assn., San Francisco Trial Lawyers Assn., No. Calif. Criminal Trial Lawyers Assn., San Francisco Bay Club, Commonwealth Club. Democrat. Office: Bushnell Caplan & Fielding 901 Market St Ste 230 San Francisco CA 94103

BUSICK, BONNIE SIGREN, nurse; b. Bklyn., Feb. 5, 1933; d. Floyd Turk and Maude Katherine (Weir) Turk Herman; m. Vincent G. Sigren, Oct. 6, 1951 (div.); children: Linda Jeanne, Eric Vincent, Krista L. Sigren Boyer, Beth Anne, Lief Carl; m. Christopher Jay Busick, June 21, 1974. BA, Mich. State U., 1967, MA, 1969; Assoc. Nursing, Kalamazoo Valley Community Col, 1974; PhD, Columbia Pacific U., 1988. RN, Colo. Asst. prof. Olivet Coll., Mich., 1969-71, Western Mich. U., Kalamazoo, 1971-75; nurse Henry Ford Hosp., Detroit, 1978-80; educator psychology Naropa Inst., Boulder, Colo., 1983-87; educator psychology grad. sch. Boulder Coll., 1981—; hospice trainer Boulder Meml. Hosp., 1987—; seminar leader, cons. and lectr. in field. Author: Ill Not Insame, 1986, Living With Cancer Workbook, 1988, Grieving as a Hero's Journey Seminar Manual, 1988; contbr. articles to profl. jours. State legisl. chair Colo. Alliance Mentally Ill, Denver, 1983—; coordinator Nat. Alliance Mentally Ill, Wash. D.C., forensics network com., 1986—. Recipient Community Service award Boulder Psychiatric Inst., 1983, Advocacy, Colo. Alliance Mentally Ill, 1985, 86, Jefferson, Am. Inst. Pub. Services, 1986. Democrat. Buddhist. Home: 1465 Ithica Boulder CO 80303 Office: 2880 Falsom Ste #104 Boulder CO 80302

BUSIG, RICK HAROLD, mining executive; b. Vancouver, Wash., June 21, 1952; s. Harold Wayne and Ramona (Riley) B. AA, Clark Coll., Vancouver, 1972; BA in Econs., U. Wash., 1974. CPA, Wash. Acct., Universal Svcs., Seattle, 1975-78; acct., acctg. mgr., controller Landura Corp., Woodburn, Oreg., 1978-80; asst. controller Pulte Home Corp., Laramie, Wyo., 1980-81; treas., controller Orcal Cable, Inc., Sparks, Nev., 1981-82; controller Saga Exploration Co., Reno, Nev., 1982—; acct. Sterling Mine Joint Venture, Beatty, Nev., 1982—. Del. Nev. State Dem. Conv., Reno, 1984, Las Vegas, 1988. Recipient Spaatz award CAP. Mem. AICPA, Wash. Soc. CPA's, Oreg. Soc. CPA's. Home: 2500 Dickerson Rd #174 Reno NV 89503 Office: Saga Exploration Co 2660 Tyner Reno NV 89503

BUSK, PATRICIA LYNN, statistics educator; b. Southampton, N.Y., Nov. 25, 1944; d. Andrew Stanley and Julia (Maziarz) Zuczek; m. Michael Christopher Busk, June 7, 1969. BA, Trenton State Coll., 1966; MA, Cath. U. Am., 1969; postgrad., Northwestern U., 1970-72; PhD, U. Wis., 1976. Intern dept. mental health NASA, Washington, summer 1969; statistician Children's Meml. Hosp., Chgo., 1969-72, project dir., 1972-73; grad. asst. Cath. U. Am., Washington, 1966-67; teaching asst. U. Wis., Madison, 1973-74, 75-76; lectr. U. Wis., Milw., 1975; asst. prof. Sch. Edn. Mich. State U., East Lansing, 1976-78; vis. assoc. prof. Sch. Edn., U. Calif., Berkeley, 1979—; assoc. prof. stats. Sch. Edn., U. San Francisco, 1980—; cons. Archdiocese San Francisco, 1981-84, Ctr. for Rsch. on Pvt. Edn., San

Francisco, 1980-81; test developer Children's Hosp., San Francisco, 1985. Contbr. articles to profl. jours. Recipient Disting. Teaching award Sch. Edn., U. San Francisco, 1986, 89, Merit award, 1987, 89; Kate D. Stout scholar, 1966; NIH fellow, 1967-69. Mem. Am. Ednl. Rsch. Assn. (sec.-treas. 1986-88), Am. Psychol. Assn., Am. Statis. Assn., Nat. Coun. on Measurement in Children, Psychometric Soc., Phi Delta Kappa (treas. U. San Francisco chpt. 1984-86, pres. 1986-87). Democrat. Roman Catholic. Home: 123 Turquoise Way San Francisco CA 94131 Office: U San Francisco Sch Edn San Francisco CA 94117-1080

BUSS, JERRY HATTEN, real estate executive, sports team owner. Children: John, Jim, Jeanie, Jane. BS in Chemistry, U. Wyo.; MS, PhD in Chemistry, U. So. Calif., 1957. Chemist Bur. Mines; past mem. faculty dept. chemistry U. So. Calif.; mem. missile div. McDonnell Douglas, Los Angeles; partner Mariani-Buss Assos.; former owner Los Angeles Strings; chmn. bd., owner Los Angeles Lakers (Nat. Basketball Assn.); until 1988 owner Los Angeles Kings (Nat. Hockey League). Office: care Los Angeles Lakers 3900 W Manchester Blvd PO Box 10 Inglewood CA 90306 *

BUSS, TERRANCE MAYNARD, insurance executive; b. Duluth, Minn., July 15, 1939; s. Maynard Mathias and Arline Ieleen (Hanson) B.; m. Barbara Merilyn Larsen, July 12, 1965; children: Whitney M., Garrett T. BA, Mankato (Minn.) State U., 1964. Mktg. rep. Aetna Casualty & Surety, San Francisco, 1964-73; owner, ins. broker Moellering Russell & Buss, Inc., San Jose, Calif., 1973—; pres. S. Coast Fieldmen's Assn., San Jose, 1971-72. With U.S. Army, 1959-60. Mem. Soc. Chartered Property Casual Underwriters, Ins. Agt.'s Assn. Calif., Almaden Athletic Club. Republican. Lutheran. Office: Moellering Russell & Buss 3880 S Bascom Ave #201 San Jose CA 95124

BUSSCHAERT, JOHN LEWIS, food products executive; b. Chgo., Oct. 17, 1960; s. Andrew William and Margaret Ellen (Lewis) B. BA in Polit. Sci., Calif. State U., Bakersfield, 1983; postgrad., Western State Coll., 1985-86. Mktg. rep. Tandy Bus. Telephone Systems, Anaheim, Calif., 1984-85; resource mgr. The Food Distbin. Ctr., Orange, Calif., 1987—. Asst. campaign mgr. Ashburn for County Supr., Bakersfield, Calif., 1984; coordinator campaign hdqrs. Reps. Orange County, Calif., 1986. Episcopalian. Home: 12712 Tunstall St Garden Grove CA 92645 Office: The Food Distbn Ctr 426A W Almond Orange CA 92666

BUSSEY, CLARK ELY, education educator; b. Hot Springs, Wyo., Aug. 9, 1937; s. Fred Glenn and Mabelle (Livingston) B. BA, U. Pa., 1959. Travel agent Am. Express, Capetown, So. Africa, 1962-65; assoc. dean admission Univ. Pa., Phila., 1965-73; dean admissions Colo. Women's Coll., Denver, 1973-74; dir. of placement Denver Inst. Tech., 1974-76, agy. counselor, 1976-86, dir. admission, 1986-88, agy. dir., 1988--. Elder, Montveiw Presbyn. Ch., Denver, 1981-83; with the U.S. Navy,. Mem. Colo. Career Devel. Assn., Nat. Assn. Rehab. Prof., Nat. Rehab. Assn. Democrat. Home: 748 Magnolia St Denver CO 80220 Office: Denver Inst Tech 7350 N Broadway Denver CO

BUSSEY, GEORGE DAVIS, psychiatrist; b. Salta, Argentina, Apr. 14, 1949; s. William Harold and Helen (Wygant) B.; m. Moira Savage, July 26, 1975; children: Andrew Davis, Megan Elizabeth. BS, U. Denver, 1969; MD, Ea. Va. Med. Sch., 1977. Intern Eastern Va. Grad. Sch. Medicine, resident; resident Vanderbilt U. Hosp., Nashville; staff psychiatrist Hawaii State Hosp., Kanpohe, 1981-82; asst. prof. dept. psychiatry U. Hawaii, Honolulu, 1982-84; dir. adult svcs. Kahi Mohala Hosp., Ewa Beach, Hawaii, 1983—; clin. dir. Queens Healthcare Plan, Honolulu, 1988—. Contbr. articles to profl. jours. Mem. Am. Psychiat. Assn., Hawaii Psychiat. Soc. (treas. 1982-83, pres. 1985-87).

BUSSINGER, ROBERT E., service executive; b. Dayton, Ohio, Jan. 26, 1932; s. Albert G. and Louise B. (Hoffman) B.; m. Doreen L. Fine, Jan. 25, 1957 (div. 1978); children: Leslie E., Daniel M., David M. Student, U. Dayton, 1955-56, U. Redlands, 1957-59. Broker Bussinger Ins., Carmel, Calif., 1962-69; broker, dealer Esper Corp., Carmel, 1969-72; owner Esperanto Coffee House, Carmel, 1971-75; gen. mgr. Gen. Store Restaurant, Carmel, 1976-77; food svc. dir. Lodge at Pebble Beach (Calif.), 1977-79; resort v.p., gen. mgr. TransAm. Corp., Big Sur, Calif., 1979—, Ventana Inn Resort, Big Sur, 1979—. With USN, 1951-55. Mem. Nat. Restaurant Assn., Calif. Hotel Assn., Monterey Peninsula Hotel Restaurant Assn., Carmel Bus. Assn., Calif. Hotel Sales Mktg. Assn., Monterey Advt. Club (v.p. 1985-87), Monterey County Restaurant Assn. (bd. dirs.). Big Sur C. of C. (pres. 1984-89), Monterey Peninsula C. of C. (bd. dirs. 1984-89). Home and Office: Ventana Big Sur CA 93920

BUSSMAN, JOHN WOOD, physician, health care administrator; b. Mankato, Minn., July 4, 1924; s. A.M. and Myrtle E. (Wood) B.; m. Muriel J. Koenck, June 17, 1950; children: David, John, Sarah, James, Rebecca, Penelope. BSc, U. Minn., 1946, MB, 1947, MD, 1948. Diplomate Am. Bd. Pediatrics, Am. Bd. Pediatric Cardiology. Intern Sioux Valley Hosp., Sioux Falls, S.D., 1948; residency in pediatrics U. Minn. Hosp., Mpls., 1949-50, pediatric cardiology fellow, 1951; gen. practice medicine The Children's Clinic-Sylvan Med. Services, Inc., Portland, Oreg., 1953—; clin. prof. pediatrics U. Oreg. Med. Sch.; cons. in pediatric cardiology; chief pediatrics Emanuel Hosp., 1966-69, health maintenance orgn. com. 1972; bd. dirs. Health Choice, Inc., 1983-86; chmn. Physicians' Health Network, 1982-83. Chmn. health services adv. com. Multnomah County Commrs., 1973-77; mem. Multnomah County Health Care Commn. 1977-82. Fellow Am. Acad. Pediatrics, Am. Coll. Chest Physicians (sec. com. myopathy in childhood 1976), Am. Coll. Cardiology (Oreg. gov. 1974-77); mem. Nat. Acad. Sci. (Inst. of Medicine), Portland Acad. Pediatrics (pres. 1963), Portland Acad. Medicine, Portland Heart Club, Oreg. Heart Assn. (chmn. 1976-77, exec. com., bd. dirs. 1960-81, chmn. community service com. 1972-74, chmn. rheumatic fever commn. 1954-77, del. Am. Heart Assn. regional heart com. 1973-80, budget com., chmn. program rev. council, 1985), Oreg. Thoracic Soc. (chmn. research com. 1966), Multnomah Found. Med. Care (pres. 1970-80, med. dir. 1972-83, treas. 1980-83), Multnomah County Med. Soc. (pres. 1970, trustee 1963-71, treas .1965, sec. 1966, v.p. 1967, pres.-elect 1969, chmn. bd. censors 1971, chmn. peer rev. commn. 1971, chmn. Portland Council Hosps. liaison com. 1971), Oreg. Med. Assn. (v.p. 1972, chmn. health manpower 1972, ad hoc com. peer rev. 1972, long-range planning com. 1972, trustee 1969-80), Oreg. Found. Med. Care (bd. dirs. 1972-77), Oreg. Comprehensive Health Planning Authority (health manpower com.), Comprehensive Health Planning Assn. (chmn. project rev. com., chmn. profl. health service com., bd. dirs. 1970-77, exec. com. 1970-74), N.W. Oreg. Health Systems (health planning com. 1978-80, diagnosis and treatment subcom. 1978-80, chmn. health care tech. assessment com. 1983), HEW (Exptl. Med. Care Rev. Orgns. 1972-73), Am. Assn. Profl. Standards Rev. Orgns. (pres. 1974-77), Nat. Prof. Standards Rev. Council (chmn. 1978-80), and others. Clubs: Portland City, Multnomah Athletic. Lodge: Rotary. Office: Sylvan Med Service Inc 5415 SW Westgate Dr Portland OR 97221

BUSSY, PATRICIA JEAN, interior designer, real estate company executive; b. Long Beach, Calif., Nov. 10, 1923; d. Charles Davenport and Nora Augustine (Bills) Hamilton; m. Henry Dillon, July 15, 1945 (dec. 1957); children: Patrick H., Michael C.; m. Frederick Ernest Bussey, Sept. 16, 1961. Student, U. Calif., San Francisco, 1963; real estate cert., Anthony's Sch., 1982. Sec. N. Am. Aviation, Inglewood, Calif., 1942-44, Juvenile and Adult Probation, Oakland, Calif., 1946-50; model May Co., Los Angeles, 1944-45; stenographer Los Angeles Hall Records, 1944-45; adminstrv. asst. ABMA Werner Von Braun, Oakland, 1950-52, Piper and Aero Commander Sales, Oakland, 1953-57; owner, pres. Paticia Bussey Interior Design, Oakland Castro Valley, Calif., 1957—; sales agt. Peter Mattie Co., San Francisco, 1982—; owner, mgr., apt. bldgs., restaurants. Bd. dirs. 4,000,000 Coop, Castro Valley, 1975-76. Republican. Clubs: Blackhawk (Danville, Calif.), Lakes (Palm Desert, Calif.).

BUSWELL, CAROL ANNE, genealogist, writer; b. Burbank, Calif., Jan. 31, 1945; d. Lloyd Raymond and Katheryn Louise (Forbes) Apperson; m. Jerry Leonard Brown, May 30, 1964 (div. May 1973); children: Terri Lynn, William Scott, Elizabeth Anne; m. Lloyd Arthur Buswell, Dec. 29, 1973. BA cum laude, Western State Coll., 1978; postgrad., Calif. State U., Northridge, 1983, Brigham Young U., 1986. Tchr. Woodland Park (Colo.) Elem. Sch., 1978-80, Baker (Oreg.) Sch. Dist., 1980-82; private research genealogist Canoga Park, Calif., 1982-87, Littlerock, Calif., 1987—; cons. So. Calif. Genealogical Soc., Burbank, 1987—; cons. and librarian Palmdale (Calif.) Br. LDS Family History Ctr. Precinct officer, Canoga Park, 1986-87. Mem. Nat. Genealogical Soc., Antelope Valley Genealogical Soc., Tex. County (Mo.) Genealogical Soc. Democrat. Mormon. Office: LDS Family History Ctr Palmdale Br 2120 E Ave R Palmdale CA 93550

BUTAC, ANNE AKIKO HIGA, accountant; b. Tokyo, Sept. 30, 1956; came to U.S., 1974; d. Harry Koei and Alice Mitomi (Matsuo) Higa; m. Reinold Terzo Butac, Oct. 31, 1981; children: Ryan Akria, Terrianne Chiaki. BA, U. Hawaii, 1978. Mem. audit staff Ernst & Whinney, Honolulu, 1979-80, mem. advanced staff, 1980-81, sr. auditor, 1981; audit sr. Arthur Young & Co., Honolulu, 1981-84, audit mgr., 1984-86; sr. intrnal auditor Queen's Health Systems, Honolulu, 1986-87, dir. internal audit, 1987—. Bd. dirs. Hawaii Mothers Milk Bank, 1981—. Mem. Am. Soc. Women Accts. (pres. 1986-87), Inst. Internal Auditors. Office: Queen's Health Systems 1301 Punchbowl St Honolulu HI 96813

BUTEYN, DONALD P., pastor, educator; b. Fond du Lac, Wis., Nov. 19, 1924; s. Cornelius and Jessie Louise (Felsman) B.; m. Marian Schroeder, June 24, 1949; children: Richard, Joyce, Jean, Carol, Douglas, Steven. BA, Hope Coll., 1948; MDiv, Western Theol. Sem., 1951; DD, Whitworth Coll., 1974. Pastor Jamestown (Mich.) Reformed Ch., 1951-53, Midland (Mich.) Reformed Ch., 1953-58; sr. pastor 1st Reformed Ch., Kalamazoo, Mich., 1958-64; assoc. pastor 1st Presbyn. Ch., Berkeley, Calif., 1964-69; exec. pastor 1st Presbyn. Ch., Hollywood, Calif., 1973-79; sr. pastor 1st Presbyn. Ch., Bakersfield, Calif., 1986—; exec. Seattle Presbery, 1969-73; chaplain L.A. Police Dept., 1975-79; Flora Lampson Hewlett prof. evangelism and mission San Francisco Theol. Sem., 1979-86; dean San Francisco Theol. Sem., San Anselma, Calif., 1983-86; prof. emeritus San Francisco Theol. Sem., 1989—; bd. dirs. Kern County Food Banks, Inc., Bakersfield, Bethany Svc. Ctr., Bakersfield, Friends Outside Agy., Bakersfield, Frontier Fellowship Presbyn. Ch.; mem. governing bd. Nat. Coun. Chs. of Christ, 1988—. Contbr. articles to profl. jours. Chmn. Hollywood Devel. Commn., L.A., 1976-79. Named Presbyn. Preacher of Yr., Gen. Assembly Presbyn. Ch., 1983. Mem. Nat. Assn. Profs. of Mission, Rotary. Democrat. Home: 9600 Lea Oak Rd Bakersfield CA 93311

BUTLER, ALDIS PERRIN, advertising agency executive; b. New Haven, Dec. 7, 1913; s. Sidney Perlin and Margaret Taylor (Simpson) B.; m. Louise B. SMith, Sept. 9, 1936; children: Louise Butler Johnson, Aldis Perrin Butler, Jr., Margaret Butler McKenna. BA, Dartmouth Coll., 1936. V.p. Young and Rubicam, Inc., N.Y.C., 1953-54; v.p., gen. mgr. Young and Rubicam, Inc., Detroit, 1954-59; v.p. J. Walter Thompson Co., N.Y.C., 1959-62; sr. v.p., dir. Benton & Bowles, Inc., N.Y.C., 1962-66; chmn. bd. Butler-Turner Advt., Vero Beach, Fla., 1966-82; v.p. mktg. Metapath, Inc., Foster City, Calif., 1984; chmn. bd. Livingston/Sirutis Advt., Belmont, Calif., 1984-85; pvt. practice cons. Sonoma, Calif., 1986—. Chmn. Am. Heart Assn., Vero Beach, Fla., 1973-75; chmn. ARC, Vero Beach, 1973-75; chmn. Civic Arts Com., Vero Beach, 1969-76. Served to lt. USNR, 1943-46, PTO. Recipient Silver Medal award Am. Advt. Fedn., 1979. Mem. Sonoma Valley C. of C. Democrat. Episcopalian. Club: Adcraft (life mem.) (Detroit). Home and Office: 202 Avenida Barbera Sonoma CA 95476

BUTLER, BYRON CLINTON, physician, gemologist; b. Carroll, Iowa, Aug. 10, 1918; s. Clinton John and Blance (Prall) B.; m. Jo Ann Nicolls; children: Marilyn, John Byron, Barbara, Denise; 1 stepdau., Marrianne. MD, Columbia Coll. Physicians and Surgeons, 1943; ScD, Columbia U., 1952; grad., Gemol. Inst. Am., 1986. Intern Columbia Presbyn. Med. Ctr.; resident Sloane Hosp. for Women; instr. Columbia Coll. Physicians and Surgeons, 1950-53; dir. Butler Research Found., Phoenix, 1953-86, pres., 1970—; pres. World Gems/G.S.G., Inc. Bd. dirs. Heard Mus., Phoenix, 1965-74; founder Dr. Byron C. Butler, G.G., Fund for Inclusion Research, Gemol. Inst. Am., Santa Monica, Calif., 1987. Served to capt. M.C. AUS, 1944-46. Grantee Am. Cancer Soc., 1946-50, NIH, 1946-50. Fellow AAAS; mem. Am. Gemstones Trade Assn., Internat. Color Gemstone Assn. Home and Office: 6302 N 38th St Paradise Valley AZ 85253

BUTLER, DOUGLAS EARLE, city official; b. Portland, Oreg., Dec. 17, 1945; s. Herbert Emery and Suzanne (Galvin) B.; m. Judith Louise West, Aug 26, 1967 (div. 1978); children: Dylan Eachan, Neely Elizabeth; m. Patricia Lynn Holman, May 31, 1981; stepchildren: Aaron Robert Gregg, Sarah Elizabeth Gregg. Student, Oregon State U., 1963-66; BSBA, Portland State U., Oreg., 1971. Lic. real estate broker, Oreg. Spl. dep. registrar Dept. Records and Elections Multnomah County, Portland, Oreg., 1969-70; sr. mgmt. analyst Fiscal Mgmt. Office Multnomah County, Portland, Oreg., 1971-73; dep. adminstr. Office Planning & Devel. City of Portland, Oreg., 1973-80; v.p. Remold Corp., Portland, Oreg., 1980-83; pres. Pinnacle Devel. Co., Portland, Oreg., 1984-85; devel. mgr. The Koll Co., Portland, Oreg., 1985-86; v.p. Met. Homes Inc., Lake Oswego, Oreg., 1987-88; dir. Oregon Film & Video Task Force, Portland, 1988-89; project coord. Portland Devel. Commn., 1989—; cons., trainer Nat. Community Devel. Assn., Washington, 1980. Founder, chmn. Portland Special Olympics, 1979-82; chmn. Multnomah County Juvenile Ct. Adv. Council Portland, 1986-87; bd. dirs. Christie Sch., Portland, 1984—. Lt. U.S. Army, 1966-69. Home: 111 NE Graham St Portland OR 97212

BUTLER, JEFFREY SHERIDAN, publisher; b. Christopher, Ill., June 19, 1939; s. Jefferson Macklin and Veneita May (Slinger) B.; B.S. in Mktg., U. Ill., 1961; m. Erin Clarke; children—Drew Sheridan, Emily Louise. With UARCO Bus. Systems Sales, Chgo., 1961-62; dir. public relations Pacific S.W. Airlines, San Diego, 1965-68; chmn. bd., chief exec. officer, founder, pub. East/West Network Inc., Los Angeles, 1968—; pub. mags. Continental Airlines, N.W. Airlines, Pan Am. Airlines, United Airlines, Eastern Airlines, TWA, S.W. Airlines. Bd. dirs. So. Calif. Visitors Council, United Service Orgn. met. N.Y. Served with M.C., AUS, 1962-65. Mem. Regency Club, Doubles Internat. Club, Westchester Country Club, Annabel's Club, Beach Club, Sigma Nu. Office: East/West Network Inc 5900 Wilshire Blvd 8th Fl Los Angeles CA 90036

BUTLER, KENT ALAN, electrical engineer; b. Payson, Utah, Aug. 31, 1958; s. Kenneth David and Cherril (Benson) B.; m. Shauna Alexander, Apr. 10, 1987. BSEE, Brigham Young U., 1983. Engr. Ford Aerospace and Communications, Inc., Palo Alto, Calif., 1983-85; sr. engr. Boeing Mil. Airplane Co., Seattle, 1985-86; hardware design engr. II, Novell, Inc., Provo, Utah, 1986—. Mem. IEEE, Tau Beta Pi, Eta Kappa Nu. Republican. Mormon. Office: Novell Inc 122 East 1700 South Provo UT 84601

BUTLER, LESLIE ANN, advertising agency owner; b. Salem, Oreg., Nov. 19, 1945; d. Marlow Dole and Lala Ann (Erlandson) Butler. Student Lewis and Clark Coll., 1963-64; BS, U. Oreg, 1969; postgrad. Portland State U. 1972-73. Creative trainee Ketchum Advt., San Francisco, 1970-71; asst. advt. dir. Mktg. Systems, Inc., Portland, Oreg., 1971-74; prodn. mgr., art dir., copywriter Finzer-Smith, Portland, 1974-76; copywriter Gerber Advt., Portland, 1976-78; freelance copywriter, Portland, 1983-84, 83-85; copywriter McCann-Erickson, Portland, 1980-81; copy chief Brookstone Co., Peterborough, N.H., 1981-83; creative dir. Whitman Advt., Portland, 1984-87; prin. L.A. Advt., 1987—. Co-founder, v.p., newsletter editor Animal Rescue and Care Fund, 1972-81. Recipient Internat. Film and TV Festival N.Y. Finalist award, 1985, 86, 87, 88, Internat. Radio Festival of N.Y. award, 1984, 85, 88, Hollywood Radio and TV Soc. Internat. Broadcasting award, 1981, TV Comml. Festival Silver Telly award, 1985, TV Comml. Festival Bronze Telly, 1986, AVC Silver Cindy, 1986, Los Angeles Advt. Women LULU, 1986, 87, Ad Week What's New Portfolio, 1986, N.W. Addy award Seattle Advt. Fedn., 1984, Best of N.W. award N.W. Seminar Film and Video, 1985, numerous others. Mem. Portland Advt. Fedn. (Rosey Finalist award 1986), Portland Art Assn., Assn. Research and Enlightenment, PETA, Nat. Wildlife Fedn., ASPCA, People for Ethical Treatment of Animals. Address: 6005 SE 21st Ave Portland OR 97202

BUTLER, LUCIUS ALBERT, education educator; b. St. Petersburg, Fla., Feb. 2, 1928; s. Lucius Albert and Mable Rose (Tubbs) B.; m. Dona Mae Medchill, Nov. 11, 1950; children: Stephen Paul, Thomas Albert, Susan Joy. BA, U. Puget Sound, 1952; BDiv, Bethel Sem., St. Paul, 1955; MA, U. Minn., 1955; PhD, 1968; MLS, U. Hawaii, 1974. Ordained to ministry Bapt. Ch., 1955. Missionary Bapt. Gen. Conf., Tokyo, 1955-66; instr. edn. U. Minn., Mpls., 1966-68; prof. edn. U. Hawaii, Honolulu, 1968-85, prof. emeritus, 1985—; edn. specialist Naval Submarine Tng. Ctr. Pacific, Pearl Harbor, Hawaii, 1985—; chief of party Hawaii Edn. Team, Vientiane, Laos, 1971-73; lectr. Nicosia, Cyprus, 1977-78. With U.S. Army, 1946-51. Fulbright scholar, 1977-78. Mem. Assn. for Ednl. Communications and Tech., AAUP, Phi Delta Kappa. Home: 1452 Liholiho St Penthouse Honolulu HI 96822 Office: Naval Submarine Tng Ctr Pacific Pearl Harbor HI 96860-6600

BUTLER, MORSE RODNEY, accountant; b. Salt Lake City, June 7, 1914; s. George Henry and Catherine (Johnson) B.; m. Miriam McFadden, Dec. 24, 1938; 1child, Beverly James. BS, U. Calif.-Berkeley, 1936, postgrad., 1937. Cert. tchr., Calif.; pub. acct., Calif. Tchr. San Luis Obispo (Calif.) City Schs., 1937-40; head dept. bus. San Luis Obispo High Sch. and Jr. Coll., 1940-43; ptnr. Hall & Butler Tax Cons., San Luis Obispo, 1948-52, Butler & Bourdon Pub. Accts., San Luis Obispo, 1969-80; prin. Morse R. Butler Pub. Acct., San Luis Obispo, 1957-69; pres. Morse & Butler, Inc., Acctg., San Luis Obispo, 1980--. Recipient Luther Gulick award Camp Fire Girls. Mem. Soc. Calif. Accts. (pres. 1969-70), Nat. Soc. Pub. Accts., Nat. Soc. Enrolled Agts., Calif. Soc. Enrolled Agts., Rotary (pres. San Luis Obispo chpt. 1971-72), Masons, Shriners (treas. San Luis Obispo chpt. 1988). Home: 1394 Andrews St San Luis Obispo CA 93401 Office: Morse R Butler Acct 694 Santa Rosa St San Luis Obispo CA 93401

BUTLER, PARLEY NARVIN, mortgage banker; b. Ogden, Utah, Dec. 22, 1928; s. Parley A. and Louisa Ardelia (Thompson) B.; grad. Weber Coll., 1950; grad. indsl. engr., 1958; m. Wilma Johansen, Sept. 11, 1950; children—Susan, Curtis, Paul, Julie, Mary. Crew foreman Ogden Union Ry. & Depot Co. (Utah), 1944-50; office mgr. Quaker Oats Co., Ogden, 1950-55, Joplin, Mo., 1955-59, Marion, Ohio, 1959-62, Chattanooga, 1962-65, St. Joseph, Mo., 1965-73; contr. Magic Pan Inc. subs. of Quaker Oats Co., San Francisco, 1973-74; asst. gen. mgr., contr. Powder River Enterprises, Provo, Utah, 1974-81; asst. sec., treas. Powder River Enterprises, Inc., Provo, 1975-83, sec., 1983-85; v.p. Provo Aviation, 1978-80, sec. 1983-85; v.p. Am. West Advt., 1978-82; sec.-treas. Powder River Motor Transport, Inc., 1977-85; sec.-treas. Stout Corp., 1981-84; pres. Quaker Oats Employees Credit Union, St. Joseph, 1971-73; trustee, adminstr. Powder River Enterprises Profit Sharing Plan, 1974-85; v.p., treas., mgr. ops. Certa Fin. Group Inc., Provo, 1986—; pres. Butler Assocs Internat., 1985—. Curator St. Joseph Archeaol. Soc., 1965-73. With U.S. Army, 1946-48. Mem. Nat. Assn. Accts. (v.p. 1972-73), Adminstrv. Mgmt. Assn. (v.p. 1964-65), Utah Taxpayers Assn. (dir. 1982-85). Republican. Mormon. Club: Lions (past pres. 1971-72). Home: 625 E 60 N Circle Orem UT 84057 Office: PO Box 758 Provo UT 84601

BUTLER, REX LAMONT, lawyer; b. New Brunswick, N.J., Mar. 24, 1951; s. Ekker and Beatrice (Curry) B.; m. Willie Ruth Harris; children: Nijel Jaibrun, Vikteria Lamontra. AA with honors, Fla. Jr. Coll., 1975; BA, U. North Fla., 1977; JD, Howard U., 1983. Bar: Alaska 1983, U.S. Dist. Ct. Alaska 1983, U.S. Ct. Appeals (9th cir.) 1984, U.S. Ct. Appeals (D.C. cir.) 1984. Assoc. M. Ashley Dickerson, Inc., Anchorage, 1983-84; profl. legis. asst. State of Alaska, Juneau, 1984; asst. atty. gen. State of Alaska, Anchorage, 1984-85; pvt. practice Anchorage, 1985—; adj. prof. law Anchorage Community Coll., 1985; bd. dirs. Akeela House, Inc. Pres. Alaska Black Caucus, Anchorage, 1986, bd. dirs. 1987-88; gen. counsel NAACP, Anchorage, 1985-87; commr. Anchorage Telephone Utility, 1985-87; trustee Anchorage Sr. Ctr., Inc., 1985-87, Shiloh Missionary Bapt. Ch., Anchorage, 1985—; bd. dirs. Ctr. for Drug Problems, Anchorage, 1985-86, Alaska Civil Liberties Union, 1987-88. Served with USN, 1969-73. Named one of Outstanding Young Men Am., 1984; recipient Cert. Appreciation, African Relief Campaign, 1985. Mem. ABA, Nat. Bar Assn., Nat. Assn. Criminal Def. Lawyers, Alaska Bar Assn., Assn. Trial Lawyers Am., Anchorage Bar Assn., Alaska Trial Lawyers Assn., Omega Psi Phi. Democrat. Home: PO Box 200025 Anchorage AK 99520 Office: 745 W 4th Ave Suite 300 Anchorage AK 99501

BUTLER, RUSSELL, artist; b. N.Y.C., Mar. 7, 1949; s. Milton W. and Dorothy Ann (Adams) B. BFA, U. Buffalo, 1971; postgrad., San Francisco Art Inst., 1977. Art dir. Annelieses Sch., Laguna Beach, Calif., 1977—, Willowbrook, Calif., 1987-88; owner Russ Butler Sch. of Art, Laguna Beach, 1981-84; artist Stein/Brief Corp., Newport Beach, Calif., 1983, Xerox, San Francisco, 1985, City of Laguna Beach, 1986, Transamerica Corp., Los Angeles, 1987, U. Calif. Irvine Med. Ctr., Orange, Calif., 1987-88. Prin. works include (commemorative murals) Legend of the Waters, 1988, Delusions of Grandeur, 1987, Dreamer, 1983, 5 major paintings U. Calif Irvine Med. Ctr.; exhibited at L.A. Art Expo, 1988; exhibited at Sheraton Rosemead, Newport Harbor Yacht Club, Magic Internat., 1989. Mem. Aliso Artists Alliance (pres. 1981-84). Home: 165 Dumond Dr Laguna Beach CA 92651

BUTTERWORTH, ROBERT ROMAN, psychologist; b. Pittsfield, Mass., June 24, 1946; s. John Leon and Martha Helen (Roman) B. BA, SUNY, 1972; MA, Marist Coll., 1975; PhD in Clin. Psychology, Calif. Grad. Inst., 1983. Asst. clin. psychologist N.Y. State Dept. Mental Hygiene, Wassaic, 1972-75; pvt. practice clin. psychology Los Angeles and Downey, Calif., 1976—; cons. Los Angeles County Dept. Health Services; staff clinician san Bernardino County Dept. Mental Health, 1983-85; staff psychologist State of Calif. Dept. Mental Health, 1985—; media interviews include NBC, CBS, ABC, Mutual Radio, Cable News Network, AP, UPI, Network 9 (Australia), LBC (London), USA Today, Christian Sci. Monitor, N.Y. Daily News, Los Angeles Times. Served with USAF, 1965-69. Mem. Am. Psychol Assn. for Media Psychology, Calif. State Psychol. Assn., Nat. Accreditation Assn. Psychoanalysis. Office: PO Drawer 76477 Los Angeles CA 90076

BUTTORFF, CURTIS DEEN, computer engineer, data processing executive; b. Alexandria, La., Nov. 7, 1948; s. Curtis Lee and Elizabeth (Deen) B.; m. Leslie Ann Cavarra, Sept. 11, 1982; 1 child, Jordan Deen. BA in Math. and Music, Colo. Coll., 1970; MS in Computer and Info. Scis., Ohio State U., 1972. Head wrangler Big Spring Ranch, Florissant, Colo., 1970-72; applications engr., program mgr., sr. programmer, mgr. tech support, info. svcs. tng. Security Life, Denver, 1968-80; mgr. mgmt. ins. svcs. Price Waterhouse & Co., Denver, 1980-83; Coopers & Lybrand, Denver, 1983-85; mng. cons. Berger & Co., Denver, 1985-87; sr. staff regional systems engr. AMDAHL Corp., Denver, 1987—. Active Big Bros. Am., Colorado Springs, Colo., 1966-70; co-chmn. allocations com. United Way, Denver, 1983-85, Univ. fellow Ohio State U., 1970-72. Mem. Capacity Mgmt. Group, Valley Country Club. Republican. Presbyterian. Home: 5238 S Geneva St Englewood CO 80111 Office: AMDAHL Corp 6400 S Fiddlers Green Cir Englewood CO 80111

BUTTS, JAMES A., real estate broker; b. Perry, Okla., Nov. 7, 1938; s. Oscar Walter and Laudie (Becquart) B.; m. Mary Schoenborn (div.); 1 child, Jill Marie. BS, Okla. State U., 1961, MS, 1962; postgrad., UCLA, 1972. Asst. dean students U. Tex., Arlington, 1964-65; merchandising mgr. Southland Corp., Dallas, 1965-69; mgr. we. div. Nat. Convenience Stores, Inc., Anaheim, Calif., 1969-73; pres. Minit Market, Inc., Anaheim, 1973-79; exec. v.p. Ladd Liquors, Inc., Santa Ana, Calif., 1979-84; owner Sunset Liquor Store, Tustin, Calif., 1984-88; sales mgr. Tarbell Realtors, Tustin, 1985-87; rep. acquisitions The Southland Corp., Tustin, 1987-88; real estate broker Re/Max, Irvine, Calif., 1988—; also bd. dirs. Re/Max. Lt. U.S. Army, 1962-68. Mem. Irvine Bd. Realtors (chmn. 1987-88), Nat. Assn. Realtors, Calif. Assn. Realtors, Internat. Coun. Shopping Ctrs. Republican. Roman Catholic. Home: 16 Prescott Irvine CA 92720 Office: Re/Max of Irvine 4482 Barranca Pkwy #210 Irvine CA 92714

BUTTS, JAMES EDWARD, travel agency executive; b. Paoli, Okla., Nov. 14, 1939; s. Archie Benjamin and Esta (Philipps) B.; m. Jeanette Olive Blaisdell, Aug. 12, 1973. Student, Texarkana Jr. Coll., 1963-65, Paris Jr. Coll., 1969. Bldg foreman Day & Zimmerman, Inc., Texarkana, Tex., 1966-69; clk., carrier U.S. Postal Service, Mt. Pleasant, Tex., 1969-71; part time clk., carrier U.S. Postal Service, Hardin, Mont., 1972-77; clk., carrier U.S. Postal Service, Devils Lake, N.D., 1981-82; part time clk. U.S. Postal Service, Tanana, Alaska, 1979; bus aide Sch. Dist. No. 1, Great Falls, Mont., 1983-87, tchr.'s aide, 1987—; owner, mgr. Beam Your Travels, Great Falls, 1988--. With USN, 1958-62. Mem. Am. Legion. Democrat. Methodist. Office: Beam Your Travels 2000 2d Ave N Great Falls MT 59401

BUTZER, MITCHELL STANLEY, computer engineer; b. Salem, Oreg., Jan. 27, 1960; s. Stanley Dwight and Keta Rea (Digby) B.; m. Denise Lucetta Landreth, Apr. 3, 1985: children: Andrew Mitchell, Adam Wade. AA, Shasta Coll., 1982; BS, Calif. State U., Chico, 1985. Lectr. Calif. State U., Chico, 1984-85; computer engr. Eurolink Inc., Redding, Calif., 1985; project engr. Hinds Internat., Hillsboro, Oreg., 1985—; owner Omnitek, Hillsboro, 1984; engr. Firesave Inc., Redding, Calif., 1985—. Mem. IEEE. Republican. Home: 1275 NE Grant St #3 Hillsboro OR 97124 Office: 5250 NE Elam Young Pkwy Hillsboro OR 97124

BUXTON, RICHARD MILLARD, financial executive; b. Denver, July 8, 1948; s. Charles Roberts and Janet (Millard) B.; m. Consuelo Gonzalez, June 15, 1974; children—Richard Fernando. B.A. with distinction, Stanford U., 1970; M.B.A., Harvard U., 1975. Mgr. ops. planning Western Fed. Savs., Denver, 1975-78; sr. fin. analyst Rocky Mountain Energy Co., Denver, 1978-83; dir. fin. analysis, treas. Frontier Devel. Group, Inc., Denver, 1983-85; treas. Frontier Holdings, Inc., Denver, 1985-86; dir. fin. services K N Energy, Inc., Denver, 1986—. Mem. Colo. Harvard Bus. Sch. Club, Rocky Mountain Stanford Club (bd. dirs. 1982-84). Presbyterian. Club: Columbine Country. Home: 17 Wedge Way Littleton CO 80123 Office: KN Energy Inc PO Box 15265 Lakewood CO 80215

BUYDOS, GEARY STEPHEN, television producer; b. Johnstown, Pa., Feb. 15, 1950; s. George Peter and Pauline Patricia (DeLasko) B. BA in Electronic Engring., Ohio State U., 1972; AA in Telecommunications, San Diego City Coll., 1978. Projectionist WOSU-TV, Columbus, Ohio, 1969-72; projectionist, cameraman WIMA-TV, Lima, Ohio, 1972-75; audio technician KFMB-TV News, San Diego, 1978-79, photographer, 1979-80; photographer, producer PM Mag., KFMB-TV, San Diego, 1980-85, sr. photographer, producer, 1985-88, exec. producer, 1988—; lectr. San Diego City High Schs., 1988—. Mem. Nat. Acad. TV Arts and Scis. (Emmy nomination 1980-88, Emmy award 1980, 82, 88), NRA, Greenpeace, Defenders of Wildlife, Harley Owners Group. Office: KFMB-TV PM Mag 7677 Engineer Rd San Diego CA 92111

BUZZELL, CALVIN ALBERT, computer company executive; b. Caribou, Maine, Nov. 1, 1942; s. Colby Wiggens and Pkyllis (Kelley) B.; m. Sue M. Yoon, Oct. 25, 1975; children: Colby, Michael, Elizabeth. BS in Physics, Calif. Poly. U., 1964; MS in Computer Sci., Kansas State U., 1979. Commd. 2d lt. U.S. Army, 1966, advanced through grades to lt. col., ret., 1985; simulation lab. project leader Lawrence Livermore Nat. Lab., Livermore, Calif., 1979-86; dir. simulation engring. Litton Applied Tech., San Jose, Calif., 1986—; also bd. dirs. Integrated Parallel Tech., Campbell, Calif. Mem. Soc. Computer Simulation. Republican. Home: 56 Longwood Ct San Ramon CA 94583 Office: Litton Applied Tech 4747 Hellyer Ave San Jose CA 95150

BUZZO, MARGARET MINNIE WALKER (MARGE BUZZO), artist; b. San Diego, Nov. 28, 1927; d. Harold Styles and Mollie (Whittman) Walker; m. Frank Ross Buzzo, Mar. 4, 1946; children—Yvonne, Marie, Wayne Bennette. AA, Long Beach City Coll., 1952; postgrad. L.A. Art Ctr. Sch. Design, 1956-58. Artist, owner Marge Buzzo Art Service, Woodland Hills, Calif., 1972—; owner Margie Ditto Creations; lectr. in field. Exhibitions include Burbank (Calif.) Pub. Library, 1977, Independence Bank, Canoga Park, Calif., 1975; invitational shows include KCET Art Auction, Hollywood, Calif., 1971, Descanso Gardens, La Canada, Calif., 1972, ARC Nat. Hdqrs., 1982, Le Salon Des Nations, Paris, 1983; group exhibits include Lemon Tree Art Gallery, 1974, Soc. Security Office (Canoga Park), 1975, Happy Eye Gallery, 1976, Shirley Meyers Art Gallery, 1977, Artists & Crafter, 1989; represented in permanent collections Burbank Pub. Lib., others. Recipient Flier Prodns. Desi award, 1980. Mem. Zonta Internat. (charter), Nat. Mus. and Gallery Registration Assn. (life), San Fernando Valley Arts Council. Roman Catholic. Juror numerous art shows and lectr. in field; illustrator numerous children's books, including: The Story of Grandma Water, 1977, The Wee River Flier, 1979. Home: 4620 Santa Lucia Dr Woodland Hills CA 91364

BYBEE, RODGER WAYNE, college director; b. San Francisco, Feb. 21, 1942; s. Wayne and Mary Genevieve (Mungon) B.; m. Patricia Ann Brovsky, May 28, 1986. BA, Colo. State Coll., 1966; MA, U. No. Colo., 1969; PhD, NYU, 1975. Tchr. sci. Greeley (Colo.) Pub. Schs., 1965-66; instr. sci. U. No. Colo., Greeley, 1966-70; teaching fellow NYU, N.Y.C., 1970-72; instr. edn. Carleton Coll., Northfield, Minn., 1972-75, asst. prof., 1975-81, assoc. prof., chmn. dept., 1981-85; assoc. dir. biol. scis. curr. study Colo. Coll., Colorado Springs, 1986—; mem. adv. bd. for sci. assessment Nat. Assessment Ednl. Progress, Princeton, N.J., 1987—; mem. adv. bd. Social Sci. Edn. Consortium, Boulder, Colo., 1987—. Author: numerous books; contbr. numerous articles to profl. jours. NSF grantee, 1986—. Fellow AAAS (mem.-at-large, prin. investigator), Nat. Assn. Rsch. Sci. Teaching (rsch. coord. 1986—). Home: PO Box 237 Cascade CO 80809

BYE, KARI, jewelry designer; b. Voss, Norway, Sept. 6, 1937; d. Knut and Gudrun (Bjorgaas) B.; m. John Tveitaraas, June 15, 1957 (div. 1975); children: Inger, Randi Anne. BA in Art Edn., U. Colo., 1971; MA in Human Ecology, Sangamon State U., 1983. Designer, owner Kari Design, Estes Park, Colo., 1973—; cons. Dept. Culture, Voss, Norway, 1984—; internat. rep. Ole Bull Music Acad., Voss, 1987—. Co-author: Emigration from Voss to U.S.A., 1985; contbr. articles to profl. jours. Co-founder Boulder (Colo.) Ctr. for Visual Arts, 1973-75, Estes Park Art Ctr. 1985-87.; docent Denver Art Museum, 1975-76; dir. Learning Exchange, Estes Park, 1984-86. Recipient Fellowship Ossabaw Found., 1980, Internat. Gold Corp. Design award, 1983, Sculpture award Sangamon State U., 1982, Norwegian Art Program award Norwegian Dept. Foreign Affairs, 1986, Exhibit Grant Boehm Found., 1988. Mem. Worl Crafts Council, Sons of Norway. Home and Office: Box 3215 Estes Park CO 80517

BYE, ROSEANNE MARIE, marketing professional; b. Chgo., Nov. 27, 1946; d. Paul David and Gwendalynn Luciell (Hipp) Forrester; BS in Foods and Nutrition, Western Ill. U., 1969; m. Richard Wayne Bye, June 14, 1969. Banquet mgr. Western Ill. U., 1967-69; new product home economist Hunt/Wesson Foods, Fullerton, Calif., 1969-73; retail and restaurant home economist Lawry's Foods, L.A., 1973-74; mgr. product devel. Carl Karcher Enterprises, Anaheim, Calif., 1974-81; v.p. R & D Denny's Restaurants, La Mirada, Calif., 1981-88; owner, cons. Roseanne Bye & Assocs., Orange, Calif., 1988-89; v.p. foodsvc. div. TG Mktg. and Advt., Anaheim, 1988—; mem. speakers bur. mktg. fast food Industry/Edn. Coun. Mem. food svc. adv. com., Calif. State U., Long Beach, Chapman Coll., adv. com. Santa Ana Jr. Coll., Garden Grove Sch. Dist. Recipient Nat. Mktg. award for devel. of Charbroiler Steak Sandwich, 1975-76, serve-yourself salad bar, 1978-79. Mem. Am. Home Econs. Assn., Calif. Home Econs. Assn. (Outstanding Economist in Bus. 1977, 79, 86, pres. 1977-79), Home Economists in Bus. (award of excellence, Western regional adv. 1976-78, nat. pub. rels. chmn. 1983-85), Women in Mgmt., Nat. Restaurant Assn. (chmn. mktg. rsch. div., nat. conf. speaker), NOW, Anaheim C. of C. (publicity chmn. 1977-78), Soc. Advancement Food Svc. Rsch. (bd. dirs. 1986-88, co-chair regional meetings 1988—, Fellowship award 1987), Internat. Food Svc. Editorial Coun., Multi Unit Food Svc. Ops., Chain Ops. Execs., Internat. Platform Assn. Republican. Presbyterian. Clubs: Tennis and Swim, Gourmet/Wine, Teddy Bear, Lit. Guild, Newport Harbor Art Mus., Bower's Art Mus., Gem Theatre Guild. Office: TG Mkting and Advt 3943 E La Palma Ave Anaheim CA 92807

BYERLY, RADFORD, JR., university policy research center official; b. Houston, May 22, 1936; s. Radford and Garvis N. (Cook) B.; m. Kathryn Jester, May 13, 1960 (div. 1980), children: Laura, Hamilton, Charles; m. Carol Ann Ries, Apr. 10, 1987. BA, Williams Coll., 1958, MA, 1960; PhD, Rice U., 1967. Sr. engr. No. Rsch. & Enging. Co., Cambridge, Mass., 1961-63; postdoctoral fellow U. Colo., Boulder, 1967-69, dir. Ctr. for Space and Geoscis. Policy, 1987—; physicist, mgr. Nat. Bur. Standards, Washington, 1969-75; mem. profl. staff com. on sci. and tech. U.S. Ho. of Reps., Washington, 1975-87; mem. space sta. adv. com., space sci. adv. com. NASA, 1988—; hon. lectr. Mid-Am. State Univs. Assn., 1988-89. Contbr. articles to profl. jours. NSF fellow, 1963-67. Mem. AIAA (chmn. civil space subcom. 1988—), Am. Phys. Soc., ASTM, Am. Astronautical Soc., AAAS, Williams Club (N.Y.C.), Phi Beta Kappa, Sigma Xi. Home: 765 15th St Boulder CO 80302 Office: U Colo Ctr for Space-Geosci Policy Campus Box 361 Boulder CO 80309

BYERS, EDWARD W., library director; b. Pitts., Jan. 2, 1948. B.A. in History, Lawrence U., 1971; M.A.L.S., U. Denver, 1972. Sci. ref. librarian Pub. Library of Cin. and Hamilton County, 1972-73; head of reference Warder Pub. Library, Springfield, Ohio, 1973, head main library, 1974-77; dir. Laramie County Library System, Cheyenne, Wyo., 1977—. Bd. dirs. Bibliog. Ctr. for Research, Denver. Mem. Wyo. Library Assn. (exec. bd., pres. pub. library sect. 1984), ALA (mem. council 1980-83), PLA, LAMA, Mountain Plains Library Assn. (v.p. pub. library sect. 1987), Am Soc. Info. Sci., Bd. editors Miami Valley List of University Serials, 1973-77. Office: Laramie County Libr System 2800 Central Ave Cheyenne WY 82001 *

BYLES, TORREY KOPPE, communications technolgy specialist; b. Los Angeles, June 12, 1957; s. Howard Douglas and Dorothy (Wardwell). BA, U. Calif., San Diego, 1979; postgrad., Calif. State U., L.A., 1981-83. Secondart tchr. Alhambra (Calif.) Sch. Dist., 1981-82, 83-84; editor Internat. Bus. Svcs., Inc., Taipei, Taiwan, 1982-83; interpreter Mandarin Chinese L.A. Olympic Organizing Com., 1984; freelance contract writer Pasadena, Calif., 1984-85; staff writer IEEE Computer Soc., Los Alamitos, Calif., 1985-87; journalist, writer Long Beach, Calif., 1987—; cons. Amtrade Internat., Los Alamitos, 1987—. Spl. correspondent, Jour. of Commerce; contbr. articles to profl. jours. Mem. Chinese Interagency Coun., Los Angeles, 1983, 84, 85, 87. Democrat. Unitarian. Office: 366 Redondo Ave #7 Long Beach CA 90814

BYNOE, PETER CHARLES BERNARD, real estate developer, legal consultant; b. Boston, Mar. 20, 1951; s. Victor Cameron Sr. and Ethel May (Stewart) B.; m. Linda Jean Walker, Nov. 20, 1987. BA, Harvard U., 1972, JD, 1976, MBA, 1976. Bar: Ill. 1982; cert. real estate broker, Ill. Exec. v.p. James H. Lowry & Assocs., Chgo., 1977-82; pres. Telemat Ltd., Chgo., 1982—; mng. dir. Howard Ecker & Co. Real Estate, Chgo., 1986—; of counsel Davis, Barnhill & Galland, Chgo., 1987—; exec. dir. Ill. Sports Facilities Authority, Chgo., 1988—; bd. dirs. Chgo. Architecture Found. Chmn. Chgo. Landmarks Commn., 1985; bd. dirs. Goodman Theatre, Chgo., 1986, Boys and Girls Clubs of Chgo., 1987, Cinema Chgo, 1988. Mem. Chgo. Architecture Found., Chgo. Bar Assn., Chgo. Bd. Realtors, Ill. Bar Assn., Ill. Preservation Council, Urban Land Inst., Harvard Bus. Sch. Alumni Council (bd. dirs. 1987). Democrat. Clubs: International (Chgo.), East Bank. Office: 1 First Nat Pla #2785 Chicago IL 60603 also: care Denver Nuggets McNichols Sports Arena 1635 Clay St PO Box 4658 Denver CO 80204

BYRD, MARC ROBERT, florist; b. Flint, Mich., May 14, 1954; s. Robert Lee and Cynthia Ann (Poland) B.; m. Bonnie Jill Berlin, Nov. 25, 1975 (div. June 1977). Student, Ea. Mich. U., 1972-75; grad., Am. Floral Sch., Chgo., 1978. Designer Olive Tree Florist, Palm Springs, Calif., 1978-79, Kayo's Flower Fashions, Palm Springs, 1979-80; owner, designer Village Florist, Inc., Palm Springs, 1980-85; pres. Mon Ami Florist, Inc., Beverly Hills, 1986-87; gen. mgr. Silverio's, Santa Monica, 1987; gen. mgr., hotel florist, creative dir. Four Seasons Hotel, Beverly Hills, 1988—. Author: Celebrity Flowers, 1989. Del. Dem. Party, Mich., 1972. Mem. Soc. Am. Florists, So. Calif. Floral Assn., Desert Mus., Robinson's Gardens. Republican. Mem. Dutch Reformed Ch. Home: 626 N Harper Ave Los Angeles CA 90048 Office: Four Seasons Hotel 300 S Doheny Dr Los Angeles CA 90048

BYRD, OTTO LEE (MIKE BYRD), minister; b. Pekin, Ill., Dec. 23, 1946; s. Luther Nathaniel and Betty Marie (Swingle) B.; m. Janet Faye Smith, June 11, 1966; children: Creighton Malachi, Ryland Micah. MS, Western Ill. U., 1972; MDiv, Denver Sem., 1977; EdD, U. No. Colo., 1979; DMinistry, Fuller Theol. Sem., 1988. Ordained to ministry Evangel. Free Ch. Am., 1976. Guidance dir. Sciota (Ill.) Northwestern High Sch., 1972-74; youth minister South Suburban Christian Ch., Littleton, Colo., 1975-76; pastor, sr. pastor Mountain View Evangel. Free Ch., Greeley, Colo., 1977-82; sr. pastor Community Bible Ch., San Bernardino, Calif., 1982—; v.p. Chinese for Christ Theol. Sem., Rosemead, Calif., 1985—. Contbr. articles to mags. With U.S. Army, 1965-68, Vietnam. Mem. Internat. Leadership Council. Republican. Office: Community Bible Ch 324 W 40th St San Bernardino CA 92407

BYRD, RONALD DALLAS, civil engineer; b. Reno, Nov. 30, 1934; s. Eugene Richard and Helen Madelyn (Hursh) B.; m. Irene Josephine Phenix, Sept. 19, 1953; children: Kevin Gregory, Helen Christine, Stephanie Irene. BSCE, U. Nev., 1960. Registered profl. engr., Nev., Calif., Oreg., Wash., Idaho., Wyo. Staff engr. Sprout Engrs., Sparks, Nev., 1960-64, design engr., 1964-67; office mgr. Sprout Engrs., Seattle, 1967-70; v.p. SE&A Engrs., Seattle, 1970-72; exec. v.p. SE&A Engrs., Sparks, 1972—; also bd. dirs. SE&A Engrs.; bd. dirs. ABS Land Co., Nev. Cons. Engrs. Fellow ASCE (sec. 1966-67); mem. NSPE (bd. dirs. 1983-86), Am. Pub. Works Assn., U. Nev. Reno Engring. Alumni Assn. (sec. 1985-86), U. Nev.-Reno Alumni Assn. (pres. 1989—), Kiwanis (pres. Sparks club 1965-66), Rotary (pres. Federal Way, Wash. club 1971-72), Elks, Masons. Republican. Methodist. Home: 50 Rancho Manor Dr Reno NV 89509 Office: SE&A Inc 950 Industrial Way Sparks NV 89431

BYRNE, GARY CECIL, banker; b. Upland, Calif., May 1, 1942; s. Cecil John Byrne and Verda Alice (Burgers) Frehe; m. Norma E. Elliott, Aug. 19, 1967; children: Silas Elliott, Tristan Oliver. BA, U. Redlands, 1965; PhD, U. N.C., 1969. Assoc. prof. San Diego State U., 1969-73; assoc. Arthur Young & Co., Washington, 1973-74; v.p. Orkand Corp., Silver Spring, Md., 1974-75; dir., ptnr. Miller and Byrne Inc., Washington, 1975-77; v.p. H.C. Elliott Inc., Sacramento, 1977-83; chmn. Meridian Nat. Bank, Concord, Calif., 1979—; chmn., pres., chief exec. officer Alex Brown Fin. Group, Sacramento, 1985—, Alex Brown Devel. Corp., Sacramento, 1986—, Bank of Alex Brown, Sacramento, 1987—; bd. dirs. Physicians Clin. Labs, Sacramento, Elliott Fin., Sacramento. Author: (with others) The Great American Convention, 1977; co-editor: Politics in Western Europe, 1972; contbr. articles to profl. jours. Trustee U. Redlands, Calif., 1983—, Sutter Hosps., Sacramento, 1983-86; bd. dirs. Boy Scouts Exec. Coun., 1980-84. Grantee NSF, 1968; fellow Rotary Internat., 1965, NIMH, 1969. Mem. Am. Bankers Assn., Calif. Bankers Assn., Western Ind. Bankers Assn., Western Mobile Home Assn. (bd. dirs. 1982-84), Sutter Club, Capital Athletic Club. Office: Bank Alex Brown 1425 River Park Dr Sacramento CA 95815

BYRNE, GEORGE MELVIN, physician; b. San Francisco, Aug. 1, 1933; s. Carlton and Esther (Smith) B.; BA, Occidental Coll., 1958; MD, U. So. Calif., 1962; m. Joan Stecher, July 14, 1956; children: Kathryne, Michael, David; m. Margaret C. Smith, Dec. 18, 1982. Diplomate Am. Bd. Family Practice. Intern, Huntington Meml. Hosp., Pasadena, Calif., 1962-63, resident, 1963-64; family practice So. Calif. Permanente Med. Group, 1964-81, physician-in-charge Pasadena Clinic, 1966-81; asst. dir. Family Practice residency Kaiser Found. Hosp., L.A., 1971-73; clin. instr. emergency medicine Sch. Medicine, U. So. Calif., 1973-80; v.p. East Ridge Co., 1983-84, sec., 1984; dir. Alan Johnson Porsche Audi, Inc., 1974-82, sec., 1974-77, v.p., 1978-82. Bd. dirs. Kaiser-Permante Mgmt. Assn., 1976-77; mem. regional mgmt. com. So. Calif. Lung Assn., 1976-77; patron L.A. County Mus. Art, The S.W. Mus., 1988; mem. pres.'s circle Occidental Coll., L.A. Drs. Symphony Orch, 1975-80. Fellow Am. Acad. Family Physicians (charter); mem. Am., Calif., L.A. County Med. Assns., Calif. Acad. Family Physicians, Internat. Horn Soc., Am. Radio Relay League (Pub. Service award), Sierra (life). Home: 528 Meadow View Dr La Canada-Flintridge CA 91011

BYRNE, JOHN PATRICK, retired state official, army officer; b. Detroit, May 25, 1929; s. George Arnold and Opal Vere (Cooper) B.; BS, Johns Hopkins U., 1958; MBA with high distinction, U. Mich., 1961; grad. Army War Coll., 1971; m. Dolores Ann Meyer, Aug. 11, 1951; children: John Patrick, David Michael, Richard Terrence, Kevin Francis. Commd. 2d lt. Chem. Corps, U.S. Army, 1950, advanced through grades to col., 1970; served with Far East Command in Japan, 1951-54; various logistic assignments Army Chem. Center, Md., 1954-58; assigned to Chem. Corps Hdqrs. and Dept. of Army, The Pentagon, Washington, 1961-65; U.S. Army exchange officer to Brit. Army, Eng., 1965-68; comdr. 2d chem. bn. Ft. McClellan, Ala., 1968-70; chief of staff Cam Ranh Support Command in Vietnam, 1970-71, dep. comdr., 1971-72; dep. comdr. Bayern Support Dist., Germany, 1972-73, exec. to comdg. gen. of Theater Army Support Command, 1973-74, dep. comdr. of 1st. Support Brigade, 1974-75; comdr. Rocky Mountain Arsenal, Denver, 1975-78; dir. emergency preparedness Denver County, 1978-79; dir. disaster emergency services State of Colo., Golden, 1979-89; dir. St. Vincent DePaul Stores, Denver, 1979—. Pres. Brookland Estates Citizens Assn., Alexandria, Va., 1963-65; bd. advisors Natural Hazards Research and Applications Info. Ctr., U. Colo., 1984-89; bd. visitors Emergency Mgmt. Inst. at Nat. Emergency Tng. Ctr., 1987-89, chmn., 1987; hon. bd. dirs. Mile High chpt. ARC. Decorated Legion of Merit, Bronze Star; Vietnam Cross of Gallantry with palm. Mem. Nat. Emergency Mgmt. Assn. (pres. 1983-84), Assn. of U.S. Army (sec. Gallant Pelham chpt. 1969-70), Nat. Def. Preparedness Assn., Nat. Ret. Officers Assn., Denver C. of C. (mil. affairs com. 1975-89), Colo. Emergency Mgmt. Assn. (sec.-treas. 1978-80), Emergency Med. Technicians Assn. of Colo. (adv. 1980-87), Beta Gamma Sigma, Delta Sigma Pi, Phi Kappa Phi. Roman Catholic. Clubs: Rotary, Denver Execs. Home: 7679 Waverly Mountain Littleton CO 80127

BYRNE, JOHN PATRICK, manufacturing executive; b. Balt., Dec. 24, 1951; s. Thomas C. and Virginia J. (Patrick) B.; m. Pamela A. Wynn, June 21, 1975; children: Jonathan, Megan. MetE, Drexel U., 1975. Metall. engr. U.S. Naval Ship Rsch. and Devel. Ctr., Annapolis, Md., 1970-76; mfg. engr. ESCO Corp., Danville, Ill., 1976-78; mgr. mfg. control ESCO Corp., Danville, 1978-80; prodn. control mgr. ESCO Corp., Portland, Oreg., 1980-82, dir. mfg. planning, 1982-84, plant mgr. tech. devel. ctr., 1984-86; pres., chief exec. officer Tiline, Inc., Albany, Oreg., 1986—. Regional chmn. United Way Campaign, Portland, 1985; mem. adv. com. Linn-Benton Community Coll., Albany, 1986—; fundraiser YMCA, Albany, 1987. Fellow Am. Prodn. and Inventory Control Soc.; mem. Am. Foundrymen's Soc., Foundry Edn. Found., Rotary, Albany C. of C. (bd. dirs.), Dakota Hills Assn. (pres. 1984-85). Home: 4454 Bramblewood Ln NW Albany OR 97321 Office: Tiline Inc 150 Queen Ave SW Albany OR 97321

BYRNE, JOHN VINCENT, academic administrator; b. Hempstead, N.Y., May 9, 1928; s. Frank E. and Kathleen (Barry) B.; m. Shirley O'Connor, Nov. 26, 1954; children: Donna, Lisa, Karen, Steven. AB, Hamilton Coll., 1951; MA, Columbia U., 1953; PhD, U. So. Calif., 1957. Research geologist Humble Oil & Refinery Co., Houston, 1957-60; assoc. prof. Oreg. State U., Corvallis, 1960-66, prof. oceanography, 1966—, chmn. dept., 1968-72, dean Sch. Oceanography, 1972-76, acting dean research, 1976-77, dean research, 1977-80, v.p. for research and grad. studies, 1980-81, pres., 1984—; adminstr. NOAA, Washington, 1981-84; Program dir. oceanography NSF, 1966-67. Recipient Carter teaching award Oreg. State U., 1964. Fellow AAAS, Geol. Soc. Am., Am. Meteorol. Soc.; mem. Am. Assn. Petroleum Geologists, Maritime Technol. Soc., Am. Geophys. Union, Sigma Xi, Chi Psi. Club: Arlington (Portland, Oreg.). Home: 3520 NW Hayes Ave Corvallis OR 97330 Office: Oreg State U Office of Pres Corvallis OR 97331

BYRNE, NOEL THOMAS, sociologist, educator; b. San Francisco, May 11, 1943; s. Joseph Joshua and Naomi Pearl (Denison) B.; m. Elizabeth Carla Rowlin, Nov. 5, 1966 (div.); 1 child, Ginger Butler. BA in Sociology, Sonoma State Coll., 1971; MA in Sociology, Rutgers U., 1975, PhD in Sociology, 1987. Instr. sociology Douglass Coll., Rutgers U., New Brunswick, N.J., 1974-76, Hartnell Coll., Salinas, Calif., 1977-78; research dir. mgmt. grads. survey projects Sonoma State U., Rohnert Park, Calif., 1983-86, 89, family bus. research project, 1987-88; from lectr. to assoc. prof. depts. sociology and mgmt. Sonoma State U., 1978—. Contbr. articles and revs. to profl. lit. Recipient Dell Pub. award Rutgers U. Grad. Sociology Program, 1976, Louis Bevier fellow, 1977-78. Mem. AAAS, Am. Sociol. Assn., Pacific Sociol. Assn., Acad. of Mgmt., N.Y. Acad. Sci., Soc. for Study Symbolic Interaction (rev. editor Jour. 1980-83), Soc. for Study Social Problems. Democrat. Club: Commonwealth. Home: 4773 Ross Rd Sebastopol CA 95472 Office: Sonoma State U Sch Bus and Econs Rohnert Park CA 94928

BYRNE, ROBERT LEE, III, computer systems analyst and programmer; b. Lorain, Ohio, Oct. 11, 1957; s. Robert Lee Jr. and Shirley Maxine (Smith) B.; m. Christine White, Sept. 2, 1988. Student, St. Edward's U., Austin, Tex., 1975-78; BA in Computer Sci., U. Tex., 1980; postgrad., U. Houston, 1981-86, Calif. State U., Chico, 1988—. Team mem. onboard space shuttle software devel.-verification NASA, Houston, 1980-85, space sta. software support environ., 1985-86, space sta. software devel., 1986-88; project coord. info. facility devel. and support IBM, San Jose, Calif., 1988—; mgr. Diamond Cutters, League City, Tex., 1982-87. Author: Reflections in a Dark Room, 1978; satirical columnist The Observer, 1974. Mem. Missoula Bicentennial Commn., 1986. Recipient Silver Snoopy award NASA-Johnson Space Ctr., 1985; named Ky. Col., Commonwealth of Ky., 1985. Mem. Assn. for Computing Machinery, Order Ky. Cols., Sierra Club, Greenpeace, Athletic Congress., IBM PC Club, IBM Running Club. Libertarian. Home: PO Box 1147 Morgan Hill CA 95037 Office: IBM Santa Teresa Lab 555 Bailey Ave San Jose CA 95161

BYRON, JUDITH ANNE, art director; b. Phila., Oct. 13, 1941; d. Joseph M. and Elizabeth (Maguiness) B.; m. Cesare M. Olivieri, Feb. 5, 1967 (div. July 1984); children: Adriana C., Stephanie L.; m. John W. Almond, June 18, 1988. BFA in Illustration, Moore Coll. Art, 1963. Art supr. Pa. Mut. Ins. Co., Phila., 1963-67; freelance artist Bennington, Vt., 1967-81; art dir. Sun Graphics, Tucson, 1981-84, Tucson Lifestyle Mag., 1984—. Recipient Addy award Tucson Ad Club, 1985, 86, awards Soc. Publ. Designers, 1989, Ariz. Press Club, 1989. Republican. Home: 1170 W Las Lomitas Tucson AZ 85704 Office: Tucson Lifestye Mag 7000 E Tanque Verde Tucson AZ 85715

BYRUM, DAVID LAWRENCE, chemistry and physics educator; b. Chgo., Nov. 1, 1948; s. Gloria Elizabeth (DeLyle) B.; m. Sylvia Gallegos Silvas, Sept. 13, 1969 (div. Mar. 1986); 1 child, Raymond David. BA in Edn., Ariz. State U., 1972; MEd, U. Ariz., 1978. Cert. tchr., Ariz., cert. community coll. tchr., Ariz. Instr. chemistry, track coach Salpointe High Sch., Tucson, 1972-77; instr. chemistry and physics, track coach Globe (Ariz.) High Sch., 1977-85; instr. chemistry Eastern Ariz. Coll., Thatcher, 1977-85; instr. chemistry and physics Flowing Wells High Sch., Tucson, 1985—; adj. instr. sci. edn. U. Ariz., 1986—; workshop leader NSF. Co-author BASIC Program Conversions, 1984. Recipient Golden Bell award Ariz. Sch. Bd. Assn., 1983, Presdl. award for Excellence in Sci. Teaching, 1988. Mem. Nat. Sci. Tchrs. Assn. (publ. com. 1983-86, speaker various locations 1979—, Search for Excellence in Sci. Edn. award 1984), Ariz. Sci. Tchrs. Assn. (regional dir. 1978-80, Search for Excellence in Sci. Edn. award 1984), Ariz. Edn. Assn., Catalina Commodore Computer Club. Republican. Roman Catholic. Home: 3301 E Fort Lowell Rd Tucson AZ 85716 Office: Flowing Wells High Sch 3725 N Flowing Wells Rd Tucson AZ 85705

CABANYA, MARY LOUISE, data processing executive; b. Denver, Nov. 3, 1947; d. Dareo and Hellen Etta (Charley) Mattivi; m. Robert L. Cabanya, Jan. 6, 1978. BS in Math., U. So. Colo., 1969; postgrad., Regis U., 1985. Flight test engr. Boeing Co., Seattle, 1969-75; computer scientist Telephone Computing Service, Seattle, 1975-77; support engr. Digital Equipment Corp., Denver, 1977-79; cons. computer systems Colorado Springs, Colo., 1979—; program mgr. Digital Equipment Corp., Colorado Springs, 1980—. Mem. Aircraft Owners Pilots Assn. Republican. Roman Catholic. Office: Digital Equipment Corp 301 Rockrimmon Colorado Springs CO 80919

CABEZAS, HERIBERTO, JR., educator; b. La Esperanza, Las Villas, Cuba, Dec. 8, 1952; s. Heriberto and Ana Rosa (Fernandez) C.; m. Isaura Vazquez, May 21, 1988. BS in Chem. Enging., N.J. Inst. Tech., Newark, 1980; MS in Chem. Enging., U. Fla., 1981, PhD in Chem. Enging., 1985. Research asst. U. Fla., Gainesville, 1980-85; asst. prof. chem. enging. U. Ariz., 1985—; cons. Nat. Bur. Standards, Boulder, Colo., 1986—. Contbr. articles in profl. jours. Mem. Am. Inst. Chem. Engrs., Am. Chem. Soc., AAAS, Cuban Soc. Tucson, Tau Beta Pi, Omega Chi Epsilon (chpt. pres. 1979-80). Republican. Roman Catholic. Office: Univ Ariz Chem Enging Dept Tucson AZ 85721

CABLE, JOHN FRANKLIN, lawyer; b. Hannibal, Mo., Dec. 22, 1941; s. John William and Dorothy (Stanley) C.; m. Leslie Gibbs, Apr. 5, 1965; children: Coventry, Tory, John. AB, Stanford U., 1964; LLB, Harvard U., 1967. Bar: Oreg. 1967. Assoc. Miller, Nash, Wiener, Hager & Carlsen, Portland, Oreg., 1967-73; ptnr. Miller, Nash, Wiener, Hager & Carlsen, Portland, 1973—. Office: Miller Nash Wiener Hager & Carlsen 111 SW 5th Ave 35th Fl Portland OR 97204

CABLE, RICHARD ALBERT, manufacturing executive; b. Port Townsend, Wash., Apr. 22, 1950; s. Anton and Josephine Elizabeth (Kiesel) C.; m. Glenda Gaye Swain, Aug. 12, 1972; children: Emily Serena, Grant Michael. B in Mgmt. Sci. and Mktg., U. Wash., 1972; MBA, U. Nev., 1974. Cert. mgmt. acct. Sr. acct. Crown Zellerbach Co., Camas, Wash., 1974-77, mgr. acctg., 1977-79; asst. controller Crown Zellerbach Co., West Linn, Oreg., 1979-82; controller Crown Zellerbach Co., Los Angeles, 1982-83; corp. controller Grant and Roth Plastics, Hillsboro, Oreg., 1983-84, corp. gen. mgr., 1984-87, also sec. bd. dirs.; proprietor Ragg, Inc., West Linn, Oreg., 1986—; chief fin. officer, sec.-treas. Dee Forest Products, Hood River, Oreg., 1987—; market researcher Swain's Gen. Store, Port Angeles, Wash., 1972, co-dir., 1980—. Cub master Boy Scouts Am., Camas, 1977-79, West Linn, 1986, asst. scoutmaster, Oreg. City, Oreg., 1982; mem. exec. adv. com. Clackamas Community Coll. Named Eagle Scout Boy Scouts Am., 1965. Mem. Am. Mgmt. Assn., Assn. MBA Execs., Nat. Assn. Accts. (bd. dirs. Portland chpt.), Soc. Plastics Engrs., Am. Soc. Quality Control, Beta Gamma Sigma. Republican. Mormon. Clubs: Clark County Kennel (Vancouver, Wash.) (bd. dirs. 1977-79), Portland Borzoi (treas. 1977-80). Lodge: Elks. Office: Dee Forest Products 4780 Dee Hwy Hood River OR 97031

CABOT, HUGH, III, painter, sculptor; b. Boston, Mar. 22, 1930; s. Hugh and Louise (Melanson) C.; m. Olivia P. Taylor, Sept. 8, 1967; student Boston Museum, 1948, Ashmolean Mus., Oxford, Eng., 1960, Coll. Ams., Mexico City, 1956, San Carlos Acad., Mexico City. Portrait, landscape painter; sculptor in bronze; one-man shows: U.S. Navy Hist. and Recreation Dept., U.S. Navy Art Gallery, The Pentagon, Nat. War Mus., Washington, La Muse de la Marine, Paris; group shows include: Tex. Tri-state, 1969 (1st, 2d, 3d prizes). Served as ofcl. artist USN, Korean War. Named Artist of Yr., Scottsdale, Ariz., 1978, 30th ann. Festival of Arts, Tubac, Ariz., 1989. Clubs: Salmagundi (N.Y.C.). Author, illustrator: Korea I (Globe).

CABRAL, EVELYN AMELIA, nurse; b. London, June 8, 1939; d. William Watts and Eveline Rose (Bygrave) Butcher; m. Luis Cano Cabral, Feb. 7, 1960; children: Michael, Stephen, Martin-Andrew. AS, Mt. San Antonio Coll., 1976; AA in Nursing, Los Angeles Trade-Tech. Coll., 1977; student, U. Laverne, 1987—. RN. Specialist ICU coronary care Intercommunity Med. Ctr., Covina, Calif., 1977—, relief cons. diabetic edn., 1982. Mem. San Jose Homeowners Assn., Valinda, Calif., 1965-68; youth leader Boy Scouts Am., La Puente, Calif., 1967-74; instr. mentally disabled Delhaven Community Ctr., La Puente, 1976. Mem. Dalmatian Club Am., Dalmatian Club So. Calif. (chmn. hospitality com. 1988), Alpha Gamma Sigma. Democrat. Roman Catholic. Home: 646 Lidford Ave La Puente CA 91744

CACCIATORE, RAYMOND F., machine tool designer, business consultant; b. Rockford, Ill., Sept. 25, 1923; s. Steve and Marianna (Caruana); m. Josephine Jean Cipolla, Aug. 20, 1947; children: Steve, Gerald, Marian, Thearesa. Engring. detailer Ingersoll Milling Machine Co., Rockford, 1946-52; engring. designer W.F. & John Barnes Co., Rockford, 1952-58, Spl. Machine Co., Rockford, 1958-74; machine tool design cons. Rockford, 1974-81, Tucson, 1981—; treas., bd. dirs. Ahead Corp., Tucson, 1981-85, St. Mary's Med. Park Pharmacy, Tucson, 1985—. With USAAF, 1943-46, ETO. Mem. Moose. Roman Catholic. Home and Office: 8724 N Arnold Palmer Dr Tucson AZ 85741

CADDELL, DEBBIE EILEEN, electrologist; b. Seattle, Nov. 24, 1957; d. Donald Arthur and Rose Julia (Clough) Garries; m. James Melford Caddell, Apr. 27, 1984. Assoc. Applied Sci., Shoreline Community Coll., Seattle, 1977; BA in Clothing, Textiles, Seattle Pacific U., 1981. Bldg. maintenance Greyhound, Seattle, 1977-80; waitress Seattle Hilton, 1981-82; electrologist Caddell's Electrolysis Clinic, Federal Way, Wash., 1982—, Bellevue, Wash., 1982—. Mem. Internat. Guild Profl. Electrologists, Am. Electrologists Assn., Calif. Electrolysis Assn., Wash. State Electrology Assn., Soroptimists. Home: 3854 S 305 Pl Auburn WA 98001

CADE, JACK CARLTON, marketing professional; b. San Mateo, Calif., Mar. 9, 1948; s. Ross Dean and Florence Evelyn (Carlton) C. AA in Vacuum Tech., San Jose City Coll., 1968; BS in Bus., San Jose State U., 1972. Budget analyst Naval Elec. Lab. Ctr., San Diego, 1972-75, Dept. of the Air Force, Sunnyvale, Calif., 1975-78; contract negotiator Dept. of the Air Force, Sunnyvale, 1978-80, staff price analyst, 1980-81, sr. contract negotiator, 1981-82, contracting officer, 1982-86; sr. contract specialist Ford Aerospace Corp., Sunnyvale, 1986—. Mem. Air and Space Mus., active cen. com. Santa Clara (Calif.) County Rep. Party, 1969-72; team mgr., league pres. El Camino Little League, Santa Clara, 1982-83; pres. council San Jose State U.; bd. dirs. Santa Clara County Big Bros., 1972. Mem. Nat. Contract Mgmt. Assn., San Jose State U. Alumni Assn., Smithsonian. Club: Yosemite Fund (Calif.). Home: 1756 Roll St Santa Clara CA 95050 Office: Ford Aerospace Corp 1260 Crossman Ave Sunnyvale CA 94089

CADE, THOMAS GRANT, manufacturing executive; b. Lakewood, Ohio, May 22, 1941; s. Ross Dean and Florence Evelyn (Carlton) C.; m. Geraldine Beth Moser, Feb. 25, 1961; children: Tammy Rona Cade Walker, Rhonda Sholeen Cade Barnes, Autumn Beth. Student, San Jose (Calif.) City Coll., 1959-61. With prodn. control dept. Sylvania EDL Labs., Mountain View, Calif., 1963-65; buyer ESL, Inc., Sunnyvale, Calif., 1965-66; product mgr. Elmar Electronics, Mountain View, 1965-69; purchasing-inventory mgr. Racal-Vadic, Sunnyvale, 1969-78; ops. mgr. Cramer Electronics, Tucson, Ariz., 1978-81; v.p. ops., ptnr. M.E.C. Internat., Tucson, 1981-85; ops. mgr. Xytec Mfg., Tucson, 1985-87; bus. unit mgr. Qualtronics Mfg., Tucson, 1987-89; v.p., gen. mgr. Cadence Techs., Inc., Tucson, Ariz., 1989—. Pres. 6th div. of silent majority March for Am., San Jose, 1971; spokesperson Homeowners Assn. for Sch. Dist. Issues, San Jose, 1976. With U.S. Army, 1961-63. Republican. Home: 12000 Jefsumark Cir Tucson AZ 85749

CADEZ, PATRICIA POWELL, state agency administrator; b. Reno, July 5, 1940; d. A.C. and Dorothy (Pope) Powell; 1 child, Tracy Cadez Bullock. BS, Colo. State U., 1966; postgrad., Cen. Mich. U. Registered occupational therapist. Occupational therapist Bethesda Psychiat. Hosp., Denver, 1967; team therapist VA Hosp., Denver, 1968; occupational therapist State Home & Tng. Sch., Denver, 1968-72; sr. occupational therapist Health Svcs. Dept., Denver, 1972-73, dir. occupational therapy, 1973-75, therapy coord., 1975-76, retardation unit leader, 1976-77, dir. tng. and therapy, 1977-81, program adminstr., 1977—, asst. supr., 1981-85, dir., 1985—; mem. adj. faculty Colo. State U., 1974; office adminstr. Western Colo. Pediatric Assocs., 1987. Contbr. articles to profl. jours. Mem. Gov.'s Devel. Disabilities Coun., 1978, Deaf/Blind Diagnostic Team, 1975, Dept. of Edn. State Instl. Libr. Com., 1983-85, chmn., 1984-85; bd. dirs. Goodwill Rehab., Inc., 1979-84, Effective Parent Project; bd. dirs., sec. Community Tng. Ctr., Inc., 1978-83; mem. admission com. Mesa Devel. Svcs., 1979-81; mem. adv. coun. Foster Grandparent Program Mesa County, 1977-81; mem. accountability com. Mesa County Valley Sch. Dist. #51, 1985; participant citizens ambassador program Women in Mgmt. Tour of China, 1988. Recipient Colo. Disting. State Svc. award, 1983; named Occupational Therapist of the Western Slope, 1977. Mem. Am. Occupational Therapy Assn., Grand Junction Area C. of C. (mem. rangers 1985—, vice-chmn. 1986, chmn. 1987, exec. bd. dirs. 1988—), Soroptomists (Grand Junction, Colo. chpt.: v.p. 1983-84, pres. 1984-86). Home: 1044 Lakeside Dr Grand Junction CO 81506

CADIGAN, JOHN JOSEPH, educator physics, math; b. Boston, Oct. 2, 1933; s. Francis Clement and Alice Louise (Vahey) C.; m. Liv Margareth Jacobsen, June 10, 1966; children: Anne-Lise, Tanja, Kristin, Jason, Mark. BA in Physics, Boston Coll., 1954; MA Edn., U. Alaska, Juneau, 1988. Cert. tchr. Mass., Alaska. Engr. Sperry, L.I., N.Y., 1954-55; enlisted USCG, 1955, advanced to capt., ret., 1984; gen. ptnr. Juneau Olde Towne Classics (doing bus. as The Irish Shop, The Russian Shop, The Nordic House and The Country Loft), 1984—; prof. physics USCG Acad., New London, Conn., 1960-64; prof. physics. Old Dominion U., Norfolk, Va., 1974-79; prof. physics U. Alaska, Juneau, 1985-86; tchr. math., sci. State Alaska Cen. Corrs. Studies, Juneau, 1987—. Author: (book) Alaska Notes for Fishermen, 1966; contbr. articles to profl. jours. Mem. U.S.-USSR Trade and Econ. Council, 1987—. Decorated Coast Guard medal. Mem. Downtown Bus. Assn. (port com.), Mil. Order of St Lazurus, Mil. Order of Loyal Legion, Sons of Norway (pres. 1986—), Am. Legion, Juneau C. of C., Juneau Lions Club (v.p. 1986—). Republican. Lutheran. Lodge: Elks. Home: 3199 Pioneer Ave Juneau AK 99801 Office: Juneau Olde Towne Classics 175 S Franklin St Juneau AK 99801

CADRA, MICHAEL EDWARD, oral and maxillofacial surgeon; b. Washington, Aug. 15, 1953; s. Paul Miro and Eddene (Chism) C.; m. Sandra Jean Hall, Aug. 16, 1980; children: Meridith Melissa, Erik Paul. BS in Biol. Sci., U. Calif., Irvine, 1975; DMD, Washington U., St. Louis, 1982. Diplomate Am. Bd. Oral and Maxillofacial Surgery. Resident in dentistry VA Med. Ctr. of San Diego, La Jolla, Calif., 1982-83; resident in oral and maxillofacial surgery U. So. Calif., Los Angeles, 1983-86; practice dentistry specializing in oral and maxillofacial surgery Sacramento, 1986—. Mem. ADA, Am. Assn. Oral and Maxillofacial Surgeons, So. Calif. Acad. Oral Pathology, Am. Dental Soc. Anesthesiology. Mem. Ch. of Christ. Office: 1901 Watt Ave Ste 1 Sacramento CA 95825

CADWELL, DAVID ROBERT, lawyer; b. Hartford, Conn., June 7, 1934; s. Robert M. and Esther (Pinsky) C.; m. Carolle Cramer, 1964 (div. 1970); children—David, Kimberly; m. Sumiko Hashigiwa, Dec. 28, 1974; children—Kenneth, Daniel. B.A. magna cum laude, U. Minn., 1956; J.D., UCLA, 1959. Bar: Calif. 1960, U.S. Dist. Ct. (cen. and so. dists.) Calif. 1960, U.S. Supreme Ct. 1968. Dep. atty. gen. Calif. Atty. Gen., Los Angeles, 1960-61; sole practice, Santa Ana, Calif., 1961-70; adminstr. Jacoby & Meyers, Los Angeles, 1972-74, assoc., 1974-82; sole practice, Los Angeles, 1982-84; mng. ptnr. Cadwell & Glenn, Los Angeles, 1984—; lectr. Practical Law Course, Los Angeles, 1975-80. Author: How to Take a Case to Court, 1975; How to Handle Personal Injury Cases, 1976; How to Evaluate a Personal Injury Case, 1978, 80. Nat. committeeman Calif. Young Democrats, Los Angeles, 1959-60; mem. host com. Dem. Nat. Conv., Los Angeles, 1960, county com. Dem. Party, Orange County, Calif., 1962-64; exec. com. Fox Hills Dem. Club, Los Angeles, 1973-78. Recipient Outstanding Legal Services award NAACP, 1963. Mem. Assn. Trial Lawyers Am. Calif. Trial Lawyers Assn., Los Angeles Trial Lawyers Assn. Jewish. Home: 3575 Green Vista Dr Encino CA 91436 Office: Cadwell & Glenn 9744 Wilshire Blvd Ste 440 Beverly Hills CA 90212

CADY, WALLACE MARTIN, research geologist; b. Middlebury, Vt.; s. Frank William and Alice Marian (Kingsbury) C.; m. Helen Johanna Raitanen, Jan. 1, 1942; children: John Wallace, Nancy Helen, Norma Louise. BS, Middlebury Coll., Vt., 1934; MS, Northwestern U., 1936; PhD, Columbia U., 1944. Registered geologist, Colo., Vt., D.C. Rsch. geologist U.S. Geol. Survey, Washington, 1939-45, Montpelier, Vt., 1945-61, Denver, 1961-85. Author: New England and Quebec, 1969; (with others) geol. maps. Fulbright lectureship, USSR, 1975; recipient Meritorious award U.S. Dept. Interior. Fellow Geol. Soc. Am., Am. Geophys. Union; mem. Colo. Sci. Soc., (pres. 1975), Soc. Econ. Geologists, Vt. Geol. Soc. Home: 3955 Douglas Mountain Dr Golden CO 80403 Office: US Geol Survey Fed Ctr Box 25046 Denver CO 80225

CADY, WILLIAM LODGE, aerospace executive; b. Palo Alto, Calif., Dec. 3, 1946; s. John Atwood and Margaret Louise (Kessler) C.; m. Maria Ester Cordillo, Oct. 13, 1979; 1 child, Leo R. Villarreal. BS in Econs., Calif. State U., Chico, 1970. Contract adminstr. Bechtel Corp., San Francisco, 1972-78; MX contract adminstr. Aerojet Strategic Propulsion Co., Sacramento, 1978-86; contract adminstr. sml. ICBMs Aerojet Nev. Rocket Ops., Sacramento, 1986—. Bd. dirs. Cien Amigos y Amigas, Sacramento, 1987—; mem. adv. bd. U. Calif., Davis, acad. enrichment program/early outreach. Mem. Nat. Contract Mgmt. Assn., Sacramento Hispanic C. of C. (sec. 1986—, bd. dirs.). Republican. Congregationalist. Office: Aerojet Nev Rocket Ops PO Box 13028 Sacramento CA 95813-4028

CAEN, HERB, newspaper columnist, author; b. Sacramento, Calif., Apr. 3, 1916; s. Lucien and Augusta (Gross) C.; m. Sally Gilbert, Feb. 15, 1952 (div. 1959); 1 step dau., Deborah; m. Maria Theresa Shaw, Mar. 9, 1963; 1 son, Christopher. Student, Sacramento Jr. Coll., 1934. Daily newspaper columnist San Francisco Chronicle, 1936-50, 1958; columnist San Francisco Examiner, 1950-58. Author: The San Francisco Book, 1948, Baghdad-by-the-Bay, 1949, Baghdad 1951, 1950, Don't Call It Frisco, 1953, Caen's Guide to San Francisco, 1957, Only in San Francisco, 1960, (with Dong Kingman) City on Golden Hills, 1968, The Cable Car and the Dragon, 1972, One Man's San Francisco, 1976. Served from pvt. to capt. USAAF, 1942-45. Decorated Medaille de la Liberation France, 1949. Democrat. Club: Calif. Tennis. Office: San Francisco Chronicle Pub Co 925 Mission St San Francisco CA 94103 *

CAHILL, EDWARD PATRICK, financial executive; b. Bklyn., Feb. 14, 1943; s. Patrick M. and Margaret (Argue) C.; m. Antoinette Pampaloni, Aug. 29, 1964; children: Edward Patrick, Lisa Ann. BBA in Acctg., St. John's U., 1967; MBA, Baldwin-Wallace U., 1976. Mktg. v.p. Banc Systems, Inc., Cleve., 1969-80, TymShare McDonnell-Douglas, Fremont, Calif., 1980-83; gen. mgr. TeleCheck, San Diego, 1983-86; acct. exec. Am. Bank Stationery, PetaLuma, Calif., 1986-87; Compliance officer First Deposit Corp, San Francisco, 1987--. Served as sgt. USMC, 1959-61. Republican. Roman Catholic. Home: 721 Sinnett Ct Danville CA 94526 Office: First Deposit Corp 88 Kearney St San Francisco CA 94108

CAHILL, PATRICIA ANN, insurance executive; b. Utica, N.Y., Oct. 11, 1950; d. Warren Harding and Hazel Augustine (Morton) Rishel; children: Matthew James, Shannon Marie. BA, Utica Coll., 1972. Tchr. St. Agnes Sch., Utica, 1972-75; with Clinton (N.Y.) Cen. Sch., 1975-76, Hartford Ins., New Hartford, N.Y., 1976-81, Utica Nat. Ins. Co., 1981—; sr. staff asst., svcs. mgr. Utica Nat. Ins. Co., Glendora, Calif., 1988—; instr. Ins. Inst. Am., 1986—. Mem. NAFE, Aims, Phi Kappa Phi. Democrat. Home: 10456 Mangrove St Alta Loma CA 91730 Office: Utica Nat Ins Co 2020 Financial Way Glendora CA 91740

CAHOON, JEAN MITCHELL, interior designer; b. San Diego, July 24, 1959; d. Carl DeWite and Elizabeth F.J. (Winter) Mitchell; m. Jack Everett Cahoon, Nov. 22, 1986. BA in Interior Design, San Diego State U., 1988. Design asst. Charlotte Jensen & Assoc., San Diego, 1985-87; interior designer Ethan Allen/Carriage House Interiors, San Diego, 1987-88; sr. project designer Gerhard Interiors, Ltd., La Costa, Calif., 1988—. Mem. Am. Soc. Interior Design (student chpt. rep., social dir. 1981-82). Republican. Home: 4772 Wilson Ave 6 San Diego CA 92116 Office: Gerhard Interiors Ltd 7630 El Camino Real Rancho La Costa CA 92009

CAHOON, RICHARD STUART, biotechnologist; b. Salt Lake City, Apr. 28, 1954; s. Reynolds Fehring and Margaret (Mothersill) C.; m. J'Nelle Hathaway, June 28, 1980; children: Lauren E., Lindsey M. BA, U. Utah, 1976, BS cum laude, 1977; MS, Mont. State U., 1983. R&D tech. Pax Co. (Cenex), Salt Lake City, 1974-78; rsch. tech. II Biology dept. U. Utah, Salt Lake City, 1978-80; rsch. specialist U.S. Geol. Survey, Salt Lake City, 1980-81; rsch. assoc. Inst. for Bioprocess Analysis Mont. State U., Bozeman, 1981-83; pres. Assoc. Biotechs., Inc., Salt Lake City, 1983-85; sales/process engr. Monroe Food Process Machinery, Inc., Salt Lake City, 1985-87; dir. bus. devel. CCE, Inc., Bozeman, 1987-88; tech. transfer dir. The R&D Inst., Bozeman, 1989—; program devel. Inst. for Bioprocess Analysis, 1988—; new projects cons. Utah State Dept. Agr., Salt Lake City, 1986-87. Author (strategic plan) Tech./Transfer Devel., 1989, IPA , 1989; patentee in field. Vol. tchr. Montessori Sch., Bozeman, 1988—, Granite Sch. Dist., Salt Lake City, 1980-81; vol. therapist Children's Ctr. United Way, Salt Lake City, 1978-80; coord. Neighborhood Tree Planning Porject, Salt Lake City, 1978-81. Rsch. Commendation award U.S. Geol Survey, Salt Lake City, 1981; Rsch. fellow Chevron, Inc., Bozeman, 1981-83, Rsch. Creativity grantee, Mont. State U., Bozeman, 1982. Mem. Pi Kappa Alpha. Office: PO Box 1409 Bozeman MT 59771

CAICEDO, SINAR ABDIEL, nurse; b. Cali, Colombia, Oct. 16, 1963; came to U.S., 1965; s. Jeorge Enrique and Luz (Passos) C. LVN, Pasadena Community Coll., Pasadena, Calif., 1984. Carpenter journeyman L.A., 1981-85; assoc. R.I. Rsch. Lab., N.Y.C., 1987; instr., translator Gnostic Assn. Anthropological Studies, L.A., 1978-89; pvt. duty nurse L.A. Translator: Occult Medicine, 1988, Introduction to Gnosis, 1987, Technique for the Yo, 1986. Republican. Home: 6414 Elging St Los Angeles CA 98042

CAIN, JAMES DOUGLAS, JR., government official; b. Oakland, Calif., July 4, 1946; s. James Douglas and Daisy Doris (DeBerry) C.; m. Joyce Mae Dilworth, Aug. 12, 1967. B.S., SUNY-Albany, 1980; postgrad. Troy State U., 1980-81; B.A. in History cum laude, U. Md., 1982. Fgn. service staff officer Office Def. Attache, Saigon, Vietnam, 1973-74; counter-intelligence ops. specialist Dept. Army, various locations, 1974-87; intelligence ops. specialist, vice counter-intelligence ops. specialist, Dept. Army, 1987—. Active Minn. Chippewa Tribe, Nat. Congress Am. Indians. From 2d lt. to capt., M.I., U.S. Army, 1967-73. Fellow Internat. Ctr. for Asian Studies, 1984. Mem. Internat. Polit. Sci. Assn., Am. Polit. Sci. Assn., Am. Econs. Assn., Nat. Geog. Soc., Middle East Inst., VFW, Vietnam Vets. Am., Alpha Sigma Lambda, Pi Alpha Theta, Pi Sigma Alpha. Democrat. Club: Masons.

CAIN, PATRICIA JEAN, accountant; b. Decatur, Ill., Sept. 28, 1931; d. Paul George and Jean Margaret (Horne) Jacka; m. Dan Louis Cain, July 12, 1952; children: Mary Ann, Timothy George, Paul Louis. Student, U. Mich., 1949-52, Pasadena (Calif.) City Coll., 1975-76; BS in Acctg., Calif. State U., L.A., 1977, MBA, 1978; M in Taxation, Golden Gate U., Los Angeles, 1988. CPA, Calif.; cert. personal fin. planner; cert. advanced fin. planner. Tax supr. Stonefield & Josephson, L.A., 1979-87; chief fin. officer Loubella Extendables, Inc., L.A., 1987—; participant program in bus. ethics U. So. Calif., L.A., 1986. Bd. dirs. Sierra Madre Girl Scout Coun., Pasadena, 1968-73, treas., 1973-75, elected nat. del., 1975; mem. Town Hall, L.A., 1987—. Listed as one of top six tax experts in L.A. by Money mag., 1987. Mem. AICPA (chairperson nat. tax teleconf. 1988), Am. Women's Soc. CPA's (bd. dirs. 1986-87, v.p. 1987—), Calif. Soc. CPAs (chairperson free tax assistance program 1983-85, high rd. com. 1985-86, chairperson pub. rels. com. 1985-89, microcomputer users discussion group, taxation com., fin. com./speaker computer show and conf. 1987-89, planning com. and speaker San Francisco Tax and Microcomputer show 1988), Internat. Arabian Horse Assn., Beta Alpha Psi. Democrat. Episcopalian. Club: Wrightwood Country (Calif.). Home: 3715 Fairmeade Rd Pasadena CA 91107 Office: Loubella Extendables Inc 2222 S Figueroa St Los Angeles CA 90007

CAIN, VIRGINIA HARTIGAN, judicial educator; b. Bklyn., May 1, 1922; d. James Gerard and H. Virginia (Williams) Hartigan; m. Edmund Joseph Cain, Dec. 3, 1944; children: Edmund Joseph III, Mary Ellen McMullen, James Michael. AB, NYU, 1943; MEd, U. Del., 1963; postgrad., U. Nev., 1972. Personnel counselor R & D Labs., Ft. Monmouth, N.J., 1943-47; elem. and secondary tchr. and counselor Reno, 1968-73; dir. children in placement project Nat. Coun. Juvenile and Family Ct. Judges, Reno, 1974-76; asst. tng. dir. Nat. Coll. Juvenile Justice, Reno, 1976-80, curriculum dir., 1980-83, child support enforcement project dir., 1983-86; cons. juvenile and family law Reno, 1987—; adj. asst. prof. U. Nev., Reno; mem. adv. bd. Com. To Aid Abused Women, Nat. Assn. Family Counselors in Juvenile Ct., 1981-82; del.-at-large White House Conf. on Families, 1980; mem. Gov.'s Adv. Com. on Youth, 1985—; mem. Washoe County Adv. Bd. Human Services, 1987—. Author numerous poems. Co-chair Nev. Friends of Gov.'s Mansion, 1989; mem. Nev. Gov.'s Commn. on Status of Women, 1966-70, 72-81; del. Nat. Dem. Convs., 1970, 72, 80; Dem. chmn. Nev. chpt. ERA, 1980-82; mem. Dem. Nat. Com., 1980-82, mem. platform accountability commn., 1982; 1st vice chmn. Nev. Dem. Com., 1980-82, mem. exec. bd. Cen. Com., 1988—; mem. adv. bd. Mental Health Assn. Nev., 1966-72; mem. Nev. Gov.'s Commn. on Girl's Tng. Sch., 1972-76; mem. exec. com. Washoe County Dem. Central Com., 1966-80; Nev. mem. Compliance Rev. Commn., 1972-76; mem. Nev. Charter Com., 1972-74; No. Nev. Coord. for Senator Edward Kennedy, 1979-80, Gov. of Nev., 1972; active campaign worker for Adlai Stevenson, John F. Kennedy, Jimmy Carter; bd. dirs. United Way No. Nev., Planned Parenthood Nev.; mem. Nat. Com. for Support Pub. Schs.; mem. Sr. Citizens Adv. Bd. Washoe County; former chmn. early childhood edn. and legis. com. Del. PTA Bd.; former mem. adv. bd. Washoe Assn. For Mentally Retarded; co-program chmn. 21st Ann. South Pacific Regional Conf., Child Welfare League Am.-Nat. Coun. Juvenile Ct. Judges, 1976; numerous other civic polit. activities. Recipient various service and profl. awards. Mem. Internat. Soc. Family Law, Children's Def. Fund, Women's Polit. Caucus, Nat. Women's Polit. Caucus, Nat. Assn. Counsel for Children, AAUW, LWV, Reno Bus. and Profl. Women (legis. chmn.), Nev. Art Gallery, Croesus Corp. Investment Club (pres.), Nat. Jud. Educators Assn., U. Club Nev. Faculty Wives, Caughlin Club. Roman Catholic. Home: 3710 Clover Way Reno NV 89509 Office: U Nev Box 8978 Reno NV 89507

CAINE, STEPHEN HOWARD, data process executive.; b. Washington, Feb. 11, 1941; s. Walter E. and Jeanette (Wenborne) C.; student Calif. Inst. Tech., 1958-62. Sr. programmer Calif. Inst. Tech., Pasadena, 1962-65, mgr. systems programming, 1965-69, mgr. programming, 1969-70; pres. Caine, Farber & Gordon, Inc., Pasadena, 1970—; lectr. applied sci. Calif. Inst. Tech., Pasadena, 1965-71, vis. asso. elec. engring., 1976, vis. asso. computer sci., 1976-84. Mem. Pasadena Tournament of Roses Assn., 1976—. Mem. Assn. Computing Machinery, Nat. Assn. Corrosion Engrs., AAAS, Am. Ordnance Assn. Clubs: Athenaeum (Pasadena); Engrs. (N.Y.C.). Home: 77 Patrician Way Pasadena CA 91105

CAINES, KENNETH L.D., management consulting executive; b. N.Y.C.; s. Clarence and Monica C.; BS in Psychology and Sociology, NYU; postgrad. Calif. State Coll., UCLA, ; m. Josephine A. Robinson. pres. People Oriented Systems, Santa Ana, Calif., 1969—; v.p. Band Aide, 1984-87; dir. Joken Human Factors Assocs. lectr. civil and social systems U. Calif.-Irvine, 1970-71. V.p. tech. adv. com. on testing Calif. Fair Employment Practices Commn., 1967-71; mem. U. Calif. at Irvine-Project 21 Com. on Population Growth, 1971-72; pres. Orange YMCA, 1973; mem. adv. bd. Orange County coun. Boy Scouts Am., 1970—; mem. Orange County Grand Jury, 1980-81. Mem. Orange Planning Commn., 1973-76. Bd. dirs. Orange County United Way, 1971-73, Orange County Community Housing Corp., 1986—. Served with USAAF. Named Citizen of Year Orange YMCA, 1972. Mem. IEEE, Am. Mgmt. Assn., Human Factors Soc. Orange County, Assn. Profl. Cons. Office: People Oriented Systems 2060 N Tustin Ave Santa Ana CA 92701

CAIRNS, SHIRLEY ANN, financial planner; b. Hundred, W.Va., Sept. 26, 1937; d. John Martin and Thelma Irene Stiles; children: John Michael, Lyle Dennis, Glynis Ann. BS, W.Va. U., 1959, MA, 1964; MPA, Harvard U., 1989. Cert. fin. planner. Tchr. public schs., Alliance, Ohio, 1958-60, Morgantown, W.Va., 1960-61; tchr., head bus. edn. dept. Sutherlin (Oreg.) High Sch., 1964-80; registered rep. IDS, 1980-83; prin. Shirley A. Cairns & Assocs., 1983—. Active Oreg. State Dem. 4th dist. Cen. Com., 1982, Oreg. Dem. Rules Com., Oreg. Dem. Exec. Com., 1985-88, Oreg. Dem. Cen. Com., 1982-89, Oreg. Orgn. Com., 1989—, Douglas County Tourist Adv. Com., Douglas County Dem. Cen. Com., 1980-88; del. Dem. Nat. Conv., 1984, mem. rules com., 1988; mem. Roseburg dist. adv. com. Bur. Land Mgmt., 1987-90; mem. Oreg. Port Adv. Com., 1988-89; bd. dirs. Calapooia Water Dist., March of Dimes; active Leadership Am., 1988. Mem. Nat. Women's Polit. Caucus, So. Oreg. Women's Polit. Caucus (v.p.). Oreg. Women's Polit. Caucus, Internat. Assn. Fin. Planners, Inst. Cert. Fin. Planners, Roseburg C. of C., Douglas County C. of C., AAUW, Lioness, Xi Tau. Home: 640 Rolling Ridge Rd PO Box 76 Oakland OR 97462 Office: 1012 SE Oak Ste 330 Roseburg OR 97470

CAKEBREAD, BRUCE ALLEN, SR., bodyguard, security advisor; b. Antioch, Calif., Mar. 27, 1949; s. Robert Harold Cakebread and Mildred Irene (McQueen) Cakebread Cowing. Dip., Security Tng. Inst., Seattle, 1973; cert., Internat. Police Congress, Seattle, 1973; dip., Wash. State Criminal Justice, 1981. Private investigator R.A.M. Enterprises, Seattle, 1973-80; security tng. officer Pvt. Body Guard Service, Seattle, 1973-80; correctional officer Dept. Corrections, Walla Walla, Wash., 1980-85; news reporter KTEL Radio, Walla Walla, 1987--. Served with U.S. Army, 1971-73. Recipient Citizen of Valor award Bellingham (Wash.) Police Dept., 1974; cert. appreciation Bellingham Police Dept., 1974. Home: 524 Chase St Walla Walla WA 99362

CALDER, ROBERT MAC, aerospace engineer; b. Vernal, Utah, Oct. 16, 1932; s. Edwin Harold and Sydney (Goodrich) C.; m. Yoshiko Iemura, Feb. 14, 1959; children—Suzanne, Alex, Irene, John. B.S. in Chem. Engring., U. Utah, 1956, M.S. in Math. and Geology (NSF grantee), 1967; postgrad. U. Wash., 1964, Utah State U., 1965, U. Iowa, 1966. Cert. secondary tchr., Utah. Tchr. Utah Pub. Schs., 1958-79; v.p. Sydney Corp., Bountiful, Utah, 1958-82; sr. engr. aero. div., Hercules Inc., Magna, Utah, 1979—; owner RMC Enterprises, Nations Imports; cons. in field, 1960—; cultural exchange participant to Israel, Egypt, 1983, 87. Active Boy Scouts Am., 1945-75, instr., Philmont Scout Ranch, 1972, asst. scoutmaster Nat. Jamboree Troop, 1973; instr. hunter safety and survival, Utah Dept. Fish and Game, 1964-74; state advisor U.S. Congl. Adv. Bd., 1982—. Served to capt. USAF, 1956-70. Mem. AIAA, Nat. Rifle Assn. (life), Am. Quarter Horse Assn., Internat. Platform Assn., Oratorio Soc. Utah, Republican Nat. Com. Mormon. Club: Hercules Toastmasters (treas. 1980, v.p. edn. 1981, pres. 1982). Home: PO Box 268 Bountiful UT 84011-0268 Office: PO Box 98 Magna UT 84044

CALDER, WILMER COYT, real estate investor; b. Apache, Okla., Mar. 25, 1933; s. Cecil William and Zelma Orthel (Wilson) C.; m. Shirley Ann Calder, Feb. 12, 1971 (dec. Jan. 1984); m. Sharon Ann Irelan, Dec. 27, 1985. Grad. high sch., Clovis, N.Mex. Switch-fireman Santa Fe R.R., Clovis, 1951-53, 55-58; prin. Constrn. & Real Estate Investment, Clovis, 1958—. With U.S. Army, 1953-55. Republican. Baptist. Home: 1008 Oakhurst Clovis NM 88101 Office: Coyt Calder Enterprises 1401 E Mabry Dr Clovis NM 88101

CALDERELLA, LEO FRANCIS, magazine editor; b. N.Y.C., July 16, 1949; s. Pasquale and Jeanne Therese (McNeil) C. BA, Columbia U., 1971; postgrad., Fordham U., 1971-72. Typographer Cardinal Type Svc., N.Y.C., 1975-78; pres. Leo Calderella Enterprises, N.Y.C., Phoenix, 1978-84; pub. relations rep. Bapt. Hosps. and Health Systems, Phoenix, 1984-86; editor, assoc. publisher Vim and Vigor mag., Phoenix, 1986—. Author: The Unguarded Moment, 1976, also short stories; contbr. articles to mags. Recipient Award of Merit Internat. Assn. Bus. Communicators, Phoenix, 1985. Mem. Phoenix Advt. Club, Pub. Relations Soc. Am., Phi Beta Kappa. Republican. Office: Vim & Vigor 8805 N 23d Ave Suite 11 Phoenix AZ 85021

CALDERON, ESTHER MORAGA, nurse; b. Kondyke, Ariz., Mar. 10, 1937; d. Juan Calderon and Angelita (Moraga) Calderon Valenzuela. Assoc. Nursing, Pima Community Coll., Tucson, 1982. RN, La. Home health nurse Catholic Social Services, Tucson, 1974-80; team leader home health Pima County Health Dept., 1979-80; surgical nurse Kino Community Hosp., 1982, Mercy Med. Ctr., Nampa, Idaho, 1982-83; staff nurse Eucharistic Missionaries Ctr., New Orleans, 1983-86, Belmont Lodge Nursing Home, Pueblo, Colo., 1986-88, Parkview Episc. Med. Ctr., 1986-88; coordinator Religious Community Central House, New Orleans, 1988—. Sister in religious community Eucharistic Missionaries St. Dominic, 1962; active various social justice activities. Democrat. Roman Catholic.

CALDERWOOD, WILLIAM ARTHUR, physician; b. Wichita, Kans., Feb. 3, 1941; s. Ralph Bailey and Janet Denise (Christ) C.; m. Nancy Jo Crawford, Mar. 31. 1979; children: Lisa Beth, William Arthur, Christopher Robert, Adam J.W. MD, U. Kans., 1968. Diplomate Am. Bd. Family Practice. Intern Wesley Med. Ctr., Wichita, 1968-69; gen. practice family medicine Salina, Kans., 1972-80, Peoria, Ariz., 1980—; pres. staff St. John's Hosp., Salina, 1976; 28th judicial dist. coroner, State of Kans., Salina, 1973-80; clins. instr. U. Kans., Wichita, 1978-80; cons. U. Ariz., 1989—. Lt., M.C., USN, 1969-70. Fellow Am. Acad. Family Physicians; mem. AMA, Ariz. Med. Soc. (physicians med. health com., exec. com. 1988—), Maricopa County Med. Soc., Ariz. Acad. Family Practice (med. dir. NW Orgn. Vol. alternatives 1988—), Am. Med. Soc. on Alcoholism and Other Drug Dependencies (cert.). Lodge: Shriners. Home: 7015 W Calavar Peoria AZ 85345 Office: 13640 N Plaza del Rio Blvd Peoria AZ 85345

CALDWELL, BETTE ALICE, educational administrator, counselor; b. L.A., May 31, 1941; d. George Joseph and Helen Gibson (Glaesmer) C. BA, UCLA, 1963; MEd, Loyola U., L.A., 1972. Cert. tchr., adminstr., counselor, in guidance, Calif. Tchr., tutor Fernald Sch., UCLA, 1962-64; tchr. English and remedial reading Marina Del Rey Jr. High Sch., L.A., 1964-67, tchr., dept. chmn., reading coord., 1967-74, tchr. journalism, grade counselor, 1967-78, dean students, 1974-78; head counselor Bethune Jr. High Sch., L.A., 1979-85; head counselor Bancroft Jr. High Sch., L.A., 1985-87, asst. prin. for secondary counseling svcs., 1987-89; cons. individual instrn. edn. dept. Loyola U., 1971-72; cons. global edn. Sch. for Internat. Tng., Brattleboro, Vt., 1985-88. Editor monthly newsletter So. Calif. Camping Assn., 1975-79. Chmn. camping com. L.A. Area coun. Camp Fire, 1980-88, v.p., 1983-87; chmn. youth coun., mem. adminstrv. bd. Westwood United Meth. Ch., L.A., 1982-88. Recipient nat. awards Campe Fire, 1983, 85, 87. Mem. Assn. Calif. Sch. Adminstrs., Assoc. Adminstrs. L.A., Secondary Head Counselors L.A., Marina Del Rey Jr. High Sch. PTA (hon. life), Delta Kappa Gamma (bd. dirs. Chi state area 1981-83, news editor 1983—, speaker profl. confs. 1984—, internat. communications com. 1986-88, scholar 1976, 78). Democrat. Home: 1200 Galapago #105 Denver CO 80204 Office: Bancroft Jr High Sch 929 N Las Palmas Ave Los Angeles CA 90038

CALDWELL, CHARLES DEWEY, history educator; b. Del Norte, Colo., June 13, 1925; s. Ralph Dewey and Anna (Ydren) C.; m. Geraldine Delores Showalter, June 15, 1947. AA, Mt. San Antonio Coll., 1965; BA, La Verne U., 1967; MA, Claremont Grad. Sch., 1969. Cert. jr. coll. tchr., Calif. Instr. history La Verne (Calif.) U., 1968-69, Kapiolani Community Coll., Honolulu, 1969-71, Honolulu Community Coll., 1970—; asst. dir. field study on Oreg. Trail and Colonial Am. La Verne U., 1967; mem. State Hawaii Found. History and Humanities com., 1971-72, Hawaii Bicentennial Commn. Publs. com., 1975-76; instr. Hoomana Sch., Honolulu, 1975-76, Lanikila Sr. Ctr., Honolulu, 1976-78. Mem. adv. com. Honolulu Community Coll. Emeritus Coll., 1988. Mem. Nat. Hist. Soc., Community Coll. Soc. Sci. Assn., Hawaiian Hist. Soc., Bishop Mus. Assn., Honolulu Acad. Arts. Republican. Mem. Christian Ch. Club: Queen Emma Hawaiian Civic. Home: 1325 Wilder Ave Mauka 6 Honolulu HI 96822 Office: U Hawaii Honolulu Community Coll 874 Dillingham Blvd Honolulu HI 96822

CALDWELL, DANIEL EDMUND, educator; b. San Francisco, Feb. 22, 1938; s. George Forrester and Bernice (Bresson) Rosselli C.; m. Karlene Louise Crockett, Oct. 4, 1981; children: Monica, Daniel Karm, Antony. BA, San Francisco State U., 1958, MA, 1966; postgrad., UCLA, 1970. Gen. Secondary Credential, Calif. Theater tchr. Tamalpais High Sch., Mill Valley, Calif., 1962—; fine arts dept chmn. Tamalpais High Sch., Mill Valley, 1988—; program dir. Ensemble Theatre Co. (ETC), Mill Valley, 1981—; dir. Marin Shakespeare Festival, San Rafael, 1965-73; dir., actor various film and TV companies, L.A., 1958—. Director/writer The Tipsters, 1976, Kids Writes, 1977. Bd. dirs. The Marin Arts Coun., Marin County, Calif., 1980—, Ensemble Theatre Co. of Marin, 1981—, Teens Kick Off, 1989—. Recipient Director's award Am. Assn. Theatre, 1988. Mem. Screen Actors Guild (v.p. 1983—, pres. San Francisco br. 1974-77). Office: Ensemble Theatre Co Miller Ave and Camino Alto Mill Valley CA 94941

CALDWELL, HOWARD BRYANT, teacher of English as a second language; b. London, Ky., Jan. 28, 1944; s. Stratton and Linda Emily (Bryant) C. BA, Berea (Ky.) Coll., 1966; MA, U. Calif., Berkeley, 1977. Cert. adult edn. tchr. Tchr. L.A. Unified Sch. Dist., 1977—. Mem. L.A. County Mus. Art, L.A. World Affairs Council. With USAF, 1966-70, The Philippines. Mem. United Tchrs. L.A. Republican. Baptist.

CALDWELL, JOHN JACK, small business owner; b. Cleve., Apr. 14, 1933; s. John Joseph and Thelma Mae (Coughlin) C.; m. Vivian Ruth Furr, Nov. 10, 1956; children: Kevin John, Kerry Scott, Kelly Ann Caldwell Olsen. BS in Biology, Loyola U., L.A., 1955. Auto body/paint tech. Hastings Chevrolet, Santa Monica, Calif., 1949-56; pharmaceutical sales Am. Cyanamid, Riverside, Calif., 1959-65; aluminum foil specialist Amax Aluminum Mill Products, Riverside, 1965-67; product mgr. Amax Aluminum Foil Products, St. Louis, 1968-69; West sales mgr. Alumax Aluminum Foil, Riverside, 1969-74; v.p. sales Metal Industries, Ontario, Can., 1974-78; sales mgr. ABC Metals Supply, Santa Ana, Calif., 1978-79; owner, pres. Autobody by Caldwell, Inc., Laguna Hills, Calif., 1979—. Pres. Saddleback Valley YMCA, El Toro, Calif., 1972-74; v.p. Orange County YMCA, Santa Ana, 1977-81. Capt. USAF, 1956-59. Named to Outstanding Young Men of America, Jaycees, Riverside, 1966, Jr. Chamber Internat. Senator, Jaycees, Riverside, 1968; recipient Chmn.'s Disting. Svc. award, Orange County YMCA, Santa Ana, 1981. Mem. Calif. Autobody Assn. (pres. 1984, Mem. of Yr. award, 1987); Automotive Svc. Assn. (bd. dirs. 1986—, chmn. awards com. 1989). Republican. Roman Catholic. Office: Autobody By Caldwell Inc 22681 Granite Way Laguna Hills CA 92653

CALDWELL, WALTER EDWARD, editor, small business owner; b. L.A., Dec. 29, 1941; s. Harold Elmer and Esther Ann (Fuller) C.; m. Donna Edith Davis, June 27, 1964; 1 child, Arnie-Jo. AA, Riverside City Coll., 1968. Sales and stock professional Sears Roebuck & Co., Riverside, Calif., 1963-65; dispatcher Rohr Corp., Riverside, Calif., 1965-67; trainee Aetna Fin., Riverside, 1967-68; mgr. Aetna Fin., San Bruno, Cal., 1968-70, Amfac Thrift & Loan, Oakland, Calif., 1970-74; free lance writer San Jose, Calif., 1974-76; news dir. Sta. KAVA Radio, Burney, Cal., 1977-79; editor-pub. Mountain Echo, Fall River Mills, Calif., 1979—. Contbg. author Yearbook of Modern Poetry, 1976. Pres. Intermountain United Way, Burney, Calif., 1979, co-chmn., 1977, chmn. 1978; disaster relief worker ARC, Redding, Calif., 1988—; bd. dirs. Shasta County Women's Refuge, Redding, 1988—; bd. dirs. Shasta County Econ. Devel. Corp., Redding, 1986-87, 89—, exec. bd. dirs., 1987; pres. Eastern Shasta County Econ. Devel. Corp., 1987-89; bd. dirs. Shasta County Econ. Devel. Task Force, 1985-86; troop leader Girl Scouts U.S., San Jose, 1973-76; announcer Intermountain Fair Parade, McArthur, Calif., 1983—, Burney Basin Days Parade, 1985—, Big Valley Days Parade, Adin, Calif., 1988; commr. Burney Fire Protection Dist., 1987—; trustee Mosquito Abatement Dist., Burney, 1978-87; pres. Burney Basin Days Com., 1985-86, 88-89; observer Eastern Shasta County Sheriff's Flying Possee, 1988—. Cpl. USMC, 1959-63. Mem. Am. Legion, Burney Basin C. of C. (advt. chmn. 1982), Rotary (chmn. bike race 1981-85), Lions (student speaker Fall River club 1983-88), Moose. (trustee 1988—). Republican. Home: 1565 Elm St Burney CA 96013 Office: Mountain Echo Main St Fall River Mills CA 96028

CALDWELL, WILLIAM MACKAY, III, business executive; b. Los Angeles Apr. 6, 1922; s. William Mackay II and Edith Ann (Richards) C.; BS, U. So. Calif., 1943; MBA, Harvard U., 1948; m. Mary Louise Edwards, Jan. 16, 1946 (dec. 1980); children: William Mackay IV, Craig Edwards, Candace Louise; m. Jean Bledsoe, Apr. 27, 1985. Sec.-treas., dir. Drewry Photocolor Corp., 1957-60, Adcolor Photo Corp., 1957-60; treas., dir. Drewry Bennetts Corp., 1959-60; sr. v.p., chief fin. officer Am. Cement Corp., 1960-67; sr. v.p. corp., 1966-70, pres. cement and concrete group, 1967-70; pres., chmn. bd., chief exec. officer Van Vorst Industries, 1969; pres. Van Vorst Corp., Washington, 1969-77; chmn. bd., pres. So. Cross Industries, U.S. Bedding Co., 1979-84, St. Croix Mfg. Co., 1979-81, Hawaiian Cement Corp.; pres. Englander Co., 1979-84; v.p., dir. Am. Cement Internat. Corp., Am. Cement Properties; chmn. Kyco Industries Inc., 1982—; pres. BHI Inc., 1984—; cons. prof. U. So. Calif. Mem. men's com. Los Angeles Med. Center; bd. dirs. Commerce Assocs., Calif. Mus. Sci. and Industry, U. So. Calif. Assocs., bd. dirs. Pres.'s Circle; bd. dirs. Am. Cement Found. Served to lt. USNR, 1943-46. Mem. Newcomen Soc., Friends Huntington Library, Los Angeles Country Club, Town Hall Club, Calif. Club (Los Angeles), Trojan Club, Annandale Golf Club, Eldorado Country Club, Marrakesh Golf Club, Harvard Bus. Sch. of So. Calif. (dir. 1960-63), Kappa Alpha, Alpha Delta Sigma, Alpha Pi Omega. Presbyterian. Office: PO Box 726 Pasadena CA 91102

CALHOON, EILEEN ZEIMET, insurance executive; b. Hot Springs, S.D., Jan. 21, 1953; d. Michael David and Sylvia Marie (Owens) Z.; m. Randy R. Calhoon, Nov. 24, 1973; children: Andrea Marie, Katlyn Grace. AA in Bus., Chadron (Nebr.) State Coll., 1973; student, U. Wyoming, 1988—. Edn. counselor F.E. Warren AFB, U. N. Colo., Cheyenne, Wyo., 1974-75, F.E. Warren AFB, Cheyenne, 1975-76; advt. mgr., adminstrv. asst. Wilson Equipment and Supply, Cheyenne, 1976-83; mgr. personnel lines Wallick & Volk Inc., Cheyenne, 1983-85, mgr. ins., 1985—; bd. dirs. Attention Homes Inc., Cheyenne. Mem. Am. Bus. Women's Assn. (sec. 1983-84, treas. 1986-87), Ind. Ins. Agts. Democrat.

CALKIN, CONSTANCE LEWIS, social work educator; b. Milo, Maine, May 10, 1933; d. Arthur Sherwood Lewis and Verna M. (Stubbs) Wilson; m. William Sommerville Calkin, Aug. 19, 1956; children: John, Ann Sauer, Amy Glenn. BA, U. Maine, 1955; MSW, U. Denver, 1968, PhD, 1982. Child welfare worker Jefferson County Dept. Pub. Welfare, Golden, 1964-66; sch. social worker Denver Pub. Schs., 1968-73; exec. dir. Big Sisters of Colo., Denver, 1973-78; cons. evaluator Big Bros./Big Sisters Am., Phila., 1978-79; dir. field edn. Grad. Sch. Social Work U. Denver, 1981—. Bd. dirs. Big Sisters of Colo., Denver, 1978—; mem. addictive behaviors adv. bd. Mile High Inst. on Alcohol, Denver, 1985—; mem. Colo. Tech. Assistance Ctr., 1988—; mem. adv. bd. Mile High United Way, Denver, 1982—. Recipient Vol. Service grant Mile High United Way, 1981. Mem. Nat. Assn. Social Workers (cert., mem. nat. program com. 1986-88, also past state v.p., and other offices), Council on Social Work Edn., Women's Found., NOW, Sigma Nu Sigma. Democrat. Office: U Denver Grad Sch Social Work 2148 S High St Denver CO 80208

CALKINS, JAMES RICHARD, sales executive; b. Los Angeles, Aug. 25, 1946; s. James William and Ernestine Marie (Abbett) C.; m. Jean Marie Calkins, Aug. 30, 1969; children: Shannan, Adrianne, Ryan. Student, So. Colo. State U., 1968, Northwest Mo. State U., 1964-70, U. Nebr., 1974, Casper Coll., 1988. Area sales mgr. Dearborn Chem., Omaha, 1974-80, Walling Chem., Omaha, 1980-82; sales rep. NL Treating Chems. div. Exxon, Casper, Wyo., 1982-88, Exxon Chem., Casper, 1988—. Served with U.S. Army, 1966-68. Mem. Soc. Mining Engrs., Soc. Petroleum Engrs., Am. Registry Radiologic Technologists. Republican. Roman Catholic. Home: 740 W 51st St Casper WY 82601

CALL, DWIGHT VINCENT, accountant, educator; b. Chgo., Mar. 19, 1934; s. Jerome V. and Ruth E. (Wright) C.; m. Claudia Louise Hand, July 13, 1956; children—Jeanene Lee, Victoria Irene, Doreen Ann, Carrie Leann, Dwayne Vincent, Michelle Antoinette. m. Christine Gail Fox, Dec. 30, 1976. B.S., UCLA, 1957, M.B.A., 1959, Ph.D., 1966. C.P.A., Calif. Prof. acctg. Calif. State U.-Northridge, 1959—; staff acct. Anderson, Gursky & Maccallum, Los Angeles, 1959-62; ptnr. Call & Call, Sherman Oaks Calif., 1962-76; owner Dwight V. Call, C.P.A., Sherman Oaks, 1976-81; ptnr. Call & Trapani, Van Nuys, Calif., 1981-83; pres. Call & Call, Van Nuys, 1983—; instr. UCLA, 1964-69; lectr. in field. Recipient Outstanding Prof. award from acctg. students Calif. State U., 1968. Mem. Nat. Assn. Accts., Calif. Soc. C.P.A.s, Am. Inst. C.P.A.s, Beta Gamma Sigma. Clubs: Lakeside Golf, Desert Island Country, Jonathan Club. Office: Call & Call 5900 Sepulveda Blvd Ste 431 Van Nuys CA 91411

CALL, JOSEPH RUDD, accountant; b. Pensacola, Fla., Oct. 18, 1950; s. Melvin Eliason and Doris Mae (Rudd) C.; m. Nola Jean Pack, Dec. 20, 1973; children—Benjamin, Jeremy, Joshua, Rebecca, Jacob. BS, Brigham Young U., 1974. CPA, Calif., Idaho; cert. fin. planner, 1986. Small bus. specialist Deloitte, Haskins & Sells, Los Angeles, 1974-78; audit mgr. Rudd, DaBell & Hill, Rexburg, Idaho, 1978-80, audit ptnr. Rudd & Co., 1980-82, ptnr. in charge Idaho Falls office, 1982—. Mem. task force Small Bus. High Tech. Devel. State of Idaho, 1983; pres. Bonneville-Idaho Falls Crimestoppers, Inc., 1984-85. Mem. Am. Inst. CPAs (hon. mention on CPA exam 1975), Calif. Soc. CPAs., Idaho Soc. CPAs (pres. S.E. Idaho chpt. 1983-84, state bd. dirs. 1984-88, pres.-elect 1987, pres. 1988-89), Internat. Assn. Fin. Planners Mcpl. Fin. Officers Assn., Healthcare Fin. Mgmt. Assn., Idaho Falls C. of C. (bd. dirs. 1984—, chmn. bd. dirs. 1986-87), Rexburg C. of C. (dir. 1981-82), MENSA, Eastern Idaho Sailing Assn. (rear commodore 1983—). Mormon. Office: Rudd & Co/Chartered 1820 E 17th St Ste 310 Idaho Falls ID 83404

CALLACI, CHARLES ANTHONY, educator; b. N.Y.C., Feb. 24, 1924; s. John B. and Mary A. (Liotta) C.; m. Peggy Jean Hall, Jan. 11, 1979. AB, Emerson Coll., Boston, 1951; MA, San Francisco State U., 1957; DD, U. Kans., 1976. Speech pathologist Sonoma County Schs., Santa Rosa, Calif., 1953-57; asst. prof. broadcasting Oreg. State U., Corvallis, 1957-59; instrl. TV adminstr. Anaheim (Calif.) City Schs., 1959-67; dir. ednl. svcs. Sta. KCET, Lafayette, Calif., 1967-69; v.p. Visual Dynamics Films, Beverly Hills, Calif., 1969-72; assoc. dean-instrn. hdqrs. Calif. State U., L.A., 1972-74; media dir. Calif. State Poly. U., Pomona, Calif., 1974-80, prof. sch. edn., 1980—; liturgy cons. Diocese of San Bernardino, Calif., 1980—; advisor Sta. KNBC. Author: (book) Learning Thru TV, 1975, Cue the Teacher, 1976, Effective Reader. With USAAF 1942-45. Recipient Outstanding Service award Acad. TV Arts and Sics. Mem. Internat. TV Assn. (pres. L.A. chpt. 1975-76), Western Radio and TV Assn. (exec. dir. L.A. chpt. 1967-72). Republican. Roman Catholic. Home and Office: 15750 Country Club Dr Chino Hills CA 91709

CALLAGHAN, G. CAL, yacht club manager; b. Chgo., June 20, 1934; s. George F. Callaghan; m. Corinne Garcia, Sept. 18, 1982. BS in Commerce, Spring Hill Coll., Mobile, Ala., 1956. Vice-pres. GAC Properties, Miami, Fla., 1960-71; sales rep. The Keyes Co., Miami, 1972-76; self-employed real estate and fin. Miami, 1977-81; dockmaster, mgr. yacht club facilities San Diego Yacht Club, 1982—; pres. Marina Cons., San Diego, 1985—; exec. dir. Dockmaster's Group, San Diego, 1988—. 1st lt. U.S. Army, 1957-59. Republican. Roman Catholic. Home: 4464 Castelar Apt 404 San Diego CA 92107 Office: San Diego Yacht Club 1011 Anchorage Ln San Diego CA 92106

CALLAHAN, DAVID L., architect; b. Washington, Jan. 7, 1947. AB, Cornell U., 1969; BArch with high honors, U. Tenn., 1978. Registered architect, N.Mex. Teaching master Peddie Sch., Hightstown, N.J., 1969-70; subs. tchr., homebound instr. Fairfax County (Va.) Secondary Sch. Systems, 1970-72; spl. asst. for laison Chief Counsel's Office IRS, Washington, 1972-73; carpenter various cos., Md., N.Y., Ariz., 1973-75; grad. teaching asst. U. Tenn., Knoxville, 1976-78, instr., 1978; design cons. Hunter-Miller Environ. Planners, Alexandria, Va., 1979; architect-in-residence N.Mex. Solar Energy Inst., Las Cruses, 1979-80; designer George Staten & Assocs., El Paso, Tex., 1980; job capt. Omar Bradley Elem. Sch., El Paso, 1980; intern with various cos., 1980-83; v.p., project architect Rowland Ptnrs., Alburquerque, 1983—; Project architect, Magdalena Elem. Sch., 1983-84, W. Las Vegas Pub. Schs., 1983-84; project mgr., Southwest Border Regional Commns. Solar Upgrading of Low Income Housing, 1979-80; architectl. designer Passive Solar Retrofits for Las Cruces Pub. Housing Auth., 1979-80; lectr. in field. Contbr. articles to profl. jours. Mem. Internat. Solar Energy Soc., AIA, Rio Grande Hist. Collections, Internat. Connoisseurs of Green and Red Chile. Home: 429 Sierra Dr SE Albuquerque NM 87108

CALLAHAN, FRANCIS XAVIER, marketing professional, educator; b. N.Y.C., Dec. 3, 1932; s. Frank and Dorothy (Knoff) C.; m. Deirdre Fiona Miurne de Berg MacDonald, Mar. 29, 1949 (dec. 1984). Cert. Far Eastern Lang., Yale U., 1952; BS, Columbia U., 1957; MA, New Sch. Social Rsch., 1971, PhD, 1971. Internat. trainee W.R. Grace Co., N.Y.C., 1956-58; copywriter Mut. Benefit Co., Newark, 1958-59; dir. advt. N.Y. Life Ins. Co., N.Y.C., 1959-62; nat. advt. mgr. Nationwide Ins. Co., Columbus, Ohio, 1962-63; dir. advt. McGraw Hill Co., N.Y.C., 1963-65; prof. Calif. State U., Chico, 1968—, now prof. emeritus; prof., South Australian Inst. Technology, Adelaide, 1980-82; sr. fellow, Nat. U. Singapore, 1983-85. Contbr. numerous articles to various publs. With USAF, 1951-55, Korea. Home: 12 Lindo Park Dr Chico CA 95926 Office: Calif State U Chico CA 95929-0522

CALLAHAN, MARILYN JOY, social worker; b. Portland, Oreg., Oct. 11, 1934; d. Douglas Quinlin and Anona Helen (Bergemann) Maynard; m. Lynn James Callahan, Feb. 27, 1960 (dec. June 1979); children: Barbara Callahan Baer, Susan Dana and Jeffrey Lynn (twins). BA, Mills Coll., 1955; degree secondary teaching, Portland State U., 1963, MSW, 1971. Cert. secondary tchr., Oreg.; diplomate Am. Bd. Clin. Social Workers, Am. Acad. Cert. Social Workers; registered clin. social worker, Oreg; cert. child welfare counselor. Child welfare counselor Clackamas County Pub. Welfare, Oregon City, Oreg., 1955-58; med. social worker U. Oreg. Med. Sch., Portland, 1958-59; counselor Multnomah County Juvenile Ct., Portland, 1959-62, Marion County Juvenile Ct., Salem, Oreg., 1965-69; devel., adminstrn. 1st ednl. program Oreg. Women's Correctional Ctr., Salem, 1966-67; mental health counselor Benton County Mental Health Clinic, Corvallis, Oreg., 1970-71; tchr. inst. Hillcrest Sch., Salem, 1975-81; social worker Mid Will Valley Sr. Service Agy., Salem, 1981-88; psychiat. social worker dept. forensics Oreg. State Hosp., 1988—; part time pvt. practice in care mgmt. of elderly/disabled; pvt. practice group therapist adult sex offenders; bd. dirs. Vols. for Srs., Tri County Area Conservator-Guardian Program, Statewide Seminar on Age Discrimination, 1985. Mem. exec. bd. South Salem Neighborhood Assn., 1982—, sch. bd. Sacred Heart Acad., 1977-81, Boys and Girls Aid Soc., past dist. v.p.; bd. dirs. Camp Fire Girls, 1971-81; appeared on MacNeil-Lehrer TV News Hour on elderly abuse, 1988, also local TV channels; panel mem. surgeon gen. N.W. Region Conf. Interpersonal Violence, 1987. Mem. Nat. Assn. Social Workers , AAUW (past v.p., past bd. dirs., directed study on family ct. bill 1967), Salem City Club (directed and published research study), U.S. Power Squadron, Catalina 22 Nat. Sailing Assn. Republican. Methodist. Club: Eugene Yacht (Oreg.). Home: 2880 Mountain View Dr S Salem OR 97302 Office: Oreg State Hosp Forensics Dept 2600 Center St Salem OR 97310

CALLEN, LON EDWARD, county official; b. Kingman, Kans., Mar. 31, 1929; s. Cleo Paul and Josephine Nell (Mease) C.; BA in Math. and Physics, U. Wichita (Kans.), 1951; m. Barbara Jean Sallee, Oct. 12, 1954; children: Lon Edward, Lynnette J. Commd. 2d lt. USAF, 1951, advanced through grades to lt. col., 1968; comdr. Tuslog Detachment 93, Erhac, Turkey, 1966-67; sr. scientist Def. Atomic Support Agy., Washington, 1967-71; ret., 1971; dir. emergency preparedness City-County of Boulder, Colo., 1976—; bd. dirs. Boulder County Emergency Med. Services Council, 1977, Boulder County Amateur Radio Emergency Services, 1978—. Mem. hon. awards com. Nat. Capital Area council Boy Scouts Am., 1971; chmn. Boulder County United Fund, 1976-82; mem. asst. staff Indian Princesses and Trailblazer programs Boulder YMCA, 1974-78. Decorated Joint Service Commendation medal; recipient cert. achievement Def. Atomic Support Agy., 1970. Mem. AAAS, Am. Ordnance Soc., Am. Soc. Cybernetics, Planetary Soc., Math. Assn. Am., N.Y. Acad. Scis., Fedn. Am. Scientists, Nat. Assn. Atomic Vets., Union Concerned Scientists, Boulder County Fire Fighters Assn., Colo. Emergency Mgmt. Assn., Ret. Officers Assn., Colo. Front Range Protective Assn., Mensa, Sigma Xi, Pi Alpha Pi. Clubs: Boulder Knife and Fork, Boulder Gunbarrel Optimists, Denver Matrix, U. Colo. Ski, U. Wichita. Author articles in field. Home: 4739 Berkshire Ct Boulder CO 80301 Office: Box 471 County Courthouse Boulder CO 80306

CALLENDER, JONATHAN FERRIS, museum director; b. L.A., Nov. 7, 1944; s. Robert Ford and Ruth Merigold (Ferris) C.; m. Cynthia E. Bennett, Aug. 16, 1967 (div. Apr. 1982); children: Katherine, Elizabeth, Jennifer, Sarah. BS, Calif. Inst. Tech., 1966; AM, Harvard U., 1968, PhD in Geology, 1975. Asst. prof. U. N.Mex., Albuquerque, 1972-77, assoc. prof., 1977-84, asst. chmn. geology dept., 1979-81, adj. prof. geology, 1985—; chief sci. programs N.Mex. Mus. Natural History, Albuquerque, 1983-84, dir., 1984—, also bd. dirs.; adj. prof. geology N.Mex. Inst. Mining and Tech., Socorro, 1985—. Editor numerous books on N.Mex. geology; author numerous tech. papers in field. Active N.Mex. First, 1986—, Hispanic Cultural Found., Albuquerque, 1986—; bd. dirs. N.Mex. Mus. Found., 1984—. Nat. Sci. Found. fellow, 1971-72; recipient Presdl. Recognition award U. N.Mex., 1982. Fellow Geol. Soc. Am.; mem. AAAS (sect. bd. mem. 1988—), Albuquerque Mus. Found., Maxwell Mus. Found., Am. Assns. Mus., Am. Assn. Petroleum Geologists, Assn. Sci. Mus. Dirs., Am. Geophys. Union (editor transl. bd. 1985—), N.Mex. Geol. Soc. (pres. 1977), Rotary. Home: 1202 Las Lomas Rd NE Albuquerque NM 87106 Office: NMex Mus Natural History PO Box 7010 Albuquerque NM 87194

CALLIHAN, C. MICHAEL, lieutenant governor, former state senator, broadcaster; b. Spokane, Wash., Aug. 1, 1947; s. Cal and Dorothy C.; m. Ann L. Duckett, 1973. BA, Western State Coll., 1973. Owner Callihan Broadcasting Group; Gunnison county assessor 1975-78; mem. Colo. Ho. of Reps., 1979-80, Colo. Senate, 1982-86; lt. gov. State of Colo., 1986—; chmn. Colo. Promotinos Assn., Colo. Commn. Indian Affairs, 1987. With USN, Vietnam. Mem. Am. Legion, Lions. Democrat. Office: Office of Lt Gov 130 State Capitol Denver CO 80203

CALLISON, NANCY FOWLER, nurse; b. Milw., July 16, 1931; d. George Fenwick and Irma Esther (Wenzel) Fowler; m. B.G. Callison, Sept. 25, 1954 (dec. Feb. 1964); children: Robert, Leslie, Linda. Diploma, Evanston Hosp. Sch. Nursing, 1952; BS, Northwestern U., 1954. RN, Calif. Staff nurse, psychiat. dept. Downey VA Hosp., 1954-55; staff nurse Camp Lejeune Naval Hosp., 1955, 59-61; obstet. supr. Tri-City Hosp., Oceanside, Calif., 1961-62; pub. health nurse San Diego County, 1962-66; sch. nurse Rich-Mar Union Sch. Dist., San Marcos, Calif., 1966-68; head nurse San Diego County Community Mental Health, 1968-73; dir. patient care services Southwood Mental Health Ctr., Chula Vista, Calif., 1973-75; program cons. Comprehensive Care Corp., Newport Beach, Calif., 1975-79; dir. Manpower Health Care, Culver City, Calif., 1979-80; dir. nursing services Peninsula Rehab. Ctr., Lomita, Calif., 1980-81; clinic supr., coordinator utilization and authorizations, acting dir. provider relations Hawthorne (Calif.) Community Med. Group, 1981-86; mgr. Health Care Delivery Physicians of Greater Long Beach, Calif., 1986-87; cons. Quality Rev. Assocs., 1988—; clinic coordinator, translator Flying Samaritans, 1965—, mem. internat. bd. dirs., 1975-77, 79-86, pres. South Bay chpt., 1975-81, v.p., 1982—, bd. dirs. San Diego chpt., 1987—. Mem. Am. Nurses Assn., Nat. Assn. Female Execs., Aircraft Owners and Pilots Assn., U.S.-Mex. Border Health Assn., Calif. Assn. of Quality Assurance Profls., Cruz Roja Mexicana (Delegacion Rosarito 1986—).

CALLISTER, LOUIS HENRY, JR., lawyer; b. Salt Lake City, Aug. 11, 1935; s. Louis Henry and Isabel (Barton) C.; B.S., U. Utah, 1958, J.D., 1961; m. Ellen Gunnell, Nov. 27, 1957; children—Mark, Isabel, Jane, Edward, David, John Andrew, Ann. Bar: Utah 1961. Asst. atty. gen. Utah, 1961; sr. ptnr. Callister, Duncan & Nebeker, Salt Lake City, 1961—; bd. dirs. Am. Stores Co., Premium Oil Co., Quailbluff Devel. Co. Vice-chmn. Salt Lake City Zoning Bd. Adjustment, 1979-84; bd. govs. Latter Day Saints Hosp., 1983—; treas. exec. com. Utah Rep. Com., 1965-69; chmn. Utah chpt. Rockefeller for Pres. Com., 1964-68; sec., trustee Salt Lake City Police Hon. Cols., 1982—; mem. U. Utah Instl. Coun., 1987—. Mormon. Home: 1454 Tomahawk Dr Salt Lake City UT 84103 Office: Callister Duncan Nebeker 800 Kennecott Bldg Salt Lake City UT 84133

CALLISTER, MARION JONES, federal judge; b. Moreland, Idaho, June 6, 1921; m. Nina Lynn Hayes, June 7, 1946; children—Nona Lynn Callister Haddock, Lana Sue Callister Meredith, Jenny Ann Callister Thomas, Tamara Callister Banks, Idonna Ruth Callister Andersen, Betty Patricia Callister Jacobs, Deborah Jean Hansen, Mary Clarice Fowler, David Marion, Nancy Irene Callister Garvin, Michelle, Kimberly Jane. Student, Utah State U., 1940-41; B.S.L., U. Utah, 1950, J.D., 1951. Bar: Idaho 1951. Dep. pros. atty. Bingham County, Idaho, 1951-52; asst. U.S. atty. Dist. of Idaho, 1953-57, U.S. atty., 1975-76; pvt. practice 1958-69; judge Idaho Dist. Ct. 4th Jud. Dist., 1970-75; judge U.S. Dist. Ct. Idaho, Boise, 1976—, chief judge, 1981-88. Served with U.S. Army, 1944-46. Decorated Purple Heart. Republican. Mormon. Office: US Dist Ct 550 W Fort St PO Box 040 Boise ID 83724

CALLOW, KEITH MCLEAN, judge; b. Seattle, Jan. 11, 1925; s. Russell Stanley and Dollie (McLean) C.; m. Evelyn Case, July 9, 1949; children: Andrea, Douglas, Kerry. Student, Alfred U., 1943, CCNY, 1944, Biarritz Am. U., 1945; BA, U. Wash., 1949, JD, 1952. Bar: Wash. 1952, D.C., U.S. Dist. Ct. (we. dist.) Wash., U.S. Ct. Appeals (9th cir.), U.S. Supreme Ct. Asst. atty. gen. Wash., 1952; law clk. to presiding justice Wash. Supreme Ct., 1953; dep. pros. atty. King County, 1954-56; ptnr. Little, LeSourd, Palmer, Scott & Slemmons, Seattle, 1957-62, Barker, Day, Callow & Taylor, 1964-68; judge King County Superior Ct., 1969-71, Wash. State Ct. of Appeals, Seattle, 1972-84; presiding chief judge Wash. State Ct. of Appeals, 1980; justice Wash. State Supreme Ct., Olympia, 1985-89, chief justice, 1989—; lectr. bus. law U. Wash., 1956-62; faculty Nat. Jud. Coll., 1980; co-organizer, sec. Coun. of Chief Judges, 1980; mem. study com. Fed. Cts., 1989—. Editor works in field. Chief Seattle coun. Boy Scouts Am.; pres. Young Men's Rep. Club, 1957. With AUS, 1943-46. Decorated Purple Heart.; recipient Brandeis award Wash. State Trial Lawyers Assn., 1981. Mem. ABA (chmn. com. on judiciary 1984—), Wash. State Bar Assn., D.C. Bar Assn., Seattle-King County Bar Assn., Estate Planning Coun., Fed. Cts. Study Com., Navy League, Rainier Club (sec. 1978), Coll. Club, Harbor Coll. Club, Forty Nine Club (pres. 1972), Masons, Rotary, Psi Upsilon, Phi Delta Phi. Office: Wash Supreme Ct Temple of Justice Olympia WA 98504-0511

CALLOWAY, DORIS HOWES, nutritional educator; b. Canton, Ohio, Feb. 14, 1923; d. Earl John and Lillian Ann (Roberts) Howes; m. Nathaniel O. Calloway, Feb. 14, 1946 (div. 1956); children: David Karl, Candace; m. Robert O. Nesheim, July 4, 1981. BS, Ohio State U., 1943; PhD, U. Chgo., 1947. Head metabolism lab., nutritionist, chief div. QM Food and Container Inst., Chgo., 1951-61; chmn. dept. food sci. and nutrition Stanford Rsch. Inst., Menlo Park, Calif., 1961-63; prof. U. Calif., Berkeley, 1963—, provost profl. schs. and colls., 1981-87; mem. expert adv. panel nutrition WHO, Geneva, 1972—; trustee Internat. Maize and Wheat Improvement Ctr., 1983-88; trustee, bd. dirs. Winrock Internat. Inst., 1986—; cons. FAO, UN, Rome, 1971,74-75,81-83; adv. coun. NIH, Nat. Inst. Arthritis, Metabolic and Digestive Diseases, Nat. Inst. Aging, Bethesda, Md., 1974-77, 78-82. Author: Nutrition and Health, 1981, Nutrition and Physical Fitness 11th edit., 1984. Recipient Meritorious Civilian Service Dept. Army, 1959; named Disting. Alumna Ohio State U., 1974, Wellcome vis. prof. Fedn. Am. Soc. Exptl. Biol., U. Mo., 1980. Fellow Am. Inst. Nutrition (pres. 1982-83, sec. 1969-72, editorial bd. 1967-72; Conrad A. Elvehjem award 1986); mem. Am. Dietetic Assn. (editorial bd. 1974-77, Cooper Meml. lectr. 1983), Inst. Medicine Nat. Acad. Scis., Sigma Xi. Office: U Calif Morgan Hall Berkeley CA 94720

CALVERT, DEBORAH SUZANNE, interior designer; b. Indpls., Apr. 21, 1956; d. Vern Singleton and Evelyn (Wainscott) C. Student, Orange Coast Coll., 1974-76. Asst. to pub. Stuart Karl/Design Living, Newport Beach, Calif., 1976-77; bus. cons., designer Braselle Design Co., Newport Beach, 1978-80, Jacqueline Olmstead Interiors, Corona del Mar, Calif., 1980-84, William S. Lund, Inc., Corona del Mar, 1984-85, Suzanne Robert Interiors, Corona del Mar, 1985-86, John Cottrell Co., L.A., 1987, Gloria Rothschild Interiors, Corona del Mar, 1987—; bus. cons., owner B-A-B Designs, Corona del Mar, 1979—; asst. to Dr. Buzz Aldrin, Laguna Beach, Calif., 1988—. Founding mem. Ctr. 500, Costa Mesa, 1985. Democrat. Home: 218 Virginia Pl Costa Mesa CA 92627 Office: B-A-B Designs 1111 Bayside Dr Corona Del Mar CA 92625

CALVERT, THOMAS LEE, telecommunications engineer; b. Moline, Ill., July 19, 1957; s. Hampton Cecil and Viola (Andon) C.; m. Lori Marie Bull, Apr. 15, 1978; children: Justin Lee, Jesus Thomas. Elec. drafter Iowa-Ill. Gas & Electric, Davenport, Iowa, 1979; drop forge crewman Moline Forge, Inc., 1979-80; elec. drafter Mainstream Engring., Santa Clara, Calif., 1980-81; elec. designer Lawrence-Livermore (Calif.) Lab., 1981-87, outside plant distbn. engr., 1987--. Served with USN, 1975-79, with USNR, 1979-81, 84. Republican. Methodist. Home: 3553 Leafwood Circle Antioch CA 94509

CALVIN, DOROTHY VER STRATE, computer company executive; b. Grand Rapids, Mich., Dec. 22, 1929; d. Herman and Christina (Plakmyer) Ver Strate; m. Allen D. Calvin, Oct. 5, 1953; children: Jamie, Kris, Bufo, Scott. BS magna cum laude, Mich. State U., 1951; MA, U. San Francisco, 1988. Mgr. data processing. Behavioral Research Labs., Menlo Park, Calif., 1972-75; dir. Mgmt. Info. Systems Inst. for Prof. Devel., San Jose, Calif. 1975-76; systems analyst, programmer Pacific Bell Info. Systems, San Francisco, 1976-81; staff mgr., 1981-84; mgr. applications devel. Data Architects Inc., San Francisco, 1984-86; pres. Ver Strate Press, San Francisco, 1986—. Instr., Downtown Community Coll., San Francisco, 1980-84, Cañada Community Coll., 1986—; mem. computer curriculum adv. council San Francisco City Coll., 1982-84. Vice pres. LWV, Roanoke, Va., 1956-58; pres. Bulliss Purissima Parents Group, Los Altos, Calif., 1962-64; bd. dirs. Vols. for Israel, 1986-87. Mem. NAFE, Assn. Systems Mgmt., Assn. Women in Computing. Democrat. Avocations: computing, gardening, jogging, reading. Office: Ver Strate Press 1645 15th Ave San Francisco CA 94122

CALVIN, DOUGLAS WAYNE, photolithography equipment manufacturing executive; b. San Diego, Calif., Jan. 28, 1942; s. Wayne Calvin and Delores Platz; m. Lena Loriene Lee, Feb. 6, 1965; 1 child, Christina. BSBA, U. Phoenix, 1984; MBA, Golden Gate U., 1988. Plant engr. Northern Telecom, Nashville, 1978-80; mgr. maintenance, plant engring. Lindsay (Nebr.) Mfg. Co., 1980-81; mgr. plant engring. Kaiser Electronics Co., San Jose, 1981-84; dir. cen. services Ultratech Stepper, Santa Clara, Calif., 1984—; mem. steering com. Internat. Semiconductor Mfg. Sci. Symposium. Pres. Glenmoor Meadows Homeowners Assn., San Jose, 1986. Served with USN, 1960-67. Mem. Assn. Plant Engrs., Planning Forum (v.p. planning forum), Risk and Ins. Mgmt. Soc., Am. Soc. Indsl. Security, Telecommunications Assn. Club: Toastmasters (San Jose). Home: 6467 Matthew Ct San Jose CA 95123 Office: Ultratech Stepper Inc 3230 Scott Blvd Santa Clara CA 95054

CALVIN, MELVIN, chemist, educator; b. St. Paul, Apr. 8, 1911; s. Elias and Rose I. (Hervitz) C.; m. Genevieve Jemtegaard, 1942; children: Elin, Karole, Noel. B.S., Mich. Coll. Mining and Tech., 1931, D.Sc., 1955; Ph.D., U. Minn., 1935, D.Sc., 1969; hon research fellow, U. Manchester, Eng., 1935-37; Guggenheim fellow, 1967; D.Sc., Nottingham U., 1958, Oxford (Eng.) U., 1959, Northwestern U., 1961, Wayne State U., 1962, Gustavus Adolphus Coll., 1963, Poly. Inst. Bklyn., 1962, U. Notre Dame, 1965, U. Gent, Belgium, 1970, Whittier Coll., 1971, Clarkson Coll., 1976, U. Paris Val-de-Marne, 1977, Columbia U., 1979, Grand Valley U., 1986. With U. Calif., Berkeley, 1937—; successively instr. chemistry, asst. prof., prof., Univ. prof., dir. Lab. Chem. Biodynamics U. Calif., 1963-80, assoc. dir. Lawrence Berkeley Lab., 1967-80; Peter Reilly lectr. U. Notre Dame, 1949; Harvey lectr. N.Y. Acad. Medicine, 1951; Harrison Howe lectr. Rochester sect. Am. Chem. Soc., 1954; Falk-Plaut lectr. Columbia U., 1954; Edgar Fahs Smith Meml. lectr. U. Pa. and Phila. sect. Am. Chem. Soc., 1955; Donegani Found. lectr. Italian Nat. Acad. Sci., 1955; Max Tishler lectr. Harvard U., 1956; Karl Folkers lectr. U. Wis., 1956; Baker lectr. Cornell U., 1958; London lectr., 1961, Willard lectr., 1982; Vanuxem lectr. Princeton U., 1969; Disting. lectr. Mich. State U., 1977; Prather lectr. Harvard U., 1980; Dreyfus lectr. Grinnell Coll., 1981, Berea Coll., 1982; Barnes lectr. Colo. Coll., 1982; Nobel lectr. U. Md., 1982; Abbott lectr. U. N.D., 1983; Gunning lectr. U. Alta., 1983; O'Leary disting. lectr. Gonzaga U., 1984; Danforth lectr. Dartmouth Coll., 1984, Grinnell Coll., 1984; R.P. Scherer lectr. U. S. Fla., 1984; Imperial Oil lectr. U. Western Ont., Can., 1985; disting. lectr. dept. chemistry U. Calgary, Can., 1986; Melvin Calvin lectr. Mich. Tech. U., 1986; Eastman prof. Oxford (Eng.) U., 1967-68. Author: (with G. E. K. Branch) The Theory of Organic Chemistry, 1940, Isotopic Carbon, (with others), 1949, Chemistry of Metal Chelate Compounds, (with Martell), 1952, Path of Carbon in Photosynthesis, (with Bassham), 1957, (with Bassham) Photosynthesis of Carbon Compounds, 1962, Chemical Evolution, 1969; contbr. articles to chem. and sci. jours. Recipient prize Sugar Research Found., 1950, Flintoff medal prize Brit. Chem. Soc., 1953, Stephen Hales award Am. Soc. Plant Physiologists, 1956, Nobel prize in chemistry, 1961; Davy medal Royal Soc., 1964; Virtanen medal, 1975; Priestley medal, 1978; Am. Inst. Chemists medal, 1979; Feodor Lynen medal, 1983; Sterling B. Hendricks medal, 1983, Melvin Calvin Medal of Distinction Mich. Tech. U., 1985. Mem. Britain's Royal Soc. London (fgn. mem.), Am. Chem. Soc. (Richards medal N.E. sect. 1956, Chem. Soc. Nichols medal N.Y. sect. 1958, award for nuclear applications in chemistry, pres. 1971, Gibbs medal Chgo. sect. 1977, Priestley medal 1978, Oesper award Cin. sect., 1981), Am. Acad. Arts and Scis., Nat. Acad. Scis., Royal Dutch Acad. Scis., Japan Acad., Am. Philos. Soc., Sigma Xi, Tau Beta Pi, Phi Lambda Upsilon. Office: U Calif Dept Chemistry Berkeley CA 94720

CAMERON, DUNCAN FERGUSON, museum director; b. Toronto, Ont., Can., Feb. 1, 1930; s. Charles Gordon and Winnifred Petrie (Peppderdene) C.; m. Nancy Tousley, Apr. 24, 1975. Adminstr. Royal Ont. Museum, Toronto, 1956-62; pres. Janus Ltd., Toronto, 1962-70; nat. dir. Can. Conf. Arts, Toronto, 1968-71; dir. Bklyn. Mus., 1971-73; prin. P.S. Ross & Partners, Toronto, 1975-77; dir. Glenbow-Alta. Inst., Calgary, 1977-88, dir. emeritus, 1988—. Author articles in field; frequent guest lectr. Mem. Internat. Council Museums, Museums Assn., Am. Assn. Museums, Can. Museums Assn., Can. Art Mus. Dirs. Orgn. (pres.), Commonwealth Assn. Museums (pres.), Exec. Coun. Assoc. Mus. Dirs., Am. Assn. Mus., Royal Can. Mil. Inst., Order of St. Lazarus of Jerusalem, Freemason, Royal Scottish Heritage Found. Anglican. Club: Ranchmen's (Calgary). Home: 3438 6th St SW, Calgary, AB Canada T2S 2M4

CAMERON, EUGENE FOSTER, advertising agency executive; b. Sleepy Eye, Minn., May 7, 1945; m. Patricia Woodard, 1964 (div.); children: Sean, Heather. BA in Polit. Sci., Princeton U., 1967; MBA, U. Pa., 1969. Asst. venture mgr. Scott Paper Co., 1969-72; account exec. Ogilvy & Mather, L.A., 1972-77; account supr. Chiat/Day Inc., L.A., 1977-79; v.p., sr. v.p., exec. v.p., pres. BBDO/West, L.A., 1988—. Office: BBDO/West 10960 Wilshire Blvd Los Angeles CA 90024 *

CAMERON, FRANKLIN DANE, magazine editor; b. Los Angeles, Jan. 30, 1947; s. James B. Cameron and Evangeline C. (Booth) Hixson. BA, U. Calif., Berkeley, 1968. Mng. editor Photographic mag., Los Angeles, 1979-83; mng. editor Small Bus. Mag. Bus. Research and Monitoring Co., Monterey, Calif., 1983-84; mng. editor Petersen's Photographic mag., Los Angeles, 1984—; pres. Beauty Mgmt., Los Angeles, 1985—. Contbr. numerous articles to popular mags. Archaelogist York (Eng.) Archeol. Trust, 1973. Mem. Wilderness Soc., World Wildlife Fund. Pantheist. Office: Photographic Mag 8490 Sunset Blvd Los Angeles CA 90069 *

CAMERON, JAMES DUKE, state justice; b. Richmond, Calif., Mar. 25, 1925; s. Charles Lee and Ruth M. (Mabry) C.; m. Suzanne Jane Pratt, Aug. 16, 1952 (div. 1982); children: Alison Valerie, Craig Charles, Jennifer Elaine. A.B., U. Calif. at Berkeley, 1950; J.D., U. Ariz., 1954; LL.M., U. Va., 1982. Bar: Ariz. 1954. Practice in Yuma, 1954-60, 61-65; judge Superior Ct. Yuma County, 1960, Ariz. Ct. Appeals, 1965-70; justice Ariz. Supreme Ct., 1970—, vice chief justice, 1971-75, chief justice, 1975-80; mem. faculty appellate judges seminar Inst. Jud. Adminstrn., 1968-80; bd. dirs. Ariz. State Justice Inst., 1986—. Author: Arizona Appellate Forms and Procedures, 1968, also article. Mem. Ariz. Bd. Pub. Welfare, 1961-64, chmn., 1963-64; Mem. Eagle Scout bd. rev. Theodore Roosevelt council Boy Scouts Am., 1968—; Alternate del. Republican Nat. Conv., 1952; treas. Ariz. Rep. Party, 1958-60; Trustee Yuma City-County Library, 1958-67. Served with AUS, World War II. Mem. ABA (chmn. appellate judges conf. Judicial Adminstrn. div. 1977-78, jud. mem.-at-large 1986-88), Ariz. Bar Assn., Yuma County Bar Assn. (past pres.), Ariz. Acad., Inst. Jud. Adminstrn., Nat. Inst. Justice (adv. com. 1984-86), Conf. Chief Justices U.S. (chmn. 1978-79), Am. Judicature Soc., Am. Law Inst., Lambda Chi Alpha, Phi Alpha Delta, Delta Theta Phi. Clubs: Mason, Shriner, Arizona. Office: Ariz Supreme Ct 1700 W Washington Ste 219 Phoenix AZ 85007

CAMERON, JUDITH LYNNE, educator, hypnotherapist; b. Oakland, Calif., Apr. 29, 1945; d. Alfred Joseph and June Estelle (Faul) Moe; m. Richard Irwin Cameron, Dec. 17, 1967; 1 child, Kevin Dale. AA in Psychol., Sacramento City Coll., 1965; BA in Psychol., German, Calif. State U., 1967; MA in Reading Specialization, San Francisco State U., 1972; postgrad., Chapman Coll.; PhD, Am. Inst. Hypnotherapy, 1987. Cert. tchr., Calif. Tchr. St. Vincent's Catholic Sch., San Jose, Calif., 1969-70, Fremont (Calif.) Elem. Sch., 1970-72, LeRoy Boys Home, LaVerne, Calif., 1972-73; tchr. Grace Miller Elem. Sch., LaVerne, Calif., 1973-80, resource specialist, 1980-84; owner, mgr. Pioneer Take-out Franchises, Alhambra and San Gabriel, Calif., 1979-85; resource specialist, dept. chmn. Bonita High Sch., LaVerne, Calif., 1984—; mentor tchr. in space sci. Bonita Unified Sch. Dist., 1988—; bd. dirs., recommending tchr., asst. dir. Project Turnabout, Claremont, Calif.; Teacher-in-Space cons. Bonita Unified Sch. Dist., LaVerne, 1987—; advisor Peer Counseling Program, Bonita High Sch., 1987—; advisor Air Explorers/Edwards Test Pilot Sch., LaVerne, 1987—; mem. Civil Air Patrol, Squadron 68, Aerospace Office, 1988—. Vol. advisor Children's Home Soc., Santa Ana, 1980-81. Mem. Council Exceptional Children, Calif. Assn. Resource Specialists, Calif. Elem. Edn. Assn., NEA, Calif. Teacher's Assn., Calif. Assn. Marriage and Family Therapists, Planetary Soc., Com. Scientific Investigation L5 Soc., Challenger Ctr. for Space Edn., Calif. Challenger Ctr. Crew for Space Edn. Republican. Clubs: Chinese Shar-Pei Am., Concord, Rare Breed Dog, Los Angeles. Home: 3257 La Travesia Dr Fullerton CA 92635 Office: Bonita High Sch 115 W Allen Ave San Dimas CA 91773

CAMERON, ROY EUGENE, scientist; b. Denver, July 16, 1929; s. Guy Francis and Ilda Annora (Horn) C.; m. Margot Elizabeth Hoagland, May 5, 1956 (div. July 1977); children: Susan Lynn, Catherine Ann; m 2d Carolyn Mary Light, Sept. 22, 1978. B.S., Wash. State U., 1953, 54; M.S., U. Ariz., 1958, Ph.D., 1961; D.D. (hon.), Ministry of Christ Ch., Delavan, Wis., 1975. Research scientist Hughes Aircraft Corp., Tucson, 1955-56; sr. scientist Jet Propulsion Lab., Pasadena, Calif., 1961-68, mem. tech. staff, 1969-74; dir. research Darwin Research Inst., Dana Point, Calif., 1974-75; dep. dir. Land Reclamation Lab. Argonne Ill. Nat. Lab., 1975-77, dir. energy resources tng. and devel., 1977-85; sr. staff scientist Lockheed Engring. and Scis. Co., Las Vegas, Nev., 1986—; cons. Lunar Recieving Lab. Baylor U., 1966-68, Ecology Ctr. Utah State U., Desert Biome, 1970-72, U. Alaska Tundra Biome, 1973-74, U. Maine, 1973-76, numerous others; mem. Nat. Agricul-ture Research and Extension Users Adv. Bd., 1986—. Contrb. articles to sci. books; participated in 7 Antarctic expdns. Served with U.S. Army, 1950-52, Korea, Japan. Recipient 3 NASA awards for tech. briefs, EPA award of Excellence for global climate program, 1988; Paul Steere Burgess fellow U. Ariz., 1959; grantee NSF, 1970-74; Dept. Interior, 1978-80. Mem. AAAS, Soil Sci. Soc. Am., Am. Chem. Soc., Am. Soc. Microbiology, Am. Soc. Agronomy, Antarctican Soc., Polar Soc. Am., Am. Scientist Affiliation, World Future Soc., Internat. Soc. Soil. Sci., Council Agrl. Sci. and Tech., Am. Inst. Biol. Sci., Am. Geophys. Union, Sigma Xi. Mem. Christian Ch.

CAMERON, TODD ELLIOTT, publishing company executive, consulting enologist; b. Des Moines, July 21, 1935; s. Robert William and Mary Janet (Elliott) C.; m. Kaye Marrianne Field (div. Oct. 1969); children: John, Leslie, Stephanie; m. Wendy Margaret Mycroft, Dec. 15, 1986. BS, Iowa State U., 196l. Mktg. researcher Standard Oil Calif., San Francisco, 196l-63; office mgr. Cameron & Co., San Francisco, 1963-66, pres., 1984—, also bd. dirs.; sales mgr. Scott Labs., Richmond, Calif., 1966-74; v.p. ops. Monterey Vineyard, Gonzales, Calif., 1974-79; gen. mgr., cons. Monterey (Calif.) Peninsula Winery, 1979-8l; owner, pres. Cameron Collection, Brisbane, Calif., 198l—; cons. winemaker Creston (Calif.) Manor Winery, 1980—. Co-author: The Drinking Man's Diet, 1965. Vol. Bush Election Campaign, San Francisco, 1988. S/Sgt. USAF, 1954-58. Mem. Am. Soc. Enologists (profl.), No. Calif. Booksellers Assn., San Francisco Conv. and Visitors Bur., Mus. Soc. San Francisco, Commonwealth Club Calif., Olympic Club. Home: 159l 34th Ave San Francisco CA 94122 Office: 543 Howard St San Francisco CA 94105

CAMERON, TRACY ANN, preschool director; b. Mpls., Dec. 24, 1953; d. Donald Shaw and Elsie Andrea (Hougen) C. BS in Child Devel., U. Wis.-Stout, Menomonie, 1976. Dir. Happy Hours Dunham Elem. Tucson (Ariz.) Assn. for Child Care, 1987; dir. Magic Yrs. Learning Ctr. Mish Inc., Tucson, 1987—, area dir., dir. personnel, 1988—. Mem. Nat. Assn. Child Care, Ariz. Child Care Mgmt. Assn. Home: 8550 E Speedway 179 Tucson AZ 85710 Office: Mish Inc 5540 E Hampton Tucson AZ 85712

CAMERON, WILLIAM WRIGHT, cosmetics executive; b. Chgo., Aug. 15, 1941; s. William Mackie and Nancy (Wright) C.; m. Janice Meredith Boardman, Apr. 22, 1966 (div. Nov. 1972); 1 child, Brian Price. Student, U. N.C., 1963; BS in Econs., Columbia U., 1966. Registered investment advisor, cert. fin. analyst. Rep. Winslow, Cohn & Stetson, N.Y.C., 1964-65; asst. dir. research Drysdale & Co., N.Y.C., 1965-66; account exec. Wall St. Cons., N.Y.C., 1966-69; v.p. Caribbean Investment Cons., St. Thomas, V.I., 1969-73; exec. v.p. Haven Investments Ltd., Oakbrook, Ill., 1973-79, pres., 1979-84; pres. Derma-Cure, Inc., Chgo., 1984-87, Portland, Oreg., 1987—. Inventor medicated shampoo. Mem. Portland C. of C. Republican. Club: Internat. (Portland). Lodge: Eagles (Portland). Office: Derma-Cure Inc 1001 SW Fifth Ave Portland OR 97204

CAMMACK, DENNIS ROBERT, real estate development company executive; b. Laramie, Wyo., Apr. 29, 1948; s. LeRoy Robert and Eleanor Marie (Hejde) C.; m. Kathleen Ann Trippel, Feb. 28, 1973; 2 children. BSBA in Mktg., Colo. State U., 197l. Lic. real estate broker, Colo. Auditor Holiday Inns Am., Ft. Collins, Colo., 1966-68; ops. mgr., mdse. mgr., dist. advt. mgr. Montgomery Ward and Co., Denver, 1968-80, Colorado Springs, Colo., 1968-80; retail store mgr. Everitt div. Weyerhaeuser Co., Colorado Springs, Colo., 1980-82; v.p. adminstrn. Nautilus Fitness Ctrs., Colorado Springs, Colo., 1982-83; ptnr., v.p. Transwestern Properties, Inc., Colorado Springs, 1983-86; v.p., gen. mgr. Craddock Devel. Co., Colorado Springs, 1986—; real estate investor, cons., Colorado Springs, 1982-83; pres. Prodec Cons., Colorado Springs, 1982-84. Mem. fin. com. Holy Trinity Parochial Sch. and Ch., 1983—; precinct rep. Colorado Springs Rep. Com., 1986-87; vice chmn. bd. trustees Pikes Peak Community Coll., Colorado Springs, 1986—; mem. Office Sch. and Community Rels., Colo. Sch. Dist. ll, Colorado Springs, 1987—; Colorado Springs Cath. Diocese Sch. Bd., 1989—. Mem. Realtors Comml. Indsl. Soc. (com. mem. 1984—), Colorado Springs C. of C. (com. chmn. econ. devel. coun.). Home: 5327 Constitution Ave Colorado Springs CO 80915 Office: Craddock Devel Co 228 N Cascade St Ste 300 Colorado Springs CO 80903

CAMMALLERI, JOSEPH ANTHONY, university administrator, retired air force officer; b. Bronx, N.Y., Feb. 2, 1935; s. Leo Anthony and Angela Marie (Mirandi) C.; B.S., Manhattan Coll., 1956; M.S., Okla. State U., 1966; postgrad. Golden Gate U., 1974—; children—Anthony R., Aaron L., Thomas K., Jeffrey A. Commd. 2d lt. USAF, 1956, advanced through grades to lt. col., 1973; trainee flight crew, 1956-58; crew mem. B-52, 1958-64; behavioral scientist Aerospace Med. Research Labs., Wright-Patterson AFB, Ohio, 1966-68; EB-66 crew mem. Tahkli AFB, Thailand, 1968-69; faculty mem. dept. life and behavioral scis. USAF Acad. (Colo.), 1969-74, assoc. prof., dir. operational psychology div., 1972-74, B-1 human factors engring. mgr. Air Force Flight Test Center, Edwards AFB, Calif., 1974-76, chief handbook devel., 1976-77; ret., 1977; account exec. Merrill Lynch, Pierce, Fenner & Smith, Sherman Oaks, Calif., 1977-80; acad. program rep. U. Redlands (Calif.), 1980-84, regional dir. admissions assessment, 1984—, mem. faculty Whitehead Ctr., 1979—, assoc. dean faculty, 1986-89; faculty Golden Gate U., 1975-80; account exec. Humanomics Ins., 1989—; spl. agt. Prudential LIfe Ins. Co., 1989—; sec., 7th Ann. Narrow Gauge Conv. Com., Pasadena, Calif., 1986. Decorated D.F.C., Air medal (5), Meritorious Service medal. Mem. Nat. Ry. Hist. Soc., Ry. and Locomotive Hist. Soc., Rocky Mountain R.R. Club, Los Angeles Live Steamers, Nat. Model R.R. Assn., Colo. R.R. Hist. Found. (life), Santa Fe Ry. Hist. Soc., USAF Acad. Athletic Assn. (life), DAV, Psi Chi. Home: 3093 Charlotte St Newbury Park CA 91320 Office: Humanomics Ins Svcs Granada Hills CA 91344

CAMMOCK, EARL E., surgeon; b. Sheridan, Wyo., Jan. 18, 1926; s. Earl and Ruth (Elarth) C.; m. Iris Nordman, June 25, 1960; children: Christopher, Caryn, Craig. BA magna cum laude, U. Minn., 1950, BS, 1952, MD, 1953; MS in Surgery, U. Wash., 1962. Diplomate Am. Bd. Surgery. Intern King County Hosp. System, Seattle, 1953-54; resident gen. practice Sacramento (Calif.) County Hosp., 1954-55; resident in surgery U. Wash., 1955-62; chief resident surgery King County Hosp., Seattle, 1959, U. Wash. Hosp. and VA Hosp., 1960; rsch. fellow U. Wash., 1960-62; instr. U. Wash. Dept. Surgery, Seattle, 1960-62, clin. instr., 1962-85, clin. asst. prof., 1985—; practice medicine specializing in gen. surgery Mt. Vernon, Wash., 1962; chief staff Skagit Valley Hosp., 1972; mem. exec. com. Skagit Valley Hosp., 1970-72, chief dept. surgery, 1969, mem. library com., 1988; med. advisor NW Ostomy Soc.; mem. endowment fund com. U. Wash. Co-author: Medicine for Mountaineering (3 edits.), 1967, 75, 85; contbr. articles to profl. jours. Bd. dirs. Lutherwood, Bellingham, Wash., 1974-76, v.p., 1976; council mem. Salem Luth. Ch., 1971-73, pres. 1973; troopmaster Cub Scout Boy Scouts Am., Mt. Vernon, 1977-78; mem. Physicians for Social Responsibility, 1982-86. With U.S. Army, 1944-47, PTO; USAR, 1947-50. Fellow ACS; mem. AMA, Am. Soc. Colon and Rectal Surgeons, Northwest Soc. Colon and Rectal Surgeons, Wash. State Med. Assn., Henry Harkins Surg. Soc. (pres. 1983-84), Pan Pacific Surg. Assn., N.W. Ostomy Soc., Sigma Xi, Phi Beta Kappa. Lodge: Rotary, Vasa. Home: 1226 Madison Park Dr Mount Vernon WA 98273 Office: 215 S 13th Mount Vernon WA 98273

CAMP, ROBERT GOUNOD, SR., real estate exchanger; b. Northumberland County, Pa., Jan. 22, 1915; s. Romeo Bianco and Laura Myrtle (Hoy) Campiglio; 4 children. AB, U. Md., 1937. Appraiser Prescott, Ariz., 1946—; chief exec. officer, real estate developer Bob Camp Agy., Inc., Prescott, 1970—; chief exec. officer, real estate appraiser, counsellor, exchanger developer Ariz. Growth Unltd. Assn., Inc., Prescott, 1972—; conservator ZAZ Corps., Prescott, 1980—. Dem. Precinct committeman Yavapai County, 1952-87. Served with USAAF, 1942-46. Mem. Ind. Profl. Agts. (state pres. 1961-63, nat. bd. dirs. 1969-70), Am. Legion (comdr. 1953-54), Delta Sigma Phi (Alpha Sigma chpt.), Beta Sigma Phi, Lions Club of Prescott (charter mem.), Elks (life). Democrat. Lodge: Elks. Home and Office: Rt 3 Camp Bountiful Prescott AZ 86301

CAMPBELL, ALLAN MCCULLOCH, bacteriology educator; b. Berkeley, Calif., Apr. 27, 1929; s. Lindsay and Virginia Margaret (Henning) C.; m. Alice Del Campillo, Sept. 5, 1958; children—Wendy, Joseph. B.S. in Chemistry, U. Calif. at Berkeley, 1950; M.S. in Bacteriology, U. Ill., 1951; Ph.D., 1953; Ph.D. hon. degree, U. Chgo., 1978, U. Rochester, 1981. Instr. bacteriology U. Mich., 1953-57; research asso. Carnegie Inst., Cold Spring

Harbor, N.Y., 1957-58; asst. prof. biology U. Rochester, N.Y., 1958-61; assoc. prof. U. Rochester, 1961-63, prof., 1963-68; prof. biol. sci. Stanford, 1968—; mem. genetics study sect. NIH, 1964-69, mem. DNA recombinant adv. com., 1977-81; mem. genetics panel NSF, 1973-76. Author: Episomes, 1969; co-author: General Virology, 1978; Editor: Gene, 1980—; assoc. editor: Virology, 1963-69, Ann. Rev. Genetics, 1969-84, editor, 1984—; editorial bd.: Jour. Bacteriology, 1966-72, Jour. Virology, 1967-75. Served with AUS, 1953-55. Recipient Research Career award USPHS, 1962-68. Mem. Nat. Acad. Scis., Am. Acad. Arts and Scis., Am. Soc. Microbiology, Soc. Am. Naturalists, Genetics Soc. Am., AAAS. Democrat. Home: 947 Mears Ct Stanford CA 94305 Office: Stanford U Dept Biol Scis Stanford CA 94305

CAMPBELL, BEN NIGHTHORSE, congressman; b. Auburn, Calif., Apr. 13, 1933; m. Linda Price; children: Colin, Shanan. BA, U. Calif., San Jose. Educator Sacramento Law Enforcement Agy.; mem. Colo. Gen. Assembly, 1983-86, U.S. Ho. Reps., 1987—; owner, trainer horse ranch, Ignacio, Colo.; jewelry designer, Ignacio. Chief No. Cheyenne Tribe. Named Outstanding Legislator Colo. Bankers Assn., 1984, Man of Yr. LaPlata Farm Bur., Durango, Colo., 1984; named one of Ten Best Legislators Denver Post/Channel 4, 1986. Mem. Am. Quarter Horse Assn., Am. Brangus Assn., Am. Paint Horse Assn., Am. Indian Edn. Assn., Colo. Pilots Assn. Democrat. Office: US Ho of Reps 1724 Longworth House Office Bldg Washington DC 20515

CAMPBELL, BILLY WILMON, librarian; b. Los Angeles, Sept. 14, 1927; s. Joe Carson and Claire Ellen (Wilmon) C.; m. Patricia Jean Cowan, Apr. 20, 1951 (div. 1971); children: Frederick William, Bruce Duane, Aisha Ellen, Cameron Clay; m. Judith Weinberg Stang, Feb. 14, 1973. AA, UCLA, 1950, BA, 1952; BLS, U. Calif., Berkeley, 1954. Periodicals and films librarian Library of Hawaii, Honolulu, 1954-56; asst. acquistions librarian Los Angeles State Coll., 1956-57; serials librarian San Fernando Valley State Coll., Northridge, Calif., 1957-63; from cataloguer to head tech. documents ctr. Hughes Aircraft Co., El Segundo, Calif., 1963-85, mgr. info. services dept., electro-optical and data systems group, 1985—. Contbr. articles to profl. jours. Served as pvt. USAAF, 1945-46. Mem. Spl. Libraries Assn., Los Angeles Regional Tech. Info. Users Council, Alpha Mu Gamma. Democrat. Presbyterian. Office: Hughes Aircraft Co-Electro Optical/Data PO Box 902 Systems Group MS E1/E109 El Segundo CA 90245

CAMPBELL, CHERIE LYNN, real estate development executive; b. Buffalo, July 15, 1950; d. Arthur Jerome and Margaret Ann (Wharton) C.; children: Ross Arthur, Wyatt Joseph. BA, Mills Coll., 1972; postgrad., U. Ariz., 1972-73. Asst. head planning dept. Jerry Jones & Assocs., Tucson, 1978-80; dir. planning and bus. devel. Johnson-Brittain & Assoc., Tucson, 1980-83; v.p. planning and devel., cons. Schomac Corp., Tucson, 1983—; cons. Nat. Self Storage, Tucson, 1987—. Mem. So. Ariz. Homebuilders Assn., Am. Planning Assn. Office: Schomac Corp 1790 E River #300 Tucson AZ 85718

CAMPBELL, COLIN HERALD, mayor; b. Winnipeg, Man., Can., Jan. 18, 1911; s. Colin Charles and Aimee Florence (Herald) C.; B.A., Reed Coll., 1933; m. Virginia Paris, July 20, 1935; children—Susanna Herald, Corinna Buford, Virginia Wallace. Exec. sec. City Club of Portland, 1934-39; alumni sec., dir. endowment adminstrn. Reed Coll., 1939-42, exec. sec. N.W. Inst. Internat. Rels. 1940-42, instr. photography, 1941-42; contract engr. Kaiser Co., Inc., 1942-45; asst. pers. dir. Portland Gas & Coke Co., 1945-48; dir. indsl. rels. Pacific Power & Light Co., Portland, 1948-76. Mem. Oreg. Adv. Com. on Fair Employment Practices Act, 1949-55; trustee, chmn., pres. Portland Symphonic Choir, 1950-54; trustee Portland Civic Theater, 1951-54; bd. dirs. Portland Symphony Soc., 1957-60, Community Child Guidance Clinic, 1966-68; active United Way, 1945-75; bd. dirs. Contemporary Crafts Assn., 1972-76, treas., 1975-76; bd. dirs. Lake Oswego Corp., 1961-65, 71-73, 74-76, corp. sec., 1964, pres., 1973-74, treas., 1975-76; mem. com. on Citizen Involvement, City of Lake Oswego, 1975-77; chmn. Bicentennial Com., Lake Oswego; sec.-treas. Met. Area Communications Commn., 1980-85; treas. Clackamas County Community Action Agy., 1980-82, chmn., 1982-85; mem. fin. adv. com. W. Clackamas County LWV, 1974-76, 78-80; councilman City of Lake Oswego, 1977-78, mayor, 1979-85; chmn. energy adv. com. League Oreg. Cities, 1982-84; mem. adv. bd., chmn. fin. com. Lake Oswego Adult Community Ctr. 1985-88. Mem. Edison Electric Inst. (exec. com.), NW Electric Light and Power Assn., Lake Oswego C. of C. (v.p. 1986-87), Portland Art Assn., Pacific N.W. Pers. Mgmt. Assn. (past regional v.p.), St. Andrews Soc., Oreg. Hist. Soc., Boone's Ferry Club (bd. dirs. 1989), Rotary. Republican. Presbyterian. Home: 1219 Maple St Lake Oswego OR 97034

CAMPBELL, CRAIG EATON, aviation consulting company executive; b. Springfield, Mass., Mar. 24, 1952; s. Gilbert M. and Patricia A. (Chapin) C.; m. Anne Marie Brown, Aug. 11, 1972; children: Melanie K., Amanda M. BS, U. Tulsa, 1974; M Pub. Adminstrn., Golden Gate U., 1981; postgrad., Air U., Maxwell AFB, 1979. Comd. 2nd lt. USAF, 1975, advanced through grades to maj.; air traffic controll officer USAF, Travis AFB, Calif., 1975-76; chief radar ops. USAF, K.J. Sawyer AFB, Mich., 1976-79; chief air traffic control USAF, Vandenberg AFB, Calif., 1979-81; dir. air traffic services USAF, Elmendorf AFB, Alaska, 1981-84; noise abatement specialist Sky Harbor Airport, Phoenix, 1984-85; chief air traffic control Calif. Air Nat Guard, Hayward, 1984--; mng. assoc. Coffman Assocs., Anchorage, 1985--; mem. policy com. Anchorage Met. Transp. Study, 1987, 88; mem. pub. selection com. Dept. Natural Resources, State of Alaska, Anchorage, 1988; mem. coastal policy council State of Alaska, Juneau, 1988; bd. dirs. Anchorage Econ. and Devel. Corp. Contbr. articles to newspapers. Assemblyman, Municipality of Anchorage, 1986--; precint chmn. Rep. Party of Alaska, Eagle River, 1984--; chmn. Eagle River Valley Community council, 1986. Mem. Eagle River C. of C. (chmn. mil. affairs com. 1985), Alaska Mcpl. League, Nat. Guard Assn. Am. Republican. Home: 18324 N Parkview Terr Loop Eagle River AK 99577 Office: Coffman Assocs 733 W 4th Ave Anchorage AK 99501

CAMPBELL, DAVID RALPH, medical systems executive, aerospace engineer; b. Cin., Aug. 20, 1945; s. Ralph William And Sophia (Gordon) C.; m. Linda Maureen Stuewe, Dec. 17, 1966; children: Alan, Kevin. BS in Aeronautical Engring., U. Notre Dame, 1967, MS in Aeronautical Engring., 1969, PhD, 1971; M. Adminstrn. in Bus., U. Calif., Riverside, 1977. Rsch. engr. Aerospace Rsch. Labs., Dayton, Ohio, 1971-73; staff scientist Sci. Applications, Inc., LaJolla, Calif., 1973-74; cons. engr. Pacific Sunland Assocs., Corona, Calif., 1974-77; regional mgr. Pall Biomed. Products, Glen Cove, N.Y., 1977-78; sales assoc. Med. Mktg., Inc., Denver, 1978-80; pres., chief exec. officer Vital/Med Systems Corp., Castle Rock, Colo., 1980—; bd. dirs. Vital/Med Systems Corp., Castle Rock. Capt. USAF, 1967-73. Undergrad. hon. scholar U. Notre Dame, 1963, U. Notre Dame scholar, 1969. Republican. Roman Catholic. Office: Vital Med Systems Corp PO Box 1177 Castle Rock CO 80104

CAMPBELL, DEMARAIS LINDSAY, scenic artist, designer; b. N.Y.C.; d. Peter Stephen II and Mary Elizabeth (Edwards) C.; m. Dale Gordon Haugo. MFA in Scenic Design. Resident scenic artist, sculptor Am. Conservatory Theatre, San Francisco, 1976—; scenic artist LucasFilm Ltd., San Rafael, Calif., 1985-88, various nat. and internat. opera cos., regional theatres and films, 1983—; art dir., designer murals and residential interiors Campbell & Haugo, 1975—. Mem. NOW, Asian Art Mus. Soc., San Francisco. Mem. United Scenic Artists, Scenic & Title Artists and Theatrical Stage Designers., Sherlock Holmes Soc. London. Office: Campbell & Haugo 3751 23d St San Francisco CA 94114-3416

CAMPBELL, DIANE MARILYN, political worker; b. Albany, Calif., Mar. 31, 1941; d. James Lester and Mary Francis (Carey) Roark; m. Robert J. Campbell, Nov. 21, 1961; children: Lisa Renea, Kirk Robert. Bank teller, svc. agt. Wells Fargo, 1961-63; mgr. ins. claims and mktg. M.A. Hayes Ins. Co., 1968-81; campaign coordinator various non-profit orgns., 1981-85; lobbyist City of San Pablo, 1985-86, City of Hercules, 1987-88. Fundraiser Juvenile Hall, Sr. Citizen Programs and Pub. Schs., 1966-77; acting chief protocol, City of Richmond, 1973-78; designer, organizer several Community Awareness Programs, 1976-78; rep. Assemblyman Bob Campbell, 1979—; active numerous other activities. Mem. NAFE, Calif. Fedn. Womens Club (officer, bd. dirs.), Bay Valley Dist. Bus. and Profl. Women, Creative Women Contra Costa, Mt. Diablo Dist. Jr. Womens Club, Richmond C. of C., Rodeo C. of C., Art Ctr. Guild, Greater Richmond Devel. Assn., numerous others. Home: 3400 Clearfield Richmond CA 94803

CAMPBELL, FREDERICK HOLLISTER, lawyer, historian; b. Somerville, Mass., June 14, 1923; s. George Murray and Irene Ivers (Smith) C.; A.B., Dartmouth, 1944; J.D., Northwestern U., 1949; postgrad. Indsl. Coll. Armed Forces, 1961-62; M.A. in History, U. Colo., 1984; m. Amy Holding Strohm, Apr. 14, 1951; 1 dau., Susan Hollister. Served with USMCR, 1944-46; joined USMC, 1950, advanced through grades to lt. col., 1962; admitted to Ill. bar, 1950, U.S. Supreme Ct. bar, 1967, Colo. bar, 1968; judge adv. USMC, Camp Lejeune, N.C., Korea, Parris Island, S.C., El Toro, Calif., Vietnam, Washington, 1950-67; asso. editor Callaghan and Co., Chgo., 1949-50; practice law, Colorado Springs, Colo., 1968—, partner firm Gibson, Gerdes and Campbell, 1969-79, Frederick H. Campbell, P.C., 1980—; hon. instr. history U. Colo., Colorado Springs, 1986—. Mem. Estate Planning Council, Colorado Springs, 1971-81, v.p., 1977-78. Republican precinct committeeman, 1971-86; del. Colo. Rep. State Conv., 1972, 74, 76, 80, alt., 1978; trustee Frontier Village Found., 1971-77; bd. dirs. Rocky Mountain Nature Assn., 1975—, pres., 1979—. Mem. Colo. Bar Assn., El Paso County Bar Assn., Am. Arbitration Assn., Marines Meml. Club, Phi Alpha Theta. Congregationalist. Club: Kiwanis (lt. gov. Rocky Mountain Dist. 1973-74, pres. Rampart Range Club 1970-71), Author: John's American Notary and Commissioner of Deeds Manual, 1950. Contbr. articles to profl. jours. Home and Office: 2707 Holiday Ln Colorado Springs CO 80909

CAMPBELL, GARY MARTIN, publisher; b. Alhambra, Calif., Nov. 17, 1932; s. Martin James and Corean Ida (Roe) C.; m. Collene Thompson, Sept. 10, 1951; 1 child, Shelly Fischermann. BA in Mktg., Woodbury U., L.A., 1956. Sr. salesman L.A. Times, 1956-61; owner Gary Campbell Advt. Co., L.A., 1961-66; v.p., acct. supr. Recht & Co., Advt., Beverly Hills, Calif., 1966-67, Speer & Mays Advt., L.A., 1967-68; advt. dir. Herbert Pub. Co., Gardena, Calif., 1968-69; asst. pub. Argus Pubs., L.A., 1969-71; sr. assoc. N.W. Gibson & Assocs., L.A., 1971-72; regional mgr. Bryan Publs., Newport Beach, Calif., 1972-78; pres. Housing Publs., Irvine, Calif., 1978—; bd. dirs. Pixel 8 Corp., Santa Ana, Calif., Mickey Thompson Entertainment Group. State co-chmn Crime Victims for Ct. Reform Calif., 1986; bd. dirs. Constrn. Industries Alliance, City of Hope, Orange County, Calif., 1979—. With USN, 1952-54, Korea. Mem. Inst. Residential Mktg., Bldg. Industry Sales and Mktg. Coun. (pres. San Diego chpt. 1977, so. Calif. chpt. 1982, Max Tipton award 1986). Republican. Office: Housing Publs 15 Studebaker Irvine CA 92718

CAMPBELL, GLORIA DAWN, consultant, educator; b. Seattle, July 13, 1929; d. Delbert Louis and Aleita Helen (Blethen) Knoph; m. Lawrence Toal Campbell, Nov. 13, 1948; children: Claudia Campbell Guilford, Hollis, Paul. BA, U. Wash., 1975, MAT, 1977. Tchr., cons. Campbell & Assocs., Kirkland, Wash., 1976—; cons. office of personnel mgmt. City of San Francisco, 1978—; lectr. U. Wash., Seattle, 1977—, Univs. Ctr., Richland, Wash., 1978—; exec. dir. Forum East, Kirkland, 1981-85; bd. dirs. Bellevue Community Coll. Found., mem. exec. bd., 1987-88. Contbr. articles to profl. publs. Mem. exec. bd. 1st Ch. Christ Scientist, Kirkland, 1987--. Mem. Bellevue Mcpl. League, Bellevue C. of C. (co-chmn. 1987-88; Recognition award 1987), Kirkland C. of C. (life), Phi Beta Kappa. Republican.

CAMPBELL, GORDON MUIR, mayor; b. Vancouver, B.C., Can., Jan. 12, 1948; s. Charles Gordon and Margaret Janet (Muir) C.; m. Nancy J. Chipperfield, July 4, 1970; children: Geoffrey Gordon, Nicholas James. AB, Dartmouth Coll., 1970; MBA, Simon Fraser U., 1978. Tchr. Can. Univ. Service Overseas, Yola, Nigeria, 1970-72; exec. asst. to mayor City of Vancouver, 1972-76, alderman, 1984-86, mayor, 1986—; project mgr. Marathon Realty Devel. Co., Vancouver, 1976-81; pres. Citycore Devel. Corp., Vancouver, 1981-86. Recipient Outstanding Alumni award Simon Fraser U., 1987. Office: City of Vancouver, 453 W 12th Ave, Vancouver, BC Canada V5Y 1V4

CAMPBELL, HARRY WOODSON, geologist, mining engineer; b. Carthage, Mo., Jan. 14, 1946; s. William Hampton and Elizabeth Verle (Legrand) C. BSEE, Kans. State U., 1969; MBA, U. Oreg., 1973, BS in Geology, 1975; MS in Geology, Brown U., 1978. Registered profl. engr., Wash.; cert. profl. geologist, Va. Geologist, mining engr. and phys. scientist U.S. Br. Mines, Spokane, 1980—. Served with U.S. Army, 1969-71. Recipient Spl. Achievement award U.S. Bur. Mines, 1983, 86, 88. Mem. Geol. Soc. Am., Soc. Mining Engrs. Office: US Bur Mines E 360 3d Ave Spokane WA 99202

CAMPBELL, HENRY LECLERC, interior designer; b. Santa Barbara, Calif., Nov. 1, 1921; s. Donald Ernest and Elisabeth (LeClerc) C. Apprentice, Miss Capitola Mills, 1936-39. Designer W.& J. Sloanes, San Francisco, 1959-1961, John Breuner Co., San Francisco, 1961-63; free-lance designer Daly City, Calif., 1963—; tchr. interior design Lincoln (Nebr.) Coll. Works exhibited in House and Garden mag. and local newspapers. Staff sgt. U.S. Army, 1942-46. Mem. Am. Soc. Interior Designers (bd. dirs., chmn. membership, hist. preservation). Home and Office: 23 Cliffside Dr Daly City CA 94015

CAMPBELL, IAN DAVID, opera company director; b. Brisbane, Australia, Dec. 21, 1945; came to U.S., 1982; m. Ann Spira; children: Benjamin, David. BA, U. Sydney, Australia, 1966. Prin. tenor singer The Australian Opera, Sydney, 1967-74; sr. music officer The Australia Council, Sydney, 1974-76; gen. mgr. The State Opera of South Australia, Adelaide, 1976-82; asst. artistic adminstr. Met. Opera, N.Y.C., 1982-83; gen. dir. San Diego Opera, 1983—; guest lectr. U. Adelaide, 1978; guest prof. San Diego State U., 1986—; cons. Lyric Opera Queensland, Australia, 1980-81; bd. dirs. Opera Am., Washington, 1986—. Recipient Peri award Opera Guild So. Calif., 1984. Mem. Australian Inst. Mgmt. (assoc.). Club: University (San Diego). Lodge: Rotary. Office: San Diego Opera PO Box 988 San Diego CA 92112-0988

CAMPBELL, JERRY LYNN, small business owner; b. Wichita, Kans., Jan. 5, 1952; s. Hugh T. and Roberta M. Campbell. Grad. high sch., El Paso, Tex. Co-owner S.E.T.L.A.B. Electronics, El Paso, 1965-78; asst. mgr. Radio Shack, El Paso, 1968-70, Dollar Systems Rent-a-Car, 1973-74; mgr. Northeast Toyota, El Paso, 1977-78; owner, operator Setlab Industries, Albuquerque, 1982--; technician Great Southwest Labs., Albuquerque, 1986--. With U.S. Army, 1970-71, Viet Nam. Home and Office: Setlab Industries 1824 Elizabeth NE Albuquerque NM 87112

CAMPBELL, JOHN DUNCAN, librarian; b. Phila., Jan. 5, 1946; s. Robert Olwell and Hazel (Maybee) C.; m. Victoria Lynn Coffey, Jan. 1977 (div. Jan. 1980). BA, U. Ariz., 1973, MLS, 1974. Libr. at large Occidental Coll. Libr., L.A., 1974-77; head circulation-extension dept. Gt. Falls (Mont.) Pub. Libr., 1977-80; dir. Pathfinder Libr. System, Montrose, Colo., 1980—. With U.S. Army, 1966-69. Mem. ALA, Colo. Libr. Assn. (pres. 1983-84, Colo. Libr. of Yr. 1987), Colo. Ednl. Media Assn., Mountain Plains Libr. Assn. Congregationalist. Office: Pathfinder Libr System 432 S 1st St PO Box 670 Montrose CO 81402

CAMPBELL, JUDITH LYNN, molecular biology educator; b. New Haven, Mar. 24, 1943; d. John Campbell. B.A., Wellesley Coll., 1965; Ph.D., Harvard U., 1974; postgrad. Harvard Med. Sch., 1969-74. Postdoctoral fellow Harvard Med. Sch., 1974-77; asst. prof. dept. chemistry Calif. Inst. Tech., Pasadena, Calif., 1977-83, assoc. prof., 1983-89, prof., 1989—, assoc. prof. biology div., 1984-89, prof., 1989—. Recipient Research Career Devel. award NIH, 1979-84; Bavarian State scholar U. Munich, 1966-67, Wellesley Coll. Pendleton scholar, 1965. Mem. Am. Soc. Biol. Chemists. Home: 625 Sierra Meadow Dr Sierra Madre CA 91024 Office: Calif Inst Tech Dept Biology and Chemistry 147-75 Pasadena CA 91125 *

CAMPBELL, MARY KATHLEEN, mortgage banker; b. Torrance, Calif., Aug. 5, 1944; d. David F. and Katherine I. (Norton) Shields; m. John Alan Campbell, Aug. 19, 1963; children—Lisa Marie Campbell Mitchell, John Andrew. B.B.A. in Acctg., Nat. U., San Diego, 1984. Head cashier Navy Exchange, San Diego, 1968-69; customer relations mgr. J.M. Fields, Norfolk, Va., 1970-72; acct. Hart Enterprises, San Diego, 1973-76; asst. treas. Midwest Pacific Fin., Inc., San Diego, 1976-80, treas., 1980-84, v.p., treas., 1984—; asst. sec. Midwest Fed. Savs. of Eastern Iowa, Burlington, 1978—, asst. v.p., 1985—; treas., dir. Burlington Fin., San Diego, 1984—. Vol. worker Girl Scouts U.S.A., San Diego, 1970-77, Boy Scouts Am., San Diego, 1972-79, Am. Cancer Soc., San Diego, 1978-82; student-family liaison Am. Field Service, Poway, Calif., 1983—. Mem. Fin. Mgrs. Soc., Assn. for Profl. Mortgage Women, Am. Bus. Women's Assn. (treas. 1980-81, Woman of Yr. Poway 1982). Office: Midwest Pacific Fin Inc 5405 Morehouse Dr San Diego CA 92121

CAMPBELL, MAYNARD THOMAS, English language educator; b. Atlanta, Ohio, Mar. 23, 1917; s. James Wiley and Florence (Thomas) C.; cert. Capital U., 1937; B.S., Ohio State U., 1942; M. Ed., U. Ariz. at Tucson, 1952, Ed.D., 1967; m. Shirley I. Hare, July 14, 1960; stepchildren—Michael R. Hare, Kathleen D. Rogers, Kevin S. Hare. Tchr., Salt Creek Twp. Schs., Pickaway County, Ohio, 1937-40; tchr.-prin. Venice (Ohio) Elem. Sch., 1942-44, Sasebo (Japan) Dependents Sch., 1954-55, Upper Secondary Comml. Japanese High Sch., Sasebo, 1954-55; tchr., counselor Tucson Pub. Schs., 1944-81; tutor in English for speakers of other langs., 1981—. Mem. NEA (life), Am. Assn. for Counseling and Devel., Ariz. Counselors Assn., George Washington Masonic Nat. Meml. Assn. (life), Ariz. State Geneal. Soc. (life), Pickaway County (Ohio) Hist. Soc., Internat. Platform Assn., Phi Delta Kappa (life, pres. chpt. 1965-66). Unitarian Universalist. Club: Masons. Author: Campbell, Evans, Hosler and Thomas Family Trees of Ohio, 1973. Home: 1310 Avenida Sirio Tucson AZ 85710

CAMPBELL, MICHAEL HARVEY, air cargo executive; b. Pasadena, Calif., Mar. 11, 1945; s. Harvey C. Flanders and Emma Elaine (Nielson) C.; m. Oct. 19, 1967 (div. Sept. 1969); 1 child, Michael John; m. Barbara Rose Adams, July 1, 1988. BA, U. San Francisco, 1975; MBA, Golden Gate U., 1983. Sales mgr. U.S. Lines, San Francisco, 1975-80; dist. mgr. Japan Lines USA Ltd., San Francisco, 1981-82; facilitations mgr. Flying Tiger Lines, Los Angeles, 1984—; atty. Self Dang Wah, Oakland, Calif., 1988—; dir. Nat. Council on Trade Facilitations, N.Y.C., 1988—. Served as lt. col. USAR, 1966—. Republican. Mormon. Home: 601 Beaumont Blvd Pacifica CA 94044 Office: Flying Tiger Lines Inc 7401 World Way W Los Angeles CA 90015

CAMPBELL, MURRAY BRUCE, quality engineer; b. Ashtabula, Ohio, Feb. 13, 1928; s. Clarence Raymond and Louise Clariss (McNutt) C.; m. Eloise June Harbaugh, Mar. 15, 1957; children: Joslyn, Steve, Marge. BS in Indsl. Tech., Kent State U., 1989. Registered profl. engr., Calif. Quality assurance rep. USN and Def. Supply Agy., Chgo. and Cleve., 1963-69; quality assurance engr. Pub. Svs. Electric and Gas Co., Newark, 1969-71; quality assurance mgr. Walsh Constrn. Co., N.Y.C., 1971-73; quality assurance program mgr. Gilbert Assocs., Inc., Reading, Pa., 1973-75; corp. quality assurance engr. Ralph M. Parsons Co., Pasadena, Calif., 1975-79; quality engr. Bechtel Power Co., Midland, Mich., 1979-80, TRW Ballistic Missiles Div., San Bernardino, Calif., 1980—. Coach, Little League Altadena, Pasadena, 1976, pres., 1977. Sgt. USAAF, 1946-47, Panama. Mem. Am. Soc. Quality Control (sr. mem.), Am. Welding Soc., Am. Soc. Nondestructive Testing, Elks. Democrat. Home: 2931 Oleta Ln Highland CA 92346

CAMPBELL, ROBERT W., transportation executive; b. Valentine, Nebr., Oct. 22, 1922; s. Harry Lee and Margaret (Haley) C. Grad., Creighton U., 1948, grad. in law, 1950. Chmn. Can. Pacific Enterprises, Calgary, Alta., Can. Pacific Ltd., Calgary, 1986—; bd. dirs. AMCA Internat. Ltd., Can. Pacific Ltd., Can. Pacific Enterprises Ltd., Can. Pacific Forest Products Ltd., Can. Pacific Hotels Corp., Can. Pacific Securities Ltd., Royal Bank Can., Pan Can. Petroleum Ltd., Westinghouse Electric Corp. Served to capt. U.S. Army, World War II. Roman Catholic. Office: Can Pacific Ltd, PO Box 6042 Sta A, Montreal, PQ Canada H3C 3E4

CAMPBELL, ROBIN TODD, county official; b. Johnstown, Pa., Feb. 17, 1939; s. Lynn D. and Phyllis Kay (Horner) C.; m. Lois Maryan Woods; children: Timothy James, Daniel Lynn, Bethany Dale. BA, U. Md., 1967; MA, Cen. Mich. U., 1974. Enlisted U.S. Air Force, 1959, commd. 2d lt., 1969, advanced through grades to maj., 1979; med. material officer U.S. Air Force Hosp. Reese, Lubbock, Tex., 1969-71, U.S. Air Force Clinic Howard, C.Z., 1971-72; asst. adminstr. U.S. Air Force Hosp. Rickenbacker, Columbus, Ohio, 1973-75, U.S. Air Force Hosp. Williams, Phoenix, 1975-77; adminstr. U.S. Air Force Hosp., Grand Forks, N.D., 1977-81; ret. 1981; adminstr. correctional health Maricopa County Dept. Health Svcs., Phoenix, 1981-87, health svcs. adminstr., 1987--; mem. adj. faculty Park Coll., Kansas City, Mo., 1977-79. Deacon Ch. of Redeemer, Mesa, Ariz., 1982-85, elder, vice chmn. bd., 1985--; bd. dirs., mem. foster care rev. bd. Ariz. Supreme Ct., Mesa, 1983--; bd. dirs. Crisis Pregancy Ctrs., Phoenix, 1985-86. Decorated Meritorious Svc. medal. Mem. Ret. Officers Assn. Republican. Home: 741 N Mesa Dr Mesa AZ 85201 Office: Maricopa County Dept Health Svcs 400 N 7th St Ste 203 Phoenix AZ 85006

CAMPBELL, ROLLA BRUCE DUNBAR, emergency physician; b. N.Y.C., Apr. 4, 1950; s. Rolla Dacres Campbell and Eunice Coit (Johnson) Winslow; m. Melissa Jane Loveless, Feb. 22, 1975; children: Caroline, Allison. BA in Psychology, Stanford U., 1972; MD, Albany Union U., 1979. Diplomate Am. Bd. Emergency Physicians. Intern U. Hawaii, Honolulu, 1979-80; emergency physician Washoe Med. Ctr., Reno, 1980-87, Mt. Grant Gen. Hosp., Hawthorne, Nev., 1986—; dir. emergency medicine Sparks (Nev.) Family Hosp., 1983—; instr. advanced cardiac life support, Reno, 1983--. Mem. Am. Coll. Emergency Physicians, Am. Coll. Sports Medicine. Republican. Episcopalian. Office: Sparks Family Hosp 7000 Prater Way Sparks NV 89431

CAMPBELL, SUELLA, equipment company executive; b. Hyannis, Mass., June 1, 1943; d. John Arthur and Mini Frances (Hillman) Ahlm; m. Walter Thomas Wendell Jr., Feb. 27, 1965 (div. May 1985); children: Lisa Ann, Mathew Thomas; m. John Russell Campbell, Feb. 14, 1987. BA in Social Studies, U. Philippines, Clark AFB, 1973. Clk. Ryder Truck Rental, Albuquerque, Dayton (Ohio), 1974-80; fiscal officer, continuing edn. and tng. Great Falls (Mont.) Native Am. Ctr., 1981-82; ops. supr. Amfac Plumbing Supply, Great Falls, 1982-86; office mgr. Normont Equipment Co., Great Falls, 1986—. Treas. St. Francis Episcopal Ch., Great Falls, 1987—. Republican.

CAMPBELL, TERRY ALLEN, avionics systems engineer; b. San Diego, Nov. 17, 1957; s. Guy Walton and Joan Viola (Shoning) C.;m. Suzanne Kay Desiderati, Mar. 14, 1987; 1 child, Grace. AA, Rio Salado Community Coll., Phoenix, 1982. Tech. rep. A.B. Dick, Phoenix, 1982-83; mfg. test engr. McDonnell Douglas Hellicopter Co., Mesa, Ariz., 1983-87; avionics systems engr. McDonnell Douglas Hellicopter Co., 1987—. With USAF, 1978-82. Republican. Office: McDonnell Douglas 5000 E McDowell Rd Mesa AZ 85205

CAMPBELL, THOMAS J., congressman; b. Chgo., Aug. 14, 1952; s. William J. and Marie Campbell; m. Susanne Martin. BA, MA in Econs. with highest honors, U. Chgo., 1973, PhD in Econs. with highest dept. fellowship, 1980; JD magna cum laude, Harvard U., 1976. Law clk. to presiding justice U.S. Ct. Appeals (D.C. cir.), 1976-77; law clk. to Justice Byron R. White U.S. Supreme Ct., Washington, 1977-78; assoc. Winston & Strawn, Chgo., 1978-80; White Ho. fellow Office Chief of Staff and White Ho. of Counsel, Washington, 1980-81; exec. asst. to dep. atty. gen. Dept. Justice, Washington, 1981; dir. Bur. Trade Competition FTC, Washington, 1981-83, head del. to OECD, Paris, com. experts on restictive bus. practices, 1982, 83; mem. 101st Congress from 12th Calif. dist., 1989—, mem. com. on sci., space and tech., com. on small bus., 1989—; prof. Stanford Law Sch., 1983-89. Referee Jour. Polit. Economy, Internat. Rev. Law and Econs. Mem. San Francisco Com. on Fgn. Relations. Mem. ABA (antitrust sect., coun. 1985-88, program chmn. 1983-84). Office: US Ho of Reps 1730 Longworth House Office Bldg Washington DC 20515 also: 599 N Mathilda Ave Ste 105 Sunnyvale CA 94086

CAMPBELL, WESLEY GLENN, economist, educator; b. Komoka, Ont., Can., Apr. 29, 1924; s. Alfred E and Delia (O'Brien) C.; m. Rita Ricardo, Sept. 15, 1946; children: Barbara Campbell Bizewski, Diane Campbell Porter, Nancy. B.A., U. Western Ont., 1944; M.A., Harvard, 1946, Ph.D.,

1948. Instr. econs. Harvard, 1948-51; research economist U.S. C. of C., 1951-54; dir. research Am. Enterprise Assn., 1954-60; dir. Hoover Instn. War, Revolution and Peace, Stanford, Calif., 1960—; Co-dir. project on Am. competitive enterprise, fgn. econ. devel. and aid program, spl. com. to study fgn. aid program U.S. Senate, 1956-57; mem. Pres.'s Commn. on White House Fellows, 1969-74, President's Com. on Sci. and Tech., 1976; mem. personnel adv. com. to Pres., 1980-81; mem. adv. bd. Ctr. for Strategic and Internat. Studies, 1980-85; dir. Hutchins Ctr. for Study Dem. Instns., 1981-87; bd. dirs. NSF, 1972-78, Com. on Present Danger, 1976—; chmn. Pres.'s Intelligence Oversight Bd., 1981—; spl. advisor U.S. Delegation to 43d Session Gen. Assembly of UN; mem. Pres.'s Fgn. Intelligence Adv. Bd., 1981—; chmn. Am. panel Joint Com. Japan-U.S. Cultural and Ednl. Coop., 1983—; chmn. Japan-U.S. Friendship Commn., 1983—; mem. UNESCO Monitoring Panel, 1984; bd. trustees Ronald Reagan Presdl. Found., 1985—, chmn., 1985-87. Co-author: The American Competitive Enterprise Economy, 1952; Editor, prin. author: The Economics of Mobilization and War, 1952; contbr. articles to profl. jours. Trustee Herbert Hoover Presdl. Library Assn.; mem. bd. visitors Bernice P. Bishop Mus.; regent U. Calif., 1968—. Fellow Royal Econ. Soc.; mem. Am. Econ. Assn., Phila. Soc. (pres. 1965-67), Mont Pelerin Soc. (dir. 1980—). Clubs: Bohemian (Cal.), Cosmos (Cal.), Commonwealth (Cal.). Home: 26915 Alejandro Dr Los Altos Hills CA 94022 Office: Stanford U Hoover Instn Stanford CA 94305

CAMPER, JOHN SAXTON, public relations and marketing executive; b. Trenton, N.J., Apr. 24, 1929; s. Thomas Emory and Mildred Ruth (Burke) C.; m. Ferne Arlene Clanton; children: Susan Jennifer, John Saxton III. BS in History and Econs., U. Nebr., 1968. Enlisted U.S. Army, 1948, commd. to 1st lt., advanced through ranks to maj., 1972, ret., 1972; regional mktg. officer First Bank System, Mont., 1978-83; lectr., instr. mktg. and advt., pub. relations; pres. Camper Communications, Helena, 1983; dir. Profl. Devel. Ctr., Mont., 1984—. Decorated Legion of Merit. Mem. Helena Advt. Fedn. (1st pres., founder). Republican. Methodist. Lodge: Rotary.

CAMPHAUSEN, FRED HOWARD, physicist; b. L.A., Aug. 23, 1933; s. Fred Henry and Eloise (Ingebretsen) C.; BA in Physics, U. Calif., 1961; m. Martina Simon, Apr. 2, 1956 (div.); children: Raymond Thomas, Karin Maria; m. 2d, Marianna P. Dembinski, Aug. 2, 1980. With Naval Weapons Cen., China Lake, Calif., 1961-88, physicist, project mgr. electronic warfare test and evaluation, 1980-88; owner, mgr., Mountain High, Ltd., 1980—. With U.S. Army, 1953-56. Mem. Naval Aviation Execs. Inst., Assn. of Old Crows, Am. Alpine Club, Sierra Club. Republican. Roman Catholic. Club: Vägmarken, Eastern Sierra Mountaineers. Contbr. articles to profl. jours. Home and Office: 2765 Sierra Vista Way Bishop CA 93514

CAMPING, WALT LEE, investment company executive; b. Denver, Dec. 28, 1943; s. John Jr. and Pauline (Nussbaum) C.; m. Judith L. Wanders, Apr. 3, 1964; children: Douglas, Kevin, Candice, Billy, Karen. AA in Bus., Phoenix Coll., 1967. Police officer City of Phoenix, 1966-71; sales cons. Lou Grubb Chevrolet, Phoenix, 1971-74; gen. mgr. Ariz. Irrigation Co., Phoenix, 1974-77; pres., chief exec. officer ServiceMaster, Phoenix, 1978-87, The Camping Cos., Phoenix, 1988—. Cons., bd. dirs. Fellowship Christian Athletes, Phoenix, 1986-87; bd. dirs. Grand Canyon counseling, Phoneix, 1986-88. With USN, 1962-66. Republican. Home: 2532 E Indianola St Phoenix AZ 85016 Office: Camping Cos ServiceMaster 2334 N 32d St Phoenix AZ 85008

CAMPISTEGUY-HAWKINS, MARIA ELENA, international marketing and sales executive; b. Montevideo, Uruguay, Sept. 22, 1961; came to U.S., 1969; d. Juan Jose Campisteguy and Martha (Perez) Gonzalez-Prats; m. Andre Rene Hawkins, Sept. 22, 1984. BS in Russian and Spanish, Georgetown U., 1983; postgrad. in internat. bus., Portland State U., 1985—. Ops. asst. Africa Intergovtl. Com. for Migration, Washington, 1983-84; dir. Hispanic services Cath. Family Services, Portland, Oreg., 1984-85; assoc. community relations, liason for minority affairs United Way Columbia-Willamette, Portland, Oreg., 1985-88; internat. mktg. and sales rep. for S.Am. Esco Corp., Portland, 1988—. Advisor Internat. Lang. Bank, Portland, Oreg., 1986-88. Mem. Oreg. Council for Hispanic Advancement (founder, exec. com. 1984--),Uruguayan-Am. Soc., Georgetown U. Alumni Assn., Alpha Sigma Nu. Home: 2445 NE 46th Ave Portland OR 97213 Office: Esco Corp 2141 NW 25th Ave Portland OR 97210

CAMPOS, SANTIAGO E., federal judge; b. Santa Rosa, N.Mex., Dec. 25, 1926; s. Ramon and Miquela Campos; m. Patsy Campos, Jan. 27, 1947; children: Teresa, Rebecca, Christina, Miquela Feliz. J.D., U. N.Mex., 1953. Bar: N.Mex. 1953. Asst., 1st asst. atty gen. State of N.Mex., 1955-57; judge U.S. Dist. Ct. N.Mex., 1st Jud. Dist., 1971-78, now chief judge. Served as seaman USN, 1944-46. Mem. State Bar N.Mex., First Jud. Dist. Bar Assn., Order of Coif. Office: US Dist Ct PO Box 2244 Santa Fe NM 87501

CANBY, WILLIAM CAMERON, JR., U.S. judge; b. St. Paul, May 22, 1931; s. William Cameron and Margaret Leah (Lewis) C.; m. Jane Adams, June 18, 1954; children—William Nathan, John Adams, Margaret Lewis. A.B., Yale U., 1953; LL.B., U. Minn., 1956. Bar: Minn. bar 1956, Ariz. bar 1972. Law clk. U.S. Supreme Ct. Justice Charles E. Whittaker, 1958-59; asso. firm Oppenheimer, Hodgson, Brown, Baer & Wolff, St. Paul, 1959-62; asso., then dep. dir. Peace Corps, Ethiopia, 1962-64; dir. Peace Corps, Uganda, 1964-66; asst. to U.S. Senator Walter Mondale, 1966; asst. to pres. SUNY, 1967; prof. law Ariz. State U., 1967-80; judge U.S. Ct. Appeals 9th Circuit, Phoenix, 1980—; bd. dirs. Ariz. Center Law in Public Interest, 1974-80, Maricopa County Legal Aid Soc., 1972-78, D.N.A.-People's Legal Services, 1978-80; Fulbright prof. Makerere U. Faculty Law, Kampala, Uganda, 1970-71. Author: American Indian Law, 1988; also articles.; Note editor: Minn. Law Rev, 1955-56. Precinct and state committeeman Democratic Party Ariz., 1972-80; bd. dirs. Central Ariz. Coalition for Right to Choose, 1976-80. Served with USAF, 1956-58. Mem. State Bar Ariz., Minn. Bar Assn., Maricopa County Bar Assn., Phi Beta Kappa, Order of Coif. Office: US Ct of Appeals 6445 US Courthouse and Fed Bldg 230 N 1st Ave Phoenix AZ 85025

CANDELARIA, LIONEL MICHAEL, military officer, dentist; b. Albuquerque, Dec. 17, 1958; s. John Julius and Agnus Victoria (Garcia) C.; m. Karil Rene Taylor, July 21, 1985. BS in Biology, U. N.Mex., 1981; DDS, U. Mo., Kansas City, 1985. Resident gen. practice Balboa Hosp., San Diego, 1986; commd. lt. USN, 1985; staff dentist 3d Dental Co. 3d FSSG USN, Okinawa, Japan, 1986-87; staff dentist 1st Dental Co. 1st. FSSG USN, Camp Pendelton, Calif., 1987-89; resident in oral and maxillofacial surgery U. Tenn., 1989—; cons. Myrons Labs. Internat., Kansas City; lectr. in field. Fellow Am. Assn. Hosp. Dentists; mem. ADA, Acad. Gen. Dentistry, Clinicians of ADA, Dive Club., Sigma Chi, Omicron Kappa Upsilon. Democrat. Roman Catholic. Home: 962 Sea Cliff Dr Carlsbad CA 92009 Office: USN 1st Dental Co 1st FSSG Camp Pendleton CA 92055

CANETTI, BRUCE NICOL, financial agency executive; b. San Pedro, Calif., Apr. 4, 1956; s. Frank John and Barbara (Glenn) C.; m. Kimberley Anne Davey, Aug. 26, 1978; children: Sarah Paige, Alexander Franklin. BS in Bus. Adminstrn., U. So. Calif., 1978; cert. in life ins. planning, The Am. Coll. Agy. mgr. Standard Ins. Co., Portland, Oreg., 1978-87, The Prin. Fin. Group, San Diego, 1987—. Rep. vol. Redondo Beach, Calif., 1972-80, San Diego, 1984—. Life Underwriting Tng. Council fellow. Mem. Nat. Assn. Life Underwriters (bd. dirs. 1985-87, Million Dollar Round Table award 1980-81, 82-83), Calif. Assn. Life Underwriters (Nat. Quality award, Nat. Sales Achievement award), Gen. Agts. and Mgrs. Assn. (bd. dirs. San Diego chpt. 1985-88, Costa Mesa, Calif. chpt. 1988—, Career Devel. award 1987). Clubs: Bernardo Heights Country (San Diego); Marbella Golf and Country (San Juan). Office: Prin Fin Group 888 N Main St PO Box 1942 4th Fl Santa Ana CA 92702

CANFIELD, GRANT WELLINGTON, JR., educational association administrator; b. Los Angeles, Nov. 28, 1923; s. Grant Wellington and Phyllis Marie (Westland) C.; m. Virginia Louise Bellinger, June 17, 1945; 1 child, Julie Marie. BS, U. So. Calif., 1949, MBA, 1958. Personnel and indsl. relations exec., Los Angeles, 1949-55; employee relations cons., regional mgr. Mchts. and Mfrs. Assn. Los Angeles, 1955-60; v.p., orgnl. devel. cons. Hawaii Employers Council, Honolulu, 1960-75; pres., dir. Hawaiian Ednl. Council, 1969—, chmn., chief exec. officer, 1989; exec. v.p. Hawaii Garment Mfrs. Assn., 1965-75, Assn. Hawaii Restaurant Employers, 1966-75; exec. dir. Hawaii League Savs. Assns., 1971-78; exec. dir. Pan-Pacific Surg. Assn., 1980-81, exec. v.p., 1982-83; exec. dir. Hawaii Bus. Roundtable, 1983—; sec., treas. Econ. Devel. Corp. Honolulu, 1984-85; sec., treas. Hawaii Conv. Park Council, Inc., 1984-86, hon. dir., 1986-88. Co-author: Resource Manual for Public Collective Bargaining, 1973. Bd. dirs. Hawaii Restaurant Assn., 1974-76, bd. dirs. Hawaii chpt. Nat. Assn. Accts., 1963-67, nat. dir., 1965-66; bd. dirs. Vol. Service Bur. Honolulu, 1965-66, pres., 1966-68; bd. dirs. Vol. Info. and Referral Service Honolulu, 1972-75, Goodwill Vocat. Tng. Ctrs. of Hawaii, 1973-81, Girl Scout council Pacific, 1961-65, 71-72; bd. dirs. Hawaii Com. Alcoholism, 1962-71, co-chmn., 1964-68; pres., dir. Friends of Punahou Sch., 1972-75; mem. community adv. bd. Jr. League Honolulu, 1968-70; exec. bd. Aloha council Boys Scouts Am., 1962-65; bd. regents Chaminade U., 1983-85. Served to 1st lt. inf. AUS, 1943-46. Decorated Bronze Star, Purple Heart, Combat Inf. badge. Mem. Am. Soc. Assn. Execs. (cert. assn. exec.), Inst. Mgmt. Cons. (cert.), Am. Soc. Tng. and Devel., Am. Soc. Personnel Adminstrn., Inst. Mgmt. Cons., Pacific Club, Rotary, Masons. Home: 1950 W Dry Creek Rd Healdsburg CA 95448 Office: PO Box 4145 Honolulu HI 96812-4145

CANFIELD, SUZANNE RENÉE, brokerage executive; b. Greensboro, N.C., July 1, 1962; d. William Norman and Ella Mae (Cashwell) Booker; m. John Charles Canfield, July 20, 1985. BA summa cum laude, U. N.C., 1982, MA, 1985. Dist. mgr. First Investors Corp., Colorado Springs, Colo., 1986-87; assoc. mgr. First Investors Corp., Denver, 1987—. Book reviewer: Asheville (N.C.) Citizen-Times, 1982-85; mem. edit. bd. Carolina Quarterly, 1983-85. Bd. dirs. Encorps/Colo. Springs Symphony Guild, 1986—. Richard N. Weaver fellow Intercoll. Studies Inst., 1985-86. Mem. Assn. Bus. Profl. Women (young career woman nominee 1988), Nat. Assn. Female Execs. (communication dir. in tng. 1986-87), Trinidad C. of C., Million Dollar Club, English Speaking Union, Phi Delta (program dir. 1980-81). Club: Linacre Coll. Boat (Oxford, Eng.). Lodge: Lions. Home: 7545 Hickorywood Dr Colorado Springs CO 80920 Office: First Investors Corp 8704 Yates Dr Ste 210 Westminster CO 80003

CANGER, JAMES ANTHONY, sales and revenue consultant; b. Paterson, N.J., May 9, 1948; s. Ralph Edward and Gloria (Petrosi) C.; m. Elaine Isabel Soubajy, Feb. 26, 1972; children: Jason Thomas, Jarod Michael. BA, St. Vincent Coll., Latrobe, Pa., 1970. Western regional mgr. Inmont Corp. div. United Tech., Anaheim, Calif., 1970-81; nat. mktg. and sales mgr. SRW Computer Compenents, Fountain Valley, Calif., 1981-83, CBJ Enterprises, Irvine, Calif., 1983-85; dir. mktg. and sales Dial Precision, Inc., Torrance, Calif., 1985--; v.p. mktg. and sales, owner Artifex Corp., Costa Mesa, Calif., 1987--; owner, pres. Bus. Network, Laguna Niguel, Calif., 1987--; western regional mktg. developer Gen. Electric Superabrasives, Laguna Niguel, 1987--; speaker, tchr. sales Calif. Poly Inst., Pomona, 1988--. Commr. Am. Youth Soccer Orgn., Region 41 div. K&G, Laguna Niguel, 1984-86; mem. Niguel Woods Homeowners Assn., 1987--; cons. St. Timothy's Roman Cath. Ch., 1986. Democrat. Roman Catholic. Office: Bus Network 30100 Town Ctr Dr Ste 195 Laguna Niguel CA 92677

CANNON, EARL NELSON, lawyer; b. Delavan, Wis., Jan. 20, 1900; s. Dan E. and Lenora (Nelson) C.; B.S., U. Wis., 1924, LL.B., 1927, J.D., 1966; m. Helen Gibson, July 23, 1926. Atty., law firm Stephens, Cannon & Cooper (now Stephens, Cannon, Bieberstein & Cooper), 1928-53; pres. Yellow Truck Lines, Inc., 1930-45; exec. dir., legal counsel Central States Area Employers Assn., 1940-53; labor counsel Central Motor Freight Assn., 1940-53; v.p. charge personnel and labor relations Greyhound Corp., Chgo., 1952-65. Pres. Idyllwild Property Owners Assn.; dir. Idyllwild County Water Dist. Industry mem. War Labor Bd., 1944-45; industry mem. Nat. WSB, 1946; v.p. Am. Trucking Assn., 1936-46 commr. Riverside County Flood Control and Water Conservation Dist.; mem. adv. com. Hemet-San Jacinto YMCA; bd. dirs. Idyllwild (Calif.) Arts Found., Hemet-San Jacinto YMCA. Mem. Theta Chi, Phi Alpha Delta. Clubs: Executive, Union League (Chgo.); Madison; Indian Wells Country (Palm Desert, Calif.); Palm Springs Country, Tennis (Palm Springs, Calif.); Idyllwild Lions (pres.); Ojai (Calif.) Country; San Jacinto Lions (Zone A chmn.), Sobobe Springs Country Soboba Springs Mens (chmn. membership com.) (San Jacinto, Calif.). Home: 42701 Main St #116 San Jacinto CA 92383 Office: Greyhound Towers 111 W Clarendon Ave Phoenix AZ 85013

CANNON, JAMES W., insurance company executive; b. 1927. With Safeco Corp., Seattle, 1948—, statistical supr., 1948-55, asst. controller, 1955-56, dir. ops., 1956-67, v.p. ops., data processing, 1967-75, sr. v.p. adminstrn., 1975-82, sr. v.p., 1982-85, exec. v.p., 1985—; also pres. Gen. Ins. Co. of Am. (subs.), Seattle, Safeco Ins. Co. of Am. (subs.), Seattle, Safeco Lloyd's Ins. Co. (subs.), Seattle, Safeco Nat. Ins. Co. (subs.), Seattle, Safeco Surplus Lines Ins. Co. (subs.), Seattle. Served with USN, 1945-47. Office: Safeco Ins Co of Am Safeco Plaza T-22 Seattle WA 98185 *

CANNON, THEODORE WILES, environmental engineer; b. Eugene, Oreg., Aug. 28, 1933; s. Clarence Dempster and Frances Alberta (Wiles) C.; m. Grace Miriam King, Dec. 23, 1969; children: Theodore Alfred, Grace April, Celeste Dorothy. BS, Oreg. State U., 1956; MS, U. Oreg., 1960; PhD, Oreg. State U., 1966. Reg. profl. engr., Colo. Elec. engr. Hanford Atomic Products Operation, Richland, Wash., 1956-58; instr. Westmont Coll., Santa Barbara, Calif., 1960-61; research asst. Oreg. State U., Corvallis, 1964-66; staff scientist Nat. Ctr. for Atmospheric Research, Boulder, Colo., 1968-79; sr. engr. Solar Energy Research Inst., Golden, Colo., 1979—; cons. in field, 1973—. Contbr. articles to profl. jours. Sec. Rocky Mountain Communications Group, Denver, 1988—. Recipient Service award Soc. Photographic Scientists and Engrs., 1975; post-doctoral fellow Nat. Ctr. for Atmospheric Research, 1966-68. Mem. Soc. Photo-optical Instrumentation Engrs., Rehab. Engring. Soc. N.Am., Inst. for Alternative and Augmentative Communication. Republican. Baptist. Home: 3345 Alkire Way Golden CO 80401 Office: Solar Energy Rsch Inst 1617 Cole Blvd Golden CO 80401

CANOVA-DAVIS, ELEANOR, biochemist, researcher; b. San Francisco, Jan. 18, 1938; d. Gaudenzio Enzio and Catherine (Bordisso) Canova; m. Kenneth Roy Davis, Feb. 10, 1957; children: Kenneth Roy Jr., Jeffrey Stephen. BA, San Francisco State U., 1968, MS, 1971; PhD, U. Calif., San Francisco, 1977. Lab. asst. Frederick Burk Found. for Edn., San Francisco, 1969-71; research , teaching asst. U. Calif., San Francisco, 1972-77, asst. research biochemist, 1980-84; NIH postdoctoral fellow U. Calif., Berkeley, 1977-80; sr. scientist Liposome Tech., Menlo Park, Calif., 1984-85; scientist Genentech, Inc., South San Francisco, 1985—. Contbr. articles to profl. jours. Recipient Nat. Research Service award NIH, 1977-80; grantee Chancellor's Patent Fund, U. Calif., San Francisco, 1976, Earl C. Anthony Trust, U. Calif., San Francisco, 1975. Mem. Am. Chem. Soc., Calif. Scholarship Fedn. Roman Catholic. Club: Sequoia Woods County (Arnold, Calif.). Home: 2305 Bourbon Ct South San Francisco CA 94080 Office: Genentech Inc 460 Point San Bruno Blvd South San Francisco CA 94080

CANSECO, JOSE, professional baseball player; b. Havana, Cuba, July 2, 1964; m. Esther Haddad, October 25, 1988. Player various minor league teams, 1982-85; outfielder Oakland (Calif.) Athletics, 1985—; mem. Am. League All-Star Team, 1986, 88; player 1988 World Series. Named Most Valuable Player So. League, 1985, Am. League Rookie of Yr. The Sporting News, 1986, Baseball Writers' Assn. Am., 1986; holds record for 40 home runs and 40 stolen bases in same season, 1988. Office: care Oakland A's Oakland-Alameda County Coliseum PO Box 2220 Oakland CA 94621 *

CANTER, STANLEY STANTON, motion picture producer; b. Plainfield, N.J., July 15, 1933; s. Benjamin and Lillian (Stanton) C.; m. Susan Ohrbach, Sept. 23, 1963 (div. Aug. 15, 1978); children: Jonathan, Jeremy. BA, UCLA, 1955, MA, 1957, postgrad., 1958; postgrad., U. So. Calif., 1963-64. Page, editor NBC-TV, Burbank, Calif., 1958-59; supr. studio facilities NBC-TV, Burbank, 1959-60, mgr. broadcast promotion, 1960-63; asst. v.p. Union Bank, Beverly Hills, Calif., 1963-66; assoc. producer E. Kadison Prodns., Los Angeles, 1966-68; pres. Triangle Prodns. Inc., Los Angeles, 1968—; Producer Hornets Nest, 1972, W.W. & The Dixie Dancekings, 1975, St. Ives, 1976, Greystoke I: Legend of Tarzan, 1984. Patron Los Angeles Museum Art, 1978—; tennis coach minority tennis players, Los Angeles, 1963—. Mem. Assn. Motion Picture & TV, Producers Guild (bd. dirs. 1963-65), Writer Guild Am., Bruin Racketeers, Phi Beta Kappa, Beverly Hills Tennis, Queens Club. Republican. Office: Triangle Prodns Inc 10550 Wilshire Blvd Ste 905 Los Angeles CA 90024

CANTOR, ROBERT FRANK, computer company executive; b. N.Y.C., Apr. 29, 1943; s. Myron David and Phyllis Jane (Singerman) C.; m. Nancy Marie Carpenter, May 3, 1970 (div.); 1 child, Michelle; m. Brenda Lee Cousins, May 5, 1984; children: Anthony, Samuel. BSBA, Pa. State U., 1965, MSBA, 1967. Indsl. engr. IBM, 1967, with software devel., 1968-72; adv. planner banking and security Kingston, N.Y., 1973-78; program mgr. strategy and bus. practices at div. hdqrs. Harrison, N.Y., 1978-80; mgr. tech. products planning Boulder, Colo., 1980-83; program mgr. OEM supplies 1983—; mem. faculty loan program Xavier U., New Orleans, 1972-73; bd. dirs. and pres. Colo. Neurodiagnostic Inst., Boulder. Inventor in field. Mem. Beta Gamma Sigma. Republican. Mem. Bahai Faith. Home: 745 Linden Ave Boulder CO 80302 Office: IBM 51Z 022 6300 Diagonal Hwy Boulder CO 80301

CANTRELLE, JOSEPH, SR., foundation administrator; b. San Francisco, June 2, 1951; s. Albert Joseph and Doris May (Cassetta) C.; 1 child from previous marriage, Julie Ann; m. Suying Luong, Jan. 11, 1985; children: Joseph Jr., Jennifer Lynn. BS, San Francisco State U., 1976. Exec. dir. employment and tng. project Sacramento Occupational Advancement Resources, Inc., 1988—; project dir. Cath. Social Services, Sacramento, 1981-88. Mem. task force GAIN, 1987-88. Mem. Program Operators Assn., Sacramento Refugee Forum. Home: 2327 Dartmouth Pl El Dorado Hills CA 95630 Office: Sacramento Occupational Advancement Resources 5450 Power Inn Rd Ste B Sacramento CA 95820

CAO, THAI-HAI, industrial engrineer; b. Saigon, Republic of Vietnam, July 8, 1954; came to U.S., 1975; s. Pho Thai and Anh Ngoc (Nguyen) C.; m. Hue Thi Iran, June 29, 1979; children: Quoc-Viet Thai, Quoc-Nam Thai, Huyen-Tran Thai. BS in Indsl. Engring., U. Wash., 1980. Mfg. engr. GE, San Jose, Calif., 1980-82; mgr. mfg. engring. and quality assurance Broadcast Microwave div. Harris Corp., Mountain View, Calif., 1982-85; mgr. mfg. engring. John Fluke Mfg. Co., Everett, Wash., 1986—; mgr. quality engring. Advanced Tech. Labs., Bothell, Wash., 1986—. Mem. Am. Soc. Quality Control (chmn. membership com. 1987—), Soc. Vietnamese Profls. (pres. 1988), Soc. Mfg. Engrs., Inst. Indsl. Engrs., Am. Prodn. and Inventory Control. Home: 23502 22d Ave SE Bothell WA 98021 Office: Advanced Tech Labs Quality Engring Dept PO Box 3003 Bothell WA 98041-3003

CAPENER, REGNER ALVIN, minister, electronics engineer; b. Astoria, Oreg., Apr. 18, 1942; s. Alvin Earnest and Lillian Lorraine (Lehtosaari) C.; divorced; children: Deborah, Christian, Melodie, Ariella; m. Della Denise Melson, May 17, 1983; children: Shelley, Danielle, Rebekah, Joshua. Student, U. Nebr., 1957-58, 59-60, Southwestern Coll., Waxahachie, Tex., 1958-59, Bethany Bible Coll., 1963-64. Ordained to ministry Full Gospel Assembly, 1971, Calif. Evangelistic Assn., 1973. Engr., talk show host Sta. KHOF-FM, Glendale, Calif., 1966-67; youth min. Bethel Union Ch., Duarte, Calif., 1966-67; pres. Intermountain Electronics, Salt Lake City, 1967-72; assoc. pastor Full Gospel Assembly, Salt Lake City, 1968-72, Long Beach (Calif.) Christian Ctr., 1972-76; v.p. Refuge Ministries, Inc., Long Beach, 1972-76; pres. Christian Broadcasting Network-Alaska, Inc., Fairbanks, 1977-83; gen.mgr. Action Sch. of Broadcasting, Anchorage, 1983-85; pres., pastor House of Praise, Anchorage, 1984—; chief engr. KTBY-TV, Inc., Anchorage, 1988—; area dir. Christian Broadcasting Network, Virginia Beach, 1977-83; cons., dir. Union Bond and Trust Co., Anchorage, 1985-86. Author: Spiritual Maturity, 1975, Spiritual Warfare, 1976, The Doctrine of Submission, 1988, A Vision for Praise, 1988; author, composer numerous gospel songs; creator numerous broadcasting and electronic instrument inventions. Sec., Christian Businessmen's Com., Salt Lake City, 1968-72; area advisor Women's Aglow Internat., Fairbanks, 1981-83; local co-chmn. campaign Boucher for Gov. , Fairbanks, 1982; campaigner for Boucher for State House, Anchorage, 1984, Clark Gruening for Senate Com., Barrow, Alaska, 1980; TV producer Stevens for U.S. Senate, Barrow, 1978; fundraiser City of Refuge, Mex., 1973-75; statewide rep. Sudden Infant Death Syndrome, Barrow, 1978-82; founder, Operation Blessing/Alaska, 1981. Mem. Soc. Broadcast Engrs., Internat. Soc. Classical Guitarists (sec. 1967-69), Alaska Broadcaster's Assn., Nat. Assn. Broadcasters, Long Beach C. of C. Republican. Office: Sta KTBY Inc 1840 S Bragaw Ste 101 Anchorage AK 99508

CAPIEL-COLLIN, SUSAN, satellite services executive; b. Van Nuys, Calif., Oct. 4, 1952; d. Joe A. and Josie (Toler) Capiel; m. Steve Collin, July 7, 1984. Student La. State U., 1973. Legal sec. Austin & Jordan, Aspen, Colo., 1978-82; ptnr., broker satellite services SAT TIME, Inc., Aspen, 1982—. Democrat. Roman Catholic. Home and Office: SAT TIME Inc Box 3057 Aspen CO 81612

CAPLIN, DAVID JOEL, statistician; b. Rochester, N.Y., Apr. 3, 1943; s. Albert David and Ruth (Moses) C.; m. Arlene E. Joseph, May 12, 1963 (div. June 1979); children: Richard, Donna; m. Paula Louise Cagney, July 6, 1979; 1 stepchild, Kent. ASEE, Rochester Inst. Tech., 1972; BS in Econ. Acctg., Rollins Coll., 1975, MS in Mgmt., 1976; MS in Engring., Cen. Fla. U., 1984. Engring. technician Stromberg Carlson, Rochester, 1966-72; owner Shell Oil Co. Svc. Sta., Winter Park, Fla., 1972-76, Ormond Beach, Fla., 1976-80; sales rep. Shell Oil Co., Tampa, Fla.; customer rels. rep. B.F. Goodrich, Ft. Myers, Fla., 1980-82; project mgr. Sparton Electronics, Deleon Springs, Fla., 1982-83, quality systems mgr., 1983-85; factory auto application engr. Hewlett-Packard Co., L.A., 1985-87, indsl. auto sales rep., 1987--. Com. mem. Save the Lighthouse, Ponce Inlet, Fla., 1983. With USN, 1961-66, Vietnam. Mem. Am. Soc. for Quality Control, Soc. Mfg. Engring., Computer Automation Systems Assn., Shriners, Masons. Republican. Jewish. Home: 700 Esplanade #31 Redondo Beach CA 90277 Office: Hewlett-Packard Co 5651 W Manchester Ave Los Angeles CA 90045

CAPLINGER, PAULA RUTH, music educator; b. Sacramento, Calif., Sept. 10, 1948; d. Gerald Lavell and Evelyn Ruth (Wanner) C.; divorced. BA, Calif. State U., Sacramento, 1973. Cert. elem. tchr., Calif. Traveling music tchr. Sacramento Unified Sch. Dist., 1973—; del. Calif. Tchr. Competency Panel, 1988. 1st trumpet Sacramento Valley Wind Ensemble, 1986—. Mem. Sacramento City Tchrs. Assn. (Golden Apple 1986), Nat. Edn. Assn. Office: Sacramento City Tchrs Assn 2564 21st St Sacramento CA 95818

CAPPA, DONALD, college instructor, management consultant; b. San Francisco, Aug. 29, 1930; s. Dominick Navarro and Ruth (Bergman) C.; m. Maryann Freer, Dec. 31, 1950 (div. June 1985); children: Janice Faye Rodondi, James Donald, Christopher Louis; m. Diana Estelle Barry, m. Aug. 21, 1986. Cert. in indsl. mgmt., Coll. San Mateo, 1960, AA, 1961; BA in Mgmt., Golden Gate U., 1973, MA, 1976. Engring. asst. Standard Oil of Calif., San Francisco, 1950-60; pres. Marina Ski Corp., San Francisco, 1960-73; instr. bus. Chabot Coll., Hayward, Calif., 1974—; co-host TV series Sta. KPIX-TV, San Francisco, 1967-71; cons. Hayward (Calif.) Park and Recreation Assn., 1985-86, Plumbers Union 44, San Leandro Calif., 1985—; regional dir. U.S. Naval Sea Cadets, San Francisco, 1985—; ski cons. Sta. KPIX-TV and Sta. KSFO , San Francisco, 1961-72. Co-advisor Arlington, Va. chpt. Distributive Edn. Clubs Am. Lodge: Lions (pres. 1981-82). Office: Chabot Coll 25555 Hesperian Blvd Hayward CA 94545

CAPPEL, CONSTANCE, consulting company executive; b. Dayton, Ohio, June 22, 1936; d. Adam Denison and Mary Louise (Henry) C.; m. R.A. Montgomery Jr., June 22, 1962 (div. Apr. 1980); children: Ramsey, Anson, Montgomery. BA, Sarah Lawrence Coll., 1959; MA, Columbia U., N.Y.C., 1961; postgrad., Union Coll. Editor Newsweek, N.Y.C., 1961-63, Vogue, N.Y.C., 1964-66; grad. prof. Goddard Coll., Plainfield, Vt., 1975-79; founder, chief exec. officer, pub. Vt. Crossroad Press, Waitsfield, 1972-82; comml. realtor Investmark, Dayton, 1985-87; prin. Cappel Cons., San Francisco, 1986—. Author: Hemingway in Michigan, 1966, Vermont School Bus Ride; editor: (children's book) Sugarcane Island, 1979. Founder Women's Rights Project/ACLU, Vt., 1973-74. McDowell Colony fellow, Peterborough, N.H., 1972, 74. Mem. Am. Mgmt. Assn., Commonwealth Club Calif. Episcopalian. Office: PO Box 553 Bodega Bay CA 94923

CAPPELLO, EVE, business consultant; b. Sydney, Australia, Dec. 4, 1922; d. Nem and Ethel Shapira; children from previous marriage: Frances Soskins, Alan Kazdin; came to U.S., 1940, naturalized, 1944; AA, Santa Monica City Coll., 1972; BA, Calif. State U.-Dominguez Hills, 1974; MA, Pacific Western U., 1977, PhD, 1978. Singer, pianist, L.A., 1958-78; pvt. practice profl. and personal devel., corp. and employee tng., L.A., 1976-85 ; instr. Calif. State U.

Extension, Dominguez Hills, 1977-86; Mt. St. Mary's Coll., U. of Judaism, U. So. Calif., Loyola Marymount U., 1976—; founder, dir. A-C-T Inst.; invited lectr. World Congress Behavior Therapy, Israel, Melbourne U., Australia; mem. Calif. Community Coll. Placement Assn. Mem. Calif. State U.-Dominguez Hills Alumni Assn., Women's Internat. Network (founder, 1st pres., chmn.), Inc., Assn. Advancement Behavior Therapy, Assn. Behavioral Analysis, Alpha Gamma. Author: Let's Get Growing, 1979, The New Professional Touch, 1983, 2d edit., 1988, Dr. Eve's Garden, 1984, Act, Don't React, 1985, 3d edit., 1988, The Game of the Name, 1985, newspaper columnist, 1976-79; contbr. articles to profl. jours. Home: 10600 Eastborne Ave #16 Los Angeles CA 90024 Office: PO Box 25544 Los Angeles CA 90025

CAPPELLO, GERARD KARAM, investment banker; b. Bakersfield, Calif., Mar. 19, 1961; s. Jerry Lee Cappello. BS, U. So. Calif., 1983. Mktg. agt. McCarter-Burke & Ptnrs., Irvine, Calif., 1983-85; sr. v.p. Swiss Am. Fin., Beverly Hills, Calif., 1985-87; mng. dir. Swiss Am. Landcorp, Beverly Hills, 1985-87; pres. Karam Capital Corp., Los Angeles, 1988—; dir., officer Cappello Family Group, Los Angeles, 1987—; from sr. v.p. to pres. Euro Am. Fin., Los Angeles, 1987—; bd. dirs. Flexsol Marble, Stone, Granite, Los Angeles; treas., bd. dirs. Coffees of Hawaii, Honolulu. Mem. U. So. Calif. Commerce Assocs., U. So. Calif. Alumni Assn., U. So. Calif. Gen. Alumni Assn. Republican. Roman Catholic. Office: Euro Am Fin 1888 Century Park E Ste 2000 Los Angeles CA 90067

CAPPS, ANTHONY THOMAS (CAPOZZOLO CAPPS), international public relations executive; b. Pueblo, Colo.; s. Nicolo and Anna (Solomone) Capozzolo; m. Theresa Cecelia Harmon, Nov. 12, 1945. Student, L.A. Bus. Coll., 1929-33; pvt. studies in arts, music. Dance dir., choreographer, producer motion pictures for TV and radio; featured profl. dance team Biltmore Bowl, Cocoanut Grove, Los Angeles, St. Catherine Hotel, Catalina, Calif., 1939-42; dance dir., producer NBC, ABC, Sta. KCOP-TV, Columbia Pictures, 20th Century Fox, Calif. Studios, 1940-60; exec. dir. activities Lockheed and Vega Aircraft Co., various locations, 1942-44; internat. pub. relations dir. Howard Manor, Palm Springs Key Club, 1960—, Country Club Hotel, Palm Springs Ranch Club, 1970-71, Kedes Radio, Cameron Ctr., 1971-73, Cameron Enterprises, Murietta Hot Springs Hotel, Health and Beauty Spa, 1972-73; numerous TV interviews on religion and politics, history of ballet and opera of last 500 yrs.; founder, pres., dir. Tony Capps Enterprises, Inc., Palm Springs, Calif., 1959—, chmn., exec. dir. golf and tennis tournaments, benefit dinners, govt. ofcls., various fund-raising events; mem. research council Scripps Clinic and Research Found.; chmn., founder NAAPS St. Martins Abbey and Coll.; founder St. Martins Abbey & Coll., Lacey, Wash., 1988. Columnist Desert Sun Newspapers, 1959—. Founder, co-chmn. Nat. Football Found. and Hall of Fame Golf Classic, Palm Springs; founder, pres. Capps-Cappazzolo Art Gallery, City of Hope, Duarte, Calif.; exec. dir. Alan Cranston for Senator Dinner, 1963, Edmund G. (Pat) Brown Testimonial Dinner, 1964, Progressive Jet Set Party-Nat.Cystic Fibrosis Research Found. fund raising, 1968, United Fund Gala Premier Ball, 1971; mem. Assistance League Palm Springs Desert Area, Desert Hosp., Palm Springs Desert Mus., Desert Art Ctr. of Coachella Valley, Mary and Joseph League, Eisenhower Med. Ctr, Women's Aux. Internat. Found., Boys Club of Palm Springs, Children Charity of the Desert; founder, pres. City of Hope Duarte. Mem. Nat. Artists and Art Patrons Soc. (chmn., founder), Am. Film Inst., Nat. Cystic Fibrosis Found. and Hall of Fame in Calif. (founder, pres. Tri-county chpt., founder, co-chmn. golf classic at Palm Springs), Internat. Platform Assn., Nat. Hist. Soc. Gettysburg, Nat. Trust for Historic Preservation, Smithsonian Instn., Jacques Cousteau Soc., Palm Springs Pathfinders (life), Internationale Philanthropique Societe de Gourmet (founder), Century Club. Home: 2715 Junipero Ave Palm Springs CA 92262

CAPRON, ALEXANDER MORGAN, lawyer, educator; b. Hartford, Conn., Aug. 16, 1944; s. William Mosher and Margaret (Morgan) C.; m. Barbara A. Brown, Nov. 9, 1969 (div. Dec. 1985); m. Kathleen West, Mar. 4, 1989; 1 child, Jared Capron-Brown. BA, Swarthmore Coll., 1966; LLB, Yale U., 1969; MA (hon.), U. Pa., 1975. Bar: D.C. 1970, Pa. 1978. Law clk. to presiding judge U.S. Ct. Appeals, Washington, 1969-70; lectr., research assoc. Yale U., 1970-72; asst. prof. law U. Pa., 1972-75, vice dean, 1976, assoc. prof., 1975-78, prof. law and human genetics, 1978-82; exec. dir. Pres.'s Commn. for Study of Ethical Problems in Med., Biomed. and Behavioral Rsch., Washington, 1980-83; prof. law, ethics and pub. policy Law Ctr. Georgetown U., Washington, 1983-84, inst. fellow Kennedy Inst. Ethics, 1983-84; Topping prof. law, medicine and pub. policy U. So. Calif., L.A., 1985-89, prof. law and medicine, 1989—; mem. policy adv. com. Joint Commn. Accreditation of Hosps., 1984-85; cons. NIH, Office Tech. Assessment; bd. advisors Am. Bd. Internal Medicine, 1985—; mem. subcom. on human gene therapy NIH, 1984—; chmn. Congl. Biomed. Ethics Adv. Commn., 1987—. Author: (with Katz) Catastrophic Diseases: Who Decides What?, 1976, (with others) Genetic Counseling: Facts, Values and Norms, 1979, Law, Science and Medicine, 1984, supplements, 1987, 89; contbr. articles to profl. jours. Bd. mgrs. Swarthmore Coll., 1982-85; bd. trustees Twentieth Century Fund. Fellow Hastings Ctr. (Inst. Soc. Ethics and the Life Scis., dir.); mem. Inst. of Medicine of Nat. Acad. Sci. (bd. dirs.), Soc. Am. Law Tchrs., AAUP (mem. exec. com. Pa. chpt.), Am. Soc. Law and Medicine (pres. 1988-89), Am. Coll. Legal Medicine (hon. fellow), Swarthmore Coll. Alumni Soc. (v.p. 1974-77). Office: U So Calif Law Ctr Univ Park Los Angeles CA 90089-0071

CAPUTO, KATHLEEN ANN, teacher; b. San Jose, Calif., Sept. 23, 1950; d. Henry Paul and Grace Margaret (Intravia) C. BA in English and History, San Jose State U., 1972. Cert. tchr., Calif. Tchr. Santa Clara (Calif.) Unified Sch. Dist., 1973-75, Evergreen Sch. Dist., San Jose, 1975—. Recipient various scholarships and grants in edn. Democrat. Mem. Christian Ch. Home: 3505 Pleasant Crest Dr San Jose CA 95148 Office: Evergreen Sch Dist 3799 Cadwallader Ave San Jose CA 95148

CAR, MICHAEL ANTHONY, educational administrator; b. Chgo., Mar. 7, 1946; s. Michael Luke and Velda Maxine (Essington) C.; m. Joyce Rae Reinhart, June 1964 (div. 1973); children: Wade Steven, Jarrod Lee; m. Mercedes Garcia Banez, Aug. 13, 1977; 1 child, Tamara Banez. AA, L.A. Harbor Coll., 1969; BA, Calif. State U., L.A., 1971; MA, Claremont Coll., 1974, PhD, 1977. Asst. dir. fin. aid L.A. Valley Coll., Van Nuys, Calif., 1972-74, UCLA, 1974-78; asst. dir. U. Hawaii, Honolulu, 1978-81; ops. mgr. San Diego State U., 1981-86, jud. coord., 1986—. Author (with B.L. Smith): Gone, 1972. Unit commr., Boy Scouts Am., Hawaii, 1979-81; bd. dirs. Windward Mental Health Ctr., Hawaii, 1980-81; res. peace officer, San Diego Police Dept., 1983-87; trustee, Calif. Ballet, San Diego, 1984-87. With USN, 1964-67, Vietnam. Decorated, Vietnam Cross (Republic Vietnam). Mem. DAV, Vietnam Veterans Am., Assn. Student Jud. Affairs. Republican. Roman Catholic. Home: 12675 Brickellia St San Diego CA 92129-3705 Office: San Diego State U Jud Procedures Office San Diego CA 92182-0718

CARDEN, ROBERT CLINTON, III, electrical engineer; b. Phila., Mar. 26, 1933; s. Robert Clinton and Mary Alice (Blanton) C.; B.E.E., Ga. Inst. Tech., 1955, M.S. in Elec. Engring., Ga. Inst. Tech., 1959; postgrad. UCLA, 1961-74, U. Calif.-Irvine, 1980-81; m. Mary Eleanore Clapp, Aug. 15, 1959; children—Robert Clinton IV, Linda Warren. Project engr. Bendix Radio div. Bendix Aviation, Towson, Md., 1950-57; mem. tech. staff Space Tech. Labs. TRW, 1959-62, El Segundo, Calif.; mem. tech. staff Marshall Labs., Torrance, Calif., 1962-68; founder, dir. Time Zero Corp., Torrance, 1968-71; founder, dir., mgr. engring. Comtec Data Systems div. Am. Micro Systems, Cupertino, Calif., 1971-75; engring. mgr., prin. engr. Ball Corp., Gardena, Calif., 1975-80, staff cons. Ball Corp., Huntington Beach, Calif., 1980-83; sr. staff engr. TRW Inc., Redondo Beach, Calif., 1983—; cons. engr. digital systems, 1980—; instr. in field. Served with AUS, 1957. Mem. Am. Rocket Soc., IEEE, Computer Soc., Ga. Tech. Alumni Assn., Tau Beta Pi, Eta Kappa Nu, Scabbard and Blade, Chi Phi. Republican. Presbyterian. Research in digital space systems. Author, producer: Space for the Everyday Man, 1978; contbr. articles to profl. jours. Home: 1217 N Kennymead St Orange CA 92669 Office: TRW Inc 1 Space Park 105/2810 Redondo Beach CA 90278

CÁRDENAS, RENÉ, television executive, demographer; b. San Francisco, Feb. 13, 1928; s. Lauro and Maria (Ball) C.; m. Doris F. Marino, June 7, 1952; children—Rene, Kevin, Gregory. Ph.D. in Cultural Anthropology, U. Calif.-Berkeley, 1970. Producer, writer Villa Alegre, Oakland, Calif., 1970-81; mgr. Kingston Trio, 1959-69; with Stanford Research, Inc., 1956, Ampex Corp., San Juan, P.R., 1957-59; pres. BCTV, San Leandro, Calif., 1969—; adj. prof. sch. edn. U. Mass., Amherst, 1986—; cons. U.S. Office Edn., 1971-72, Office Mgmt. and Budget, 1972-73, White House, 1974-75, also fed. govt. agys. Served with USNR, 1941-48. Grantee Exxon USA Found., 1973-76, Ford Found., 1972, Lilly Endowment Found., 1975-76, HUD, 1978, Dept. Labor, 1972-73, Levi Strauss Corp., 1975; named Hon. Col. N.Mex.; Hon. Citizen Okla.; recipient Tex. Silver Spur award, 1975; NEA Humanitarian award, 1974; recognition Calif. State Legislature for outstanding ednl. achievement in broadcasting; 4 Emmys, 1977, 79, 80, 81. Mem. Nat. Acad. TV Arts and Scis. Democrat. Club: Oakland Athletic. Author: Parenting in a Multi Cultural Society, 1980; contbr. numerous articles on edn. of culturally disadvantaged child to profl. jours. Home: 4265 Bemis St Oakland CA 94605 Office: BCTV 155 Callan Ave San Leandro CA 94605

CARDINE, GODFREY JOSEPH, state supreme court chief justice; b. Prairie Du Chien, Wis., July 6, 1924; s. Joseph Frederick and Mary (Kasparek) C.; m. Janice Irene Brown, Sept. 14, 1946; children—Susan, John, Lisa. B.S. in Engring., U. Ill., 1948; J.D. with honors, U. Wyo., 1954. Bar: Wyo. 1954, U.S. Dist. Ct. Wyo. 1954, U.S. Ct. Appeals (10th cir.) 1954. Assoc. Schwartz, Bon & McCrary, Casper, Wyo., 1954-66; dist. atty. Natrona County, Wyo., 1966-70; ptnr. Cardine, Vlastos & Reeves, Casper, 1966-77; prof. law U. Wyo., Laramie, 1977-83; justice Wyo. Supreme Ct., Cheyenne, 1983-88, chief justice, 1988—; mem. Wyo. State Bd. Law Examiners, 1973-77; faculty, dir. Western Trial Advocacy Inst., Laramie, 1981—; bd. advisors Land and Water Law Rev., 1985—; mem. ad hoc com. to rev. bar assn. rules and by-laws, 1987-88. Contbr. articles to profl. jours. Active Little League Baseball, Casper, 1960-62; mem. Gov.'s Com. on Dangerous Drugs, 1968-71. Served to 1st lt. USAF, 1943-46, PTO. Fellow Internat. Soc. Barristers; mem. ABA (judicial adminstrn. div.), Assn. Trial Lawyers Am., Wyo. State Bar (pres. 1977-78, minor cts. com. 1968-71), Chi Epsilon, Phi Alpha Delta. Club: Potter Law (pres. 1953-54). Lodge: Rotary. Home: PO Box 223 Cheyenne WY 82003 Office: Wyo Supreme Ct Supreme Ct Bldg Cheyenne WY 82002

CARDOZA, DESDEMONA, academic administrator; b. Copenhagen, Denmark, Dec. 13, 1953; d. Ricardo Seañez and Minna Ploug (Christoffersen) C.; m. Rodolfo Morales Jr., Nov. 25, 1978. BA, U. Calif., Berkeley, 1975; MA, U. Calif., Riverside, 1979, PhD, 1982. Dir. of research Nat. Ctr. for Bilingual Research, Los Alamitos, Calif., 1982-86; dir. of research and evaluation UCLA, 1986-87; dir. analytical studies Calif. State U., Los Angeles, 1987-88, asst. v.p. info. resource mgmt., 1988—; cons. L.A. County Mental Health, 1985-86, Market Opinion Research, Detroit, 1982-85. Contbr.: book, In Times of Challenge: Chicanos and Chicana in American Society, 1988. Mem. Am. Psychol. Assn., Am. Edn. Research Assn., Evaluation Research Soc., Soc. for the Psychol. Study of Social Issues, Phi Beta Kappa. Office: Calif State U 5151 State University Dr Los Angeles CA 90032

CARDOZA, FRANK RICHARD, III, social services administrator, cattle rancher; b. Hayward, Calif., May 8, 1949; s. Frank Richard Sr. and Adeline Mary (Klinkhammer) C. AB, St. Mary's Coll., Moraga, Calif., 1971; MA, So. Oreg. State Coll., 1989. Cert. alcohol and drug counselor. Continuing care coordinator Siskiyou County Mental Health, Yreka, Calif., 1975-82; substance abuse program coordinator Siskiyou County Alcohol and Drug Abuse Services, Yreka, 1982—; ptnr. Cardoza Ranch, Big Springs, Calif., 1974—; bd. dirs. Siskiyou Perinatel Task Force, Mt. Shasta, Calif., Klamath River Service Providers Interagy. Task Force, Happy Camp, Calif., Ancient Forest League. Mem. Calif. Assn. Alcohol and Drug Abuse Counselors, Calif. Assn. Drug Adminstrs., Calif. Cattleman's Assn., Mt. Shasta Trail Assn. (sec. 1988), Marble Mountain Audobon Soc., Siskiyou County Cattleman's Assn., Siskiyou County Employees Assn. (v.p. 1988—). Democrat. Buddhist. Home: 3702 Louie Rd Montague CA 96064 Office: Siskiyou County Alcohol and Drug Svcs 804 S Main St Yreka CA 96064

CARDWELL, WILLIAM RICHARD, engineering executive; b. Nashville, Mar. 25, 1934; s. Arthur Henry and Margaret Lucille (Kimbrough) C.; m. Sharon Gay Little, June 6, 1960 (div. Jan. 1976); children: Lee Ellen Koch, Leslie Susan, Scott William, Matthew Richard. BSEE, U. Tenn., 1960; MSEE, MIT, 1963. Engring. area mgr. IBM Corp., Lexington, Ky., 1960-73; mgr. engring. copier systems IBM Corp., Boulder, Colo., 1973-79; v.p. engring. Mead Office Systems, Dallas, 1979-84, Savin Corp., Binghamton, N.Y., 1984-86; chmn., chief exec. officer Sunburst Tech., Inc., Binghamton, N.Y., 1986-87; v.p. engring. Office Automation Systems, San Diego, 1987—. Author and patentee: Support for Planar Electronics, 1967, Document Feeder, 1977. Served with USN, 1952-56. Mem. Sigma Phi Epsilon. (v.p. 1958-59). Office: Office Automation Systems 9940 Barnes Cnyn Rd San Diego CA 92121

CAREY, DIANE LEWIS, nurse; b. Tucson, July 15, 1937; d. Donald Burns and Harriet (Barcroft) Lewis; m. Lawrence Lattomus, Mar. 15, 1960 (div. 1973); children: Jennifer Lattomus Donley, Jeffrey Lewis. BS in Nursing, U. Penn., Phila., 1959. Office nurse Pvt. Doctors Office-Dermatology, Beverly Hills, Calif., 1959; nurse Reese Stealy Clinic, San Diego, 1960-62; nurse cons. Head Start Program, Muncie, Ind., 1967-69; elem. jr. high nurse Tucson Unified Sch. Dist., 1969-79; high sch. nurse Tucson Unified Sch. Dist., 1979—; team coord. Substance Abuse Com., Sabino High Sch., Tucson, 1983—. Recipient Outstanding Women's Eastern A.A.U. Diver Helen C. Morgan Meml. Mem. Tucson Edn. Assn., Ariz. Sch. Health Assn., Sch. Nurses Orgn. Ariz. Republican. Presbyterian. Home: 8543 Haverhill Ln Tucson AZ 85715

CAREY, KATHRYN ANN, corporate philanthropy, advertising and public relations executive, editor, consultant; b. Los Angeles, Oct. 18, 1949; d. Frank Randall and Evelyn Mae (Walmsley) C.; m. Richard Kenneth Sundt, Dec. 28, 1980. BA in Am. Studies with honors, Calif. State U.-Los Angeles, 1971. Tutor Calif. Dept. Vocat. Rehab., Los Angeles, 1970; teaching asst. U. So. Calif., 1974-75, UCLA, 1974-75; claims adjuster Auto Club So. Calif., San Gabriel, 1971-73; corp. pub. relations cons. Carnation Co., Los Angeles, 1973-78; cons., adminstr. Carnation Community Service Award Program, 1973-78; pub. relations cons. Vivitar Corp.; sr. advt. asst. Am. Honda Motor Co., Gardena, Calif., 1978-84; exec. dir. Am. Honda Found., 1984—; mgr. Honda Dealer Advt. Assns.; cons. advt., pub. relations, promotions. Editor: Vivitar Voice, Santa Monica, Calif., 1978, Honda Views, 1978-84, Found. Focus, 1984—; asst. editor Friskies Research Digest; contbg. editor Newsbriefs, Am. Honda Motor Co., Inc. employees mag.; Calif. Life Scholarship Found. scholar, 1967. Mem. Advt. Club Los Angeles, Pub. Relations Soc. Am., So. Calif. Assn. Philanthropy, Council Founds. of Washington, Aircraft Owners and Pilots Assn., Ninety-Nines, Am. Quarter Horse Assn., Los Angeles Soc. for Prevention Cruelty to Animals, Greenpeace, German Shepherd Dog Club Am., Ocicats Internat., Am. Humane Assn., Elsa Wild Animal Appeal. Avocation: private pilot. Democrat. Methodist. Office: Am Honda Found 700 Van Ness Ave Torrance CA 90509-2205

CAREY, MARCIA J., service executive; b. Willmar, Minn., Feb. 13, 1941; d. Franklin N. and Thelma L (Portinga) Fanberg; m. Donald L. Carey, June 23, 1962 (div. May 1976); children: Michelle C., Matthew S. Student, Trinity Coll., 1959-61, Calif. State U., Chico., 1961-62. Cert. med. transcriptionist; accredited record technician. Med. transcriptionist Hillcrest Hosp., Petaluma, Calif., 1972-73; med. care evaluation coordinator Santa Teresa Community Hosp., San Jose, Calif., 1973-79; med. transcriptionist San Jose, 1979-84; dir. pub. relations Dictation West, South San Francisco, Calif., 1984-85, dir. ops., 1985-87; pres. United Transcription Services, San Jose, 1987—. Mem. Am. Assn. Med. Transcription, (treas. 1981, v.p. 1982, bd. dirs. 1979-82, pres. South Bay chpt. 1979-81, 85-86), Am. Med. Record Assn. Home: 6283 Channel Dr San Jose CA 95123 Office: United Transcription Svcs 5899 Santa Teresa Blvd San Jose CA 95123

CAREY, PETER KEVIN, reporter; b. San Francisco, Apr. 2, 1940; s. Paul Twohig and Stanleigh M. (White) C.; m. Joanne Dayl Barker, Jan. 7, 1978; children: Brendan Patrick, Nadia Marguerite. BS in Econs., U. Calif., Berkeley, 1964. Reporter San Francisco Examiner, 1964; reporter Livermore (Calif.) Ind., 1965-67, editor, 1967; aerospace writer, spl. projects and investigative reporter San Jose (Calif.) Mercury, 1967—. Recipient Pulitzer Prize for Internat. Reporting, Columbia U., 1986, George Polk award L.I. U., 1986, Investigative Reporters and Editors award, 1986, Jessie Meriton White Service award Friends World Coll., 1986, Calif.-Nev. UPI Editors Assn. Newspaper award, 1985, Mark Twain award Calif.-Nev. AP, 1983, Best Bus. Story award San Francisco Press Club, 1984, Best Daily News Story award San Francisco Press Club, 1982; profl. journalism fellow NEH, 1983-84. Mem. Soc. Profl. Journalists. Office: San Jose Mercury-News 750 Ridder Park Dr San Jose CA 95190

CARGILE, PAT KAYE, insurance agency executive; b. Hobbs, N.Mex., Aug. 31, 1938; d. Ralph Eugene and Virgie Augusta (Denton) Beard; m. Hulin Woodrow Cargile, Sept. 21, 1957 (div. 1987); children: Zane Edward, Colleen Elaine, Melissa Evelyn. Grad. high sch. Cert. ins. counselor; assoc. in risk management. With Daniels Ins., Inc., Hobbs, N.Mex., 1962—; sr. v.p. Daniels Ins., Inc., 1980—. Mem. Lea County Insurers (pres.), Lea County Ins. Women (pres.), Soc. Cert. Ins. Counselors Ins. Inst. Am. Office: Daniels Ins Inc 300 N Linam St Hobbs NM 88240

CARIÑO, FELIPE, computer scientist; b. Bronx, N.Y., Feb. 5, 1956; s. Felipe and Manuela (Rios) C. BA in Math. and Computer Sci., NYU, 1977, MS in Computer Sci., 1979. Mem. tech. staff AT&T Bell Labs, Piscataway, N.J., 1977-80; sr. systems programmer Fairchild Test Systems, San Jose, Calif., 1980-81; staff engr. Ampex Corp., Redwood City, Calif., 1982-84; program mgr. CounterPoint Computers, Sunnyvale, Calif., 1984-86; pres., chief exec. officer HeteroLink Corp., Sunnyvale, 1986-87; advisor, chief scientist Teradata Corp., L.A., 1987—. Contbg. author Office Systems: Methods and Tools, 1986. Founding mem. Puerto Rican Western Region Polit. Action Com., San Jose, 1988. Mem. IEEE, Am. Assn. for Artificial Intelligence, Assn. for Computing Machinery, Math. Assn. Am., Soc. Hispanic Profl. Engrs. Republican. Roman Catholic. Office: Teradata Corp 12945 Jefferson Blvd Los Angeles CA 90066

CARLE, HARRY LLOYD, social worker, career devel. specialist; b. Chgo., Oct. 26, 1927; s. Lloyd Benjamin and Clara Bell (Lee) C.; B.S.S., Seattle U., 1952; M.S.W., U. Wash., 1966; m. Elva Diana Ulrich, Dec. 29, 1951; adopted children: Joseph Francis, Catherine Marie; m. 2d, Karlen Elizabeth Howe, Oct. 14, 1967; children: Kristen Elizabeth and Sylvia Ann (twins), Eric Lloyd. Indsl. placement and employer relations rep. State of Wash., Seattle, 1955-57, parole and probation officer, Seattle and Tacoma, 1957-61, parole employment specialist, 1961-63, vocat. rehab. officer, 1963-64; clin. social worker Western State Hosp., Ft. Steilacoom, Washington and U.S. Penitentiary, McNeil Island, Wash., 1964-66; exec. dir. Community Action Council/Social Planning Council, Everett, Wash., 1966-77; career devel. counselor, 1962—; employment and edn. counselor Pierce County Jail Social Services, Tacoma, 1979-81; dir. employment devel. clinic North Rehab. Facility, King County Div. Alcoholism & Substance Abuse, Seattle, 1981—; community orgn./agy. problems mgmt. cons., 1968—; mem. social service project staff Pacific Luth. U., Tacoma, 1979-81. Olympia (Wash.) Japanese Garden; cons. to pres. Geneal. Inst., Salt Lake City, 1974-78. Served with USN, 1944-46. U.S. Office Vocat. Rehab. scholar, 1965-66. Mem. Seattle Geneal. Soc. (pres. 1974-76), Soc. Advancement Mgmt. (chpt. exec. v.p. 1970-71), Acad. Cert. Social Workers, Nat. Assn. Social Workers, Pa. German Soc., Henckel Family Nat. Assn., various hist. and geneal. socs. in Cumberland, Perry and Lancaster counties, Pa., Peoria and Fulton Counties, Ill., Seattle Japanese Garden Soc., Olympia-Yashiro Sister City Assn., Puget Sound Koi Soc., Dr. Sun Yat-sen Garden Soc. Vancouver. Roman Catholic. Home: 1425 10th Pl N Edmonds WA 98020-2629 Office: North Rehab Facility 2002 NE 150th St Seattle WA 98155-7399

CARLEONE, JOSEPH, mechanical engineer; b. Phila., Jan. 30, 1946; s. Frank Anthony and Amelia (Ciaccia) C.; m. Shirley Elizabeth Atwell, June 29, 1968; children: Gia Maria, Joan Marie. BS, Drexel U., 1968, MS, 1970, PhD, 1972. Civilian engring. trainee, mech. engr. Phila. Naval Shipyard, 1963-68; grad. asst. in applied mechanics Drexel U., Phila., 1968-72, postdoctoral rsch. assoc., 1972-73, NDEA fellow, 1968-71, adj. prof. mechanics, 1974-75, 77-82; chief rsch. engr. Dyna East Corp., Phila., 1973-82; chief scientist warhead tech. Aerojet Ordnance Co., Tustin, Calif., 1982-88. v.p., gen. mgr. warhead systems div. GenCorp. Aerojet Precision Weapons, Tustin, 1988— . Mem. ASME, Sigma Xi, Tau Beta Pi, Pi Tau Sigma, Phi Kappa Phi. Contbr. articles to profl. jours.; researcher explosive and metal interaction, ballistics, projectile penetration, impact of plates. Home: 19741 Marsala Dr Yorba Linda CA 92686 Office: Aerojet Precision Weapons 2521 Michelle Dr Tustin CA 92680

CARLEY, JOHN BLYTHE, retail grocery executive; b. Spokane, Wash., Jan. 4, 1934; s. John Lewis and Freida June (Stiles) C.; m. Joan Marie Hohenleitner, Aug. 6, 1960; children: Christopher, Kathryn, Peter, Scott. AA, Boise Jr. Coll., 1955; student, U. Wash., 1956-57, Stanford U. Exec. Program, 1973. Store dir. Albertson's Inc., Boise, Idaho, 1961-65, grocery merchandiser, 1965-70, dist. mgr., 1970-73, v.p. gen. mdse., 1973, v.p. corp. merchandising, 1973-75, v.p. retail ops., 1975-76, sr. v.p. retail ops., 1976-77, exec. v.p. retail ops., 1977-84, pres., 1984—, also dir. Active fund-raising drives United Way. Served with U.S. Army, 1957-59. Mem. Am. Mgmt. Assn., Food Mktg. Inst. Republican. Roman Catholic. Clubs: Arid, Hillcrest Country (Boise). Office: Albertson's Inc 250 Parkcenter Blvd PO Box 20 Boise ID 83726 *

CARLEY, KAREN FAY, fabric shop owner; b. Malta, Mont., June 23, 1958; d. Lowell A. and Fay B. (Smith) Smith; m. John A. Carley, Oct. 20, 1984. BSBA, Adams State Coll., 1979. Mgr. trainee K-Mart, Denver, 1979-80; acctg. supr. San Juan Coll., Farmington, N.Mex., 1980-83; owner, mgr. The Fabric and Drapery Shop, Truth or Consequences, N.Mex., 1983—. Republican. Methodist. Home and Office: 4601 Woodlands Apt 111 Vernon TX 76384

CARLIN, BRUCE MICHAEL, financial executive; b. Los Angeles, Jan. 8, 1952; s. Robert and Esther (Jayne) C.; m. Marilyn Gurevitch, May 9, 1976; children: Rita, Valerie. BS, U. Calif., Berkeley, 1974, MBA, 1975. Mgr. corp. fin. planning Pacificorp, Oreg., 1976-84; mgmt. cons. Mgmt. Analysis Co., San Diego, 1984-88; pres. Nielsen Capital Group, Inc., 1989; cons. in field. Author: Testimony, 1987. mem. Constrn. Fin. Mgmt. Assn.

CARLISLE, KEVIN BRUCE, choreographer, director, producer; b. Bklyn., Dec. 24, 1935; s. Theodore Daily and Ruth (Bardell) C. Degree, Juilliard Sch. Music, N.Y.C., 1956, Doctorate Sierra U., 1987. Choreographer Garry Moore Show, Dean Martin Show, Bell Telephone Hour; producer, dir., choreographer numerous TV series and variety spls. including Barry Manilow, Rich Little, Dionne Warwick, Michael Landon, Herb Alpert, Doris Day, Bea Arthur, Bob Hope, Bill Cosby, Sha Na Na, Mother/Daughter Pageant, 1987, John Sebastian Special, 1986, Barry Manilow in Japan, 1985, Dream Girl USA, Siempre Domingo Show, Vienna TV spl.; dir., choreographer live shows including Paul Anka, Shaun Cassidy, Melissa Manchester, Barry Manilow, Shields and Yarnell, Liberace, George Burns, Judy Garland, Barry Manilow Tour 1979, 86, Robert Guillaume, 1985-87, Marilyn McCoo, 1984-87, Cathy Rigby, 1985-86, Solid Gold in Veyas, 1984, 85; creator Solid Gold Dancers, 1979; pres. Kevin Carlisle and Assocs., Hollywood, Calif.; choreographer, dir. Broadway, Barry Manilow on Broadway, 1983, Harry Blackstone Jr. On Broadway, 1980, Hallelujah Baby, Happy Time, Tammy Wynette, 1984, Melissa Manchester, 1984, Marilyn McCoo, 1984-89, Solid Gold Las Vegas Riviera, 1984, Videos, Debbie Reynolds Exercise Video, 1983, Barry Manilow, 1983, Solid Gold Dancers 5 Day

Workout, 1984, Exercise in the Flesh, 1984, Suzanne Somers Exercise Video, 1987, Joe Tremaine's Dance, 1985, 86, 87, 88, 89 (Am. Video Conf. award for best dance instrn. 1988), Barry Manilow: Big Fun on Swing Street, 1987, Pee Wee's Christmas Spl., 1988, Julie and Carol: Together Again, 1989; , Barry Manilow: Barry at the Gershwin Showtime Spl., 1989, Barry Manilow: Broadway Show at the Gershwin, 1989; dir., choreographer stage and TV in Can., Belgium, Germany, France, Eng., Italy, Mex., Spain, Bora Bora; dir., choreographer various commls. and indsl. shows. Recipient Emmy award for Third Barry Manilow TV Spl., 1979; creator book and video The 5 Midnight Worker with Sandy Duncan, 1989. Home and Office: 1647 Woods Dr Los Angeles CA 90069

CARLSBERG, RICHARD PRESTEN, real estate corporation executive; b. Stockton, Calif., Mar. 2, 1937; s. Arthur Walter and Lillian Marie (Presten) C.; m. Barbara Ann Hearn, June 28, 1959; children: David Arthur, Rebecca Jane, Dawn Marie. Student, City Coll. San Francisco, 1954-56, U. San Francisco, 1955; BA in Geology, UCLA, 1959. Lic. broker securities, real estate. Officer and/or dir. various pvt. corps. in fields of real estate, fin., devel., research, petroleum 1961—; pres., founder Carlsberg Fin. Corp., Santa Monica, Calif., 1972—; pres. Carlsberg Corp., 1971-86; founder Carlsberg Mgmt. Co., 1975-85. Contbr. articles to profl. jours. Bd. dirs. UCLA Found., Calif. Pines Youth Found., Soc. of Blue Shield; past trustee Hollywood Presbyn. Hosp., L.A. Mus. Natural History; mem. UCLA Assocs., Pepperdine U. Assocs., L.A Craft and Folk Art Mus.; numerous others. Served with Air Force N.G., 1959-65. Recipient awards Los Angeles County, 1965, resolution Calif. Legislature, 1965, 71, commendations County of Los Angeles, 1971, commendations U.S. Dept. Interior, 1971; named one of Outstanding Young Men in Am., 1971. Mem. Mem. World Bus. Council. Presbyterian. Clubs: So. Calif. Safari, Safari Club Internat, Game Coin, Boone, Crockett, various conservation groups including Ducks Unlimited. Office: 2800 28th St Santa Monica CA 90405

CARLSEN, DOUGLAS MICHAEL, dentist; b. Yakima, Wash., Nov. 26, 1950; s. Joseph B. and Eleanore A. (Berner) C.; m. Lynette M. Degani, Aug. 18, 1984. AB in Chemistry, Occidental Coll., 1972; DDS, UCLA, 1977; resident cert., U. of the Pacific, 1978. Dental lic., Calif., N.Mex. Pvt. practice dentistry Albuquerque, 1979—; dental cons. Manzano Del Sol Hosp., Albuquerque, 1979-84. Mem. Civitan, Rio Rancho, N.Mex., 1980-83, Elks Club, Rio Rancho, 1980-81; singer N.Mex. Symphony Orch., Albuquerque, 1980-86. Lt. USPHS, 1978-79. Project Link-Inner City Child Devel. Program grantee Occidental Coll., 1971-72. Mem. N.Mex. Acad. Dental Implantology, Horizon Dental Acad. Soc. (pres. 1985-86), Albuquerque Dental Soc., N.Mex. Dental Soc., Am. Dental Soc., Delta Sigma Delta. Home: 1563 Eagle Ridge Ct NE Albuquerque NM 87122 Office: 3615 Rio Rancho Blvd NW Corrales NM 87048

CARLSMITH, LYN KUCKENBERG, psychologist; b. Portland, Oreg., Oct. 7, 1932; d. Henry Andrew and Harriet Anne (Casey) Kuckenberg; m. James Merrill Carlsmith, July 27, 1963 (dec. 1984); children: Christopher, Kimberly, Kevin. BA in Internat. Relations, Stanford U., 1954, MA in Psychology, 1959; PhD in Psychology, Harvard U., 1963. Manuscript editor Mid-European Studies, N.Y.C., 1955-57; research assoc. Yale U., New Haven, 1963-64; research assoc. Stanford (Calif.) U., 1964-68, lectr. psychology, 1969-71, sr. lectr. psychology, 1978—; counseling psychologist Social Advocates for Youth, Mountain View, Calif., 1973-79; adv. bd. The Bridge Counseling Ctr., Stanford, 1983—, Action Research Liaison Office, Stanford, 1977-79. Bd. dirs. Ladera Community Assn., Portola Valley, Calif., 1975-78. Mem. Sierra Club. Office: Stanford U Dept Psychology Bldg 420 Stanford CA 94305

CARLSON, DALE ARVID, university dean; b. Aberdeen, Wash., Jan. 10, 1925; s. Edwin C.G. and Anna A. (Anderson) C.; m. Jean M. Stanton, Nov. 11, 1948; children—Dale Ronald, Gail L. Carlson Manahan Joan M. Carlson Lee, Gwen D. Carlson Elliott. A.A., Grays Harbor Coll., 1947; B.S. in Civil Engring, U. Wash., 1950, M.S., 1951; Ph.D., U. Wis., 1960. Registered profl. engr., Wash. Water engr. City of Aberdeen, 1951-55; asst. prof., assoc. prof., prof., chmn. dept. civil engring. U. Wash., Seattle, 1955-76; dean (Coll Engring.) U. Wash., 1976-80, dean emeritus, 1980—, dir. Valle Scandinavian Exchange Program, 1980—; chmn. dept. civil engring. Seattle U., 1983-88; vis. prof. Tech. U. Denmark, Copenhagen, 1970, Royal Coll. Agr., Uppsala, Sweden, 1976, 78. Contbr. articles to profl. jours. Mem. exec. bd. Pacific N.W. Synod Luth. Ch. in Am., chmn. fin. com., 1980-84, treas., 1986-87; bd. edn., fin. com. Evang. Luth. Ch. in Am., 1987—; v.p. Nat. Luth. Campus Ministry, 1988—; mem. exec. bd. Nordic Heritage Mus., 1981-86; bd. dirs. Evergreen Safety Council, 1980-86. Served with AUS, 1943-45. Named Outstanding Grad. Weatherwax High Sch., Aberdeen, 1972, Outstanding Grad. Grays Harbor Coll., 1947; guest of honor Soppeldagene, Trondheim, 1978. Mem. Water Pollution Control Fedn., ASCE, Am. Water Works Assn., Am. Scandinavian Found., Swedish Water Hygiene Assn. Club: Rotary. Home: 9235 41st St NE Seattle WA 98115 Office: U Wash 335 More Hall Seattle WA 98195

CARLSON, GARY LEE, public relations executive, director, producer; b. Yakima, Wash., Oct. 15, 1954; s. Glenn Elmer and Helen Mary (McLean) Carlson. AA, Yakima Community Coll., 1975; BA in Communications, U. Wash., 1977. Dir. pub. affairs Sta. KCMU, Seattle, 1976-77; dir. programming and promotions Sta. KAPP-TV, Yakima, 1978-80; dir. promotions Sta. WBZ-TV, Boston, 1980-84; producer Sta. KCBS-TV, Los Angeles, 1985; dir. creative services Metromedia Producers, Los Angeles, 1985-86; dir. promotion publicity 20th Century Fox, Los Angeles, 1986—. Producer, dir.: M*A*S*H* 15th Ann. Campaign, 1987 (Internat. Film and TV Festival N.Y. award), The Fox Tradition, 1988 (Internat. Film and TV Festival N.Y. award, Clio Finalist award, 1988, Telly award, 1988, B.P.M.E. award, 1988); producer, writer, dir. Consumer Reports, 1983 (Internat. Film and TV Festival N.Y. award, Houston Internat. Film and TV award). Mem. Broadcast Promotion and Mktg. Execs., Nat. Assn. TV Program Execs., Beta Theta Pi. Home: 1510 Rockglen Ave Glendale CA 91205 Office: 20th Century Fox Film Corp 10201 W Pico Blvd Century City CA 90035

CARLSON, GEORGE ARTHUR, artist; b. Elmhurst, Ill., July 3, 1940; s. William Emanuel and Mathilda Katherine (Jorgensen) C.; m. Pamela Gustavson Hatzenbiler, May 9, 1981; children: Solon Emil, Andra Sean, Erin Hatzenbiler Vaughan, Eric Hatzenbiler. Student, Art Inst. Chgo., Am. Acad. Art, Chgo., U. Ariz., Tucson. One man exhbns. include Indpls. Mus. Art, 1979, 85, Smithsonian Inst., Washington, 1982, Southwest Mus., L.A., 1988; one man shows include Saks Gallery, Colorado Springs, Colo., 1972, Kennedy Galleries, N.Y.C., 1976, Bishop Galleries, Scottsdale, Ariz., 1977, Stremmel Galleries, Reno, 1978, 81, Grand Cen. Galleries, N.Y.C., 1980, O'Grady Galleries, Chgo., 1983, Gerald Peters Gallery, Santa Fe, N.Mex., 1985, Gerald Peters Gallery, Dallas, 1987; featured in group exhbns. including Phoenix Art Mus., Denver Art Mus., Denver Natural History Mus., Penrose Library at U. Denver, Gillette Pub. Library, Wyoming, Nat. Acad. Western Art, Oklahoma City, 1973-87, The Peking Exhibit, Beijing, Peoples Republic of China, 1981, Artists of Am. Show, Denver, 1981-87, Nat. Sculpture Soc., N.Y.C., 1982-83, 86, Mus. Western Art, Denver, 1985, Gilcrease Mus., Tulsa, 1985, Ft. Smith (Okla.) Art Ctr., 1986, Kyoto (Japan) World Expn. Hist. Cities, 1987, Sonoma County Mus., Santa Rosa, Calif., 1987, Western & Wildlife Mus., Jackson Hole, Wyo., 1988; represented in pub. and corp. collections including Indpls. Mus., Genesee Mus., Rochester, N.Y., Denver Pub. Library, Denver Natural History Mus., Los Angeles Athletic Club, Cherokee Nat. Hist. Soc., Chakota, Okla., Corning (N.Y.) Mus., Anshutz Collection, Denver, Outdoor Mus. Art, Denver, Rockwell Mus., Pitts., Valley Bank of Nev., Las Vegas, Boatmans Bankshare, Inc., St. Louis, Brownsville (Tex.) Nat. Bank, Mountain States Bank, Denver, Rocky Mountain Bank, Denver, Sierra Nev. Arts Mus., Reno, Nat. Cowboy Hall of Fame, Oklahoma City; represented in various pvt. collections; sculptures include Bill Cosby, 1979, Bill Harrah, 1981, Early Day Miner, Washington Park, Denver, 1980, Of One Heart, Genesee Country Mus., 1982, Of One Heart, Mus. of Outdoor Arts, Englewood, Colo., 1985, I'm the Drum, Gerald Peters Gallery, Santa Fe, 1987, The Greeting, Genesee Mus., 1988, Eiteljorg Mus., 1989; featured in various bibliographies and films. Served with USAR, 1963-69. Mem. Nat. Sculpture Soc., Nat. Acad. Western Art (Gold medal 1974, 78, 80, 85, Best of Show 1975, Silver medal 1976, 81, 88). Address: Route 2 Box 283 Saint Maries ID 83861

CARLSON, HELEN MARIE, health care administrator; b. St. Paul, Oct. 3, 1950; d. Paul Arnold and Eleanor (Jacobson) C. BA in Psychology, San Diego State U., 1976; MBA, Nat. U., 1984. Analyst U. Calif., San Diego, 1980-82; dir. outpatient services U. Calif. Med. Ctr., San Diego, 1982-85; adminstr. immed. care svcs. Eisenhower Med. Ctr., Rancho Mirage, Calif., 1985—. Named Woman of Distinction, Soroptimist Internat., La Quinta, Calif., 1988. Mem. La Quinta C. of C., Assn. Western Hosps., Med. Group Mgmt. Assn., Employers Adv. Group, Riverside County, Assn. Ambulatory Care Profls., Calif. Employer Council (legis. rep. region 7). Republican. Office: Eisenhower Med Ctr 39000 Bob Hope Dr Rancho Mirage CA 92270

CARLSON, KENNETH ALVIN, investment company executive, consultant; b. Deadwood, S.D., July 11, 1943; s. Leonard Eric and LeRoye C. (Crane) C.; m. Dana Holst, Dec. 27, 1964; children: Slade, Heath, Britt. BS, Iowa State U., 1965. Lic. real estate broker, Ariz. Sales engr. Hupp Corp.; owner Lewis & Kiriceby Real Estate; broker Realty Execs., Scottsdale, Ariz., 1984-86; pres. Sun Country Group Inc., Scottsdale, 1986—. Contbr. articles to trade mags. Mem. Ariz. Multihousing Assn. (bd. dirs. 1986-88), Nat. Corvette Restorers Soc. (pres. Phoenix 1984-88), Toastmasters, Epsilon Pi Tau. Home and Office: 8lll E Carol Way Scottsdale AZ 85260

CARLSON, MARC R(OLAND), lawyer; b. Pensacola, Fla., Jan. 21, 1946; s. Maurice Raymond and Edna Alvina (Schneider) C.; m. Donna Kay Reese, Mar. 21, 1970; children: Matthew Ryan, Katherine Nicole. BS with distinction, U. Kans., 1968; JD, U. Colo., 1973. Bar: Colo. 1973. Tchr. Oak Park High Sch., North Kansas City, Mo., 1968-69, Ft. Collins (Colo.) High Sch., 1969-70; dep. dist. atty. City of Denver, 1973-75; assoc. Moore & Carlson, Ft. Collins, 1975, Atler, Zall & Haligman, Denver, 1976-78; ptnr. Grant, McCarren & Bernard, Longmont, Colo., 1978-83, Hopp, Carlson & Beckmann, Longmont, 1984—; lectr. on revelations, cults, resurrection, wills, trusts, and estate planning, Longmont and Boulder, Colo. Adult Sunday sch. tchr. 1st Christian Ch., Longmont. Mem. ABA, Colo. Bar Assn., Boulder County Bar Assn., Colo. Trial Lawyers Assn., Longmont C. of C., Men's Golf Assn. (past pres.), Fox Hill Country Club, Rotary. Republican. Home: 81 Baylor Dr Longmont CO 80501 Office: 2130 Mountain View Ave Longmont CO 80501

CARLSON, MARY REBECCA, university administrator; b. Seattle, July 5, 1955; d. Paul Benjamin and Ruth (Fulton) Carlson. BA in Bus. Adminstrn. and Acctg. magna cum laude, U. Wash., 1976. CPA, Alaska. Staff acct. Bigler, Hawkins & Obendorf, CPA's, Anchorage, 1976-78; sr. acct. Coopers & Lybrand, Anchorage, 1978-80; acctg. svcs. mgr. U. Alaska, Anchorage, 1980-83; fin. statement acct. U. Alaska, Fairbanks, 1983, dir. acctg. svcs., 1983-87; dir. fiscal svcs. We. Wash. U., Bellingham, 1987--. Bd. dirs. YWCA, Bellingham, 1988--. Mem. Am. Soc. Women Accts., Am. Inst. CPA's, Alaska Soc. CPA's, AAUW, Soroptomist club. Lutheran.

CARLSON, NANCY LEE, English language educator; b. Spokane, Wash., June 1, 1950; d. Alfred William and Geneva May (Conniff) C. BS, Wash. State U., 1973; MEd, curriculum specialist, Ea. Wash. U., 1987. Tchr. Stevenson-Carson Sch. Dist., Wash., 1973-74, Spokane Sch. Dist., 1974—. Spokane County co-chmn. Sen. Slade Gorton campaign, 1988; Rep. precinct committeeperson, 1988; bd. dirs. Spokane Civic Theater, 1986—, Spokane Human Services Adv. Bd., 1986—; treas. Inland Empire for Africa, Spokane, 1985-86; vice chmn. ea. Wash. phone bank for Sen. Dan Evans, Spokane, 1984. Mem. NEA, Nat. Council Tchrs. English, Wash. Council Tchrs. English, Assn. for Supervision and Curriculum Devel., Am. Mgmt. Assn., Wash. State U. Alumni Assn. (area rep. 1987—). Republican. Presbyterian. Office: Sch Dist #81 Rogers High Sch E 1622 Wellesley Spokane WA 99207

CARLSON, PAUL EDWIN, real estate developer, writer; b. San Francisco, June 29, 1944; s. Carl John and Marguerite Eutha (Kovatch) C.; m. Sharon Raye Hammond, Nov. 14, 1964; children: Kimberley, Davin, Christina. AA, Yosemite Coll., 1964; BA, Calif. State U., Long Beach, 1971; cert. shopping ctr. mgr., Internat. Council of Shopping Ctrs. Mgmt. Sch., 1981. Vice and narcotics officer Modesto and Los Angeles Police Depts., Calif., 1964-69; owner Universal Prodns., N.Y.C. and Modesto, 1963-73; gen. mgr. City Investing Co., N.C.Y. and Beverly Hills, Calif., 1973-75; v.p. The Koll Co., Newport Beach, Calif., 1975-79, Irvine Co., Newport Beach, 1979-80; owner Willows Shopping Ctr., Concord, Calif., 1980-83; sr. v.p. Lee Sammis Co., Irvine, 1983-85; pres. Am. Devel. Co., Costa Mesa, Calif., 1985-86; chmn. bd. The Carlson Co., Huntington Beach, Calif., 1986—; guest lectr. U. So. Cal., U. Calif., Los Angeles, Orange Coast Coll.; real estate cons. Bank of Am., Union Bank, Chevron U.S.A., Aetna Life Ins. Co., James Lang Wooten, Eng., Peoples Republic of China. Author three screen plays for Police Story; comedy contbr. to The Tonight Show, Sat. Night Live, Late Night with David Letterman; pub. Property Mgrs. Handbook. mem. Calif. State Juvenile Justice Commn., Rep. Senatorial Inner circle, Washington; past chmn. City of Newport Beach Traffic Commn.; pres. bd. trustees Mt. Diablo Hosp.; v.p. bd. dirs. City of Concord Pavillion; bd. dirs. Concord Visitors and Conv. Bur. Mem. Am. Cancer Soc. (bd. dirs. Contra Costa Co.). Republican. Home: 1830 Port Barmouth Pl Newport Beach CA 92660 Office: The Carlson Co 19900 Beach Blvd Ste C Huntington Beach CA 92646

CARLSON, RIA MARIE, public relations executive, writer; b. Los Angeles, Apr. 8, 1961; d. Erick Gustaf and Roberta Rae (Bandelin) C.; m. James Bradley Gerdts, May 19, 1985. BA cum laude, U. So. Calif., 1983. Assoc. producer NBC, Burbank, Calif., 1982-85; account exec. Kerr & Assocs. Pub. Relations, Huntington Beach, Calif., 1985-86; pub. relations mgr. Orange County Performing Arts Ctr., Costa Mesa, Calif., 1986-88; dir. pub. relations and mktg. Bowers Mus., Santa Ana, Calif., 1988—; free lance writer, 1985—. Scriptwriter award ceremony Latin Bus. Assn., 1985; author, editor newsletter Am. Sch. Food Service Assn. Bus. Report, 1985-86; assoc. editor Revue mag., 1987; editor Artifacts mag., 1988—; contbr. articles to publs; cast mem. Disneyland, Anaheim, Calif. Prodn. asst. Profiles in Pride, Black History Month, Burbank, 1985. Named one of Outstanding Young Women in Am., 1985. Mem. AAUW (dir. pub. relations, br. officer), Women in Communications, Nat. Assn. Female Execs., Am. Film Inst., U. So. Calif. Alumni Assn., Blackstonians Pre-Law Hon. Soc. (life), Calif. Scholarship Fedn. (sealbearer, life). Republican. Roman Catholic. Avocations: writing short stories, reading, skiing, softball, travel. Office: Bowers Museum 2002 N Main St Santa Ana CA 92706

CARLSON, RICHARD FREDERICK, physicist, educator; b. St. Paul, June 19, 1936; s. Richard E. and Margaret D. (Kaercher) C.; m. Sandra Johnson, Sept. 7, 1957; children: Karen Jean Carlson Muyskens, Kristin Ann, Keith Richard. BS, U. Redlands, 1957; MS, U. Minn., 1962, PhD, 1964. Asst. rsch. physicist UCLA, 1963-67; prof. physics U. Redlands, Calif., 1967—. Author numerous rsch. papers. Mem. adv. bd., Redlands Salvation Army, 1982-86. Recipient 6 grants, Rsch. Corp., Tucson, 1969-85. Mem. Am. Phys. Soc., Am. Sci. Affiliation. Office: Dept Physics U Redlands Redlands CA 92373-0999

CARLSON, ROBERT ERNEST, freelance writer, architect, lecturer; b. Denver, Dec. 6, 1924; s. Milton and Augustine Barbara (Walter) C.; m. Jane Frances Waters, June 14, 1952 (div. June 1971); children: Cristina, Bob, Douglas, Glenn, James. BS in Archtl. Engring., U. Colo., 1951. Registered architect, Colo. Architect H.D. Wagener & Assocs., Boulder, Colo., 1953-75; pvt. practice architect Denver, 1975-82; health and promotion cons. Alive & Well Cons., Denver, 1982-85; freelance writer Denver, 1985—; mem. Colo. Gov.'s Coun. for Health Promotion and Phys. Fitness, Denver, 1975—; state race walking chmn. Athletics Congress U.S.A., Denver, 1983—; bd. dirs. Colo. Found. for Health Promotion and Phys. Fitness, Denver; lectr. in field. Author: Health Walk, 1988. Vol. Colo. Heart Assn., 1985-88, Better Air Campaign, 1986-87, Multiple Sclerosis Soc., 1988—. With U.S. Army, 1943-46, Overseas combat in Itlay. Named One of Ten Most Prominent Walking Leaders in U.S.A. Rockport Shoe Co., 1989. Mem. Colo. Author's League, Phidippides Track Club (walking chmn. 1981-85), Rocky Mountain Rd. Runners (v.p. Denver chpt. 1983-84), Front Range Walkers Club (founder, pres. Denver chpt. 1985—). Episcopalian. Home and Office: 2261 Glencoe St Denver CO 80207

CARLSON, SHARON LEE, data processing executive; b. East Liverpool, Ohio, May 7, 1949; d. Samuel Sander and Harriette (Simon) Seltzer; m. Kenneth James Hoover (div. July 16, 1979); m. Dewey Leroy Carlson, Nov. 28, 1981; stepchildren: Sonia Louise, Kurt Dewey. BA in English, Calif. State U., Long Beach, 1976, MPA, 1981; postgrad., West Coast U., Orange, Calif., 1989. Worker, supr. County of L.A., Dept. Pub. Social Svcs., L.A., 1970-76, systems analyst, 1976-79; systems analyst City of Anaheim, Utilities, Calif., 1979-80; sr. systems analyst Carter, Hawley, Hale Stores, Anaheim, 1980-82, project leader, 1982; project mgr. St. Joseph Health System, Orange, Calif., 1982-85; sr. mgr. St. Joseph Health System, Orange, 1985—. Bd. dirs. Health Assocs. Fed. Credit Union, Orange, Calif., 1987-89, Care of the Poor Com., Orange, 1988-90; mem. commn. City of Fountain Valley Improvement Authority, Fountain Valley, Calif., 1988-90; fund raiser, chmn. Friends of Guaymas, Orange, Calif. Named Honoree Woman in History City of Fountain Valley, 1988. Mem. NAFE. Democrat. Jewish. Home: 10787 Chere Ct Fountain Valley CA 92708 Office: St Joseph Health System 505 S Main St Ste 400 Orange CA 92668 Address: PO Box 8611 Fountain Valley CA 92728

CARLSON, STEVEN A., geography educator; b. Borger, Tex., Aug. 13, 1948; s. Roland A. and Betty G. (Shorb) C.; m. H. Lorraine Stark; children: Derek G., Justin D. BA, U. Mont., 1971, MA, 1973; PhD, U. Wash., 1977. From asst. prof. to assoc. prof. Dept. Geography, Earth Sci. & Conservation, No. Mich. U., Marquette, 1976-83; from assoc. prof. to prof. Humboldt State U., Arcata, Calif., 1983—; chmn. Marquette County Planning Commn., Marquette, 1980-83; cons. on land use matters, Marquette, Arcata, 1976—; active geographic info. systems workshops, Mich, Calif., 1976—. Author several papers and reports. Treas. Humboldt Habitat for Humanity, Arcata, 1988—; bd. dirs. Arcata Little league, 1988—, Upper Peninsula Environ. Coalition, Marquette, 1978-83, Lanphere Christensen Dunes Mgmt. Commn., Arcata, 1985—. Mem. Assn. Am. Geographers, Soil Conservation Soc. Am., Am. Soc. for Photogrammetry and Remote Sensing, The Nature Conservancy, Redwoods Flying Club (Eureka, Calif.). Home: 1137 Vista Dr McKinleyville CA 95521 Office: Humboldt State U Arcata CA 95521

CARLSON, ZEKE, liquid waste disposal company executive; b. Evanston, Ill., May 1, 1953; s. Henry C. and Jean (Elliott) C. Student, Lehigh U., 1971-74, U. Ariz., 1975. Owner, operator Mad Merlin's Hot rod Co., Tucson, 1975-79; pres. Pacific Plumbing co., Tucson, 1979-85; pres., chief exec. officer Carlson-Fehser Corp., Tucson, 1985—. Office: 3231 E Columbia Tucson AZ 85714

CARLTON, RICHARD ANTHONY, management consultant, educator; b. Henderson, N.C., Feb. 4, 1951. BA, U. Mo., 1972. Prin. Loadmaster Magnetics, Wichita, Kans., 1975-77; dir. music svcs. Bellestreet Prodns., Kansas City, Mo., 1977-78; prin. Carlton Unltd., Costa Mesa, Calif., 1978-82; pres. Desert Wind Communications, Inc., Costa Mesa, 1982-85; sr. assoc. R.A. Carlton Consultancy, Costa Mesa, 1985—. Feature writer periodical Kitchen Bath Design, 1986; contbg. editor periodical Furniture Design and Manufacturing, 1987—, Cabinet Maker, 1988—. Sustaining mem. Rep. Nat. Com., Washington, 1987—, CAP, Costa Mesa, 1987—; mem. Whale Addition Project, Woods Hole, Mass., 1988—; charter mem. Battle of Normandy Mus., Caen, France, 1988—. With USAF, 1971-75, SEA, ETO. Mem. Am. Mgmt. Assn., AIAA, Nat. Assn. Broadcasters, Am. Helicopter Soc., Vietnam VA's of Am., Image IV Soc., IEEE, Helicopter Assn. Internat., Assn. Computing Machinery. Republican.

CARMAZZI, ARTHUR FRANCISCO, automobile company executive; b. Reno, Aug. 21, 1962; d. Arthur Anthony and Luz Maria (Villa) C. Student, Pacific U., 1981, Mont. State U., 1982, U. Nev., Reno, 1982-86. Pres. Carmazzi Coachworks/Advanced Automotive Techs., Sparks, Nev., 1982-88, DECO Internat., Reno, 1988—; cons. Interlude Internat., Incline Village, Nev., 1987-88, Jac Pot Promotions, Sparks, 1986-87, Pro Golf Specialities, Inc., Incline Village, 1988. Author (poetry): Accent on Romance, 1988. Active Econ. Devel. Authority of Western Nev., Reno; instr. in fencing YWCA, Reno, 1986. With USAR, 1981-88. Mem. Soc. for the Advancement Materials Processing Engrs., Profl. Assn. Diving Inst. Republican. Roman Catholic. Clubs: Ches (Reno) (v.p. 1980-81), Silver Blades. Home: 2945 Kietzke #2 Reno NV 89502 Office: DECO Internat 335 W 1st St Reno NV 89503

CARMICHAEL, JAMES EDWIN, company executive; b. Spokane, Wash., May 23, 1942; s. Edwin Harold and Isabel (Urquhart) C.; m. Margo Jean Moran, June 28, 1969; children: Andrew, Ryan. BS in Forestry, U. Idaho, 1966. Analyst Boise (Idaho) Cascade Corp., 1967; pilot, staff mem. Carson Helicopters, Wenatchee, Wash., 1972; mem. staff Weyerhaeuser Co., Tacoma, 1972-82; ptnr. Internat. Resource and Industry Svcs. Co., Federal Way, Wash., 1982-83; account exec. Dean Witter Reynolds, Tacoma, 1982-85; gen. mgr. Afognak Native Corp., Kodiak, Alaska, 1985—. Mem. Tacoma Econ. Devel. Coun., 1984-85, Kodiak Parks & Recreation Bd., 1985—, Kodiak Bus. Devel. Coun., 1987—. Lt. USNR, 1967-71, Vietnam. Mem. Rotary. Republican. Office: Afognak Native Corp 203 Marine Way Kodiak AK 99615

CARMONY, KEVIN BRACKETT, computer software manufacturing company executive; b. Ogden, Utah, Sept. 26, 1959; s. Clifford Conrad and Marion Janette (Fletcher) C.; m. Sandra Allen, July 16, 1982; children: Justin, Brackett, Bryce. BA in Bus. and Econs., Weber State Coll., 1983. Dist. mgr. Consol. Theatres, Salt Lake City, 1980-82; founder, chief exec. officer Streamlined Info. Systems, Inc., Ogden, 1982—; bd. dirs. Pro Image, Inc., Salt Lake City. Elder's pres. LDS Ch., Ogden, 1987—. Republican. Home: 5972 S Skyline Dr Ogden UT 84403 Office: Streamlined Info Systems 4155 Harrison Blvd Ste 110 Ogden UT 84403

CARNAHAN, ROBERT DANIEL, fire chief, instructor; b. Placerville, Calif., Mar. 24, 1949; s. Edward Bruce and Shirley Alzada (Dixon) C.; m. Rebecca Lynn Kelly, Nov. 21, 1970; children: Kevin, Jason, Bryan. AA in Polit. Sci., Mt. Hood Community Coll., Gresham, Oreg., 1971; BS in Social Sci., Portland (Oreg.) State U., 1975. Title examiner Transamerica Title Ins., Oregon City, Oreg., 1970-72; firefighter, paramedic Molalla (Oreg.) Fire Dist., 1974-81; with Clackamas County Fire Dist., Oregon City, 1977—, asst. fire chief, 1983-86, fire chief, 1986—; instr. Wester Oreg. State Coll., Monmouth, 1984—, Clackamas Community Coll., 1984—; cons. in field; bd. dirs. Shepherd Ministries, Tualatin, Oreg. Contbr. articles to profl. jours. Mem. legis. com. Oreg. Fire Med. Adminstrs., Salem, 1985, 87; chmn. adv. bd. Clackamas County Emergency Med. Svc., Oregon City, 1977-79. Mem. Oreg. Fire Chief Assn. (com. chair 1979-80), Nat. Fire Acad. (exec. officer 1989—), Internat. Assn. Fire Chiefs, Nat. Fire Protection Assn., Tri-City C. of C. (fellow), Clackamas County Fire Def. Bd. (sec., treas.), Toastmasters, Inc., Exch. Club (sec., treas. Oregon City chpt.). Republican. Home: 18490 S Holly Ln Oregon City OR 97045 Office: Clackamas County Fire Dept PO Box 358 Clackamas OR 97015

CARNEGIE, DEBORAH MARY, litigation case management and document control company executive; b. Corry, Pa., Nov. 26, 1952; d. Thomas Edward and Genevieve Mary (Wascak) Reed; m. Roger Earl Bailey, Dec. 18, 1971 (div. 1974); 1 child, Joel Scott; m. Charles Barton Carnegie II, Jan. 26, 1980; 1 child, Charles Thomas. Cert. lab. asst., Hamot Hosp., Erie, Pa., 1971; cert., Parks Bus. Sch., Denver, 1979; student, U. Calif., San Diego, 1986-87. Lab. asst. Corry Meml. Hosp., 1974-76, Wheatridge (Colo.) Hosp., 1976-79, Broomfield (Colo.) Clin. Lab., 1979-80; lab. office mgr. Coronado (Calif.) Hosp., 1980-81; paralegal Luce, Forward, Hamilton & Scripps, San Diego, 1981-87; pres., paralegal Litigation Support Svcs., San Diego, 1987—. Vol. support group for parents premature infants Sharp Meml. Hosp., San Diego, 1988. Mem. NAFE. Republican. Roman Catholic. Office: Litigation Support Svcs 1335 Hotel Circle S Ste 110 San Diego CA 92108

CARNER, BRADFORD ALLEN, real estate broker; b. Anderson, Ind., June 17, 1947; s. Herbert Allen and Hilda (Simpson) C.; m. Kaye Wood, Sept. 25, 1977; children: Fearon, Tyler, Ned. Student, Ind. State U., Terre Haute, 1966-68; BS, Ind. U., 1970-72. Comml. brokerage Coldwell Banker, Denver, 1973-83; dir. mktg. Stan Miles Properties, Denver, 1983-85, Wright Runstad & Co., Seattle, 1985-88; comml. brokerage Grubb & Ellis, Seattle, 1987—. Mem. Valley Area Transp. Authorityk, Seattle, 1986-88, Seattle Zoning Com., 1985-86; chmn. Downtown Devel., Boulder, 1973-74, Arapahoe Corridor Devel., Denver, 1983-85. With U.S. Army, 1969-70. Mem. VADA, CCIM, Wing Point Athl ric, Seattle, 1983-85, Toastmasters, Elephant Club. Republican. Methodist. Home: 7068 Wingpoint Rd Bainbridge Island WA 98110 Office: Grubb & Ellis 1800 One Union Rd Seattle WA 98101

CARNES, WILLIAM GRAY, retired landscape architect, educator; b. La Plata, Mo., Jan. 7, 1907; s. Percy Thomas and Annie Mary (Nichols) C.; m. Hazel Marian Troutwine, Feb. 2, 1938 (dec.); 1 child, Karen Diane Carnes Debley; m. Vera Elizabeth Okeson, Mar. 29, 1972. BS, U. Calif., Berkeley, 1930. Landscape architect Nat. Park Service, San Francisco, 1930-36; chief landscape architect Nat. Park Service, Washington, 1936-55, chief of planning, 1955-60; dep. asst. dir. Nat. Park Service, 1960-62; prof. landscape architecture, chmn. dept. U. Ill., Urbana, 1962-70; cons. State of Wis., State of Utah Parks, 1955-60, City of Chgo., 1962-66, Nat. Sand Gravel Assn., 1961-70. Author: (with others) Accreditation in Higher Education, 1959, Modern Land Planning, 1960; contbr. articles to profl. jours. bd. dirs. Keep America Beautiful, N.Y.C., 1953-56. Recipient Alfred B. Lagasse Medal Landscape Archtl. Found., 1984. Fellow Am. Soc. Landscape Architects.

CARNESE, DANIEL J., artificial intelligence researcher; b. Amityville, N.Y., Mar. 4, 1954; s. Daniel J. Carnese and Josephine (Condello) Yerger; m. Angela Margaret Sutton, June 25, 1988. AB, U. Calif., Berkeley, 1974; SM, MIT, 1984. Mem. rsch. staff Schlumberger Palo Alto (Calif.) Rsch., 1984--. Co-dir. Computer Profls. for Social Responsibility, Palo Alto, 1985--. Mem. Am. Assn. for Artificial Intelligence, Assn. for Computing Machinery, IEEE, Computer Soc., Phi Beta Kappa, Sigma Xi. Home: 19 Mercedes Ct Los Altos CA 94022 Office: Schlumberger Palo Alto Rsch 3340 Hillview Ave Palo Alto CA 94304

CARNEY, HEATH JOSEPH, aquatic ecologist, educator; b. Lyon, France, Aug. 7, 1955; s. Stephen McLure and June (Kempf) C. BS, Coll. William and Mary, 1979; MS, U. Mich., 1981; PhD, U. Calif., Davis, 1987. Research asst. U. Mich., Ann Arbor, 1979-82; aquatic ecology fellow U. Calif., Davis, 1982-87; asst. prof., research fellow Dept. Biol. Ind. U., Bloomington, 1987—; cons. U. Mich., 1980-81, Harvard U., 1988—, U. Calif. Berkeley, 1989—. Contbr. articles to profl. jours. Grantee EPA, NOAA, NSF. Mem. AAAS, Am. Soc. Limnology and Oceanography, Ecol. Soc. Am. Phycol. Soc. Am., Soc. Internat. Limnologiae, Internat. Assn. Ecology, Union Concerned Scientists, Sierra Club, Sigma Xi, Phi Beta Kappa. Office: U Calif Inst Ecology Davis CA 95616

CARNEY, JAMES F., archbishop; b. Vancouver, B.C., Can., June 28, 1915; s. John and Ethel (Crook) C. Ed., Vancouver Coll., Jr. Sem. of Christ the King, 1930-38, St. Joseph's Sem., Alta., Can., 1938-42. Ordained priest Roman Catholic Ch., 1942; pastor Corpus Christi Ch., Vancouver; later vicar gen., domestic prelate; consecrated bishop Corpus Christi Ch., 1966; ordained titular bishop of Obori and aux. bishop of Vancouver, 1966-69, installed as archbishop, 1969—. Office: 150 Robson St, Vancouver, BC Canada V6B 2A7 *

CARNEY, PATRICIA, Canadian legislator; b. Shanghai, China, May 26, 1935; d. John James and Dora (Sanders) C.; two children. B.A. in Econs. and Polit. Sci., U. B.C., Can., 1960, M.A. in Comml. and Regional Planning, 1977. Econ. journalist various publs. 1955-70; owner, cons. Gemini North Ltd., Vancouver, B.C., Can., 1970-80, Yellowknife, N.W.T., Can., 1971, Alta., Can., 1971; mem. Can. Ho. of Commons, Ottawa, Ont., 1980-89, minister of state, 1981, minister fin., 1983, minister energy, mines and resources, 1984-86, minister for internat. trade, 1986-88, pres. Treas. Bd., 1988-89; mem. planning and priorities com.; mem. fgn. def. cabinet com. Recipient Can. Women's Press award, 1968, 3 MacMillan Bloedel Ltd. awards. Mem. Assn. Profl. Economists B.C., Can. Inst. Planners. Office: House Commons, Parliament Bldgs, Ottawa, ON Canada K1A 0A6 *

CARNIGLIA, STEPHEN DAVIS, accountant, real estate consultant; b. Kentfield, Calif., Dec. 1, 1950; s. Stephen Charles and Phebe Ruth (Davis) C. BA in Econs., Pomona Coll., Claremont, Calif., 1972; JD, U. Calif., San Francisco, 1975. Bar: Calif.; CPA, Calif. Tax mgr. Coopers & Lybrand, San Francisco, 1975-80, Minihan Kernut Stokes & Co., Eugene, Oreg., 1981; div. contr. Carma Developers, San Francisco, 1981-82; ptnr. Peat Marwick Main & Co., San Francisco, 1982—; guest lectr. Hastings Coll. Law U. Calif. San Francisco, 1983—, U. Calif., Berkeley, 1986—, Golden Gate U., San Francisco, 1987—; columnist San Francisco Bus. Times, 1987—. Mem. Bay Area Mortgage Assn., Berkeley Real Estate Assocs., Real Estate Syndication Securities Inst., Urban Land Inst., Bankers Club. Home: 2321 Scott St Apt 5 San Francisco CA 94115 Office: Peat Marwick Main & Co 3 Embarcadero Ctr San Francisco CA 94111

CARNS, CAROLYN FAITH, industrial specialist; b. San Diego, May 1, 1947; d. James Franklin and Beryl Agnes (Slocum) McDade; m. L. Thomas Carns, Mar. 26, 1966; children: Shawndel, Michael, William. Grad. high sch., San Diego. Corp. officer Speedy Print, Inc., Las Vegas, Nev., 1980-81; corp. v.p. PDQ Printing, Inc., Las Vegas, 1981—. Leader Camp Fire Girls, Edmonds, Wash., 1972-79, Boy Scouts Am., Edmonds, 1975-80. Mem. Nat. Assn. Quick Printers. Republican. Mem. Christian Ch. Home: 1500 Eaton Dr Las Vegas NV 89102

CARO, IVOR, dermatologist; b. Johannesburg, South Africa, June 2, 1946; came to U.S., 1975; s. Herbert and Rachel (Eisenstein) C.; m. Sheryl Helaine Marsden, Dec. 14, 1969; children: Howard Seth, Glen. MB, BCh, U. Witwatersrand, 1969. Diplomate, Am. Bd. Dermatology. Resident U. Witwatersrand, Johannesburg, 1971-74; fellow St. John's Hosp., London, 1974-76; asst. prof. U. N.C., Chapel Hill, 1975-78; pvt. practice Seattle, 1978—; clin. assoc. prof., U. Wash., Seattle, 1978-89; attending dermatologist, Virginia Mason Med. Ctr., Seattle, Swedish Hosp. Med. Ctr., Seattle. Contbr. to profl. publs. and textbooks. Fellow Am. Acad. Dermatology; mem. Seattle Dermatologic Soc. (pres. 1987-88), Pacific Dermatologic Soc., Soc. Investigative Dermatology, Noah Worcester Dermatologic Soc. Office: 1229 Madison St Ste 1010 Seattle WA 98104

CARO, JOSEPH JAMES, marketing consultant; b. Plainfield, N.J., July 9, 1942; s. James Carl and Helen (Tkach) C.; m. Charlotte Craig, Nov. 15, 1979 (div. 1982). BA in Bus. Adminstrn., Seton Hall U., Orange, Calif., 1964; AB in Bus. Mgmt., La Salle U., Chgo., 1975; MA in Communications, Windsor U., Los Angeles, 1978. Mktg. supr. GE, L.A., 1971-74; mktg. dir. small projects program SBA, Van Nuys, Calif., 1974-77; exec. v.p. RMA Archtl. Group, Costa Mesa, Calif., 1977-82; prin. J. Caro & Assoc., Long Beach, Calif., 1982—; cons. SBA. Author: Consumers Guide to the California Lemon Law, 1989; photographs exhibited in Long Beach Mus. Art, 1988, Long Beach Centennial Exhibit, 1988. Apptd. airport commr., Long Beach, 1986-88; apptd. Mayor's Exec. Task Force City of Long Beach, 1988—; environ. co-chmn. Long Beach Area Citizens, 1984—. Served with USMC, 1964-67. Mem. Am. Arbitrators Assn., Nat. Panel Consumer Arbitrating, Nat. Panel Am. Arbitrators. Lodge: Rotary (pub. editor 1980-82). Office: J Caro & Assocs PO Box 7486 Long Beach CA 90807

CAROLLO, JOHN ROBERT, electrical engineer; b. Bklyn., Aug. 28, 1950; s. John Nicholas and Rosalie Grace (Ferraro) C.; m. Debra Jean Cancilla, apr. 6, 1974; children: Marisa Danielle, John Salvadore. AS in Electronic Tech., S.I. Community Coll., 1971; BSEE, Okla. State U., 1973. Low noise engrng. mgr. Varian Assocs., Palo alto, Calif., 1973-81; western & internat. sales mgr. C.E.L., Santa Clara, Calif., 1981-84; v.p. mktg. & sales C.T.T., Inc., Santa Clara, Calif., 1984-85; sr. applications engr. Teledyne-Counter Measures Equipment, Santa Clara, Calif., 1985-88; product line mgr. F.E.I. Microwave, Inc., Sunnyvale, Calif., 1989—. Fellow Assn. Old Crows; mem. Nat. TrustHistoric Preservation, Santa clara Sheriff's Assn. Home: 2226 Central Park Dr Campbell CA 95008 Office: 865 Stewart Dr Campbell CA 95008

CAROSELLI, PATRICIA ANN, film production executive; b. Rochester, N.Y., Feb. 21, 1954; d. Patrick Renato and Elvira Josephine (Ciaccia) C.; m. Jonathan Barnet Rintels, Feb. 11, 1989. BA, SUNY, Buffalo, 1975; MBA, U. Conn., 1977. Asst. project dir. Grey Advt., L.A., 1977-79; from prodn. assoc. to v.p. prodn. Blake Edwards Co., L.A., 1979—. Assoc. producer: (films) Micki and Maude, A Fine Mess, That's Life, Blind Date, Justin Case, Skin Deep, Peter Gunn. Mem. Conn. Commn. on Arts, Hartford, 1977, Operation Calif., L.A., 1979—. Mem. Am. Film Inst., Women in Film, Assn. MBA Execs., ACLU. Democrat. Office: Blake Edwards Co 9336 W Washington Blvd Culver City CA 92030

CAROTHERS, RICHARD ALTON, landscape architect; b. Seattle, Feb. 21, 1935; s. Max Amillion and Alyce Roberta (Napier) C.; m. Myra Ann Bush, March 22, 1958 (div. 1978); children: Mishelle Ane, Corinne Marie, Richard Jr.; m. Barbara Carol Dickinson, Feb. 18, 1978. B in Landscape Architecture, U. Oreg., 1960. Lic. landscape architect Wash., Oreg., Idaho, Mont., Nev., Ariz., N.Mex., Tex., Okla., S.C., Ga. Founder Richard Carothers Assocs., Eugene, Oreg., 1960-63; pres., chief exec. officer Richard Carothers Assocs., Seattle, 1963—. Contbr. articles to profl. jours. Active Civil Svc. Exam Bd., Seattle, 1966-70; juror King County Environ. Awards Program, Seattle, 1972. Recipients 8 awards Am. Nurserymen Assn., 1971-88, 4 awards King County Environ., 1970-82, Nat. Grand award Am. Landscape Architects Assn., 1978. Mem. Am. Soc. Landscape Architects (pres. 1977-80, Achievement award 1982), Am. Arbitration Assn. (bd. dirs. 1969—), Construction Specifications Inst. (bd. dirs. 1971—), Am. Planning Assn. (bd. dirs. 1981—), Wash. Council Landscape Architects (founder, pres. 1972-73). Episcopalian. Office: 814 E Pike St Seattle WA 98122

CARPENTER, BETTY LOU, management consultant; b. Winfield, Kans., Aug. 28, 1934; d. George Owen and Louise Watson; m. E. Reid Graves, June 17, 1952 (div. June 1970); children: G. Micheal, Laurie L. Livesay, Betsy M. Goodell, David L.; m. Lester G. Carpenter Jr., Sept. 17, 1971. Student, U. Kans., 1952-55; BSBA, Regis Coll., 1983. V.p. Midland Fed. Savs., Denver, 1967-70, Cen. Bank of Denver, 1973-83; acct. mgr. Broyles, Allebaugh & Davis, Denver, 1970-72; pvt. practice cons. Denver, 1983—; mgmt. cons. West Hudson, Century City, Calif. Bd. Commrs., vice chmn. Denver Housing Auth., 1976—; mem. subcom. Mayor's Comprehensive Plan Task Force, Denver, 1988. Mem. Nat. Assn. Housing and Redevel. Offls. (nat. com. 1978—), Colo. Bank Mktg. Assn. (bd. dirs. 1982-83), Colo. Affordable Housing Partnership, Denver Advt. Fedn. (bd. dirs. 1970-72). Democrat. Methodist. Home and Office: 915 S Jackson Denver CO 80209

CARPENTER, DANIEL EDWIN, insurance company administrator; b. Redlands, Calif., Apr. 5, 1946; s. Clayton Arnold and Virginia (Pettit) C.; m. Mildred Mae Glaw, Aug. 15, 1970; children: Daniel E. Jr., Sarah N. BS in Indsl. Mgmt., U. Nev., 1969; MBA, U. Pepperdine, 1972. CPCU; CLU. Underwriter comml. lines Fireman's Funds Ins. Co., Reno, 1972-77; dist. adminstrv. asst. Farmers Ins. Group, Reno, 1977—. Served to lt. col. USAR, 1969—. Mem. CPCU Assn. (pres. Sierra, Nev. chpt. 1986-88), CLU Assn. (bd. dirs. Sierra chpt. 1983—). Methodist. Home: 3321 Saratoga Ct Sparks NV 89431 Office: Farmers Ins Group 100 W Grove Rd Suite 200 Reno NV 89509

CARPENTER, DAVID ROLAND, life insurance executive; b. Fort Wayne, Ind., Mar. 24, 1939; s. Geary W. and Rita (Ueber) C.; m. Karen Woodard, Oct. 20, 1963 (div. Apr. 1975); children: Kimberly, Clayton; m. Leila E.M. Sjogren, Sept. 20, 1980; 1 dau., Michelle. BBA, U. Mich., 1961, MS, 1962. Sr. v.p. Booz, Allen Cons., Newport Beach, Calif., 1976-77; v.p. Tillinghast, Nelson & Warren, Newport Beach, Calif., 1977-80; chief mktg. officer Transam. Occidental Life Ins. Co., L.A., 1980-81, exec. v.p., chief mktg. officer, 1981-82, pres., 1982—, chief operating officer, 1982-83, chief exec. officer, 1983—, now chmn., dir.; dir. Transam. Life & Annuity Co., Transam. Assurance Co., Transam. Ins. Corp., Transam. Internat. Ins. Services. Trustee, nat. chmn. Alliance for Aging Rsch., 1986—; chmn., bd. dirs. Calif. Med. Ctr. Fedn., 1985—; bd. dirs. Cen. City Assn., 1985, chmn., 1987-88; bd. dirs. Greater L.A. Partnership for the Homeless, 1986—, Ind. Colls. So. Calif., 1988—; vice-chmn. UniHealth Am., 1988—, chmn., 1985-88; gov. Ford's Theatre, 1985—; trustee Mus. Contemporary Art, 1986—. Fellow Soc. Actuaries (bd. dirs. 1978-81); mem. Am. Acad. Actuaries (v.p. 1981-83), Internat. Ins. Soc. (gov. 1987—), L.A. C. of C. (bd. dirs. 1984—). Presbyterian. Office: Transam Occidental Life Ins Co 1150 S Olive St Los Angeles CA 90015

CARPENTER, DONALD BLODGETT, real estate appraiser; b. New Haven, Aug. 20, 1916; s. Fred Donald and Gwendolen (Blodgett) C.; PhB, U. Vt., 1938; m. Barbara Marvin Adams, June 28, 1941 (dec. Aug. 1978); m. 2d, Lee Burker McGough, Dec. 28, 1980 (div. Apr. 1987); children—Edward G., John D., William V., Andrew J., Dorothy J. and James J. McGough. Reporter Burlington (Vt.) Daily News, 1938-39; guide chair operator Am. Express Co., N.Y. World's Fair, 1939; underwriter G.E.I. Corp., Newark, 1939-40; Sales corr. J. Dixon Crucible Co., Jersey City, 1940-41, asst. office mgr., priorities specialist, 1941-42, sales rep., San Francisco, 1946-52; field supr. Travelers Ins. Co., San Francisco, 1952-58; gen. agt. Gen. Am. Life Ins. Co., San Francisco, 1958-59; Western Supr. Provident Life & Accident Ins. Co., San Francisco, 1959-60; brokerage supr. Aetna Life Ins. Co., San Francisco, 1960-61, maintenance cons. J.I. Holcomb Mfg. Co., Mill Valley, Calif., 1961-68; ednl. svc. rep. Marquis Who's Who, Inc., Mill Valley, 1963-68; sales rep. Onox, Inc., Mendocino, Calif., 1965-68; tchr., coach Mendocino Jr.-Sr. High Sch., 1968; real property appraiser, Mendocino County, Calif., 1968-81; instr. Coll. of Redwoods, 1985-87; ret. 1988. Active numerous civic orgns.; co-chmn. Citizens for Sewers, 1971-72; mem. Mendocino County Safety Coun., 1981. With USNR, 1942-46; lt. comdr., comdg. officer res. unit, 1967-68, now ret. Recipient Community Sportsman-of-Year award, 1971; Sec. of Navy Commendation with ribbon, 1946, other awards, certificates; companion Mil. Order World Wars. Mem. Reserve Officers Assn. U.S. (life; chpt. pres. 1954, 56, state v.p. 1958-61), Ret. Officers Assn. (life, chpt. survivors assistance area counselor 1979—, chpt. scholarship com. 1986-87), Mendocino Art Ctr. (sponsor mem.), Save-The-Redwoods League, Marines Meml. Assn., Mendocino County Employees Assn. (dir. 1981), Mendocino County Hist. Soc., Mendocino Hist. Rsch. Inc. (docent 1982-88), Nat. Assn. Uniformed Svcs. (life), Nat. Ret. Tchrs. Assn., Calif. Ret. Tchrs. Assn., Naval Order of U.S. (life), Naval Res. Assn. (life), Navy League of U.S. (life), U.S. Naval Inst. (life), Am. Diabetes Assn., Alumni Assn. U. Vt. (founding pres. San Francisco Alumni Club 1964), Mendocino Coast Stamp Club (charter; dir. 1983—), Kappa Sigma (scholarship leadership award 1937-38), Rotary Internat. (club pres. 1975-76, dist. gov. area rep. 1977-78, Dist. Gov. awards 1974, 76, dist. ednl. awards com. 1978-81, 89—, dist. group study exchange com. 1981-88; Paul Harris fellow 1979—, Rotarian of the Yrs. 1969-88), Am. Legion (post comdr. 1972-73, state citation for outstanding community svc. 1972), Am. Legion Past Comdrs. Calif. (life), Mendocino Cardinal Booster Club (charter, life mem., pres. 1971), U. Vt. Catamount Club (charter), Old Mill Club. Republican. Congregationalist. Home: Box 87 10801 Gurley Ln Mendocino CA 95460-0087

CARPENTER, FRANK CHARLES, JR., retired electronics engineer; b. Los Angeles, June 1, 1917; s. Frank Charles and Isobel (Crump) C.; A.A., Pasadena City Coll., 1961; B.S. in Elec. Engrng. cum laude, Calif. State U.-Long Beach, 1975, M.S. in Elec. Engrng., 1981; m. Beatrice Josephine Jolly, Nov. 3, 1951; children—Robert Douglas, Gail Susan, Carol Ann. Self-employed design and mfgr. aircraft test equipment, Los Angeles, 1946-51; engr. Hoffman Electronics Corp., Los Angeles, 1951-56, sr. engr., 1956-59, project mgr., 1959-63; engr.-scientist McDonnell-Douglas Astronautics Corp., Huntington Beach, Calif., 1963-69, spacecraft telemetry, 1963-67, biomed. electronics, 1967-69, flight test instrumentation, 1969-76; lab. test engr. Northrop Corp., Hawthorne, Calif., 1976-82, spl. engr., 1982-83; mgr. transducer calibration lab. Northrop Corp., Pico-Rivera, Calif., 1983-86. Served with USNR, 1941-47. Mem. IEEE (sr.), Amateur Radio Relay League. Contbr. articles to profl. jours. Patentee transistor squelch circuit; helicaland whip antenna. Home: 2037 Balearic Dr Costa Mesa CA 92626

CARPENTER, JOHN EVERETT, retired prinicipal; b. Tarrytown, N.Y., Nov. 27, 1923; s. Everett Birch and Mary (Avery) C.; student Union Coll., 1943; B.A., Iona Coll., 1946; M.A., Columbia, 1949, profl. diploma, 1961; m. Marie F. McCarthy, Nov. 14, 1944; 1 son, Dennis Everett. Tchr., Blessed Sacrament High Sch., New Rochelle, N.Y., 1946-50; tchr., adminstr. Armonk (N.Y.) pub. schs., 1950-62; dir. guidance Ridge Street Sch., Port Chester, N.Y., 1962-64; counselor Rye (N.Y.) High Sch., 1964-66, prin., 1966-78, ret.; guest lectr. Served to lt. USNR; now lt. comdr. ret. Res. Decorated Bronze Star medal. Mem. Middle States Assn. Colls. and Schs. (commn. on secondary schs.), Am. (life), Westchester-Putnam-Rockland (past pres.) personnel and guidance assns., NEA, Am. Legion (past comdr.), Phi Delta Kappa, Kappa Delta Pi. Rotarian (past pres., Paul Harris fellow). Clubs: Tarrytown Boat (past commodore), Green Valley Elks. Home: 321 Paseo de los Conquistadores Green Valley AZ 85614

CARPENTER, KENT RICHARD, pharmaceutical company executive; b. Decar, Utah, May 20, 1942; s. Paul James and Dorothy (Prince) C.; m. Mary Sander, June 10, 1961; children: Michael, K. Todd, Gregory, Danielle. BS in Mktg., U. Utah, 1970. Sales mgr. I.T.T. Continental Baking, Salt Lake City, 1963-71; regional sales mgr. Sandoz Pharm. Co., East Hanover, N.J., 1971-72; v.p. sales and mktg. Murdock Internat., Provo, Utah, 1982-84; pres. Puget Sound Fin. Group, Seattle, 1984-86; regional dir. sales, Western U.S. Connaught Labs., Seattle, Swiftwater, Pa., 1986—; cons. Bread Garden, Seattle, 1983-84, Health Care-H.M.O., Seattle, 1982. Conv. del. Republican Party, Utah, 1968; voting dist. chmn., Midvale, Utah, 1967-71; pres. Booster Club, Redmond (Wash.) High Sch., 1986-87; leader Boy Scouts Am., Utah, Wash., 1960— (nat. pres. unit award 1976). Mem. Brigham Young U. Mgmt. Soc., Bellevue C. of C., Rotary. Mormon. Home: 18311 NE 25th St Redmond WA 98052 Office: Connaught Labs Inc 800 Koll Ctr Ste 814 500 108th Ave NE Bellevue WA 98004-5560

CARPENTER, PETER ROCKEFELLER, bank executive; b. Sunbury, Pa., Apr. 18, 1939; s. Alvin Witmer and Katherine (Rockefeller) C.; m. Janet Ross Buck, Aug. 24, 1963; children: Karen Louise Althaus, Jean Ellen, Peter Alvin. BA, Pa. State U., 1962. Mgr. J.C. Penney Co., Menlo Park, N.J., 1964-67; ops. mgr. Allstate Ins. Co., Summit, N.J., 1967-73; adminstrv. mgr. Prudential Property & Casualty, Scottsdale, Ariz., 1973-75; v.p. Fortune Properties, Scottsdale, 1975-76; life underwriter Conn. Mutual Life, Phoenix, 1976-81; v.p. and dir. sales and mktg. No. Trust Bank, Phoenix, 1981—. Sec. exec. bd. Samuel Gompers Rehab. Ctr., 1981-84, chmn. bd., 1984—; div. chmn. Phoenix United Way, 1981, 82, 86—; Rep. committeeman, Phoenix, 1978-86 . With USN, 1962-64. Mem. Nat. Assn. Life Underwriters, Am. Inst. Banking, Internat. Platform Assn., Pa. State U. Alumni Assn. (dir. 1979-86), Son of Am. Revolution, Ariz. Club, U.S. Navy League, Mansion Club, Kiwanis (Disting. lt. gov.), Masons, Sigma Alpha Epsilon. Lutheran. Home: 5817 E Cochise Rd Scottsdale AZ 85253 Office: No Trust Bank Ariz 4350 E Camelback Rd Ste G-100 Phoenix AZ 85018

CARPENTER, RON DUANE, dentist; b. Porterville, Calif., Dec. 7, 1946; s. Orville J. and Mary I. (Rider) C.; m. Connie Jo Stewart, June 1977; children: Debbie, Shannon, Sarah. BS, U. Okla., 1979; postgrad., Boise (Idaho) State U., 1979-81; DDS, U. Okla., Oklahoma City, 1986. Physician's assoc. Boise Vets. Med. Ctr., 1979-82; pvt. practice Boise, 1987—. Contbr. articles to profl. jours. Mem. ADA, Idaho State Dental Assn., Southwest Idaho Dental Assn., Okla. Dental Assn., Am. Acad. of Physicians Assts. Office: Warm Springs Family Dentistry 100 Warm Springs Boise ID 83702

CARPENTER, SUNNY LYNNE, oil company executive; b. Portland, Oreg., Feb. 4, 1950; d. Hubert Frank and Yvonne D. (Miner) Behm; m. Larry Dean Carpenter, Nov. 29, 1969 (div.); 1 child, Kevin Scott. Bachelors degree, U. Alaska, 1978. Cert. secondary tchr., Alaska, Ariz. Broadcaster CBS Affiliate Stas. KTVF/KFRB TV, Fairbanks, Alaska, 1970-75; office mgr. Interior Energy Corp., Fairbanks, 1980-81, v.p. adminstrn., 1981-84, sr. v.p., 1984-87; pvt. practice Carpenter Cons., Fairbanks, 1987—; case mgmt. coord. Mesa (Ariz.) Community Coun., 1987—; mem. Credit Women Internat., Fairbanks, 1982-84; v.p. Airwaves, Ltd., Anchorage, 1984-86; sr. v.p. Churchill Group Ltd., Fairbanks, 1984-87. Mem. Tanana Valley Sportsman Assn., Fairbanks, 1987—; assemblywoman, 1970-76, presiding officer Fairbanks Borough, 1975-76. Mem. Fairbanks C. of C. Office: Mesa Community Coun 7 S Hibbert Mesa AZ 85202

CARPENTER, THOMAS NELSON, computer systems developer; b. Wenatchee, Wash., June 7, 1943; s. Virgil Nelson and Cozette Marcelle (Beckley) C.; m. Laurie Anne Schirmer, May 16, 1966; children: Stephanie Anne, Christine Elise. BS in Computer Sci., Metro State Coll., Denver, 1984. Various jr. profl. positions Ideal Basic Industries, Inc., Denver, 1969-74, various sr. profl. positions, 1976-86, systems devel. mgr., 1986—; sr. analyst mgmt. info. systems Diners Club Internat., Denver, 1974-76. With USAF, 1963-67. Mem. Am. Rose Soc., Denver Rose Soc. (treas. 1987—). Avocations: stained glass, golf. Home: 1730 Albion St Denver CO 80220

CARPENTER, WAYNE LEWIS, psychotherapist; b. Alamosa, Colo., Oct. 24, 1945; s. Harold George and Margaret Joetta (Herrmann) C.; m. I. Jean Masterson, June 3, 1979; 1 child, Graham Matthew. BA, U. Colo., 1968; M Div., San Francisco Theol. Sem., Berkeley, Calif., 1971; MA, San Francisco Theol. Sem., San Anselmo, Calif., 1974. Ordained to ministry Prebyn. Ch., 1971. Asst. pastor Saratoga (Calif.) Presbyn. Ch., 1974-76; pastor Creede (Colo.) Community Ch., 1978-79; prin. Library Park Psychotherapy Group, Ft. Collins, Colo., 1979—. Mem. candidates com. Presbytery of Boulder Presbyn. Ch., 1986-87; bd. dirs. United Ministries in Higher Edn., Colo. State U., 1984. Mem. Internat. Transactional Analysis Assn. (provisional teaching, Honored Mem. 1981, mem. ethics com. 1983—, trustee 1988), Am. Assn. Marriage and Family Therapy (clin., v.p. Colorado chpt. 1980), Internat. Transactional Assn. (mem. tng. standards com.). Democrat. Office: Libr Park Psychotherapy Group 218 Peterson St Fort Collins CO 80524

CARPENTER, WILLIAM WARD, judicial administrator; b. Greeley, Colo., Apr. 28, 1949; s. Donald A. and Evelyn Ward. BA, U. Colo., 1971; MS in Judical Adminstrn., U. Denver, 1972. Judicial dist. adminstr. Colo. Jud. Dept., Lamar, 1972-73, Brighton, 1973—. Mem. Colo. State Mgrs. Assn., Colo. Ct. Mgrs. Assn., Masons, Elks. Office: Colo Jud Dept Hall of Justice 1931 Bridge St Brighton CO 80601

CARR, ALLAN, film and stage producer, celebrity representative; b. Chgo., May 27. BA, Lake Forest Coll., 1962; postgrad., Northwestern U. Formed Rogallan Prodns., 1966; became mgr. Ann-Margret's career, 1966; formed Allan Carr Enterprises, 1971; mgr. careers of Peter Sellers, Marvin Hamlisch, Rosalind Russell, Paul Anka, Mama Cass, others, producer nightclub extravaganzas, TV spls., motion pictures; creative cons. for motion picture and TV prodn. including Tommy, 1975, Bugsy Malone, Deer Hunter, The Natural; producer: The First Time, 1969, C.C. & Company, 1970, Can't Stop the Music, 1980; co-writer, producer motion picture Grease; producer Broadway show La Cage Aux Folles, 1983; producer motion pictures: Survive, 1976, Grease II, 1982, Where the Boys Are, 1984, Cloak and Dagger, 1984. Office: Allan Carr Enterprises PO Box 691670 Los Angeles CA 90069

CARR, DEREK COOPER, Spanish educator; b. Darlington, Durham, Eng., Feb. 26, 1944; came to Can., 1966; s. Clarence and Ethel Maud (Cooper) C.; m. Silvana Ester Minuto, July 18, 1970; children—Catherine Elizabeth, Paul Antony. B.A. with honors, U. Newcastle upon Tyne, 1965, Dip.Edn., 1966; Ph.D., U. B.C., 1972. Asst. prof. Spanish, U. B.C., Vancouver, 1974-79, assoc. prof. Spanish, 1979—, head Dept. Spanish and Italian, 1981—. Author: Enrique de Villena: Tratado de la Consolacion, 1979. Contbr. articles to profl. jours. U. B.C. grantee, 1981, 82; Social Scis. and Humanities Research Council Can. grantee, 1985. Mem. Internat. Assn. Hispanists, Can. Assn. Hispanists, MLA, Medieval Assn. Pacific. Roman Catholic. Avocations: walking; motoring; drawing; model railways. Home: 4424 Maple St, Vancouver, BC Canada V6J 3W2 Office: Univ BC, 2075 Wesbrook Mall, Vancouver, BC Canada V6T 1W6

CARR, FRED, insurance company executive; b. 1931; married. Student, UCLA. Former pres. Shareholders Mgmt. Corp., Los Angeles; fin. advisor Cons. Assocs. Inc., Los Angeles, 1970-71; pres. Carr Mgmt. & Research Corp., Los Angeles, 1971-74; with First Exec. Corp., Los Angeles, 1974—, chmn., 1974—; pres., chmn. Exec. Life Ins. Co. (subs. First Exec. Corp.), Los Angeles. Office: Exec Life Ins Co 11444 W Olympic Blvd Los Angeles CA 90064 *

CARR, LUTHER JAMES, construction executive; b. Atlanta, May 7, 1936; s. Luther James and Mary Elizabeth (Jackson) C.; m. Frances Jean Ross, Aug. 16, 1958; children: Brenda Elaine, Dana Maria, Luther James III. BA in Sci., U. Wash., 1961. Buyer Boeing Corp., Seattle, 1960-63; sales rep. Waddell & Reed, Seattle, 1963-66; broker Dow-Laney, Seattle, 1966-70, Frank B. of Wash., Seattle, 1970-76; pres. Urban Industries, Seattle, 1976—; pres. Leaf Corp.; mng. gen. ptnr. JAK Assocs.; mem. adv. council SBA; mem. gov's com. on econ. devel., State of Wash.; founder Cen. Area Fed. Credit Union. Pres., United Way of King County, 1979-80; bd. dirs. Seattle-King County Econ. Devel. Council; founder, chmn. bd. dirs. Madison-Jackson Econ. Devel. Council; pres. Seattle Housing Authority, Medina

Children's Service; mem. fin. com. Brock Adam for Senate, 1987. Mem. Am. Gen. Contracts, Seattle Urban League (pres.), Seattle Jaycees (v.p.), U. Wash. Alumni Assn. (treas.), Seattle C. of C., Wash. Athletic Club (Seattle, bd. dirs. 1981-85), Rainier Club (Seattle, house com.).

CARR, NOLY CRUZ, real estate broker, notary public; b. Mabalacat, Pampanga, Philippines, Jan. 31, 1940; came to U.S., 1970; s. Efipanio and Isabel (DelaCruz) Carreon; m. Libby C. Carr, June 21, 1967; children: Beth C., Cathy C. BS in Elem. Edn., Philippine Normal Coll., Manila, 1964. Tchr. Mabalacat Elem. Sch., Pampanga, 1964-65; prin. elem. dept. and dean St. Peter's Coll., Iligan City, Philippines, 1965-67; stock clk. J.W. Robinson, Pasadena, Calif., 1970-71; supr. mailroom Clinton E. Frank Advt., Los Angeles, 1971-73; supr. shipping Eldon Office Products, Carson, Calif., 1974-80; traffic mgr. Internat. Rectifier, El Segundo, Calif., 1980-81; assoc. realtor Century 21-Crown Equitites, Long Beach, Calif., 1981-88; real estate broker and owner Realty Square, Long Beach, 1988—. Pres. Mabalacat Residents of So. Calif., Gardena, 1986. Mem. Long Beach Dist. Bd. Realtors. Home: 313 W 230th St Carson CA 90745 Office: Realty Square 1736 W Willow St Long Beach CA 90810

CARR, RICHARD LLOYD, construction executive; b. Valentine, Nebr., Nov. 9, 1937; s. Gerald Rodney and Winifred Jean (Harse) C.; m. Mary Sharon Tyler, Dec. 20, 1959; children: Tori, John. BCE, S.D. U., 1960; postgrad., Stanford U., 1985. Registered profl. engr., Ariz., N.M., Nev., Nebr., N.D., S.D. Engr. Internat. Harvester, Sioux Falls, S.D., 1960-63; ptnr. Carr & Sons Constrn., Pierre, S.D., 1963-70, Dana, Larson, Roubal & Assocs., Omaha, 1970-77, Lescher & Mahoney (affiliate Dana, Larson, Roubal & Mahoney), Phoenix, 1974-82; pres., chief exec. officer Reese-Carr, Inc. (name now Project Control Co.), Phoenix, 1982—. Chmn. bd. dirs. Handicapped Village of Ariz., 1985—; bd. dirs. Scottsdale (Ariz.) Boys Club; elder Presbyn. Ch. Mem. Am. Arbitration Assn., Am. Inst. of Contractors, Nat. Soc. Profl. Engrs., Ariz. Soc. Profl. Engrs., Phoenix C. of C. Office: Project Control Co 4343 E Camelback Rd #300 Phoenix AZ 85018

CARR, ROBERT LOCKE, museum executive; b. Covington, Ky., Nov. 9, 1930; s. Ralph Fillmore Carr and Laura Lemarian (Locke) Bennett. Student, James Millikin U., 1950, San Francisco State U., 1954-57, U. Calif., Berkeley, 1958-70. Field acct. Pacific Gas & Electric Co., San Francisco, 1953-55; supr. Wells Fargo Bank, N.A., San Francisco, 1955-64; contr. Wax Mus. at Fisherman's Wharf, San Francisco, 1964—, Movieland Wax Mus., Buena Park, Calif., 1985—; actor, entertainer Living History Ctr., Novato, Calif., 1970-78; cons. Thomas Fong Enterprises, San Francisco, 1974—. Asst. Stevenson-Kefauver Campaign, San Francisco, 1956. With USAF, 1950-51. Mem. Am. Guild Mus. Artists, AFTRA, SAG, Am. Humanist Assn. (counselor, treas. div. humanist counselling, 1984-87), U. Calif. Alumni Assn., Masons. Democrat. Home: PO Box 1321 Paradise CA 95967 Office: Wax Mus at Fishermans Wharf 145 Jefferson St San Francisco CA 94133

CARR, WILLARD ZELLER, JR., lawyer; b. Richmond, Ind., Dec. 18, 1927; s. Willard Zeller and Susan (Brownell) C.; m. Margaret Paterson, Feb. 15, 1952; children: Clayton Paterson, Jeffrey Westcott. BS, Purdue U., 1948; JD, Ind. U., 1951. Bar: Calif. 1951, U.S. Supreme Ct. 1963. Ptnr. Gibson, Dunn & Crutcher, Los Angeles, 1952—; mem. nat. panel arbitrators Am. Arbitration Assn.; former labor relations cons. State of Alaska; lectr. bd. visitors Southwestern U. Law Sch.; mem. adv. council Southwestern Legal Found., Internat. and Comparative Law Ctr. Trustee Calif. Adminstrv. Law Coll.; bd. dirs. Mchts. and Mfrs. Assn., Greater Los Angeles Zoo Assn., Los Angeles council Boy Scouts Am.; mem. Mayor's Econ. Devel. Policies Com.; trustee, past chmn. Pacific Legal Found.; past chmn. men's adv. com. Los Angeles County-USC Med. Ctr. Aux. for Recuitment, Edn. and Service; past chmn. bd. Wilshire Republican Club; past mem. Rep. State Central Com.; past mem. pres.'s council Calif. Mus. Sci. and Industry; mem. Nat. Def. Exec. Res., Los Angeles World Affairs Council; bd. dirs., sec. Los Angeles Police Meml. Found.; past chmn. Los Angeles sect. United Way; mem. adv. com. Los Angeles County Human Relations Commn.; Los Angeles chpt. ARC; mem. Fellow Am. Bar Found.; mem. ABA (co-chmn. com. benefits to unemployed persons, past chmn. econ. and resources controls com. of corp., banking and bus. law sect.; internat. labor relations law com. of labor and employment law sect., also com. devel. of law under Nat. Labor Relations Act), Internat. Bar Assn. (past chmn. labor law com. of bus. law sect.), Calif. State Bar, Los Angeles County Bar Assn., Los Angeles C. of C. (chmn. 1980). Home: 2185 Century Hill Los Angeles CA 90067 Office: Gibson Dunn & Crutcher 333 S Grand Ave 49th Floor Los Angeles CA 90071

CARRAHER, DANIEL PETER, accountant; b. Hawthorne, Nev., Dec. 27, 1953; s. Martin William and Pernina (Cadwell) C.; student U. Nev., 1971-72; BS in Bus. Adminstrn., U. San Francisco, 1975; postgrad. Golden Gate U., 1978—; m. Pamela Marie Peterson, Mar. 22, 1975; children: Tiffin, Kyle, Alexandria. CPA, Calif. Adminstrv. asst. U. San Francisco, 1974-75; staff acct. Alexander Grant & Co., San Francisco, 1975-78; ptnr. Carraher & Carraher, Ltd., CPAs, Reno, 1978-81; pvt. practice, 1981-82; chief fin. officer Oiltech, Reno, 1982-85, sec., 1984-85; chief fin. officer Mushroom King, Inc., Santa Rosa, Calif., 1985-86; controller Marine Terminals Corp., San Francisco, 1986—; sec. Majestic Ins. Co., San Francisco, 1987—; instr. Western Nev. Community Coll., Reno, 1978. Treas., bd. dirs. John Mark Christian Sch., Santa Rosa, 1986—; mem. Healdsburg Community Band, 1985—. Recipient The Wall St. Jour. award, U. San Francisco, 1975. Mem. Ins. Accts. and Systems Assn., Calif. Soc. CPAs. Republican. Avocations: trumpet, chess, golf. Home: 36 Grande Paseo San Rafael CA 94903 Office: Marine Terminals Corp 289 Steuart St San Francisco CA 94105

CARREY, NEIL, lawyer, educator; b. Bronx, N.Y., Nov. 19, 1942; s. David L. and Betty (Kurtzburg) C.; m. Karen Krysher, Apr. 9, 1980; children—Jana, Christopher; children by previous marriage—Scott, Douglas, Dana. B.S. in Econs., U. Pa., 1964; J.D., Stanford U., 1967. Bar: Calif. 1968. Mem. firm, v.p. corp. DeCastro, West, Chodorow & Burns, Inc., Los Angeles, 1967—; instr. program for legal paraprofls. U. So. Calif., 1977—; lectr. U. So. Calif. Dental Sch., 1987—. Author: Nonqualified Deffered Compensation Plans-The Wave of the Future, 1985. Officer, Vista Del Mar Child Care Center, Los Angeles, 1968-84; treas. Nat. Little League of Santa Monica, 1984-85, pres., 1985-86, coach Bobby Sox Team, Santa Monica, 1987—, bd. dirs. 1988; curriculum com. Santa Monica Sch. Dist., 1983-84, community health adv. com., 1988—, athletic adv. com., 1989—. Mem. U. Pa. Alumni Soc. So. Calif. (pres. 1971-79, dir. 1979-87), The Group (bd. dirs. 1989—), Alpha Kappa Psi (disting. life). Republican. Jewish. Club: Mountaingate Tennis (Los Angeles). Home: 616 23d St Santa Monica CA 90402 Office: 10960 Wilshire Blvd Ste 1800 Los Angeles CA 90024

CARRICO, DONALD JEFFERSON, vehicle fleet manager; b. Dallas, June 15, 1944; s. Ivan and Helen Mae (Jefferson) C.; m. Prudence Louise Cornish, Aug. 17, 1968; children: Bryan Jefferson, Alan Jefferson. BSBA, Ohio State U., 1967; MA in Bus. Mgmt., Cen. Mich. U., 1977. Commd. 2d lt. USAF, 1967, advanced through grades to maj., 1979; various supervisory positions USAF Air Freight Terminals, 1967-72; mgr. passenger travel and cargo br. USAF Transp. Div., Rickenbacker AFB, Ohio, 1972-74; transp. and air terminal insp. USAF Insp. Gen. Team, Hawaii, 1974-76; liaison officer US Naval Supply Ctr., Pearl Harbor, Hawaii, 1976-78; transp. staff officer USAF Hdqrs. Tactical Air Command, Langley AFB, Va., 1978-83; chief transp. USAF Transp. Div., Incirlik AFB, Turkey, 1983-85, Williams AFB, Ariz., 1986-88; vehicle fleet mgr. V&B Svcs., Phoenix, 1989—. Logistics chief Gilbert Food Bank Community Food Dr., Gilbert, Ariz., 1987, chmn. 1988; asst cubmaster Pack 282 Boy Scouts Am., Gilbert, 1987. Decorated Bronze Star. Home: 683 E Washington Dr Gilbert AZ 85234

CARRIER, KATHRYN EARLENE, sales manager; b. Monroe, Mich., Oct. 19, 1945; d. Earl Lamoine and Rubye Lee (Guest) Lewis C.; m. Ronald William Kodman, Oct. 17, 1964 (div. May 1970); children: Kathalene Kae, Kelli Rene. Grad. high sch., Compton, Calif. Receptionist, bookkeeper Rontells Nissan, Fresno, Calif., 1976-77; DMV car desk Decker Ford, Fresno, 1977-79, office mgr., 1979-84, fin. mgr., 1984-85; sales mgr. Swanson Fahrney Ford, Selma, Calif., 1985-87; gen. sales mgr. Fresno (Calif.) Dodge, 1987-88; sales mgr. Herwaldt Oldsmobile GMC, Fresno, 1988—. Democrat.

CARRILLO, GILBERTO, engineer; b. San Diego, Sept. 22, 1926; s. Manuel C. and Francisca (Ruiz) C.; m. Maria de Lourdes Paez, Jan. 21, 1957; children: Gilbert A., Elizabeth, Evelyn, Fernando, Mary Lou. BS with honors, San Diego State U., 1951. Materials and process engr. Convair Div. Gen. Dynamics, San Diego, 1950-56, Douglas Aircraft Co., El Segundo, Calif., 1956-60; tech. dir. Torco Products, Inc., Mexico City, 1960-68; mgr., environ. engr. Rohr Industries, Riverside, Calif., 1969—. Contbr. articles to profl. jours.; patentee in field. Served as sgt. USAAF, 1945-46, Japan. Mem. Soc. for Advancement Materials and Process Engring. (nat. chpt.: gen. chmn., internat. symposium and tech. conf. 1988; Inland Empire chpt.: chmn. arrangements com. 1972-76, chmn. scholarships 1976-82, gen. chmn. 1982-83, Best Paper award, 1983), VFW. Republican. Roman Catholic. Home: 5535 Montero Dr Riverside CA 92509 Office: Rohr Industries Materials Engring 8200 Arlington Ave Riverside CA 92503

CARRIVEAU, RICHARD CHARLES, teacher; b. Oconto Falls, Wis., Sept. 6, 1959; s. Walter Anthony and Grace Elizabeth (Smith) C. BA magna cum laude, St. Norbert Coll., 1981; postgrad., Oxford U., 1983, U. Wyo., 1983-87. Cert. tchr. Elem. Edn., English, World History. Tchr. Cath. Cen. Grade Sch., Green Bay, Wis., 1982, Rawhide Elem. Sch., Gillette, Wyo., 1982-86, Sage Valley Jr. High Sch., Gillette, 1986-88, Sunflower Elem. Sch., Gillette, 1988—; coach intramural sports, Rawhide Elem., Gillette, 1982-86, high sch. speech, debate team, Gillette, 1987—; workshop leader Campbell County Sch. Dist., Gillette, 1984-85, editor sch. newspapers Rawhide, Sage Valley, Sunflower, Gillette, 1982—. Author, compiler various ednl. materials Campbell County Sch. Dist., 1984—. Named One of Outstanding Young Men of Am., 1987. Mem. Nat. Forensic League, Amnesty Internat., Nat. Geographic Soc., Smithsonian Instn. Soc., Delta Epsilon Sigma. Roman Catholic. Home: 707 W 9th St Gillette WY 82716 Office: Sunflower Elem Sch Gillette WY 82716

CARROLL, DAVID TODD, computer engineer; b. West Palm Beach, Fla., Apr. 8, 1959; s. David Irwin and Lois Ellen (Spriggs) C. Student, U. Houston, 1978-81. Lab. technician Inst. for Lipid Rsch., Baylor Coll. Medicine, Houston, 1978-81; software specialist Digital Equipment Corp., Colorado Springs, Colo., 1982-86; systems engr. Digital Equipment Corp., Colorado Springs, 1986—. Mem. Digital Equipment Corp. Users Soc. Home: 7332 Aspen Glen Ln Colorado Springs CO 80919 Office: Digital Equipment Corp 305 Rockrimmon Blvd S Colorado Springs CO 80919

CARROLL, EARL HAMBLIN, judge; b. Tucson, Mar. 26, 1925; s. John Vernon and Ruby (Wood) C.; m. Louise Rowlands, Nov. 1, 1952; children—Katherine Carroll Pearson, Margaret Anne. BSBA, U. Ariz., 1948, LLB, 1951. Bar: Ariz., U.S. Ct. Appeals (9th and 10th cirs.), U.S. Ct. of Claims, U.S. Supreme Ct. Law clk. Ariz. Supreme Ct., Phoenix, 1951-52; assoc. Evans, Kitchel & Jenckes, Phoenix, 1952-56, ptnr., 1956-80; judge U.S. Dist. Ct. Ariz., Phoenix, 1980—; spl. counsel City of Tombstone, Ariz., 1962-65, Maricopa County, Phoenix, 1968-75, City of Tucson, 1974, City of Phoenix, 1979. Mem. City of Phoenix Bd. of Adjustment, 1955-58; trustee Phoenix Elem. Sch. Bd., 1961-72; mem. Gov.'s Council on Intergovtl. Relations, Phoenix, 1970-73; mem. Ariz. Bd. Regents, 1978-80. Served with USNR, 1943-46; PTO. Recipient Nat. Service awards Campfire, 1973, 75, Alumni Service award U. Ariz., 1980, Disting. Citizen award No. Ariz. U., Flagstaff, 1983, Bicentenial award Gergetown U., 1988. Fellow Am. Coll. Trial Lawyers, Am. Bar Found.; mem. ABA, Ariz. Bar Assn., U. Ariz. Law Coll. Assn. (pres. 1975), Phoenix Country Club, Sigma Chi, Phi Delta Phi. Democrat. Office: US Dist Ct US Courthouse and Fed Bldg 230 N 1st Ave Rm 6000 Phoenix AZ 85025

CARROLL, JAMES FRANCIS, corporate executive; b. Newark, July 12, 1929; s. James Francis and Marguerite Ann (Gahr) C.; m. Ann Marie Brennan, Sept. 15, 1953 (div. 1972); children: Robert, Richard, Eileen, William; m. Georgia Ann Leuth, June 9, 1973; children: Alexis, James F. III. BS, Seton Hall U., 1952; MS, USN Postgrad Sch., 1966; postgrad., Naval War Coll., Newport, R.I., 1968-69. Commd. ensign USN, 1954, advanced through grades to comdr., 1967; rsch. dir. B-K Dynamics, Inc., San Diego, 1974-84; pres. Data Disposal, Inc., La Mesa, Calif., 1985—; chmn. bd. Valle de Oro Bank, Spring Valley, Calif., 1983—. Mem. Naval Aviaton Soc., Assn. Naval Aviation, VFW. Home: 9443 Mesa Vista La Mesa CA 92041 Office: Valle de Oro Bank 9832 Campo Rd Spring Valley CA 92077

CARROLL, JOHN MOORE, electrical engineer; b. Butte, Mont., Oct. 27, 1911; s. William Craig and Harriet Lane (McKay) C.; m. Kathleen McClintock, Apr. 18, 1938 (div. 1964); children: Susan, William; m. Virginia Lee Roberts, Dec. 31, 1966; stepchildren: Thomas Gilbert, Rodney Gilbert, Gary Gilbert. Student, Oreg. State U., 1931; BA in Engring., N.W. Schs., 1958. Elec. supt. Harvey Aluminum Co., The Dalles, Oreg., 1957-62; sr. elec. engr. Aetron-Blume-Atkinson, Stanford, Calif., 1962-66, Bechtel Power Corp., San Francisco, 1968-75; sr. cost engr., contract adminstr. Burns & Roe, Inc., Paramus, N.J., 1975-79; sr. elec. engr. J.A. Jones, Inc., Hanford, Wash., 1979-88; cons., elec. estimator Kennewick, Wash., 1988–; elec. estimator Tempest Co., Omaha, 1985; elec. engr. Metcalf & Eddy, Inc., Long Beach, Calif., 1987. Capt. U.S. Army, 1942-46, PTO. Decorated Bronze Star. Mem. Nat. Soc. Profl. Engrs., IEEE, Am. Assn. Cost Engrs., Am. Arbitration Assn., Masons, Shriners. Republican. Presbyterian. Address: 312 S Columbia Center Blvd Apt 18 Kennewick WA 99336

CARROLL, PAULA MARIE, security company executive; b. Fresno, Calif., July 17, 1933; d. Paul Edward Mikkelsen and Helen Marie (Anderson) Mack; m. Herman S. Carroll Jr., April 25, 1954. V.P., co-owner Cen. Valley Alarm Co., Inc., Merced, Calif., 1963—; pres., co-owner Cen. Valley Alarm Co., Inc., Merced, 1988—. Author: Life Wish, 1986. Mem. Hospice of Merced and Mariposa Counties, Calif., 1979; pres., founder Consumers for Med. Quality Inc., Merced, 1981; chair Ombudsman, Merced, 1982-85. Recipient Celebrating Women award Merced County, 1987, Pres.'s award Calif. Trial Lawyers Assn., 1987; named Woman Distinction Soroptimist Internat., 1986; Consumers for Med. Quality grantee Calif. Trial Lawyers Assn., 1987. Mem. Western Burglar and Fire Alarm Assn., Soc. Law and Medicine, Hastings Ctr. Inst. of Soc., NAFE, Internat. Platform Assn., Beta Sigma Phi. Home: 3271 Alder Ave Merced CA 95340 Office: Cen Valley Alarm Co Inc 620 W 14th St Merced CA 95340

CARROLL, SCOTT MARSHALL, electrical design engineer; b. Sun Valley, CA, June 12, 1956; s. Robert Edward and Janet Lee (Marshall) C.; m. Mary Ileana Schissler, Apr. 1, 1984; children: Jennifer Allison, Andrew Robert. AA, Golden West Coll., Hungtington Beach, Calif., 1979; BSEE, Calif. State U.-Long Beach, 1982; MSEE, Calif. State U., Fullerton, 1988. Lighting designer Long Beach, 1979-82; circulation mgr. Daily 49er' Newspaper, Long Beach, 1980-82; mem. tech. staff Hughes Aircraft Co., Fullerton, 1982–. Mem. Audio Engring. Soc., Opossum Soc. Calif. (data base mgr. 1987–), Alpha Phi Omega. Home: 1301 W Woodcrest Ave Fullerton CA 92633

CARROTT, JOHN ARDEN, manufacturing executive; b. Columbus, Ohio, Dec. 18, 1947; s. Donald Forwein and Marion Randall (Miller) C.; m. Nancy Elizabeth Loftus, Oct. 2, 1970 (div. Sept. 1986); children: Andrew Alan, Christopher Thomas; m. Jerri Lynn Stetler, May 22, 1987. ASEE, Capital Radio Engring. Inst., Washington, 1973; BTCT, N.Y. Inst. Tech., Old Westbury, 1976; ASCS, R.I. Jr. Coll., Warwick, 1981; postgrad., Kennedy-Western U. Research specialist U. R.I. Sch. Oceanography, Narragansett, 1974-78; sr. engr. Data Gen., Providence, 1978-81; pres. Sequoia Computers, Cranston, R.I., 1981-83; dir. research & devel. SCI, Inc., Huntsville, Ala., 1983-84; pres. Diversified Digital Systems, Huntsville, 1984, Universal Systems of Ala., Albertville, 1985; dir. engring. Mets, Inc., Pompano Beach, Fla., 1985-87; v.p. Fairview, Inc., Orlando, Fla., 1987; chief exec. officer Ocean Electronic Systems, Sunnyvale, Calif., 1988—. Patentee security monitoring and tracking systems. Served with USN, 1967-73. Mem. World Trade Ctr., VFW, Smithsonian Assn. Democrat. Roman Catholic. Home: 160 Aries Way #19 Sunnyvale CA 94086 Office: Ocean Electronic Systems 1250 Oakmead Pkwy Ste 210 Sunnyvale CA 94088

CARRUTHERS, ANNETTE RENEE, air toxics specialist, medical technologist; b. Buffalo, N.Y., Nov. 4, 1952; d. Rene and Regina Victoria (Staskiewicz) Blanc; m. Anthony David Carruthers, Aug. 26, 1972 (div. Jan. 1987); children: Michael Anthony, Ryan Scott. BS, Calif. State U., Sacramento, 1980. Cert. med. technologist, Calif. Ward clk. U. Calif. Med. Ctr., Sacramento, 1973-77; lab. technologist Petaluma (Calif.) Valley Hosp., 1981-85; lab. mgr. Sonoma (Calif.) Valley Hosp., 1984-86; computer tng. specialist Barrett Lab., Sacramento, 1986-87; air toxics specialist Sacramento County Air Pollution Control Dist., 1987—. Mem. No. Calif. Asbestos Task Force, San Francisco, 1988-89, Calif. Air Resources Bd., Tech. Adv. Com., Sacramento, 1988-89, Mather Toxic Cleanup/Superfund Site, Mather AFB, Calif., 1987-89, Cleaner Air Partnership, Sacramento, 1987-89; precinct leader, Dem. Campaign, Sacramento, 1988. Mem. Sierra Club. Democrat. Office: Sacramento County Air Poll 8475 Jackson Rd Ste 215 Sacramento CA 95826

CARRUTHERS, GARREY EDWARD, governor of New Mexico; b. Alamosa, Colo., Aug. 29, 1939; s. William Core and Frankie Jane (Shoults) C.; m. Katherine Thomas, May 13, 1961; children: Deborah Ann Carruthers Joyce, Carol Lynn, Stephen Edward. BS in Agr., N.Mex. State U., 1964, MS in Agrl. Econs., 1965; PhD in Econs., Iowa State U., 1968. From asst. prof. to assoc. prof. dept. agrl. econs. and agrl. bus. N.Mex. State U., Las Cruces, 1968-76, 78-79, prof. agrl. econs. and agrl. bus., 1979-81, 84-87; spl. asst. U.S. Sec. of Agr., Washington, 1974-75; acting dir. N.Mex. Water Resources Research Inst., 1976-78; asst. sec. interior for land and water resources Dept. Interior, Washington, 1981-83, asst. sec. interior for land and minerals mgmt., 1983-84; Gov. State of N.Mex., 1987—; pres. Garrey Carruthers Assocs., Inc., 1979—; while serving on Pres. Ford's campaign com., coordinator N.Mex.'s 2d Congrl. Dist., 1976, co-chmn. Dona Ana County; Dallas panel commn. White House Fellowships, 1976. Contbr. articles to profl. jours. Mem. Am. Agrl. Econs. Assn., Western Agrl. Econs. Assn., Am. Acad. Polit. and Social Services, Univ. Golf Assn. (former v.p., pres.), Sigma Xi, Omicron Delta Kappa. Lodge: Optimist of Las Cruses (former v.p., pres.). Office: State Capitol Office of Gov Santa Fe NM 87503

CARRUTHERS, PETER AMBLER, physicist, educator; b. Lafayette, Ind., Oct. 7, 1935; s. Maurice Earl and Nila (Ambler) C.; m. Jean Ann Breitenbecher, Feb. 26, 1955; children: Peter, Debra, Kathryn; m. Lucy J. Marston, July 10, 1969; m. Cornelia B. Dobrovolsky, June 20, 1981 (div. Dec. 1985). B.S., Carnegie Inst. Tech., 1957, M.S., 1957; Ph.D., Cornell U., 1960. Asst. prof. Cornell U., N.Y., 1961-63, assoc. prof., 1963-67, prof. physics, atomic and solid state physics, nuclear studies, 1967-73; div. leader, theoretical div. Los Alamos (N.Mex.) Sci. Lab., 1973-80, group leader of elem. particles and field theory, 1980-85, sr. fellow, 1980-86; prof., dept. head physics U. Ariz., Tucson, 1986-87, dir. ctr. for study of complex systems, 1987—; vis. asso. prof. Calif. Inst. Tech., 1965, vis. prof., 1969-70, 77-78; mem. physics adv. panel NSF, 1975-80, chmn., 1978-80; trustee Aspen Center for Physics, 1976-82, chmn. exec. com., 1977-79, chmn. bd. trustees, 1979-82, advisor, 1982—; mem. High Energy Physics Adv. Panel, 1978-82; mem. com. on U.S.-USSR cooperation in physics Nat. Acad. Scis., 1978-82; cons. SRI Internat., 1976-81, MacArthur Found., 1981-82, 84-88, Inst. for Def. Analysis, 1985-89; chmn. Ariz. Superconducting Super Collider Tech. Com., 1986-89; editor Multiparticle Prodn. Dynamics, 1988. Author: (with R. Brout) Lectures on the Many-Electron Problem, 1963, Introduction to Unitary Symmetry, 1966, Spin and Isospin in Particle Physics, 1971; editor: (with D. Strottman) Hadronic Matter in Collision, 1986, Hadronic Multiparticle Dynamics, 1988; cons. editor Harwood Soviet Physics Series. Trustee Santa Fe Inst., 1984-86, v.p., 1985-86, mem. sci. bd. 1986—. Recipient Merit award Carnegie Mellon U., 1980; Alfred P. Sloan research fellow, 1963-65; NSF sr. postdoctoral fellow U. Rome, 1967-68; Alexander von Humboldt sr. fellow, 1987—. Fellow Am. Phys. Soc. (panel on pub. affairs 1984-86), AAAS. Home: 2220 E Camino Miraval Tucscon AZ 85718 Office: U Ariz Dept Physics Tucson AZ 85721

CARRUTHERS, RODERICK WILLIAM, educator, management consultant; b. White Horse, Can., Dec. 27, 1933; came to U.S., 1957; s. William Richard and Mildred Eva (Perchie) C.; m. Joan Louise Carstens 1955 (div. Apr. 1986); children: Scott, Sandra, Suzanne, Steven; m. Barbara Joan Lutter, Aug. 23, 1986. BS, St. Martin's Coll., Lacey, Wash., 1964; postgrad., Wis. State U., 1965-66. Dept. chmn. Calif. State Poly. U., San Luis Obispo, Calif., 1965-70; dir. programming Graphic Arts Technical Found., Pitts., 1970-73; v.p. Autographics, Inc., L.A., 1973-75; pres. Ronprint Data, Ltd., Montreal, Can., 1975-77; v.p., gen. mgr. Imprimerie Ronald, Ltd., Montreal, 1977-79; corp. v.p. Ronalds-Federated, Ltd., Toronto, Can., 1981-82; pres. communications div. Ronalds-Federated, Toronto, 1981-82, Strategic Mgmt. Consulting, St. Albans, Vt., 1982-85; disting. prof. chair Ariz. State U., Tempe, 1985-87; pres. Carruthers & Assocs., Sun Lakes, Ariz., 1987—. Author: Quality Management for Printing, 1987; contbr. articles to Graphic Arts Monthly, 1985, 87. Sec. Campbell River C. of C., Campbell River, B.C., Can., 1956-57. Mem. Printing Industries Am. (bd. dirs. 1981-88, chmn. 1987-89), Graphic Arts Tech. Found., Printing Industries So. Calif., Rotary. Republican. Episcopalian. Home and Office: Carruthers & Assocs 26249 Lakeview Dr Sun Lakes AZ 85248

CARSON, BRIAN ALLAN, architect; b. Moscow, Idaho, Apr. 2, 1957; s. Allan Newnan and Nina MayBelle (Gardner) C.; m. Kimberly Patricia Ann Calhoun, Oct. 25, 1986. Student, Idaho State U., 1975-78; degree in architecture, U. Ariz., 1983; hon. degree in architect, U. LaSalle, Mexico City, 1981. Registered architect, Ariz. Tchr.'s aide U. Ariz., 1980, 83; draftsman Rebaque & Belmont, Architects, Mexico City, 1981, H.S. Pederson Architects, Inc., Tucson, 1982; designer, draftsman Whitaker Pools, Tucson, 1982-83; architect, designer Cullen/Burr Assoc., Architects, Ltd., Phoenix, 1983—. Office: Cullen Burr Assocs 4020 N 24th St Phoenix AZ 85016

CARSON, EDWARD MANSFIELD, banker; b. Tucson, Nov. 6, 1929; s. Ernest Lee and Earline M. (Mansfield) C.; m. Nadine Anne Severns, Dec. 13, 1952; children: Dawn, Tod. BSBA, Ariz. State U., 1951; grad. in banking, Rutgers U., 1963. With First Interstate Bank of Ariz., Phoenix, 1951-85, exec. v.p., 1969-72, chief adminstrv. officer, 1972-75, vice chmn. bd., 1975-77, pres., chief exec. officer, 1977-85, also bd. dirs.; pres. First Interstate Bancorp, Los Angeles, 1985—, also bd. dirs.; bd. dirs. Inspiration Resources Corp., Ramada Inns, Inc., First Interstate Bank of Oreg. Bd. fellows Am. Grad. Sch. Internat. Mgmt. Recipient Service award Ariz. State U. Alumni Assn., 1968; named to Ariz. State U. Alumni Assn. Hall of Fame, 1977. Mem. Assn. Res. City Bankers, Assn. Bank Holding Cos. (bd. dirs.). Clubs: Paradise Valley Country, Thunderbirds, Los Angeles Country, Calif.; Phoenix Country. Office: 1st Interstate Bancorp 707 Wilshire Blvd Los Angeles CA 90017 *

CARSON, MARVIN WAYNE, city official; b. Henryetta, Okla., Apr. 20, 1955; s. William Walter and Pauline Janet (Gasaway) C. Student, U. Alaska, 1986. Data tech. Veco Inc., Prudhoe Bay, Alaska, 1979-81; engring. aide Arco Alaska, Inc., Anchorage, 1981, info. systems coordinator, 1981-82; systems analyst Municipality of Anchorage, 1982-85, data and system security officer, 1985–; distbr. Amway Corp., 1987–. Pres. Jr. Achievement, Bellingham, Wash., 1973. With USAF, 1973-79. Decorated USAF Commendation medal. Mem. Assn. Records Mgrs. (bd. dirs. 1982-83), Data Processing Mgmt. Assn., Masons. Home: PO Box 100535 Anchorage AK 99510 Office: Municipality of Anchorage 632 W 6th Ave Anchorage AK 99502

CARSTENS, DIANE YVONNE, retirement housing consultant; b. Vancouver, B.C., Can., Apr. 9, 1955; d. Hans Wilfred Otto Carstens and Louise Marie (Kennedy) Voloshin; m. Edward Christie Lubieniecki, Mar. 24, 1983. Student, Stanford U., 1976; BA, Mills Coll., 1979; M in Landscape Architecture, U. Ill., 1982; postgrad., UCLA, 1980. Researcher U. Ill. Housing Research Program, Champaign, 1981-83; project mgr. Project for Pub. Spaces, N.Y.C., 1983-85; dir. planning and research Leisure Tech. and Care Inc., Lakewood, N.J., 1985-86; v.p. planning and design Gerontol. Services, Inc., Santa Monica, Calif., 1986—; cons., manuscript reviewer Van Nostrand Reinhold, N.Y.C.; lectr., speaker at various univs.; conductor seminars in field. Author: Site Planning and Design for the Elderly, 1985, (with others) Housing the Elderly: A Review of Selected References, (contbg.) Retirement Housing in Australia, 1986. Mem. ad hoc com. Dept. of Health, Bur. Licensure and Certification- State of Ala., 1986. Recipient Honor award Am. Soc. Landscape Architects, Ill., 1981. Mem. Am. Assn. Homes for Aging, Am. Soc. Aging, Environ. Design Research Assn. (Honor award 1986), Gerontol. Soc. Am., Nat. Assn. Sr. Living Industries. Home:

1737 Robson St Santa Monica CA 90405 Office: Gerontol Svcs Inc 204 Santa Monica Blvd #A Santa Monica CA 90401

CARTÉ, GEORGE WAYNE, geophysicist, mayor; b. Buhl, Idaho, Sept. 8, 1940; s. Harold D. Carte and Reba E. (Lammert) Magoon; m. Katherine I. Williams, Sept. 8, 1962; children: Charles M., Theresa L., Jeannette M., Suzanne I. AAS, Columbia Basin Coll., Wash., 1962; BS in Geol. Engring., U. Idaho, 1964; postgrad. U. Hawaii, 1978-79. Hydraulic engr. U.S. Geol. Survey, Anchorage, 1964-66; seismologist AK Tsunami Warning Ctr., Palmer, Alaska, 1966—; instr. Mat-Su Community Coll., Palmer, 1971-72, 81. Mayor City of Palmer, 1981—; chmn. Palmer Planning and Zoning Commn., 1968-78; mem. Mat-Su Borough Planning Commn., 1975-78. Mem. Alaska Conf. of Mayors, 1982—; chmn. Palmer-Saroma Japan Sister City. Recipient cert. of achievement Anchorage Fed. Exec. Assocs., 1981, 87. Mem. Alaska Mcpl. League (bd. dirs. 1983—, pres. 1986-87), Earthquake Engring. Research Inst., Seismol. Soc. Am., Am. Geophys. Union, Tsunami Soc., Alaska Geol. Soc. Mem. Pentecostal Ch. Home: 367 N Valley Way Palmer AK 99645 Office: 910 S Felton St Palmer AK 99645

CARTEE, ROGER LEE, electrical engineer; b. Sutton, W.Va., Feb. 20, 1953; s. Lewis Dean and Martha Pearl (Hutchison) C.; m. Margaret Ellen Mullaly, Sept. 28, 1976 (div. 1982); m. Brenda Lee Post, June 28, 1986; 1 child, Danielle Pearl. BEE, Syracuse U., 1974. Elec. engr. Dept. Interior/Labor, Denver, 1975-79, Anamax Mining Co., Sahuarita, Ariz., 1979-80, Aztec Elec. and Engring. Co., Tucson, 1980-83; elec. project engr. Niagara Mohawk Power Corp., Syracuse, N.Y., 1983-84; elec. engr. Western Area Power Adminstrn., Denver, 1985-87; power mgr. San Carlos Irrigation Project, Coolidge, Ariz., 1988—. Mem. IEEE. Democrat. Methodist. Home: 2407 E Manhatton Dr Tempe AZ 85282 Office: San Carlos Irrigation Coolidge AZ 85282

CARTER, AARON LOUIS, aerospace company executive; b. Center, Tex., Dec. 6, 1944; s. John Robert and Mary (Dupree) C.; m. Mary Alice Jones, Aug. 20, 1967; children: Carol, Cheryl, Candice. BSME, Calif. State U., Fullerton, 1968, MSME, 1971; EDCE, U. So. Calif., 1978, PhDME, 1981. Mem. tech. staff Rockwell Internat. Inc., Anaheim, Calif., 1968-72; mgr. engring. div. Holmes & Narver Inc., Orange, Calif., 1972-83; lctr. UCLA, 1981-83, Calif. State U., Fullerton, 1982—. Mem. ASME. Office: Hughes Aircraft Co 1610 Forbes Way Long Beach CA 90810

CARTER, BLANCHARD LEE, data processing executive, consultant; b. L.A., Aug. 25, 1964; s. Aldridge Evans and Amelia Sylvia (Lee) C. BS in Computer Sci., Calif. State U., L.A., 1987. Programmer Orient-U.S. Leasing Corp., L.A., 1985-87, Calif. State U., L.A., 1982-87; chief exec. officer Compuplex, L.A., 1988—; ADP systems software specialist skill level 2 Planning Rsch. Corp. Govt Info. Systems, L.A., 1988—; cons. BCM Corp., Northridge, Calif., 1986—. Democrat. Methodist. Home and Office: Compuplex 3910 Wisconsin St Los Angeles CA 90037-1507

CARTER, CONNIE BERNICE, small business owner; b. Idaho Falls, Idaho, Jan. 30, 1943; d. James Lazelle Carter and Bernice (Collier) Carter Buttars; m. Welby L. Huffaker, July 4, 1961 (div. 1972); children: Kim Huffaker Walker, Rayna Huffaker Williams. Grad. high sch., Rigby, Idaho. Sales rep. Sta. KUPI, Idaho Falls, 1968-70; sales mgr. Holiday Office Products, Idaho Falls, 1972-77; cons. Snelling & Snelling, Idaho Falls, 1977-81; sales rep. Martin Stationers, Idaho Falls, 1981-84; owner, mgr., counselor Carter Personnel Agy., Idaho Falls, 1984—; cons. Ideal Hardware, Idaho Falls, 1985—, Vo-Tech, Idaho Falls, 1987—. Mem. Idaho Falls C. of C., Achievers Club. Republican. Mormon. Office: Carter Pers Agy 482 Constitution Way Idaho Falls ID 83404

CARTER, DAVID J., Canadian provincial government official; b. Moose Jaw, Sask., Can., Apr. 6, 1934. BA, U. Manitoba, 1958; Licentiate in Theology, St. John's Coll., Winnipeg, 1960; D.Div., St. John's Coll., 1968; B. in Sacred Theology, U. B.C., 1968. Chaplain U. Calgary, 1965-69, So. Alta. Inst. Tech., 1965-69, Mount Royal Coll., 1965-69; dean Anglican Diocese of Calgary, 1969-79; with NOVA, Alta., 1982-86; rep. for Calgary Millican Alta. Legislature, 1979-82, rep. for Calgary Egmont, 1982—, speaker, 1986—; archivist Anglican Diocese of Calgary, 1966-88; senator U. Calgary, 1971-77. Rector Cathedral Ch. of the Redeemer, Calgary; hon. chmn. Lupus Erythematosus Soc. Alta.; dir. Trinity Place Found. Alta., Calgary Canucks Jr. Hockey Team, Calgary Exhbn. & Stampede; founding chmn. Alta. Social Care FAcilities Rev. Com., 1979-82; mem. numerous govt. and legis. coms.; spl. advisor Minister of Edn. Mem. Calgary C. of C., Commonwealth Parliamentary Assn. (pres. Alta. br., mem. exec. com. Can. region). Office: Alta Legislature, Legislature Bldg, Edmonton, AB Canada T5K 2B6

CARTER, EDWARD WILLIAM, retail executive; b. Cumberland, Md., June 29, 1911; s. S. and Rose P. C.;m. Christine Dailey; children: William Dailey, Ann Carter Huneke; m. Hannah Locke Caldwell, 1963. AB, UCLA, 1932; MBA cum laude, Harvard, 1937; LLD (hon.), Occidental Coll., 1962. Account mgr. Scudder, Stevens & Clark, L.A.; mdse. mgr. May Co., L.A.; chmn. emeritus bd. dirs. Carter Hawley Hale Stores, Inc., Los Angeles; bd. dirs. Stamford Rsch. Inst., Palo Alto, Calif., Businessmen's Council, N.Y.C., chmn. bd. regents U. Calif., Berkeley. Trustee Occidental Coll., Brookings Instn., Los Angeles County Mus. Art,Nat. Humanities Ctr. Com. Econ. Devel.; bd. dirs. Assocs. Harvard Grad. Sch. Bus., Stanford Research Inst., James Irvine Found., Santa Anita Found., Los Angeles Philharm. Assn.; mem. vis. com. UCLA Grad. Sch. Mgmt.; mem. Woodrow Wilson Internat. Center Council, Harvard Bd. Overseers Com. Depts. Econs., Art Mus. and Univ. Resources, Council on Fgn. Relations. Mem. Bus. Council, Conf. Bd., Council on Fgn. Relations, Harvard U. Bus Sch. Alumni Assn. (bd. dirs.). Clubs: Calif. (Los Angeles), Los Angeles Country; Pacific Union, Bohemian, Burlingame Country (San Francisco); Cypress Point (Pebble Beach). Office: Carter Hawley Hale Stores 550 S Flower St Los Angeles CA 90071

CARTER, GEORGE HENRY, IV, marketing executive; b. Quincy, Mass., Feb. 17, 1955; s. George Henry III and Shirley (MacLean) C. BSBA, U. Richmond, 1977. V.p., dir. mktg. research and new bus. devel. TNT Mktg. Inc., Acton, Mass., 1976-82; dir. mktg. research Home Fed. Savs. and Loan, San Diego, 1982-86; pres., mgr. TNT West Mktg., San Diego, 1986—. Author: (research study jour.) San Diego County Builders/Development Primary Research, 1982. Mem. Am. Mktg. Assn., Bank Mktg. Assn., Ad Club (San Diego). Republican. Office: TNT Mktg Box 203444 San Diego CA 92120

CARTER, JACK RALPH, broadcasting administrator, television personality; b. Pueblo, Colo., Nov. 4, 1948; s. Jack R. Sr. and Billie Carter; m. Virginia Carter, May 10, 1988. BS, U. Southern Colo., 1970. Sta. mgr. KDZA TV, Pueblo, Colo., 1967-76; sales program mgr. Cetec Broadcast Group, Goleta, Calif., 1976-77; gen. mgr. Sta. KSPN-FM, Aspen, Colo., 1977; weatherman KOAA-TV, Pueblo and Colorado Springs, 1979-87; cons. KCCY-FM, Pueblo, 1980-86, v.p., gen. mgr., 1986—; host program "Matchwits" Sta. KTSC-TV, Pueblo, 1980-84, 86—; broadcasting and bus. cons. Pueblo, 1981—; instr. U. So. Colo., Pueblo, 1970-76, 77-82. Home: 2429 7th Ave Pueblo CO 81003 Office: Sta KCCY-FM 106 W 24th St Pueblo CO 81003

CARTER, JANE FOSTER, agriculture industry executive; b. Stockton, Calif., Jan. 14, 1927; d. Chester William and Bertha Emily Foster; m. Robert Buffington Carter, Feb. 25, 1952; children: Ann Claire Carter Palmer, Benjamin Foster. BA, Stanford U., 1948; MS, NYU, 1949. Pres. Colusa (Calif.) Properties, Inc., 1953—; owner Carter Land and Livestock, Colusa, 1965—; sec.-treas. Carter Farms, Inc., Colusa, 1975—. Author: If the Walls Could Talk, Colusa's Architectural Heritage, 1988; author and editor: Colusa County Survey and Plan for the Arts, 1981, 82, 83, Implementing the Colusa County Arts Plan, 1984, 85, 86. Mem. agrl. adv. com. Yuba Coll., Marysville, Calif., 1976—, Gov's. Commn. Agriculture, Sacramento, 1979-82; del. Rep. Nat. Conv., Kansas City, Mo., 1976, Detroit, 1980, Dallas, 1984; mem. bd. trustees Calif. Hist. Soc., San Francisco, 1979—, regional v.p. 1984—; sec. State of Calif. Reclamation Bd., 1983—. Mem. Sacramento River Water Contractors Assn. (exec. com. 1974—). Episcopalian. Club: Francisca (San Francisco). Home and Office: 909 Oak St Colusa CA 95932

CARTER, JANICE JOENE, telecommunications executive; b. Portland, Oreg., Apr. 17, 1948; d. William George and Charline Betty (Gilbert) P.; m. Ronald Thomas Carter, June 13, 1968; children: Christopher Scott, Jill Suzanne. Student, U. Calif., Berkeley, 1964, U. Portland, 1966-67, U. Colo., Boulder, 1967-68; BA in Math, U. Guam, 1970. Computer programmer Ga.-Pacific Co., Portland, 1972-74; systems analyst ProData, Seattle, 1974-79; systems analyst, mgr. Pacific Northwest Bell, Seattle, 1979-80; data ctr. mgr. Austin Co., Reston, Wash., 1980-83; developer shared tenent svcs. Wright-Runstad, Seattle, 1983-84; system adminstr. Hewlett-packard, Bellevue, Wash., 1984; telecommunications dir. Nordstrom, Seattle, 1984—; mem. large customer panel AT&T, Seattle, 1987—. Ski instr. Alpental, Snoqualmie Pass, Wash., 1984-87; bd. dirs. Educationally Gifted Children, Mercer Island, Wash., 1978-80. Mem. Telecommunications Assn., Internat. Communications Assn., System 85/ETN User Group. Office: Nordstrom Inc 1321 2d Ave Seattle WA 98101

CARTER, JOY EATON, electrical engineer, consultant; b. Comanche, Tex., Feb. 8, 1923; d. Robert Lee and Carrie (Knudson) Eaton; m. Clarence J. Carter, Aug. 22, 1959; 1 child, Kathy Jean. Student, John Tarleton Agrl. Coll., 1939-40; B Music cum laude, N. Tex. State Tchrs. Coll., 1943, postgrad., 1944-45; postgrad., U. Tex., 1945; MSEE, Ohio State U., 1949, PhDEE and Radio Astronomy, 1957. Engr. aide Civil Service Wright Field, Dayton, Ohio, 1945-46; instr. math. Ohio State U., Columbus, 1946-48, research asst., assoc.Research Found., 1947-49, from instr. to asst. prof. elec. engring., 1949-58; research engr. N. Am. Aviation, Columbus, 1955-56; mem. tech. staff Space Tech. Labs. (later TRW Inc.), Redondo Beach, Calif., 1958-68; sect. head, staff engr. electronics research labs. The Aerospace Corp., El Segundo, 1968-72, staff engr. and mgr. system and terminals, USAF Satellite Communications System Program Office, 1972-77, mgr. communications subsystem Def. Satellite Communications System III Program Office, 1978-79; cons. Mayhill, N.Mex., 1979—. Active Mayhill Vol. Fire Dept.; Mayhill Community Assn. (bd. dirs. 1988—, sec. bd. dirs. 1988—); mem. music com. Mayhill Bapt. Ch., 1988—; bd. dirs. Otero County Farm Bur., 1987—. Mem. Am. Astron. Soc., IEEE (sr.), Am. Nat. Cattle Women (sec. Otero CowBelles chpt. 1986-87, 1st v.p. 1988, historian 1989), Sacramento Mountains Hist. Soc. (bd. dirs. 1986—), Sun Country Walking Horse Assn., Calif. Rare Fruit Growers, Native Plant Soc. N.Mex., Sigma Xi (life), Eta Kappa Nu (life), Sigma Alpha Iota (life), Alpha Chi, Kappa Delta Pi, Pi Mu Epsilon, Sigma Delta Epsilon. Home and Office: PO Box 23 Mayhill NM 88339

CARTER, LARRY ALEXANDER, brokerage firm executive; b. Joplin, Mo., Nov. 9, 1940; s. Samuel E. and Laura L. (House) C.; m. Jan. 24, 1962; children: Larry Vince, Donna Diane, Mitchell Alexander; m. Gail Carter, Apr. 28, 1989; children: Jacques, Gabriella. Student, Cerritos Coll., Long Beach State Coll., UCLA, Calif. Orange Coast Coll. Police officer South Gate (Calif.) Police Dept., 1963-65; narcotics expert Long Beach (Calif.) Police Dept., 1965-75; pvt. practice constrn. 1975-76; v.p., office mgr. Diversified Securities, Inc., El Toro, Calif., 1976—; speaker in field. Recipient Calif. Commn. on Police Officer Standards and Tng. Advanced cert., 1974. Mem. Saddleback C. of C., Lake Arrowhead C. of C., Crestline C. of C., Narcotics Officers Assn., Crest Forest Community Assn. (dir.), Rotary. Republican. Baptist. Home: 396 Hartman Circle PO Box 3271 Crestline CA 92325 Office: 24028 Lake Dr Ste C PO Box 3271 Crestline CA 92325

CARTER, LARRY ERNEST, automotive executive; b. Humboldt, Tenn., Sept. 12, 1941; s. Ernest Richard and Mary Sue (Stegal) C.; m. Marilyn Wendt, Sept. 15, 1963 (div. July 1976); children: Kirsten, Kimberly, Dana; m. DeEtte Carlson, Aug. 27, 1977. BS in Mktg., Ferris State U., 1966. Various positions GMC, Los Angeles and Pontiac, Mich., 1966-73; pres., gen. mgr. Desert White GMC, Inc., Las Vegas, Nev., 1973—; pres. Kawasaki West, Inc., Las Vegas, 1981-87, Econo Rental & Leasing, Las Vegas, 1983—, Popeye's Car Rental, Las Vegas, 1986—; sec., treas. Truck Wholesalers of Nev., Las Vegas, 1985—; owner West Sahara Properties, Las Vegas, 1986—; pres. Desert GMC Inc. East, Las Vegas, 1988—; pres. GMC council, 1988, nat. dir., 1986—, nat. dir. chmn., 1989. Mem. Citizens for Pvt. Enterprise; chmn. projects campaign Boy Scouts Am., bd. dirs. Mem. Better Bus. Bur., Nev. Franchised Dealers Assn., Las Vegas Franchised Dealers Assn., Nev. Motor Transport Assn., Las Vegas Exec. Assn. (chmn. various coms., v.p., bd. dirs., Las Vegas C. of C., Lambda Chi Alpha (chmn. various coms., sec., treas.), Nat. Auto Dirs. Assn. (elected rep. GMC/Chevrolet dirs.). Club: U. Nev. Athletic. Office: Desert GMC Inc 3655 W Tropicana Las Vegas NV 89103

CARTER, LARRY VINCE, financial planner; b. Long Beach, Calif., July 5, 1962; s. Larry Alexander and Patricia Ruth (Gabriel) C. Grad. high sch., El Toro, Calif. Lead technician Mini Lab Maintenance, Inc., Laguna Hills, Calif., 1983-85, Taylor Photo/Technician Support, Cypress, Calif., 1985-87; fin. planner Diversified Securities Inc., Crestline, Calif., 1987—. Mem. Crestline Resorts C. of C., Saddleback Valley C. of C., Rotary, Crest Forest Hist. Soc. Republican. Home: 392 Hartman Circle Cedarpines Park CA 92322 Office: Diversified Securities Inc PO Box 3271 24028 Lake Dr Ste #C Crestline CA 92322

CARTER, MARY JO, educator; b. Buckville, Ark., Sept. 2, 1939; d. Joe Southard and Mary Mathalene (Bratton) Breashears; m. Lou Carter, May 26, 1958 (div. 1971); children: Laura, Libby. BA, Calif. State U., Long Beach, 1963. Tchr. Norwalk (Calif.)-La Mirada Sch. Dist., 1963—; owner, mgr. Night Owls Cleaning Svc., Anaheim, Calif., 1984—. Recipient cert. of achievement Norwalk-La Mirada Sch. Dist., 1987. Mem. NEA, Calif. Tchrs. Assn., Tchrs. Assn. Norwalk-La Mirada Area, NAFE, Audubon Soc., Smithsonian Assocs. Libertarian. Home: 2207 E Alden Ave Anaheim CA 92806 Office: Foster Read Sch 13930 E Foster Rd La Mirada CA 90638

CARTER, MICHAEL RAY, freelance artist; b. L.A., Dec. 2, 1953; s. Richard Eugene and Sarah Ann (Carter) C.; m. Janet Lynette Siefman, Sept. 15, 1978 (div. Apr. 1987); m. Susan Rebecca Harper, Apr. 16, 1988; stepchildren: Douglas Charles Davey, Paul Allen Davey. Student, Cypress (Calif.) Jr. Coll. Ind. collector, appraiser memorabilia and Am. oak antiques San Diego, 1965—; freelance artist San Diego and Escondido, Calif., 1976—; pres., founder M.R. Carter's Am. Character Co., Valley Center, Calif., 1988—. Author poetry. Charter and founding mem. Gene Autry Western Heritage Mus., L.A., 1988; patron, mem. Buffalo Bill Hist. Ctr., Cody, Wyo.; asst. nat. foreman Buck Jones Western Corral #1, Lompoc, Calif., 1989—. Winner 2d Pl. Ft. Verde Days Assn., Inc., 1985, Art Placement in Roy Rogers-Dale Evans Mus., 1986, Best of Show, UNISYS Corp., 1987. Mem. Western Music Assn., Inc. (founding and voting mem. 1988), NRA, N.Am. Hunting Club, Inc. (charter and founding mem. 1980), Statue Liberty-Ellis Island Found., Inc. (charter mem., contbr. 1985—). Republican. Office: PO Box 27464 San Diego CA 92128

CARTER, PAUL RICHARD, physician; b. St. Louis, Apr. 14, 1922; s. Paul William and Lily Edith (Kreutzer) C.; m. Lenora Martha Parker, Dec. 24, 1944; children: Richard Brian, Janet Carol Becker. BA in English and History, Union Coll., 1944; MD, Loma Linda U., 1947. Diplomate Am. Bd. Family Practice, Nat. Bd. Med. Examiners. Head physician surgery L.A. County General Hosp., L.A., 1957-67; chief of surgery Rancho Los Amigo Hosp., Downey, Calif., 1967-69; prof. of surgery Loma Linda (Calif.) U., 1960—; clin. prof. of surgery U. Calif., Irvine, 1960—; pvt. practice surgery Covina, Calif., 1960—; chief thoracic surgery Pettis VA Hosp., Loma Linda, 1978—. Author about 80 articles and book chpts. in field; co-author: (2 vol.) History of the Pacific Coast Surgical Association, 1982, 88. Capt. USAMC, 1952-54, Korea. Recipient Fulbright scholarship, Oxford, 1959; named to editorial bd., Annals of Thoracic Surgery for 11 yrs. Fellow. Am. Coll. Surgeons; mem. So. Calif. Chpt. Am. Coll. Surgeons (recorder, sec., treas., pres. 1989), Pacific Coast Surgical Assn. (v.p. 1987—, historian), Am. Assn. Thoracic Surgery, Soc. Thoracic Surgeons, Western Surgical Assn., Societe Internat. Chirurgie, Coll. Chest Physicians. Republican. Home: 1421 Alpine Dr West Covina CA 91791 Office: 238 W Badillo Covina CA 91723

CARTER, RICHARD BERT, church official, retired government official; b. Spokane, Wash., Dec. 2, 1916; s. Richard B. and Lula Selena (Jones) C.; BA in Polit. Sci., Wash. State U., 1939; postgrad. Georgetown U. Law Sch., 1941, Brown U., 1944, Brigham Young U. Extension, 1975-76; m. Mildred Brown, Sept. 6, 1952; children: Paul, Mark, Janis, David. Advt. credit mgr. Elec. Products Consol., Omaha, 1939-40; pub. communications ofcl., investigator FBI, Washington, 1940-41, Huntington, W.Va., 1941, Houston, 1942, Boston, 1943, S. Am., 1943, Providence, 1944-45, N.Y.C., 1945, Salt Lake City, 1945, P.R., 1946-48, Phoenix, 1948-50, Washington, 1950-51, Cleve., 1952-55, Seattle, 1955-75, ret., 1975; assoc. dir. stake and mission pub. communications dept. Ch. Hdqrs., Ch. of Jesus Christ of Latter-day Saints, Salt Lake City, 1975-77. Dist. chmn. Chief Seattle coun. Boy Scouts Am., 1967-68, coun. v.p., 1971-72, coun. commr., 1973-74, nat. coun. rep., 1962-64, 72-74, dir. pub. rels., area II, Eagle Scout Assn., 1984—. Mem. Freedoms Found. Valley Forge, Utah chpt., 1988—; bd. dirs. Salvation Army, 1963, United Way, 1962-63, mem. allocations com., 1962, 1987-88. Served to 1st lt., Intelligence Corps, U.S. Army, 1954. Recipient Silver Beaver award Boy Scouts Am., 1964, Vigil Honor, 1971, Meritorious Svc. medal, 1989; named Nat. Media Man-of-Month Morality in Media, Inc., N.Y.C., 1976. Mem. Profl. Photographers Am., Internat. Assn. Bus. Communicators, Am. Security Council (nat. adv. bd.), Internat. Platform Assn., Sons Utah Pioneers (pres. 1982), SAR (pres. Salt Lake City chpt. 1987-88, Law Enforcement Commendation medal 1987), Utah State Soc. (pres. 1989—), Amicus Club (chmn. membership com. Deseret Found. 1988—, world sr. games adv. com. 1987—), William Carter Family Orgn. (nat. pres.), Nat. Assn. Chiefs of Police, Scabbard and Blade, Am. Media Network (nat. adv. bd.), Assn. Former Intelligence Officers, Alpha Phi Omega, Pi Sigma Alpha, Sigma Delta Chi, Phi Delta Theta. Mormon (coordinator pub. communications council Seattle area 1973-75, br. pres. 1944-45, dist. pres. 1954-55, high priest 1958—, pres. stake 1959-64, stake Sunday Sch. pres. 1980-81). Clubs: Bonneville Knife and Fork (bd. dirs. 1982—), Rotary (dir., editor The Rotary Bee, 1982-83, Paul Harris fellow 1982, Richard L. Evans fellow 1987, Best Club History in Utah award 1988, Best Dist. Newsletter award 1983, Rotarian of Month 1988). Author: The Sunbeam Years-An Autobiography, 1986; assoc. editor FBI Investigator, 1965-75; contbg. author, editor: Biographies of Sons of Utah Pioneers, 1982; contbr. articles to mags. Home: 2180 S Elaine Dr Bountiful UT 84010

CARTER, ROBERTA ECCLESTON, educator, therapist; b. Pitts.; d. Robert E. and Emily B. (Bucar) Carter; (div.); children: David Michael, Daniel Michael. Student Edinboro State U., 1962-63; BS, California State U. of Pa., 1966; MEd, U. Pitts., 1969; MA, Rosebridge Grad. Sch., Walnut Creek, Calif., 1987. Tchr., Bethel Park Sch. Dist., Pa., 1966-69; writer, media asst. Field Ednl. Pub., San Francisco, 1969-70; educator, counselor, specialist Alameda Unified Sch. Dist., Calif., 1970—; master trainer Calif. State Dept. Edn., Sacramento, 1984—; personal growth cons., Alameda, 1983—. Author: People, Places and Products, 1970, Teaching/Learning Units, 1969; co-author: Teacher's Manual Let's Read, 1968. Mem. AAUW, Calif. Fedn. Bus. and Profl. Women (legis. chair Alameda br. 1984-85, membership chair 1985), NEA, Calif. Edn. Assn., Alameda Edn. Assn., Charter Planetary Soc., Oakland Mus., Exploratorium, Big Bros. of East Bay, Alameda C. of C. (svc. award 1985). Republican. Club: Commonwealth. Avocations: aerobics, gardening, travel, tennis. Home: 1516 E Shore Dr Alameda CA 94501

CARTER, RONALD DALE, marketing professional; b. Wichita, Kans., Mar. 26, 1948; s. Ivan Dale and Francis Earlene (Culp) C. BS, U. Kans., 1971, MS, 1972. Account svc. coord. Assoc. Advt. Agy., Wichita, 1972-74; account mgr. Broyles, Allebaugh & Davis Inc., Englewood, Colo., 1974-85; dir. mktg. Am. Assn. Critical-Care Nurses, Newport Beach, Calif., 1987—; guest instr. mktg. Metro State Coll., Denver, Colo., 1982-83. Mem. Am. Soc. Assn. Execs., Am. Birding Assn., Nat. Audubon Soc., Western Field Ornithologists, Colo. Field Ornithologists, Kans. Ornithol. Soc., Denver Field Ornithologists, Alpha Delta Sigma, Kappa Tau Alpha. Office: Am Assn Critical Care Nurses 1 Civic Plaza Newport Beach CA 92660

CARTER, VICTOR M., private investor; b. Rostov-on-Don, Russia, Aug. 21, 1910; s. Mark and Fanya (Rudnick) C.; m. Adrea Zucker, July 15, 1928; 1 dau., Fanya. Dir., 1st Interstate Bank, Nat. Lumber, Ampal-Am. Israel Corp.; mem. exec. com. IDB Bankholding Co.; v.p., dir. So. Calif. Theatre Assn. Past pres. United Way, City of Hope, Japan Am. Soc., Japanese Philharmonic Soc. Bd. dirs. Fedn. Jewish Welfare Orgns., World Affairs Council, Century City Cultural Commn.; hon. chmn. bd. Israel Devel. Corp., CLAL (Israel) Ltd. (exec. com.), Teva Pharm.; bd. govs. Jewish Agy., Inc. Democrat. Mem. Masons, B'nai B'rith, Hillcrest Country Club. Home: 10375 Wilshire Blvd Penthouse A Los Angeles CA 90024 Office: 10375 Wilshire Blvd Penthouse D Los Angeles CA 90024

CARTER-SCOTT, CHERIE UNTERMEYER, entrepreneur, management consultant, designer; b. Long Branch, N.J., May 30, 1949; d. Milton Frederick and Mary (Kelly) Untermeyer; m. John Carter-Scott, July 17, 1976 (div. 1984); 1 child, Jennifer Hayden. AA, Bradford Coll., 1969; BA, U. Denver, 1971; postgrad., Fielding Inst., 1989—. Chmn. bd. Motivation Mgmt. Svc., San Francisco, 1974—, The MMS Inst., L.A., 1985—; cons., tchr. AMI Corp. Coll., Beverly Hills, Calif., 1985; cons. Rep. Indemnity, San Francisco and Encino, Calif., 1985-88, GTEL/GTE, Thousand Oaks, Calif., 1985—, Better Homes & Gardens mag., Des Moines, Iowa, 1988—. Author: The New Species, 1977, Negaholics: How to Recover From Your Addiction to Negativity and Turn Your Life Around, 1989. Mem. Am. Soc. Tng. and Devel. (trainer, cons. dir.).

CARUFEL, JOAN PATRICIA, travel films company executive; b. Everett, Wash., Jan. 4, 1935; d. George Alexander and Alice Margaret (Miller) Hatchell; m. John Bradfield Carufel, Sept. 6, 1958; children: Michelle, Bradfield, Suzanne. BA in Humanities, Seattle U., 1957. Ind. cons. in art and advt. Seattle, 1973-85; ind. cons. World Adventure Tours Films, Vancouver, B.C., Can., 1985-87; mktg. dir. World Cavalcade Seattle, 1973—; dir., owner World Cavalcade Travel Films, Portland, Oreg., 1987—. Mem. Women in Communications (bd. mem. 1983-84), Pub. Relations Round Table (pres. 1983-84), Profl. Travel Film Sponsors Assn., Toastmasters (Redmond). Roman Catholic. Home: 14312 NE 71st St Redmond WA 98052 Office: World Cavalcade Travel 500 Union Ste 404 Seattle WA 98101

CARUSO, WILLIAM JOSEPH, food service management consultant; b. Summit, N.J., July 25, 1948; s. Joseph R. and Mary (Crane) C.; m. Linda Ann Renn, Apr. 26, 1972; children: Kristin Ann, Tara Lee. BS, Cornell U., 1970; MBA, U. Colo., 1974. Prin. The LFL Cons. Group, Toronto, Ont., Can., 1974-82, The Ricca, Colburn & Caruso Group, Englewood, Colo., 1982-87; pres. William Caruso & Assocs. INc., Littleton, Colo., 1987—. Contbr. articles to profl. jours. Served as sgt. USAR, 1970-76. Fellow Foodservice Cons. Soc. Internat. (bd. dirs. 1980-86, pres. 1985-86, pres.-elect 1984-85, treas. 1983-84, sec. 1982-83); mem. Cornell Soc. Hotelmen (2d v.p. 1987, pres. 1987-88, award of service 1986), Cornell Alumni Assn. (v.p., dir.), Cornell U. Council (elected), Sigma Chi Alumni Assn. (bd. dirs. 1983—). Republican. Roman Catholic. Home: 7819 Waverly Mountain Littleton CO 80127 Office: William Caruso & Assocs Inc 7819 Waverly Mountain Littleton CO 80127

CARVELLI, JOHN JOSEPH, JR., real estate executive; b. Bklyn., Mar. 13, 1962; s. John Joseph and Theresa Marie (Shand) C. BA, Cath. U. Am., 1984. V.p. Inland Group, Inc., Newport Beach, Calif., 1989—; mem. Project 90 Co., 1988—. Calif. Rep. del., 1989—, mem. fin. com. Orange County, 1988—, state assemblyman Gil Ferguson, Newport Beach, 1985; press aide U.S. Sen. Bill Bradley, Washington; campaign mgr. lt. gov. Calif., state Sen. H.L. Richardson, 1986; mem. Orange County Am. Italian Renaissance Found. Mem. Cath. U. Alumni Assn. Roman Catholic. Home: 1542 Valencia Newport Beach CA 92660 Office: Inland Group Inc South Tower #606 3501 Jamboree Rd Newport Beach CA 92660

CARVER, DOROTHY LEE ESKEW (MRS. JOHN JAMES CARVER), educator; b. Brady, Tex., July 10, 1926; d. Clyde Albert and A. Maurine (Meadows) Eskew; student So. Ore. Coll., 1942-43, Coll. Eastern Utah, 1965-67; B.A., U. Utah, 1968; M.A., Cal. State Coll. at Hayward, 1970; postgrad. Mills Coll., 1971; m. John James Carver, Feb. 26, 1944; children—John James, Sheila Carver Bentley, Chuck, David. Instr., Rutherford Bus. Coll., Dallas, 1944-45; sec. Adolph Coors Co., Golden, Colo., 1945-47; instr. English, Coll. Eastern Utah, Price, 1968-69; instr. speech Modesto (Calif.) Jr. Coll., 1970-71; instr. personal devel. men and women Heald Bus. Colls., Oakland, Calif., 1972-74, dean curricula, Walnut Creek, Calif., 1974-86; instr. Diablo Valley Coll., Pleasant Hill, Calif., 1986—; communications cons. Oakland Army Base, Crocker Bank, U.S. Steel, I. Magnin, Artec Internat. Author: Developing Listening Skills. Mem. Gov's. Conf. on Higher Edn. in

Utah, 1968; mem. finance com. Coll. Eastern Utah, 1967-69; active various community drives. Judge election Republican party, 1960, 64. Bd. dirs. Opportunity Center, Symphony of the Mountain. Mem. AAUW, Bus. and Profl. Womens Club, Nat. Assn. Deans and Women Adminstrs., Delta Kappa Gamma. Episcopalian (supt. Sunday Sch. 1967-69). Clubs: Soroptimist Internat. (pres. Walnut Creek 1979-80 sec., founder region 1978-80); Order Eastern Star. Home: 20 Coronado Ct Walnut Creek CA 94596

CARVER, JUANITA, plastic company executive; b. Indpls., Apr. 8, 1929; d. Willard H. and Golda M. Ashe; children: Daniel Charles, Robin Lewis, Scott Alan. Cons. MOBIUS, 1983— ; pres. Carver Corp., Phoenix, 1977—. Bd. dirs. Scottsdale Meml. Hosp. Aux., 1964-65, now assoc. Republican. Methodist. Patentee latch hook rug yarn organizer. Home: 6255 E Avalon St Scottsdale AZ 85251

CARWELL, HATTIE V., health physicist; b. Bklyn., July 17, 1948; d. George and Fannie (Tunstall) C. BS in Chemistry/Biology, Bennett Coll., 1970; MS in Radiation Sci., Rutgers U., 1971; postgrad., U. Calif., Berkeley, 1973-75. Rsch. asst. Thomas Jefferson U. Hosp., Phila., 1970-72; health physicist AEC, Upton, N.Y., 1972-73, Energy Rsch. Adminstrn., Oakland, Calif., 1973-80; internat. nuclear safeguards insp. and group leader Internat. Atomic Energy Agy., Vienna, Austria, 1980-85; health physicist U.S. Dept. Energy, Oakland, Calif., 1985—; asst. environ. survey team leader Dept. Energy, Washington, 1987; lectr. U. Calif.-Berkeley, Stanford U., Cabrillo Coll., Can. Coll., Tougaloo Coll. Author: Blacks In Science: Astrophysicist to Zoologist; contbr. sci. articles to profl. jours. Co-founder, chmn. Devel. Fund for Black Students in Sci. and Tech., Washington, 1983—; regional dir., mem. Nat. Tech. Assn., Washington, 1977-80. Recipient Fed. Community Svc. award, 1977. Mem. Nat. Health Physics Soc., Inst. Materials Mgmt. (treas. Vienna chpt. 1985), No. Calif. Coun. Black Profl. Engrs. (pres. 1986, 87, sec. 1988), NAACP (life). Home: 4633 Allendale Ave Oakland CA 94619

CARY, CLAYTON LEWIS, vocational educator; b. Kirby, Ohio, May 17, 1932; s. Clayton Lewis and Mildred (Pfeiffer) C.; m. Mary Irene Smith, Feb. 10, 1952; children: JoAnne, Robert, Christopher, Gregory. BS in Edn., Ohio No. U., 1969; MS in Edn., Colo. State U., 1973. Cert. tchr., Ohio, Wyo., Colo. With quality control dept. Westinghouse Electric Co., Upper Sandusky, Ohio, 1955-65; tchr. Upeer Sandusky High Sch., 1968-73, Rock Springs (Wyo.) High Sch., 1974—. Dep. comdr. CAP, Rock Springs, 1987—. With USN, 1950-54. Named Tchr. of Yr., State of Wyo., 1985, Outstanding Alumnus, Ohio No. U., 1987. Mem. Internat. Tech. Edn. Assn., Am. Vocat. Assn., Wyo. Vocat. Assn., Wyo. Tech. Edn. Assn. (pres. 1986-87), Elks (treas. 1975-79). Democrat. Methodist. Home: 302 Agate Rock Springs WY 82901 Office: Rock Springs High Sch James Dr Rock Springs WY 82901

CARY, MICKEY DOUGLAS, savings and loan executive, information systems specialist; b. Carrollton, Mo., Oct. 20, 1949; s. Robert William and Glenn Dell (Willis) C.; m. Sandra Kay Lotspeich, Jan. 19, 1970; 1 child, Michael Douglas. Student bus. adminstrn., U. Mo., Kansas City, 1967-70. System programmer Electronic Data Systems, Atlanta and Cin., 1969-72; systems programming supr. Commerce Bank Kansas City (Mo.), 1972-75; mgr. data ctr. Massey-Ferguson Ltd., Des Moines, 1975-79; dir. mgmt. info. systems Carlson Co. Inc. div. Ardans and Naums, Rochester, N.Y., 1979-81; systems and programming mgr. Central Bank Denver, 1981-84; v.p. info. systems, chief info. officer Capitol Fed. Savs., Denver, 1984--. Cons. Colo. Assn. Home and Services Aged, 1984-87. Mem. Am. Mgmt. Assn., Fin. Mgmt. Soc., Assn. Info. Mgrs., Data Processing Mgmt. Assn.

CASALASPRO, DEBRA ANN, nurse; b. Barksdale AFB, La., Sept. 30, 1956; d. Joseph Ronald and Pauline Josephine (Bichanich) C. BSN, Molloy Coll., Rockville Centre, N.Y., 1979. Pvt. duty nurse Lynbrook, N.Y., 1979-80; team leader, nurse Med. Meml. Ctr., Ashland, Wis., 1980-81; nurse intern Wilford Hall, USAF, San Antonio, Tex., 1981; commd. USAF, 1981, advanced through grades to capt.; staff nurse USAF Hosp. KI Sawyer AFB, Gwinn, Mich., 1981-84; flight nurse, instr., res. affairs officer 2 AES Rhien Maim AFB, Frankfurt, Fed. Republic Germany, 1984-86; staff nurse Air Force Acad. Hosp., Colorado Springs, 1986-87, asst. charge nurse, mem. staff nurse com., 1987--. Decorated Air Force Commendation medal. Mem. Air Force Assn., Orgn. for Ob-Gyn. and Neonatal Nurses, Aerospace Med. Assn., Co. Grade Officers (adv. coun.), Air Force Acad. Booster. Republican. Roman Catholic. Home: 8260 Camfield Circle Colorado Springs CO 80920

CASANI, EDWARD KANE, aerospace research and development manager; b. Phila., June 17, 1935; s. John C. and Julia J. (Bateman) C.; children: Anita, Andrea. CE, U. Pa., 1959, postgrad.; postgrad. U. So. Calif., UCLA. With Jet Propulsion Lab., Pasadena, Calif., 1958—, mgr. spacecraft system design and integration sect., 1973-76, project mgr. infrared astron. satellite, 1976-80, dep. mgr. Observational Systems div., 1980-81, div. mgr., 1981—; tchr. various colls., guest lectr., cons.; cons. movie Andromeda Strain; v.p. JETS, Ltd.; active design and devel. of Ranger, Mariner, Viking, Voyager and Galileo spacecraft. Mem. YMCA. Recipient Exceptional Svc. medal NASA. Mem. AIAA, Sigma Xi. Contbr. articles profl. jours.

CASANOVA, ALDO JOHN, sculptor; b. San Francisco, Feb. 8, 1929; s. Felice and Teresa (Papini) C.; children: Aviva, Liana, Anabelle. B.A., San Francisco State U., 1950, M.A., 1951; Ph.D., Ohio State U., 1957. Asst. prof. art San Francisco State U., 1951-53; asst. prof. Antioch (Ohio) Coll., 1956-58; asst. prof. art Tyler Sch. Art, Temple U., Phila., 1961-64, Tyler Sch. Art, Temple U. (Italy campus), Rome, 1968-70; prof. art Scripps Coll., Claremont, Calif., 1966—; chmn. art dept. Scripps Coll., 1971-73; vis. prof. SUNY, 1981; faculty mem. Skowhegan Sch. Painting and Sculpture, Maine, summers 1973-74. One-man shows include, Esther Robles Gallery, Los Angeles, 1967, Santa Barbara (Calif.) Mus., 1967, Calif. Inst. Tech., 1972, Carl Schlosberg Fine Arts, Los Angeles, 1977, SUNY, 1981; represented in permanent collections, Whitney Mus., San Francisco Mus. Art, Hirshhorn Collection, Cornell U., Columbus (Ohio) Mus., UCLA Sculpture Garden, Calif. Inst. Tech., Pasadena, Univ. Judaism, Los Angeles, Air and Space Mus., Washington. Recipient Prix-de-Rome Am. Acad. in Rome, 1958-61; Louis Comfort Tiffany award, 1970. Fellow Am. Acad. in Rome; mem. Sculptors Guild. Democrat. Roman Catholic. Office: Scripps Coll Claremont CA 91711

CASCINO, JAMES MADISON, consumer products fund raising executive; b. Balt., Apr. 1, 1951; s. Alfred M. and Mona (Madison) C.; m. Debora C. Chapman, Apr. 10, 1976; children: Taylor C., Thomas J. AB, Mercer U., 1974. Dir. ann. fund Mercer U., Macon, Ga., 1974-75; dir. planned giving Cystic Fibrosis Found., Atlanta, 1975-78; dir. recruiting, sales dir. HBO, Atlanta, 1978-81; div. mgr. Avon Products, Atlanta, 1981-83; mgr. sales productivity, dir. field planning Avon Products, N.Y.C., 1983-85, dir. bus. planning and sales productivity; founder, v.p. Wynmere Ltd., Houston, 1985-87; sr. v.p. Instnl. Financing Svcs., San Francisco, 1987—. Office: Instnl Financing Svcs 5100 Park Rd Benicia CA 94510

CASE, JOHN PHILIP, real estate corporation officer; b. Marquette, Mich., Jan. 25, 1952; s. Kenneth Carroll and Judith (Paul) C.; m. Patricia Lee Sullivan, July 5, 1985. BS, No. Mich. U., 1974, MA, 1979. Instr. Engadine (Mich.) Sch. Dist., 1974-85; pres. The Carroll Paul Forests, Inc., Marquette, 1976—, The Longyear Realty Co., Marquette, 1987—, Ashland Mining Corp., Marquette, 1987—, Gogebic & Ontonagon Land Co., Marquette, 1987—; also bd. dirs. Gogebic & Ontonagon Land Co.; bd. dirs. UP Forest Mktg. Corp., Longyear Realty Corp., J.M. Longyear Heirs, Inc., Ashland Mining Corp.; instr. Scottsdale Sch. Dist., Ariz., 1985—. Mem. Ariz. Hist. Soc., The Nature Conservancy, The Forest History Soc. Mem. Newcomen Soc., Iron Ore Lessors Assn. Republican. Episcopalian. Club: Ives Lake Sailing (Mich.) (treas. 1988-89). Home: 5029 E Hearn Rd Scottsdale AZ 85254 Office: Longyear Cos 210 N Front St Marquette MI 49855

CASE, KAREN LOUISE, nurse; b. L.A., Nov. 3, 1954; d. Gordon Grant and Mary Jayne (Stokes) C.; m. Conrad Israel Castillo, Apr. 23, 1981 (div. 1985). AA in Socilogy, L.A. Pierce Coll., 1975; BA in Social Welfare, Calif. State U., Northridge, 1978; AS in Nursing, L.A. Pierce Coll., 1985. RN, Calif. Nurse St. Joseph Med. Ctr., Burbank, Calif., 1986-87, Reg. Med. Ctr., Canoga Park, Calif., 1987--, Tarzana Reg. Med. Ctr., Calif., 1986--. Democrat. Home: 7038 Farmdale Ave Van Nuys CA 91406

CASE, LEE OWEN, JR., college official; b. Ann Arbor, Mich., Nov. 5, 1925; s. Lee Owen and Ava (Comin) C.; m. Dolores Anne DeLoof, July 1950 (div. Feb. 1958); children—Lee Douglas, John Bradford; m. Maria Theresia Breninger, Feb. 27, 1960; 1 adopted dau., Ingrid Case Dunlap. A.B., U. Mich., 1949. Editor Washtenaw Post-Trib, Ann Arbor, 1949; dir. pub. relations Edison Inst., Dearborn, Mich., 1951-54; field rep. Kersting, Brown, N.Y.C., 1954-58; campaign dir. Cumerford Corp., Kansas City, Mo., 1958-59; v.p. devel., pub. relations U. Santa Clara, 1959-69; v.p. planning, devel., Occidental Coll., Los Angeles, 1969—; bd. visitors South Western U. Law Sch., Los Angeles, 1981—. Chmn. Santa Clara City Proposition A, 1966; mem. Santa Clara County Planning Com. on Taxation and Legis., Santa Clara, 1968. Served to 1st lt. USAAF, 1943-46. Mem. Am. Coll. Pub. Relations Assn. (bd. dirs. 1968-74), Council for Advancement and Support Edn. (founding bd. dirs. 1974-75), 1st Tribute for Distinction in Advancement, Dist. VII, 1985), Santa Clara C. of C. (pres. 1967), Santa Clara County C. of C. (founding bd. dirs. 1968), Town Hall. Republican. Club: University (Los Angeles). Lodge: Rotary. Home: 2633 Risa Dr Glendale CA 91208 Office: Occidental Coll 1600 Campus Rd Los Angeles CA 90041

CASE, RICHARD THOMAS, health care company executive; b. Chgo., June 24, 1949; s. Thomas Case and Betty Mae (Gately) Steenstry; m. Linda Marie Smith, June 13, 1970; children: Christina, Michelle, Peter. BS, Bradley U., 1971; MBA, U. So. Calif., 1972; MA, Trinity Div. Sch., Deerfield, Ill., 1976. Mktg. mgr. Baxter Labs., Costa Mesa, Calif., 1972-73; new bus. devel. mgr. Corning (N.Y.) Glass Works, 1973-75; dir. bus. devel. Am. Hosp. Supply, Evanston, Ill., 1975-80, v.p. mktg., 1980-81; pres. Scientech, Boulder, Colo., 1981-82, Benchmark Assocs., Boulder, 1982-88; sr. v.p. Hycor Biomed., Fountain Valley, Calif., 1988—; bd. dirs. G.L. Lewis Co., Anaheim, Calif.; speaker in field. Author: Money Diet, How to Interview, Practical Accountant. Elder Calvary Evang. Free Ch., Boulder, 1986-87, Christ Ch. Lake Forest (Ill.), 1979-81; cons. Christian Bus. Men's Com., Chattanooga, 1975-87, Campus Crusade for Christ, Boulder, 1984-88. Mem. Biomed. Mktg. Assn., Med. Mktg. Assn., U. So. Calif. Bus. Assocs. Republican. Presbyterian. Office: Hycor Biomed 7272 Chapman Ave Garden Grove CA 92641

CASEBOLT, MARK WILLIAM, electronics company executive; b. Ankara, Turkey, Nov. 10, 1953; came to U.S., 1959; s. William Oscar and Berniece Casebolt; m. Patricia Lynn Paulson, Jan. 18, 1986. BSEE, Oreg. State U., 1976. Cert. profl. engr., Wash. Design engr. Boeing Aerospace Co., Seattle, 1977-83; project engr. Honeywell Marine Systems, Seattle, 1983-84; chief engr. Rapid Systems, Inc., Seattle, 1984—, gen. ptnr., 1985—. Home: 210 NW 55th St Seattle WA 98107 Office: Rapid Systems Inc 433 N 34th St Seattle WA 98103

CASEY, DON, professional basketball coach. M. Dwynne Casey; 3 children: Leann, Michael, Sean. Formerly head coach Temple U., Phila.; asst. coach Chgo. Bulls (NBA), 1982-83, Los Angeles Clippers (NBA), 1983-84; head coach in Italian profl. basketball league 1984-85; asst. coach Los Angeles Clippers, 1985-89, head coach, 1989—. Office: care Los Angeles Clippers Meml Sports Arena 3939 S Figueroa St Los Angeles CA 90037 *

CASEY, MICHAEL HARRINGTON, sculptor, restoration sculptor, consultant designer; b. San Jose, Calif., Mar. 6, 1947; s. Jocelyn Gaudielle; m. Cynthia Jane Mark, Feb. 28, 1987. BFA, R.I. Sch. of Design, 1969. Resident artist State Capitol Restoration Project, Sacramento, 1976-83; supt. ornamental div. Western Art Stone, Brisbane, Calif., 1983-87; dir. Michael H. Casey Designs, San Francisco, 1987-88. Prin. works include Minerva sculpture, Calif. State Senate, 1982. Office: Michael H Casey Designs 1510 Indiana St San Francisco CA 94107

CASEY, STEPHEN JAMES, administrative electrical engineer; b. Hanford, Calif., Aug. 20, 1948; s. James Alfred and Juanita Alice (Spanke) C.; m. Maureen Patricia Kearney, May 26, 1985. AA, Southwestern Coll., Chula Vista, Calif., 1968; BSEE, San Diego State U., 1972; MBA, Pepperdine U., 1985. Assoc. elec. engr. Lockheed Calif. Co., Burbank, 1973-74, mgmt. trainee, mfg. br., 1974-75, engr., functional test, 1975, supr. mgr. test equipment engring., 1975-84, supr. and group engr., mfg. research automation technology dept., 1984—. Mem. Nat. Mgmt. Assn., Pepperdine Alumni Assn. Republican. Home: 1304 N Sparks St Burbank CA 91506

CASEY, WALTER PEVEAR, JR., reverse osmosis equipment manufacturing executive; b. Glendora, Calif., Aug. 4, 1918; s. Walter Pevear and Anna Irene (LaFetra) C.; m. Margaret Lehr Perkins, Nov. 28, 1946; children: Steven Shannon, Michael Andrew, Ann LaFetra. BA, U. Calif., Berkeley, 1942. Air freight specialist United Air Lines, Chgo, 1945; cargo sales mgr. United Air Lines, Portland, Oreg., 1946-48; owner, mgr. Servisoft, Las Vegas, 1954-70; pres. Universal Water Corp., Del Mar, Calif., 1965-74; Wetco, Inc. (acquired by BioLab 1988) Las Vegas, 1974-88; owner, mgr. Walt Casey Water Conditioning, 1970—; cons. BioLab, Las Vegas, 1988—. Vice chmn. Colorado River Commn., Las Vegas, 1969-71; chmn. Nev. Rep. Central Com., 1972-74; bd. dirs. Las Vegas Conv. Authority, 1972-74. Ensign USN, 1942-45. Mem. Water Quality Assn. (conv. chmn. 1964, 72; nat. bd. govs. 1982-84; dir. group ins. 1984—; Regents award 1980), Pacific Water Quality Assn. (pres. 1964, Hall of Fame award 1981), Las Vegas C. of C. (pres. 1964), NAM (nat. bd. dirs. 1965-72, 85—), Masons, Shriners, Jesters, Kiwanis, Sigma Nu. Office: Walt Casey Water Cond 2661 Western St Las Vegas NV 89109

CASH, KATHLEEN MCCARTHY, television broadcast technician; b. Omaha, Nov. 30, 1958; d. William Henry and Andrea (Powell) McC.; m. Kevin Marshal Cash, Oct. 4, 1986 (div.). Cert. completion, L.H. Bates, Tacoma, 1982. Prodn. clk. Tektronix, Beaverton, Oreg., 1978-79; shipping clk. NIKE, Portland, Oreg., 1980-81; cashier Pacific N.W. Bell, Seattle, 1981; video tape operator Sta. KOIN-TV, Portland, 1983-88, NBC Inc., Burbank, Calif., 1988—. Mem. Internat. Brotherhood Electrical Workers, Nat. Assn. Broadcast Employees and Technicians. Republican. Roman Catholic. Home: 530 Palm Dr #205 Glendale CA 91202

CASH, R(OY) DON, gas and petroleum company executive; b. Shamrock, Tex., June 27, 1942; s. Bill R. and Billie Mae (Lisle) C.; m. Sondra Kay Burleson, Feb. 20, 1966; 1 child, Clay Collin. BSIndslE, Tex. Tech U., 1966. Former engr. Amoco Prodn. Co.; v.p. Mountain Fuel Supply, Salt Lake City, 1976-79; pres. Wexpro Co., Salt Lake City, 1979-80; pres., chief exec. officer Mountain Fuel Supply Co., Salt Lake City, 1980-84; pres., chief exec. officer Questar Corp., Salt Lake City, 1984-85, pres., chmn., chief exec. officer, 1985—, also bd. dirs.; bd. dirs. Zions First Nat. Bank, Salt Lake City; trustee Inst. Gas Technology, Chgo., 1986—. Trustee Holy Cross Hosp.; bd. dirs. Utah Symphony Orch., Salt Lake City, 1983-86. Mem. Soc. Petroleum Engrs., Rocky Mountain Oil and Gas Assn. (bd. dirs., pres. 1982-84), Utah Mfrs. Assn. (bd. dirs., chmn. 1986), Pacific Coast Gas Assn. (bd. dirs. 1981-85, 87—), Am. Gas Assn., Am. Petroleum Inst., Nat. Petroleum Council, Ind. Petroleum Assn. of Am. Club: Alta (Salt Lake City), Fort Douglas Country. Office: Questar Corp 180 E 1st South St Salt Lake City UT 84147

CASH, WEBSTER COFIELD, JR., astrophysics educator; b. Washington, Aug. 22, 1952; s. Webster Cofield and Mary Ann (Thomas) C.; m. Cynthia Smith, Sept. 20, 1980; children: Lindsey Jacqueline, Christine Annmarie, Webster Cofield III. BS, MIT, 1973; PhD, U. Calif., 1978. Asst. rsch. physicist U. Calif. Space Sci. Lab., Berkeley, 1978-79; rsch. assoc. U. Colo., Boulder, 1979-82, asst. prof., 1982-85, assoc. prof., 1985—; pres. CW Optics, Inc., Boulder, 1989—; assoc. dir. Cen. for Astrophysics and Space Astromony U. Colo., 1986—. Author (software): Interactive Raytrace; contbr. articles to profl. jours. Rsch. grantee NASA. Mem. Internat. Astromonical Union, Am. Astronomical Soc. (head exec. com 1986-88), Optical Soc. Am. Office: U Colo CASA CB-391 Boulder CO 80309

CASHATT, CHARLES ALVIN, hydro-electric power generation company executive; b. Jamestown, N.C., Nov. 14, 1929; s. Charles Austin and Ethel Buren (Brady) C.; m. Wilma Jean O'Hagan, July 10, 1954; children: Jerry Dale, Nancy Jean. Grad. high sch., Jamestown. Bldg. contractor, Jamestown, 1949-50; 1954-58; powerhouse foreman Tri-Dam Project, Strawberry, Calif., 1958-66; power project mgr. Merced Irrigation Dist., Calif., 1966—. Contbr. articles to ASCE pub. and books. Pres. Merced County Credit Union, 1981-82. Served with USAF, 1950-54. Mem. Am. Legion. Republican. Lodge: Elks, Odd Fellows. Office: Merced Irrigation Dist 9188 Village Dr Snelling CA 95369

CASHMAN, MICHAEL RICHARD, small business owner; b. Owatonna, Minn., Sept. 26, 1926; s. Michael Richard and Mary (Quinn) C.; m. Antje Katrin Paulus, Jan. 22, 1972 (div. 1983); children: Janice Katrin, Joshua Paulus, Nina Carolin. BS, U.S. Mcht. Marine Acad., 1947; BA, U. Minn., 1951; MBA, Harvard U., 1953. Regional mgr. Air Products & Chems., Inc., Allentown, Pa.; then pres. so. div. Air Products & Chems., Inc., Washington; mng. dir. Air Products & Chems., Inc., Europe and Brussels, 1959-72; internat. v.p. Airco Indsl. Gasses, Brussels, 1972-79; pres. Continental Elevator Co., Denver, 1979-81; assoc. Moore & Co., Denver, 1981-84; prin. Cashman & Co., Denver, 1984—. Creator continental walking baton, 1987. Committeeman Denver Rep. Com., 1986—, congl. candidate, 1988. Lt. (j.g.) USN, 1953-55; co-chmn. "Two Forks or Dust" Ad Hoc Citizens Com. Mem. Bdlg. Owners and Mgrs. Assn., Colo. Harvard Bus. Sch. Club, Royal Golf de Begigue, Belgian Shooting Club, Rotary, Phi Beta Kappa. Home: 2512 S University Blvd Apt 802 Denver CO 80210

CASKIE, WILLIAM WIRT, accountant, securities broker; b. N.Y.C., May 9, 1945; s. John Minor and Rosa Maria (Marchese) C.; BS in Physics, Georgetown U., 1967; MBA in Ops. Research, NYU, 1970; BS magna cum laude in Acctg., Golden Gate U., 1976. Tchr. math. N.Y.C. pub. schs., 1968-71; statistician Fed. Res. Bank of San Francisco, 1972-74; pvt. practice acctg., Marina Del Rey, Calif., 1977—; registered rep. Fin. Network Investment Corp., 1986—. Mem. Assn. Bus. and Tax Cons., Nat. Assn. Enrolled Agts., Calif. Soc. Enrolled Agts., Mensa, Fin. Network Investment Corp. (registered rep.). Home and Office: 557 1/2 Washington St Marina Del Rey CA 90292

CASORLA, RODRIGO CHAVES, nurse; b. Iloilo, Philippines, Mar. 13, 1950; came to U.S., 1974; s. Solomon C. and Esther (Chavez) C. AA in Liberal Arts, U. San Agustine, Iloilo City, 1970; degree in nursing, Riverside Coll., Bacolod City, Philippines, 1973, BS in Nursing with honors, 1974; MS in Health Care Adminstrn., U. La Verne (Calif.), 1983. Staff nurse pediatrics unit U. Ark. Med. Ctr., Little Rock, 1974-75; staff nurse ICU, pedicatrics, neonatal Kaiser Permanente Med. Ctr., Hollywood, Calif., 1975-79; supr. med./surg. unit West Hollywood (Calif.) Hosp., 1979-80, assoc. dir. nursing, in-svc. edn., 1980-83, dir. nursing svc., 1983—, assoc. adminstr., 1987—; clin. instr. Pacific Coast Coll., L.A., 1982—; cons., lectr. nursing edn. Queen of Angels Med. Ctr., L.A., 1984-85; cons. nursing edn. San Fernando (Calif.) Valley Community Hosp., 1985-86; moderator minority nursing UCLA, 1980—. Vol. Hypertension Clinic Philippines Community Ctr., L.A., 1985—; coord. Sr. Citizens Flu Vaccinations Clinic, West Hollywood, 1984—; bd. dirs. minority edn. com. AIDS Project, L.A., 1987—. Named an Outstanding Nurse Internat. Nursing Hall of Fame, 1987. mem. Philippine Nurses Assn. (pres. So. Calif. chpt. 1986—), Philippine Nurses Assn. U.S. (chpt. local chpt. 1985), Asian Pacific Rim Nurses Assn., Confedn. of Philippine-U.S. Organ., Calif. Bd. Registered Nurses (standardized task force 1985), Amona Found. Office: West Hollywood Hosp 1233 N La Brea Ave West Hollywood CA 90038

CASS, MAXINE HARRIET, photojournalist; b. Palo Alto, Calif., Jan. 27, 1952; d. Harry and Alma Lyndell (Thorup) C.; m. Lloyd Frederick Gebhart II, Sept. 24, 1974. BA in History and Medieval Studies, U. Calif., Santa Barbara, 1973. Claims rep., ops. analyst Social Security Adminstrn., San Francisco, 1973-78; vol. ACTION-Peace Corps Senegal, 1978-80; field examiner NLRB, San Francisco, 1981-85; freelance photojournalist San Francisco, 1983—. Photography exhbns. include one-woman show In the Eye of the Beholder, Expose Gallery, San Francisco, 1985, group show Camerawork Gallery, San Francisco, 1987; led photo workshop Jarbidge Nat. Wilderness, 1988; contbg. photographer: (travel book series) Insight Guides to Alaska, the Bahamas, Northern California, Canada, Indian Wildlife, (books) Remembering Pearl Harbor, 1986, Hawaiian National Parks, 1986, Death Valley National Monument, 1986, California State Parks, 1987, Alaska's Inside Passage, 1987, Exploring the Southwest's Grand Circle, 1988. Active Media Alliance San Francisco. Mem. Profl. Photographers of Am., Profl. Photographers of San Francisco (adv. com. 1988—). Home and Office: 223 Douglass St San Francisco CA 94114

CASSADY, JANIS NORA, marketing professional; b. St. Johnsbury, Vt., Apr. 4, 1951; d. George Robert and Irene Doris (Normand) J.; m. Gary Charles Cassady, Apr. 3, 1971; children: Christopher Colin, Jessica Lynn. Student, Champlain Coll., 1969-71. With Caldera Spas, El Cajon, Calif., 1981--; nat. sales coord. Caldera Spas, 1983-84, v.p. mktg., 1984--. Mem. Nat. Assn. Female Execs., Nat. Spa and Pool Inst. Presbyterian. Office: Caldera Spas 1080 W Bradley Ave El Cajon CA 92020

CASSANO, RONALD MICHAEL, accountant; b. Santa Rosa, Calif., June 29, 1940; s. Marion and Mary (Moschetti) C.; m. Karen L. Bryan, Feb. 8, 1964; children: Kathryn, Kristina, Kassandra. AA, Santa Rosa Community Coll., 1960; BS, U. Calif., Berkeley, 1963. CPA, Calif. Mem. staff Peat Marwick Main, San Francisco, 1963-67, mem. sr. staff, 1967-68, tax mgr., 1968-70, mgr. small bus., 1970-78; owner, mgr. Ronald M. Cassano, CPA, Pleasant Hill, Calif., 1978—; owner, founder 4 K's ARt, Walnut Creek, Calif., 1983—. Paintings represented in pvt. collections. Treas. Brooktree Assn., Walnut Creek, 1971-72; chmn. budget panel 6, United Way, San Francisco, 1973-74; treas. Castle Rock Parents Club, Walnut Creek, 1976-78, pres., 1979; mem. adv. panel Assistance League Diablo Valley, Walnut Creek, 1984—; mem. steering com. class of 1963 gift campaign U. Calif., Berkeley, 1987—; pres. Northgate High Sch. Parents Club, Walnut Creek, 1987-88. Mem. AICPA, Calif. Soc. CPA's, Soc. Calif. Accts.-Diablo (sec.-treas. 1986-87, v.p. 1987-88, pres. 1988-89), Kiwanis (pres. Ygnacio Valley 1982-83), Alpha Kappa Lambda (life, bd. dirs., treas. 1984—), Alpha Kappa Psi (life). Home: 2841 Bowling Green Dr Walnut Creek CA 94598 Office: 3333 Vincent Dr Ste 205 Pleasant Hill CA 94523

CASSENS, NICHOLAS, JR., ceramics engineer; b. Sigourney, Iowa, Sept. 8, 1948; s. Nicholas and Wanda Fern (Lancaster) C.; B.S., Iowa State U., 1971, B.S. in Chem. Engring., 1971; M.S. in Material Sci. and Engring., U. Calif., Berkeley, 1979; m. Linda Joyce Morrow, Aug. 30, 1969; 1 son, Randall Scott, Jr. research engr. Nat. Refractories and Minerals Corp., Pleasanton, Calif., 1971-72, research engr., 1972-74, sr. research engr., 1974-77, staff research engr., 1977-84, sr. staff research engr., 1984—. Mem. Am. Ceramic Soc. Democrat. Patentee in field, U.S., Australia, S.Am., Japan, Europe. Home: 4082 Suffolk Way Pleasanton CA 94566 Office: PO Box 877 Pleasanton CA 94566

CASSIDY, CHARLES PHILIP, aviation maintenance specialist, educator; b. Needham, Mass., Aug. 31, 1937; s. Philip Irving and Viola Dorathea (Lindoff) C.; m. Pat Chaingtong, July 16, 1976 (div. July, 1981); 1 child, William; m. Billie Sue Llewellyn, Sept. 12, 1981; children: Crystal, Christopher. Grad., Air War Coll., 1976; BA, Chapman Coll., 1977; M in Aero. Sci., Embry-Riddle Aero. U., 1986. Commd. 2d lt. USAF, 1958, advanced through grades to lt. col., 1975, served as pilot, world wide, Vietnam Vet., 1958-75, ret., 1975; comdr. 376th Field Maintenance Squadron, Okinawa, Japan, 1976-77; wing maintenance officer 376th Strategic Wing, Okinawa, 1978-79; chief wing standardization 22d Bomb Wing, March AFB, Calif., 1979; deputy base comdr. 22d Combat Support Group, March AFB, 1979-80; asst. chief maintenance 21st Tactical Fighter Wing, Anchorage, 1981-83; info. systems dir. Hdqrs. Alaskan Air Command, Anchorage, 1983-84; chief command and control 81st Tactical Fighter Wing, RAF, Bentwaters, Eng., 1984-87; asst. mgr. Mosesian Farms, Anchorage, 1988; acct. rep. Met. Life, Anchorage, 1989—; adj. instr. Embry-Riddle Aero. Univ., internationally, 1987—. Author tng. manual for B-52 maintenance officers, 1980. Decorated Air medal with one oak leaf cluster, 1969. Mem. Data Processing Mgmt. Assn. Republican. Episcopalian. Club: Elemendorf Aero. (Anchorage). Home: 10917 Gakona Circle Eagle River AK 99577 Office: Met Life Frontier Bldg 3601 C St Ste 298 Anchorage AK 99503

CASSIDY, DONALD LAWRENCE, aerospace company executive; b. Stamford, Conn., May 26, 1933; s. John Dingee and Ursula Agnes (Lynch)

C. BS, MIT, 1954; grad. mgmt. policy inst., U. Southern Calif., L.A., 1973. Jr. exec. Johns-Manville Corp., N.Y.C., 1954-55; contracting officer U.S. Army Signal Corps Electric Lab., Ft. Monmouth, N.J., 1955-57; with contract dept. field svc. and support div. Hughes Aircraft Co., L.A., 1957-69, mgr. contracts support systems, 1969-78, staff v.p., chief contracts officer, 1987—; dir. contracts Hughes Aircraft Co., Long Beach, Calif., 1978-87, group v.p. bus. ops., 1987. 1st lt. U.S. Army, 1955-57. Mem. Am. Def. Preparedness Assn. (L.A. chpt. bd. dirs.), Nat. Contract Mgmt. Assn., Nat. Security Indsl. Assn. Republican. Office: Hughes Aircraft Co 7200 Hughes Terr Westchester CA 90045

CASSIDY, JACK P., marketing executive; b. Mineola, N.Y., Oct. 25, 1942; s. John W. and Marion L. (Carota) C.; divorced; children: Colleen Marie, Adam Joseph. BS in Indsl. Mgmt., L.I. U., 1969. Asst. product mgr. Crest/Good, Syosset, N.Y., 1963-67, dist. mgr., 1967-70; dir. ops. P&M Mfg. Co., L.A., 1970-75; gen. mgr. Steamsearch Corp., Gardena, Calif., 1975-77; v.p. Walter Plumbing Parts Mfg. Co., Pacoima, Calif., 1977-78, Ex-L-Co., Inc., Tarzana, Calif., 1978-81, Kiener Co., L.A., 1981-83; pres. R-C Mktg., Inc., Woodland Hills, Calif., 1983—; cons. Permabilt Industries, Torrance, Calif., 1976-77, Kiener Plumbing Specialties, L.A., 1979-80. Troop leader Boy Scouts Am., Woodland Hills, 1985-86. Sgt. U.S. Army, 1965-67, Vietnam. Recipient Achievement award City of L.A., 1973. Republican. Roman Catholic. Home and Office: 22374 Macfarlane Dr Woodland Hills CA 91364

CASSIDY, JOHN ROBERT, logistics specialist, educator; b. Salt Lake City, Sept. 20, 1933; s. Robert and Grace Louise (Holder) C.; m. Carol Ann Hansen, Feb. 10, 1956; children: Jeff, Steve, Connie, Christy, Cathy. Student, Long Beach City Coll., 1951-53, LaSalle U., 1964; grad., Indsl. Coll. of the Armed Forces, 1964; student, Cerritos Coll., 1983—; D of Sci Logistics (hon.), Pacific States U., 1980. With Rockwell Internat., 1955-89, 72—; logistics mgr. Minuteman Missiles, Anaheim, Calif., 1958-69, F-111 Aircraft, Anaheim, 1972-73; logistics contract mgr. B-1 Bomber Program, Los Angeles, 1974-77; logistics program mgr. Newport Beach, Calif., 1978-80; dir. div. logistics Space Shuttle Program, Downey, Calif., 1981-86, dir. logistics program, 1987—; dir. ops. Apollo Corp., Salt Lake City, 1970-71; prof., chmn. logistics dept., Pacific States U., Los Angeles, 1971—; instr., advisor Cerritos (Calif.) Coll., 1983—, Northrup U., Los Angeles, 1986—, Weber State Coll., Cerritos, 1987—; advisor Nat. U., Los Angeles, 1982, instr., 1986—; lectr. in field Austria, Luxemberg, Eng., 1982—. Author: Introduction to Logistics, 1982, Repair Management, 1983, Logistics Simulator, 1984. Served to cpl. U.S. Army, 1953-55. Fellow Soc. Logistics Engrs. (sr., cert. profl., charter mem. Orange County cpht., Cert. of Achievement award, ECCLES award 1989), Nat. Mgmt. Assn. (advisor, Silver Knight award 1987), NASA (Pub. Svc. award 1989). Republican. Mormon. Home: 18782 Oriente Ln Yorba Linda CA 92686 Office: Rockwell Internat Space Shuttle Program 12214 Lakewood Blvd Downey CA 90242

CASSIDY, RICHARD ARTHUR, environmental engineer, governmental water resources specialist; b. Manchester, N.H., Nov. 15, 1944; s. Arthur Joseph and Alice Ethuliette (Gregoire) C.; m. Judith Diane Maine, Aug. 14, 1971; children—Matthew, Amanda, Michael. B.A., St. Anselm Coll., 1966; M.S., U. N.H., 1969, Tufts U., 1972. Field biologist Pub. Service Co. of N.H., Manchester, 1968; jr. san. engr. Mass. Div. Water Pollution Control, Boston, 1968-69; aquatic biologist Normandeau Assocs., Bedford, N.H., 1969-70; hydraulic engr. New Eng. div. U.S. Army C.E., Waltham, Mass., 1972-77, environ. engr., Portland Dist., Oreg., 1977-81, supr., environ. engr., 1981—. Contbr. articles to profl. jours. Den leader Pack 164 Columbia Pacific council Cub Scouts Am., Beaverton, Oreg., 1982-83, Webelos leader, 1984-85, troop 764 committeeman, 1985-87, Columbia Pacific council Boy Scouts Am., 1985-87; mem. Planning Commn. Hudson, N.H., 1976-77. Recipient commendation for exemplary performance Mo.-Miss. flood, 1973, commendation for litigation defense, 1986, commendation for mgmt. activities, 1987. Mem. Am. Inst. Hydrology (cert., profl. ethics com. 1986, v.p. Oreg. sect. 1987-89), Am. Soc. Limnology and Oceanography. Democrat. Roman Catholic. Home: 7655 SW Belmont Dr Beaverton OR 97005 Office: Portland Dist CE Chief Reservoir Reg & Water Quality Sect PO Box 2946 Portland OR 82946

CASTAGNINI, GENE JOSEPH, laboratory executive and administrator; b. Oakland, Calif., Sept. 6, 1949; s. Silvio P. and Anna M. (Del Rio) C.; m. Janice Rose De Santi, July 22, 1972; children: Kenneth, Cristina, Mark. BSBA in Acctg., Calif. State U., 1972; MBA in Human Resources, Calif. Coast U., 1983. Registered tax preparer, Calif. Acct. Nakahama and Arnold, Oakland, 1972-73; br. acct. Medi-Physics Inc./Hoffman La Roche, Emeryville, Calif., 1974-76, corp. acct., 1974-76, sr. acct., 1976-77, sr. supervising acct., fleet mgr., 1977-78, corp. acctg. mgr., 1978-82; corp. officer, dir. fin. and acctg. Medi-Physics Inc./Hoffman La Roche, Richmond, Calif., 1982-88; v.p., chief fin. officer, chief adminstrv. officer, corp. dir. Biogenex Labs. Inc., San Ramon, Calif., 1988—; tax preparer, cons. Oakland and Walnut Creek, Calif., 1972—. Mem. Am. Mgmt. Assn., Nat. Assn. Accts., Nat. Assn. Tax Cons. Republican. Roman Catholic. Office: Biogenex Labs Inc 4600 Norris Canyon Rd San Ramon CA 94583

CASTANIA-SMITH, DEBORAH LYNN, management executive; b. Long Beach, Calif., Jan. 2, 1963; d. Howard Dodson Lloyd and Lina Ann (Deneault) Castania; m. J. Rick Smith, Apr. 21, 1984; 1 child, Brittany Nicole. Cert., Plaza Three Acad., Phoenix, 1982; AS in mgmt., Glendale Community Coll., 1984. Econ. security specialist Dept. Econ. Security, Lake Havasu City, Ariz., 1978-81; staff support mgmt. Storer Cable Communications, Glendale, Ariz., 1981-85; bus. devel. mgr. Stewart Title and Trust, Phoenix, 1985-87, Founders Title Co., Phoenix, 1985-89; pvt. investigator G.S.I. Investigations, Phoenix, 1984—; bus. devel. mgr. Transamerica Title, Phoenix, 1989—. Mem. Phoenix Bd. Realtors (vice chair 1988—), Mesa Bd. Realtors, Chandler Bd. Realtors, Tempe Bd. Realtors, Women's Council Realtors (publicity chair 1988—), Ariz. Assn. Lic. Pvt. Investigators. Home: 4397 W Bethany Home Rd Ste 1085 Glendale AZ 85301 Office: Transamerica Title Co 11209 N Tatum Blvd Phoenix AZ 85029

CASTBERG, ANTHONY DIDRICK, political science professor, researcher; b. San Francisco, Apr. 1, 1941; s. Robert Stabell and Juliet Louise (Evans) C.; m. Harolyn Dang, Dec. 22, 1963 (div. Feb. 1977); 1 child, Beth Kehaulani Mei-Lin; m. Joan Kazu Eguchi, Dec. 30, 1977. BA, U. Hawaii, 1963, MA, 1966; PhD, Northwestern U., 1968. Asst. prof. polit. sci. Calif. State U., L.A., 1968-72, assoc. prof. polit. sci., 1972-76; prof. polit. sci. U. Hawaii, Hilo, 1974—. Author: Cases on Constitutional Law, 1973; contbr. articles to profl. jours. Russell Sage Found. fellow Northwestrn U., 1966-68, Fulbright Found. fellow, 1987-88. Mem. Law and Soc. Assn., Res. Officers Assn., U.S. Naval Inst. Office: U Hawaii at Hilo Hilo HI 96720-4091

CASTEEL, ROBERTA LYNN, nurse; b. Houston, May 21, 1960; d. Arthur Irvin and Margaret LaVon (Bellotte) Kriss; m. Dennis Wayne Casteel, July 12, 1980; children: William Arthur, David Wayne. AA in Nursing, U. Nev., 1981. Staff nurse Children's Clinic, Las Vegas, Nev., 1981—, Univ. Med. Ctr., Las Vegas, Nev., 1985—. Republican. Methodist. Lodges: Order Eastern Star, Order Rainbow for Girls. Home: 2720 Daley St Las Vegas NV 89030 Office: Childrens Clinic 2200 Rancho St Las Vegas NV 89102

CASTILLO, JESS LAGOY, insurance sales agent; b. Dapugan City, Philippines, Dec. 25, 1949; came to U.S., 1979; s. Luis Biagtan and Petra Iglesias (Lagoy) C.; m. annabella Cunanan de Venecia, 1975; children: Jesse, Jason Bo, Jena Hanna, Pinky Jean. BA, U. East, Manila, 1973. Radio announcer Sta NBC-DZRD, Dagupan City, Philippines, 1973-76; sta. mgr. Sta NBC-DZRD, 1976-78, Sta. ABC-DWPR, 1978-79; mgr. trainee Holyway Cleaners & Laundry Co., Westwood, Calif., 1979; ins. agt. Nat. Life & Accident Ins., L.A., 1979-81, staff mgr., 1981-83, svc. mgr., 1983-84; gen. agt. J.L. Castillo Ins. Agy., L.A., 1984—. Recipient City Mayor's Appreciation award, City of Dagupan, 1977, Meritorious Svc., United Way, 1976. Mem. Jaycees (recipient numerous awards, past officer different chpts., life), Lions, Toastmasters (charter), Gun Club So. Calif. (dirs. 1983-85), Optimist Club, Alpha Phi Omega. Democratic. Roman Catholic.

CASTILLO, RAFAEL ERNEST, beer company official; b. Ann Arbor, Mich., July 23, 1952; s. Rafael and Betty Louise (Blomquist) C.; m. Anita Margrethe Halvorssen, Sept. 3, 1988. BA in Govt., Dartmouth Coll., 1974; MPhil Latin Am. Studies, Oxford U., 1976, DPhil in Modern History, 1981; cert. in fin., Instituto de Estudios Superiores de Administracion, Caracas, Venezuela, 1983. Asst. to v.p. adminstrn. Cerveceria Polar, C.A., Caracas, 1981-83, corp. risk mgr., 1984-87, dir. risk and ins., 1987; mgr. risk and ins. Adolph Coors Co., Golden, Colo., 1987—, mem. supervisory com. credit union, 1989—; assoc. risk mgmt. Brit. Safety Coun. Author: Monagas Family and Its Role, 1976, Jose Tadeo Monagas, 1987; contbr. articles to profl. publs. Bd. dirs. Andres Bello Fellowship, Oxford, Eng., 1984-87, Venezuelan-Brit. C. of C., 1985-87. Nat. Acad. History grantee, 1977, Oxford U. Latin Am. Ctr. grantee, 1980, Gasparian Fund grantee, 1980. Mem. Risk and Ins. Mgmt. Soc. (chmn. beverage industry 1985-87, co-chmn. 1987-89), Internat. Inst. Risk and Safety Mgmt., Oxford Soc. (chmn. Caracas chpt. 1984-87), St. Antony's Coll. Soc. (chmn. Caracas chpt. 1986-87), Caracas Country Club, Oxford and Cambridge Club (London). Office: Adolph Coors Co Mail BC 210 Golden CO 80401

CASTLEBERRY, ARLINE ALRICK, architect; b. Mpls., Sept. 19, 1919; d. Bannona Gerhardt and Meta Emily (Veit) Alrick; m. Donald Montgomery Castleberry, Dec. 25, 1941; children: Karen, Marvin. B in Interior Architecture, U. Minn., 1941; postgrad., U. Tex., 1947-48. Designer, draftsman Elizabeth & Winston Close, Architects, Mpls., 1940-41, Northwest Airlines, Mpls., 1942-43, Cerny & Assocs., Mpls., 1944-46; archtl. draftsman Dominick and Van Benscotten, Washington, 1946-47; ptnr. Castleberry & Davis Bldg. Designers, Burlingame, Calif., 1960-65; prin. Burlingame, 1965—. Smith Coll. scholar, Cambridge, Mass., 1941. Mem. AIA, Am. Inst. Bldg. Designers (chpt. pres. 1971-72), Commaisini, Alpha Alpha Gamma, Chi Omega. Democrat. Lutheran. Home and Office: 3004 Canyon Rd Burlingame CA 94010

CASTOR, WILBUR WRIGHT, corporate marketing executive; b. Harrison Twp., Pa., Feb. 3, 1932; s. Wilbur Wright and Margaret (Grubbs) C.; m. Donna Ruth Schwartz, Feb. 9, 1963; children: Amy, Julia, Marnie. BA, St. Vincent Studies, 1959; postgrad., Calif. U. Advanced Studies, 1986—. Sales rep. IBM, Pitts. and Cleve., 1959-62; v.p. data processing ops. Honeywell, Waltham, Mass., 1962-80; pres., chief exec. officer Aviation Simulation Tech., Lexington, Mass., 1980-82; sr. v.p. Xerox Corp., El Segundo, Calif., 1982—. Author: (play) Un Certaine Soirire, 1958, (mus. comedy) Breaking Up, 1960; contbr. articles to profl. jours. Mem. Presdl. Rep. Task Force; trustee Info. Inst., Santa Barbara, Calif.; pres. bd. dirs. Internat. Acad., Santa Barbara; active Town Hall Calif. Served to capt. USN, 1953-58, with USAFR, 1958-76. Mem. Internat. Platform Assn., World Future Soc., Aircraft Owners and Pilots Assn. Clubs: Manhattan Country (Manhattan Beach, Calif.); Caballeros, Rolling Hills (Calif.) Tennis; U.S. Senator's. Home: 19 Georgeff Rd Rolling Hills CA 90274 Office: Xerox Corp ES XC15-B 101 Continental Blvd El Segundo CA 90245

CASTRO, JOSEPH ARMAND, musical director, pianist, composer, orchestrator; b. Miami, Ariz., Aug. 15, 1927; s. John Loya and Lucy (Sanchez) C.; m. Loretta Faith Haddad, Oct. 21, 1966; children: John Joseph, James Ernest. Student, San Jose State Coll., 1944-47. Mus. dir. Herb Jeffries, Hollywood, Calif., 1952, June Christy, Hollywood, 1959-63, Anita O'Day, Hollywood, 1963-65, Tony Martin, Hollywood, 1962-64, Tropicana Hotel, Las Vegas, Nev., 1980-; orch. leader Mocambo Night Club, Hollywood, 1952-54; soloist Joe Castro Trio, L.A., N.Y.C., Honolulu, 1952-65, Sands Hotel, Desert Inn, Las Vegas, 1975-80; mus. dir. Folies Bergere, 1980-89. Recs. include Cool School with June Christy, 1960, Anita O'Day Sings Rodgers and Hart, 1961, Lush Life, 1966, Groove-Funk-Soul, Mood Jazz, also albums with Teddy Edwards, Stan Kenton, Honolulu Symphony concerts. With U.S. Army, 1946-47. Roman Catholic. Home: 2812 Colanthe Ave Las Vegas NV 89102-2026 Office: Tropicana Hotel 3801 Las Vegas Blvd Las Vegas NV 89109

CASTRO, LEONARD EDWARD, lawyer; b. Los Angeles, Mar. 18, 1934; s. Emil Galvez and Lily (Meyers) C.; 1 son, Stephen Paul. A.B., UCLA, 1959, J.D., 1962. Bar: Calif. 1963, U.S. Supreme Ct. 1970. Assoc. Musick, Peeler & Garrett, Los Angeles, 1962-68, ptnr., 1968—. Mem. ABA, Internat. Bar Assn., Los Angeles County Bar Assn. Office: Musick Peeler & Garrett 1 Wilshire Blvd Ste 2000 Los Angeles CA 90017

CASTRO, LILLIANA, dentist; b. San Jose, Costa Rica, Aug. 29, 1949; d. Abdenago and Mireya (Blanco) Villalobos; m. Luis Diego Castro, Feb. 14, 1975; children: Vivian, Brenda Isabel, Andrea Maria. BS, Maria Auxiliadora Coll., San Jose, 1967; DDS, U. Costa Rica, 1975; postgrad., UCLA, 1980-81, diploma, 1981. Assoc. Dr. Euler Ferrer Paulet, DDS, Santa Ana, Calif., 1981-83; pvt. practice Corona, Calif., 1982—; mem. staff Circle City Hosp., Corona, 1982—; columnist Corona-Norco Daily Ind.,1987—. Mem. civic adv. bd. Corona Community Hosp., 1986—. Recipient Gold Hammer award C. of C., 1982, award of merit Costa Rica Rotary, 1988; named Woman of Yr. Hispanic Community mag., 1988. Mem. ADA, Calif. Dental Assn., Tri-County Dental Soc., Am. Bus. Women's Assn. (v.p. 1988, Woman of Yr. 1988), Circle City Rotary Club (chmn. internat. affairs com. 1988). Republican. Roman Catholic. Home: 1521 Marshall Ln Corona CA 91719 Office: Lilliana Castro DDS Inc 800 Magnolia Ave Corona CA 91719

CASTRO, LORETTA FAITH, singer, pianist; b. Whitesville, W.Va., Mar. 23, 1930; d. Joseph and Amelia (Gossen) Haddad; m. Joseph Armand Castro, Oct. 21, 1966; children: John Joseph, James Ernest. BA, Marshall U., 1953. Singer, pianist Greenbriar Hotel, White Sulphur Springs, Hawaii, 1957-64, Outrigger Canoe Club, Honolulu, 1966, Sorrentino's, Toluca Lake, Calif., 1968, Flamingo Hotel, Las Vegas, Nev., 1971, Desert Inn Motel, Las Vegas, 1977, Tropicana Hotel, Las Vegas, 1981-87, Bistro, Las Vegas. Republican. Home and Office: 2812 Colanthe Ave Las Vegas NV 89102

CASWELL, CHARLES WILLIAM, company executive, transportation consultant; b. Detroit, Aug. 2, 1954; s. Peter John and Rosemary I. (English) C. BA, San Francisco State U., 1980, MBA, 1983. Transp. cons. Edgar, Inc., Palo Alto, Calif., 1983-84; bus. mgr. Edgar, Inc., Palo Alto, 1984—. Mem. Calif., Assn. Sch. Bus. Ofcls., Calif. Assn. for Coordinated Transp., Uniform user/group. Democrat. Office: Edgar Inc 9530 Imperial Hwy Ste M Downey CA 90242

CATALAN URIEL, JOSE, small business executive; b. Havana, Cuba, Dec. 23, 1944; came to U.S., 1961; s. Rafael and Joya (Uriel) Catalan. Degree in mgmt., Ecole Hoteliere de la Societe Suisse des Hoteliers, Lausanne, Switzerland, 1968; BA in Journalism, Ariz State U., 1973. Gen. mgr. Montemar Resort, Aquadilla, P.R., 1961-70; gen. mgr. Castle Hot Springs, Morristown, Ariz., 1973-74, The Wickenburg (Ariz.) Inn Tennis & Guest Ranch, 1974-76; pres. Fifth Avenue Travel & Tours, Scottsdale, Ariz., 1976--. Mem. Fifth Ave. Merchants Assn. (v.p. 1979), Fifth Ave. Property Owners Assn. (pres. 1986--). Alliance Francaise (pres. 1969-70). Office: Fifth Ave Travel & Tours 7007 5th Ave Scottsdale AZ 85251

CATE, FLOYD MILLS, electronic components executive; b. Norfolk, Va., Aug. 2, 1917; s. Floyd Mills and Ellen (Lewis) C.; m. Ann Willis, Jan. 31, 1943; 1 child Carol Cate Webster. B.A. U. Tenn., 1940; student exec. program UCLA, 1958; B.A. (hon.) Calif. Inst. Tech., 1947. With special sales dept. Cannon Electric Co., Los Angeles, 1930-46, western sales mgr., 1946-50, with internat. sales dept., 1950-57, v.p. sales, mktg., 1957-62, pres. internat. sales, 1958-62; v.p. sales, mktg. Zemco, Irvine, Calif., 1977-80, cons., 1977-80; pres., owner F.E.S. Cons., San Clemente, Calif., 1968—; 2R engring. cons. dir., San Marcos, Calif., 1987— . Co-chmn. Ron Packard for Congress, San Clemente, 1984; chmn. adhoc com. Seascape Village, 1986—; pres. Assn. Shorecliffs Residence, San Clemente, 1986—. Mem. Internat. Electric Electronic Engrs., IEEE. Democrat. Roman Catholic. Club: Shorecliff Golf (bd. dirs. San Clemente). Office: 205 Via Montego San Clemente CA 92672

CATE, WILLIAM BURKE, religious organization administrator; b. Itasca, Tex., Mar. 25, 1924; s. Emmet Cate and Irene N. (Kincaid) Moberly; m. Janice McLeod Patterson, Aug. 20, 1946; children: Lucy, Nancy, Michael, Sara, Rebecca, Mary. BA, Willamette U., 1945; STB, Boston U., 1948, PhD, 1953; DD (hon.), Lewis and Clark U., 1965. Ordained minister United Meth. Ch., 1952. Exec. dir. Interchurch Council of Greater New Bedford, Mass., 1953-58, Greater Portland (Oreg.) Council of Chs., 1958-70; pres., dir. Ch. Council of Greater Seattle, 1970—; v.p. Nat. Council of Chs., N.Y.C., 1970-73; pres. Nat. Assn. of Ecumenical Staff, 1972-73. Served with USN, 1943-46. Recipient Disting. Alumni award Boston U. Sch. Theology, 1968. Lodge: Rotary. Home: 12642 NE 5th Bellevue WA 98005 Office: Church Coun Greater Seattle 4759 15th Ave NE Seattle WA 98105

CATES, REBECCA ANN, accountant; b. Mpls., Aug. 7, 1960; d. Lawrence Joseph and Beatrice Louise (Ludowese) C. BA, with honors, Gonzaga U., 1982. CPA, Wash. Asst. acct. Peat, Marwick, Main & Co., Seattle, 1982-83; staff acct. KPMG Peat Marwick, Seattle, 1983-84, sr. acct., 1984-85, supervising sr. acct., 1985-87, mgr., 1987—. Mem. Am. Women's Soc. CPA's, Women CPA's of Seattle, NAFE, Women & Bus. Exch., Wash. State Soc. CPA's. Roman Catholic. Office: KPMG Peat Marwick 1301 5th Ave Ste 2600 Seattle WA 98101

CATHCART, MARGARET E., publications executive; b. San Diego, Aug. 16, 1945; d. Harry and Margaret (Eller) Biszmaier; m. John G. Cathcart, May 22, 1971. BA, San Diego State U., 1967. Tech. writer Naval Elec. Lab, San Diego, 1968-70; tech. writer Naval Undersea Ctr., San Diego, 1970-73, mgr. reports grp., 1973-77; mgr. reports br. Naval Ocean Sys. Ctr., San Diego, 1977-79, mgr. pubs. div., 1979—. Contbr. articles to profl. jours. Mem. San Diego State U. adv. com. on tech. com., 1982—. Mem. Soc. Tech. Communication (chpt. pres.), Am. Def. Preparedness Assn. Home: 5370 Wilshire Dr San Diego CA 92116

CATHEY, SHARON SUE, teacher; b. Reed City, Mich., June 11, 1940; d. Sherwood and Ellen (Hutson) Rinn.; m. Jerry A. Cathey, June 25, 1960; children: Joel A., Julie A. BA in Edn., San Francisco State U., 1962; postgrad., U. Mich., 1972-74, U. Calif., 1975-77; MA in Edn., U. Nev., 1988. Tchr. Laguna Salada Union Sch. Dist., Pacifica, Calif., 1962-64, Redwood City (Calif.) Sch. Dist., 1964-66, Lapeer (Mich.) Sch. Dist., 1970-74, Washoe County Sch. Dist., Reno, 1983--; diagnostician Thompson Learning Ctr., Reno, 1987--; asst. U. Nev., Reno, 1988--. Nev. ESSA grantee, 1977. Mem. AAUW (pres. 1976-78), Washoe County Tchrs. Assn., Phi Kappa Phi, Delta Kappa Gamma (state pres. 1989--). Republican. Episcopalian. Home: 814 Glen Meadow Sparks NV 89431

CATRAMBONE, EUGENE DOMINIC, public relations consultant; b. Chgo., June 5, 1926; s. Nicola and Maria Theresa (Catrambone) C.; m. Mary Gloria Gaimari, Mar. 26, 1951; children: Mary, Eugene Jr., Jane, David, Jill. BA, St. Benedict Coll., 1950; postgrad., Kans. State U., 1952-54; MA, DePaul U., 1960; postgrad., UCLA, 1962-63. Cert. secondary tchr., coll. instr., Calif. Tchr. high schs. Chgo., 1950-62, L.A., 1963-88; cons. pub. rels. Westlake Village, Calif., 1986—; tech. writer U. Chgo., 1956-59, Douglas Missile div. USN, L.A. and Ventura, Calif., 1962-75; reporter, editor Las Virgenes Enterprise, Calabasas, Calif., 1968-75; evening instr. L.A. City Coll., 1965-68. Author: The Golden Touch: Frankie Carle, 1981; contbr. articles on edn. to profl. publs., 1959-60, feature stories to local newspapers, 1968-75. Sgt. U.S. Army, 1944-46. Mem. NEA (life), Calif. Tchrs. Assn., Book Publicists So. Calif., United Tchrs. L.A., Am. Legion, Westlake Village Men's Golf Club (pub. rels. editor 1986—, bd. dirs., pres. 1989—). Democrat. Roman Catholic. Home: 31802 Tynebourne Ct Westlake Village CA 91361 Office: Golden Touch Assocs PO Box 1064 Agoura Hills CA 91301

CATTANEO, JACQUELYN ANNETTE KAMMERER, artist, educator; b. Gallup, N.Mex., June 1, 1944; d. Ralph John and Gladys Agnes (O'Sullivan) Kammer; m. John Leo Cattaneo, Apr. 25, 1964; children: John Auro, Paul Anthony. Student Tex. Woman's U., 1962-64. Portrait artist, tchr. Gallup, N. Mex., 1972; coordinator Works Progress Adminstrn. art project renovation McKinley County, Gallup, Octavia Fellin Performing Arts wing dedication, Gallup Pub. Library; formation com. mem. Multi-modal/Multi-Cultural Ctr. for Gallup, N.Mex.; one-woman shows: Gallup Pub. Libr., 1963, 66, 77, 78, 81, 87, Gallup Lovelace Med. Clinic, Santa Fe Station Open House, 1981, Gallery 20, Farmington, N.Mex., 1985—, Red Mesa Art Gallery, 1989; group shows include: Navajo Nation Library Invitational, 1978, Santa Fe Festival of the Arts Invitational, 1979, N.Mex. State Fair, 1978, 79, 80, Catharine Lorillard Wolfe, N.Y.C., 1980, 81, 84, 85, 86, 87, 88, 4th ann. exhbn. Salmagundi Club, 1984, 3d ann. Palm Beach Internat., New Orleans, 1984, Fine Arts Ctr. Taos, 1984, The Best and the Brightest O'Brien's Art Emporium, Scottsdale, Ariz., 1986, Gov.'s Gallery, 1989, N.Mex. State Capitol, Santa Fe, 1987, Pastel Soc. West Coast Ann. Exhbn. Sacramento Ctr. for Arts, Calif., 1988; represented in permanent collections: Zuni Arts and Crafts Ednl. Bldg., U. N.Mex., C.J. Wiemar Collection, McKinley Manor, Gov.'s Office, State Capitol Bldg., Santa Fe, Historic El Rancho Hotel, Gallup, N.Mex., Sunwest Bank. Fine Arts Ctr., En Taos, N.Mex., Armand Nammer Pvt. Collection. Mem. Internat. Fine Arts Guild, Am. Portrait Soc. (cert.), Pastel Soc. of W. Coast (cert.), Mus. N.Mex. Found., Mus. Women in the Arts, Fechin Inst., Artists' Co-op. (co-chair), Gallup C. of C., Gallup Area Arts and Crafts Council, Catharine Lorillard Wolfe Art Club of N.Y.C. (oil and pastel juried membership), Chautaugua Art Club. Soroptimists. Address: 210 E Green St Gallup NM 87301

CATTANI, DAVID ARTHUR, aerospace engineer; b. Milw., July 25, 1953; s. Henry E. and Ruth E. (Peterson) C.; m. Deborah Ann Reynolds, Feb. 18, 1978. BSEE, Mich. Tech. U., 1975, MSEE, 1978. Engr. Motorola Communications Group, Schaumburg, Ill., 1977-78; sr. staff engr. Martin Marietta Space Systems, Denver, 1978—. Office: Martin Marietta PO Box 179 Denver CO 80201

CATTANI, MARYELLEN B., lawyer; b. Bakersfield, Calif., Dec. 1, 1904; d. Arnold Theodore and Coorinne Marilyn (Kovacevich) C.; m. Frank C. Herringer; 1 child, Sarah. AB, Vassar Coll., Poughkeepsie, N.Y., 1965; JD, U. Calif. (Boalt Hall), 1968. Assoc. Davis Polk & Wardwell, N.Y.C., 1968-69; assoc. Orrick, Herrington & Sutcliffe, San Francisco, 1970-74, ptnr., 1975-81; v.p., gen. counsel TransAmerica Corp., San Francisco, 1981-83, sr. v.p., gen. counsel, 1983-89; ptnr. Morrison & Foerster, San Francisco, 1989—; chmn. exec. com. bus. law sect. Calif. State Bar Assn., 1980-81; regent St. Mary's Coll. Calif., Moraga, 1985—; trustee Vassar Coll., 1985—; bd. dirs. The Exploratorium, 1988—. Author: Calif. Corp. Practice Guide, 1977, Corp. Counselors. Mem. Ctr. Pub. Resources San Francisco. Mem. San Francisco Bar Assn. Democrat. Roman Catholic.

CATTERTON, MARIANNE ROSE, occupational therapist; b. St. Paul, Feb. 3, 1922; d. Melvin Joseph and Katherine Marion (Bole) Maas; m. Elmer John Wood, Jan. 16, 1943 (dec.); m. Robert Lee Catterton, Nov. 20, 1951 (div. 1981); children: Jenifer Ann Dawson, Cynthia Lea Uthus. Student, Carleton Coll., 1939-41, U. Md., 1941-42; BA in English, U. Wis., 1944; MA in Counseling Psychology, Bowie State Coll., 1980; postgrad., No. Ariz. U., 1987—. Registered occupational therapist. Occupational therapist VA, N.Y.C., 1946-50; cons. occupational therapist Fondo del Seguro del Estado, Puerto Rico, 1950-51; dir. rehab. therapies Spring Grove State Hosp., Catonsville, Md., 1953-56; occupational therapist Anne Arundel County Health Dept., Annapolis, Md., 1967-78; dir. occupational therapy Eastern Shore Hosp. Ctr., Cambridge, Md., 1979-85; cons. occupational therapist Kachina Point Health Ctr., Sedona, Ariz., 1986; regional chmn. Conf. on revising Psychiat. Occupational Therapy Edn., 1958-59; instr. report writing Anne Arundel Community Coll., Annapolis, 1974-78. Editor Am. Jour. Occupational Therapy, 1962-67. Active Md. Heart Assn., 1959-60; mem. task force on occupational therapy Md. Dept. of Health, 1971-72; chmn. Anne Arundel Gov. Com. on Employment of Handicapped, 1959-63; mem. gov.'s com. to study vocat. rehab., Md., 1960; com. mem. Annapolis Youth Ctr., 1976-78; mem. ministerial search com. Unitarian Ch. Anne Arundel County, 1962; curator Dorchester County Heritage Mus., Cambridge, 1982-83; v.p. Unitarian-Universalist Fellowship Flagstaff, 1988—. Mem. Puerto Rico Occupational Therapy Assn. (co-founder 1950), Am. Occupational

Therapy Assn. (chmn. history com. 1958-61), Md. Occupational Therapy Assn. (del. 1953-59), Dorchester County Mental Health Assn. (pres. 1981-84), Internat. Platform Assn., Delta Delta Delta. Republican. Clubs: Severn Town (treas. 1965), International (publicity chmn. 1966) (Annapolis); Toastmasters, Newcomers (pres. 1986) (Sedona). Home: 100 Canyon Circle Dr #4 Sedona AZ 86336

CATZ, BORIS, physician; b. Troyanov, Russia, Feb. 15, 1923; s. Jacobo and Esther (Galbmilion) C.; came to U.S., 1950, naturalized, 1955; B.S., Nat. U. Mexico, 1941, M.D., 1947; M.S. in Medicine, U. So. Calif., 1951; m. Rebecca Schechter; children—Judith, Dinah, Sarah Lea, Robert. Intern, Gen. Hosp., Mexico City, 1945-46; prof. adj., sch. medicine U. Mexico, 1947-48; research fellow medicine U. So. Calif., 1949-51, instr. medicine, 1952-54, asst. clin. prof., 1954-59, assoc. clin. prof., 1959-83, clin. prof., 1983—; pvt. practice, Los Angeles, 1951-55, Beverly Hills, Calif., 1957—; chief Thyroid Clinic Los Angeles County Gen. Hosp., 1955-70; sr. cons. thyroid clin. U. So. Calif.-Los Angeles Med. Center, 1970—; clin. chief endocrinology Cedars-Sinai Med. Ctr., 1983-87. Served to capt. U.S. Army, 1955-57. Boris Catz lectureship named in his honor Thyroid Research Endowment Fund, Cedars Sinai Med. Ctr., 1985. Fellow ACP, Am. Coll. Nuclear Medicine (pres. elect 1982); mem. AMA, Cedars Sinai Med. Ctr. Soc. for History of Medicine (chmn.), L.A. County Med. Assn., Calif. Med. Assn., Endocrine Soc., Am. Thyroid Assn., Soc. Exptl. Biology and Medicine, Western Soc. Clin. Research, Am. Fedn. Clin. Research, Soc. Nuclear Medicine, So. Calif. Soc. Nuclear Medicine, AAAS, N.Y. Acad. Scis., Los Angeles Soc. Internal Medicine, Am. Soc. Internal Medicine, Calif. Soc. Internal Medicine, The Royal Soc. Medicine (affiliate), Collegium Salerni, Cedar Sinai Soc. of History of Medicine, Beverly Hills C. of C., Phi Lambda Kappa. Jewish. Mem. B'nai B'rith. Club: The Profl. Man's (past pres.). Author: Thyroid Case Studies, 1975, 2d edit., 1981. Contbr. numerous articles on thyroidology to med. jours. Home: 300 El Camino Dr Beverly Hills CA 90212 Office: 435 N Roxbury Dr Beverly Hills CA 90210

CAUDRON, JOHN ARMAND, safety engineer, technical forensic investigator; b. Compton, Calif., Sept. 26, 1944; s. Armand Robert and Evelyn Emma (Hoyt) C.; m. Marilyn Edith Fairfield, Mar. 16, 1968; children: Melita, Rochelle. AA, Ventura Coll., 1965; BA, Calif. State U., Fullerton, 1967; postgrad., U. Nev., 1975-78; MS, U. So. Calif., 1980. Dist. rep. Gen. Motors Corp., Reno, 1969-75; mgr. Snyder Rsch. Lab., Reno, 1976-78, v.p., El Monte, Calif., 1978-82, pres., 1982-85; prin. Fire and Accident Reconstruction, Rowland Heights, Calif., 1985—. Pub. accident reconstrn. newsletter. With U.S. Army, 1967-69. Mem. ASCE, Am. Soc. Safety Engrs., Nat. Fire Protection Assn., Geol. Soc. Am., Firearms Research and Identification Assn. (pres. 1978—), Am. Soc. Metals, Nat. Safety Council, Ft. Tejon Hist. Assn. (info. adviser 1983—). Republican. Baptist. Avocations: hiking, traveling, photography. Office: Fire & Accident Reconstrn 17524 Colima Rd Ste 360 Rowland Heights CA 91748

CAUGHLIN, STEPHENIE JANE, futures company executive, metals company executive; b. McAllen, Tex., July 23, 1948; d. James Daniel and Betty Jane (Warnock) C. BA in Family Econs., San Diego State U., 1972, MEd, 1973; M. in Psychology, U.S. Internat. U., San Diego, 1979. Cert. secondary life tchr., Calif. Owner, mgr. Minute Maid Svc., San Diego, 1970-75; prin. Rainbow Fin. Svcs., San Diego, 1975-78; tchr. San Diego Unified Sch. Dist., 1973-80; mortgage broker Santa Fe Mortgage Co., San Diego, 1980-81; commodity broker Premex Commodities, San Diego, 1981-84; pres., owner Nationwide Futures Corp., San Diego, 1984-88; owner, sec. Nationwide Metals Corp.; owner gen. mgr. Seabreeze Organic Farm, 1984-88. Sec. Arroyo Sorrento Assn., Del Mar, Calif., 1978—. Mem. Greenpeace Nature Conservancy, DAR, Sierra Club. Republican. Avocations: horseback riding, swimming, skiing, gardening. Lodge: Jobs Daus. Home and Office: 3909 Arroyo Sorrento Rd San Diego CA 92130

CAULPETZER, DANIEL BRUCE, electrical engineer; b. Benton Harbor, Mich., May 24, 1950; s. Donald Lawrence and Joretta Marie (Fay) C.; m. Grace Godden, Aug. 16, 1972 (div. Sept., 1973); m. Irene Carol Lakner Feb. 13, 1982. BSEE, U. Wash., 1972; MBA in Info. Systems, City U., Bellevue, Wash., 1987. Reg. profl. engr., Wash. Mgr. gen. constrn. Rustic Mobile Sales, Oak Harbor, Wash., 1972-78; quality control rep. Quality Cons., Federal Way, Wash., 1978-79; elec. engr. Pan Am World Svcs., Bremerton, Wash., 1979-87; engring. supr. Flight Safety Svcs. Corp., Bremerton, 1987—. Scoutmaster Boy Scouts Am., Oak Harbor, Wash., 1973-74. Recipient Letter of Appreciation Naval Submarine Base Bangor, Bremerton, Wash., 1984. Mem. Pan Am. Mgmt. (treas. 1983-87), Lake Symington Community Club (v.p. 1984-89). Republican. Mem. United Ch. of Christ. Home: 3908 Redwing Trail Bremerton WA 98312 Office: Flight Safety Svcs Sys/Maint Engring/MS U-32 Navy Submarine Base Bangor Bremerton WA 98315

CAUWELS, PAUL STEVEN, real estate developer; b. Denver, Aug. 10, 1962; s. David Edward and Charlotte (Jones) C. BA in Bus. cum laude, Westmont Coll., 1985. Exec. v.p. Cauwels and Davis Devel. Co., Albuquerque, N.M., 1985--. Bd. dirs. New Mex. Fellowship of Christian Athletes. Mem. Execs. Assn. Greater Albuquerque (bd. dirs.), Inst. Real Estate Mgmt., Apt. Assn. New Mex. (bd. dirs. 1985-87). Republican. Baptist. Office: Cauwels & Davis Devel 1116 Pennsylvania Albuquerque NM 87110

CAVAKIS, ROBERT ALLAN, state official; b. Reno, Nev., June 6, 1947; s. Robert Joseph Cavakis and Beverly Ann (Brace) Hughes; m. Gaye Marie Savage, Aug. 31, 1968 (div. Jan. 1976); m. Michelle Marie Pitts, May 20, 1978. BS in Edn., U. Nev., Reno, 1973; grad., Nat. Coll. Juvenile Justice, 1978. Cert. juvenile justice adminstr. Detention supr. Washoe County Juvenile Detention, Reno, 1968-70; juvenile probation officer Washoe County Juvenile Probation, Reno, 1970-77; chief juvenile probation officer 6th Jud. Dist., Winnemucca, Nev., 1977-87; juvenile justice specialist State Nev., Carson City, 1987; adminstr. State Nev. Youth Svcs. Div., Carson City, 1987—; mem. faculty Nat. Coll. Juvenile Justice, Reno, 1986. Pres. Winnemucca Vol. Fire Dept., 1986-87; chmn. Winnemucca Parks & Recreation Commn., 1981-82; mem. nat. adv. panel Child Care Action Campaign, N.Y.C., 1988. Mem. Nat. Juvenile Ct. Svcs. Assn. (chmn. cert. com. 1986—, Far West regional rep. 1987—), Nat. Assn. Juvenile Correctional Agys., Nat. Assn. Juvenile and Famliy Ct. Judges, Kiwanis (pres. 1984-85). Office: State Nev Youth Svcs 505 E King St Ste 606 Carson City NV 89710

CAVALLERO, HAZEL HELEN, properties corporation executive; b. Burntmill, Colo., Mar. 18, 1913; d. Walter Merwin and Elizabeth Belle (Donley) Heller; m. John Walter Miller, June 4, 1937 (dec. Dec. 1943); m. Robert Angelo Cavallero, May 10, 1950; 1 child, Robert Clive. BA, U. Ill., 1941; MA, Stanford U., 1950. Pres. CSI, Inc., San Mateo, Calif., 1979—. Bd. dirs. Peninsula Vols., Menlo Park, Calif., 1962-74. Lt. (j.g.) USN, 1943-45. Republican. Episcopalian. Home: One Baldwin Ave #323 San Mateo CA 94401 Office: Mills Sq Tower 100 S Ellsworth #401 San Mateo CA 94401

CAVALLI-SFORZA, LUIGI LUCA, genetics educator; b. Genoa, Italy, Jan. 25, 1922; s. Pio and Attilia (Manacorda) C.; M.D., U. Pavia (Italy), 1944; M.A., Cambridge U. (Eng.), 1950; D.Sc. (hon.), Columbia U., 1980; m. Albamaria Ramazzotti, Jan. 12, 1946; children—Matteo, Francesco, Tommaso, Violetta. Came to U.S., 1970. Asst. research Istituto Sieroterapico Milanese, Milan, Italy, 1945-48, dir. research, 1950-57; prof. genetics U. Parma, 1958-62; prof. genetics, dir. Istituto di Genetica, U. Pavia, 1962-70; prof. genetics Stanford, 1970—. Vice-pres. Internat. Congress Genetics, Tokyo, Japan, 1968. Served as med. officer, Italian Army, 1947-48. Recipient T.H. Huxley award in anthropology, 1972, Weldon award in biometry, 1975. Fellow AAAS; mem. Am. Assn. Phys. Anthropology, Am. Soc. Human Genetics, Associazione Genetica Italiana, Behavioral Genetic Assn., Biometric Soc. (pres. 1967-68), Genetical Soc. Gt. Britain, Institut Internat. de Statistique, Soc. for Study Evolution, Union Internat. pour L'Etude Scientifique de la Population, Royal Statis. Soc., Am. Acad. Arts and Scis. (fgn. hon.), Japanese Soc. Human Genetics (fgn. hon.), U.S. Nat. Acad. Sci. (fgn. hon.). Author: (with W. Bodmer) The Genetics of Human Populations, 1971; Genetics, Evolution and Man, 1976; (with M. Feldman) Cultural Transmission and Evolution, 1981. Office: Stanford U Dept Genetics Room S-337 Stanford CA 94305-5120 *

CAVANAUGH, KENNETH CLINTON, housing consultant; b. Fremont, Mich., Apr. 30, 1916; s. Frank Michael and Buryll Marie (Preston) C.; m. Barbara Blythe Boling, Feb. 24, 1979; children from previous marriage: Patricia Ann, James Lee, John Thomas. BS in Forestry, Mich. State U., 1939. County supr. Farm Security Adminstrn., USDA, Kalamazoo, 1939-43; community mgr. PHA, Willow Run, Mich., 1946-49; dir. fiscal mgmt. PHA, Washington, 1949-55, dir. elderly housing Housing & Home Fin. Agy., 1955-57; reg. dir. PHA, San Juan, P.R., 1957-58; dir. housing progs. Housing & Urban Devel. Agy. PHA, Washington, 1958-73; controller/dep. dir. San Francisco Housing Authority, 1973-78; pres. Ken C. Cavanaugh & Assocs., pvt. internat. housing and community devel. cons., Vista, Calif., 1978—; fin. finder Merrill Lynch-Huntoon Paige Co., San Francisco, 1979-81, Western Pacific Fin. Co., Newport Beach, Calif., 1981-83; gen. ptnr. The Knolls, Rogers, Ark., 1980—. Exec. dir. Arlington (Va.) Youth Found., 1950-58; advisor Salvation Army adv. bd., Honolulu, 1985-88. Served to capt. USN, 1943-46, USNR, 1946-73. Recipient Superior Svc. award, Pub. Housing Adminstrn., 1956. Mem. Nat. Assn. Housing & Redevel. Ofcls., Ret. Officers Assn., Res. Officers Assn., Naval Res. Assn., Shadowridge Golf Club (Vista), Elks, Masons. Home: PO Box 749 Vista CA 92083

CAVAZOS, DAVID, areospace engineer, real estate agent; b. Harbor City, Calif., May 22, 1964; s. David Ramirez and Eduviges (Rodriguez) C. BS in Aerospace Engring., Calif. Poly., Pomona, 1986. Tech. writer Hughes Aircraft Co., Long Beach, Calif., 1984; engr. McDonnell Douglas Corp., Long Beach, 1985—; real estate agt. Century 21, Carson, Calif., 1987—. Recipient of 2d place in Aircraft Design Prat & Whitney/United Tech., 1986. Mem. Am. Inst. Aero. and Astronautics, Nat. Assn. Realtors, Calif. Assn. Realtors. Republican. Roman Catholic. Home: 22129 Ravenna Ave Carson CA 90745

CAVIN, LYLE CHRISTOPHER, JR., lawyer; b. Oakland, Calif., July 27, 1944; s. Lyle Christopher Sr. and Madeline E. (Selna) C.; m. Geraldine A. Cavin, July 8, 1967 (div. 1979); children; Lyle C. III, Gretchen Mitchell. BA, St. Mary's Coll., 1965; JD, Golden Gate U., 1969. Bar: Calif. 1970. Assoc. Sullivan & Johnson, San Francisco, 1970-72; ptnr. Sullivan, Johnson, Graham & Cavin, San Francisco, 1972-74; pvt. practice San Francisco, 1974--; lectr. at profl. confs. Mem. Calif. Bar Assn., San Francisco Trial Lawyers Assn., Assn. Trial Lawyers Am., Calif. Trial Lawyers Assn. Democrat. Roman Catholic. Office: 122 World Trade Ctr San Francisco CA 94111

CAVINESS, JAMES DONALD, state government official; b. Raton, N.Mex., Oct. 6, 1942; s. James Olen and Opal Belle (Thompson) C. BBA, N.Mex. State U., 1966, BS in Agrl. Econs., 1969, MS in Agrl. Econs., 1970. Pub. rels. asst., then dir. pub. rels. Wichita (Kans.) Bank for Coops., 1970-81, v.p. corp. svcs., 1981-85; asst. v.p. pub. affairs Farm Credit Svcs., Wichita, 1985-87; adminstrv. asst., pub. info. officer N.Mex. Dept. Corrections, Santa Fe, 1987-88; dep. for pub. affairs Office of Gov., State of N.Mex., Santa Fe, 1988—. Mem. Nat. Agri-Mktg. Assn., Am. Corrections Assn., Nat. Govs. Assn., C. of C., Classic Chevy Car Club. Republican. Methodist. Home: 1878 Camino Lumbre Santa Fe NM 87505 Office: Office of Gov State Capitol Bldg Santa Fe NM 87503

CAVNAR, SAMUEL MELMON, author, publisher, activist; Denver, Nov. 10, 1925; s. Samuel Edward and Helen Anita (Johnston) C.; m. Peggy Nightengale, Aug. 14, 1977; children by previous marriage—Dona Cavnar Hambly, Judy Cavnar Bentrim; children—Heather Anne, Heide Lynn. Student pub. schs., Denver. Dist. mgr. U.S. C. of C., various locations, 1953-58; owner Cavnar & Assocs., mgmt. cons., Washington, Las Vegas, Nev., Denver and Reseda, Calif., 1958—; v.p. Lenz Asso. Advt., Inc., Van Nuys, Calif., 1960—; dist. mgr. Western States Nu-Orm Plans, Inc., Los Angeles, 1947-52; cons. to architect and contractor 1st U.S. Missile Site, Wyo., 1957-58; prin. organizer Westway Corp. and subsidiaries, So. Calif. Devel. Co., 1958—; chmn. bd. Boy Sponsors, Inc., Denver, 1957-59; pres. Continental Am. Video Network Assn. Registry, Inc., Hollywood, Calif., 1967—; pres. United Sales Am., Las Vegas and Denver, 1969—; sr. mgmt. cons. Broadcast Mgmt. Cons. Service, Hollywood, Las Vegas, Denver, Washington, 1970—; pres., dir., exec. com. Am. Ctr. for Edn., 1968—; pub. Nat. Ind., Washington, 1970—, Nat. Rep. Statesman, Washington, 1969—, Nat. Labor Reform Leader, 1970—, Nat. Conservative Statesman, 1975—; owner Ran Vac Pub., Las Vegas and Los Angeles, 1976—; ptnr. P.S. Computer Services, Las Vegas, 1978—, C & A Mgmt., Las Vegas, 1978—, Westway Internat., 1983—; lectr. in field; spl. cons. various U.S. senators, congressmen, 1952—. Author: Run, Big Sam, Run, 1976, The Girls on Top, 1978, Big Brother Bureaucracy, The Cause and Cure, 1979, Kiddieland West, 1980, Games Politicians Play: How to Clean Up Their Act, 1981, A Very C.H.I.C. President, 1981, How to Clean Up Our Act, 1982, Assassination By Suicide, 1984, How to Get Limited Government, Limited Taxes, 1985, Tax Reform or Bust, 1985, At Last: Real Tax Reform, 1986. Nat. gen. chmn. Operation Houseclean, 1966-81; nat. candidate chmn. Citizens Com. To Elect Rep. Legislators, 1966, 68, 70, 72-74, 85—; mem. Calif. and Los Angeles County Rep. Cen. Coms., 1964-70; nat. gen. chmn. Project Prayer, 1962—; exec. dir. Project Alert, 1961—; nat. chmn. Nat. Labor Reform Com., 1969—; sustaining mem. Rep. Nat. Com., 1964—; Western states chmn. and nat. co-chmn. Am. Taxpayers Army, 1959—; area II chmn. Calif. Gov.'s Welfare Reform Com., 1970; chmn. Com. Law and Order in Am., 1975; mem. Nev. State Rep. Com., 1972—; mem. Clark County Rep. Com., 1972—; bd. dirs. Conservative Caucus, Las Vegas, 1980—; Rep. candidate for U.S. Senate from Nev., 1976, 82; Rep. candidate for U.S. Congress from 30th dist. Calif., 1968, 70; nat. chmn. Return Pueblo Crew, 1968, Citizens League for Labor Reform, 1984—; nat. co-chmn. U.S. Taxpayers Forces, 1985—; pres., trustee Community Youth Activities Found., 1977—; nat. chmn. Operation Bus Stop, 1970—, P.R.I.D.E. Com., 1981—, Positivics Program, 1982—; co-chmn. Question 8 Com., 1980-82, S.H.A.F.T.E.D. Tax Repeal Com., 1982 C.H.I.C. Polit. Edn. Com., 1977—, People Against Tax Hikes Com., 1983—; state chmn., pres. Reagan,s Tax Reform Com., 1985-86. Served with USN, 1942-45, USAF, 1950-53, Korea; comdr. USCG Aux., 1959-60. Recipient Silver medal SAR. Mem. Am. Legion (comdr. 1947-48, mem. nat. conv. disting. guest com. 1947-52), DAV, VFW, Am. Security Council (nat. adviser 1966—). Home: 301A Misty Isle Ln Las Vegas NV 89107 Office: PO Box 26073 Las Vegas NV 89126

CAWOOD, JAMES SCOTT, security professional; b. Lansing, Mich., May 6, 1956; s. James Humes and Joan Patricia Cawood; m. Anne Virginia Capron, Aug. 28, 1982. BA, U. Calif., Berkeley, 1978. Cert. protection profl. Security officer St. Francis Hotel, San Francisco, 1980-82; investigator W.J. Weaver Co., Hayward, Calif., 1982; dir. corp. security IMI, San Francisco, 1983; security ops. mgr. BankAmerica Data Ctr., San Francisco, 1984; pres. Factor One Security and Investigative Service, Inc., San Leanrdo, Calif., 1985—; instr. Golden Gate U., 1987—. Spl. asst. U.S. delegation UN, N.Y.C., 1977. Mem. Am. Soc. Indsl. Security, Calif. Assn. Licensed Investigators, Internat. Assn. Arson Investigators. Republican. Mem. Taoist faith. Office: Factor One Security & Investigative Svce Inc PO Box 1772 San Leandro CA 94577

CAYETANO, BENJAMIN JEROME, lieutenant governor, former state senator and representative; b. Honolulu, Nov. 14, 1939; s. Bonifacio Marcos and Eleanor (Infante) C.; m. Lorraine Gueco, Sept. 20, 1958; children: Brandon, Janeen, Samantha. B.A., UCLA, 1968; J.D., Loyola U., 1971. Bar: Hawaii 1971. Practiced in Honolulu, 1971-86; mem. Hawaii Ho. of Reps., 1975-78, Hawaii Senate, 1979-86; lt. gov. State of Hawaii, 1986—; bar examiner Hawaii Supreme Ct., 1976-78, disciplinary bd., 1982-86; arbitration panel 1st Cir. Ct. State of Hawaii, 1986; adv. U. Hawaii Law Rev., 1982-84. Mem. bd. regents Chaminade U., 1980-83; mem. adv. council U. Hawaii Coll. Bus. Administrn., 1982-83. Democrat. Office: Office of Lt Gov State Capitol Honolulu HI 96813

CAZIER, BARRY JAMES, electrical engineer, software developer; b. Phoenix, May 10, 1943; s. James Henry and Dorothy Marie (Lynton) C.; m. Susan Arline Shewey, June 13, 1964 (div. July 1979); children: Suzanne, Bryan. Student, Colo. Sch. Mines, 1961-62; BSEE, U. Colo., 1965; student advanced bus. adminstrn., Ariz. State U., 1974-77. Mfg. mgmt. Gen. Electric, Richland, Wash., 1965-66, Warren, Ohio, 1966-67; system engr. Gen. Electric, Schenectady, N.Y., 1967-69; project mgr. Honeywell, Phoenix, 1970-80, dir. field ops., 1980—; prin. Cazier Software Designs, Scottsdale, Ariz., 1985—. adv. Jr. Achievement, Phoenix, 1972. Club: IBM PC Users (Phoenix). Home: 6616 E Desert Cove Scottsdale AZ 85028 Office: Honeywell 16404 N Black Canyon Hwy Phoenix AZ 85023

CAZIER, STANFORD, university president; b. Nephi, Utah, June 11, 1930; m. Shirley Anderson, 1952; children: David, John, Paul. B.S. in Philosophy, U. Utah, 1952, M.A. in History, 1956; Ph.D. in History, U. Wis., 1964. Reader, U. Utah, 1954-56; teaching asst. U. Wis., 1957-58, research asst., 1959; instr. Bronx Community Coll., 1959-60; mem. faculty Utah State U., 1960-71, instr., 1960-62, asst. prof. history, 1962-67, asso. prof., 1968-69, prof., 1969-71, asst. to pres., 1968-69, chmn. dept. history, 1969, vice provost, 1969-71; Am. Council on Edn. fellow in acad. adminstrn. NYU, 1967-68; pres. Calif. State U., Chico, 1971-79, Utah State U., Logan, 1979—; chmn. council of pres. Calif. State Univs. and Colls., 1978-79, mem. exec. com. council pres., 1976-79; chmn. Utah Rhodes scholars com., 1980-88. Contbr. articles to profl. publs.; author: Student Discipline in Higher Education, 1973; also articles; bibliography editor history div.: Am. Quar., 1968-71. Served as ensign USN, 1952-53. Named Tchr. of Year, Robin's award, 1966; Danforth Found. asso., 1966—. Mem. Am. Assn. Higher Edn., Nat. Assn. Colls. and Univs., Soc. Coll. and Univ. Planning, Phi Kappa Phi, Phi Alpha Theta. Office: Utah State U Office of Pres Logan UT 84322

CECH, THOMAS ROBERT, chemistry and biochemistry educator; b. Chgo., Dec. 8, 1947; m. Carol Lynn Martinson; children: Allison E., Jennifer N. BA in Chem., Grinnell Coll., 1970; PhD in Chem., U. Calif., Berkeley, 1975. Postdoctoral fellow dept. biology MIT, Cambridge, Mass., 1975-77; from asst. prof. to assoc. prof. chemistry U. Colo., Boulder, 1978-83, prof. chemistry and biochemistry also molecular cellular and devel. biology, 1983—; research prof. Am. Cancer Soc., 1987—; investigator Howard Hughes Med. Inst., 1988—; investigator Howard Hughes Med. Inst., 1988—; Phillips disting. visitor Haverford Coll., 1984; Vivian Ernst meml. lectr. Brandeis U., 1984, Cynthia Chan meml. lectr. U. Calif., Berkeley; mem. Welch Found. Symposium, 1985; Danforth lectr. Grinnell Coll, 1986; Pfizer lectr. Harvard U., 1986; Verna and Marrs McLean lectr. Baylor Coll. Medicine, 1987; Harvey lectr., 1987; Mayer lectr. MIT, 1987; Martin D. Kamen disting. lectureship, U. Calif., San Diego, 1988; Alfred Burger lectr. U. Va., 1988; Berzelius lectr. Karolinska Inst., 1988; Osamu Hayaishi lectr. Internat. Union Biochemistry, Prague, 1988; co-chmn. Nucleic Acids Gordon Conf., 1984. Assoc. editor Cell, 1986-87; mem. editorial bd. Genes and Development. NSF fellow, 1970-75, Pub. Health Service research fellow Nat. Cancer Inst. 1975-77, Guggenheim fellow, 1985-86; recipient medal Am. Inst. Chemists, 1970, Research Career Devel. award Nat. Cancer Inst., 1980-85, Young Sci. award Passano Found., 1984, Harrison Howe award, 1984, Pfizer award, 1985, U.S. Steel award, 1987, V.D. Mattia award, 1987, Louisa Gross Horowitz prize, 1988, Newcombe-Cleveland award AAAS, 1988, Heineken prize Royal Netherlands Acad. Arts and Scis., 1988, Gairdner Found. Internat. award, 1988, Lasker Basic Med. Rsch. award, 1988, Rosenstiel award, 1989; named to Esquire Mag. Register, 1985, Westerner of Yr. Denver Post, 1986. Mem. AAAS, Am. Soc. Biol. Chemists, Nat. Acad. Scis., Am. Acad. Arts and Scis. Office: U Colo Dept Chemistry & Biochemistry Boulder CO 80309

CEDAR, PAUL ARNOLD, minister; b. Mpls., Nov. 4, 1938; s. C. Benjamin and Bernice P. Cedar; m. Jean Helen Lier; children: Daniel Paul, Mark John, Deborah Jean. BS, No. State Coll., S.D., 1960; postgrad., Trinity Div. Sch., 1962, Wheaton Grad. Sch., 1962, U. Iowa Grad. Sch. of Religion, 1965; M Div., No. Baptist Theol. Sem., 1968; postgrad., Calif. State U., Fullerton, 1971; D Ministry, Am. Baptist Sem., 1973. Ordained to ministry, 1966. Crusade dir. Leighton Ford Team, 1967-69; sr. pastor Evang. Free Ch. of Yorba Linda, Calif., 1969-73; exec. pastor of evangelism 1st Presbyn. Ch. of Hollywood, Calif., 1975-80; sr. pastor Lake Ave. Congl. Ch., Pasadena, Calif., 1981—; pres. Dynamic Communications, Pasadena, Calif., 1973—; mem. adv. bd. World Wide Pictures, Mpls., 1982-86; guest dean Billy Graham Sch. Evangelism, Mpls., 1983—; adj. prof. Fuller Theol. Sem., Pasadena, 1978—, Talbot Theol. Sem., LaHabra, Calif., 1978—. Author: Seven Keys to Maximum Communication, 1980, Servant Leadership in The Church, 1986. Vice chmn. Billy Graham So. Calif. Crusade, 1984-85. Mem. Lausanne Com. for World Evangelization, Phi Kappa Delta (life). Club: University. Home: 848 W Huntington Dr Arcadia CA 91006 Office: Lake Ave Congl Ch 393 North Lake Ave Pasadena CA 91101

CEDERBLOM, RODNEY PAUL, accountant; b. Spokane, Wash., June 6, 1949; s. Volney David and Mildred Marion (Miller) C.; m. Rose Marie Fink, Nov. 8, 1975; children: Eric Paul, Nicole Marie. BBA, U. Wash., 1971. CPA, Wash. Acct. Arthur Young & Co., Seattle, 1970-71, Warren K. Smith CPA, Seattle, 1972; internal auditor Smyth Greyhound, Seattle, 1972-74; asst. controller Tacoma Boatbuilding Co. Inc., 1974-78, mgmt. info. systems dir., 1978-79; group controller The NBBJ Group, Seattle, 1979-86, dir. automated systems, 1986—; treas. Streeter Dermanis/NBBJ, Seattle, 1980-82. Water commr. King County Water Dist. #57, Seattle, 1980—. Served as sgt. Air N.G., 1971-77. Mem. Am. Inst. CPAs, Wash. Soc. CPAs., Western Cascade Tree Fruit Assn. Luthern. Office: The NBBJ Group 111 S Jackson St Seattle WA 98104

CEDOLINE, ANTHONY JOHN, psychotherapist; b. Rochester, N.Y., Sept. 19, 1942; s. Peter Ross and Mary J. (Anthony) C.; m. Clare Marie De Rose, Aug. 16, 1964; children: Maria A., Antonia C., Peter E. Student, U. San Francisco, 196062; BA, San Jose State U., 1965, MS, 1968; PhD in Ednl. Pscyhology, Columbia Pacific U., 1983. Lic. ednl. psychologist, sch. adminstr., marriage, family, child counselor, sch psychologist, sch. counselor, social worker, Calif.; Lic. real estate broker, Calif. Mng. ptnr. Cienega Valley Vineyards and Winery and Comml. Shopping Ctr., Hollister and others, Calif., 1968—; coordinator of psychological svcs. Oak Grove Sch. Dist., San Jose, Calif., 1968-61; asst. dir. pupil svcs. Oak Grove Sch. Dist., San Jose, 1977-81, dir. pupil svcs., 1981-83; pvt. practice, ednl. psychologist Ednl. Assocs., San Jose, 1983—; co-dir. Biofeedback Inst. of Santa Clara County, San Jose, 1976-83; ptnr. in Cypress Ctr.-Ednl. Psychologists and Consultancy, 1978—; cons. Morgan Hill Unified Sch. Dist., Modoc County Schs., Campbell Union Sch. Dist., Newark Sch. Dist.; spl. program auditor for Calif. State Dept. Edn.; instr. U. Calif., Santa Cruz and LaVerne Coll. Ext. courses; guest spkr. San Jose State U.; lectr., workshop presenter in field. Author: Occupational Stress and Job Burnout, 1982, A Parents Guide to School Readiness, 1971, The Effect of Affect, 1975; contbr. articles to profl. jours. and newspapers. Founder, bd. dirs. Lyceum of Santa Clara County, 1971. Recipient award from Optimist Club of San Jose, Special Recognition award, Almaden Preschool. Mem. NEA, Calif. Tchrs. Assn., Calif. Assn. Sch. Psychologists, Nat. Assn. Sch. Psychologists, Council for Exceptional Children, Calif. Assn. for the Gifted, Assn. Calif. Sch. Adminstrs., Calif. Personnel & Guidance Assn., Biofeedback Soc. Am., Nat. Assn. Realtors, Calif. Assn. Realtors, San Jose Realty Bd., Tau Delta Phi and others. Home and Office: 1183 Nikulina Ct San Jose CA 95120

CEGELSKY, MIKE, language professional; b. Wroclaw, Poland, Feb. 5, 1951; arrived in Demark, 1972; came to U.S., 1974; s. Adam and Maria (Zielinska) Cegielski; m. Birgit Bech, Jan. 18, 1975; children: Christine Cynthia, Brian Scott. BA in Russian Lang. Studies, U. Tex., 1980; MA in Fgn. Lang. Edn., U. Md., 1986. With AFSAC/AFIS, Ft. Belvoir, 1981-85; asst. prof. Fgn. Lang. Dept. USAF Acad., Colorado Springs, Colo., 1986—. Active Am. Wildlife Assn. Mem. Am. Council on Teaching Fgn. Langs., Colo. Consortium Russian Studies, Colo. Congress of Fgn. Lang. Tchrs., Air Force Assn., Nat. Rifle Assn. Republican. Roman Catholic. Lodge: Sertoma. Home: 8455 Sweetgum Terr Colorado Springs CO 80920-5744 Office: Hdqrs USAF Acad/DFF Fairchild Hall Colorado Springs CO 80840

CELANO, BRYAN W., communications executive; b. Syracuse, N.Y., May 29, 1964; s. E. William and Margaret D. (Donegan) C. BS in Computer Science, SUNY, Potsday, N.Y., 1986. Dist. mgr. Monaras Bartending Sch., Syracuse, N.Y., 1983-84; sound engr., programmer THWK Ednl. Software, Potsdam, N.Y., 1983-86; sales, mktg. Hybrid Arts, Inc., L.A., 1986-87, pub. dir., 1987-88, product support dir., 1987—; pres. BC Consulting, N. Hollywood, Calif., 1986—; co-owner Video Studio Internat., North Hollywood, 1988—; drummer Haley-Scott Band, 1987—. Mem. Phi Mu Alph Sinfonia. Republican. Roman Catholic. Home: 12643 Collins St North Hollywood CA 91607 Office: Hybrid Arts Inc 11920 W Olympic Blvd Los Angeles CA 90064

CELENZA, JOHN PATRICK, engineering manager; b. N.Y.C., Dec. 2, 1943; s. John James and Mary (Dunne) C.; m. Jacqueline Jean Dever, June 20, 1987; 1 child, Audrey. BS, Manhattan Coll., 1965. Construction worker John Barba & Sons, N.Y.C., 1969-71; recording engr. Airwaves Studio, San Francisco, 1971-72; restaurant mgr. James Reisdorf's, Berkeley, Calif., 1972-73; devel. engr. Chemeley, Redwood City, Calif., 1973-77, Nicolet CAD, Berkeley, 1977-81; engring. mgr. GENRAD, Milpitas, Calif., 1983-88, KLA Instruments, Santa Clara, Calif., 1988—. Founder, Miss. Civil Liberties Union, 1969; worker Lawyers Constitutional Def. Com., Miss., 1968-69; mem. ACLU, 1963—. 2nd Lt. USAF, 1967-69. Mem. AAAS, Math. Assn. Am.

CELLIER, ALFRED, electronics engineering project manager; b. Alameda, Calif., Oct. 3, 1938; s. Alfred Jr. and Alice (Klump) C.; m. Nancy Ann Lee, Mar. 5, 1939 (div. May 1987); children: David Michael, Susann. BSEE, So. Meth. U., 1961; MSEE, Stanford U., 1966. Engr. Tex. Instruments, Dallas, 1957-61, lead engr., 1961-64, sr. engr., 1964-67; mem. tech. staff TRW Space & Defense, Redondo Beach, Calif., 1967-68, sect. head, 1968-73, dept. mgr., 1973-78, asst. project mgr., 1978-82, advanced systems mgr., 1982-86, project mgr., 1986—. Inventor and patentee in field. Reader Recording for the Blind, L.A., 1988—. Republican.

CENARRUSA, PETE T., state official; b. Carey, Idaho, Dec. 16, 1917; s. Joseph and Ramona (Gardoqui) C.; m. Freda B. Coates, Oct. 25, 1947; 1 son, Joey Earl. B.S. in Agr., U. Idaho, 1940. Tchr. high sch. Cambridge, Idaho, 1940-41, Carey and Glenns Ferry, Idaho, 1946; tchr. vocat. agr. VA, Blaine County, Idaho, 1946-51; farmer, woolgrower, nr. Carey, 1946—; mem. Idaho Ho. of Reps., 1951-67, speaker, 1963-67; sec. state Idaho, 1967—; mem. Idaho Bd. Land Commrs., Idaho Bd. Examiners; pres. Idaho Flying Legislators, 1953-63; chmn. Idaho Legis. Council, 1964—, Idaho Govt. Reorgn. Com.; Idaho del. Council State Govts., 1963—. Republican adminstr. Hall of Fame, 978. Served to maj. USMCR, 1942-46, 52-58. Named Hon. Farmer Future Farmers Am., 1955; named to Agrl. Hall of Fame, 1973; Idaho Athletic Hall of Fame, 1976, Basque Hall of Fame, 1983. Mem. Blaine County Livestock Mktg. Assn., Blaine County Woolgrowers Assn. (chmn. 1954), Carey C. of C. (pres. 1952), U. Idaho Alumni Assn., Gamma Sigma Delta. Republican. Office: Office of Sec State State Capitol Rm 203 Boise ID 83720 *

CEPPOS, JEROME MERLE, newspaper editor; b. Washington, DC, Oct. 14, 1946; s. Harry and Florence (Epstein) C.; m. Karen E. Feingold, Mar. 7, 1982. B.S. in Journalism, U. Md., 1969. Reporter, asst. city editor, night city editor Rochester Democrat & Chronicle, N.Y., 1969-72; from asst. city editor, to nat. editor, to asst. mng. editor The Miami Herald, Fla., 1972-81; assoc. editor San Jose Mercury News, Calif., 1981, mng. editor, 1983—; mem. adv. bds. to journalism depts. San Jose State U. and Santa Clara U., nat. adv. bd. Knight Ctr. Specialized Reporting U. Md. Mem. Am. Soc. Newspaper Editors, AP Mng. Editors, Sigma Delta Chi. Home: 14550 Pike Rd Saratoga CA 95070 Office: San Jose Mercury News 750 Ridder Pk Dr San Jose CA 95190

CERANSKI, MICHAEL EDWIN, software development executive; b. Missoula, Mont., Nov. 4, 1957; s. Lawrence E. and Nora Lynn (Zirbes) C.; m. Julie Ann Kovash, July 22, 1979; 1 child, Aaron Michael. BA, U. Colo., 1982. V.p., ptnr. Sophco, Inc., Boulder, Colo., 1983-89; founder, pres. Ctr. for Computer Disease Control, Boulder, 1989—. Office: Sophco Inc PO Box 7430 Boulder CO 80306

CERMAK, JACK EDWARD, engineer, educator; b. Hastings, Colo., Sept. 8, 1922; s. Joseph and Helen (Herman) C.; m. Helen Jane Carlson, Dec. 17, 1949; children: Douglas Karl, Jonathan Joel. B.S., Colo. State U., 1947, M.S., 1948; Ph.D., Cornell U., 1959; NATO postdoctoral fellow, Cambridge U., Eng., 1961-62. Mem. faculty Colo. State U., Ft. Collins, 1948—; prof. charge fluid mechanics and wind engring. program, also dir. Fluid Dynamics and Diffusion Lab. Colo. State U., 1960-85, univ. disting. prof., 1986—, chmn. engring. sci. maj. program, 1963-72; pres., dir. Colo. State U. (Research Found.), 1965-72; pres. Cermak Peterka Petersen Inc., 1982—; cons. in field. Mem. bd. mems. Univ. Corp. Atmospheric Research, 1966-67; pres., chmn. 10th Midwestern Mechanics Conf., 1966-67; dir. summer inst. fluid mechanics NSF, 1963, 65, 68, 72; chmn. 2d U.S. Nat. Conf. Wind Engring. Research, 1975, 5th Internat. Conf. Wind Engring., 1979; pres. Wind Engring. Research Council, Inc., 1979-85; co-chmn. U.S.-Japan Seminar Lab. Simulation of Stratified Shear Flows; mem. Colo. Gov.'s Sci. and Tech. Adv. Council, Com. on Army Basic Research, NRC, 1979-83. Mem. editorial adv. bd. Indsl. Aerodynamics Abstracts, Mechanics Research Communications; regional editor for U.S., Internat. Jour. Wind Engring; mem. editorial bd. Meteorology and Atmospheric Physics; contbr. articles to profl. jours. Fellow ASCE (chmn. engring. mechanics div. 1965), Am. Acad. Mechanics, AIAA (assoc.); mem. Am. Soc. Engring. Edn. (chmn. mechanics div., Sr. Rsch. award 1987), Nat. Acad. Engring. (chmn. com. natural disasters, chmn. panel on wind engring. research), Internat. Assn. Wind Engring. (chmn. bd. 1975-79, regional sec. North and S.Am. 1983—), Am. Meteorol. Soc., Am. Geophys. Union, ASME (Freeman scholar 1974, disting. lectr. 1987—), AAAS, ASHRAE (mem. com. flow around bldgs.), Air Pollution Control Assn., NSPE (Outstanding Profl. Achievement award), N.Y. Acad. Scis., Sigma Xi (nat. lectr. 1976-77). Home: 407 E Prospect St Fort Collins CO 80525

CERRITO, ORATIO ALFONSO, real estate investor, financial advisor; b. Cleve., Mar. 10, 1911; s. Carl and Lillian (DiVita) C.; m. Rita McCue, Oct. 9, 1931 (div. 1946); children: Lillian, Rita-Diane; m. Maria Capri, Dec. 18, 1947; children: Miriam, Linda, Claudia. BA, John Carroll U., 1935; LLB, Cleve. Law Sch., 1940. Bar: Ohio, 1941, U.S. Dist. Ct. (no. dist.) Ohio, 1950. Foreman Chase Brass and Copper Co., Euclid, Ohio, 1931-41; assoc. Sindell & Sindell, Cleve., 1941-42; law violations investigator Wage-Hour div. U.S. Dept. Labor, Cleve., 1942-44; price officer Allied Control Commn. of Allied Mil. Govt., Rome, 1944-45; hdqs. distbn. officer UNRRA, Athens, 1945-46; pres., gen. mgr. U.S. Store Fixture Co., Cleve., 1946-52; account exec. Research Inst. Am., Cleve., 1952-54, So. Calif., 1954-60; regional mgr. indsl. div. Marlin, So. Calif., 1960-81; fin. advisor, mgr. O.A. Cerrito Family Trust, Fountian Valley, Calif., 1981—. Home and Office: 18173 Santa Cecilia Circle Fountain Valley CA 92708

CERVANTES, MICHAEL ANTHONY, bilingual and computer educator; b. Altadena, Calif., July 27, 1949; s. John G. and Anita (Muro) C. BA in English, Calif. State Coll., L.A., 1971, MA in Edn., 1978; MA in Chicano Studies, Calif. State U., L.A., 1985. Cert. elem. tchr., Calif., bilingual specialist, Calif. 5th grade tchr. Valle Lindo Sch. Dist., South El Monte, Calif., 1972-75, bilingual tchr., 1974-75, 3d grade tchr., 1975-76; 3d grade tchr. El Rancho Unified Sch. Dist., Pico Rivera, Calif., 1976-78, kindergarten tchr., 1978-83, 2d grade tchr., 1983—, computer tchr., 1986, computer tchr. Gifted and Talented Edn., 1988—; sch. rep. to computer and tech. com. El Rancho Unified Sch. Dist., 1984—, prin. judge computer contest, 1985—, co-chmn. parent participation component, 1988, computer participation component, 1988; judge dist.-wide finals computer contest, 1984—. Co-coord. benefit for homeless and orphans of El Salvador San Gabriel (Calif.) Mission Parish, 1984—, treas. peace and justice com., 1988—, co-coordinator legalization program for undocumented, 1986-87, co-chmn. subcom. of human rights, 1984—, chmn. accion catolica juvenil youth group, 1983-84, chmn. religious high sch. youth program, 1981-82, chmn. 5th grade religious edn., 1978-79, chmn. religious elem. edn., 1974-76, eucharistic minister, 1983—; mem. L.A. County Mus. of Art, 1984—, L.A. County Mus. of Nat. History, 1985—, Peace and Justice Ctr. of So. Calif., 1987—. Grantee in field. Mem. Internat. Reading Assn., NEA, Valle Lindo Ednl. Assn., AFT. Democrat. Roman Catholic. Home: 127 Fisk Ave San Gabriel CA 91776 Office: El Rancho Unified Sch Dist 5241 S Passons Blvd Pico Rivera CA 90660

CHA, CHUNG-HWA, dentist; b. Seoul, Apr. 14, 1960; d. Bong-Hwoe and Chung-Min (Lee) C. BS in Biology, U. Tex., San Antonio, 1981; DDS, Marquette U., 1986. Pvt. practice San Francisco and Sunnyvale, Calif., 1987—. Mem. ADA, Am. Assn. Women Dentists, Acad. Gen. Dentistry. Home: 2719 S Norfolk #303 San Mateo CA 94403

CHABOT-FENCE, DENE, industrial engineer; b. Long Beach, Calif., Dec. 20, 1932; s. Marvin Carl and Jessica May Castelberry (Albrecht) Fence. AA, Am. River Coll., Sacramento, 1965; BS, Calif. Inst. Tech., 1966, U. San Francisco, 1983; MS, U. San Francisco, 1985. Research technician Calif. Inst. Tech., Pasadena, 1960-66; engr. various firms, Calif., 1966-80; design engr. J.R. Simplot, Helm, Calif., 1980-85; project engr. J. Oakley & Assocs., Fresno, Calif., 1985-86; prin. engr. Handypersons, Fresno, 1986-87; design engr. Heublein Wines, Madera, Calif., 1987-88, Bruce Industries, Dayton, Nev., 1988—. Patentee in field. Mission pilot Airlifeline, Sacramento. Served with USAF, 1950-54, Korea. Mem. Am. Assn. Indsl. Hygiene (cert.), 99's (chmn. local chpt. 1985-86). Democrat. Home: 5959 Sedge Rd Carson City NV 87901

CHACE, ALDEN BUFFINGTON, JR., ocean engineer; b. San Francisco, Dec. 13, 1939; s. Alden Buffington Sr. and Naomi (Wingfield) C.; m. Diane Budde, June 13, 1967; children: Tara F., David W., Adam B. BS in Naval Sci., U.S. Naval Acad., 1962; MS in Oceanography, Naval Postgrad. Sch., Monterey, Calif., 1969; PhD in Ocean Engring., U. R.I., 1975. Registered profl. engr., R.I. Commd. ensign USN, 1962, advanced through grades to lt. comdr., submarine officer, 1962-70, oceanographer, 1975-82, ret., 1982; ops. analyst Summit Rsch. Corp., Gaithersburg, Md., 1982-83; sr. rsch. scientist Sci. Applications Internat. Co., Monterey, 1983-84; supervising engr. Brown & Caldwell Cons. Engrs., Walnut Creek, Calif., 1984-85; prin. engr. Boeing Co., Seattle, 1985—. Contbr. articles to profl. jours. Mem. Marine Tech. Soc. chpt. sec. 1982-83, tech. program com. oceans 89 conf. 1988-89), Am. Meteorol. Soc., ASCE, U.S. Naval Inst., Hawaii Bicycle League (treas. 1982), Boeing Employees Bicycle Club (treas. 1989), Sigma Xi. Home: 3250 S 164th St Seattle WA 98188-3036 Office: Boeing Co PO Box 3999 M/S 82-99 Seattle WA 98124-2499

CHACKEL, CHARLES VICTOR, communications executive; b. San Francisco, Nov. 20, 1947; s. Reno D. and Betty J. Chackel; m. Kathryn A. Fitzhugh, Aug. 30, 1969; children: Geoffrey C., Ryan R. BSBA, U. Oreg., 1970. Dist. mgr. Kraft Foods, Inc., Eugene, Oreg., 1970-72; design cons. Obie Communications Corp., Eugene, 1972-74; account exec. Sta. KUGN-AM, Eugene, 1974-76, sales mgr., 1976-81; gen. mgr. Sta. KUGN-FM, Eugene, 1981-83; v.p., gen. mgr. Sta. KUGN-AM-FM, Eugene, 1983—; bd. dirs. CBS Radio Affiliates, N.Y.C., 1986—, Arbitron Radio, Beltsville, Md., 1988—. Bd. dirs. Youth for Christ, Eugene, 1985—, Community Substance Abuse, 1987—, Children's Relief Nursery, 1981-83, Oreg. Bach Festival, 1981-83. Mem. Oreg. Assn. Broadcasters (bd. dirs. 1987—), Mid-Oreg. Advt. Club, Eugene Arts Found., Rotary, Eugene Country Club. Republican. Office: Sta KUGN 4222 Commerce St Eugene OR 97402

CHACON, EDILIA LORETTO, cement construction executive; b. Harshaw, Ariz., Apr. 6, 1938; d. Manuel Salcedo and Stella Andrade (Acevedo) Loretto; m. Mike Nieto Chacon, Apr. 2, 1958; children: Sylvia, Michael, Mona. Student pub. schs., Salinas, Calif. Head cashier, buyer Washington Wholesalers, Salinas, 1968-71; office mgr. Diamond Cement Contractor, Salinas, 1971—; constrn. contractor New Comdr. Constrn., Salinas. Author: One Woman Saga, Fear of Life and Fear of Death, 1980. Home: 773 Galindo St Salinas CA 93905 Office: Diamond Cement Contrator 320 John St Ste 324 Salinas CA 93901

CHADEY, HENRY F., museum director; b. Superior, Wyo., Feb. 20, 1924; s. Frank and Anna (Glogovsek) C.; m. Helen Putz, Aug. 3, 1957; children: Michael, Katherine, Mary Jo, Jeanne. BA, U. Wyo., 1949, MA, 1955. Tchr. Dist. No. 7, Reliance, Wyo., 1956; sch. supt. Dist. No. 7, Reliance, 1956-59; asst. supt. Wyo. State Dept. Edn., Cheyenne, Wyo., 1959-61; high sch. prin. Dist. No. 8, Glenrock, Wyo., 1961-62, Dist. No. 4, Rock Springs, Wyo., 1962-67; museum dir. Sweetwater City Museum, Green River, Wyo., 1967—; instr. in field. Author: Rock Springs Chinese, 1985; author jour. Wyoming Geological Assistant Guidebook, 1973, Annals of Wyoming, 1978. Clk. Sch. Dist. No. 1, Sweetwater County, 1967—; pres. Wyo. State Hist. Soc., 1972-73; chmn. Wyo. Sch. Bd. Assn., 1977-78; mem. Wyo. State Sch. Bd., 1977-78. Mem. Am. Assn. Museums, Am. Assn. for State and Local History, Mt. Plains Museum Assn., Colo.-Wyo. Museum Assn. (dir. 1986-88), Lions (pres. 1976-77, clk. 1980—). Democrat. Roman Catholic. Home: 413 Fremont Ave Rock Springs WY 82901 Office: Sweetwater Hist Museum 80 W Flaming Gorge Way Green River WY 82935

CHADSEY, HELEN JEAN, teacher; b. Hudsonville, Mich., Apr. 18, 1936; d. Raymond and Dorothy (Ann) Van Dyke; m. Phillip Duke Chadsey, June 26, 1962; children: Phillip Duke II, Dana Lea, Jeffrey Dyke. BA, Hope Coll., 1958; MEd, West Oreg. Coll., 1966; postgrad., Portland State U., 1980. Tchr. Grand Haven (Mich.) Schs., 1958-60, Holland (Mich.) Pub. Schs., 1960-61, USAF, Novaseur, Morocco and Chatcauroux, France, 1961-63, Salem (Oreg.) Pub. Schs., 1963-66; freelance tutor of dyslexics Portland and Beaverton, Oreg., 1980-83; co-coord. cultural programs Ikebana Internat., Portland, 1983—. Treas. Ikebana Internat., Portland, 1977; Sunday Sch. tchr. Unitarian Ch., Portland, 1970-79, symphony aux. Mem. Lang. Skills Therapy (bd. dirs. 1986-88), Orton Dyslexia Soc. (librarian 1987—), Assn. for Children with Learning Disabilities. Democrat. Unitarian. Home: 2705 SW Summit Dr Portland OR 97201

CHADWICK, SHARON STEVENS, librarian; b. Syracuse, N.Y., June 1, 1951; d. Robert Harold and Melba Frances (Hurlburt) Stevens; m. Gary Robert Chadwick, May 27, 1972. BS in Chemistry, Clarkson Coll. Tech., 1973; MSLS, Syracuse U., 1975; MS in Chemistry, SUNY, Oswego, 1980. Asst. librarian SUNY, Oswego, 1977-78; chemistry, physics bibliographer Syracuse U., 1978-79; sci. librarian Humboldt State U., Arcata, Calif., 1980—. Mem. AAAS, ALA, Am. Chem. Soc., Calif. Libr. Assn., Med. Libr. Assn., Alexander Graham Bell Assn. for Deaf. Home: 190 Willow Ln Arcata CA 95521 Office: Humboldt State U The Libr Arcata CA 95521

CHAFFEE, PAUL STANLEY, veterinarian, zoo administrator; b. Port Huron, Mich., Jan. 23, 1928; s. Walter Henry and Leland Elizabeth (Green) C.; children: David P., Daniel P., Richard P., Denise J. AS, Port Huron Jr. Coll., 1949; BS, DVM with honors, Mich. State U., 1953. Asst. veterinarian Peigh Animal Hosp., 1953-54; owner, veterinarian McKinley Pet Hosp., Fresno, Calif., 1955-65; veterinarian Fresno Zoo, 1960—, zoo dir., 1965—. Contbr. numerous articles to profl. publs. Bd. dirs. Am. Assn. Zoological Parks and Aquariums. Served as cpl. U.S. Army, 1946-48. Mem. Am. Assn. Zoo Veterinarians (pres. 1972), Zoo Act (pres.), Am. Assn. Zool. Parks and Aquariums (pres. 1980-81, past chmn. ethics com., current bd. dirs.), Fresno Zool. Soc., Calif. Acad. Vet. Medicine, Phi Zeta. Republican. Lodge: Rotary (pres. Fresno club 1978-79). Office: Fresno Zoo 894 W Belmont Ave Fresno CA 93728

CHAI, WINBERG, political science educator; b. Shanghai, China, Oct. 16, 1932; came to U.S., 1951, naturalized, 1973; s. Ch'u and Mei-en (Tsao) C.; m. Carolyn Everett, Mar. 17, 1966; children: Maria May-lee, Jeffrey Tien-yu. Student, Hartwick Coll., 1951-53; BA, Wittenberg U., 1955; MA, New Sch. Social Rsch., 1958; PhD, NYU, 1968. Lectr. New Sch. Social Rsch., 1957-61; vis. asst. prof. Drew U., 1961-62; asst. prof. Fairleigh Dickinson U., 1962-65; asst. prof. U. Redlands, 1965-68, assoc. prof., 1969-73, chmn. dept., 1970-73; prof., chmn. Asian studies CCNY, 1973-79; disting. prof. polit. sci., v.p. acad. affairs, spl. asst. to pres. U. S.D., Vermillion, 1979-82; prof. polit. sci., dir. internat. programs U. Wyo., Laramie, 1988—; chmn. Third World Conf. Found., Inc., Chgo., 1982-88. Author: (with Ch'u Chai) The Story of Chinese Philosophy, 1961, The Changing Society of China, 1962, rev. edit., 1969, The New Politics of Communist China, 1972, The Search for a New China, 1975; editor: Essential Works of Chinese Communism, 1969, (with James C. Hsiung) Asia in the U.S. Foreign Policy, 1981, (with James C. Hsiung) U.S. Asian Relations: The National Security Paradox, 1983, (with Cal Clark) Political Stability and Economic Growth, 1988, (with Carolyn Chai) Beyond China's Crisis, 1989; co-translator: (with Ch'u Chai) A Treasury of Chinese Literature, 1965. Ford Found. humanities grantee, 1968, 69; Haynes Found. fellow, 1967, 68; Pacific Cultural Found. grantee, 1978, 86; NSF grantee, 1970; Hubert Eaton Meml. Fund grantee, 1972-73; Field Found. grantee, 1973, 75; Henry Luce Found. grantee, 1978, 80; S.D. Humanities Com. grantee, 1980; Asian Pacific Fund grantee, 1987. Mem. Am. Assn. Chinese Studies (pres. 1978-80), AAAS, AAUP, Am. Polit. Sci. Assn., N.Y. Acad. Scis., Internat. Studies Assn., NAACP. Democrat. Home: 1071 Granite Dr Laramie WY 82070 Office: PO Box 4098 Laramie WY 82071

CHAIM, ROBERT ALEX, academic administrator, educator; b. Stockton, Calif., Oct. 25, 1947; s. Alex Jr. and Carmen Lorraine (Rodriques-Lopez) C.; m. Diane Leonora Gregonis, May 30, 1971 (dec. 1973); m. Linda Jean Riley, Dec. 22, 1976. AA, San Joaquin Delta Coll., 1967; BA, Sacramento State Coll., 1970; cert. in secondary teaching, U. Pacific, 1972, ArtsD, 1980. Instr. English lang. U. Pacific, Stockton, 1973-77; lectr. lang. of law U. Pacific, Sacramento, 1977—; asst. to dean McGeorge Sch. Law, Sacramento, 1977-81, asst. dean students, 1981—; cons. grammar, usage and linguistics numerous law orgns. and pvt. law firms, Calif., 1978—; mem. curriculum com. law sch. U. San Fernando, Calif., 1979. Editor-in-chief Stauffer Legal Rsch. Series, 1978—; contbr. articles to scholarly books and profl. jours. Mem. Elk Grove (Calif.) Community Planning Adv. Couns., 1986-88, vice-chmn., 1987; mem. scholarship com. Centro Legal de Calif., Sacramento, 1987—, curriculum adv. com. Elk Grove Unified Sch. Dist., 1988, scholarship com. Sacramento Country Day Sch., 1988. Recipient Meritorious Svc. award Asian-Am. Law Students Assn., Sacramento, 1986, 87, Outstanding Svc. award La Raza Law Students Assn., 1988. Mem. ABA (assoc., legal edn. and bar admissions sect.), Nat. Assn. Fgn. Student Affairs, Assn. Am. Law Schs. (mem. legal rsch. and writing sect.). Office: U of the Pacific McGeorge Sch Law 3200 5th Ave Sacramento CA 95817

CHAIRES, ANGEL HERNANDEZ, insurance agency executive; b. Lordsburg, N.Mex., Dec. 5, 1933; s. Francisco H. and Concepcion (Neverez) C.; m. Yolanda Randall, Aug. 10, 1952 (div. 1958); children: Charles, Steve, Susan; m. Ofelia Dorantes, Aug. 29,1959; children: Angel Jose, Marianne, Debra, Ruben. Student in acctg., Phoenix Coll. Agt. Farmers Ins. Co., Phoenix, 1967—; acct., tax acct. Income Tax Svc. Systems, Phoenix, 1969—; prin. Chaires Ins. Ctr., Phoenix. With USN, 1955-57. Democrat. Roman Catholic. Home: 4913 W Seldon Ln Glendale AZ 85302 Office: Chaired Ins Ctr 326 N 35th Ave Phoenix AZ 85009

CHALFIN, NORMAN LEONARD, electronics engineer; b. Phila., Oct. 16, 1913; s. Nathan M. and Katherine M. (Tinkelman) C.; m. Ethel Friedman, Jan. 22, 1937; 1 son, Gregory Thomas. Student, NYU, 1931-33; BS, U. Ga., 1936; postgrad., Columbia U., 1936-41; JD, Southwestern U., 1960. Bar: U.S. Patent Office 1955, Can. Patent Office 1955. Instr. communications tng. project Nat. Youth Adminstrn., 1941-42; sr. elec. engr. Western Electric Co., Clifton, N.J., 1942-43; chief radio engring. Crystal Rch. Labs., Hartford, Conn., 1943; project engr. Am. Type Founders, N.Y.C., 1944; sr. applications engr. N.Am. Phillips Co., Dobbs Ferry, N.J., 1945; sr. devel. engr. Daven Co., Newark, 1946; chief engr. Eastern Ed. Radio News, N.Y.C., 1947-48, Eastern Ed. radio and TV maintenance, 1950; chief engr. Crystal Devices Corp., Freeport, N.Y., 1949-51; tech. editor Hughes Aircraft Co., Culver City, Calif., 1951-52, 1952-57, 58-61; patent engr. Litton Industries, Beverly Hills, Calif., 1957-58; tech. editor Hughes Aircraft Co., Fullerton, Calif., 1958-61; sole practice 1961-63; instr. Manpower Devel. and Tng. Act courses Solar Electronics Schs., Monrovia, Calif., 1963-64; patent agt. Aerojet Gen. Corp., Azusa, Calif., 1964; instr., coord. Agy. for Internat. Devel. communications tng. project Pasadena (Calif.) City Coll., 1964-66; mem. staff Office of Patent Counsel Jet Propulsion Lab., Pasadena, 1966-77; mem. staff Office of Patents and Tech. Utilization Calif. Inst. Tech., Pasadena, 1977—, mgr. Office Tech. Utilization, 1985—; lectr. UCLA, Calif. Inst. Tech. Contbr. articles to profl. jours. Fellow Radio Club Am.; mem. Los Angeles Patent Law Assn. (historian 1966—), IEEE (life), Audio Engring. Soc. (life, chmn. Los Angeles sect. 1959, 69), Am. Radio Relay League, Radio Amateur Satellite Corp. (life). Office: Calif Inst Tech Jet Propulsion Lab 4800 Oak Grove Dr Pasadena CA 91109

CHALMERS, JACQUELINE LOUISE, art gallery owner; b. Calgary, Alta., Can., Aug. 25, 1952; d. Robert John and Doreen Jeanette (Nichols) C. Student, Mont. State U., 1973-75, U. Calgary, 1976. Media coordinator Spruce Meadows Internat. Equestrian Ctr., Calgary, 1975-77; adminstr. agr. dept. Calgary Exhibition and Stampede, Calgary, 1978; asst. sales mgr. Transcon/Charcan Livestock services, Calgary, 1978-79; prodn. mgr. Simmental County, Calgary, 1979-80; asst. coordinator Stockmen's Found., Calgary, 1980-82; mktg. and public relations cons. Best Plumbing and Heating, Edmonton, Atla., 1983-84; cons. Suicide Prevention Provincial Adv. Com., Calgary, 1983-84; owner Gallery West, Calgary, 1985—, Trails West Galleries, Calgary, 1987—. Contbr. articles to profl. jours. Home: Millarville, AB Canada T0L 1K0 Office: Gallery West, 476 10816 Macleod Terr S, Calgary, AB Canada T2J 5N8

CHALMERS, JAMES A., II, consulting company executive; b. Ithaca, N.Y., Jan. 10, 1942. BA in Econs., U. Wyo., 1963; PhD in Econs., U. Mich., 1969. Cert. real estate counselor. Asst. prof. econs. Amherst (Mass.) Coll., 1966-70; field staff Rockefeller Found., Bangkok, 1970-72; assoc. prof. econs. Ariz. State U., Tempe, 1972-79; prin., pres. Mountain West, Inc., Phoenix, 1974—, chmn. bd. dirs. Bd. dirs., sec. East Valley Partnership, Ariz., Phoenix City Club. Mem. Am. Soc. of Real Estate Counselors, Lambda Alpha (pres. 1987-88). Office: Mountain West Rsch SW Inc 432 N 44th St Ste 400 Phoenix AZ 85008

CHALTIEL, VICTOR M.G., health care products executive; b. Tunis, Tunisia, Sept. 8, 1941; s. Jean Joseph and Alice (Cohen) C.; m. Rosita Lelievre, Feb. 23, 1976; 1 child, Edouard. MA in Econs., Ecole Superieure des Sciences Economiques et Commerciales, Paris, 1965; MBA, Harvard U., 1967. Staff asst. internat. mktg. Baxter Travenol Labs., Inc., Deerfield, Ill., 1967-68; product and sales mgr. Europe Baxter Travenol Labs., Inc., Brussels, 1968-70; pres. Travenol France, Paris, 1970-75; v.p. internat. div. Baxter Travenol Labs., Inc., Deerfield, 1975-77, pres. artificial organs div., 1977-79, corp. v.p., 1979-81, corp. group v.p., 1981-83; chmn., pres., chief exec. officer Omnis Surg. Inc. affiliate Baxter Travenol Labs., Inc., Deerfield, 1983-85; pres., chief operating officer Salick Health Care, Inc., Beverly Hills, Calif., 1985—. Recipient Health Advancement award Nat. Kidney Found., 1982; apptd. Conseiller du Commerce Exterieur de la France, 1982. Office: Salick Health Care Inc 407 N Maple Dr Beverly Hills CA 90210

CHAMBERLAIN, DAVID M., consumer products company executive; b. Ft. Benning, Ga., 1943; m. Karin Chamberlain; children: Pamela, Katheryn. BS, U. Pa., 1965; MBA, Harvard U., 1969. With Quaker Oats Co., Chgo., 1969-74, v.p., gen. mgr., 1974-77, pres. frozen foods div., 1977-80; pres. margarine and desserts div. Nabisco Brands, Inc., N.Y.C., 1980-82; sr. v.p. Nabisco Brands, Inc., Toronto, Can., 1982-83; pres., chief op. officer Shaklee Corp., San Francisco, 1983-85, pres., chief exec. officer, 1985—. Bd. dirs. San Francisco Boys and Girls Club, San Francisco Opera, U.S. C. of C., Washington, Calif. Roundtable; pres. San Francisco C. of C. Served to 1st lt. U.S. Army, 1965-67. Mem. St. Francis Yacht Club, University Club, Apawamin Club, Larchmont (N.Y.) Yacht Club, Royal Canadian Yacht Club. Republican. Office: Shaklee Corp 444 Market St San Francisco CA 94111

CHAMBERLAIN, OWEN, nuclear physicist; b. San Francisco, July 10, 1920; divorced 1978; 4 children; m. June Steingart, 1980. AB (Cramer fellow), Dartmouth Coll., 1941; PhD, U. Chgo., 1949. Instr. physics U. Calif., Berkeley, 1948-50, asst. prof., 1950-54, assoc. prof., 1954-58, prof., 1958-89, prof. emeritus, 1989—; civilian physicist Manhattan Dist., Berkeley, Los Alamos, 1942-46. Guggenheim fellow, 1957-58; Loeb lectr. at Harvard U., 1959; Recipient Nobel prize (with Emilio Segré) for physics, for discovery anti-proton, 1959. Fellow Am. Phys. Soc., Am. Acad. Arts and Scis.; mem. Nat. Acad. Scis. Office: U Calif Physics Dept Berkeley CA 94720

CHAMBERLAIN, ROBERT WAYNE, financial planner; b. Flint, Mich., Feb. 28, 1951; s. Wayne J. and Elaine E. (Scheidler) C.; m. Janet Munoz Ching, Aug. 1, 1987; 1 child, Andrea Kristin. Student, Flint Jr. Coll., 1969, Honolulu Community Coll., 1975, N.Y. Inst. Fin., 1976, Coll. Fin. Planning, 1981. Cert. fin. planner. Registered rep. Blyth Eastman Dillon & Co., Inc., Honolulu, 1976-78; registered rep., regional dir. personal fin. mgmt. E.F. Hutton & Co., Inc., Honolulu, 1978-81; pres. Chamberlain & Assocs., Inc., Honolulu, 1981—; dir. securities prin. Associated Planners Securities Corp., L.A., 1983-88; adj. faculty Coll Fin. Planning, Denver, 1981-86. Staff sgt. USAF, 1970-74. Named one of Best Fin. Planners in the nation Money Mag., 1987. Mem. Internat. Assn. Fin. Planning (bd. dirs. 1985-87, registry appeals bd. 1985-87, chmn., 1986-87, legis. liaison Honolulu chpt. 1984—), Inst. Cert. Fin. Planners (ethics com. 1985-86—, legis. liaison Honolulu chpt. 1984-85), Am. Arbitration Assn. (panel mem. 1983—), Hawaii C. of C.

(chmn. Small Bus. Council 1983-87, v.p. 1984-87). Republican. Office: Chamberlain & Assocs 737 Bishop St Ste 2770 Honolulu HI 96813

CHAMBERLAIN, VIRGIL RALPH, petroleum consultant; b. Calgary, Alta., Can., Feb. 5, 1916; (parents Am. citizens); s. Ralph Eugene and Blance Louise (Hardy) C.; m. Elsie Elizabeth Dalry, Nov. 18, 1949; children: Sally Elizabeth, Sue Anne, Virgil Ralph, Cindy Lu. Student, Mont. State U., 1934-35; BS in Geol. Engring., Mont. Tech., 1938; MS in Petroleum Geology, Stanford U., 1950. Cert. profl. geol. scientist; registered profl. engr., Mont., Alta. With various oil/mining cos., Wyo. and Mont., 1933-35; jr. geologist U.S. Geol. Survey, S.E. Mont. and North Wyo., 1938-39; mine geologist Tha Anaconda Co., Mont. and Calif., 1939-43; field geologist, party chief Union Mines Devel. Corp., 1941-45; geologist Union Oil of Calif., Mont., 1945-47; field geologist Irvine (Calif.) Steward & Assocs., Why. and Mont., 1947-49 summers; stratigrapher/geologist Mobil Oil, 1949-50; cons. geologist, engr, owner Geo Rsch. & Engring., Great Falls, Mont., 1950—, pres., 1953—; chmn. bd., chief exec. officer N.W. Geo Rsch. Geo Rsch. & Engring., Calgary, Alta., Can., 1955-65; cons. Grae Exploration, Inc., Great Falls, 1979-87, cons. geologist, engr., 1987—. Merit badge councilor Boy Scouts Am., Great Falls, 1966—. Mem. Am. Assn. Petroleum Geologists (mem. edn. com. 1986—), Assn. Profl. Geologists, Soc. Petroleum Engrs., Geol. Soc. Am., Mont. Geol. Soc., Meadow Lark Country Club, Baypoint Owners Club, Masons (32d degree), Shriner. Home: 3615 7th Ave S Great Falls MT 59405 Office: Geo Rsch & Engring 13th Ave S Village Pla Ste A914 Great Falls MT 59405

CHAMBERLAIN, WILLIAM EDWIN, JR., management consultant; b. St. Louis, June 8, 1951; s. William Edwin Sr. and Grace (Salisbury) C. AA in Bus. Mgmt., Mesa (Ariz.) Community Coll., 1983; BBA, U. Phoenix, 1988. Tng., human resources devel. specialist Motorola, Inc., Phoenix, 1979-87; pres., seminar speaker Chamberlain Cons. Svcs., Scottsdale, Ariz., 1987—. Mem. Am. Soc. Tng. and Devel., Network for Profl. Devel. Office: Chamberlain Cons Svcs PO Box 3247 Scottsdale AZ 85257

CHAMBERLIN, EUGENE KEITH, historian, educator; b. Gustine, Calif., Feb. 15, 1916; s. Charles Eugene and Anina Marguerite (Williams) C.; B.A. in History, U. Calif. at Berkeley, 1939, M.A., 1940, Ph.D., 1949; m. Margaret Rae Jackson, Sept. 1, 1940; children—Linda, Thomas, Rebecca, Adrienne (dec.), Eric. Tchr. Spanish, Latin, Lassen Union High Sch. and Jr. Coll., Susanville, Calif., 1941-43; tchr. history Elk Grove (Calif.) Joint Union High Sch., 1943-45; teaching asst. history U. Calif., Berkeley, 1946-48; instr. history Mont. State U., Missoula, 1948-51, asst. prof., 1951-54; asst. prof. to prof. San Diego City Coll., 1954-78; cab driver San Diego Yellow Cab Co., 1955-74, 79, 86; vis. prof. history Mont. State Coll., Bozeman, summer 1951, U. Calif. Extension, 1965-68, San Diego State Coll., 1965-68, others; instr., coordinator history lectures San Diego Community Colls.-TV, 1969-77; prof. San Diego Miramar Coll., 1978-83; prof. history San Diego Mesa Coll., 1983-86; mem. adv. com. Quechan Crossing Master Plan Project, 1989—. Huntington Library-Rockefeller Found. grantee, 1952; Fulbright-Hays grantee, Peru, 1982; recipient merit award Congress of History San Diego County, 1978; Outstanding Educator award, San Diego City Coll., 1970. Mem. AAUP (various coms., nat. council 1967-70, pres. Calif. conf. 1968-70, acting exec. sec. 1970-72), San Diego County Congress of History (pres. 1976-77, newsletter editor 1977-78), Am. Hist. Assn. (Beveridge-Dunning com. 1982-84, chmn. 1984), Pacific Coast Council on Latin-Am. Studies, Cultural Assn. of the Californias, The Westerners (Calafia chpt.), E Clampus Vitus (historian 1970—, chpt. pres. 1972-73, dir. 1983-89, grand council mem. 1972—, dir. T.R.A.S.H 1979—, pres. 1983-84), Phi Alpha Theta (sec. U. Calif. Berkeley chpt. 1947-48, organizer and faculty adv., Mont. State U. chpt. 1948-54). Democrat. Mem. Ch. of the Brethren (del. 200th Annual Conf. 1986). Author numerous booklets on SW Am. history and numerous articles on Mexican NW to profl. jours. Home: 3033 Dale St San Diego CA 92104

CHAMBERS, ALAN B., science administrator; b. Sacramento, Calif., Jan. 7, 1940; s. Jack Valentine and Eleanor (Derby) C.; m. Coeta Jean Chambers, June 23, 1962; children: Kristin, Shelly. BA in Biology, Stanford U., 1961, BS in Engring., 1962; MS in Bioengring., Oreg. State U., 1964, PhD in Mechan. Engring., 1967. Res. scientist Ames Res. Ctr. NASA, Moffett Field, Calif., 1967-73, tech. asst. to dir. Ames Res. Ctr., 1973-76, div. chief human factors Ames Res. Ctr., 1976-84, dir. for space res. Ames Res. Ctr., 1984—; spl. asst. OSTP White House, Washington, 1988. Mem. ASMA, Sigma Xi, Phi Kappa Phi. Office: NASA Ames Res Ctr MS 200-7 Moffett Field CA 94035

CHAMBERS, CAROLYN SILVA, communications company executive; b. Portland, Oreg., Sept. 15, 1931; d. Julio and Elizabeth (McDonnell) Silva; widowed; children: William, Scott, Elizabeth, Silva, Clark. BBA, U. Oreg. V.p., treas. Liberty Communications Inc., Eugene, Oreg., 1960-83; pres. Chambers Communications Corp., Eugene, 1983—; bd. dirs., dep. chair of bd. Fed. Res. Bank of San Francisco, with Portland br., 1982-84. Mem. Sacred Heart Med. Found., Gen. Hosp. Gov. Bd., 1987—; chair U. Oreg. Found. The Campaign for Oreg., 1988-89; pres., bd. dirs. Eugene Arts Found.; bd. dirs., treas., dir. search com. Eugene Symphony; mem. adv. bd. Eugene Hearing and Speech Ctr., Alton Baker Park Commn., Pleasant Hill Sch. Bd.; chmn., pres., treas. Civic Theatre, Very Little Theatre; negotiator, treas., bd. dirs., mem. thrift shop Jr. League of Eugene. Recipient Webfoot award U. Oreg., 1986, Pioneer award, 1983. Mem. Nat. Cable TV Assn. (mem. fin. com., chmn. election and by-laws com., chmn. awards com., bd. dirs. 1987—, Vanguard award for Leadership 1982), Pacific Northwest Cable Communications Assn. (conv. chmn., pres.), Oreg. Cable Communications Assn. (v.p., pres., chmn. edn. com., conv. chmn., Pres.'s award 1986), Calif. Cable TV Assn. (bd. dirs., conv. chmn., conv. panelist), Women in Cable (charter mem., treas., v.p., pres.), Wash. State Cable Communications Assn., Idaho Cable TV Assn., Community Antenna TV Assn., Cable TV Pioneers. Home: PO Box 640 Pleasant Hill OR 97455 Office: Chambers Communications Corp PO Box 7009 Eugene OR 97401

CHAMBERS, DOROTHY ROSE, educator; b. Yakima, Wash., May 8, 1941; d. George Milford and Blance Mary (McCarthy) Hollenbeck; B.S. in Speech and Lang. Therapy, Marquette U., 1964; M.A. in Spl. Edn., San Francisco State U., 1969; m. Thomas M. Chambers, Aug. 14, 1971; adopted children—David, Monique, Christopher, George, Elizabeth. Speech pathologist Mpls. Pub. Schs., 1964-65, Milbrae (Calif.) Sch. Dist., 1965-68; reading specialist Dept. Def., Landstuhl, Germany, 1970-71; tchr. children with extreme learning problems Portland (Oreg.) Public Schs., 1971-80, dept. chmn. spl. edn., 1980-84, program specialist program devel., 1984-86; diagnostic specialist assessment program spl. edn., 1986—; cert. instr. develop. therapy U. Ga., 1982; instr. Portland State U., D.C.E., 1982, 83. HEW Dept. Rehab. fellow, 1969. Mem. Am. Speech and Hearing Assn. (cert. in clin. competence), Common Cause, Cousteau Soc., NEA, Oreg. Edn. Assn., Nat. Council Exceptional Children (presenter nat. conv. 1984). Democrat. Roman Catholic. Author: PEACHES (Pre-Sch. Ednl. Adaptation for Children Who Are Handicapped), 1978. Home: 12414 SE Oatfield Rd Milwaukie OR 97222 Office: Portland Pub Schs 501 N Dixon St Portland OR 97227

CHAMBERS, LOIS IRENE, insurance agency executive; b. Omaha, Nov. 24, 1935; d. Edward J. and Evelyn B. (Davidson) Morrison; m. Peter A. Mscichowski, Aug. 16, 1952 (div. 1980); 1 child, Peter Edward; m. Frederick G. Chambers, Apr. 17, 1981. Clk. Gross-Wilson Ins. Agy., Portland, Oreg., 1955-57; sec., bookkeeper Reed-Paulsen Ins. Agy., Portland, 1957-58; office mgr., asst. sec., agt. Don Biggs & Assocs., Vancouver, Wash., 1958-88, v.p. ops., 1988—; automation cons. Chambers & Assocs., Tualatin, Oreg., 1985—; chmn. adv. com. Clark Community Coll., Vancouver, 1979—. Mem. citizens com. task force City of Vancouver, 1976-78, mem. Block Grant rev. task force, 1978—. Mem. Ins. Women of S.W. Wash. (pres. 1978, Ins. Woman of Yr. 1979), Nat. Assn. Ins. Women, Nat. Users Agena Systems (charter; pres. 1987-88), Soroptimist Internat. (Vancouver)(pres. 1978-79, Soroptimist of the Year 1979-80, charter pres. 1987—). Democrat. Roman Catholic. Office: Don Biggs & Assocs 916 Main St PO Box 189 Vancouver WA 98666-0189

CHAMBERS, PETER R., psychologist; b. L.A., Aug. 23, 1953; s. Ralph James and Eileen Lucy (Allsworth) C.; m. Renee Chambers; children: Morgan, Mason. Student U. Calif., Riverside, 1975-77; BA, Chapman Coll., 1978; MA, U.S. Internat. U., 1980, PhD, 1982. Researcher, Rancho Los Amigos Hosp., Downey, Calif., 1972-76; counselor educator Free Clinic of Orange County, Anaheim, Calif., 1976-78; psychotherapist Care Manor Hosp., Orange, Calif., 1978-80; asst. adminstr. Cabrillo Med. Center, San Diego, 1980-81, psychologist Cabrillo Mental Health Group, 1982, prof. Nat. U.; evaluation and guidance unit Orange County Mental Health, Orange, 1982—; instr. Calif. Community Coll.; adj. clin. instr. medicine U. Calif., Irvine, 1987. Mem. Am. Psychol. Assn. Republican.

CHAMBERS, THOMAS DOANE, professional basketball player; b. Ogden, Utah, June 21, 1959; m. Erin C.; children: Ericka, Skylar. Attended, U. Utah. Player San Diego Clippers, 1981-83, Seattle SuperSonics, 1983-88, Phoenix Suns, 1988—. Mem. Nat. Basketball Assn. All-Star Team, 1987; Most Valuable Player, Nat. Basketball Assn. All-Star Game, 1987. Office: care Phoenix Suns 2910 N Central Phoenix AZ 85012 *

CHAMBERS, VIRGINA ELLEN, retired photographer, community volunteer; b. St. Paul, Apr. 17, 1927; d. Carlton Gardner and Lillian (Cox) Annable; m. Newell LeMoine Bradley, Oct. 26, 1946 (dec. Aug. 1968); children: Rosalind, Newell Jr., Lawrence, Stephan; m. Stanley Lancaster Chambers, July 22, 1979. Student, Morningside Coll., Sioux City, Iowa, 1945, Nebr. U., 1961-62. Telephone operator Northwestern Bell, Sioux City, 1946-48, Norfolk, Nebr., 1949-52, Des Moines, 1962-67; owner cocktail lounge Tucson, 1968-72; photographer Jones & Presnell, Charlotte, N.C., 1975-79. Founder, active Gen. Fedn. Women's Clubs-Ariz. London Bridge Woman's Club, Lake Havasu; v.p. Homemakers Extension Club, Lake Havasu, 1988; vol. Festival Arts Assn., Lake Havasu, Cancer Soc., Easter Seal Soc., Heart Fund; mem. state legis. com. Am. Assn. Ret. Persons; sec. Mohave County (Ariz.) Dem. Cen. Com., 1988—; mem. Dem. Women's Assn., Havasu, Apple Users Club. Home: 165 Willow Ave Lake Havasu City AZ 86403

CHAMBERS-MEYERS, TRESSA, consultant, writer; b. Lyon, Miss., Apr. 26, 1942; d. James W. and Anna L. (Dorsey) Chambers; m. Joseph R. Meyers, Mar. 18, 1961 (div. Apr. 1983); children—Monica Denise Meyers, Jon Raymond Meyers. B.A., Eastern Wash. U., 1965. Cert. sch. tchr., Calif. Tchr., San Francisco Unified Schs., 1969-75; freelance writer, San Francisco, 1975-81; writer-cons., 1981-83; founder, pres. Thought Motivation Inst., San Francisco, 1983—. Author: Balanced Living Program 1986; contbg. author: The Stress Strategists, 1986. Mem. Mayor's San Francisco Host Com., 1979—; mem. host. com. 1984 Democratic Conv., 1983; mem. Dem. Women's Forum, 1978—. Mem. Bus. Execs. for Nat. Security (charter), World Affairs Council No. Calif. (membership com.), Nat. Assn. Female Execs., Nat. Speakers Assn., Internat. Platform Assn., Assn. Continuing Higher Edn. Roman Catholic. Club: Circlets (v.p. 1978-84). Office: Thought Motivation Inst 2966 Diamond St Se 151 San Francisco CA 94131

CHAMPIE, ELLMORE ALFRED, historian, writer; b. Eden, Tex., Sept. 11, 1916; s. Sam Houston and Nora Louise (Sorrell) C.; student Tex. Coll. Mines and Metallurgy, 1941-42; BA with highest honors, U. Tex, Austin, 1947, MA (Univ. Scholar), 1948; PhD in History (Bayard Cutting Scholar), Harvard U., 1967; m. Rosemary Erter, Sept. 7, 1947 (dec. Nov. 1962); children—Ellmore Alfred, Nora Beatrice; m. 2d, Miriam Helene Boysen Mann, Aug. 28, 1971 (div. Oct. 1974). Archivist, Nat. Archives, 1952-55; historian U.S. Marine Corps Hdqrs., 1955-56, Joint Chiefs of Staff, U.S. Dept. Def., 1956-61; asso. agy. historian Fed. Aviation Agy., 1961-67; agy. historian FAA, Dept. of Transp., 1967-72; hist. researcher and writer, 1972—; mem. tech. com. on history U.S. Inst. of Aeros. and Astronautics, 1970-72; editorial cons. history of FAA and predecessor agys., 4 vols. With USN, 1936-40, 1st lt. USAAF, 1942-45. Mem. Am. Hist. Assn., Am. Soc. for Eighteenth-Century Studies, Am. Soc. for Pub. Adminstrn., Phi Beta Kappa. Democrat. Club: Harvard (So. Ariz.). Lodge: Masons. Author: The Federal Turnaround on Aid to Airports, 1926-38, 1973. Home: 7480 E Rio Verde Dr Tucson AZ 85715

CHAN, ALLEN FONG, protective services official; b. Union City, Calif., Mar. 9, 1957; s. Herbert Quai and Christine (Lee) C. Student, Ohlone Coll., Fremont, Calif., 1975-79; BS in Recreation Adminstrn., Calif. State U., Hayward, 1979. Recreation specialist City of Newark (Calif.) Recreation Dept., 1973-79, police aide, 1981-83, police officer, 1983—; supervising recreation coordinator City of Fremont (Calif.) Community Services, Recreation, 1978-79, park ranger, 1979-83; communication operator City of Hayward (Calif.) Police Dept., 1980-81. Advisor Newark Police Explorers, Boy Scouts Am., 1983—; coordinating officer, Sch. Safety Patrol, Newark, 1987—; basketball ofcl. Mission Valley Athletic League, Fremont, Calif., 1975-79; site ofcl. Cath. Youth Orgn., Fremont, 1975-79; active Alameda County (Calif.) Spl. Olympics, 1981; chmn. local chpt. Internat. Spl. Olympic Winter Games, 1989; chmn. law enforcement torch run Calif. Spl. Olympics, 1989; bd. dirs. Fremont Softball League, 1979-80. Named Outstanding Young Men. Am., 1982. Mem. Police Officers Research Assn. Calif., Calif. Orgn. Police and Sheriffs, Caif. Parks and Recreation Soc., Newark Police Assn. (sec. 1985-88, pres. 1988—). Democrat. Office: City of Newark Police Dept 37101 Newark Blvd Newark CA 94560

CHAN, JOSEPH P.H., mechanical engineer; b. Hong Kong, Feb. 1, 1959; s. Chak and Siu-Ping (Chung) C. BS, U. Calif., Berkeley, 1982; MS, Stanford U., 1984. Rsch. asst. Stanford (Calif.) U., 1982-83; system integration and project mgr. machine vision and motion control systems Newport Corp., Fountain Valley, Calif., 1983—. Designer video instruction system, 1983. Mem. ASME, Soc. Automotive Engrs., Pi Tau Sigma. Home: 41 Hillgrass Irvine CA 92715 Office: Newport Corp 18235 Mt Baldy Circle Fountain Valley CA 92708

CHAN, LOREN BRIGGS, technical writing specialist; b. Palo Alto, Calif., Sept. 10, 1943; s. Shau Wing and Anna Mae (Chin) C.; m. Frances Anastasia Chow, Apr. 19, 1975 (div. Jan. 1988); children: Karen Monique, Pierre Bénédict, Marc Henri. AB, Stanford U., 1965, AM, 1966; MS, Golden Gate U., 1988; PhD, UCLA, 1971. Teaching asst. UCLA, 1968-69, teaching assoc., 1969-70; lectr. in history Calif. State U., Northridge, 1970-71; lectr. in history San Jose (Calif.) State U., 1971-72, asst. prof. history, 1972-76, assoc. prof. history, 1976-80; lectr. history Calif. State U., Hayward, 1980-81; prodn. test technician Nicolet Paratronics Corp., Fremont, Calif., 1982; computer svc. technician Bell-Northern Rsch., Mountain View, Calif., 1982-83; rsch. analyst Bell-No. Rsch., Mountain View, Calif., 1984-85, tech. writer, 1985-87; sr. tech. writer StrataCom, Inc., Campbell, Calif., 1987-88; tech. writer Sun Microsystems, Inc., Mountain View, Calif., 1988—. Author: Sagebrush Statesman, 1973, APARC station 1 Installation Guide, 1989; editor: Chinese-American History Reader, 1976, Collected Technical Support Notes, 1988; contbr. articles to profl. jours. Radio sta. trustee ARC, Menlo Park, Calif., 1975-80. Recipient Presdl. Sports award Pres.'s Coun. on Phys. Fitness and Sports, 1973. Mem. Nat. Geog. Soc., Chinese Inst. Engrs., Am. Radio Relay League, Buick Club of Am., San Jose Aquatics Masters Swim Club. Republican. Christian Scientist. Home: 5719 Makati Circle Apt D San Jose CA 95123-6211

CHAN, MARIE YEE, fiber company executive; b. Braddock, Pa., Mar. 8, 1956; d. Y. Chuck and Jean B. (Chu) Wong; m. Ignatius Y. Chan, Sept. 27, 1986. AA, U. Md., Fed. Republic Germany, 1978; BS in Chemistry, Coll. of Charleston, 1981. Chem. sales rep. Allied div. Signal Corp., Pitts., 1981-84, San Francisco, 1984-86; exec. recruiter Fortune Co., Novato, Calif., 1986; sales rep. Citicorp, San Francisco, 1986; sales coord. Longview Fibre Co., San Francisco, 1987, mktg. svcs. mgr., 1988--. Bd. dirs., pres. Crossroads Townehomes Assn., Novato, 1986-88. Grantee U. Pitts., 1974, State of Pa., 1974. Mem. Adminstrv. Mgmt. Soc., Rolling Hills Club. Presbyterian. Office: Longview Fibre Co 120 Montgomery St Ste 2200 San Francisco CA 94104

CHAN, PATRICK JOHN, ophthalmologist; b. Hong Kong, Apr. 8, 1939; s. Edward Yew-Wah and Cecilia (Fok) C.; m. Christine Hai-Chau Tran Chan. BA, Carroll Coll., 1962; MD, Loyola U., Chgo., 1966. Intern Cook County Hosp., Chgo., 1966-67, resident in ophthalmology, 1967-70; ophthalmologist The Eye Clinic, P.C., Portland, Oreg., 1972—. Fellow Am. Acad Ophthalmology; mem. AMA, Oreg. Med. Assn., Multnumah. Republican. Presbyterian. Office: The Eye Clinic 1511 SW Park Ave Ste 100B Portland OR 97201

CHAN, PETER WING KWONG, pharmacist; b. L.A., Feb. 3, 1949; s. Sherwin T.S. and Shirley W. (Lee) C.; BS, U. So. Calif., 1970, D in Pharmacy, 1974; m. Patricia Jean Uyeno, June 8, 1974; children: Kristina Dionne, Kelly Alison, David Shoichi. Clin. instr. U. So. Calif., 1974-76; staff clin. pharmacist Cedars-Sinai Med. Ctr., Los Angeles, 1974-76; 1st clin. pharmacist in ophthalmology Alcon Labs., Inc., Ft. Worth, 1977—, formerly in Phila. monitoring patient drug therapy, teaching residents, nurses, pharmacy students, then assigned to Tumu Tumu Hosp., Karatina, Kenya, also lectr. clin. ocular pharmacology tng. course, Nairobi, Cairo, Athens, formerly dist. sales mgr. Alcon/BP, ophthal. products div. Alcon Labs., Inc., Denver; v.p., gen. mgr. Optikem Internat., Sereine Products Div., Optacryl, Inc., Denver; formerly product mgr. hosp. pharmacy products Am. McGaw div. Am. Hosp. Supply Corp.; past internat. market mgr. IOLAB subs. Johnson & Johnson, past dir. new bus. devel. Iolab Pharms., dir. Internat. Mktg., dir. new products mktg.; bd dirs. SUDCO Internat., L.A.; del. Am. Pharm. Assn. House of Dels., 1976-78; bd. dirs. Calif. Youth Theatre, 1986-87. Recipient Hollywood-Wilshire Pharm. Assn. spl. award for outstanding svc., 1974; licensed pharmacist, Calif. Mem. Chinese Am. Pharm. Assn., Am. Pharm. Assn., Calif. Pharm. Assn., Hollywood-Wilshire Pharm. Assn. (bd. dirs. 1972-76), Am. Soc. Hosp. Pharmacists, Am. Pharm. Assn. Acad. of Pharmacy Practice, U. So. Calif. Gen. Alumni Assn., OSAD Centurions, Phi Delta Chi. Democrat. Home: 10251 Van Alden Ave Northridge CA 91324 Office: IOLAB 500 Iolab Dr Claremont CA 91711

CHAN, STANLEY, graphic designer; b. Oakland, Calif., Mar. 25, 1945; s. Yuen Hee and Ah Hoo . BFA, Calif. Coll. of Arts & Crafts, Oakland, 1967; MA, Calif. Coll. of Arts & Crafts, 1972. sec. credential, 1972. Newspaper paste-up artist Calif. Jewish Record, Oakland, Calif., 1965-68; art materials clk. Calif. Coll. of Arts & Crafts Student Store, Oakland, Calif., 1970-72; sub. art tchr. Oakland Pub. Schs., 1972-73; asst. graphic mgr. Flax's Art Materials, San Francisco, 1973—; represented by Hank Baum Gallery, Oakland Mus. Collector's Gallery, San Francisco Mus. of Modern Art Rental Gallery; illustrator, bookjackets, White Oxen, U. Calif. Press, Transforming Childhood, 1988; cover illustrator Callboard Mag.; poster designer One Act Theatre Co. of San Francisco, 1978-82. Works in several exhibitions 1965— . Served with U.S. Army, 1968-70, Germany. Office: Flax Artist Materials 1699 Market St San Francisco CA 94103

CHAN, TONY CHI-HUNG, data processing executive; b. Hong Kong, Sept. 4, 1954; came to U.S., 1980; s. Ho Yue and Sap Kan (Leung) C. BS in Elec. and Electronics Engring. cum laude, Calif. State Polytech. U., 1985; postgrad., Calif. State U. Cert. reliability engr., quality engr. With aircraft engring. Hong Kong Aircraft Engring. Co., 1973-80; assoc. engr. hardware assurance Burroughs Corp., Mission Viejo, Calif., 1985-87; engr. hardware assurance UNISYS Corp., Mission Viejo, 1987-89; quality assurance engr. Baxter Healthcare Corp., 1989—. Mem. Am. Soc. Quality Control, Nat. Mgmt. Assn., Tau Beta Pi, Eta Kapa Nu. Office: Baxter healthcare Corp 9500 Feronimo Rd Irvine CA 92718

CHAN, YEE-WAI, chemist; b. Hong Kong, Apr. 8, 1952; came to U.S., 1979; s. Leung and Seim (Seiu) C.; m. Annette Ke-Lee Hu, Dec. 25, 1976. BS, Nat. Taiwan Normal U., 1974; MA, Mankato State U., 1981; PhD, U. Calif., Davis, 1985. Teaching asst. U. Calif., 1981-82, rsch. asst., 1982-85; postdoctoral fellow, chemist SRI Internat., Menlo Park, Calif., 1985-87; chemist SRI Internat., Menlo Park, 1987—. Contbr. articles to profl. jours. Scholar U. Calif., Davis, 1981-85; Dow Chemical Co. Graduate Merit award, 1983. Mem. Am. Chem. Soc., Chinese Am. Chem. Soc., Phi Kappa Phi. Home: 34819 Lilac St Union City CA 94587 Office: SRI Internat 333 Ravenswood Ave Menlo Park CA 94025

CHANANI, MADHU SUDAN, corporate controller, consultant; b. Raniganj, West Bengal, India, Apr. 10, 1952; s. Mali Ram and Jasoda Devi (Munka) C.; m. Sudha-Murarka, June 21, 1977; children: Neera, Alok, Rama. BA in Commerce with honors, Burdwan U., Raniganj, 1971. CPA, Calif. 1983. Acct. various mfg. cos., India, 1968-71; acct. sr. auditor various acctg. firms, India, 1971-76; accounts officer E.C.L. (Coal India Ltd.), Raniganj, 1977-80; auditor Price-Waterhouse, L.A., 1983; sr. acct. Western Waste Industries, Carson, Calif., 1980-82; asst. corp. contr. Western Waste Industries, Carson, 1982-85, corp. contr., 1985-88, v.p., corp. contr., 1988—. Mem. AICPA, Calif. Soc. CPAs, Inst. Chartered Accts. of India (chartered acct. 1977), The Acctg. Circle U. So. Calif. Hindu. Home: 22808 Ladeene Ave Torrance CA 90505 Office: Western Waste Industries 19803 S Main St Carson CA 90745

CHANDLER, CALEB JOHN, state senator, city official; b. Clovis, N.Mex., Jan. 4, 1943; s. John Caleb and Myrtle Marie (Bishop) C.; student Eastern N.Mex. U., 1962-63; grad. N.Mex. Law Enforcement Acad., 1967, FBI Nat. Acad., 1974; m. Donna Marie Murray, Jan. 8, 1971; children—Sandra Michelle, Tammy Annette, John Caleb, Matthew Edward. Switchman, Santa Fe R.R., 1961-63; foreman Trans-Pecos Dairy, Pecos, Tex., 1963-67; with Dept. Police, City of Clovis, 1967—, dep. police chief, 1977-83, police chief, 1983—; mem. N.Mex. Senate, 1976—, chmn. interim criminal justice study com., 1981—, vice chmn. fin. com., 1985; chmn. interim criminal justice study com., Western Council State Govts., 1981-84. Bd. dirs. YMCA, Clovis, N.Mex. Outdoor Drama Assn. Democrat. Baptist. Club: Rotary. Office: PO Box 862 Clovis NM 88101

CHANDLER, DOROTHY BUFFUM, civic worker; b. Lafayette, Ill.; d. Charles Abel and Fern (Smith) Buffum; m. Norman Chandler, Aug. 30, 1922; children: Camilla (Mrs. F. Daniel Frost), Otis. Student, Stanford U., 1919-22; LHD (hon.), U. Calif., U. Judaism, U. Redlands, Hebrew Union Coll.; LLD (hon.), Occidental Coll., Mt. St. Mary's Coll., U. So. Calif.; DFA (hon.), U. Portland, Pepperdine Coll., Loyola Marymount U.; D of Arts (hon.), Art Inst. Los Angeles County. Hon. life chmn. Los Angeles Philharmonic Assn.; chmn. bd. govs. Performing Arts Council, Music Ctr. Los Angeles County; chmn. The Amazing Blue Ribbon of Music Ctr., Music Ctr. Found.; former regent U. Calif.; hon. life trustee Occidental Coll., Calif. Inst. Tech. Recipient Herbert Hoover medal Stanford Alumni Assn., Humanitarian award Variety Clubs Internat., 1974. Address: care Los Angeles Philharm Assn 135 N Grand Avenue Blvd Los Angeles CA 90012 *

CHANDLER, EDWARD WILLIAM, communications systems engineer; b. Milw., Oct. 10, 1953; s. Donald Harold and Helen Aliedia (Wonders) C.; m. Christine Anne Wohl, June 23, 1987. BS, U. Wis., Milw., 1975; MSEE, Ill. Inst. Tech., 1978; PhD, Purdue U., 1985. Registered profl. engr., Wis. Electronics engr. Communications and Electronics div. Motorola Inc., Schaumburg, Ill., 1976-77; instr. elec. engring. Milw. Sch. Engring., 1977-79, asst. prof., 1979-80, assoc. prof., 1982-84, acting head electronic communications engring. tech. program, 1978-79, head, 1979-80, dir. elec. engring. program, 1982-84; asst. prof. elec. engring. Marquette U., Milw., 1984-86; sr. engr. govt. systems div. M/A-COM, Inc., San Diego, 1986-88, mem. tech. staff, 1988—; lectr. U. Wis., Milw., part-time 1979-83; grad. instr. rsch. Purdue U., West Lafayette, Ind., 1980-82; rsch. cons. Naval Ocean Systems Ctr., San Diego, 1988. Contbr. articles to profl. jours. David Ross summer grantee Purdue U., 1981, summer faculty rsch. grantee Milw. Sch. Engring, 1983. Mem. IEEE (sr., newsletter editor Milw. sect. 1985-86), Am. Soc. Engring. Edn., Armed Forces Communications Electronics Assn., Triangle Club, Sigma Xi, Tau Beta Pi, Eta Kappa Nu. Home: 13676-C Ruette Le Parc Del Mar CA 92014 Office: M/A-COM Govt Systems Div 3033 Science Park Rd San Diego CA 92121

CHANDLER, GEORGE DENNIS, electrical engineer; b. Port Jervis, N.Y., Apr. 15, 1943; s. George Eugene and Doris Elanor (Talcott) C.; m. Ruth Estelle Edwards, July 13, 1964 (dec. Oct. 1976); m. Marie Carolyn Fairchild, Nov. 4, 1977; 1 child, Nicholas George. BSEE, Syracuse U., 1970; MSEE, Calif. State U., Fullerton, 1984. Elec. engr. Westinghouse Corp., Balt., 1971-76; chief engr. Magnetic Pulse Tech., Riverside, Calif., 1976-81; mem. tech. staff Rockwell Internat., Anaheim, Calif., 1981—. Served with U.S. Army, 1965-67. Mem. Tau Beta Pi, Eta Kappa Nu. Home: 400 W Patwood Dr La Habra CA 90631 Office: Rockwell Internat 3370 Miraloma Ave MS DC 21 Anaheim CA 92803

CHANDLER, JOHN HERRICK, college president; b. San Francisco, Aug. 7, 1928; s. Ralph William and Gwen Thornton (Herrick) C.; m. Nancy Gordon Phillips, Dec. 10, 1955; children: John, Seth, Will. A.B., U. Calif., Los Angeles, 1952; B.D. (Danforth fellow), U. Chgo., 1958, Ph.D. (fellow),

1963. Ordained to ministry Episcopal Ch., 1960. Instr. English Dartmouth Coll., 1961-63; asst. prof. U. Calif., Los Angeles, 1963-64; assoc. prof., dean spl. programs Ohio U., 1964-67; v.p. Danforth Found., St. Louis, 1967-71; pres. Salem Coll. and Acad., Winston-Salem, N.C., 1971-76, Scripps Coll., Claremont, Calif., 1976-89. Trustee Newton Coll. Sacred Heart, 1970-75, Thacher Sch., 1977-85; bd. dirs. Clayton (Mo.) Bd. Edn., 1970-71, Ctr. Theater Group, 1985-88. Clubs: University (Los Angeles); Twilight, Bohemian.

CHANDLER, JUDITH ANNE, teacher; b. Pueblo, Colo., Sept. 1, 1948; d. Joseph Anthony and Lucille Evelyn (Ercul) Jesik; m. DeWitt Spencer Chandler, Sept. 10, 1966; children: Kristine Marie, Kerrie Susan, Kurt Spencer. BS, So. Colo. State Coll., 1972; MA, U. So. Colo., 1976. Tchr. Columbian Elem. Sch., Pueblo, 1972—; mem. Lang. Arts Com. and CRT Writing Team Sch. Dist. 60, Pueblo, 1982—. Recipient Outstanding Tchr. award, 1989. Mem. Am. Assn. U. Women (ednl. rep. 1986-88), Delta Kappa Gamma (sec. 1982-84), Alpha Omicron (2d v.p. 1984-86). Democrat. Roman Catholic. Home: 165 Encino Dr Pueblo CO 81005 Office: Columbian Elem Sch 1202 Bragdon Pueblo CO 81004

CHANDLER, KRISTIAN, computer consultant, educator; b. Cleveland Heights, Ohio, June 26, 1948; d. Gerhard A. and Hanna R. (Rittmeyer) Hoffmann; children: Karen, Heidi. BSBA with honors and spl. distinction U. So. Colo., 1984, postgrad., 1984-85; MBA, U. Ark., 1987. Owner, mgr. V&W Fgn. Car Service, Canon City, Colo., 1970-80; prin. The Chandlers, Computer Cons., Pueblo, Colo., 1982—; ptnr. Rabbit Enterprises, 1989/6; faculty Pikes Peak Community Coll., U. So. Colo., also mgr. Sch. Bus. microcomputer lab. Bd. dirs. Canon City Community Service Ctr., 1978-80, Canon City chpt. ARC, 1978-81. Mem. Assn. for Computing Machinery, Data Processing Mgmt. Assn. (advisor student chpt. Pikes Peak Community Coll. 1989—), U. So. Colo. Honors Soc. (pres.), U. So. Colo. Grad. Assn. (founder), Alpha Chi, Sigma Iota Epsilon. Home and Office: 401 Neilson Ave Pueblo CO 81001

CHANDLER, MARY VOELZ, journalist; b. St. Louis, June 14, 1948; d. Earl Frederick and Doris (Vaughan) Voelz; m. Michael Dissen, Sept. 18, 1971 (div. 1981); m. David Leon Chandler, Sept. 8, 1981. BJ, U. Mo., 1970. Reporter Jour., Flint, Mich., 1970-72, Times-Union, Rochester, N.Y., 1972, Rocky Mountain News, Denver, 1987--; editor, reporter Ledger-Star, Norfolk, Va., 1973-81; editor Sunday dept. Miami (Fla.) Herald, 1981-84. Co-author: Greater Miami Opera, 1985, Binghams of Louisville, 1987; contbr. articles to People mag. Home: 390 Holly St Denver CO 80220 Office: Rocky Mountain News 400 W Colfax Ave Denver CO 80204

CHANDLER, OTIS, publisher; b. Los Angeles, Nov. 23, 1927; s. Norman and Dorothy (Buffum) C.; m. Marilyn Brant, June 18, 1951 (div.); children: Norman, Harry, Cathleen, Michael, Carolyn; m. Bettina Whitaker, Aug. 15, 1981. Grad., Andover Acad., 1946; B.A., Stanford U., 1950. Joined Times Mirror Co., 1953; pub. Los Angeles Times, 1960-80; chmn. bd., editor-in-chief Times Mirror Co., Los Angeles, 1980-86, chmn. exec. com., 1986—. Served to 1st lt. USAAF, 1951-53. Mem. Am. Soc. Newspaper Editors, Am. Newspaper Pubs. Assn. Club: California. Office: The Times Mirror Co Times Mirror Sq Los Angeles CA 90053 *

CHANDLER, RICHARD HILL, health science administrator; b. N.Y.C., Mar. 25, 1943; s. Marvin and Carmen (Arguedas) C.; m. Linda Boerner, Aug. 21, 1965; Children: Lauren, Christy, Karen. BA, Princeton U., 1964; MBA, U. Chgo., 1966; Masters Internat. Econs., U. Louvain, Belgium, 1967. Various exec. positions Bell & Howell Co., Chgo., 1967-72; pres. retail div. Harvey Group, Melville, N.Y., 1972-74; v.p. planning & devel. Sara Lee Corp., Chgo., 1974-77, group v.p., 1978-79; pres. Abbey Med. Inc., Los Angeles, 1977-78, pres., owner, 1979-82; chmn., pres. Sunrise Med. Inc., Torrance, Calif., 1983—; bd. dirs., founder, vice chmn. Chgo. Community ventures, Inc., 1970-73. Del. White House Conf. Youth, 1970; trustee Chadwick Sch., Palos Verdes, Calif., 1983—. Mem. Young pres's. Orgn., 1980—, Princeton Club of N.Y., J. Kramer Tennis. Republican. Episcopalian. Office: Sunrise Med Inc 2355 Crenshaw Blvd Ste 150 Torrance CA 90501

CHANDLER, ROD D(ENNIS), congressman; b. La Grande, Oreg., July 13, 1942; s. Robert John and Edna Pearl (Hagey) C.; m. Joyce Elaine Laremore, Aug. 3, 1963; children: John Gifford, Amanda Joy. B.S.in history, Oreg. State U., 1968. News corr. Sta. KOMO-TV News, Seattle, 1968-73; mktg. officer Wash. Mut. Savs. Bank, Seattle, 1973-77; mem. Wash. State Ho. of Reps.,.1975-82, 98th-101st Congresses from 8th Wash. Dist., 1983—; mem. King County Metro Coun. 1973-75; ptnr. Chandler & Corcoran Communications Inc., Seattle, 1977-82. Recipient Sigma Delta Chi award, 1971, Guardian of Small Business award (Nat. Fedn. Ind. Business), 1984, 1986, 88, Excellence in Pub. Svc. award (Am. Acad. Pediatrics), 1984, Humanitarian of the Yr. award (Seattle-King Co. Humane Soc.), 1984, Golden Bulldog award (Watchdogs of Treas. Inc.), 1984, 86, 87, 88 Legislator of Yr. award (Washington Vocat. Assn.), 1984, 85, Employee Benefit award Pension Word Mag., 1988, Nat. Security Leadership award Am. Security Coun. Found., 1987, Taxpayers' Friend Award Nat. Taxpayers Union, 1987. Mem. Rotary. Republican. Office: 233 Cannon House Office Bldg Washington DC 20515

CHANDLER, STEPHEN RAY, musical instrument company executive; b. Berkeley, Calif., Feb. 8, 1949; s. Allen Stephen and Edna (Erickson) C.; m. Barbara Louise Gunn, Jan. 28, 1972; children: Jane, David. BA magna cum laude, Utah State U., 1979. Pres. R. Chandler & Co., Salt Lake City, 1979-84; tech. dir. Young Chang Piano Co., Cerritos, Calif., 1984-87, Kawai Am. Corp., Compton, Calif., 1987—; chief technician Utah Symphony, Salt Lake City, 1979-84, Internat. Bachauer Piano Competition, Salt Lake City, 1982; founder, dir. Friends and Music Concerts, Salt Lake City, 1979-82. Mem. Salt Lake Tabernacle Choir, 1982-84; organ recitalist, 1982-83; asst. organist St. Basil's Ch., L.A., 1988—. Recipient Presdl. citation Brigham Young U., 1983. Mem. Am. Guild Organists, Royal Sch. Ch. Music, Am. Choral Dirs. Assn., Piano Technicians Guild (craftsman), Nat. Piano Found. (v.p. 1988—), Dallas. Home: 9822 Kite Dr Huntington Beach CA 92646 Office: Kawai Am Corp 2055 E University Dr Compton CA 90220

CHANDOLA, ANOOP C., educator, writer; b. Pauri, U.P., India, Dec. 24, 1937; came to U.S., 1959; s. Satya Prasad and Kishori Devi (Ghildyal) C.; m. Sudha Nautiyal, July 14, 1963; 1 child, Varn. BA, Allahabad (Uttar Pradesh, India) Univ., 1954; MA, Lucknow U., India, 1956, U. Calif., Berkeley, 1961; PhD, U. Chgo., 1966. Tutor, lectr. S.V. Patel Univ., Vallabh Vidyanagar, India, 1956-58; lectr. MS Univ. of Baroda, India, 1958-59; asst. prof. U. Ariz., Tucson, 1963-66, assoc. prof., 1967-71, prof. comparative lit. and religions, 1971—; vis. assoc. prof. U. Calif., Berkeley, summers 1967, 68; vis. prof. U. Tex., 1972, U. Wis., 1973. Author: Folk Drumming in the Himalayas, 1977, Situation to Sentence, 1979, Mystic and Love Poetry of Hindi, 1982. Ford Found. scholar, U. Chgo., 1961; NSF grantee, 1973. Mem. Assn. for Asian Studies, Am. Anthrop. Assn., Linguistic Soc. Am., Internat. Platform Assn., Linguistic Soc. India. Hindu. Home: 6041 N Calle Culebra Tucson AZ 85718

CHANDRAMOULI, RAMAMURTI, electrical engineer; b. Sholinghur, Madras, India, Oct. 2, 1947; s. Ramamurti and Rajalakshmi (Ramamurti) Krishnamurti; m. Ranjani; 1 child, Suhasini. BSc, Mysore U., 1965, BE, 1970, MEE, Pratt Inst., 1972; PhD, Oreg. State U., 1978; m. Ranjani, Dec. 4, 1980. Instr., Oreg. State U., Corvallis, 1978; sr. engr. R & D group, mem. tech. staff spacecraft datasystems sect. Jet Propulsion Lab., Pasadena, Calif., 1978-81; staff engr., design automation group Am. Microsystems Inc., Santa Clara, Calif., 1982-83; staff software engr. corp. computer-aided design Intel, Santa Clara, 1983-86; project leader computer-aided design Sun Microsystems, Mountain View, Calif., 1986—; adj. lectr. Calif. State U.-Fullerton, 1987—. Sec., South India Cultural Assn., L.A., 1980-81; bd. dirs. Am. Assn. East Indians. Mem. IEEE, IEEE Computer Soc., Sigma Xi, Eta Kappa Nu. Home: 678 Tiffany Ct Sunnyvale CA 94087 Office: Sun Microsystems 2550 Garcia Ave Mountain View CA 94043

CHANEY, FREDERICK BENNETT, management education company executive; b. Boulder, Colo., Sept. 8, 1936; s. Marjorie (Elliott) Hendrickson; m. Linda S. Spearman; children: Melanie, Andrew, Kira, Ari. BS in Psychology, Purdue U., 1959, MS in Exptl. Psychology, 1960, PhD in Managerial Psychology, 1962. Research asst. The Boeing Co., Seattle, 1962-63, N.Am. Ops. div. Rockwell Internat. Corp., 1964-68; pres. Continuing Edn. Corp., 1968-81; pres., chief exec. officer successor firm Vedax Scis. Corp., Santa Ana, Calif., 1981—; instr. managerial psychology U. So. Calif., 1969-70; adj. prof. mgmt. Pepperdine U., 1970-74; cons. Xerox Corp., Collins Radio, Lockheed Corp., State of Calif., 1969—. Author: (with D.H. Harris) Human Factors in Quality Assurance, 1969; contbr. articles to profl. jours. NSF fellow, 1964. Office: Vedax Scis Corp 5000 Birch #6200 Newport Beach CA 92660

CHANEY, VICTOR HARVEY, teacher, historical dramatist; b. Chgo., Nov. 11, 1940; s. Charles and Libby (Siegel) C.; m. Meta Bowman, July 14, 1973; 1 child, Dana; stepchildren: Gary, Rick, Randy. BA in Polit. Sci., UCLA, 1963; MEd, Calif. State U., Northridge, 1973. Tchr. Simi Valley (Calif.) Unified Sch. Dist., 1972-89, Beaverton (Oreg.) Sch., 1989—. Author: Passing Through, 1984; portrayer and creator of one-man plays and guest speaker presentations. Mem. NEA, ARC (instr.). Home: 6940 SW 160th Ave Beaverton OR 97007 Office: Beaverton Schs Beaverton OR 97007

CHANG, DONALD MARK, law and economics educator, consultant; b. Honolulu, Nov. 30, 1927; s. Y.K. and L.K. (Leong) C.; m. Mildred Sachiko Matsunaga, July 6, 1957. BA cum laude, U. Nebr., 1950; JD, Yale U., 1953; PhD in Econs. and Ethics and Law, U. Chgo. and Claremont Sch. Theology, U. So. Calif., 1961; student U. Hawaii, 1945-46, 47-48. Jr. exec. Castle & Cooke Co., Honolulu, 1953-54; gen. counsel Hawaii AFL-CIO, Honolulu, 1954-56; spl. asst. to chmn. NLRB, Washington, 1961-62; minority, gen. counsel Com. on Judiciary, U.S. Senate, Washington, 1962-71; prof. law and econs. U. Hawaii, Honolulu, 1971—; cons. Calif. Western Sch. Law, San Diego, 1978-81, Patton, Boggs & Blow, Washington, 1978-80. Bd. dirs. Honolulu Symphony Soc., 1973-78; chmn. Gubernatorial Candidacy Com., Honolulu, 1972; pres. Waialee Nui Assn., Honolulu, 1972-79. Recipient Outstanding Accomplishment award Moot Ct. Program, U. Hawaii, 1983. Fellow Ethics and Society Colloquium (dir. 1976-85; gold award 1984); mem. Am. Bus. Law Assn., U. Hawaii Law, Ethics and Society Colloquium (dir. 1985—), Am. Econ. Assn., Am. Indsl. and Labor Relations Assn., Am. Immigration and Nationality Conf., Phi Alpha Delta (pres. 1972-73), Acacia. Democrat. Methodist. Home: 1803 Halekoa Dr Honolulu HI 96821 Office: U Hawaii 96-045 Ala Ike Pearl City HI 96782

CHANG, DONG HYUN, chiropractor, acupuncturist; b. Buan, Republic of Korea, Sept. 13, 1944; came to U.S., 1977; s. Joon-Yeol and Guim Gui (Chae) C.;m. Bu-Weol Kim, Dec. 31, 1973; children: Jessica, Daniel, Sarah, David. DVM, Jeon-Bug Nat. U., Jeon-Ju, Republic of Korea, 1967, MBA, 1972; D.C., L.A. Coll. Chiropractic, Whitier, Calif., 1981; O.M.D., S. Baylo U., 1984, PhD, 1985. Diplomate Benezolana Acupuncture Assn. Dr. of chiropractic Calif. State Bd. Chiropractic Examiners, Sacramento, 1981; cert. acupuncturist Calif. Dept. Consumer Affairs, Sacramento, 1983; pvt. practice, L.A., 1985-89, Reseda, Calif., 1989—; mem. acupuncture examining com. Bd. Med. Quality Assurance, 1988. Elder Korean Christian Ch., Pasadena. Mem. Kowloon Chinese Herbalist Assn., S.O.T. Technique from SORSI. Home: 32070 Canterhill Pl Westlake Village CA 91361 Office: Changs Chiropractic Clinic 18625 Shermanway #109 Reseda CA 91335

CHANG, ERNEST SUN-MEI, endocrinology and aquaculture educator; b. Berkeley, Calif., Dec. 7, 1950; s. Shu-Chi and Helen (Fong) C.; m. Sharon A. Chang. BA, U. Calif., Berkeley, 1973; PhD, UCLA, 1978. Postdoctoral fellow U. Chgo., 1978; asst. prof. endocrinology U. Calif., Davis, 1978-85, assoc. prof., 1985—; vis. prof. Sonoma (Calif.) State U., 1986—. Contbr. numerous articles to profl. jours. Chief Jenner (Calif.) Fire Dept., 1986—. Recipient Research medal, UCLA, 1978; grantee Am. Cancer Soc., 1979-81, Sea Grant Coll. Program grantee, 1978—. Mem. Am. Soc. Zoologists, Western Soc. Naturalists, World Aquaculture Soc., Nat. Shellfisheries Assn., Sonoma County Fire Chiefs Assn. Office: Bodega Marine Lab PO Box 247 Bodega Bay CA 94923

CHANG, LOIS LEILANI See CHUR-OGURA, LOIS LEILANI

CHANG, LORENE ANASTASI, real estate broker; b. Harlan, Iowa, Sept. 26, 1936; d. Gerald Carl and Angeline Theresa (Arkfeld) Anastasi; m. Hing Chang, Sept. 9, 1967; children: Steven, Alan, Julie. BS, Creighton U., 1958, MD, 1963; MS, U. Minn., 1967. Pvt. practice physician Honolulu, 1968—; real estate broker Gecko Realty, Inc., Honolulu, 1988—. Office: Gecko Realty Inc 1314 S King St #417 Honolulu HI 96814

CHANG, MARY HSUEH-MEI, hotel executive; b. Tainan, Taiwan, Mar. 23, 1935; d. Ti and Yulan (Hsieh) Yang; m. Joseph Juifu Chang, Jan. 1, 1954; children—Judy, Howard, Mona. Pres., Trade Internat. Inc., Berkeley Heights, N.J., 1961-65; owner, gen. mgr. Dorchester Motor Lodge, Poughkeepsie, N.Y., 1973-78; owner Holiday Inn, Springfield, Mass., 1978—; pres. Yangti Hotel Corp., 1980—; owner, gen. mgr. Ramada Inn, Chicopee, Mass., 1980—; pres. Yulan Hotel Corp., 1985—. Home and Office: 4600 Swenson St Ste 201 Las Vegas NV 89119-6675

CHANG, MERTON K. W., chemical company executive; b. Honolulu, Feb. 20, 1943; s. Kam Yee and Lily (Wong) C.; m. Genevive Ching Chang, July 27, 1968; children: Yvette, Ryan. BA, U. Hawaii, 1966. Sales rep. Dearborn Chemical Div., Honolulu, 1968-76, area mgr., 1976-80, dist. mgr., 1980-88; tech. dir. Dearborn Chemical Div., Honolulu, 1989—. Bd. dirs. Moiliili Community Ctr., Honolulu, Neighborhood Bd., Honolulu. With U.S. Army, 1966-68. Named Honor grad. U.S. Army Vet. Svc., 1968. Mem. Bldg Owners Mgmt. Assn., ASHRAE, Chang Soc. (v.p. Honolulu 1975-86). Republican. Home: 658 Hausten St Honolulu HI 96826 Office: Dearborn Chemical Co 1405 N King St 300 Honolulu HI 96817

CHANG, RODNEY EUI JOON, artist, dentist; b. Honolulu, Nov. 26, 1945; s. Alfred Koon Bo and Mary Yet Moi (Char) C.; m. Erlinda C. Feliciano, Dec. 4, 1987; 1 child, Bronson York. BA in Zoology, U. Hawaii, 1968; AA in Art, Triton U., 1972; DDS, Loyola U., 1972; MS in Edn., U. So. Calif., 1974; MA in Painting and Drawing, U. No. Ill., 1975; MA in Community Leadership, Cen. Mich. U., 1976; BA in Psychology, Hawaii Pacific Coll., 1977; MA in Psychology of Counseling, U. No. Colo., 1980; PhD in Art Psychology, Union Grad. Sch., 1980; MA in Computer Art, Columbia Pacific U., 1988. Pvt. practice dentist Honolulu, 1975—; dir. SOHO too Gallery and Loft, Honolulu, 1985-86; freelance artist Honolulu, 1982—; speaker on art psychology and computer art various orgns., also numerous TV and radio interviews. Author: Mental Evolution and Art, 1980, Rodney Chang: Computer Artist, 1988, Commentaries on the Psychology of Art, 1980; host (radio show) Disco Doc Hour, Sta. KISA; one-man shows: Honolulu Acad. Arts, 1986, Shanghai State Art Mus., People's Republic of China, 1988, Hawaii Med. Assn. Art Gallery, 1989; exhibited in group shows at AmFac Exhbn. Hall, Honolulu, 1986, Ramsay Chinatown Gallery, Honolulu, 1987, Visual Encounters Gallery, Denver, 1987, The Bronx Mus. of the Arts, N.Y.C., 1987, Royal Culture Art Gallery, Honolulu, 1987, Nishi Noho Gallery, Manhattan, N.Y., 1987, The Adler Cultural Ctr., Libertyville, Ill., 1988, Eastern Wash. U. Gallery of Art, 1988, Southwestern Coll. Art Gallery, 1988. Judge Jr. Miss Contest, Honolulu, 1981. Served to capt., U.S. Army, 1973-74. Mem. ADA, Hawaii Dental Assn., Assn. of Honolulu Artists, Nat. Computer Graphics, Hawaii Craftsmen, Windward Artists Guild. Roman Catholic. Office: 2119 N King St Ste 206 Honolulu HI 96819

CHANG, TSU-SHUAN, electrical engineering educator; b. Republic of China, Feb. 10, 1950; came to U.S., 1976; s. Tao-Ming and Erh-Chun (Teng) C. BS, Nat. Chiao Tung U., Taiwan, Republic of China, 1971, MS, 1973; SM, PhD, Harvard U., 1981. Instr. Chinese Navy Communication and Electronic Sch., Taiwan, 1974-75, Nat. Chiao Tung U., Hsinchu, Taiwan, 1975-76; research asst. IBM T.J. Watson Research Ctr., Yorktown Heights, N.Y., 1977; asst. prof. elec. engring. SUNY, Stony Brook, 1981-84; asst. prof. elec. engring. U. Calif., Davis, 1984-88, asst. prof. dept. elec. engring & computer sci., 1988—; cons. Harvard U., Cambridge, 1981, 82; assoc. visiting prof. U. Ill., Urbana and Champaign, 1988. Contbr. articles to profl. jours. Served to 2d lt. Chinese Navy, 1973-75. Fellow Harvard U., 1977, NSF, 1984, 85, 88, U. Calif. and FMC Corp., 1985, 86, 87. Mem. Control Systems Soc. of IEEE, Computer Soc. of IEEE, Communications Soc. of IEEE, Phi Tau Phi. Office: U Calif Dept Elec Engring & Computer Sci Davis CA 95616

CHANG, YEPING, computer company executive; b. Taipei, Republic of China, May 20, 1959; d. Tze-Shiow and Wen-Shiang (Wang) C.; m. Robert F. Wan, Mar. 21, 1987. BS, Nat. Taiwan U., 1981; MA, U. Calif., Riverside, 1982; PhD, U. Calif., 1988. Lic. real estate broker, Calif. Rsch. asst. U. Calif., Riverside, 1982-83, adminstrv. analyst, 1984-85, teaching asst., 1984; v.p. Masters Systems Co., Alhambra, Calif., 1985—; real estate broker, Masters Systems Co., Alhambra, Calif., 1987, computer software design svc. rep. Author software: My Schedule and Office Master. Regents fellow U. Calif., 1983-84. Mem. Am. Econ. Assn., Nat. Geog. Soc., San Gabeiel Valley Bd. Realtors. Baptist. Home and Office: 501 Westmont Dr Alhambra CA 91803

CHAO, CHIH HSU, research mechanical engineer; b. Shantung, China, Aug. 2, 1939; s. Ching Fung and Ching Chih (Lin) C.; B.S., Nat. Taiwan U., 1962; M.S., U. Calif.-Berkeley, 1965, Ph.D., 1972; m. Grace Yng Chu, Apr. 15, 1967; children—Henry Shaw, Lily Yuin. Research asst., applied mechanics U. Calif.-Berkeley, 1965-72; research engr. Boeing Co., Seattle, 1966-67; research scientist, mgr. engring. analysis, chief engr. Physics Internat. Co., San Leandro, Calif., 1969—; cons. engr. Registered profl. engr., Calif. Mem. ASME (sect. chmn.), Nat. Soc. Profl. Engrs., Calif. Soc. Profl. Engrs., Nat. Apt. and Property Owners Assn. Democrat. Roman Catholic. Contbr. research papers in field to profl. jours. Home: 1018 Contra Costa Dr El Cerrito CA 94530

CHAO, JAMES MIN-TZU, architect; b. Dairen, China, Feb. 27, 1940; s. T. C. and Lin Fan (Wong) C.; came to U.S., 1949, naturalized, 1962; m. Kirsti Helena Lehtonen, May 15, 1968. BArch, U. Calif., Berkeley, 1965. Cert. architect, Calif.; cert. instr. real estate, Calif. Intermediate draftsman Spencer, Lee & Busse, Architects, San Francisco, 1966-67; asst. to pres. Import Plus Inc., Santa Clara, Calif., 1967-69; job capt. Hammaberg and Herman, Architects, Oakland, Calif., 1969-71; project mgr. B A Premises Corp., San Francisco, 1971-79; constrn. mgr. The Straw Hat Restaurant Corp., 1979-81, mem. sr. mgmt., dir. real estate and constrn., 1981-87; pvt. practice architect, Berkeley, Calif., 1987—; pres. Food Svc. Cons. Inc., 1987-89; pres., chief exec. officer Stratsac, Inc., 1987—; lectr. comml. real estate site analysis and selection for profl. real estate seminars; coord. minority vending program, solar application program Bank of Am.; guest faculty mem. Northwest Ctr. for Profl. Edn. Patentee tidal electric generating system; author first comprehensive consumer orientated performance specification for remote banking transaction. Recipient honorable mention Future Scientists Am., 1955. Mem. AIA, Encinal Yacht Club (dir. 1977-78). Republican.

CHAPDELAINE, ROLAND JOSEPH, academic administrator; b. Springfield, Mass., Aug. 23, 1946; s. Roland George and Therese Rose (LaRose) C.; m. Pamela Jeanne Mearns, Aug. 24, 1968; children: Eric Roland, Denise Elizabeth. BA, Providence Coll., 1968; MS, Ball State U., 1969, EdD, 1976. Instr. biology Ball State U., Muncie, Ind., 1969-72; assoc. prof. Howard Community Coll., Columbia, Md., 1972-78, div. chmn., 1975-80, coordinator faculty devel., 1978-80, acting dean students, 1982-83, dean instrn., 1980-86; v.p. acad. affairs Mohave Community Coll., Kingman, Ariz., 1986—; co-chmn. adv. com. Columbia Assn. Urban Lake Water Quality Project, 1976-86; advisor Solar Energy Ednl. Project State of Md., 1977; cons. various community colls., Md., Pa., N.J., 1974—; lectr. Md. Acad. Scis., Balt., 1976-80; mem. Project Cooperation Task Force on Value added Instrn., 1988—. Contbr. articles to profl. jours. Vice-chmn. AYRA Youth Baseball, Howard County, Md., 1982; bd. dirs. St. John's Parish, Howard County, 1980-84; co-chmn. Citizens Adv. Com. Critical Areas Planning, Howard County, 1976-77; edn. coordinator Middle Patuxent Environ. Assn., Howard County, 1974-78; appointed State Commn. for Study of Future of Md. Community Coll., 1985-86; bd. dirs. Industry Edn. Alliance Council, Howard County, 1984-86, Hist. Savage Mill Mus., 1985-86; mem. Cholesterol Edn. Task Force, 1988—; selected participant Rising Star League for Innovation Leadership Inst., 1988; mem. Ariz. Task Force on Awarding Credit, 1988-89. Recipient Cert. Appreciation, Md. Dept. Vocat. Edn., 1982, Spl. Achievement award Howard Community Coll., 1986; grantee NSF, 1981, FIPSE, 1984, 85. Mem. Ariz. Acad. Adminstrs. (exec. com. 1988-89), Nat. Council Staff Program and Orgnl. Devel. (regional dir. 1984-85, Cert. Appreciation 1985), Nat. Council Instructional Adminstrs. (regional dir. 1980-85, dir. nat. issues 1985-86, sec. 1986, v.p., pres. elect 1987-88, pres. 1988—, co-chair Project Cooperation, 1988-89), Council Md. Deans (pres. 1983-84), Nat. Council for Staff, Program and Orgnl. Devel. (regional dir.), Md. Consortium of Biol. Scientists (steering com. 1973-80), Howard County C. of C. (leadership tng. program 1986); Ariz. Media Assn. (adminstr. of Yr. 1987). Democrat. Roman Catholic. Lodges: Rotary (sec. Kingman Rt.66, 1988—, program chair 1987-88, mem. exec. leadership inst. 1988—), Elks (Kingman Lodge 468, chaplain 1988-89). Home: 3705 Martingdale Dr Kingman AZ 86401 Office: Mohave Community Coll Kingman AZ 86401

CHAPIN, ROSS HIATT, infosystems specialist; b. Woodland, Calif., Dec. 12, 1953; s. Robert Lee and Dorothy Ann (Roller) Brewer. BA in English, Monmouth (Ill.) Coll., 1978. Sales rep. Xerox Corp., Chgo., 1980-83; account mgr. Digital Equipment Corp., San Francisco, 1983-84; account exec. Interleaf, Inc., San Francisco, 1984-85; we. region mgr. Dest Corp., Milpitas, Calif., 1985-88, Computer Consoles, Inc., San Mateo, Calif., 1988-89; mgr. territory acct. Xerox Imaging Systems, Mountain View, Calif., 1989—. Mem. Profl. Rodeo Cowboy Assn. Home: 639 Carolina St San Francisco CA 94107

CHAPLIN, GEORGE, editor; b. Columbia, S.C., Apr. 28, 1914; s. Morris and Netty (Brown) C.; m. Esta Lillian Solomon, Jan. 26, 1937; children—Stephen Michael, Jerry Gay. B.S., Clemson Coll., 1935; Nieman fellow, Harvard U., 1940-41. Reporter, later city editor Greenville (S.C.) Piedmont, 1935-42; mng. editor Camden (N.J.) Courier-Post, 1946-47, San Diego Jour., 1948-49; mng. editor, then editor New Orleans Item, 1949-58; asso. editor Honolulu Advertiser, 1958-59, editor in chief, 1959-86, editor at large, 1986—; Pulitzer prize juror, 1969, 83; mem. selection com. Jefferson fellowships East-West Ctr.; Chmn. Gov.'s Conf. on Year 2000, 1970; chmn. Hawaii Commn. on Year 2000, 1971-74; co-chmn. Conf. on Alt. Econ. Future for Hawaii, 1973-75; charter mem. Goals for Hawaii, 1979—; alt. U.S. rep. South Pacific Commn., 1978-81; chmn. search com. for pres. U. Hawaii, 1983; chmn. Hawaii Gov.'s Adv. Council on Fgn. Lang. and Internat. Studies, 1983—; rep. of World Press Freedom Com. on missions to Sri Lanka, Hong Kong, Singapore, 1987. Editor, officer-in-charge: Mid-Pacific edit. Stars and Stripes World War II; Editor: (with Glenn Paige) Hawaii 2000, 1973. Bd. dirs. U. Hawaii Research Corp., 1970-72, Inst. for Religion and Social Change, Hawaii Jewish Welfare Fund; bd. govs. East-West Ctr., Honolulu, 1980—, chmn., 1983-89, Pacific Health Research Inst., 1984—, Hawaii Pub. Schs. Found., 1986-87—; Am. media chmn. U.S.-Japan Conf. on Cultural and Ednl. Interchange, 1978-86; co-founder, v.p. Coalition for A Drug-Free Hawaii, 1987—. Served as capt. AUS, 1942-46. Decorated Star Solidarity (Italy), Order Rising Sun (Japan), Prime Minister's medal (Israel); recipient citations Overseas Press Club, 1961, 72, Headliners award, 1962, John Hancock award, 1972, 74, Distinguished Alumni award Clemson U., 1974, E.W. Scripps award Scripps-Howard Found., 1976, Champion Media award for Econ. Understanding, 1981, Judah Magnes Gold medal Hebrew U. Jerusalem, 1987; inducted Honolulu Press Club Hall of Fame, 1987. Mem. Soc. Nieman Fellows, Honolulu Symphony Soc., Pacific and Asian Affairs Council (dir.), Internat. Press Inst., World Future Soc., Japan-Am. Soc. Honolulu, Am. Soc. Newspaper Editors (dir., treas. 1973, sec. 1974, v.p. 1975, pres. 1976), Friends of East-West Center, Sigma Delta Chi. Clubs: Pacific, Waialae Country. Home: 4437 Kolohala St Honolulu HI 96816 Office: care Honolulu Advertiser PO Box 3110 Honolulu HI 96802

CHAPMAN, CARL EDWARD, director, consultant; b. San Antonio, Nov. 3, 1959; s. Phillip Allen and Barbara Ann (Stafford) C.; m. Tanya Lapierre; children: Brooke, Robert. BA, No. Ariz. U., 1982. Dir. telecommunications Mohave Community Coll., Kingman, Ariz., 1986—; cons. Hale Communications, Parker, Ariz., 1983—, Group Seven, Lake Havasu City, Ariz., 1986—, Ariz. Dept. Health, Phoenix, 1987—; photographer Ariz. Coast Photography; bd. dirs. ops. Ariz. Ednl. Telecommunications Consortium; exec. bd. dirs. Ariz. Ednl. Media Assn. Rep. Committeeman, Kingman,

1986—. Mem. Community Colls. Assn. for Instruction Tech., No. Ariz. Alumni Assn. (bd dirs.). Home: PO Box 4267 Kingman AZ 86402-4267

CHAPMAN, CAROLYN, music educator; b. Oak Park, Ill., Sept. 8, 1942; d. Edmund Earle Jr. amd Ella Mae (Bryant) C.; m. Gene Paul Cech, July 6, 1963 (div. 1980); children: Geoffrey Paul, Gary Peter, Nancy Carolyn; m. Melvin LeRoy Flood, Apr. 1980 (div. 1982); 1 child, Erik Louis. BS in Music Edn., U. Ill., 1964, MS in Music Edn., 1968; Cert., Point Loma Coll., 1983; JD, Western State U., 1988. Cert. tchr., Ill., Calif. Tchr. music Barrington and Addison (Ill.) Pub. Schs., 1964-67; tchr. history, music, math., English, band, orch., chorus San Diego City Schs., 1971-87; law clk. U.S. Atty.'s Office, San Diego, 1986-88, Law Offices of Eugene G. Iredale, San Diego, 1988—; curriculum developer moot ct. program Western State U., San Diego, 1985-86; organizer string orch. Dana Jr. High Sch., San Diego, 1972-80. Mem. law rev. staff Western State U., 1986; mem. moot ct. Nat. Semi-Final Am. Jury, Corpus Juris Secundum. Foster parent; sponsor fgn. student exchange program. T.J. Smith scholar, McDowell scholar. Mem. Calif. Tchrs. Assn., San Diego Tchrs. Assn., NEA, Am. Trial Lawyers Assn., Calif. Women Lawyers, Lawyers Club San Diego, CWL, Delta Theta Phi, Sigma Alpha Iota, Delta Delta Delta. Republican. Home: 7856 Carter Pl La Mesa CA 92041

CHAPMAN, JAMIE SUE, chemical engineer; b. Denver, Feb. 19, 1964; d. Richard John and Lorraine (Stap) K. BSChemE, Colo. State U., Ft. Collins, 1986. Cert. Bldg. Inspector and Mgmt. Planner, Calif. Chem./process engr. Sci. Applications Internat. Corp., San Diego, 1987—. Mem. NAFE, Am. Inst. Chem. Engrs. Home: 6576 Friars Rd #105 San Diego CA 92108 Office: Sci Applications Internat Corp 10240 Sorrento Valley Rd #204 San Diego CA 92121

CHAPMAN, LORING, psychologist, neuroscientist; b. Los Angeles, Oct. 4, 1929; s. Lee E. and Elinore E. (Gundry) Scott; children: Robert, Antony, Pandora. B.S., U. Nev., 1950; Ph.D., U. Chgo., 1955. Lic. psychologist, Oreg., N.Y., Calif. Research fellow U. Chgo., 1952-54; research asso., asst. prof. Cornell U. Med. Coll., N.Y.C., 1955-61; asso. prof. in residence, mem. Neuropsychiat. Inst., UCLA, 1961-65; research prof. U. Oreg., Portland, 1965; br. chief NIH, Bethesda, Md., 1966-67; prof., chmn. dept. behavioral biology Sch. Medicine U. Calif., Davis, 1967-81; prof. psychiatry Sch. Medicine U. Calif., 1977—, prof. neurology, 1977-81, prof. human physiology, 1977-81; vice chmn. div. of sci. basic to medicine 1976-79; condr. research in field of behavioral and sensory physiology, brain function, neuropharmacology; vis. prof. U. Sao Paulo, Brazil, 1959, 77, Univ. Coll., London, 1969-70, U. Florence, Italy, 1979-80; clin. prof. Georgetown U., 1966-67; mem. Calif. Primate Research Center, 1967—; dir. research Fairview Hosp., 1965-66; cons. Nat. Inst. Neurol. Disease and Stroke, 1961—, Nat. Cancer Inst., 1977—, Nat. Inst. Child Health Devel., 1967—, mem. research and tng. com., 1968-72. Author: Pain and Suffering, 3 vols, 1967, Head and Brain 3 vols, 1971, (with E.A. Dunlap) The Eye, 1981; contbr. sci. articles to publs. Recipient Thornton Wilson prize, 1958, Career award USPHS, 1964, Commonwealth Fund award, 1970; grantee NASA, 1969—; grantee NIH, 1956—; grantee Nat. Inst. Drug Abuse, 1971—; Forgarty Sr. Internat. fellow, 1980. Mem. Am. Acad. Neurology, Am. Physiol. Soc., Am. Psychol. Assn., Royal Soc. Medicine (London), Am. Neurol. Assn., Am. Assn. Mental Deficiency, Aerospace Med. Assn., Soc. for Neurosci. Home: 205 Country Pl Sacramento CA 95831 Office: U Calif Med Ctr Dept Psychiatry 2315 Stockton Blvd Sacramento CA 95817

CHAPMAN, MATTHEW WILLIAM, lawyer; b. Portland, Oreg., Aug. 7, 1950; s. James Don and Regan Mary (McCoy) C.; m. Lillian Louise Richards, Sept. 21, 1985; 1 child, Richard Scott. BA in Econs., U. Portland, 1971; JD, U. Oreg., 1974. Bar: U.S. Dist. Ct. Oreg. 1974, Wash. 1985. Assoc. Stoel, Rives, Boley, Fraser & Wyse, Portland, 1974-80; ptnr. Martin, Bischoff, Templeton, Biggs & Ericsson, Portland, 1980-81, Waggoner, Chapman, Farleigh, Wada & Bogrand, Portland, 1981-87; pres. CFI Bankers Service Group, Portland, 1987—; Lectr. numerous bus. assn. seminars. Editor Oreg. Law Rev., 1973-74; contbr. articles to profl. jours. Paul Patterson fellow. Mem. ABA (subcom. credit unions, comml. fin. services com. sect. corp. banking and bus., consumer fin. services), Oreg. Bar Assn., Wash. State Bar Assn., Multnomah Bar Assn., Order of Coif, Oreg. Mortgage Bankers Assn. Republican. Roman Catholic. Clubs: Arlington, Multnomah Athletic. Lodge: Rotary. Home: 615 Burlingame Terr Portland OR 97201 Office: CFI Bankers Svc Group Inc 220 NM 2nd Portland OR 97201

CHAPMAN, RICHARD LEROY, public policy researcher; b. Yankton, S.D., Feb. 4, 1932; s. Raymond Young and Vera Everette (Trimble) C.; m. Marilyn Jean Nicholson, Aug. 14, 1955; children: Catherine Ruth, Robert Matthew, Michael David, Stephen Raymond, Amy Jean. BS, S.D. State U., 1954; postgrad., Cambridge (Eng.) U., 1954-55; MPA, Syracuse U., 1958, PhD, 1967. Profl. staff mem. com. govt. ops. Sec. of Def., 1958-59, 61-63, U.S. Ho. Reps., Executive Office of Pres. (Bur. of Budget), Washington, 1960-61, U.S. Ho. Reps., 1966; program dir. NIH, Bethesda, Md., 1967-68; sr. research assoc. Nat. Acad. Pub. Adminstrn., Washington, 1968-72, dep. exec. dir., 1973-76, v.p., dir. research, 1976-81; sr. research scientist Denver Research Inst., 1982-86; mem. adv. com. Denver Research Inst. U. Denver, 1984-86; ptnr. Milliken Chapman Rsch. Group Inc., Denver, 1986-88; prin., v.p. Chapman Rsch. Group, Inc., Denver, 1986-88; v.p. Chapman Research Group, Inc., Littleton, 1988—; cons. U.S. Office Personnel Mgmt., Washington, 1977-81, Denver, 1986—; cons. CIA, Washington, 1979, 80, 81, Arthur S. Fleming Awards, Washington, 1977-81. Contbr. articles to profl. jours. Mem. aerospace com. Colo. Commn. Higher Edn., Denver, 1982-83; chmn. rules com. U. Denver Senate, 1984-85; bd. dirs. S.E. Englewood Water Dist., Littleton, 1984-88, pres. 1986-88. Capt. U.S. Army, 1955-57, Korea. Brookings Inst. fellow, 1964-65. Mem. Tech. Transfer Soc. (bd. dirs.), Am. Soc. Pub. Adminstrn., AAAS, IEEE, Engring. Mgmt. Soc., Futures Soc. Republican. Lodges: Masons, Commandery, Order of DeMoley (Cross of Honor 1982). Office: Chapman Rsch Group 6631 S University Blvd Ste 212 Littleton CO 80121

CHAPMAN, RON DUANE, financial services executive; b. Portland, Oreg., Dec. 29, 1958; s. Ron A. and Marjorie May (Sanders) C.; m. Mara Suzanne Caler, Jan. 15, 1983. BA in Polit. Sci. and Econs., U. Calif., Riverside, 1981; MBA, U. Calif., Irvine, 1988. Credit trainee 1st Interstate Bank, Los Angeles, 1982; loan officer Sumitomo Bank Calif., San Diego, 1983-86, officer fin. services, 1988—. Mem. Am. Mgmt. Assn., Fin. Mgmt. Assn., Assn. MBA Execs., U. Calif. at Riverside Alumni Assn. Democrat. Lutheran. Home: 945 Chardonney Way Escondido CA 92025 Office: Sumitomo Bank Calif 410 A St San Diego CA 92101

CHAPMAN, THOMAS BARCLAY, retail executive; b. Eugene, Oreg., May 2, 1929; s. Thomas Ignations and Marion (Lawrence) C.; m. Phyllis Loreen Gardner, May 11, 1952; children: David, John, Dan, Steven. BS in Political Sci., U. Oreg., 1951. Salesman Koke-Chapman Co., Eugene, Oreg., 1953-62; pres. Chapman Bros. Stationery and Office Equipment Co., Eugene, Oreg., 1962—; gov. Nat. Office Products Assocs., Northwest Area, 1964-65; chmn. bd. dirs. Northwest Wholesale Stationers, Portland, Oreg., 1986—. Pres. bd. dirs. Jr. Achievement, 1963-73. Cpl. U.S. Army, 1951-53. Mem. Eugene C. of C. (bd. dirs. 1980-82), Rotary (pres. 1973-74, bd. dirs. 1973-74). Republican. Home: 2281 Rose Ln Eugene OR 97403

CHAPMAN, VAUGHN VICKERS, dentist; b. Seattle, Mar. 14, 1921; s. Asa B. and Emma (Woodhouse) C.; m. Mildred Fyfe, Dec. 28, 1949; 1 child, Melissa. Student, Wheaton (Ill.) Coll., 1939-41, U. Wash., 1941; BS, U. Ill., 1942, DDS, 1944. Gen. practice dentistry Seattle, 1944—; bd. dirs. Worldwide Dental Health Service, Seattle, 1950—, Missionary Dentists Overseas Tng. Seminars, 1957—. Editor News Report, 1950—, Dental Evangelism Heartbeat, 1983—; editor: Missionary Dentistry, 1969; producer radio broadcast The Dental Story, 1955-59. Bd. dirs. Internat. New Life Ministries, 1986—. Served to capt. U.S. Army, 1942-47, ETO. Named Man of Year Wash. Acad. Gen. Dentistry, 1988. Mem. Christian Med. Soc. (house of dels.), ADA, Seattle-King County Dental Soc. , Wash. State Dental Assn., Internat. Assn. for Orthodontics. Presbyterian. Club: Wash. Athletic. Office: Worldwide Dental Health Svc 5116 196th SW Lynnwood WA 98036

CHARCA, BERNARDO CLAUDIO, architect; b. Buenos Aires, Nov. 22, 1959; s. Marcos Enrique and Aida (Rabinovich) C. BArch, So. Calif. Inst. Architecture, Santa Monica, 1983. Prin. Bernardo Charca Architect, L.A., 1983-84; pvt. practice designing, project mng., prodn. designing Barcelona, Spain, 1984-86; designer, project mgr. Lise Matthews & Assocs., L.A., 1986-87; project mgr. Breidenbach Cuen Architects, L.A., 1987-88; prin. Bernardo Charca Architect, L.A., 1988, Venice, 1988—; Prin. works include Otto Zutz Club, Barcelona, 1985-86, Tokio SA, Barcelona, 1985-86. Woman's Archtl. League scholar, 1981. Jewish. Home: 1018 20th St Apt K Santa Monica CA 90403 Office: 1114 W Washington Blvd Venice CA 90291

CHARD, FREDERICK HARRISON, chiropractor; b. Oakland, Calif., Apr. 24, 1947; s. Chester Brooks-Stevens and Elizabeth (Walter) C.; m. Virginia Yuponce, Mar. 15, 1973; 1 child, Yuri Miguel. BA, U. San Francisco, 1972; D Chiropractic Medicine, Western States Chiropractic Coll., Portland, Oreg., 1977. Diplomate Nat. Bd. Chiropractic Examiners; lic. chiropracter, Hawaii. Mental health therapist Woodland Park Mental Health Ctr., Portland, 1976-77; chiropracter Kailua-Kona, Hawaii, 1981-87, Hilo, Hawaii, 1981-82, Kamuela, Hawaii, 1982-87, Kaneoehe, Hawaii, 1983-87, Honolulu, 1982—; mental health therapist Hoikka House Extend Care Facility, St. Paul, 1985-86; hosp. and rsch. asst. Spears Chiropractic Hosp., Denver; dep. state fiscal officer Wailuku, Maui, Hawaii, Pub. Welfare, 1987; assoc. chief physician for hospitality Internat. Olympic Soc., Seoul, Republic Korea, 1987—. Contbr. editor health newspapers, 1979-87. Prin. contbr., advisor Key Project Community Ctr., Kanoehe, 1983-87. Served with U.S. Army 1966-68. Mem. Hawaii State Chiropractic Assn. Democrat. Home and Office: 350 Ward Ave #106 Honolulu HI 96814

CHARETTE, STEVE VERN, interior designer; b. Pleasanton, Calif., Oct. 27, 1952; s. Vern and Shirley (Dimond) C. BS in Design, Ariz. State U., 1980. Sr. designer Marshall Brown Interior Design, San Diego, 1980-83; dir. of design Austin Hansen Fehlman Group, San Diego, 1983-87; pres. Charette Inc., San Diego, 1987—. Mem. Pacific Beach Planning Com., San Diego, 1986-87. Mem. AIA (profl. affiliate, Interior Design award, 1985), Am. Soc. Interior Designers, Inst. Bus. Designers, Greater San Diego C. of C. Democrat. Office: 800 W Ivy St Ste C San Diego CA 92101

CHARLES, MARY LOUISE, newspaper reporter, photographer, editor; b. L.A., Jan. 24, 1922; d. Louis Edward and Mabel Inez (Lyon) Kusel; m. Henry Loewy Charles, June 19, 1946; children: Susan, Henry, Robert, Carol. AA, L.A. City Coll., 1941; BA, San Jose (Calif.) State U., 1964. Salesperson Roos Bros., Berkeley, Calif., 1945-46; ptnr. Charles-Martin Motors, Marysville, Calif., 1950-54; farm editor Indep. Herald, Yuba City, Calif., 1954-55; social worker Sutter County, Yuba City, 1955-57; social worker Santa Clara County, San Jose, 1957-61, manual coordinator, 1961-73, community planning specialist, 1973-81; columnist Sr. Grapevine various weekly newspapers, Santa Clara, 1981-86; editor Bay area Sr. Spectrum Newspapers, Santa Clara, 1986—; founder, pres. Triple-A Council of Calif., Sacramento, 1978-80. Vice chmn. Santa Clara County Sr. Care Commn., 1987—; mem. Calif. Legis. Roundtable, 1975—, editor newsletter, 1968-74. With USN Women's Res., 1942-45. Recipient Social Welfare award Daniel E. Koshland Found., 1973. Mem. Nat. Council of Sr. Citizens (bd. dirs. 1988—), Congress of Calif. Srs. (bd. dirs. 1987—), Older Women's League of Calif. (edn./resource coord. 1987—), Nat. Assn. Social Workers, Am. Soc. on Aging (program com. 1985-88), Nat. Council on Aging, Calif. Specialists on Aging (treas. 1985—), Calif. Srs. Coalition (chmn. 1986). Democrat. Jewish. Home and Office: 2527 Forbes Ave Santa Clara CA 95050

CHARLES, ROLAND SCOTT, accountant; b. Sacramento, Apr. 23, 1947; s. Ray Donobedian and Ernestine Fay (Scott) Charles; m. Dawn Patricia Taylor, Apr. 22, 1964 (div. June 1982); children: Deborah, Jennifer, Alfred; m. Christel Margarete Kauffeldt, Nov. 25, 1987. AA, Coll. San Mateo, Calif., 1965; BA, Stanford U., 1967; postgrad., Golden Gate U., 1970. Asst. controller R.F. Jones Co., San Francisco, 1965-67; systems analyst Interior Computer Control Company, Ltd., Chilliwack, B.C., Can., 1967-69; chief acct. Presbyn. Hosp., San Francisco, 1969-72; cons. medicare/medicaid Hosp. Reimbursement Assocs., Dallas, 1972-75; auditor A.S. Barnhill, CPAs, Dallas, 1975-77; controller European Motors, Ltd., Oakland, Calif., 1977-79; mgr. internal audit San Jose (Calif.) Hosp., 1979-81; pvt. practice cons. Spokane, Wash., 1987—; lectr. in field, 1970-86. Rep. nominee U.S. Ho. Reps., San Francisco, 1970; city chmn. Ford for Pres. Com., Dallas, 1976; mem. Rep. State Cen. Com. Calif., 1965-68, 70-72, San Francisco County Rep. Cen. Com., 1970-72. Mem. Stanford Alumni Assn., Nat. Assn. Accts., Hosp. Fin. Mgmt. Assn. (bd. dirs. 1970-72), Kiwanis, NRA (life), Phi Rho Pi (life). Presbyterian. Office: PO Box 14894 Spokane WA 99214-0894

CHARLTON, BRIAN, service executive; b. Newbiggin, Eng., Apr. 14, 1950; came to U.S., 1975; s. Clement Wilson and Eva (Norman) C.; m. Kimberly Anne Doney, July 29, 1981; children: Jovan Anthony, Larissa Gayle, Eva-Marie Catrisse, Brianna Reece. Student, Keogh Mil. Acad., Ash Vale, Eng., 1966-67. Pub. rels. officer CINDUSTA, Copenhagen, Denmark, 1968-70; dir. Ops. & Transps. Corp., Lisbon, Portugal, 1970-75; asst. gen. mgr. Ft. Harrison Hotel, Clearwater, Fla., 1975-80; dir. community and vocat. edn. Salmon (Idaho) Sch. Dist., 1980-81; resident mgr. Properties, Inc., Missoula, Mont., 1981-83; gen. mgr. Aladdin Motor Inns, Helena, Mont. and Newport, Oreg., 1983-88, Village Resorts, Inc., Winthrop, Wash., 1988—; cons. Sun Mountain Resorts, Winthrop., 1988—. Contbg. author: Chess, 1965. Mem. Rep. Task Force, Washington, 1985—; bd. dirs. community edn. com. Salmon Sch. Dist., 1980, bd. dirs. vocat. edn. com., 1981. With English Army, 1966-67. Idaho State U. grantee, 1980. Home: RR 2 Box 662 Winthrop WA 98862 Office: Sun Mountain Lodge PO Box 1000 Winthrop WA 98862

CHARLTON, JAMES WILLIAM MARK, cable television executive; b. Klammath Falls, Oreg., Feb. 9, 1948; s. James William Herbert and Ruth Estelle (Richardson) C.; m. Dawn Cecelia Tibus; children: Robert Carl, John William. Student, Calif. State U., Northridge; JD, Whittier Coll., 1989. Founder, co-owner HFU Mfg., North Hollywood, Calif., 1972-82, HFU TV, Coleville, Calif., 1979—, Sierra Pines Apts., Coleville, 1979—; founder, owner New Dawn Electric Co., Westlake Village, Calif., 1985—; founder, pres. HFU Investments, Inc., Reno, Nev., 1983—. Contbr. articles Law Rev. Chmn. Buhs High Sch. Class Reunion Com., Bishop, Calif., 1986. Served with U.S. Army, 1968-70, Vietnam. Mem. VFW, Nat. Rifle Assn. Office: New Dawn Electric Co 30941 Agoura Rd #314 Westlake Village CA 91361

CHARLTON, JOHN KIPP, pediatrician; b. Omaha, Jan. 26, 1937; s. George Paul and Mildred (Kipp) C.; A.B., Amherst Coll., 1958; M.D., Cornell U., 1962; m. Susan S. Young, Aug. 15, 1959; children—Paul, Cynthia, Daphne. Intern, Ohio State U. Hosp., Columbus, 1962-63; resident in pediatrics Children's Hosp., Dallas, 1966-68, chief pediatric resident, 1968-69; nephrology fellow U. Tex. Southwestern Med. Sch., Dallas, 1969-70; practice medicine specializing in pediatrics, Phoenix, 1970; chmn. dept. pediatrics Maricopa Med. Ctr., Phoenix, 1971-78, 84—, assoc. chmn. dept. pediatrics, 1979-84; med. dir., bd. dirs. Crisis Nursery, Inc., 1977—; sr. clin. lectr. dept. pediatrics U. Ariz. Pres. Maricopa County Child Abuse Coun., 1977-81; bd. dirs. Florence Critenton Svcs., 1980-83, Ariz. Children's Fund, 1987—; mem. Gov.'s Coun. on Children, Youth and Families, 1984-86. Officer M.C., USAF, 1963-65. Recipient Hon Kachina award for volunteerism, 1980, Jefferson award for volunteerism, 1980. Mem. Am. Acad. Pediatrics, Ariz. Pediatric Soc., Maricopa County Pediatric Soc. (past pres.). Author articles, book rev. in field. Home: 6230 E Exeter St Scottsdale AZ 85251 Office: Maricopa County Gen Hosp 2601 E Roosevelt St Phoenix AZ 85008

CHARTIER, VERNON LEE, electrical engineer; b. Ft. Morgan, Colo., Feb. 14, 1939; s. Raymond Earl and Margaret Clara (Winegar) C.; m. Lois Marie Schwartz, May 20, 1967; 1 child, Neal Raymond. B.S. in Elec. Engring., U. Colo., 1963, B.S. Bus., 1963. Registered profl. engr., Pa. Research engr., cons. Westinghouse Electric Co., East Pittsburgh, Pa., 1963-75; chief high voltage engr. Bonneville Power Adminstrn., Vancouver, Wash., 1975—. Contbr. articles to profl. jours. Fellow IEEE (past chmn. transmission and distbn. com.); mem. Internat. Conf. Large High Voltage Electric Systems, Acoustical Soc. Am., Internat. Electrotech. Commn., Club: Chartier Family Assn. Baptist. Home: 5190 SW Dover Ln Portland OR 97225 Office: Bonneville Power Adminstrn PO Box 491 Vancouver WA 98666

CHASE, CHARLES ANTHONY, aerospace engineer; b. Detroit, June 27, 1939; s. Joseph Leon and Marion Katherine (Lukowiak) C.; m. Carole Ann Chaikin, June 10, 1961; children: Carlton, William. BSAE, U. Mich., 1961, MSAE, 1962; D. of Engring. AE, Stanford U., 1968. Design engr. Chem. Systems div. United Technologies Corp., San Jose, Calif., 1962-68, project engr., 1968-71, chief solid propulsion advanced design, 1971-74, chief engr. space motor programs, 1974-86, chief engr. space propulsion systems, 1986—; guest lectr. Stanford U., Naval Postgrad. Sch., AAIA student lectr. series. Mem. Monte Sereno Sch. Bd., 1972-77. Recipient Outstanding Svc. award United Techs. Corp., 1981. Assoc. fellow AIAA (solid rocket com.); mem. AAAS, ASME, Solid Propulsion Industry (reliability bd.), Courtdise Racquet Club. Republican. Roman Catholic. Contbr. numerous articles to profl. jours. Patentee in field.

CHASE, JACOLINE B., career educator, consultant; b. Richmond Heights, Mo., Oct. 10, 1953; d. Thomas Joseph and Dorothea Mae (Pilgrim) S. B of Liberal Studies, magna cum laude, St. Louis U., 1978; MA, UCLA, 1989. Cert. community coll. tchr. (life), Calif. Office mgr., sec. Investors Planning Group, Clayton, Mo., 1978; substitute tchr. Vashon High Sch., St. Louis, 1978; pres., creative dir. Chase and Assocs., Goleta, Calif., 1979-81; chief exec. officer Personal Paackaging, Inc., Thousand Oaks, Calif., 1981—; cons. Ventura (Calif.) Unified Sch. Dist., 1986; instr. adult edn. Santa Barbara (Calif.) City Coll., 1984; pub. speaker, conductor seminars in field, 1985—. Producer ednl. videotapes; tech. writer, editor numerous govt. proposals. Pub. rels. dir. United Boys' Clubs Greater Santa Barbara, 1980; vol. coach Spl. Olympics, Santa Barbara, 1979—. Grad. Fellow State of Calif., 1987-89. Mem. Am. Assn. Counseling Devel., Nat. Career Devel. Assn., Nat. Employment Counselors Assn. Home: 340 Rutherford Dr #8 Santa Barbara CA 93117 Office: Personal Paackaging Inc 665 N Shadow Lake Dr Thousand Oaks CA 91360

CHASE, JEFFREY MICHAEL, traffic safety institute executive; b. Port Angeles, Wash., Aug. 12, 1947; s. Hal E. and Barbara (Hendrick) C.; m. Sara E. Struble, Aug. 1, 1982 (Jan. 1989); children: Matthew, Patrick. Student, West Valley Coll., 1969; BA in Polit. Sci., San Jose State U., 1974, MPA, 1976; PhD in Human Behavior, Newport U., 1978. Firefighter, emergency med. tech. Santa Clara County (Calif.) Fire Dept./Ambulance Svc., 1965-72; safety dir. Marriott Corp., Santa Clara, Calif., 1972-74; pres., chief exec. officer Nat. Traffic Safety Inst., Salem, Oreg., 1974—. Editor Interchange mag., 1986—. Mem. Santa Clara County Emergency Med. Svcs. Commn., 1976-78. Mem. Am. Soc. Safety Engrs., Nat. Judges Assn., Am. Assn. Motor Vehicle Adminstrs. Republican. Office: Nat Traffic Safety Inst 1235 Woodrow St Salem OR 97303

CHASE, JUDITH HELFER, librarian, educator, musician; b. Elizabethton, Tenn., Feb. 19, 1939; d. Edward Conley and Faith (Clemons) Helfer; m. William Clark Chase, Aug. 8, 1970. BS in Music Edn., East Tenn. State U., 1962; postgrad., Bradley U., 1963-64; student, German Ctr. for Internat. Music Edn., 1969-70; postgrad., Oreg. Inst. Tech., 1975-77; M in Music, U. Oreg., 1984; ML, U. Wash., 1986. Music specialist Morristown (Tenn.) City Schs., 1962-63, Peoria (Ill.) County Schs., 1963-64, Anne Arundel County Bd. Edn., Annapolis, 1964-69, 70-73; ch. organist, pvt. practice piano Elizabethtown Tenn. and Klamath Falls, Oreg., 1973-77; with med. records dept. Merle West Med. Ctr., Klamath Falls, 1977-79; media svcs. cataloger, library aid, music specialist Klamath County Sch. Dist., 1977-85; med. library aid of aux. 1987-89; asst. prof., reference and documents librarian Oreg. Inst. Tech., Klamath Falls, 1987—; bassoonist, counselor Brevard (N.C.) Music Ctr., summer 1961; unit leader Nat. Music Camp, Interlochen, Mich., summer 1964. Dirs youth choir St. Paul's Episcopal Ch., Klamath Falls, 1975-84; mem. aux. Klamath Arts Coun., 1976—, Interinstitutional Libr. Coun. Oreg. State Systems Higher Edn., 1989—; soprano Klamath Symphonic Choir, 1977-84; librarian Plum Ridge Symphony, Klamath Falls, 1979-84, v.p. guild, 1980-82; bd. dirs., librarian Klamath Youth Symphony, 1983—. Bassoon scholar, 1957, 58-62, 63, 63-64. Mem. ALA (govt. documents roundtable 1987--, resources and tech. svcs. div. 1988--), Med. Library Assn. (pub. svcs. sect. 1988--), Music Library Assn., Pacific NW Library Assn., Oreg. Library Assn., AAUW, Delta Omicron (pres. alumni chpt. 1967-68, Mae Chenoweth Grannis grantee 1984), Kappa Delta Pi. Episcopalian. Office: Oreg Inst Tech LRC 3201 Campus Dr Klamath Falls OR 97601

CHASE, JULIA P., public relations and advertising company executive, editor; b. Riverside, Calif., May 21, 1942; d. Harold W. Peebles and Jean M. Smith. BA, San Francisco State U., 1965; postgrad. Calif. State U., Long Beach, U. Calif., Berkeley, U. Calif., Irvine, U. So. Calif. Tchr. English, Calif. high schs., 1966-70; assoc. editor Videorecord World mag., Newport Beach, Calif., 1970-71; advt. promotion dir. Technicolor, Inc., 1971-72; pub. relations account exec. Cochrane Chase & Co., Inc., Orange County, Calif., 1973; community relations dir. McGaw Labs., Irvine, 1976-77; pres. J.P. Chase & Co., Inc. Advt. & Pub. Relations, Newport Beach, 1977-83; pres. MedComm Mktg., Newport Beach, 1984—. Rep. council agys., allocations and communications United Way, 1976-83; bd. dirs. United Way North/South, 1980-81; Recipient award Am. Advt. Fedn., 1978; award of merit Western Art Dirs.; award of excellence Creative Arts mag., N.Y. Art Dirs.; award of merit/communication excellence So. Calif. Bus. Communicators; Mem. Orange County Ad Club, Orange County Sportswriters, So. Calif. Assn. Hosp. Devel., Newport Harbor Art Mus., Laguna Beach Mus. Art. Democrat. Presbyterian. Clubs: Orange County Press (life mem.; dir. 1979), Newport Beach Tennis. Editor, pub.: Newport Set mag.; art editor Orange County Illustrated; editor: Add One, 1983, 84. Office: PO Box 8343 Newport Beach CA 92658

CHASE, LARRY J., communications executive; b. Akron, Ohio, May 5, 1945; m. George Ramsey and Phyllis (Bugh) Chase; m. Patricia A. Alexander, Aug. 26, 1967 (div. 1980); children: Benjamin, Jeremy; m. Sara A., July 2, 1982; 1 child, Kerri. Student, Kent State U., 1963-65; BA in Communications, Boise State U., 1972. Radio announcer, TV weatherman KBOI Radio and TV, Boise, Idaho, 1969-84; promotion mgr. KBCI TV, Boise, Idaho, 1974-76, account exec., 1976-78; local sales mgr. KPCI-TV, Pocatello, Idaho, 1978-79, sta. mgr., 1979-81; ops. mgr. KIVI-TV, Boise and Nampa, Idaho, 1981-82; gen. mgr. KIVI-TV, Boise and Nampa, 1982—. Pres. bd. dirs. YMCA, Boise, 1987—, Big Sky Cluster YMCA, Idaho, Utah, Mont., Wyo., 1986—; bd. dirs. Idaho Children's Trust Fund, Boise, 1985—. With USAF, 1965-69. Named Distin. Citizen Idaho Statesman newspaper, Boise, 1985, Exec. of the Yr., Exec. Women Internat., 1985. Mem. Idaho Advt. Fedn. (vice-chmn. 1986-88), Idaho State Broadcasters (legis. chmn. 1987-88), Am. Advt. Fedn. (lt. gov. 1984-86), Boise Area C. of C. (chmn. 1987), Rotary Club. Home: 1530 Knights Dr Boise ID 83712 Office: KIVI-TV 1866 E Chisholm Dr Nampa ID 83651

CHASE, LORIENE ECK, psychologist; b. Sacramento; d. Walter and Genevieve (Bennetts) Eck; A.B., U. So. Calif., 1948, M.A., 1949, Ph.D., 1953; m. Leo Goodman-Malamuth, 1946 (div. 1951); 1 son, Leo; m. 2d, Allen Chase, Mar. 4, 1960 (div.); m. 3d, Clifton W. King, 1974. Psychologist Spastic Children's Found., Los Angeles, 1952-55, Inst. Group Psychotherapy, Beverly Hills, Calif., 1957-59; pvt. practice, 1953—; v.p. VSP Exec. Relocation Consultants. Condr., Dr. Loriene Chase Show, ABC-TV, Hollywood, Calif. 1966—. Cons., Camarillo State Hosp.; bd. dirs., pres.'s circle U. So. Calif.; founding mem. Achievement Rewards for Coll. Scientists; bd. dirs. Chase-King Personal Devel. Center, Los Angeles; v.p. Chase-King Prodns. Inc., Los Angeles, Shell Beach, Calif.; exec. bd. Cancer Research Center, Los Angeles. Writer syndicated newspaper column Casebook of Dr. Chase. Served with Waves World War II. Recipient Woman of Year in Psychology award Am. Mothers Com. Mem. Diadames, Assn. Media Psychologists, Les Dames de Champagne, Dame de Rotisseur, Nat. Art Assn., AFTRA, Screen Actors Guild, Internat. Platform Assn. Clubs: Regency, Lakeside Country, Santa Maria Country. Author: The Human Miracle; columnist Westways mag. Home: 375 Palomar Shell Beach CA 93449

CHASE, ROBERT CHESEBROUGH, real estate broker; b. Balt., Nov. 19, 1946; s. Philip Williams and Nancy Jane (Ensor) C.; m. Christine Wasmuth, Apr. 10, 1976. BA in Econs., Princeton (N.J.) U., 1968. Real estate assoc. Mahoney and Co., Denver, 1973-75, Perry and Butler, Denver, 1975-78, Distinctive Properties, Ltd., Denver, 1978-80, Premier, The Real Estate Group, Denver, 1980-88, Re/Max of Cherry Creek, Inc., Denver, 1988—.

Mem. Denver Bd. Realtors (chmn. urban housing task force 1988—), Colo. Assn. Realtors, Nat. Assn. Realtors. Republican. Club: Denver Athletic. Home: 1200 Humboldt St #1104 Denver CO 80218 Office: Re/Max Cherry Creek Inc 3700 E Alameda Denver CO 80209

CHASEY, WILLIAM CARMAN, lobbyist; b. Trenton, N.J., Feb. 11, 1940; s. William Carman Sr. and Hazel (Kinsler) C.; m. Virginia Marie Borys, Feb. 1, 1980; 1 child, Kathryn Kinsler. BS, Springfield (Mass.) Coll., 1962; BA, East Carolina U., 1965; PhD, U. MD., 1969; hon. LDH, Nat. U., 1987. Registered lobbyist. Instr. U. Md., College Park, 1965-67; asst. prof. Delta State U., Cleveland, Miss., 1967-69; assoc. prof. U. Tex., Austin, 1969-72; prof. Peabody Coll., Vanderbilt U., Nashville, 1972-75; pres. William Chasey Orgn., Washington, 1975—; lobbyist City U., Preuss Found., Taylor Assocs., TAK Communications, Ehrenborg Found. 3d World Prosthetic Found., RDL, Palomar Hosp.; fgn. agt. Embassy of India, Washington, Govt. of Costa Rica, Washington. Editor numerous profl. jours., contbr. articles to profl. jours. 1st lt. USMC, 1962-65. Named to Endowed Chair Joseph P. Kennedy Found., 1972. Mem. Am. League Lobbyists (v.p. 1983-84, founder), Christian Exec. Officers (pres. 1984-85, founder), LaJolla Beach and Tennis Club, Fairbanks Riding Club, Capitol Hill Club, Internat. Club. Presbyterian. Home: 855 La Jolla Corona Ct La Jolla CA 92037 Office: William Chasey Orgn 1015 33rd St NW #509 Washington DC 20007

CHASON, LLOYD RALPH, corporate educator; b. Rocky Mount, N.C., Oct. 14, 1934; s. Charles Franklin and Katie Vera (Rich) C.; m. Joan Carolyn McKenzie, June 16, 1957; children: Allison Lynn, Michael Ralph. BS, East Carolina U., 1957; MA, Baylor U., 1962, PhD, 1968. Commd. 2d lt. USAF, 1957, advanced through grades to col., 1982, ret., 1982; mgr. tech. edn. and tng. Northrop Aircraft Svcs. Div., Hawthorne, Calif., 1982-85; dir. corp. edn. and tng. Northrop Corp., L.A., 1985-89; v.p., mgr. career devel. and tng. Betchel Corp., San Francisco, 1989—. Contbr. articles to profl. jours. Mem. Am. Psychol. Assn., Am. Soc. Tng. and Devel., Inter-U. Seminar on Armed Forces, Sigma Xi, Alpha Chi, Phi Mu Alpha. Republican. Methodist. Home: 81 Amanda Ct Danville CA 94526 Office: Betchel Corp 50 Beale St San Francisco CA 94119

CHATARD, PETER RALPH NOEL JR., aesthetic surgeon; b. New Orleans, June 25, 1936; s. Peter Ralph Sr. and Alberta Chatard; m. Patricia Myrl White, Jan. 31, 1963; children: Andrea Michelle, Faedra Noelle, Tahra Deonne. BS in Biology, Morehouse Coll., 1956; MD, U. Rochester, 1960. Diplomate Am. Bd. Plastic Surgery, Am. Bd. Otolaryngology. Intern Colo. Gen. Hosp., 1960-61; asst. resident in gen. surgery Highland Gen. Hosp., Rochester, N.Y., 1963-64; resident in otolaryngology Strong Meml. Hosp., Rochester, 1964-67; resident in plastic and reconstructive surgery U. Fla., 1980-82; staff otolaryngologist Group Health Corp. of Puget Sound, Seattle, 1967-68; practice medicine specializing in otolaryngology Seattle, 1968-80, practice medicine specializing in plastic surgery, 1982—; clin. asst. prof. otolaryngology, head and neck surgery U. Wash., Seattle, 1975—; plastic surgery cons. western sec. Maxillofacial Review Bd. State of Wash., 1982—, cons. Conservation of Hearing Prog., 1968-80; trustee Physicians and Dentist Credit Bur., 1974-80, 84-87, pres. 1976-77, 84-85; attending staff mem. N.W. Hosp., Seattle, Northgate Gen. Hosp., Seattle; courtesy staff Swedish Hosp. Med., Ctr., Children's Hosp. and Med. Ctr., Seattle, Providence Hosp., Seattle, Stevens Meml. Hosp., Edmond, Wash., St. Cabrini Hosp., Seattel, Fifth Ave Med. Ctr., Seattle, Overlake Meml. Med. Ctr., Bellevue, Wash.; cons. staff Group Health Hosp. , Seattle, Virginia Mason Hosp., Seattle. Capt. USAF, 1961-63. Fellow Am. Rhinologic Soc., Seattle Surg. Soc., ACS, Am. Acad. Facial Plastic and Reconstructive Surgery, Am. Acad. Otolaryngology-Head and Neck Surgery, Northwest Acad. Otolaryngology and Head and Neck Surgery, Soc. for Ear, Nose and Throat Advances in Children, Pacific Oto-Ophthalmological Soc.; mem. AMA, Am. Soc. Plastic and Reconstructive Surgeons, Lipoplasty Soc. N. Am., Wash. Soc. Plastic Surgeons, Nat. Med. Assn., King County Med. Soc., Wash. Med. Assn., N.W. Soc. of Plastic Surgeons. Home: 20914 39th Ave SE Bothell WA 98021 Office: AEsteem Aesthetic Plastic 1570 N 115th St #10 Seattle WA 98133

CHATFIELD, CHERYL ANN, stock brokerage firm executive, writer; b. King's Park, N.Y., Jan. 24, 1946; d. William David and Mildred Ruth (King) C.; m. Gene Allen Chasser, Feb. 17, 1968 (div. 1979); m. James Bernard Arkebauer, Apr. 16, 1983 (div. 1987). BS, Cen. Conn. Coll., 1968, MS, 1972; PhD, U. Conn., 1976. Cert. gen. prin. securities. Tchr. Bristol East High Sch., Conn., 1968-77; adminstr. New Britain Schs., Conn., 1977-79; prof. Ariz. State U., Phoenix, 1979; stockbroker J. Daniel Bell, Denver, 1980-83, Hyder and Co., Denver, 1983-84; stockbroker, pres. Denari Securities, Denver, 1984—; tchr. investment seminars Front Range Community Coll., Denver, 1984-86; speaker women's groups, Denver, 1983-86. Author: Low-Priced Riches, 1985, Selling Low-Priced Riches, 1986, (newspaper columns) For Women Investors, 1982-84, Commentary, 1985-86; editor, founder (newsletter) Women in Securities . Project bus. cons. Jr. Achievement, Denver, 1986; trustee Orchestra of Santa Fe. Mem. Nat. Assn. Female Execs., Aircraft Owners and Pilots Assn., AAUW, N.Mex. Venture Capital Club (treas.), Kappa Delta Pi. Republican. Roman Catholic. Avocation: flying. Office: Chatfield Dean & Co 7935 E Prentice Ave Ste 300 Englewood CO 80111

CHATO, DONNA MAE, computer scientist; b. Oakland, Calif., Mar. 13, 1949; d. William John and Florence Alberta (Shunk) C.; 1 child, Care'n Kapell Chato. BA in Computer Sci., U. Calif., Berkeley, 1971. Computer scientist Lawrence Livermore (Calif.) Nat. Lab., 1974—. Performer, organizer Festival of the Arts, 1970's, 80's; co-founder Kids Deserve Dads Sharing, 1985-89, Sci. and Engring. Explorer Post, 1986-89. Mem. Soc. Profl. Women Engrs., Tri-Valley Deaf Awareness, Sign Lang. Club (v.p. 1985-86). Office: Lawrence Livermore Nat Lab East Ave L-281 Livermore CA 94550

CHATO, JOSEPH EDWARD, civil engineer; b. Albuquerque, Nov. 23, 1950; s. Edgar J. and Mary R. (Begay) C.; m. Barbara J. Moot, Oct. 11, 1975; children: Joshua Joseph, Jeremy James. BCE, U. N.Mex., 1973. Registered profl. engr., N. Mex., Ariz. Structural engr. Krause Engring., Santa Fe, N. Mex., 1973-74; project engr. FAA, Chgo., 1974-77; town engr. Town of Silver City, N.Mex., 1977-80; project engr. Sullivan Design Group, Inc., Santa Fe, 1980-86, v.p., chief engr., 1986-88; prin. Chato Engring., Santa Fe, 1988—. Cubmaster local pack Boy Scouts Am., Santa Fe, 1988—; pres. Kaune PTA, 1989—. Mem. N. Mex. Soc. Profl. Engrs. (chpt. pres. 1984-85, chmn. legis. affairs 1988—), Sangre de Christo Flyfishers Club. Home: 1407 Santa Rosa Dr Santa Fe NM 87501 Office: Chato Engring PO Box 16115 Santa Fe NM 87506-6115

CHATZIPETROU, NICK THEODORAKI, electronics executive; b. Athens, Greece, Nov. 24, 1943; came to U.S. 1968; s. Demetrios and Helen C.; m. Catherine Koutzoukis, Aug. 28, 1971; children: Eleana, Christina. BSEE, Calif. State Poly. U., Pomona, 1975, MBA, 1985. Registered profl. engr., Calif., Oreg. Computer engr. Hewlett-Packard Corp., Fullerton, Calif., 1976-78; engring. mgr. Tektronix Corp., Beaverton, Oreg., 1978-82; sales exec. Racal-Dana, Irvine, Calif., 1982-84; sales mgr. Genrad, Inc., Irvine, Calif., 1984-86; pres., chief executive officer Nikotron Internat. Corp., Santa Fe Springs, Calif., 1986-; bd. dirs. Micronet Computer Systems, Santa Fe Springs. Design engr. and inventor electronic currency counter, 1976. Home: 6571 Fairlynn Blvd Yorba Linda CA 92686

CHAUHAN, HEMRAJ, consulting engineer; b. Chakradharpur, India, Jan. 2, 1941; came to U.S., 1962; s. Vishram Ratna and Ratan C.; m. Linda Jean Chauhan, Dec. 31, 1966; children: Sunita, Rajesh, Krishna, Ajit. BSc, Calcutta (India) U., 1962; BSME, Marquette U., Milw., 1966; MBA, West Coast U., L.A., 1972. Design engr. Boeing Co., Seattle, 1966-69, 73-78; master engr. TWA, Kansas City, Mo., 1978-84; consulting engr. Braniff Airlines, Dallas, 1984-85, Western Airlines, L.A., 1985-87, McDonnell Douglas Aircraft, Long Beach, Calif., 1987—; engring. cons. to airlines, bus. cons. to mfg. cos., 1985—. Republican. Hindu. Home: 22114 Califa St Woodland Hills CA 91364

CHAUNCEY, TOM, retired radio and television executive.; b. Houston, Jan. 20, 1913; s. Brinkley and Lucille Dunn (Weber) C.; 6 children; student pub. schs.; LHD (hon.) Ariz. State U., 1983. Owner, Tom Chauncey Jeweler, 1940-61; v.p., gen. mgr. Sta KPHO, 1941-48; pres. Sta. KOPO, Tucson, 1947-76; v.p., mng. dir. KOOL Radio-TV, Inc., 1948-55, exec. v.p., gen. mgr., 1955-57, pres., gen. mgr., 1957-61, pres., 1961-81, chmn. bd., pres., chief exec. officer, 1981-82, owner, chief exec. officer Sta. KOOL-AM-FM, 1982-86; owner H Lazy A Ranches, Tom Chauncey Arabians, Tom Chauncey Properties; pres., mng. dir. Old Pueblo Broadcasting Co., (KOLD-TV), Tucson, 1957-69; daily columnist TV Views, Ariz. Republic, Phoenix Gazettè, (weekly) Broadcasting mag., 1960-61; former chmn. bd. CBS TV Network Affiliates 1961-62; dir. Valley Nat. Bank; mem. nat. com. Support Free Broadcasting; rep. of pres. U.S., ambassador, Nigeria, 1960. Grand marshal J.C. World Championship Rodeo and Parade, 1963; former nat. trustee City of Hope; former mem. Ariz. Nat. Livestock Show; past Ariz. chmn. Radio Free Europe; former mem. bd. Phoenix Symphony Assn., Phoenix Art Mus., Muscular Dystrophy Assn. Am.; gen. campaign. chmn. Greater Phoenix-Scottsdale United Fund Campaign; former mem. bd., v.p., pres. Phoenix Better Bus. Bur.; mem. Citizen's Action Com.; voting mem. Ariz. State U. Found.; former mem. Phoenix Baseball Stadium Com., U. Ariz. Found., chmn. Ariz. com. A.R.C.; past dir. at large for Ariz. Am. Cancer Soc.; past dir. and pres. Community Council; exec. v.p., mem. bd., Incorporator, co-founder Barrow Neurol. Inst.; mem. Com. for Phoenix Civic Plaza Dedication Ceremonies, 1972, Ariz. Commn. on Nat. and Internat. Commerce; past nat. chmn. Broadcaster's adv. com. U.S. Savs. Bonds; past dir. United Cerebral Palsey Assn. Central Ariz.; past mem. Phoenix All-Am. City Com.; chmn. Ariz. Motion Picture Adv. Bd.; past chmn. adv. bd. on radio and TV, Ariz. State U.; bd. dirs. Central Ariz. Water Conservation Dist.; Nat. Cowboy Hall of Fame bd. dir. 1979—; pres., bd. dirs. Ariz. Children's Found. Named Man of Yr., City of Hope, 1962, NCCJ, 1967, B'nai B'rith Anti-Defamation League, 1975; Citizen of Yr., Phoenix Real Estate Bd., 1965; recipient Nat. Sch. Bell award, 1961; award U.S. Treasury Dept., 1961; Tom Chauncey award United Fund, 1962; Jesse Owens award; George Foster Peabody award, Disting. Achievement award Coll. Pub. Programs Ariz. State U., 1984. Mem. Ariz. (past pres., past dir., past mem. legis. com.), Met. Phoenix (past pres., dir.) broadcasters assns., Nat. Assn. Broadcasters, Nat. Acad. TV Arts and Scis. (Bd. Govs. award Phoenix chpt. 1962, past Ariz. bd. gov.), Mus. Broadcasting (hon.), Nat. Retail Jewelers Assn. (past dir.), Phoenix C. of C., Ariz. Quarterhorse Breeders Assn., Ariz. State Horseman's Assn., Ariz. Heart Inst. 1974—, Arabian Horse Assn. Ariz. (dir. 1972), Ariz. Hereford Assn., Ariz. Retail Jewelers Assn., Am. Gem Soc., TV Pioneers, Phoenix Press Box Assn. (life), Phoenix Thunderbirds, Navy League, Newcomen Soc. N. Am., Sigma Delta Chi. Elk. Clubs: Phoenix Country, Phoenix Execs.; Paradise Valley Country; Rancheros Vistacores; Cowman's. Author: Educational Contributions of Commercial Television, 1960. Tom and Dorothy Chauncey Student Loan Fund established at Ariz. State U. Home: 18000 N Scottsdale Rd Scottsdale AZ 85255

CHAUNCEY, TOM WEBSTER, II, lawyer; b. Phoenix, May 30, 1947; s. Tom Webster and Kathryn (Geare) C.; m. Mary Kathleen LaCroix, Dec. 28, 1972. BA in Sociology with honors, Northwestern U., 1970; JD, Ariz. State U., 1973. Bar: Ariz. 1973, U.S. Dist. Ct. Ariz. 1973. Assoc. Gust, Rosenfeld & Henderson, Phoenix, 1972-76; exec. v.p., counsel KOOL Radio-TV, Inc., Phoenix, 1972-82; gen. counsel, sta. mgr. KOOL-AM-FM, Phoenix, 1982-86; chmn. Cameras in the Courtroom Com., 1979-86; mem. bd. CBS RadioRadio Network Affiliates, 1984-86. V.p. 1st Amendment Coalition, 1981-83, pres., 1984-85; bd. dirs. Park Found. of Phoenix, 1980-84, NCCJ, 1978—, nat. exec. bd. 1986—; bd. dirs. Ariz. Bus.-Industry-Edn. Council, Inc., 1979-83, Friendly House, 1983-84, Ariz. Community Found., 1981-85, Sands North Townhouse Homeowners Assn., 1973-77; mem. task force on ct. productivity Ariz. Supreme Ct.; met. fin. com. YMCA Phoenix and Valley of Sun, 1974-80, mem. camp com., 1978-80; bd. dirs., mem. Project Pool It, Valley Forward Assn., 1977-83; mem. media adv. bd. Traffic Accident Reduction Task Force, 1980; bd. dirs. Meml. Hosp. Found., 1978-83, planning com., 1980-83, community rels. com., 1982-83; bd. dirs. Barrow Neurol. Found., 1979—, mem. exec. com., 1980—, v.p., 1983-85, pres., 1986—, mem. investment com. 1985—; bd. dirs. Ariz. Hist. Soc., 1982-84, mem. bldg. com., 1983, bylaws com., 1983, bd. dirs. Cen. Ariz. Mus. chpt., 1979-84; mem. Crisis Nursery, 1988—; mem. Walter Cronkite Found. for Journalism and Telecommunications, Ariz. State U., 1982—, Ariz. Supreme Ct. Commn. Cts., 1988—; mem. Maricopa City voter awareness com. 1986—. Fellow Ariz. State Bar Found.; mem. ABA, Ariz. Bar Assn. (pub. rels. com. 1975-86, fee arbitration com. 1976-86), FCC Bar Assn., Maricopa County Bar Assn. (past dir. Young Lawyers sect.), Ariz. Trial Lawyers Assn., Phoenix Assn. Def. Counsel, Orme Sch. Alumni Assn., Northwestern U. Alumni Assn. Phoenix (pres. 1975-76), Ariz. State U. Alumni Assn., Ariz. State U. Law Alumni Assn., Phoenix Press Club, Nat. Assn. Broadcasters, Ariz. Broadcasters Assn. (bd. dirs. 1985-86), Met. Phoenix Broadcasters (bd. dirs. 1976-86, pres. 1985-86), Phi Delta Phi, Sigma Delta Chi, Phi Gamma Delta. Office: Gust Rosenfeld & Henderson 3300 Valley Bank Ctr Phoenix AZ 85073

CHAUSSEE, MICHAEL DEAN, lawyer, financial consultant; b. Denver, Mar. 8, 1952; s. Dean F. and Para Lee Chaussee. BA, U. Colo., 1974; JD, Pepperdine U., 1977. Bar: Colo. 1977, Supreme Ct. Colo. 1977. Sole practice, fin. cons. Colorado Springs, 1977—; pres. Four Strong Winds, Inc., Colorado Springs, 1985—. Mem., founder Pikes Peak Children Advocates, Colorado Springs, 1978-82; dir., counsel Make A Wish, Colorado Springs, 1986-87; sec., dir. Chins Up Youth, Colorado Springs, 1977-80; pres. Big Hearted Rabbits, Colorado Springs, 1977-88. Office: Four Strong Winds 1607 Ridgeway Ave Colorado Springs CO 80906

CHAUVIN, RICHARD LUCIEN, software executive; b. Manchester N.H., Apr. 6, 1949; s. Lucien F. and Violette G. (LeMay) C.; m. Theresa Ann Pachtner, June 20, 1977; children—Christopher Scott, Michael Andrew. Computer supr. Nat. CSS, San Francsico 1974-76, tech. rep., 1976-77, computer systems programmer, 1977-78, sr. systems programmer, 1978-79; with Fireman's Fund Ins. Co., San Rafael, Calif., 1979-80; with Magnuson Computer Systems, San Jose, Calif., 1979-80, systems software specialist, 1980, mgr. systems software, 1980-82; owner Chauvin Cons., 1982—; chmn. bd., chief fin. officer, sr. exec. v.p. Dovetail Systems, Inc., Sunnyvale, Calif., 1982-85; pres. Software Assistance, Sunnyvale, 1984-85. With U.S. Air Force, 1968-74. Mem. Assn. Computing Machinery, Aircraft Owners and Pilots Assn. Home and Office: 418 Ridge Rd San Carlos CA 94070

CHAVEZ, CESAR ESTRADA, union official; b. nr. Yuma, Ariz., Mar. 31, 1927; married; 8 children. Mem. staff Community Service Orgn., Calif., 1952-58; gen. dir. Community Service Orgn., 1958-62; organized Nat. Farm Workers Assn., 1962; merged 1966 with Agrl. Workers Organizing Com. of AFL-CIO to form United Farm Workers Organizing Com., dir. 1966-73, Delano, Calif.; now pres. United Farm Workers Am. AFL-CIO, Keene, Calif. Served with USNR, 1944-45. Roman Catholic. Office: United Farm Workers Am PO Box 62 La Paz Keene CA 93531 *

CHAVEZ, CESAR TIZOC, ophthalmologist, eye and facial cosmetic surgeon; b. Mexicali, Mexico, Aug. 3, 1952; s. Felipe and Norbertha (Tizoc) C.; m. Teresa Cardenas, June 1977; children: Elena, Esteban. BA, UCLA, 1973; MD, U. Wash., 1977, MPH, 1977. Diplomate Nat. Board of Med. Examiners, Am. Board Ophthalmology. Div. chief Comprehensive Ophthalmology, UCLA, 1985-88; med. dir. Jules Stein Eye Inst. OPD, UCLA, 1985-88, U. Ophthalmology Assocs., Los Angeles, 1986-88; asst. prof. ophthalmology UCLA, 1985-88; med. dir. Camino Coastline Eye Surgeons, Encinitas, Calif., 1988—; cons. Rand Corp., Santa Monica, Calif, 1986-88. Contbr. articles to profl. jours. Served to lt. USPHS, 1978-81. Fellow Am. Acad. Ophthalmology; mem. Med. Group Mgmt. Assn., San Diego County Med. Soc., Calif. Assn. of Ophthalmologists, Calif. Med. Assn. Roman Catholic. Office: Camino Coastline Eye Surgeons 477 N El Camino Real Ste C-200 Encinitas CA 92024

CHAVEZ, CYNTHIA LOUISE, graphics company executive; b. Pasadena, Calif., Nov. 5, 1957; d. Frank Cleland and Marian Elinor (Morgan) Vejar; m. Lloyd Chavez (div. 1980). BS, San Jose State U., 1980. Sales clk. Peoples Pants Store, San Jose, 1972-73; bindery journeywoman San Jose Graphics, 1973-80; account rep. Arrow Graphics, San Jose, 1980—; agt. Morgan Properties/Better Homes and Gardens, Morgan Hill, Calif., 1987—. Mem. San Jose Real Estate Bd., Sales and Marketing Council (treas. San Jose 1985—, bd. dirs., judging com. chmn. 1986-87), Bldg. Industry Assn. (bd. dirs. 1988—). Home: 16605 Rustling Oak Ln Morgan Hill CA 95037

CHAVEZ, GILBERT ESPINOZA, bishop Roman Catholic Church; b. Ontario, Calif., Mar. 19, 1932; Educated St. Francis Sem., El Cajon, Calif., Immaculate Heart Sem., San Diego, U. Calif., San Diego. Ordained priest Roman Cath. Ch., 1960; titular bishop of Magarmel and aux. bishop Diocese of San Diego, 1974—. Office: 1535 3rd Ave San Diego CA 92101 *

CHAVEZ, RODRIGO GUTIERREZ, research chemist, educator; b. Mexico City, Feb. 7, 1955; came to U.S., 1980; s. Demetrio Z. and Maria (Gutierrez) C. Student, Southwestern Coll., 1972-75; BS in Chemistry, San Diego State U., 1978, MS in Chemistry, 1981. Organic chemist Bachem, Inc., Torrance, Calif., 1982; research chemist Behring Diagnostics, La Jolla, Calif., 1982-88, Calbiochem, La Jolla, 1988--; instr. chemistry San Diego City Coll., 1981-82, 1986--, U. Calif.-San Diego, La Jolla, 1987. Pantentee, amylase substrate. Mem. Am. Chem. Soc. Roman Catholic. Home: 8292 Gilman Dr # 49 La Jolla CA 92037 Office: Calbiochem Corp 10933 N Torrey Pines Rd La Jolla CA 92037

CHAVIS-BUTLER, GRACE LEE, educator; b. Charleston, S.C., Aug. 26, 1916; d. Thomas and Sarah (Lafayette) Chavis; m. E. Hardy Butler, June 15, 1974 (div. Feb. 1984); remarried, Sept. 17, 1985. Diploma in Teaching, Avery Normal Inst., 1938; BA, Am. U., 1954, MA, 1955; PhD, U. Beverly Hills, 1982. Educator Washington high schs., 1955-73; chmn. history dept. Western High Sch., Washington, 1971-73; substitute tchr. Oakland (Calif.) Pub. Schs., 1973-74; substitute instr. Los Angeles Community Coll. Dist., 1974-80, 82—. Author: Reflections on Africa, 1975; contbr. articles to newspapers, profl. jours. Mem. Friends of Vernon Br. Library, Los Angeles, 1978—, v.p., 1980-81; vol. asst. mgr. The Mankind Ctr., Los Angeles, 1978-79; coordinator Los Angeles-Lusaka Sister City Com., 1980. Served as sgt. WAC, 1943-46. Recipient Cert. of Merit Human Relations Commn., Los Angeles, 1982, Martin Luther King award So. Christian Leadership Conf. West, 1978, Annual Fin. Support award Am. U. John Fletcher Hurst Soc., Washington, 1981-82. Mem. AAUW (life mem., 1st v.p. Los Angeles br. 1978-80, Recognition of Service award Los Angeles chpt. 1979, Significant Contbn. to Edn. Found. award State div. 1984, pres. 1988-90), Am. Inst. Parliamentarians (adminstrv. lt. gov. region 7 1984-85, pres. El Camino Real chpt., Los Angeles, 1982-84, chmn. region ann. conf. 1985), Nat. Council of Negro Women (life, chmn. ann. festival com. 1976-77), Seeds of Sequoia (v.p. 1983—), Am. U. Alumni Assn. (Recognition award 1987). Democrat. Roman Catholic. Home: 3465 W 54 St Los Angeles CA 90043

CHEADLE, WILLIAM GRAHAM, software engineering manager; b. Tulsa, Okla., Feb. 1, 1934; s. John Alexander and Nina (Sinnett) C.; m. Janet Roberta Petersen, Sept. 15, 1962; children: Lisa Anne, James Bradley. BA, U. Okla., 1956. Engr. Martin Marietta Astronautics, Denver, 1958-69, 1970-77, sect. chief, 1978-84, mgr., 1985-87, software mgr., 1988—; speaker and instr. in field. Developer numerous software programs; contbr. numerous articles to profl. jours. Deacon Sunday sch. tchr. Bapt. Ch. Col. USMCR, 1956-87. Recipient Frank R. Freiman award Internat. Soc. Parametric Analysts, 1985. Mem. Denver Marine Corps Meml. Assn. (pres. 1971, bd. dirs. 1972-86), Marine Corps Res. Officers Assn. (pres. 1970, bd. dirs. 1971-86). Home: 2825 Eldridge St Golden CO 80401 Office: Martin Marietta Astronaut PO Box 179 Denver CO 80201

CHEAH, JONATHON YOO CHONG, electrical engineer; b. Penang, Malaysia, Aug. 17, 1951; came to the U.S., 1984; s. Kheng Kok and Siew Eng (Lee) C; m. Mary Joan Crutchley, Nov. 12, 1977. BE (with honors), Auckland U., New Zealand, 1976, ME, 1977; PhD, Wollongong U., 1986. Reg. profl. engr., Calif. Assoc engr. New Zealand P.O. Engr., Wellington, 1978-82; tutor Wollongong U., Australia, 1982-84; sr. engr. MA COM Linkabit, San Diego, 1984-87; prin. engr. Hughes Newwork Systems, San Diego, 1987—. Mem. IEEE, Instn. Profl. Engrs. New Zealand. Home: 8746 49 Villa La Jolla Dr San Diego CA 92037 Office: Hughes Network Systems 10790 Roselle St San Diego CA 92121

CHEAL, BERYL IRENE, educational administrator; b. Riverside, Calif., Aug. 12, 1935; d. Alvin William and Carolyn Elizabeth (Taggart) Bullard. BA in Edn., U. La Verne, 1959; MA in Early Childhood Edn., U. Wash., 1973, MS in Mid. Ea. Studies, 1985. Tchr. elem. schs. La Puente (Calif.) and La Verne Sch. Dist., 1959-61; adminstr. Am. Friends Svc. Com., Calif., 1961-66, Gaza, Israel, 1980-82, 86; tchr. Crescent (Wash.) Sch. Dist. and Forks Sch. Dist., 1966-68; head start tchr. Neighborhood House, Seattle, 1968-70; head start program analyst HHS, Seattle, 1970-73; mgr. day care Wash. State Dept. Social and Health Svcs., Olympia, 1975-78; dir pre-schs. UNRWA, Gaza, 1980-82; dir. head start Ednl. Svc. Dist. No. 121, Seattle, 1986—; cons. various ogns. Wash., Oreg., Idaho, 1978-80, 82-85; day care cons., Cairo, 1984; lectr., seminar presenter on Mid. East Issues. Author: Refugees in the Gaza Strip, December 1948-May 1950, 1988; contbr. articles to profl. jours. Founding mem. Seattle Com. for Isreaili Palestinian Peace, 1984—; mem. Arab Anti-Discrimination Com., Seattle. NSF scholar Yarmouk U., Irbid, Jordan, 1984. Mem. Nat. Assn. for Edn. Young Children, Wash. Assn. for Edn. Young Children (treas. 1976, 88), World Orgn. for Early Childhood Edn., Assn. Supervision and Curriculum Devel. Democrat. Home: 331 NW 75th St Seattle WA 98117 Office: Ednl Svc Dist #121 12320 80th Ave S Seattle WA 98178

CHEATHAM, DAVID TODD, software company executive; b. L.A., June 2, 1956; s. Robert Tracy and Jane C.; m. Sharon Bond, Sept. 9, 1079; 2 children: Michael, Alyssa. BA in Bus. Adminstrn., Principia Coll., 1979; MBA in Mgmt., Pepperdine U., 1984. Ops. mgr. Microcheck, Inc., Long Beach, Calif., 1979-81; chief fin. officer Data Trek, Inc., Encinitas, Calif., 1981-84, pres., chief exec. officer, 1984—. Author card datalog-libr. automation software. Recipient Outstanding Tech. award Assn. Info. Mgrs., 1985. Mem. Internat. Interactive Communications Soc. Republican. Christian Scientist. Officek: Data Trek Inc 167 Saxony Rd Encinitas CA 92024

CHECKETTS, DAVID WAYNE, professional sports team executive; b. Salt Lake City, Sept. 16, 1955; s. Clyde Alvin and Edith (Jones) C.; m. Deb Leishman, June 2, 1977; children: Spencer, Katie, Nathaniel, Andrew, Benjamin. BS, U. Utah, 1979; MBA, Brigham Young U., 1981. Mgmt. cons. Bain and Co., Boston, 1980-83; exec. v.p. Utah Jazz, NBA, Salt Lake City, 1983-84, pres., 1984-87, pres., gen. mgr., 1987-88, gen. mgr., 1988-89. Trustee Salt Lake Visitor and Conv. Bur., 1986. Mormon. Lodge: Rotary. Office: care Denver Nuggets McNichols Sports Arena PO Box 4658 Denver CO 80204

CHEDID, JOHN G., bishop Roman Catholic Church; b. Eddid, Lebanon, July 4, 1923. Educated, Sems. in Lebanon and Pontifical Urban Coll., Rome. Ordained priest Roman Cath. Ch., 1951. Titular bishop of Callinico and aux bishop St. Maron of Bklyn., 1981. Office: Our Lady Mount Lebanon Ch 333 S San Vicente Blvd Los Angeles CA 90048 *

CHEE, PERCIVAL HON YIN, ophthalmologist; b. Honolulu, Aug. 29, 1936; s. Young Sing and Den Kyau (Ching) C.; B.A., U. Hawaii, 1958; M.D., U. Rochester, 1962; m. Carolyn Siu Lin Tong, Jan. 27, 1966; children—Lara Wai Lung, Shera Wai Sum. Intern, Travis AFB Hosp., Fairfield, Calif., 1962-63; resident Bascom Palmer Eye Inst., Miami, Fla., 1965-68, Jackson Meml. Hosp., Miami, 1965-68; partner Straub Clinic, Inc., Honolulu, 1968-71; practice medicine specializing in ophthalmology, Honolulu, 1972—; mem. staffs Queen's Med. Center, St. Francis Hosp., Kapiolani Children's Med. Center, Honolulu; clin. assoc. prof. surgery U. Hawaii Sch. Medicine, 1971—; cons. Tripler Army Med. Center. Mem. adv.

bd. Services to Blind; bd. dirs. Lions Eye Bank and Makana Found. (organ bank), Multiple Sclerosis Soc. Served to capt. USAF, 1962-65. Fellow Am. Acad. Ophthalmology, ACS; mem. AMA, Pan Am. Med. Assn., Pan Pacific Surg. Assn., Am. Assn. Ophthalmology, Soc. Eye Surgeons, Hawaii Ophthal. Soc. Pacific Coast Ophthal. Soc., Am. Assn. for Study Headache, Pan Am. Ophthal. Found. Contbr. articles to profl. pubs. Home: 3757 Poka Pl Honolulu HI 96816 Office: Kukui Plaza 50 S Beretania St Honolulu HI 96813

CHEESEMAN, DOUGLAS TAYLOR, JR., wildlife tour company executive, photographer; b. Honolulu, July 16, 1937; s. Douglas Taylor Cheeseman and Myra (Bettencourt) Ehrlich; m. Gail Macomber, Apr. 7, 1963; children: Rosie M., Ted F. BA, San Jose (Calif.) State U., 1959, MA, 1964. Cert. secondary tchr., Calif. Naturalist Crater Lake (Oreg.) Nat. Park, summers 1959-60; tchr. biology Woodside High Sch., Redwood City, Calif., 1961-65; teaching asst. U. Colo., Boulder, 1966-67; prof. biology De Anza Coll., Cupertino, Calif., 1967—, dir. environ. study area, 1970—; pres. Cheeseman's Ecology Safaris, Saratoga, Calif., 1981—; instr. wildlife and natural history photography, Saratoga, 1984—; rsch. cooperator Fish and Wildlife Svc., 1972—; guest lectr. numerous conservation groups, No. Calif., 1978—. Photographs represented in books and on calendars. Recipient Outstanding Svc. and Tchr. award, Pres.'s award De Anza Coll., 1988; NSF fellow, 1969, 71; NDEA Title III grantee, 1970. Mem. Ecol. Soc. Am., Am. Ornithologists Union, Am. Soc. Mammalogists, Brit. Trust Ornithology, Brit. Ornithologists Union, African Wildlife Soc. (bd. dirs.), Marine Mammal Soc. (founding), Calif. Native Plants Soc., Bay Area Bird Photographers (co-founder), Santa Clara Valley Audubon Soc. (bd. dirs. v.p., program chmn. 1983—), Cooper Soc. Home: 20800 Kittredge Rd Saratoga CA 95070 Office: De Anza Coll Dept Biology Cupertino CA 95014

CHEINSTEIN, JULIAN EDWARD, government official; b. Boston, Apr. 14, 1950; s. Lawrence George and Blanche (Adler) C. BA in Polit. Sci., Case Western Res. U., 1972. Social ins. rep. Social Security Adminstrn., Boston, 1973-78, quality rev. analyst, 1978-85; supr. Social Security Adminstrn., Glendale, Calif., 1985–, trainer, 1977-78, 88. Mem. Orono (Maine) Conservation Commn., 1976-77. Home: 2971 Avenel Terr Los Angeles CA 80039 Office: Social Security Adminstrn 425 E Colorado St Glendale CA 91205

CHEL, FREDERIK WILLEM, manufacturing executive, lawyer; b. Rotterdam, The Netherlands, Nov. 30, 1929; Came to U.S., 1946; s. Cornelis and Elizabeth Francina (DeLooze) C.; m. Elizabeth June Malak, Oct. 26, 1952; children: Frederick W., Lisette F. BA, Pepperdine U., 1952; JD, UCLA, 1955. Bar: Calif. 1955, U.S. Dist. Ct. (so. dist.) Calif. 1956. Sole practice Long Beach, Calif., 1956-74; legislator Calif. Legislature, Sacramento, 1974-78; v.p., legal counsel Custom Fiberglass Mfg. Co., Long Beach, 1979-85, pres., chief exec. officer, 1985—; bd. dirs. Blando Corp., Long Beach, Snugtop Southbay Corp., Long Beach, Kit Mfg. Co., Long Beach, Custom Fibreglass Mfg. Co., Long Beach. Assoc. editor UCLA Law Rev., 1954-55; contbr. articles to profl. jours. Mem. Calif. Assembly, Sacramento, 1974-78. Mem. ABA, Calif. State Bar, Los Angeles County Bar Assn., Long Beach Bar Assn. Democrat. Episcopalian. Office: Custom Fiberglass Mfg Co 1711 Harbor Ave PO Box 121 Long Beach CA 90801

CHELEY, DONALD SCOTT, camp director; b. Denver, Apr. 28, 1943; s. John Austin and Eleanor (Clark) C.; m. Susan K. Birchmier, Aug. 31, 1968 (div.); children: Jeff Harrison, Brooke Alison; m. Carole Ann Tyer, Jan. 2, 1982; 1 child, Austin Scott. BS in Bus., Menlo Sch. Bus., Menlo Park, Calif., 1968; student, Colorado Coll., 1964. Supr. Sky Chef, Inc. Am. Airlines, Denver and others, 1964-67, Saga Food Svc., Menlo Park, Calif., 1967-69; dir. Cheley Colo. Camps, Estes Park, 1969—. With Air Nat. Guard, 1964-70. Mem. Am. Camping Assn. (pres. Rocky Mt. Sect. 1980-81, regional honor award 1984, sect. outstanding svc. 1988), Estes Park Liveryman's Assn. (mgmt. treas. 1980—), Western Assn. Independent Camps (pres. 1988—). Republican. Lutheran. Office: Cheley Colo Camps 601 Steele Dr Denver CO 80206

CHEN, CHUAN FANG, mechanical engineering educator; b. Tientsin, China, Nov. 15, 1932; came to U.S., 1950, naturalized, 1963; s. Kwang Yuan and Chin Han (Wang) C.; m. Frances Ya-Kiang Liu, Aug. 10, 1957; children: Peter Peishan, Paul Peichuan, Philip Peihai. B.Sc., U. Ill., 1953, M.Sc., 1954; Ph.D., Brown U., 1960. Asst. to chief engr. Hydronautics, Inc., Laurel, Md., 1960-63; asst. prof. mech. and aerospace engring. Rutgers U., New Brunswick, N.J., 1963-66; asso. prof. Rutgers U., 1966-69, prof., 1969—, chmn. dept., 1976-80; prof., head aerospace and mech. engring. dept. U. Ariz., Tucson, 1980—; cons. Vitro Labs., Silver Spring, Md., Hydronautics, Inc., Laurel, C.R. Bard, Inc., Murray Hill, N.J.; Am. Soc. Engring. Edn.-NASA fellow, summers 1968, 69, Rutgers Research Council Faculty fellow, 1971-72; sr. visitor DAMTP, Cambridge (Eng.) U.; vis. fellow Research Sch. Earth Scis., Australian Nat. U., Canberra, summer 1978. Contbr. articles to profl. jours. Clare Hall vis. fellow Cambridge U., 1987. Fellow Am. Inst. Aeros. and Astronautics (asso.), ASME; mem. AAAS, Am. Phys. Soc., Am. Soc. Engring. Edn., Sigma Xi, Tau Beta Pi, Pi Tau Sigma. Home: 4266 E Coronado Dr Tucson AZ 85718 Office: U Ariz Dept Aero and Mech Engring Tucson AZ 85721

CHEN, GEORGE KOWN-HOW, electrical engineer; b. Taipei, Taiwan, Feb. 7, 1962; came to U.S., 1968.; s. Paul Tsong and Barbara Char-Fan (Hwang) C.; m. Amy Seng-Huei, July 12, 1986; 1 child, Serena Abigail. BEE, UCLA, 1986. Tech. staff Hughes Aircraft Co., Los Angeles, 1984—. Republican. Office: Hughes Aircraft Co PO Box 92426 Los Angeles CA 90009-2426

CHEN, LARRY LUNG-FENG, structural engineer; b. Kaohsiung, Taiwan, Republic of China, July 17, 1953; came to U.S., 1978; s. Shan-Shi and Chin (Hung) C. BS, Nat. Cheng-Kung U., Tainan, Taiwan, Republic of China, 1975; MS, U. Utah, 1979. Structural engr. Tams Cons. Engrs., Seattle, 1979-80; stress engr. Boeing Co., Seattle, 1980-87; contract engr. McDonald Douglas Co., Long Beach, Calif., 1987-88; cons. structural engr. Long Beach, 1988—. Lt. Republic of China Army, 1975-77. Mem. Soc. Chinese Engrs., Formosa Soc. Home: 11237 Lucas St Cerritos CA 90701 Office: 552 N Bellflower Blvd No 117 Long Beach CA 90814

CHEN, MARJORIE WONG, aviation and marketing consultant; b. Los Angeles, Oct. 28, 1940; d. Thomas A. and Mayme M. (Moe) Wong; children: Barbara Joanne, Cynthia Anne. BA, Goucher Coll., 1962; MA, U. Calif. at Berkeley, 1965. Research economist Fed. Reserve Bank San Francisco, 1964-65; bus. cons., travel industry, 1968-74; marketing analyst The Flying Tiger Line Inc., Los Angeles, 1974-76, systems analyst, 1976-77, mgr. mgmt. reporting and performance analysis, 1977-78; dir. passenger pricing and fare devel. Continental Airlines, 1978-80, dir. internat. pricing, 1980-83; aviation and mktg. cons. Chen and Assocs., 1983—; fin. cons. Shearson Lehman Hutton; bd. dirs. Continental Fed. Credit Union. Mem. Calif. Republican Assembly, 1976; trustee, chmn. devel. Marlborough Sch.; trustee, v.p. Los Angeles Library Assn.; trustee, deacon 1st Congl. Ch. of Los Angeles; mem. evaluation com. Am. Heart Assn. Danforth Found. assoc., 1968-79. Mem. Nat. Mgmt. Assn. (membership chmn.), World Affairs Council Los Angeles, Town Hall Calif., U. Calif., Marlborough alumni assns. Republican. Conglist. Club: Goucher. Home: 640 N June St Los Angeles CA 90004

CHEN, PETER WEI-TEH, mental health services administrator; b. Fuchow, Republic of China, July 20, 1942; came to U.S., 1966; s. Mao-Chuang and Sheu-Lin (Wang) C.; m. Lai-Wah Mui, Nov. 8, 1969; children: Ophelia Mei-Chuang, Audrey Mei-Hui. BA, Nat. Chung Hsing U., Taipei, Republic of China, 1964; MSW, Calif. State U., Fresno, 1968; D of Social Work, U. So. Calif., 1976. Case worker Cath. Welfare Bur., L.A., 1968-69; psychiat. social worker L.A. County Mental Health Svcs., 1969-78, mental health svcs. coordinator, 1978; sr. rsch. analyst Jud. and Legis. Bur. L.A. County Dept. Mental Health, 1978-79; Forensic In-Patient Program dir. L.A. County Dept. Mental Health, 1979-86, chief Jail Mental Health Svcs., 1986-89, asst. dep. dir., 1989—; pres. Orient Social and Health Soc., Los Angeles, 1973-75; bd. dirs. Am. Correctional Health Assn., 1986-87. Author: Chinese-Americans View Their Mental Health, 1976. Bd. dirs. San Marino (Calif.) Community Chest, 1986-87; trustee San Marino Schs. Found., 1987—. Served to 2d lt. Chinese Marine Corps, Taiwan, People's Republic of China, 1964-65. Recipient several community service awards. Mem. Nat. Assn. Social Workers (bd. dirs. Calif. chpt. 1979-80), Nat. Correctional Health Assn., Forensic Mental Health Assn. Calif. Clubs: Chinese of San Marino (pres. 1987-88), San Marino City. Home: 2161 E California Blvd San Marino CA 91108 Office: LA County Dept Mental Health 505 S Virgil Ave Los Angeles CA 90020

CHEN, WEN, trading company executive; b. Beijing, Mar. 5, 1939; came to U.S., 1964; d. Kan-I and Chao-Yo Chen; divorced; children: Steven Han Yang, Wenni Lynn Yang. AA, Shi Chien Coll., Taipei, Republic China, 1962; BS, Radford U., 1967; MA, Seton Hall U., 1975. Comml. artist, designer Burlington Industries, Duet Design, N.Y.C., 1967-76; instr. Clark Coll., Vancouver, Wash., 1976-81; China liaison mgr. Nike Inc., Portland, Oreg., 1981-83; sr. trader, asst. to pres. U.S. World Trade Corp. subs. U.S. Bankcorp, Portland, 1983-85; mng. dir. Asia Pacific region North Pacific Trading Co., Portland, 1985—; contract interpreter Nat. Council for U.S.-China Trade, Washington, 1978-81, Oreg. China Council, Portland, 1978-81, North Pacific Cons. Co., Portland, 1978-81; lectr. Lewis & Clark Coll., Portland, 1979-81. Bd. dirs. Clark County Social Service Adminstrv. Bd., 1978-80, Vancouver-Clark County YWCA, 1980-82, Northwest Regional China Council, 1982-86, Wash. State Adv. Council on Internat. Trade and Devel., 1984-86; trustee Wash. Commn. for Humanities, 1986--. Office: North Pacific Trading Co 1505 SE Gideon St Portland OR 97208

CHENEY, DICK (RICHARD BRUCE CHENEY), secretary of defense, former congressman; b. Lincoln, Nebr., Jan. 30, 1941; s. Richard Hebert and Marjorie Lauraine (Dickey) C.; m. Lynne Anne Vincent, Aug. 29, 1964; children—Elizabeth, Mary Claire. B.A., U. Wyo., 1965, M.A., 1966; postgrad., U. Wis., 1966-68. Staff aide to Gov. Warren Knowles, Wis., 1966; mem. staff Congressman William A. Steiger, 1969; spl. asst. to dir. OEO, Washington, 1969-70; dep. to counsellor to Pres. The White House, Washington, 1970-71; asst. dir. Cost of Living Council, 1971-73; dep. asst. to Pres. The White House, Washington, 1974-75, asst. to Pres., 1975-77; ptnr. Bradley, Woods and Co., 1973-74; mem. 96th-100th Congresses from Wyo., 1979-89; sec. U.S Dept. of Defense, Washington, 1989—; chmn. Rep. Conf. Com. Named One of 10 outstanding young men in Am., U.S. Jaycees, 1976; Congl. fellow Am. Polit. Sci. Assn., 1968-69. Mem. Am. Polit. Sci. Assn. Republican. Office: US Dept Def The Pentagon Washington DC 20301

CHENG, EDMUND KAI-LIEN, electrical engineer; b. Kowloon, Hong Kong, July 7, 1949; came to U.S. 1968; s. Chung Hao and Zing San Cheng; m. Kitty Wai-Sing Chang; children: Daniel Wai, Eric Ben. BSEE, Ohio U., 1972; MSEE, Calif. Inst. Tech., 1973, PhD, 1976. Design engring. mgr. Intel Corp., Santa Clara, Calif., 1975-81; v.p. Silicon Compiler Systems Corp., San Jose, 1981—; adv. com. NSF, Washington, 1987—. Contbr. to book: Silicon Compilation, 1988. Mem. IEEE, ACM. Office: Silicon Compiler Systems 2045 Hamilton Ave San Jose CA 95125

CHENG, PETER YU-HUNG, electronics engineer; b. Hong Kong, Feb. 4, 1952; came to U.S., 1970, naturalized, 1984; s. Yuk Kwan and Sussy Shui-Wan (Kao) C.; m. Pearl Po-Yee Li, Mar. 21, 1981. BSEE summa cum laude, Wash. State U., 1974; MSEE, U. Pa., 1976; postgrad., Stanford U., 1982. Design engr. Tex. Instruments, Houston, 1977-78; design engr. Intel, Santa Clara, Calif., 1978-79, sr. design engr., 1980-81; sr. design engr. Intersil, Cupertino, Calif., 1979-80; devel. engr. Hewlett Packard, Cupertino, Calif., 1981-82, project mgr., 1982—, chmn. design tech. conf., 1983—. Contbr. tech. articles to profl. confs. S. Town Stephenson scholar Wash. State U., Pullman, 1974; fellow U. Pa., Phila., 1975-76. Mem. IEEE, AAAS, Am. Mgmt. Assn., Am. Assn. Artificial Intelligence, Stanford Alumni Assn. (life), Tau Beta Pi (treas. 1973-74), Phi Kappa Phi. Republican. Home: 10229 Palo Vista Rd Cupertino CA 95014 Office: Hewlett Packard 19447 Pruneridge Ave Cupertino CA 95014

CHERBERG, JOHN ANDREW, former lieutenant governor Washington; b. Pensacola, Fla., Oct. 17, 1910; s. Fortunato and Annie (R) C.; m. Elizabeth Anne Walker, Aug. 17, 1935; children—Kay Elizabeth (Mrs. Ray Cohrs), Barbara Jean (Mrs. Dean Tonkin), James Walker. B.A., U. Wash., 1933. Cert. tchr., Wash. High sch. tchr., athletic coach 1934-46; football coach U. Wash., 1946-56; lt. gov. Wash., 1957-89; Chmn. Nat. Conf. Lt. Govs., 1968-69. Mem. NEA, AFTRA, Nat. Acad. TV Arts and Scis., Wash. State Assn. Broadcasters (hon. life), Sigma Nu. Club: Variety. Home: 515 Howe St Seattle WA 98109 Office: Office of Lt Gov 304 Legis Bldg AS-31 Olympia WA 98504-0431

CHERIN, LOTTE, artist; b. Detroit. BA, Mills Coll., Oakland, Calif., 1969; MFA, Calif. State U., Long Beach, 1980. Teaching asst. San Francisco Mus. of Art, 1972-74; grad. asst. art history dept. Calif. State U., Long Beach, 1975-77, art instr., 1978-79; artist-in-residence City of Long Beach, 1977-78; owner, pres. Archtl. Sculpture, Malibu, Calif., 1978—; art dir. Rhythms Prodns., L.A., 1980—. Commd. Fullerton (Calif.) Coll. Dance Dept., 1979, Long Beach Pub. Libr., 1979, C.G. Jung Inst.-M. McClean Fund, L.A., 1982, Dr. Armand Hammer-United World Coll., L.A., 1985, Universal/MCA, L.A., 1989; prin. works include sculpture for Gallery of Contemporary Metalsmithing, Rochester, N.Y., 1980, Kohler Art Ctr., Wis., 1983, Mitchell Mus., Wis., 1985, Downey Mus., Calif., 1987, Third Internat. Sculpture Exhibit-Traveling Show, 1988. Active U.N. World Conf., Nairobi, Kenya, 1985, "Catch a Rising Artist" scholarship benefit L.A. Arts Coun., Century City, Calif., 1988; mem. L.A. Mus. Contemporary Art. Task Force grantee U. Calif., Santa Cruz, 1975; named one of 6 Americans to exhibit Fachverband Metall Bayern, Lindau-Bodensee, Fed. Republic Germany, 1980; recipient Achievement award Internat. Art Competition, Los Angeles, 1984, Honorable Mention Product Design Letraset Internat., Paramus, N.J., 1986. Mem. Internat. Sculptors Assn., Soc. North Am. Goldsmiths, AIA (affiliate, urban design com. 1986, city room com. 1987), Am. Crafts Council, Artists Equity Assn. (bd. dirs. 1983-85, newsletter editor 1984-85), Artists Blacksmiths Assn. of North Am., Sierra Club, Wilderness Soc., Animal Welfare Inst. Office: Archtl Sculpture PO Box 786 Malibu CA 90265-0786

CHERIS, SAMUEL DAVID, lawyer; b. Bklyn., Nov. 14, 1945; s. Hyman and Gertrude Eunice (Perlman) C.; m. Judith Lynn Jones, 1972 (div. 1976); 1 child, Aaron Joseph; m. Elaine Gayle Ingram, June 8, 1980. BS in Acctg., Bklyn. Coll., 1967; MBA, JD, Stanford U., 1971. Bar: Calif. 1972, Colo. 1973, U.S. Tax Ct. 1972, U.S. Ct. Appeals (fed. cir.) 1972. Law clk. to justice U.S. Ct. Appeals (fed. cir.), Washington, 1971-72; ptnr. Hall & Evans, Denver, 1972—; bd. dirs. Petrofiche, Inc. Author: (book) Estate Planning and Administration in Colorado, 1987; editor Stanford Jour. of Internat. Studies, 1970-71, Stanford Law Rev., 1968-71. Bd. dirs. U.S. com. Sports for Israel, Phila., 1982—, Internat. Hearing Dog., Henderson, Colo., 1981—; pres. of jury Fed. Internat. d'Escrime, Paris, France, 1980—; mem. Leadership com., Denver, 1987-88; del. U.S. Olympic Com., Colorado Springs, Colo., 1988—. Fellow Am. Coll. Probate Counsel, mem. ABA (com. chmn. real property probate and trust 1985—), Denver Estate Planning Council, Denver C. of C. (membership council 1986—, task force chmn. 1987-88), Am. arbitration Assn. (comml. arbitrator 1983—), Asia Pacific Lawyers Assn., U.S. Fencing Assn. (pres. 1988—), Cheyenne Fencing Soc. (pres. 1981—). Jewish. Home: 5730 Monview Blvd Denver CO 80207 Office: Hall & Evans 1200 17th St #1700 Denver CO 80202

CHERNESKY, JOHN JOSEPH, JR., naval officer; b. Hartford, Conn., July 6, 1944; s. John Joseph and Mary (Milewski) C.; m. Patricia Ann Wolf, Oct. 9, 1967 (div. June, 1988); children: Karen Elizabeth, John David. BS, Miami U., 1967. Commd. ensign U.S. Navy, 1967, advanced through grades to capt., 1985; flag lt., aide Commander Submarines Pacific, Pearl Harbor, Hawaii, 1971-73; engr. officer USS Blueback, Pearl Harbor, 1973-75; exec. officer USS Bonefish, Pearl Harbor, 1975-77; head officer retention Bur. Naval Personnel, Washington, 1977-79; exec. officer USS Dale, commanding officer USS Patterson Mayport, Fla., 1979-83; exec. officer USS Iowa, Norfolk, Va., 1983-85; dir. navy programs Office of Legisl. Affairs, Washington, 1985-88; commanding officer USS Missouri, Long Beach, Calif., 1988—. Decorated with Legion of Merit, President of U.S., 1985, USS Iowa (at sea), 1988, Washington. Mem. U.S. Naval Inst., Am. Legion, Delta Tau Delta, Soc. of Philatelic Ams. Republican. Roman Catholic. Office: USS Missouri (BB-63) FPO San Francisco CA 96689

CHERNOF, DAVID, internist; b. Chgo., Dec. 6, 1935; s. Joseph and Fannie (Cassata) C.; m. Lorna Jean Laff, Mar. 30, 1958; children: Bruce, Steven, Kenneth. AB, Harvard U., 1957; MD, UCLA, 1961. Diplomate Am. Bd. Internal Medicine. Staff physician City of Hope, Duarte, Calif., 1967-68; pvt. practice Northridge, Calif., 1968—; pres. med. staff, Northridge Hosp., 1980-81; assoc. prof. medicine, UCLA, 1984—; bd. dirs. Blue Cross Calif., L.A., 1987—. Contbr. articles to sci. jours. Fellow ACP; mem. So. Calif. Ind. Practice Assn. (founding pres. 1985-87), Northridge Physicians Preferred Provider Assn. (founding pres. 1983—), Calif Med. Assn. (bd. dirs. polit. action com. 1989—), L.A. County Med. Assn. (treas. 1987-88, sec. 1988-89, bd. dirs. polit. action com. 1987—, pres.-elect 1989—). Democrat. Jewish. Office: 18350 Roscoe Blvd Ste 500 Northridge CA 91324

CHERNY, WALTER B., obstetrician, gynecologist, educator; b. Montreal, Que., Can., Apr. 13, 1926. BSc, McGill U., 1948, MD, CM, 1950. Diplomate Am. Bd. Ob-Gyn. Rotating intern Montreal Gen. Hosp., 1950-51, asst. resident in gen. surgery, 1951-52; resident in ob-gyn Duke U., Durham, N.C., 1952-55; prof. ob-gyn Duke U. Sch. Medicine, 1955-70, U. Ariz., Tucson, 1971-88; dir. ob-gyn edn. Good Samaritan Med. Ctr., Phoenix, 1970—; mem. cons. staff, 1955—. Fellow Am. Coll. Obstetricians and Gyncologists (coun. on residency edn. 1981-87), Cen. Assn. Ob-Gyn (v.p. 1986-87). Office: Good Samaritan Med Ctr 1111 E McDowell Rd PO Box 2899 Phoenix AZ 85062

CHERRY, DENISE EDYTHE, association executive; b. Renton, Wash., July 6, 1953; m. Raymond L. Cherry, Aug. 2, 1973. BS, U. Wash., 1977. Registered pharmacist, Wash. Pharmacist Ray's Rexall Drugs, Seattle, 1977-85; dir. Wash. State Pharmacists Assn., Renton, 1985—, dir. pub. rels., 1986—. Mem. King TV Drug Abuse Task Force, Seattle, 1986—, Pharmacists Polit. Action Com.; mem. com. Arthritis Found., Seattle, 1985—; vol. Leukemia Soc., Kent, Wash., 1986-88. Mem. Am. Pharm. Assn., South King County Pharmacists Assn. (pres. 1985-86), Wash. Pilots Assn. (pres. Green River chpt.). Office: Wash State Pharmacists Assn 1420 Maple Ave SW #101 Renton WA 98055

CHERRY, JOHN THOMAS, chemist; b. Houston, Mar. 18, 1951; s. Roy Wilson and Francis (Johns) C.; m. Anne Janette Kemp (dec. Dec. 1977). 1 child, Tressa Anne. BA in Biology, U. Houston, 1976, BS in Chemistry, 1981. Head extracorporeal tech./surgery M.D. Anderson Hosp., Houston, 1970-73, 75-76, 80; microbiologist Baylor Coll. Medicine, Houston, 1977-79; chemist Tex. City (Tex.) Refining, 1980-82; sr. chemist Unocal-Oil Shale Ops., Parachute, Colo., 1982—. Mem. Am. Chem. Soc., Petroleum div. Am. Chem. Soc. Republican. Baptist. Home: 361 Tamarisk Parachute CO 81635 Office: Unocal 2717 County Rd 215 Parachute CO 81635

CHERRY, MICHAEL RAY, computer systems analyst; b. Cedar Rapids, Iowa, July 31, 1955; s. Raymond Forrest and Ardyth Sue (Randa) C.; m. Susie Q. June Thumma, July 8, 1978; children: Alyssa Queue, Troy Michael, Robyn Michelle. AAS, Kirkwood Coll., 1975. Computer programmer Exec. Data Systems, Cedar Rapids, 1975-76, Health Mgmt. Svcs., Cedar Rapids, 1976-78, N.Am. Rockwell, Cedar Rapids, 1978, McDonnell Douglas Co., St. Louis, 1978-79; with Valley Nat. Bank, Phoenix, 1979—, data communications systems analyst, 1985—; cons. in field. Republican. Office: Valley Nat Bank Q580 PO Box 71 Phoenix AZ 85001

CHESHER, HOWARD L., small business owner; b. Lubbock, Tex., May 19, 1936; s. Dallas Reid and Flora Josephine (Young) C.; m. Lia Kuhagen, Dec. 20, 1958 (div. 1974); 1 child, Detlef Walter; m. Ruth Irene Peter, Dec. 3, 1976. Student, Mt. San Antonio Coll., Walnut, Calif., 1954-55. Owner, operator Blvd. Cleaners, Lakewood, Calif., 1959-74, Dutch Dry Cleaners, Temecula, Calif., 1974—; cons. Dutch Enterprises, Temecula, 1987-88. Pres. Lakewood C. of C., 1972; vol. Lakewood Pan Am. Assn., 1973, Lakewood Rose Float Assn., 1974. Recipient Pres. award Lakewood Pan Am. Assn., 1972. Mem. Internat. Fabricare Inst., Calif. Fabricare Inst., Temecula Valley C. of C. (v.p. 1987-88). Republican. Presbyterian. Lodge: Moose. Office: Dutch Enterprises 27461 Jefferson Ave Temecula CA 92390

CHESNUT, CAROL FITTING, economist; b. Pecos, Tex., June 17, 1937; d. Ralph Ulf and Carol (Lowe) Fitting; m. Dwayne A. Chesnut, Dec. 27, 1955; children: Carol Marie, Michelle, Mark Steven. BA magna cum laude, U. Colo., 1971. Research asst. U. Colo., 1972; head quality controller Mathematica, Inc., Denver, 1973-74; cons. Mincome Man., Winnipeg, Can., 1974; cons. economist Energy Cons. Assocs. Inc., Denver, 1974-79; exec. v.p. tng. ECA Intercomp, 1980-81; gen. ptnr. Chestnut Consortium, Las Vegas, 1981—; sec., bd. dirs. Critical Resources, Inc., 1981-83. Rep. Lakehurst Civic Assn., 1968; staff aide Senator Gary Hart, 1978; Dem. precinct capt., 1982-88. Mem. Am. Mgmt. Assn., Soc. Petroleum Engrs., Am. Nuclear Soc. (chmn. conv. space activities for 1989), Am. Geophys. Union, Assn. Women Geoscientists (treas. Denver 1983-85), ACLU, NOW, AAUW (1st v.p. 1989—), Century Club, Phi Beta Kappa, Phi Chi Theta. Unitarian. Office: 3416 Biscaya Circle Las Vegas NV 89121

CHESTER, ARTHUR NOBLE, physicist; b. Seattle, Aug. 5, 1940; s. Arthur Malbridge and Marjorie (Stenberg) C.; m. Cynthia Anne Ashford, Sept. 6, 1961 (div. June 1968); m. Catherine Rogers Buchanan, Aug. 10, 1969. BS in Physics, U. Tex., 1961; PhD in Theoretical Physics, Calif. Inst. Tech., 1965. Mem. tech. staff Bell Labs., Murray Hill, N.J., 1965-69; mem. tech. staff Hughes Research Labs., Malibu, Calif., 1969-73, mgr. laser dept., 1973-75, assoc. dir., 1975-80; program mgr. very high speed integrated circuits Hughes Aircraft Co., El Segundo, Calif., 1980-83, mgr. tactical engring. div., 1984-85; group v.p., mgr. space and strategic systems div. Hughes Aircraft Co., 1985-88; v.p. and dir. research labs. Hughes Aircraft Co., Malibu, Calif., 1988—; cons. U.S. Dept. Def., Washington, 1975-79; co-dir. Internat. Sch. Quantum Electronics, Erice, Sicily, Italy, 1980—; bd. dirs., chmn. exhbn. comm. Fellows Contemporary Art, Los Angeles. Co-editor: Integrated Optics: Physics and Applications, 1983, Free Electron Lasers, 1983, Analytical Laser Spectroscopy, 1985, Laser Photobiology and Photomedicine, 1985, Optical Fiber Sensors, 1986; contbr. articles to publs. Pres. Masterwork Chorus, Morristown, N.J., 1968-69; bd. dirs. Fellows Contemporary Art, Los Angeles. Recipient A.A. Bennett Calculus prize U. Tex., 1959; recipient Nat. Merit scholar, 1957; NSF fellow, 1961; Howard Hughes doctoral fellow, 1963. Fellow IEEE (chmn. com. 1982—, Centennial Medal 1984); mem. IEEE Lasers and Electro-Optics Soc. (pres. 1980), Optical Soc. Am., Am. Phys. Soc., AAAS, Sigma Xi. Office: Hughes Rsch Labs 3011 Malibu Canyon Rd Malibu CA 90265

CHESTER, SHARON ROSE, photographer, natural history educator; b. Chgo., July 12, 1942; d. Joseph Thomas and Lucia Barbara (Urban) C. BA, U. Wis., 1964; postgrad., Coll. San Mateo, 1972-74, U. Calif., Berkeley, 1977; grad., San Francisco State U., 1989. Flight attendant Pan Am. World Airways Inc., San Francisco, 1965; free lance photographer San Mateo, Calif., 1983—; stock photographer Comstock, N.Y.C., 1987—; lectr. Soc. Expdns., Seattle, 1985—. Author (checklist) Birds of the Antarctic and Sub-Antarctic, 1986; translator Field Guide to the Birds of Chile, 1989; photographer mag. cover King Penguin and Chick for Internat. Wildlife mag., 1985, Sierra Club Calendar, 1986; exhibited photos at Royal Geog. Soc., London, 1985. Mem. Audubon Soc., Am. Soc. Mag. Photographers, Calif. Acad. Sci. Home: 724 Laurel Ave #121 San Mateo CA 94401

CHESTERFIELD, RHYDONIA RUTH EPPERSON, financial company executive; b. Dallas, Tex., Apr. 23, 1919; d. Leonard Lee and Sally E. (Stevenson) Griswold; m. Chad Chesterfield, Apr. 21, 1979. BS Southwestern U., 1952; BS, N. Tex. U., 1954, ME, 1956; PhD, Bernardean U., 1974, Calif. Christian U., 1974, LLD (hon.), 1974. Evangelist with Griswold Trio, 1940-58; tchr., counselor Dallas public schs., 1952-58, Los Angeles public schs., 1958-74; pres. Griswold-Epperson Fin. Enterprise, Los Angeles, 1974—; pres. GEC Enterprises, 1979—; guest speaker various schs., chs. and civic orgns. in U.S. and Can. Author: Little Citizens series, Cathedral Films; contbr. articles on bus. to profl. pubs. Fellow Internat. Naturopathic Assn.; mem. Los Angeles Inst. Fine Arts, Assn. of Women in Edn. (hon.), Internat. Bus. and Profl. Women, Calif. C. of C., Los Angeles C. of C., Pi Lambda Theta (hon.), Kappa Delta Pi (hon.). Office: 10790 Wilshire Blvd 202 Los Angeles CA 90024

CHETKOWSKI, RYSZARD JERZY, obstetrician and gynecologist; b. Gliwice, Poland, Mar. 26, 1948; came to U.S., 1965; s. Jozef Konrad and Maria (Gordon) C.; m. Robin Beth Rollens, Mar. 25, 1972; 1 child, Adam

Julian. BA, U. Calif., Berkeley, 1970; MA, U. Calif., 1973; MD, U. Calif., San Francisco, 1978. Diplomate Am. Bd. Ob-Gyn, Nat. Bd. Med. Examiners. Resident in ob-gyn Yale-New Haven Hosp., 1979-82; fellow in reproductive endocrinology UCLA, 1982-84, asst. prof. ob-gyn, 1983-84; dir. in vitro fertilization Alta Bates Hosp., Berkeley, 1984--. Contbr. articles to med. jours. Woodrow Wilson fellow, 1970. Fellow Am. Coll. Ob-Gyn; mem. AM. Fertility Soc., Telluride Assn., Phi Beta Kappa, Alpha Omega Alpha. Office: Alta Bates Hosp 3001 Colby St Berkeley CA 94705

CHETWYND, LIONEL, screenwriter, producer, director; b. London, Jan. 29; s. Peter and Betty (Dion) C.; m. Gloria Carlin, June 2; children: Michael Anthony, Joshua Stephen. BA with honors, Sir George Williams U., Montreal, Que., 1963; B in Civil Law, McGill U., Montreal, Que., 1967; postgrad., Trinity Coll. of Oxford (Eng.) U., 1968. Bar: PQ 1967. With acquisition/distbn. dept. Columbia Pictures, London, 1968-72; screenwriter 1971—; mem. faculty Grad. Film Sch., NYU; lectr. screenwriting Frederick Douglass Ctr., Harlem. Writer: (stage prodns.) Maybe That's Your Problem, 1971, Bleeding Great Orchids, 1971, (feature films) The Apprenticeship of Duddy Kravitz, 1974 (also adaptor, Acad. award nomination 1974), Morning Comes, 1975 (also dir.), Two Solitudes, 1978 (also producer, dir., Grand award Salonika 1979), Quintet, 1978, Hot Touch, 1981 (Genie nomination), The Hanoi Hilton, 1987 (also dir.), (TV films) Johnny, We Hardly Knew Ye, 1976 (also producer, George Washington Honor medal Freedom Found. 1976), It Happened One Christmas, 1977 (citation Am. Women in Film and TV 1979), Goldenrod, 1977 (also producer), A Whale for the Killing, 1980, Miracle on Ice, 1981 (Christopher award 1981), Escape From Iran: The Canadian Caper, 1981, Sadat, 1983 (NAACP Image award 1983), Children in the Crossfire, 1984 (Prix D'Association Mondiale des Amis de L'Enfants 1985, award Monte Carlo Internat. TV Festival 1985), To Heal a Nation, 1988 (also producer, Vietnam Vets. Meml. Fund Patroits award), The American 1776 (official U.S. bicentennial film); co-writer, co-producer (stage prodn.) We The People...200, 1987; exec. producer (TV film) Evil in Clear River, 1988 (Spl. award Am. Jewish Com., Christopher award). Co-chair Arts and Entertainment Commn. for Reagan/Bush, Los Angeles, 1978-80; exec. bd. dirs. Can. Ctr. for Advanced Cinema Studies, Toronto, 1986—; mem. exec. bd. LA chpt. Am. Jew. Com. Served as sgt. Black Watch of Can., 1956-58. Mem. Acad. Motion Picture Arts and Scis., Acad. TV Arts and Scis., Writers Guild Am. (exec. bd. 1972-76, nat. exec. 1975, Writers Guild award 1974), Writers Guild Britain, Can. Bar Assn., Dirs. Guild Am., Broadcast Music, Inc., Assn. Can. TV and Radio Artists. Jewish. Office: care Gang Tyre Raymer 6400 Sunset Blvd Los Angeles CA 90028

CHEUNG, TAK KEE, atmospheric science research scientist; b. Kowloon, Hong Kong, Oct. 29, 1955; came to U.S., 1974; s. Nien-Cho and Wai-Chun (Chan) C. BS, Johns Hopkins U., 1977; MS, Stanford U., 1979, PhD, 1984. Rsch. predoctoral fellow Stanford (Calif.) U., 1978-84; asst. prof. Rutgers U., New Brunswick, N.J., 1984-86; rsch. scientist U. Corp. for Atmospheric Rsch., Boulder, Colo., 1987—; dir. microprocessor lab. mech. engring. dept. Rutgers U., New Brunswick, 1985-86; cons. civil engring. dept. Stanford U., 1985-87. Vol. guide Monterey (Calif.) Aquarium, 1987. Recipient Marx & Moreno fellow Stanford U., 1979-84. Mem. IEEE, ASME, AAAS, Phi Beta Kappa, Sigma Xi, Tau Beta Pi, Eta Kappa Nu. Home: 300 Glenwood Circle #238 Monterey CA 93940 Office: UCAR/NEPRF Monterey CA 93943

CHEW, DENNIS W., labor relations and fund raising consultant; b. Hong Kong, Jan. 1, 1941; s. Stephen and Wai (Mui) C.; B.S., U. Redlands, 1963; postgrad. U. Calif.-Riverside, 1965; m. Linda Lee Olson, July 23, 1965; children—Stephanie L.S., Erica L.S. Tchr., Riverside (Calif.) Unified Sch. Dist., 1965-71; asst. exec. dir. Sacramento City Tchrs. Assn., 1971-73; negotiations cons. Calif. Tchrs. Assn., Burlingame, 1973-77, asst. exec. dir., 1977-78, assoc. exec. dir., 1979-82, cons., 1982—; instr. U. Calif. Extension. Bd. dirs. Redlands Winter Concerts, 1969-71, San Francisco council Girl Scouts Am., 1986—. Mem. AAAS, Am. Arbitration Assn., Nat. Soc. Fund Raising Execs. Office: Chew Assocs 3211 Crow Canyon Pl Ste A-29 San Ramon CA 94583

CHEW, JAMES SOONG BILL, rocket propulsion engineer, automobile consultant; b. Lancaster, Calif., Nov. 21, 1961; s. Thomas Ju Chu and Shirley Hang Ying (Yu) C.; m. Cynthia Jeanne Bixby, Dec. 29, 1984. AS, Antelope Valley Coll., 1982, AA, 1983; BS, Calif. State Poly U., 1984; postgrad., U. Wash., 1985. Community coll. tchng. credential, Calif. Student engr. USAF Rocket Propulsion Lab., Edwards AFB, Calif., 1980-84; lab. asst. Antelope Valley Coll., Lancaster, 1980-81, instr. engring., 1988--; tchng. asst. Calif. State Poly. U., Pomona, 1981-84; sr. research engr. Boeing Aerospace Co., Seattle, 1984-86; sr. propulsion engr. Sparta, Inc., Edwards AFB, 1986-88; program mgr. USAF Astronautics Lab., 1988--; product cons. Chrysler Motors Corp., Highland Park, Mich., 1986--. Contbr. articles to tech. publs. Mm. ASME, Soc. Automotive Engrs. Republican. Home: 44835 N Caboose Dr Lancaster CA 93535 Office: USAF Astronautics Lab AFAL/RKA Edwards AFB CA 93523-5000

CHEW, KA-WING, dentist; b. Hong Kong, Mar. 16, 1957; s. Pui-Wan and Shun-Chuk (Chan) C. AS, City Coll. of San Francisco, 1978; BS, San Francisco State U., 1981; DDS, Northwestern U., 1985. Assoc. dentist Stanley Lee, DDS, San Jose, Calif., 1986-87; staff dentist N.E. Med. Svc., San Francisco, 1987—. Mem. ADA, Calif. Dental Assn., San Francisco Dental Soc., Acad. Gen. Dentistry, full Gospel Businessmen's Fellowship Internat., Assemblies of God Chinese Christian Ctr. Mem. Assemblies of God Ch. Home: 861 1/2 Union St San Francisco CA 94133

CHEW, KENNETH WARREN, manufacturing executive; b. L.A., May 7, 1939; s. Paul Cedric and Anne Martha Ida (Wichers) C.; m. Elaine Jeanette Michael, June 10, 1961; children: Lynn Anne, Debra Jean, Paul Kenneth. AA, L.A. Pierce Coll., 1966; BA, Calif. State U., Northridge, 1971; MA, Calif. State U., 1987. Mgr. pubs. and illustrations Rocketdyne div. of Rockwell Internat., Canoga Park, Calif., 1978-81; mgr. documentation repro services Rocketdyne div. of Rockwell Internat., Canoga Park, 1981-86, project coordinator engring. ops., 1987—. Exec. adviser Jr. Achievement, North Hollywood, Calif., 1978-79, coordinator, 1979-81; sec., team mgr. Reseda (Calif.) Baseball Assn., 1975-83. Petty officer USN, 1956-62. Mem. Nat. Mgmt. Assn. Republican. Home: 19754 Bassett St Canoga Park CA 91306 Office: Rockwell Internat Rocketdyne Div 6633 Canoga Ave Canoga Park CA 91303

CHEW, LINDA LEE, fund raising and management consultant, public relations executive; b. Riverside, Calif., Mar. 3, 1941; d. LeRoy S. and Grace (Ham) Olson; m. Dennis W. Chew, July 23, 1965; children—Stephanie, Erica. B.Mus., U. Redlands, 1962. Cert. fund raising exec. Dir. pub. events U. Redlands (Calif.), 1962-69; dir. fin. and communications San Gorgonio council Girl Scouts U.S., Colton, Calif., 1969-71; exec. dir. United Cerebral Palsy Assn. Sacramento-Yolo Counties, 1972-73; fin. devel. dir. San Francisco Bay council Girl Scouts U.S.A., 1973-76; chief devel. and pub. info. East Bay Regional Park Dist., Oakland, Calif., 1976-86; cons. Chew & Assocs., San Ramon, Calif., 1986—. Bd. dirs. Planned Parenthood Contra Costa County, 1980-82, San Ramon Valley Edn. Found., 1984-88; Calif. Conservation Corps Bay Area Ctr. Adv. Bd., 1988—. Mem. Nat. Soc. Fund Raising Execs. (nat. bd. dirs. 1981—, nat. vice chmn. 1982-84, pres. Golden Gate chpt. 1979-80, bd. dirs. 1987—, Abel Hanson Meml. award 1977, Outstanding Fund Raising Exec. 1988), Pub. Relations Soc. Am., Calif. Park and Recreation Soc., AAUW (pres. Redlands br. 1968-69), Am. Guild Organists (dean Riverside-San Bernardino chpt. 1969-71), Nat. Assn. Hosp. Devel., 1986—. Office: 3211 Crow Canyon Pl Ste A-29 San Ramon CA 94583

CHIANG, ALBERT CHIN-LIANG, electrical engineer; b. Putai, Taiwan, Jan. 25, 1937; s. San Chi and Chiu (Hsu) C.; BS in Elec. Engring., Nat. Taiwan U., 1959; MS in Elec. Engring., Chiaotung U., Taiwan, 1963; PhD, U. So. Calif., 1968; m. Steffie F.L. Huang, Dec. 24, 1966; children: Margaret, Stacy, Kathy, George. Came to U.S., 1963, naturalized, 1973. Research asst. U. So. Calif., Los Angeles, 1963-68; engr. specialist Litton Industries, Woodland Hills, Calif., 1968-70; dir. internat. sales Macrodata Co., Woodland Hills, Calif., 1970-77; pres. Tritek Internat. Co., Northridge, Calif., 1977—. Mem. IEEE, Sigma Xi, Eta Kappa Nu. Home: 24132 Lupin Hill Rd Hidden Hills CA 91302 Office: Tritek Internat Co 8345 Reseda Blvd Northridge CA 91324

CHIANG, MARTIN KUANG PING, computer and electronic engineer, real estate investor; b. Peiping, Republic of China, Nov. 22, 1933; came to U.S., 1951; s. S.T. and Shu Chun (Chen) C.; m. Jane Chang, June 18, 1955; children: Lucy Sung, Virginia Huang, Mason. BS in Civil and Elec. Engring., U. Wash., 1964; MSEE, Pratt Inst., 1968; advanced engr.'s degree, U. So. Calif., 1975; PhD in Elec. Engring., Pacific W. U., 1985. Design engr. Boeing Co., Renton, Wash., 1958-65; cons. engr. Lockheed Aircraft Co., Marietta, Ga., 1965-66; instr. Pratt Inst., Bklyn, 1966-67; sr. engr. Grumman Aircraft Corp., Long Island, N.Y., 1967-69; sr. staff engr. Hughes Aircraft, L.A., 1969—. Mem. Rep. Senatorial Inner Circle, Washington, D.C., 1985—. Mem. IEEE, Apt. Owners Assn., Hughes Fullerton Mgmt. Club, Hughes Mgmt. Club. Home: 20 Country Ln Rolling Hills Estate CA 90274 Office: Hughes Aircraft Co PO Box 92426 R1 6A27 Los Angeles CA 90009

CHIANG, YAWEN LEE, research molecular biologist; b. Taipei, Taiwan, Republic of China, May 26, 1950; came to U.S., 1971; d. Stanley Y.C. and Chieh Fang (Ou) L.; m. Nelson N.C. Chiang, Aug. 10, 1972; children: David, Andrew. BS, U. Md., 1974; MS, George Washington U., 1979, PhD, 1983; MA, Cen. Mich. U., 1981. Clin. chemist, med. technologist Holy Cross Hosp., Silver Spring, Md., 1974-84; chemist NIH/George Washington U., Bethesda, Md., 1978-83; chemist, postdoctoral fellow Uniform Service Univ. of Health Scis., Bethesda, 1983-84; assoc. scientist Cetus, Palo Alto, Calif., 1984-88; scientist Genetic Therapy, Inc., Gaithersburg, Md., 1988—. Mem. AAAS, Am. Soc. Med. Technologists, Am. Soc. Clin. Pathologists, Clin. Lab. Technologists Calif., Am. Soc. Clin. Chemistry, Am. Soc. Microbiologists, N.Y. Acad. Sci., Columbian Women Assn. (corr. sec. 1983-85).

CHIAVERINI, JOHN EDWARD, construction company executive; b. Providence, Feb. 6, 1924; s. John and Sadie (Ginsberg) C.; m. Cecile Corey, Mar. 31, 1951; children—Caryl Marie, John Michael. Cert. advanced san. engring. U. Ill., 1945; B.S., U. R.I., 1947. Registered profl. engr., Mass., R.I. Project engr. Perini Corp., Hartford, Conn., 1950-51, project mgr., 1951-55, asst. project mgr., Pitts. and Que., 1955-61, v.p., Framingham, Mass., 1965-84, sr. v.p., San Francisco, 1984—; pres., dir. Compania Perini S.A., Colombia, 1961—; v.p., exec. mgr. Perini Yuba Assocs., Marysville, Calif., 1966-70, v.p. Western ops., 1970-78, 79-84, group v.p., 1978-79; sr. v.p. spl. projects Perini Corp., 1984—; dir. Perini Corp.; mem. U.S. com. Internat. Commn. on Large Dams. Served to 2d lt. USAAF, 1944-46. Recipient Golden Beaver award, 1989. Fellow ASCE; mem. Nat. Soc. Profl. Engrs., Calif. Soc. Profl. Engrs., Soc. Am. Mil. Engrs. (bd. dirs.), Beavers (bd. dirs.), Moles, Commonwealth Club of Calif. Democrat. Roman Catholic. Lodges: K.C., Rotary. Home: 37 Dutch Valley Ln San Anselmo CA 94960 Office: Perini Corp 75 Broadway San Francisco CA 94111

CHICHESTER, SUSAN MARY, counselor; b. Racine, Wis., Oct. 21, 1936; d. Chester Thomas and Mercedes Margaret (Strewler) Organ; m. Norman James Chichester, Aug. 7, 1983. BS, U. Colo., 1965, MA, 1968. Cert. nat. bd. for cert. counselors. Tchr. Jefferson (Colo.) County Pub. Schs., 1965-68; sch. counselor Alameda (Colo.) Jr. High Sch., 1968-87, Arvada (Colo.) Jr. High Sch., 1987—. Sr. v.p. Lakewood (Colo.) on Parade Com., 1981-82; chmn. music scholar exch. com. Lakewood Sister City Program, 1985—; coord. radio communication Mile High chpt. ARC, Denver, 1988; committeewoman Lakewood Rep. Com., 1972-74, 88; unit chmn. LWV, 1977-78; pres. UNESCO, Colo. 1982-83. Recipient Disting. Tchr. award Jefferson County chpt., 1985, Outstanding Achievement award Lakewood Sister City, 1986, Humanities award Jefferson County Pub. Schs., 1989. Mem. NEA, Colo. Edn. Assn., Jefferson County Edn. Assn., AAUW (telephone chmn. Lakewood br. 1987-88, roster editor 1988, chmn. home fair workers, 1987, fin. chmn. 1988, others), UN Assn. U.S. (Disting. Svc. award 1978), Denver Radio Club (program chmn. 1987-88), Toastmasters (membership chmn. 1988, area gov. 1989, Competent Toastmaster award 1987), Alpha Delta Kappa (pres. Psi chpt. 1983-84). Episcopalian. Home: 5822 W Atlantic Pl Lakewood CO 80227 Office: Arvada Jr High Sch 5751 Balsam St Arvada CO 80002

CHIEFFALO, MARIO VICTOR (VIC CHIEFFALO), advertising executive; b. Italy, Aug. 24, 1934; came to U.S. from Uruguay, 1948, naturalized 1954; s. Rosario and Teresa C.; m. Mary Ruth Rector, June 3, 1958; 1 child, Belinda. BS, La. State U., 1961; B in Fgn. Trade, Am. Inst. Fgn. Trade, 1962. Mgr. export sales Cotton Producers Assn., Atlanta, 1963-66; mem. advt. sales staff This Week mag., N.Y.C., 1966-69, Am. Home mag., N.Y.C., 1969-71, Reader's Digest, N.Y.C., 1971-74; mgr. advt. Iberian edit., Spain, 1974; mgr. west coast advt. sales So. Living mag., San Francisco, 1975—. Served to petty officer U.S. Navy, 1955-58. Mem. San Francisco Mag. Reps., Moraga Country Club. Office: 90 New Montgomery #905 San Francisco CA 94105

CHIEN, KUEI-RU, physicist; b. Nantung, Kiangsu, China, Dec. 14, 1945; came to U.S. 1969; s. Hun-Wen and Jang-Jen (Tsao) C.; m. Ming-Hsia Lee, July 25, 1983. BS, Nat. Taiwan Normal U., 1968; PhD, MIT, 1973. Research assoc. MIT, Cambridge, Mass., 1973-74, Cornell U., Ithaca, N.Y., 1974-76; with TRW, Redondo Beach, Calif., 1976-83; sr. staff engr. Hughes Aircraft, El Segundo, Calif., 1983-85; sect. head Hughes Aircraft, 1985-87, sr. scientist, 1987-88, dept. mgr., 1988—. Contbr. articles to profl. jours.; inventor in field. Mem. Optical Soc. Am., Sigma Xi. Home: 17310 S Eveningstar Ave Cerritos CA 90701 Office: Hughes Aircraft 2000 El Segundo Blvd El Segundo CA 90245

CHIEN, NORBERT WEI, electronic design automation company executive; b. Taipei, Taiwan, Apr. 11, 1955; came to U.S., 1984; s. Shiow Bin and Hsing Chu (Li) C.; m. Christina Pong, Feb. 9, 1980; children: Lucy, William. BSEE, State U. Campinas, 1979. Design engr. R&D Telebras, Campinas, Sao Paolo, Brazil, 1979-80, testability engr., 1980-81, simulation engr., 1981-82, design automation staff mem., 1981-84; project mgr. Control Data Corp., Bloomington, Minn., 1984-86, Mentor Graphics Corp., Beaverton, Oreg., 1987; design automation mgr. Floating Point Systems, Beaverton, 1986-87, project mgr. electronic design automation, 1987—; cons. Control Data Corp Brazil, Sao Paulo, 1983-84. Author ednl. video. Creator Tech. Applied to Me (T.E.A.M.) contest Robotices Applied to Handicap, 1989; judge Saturday sci. fair Oreg. Mus. of Sci. and Industry, 1989. Recipient Jack Chase award , 1987. Mem. IEEE, Northcon (bd. dirs. 1987, chmn. exhibit 1987). Home: 15005 SW 105th Ct Beaverton OR 97007 Office: Mentor Graphics Corp 8500 SW Creekside Pl Beaverton OR 97005

CHIEN, RING-LING, physical chemistry research scientist; b. Kaohsiung, Republic of China, May 20, 1952; came to U.S., 1976; s. Chiao-Chung and Shi-Wei (Hwuang) C.; m. Jin Tsao, Oct. 10, 1981; children: Jessie, Victoria. BS, Nat. Taiwan U., 1974; MS, U. Chgo., 1977, PhD, 1983. Research assoc. Princeton (N.J.) U., 1983-86; engr. Varian Assocs., Inc., Palo Alto, Calif., 1986--. Contbr. articles to profl. jours. Mem. Am. Chem. Soc., Am. Phys. Soc., AAAS. Home: 422 W Campbell Ave Campbell CA 95008 Office: Varian Assocs 6ll Hansen Way K-3l2 Palo Alto CA 94303

CHIGOS, DAVID, university president; b. Scranton, Pa., Mar. 29, 1933; s. Andrew D. and Emma (Kossmann) C.; m. Ruth Elizabeth Chamberlain, May 22, 1954; children: Catherine Mary Chigos Bradley, Carla Jane Chigos Sotelo, Lisa Anne, Laura Elizabeth. B.S. in Chemistry, W.Va. Wesleyan Coll., 1954, LL.D., 1980; M.A. in Counseling and Guidance, U.S. Internat. U., 1968, Ph.D., 1972. Teaching asst. U. Tex., 1954-56; commd. ensign USN, 1957, advanced through grades to capt., 1983; indsl. relations Convair Aerospace div. Gen. Dynamics Corp., San Diego, 1967-70; faculty U. Calif. Extension at San Diego, 1967-83, San Diego State U. Extension, 1968-71, San Diego Evening Coll., 1967-71; pres. Nat. U., San Diego, 1971—. Bd. dirs. Nat. Def. U. Found., San Diego council Boy Scouts Am. Recipient Citizenship of Yr. award, 1988. Mem. Nat. Mgmt. Assn. (exec. adv. com., Golden Knight award 1979), Convair Nat. Mgmt. Assn. (hon. life), Am. Assn. of Presidents of Ind. Colls. and Univs., Naval Res. Assn. (life), Navy League U.S. (life, nat. dir.; Scroll of Honor 1979), Res. Officers Assn. (life, mem. pvt. sector council Washington). Clubs: San Diego Yacht, Kona Kai, University (San Diego), Army-Navy, Capitol Hill (Washington). Office: Nat U University Park San Diego CA 92108-4194

CHIKALLA, THOMAS DAVID, science facility administrator; b. Milw., Sept. 9, 1935; s. Paul Joseph and Margaret Ann (Dittrich) C.; m. Ruth Janet Laun, June 20, 1960; children: Paul, Mark, Karyn. BS in Metallurgy, U. Wis., 1957, PhD in Metallurgy, 1966; MS in Metallurgy, U. Idaho, 1960. Research scientist Gen. Electric Co., Richland, Wash., 1957-62; sr. research scientist Battelle Pacific N.W. Labs., Richland, 1964-72, sect. mgr., 1972-80, programs mgr., 1980-83, dept. mgr., 1983-86, assoc. dir., 1986—; tchr. U. Wis., Madison, 1962-64. Contbr. articles to profl. jours. Fellow AEC. Fellow Am. Ceramic Soc. (counselor 1974-80); mem. AAAS, Am. Nuclear Soc., Sigma Xi. Republican. Roman Catholic. Clubs: Desert Ski (pres. 1958-59), Alpine. Home: 2108 Harris Richland WA 99352 Office: Battelle Pacific NW Labs Battelle Blvd Richland WA 99352

CHILD, GARY RICHARD, photographer; b. Portland, Oreg., Sept. 8, 1935; s. Richard P. and Eleanor J. (Johnson) C.; m. Darlene F. Gottfried, Apr. 8, 1956; children: David, Richard, Sarah, Lisa. Student, Portland State U., 1955, Calif. Coast U., 1978. Cert. profl. photographer. Mgr. Bruno Studies, Vancouver & Aberdeen, 1957-59; gen. mgr. Yuen Lui Studios, Portland, 1959-64; pres. G.R. Child, Inc. Child's Photographers, Redmond and Bend, Oreg., 1964—. Named Outstanding Club Pres. Kiwanis Club, 1981; recipient Meritorious Service Citation Oreg. State U., 1968. Mem. profl. Photographers Oreg. (dir. 1966-88, pres. 1979-80), Profl. Photographers Am. Inc., Redmond C. of C. Republican. Club: Bend Golf and Country. Lodges: Rotary, Elks. Home: 20435 Illahee Dr Bend OR 97702 Office: GR Child Inc Child's Photographers 1554 NE 4th St Bend OR 97701

CHILDRESS, DENNIS ROBERT, municipal protective service administrator; b. South Gate, Calif., Oct. 3, 1945; s. Robert Wier and Janice Alicia (Sayles) C.; m. Suzanne Dietrich, Dec. 12, 1970; children: Bryan, Scott, Lara. AA in Fire Sci., Long Beach City Coll., 1975; BS in Indsl. Tech.-Fire Protection Adminstrn., Calif. State U., Los Angeles, 1978. Cert. fire officer, tchr., Calif. Firefighter Lynwood (Calif.) Fire Dept., 1967-76, apparatus engr., 1976-79, fire capt., battalion chief, 1970-85; dir. tng. and safety Buena Park (Calif.) Fire Dept., 1985—; instr. Rancho Community Coll., Santa Ana, Calif., 1981—, State Fire Marshal, Santa Ana, 1984—; cons., 1979—. Author articles in field. Coach Am. Youth Soccer Orgn., Orange County, 1979-85; chmn. Orange County Tng. and Edn. Master Plan com., 1986—, Orange County Mass Casualty Drill com.; instr. CPR Orange County ARC; developer, coordinator Smoke Detector Program for Sr. Citizens, Lynwood, Fire Flow Research Program, Lynwood. Mem. So. Calif. Tng. Officers Assn. (dir. Div. II), Orange County Fire Chief's Tng. Officers Assn. (v.p., bd. dirs. 1987—, pres. 1989), Calif. State Firefighter's Assn., Safety Standard Com. (vice-chmn.), Lynwood Firefighters Assn. (bd.dirs. 1979-82, v.p. 1980, pres. and chmn. bd. dirs. 1981), Epsilon Pi Tau. Republican. Office: Buena Park Fire Dept 8081 Western Ave Buena Park CA 90622

CHILDRESS, PHYLLIS ANN, construction executive; b. Fort Wayne, Ind., Feb. 28, 1937; d. Paschal J. and Pietrina M. (Ceccanese) Pallone; m. Kelly W. Childress, Aug. 24, 1973; children: Patricia, William, Jeffrey. BS in Commerce, Internat. Coll., 1955; postgrad. Pima Community Coll., 1978-80. Cert. constrn. mgr., 1987. Sec. to v.p. trust dept. Lincoln Nat. Bank, Ft. Wayne, Ind., 1955-57; sec. to pres. adminstrn. dept. Internat. Coll., Ft. Wayne, 1957-60; dir., sec. Lightning Homes, Inc., Homebuilders and Developers, Ft. Wayne, 1960-63; sec. to v.p., fin. dept., office mgr. fleet maintenance dept. N.Am. Van Lines, Inc., Ft. Wayne, 1963-71; asst. mktg. dir. ITT Electro-Optical Products, Ft. Wayne, 1972-76; asst. v.p. Empire West Builders, Inc., Tucson, 1977-80; staff constrn. mgmt. Akins Co., Tucson, 1981-82; constrn. mgr. Archtl. Div., City of Tucson, 1982-85; pres. Construction Techniques, Inc., Tucson, 1985—. Block grants advisor Tucson Community Devel. Commn., 1983—. Recipient Appreciation Cert. Nat. Assn. Women Constrn., 1978; named Sec. of Yr. Tawasi chpt. Nat. Secs. Assn., 1967; recipient plaque for outstanding service, 1977. Mem. Cholla Bus. and Profl. Women (past chpt. pres., Woman of Yr. 1986), Nat. Assn. Women Constrn. (past pres.). Democrat. Baptist. Contbr. articles to various publs. Home and Office: 2833 N Laurel Ave Tucson AZ 85712

CHILDS, JOHN DAVID, computer hardware and services company executive; b. Washington, Apr. 26, 1939; s. Edwin Carlton and Catherine Dorothea (Angerman) C.; m. Margaret Rae Olsen, Mar. 4, 1966 (div.); 1 child, John-David. Student Principia Coll., 1957-58, 59-60; BA, Am. U., 1963. Jr. adminstr. Page Communications, Washington, 1962-65; account rep. Friden Inc., Washington, 1965-67; Western sales dir. Data Inc., Arlington, Va., 1967-70; v.p. mktg. Rayda, Inc., Los Angeles, 1970-73, pres., 1973-76, chmn. bd., 1976-84; sr. v.p. sales Exec. Bus. Systems, Encino, Calif., 1981—; sr. assoc. World Trade Assocs., Inc., 1976—. Pres. Coll. Youth for Nixon-Lodge, 1959-60, dir. state fedn.; mem. OHSHA policy formulation com. Dept. Labor, 1967. Served with USAFR, 1960-66. Mem. Assn. Data Ctr. Owners and Mgrs. (chmn. privacy com. 1975, sec. 1972-74, v.p. 1974). Democrat. Christian Scientist. Office: 15760 Ventura Blvd #700 Encino CA 91436

CHILSON, OLIN HATFIELD, U.S. judge; b. Pueblo, Colo., Nov. 22, 1903; s. Leonard and Annie (Mills) C.; m. Marian Cole, Aug. 18, 1929; 1 son, John Hatfield. LL.B., U. Colo., 1927. Bar: Colo. bar 1927. Practiced in Greeley, Loveland and Denver, 1927-36; city atty. Estes Park, 1928-56, Loveland, 1931-36; dist. atty. 8th Jud. Dist. Colo., 1940-48; mem. firm Grant, Shafroth, Tell, Chilson & McHendrie, Denver, 1959-60; U.S. dist. judge Colo. Denver, 1960—; Mem. Colo. Bd. Law Examiners, 1951-54. Organizer, sec. 2Big Thompson Soil Conservation Dist., 1940-47; asst. sec. pub. land mgmt. Dept. Interior, 1956-57, under sec. interior, 1957- 58; dir. No. Colo. Water Conservancy Dist., 1951-55; legal cons. Colo. Water Conservation Bd., 1954-56; mem. Loveland Sch. Bd., 1945-55; Trustee Boettcher Found. Mem. ABA, Colo. Bar Assn. (past pres.), Larimer County Bar Assn. (past pres.), Alumni Assn. U. Colo. (past pres.), Phi Alpha Delta, Alpha Tau Omega. Methodist. Clubs: Mason, Rotarian, Denver Country. Home: 2101 S Garfield Ave Apt 424 Loveland CO 80537 Office: US Dist Ct US Courthouse Rm C-566 1929 Stout St Denver CO 80294

CHIMY, JEROME ISIDORE, bishop; b. Radway, Alta., Can., Mar. 12, 1919; s. Stanley and Anna (Yahnij) C. J.C.D., Lateran U., Rome, 1966. Ordained priest Ukrainian Cath. Ch., 1944; consecrated bishop 1974; consultor to Provincial Superior, 1958-61; sec. to Superior Gen. of Basilian Order, Rome, 1961-63; consultor Superior Gen. of Basilian Order, 1963-74; rector St. Josaphat Ukrainian Pontifical Coll., Rome, 1966-74; former consultor to Sacred Congregation for Eastern Chs.; former commissario for matrimonial cases at Sacred Congregation for Doctrine of Faith; bishop of New Westminster B.C., Can., 1974—; consultor to Pontifical Comm. for Revision Oriental Canon Law. Author: De Figura Luridica Archiepiscopi Maioris in Iure Canonico Orientali Vigenti, 1968. Home and Office: 502 5th Ave, New Westminster, BC Canada V3L 1S2 *

CHIN, ANGELA MERICI AUDREY, dentist; b. Mandeville, Jamaica, W.I.; came to U.S., 1973; d. Lester Aubrey Donald and Jean Evelyn (Chung) C. BS in Biology, Ga. Tech. U., 1977; DMD magna cum laude, Tufts U., 1981. Resident in gen. dentistry Queen's Med. Ctr., Honolulu, 1981-82; pvt. practice Aiea, Hawaii, 1982—. Fellow Acad. Gen. Dentistry (sec. Hawaii chpt. 1984-85); mem. Hawaii Dental Assn. (mem. speakers bur., numerous coms.), Honolulu County Dental Soc., ADA, Am. Assn. Women Dentists, South Shore Dental Soc., Omicron Kappa Upsilon, Omicron Delta Kappa. Office: Ste 103 98-1247 Kaahumanu St Aiea HI 96701

CHIN, ARK GEOW, civil engineering executive; b. Toishan, Republic of China, Feb. 9, 1924; came to U.S., 1934; s. Jing Teung and Yu Sung (Lim) C.; m. Winifred Chung, May 6, 1948; children: Candace, Curtis, Patrick, Phoebe, Colin, Wilson. BS in Civil Engring., U. Wash., 1950, MS in Civil Engring., 1952. Registered profl. engr., Wash., Oreg., Alaska, Mich., Wis., Iowa, Ill., N.Y., S.C., Kans. Design engr. Richardson Assocs., 1951-52; design engr. Carey & Kramer, Seattle, 1953-61, ptnr., 1961-72; pres. Kramer, Chin & Mayo, Inc., Seattle, 1972—; vis. com. mem. U. Wash. Coll. Engring., 1976-79. Contbr. articles to profl. jours. Mem. Am. Cons. Engrs. Coun.'s Minority Affairs Com., 1979-81; chmn. bd. trustee Western Washington U. Sft. U.S. Army, 1943-46. Named Engr. of Yr. Seattle Chinese Engrs. Soc., 1984; selected Engr. of Yr. Consulting Engrs. Coun. of Washington. Fellow Am. Concrete Inst.; mem. ASCE, Nat. Panel Am. Arbitration Assn., Structural Engrs. Assoc. Wash., Pre-Stress Concrete Inst., Am. Pub. Works. Assn., Cons. Engring. Coun. Wash. (pres. 1982-83), Gee How Oak Tin Assn. (pres. 1960—), Wash. Athletic Club. Office: Kramer Chin May Inc 1917 First Ave Seattle WA 98101

CHIN, SUE S. (SUCHIN CHIN), artist, photographer, community affairs activist; b. San Francisco; d. William W. and Soo-Up (Swebe) Chin; grad. Calif. Coll. Art, Mpls. Art Inst., (scholar) Schaeffer Design Ctr.; student Yasuo Kuniyoshi, Louis Hamon, Rico LeBrun. Photojournalist, All Together Now show, 1973, East-West News, Third World Newscasting, 1975-78, KNBC Sunday Show, Los Angeles, 1975, 76, Live on 4, 1981, Bay Area Scene, 1981; graphics printer, exhbns. include Kaiser Ctr., Zellerbach Plaza, Chinese Culture Ctr. Galleries, Capricorn Asunder Art Commn. Gallery (all San Francisco), Newspace Galleries, New Coll. of Calif., Los Angeles County Mus. Art, Peace Plaza Japan Ctr., Calif. Mus. Sci. and Industry, Lucien Labaudt Gallery, Salon de Medici, Madrid, Salon Renacimento, Madrid, Sacramento State Fair, AFL-CIO Labor Studies Ctr., Washington, Asian Women Artists (1st prize for conceptual painting, 1st prize photography), 1978, SFWA gallery-imprint show, 1989; represented in permanent collections Los Angeles County Fedn. Labor, Calif. Mus. Sci. and Industry, AFL-CIO Labor Studies Ctr., Australian Trades Council, Hazeland and Co., also pvt. collections. Del. nat., state convs. Nat. Women's Polit. Caucus, 1977-83, San Francisco chpt. affirmative action chairperson, 1978-82, nat. conv. del., 1978-81, Calif. del., 1976-81. Recipient Honorarium AFL-CIO Labor Studies Ctr., Washington, 1975-76; award Centro Studi Ricerche delle Nazioni, Italy, 1985; bd. advisors Psycho Neurology Found. Bicentennial award Los Angeles County Mus. Art, 1976, 77, 78. Mem. Asian Women Artists (founding v.p., award 1978-79, 1st award in photography of Orient 1978-79), Calif. Chinese Artists (sec.-treas. 1978-81), Japanese Am. Art Council (chairperson 1978-84, dir.), San Francisco Women Artists, San Francisco Graphics Guild, Pacific/Asian Women Coalition Bay Area, Chinatown Council Performing and Visual Arts. Chmn., Full Moon Products; pres., dir. Aumni Oracle Inc. Featured in Calif. Living Mag., 1981. Address: PO Box 1415 San Francisco CA 94101

CHIN, SUSAN WONG, educator; b. Stockton, Calif., Mar. 14, 1946; d. Wee Poy and Yik Gee (Fong) Wong; m. Harvey Victor Chin, Sept. 8, 1968; children: Christina, Cherilyn. BA, U. Calif., Berkeley, 1968; secondary credential, U. San Francisco, 1970; cert. data processing, Merritt Coll., 1984; MBA with distinction, Nat. U., 1988. Office mgr. J.L. Burke, CPA, Oakland, Calif., 1983; instr. Coll. Alameda (Calif), 1984—; faculty senator Coll. Alameda Faculty Senate, 1987—. Sch. vol. Joaquin Miller Sch., Oakland, 1971-87. Recipient Cert. of Leadership, Nat. U., Oakland, 1987. Mem. Assn. Computing Machinery, East Bay Users Group, Peralta Fedn. of Tchrs. Democrat. Methodist. Office: Coll Alameda 555 Atlantic Ave Alameda CA 94501

CHIN, WILLIAM MOON, JR., engineering specialist; b. Oakland, Calif., May 21, 1953; s. Bill H. Fong and Mee (Yee) Chin; m. Anita Kay Hernandez, June 23, 1984. BSME, U. Nev., 1975. Cert. reliability engr. Mech. engr. U.S. Army Mgmt. Engr. Tng. Act, Rock Island, Ill., 1976-77, U.S. Army Aviation Systems Command, St. Louis, 1977; gen. engr. Fleet Analysis Ctr., USN, Corona, Calif., 1977-80; research and design engr. Brunswick Def. Div., Costa Mesa, Calif., 1980-83; sr. engr. Gen. Dynamics, Pomona, Calif., 1983-85; design specialist Gen. Dynamics, Pomona, 1985-88; engring. specialist Gen. Dynamics Valley Systems Div., Rancho Cucamonga, Calif., 1988—. Mem. Am. Soc. Quality Control, Nat. Mgmt. Assn., Sports Car Club Am. (pres. Denver 1977—). Office: Gen Dynamics Valley Systems 10900 E 4th St MZ801-11 Rancho Cucamonga CA 91730

CHING, ERIC SAN HING, health care and insurance administrator; b. Honolulu, Aug. 13, 1951; s. Anthony D.K. and Amy K.C. (Chong) C. BS, Stanford U., 1973, MS, MBA, 1977. Fin. analyst Mid Peninsula Health Service, Palo Alto, Calif., 1977; acting dep. exec. dir. Santa Clara County Health Systems Agy., San Jose, Calif., 1977-78; program officer Henry J. Kaiser Family Found., Menlo Park, Calif., 1978-84; dir. strategic planning Lifeguard Health Maintenance Orgn., Campbell, Calif., 1984—; v.p. strategic planning and dir. ops. Found. Life Ins. Co., Milpitas, Calif., 1986—; cons. El Camino Dialysis Service, Mountain View, Calif., 1984. Mem. vol. staff Los Angeles Olympic Organizing Com., 1984; mem. panel United Way of Santa Clara County, 1985, panel chmn., 1986-87, mem. com. priorities and community problem solving, 1987—, Project Blueprint, 1988—. Mem. Stanford U. Alumni Assn., Stanford U. Bus. Sch. Alumni Assn., Stanford U. Swordmasters (pres. 1980—). Office: Lifeguard HMO Inc 1851 McCarthy Blvd Milpitas CA 95035

CHINN, ROGER, architect; b. Isleton, Calif., May 22, 1933; s. Gee and Bessie (Toy) C.; m. Rachel Han, Feb. 10, 1961; children: Annette Diane, Robert Michael. AB in Architecture, U. Calif., Berkeley, 1957. Registered architect, Calif. Pvt. practice San Francisco, 1968-72, 77—; gen. ptnr. Hertzka & Knowles Architects, San Francisco, 1972-77. Mayor Foster City, Calif., 1981, 84-85. With U.S. Army 1958-60. Mem. AIA, Lions (dist. gov. 1983-84, Lion of Yr. 1970), Chinese Club (pres. 1974-75). Republican. Methodist. Home: 833 Constitution Dr Foster City CA 94404 Office: Roger Chinn Architect AIA 1485 Bayshore Blvd San Francisco CA 94124

CHINN, THOMAS WAYNE, typographic company executive; b. Marshfield, Oreg., July 28, 1909; s. Wing Chin and Shee Lee; student U. Calif.; m. Daisy Lorraine Wong, June 8, 1930; 1 son, Walter Wayne Chinn. Propr., Chinn Linotype Co., San Francisco, 1937-42; owner Calif. Typesetting Co., 1949-56; typographer, 1956-71; pres. Gollan Typography, Inc., San Francisco, 1971-80. Mem. San Francisco Mayor's Citizens Com., 1958—; mem. San Francisco Twin Bicentennial History Com., 1974-76; mem. Nat. Am. Revolution Bicentennial Advisory Com. on Racial, Ethnic and Native Am. Participation, 1974-76; governing mem. San Francisco YMCA, 1972-82; founding pres., Chinese Hist. Soc. Am., San Francisco, 1963, pres., 1964-66, 75; foreman Civil Grand Jury, City and County of San Francisco, 1983-84. Author: Bridging the Pacific: San Francisco Chinatown and Its People, 1989. Recipient awards of merit Conf. Calif. Socs., 1976, 81, Am. Assn. State and Local History, 1976. Mem. Calif. Hist. Soc. (award of merit 1970, trustee 1981-83), E Clampus Vitus, The Westerners. Clubs: Masons (32 deg.) (past master lodge), Shriners. Editor: A History of the Chinese in California-A Syllabus, 1969; editor, co-pub. 1st newspaper in English for Chinese-Ams., 1935-37; contbr. articles to hist. jours.

CHIOLIS, MARK JOSEPH, television producer, video consultant; b. Walnut Creek, Calif., Dec. 29, 1959; s. Richard Spiro and Muriel Marie (Kottinger) C. Student aeronautics, Sacramento Community Coll., 1980-82; student, American River Coll., 1982. With on air ops. Sta. KRBK-TV, Sacramento, 1978-81, trainer on air ops., ops. crew chief, 1981-84, producer, dir., ops. crew chief, 1984-87, production mgr., producer, dir. spl. programs, comml. productions, 1987—; with on air ops. Sta. KVIE-TV, Sacramento, 1980-82; promotion chmn. Capitol Concour d'Elegance, Sacramento, 1984—, gen. chmn., 1987-89. Producer (music videos) Running Wild, Running Free, 1984, Rocket Hot-/The Image, 1984 (Joey award 1985); dir. (documentary) Behind Closed Doors, 1984; producer, dir. FLIGHTLOG, The Jerry Reynolds Show. Video producer Calif. N.G., 1980-82; video trainer Am. Cancer Soc., Sacramento, 1983-85; cons. Sacramento Sheriff's Dept., Sacramento, 1984—, United Way-WEAVE, Sacramento, 1984-85; bd. dirs. Woodside Homeowners Assn., 1989—. Recipient Gold Addy award, 1986, 87. Mem. Am. Advt. Fedn., Sacramento Advt. Club (awards video producer 1984—, chmn. judging 1988-89, bd. dirs. 1989—), Aircraft Owners and Pilots Assn., Computer Users Group. Republican. Office: Sta KRBK-TV 500 Media Pl Sacramento CA 95815

CHISUM, EMMETT DEWAIN, historian, archeologist, researcher; b. Monroe, La., Mar. 19, 1922. BA in Social Sci., Northwestern State U., 1942; MA in Social Sci., La. State U., 1946; MA in History, U. Wyo., 1952, MA in Polit. Sci. an dAnthropology, 1961. Tchr. sci. Cameron (La.) Parish Sch. System, 1947-51; tchr. English Welsh (La.) High Sch., 1946-47; social sci. librarian U. Wyo., Laramie, 1954-77, prof. rsch. history, archeology, 1977—; mem. faculty senate U. Wyo., 1986—. Author: (books) Guide to Library Research, 1969, Guide to Research in Political Science, 1970, Guide to Research in Education, 1974, Memories: University of Wyoming 1886-1986, 1987; contbr. articles to Ency. of Lir. and Info. Sci. (45 vols.), 1986—, profl. jours. Mem. ALA, Am. Archeol. Soc., Western Pol. Sci. Assn., AAUP, Phi Delta Kappa. Home: 2032 Holliday Dr Laramie WY 82070

CHITTENDEN, CORA LEA, clinical social worker; b. Denver, July 11, 1942; d. Clarence Pinkerton Hearn and Grace Edwina (Thornton) Lovisone; m. Michael F. Chittenden, Apr. 2, 1967 (div/ Apr. 1981). BA in Psychology and Sociology, Ottawa U., 1965; MSW, U. Kans., 1968. Lic. social worker, Colo. Clin. social worker Marillac Ctr. for Children, Kansas City, Mo., 1968-71; clin. dir. day treatment program Hearnes Youth Ctr., Mo., 1971-75; clin. social worker Pikes Peak Family Counseling & Mental Health Ctr., Colorado Springs, Colo., 1975-77, Colorado Springs Pub. Schs., Colorado Springs, Colo., 1977-79; pvt. practice child, adult, family and marital psychotherapy Colorado Springs, 1979—; instr. Grad. Sch. of Social Work U. Mo., 1974-75, U. Denver, 1976-77; cons.Pediatrics Day Treatment Program Penrose Community Hosp., 1981. Contbr. articles to Internat. Jour. Psychoanalytic Psychotherapy. Mem. Colo. Soc. Clin. Social Workers (sec. local chpt. 1977-81, pres. 1981, chmn. ethics com. 1982—), El Paso County Interdisciplinary Mental Health Profl. Afairs Com. (chmn. 1982-83, 86-87), Nat. Assn. Social Workers (bd. cert. in clin. social work). Office: 1127 N Weber Colorado Springs CO 80903

CHITTENDEN, MICHAEL FENN, social worker; b. Meridan, Conn., Feb. 5, 1942; s. Donald Fenn Chittenden and Gloria Ann (Parsons) Sacco; m. Cora Lea Lovisone, Apr. 2, 1967 (div. 1981); m. Alberta Bernadine Romero, Nov. 27, 1981; children: Michelle, Jennifer, Joe. BS in Psychology, U. Mo., Kansas City, 1970; MS in Social Work, U. Mo., Columbia, 1973. Lic. social worker, Colo. Resident supr. Colo. Youth Ctr., Denver, 1965-67; aid and activity therapist Western Mo. Mental Health Ctr., Kansas City, 1967-70, social worker, 1970-71; psychiatric social worker Fulton (Mo.) State Hosp., 1971-75; program coordinator Adult Forensic Svcs. mental health ctr., Colorado Springs, Colo., 1975-76; psychiatric social worker Colo. State Hosp., Pueblo, 1976-80, clin. adminstr., 1980—. Mem. Cong. Racial Equality, New Haven, 1962-63; campaign worker McGovern for Pres., Kansas City, McCarthy for Pres., Kansas City; mem. Colo. Sanity Law Task Force, Denver, 1977; mem. demonstration project Greater Kansas City Coun. on Race and Religion, 1970. With USN, 1959-61. Recipient Recognition award U.S. Atty. Gen. Mitchell, 1970. Mem. Nat. Assn. Social Workers. Democrat. Office: Colo State Hosp 1600 W 24th St Pueblo CO 81003

CHIU, ARTHUR NANG LICK, engineering educator; b. Singapore, Mar. 9, 1929; came to U.S., 1948; s. S.J. and Y.N. (Wong) C.; m. Katherine N. Chang, June 12, 1952; children: Vicky, Gregory. BSCE, BA, Oreg. State U., 1952; MSCE, MIT, 1953; PhD in Structural Engring., U. Fla., 1961. Instr. U. Hawaii, Honolulu, 1953-54, asst. prof., 1954-59, assoc. prof., 1959-64, chmn. dept. civil engring., 1963-66; prof. structural engring. Colo. State U. (on assignment to Asian Inst. Tech., Bangkok, Thailand), 1966-68; acting assoc. dean research, tng. and fellowships grad. div. U. Hawaii, Monoa, 1968; assoc. dean research, tng. and fellowships grad. div. U. Hawaii, Manoa, 1972-76, prof. civil engring., 1964—; research specialist Space and Info. Systems div. N.Am. Aviation, Inc. (now Rockwell Internat.), Downey, Calif.; vis. scholar UCLA and vis. assoc. Calif. Inst. Tech., Pasadena, 1970; vis. research scientist Naval Civil Engring. Lab., Port Hueneme, Calif., 1976-77; mem. several univ. coms., U. Hawaii; co-chmn. Indo-US Workshop on Wind Disaster Mitigation, 1985; chmn. US-Asia Conf. on Engring. for Mitigating Natural Hazards Damage, 1987. Contbr. articles to profl. jours. NSF research grantee 1970—. Fellow ASCE (mem. team that surveyed damage caused by Kaoiki earthquake, 1983, mem. task com. on turbulence, past. pres. Hawaii sect.); mem. NSPE, NRC (leader of team that surveyed and reported damage caused by Hurricane Iwa 1982, mem. com. on natural disasters 1985-88, com. vice-chmn. 1986-87, chmn. 87-88), Am. Concrete Inst. (assoc. mem. Response of bldgs. to lateral forces com.), Structural Engrs. Assn. of Hawaii (coordinator, lectr. Wind Engring. Design Seminar 1984, co-chmn. annual state convs. 1983, 84, Conv. of Western State Council of Structural Engrs. Assns. 1979, v.p. 1981, pres. 1982), Am. Soc. Engring. Edn., Earthquake Engring. Research Inst., Wind Engring. Research Council Inc., Internat. Conf. on Engring. for Protection Against Natural Disasters (mem. internat. steering com. 1980), Pan-Pacific Tall Bldgs. Conf. (gen. chmn. 1975), Hawaii State Dept. Transp. Research Com., Sigma Xi (mem. com. internat. membership 1978-85), Chi Epsilon (nat. pres. 1986—, Pacific dist. councilor 1982—, faculty advisor to U. Hawaii chpt.), Kappa Mu Epsilon, Phi Eta Sigma, Tau Beta Pi, Phi Kappa Phi (Hawaii Engr. of Yr. 1989). Home: 1654 Paula Dr Honolulu HI 96816 Office: U Hawaii Manoa Dept Civil Engring 2540 Dole St Honolulu HI 96822

CHIU, PETER YEE-CHEW, physician; b. Republic of China, May 12, 1948; came to U.S., 1965; naturalized, 1973; s. Man Chee and Yiu Ying (Cheng) C. BS, U. Calif., Berkeley, 1969, MPH, 1970, DrPH, 1975; MD, Stanford U., 1983. Diplomate Am. Bd. Family Practice; registered profl. engr., Calif.; registered sanitarian, Calif. Asst. civil engr. City of Oakland, Calif., 1970-72; assoc. water quality engr. Bay Area Sewage Services Agy., Berkeley, 1974-76; prin. environ. engr. Assn. Bay Area Govts., Berkeley, 1976-79; resident physician San Jose (Calif.) Hosp., 1983-86; ptnr. Chiu and Crawford, San Jose, 1986—; adj. prof. U. San Francisco, 1979—; clin. prof. Stanford U. Med. Sch., 1987—. Contbr. articles to profl. publs.; co-authored one of the first comprehensive regional environ. mgmt. plans in U.S.; composer, publisher various popular songs Southeast Asia, U.S. Mem. Chinese for Affirmative Action, San Francisco, 1975—; bd. dirs. Calif. Regional Water Quality Control Bd., Oakland, 1979-84, Bay Area Comprehensive Health Planning Council, San Francisco, 1972-76; mem. Santa Clara County Cen. Dem. Com., 1987—; mem. exec. bd. Calif. State Dem. Cen. Com. Recipient Resident Tchr. award Soc. Tchrs. Family Medicine, 1986, Resolution of Appreciation award Calif. Regional Water Quality Control Bd., 1985. Mem. Am. Acad. Family Physicians, Am. Pub. Health Assn., Chi Epsilon, Tau Beta Pi. Democrat. Office: Chiu & Crawford 1610 Westwood Dr San Jose CA 95125

CHIU, TIEN CHENG, physician; b. Canton, Peoples Republic of China, Jan. 25, 1950; came to U.S., 1973; s. Ting-Chung and Shio-Chuang (Ning) C.; m. Peggy Pai-Tzu Hsiao, Dec. 12, 1976; children: Yucan, Sanjung, Yumming. BS, Taiwan U., 1971; MAT, Tex. Christian U., 1974, PhD, 1977; MD, U. Utah, 1983. Diplomate Am. Bd. Med. Examiners. Lab. instr. dept. chemistry Tex. Christian U., Ft. Worth, 1973-74, predoctoral fellow dept. chemistry, 1974-77; rsch. assoc. Brain Rsch. Ctr. U. Chgo., 1977-78; rsch. assoc. Biomed. Engring. Ctr. U. Utah, Salt Lake City, 1978-82; resident U. Wis. Hosp., Madison, 1983-87; attending and fellow U. Calif., San Diego, 1987—; spl. scientist for polymer implant, Biomed. Engring. Ctr., U. Utah, 1980-83. Contbr. articles and rsch. papers to profl. jours. Robert A. Welch fellow, Tex., 1974, Andrew W. Mellon Found. fellow, Calif., 1987. Fellow Am. Coll. Ob-gyn.(jr.). Republican. Baptist. Office: U Calif Med Ctr 225 Dickinson St San Diego CA 92103

CHMELIR, JOHN DAVID, engineer, consultant; b. Chgo., June 30, 1949; s. John Joseph and Dolores Margaret (Suehla) C.; m.Kathryn Elizabeth Davis; children: John Matthew, William Jason. BS in Civil Engring., St. Martins Coll., Olympia, Wash., 1976; postgrad., U.S. Army Command and Gen. Staff Coll., Ft. Leavenworth, 1985. Registered profl. engr., Colo., Oreg., Wash., Nev., Ariz. Enlisted U.S. Army, 1969, advanced through ranks to maj., 1980, platoon leader Corps of Engrs., 1969-76; commdr. Co. C 44th Engrs. U.S. Army, Republic of Korea, 1976-77; asst. to area engrs. CE U.S. Army, Jacksonville, Oreg., 1977-80; ret. U.S. Army, 1980; owner, pres. John Chmelir's Sons Co., Ashland, Oreg., 1980-85; project mgr. URS Corp., Colorado Springs, Colo., 1985-87; v.p. URS Corp., Colorado Springs, 1988—. Mem. Citizens Budget Com., Ashland, 1983-85, Colorado Springs Citizens Goals, 1987-88; bd. dirs. Ptnrship for Community Design, Colorado Springs, 1983-85. Mem. ASCE, Am. Soc. Mil. Engrs. (v.p. 1987-89), Rotary. Republican. Methodist. Home: 135 Palm Springs Rd Colorado Springs CO 80921 Office: URS Cons 1040 S 8th St Colorado Springs CO 80906

CHMELL, SAMUEL JAY, orthopedic surgeon; b. Chgo., Aug. 21, 1952; s. Samuel and Elsie (Wauterlek) C.; m. Nancy Jean Aumiller, June 22, 1974; children: Jessica, Carson, Alexis, Lesley. BS, U. Notre Dame, 1974; MD, Loyola U., 1977. Diplomate Am. Bd. Orthopedic Surgery. Intern Loyola U. Med. Ctr., Maywood, Ill., 1977-78, resident in orthopedic surgery, 1980-84; emergency room physician USPHS Indian Health Service, Chinle, Ariz., 1978-80; attending surgeon Hines (Ill.) VA Hosp., 1984—, Shriners Hosp. for Crippled Children, Chgo., 1985—; clin. instr. orthopedic surgery Loyola U. Med. Ctr., Maywood, 1985—. Contbr. articles on orthopedic surgery to profl. jours. Sofield Travelling Fellow Orthopedic Research Soc. Great Britain, 1985. Mem. AMA, Ill. State Med. Soc., Chgo. Med. Soc., Olmsted Hist. Soc. Riverside (Ill.), Alpha Omega Alpha.

CHOE, JOSEPH JONG KOOK, mortgage banker; b. Seoul, Republic of Korea, Mar. 15, 1961; s. Eung S. and Koja (Lee) C. Student, Santa Monica (Calif.) Coll., 1981, UCLA, 1982. Loan officer Southwest Savs. & Loan, Los Angeles, 1984-85; v.p. I.G.F.S. Inc., Los Angeles, 1986-87; pres. Investree, Inc., Los Angeles, 1985-87; sr. loan cons. Merchant Bank of Calif., Beverly Hills, 1987-88; pres. Fin. Am., Los Angeles, 1988—. Mem. Korean Jr. League Am. (Los Angeles) (treas., counselor, 1982-83), Wooriro Club (Los Angeles) (treas. 1987—). Office: Fin Am 3325 Wilshire Blvd #1006 Los Angeles CA 90010

CHOE, WON-GIL, electronics executive; b. Gang-Nung, Korea, Apr. 24, 1932; s. Chan-Jang and Sook-Ja (Shim) C.; came to U.S., 1957, naturalized, 1970; BS, Ariz. State U., 1960; MS, Stanford U., 1962, PhD, 1975; m. Mirang Wonne. children: Iliad, Christopher, Charlotte, Scott, Julia. Engr. Fairchild Semiconductor, 1962-64; project mgr. Memorex Corp., 1966; mgr. indsl. engring. Internat. Video Corp., 1967-68; v.p. ops. Dole Electro-Systems, Inc., Palo Alto, Calif., 1968-70; v.p. ops. Intellex Corp., Palo Alto, 1970-72; v.p. fin. Vacu-Blast Corp., Belmont, Calif., 1972-74, exec. v.p., 1977-79; pres. Tronic Corp., Belmont, 1973-79; v.p. Applied Implant Tech, Santa Clara, Calif., 1979-81; pres., chief exec. officer Video Logic Corp., Sunnyvale, Calif., 1982-87, v.p., chief fin. officer Mass Micro Systems, Inc., Sunnyvale, 1987-88; sr. v.p., chief fin. officer Televideo Systems Inc., San Jose, Calif., 1988—; bd. dir. EEI, Inc., TRI, Inc., Visidata, Inc., Adivan Tech, Inc., Chexel Internat., Inc., Gold Tech., Inc., PSI, Inc., Video Logic Corp. Mem. Am. Mgmt. Assn., Inst. Indsl. Engring. Assn. Republican. Presbyterian. Author: Quality of Profit in Non-Financial Cos., 1975. Home: 11 Cowell Ln Atherton CA 94025 Office: Televideo Systems Inc 550 E Brokaw Rd San Jose CA 95112

CHOI, PAUL SOO-WOONG, metallurgical engineer; b. Song-Jung, Republic of Korea, Oct. 9, 1943; came to U.S., 1975; s. Gou-Doo and Nam-Rae (Park) C.; m. Keum R. Kang, June 13, 1972; children: Michael M., Gina M. BS, Han Yang U., Seoul, Republic of Korea, 1968, MS, 1970; MS, Ohio State U, 1981; PhD, U. Cin., 1985. Capt., instr. Korea Mil Acad., Seoul, 1970-75; testing inst. R.R. Rsch. Lab., Columbus, Ohio, 1976-78; mfg. engr. Westinghouse Electric Corp., Cin., 1981-82; scientist mfg. rsch. and devel. McDonnell Douglas, Culver City, Calif., 1986-87, Long Beach, Calif., 1987—; instr. Pierce Coll. 1987, mfg. tech. UCLA, 1988, West Coast U., L.A., 1989—. Mem. Soc. Mfg. Engrs., Metallurgy sect. of Am. Soc. Metals. Home: 13750 Beach St Cerritos CA 90701

CHONG, GERALD H. W., real estate developer; b. Honolulu, Aug. 4, 1940; s. Jared Young and Ruby (Lin) C.; m. Mona Katherine Lee, Dec. 30, 1967. BA, U. of the Pacific, 1962; MA, Cornell U., 1963. Div. credit and office mgr. Zellerback Paper Co. div. Crown Zellerbach Corp., L.A., Salt Lake City, 1963-65; project mgr. Property Rsch. Corp., L.A., 1965-66; mgr. devel. Kaluakoi Corp., Honolulu, 1966-68; v.p. ops. Urbanetics Fin., L.A., 1968-70; mgr. acquisitions and devel. Coldwell Banker Mgmt. Corp., L.A., 1970-75; owner The Royce Co., L.A., 1975-83, Gerald Chong and Assocs., Beverly Hills, Calif., 1983—; mgr. western div. Latigo Corp., Beverly Hills, 1988—; cons. Allied Parking Co., Beverly Hills, Calif., 1986-87, Sumitomo Constrn. Co., L.A., 1984-85, Keller Constrn. Co., El Monte, Calif., 1986-87. Mem. City Land Use Commn., El Segundo, Calif., 1986, Santa Monica Traffic Task Force, 1988, Santa Monica Land Use Com., 1988, Santa Monica Mid-Cities Homeowners, 1988. Mem. Nat. Assn. Corp. Real Estate Execs., Calif. Real Estate Brokers, L.A. Athletic Club. Republican. Methodist. Office: Latigo Corp 9440 Santa Monica Blvd Ste 500 Beverly Hills CA 90210

CHONG, IAN MARK, ergonomist, methods analyst; b. Seattle, July 8, 1948; s. Frank Locke and Dora (Kwan) C.; m. Sally Bowen, Sept. 6, 1986; 1 child, Alexis Nicole Bowen. B Archtl. Engring., U. Wash., 1972; M Indsl. Design, Pratt Inst., 1978; M in Occupational Biomechanics and Ergonomics, NYU, 1982. Ops. dir. Theater Planning-CBL Engrs., N.Y.C., 1975-80, Metra Electronics, N.Y.C., 1979-80, Unicube Corp., N.Y.C., 1980-81; project dir. Cannan Croup, N.Y.C., 1982-84, APC Internat., Chgo., 1984-87; mgr. Tri Tech Inc., N.Y.C., 1987-88; mgmt. biomechanics and ergonomics cons. Peat Marwick Main, Seattle, 1988—. Contbr. articles to profl. publs.; patentee orthodontic and sterilizing equipment, solar drapery mechanism. Mem. Indsl. Design Soc. Am., Human Factors Group. Home: 22802 64th Pl W Mountlake Terrace WA 98043 Office: Peat Marwick Main 2030 lst Ave Seattle WA 98100

CHONG, RICHARD DAVID, architect; b. Los Angeles, June 1, 1946; s. George and Mabel Dorothy (Chan) C.; m. Roze Gutierrez, July 5, 1969; children: David Gregory, Michelle Elizabeth. BArch, U. So. Calif., 1969; MArch, UCLA, 1974. Registered architect, Utah, Calif., Wyo. Assoc. Pulliam, Matthews & Assocs., Los Angeles, 1969-76; dir. asst. Community Design Ctr., Salt Lake City, 1976-77; prin. Richard D. Chong & Assocs., Salt Lake City, 1977—; planning cons. Los Angeles Harbor Dept., 1974-76; asst. instr. So. Calif. Inst. Architecture, Santa Monica, 1973-74; vis. design critic Calif. State Poly. U., Pamona, 1975, U. Utah, Salt Lake City, 1976-78; design instr. Calif. State Poly. U., 1975-76; adj. asst. prof. urban design, U. Utah, 1980-84; bd. dirs. Utah Housing Coalition, Salt Lake City; Salt Lake City Housing Adv. and Appeals Bd., 1976-80. Author: Design of Flexible Housing, 1974; prin. works include Airmen's Dining Hall, 1985 (1st Pl. Mil. Facility Air Forces Escape and Evasion Soc. 1986), Oddfellows Hall, 1984 (Heritage Found. award 1986). Mem. Task Force for the Aged Housing Com. Salt Lake County, Salt Lake City, 1976-77; Salt Lake City Mortgage Loan Instns. Rev. Com., 1978; bd. dirs. Neighborhood Housing Services of Fed. Home Loan Bank Bd., Salt Lake City, 1979-81, devel. com.; vice chmn. Water Quality Adv. Council, Salt Lake City, 1981-83; vice-chair Salt Lake City Pub. Utilities Bd., 1985—; mem. adv. bd. Pub. Utilities Commn., Salt Lake City, 1986-87. Served as staff sgt. N.G., 1969-75. Mem. AIA (jury mem. Am. Soc. Interior Designers Annual awards 1981-82), Am. Inst. Planning (juror Annual Planning award 1984-85), Am. Planning Assn., Am. Arbitration Assn., Nat. Panel Arbitrators, Salt Lake City C. of C. (mem. housing com. 1977). Democrat. Club: Ft. Douglas Country (Salt Lake City). Office: Richard D Chong & Assocs 248 Edison St Salt Lake City UT 84111

CHOPRA, AJAY, electrical engineer, computer company executive; b. New Delhi, Jan. 2, 1957; s. Balraj and Mohini Chopra; m. Shyamoli Banerjee, June 25, 1984. BSEE, Birla Inst. Tech., Pilani, India, 1978; MSEE, SUNY, Stony Brook, 1979. Engr. Burroughs Corp., Danbury, Conn., 1979-81, Atari Inc., San Jose, Calif., 1982-84; engring. mgr. Mindset Corp., Sunnyvale, Calif., 1984-86; pres. Pinnacle Systems Inc., Santa Clara, Calif., 1986—. Office: Pinnacle Systems Inc 2380 Walsh Ave Santa Clara CA 95051

CHOQUETTE, PHILIP WHEELER, geologist, educator; b. Utica, N.Y., Aug. 16, 1930; s. Charles Auguste and Lucy (Wheeler) C.; m. Jean Henry, July 4, 1959; children: Steven Charles, Janine Tiffany. Cert., Inst. Cath., Paris, 1952; BA in Geology with honors, Allegheny Coll., 1952; MA, Johns Hopkins U., 1954, PhD, 1957. Geologist U.S. Geol. Survey, Washington, 1956-58; rsch. geologist Denver Rsch. Ctr. Marathon Oil Co., Littleton, Colo., 1958-63, advanced rsch. geologist, 1963-70, sr. rsch. geologist, 1970-85, rsch. assoc., 1985-86, ret., 1986; adj. prof. dept. geol. scis. U. Colo., Boulder, Colo., 1987-89, rsch. prof., 1989—; vis. prof. SUNY, Stony Brook, 1987-88. Assoc. editor Geology, 1970-74, Jour. Sedimentary Petrology, 1974-82; editor: (with P. Roehl) Carbonate Petroleum Reservoirs, 1985, (with N. James) Paleokarst, 1988. Fellow Geol. Soc. Am., AAAS; mem. Am. Assn. Petroleum Geologists (co-recipient Levorsen award 1965), Internat. Assn. Sedimentologists, Soc. Econ. Paleontologists and Mineralogists (Coun. for Sedimentology, 1981-83), Phi Beta Kappa. Democrat. Home: 5111 S Franklin St Littleton CO 80121 Office: U Colo Dept Geol Scis Boulder CO 80309-0250

CHOSAK, SHELLI, psychotherapist; b. Detroit, Dec. 29, 1937; d. Jack M. and Emily (Gelman) Berke; m. Arnold H. Chosak, Feb. 14, 1960 (dec. Sept. 1974); children: Mark, Jodi, Jamie; m. Alan Sieroty, Oct. 2, 1982. BA in Psychology, UCLA, 1959; MA in Psychology, Pepperdine U., 1975; Phd in Psychology, William Lyon U., San Diego, 1987. Personnel dir. Charles Luckman Assoc., L.A., 1959-61; bus. owner Chosak's Women's Wear, L.A., 1961-71; with bus. mgmt. Arnold H. Chosak, CPA, L.A., 1971-74; field rep. congressman Anthony Beilenson, L.A., 1976-78; pvt. practice L.A., 1976—; co-dir. human svcs. tng. Wagner Program, U. Judaism, L.A. Bd. dirs.

Alternatie Living for the Aging, L.A., Am. Jewish Com. Honoree Wagner Program, U. Judaism, 1986, Alternative Living for the Aging, 1985. Mem. Women in Bus., Organizational Devel. Network, Am. Soc. Tng. and Devel., L.A. County Psychol. Assn., Calif. Assn. Marriage and Family Therapists. Democrat. Jewish. Home: 620 Warner Ave Los Angeles CA 90024 Office: 405 S Beverly Dr #350 Beverly Hills CA 92012

CHOTINER, KENNETH LEE, judge; b. Los Angeles, Aug. 14, 1937; s. Murray M. and Phyllis Sylvia (Levenson) C.; m. Florence Helene Penney, May 29, 1964; children—Dana Lynne, Cara Lee. BA in Polit. Sci. with honors, UCLA, 1959; JD with honors, Loyola U., Los Angeles, 1969; grad. Hastings Coll. Law Coll. Criminal Advocacy, San Francisco, 1980, Calif. Jud. Coll., U. Calif., Berkeley, 1981. Bar: Calif. 1970, U.S. Ct. Customs and Patent Appeals 1971, U.S. Ct. Mil. Appeals 1974, U.S. Sup. Ct. 1975. Instr. Am. govt. U. Alaska, 1962; dep. city atty., Los Angeles, 1970-71; sole practice, Santa Monica, Calif., 1971-81; spl. counsel City of Hawthorne (Calif.), 1973-80; judge pro tem Los Angeles Mcpl. Ct., 1975-81, Santa Monica Mcpl. Ct., 1977-81; judge Los Angeles Mcpl. Ct., 1981—, supervising judge valley div., 1983, Van Nuys-Encino br., 1983-84; justice pro tem Calif. Ct. Appeal, 1982; adj. prof. U. West Los Angeles Sch. Law, 1981-82; faculty Calif. Jud. Coll., Earl Warren Legal Inst., U. Calif., Berkeley, 1982, Calif. Ctr. Jud. Edn. and Research, Berkeley, 1982—, Media Workshop on Calif. Cts., 1982—; chmn. Media Conf. on Calif. Cts., 1986; conf. del. State Bar Calif., 1972, 73, 76-80. Author: Restricting Handguns, 1979; contbr. articles to legal jours. Mem. exec. com. Los Angeles Mcpl. Ct., 1985, 88. Bd. dirs. So. Calif. ACLU, 1972-81, v.p., 1978-81; dir. ex-officio Legal Aid Soc. Santa Monica, 1979-80; bd. dirs. Friends of the Santa Monica Mountains, Parks and Seashore, 1979-81; mem. dean's council UCLA Coll. Letters and Sci.; mem. wildlife adv. com. Los Angeles County Fish and Game Commn., 1973-75, chmn., 1974; mem. Los Angeles County Interdepartmental Drinking Driver Program task force, 1985-87; mem. PTA, 1973-81, Los Angeles Olympic Organizing Com. Criminal Justice System Subcom., 1983-84. Served to capt. USAF, 1961-66. Recipient recognition awards Calif. Trial Lawyers Assn. (trial lawyer and criminal def.), 1980, U. W. Los Angeles Sch. Law award for Outstanding Service, 1984, Nat. Council on Alcoholism award of Appreciation, 1984, Eagle Scout award Boy Scouts Am., Order of the Arrow. Mem. Nat. Conf. State Trial Judges, Nat. Conf. Spl. Ct. Judges (del. 1985), Calif. Judges Assn., Nat. Conf. Bar Pres., ABA (presdl. showcase program, Washington 1985), Nat. Eagle Scout Assn., Mcpl. Ct. Judges Assn. Los Angeles County, Irish Am. Bar Assn., Am. Arbitration Assn. (panel 1970-81), Santa Monica Bay Dist. Bar Assn. (pres. 1979), Assn. Trial Lawyers Am., Women's Lawyers Assn. Los Angeles, Criminal Ct. Bar Assn., Los Angeles County Bar Assn., St. Thomas More Law Soc., UCLA Alumni Assn., UCLA Blue and Gold Circle, U. Calif. Santa Cruz Fiat Lux Soc., Am. Judicature Soc., Ephebian Soc., Quill and Scroll Soc., Santa Monica C. of C., Sealbearer Soc., Phi Alpha Delta. Lodge: Lions (zone chmn. 1975-76). Office: Los Angeles Mcpl Ct 110 N Grand Ave Los Angeles CA 90012-3055

CHOU, ERWIN C., economist; b. San Francisco, July 12, 1952; s. George H. and Suet F. (Yim) C. BA, U. Calif., 1974; PhD, Stanford U., 1986. Economist World Bank, Washington, 1977-84; internat. economist U.S. Treasury/IRS, San Francisco, 1987—; economic cons. Pacific Gas & Electric Co., San Francisco, 1986-87. Mem. Am. Econ. Assn. Democrat. Home: 2921 Privet Dr Hillsborough CA 94010 Office: US Treasury IRS 450 Golden Gate Ave Rm 12118 San Francisco CA 94102

CHOU, NELSON NAN-SAN, engineer; b. Hen-Sun, Hunan, China, July 2, 1948; came to U.S., 1973; s. Shih-Fu and Su-Ching (Q) C.; m. Grace C. Lee, March 29, 1975; children: Andy, Dennis. BS, Nat. Cheng-Kung U., Tainan, Taiwan, 1971; MS, U. S.C., 1975. Registered profl. engr., Colo. Soil lab mgr. Law Engrng. Testing Co., Columbia, S.C., 1975-77; project engr. China Engrng. Cons., Taipei, Taiwan, 1977-79; sr. project engr. Geotek, Inc., Denver, 1979-83; sr. hwy. engr. Colo. Dept. of Hwys., Denver, 1983—. Editor: Proceedings of Lateral Load Capacity of Piles, 1988, Manual of Embankment; contbr. articles to profl. jours. Chmn. Taiwan's Nat. Day Com., Denver, 1986. Recipient Outstanding Presentation award, Lateral Capacity of Piles Symposium, Denver, 1988. Mem. Am. Soc. Civil Engrs., Colo. Chinese Soc. Science and Engrng. (pres. 1987-88, outstanding service award, 1988), Internat. Soc. Soil Mechanics and Found. Engrng. Office: Colo Dept of Hwys 4340 E Louisiana Ave Denver CO 80222

CHOU, TIMOTHY CHEN KUANG, computer engineer; b. Wooster, Ohio, June 23, 1954; s. David Yuan-Pin and Mary Ann Mei-En (Sung) C. BSEE, N.C. State U., 1975; MSEE, U. Ill., 1977, PhD, 1981. Sr. software architect Tandem Computers, Cupertino, Calif., 1981-85; mgr. secure operating systems Tandem Computers, Cupertino, 1985—; lectr. Stanford U., Palo Alto, Calif., 1982—; cons. Constrn. Engrng. Rsch. Lab., Urbana, Ill., 1979. Author/contbr.: Fault-Tolerant Systems, 1986; contbr. articles to profl. jours. Mem. IEEE. Home: 3326 Emerson St Palo Alto CA 94306 Office: Tandem Computers 19333 Vallco Pkwy Cupertino CA 95014

CHOUINARD, YVON, small business owner; b. Lewiston, Maine, Nov. 9, 1938; s. Gerard and Yvonne (Lizzotte) C.; m. Carol Lamb, 1962 (div. 1963); m. Malinda Pennoyer, Dec. 25, 1970; children: Fletcher, Claire. Founder Chouinard Equipment, Burbank, Calif., 1957, Great Pacific Iron Works, Inc., Ventura, Calif., 1970, Lost Arrow Corp., Ventura, 1974, Patagonia Software, Inc., 1975. Author: Climbing Ice, 1978. Active Surf Rider Orgn., various environ. orgns. worldwide. With U.S. Army, 1962-64, Korea. Mem. Am. Alpine Club. Democrat. Office: Lost Arrow Corp 235 W Santa Clara St Ventura CA 93002

CHOUTEAU, WALTER C(HRISTY), utility company executive, researcher; b. San Francisco, Mar. 3, 1950; s. Walter Cerre and Francesca (Young) C. Student, Dartmouth Coll., 1969, U. Wash., 1970-73; AB in Biology, U. Calif., Berkeley, 1974, MS in Resource Science, 1975. Biologist Pacific Gas & Electric Co., San Ramon, Calif., 1977-80, research advisor, 1980-81, sr. research advisor, 1981-83, supr. research, 1983, acting dir. research and devel., 1984-86; asst. to v.p., elec. resource planning and devel. Pacific Gas & Electric Co., San Francisco, 1986-88, dir. retail mktg., 1988—. Myers scholar U. Wash., 1971-72; Needham fellow U. Calif. Berkeley, 1975; grantee U. Calif., Berkeley, 1972-73. Mem. AAAS, Electric Power Research Inst. (utility advisor task force on environment, 1984-86, chmn. ecol. studies program com. 1986), Sigma Xi (research honor soc. 1975). Club: Olympic (San Francisco). Office: Pacific Gas & Electric 77 Beale St San Francisco CA 94106

CHOW, CONROY YET FARN, state agency administrator; b. Honolulu, Oct. 31, 1944; s. Tim Kau and Alice Fong (Chow); m. Susan Shu Wai Chen, Sept. 23, 1972; children: Vivian, Winston. BA, U. Redlands, 1966; MA, U. Minn., 1968. Instr. U. Minn. Extension Div., Mpls., 1970-71; project dir. Hawaii Dept. Ctr. Social Services, Honolulu, 1971-75, chief rsch. and statis. bur., 1984-86; rsch., info. systems chief Hawaii State Intake Service, Honolulu, 1975-84; planning chief Hawaii Dept. Human Services, Honolulu, 1986. Named Gov.'s Office Employee of Yr., Boss of Yr. Honolulu Japanese Jaycees. Mem. Am. Pub. Welfare Assn., Hawaii Statis. Assn., Lin Yee Chung Assn. (v.p. 1988), Correctional Res. Assn. (pres. 1982-83). Democrat. Office: Hawaii Dept Human Svcs 1390 Miller St Honolulu HI 96813

CHOW, FRANKLIN SZU-CHIEN, obstetrician, gynecologist; b. Hong Kong, Apr. 15, 1956; came to U.S., 1967; s. Walter Wen-Tsao and Jane Ju-Hsien (Tang) C. BS, CCNY, 1977; MD, U. Rochester, 1979. Diplomate Am. Bd. Ob-Gyn. Intern Wilmington (Del.) Med. Ctr., 1979-80, resident in ob-gyn, 1980-83; practice medicine specializing in ob-gyn Vail (Colo.) Valley Med. Ctr., 1983—, chmn. obstetrics com., 1984-85, 86-87, chmn. surg. com., 1987-88, vice chief of staff, 1989—. Named to Athletic Hall of Fame, CCNY, 1983. Fellow Am. Coll. Ob-Gyn's; mem. AMA, Colo. Med. Soc., Intermountain Med. Soc. (pres. 1985-86), Internat. Fedn. Gynecol. Endoscopists, Am. Assn. Gynecol. Laparoscopists, Gynecologic Laser Soc. Home: 0746 N Deer Blvd PO Box 3257 Vail CO 81658 Office: Vail Valley Med Ctr 181 W Meadow Dr Ste 600 Vail CO 81657

CHOW, WINSTON, chemical engineer; b. San Francisco, Dec. 21, 1946; s. Raymond and Pearl C.; m. Lilly Fah, Aug. 15, 1971; children: Stephen, Kathryn. BSChemE, U. Calif., Berkeley, 1968; MSChemE, Calif. State U., San Jose, 1972; MBA with honors, Calif. State U., San Francisco, 1985. Registered profl. chem. and mech. engr.; instr.'s credential Calif. Community Coll. Chem. engr. Sondell Sci. Instruments, Inc., Mountain View, Calif., 1971; mem. research and devel. staff Raychem Corp., Menlo Park, Calif., 1971-72; supervising engr. Bechtel Power Corp., San Francisco, 1972-79; sr. project engr. water quality and toxic substances control program Electric Power Research Inst., Palo Alto, Calif., 1979—. Contbr. author Water Chlorination, vol. 4; contbr. articles to profl. publs. Pres., chief exec. officer Directions, Inc., San Francisco, 1985-86, bd. dirs. 1984-87, chmn. strategic planning com., 1984-85; mem. industry com. Am. Power Conf., 1988—; bd. dirs., treas. Calif. State 2. Alumni Assn., San Francisco, 1989—. Recipient Grad. Disting. Achievement award, 1985; Calif. Gov.'s Exec. fellow. Mem. Am. Inst. Chem. Engrs. (Profl. Devel. Recognition cert.), NSPE, Calif. Soc. Profl. Engrs. (pres. Golden Gate chpt. 1983-84, v.p. 1982-83, state dir.), Water Pollution Control Fedn., Calif. Water Pollution Control Assn., ASME, Calif. Alumni Assn., Beta Gamma Sigma. Democrat. Presbyterian. Office: Electric Power Rsch Inst 3412 Hillview Ave Palo Alto CA 94303

CHOY, HERBERT YOUNG CHO, judge; b. Makaweli, Kauai, Hawaii, Jan. 6, 1916; s. Doo Wook and Helen (Nahm) C.; m. Dorothy Helen Shular, June 16; 1945. B.A., U. Hawaii, 1938; J.D., Harvard U., 1941. Bar: Hawaii bar 1941. Practiced in Honolulu, 1946-57, 58-71; atty. gen. Ter. Hawaii, 1957-58; judge U.S. Ct. Appeals, 9th circuit, Honolulu, 1971—. Trustee Hawaii Loa Coll., 1963-79. Served with AUS, 1942-46. Decorated Order Civil Merit Korea). Fellow Am. Bar Found.; mem. Am., Hawaii bar assns., World Peace Through Law Center. Home: 3964 Monterey Pl Honolulu HI 96816 Office: US Ct Appeals PO Box 50127 Honolulu HI 96850

CHOY, RUDOLPH C., catamaran designer, business executive; b. Kauai, Hawaii, July 12, 1923; s. Kun Ha and Katherine (Kim) C.; children: Robin M., W. Barry. BA, U. Hawaii, 1951. Tech. editor Jet Propulsion Lab., Pasadena, Calif., 1958-58, Interstate Electronics, Gardena, Calif., 1960-86; sr. ptnr. Rudy Choy Designs, Honolulu, 1987—; tech. cons., voyage coordinator, chief designer Polynesian Voyaging Soc., Honolulu, 1974-76; bd. dirs. Hawaii's Visitor's Bur., Honolulu, 1976. 1st lt., USAF, 1945-53, Europe, Korea. Recipient Air Medals Oak Leaf, Disting. Flying Cross; named Entrepreneur of the Yr., Hawaii Bus. Mag., Honolulu, 1988. Mem. Skal Club (pres. 1983-84), Hawaii Cruise Boat Owner's Assn. (pres. 1988—), Soc. of Naval Architects and Marine Engrs. Outrigger Canoe Club (Honolulu), Balboa Yacht Club, Am. Soc. of Travel Agts. (assoc.), Japan Assn. Travel Agts., Hawaii Yacht Club, Pacific Area Travel Assn. Office: Aikane Catamarans 677 AlaMoana Blvd Ste 502 Honolulu HI 96813

CHRISMAN, WILLIAM HERRING, property tax cons.; b. Evanston, Ill., June 28, 1932; s. Roswell Herring and Virginia Ruth (Haynes) C.; m. Margaret Baker Craig, Apr. 17, 1989; children: Katherine Anne, Emily Louise. AB, Harvard U., 1955. Media buyer Leo Burnett Co., Chgo., 1958-60; account exec. Lennen & Newell Inc., N.Y.C., 1960-63; subsidiary pres. Clairol Inc., N.Y.C., 1963-72; exec. v.p. Metalware Corp., Chandler, Ariz., 1973-75; pres. Chrisman Farms, Inc., Scottsdale, Ariz., 1975-80, E. Allen Mgmt. Corp., Phoenix, 1980-85; gen. mgr. Oasis Family Water Park, Phoenix, 1985; asset mgr. Evans Withycombe Inc., Phoenix, 1985-87; prin. Real Estate Valuation Cons., Phoenix, 1987—; advt. instr. Katherine Gibbs Sch., N.Y.C., 1963-65. 1st lt. U.S. Army, 1955-57. Mem. Ariz. Tax Research Assn., Inst. Property Taxation, Christmas Cove Improvement Assn., Spa at Camelback Inn. Democrat. Methodist. Home: 6235 E Catesby Rd Paradise Valley AZ 85253 Office: Real Estate Valuation Cons 1212 E Osborn Rd Phoenix AZ 85014

CHRISS, DIANE ALTMAN, social worker, psychotherapist; b. N.Y.C., June 23, 1946; d. Samuel David and Edna (Birnbach) Altman; m. Nathan J. Sambul, June 9, 1968 (div. 1976); m. Charles Bernhard Chriss, Mar. 25, 1979; stepchildren: Roger Bennett, Neil Andrew. BA in Psychology, CUNY, 1968; AM in Devel. Psychology, U. Mich., 1970; postgrad., NYU, 1972-76; MSW in Clin. Social Work, U. So. Calif., 1988. V.p. devel. The Systems Guild, Inc., Thornwood, N.Y., 1976-80; mgr. distbn. systems Savin Corp., Stamford, Conn., 1980-84; v.p. devel. Chriss Cons., Inc., Ridgefield, Conn., 1984-86; social work intern Family & Children's Aid, Norwalk, Conn., 1986-87, San Fernando Valley Child Guidance Clinic, Northridge, Calif., 1987-88; pvt. practice Calabasas, Calif., 1988-. Mem. Monte Nido Homeowners Assn., Calabasas, 1987-88. Mem. Nat. Assn. Social Workers, Soc. for Clin. Social Work.

CHRISTEN, MONICA SUE, university administrator; b. Appleton, Wis., May 1, 1953; d. Wilbert Frank and Marjorie Louise (Wentzel) C. BS, U. Wis., Stevens Point, 1975; MA, Ball State U., 1977. Residence hall dir. Northeast Mo. State U., Kirksville, 1977-79; asst. area coordinator Tex. A&M U., College Station, 1979-81, area coordinator, 1981-86; dir. student live Inst. for Shipboard Edn., Colo. State U., 1986-87; with Advanced Energy, Ft. Collins, Colo., 1987—. Helper Crisis Hotline, Bryan, Tex., 1985-86. Avocations: reading, needlework, biking, travel. Home: 3430 Colony Dr Fort Collins CO 80526 Office: Advanced Energy 1600 Prospect Pkwy Fort Collins CO 80525

CHRISTENSEN, ALBERT SHERMAN, judge; b. Manti, Utah, June 9, 1905; s. Albert H. and Jennie (Snow) C.; m. Lois Bowen, Apr. 4, 1927; children: A. Kent, Karen D., Krege B. Student, Brigham Young U., intermittently 1923-27; J.D., Nat. U., 1931. Bar: D.C. 1932, Utah 1933. Asst. bus. specialist U.S. Dept. Commerce, 1930-32; practiced in Provo, Utah, 1933-42, 45-54; U.S. dist. judge Salt Lake City, 1954—; mem. com. on revision laws Jud. Conf. U.S., 1960-68, com. on ct. adminstrn., 1968-75, mem. adv. com. rules of civil procedure, 1972-82, mem. rev. com., 1977-78, jud. ethics com., 1978-82; mem. Temporary Emergency Ct. Appeals, 1972—; mem. bd. Utah Bar Examiners, 1939-42. Republican congressional candidate, 1939. Served from lt. to lt. comdr. USNR, 1942-45. Mem. ABA, Utah Bar Assn. (pres. 1951-52), Utah Jr. Bar Assn. (pres. 1937-38), Utah County Bar Assn. (pres. 1936-37, 47-48). Mem. Ch. Jesus Christ of Latter-day Saints.

CHRISTENSEN, ALLEN CLARE, agriculturalist, educator; b. Lehi, Utah, Apr. 14, 1935; s. Clare Bernard and Relia Sarah (Allen) C.; m. Kathleen Ruth Atwater, Dec. 19, 1958; children: Ann Marie, Allen Clare Jr., James Lynn, Niel Daniel, Eric Wayne. BS with Honors, Brigham Young U., 1957; MS, U. Calif.-Davis, 1960; PhD, Utah State U., 1979. Cert. Am. Registry Profl. Animal Scientists. Vocat. agr. tchr. White Pine County Schs., Lund, Nev., 1961-64; from asst. to assoc. prof. agr. Calif. State Poly. U., Pomona, 1964-73, prof., 1973—, dean coll. agr., 1980-85, 87—; acting provost and acad. v.p., 1985-87; cons. Agrl. Edn. Found., Davis, Calif., 1971-85, AID, Washington, 1983—, W.K. Kellogg Found., Battle Creek, Mich., 1984; trustee Consortium for Internat. Devel., Tucson, Ariz., 1980—, vice chair of bd., 1988—; mem. deans' coun. Calif. Agr. Leadership Program, Davis, 1980-85, 87—; mem. joint com. on agr. rsch. and devel., AID, 1982-87, chmn. strengthening grant panel bd. internat. food and agrl. devel., 1983-87; chair BIFAD panel Humane Capital Devel., 1985-87. Author: (with others) Working in Animal Science, 1978. Contbr. articles to profl. jours. Pres. Chino, Calif Latter-day Saint Stake, 1979-88, mem. exec. bd. Old Baldy coun. Boy Scouts Am., 1988-89; bd. dirs. So. Calif. Agrl. Land Found., 1988—. Recipient Hon. State Farmer Degree, Calif. Assn. Future Farmers Am., 1983. Mem. Am. Soc. Animal Scis., Poultry Sci. Assn., Golden Key Nat. Honor Soc. (hon.), Phi Beta Delta, Phi Kappa Phi, Gamma Sigma Delta (Outstanding Faculty award of Merit, 1976, pres. 1969-70), Alpha Zeta. Republican. Mormon. Office: Calif State Poly U Coll Agr 3801 W Temple Ave Pomona CA 91768

CHRISTENSEN, CAROLINE, college instructor; b. Lehi, Utah, Oct. 5, 1936; d. Byam Heber and Ruth (Gardner) Curtis; m. Marvin Christensen, June 16, 1961; children: Ronald, Roger, Robert, Corlyn, Richard, Chad. BS, Brigham Young U., 1958, MS, 1964. Sec. Brigham Young U., Provo, Utah, 1954-58; instr. bus. Sevier Valley Area Vocat. Ctr., Richfield, Utah, 1970—. Historian, Sevier Sch. Dist. PTA, 1968, 69; chmn. Heart Fund Dist., 1983, Voting Dist., 1988—. Mem. Utah Edn. Assn., Am. Vocat. Assn., Utah Vocat. Assn., Nat. Bus. Edn. Utah Bus. Edn. Assn. (sec. 1986-87), NEA, Western Bus. Edn. Assn., Sevier Valley Tech. Tchrs. Assn. (sec. 1971—, pres. 1986-87), Delta Pi Epsilon, Delta Kappa Gamma (treas. 1975—).

CHRISTENSEN, DONN WAYNE, insurance executive; b. Atlantic City, Apr. 9, 1941; s. Donald Frazier and Dorothy (Ewing) C.; BS, U. Santa Clara, 1964; m. Marshella Abraham, Jan. 26, 1963 (div.); children: Donn Wayne, Lisa Shawn; m. Mei Ling Fill, June 18, 1976 (div.); m. Susan Kim, Feb. 14, 1987; stepchildren: Don Kim, Stella Kim. West Coast div. mgr. Ford Motor Co., 1964-65; agt. Conn. Mut. Life Ins. Co., 1965-68; pres. Christensen & Jones, Inc., L.A., 1968—; v.p. Rsch. Devel. Systems Inc.; investment advisor SEC, 1985—. Pres. Duarte Community Drug Abuse Coun., 1972-75; pres. Woodlyn Property Owners Assn., 1972-73; mem. L'Ermitage Found., 1985—, Instl. Rev. Bd. White Meml. Hosp., L.A., 1975—. Recipient Man of Yr. award L.A. Gen. Agts. and Mgrs. Assn., numerous. Mem. Nat. Life Underwriters Assn., Calif. State Life Underwriters Assn., Investment Co. Inst. (assoc.), Soc. Pension Actuaries, Foothill Community Concert Assn. (pres. 1970-73). Registered investment advisor, SEC, 1984. Office: 709 E Colorado Blvd Ste 270 Pasadena CA 91101

CHRISTENSEN, DUANE LEE, seminary educator; b. Park Rapids, Minn., May 27, 1938; s. John William and Elsie Annabelle (DeFoer) C.; m. Carol Russell Christensen, June 10, 1960; children: Beth, Sharon, Julie. BS, MIT, 1960; MDiv, Am. Bapt. Sem., 1963; ThD, Harvard U., 1972. Ordained to ministry, Bapt. Ch. Min. of edn. First Bapt. Ch., Melrose, Mass., 1965-68; instr. Bridgewater (Mass.) State Coll., 1969-71, asst. prof., 1971-74, assoc. prof., 1974-78; pastor Winter Hill Bapt. Ch., Somerville, Mass., 1972-78; prof. O.T. Am. Bapt. Sem., Berkeley, Calif., 1978—; vis. prof. U. Calif., Berkeley, 1984; pres. Berkeley Inst. of Bible, Archaeology & Law Bibal Corp., 1987—; bd. trustees Am. Schs. Oriental Rsch., Balt., 1986—. Author: Transformations of War Oracle, 1975; editor: Experiencing the Exodus, 1988; contbr. articles to profl. jours. Grantee Hebrew U., Inst. for Adv. Studies, 1983, Assn. Theol. Schs., Vienna, Austria, 1980; Zion Rsch. Found. fellow, 1976. Mem. Cath. Bibl. Assn. (task force com. 1984-89), Soc. Bibl. Lit., Am. Oriental Soc., Internat. Orgn. for Study of O.T. Democrat. Baptist. Home: 845 Bodega Way Rodeo CA 94572 Office: American Bapt Sem 2606 Dwight Way Berkeley CA 94704

CHRISTENSEN, HOWARD ALAN, consulting firm executive; b. Atlantic, Iowa, Aug. 15, 1933; s. J. Chris and S. Christena (Gustafsen) C.; m. Verla Suhr, May 10, 1953; children—Debra, Jo Elyn, Jeffrey. B.S., State U. Iowa, 1959. C.P.A., Kans., Mo. Mgr. Arthur Andersen & Co., Kansas City, Mo., 1959-65; v.p., sec., treas. St. Joseph Light & Power Co., St. Joseph, Mo., 1965-76; treas. Mich. Wis. Pipe Line Co., Detroit, 1976-78; dir. investor relations Am. Natural Resources Co., Detroit, 1978-80, v.p. corp. planning and investor relations, 1980-82; pres. Christensen & Assocs. Ltd., 1982—. Bd. dirs. United Fund, 1972-76. Served with U.S. Army, 1953-55. Mem. Am. Inst. C.P.A.s, Fin. Analyst Fedn., Nat. Investor Relations Inst., C. of C. (dir. 1972-76, 1st v.p. 1975-76), Fin. Exec. Inst., City Miday Lodge, Boardroom Lodge, Rotary (pres. 1968-76), Renaissance Club, Kansas City Athletic Club. Lutheran. Office: Christensen & Assocs Ltd PO Box 4790 Scottsdale AZ 85261

CHRISTENSEN, JEFFREY PAUL, real estate broker; b. Tacoma, Feb. 4, 1952; s. Theodore Christensen and Patricia Molloy (Wittenberg) Murray; m. Linda Joy Ash, Jan. 5, 1974; children: Calvin, Alex. BS, Seattle Pacific U., 1973; student, U. Wash., 1973-75. Assoc. broker Crescent Realty, Spanaway, Wash., 1976-79, Moore Profl. Realty, Tacoma, 1979-87; real estate broker Jeff Christensen, Realtor, Tacoma, 1987—. Mem. Tacoma Bd. Realtors (vice chmn. 1985, com. chmn. 1986-88), South Sound Land Use Assn. (exec. v.p. 1988). Home: 3930 260 St E Spanaway WA 98387 Office: Jeff Christensen Realtor 14208 Pacific Ave Tacoma WA 98444

CHRISTENSEN, JULIE MERCER, association executive, realtor; b. Prosser, Wash., Jan. 28, 1956; d. Milton Thorpe and Freda Wilma (Wagener) Mercer; m. Gordon Christensen, July 6, 1982 (div. 1988); children: Jennifer Lee, Michelle Lynn. Student, Columbia Basin Coll., Washington, 1980-81; pesticide applicator lic., Blue Mountain Coll., 1981. Tchr. Meredith Manor, Waverly, W.Va., 1977; pesticide mgr. Mercer Ranches, Inc., Prosser, Wash., 1977-81; owner, mgr. Horse Heaven Hay Co., Prosser, 1983-88; realtor Century 21 Frontier Brokers, Prosser, 1986—; coord. econ. devel Prosser Econ. Assn., 1988—. Leader Horse Heaven Stockmasters 4-H Club, 1984-87; v.p. Wash. Women for Survival Agr., 1986-77, sec. 1987-88; county rep. Team Washington, 1987. Recipient awards Western Wash. State Fair, 1986, Portland Internat. Expn., 1987. Mem. Prosser Jaycees (v.p. 1987-88), TRI DEC Assn. Devel. Orgn. (bd. dirs. 1988), TRI Cities Diversifaction Leadership Coun. Republican. Mem. Brethren Ch. Home: PO Box 483 Prosser WA 99350 Office: Prosser Econ Devel Assn 519 6th St Prosser WA 99350

CHRISTENSEN, ODIN DALE, geologist; b. Duluth, Minn., Dec. 12, 1947; s. Clarence Henry and Doris Grace (Bahls) C.; m. Brenda Haglund, Mar. 21, 1971 (div. June, 1982). BA, U. Minn., Duluth, 1970; PhD, Stanford U., 1975. Asst. prof. U. N.D., Grand Forks, 1975-78; rsch. geochemist U. Utah Rsch. Inst., Salt Lake City, 1978-81; rsch geologist Newmont Exploration Ltd., Reno, 1981-85; mgr. exploration Newmont Exploration Ltd., Elko, Nev., 1985-88; dir. U.S. exploration Newmont Exploration Ltd., Denver, 1988—. Mem. AIME, Nev. Mining Assn., Soc. Econ. Geologists, Assn. of Exploration Geochemists, Geol. Soc. Am. Office: Newmont Mining Corp One United Bank Ctr 1700 Lincoln Denver CO 80203

CHRISTENSEN, ROBERT WAYNE, JR., financial and leasing company executive; b. Chester, Calif., Nov. 11, 1948; s. Robert Wayne and Ann (Forsyth) C.; m. Debra Schumann, Dec. 6, 1988; 1 child, Heather. BA with honors, Coll. Gt. Falls, 1976; MBA, U. Puget Sound, 1978. Cert. flight instr. Corp. pilot Buttrey Food Stores, Gt. Falls, Mont., 1972-74; asst. to pres. Pacific Hide & Fur, Gt. Falls, 1974-76; fin. analyst Olympia Brewing Co., Olympia, Wash., 1977; pres., chief exec. officer Republic Leasing, Olympia, 1978—; pres. PacWest Fin. Corp., Olympia, 1984—; dir. Republic Leasing, Olympia, 1978—, Wash. Independent Bancshares, Olympia, 1982, PacWest Fin. Corp., Olympia, 1984—, Heritage Fed. Savs. and Loan Assn. Served to sgt. USAF, 1969-72. Mem. Nat. Vehicle Leasing Assn. (bd. dirs. 1978—, 2d. v.p. 1984, pres. 1986), Western Assn. Equipment Lessors, Western Leasing Conf., Mensa. Lodge: Rotary (bd. dirs. 1982—, v.p. 1986-88, pres. 1988—). Office: Republic Leasing The Republic Bldg PO Box 737 Olympia WA 98507

CHRISTENSEN, ROGER GLEN, controller; b. Salt Lake City, Nov. 17, 1953; s. Sheron G. and Colleen (Cloward) C.; m. Christine Cecilia Baker, Dec. 19, 1975; children: Stephen L., Ryan G., Ashlie, Megan, Michelle, Scott D., Jennifer. BS, Brigham Young U., 1977. CPA, Calif., Idaho. Acct. Coopers & Lybrand, San Francisco, 1977-79, Boise, Idaho, 1979-82; audit mgr. Morrison-Knudsen Internat., Barranquilla, Colombia, 1982-86; acctg. mgr. Micron Technology, Boise, 1986-87; internal audit mgr. Associated Food Stores, Inc., Salt Lake City, 1987-88, corp. controller, 1988—. Asst. scout master, Boy Scouts Am., Boise, 1986, unit commr., Salt Lake City, 1987—. Mem. AICPA, Idaho Soc. CPAs. Republican. Mormon. Office: Associated Food Stores Inc 1812 Empire Rd Salt Lake City UT 84104

CHRISTENSEN, RON L., data processing coordinator; b. Hutchinson, Minn., Jan. 1, 1944; s. Ben f. and Lucylle F. (Fisher) C.; m. Mauretta V. Chrispens, Aug. 6, 1967; children: Keith Lee and Mark Randal. BS in Acctg., Union Coll., Lincoln, Nebr., 1966; cert., IBM Sch., Boston, 1967. Computer operator New Eng. Meml. Hosp., Stoneham, Mass., 1967-68, programmer, 1968-70, data processing mgr., 1970-74; programmer N.W. Med. Found., Portland, Oreg., 1974-78; dir. info. services Cascade Health Care, Portland, 1978-80; cons. data processing Portland, 1980-81; data processing coordinator Home Health Edn. Service, Portland, 1981—; Lic. taxpreparer, State of Oreg., Portland, 1976-79; instr. Hood View Jr. Acad., Boring, Oreg., 1986-87. Mem. Common. Avocation: gardening. Home: 14190 SE 177th Ct Boring OR 97009

CHRISTENSEN, STEVEN BRENT, data processing executive; b. Salt Lake City, Feb. 26, 1959; s. Raymond David and Marlene Kay (Manheim) C. BA in Human Resource Devel. cum laude, Brigham Young U., 1983, postgrad. Tng. specialist Am. Express Co., N.Y.C., 1983; mgr. C&J Clark Inc., Orem, Utah, 1984-86; mgr. computer svc. Valcom Computers, Provo, Utah, 1987; cons. Castle Computer Systems, Orem, 1988—. Com. leader Broke Human Domino Record, Guiness Book of World Records, 1981. Vol. asst. Found. Ancient Rsch., Provo, 1987-88; active Mormon Ch. Named one of Outstanding Young Men Am., 1983. Mem. ALA, Spl. Libraries Assn.,

Am. Soc. Tng. and Devel. Republican. Home: 724 W 1720 N #108D Provo UT 84604 Office: Castle Computer Systems Nc 1799 N State Orem UT 84057

CHRISTENSEN, THOMAS MICHAEL, surface physicist; b. Mpls., Dec. 9, 1956; s. Raymond Paul and Ramona Jane (Kinnett) C.; m. Ann Leahigh, June 10, 1989. BS in Physics, U. Minn., 1979, BS in Astrophysics, 1979; MS in Applied Physics, Cornell U., 1981, PhD in Applied Physics, 1985. Grad. rsch. asst. Cornell U., Ithaca, N.Y., 1980-85; mem. tech. staff Sandia Nat. Labs., Albuquerque, 1985-89; asst. prof. physics U. Colo., Colorado Springs, 1989—. Contbr. articles to profl. jours. Pres. bd. dirs. Albuquerque Philharm. Orch., 1987-89. Mem. Am. Vacuum Soc. (local symposium com. 1987-89), Phi Beta Kappa, Tau Beta Pi, Sigma Pi Sigma. Office: Physics Dept Univ Colo PO Box 7150 Colorado Springs CO 80933

CHRISTIAENS, CHRIS (BERNARD F. CHRISTIAENS), financial analyst, senator; b. Conrad, Mont., Mar. 7, 1940; s. Marcel Jules and Virgie Jeanette (Van Spyk) C. BA in Chemistry, Coll. Gt. Falls, 1962, postgrad., 1984—. Fin. and industry mgr. Rice Motors, Gt. Falls, Mont., 1978-84; senator State of Mont., 1983—, majority whip 49th legis., 1985-86; fin. planner Jack Stevens CPA, Gt. Falls, 1984-85; adminstr., fin. analyst Gt. Falls Pre-Release, 1986—. Chmn. Balance of State Pvt. Industry Council, Mont. 1984—; mem. Mont. Human Rights Commn., 1981-84; bd. dirs. St. Thomas Child and Family Ctr., Gt. Falls, 1983—, Coll. Gt. Falls, 1984—; bd. dirs., treas. Gt. Falls Community Food Bank, 1984-86; Dem. committeeman, Cascade County, Mont., 1976-82; Mont. del. to Nat. Rules Conv., 1980; pub. chmn. Cascade County chpt. ARC, 1986; mem. adv. bd. Cambridge Court Sr. Citizen Apt. Complex, 1986; bd. dirs. Cascade County Mental Health Assn., 1986—; treas. Cascade County Mental Health Ctr.; vice-chmn. Gov.'s Task Force on Overcrowding; mem. regional jail com. Named one of Outstanding Young Men of Am., Jaycees, 1976; recipient Outstanding Young Alumni award Coll. Gt. Falls, 1979. Roman Catholic. Clubs: Gt. Falls Ski, Toastmasters. Lodge: Optimists. Home: 210 36th St N Great Falls MT 59401 Office: Great Falls Pre-Release Svcs Inc 1019 15 St N Great Falls MT 59401

CHRISTIAN, MARY NORDEAN, educator; b. Montgomery, Ala., Oct. 28, 1944; d. Gwyn Thomas and Lillie (Beasley) Wilburn; m. Thurmal Christian, June 1, 1984 (div. Aug. 1981). Student, Tuskegee Inst., 1962-64; BS, Ala. State U., 1967; MA, George Washington U., 1981. Cert. tchr. biology, phys. edn. and English. Tchr. Talladego County Bd. Edn., Talladego, Ala., 1967-70; tchr., coach Charles County Bd. Edn., LaPlata, Md., 1970-84, Garvey Sch. Dist., Rosemead, Calif., 1984—; mem. Md. State Track Com., Balt., 1975-84; chmn. So. Md. Athletic Conf. Girls Track Com., 1974-84; mem. Middle States Vis. Coms., 1976, 77, 82, 84. Dir. summer youth program East Washington Heights Bapt. Ch., Washington, 1981; mem. Coun. of Chs. of Greater Washington, 1976-84. Named Coach of Yr., So. Md. Athletic Conf., 1981, 84, Md. Ind. Newspaper, Waldorf, Md., 1984. Mem. NEA, Nat. Congress Parents and Tchrs., Calif. Tchrs. Assn., Garvey Edn. Assn., Alpha Kappa Alpha (parliamentarian 1980-84). Democrat. Baptist. Home: 616 S Glendora Ave Apt A West Covina CA 91790 Office: Fern Intermediate Sch 8470 E Fern Ave Rosemead CA 91770

CHRISTIAN, ROLAND CARL (BUD CHRISTIAN), English and speech communications educator; b. LaSalle, Colo., June 7, 1938; s. Roland Clyde and Ethel Mae (Lattimer) C.; m. Joyce Ann Kincel, Feb. 15, 1959; children: Kathleen Marie Christian-Davis, Kristine May Sweet. BA in English and Speech, U. No. Colo., 1962, MA, 1966. Cert. tchr., N.Y., Colo. Tchr. Southside Jr. High Sch., Rockeville Ctr., N.Y., 1962-63, Plateau Valley High Sch., Collbran, Colo., 1963-67; prof. English Northeastern Jr. coll., Sterling, Colo., 1967—; presenter seminars, workshops, Sterling, 1967—; emcee/host Town Meeting of Am., Sterling, 1976. Author: Be Bright! Be Brief! Be Gone! A Speaker's Guide, 1983, Potpourrivia, A Digest of Curious Words, Phrases and Trivial Information, 1986, Nicknames in Sports: A Quiz book, 1986; lit. adv. New Voices mag., 1983—; contbr. Ways We Write, 1964, The Family Treasury of Great Poems, 1982, Our Twentieth Century's Greatest Poems, 1982, Anti-War Poems; vol. II, 1985, Impressions, 1986, World Poetry Anthology, 1986, American Poetry Anthology, 1986, Chasing Rainbows, 1988, The Poetry of Life, 1988, Hearts on Fire, 1988, Wide Open Magazine, 1986, 87, 88. Served with U.S. Army, 1956-59. Recipient Colo. Recognition of Merit scholarship, 1956, Merit cert. Poets Anonymous, 1983, Award of Merit (9), 1985, 86, Golden Poet of Yr. award World of Poetry Press, 1985, 86, 87, 88, Joel Mack Tchr. of Yr. award Northeastern Jr. Coll., 1986; Jr. Coll. Found. grantee, 1986, 87. Mem. NEA, AAUP, Jr. Coll. Faculty Assn. (sec./treas. 1970-72), Colo. Edn. Assn., Nat. Council Tchrs. of English, Poets of Foothills. Roman Catholic. Home: 1027 Park St Sterling CO 80751 Office: Northeastern Jr Coll Dept Gen Studies Sterling CO 80751

CHRISTIAN, THOMAS EMBREE, pharmacist; b. Waterloo, Iowa, Dec. 6, 1953; s. James Embree and Verna Ione (Harvey) C., Dorothy Schmidt (stepmother); m. Ann Seger, July 21, 1978. BS in Pharmacy with distinction, U. Iowa, 1977. Staff pharmacist unit dose clin. div. U. Iowa Hosps. and Clinics, Iowa City, 1977-80; staff pharmacist SW Wash. Hosps., 1980—; cons. SW Wash. Hosps. Pharmacy & Therapeutics Com., 1982. Mem. Ctr. for Environ. Edn., com. polit. action PharmPAC Wash. Mem. Am. Soc. Hosp. Pharmacists, Wash. Soc. Hosp. Pharmacists, U. Iowa Alumni Assn., U. Iowa Coll. Pharmacy Second Century Fund, Vancouver Humane Soc., Amnesty Internat., Nat. Geog. Soc., Planetary Soc., Cousteau Soc., Greenpeace, Physicians for Social Responsibility, Com. for Sci. Investigation Claims Paranormal, Union Concerned Scientists, Rho Chi. Home: 4114 Idaho St Vancouver WA 98661 Office: St Joseph Community Hosp Pharmacy Dept 600 NE 92d Ave Vancouver WA 98664

CHRISTIANSEN, CHERYL L., motion picture production company executive, food company executive, music publisher, composer; b. Washington, June 10, 1945; d. Frederick Alvin and Lucy Rita (Morelli) C. Student Bus. Mgmt., San Francisco State Coll., 1963; student bus., Heald's Bus. Coll., 1964; student Fine Arts, Otis, Parsons Design Sch., 1989. Dancer Harrah's Club, Lake Tahoe, Calif., 1965-66; actress, dancer Hollywood Studios, L.A., 1966—; dancer, singer The Dean Martin Show NBC TV, L.A., 1969-72; songwriter, singer various recording studios, L.A., 1979—; owner Cee Lu Music Pub., L.A., 1979—; actress Santa Barbara TV Show, L.A., 1985; producer Robert Shields Show, L.A., 1986; pres., bd. chmn. Certified Nuts of Beverly Hills Ltd., L.A., 1985—; sec., treas. DeathRider, Inc., L.A., 1988—; exec. v.p., bd. dirs. Pegasus Entertainment Group, Inc., L.A., 1989—. Composer: You Bring Out The Best in Me, Best Thing We Can Do Is Say Goodbye, Best Days of My Life, 1980, Sweet Surrender, 1981 (Platinum Album). Active in MIA-POW lobby, United Vets. Fund, L.A., Concerned Ams., N.C. Mem. AFTRA, AGVA, SAG, Club Davinci. Republican. Roman Catholic.

CHRISTIANSEN, DALE H., finance executive; b. Pocatello Idaho, Nov. 3, 1951; s. JY and Betty Mae (Hansen) C.; m. Mary Jean Apple, Aug. 5, 1974; children: Matthew, Steven, Nathalie, Karen. BS in Fin., Brigham Young U., 1975; M of Mgmt., Northwestern U., 1977. With mgmt. devel. program Chrysler Corp., Highland Park, Mich., 1977-78; area fin. rep. Chrysler Corp., Highland Park, 1978-80; mgr. fin. planning and analysis Niassan Motor Corp., Carson, Calif., 1980-86; chief fin. officer J.D. Power & Assocs., Agoura Hills, Calif., 1986-88, fin. mgmt. cons., 1988—. Explorer, advisor Ventura Coun. Boy Scouts Am., Fillmore, Calif., 1986-88. Mem. L.A. C. of C. Republican. Mormon. Home: 223 Parkhaven Ct Fillmore CA 93015

CHRISTIANSEN, JOYCE L. SOELBERG, newspaper editor; b. Salt Lake City, May 25, 1924; d. Lloyd LeRoy and Irene (Lindberg) Soelberg; student public schs.; m. Ernald Christiansen, Sept. 7, 1947; children: Melodie Joyce, Lynda Lee, Lloyd Randall, Catherine Jill. Sec., COBUSCO Steel, Salt Lake City, 1941-42, Universal Film, Inc., Salt Lake City, 1942-43, Delivery Service Co., Salt Lake City, 1946-47; legal sec. Clearfield Naval Supply (Utah), 1943-45; editor Sunset News, Bountiful, Utah, 1972-75; religion writer Deseret News, Salt Lake City, 1976-82, photographer, feature writer, 1976—; editor, writer, photographer South Salt Lake Bugle, Salt Lake City, 1982-83. Pres., Backman Elem. Sch. PTA, 1958-60; 2 v.p. N.W. Jr. High Sch. PTA, 1961-62; active Girl Scouts U.S.A., 1965—, originator Girl Scout Baby award, Utah, 1980; mem. adv. bd. N.W. Multi-Purpose Ctr., 1972-82, sec., 1973-82, substitute day care tchr., 1982—; host radio show Get Me to the Church on Time, 1977; mem. Utah Rose Park Latter-day Saint Stake, 1986, pub. relations specialist, 1986—; mem. Salt Lake Library Bd., 1980-86, sec. bd. 1982, mem. ops., bldgs. and grounds coms.; appointed by gov. Utah State Bldg. Bd., Utah State Bldg. ownership Authority. Recipient 3rd place award Nat. Fedn. Press Women Communication Contest, 1977; numerous first and second place awards Utah Press Women. Mem. Nat. Fedn. Press Women, Utah Press Women (sec. 1978-82, corr. sec. 1982—, 2d v.p. 1980-82, 1st v.p. 1986—, pres.-elect 1987—). Mem. Ch. Jesus Christ of Latter-day Saints (mem. Sunday sch. bd. Riverside Stake 1955). Clubs: Women's Dem., Jane Jefferson, Lady Lions (2d v.p. 1979-80). Contbr. articles to Utah Life mag. Home: 755 N 1400 W Salt Lake City UT 84116 Office: Deseret News 30 E 1st St S Salt Lake City UT 84110

CHRISTIANSON, ROGER GORDON, biology educator; b. Santa Monica, Calif., Oct. 31, 1947; s. Kyle C. and Ruby (Parker) C.; m. Angela Diane Rey, Mar. 3, 1967; children: Lisa Marie, David Scott, Stephen Peter. BA in Cell and Organismal Biology, U. Calif., Santa Barbara, 1969, MA in Biology, 1971, PhD in Biology, 1976. Faculty assoc. U. Calif., Santa Barbara, 1973-79, staff research assoc., 1979-80; asst. prof. So. Oreg. State Coll., Ashland, 1980-85, assoc. prof., 1985—. Contbr. articles to profl. jours. Active Oreg. Shakespeare Festival Assn., Ashland, 1983-87; mem. bikeway com. Ashland City Council, 1986-88; coordinator youth program First Bapt. Ch. Ashland, 1981-85, mem. church life commn., 1982-88, organizer Bike Oreg., 1982—, Frontline staff, 1985—; youth leader jr. and sr. high sch. students Grace Ch., Santa Barbara, Calif., 1973-80. Mem. AAAS (coordinator Pacific div. edn. sect. 1985—, council mem. Pacific div. 1985—), Am. Mus. Natural History, Oreg. Sci. Teacher's Assn., Oreg. Acad. Scis. Republican. Home: 430 Reiten Dr Ashland OR 97520 Office: So Oreg State Coll Dept Biology Ashland OR 97520

CHRISTIE, H. FREDERICK, utility company subsidiaries executive; b. Alhambra, Calif., July 10, 1933; s. Andreas B. and Sigrid (Falk-Jorgensen) C.; m. Susan Earley, June 14, 1957; children—Brenda Lynn, Laura Jean. B.S. in Fin., U. So. Calif., 1957, M.B.A., 1964. Treas. So. Calif. Edison Co., Rosemead, 1970-75, v.p., 1975-76, sr. v.p., 1976-80, exec. v.p., 1980-84, pres., dir., 1984-87; pres., chief exec. officer The Mission Group (non-utility subsidiaries SCEcorp.), Seal Beach, CA, 1987—; bd. dirs. Gt. Western Fin. Corp., Beverly Hills, Calif., Ducommun Inc., L.A., Am. Mut. Fund, Inc., L.A., Bond Fund Am., Inc., L.A., Tax-Exempt Bond Fund Am., L.A., Capital Income Builder, L.A., Capital World Bond Fund, L.A., Intermediate Bond Fund Am., L.A.; Assoc. Electric and Gas Ins. Svcs. Ltd., Jersey City; trustee Cash Mgmt. Trust Am., New Economy Fund, Am. Funds Income Series, L.A., The Am. Funds Tax-Exempt Series II; trustee Am. High Income Trust, L.A. Vice chmn. United Way L.A., 1985-88, bd. dirs. 1983-87; trustee Occidental Coll., L.A., Nat. History Mus. Los Angeles County. With U.S. Army, 1953-55. Named Outstanding mem. Arthritis Found., L.A., 1975, Outstanding Trustee, Multiple Sclerosis Soc. So. Calif., 1979. Mem. Pacific Coast Elec. Assn. (bd. dirs. 1981-87 , treas. 1975-87), L.A. C. of C. (bd. dirs. 1983-87). Republican. Club: California. Home: 548 Paseo Del Mar Palos Verdes Est CA 90274 Office: The Mission Group Ste 400 3010 Old Ranch Pkwy Seal Beach CA 90740-2750

CHRISTMAN, HELEN DOROTHY NELSON, resort executive; b. Denver, Nov. 25, 1922; d. Hector C. and Dorothy C. (Hansen) Russell; m. James Ray Christman, Aug. 7, 1942 (dec. June 1986); children: J. Randol, Linda Rae. Student, Colo. U., 1940-42. Producer Sta. KRMA-TV, Denver, 1960-62; resident mgr. Mana Kai Maui, Maui, Hawaii, 1974-76, exec. coord., 1976-78; pres. Resort Apts., Inc., 1986—; bd. dirs. Kihei Community Assn. Pres. Stephen Knight PTA, Denver, 1957; radio and TV chmn. Colo. PTA, 1958-59; producer ednl. TV programs for PTA, Denver County, 1960-61; bd. dirs. Maui United Way, 1983—; precinct pres. Maui Reps.; chmn. Maui County Rep. Com., 1989-91. Mem. Delta Delta Delta, Women's Golf Club (chmn. Silverswood chpt.), Maui Country Club (chmn. women's golf assn. 1987). Address: 3448 Hookipa Kihei HI 96753

CHRISTMAS, JANICE JEAN, multimedia producer; b. Monroe, Wis., Apr. 4, 1946; d. Walter Dean and Helen Isabel (Lanz) Lavasseur; divorced; children: Ianthe Ingham, Anna Elissa. BS in Art Edn., U. Wis., 1974. Guest fashion editor Mademoiselle mag., N.Y.C., 1967; fashion designer N.Y.C., 1967-69; broadcast prodn. coordinator McCann-Erickson, Chgo., 1975-77; prodn. mgr. Laurence Deutsch Design, Los Angeles, 1978-80; producer, v.p. Kevin Biles Design, Venice, Calif., 1980—. Author, producer, dir. videotape Wood Heat, 1975. Troop leader Girl Scouts, Los Angeles U.S., Los Angeles, 1979-80. Mem. Venice C. of C. Home: 12922 Stanwood Dr Los Angeles CA 90066 Office: Kevin Biles Design 13360 Beach Ave Marina Del Rey CA 90292 also: 5 E 16th St 8th Fl New York NY 10003

CHRISTOFFERSEN, JON M., banker; b. Coeur d'Alene, Idaho, Sept. 18, 1942; s. Arne Birger and Mary Louis (Chaney) C.; m. B. Joan Bigley, Apr. 8, 1965; children—Eric Stephen, Lisa M. Student, Wash. State U., 1961; BA, U. Wash., 1964, MBA, 1969; postgrad. advanced mgmt., Harvard U., 1979. With Citibank, 1970-81; v.p. Citibank, Tokyo, 1970-71, Seoul, Republic of Korea, 1971-73, Taipei, Republic China, 1974-76; mng. dir. Citibank, Sydney, Australia, 1976-81; exec. v.p. Rainier Nat. Bank, Seattle, 1981-86, pres., 1986-88, also bd. dirs.; pres. Ranierbancorp., 1986-88, bd. dirs.; pres. Visa USA, San Mateo, Calif., 1988—; bd. dirs. Visa USA, San Mateo; chmn. Oreg. Bank. Portland. Mem. adv. bd. Grad. Sch. Bus. Adminstrn. U. Wash.; bd. dirs. United Way King County, Seattle, 1988. Capt. U.S. Army, 1964-68.

CHRISTOFFERSON, THOMAS LEE, counselor; b. Compton, Calif., Sept. 19, 1949; s. Kenneth L. and Kathleen W. (Stewart) C.; m. Victoria D. Flores; 1 child, Justin Matthew. AA, El Camino Jr. Coll., 1969; BA, San Diego State U., 1972, MS, 1975. Nat. cert. counselor. Career counselor aide San Diego City Schs., 1972-76; counselor Los Alamos (N.Mex.) Schs., 1976—; facilitator group First Jud. Dist., Santa Fe, 1980—; instr. continuing edn. U.N. Mex., 1980-82, 87—; counselor summer sci. Los Alamos Nat. Lab., 1984-86; coordinator test ctr. Ednl. Testing Service, Princton, N.J., 1986—. Mem. steering com. Developing Tomorrows Leaders, Los Alamos County, 1986—; sponsor Los Alamos High Sch. Peer Counselors, 1984—. Grantee Dept. Edn. N.Mex. State, 1977-80. Mem. N.Mex. Sch. Counselor Assn. (chair interprofl. relations 1986-87, pres. 1988-89, named Counselor of Yr. 1987), Am. Sch. Counselor Assn., Assn. Counseling and Devel., Nat. Bd. Cert. Counselors. Democrat. Mem. United Ch. Home: 414 Rover Blvd White Rock NM 87544 Office: Los Alamos High Sch 1300 Diamond Dr Los Alamos NM 87544

CHRISTOPH, CHRISTINE ELIZABETH, real estate professional; b. Oak Park, Ill., July 18, 1951; d. Gustuv William and Elizabeth Christine (Gartmann) C. BS in Interior Design, Purdue U., 1973. Lic. real estate broker, Ill., Kans., Mo. Property mgr. Partnership Concepts, Hinsdale, Ill., 1975-81, Gillingwater Mgmt., Austin, Tex., 1981-82; v.p. acquisitions Encom Properties, Ltd., Mission, Kans., 1982-83; pres., owner Combro Corp., Chgo., 1983-87; real estate agt. The Prudential Lefferdink Peal Estate Co., San Diego, 1987—. Bd. dirs. San Diego unit Am. Cancer Soc., 1988. Mem. Inst. Real Estate Mgmt., San Diego Bd. Realtors. Republican. Presbyterian. Home: 7105 Mimosa Dr Rancho La Costa CA 92009

CHRISTOPHER, GAYLAIRD WILEY, architect; b. L.A., Dec. 14, 1951; s. Wiley S. and Eleanor A. (Smith) C.; m. Gayle Ann Gibbons, Sept. 25, 1976; children: Katie Marie, Whitney Gayle, Hayley Suzanne. AA, Pasadena City Coll., 1972, BArch, Calif. Poly. State U., 1976. Registered architect, Calif. Designer M.R.C. Architects, L.A., 1976-77; designer, architect assoc. Barmakian Wolff & Assocs., Upland, Calif., 1977-81; pres. Wolff, Lang, Christopher Architects Inc., Rancho Cucamonga, Calif., 1981—; adj. educator Chaffey Coll., Rancho Cucamonga, 1982, 83; lectr. and juror in field. Chmn. Upland Archtl. Commn., Calif., 1982-83; mem. State of Calif. Allocation Bd. Legis. Implementation com.; mem. vestry St. Marks Episcopal Ch., Upland, 1984-85. Recipient Honorable Mention design Soc. Am. Registered Architects for Yucca Valley Sr. Ctr., 1983; Honor award Soc. Am. Registered Architects for Long Beach Child Care Ctr., 1984, Nat. Honor award Soc., Design award Am. Registered Architects, 1987, Design award Council Ednl. Facility Planners, 1987, Merit award Ruben & Ayala High Sch., 1987. Mem. AIA (architecture for edn. com., design award Am. Assn. Sch. Adminstrs. for Pomona Vocat. Ctr., Pomona Unified Sch. Dist. 1984, citation for design Foothill chpt. Eagle Canyon Elem. Sch. and Southridge Village Jr. High Sch., Fontana, Calif. 1986), Soc. Am. Registered Architects C. of C., Coalition for Adequate Sch. Housing, Cultural League Advocating Support Arts in Soc. Democrat. Episcopalian. Home: 1055 W 25th St Upland CA 91786 Office: 10470 Foothill Blvd Virginia Dare Tower Rancho Cucamonga CA 91730

CHRISTOPHER, IRVIN WALLACE, dentist; b. Irvine, Ky., June 12, 1925; s. Irvin Wesley and China (Cornelison) C.; m. Helen Judith Bagda, 1949 (dec. 1970); children: Craig Irving, Stacy June. BFA, U. Ariz., 1952; DDS, Northwestern U., 1967. Lic. dentist Ariz., Calif. Sales mgr. Fine Arts Sterling Silver, Louisville, 1948-49, Royal Crest Sterling Silver, Columbus, Ohio, 1950; pilot Coyner Crop Dusters, Phoenix, 1952-55; prin., pilot Christopher Enterprises, Casa Grande, Ariz., 1955-67; pvt. practice Mesa, Tempe, Aria., 1968-83, Gilbert, Ariz., 1983—. Founder Profl. Aid to Handicapped, Tempe, 1975-85. Flight officer USAAF, 1943-45. Fellow Acad. of Dentistry Internat., Acad. Gen. Dentistry; mem. Am. Dental Assn., Fedn. Dentaire Internat., Am. Equilibration Soc., Cranio-Facal Pain Ctr. Assn., Gilbert C. of C. Republican. Methodist. Office: 610 N Gilbert Rd #300 Gilbert AZ 85234

CHRISTOPHER, R. PATRICK, architect; b. New Orleans, June 1, 1950; s. Robert L. and Miriam (Parke) C. BA in Arch., U. Calif., 1972; MS in, Columbia U., N.Y., 1974; attended, Internat. Ctr. for Conservation, Rome, 1976. Archl. historian Conron & Lent, Architects, Santa Fe, N.M., 1975-77; preservation architect Nat. Park Service, Denver, 1977-79; park architect Golden Gate Nat. Recreation Area, San Francisco, 1979—; cons. Mus. New Mex., Santa Fe 1975, Historic Am. Bldgs. Survey, Wash. Co-author: Book, Historic Styles of Santa Fe 1977. Chmn. Sausalito Historic Landmarks Bd., Calif. 1987—; mem. Free Daist Communion Ch. Mem. Nat. Trust for Historic Preservation, Assn. for Preservation. Home: 639 Main St Sausalito CA 94965 Office: Nat Park Service Fort Mason Bldg 201 San Francisco CA 94123

CHRISTOPHER, RAYMOND KEITH, scientific programmer; b. Richmond, Australia, Mar. 9, 1947; came to U.S. 1980; s. William Clarence and Marian Elsa (Donaldson) C. Grad., Royal Melbourne Inst. Tech., Australia, 1968; PhD in Biotech., U. N.S.W., Sydney, 1980. Chem. engr. Chem. Plant & Engring. Co., Melbourne, 1964-68, Unilever Pty. Ltd., Sydney, 1969; profl. officer U. N.S.W., Sydney, 1970-80; sci. programmer Finnigan Corp., San Jose, 1980—. Recipient Australian Synthetic Rubber Co. prize in chem. engring., 1969; Conzinc Riotinto Ltd. research award, 1970-73. Fellow Royal Melbourne Inst. Tech. in Chem. Engring.; mem. Am. Soc. Mass Spectrometry. Anglican Ch. Office: Finnigan Corp 355 River Oaks Pkwy San Jose CA 95134

CHRISTY, JAMES T., minister, writer; b. Leavenworth, Kan., Dec. 3, 1936; s. Peter Frederick Christiansen and Frances Grace (Somers) Christy; m. Velma June Snodgrass, July 17, 1962; children: Jamey, Greg. BA, Southern Nazarene U., 1959, Nazarene Theological Seminary, Kansas City, Mo., 1962; MA, Nazarene Theological Seminary, Kansas City, Mo., 1972, DM, 1978. Pastor Ch. of the Nazarene, Drexel, Mo., 1960-62; pastor Ch. of the Nazarene, Kimball, Nebr., 1962-65, Rochester, Minn., 1965-72, Greeley, Colo., 1972—; chaplain Ch. of the Nazarene to The Mayo Clinic, Rochester 1965-72; counselor Northeast Health Assn., Greeley 1975-85; regent Northwest Nazarene Coll. Nampa, Idaho 1982—; bd. dirs. several orgns. with Ch. of the Nazarene 1962—. Author: book, The Puppet Ministry 1978, dozens of articles and writing contests. Chmn. Centennial-Bi-Centennial Religious Heritage, Greeley, Colo. 1976; dir. Budget Counseling, Greeley, 1980, Food/Aid, Greeley, 1986. Mem. Greeley Area Ministeral Assn. (pres. 1978), Long's Peak Council. Office: SunnyView Nazarene 4100 W 20th St Greeley CO 80634

CHRISTY, THOMAS PATRICK, banker; b. Urbana, Ill., May 18, 1943; s. Edward Michael and Iona Theresa (Rogers) C.; m. Marjorie Anne McIntyre, June 1966 (div. May 1973); children: Thomas Patrick Jr., Derek Edward; m. Sandra Allen Stern, May 19, 1984; 1 child, Patrick Edward. BA in Psychology, Adams State Coll., 1965. Tchr. Colorado Springs Pub. Sch., 1965-69; regional personnel dir. Forest Service USDA, Washington, 1969-81; sr. account exec. Mgmt. Recruiters Inc., Costa Mesa, Calif., 1981-84; v.p. Coleman & Assoc. Inc., Santa Monica, Calif., 1984; asst. v.p. Union Bank, Los Angeles, 1984—; adj. prof. grad. sch. bus. Northrop U., Los Angeles. Arbitrator Bus. and Consumer Arbitrator program Better Bus. Bur., Los Angeles and Orange County; mem. Pasadena Area Young Reps. Mem. Personnel and Indsl. Relations Assn. (chmn. fed. issues com, govtl. affairs com.), Employment Mgrs. Assn. (co-chmn. regional com.), Am. Soc. of Personnel Adminstrs., Soc. of Profls. in Dispute Resolution, Sigma Pi Alumni Assn., Adams State Coll. Alumni Assn. (Calif. state pres.), AAUP. Episcopalian. Clubs: Athletic (Los Angeles), Beach (Santa Monica). Home: 1730 Banning Way San Marino CA 91108-1714 Office: Union Bank Corp Staffing Dept 445 S Figuroa St Los Angeles CA 90071

CHRISTY, WILLIAM O., food products company executive; b. 1931. With Certified Grocers of Calif. Ltd., 1952-60; owner Rancho Mirage, Calif., 1960-62; with Certified Grocers of Calif., 1962—, asst. treas., 1971-72, treas., 1972-74, sr. v.p., 1974-75, exec. v.p., 1975-77, chief exec. officer, 1977—, now pres., dir. Office: Cert Grocers of Calif Ltd 2601 S Eastern Ave Los Angeles CA 90040 *

CHRYSSANTHOU, ALINA HELEN, advertising and public relations executive; b. N.Y.C., May 11, 1962; d. Chrys and Effie (Fotiades) C. BSBA, Ariz. State U., 1984, BA in Mass Communications, 1984, MBA, 1986. Media buyer Martz & Assoc., Scottsdale, Ariz., 1985-87; sales coord. United TV/KUTP-TV45, Phoenix, 1985-87; advt. dir. Sun Lakes Mktg., Phoenix, 1987—; cons. in field. Mem. North Shore Animal League, Washington, 1984. Named 1st Runner-up Music Video Wavelength/KTVK-TV13, 1983. Mem. Sigma Iota Epsilon. Home: 4424 E Baseline Rd #2107 Phoenix AZ 85044 Office: Sun Lake Mktg 25612 EJ Robson Blvd Sun Lakes AZ 85248

CHU, EUGENE YUN-CHING, engineer; b. Taipei, Taiwan, May 22, 1959; came to U.S., 1968; s. George P.C. and Jane C.; m. Susan Maxwell, Aug. 1, 1987. BEE, U. Detroit, 1982; MEE, Calif. Inst. of Tech., Pasadena, 1983. Engring. trainee Ford Motor Co., Dearborn, Mich., 1979-80, Environ. Research Inst. of Mich., Ann Arbor, 1980-82; sr. engr. Jet Propulsion Lab., Pasadena, Calif., 1983—. Recipient design award U. of Detroit, 1982. Home: 585 Avocado Ave Pasadena CA 91107 Office: Jet Propulsion Lab 4800 Oak Grove Dr M/S 300-243 Pasadena CA 91109

CHU, TONY YELING, business executive. financial consultant; b. Shanghai, Republic of China, Dec. 21, 1936; came to U.S., 1974; s. Victor and Laura (Chang) C.; m. Grace Chow, Nov. 21, 1965; children: Johnny Tony Yung-Wai Jr., Pai-Ling. BA in Western Lit., Tamkong U., Taipei, Republic of China, 1965; MBA, City U., Bellevue, Wash., 1983, MPA, 1984; BS in Computer Sci., Seattle Pacific U., 1985; postgrad., Nova U., 1987—. Computer programmer Wash. Community Coll. Computing Consortium, 1977-78, with data control, 1980-85; acctg. supr. Mars Express Co., Seattle, 1979-80; instr. Seattle Cen. Community Coll., 1983-84; contr. Ocean City Co. Ltd., Seattle, 1985—. Mem. Am. Acad. Mgmt., United Comml. Travelers. Democrat. Roman Catholic. Home: 2110 NE 137th St Seattle WA 98125

CHUANG, TUNG JUNG, chemist; b. Chiayi, Taiwan, Apr. 25, 1940; came to U.S., 1964; s. King T. and Kuei-Li (Chang) C.; m. Betty Y. Chiang, Dec. 30, 1969; 1 child, Henry H. BS, Nat. Taiwan U., 1963; MS, U. Ill., 1966; PhD, U. Calif., Berkeley, 1970. Postdoctoral fellow IBM Research Lab., San Jose, Calif., 1970-71, mem. research staff, 1971—; adj. prof. San Diego State U., 1984—; vis. prof. U. Munich, 1985-86. Contbr. articles to profl. jours.; patentee in field. Grantee NSF, 1985; recipient IBM Outstanding Innovation award, 1982, 87, Alexander Von Humbold Sr. U.S. Scientist award Alexander Von Humboldt Found., 1985. Mem. Am. Chem. Soc., Am. Vacuum Soc., Am. Inst. Physics. Democrat. Office: IBM Almaden Rsch Ctr K33/801 650 Harry Rd San Jose CA 95120-6099

CHUCK, MARILYN, advertising executive; b. N.Y.C., Aug. 25, 1935; d. Samuel and Dorothy (Finklestein) Dunayer; m. Robert Alan Chuck, Feb. 9, 1956 (separated); children: Adam R., Matthew L., Deborah L. BS in Math., Hunter Coll., 1956; postgrad., UCLA, 1977-79. Dir. of staff SmokEnders

Inc., Woodland Hills, Calif., 1976-79; regional dir. SmokEnders Inc., Reseda, Calif., 1979-80, nat. v.p., 1980-81, nat. pres., 1981-82; ptnr. WO is Me, Northridge, Calif., 1982-84, Ready to Show, Northridge, 1983-84, Chellor Mktg. Coop., Northridge, 1984—; v.p. Direct Mail Mktg. Co. Los Angeles, Sherman Oaks, 1985—; chief exec. officer DMMC Inc., Sherman Oaks, 1987—; also bd. dirs. DMMC Inc. Mem. Direct Mktg. Assn., Pi Mu Epsilon. Democrat. Jewish. Office: DMMC Inc 16005 Sherman Way Ste 300 Van Nuys CA 91406

CHUCK, WALTER G(OONSUN), lawyer; b. Wailuku, Maui, Hawaii, Sept. 10, 1920; s. Hong Yee and Aoe (Ting) C.; m. Marian Chun, Sept. 11, 1943; children: Jamie Allison, Walter Gregory, Meredith Jayne. Ed.B., U. Hawaii, 1941; J.D., Harvard U., 1948. Bar: Hawaii 1948. Navy auditor Pearl Harbor, 1941; field agt. Social Security Bd., 1942; labor law insp. Terr. Dept. Labor, 1943; law clk. firm Ropes, Gray, Best, Coolidge & Rugg, 1948; asst. pub. prosecutor City and County of Honolulu, 1949; with Fong, Miho & Choy, 1950-53; ptnr. Fong, Miho, Choy & Chuck, 1953-58; pvt. practice law Honolulu, 1958-65; ptnr. Chuck & Fujiyama, Honolulu, 1965-74; ptnr. firm Chuck, Wong & Tonaki, Honolulu, 1974-76, Chuck & Pai, Honolulu, 1976-78; sole practice Honolulu, 1978-80; pres. Walter G. Chuck Law Corp., Honolulu, 1980—; dist. magistrate Dist. Ct. Honolulu, 1956-63; gen. ptnr. M & W Assocs., Tripler Warehousing Co., Kapalama Investment Co.; dir. Aloha Airlines, Inc., Honolulu Painting Co., Ltd., Negov Inc. subs. Volkswagen of Am. Inc. Chmn. Hawaii Employment Relations Bd., 1955-59; bd. dirs. Nat. Assn. State Labor Relations Bd., 1957-58, Honolulu Theatre for Youth, 1977-80; chief clk. Ho. of Reps., 1951, 53; chief clk. Hawaii senate, 1959-61; govt. appeal agt. SSS, 1953-72; mem. jud. council, State of Hawaii; exec. com. Hawaiian Open; dir. Friends of Judiciary History Ctr. Inc., 1983—; former bd. dirs. YMCA. Served as capt. inf. Hawaii Territorial Guard. Fellow Internat. Acad. Trial Lawyers (dir.); mem. ABA (chmn. Hawaii sr. lawyers div.), Hawaii Bar Assn. (pres. 1963), Am. Trial Lawyers Assn. (editor), U. Hawaii Alumni Assn. (Distinguished Service award 1967, dir., bd. govs.), Law Sci. Inst., Assoc. Students U. Hawaii (pres.), Am. Judicature Soc., Internat. Soc. Barristers, Am. Inst. Banking, Chinese C. of C. Republican. Clubs: Harvard of Hawaii, Waialae Country (pres. 1975), Pacific, Oahu Country. Home: 2691 Aaliamanu Pl Honolulu HI 96813 Office: Ste 1814 745 Fort St Honolulu HI 96813

CHUKS-ORJI, AUSTIN OGONNA, automotive executive; b. Enugu, Anambra, Nigeria, May 29, 1943; came to U.S., 1964; s. Arum Okosisi and Maria Nneze (Ogbuonye) C.-O; m. Mabel Eke Nnatu, Feb. 12, 1972 (div. Oct. 1978); children: Loretta, Leslie Austin Jr.; m. Gloria Nnenna Nkwonta; children: Nancy, Brenda, Michael, Robert. AA, Coll. of Marin, Kentfield, Calif.; BA, San Francisco State U., 1968; MBA, U. San Francisco, 1970; PhD, Oxford (Calif.) U., 1976. Franchise owner McDonald's, Oakland, Calif., 1971-85; founder Martins Fast Foods, Enugu and Lagos, Nigeria, 1979-84; chmn. Macon's, Lagos, Nigeria, 1979-86; pres. Real Co., Ltd., San Francisco, 1973—; chmn. Am. Investrade, Oakland, Calif., 1984—; pres. Mission Blvd Lincoln-Mercury, Hayward, Calif., 1985—. Author: Names from Africa, 1972, African Wise Sayings, 1973. Senatorial chmn. Nat. Polit. Party, Enugu, 1979, deputy chmn. Anambra state br. 1980, v.p., nat. chmn. 1979-83; chmn. Housing Corp., Enugu, 1979-83. Named one of Top 100 Black-owned Bus. in USA Black Enterprise mag., N.Y.C., 1986, one of Top 2 Black-owned Bus. in San Francisco, 1986. Mem. Black Automobile Dealers Assn., Nat. Automobile Dealers Assn., Lincoln-Mercury Dealers Assn., Ford Dealers Assn., NAACP. Democrat. Baptist. Office: Mission Blvd Lincoln-Mercury 24644 Mission Blvd Hayward CA 94544

CHUN, LOWELL KOON WA, architect; b. Honolulu, Sept. 2, 1944; s. Kwai Wood and Sara Lau C. BA in Eng., U. Hawaii, 1967; BArch, Cornell U., 1971. Registered profl. architect, Hawaii. Archtl. designer Wilson, Okamoto & Assocs., Honolulu, 1972-74; architect, planner Aotani & Assocs., Inc., Honolulu, 1974-82; design planner Daniel, Mann, Johnson & Mendenhall, Manila and Honolulu, 1982-84; architect, planner Alfred A. Yee div. Leo A. Daly Co., Honolulu, 1984-87; prin. Lowell Chun Planning & Design, Honolulu, 1987-89; dir. of planning Daniel, Mann, Johnson & Mendenhall, Honolulu, 1989—. Prin. author: Kauai Parks and Recreation Master Plan, 1978, Hawaii State Recreation Plan (Maximum Federal Eligibility award, 1980), Maui Community Plans, 1981, Hilo Civic Ctr. Master Improvements Plan, 1989. Advisor, locations officer Maitreya Inst., Honolulu, 1983-84; v.p., treas. Kagyu Theg Chen Ling Tibetan Ctr., Honolulu, 1982, 84; rep. Environ. Coalition to Hawaii State Legislature, 1974. Recipient Master Plan award Nat. Assn. Counties, 1975. Mem. Am. Planning Assn. (local exec. com. mem.-at-large 1987-88), Sierra Club (local vice-chmn. 1974-76). Buddhist. Club: Cornell of Hawaii (Honolulu). Home: 456 N Judd St Honolulu HI 96817 Office: DMJM Hawaii Cen Pacific Pla 220 S King St Ste 1570 Honolulu HI 96813

CHUN, WENDY SAU WAN, investment company executive; b. China, Oct. 17, 1951; came to U.S., 1975, naturalized, 1988; d. Siu Kee and Lai Ching (Wong) C.; m. Wing Chiu Ng, Aug. 12, 1976. B.S., Hong Kong Bapt. Coll., 1973; postgrad. U. Hawaii-Manoa, 1975-77. Real estate saleswoman Tropic Shores Realty Co., Honolulu, 1977-80; pres., prin., broker Advance Realty Investment Co., Honolulu, 1980—; owner Video Fun Centre, Honolulu, 1981-83; pres, Asia-Am. Bus Cons., Inc., Canada, 1986—; co-owner, dir. H & N Tax, Honolulu, 1983—; bd. dirs. B.P.D. Internat., Ltd., Hong Kong; exec. dir. Asia-Am. Investment Inc., Hong Kong and Taipei, Taichung and Kao Hsiung brs., 1985—; pres. Asia-Am. Internat., Ltd., Honolulu, 1989. Mem. Nat. Assn. Realtors. Avocations: singing; dancing; swimming; dramatic performances. Home: Apt 3302 2333 Kapiolani Blvd Honolulu HI 96826

CHUNG, JAY HOON, aerospace company executive; b. Seoul, Republic of Korea, May 8, 1947; came to U.S., 1977; s. Il S. and Chung H. (Kim) C.; m. Sue Chungsook Roh, Apr. 10, 1971; children: Julie J., Connie Y. BS in Engring., Seoul Nat. U., 1968; MS in Engring., Calif. State U., Long Beach, 1982; PhD, U. Calif., Irvine, 1988. Chief engr. Taihan Electric Wire Co., Ltd., Seoul, 1970-74; exec. mgr. Ah-Seong Internat., Inc., Seoul, 1974-77; v.p. Tayo Engring., Inc., Long Beach, 1978—. Inventor O-Ring Heating System for Space Shuttle, Infrared Calibration Source for Space Surveillance Satellite. Mem. L.A. Philanthropic Found., 1985. Recipient Indsl. Achievement award Dept. Trade and Industry, Republic of Korea, 1988. Mem. AIAA, ASME, Am. Soc. Metals, Korean Scientists and Engrs. Assn. in Am., Long Beach Korean C. of C. (chmn. 1987), Long Beach Area C. of C. (bd. dirs. 1988). Home: 6762 Vista Del Sol Dr Huntington Beach CA 92647 Office: Tayco Engring Inc 441 E 4th St Long Beach CA 90801

CHUNG, STEWART, architect; b. Hong Kong, Sept. 2, 1956; came to U.S., 1973; s. Shek-Chuen and Alice (Wong) C. BArch, U. So. Calif., 1979; MArch, UCLA, 1981. Architect Jarvis & Murray AIA, Newport Beach, Calif., 1979-81; prin. Chung & Assocs., South Pasadena, Calif., 1981—; chmn. Com. to Rebuild South Pasadena, 1984-85; mem. adv. com. Cerritos Coll., Norwalk, Calif., 1985—. Served to lt. USNR, 1985—. Mem. AIA. Republican. Home and Office: 2000 Hanscom Dr South Pasadena CA 91030

CHURCH, A. MAUDE, artist; b. Berkeley, Calif., June 15, 1949; d. Edwin Sears and Adelaide Maude (Barton) C. Student, Antioch Coll., Yellow Springs, Ohio, 1969-70; BFA, Calif. Coll. Arts and Crafts, 1972; MA, Byam Shaw Coll. Art, London, 1973. Freelance artist Oakland, Calif., 1973—; adj. instr. humanities dept. Calif. Sch. Profl. Psychology, Alameda, Calif., 1974—, San Francisco Art Inst., 1982-83. Exhibited in one-woman shows including Pacific Grove (Calif.) Art Ctr., 1987, Maud Kerns Art Ctr., Eugene, Oreg., 1987, So. Exposure Gallery, San Francisco, 1987, Barlett Gallery, Pleasonton, Calif., 1987, Coos Bay (Oreg.) Art Mus., 1987, Artists Against AIDS, San Francisco, 1988, Wrubel Gallery, Berkeley, 1988 and numerous others; represented in numerous pvt. collections; edit. bd.: Dialogue Journal, 1987—; designer of several book and album covers. Bd. dirs. Friends of San Francisco Psychoanalytic Inst., 1984—. Named one of Outstanding Young Women of Yr., City of Montgomery, Ala., 1979. Mem. No. Calif. Women's Caucus for Art (v.p. 1987-89, program chmn. 1989), No. Calif. Artist's Equity Assn. (pres. 1977-79, bd. dirs. 1974-76), Calif. Lawyers for Arts (adv. bd. 1977-79). Democrat.

CHURCH, BRUCE EDWARD, propulsion devices manufacturing company executive; b. Cleve., Feb. 29, 1936; s. Donald Leroy and Isobel (Heath) C.; m. Jeanne Gilmore, June 9, 1956 (div. Mar. 1983); children: Christopher, Bonnie, Bruce, Michael. BSME, Akron U., 1958. Registered profl. engr., Ohio, Ariz. Aerospace engr. Lewis Rsch. Ctr., NASA, Cleve., 1959-63; project engr. Rocket Power Inc., Mesa, Ariz., 1963-66; sr. project engr. Quantic Industries, San Carlos, Calif., 1968-70; dir. advanced projects Universal Propulsion Co., Phoenix, 1970—. Capt. USAF, 1959-62. Mem. Nat. Soc. Profl. Engrs., Am. Def. Preparedness Assn., Safety and Flight Equipment Assn., Sigma Tau, Phi Delta Theta. Republican. Office: Universal Propulsion Co 25401 N Central Phoenix AZ 85029

CHURCH, JOHN S., economist; b. Ilwaco, Wash., Dec. 15, 1948; s. James Stewart and Frieda Carolyn (Zinn) C.; m. Kathleen Ann Spencer, July 6, 1971; children: Nathan, Shanna, Nicholas, Daniel, Sarah. BBA, Boise State U., 1979; MA in Econs., U. Idaho, 1981. Economist Idaho Power Co., Boise, 1980—; instr. econs. Boise State U., 1981—. Office: Idaho Power Co PO Box 70 Boise ID 83707

CHURCH, LORENE KEMMERER, government official; b. Jordan, Mont., Oct. 18, 1929; d. Harry F. and Laura (Stoller) Kemmerer; m. Scott Johnston, Sept. 8, 1948 (div. 1953); children: Linda M., Theodore O.; m. Fred C. Church, May 9, 1956; children: Ned B., Nia J. Student, Portland Community Coll., 1973-76, Portland State U., 1978-79. Sec. intelligence div. IRS, Portland, Oreg., 1973-75; trade asst. Internat. Trade Adminstrn., U.S. Dept. Commerce, Portland, 1975-84, internat. trade specialist, 1984—. Recipient high performance award U.S. Dept. Commerce, 1986, spl. act and svc. award, 1987. Mem. NAFE, World Affairs Coun., N.W. China Coun., Portland C. of C. (Europe 1992 com. 1988-89, internat. trade adv. bd. 1988-89). Democrat. Roman Catholic. Home: 19725 SW Pike St Beaverton OR 97007 Office: US Dept Commerce US&FCS 1200 SW 3d Ave Rm 618 Portland OR 97204

CHURCHILL, WILLIAM DELEE, retired educator, psychologist; b. Buffalo, Nov. 4, 1919; s. Glenn Luman and Ethel (Smith) C.; AB, Colgate U., 1941; MEd, Alfred U., 1951; EdD, U. Rochester, 1969; m. Beulah Coleman, Apr. 5, 1943; children: Cherylee, Christie. Tchr. secondary sci., Canaseraga, N.Y., 1947-56; dir. guidance Alfred-Almond Sch., Almond, N.Y., 1956-63; grad. asst. U. Rochester, 1963-65; asst. prof. psychology Alfred (N.Y.) U., 1965-66; assoc. prof. edn. Ariz. State U., Tempe, 1966-86. Lt. col. USAAF, 1942-46, PTO. Mem. Am. Psychol. Assn., Western Psychol Assn., Ariz. Psychol. Assn., Am. Ednl. Rsch. Assn. Author: Career Survey of Graduates, 1973. Home: 11454 N 85th St Scottsdale AZ 85260

CHURCHMAN, ARTHUR DAVID, aerospace analyst; b. London, Mar. 4, 1952; came to U.S., 1976; s. Arthur Alfred and Monica Mary (Power) C.; m. Sharon Kay Iverson, Dec. 20, 1975; children: Michael David, Kimberly Marie. BSc in Engring., Cambridge U., 1972; MSc in Math., London U., 1974. Sr. engr. Internat. Computers, London and eastern Europe, 1969-76; computer engr. Honeywell, Seattle, 1976-78; computer analyst Wang Labs., Lowell, Mass., 1978-79; tech. dir. Am. Concrete, Seattle, 1979-80; aerospace analyst Boeing Advanced Systems, Seattle, 1980—. Republican. Episcopalian. Home: 1409 Valley View Dr Puyallup WA 98372 Office: Boeing Advanced Systems PO Box 3707 Seattle WA 98124

CHUR-OGURA, LOIS LEILANI (LOIS LEILANI CHANG), interior floral designer, real estate development consultant, business researcher; b. Yokohama, Japan, Aug. 31, 1955; came to U.S., 1973; d. John Joseph and Reiko (Ogura) Chur; m. Fu-Lien (Henry) Chang, Apr. 28, 1978 (div. July 1986); 1 child, Vincent Eugene. Cert. in music, Kawai Music Sch., Japan, 1973; Assoc. in Social Sciences, Indian Valley Colls., 1975; BA in Mgmt., Sonoma State U., 1978; MBA, Golden State U., 1981; grad., Indian Valley Colls., Anthony Sch. of Real Estate, 1975-88. Reg. Calif. life ins. underwriter. Credit analyst Fed. Home Loan Bank of San Franciso, 1975-76; research officer in office of the pres. Calif. First Bank, San Francisco, 1978-82; assoc. structural engr. Henry Chang & Assocs., San Francisco, 1978-82; rep. A.L. Williams, Inc., Burlingame, Calif., 1986—; designer, owner Leilani Designs, Redwood City, Calif., 1986—; pvt. practice choral and piano instrn., San Francisco, 1973-85; real estate and investment cons. to various cos. and individuals, Redwood City, 1979—; cons. Living Data Systems, Redwood City, 1987—; children educator Kiddieland Play Nursery, San Francisco, 1984—. Fund-raiser to various orgns., 1973-86. Recipient recognition award Chase Manhattan Bank, Japan, 1971. Mem. Japan Soc., Smithsonian Instn., Nichiren Shoshu of Am. (recognition awards 1975-85), Nat. Assn. for Female Execs., San Francisco Zool. Soc., Williams Ltd. Buddhist. Office: Leilani Designs 802 Newport Circle Redwood City CA 94065

CHUTE, DONALD DEAN, leasing company executive; b. Creston, Iowa, Dec. 25, 1944; s. Paul Clifford and Harriet Ann (Lawrence) S.; m. Helen Elaine Hogan, Aug. 27, 1966; children: Dawn M., Robin A. BA in Bus. Mgmt., Sonoma State U., 1974. Spl. asst. So. Pacific Transp. Co., San Francisco, 1974, car hire acctg. mgr., 1975-78; car hire acctg. mgr. Itel Rail Corp., San Francisco, 1978-80; car hire acctg. dir. Itel Rail Corp. div. Itel Corp., San Francisco, 1981, car hire & system services dir., 1982-83, car hire, bus. systems planning and ops. dir., 1983, dir. ops., 1983-87, chmn. Vista user liaison com., 1987—. Served as master sgt. Calif. Air N.G., 1966-88. Mem. Nat. and Southwestern Care Hire and Car Service Assns., Am. Short Line Assn., Internat. Platform Assn., Enlisted Assn. Nat. Guard U.S. (life-time). Republican. Roman Catholic. Office: Itel Rail Corp 55 Francisco San Francisco CA 94133

CICCIARELLI, JAMES CARL, immunology educator; b. Toluca, Ill., May 26, 1947; s. Maurice Cicciarelli and Helen Ippolito; divorced; 1 child, Nicola. BS, Tulane U., 1969; PhD, So. Ill. U., 1977. Lic. clin. lab. dir., Calif. Postdoctoral fellow dept. surgery UCLA, 1977-79, asst. prof. immunology, 1980-87, assoc. prof., 1987—; staff lab. Metic Transplant Lab., Inc., L.A., 1984—. Contbr. articles to sci. jours., chpts. to books. Councillor Hermosa Beach (Calif.) Sch. Site Coun., 1987. NIH rsch. grantee, 1985-88. Mem. Am. Soc. Histocompatibility and Immunogenetics, Internat. Transplant Soc., Am. Soc. Transplant Physicians. Republican. Roman Catholic. Home: 1527 Manhattan Ave Hermosa Beach CA 90254 Office: UCLA Dept Surgery Rehab Ctr 1000 Veteran Ave Los Angeles CA 90024

CICCONE, AMY NAVRATIL, art librarian; b. Detroit, Sept. 19, 1950; d. Gerald R. and Ruth C. (Kauer) Navratil. BA, Wayne State U., 1972; AM in Library Sci., U. Mich., 1973. Rsch. librarian Norton Simon Mus., Pasadena, Calif., 1974-81; chief librarian Chrysler Mus., Norfolk, Va., 1981-88; head librarian Architecture and Fine Arts Library U. So. Calif., L.A., 1988—. Contbr. articles to profl. jours. Mem. Art Libraries Soc. N.Am. (facilities standards com. 1986—, vice-chmn. So. Calif. chpt. 1989—). Office: U So Calif Library Architecture and Fine Arts Los Angeles CA 90089-0182

CICHOKE, ANTHONY JOSEPH, JR., chiropractor; b. Peoria, Ill., Nov. 23, 1931; s. Anthony Joseph Sr. and Margaret Mary (Conwell) C.; m. Margaret A. Kovner, Feb. 24, 1962; children: Anthony Joseph III, Michael David, William F., Margaret Kathleen. BS in Social Sci., John Carroll U., 1954; student, Army Lang. Sch., Monterey, Calif., 1955; MA in Speech and Theater, St. Louis U., 1964; MA in Speech Sci. Pathology and Audiology, U. Minn., 1967; postgrad., Case Western Res. U., 1969; D. Chiropractic, Nat. Coll. Chiropractic, Lombard, Ill., 1973; postgrad., Western States Chiropractic Coll., 1975. Diplomate Nat. Bd. Chiropractic Examiners, Am. Chiropractic Bd. Nutrition. Actor, promoter Schubert Orgn., N.Y.C., 1960-61; entertainment dir., producer U.S. Army and 2d Army, Ft. Eustis, Va., 1961-62; actor, tchr. radio announcer U. Minn., Mpls., 1964-67; tchr., researcher Eastman Dental Ctr., Rochester, N.Y., 1967-68; team physician Portland State U. Amateur Athletic Union, 1975-84; instr. and lectr. on sports medicine, nutrition, and chiropractic medicine at seminars, convs. and various colls. and univs; researcher. Contbr. over 100 articles to profl. journals; editor Nutritional Prospectives mag, 1979; producer Blockheads, London, 1984-85, This was Burlesque, L.A., 1985. Chmn. sports medicine com. Amateur Athletic Union, 1975—; mem. postgrad. faculty numerous chiropractic colls. 1st lt. U.S. Army, 1955-59. Grantee U.S. Office Edn., 1965-67, Case We. Res. U., 1968-69, U. Minn., 1965-67, NIH, 1968-69. Fellow Internat. Assn. Study of Pain (diplomate), Internat. Coll. Chiropractic; mem. Am. Chiropractic Assn. (council on orthopedics, 3 man posture com., council on sports injuries, past pres. and v.p. council on nutrition), Oreg. Chiropractic Physicians Assn., New York Acad. Scis., Orthomolecular Med. Soc., Acad. Orthomolecular Psychiatry, Acad. Sports Medicine, U.S. Sports Acad., Found. Chiropractic Edn. and Research, Metabolic Research Found., Portland C. of C. (edn. com.). Republican. Roman Catholic. Lodges: Kiwanis, KC, Elks. Office: Cichoke Chiropractic Clinic 15925 SE Stark St Portland OR 97233

CIELLE, CYNTHIA ELIZABETH, management consultant; b. Phoenix, June 15, 1949; d. Elmer Smith and Olive Elizabeth (Goman) Green; m. Carl Dean Southard, Apr. 29, 1972 (div. May 1978). BA, U. Ariz., 1971; Master of Internat. Mgmt., Am. Grad. Sch. Internat. Mgmt., 1980. Asst. buyer Macy's, San Francisco, 1971-73; supr. Calif. Social Svcs., Vallejo, 1973-78; gen. mgr. Phoenix Export Systems, Scottsdale, Ariz.-, 1980-81; ops. mgr. Bell Industries, Tempe, Ariz., 1981-83; dir. ops. Euro-Dip, Inc., Tempe, 1983-85; pres. Cielle & Assocs., Phoenix, 1986—. Author: Fun in a Foreign Language, 1985. Gen. mem. by mayoral appointment Phoenix Local Devel. Corp., 1986—; vol. World Affairs Coun., Phoenix, 1984—. Mem. Mensa (pres. Phoenix chpt. 1983-85), Intertel. Republican. Office: Cielle & Assocs PO Box 17088 Phoenix AZ 85011

CIERNIA, JAMES RICHARD, financial advisor; b. St. Paul, Sept. 22, 1933; s. Albert Joseph and Lillian Caroline (Kemski) C.; m. Mary Elizabeth Friese, Aug. 4, 1956; children: Karen M., Mark J., Jennifer M., Scott W. BA, Calif. State U., Long Beach, 1954; PhD, Clayton U., 1983. CLU. Group ins. mgr. Conn. Gen. Life Ins. Co., Long Beach, 1957-60; account exec. Johnson and Higgins, L.A., 1960-65; v.p. Behrendt-Levy, L.A., 1965-67; pres., owner Ciernia Co., Denver, 1967-73; sr. v.p. Frank B. Hall Inc., Denver, 1973-75; owner, mgr., cons. Cernia Co., Investment Account Svcs. Corp., San Luis Obispo, Calif., 1975—; with mktg. RNC Capital Mgmt., L.A., 1978-85. Bd. dirs. Colo. Comprehensive Planning Coun., 1970, Cen. City Opera House Assn., 1973. Lt. (j.g.) USN, 1951-53. Mem. Nat. Assn. Securities Dealers, Mensa, San Luis Obispo Country Club (bd. dirs. 1979-80). Home and Office: 153 Country Club Dr San Luis Obispo CA 93401

CILANO, JAMES ALLEN, avionics test engineer; b. Rochester, N.Y., July 18, 1955; s. Joseph Emilio and Dorothy May (Bush) C.; m. Peggy Ann Saunders, Nov. 7, 1979. AS Elec. Engring. Tech., Ohio Inst. Tech., 1977, BS Elec. Engring. Tech., 1978; MS Bus. Orgnl. Mgmt., U. LaVerne, 1988. Field svcs. engr. Itek Corp. (OSD), Sunnyvale, Calif., 1978-80; liaison engr. Lockheed Calif. Co., Palmdale, 1980-81; design engr. Lockheed Calif. Co., Burbank, 1981-82; liaison engr. Northrop Corp., Palmdale, 1982-85; sr. test engr. Northrop Corp., Hawthorne, Calif., 1985—. Mem. IEEE (assoc.), Engring. Mgmt. Soc., Aerospace and Elec. System Soc. Democrat. Roman Catholic. Home: 8207 Mammoth Circle Buena Park CA 90621

CIMINO, RICHARD ANGELO, broadcasting personality, actor; b. Gilroy, Calif., Dec. 17, 1929; s. Angelo and Laura Maria (Macchione) C.; student Hartnell Coll., 1948-50; m. Enid Lucile Kilburn, Dec. 9, 1962. Program mgr. Sta. KCRA, Sacramento, 1966-68; morning program host Sta. KNEW, Oakland, 1968-72; afternoon program host Sta. KSFO, San Francisco, 1974-77; ptnr. Charles Jewelry; pres. Rick Cimino, Inc.; developer and chief exec. officer Compu-Cast; owner comml. fishing vessel African Queen; instr. voice, acting; freelance advt. voice. Served with U.S. Army, 1951-53. Recipient Best Radio Personality award TV-Radio Mirror mag., 1969; 9 CLIO awards, 1976-83, Gold Clio award, 1985; 2 Nat. Acad. TV Arts and Scis. awards, 1981; Gold medal 1982 Internat. Film Festival; Addy award, 1983. Mem. Am. Advt. Fedn. (radio div. chmn. Am. Advt. Best in West awards), AFTRA, Screen Actors Guild, Il Cenacolo, Cousteau Soc., Oceanic Soc., Internat. Platform Assn. Home: 7352 Stockton Ave El Cerrito CA 94530

CIMOCHOWICZ, DIANE MARIE, naval petty officer; b. Jacksonville, Fla., Aug. 13, 1955; d. Richard Clarence and Edith Darlene (Johnson) C. AS in Mgmt., Hawaii Pacific Coll., 1986, BSBA, 1986. Enlisted USN, 1974, advanced through grades to petty officer first class; ops. specialist USN, Naples, Italy, 1975-77; ops. specialist, instr. USN, Dam Neck, Va., 1977-78; resigned USN, 1978, reenlisted, 1980; photographer USN, San Diego, 1980-82, Honolulu, 1982—; owner ICON, Columbia, Md., 1978-79; owner, operator In Other Words, Honolulu, 1988—. Mem. Federally Employed Women, Fleet Res. Assn., Associated Photographers Internat., Hawaii Pacific Coll. Student Bus. Orgn., Nat. Honor Frat. Bus. Adminstrn., Delta Mu Delta. Democrat. Clubs: Lokahi Canoe, Koa Kai (Honolulu). Home: 3110 Woodward SW Wyoming MI 49509 Office: Fleet Intelligence Ctr Pacific Box 500 Pearl Harbor HI 96860

CIMOLINO, MARC CHRISTOPHER, physicist, educator; b. Glendale, Calif., Dec. 23, 1954; s. Gerald N. and Jane (Collinge) C.; m. Carolyn Campbell, Aug. 13, 1983. BS, Calif. Inst. Tech., 1976; MS, U. Calif., San Diego, 1978, PhD, 1982. Cert. tchr. Teaching asst. U. Calif.-San Diego, La Jolla, 1976-81; rsch. assoc. U. So. Calif., L.A., 1982-84; mem. tech. staff TRW Space and Tech. Group, Redondo Beach, Calif., 1985-87; physics instr. L.A. City Coll., 1987; scientist Northrop Electronics Div., Hawthorne, Calif., 1987-88; sr. rsch. scientist Spectron Devel. Labs. div. Titan Corp., Costa Mesa, Calif., 1988—; cons. U. So. Calif., 1984-88. Judge High Sch. Sci. Fair, Inglewood Sch. Dist., 1987, Orange County Sci. and Engring. Fair, 1989. Mem. Am. Chem. Soc., Optical Soc. Am., Laser Inst. Am., IEEE, Lasers and Electro-Optics Soc. Office: Spectron Devel Labs 3535 Hyland Ave Ste 102 Costa Mesa CA 92626-1439

CINCO, MARIA ASUNCION, real estate professional; b. Manila, Aug. 15, 1950; came to U.S., 1974; d. Romulo C. and Remedios (Cruz) Caoile; m. Renato Magpile Cinco, June 5, 1971; 1 child, Jose Rommel. Student, U. Santo Tomas, Manila, 1967-68. Lic. real estate broker, Calif. Sec. Toyo Menka Kaisha, Ltd., Makati, Rizal, Philippines, 1967-68, Yutivo & Sons, Manila, 1968-71, Japan-Calif. Bank, L.A., 1974-75; sales rep. Taiping Carpets, Makati, 1971-74; real estate assoc. Spring Realty, Torrance, Calif., 1975-79, Carriage Realty, Torrance, 1979-88, ReMax Beach Cities, Torrance, 1988—. Home: 16 Horseshoe Ln Rolling Hills Estate CA 90274 Office: ReMax Beach Cities 2822 Sepulveda Blvd Torrance CA 90505

CIPRIANO, PATRICIA ANN, teacher, consultant; b. San Francisco, Apr. 24, 1946; d. Ernest Peter and Claire Patricia (Croak) C. BA in English, Holy Names Coll., Oakland, Calif., 1967; MA in Edn. of Gifted, Calif. State U.-L.A., 1980. Cert. tchr., tchr. spl. edn., adminstrv. svc., Calif. Tchr. English, math. and bus. Bancroft Jr. High Sch., San Leandro, Calif., 1968-79, 83-85, coord. gifted edn., 1971-79; tchr. English, math., computers San Leandro High Sch., 1979-83, 85—, coord.gifted and talented edn., 1981-83; cons. Calif. State Dept. Edn., various Calif. sch. dists. Recipient Hon. Svc. award Tchr. of Yr., Bancroft Jr. High Sch. PTA, 1973. Mem. NEA, Calif. Assn. for Gifted (rep. Region 3 tchr. com.), Assn. for Gifted, Nat. Assn. for Gifted, World Coun. Gifted and Talented, Cen. Calif. Coun. Tchrs. English (past pres.), Calif. Assn. Tchrs. English (bd. dirs., treas.), Nat. Coun. Tchr. English (bd. dirs.), San Leandro Tchrs. Assn., Calif. Tchrs. Assn., Delta Kappa Gamma (past pres.). Roman Catholic. Avocations: reading, piano, calligraphy, tennis, racquetball. Contbr. articles to profl. jours. Office: San Leandro High Sch 2200 Bancroft Ave San Leandro CA 94577

CIRKET, MORGAN TREVOR, engineer; b. London, Eng., Jan. 20, 1962; came to U.S., 1973; s. Raymond Frank and Annelise Leontine (Lichte) C.; m. Barbara Ann Young, Nov. 20, 1981; 1 child, Brandon Paul. Design mgr. Soniform, Inc., El Cajon, Calif., 1982-88; pres. Westek Engring. Svcs., La Jolla, Calif., 1988—; bd. dirs. MTC Enterprises, Spring Valley, Calif. Designer: Easy-Cam SCUBA Buckle, 1987, SCUBA Power Exhaust Valve, 1986, SCUBA 2-Way Inflate Valve, 1986, 3-D buoyancy Compensator, 1986. Mem. Nat. Assn. Temporary Svcs., Nat. Assn. Underwater Instrs. Republican. Anglican. Home: 9766 Kenora Woods Ln Spring Valley CA 92077 Office: Westek Engring Svcs 4275 Executive Square La Jolla CA 92037

CISNEROS, CARLOS R., state senator. Office: Office of State Senate State Capitol Santa Fe NM 87503

CIVER, MARILYN GARRETT, alcohol and drug abuse prevention consultant; b. Douglas, Ariz., Feb. 25, 1942; s. Albert Avery Wilkins and Marjorie Lee (Garrett) Paullin; m. Anthony J. Gallo, June 20, 1963 (div. Sept. 1974); children: Teresa Gallo, Tana Gallo, A.J. Gallo. BS, Ariz. State U., 1977. Comml. rep. Salt River Project, Phoenix, 1978-80; real estate saleswoman Coldwell Banker, Scottsdale, Ariz., 1980-82; account exec. Chambers Mayflower, Phoenix, 1982; owner, mgr. Dance Ctr., Tucson, 1982-

84; health coord. Manana Health Ctr., Manara, Ariz., 1985-86; owner, cons. Energy Plus, Tucson, 1986—; dir. community Gov.'s Office Substance Abuse, Phoenix, 1987; conf. cons. Ariz./Mex. Border Health Found., Phoenix, 1988; state Red Ribbon coord. Arizonans Drug Free Youth, Phoenix, 1988; cons. Durg Abuse Prevention and Wellness, Scottsdale, Ariz., 1989—; seminar leader Intergroup Ariz., Tucson, 1986-88, Ariz. Mex. Border Health Found., Phoenix, 1988; exec. bd. Arizonans for Drug Free Youth, Phoenix, 1986-88. Contbr. articles to profl. jours. Founder Arizonans for Drug Free Youth, Phoenix, 1986; coord. Chem. People Project, P.B.S., Ariz., 1983; founder Tucsonans Say No to Drugs, Tucson, 1986; bd. dirs. Nat. Fedn. Parents, 1984, Tucson Issues Forum, 1987-88; pres. PTA, Safford, Ariz., 1970. Named for Outstanding Svc. to Youth, Nat. Fedn. Parents, 1983; recipient svc. award Ariz. Dept. Edn., 1988, cert. appreciation Nat. Fen. Parents., 1986. Mem. Tucson Issues Forum (bd. dirs. 1987-89), Arizonans for Drug Free Youth, Toastmasters. Democrat. Roman Catholic. Home and Office: 6726 E 6th St Scottsdale AZ 85251

CLACK, DICK SCOTT, international trade consultant; b. Celina, Tex., Nov. 13, 1927; s. Clyde William and Tink (Blakemore) C.; BS in Wildlife Conservation, Okla. State U., 1952; postgrad. Hokkaido U., Sapporo, Japan, 1953-54, U. Hawaii, 1979; m. Yoshiko Eguchi, Oct. 1, 1955; children: Michael Bruce, Meiling Jade. Served as enlisted man U.S. Army, 1945-48, commd. 2 lt., 1952, lt. col., 1967, ret., 1970; asst. v.p. Makaha Surfside Devel. Co., Honolulu, 1970-72; pres. D. Clack Inc., pub. relations cons., Honolulu, 1972-74; v.p. PCO Inc., Honolulu, 1974-76; Chmn. of founding com., exec. trustee Hawaii Army Museum Soc., Honolulu, 1976-78, trustee, 1976-84; v.p., dir. mktg. Traders Pacifica Ltd., Honolulu, 1979-81; dir. Société Tahitienne de Developpement Agri-Industrielle et Touristique, Papeete, 1982-85; propr. C & S Imports, Honolulu, 1981-86, bd. dirs. C.S.W. Holdings, Nadi, Fiji, Kaikoo Devel. Co., Inc., 1983—; v.p. K.N. Devel. Co., 1983—; internat. rep. COPABAM, Moorea, Tahiti, 1982-83; dir. Pacific Trade and Devel. Decorated Legion of Merit, Army Commendation medal with 3 oak leaf clusters; named hon. mem. City Council Kumagaya (Japan), 1954; recipient cert. of commendation Gumma Prefectural Govt. Japan, 1955, Saitama Prefecture Govt. Japan, 1955; named Okla. Col., 1957, Ark. Traveler, 1962, La. Col., 1963, Hon. Citizen New Orleans, 1964. Mem. Assn. U.S. Army (exec. com. Hawaii chpt. 1967—), Navy League, Mil. Order World Wars, War Mus. Can., VFW (chief of staff Hawaii 1973), Regent Clan Buchanan Soc. Am., Caledonian Soc., Polynesian Voyaging Soc., Rotary (dir. public relations Dist. 500, 1974, 79, dir. internat. relations Dist. 500, 1980, mem. Internat. Yachting Fellowship chpt.), Adventurers Honolulu Club, Cook Island Game Fishing Club. Office: 1507 Kapiolani Ste 6 Honolulu HI 96814

CLACK, SIDNEY ROSS, electronics executive; b. Whittier, Calif., Oct. 5, 1936; s. Jeffie Ross and Evelyn Fern (Ruhl) C.; m. Yoko Uehigashi, Dec. 4, 1957; children: Susan Marie, Donald Almond. Enlisted USMC, 1954, technician, 1954-62, resigned, 1962; technician Progress Electronics, Portland, Oreg., 1962-66, design engr., 1966-68, project engr., 1968-79, engring. mgr., 1979—; pres. Automotive Design Group, Vancouver, Wash., 1987—. Democrat. Home: 13838 S Vick Rd Molalla OR 97038 Office: Progress Electronics PO Box 11008 Portland OR 97211

CLAES, DANIEL JOHN, physician; b. Glendale, Calif., Dec. 3, 1931; s. John Vernon and Claribel (Fleming) C.; A.B. magna cum laude, Harvard U., 1953, M.D. cum laude, 1957; m. Gayla Christine Blasdel, Jan. 19, 1974. Intern, UCLA, 1957-58; Bowyer Found. fellow for research in medicine, Los Angeles, 1958-61; practice medicine specializing in internal medicine, Los Angeles, 1962—; v.p. Am. Eye Bank Found., 1978-83, pres., 1983—, dir. research, 1980—; pres. Heuristic Corp., 1981—. Mem. Los Angeles Mus. Art, 1960—. Mem. AMA, Calif. Med. Assn., Los Angeles County Med. Assn., Am. Diabetes Assn., Internat. Diabetes Fedn. Clubs: Harvard and Harvard Med. Sch. of So. Calif.; Royal Commonwealth (London). Contbr. papers on diabetes mellitus, computers in medicine to profl. lit. Office: 845 Via de la Paz Ste A236 Pacific Palisades CA 90272

CLAGETT, LESLIE PLUMMER, editor; b. Providence, Apr. 30, 1956; d. Robert Eugene and Peg (Hassett) Plummer; m. John Stephen Clagett, June 10, 1982. BA in English, Denison U., 1978. Mng. editor N.Y. Arts Jour., N.Y.C., 1978-81, Arts & Architecture, Los Angeles, 1981-85; assoc. editor architecture Home mag., Los Angeles, 1985—. Mem. Archtl. League, Nat. Trust for Hist. Preservation. Office: Home Mag 5900 Wilshire 15th Fl Los Angeles CA 90036

CLAGETT, ROBERT, semiconductor manufacturing company executive; b. Phila., Aug. 8, 1952; s. Cornelius and Bianca Maria (Fischer) Zwart; m. Janet Lynn Epperson, Nov. 3, 1979; 1 child, Casey Allen. BS in Biology, Rensselaer Poly. Inst., 1974; MBA, Pepperdine U., 1983. Prodn. supr. Nat. Semicondr. Corp., Santa Clara, Calif., 1978-80, with prodn. control dept., 1980-83, systems support mgr., 1983-87, sr. program mgr., 1987--. 1st lt. USMC, 1974-78, maj. Res. Republican. Episcopalian. Home: 525 Stewart St Boulder Creek CA 95006 Office: Nat Semicondr Corp 2900 Semiconductor Dr Mail Stop C2500 Santa Clara CA 95052

CLAGHORN, KATHY LORRAINE, electrical engineer; b. Albuquerque, Nov. 21, 1964; d. Chester Gerald and Augustina Romo (Holguin) C. BA, N. Mex. State U., 1987. Elec. engr. trainee Naval Underwater Systems Ctr., New London, Conn., 1983-84, Naval Surface Weapons Ctr., Dahlgren, Va., 1985-86; elec. engr. TRW-WSGT, Las Cruces, N. Mex., 1987--. Democrat. Roman Catholic. Home: 830 Stagecoach Dr Las Cruces NM 88001

CLAIR, THEODORE NAT, psychologist; b. Stockton, Calif., Apr. 19, 1929; s. Peter David and Sara Renee (Silverman) C.; A.A., U. Calif. at Berkeley, 1949, A.B., 1950; M.S., U. So. Calif., 1953, M.Ed., 1963, Ed.D., 1969; m. Laura Gold, June 19, 1961; children—Shari, Judith. Tchr., counselor Los Angeles City Schs., 1957-63; psychologist Alamitos Sch. Dist., Garden Grove, Calif., 1963-64, Arcadia (Calif.) Unified Sch. Dist., 1964-65; head psychologist Wiseburn Sch. Dist., Hawthorne, Calif., 1966-69; asst. prof. spl. edn., coordinator sch. psychology program U. Iowa, Iowa City, 1969-72; dir. pupil personnel services Orcutt (Calif.) Union Sch. Dist., 1972-73; adminstr. Mt. Diablo Unified Sch. Dist., 1973-77; program dir., psychologist San Mateo County Office of Edn., Redwood City, 1977—; assoc. prof. John F. Kennedy U. Sch. Mgmt., 1975-77; pvt. practice as ednl. psychologist and marriage and family counselor, Menlo Park, Calif., 1978—, Menlo Park, Calif., 1977—; dir. Peninsula Vocat. Rehab. Inst., 1978—. Served with USNR, 1952-54. Mem. Am. Assn. Counseling and Devel., Calif. Assn. Marriage and Family Counselors, Am. Psychol. Assn., Nat. Rehab. Assn., Phi Delta Kappa. Club: Palo Alto B'nai B'rith (pres.). Author: Phenylketonuria and Some Other Inborn Errors of Amino Acid Metabolism, 1971; mem. editorial adv. bd. Psychology in Schs., 1972—; contbr. articles to profl. jours. Home and Office: 56 Willow Rd Menlo Park CA 94025

CLAIRE, FRED, professional baseball team executive. A.A., Mt. San Antonio Coll.; B.A. in Journalism, San Jose State Coll., 1957. Formerly sports writer and columnist Long Beach Ind. Press Telegram and Whittier News; sports editor Pomo Progress-Bull, Calif., until 1969; dir. publicity Los Angeles Dodgers, Nat. League, 1969-75, v.p. pub. relations and promotions, 1975-82, exec. v.p., from 1982, now exec. v.p. player personnel, 1987—; bd. dirs. Major League Baseball Promotion Corp. Bd. dirs. Greater Los Angeles Vistors and Conv. Bur. Named The Sporting News Major League Exec. of Yr., 1988. Mem. Echo Park C. of C. Lodge: Los Angeles Rotary. Office: Los Angeles Dodgers 1000 Elysian Park Ave Los Angeles CA 90012 *

CLANCY, RAYMOND EDWARD, transportation executive; b. Springfield, Ill., Nov. 10, 1926; s. Patrick Edward and Anna Marie (Hartwig) C.; m. Jamie Haven Horn, July 17, 1953; 1 child, Thomas. BSCE, U. Ill., 1947; MS, MIT, 1963. Registered profl. engr., Tex. Dist. engr. Santa Fe R.R., Amarillo, Tex., 1947-65; v.p. Sharp & Fellows Constrn., Torrance, Calif., 1965-67, M. Lummus, Inc., Torrance, Calif., 1967-75; pres. Pacific R.R. Constrn., Torrance, Calif., 1975-86; sec.-treas. So. Pacific R.R., Inc., Torrance, Calif., 1986—. Mem. Planning Commn., Manhattan Beach, Calif., 1985-86. Lt. USN, 1951-53. Mem. Am. R.R. Engr. Assn., Sembradores Club (pres. 1980-81). Home: 852 6th St Manhattan Beach CA 90266 Office: So Pacific RR Inc 1450 W 228 Unit 33 Torrance CA 90501

CLAPPER, LINDA CHERYL, horse trainer; b. Washington, Dec. 6, 1954; d. Thomas Winford Sr. and Dorothy (Coomes) Hoffman; m. Jeffrey W. Clapper, Apr. 21, 1979. Grad. high sch., Wheaton, Md. Cert. riding master. Asst. barn mgr. Circle N Ranch, Silver Spring, Md., 1976-78; riding instr., barn supr. Valley View/Golden Rose Thoroughbreds, Damascus, Md., 1978; barn supr. Merry Mount Equitation Ctr., Upper Marlboro, Md., 1979-80; show rider Panama, 1980-82; show rider, judge Sacramento, Calif., 1986-87, S&H Horse Hotel, Rio Linda, Calif., 1986-87; cake decorator Cake Castle, Sacramento, 1987—. Mem. Ismithian Horsemen's Assn. (Western Pleasure Horse Champion, 1982, Stockseat Equitation 18 and over Champion, 1982, rep. to Howard Riding Club, 1980-82, Western Pleaseure pony stockseat equitation 14 and 17 Panama), Equestrian Tng. Club (refreshment com. chmn. 1987—).

CLARK, ALAN B., library director. Dir. Albuquerque Pub. Library. Office: Albuquerque Pub Libr 501 Copper Ave NW Albuquerque NM 87102 *

CLARK, ARTHUR JOSEPH, JR., mechanical and electrical engineer; b. West Orange, N.J., June 10, 1921; s. Arthur Joseph and Marjorie May (Courter) C.; B.S. in Mech. Engring., Cornell U., 1943; M.S., Poly. Inst. Bklyn., 1948; M.S. in Elec. Engring., U. N.Mex., 1955; m. Caroline Katherine Badgley, June 12, 1943; children—Arthur Joseph, III, Durward S., David P. Design engr. Ranger Aircraft Engines Co., Farmingdale, N.Y., 1943-46; sr. structures engr. propeller div. Curtis Wright Co., Caldwell, N.J., 1946-51; mgr. space isotope power dept., also aerospace nuclear safety dept. Sandia Labs., Albuquerque, 1951-71, mgr. environ. systems test lab., 1971-79, mgr. mil. liaison dept., 1979—; mem. faculty U. N.Mex., 1971-75; invited lectr. Am. Mgmt. Assn. Pres. Sandia Base Sch. PTA, 1960-61; chmn. finance com. Albuquerqe chpt. Am. Field Service, 1964-66; chmn. Sandia Labs. div. U.S. Savs. Bond drive, 1972-74, chmn. employee contbn. drive, 1973-75; active local Boy Scouts Am., 1958-66. Recipient Order Arrow, Boy Scouts Am., 1961, Order St. Andrew, 1962, Scouters Key award, 1964; cert. outstanding service Sandia Base, 1964. Fellow ASME (nat. v.p. 1975-79, past chmn. N.Mex. sect.); mem. IEEE (sr.), Cornell Engring. Soc., Theta Xi. Clubs: Kirtland Officers, Four Hills Country. Home: 905 Warm Sands Trail Albuquerque NM 87123 Office: Sandia Labs Dept 7210 Albuquerque NM 87185

CLARK, BILLY RAY, insurance executive; b. Little Falls, Minn., Mar. 18, 1928; s. William Edward and Cora Esther (Crabtree) C.; B.A. in Bus. Adminstrn., Bemidji State U., 1953; m. Elsie Helen Torgerson, Oct. 28, 1951; children—Nancy Jo, Kathryn Jean, Julie Rae, Janice Renee. Field supr., supt. Fidelity and Surety Lines, Travelers Ins. Co., Mpls., Denver, 1953-63; account exec. Talbert Corp., Denver, 1963-65, v.p. sales, 1965-73, pres., chmn. bd., 1973—; lectr. engring. dept. U. Colo., 1972-79; lectr. constrn. mgmt. Colo. State U., 1972-79. Mem. panel of arbitrators Am. Arbitration Assn.; adv. com. Indsl. Constrn. Mgmt. Program, Colo. State U., also mem. constrn. com. Bus.-Econ. Outlook Forum. Served with USN, 1946-48, 51-53. Named Agt. of Yr., Travelers Ins. Co., 1981. Mem. Nat. Assn. Surety Bond Producers (past pres.), Nat., Colo. assns. ins. agts., Profls. for Colo. Contractors Council (past pres.), Colo. Transp. Assn. Republican. Lutheran. Club: Columbine Country (Littleton, Colo.). Home: 5186 Tule Lake Dr Littleton CO 80123 Office: Talbert Corp 1001 Lincoln St Denver CO 80203

CLARK, BRIAN THOMAS, mathematical statistician, operations research analyst; b. Rockford, Ill., Apr. 7, 1951; s. Paul Herbert and Martha Lou (Schlensker) C. B.S. cum laude, No. Ariz. U., 1973; postgrad. Ariz. State U., 1980-82. Math. aide Center for Disease Control, Phoenix, 1973-74, math. statistician, 1979-83; math. Statistician Ctrs. for Disease Control, Atlanta, 1983-84 ops. research analyst U.S. Army Info. Systems Command, Ft. Huachuca, Ariz., 1984—; math. statistician U.S. Navy Metrology Engring. Center, Pomona, Calif., 1974-79. Mem. Am. Statis. Assn., Ops. Rsch Soc. Am., Am. Soc. Mil. Comptrs. Republican. Lutheran. Office: US Army Info Systems Command Dep Chief Staff Resource Mgmt Chargeback Test Div Fort Huachuca AZ 85613

CLARK, CALEB MORGAN, political scientist, educator; b. Washington, June 6, 1945; s. Tanner Morgan and Grace Amanda (Kautzmann) C.; B.A., Beloit Coll., 1966; Ph.D., U. Ill., 1973; m. Janet Morrissey Sentz, Sept. 28, 1968; children—Emily Claire, Grace Ellen, Evelyn Adair. Lectr., N.Mex. State U., Las Cruces, 1972-75, asst. prof., 1975-78, assoc. prof. govt., 1978-81; assoc. prof. polit. sci. U. Wyo., Laramie, 1981-84, prof., 1984—. NDEA fellow, 1966-69; Woodrow Wilson dissertation fellow, 1969-70; grantee N.Mex. Humanities Council, 1975, Wyo. Council for Humanities, 1982, U.S. Dept. Edn., 1983-85, Pacific Cultural Found., 1984-86. Am. Council Learned Socs., 1976, Met. Life Edn., 1978-80, NEH, 1978, NSF, 1981. Mem. Am. Polit. Sci. Assn., Am. Assn. Advancement Slavic Studies, Rocky Mountain Assn. Slavic Studies, Western Polit. Sci. Assn., Western Social Sci. Assn., Internat. Studies Assn. (exec. dir. West 1981-84), Phi Beta Kappa (treas. 1983—), Pi Eta Sigma, Phi Kappa Phi. Author: (with Robert L. Farlow) Comparative Patterns of Foreign Policy and Trade, 1976; (with Karl F. Johnson) Development's Influence on Yugoslav Political Values, 1976; Taiwan's Development, 1989; mng. editor IS Notes, 1984—; co-editor: North/South Relations, 1983, State and Development, 1988, Polit. Stability and Economic Development, 1989; cons., assoc. editor Soviet Union, 1974-77, World Affairs, 1975-84, Social Sci. Jour., 1978-80; contbr. articles to profl. jours. Home: 519 S 12th St Laramie WY 82070 Office: U Wyo Dept Polit Sci Laramie WY 82071

CLARK, CHARLES JOSEPH (JOE CLARK), Canadian government official, former prime minister; b. High River, Alta., Can., June 5, 1939; s. Charles A. and Grace R. (Welch) C.; m. Maureen McTeer, June 30, 1973; 1 dau., Catherine Jane. B.A. in History, U. Alta., 1960, M.A. in Polit. Sci., 1973; LL.D. (hon.), U. N.B., 1976, U. Calgary, 1984. Lectr. polit. sci. U. Alta., 1965-67; journalist CBC Radio and TV, Calgary Herald, Edmonton Jour., 1966; exec. asst. in Ottawa to Robert L. Stanfield, 1967-70; M.P. for Rocky Mountain 1972-79, M.P. for Yellowhead, 1979—; leader Progressive Conservative Party, 1976-83; prime minister Can., 1979-80; leader of opposition 1976-79, 80-83, sec. of state for external affairs, 1984—. Roman Catholic. Office: House of Commons, Rm 165 E Block, Ottawa, ON Canada K1A 0A6 *

CLARK, CHARLES RUSSELL, insurance company executive; b. Chgo., Aug. 18, 1931; s. Aud J. and Catherine (Miller) C. BSBA, U. Ariz., 1954. Pres., owner Clark McWilliam & Assoc., Tuscon, 1987, Clark Swano Ins. Inc., Tucson, 1959-87. Office: Clark McWilliam & Assoc 4727 E 5th St Tucson AZ 85711

CLARK, CHARLES SUTTER, interior designer; b. Venice, Calif., Dec. 21, 1927; s. William Sutter and Lodema Ersell (Fleeman) C. Student Chouinard Art Inst., Los Angeles, 1950-51. Interior designer LM.H. Co., Gt. Falls, Mont., 1956-62, Andreason's Interiors, Oakland, Calif., 1962-66, Western Contact Furnishers Internat., Oakland, 1966-70, Design Five Assocs., Lafayette, Calif., 1972-73; owner, interior designer Charles Sutter Clark Interiors, Greenbrae, Calif., 1973—. Served with USAF, 1951-55. Recipient prizes Mont. State Fair, 1953-55. Mem. Am. Soc. Interior Designers. Home: 61 Via Belardo #11 Greenbrae CA 94904

CLARK, CORNELIOUS, electronics executive, consultant; b. Birmingham, Ala., Dec. 14, 1940; s. George Clark and Ora (Porter) Gatlin; m. Audrey Mae Luke, Mar. 13, 1960; children: Michael, Alisa, Dennis. AS in Computer Sci., Pikes Peak Community Coll., Colo. Springs, 1981; AS in Electronic Tech., Pikes Peak Community Coll., 1983; BS in Indsl. Mgmt., Colo. Tech. Coll., 1986. Enlisted U.S. Army, 1956, advanced through grades to 1st sgt., 1956-73, ret., 1976; electronic technician Digital Equipment Corp., Colo. Springs, 1983-84, employee devel. specialist, 1984-87, employee devel. supr., 1987–; mem. electronic bd. Pikes Peak Community Coll.; electronic bd., quality bd., Tech. Trades Inst.; electronic bd. black leadership group Digital Equipment Corp., 1987—. Exec. bd. dirs. Emmanuel Missionary Bapt. Ch., Colo. Springs, 1988. Mem. NAACP, Soc. Mfg. Engrs., Urban League, Sickle Cell Anemia Assn., Spl. Forces Assn., Airborne Assn., Masons (sr. deacon 1962-65), Edward Edwards (prince 1963—), Negro Hist. Assn. Democrat. Home: 6855 Omaha Blvd Colorado Springs CO 80915

CLARK, DEANNA DEE, civic leader; b. Cedar Rapids, Iowa, June 1, 1944; d. Cyrus Dean and Isabelle Esther Thomas; m. Glen Edward Clark, July 16, 1966; children: Andrew Curtis, Carissa Jane. AA, Coll. of the Desert, 1964; BA, Coe Coll., 1966. Co-chairperson Nat. Conf. of Christians & Jews, Utah Chpt., 1988—; pres. League Women Voters of Utah, 1981-83; bd. dirs. Assistance League of Salt Lake City, 1988-89, Provo-Jordan River Pkwy. Found., 1984—; sustaining mem. Jr. League of Salt Lake City. Home: 2102 Pheasant Way Salt Lake City UT 84121

CLARK, DONALD CLAYTON, secondary education educator; b. L.A., Feb. 28, 1937; s. John Clayton and Grace Eleanor (Link) Clark; m. Sally Mae Newbert, Jan. 26, 1957; children: Susan Lynn, Janet Kathleen May. BA, Pasadena Coll., 1959; MA, Calif. State U., 1963; EdD, U. So. Calif., 1971. Tchr. Duarte Unified Sch. Dist., Duarte, Calif., 1959-65; dir. cuuriculum Monrovia Unified Sch. Dist., Monrovia, Calif., 1965-71; asst. prof. secondary edn. U. Ariz., Tucson, 1971-74, assoc. prof. secondary edn., 1974-79, prof. secondary edn., 1979—; mem. research team NAASP-Dodge Found. Nat. Study of Schs. in the Middle, Reston, Va., 1980-84; exec. dir. So. Ariz. Middle Level Assn., Tucson, 1980—; mem. NASSP Middle Level Coun., Reston, 1988—; co-dir. Nat. Study of 8th Grade, Reston, 1988-89. Author: The Middle Level School, Vol. I, 1981, The Middle Level School, Vol. II, 1983; co-editor: Models for Individualized Instruction, 1974; contbr. articles to profl. jours. Mem. Nat. Assn. Secondary Sch. Prins., Nat. Middle Sch. Assn. (research com. 1988—), Assn. for Supervision and Curriculum Devel., We. Region Middle Level Consortium, Ariz. Sch. Adminstrs., Inc. Republican. Mehtodist. Office: Univ of Arizona Coll of Education 304 Tucson AZ 85721

CLARK, DOUGLAS BERNARD, computer company executive; b. Rochester, N.Y., Sept. 3, 1951; s. Frederick R. and Anne (Murray) C. BS in Fin. with Honors, U. Ariz., 1975; MBA, Ariz. State U., 1976. Mgr. continuity Sta. KTVK-TV, Phoenix, 1977-78; mgr. inventory control Revlon, Phoenix, 1979-82; pres. DATAPOL, Phoenix, 1982—. Author, pub. Ariz. Trivia, 1985; columnist Ariz. Thoroughbred, 1987. Trustee Leukemia Soc. Am., 1987—, v.p. Ariz. chpt., 1983-85, pres., 1985-86. Mem. Ariz. Thoroughbred Breeders Assn. Roman Catholic. Home: PO Box 35022 Phoenix AZ 85069 Office: DATAPOL 3443 N Central #1509 Phoenix AZ 85012

CLARK, DWIGHT WILLIAM, lawyer; b. Gothenburg, Nebr., Sept. 24, 1944; s. William Elwood Clark and Christina Antina Koster; m. Sharon Louise Anderson, Aug. 31, 1968; children: Andrea Christine, Nathan William. BS, U. Nebr., 1967; JD, Calif. Western Law Sch., 1974; MPA, U. So. Calif., 1976. Bar: Calif. 1975; cert. specialist in jud. adminstrn. Adminstrv. intern U.S. Probation Office, L.A., 1975-76; exec. asst. San Francisco Mcpl. Ct., 1976-84, clk.-adminstr., 1984-89; com. justice systems IBM, 1989—; moot ct. judge U. San Francisco Sch. Anthropology, 1977; dir. Corp. Bus. Brokers No. Calif., Inc.; user rep. EDP priority com. City and County San Francisco, 1979, electronic info. steering com., 1983-86; assoc. faculty Nat. Judges Coll., Reno, 1985-88; lectr. in law and computer related fields. Mem. adv. bd. Coll. Bus. Adminstrn. U. Nebr., Lincoln, 1966, 67, chmn. placement bd. program, 1967; chmn. honor code revision com. Calif. Western Law Sch., San Diego, 1968, 69; trustee San Mateo Elem. Sch. Dist. (Calif.), 1983—; San Mateo PTA. Recipient Am. Jurisprudence Scholastic award, 1969, Tech. Achievement award Fin., Pub. Tech., Inc., Washington, 1984, Hon. Svc. award PTA, 1986. Mem. ABA, Am. Judicature Soc., Calif. State Bar, Calif. Mcpl. Ct. Clks. Assn., San Mateo County Bar Assn., Nat. Assn. Ct. Mgrs., Western Internat. Law Soc. (founding mem.), Calif. Western Law Sch. Alumni Club, U. So. Calif. Alumni Club, Lawyers Club, Phi Delta Phi, Delta Sigma Pi (life). Democrat. Lutheran. Avocations: woodcrafts, music, reading. Home: 312 Cupertino Way San Mateo CA 94403 Office: IBM 425 Market PO Box 7820 San Francisco CA 94105

CLARK, EARNEST HUBERT, JR., tool company executive; b. Birmingham, Ala., Sept. 8, 1926; s. Earnest Hubert and Grace May (Smith) C.; m. Patricia Margaret Hamilton, June 22, 1947; children: Stephen D., Kenneth A., Timothy R., Daniel S., Scott H., Rebecca G. BS in Mech. Engring, Calif. Inst. Tech., 1946, MS, 1947. With Baker Hughes, Inc. (formerly Baker Oil Tools, Inc.), L.A., 1947-89, v.p., asst. gen. mgr., 1958-62, pres., chief exec. officer, 1962-69, 75-79, chmn. bd., 1969-75, 79-89, chief exec. officer, 1979-87, ret., 1989; chmn., chief exec. officer The Friendship Group, Newport Beach, Calif., 1989—; bd. dirs. CBI Industries, Inc., Honeywell Inc., Kerr-McGee Corp., Beckman Instruments Inc. Bd. dirs. YMCA of U.S.A., YMCA for Met. L.A.; mem. nat. coun. YMCA; chmn. bd. trustees Harvey Mudd Coll. With USNR, 1944-46, 51-52. Mem. Am. Inst. M.E., Am. Petroleum Inst., Petroleum Equipment Suppliers Assn. (bd. dirs.), Calif. C. of C. (mem. exec. com.), Tau Beta Pi. Office: The Friendship Group 5000 Birch St West Tower #3000 Newport Beach CA 92660

CLARK, EDGAR SANDERFORD, insurance broker, consultant; b. N.Y.C., Nov. 17, 1933; s. Edgar Edmund, Jr., and Katharine Lee (Jarman) C.; student U. Pa., 1952-54; BS, Georgetown U., 1956, JD, 1958; postgrad. INSEAD, Fountainbleau, France, 1969, Golden Gate Coll., 1973, U. Calif., Berkeley, 1974; m. Nancy E. Hill, Sept. 13, 1975; 1 dau., Schuyler; children by previous marriages—Colin, Alexandra, Pamela. Staff asst. U.S. Senate select com. to investigate improper activities in labor and mgmt. field, Washington, 1958-59; underwriter Ocean Marine Dept., Fireman's Fund Ins. Co., San Francisco, 1959-62; mgr. Am. Fgn. Ins. Assn., San Francisco, 1962-66; with Marsh & McLennan, 1966-72, mgr. for Europe, resident dir. Brussels, Belgium, 1966-70, asst. v.p., mgr. captive and internat. div., San Francisco, 1970-72; v.p., dir. Risk Planning Group, Inc., San Francisco, 1972-75; v.p. Alexander & Alexander Inc., San Francisco, 1975—; lectr. profl. orgns.; guest lectr. U. Calif., Berkeley, 1973, Am. Grad. Sch. Internat. Mgmt., 1981, 82. Served with USAF, 1956-58. Mem. Am. Mgmt. Assn., Am. Risk and Ins. Assn., Chartered Ins. Inst., Am. Soc. Internat. Law, Soc. Calif. Pioneers (San Francisco), Meadow Club (Fairfax, Calif.), World Trade (San Francisco). Episcopalian. Mem. editorial adv. bd. Risk Mgmt. Reports, 1973-76. Home: 72 Millay Pl Mill Valley CA 94941 Office: Alexander & Alexander Inc Ste 1280 2 Embarcadero Ctr San Francisco CA 94111

CLARK, EDWARD EASTERS, III, retired air force non-commissioned officer; b. Dallas, Aug. 29, 1935; s. Edward Easters Jr. and Mary (Belt) C.; m. Wanda Lavon Wooten, Nov. 26, 1955 (div. 1970); children: Edward E. IV, Mary C. Vineyard; m. Gertrude Helene Von Hentschel, Feb. 14, 1975; children: Kimberele Kae Paisley, Donald Paisley. BS in Animal Husbandry, Tex. A&M U., 1957. Asst. sales mgr. Flexsteel Furniture Industries, Waxahachie, Tex., 1957-59; enlisted USAF, 1959, advanced through grades to master sgt.; loadmaster supt. spl. ops. McChord AFB, Washington, 1981, ret., 1981; ops. mgr. Valero Energy Co., Tyler, Tex., 1982-84; carrier U.S. Postal Service, Sacramento, Calif., 1985—; instr./flight examiner spl. ops., USAF, 1970-81. Mem. safety com. and community planning com. Community Service Dist., El Dorado Hill, Calif., 1988—. Decorated Purple Heart, Meritorious Svc. Medal; Vietnamese Cross of Gallantry with palm leaf, Disting. Flying Cross Air Medal. Mem. Nat. Assn. Letter Carriers, DAV., Nat. Rifle Assn., Elks. Republican. Lutheran. Home: 2869 Canterbury Circle El Dorado Hills CA 95630 Office: US Postal Svc St Sutter Sta Sacramento CA 95816

CLARK, ELLEN WILSON, chamber of commerce executive; b. Mesa, Ariz., Apr. 14, 1934; d. Marion Bert and Hazel (Pittman) Wilson; m. Paul M. Clark, Sept. 8, 1948; children: Edmund, Barbara, Robert. AA, Cochise Coll., Douglas, Ariz., 1980. Adminstrv. asst. USDA-ASCS, Willcox and Tucson, Ariz., 1962-75; exec. dir. Willcox C. of C. and Agr., 1976—. Mem. Ariz. Chamber Execs., Ariz. Assn. for Indsl. Devel., Cochise Cooperative Extension Service Adv. Bd. (chmn. 1987-88). Democrat. Home: 348 S Curtis Willcox AZ 85643 Office: Willcox C of C and Agr 1500 N Circle I Rd Willcox AZ 85643

CLARK, JAMES A., banker; b. 1930. Grad., Rutgers U. Stonier Grad. Sch. of Banking, 1963. With Citizens Bank of Clovis Clovis, N. Mex., 1948-55; with Southwest Nat. Bank El Paso, Tex., 1955-64; pres. Security Bank of Roswell, Roswell, N. Mex., 1964-73; exec. v.p. Albuquerque Nat. Bank, Albuquerque, N. Mex., 1973-74; pres. First Nat. Bank, Albuquerque, N. Mex., 1974-75, First City Bank of Dallas, Dallas, Tex., 1975-79; chmn. bd. First City Fin. Corp., Dallas, Tex., 1979-80; pres., chief exec. officer United N. Mex. Fin. Corp., Albuquerque, N. Mex., 1980-85; chmn. bd. United N.

Mex. Bank of Albuquerque, Albuquerque, N. Mex.; pres., chief exec. officer First Interstate Bank, Albuquerque, N. Mex., 1985—, now also chmn. bd., dir. Office: 1st Interstate Bank Office of Chmn 320 Gold Ave SW Albuquerque NM 87103 *

CLARK, JAMES ENES, health science administrator; b. Olympia, Wash., Nov. 25, 1943; s. Evan Allred and Margaret (Enes) C.; m. Martie Gayle Quick, Dec. 20, 1986; 1 child, Cedar Gayle Jones. Cert. respiratory therapy, St. Mary's Hosp., Reno, 1975. Cert. Respiratory Therapy Practitioner. Respiratory therapist St. Mary's Hosp., 1975-78, asst. dir. respiratory care, 1978-79; respiratory therapist Washoe County Med. Ctr., Reno, 1979-84; owner, chief exec. officer, pres. VAS Inc. dba Vital Air Supply, Cody, Wyo., 1984—; appointed West Park Hosp. Cody, Wyo.,Long Range Strategic Planning Com. Exec. Sec. Elders Quorum Ch. Jesus Christ Latter Day Saints, Cody, 1987—. Mem. Am. Assn. Respiratory Care, Nat. Bd. Respiratory Care. Democrat. Office: PO Box 848 Cody WY 82414

CLARK, JAMES ROBERT, broadcast executive; b. Ganado, Ariz., Nov. 6, 1953; s. David Howard and Manie Regina (Mathis) C.; m. Cynthia Corley, July 20, 1974; children: Krista, Erin, Audrey. BA, John Brown U., 1976. Mgr. Sta. WTIS, Tampa, Fla., 1976-79; account exec., radio sales cons. David Benware and Assocs., Dallas, 1979-80; nat. sales mgr. Forus Communications, St. Petersburg, Fla., 1980-85; exec. v.p., gen. mgr. Sta. KFIA, Sacramento, 1985—; v.p. Regal Prodns., 1984-85. Mem. Nat. Religious Broadcasters (sec. western chpt. 1986—). Republican. Office: Sta KFIA 5705 Marconi Ave Carmichael CA 95608

CLARK, JANET EILEEN, political scientist, educator; b. Kansas City, Kans., June 5, 1940; d. Edward Francis and Mildred Lois (Mack) Morrissey; A.A., Kansas City Jr. Coll., 1960; A.B., George Washington U., Washington, 1962, M.A., 1964; Ph.D., U. Ill., 1973; m. Caleb M. Clark, Sept. 28, 1968; children—Emily Claire, Grace Ellen, Evelyn Adair. Staff, U.S. Dept. Labor, Washington, 1962-64; instr. social sci. Kansas City (Kans.) Jr. Coll., 1964-67; instr. polit. sci. Parkland Coll., 1970-71; asst. prof. govt., N.Mex. State U., Las Cruces, 1971-77, assoc. prof., 1977-80; assoc. prof. polit. sci. U. Wyo., 1981-84, prof., 1984—. Co-author: Women Elections and Representation and Equality State. Wolcott fellow, 1963-64, NDEA Title IV fellow, 1967-69. Mem. Internat. Soc. Polit. Psychology Gov. Coun., 1987-89. Mem. NEA (pres. chpt. 1978-79), Am. Polit. Sci. Assn., Western Polit. Sci. Assn. (exec. council 1984-87), Western Social Sci. Assn. (exec. council 1978-81, v.p. 1982, pres. 1985), Women's Caucus for Polit. Sci. (treas. 1982, pres. 1987), LWV (exec. bd. 1980-83, treas. 1986—), Women's Polit. Caucus, Beta Sigma Phi (v.p. chpt. 1978-79), Phi Beta Kappa, Chi Omega (prize 1962), Phi Kappa Phi. Democrat. Lutheran. Book rev. editor Social Sci. Jour., 1982-87. Contbr. articles to profl. jours. Home: 519 S 12th St Laramie WY 82070

CLARK, JEFFRY RUSSELL, counseling psychologist, consultant, researcher; b. Wareham, Mass., Oct. 12, 1950; s. John Russell and Barbara Jean (Roberts) C.; children—Stephen Russell, Jeffry John Taylor. B.S., Trinity Coll., 1975; M. Ed., Am. U., 1979; Ph.D., Stanford U., 1989. Social worker Monmouth Family Ctr., Middletown, N.J., 1975-76; counselor Annandale Correctional Ctr., Annandale, N.J., 1977, Temple Hills Counseling (Md.) Ctr., 1977-79; adminstrv. dir. Stanford (Calif.) Counseling Inst., 1979-82, counselor Emergency Treatment Ctr., Palo Alto, Calif., 1981-87, dir. tng., 1985-86; dir. adolescent and family services Mid Peninsula Family Service, Palo Alto, 1986—; pvt. practice family counseling, Palo Alto, 1986—; cons. Peninsula Children's Ctr. Served with USMC, 1969-71. Mem. Am. Psychol. Assn., Am. Assn. for Counseling and Devel., Assn. Advancement Behavior Therapy, Western Psychol. Assn., Annandale Jaycees (pres. 1978-79). Democrat. Research on children of divorce, stress, insomnia. Home: 114D Escondido Village Stanford CA 94305

CLARK, JOE See CLARK, CHARLES JOSEPH

CLARK, JOHN ELWOOD, mayor; b. Nampa, Idaho, Dec. 19, 1931; m. Sigrid Fehrenbacher; 4 children. Student, Oreg. State Coll., 1950, Reed Coll., 1954. Owner, operator Aardvark Pest Control, 1959; owner, operator Goose Hollow Inn, 1961—, Mother Goose Antiques, 1974—; founder local newspaper The Neighbor, 1974—; co-owner, operator Forsstrom & Clark Waterfowl Spltys. and Duck Stuff, Portland, 1982-85; mayor City of Portland, 1985—; mem. Portland Waterways Adv. Com., 1978, Portland Cen. Precinct Police Adv. Com., 1975-76. Bd. dirs. Goose Hollow Neighborhood Assn., 1977-81, Planned Parenthood, 1979-80, Restaurants of Oreg. Assn., 1977-78; mem. planning com. Portland-Multnomah Area Agy. on Aging, 1974-76; mem. United Good Neighbor Policy and Devel. Com., 1975-76; mem. Multnomah County Venereal Disease Action Com., 1973-77; treas. N.W. Dist. Assn., 1972-75; vol. Meals-On-Wheels, 1971-82. Served with USMC, 1951-54. Office: Mayor's Office 1220 SW 5th Ave Portland OR 97204

CLARK, KAREN ELIZABETH, industrial engineer, consultant; b. Battle Creek, Mich., Feb. 28, 1955; d. Charles Grafton and Thelma Elizabeth (Robertson) C. BS in Indsl. Engring., Purdue U., 1978; MBA, Pepperdine U., 1986. Registered profl. engr., Calif. Ops. analyst Gen. Dynamics Co., Ft. Worth, 1978-80; indsl. engr. assembly div. GM, Arlington, Tex., 1980-82, David Crystal Co., Reading, Pa., 1982; sr. indsl. engr. Emhart Industries, Commerce, Calif., 1983, Northrop Electronics, Hawthorne, Calif., 1983-84; sr. ops. analyst Glendale (Calif.) Fed. Savs. & Loan, 1984-85; sr. mfg. systems engr. Douglas Aircraft Co., Long Beach, Calif., 1985-87; sr. mfg. applications cons. Honeywell Indsl. Automation Systems div., Phoenix, 1987—; speaker in field. Contbr. articles to profl. publs. Mem. citizens adv. bd., Ft. Worth Planning Coun., 1979-81; treas., Cameo Woods Homeowners Assn., L.A., 1985, 86. Mem. Inst. Indsl. Engrs. (sr., bd. dirs. L.A. chpt. 1984-86, sec. Phoenix chpt. 1988—, editor newletter 1984-85), Soc. Mfg. Engrs., Alpha Pi Mu. Republican. Home: 3816 W Carol Ann Way Phoenix AZ 85023 Office: Honeywell Indsl Automation Systems Div 16404 N Black Canyon Frwy Phoenix AZ 85023

CLARK, KAREN SUE, editor; b. Spokane, Wash., Aug. 15, 1952; d. Clifford French and Patty Ann (Ellis) C. BS in Wildlife Biology, Wash. State U., Pullman, 1974; postgrad., Ea. Wash. U., Cheney, 1987—. Lab. technician molecular genetics dept., plant pathology dept. U. Wash., Spokane, 1972-75; accounts payable supr. Gen. Store, Spokane, 1975-77; purchasing bookkeeper B.J. Carney & Co., 1977-81; supr. accounts payable Ramae Corp., Spokane, 1981-82; bookeeper lodge #228 Elks, Spokane, 1982-84; copy editor Internat. Ambassador Programs, Spokane, 1984-86, sr. sci. editor, 1986-88, dir. publs. dept., 1988—. Editor: Aerospace Education, 1988, Wildlife Management, 1988, Automatic Control Technology, 1988, Shellfish Production, 1987. Sch. bd. dir. Dist. 325/179, 9 Mile Falls, Wash., 1988—; acad. coach, Wash. State Nat. 4-H Horse Bowl Team, Washington, Denver, 1981, 83, 85; Spokane County alt. del. Rep. Convention, 1986, 88. Mem. Wash. State Sch. Dirs. Assn. (rep. 5th legis. dist. network 1989), Nature Conservancy Club, 9 Mile Falls Booster Club.

CLARK, KATHLEEN ANN, medical group administrator; b. Chgo., Aug. 17, 1951; d. Louis Bakondy and Lenore Kathryn (Mateer) Comon; m. Roger Lee Clark, Aug. 17, 1985 (div. May 1988); children: Amy Lynn Beckett, John Donald Beckett, Dawne Kathryn Beckett. Asst. office mgr. Neurol. Neurosurgical Assocs., Gurnee, Ill., 1974-79; billing supr. Neurology Neurosurgery Assocs., Phoenix, 1980-83; asst. adminstr. Neurosurgical Assocs., Phoenix, 1983—. Sec. West Miltmore Assn., Lake Villa, Ill., 1976-79; mem. campaign com. W. Thompson, Lake Villa, 1974. Mem. Med. Group Mgmt. Assn., Ariz. Med. Group Mgmt. Assn., Am. Hosp. Assn., Nat. assn. Female Execs. Republican. Lutheran. Office: Neurosurg Assocs Ltd 2910 N 3d Ave Phoenix AZ 85013

CLARK, LINDA JEAN, corporate professional; b. Sidney, Nebr., Apr. 20, 1961; d. Robert Arthur and Marilyn Lou (Opperman) C. BSBA, Colo. State U., 1983. Sec. radiology dept. Colo. State U., Ft. Collins, 1979-80; sec. Scuba Sch. Internat., Ft. Collins, 1980-82; salesperson, mgr. Caribbean Sea Adventures, St. Croix, V.I., 1982; scuba instr. Midwest Divers Supply, Ft. Collins, 1982-83; office mgr. Scuba Sch. Internat., Concept Systems Inc., Ft. Collins, 1984—, also bd. dirs. Vol. Power Plant Visual Arts Ctr., Ft. Collins, 1986; collection person Am. Canser Soc., 1988, 89. Republican. Home: 2618 Canterbury Dr Fort Collins CO 80526 Office: Scuba Sch Internat 2619 Canton Ct Fort Collins CO 80525

CLARK, LLOYD, historian, educator; b. Belton, Tex., Aug. 4, 1923; s. Lloyd C. and Hattie May (Taylor) C.; m. Jean Reeves, June 17, 1950; children: Roger, Cynthia, Candyce. BSJ, So. Meth. U., 1948; B in Fgn. Trade, Am. Grad. Sch. Internat. Mgmt., 1949; MPA, Ariz. State U., 1972. String corr. A.P., Dallas, 1941-42; editor, pub. Ex-Press, Arlington, Tex., 1945-48; publicity mgr. Advt. Counselors Ariz., Phoenix, 1949; reporter Phoenix Gazette, 1949-65; asst. pub. Ariz. Weekly Gazette, 1965-66; founder Council on Abandoned Mil. Posts-U.S.A., 1966; project cons. City of Prescott, Ariz., 1971-72; dep. dir. adminstrv. services No. Ariz. Council Govts., Flagstaff, 1972-73; regional adminstr. South Eastern Ariz. Govts. Orgn., Bisbee, 1973-75; local govt. assistance coordinator Ariz. Dept. Transp., Phoenix, 1975-80, program adminstr., 1980-83; history instr. Rio Salado Community Coll., Phoenix, 1983—; editor and pub. Clark Biog. Reference, 1956-62. Bd. dirs. Friends of Channel 8, 1984-86; Phoenix del. Papago Park Prisoner of War Camp Commn., 1985; mem. transit planning com. Regional Pub. Transit Authority, 1988, Phoenix Citizen's Bond Com., 1987. Served to lt. AUS, 1942-46; maj., 1966-70; col. Res. Recipient Ariz. exemplary gen. news coverage award, 1960, outstanding news reporting, 1961. Mem. Am. Grad. Sch. Internat. Mgmt Alumni Assn. (pres. Phoenix chpt. 1965), Ariz. Hist. Soc., Sharlot Hall Hist. Soc. (life mem.), Res. Officers Assn., Ex-Students Assn. U. Tex. at Arlington (life mem., pres. 1946-48), The Westerners (sheriff Phoenix Corral 1986-88), Sigma Delta Chi (pres. Valley of Sun chpt. 1964). Club: University (Phoenix). Author: Lloyd Clark's Scrapbook, Vol. 1, 1958, Vol. 2, 1960. Address: PO Box 13344 Phoenix AZ 85002

CLARK, MARK THOMAS, defense policy analyst, Soviet foreign and; b. Pasadena, Calif., Sept. 1, 1955; s. John Thomas and Patricia Mary (Eitner) C. Student, U. Houston, 1979-82; BA, Calif. State Poly U., 1984; MA, U. So. Calif., 1986, PhD, 1989. Pvt. practice Houston, 1979-81, Arcadia, Calif., 1982-84; cons. U.S. Naval Postgrad. Sch., Monterey, Calif., 1985-86; researcher U. So. Calif., L.A., 1987-88, lectr., 1988, prof., 1988—; vis. scholar Hoover Instn. Stanford U., summer 1986. Contbr. articles to profl. jours. Pub. speaker, 1986--. Served with USMC, 1973-77. Smith-Richardson fellow, 1986-87. Mem. Com. on Present Danger, Security and Intelligence Found., Air Force Assn., Phi Alpha Theta. Home and Office: 606 E Camino Real Arcadia CA 91006

CLARK, MARY ELLON, historian, writer; b. Norton, N.Mex., Dec. 22, 1934; d. Edward and Delia (Kingston) Brown; m. Donald G. Clark, June 11, 1981; children: Elaine, Terry, Johnny, Joe. Society editor Tucumcari (N.Mex.) News, 1969-70, correspondent, 1970-75, editor, 1975-76; anchorwoman Sta. KTNM Radio, Tucumcari, 1975-80, reporter, history program hostess, 1976-80; news correspondent Amarillo (Tex.) Globe & TV, 1976-80. Author: El Chaparito, 1976 (DAR Bicentennial award), A Mark of Time, 1984; author numerous poems; contbr. articles to mags. Mem. Dem. Campaign Com., Tucumcari, 1979; active with Tucumcari Hist. Mus., 1974-75. Recipient N.Mex. N.G. cert. 1976, Col. Aide-de-Camp award Exec. Staff of State of N.Mex. bestowed by the gov. Bruce King and lt. gov. Roberto Mondragon, 1979. Baptist. Home: PO Box 946 Tucumcari NM 88401

CLARK, PATRICIA ANN, federal judge; b. Buffalo, July 26, 1936; d. Andrew A. and Mary (Gardner) Zacher; m. James A. Clark, Mar. 25, 1960; B.A., Goucher Coll., Towson, Md., 1958; postgrad. Duke U., 1958-60; LL.B., U. Colo., 1961. Bar: Colo. 1961, U.S. Dist. Ct. D.C. 1961. With Transamerica Title Ins. Co., 1962-65; assoc. Holme, Roberts and Owen, 1965-70, ptnr., 1970-74; judge U.S. Bankruptcy Ct., Denver, 1974—. Commr., Colo. Civil Rights Commn., 1969-72; trustee Waterman Fund, 1978—; mem. transition adv. com. U.S. Cts., 1980-84, com. jud. resources, 1987—. Recipient Disting. Alumni award U. Colo. Sch. Law, 1984. Mem. Colo. Bar Assn., Denver Bar Assn. Office: US Dist Ct 1845 Sherman St 400 Columbine Bldg Denver CO 80203

CLARK, PETER BRUCE, newspaper executive; b. Detroit, Oct. 23, 1928; s. Rex Scripps and Marian (Peters) C.; m. Lianne Schroeder, Dec. 21, 1952; children: Ellen, (Mrs. Fowler M.S. Brown), James. B.A., Pomona Coll., 1952, LL.D. (hon.), 1972; M.P.A., Syracuse U., 1953; Ph.D., U. Chgo., 1959; H.H.D., Mich. State U., 1973, Lawrence Inst. Tech., 1982; LL.D. (hon.), U. Mich., 1977. Research assoc., then instr. polit. sci. U. Chgo., 1957-59; asst. prof. polit. sci. Yale U., 1959-61; with Evening News Assn., Detroit, 1960-86, corp. sec., 1960-61, v.p., 1961-63, pres., 1963-86, chmn. bd., chief exec. officer, dir., 1969-86; pub. Detroit News, 1963-81, also dir.; Regent's prof. UCLA Grad. Sch. Mgmt., 1987; chmn. Fed. Res. Bank Chgo., 1975-77, former chmn. br. Fed. Res. Bank Detroit; former mem. vis. coms. Harvard U. Dept. Govt., Govtl. Studies program Brookings Instn., U. Mich. Sch. Bus. Adminstrn., U. Chgo. div. Social Scis.; mem. adv. council Woodrow Wilson Internat. Ctr. for Scholars; bd. dirs. Gannett Co., Inc. Bd. dirs. Harper-Grace Hosps. Detroit, Earhart Found.; trustee Pomona Coll., 1981—; past bd. dirs. United Found. Met. Detroit. Served with AUS, 1953-55. Mem. Am. Newspaper Pubs. Assn. (dir. 1966-74), Am. Soc. Newspaper Editors. Clubs: Detroit Country, Detroit. Home: 193 Stephens Rd Grosse Pointe Farms MI 48236 also: 73220 Foxtail Ln Palm Desert CA 92260

CLARK, RAYMOND OAKES, banker; b. Ft. Bragg, N.C., Nov. 9, 1944; s. Raymond Shelton and Nancy Lee (McCormick) C.; m. Patricia Taylor Slaughter, Jan. 23, 1988; children: Matthew Patrick, Geoffry Charles. BBA, U. Ariz., 1966; postgrad., U. Wash., 1984-86. Mgmt. trainee First Interstate Bank, Phoenix, 1966, credit analyst, 1968-69, asst. br. mgr., Scottsdale, Ariz., 1969-72, asst. v.p., br. mgr., Tempe, Ariz., 1972—. Pres., bd. dirs. Sun Devil Club, Tempe, 1975—; pres. Tempe Diplomats, 1979—; pres. Tempe Diablos, 1975—; major chmn. Fiesta Bowl, Tempe, 1975-79; bd. dirs. Maricopa County Bd. Mgrs., Phoenix, 1973, YMCA, Tempe, 1974, Tempe Design Rev. Bd., 1983-87. Named one of Outstanding Young Men of Am., Tempe Jaycees, 1977, Ariz. Jaycees, 1978, U.S. Jaycees, 1979. Bd. dirs. East Valley div. Am. Heart Assn., 1989—. Served with U.S. Army, 1966-68. Mem. Tempe C. of C. (pres. 1979-80). Republican. Episcopalian. Lodge: Kiwanis (dist. lt. gov. 1980).

CLARK, RICHARD JAMES, advertising and marketing executive, designer, artist; b. Attica, N.Y., Aug. 19, 1945; s. Claude Jonas and Rita Elizabeth (McKernan) C.; m. Margo E. Clark, Mar. 19, 1989. BS, SUNY-Buffalo, 1964, BA, 1969; postgrad. Yale U., summer 1965; MFA, SUNY, Buffalo, 1970. Designer, Calspan Corp., Buffalo, 1966-69; mktg. exec. Erie Bank, Buffalo, 1969-71; designer Design for Industry, Buffalo, 1972-77; v.p. creative dir., 1978—; ptnr. Design Graphics, Buffalo, 1977—; pres., chmn. bd. Nat. Design Concepts, Huntington Beach, Calif., 1979-84; pres., chmn. Clark Meyer Charters & Howell, 1984—; chmn. bd. Design for Industry, 1985—; cons., tchr. SUNY. Recipient Western N.Y. Communicators award, 1981, 82, 83; Clio award. Mem. Orange County Advt. Fedn., Bus. and Profl. Advt. Assn., Western N.Y. Communicators, Huntington Beach C. of C. Art editor Scene Mag.; exhibited several one-man shows. Office: Clark Meyer Charters & Howell Ste 263 N 16052 Beach Blvd Huntington Beach CA 92647

CLARK, RICHARD LEFORS, systems research scientist; b. Aberdeen, S.D., Oct. 29, 1936; s. Robert Montgomery and Marion (Shook) C.; m. Barbara Louise Battersby, Mar. 28, 1980; 1 child, Robert James. BA, Pacific Western U., 1974, MS, 1975, PhD, 1978; BS in Engring. and Applied Sci., Jackson State Coll., 1968, MA in Bus. Mgmt., 1972. Technician Honeywell Co., 1957-58; quality assurance Martin Co., 1958-59, Remington Rand, 1959; engr. Gen. Dynamics/Electronics, 1959-68; supr. Graco, Inc., 1971-74; with Internat. Harvester, 1975-81, Caterpiller Tractor Co., 1981—, Solar Turbines subs. Caterpiller Tractor Co.; systems research in fusion power, parapsychology and physics, over unity elec. generators, archeol. research and gravity research, San Diego, 1975—; lectr. gravity/Maxwell-Faraday physics systems and devices. Inventor vortex fusion engine; author tech. papers. Served with U.S. Army, 1954-57.

CLARK, RICHARD WARREN, lawyer; b. Lampasas, Tex., Dec. 17, 1943; s. Richard Sargent and Mary Ellen (Hobby) C.; m. Joyce Elaine Moses, Apr. 17, 1965; children: Lisa, Doug. BS, U. Wyo., 1965; JD, U. Ariz., 1972. Bar: Ariz. Pvt. practice Phoenix, 1972-84; sr. ptnr. Ellis, Baker, Clark & Porter P.C., Phoenix, 1984—; bd. dirs. The Breakfast Club, Inc. Contbg. editor Ariz. Advocate, 1971-72. Pres., gov. bd. Scottsdale Unified Sch. Dist., 1976-82; mem. Scottsdale Charros, 1977—, pres. 1977; active Fiesta Bowl, Phoenix, 1982—; bd. dirs. Scottsdale Boys Club, Scottsdale Girl's Club, 1987—, Scottsdale Charro Community Found., 1986—; dir. Scottsdale YMCA. Served to capt. U.S. Army, 1965-67, Vietnam. Decorated Purple Heart with oak leaf cluster, Bronze Star valor device with oak leaf cluster. Named Outstanding Yong Man Ariz. Jaycees, Charro of Yr. Scottsdale Charros, 1982-83. Mem. ABA, Ariz. State Bar Assn., State Bar Ariz. (corp. banking and bus. sect.), Scottsdale C. of C. (past pres.), Scottsdale Savs. & Loan Assn. (chmn.). Republican. Clubs: Paradise Valley (Ariz.) Country; Ariz. (Phoenix). Office: Ellis Baker Clark & Porter PC 4444 N 32d St Ste 200 Phoenix AZ 85018

CLARK, RONALD WILLIAM, civil engineer; b. Los Angeles, Aug. 7, 1934; s. William Bishop and Maxine (Wilson) C.; m. Bonnie Jean Clark, Aug. 31, 1957; children: Donald Bishop, Sandra Jean, Nancy Ann, Dennis Lee. BS in Geol. Engring., Colo. Sch. Mines, 1957; cert. in indsl. supervision, Mt. Sac Jr. Coll., Calif., 1975, Rio Hondo (Calif.) Jr. Coll., 1975. Registered civil engr., registered geotech. engr. Calif. Engr. asst. st. design Bur. Engrs. City of Los Angeles, 1959-61, engr. asst. sewer design, 1961-63, assoc. engr. soils, 1963-67, engr. soils, 1967-68; engr. soils Bur. Standards City of Los Angeles, 1968-86; div. head Standards Div. City of Los Angeles, 1986—; pres. Mineral Enterprises Inc., Colo. Mem. com. Boy Scouts Am., Whittier, Calif.; mgr. Little League, Whittier. Mem. ASCE (assoc.), Am. Soc. Testing and Materials. Republican.

CLARK, ROSS GODFREY, producer; b. Martinsburg, W.Va., Apr. 7, 1949; s. Edgar Godfrey and Mary Patricia (Ross) C.; m. Eileen Frances Bonewitz, Sept. 27, 1975. Student, Northwestern U., 1966-67, Purdue U., 1967-68; BFA, Pasadena (Calif.) Playhouse, 1970; MFA, U. So. Calif., Los Angeles, 1973. Theater arts specialist Los Angeles County dept. Parks and Recreation, 1971-73; asst. mgr. entertainment Busch Gardens, Van Nuys, Calif., 1974-76; owner Wings of Fame Prodns., Azusa, Calif., 1976-83; gen. mgr. Cable Services of Azusa, 1978-81; dir. Mickey Rooney's Talent Town USA, N.Y.C., 1981-84; dir., producer Finesse With a Plum Prodns., Azusa, 1984—; organizing dir. Diamond Bar (Calif.) Children's Theater, 1970-80, (bd. dirs. 1970-82); artist-in-residence Calif. Arts Commn., Los Angeles, 1977-78; cons. Pomona (Calif.) Sch. Dist., 1977-79, West Covina (Calif.) Sch. Dist., 1978-80. Child actor on Broadway and nat. tours of numerous shows including Take Me Along, Music Man, Bye Bye Birdie, Gypsy, Lion in Winter, Mame, Oliver!, 1959-66; writer numerous children's shows, 1973—, amusement park shows, 1974—. Recipient Arts in Community award Calif. Arts Commn., 1976. Mem. Soc. for Preservation Variety Arts (life), Acad. Magical Arts, Actors Equity Assn., Internat. Assn. Amusement Park Operators, Azusa C. of C. (bd. dirs. 1980-83). Republican. Mem. United Ch. of Christ. Home: 807 E Gladstone St LaVerne CA 91750 Office: Finesse With a Plum Prodns 527 N Azusa Ave Ste 296 Covina CA 91722

CLARK, R(UFUS) BRADBURY, lawyer; b. Des Moines, May 11, 1924; s. Rufus Bradbury and Gertrude Martha (Burns) C.; m. Polly Ann King, Sept. 6, 1949; children: Cynthia Clark Maxwell, Rufus Bradbury, John Atherton. BA, Harvard U., 1948, JD, 1951; diploma in law, Oxford U., Eng., 1952; D.H.L., Ch. Div. Sch. Pacific, San Francisco, 1983. Bar: Calif. 1952. Assoc. O'Melveny & Myers, L.A., 1952-62, sr. ptnr., 1961—, mem. mgmt. com., 1983-89; bd. dirs. So. Calif. Water Co., Econ. Resources Corp., Brown Internat. Corp., Automatic Machinery & Electronics Corp., John Tracy Clinic, also pres. 1982-88. Editor: California Corporation Laws, 6 vols, 1976—. Chancellor Prot. Episcopal Ch. in the Diocese of L.A., 1967—, hon. canon, 1983—. Capt. U.S. Army, 1943-46. Decorated Bronze star with oak leaf cluster, Purple Heart with oak leaf cluster; Fulbright grantee, 1952. Mem. ABA (subcom. on audit letter responses, com. on law and acctg., task force on legal opinions), State Bar Calif. (chmn. drafting com. on gen. corp. law 1973-81, chmn. drafting com. on nonprofit corp. law 1980-84, mem. exec. com. bus. law sect., 1977-78, 84-87, sec. 1986-87), L.A. County Bar Assn., Calif. Club (L.A.), Harvard Club (L.A.), Chancery Club (L.A.), Alamitos Bay Yacht Club (Long Beach). Republican. Office: O'Melveny & Myers 400 S Hope St Los Angeles CA 90071-2899

CLARK, SUSAN INGRID, small business owner; b. Iowa City, Mar. 15, 1951; d. Edward Cargile and Doris Arlene (Gordon) C.; m. John Roscoe Lindh, Mar. 24, 1975; children: Teman David, Connor Andrew. BA in Edn., Western Wash. U., 1975. Supr. film library Maharishi Internat. U., Fairfield, Iowa, 1976-77; retail salesperson Fairhaven Books, Bellingham, Wash., 1975, 77-79; owner A-Assist, Bellingham, Wash., 1981—. V.p. Samish Neighborhood Assn., Bellingham, 1981; publicity chmn. Whatcom Literacy Coun., Bellingham, 1985. Mem. United Ch. Christ. Home: 505 W Bakerview #66 Bellingham WA 98226

CLARK, SYLVIA MARGARET, healthcare service administrator; b. St. Anthony, Idaho, Oct. 4, 1937; d. Paul James and Jennie (Dorrance) Shank; m. Paul Wilson Clark, July 4, 1958 (div. 1981); children: Geoffrey Wilson, Courtney Anne. Nursing diploma, Johns Hopkins Hosp., Balt., 1958; BA in Healthcare Mgmt., Antioch U. West, 1983. RN, Colo.; cert. nurse midwife. Nurse Pvt. physician, Monroeville, Pa., 1963-65; clin. supr. Planned Parenthood Rocky Mtns., Colorado Springs, Colo., 1967-70; area adminstr. Planned Parenthood Rocky Mtns., Denver, 1970-74; program devel. con. Planned Parenthood Rocky Mtns., Aurora, Colo., 1978-80; dir. tng. and edn. Planned Parenthood Rocky Mtns., Aurora, 1980-81, assoc. dir., 1981-86, exec. dir., 1986—; adminstrv. asst. Family Planning Assn., London, 1974-75; nurse Marie Stopes Well Woman Health Ctr., London, 1977-78. Mem. editorial bd. jour. Ob-Gyn and Neonatal Nursing, 1981-84; contbr. articles to profl. jours. Mem. Nat. Assn. Nurse Practitioners Reproductive Health (pres. 1980-83), Am. Coll. Nurse Midwives, Assn. Reproductive Health Profls., Am. Pub. Health Assn., Am. Nurses Assn. Home: 195 Pinewood Loop Monument CO 80132

CLARK, TERRENCE ANDREW, dentist, educator; b. Provo, Utah, Feb. 27, 1956; s. Selby Gamette and Alice (Thompson) C.; m. Laraine Marie Sykes, May 28, 1977; children: Wendy Kay, Thomas Evans, Leah Marie. BS, Portland State U., 1987; DMD, Oreg. Health Scis. U., 1986. Small bus. owner, operator Earthcraft Products, Portland, Oreg., 1978-82; intern and resident Oreg. Health Sci. U., 1986-87; hosp. dentist Vancouver (Wash.) VA Hosp., 1986-87, Oreg. Health Sci. U., Portland, 1986-87; pvt. practice Wilsonville, Oreg., 1987—; v.p., program chmn. Oreg. Implant Rsch. Seminar, 1987-88, v.p., 1988—; guest lectr. Oreg. Health Scis. U., 1986—. Mem. Oreg. State Bd. of Higher Edn., 1984-86; scout master Boy Scouts Am., Portland, 1978-80; vol. paramedic Tualitan Valley Ambulance, Portland, 1980-82; sem. instr., Ch. Jesus Christ of Latter Day Saints, 1987—, missionary La. and Miss., 1975-77. Recipient Disting. Service award Oreg. State Bd. Higher Edn., 1986. Mem. Am. Dental Assn., Am. Acad. of Implant Dentistry, Oreg. Dental Assn., Am. Soc. Dentistry for Children, Clackamus County Dental Soc. (rep. to state bd. 1987—), Predental Club (pres. 1981-82). Republican. Office: Wilsonville Dental Group 8890 Holly Ln Ste B Wilsonville OR 97070

CLARK, THOMAS LLOYD, English linguistics educator; b. Havre, Mont., July 10, 1939; s. Lloyd Thomas and Loretta Margaret (LaPlante) C.; m. H. Jeanne Wilson, Apr. 8, 1960; children—Tim, Helen-Margaret, Kristin. B.A., U. Utah, 1964, M.A., 1966; Ph.D., Ohio U., 1970. Prof. U. Nev., Las Vegas, 1970—; dir. Nev. Lang. Survey, 1974-84; cons. Lexik House Pubs., Barnhart Books, Prentice-Hall Pubs., U. Nev. Press; lectr. lang., names, lexicography, Am. English. Author: Language: Structure and Use, 1981; (monograph) Marietta, Ohio; Erosion of a Speech Island, 1972, Dictionary of Gambling and Gaming, 1987; contbr. articles to Am. Speech, Names, Dictionaries, Jour. of English Linguistics, Conn. English Jour., Verbatim, Halcyon, Language and Speech, Elem. English jours., others. Active Nev. Humanities Com. Programs, Sta. KNPR shows, Credit Com. for Silver State Schs. Fed. Credit Union. Served with USN, 1959-61. NDEA, 1966-70, Dictionary of Am. Regional English, 1967-68; NEA grantee. Mem. Am. Dialect Soc. (pres. 1985-87), Nat Council Tchrs. English. (dir. Commn. on English Lang. 1974-78), Dictionary Soc. N.Am., Am. Name Soc. (bd. mgrs. 1977-80), MLA, Rocky Mountain MLA, Internat. Conf. on Methods in Dialectology (mem. steering com. 1974-84), So. Nev. Tchrs. English (pres. 1974). Roman Catholic.

CLARK, THOMAS RYAN, retired federal agency executive, business and technical consultant; b. Aberdeen, Wash., Sept. 16, 1925; s. George O. and Gladys (Ryan) C.; m. Barbara Ann Thiele, June 14, 1948; children: Thomas R. III, Kathleen A., Christopher J.T. Student, U. Kans., 1943-44; BS, U.S. Mil. Acad., 1948; MSEE, Purdue U., 1955; cert., U.S. Army Command and Gen. Staff Coll., 1960, Harvard U., 1979. Commd. C.E., U.S. Army, 1948, advanced through grades to col., 1968; ret. U.S. Army, 1968; program mgr. U.S. AEC, Washington, 1968-75; dep. mgr. Dept. of Energy, Albuquerque, 1976-83; mgr. Nev. ops. Dept. of Energy, Las Vegas, 1983-87, ret., 1987; cons. in field Las Vegas and Albuquerque, 1987—; mem. adv. bd. Dept. Chem. and Nuclear Engring., U. N.Mex., 1984—; mem. statewide adv. bd. Desert Research Inst., U. Nev., 1985-88. Editor, co-author: Nuclear Fuel Cycle, 1975. Trustee Nev. Devel. Authority, Las Vegas, 1984-88. Decorated Legion of Merit, Bronze Star; named Disting. Exec., Pres. of U.S., 1982. Mem. Las Vegas C. of C. (bd. dirs. 1983-87), Sigma Xi, Tau Beta Pi, Eta Kappa Nu. Episcopalian. Lodge: Rotary.

CLARK, THOMAS SULLIVAN, lawyer; b. Bakersfield, Calif., Dec. 12, 1947; s. Walter J. and Ruth Virginia (Sullivan) C.; m. Barbara H. Langston, June 14, 1969. BA in History, U. So. Calif., 1969, JD, 1973. Gen. counsel Income Equities Corp., Los Angeles, 1972-74; campaign cons. Huntington Beach, Calif., 1974-75; prosecutor Office of Kern County Dist. Atty., Bakersfield, 1975-78; ptnr. Arrache, Clark & Potter (formerly Rudnick, Arrache & Clark), Bakersfield, 1978—; cons. Vol. Attys. Program, Bakersfield, 1985—. Pres. Kern Bridges Youth Found., Bakersfield, 1987—; mem. Kern County Dem. Cen. Com., 1976-80. Served with Calif. N.G., 1970-76. Mem. Calif. Bar Assn., Kern County Bar Assn. (client cons. 1984—), Community Assns. Inst., Kern County Hist. Soc., Kern County U. So. Calif. Alumni Assn. (bd. dirs., v.p. 1985-88, pres. 1988—). Republican. Roman Catholic. Club: Petroleum. Lodge: Rotary (bd. dirs. Bakersfield club 1982). Office: Arrache Clark & Potter 5401 California Ave Ste 301 Bakersfield CA 93309

CLARK, WILLIAM ALLEN, lawyer; b. Long Beach, Calif., Aug. 22, 1947; s. Ray Miller and Lillian Maureen (Bjorstrom) C.; m. Mary Alice Smith, Dec., 1967 (div. 1980); children: Heather Elizabeth, Anthea Marie; m. Sandra Ann Hill, May 18, 1980; 1 child, William Allen. Student, Loyola U., L.A., 1967-69; JD, U. San Fernando Valley, 1976. Bar: Calif. 1977, U.S. Dist. Ct. 1977. Golf professional Antelope Valley Country Club, Palmdale, Calif., 1968-70; automobile salesman Pioneer Lincoln Mercury, Lancaster, Calif., 1970-71, Martin Pontiach-Cadillac, Lancaster, 1971-73; pvt. practice Palmdale, Calif., 1976—; atty. City of Maricopa, Calif., 1976-77. Mem. ABA, Calif. State Bar, Los Angeles County Bar Assn., Antelope Valley Bar Assn., Elks (trustee Lancaster 1985-89, chmn. 1987-88). Republican. Methodist. Office: William Allen Clark Atty 44421 N 10th St W Ste G Lancaster CA 93534

CLARK, WILLIAM SACKETT, JR., electronic engineer; b. Columbus, Ohio, Aug. 16, 1953; s. William Sackett and Phyllis H. (Hansberger) C.; m. Merrilynn Bills, Mar. 1, 1980; children: William Sackett III, Grant Trowbridge. BSEE, Carnegie-Mellon U., 1975. Sr. engr. Coded Communications Corp., San Marcos, Calif., 1976-80, Electron Inc., San Diego, 1980-81; mgr. new product devel. Distributed Networks, Inc., Carlsbad, Calif., 1981; dir. computer engring. Epic Computer Products,Inc., San Diego, 1981-83; sr. engr. Cipher Data Products, Inc., San Diego, 1983-87; mgr. hardware engring. Meridian Data, Inc., San Marcos, 1987—. Patentee, digital data transferral system. Mem. Kappa Sigma. Home: 2625 Pasatiempo Glen Escondido CA 92025 Office: Meridian Data Inc 1239 Linda Vista Dr San Marcos CA 92069

CLARKE, FRANK, family physician, educator; b. Blythe, Calif., Nov. 11, 1921; s. Francis Dodsworth; grad. cum laude Los Angeles City Coll., 1942; BS, UCLA, 1946; MD, St. Louis U., 1950; postgrad. U.S. Naval Med. Sch., 1951-52; MPH, U. Calif.-Berkeley; m. Pearl Tucker, children: Michael A., Timothy L., Stephen, Teressa, M. Robert, Sha-ni. Diplomate Am. Bd. Family Practice. Intern, USN Hosp., Oakland, Calif., 1950-51; resident Tulare County Gen. Hosp., Tulare, Calif., 1953-54; practice medicine and surgery, Woodlake, Calif., 1974-75; mem. staff Kaweah Delta Dist. Hosp.; chief staff Exeter Meml. Hosp., 1954-56; team physician Coll. of Sequoias, 1968-75; med. dir. USPHS (ret. 1986); clin. dir. Albuquerque Indian Hosp., 1975-80; lecturer U. Calif. at Santa Cruz, 1971-73; asst. clin. prof. dept. family and community medicine Georgetown U., 1980—; adj. faculty Sch. Allied Health Profls. Idaho State U. Trustee, Woodlake Union Elem. Sch. Dist., 1956-60, pres. bd. trustees, 1958-60; chmn. Citizens Adv. Com., Title I Funds, 1969-73. Bd. dirs. D-Q. U., 1971. Served with USN, 1942-46, 50-53. Recipient fellowship and grant John Hay Whitney Found., 1950; Indian achievement award Indian Council Fire Chgo., 1961; named Man of Year, City of Woodlake, 1962. Charter fellow Am. Acad. Family Physicians; mem. Assn. Am. Indian Physicians (pres. 1973-74), Nat. Council Clin. Dirs. (chmn. 1977-79), Phi Chi, Tau Alpha Epsilon. Home: PO Box 309 Woodlake CA 93286

CLARKE, GREGORY RAY, data processing executive; b. Huntington Park, Calif., July 21, 1942; s. Harvey Rae and Dorothy Louise (Cooke) C.; m. Janet Carole Clack, Sept. 28, 1974; children: Jennifer, Kendra. BA, U. Calif., Berkeley, 1965. Owner, operator Bioexotica, Berkeley, 1965-70; computer operator Bergen Brunswig, South San Francisco, 1970-71; asst. fin. dir. City of Redwood City, Calif., 1971-76; owner, operator Aku Hale, Mountain View, Calif., 1972-80; pres. Creative Computer Solutions, Inc., Fremont, Calif., 1976—. Republican. Office: Creative Computer Solutions Inc 39350 Civic Ctr Dr Fremont CA 94538

CLARKE, IAN CAMERON, mechanical engineer, researcher, educator; b. Kilmarnock, Scotland, Mar. 17, 1946; came to U.S., 1972, s. Donald L. and Elizabeth Clarke, m. Anne Clarke, June 30, 1967; children: Lynne C., Alan C. BS in Mech. Engring., U. Strathclyde, Glasgow, Scotland, 1968, PhD, in Bioengring., 1972. Bioengring. research tech. U. Strathclyde, 1968, bioengring. research asst., 1971-72; asst. research bioengr. UCLA, 1972-73, asst. adj. prof., 1973-79; assoc. prof. mech. engring. and orthopaedics U. So. Calif., Los Angeles, 1979-83, dir. Orthopaedic Biomechanics Lab., Orthopaedic Hosp., 1979-83; pres. Bioengring. Research Inst., Los Angeles, 1983-87; pres. Kinamed, Inc., Los Angeles, 1987—. Contbr. articles to profl. jours., also reviewer various jours; mem. arthroplasty editorial bd. Techniques in Orthopaedics, 1982—; mem. editorial bd. Anns. Biomed. Engring., 1975—; mem. U.S. bd. editors Biomaterials Jour., 1982—. Numerous research grants including NIH, NASA, NSF. Mem. Inst. Mech. Engrs. (grad. mem.), ASME, Biomed. Engring. Soc., Orthopaedic Research Soc., ASTM (F-4 com. on med. devices), Biomaterials Soc., Hip Soc. (John Charnley award for paper 1977, Otto AuFrance award for paper 1979). Home: 2215 23d St Santa Monica CA 90405 Office: Kinamed Inc 10780 Santa Monica Blvd Ste #100 Westwood CA 90025

CLARKE, JAMES PHILIP, medical educator, physician; b. Denver, Nov. 25, 1922; s. Philip and Grace (Lilly) C.; m. Doris Jean O'Brien, Jan. 5, 1946; children: Philip, Bernard, Nancy, Ted, Paul, Maureen, Mark, Mary, Patricia, Peggy, Libby. BS, U. Notre Dame, 1945; MD, U. Colo., 1946. Diplomate Am. Bd. Internal Medicine, 1955, 74. Co-founder Denver Clinic, 1956, ptnr., 1956-85; clin. prof. U. Colo. Sch. Medicine, Denver, 1977—, assoc. dean, 1985—; bd. dirs. Nat. Alumni Bd., U. Notre Dame; founder Conf. Med. Ethics U. Notre Dame, 1986—. Contbr. articles to profl. jours. Mem. Nat. Commn. on Future Regis Coll., Denver, 1980-82; bd. dirs. Denver Bd. Health and Hosp. (chmn.), 1973-75. Lt. U.S. Navy, 1947-49. Recipient Robins award Colo. Med. Soc., 1972, Outstanding Clin. Faculty award U. Colo. Health Sci. Ctr., Denver, 1983, Edward Sorin award U. Notre Dame, 1987. Fellow AMA, Am. Coll. Physician (gov. 1981-85, chmn. 1985-86, regent 1986—), Am. Soc. Internal Medicine, Denver Med. Soc., Colo. Med. Soc., Serra (pres. 1968), Denver Country Club. Democrat. Roman Catholic. Home: 3921 S Bellaire Englewood CO 80110 Office: U Colo Health Scis Ctr S2C-295 4200 E 9th Ave Denver CO 80262

CLARKE, RICHARD ALAN, electric and gas utility company executive, lawyer; b. San Francisco, May 18, 1930; s. Chauncey Frederick and Carolyn (Shannon) C.; m. Mary Dell Fisher, Feb. 5, 1955; children: Suzanne, Nancy C. Stephen, Douglas Alan. AB Polit. Sci. cum laude, U. Calif., Berkeley, 1952, JD, 1955. Bar: Calif. 1955. Atty. Pacific Gas and Electric Co., San Francisco, 1955-60, sr. counsel, 1970-74, asst. gen. counsel, 1974-79, v.p., asst. to chmn., 1979-82, exec. v.p., gen. mgr. utility ops., 1982-85, pres., 1985-86, chmn. bd., chief exec. officer, 1986—; ptnr. Rockwell, Fulkerson and Clarke, San Rafael, Calif., 1960-69; bd. dirs. Potlach Corp.; dir. exec. com. Edison Elec. Inst., Invest in Am. Dir. exec. com. Bay Area Coun.; mem. Bay Area Econ. Forum, Calif. Bus. Roundtable; trustee Com. for Econ. Devel., Boalt Hall Trust-U. Calif.-Berkeley Sch. Law; bd. govs. San Francisco Symphony; exec. com. San Francisco Edn. Fund, United Way of Bay Area, Campaign Cabinet, 1988. Mem. State Bar Calif., Pacific Coast Elec. Assn., Pacific Coast Gas Assn., Edison Electric Inst. (dir., mem. exec. com.), Calif. C. of C. (past dir.), San Francisco C. of C. (past dir., v.p. econ. devel.), Pacific-Union Club, Marin Tennis Club. Office: Pacific Gas & Electric Co 77 Beale St San Francisco CA 94106

CLARKE, ROBERT EMMETT, writer, poet; b. Cleve., May 28, 1906; s. Robert Emmett and Mary Bernadette (Paquette) C. Student schs. Lakewood, Ohio. Reporter, Cleve. Times, 1925; asst. mgr. UP, Cleve., 1925-26; police reporter Canton Daily News (Ohio), 1926-27; courthouse and police reporter, asst. sports editor Akron Times-Press (Ohio), 1927-30; with Thompson Products, 1943-45, Erie R.R., 1945-46; hotel cashier, 1937-38; with Grant Photo Products, 1946-55. With USN, 1942. Author: polit. satire: Charley Horse, 1944, 4 line poetry: Rhyming Robert, 1966, Violets, Tulips, Rosebuds, Buttercups, 1971; works included in World of Poetry Anthology, 1984, Am. Poetry Anthology, Vol. III, No. 3-4, 1984, Ashes to Ashes, Vol. V, 1985, The Art of Poetry, 1985, The National Poetry Anthology, 1985, Masterpieces of Modern Verse, 1985, Our Wold's Most Beloved Poems, 1984, Our Western World's Most Beautiful Poems, 1985, Moods and Mysteries (Poetry Press vol. 3), Pauses in Time, 1986, American Poetry Anthology, 1986, 87, numerous editions of Am. Poetry Assn. and Poetry Press, 1986, Words of Praise Vol. II, 1986, Peace on Earth Poetry Anthology, 1986, World of Poetry--American Poetry Anthology, vol. 6, no. 1, 1986, Pleasant Journeys, 1986, Riders of the Rainbow, 1986, The New York Poetry Foundation Anthology, 1986, The World's Most Cherished Poems, 1986, Celebrations of Life, 1987, The Poet's Hand, 1987, Words of Praise III, 1987, American Poetry Anthology Vol. VI, No. 5 (Golden Poet award, 1986, 87), World of Poetry Anthology, 1986, N.Y. Poetry Anthology, 1988, 89, Sparrowgrass Anthology, 1989, Of Diamonds and Rust, 1989, numerous others. Precinct committeeman Democratic Party, Ohio, Cuyahoga County, 1944-48; candidate Ohio Senate Primary, 1944. Recipient Golden Poetry award World of Poetry, 1986, 88; named one of Best Poets of 1988 Am. Poetry Assn., editor's choice, 1988. Roman Catholic. Home: 212 S 6th St Apt B Alhambra CA 91801

CLARKE, ROBERT FRANCIS, metallic ore processing research executive; b. Mpls., Mar. 20, 1915: s. Charles Patrick and Maurine Elizabeth (Clark) C.; B.S. with honors, U. Fla., 1948; M.S., U. Ariz., 1971; m. Charlotte Adele Radwill, July 24, 1966; children—Robert, Carol, David. Meteorologist, U.S. Weather Bur., 1940-42, 48-50, 52-55; supervisory electronics engr., chief navigation br. aviation dept. U.S. Army Electronics Proving Ground, 1956-58, nuclear physicist, chief scientist nuclear surveillance div., 1958-62; aerospace engr. NASA, Lewis Research Ctr., 1962-66; physicist Hughes Aircraft Co., 1966-68; instr. Math. Pima Community Coll., 1969-74, and San Juan campus N.Mex. State U., 1974-75; instr. math. Am. Internat. Sch., Kabul, Afghanistan, 1976-78; dir. Polaris Internat. Metals Corp., Tucson. Radiol. def. officer Fed. Emergency Mgmt. Agy., CAP. Trustee Rep. Presdl. Task Force; mem. mayor's com. Celebration of Bicentennial of Constn., 1987. Served with U.S. Army, 1942-46, USAF, 1950-52; res. ret. as col., 1975. Recipient nat. award for best articles in Officer Rev.; honor cert. for excellence in published works Freedoms Found. of Valley Forge; recipient Presdl. Medal of Merit. Sr. mem. IEEE (plasma physics and computer sects.), AIAA; mem. Am. Nuclear Soc. (fusion power and reactor physics sect.), Space Studies Inst., Internat. Platform Assn., Fusion Power Assocs., Soc. Photo-Optical Instrumentation Engrs., Am. Meteorol. Soc., Am. Optical Soc., Soc. Unmanned Vehicle Systems, Arctic Inst. N.Am., AAUP, Assn. Former Intelligence Officers, Am. Def. Preparedness Assn., Scientists and Engrs. for Secure Energy, N.Y. Acad. Scis., Ariz.-Nev. Acad. Scis., Navy League, Am. Legion, VFW, (pres. 1986, honor degree), AMVETS, Ret. Officers Assn. (pres. Tucsonchpt. 1986), U.S. Naval Inst., Assn. U.S. Army (chpt. pres. 1982-83), Air Force Assn., Mil. Order World Wars (chpt. commdr. 1987—), Am. Security Council, Vets. Affairs Tucson (com. chmn. 1986), Inst. Polit. Sci. Club: Army and Navy. Lodges: Odd Fellows, Kiwanis, Elks. Contbr. articles in aerospace and nat. def. to mags., jours. Home: 5846 E South Wilshire Dr Tucson AZ 85711 Office: 1745 E Factory Ave Tucson AZ 85719

CLARKE, URANA, musician, writer, educator; b. Wickliffe-on-the-Lake, Ohio, Sept. 8, 1902; d. Graham Warren and Grace Urana (Olsaver) C.; artists and tchrs. diploma Mannes Music Sch., N.Y.C., 1925; cert. Dalcroze Sch. Music, N.Y.C., 1950; student Pembroke Coll., Brown U.; BS, Mont. State U., 1967, M of Applied Sci., 1970. Mem. faculty Mannes Music Sch., 1922-49, Dalcroze Sch. Music, 1949-54; adv. editor in music The Book of Knowledge, 1949-65; v.p., dir. Saugatuck Circle Housing Devel.; guest lectr. Hayden Planetarium, 1945; guest lectr., bd. dirs. Roger Williams Park Planetarium, Providence; radio show New Eng. Skies, Providence, 1961-64, Skies Over the Big Sky Country, Livingston, Mont., 1964-79, Birds of the Big Sky Country, 1972-79, Great Music of Religion, 1974-79; mem. adv. com. Nat. Rivers and Harbors Congress, 1947-58; instr. continuing edn. Mont. State U. Chmn., Park County chpt. ARC, co-chmn. county blood program, first aid instr. trainer, 1941—; instr. ARC cardio-pulmonary resuscitation, 1976—; mem. Mont. Commn. Nursing and Nursing Edn., 1974-76; mem. Park County Local Govt. Study Commn., 1974-76, chmn., 1984-86; mem. Greater Yellowstone Coalition. Mem. Am. Acad. Polit. Sci., Am. Musicol. Soc., Royal Astron. Soc. Can., Inst. Nav., Maria Mitchell Soc. Nantucket, N.Am. Yacht Racing Union, AAAS, Meteoritical Soc., Internat. Soc. Mus. Research, Skyscrapers (sec.-treas. 1960-63), Am. Guild Organists, Park County Wilderness Assn. (treas.), Trout Unlimited, Nature Conservancy, Big Sky Astron. Soc. (dir. 1965—), Sierra Club. Lutheran. Club: Cedar Point Yacht. Author: The Heavens are Telling (astronomy), 1951; Skies Over the Big Sky Country, 1965; also astron. news-letter, View It Yourself, weekly column Big Skies; contbr. to mags, on music, nav. and astronomy. Pub. Five Chorale Preludes for Organ, 1975; also elem. two-piano pieces. Inventor, builder of Clarke Adjustable Piano Stool. Address: Log-A-Rhythm 9th St Island Livingston MT 59047

CLARKE, WILLIAM BURTON, academic director; b. Detroit, Aug. 14, 1947; s. William B. and Dorothy M. Clarke; m. Clarice E. Beene; children: Asha, William, Ashton. Student, Tenn. State U., 1965-66, Glendale Community Coll., 1967; BA in Sociology, So. Ill. U., 1973; MA in Mgmt., Webster U., 1981. Asst. to registrar and fin. aid officer So. Ill. U., Edwardsville, 1973-74, coord. student svcs., 1974-76; bus. mgr. Performing Arts Tng. Ctr., East St. Louis, Ill., 1973-76; tour mgr. African Diaspora Smithsonian Instn., Washington, 1976; student affairs officer U. Calif., San Diego, 1977-78; asst. dir. U. Calif., La Jolla, 1978-80; dir. edn. opportunity program Sonoma State U., Rohnert Park, Calif., 1979-80, dir. edn. support programs, 1980—. Co-author artistic activities Nemesis '76 for Community Arts Coun., 1975-76. Bd. dirs. Sonoma County People for Econ. Opportunity, 1988; active NAACP. Served with USAF, 1966-70. Artist-in-residence grant, Calif. Mem. Calif. Assn. Student Fin. Aid Adminstrs., Calif. Community Coll. Extended Opportunity Program and Svcs. Assn., So. Ill. U. Alumni Assn. (life), Nat. Assn. for Devel. Edn., Am. Assn. Coll. Registrar and Admissions Officers, Nat. Assn. Student Pers. Adminstrs. Home: 7708 Blair Ave Rohnert Park CA 94928 Office: Sonoma State U 1801 E Cotati Rohnert Park CA 94928

CLARK-MAHONEY, JOHN PAUL, nurse; b. Coldwater, Ohio, July 10, 1955; s. Thomas William and Roselyn (Fox) Mahoney; m. Charlotte Ennis Clark, Aug. 18, 1979; children: Merlin Ennis, Kelty Brendan. BSN, Wright State U., 1980. RN, Ohio, Wash.; cert. rehab. nurse. Staff nurse St. Elizabeth's Med. Ctr., Dayton, Ohio, 1980-82; nurse practitioner U. Wash. Hosp., Seattle, 1982—. Contbr. articles to profl. jours. Mem. Am. Nurses Assn., Rehab. Nurses Assn. Home: 4356 NE 56th St Seattle WA 98105

CLARKSON, LAWRENCE WILLIAM, airplane company executive; b. Grove City, Pa., Apr. 29, 1938; s. Harold William and Jean Henrietta (Jaxtheimer) C.; m. Barbara Louise Stevenson, Aug. 20, 1960; children: Michael, Elizabeth, Jennifer. BA, DePauw U., 1960; JD, U. Fla., 1962. Counsel Pratt & Whitney, West Palm Beach, Fla., 1967-72, program dep. dir., 1972-75, program mgr., 1974-75; v.p., mng. dir. Pratt & Whitney, Brussels, Belgium, 1975-78; v.p. mktg. Pratt & Whitney, West Palm Beach, 1978-80; v.p. contracts Pratt & Whitney, Hartford, Conn., 1980-82, pres. comml. products div., 1982-87; sr. v.p. govt. and internat. affairs Boeing Comml. Airplanes, Seattle, 1988—; dir. Partnership for Improved Air Travel, Washington, 1988—. Trustee DePauw U., Greencastle, Ind., 1987; corp. council Interlochen (Mich.) Ctr. for the Arts, 1987. Served to capt. USAF, 1963-66. Episcopal. Clubs: N.Y. Yacht, Met. Opera, Wings (bd. govs. 1987—). Home: 15502 SE 53d Pl Bellevue WA 98006 Office: Boeing Comml Airplanes PO Box 3707 Seattle WA 98124

CLASS, JOHN BROMMER, information systems specialist; b. Madison, Wis., July 31, 1941; s. George Michael and Catherine Ann (Hand) C.; m. Elizabeth Ann Butcher, June 15, 1963; children: Kathryn, John G., Karen. BS, U. Nebr., Omaha, 1969; MS in Systems Engring., AT&T, Fort Monmouth, N.J., 1974; MBA, N.Y. Inst. Tech., 1975. Sr. engr. U.S. Army, 1963-83; dir. spl. ops. Mandex, Inc., Sierra Vista, Ariz., 1983-86; dir. P&A Advance Tech. Info. Systems, Sierra Vista, 1983—; bd. dirs. Advanced Tech. Info. Systems, Sierra Vista, 1983—, chief operating officer info support system, 1987—; dept. mgr., sr. engr. Bell Tech. Ops., Sierra Vista, 1986-87. Asst. leader Boy Scouts Am., Girl Scouts U.S., N.J., Ariz., N.B., Belgium, 1970-80; baseball coach various Little Leagues, N.J., Ariz., Belgium, 1972-78. Lt. col. U.S. Army, 1963-83. Decorated Bronze Star, Purple Heart, Legion of Merit. Mem. Nat. Contract Mgmt. Assn. (pres. 1987-88, Cert. of Appreciation 1988), Armed Forces Communications (chmn. tech. seminars 1988—, Certs. of Appreciation 1986-88), Electronics Assn. Republican. Episcopalian. Home: 4854 Cherokee Ave RR #1 Box 2178 Sierra Vista AZ 85635 Office: Advance Tech Info Systems 333 W Wilcox Dr Ste 301 Sierra Vista AZ 85635

CLAUSEL, NANCY KAREN, clergywoman; b. Jackson, Tenn., Jan. 1, 1948; s. Clinton Prentice and Martha Juanita (Felker) C.; children: Richard D. Harwood Jr., Kara Denise Harwood. Student Lambuth Coll., 1966-67, George Peabody Coll. for Tchrs.; BEd, Memphis State U., 1971; MDiv summa cum laude, Memphis Theol. Sem., 1980. Ordained to ministry United Meth.; lic. counselor Tenn. Ch. Dir. Christian edn. Grimes United Meth. Ch., Memphis, 1977-79, Wesleyan Hills United Meth. Ch., Memphis, 1979-80; assoc. minister St. James United Meth. Ch., Memphis, 1981-82; dir. Wesley Pastoral Counseling Ctr., Memphis, 1982-85; co-dir. Connection: Holistic Counseling Ctr., Memphis, 1985-87; co-founder, co-minister The Connection Ch., 1986—; bd. dirs. Wesley Found.-Memphis State, 1979-80, 82-84; vice chmn. commn. on status and role of women Memphis Ann. Conf., 1980-86; chmn. work area on worship McKendree Dist. Memphis Ann. Conf., 1980-84; mem. Bd. Pensions Memphis Ann. Conf., 1983-84; supervising pastor Candidacy for Minister program Memphis Ann. Conf., 1984-86. Vol. Johnson Aux. City of Memphis Hosp., 1975; sec. Peacemakers Memphis, 1979; clergy rep. adv. bd. Memphis chpt. Parents Without Ptnrs., 1984-85; mem. Network, Memphis, 1984-87. Mem. Internat. Transactional Analysis Assn. (clin. mem. 1981—, provisional teaching mem. 1982—), Assn. for Specialists in Group Work, Memphis Ministers Assn. (treas. 1985-86), Altrusa Internat., Phi Kappa Phi. Columnist: The Light (newspaper). Avocations: aerobics, music. Home: 15808 Vail Cut Off Rd Rainier WA 98576

CLAUSEN, ALDEN WINSHIP, banker; b. Hamilton, Ill., Feb. 17, 1923; s. Morton and Elsie (Kroll) C.; m. Mary Margaret Crassweller, Feb. 11, 1950; children: Eric David, Mark Winship. B.A., Carthage Coll., 1944, LL.D., 1970; LL.B., U. Minn., 1949; grad., Advanced Mgmt. Program, Harvard U., 1966. Bar: Minn. 1949, Calif. 1950. With Bank Am. (NT & SA), San Francisco, 1949-81, 1986—; v.p. Bank Am. (NT & SA), 1961-65, sr. v.p., 1965-68, exec. v.p., 1968-69, vice chmn. bd., 1969, pres., chief exec. officer, 1970-81, chmn., chief exec. officer, 1986—; pres. World Bank, 1981-86; now chmn., pres., chief exec. officer BankAmerica Corp.; past pres. Internat. Monetary Conf., San Francisco; Clearing House Assn. Past pres. Fed. Adv. Council, 1972; past chmn. Bay Area Council; past bd. govs. United Way of Am.; past chmn. United Way of Bay Area; past mem. Bus. Roundtable; mem. Bus. Council; past mem. Japan-U.S. Adv. Council; past bd. dirs. Conf. Bd., San Francisco Opera; past bd. dirs., mem. adv. council SRI Internat.; mem. adv. council Stanford U. Grad. Sch. Bus.; bd. dirs. Harvard Bus. Sch.; trustee Carthage Coll., Brookings Instn. Mem. Res. City Bankers Assn. (hon.), Calif. Bar Assn. Clubs: Bankers of San Francisco, Pacific Union, Burlingame Country; Bohemian, Links (N.Y.C.); Metropolitan (Washington); Chevy Chase (Md.). Office: BankAm Corp 555 California St San Francisco CA 94104 *

CLAUSEN, ALF HEIBERG, composer; b. Mpls., Mar. 28, 1941; s. Alf and Magdalene (Heiberg) C.; m. Judy Kaye Landstrom, June 5, 1965; children: Karen Leigh, Scott Owen, Kyle Evan. BA, N.D. State U., 1963; postgrad., U. Wis., 1963; diploma in music composition and arranging, Berklee Coll. Music, 1966; studies with John Bavicchi, William Maloof, Herb Pomeroy, Earle Hagen. Composer, orchestrato; pres. Karleigh Music Co.; instr. music The Dick Grove Music Workshops; instr. music arranging and composition UCLA; adjudicator Playboy All-Star Intercollegiate Jazz Festival Competition, Western Div. Intercollegiate Jazz Festival Competition; composer Los Angeles Neophonic Orch. Concert Series, 1968. Composer, orchestrator (films) Mr. Mom, Force Five, An Eye for an Eye, Fast Walking, Forced Vengeance, Airplane II: The Sequel, Natty Gann, Splash, Micki & Maude, Weird Science, Dragnet, Number One With a Bullet, (TV shows) Father Murphy, Little House on the Prairie, Shell Game, The Mississippi, Fame, Wizards & Warriors, Partners in Crime, Dads, Lime Street, Harry, Alf, Moonlighting (4 Emmy award nominations), (TV films) Happy Endings, Rememberance of Love, Miss All-American Beauty, This is Kate Bennett, For Ladies Only, The Other Lover, Letting Go, The Long Way Home, Double Agent, Murder in Three Acts, My First Love, Police Story, She Knows Too Much, Stranded; orchestrator (films) Buddy, Buddy, Jinxed, The Beastmaster, Table for Five, Up the Creek, Miracles, My Science Project, Wise Guys, Into the Night, Lots of Luck, The Last Starfighter, Ferris Bueller's Day Off, (TV shows) Bronk, Jigsaw, The FBI, Ripley's Believe It Or Not, Scene of the Crime, Trauma Center (TV movies) Sparkling Cyanide, Princess Daisy, Quarterback Princess, Caribbean Mystery, I Want to Live, Legs, Six Months With an Older Woman, Two of a Kind (Emmy award), Listen to Your Heart, Mirrors; composer, arranger, producer (albums) Into the Night, Moonlighting, The Beastmaster, The Last Starfighter, North Tex. State Lab Band (Grammy nomination), numerous others. Recipient Clio nomination, N.Y.C., 1979, One O'Clock award North Tex. State U., Denton, 1978, 79, 80, Alumnus Recognition award Berklee Coll. Music, 1984, Alumni Achievement award N.D. State U., 1986; U. Wis. scholar; Nat. Endowment Arts, Berklee Coll. Music fellow. Mem. ASCAP, Am. Soc. Music Arrangers, Nat. Assn. Jazz Educators, Dramatists Guild, Songwriters Guild, Soc. Composers and Lyricists, Nat. Acad. Rec. Arts and Scis. (mem. jazz crafts com.), Acad. TV Arts and Scis. (5 Emmy nominations), Am. Fedn. Musicians, Screen Actors Guild, Blue Key, Phi Kappa Phi, Kappa Kappa Psi. Republican. Lutheran.

CLAUSEN, BRET MARK, safety engineer; b. Hayward, Calif., Aug. 1, 1958; s. Norman E. and Barbara Ann (Wagner) C.; m. Cheryl Elaine Carlson, May 24, 1980; children: Kathrine, Eric, Emily. BS, Colo. State U., 1980, MS, 1983. Diplomate Am. Acad. Indsl. Hygiene; cert. indsl. hygienist; cert. safety profl.; cert. hazard control mgr. Indsl. hygienist, safety rep., assoc. risk mgmt. Samsonite Corp., Denver, 1980-83, mgr. loss prevention, 1984-88; health, safety and environment rep. Storage Tech., Longmont, Colo., 1984; sr. project cons. Occusafe Inc., Denver, 1988; prin. program adminstr. indsl. hygiene Rockwell Internat., Golden, Colo., 1988—. Mem. Am. Indsl. Hygiene Assn. (pres. Rocky Mtn. section 1988-89), Am. Soc. Safety Engrs. (profl.), Am. Bd. Indsl. Hygiene (cert.), Bd. Cert. Safety Profls. (cert.), Bd. Hazard Control Mgmt. (cert.), Ins. Inst. Am. (assoc. risk mgmt.). Republican. Lutheran. Home: 1568 S Elkhart St Aurora CO 80012 Office: Rockwell Internat PO Box 464 Mail Stop T452D Golden CO 80402

CLAUSON, STEVEN LLOYD, chiropractor; b. Alamagordo, N.Mex., Aug. 2, 1955; s. Lloyd Allen and Shirley Ann (Hughes) Clauson; m. Lauren Rose Karam- Mooney, Apr. 3, 1982. Student biol. scis., San Bernardino Valley Coll., 1981-83; DChiropractic, Life-Chiropractic West, San Lorenzo, Calif., 1986. Co. mgr. Home Bldg. Ctr., San Bernardino, Calif., 1975-81; pvt. practice Sacramento, 1986--. Named Chiropractic Humanitarian, Gibson Cons., 1988. Mem. Internat. Chiropractic Assn., Calif. Chiropractic Assn., Sacramento Valley Chiropractic Assn. Republican. Episcopalian. Home: 2889

Wiese Way Sacramento CA 95833 Office: 7000 Franklin Blvd Ste 190 Sacramento CA 95823

CLAUSSEN, BONNIE ADDISON, II, aerospace company executive; b. Pueblo, Colo., Jan. 11, 1942; s. Bonnie A. I and Gertrude A. (Poe) C.; m. Charlotte J. Dipert, July 11, 1961; children: Christopher Addison, Raymond Dale. BS in Math., U. So. Colo., 1967; postgrad., Pa. State U., King of Prussia, 1968-69. Programmer Gen. Electric Corp., King of Prussia, 1967-69, sr. programmer, 1969-71; project mgr. Martin Marietta Aerospace Co., Denver, 1971-79; co-founder, exec. v.p. CTA, Inc., Englewood, Colo., 1979—, also bd. dirs. Designer: (software) Real-Time Flight, 1967-78, Viking Mars Lander Flight, 1975; contbr: Real-Time Simulation Publs., 1975-78. Served with USAF, 1962-65. Recipient Pub. Service medal Nat. Aeronautics and Space Adminstrn., 1976. Republican. Office: CTA Inc 900 Heritage Dr Ridgecrest CA 93555

CLAUSSEN, RONALD VERNON, federal transportation agency administrator; b. Davenport, Iowa, Feb. 6, 1938; s. Elmer Arthur and Mary Elizabeth (Negus) C.; m. Martha Elizabeth Walls, Jan. 26, 1961 (div. 1988); children: Terry, Traci. AA in Bus. Adminstrn., Palmer Jr. Coll., 1970; BA in Pub. Adminstrn., Upper Iowa U., 1974; MBA, Cen. Mich. U., 1977. Police officer City of Davenport, 1961-67; transp. specialist Rock Island (Ill.) Arsenal Activity U.S. Dept. Def., 1967-69, traffic mgr. Savanna (Ill.) Army Depot, 1969-70; storage specialist personal property U.S. Dept. Def., Chgo. and Atlanta, 1970-73; traffic mgmt. specialist Rock Island Arsenal U.S. Dept. Def., 1973-74; sr. storage specialist personal property U.S. Dept. Def., Falls Church, Va., 1974-82; chief of transp. Army Aviation Ctr. U.S. Dept. Def., Ft. Rucker, Ala., 1982-85; dep. dir. personal property U.S. Dept. Def., Oakland, Calif., 1985-88; dep. dir. inland traffic U.S. Dept. Def., Oakland, 1988—; bus. instr., Fairfax County (Va.) Adult Edn., 1977-83; seminar instr., George Mason U., Fairfax, 1977-83; adj. faculty, U. Va. Falls Church, 1977-83, Embry-Riddle Aero. U., Daytona Beach, Fla., 1983—. Co-author: Warehouse Emergency Operations, 1982; contbr. to profl. orgns. Sgt. USAF, 1956-60. Mem. Meeting Planners Internat., Nat. Def. Transp. Assn. (bd. dirs. 1987—), Soc. Govt. Meeting Planners (pres. 1987-89)No. Calif. Meeting Planners Internat., Am. Legion, Shriners, Mason (32 degree), Scottish Rite, Delta Nu Alpha. Republican. Lutheran. Home: 1009 Cedar Terr San Pablo CA 94806 Office: Mil Traffic Mgmt Command Western Area Oakland Army Base Oakland CA 94626-5000

CLAWSON, RAYMOND WALDEN, independent oil producer; b. San Jose, Calif.; s. Benjamin B. and Mae Belle (Names) C.; LL.B., Am. U., 1936; m. Barbara M. Robbins, 1965. Ind. operator, exploration and devel. oil properties, 1936—; pub. Los Angeles Mirror, 1945-47; pres. Ariz. Securities, Phoenix, 1947-50, Transcontinental Oil Co., Los Angeles, 1947-49; geophys. cons. in offshore drilling ops. Gulf of Mexico, 1963—, North Sea, 1970—; chmn., chief exec. officer Clawco Petroleum Corp., Newport Beach, Calif., 1979—. Clubs: Balboa Bay, Acapulco Yacht. Office: PO Box 2102 Newport Beach CA 92659

CLAYTON, STEPHEN JOHN, respiratory therapist; b. Bremerton, Wash., Dec. 17, 1946; s. William Arthur and Eunice Frances (Van Laanen) C.; m. Carole Adrienne Phipps, May 3, 1969 (div. Mar. 1977); m. Patricia Nancy Miller, Sept. 20, 1980. AS, Highline Coll., 1974; BA summa cum laude, Western Wash. State U., 1976. Respiratory dept. mgr. Overlake Meml. Hosp., Bellevue, Hosp., 1975-77; staff respiratory therapist Harborview Med. Ctr., Seattle, 1977-78; asst. dept. mgr. Pacific Med. Ctr., Seattle, 1978-79, Ballard Community Hosp., Seattle, 1979-83; clin. respiratory therapist, mktg. rep. Foster Med. Corp., Seattle, 1983-87; v.p. ops. Staff Specialists, Inc., Bellevue, 1987—; bd. dirs. Weight Mgmt. Ctr., Bellevue. Bd. dirs. East King County unit Am. Cancer Soc., Kirkland, Wash., 1987—, orgnl. chair. With USN, 1969-73. Mem. Am. Assn. for Respiratory Care, Wash. State Soc. of Respiratory Care, Home Health and Staffing Svcs. Wash. (v.p., pres. 1989), 1861 Club, Tyce Club. Roman Catholic. Home: 7539 41st Ave NE Seattle WA 98115 Office: 12509 Bel-Red Rd Ste 102 Bellevue WA 98005

CLEARS, ARTHUR LAWRENCE, teacher; b. N.Y.C., Mar. 9, 1943; s. Arthur and Dora (D'Agostino) C. BS, Adelphi U., 1968, MA, 1975; postgrad., San Francisco State U. Tchr., tchr. in charge Waverly Pk. Sch., Lynbrook, N.Y., 1968-84; sci. tchr. Abbott Mid. Sch., San Mateo City, Calif., 1984-85; math. tchr. J.F. Kennedy Mid. Sch., Redwood City, Calif., 1985—. Mem. NEA, Math. Tchrs. Assn., Calif. Adminstrs. Assn., Calif. Tchrs. Assn., Mid. Sch. Assn., Calif. League Mid. Schs. Home: 155 Hancock St #5 San Francisco CA 94114

CLEARY, JAMES W., university president; b. Milw., Apr. 16, 1927; married, 1950. PhB, Marquette U., 1950, MA, 1951; PhD, U. Wis., 1956. Instr., dir. forensics high sch. Wis., 1949-51; instr. speech, head coach debate Marquette U., 1951-53; from instr. to prof. speech U. Wis., 1956-63, vice chancellor academic affairs, 1966-69; pres. Calif. State U., Northridge, 1969—; mem. Pres.'s Commn. NCAA. Author: books in field including Robert's Rules of Order Newly Revised, 1970, 80; editor: books in field including John Bulwer's Chirologia . . . Chironomia, 1644, 1974; co-editor: books in field including Bibliography of Rhetoric and Public Address, 1964. Served to 2d lt. AUS, 1945-47. Named one of the 100 Most Effective Coll. Pres. in the U.S., Exxon Edn. Found., 1986; U. Wis. fellow, 1954-55. Mem. Speech Assn. Am., Am. Assn. State Colls. and Univs. (chmn. 1983), NCAA (pres.' commn. 1984—, chmn. div. II com.). Address: Calif State Univ Office of the Pres 18111 Nordhoff St Northridge CA 91330 *

CLEARY, MICHAEL FRANKLIN, manufacturing company executive; b. San Francisco, Sept. 3, 1947; s. Thomas William and Florence Georgina (Cunningham) C.; m. Kathleen Cheryl Pfeifer, Mar. 22, 1969; children: Jason Andrew, Erin Thomas, Colin Matthew, Megan Joseph. BS, U. Calif., L.A., 1969; PhD, Oreg. State U., Corvallis, 1975. Research assoc. I Spreckels Sugar Co., Woodland, Calif., 1976-77; research assoc. II Spreckels Sugar Co., Woodland, 1977-79; sr. research chemist Am. Crystal Sugar Co., Moorhead, Minn., 1979-82; mgr. chem. research Am. Crystal Sugar Co., Moorhead, 1982-88; mgr. tech. svcs., Western div. Holly Sugar Corp., Emeryville, Calif., 1988—; consulting instr. Beet Sugar Devel. Found., Ft. Collins, Colo., 1982—. Co-author: Processing of Beet Sugar and Cane Sugar, 1988; contbr. articles to profl. jours. Troop leader, Boy Scouts Am., Woodland, 1978-79; lector Holy Spirit Ch., Fargo, N.D., 1980-88; coord. United Fund Annual Drive, Fargo, 1984. Mem. Am. Chem. Soc. (chmn. Red River Valley sect. 1988), Royal Soc. Chemistry. Democrat. Roman Catholic. Office: Holly Sugar Corp 2000 Powell St Ste 800 Emeryville CA 94608

CLEARY, WILLIAM JOSEPH, JR., lawyer; b. Wilmington, N.C., Aug. 14, 1942; s. William Joseph and Eileen Ada (Gannon) C.; AB in History, St. Joseph's U., 1964; JD, Villanova U., 1967. Bar: N.J. 1967, U.S. Ct. Appeals (3d cir.) 1969, Calif. 1982, U.S. Ct. Appeals (9th cir.) 1983. Law sec. to judge N.J. Superior Ct. Jersey City, 1967-68; assoc. Lamb, Blake, H&D, Jersey City, 1968-72; dep. pub. defender State of N.J., Newark, 1972-73; 1st asst. city corp. counsel, Jersey City, 1973-76; assoc. Robert Wasserwald, Inc., Hollywood, Calif., 1984-86, 88—, Gould & Burke, L.A., 1986-87. Mem. ABA, N.J. State Bar, Calif. Bar Assn., L.A. County Bar. Democrat. Roman Catholic. also: Robert Wassewald Inc 315 W 9th St Ste 600 Los Angeles CA 90015

CLECAK, DVERA VIVIAN BOZMAN, psychotherapist; b. Denver, Jan. 15, 1944; d. Joseph Shalom and Annette Rose (Dveirin) Bozman; m. Pete Emmett Clecak, Feb. 26, 1966; children: Aimée, Lisa. BA, Stanford U., 1965; postgrad., U. Chgo., 1965; MSW, UCLA, 1969. Lic. clin. social worker, Calif., marriage, family and child counselor, Calif. Social work supr. Harbor City (Calif.) Parent Child Ctr., 1969-71; therapist Orange County Mental Health Dept., Laguna Beach, Calif., 1971-75, area coordinator, 1975-79; pvt. practice psychotherapy Mission Viejo, Calif., 1979—; founder, exec. dir. Human Options, Laguna Beach, 1981—; mem. co-chmn. domestic violence com. Orange County Commn. on Status of Women, 1979-81; mem. mental health adv. com. extension U. Calif., Irvine, 1983, counseling psychologist, 1980, lectr., 1984-85; lectr. Saddleback Community Coll., Mission Viejo, 1981-82, Chapman Coll., Orange, 1979; field instr. UCLA, 1970-71, 77-78. Recipient Women Helping Women award Saddleback Community Coll., 1987, Cert. Commendation State of Calif. Dept. Social Svcs., 1988. Mem. Nat. Assn. Social Workers, Calif. Marriage Family Child Counselors' Assn., Phi Beta Kappa. Office: 28261 Marguerite Pkwy #255 Mission Viejo CA 92692

CLEIN, A. MICHAEL, lawyer; b. Miami, Fla., Aug. 30, 1937; s. Reubin J. and Hannah (Berner) C.; m. Nancy Ann Ball, July 14, 1988; children from previous marriage: Stephen, Jeffery, Michael, Savannah, Catherine. BA, U. Miami, 1958; LLB, Boston Coll., 1961. Pvt. practice Miami, 1961—, L.A., 1982—, Las Vegas, Nev., 1985—; judge, Florida City, Fla., 1966. Named World Poker Champion, Profl. Gamblers Assn., Las Vegas, 1972-73, 83-84. Mem. Fla. Bar Assn., Calif. Bar Assn. Office: 1541 Ocean Ave Santa Monica CA 90401

CLEMENT, RICHARD WILLIAM, plastic and reconstructive surgeon; b. Pontiac, Mich., Nov. 10, 1953; s. William Henry and Jean Elizabeth (Girst) C.; m. Phyllis Jean Hobson, Aug. 15, 1981; children: Nicholas William, Kimberly Ashley, Christopher Richard. BS, Alma Coll., 1975; MD, U. Va., 1979. Diplomate Am. Bd. Plastic Surgery; fellow Am. Coll. Surgeons. Asst. prof. surgery Washington U., St. Louis, 1984-88; dir. Southwest Plastic Surgeons, Paradise Valley, Ariz., 1988—. Contbr. articles to profl. jours.; co-author: Essentials of Plastic Surgery, 1987. Fellow Am. Coll. Surgeons; mem. AMA, Am. Soc. Plastic and Reconstructive Surgeons., Bellerive Country Club. Republican. Presbyterian. Office: Southwest Plastic Surgeons 7101 E Jackrabbit Rd Paradise Valley AZ 85253

CLEMENT, WALTER HOUGH, retired railroad executive; b. Council Bluffs, Iowa, Dec. 21, 1931; s. Daniel Shell and Helen Grace (Hough) C.; AA, San Jose (Calif.) City Coll., 1958; PhD, World U., 1983; m. Shirley Ann Brown, May 1, 1953; children: Steven, Robert, Richard. Designer, J.K. Konerle & Assocs., Salt Lake City, 1959-62; with U.P. R.R. Co., 1962—, class B draftsman, Salt Lake City, 1971-75, sr. right of way engr. real estate dept., 1975-80, asst. dist. real estate mgr., 1980-83, asst. engr. surveyor, 1983-87; Mem. Republican Nat. Com., Rep. Congl. Com. With USN, 1950-54, Korea. Lic. realtor, Utah. Mem. Am. Ry. Engring. Assn., Execs. Info. Guild (assoc.), Bur. Bus. Practice. Republican. Methodist. Home: 290 West 1200 North Bountiful UT 84010 Office: 406 West 100 South Salt Lake City UT 84101

CLEMENTE, CARMINE DOMENIC, anatomist, educator; b. Penns Grove, N.J., Apr. 29, 1928; s. Ermanno and Caroline (Friozzi) C.; m. Juliette Vance, Sept. 19, 1968. A.B., U. Pa., 1948, M.S., 1950, Ph.D., 1952; postdoctoral fellow, U. London, 1953-54. Asst. instr. anatomy U. Pa., 1950-52; mem. faculty UCLA, 1952—, prof., 1963—, chmn. dept. anatomy, 1963-73, dir. brain research inst., 1976-87; hon. rsch. assoc. Univ. Coll., U. London, 1953-54; vis. scientist Nat. Inst. Med. Rsch., Mill Hill, London, 1988-89; cons. Sepulveda VA Hosp., NIH; mem. med. adv. panel Bank Am.-Giannini Found.; chmn. sci. adv. com., mem. bd. dirs. Nat. Paraplegia Found.; bd. dirs. Charles R. Drew Univ., 1985—. Author: Aggression and Defense: Neurol Mechanisms and Social Patterns, 1967, Physiological Correlates of Dreaming, 1967, Sleep and the Maturing Nervous System, 1972, Anatomy, An Atlas of the Human Body, 1975, 3d edit., 1987; editor: Gray's Anatomy, 1973—, 30th Am. edit., 1985, also Exptl. Neurology; asso. editor: Neurol. Research; contbr. articles to sci. jours. Recipient award for merit in sci. Nat. Paraplegia Found., 1973; 23d Ann. Rehfuss Lectr. and recipient Rehfuss medal Jefferson Med. Coll., 1986; John Simon Guggenheim Meml. Found. fellow, 1988-89. Mem. Pavlovian Soc. N.Am. (Ann. award 1968, pres. 1972), Brain Research Inst. (dir. 1976-87), Am. Physiol. Soc., Am. Assn. Anatomists (v.p. 1970-72, pres. 1976-77), Am. Acad. Neurology, Am. Acad. Cerebral Palsy, Am. Neurol. Assn., Assn. Am. Med. Colls. (exec. com. 1978-81, disting. service mem. 1982), Council Acad. Socs. (adminstrv. bd. 1973-81, chmn. 1979-80), Assn. Anatomy Chairmen (pres. 1972), Biol. Stain Commn., Inst. Medicine of Nat. Acad. Scis. (sci. adv. bd.), Internat. Brain Research Orgn., AMA-Assn. Am. Med. Colls. (liaison com. on med. edn. 1981-87), Med. Research Assn. Calif. (dir. 1976—), N.Y. Acad. Sci., Nat. Bd. Med. Examiners, Nat. Acad. Sci. (mem. com. neuropathology, BEAR coms.), Japan Soc. Promotion of Sci. (Research award 1978), Sigma Xi. Democrat. Home: 11737 Bellagio Rd Los Angeles CA 90049 Office: UCLA Brain Rsch Inst Ctr Health Scis Los Angeles CA 90024

CLEMENTE, PATROCINIO ABLOLA, psychology educator; b. Manila, Philippines, Apr. 23, 1941; s. Elpidio San Jose and Amparo (Ablola) C.; came to U.S., 1965; B.S.E., U. Philippines, 1960; postgrad. Nat. U., Manila, 1961-64; M.A., Ball State U., 1966, Ed.D., 1969; postgrad. U. Calif., Riverside, 1970, Calif. State Coll., Fullerton, 1971-72. High sch. tchr. gen. sci. and biology, div. city schs., Quezon City, Philippines, 1960-65; doctoral fellow dept. psychology Ball State U., Muncie, Ind., 1966-67, dept. spl. edn., 1967-68, grad. asst. dept. gen. and exptl. psychology, 1968-69; tchr. educable mentally retarded high sch. level Fontana (Calif.) Unified Sch. Dist., 1969-70, intermediate level, 1970-73, dist. sch. psychologist, 1973-79, bilingual edn. counselor, 1979-81; resource specialist Morongo (Calif.) Unified Sch. Dist., 1981-83, spl. day class tchr., 1983—; adj. assoc. prof. Chapman Coll., Orange, Calif., 1982—. Adult leader Girl Scouts of Philippines, 1963-65; mem. sch. bd. Blessed Sacrament Sch., Twentynine Palms, Calif. State bd. scholar Ball State U., 1965-66. Fellow Am. Biographical Inst. (hon. mem. research bd. advisors, life); mem. Council for Exceptional Children, Am. Assn. on Mental Deficiency, Am. Assn. Psychiat. Services for Children, Nat. Assn. of Sch. Psychologists, Found. Exceptional Children, Assn. for Children with Learning Disabilities, N.Y. Acad. Scis., AAAS, Assn. for Supervision and Curriculum Devel., Roman Catholic. Home: PO Box 637 Twentynine Palms CA 92277

CLEMENTS, JOHN ROBERT, real estate professional; b. Richmond, Ind., Nov. 2, 1950; s. George Howard and Mary Amanda (McKown) C. Grad. high sch., Phoenix. Sales assoc. Clements Realty, Inc., Phoenix, 1973-75; office mgr. Clements Realty, Inc., Mesa, Ariz., 1975-78; v.p., co-owner Clements Realty, Inc., Phoenix, 1978-80; broker, assoc. Ben Brooks & Assocs., Phoenix, 1980-88; pres. John R. Clements, P.C., 1984—; broker, assoc. Prince Realty, Inc., Phoenix and Mesa, Ariz., 1988—. Bd. dirs., v.p. Big Sisters Ariz., Phoenix, 1974-80; trustee, Ariz. Realtors Polit. Action Com., 1975-85, Realtors Polit Action Com., Ill., 1985-88; appointee Govtl. Mall Com., Ariz., 1986—; commr., chmn. Urban Plan Implementation Subcom. With USN, 1969-73. Mem. Ariz. Assn. Realtors (bd. dirs., pres. 1981), Mesa-Chandler-Tempe Bd. Realtors (bd. dirs., pres. 1978), Nat. Assn. Realtors (certified, past bd. dirs.), Residential Sales Coun. Realtors (bd. govs. 1986—, v.p. 1990), Nat. Mktg. Inst., Nat. Assn. Realtors, Ariz. Country Club. Republican. Presbyterian. Home: 3618 N 60th St Phoenix AZ 85018 Office: Prince Realty Inc 4402 E Camelback Rd Phoenix AZ 85018

CLEMENTS, PATRICIA LYN, nurse; b. Chgo., Nov. 7, 1951; d. Frederick Herman and Mae Lucille (Williams) Mentemeyer; m. D.J.M. Foussat, Apr. 27, 1973 (div. 1976); m. William Lawrance Clements, May 13, 1979; children: Jennifer Lea, Christopher Lee. Team leader Palomar Hosp., Escondido, Calif., 1972-76; registry nurse Profl. Nurses Bur., Vista, San Diego and Oceanside, Calif., 1977-87; operating room nurse MediVision, Vista, 1985-87; CPR instr. Nat. U., Vista, 1988—.

CLEMONS, J. KING, insurance executive; b. Columbus, Ohio, Jan. 21, 1936; s. Frank M. and Ethel K. Clemons; B.S. in Physics, Colorado Coll., 1958; M.S. in Stats., U. Iowa, 1966; m. Ann Douglass, June 2, 1959; children—Mike, Steve, Karl. Research physicist White Sands Missile Range, N.Mex., 1958; actuarial asst. A.S. Hansen, Inc., Lake Bluff, Ill., 1966-67, cons. in tng., Lake Bluff, 1967-69, subject cons., Milw., 1969-70, subject cons., Los Angeles, 1970-72; pres. Western Res. Life Ins. Co., Grand Junction, Colo., 1972—; elected pres. Colo. Life Conv., 1986. Pres., Grand Junction Eagles Baseball, 1976-83; active YMCA Fund Drive, Milw., 1969; chmn. Grand Junction/Mesa County Indsl. Devel. Revenue Bond Com., 1981—; mem. pres.'s adv. bd. Mesa Coll., 1980—; mem. Mesa County Revolving Loan Fund Com., 1985—. Served to capt., Ordnance Corps, U.S. Army, 1958-64. Recipient Disting. Service award YMCA, 1969; named Businessman Yr. for Colo. and USA, Phi Beta Lambda, 1986. Mem. Western Colo. Estate Planning Council, North Ave. Trade Assn. (dir. 1978-82), Grand Junction C. of C. (pres. 1980). Republican. Club: Lions. Home: 2561 I Rd Grand Junction CO 81501 Office: Western Res Life Ins Co 2755 North Ave Grand Junction CO 81501

CLENDENEN, BRIAN, film sales and marketing executive; b. New London, Conn., Mar. 4, 1946; s. William H. and Ethel Lorraine (Clifford) C.; m. Karen Van Vleet, Nov. 21, 1980 (div.). BS in Bus., U. Conn., New Brittain, 1968. Lic. radio broadcaster. Regional sales rep. ARTEC Distbn., Burlington, Vt., 1979-81; owner Video Realm Computer, Computer Realm, Realm of the Coin, Saratoga Springs, N.Y., 1981-83; regional sales mgr. Thorn EMI, N.Y.C., 1982-86; sr. v.p. Ingram Video, Nashville, 1986-88; v.p. sales and mktg. Imperial Entertainment Corp., Hollywood, Calif., 1988—; bd. dirs. Ingram Distbn., Nashville. Author: (movie) Demon Cop, 1988. Active Santa Fund for Kids Downtown Merchants Assn., Saratoga Springs, 1981, 82; fund raiser United Way, Nashville, 1986-88. Mem. Nat. Assn. Video Distbrs., Video Software Dealers Assn., Antique Auto Club Am., Theta Alpha Phi. Home: 13912 Old Harbor Ln Apt # 204 Marina Del Rey CA 90292 Office: Imperial Entertainment Corp 6430 Sunset Blvd Ste 1500 Hollywood CA 90028

CLEVELAND, GERALD LLOYD, university dean; b. Conde, S.D., Apr. 18, 1931; s. Lloyd Edward and M. Frances (Miesen) C.; m. Ramona June Morgan, Sept. 11, 1952; children: Debra, Linda, Sara. BBA in Acctg. summa cum laude, U. S.D., 1953; MBA, U. Minn., 1957; PhD, U. Wash., 1965. Assoc. prof. U. S.D., Vermillion, 1956-59; asst. prof. U. Wash., Seattle, 1959-67; assoc. prof. Seattle U., 1967-69, prof. acctg., dean Sch. Bus., 1969-76; prof. acctg., dean Coll. Bus. and Econs. U. Idaho, Moscow, 1976-77; chmn. dept. acctg. Seattle U., 1978-84; dean. Sch. Bus. and Econs., prof. acctg. Cen. Wash. U., Ellensburg, 1987—; lectr., asst. prof. U. Wash., 1959-67; adv. com. Accounting Career Awareness, Seattle, 1981-88; Wash. adv. com. for Acctg. Transfer Edn., 1973-75; mem. exec. com. Western Assn. Collegiate Schs. Bus., 1975-77; vis. lectr. acctg. and fin. Bristol (Eng.) Poly. Inst., 1984-85; vis. prof. Massey U., New Zealand, 1985; cons., expert witness for FTC, 1978-79, pvt. cons., 1963—; inst., asst. prof. U. S.D.; frequent speaker in field. Contbr. chpts. to books, articles to profl. jours. Mem. Lake Forest Park Civil Service Commn., Seattle, 1982-84, regional selection panel White House Fellows program, 1974; acctg. advisor Shoreline Community Coll., Seattle, 1969-75. Served to 1st lt. U.S. Army, 1954-56, capt. Res. Mem. Am. Acctg. Assn., Fin. Execs. Inst. (bd. dirs. Seattle chpt. 1974-76, 78-80, edn. com. 1971-74), Phi Eta Sigma, Beta Gamma Sigma, Beta Alpha Psi. Office: Cen Wash U Sch Bus and Econs Ellensburg WA 98926

CLEVER, JOHN JOSEPH, computer scientist; b. Lackawanna, N.Y., Nov. 26, 1942; s. Joseph Clarence and Ruth (Costigan) C.; m. Catherine Rosling, Sept. 9, 1966 (div. Feb. 1975); children: Cathleen Ruth, Deanna Elizabeth; m. Carolyn Chieno Arashiro, July 12, 1975. AA, St. Johns River Jr. Coll., Palatka, Fla., 1962; BA, U. Md., 1973; MS, Fairleigh Dickinson U., 1986. Enlisted U.S. Army, 1964, spl. agt. intelligent dept., 1964-80; automation mgmt. officer U.S. Army, N.J., 1981-85, Fed. Republic Germany, 1981-85; retired U.S. Army, 1985; sr. systems analyst Planning Research Corp., N.J., 1985-86; mem. tech. staff Sandia Nat. Labs., Albuquerque, 1986—; instr. in computer sci. Champman Coll., Albuquerque, 1986—. Mem. allocation panel United Way, Albuquerque, 1988. Decorated Bronze Star. Mem. IEEE, ACM, Elks, Masons. Republican. Home: 3012 Camino de la Sierra NE Albuquerque NM 87111 Office: Sandia Nat Labs PO Box 5800 Albuquerque NM 87185

CLIFF, MOLLY PORTER, interior designer; b. Palo Alto, Calif., Feb. 20, 1958; d. Lee Harker and Nell (Sesnon) C.; m. John Lawrence Cunniff, Sept. 25, 1982 (div. June 1986). Student, U. Oreg., 1979-81; BFA, U. Calif., Santa Cruz, 1981; postgrad., Cabrillo Coll., 1982, U. Calif., San Francisco, 1983, W. Valley Coll., 1983. Jr. designer Britton & Franks, Architects, Santa Cruz, 1981-83; bldg. designer, owner Molly Cliff Cunniff Design, Santa Cruz, 1983-84; space planner Kravitz Group, San Jose, Calif., 1984-85; owner, space planner, contract furnisher Integated Environs., San Jose, Calif., 1985-87; comml. and residential interior designer Hurst Cliff Group, Las Vegas, Nev., 1987—; comml. project interior designer Jerome King, AIA and Assoc., Santa Cruz, 1984; residential project interior designer Vantress Derign Assoc., Aptos, Calif., 1984; graphic designer Christmas cards, W. coast, 1976—; sales rep. Laughing Willows Furniture, Big Sur, Calif., 1983—; with mktg. staff John Renton Young Lighting Co., Las Vegas, 1988. One-woman show include photography exhibit Images, 1981. Mem. mus. architects com. Nev. Inst. Contemporary Art, 1988, com. Am. Cancer Soc., Las Vegas, 1987—, D'Art, San Jose, 1986-87; vol. Santa Cruz Mus. Art, 1984. Honored for outstanding design svcs. Planned Parenthood, San Francisco, 1986; recipient Santa Cruz Orgn. for Progressive Euthenics award, 1984. Mem. Internat. Soc. Interior Designers (assoc.), Nat. Assn. Indsl. Office Parks, Am. Soc. Interior Designers (assoc.), Network (Las Vegas) (founder), Las Vegas Art Dirs. and Creative. Democrat. Office: Hurst Cliff Group 3665 W Diablo Dr Las Vegas NV 89118

CLIFFORD, ROBERT ANDERSON, real estate investment executive; b. L.A., Sept. 29, 1957; s. Robert Paul Clifford and Jane (Anderson) Barrett. BA in Communications, Pepperdine U., 1981. Mgr. C.H.E., Inc., Westwood, Calif., 1977-81; sales Charles Dunn Co., L.A., 1981-88; founder, ptnr. Western Holdings, Santa Monica, Calif., 1988—. Mem. Assn. Indsl. Realtors, Belair Bay Club (Pacific Palisades). Home: PO Box 84528 Los Angeles CA 90073 Office: Western Holdings 3301 Ocean Park Blvd #208 Los Angeles CA 90405

CLIFTON, MICHAEL EDWARD, English educator; b. Reedley, Calif., Jan. 6, 1949; s. Edward Eugene and Helen May (Peters) C.; m. Anita May Bernardi, June 22, 1973. BA, Calif. State U., Fresno, 1971, MA with distinction, 1977; PhD, Ind. U., 1984. Tchr. English Hoover High Sch., Fresno, 1971-74; assoc. instr. Ind. U., Bloomington, 1978-80; lectr. Calif. State U., Fresno, 1982—; reader, presenter Internat. Assn. Fantastic in Arts, Ft. Lauderdale, Fla., 1988, Houston, Tex., 1987, Am. Imagery Assn., San Francisco, 1986, Eaton Conf., U. Calif. Riverside, 1985. Contbr. articles to popular mags. and profl. jours. Mem. MLA, AAUP. Democrat. Home: 921 N San Pablo Fresno CA 93728 Office: Calif State U Dept Engring Peters Bldg Fresno CA 93740

CLIFTON, ROBERT BLAINE, educator, aviation maintenance training consultant; b. Sabina, Ohio, Dec. 1, 1937; s. Ulysis Blaine and Olive Imogene (Storer) C.; m. Regina Esposito, Aug. 26, 1961; children: Christopher Blaine, Jennifer Regina. Cert. teaching, UCLA, 1970; B in Vocat. Edn., Calif. State U., Long Beach, 1971, MA, 1973. Mechanic Los Angeles Airways, 1959-62, 63-66, ERA Helicopters, Anchorage, 1962; FAA designee, engring. flight test technician Hughes Tool Co., Culver City, Calif., 1966-69; asst. prof. aviation tech. Orange Coast Coll., Costa Mesa, Calif., 1969-74, assoc. prof., 1974-79, prof., 1979—, asst. div. chmn. tech., 1979-84; designated mech. examiner, FAA, Long Beach, 1971—; exec. com. mem. Aviation Tech. Edn. Council, 1986—. Creator (films) Aviation Tech. Tng., 1974. coach Huntington Beach (Calif.) Youth Soccer Club, 1985-86, Am.Youth Soccer Orgn., 1978-85, Westminster (Calif.) Lil' Miss Softball, 1979-83, Little League Baseball, Huntington Beach, 1972-79. Served with U.S. Army, 1956-59. Mem. Am. Vocat. Assn., Calif. Assn. Vocat. Edn., Am. Helicopter Soc., Calif. Internat. Tech. Edn. Commn., 101st Airborne Div. Assn., Orange Coast Coll. Airframe and Powerplant Club (chmn. 1976-86), Kappa Delta Pi. Republican. Roman Catholic. Office: Orange Coast Coll 2701 Fairview Rd Costa Mesa CA 92626

CLINE, CAROLYN JOAN, plastic and reconstructive surgeon; b. Boston; d. Paul S. and Elizabeth (Flom) Cline. BA, Wellesley Coll., 1962; MA, U. Cin., 1966; PhD, Washington U., 1970; diploma Washington Sch. Psychiatry, 1972; MD, U. Miami (Fla.) 1975. Diplomate Am. Bd. Plastic and Reconstructive Surgery. Rsch. asst. Harvard Dental Sch., Boston, 1962-64; rsch. asst. physiology Laser Lab., Children's Hosp. Research Found., Cin., 1964, psychology dept. U. Cin., 1964-65; intern in clin. psychology St. Elizabeth's Hosp., Washington, 1966-67; psychologist Alexandria (Va.) Community Mental Health Ctr., 1967-68; research fellow NIH, Washington, 1968-69; chief psychologist Kingsbury Ctr. for Children, Washington, 1969-73; sole practice clin. psychology, Washington, 1970-73; intern internal medicine U. Wis. Hosps., Ctr. for Health Sci., Madison, 1975-76; resident in surgery Stanford U. Med. Ctr., 1976-78; fellow microvascular surgery dept. surgery U. Calif.-San Francisco, 1978-79; resident in plastic surgery St. Francis Hosp., San Francisco, 1979-82; practice medicine, specializing in plastic and reconstructive surgery, San Francisco, 1982—. Contbr. articles to profl. jours. Mem. Am. Bd. Plastic and Reconstructive Surgery (cert. 1986). Address: 450 Sutter St Ste 2433 San Francisco CA 94108

CLINE, CRAIG EMERSON, editor; b. Hagerstown, Md., Aug. 29, 1951; s. Robert Warron and Grace Allan (Mercereau) C.; m. Wondy A. Kupferman, Aug. 22, 1976 (div. Dec. 1984); children: Matthew D., Dylan G., Ian G.; m. Gail Elizabeth Harrison, July 20, 1985; children: Aliyah M., Ryan Walton, Robert Walton. BA cum laude, Amherst Coll., 1973. Editorial asst. MIT Press, Cambridge, Mass., 1973-75; instr. bus. sch. Harvard U., Boston, 1975-79; sr. mktg. mgr. Atex Inc., Bedford, Mass., 1979-87; assoc. editor Seybold Publs., Malibu, Calif., 1987—; cons. Seybold Consulting Group, Malibu, 1987—; program dir. Seybold Seminars, Malibu, 1987—. Contrb. author: Problems in Marketing. Office: Seybold Publications 6922 Wildlife Rd Malibu CA 90265

CLINE, JACK L., sales executive; b. Sioux Rapids, Iowa, Oct. 1, 1941; s. Patrick M. and Marie E. (Streed) C.; m. Sheila K. Rommel, Jan. 19, 1975 (dec. 1980); m. Cari M. Zatco, June 10, 1984; children: Michael J., Christopher D. BS, Nat. Bus. Coll., Sioux City, 1961. Salesman Cook Paint & Varnish Co., Sioux City, 1961-62; asst. store mgr. Cook Paint & Varnish Co., Rochester, Minn., 1962-64; constrn. foreman Cherokee (Iowa) Concrete Co., 1964-65; prodn. supr. Vilas & Co., Storm Lake, Iowa, 1965-66; rt. supr. Karls Dairy, Denver, 1966-68; asst. mgr., rt. supr. Landshire Food Systems, Denver, 1968-75; br. mgr., auditor, area rt. supr. Universal Foods Corp., Denver, 1975—. Treas., bd. dirs. Beyond Divorce Inc., Denver, 1982-85; coach Arvada Colo. Mem. Nebr. Bakers Assn., Kansas City (Mo.) Bakers Assn. Club: Eagles Soccer (tournament com. 1985—). Office: Universal Foods Corp 4390 Glencoe Denver CO 80216

CLINE, ROBERT CORDÉ, governmental relations advocate; b. San Francisco, May 6, 1933; s. John Wesley and Edith Bertha (Cordé) C.; m. Betty Robison, Aug. 24, 1955 (div. 1979); children: Bruce Cordé, Caren J. Claus. AB, U. Calif., Berkeley, 1955, MBA in Finance, 1961. Fin. analyst Litton Ind., Inc., Beverly Hills, Calif., 1961-65; owner Robert C. Cline Co., Canoga Park, Calif., 1965-70; ptnr. Cline Holzberg, Woodland Hills, Calif., 1970-77; state legislator Calif. Assembly, Sacramento, 1970-80; owner, pres. R.C. Cline Co., Sacramento, 1980—; lobbyist Assoc. Builders and Contractors Calif. Inc., Calif. Ind. Petroleum Assn., N.Am. Assn. Inventory Svcs., Boxers/Wrestlers Benefit Fund, Calif. Sch. Bus. Contractors, Gary Drilling Co., Union Pacific Resources Co. Rep. cen. committeeman, Sacramento, 1962-80. Served with U.S. Army, 1956-58. Mem. Inst. Govtl. Advs., Assoc. Builders and Contractors, Calif. Waterfowl Assn. (bd. dirs. 1985-89), Butte Sink Waterfowl Assn. (bd. dirs. 1983—, sec./treas.), Colusa Shooting Club. Episcopalian. Home: 1596 Newborough Dr Sacramento CA 95833 Office: 1127 11th St #544 Sacramento CA 95814

CLINE, ROBERT STANLEY, air freight company executive; b. Urbana, Ill., July 17, 1937; s. Lyle Stanley and Mary Elizabeth (Prettyman) C.; m. Judith Lee Stucker, July 7, 1979; children: Lisa Andre, Nicole Lesley, Christina Elaine, Leslie Jane. B.A., Dartmouth Coll., 1959. Asst. treas. Chase Manhattan Bank, N.Y.C., 1960-65; v.p. fin. Pacific Air Freight Co., Seattle, 1965-68; exec. v.p. fin. Airborne Freight Corp., Seattle, 1968-78, vice chmn., chief fin. officer, dir., 1978-84, chmn., chief exec. officer, dir., 1984—; bd. dirs. Rainier Bancorp, Rainier Nat. Bank. Trustee Seattle Repertory Theatre, 1974—, Children's Orthopedic Hosp. Found., 1983—, Corp. Council of the Arts, 1983—, Wash. Gives, 1983—; chmn. bd. Seattle Repertory Theatre, 1979-83; bd. dirs. Washington Roundtable, 1985—; chmn. bd. Children's Hosp. Found, 1987—. Served with U.S. Army, 1959-60. Home: 1209 39th Ave E Seattle WA 98112 Office: Airborne Freight Corp 3101 Western Ave PO Box 662 Seattle WA 98121

CLINE, WILSON ETTASON, retired judge; b. Newkirk, Okla., Aug. 26, 1914; s. William Sherman and Etta Blanche (Roach) C.; student U. Ill., 1932-33; A.B., U. Okla., 1935, B.S. in Bus. Adminstrn., 1936; J.D., U. Calif., Berkeley, 1939; LL.M., Harvard U., 1941; m. G. Barbara Verne Pentecost, Nov. 1, 1939 (div. Nov. 1960); children—William, Catherine Cline MacDonald, Thomas; m. Gina Lana Ludwig, Oct. 5, 1969; children—David Ludwig, Kenneth Ludwig. Admitted to Calif. bar, 1940; atty. Kaiser Richmond Shipyards, 1941-44; pvt. practice, Oakland, 1945-49; atty., hearing officer, asst. chief adminstrv. law judge, acting chief adminstrv. law judge Calif. Pub. Utilities Commn., San Francisco, 1949-80, ret., 1981, dir. gen. welfare Calif. State Employees Assn., 1966-67, chmn. retirement com., 1965-66, mem. member benefit com., 1980-81, mem. ret. employees div. council dist. C, 1981-82. Trustee Cline Ranch Trust, various family trusts. Mem. ABA, State Bar Calif., Conf. Calif. Pub. Utility Counsel (steering com. 1967-71), Am. Judicature Soc., Boalt Hall Alumni Assn., Phi Beta Kappa (pres. No. Calif. assn. 1969-70), Beta Gamma Sigma, Delta Sigma Pi (Key award, 1936), Phi Kappa Psi, Phi Delta Phi, Pi Sigma Alpha. Republican. Mem. United Ch. Christ. Clubs: Harvard, Commonwealth (San Francisco); Sleepy Hollow Swim and Tennis (Orinda, Calif.); Masons (Orinda-Plymouth lodge past master 1949, sec. 1951-55), Sirs (Peralta chpt. 12). Home: 110 St Albans Rd Kensington CA 94708 Office: 1400 Webster St Ste 212 PO Box 526 Alameda CA 94501

CLINTON, GORDON STANLEY, lawyer; b. Medicine Hat, Alta., Can., Apr. 13, 1920; s. John H. and Gladys (Hall) C.; m. Florence H. Vayhinger, Dec. 19, 1942; children: Barbara H. Clinton Tompkins, Gordon Stanley Jr., Deborah. A.B. in Polit. Sci., U. Wash., 1942, J.D., 1947; postgrad., Harvard U., 1945; LL.D. (hon.), Coll. Puget Sound, 1957, Seattle Pacific Coll., 1960. Bar: Wash. 1947. Spl. agt. FBI, 1942-44; pvt. practice Seattle, 1949—; firm Clinton, Fleck & Glein; dep. pros. atty. King County, 1947-49; judge pro tem Mcpl. Ct., Seattle, 1949-52; spl. atty. City Council of Seattle, 1953; mayor City of Seattle, 1956-64; chmn. exec. com. Japan-Am. Conf. Mayors; adv. bd. U.S. Conf. Mayors, 1956-64; mem. Presdl. Commn. Intergovtl. Relations, 1959-60, adv. bd. Pacific Ctr. Internat. Studies, Edmonds Community Coll.; v.p. Western region, civic com. People to People; founder, chmn. Kobe-Seattle Affiliation Com., Marine Employees Commn. Mem. Wash. Bd. Edn., 1969-70; trustee Seattle Pacific Coll., 1964-70, Alaska Meth. U., 1979-84; bd. dirs. YMCA, Wesley Found., 1968—, Town Affiliation Assn.; pres. First Methodist Home, Inc., 1969-72, Philippines-Am. Soc. Pac N.W.; del. Gen. Conf. Meth. Ch.; pres., chief Boy Scouts Am., Seattle, 1988. Lt. (j.g.) USNR, 1944-46. Recipient Silver Beaver award, Disting. Service award Chief Seattle council Boy Scouts Am., Disting. Grad. award Roosevelt High Sch., 1960, Newsmakers of Tomorrow award Time Mag. and Seattle C. of C., 1953, citation of honor Wash. State chpt. AIA, 1957, Human Relations award Seattle Civic Unity Commn., 1963, citation NCCJ, 1964, Outstanding Pub. Ofcl. award Mcpl. League, 1964, Eisenhower award Sister Cities Internat., 1985; decorated Order of Sikatunah (Philippines), 3d Class Order of Rising Sun (Japan). Mem. Am. Mcpl. Assn. (exec. com. 1957—, pres. 1962), ABA, Wash. State Bar Assn., Seattle Bar Assn., NCCJ, Japan-Am. Soc. Seattle (pres. 1973), Phillipine-Am. Soc. Pacific N.W. (pres. 1988), Phi Delta Phi. Republican. Methodist (bd. missions). Lodges: Masons (32 degree Knight Comdr. Ct. of Honor), Shriners. Home: 7733 58th Ave NE Seattle WA 98115 Office: Third-Lenora Bldg Seattle WA 98121

CLINTON, JOHN HART, lawyer, editor; b. Quincy, Mass., Apr. 3, 1905; s. John Francis and Catherine Veronica (Hart) C.; m. Helen Alice Amphlett, Feb. 18, 1933 (dec. 1965); children: Mary Jane (Mrs. Raymond Zirkel), Mary Ann (Mrs. Christopher Gardner, Jr.), John Hart; m. Mathilda A. Schoorel van Dillen, Feb. 22, 1969. A.B., Boston Coll., 1926; J.D., Harvard U., 1929. Bar: Calif. 1930, Mass. 1930. Since practiced in San Francisco; assoc. Morrison, Foerster, Holloway, Clinton & Clark, and predecessor, 1929-41, ptnr., 1941-72; of counsel Morrison & Foerster, 1972—; Vice pres., gen. counsel Indsl. Employers and Distbrs. Assn., Emeryville, 1944-72; pres. Leamington Hotel, Oakland, Calif., 1933-47, Amphlett Printing Co., San Mateo, Calif., 1943—; pub. San Mateo Times, 1943-87, editor, 1960—. Hon. mem. exec. com. San Mateo County council Boy Scouts Am.; bd. dirs., pres. Bay Meadows Found.; regent emeritus Notre Dame Coll., Belmont, Calif. Decorated Knight Equestrian Order of Holy Sepulchre of Jerusalem. Mem. FCC, Am., San Francisco, San Mateo County bar assns., State Bar Calif. (past chmn. fair trial/free press com., past co-chmn. Calif. bench/bar media com.), Am. Judicature Soc., Nat. Lawyers Club, Am. Law Inst., San Mateo County Devel. Assn (pres. 1963-65), San Mateo County Hist. Assn. (pres. 1960-64), Calif. Press Assn. (pres. 1970, chmn. membership com.), Am. Newspaper Pubs. Assn. (govt. affairs com., press/bar relations com.; Am. Bar Assn.-Am. Newspapers Pubs. Assn. task force), Calif. Newspaper Pubs. Assn. (pres. 1969), Wine and Food Soc. San Francisco, Am. Soc. Newspaper Editors, Assn. Cath. Newsmen, Nat. Press Photographers Assn., Internat. Platform Assn., Newcomen Soc. Clubs: Commonwealth of Calif. (San Francisco) (past pres.), San Francisco Comml. (San Francisco), Bohemian (San Francisco); Bombay Bicycle Riding (Burlingame, Calif.); Sequoia (Redwood City, Calif.). Lodges: Elks; Rotary (San Mateo past pres.). Home: 131 Sycamore Ave San Mateo CA 94402 Office: 1080 S Amphlett Blvd San Mateo CA 94402

CLODIUS, ALBERT HOWARD, educator; b. Spokane, Wash., Mar. 26, 1911; s. William Sr. and Mary Hebner (Brown) C.; m. Wilma Charlene Candler, June 3, 1961; children: Helen Lou Namikas, John Charles Parker. BA in Edn., Ea. Wash. State U., 1937; postgrad., Stanford U.; MA in History, Claremont (Calif.) Coll., 1948, PhD in History, 1953. Cert. secondary edn. tchr., Calif. Editorial asst. Pacific N.W. Quarterly, U. Wash., Seattle, 1938-40; reader Stanford U., Palo Alto, Calif., 1940-42; instr. Claremont-McKenna Coll., 1946-50; asst. prof. Pepperdine U., L.A., 1952-53; instr. Ventura (Calif.) Community Coll., 1953-76; adj. prof. Northrop U., L.A., 1977-85; prof. Nat. U., San Diego, 1987-88; ret. 1988. English conversation tchr., vol. internat. student ctr. U. Calif., L.A., 1979—. John R. and Dora F. Haynes Found. fellow, 1950-52; Clarence D. Martin scholar Ea. Wash. State U., 1936-37. Mem. Plato Soc. U. Calif. Democrat. Unitarian. Home: 4838 Salem Village Pl Culver City CA 90230-4324

CLOE, JOHN HAILE, military historian; b. Fredericksburg, Va., May 11, 1938; s. William Weedon and Elizabeth (Haile) C.; m. Harrieth Cathorine Hill. BA in History, Va. Mil. Inst., 1963; student, Comman and Gen. Staff Coll., 1976, U.S. Army War Coll., 1985. Commd. officer USAR, 1963, advanced through grades to maj., 1973; company commdr., sr. advisor Republic Vietnam; transfered to Alaska Army Nat. Guard, 1973, advanced through grades to col., 1983—; historian 21st Tactical Fighter Wing, Elmendorf AFB, Alaska, 1973-75; asst. historian Alaskan Air Command, Elmendorf AFB, 1975-76, intelligence analyst, dep. chief of staff intelligence, 1978, historian, 1978—; tech. writer 1931st Communications Group, Elmendorf AFB, 1976-78. Co-author: Top Cover for America The Air Force in Alaska 1920-83, 3rd edit. 1985; contbr. articels and papers to profl. jours. Decorated Bronze Star medal, Vietnamese Cross of GAllantry, Combat Infantryman's Badge. Mem. Air Force Assn. (mem. exec. coun. Anchorage chpt.), Cook Inlet Hist. Soc. (bd. dirs.), Alaska Hist. Soc. (Trailblazer award 1988), Am. Aviation Hist. Soc., Nat. Guard Officers Assn. (life), Alaska Nat. Guard Officers Assn. (life), Alaska Press Club. Episcopal. Home: 10705 Chataniha Loop Eagle River AK 99577 Office: Office of History Alaska Air Command Elmendorf AFB AK 99577

CLOSSON, JOHN EUGENE, JR., insurance company executive; b. Oklahoma City, Aug. 6, 1947; s. John E. and Ann Laura (Smith) C.; m. Nancy Kay Green, July 16, 1988. AA, Orange Coast Coll., 1974. Ins. rep. Auto Club of So. Calif., South Laguna, 1967-75; salesman Regent Realty, South Laguna, 1975-76, Lingo Real Estate, South Laguna, 1976-79; dir. membership Newport Harbor/Costa Mesa Bd. Realtors, Newport Beach, Calif., 1979-85; pres., adminstrv. officer Escrow Agts. Fidelity Corp., Newport Beach, 1985-89, Sherman Oaks, Calif., 1989—. Author, editor newsletter, 1985—. Mem. Escrow Inst. Calif., Calif. Escrow Assn., Orange County Escrow Assn. Republican. Home: 10411 Des Moines Ave Northridge CA 91326 Office: Escrow Agts Fidelity Corp 15456 Ventura Blvd Ste 200 Sherman Oaks CA 91403

CLOUD, PRESTON, geologist, author, consultant; b. West Upton, Mass., Sept. 26, 1912; s. Preston E. and Pauline L. (Wiedemann) C.; m. Janice Gibson, 1972; children by previous marriage: Karen, Lisa, Kevin. B.S., George Washington U., 1938; Ph.D., Yale U., 1940. Instr. Mo. Sch. Mines and Metallurgy, 1940-41; research fellow Yale U., 1941-42; geologist U.S. Geol. Survey, 1942-46, 48-61, 74-79, chief paleontology and stratigraphy br., 1949-59; research geologist 1959-61, 74-79; asst. prof., curator invertebrate paleontology Harvard U., 1946-48; prof. dept. geology and geophysics U. Minn., 1961-65, chmn., 1961-63; prof. geology UCLA, 1965-68; prof. biogeology and environ. studies dept. geol. scis. U. Calif., Santa Barbara, 1968-74, prof. emeritus, 1974—; vis. prof. U. Tex., 1962, 78; H.R. Luce prof. cosmology Mt. Holyoke Coll., 1979-80; Sr. Queens fellow Baas-Becking Geobiology Lab., Canberra, Australia, 1981; internat exchange scholar Nat. Sci. and Engring. Research Council Can., 1982; hon. vis. prof. U. Ottawa (Ont. Can.), 1982; Nat. Sigma Xi lectr., 1967; Emmons lectr. Colo. Sci. Soc.; Bownocker lectr. Ohio State U.; French lectr. Pomona Coll.; Dumaresq-Smith lectr. Acadia Coll., N.B., Can.; A.L. DuToit Meml. lectr. Royal Soc. and Geol. Soc. of South Africa; mem. governing bd. NRC, 1972-75; mem. Pacific Sci. Bd., 1952-56, 62-65; del. internat. sci. congresses; cons. to govt., industry, founds. and agys. Author: Terebratuloid Brachiopoda of the Silurian and Devonian, 1942; (with Virgil E. Barnes) The Ellenburger Group of Central Texas, 1948; (with others) Geology of Saipan, Mariana Islands, 1957; Environment of Calcium Carbonate Deposition West of Andros Island, Bahamas, 1962, Cosmos, Earth and Man, 1978, Oasis in Space, 1988; editor and co-author: (with others) Resources and Man, 1969, Adventures in Earth History, 1970; Author articles. Recipient A. Cressey Morrison prize natural history, 1941, Rockefeller Pub. Service award, 1956, U.S. Dept. Interior Distinguished Service award and gold medal, 1959, Medal, Paleontol Soc. Am., 1971, Lucius W. Cross medal Yale U., 1973, Penrose medal Geol. Soc. Am., 1976, C.D. Walcott medal Nat. Acad. Scis., 1977, R.C. Moore medal Soc. Econ. Paleontologists and Mineralogists, 1986; J.S. Guggenheim fellow, 1982-83. Fellow Am. Acad. Arts and Scis. (com. on membership 1978-80, council 1980-83); mem. Am. Philos. Soc., Nat. Acad. Scis. (com. on sci. and pub. policy 1965-69, mem. council 1972-75, exec. com. 1973-75, chmn. com. on resources and man 1965-69, chmn. ad hoc com. nat. materials policy 1972, chmn. study group on uses of underground space 1972, chmn. com. mineral resources and environment 1972-73, chmn. com. geology and climate 1977, chmn. sect. geology 1976-79, mem. assembly math. and phys. scis. 1976-79), Polish Acad. Scis. (fgn. assoc.), Geol. Soc. Am. (council 1972-75), Paleontol. Soc. Am., Paleontol. Soc. India (hon.), AAAS, Geol. Soc. Belgium (hon. fgn. corr.), Paläont. Soc. Deutschland (hon., corresponding mem.), Phi Beta Kappa, Sigma Xi, Sigma Gamma Epsilon. Home: 400 Mountain Dr Santa Barbara CA 93103 Office: U Calif Dept Geol Scis Santa Barbara CA 93106

CLOUSE, JAN LOUISE, teacher, illustrator; b. San Francisco, Feb. 1, 1945; d. John Harwood and JoEllen (Gladden) Parker; m. Charles Hercel Clouse, Aug. 3, 1968. BA in English, U. Calif., Santa Barbara, 1966. Tchr. Santa Barbara (Calif.) High Sch. Dist., 1967—; tchr., chmn. English dept. Dos Pueblos High Sch., Goleta, Calif., 1988—. Illustrator: Alumnus mag., 1976-78, The Weekly, 1984-86.

CLOUTIER, JAMES THOMAS, data processing executive; b. Cloquet, Minn., June 17, 1940; s. Milton J. and Marquerite C. BA in Math., U. Minn., 1962. Systems and programming mgr. Potlatch Corp., Cloquet, 1962-73; corp. analyst Potlatch Corp., Lewiston, Ida., 1973-86; dir. info. sys. Potlatch Corp., Lewiston, 1986--. Mem. Data Processing Mgmt. Assn., Soc. Info. Mgmt. Office: Potlatch Corp PO Box 1016 Lewiston ID 83501

CLUSE, SUSAN MARIE, accountant, actress; b. Lafayette, La., June 11, 1959; d. Gustave and Betty Jo (Anderson) Dural; m. Kevin Ray Cluse, Jan. 12, 1980. AA in Acctg., Delta Sch. of Bus.; student, U. Southwestern La., Van Mak Acad. Acct. Soloco Oil Co., Lafayette, 1980-83; clk. carrier U.S. Postal Svc., Lafayette, 1983-85; acct., bookkeeper Accts. Overload, Beverly Hills, Calif., 1985-88; owner Prompt Bookkeeping and Secretarial Svc., Fontana, Calif., 1988—. Mem. SAG, AFTRA. Democrat. Episcopalian. Home: 1531 W Rialto Ave #503 Fontana CA 92335

CLYDE, MILES LEE, metallurgical engineer; b. Heber City, Utah, Apr. 8, 1953; s. Lynn M. and Ann (Huber) C.; m. Joanne Kaye Rathbone, Sept. 23, 1973; children: Lynda Marie, Aaron Lee, Allison Kaye, Sara Ann. BS in Phys. Oceanography, U. Wash., 1975, BSME, 1978. Registered profl. engr., Utah, Ariz. Sr. reator operator PUNGS Utah Internat., Riverton, Wyo., 1971-74; traffic engring. technician City of Seattle, 1974-75; prodn. foreman White Metal Fabricating, Seattle, 1975-77; nuclear plant engr. Bettis Applied Physics Lab--Westinghouse Electric, Idaho Falls, Idaho, 1978-81; shift tech. advisor, plant review bd. chmn. Ariz. Pub. Svc., Phoenix, 1981—. Active Boy Scouts Am. (cubmaster 1985-86). With USCG, 1975. Mem. Am. Soc. Metals, Tau Beta Pi. Republican. Mormon. Home: 11408 N 45th Ln Glendale AZ 85304 Office: Arizona Nuclear Plant Project PO Box 21666 Sta 6079 Phoenix AZ 85036

COAD, LYNN SANFORD, biologist; b. Minot, N.D., Jan. 28, 1945; s. Melvin Sanford and Ione A. (Graves) C; m. D. Renée Kummer, Aug. 13, 1967; children: Carol Ann, John Adam. BS, Minot State U., 1967; postgrad., Wells & Water Sch., Jan.-Mar. 1972. Tchr. Great Falls (Mont.) Sch. System, 1967-68, Ft. Laramie (Wyo.) Schs., 1968-69. Leader Boy Scouts Am., Anchorage, 1977-83, eagle scout; coach Little League, 1977-80; elder 1st Presbyn. Ch., 1977-80 (deacon moderator 1988—), Anchorage. Home: 13427 Stephenson Anchorage AK 99515

COATES, DAVID JOHN, metallurgical consultant; b. Weston-Super-Mare, Somerset, Eng., Aug. 12, 1953; came to U.S., 1980; s. Ronald Charles and Norma (Stott) C.; m. Patricia Eileen Nagle, Sept. 24, 1977. BSc, U. Newcastle Upon Tyne, Eng., 1977, PhD, 1980. Dir. lab. ops. Mettek Labs., Santa Ana, Calif., 1982-85; assoc. cons. L. Raymond & Assocs., Irvine, Calif., 1985-86; prin. engr. Gen. Electric Nuclear Energy, San Jose, Calif., 1987-88; owner Coates Engring. Svcs., Corona Del Mar, Calif., 1988—. Contbr. articles to sci. jours. Recipient Galloway award Instn. Corrosion Sci. and Tech., Eng., 1978. Mem. Am. Soc. Metals, Nat. Assn. Corrosion Engrs., The Metall. Soc. Home: 713 Marguerite Ave Corona Del Mar CA 92625 Office: Coates Engring Svcs 713 Marguerite Ave Corona Del Mar CA 92625

COATES, MICHAEL ANDREW, investment broker; b. Pitts., Oct. 14, 1958; s. Russell Stephen and Phyllis (Romano) C.; m. Sherrie Willox, Feb. 28, 1982 (div. Dec. 1986); children: Tiffany, Amanda Rae. Sales mgr. Kale-Riok Radio, Tri-Cities, Wash., 1977-81; v.p. Shearson-Lehman, Tri-Cities, 1981-85, Prudential Bache, Seattle, 1985-86; gen. mgr. Celebrity Bar & Grill, Seattle, 1986-88; fin. cons. Shearson-Lehman-Hutton, Seattle, 1988—. Republican. Office: Shearson Lehman Hutton 999 3rd Ave Ste 2800 Seattle WA 98104

COATS, HUBERT S., JR., banker; b. Julesberg, Colo., Feb. 26, 1927; s. Hubert S. and Ruth (Lang) C.; pre-standard cert. Am. Inst. Banking, 1951, standard cert., 1955; grad. Pacific Coast Bankers Sch., 1970; m. Edna Mae, July 13, 1946; children—Larry Dale, Matthew Daniel. With First Security Bank, Jerome, Idaho, 1946-55, 57-59, asst. mgr. timeway credit, 1953-55, asst. mgr., 1957-59; asst. mgr. Hailey (Idaho) First Security Bank, 1955-57; v.p., cashier First Security Bank Twin Falls (Idaho), 1959-67; mgr. First Security Bank, Rupert, Idaho, 1967-69; v.p. ops. eastern div. First Security Bank, Pocatello, Idaho, 1967-72, v.p., asst. mgr., 1972-73, mgr., 1977; mgr., v.p. First Security Bank, Coeur d'Alene, Idaho, 1973-77; v.p., area mgr. Idaho Bank & Trust Co., Boise, 1977-78, sr. v.p., 1978—. Pres. PTA, Hailey, Idaho, 1955-56; treas. Pocatello Jr. Achievement, 1970-71, pres., 1969-70; chmn. bd. trustees First Methodist Ch., Coeur d'Alene; treas. Kootenai County (Idaho) YMCA, 1972-75, dir., 1972—; chmn. Idaho Housing Agy.; chmn. St. Luke's Charity Ball, 1983; bd. dirs., chmn. gen. div. United Way, Boise; vice chmn. Idaho Council on Econ. Edn.; treas. Funday. Served with USN, 1944-46. Named Businessman of Yr., Twin Falls Credit Women's Club, 1954, Man of Yr., Kootenai Family YMCA, 1975; recipient Disting. Service award Coeur d'Alene C. of C., campaign award Kootenai County United Way, 1976. Mem. Idaho Bankers Assn. (chmn. public relations com. 1979-80), Sales and Mktg. Execs. of Boise (2d v.p.). Boise C. of C. Clubs: Hillcrest Country, Arid (Boise), Boise Southwest Rotary (pres.-elect). Home: 817 Argyll Dr Boise ID 83702 Office: PO Box 2800 Boise ID 83701

COBB, ALONZO FLOYD, JR., chemical company executive; b. N.Y.C., Jan. 12, 1947; s. Alonzo Floyd Sr. and Lorene (Brown) Cobb; m. Ernestine Mitchell (div.); children: Tarik Walden, Tammy Melissa. AS in Chemistry, Nassau Community Coll., 1976; BBA in Finance, Baruch Coll., 1979; MA in Econs. and Bus., Stanford U., 1983. Internal auditor Crocker Bank, San Francisco, 1979-80; fin. analyst Castle & Cooke, San Francisco, 1981-82; fin. planner Childers, Swan & Co., Fremont, Calif., 1983-85; mktg. analyst Pacific Bell Directory, San Francisco, 1985-87; sr. fin. analyst Pacific Bell, San Ramon, 1987-88; pres. Cobb Chemicals Société Privée À Résponsabilité Limitée, Kinshasa, Zaire, 1989—. Tutor San Francisco Sch. Vols., 1986—; com. mem. Corp. Action in Pub. Schs., 1986—. Served with U.S. Army, 1966-70. Republican. Adventist. Home: 537 16th Ave San Francisco CA 94118 Office: Cobb Chemicals SPRL, 10 B Ave, Bakongo Republic of Zaire

COBB, DONALD DEAN, physicist; b. Atlantic, Iowa, May 4, 1943; s. Leland D. and Betty J. (Nissen) C.; m. Constance M. Olson, Aug. 3, 1963; children: Paula M., Allison K. BS, No. Ill. U., 1965; MS, U. Iowa, 1968, PhD, 1970. Sr. scientist EG&G, Inc., Los Alamos, N.Mex., 1970-75; staff mem. Los Alamos Nat. Lab., 1976-80, group leader, 1981-85, dep. div. leader, 1986--. Contbr. articles to profl. publs. Mem. Am. Phys. Soc., Am. Geophys. Union. Office: Los Alamos Nat Lab M D446 Los Alamos NM 87545

COBB, JEWEL PLUMMER, college president; b. Chgo., Jan. 17, 1924; divorced; 1 child. A.B., Talladega Coll., 1944; M.S., N.Y. U., 1947, Ph.D. in Biology, 1950. Fellow Nat. Cancer Inst., 1950-52; instr. anatomy U. Ill. Coll. Medicine, 1952-54; research surgery Postgrad. Med. Coll., N.Y. U., 1955, asst. prof., 1955-60; Cancer Research Found. prof. biology Sarah Lawrence Coll., 1960-69; prof. zoology, dean Conn. Coll., 1969-76; prof. biology, dean Douglass Coll., Rutgers U., 1976-81; pres. Calif. State U.-Fullerton, 1981—; condr. research on tissue culture, changes produced by promising chemotherapeutic agents, normal and abnormal pigment cell metabolism; dir. Travelers Ins. Co.; Former mem. commn. on acad. affairs Am. Council on Edn.; Bd. dirs. 21st Century Found., Nat. Center Resource Recovery, Nat. Sci. Bd., 1974-80, Nat. Inst. Medicine, CPC Internat., Inc., Allied/Signal Corp., First Interstate Bancorp. Recipient Alumnae Woman of Yr. award N.Y. U., 1979. Fellow N.Y. Acad. Scis., Tissue Culture Assn.; mem. AAUW, Sigma Xi. Office: Calif State U-Fullerton Office of Pres Fullerton CA 92634 *

COBB, KATRINA KEES, artist; b. Erie, Pa., July 12, 1947; d. Arthur Raymond and Marian Mae (Springetie) Collenburg; m. Terry Vani, Feb. 23, 1969 (div. 1985); children: Nicole Mae, Aarow Nathen; m. Michael Eugene Cobb, Dec. 21, 1985. Student, Pasadena (Calif.) City Coll., 1966. Interior designer 1971-75, clothing designer, 1975-85, artist, 1985—; distributes art work through Picture Source N.W. One-woman show in Bellevue, Wash., 1987-88, San Francisco, 1988; exhibiting in conjunction with Son of Heaven Show from China Tour.

COBB, ROWENA NOELANI BLAKE, real estate broker; b. Kauai, Hawaii, May 1, 1939; d. Bernard K. Blake and Hattie Kanui Yuen; m. James Jackson Cobb, Dec. 22, 1962; children: Shelly Ranelle Noelani, Bret Kimo Jackson. BS in Edn., Bob Jones U., 1961; broker's lic., Vitousek Sch. Real Estate, Honolulu, 1981. Lic. real estate broker, Honolulu. Prin. broker Cobb Realty, Lihue, Hawaii, 1983—; sec. Neighbor Island MLS Svc., Honolulu, 1985-87, vice chmn., 1987-88; chmn. MLS Hawaii, Inc., Honolulu, 1988—. Sec. Koloa Community Assn., 1981-89, pres., 1989; mem. Kauai Humane Soc. Mem. Nat. Assn. Realtors (grad. Realtors Inst., cert. residential specialist), Hawaii Assn. Realtors (cert. tchr., state bd. dirs. 1984, v.p. 1985), Kauai Bd. Realtors (v.p. 1984, pres. 1985, Realtor Asssoc. of Yr. award 1983, Realtor of Yr. award 1986), Kauai Mus., Soroptimists (bd. dirs. Lihue 1986-89, treas. 1989). Republican. Office: 3016 Umi St Ste 205 Lihue HI 96766

COBB, ROY LAMPKIN, JR., professional services company executive; b. Oklahoma City, Sept. 23, 1934; s. Roy Lampkin and Alice Maxine (Ellis) C.; B.A., U. Okla., 1972; postgrad. U. Calif., Northridge, 1976-77; m. Shirley Ann Dodson, June 21, 1958; children—Kendra Leigh, Cary William, Paul Alan. Naval aviation cadet U.S. Navy, 1955, advanced through grades to comdr., 1970; ret., 1978; mktg./project staff engr. Gen. Dynamics, Pomona, Calif., 1978-80; prin. engr. Advanced Tech., Inc., Camarillo, Calif., 1980—. Decorated Navy Commendation medal, Air medal. Mem. Assn. Naval Aviators, Soc. Logistic Engrs. Republican. Methodist. Club: Las Posas Country. Home: 2481 Brookhill Dr Camarillo CA 93010 Office: Advanced Tech Inc 1000 Paseo Camarillo Camarillo CA 93010

COBB, SHIRLEY ANN, public relations specialist, journalist; b. Oklahoma City, Jan. 1, 1936; d. William Ray and Irene (Fewell) Dodson; m. Roy Lampkin Cobb, Jr., June 21, 1958; children: Kendra Leigh, Cary William, Paul Alan. BA in Journalism with distinction, U. Okla., 1958, postgrad., 1972; postgrad., Jacksonville U., 1962. Info. specialist Pacific Missle Test

Ctr., Pt. Mugu, Calif., 1975-76; corr. Religious News Service, N.Y.C., 1979-81; splty. editor fashion and religion Thousand Oaks (Calif.) News Chronicle, 1977-81; pub. relations cons., Camarillo, Calif., 1977—; sr. mgmt. analyst pub. info City of Thousand Oaks, 1983—. Contbr. articles to profl. jours. Trustee Ocean View Sch. Bd., 1976-79; pres. Pt. Mugu Officers' Wives Club, 1975-76; bd. dirs. Camarillo Hospice, 1983-85. Recipient Spot News award San Fernando Valley Press Club, 1979. Mem. Pub. Relations Soc. Am., Sigma Delta Chi, Phi Beta Kappa, Chi Omega. Republican. Clubs: Las Posas Country, Town Hall of Calif. Home: 2481 Brookhill Dr Camarillo CA 93010 Office: 2150 W Hillcrest Dr Thousand Oaks CA 91320

COBB, STEPHEN HENRY (STEVE COBB), state senator; b. Honolulu, Dec. 5, 1942; s. William B. and Olivine (Steffens) C.; married; 1 child; student U. Hawaii, 1961-64; BA in Journalism, Calif. State U.-Los Angeles, 1966. With mktg. and loans dept. Bank of Hawaii, 1970-72; corp. policy coordinator Pacific Resources Inc., 1976—; mem. Hawaii Ho. of Reps. from 8th Dist., 1972-78, Hawaii Senate from 7th, 12th Dists., 1978—, chmn. consumer protection and commerce com., 1979—, majority floor leader, 1981-86. Treas., Hawaii Little League Baseball, 1971-75. active numerous Dem. campaigns, 1960—; mem. Citizens Against Noise; advisor Big Bros.; bd. dirs. Hawaii Vietnam Vets. Leadership Program. Served with AUS, 1966-70; Vietnam. Decorated Silver Star, Bronze Star medal, Army Commendation medal, Purple Heart, Air medal. Named Kiwanis Vet. of Yr., Hawaii, 1970. Mem. Vietnam Vets. of Am., DAV, Sigma Delta Chi. Roman Catholic. Office: Office of State Senate State Capitol Honolulu HI 96813

COBB, THOMAS CHARLES, construction executive; b. Belleville, Kans., Aug. 28, 1930; s. Orval Francis and Edith Louella (Collins) C.; m. LaDonna Jean Todd, Nov. 19, 1950; children: Charles Brian, Sheryl Sue, Scott Alan. AA, Gen. Motors Inst., 1951. Svc. rep.Buick Motor div. Gen. Motors Corp., Denver, 1955-60; owner, mgr. Cobb Motor Supply, Longmont, Colo., 1960-73, Cobb Tractor Supply, Longmont, Colo., 1973-77, T-L Constrn., Longmont, Colo., 1977—. Leader Cloverleaf Riders 4-H Club, Longmont, 1969-85; mem. parent adv. com. Mead Jr. High Sch., Longmont High Sch., 1970-80; ad hoc com. City of Longmont, 1985—. With USAF, 1951-55. Named Leader of Yr. Boulder County 4-H, 1978, Entrepreneur of Yr., Salesman with a Purpose Orgn., 1987. Mem. Longmont Builders Assn. (reporter 1988, polit. action com. 1989), Longmont Area C. of C. (bd. dirs. 1989, site devel. coun. 1988, 89), Knife & Fork Club (Boulder, bd. dirs. 1983—), Elks. Republican. Methodist. Home: 13651 N 115th St Longmont CO 80501 Office: 500 9th Ave Ste 13A Longmont CO 80501

COBBS, HARTZELL JAMES, insurance marketing executive; b. Eugene, Oreg., Oct. 17, 1942; s. Hartzell Miller and LaVancy May (Hoffman) C.; m. Joy Ann Harter, Aug. 27, 1965; children: Justine, Stephen. BTh, N.W. Christian Coll., 1966; D of Religion, Claremont Sch. of Theology, 1970. Assoc. minister First Christian Ch., Sacramento, 1970-71; sr. minister South Bay Christian Ch., Redondo Beach, Calif., 1971-76; exec. v.p. Idaho Health Care Assn., Boise, Idaho, 1976-81; exec. dir. Oreg. Health Care Assn., Portland, 1981-87; sr. v.p. C&M Assocs., Portland, 1987—; internat. lectr. Intercare, 1984—; mem. Govs. Commn. on Fin. Long-Term Care, Salem Oreg., 1988—; v.p. Mountain State Health Corp, Boise, 1984—. Pres. Redondo Beach Coordinating Coun., Redondo Beach, Calif., 1975; drug counselor The Center, Honolulu, 1970; bd. dirs. Emergency Housing Ctr., Sacramento, 1970-71. Mem. Am. Soc. Health Care Assn. Execs. (pres. 1986-87), Am. Health Care Assn. (bd. dirs. 1986-87). Democrat. Disciples of Christ. Home: 7160 SW Ralieghwood Ln Portland OR 97225

COBE, LORI, casting director; b. N.Y.C., Jan. 20, 1957; d. Sandy Cobe and Marianne (Findler) Bobick. Office, personnel mgr. Calif. Mag., Los Angeles, 1979-85; dir. bus. affairs, casting dir. Intercontinental Releasing, Los Angeles, 1985-87; ind. casting dir. Lori Cobe Casting, Los Angeles, 1987—. Producer: (feature film) Nicky and the Mack, (play) Rocket to the Moon by Clifford Odets; casting dir.: Open House, The Jigsaw Murders, Eyewitness to Murder, Black Snow, Riding the Edge. Recipient Los Angeles Dramalogue award for prodn. "Rocket to the Moon", 1988. Mem. Women in Film, Women in Theatre. Office: Lori Cobe Casting 10351 Santa Monica Blvd Los Angeles CA 90025

COBERLY, DONALD EDWARD, educator; b. Washington, Oct. 18, 1955; s. James E. and Imelda E. (Gagnon) C.; m. Shannon Renae Elledge, Oct. 17, 1986; children: Marcie, Heather. BA in History, BE, U. Idaho, 1977; MA in Reading Edn., Boise State U., 1982; PhD in Adminstrn., U. Idaho, 1985. Cert. tchr., Idaho. Tchr. Lewiston (Idaho) Head Start Program, 1977-78; tchr., asst. prin. Kuna (Idaho) Sch. Dist., 1978-82; instr. U. Idaho, Moscow, 1982-84; tchr. Boise (Idaho) Sch. Dist., 1984-85, supr. lang. arts, 1985—. Mem. Nat. Coun. Tchrs. English, Nat. Reading Assn., Idaho Coun. Tchrs. English (bd. dirs. 1988), Idaho Reading Consortium (bd. dirs. 1986), U.S. Slo Pitch Softball Assn. (asst. Idaho commr. 1988), Elks, Kiwanis, Phi Delta Kappa. Republican. Roman Catholic. Home: 4071 Law Ave Boise ID 83706 Office: Boise Sch 1207 Fort St Boise ID 83702

COBERT, ROBERT WILLIAM, composer; b. N.Y.C., Oct. 26, 1924; s. Irving and Rose (Stone) C.; m. Helen Elizabeth Fosse, July 7, 1950; children: Holly, Suzy, William. Student, CCNY, 1940-43, Juilliard, 1944-46, Columbis U., 1947. tchr. film composing, U. So. Calif. Grad. Sch., Los Angeles, 1985-87. Composer numerous soundtracks including: The Last Ride of the Dalton Gang (winner of the Wrangler award), Heaven Can Wait, Black Widow, Dark Shadows, Burnt Offerings, Bonanza: The Next Generation; (mini-series) War and Remembrance, The Winds of War; (game shows) Password, The Price is Right, The $25,000 Pyramid, The $100,000 Pyramid, many others. Recipient Wrangler award for best film score Last Ride of the Dalton Gang. Mem. Broadcast Music Inc., Musicians Union Local 47, Songwriters Guild, Nat. Acad. of TV Arts and Scis.

COBEY BLACK, journalist, corporate executive; b. Washington, June 15, 1922; d. Elwood Alexander and Margaret (Beall) Cobey; m. Edwin F. Black; children: Star, Christopher, Noel, Nicholas, Brian, Bruce. BA, Wellesley Coll., 1944; postgrad., U. Hawaii. Exec. sec. to Irene, designer Metro-Goldwyn-Mayer, 1944; actress Fed. Republic Germany, 1945-46; women's editor Washington Daily News, 1947-50; columnist Honolulu Star Bull., 1954-65, Honolulu Advertiser, 1972-84; pres. Black & Black, Honolulu, 1988—; cons. HEW, Peace Corps, 1960-61; v.p. Mandalay Imports Corp.; bd. dirs. Pacific and Asian Affairs Coun., 1986—, Honolulu Com. on Fgn. Rels., 1987—. Author: Birth of A Princess, 1962, Iolani Luahine, 1986; travel editor Bangkok World, 1968-69; publicist CBS-TV series Hawaii Five-O, 1978. Mem. Hawaii State Commn. on Status of Women, 1978-86. Democrat. Episcopalian. Clubs: Nat. Press, Royal Bangkok Sports, Outrigger Canoe, Waialae Country. Office: Black & Black Inc 1152 Koko Head Ave Ste 102 Honolulu HI 96816

COBIANCHI, THOMAS THEODORE, engineering and marketing executive, educator; b. Paterson, N.J., July 7, 1941; s. Thomas and Violet Emily (Bazzar) C.; m. Phyllis Linda Asch, Feb. 6, 1964; 1 child, Michael. Student, Clemson U., 196-62; BS, Monmouth Coll., 1968, MBA, 1972; postgrad., U. Pa., 1988. Sales mgr. Westinghouse Electric Corp., Balt., 1968-74; sr. internat. sales engr. Westinghouse Electric Corp., Lima, Ohio, 1975-77; program mgr. Westinghouse Electric Corp., Pitts., 1977-78, mgr. bus. devel., 1978-82; dir. mktg. Westinghouse Electric Corp., Arlington, Va., 1982-86; acting dir., engring. mgr. General Dynamics Corp., San Diego, 1986-89; dir. bus. devel. RPV Programs Teledyne Ryan Aero., San Diego, 1989—; instr., lectr. various ednl. instns. Active various polit. and ednl. orgns. Mem. Armed Forces Communications and Electronics Assn. (acting chmn. 1988), Princeton Club of Washington, Nat. Aviation Club, General Dynamics Health Club, Delta Sigma Pi. Home: 16468 Calle Pulido San Diego CA 92128 Office: Teledyne Ryan Aero 2701 Harbor Dr San Diego CA 92101

COBURN, MARJORIE FOSTER, psychologist, educator; b. Salt Lake City, Feb. 28, 1939; d. Harlan A. and Alma (Ballinger) Polk; m. Robert Byron Coburn, July 2, 1977; children—Robert Scott Coburn, Kelly Anne Coburn, Polly Klea Foster, Matthew Ryan Foster. B.A. in Sociology, UCLA, 1960; Montessori Internat. Diploma honor grad. Washington Montessori Inst., 1968; M.A. in Psychology, U. No. Colo., 1979; Ph.D. in Counseling Psychology, U. Denver, 1983. Licensed clin. psychologist. Probation officer Alameda County (Calif.), Oakland, 1960-62, Contra Costa County (Calif.), El Cerrito, 1966, Fairfax County (Va.), Fairfax, 1967; dir. Friendship Club, Orlando, Fla., 1963-65; tchr. Va. Montessori Sch., Fairfax, 1968-70; spl. edn. tchr. Leary Sch., Falls Church, Va., 1970-72, sch. administr., 1973-76; tchr. Aseltine Sch., San Diego, 1976-77, Coburn Montessori Sch., Colorado Springs, Colo., 1977-79; pvt. practice psychotherapy, Colorado Springs, 1979-82, San Diego, 1982—; cons. spl. edn., agoraphobia, women in transition. Mem. Am. Psychol. Assn., Am. Orthopsychiat. Assn., Phobia Soc., Council Exceptional Children, El Paso Psychol. Assn., Calif. Psychol. Assn., Acad. San Diego Psychologists, AAUW, NOW, Mensa. Episcopalian. Lodge: Rotary. Contbr. articles to profl. jours.; author: (with R.C. Orem) Montessori: Prescription for Children with Learning Disabilities, 1977. Office: 826 Prospect Suite 201 La Jolla CA 92037

COBURN, WILLIAM PIERCE, architect; b. Melrose, Mass., May 10, 1944; s. Frank Sewall and Rachel (Pierce) C.; m. Subhashini Singh, 1988. BFA, Mass. Coll. Art, 1966; M. in architecture, Harvard U., 1971. Registered architect, Calif. Owner William P. Coburn AIA, Oakland, Calif., 1978—; cectr. grad. sch. dept. design Harvard U., Cambridge, Mass., 1988, vis. critic grad. sch. dept. landscape architecture; lectr. Chabot Coll., Hayward, Calif., 1988; bd. dirs. W. Oakland (Calif.) Economic Devel. Corp. Furniture exhibit dept. architecture U. Calif., Berkeley, 1989. Co-founder W. Oakland Prescott Neighborhood Assn., 1987. Recipient merit award San Francisco Landscape Design Show, 1987. Mem. AIA. Democrat. Office: 1224 Center St Oakland CA 94607

COCANOWER, LIANA CHERYL, lawyer; b. Salt Lake City, June 19, 1953; d. Elbert Ernest and Dorothy June (Smith) Miller; m. Michael A. Thiessen, Aug., 1973 (div. 1975); m. Michael Andrew Maher, Oct. 15, 1975 (div. Feb. 1981); m. David Lehman Cocanower, Sept. 21, 1983; children—Michael Whitten, Joseph Charles, Emily Elizabeth. B.E., Western Wash. State Coll., 1973; J.D., McGeorge Sch. Law, U. Pacific, 1979; LL.M. in Taxation, NYU, 1980. Bar: Calif. 1979, Ariz. 1980. Assoc. Lewis and Roca, Phoenix, 1980-85, ptnr., 1985-87; assoc. Storey & Ross, 1987—. Served with USAF, 1975-76. Mem. ABA (tax sect., com. small bus., chmn. subcom. on publs.. real property, probate and trust div., vice chmn. com on spl. problems of bus. owners), Calif. State Bar, Ariz. State Bar (cert. tax specialist, tax sect.), Phi Delta Phi. Republican. Presbyterian. Home: 202 E McLellan Blvd Phoenix AZ 85012 Office: Storey & Ross 4742 N 24th St Ct 1 4th Fl Phoenix AZ 85016

COCHRAN, BRIAN B., banker, real estate; b. Los Angeles, Oct. 15, 1953; s. Burke B. and Barbara Jane (Wilson) C. BS in Fin., USC, Los Angeles, 1975; MBA, Pepperdine U., 1989. Pilot Braniff Airways, Dallas, 1977-80; sls. cons. Coldwell Banker, Houston, 1980-84; vp/mktg. dir. Coldwell Banker, Los Angeles, 1984-86; vp/sls. mgr. Coldwell Banker, Beverly Hills, Calif., 1987—; dir. Stewart Title of Los Angeles, Glendale, Calif. 1985—, dir. bus. property council, Los Angeles 1986—. Mem. Jonathan Club, King Harbor Yacht Club. Republican. Protestant. Office: Coldwell Banker 1840 Century Park East Los Angeles CA 90067

COCHRAN, PATRICIA LUELLA, small business owner; b. Modesto, Calif., Nov. 13, 1944; d. L.V. and Mary Pauline (Wilson) Ingram; m. Ronald Lee Campbell, May 13, 1961 (div. Apr. 1984); children: Rebecca Lyn, Ronald Lee Jr., Patrick Lawrence, Sherri Anne; m. Adrian Lester Cochran, June 20, 1984. Student, Modesto Jr. Coll., 1971-72, diploma, 1981; diploma, CLS Design Acad., 1983; student, U. Calif., Berkeley, 1983—; cert., Keye Productivity Ctr., 1984; mem. Lic. cosmetologist and instr., Calif. Foreclosure officer Cen. State Title Ins. Co., Modesto, 1974-79; bookkeeper North Adrians, Modesto, 1979-82; instr. Adrians Beauty Coll., Modesto, 1982-84, also bd. dirs. Author: Adrians Beauty College Student Handbook, 1985. Mem. Nat. Assn. Cosmetology Schs. (diploma 1985), Calif. Cosmetology Assn., Calif. Assn. Regional Occupational Program Commn., World Internat. Nail and Beauty Assn. (nat. and internat. Olympic judge 1985). Democrat. Office: 950 Oakdale Rd Ste N Modesto CA 95350

COCHRANE, ROBERT H., bishop; s. William Arthur H. and Raven (Hume) C.; m. Theresa M. Tripi; two children. BA, CUNY, 1948; STB, Gen. Theol. Sem., N.Y., 1951, DD, 1976. Ordained to ministry, Episcopal Ch., 1951; consecrated bishop coadjutor, Diocese of Olympia, Wash., 1976. Vicar Redeemer Ch., Delano, Calif., 1951-52; curate Trinity Ch., Reno, 1952-54; vicar St. Timothy Ch., Henderson, Nev., 1954-60; rector All Saints Ch., Salt Lake City, 1960-69, Christ Ch., Tacoma, Wash., 1969-76; bishop, Olympia, 1976—. Office: Diocese of Olympia PO Box 12126 Seattle WA 98102 *

COCKE, JAMES WILL, banker; b. Clarksville, Tenn., Apr. 6, 1917; s. James Gordon and Kate (Powell) C.; m. Marjorie Warwick, Oct. 26, 1941 (dec. 1961); 1 child, Robert D.; m. Joan Waterson, Oct. 31, 1964; stepchildren: David Hopping, Spencer B. Hopping, Ann Louise Hopping, Amy Louise Hopping Horton. Student Vanderbilt U., 1938-54; BS, U. Md., 1958; postgrad., U. Ariz., 1961-63; student Indsl. Coll. Armed Forces, 1960-61. Commd. 2d. lt., U.S. Army, 1940, advanced through grades to lt. col., 1961; instr. U.S. Army Cavalry Sch., 1945-46, U.S. Army Ground Gen. Sch., 1947-49, U.S. Army Armor Sch., 1959-61; prof. mil. sci. Vanderbilt U., 1954-57; with Valley Nat. Bank, Tucson, 1963-84; asst. v.p., 1968-73, v.p. econ. div. dept., 1973-83, v.p. corp. affairs, 1983-84; prin. James W. Cocke & Assocs., devel., mktg. and pub. affairs svcs. cons., 1984—; lectr. mktg. and pub. relations, econ. devel. to various civic and coll. groups; mem. assoc. faculty Pima Community Coll. Bus. and Mgmt. Contbr. articles to mil. jours. Bd. dirs. Tucson Festival Soc., 1963-69, Jr. Achievement Tucson, 1963-69; chmn. community growth and devel. and objectives sub-com. Pima Community Coll. Found., pres. 1983-85, 1966; pres. Tucson Child Guidance Clinic, 1968-69, Tucson Council of the Arts, 1968-70; bd. dirs. Pima County Real Estate Research Council, 1969—, chmn. 1973-74, sec. treas. emeritus 1985—; pres. Tucson Trade Bur., 1970-71, Ariz. Tng. Ctr. for The Handicapped, 1971-73; mem. Tucson Regional Planning Bd., 1972—, Ariz. Assn. for Indsl. Devel., 1973-86, water com. Pima Assn. of Govts., 1977-78, Tucson Com. on Foreign Relations, 1978-80, 87, Citizens Water Adv. Com. City of Tucson, 1979-83, Community Adv. Bd. Stas. KUAT-TV AM-FM Pub. Radio, 1979-82, Ariz. Dist. Export Council, U.S. Dept. Commerce, 1983—; bd. dirs. Ariz. Econ. Devel. Council, 1973-84, chmn., 1978; mem. City of Tucson Overall Econ. Planning Com., CETA Adv. Com., 1978-83; v.p. OEPC, 1979-82, chmn. 1982—; chmn. Trunk 'N' Tusk com. Pima County Republican Club, 1979-80; pres. Pima Coll. Found., 1983—, hon. bd. dirs.; treas. So. Ariz. Water Resources Assn. Bd., 1982-84; v.p. Pima County Acad. Decathlon Assn., 1983-85. Mem. Flecha Caida Homeowners Assn. (pres. 1970-76), Mil. Order of World Wars and Retired Officers Assn. (life), U. Md. Alumni Assn. (life), Tucson Met. C. of C. (gen. chmn. Tucson Town Hall on Community Devel. 1974, chmn. task force on comprehensive planning 1973-74, chmn. 1967-68, chmn. Internat. Trade com. 1986-88, bd. dirs. 1973-74, Chmn. of Yr. 1968, Outstanding Achievement award 1987-88), Tucson Ret. Officers Assn. (pres. 1981), U.S. Army Assn. So. Ariz., U. Md. Alumni Assn., Vanderbilt U. Alumni Assn., Davis Monthan AFB Officers Club, Rotary. Presbyterian. Home and Office: 4045 La Cadena Ave Tucson AZ 85702

COCKLIN, ROBERT L., emergency medicine physician; b. Phoenix, July 4, 1953; s. Hubert W. and Anna L. (Wallace) C. BA, N.Mex. State U., 1975; MD, U. Ariz., 1979. Intern Maricopa Med. Ctr, Phoenix, 1979-80, residency, 1980-81; residency Sacred Heart Med Ctr. Deaconess Hosp., Spokane, Wash., 1981-83; practice medicine specializing in internal medicine Phoenix, 1983-84; mem. staff emergency dept. Maricopa Med. Ctr.; practice medicine specializing in emergency medicine Phoenix, Chandler, Ariz., 1984-87; mem. staff emergency dept. Chandler Regional Hosp.; mem. staff urgent care unit Cigna Healthplan of Ariz.; practice medicine specializing in emergency medicine Tempe, Ariz., 1987—; mem. staff emergency dept. Tempe Saint Luke's Hosp. Republican. Episcopalian.

COCKRELL, FRANK BOYD, II, oil executive; b. Redding, Calif., May 3, 1948; s. Alfred Marion Sr. and Blanche Delma (Webb) C.; m. Grace Marie Louise Whest, Sept. 20, 1986; children: Catherine, Francis V, Ross, Sabrina, Brooke. AA, Shasta Jr. Coll., 1968; BS, Sacramento (Calif.) State U., 1970; postgrad., U. Pacific, 1970-72. Pres., chmn. Als Towing & Storage Co., Sacramento, 1976-78, Compacts Only Rental Cars, Sacramento, 1976-78; film producer, actor, comedian Sacramento, Los Angeles and Las Vegas, Nev., 1976—; pres., chmn. Cockrell Prodns., Inc., Los Angeles, 1984—, Palm Spring Employment Agy., Inc., Palm Desert, Calif., 1986. Author: Vietnam History, 1970. Candidate Assembly 6th Dist. Rep. Party, Sacramento, 1974; mem. Sacramento Rep. Cen. Com., 1975-76, Calif. State Cen. Rep. Com., 1974-76. Bank of Am. scholar, 1966, Shasta Coll. scholar, 1967. Lodge: Optimists (pres. Sacramento chpt. 1975-76, lt. gov. 1976-77). Office: Cockrell Prodns Inc PO Box 1731 Studio City CA 91604

COCKRELL, WILLIAM JASPER, III, accountant; b. Jacksonville, Fla., July 7, 1942; s. William Jasper and Bethel Aurora (Hughes) C.; BSBA, Calif. State Coll., Los Angeles, 1968; MBT, U. So. Calif., 1974; MBA, Pepperdine U., 1978; m. Sharon Lee Gerrie, Sept. 9, 1967. Tax supr. Laventhol & Horwath, Los Angeles, 1973-74; prin. Palmer, Wiggs & Heston, Agana, Guam, 1974-75; tax supr. Laventhol & Horwath, Los Angeles, 1975-76; tax mgr. Arthur Young & Co., Beverly Hills, Calif., 1977-78, Price, Waterhouse & Co., Newport Beach, Calif., 1978-79; pvt. practice acctg., Newport Beach, 1979—; bd. dirs. MBAN V, Inc., Newport Beach, CCC Steel, Inc., Compton, Calif.; instr. Northrop U., 1976-77. Co-trustee T.F. Haller Trust, 1978—. Served with USN, 1960-61. CPA, Calif., Guam. Mem. Am. Inst. CPA's, Calif. Soc. CPA's (ethics com., taxation com.), U. So. Calif. Alumni Assn., Newport Beach-Irvine Estate Planning Council, Phi Kappa Tau. Clubs: Athletic (Los Angeles), 1000, Acctg. Circle (U. So. Calif.). Contbr. articles to profl. jours. Office: PO Box 337 Balboa Island CA 92662

COCKRIEL, STEPHEN EUGENE, lawyer; b. Long Beach, Calif., June 9, 1948; s. John Robert and Patricia D. (Carroll) C.; m. Helen K. Mulford, Dec. 19, 1968 (div. Feb. 1988); children: Jonathan Ryan, Timothy; m. Dee Ann Kahler, Apr. 17, 1987; stepchildren: John Brandon Kahler, Zachary Robert Kahler, Sara Courtney. BS, U. So. Calif., 1970; JD, Loyola U., L.A., 1973. Bar: Calif. 1973. Assoc. Munns, Kofford, Hoffman, Hunt & Throckmorton, Pasadena, Calif., 1973-74; atty. Thrify Drug Stores Co., Inc., L.A., 1974-75; pvt. practice Long Beach, 1975-81, 87—; ptnr. Bergmann, Cockriel & Forrester, Long Beach, 1975-87; assoc. legal counsel U.S. Jaycees, Tulsa, 1978-79, legal counsel, 1979-80. Pres. Grand Prix Charities Found., Long Beach, 1979-80, Local Devel. Corp., Long Beach, 1987-89; chmn. bd. Community Svcs. Devel. Corp., Long Beach, 1986—. Mem. Long Beach Jaycees (pres. 1978-79). Republican. Methodist. Office: 2105 E 4th St Long Beach CA 90814

COCKRUM, ELMER LENDELL, biology educator; b. Sesser, Ill.; s. Ernest Elmer and Alta May (Quillman) C.; m. Irma Pauline Schutte, Nov. 9, 1943; children: David Lendell, Ward Andrew. BEd, So. Ill. U., 1942; PhD, U. Kans., 1951. Postdoctorate research assoc. U. Kans., Lawrence, 1951-52; asst. prof. zoology U. Ariz., Tucson, 1952-55, curator of mammals, 1955-76, assoc. prof., 1959-63, prof., 1963—, dir. Desert Biology Sta., 1966-67, prof. biol. scis., 1967-76, mammalogist Agrl. Experiment Sta., 1971-76, acting head dept. ecology and evolutionary biology, 1976-77, head dept., 1977-85; desert ecologist U.S. AID/MIT Sahel Drought Project, 1973-74. Author: Mammals of the Southwest 1982; cons. editor Encyclopedia Americana, 1980—; contbr. articles to profl. jours. Served to lt. USNR, 1942-45. Research grantee Smithsonian Inst., 1972-75. Fellow AAAS, Ariz.-Nev. Acad. Sci.; mem. Am. Soc. Mammalogists (life). Presbyterian. Club: Ariz. Philatelic Rangers. Lodge: Elks. Home: 846 W Palma de Coco Tucson AZ 85704 Office: U Ariz Dept Ecology & Evolutionary Biology Tucson AZ 85721

COCKRUM, WILLIAM MONROE, III, investment banker, consultant, educator; b. Indpls., July 18, 1937; s. William Monroe C. II and Katherine J. (Jaqua) Moore; m. Andrea Lee Deering, Mar. 8, 1975; children: Catherine Anne, William Monroe IV. AB with distinction, DePauw U., 1959; MBA with distinction, Harvard U., 1961. With A.G. Becker Paribas Inc., L.A., 1961-84, mgr. nat. corp. fin. div., 1968-71, mgr. pvt. investments, 1971-74, fin. and adminstrv. officer, 1974-80, sr. v.p., 1975-78, vice chmn., 1978-84, also dir.; mem. faculty Northwestern U., 1961-63; vis. lectr. grad. sch. mgmt. UCLA, 1984-88, adj. prof., 1988; bd. dir. Knapp Communications Corp., Cinema Capital Mgmt., Inc. Mem. Delta Kappa Epsilon, Univ. Club (Chgo.), Monterey Club (Palm Desert, Calif.), Deke Club (N.Y.C.), Alisal Golf Club (Solvang, Calif.).

COE, DAVID KELLY, local government association manager, educator, philosopher, author; b. Seattle, Oct. 31, 1941; s. Foster Witham and Maxine Milton (Kelly) C.; m. Patricia Grace Smith, 1970 (div. 1973); m. Barbara Ann Wright, May 31, 1975. BA, U. Hawaii, 1969, MA, 1971, PhD, 1981. Grad. teaching asst. in philosophy U. Hawaii at Manoa, Honolulu, 1970-73; dir. human resources coordination Colo. R-9 Commn., Durango, 1975-77; dir. Colo. INVEST program Colo. State Bd for Community Colls., Denver, 1977-81; dir. adult edn. Regis Coll., Denver, 1982-83; dir. Rocky Mountain mgmt. series U. Colo., Denver, 1983-86; dir. Assn. Bay Area Govts. Tng. Inst., 1986—; pres. Denver chpt. Am. Soc. Pub. Adminstrn., 1981-82, pres. Colo. chpt., 1976-80; adj. prof. pub. mgmt. Calif. State U., Hayward, 1988—. Author: Angst and the Abyss, 1985; contbr. articles to profl. jours. Mem. Colo. Right-to Read Acad., 1978-80; bd. dirs. high cardinal Lifespring, Inc. Leadership program, Denver, 1985—. Mem. Am. Soc. Tng. and Devel., Denver Art Mus. Home: 3155 Gilbert Ln Alameda CA 94501 Office: Assn Bay Area Govts Tng Inst PO Box 2050 Oakland CA 94604

COELHO, DUANE CHRYSLER, writer; b. Richmond, Calif., May 8, 1940; d. Claude Walter and Kindness Leota (Hale) Chrysler; m. William Martin Coelho, Dec. 21, 1957; children: William Martin Jr., Blake Edward. BA with distinction, U. Colo., 1981. Tech. writer Primewriter, Englewood, Colo., 1981, J.D. Edwards & Co., Englewood, 1981-82; supr. written communications COBE Labs., Inc., Lakewood, Colo., 1982—. Mem. Soc. Tech. Communication (sr.), Am. Med. Writers Assn., Phi Beta Kappa. Republican. Presbyterian. Home: 154 Flora Way Golden CO 80401 Office: COBE Labs Inc 1185 Oak St Lakewood CO 80215

COELHO, TONY, former congressman; b. Los Banos, Calif., June 15, 1942; s. Otto and Alice (Branco) C.; m. Phyllis Butler, June 10, 1967; children: Nicole, Kristin. B.A., Loyola U., Los Angeles, 1964. Agr. asst. to Rep. B.F. Sisk, 1965-70, adminstrv. asst., 1970-78; mem. 96th-101st Congresses from 15th Calif. Dist., 1979—; majority whip 100th, 101st Congress, 1987-89; resigned 1989; sec.-treas. United Democrats for Congress; chmn. Dem. Congressional Campaign Com.; mem. Dem. Steering and Policy Com. Mem. nat. implementation task force Epilepsy Found. Am. Roman Catholic. Office: 403 Cannon House Office Bldg Washington DC 20515 *

COEN, LODEWIJK KAREL CELINA, graphic designer; b. Antwerp, Belgium, Oct. 9, 1952; came to U.S. 1987; s. Karel Constantijn Renaat and Margaretha C.E. (Geysen) C.; m. Melanie Hubertine Pauwels, Dec. 10, 1983. Diploma Higher Art Edn., Royal Acad. Fine Arts, Antwerp, 1976; Pedagogical Dipl., Royal Acad. Fine Arts, 1976; dipl. continued Higher Ed, Nat. Higher Inst., Antwerp, 1979. Tchr. art St. Michaels Art Acad., Brasschaat, Belgium, 1976-79; art/design prof. St. Luke's Coll. Art, Antwerp, 1980-87; coordinator dept. graphic design St. Luke's Coll. Art, 1982-87; freelance designer Antwerp, 1976-87; sr. designer Hasbro Electronics, Foster City, Calif., 1987-88; computer graphics dir. HyperPro, Cupertino, Calif., 1989—; cons. in field. With Belgium Army, 1979-80. Named Desktop Pubr. of the Yr., Mac User Europe, 1987; award. Royal Acad., Antwerp, 1975, others.

COEN, VICTORIA LYNN, psychotherapist, group and private consultant, psychology educator; b. Seattle, Jan. 8, 1954; d. Thomas Judson and Janet (Dunn) C. BA, Wagner Coll., Bregenz, Austria, 1975, Western Wash. U., 1976; MSW, U. Wash., Seattle, 1981. Cert. social worker, Wash. Med. social worker Children's Hosp., Seattle, 1976; psychiat. social worker St. John's Hosp., Longview, Wash., 1976-77, mental health profl., 1977-79; Adminstr. King County div. Human Svcs., Seattle, 1979-80; med. social worker Harborview Hosp., Seattle, 1980; instr., researcher U. Wash., Wash. Dept. Licensing, Seattle, 1980-81; psychotherapist Eastside Mental Health, Bellevue, Wash., 1980-85, Divorce Lifeline, Seattle, 1986-88; pvt. practice psychotherapist Seattle, 1982—; group cons. Parents Anonymous, Longview, 1976-78; co-founder ADAPT: Battered Women's shelter, Longview, 1978-79; media interviewee Seattle Times, KING, KIRO Radio stas., KING-TV, KOMO-TV, 1984—. Author numerous pub. poems. Mem. Seattle Art Mus., 1987. Mortar Bd. scholar U. Wash., 1980. Mem. Nat. Assn. Social Workers, Phobia Soc. Am., Am. Assn. Behavioral Therapists, Jungian Soc.,

Green Peace (vol.), Sierra Club (vol.). Home: 737 N 71st St Seattle WA 98103 Office: 2808 II E Madison Ste 200 Seattle WA 98112

COFER, BERDETTE H., consulting company executive; b. Las Flores, Calif.; s. William Walter and Violet Ellen (Elam) C.; m. Ann M. Cofer, July 27, 1954; children: Sandra Lea Cofer-Oberle, Ronald William. AB, Calif. State U., Chico, 1950; MA, U. Calif., Berkeley, 1960. Tchr. Westwood (Calif.) Jr.-Sr. High Sch., 1953-54, Alhambra High Sch., Martinez, Calif., 1954-59; prin. adult and summer sch. Hanford (Calif.) High Sch., 1959-60, asst. supt. bus., 1960-67; dean bus. svcs. West Hills Coll., Coalinga, 1967-76; vice chancellor Yosemite Community Coll. Dist., Modesto, 1976-88; pres. BHC Assocs., Inc., Modesto, 1988—; chmn. Valley Ins. Program Joint Powers Agy., Modesto, 1986-88. Contbr. articles to profl. publs. Pres. Coalinga Indsl. Devel. Corp., 1972-74, Assn. for Retarded Citizens, Modesto, 1985; mayor City of Coalinga, 1974-76; foreman Stanislaus County Grand Jury, Modesto, 1987-78. 1st lt. USAF, 1951-53. Recipient Outstanding Citizen award Coalinga C. of C., 1976, Walter Starr Robie Outstanding Bus. Officer award Assn. Chief Bus. Officers Calif. Community Colls., 1988. Mem. Assn. Calif. Community Coll. Adminstrs. (life), Commonwealth Club Calif. (San Francisco), Elks, Phi Delta Kappa (pres. Kings-Tulare chpt. 1962-63). Democrat. Home and Office: 3608 Bellwood Ct Modesto CA 95356

COFFELT, RALPH WENDELL, pediatrician; b. Junction City, Kans., Nov. 5, 1910; s. Ralph M. and Alice M. (Haworth) C.; m. Claribel Coffelt, June 10, 1933 (div. 1952); m. Dolores Storm, June 24, 1954. BS, U. Kans., 1933, MS, 1934, MD, 1938; BA (hon.), Pierce Coll., 1976. Diplomate Am. Bd. Pediatrics. Intern Hunnington Hosp., Pasadena, Calif., 1938-39; resident Children's Hosp., L.A., 1939-40, 45; practice medicine specializing in pediatrics Burbank, Calif., 1946--. Lt. col. M.C., U.S. Army, 1940-46, CBI. Mem. Am. Acad. Pediatrics (dist. chmn. 1976). Democrat. Home: 1631 Valley View Rd Glendale CA 91202 Office: 2409 W Magnolia St Burbank CA 91506

COFFEY, GEORGE LYLE, financial executive, property consultant; b. Chgo., Oct. 2, 1953; s. Ray Leonard and Theresa (Wahl) C. BS in Indsl. Engring., N.Y. Inst. Tech., 1975. Engr. Bethleheim Steel, Burns Harbor, Ind., 1975-80; engring. contractor McCabe S. Dalton, Las Vegas, Nev., 1980-83; pres., chief exec. officer Foreclosure Stoppers and Property Cons., Mission Viejo, Calif., 1984—; advisor Calif. Savs. and Loans. Advisor Diebetic Children's Fund. Home: 23902 Villena Mission Viejo CA 92692

COFFEY, JENNESS HALL, biologist, natural resource specialist; b. Washington, Apr. 1, 1951; d. Kenneth Delos and Jane (Thoma) Hall; m. Michael Allen Coffey. BS, U. Md., 1976; grad. natural resource specialist masters program, Nat. Park Service, 1986. Park ranger C&O Canal Nat. Hist. Park, Sharpsburg, Md., 1978-82; supr. White House tours and spl. events Nat. Park Service, Washington, 1982-83; resource mgr. Nat. Park Service, Triangle, Va., 1983-84; natural resource specialist Nat. Park Service, Twentynine Palms, Calif., 1986-88, Boulder City, Nev., 1988—; leader Interagy. Task Force on Natural Resources, Dept. Interior and Dept. Navy, Quantico, Va., 1984; symposium presenter various natural resource councils. Contbr. articles to profl. journals. Mem. Park Arts Assn., Evergreen, Colo. Fellow Phi Kappa Phi; mem. Nat. Parks and Conservation Assn., George Wright Soc., Assn. Nat. Park Rangers, Wilderness Soc. Office: Nat Park Svc 601 Nevada Hwy Boulder City NV 89005

COFFEY, MELVIN WILLIAM, metallurgical engineer; b. Portland, Oreg., May 19, 1949; s. Melvin William and Lenora (Peterson) C.; m. Eileen JoAnne Schuba, Aug. 19, 1988. BS, Oreg. State U., 1972; MS, Oreg. Grad. Ctr., 1985. Technician N.W. Testing Labs., Portland, 1974-75; metallurgist ESCO Corp., Portland, 1975-78, electron microscopist, 1978-83; rsch. metallurgist Precision Castparts Corp., Portland, 1983-87, process engring. mgr., 1987—. Mem. ASTM, Am. Soc. for Metals, Internat. Metallographic Soc., N.Y. Acad. Scis. Democrat.

COFFEY, PHILIP JOHN, civil engineer; b. Holyoke, Mass., Dec. 6, 1910; s. John and Mildred (Knappett) C.; B.S. in Civil Engring. (scholar 1930-32). MIT, 1933; M.A. in Journalism, U. Colo., 1970; m. Lydia Spomer, Aug. 15, 1942; 1 son, Cecil. With USPHS, Chgo., San Francisco, Addis Ababa, Ethiopia. Cin., Denver, 1936-42, 57-68, san. engr. dir., until 1968; san. hydraulic engr. Calif. Depts. Fin. and Water Resources, San Francisco, Sacramento, 1946-48, 51-57; engr. Inst. Inter-Am. Affairs, Asuncion, Paraguay, 1949-51; spl. exam. commr. Calif. Bd. Registration for Profl. Engrs., Sacramento, 1952; mem. tech. adv. com. Calif. Senate Com. Radiation Protection, Sacramento, 1956-57; mem. faculty Water and Sewage Plant Operators' Sch., U. Colo., 1966-67. Served to lt. col., C.E., AUS, 1942-46. Registered profl. engr., Calif., Colo. Mem. Ret. Officers Assn., DAV, Kappa Tau Alpha. Lodge: Masons. Contbr. articles to tech. publs. Address: 10555 W Jewell Ave #26 207 Lakewood CO 80226

COFFILL, MARJORIE LOUISE, civic leader; b. Sonora, Calif., June 11, 1917; d. Eric J. and Pearl (Needham) Segerstrom; A.B. with distinction in Social Sci., Stanford U., 1938, M.A. in Edn., 1941; m. William Charles Coffill, Jan. 25, 1948; children—William James, Eric John. Asst. mgr. Sonora Abstract & Title Co. (Calif.), 1938-39; mem. dean of women's staff Stanford, 1939-41; social dir. women's campus Pomona Coll., 1941-43, instr. psychology, 1941-43; asst. to field dir. ARC, Lee Moore AFB, Calif., 1944-46; partner Riverbank Water Co., Riverbank and Hughson, Calif., 1950-68. Mem. Tuolumne County Mental Health Adv. Com., 1963-70; mem. central advisory council Supplementary Edn. Center, Stockton, Calif., 1966-70; mem. advisory com. Columbia Jr. Coll., 1972—, pres., 1980—; pres. Columbia Found., 1972-74, bd. dirs., 1974-77; mem. Tuolumne County Bicentennial Com., 1974—; active PTA, ARC. Pres., Tuolumne County Republican Women, 1952—, asso. mem. Calif. Rep. Central Com., 1950. Trustee Sonora Union High Sch., 1969-73, Salvation Army Tuolumne County, 1973—; bd. dirs. Lung Assn. Valley Lode Counties, 1974—. Recipient Pi Lambda Theta award, 1940; Outstanding Citizen award C. of C., 1974, Citizen of Yr. award, 1987. Mem. AAUW (charter mem. Tuolumne County br., pres. Sonora br. 1965-66). Episcopalian (mem. vestry 1968, 75). Home: 376 E Summit Ave Sonora CA 95370

COFFMAN, GARY L., sales executive; b. Chariton, Iowa, Dec. 18, 1949; s. Bernard Ray and Donna Jean (Shore) C. BS, Iowa State U., 1972. Mgr. trainee First State Bank, Chariton, 1972-74; ops. mgr. Riekes Container Co., Des Moines, 1974-75, Mpls., 1975-80; sales rep. Riekes Container Co., Houston, 1980-86; dist. mgr. Alco Packaging (formerly Riekes Container Co.), Phoenix, 1986-87; dist. mgr. Alco Packaging (formerly Riekes Container Co.), L.A., 1987-89, gen. mgr. pacific region, 1989—. Leader 4-H sr. group, Des Moines, 1975; precinct chmn. Whitmore for Mayor, Houston, 1982; vol. M.D. Anderson Hosp., Houston, 1984-85; mem. City of Hope, 1986—; DFL party worker, Mpls. Mem. Iowa State Alumni Assn. Democrat. Methodist. Clubs: Sequioa Athletic (Buena Park, Calif.), Calhoun Beach (Mpls.). Office: Alco Packaging 6270 Caballero Blvd Buena Park CA 90620

COFFMAN, WILLIAM BRENT, dentist; b. Wytheville, Va., Nov. 6, 1945; s. William Henry and Esther Virginia (Brent) C.; m. Louise Roberta Hillegas, Apr. 30, 1967; children: William Brent, Amy Louise. BA, Columbia Union Coll., 1969; MA, Andrews U., 1971; DDS, Loma Linda (Calif.) U., 1983. Pastor Ohio Conf. SDA Ch., Kettering, 1969-73, SE Calif. Conf. U. Ch., Loma Linda, 1974-80; pvt. practice Yucaipa, Calif., 1983—. Mem. ADA (internat. svc. award 1983), Columbia Union Coll. Alumni Assn. (pres. 1983—), Calif. Dental Assn., TriCounty Dental Assn., Assn. Adventist Forums, Andrew Soc. for Religious Studies. Home: 11422 Loma Vista Dr Loma Linda CA 92354 Office: Bryant Profl Ctr 11834 Bryant St Ste 101 Yucaipa Valley CA 92399

COFIELD, PHILIP THOMAS, educational association administrator; b. Monmouth, Ill., July 3, 1951; s. Earl Crescant and Vera (Shunick) C.; m. Louise Ann Trapkus, June 13, 1981; children: Calla, Megan. BA in English, St. Ambrose U., 1973. Dir. Jr. Achievment of Quad Cities, Davenport, Moline, Iowa, Ill., 1980-83; account exec. Jr. Achievment Inc., 1983-85; pres. Jr. Achievment of Utah, Salt Lake City, 1985—. Mem. Utah Coun. on Economic Edn. (bd. dirs.), Salt Lake area C. of C., Rotary Club, (com. co-chmn. Salt Lake City). Office: Jr Achievment of Utah 182 S 600 E Salt Lake City UT 84102

COGAN, RONALD JAMES, writer, editor, producer; b. Cleve., Dec. 5, 1952; s. John Patrick and Alice Marie (Zollner) C.; m. Sheree K. Gardner, Nov. 20, 1982; children: Stefanie, Caitlin. Student, Calif. State Poly. U., Pomona, 1971-74. Staff writer newsletter Biomed. Safety and Standards, City of Industry, Calif., 1974; sr. staff writer Select Promotions, Irvine, Calif., 1975; sr. editor Petersen's Vans and Pickups/4 Wheel and Off-Road/Hot Rod Specialty Publs., Los Angeles, 1977-80; editor Custom Rodder mag., Anaheim, Calif., 1980; prin. R.J. Cogan and Assocs., Montclair, Calif., 1980—; editor Petersen Specialty Publs., 1982-89; feature editor Motor Trend mag., 1989—; prin. Level One Prodns., Rancho Cucamonga, Calif., 1987—; cons. to mags. Editor: Hot Rod's Kit Car Ann. #2, 1981, Hot Rod's VW Classics Ann. #1, 1981, Petersen's Big Book of Volkswagens, 1981, Motor Trend's Road Tests, 1986—, Motor Trend's Truck and Van Buyer's Guide, 1986—, Musclecar Classics, 1986-87, 4 Wheel and Off-Road Ann., 1986-88, Car Craft Ann., 1986-88, RV Wheels Afield, 1988.

COGBURN, MARTIN ARTHUR, accountant, real estate broker; b. Fancy Hill, Ark.; s. Francis Marion and Mary Isabell (Beezeley) C.; student U. Calif. at Berkeley, 1932-34; BS, Golden Gate U., 1940; grad. Realtors Inst.; m. Metta Naomi Stockdal, Feb. 18, 1956; children: Martin Arthur, Thomas Stockdal; children from previous marriage: Robert F., Nancy Ann. Instr., Golden Gate U., 1945-49; accountant, San Francisco, 1944—; prin. Cogburn Comml. Brokerage, San Francisco, 1963—, Cogburn Mortgage & Investment Co., San Francisco, 1963—. Councilman, City of Lafayette (Calif.), 1968-70; treas. Springhill Valley Assn., 1967; pres. Lafayette-Morage-Orinda Republican Assembly, 1967-68, 1970-73, congressional dist. state dir., 1971-73. C.P.A., Calif.; cert. comml. investment mem. Realtors Nat. Mktg. Inst. Mem. Calif. Soc. C.P.A.s, Calif., Nat. assns. realtors, San Francisco Bd. Realtors, Contra Costa Bd. Realtors, Sierra Club, Tower and Flame, Beta Alpha Phi. Republican. Clubs: Commonwealth, Masons, Shriners. Home: 3447 Black Hawk Rd Lafayette CA 94549 Office: 1910 Olympic Blvd Ste 314 Walnut Creek CA 94596

COGGIN, CHARLOTTE JOAN, cardiologist, educator; b. Takoma Park, Md., Aug. 6, 1928; d. Charles Benjamin and Nanette (McDonald) Coggin; BA, Columbia Union Coll., 1948; MD, Loma Linda U., 1952, MPH, 1987; Intern, Los Angeles County Gen. Hosp., Los Angeles, 1952-53, resident in medicine, 1953-55; fellow in cardiology Children's Hosp., Los Angeles, 1955-56, White Meml. Hosp., Los Angeles., 1955-56; research assoc. in cardiology, house physician Hammersmith Hosp., London, 1956-57; resident in pediatrics and pediatric cardiology Hosp. for Sick Children, Toronto, Ont., Can., 1965-67; cardiologist, co-dir. heart surgery team Loma Linda (Calif.) U., asst. prof. medicine , 1961-73, asso. prof., 1973—, asst. dean Sch. Medicine Internat. Programs, 1973-75, assoc. dean, 1975—, co-dir., cardiologist heart surgery team missions to Pakistan and Asia, 1963, Greece, 67, 69, Saigon, Vietnam, 1974, 75, to Saudi Arabia, 1976-87, China, 1984, Hong Kong, 1985, Zimbabwe, 1988, Kenya, 1988; mem. Pres's. Advisory Panel on Heart Disease, 1972—. Apptd. Med. Quality Rev. Com.-Dist. 12, 1976-80. Recipient award for service to people of Pakistan City of Karachi, 1963, Medallion award Evangelismos Hosp., Athens, Greece, 1967, Gold medal of health South Vietnam Ministry of Health, 1974, Charles Elliott Weinger award for excellence, 1976, Wall Street Jour. Achievement award, 1987; named Honored Alumnus Loma Linda U. Sch. Medicine, 1973, Outstanding Women in Gen. Conf. Seventh-day Adventists, 1975, Alumnus of Yr., Columbia Union Coll., 1984. Diplomate Am. Bd. Pediatrics. Mem. Am. Coll. Cardiology, AMA (physicians adv. com. 1969—) Calif. Med. Assn. (com. on med. schs., com. on member services), San Bernardino County Med. Soc. (chmn. communications com. 1975-77, mem. communications com. 1987-88, editor bull. 1975-76), Am. Heart Assn., AAUP, Med. Research Assn. Calif., Calif. Heart Assn., AAUW, Am. Acad. Pediatrics, World Affairs Council, Internat. Platform Assn., Calif. Museum Sci. and Industry MUSES (Outstanding Woman of Year in Sci. 1969), Am. Med. Women's Assn., Loma Linda Sch. Medicine Alumni Assn. (pres. 1978), Alpha Omega Alpha, Delta Omega. Author: Atrial Septal Defects, motion picture (Golden Eagle Cine award and 1st prize Venice Film Festival 1964); contbr. articles to med. jours. Democrat. Home: 11495 Benton St Loma Linda CA 92354 Office: Loma Linda U Med Ctr Loma Linda CA 92354

COGHILL, JOHN B., state senator; b. Fairbanks, Alaska, Sept. 24, 1925; m. Francis Coghill; children: Patricia, John Jr., James, Jerald, Paula, Jefferey. Grad. high sch., Nenana, Alaska. Mem. from senate dist. J Alaska State Legislature, Juneau, 1959-64, 85—; chmn. resources com., chmn. majority caucus, vice chmn. transp., mem. oil and gas com., spl. joint com. on tax policy, nre revenue work group and fin. budget subcommittees on DNR, DEC and fish & game; mayor City of Nenana, 1962-84; sec. Coghill's, Inc., Nenana Fuel Co. Mem. sch. bd., 1948-59; mem. Alaskan territorial Ho. of Reps., 1953, 57, Alaska Constl. Conv., 1955; spl. asst. to gov. State of Alaska, 1967; sec. North Commn., 1968-72; chmn. Alaska Statehood Commn., 1980-83. Sgt. Alaska Command U.S. Army, 1944-46. Mem. Am. Legion, Eagle Hist. Soc., Pioneers of Alaska, VFW, Lions Club, Masons. Office: Office of State Senate State Capitol Juneau AK 99811

COGLEY, SUZANNE MARY, art gallery owner; b. Berkeley, Calif., Dec. 7, 1933; d. Esley Foster Salsbury and Mary-Louise (Fitkin) Hooper; m. Lloyd David Cogley, Dec. 26, 1950; children: Michael, James, William, Thomas, Jack. Grad. high sch., Carmel, Calif. Dir. The Mosaic Gallery, Carmel, 1956-58; co-owner, mgr. Galiban Western Emporium, San Juan Bautista, Calif., 1959-63, Cogley's Klamath Kennels, Klamath Falls, Oreg., 1970-79; prof. dog show handler Klamath Falls, 1972-80; co-trustee Mary-Louise Hooper Trust, N.Y.C., 1970-87; sec., estimator Cogley Enterprises, Klamath Falls, 1979-85; sec., treas. Wiramal Corp., Klamath Falls, 1982-84; owner, mgr. Cogley Art Ctr., Klamath Falls, 1985—; judge Photo Contest, Audoban Soc. High Sch. Art Show, Klamath Falls; bd. dirs. Klamath Arts Coun. Art Show, 1988. Editor: newsletters Klamath Dog Prints, 1972-79, For Art's Sake, 1985—; writer monthly column Gallery News for Herald and News. Mem. San Juan Bautista C. of C., Klamath County C. of C., Klamath Dog Fanciers (pres. 1972-75, bd. dirs. 1975-78), Klamath Arts Coun. (bd. dirs. 1987—), Klamath Art Assn., Am. Chespeake (nat. bd. dirs. 1979-82), Irish Water Spaniel. Republican. Home: 6210 Cherry Way Klamath Falls OR 97063 Office: Cogley Art Ctr 4035 S 6th St Klamath Falls OR 97603

COHAN, MARC PHILIP, accountant; b. Indpls., Nov. 27, 1953; s. Edwin Harold and Lorraine (Wexler) C. BS in Acctg., San Diego State U., 1976. CPA, Calif. Fin. analyst Handyman of Calif., Inc., San Diego, 1972-77; contr. Sandico, Inc., El Cajon, Calif., 1977-79; staff acct. Steres, Alpert & Carne, CPA's, San Diego, 1979-80; with Sussman & Siegel CPA's, 1980-83; pvt. practice San Diego, 1983—. Mem. Am. Inst. CPA's, Calif. Soc. CPA's. Democrat. Jewish. Office: 1033 Grand Ave Ste B San Diego CA 92109

COHEN, DANIEL MORRIS, museum administrator, marine biology researcher; b. Chgo., July 6, 1930; s. Leonard U. and Myrtle (Gertz) C.; m. Anne Carolyn Constant, Nov. 4, 1955; children—Carolyn A., Cynthia S. B.A., Stanford U., 1952, M.A., 1953, Ph.D., 1958. Asst. prof., curator fishes U. Fla., Gainesville, 1957-58; systematic zoologist Bur. Comml. Fisheries, Washington, 1958-60; dir. systematics lab. Nat. Marine Fisheries Service, Washington, 1960-81; sr. scientist Nat. Marine Fisheries Service, Seattle, 1981-82; chief curator life scis. Los Angeles County Mus. of Natural History, Los Angeles, 1982—; adj. prof. biology U. So. Calif., 1982—. Contbr. numerous articles to profl. jours. Fellow AAAS; mem. Am. Soc. Ichthyologists and Herpetologists (v.p. 1969, 70, pres. 1985), Biol. Soc. Washington (pres. 1971-72), Soc. Systematic Zoology (mem. council 1976-78). Home: 3667 Greve Dr Rancho Palos Verdes CA 90274 Office: Los Angeles County Mus Nat History 900 Exposition Blvd Los Angeles CA 90007

COHEN, DAVID ANDREW, naval officer; b. N.Y.C., Aug. 31, 1962; s. Robert Irwin and Marjorie E. (Winneg) C. BA in Econs., U. Rochester, 1984. Commd. lt. U.S. Navy, 1984; machinery div. officer, then communications officer USS Fox U.S. Navy, San Diego, 1985-87; adminstrv. officer USS St. Louis U.S. Navy, Sasebo, Japan, 1988--. Mem. U.S. Naval Inst., Nat. Eagle Scout Assn. Jewish.

COHEN, DAVID WALTER, health facility administrator; b. Bklyn., Oct. 18, 1947; s. Stanley Martin and Evelyn (Lang) C.; m. Dorene Ann Sanders, May 8, 1983. BA, Rutgers U., 1969; MA, U. Redlands, 1986. Blood bank officer U.S. Naval Hosp., St. Albans, N.Y., 1971-73; lab. officer U.S. Naval Hosp., Groton, Conn., 1974; student sch. blood bank tech. Irwin Meml. Blood Bank, San Francisco, 1975; blood bank supr. Valley Children's Hosp., Fresno, Calif., 1976-78; supr. reference and cons. lab. Blood Bank San Bernardino and Riverside Counties (Calif.), 1978—; surg. bone bank coordinator Blood Bank San Bernadino and Riverside Counties (Calif.), 1988; restaurant critic Sta. KDUO Radio, San Bernadino, Calif., 1987—. Dining out columnist The Press Enterprise, Riverside, 1986-88; restaurant editor: Inland Bus. Mag., 1986—; author: (with others) Laboratory Investigation of Hemolytic Transfusion Reactions, 1982; contbr. articles to profl. jours., newspapers, and popular mags. Lt. USNR, 1971-74; capt. USAFR, 1985—. Mem. Am. Assn. Blood Banks (inspector 1978—), Calif. Blood Bank Soc. (chmn. sci. program com. 1988—), So. Calif. Restaurant Writers (chmn. familiarization, 1987, trips 1987—), Internat. Food, Wine & Travel Writers, Am. Inst. Wine & Food. Jewish. Office: Blood Bank San Bernardino & Riverside Counties PO Box 5729 San Bernardino CA 92412

COHEN, DEAN BRIAN, dentist, military officer; b. Springfield, Mass., Dec. 3, 1959; s. Shepard and Arlene Sylvia (Cohen) C. BS in Biology, Syracuse (N.Y.) U., 1981, BA in Psychology, 1981; DMD, Tufts U., 1985. Sec. Gamma chpt. Alpha Omega Dental Fraternity, Boston, 1984-85; chief dental resident Western Mass. Hosp., Westfield, 1985-86; dental officer Long Beach (Calif.) Dental Clinic, 1986-89; support instr. cordiopulmonary Long Beach Naval Dental Clinic, 1987-89. Counselor dentistry merit badge com. Boy Scouts Am., South Bay of L.A., 1987—; active Vol. Jewish Big Brother Com. of Greater L.A., 1987—, mem. vol. com.; interviewer Tufts Alumni Asst. Program, L.A., 1988—. Recipient Brotherhood award Jewish War Vets. USA, 1977, Cert. Appreciation, Jewish Big Bros. Greater L.A., 1987, Trophy Jewish Big Bros. Greater L.A., 1988. Fellow Acad. Gen. Dentistry; mem. ADA, Alpha Omega Dental, Table Tennis (N.Y.C.). Home: 20 Club View Ln Rolling Hills Estate CA 90274 Office: Long Beach Naval Sta Long Beach Naval Dental Clinic Long Beach CA 90822-5096

COHEN, EDITH TARTASKY, travel consultant; b. Bklyn., July 2, 1953; d. Sol and Sarah (Ornstein) Tartasky; m. Gerard Dominique Cohen, Feb. 15, 1978. BA in Linguistics, SUNY, Binghamton, 1975. Travel agt. Wayfarer Travel Agy., Bklyn., 1967-71, Am. Express Co., N.Y.C., 1973, Murray's Tours & Travel, Los Angeles, 1975, Architects of Travel, Beverly Hills, Calif., 1975-76, Travel Ctr. Pasadena (Calif.), 1978-83, The Travel Corner (formerly Ask Mr. Foster-Travel Corner), Montrose, Calif., 1984—; reservationist, ship dispatcher Princess Cruises, Los Angeles, 1976-77. N.Y. State Regents scholar, 1970. Mem. B'nai B'rith Women (treas. Verdugo Hills, Calif., 1986-88). Democrat. Jewish. Office: The Travel Corner 2200 Honolulu Ave Montrose CA 91020

COHEN, ELAINE L., college dean; b. Phila., Nov. 7, 1939; d. Herman and Goldie (Greenberg) Linenberg; m. George Harris Cohen, June 19, 1960; children: Sheryl L. Greenberg, Jeffrey Michael, Jonathan Marc. BS in Edn., U. Pa., 1960; MEd in Adminstrn. and Supervision, Trinity U., 1969; EdD in Orgn. and Leadership, U. San Francisco, 1978. Tchr. Lower Merion, Pa., 1960-63, Wyndmoore, Pa., 1966-67; tchr. San Antonio Unified Sch. Dist., 1968-69, Laguna Salada Sch. Dist., Pacifica, Calif., 1969-70, Millbrae (Calif.) Sch. Dist., 1970-74; instr., supr. student tchrs. U. San Francisco, 1974-77; from instr. adminstrn. and tchr. edn. to prof. Coll. Notre Dame, Belmont, Calif., 1975-84; dir. MPA program Coll. Notre Dame, Belmont, 1980-84, acting head dept. edn., summer 1981, dean Grad. Sch., 1984--; presenter in field; mem. task force on women Council Grad. Schs., 1984--. Mem. Upper Peninsula League bd. San Francisco Symphony, 1972—; founding bd. dirs. Hillsborough Schs. Found., 1980-82; trustee Mills-Peninsula Hosp. Found., 1986—; assoc. trustee pres.' coun. U. Pa., 1989—; chmn. San Francisco Bay Area secondary schs. com. U. Pa., 1982—. Mem. AAUW (chmn. ednl. found. program 1983), Am. Bus. Women's Assn. (founding Hilsborough chpt., ednl. chmn.) San Mateo County Med. Aux. (pres. 1979-80, chmn. computer program 1984), Phi Delta Kappa (organizer Coll. Notre Dame chpt., pres.). Republican. Jewish. Home: 1350 Brandt Rd Hillsborough CA 94010 Office: Coll Notre Dame 1500 Ralston Ave Belmont CA 94002

COHEN, JEREMY BENJAMIN, real estate executive, former professional tennis player; b. Chgo., Feb. 13, 1955; s. Robert Irwin and Shifrette Diane (Bode) C.; m. Marscee Beth Kaden, Oct. 29, 1978; children: Brandon, Jordan. Student, Ariz. State U., 1973-77. Lic. real estate broker, mortgage broker. Profl. tennis player Assn. Tennis Profls., 1977-81; World Team Tennis player Phoenix Sunsets, 1982; sales assoc. The August Group, Scottsdale, Ariz., 1982-85; v.p. Provident Properties, Inc., Tempe, Ariz., 1985-88; pres. Jeremar Corp., Scottsdale, Ariz., 1988—; instr. Ariz. Sch. Real Estate, Scottsdale, 1983—. Chmn. Fiesta Bowl Invitaional Tennis Tournament. Mem. Nat. Realtor Assn., Ariz. Realtor Assn. Jewish. Office: Jeremar Corp 8580 E Thoroughbred Tr Scottsdale AZ 85258

COHEN, JON STEPHAN, lawyer; b. Omaha, Nov. 9, 1943; s. Louis H. and Bertha N. (Goldstein) C.; m. Maxine B. Turetsky, Dec. 1, 1968; children: Carolyn, Sherri, Barbara. Student, London Sch. Econs., 1963-64; BA, Claremont Men's Coll. (now Claremont McKenna Coll.), 1965; JD, Harvard U., 1968. Bar: Ariz. 1968. Assoc. Snell & Wilmer, Phoenix, 1968-73, ptnr., 1973—; bd. dirs. Lincoln Laser Co., Phoenix, Vika Corp., Phoenix, Lex Mundi, Houston. Fellow Ariz. Bar Found.; mem. ABA, Ariz. Bar Assn., Maricopa County Bar Assn., Village Tennis Club, La Mancha Athletic Club. Home: 5318 N 46th St Phoenix AZ 85018 Office: Snell & Wilmer 3100 Valley Bank Ctr Phoenix AZ 85073

COHEN, JOYCE E., state senator, investment executive; b. McIntosh, S.D., Mar. 27, 1937; d. Joseph and Evelyn (Sampson) Petik; children: Julia Jo, Aaron J. Grad., Coll. Med. Tech., Minn., 1955; student, UCLA, Minn., 1957-78, Santa Ana Coll., Minn., 1961-62. Med. rsch. technician dept. surgery U. Minn., 1955-58; dept. tech. U. Calif., 1958-59, dept. bacteriology, 1959-61; med. rsch. scientist Allergan Pharms., Santa Ana, Calif., 1961-70; ptnr. Co-Fo Investments, Lake Oswego, Oreg., 1978—; mem. Oreg. Ho. of Reps., from 1979, now state senator. Mem. Jud. Com., Ho. of Reps. and Senate, 1979—, chmn. 1989—; mem. banking and pub. fin. com., Ho. of Reps. and Seante, 1981—; co-chmn. Joint Trade and Econ. Devel. coms., 1985-87; mem. hazardous waste com., agr. and nat. resources coms., environ. and energy coms., housing and urban devel. coms., ins. and arson coms. task force on ethics; chmn. Vet.'s Task Force; chmn. jud. com.; vice chmn. trade and econ. devel. and health ins. and biologic coms.; mem. Oreg. Criminal Justice Coun.; mem. Jud. Br. State Energy Policy Rev. Com., 1979; mem. Gov.'s Commn on child Support. Woodrow Wilson Lecture series fellow, 1988. Mem. Assn. Family Conciliation Cts., Citizens Coun. of Cts., LWV, Oreg. Environ. Coun., Oreg. Women's Polit. Caucus. Democrat. Office: Oreg State Senate State Capitol Salem OR 97310

COHEN, JULIUS MILTON, retired association executive; b. Rochester, N.Y., Feb. 14, 1914; s. Abraham V. and Lillian (Pontesof) C.; BA, Cornell U., 1935; postgrad. Rochester Bus. Inst., 1939, Columbia, 1943, U. N.C., 1948, Stanford, 1954; m. Sophie Katz, Feb. 14, 1956. Mng. editor, columnist Jewish Ledger Publs., Rochester, 1935-43; area dir. U.S.O.-Nat. Jewish Welfare Bd., 1943-63, So. Calif. area, Los Angeles, 1952-63; community devel. dir. Gateways Hosp., Los Angeles, 1963-65; exec. dir. Western region Am. Jewish Congress Los Angeles, 1965-81, ret., 1981; investment officer

Am. Savs. & Loan, Seal Beach, 1984-89, Union Fed., Seal Beach, 1989—. Mem. Los Angeles City Atty.'s Task Force Nursing Home Reform, 1972-74; bd. dirs. Inter-racial Council Bus. Opportunity, 1966-78, Bus. Devel. Center, 1979—, North Seal Beach Sr. Citizens Ctr., 1981—; pres. council presidents Pacific S.W. region United Synagogue Am., 1984—; pres. Leisure World Congregation Sholom, 1981-84. Recipient USMC award, Los Angeles, 1960; 6th Army award, 1963; Gateways award, 1965; City of Los Angeles Bicentennial Salute, 1980; 40th Anniversary award USO, 1981, Adv. Council award for disting. service to sr. citizens of Orange County, 1983, others; Disting. Service award Leisure World Congregation Sholom, 1985, Mem. Nat. Assn. Jewish Center Workers (past pres. Western states sect.), Acad. Certified Social Workers (charter), Nat. Assn. Social Workers (charter), Nat. Assn. Inter-Group Relations Ofcls. (v.p. So. Calif.), Assn. for Study Community Orgn. (sec.). Mem. B'nai B'rith (past pres. Rochester, Distinguished Service award 1961). Columnist Seal Beach Jour., Huntington Harbour Sun, 1981-86, Orange County Register, 1987—. Home: 13200 Del Monte Dr Seal Beach CA 90740

COHEN, KENNETH BRUCE, hospital administrator; b. Springfield, Mass., Jan. 19, 1950; s. Samuel A. and Shirley F. (Austin) C.; m. Deborah F. Roberts, Aug. 3, 1975; children: Kimberly A., Lauren B., Meredith L. BS, Ithaca Coll., 1971; M in Hosp. Adminstrn., George Washington U., 1975. Budget dir. Meml. Hosp., Hollywood, Fla., 1976-77; asst. adminstr. Meml. Hosp., Hollywood, 1977-78, sr. asst. adminstr., 1978-83; chief ops. officer Hollywood (Fla.) Med. Ctr., 1983-85; adminstr. Riverside (Calif.) Gen. Hosp., 1985—. Mem. Health Planning and Devel Council, Fla., 1985, bd. Nursing Home Adminstrs., Fla., 1981-84. Mem. Health Care Fin. Mgmt. Assn., Am. Hosp. Assn., Calif. Hosp. Assn., Calif. Assn. Pub. Hosps., Nat. Assn. Pub. Hosps., Am. Coll. Health Care Execs. Home: 5342 Lescoe Ct Riverside CA 92503 Office: Riverside Gen Hosp 9851 Magnolia Ave Riverside CA 92506

COHEN, LEONARD, hospital management company executive; b. 1925; married. BS, UCLA, 1948; LLB, Loyola U., 1951. Ptnr. Ervin, Cohen & Jessup, 1952-68; with Nat. Med. Enterprises, Los Angeles, 1968—, pres., chief operating officer, 1983—, now also vice-chmn., dir. With U.S. Army, 1942-46. Office: Nat Med Enterprises Inc 11620 Wilshire Blvd Los Angeles CA 90025

COHEN, MICHAEL HARRIS, computer scientist; b. Bklyn., Mar. 20, 1953; s. Paul and Henrietta (Precker) C. BMus, Berklee Coll. Music, Boston, 1977; MS, Boston U., 1983; PhD, U. Calif., Berkeley, 1989. Composer, musician, conductor Boston, San Francisco, 1974—; sci. systems analyst Tufts-New Eng. Med. Ctr., Boston, 1980-83; computer scientist SRI, Internat., Menlo Park, Calif., 1984—; cons. in field; organizer computer music seminar series, U. Calif.-Berkeley, 1985-87. Contbr. articles to sci. jours.; composer, conductor, guitarist 3 record albums. Mem. IEEE, Assn. Computing Machinery, Assn. Computational Linguistics. Democrat. Home: 1032 Henderson Ave Menlo Park CA 94025 Office: SRI Internat 333 Ravenswood Ave Menlo Park CA 94025

COHEN, RANDAL LEE, air force officer; b. March AFB, Calif., Jan. 13, 1953; s. Herbert Jack and Virginia Eloise (Carson) C.; m. Linda Evonne Huber, June 12, 1976; children: Timothy Lee, Brian Douglas, Christopher Sean. BSEE, U. Wash., 1977; MSEE, Northrop U., Inglewood, Calif., 1987. Systems test engr. Boeing Aerospace Co., Seattle, 1977-78; commd. USAF, 1979, advanced through grades to capt., to date; mgr. spacecraft ops. Air Force Satellite Control Facility, Onizuka AFB, Colo., 1979-82; integration engr. Air Force Satellite Control Facility, 1982-83; chief elec. engr. payload br. SAF/Spl. Projects, Los Angeles AFB, 1983-87; dep. chief Tencap div. Air Force Space Command, Peterson AFB, Colo., 1987—. Home: 1224 Piros Dr Colorado Springs CO 80922

COHEN, SEYMOUR I., lawyer; b. N.Y.C., Apr. 15, 1931; s. Fred and Nettie (Sederer) C.; m. Rhoda Goldner, July 22, 1956; children: Cheryl Lynn, Marcy Ann, Lori Beth. BBA cum laude, CCNY, 1951; LLB, Bklyn. Law Sch., 1954, JD, 1967; MBA, NYU, 1960. Bar: N.Y. 1954, Calif. 1973, U.S. Dist. Ct. (cen. dist.) Calif., U.S. Ct. Appeals (9th cir.), U.S. Tax Ct., U.S. Supreme Ct.; CPA, Ohio, Calif. Staff acct. S.D. Leidesdorf, N.Y.C., 1958-61; mgr., acct. Rockwell, Columbus, Ohio, and L.A., 1961-69; mgr. contracts Logicon, L.A., 1970-71; mgr. internal audit Daylin, 1971-72; controller NYSE Co., 1972-73; pvt. practice, Torrance, Calif., 1973—. Mem. AICPA, Los Angeles County Bar Assn. (appellate ct. com. 1979—, svcs. com. 1981-82), S. Bay Bar Assn. (pres. 1986-87, chmn. referral svc. 1977-81), State Bar Calif. (client trust fund commr. 1983, 84), Ohio Inst. CPAs, N.Y. Inst. CPAs, Calif. Inst. CPAs, Nat. Assn. Accts., L.A. Trial Lawyers Assn., N.Y. State Bar Assn., Calif. State Bar Assn. Jewish. Republican. Home: 30691 Via La Cresta Rancho Palos Verdes CA 90274 Office: 18411 Crenshaw Blvd #411 Torrance CA 90504

COHEN, STANLEY NORMAN, geneticist, educator; b. Perth Amboy, N.J., Feb. 17, 1935; s. Bernard and Ida (Stolz) C.; m. Joanna Lucy Wolter, June 27, 1961; children: Anne, Geoffrey. B.A., Rutgers U., 1956; M.D., U. Pa., 1960. Intern, Mt. Sinai Hosp., N.Y.C., 1960-61; resident Univ. Hosp., Ann Arbor, Mich., 1961-62; clin. asso. arthritis and rheumatism br. Nat. Inst. Arthritis and Metabolic Diseases, Bethesda, Md., 1962-64; sr. resident in medicine Duke U. Hosp., Durham, N.C., 1964-65; Am. Cancer Soc. postdoctoral research fellow Albert Einstein Coll. Medicine, Bronx, 1965-67, asst. prof. devel. biology and cancer, 1967-68; mem. faculty Stanford (Calif.) U., 1968—, prof. medicine, 1975—, prof. genetics, 1977, chmn. dept. genetics, 1978-86; mem. com. recombinant DNA molecules Nat. Acad. Sci.-NRC, 1974; mem. com. on genetic experimentation Internat. Council Sci. Unions, 1977—. Mem. editorial bd.: Jour. Bacteriology, 1973-79; asso. editor: Plasmid, 1977-86. Served with USPHS, 1962-64. Guggenheim fellow, 1975; Josiah Macy Jr. Found. faculty scholar, 1975-76; recipient Burroughs Wellcome Scholar award, 1970, Mattia award Roche Inst. Molecular Biology, 1977, Albert Lasker basic med. research award, 1980, Wolf prize, 1981, Marvin J. Johnson award, 1981, Disting. Grad. award U. Pa. Sch. Medicine, 1986, Disting. Service award Miami Winter Symposium, 1986, LVMH Institut de la Vie prize, 1988, Nat. Medal of Sci., 1988, City of Medicine award, 1988. Mem. Nat. Acad. Sci., Inst. Medicine, Am. Acad. Arts and Sci., Am. Soc. Biol. Chemists, Genetics Soc. Am., Am. Soc. Microbiology (Cetus award 1988), Am. Soc. Pharmacology and Exptl. Therapeutics, Am. Soc. Clin. Investigation, Phi Beta Kappa, Sigma Xi, Alpha Omega Alpha. Office: Stanford U Sch Med Dept Genetics S-337 Stanford CA 94305

COHEN, STEPHEN MICHAEL, physician's assistant; b. Washington, Dec. 27, 1957; s. Herbert Jay and Lucille (Walter) C. Cert. emergency med. tech, Santa Fe Community Coll., Gainesville, Fla., 1978, AA, cert. paramedic, 1981; BS in Allied Health, U. Ala., 1984. Firefighter, paramedic City of Gainesville Fire Dept., 1980-81; hyperbaric chamber diver, critical care technician Shard's Hosp., U. Fla., Gainesville, 1981-82; paramedic instr. Santa Fe Community Coll., 1981-82; surg. and trauma physician's asst. Halifax Hosp. Med. Ctr., Daytona Beach, Fla., 1985-86; surg. and orthopedics physician's asst. U. Ala., Birmingham, 1986-88; surg. physician's asst. Maui Plastic Surgery, Kahului, Hawaii, 1988—; instr. anatomy and physiology, Maui Acad. Healing Arts, 1989—. Author poetry. Mem., sponsor Pacific Whale Found., Maui, 1988—. Fellow Am. Assn. Physician's Assts. (bd. sec. Birmingham chpt. 1987-88, vice chmn. surg. coun. nat. 1987), Am. Assn. Surgeons Assts. (sec. 1985-86), Hawaii Assn. Physician Assts.; mem. Magic City Triathlon Club, Maui Macintosh Users Group, Maui Humane Soc., Phi Kappa Phi. Office: PO Box 2291 Kihei HI 96753

COHN, LAWRENCE STEVEN, physician, educator; b. Chgo., Dec. 21, 1945; s. Jerome M. and Francis C.; BS, U. Ill., 1967, MD, 1971; m. Harriett G. Rubin, Sept. 1, 1968; children: Allyson and Jennifer (twins). Intern, Mt. Zion Hosp., San Francisco, 1971-72, resident, 1972-73; resident U. Chgo., 1973-74; practice medicine specializing in internal medicine, Paramount, Calif.; pres. med. staff Charter Suburban Hosp., 1981-83; mem. staff Long Beach Meml. Hosp., Harbor Gen. Hosp; assoc. clin. prof. medicine UCLA. Maj. USAF, 1974-76. Recipient Disting. Teaching award Harbor-UCLA Med. Ctr., 1980; diplomate Am. Bd. Internal Medicine. Mem. A.C.P., AMA, Calif. Med. Assn., L.A. County Med. Assn., Am. Heart Assn., Soc. Air Force Physicians, Phi Beta Kappa, Phi Kappa Phi, Phi Lambda Upsilon, Phi Eta Sigma, Alpha Omega Alpha. Home: 6608 Via LaPaloma Rancho Palos Verdes CA 90274 Office: 16243 Colorado Ave Paramount CA 90723

COHN, MILTON HERBERT, JR., financial analyst, consultant; b. West Point, Ga., Sept. 30, 1948; s. Milton Herbert Sr. and Jean (Herzfeld) C.; m. Janet Frank, Oct. 11, 1973; children: Jenoa M., J. Michael. BA, U. Colo., 1970; MA, West Ga. Coll., 1973. CLU, chartered fin. cons. Coord. Am. Found. for Sci., L.A., 1973-76; assoc. Capital Analysts, Inc., Bethlehem, Pa., 1976-82; prin. Engle, Erickson, Garson, Gold & Cohn Ltd., Phoenix, 1082-87; pres., chief exec. officer The Cohn Fin. Group, Inc., Phoenix, 1987—; mem. exec. com. Fidelity Mut. Life Ins. Co., Radnor, Pa., 1980, 83-85, 87, Nat. Security Reassurance Co., Phoenix, 1986—. Contbr. articles to profl. jours. Mem. Family Firm Inst., Internat. Assn. Fin. Planners, Ariz. Estate Planning Coun. Jewish. Office: The Cohn Fin Group Inc 5058 N 40th St Ste 235 Phoenix AZ 85018

COIT, R. KEN, financial planner; b. L,A., Aug. 26, 1943; s. Roger L. and Thelma D. C.; BS, U. Ariz., 1967; MBA, Pepperdine U., 1981; m. Donna M. Schemanske, Oct. 8, 1977; children—Kristin M., Shannon, Darren, Lauryn. Co-founder, pres. Coit-Gemmer Fin. Inc., 1981; mem. adj. faculty Coll. Fin. Planning, Denver, 1978-79; pres. Walnut Creek adv. bd. Summit Bank, 1987—. Mem. dean's adv. bd. Pepperdine U., 1988—; bd. dirs., mem. investment com. East Community Found. Recipient Outstanding Alumnus award Pepperdine U. Sch. Bus. and Mgmt., 1986. Mem. Internat. Assn. Fin. Planners (chpt. pres. 1978-79), Inst. Cert. Fin. Planners, Am. Investors Co., East Bay Gourmet Club, Blackhawk Country Club. Office: 1655 N Main St Ste 270 Walnut Creek CA 94596

COKER, MARCIA LEE, college administrator; b. Atascadero, Calif., Sept. 18, 1944; d. Keith Allen and Nita (Chard) Burbidge; m. Alan Wayne Myers, Sept. 18, 1971 (div. 1982); m. Gary Lynn Coker, Feb. 13, 1987. BA, U. Calif., Santa Barbara, Calif., 1966, MA, 1968. Instr. Marymount High Sch., Santa Barbara, 1968-69, Clackamas Community Coll., Oregon City, Oreg., 1969-84; com. adminstr. Oreg. State Legisl. Assembly, Salem, 1981, 1983; dept. chmn. Clackamas Community Coll., Oregon City, 1984-88, asst. dean, 1988--. Mem. Am. Soc. Tng. and Devel., Milw. Rotary Internat. Democrat. Home: 3566 Halifax Sq SE 13 Salem OR 97302 Office: Clackamas Community Coll 19600 S Molalla Ave Oregon City OR 97045

COLANGELO, JERRY JOHN, professional sports executive; b. Chicago Heights, Ill., Nov. 20, 1939; s. Larry and Sue (Drancek) C.; m. Joan E. Helmich, Jan. 20, 1961; children: Kathy, Kristen, Bryan. B.A., U. Ill., 1962. Partner House of Charles, Inc., 1962-63; assoc. D.O. Klein & Assocs., 1964-65; dir. merchandising Chgo. Bulls basketball club, 1966-68; gen. mgr. Phoenix Suns basketball club, 1968-87, now also exec. v.p., until 1987, pres., chief exec. officer, 1987—. Mem. Basketball Congress Am. (exec. v.p., dir.), Phi Kappa Psi. Republican. Baptist. Clubs: University, Phoenix Execs. Office: Phoenix Suns 2910 N Central Ave PO Box 1369 Phoenix AZ 85012 *

COLBERT, ELBERT LYNN, dentist, recording artist; b. Stillwater, Okla., July 11, 1952; s. Oscar James and Hazel Elizabeth (Summit) C.; m. Denise Annette Wilson (div. July 1980); m. Gayla Janyce Burpo, Feb. 27, 1982; 1 child, Shane Michael Cheatham. BS in Pre-Medicine, Okla. State U., 1976; DMD cum laude, Washington U., 1977. Pvt. practice dentistry Woodward, Okla., 1977-82, Bear Creek Dental Group, Boulder, Colo., 1982—. Composer, musician, producer Zuriel the Rock of God, 1987, Crown of Thorns, 1986; composer, producer, singer First Born, 1985, Delorean's Ride/Lead the Way, 1984, Flyers, 1978-82. Regional coordinator Am. Student Dental Assn., midwestern states, 1976-77. Mem. Omicron Kappa Upsilon, Alpha Epsilon Delta. Home: 4445 Squires Circle Boulder CO 80303 Office: 3400 Table Mesa Dr Boulder CO 80303

COLBERT, LESTER LUM, JR., technology company executive; b. Detroit, Feb. 6, 1934; s. Lester Lum Sr. and Daisy (Gorman) C. AB, Princeton U., 1955; MBA, Harvard U., 1961. V.p., dir. Reichhold Chemicals, Inc., White Plains, N.Y., 1961-72; chmn., pres., chief exec. officer Xidex Corp., Palo Alto, Calif., 1972-87, chmn., 1987-88. Bd. dirs. Castle Convertible Fund, N.Y.C., 1974—. Lt. (j.g.) USN, 1955-57. Mem. Bohemian Club, Knickerbocker Club, Phi Beta Kappa. Office: care Am Indsl Ptnrs 1 Maritime Pla 23rd Fl San Francisco CA 94111

COLBURN, GENE LEWIS, insurance and industrial psychology consultant; b. Bismarck, N.D., July 12, 1932; s. Lewis William and Olga Alma (Feland) C.; PhD, UCLA, 1982. Pres., gen. mgr. Multiple Lines Ins. Agy., Auburn, Wash., 1953-79; ins. and risk mgmt. cons., Auburn, Wash., 1980—; pres. Feland Safe Deposit Corp.; bd. dirs. Century Service Corp. sub. Capital Savs. Bank, Olympia, Wash.; mem. exec. com. Great Republic Life Ins. Co., Portland, Oreg., 1971-75; mem. Wash. State Ins. Commrs. Test Devel. Com., 1986—. cons. indsl. risk mgmt. and psychology. Councilperson Auburn City, 1982-85; mayor-pro tem, City of Auburn, 1984; co-incorporator, chmn. bd. SE Community Alcohol Ctr., 1971-75; mem. Wash. State Disaster Assistance Council, 1981—, founding mem.; pres. Valley Cities Mental Health Center, 1980; mem. instn. rev. com. Auburn Gen. Hosp., 1978—; prin. trustee Dr. R. B. Bramble Med. Research Found., 1980—; bd. dirs. Wash. Assn. Chs. (Luth. Ch. in Am.), Asian Refugee Resettlement Mgmt. div., 1981-83, Columbia Luth. Home, Seattle, 1985—, Wash. Law Enforcement Officers and Fire Fighter's Pension Disability Bd., Auburn, 1980-84. Cert. ins. counselor, 1978. Recipient Disting. Alumni award Green River Community Coll., 1982. Fellow Acad. Producer Ins. Studies (charter); mem. Internat. Platform Assn. Lodge: Auburn Lions (past pres.). Office: 201 A St NW Auburn WA 98002

COLBURN, HERBERT WILLIAM, financial planner; b. Huntington Park, Calif., Feb. 20, 1926; s. Maurice Eugene and Helen Ernestine (Witmer) C.; m. Barbara Worthen, Feb. 25, 1950; 1 child, Cynthia Anne. BS, U. Calif., Berkeley, 1949. CPCU; cert. fin. planner. Agrl. economist U.S. Bur. Reclamation, Minot, N.D., 1949-50; co-ptnr., ins. broker Colburn & Co., Van Nuys, Calif., 1951-87; owner, mgr. Colburn & Co., 1987-88; fin. planner Titan Capital Corp., Wrightwood, Calif., 1988—. With USAAF, 1944-45. Mem. Internat. Assn. Fin. Planning, Van Nuys C. of C., Sierra Club., Rotary. Christian Scientist. Office: Titan Capital Corp 1751 Outer Hwy 2 Wrightwood CA 92397

COLBURN, PAUL LEROY, healthcare administrator; b. San Pedro, Calif., Mar. 23, 1948; s. Francis Hervey and Lois Katherine (Egner) C.; m. Lorraine Nares, June 1, 1974 (div. Mar. 1982); 1 child, Jessica Lynne; m. Krista Sue Kline, Oct. 9, 1982; children: Sean Michael Kline, Christian Eric Kline. AS, Long Beach City Coll., 1977; BS, U. Phoenix, Costa Mesa, Calif., 1986. Cert. diagnostic radiology, Nat., Calif. Supr. computed tomography Torrance Meml. Hosp. Med. Ctr., Calif., 1978-86; dir. dept. radiology Coastal Communities Hosp., Santa Ana, Calif., 1986—; instr. Long Beach City Coll., Calif., 1987—. Contbr. tech. manual for stereotactic neurosurgery, 1984. With USAF, 1966-68. Mem. Am. Soc. Radiologic Technologists, Calif. Soc. Radiologic Technologists (mem. Nominations Com. 1986-87, sec. and treas. 1987-88, pres. 1988—, 1st place award Technologist Essay Competition 1984). Republican. Lutheran. Home: 15232 Vichy Cir Irvine CA 92714 Office: Coastal Communities Hosp 2701 S Bristol St Santa Ana CA 92704

COLBY, BARBARA DIANE, interior designer, consultant; b. Chgo., Dec. 6, 1932; d. Raymond R. and Mertyl Shirley (Jackson) C.; 1 son, Lawrence James. Student Wright Jr. Coll., 1950, Art Inst. Chgo., UCLA. Owner, F.L.S., Los Angeles, 1971-77; ptnr. Ambiance Inc., Los Angeles, 1976-77; owner Barbara Colby, Ltd., Los Angeles, 1977-81; bus. adminstr. Internat. Soc. Interior Designers, Los Angeles, 1982—; owner Chromanetics, Glendale, Calif., 1981—; instr. Otis/Parsons Sch. Design, Los Angeles Fashion Inst. Design and Merchandising; dir. color Calif. Coll. Interior Design, Costa Mesa, Calif., 1987; also lectr. in field. Contbg. editor Giftware News. Recipient award for Best Children's Room, Chgo. Furniture Show, 1969, award Calif. Design Show '76, 1976. Mem. Am. Soc. Interior Designers (cert.), Color Mktg. Group of U.S., Women's Internat. Network. Contbr. to profl. jours. Home and Office: 101 E Stocker St Glendale CA 91207

COLBY, CAROLYN ANNE, business executive; b. St. Louis; d. Leonard and Iselena Anne Savage. B.S., Edgewood Coll.-St. Mary's Coll., 1970. Head nurse U. Chgo., 1975; clin. specialist Michael Reese Hosp., Chgo., 1976; br. mgr. Kimberly Services Inc., Overland Park, Kans., 1979-80, regional dir., 1980-82, regional mgr., 1982-83, ops. cons., 1983—; exec. dir. Am. Nursing Resources, Marina Del Rey, Calif., 1982—. Mem. Nat. Assn. Female Execs. Buddhist. Office: 4551 Glencoe Stes 215 217 Marina Del Rey CA 90292

COLE, CATHY JOYCE, nurse; b. Wilmington, N.C., Mar. 26, 1953; d. Seymour and Marilyn B. (Sachs) Friedlander; m. Larry Alfred Cole, Apr. 21, 1979. BS in Biology, Rutgers U., 1975; AA in Nursing Sci., Pierce Coll., Woodland Hills, Calif., 1978. Teaching cert., L.A., nurse practitioner cert., L.A. Adminstrv. asst. Adams-Crenshaw Med. Group, L.A., 1976-78; nursing instr. Conejo Unified Sch. Dist., Thousand Oaks, Calif., 1980-81; nurse labor-delivery Valley Presbyn. Hosp., Van Nuys, Calif., 1978-80, clin. educator, 1980-82, childbirth educator, 1980-84; ob-gyn nurse practitioner Jack S. Galloway, M.D., Van Nuys, 1982-84, Facey Med. Group, Inc., Mission Hills, Calif., 1984—; pvt. practice cons., lectr., 1983—. Vol. Am. Cancer Soc., Ventura County, Calif., 1981—; co-founder Gregory Mus., Long Island, N.Y., 1965; sec. Dem. Club Conejo Valley, Thousand Oaks, 1982-85. Recipient Cert. Appreciation Am. Cancer Soc., 1982. Mem. Nurses Assn. of Am. Coll. Obstetricians and Gynecologists (cert. nurse practitioner), Calif. Coalition Nurse Practitioners (sec. 1982-83), AAUW. Jewish. Office: Facey Med Group Inc 11211 Sepulveda Blvd Mission Hills CA 91345

COLE, CHRISTOPHER ANTHONY, medical building developer; b. San Francisco, Dec. 24, 1938; s. Andrew M. Cole and Marjorie (Eiger) Brand; m. Brend J. Cox, Sept. 2, 1978; children: Deborah, Andrew, Kandee. BA in Polit. Sci., Stanford U., 1960; postgrad., Pepperdine U., 1976. V.p. First Calif. Title Co., San Diego, 1962-77; devel. dir. Mediplex Med. Bldg., San Diego, 1982-87, Cabot, Cabot & Forbes, San Diego, 1987—; pres. The Brandekan Co., San Diego, 1985—. Mem. Nat. Assn. Securities Dealers, Nat. Assn. Realtors. Office: Cabot Cabot 7 Forbes 401 West A St Ste 1806 San Diego CA 92101

COLE, DIANA BARAJON, communications executive; b. Milan, Italy, Aug. 6, 1938; came to U.S., 1959; d. Bruno and Anna Maria (Cialvi) Barajon; m. David G. Cole; 1 child, Valerie. BS, Cambridge U.; postgrad., Miami U., Ohio. Asst. to internat. v.p. C&I Girdler, Louisville, 1963-67; asst. mgr. export div. Thomas Industries, Louisville, 1967-69; mgr. comml. research Champion Internat., Hamilton, Ohio, 1969-78; dist. sales mgr. Avon Products, Cin., 1978-81; country planner, A/V writer Avon Products, N.Y.C., 1981-82; sales, mktg. mgr. Warner Amex, Pitts., 1982-83; br. mgr. MCI Telecommunications Inc., Denver, 1983-84, area sales mgr., 1984-85, area mgr. P&L responsibilities, 1985-86; customer svc. div. mgr. MCI Telecommunications Inc., Phoenix, 1987, customer svc. div. mgr. Southwest region, 1987—. Democrat. Roman Catholic. Home: 5720 N Via Umbrosa Tucson AZ 85715 Office: MCI Telecommunications 3300 N Central Ave Phoenix AZ 85012

COLE, FRANK MAURICE, civil engineer; b. Cheyenne, Wyo., July 28, 1935; s. George Lee and Mary Kate (Heacock) C.; m. Frieda Louise Christensen, June 2, 1957; children: Caroline Kate Cole Tietjen, Frank M. Jr. BSCE, U. Wyo., 1957. Registered profl. engr., Wyo. Hwy. designer Calif. Hwy. Dept., San Francisco, 1957-58; bridge designer Wyo. Hwy. Dept., Cheyenne, 1958-61; pres. Cole Corp., Cheyenne, 1961—. Mem. regional planning commn. Cheyenne Laramie County, 1981-83. Mem. ASCE, NSPE, Urban Land Inst. (assoc.), Nat. Homebuilders Assn., Internat. Coun. Shopping Ctrs. (cert., bd. dirs. Wyo. chpt. 1968-71), Nat. Retail Mchts. Assn. (trustee 1975—), Cheyenne C. of C. (chmn. coms. transp. and local affairs), Kiwanis. Office: Cole Corp 425 Cole Shopping Ctr Cheyenne WY 82001

COLE, HOWARD PARKER, realtor, religious organization executive; b. Fresno, Calif., Aug. 28, 1946; s. Nathaniel Parker and Helena (Howard) C.; m. Patricia Jeanne Selby, Aug. 24, 1968; children: Jason Nathaniel, Michelle Linda, Brent Parker. AA, Foothill Jr. Coll., 1966; BS in Sociology, U. Oreg., 1968; cert. completion, Young Life Inst., 1971; grad., Realtors Inst. Youth minister Young Life Campaign, Seattle, 1968-69, Yakima, Wash., 1969-75; Youth minister Young Life Campaign, Eugene, Oreg., 1975-78, com. chmn., 1985—; realtor RE/Max Eugene, Inc., 1978—; franchise devel. rep. Stretch and Sew, Inc., Eugene, 1980-81. Coach Eugene Sports Program, 1981--; lay counselor, mem. coun. Faith Ctr., Eugene, 1987--. Mem. Nat. Assn. Realtors, Oreg. Assn. Realtors, Eugene Bd. Realtors (Million Dolar Club 1983--), Eugene C. of C. Home: 2150 Keith Way Eugene OR 97401 Office: RE/Max of Eugene Inc 1200 Executive Pkwy Ste 320 Eugene OR 97401

COLE, JACK, film and video director; b. Bklyn., Jan. 14, 1943; s. Robert and Gerrie (Walzer) C.; m. Carole Ann Kane (div. 1976); children: Tristina, Christopher. Student, Sch. Visual Arts, N.Y.C. Graphic designer Dick Clark Prodns., L.A., 1964-65; film designer Nat. Screen Service, L.A., 1965-67; dir. The Spungbuggy Works, L.A., 1967-68; dir., designer The Jack Cole Film Group, L.A., 1968-75; dir. N. Lee Lacy and Assocs., L.A., 1975-82; dir. freelance L.A., 1981-83; dir. Picture Music Internat., N.Y.C., 1983-85; dir., co-founder Split Screen Prodns., L.A., 1985-86; dir. One Heart Corp., L.A., 1986—; guest lectr. UCLA Extension Sch., 1982—. Dir. numerous TV comml s. and programs. Recipient Best Dir. Am. Music Awards, L.A., 1988; Best Dir. and Best Music Video, Acad. Country Music, L.A., 1988; Best Dir. Music Row Pub., Nashville, 1988, Best Music Video, The Nashville Network, 1988, Dove award, Nashville, 1988. Democrat. Jewish.

COLE, JO ELLEN, appraiser, gemologist; b. Long Beach, Calif., Aug. 19, 1958; d. Henry Samuel and Lillian (Vogel) Cole. Grad., Gem Inst. Am., 1979. Gemologist/lab. tech. U.S. Gemological Svcs., Inc., Santa Ana,, Calif., 1980-82; with Shanes Jewelry, Inc.,, Westwood,, Calif., 1984-85; mgr. Guild Labs., Inc., L.A., 1986—. Mem. Gemological Inst. of Am. Alumni Assn. Democrat. Jewish. Office: Guild Laboratories Inc 606 S Hill St #304 Los Angeles CA 90014

COLE, KAREN LORRAINE, operating engineer; b. Norco, Calif., Apr. 12, 1954; d. William G. Willis and Lorraine Ruth (Buratti) Willis-Beisner; children: Cirdon Brion, Vanna Alia. Apprentice, Trade Tech. Coll., L.A., 1980-84, Journeyman Grad., 1984. Apprentice engr. Cushman & Wakefield, L.A., 1980-83, asst. chief engr., 1988— , Bank of Calif., 1983-84, chief operating engr., 1984-88. Active Boy Scouts Am. Mem. NAFE, Bldg. Owners and Mgrs. Assn., Local 501 Internat. Union Operating Engrs. (Apprentice of Yr. award 1984). Avocations: design and constrn. of stained-glass windows, scuba diving, off-road driving. Office: Cushman & Wakefield Calif Inc 515 S Flower St Ste 2200 Los Angeles CA 90071

COLE, LEE ARTHUR, computer information systems executive; b. Pitts., May 2, 1953; m. Loni Kay Chestor, May ll, 1985. BS, Indiana U. Pa., 1975; PhD, Dartmouth Coll., 1979. Postdoctoral fellow physics dept. Tulane U., New Orleans, 1979-8l; project mgr. Solar Energy Rsch. Inst., Dept. Energy, Golden, Colo., 198l-85; program mgr. Solid State Elec. div. Honeywell Co., Colorado Springs, Colo., 1985-87; R & D mgr. Unisys CAD-CAM, Inc., Boulder, Colo., 1987—. Contbr. articles to profl. jours. Mem. Am. Phys. Soc. Home: 565 Mohawk Dr Boulder CO 80303 Office: Unisys CAD-CAM Inc 2970 Wilderness Pl Boulder CO 80301

COLE, MALVIN, neurologist, educator; b. N.Y.C., Mar. 21, 1933; s. Harry and Sylvia (Firman) C.; A.B. cum laude, Amherst Coll., 1953; M.D. cum laude, Georgetown U. Med. Sch., 1957; m. Susan Kugel, June 20, 1954; children: Andrew James, Douglas Gowers. Intern, Seton Hall Coll. Medicine, Jersey City Med. Ctr., 1957-58; resident Boston City Hosps., 1958-60; practice medicine specializing in neurology, Montclair and Glen Ridge, N.J., Montville, N.J., 1963-72, Casper, Wyo., 1972—; teaching fellow Harvard Med. Sch., 1958-60; Research fellow Nat. Hosp. for Nervous Diseases, St. Thomas Hosp., London, Eng., 1960-61; instr. Georgetown U. Med. Sch., 1961-63; clin. assoc. prof. neurology N.J. Coll. Medicine, Newark, 1963-72, acting dir. neurology, 1965-72; assoc. prof. clin. neurology U. Colo. Med. Sch., 1973-88, prof., 1988—; mem. staff Martland Hosp., Newark, Wyo. Med. Ctr., Casper, U. Hosp., Denver. Served to capt. M.C., AUS, 1961-63. Licensed physician, Mass., N.Y., Calif., N.J., Colo., Wyo.; diplomate Am. Bd. Psychiatry and Neurology, Nat. Bd. Med. Examiners. Fellow

ACP, Am. Acad. Neurology, Royal Soc. Medicine; mem. Assn. Research Nervous and Mental Disease, Acad. Aphasia, Am. Soc. Neuroimaging, Internat. Soc. Neuropsychology, Harveian Soc. London, Epilepsy Found. Am., Am. Epilepsy Soc., Am. EEG Soc., N.Y. Acad. Sci., Osler Soc. London, Alpha Omega Alpha. Contbr. articles to profl. jours. Office: 246 S Washington St Casper WY 82601

COLE, MICHAEL L., insurance company broker; b. Detroit, Aug. 15, 1945; s. Ralph Cole and Juanita Esteen (Westbrook) McCay; m. Ruth Marion Barthel, Oct. 29, 1966; children: Jessica Katherine, Michael Thomas. Grad. high sch., Hacienda Hgts., Calif. Registered life ins. rep. Group ins. broker N.Y. Life Ins. Co., San Diego, 1969—. Contbr. numerous articles in field. Active Just Say No, Poway, Calif., 1988. With USAF, 1965-69. Mem. Nat. Assn. Life Underwriters. Office: NY Life Ins Co 8880 Rio San Diego Dr Ste 700 San Diego CA 92108

COLE, RICHARD GEORGE, public administrator; b. Irvington, N.J., Mar. 11, 1948; s. Warner W. and Laurel M. (Wilson) C. AS in Computer Sci., Control Data Inst., Anaheim, Calif., 1972; BA in Sociology with high honor, Calif. State U., Los Angeles, 1974; MA in Social Ecology, U. Calif., Irvine, 1976; postgrad., So. Oreg. State Coll., 1979. Computer operator Zee Internat., Gardena, Calif., 1971; teaching asst. U. Calif., Irvine, 1974-75; planner Herman Kimmel & Assocs., Newport Beach, Calif., 1976-78; program analyst The Job Council, Medford, Oreg., 1980-81, compliance officer, 1981-82, mgr. adminstrv. services, 1982—; instr. Calif. Community Coll.; chmn. bd. trustees Job Council Pension Trust, Medford, 1982—; mem. curriculum adv. com. Rogue Community Coll., Grants Pass, Oreg., 1986; mgr. computer project State of Oreg., Salem, 1983-84; mem. Oreg. Occupational Info. Coordinating Com., Salem, 1982-84. Pres. bd. trustees Vector Control Dist., Jackson County, Oreg., 1985, treas., 1986, bd. dirs., 1984-87, sec. buget com., 1988—; candidate bd. dirs. Area Edn. Dist., Jackson County, 1981; treas. Job Svc. Employer Com., Jackson County, 1987—; dir. fin. joint pub. venture System Devel. Project, Oreg., Salem, 1986—; mem. adv. bd. New Jobs Planning, Medford, Oreg., 1987-88, Fin. Audit and Risk Mgmt. Task Force, 1987—, chmn. 1989—; treas., bd. dirs. Medford Edn. and Resource Ctr., 1989. With U.S. Army, 1968-69. Fellow LaVerne Noyes, U. Calif., Irvine, 1974; Dr. Paul Doehring Found. scholar, Glendale, Calif., 1973; Computer Demonstration grantee State of Oreg., Salem, 1983. Mem. Am. Soc. Personnel Adminstrn., Assn. So. Oreg. Pub. Adminstrs., Oreg. Employment and Tng. Assn., Pacific N.W. Personnel Mgmt. Assn. (chpt. treas. 1985-87, orgnl. liaison dir. 1988-89, Appreciation award 1985), Govt. Fin. Officers Assn., Oreg. Mcpl. Fin. Officers Assn., The Nature Conservancy. Home: 575 Morey Rd Talent OR 97540 Office: The Job Coun 3069 Crater Lake Ave Medford OR 97504

COLE, ROBERT STANLEY, JR., company executive; b. Tacoma, Wash., Dec. 25, 1946; s. Robert Stanley and Alice (Bradshaw) C.; m. Carolyn Dianne Hook, Dec. 10, 1966; children: Leanne, Deanne, Mary Alice, Lisa. Prodn.control supr. Boeing Comml. Aircraft Co., Auburn, Wash., 1973-75, mem. acquisition team, 1976-77, tooling off-loan mgr., 1978-80; indsl.engr., facility mgr. Boeing Products, Inc., Macon, Ga., 1981-82; v.p. Macro Inc., Walnut, Calif., 1983-85; gen. mgr. Alva Gwyn Co., Inc., Auburn, 1986—; sales cons. Stellar Engring., Detroit, 1986-88, Formative Products, Detroit, 1986-87, A.A.R. Corp., Detroit, 1987, Bosh, Bridgman, Mich., 1988. Named Indsl. Engring. Supr. of Yr. Boeing Airplane Co., 1980. Mem. Elks. Republican. Baptist. Office: Alva Gwyn Co Inc 912 Harvey Rd Auburn WA 98002

COLE, STEVE PAUL, transportation company executive; b. Lynwood, Calif., May 6, 1952; s. Jerry Lee Cole and Virginia Lee (Roberts) Calkins; m. Catherine Louise Barela, Feb. 3, 1973; children: Cherilyn Lee, Steven Paul. BS in Mktg., Woodbury Coll., 1973. Br. mgr. Avco Corp., Newport Beach, Calif., 1973-77; zone sales mgr. Avis Leasing Corp., Los Angeles, 1977-82; sales dir. Hertz Corp., Los Angeles, 1982-86; v.p., regional mgr. Idealease, Inc., Chgo., 1986—. Exec. dir. Woodbury Coll. Jaycees, 1973; active St. Margaret Mary Sch. Bd., Chino, Calif., 1988—. Mem. Truck Rental and Leasing Assn. Republican. Roman Catholic. Home: 2443 S Imperial Pl Ontario CA 91761

COLE, WILLIAM L. WADE, real estate broker, attorney; b. Nashville, Sept. 9, 1944; s. Fred Ealy and Sara (Harwood) C.; m. Theresa L. McCord, Aug. 13, 1977; 1 child, Lisa Victoria. BA, Yale U., 1966; JD, U. Puget Sound, 1975. Asst. dir. admissions Yale U., 1967-70; pvt. practice Seattle, 1975-81; assoc. broker and br. mgr. Kidder, Mathews & Segner, Inc., Seattle, 1981—; Bar: Wash. 1975. Mem. Wash. State Bar Assn., Seattle King County Bar Assn., Seattle King County Assn. Realtors. Office: Kidder Mathews & Segner Inc 1600 Key Bank Tower Seattle WA 98104

COLEMAN, DOROTHY IRENE HART, public relations executive; b. Juneau, Alaska, Nov. 9, 1924; d. Julius Harold and Dorothy (Canfield) Hart; m. Don Coryell, May 20, 1952 (div. 1957); m. 2d, Patrick Coleman, Dec. 15, 1957 (dec. 1983); children: Mary Patricia and Anne Dorothy (twins). BA, U. Wash., 1947, postgrad., 1947-50; postgrad. UCLA, 1956-60. Asst. to dir. U. Wash. Sch. Journalism, Seattle, 1947-50; reporter Seattle Post-Intelligencer, 1945-57, 50-52; columnist Honolulu Star-Bull., 1952-53; women's editor Vancouver (B.C.) News Herald, 1953-54; pub. relations dir. U. B.C., Vancouver, 1954-55; news editor Wenatchee (Wash.) Daily World, 1955-56; feature writer Los Angeles Mirror, 1956-59, women's editor, 1959-62; asst. family sect. editor Los Angeles Times, 1962; women's editor Los Angeles Herald-Examiner, 1963-68; pub. relations dir. Hollywood Presbyn. Hosp., 1968-72; pres. Dorothy Coleman Pub. Relations, Los Angeles, 1972-73; dir. communications Braille Inst. Am., Inc., 1973-82; dir. community relations Meml. Med. Centers, Inc., 1982—. Served to lt. comdr., USNR, 1950-65. Mem. Los Angeles Press Club, San Francisco Press Club, Honolulu Press Club, Wash. State Press Club, Can. Women's Press Club, Am. Women in Radio and TV, Am. Coll. Pub. Relations Assn., Women in Communications (chpt. pres. 1964), Pub. Relations Soc. Am., Los Angeles Advt. Women, Los Angeles Publicity Club, Gifted Children's Assn., Kappa Alpha Theta. Home: 14 Shiloh Irvine CA 92620 Office: 1111 W La Palma Ave Anaheim CA 92803

COLEMAN, JASON CHANDLER, petroleum and minerals company executive; b. Compton, Calif., May 18, 1958; s. James C. and Frances E. (Barr) C.; m. Julia H. Burbank, Oct. 29, 1988. BS in Bus., Calif. State U., Chico, 1980, MBA, 1982. Investment analyst J.C. Coleman Real Estate, Chico, 1978-82; profl. acct. Standard Oil Co. Calif., San Francisco, 1982-83; assoc. fin. analyst Chevron Overseas Petroleum, Inc., San Francisco, 1983-85; systems analyst Chevron Overseas Petroleum, Inc., San Ramon, Calif., 1985-86; fin. analyst Chevron Resources Co., San Ramon, Calif., 1986-88; supr. bank controls Chevron Corp., San Francisco, 1988—; chmn. bd. dirs. Chevron Fed. Credit Union, San Francisco; cons. Scholars Press, Chico, 1981-82; lectr. Sch. Bus. Calif. State U., Chico, 1980-82. Mem. Calif. State U.-Chico Alumni Assn., Beta Gamma Sigma, Phi Kappa Phi, Phi Eta Sigma, Sigma Phi Epsilon. Republican. Presbyterian. Club: Commonwealth (San Francisco). Office: Chevron 225 Bush St San Francisco CA 94104

COLEMAN, LAMAR WILLIAM, physicist, researcher; b. Phila., Feb. 19, 1934; s. William Francis and Henrietta Kiefer (Grookett) C.; m. Rosemary Ann Scott, Aug. 18, 1962; children: William Scott, Christopher Lamar. BS in Physics, Va. Mil. Inst., 1955; postgrad., Carnegie Inst. Tech., 1955-56; MS, PhD in Physics, Oreg. State U., 1963. Rsch. physicist Lawrence Livermore (Calif.) Nat. Lab., 1964-69, physicist, group leader, 1969-78, dep. assoc. program leader, 1981-83, assoc. program leader, 1981-83, asst. program leader, 1983-86, dep. program leader, 1986--; mem. internat. sci. com. Internat. Sch. Plasma Physics Piero Caldirola, Milan, 1988--; speaker, presenter in field. Contbr. numerous articles to profl. jours. Mem. Am. Phys. Soc. Republican. Presbyterian. Office: Lawrene Livermore Nat Lab PO Box 5508 Livermore CA 94550

COLEMAN, MARY ANN, nurse; b. Meridian, Miss., Nov. 3, 1946; d. Herschel Lee and Jessie Mae (Franklin) Bolden; m. Harvie Lee Coleman, July 29, 1967; children: Brantley, Mandi, Creighton. BS in Nursing, Fresno State U., Calif., 1972. Staff nurse Saint Agnes Med. Ctr., Fresno, 1972-74, critical care nurse, 1974-77, lab. staff nurse, 1977-85, Cath. lab coord., 1985—. Mem. Nat. Council Negro Women, Calif., 1975-79, Black Nurses Assn., Calif., 1985-86. Mem. Am. Coll. Cardiovascular Invasive Specialists, Am. Radiol. Nurses Assn. Democrat. Home: 1209 E Kaviland Ave Fresno CA 93706 Office: Saint Agnes Med Ctr 1303 E Herndon Fresno CA 93710

COLEMAN, MATTISON BARR, real estate corporation officer; b. Burbank, Calif., Apr. 8, 1934; s. Eugene and Christene C.; m. Pamela Miles, July 1, 1984 (div.), 1 child, Marcos Barr. BA, U. So. Calif., 1956. Pvt. practice gen. contracting L.A., 1956-77; chief exec. officer Marc-O-Matt Corp., L.A., 1971—. Sec. Venice Town Coun., 1972. Mem. Marina City Club. Home and Office: 27 Ketch St Marina Del Rey CA 90292-5951

COLEMAN, PAUL JEROME, JR., physicist, educator; b. Evanston, Ill., Mar. 7, 1932; s. Paul Jerome and Eunice Cecile (Weissenberg) C.; m. Doris Ann Fields, Oct. 3, 1964; children: Derrick, Craig. BS in Engring. Math., U. Mich., 1954, BS in Engring. Physics, 1954, MS in Physics, 1958; PhD in Space Physics, UCLA, 1966. Research scientist Ramo-Wooldridge Corp. (now TRW Systems), El Segundo, Calif., 1958-61; instr. math. U. So. Calif., L.A., 1958-61; mgr. interplanetary scis. program NASA, Washington, 1961-62; research sci. Inst. Geophysics and Planetary Physics UCLA, 1962-66, prof. geophysics, space physics Inst. Geophysics and Planetary Physics, 1966—; pres. Univs. Space Rsch. Assn., Columbia, Md., 1981—; vis. scholar U. Paris, 1975-76; vis. scientist Lab. for Aeronomy Ctr. Nat. Research Sci., Verrieres le Buisson, France, 1975-76; asst. lab. dir., mgr. Earth and space scis. div., chmn. Inst. Geophysics and Planetary Physics Los Alamos (N.Mex.) Nat. Lab., 1981-86; com. mem. numerous scientific and ednl. orgns., cons. numerous fin. and indsl. cos. Co-editor (books) Solar Wind, 1972, Pioneering the Space Frontier, 1986; mem. editorial bd. Geophysics and Astrophysics Monographs, 1970—; assoc. editor Cosmic Electrodynamics, 1968-72; contbr. reviews to numerous profl. jours. Appointed Nat. Commn. on Space, Pres. U.S., 1985; mem. Fraternity of Friends of the Los Angeles Music Ctr., 1987—, Los Angeles County Mus. Nat. History, 1980—, Los Angeles County Mus. Art, 1968; bd. dirs. St. Matthew's Sch., Pacific Palisades, Calif., 1979-82, v.p. 1981-82. 1st lt. USAF, 1954-56, Korea. Recipient Exceptional Sci. Achievement Medal NASA, 1970, 1972, spl. recognition for contributions to the Apollo Program, 1979; Guggenheim fellow 1975-76, Fulbright scholar, 1975-76, Research grantee NASA, NSF, Office Naval Research, Calif. Space Inst., Air Force Office Sci. Research, U.S. Office Geol. Survey. Mem. AAAS, AIAA, Am. Geophys. Union, Am. Phys. Soc., Soc. Exploration Geophysicists, Internat. Acad. Astronautics, Bel Air Bay Club (L.A.) Birnam Wood golf Club (Santa Barbara, Calif.), Cosmos Club (Washington), Explorers Club (N.Y.C.), Tau Beta Pi, Phi Eta Sigma. Home: 1323 Monaco Dr Pacific Palisades CA 90272 Office: UCLA Inst Geophysics and Planetary Physics 405 Hilgard Ave Los Angeles CA 90024-1567

COLEMAN, Q. PATRICK, accountant; b. Mabridge, S.D., Dec. 14, 1963; s. Q.P. and Nadine Marie (Gill) C. BSBA, San Diego State U., 1986. Mgr. fin. dept. Kiyomura & Assocs., L.A., 1987-88; project mgr. Rodin/Neil Constrn., L.A., 1988--. Republican. Roman Catholic. Home: 100 N Catalina St Apt 202 Los Angeles CA 90004 Office: Rodin/Neil Constrn Inc Los Angeles CA 90017

COLEMAN, ROBERT TRENT, social worker; b. Gary, Ind., Feb. 4, 1936; s. Robert Clinton and Lucille Verna C.; m. Dorothy Agnes, Aug. 1957; children: Sean, Bryce, Daniel; m. 2d, Patricia Lou, June 13, 1976; m. 3d Polly Anderson, Sept. 15, 1984. BA in Speech Therapy, U. Wash., Seattle, 1962; postgrad. in speech U. Redlands, 1963-64; MS in Rehab. Counseling, U. Oreg., 1971. Cert. rehab. counselor, cert. ins. rehab. specialist; nat. cert. counselor. Social worker, San Bernardino City Welfare Dept., 1963-64; correctional counselor Calif. Rehab. Center, Norco, 1964-67; sr. counselor Job Corps, Clearfield, Utah, 1967; assoc. dir. Ednl. Systems Corp., Washington, 1968-69; ptnr. Black Fir Jade Mines, Big Sur, Calif., 1971-76; vocat. specialist Internat. Rehab. Assn., San Diego, 1976-77; vocat. rehab. counselor Sharp Hosp., San Diego, 1977-80; clin. coord. San Diego Pain Inst., 1981; cons. in rehab. counseling, career guidance, human rels., Carlsbad, Calif., 1981-83; propr. R.T.C. Cons. Svcs., Escondido and San Diego, 1983—. Commr., Handicapped Appeals Commn., San Marcos, Calif., 1981-83. Served with U.S. Army, 1955-58. Mem. Am. Assn. for Counseling and Devel. (pres.), San Diego Career Guidance Assn. (pres. 1984), Assn. Indsl. Rehab. Reps. (pres. 1983), Am. Rehab. Counseling Assn., Nat. Assn. Rehab. Profls. in Pvt. Sector (standards and ethics com. 1986—, chmn. 1988-90). Republican. Home: 538 Glenheather Dr San Marcos CA 92069 Office: 210 S Juniper St Ste 100 Escondido CA 92025

COLEMAN, ROGER DIXON, bacteriologist; b. Rockwell, Iowa, Jan. 18, 1915; s. Major C. and Hazel Ruth Coleman; A.B., UCLA, 1937; postgrad. Balliol Coll., Oxford (Eng.) U., 1944; M.S., U. So. Calif., 1952, Ph.D., 1957; m. Lee Aden Skov, Jan. 1, 1978. Sr. laboratorian Napa (Calif.) State Hosp., 1937-42; dir. Long Beach (Calif.) Clin. Lab., 1946—, pres., 1980—; mem. Calif. State Clin. Lab. Commn., 1953-57. Served as officer AUS, 1942-46. Diplomate Am. Bd. Bioanalysts. Mem. Am. Assn. Bioanalysts, Am. Assn. Clin. Chemists, Am. Soc. Microbiologists, Am. Chem. Soc., Am. Venereal Disease Assn., AAAS (life), Calif. Assn. Bioanalysts (past officer), Med. Research Assn. Calif., Bacteriology Club So. Calif., Sigma Xi, Phi Sigma (past chpt. pres.). Author papers in field. Home: 30041 Running Deer Ln Laguna Beach CA 92677 Office: PO Box 7073 Laguna Niguel CA 92677

COLEMAN, ROGER W., institutional food distribution company executive; b. Newark, Mar. 30, 1929; s. Bernard Simpson and Evelyn (Bornstein) C.; m. Ruth Rykoff (div. Apr. 1982); children—William, Wendy, Paul, Eric; m. Francesca Marie Wessilius, Sept. 1983. B.S., UCLA, 1950. Gen. mgmt. positions Rogay Food Supply div. S. E. Rykoff & Co., Los Angeles, 1951-58; purchasing and gen. mgmt. positions S.E. Rykoff & Co., Los Angeles, 1958-63, gen. mgr., 1963-67, pres., chief exec. officer, 1967-86; pres., chief exec. officer John Sexton Inc., 1983-86, Rykoff-Sexton, Inc., 1986—. Bd. dirs. Los Angeles Conv. Ctr., Reiss-Dis Child Study Ctr., Los Angeles, ARC (Los Angeles chpt.). Mem. Nat. Inst. Food Service (bd. dirs.), L.A. C. of C. (bd. of dirs.). Clubs: Los Angeles Athletic, Hillcrest Country, Regency, Met., Carlton, World Trade and Stock Exchange, Pebble Beach, Beach and Tennis of Pebble Beach, La Costa Country. Home: 515 Homewood Rd Los Angeles CA 90049 Office: Rykoff-Sexton Inc 761 Terminal St Los Angeles CA 90021

COLEMAN, STEVEN LEROY, endodontist; b. Lincoln, Nebr., June 30, 1944; s. Edgar LeRoy and Janet (Coussins) C.; m. Kristin Luepke, July 21, 1973. DDS, Baylor U., 1969. Endodontist Landeen and Golden, Tucson, 1975-76, Assocs. Peridontics & Endodontics, Tucson, 1976—. Mem. Pima Dental Study Club, Tucson, 1978—, N.W. Dental Study Club, Tucson, 1984—, Nature Conservancy, Tucson, Citizens Alliance for Change, Tucson. Served as capt. USAF, 1969-73. Mem. Ariz. Endodontic Assn. (treas. 1985-88), So. Ariz. Dental Soc., Ariz. State Dental Assn., Am. Dental Assn. Office: Assoc in Periodontics & Endodontics 1601 N Tucson Blvd Tucson AZ 85716

COLES, CHRISTOPHER BARRETT, marketing executive; b. Rochester, Minn., Dec. 31, 1959; s. Douglas Terry and Janet (Ayres) C.; m. Deborah Lynn Daniels, Dec. 31, 1983; children: Brittany Elizabeth, Chelsey Barrett. BA, Colo. Coll., 1981; MBA, U. Denver, 1986. Asst. mgr. bus. office Mountain Bell, Boulder, Colo., 1981-83; asst. mgr. budgeting Mountain Bell, Denver, 1983-84; asst. mgr. fin. assurance Mountain Bell, 1984-85, mgr. product devel., 1985, mgr. strategic planning, 1985-86; dir. strategic mktg. U.S. West, Englewood, Colo., 1986-88; strategic alliance dir. U.S. West, Bellevue, Wash., 1988—. Mem. Phi Gamma Delta. Republican. Presbyterian. Home: 24000 SE 47th St Issaquah WA 98027

COLES, DAVID GEORGE, environmental chemist; b. Baker, Oreg., Jan. 8, 1948; s. James Bernal and Lois Irene (Inskeep) C.; m. Barbara Laura Brown, July 10,1971. BS in Chemistry, Oreg. State U., 1970, MS in Nuclear Chemistry, 1973. Chemist Lawrence Livermore Nat. Lab., Livermore, Calif., 1972-81; research chemist Battelle Pacific NW Labs., Richland, Wash., 1981-88; environ. chemist, dir. containment assessment/mgmt. svcs. Beak Consultants, Inc., Portland, Oreg., 1988--. Mem. Geol. Soc. Am., Am. Chem. Soc., Nat. Water Well Assn., Antarctican Soc. Office: Beak Cons Inc 317 SW Alder 8th Fl Loyalty Bldg Portland OR 97204-2583

COLETTI, GERALD PETER, controller; b. Boston, Aug. 6, 1946; s. Nino L. Coletti and Julia M. (Abate) Walker. BS in Mktg., U. R.I., 1968, BS in Indsl. Mgmt., 1968. Controller Evans & Co., Hartford, Conn., 1968-80; payroll mgr. Able Bldg. Maintenance, San Francisco, 1980-82; controller Mattison/Shidler Investment Corp., San Francisco, 1982—; restaurant owner The Galleon Bar & Restaurant, San Francisco, 1985—. Mem. adv. bd. San Francisco Lesbian/Gay Chorus, 1982—. Mem. Nat. Restaurant Assn., Golden Gate Restaurant Assn., Nat. Notary Assn., San Francisco C. of C., Golden Gate Bus. Assn. Democrat. Roman Catholic. Home: 714 14th St Apt 2 San Francisco CA 94114 Office: Mattison Shidler Investment 4 Embarcadero Ste 3150 San Francisco CA 94111

COLEY, SORAYA MOORE, social work educator; b. Wilmington, N.C., Nov. 25, 1950; d. John H. Moore and Majoria (McWilliams) Morgan; m. Ron T. Coley, Aug. 18, 1979. BA, Lincoln U., 1972; MSW, Bryn Mawr Coll., 1974, PhD, 1981. Project dir. Nat. Urban League, N.Y.C., 1975-76, research cons., 1976—; survey mgr. Mathematica Policy Research, Princeton, N.J., 1979-81; assoc. prof. Calif. State U., Fullerton, 1981—; research cons. Planned Parenthood, Santa Ana, Calif., 1984-85; acad. panel chmn. Coalition Concerned with Adolescent Pregnancy, Santa Ana, 1986—. Mem. United Way, Garden Grove, Calif., 1984—, Orange County Health Planning Council, Tustin, Calif., 1984-85. Recipient Vol. award United Way, 1983, 84, faculty research award Calif. State U., 1983; NIMH fellow U. Mich., 1984. Mem. Nat. Assn. Social Workers, Nat. Coalition Against Domestic Violence, Black Women's Forum, Delta Sigma Theta. Club: Links (Orange County). Office: Calif State U Human Svcs 800 N State College Blvd Fullerton CA 92634

COLEY, TRAVIS CARL, fisheries biologist, estuarine ecologist; b. Holly Springs, Miss., May 18, 1947; s. William Travis and Corrine (Fitch) C.; m. Patricia Ann Gladney, Dec. 20, 1969; children: Angela, Amy, Drew, Caleb. BS, Miss. State U., 1976; MS, U. Idaho, 1979. Fisheries rsch. biologist Nat. Marine Fisheries Svc., Hammond, Oreg., 1978-86; asst. project leader U.S. Fish and Wildlife Svc., Ahsahka, Idaho, 1986—; regional diving supr. U.S. Fish and Wildlife Svc., Portland, Oreg., 1988—; contract diver. Leader youth group Warrenton (Oreg.) lst Bapt. Ch., 198l-85; bd. dirs. Astoria (Oreg.) Union Gospel Mission, 1985-86. With USN, 1969-73; lt. (j.g.) USCGR. Mem. Am. Inst. Fishery Rsch. Biologists (assoc.), Am. Fishery Soc., Nat. Assn. Diver Med. Technicians, Pacific Fisheries Biologists Assn., Xi Sigma Pi. Home: 2594 Grangemont Rd PO Box 2l04 Orofino ID 83544 Office: US Fish and Wildlife Svc PO Box l8 Ahsahka ID 83520

COLFAX, J(OHN) DAVID, educator; b. Pitts., May 13, 1936; s. John D. and Margaret E. (Pristas) C.; m. Mary-Alice Nash, June 13, 1959; children: Grant, Drew, Reed, Garth. BS, Pa. State U., 1958; MA, U. Pitts., 1960; postgrad. fellow, London Sch. Econs., 1960-61; PhD, U. Chgo., 1964. Asso. prof. U. Conn., Storrs, 1963-69, Washington U., St. Louis, 1969-72; regional dir. NCAT, Boonville, Calif., 1977-81; exec. dir. Colfax Assocs., Boonville, 1972—; bd. dirs., The Mountain Sch., Boonville, Black Fox Prodns., Boonville, Mountain House Press, Philo, Calif.; sr. cons., Policy Rsch. Group, Winchester, Mass., 1979-81. Author: Homeschooling for Excellence, 1988; editor: Radical Sociology, 1971; editor, Goat Notes, 1986—; contbg. editor, Anderson Valley Advertiser, Boonville, 1983—; contbr. to various profl. and gen. interest publs. Vice pres. Mendocino County Dem. Cen. Com., Ukiah, Calif., 1983-87; v.p., trustee Mendocino County Office Edn., Ukiah, 1986—; bd. dirs. Fern Hill Sch., Boonville, 1987—. Home: 246 Redwood Ridge Rd Boonville CA 95415 Office: Colfax Assocs PO Box 246 Boonville CA 95415

COLGAN, HOWARD WILLIAM, JR., electronics company executive; b. Hutchinson, Kans., Jan. 23, 1937; s. Howard William and Viola May (Collins) C.; m. Carol Ann King, June 10, 19612 (div. 1973);l children: Howard William III, Carrie Elaine. Grad., U. San Francisco, 1986. Sr. operator data processing Johnson & Johnson, Dallas, 1960-62; programmer Johnson & Johnson, Sherman, Tex., 1962-68; sr. programmer, analyst Motorola Co., Phoenix, 1969-71; sr. analyst Motorola Co., 1971-74; sr. cons. MIS Fairchild Semiconductor Co., Mt. View, Calif., 1975-78; project mgr. Fairchild Semiconductor Co., 1978-82; sr. specialist procurement and custom products GE, San Jose, Calif., 1982-85; program mgr. custom products GE, 1985--. With U.S. Army, 1956-59. Mem. Am. Prodn. and Inventory Control Soc., Tex. Bas Club (pres. 1967-68). Republican. Baptist. Home: 395 Via Prima Vera San Jose CA 95111 Office: GE Corp 175 Curtner St San Jose CA 95125

COLHOUR, DONALD BRUCE, producer, director; b. Ellsworth, Kans., May 28, 1946; s. Bruce and Ruth (Williams) C. BSJ, U. Kans., 1969. Unit prodn. mgr. ABC, Inc., Los Angeles, 1969-80; mgr. spl. projects ABC Entertainment, Los Angeles, 1980-83, dir. spl. projects, 1983—; exec. producer L.A. Bach Festival, L.A., 1985-89; cons. Claremont Sch. Theology, 1986—; sponsor The Am./Soviet Film Initiative, 1988; chmn. Commonwealth Theatre, L.A., 1987-89; chmn., founder Am. Pilgrim Chorus, 1988; with M.C.H. Entertainment, Hollywood, Calif., 1989—. Producer theatrical concerts Dionne Warwick, 1984, Dudley Moore, 1983, John Denver, 1983, Wayne Newton, 1983, Perry Como, 1982; theatrical rev. You'll Love It, 1986; exec. producer and dir. Tribute to George Gershwin, 1987; producer, dir. Tribute to Neil Simon, 1988; creator Star Spangled Celebration to Promote Literacy in America, St. Louis, 1987-88. Lay minister 1st Congl. of Los Angeles; communicator on ministry Nat. Assn. Congregation Chs., Los Angeles, 1986—; producer AIDS Project, Los Angeles, 1985, Beverly Hills B'nai B'rith, 1985, Devereux Found., 1983, 84, 85, United Jewish Fund, 1984, Boys Club of Am., 1984, Am. Jewish Com., 1984, Nat. Conf. Christians and Jews, 1984, 86, 88, United Cerebral Palsy Tennis Festival, 1983-88, Entertainment Industries Council Drug Abuse, 1986; mem. U.S. Project Literacy, 1987—; founder, pres. Los Angeles Project Literacy, 1987—, ABC-TV West Coast rep.; sponsor Am. and Soviet Film Initiative, 1988, Nat. Ctr. for Hyperactive Children, 1988; exec. producer, dir. YWCA Leader's Luncheon, 1989—; chmn. Ecumenical Coun. Drama & Arts, L.A., 1989—. Recipient Leadership in Literacy award Laubach Literacy Action, 1987. Mem. Hollywood Radio and TV Soc., Acad. TV Arts and Scis. Lodge: Masons. Office: ABC Entertainment 2040 Ave of the Stars Los Angeles CA 90067

COLL, COLLEEN, city council member. BA, U. of the Pacific; student, John F. Kennedy Law Sch., U. Santa Clara. Correctional counselor Solano County Criminal Justice System; mem. Concord (Calif.) City Coun., 1982—; now mayor City of Concord. Chairperson Concord Child Care Task Force; bd. dirs. Concord Citiznes for Improved Quality Water, Child Assault Prevention Coun.; mem. Downtown Bus. Merchants Assn. Office: Office of Mayor 1950 Parkside Dr Concord CA 94519

COLLAZOS, ALVARO GABRIEL, computer systems analyst; b. Bogota, Colombia, July 4, 1958; s. Gabriel and Leonor (Angulo) C.; m. Maria de Lourdes Ward, July 19, 1983; 1 child, Raquel Elizabeth. Grad. in data processing, U. Bogota, 1982. Computer operator Computec S.A., Bogota, 1978; programmer Aseguradora Grancolombiana, Bogota, 1978-79; systems devel. mgr. Internat. Computer Processing Inc., Bogota, 1979-83; regional dir. Campus Crusade for Christ Internat., Brasilia, Brazil, 1983-86; dispatcher, receiving mgr. U-Haul Co., Pasadena, Calif., 1986-87; enlisted USN, 1987—. Home: 3700 10th Ave Apt 2-R San Diego CA 92103 Office: USN AIMD/SE 900 Naval Air Sta N Island San Diego CA 92135-5040

COLLEGEMAN, LEROY H., retired aerospace executive, civic affairs volunteer; b. Wahington, Mar. 8, 1925; m. Maybelle O. Elder, Feb. 1986; children: Adam P., Ethan S. BSCE, Villanova U., 1945; advanced mgmt. course, U. Hawaii, 1979. Oil refinery, power plant and heavy constrn. engr. and supr. for varios cos. U.S., Venezuela, India, Republic of South Africa and Baghdad, Iraq, 1946-59; engr. Aerospace and Mil. Airplanes div. Boeing, 1959, Bomarc and Minuteman project mgr., mgr. of Ballistic Missile Advanced Devel., proposal mgr. on Air Force One, dep. mgr. of nat. aerospace plane project, ret., 1987. Mem. Wash. State Gov.'s Com. on Disability Issues and Employment; vice-chmn. Elderly/Handicapped Transit Adv. Com. Seattle Metro Transit; mem. Speaker's Bur. for Ret. Sen. Vol. Program; vol. arbitrator Better Bus. Bur.; active Wash. State Spl. Olympics. Lt. (j.g.) USN, 1943-46. Fellow AIAA (assoc., Aerospace Contribution to

Soc. award 1989, mem. Missle Tech. Com., mem. Soc. and Aerospace Tech. Com.); mem. MENSA, Audubon Soc. Address: 410 W Roy St #E301 Seattle WA 98119

COLLIAT, GEORGE HENRI, computer executive, director; b. Lyon, France, Aug. 1, 1946; s. Rene Francois and Marie Louise (Venet) C.; m. Marcia Dee McDonald, Dec. 28, 1969 (div. July 1988); children: Philippe, Karina. Ingenieur, I.N.S.A., Lyon, 1968; MSEE, Stanford (Calif.) U., 1969. Assoc. prof. Sherbrooke (Can.) U., 1969-70; systems engr. Honeywell Bull, Paris, 1970-73; network mgr. Honeywell Info. Systems, Phoenix, 1973-80; software engr. mgr. A.B. Dick, Scottsdale, Ariz., 1980-83; v.p. engring. div. Alcatel Info. Systems, Tempe, Ariz., 1983-88; mission dir. Bull-HN, Phoenix, 1989—. Mem. Assn. For Computing Machinery. Office: Bull-HN 13430 N Black Canyon Hwy Phoenix AZ 85023

COLLIER, ERICH EDWARD, screenwriter; b. Boston; s. Hugh Talmadge and Eleanor Frances (Kenneally) C.; m. Mary Ann Jensen, May 31, 1980; children: Breanna, Matthew. Student, Boston U., 1969-71; BA, Bard Coll., 1974. Freelance screenwriter L.A., 1979—; instr. Hollywood (Calif.) Scriptwriter Inst., 1981—. Writer (TV script) Cagney and Lacey, Family Tree, Partners in Crime, Another World, Capitol, (play) Priority Girl, 1981, The Squirrel's Nest, 1983, Quincy. Mem. Writers Guild Am. Democrat.

COLLIER, PATRICIA FRANCES, nurse; b. Queens, N.Y., Sept. 12, 1943; d. Harold and Frances (Naldrett) Entenmann; m. John Collier, May 9, 1970; children: Shannon, Christina. AA, Los Angeles City Coll., 1977. Staff nurse USC-LAC Med. Ctr., Los Angeles, 1977-79, Group Health Cooperative, Seattle, 1980-88; hospice case mgr. Hospice Snohomish County, Everett, Wash., 1988; com. mem., emcee Conf. on Chem. Dependency and Codependency, Seattle, 1988. Com. mem. Eastside Unitarian Ch. Sanctuary, Bellvue, Wash., 1984-88. Mem. Nat. Union Hosp. and Health Care Employees. Democrat. Home: 18824 67th Ave SE Seattle WA 98290

COLLIER, RICHARD BANGS, foundation executive; b. Hastings, Nebr., Aug. 12, 1918; s. Nelson Martin and Stella (Butler) C. BA, U. Wash., 1951. Fgn. aid officer GS14, civil aviation Am. embassy, Bangkok, Thailand, 1958-63; founder, dir. Pleneurethics Society, Tacoma, 1963—; founder Inst. Ethics & Sci., Tacoma, 1988—. Carnegie fellow Inst. Pub. Affairs, Grad. Sch., U. Wash., 1950-51. Nat. adv. bd. Am. Security Council. Capt. USAF, 1965-66. Mem. AAAS, Assn. Supervision & Curriculum Devel., Soc. Health & Human Values, Internat. Platform Assn., Acad. of Polit. Sci., Royal Inst. Philosophy (Eng.), Senatorial Club. Republican. Author Pleneurethic, 15 vols., 1964-81. Home: PO Box 1256 Tacoma WA 98401

COLLIER, WILLIAM J., III, dentist; b. Oakland, Calif., Aug. 18, 1953; s. William J. and Mary Evelyn (Fisher) C. BS in Agr., Kans. State U., 1976; DDS, U. Mo., Kansas City, 1983. Pvt. practice dentistry Juneau, Alaska, 1983—. Mem. Am. Dental Assn., Juneau Dental Soc., S.E. Alaska Dental Soc., Acad. Gen. Dentistry, Elks. Office: 1600 Glacier Hwy Juneau AK 99801

COLLIER-EVERNDEN, MARSHA ANN, publishing executive; b. N.Y.C., Dec. 4, 1950; d. Samuel Schleimer and Claire (Schmelzer) Tracy; m. Blake Ian Evernden, Dec., 11, 1987; 1 child from previous marriage, Susan Marie. Student, Miami Dade Jr. Coll., 1968-70, U. Miami, 1970-72. Advt. account exec. Miami (Fla.) Herald, 1977; spl. projects mgr. Daily News, Los Angeles, 1977-84; pres. Collier Advt. & Promotion inc., Northridge, Calif., 1984—; bridal show dir. Daily News, Los Angeles, 1978-83; gen. mgr. Dodger Blue, Los Angeles, 1982-83; pub. So. Calif. Autoracing Newspaper, 1985-88, Score News-(official pub. of Score Internat.), 1986—, Northridge Bus. News. Mem. Am. Autoracing Writers and Broadcasters Assn., Advt. Club Los Angeles, So. Calif. Mktg. Dirs. Assn., Internat. Council Shopping Ctrs., Northridge C. of C. (bd. dirs.), Rotary. Republican. Office: 18620 Plummer St Northridge CA 91324

COLLINGE, GAIL JOAN, teacher, consultant; b. Glendale, Calif., Jan. 28, 1941; m. Michael W. Milne Sr., Dec. 16, 1962 (div. 1971); children Michael Jr., Mark William, Matthew Wayne. BA in Elem. Edn., Calif. State U., Northridge, 1962. Cert. elem. tchr., Calif. Tchr. Long Beach (Calif.) Sch. Dist., 1962-64; substitute tchr. Rowland (Calif.) Sch. Dist., 1969-71, Walnut (Calif.) Sch. Dist., 1969-71; asst. mgr. tng. Household Fin., Pomona, Calif., 1971-72; tchr. Chino (Calif.) Sch. Dist., 1972—, kindergarten mentor, 1986—; presentor U. Calif. Riverside (Calif.) Kindergarten Conf., 1987, Corona (Calif.) Unified Sch. Dist., 1988, Calif. Assn. for the Edn. Young Children, 1989, Tchrs. Are #1 Conf., 1988, So. Calif. Kindergarten Conf., Riverside, 1987, 88, No. Calif. Kindergarten Conf., San Francisco, 1989. Named Chino Tchr. of Yr., San Bernardino County Schs., 1988, San Bernardino County Tchr. of Yr., 1988. Mem. AAUW, Nat. Assn. Edn. Young Children (presentor nat. conf. 1988), Assn. Childhood Edn. Internat., Assn. Supervision and Curriculum Devel. Congregationalist. Home: 13631 Preciado Ave Chino CA 91710 Office: Chino Sch Dist 5550 Walnut Ave Chino CA 91710

COLLINGS, CELESTE LOUISE, marketing executive, professional artist; b. Highland Park, Ill., Dec. 9, 1948; d. Robert Zane Jr. and Laura (Vasaly) C.; m. John Austin Darden III, July 17, 1971 (div. July 1975); 1 child, Desiree Anne; m. John Cochran Barber, Dec. 13, 1984. BA, U. Ariz., 1970; postgrad., N.Mex. State U., 1975; completed mktg. mgr. seminar, U. Calif., Irvine, 1978; cert. of achievement, Wilson Learning Course, 1983. Art tchr. Devargas Jr. High Sch., Santa Fe, 1971; artist, pvt. tchr. Las Cruces, N.Mex., 1971-75; sales rep. Helpmates Temp. Services, Santa Ana, Calif., 1975-76; sales account mgr. Bristol-Myers Products, N.Y.C., 1976-82; sales mgr. Profl. Med. Products, Greenwood, S.C., 1982-85; mktg. mgr. med. products Paper-Pak Products, La Verne, Calif., 1985-88; owner Multi-Media West, Newport Beach, Calif., 1988—; mgmt. trainee Bristol-Myers, Kansas City, Mo., 1978; sales trainee Profl. Med. Products, Greenwood, 1983, product strategy, 1984, chmn. nat. adv. com., 1983-84; owner and pres. Accent Shoji Screens, Newport Beach, Calif., 1981—. Exhibited in one-woman art shows at Nancy Dunn Studio and Gallery, San Clemente, Calif., 1980, The Collectables, San Francisco, 1980, Laguna Beach (Calif.) Festival of the Arts Art-A-Fair, 1981, Ariz. Inter-Scholastic Hon. Exhibit, 1st place award, 1962-66, Glendale Fed. Savs. Art Exhibition, 1982; numerous others. Mem. Orange County Performing Arts Ctr., Corona Del Mar, Calif., 1981. Recipient 10 sales awards Bristol-Meyers, 1976-82, Western Zone Sales Rep. award Profl. Med. Products, 1984, Gainers Club award, 1984; named Nat. Sales Rep. of Yr. Profl. Med. Products, 1984. Mem. U. Ariz. Alumni Assn., Kappa Alpha Theta Alumni. Roman Catholic.

COLLINGS, CHARLES LEROY, supermarket executive; b. Wewoka, Okla., July 11, 1925; s. Roy B. and Dessie L. C.; m. Frances Jane Flake, June 28, 1947; children—Sandra Jean, Dianna Lynn. Student, So. Methodist U., 1943-44, U. Tex., 1945. Sec., contr., dir. Noble Meat Co., Madera, Calif., 1947-54; chief acct. Montgomery Ward & Co., Oakland, Calif., 1954-56; with Raleys, Sacramento, 1956—; sec. Raleys, 1958—, pres., 1970—, also dir. Bd. dirs. Pro Athlete Outreach, Youth for Christ. With USNR, 1943-46. Mem. Calif. Grocers Assn. (dir., officer, past chmn.), Calif Retailers Assn. (bd. dir.). Republican. Baptist. Home: 6790 Arabela Way Sacramento CA 95831 Office: Raleys 500 W Capitol Ave Broderick CA 95605

COLLINGS, TAYLOR, insurance executive; b. Seattle, Oct. 28, 1947; s. William and Gloria (Geisert) Burch; m. Anita L. Taylor, Aug. 2, 1980; 1 child, Zachary. BSBA cum laude, Denver U., 1974; MIM, Thunderbird Coll., Glendale, Ariz., 1975. Broker J. H. Minet, London, 1975-78; treaty producer Sullivan Payne Co., Seattle, 1978-82; asst. v.p. Sullivan Payne Co., 1982-84, v.p., 1984-86, sr. v.p., 1986—. With U.S. Army, 1965-68. Mem. Broadmoor Club, Tower Club. Home: 2306 16th Ave E Seattle WA 98112 Office: Sullivan Payne Co Century Square Bldg 1501 4th Ave Ste 1400 Seattle WA 98101

COLLINS, BERNHARDT WILLIAM, accountant; b. St. Louis, Dec. 28, 1932; s. Robert Leo and Alive Mae (Klute) C.; children: Kimberley Ann, Bernhardt William II, Danita Marie, Patricia Mae. BS in Commerce, St. Louis U., 1954. CPA, Ariz. Staff acct. Sarrells & Riordon, Tucson, 1956-61, Donald Gill & Co., Madison, Wis., 1961; asst. corp. controller Parker Pen Co., Janesville, Wis., 1962; ptnr. Riordon, Crouse & Collins, Tucson, 1963-75, Bernhardt Collins & Co., Tucson, 1979-82, Turigliatto, Collins, Bittner & Palm, P.C., Tucson, 1981-84, Coopers & Lybrand, Tucson, 1984--; owner, mgr. Bernhardt Collins, CPA,, Tucson, 1976-78; presdl. del. White House Small Bus. Conf., 1986. Author: An Accounting Manual for Catholic Parishes of the Diocese of Tucson and Phoenix, 1970. Trustee, St. Joseph's Found., Tucson, 1978--, Stonewall Found., Tucson, 1979--; bd. dirs. Carondelet Healthcare Corp., Tucson, 1986--; trustee, treas. Case de los Ninos, Tucson, 1986--. 1st lt. USAF, 1954-56. Mem. AICPA, Ariz. Soc. CPA's (ethics com. 1970-71, educator com. 1978-79), Old Pueblo Club, Tucson Country Club. Republican. Roman Catholic. Office: Coopers & Lybrand 33 N Stone Ave Ste 1900 Tucson AZ 85701

COLLINS, BRUCE ALAN, coal company executive; b. Greensboro, N.C., Dec. 27, 1944; s. Alan Charles and Beattrice (Irene) Bramble C.; m. Betty Jeanne Estes, Aug. 19, 1966; children: Brian Scott, Bethany Alana. BA, Coll. of Wooster, 1966; MS, Colo. Sch. of Mines, 1971, PhD, 1975. Cert. profl. geologist. Geologist Ea. Associated Coal Corp., Pitts., 1971-73, Mid-Continent Coal & Coke Co., Carbondale, Colo., 1974-78; dir. prospect devel. Western Associated Coal Corp., Denver, 1978-81; supt. Blue Ribbon Coal Co., Paonia, Colo., 1981; dir. property devel. Western Assoc. Coal Corp., Delta, Colo., 1982-83; geology cons. Paonia, 1983-86; asst. to pres. Mid-Continent Resources, Inc., Carbondale, 1986—. Contbr. articles to profl. jours. Contbr. mem. Colo. Railroad Hist. Found., Golden, 1981—. Gulf Oil Co. fellow, 1969-71. Mem. Soc. Mining Engrs., Geol. Soc. Am., Am. Inst. Profl. Geologists, Am. Assn. Petroleum Geologists, Rocky Mountain Assn. Geologists, Railway Hist. Soc., Railway and Locomotive Hist. Soc. Methodist. Office: Mid-Continent Resources Inc PO Box 500 Carbondale CO 80623

COLLINS, CARTER COMPTON, research scientist, inventor; b. San Francisco, Aug. 3, 1925; s. Carter and Clella (Reeves) C.; m. Patricia Burns, Aug. 12, 1961; children: Carter Compton, Diana Reeves. BS in Engring. Physics, U. Calif., Berkeley, 1949, MSEE, 1953, PhD in Biophysics, 1966. R&D engr. Donner Sci. Co., Concord, Calif., 1953-55; chief bioastronautics div. Aviation Med. Acceleration Lab., Naval Air Devel. Ctr., Johnsville, Pa., 1958-59; dir. R&D lab. U. Calif. Med. Ctr., San Francisco, 1959-63; assoc. prof. U. Pacific, San Francisco, 1969-83; assoc. dir. Smith Kettlewell Inst., San Francisco, 1975-88—; sr. scientist Med. Rsch. Inst., San Francisco, 1963-88; sr. rsch. scientist Smith-Kettlewell Eye Rsch. Found., San Francisco, 1964—; cons. biomechanics group U. Calif. Med. Ctr., San Francisco, 1951-54; cons. Neurol. Inst., Mt. Zion Hosp., San Francisco, 1953-55; cons. physiology dept. U. Pa. Med. Sch., 1957-59; lectr. cardiology U. Calif. Med. Ctr., San Francisco, 1960-80. Patentee, author in field; editor Jour. Biomed. Systems, 1971-75. Mem. BMUG, NRC Com. on Vision, Nat. Acad. Sci., 1975-80; mem. fundamental neuroscis. adv. com. Nat. Inst. Neurol. and Communicative Disorders and Stroke, 1979—, mem. sci. programs adv. com., 1982—, sci. programs adv. com. 1984—. Recipient Hektoen Silver medal AMA, 1972, Hektoen Bronze medal, 1976; NIH, NSF, Fight for Sight, Fleischman Found. grantee 1969-84; Erskine fellow 1977. Mem. IEEE, AAAS, Assn. Rsch. in Vision and Opthalmology, Am. Assn. Artificial Intelligence, MENSA, San Francisco Macintosh Group, Sigma Xi. Home: 8 Ridge Ave Mill Valley CA 94941 Office: Smith-Kettlewell Inst Visual Scis 2232 Webster St San Francisco CA 94115

COLLINS, GEORGE TIMOTHY, computer software consultant; b. Connersville, Ind., Aug. 21, 1943; s. Robert Emerson and Oma (Richie) C.; m. Martha Elizabeth Holt, Apr. 30, 1966; children: Kirsten Stephanie, Eowyn Erika. BA in Math., Ind. U., 1966; MS in Computer Sci., Rensselaer Poly. Inst., 1971. Engr. program analyst Sikorsky Aircraft, Stratford, Conn., 1966-70; research mathematician Peter Eckrich, Ft. Wayne, Ind., 1970-75; sr. systems analyst Pyrotek Data Service, Ft. Walton Beach, Fla., 1975-77; sr. aerosystems engr. Gen. Dynamics, Ft. Worth, 1977-79; sr. specialist Electronic Data Systems, Las Vegas, Nev., 1979-81; sr. assoc. CACI Fed., San Diego, 1981-82; prin., gen. mgr. Structured Software Systems, Escondido, Calif., 1982—; cons. Hi-Shear Corp., Los Angeles, 1973-75. Developer (computer model and data base) Aircraft Stores Interface, 1975; (computer model) TAC Disrupter, 1981; co-developer (computer model) Tactical Air Def. Battle Model, 1978, Tactical Air and Land Ops., 1980. Bd. dirs. Family and Children's Service, Ft. Wayne, 1974. Mem. Assn. Computing Machinery (assoc.). Unitarian. Club: North County Chess (Escondido). Home: 121 W 8th Ave Escondido CA 92025

COLLINS, GERALD CHESTER, savings and loan executive; b. L.A., July 28, 1946; s. Chester Walter and Harriet Iva (Hart) C.; m. Midge A. Bigham, May 31, 1968; children: Julie L., Bart C. BA, Calif. State U., Northridge, 1970. Appraiser, v.p., regional mgr. Calif. Fed., L.A., 1970-85; v.p., loan mgr. no. Calif. Gibraltar Savs., San Francisco, 1985-87; sr. v.p. lending Gibraltar Savs., Simi Valley, Calif., 1987-88; with Wells Fargo Bank, Tulare, 1988—; bd. dirs. VCP, Inc., Visalia, Calif.; tchr. Coll. Sequoias, Visalia, 1988-89. Pres. Calif. Polit. Action Com., L.A.; with U.S. Army, 1966-69, Korea. Recipient Cert. of Merit, HUD, Visalia, 1984. Mem. Builders Industry Assn., Christian Bus. Men's Com. Republican. Methodist. Home: 1313 Chatham St Visalia CA 93277 Office: Wells Fargo Bank 229 E Tulare Ave Tulare CA 93274

COLLINS, JIM H., marriage and family therapist; b. Enid, Okla., Nov. 14, 1934; s. Carl V. and Wanda Mae (Ethridge) C.; m. Marion Elizabeth Craig, Sept. 3, 1965; children: Elizabeth Dawn, Candace Rochelle. BA, Tulsa U., 1968, M in Teaching Arts, 1972; EdD, George Washington U., 1985. Psychologist intern U.S. Penitentiary, Marion, Ill., 1973-74; asst. prof. Correction and Law Enforcement So. Ill. U., Carbondale, 1974-75; dir. Christian Counseling and Guidance Service Inc., Englewood, Colo., 1975—. Republican. Lodge: Kiwanis. Office: Christian Guidance & Counseling Svc Inc Ste 208 5660 Greenwood Plaza Blvd Englewood CO 80111

COLLINS, JOHN ADDISON, electrical engineer, consultant; b. Midway, Pa., Jan. 6, 1929; s. John William and Clodya (Boyles) C.; Lois Gregory, May 2, 1953; children: Lisa Margaret, Sean Gregory, John Patrick. BA, Washington and Jefferson Coll., 1951; BSEE, MIT, 1957. Staff engr. Jet Propulsion Lab., Pasadena, Calif., 1957-59, group supr., 1961-64; staff engr. instrumentation lab. MIT, Cambridge, 1959-61; engr. product devel. IBM, San Jose, 1964-67; mgr. electronic div. Analog Tech. Group, Pasadena, 1967-72; sr. staff engr. Hughes Aircraft Co., Torrance, Calif., 1973-77, asst. dept. mgr., 1977-81, sr. scientist, 1981-88; cons. engr. high voltage power conversion Cow Creek Enterprises, Azalea, Oreg., 1988—; cons. Hughes Aircraft Co., Torrance, 1988; lectr. Cow Creek Enterprises, Azalea, 1986-88. Served to lt.(j.g.) USNR, 1951-54, Korea. Mem. IEEE, AIAA. Home and Office: 14671 Upper Cow Creek Rd Azalea OR 97410

COLLINS, JOHN JOSEPH, lawyer; b. Los Angeles, Calif., Dec. 13, 1936; s. James Edward Collins and Helen Agnes Howard; m. Patricia Lynn Stephens; children: James H., Cynthia A., Robert J., Pamela M. Birmingham, John J. Jr., Lauren P., Williams, Andrea E. AB, U. Santa Clara, Santa Clara, 1958; LLB, Loyola U., L.A., 1961. Dep. county counsel Office of County Counsel, L.A., 1961-64; assoc. ptnr. mg. ptnr. Collins and Collins, L.A., 1964-81, Pasadena, Calif., 1981-84; mg. ptnr. Collins Collins Muir Traver, Pasadena, 1984—. Dir., pres., Soc. Friendly Sons of St. Patrick, L.A., 1964—; Mem. Calif. Def. Counsel (treas., dir.), Pasadena Bar Assn. (pres. elect 1989), Am. Bd. Trial Advocates (pres. L.A. chpt. 1989, nat. bd. dirs. 1985—, diplomate). Home: 979 Fallen Leaf Rd Arcadia CA 91006 Office: Collins Collins Muir & Traver 265 N Euclid Ave #300 Pasadena CA 91101

COLLINS, JOHN WENDLER, consumer products company executive; b. Rutherford, N.J., Nov. 7, 1930; s. Nelson Haley and Agnes Lucinda (Maier) C.; m. Martha E. Raiff, Oct. 26, 1952; children: Bruce, Nancy, Susan; m. Janet Doyle, July 17, 1975. B.A., Dartmouth Coll., 1952. V.p. Procter & Gamble Co., Cin., 1955-76; group v.p. Clorox Co., Oakland, Calif., 1976—, exec. v.p. ops., 1984, exec. v.p., chief operating officer, 1985-86, pres., chief operating officer, 1986—, dir., 1983—. Trustee East Oakland Youth Devel. Ctr., Oakland, 1976—; com. mem. United Way, Bay Area, 1976—. Served to lt. USNR, 1952-55. Mem. Phi Beta Kappa. Democrat. Home: 19 Honey Hill Rd Orinda CA 94563 Office: Clorox Co 1221 Broadway Oakland CA 94612 *

COLLINS, JUDITH ANN, librarian; b. San Francisco, Aug. 12, 1941; d. Walter George and Dorothy Louise (Eisenhut) Petersen; m. Curtis Allan Collins, Dec. 22, 1962; children: Nathaniel Christopher, Hillary Victoria. AA, Modesto Jr. Coll., 1962; BS, Oreg. State U., 1967; MS, Cath. U. Am., 1983. Library cons. World Bank, Washington, 1983-84; reference librarian Am. Bankers Assn., Washington, 1984-87, Monterey (Calif.) County Library, 1987—; circulation librarian Nat. Rural Electric Coop. Assn., Washington, 1984-87; tech. services librarian Zimmerman Assocs., Inc., Washington, 1986-87; substitute sch. librarian Fairfax County Schs., Va., 1986-87; media librarian Hartnell Community Coll., Salinas, Calif., 1987—, instr., 1988—; cons. AID, 1984-85. Ruling elder Presbyn. Ch., Springfield, Va., 1981-83; election ofcl. Fairfax Electoral Bd. (Va.), 1980-87, Monterey County Electoral Bd., 1987—. Mem. ALA, Spl. Libraries Assn., AAUW, Calif. Library Assn. Lodge: Order Eastern Star. Home: 24010 Ranchito del Rio Ct Salinas CA 93908

COLLINS, MARK STEVEN, naturalist, travel service owner; b. Norfolk, Va., Apr. 1, 1952; s. Marion C. and Johnie L. (Ray) C.; m. Marian E. Berger, June 1975 (div. Oct. 1979). BS in Wildlife Mgmt., Humboldt State Coll., 1975. Wildlife biologist U.S. Fish and Wildlife Svc., Hawaii Volcano National Park, 1976-78, Inst. Pacific Island Forestry, Honolulu, 1978-82; naturalist, owner Hawaiian Sunrise Excursions, Honolulu, 1983—; bd. dirs. Internat. Expeditions, Inc. Charter pres. Hawaiian Orchid Island Community Assn., Volcano, 1984. Recipient Spl. Achievement award U.S. Fish and Wildlife Svc., 1980. Office: Hawaiian Sunrise Excursions 3081-E Paty Dr Honolulu HI 96822 also: PO Box 62011 Honolulu HI 96839

COLLINS, MEGHAN ROBBINS, writer and storyteller; b. New Orleans, June 7, 1926; d. Maude Elsie (Gamble)Robbins; m. Sterrett Austin Burges, Mar. 24, 1945 (div. 1974); children: Peter Cameron, Laura, Elizabeth Burges Kahn; m. John S. Collins, Jan. 27, 1974. BA, Calif. State U.-Hayward, 1971. Freelance writer, storyteller Benicia, Calif., 1973—; garden columnist Benicia Herald, 1984-88. Author: Maiden Crown, 1979, Willow Maiden, 1985 (Parents mag. award 1985, Commonwealth Club award 1986); contbr. articles to various publs. Mem. Native Plant Soc., Master Gardeners Soc., Garden Writers Am., Children's. Democrat. Home: 1749 Valerie Ct Benicia CA 94510

COLLINS, MICHAEL SEAN, obstetrician, gynecologist; b. Yankton, S.D., Sept. 8, 1951; s. Edward Daniel and Joyce (Slatky) C.; m. Judy Furman, Sept. 20, 1975; children: Lauren, Sean, Carolyn. BS, Davidson Coll., 1973; MD, Med. U. S.C., 1977. Diplomate Am. Bd. Ob-Gyn. Chief resident in ob-gyn Med. U. S.C., Charleston, 1980-81; instr. in ob-gyn U. Oreg. Health Scis. Ctr., Portland, 1981—; chmn. dept. ob-gyn Good Samaritan Hosp., Portland, 1983-85; cons. Prepared Childbirth Assn., Portland, 1981—, Triplet Connection, L.A. , 1985—. Fellow Am. Coll. Ob-Gyn; mem. AMA, Oreg. Med. Assn., Oreg. Ob-Gyn Soc., Am. Fertility Soc., Porsche Club Am. Republican. Roman Catholic. Home: 716 NW Rapidan Terr Portland OR 97210 Office: NW Women's Clinic 2222 NW Lovejoy Portland OR 97210

COLLINS, MOSELEY CARY, III, lawyer; b. Tallahassee, Apr. 8, 1947; s. Mosely Cary II and Mary L. Palmer; m. Nancy G. Sugg, Dec. 6, 1975; children: Rod, Parris, Casey, Beau. BA, U. Fla., 1969, postgrad., 1970; student, Holy Word Bible Sch., 1975; JD, La Salle Extension, 1980. Bar: Calif., 1980. Atty., pres. Moseley Collins, III a Profl. Corp., San Jose, Calif., 1980—. Founder, pres. Mothers Against Drunk Drivers, San Jose, 1983; vol. asst. dist. atty Santa Cruz County (Calif.), 1984—, vol. asst. dist. atty. Santa Clara County (Calif.), 1987. Mem. ABA, Assn. Trial Lawyers Am., Calif. Trial Lawyers Assn. Republican. Office: Moseley Collins 1611 The Alameda San Jose CA 95126

COLLINS, PATRICIA ELAINE, counselor; b. L.A., Aug. 6, 1932; d. Sidney Willis and Marguerite (Wallace) French; m. Richard Bryan Collins, Dec. 28, 1958; children: Kathryn L., Lisa D., Erin S. BA in English, U. Calif., Berkeley, 1955; MA, Calif. State U., Dominguez, 1978. Cert. marriage, family, child counselor; lifetime cert. elem. tchr.; cert. gen. secondary tchr. Tchr. Los Angeles and El Segundo (Calif.) Schs., 1956-63; pvt. practice counseling, Torrance, Calif., 1984—; dir. youth programs St. Luke's Presbyn. Ch., Rolling Hills Estates, Calif., 1970-72; early childhood coordinator Palos Verdes (Calif.) Sch. System, 1976—; tutor Calif. State U., Dominguez, 1977-78. Pres. Rancho Vista PTA, Rolling Hills Estates, 1975; 1st v.p. South Bay Law Wives, Rolling Hills Estates, 1970; pres. Project Choice Com., Rancho Palos Verdes, Calif., 1987-88; mem. Nat. Charity League, Palos Verdes Estates. Recipient Hon. Service award Miraleste High Sch. PTA, Rancho Palos Verdes, 1987. Mem. Calif. Assn. Marriage and Family Therapists (clin.). Democrat. Office: 24586 Hawthorne Blvd Torrance CA 90505

COLLINS, PATRICK W., grocery stores company executive. Pres. Ralph's Grocery Co., Compton, Calif. Office: Ralph's Grocery Co 1100 W Artesia Blvd Compton CA 90220 *

COLLINS, PEGGY JANET, nurse; b. Wichita Falls, Tex., Dec. 13, 1920; d. James Alfred and Vera Mavourneen (McKinley) Stevens; m. Chester Francis Collins, Dec. 21, 1985. Diploma, Harris Nursing Sch., Ft. Worth, 1942; BS in Nursing, U. Calif., Calif., 1962; M, U. Calif., San Francisco, 1965; AA in Interior Design, Phoenix Coll., 1982. RN, Ariz., Calif., Tex. Pvt. duty nurse Harris Hosp., Ft. Worth, 1942-43; head nurse Eagle Pass Army Hosp., Tex., 1943-45; RN Doctors Pvt. Clinic, Santa Ana, Calif., 1965; staff nurse Fitzsimmons Army Hosp., Aurora, Colo., 1947-49; head nurse VA Hosp., Livermore, Calif., 1950-60, supr., 1961-65; assoc. chief nursing VA Hosp., Phoenix, 1966-77; night supr. VA Med. Ctr., Phoenix, 1977-79; pvt. practice Designer Interior and Apparel, Sedona, Ariz., 1985—. With USN. Mem. Ret. Tchrs. Assn., Doll Club Ariz. Republican. Home: 1061 Palisades Dr N Sedona AZ 86336

COLLINS, ROBERT OAKLEY, history educator; b. Waukegan, Ill., Apr. 1, 1933; s. William George and Louise Van Horsen (Jack) C.; m. Janyce Hutchins Monroe, Oct. 6, 1974; children by previous marriage: Catharine Louise, Randolph Ware, Robert William. B.A., Dartmouth Coll., 1954; A.B. (Marshall scholar 1954-55), Balliol Coll., Oxford U., 1956, M.A., 1960; M.A. (Ford fellow), Yale U., 1958, Ph.D., 1959. Instr. history Williams Coll., Williamstown, Mass., 1959-61; lectr. U. Mass. Extension, Pittsfield, 1960-61; vis. asst. prof. history Columbia U., N.Y.C., 1962-63; asst. prof. history Williams Coll., 1963-65; mem. faculty U. Calif., Santa Barbara, 1965—; prof. history U. Calif., 1969—; dir. U. Calif. (Center for Study Developing Nations), 1967-69, acting vice chancellor for research and grad. affairs, 1970-71, dean grad. div., 1971-80; vis. sr. assoc. fellow Oxford U., Eng., 1980-81; Trevelyan fellow Durham U., 1986—; vis. fellow Balliol Coll., Oxford (Eng.) U., 1987. Author: The Southern Sudan, 1883-1898, 1962, King Leopold, England and the Upper Nile, 1968, Problems in African History, 1968, The Partition of Africa, 1969, Land Beyond the Rivers: The Southern Sudan, 1898-1918, 1971, Europeans in Africa, 1971, An Arabian Diary, 1969, The Southern Sudan in Historical Perspective, 1975, Shadows in the Grass: Britain in the Southern Sudan, 1983, The British in the Sudan, 1898-1956, 1984. NDEA lang. fellow, 1960-61; Social Sci. Research Council fellow, 1962-63; Rockefeller Found. scholar-in-residence Bellagio, Italy, 1979, 87; Ford Found. fellow, 1979-81; Fulbright sr. research fellow, 1982; Woodrow Wilson fellow, 1983; Nat. Endowment for Humanities fellow, 1989; recipient Gold class award Order Scis. and Arts Dem. Republic of Sudan, 1980; John Ben Snow Found. prize, 1984; Trevelyan fellow Coll. Fellows Durham U., 1986, fellow Balliol Coll., Oxford U., 1986-87. Mem. Am. Hist. Assn., African Studies Assn., Western River Guides Assn., Sudan Studies Assn., Explorers Club, Phi Beta Kappa. Home: 735 Calle De Los Amigos Santa Barbara CA 93105 Office: U Calif Dept History Santa Barbara CA 93106

COLLINS, TERRENCE LEE, human resources executive, retired army officer; b. Los Angeles, Aug. 31, 1942; s. Albert Newton and Martha Zeta (Merrill) C.; m. Cheryl Jean Brokaw, Jan. 25, 1978; children—Sean Alexander, Patrick Dean, Michael Paul, Christopher Lee. B.S. in Bus. Adminstrn., Columbia Coll., 1977; grad. exec. program in mgmt., UCLA, 1987; cert. instr. effectiveness mgmt., U.S. Army Organizational Tng. Inst. Enlisted U.S. Army, 1960, commd. capt., 1977, advanced to maj., 1979; multiple assignments primarily in human resources mgmt.; ret., 1980; profl. relations mgr. Nat. Med. Enterprises Inc., Los Angeles, 1980-81; personnel dir. HR Textron Inc., Valencia, Calif., 1981-86; v.p. human resources VSI Aerospace

Products div. Fairchild, Inc., Culver City, Calif., 1986—. Decorated Legion of Merit, 2 Bronze Stars, 4 Meritorious Service medals, Air medal, Army Commendation medal, Nat. Def. Service medal; Vietnam Cross Gallantry, Vietnam Service medal. Mem. Am. Soc. Tng. and Devel., Employment Mgmt. Assn., Am. Soc. Personnel Adminstrs., Army Assn. U.S., Nat. Mgmt. Assn. Republican. Methodist. Author textbook for sr. Army ednl. tng. course. Home: 6184 E Palomino Circle Somis CA 93066 Office: Fairchild Inc VSI Aerospace Products Div 3630 Eastham Dr Culver City CA 90232

COLLINS, THEODORE JOHN, lawyer; b. Walla Walla, Wash., Oct. 2, 1936; s. Robert Bonfield and Catherine Roselle (Snyder) C.; m. Patricia Spengler Pasieka, May 11, 1968; children: Jonathan, Caitlin, Matthew, Patrick, Flannery. BA, U. Notre Dame, 1958; postgrad., U. Bonn, Fed. Republic Germany, 1959; LLB, Harvard U., 1962. Bar: Wash. 1962, U.S. Supreme Ct. 1982, U.S. Ct. Appeals (fed. cir.) 1982, U.S. Dist. Ct. (ea. dist.) Wash. 1965, U.S. Dist. Ct. (we. dist.) Wash. 1962. Ptnr. Perkins Coie Law Firm, Seattle, 1962-86; v.p., gen. counsel The Boeing Co., Seattle, 1986—. Mem. ABA, Boeing Mgmt. Assn., Wash. State Bar Assn., King County Bar Assn., Wash. Athletic Club, Columbia Tower Club. Office: The Boeing Co PO Box 3707 M/S 13-08 Seattle WA 98124

COLLINS, WILLIAM LEROY, telecommunications engineer; b. Laurel, Miss., June 17, 1942; s. Henry L. and Christene E. (Finnegan) C. Student, La Salle U., 1969; BS in Computer Sci., U. Beverly Hills, 1984. Sr. computer operator Dept. Pub. Safety, Phoenix, 1975-78, data communications specialist, 1978-79, supr. computer ops., 1981-82; mgr. network control Valley Nat. Bank, Phoenix, 1979-81; mgr. data communications Ariz. Lottery, Phoenix, 1982-85; mgr. telecommunications Calif. Lottery, Sacramento, 1985—. Served as sgt. USAF, 1964-68. Mem. Soc. Mfg. Engrs., Data Processing Mgmt. Assn., Am. Mgmt. Assn., Assn. Computing Machinery. Roman Catholic. Lodge: K.C. Home: 610 Howe Ave #44 Sacramento CA 95825 Office: Calif State Lottery 600 N 10th St Sacramento CA 95814

COLLINSON, BRENT PATRICK, lawyer; b. Merced, Calif., Jan. 9, 1952; s. Roger Whitfield and Aileen June C.; m. Dianne Louise West, June 22, 1974. AB, U. Calif., Davis, 1974; JD, U. Pacific, 1985—. Bar: Calif. 1979, U.S. Dist. ct. (ea. dist.) Calif. 1979. Assoc. Law Offices of George L. Pifer, Truckee, Calif., 1979-80, Richard J. Schneider P.C., Truckee, 1981-82; ptnr. Schneider, Collinson & Lange, Truckee, 1983-84; pvt. practice law Truckee, 1985—; instr. Sierra Jr. Coll., Truckee, 1981. County chairperson McCloskey for Pres., 1971. Recipient Outstanding Community Participation recognition Sacramento Blood Found., 1987. Mem. Truckee Donner C. of C., Truckee Donner Hist. Soc., Tahoe Truckee Bar Assn. (bd. dirs. 1981-83, pres. 1982), Truckee Rotary (bd. dirs. 1984-87, v.p. found. 1988-89, Paul Harris fellow). Office: PO Box 8550 Truckee CA 95737

COLLMAN, JAMES PADDOCK, chemistry educator; b. Beatrice, Nebr., Oct. 31, 1932; married. B.Sc., U. Nebr., 1954, M.S., 1956; Ph.D. (NSF fellow), U. Ill., 1958; Ph.D. (hon.), U. Nebr., 1988; Docteur Honoris Causa, U. Dijon, France, 1988. Instr. chemistry U. N.C., Chapel Hill, 1958-59; asst. prof. U. N.C., 1959-62, asso. prof., 1962-67; prof. chemistry Stanford U., 1967—, George A. and Hilda M. Daubert prof. chemistry, 1980—; Frontiers in Chemistry lectr., 1964, Nebr. lectureship, 1968; Venable lectr. U. N.C., 1971; Edward Clark Lee lectr. U. Chgo., 1972; vis. Erskine fellow U. Canterbury, 1972; Plenary lectr. French Chem. Soc., 1974; Dreyfus lectr. U. Kans., 1974; distinguished inorganic lectr. U. Rochester, 1974; Reilley lectr. U. Notre Dame, 1975; William Pyle Philips lectr. Haverford Coll., 1975; Merck lectr. Rutgers U., 1976; FMC lectr. Princeton, 1977; Julius Stieglitz lectr. Chgo. sect. Am. Chem. Soc., 1977; Pres.'s Seminar Series lectr. U. Ariz., 1980; Frank C. Whitmore lectr. Pa. State U., 1980; Plenary lectr. 3d IUPAC Symposium on Organic Synthesis, 1980, 2d Internat. Kyoto Conf. on New Aspects Inorganic Chemistry, 1982, Internat. Symposium on Models of Enzyme Action, Brighton, Eng., 1983, Internat. Symposium, Italy, 1984; Brockman lectr. U. Ga., 1981; Samuel C. Lind lectr. U. Tenn., 1981, Syntex Disting. lectr. Colo. State U., 1983; disting. vis. lectr. U. Fla., 1983; vis. prof. U. Auckland, New Zealand, 1985; Nelson J. Leonard lectr. U. Ill., 1987. Recipient Disting. Teaching award Stanford U., 1981, Calif. Scientist of Year award, 1983, Allan V. Cox medal for excellence in fostering undergrad. rsch., 1988; named George A. and Hilda M. Daubert Prof. Chemistry (endowed chair, Stanford U.), 1980; Guggenheim fellow, 1977-78, 85-86. Mem. Am. Chem. Soc. (Calif. Sect. award 1972, soc. award in inorganic chemistry 1975, Arthur C. Cope award 1986), N.Y. Acad. Sci., Chem. Soc. (London), Nat. Acad. Sci., Am. Acad. Arts and Scis., Phi Beta Kappa, Sigma Xi, Phi Lambda Upsilon, Alpha Chi Sigma.

COLLMER, RUSSELL CRAVENER, data processing executive, educator; b. Guatemala, Jan. 2, 1924; s. G. Russell and Constance (Cravener) C.; B.S., U. N.M., 1951; postgrad. Calif. Inst. Tech., 1943-44; M.S., State U. Iowa, 1955; m. Ruth Hannah Adams, Mar. 4, 1950; 1 son, Reed Alan. Staff mem. Mass. Inst. Tech., Lincoln Lab., Lexington, 1955-57; mgr. systems modeling, computer dept. Gen. Electric, Phoenix, 1957-59; mgr. ARCAS Thompson Ramo Wooldridge, Inc., Canoga Park, Cal., 1959-62; asso. mgr. tech. dir. CCIS-70 Bunker-Ramo Corp., 1962-64; sr. asso. Planning Research Corp., Los Angeles, 1964-65; pres. R. Collmer Assos., Benson, Ariz., 1965—; pres. Benson Econ. Enterprises Corp., 1968-69. Lectr. computer scis. Pima Community Coll., Tucson, 1970—. Served with USAAC, 1942-46, to capt. USAF, 1951-53. Mem. IEEE, Am. Meteorol. Soc., Assn. for Computing Machinery, Phi Delta Theta, Kappa Mu Epsilon. Republican. Baptist. Office: R Collmer Assocs PO Box 864 Benson AZ 85602

COLLOM, THOMAS LINDELL, architect, landscape designer; b. San Francisco, Aug. 18, 1962; s. Arthur Burton and Birgitta Maria (Lindell) C. BArch, U. Calif., Berkeley, 1985. Architect, designer DeTienne Assocs., San Francisco, 1987—; landscapr designer City of Burlingame, Calif., 1986. Recipient 1st Place award NEA City of St. Paul, 1985, Hon. award City of Burlingame, 1986; 1st Place award Nat. Furniture as Art Competition, 1988. Home: 456 8th Ave San Francisco CA 94118

COLN, WILLIAM ALEXANDER, III, transportation executive; b. Los Angeles, Mar. 20, 1942; s. William Alexander and Aileen Henrietta (Shimfessel) C.; m. Lora Louise Getchel, Nov. 15, 1969 (div. July 1979); 1 child, Caryn Louise. BA in Geography, UCLA, 1966. Cert. airline transport pilot, flight engr. Commd. USN, Pensacola, Fla., 1966; pilot, officer USN, Fighter Squadron 102, 1969-71, Port Mugu, Calif., 1975-77; pilot, officer USNR, Port Mugu, Calif., 1971-75, advanced through grades to lt. comdr., 1978; ret. USNR, 1984; airline pilot Delta Airlines, Inc. (formerly Western Airlines Inc.), Los Angeles, 1972—. Recipient Nat. Def. medal USN, 1966. Mem. Nat. Aero. Assn., Airline Pilots Assn., Aircraft Owners and Pilots Assn., UCLA Alumni Assn., Am. Bonanza Soc. Democrat. Club: Santa Barbara (Calif.) Athletic. Home: 519 West Quinto St Santa Barbara CA 93105 Office: Delta Air Lines Inc Los Angeles Internat Airport Los Angeles CA 90009

COLÓN, ALY ANTONIO, journalist; b. Santurce, P.R., Mar. 6, 1952; s. Juan Antonio and Maria Magdalena (DelValle) C.; m. Deborah Sum Colón, June 1, 1974 (dec.). BA in Journalism, Loyola U., New Orleans, 1974; MA in Journalism, Stanford U., 1975; cert., Columbia U., 1983. Northwest bur. chief Fairchild News Service, Seattle, 1977-79; asst. mag. editor The Oakland Press, Pontiac, Mich., 1979, spl. projects writer, 1980, inflation columnist, 1980, regional reporter, 1980-81; bus. reporter The Oakland Press, Pontiac, 1981-82; asst. economy editor The Herald, Everett, Wash., 1983-86, economy editor, 1987—. Author: (with others) Main Street and the Third World, 1986. Bagehot fellow Columbia U., N.Y.C., 1982-83, NEH fellow U. Kans., Lawrence, 1981, Am. Bankers Assn. Communications fellow U. Del., 1987. Mem. Soc. Profl. Journalists, Soc. Am. Bus. Editors and Writers. Office: The Herald California and Grand Ave Everett WA 98201

COLPRON, MERLYN DALLAS, insurance executive; b. Newfolden, Minn., June 25, 1933; s. Ismael Charles and Freda Olivia (Nesterud) C.; m. Patricia Rose Gilbert, May 26, 1960; children: Cynthia Jean, David Allen. AA in Bus. Adminstrn., Lower Columbia Jr. Coll., 1953; BA in Fin., U. Wash., 1955. CPCU Ins. mgr. United Grocers Inc., Portland, Oreg., 1970-75; bur. chief Idaho Bur. Risk Mgmt. Boise, 1975-76; v.p., cons. Diversified Risk Mgmt. Services Inc., Boise, 1976-80; sec. Assoc. Loggers Mgmt. Corp., Boise, 1979—; v.p. Bayly, Martin & Faye Inc., Boise, 1980-82; pres. U.S. Risk Mgmt. Services Inc., Boise, 1982-86; pres. North/South Ins. Cons., Inc., Miami/Boise, 1986; risk mgr., cons. Stein-McMurray Ins. Svs., Boise, Idaho, 1986—; dir. Assoc. Loggers Exchange, Boise, 1979—. With U.S. Army, 1955-57. Mem. Soc. CPCU. Methodist. Home: 4014 Kingswood Dr Boise ID 83704

COLT, JAMES STEWART, dentist, educator; b. Salt Lake City, Mar. 27, 1944; s. Benjamin Johnand Verginia Marie (Hopkin) C.; m. Leslie Ann Ford, Aug. 26, 1966; children: Christopher, Deborah, Robert. BA, U. Utah, 1969; DDS, U. Nebr., 1973. Pvt. practice dentistry, Lakewood, Colo., 1973—; asst. prof. U. Colo., Denver, 1984—, dir. Temperomandibular Joint Disorder Clinic, 1988—. Del. Colo. Republican Com., 1986. U. Colo. grantee, 1988. Mem. ADA, Colo. Dental Assn., Brigham Young U. Acad. Dentists (nat. bd. dirs. 1975—), Acad. Gen. Dentistry, Met. Denver Dental Soc., Am. Assn. for Functional Orthodontics. Mormon. Office: Craniofacial Pain Diagnostics Ste 309 3333 S Wadsworth Blvd Lakewood CO 80227

COLTON, JOYCE PHYLLIS, interior designer; b. Los Angeles, Dec. 17, 1925; d. Sam and Syd (Woolf) Wurtzel; m. Herbert Lloyd Colton, June 16, 1946 (div. 1978); children: Christine Dana, Pamela Jan. Student, Chouinard Art Inst., 1941, U. N.Mex., 1946; AA, UCLA, 1946; BA, Immaculate Heart Coll., 1977. Interior designer Lloyd Kent Interiors, Los Angeles, 1954-61, Blackmans Interiors, Van Nuys, Calif., 1961-62, Taylor's Fine Furniture, Van Nuys, 1962-65, Glabman's, Los Angeles, 1965, Fran Sanders Interiors, Encino, Calif., 1965-66; interior designer Joyce Colton & Assocs., Van Nuys, 1966-87, Eastsound, Wash., 1987—; cons. Syverson & Son, Eastsound, 1988—. Researcher: Materials of Design, 1977; contbr. articles to profl. jours.; works include: Immaculate Heart Coll., Monica Hotel, VA Hosp. Sylmar, Monte Sano Hosp., Los Angeles, Rapisardi Restaurant, Santa Monica and numerous corp. and pvt. facilities. Designer Heritage Square Com., Los Angeles, 1970's, Banning House Restoration, Wilmington, Calif., 1970's; mem. Los Angeles Olympics Organizing Com., 1984, adv. com. Channel 50 TV Video Series, Costa Mesa, Calif., 1977. Fellow Internat. Soc. Interior Designers, 1981. Mem. AAUW (v.p. 1988—), Am. Soc. Interior Designers (pres. L.A. chpt. 1977), Nat. Soc. Interior Designers (numerous offices), Art Deco Soc. L.A. (founder, pres.). Republican. Home and Office: PO Box 729 Eastsound WA 98245

COLTON, ROY CHARLES, management consultant; b. Phila., Feb. 26, 1941; s. Nathan Hale and Ruth Janis (Baylinson) C.; B.A., Knox Coll., 1962; M.Ed., Temple U., 1963. With Sch. Dist. of Phila., 1963-64; systems analyst Wilmington Trust Co., 1967-69; exec. recruiter Atwood Consultants Inc., Phila., 1969-71; pres. Colton Bernard Inc., San Francisco, 1971—; occasional lectr. Fashion Inst. Tech., Phila. Coll. Textiles and Scis. Served with AUS, 1964-66. Mem. San Francisco Fashion Industries, San Francisco C. of C., Calif. Exec. Recruiter Assn., Nat. Assn. Exec. Recruiters, Am. Apparel Mfrs. Assn., Am. Arbitration Assn. (panel arbitrators), Am. Mgmt. Assn. Office: Colton Bernard Inc 417 Spruce St San Francisco CA 94118

COLUMBO, JOHN A(RTHUR), industrial executive; b. Spokane, Wash., Dec. 7, 1951; s. James D. Columbo and Joan L. (Jury) DeHaan; m. Cathy L. Asher, Nov. 20, 1971 (div. 1979); 1 child, Jonquil; m. Dawn A. Smith; 1 child, Jessica. AA, Portland Community Coll., 1973; student, Pacific U., 1973-74. With prodn. RTE Transformer, Tigard, Oreg., 1973-76; mgr. sales WTC Airfreight, Portland, 1976-77; dist. mgr. Coast Carloading Co., Portland, 1977-80; regional mgr. A.W. Chesterton Co., Stoneham, Mass., 1980—. Coach Men's Softball Teams, Portland, 1978-87; pres. Tualatin Hills Park & Recreation Dist., Beaverton, Oreg., 1982-83. Served with U.S. Army, 1970-72. Mem. Nat. Assn. Power Engrs. (assoc.), Tech. Assn. Pulp and Paper Industry, Nat. Assn. Petroleum ReRefiners (speaker 1985), Weyerhauser Corp. Maintenance Engring. Mfrs., Paper and Pulp Industry Mgmt. Assn. (speaker 1985-86), Pacific Energy Assn. Roman Catholic. Office: AW Chesterton Co 6125 N Basin Portland OR 97217

COLVIN, CLARK SHERMAN, management consultant; b. Seattle, Oct. 26, 1958; s. Henry Alfred and Dorothy Angie (Tigner) C.; m. Patricia Ann Stanford, Mar. 12, 1989. BA, U. Wash., 1984; MPA, Seattle U., 1986; postgrad., Golden Gate U., 1986—, Oxford U., 1989. Owner, mgr. COMCAR Computerized Auto Network, Bellevue, Wash., 1981-82; spl. asst. Wash. State Senate, Olympia, 1983-84; state chmn., pres. Wash. State Pub. Lands Assn., Seattle, 1984-86; master tchr. Independent Learning High Sch., Berkeley, Calif., 1986-87; gen. ptnr. Armand E.R. Mulden & Assoc., Livermore, Calif., 1987—; adj. prof. Chapman Coll., Vallejo, Calif., 1987-88; legis. liaison Ken Selander, Atty., Burien, Wash., 1984; faculty assoc. Intercollegiate Studies Inst., Bryn Mawr, Pa., 1988. Author: Where Jurisdictions Meet, 1984, (with others) Conflict Analysis and Resolution, 1988. Mgr. Danville (Calif.) City Coun. campaign, 1987. Lt. USNR, 1977-81, 86—; mem. Rep. Nat. Com., Washington; mem. Woodrow Wilson Internat. Ctr. for Scholars. Mem. Soc. for U.S. Constitution, Assn. Mil. Surgeons U.S. (medal), Nav. Res. Assn., Ctr. for Study of Presidency, As. Soc. Pub. Adminstrn., Oxford Ctr. Mgmt. Studies Assn. Methodist. Home: 20 Cascade Key Bellevue WA 98006 Office: Armand E R Mulder & Assocs PO Box 2296 Livermore CA 94550

COLVIN, ROBERT ALLAN, health facility administrator; b. Idaho Falls, Idaho, Mar. 18, 1952; s. Charles R. Colvin and Ruth A. (Young) Gray; m. Susan Linda Knauss, Dec. 27, 1969; children: Heather Marie, Kristopher Patrick. BBA, Idaho State U., 1975, MBA, 1980. Sales mgr. Boise Cascade Corp., Pocatello, Idaho, 1980-82; dir. een., admissions and projects Ea. Idaho Regional Med. Ctr., Idaho Falls, Idaho, 1982-84; asst. adminstr. West Valley Med. Ctr., Caldwell, Idaho, 1984-86; chief exec. officer Gritman Meml. Hosp., Moscow, Idaho, 1986—. Bd. dirs. Washington/Idaho Symphony, Moscow, Idaho, 1986-88. Recipient Orgn. Innovator award, Healthcare Forum/3M Corp., San Francisco, 1988, President's Outstanding Achievement award, Idaho State U., Pocatello, 1975. Mem. Am. Coll. Healthcare Execs. (regent's adv. coun., 1987-89), Idaho Hosp. Assn. (sec., treas., 1988-89), No. Conf. of the Idaho Hosp. Assn. (pres. 1988-89), Health Orgn. for Polit. Effectiveness (chmn. 1988-89), Rotary. Episcopalian. Home: 524 N Blaine Moscow ID 83843

COMBS, ARTHUR WRIGHT, psychology educator; b. Newark, June 3, 1912; s. Arthur Wright and Charlotte (Vyse) C.; m. Mildred Janet Mitchell, Sept. 23, 1934 (div.); children—Carol Andrea, Peter Arthur; m. Susan Jane Kannel, Dec. 27, 1976; children—Lynn Ann, Erin Elizabeth. B.S., Ohio State U., 1935, M.A., 1942, Ph.D., 1945. Diplomate Am. Bd. Examiners Profl. Psychology. Tchr., sch. psychologist Alliance (Ohio) Pub. Schs., 1935-41; teaching asst. Ohio State U., 1941-43; asst., assoc. prof., head personal counseling service, dir. clin. tng. Syracuse U., 1943-54; prof. edn., founds. in edn. dept. U. Fla., Gainesville, 1954-76; cons. edn. and psychology, Greeley, Colo., 1976—; ptnr. Community Counseling Assocs., Greeley; disting. prof. U. No. Colo., 1978-81. Author: (with others) Casebook of Nondirective Counseling, 1947; (with D. Snygg) Individual Behavior: A New Frame of Reference for Psychology, 1949; Individual Behavior: A Perceptual Approach to Behavior, 1959; Human Relations, Instructor's Handbook including Suggested Discussion Material, 1953; (with R. S. Fisk) Human Relations Training for School Administrators, 1954; Instructor's Handbook for NCO Human Relations Course, 1954; (with D. W. Soper) The Relationship of Child Perceptions to Achievement and Behavior in the Early School Years, 1963; The Professional Education of Teachers; A Perceptual View of Teacher Preparation, 1965, rev. edit., 1972; (with D. Avila and W. Purkey) Helping Relationships: Basic Concepts for the Helping Professions, 1971, rev., 1977, 85; Helping Relationships Sourcebook, 1971, rev., 1977; (with H. Wass, R. Blum and W. Hedges) Humanistic Teacher Education: An Experiment in Systematic Curriculum Innovation, 1974. Editor: Perceiving, Behaving, Becoming: A New Focus for Education, 1962; (with A. C. Richards and F. Richards) Perceptual Psychology: A Humanistic Approach to the Study of Persons, 1976; Myths in Education, 1979; A Personal Approach to Teaching: Beliefs That Make a Difference, 1983, A Theory of Therapy: Guideline to Counseling Practice, 1989. Contbr. articles to profl. jours. Recipient Am. Personnel and Guidance Assn. commendation for outstanding research, 1963, John Dewey Soc. award for outstanding contbns. to contemporary edn., 1967. Fellow Am. Psychol. Assn.; mem. NEA, Fla. Edn. Assn., Soc. Psychol. Study Social Issues, Assn. Supervision and Curriculum Devel. (past nat. pres.), Fla. Assn. Sch. Psychologists (past pres.), Sigma Xi, Phi Delta Kappa. Home: 2327 19th Ave Greeley CO 80631 Office: Community Counseling Assocs 2525 16th St Greeley CO 80631

COMBS, CHARLES CLAYTON, JR., aerospace engineer; b. Lexington, Ky., Apr. 20, 1953; s. Charles Clayton and Betty-jo (Clark) C.; m. Elaine Marie Wolk, Apr. 9, 1977. BS, USAF Acad., 1976; MS, Ariz. State U., 1983. Commd. 2nd lt. USAF, 1976, advanced through grades to capt., 1980; served as B-52 pilot 319th Bomb Wing USAF, Grand Forks, N.D., 1976-79; T-38 instr. pilot, Williams Airfield Mgr. USAF, Williams AFB, Ariz., 1979-82; resigned USAF, 1982; flight test engr., analyst McDonnell Douglas Helicopters, Tempe, Ariz., 1982-84; ops. analysis supr. Gen. Dynamics Space Systems, San Diego, 1985-87; air-to-surface mission analysis mgr. Northrop Aircraft, Hawthorne, Calif., 1987--. Active Young Repubs., San Diego, 1987, St. Joseph's Parish, San Diego, 1986. Mem. AIAA, Air Force Assn. (life), USAF Acad. Assn. Grads. (life). Roman Catholic.

COMBS, CONNIE, bank executive, human resources manager; b. Prescott, Ariz., Mar. 6, 1937; d. Clarence William and Mildred Cornelius (Storey) Baller; m. Norman R. Combs (dec. Nov. 1982). A in Philosophy, Glendale Community Coll., 1969. Teller First Nat. Bank of Ariz., Phoenix, 1955-59, Valley Nat. Bank, Prescott, 1959-60; adminstrv. asst. Valley Nat. Bank, Phoenix, 1960-67, liaison, analyst, 1967-71, asst. v.p., mgr. personnel services, 1971-78, v.p., mgr. career services, 1978-85, v.p., mgr. recruiting, tng., and compensation, 1985-87, v.p., mgr. performance mgmt., 1987-88, v.p., mgr. benefits and exec. compensation, 1988—. Contbr. articles to bus. jour., 1985. Mem. Nat. Assn. of Bank Women, Ariz. Bankers Assn. (com. chmn. 1984), Am. Inst. of Banking (chmn. nat. com. 1979), Phoenix City Club, Soc. for the Arts. Republican. Office: Valley Nat Bank PO Box 71 (B303) Phoenix AZ 85001

COMBS, JOHN G., real estate executive; b. Odessa, Tex., Dec. 26, 1958; s. Bob Joe and Dorris Louise (Summers) C.; m. Andrea Lyn Johnson, June 12, 1982; 1 child, Brittney Lyn. BBA, So. Meth. U., 1981; MBA, U. Dallas, 1987. Cert. property mgr. Asst. property mgr. Vantage Cos., Dallas, 1980-81; property mgr. Vantage Cos., 1981-83, sr. property mgr., 1983-84, asst. v.p., 1984-86, v.p., 1986-87; dir. asset mgmt. O'Donnell Armstrong Brigham & Ptnrs., Costa Mesa, Calif., 1987-88; exec. dir. asset mgmt. O'Donnell Armstrong & Ptnrs., Irvine, Calif., 1988—, O'Donnell Hopkins & Ptnrs., Irvine, 1988—, O'Donnell Investment Ptnrs., Irvine, 1988—; guest lectr. U. Calif., Irvine, 1989. Named Property Mgr. of the Yr., Vantage Mgmt. Co., Dallas, 1984. Mem. Inst. Real Estate Mgmt. (prog. chmn. Orange County, Calif. 1989, exec. coun. 1989), Bldg. Owners and Mgrs. Assn. Republican. Christian Ch. Home: 25022 Whitespring Mission Viejo CA 95672

COMEAU, PAUL THEODORE, foreign language educator. Student, Joliette (Quebec) Seminary, 1943-44; BA, Assumption Coll., 1949; MA, Princeton U., 1964, PhD, 1968. Cert. translator. Enlisted USAF, 1950-52, advanced through grades to lt. col., 1968, ret., 1975; instr. of French USAF Acad., 1964-66, asst. prof. of French, 1967, assoc. prof. of French, 1968-70; dir. of curriculum AFROTC Hdqrs., Maxwell AFB, 1970-72; prof. head dept. aerospace studies AFROTC Hdqrs., 1972-75; vis. assoc. prof. Latin N.Mex. State U., 1975-76, assoc. prof. French/Latin, 1976-88, prof. fgn. langs., 1988-89, ret., July, 1989; grad. Dean's Rep. Final Exam. Com., 1976—; sec. grad. coun. N.Mex. State U., 1988—, mem. planning com., 1988—. Author: Diehards and Innovators. The French Romantic Struggle: 1800-1830., 1988, Workbook for Wheelock's Latin: An Introductory Course, 1980; contbr. articles to profl. jours. and publs. bd. dirs. United Way of Dona Ana County, 1978-80, chmn. spl. gifts div. 1974; bd. dirs. Newman Ctr. 1980-82. Rsch. grantee N.Mex. State U., 1978, Can. Embassy, 1985. Mem. Modern Lang. Assn., Am. Coun. on the Teaching of Fgn. Langs., Am. Assn. of Teachers of French, Rocky Mountain Modern Lang. Assn., Nineteenth Century French Colloquium, Am. Translators Assn., Am. Literary Translators Assn., Am. Coun. for Quebec Studies, Rotary (pres. Las Cruces 1979-80), Rotary Internat. (Paul Harris fellow 1989). Home: 1023 Avondale Dr Las Cruces NM 88005

COMELIN, JEAN PAUL, choreographer, artistic director; b. Vannes, France, Sept. 10, 1936; came to U.S., 1967.; s. Albert Comelin; m. Marilyn Burr (div.); m. Leslie McBeth, July 24, 1986. Student, Paris Conservatoire, 1951-55. Dancer Paris Opera Ballet, 1955-60; prin. dancer London Festival Ballet, 1963-67; prin. dancer, choreographer Washington Ballet, 1967-69; choreographer Pa. Ballet, Phila., 1969-73; artistic dir., choreographer Milw. Ballet, 1974-81; balletmaster, choreographer Stuttgart (Fed. Republic Germany) Ballet, 1981-83; dir., choreographer Ballet Ariz., Phoenix, 1983—. Choreographer numerous ballets. Nat. Endowment Arts grantee, 1975, 76, 77, 78. Mem. Ariz. for Cultural Devel. (bd. dirs.). Office: Ballet Ariz 3645 E Indian School Rd Phoenix AZ 85018

COMES, ROBERT GEORGE, research scientist; b. Bangor, Pa., July 7, 1931; s. Victor Francis and Mabel Elizabeth (Mack) C.; student U. Detroit, 1957-58, Oreg. State Coll., 1959-60, U. Nev., 1960, Regis Coll., 1961-62; m. Carol Lee Turinetti, Nov. 28, 1952; children: Pamela Jo, Robert G. II, Shawni Lee, Sheryl Lynn, Michelle Ann. Tech. liaison engr. Burroughs Corp., Detroit, 1955-60, mgr. reliability and maintainability engring., Paoli, Pa., 1962-63, Colorado Springs, Colo., 1963-67; sr. engr. Martin Marietta Corp., Denver, 1960-62; program mgr., rsch. scientist Kaman Scis. Corp., Colorado Springs, 1967-75; dir. engring. Sci. Applications, Inc., Colorado Springs, 1975-80; mgr. space def. programs Burroughs Corp., Colorado Springs, 1980-82; tech. staff Mitre Corp., Colorado Springs, 1982-85; dir. Colorado Springs opn. Beers Assoc., Inc., 1985; dir. space programs Electro Magnetic Applications, Inc., Colorado Springs, 1985-87; dir. Space Systems, Profl. Mgmt. Assocs., Inc., 1987-88; mgr. Computer Svcs., Inc., Colorado Springs, 1989—; chmn. Reliability and Maintainability Data Bank Improvement Program, Govt.-Industry Data Exch. Program, 1978-80—; cons. in field. Youth dir. Indian Guides program YMCA, 1963-64; scoutmaster Boy Scouts Am., 1972-73; chmn. bd. dirs. Pikes Peak Regional Sci. Fair, 1972-84. Served with USAF, 1951-55. Mem. AAAS, IEEE, Inst. Environ. Scis., Soc. Logistics Engrs., Am. Soc. Quality Control. Lutheran. Club: Colorado Springs Racquet. Author: Maintainability Engineering Principles and Standards, 1962. Inventor Phase Shifting aircraft power supply, 1957. Home: 4309 Tipton Ct Colorado Springs CO 80915 Office: Computerware Svcs Inc 4309 Tipton Ct Colorado Springs CO 80915

COMPTON, JAMES MARTIN, manufacturing executive, corporate professional; b. Salem, Oreg., May 19, 1942; s. Otis Charles and Ruth Fay (Star) C.; m. Gail Louise Terzenbach, June 14, 1963; children: Lisa, Scott. BA, Western Oreg. State Coll., Mommouth, 1966. Mgr. bldg. materials div. Jack Largent Co., Salem, Oreg., 1967-73; sales mgr. Evans Products Co., Permaglas Div., Corvallis, Oreg., 1973-75, plant mgr., 1975-78, gen. mgr., 1978-80; v.p. and gen. mgr. Evanite Permaglas, Inc., Corvallis, Oreg., 1980-88; pres. Evanite Fiber Corp., Permaglas Div., Corvallis, Oreg., 1988--; faculty mem. Roofing Industry Edn. Inst., Englewood, Colo.; com. mem. Underwriters Labs Industry Council, Northbrook, Ill. Author: tech. manuals, Built-up Roofing Systems, 1978, Roof Maintence 1980, EPDM Roofing Systems, 1982, Modified Asphalt Roofing Systems, 1984. Dir. Corvallis YMCA, 1977, Boys and Girls Club, 1980, Am. Youth Soccer Orgn., 1981. Mem. Asphalt Roofing Mfgs. (dir. 1983-88), Constrn. Specifications Inst. (Roofing Com. 1986-88), Western Roofing Constrns. Assn., Nat. Roofing Contractors Assn. (Industry Cons.), Hawaii Roofing Contractors Assn. (cons. and guest speaker bureau), Single Ply Roofing Inst., Corvallis Country Club, Corvallis Elks. Home: 4170 NW Dale Dr Corvallis OR 97330 Office: Evanite Fiber Corp PO Box E Corvallis OR 97339

COMSTOCK, JAMES WILLIAM, pension plan consultant; b. Grand Rapids, Mich., Sept. 27, 1946; s. William Charles and Marjorie Jean (Lovell) C.; m. Mary Jo Comstock, June 10, 1972 (div. 1977); m. Catherine Ann Comstock, May 31, 1980. BA in Mktg., Mich. State U., 1969; postgrad., Ga. State U., 1971-72. CLU; chartered fin. cons. Reg. mgr. spl. mkts. Lincoln Nat. Life Ins. Co., Balt., 1972-73; reg. equities mgr. Lincoln Nat. Life Ins. Co., Washington, 1973-74; v.p. Nat. Career Ctrs., Washington, 1974-75; group and pension mgr. Lincoln Nat Life Ins. Co., Columbus, Ohio, 1975-79; agt. Lincoln Nat Life Ins. Co., L.A., 1979; sales mgr. Am. Employee Ins. Agy., L.A., 1979-82; reg. pension cons. Am. Employee Ins. Co., L.A., 1982—. Capt., U.S. Army, 1969-72; col. USAR, 1987—. Named Outstanding Student Assn. of the U.S. Army, 1980. Mem. Res. Officers Assn., Assn. of U.S. Army, First Cav. Assn., Phi Kappa Tau (treas.), Masons. Republican. Methodist. Home: 983 Jungfrau Crestline CA 92325 Office: Am Nat Ins Co PO Box 3249 Crestline CA 92325

COMSTOCK, JOSEPH EDMUND, administrator, civil engineer; b. Butte, Mont., Nov. 11, 1940; s. Wilbur Cecil and Luella Maude (Ogle) C.; m. Joyce Eileen Herman, Dec. 18, 1965; children: Jeffrey Alan, Jennifer Alyssa. BCE, Calif. State U., 1965; BS in Pub. Adminstrn., West Coast U., Los Angeles, 1974. Engr. aide Div. of Hwys., Los Angeles, 1961-64; engr. assoc. City of Covina (Calif.), 1964-69; asst. dir. pub. works, city engr. City of San Fernando (Calif.), 1969-77, city adminstrv. officer, 1977-80; city adminstr. City of Clayton (Calif.), 1980-83; dep. gen. magr. Las Vegas (Nev.) Valley Water Dist., 1983-85; constrn. mgr. Montcom. Corp., San Dimas, Calif., 1985-87; adminstrv. services officer Kern County Pub. Works, Bakersfield, Calif., 1987—. Dist. chmn. Boy Scouts Am., San Fernando, 1973-77. Recipient Engr. Merit award San Fernando Valley Engr.'s Council, Los Angeles, 1970; named one of Outstanding Young Men of Am., San Fernando Jaycees, 1971. Mem. Am. Soc. Pub. Adminstrn., Am. City Mgr.'s Assn., Am. Pub. Works Assn. (chmn. fin. com. 1973-79). Lodge: Masons. Office: Kern County Pub Works Dept 2700 M St Suite 500 Bakersfield CA 93301

CONANT, HOWARD SOMERS, artist, educator; b. Beloit, Wis., May 5, 1921; s. Rufus P. and Edith B. (Somers) C.; m. Florence C. Craft, June 18, 1943; children: Judith Lynne Steinbach, Jeffrey Scott. Student, Art Students League of N.Y., 1944-45; B.S., U. Wis.-Milw., 1946; M.S., U. Wis.-Madison, 1947; Ed.D., U. Buffalo, 1950. Instr. art, asst. head housefellow U. Wis., 1946-47; asst. prof. art SUNY, Buffalo, 1947-50, prof. art, 1950-55; chmn. dept. art and art edn. also chmn. art collection NYU, 1955-76; head dept. art U. Ariz., Tucson, 1976-86, prof. art, 1986-87; artist 1987—; art edn. cons. NBC-TV, also Girl Scouts Am. TV series, 1958-60; field reader, also Title III program cons. U.S. Office of Edn.; adviser N.Y. State Council on Arts, 1962-63, Conn. Commn. on Arts, 1967-68; cons. Ford Found., 1973, Children's Theatre Assn., 1973, Getty Trust, 1985. Moderator: weekly TV program Fun to Learn About Art, WBEN-TV, Buffalo, 1951-55; numerous one man shows; represented maj. group exhbns. and coll. art collections represented by Isis Gallery, Manhasset, N.Y. , Sol Del Rio Gallery, San Antonio, Art Collections Inc., Tulsa, Davis Gallery, Tucson; executed mural, Sperry High Sch., Henrietta, N.Y., 1971, Good Samaritan Med. Ctr., Phoenix, 1982, Valley Nat. Bank, Tucson, 1983; one-man retrospective, Amarillo (Tex.) Art Ctr., 1989; Author: (with Arne Randall) Art in Education, 1959, 63; Author, editor: Vol. 4, Masterpieces of the Arts, New Wonder World Cultural Library, 1963, Seminar on Elementary and Secondary School Education in the Visual Arts, 1965, Art Education, 1964, Art Workshop Leaders Planning Guide, 1958, Lincoln Library of the Arts (2 vols.), 1973; art editor: Intellect, 1975-78; Art editor: USA Today, 1978-85; assoc. editor: Arts mag., 1973-75; contbr. articles profl. publs. Dept. State lectr., India, 1964; Dir. Waukesha County (Wis.) YMCA Art Program, 1946-48; pres., dir. Children's Creative Art Found., 1959-60; mem. adv. com. Coll. of Potomac, 1966; mem. cultural exchange mission to Mex., Ptnrs. of the Ams., 1988; Lt. USAAF, 1943-46. Recipient 25th Ann. medal Nat. Gallery Art, 1966; Disting. Alumnus award U. Wis.-Milw., 1968; Disting. fellow Nat. Art Edn. Assn., 1985; Nat. Endowment Arts sr. fellow in painting, 1985. Mem. Coll. Art Assn., Internat. Art Critics Assn., Alliance for Arts in Edn., Nat. Assn. Schs. Art and Design, AAUP, Nat. Com. Art Edn. (council, chmn. 1962-63), Inst. Study of Art in Edn. (bd. govs. 1965-72, pres. 1965-68). Club: Torch (N.Y.C.) (pres. 1965-66). Studio: 1721 Entrada Doce Tucson AZ 85718

CONARTY, MURRAY ROGERS, electrical engineer; b. Anchorage, Alaska, June 11, 1963; s. Roger Leon and Anna May Campbell. Diplome de Langue et civilization Françaises, U. Paris Sorbonne, 1985; BS in Elec. engring., U. New Mex., 1986, BA in French, 1986. Tchr. Coll. St. Michel, Paris, 1984-85; lead design engr. aviation div. Honeywell Co., Albuquerque, 1985—; translator Immigration and Naturalization Service, Albuquerque, 1985. Author: Font Generation Techniques, 1987. Info. specialist Nat. Forest Service, Tijeras, N.Mex., 1985-87. Mem. Alliance Francaise (scholar 1985), Am. Inst. Individual Investors, Blue Key. Republican. Roman Catholic. Home: 4401 Rabbit Brush Ave NW Albuquerque NM 87120 Office: Honeywell Co Def Avionics Div 9201 San Mateo NE Albuquerque NM 87113

CONAWAY, JACK WYNN, manufacturing company executive; b. Toledo, Nov. 19, 1937; s. Jack W. and Lavern Gertrude (Puls) C.; m. Barbara Ann Kolacki, July 13, 1957; children: Jay, Scott, Cynthia, Deborah. BEE, U. Toledo, 1960; MEE, West Coast U., 1968. Various engring. positions Honeywell, West Covina, Calif., 1960-81, chief engr., 1981-83, assoc. dir. programs, 1983-86; dir. programs oceanics div. Allied Signal Co., Sylmar, Calif., 1986-88, dir. contracts and program mgmt., 1988--. Active Calif. Republican Cen. Com., 1978--; sec. West Covina Jaycees, 1965. Mem. Elks. Office: Ocean Def Corp 15825 Roxford St Sylmar CA 91342

CONBOY, MICHAEL EDWARD, banker; b. San Diego, July 19, 1958; s. Martin Edward and Marie Teresa (Castro) C.; m. Amy Lusk, June 20, 1961; children: Cameron, Courtney, Cassandra. BS in Fin., San Diego State U., 1981. Mgmt. trainee, loan officer Bank Am., San Diego, 1981-83; loan officer, asst. mgr. San Diego Trust & Savs. Bank, 1983-85; corp. banking official 1st Bank, San Diego, 1985-86, asst. v.p., mgr., 1986--. Mem. San Diego C. of C., San Diego State U. Alumni Assn., Kiwanis. Republican. Home: 8239 Tommy Dr San Diego CA 92119 Office: Calif 1st Bank 344 Laurel St San Diego CA 92103

CONCANNON, KEVIN WILLIAM, state agency administrator; b. Portland, Maine, Dec. 17, 1940; s. Stephen Patrick and Katherine Anne (Feeney) C.; m. Eileen Mary Mackasey, Aug. 21, 1965; children: Timothy, Michael, Stephen, John. BA, St Francis Xavier Univ., Antigonish, N.S., 1964; MSW, Maritime Sch. Social Work, 1966; postgrad. U. Conn., 1973, Harvard U., 1987. Cert. social worker, rehab. specialist. Psychiat. social worker N.B. Govt., Saint John, 1966-68; assoc. dir. Diocesan Human Relations Svc., Portland, Maine, 1968-75; dir. of C & YSPP Exec. Dept. Augusta, Maine, 1975-77; dir. mental retardation Maine Dept. Mental Health, Augusta, 1977-80, commr. corrections, 1980-82; commr. Maine Dept. Mental Health and Mental Retardation, 1980-87; adminstr. Oreg. Mental Health Div., 1987; dir. Oreg. Dept. Human Resources, Salem, 1987—; adj. prof. social work Portland State U., 1987—; treas. Nat. Assn. Commn. of Mental Health, Washington, 1983—; dir., 1982—; treas. Nat. Assn. State Mental Health Program Dirs., 1983-86, pres.-elect, 1986-87, pres. 1987-88; cons. State of Ala., Montgomery, 1983, Atty. Gen. N.H., 1980-81. Chmn. Citizens for Mcpl. Reform, Portland, 1975; chmn. U. Conn. adv. com., Concord, N.H., 1983-84; chmn. Legis. Commn. of Children, Augusta, 1983-84; bd. dirs. United Way Greg., 1988-89, Greater Portland United Way, 1985-87; mem. nat. adv. bd. Boston U. Psychiat. Rsch. and Tng. Ctr., 1984-87, Children's Mental Health of Robert Woods Johnson Found., 1988—; trustee Maine Council on Devel. Disabilities, 1977-87; bd. dirs. Project Mainstay, Inc., 1984-87; mem., trustee Mid-Maine Med. Ctr., Waterville, 1973—. Recipient Trustee Svc. award Seton Hosp., 1975, Community Mental Health award Area V Mental Health, 1982, Outstanding Svc. award Maine Devel. Disability Council, 1983, Leadership award Maine State Prison Staff, 1981, Pub. Leadership award Maine State Legislature, 1987, Award Maine State Alliance for the Mentally Ill, 1987, First Pub. Policy Leadership award Opportunity Housing of Bangor, 1987, Engstrom award for U.S. Leadership Nat. Assn. Private Residential Facilities for MR/DD, 1987, Leadership award Oreg. Alliance for Mentally Ill, 1988. Mem. Am. Coll. Mental Health Adminstrn., Am. Assn. Mental Deficiency, Nat. Assn. State Mental Health Program Dirs., Maine Rehab. Assn., Centerboard Yacht Club, St. Francis Xavier Alumni. Democrat. Roman Catholic. Office: Oreg Dept Human Resources 318 Pub Svc Bldg Salem OR 97310

CONDELLO, DANA JOSEPH, photographic services executive; b. Canton, Ohio, Feb. 18, 1948; s. Anthony Joseph and Betty (Yeagy) C.; m. Sandra Kay Osborne, Feb. 14, 1970; children: Tiffany, Anthony. BS, Kent State U., 1973. Sales rep. Am. Greeting Corp., Cleve., 1971-75; mktg. mgr. Progressive Industries, Dayton, Ohio, 1975-77; gen. mgr. Phototron Corp., Rialto, Calif., 1977-79; v.p. sales Berkey Film Processing, White Plains, N.Y., 1979-83, Qualex/Am. Photo Group Inc., San Clemente, Calif., 1983—; cons. Miller-Heiman, Berkeley, Calif., 1986—. Asst. coach Saddleback Valley (Calif.) Soccer League, 1987-88. Served to cpl. USMC, 1967-68. Mem. Photo Mktg. Assn. Internat. Democrat. Methodist. Office: Qualex/Am Photo Group 629 Camino Los Mares Suite 208 San Clemente CA 92672

CONDIT, MADELEINE K. BRYANT, industry executive; b. Indpls., May 1, 1941; d. H. Herschel and Helen L. (McDaniel) Bryant; m. Philip Murray Condit, Jan. 25, 1963 (div. 1981); children: Nicole Lynn, Megan Anne. BA, U. Calif., Berkeley, 1963; MBA, U. Colo., 1983. Exec. fellow Sloan Sch., MIT, Cambridge, 1975; seminar coord. ID Ctr., Seattle, 1975-78; editor Puget Soundings mag., Seattle, 1981-83; v.p. Boettcher & Co., Denver, 1983-85; prin. Korn-Ferry Internat., Denver, 1985—. Bd. dirs. Heads Up, Bellevue, Wash., 1972-74, A Contemporary Theatre, Seattle, 1976-81, Jr. League Seattle, 1976, 78, 80, Mercer Island (Wash.) Youth Svcs., 1980-81, Big Sisters Colo., Denver, 1983-87, Kent Denver Sch., 1985—; chmn. Wash. Commn. on Community Affairs and Continuing Edn., Olympia, 1977-81; mem. nat. evaluation task force Girl Scouts U.S.A., 1980; mem. Colo. Efficiency and Mgmt. Com., 1986; found. mem. Pacific Sci. Ctr., Seattle, 1980—; chmn. bus. adv. coun. U. Denver, 1988—, mem. bd. fellows, 1987—; mem. adv. coun. Colo. Advanced Tech. Inst., 1986—. Mem. Securities Industry Assn., Investment Assn. N.Y., Women in Syndicate, Syndicate Round Table, Denver Athletic Club. Episcopalian. Office: Korn-Ferry Internat 1600 Broadway Ste 1850 Denver CO 80202

CONDON, WILLIAM EDWARD, marketing consultant; b. Tampa, Fla., Jan. 30, 1949; s. Alwin J. and Patricia B. Condon; m. Carol J. Moskal. Student, Broward Community Coll., 1973-74. Lic. real estate broker; cert. police officer, Fla. Pres. Southwest Mktg. Assocs., Phoenix, 1981—; mktg. cons. DashMat Co., Phoenix, 1982—. Named Man of Yr. Automotive Accessory Industry-Automotive Mdse. News mag., 1984, 85; Mfrs. Rep. of Yr., Western Internat. Distbn., 1982, Auto Merc. News mag., 1987; nominated Man of Yr. Sales and Mktg. Mgmt. mag., 1985. Mem. Sales and Mktg. Execs. of Greater Phoenix, Mfrs. Agts. Assn. of Am. Republican. Presbyterian. Office: Southwest Mktg Assocs PO Box 37338 Phoenix AZ 85069

CONGDON, ROGER DOUGLASS, theology educator, minister; b. Ft. Collins, Colo., Apr. 6, 1918; s. John Solon and Ellen Avery (Kellogg) C.; m. Rhoda Gwendolyn Britt, Jan. 2, 1948; children: Rachel Congdon Lidbeck, James R., R. Steven, Jon B., Philip F., Robert N., Bradford B., Ruth A. Mahner, Rebecca Congdon Skones, Rhoda J. Miller, Marianne C., Mark Alexander. BA, Wheaton Coll., 1940; postgrad, Eastern Bapt. Sem., 1940-41; ThM, Dallas Theol. Sem., 1945; ThD, Dallas Theology Sem., 1949. Ordained to ministry Bapt. Ch., 1945. Exec. sec., dean Altanta Bible Inst., 1945-49; prof. theology Carver Bible Inst., Atlanta, 1945-49; prof. Multnomah Sch. of the Bible, Portland, Oreg., 1950-87; pastor Emmanuel Bapt. Ch., Vancouver, Wash., 1985—; served as past dean of faculty, dean of edn., v.p., chmn. library com., chmn. achievement-award com., chmn. lectureship com., advisor grad. div. and mem. pres.'s cabinet all at Multnomah Sch. of the Bible; chmn. Chil Evang. Fellowship of Greater Portland, 1978—; founder, pres. Preaching Print Inc., Portland, 1953—. Author: the Doctrine of Conscience, 1945. Chmn. Citizen's Com. Info. on Communism, Portland, 1968-75. Recipient Outstanding Educators of Am. award, 1972, Loraine Chafer award in Systematic Theology, Dallas Theol. Sem. Mem. Am. Assn. Bible Colls. (chmn. testing com. 1953-78), N.Am. Assn. Bible Colls. (N.W. rep. 1960-63), Near East Archaeol. Soc., Evang. Theol. Soc. Republican. Home: 16539 NE Halsey St Portland OR 97230 Office: Emmanuel Bapt Ch 14810 NE 28th St Vancouver WA 98662

CONGER, JOHN JANEWAY, psychologist, educator; b. New Brunswick, N.J., Feb. 27, 1921; s. John C. and Katharine (Janeway) C.; m. Mayo Trist Kline, Jan. 1, 1944; children: Steven Janeway, David Trist. BA magna cum laude, Amherst Coll., 1943; MS, Yale U., 1947, PhD, 1949; DSc (hon.), Ohio U., 1981, Amherst Coll., 1983, U. Colo., 1989. Asst. prof. psychology Ind. U., 1949-53; chief staff psychologist U.S. Naval Acad., 1951-52; mem. faculty U. Colo. Sch. Medicine, prof. psychology, 1957-88, assoc. dean, 1961-63, v.p. for med. affairs, 1963-70, dean, 1963-68, acting chmn. dept. psychiatry, 1983-84, acting chancellor, 1985-86, prof. emeritus, 1988—; fellow Ctr. for Advanced Study in Behavioral Scis., Stanford, Cal., 1970-71; vis. scholar Inst. Human Devel., U. Calif., Berkeley, 1978; v.p., dir. health program John D. and Catherine T. MacArthur Found., 1980-83, cons., 1983-85; cons. to NIH, VA, USPHS; vice chmn. Colo. Bd. Psychology Examiners, 1961-64; mem. Gov. Colo. Com. Mental Health, 1957; chmn. mental health adv. council Colo. Dept. Pub. Health, 1957-61; mem. tng. com. Nat. Inst. Mental Health, 1959-62; mem. Western council mental health research and tng. Western Interstate Commn. Higher Edn., 1959-66; chmn. research com. President's Com. Traffic Safety, 1960-63; vice chmn. nat. motor vehicle safety adv. council Dept. Transp., 1967-70; mem. inter-council com. constrn. univ.-affiliated facilities for mentally retarded Dept. Health, Edn. and Welfare, 1967-70, mem. sec.'s adv. com. traffic safety, 1966-69; council research and planning Am. Hosp. Assn., 1965-68; nat. adv. mental health council USPHS, 1965-69; nat. adv. com. John F. Kennedy Center for Research on Edn. and Human Devel., 1965-76, chmn., 1970-74; mem. adv. com. on undergrad med. edn. AMA, 1969-70; adv. com. on casualty ins. Dept. Transp., 1970; mem. Pres.'s Task Force on Hwy. Safety, 1970, President's Commn. on Mental Health, 1977-78; mem. com. study nat. needs for biomed. and behavioral sci. research personnel Nat. Acad. Scis., 1976-80; mem. Inst. Medicine/Nat. Acad. Scis., 1983—, bd. mental health and behavioral medicine, 1986—. Author: Child Development and Personality, 6th edit, 1984, Readings in Child Development, 1964, 3d edit., 1984, Personality, Social Class and Delinquency, 1965, Adolescence and Youth: Psychological Development in a Changing World, 3d edit., 1984, Basic and Contemporary Issues in Developmental Psychology, 1975, Contemporary Issues in Adolescent Development, 1975, Psychological Development: A Life-Span Approach, 1979, Adolescence: Generation Under Pressure, 1979, Essentials of Child Development and Personality, 1980, also articles. Served to lt. USNR, 1944-46, 51-52. Recipient Stearns Alumni medal for extraordinary service U Colo., 1970, U. Colo. medal, 1986, disting. profl. achievement award Am. Bd. Profl. Psychology, 1979. Fellow Am. Psychol. Assn. (mem. policy and planning bd. 1967-70, rec. sec., dir. 1974-79, pres. 1980-82, award for outstanding contbns. health psychology 1983, award for disting. contbns. psychology in pub. interest 1986), AAAS, Soc. Research in Child Devel. (program chmn. 1975); mem. Am. Psychol. Found. (pres. 1985-86, bd. dirs.), Denver Med. Soc. (hon. mem.), Colo. Psychol. Assn. (pres. 1959, disting. service award 1963, 84), Colo. Med. Soc. (disting. Service award 1970), Phi Beta Kappa, Sigma Xi, Alpha Omega Alpha (hon.). Home: 130 S Birch St Denver CO 80222

CONGREVE, MARIO RICARDO, producer, television editor, educator; b. Concepcion, Chile, Nov. 27, 1957; came to U.S., 1979; s. Mario Congreve Wilson and Iris (Stratta) Trabucco. BA in Cinema and Photography, So. Ill. U., 1982; MA, Calif. State U.-Dominguez Hills, 1988. Prodn. asst. Polycom Teleprodns., Mission Viejo, Calif., 1985; TV editor Christian Family Movement, L.A., 1985; prodn. coordinator Stanton Films, Redondo Beach, Calif., 1985-87; videographer Cole, Green and Assocs., Lomita, Calif., 1985—; chyron operator Shop TV Network, Hollywood, Calif., 1987—; instructional support asst. Calif. State U., Carson, Calif., 1985—; chyron operator Metroplex, 1989; cameraman Ford Motors, 1989. Dir. award winning TV commls., Concepcion, 1986, 87. Fulbright scholar, 1979; grad. equity fellow Calif. State U., 1988. Mem. Soc. Motion Picture and TV Engrs., Am. Film. Inst., Rotary (Dist. 651 scholarship 1981). Home: PO Box 1092 Redondo Beach CA 90278 Office: Calif State U Dominguez Hills 1000 E Victoria St Carson CA 90747

CONKLIN, JANIS KOPF, protective services official; b. Plainfield, N.J., Nov. 2, 1948; d. George Emil and Gladys (Wey) Kopf; m. John Harrison Conklin, June 20, 1970. BS in Math., James Madison U., 1970. Tchr. Shreveport (La.) Schs., 1970-71; programmer-analyst Amax Aluminum, Riverside, Calif., 1971-72; data control clk. The 7-Up Co., St. Louis, 1972-73; inventory clk. Certain-Teed Products, Riverside, Calif., 1973-74; staff acct. Rodgers, Hall & Macher, Riverside, 1974-77; corp. controller Com-Ser Co., Riverside, 1976-77; staff acct. Morris & Price, Riverside, 1977-78; from staff acct. to adminstrv. svcs. officer Riverside County Sheriff's Office, 1978—. With USAF, 1974. Republican. Presbyterian. Home: 29820 Del Rey Rd Temecula CA 92390 Office: Riverside County Sheriff 4129 Main St Riverside CA 92501

CONKLIN, KENNETH FRANK, marketing executive; b. Glendale, Calif., July 1, 1947; s. Frank Leslie and Ruth Lois (Rasmussen) C.; children by previous marriage: Michele Lynn, Dale Ernestine, Kristina Lee, Timothy Jensen; m. Barbara Shirley Henry, Mar. 24, 1987. BSEE, Northrop U., Inglewood, Calif., 1974. Assoc. engr. Lockheed Calif. Co., Burbank, 1974-76; sr. mem. tech. staff Dynamic Scis., Inc., Van Nuys, Calif., 1976-83; mktg. mgr. Hughes Aircraft Co., Torrance, Calif., 1983—. Served with U.S. Army, 1966-69. Mem. IEEE, Assn. Old Crows, Armed Forces Communications and Electronics Assn., Individual Investors. Republican. Home: 501 4th St Hermosa Beach CA 90254

CONKLIN, SUSAN JEAN, film producer; b. Scottsbluff, Nebr., May 18, 1950; d. John Edward and Betty Sue (Myers) C. BA, U. No. Colo., 1973, MA, 1975. Announcer Radio sta. KZEL-FM, Eugene, Oreg., 1975-76; producer, dir. Oreg. Pub. Broadcasting, Salem, Portland, Oreg., 1976-80; film coordinator self-employed, Portland, 1980-82; producer Mincey Prodns., Portland, 1982-85, Signature Prodns., Portland, 1985—. Founder: solar-powered vending cart, 1980. Producer Oreg. Media Prodn. Assn., Haunted House, Children's Trust Fund, Portland, 1987. Recipient bronze award N.Y. Internat. Film and TV Festival, 1984. Mem. Oreg. Media Prodn. Assn. (pres. 1986, 88). Democrat. Home: 2235 NE 43d Ave Ct Portland OR 97213 Office: Signature Prodns 5253 NE Sandy Blvd Portland OR 97213

CONLEY, GENE RAYMOND, internist, urologist; b. Spokane, Wash., Feb. 28, 1952; s. Donald Eugene and Kathryn (Dizney) C.; m. Annette Louise Warner, June 7, 1982; children: Kimberly Elyse, Gene Raymond. BS, Loma Linda U., 1976, MD, 1976. Diplomate Am. Bd. Internal Medicine, Am. Bd. Urology. Resident in internal medicine USPHS Hosp., Boston, 1976-79; resident in gen. surgery Loma Linda (Calif.) U. Med. Ctr., 1979-80; resident in urology Tufts New Eng. Med. Ctr., Boston, 1980-83; pvt. practice medicine speializing in urology, internal medicine Hanford, Calif., 1983—. Fellow ACS; mem. ACP, Assn. Med. Surgeons U.S., Am. Urol. Assn., Naval Res. Assn. Mem. Bible Christian Ch. Office: 460 N Greenfield Ste 5 Hanford CA 93230

CONLEY, ROBERT FRANCIS, aircraft and space industry executive; b. Beatrice, Neb., 1923. Grad., San Diego State Coll., 1950, U. Calif., 1953. Pres. Lockheed Corp. Internat., Calabasas, Calif.; dir. Lockheed Arabia, Ltd. Office: Lockheed Corp 4500 Park Granada Blvd Calabasas CA 91399 *

CONLEY, ZEB BRISTOL, JR., art gallery director; b. Andrews, N.C., Feb. 12, 1936; s. Zeb Bristol and A. Elizabeth (Faircloth) C.; student N.C. State Coll., 1954-55, Mars Hill Coll., 1955-57, Coll. William and Mary, 1957-61; m. Betty Ann Wiswall, May 25, 1974; stepchildren—Peter Wiswall Betts, Stephen Wood Betts, Frederick Beale Betts, III. Designer, Seymour Robins, Inc., N.Y.C., 1961; with First Nat. Bank, Las Vegas (N.Mex.), 1964-65; gen. mgr. Swanson's Inc., Las Vegas, 1965-73, v.p., 1969—; dir. Jamison Galleries, Santa Fe, 1973—, guest curator Alfred Morang: A Retrospective at Mus. of S.W. Midland, Tex., 1985; sec. Marbasconi, Inc., d.b.a. Jamison Galleries, 1974-80, pres., 1980—. Republican. Home: #16 White Oak Rd Asheville NC 28803 Office: The Jamison Galleries 111 E San Francisco St Santa Fe NM 87501

CONN, CAROL, television producer and writer; b. Atlanta, May 21, 1952; m. Walter F. Maibaum, 1984. BA, George Washington U., 1975. Journalist Washington Post, 1973-79; freelance writer San Francisco, 1980-87; producer, writer Art Market Report, TV show, N.Y.C., 1987—; v.p. prodns. A.M.R. Prodns., Inc., N.Y.C., 1989—. Author: (anthology) Pleasures, 1984; editor: Weight No More, 1985. Office: AMR Prodns 320 Park Ave 3rd Fl New York NY 10021

CONN, GISELE CHRISTIAN, graphic artist, illustrator, designer; b. Bronx, N.Y., Dec. 25, 1958; d. Paul and Luisa (Espada) Velez; m. Ronald William Conn, Apri. 12, 1986. AA in Advt., U. P.R., 1978, student, 1978-80; student in fine arts, Sch. Plastic Arts, Old San Juan, P.R., 1980-81. Comml. artist, asst. to art dir. N.Y. Advt. Hato Rey, P.R., 1981-83; jr. graphic artist, designer Atlantic Orgn., Old San Juan, P.R., 1983-84; asst. art dir., graphic artist, designer Orange County Register, Santa Ana, Calif., 1985--; graphics designer Nat. Hispanic Heritage Week, Congl. Hispanic Caucus Inst. Inc., 1986-87, City of Orange Centennial, 1988; judge Bear awards Calif. Newspaper Advt. Execs. Assn., 1987, 88. Contbr. articles to profl. jours. Home: 75 Lakepines Irvine CA 92720 Office: Orange County Register 625 N Grand Ave Santa Ana CA 92701

CONNELL, JAMES JOSEPH, JR., international trading company executive; b. Balt., Aug. 6, 1928; s. Joseph James and Katherine Evelyn (Dietrich) C.; m. Elaine Therese Elvig, Oct. 14, 1950; children: Katherine, James, Elizabeth. BA, U. Kans., 1950; MS, San Francisco State U., 1967. Credit analyst Anglo Calif. Nat. Bank, San Francisco, 1953-54; export trader Mark Ross & Co. Internat., San Francisco, 1954-66, export mgr., 1966-72, v.p., 1987—; v.p. Global Mdsing. Corp., San Francisco, 1966—. Pres. Soc. for Asian Art, San Francisco, 1984-86; v.p. San Francisco Craft and Folk Art Mus., 1982—; bd. dirs. Rudolph Schaeffer Sch. of Design, San Francisco, 1981—. Served to lt. (j.g.) USN, 1950-53. Mem. Internat. Mgr.'s Assn. (pres. 1972). Office: Mark Ross & Co Internat 3131 19th St San Francisco CA 94110

CONNELL, KAREN ALISON, social services administrator; b. Inglewood, Calif., Jan. 4, 1945; d. Edward Frank and Phyllis Arlene (Dickerson) Schmitt; m. Michael W. Connell, Jan. 11, 1968 (dec. 1982); 1 child, Ward Christian. Student, UCLA, 1962-63, Santa Monica City Coll., 1964-65, Valley Coll., 1975-76. Community edn. coord. Sojourn, Santa Monica, Calif., 1984-87; area rep. Calif. Alliance Against Domestic Violence, 1985-87; domestic violence victim advocate coord. City of L.A., 1987-88; facilitator Connexxus-Battered Lesbians, West Hollywood, Calif., 1988—; organizer Women's Support Svcs., Van Nuys, Calif., 1988—; chmn. Survivors' Task Force, Santa Monica, 1988—; trainer Police Acad., L.A., 1986-87, Law Enforcement Response Domestic Violence Calif.; mem. Atty. Gen. Task Force, 1985; speaker in field; organizer Women's Action Group, Van Nuys, Calif. Contbr. articles to ednl. jours. Lobbyist Calif. Alliance Against Domestic Violence, 1985-87. Recipient Svcs. to Victims award Gov. of Calif., 1987, L.A. Commn. on Status of Women, 1987, Humanitarian award L.A. Commn. on Assaults Against Women, 1986. Mem. L.A. County Domestic Violence Coun., So. Calif. Coalition on Battered Women. Office: Womens Support Svcs 13930 Leadwell St Van Nuys CA 91405

CONNELLEE-CLAY, BARBARA, laboratory administrator; b. Hereford, Tex., Dec. 4, 1929; d. Herman and Audrey Stella (Carroll) Galbraith; m. Edward Lee Clay, 1983; children: Alison Elaine Stephens, Rebecca Diane Connellee Crabtree, Calvin Clay, Larry Clay, Becky Gibson. BS, U. N.Mex., 1976, MBA, 1981. Mem. adminstrv. staff U. Calif. Los Alamos Nat. Lab., 1976—. Pres., Wesleyan Service Guild, 1958. Recipient Women at Work award region 8 Dept. Labor Council on Working Women, 1983, N.Mex. Women at Work Spl. award Coun. Working Women Inst. Women and Minority Affairs, 1985. Mem. NAFE, Laser Inst. Am., Optical Soc., Women in Sci., Assn. for Quality and Participation (cert. facilitator), Assn. for Quality and Participation. United Methodist (past dir. edn.). Office: PO Box 1663 MS E583 Los Alamos NM 87544

CONNELY, ROBERT ROSS, marketing executive; b. Salt Lake City, July 29, 1935; s. William Ivor and Alice (Croft) C.; m. Patty Meacham, July 18, 1959; children: Eric, Russell. Course in exec. sales mgmt., Stafford U., 1966. Div. mgr. W.N. Bintz Co., 1961-72; owner Elec. Systems, Inc., 1975-83; v.p. mktg. Standard Supply Co., Salt Lake City; tng. instr. Mining Enforcement and Safety Adminstrn. With USAF, 1953-61. Mem. Alpine Country Club (pres. 1982-83). Mormon. Office: Standard Supply Co 3424 S Main St Salt Lake City UT 84115

CONNER, JACK EDWARD, English philology educator; b. Marfa, Tex., Jan. 16, 1921; s. John Edwin and Frances Edith (Johnson) C.; m. Sara Frances Zimmerman, Aug. 18, 1947; children: Kay Ann, Edward Cash. BA, Tex. A&I U., 1939, BS, 1941; PhD, Stanford U., 1952. With Fgn. Svc. Dept., 1946, resignd, 1949; assoc. prof. Rice U., Houston, 1952-62; prof. English philology Calif. State U., Hayward, 1962—, prof. emeritus, 1986—; mem., chmn. Calif. Commn. Tchr. Preparation and Licensing, 1970-74. Coeditor anthology Speaking of Rhetoric, 1966; author: Grammar of Standard English, 1968; monograph, 1974. Lt. USNR, 1943-46. Mem. AAUP, Calif. Faculty Assn. (organizing mem. 1970-78). Democrat. Home: 2741 Jennifer Dr Castro Valley CA 94546 Office: Calif State U Hayward CA 94542

CONNER, JOHN CALVIN, chemistry instructor; b. Lubbock, Tex., June 9, 1944; s. John Thomas and Nathalene (Hendricks) C.; m. Carolyn Brooks Clarkson, Nov. 20, 1981; children: Kevin, Tyler, Kim, Meghan. AS, Brazosport Coll., 1978; BS, U. Houston, 1981. Technician Monsanto, Texas City, Tex., 1969-72; project chemist Dow Chemical, Freeport, Tex., 1972-83; chemist Process Operators, Inc., Beulah, N.D., 1984-85; safety supr. Catalytic, Inc., Beulah, 1985; lab. supr. Jetline of Lowell, Lowell, Mass., 1986; tech. instr. III Palo Verde Nuclear Generating Sta., Wintersburg, Ariz., 1986—. Recording sec. Kachina Kennel Club, Glendale, Ariz., 1988; treas. Palo Verde Employees Club, Wintersburg, 1988-89. Mem. Am. Inst. Chemists, Am. Chem. Soc. Republican. Home: 5908 W Highland Phoenix AZ 85073 Office: Palo Verde Nuclear Gen Sta PO Box 52034 Sta 6927 Phoenix AZ 85072-2034

CONNICK, ROBERT ELWELL, chemistry educator; b. Eureka, Calif., July 29, 1917; s. Arthur Elwell and Florence (Robertson) C.; m. Frances Spieth, Dec. 19, 1952; children—Mary Catherine, Elizabeth, Arthur, Megan, Sarah, William Beach. B.S., U. Calif. at Berkeley, 1939, Ph.D., 1942. Mem. faculty U. Calif., Berkeley, 1942-88, researcher Manhattan project, 1943-46, asst. prof. then assoc. prof. chemistry, 1945-52, prof., 1952-88, chmn. dept. chemistry, 1958-60, dean Coll. Chemistry, 1960-65, vice chancellor acad. affairs, 1965-67, vice chancellor, 1969-71, acting dean Coll. Chemistry, 1987-88. Contbr. articles profl. jours. Guggenheim fellow, 1949, 59. Mem. Am. Chem. Soc., Nat. Acad. Scis., Phi Beta Kappa, Sigma Xi, Pi Mu Epsilon. Home: 50 Marguerita Rd Berkeley CA 94707

CONNOLLY, JOHN EARLE, surgeon, educator; b. Omaha, May 21, 1923; s. Earl A. and Gertrude (Eckerman) C.; m. Virginia Hartman, Aug. 12, 1967; children: Peter Hart. John Earle, Sarah. A.B., Harvard U., 1945, M.D., 1948. Diplomate: Am. Bd. Surgery (bd. dirs. 1976-82), Am. Bd. Thoracic and Cardiovascular Surgery, Am. Bd. Vascular Surgery. Intern. in surgery Stanford U. Hosps., San Francisco, 1948-49, surg. research fellow, 1949-50, asst. resident surgeon, 1950-52, chief resident surgeon, 1953-54, surg. pathology fellow, 1954, instr. surgery, 1957-60, John and Mary Markle Scholar in med. scis., 1957-62; surg. registrar professional unit St. Bartholomew's Hosp., London, 1952-53; resident in thoracic surgery Bellevue Hosp., N.Y.C., 1955; resident in thoracic and cardiovascular surgery Columbia-Presbyn. Med. Ctr., N.Y.C., 1956; from instr. to assoc. prof. surgery Stanford U., 1957-65; prof. U. Calif.-Irvine, 1965—, chmn. dept. surgery, 1965-78; attending surgeon Stanford Med. Ctr., Palo Alto, Calif., 1959-65; chmn. cardiovascular and thoracic surgery U. Calif.-Irvine Med. Ctr., 1968—; attending surgeon St. Joseph's Children's Hosp., Orange, Calif., 1968—, Anaheim Meml. Hosp. (Calif.), 1970—; A.H. Duncan vis. prof. U. Edinburgh, 1984; Hunterian prof. Royal Coll. Surgeons Eng., 1985-86; Kinmonth lectr. Royal Coll. Surgeons, Eng., 1987; mem. adv. coun. Nat. Heart, Lung, and Blood Inst.-NIH, 1981-85; cons. Long Beach VA Hosp., Calif., 1965—, Long Beach Naval Hosp., Calif. Contbr. articles to profl. jours.; editorial bd.: Jour. Cardiovascular Surgery, 1974—, chief editor, 1985—; editorial bd. Western Jour. Medicine, 1975—, Jour. Stroke, 1979—, Jour. Vascular Surgery, 1983—. Bd. dirs. Audio-Digest Found., 1974—; bd. dirs. Franklin Martin Found., 1975-80. Served with AUS, 1943-44. Recipient Cert. of Merit, Japanese Surg. Soc., 1979. Fellow ACS (gov. 1964-70, regent 1972-82, vice chmn. bd. regents 1980-82, v.p. 1984-85), Royal Coll. Surgeons Eng. (hon.), Royal Coll. Surgeons Ireland (hon.), Royal Coll. Surgeons Edinburgh (hon.); mem. Am. Surg. Assn., Soc. Univ. Surgeons, Am. Assn. Thoracic Surgery (coun. 1974-78), Pacific Coast Surg. Assn. (pres. 1985-86), San Francisco Surg. Soc., L.A. Surg. Soc., Soc. Vascular Surgery, Western Surg. Assn., Internat. Cardiovascular Soc. (pres. 1977), Soc. Internat. Chirurgie, Soc. Thoracic Surgeons, Western Thoracic Surg. Soc. (pres. 1978), Orange County Surg. Soc. (pres. 1984-85), James IV Assn. Surgeons (councillor 1983—). Clubs: California (Los Angeles); San Francisco Golf, Pacific Union, Bohemian (San Francisco); Cypress Point (Pebble Beach, Calif.); Harvard (N.Y.C.); Big Canyon (Newport Beach). Home: 7 Deerwood Ln Newport Beach CA 92660 Office: U Calif Dept Surgery Irvine CA 92717

CONNOLLY, KATHY ANN SCHULTZ, nurse; b. Green Bay, Wis., Dec. 26, 1952; d. Herbert Albert Carl and Enid Margaret (Malach) S.; m. Patrick Connolly, Sept. 24, 1988. Diploma in nursing, Columbia Hosp., Milw., 1974; BSN, Calif. State U., L.A., 1984. RN, Wis., Calif. Staff nurse Columbia Hosp., 1974-78; staff nurse Cedars-Sinai Med. Ctr., L.A., 1978-80, nursing supr., 1980-82, staff nurse emergency dept., 1982-85, acting trauma and pediatric liaison person, 1984-85, clin. instr., IV team ambulatory care and pain mgmt. ctrs., 1985—. Vol. nurse ARC, 1982--; vol. Spl. Olympics, L.A., 1988--. Mem. Am. Assn. for Critical Care Nurses (cert.), Edelweiss Ski Club (Van Nuys, Calif.). Lutheran. Office: Cedars-Sinai Med Ctr 8700 Beverly Blvd Rm 147l Los Angeles CA 90048

CONNOLLY, SHERRY PATTERSON, accountant; b. Ft. Eustus, Va., Apr. 8, 1954; d. John Burford and Sue Ann Patterson; m. Richard William Connolly, June 10, 1978; children: Christine Anne, Sean Richard, Mary Kathleen. AA, Orange Coast Coll., 1975; BA, Calif. State U., Fullerton, 1979. Lic. tax preparer, Calif. Bookkeeper IMS Equipment, Irvine, Calif., 1974; specialist acctg. Hyland Div. Baxter/Travenol, Costa Mesa, 1974-78; pvt. con. Irvine, 1980-82; owner, pres. The Tender Tender Agy., Irvine, 1982-84; owner Connolly Acctg. & Tax Svc., Irvine, 1984—. Pres. Irvine Ednl. Found., 1985-87, Child Identification Program, Irvine, 1983-85; v.p. Irvine Jr. Women's Club, 1987-88, pres. GFWC, 1989—; v.p. Irvine Assn. Coord. Child Care, 1981-82; chmn. Symposium to Advance the Future of Edn. County of Orange, Calif., 1984-85; sec. Irvine Civic League, 1983; treas. Friends of the Homeless, Irvine, 1987-88; chmn. com. Irvine Unified Sch. Dist, 1984-85 (Exemplary Svc. award 1983, 84), El Camino Real Sch. Site Coun., Irvine, 1985-88. Mem. Irvine Bus. and Profl. Women, Gen. Fedn. of Women's Clubs (treas. , v.p. Irvine Jr. Women's chpt. 1986-88). Republican. Presbyterian. Office: Connolly Acctg & Tax Svc 4200 Trabuco Rd Ste 214 Irvine CA 92720

CONNOLLY, STEVE JAMES, music educator; b. Santa Rosa, Calif., Apr. 29, 1919; s. Charles Lawrence and Helen Maude (Keegan) C.; m. Winifred Blanche Meiners, May 2, 1946; children: Kathleen, Susan, Linda. BA, San Jose State Coll., 1947. Music tchr. Cloverdale (Calif.) Unified Sch. Dist., 1947--; city, county and regional honor band conductor, cen. and no. Calif., 1960-88. Recipient Calif. Educator award, Calif. Dept. Edn., 1987, Citation of Merit, U.S. Congl. Record, 1978. Mem. Nat. Band Assn. (citation of excellence 1983), Calif. Band Dirs. Assn. (bd. dirs. 1981-82), Calif. Music Educators Assn. (past pres., bd. dirs. Bay sect., adjudicator, clinician 1965--; named Outstanding Calif. Music Educator 1979), No. Calif. Band Dirs. Assn., Sonoma County Music Educators (bd. dirs. 1955-70). Office: Cloverdale High Sch 506 N Cloverdale Blvd Cloverdale CA 95425

CONNOLLY, THOMAS JOSEPH, bishop; b. Tonopah, Nev., July 18, 1922; s. John and Katherine (Hammel) C. Student, St. Joseph Coll. and St. Patrick Sem., Menlo Park, Calif., 1936-47, Catholic U. Am., 1949-51; JCD, Lateran Pontifical U., Rome, 1952; DHL (hon.), U. Portland, 1972. Ordained priest Roman Cath. Ch., 1947. Asst. St. Thomas Cathedral, Reno, 1947, asst., rector, 1953-55; asst. Little Flower Parish, Reno, 1947-48; sec. to bishop 1949; asst. St. Albert the Gt., Reno, 1952-53; pastor St. Albert the Gt., 1960-68, St. Joseph Ch., Elko, 1955-60, St. Theresa's Ch., Carson City, Nev., 1968-71; bishop Baker, Oreg., 1971—; Tchr. Manogue High Sch., Reno, 1948-49; chaplain Serra Club, 1948-49; officialis Diocese of Reno; chmn. bldg. com., dir. Cursillo Movement; moderator Italian Cath. Fedn.; dean, mem. personnel bd. Senate of Priests; mem. Nat. Bishops Liturgy Com., 1973-76; region XII rep. to adminstrv. bd. Nat. Conf. Cath. Bishops, 1973-76, 86-89, mem. adv. com., 1974-76; bd. dirs. Cath. Communications Northwest, 1977-82. Club: K.C. (state chaplain Nev. 1970-71). Home: 63255 Overtree Rd Bend OR 97701 Office: 911 SE Armour PO Box 5999 Bend OR 97708

CONNOLLY-O'NEILL, BARRIE JANE, interior designer; b. San Francisco, Dec. 22, 1943; d. Harry Jr. and Jane Isabelle (Barr) Wallach; m. Peter Smith O'Neill, Nov. 27, 1983. Cert. of design, N.Y. Sch. Interior Design, 1975; BAF in Environ. Design, Calif. Coll. Arts and Crafts, 1978. Profl. model Brebner Agy., San Francisco, 1963-72; TV personality KGO TV, San Francisco, 1969-72; interior designer Barrie Connolly & Assocs., Boise, Idaho, 1978—. Recipient Best Interior Design award Mktg. and Merchandising Excellence, No. Calif., 1981, 1984, Best Interior Design award Sales and Mktg. Council, San Diego, 1985, 86, Best Residential Design award Boise Design Revue Com., 1983, Grand award Best in Am. Living Nat. Assn. Homebuilders, River Run, Boise, 1986. Mem. Mannequin League of Marin. Home and Office: 2188 Bluestem Ln Boise ID 83706

CONNOR, GARY EDWARD, manufacturing company marketing executive; b. S.I., N.Y., Nov. 13, 1948; s. Everett M. and Josephine (Amato) C.; B.S. in Elec. Engring., U. Md., 1973; M.B.A., U. Santa Clara (Calif.), 1979. Quality assurance engr. Frankford Arsenal, 1973; quality assurance engr., field service engr. Lockheed Electronics Co., 1973-74; group leader memory test engring. sect. head bipolar product engring. Nat. Semicondr. Corp., 1975-79; internat. mktg. mgr. Am. Microsystems Inc., 1979-80; mktg. mgr. GenRad-STI, Santa Clara, 1980-82; prodn. mktg. exec. AMD, Sunnyvale, Calif., 1982-86; mktg. mgr. IDT, Santa Clara, Calif., 1986—. Mem. IEEE, Electronics Internat. Adv. Panel, Am. Security Council (nat. adv. bd.), Franklin Mint Collectors Soc. Republican. Home: 5121 Kozo Ct San Jose CA 95124 Office: IDT 3236 Scott Blvd PO Box 58015 Santa Clara CA 95052

CONNOR, JONATHAN PETER, public administrator; b. L.A., Feb. 28, 1949; s. Johnnie Bee and Lydia Marie (LeBlanc) C.; m. Rose Therese Madden, July 27, 1974; children: Sara, Jonas, Rachael. BA in Govt., U. San Diego, 1971; MA in Social Sci., Boston U., 1975; PhD in Psychology, Internat. Coll., 1985. Equal opportunity officer Pension Benefit Guaranty Corp., Washington, 1975-77; human rels. dir. Allstate Ins. Co., San Diego, 1977-80; employee rels. mgr. CIGNA Cos., San Diego, 1980-84; mgmt. cons. Madden-Connor Assocs., San Diego, 1985-86; ch. adminstr. Roman Cath. Diocese, San Diego, 1986-87; equal opportunity officer San Diego Housing Commn., 1987--; mem. adj. faculty La Jolla (Calif.) U., 1985--; mediator Community Mediation San Diego; cons. Eagle Internat., Irvine, Calif., 1985-86. Chmn. Calif. adv. com. to Selective Svc., Sacramento, 1971-73; legis. aide Mass. Black Caucus, Boston, 1974-75; candidate for San Diego City Coun., 1984. Ford Found. fellow, 1974. Mem. Internat. Personnel Mgmt. Assn. Democrat. Roman Catholic. Office: San Diego Housing Commn 1625 Newton Ave San Diego CA 92113

CONOVER, CHARLES TODD, management consultant; b. Bronxville, N.Y., Oct. 13, 1939; s. John Charles and Mary Dabney (Marshall) Schneider; m. Sally Jean Dillon, Dec. 12, 1961; children: Kirsten Marshall, Alison Jean. BA, Yale U., 1960; MBA, U. Calif.-Berkeley, 1965. Trainee Seattle First Nat. Bank, 1962-63; mgmt. cons. McKinsey & Co., Inc., San Francisco, also Amsterdam, Netherlands, 1965-72; v.p. corp. devel. U.S. Bancorp, Portland, 1972-74; ptnr. Touche Ross & Co., San Francisco, 1974-78; founding ptnr. Edgar, Dunn & Conover Inc., 1978-81, prin., 1987-88; U.S. Comptr. of the Currency, Washington, 1981-85; vice-chmn. Equitec Fin. Group, 1985-86; chmn., chief exec. officer Equitec Savs. Bank, 1985-86; prin. Conover & McNamar Inc., San Francisco and L.A., 1986-88; prin., nat. cons. practice dir. for Banking Peat, Marwick, Main & Co, 1988—; bd. dir. PacifiCorp, 1986-88, FDIC, 1981-85; chmn. adv. bd. Nat. Ctr. on Fin. Svcs., U. Calif. at Berkeley, 1984—; mem. Quadrennial Commn., 1986-87. Lt. (j.g.), USN, 1960-62. Mem. Calif. Bus. Alumni Assn., Inst. Mgmt. Cons., Beta Gamma Sigma. Club: Bankers (San Francisco).

CONOVER, ROBERT WARREN, librarian; b. Manhattan, Kans., Oct. 6, 1937; s. Robert Warren and Grace Darline (Grinstead) C.; BA, Kans. State U., 1959; MA, U. Denver, 1961. Librarian, supervising librarian County of Fresno, Calif., 1961-66; county librarian County of Yolo, Woodland, Calif., 1967-68; dir. City of Fullerton (Calif.) Pub. Library, 1968-73, City of Pasadena (Calif.) Pub. Library, 1973-80, Palos Verdes Library Dist., Palos Verdes Peninsula, Calif., 1980-85, City of Commerce (Calif.) Pub. Library, 1985—. Recipient Pres.'s award Fresno Jaycees, 1963. Mem. ALA, Orange County Library Assn. (pres. 1971), Spl. Libraries Assn., Calif. Library Assn. (pres. Yosemite chpt. 1965, mem. council 1981), Santiago Library System Council (pres. 1972), University Club, L.A. Athletic Club, Pi Kappa Alpha. Republican. Office: City of Commerce Pub Libr 5655 Jillson St Commerce CA 90040

CONRAD, BARBARA ANN, association executive; b. El Paso, Tex., Aug. 2, 1942; d. Gordon Andrew and Jewel Charlotte (Wilbanks) Jones; m. Robert G. Conrad,. BA, U. Tex., Austin, 1965; postgrad., Tex. Women's U., 1970-73, So. Meth. U., 1974. Caseworker Austin State Hosp., 1965-66; floor mgr. Titche-Goettingen Dept. Store, Dallas, 1966-68; dir. adult activity ctr. Dallas Assn. Retarded Citizens, 1968-70; supr. adult svcs. San Antonio Assn. Retarded Citizens, 1970-71; recreation therapist Children's Devel. Ctr., Dallas, 1975-80; devel. specialist Ida. Dept. Health & Welfare, Nampa, 1980-83; exec. asst. to pres. Coll. of Ida., Caldwell, 1982-83, dean students, 1983-86; field svc. dir. Silver Sage Girls Scouts, Boise, 1986-88; dir. Community Edn., Lewistown, Mont., 1988; lectr. in field; cons. in field. Active in various charitable orgns. Named Ida. Vol. of the Yr., 1983, Disting. Vol. award, HHS, 1984. Mem. Lewistown C. of C. (bd. dirs.), Soroptomist. Methodist. Home: 204 9th Ave N Lewistown MT 59457 Office: Office of Community Edn 215 7th Ave S Lewistown MT 59457

CONRAD, DENNIS ASHLEY, accountant; b. Seattle, Sept. 16, 1946; s. Robert Walker and Berta Maxine (Ashley) C.; m. Janice Lynn Maloney, Dec. 16, 1967; children: Rachelle Lynn, Robert Dale, Nicole Marie. BBA, U. Wash., 1968. CPA, Wash. Acct. Price Waterhouse, Seattle, 1968-80; sr. mgr., ptnr. Price Waterhouse, Manchester, Eng., 1975; ptnr. Sweeney Conrad, Bellevue, Wash., 1980—. Bd. dirs., mem. exec. com. Bellevue Downtown Assn., 1987—; past pres., bd. dirs. Bellevue Art Mus., 1982-83; mem. adv. panel U. Wash. Acctg. Dept., 1989. Mem. AICPA, Wash. Soc. CPAs, Bellevue Transp. Mgmt. Assn. (mem. policy bd. 1987—), Bellevue C. of C., Overlake Golf and Country Club (mem. fin. com. 1988, house com. 1987), Lakes Club (mem. house com. 1988-89). Office: Sweeney Conrad 1416 112nd NE Bellevue WA 98004

CONRAD, PAUL FRANCIS, editorial cartoonist; b. Cedar Rapids, Iowa, June 27, 1924; s. Robert H. and Florence G. (Lawler) C.; m. Barbara Kay King, Feb. 27, 1954; children: James, David, Carol, Elizabeth. B.A., U. Iowa, 1950. Editorial cartoonist Denver Post, 1950-64, Los Angeles Times, 1964—; cartoonist Los Angeles Times Syndicate, 1973—; lectr. Cooke-Daniels Lecture Tours, Denver Art Mus., 1964; Richard M. Nixon chair Whittier Coll., 1977-78. Exhibited sculpture and cartoons, Los Angeles County Mus. Art, 1979; recipient Editorial Cartoon award Sigma Delta Chi 1963, 69, 71, 81, 82, 87, Pulitzer prize editorial cartooning 1964, 71, 84; author: The King and Us, 1974, Pro and Conrad, 1979, Drawn and Quartered, 1985. Served with C.E. AUS, 1942-46, PTO. Recipient Journalism award U. So. Calif., 1972, Overseas Press Club award, 1970, 81, Robert F. Kennedy Journalism award, 1st Prize, 1985. Fellow Soc. Profl. Journalists; mem. Phi Delta Theta. Democrat. Roman Catholic. Office: Los Angeles Times Syndicate Times Mirror Sq Los Angeles CA 90053

CONRAD, SUSAN BOESCH, nurse, educator; b. Waukegan, Ill., Dec. 14, 1959; d. James J. and Mae (Britt) Boesch; m. John Paul Conrad, Oct. 23, 1985; 1 child, Amanda Christine. BSN, Marquette U., 1982; postgrad., Norwestern U., 1983. RN, Calif., Ill. Staff nurse, patient educator Northwestern Meml. Hosp., Chgo., 1982-84; staff nurse Evanston (Ill.) Hosp., 1984-85, Vis. Nurses Assn., San Diego, 1985-86, Mercy Hosp., 1986-87; staff nurse Grossmont Hosp., La Mesa, Calif., 1987, instr. Lamaze method and child devel., 1987—; nurse, Ask a Nurse, National City, Calif., 1988; maternal child transporter, Evanston Hosp., 1982-85, Northwestern Hosp., 1982-85; nurse preceptor Mercy Hosp., 1983-87, Evanston Hosp., 1983-87, Northwestern Hosp., 1983-87. Mem. Nat. Assn. Ob/gyn. Nursing, Children's Play Group (San Diego) (coordinator 1986-88). Roman Catholic. Home: 1434 San Altos Pl Lemon Grove CA 92045 Office: Ask a Nurse PO Box 390130 San Diego CA 92139

CONRATH, ROBERT ROY, insurance agent; b. Indiana, Pa., July 11, 1948; s. Kenneth William and Jean Katheryn (Miller) C.; m. Barbara Frances Finn, June 6, 1970; 1 child, Audrey Jean. AA, Ariz. Western U., 1968; BS, No. Ariz. U., 1970. Career agt. Conn. Mutual Life, Kingman, Ariz., 1970-75; ind. agt. Mohave Ins. Ctr., Kingman, 1975—, pres., 1979—; ptnr. SHC Properties, Kingman, 1987—. Chmn. Parks and Recreation City Kingman, 1980; councilman City of Kingman, 1982-86. Mem. Ind. Ins. Agts., Nat. Assn. Life Underwriters., Mohave Lions (pres. 1988-89). Republican. Roman Catholic. Office: Mohave Ins Ctr Inc 2116 Stockton Hill Rd Kingman AZ 86401

CONSIDINE, SHARON CULVER, restaurant executive; b. San Diego, June 6, 1942; d. Harold and Elaine Culver; m. Timothy Malcolm Considine, 1962; children: Kevin, Ken, Kelly. Student, San Diego State U., 1960-63. Lic. real estate saleswoman, Calif. Owner, operator Mexican Village Restaurant, Coronado, Calif., 1973—; owner, agt. TNT Travel Agy., San Diego, 1975-82; bd. dirs. Bank So. Calif., Point Loma; mem. industry coun. for hotel and restaurant mgmt. U.S. Internat. U., 1985-86. Pink lady Mercy Hosp. Aux., 1964-69; mem., pres. Ladies Aux. for Retarded Children, 1970-76; founder Las Ayudantes, 1973-75; leader Cub Scouts Am., Point Loma, 1974-75, Girl Scouts U.S., Point Loma, 1980-82; tchr.'s asst. Sunset View, 1978-79; bd. dirs., pres. Aztec Athletic Found., 1981-85; rep. San Diego Super Bowl Com., 1984-88; bd. dirs. Coronado Hosp. Found., 1984-88; mem. pres.' coun. San Diego State U., 1984-86; bd. dirs., treas. USO, 1986—. Recipient cert. of Merit San Diego County, 1974, Woman of Yr. award Peninsula YMCA, 1986. Mem. Calif. Restaurant Assn. (bd. dirs. 1983—), San Diego Restaurant Assn. (founder, pres. 1981-85), Coronado C. of C. (exec. bd. 1974-78, v.p. 1989), San Diego State U. Alumni Assn. (bd. dirs. 1980-84), Pi Beta Phi (past alumni pres.). Home: 545 Ocean Blvd Coronado CA 92118

CONSTABLE, RONALD LEE, aerospace engineer; b. Kansas City, Mo., Feb. 23, 1944; s. Erle M. and Eugenia P. (Goff-Cleve) C.; m. Linda Ann Renn, May 20, 1972; children: Jennifer Christine, Christopher Lee. BS in Engring., Calif. Inst. Tech., 1966; postgrad., Calif. State U., L.A., 1966-68. Avionics software systems engr., group engr. avionics systems requirements, mgr. tactical systems Advanced Systems Devel. Ctr.; mgr. unmanned aircraft avionics systems dept. Lockheed-Calif. Co., Burbank, 1967-87; mgr. systems integration Ventura unit Northrop Co., Newbury Park, Calif., 1987-89; dir. test and evaluation, missiles and unmanned vehicles div. Northrop Aircraft, Newbury Park, Calif., 1989—. Republican. Office: Northrop Co Ventura Unit 1515 Rancho Conejo Newbury Park CA 91320

CONSTANT, CLINTON, chemical engineer; b. Nelson, B.C., Can., Mar. 20, 1912; came to U.S., 1936, naturalized, 1942; s. Vasile and Annie (Hunt) C.; m. Margie Robbel, Dec. 5, 1965. B.Sc. with honors, U. Alta., 1935, postgrad., 1935-36; Ph.D., Western Res. U., 1939. Registered profl. engr. Devel. engr. Harshaw Chem. Co., Cleve., 1936-38, mfg. foreman, 1938-43, sr. engr. semi-works dept., 1948-50; supt. hydrofluoric acid dept. Nyotex Chems., Inc., Houston, 1943-47, chief devel. engr., 1947-48; mgr. engring. Ferro Chem. Co., Bedford, Ohio, 1950-52; tech. asst. mfg. dept. Armour Agrl. Chem. Co. (name formerly Armour Fertilizer Works), Bartow, Fla., 1952-61, mfg. research and devel. div., 1961-63, mgr. spl. projects Research div. (co. name changed to USS Agri-Chems 1968), 1963-65, project mgr., 1965-70; chem. adviser Robert & Co. Assocs., Atlanta, 1970-79; chief engr. Almon & Assocs., Inc., Atlanta, 1979-80; project mgr. Engring. Service Assocs., Atlanta, 1980-81; v.p. engring. ACI Inc., Hesperia, Calif., 1981-83; sr. v.p., chief engr. MTI (acquisition of ACI), Hesperia, 1983-86; engring. cons. San Bernardino County APCD, Victorville, Calif., 1986—. Fellow AAAS, Am. Inst. Chemists, Am. Inst. Chem. Engrs., N.Y. Acad. Scis., AIAA (assoc.); mem. Am. Chem. Soc., Am. Astron. Soc., Astron. Soc. Pacific, Royal Astron. Soc. Can., NSPE, Am. Water Works Assn., Calif. Water and Pollution Control Assn., Air Pollution Control Assn., Soc. Mfg. Engrs., Calif. Soc. Profl. Engrs. Author tech. reports, sci. fiction; patentee in field.

CONSTANTINEAU, CONSTANCE JULIETTE, banker; b. Lowell, Mass., Feb. 18, 1937; d. Henry Goulet and Germaine (Turner) Goulet-Lamarre; m. Edward Joseph Constatnineau; children: Glen Edward, Alan Henry. Student, Bank Adminstrn. Inst. and Am. Inst. Banking, 1975-87. Mortgage sec. The Cen. Savs. Bank, Lowell, 1955-57; head teller First Fed. Savs. & Loan, Lowell, 1957-59, Lowell Bank & Trust Co., Lowell, 1973-74; br. mgr. Century Bank & Trust Co., Malden, Mass., 1975-78; v.p. purchasing, mgr. support svcs. First Nat. Bank Albuquerque, 1983—; mem. planning purchasing mgr.'s conf. Bank Adminstrn. Inst., San Antonio; treas.polit. action com. First Nat. Bank, 1986. Bd. dirs., historian Indian Pueblo Cultural Ctr., Albuquerque, 1986—. Mem. Nat. Assn. bank Women, In-Plant Mgmt. Assn. (charter). Home: 13015 Deer Dancer Trail NE Albuquerqué NM 87112 Office: First Nat Bank Albuquerque 40 First Pla Albuquerque NM 87103

CONSTON, STANLEY ROSS, manufacturing executive; b. Somerville, N.J., Sept. 21, 1958; s. Alfred Sydney and Charlotte (Stern) C. BS in Physics, U. Calif., Santa Barbara, 1981. Research and devel. assoc. Am. Heyer-Schulte Co., Santa Barbara, 1981-83; designer Flexion Corp., Santa Barbara, 1983-85; mgr. materials engring. research and design Vitaphore Corp., Menlo Park, Calif., 1985—. Patentee in field. Democrat. Taoist. Office: Vitaphore Corp 1505 O'Brien Dr Menlo Park CA 94025

CONTE, JULIE VILLA, nurse, administrator; b. Manila, July 4, 1951; came to U.S., 1970; d. Gregorio Cortes and Lourdes (Villa) Dirige; m. Michael Don Conte, Jan. 22, 1983. BSN, Calif. State U., L.A., 1974; postgrad., Calif. State U., Long Beach, 1986. RN, Calif. Staff nurse Santa Monica (Calif.) Hosp., 1976-78; pub. health nurse Kaiser Found. Hosp., Panorama City, Calif., 1978-85; nursing supr. Nat. Med. Homecare, L.A., 1985-86; dir. home health Holy Cross Hosp., Mission Hills, 1986-88; dir. profl. svcs. Care Home Health, San Diego, 1988—; pub. health nurse cons. Able Home Health Care, Wilmington, Calif., 1984; bd. dirs. nursing Health Prime, Inc. Mem. NAFE, Nat. Assn. Home Care, Home Health Dirs. Coun. (sec. 1986-88), Calif. Assn. Health Svcs. at Home (orgn. rep. 1986—), Alpha Delta Chi. Republican. Baptist. Home: 4444 Bancroft St San Diego CA 92116

CONTI, DANIEL JOSEPH, health management executive; b. Somerville, N.J., Feb. 22, 1949; s. Daniel A. and Helen (Glab) C.; m. Carolynn E. Frush, Aug. 10, 1982; 1 child, Jonathan Daniel. BS, St. Bonaventure U., 1970; MS, U. Ariz., 1979. Sr. physiologist Los Angeles County Occupational Health Dept., 1979-80; exec. dir. Inst. Health Mgmt., San Francisco, 1980-82; owner, pres. Health Mgmt. Cons., San Francisco, 1982-86; v.p., chief ops. officer Nat. Inst. Cardiovascular Tech., Inc., Newport Beach, Calif., 1986-87; also bd. dirs. Nat. Inst. Cardiovascular Tech., Inc., Newport Beach; pres., chief exec. officer Nat. Inst. Cardiovascular Tech., Inc., Newport Beach, Calif., 1987-89; founder, ptnr. Health Resource Group, 1989—; chmn. heart at work com. Orange County chpt. Am. Heart Assn., 1988—. Pub. wellness newsletter The Pulse, 1989—; editor Health Mgmt. Newsletter, 1982-84. Mem. Am. Coll. Sports Medicine, Assn. Fitness in Bus. Democrat. Office: Health Resource Group PO Box 19654-166 Irvine CA 92713

CONTO, ARISTIDES, advertising agency executive; b. N.Y.C., Feb. 10, 1931; s. Gus Dimitrios and Osee (Kenney) C.; B.A., Champlain Coll., 1953; M.S. in Journalism, UCLA, 1958, certificate in indsl. relations, 1965; m. Phyllis Helen Wiley, June 22, 1957; 1 son, Jason Wiley. Reporter, City News Service, Los Angeles, 1958; dir. pub. relations Galaxy Advt. Co., Los Angeles, 1959-60; news media chief Los Angeles County Heart Assn., 1960-61; pub. relations asso. Prudential Ins. Co., Los Angeles, 1961-64; advt. mgr. Aerospace Controls Co., Los Angeles, 1964-65; comml. sales promotion coordinator Lockheed-Calif. Co., Burbank, 1965-73; pres. Jason Wiley Advt. Agy., Los Angeles, 1973—; dir. Tower Master, Inc., Los Angeles. Served with U.S. Army, 1955-56. Recipient advt. awards. Mem. Nat. Soc. Published Poets, Los Angeles Press Club, Bus.-Profl. Advt. Assn. Los Angeles, Public Relations Soc. . Author: The Spy Who Loved Me, 1962; The Diamond Twins, 1963; author screenplays: Lannigan, 1973; Haunted Host, 1976; Captain Noah, 1977; (screenplay) Government Surplus, 1983. Office: 1506 W 12th St Los Angeles CA 90015

CONTOS, PAUL ANTHONY, engineer, investment advisor; b. Chgo., Mar. 18, 1926; s. Anthony Dimitrios and Panagiota (Kostopoulos) C.; m. Lilian Katie Kalkines, June 19, 1955 (dec. Apr. 1985); children: Leslie, Claudia, Paula, Anthony; m. Shirley Elsa Saxton, Mar. 7, 1987. Student, Am. TV Inst., Chgo., 1946-48, U. Ill., 1949-52, 53-56, Ill. Inst. Tech., 1952-53, U. So. Calif., 1956-57. Engr. J.C. Deagan Co., Inc., Chgo., 1951-53, Lockheed Missile and Space Co., Inc., Sunnyvale, Calif., 1956-62; engring. supr. Lockheed Missile and Space Co., Inc., Sunnyvale, 1962-65, staff engr., 1965-88; pres. PAC Investments, Saratoga, Calif., 1984-88; pres. PAC Investments, San Jose, Calif., 1988—, also advisor, 1984—. Served with U.S. Army, 1944-46, ETO. Decorated Purple Heart. Mem. DAV (commdr.

Chgo. unit 1948-51), Pi Sigma Phi (pres. 1951-53). Republican. Greek Orthodox. Home and Office: 2254 Starbright Dr San Jose CA 95124

CONTRACTOR, DINSHAW N., civil engineer, educator; b. Bangalore, India, Apr. 23, 1933; came to U.S., 1958.; s. Nariman C. and Goola N. (Engineer) C.; m. Hutoxy R. Hirjibehdin, Sept. 18, 1958; children: Rashna, Shernaz, Yasmin, Yazdi, Arnavaz. BE in civil engring., U. Baroda, India, 1956; MS, U. Iowa, 1959; PhD, U. Mich., 1963. Registered profl. engr., Ariz. Research scientist Hydronautics, Inc., Laurel, Md., 1963-68; asst. prof. Va. Poly. Inst. & State U., Blacksburg, 1968-75, assoc. prof., 1975-81; visiting prof. Water & Energy Res. Inst. Univ. Guam, 1980-81; prof. U. Ariz., Tucson, 1981—; cons. United Nations Dev. Program, Baroda, 1984. Contbr. articles to profl. jours. Mem. ASCE, ASME, Am. Geophysical Union, Am. Water Resources Assn., Jaycees. Democrat. Zoroastrian. Lodge: Civitan (Blacksburg). Office: U Ariz Dept Civil & Engring Mech Tucson AZ 85721

CONWAY, JAMES VALENTINE PATRICK, forensic document examiner, former postal service executive; b. Scottdale, Pa., July 16, 1917; s. James Aloysius and Mary Margaret (Yahner) C.; m. Mildred E. Garypie, Aug. 6, 1936; children: James W., Ruth A. Conway Masonek, Colleen L. Conway Weyland, Judith Conway Henderson. Student, St. Vincent Coll., Latrobe, Pa., 1931-34, Cambria-Rowe Bus. Coll., Greensburg, Pa., 1935-36. Diplomate: Am. Bd. Forensic Document Examiners. With U.S. Postal Svc., 1939-80; regional chief insp. U.S. Postal Svc., San Francisco, 1971-73; exec. asst. to Postmaster Gen., Washington, 1973-75; sr. asst. postmaster gen. for employee and labor rels. 1975-78; dep. Postmaster Gen., 1978-80, bd. govs., 1978-80; forensic document examiner Alameda, Calif., 1980—. Author: Evidential Documents, 1959; contbr. articles to profl. jours. Bd. dirs. Regional Civil Def. Bd., Santa Rose, Calif., 1964-69. Recipient Benjamin Franklin award Postmaster Gen.'s, 1980; named Staff Man of Yr. Fed. Bus. Assn., San Francisco, 1957. Fellow Am. Acad. Forensic Scis. (chmn. document sect. 1960-61, chmn. adv. council 1960-61); mem. Internat. Assn. Chiefs Police (life), Internat. Assn. Identification (chmn. subcom. questioned document 1953-56), Am. Soc. Questioned Document Examiners (v.p. 1986-88, pres. 1988—). Democrat. Roman Catholic. Lodge: Elks.

CONWAY, LOUIS WILLIAM, surgeon; b. London, Feb. 25, 1933; came to U.S., 1947; s. William Arthur and Netta (Green) C.; m. Marjorie Anne Kryder. AB magna cum laude, UCLA, 1952, MD cum laude, 1956. Intern Johns Hopkins Hosp., Balt., 1956-57, resident, 1957-58; resident in neurological surgery UCLA, 1958-62, clin. instr., 1962-63; from asst. to assoc. prof. Med. Coll. Va., Richmond, 1963-67; assoc. prof. U. Calif., Davis, 1967-72; dir. neurological surgery Arnett Clinic, Lafayette, Ind., 1972-88; chief dept. neurosurgery, assoc. dir. dept. surgery Valley Med. Ctr., Fresno, Calif., 1988—. Contbr. articles to profl. jours. Mem. Am. Assn. Neurological Surgeons, Am. Coll. Surgeons, Congress of Neurological Surgeons, Neurosurgical Soc. Ind. (pres. 1977-80), Ind. State Med. Soc. (chmn. neurosurgery sect. 1977-80), Fresno Madera Med. Soc., Calif. Med. Assn. Office: Cen Calif Med Group 2212 N Winery Ave Fresno CA 93703

COOK, ALBERT THOMAS THORNTON, JR., financial advisor; b. Cleve., Apr. 24, 1940; s. Albert Thomas Thornton and Tyra Esther (Morehouse) C.; m. Mary Jane Blackburn, June 1, 1963; children: Lara, Thomas, Timothy. BA, Dartmouth Coll., 1962; MA, U. Chgo., 1966. Asst. sec. Dartmouth Coll., Hanover, N.H., 1972-77; exec. dir. Big Brothers, Inc., N.Y.C., 1977-78; underwriter Boettcher & Co., Denver, 1978-81; asst. v.p. Dain Bosworth Inc., Denver, 1981-82, Colo. Nat. Bank, Denver, 1982-84; pres. The Albert T.T. Cook Co., Denver, 1984—; arbitrator Nat. Assn. Securities Dealers, N.Y.C., 1985—, Mcpl. Securities Rulemaking Bd., Washington, 1987—. Pres. Etna-Hanover Ctr. Community Assn., Hanover, N.H., 1974-76; mem. Mayor's Task Force, Denver, 1984; dir. Rude Park Community Nursery, Denver, 1985-87; trustee The Iliff Sch. Theol., Denver, 1986—. Mem. Dartmouth Alumni Council (exec. com., chmn. nominating and trustee search coms. 1987-89), Delta Upsilon. Congregationalist. Clubs: University, Cactus (Denver); Dartmouth of N.Y.C., Yale. Lodge: Lions (bd. dirs. Denver chpt. 1983-85, treas. 1986-87, pres. Denver Found., 1987-88). Home: 7099 E Hinsdale Pl Englewood CO 80112 Office: 1225 Seventeenth St 23rd Floor Denver CO 80202

COOK, ANTHONY MALCOLM, aerospace engineer; b. Liverpool, Eng., Jan. 10, 1936; came to U.S., 1948; s. Edward George Cook; m. Dianne Lorene Combest, July 22, 1956; children: Robert L., Barbara L. BS in Engring., San Jose State U., 1958. Aero. rsch. engr. NASA Ames Rsch. Ctr., Moffett Field, Calif., 1962-68, aero. project engr. advanced aircraft office, 1968-70, tech. asst. to dir. aeronautics, 1970-74, asst. chief Flight Systems & Simulation Rsch. div., 1974—; chmn. flight simulation lab. adv. com. Calif. Poly. State U., San Luis Obispo, 1983—. Adviser, Los Gatos (Calif.) High Sch. Dist., 1978-79. Capt. USAF, 1958-60. Mem. Am. Arbitration Assn., AIAA (chmn. working group on r&d flight simulation 1982-83). Office: NASA Ames Rsch Ctr Flight Systems & Simulation Rsch Div Bldg 243-1 Moffett Field CA 94035

COOK, APRIL JOY, investigator; b. Sacramento, Apr. 2, 1953; d. Lee Roy and Lavina Margarite (Johnson) C.; m. Mark Pestal Worcester, Feb. 6, 1987; 1 child, Fiona Rose. Student, Sacramento City Coll., 1971-72, Cosumnes River Coll., 1973-75, Anchorage Community Coll., 1978. Criminal intelligence specialist trainee State of Calif. Dept. Justice, Sacramento, 1975-77; corrections officer Dept. Corrections State of Alaska, Anchorage, 1978-81, investigator Pub. Defender Agy., 1981-83, investigator Office of Atty. Gen., 1984—; pvt. practice, Anchorage, 1984. Democrat. Clubs: Knik Canoers and Kayakers (Anchorage) Royal Order of Grand Troglodytes (Sacramento). Office: State of Alaska Office of Atty Gen 1031 W 4th Ave Ste 200 Anchorage AK 99501

COOK, AUDELLA, child protection social worker; b. El Centro, Calif., Aug. 6, 1948; d. Oscar Patterson and Geneva (Evans) White; m. Richard Glenn Cook, May 26, 1969; children: Michael, David, Melinda. BA, U. Calif., Riverside, 1971; MA, U. Redlands, 1975. Cert. life. tchr. Tchr. Riverside (Calif.) Sch. Dist., 1971-75; social worker Guadalupe Home for Boys, Yacaipa, Calif., 1979-82; child protective svcs. social worker San Bernardino County, 1982-89; dir. Adv. Schs., San Bernardino, 1989—. Mem. Am. Transplant Coun., Children's Transplant Assn., West Mountain Mental Health Assn. (bd. mem.). Democrat. Office: Adv Schs 1248 Waterman Ave San Bernardino CA 92404

COOK, DIANE PENNELL, insurance executive; b. Trenton, N.J., Apr. 15, 1947; d. Eric Leslie and Edith Jean (Shearer) Pennell; m. Stephen Hale Cook, Mar. 21, 1970 (div. Jan. 1979). BA, Swarthmore Coll., 1969; MA, Northwestern U., 1970. Claim examiner Washington Nat. Ins. Co., Evanston, Ill., 1970-73, supr. field svcs., 1973-74, supr. claim ops., 1974-77, asst. mgr. claim support, 1978-79; mgr. adminstrn. Jordan Jones & Assoc., Inc., Sacramento, 1979-82, mgr. adminstrn. and claims, 1982-84, v.p. ops., 1984-88, sr. v.p., sec., 1988—. Fellow: Life Mgmt. Inst.; mem. Soc. of Profl. Benefit Adminstrs., Ind. Adminstrs. Assn. (legis. analyst 1987—), Sierra Club. Office: Jordan Jones & Assoc Inc PO Box 160128 631 Elverta Rd Sacramento CA 95816

COOK, DONALD CARL, aerospace engineer; b. Chgo., Sept. 19, 1928; s. Edward Clarence and Lucena Wilhelmina (Tascher) C.; m. Ellen Lucille Deckert, Feb.13, 1953; chldren: Jennifer Lyn, Jeremy Allen. Student, U. Ill., 1947-48, 54-57; AA in Math., San Diego Evening Coll., 1966; BS in Physics, San Diego State U., 1970. Applications engr. Cohu Electronics, San Diego, 1957-58; flight test engr. Gen. Dynamics Convair, San Diego, 1959-70; sr. engr. Fed. Electric Corp., Vandenberg AFB, Calif., 1970-76; sr. field engr. Martin Marietta Corp., Vandenberg AFB, 1976-86; sr. engr. specialist Lockheed Space Ops. Co., Vandenberg AFB, 1986—. 1st lt. U.S. Army, 1948-54, Korea; lt. col. USAR, ret. Mem. Res. Officers Assn. (life), U.S. Chess Fedn. (cert. tournament dir.). Republican. Baptist. Home: 895 Blake St Santa Maria CA 93455 Office: Lockheed Space Ops Co Vandenberg AFB CA 93437

COOK, DONALD E., pediatrician; b. Pitts., Mar. 24, 1928; s. Merriam E. and Bertha (Gwin) C.; BS, Colo. Coll., 1951; MD, U. Colo., 1955; m. Elsie Walden, Sept. 2, 1951; children: Catherine, Christopher, Brian, Jeffrey. Intern, Fresno County Gen. Hosp., Calif., 1955-56; resident in gen. practice Tulare (Calif.) County Gen. Hosp., 1956-57; resident in pediatrics U. Colo., 1957-59; practice medicine specializing in pediatrics, Aurora, Colo., 1959-64, in pediatrics, Greeley, Colo., 1964—; clin. faculty U. Colo., clin. prof., 1977—; mem. adv. bd. Nat. Center Health Edn., San Francisco, 1978-80; mem. adv. com. on maternal and child health programs Colo. State Health Dept., 1981-84, chmn., 1981-84; preceptor Sch. Nurse Practitioner Program U. Colo., 1978—. Mem. Weld County Dist. 6 Sch. Bd., 1973-83, pres., 1973-74, 76-77, chmn. dist. 6 accountability com., 1972-73; mem. adv. com. dist. 6 teen pregnancy program, 1983-85; mem. Weld County Task Force on teenaged pregnancy, 1986—, Dream Team Weld County Task Force on sch. dropouts, 1986—, Weld County Interagy. Screening Bd., Weld County Community Ctr. Found., 1984—, Weld County Task Force Speakers Bur. on AIDS, 1987—; group leader neonatal group Colo. Action for Healthy People Colo. Dept. Pub. Health, 1985-86; co-founder Colorodoans for seatbelts on sch. buses, 1985—; co-founder, v.p. Coalition of primary care physicians, Colo., 1986; mem. adv. com. Greeley Cen. Drug and Alcohol Abuse, 1984-86, Rocky Mtn. Ctr. for Health Promotion and Edn., 1984—; rep. counc. on med. specialty soc., AAP, 1988—, mem. coun. pediatric rsch., 1988—. With USN, 1946-48. Recipient Disting. Service award Jr. C. of C., 1962, Disting. Citizenship award Elks, 1975-76, Service to Mankind award Sertoma Club, 1972; Community Service award Phi Delta Kappa, 1981, Spark Plug award U. No. Colo., 1981. Diplomate Am. Bd. Pediatrics. Mem. Colo. Soc. Sch. Health Com. (chmn. 1967-78), Am. Acad. Pediatrics (alt. dist. chmn. 1987—, chmn. sch. health com. 1975-80, chmn. Colo. chpt. 1982-87, mem. task force on new age of pediatrics 1982-85, Ross edn. and award com. 1985-86; media spokesperson Speak Up for Children 1983—), AMA (chmn. sch. and coll. health com. 1980-82, James E. Strain Community Svc. award 1987), Adams Aurora Med. Soc. (pres. 1964-65), Weld County Med. Soc. (pres. 1968-69), Colo. Med. Soc. (com. on sports medicine, 1980—, com. chmn. 1986—, A.H. Robbins Community Service award 1974), Centennial Pediatric Soc. (pres. 1982-86), Rotary (bd. dirs. Greely chpt. 1988—). Republican. Methodist. Home: 1710 21st Ave Greeley CO 80631 Office: Greeley Med Clinic Greeley Sports Medicine Clinic 1900 16th St Greeley CO 80631

COOK, FRANCES JEFFRIES, academic administrator; b. Gastonia, N.C., Feb. 9, 1940; d. Murrell Moore and Frances Elizabeth (Moore) Jeffries; m. Edward Louis Lamie, Jan. 2, 1988; children: William Lamie, Jennifer Cook, David Lamie, Katherine Cook, Andrew Cook, Marla Lamie, Melissa Lamie. AB, Lake Erie Coll., 1960; EdM, Boston U., 1961; PhD, Kent State U., 1970. Asst. prof. Kent (Ohio) State U., 1970-75; dir. admissions Old Trail Sch., Bath, Ohio, 1975-80, Lake Erie Coll., Painesville, Ohio, 1980-82, Guilford Coll., Greensboro, N.C., 1982-83; dean admissions and fin. aid Guilford Coll., Greensboro, 1983-86; dir. admissions Calif. State U., Turlock, 1986-87, dean enrollment svcs., 1988—; mem. Chancellor's outreach and recruitment adv. com. Calif State U., Turlock. mem. Community Svc. Network, Modesto, Calif., 1986—. Fellow Kent State U., 1967-69; recipient Outstanding Bd. Svc. award Big Bros. & Sisters, Akron, Ohio, 1973-75. Mem. Nat. Assn. Coll. Admissions Counselors, Western Assn. Coll. Admission Counselors, Am. Assn. Collegiate Registrars and Admissions Officers, Pacific Assn. Collegiate Registrars and Admissions Officers, Higher Edn. Consortium, Calif. Women in Higher Edn., Calif. Edn. Roundtable (intersegmental coord. coun.), Pi Lambda Theta, Rotary. Home: 1713 Fairington Ln Modesto CA 95355 Office: Calif State U 801 W Monte Vista Ave Turlock CA 95380

COOK, GARY MORRIS, energy corporation executive; b. Lincoln, Nebr., Apr. 11, 1942; s. Eugene E. and Mary Margaret (Morris) C.; m. Diane Grafe, Sept. 3, 1966 (div. 1989); children: Christian M., Lauren S. BA in Econs. with honors, Wesleyan U., 1964; JD (hon.), Harvard U., 1967. Mgmt. cons. McKinsey & Co. Inc., N.Y.C., 1967-70; spl. asst. to sec., dep. asst. sec. HEW, Washington, 1970-72; dep. asst. sec., acting dir. Bur. Domestic Commerce, Dept. Commerce, Washington, 1972-74; sr. v.p. Agrico Chem. Co., Tulsa, 1974-78; chmn. Trend Constrn. Corp., Tulsa and Oklahoma City, 1978-82; pres., chief operating officer Barringer Resources Inc., Golden, Colo., 1983-84; mng. dir. Gary M. Cook Interests., Denver, 1980—; mng. ptnr. Kimbrel & Cook Inc., Tulsa and Denver, 1985—; pres. chief exec. officer, dir. Kimce Energy Corp., Dallas, Denver, 1987—; vice-chmn. OECD Industry Com., Paris 1973-74. Contbr. articles to profl. jours. Mem. Coun. on Fgn. Rels. Clubs: Sankaty Golf (bd. dirs 1982), Sankaty Casino (Nantucket); Harvard (N.Y.); Univ. (Washington), Denver. Home: 7355 E West Kentucky Dr Lakewood CO 80226 Office: Kimco Energy Corp 1801 Broadway Ste 300 Denver CO 80202

COOK, GREGORY ALDEN, financial analyst; b. St. Louis, Dec. 1, 1955; s. Alfred A. and Leath (Koesterer) C.; m. Barbara Jean Cook, Aug. 21, 1982; 1 child, Lindsay Reneé. BSBA in Acctg., U. Mo., 1978; MBA, U. Mo., St. Louis, 1981. CPA, Ill. Cost analyst Granite City (Ill.) Steel Co. div. Nat. Steel, 1978-83, div. cost analyst, 1987-88, fin. analyst, 1989—; fin. planning analyst Nat. Steel Corp., Pitts., 1983-85, supr. accts. payable, 1985-87; chmn. supr. com. fed. credit Union Granite City Steel, 1988. Mem. Nat. Assn. Accts., Mo. Soc. CPAs. Methodist.

COOK, HARRY LEE, lawyer; b. Alhambra, Calif., July 3, 1956; s. Harry Leroy and Lue Anne (King) C.; m. Julie Ann Carter, Mar. 5, 1988. BA, U. Oreg., 1979, JD, 1986. Bar: Oreg. 1986, Wash. 1987. Assoc. Stafford, Frey, Cooper & Stewart, Portland, 1986—. Articles editor Oreg. Law Rev., 1985-86. Mem. ABA, Oreg. State Bar Assn., Wash. State Bar Assn., Multnomah County Bar Assn., Phi Delta Phi. Democrat. Office: Stafford Frey Cooper & Stewart 1700 Benjamin Franklin Pla 1 SW Columbia Portland OR 97258

COOK, JAMES JAY, finance company executive; b. St. Paul, Nov. 2, 1940; s. Arleigh Jay and Myrtle Marie Cook; m. Christiane Augustine Seitz. July 17, 1971; 1 child, Jason. AB, Stanford U., 1962; JD, U. Calif, San Francisco, 1967. Bar: Calif. 1968, U.S. Dist. Ct. (so. dist.) Calif.; cert. fin. planner. Ptnr. Richards, Watson & Gershon, L.A., 1967-81; pres. Cook-Holman, Inc., San Marino, Calif., 1982—; state dir. Calif. Assn. of Realtors, 1984. Contbr. articles to profl. jours. Mem. Apt. Assn. Greater L.A. (dir. 1982—, pres. 1987, pres. award 1984), Pasadena Bd. of Realtors (dir. 1982-86). Lutheran. Office: Cook-Holman Inc San Marino CA 91108

COOK, JOHN EDWARD, small business owner; b. Martins Ferry, Ohio, Apr. 1, 1931; s. Jess Ambrose and Chala Elizabeth (Wright) C.; m. Carol Ann Rydberg, Nov. 22, 1951; children: Theresa, Cathy, Betty, Sally, Carolyn. Grad. high sch., Anchorage. Electrician, lineman Local 1547 IBEW, Anchorage, 1951-78; owner Sterling (Alaska) Tesoro - Cooks Cafe, 1978—. Bd. mem. rd. svc. Kenac Peninsula Borough, Soldotna, 1986-89. With USAF, 1947-49, Alaska Guard, 1950-55. Mem. Lions (pres. 1986-88), Elks, Masons, Shriners, Internat. Brotherhood Electrical Workers. Home: Box 49 Mile 76 Sterling AK 99672 Office: Sterling Tesoro-Cooks Cafe Box 49 Mile 81 Sterling Hwy Sterling AK 99672

COOK, LODWRICK MONROE, petroleum company executive; b. Castor, La., June 17, 1928; married. B.S., La. State U., 1950, B.S. in Petroleum Engring., 1955; M.B.A., So. Meth. U., 1965. Petroleum engr. Union Producing Co., 1955-56; with Atlantic Richfield Co., Los Angeles, 1956—; engring. trainee Atlantic Richfield Co., Inc., Los Angeles, 1956-61, adminstrv. asst., 1961-64, sr. personnel dept., then personnel mgr., 1964-67, labor reins. con., 1967-69, mgr. labor reins. dept., 1969-70, v.p., gen. mgr. product div. Western area, 1970-72, v.p. mktg. products div., 1972-73, v.p. corp. planning div., 1973-74, v.p. products div., 1974-75, v.p. transp. div., 1975-77, sr. v.p. transp. div., 1977-80, exec. v.p., dir., 1980-85, pres., chief exec. officer, 1985, chmn., chief exec. officer, 1986—. Chmn. bd. dirs. Nat. Jr. Achievement; bd. regents Pepperdine U., La. State U. Found; bd. govs. Music Ctr. Los Angeles. Served to 1st lt. U.S. Army, 1950-53. Mem. Nat. Petroleum Council, Am. Petroleum Inst. (dir.). Office: Atlantic Richfield Co 515 S Flower St Los Angeles CA 90071

COOK, LYLE EDWARDS, fund-raising executive, consultant; b. Astoria, Oreg., Aug. 19, 1918; s. Courtney Carson and Fanchon (Edwards) C.; m. Olive Freeman, Dec. 28, 1940; children: James Michael, Ellen Anita Cook Otto, Mary Lucinda Cook Vaage, Jean Victoria. A.B. in History, Stanford U., 1940, postgrad., 1940-41. Instr. history Yuba Jr. Coll., Marysville, Calif., 1941-42; methods analyst Lockheed Aircraft Corp., 1942-45; investment broker Quincy Cass Assocs., Los Angeles, 1945-49; mem. staff Stanford U., 1949-66, asso. dean Sch. Medicine, 1958-65; sr. staff mem. Lester Gorsline Assos., Belvedere, Calif., 1966-72, v.p., 1967-70, exec. v.p., 1970-72; v.p. univ. relations U. San Francisco, 1973-75; fund-raising and planning cons. 1975; dir. fund devel. Children's Home Soc. Calif., 1976-78; exec. dir. That Man May See, Inc., San Francisco, 1978-87; trustee, chmn. bd. The Fund Raising Sch., 1967-86; spl. cons. NIH, 1960-62. Mem. Nat. Soc. Fund Raising Execs. (bd. dirs. 1976-88, chmn. certification bd. 1988—), Stanford Assos., Belvedere Tennis Club, Theta Delta Chi. Democrat. Episcopalian. Home: 25 Greenwood Bay Dr Tiburon CA 94920

COOK, PAUL CHRISTOPHER, engineering psychologist; b. Corpus Christi, Tex., Mar. 24, 1953; s. William Eckford and Nelle (Gladney)C. AA, Ocean City Coll., Md., 1973; BA, U. Ariz., Tucson, 1978; MA, U. Ariz., 1981, PhD, 1987. Oceanographer Dept. Natural Resources, State of Md., Annapolis, 1973-75; researcher Child Psychology Lab., Tucson, 1977-78; behavioral and video cons. Intermt. Ctrs. for Human Devel., Tucson, 1978-79; research assoc. Family & Community Medicine, Ariz. Health Sci. Ctr., Tucson, 1982-84; research and analysis assoc. U. Ariz., Tucson, 1980-87; sr. human factors engr. U.S. Army Electronic Proving Ground, Ft. Huachuca, Ariz., 1986-87; engring. psychologist U.S. Army Yuma Proving Ground, Ariz., 1988; cons. engr. Cook3, Tucson, 1989—; divemaster, Tucson, 1985—. Scuba diver Pima County Sheriff's Dept., Pima County, 1985—. Mem. U.S. Navy League, U.S. Naval Inst., Human Factors Soc., Profl. Assn. Diving Instrs. Republican. Methodist. Home: 6537 E Santa Elena Tucson AZ 85715-3132 Office: Cook3 6537 E Santa Elena Tucson AZ 85715

COOK, PAUL M., chemical manufacturing company executive; b. Ridgewood, N.J.. B.S. in Chem. Engring, M.I.T., 1947. With Stanford Research Inst., Palo Alto, Calif., 1949-53, Sequoia Process Corp., 1953-56; with Raychem Corp., Menlo Park, Calif., 1957—, former pres., now chmn., chief exec. officer, bd. dirs. Recipient Nat. Medal Tech., 1988. Office: Raychem Corp 300 Constitution Dr Menlo Park CA 94025 *

COOK, RICHARD LOUIS, forensic engineer; b. Seattle, Dec. 8, 1948; s. James Louis and Margaret Edna (Alsager) C. BSME, U. Wash., 1971. Registered profl. engr. Cons. engr. NW Lab., Inc., Seattle, 1975-82, R.L. Cook Engring, Inc., Seattle, 1982, Forensic Engring, Inc., Seattle, 1983-86; pres. Forensic Cons., Inc., Kent, Wash., 1983—. Mem. Am. Acad. Forensic Scis. (student acad. faculty 1987—), Nat. Acad. Forensic Engrs., Nat. Soc. Profl. Engrs., Soc. Automotive Engrs., Aircraft Owners and Pilots Assn. Office: Forensic Cons Inc 26525 114th Ave SE Kent WA 98031

COOK, RITA LEILANI, probation director; b. Berkeley, Calif., Sept. 21, 1943; d. John Fischer and Mary Ardeane (Mariani) Raab; m. Harold Milton Cook, July 30, 1971; stepchildren: Wendy, Mandy. BA in Psychology, Chapman Coll., 1973, MA in Marriage, Family, Child Counseling, 1976. Probation counselor Orange County Probation Dept., Santa Ana, Calif., 1967-75; dep. probation officer Orange County Probation Dept., Orange, Calif., 1975-82, supervising probation officer, 1982-86, probation div. dir., 1986—; vol. counseling Orange County Breast Care Ctr., 1988; chmn. Juvenile Probation Suprs. Ops. Com., Orange, 1988; implementor, developer numerous correctional and treatment programs. Author: Probation Sujpervisor's Handbook, 1984. Democrat. Roman Catholic. Office: Orange County Probation 301 The City Dr Orange CA 92668

COOK, ROBERT SHERMAN, medical products company executive; b. Evanston, Ill., Feb. 27, 1954; s. John D. and Sybilla Pomeroy (Avery) C.; m. Carolyn Ruth Stevens, Apr. 23, 1977; children: Averie Michelle, Matthew Stevens. BS, Brigham Young U., 1977. Zoning adminstr. Douglas County Planning Dept., Roseburg, Oreg., 1977-80; sales rep. Signode Corp., Glenview, Ill., 1980-8l, Davis & Geck, Wayne, N.J., 198l-86; nat. sales mgr. Shur Med., Beaverton, Oreg., 1986; assoc. W.L. Gore and Assocs., Elkton, Md., 1986-87, Flagstaff, Ariz., 1987—. Democrat. Mormon. Home: 1821 N Raintree Rd Flagstaff AZ 86004 Office: WL Gore & Assocs PO Box 900 Flagstaff AZ 86002

COOK, ROGER NOLAN, safety consultant; b. Helen, W. Va., Aug. 18, 1945; s. Raleigh Newson and Erma Lois (Cook) C.; m. Saundra Dianne Cook, Aug. 17, 1971; children: John Andrew, Ian Philip. BS, Concord Coll., 1971; cert. mining, W.Va. U., 1973; cert. radiation, Colo. Sch. Mines, 1982; postgrad., Utah State U., 1984. Saftey inspector, tng. Pittston Corp., Beckley, W. Va., 1972-77; sr. safety specialist Syncrude Can., Ft. McMurry, Alta., 1977-79; advisor safety, security Getty Oil, Salt Lake City, 1979-85; mgr. safety, security Titanium Metals Corp. Am., Henderson, Nev., 1985—. Scout master Boy Scouts Am., Henderson, 1985-86; bd. dirs. Casper (Wyo.) Youth Hockey Assn., 1980-81, Spl. Olympics, W. Va., 1974-76; pres. Syncrude Softball Assn., Ft. McMurray, 1978-79. Served with USN, 1963-66. Named one of Outstanding Young Men of Am., Jaycees, Utah, 1982. Mem. Nev. Safety Council (bd. dirs. 1986—), Am. Soc. Safety Engrs. (profl., sec. 1986—, v.p. 1987), World Safety Orgn. (cert.), Am. Soc. Indsl. Security (profl., treas. 1983), Nat. Intelligence and Counter Intelligence Assn., Nat. Safety Council (com. health and hygiene 1984—). Republican. Episcopalian. Home: 2349 Red Willow Ln Henderson NV 89105 Office: SIS Adminstrs PO Box 2128 Henderson NV 89015

COOK, SHARON EVONNE, academic administrator, educator; b. Pocatello, Idaho, July 16, 1941; d. Willard Robert and Marian (Bartlett) Leisy; m. John Fred Cook, June 19, 1971 (div. Nov. 1980). BEd, No. Mont. Coll., 1970; M in Secondary Edn., U. Alaska, Juneau, 1980; EdD, U. San Francisco, 1987. Cert. secondary sch. tchr., Alaska. Loan officer 1st Nat. Bank, Havre, Mont., 1964-68; adminstrv. asst. Alaska State Legis., Juneau, 1970-71; tchr. Juneau Dist. High Sch., 1971-75; instr. Juneau Dist. Community Coll., 1975-79; assoc. prof. U. Alaska, Juneau, 1979—, dean Sch. Bus. and Pub. Adminstrn., 1986—; editor in chief office tech. McGraw Hill Book Gregg Div., N.Y.C., 1983-84; mem. exec. bd. statewide assembly U. Region V Vocat. Assn., 1978-80, del. 1982. Treas. Alaska State Vocat. Assn., 1980-82, pres.-elect, 1986, pres., 1987; pres. U. Alaska Juneau Assembly, 1978-80, v.p., 1980-82. No. Mont. Coll. scholar, Havre, 1968-70; named Outstanding Tchr., U. Alaska, 1976. Republican. Home: 2400 Douglas Hwy #5 Juneau AK 99801 Office: U Alaska Sch Bus and Pub Adminstrn 1108 F St Juneau AK 99801

COOK, SID FRANK, marine biologist; b. Reno, Dec. 14, 1953; s. Harold Raymond Cook and Doramae Catherine (Deal) Jakobson. BS in Vertebrate Zoology, U. Pacific, 1977; postgrad., Oreg. State U., 1978-80. Project mgr. Cook, Stolowitz and Frame, Visalia, Calif., 1978-81; cons. Argus-Mariner Cons. Scientists Inc., Corvallis, Oreg., 1981—; cons. Calif. Cedar Products Co., Stockton, 1977, UN Indsl. Devel. Orgn., 1986—, UN Food and Agrl. Orgn., 1987—; fgn. observer Nat. Marine Fisheries Service, Bering Sea, Alaska, 1979. Author: Cook's Book: A Guide to the Handling and Eating of Sharks and Skates, 1985; author, prin. artist (poster) Sharks of the U.S., 1989; pen and ink illustrator, author note card design, 1989; contbr. articles to profl. jours.; patentee underwater storage facilities. Active Community Foodbank, Corvallis, 1985-87; advisor Luth. Campus Ministries, Corvallis, 1985; bd. dirs. Grace Luth Ch. Food Gleaning Project, Corvallis, 1985. Mem. Am. Elasmobranch Soc., Desert Fishes Council, Internat. Inst. Fisheries Econ. and Trade, Am. Soc. Photogrammetry, Am. Soc. Ichthyologists and Herpetologists. Home: 801 NW 27th St #2 Corvallis OR 97330-4365 Office: 801 NW 27th #2 Corvallis OR 97330-0393

COOK, STANLEY JOSEPH, linguist; b. Spicer, Minn., June 9, 1935; s. William Joseph and Lillie Esther (Feeland) C.; B.A., U. Minn., 1957; M.A., U. Utah, 1966, Ph.D. (NDEA fellow), 1969; m. Janet Lucille Terry, Oct. 9, 1964; children—John Hildon, Laurel Erin. Project specialist in English, U. Wis., Madison, 1967; instr. English, U. Utah, Salt Lake City, 1968-69; prof. English and modern langs. Calif. State Poly. U., Pomona, 1969—; cons. communications. Served with USMCR, 1958-64. NSF grantee, 1966; Calif. State U. and Colls. grantee, 1973-74. Mem. Dialect Soc., Western Photog. Soc., Phi Beta Kappa. Democrat. Roman Catholic. Editor: Language and Human Behavior, 1973, Man Unwept: Visions from the Inner Eye, 1974; author: (with others) The Scope of Grammar: A Study of Modern English, 1980. Home: 1744 N Corona Ave Ontario CA 91764 Office: Calif State Poly U 3801 W Temple Ave Pomona CA 91768

COOK, THOMAS H., moving and storage company executive; b. Hardin, Mont., Sept. 21, 1932; s. Thomas H. and Mabel (Halin) C.; m. Nancy L.

Jones, Sept. 18, 1955; children: Pamela, Rick, Carol. BS, Mont. State Coll., 1956. Planning engr. Boeing Airplane Co., Seattle, 1956-60; bus. rep. Dick Jones Trucking, Powell, Wyo., 1960-70; pres. Cook Moving and Storage, Cody, Wyo., 1970—. Mem. Cody Economic Devel. Coun., 1986—, pres. 1988-89. Mem. Lions. Republican. Methodist. Office: Cook Moving and Storage PO Box 1357 Cody WY 82414

COOK, WILBUR SCHUYLER, airline and business consultant; b. Wadsworth, Ohio, Aug. 1, 1925; s. Wilbur Earl and Miriam Lydia (Durling) C.; m. Ruth Arlene Koppes, Feb. 19, 1949 (div. Sept. 1971); children: Bruce Alan, Debra Sue, Candice Lue, Scott Earl; m. Nell Louise Walker, Aug. 17, 1972. Lic. 1st class radiotelephone operator, Ohio. Head, pub., pres. Hughes Aircraft Co., Culver City, Calif., 1961-63; acting mgr. proposal svcs. Lockheed-Calif. Co., Burbank, 1963; staff engr. Litton Systems, Inc., Woodland Hills, Calif., 1963; co-mgr. corp. info. Rockwell Internat., El Segundo, Calif., 1963-74; mktg. rep. Proprietary Computer Systems, Van Nuys, Calif., 1974-75; regional mgr. APL service div. The Computer Co., Marina Del Rey, Calif., 1975-79; tech. staff Telos Computing, Inc., Santa Monica, Calif., 1981; asst. prof. West L.A. Coll., Culver City, 1974-88; gen. ptnr. TCP, Marina Del Rey, 1979—. Author: (with others) A Sub-Audio Time Delay Circuit, 1951, MIL-C-16279A (SHIPS), 1952. Served to lt. JG, USN, 1943-46. Westinghouse scholar, Pitts., 1943. Mem. So. Calif. Spl. Interest Group. Republican. Mem. Ch. Christ. Home and Office: TCP 4201 Via Marina Way Ste 71 Marina Del Rey CA 90292-5239

COOKE, JACK KENT, diversified company executive; b. Hamilton, Ont., Can., Oct. 25, 1912; s. Ralph Ercil and Nancy (Jacobs) C.; m. Barbara Jean Carnegie, May 5, 1934 (div.); children: Ralph Kent, John Kent; m. Jeanne Maxwell Williams, Oct. 31, 1980 (div.). Student, Malvern Collegiate. Joined No. Broadcasting and Pub. Ltd., Can., 1937; ptnr. Thomson Cooke Newspapers, 1937-52; pres. Sta. CKEY, Toronto, Ont., Can., 1944-61, Liberty of Can. Ltd., 1947-61, Toronto Maple Leaf Baseball Club Ltd., 1951-64, Micro Plastics, Ltd., Acton, Ont., Can., 1955-60, Robinson Indsl. Crafts, Ltd., London, Ont., Can., 1957-63, Precision Die Casting Ltd., Toronto, Ont., 1955-60, Consol. Frybook Industries, Ltd., 1952-61; chmn. bd., pres. Consol. Press Ltd., 1952-61; pres. Aubyn Investments, Ltd., 1961-68, Continental Cablevision Inc., 1965-68; chmn. Jack Kent Cooke Inc., 1976—; chmn. bd. Transamerica Microwave, Inc., 1965-69; chmn. Pro-Football Inc., Washington Redskins, NFL, 1960—; pres. Calif. Sports, Inc. (Los Angeles Lakers, NBA, Los Angeles Kings, NHL), 1965-79, The Forum of Inglewood, Inc., 1966-79; dir., chmn. exec. com. H&B Am. Corp, 1969-70; chmn., chief exec. officer Teleprompter Corp., 1974-81; chmn. Group W Cable Inc. (formerly Teleprompter Corp.), 1981-85, Cooke Properties Inc., N.Y.C., 1966—, Kent Farms, 1979—, Byrnley Farms, 1979-88, Cooke Media Group, Inc. (Daily News), Los Angeles, 1985—, Cooke CableVision Inc., Warner Ctr., Calif., 1986—, Ercil Pub. Inc., 1976—, Kent Plaza, Phoenix, 1983-85, Elmendorf Farm, Inc., Lexington, Ky., 1984—, Video Tape Enterprises, 1976-85, Raljon Pub. Co., Inc., 1988—. Trustee Little League Found. Mem. Nat. Athletic Inst. (bd. dirs.). Office: Washington Redskins Dulles Internat Airport PO Box 17247 Washington DC 20041

COOKE, JAMES ALLEN, printing company executive; b. Columbus, Ohio, July 17, 1948; s. Daniel Edward and Evelyn Juanita (Townsend) C.; m. Gail Ardith Fugate, June 30, 1979; 1 child, Christina Louise. BA in Social Scis., Calif. State U., Chico, 1970, MBA, 1989. Tchr. Lake Ridge High Sch., Lake Oswego, Oreg., 1971-75; owner Lake Grove Printing Co., Lake Oswego, 1975—, On the Spot Printing, Tualatin, Oreg., 1986—. Mem. Pacific Printing Industries (bd. dirs. 1986-89), Nat. Assn. Printers and Lithographers (Silver award 1986), Graphic Arts Tech. Found., Tualatin Lions, Lake Oswego C. of C. Democrat. Office: Lake Grove Printing 17394 SW Boones Ferry Lake Oswego OR 97035

COOKE, JAMES FISHER, architect; b. Taft, Calif., Sept. 28, 1948; s. Richard Joseph and Elma Jean (McGinley) C.; m. Christina B. Buechler, Dec. 20, 1969; 1 child, Michael Andrew. BArch, Calif. State Polytech. Coll., 1971. Registered architect, Calif. Job capt., designer King and King Architects, Syracuse, N.Y., 1971-73; job capt., architect The Perkins & Will Partnership, Washington, 1973-75; project dir., architect John Carl Warnecke & Assocs., Washington, 1975-80; v.p., ops. mgr. CM Constructors and Mgrs., L.A., 1980-82; pres., architect RTA Architecture Planning Interiors, Pasadena, Calif., 1982-84; prin., architect Bobrow/Thomas and Assocs., L.A., 1984-86; nat. facilities devel. mgr. Toyota Motor Sales-USA, Inc., Torrance, Calif., 1986—. Mem. Foothill Blvd. Commn., La Verne, Calif., 1983-85, Bonelli Pk. Liaison Com., La Verne, 1987; chmn. Environ. Quality Commn., La Verne, 1985-86. Mem. AIA (bd. dirs. Pasadena chpt. 1988—), Soc. for Mktg. Profl. Svcs. (bd. dirs. L.A. chpt. 1982-86, v.p. 1985), Calif. Scholastic Fedn. (life), Scarab Archtl. Soc. (hon.). Democrat. Methodist. Home: 1440 Via Camino La Verne CA 91750

COOKE, MARIAN GOPPERT, furniture company executive; b. Powell, Wyo., May 6, 1923; d. Ernest John and Estelle Vee (Butcher) Goppert; widowed; children: Patricia, John. Student, MacMurray Coll., 1941-43, Ea. Mont. Coll., 1968-69; diploma, St. Vincent's Sch. Nursing, Billings, Mont., 1946. RN, Mont. Nurse St. Vincent's Hosp., 1949-51, 54-64, Deaconess Hosp., 1951-52; owner, mgr. Holliday Furniture Co., Inc., 1964—. Mem. Downtown Interest Group, Billings, 1986—; bd. dirs. 200 Mont., 1987—, Spl. Transp. Commn., Billings, 1987—. Mem. Nat. Home Furnishing Assn., Billings Downtown Bus. Assn. (bd. dirs. 1988—), Associated Merchandisers Inc. Buying Group, MacMurray Alumnae Assn., St. Vincent's Alumnae Assn., Soroptimist (Outstanding Mem. award Billings 1982). Republican. Methodist. Home: 3208 Country Club Circle Billings MT 59102 Office: Holliday Furniture Co Inc 3301 1st Ave N Billings MT 59101

COOL, KARLA SUMMER, real estate broker; b. N.Y.C., Apr. 7, 1942; d. Henry and Muriel (Simon) Summer; m. Stephen Neville Cool, June 21, 1964; children: Jeffrey Barnum, Lara, Monte James. BA, UCLA, 1963. Tchr. Timber Sch. Dist., Newbury Park, Calif., 1963-64, Los Angeles Sch. dist., 1964-65; broker, owner Karla Cool Realty, Arroyo Grande, Calif., 1987—. Co-founder Mesa Property Owners, Arroyo, 1974; foreman San Luis Obispo County Jury, 1988—. Mem. Nat. Assn. Realtors, Calif. Assn. Realtors, Pismo Coast Bd. of Realtors. Clubs: Columbia (bd. dirs. 1988) (San Luis Obispo), Altrusa (Arroyo Grande). Office: Karla Cool Realty 1375 Grand Ave Arroyo Grande CA 93420

COOL, LEROY THOMAS, engineering executive; b. Horton, Kans., July 7, 1940; s. George Leroy and Genevieve Rosina (Stone) C.; m. Janice Ellen Koball, July 19, 1969; children: Susan L., Richard B. BA in Psychology, U. S.D., 1964; MS in Engring. Mgmt., U. Mo., Rolla, 1971. Registered profl. engr., Wis. Commd. officer U.S. Army, 1964, advanced through grades to maj., 1973; dir. facilities engring. U.S. Army, Ft. Ritchie, Md., 1976-80; asst. facilities engr. U.S. Army, Ft. Knox, Ky., 1982-84; dir. facilities United of Omaha, 1984; mgr. facilities The Slosburg Corp., Omaha, 1984-85; dir. maintenance, harbor engr. Oxnard (Calif.) Harbor Dist., 1985-87; facilities planning cons. CDI/ABEX Aerospace Corp., Oxnard, 1987—; cons. in field. Mem. Am. Soc. Engring. Mgmt., Soc. Am. Mil. Engrs. (chpt. sec. 1960-61), Masons, Shriners. Home and Office: 1635 N Dara St Camarillo CA 93010

COOLEY, DAVID LEWIS, banker; b. Cleve., Aug. 18, 1959; s. Robert Allen and Margaret Lorraine (Lewis) C. BS, U. Nev., Las Vegas, 1981; postgrad., Princeton U., 1984. Investment offer Fin. Corp. Am., L.A., 1982-84; fin. cons., stock broker Merrill Lynch, Pierce, Fenner & Smith, Beverly Hills, Calif., 1984-87; v.p., br. mgr. Wells Fargo Bank, L.A., 1987—; real estate developer, L.A., 1984—. Mem. Alpha Kappa Psi. Home: 575 Esplanade #301 Redondo Beach CA 90277 Office: Wells Fargo Bank 245 N Larchmont Blvd Los Angeles CA 90004

COOLEY, LELAND FREDERICK, writer, prose, news and commentary; b. Oakland, Calif., June 8, 1909; s. Arthur Montague and Anita Beatrice (Lewis) C.; m. Regina Francoise Verreth; children: Pamela Lee, Allison Smith Cooley; step-children: Michael Dunn, Elizabeth Dunn. With Mcht. Marine, South Pacific and worldwide, 1926-29; assoc. editor Sta. KNX News Dept., Hollywood, Calif., 1932-36; corr. Transradio Press, Europe, 1936; newscaster sports and spl. events Sta. KHJ Mut. Netword, L.A., 1937; tech. dir. Paramount Pictures, Hollywood, Calif., 1937-38; writer and master of ceremonies Andre Kostelanetz Show, Sta. CBS Radio, N.Y.C., 1939-40; dir. daytime radio and experimental TV Ruthrauff & Ryan, Advt., N.Y.C., 1946-50; producer-dir.-writer Perry Como Show, CBS TV Network, N.Y.C., 1950-56; exec. producer Paramount TV, Sta. KTLA, Hollywood, Calif., 1957-58. Author: (novels) The Run For Home, 1958, God's High Table, 1973, The Richest Poor Folks, 1963, (named to One Hundred Best Books List 1963), The Trouble With Heaven, 1966, Condition Pink, 1967, California, 1973 (awarded U. Calif. F.O.L. Hist. Fiction award, The Americana award, 1973, Stein & Day Publ. 1984), The Art Colony, 1975, The Dancer, 1978, Imaginology, 1984. With USCGR, 1942-46. Recipient Christopher award, N.Y.C., 1956. Mem. Radio & TV Dirs. Guild (founding mem.), Dutch Treat Club-West (founding mem.), Acad. of TV Arts and Scis., Writers Guild of Am. West, Authors League and Authors Guild, PEN (past pres.).

COOLEY, RICHARD PIERCE, banker; b. Dallas, Nov. 25, 1923; s. Victor E. and Helen (Pierce) C. B.S., Yale, 1944. With Wells Fargo Bank, San Francisco, 1949-82; exec. v.p. Wells Fargo Bank, 1965-66, pres., chief exec. officer, 1966-79, chmn. bd., chief exec. officer, 1979-82, also dir.; chmn., chief exec. officer, pres. Seattle-1st Nat. Bank (now Seafirst Corp.),, 1983-86, chmn., chief exec. officer, 1986—; chmn. bd., chief exec. officer, dir. Wells Fargo & Co., 1968-83; dir. UAL, Inc., Howmett Turbine Components Corp., Pechiney Ugine Kuhlmann Corp. Trustee Children's Hosp., San Francisco, Rand Corp., Calif. Inst. Tech., Pasadena. Served to 1st lt. Armed Services. Decorated Air medal. Mem. Assn. Res. City Bankers, Smithsonian Instn. Nat. Assn. (bd. dirs.), Calif. C. of C. (bd. dirs.). Office: Seafirst Corp PO Box 3977 Seattle WA 98124 also: Bank of Amer Nat Trust & Savs Bank of America Ctr San Francisco CA 94104 *

COOLIDGE, CARLTON CROMER, financial consultant; b. Cin., Apr. 5, 1943; s. James Henry and Emily (Mashburn) C.; m. Nancy Belden, Aug. 15, 1965 (div. Apr. 1974); children: Courteney Mashburn, Lindsay Vliet, K. Whitney; m. Cynthia Antoniello, Sept. 15, 1976. Student, U. Va., 1961-63; BSBA, Babson Inst., 1966. Registered rep. Smith Barney & Co., Cleve., 1966-72; pres. Daley Coolidge & Co., San Francisco, 1972-76, Coolidge & Co., San Francisco, 1976-79; v.p. Fidelity Brokerage, San Francisco, 1979-84; fin. cons. Shearson Lehman Bros., San Francisco, 1984-86; cons. New Enterprise Assocs., San Francisco, 1986—. Trustee Cleve. Zoo, 1968-72; bd. dirs. San Francisco Opera Assn. Mem. Nat. Assn. Securities Dealers. Republican. Episcopalian. Clubs: Union (Cleve.); St. Francis Yacht (San Francisco). Home: 65 Normandie Terr San Francisco CA 94115 Office: New Enterprise Assocs 235 Montgomery St #1025 San Francisco CA 94104

COOLIDGE, WESTON J., sales executive; b. Bay Shore, N.Y., Nov. 13, 1944; s. Homer W. and Louise M. (Capie) C.; m. Juanita L. (Mancuso), May 20, 1973; children: Connie L., Thomas W. BA, U. San Francisco, 1967; MBA, Golden Gate U., 1972. Asst. adminstrv. mgr. ESCO Corp., Emeryville, Calif., 1969-74; gen. mgr. Ben R. Feathers Co., Oakland, Calif., 1974-76; asst. gen. mgr. Rylock Co., Union City, Calif., 1976-79; chief exec. officer Quality Packaging, Inc., Union City, 1979-83; pres., chmn. of bd. Western Capital Leasing Corp., Fremont, Calif., 1983—; pres. EBBC Investments, Inc., Fremont, 1985—. Pres. Rep. Profl. Club, Hayward/Castro Valley, 1981-82, Chabet Rep. Assembly, 1983-84. With U.S. Army, 1967-69. Mem. Western Assn. Equipment Lessors, Hayward C. of C. (bd. dirs. 1988—, chmn. govt. relations com., 1988-89). 1st Dist. Agrl. Assn. (pres. 1988-89, Alameda County, Calif.), Rotary, Lions (chaplain, Union City chpt. 1978-83), BPOE (exalted ruler 1978-79). Roman Catholic. Home: 24532 2nd St Hayward CA 94541 Office: Western Capital Leasing Co 36640 Fremont Blvd Fremont CA 94536

COOMBE, GEORGE WILLIAM, JR., lawyer, banker; b. Kearny, N.J., Oct. 1, 1925; s. George William and Laura (Montgomery) C.; A.B., Rutgers U., 1946; LL.B., Harvard, 1949; m. Marilyn V. Ross, June 4, 1949; children—Susan, Donald William, Nancy. Bar: N.Y. 1950, Mich. 1953, Calif. 1976, U.S. Supr. Ct. Practice in N.Y.C., 1949-53, Detroit, 1953-69; atty., mem. legal-staff Gen. Motors Corp., Detroit, 1953-69, asst. gen. counsel, sec., 1969-75; exec. v.p., gen. counsel Bank of Am., San Francisco, 1975—. Served to lt. USNR, 1942-46. Mem. Am., Mich., Calif., San Francisco, Los Angeles, N.Y.C. bar assns., Phi Beta Kappa, Phi Gamma Delta. Presbyterian. Home: 2190 Broadway #2E San Francisco CA 94115 Office: BankAm Corp Bank Am Ctr 555 California St San Francisco CA 94104

COOMBS, C'CEAL PHELPS (MRS. BRUCE AVERY COOMBS), air company executive, civic worker; b. nr. Portland, Oreg.; d. Perry Edwin and Flora (Gowey) Phelps; B.S., U. Idaho, 1929; student Wash. State Coll., 1941; m. Bruce Avery Coombs, Nov. 28, 1929; children: Keith Avery, Glinda C'Ceal (Mrs. Nick E. Mason). Tchr. pub schs., Idaho, 1929-30; adminstrv. asst. Coombs West-Air Co. and Coombs Flying C Ranches, Yakima, Wash., 1945—; lobbyist, genealogist for civic activities Wash. Legislature, 1947—; notary pub., Wash., 1960—. Del. White House Conf. on Children and Youth, 1960, Wash. State White House Conf. on Edn., 1955; mem. Wash. Citizens Coun., Nat. Coun. Crime & Delinquency, 1956—; bd. dirs., mem. exec. com. Wash. State Coun. Crime & Delinquency, 1956—, chmn., 1970-71, recipient Spl. State award, 1972, 76; mem. Allied Sch. Council Wash. 1951-53; mem. Western regional scholarship com. Ford Found., 1955-57; chmn. regional dist. Wash. Cities Legislation, 1960; chmn. Yakima County Sch. Bd., 1957-59; mem. Yakima County Health Dept., 1959-60; city councilwoman Yakima, 1959-61, asst. mayor, 1960; mem. Wash. Libr. Commn., 1960, 64-68, 72— , vice chmn., 1965-70, 75-76, recipient gov's. citation, 1976; del. UNESCO Conf. Crime & Delinquency, Kyoto, Japan, 1970, Caracus, Venezuela, 1980; del. to Internat. Library Assn., Toronto, 1968, Washington, 1975, del. to worldwide seminar, Seoul, 1976, London, Brussels, 1977; del. Internat. Fedn. Libraries, Manila, 1980; trustee Wash. 4-H Found., 1960-79, chmn., 1969—, hon. trustee, 1979—; bd. mem. Wash. State Friends of Libraries, 1976, pres., 1977; mem. bd. Yakima County Law and Justice. Recipient Outstanding Citizen award Western Correctional Assn., 1974. Mem. Am. Libr.Trustee Assn. (regional dir. 1962—, pres. 1967-68), C. of C., Oreg., Idaho, Elmore County, Washington County, Calif. hist. socs., Windsor (Conn.) Hist. Assn. (life), Friends of Tewkesbury Abbey Eng. (life), Daus. Am. Colonists, Founders and Patriots, New Eng. Hist. Geneal. Soc., Conn. Hist. Soc., Dorchester (Mass.) Antiquarian and Hist. Soc., Conn. Soc. Genealogists, Ft. Simcoe Restoration Soc. (life), ALA (internat. trustee citation 1966, mem. bd. 1972—, coun. 1967-68, 71-72), Pacific N.W. (chmn. trustee sect. 1962-63), Wash. (chmn. 1960, trustee award 1967) library assns., Nat. Soc. Crown of Charlemagne, LWV, Allied Arts Council, Broadway Theatre League, Nat., Am., aviation assns., P.E.O., Federated Women, Colonial Dames (state rec. sec., pres. local chpt.), Altrusa, Nat. Soc. Magna Charta Dames, Descs. of Conqueror and His Companions, Friends of N.Y.C. Library. Home: 11430 Mieras Rd Yakima WA 98901

COON, DAREN ROSS, data processing executive; b. Gooding, Idaho, July 11, 1953; s. William Joseph and Roberta Elaine (Gifford) C.; m. Kathleen M. Simer, Aug. 22, 1981; children: Heidi M., Heather E. BA, Boise State U., 1975. Asst. sec.-treas. Nampa & Meridian Irrigation Dist., Nampa, Idaho, 1976-89, data processing mgr., 1984--; sec. treas. Nampa & Meridian Irrigation Dist., Nampa, 1989—. Sec., bd. dirs. Treasure Valley Fed. Credit Union, Caldwell, Idaho, 1976-80, Idaho div. Fed. Credit Union, Nampa, 1986-89. Mem. Idaho Pub. Employees Assn. (bd. dirs. 1987-89), Digital Equipment Computer User Soc., Idaho Water Users Assn., N.W. Irrigatiors Ops. Conf. Home: 579 Fairview Ave Nampa ID 83651 Office: Nampa & Meridian Irrigation 1503 1st St S Nampa ID 83651-4395

COONEY, MIKE, state official; b. Washington, Sept. 3, 1954; s. Gage Rodman and Ruth (Brodie) C.; m. Dee Ann Marie Gribble; children: Ryan Patrick, Adan Cecelia. BA in Polit. Sci., U. Mont., 1979. State rep. Mont. Legislature, Helena, 1976-80; exec. asst. U.S. Sen. Max Baucus, Butte, Mont., 1979-82, Washington, 1982-85, Helena, Mont., 1985-89; sec. of state State of Mont., Helena, 1989—. Committeeman Lewis & Clark Dem. Cen. Com., Helena, Mont., 1986-88. Mem. Nat. Secs. of State. Roman Catholic. Home: PO Box 754 Helena MT 59624 Office: Office Sec of State 225 State Capitol Helena MT 59620

COONS, WILLIAM ELLSWORTH, research company executive; b. Springfield, Mass., Oct. 25, 1949; s. William Ellsworth and Beverly (Allen) C.; divorced; children: Amy Marie, Meaghan Christine. BSc., St. Lawrence U., 1971; MSc., We. Mich. U., 1975; PhD, Ariz. State U., 1976. Mem. rsch. faculty U. Chgo., 1976-78; sr. geochemist Rockwell Internat., Richland, Wash., 1978-80; sr. cons., geochemist D'Applonia Cons. Engrs., Albuquerque, 1980-82; dir. bus. devel. IT Corp., Albuquerque, 1982-84, group mgr., 1984-87, ops. mgr., 1987-88; pres., chief exec. officer RE/SPEC Inc., Albuquerque, 1988—, also bd. dirs.; bd. dirs. Grant-Lee, Inc., Springfield, 1986—,. Contbr. articles to profl. jours. Expert witness House Subcom. on Energy and Environment, Washington, 1982; career advisor, St. Lawrence U., 1988-89; U.S. Tech. rep. to OECD/NEA, mem. task force on sealing, 1986—, performance assess and adv. group, 1986-89. Presdl. scholar St. Lawrence U., 1967. Mem. Am. Nuclear Soc., Am. Geochme. Soc. Roman Catholic. Office: RE/SPEC Inc 3815 Eubank NE Albuquerque NM 87111

COOPER, ANNE RITCHIE, school principal; b. Grants Pass, Oreg., July 1, 1944; d. William Riley Jr. and Allie Brown (Clark) R.; m. Charles James Cooper, Sept. 4, 1968 (div. 1985); children: Holly Anne, Wendy Nicole. BA in Edn. with honors, Calif. State U., Sacramento, 1981. Cert. elem. tchr., Calif. Prin., dir. El Rancho Schs., Inc., Carmichael, Calif., 1981—. Mem. Republican Senatorial Inner Circle, Washington, 1989. Mem. Nat. Assn. Edn. for Young Children, Profl. Assn. Childhood Educators, Assn. for Supervision and Curriculum Devel., Sacramento Symphony Assn., AAUW, Crocker Art Museum. Episcopalian. Home: 4640 Sagar Ave Sacramento CA 95821

COOPER, AUSTIN MORRIS, chemist, chemical engineer, consultant, researcher; b. Long Beach, Calif., Feb. 1, 1959; s. Merril Morris and Charlotte Madeline (Wittmer) C. BS in Chemistry, Baylor U., 1981; BSChemE, Tex. Tech U., 1983, MSChemE, 1985. Solar energy researcher U.S. Dept. Energy, Lubbock, Tex., 1983-85; advanced mfg. and chem. process line mgr., mech. cons. and researcher McDonnell-Douglas Astronautics Co., Huntington Beach, Calif., 1986—. Contbr. articles to profl. jours. Mem. Am. Inst. Chem. Engrs., Am. Chem. Soc., Sigma Xi, Omega Chi Epsilon, Kappa Mu Epsilon, Beta Beta Beta.

COOPER, GAIL ANN, realtor; b. Mpls., Oct. 6, 1942; d. Edwin A. and Phyllis J. (Eddy) Grotjahn; m. H.A. Cooper Jr., Oct. 3, 1964; children: Camille Ann, Craig Changler. BA, N. Cen. Coll., 1964; postgrad., San Diego State U., 1966-67. Substitute tchr. Pensacola, Fla., 1964-65; tchr. Corpus Christi, Tex., 1965, S. Bay Unified Sch. Dist., Imperial Beach, Calif., 1967-68, Las Virgenes Sch. Dist., Agoura, Calif., 1973-75; assoc. realtor Century 21, Thousand Oaks, 1979-82, Merrill Lynch Realty, Westlake Village, 1983—. Mem. Los Anillos sustaining chpt. Nat. Charity League, Thousand Oaks, bd. dirs., 1979-88, treas., Conejo Valley; mem. United Meth. Ch.; active children's choirs. Mem. Calif. Assn. Realtors, Nat. Assn. Realtors, Rotary. Republican. Office: Merrill Lynch Realty 3967 B Thousand Oaks Blvd Westlake Village CA 91362

COOPER, GEORGE DANIEL, export logging and investment company executive; b. Cotopaxi, Colo., Dec. 24, 1923; s. Irvin Samuel and Helen Margaret (Callicotte) C.; m. Phyllis Mae McCrea, Mar. 1, 1944; children: Kathryn (dec.), Marilou, George D. Jr., Gregory. Pres. No. Ready-Mix Co., Inc., Fairbanks, Alaska, 1949-64, DicroLite Co., Edmonds, Wash., 1966-70, Scenic Constrn. Co., Camano Island, Wash., 1978-84; gen. ptnr. No. Light Co., Edmonds, 1964-66; gen. mgr. Alaska Brick Co., Anchorage, 1971-73; project mgr. Ahtna R & B, Anchorage, 1973-78; chief exec. officer Huna Totem Corp., Juneau, Alaska, 1984—. Patentee in U.S. and fgn. countries. Del. Alaska Constn. Conv., 1955; chmn. Alaska Rep. Com., 1962-63. 1st lt. USAAF, 1942-47, ETO. Recipient Barusch trophy Internat. Power Boat Assn., 1969, Founder of Alaska Statehood award, State of Alaska, 1984. Mem. Washington Athletic Club, Masons, Shriners. Office: Huna Totem Corp 2075 Jordan Ave Ste 201 Juneau AK 99801

COOPER, JOHN ANTHONY, convention and visitors bureau executive; b. Encino, Calif., Aug. 5, 1959; s. George Edward and Viola Jane (Fendley) C.; m. Marla Diane Gumbish, May 10, 1986. BS, U. Oreg., 1982. Asst. to dir. Am. Assn. Leisure and Recreation, Reston, Va., 1982; dir. pub. rels. Safari Game Search Found., Winston, Oreg., 1983-88; exec. dir. Corvallis (Oreg.) Conv. and Visitors Bur., 1988—; asst. chmn. Douglas County Tourism Commn., Roseburg, Oreg., 1986-88. Author: Wildlife Safari Visitors Guide, 1983. Bd. dirs. Greater Douglas County United Way, 1985-87; pres. Umpqua coun. Camp Fire, 1988. Mem. Oreg. Assn. Conv. and Visitors Burs. (bd. dirs.), Roseburg C. of C. (greeters com. 1984-88), Rotary. Democrat. Roman Catholic. Office: Conv & Visitors Bur 420 NW 2d St Corvallis OR 97330

COOPER, JON HUGH, public television executive; b. Wynnewood, Okla., Aug. 6, 1940; s. John Hughes and Sarah Edna (Ray) C.; m. L. Ilene Batty, Dec. 16, 1961 (div. Jan. 1984); children: Jon Shelton, Geoffrey Harold; m. Patricia Carol Kyle, Jan. 28, 1989; children: Cynthia Lynne, Jennifer Jon Kyle. BA, Okla. State U., 1962. Mgmt. positions with Evening Star Broadcasting, Washington and Lynchburg, Va., 1962-67, Sta. KUAT-AM-TV, Tucson, 1967-73; exec. dir. Rocky Mountain Network, Denver, 1973-77; exec. dir. Pacific Mountain Network, Denver, 1977-79, also bd. dirs.; gen. mgr. Sta. KNME-TV, Albuquerque, 1979—; mem. interconnection com. PBS, Washington, 1983—, bd. dirs., 1986—, exec. com. 1988—; exec. com. Pub. Broadcasting Service, 1988—, chmn. membership com., 1989; panel judge N. Mex. Moot Ct. Competition, 1986, 87; bd. dirs. Native Am. Pub. Broadcasting Consortium, Inc.; bd. dirs., mem. Japan Survey Team Pacific Mountain Network. Bd. dirs., co-chmn. cultural devel. Sisters Cities Albuquerque, 1987—; host N.Mex. Internat. Student Program; bd. dirs., v.p., pres. Pueblo Los Cerros Homeowners Assn., 1987-88; bd. dirs. Samaritan Counseling Ctr. Albuquerque, 1987, Albuquerque Council for Internat. Visitors; bd. advisors U. N.Mex. Cancer Ctr., 1989—.

COOPER, KENNETH DEAN, data processing executive; b. Pitts., Dec. 20, 1943; s. Robert Lee and Lois Mae (Shoup) C.; children: Dawn Lynn, Bucknell Dean. BS in Computer Sci., Sussex U., 1964; PhD in Mgmt. and Computer Sci., Met. Coll., London, 1969. Supr. Mellon Bank, Pitts., 1963-64; program supr. Mobay, Pitts., 1964-67; analyst Martin-Marietta, Orlando, Fla., 1967-69; v.p. Innovative Systems, Pitts., 1969-71; mgr. Garfinckles, Richmond, Va., 1971-75; regional mgr. Cutler-Williams, Dallas, 1975-85; tech. mgr. CSC, Los Angeles, 1985-87; regional mgr. Sterling Software, Los Angeles, 1987—. Author: Mobility and Motivation, 1969, The Evaluation Process, 1974. Served USAF, 1961-68. Mem. Data Processing Mgmt. Assn. (Speaker of Yr. 1978), Assn. Data Processing Service Cos., Assn. Data Processing Cos. (bd. dirs. 1981), Calif. Hypnotist Assn. (v.p. 1986), Nat. Assn. Hypnoanasthesiologist (v.p. 1986). Republican. Baptist. Club: Toastmasters (Tex.) (lt. gov., area gov.). Home: 2616 Voorhees Ave Unit 1 Redondo Beach CA 90278

COOPER, LAURA DENISE, lawyer; b. Corvallis, Oreg., Mar. 14, 1956; d. Lowell Everett and Grace Beatrice (Scribner) C. BS, U. Oreg., 1978; JD, U. Washington, 1986. Bar: Oreg. 1986, Calif. 1987. Staff atty. U.S. Ct. Appeals (5th cir.)ú La., 1986-87; assoc. Pettit & Martin, San Francisco, 1987—. Calif. state chmn. Dole for Presidential Disability Coalition, 1987-88; nat. co-chmn. Bush for Pres., 1988. Mem. ABA (regional moot ct. champion, 1982), Oreg. State Bar Assn., State Bar of Calif., San Francisco Bar Assn. Republican. Office: Pettit & Martin 101 California St 35th Flr San Francisco CA 94111

COOPER, LAWRENCE ANDREW, military officer; b. Culver City, Calif., Apr. 5, 1964; s. Malcolm and Carol Joan (Mistachkin) C. BS in Physics with hons., USAF Acad., 1986; MBA, Webster U., 1989. Commd. 2nd lt. USAF, 1986, advanced through grades to 1st lt, 1986-88; student pilot USAF, Reese AFB, Tex., 1986; space systems physicist USAF Weapons Lab., Kirtland AFB, N.Mex., 1986—. Author: Fledging, 1986; editor: Icarus Mag., 1985. Asst. coach Duke City Soccer League, Albuquerque, 1988-89. Mem. Armed Forces Communication and Electronics Assn., Air Force Assn., Assn. Grads. USAF Acad., Albuquerque Off-Road Runners Assn. Republican. Jewish. Home: 5741 Osuna NE #614 Albuquerque NM 87109 Office: Air Force Weapons Lab AFWL/NTCAS Kirtland AFB NM 87117

COOPER, LYNN DALE, minister, retired navy chaplain; b. Aberdeen, Wash., Aug. 11, 1932; s. Lindsey Monroe and Mattie Ann (Cattron) C.; m. Doris Marlene Aydelott, June 2, 1956; children: Kevin Dale, Kathy Lois, Karen Doris Cooper Henthorn. Student, Gray's Harbor Coll., 1950-51; BTh, Northwest Christian Coll., 1955; MDiv, Phillips U., 1961, DD, 1977. ordained minister, 1955. Commd ensign USN, 1965, advance through grades to comdr., 1988, ret., 1988; assoc. minister First Christian Ch., Olympia, Wash., 1955-57; minister First Christian Ch., Aline, Okla., 1957-61, Sumner, Wash., 1961-66; chaplain U.S. Navy, 1966-88; minister Cen. Christian Ch., Prosser, Wash., 1988—; bd. dirs. Jubilee Ministries, Prosser, Wash., 1988—. Recipient many Navy and Marine Corps awards and medals; decorated Bronze Star medal. Mem. Mil. Chaplains Assn. U.S.A. (life mem.), Disciples of Christ Hist. Soc. (life mem.), Kiwanis Club (sec., treas. Prosser, Wash.) De Molay Lodge (past master, councilor 1950—). Home: 1818 Benson Ave Prosser WA 99350 Office: Cen Christian Ch 1000 Sixth St Prosser WA 99350

COOPER, MARSHA LYNN, principal; b. L.A., Jan. 23, 1943; d. Joseph and Beatrice (Caplan) B.; m. Cary David Cooper, June 28, 1964; children: Glenn Howard, Erin Denise. BA, UCLA, 1964; MA, Immaculate Heart, 1979. Elem. sch. tchr. Culver City Schs., Calif., 1963-70; instr. adult edn. UCLA Extension, 1970-74; remediation tchr., owner Studio for Acad. Improvement, Studio City, CA, 1970-78; elem. tchr. gifted children Gifted Children's Assn., L.A., 1974-77; asst. prin. Stephen S. Wise Elem. Sch., L.A., 1979—; cons. Bur. Jewish Edn., L.A., 1979—, League Pvt. Schs., L.A., 1979—. Active Adv. Coun. L.A. Pub. Schs., Sherman Oaks, 1974-79. Mem. Assn. Supervision and Curriculum Devel., Internat. Reading Assn., Women in Ednl. Leadership, Calif. Elem. Edn. Assn. Home: 3906 Mary Ellen Studio City CA 91604 Office: Stephen S Wise Schs 15500 Stephen S Wise Dr Los Angeles CA 90077

COOPER, STEPHEN ROBERT, exploration geologist, geohydrologist; b. New Haven, Apr. 9, 1957; s. Robert William Cooper and Mary Ann (Wheaton) Cooper Webb; m. Leslie Dawn Williams, Aug. 28, 1983; 1 child, Kristi Nicole. AS Arapahoe Community Coll., 1979; student Calif. State U., Arcada, 1980; BS in Geology, Wichita State U. 1982; postgrad. Colo. Sch. Mines. Ski technician, asst. mgr. Maison De Ski, Idaho Springs, Colo., 1973-79; acrobatic skier, instr. Mid West Ski Shows, Wichita, Kansas, 1980-81; with Kennedy and Mitchell, Inc., Denver, 1979—, exploration geologist, 1982-87; geohydrologist, Jacobs Engring. Group, Inc., 1987—; snow ski instr., Colo., 1979—; scuba diving instr., 1982-83; vol. World Vision, Pasadena, Calif., 1983—; counselor Arapahoe Vols. Inc. div. United Way, Littleton, Colo., 1984; vol. instr. cardiopulmonary resuscitation and 1st aid emergency med. technician. With aviation, USAR, 1987—. Grantee Kennedy Found, 1979. Mem. Am. Assn. Petroleum Geologists, Soc. Econ. Paleontologists, Profl. Assn. Diving Instrs., Am. Army Aviation Assn., Nat. Water Well Assn., Delta Upsilon. Mem. Ch. of God.

COOPER, STEVEN JON, health care management consultant, educator; b. Oct. 19, 1941; B.A., U. Calif., Los Angeles, 1966; M.Ed., Loyola U., 1973; postgrad. Union Sch., 1977—; m. Sharon M. Lepack; children—Robin E., Erik S. Ednl. coordinator dept. radiology Mt. Sinai Hosp. Med. Center, Chgo., 1969-72; chmn. dept. radiol. scis. U. Health Scis., Chgo. Med. Sch., VA Hosp., North Chicago, 1972-79; v.p. C&S Inc., Denver, 1980-81; pres. Healthcare Mktg. Corp., Denver, 1981-84; corp. officer Sharon Cooper Assocs. Ltd., Englewood, Colo., 1984—; cons. HEW; lectr. in field. Served with USAF, 1960-64, USAFR, 1964-66. Mem. W.K. Kellogg Found. grantee. Mem. Am. (mem. edn., curriculum review coms., task force), Ill. (chmn. annual meeting 1976, program Midwest conf., 1977) socs. radiol. tech., Coll. Radiol. Scis., Am. Hosp. Radiology Adminstrs. (mem. edn. com., treas. Midwest region, nat. v.p.), AMA (com. on allied health edn. and accreditation), Sigma Xi. Author numerous publs. in field. Home: 8522 E Dry Creek Pl Englewood CO 80112 Office: 9085 E Mineral Circle Ste 160 Englewood CO 80112

COOPER, SUSAN CAROL, environmental, safety and health professional; b. Milw., Dec. 25, 1939; d. Carroll Arthur and Edith Estelle (Hicks) Brooks; m. William Randall Cooper, June 20, 1964; children: Darin Benbrook, Carol Kimberly, Ryan Randall. BS in Biology, U. Wis., Milw., 1962; MS in Physiology, Wash. State U., 1966; PhD in Physiology, U. Idaho, 1972. Sr. lab. technician Dept. Vet. Pathology, Wash. State U., Pullman, 1965-68; postdoctoral assoc. dept. chemistry U. Idaho, Moscow, 1972-74, vis. prof. chemistry, 1974; instr. facilitator for gifted/talented Highland Sch. Dist., Craigmont, Idaho, 1975-76; program dir. YWCA, Lewiston, Idaho, 1977-78; support asst. Exxon Nuclear Idaho Corp., Idaho Falls, 1983; engr. Exxon Nuclear Idaho Corp. and Westinghouse Idaho Nuclear Co. Inc., Idaho Falls, 1983-84; environ. engr. Westinghouse Idaho Nuclear Co. Inc., Idaho Falls, 1984-86, mgr. environ., safety and health, 1986—. Contbr. articles to profl. jours. Mem. presenting team Marriage Encounter, 1980—; preacher, lay reader, lay Eucharistic minister Episc. Ch., Idaho, 1984—; singer Idaho Falls Opera Theater, 1983-85, St. John's, Idaho Falls, 1983—, St. Mark's, Idaho Falls, 1985—; mem., historian Mayors Com. for Employment Handicapped and Older Worker, Idaho Falls, 1983-86; campaigner United Way, Idaho Falls, 1985-86, group leader, 1986-87; del. Dem. Conv., Boise, Idaho, 1976; group leader United Way Campaign, 1986-87, campaigner, 1985-86. NSF fellow, 1963, NDEA fellow, 1963-65; Nat. Assn. Geology Tchrs. scholar, 1980. Mem. Assn. Engring. Geologist, Am. Nuclear Soc. (mem. environ. affairs subcom. Idaho chpt. 1986—), NAFE, Idaho Assn. Profl. Engrs., Idaho Acad. of Sci., Am. Nuclear Soc., Am. Soc. for Quality Control, Platinum/Uranium Conf. Clubs: Snow Dragon Judo (Idaho Falls), Toastmasters (pres. and founder local chpt.). Home: 582 Cambridge Dr Idaho Falls ID 83401 Office: Westinghouse Idaho Nuclear Co Inc Box 4000 WCB E2 MS-3412 Idaho Falls ID 83403-3412

COOPER, WILLIAM CLARK, physician; b. Manila, P.I., June 22, 1912 (father Am. citizen); s. Wibb Earl and Pearl (Herron) C.; MD, U. Va., 1934; MPH magna cum laude, Harvard U., 1958; m. Ethel Katherine Sicha, May 1, 1937; children: Jane Willoughby, William Clark, David Jeremy, Robert Lawrence. Intern, asst. resident U. Hosps., Cleve., 1934-37; commd. asst. surgeon USPHS, 1940, advanced through grades to med. dir., 1952; chief occupational health Field Hqrs., Cin., 1952-57; mem. staff div. occupational health USPHS, Washington, 1957-62, chief div. occupational health, 1962-63; ret., 1963; rsch. physician, prof. occupational health in residence Sch. Pub. Health, U. Calif.-Berkeley, 1963-72; med. cons. AEC, 1964-73; sec.-treas. Tabershaw-Cooper Asso., Inc., 1972-73, v.p., sci. dir., 1973-74; v.p. Equitable Environ. Health Inc., 1974-77; cons. occupational medicine, 1977—. Served to 1st lt. M.C., U.S. Army, 1937-40. Diplomate Am. Bd. Internal Medicine, Am. Bd. Preventive Medicine, Am. Bd. Indsl. Hygiene. Fellow AAAS, Am. Pub. Health Assn., Am. Coll. Chest Physicians, Am. Coll. Occupational Medicine, Royal Soc. Medicine (London); mem. Internat. Commn. on Occupational Health, Western Occupational Med. Assn., Am. Indsl. Hygiene Assn., Cosmos Club. Contbr. articles to profl. jours. Home: 8315 Terrace Dr El Cerrito CA 94530 Office: 3687 Mt Diablo Blvd Ste 320 Lafayette CA 94549

COORS, JEFFREY H., brewery company executive; b. Denver, Feb. 10, 1945; s. Joseph Coors. B.Chem. Engring., Cornell U., 1967, M.Chem. Engring., 1968. With Coors Porcelain Co., 1968-70; with Adolph Coors Co., Golden, Colo., 1970—; pres. Adolph Coors Co., 1985—. Office: Adolph Coors Co Golden CO 80401 *

COORS, PETER HANSON, beverage company executive; b. Denver, Sept. 20, 1946; s. Joseph and Holly (Hanson) C.; m. Marilyn Gross, Aug. 23, 1969; children: Melissa, Christien, Carrie Ann, Ashley, Peter, David. B.S. in Idsl. Engring., Cornell U., 1969; M.B.A., U. Denver, 1970. Prodn. trainee, specialist Adolph Coors Co., Golden, Colo., 1970-71, dir. fin. planning, 1971-75, dir. market research, 1975-76, v.p. self distbn., 1976-77, v.p. sales and mktg., 1977-78, sr. v.p. sales and mktg., 1978-82, div. pres. sales, mktg. and adminstrn., 1982-85, now pres. brewing div.; pres. Coors Distbn. Co., 1976-82, 1976-81, chmn., from 1981, dir.; dir. Adolph Coors Co., 1973—, asst. sec.-treas., 1974-76; dir. CADCO, 1975-85. Bd. dirs. Nat. Wildlife Fedn., 1978-81, Wildlife Legis. Fund, 1987—; hon. bd. dirs. Colo. Spl. Olympics Inc., 1978—; trustee Colo. Outward Bound Sch., 1978—, Adolph Coors Found., Pres.'s Leadership Com., U. Colo., 1978—; chmn. Nat. Commn. on the Future of Regis Coll., 1981-82, chmn. devel. com., 1983—, now trustee. Mem. Nat. Indls. Adv. Council, Opportunities Ctrs. of Am., Young Pres.' Orgn., Ducks Unlimited (nat. trustee 1979, sr. v.p., mem. mgmt. com., exec. com. 1982—, dir. Can. 1982—, pres. 1984-85, chmn. bd. 1986—). Club: Met. Denver Exec. (dir 1979, pres. 1981—). Office: Adolph Coors Co Golden CO 80401 *

COORS, WILLIAM K., brewery executive; b. Golden, Colo., 1916. Chmn. bd. Adolph Coors Co., Golden, Colo. Office: Adolph Coors Co Golden CO 80401 *

COPE, ROBERT GARY, management educator, consultant; b. Chgo., June 13, 1936; s. Henry Jasper and Alicia (Vecellio) C.; m. Claudette Holm, June 16, 1961 (div. Mar. 1985); children: Kathryn, Robin, Peter, Michael, Linda; m. Nancy Louise Junak, Aug. 1, 1987. BBA, U. Mich., 1959, AM, 1961, PhD, 1967. Dir. instl. research and planning U. Mass., Amherst, 1966-69; prof. U. Wash., Seattle, 1969—; lectr. Snowmass (Colo.) Inst., 1981—; cons. in field, 1972—. Author: Strategic Policy Planning (1978), Strategic Planning Management and Decision-Making (1981), Enterprise and Environment (1989), Opportunity from Strength (1987). Vis. fellow U. Melbourne (Australia), 1977, Australian Nat. U., Canberra, 1976, Nat. Ctr. for Mgmt. Systems, Boulder, Colo., 1981. Mem. Acad. Mgmt., Am. Assn. for Higher Edn., Assn. for Instl. Research. Home: 615 37th Ave Seattle WA 98122

COPELAND, EUGENE LEROY, lawyer; b. Fairfield, Iowa, Mar. 5, 1939; BA, Parsons Coll., 1961; JD with distinction, U. Iowa, 1965. Admitted to Colo. bar, 1965, Iowa bar, 1965, U.S. Supreme Ct. bar, 1966; individual practice law, Denver, 1965-66; sr. v.p., gen. counsel, sec. Security Life of Denver, 1966—; gen. counsel Nationale Nederlanden U.S. Corp., 1986—; lectr., speaker at legal and industry convs., seminars, meetings; participant contemporary issue program Today show NBC, 1980. Bd. dirs. Colo. Pub. Expenditures Council, 1988-89. Bd. dirs. Buffalo Mountain Met. Dist., Summit County, Colo.; bd. dirs. Friends Found. of Denver Pub. Library; v.p. Denver Pub. Library Commn.; bd. dirs. Colo. Pub. Expedition Council. Served with U.S. Army. Fulbright scholar (alt.). Mem. ABA, Colo. Bar Assn., Denver Bar Assn., Iowa Bar Assn., Assn. Life Ins. Council, Am. Council Life Ins. (state v.p. 1973-83, legis. com., reins. com., policyholder tax com., litigation com.), Colo. Life Conv. (pres. 1988-89, v.p. 1987-88, legis. chmn. 1973-86), Colo. Assn. Corp. Counsel, Denver Estate Planning Council, Colo. Assn. Life Underwriters (co-author learning guide 1978), Law Club Denver, Phi Kappa Phi. Unitarian. Author: Preventive Law for Medical Directors and Underwriters, 1973; Underwriting in a New Age of Legal Accountability, 1978; Insurance Law, 1982; bd. editors Iowa Law Rev., 1965. Office: Security Life Ctr 1290 Broadway Denver CO 80203

COPELAND, PHILLIPS JEROME, former university administrator, former air force officer; b. Oxnard, Calif., Mar. 22, 1921; s. John Charles and Marion Moffatt) C.; student U. So. Calif., 1947-49; BA, U. Denver, 1956, MA, 1958; grad. Air Command and Staff Coll., 1959, Indsl. Coll. Armed Forces, 1964; m. Alice Janette Lusby, Apr. 26, 1942; children: Janette Ann Copeland Bosserman, Nancy Jo Copeland Briner. Commd. 2d lt. USAAF, 1943, advanced through grades to col. USAF, 1964, pilot 8th Air Force, Eng., 1944-45; various flying and staff assignments, 1945-51; chief joint tng. sect. Hdqrs. Airsouth (NATO), Italy, 1952-54; asst. dir. plans and programs USAF Acad., 1955-58; assigned to joint intelligence, Washington, 1959-61; plans officer Cincpac Joint Staff, Hawaii, 1961-63; staff officer, ops. directorate, then team chief Nat. Mil. Command Center, Joint Chiefs Staff, Washington, 1964-67; dir. plans and programs USAF Adv. Group, also adviser to Vietnamese Air Force, Vietnam, 1967-68; prof. aerospace studies U. So. Calif., L.A., 1968-72, exec. asst. to pres., 1972-73, assoc. dir. office internat. programs, 1973-75, dir. adminstrv. services Coll. Continuing Edn., 1975-82, dir. employee relations, 1982-84. Decorated D.F.C., Bronze Star, Air medal with 3 clusters; Medal of Honor (Vietnam). Mem. Air Force Assn., Order of Daedalians. Home: 81 Cypress Way Rolling Hills Estates CA 90274

COPLEY, HELEN KINNEY, newspaper publisher; b. Cedar Rapids, Iowa, Nov. 28, 1922; d. Fred Everett and Margaret (Casey) Kinney; m. James S. Copley, Aug. 16, 1965 (dec.); 1 child, David Casey. Attended, Hunter Coll., N.Y.C., 1945. Assoc. The Copley Press, Inc., 1952—, chmn. exec. com., chmn. corp., dir., 1973—, chief exec. officer, sr. mgmt. bd., 1974—; chmn. bd. Copley News Service, San Diego, 1973—; chmn. editorial bd. Union-Tribune Pub. Co., 1976—; pub. The San Diego Union and The Tribune, 1973—. Chmn. bd., trustee James S. Copley Found., 1973—; life mem. Friends of Internat. Center, La Jolla, San Diego Hall of Sci., Scripps Meml. Hosp. Aux., Star of India Aux., Zool. Soc. San Diego; mem. La Jolla Mus. Contemporary Art, La Jolla Town Council, Inc., San Diego Soc. Natural History, YWCA; life patroness Makua Aux.; mem. YWCA; hon. chmn., bd. dirs. Washington Crossing Found.; trustee, mem. audit and compensation com. Howard Hughes Med. Inst.; co-chmn. San Diego Coun. Literacy. Mem. Inter Am. Press Assn., Am. Newspapers Pubs. Assn., Calif. Press Assn., Am. Soc. Newspaper Editors, Am. Press Inst., Calif. Newspaper Pubs. Assn., Greater Los Angeles, Nat., San Diego, San Francisco press clubs, Sigma Delta Chi. Republican. Roman Catholic. Clubs: Aurora (Ill.) Country; Army and Navy (D.C.); San Diego Yacht, Univ., La Jolla Beach and Tennis, La Jolla Country, Kona Kai (San Diego). Office: Copley Press Inc 350 Camino de la Reina San Diego CA 92108

COPLEY, W(ILLIAM) DOUGLAS, manufacturing company executive; b. Indpls., July 6, 1961; s. William Chambers and Madeline June (DeRoberts) C.; m. Missy G. Gantt, Nov. 12, 1983; 1 child, Christopher Douglas. BS in Mktg., Ind. U., 1983; postgrad., U. Denver, 1988—. With Black & Decker Corp., various locations, 1983—; account exec. Black & Decker Corp., Balt., 1984-85; nat. sales adminstr. Black & Decker Corp., 1985-86; retail unit mgr. Black & Decker Corp., L.A., 1987-88; dist. sales mgr. Black & Decker Corp., Denver, 1988—; cons. Careers Unltd., L.A., 1986-87, Denver, 1988—. Vol. campaign Bush for Pres., Denver, 1988; mem. steering com. Fight Found., 1983. Roman Catholic. Office: Black & Decker 6551 S Revere Pkwy Ste 115 Englewood CO 80111

COPMAN, LOUIS, naval officer, radiologist; b. Phila., Jan. 17, 1934; s. Jacob and Eve (Snyder) C.; m. Avera Schuster, June 8, 1958; children: Mark, Linda. BA, U. Pa., 1955, MD, 1959. Diplomate Am. Bd. Radiology; Nat. Bd. Med. Examiners. Commd. ensign Med. Corps USN, 1958; advanced through grades to capt. Naval Hosp., 1975; asst. chief radiology dept. Naval Hosp., Pensacola, Fla., 1966-69; chief radiology dept. Doctors Hosp., Phila., 1969-73; radiologist Mercer Hosp. Ctr., Trenton, N.J., 1973-75; chmn. radiology dept. Naval Hosp., Phila., 1975-84; chief. radiology dept. Naval Med. Clinic, Pearl Harbor, Hawaii, 1984-89; ret. USN, 1989; pvt. practice Honolulu, 1989—; cons. Radiology Services, Wilmington, Del., 1978-84, Yardley (Pa.) Radiology, 1979-84. Author: The Cuckold, 1974. Recipient Albert Einstein award in Medicine, U. Pa., 1959. Mem. AMA, Assn. Mil. Surgeons of the U.S., Royal Soc. Medicine, Radiol. Soc. N.Am., Am. Coll. Radiology, Photographic Soc. Am., Sherlock Holmes Soc., Phi Beta Kappa, Alpha Omega Alpha. Jewish. Home: 1774 Akaakaawa St Kailua HI 96734 Office: 1010 S King St Rm 8 Honolulu HI 96814

COPPEDGE, ROBERT ONEAL, college administrator; b. Rotan, Tex., Jan. 13, 1942; d. Oneal O. and Onez (Whitlock) C.; m. Marie Oates, Dec. 29, 1961; children: Johnny, Gary, Lia. BBA, N.Mex. State U., 1965, MS in Econs., 1967; PhD in Econs., Oreg. State U., 1974. Economist U.S. Dept. Agriculture, Salt Lake City, 1967-68; extension economist Oreg. State U., Corvallis, 1968-74; asst. prof. U. Fla., Gainesville, 1974-76; bus. and econ. devel. specialist Coop. Extension Svc., N.Mex. State U., Las Cruces, 1976-88, leader econ. devel. project, 1988—; bd. dirs. Enchanted Land Cert. Devel. Co., Albuquerque; mem. Gov.'s Strategic Planning Comm., Santa Fe, 1987-88. Contbr. articles to profl. jours. Mem. Lt. Gov.'s Main St. adv. com., Santa Fe, 1985-88; bd. dirs. Las Cruces Econ. Devel. Council, 1984. Economic devel. grantee Mountain Bell, 1987-88, Western Rural Devel. Ctr., 1984—, community devel., 1986-88; retail trade study grantee State N.Mex., 1987. Mem. N.Mex. Assn. Commerce and Industry (bd. dirs. 1986—), Community Devel. Soc. (nominations com. 1987-88), N.Mex. Indsl. Devel. Execs. Assn. (bd. dirs. 1976—), N.Mex. Extension Specialists Assn., Las Cruces C. of C. (chmn. coms. 1986-88). Office: NMex State U Box 3AE Las Cruces NM 88003

COPPESS, LEE PIERCE, dentist; b. Middletown, Ohio, Dec. 1, 1940; s. Walter Hugh and Elizabeth Jane (Pierce) C.; m. Karen Stevens, June 13, 1964 (div. Dec. 1973); children: Ann Elizabeth, Linda Jane, Mark Stevens; m. Donna Marjorie Robinson, Jan. 1, 1974; children: Bret Robinson, Bruce Lee. DDS, Ohio State U., 1965. Pvt. practice family preventive dentistry Coeur d'Alene, Idaho, 1967-. Bd. dirs. Hayden Lake (Idaho) Recreational Water and Sewer Dist., 1976-80. Served to capt. Dental Corps. USAF, 1965-67. Recipient cert. of appreciation Coeur d'Alene Dept. Recreation, 1986, 1987, 1988. Mem. ADA, Idaho Dental Assn., North Idaho Dental Soc., Coeur d'Alene Dental Soc. (pres. 1972-73), Spokane Dist Dental Soc., North Idaho Fly Casters (pres. 1980, treas. 1981--, trustee 1980--, Fisherman of Yr. award 1981, Golden Nymph Award 1987), Steering com. Idaho Wildlife Congress 1988--. Home: Rte 2 Box 224 Hayden Lake ID 83835 Office: 2201 Government Way Coeur d'Alene ID 83814

COPPIN, AL, real estate corporation executive; b. Hayward, Calif., Oct. 10, 1943; s. Ray and June (Langerman) C.; m. Sharron Lee Graves, Jan. 22, 1966 (div. Mar. 1982); children: Shawn, Daniel, Michael. BS in Ops. Mgmt., U. Calif., Berkeley, 1969, MBA, 1970. Construction mgmt. Johnson Controls, San Francisco, 1963-69; comml. agt. Grubb & Ellis, various, Calif., 1971-76; founder Keegan & Coppin Co., Inc., Santa Rosa, San Rafael, Calif., 1976—; instr. Golden Gate U., San Francisco, 1971. Served in USAR, 1962-68, San Francisco. Recipient Doyle Scholarship, Exchange Bank, Santa Rosa, Calif., 1961. Mem. Calif. Alumni Assn., Calif. Bus. Alumni Assn., Local Calif. Nat. Assn. Realtors, Bus. Ind. Assn., Phi Beta Kappa. Republican. Presbyterian. Home: 3024 Santa Margarita Santa Rosa CA 95405 Office: Keegan & Coppin Co Inc 1355 N Dutton Ave Santa Rosa CA 95401

COPPIN, DAVID FRANK, obstetrician, gynecologist; b. Provo, Utah, Jan. 22, 1943; s. Thomas Frank and Elisabeth (Schinkel) C.; m. Kathy Butler, July 8, 1966; children: Frank, Julie, John, Michael. BS, Utah State U., 1966; MD, U. Utah, 1970. Diplomate Am. Bd. Ob-Gyn. Intern, resident Madigan Army Med. Ctr., Tacoma, Wash., 1970-74; chief ob-gyn. U.S. Army Hosp., Ft. Huachuca, Ariz., 1974-79; ob-gyn. physician Budge Clinic, Logan, Utah, 1979—; bd. dirs. Budge Clinic, Logan; pres. med. staff Logan Regional Hosp., 1989, governing bd. trustees, 1988-89. Lt. col. U.S. Army, 1966-79. Named Outstanding Ob-Gyn. resident Madigan Army Med. Ctr., Tacoma, 1974. Fellow Am. Coll. Ob-Gyn.; mem. AMA, Utah Med. Assn., Utah Ob-Gyn. Soc. Republican. Mormon. Home: 1665 E 1185 N Logan UT 84321 Office: Budge Clinic 225 E 400 N Logan UT 84321

COPPOCK, RICHARD MILES, nonprofit foundation administrator; b. Salem, Ohio, Mar. 17, 1938; s. Guy Lamar and Helen Angeline (Johnston) C.; m. Rita Mae McArtor, June 20, 1961 (div. 1973); 1 child, Carole; m. Trelma Anne Kubacak, Nov. 21, 1973; children: James, Lori. BA, USAF Acad., 1961; MSME, U. Colo., 1969. Commd. 2d lt. USAF, 1961, advanced through grades to lt. col., 1983, ret., 1983; exec. v.p., treas. Assn. Grads. USAF Acad., Inc., Colo., 1983—; bd. dirs. Air Acad. Nat. Bank, Colo. Decorated D.F.C., Air medal; named Outstanding Alumnus Salem High Sch., 1980. Mem. Colo. Springs. C. of C. (Mil. Affairs Council 1985—), VFW (life), Am. Legion, Air Force Assn., Ret. Officers Assn. Republican. Methodist. Lodges: Elks. Home: 2513 Mirror Lake Ct Colorado Springs CO 80919 Office: USAF Acad Assn Grads Rm 3A44 Sijan Hall Colorado Springs CO 80840

COPPOLA, ALAN CARL, company executive; b. San Francisco, Sept. 25, 1947; s. Carlo Dominic and Eileen Josephine (Nannini) C.; m. Susan Jean Irvin,. Associates, Coll. San Mateo, 1970; Baccalaureate, Notre Dame, 1972; cert., Antioch, Los Medanos, 1981. Artist Merlyns Glass, Concord, Calif., 1976-81, owner, 1981-83; agt. Lustig Travel, Burlingame, Calif., 1983-84, gen. mgr., 1984-86; v.p. Impulse Travel, Inc., Burlingame, Calif., 1986-87, pres., chief exec. officer, 1987--; Pres. ACI Consulting, Burlingame, 1987--, Travel Agent Credientals. Author: Fit and Trim, 1987; In Defense of Dragons, 1988. mem. Cousteau Soc., Wash., 1987-89, Nat. Wildlife Fedn., Wash., 1988-89,. Recipient: Certi. of Merit, Spl. Olympics, 1982-86; Certi., Air Travel. mem. Certi. Travel Cons., Pacific Assn. Travel Agts., Internat. Assn. Democratic. Roman Catholic. Office: Impulse Travel Inc 205 Park Rd Ste 200 Burlingame CA 94010

COPPOLA, FRANCIS FORD, director, producer, film writer; b. Detroit, Apr. 7, 1939; s. Carmine C.; m. Eleanor Neil; children: Gian-Carlo (dec.), Roman, Sofia. B.A., Hofstra U., 1958; Master of Cinema, UCLA, 1968. Artistic dir., Zoetrope Studios.; dir. motion pictures including Tonight for Sure, 1961, Dementia 13, 1964, You're a Big Boy Now, 1967, Finian's Rainbow, 1968, The Rain People, 1969, One from the Heart, 1981; writer: motion pictures This Property Is Condemned, 1966, Reflections In a Golden Eye, 1967, The Rain People, 1969, Is Paris Burning, 1966, Patton, 1970, The Great Gatsby, 1974, Peggy Sue Got Married, 1986, Tucker, 1988; writer, producer and dir. motion pictures The Godfather (Acad. awards for Best Screenplay and Best Picture, nominee for Best Dir., Film Dir.'s award Dirs. Guild Am. 1972), The Godfather, Part II, 1974 (Acad. awards for Best Screenplay, Best Dir. and Best Picture), The Conversation, 1974 (Golden Palm award Cannes Film Festival 1974), Apocalypse Now, 1979; producer TV movie The People; co-writer, producer, dir. motion picture The Outsiders, 1983, Rumble Fish, 1983; producer: motion pictures THX 1138, 1971; exec. producer motion picture Black Stallion, 1979; producer motion picture The Black Stallion Returns, 1983; co-writer, producer, dir. motion picture The Escape Artist, 1982; exec. producer motion picture Hammett; dir., co-screenwriter The Cotton Club, 1984; co-exec. producer Mishima, 1985; dir. Gardens of Stone, 1987, Tucker: The Man and His Dream, 1988; dir. play Private Lives, opera The Visit. Mem. Dirs. Guild Am. Inc. Office: Zoetrope Studios 916 Kearny St San Francisco CA 94133

COPSEY, REED DENNIS, aerospace development and research executive; b. Encino, Calif., Mar. 7, 1956; s. Wallace Gene and Ann Reed (Zimmerman) C.; m. Cherie E Bright, June 4, 1983; children: Reed Dennis Jr., Stephanie Anne, Beau Jeffrey Reed. Student, MIT, 1973-74; BS in Engring., Applied Sci., Calif. Inst. Tech., 1977. Engring asst. Jet Propulsion Lab., Pasadena, Calif., 1976; assoc. mem. tech. staff Aerojet Electro Systems Co., Azusa, Calif., 1977-78, mem. tech. staff, 1978-80, project engr., 1980-83, supr. advanced weapon systems, 1983-85; prin. investigator Sparta, Inc., Anaheim, Calif., 1987-88, gen. mgr., 1988—. Inventor warheads. Republican. Lutheran. Home: 185 S Eucalyptus Dr Anaheim Hills CA 92808 Office: Sparta Inc 5401 La Palma Ave Anaheim CA 92807

CORAY, JEFFREY WARREN, principal, instructor; b. Chgo., July 16, 1958; s. Warren George and Rose (Paul) C. Student, U. Calif., Berkeley, 1976-77; BA, Occidental Coll., 1980. Instr. Damien High Sch., La Verne, Calif., 1982—, dir. student activities, 1983-87, chair social sci. dept., 1986-88, asst. prin. student activities, 1987-88, asst. prin. acad. affairs, instr. social sci., 1988—; cons. advanced placement program N.J. Coll. Bd., 1987—, exam reader, 1988—. Mem. Omicron Delta Epsilon. Republican. Roman Catholic. Home: PO Box 116 La Verne CA 91750 Office: Damien High Sch 1124 Bonita Ave La Verne CA 91750

CORBETT, LOUISE ANN, interior and product designer; b. Detroit, July 13, 1944; d. Thaddeus Frank and Tadzia (Eminowicz) Markiewicz; m. Robert William Corbett, July 5, 1975. B Indsl. Design, Pratt Inst., 1968. Furniture designer Schnadig Corp., Chgo., 1968-69; freelance product designer Chgo., 1969-70; interior design dir. Stella Products, Detroit, 1970-75; staff interior designer Ranch View Interiors, Leawood, Kans., 1975-76; prin., owner Louise Corbett-Designer, Overland Park, Kans., 1976-84; sr. designer Design Trend Internat. Interiors, Scottsdale, Ariz., 1984-87; product and interior designer Scottsdale, 1988--; design rev. cons. Genon Corp., Boston, 1985; pres. Sonoran Resources, Scottsdale, 1987-88; design dir. Made in the Shade, Scottsdale, 1988—. Contbr. articles to trade publs. Lobbyist Ariz. Designers Effort for Ariz. Legis., 1986. Recipient Presidential Citation, 1986, 87, 88; Dean's scholar, 1965; GM grantee, 1966-68. Mem. Am. Soc. Interior Designers (assoc., Presdl. citation 1987), Nat. Trust for Historic Preservation. Roman Catholic. Home and Office: 9083 E Sahuaro Dr Scottsdale AZ 85260

CORBETT, THOMAS JOHN, protective services official; b. Chelsea, Mass., Feb. 17, 1951; s. Thomas Francis and Margaret Elizabeth (Murray) C.; m. Margaret Alice McKinnon, Jan. 7, 1984; children: Chris Kosena, Marc Kosena. BA, Carroll Coll., 1973; MA, Fordham U., 1984. Cert. chemical dependancy counselor, Mont. Probation officer Dept. of Insts., State of Mont., Billings, Kalispell and, Missoula, 1976-80, U.S. Probation Svc., Great Falls, Helena, Mont., 1980—; lectr. U. Mont., Missoula, 1979, 83, Carroll Coll., Helena, Mont., 1987; geust lectr. No. Mont. Coll., 1982, Coll. Great Falls, 1982; drug specialist U.S. probation, D.C. Advisor Youth Sports Programs, YMCA, Helena, 1985-89; mem. Helena Arts Coun., 1987—; mem. human svcs. adv. com. Flathead Valley Community Coll.,

Kalispell, Mont.; adv. bd. Missoula Alchohol/Drug program, 1979, Transition Ctr., Great Falls, 1981-82. Mem. Mont. Corrections Assn. (bd. dirs. 1980-83, 85-86), Fed. Probation Officers Assn. (dist. liason, 1984-86). Office: US Probation 301 S Park 164 Helena MT 59626-0121

CORBIN, BARRY, actor, writer; b. Lamesa, Tex., Oct. 16, 1940; s. Kilmer Blaine and Alma LaMerle (Scott) C.; m. Marie Elyse Soape, Mar. 15, 1965 (div. Apr. 1972); m. Susan James Berger, May 29, 1976; children: James Barry, Christopher Clayton. Student, Tex. Tech. U., 1959-64, U. Colo., summer 1964. Freelance actor 1965—; faculty N.C. State U., Raleigh, 1966-67. Playwright: Suckerrod Smith and the Cisco Kid, 1974 (Theater U.S.A. award 1974), Throckmorton, Tx., 76083, 1983; screenwriter The Wildcatters, 1986. Served as pvt. USMCR, 1962-64. Mem. Screen Actors Guild (bd. dirs. 1985, 87-90), Actors Equity Assn., AFTRA, Dramatists Guild, Acad. Motion Picture Arts and Scis. Democrat. Office: care Writers and Artists Agy 11726 San Vincente #300 Los Angeles CA 90049

CORBIN, DAVID ROGER, small business owner; b. Blackwell, Okla., Nov. 15, 1944; s. Lewis Irving and Dorothea E. (Mills) C.; m. Katherine May O'Connell, June 15, 1979; children: Christopher, Mary Beth, Cynthia. Student, Southwestern Coll., Winfield, Kans., 1963-65. With service dept. Gen. Communications Co., Witchita, Kans., 1967-69; communoication engr., technician Max-Sig Inc., Medford, Oreg., 1969-70; founder, pres. Teletron Inc., Coos Bay, Oreg., 1970-75, Corbin Mfg. and Supply Inc., White City, Oreg., 1976—; founder, prin. Corbin Computers, White City, 1985—; bd. dirs., v.p. Palmer Methods Inc., Ashland, Oreg.; bd. dirs., ptnr. PC Products, Ashland; prin. Corbin Software Inc., While City; cons. in field. Author: Discover Swaging, 1980, World Directory of Custom Bullet Makers, 1987, (software) Bullet Simulation Package, 1979; conbr. articles to profl. jours. Served with USN, 1965-67, MTO. Republican. Home: PO Box 2171 White City OR 97503 Office: Corbin Mfg & Supply Inc 600 Industrial Circle White City OR 97503

CORBIN, KRESTINE MARGARET, manufacturing company executive, author, fashion designer, columnist; b. Reno, Apr. 24, 1937; d. Lawrence Albert and Judie Ellen (Johnston) Dickinson; m. Lee D. Corbin, May 16, 1959 (div. 1982); children: Michelle Marie, Sheri Karin. BS, U. Calif., Davis, 1958. Asst. prof. Bauder Coll., Sacramento, 1974—; columnist Sacramento Bee, 1976-81; owner Creative Sewing Co., Sacramento, 1976—; pres., chief exec. officer Sierra Machinery Inc., Sparks, Nev., 1984, bd. dirs. 1980—; nat. sales and promotion mgr. Westwood Retail Fabrics, N.Y.C., 1985—; bd. dirs. F.S.C. Mgmt. Svcs. Ltd., No. Internat. Bank, England, Exim Factors, Ltd.; cons. in field. Author: Suede Fabric Sewing Guide, 1973, Creative Sewing Book, 1978, (audio-visual) Fashions in the Making, 1974; producer: (nat. buyers show) Cream of the Cream Collections, 1978—, Style is What You Make It!, 1978-83. Named Exporter of Yr. State of Nev., 1989. Mem. Crocker Art Gallery Assn., 1960-78, Rep. Election Com., Sacramento, 1964, 68. Mem. Home Economists in Bus., Am. Home Econs. Assn., Internat. Fashion Group, Women's Fashion Fabrics Assn., Nat. Tool Builders Assn., Nat. Fluid Power Assn., Nev. World Trade Coun., Omicron Nu. Address: PO Box 435 Reno NV 89504 Office: Sierra Machinery Inc 1651 Glendale Rd Sparks NV 89431

CORBIN, LEROY HENRY, airline pilot; b. Morristown, N.J., Jan. 26, 1954; s. Lionel Henry and Marie LaVerne (Gilbert) C.; m. Margaret Leslie Orphan, Oct. 18, 1987. AAS in Flight Engring., Community Coll. of Air Force, 1979; BS in Aviation Tech., Thomas A. Edison Coll., 1979; postgrad., U. Wash., 1983-84. Aircraft mechanic Somerset Hills Aviation, Basking Ridge, N.J., 1976-77; flight engr. USAFR, McGuire AFB, N.J., 1977-80, pilot, 1980-82; pilot USAFR, McChord AFB, Wash., 1982—; rsch. pilot Data-Flight Corp., Everett, Wash., 1985—; pilot Delta Airlines, Seattle, 1986—. Served with USN, 1972-76. Mem. Air Line Pilots Assn. Republican. Roman Catholic.

CORBIN, ROBERT KEITH, state attorney general; b. 1928; married; 3 daus. B.S., Ind. U., 1952, J.D., 1956. Bar: Ind. 1957, Ariz. 1958. County atty. Maricopa County, 1965-69; chmn. Maricopa County Bd. Suprs., 1974-77; atty. gen. State of Ariz., Phoenix, 1979—; former mem. stats. adv. bd. U.S. Bur. Justice; former chmn. Ariz. Criminal Justice Commn. Served with USN, 1946-48. Mem. Ariz. State Bar Assn. (past mem. ethics com.), Ariz. County Attys. Assn., NRA (bd. dirs.), Nat. Assn. Attys. Gen. (chmn. anti-trust com. 1981-83), Americans for Effective Law Enforcement (pres. 1974), Conf. Western Attys. Gen. (chmn. 1982). Republican. Club: Masons. Home: 1275 W Washington Phoenix AZ 85007 Office: Law Dept State Capitol Office of Atty Gen 1275 W Washington Phoenix AZ 85007

CORBIN, ROSEMARY MAC GOWAN, civic worker, librarian; b. Santa Cruz, Calif., Apr. 3, 1940; d. Frederick Patrick and Lorena Maude (Parr) MacGowan; m. Douglas Tenny Corbin, Apr. 6, 1968; children: Jeffrey, Diana. BA, San Francisco State U., 1961; MLS, U. Calif., Berkeley, 1966. Libr. Stanford (Calif.) U., 1966-68, Richmond (Calif.) Pub. Libr., 1968-69, Kaiser Found. Health Plan, Oakland, Calif., 1976-81, San Francisco Pub. Libr., 1981-82, U. Calif., Berkeley, 1982-83; elected mem. coun. City of Richmond, 1985—, vice mayor, 1986-87; mem. Solid Waste Mgmt. Authority, 1985—, Contra Costa Hazardous Materials Commn., Martinez, Calif., 1987—, San Francisco Bay Conservation and Devel. Commn., 1987—. Contbr. articles to profl. publs. Pres. Richmond PTA, 1979-80; dist. mgr. fundraising event KQED-TV, San Francisco, 1975-77; pres. Bancroft Nursery Sch., Berkeley, 1974-76. Mem. Calif. Libr. Assn., Local Govt. Commn., League Calif. Cities, Nat. League Cities, LWV,, Women's Forum West Contra Costa County, Nat. Women's Polit. Caucus. Democrat. Home: 114 Crest Ave Richmond CA 94801 Office: Richmond City Hall 2600 Barrett Ave Richmond CA 94804

CORBOY, JAMES MCNALLY, investment banker; b. Erie, Pa., Nov. 3, 1940; s. James Thomas and Dorothy Jane (Schluraff) C.; BA, Allegheny Coll., 1962; MBA, U. Colo., 1986. m. Suzanne Shaver, July 23, 1965; children: Shannon, James McNally. Sales staff Boettcher & Co., Denver, 1964-70; sales staff Blyth Eastman Dillon, Denver and Chgo., 1970-74; sales staff William Blair & Co., Chgo., 1974-77; mgr. corp. bond dept. Boettcher & Co., Denver, 1977-79; ptnr. in charge William Blair & Co., Denver, 1979-86; first v.p. Stifel, Nicolaus & Co., 1986-88; pres., chief exec. officer J.M. Corboy, Inc., 1988—; gen. ptnr. Corboy & Co., L.P. Served with USMC, 1962-67. Mem. Securities Industry Assn., Nat. Assn. Securities Dealers (bd. arbitrators). Republican. Presbyterian. Clubs: The Attic (Chgo.), The Denver, Glenmoor Country, Metropolitan. Home: 60 Meade Ln Englewood CO 80110-6024 Office: 4643 S Ulster St Ste 1120 Denver CO 80237

CORBRIDGE, JAMES NOEL, JR., chancellor, educator; b. Mineola, N.Y., May 27, 1934; s. James Noel Sr. and Edna (Springer) C.; m. Charlotte Ivans Mixon, July 18, 1938; children: Lisa, Stuart. AB, Brown U., 1955; LLB, Yale U., 1963. Assoc. Lord, Day & Lord, N.Y.C., 1963-65; asst. prof. law U. Colo., Boulder, 1965-67, assoc. prof., 1967-73, prof., 1973—, v.p. student affairs, 1970-72, v.p. student and minority affairs, 1972-74, vice chancellor acad. affairs, 1974-77, interim vice chancellor acad. services, 1979-81, acting vice chancellor acad. affairs, 1986, chancellor, 1986—; vis. scholar Inst. for Advanced Legal Studies U. London, 1977, 85, Univ. Linkoping, Sweden, 1985. Contbr. articles to profl. jours. Served to lt. (j.g.) USNR, 1957-60. Mem. Colo. Bar Assn., Boulder County Bar Assn., Internat. Assn. Water Lawyers, Internat. Water Resources Assn. Episcopalian. Club: Boulder Country. Home: 7112 Old Post Rd Boulder CO 80301 Office: U Colo Campus Box 17 Boulder CO 80309

CORCORAN, CLIFFORD WAYNE, grocery chain consultant; b. Seattle, June 19, 1950; s. William G. and Elizbeth I. (Klein) C.; m. Carol Ann Rendahl, Sept. 16, 1972; children: Scott, Robyn, Patrick, Bradley. Student, U. Wash., 1968-72. Clk. Safeway Stores, Seattle, 1966-68; warehouseman Safeway Stores, Bellevue, Wash., 1968-80; asst., distbn. ctr. Safeway Stores, Bellevue, 1980-86; staff cons., adminstrv. offices Safeway Stores, Oakland, Calif., 1986—; ind. cons. in transp. ops., freight mgmt. Vallejo, Calif., 1987--. Author software systems for billing and order monitoring. Mem. CAP. Mem. San Francisco Clipper Developers. Office: Safeway Stores 430 Jackson St Oakland CA 94660

CORCORAN, LAWRENCE JOSEPH, traffic engineer, state official; b. New Haven, Jan. 11, 1944; s. Milton Joseph and Edna May (Hall) C; m. Virginia E. Couch, Jan. 27, 1968. BS in Mech. Engring., U. Conn., 1970; MS in Civil Engring., U. Colo., 1983. Registered profl. engr., Colo. Traffic and transp. engr. Colo. Div. Hwys., Denver, 1971-78, traffic ops. engr., 1979--. Contbr. articles to profl. publs. With U.S. Army, 1965-67. Mem. Inst. Transp. Engrs., Samoyed Club Am. (bd. dirs. 1981-83), Plum Creek Kennel Club (v.p. 1986-87, treas. 1987--). Office: Colo Div Hwys 2000 S Holly St Denver CO 80222

CORCORAN, WILLIAM PATRICK, electrical engineer, consultant; b. Assumption, Minn., Apr. 14, 1922; s. James Benedict and Bridget Cecelia (Colbert) C.; m. Margaret Ruth Norgaarden, May 29, 1945; children: Anthony, Timothy, Thomas, Patrick, Gerard, Theresa, Cecelia. BEE, U. Minn., 1948. Registered profl. engr., N.Y. State, Ind., Calif. Engr. Am. and Fgn. Power Co., N.Y.C., 1948-56; supr. Atomics Internat., Canoga Park, Calif., 1956-62; br. chief Gen. Motors Corp., Indpls., 1962-75; assoc. dir. Indpls. Ctr. Advanced Research, 1975-78, 80-83; sr. analyst Solar Energy Research Inst., Golden, Colo., 1978-80; pres. Advanced Energy Systems, Tucson, Ariz., 1983—; lectr. UCLA, 1959-61, Purdue U. 1981; mem. design com. AEC, Washington, 1960, AIEE, N.Y.C., 1959-60. Com. chmn., cubmaster Boy Scouts Am., Canoga Park, Calif., 1958-61; active energy com. LWV, 1978-80. Served as ensign, USMC, 1943-45. Roman Catholic. Home: 7042 E 2d St Tucson AZ 85710 Office: Advanced Energy Systems 7042 E 2d St Tucson AZ 85710

CORDIER, HERBERT, interior designer; b. Bad Kissingen, Germany, Apr. 22, 1925; came to U.S., 1949; s. Felix Kugelmann-Cordier and Alice (Plaut) Cordier. Diploma in interior design, Ecole Boulle, Paris, 1939. Owner Continental House, Palm Springs, Calif., 1958—; art and music critic; mem. Santa Fe Opera press corps; instr. U. Calif., Riverside, 1984-85, Coll. of the Desert, 1984-85; seminar speakerat first Asian Interior Design Conf., Singapore, 1982. Contbr. articles to newspapers and mags. Bd. dirs. Palm Springs Community Concerts, 1987—. Fellow Am. Soc. Interior Designers (chmn. So. Calif. regional conf. 1987). Home and Office: 2425 Tuscan Rd Palm Springs CA 92262

CORDOVA, DAVID EUGENE, accountant; b. Denver, Jan. 7, 1960; s. Eugene and Marguerite Gladys (Cronstedt) C. BS, U. Denver, 1981. CPA, Colo. Acct. Nelson & Zaveral, Denver, 1982—. Treas. Broadway Assistance Ctr., Denver, 1984-86, Colo. Conservative Union, Denver, 1984-87, Where Grace Abounds, Denver, 1986—, First Denver Friends Ch., 1989—; chmn. of stewards First Denver Friends Ch., 1984-88, chmn. of stewards Rocky Mt. Yearly Meeting of Friends Ch., Colorado Springs, 1986—, chmn. Little Friends Pre-school, 1987—. Mem. Am. Inst. of CPA's, Colo. Soc. of CPA's. Republican. Mem. Soc. of Friends. Home: 2915 W 49th Ave Denver CO 80221 Office: Nelson & Zaveral 7935 E Prentice Ste 301 Englewood CO 80111

CÓRDOVA, LU MARIE, financial markets economist; b. San Marino, Calif., Feb. 19, 1955; d. Fredrick Benedict and Joan M. Córdova; m. Michael Rossi Englund. BA in Polit. Sci., U. Calif., Berkeley, 1981, BA in Econs., 1983, PhD in Econs., 1989. Asst. research Atty. Gen. State of Calif., San Francisco, 1984; editor Market News Svc., Belmont, Calif., 1985; dir. Ctr. Econ. and Monetary Affairs, San Francisco, 1985—; pres., chief exec. officer Internat. Inst. Econ. Advancement, San Francisco, 1985—; bd. govs. Fed. Res. System, 1989. Editor Jour. Econ. and Monetary Affairs, 1987—, The Power of Coinage, 1987, Corporate Development, 1988; contbr., editor numerous articles Marketwire, 1985. Recipient fellowship Rockefeller Found., 1986-87, scholarship AEA/Fed. Reserve Bd., U. Wis., 1983. Mem. Nat. Assn. Bus. Econs. (chpt. pres. 1988-89), Am. Econ. Assn. (fellowship 1987-88), We. Econ. Assn., Am. Fin. Assn., Am. Assn. Indivisual Investors, Commonwealth Club.

CORDOVA, MARK ALLAN, fastener distributing company executive; b. Orange, Calif., Aug. 23, 1956; s. Moses Efren and Rachel (Martinez) C.; m. Krisandra Anne Panting, Apr. 5, 1986; 1 child, Mark Thomas. BBA, U. San Diego, 1978. Pres. Centennial Bolt Co., Denver. Mem. campaign cabinet United Way, Denver, 1986—; bd. dirs. Jr. Achievement. Mem. Rotary. Office: Centennial Bolt Co 5550 Joliet St Denver CO 80239

CORDRAY, RICHARD LYNN, electronics engineering executive; b. Tulsa, Jan. 27, 1952; s. Austin Edwin and Barbara Lee (Kline) C.; m. Barbara Scott Lamb, May 9, 1975; children: Michael Scott, Carol Ann. BS in Elec. Engring., Rice U., 1974, MEE, 1975, PhD, 1978. Rsch. engr. Tektronix, Inc., Beaverton, Oreg., 1978-81, program mgr., 1981; v.p. N.W. Instrument Systems, Beaverton, 1981-84; program mgr. Intel, Hillsboro, Oreg., 1984-85, Spacelabs, Inc., Redmond, Wash., 1985—. Bd. dirs. English Hill Homeowners Assn., Redmond, 1987-89. Mem. IEEE, Am. Heart Assn., Assn. for Advancement of Med. Instrumentation. Home: 17613 NE 142nd St Redmond WA 98052 Office: Spacelabs Inc 4200 150th Ave NE Redmond WA 98052

COREY, CONSTANCE MARCIA, librarian; b. Springfield, Ill., Apr. 10, 1936; d. Paul Eugene and H. Celestine (McCarver) Howey; m. John Douglas Corey, Oct. 11, 1958. BA in Theatre Arts, Denison U., 1958; MLS, U. Ariz., 1972; MBA, Ariz. State U., 1977. Sec. Dept. Def. and Def. Intelligency Agy., Ft. Gordon, Ga., 1961-63, Washington, 1963-64, 66-67, Kinshasa, Zaire, 1964-66, Bangkok, Thailand, 1967-68; bus. ref. librarian Ariz. State U. Libraries, Tempe, 1973-78, asst. univ. librarian for mgmt. svcs., 1978-88, assoc. dean univ. libraries, 1988—. Contbr. articles to profl. jours. Mem. ALA, Assn. Coll. and Rsch. Libraries (chmn. personnel adminstrs. and staff devel. officers discussion grp. 1986-87), Library Adminstr. and Mgmt. Assn., Ariz. State Library Assn. Home: 19 E Redondo Dr Tempe AZ 85282-2143 Office: Ariz State U Hayden Libr Tempe AZ 85287-1006

CORLESS, ELIZABETH ANN, interior design professional; b. Olds, Alta., Can., Oct. 18, 1959; came to U.S., 1978; d. Larry and Shirley Ann (Herdman) C.; m. Warren Anthony Davis, Dec. 5, 1987. BS in Interior Design, Woodbury U., 1980. Sr. designer Judith Wilson Design, Studio City, Calif., 1980-84; design dir. Impact Images, Santa Ana, Calif., 1984-85; mgr. environ. resources Pacific Bus. Interiors, Los Angeles, 1985—; instr. Brooks Coll., Long Beach, Calif., 1986-87; lectr. Woodbury U., Los Angeles, 1985-86. Mem. Inst. Bus. Designers (profl. treas. 1981-83, v.p. programs 1983-85, nat. trustee 1985-87, recipient Appreciation award 1983, 85, 87), Internat. Facility Mgmt. Assn., Nat. Trust Hist. Preservation. Episcopalian. Office: Pacific Bus Interiors 8687 Melrose Ave M-3 Los Angeles CA 90069

CORLISS, DOUGLAS RALPH, politician; b. Bremerton, Wash., Oct. 29, 1930; s. Verne Francis and Thora Ingrid (Hansen) C.; m. Lucille Joan Davis, Oct. 2, 1949; children—Roni, Randal, Rockford, Rene, Ragan, Robin, Roger. A.A., Olympic Coll., 1955; B.A., Central Wash. U., 1957; postgrad. U. Puget Sound, 1962. Music dir. pub. schs., Belfair, Wash. and Federal Way, Wash., 1957-72; owner, operator Corliss Trucking Co., 1972-73; mgr. constrn. Blazing Tree Ranch, Friday Harbor, Wash., 1973-77; owner, operator Harbor Rental Equipment, Friday Harbor, 1977; heavy equipment operator F.H. Gravel, Friday Harbor, 1977-80; gen. mgr. Friday Harbor Motor Inn, 1980-84; pres. North Mason Investment Group, Belfair, Wash., 1960-62; chmn. North Mason Edn. Assn., 1963, pres. 1964. Chmn. salary com. North Mason Schs., Belfair, 1962-63; commr. San Juan County, 1985—, freeholder, 1983; bd. dirs. San Juan Island Whale Mus.; organizer mcpl. adv. council San Juan Island, 1988—. Leader Community Stage Band, Friday Harbor, 1978-85; v.p. Community Youth Council, Friday Harbor, 1982; chmn. City Parks Action Com., Friday Harbor, 1983-84; counsel San Juan County Ferry Adv. Com.; mem. N.W. Regional Council; mem. blue ribbon com. Wash. Dept. Transp., 1985; sec., v.p. Wash. State Ferry Riders Coalition, 1985-86; ambassador State of Wash., 1986. Served with USN, 1947-51. Mem. NEA, Wash. State Edn. Assn., Wash. State Assn. of Counties legis. steering com., Music Edn. Assn., San Juan C. of C. (pres. 1984, bd. dirs. 1985), Am. Legion, Assn. Counties. Republican. Lodge: Lions (bd. dirs. 1982-84). Home: PO Box 286 Friday Harbor WA 98250

CORMIE, DONALD MERCER, investment company executive; b. Edmonton, Alta., Can., July 24, 1922; s. George Mills and Mildred (Mercer) C.; m. Eivor Elisabeth Ekstrom, June 8, 1946; children: John Mills, Donald Robert, Allison Barbara, James Mercer, Neil Brian, Buce George, Eivor, Robert. BA, U. Alta., 1944, LLB, 1945; LLM, Harvard U., 1946. Bar: Alta. 1947. With Queens counsel, 1964; sessional instr. faculty law U. Alta., 1947-53; sr. ptnr. Cormie, Kennedy & Edmonton, Barristers, 1954-87; instr. real estate law Dept. of Extension, U. Alta., 1958-64; pres., bd. dirs. Collective Securities, Ltd., Cormie Ranch, Inc., Sea Investors Corp.; bd. dirs. Sea Mgmt., Inc. With Can. Mcht. Marine, 1943-44. Recipient Judge Green Silver medal in law. Mem. Law Soc. Alta., Dean's Council of 100 Ariz. State U., World Bus. Council, Chief Execs. Forum (bd. dirs. 1976-79), Can. Bar Assn. (mem. council 1961-76, chmn. adminstrv. law com. 1963-66, chmn. taxation 1972-82, v.p. Alta. 1968-69). Home: 6301 E Yucca Rd Paradise Valley AZ 85258 Office: 10405 Jasper Ave, #216-21, Edmonton, AB Canada T5J 3S2

CORNABY, KAY STERLING, lawyer, state senator; b. Spanish Fork, Utah, Jan. 14, 1936; s. Sterling A. and Hilda G. (Stoker) C.; m. Linda Rasmussen, July 23, 1965; children: Alyse, Derek, Tara, Heather, Brandon. AB, Brigham Young U., 1960; postgrad. law Heidelberg (W.Ger.), 1961-63; JD, Harvard U., 1966. Bar: N.Y. 1967, Utah 1969, U.S. Patent and Trademark Office 1967. Assoc. Brumbaugh, Graves, Donahue & Raymond, N.Y.C., 1966-69; ptnr. Mallinckrodt & Cornaby, Salt Lake City, 1969-72; sole practice, Salt Lake City, 1972-85; assoc. Jones, Waldo, Holbrook & McDonough, Salt Lake City, 1985—; mem. Utah State Senate, 1977—, majority leader, 1983-84. Chmn. 2d Congl. Dist., Utah Rep. Party, 1973-77; mem. council legal advisers Rep. Nat. Com., 1981—. chmn. North and East Regional Council of Neighborhoods, 1976-77, Nat. Commn. on Uniform State Laws, 1979-88; mem. Salt Lake County Commn. on Youth, 1979-88; mem. Utah Health Cost Found., 1979-86, chmn., 1979-84; mem. Utah State Jud. Conduct Commn., 1983—, chmn. 1984-85; bd. dirs. KUED-KUER Pub. TV and Radio, 1982—, chmn. 1985-87, mem. adv. bd., 1988—; bd. dirs. Salt Lake Conv. and Visitors Bur., 1985—; mem. adv. council Salt Lake dist. Small Bus. Adminstrn.; pres. Utah Opera Co., 1985-86. Mem. Utah Bar Assn., Utah Harvard Alumni Assn. (pres. 1977-79), Harvard U. Law Sch. Alumni Assn. (v.p. 1979—). Mormon. Club: Alta (Salt Lake City). Office: Jones Waldo Holbrook & McDonough 1500 1st Interstate Pla 170 S Main St Salt Lake City UT 84101

CORNELIUS, BYRON GRANT, lawyer; b. Tallahassee, Nov. 8, 1951; s. Curtis Harding and Kathryn Louise (Laury) C.; m. Hilda O. Cornelius, July 28, 1973; 1 child, Camille Renee. AA, Grossmont Coll., 1979; BSL, Western State U., 1981, JD, 1982. Bar: Calif. 1983, U.S. Dist. Ct. (eas. dist., so. dist.) Calif. 1983, U.S. Ct. Appeals (9th cir.) 1983, U.S. Supreme Ct., 1986. Assoc. Davies, Barwick & Knowlton, Lemon Grove, Calif., 1983-84, Vaughan de Kirby, A.P.C., San Diego, 1984-86; ptnr. Epsten, Cornelius & Grinnell, San Diego, 1986—; tchr. legal analysis Western State U., San Diego, 1983-85, profl. respon, 1985—; tutor BAR/BRI Bar Rev., San Diego, 1984-85; tchr. law., jurisprudence Barpassers Bar Rev., Los Angeles, 1985-86. Author, editor: Professional Responsibility, 1985; editor: Criminal Justice Jour., 1981. Minister, elder Lamar Congregation Jehovah's Witnesses, Spring Valley, Calif., 1983—. Served with USN, 1969-73. Mem. San Diego County Bar Assn., San Diego Trial Lawyers, Assn. Trial Lawyers of AM. Home: 8728 Harness St Spring Valley CA 92077 Office: Epsten Cornelius & Grinnell 555 W Beech St Ste 200 San Diego CA 92101

CORNELL, IAN BEAUMONT, public relations and advertising agency executive; b. Sacramento, June 7, 1960; s. Hubert Raoul and Isabel Cornell; 1 child, Ian B. Jr. AA, American River Coll., 198l; BA, Calif. State U., Sacramento, 1983. News bur. specialist Calif. State Fair, Sacramento, 1982-83; account exec. Hedicke-Latimer Pub. Rels., Sacramento, 1983-85; prin. Ian Cornell Pub. Rels., Sacramento, 1985--. Bd. dirs. Sacramento Sheriff's Community Coun., 1985-86; mem. publicity com. Soroptimists Sacramento-San Juan, 1985--. Mem. Calif. Amateur Racquetball Assn. (exec. dir. 1985-86), Stress Busters Club (bd. dirs. 1987--). Democrat. Home: PO Box 10ll Fair Oaks CA 95628-1011 Office: 7919 Folsom Blvd Ste Ste 150 Sacramento CA 95626

CORNETT, CHARLIE LONNIE, electrical engineer; b. Welch, W.Va., June 6, 1938; s. Charlie Peyton and Virginia Elizabeth (White) C.; m. (div.); 1 child, Carrol Lynn. BS in Elect. Engring., West Vir. U., 1962; MA in Soc. Sci., Pacific Lutheran, Tacoma, Wash., 1975. Registered Engr. in Training, W.Va. Tactical Command Officer 169th Signal Co., Ft. Polk, La., 1962-64; procedures officer Supreme Hdqrs. Allied Powers, Paris, 1964-67; ops. officer 13th Signal Battalion, 1st Cav., Republic of Vietnam, 1968-69; Systems Control Officer Defense Command Agy., Washington, 1969-70, Switched Networks Officer, 1970-72; Exec. Officer 58th Signal Battalion, Ft. Lewis, Wash., 1972-74; Logistics Officer Joint U.S. Mil. Adv. Group, Udorn, Thailand, 1974-75; supr. elect. engring. U.S. Army Info. Systems Engring. Command, Ft. Huachuca, Ariz., 1975—. Named Supr. of the Month, Fed. Womens Program, Ft. Huachuca, 1988. Mem. Am. Soc. of Satellite Profls., Arizona Skeet Shooting Assn. (pres. 1986-88). Republican. Methodist. Home: PO Box 334 Fort Huachuca AZ 85613 Office: USAISEC/ASBQ-SET-S Fort Huachuca AZ 85613-5300

CORNETT, LAUREEN ELIZABETH, small business owner, photographer; b. San Diego, Nov. 14, 1946; d. Clarence Alex and Barbara Ann (Mesku) Lane; m. Bruce Walter Cornett, Oct. 17, 1981; children: Cherie Ann, Robert Michael, John David. Student, San Diego State U., 1964-70. Exec. sec. Boyle Engring., San Diego, 1964-69, Design Cons., San Diego, 1969-71; owner Laureen's Secretarial Service, San Diego, 1979-83; exec. sec. Covi Corp., San Diego, 1979-83; owner Laureen Cornett Word Processing, San Diego, 1982—; owner, photographer Panoramix, San Diego, 1984—. Photographer for brochures, newspaper ads. Office: Panoramix PO Box 15323 San Diego CA 92115

CORNFIELD, RANDOLPH BARNETT, teacher, consultant; b. Parris Island, S.C., Aug. 18, 1947; s. Dr. Leslie Sidney and Sylvia (Samuels) C. BA, U. Calif., Santa Barbara, 1972, Edn. cert., 1973, MA, 1973. Lectr. U. Calif.-Irvine, Irvine, Calif., 1987-88; substance abuse coord. Newport-Mesa Schs., Newport Beach, Calif., 1988; sales mgr. Sea-Coast Yacht Sales, Santa Barbara, 1980-81; mentor tchr. L.A. Unified Schs., 1982—; cons. Levy/Pazanti, L.A., 1984—, Jordano's, Santa Barbara; pres. Libr. Assocs. Calif. State L.A., 1985—, Lectr. Donner Mus. Lake Tahoe, Calif. 1976-77. Co-author: Substance Abuse Infusion into the Social Sciences, 1988. Commr. Small Bus. Adv. Coun., Sacramento, 1984—. Sgt. USAF, 1967-70, N. Africa. Named Fellow, U. Calif.-Irvine in Tech. 1987. Mem. Kappa Delta Pi. Democrat. Home: 8131 Manitoba #1 Playa Del Rey CA 90293

CORNYN, JOHN EUGENE, III, management consultant; b. Evanston, Ill., May 5, 1945; s. John Eugene and Virginia Ryder (Shannahan) C.; m. Alice Patricia Sellers, May 8, 1965 (div. Apr. 1974) 1 child, Kelly. B.S. in Hotel and Restaurant Adminstrn., Okla. State U., 1968. Mgr. Indian Trail Restaurant, Winnetka, Ill., 1970-71; employee services mgr. Zenith Corp., Chgo., 1971-72; mgr. Red Lion Corp., Portland, Oreg., 1973; cons. Pannell, Kerr, Forster, Chgo., 1973-75; pres., owner John Cornyn & Assocs., Portland 1976—; v.p. Seven Seas, Inc., Winnetka, Ill., 1978—, All Seas, Inc., Winneka, 1980—. Served to 1st lt. U.S. Army, 1968-70. Mem. Foodservice Cons. Soc. Internat. (chmn. mgmt. cons. com. 1983—), Inst. Mgmt. Cons. Republican. Club: Portland City. Home: 3350 NE Holladay St Portland OR 97232 Office: John Cornyn & Assocs 917 SW Oak St Ste 312 Portland OR 97205

CORNYN-SELBY, ALYCE PATRICIA, publishing company executive; b. Dayton, Ohio, Nov. 22, 1946; d.William Bain and Alice Ruth Sellers; 1 child, Kelly Alexandre. BA, Marylhurst Coll., Oreg. Prodn.mgr. Instrumentalist Pub., Evanston, Ill., 1971-72; visual communications mgr. Port of Portland, Oreg., 1976-85; owner AEnterprise, Portland, 1979-86, Paris Opera Co., Portland, 1988—; pubr. Beynch Press Pub. Co., Portland, 1986—; speaker in field. Contbr. articles to profl. jours. Recipient numerous awards for script/copy writing, design, photography and film prodn. Mem. Pubrs. Mktg. Assn., N.W. Book Pubrs. Assn., Willamette Writers, Oreg. Writers Colony. Address: 1928 SE Ladd Ave Portland OR 97214

CORP, WESLEY EARL, business executive; b. Chehalis, Wash., Apr. 18, 1952; s. Alonzo Gilmore and Vivian A. (Lowry) C.; m. Sheila Lynn Roche, July 20, 1985. Student, Boise State U., 1974-76. Owner, mgr. Wesley Corp Constrn. Co., Boise, Idaho, 1976-78; owner, mgr. Wesley Corp Farms, Sunnyside, Wash., 1978-80; pres., bd. dirs. Starpoint Inc., Boise, 1981—, Starpoint Solar Inc., Boise, 1985—, SWC Holding Inc., Boise, 1986—; v.p., bd. dirs. Keyfield Internat. Ltd., Osaka, Japan, 1985—. Inventor game Spacer. With USAF, 1970-74. Office: SWC Holding Inc PO Box 4151 Boise ID 83711

CORPANY, B. W., fund raising executive; b. Wichita Falls, Tex., June 8, 1934; s. Herbert L. and Sarah Ellen (Sisk) C.; m. Carol Lorraine Seaberg, Feb. 24, 1956; 1 child, John Frederic. BS, Baylor U., 1961; MEd, U. Houston, 1970. Tchr./coach Galvestonn (Tex.) pub. schs., 1961-63; bus. adminstr. Div. Fgn. Missions, Assemblies of God, various locations, 1963-77; mktg. mgr. Singer Sewing Machine Co., Beirut, Lebanon, 1977-78; asst. Wayne Shabaz & Assocs., Houston, 1978-80; exec. dir. Mission of Mercy, Tacoma, Wash., 1980—. Bd. dirs. Goodwill Industries, Tacoma, 1986—, Tacoma YMCA, 1986—, div. capt. fund-raising dr., 1986—. Mem. Rotary. Republican. Assemblies of God. Home: 3435 Narrows Dr Tacoma WA 98407

CORPUZ, TERESA AGRIFINA, school principal; b. San Francisco, Apr. 4, 1951; d. Faustino Ceria and Virginia (Baltazar) C. BA in English, San Francisco State U., 1972; MS in Counseling, Calif State U., Hayward, 1981. Cert. secondary tchr., Calif. Tchr. Mendota (Calif.) Sch. Dist., 1973-75, Tracy (Calif.) Sch. Dist., 1975-82; counselor Livermore (Calif.) Sch. Dist., 1982-83; vice-prin. Albany (Calif.) Unified Sch. Dist., 1983-85, prin., 1987—; prin. Sunnyvale (Calif.) Elem. Sch. Dist., 1985-87; cons. sch. edn. U. Calif., Berkeley, 1987-88. Bd. dirs. Albany-Berkeley YMCA, 1987—. Recipient Calif. Educator award Calif. State Dept. Edn. and Milken Family Found., 1987. Mem. Assn. Calif. Sch. Adminstrs., Assn. Supervision and Curriculum Devel., Phi Delta Kappa, Delta Kappa Gamma. Democrat. Roman Catholic. Office: Albany Mid Sch 1000 Jackson St Albany CA 94706

CORTES, WILLIAM PATRICK, telecommunications executive; b. Ellenville, N.Y., Apr. 23, 1955; s. Robert Paul and Joan Helen (Whitstock) C. AB, Stanford U., 1977; MBA, U. Wash., 1983, JD, 1984. Bar: Wash. 1984; CPA, Wash. Accts. payable mgr. Cen. Distbrs., Inc., Portland, Oreg., 1977-78; fin. instr. Sch. Bus. Adminstrn. U. Wash., Seattle, 1980-83; strategic planning analyst Burlington No., Inc., Seattle, 1982, 83; sr. cons. Ernst & Whinney Telecommunications Group, Tacoma, 1985-86; fin. mgr. spec. projects US WEST NewVector Group Inc., Bellevue, Wash., 1986-88, dir. investor rels. and bus. fin. analysis, 1988—. Treas. Erxleben for State Rep. Campaign, Bellevue, 1982. Mem. ABA, AICPA, Wash. State Bar Assn., Fed. Communications Bar Assn., Wash. Soc. CPA's, U. Wash. Grad. Sch. Bus. Adminstrn. Alumni Assn. (bd. dirs. 1985-87). Democrat. Roman Catholic. Office: US WEST NewVector Group Inc 3350 161st Ave SE Bellevue WA 98008

CORTEZ, JOSE ONESIMO, college administrator, vocational educator, consultant; b. Laredo, Tex., Jan. 20, 1942; s. Onesimo and Herminia (Obregon) C.; m. Bonnie Jean Frampton, Jan. 4, 1964 (div.); children—Sonya, Mathew, Carl. BA cum laude, Calif. State U., Long Beach, 1976, MA, 1980. Tool and die maker Huck Mfg. Co., Carson, Calif., 1971-76; indsl. engr. ITT Cannon Electric, Santa Ana, Calif., 1976-78; asst. prof. metals tech. Los Angeles Trade Tech. Coll., 1978-83, asst. dean, 1983—, instr. tool and die making, numerical control, 1978—; cons. in field; mem. com. on gen. edn. Community Coll. State Chancellor, Sacramento, 1982, mem. task force on acad. quality, 1983. Los Angeles Trade Tech. Coll. Pres.'s grantee, 1981. Mem. Computer Assisted Systems Assn., Soc. Mfg. Engrs., Am. Vocat. Assn., Phi Kappa Phi, Epsilon Pi Tau. Democrat. Roman Catholic. Office: LA Trade Tech Coll 400 W Washington Blvd Los Angeles CA 90015

CORTEZ, MILES COGLEY, JR., lawyer; b. Chgo., Dec. 7, 1943; s. Miles and Carol (Sandstrom) C.; m. Janice Lynn Gillespie; children: Miles III, Amy, Jeff Salzenstein, Drew. BA in Econs., Trinity U., San Antonio, 1964; JD, Northwestern U., 1967. Bar: Ill. 1967, Colo. 1970, U.S. Dist. Ct. Colo. 1970, U.S. Ct. Appeals (10th cir.) 1970, U.S. Ct. Appeals (3d cir.) 1974. Ptnr. Welborn, Dufford & Brown, Denver, 1970-84; pres. Cortez & Friedman, P.C., Denver, 1984—; lectr. Continuing Legal Edn. Seminars, Colo., 1978—. Contbr. articles to profl. jours. Bd. dirs. Colo. Youth Tennis Found., Denver, 1982-84, 88—. Served to capt. U.S. Army, 1967-69. Fellow Colo. Bar Found., Am. Bar Found.; mem. ABA, Denver Bar Assn. (pres. 1982-83), Colo. Bar Assn. (bd. govs. 1976-78, 81-83), Nat. Conf. Bar Pres., Colo. Supreme Ct. Bd. Law Examiners, Colo. Hispanic Bar Assn. Home: 7025 E Costilla Dr Englewood CO 80112 Office: Cortez & Friedman P.C. 5251 DTC Pkwy Denver CO 80111

CORTINES, RAMON, school superintendent. Supt. of schools city of San Francisco. Office: San Francisco Sch Dist 135 Van Ness Ave San Francisco CA 94102 *

CORWIN, BRUCE JAMES, civil engineer; b. Lawrence, Kans., Sept. 8, 1947; s. Robert A. Corwin Sr. and Roberta J. (Hartman) Swigart; m. Rita Jean Throop, Aug. 31, 1968; children: Christina G., Troy G. AA in Engring., Longview Community Coll., 1973; BS in Civil Engring., U. Kans., 1976. Registered profl. engr., Alaska, Mo., Ohio. Drafter, technician Black & Veatch Cons. Engrs., Kansas City, Mo., 1968-73; project engr. Black & Veatch Cons. Engrs., Kansas City, 1973-81; project mgr. Quadra Engring., Inc., Anchorage, 1981-83; pres., civil engr. Corwin & Assocs., Inc., Anchorage, 1983—; cons. Arctic & Value Engring. Teams, Anchorage. Contbr. articles to profl. jours. Auditor, judge Miss Alaska Pageant Program, Anchorage, 1987—. With USN, 1965-68, Vietnam. Named Young Engr. of the Month Mo. Soc. of Profl. Engrs., Kansas City, 1979. Mem. Soc. Am. Mil. Engrs. (pres. Anchorage post), Am. Soc. Civil Engrs. (Zone III Daniel W. Mead prize 1981), Am. Water Works Assn., Am. Concrete Inst., Water Pollution Control Fedn., Alaskan C. of C., Alyeska Ski Club. Republican. Home: 12000 Forelands Circle Anchorage AK 99515 Office: Corwin & Assocs Inc 1000 E Dimond Blvd Anchorage AK 99515

COSH, JOHN MORTON, banker; b. Mimico, Ont., Can., Dec. 28, 1924; s. George Morton and Margaret (Brown) C.; m. Marjorie Bernice Cosh, Apr. 20, 1952; children: George M., John Michael, Jayne Ann, Robert Alan. Cert. banking, U. Wis., 1971. Asst. cashier First Nat. Bank Vista, Calif., 1946-51; escrow officer, asst. mgr., mgr. security First Nat. Bank Vista, 1951-70; exec. v.p., pres., vice chmn. W. Coast Nat. Bank, 1970-77; pres. Palomar Ind. & Comml. Realtors Inc., 1977-83; v.p. Torrey Pines Bank, 1983—. Bd. dirs., past pres. Tri-City Hosp.; vice chmn. Oceanside Econ. Devel. Corp.; bd. dirs. Overall Econ. Devel. Commn. San Diego County; past pres. Greater San Luis Rey Council; past bd. dirs., chmn. guarantors fund North County Concert Assn.; vol. Vista Boys Club; life mem. San Luis Rey Council PTA's. Served with USAAF, 1943-46. Recipient Silver Keystone, Golden Boy, Bronze Medallion, Man Behind the Boy awards Boys Clubs Am.; named Disting. Citizen Jaycees, Man of Yr. North County Associated C. of C.'s, 1965, Banker of Yr. Am. Bankers Assn., 1984, Hon. Officer Vista League Cancer Socs. Mem. Vista Hist. Soc., Vista C. of C. (bd. dirs.), Indsl. Devel. Bond Authority (chmn.), Vista Econ. Devel. Assn. (past chmn.), Elks, Lions, Masons, Rotary. Republican. Presbyterian. Home: 1638 Alta Vista Dr Vista CA 92084

COSS, JAMES ROBERT, physicist; b. Newark, Ohio, June 3, 1936; s. Bert Andrew and Mary Margaret (Pickering) C.; m. Patricia Lee Schweikert, Nov. 22, 1958 (div. Apr. 1976); children: Michael Alan, David Owen; m. Maria Clara Marin, Dec. 28, 1985. BSc, Ohio U., 1958; MA, U. Calif., Santa Barbara, 1980. Physicist Wright Air Devel. Ctr., Dayton, Ohio, 1958-61; mem. tech. staff GE, Syracuse, N.Y., 1961-62; tech. staff mem. Northrop Corp., Hawthorne, Calif., 1962-69; quality assurance mgr. TRW Semiconductors, Lawndale, Calif., 1969-70; tech. staff mem. Hughes Aircraft Co., Culver City, Calif., 1971-75; geologic draftsman McClellan Engring., Ventura, Calif., 1978-79; project geologist Dames & Moore, L.A., 1980-81; staff geologist Ertec Western, Inc., Long Beach, Calif., 1981-82; tech. staff mem. TRW, Redondo Beach, Calif., 1982-83; tech. group leader, radiation effects Jet Propulsion Lab., Pasadena, Calif., 1983—. Contbr. articles to profl. jours. Fellow Inst. for Advancement of Engring.; mem. IEEE (sr., vice chmn., nuclear and plasma scis. sect. 1984-85, chmn. 1985-86). Republican. Office: Jet Propulsion Lab 4800 Oak Grove Dr M/S 303-220 Pasadena CA 91109

COSSABOON, NANCY TOURI, human resources executive; b. Port Chester, N.Y., Dec. 9, 1946; d. Joseph Ralph and Rose Mary (Christiano) Touri; m. H. Richard Cossaboon, Dec. 7, 1974 (dec. 1981). BBA cum laude, Boston U., 1979; MBA, Coll. Notre Dame, Belmont, Calif., 1982. With Am. Can Co., Greenwich, Conn., 1969-71, Bus. Machines div. The Singer Co., N.Y.C., 1971-76; employment mgr. Digial Equipment Corp., Maynard, Mass., 1976-77; personnel mgr. fin. and adminstrn. Digital Equipment Corp., Maynard, 1977-80; with Varian Assocs., Palo Alto, Calif., 1980—; corp. human resources and employment mgr. Varian Assocs., Palo Alto, 1984-86, dir. human resources devel., 1987—; instr. Resource Ctr. for Women, Palo Alto, 1982—; MBA instr. Coll. Notre Dame, 1985—. Mem. Am. Soc. Tng. and Devel., No. Calif. Human Resources Coun., Nat. Orgn. and Devel. Network, Bay Area Orgn. and Devel. Network, Employment Mgmt. Assn. Office: Varian Assocs 611 Hansen Way Palo Alto CA 94303

COSTA, DANIEL JOSEPH, electronics company executive; b. Fall River, Mass., Feb. 20, 1948; s. Daniel Da Pont and Gilda (Carvalho) C.; m. Martha Jane Bloomstine, Feb. 20, 1971; 1 child, Jennifer Elizabeth. AA, West Valley Coll., 1970; BA, San Jose State U., 1975; MA, U. Phoenix, 1981. Quality assurance supr. Sperry-Univac, Cupertino, Calif., 1971-77; quality assurance mgr. Advanced Electronics Design, Sunnyvale, Calif., 1977-78; dir. quality Nat. Semiconductor, Santa Clara, Calif., 1978-80; quality assurance mgr. Two Pi Corp., Santa Clara, 1980-82; dir. quality Osborne Computer Corp., Hayward, Calif., 1982-83; dir. ops. Liberty Electronics USA, San Francisco, 1983-85; pres. D.J. Costa Assocs., Campbell, Calif., 1985-89; quality assurance mgr. Tandem Computers, Cupertino, 1987—. Co-author: Quality Pays, 1988. Republican.

COSTA, REBECCA DAZAI, advertising executive; b. San Mateo, Calif., Apr. 11, 1955; d. Clifford Agnew Costa and Yoshiko (Kikuchi) Graves. BA, U. Calif., Santa Barbara, 1977; MBA, U. Santa Clara, 1980. Asst. mgr. RLS Mgmt., Los Gatos, Calif., 1977-79; mgr. mktg. Gen. Electric, Calma Co., Santa Clara, Calif., 1979-82; dir. mktg. Omex Corp., Santa Clara, 1982-83; v.p. mktg. Tera Corp., Berkeley, Calif., 1983-84; pres., chief exec. officer Dazai Advt., Campbell, Calif., 1984—; sec., bd. dirs. Coral, Inc., San Jose, Calif., 1986—; v.p., bd. dirs. Ascent, Inc., San Jose, 1986—; bd. dirs. Bayou Oil and Gas, Inc. Contbr. articles to profl. jours. Recipient Western Art Dirs. Club award, 1981. Home: PO Box 2054 Los Gatos CA 95031 Office: Dazai Advt Inc Pruneyard Towers II 6th Fl Campbell CA 95008

COSTACOS, JOHN ARISTOTLE, sports marketing executive; b. Seattle, Nov. 29, 1960; s. Jerry Alexander and Eva (Tsalaky) C. BS, U. Wash., 1984. Pres., founder Costacos Bros. Sports, Seattle, 1985—; pres. N.W. Sports Rev. mag., Seattle, 1988—. Mem. Wash. Athletic Club, Zeta Psi. Greek Orthodox. Home: 3707 SW Prescott Pl Seattle WA 98126 Office: Costacos Bros Sports Harbor Marina Corp Ctr 10001 Klickitat SW Ste 201 Seattle WA 98134

COSTANTINI, LANA ELLEN, textbook editor; b. San Francisco, Feb. 9, 1955; m. Everett Rhodes Castle III, Oct. 28, 1984. BA in Philosophy, Calif. State U., Sonoma, 1979; MFA in Creative Writing, U. Mont., 1983. Writing instr. U. Mont., Missoula, Mont., 1981-83; textbook writer Quercus Corp., Castro Valley, Calif., 1983-85; freelance editor Houghton Mifflin Co., San Francisco, 1985-86; supervising editor Straight Line Editorial Devel., San Francisco, 1986-89; cons. in field. Author of short story in CalQuarterly, 1986. Recipient Bank of Am. Award for English, 1973. Mem. Media Alliance, Calif. Poets in the Schs., Internat. Reading Assn. Office: Straight Line Editorial 555 DeHaro Suite 390 San Francisco CA 94107

COSTANZA, MARGARET MIDGE, political consultant, public service administrator; b. Rochester, N.Y., Nov. 28, 1932; d. Philip Joseph and Concetta (Granata) C. LLD (hon.), Framingham State Coll., 1979. Exec. asst. to pres. John J. Petrossi Enterprises, Rochester, N.Y.; asst. to James E. Carter Exec. Office of the Pres., Washington; speaker on human rights, fgn. policy, econs. various orgns. including John F. Kennedy Sch. Politics, Harvard U., Ford Hall Forum, Mass., The Econs. Club of Southwestern Mich., Inst. of Internal Auditors; exec. dir. Shirley Maclaine Enterprises, Los Angeles; v.p. Alan Landsburg Prodns. Talent coordinator, segment producer (TV series) America; spl. corr., segment producer (TV series) America Talks Back, Woody Fraser Prodns. Mem. exec. com. 22d Ward, 1959-64; mgr. Robert F. Kennedy Senatorial campaign, Monroe County, N.Y., 1964; vice-chmn. Monroe County Dem. com., 1966-70; mem. County Com., 1966-70, Dem. State Com., 1967-79; Dem. Nat. C, 1972-80, Rochester City Council, 1974-77 (1st woman to be elected); Dem. Congl. cand., 35th dist., N.Y., 1974; co-chairperson N.Y. State Carter campaign, 1975-76, N.Y. State Platform com., 1976; mem. com. Nat. Dem. Platform, 1976; del. Nat. Conv., 1976; pres. Nat. Coalition to End Pound Seizure, Los Angeles, 1988; bd. dirs. Nat. Gay Rights Advocates, San Francisco, 1988, New Hope for Animals, Los Angeles, 1988. Roman Catholic.

COSTELLO, SHARON YEVONNE, communications management consultant; b. L.A., Mar. 11, 1944; d. Robert Joseph and Virginia Gladys (Conroy) C. BA in Psychology, U. So. Calif., 1979, MA in Communication Mgmt., 1984, postgrad., 1987—. Owner Costellos Property Mgmt., Mammoth Lakes, Calif., 1971-80; mgmt. cons. Annenbert Sch. Communications and U. So. Calif., 1982-84; dir. corp. communications Benchmark Tech., Houston, 1984-85; mgmt. cons. The Murrieta Group, Rancho, Calif., 1985—. Contbr. articles to profl. jours.; writer, producer 13 part cable TV show Executive Choices in A Technological World. Mem. NAFE, NOW, U. So. Calif. Alumni Assn., Annenberg Sch. Alumni Assn. (speakers and events com., seminar speaker), Newport Beach Tennis. Republican. Roman Catholic. Office: The Murrieta Group 27475 Ynez Rd Ste 204 Temecula CA 92390

COTA, MERCEDES ELIZABETH, ambulance service company official, educator; b. Camden, N.J., Jan. 22, 1951; d. Burton Lloyd Anderson and Doris Ruth (Young) Brigham; m. Gilbert David Cota, Jan. 10, 1981; stepchildren: Stephanie Ann, Gilbert Damian. BA, San Diego State U., 1973; MA, U. Redlands, 1986. mem. faculty dept. bus. and human resource mgmt. Whitehead Ctr. for Lifelong Learning, U. Redlands (Calif.), 1986—. Adminstv. liaison to med. staff Hemet (Calif.) Valley Hosp. Dist., 1980-87; employee resource mgr. Hemet Valley Ambulance Svc., Inc., 1987—. Participant Valley Emergency Svc. Com., Hemet, 1980—. Mem. Soroptimists (bd. dirs. Hemet 1988-89, Woman of Distinction award 1988). Republican. Office: Hemet Valley Ambulance Svc 41889 E Florida Ste E Hemet CA 92344

COTE, RALPH WARREN, nuclear engineer, consultant; b. Berkeley, Calif., Oct. 5, 1927; s. Ralph Warren and Clara Maria (Neves) C.; m. Lois Lydia Maddox, Aug. 8, 1950; children: Ralph Warren III, Michele Marie. BSME, N.Mex. Inst. Mining and Tech., 1952. Registered profl. nuclear engr., Calif. Resident engr. Am. Smelting and Refining Co., Page, Idaho, 1952-54; shift boss Bunker Hill Co., Kellogg, Idaho, 1954-57, gen. mine foreman, 1958-60; project engr. Union Carbide Nuclear Co., Grand Junction, Colo., 1957-58; shift supr. Gen. Electric Co., Richland, Wash., 1960-63; shift supr. Gen. Electric Co., Vallecitos, Calif., 1963-66, maintenance mgr., 1966-67; supt. start up shift Gen. Electric Co., San Jose, Calif., 1967-71; mgr. project start up Bechtel Power Corp., San Francisco, 1971—. Served to 2d lt. USNG, 1946-50. Mem. Am. Nuclear Soc., VFW. Republican. Home: 3478 Silver Maple Dr Danville CA 94526 Office: Bechtel Power Corp 50 Beale St San Francisco CA 94119

COTNER, ROBERT B., dentist; b. Bozeman, Mont., Mar. 26, 1930; s. Frank Boyd and Anita (Clark) C.; m. Kathleen Wolfe, June 7, 1952; children: Robert B., Thomas W., David B., Caroline E., John C. BS, Mont. State U., 1952, MS, 1953; DDS, U. Mich., 1957. Pvt. practice Columbia Falls, Mont., 1960-; dentist Mont. Vets. Home, Columbia Falls, Mont., 1980-. Bd. trustees Sch. Dist. #6, Columbia Falls, Mont., 1969-77; dental adv. team Bd. Health, Flathead Co., 1986-; bd. dirs. St. Richard's Parish, Columbia Falls, 1968-71; bd. dirs. MODPAC,Mont. Polit. Action Com., 1979-85; mem. Bd. Dentistry, State Mont., 1986-. Capt. AUS, 1956-60. Fellow Am. kColl. Dentistry, Internat. Coll. Dentistry; mem. Mont. Dental Assn. (pres. 1976-77), Am. Dental Assn. (nat. del. 1966, 74, 75, 76, 77), Acad. Gen. Dentistry (chpt. pres. 1969-72). Roman Catholic. Home: 125 Larch Hill Dr Columbia Falls MT 59912 Office: 640 1st Ave W Columbia Falls MT 59912

COTTER, LAWRENCE RAFFETY, management consultant; b. Albany, Calif., Aug. 13, 1933; s. Malcolm Thompson Cotter and Una Elyse Raffety. AA, U. Calif., Berkeley, 1953, BA in Astronomy, 1956; MS in Bus. Adminstrn., The George Washington U., 1967; PhD in Mgmt. Theory, UCLA, 1977. Commd. 2nd lt. USAF, 1956, advanced through grades to col., 1975, ret., 1982; orbital analyst, network controller Project Space Track USAF, Bedford, Mass., 1958-61; staff scientist Hdqs. N.Am. Air Def. Command, Colorado Springs, Colo., 1962-66, Hdqrs. USAF, Washington, 1967-70; dir. test and deployment DEF. Support program USAF, Los Angeles, 1975-76; commdr. detachment 1 Electronic Systems Div. USAF, Tehran, Iran, 1976-78; system program dir. Electronic Systems div. USAF, Bedford, Mass., 1978-79; dep. commdr. network plans and devel. AF Satellite Control Facility USAF, Sunnyvale, Calif., 1979-82; mgmt. cons. Berkeley, 1982—; adminstrv. asst. Arnold Air Soc., Washington, 1959-72. Co-author: The Arnold Air Soc. Manual, 1956; (computer program) SPACE, 1970; editor: The Arnold Air Soc. Manual 1964-72. Recipient Departmental Citation U. Calif. Berkeley, 1955, Citation of Honor, Arnold Air Soc., 1967. Mem. AF Assn., The Royal AF Club, Beta Gamma Sigma.

COTTERMAN, MYRON LEE, realtor; b. Rushville, Ohio, Sept. 21, 1918; s. Guy Renard and Lottie May (Palmer) C.; m. Evelyn Teresa Tateosian, Mar. 16, 1952 (div. 1977); children: Karen Lee, Mark Steven; m. Jacqueline Ann Tiller, Apr. 29, 1979. Student, Bliss Coll., 1936-38, George Washington U., 1963-64. Lic. realtor, Ohio, Calif. Staff officer U.S. Fgn. Service, Washington, London, Buenos Aires, 1941-54; Am. consul Am. Consulate Gen., Hamburg, Fed. Republic Germany, 1954-57; prin. officer Am. Consulate Gen., Nuevo Laredo, Mex., 1968-73; adminstrv. officer Am. Embassy, Santo Domingo, Dominican Republic, 1957-62; supr., adminstrv. officer U.S. Dept. State, Washington, 1962-66, exec. dir., 1973-76; dir. fin. Cen. Treaty Orgn., Ankara, Turkey, 1966-68; realtor Sawmill Homes, Century 21, Columbus, Ohio, 1979-84, Cal-Rancho Properties, Century 21, Carlsbad, Calif., 1985—; Am. consul Am. Embassy, Tel Aviv, Israel, 1976, Am. Consulate Gen., Tijuana, Mex., 1980. Mem. Nat. Assn. Realtors, Calif. Assn. Realtors, Carlsbad Bd. Realtors, Diplomatic and Consular Officers Retired, Am. Fgn. Service Assn., Sertoma (treas. 1983-84, Sertoman of Yr. 1983, 84), Rotary. Republican. Lutheran. Home: 6571 Via Barona Carlsbad CA 92009 Office: Century 21 Cal-Rancho Properties 2588-F El Camino Real Carlsbad CA 92008

COTTINGHAM, SUSAN MARIE, infosystems specialist; b. Denver, July 14, 1950; d. Cyril Francis and Nancy Lee (Meyer) Kipp; m. Ronald Lynn Cottingham, Apr. 26, 1973. BFA, Colo. State U., 1972; postgrad., R.I. Sch. Design, 1972-73. Programmer Larimer County Govt., Ft. Collins, Colo., 1978-81, lead analyst, 1981-84, mgr., 1984—. Mem. Am. Mgmt. Assn., Data Processing Mgmt. Assn., Inst. Cert. Computer Profls. (cert., assoc.), Career Women's Roundtable (co-founder), Am. UNIVAC Users Assn., AAU, Ft. Collins Potter's Guild (v.p. 1977-78). Democrat.

COTTON, DANIEL FRANCIS LEIGH, healthcare management executive; b. Mt. Vernon, N.Y., Jan. 16, 1931; s. Harold Heath and Dorothy Submit (Avery) C.; B.A., Pacific Union Coll., Angwin, Calif., 1952; M.A., Andrews U., Berrien Springs, Mich., 1954, B.D., 1956; m. Marilyn Dillow, Feb. 27, 1955; children—Patrice Lynn, Jennifer Leigh, Elizabeth Anne, Lori Jean. Assoc. prof. religion Columbia Union Coll., Takoma Park, Md., 1959-62; assoc. prof. religious philosophy Loma Linda (Calif.) U., 1962-69; developer, pres. Heritage Health Care Inc. Loma Linda, 1966—; developer, pres. Loma Linda Community Hosp., 1972-82; pres. Colorado Springs Community Hosp., 1974-78; chmn. bd., chief exec. officer United Med. Mgmt. Inc., 1978—. Chmn. bd. Nat. Child Health Council, 1977-82; chmn. bd., chief exec. officer The Am. Heritage Group, 1986—; pres. Loma Linda Health Care Found., 1979-82; dir., sec. Health Care Funding Corp., 1986—. Fellow Am. Coll. Health Care Adminstrs.; mem. AAUP, Hosp. Fin. Mgmt. Assn., Loma Linda C. of C. (past dir.). Republican. Club: Rotary. Home: 1300 Propsect Dr Redlands CA 92373 Office: 25271 Barton Rd Loma Linda CA 92354

COTTON, LINDA ANN, company official; b. Gloversville, N.Y., Mar. 31, 1944; d. August and Christine (Iavarone) Minasi; children: Robin Cotton, Jamie Cotton. BA in Psychology, U. So. Calif., 1971. Psychologist/social worker VA Hosp., Albany, N.Y., 1971-75; v.p. Gold Co., Jeddah, Saudi Arabia, 1975-80; project mgr. Diamond Diversified Ltd., Sao Paulo, Brazil, 1980-83, Cotton Enterprises, Aspen, Colo., 1979—; tchr./lectr./counselor, Colo. Mountain Coll., Aspen, 1981-85. Bd. dirs. Les Dames d'Aspen, 1983-86; pres. bd. dirs., Grass Roots TV Network, Aspen, 1984-86. Mem. Nat. Assn. Female Execs., Am. Arbitration Assn. Roman Catholic. Home and office: 0412 Summit Dr Carbondale CO 81623

COUCH, GEORGE WALTER, III, beverage distributor; b. Washington, Sept. 22, 1947; s. George W. Jr. and Geraldine Catherine (Glockner) C. AB in Econs., Stanford U., 1969; MBA, Harvard U., 1971. Securities analyst Fidelity Mgmt., Boston, 1971-73; chmn., pres. Couch Distbg. Co., Watsonville, Calif., 1973—; bd. dirs. Trammell Crow Hotel, Dallas, 1984-87. Chmn. governing bd. Cabrillo Community Coll., Aptos, Calif., 1985-87, mem. governing bd., 1985—; bd. govs. State Bar of Calif., 1982-85; bd. dirs. Santa Cruz Soc. for the Prevention of Cruelty to Animals, 1988—. Mem. Calif. Beer and Wine Wholesalers Assn. (bd. dirs. 1984—, vice chair 1988), Phi Beta Kappa. Democrat. Home: 100 Merk Rd Watsonville CA 95076 Office: Couch Distbg Co Inc 104 Lee Rd PO Box 183 Watsonville CA 95077

COUCH, JOHN CHARLES, diversified company executive; b. Bremerton, Wash., May 10, 1939; s. Richard Bailey and Frances Harriet (Gilmore) C. BS in Engring., U. Mich., 1963, MS, 1964; MBA, Stanford U., 1976. With Ingalls Shipbldg. div. Litton Industries, 1967-74; exec. v.p. Alexander and Baldwin Inc., Honolulu, 1976-85; asst. to sr. v.p. engring. and marine ops. Matson Navigation Co. subs. Alexander and Baldwin., San Francisco, 1976-84, exec. v.p., chief operating officer, 1984; pres., chief operating officer Alexander and Baldwin Inc., Honolulu, 1985-88; pres., chief exec. officer Alexander and Baldwin Hawaii Inc., Honolulu, 1989—; pres., chief operating officer Matson Navigation Co., 1985; bd. dirs. A&B Devel. Co., Calif., A&B Properties, Inc., Alanui Corp., East Maui Irrigation Co., Ltd., Kahului Trucking & Storage, Inc., McBryde Sugar Co., Ltd., Ohanui Corp., Princess Orchards, Wailea Devel. Co., Inc., WDCI Inc., Calif. and Hawaiian Sugar Co., First Hawaiian Bank, Hawaiian Sugar Transp. Co., Inc., Hawaiian Western Steel, Ltd. Bd. dirs. Kauai Econ. Devel. Bd., 1985—, Maui Econ. Devel. Bd., 1986—; mem. exec. bd. Aloha coun. Boy Scouts Am., 1986—; bd. dirs., mem. exec. com. Aloha United Way, 1988, chmn., 1988. Mem. Hawaiian Sugar Planters' Assn. (bd. dirs. 1985—), C. of C. of Hawaii (bd. dirs. 1986—), Hawaii Bus. Roundtable, Inc., Hawaii Maritime Ctr. (vice-chmn. 1988), Honolulu Club, Oahu Country Club, Plaza Club. Office: Alexander & Baldwin Inc 822 Bishop St Honolulu HI 96813

COUCH, REX DEE, pathologist, medical executive; b. Fairmount, Ind., July 7, 1930; s. James Alva and Velma Elizabeth (Briles) C.; m. Patricia Alice Hynes, Feb. 19, 1955; children: Denis, Philip, Meredith, Patrick, Marie, Brian. AB, Ind. U., 1952; MD, Ind. U., Indpls., 1956. Diplomate Am. Bd. Pathology; cert. anatomic and clin. pathologist, forensic pathologist, Hawaii. Intern Upstate Med. Ctr. SUNY, Syracuse, 1956-57; resident instr. Med. Ctr. Ind. U., Indpls., 1957-58, 60-62; chief of lab. svc. Ft. Sill, Lawton, Okla., 1958-60; asst. to assoc. prof. Coll. of Med. U. Vt., Burlington, Vt., 1962-68; pvt. practice Christie-Couch Prof. Assn., Lancaster, N.H., 1968-75; dir. of lab. G.N. Wilcox Meml. Hosp., Lihue, Hawaii, 1975—; also bd. dirs. G.N. Wilcox Meml. Hosp., Lihue; med. dir. Kauai Med. Group, Lihue, 1975—, also bd. dirs.; bd. dirs. G.N. Wilcox Health Found. Editor Am. Soc. Clin. Pathologists Summary Report, Chgo., 1968—; contbr. articles to profl. jours. Mem. and soloist Kauai Chorale, Lihue, 1975—; bd. dirs. Hale Opio Children's Home, 1975—, Mayors Task Force Substance Abuse, 1984-86, Kauai Community Players, 1975-84. Capt. M.C., U.S. Army, 1958-60. Student fellow Nat. Polio Found., 1954, clin. fellow Am. Cancer Soc., 1960-61: named best actor Kauai Community Players, 1980. Fellow Am. Soc. Clin. Pathologists (bd. dirs. 1970-73, disting. svc. award 1979), Coll. Am. Pathologists, Nat. Assn. Med. Examiners, Am. Acad. Forensic Scis.; mem Hawaii Soc. Pathologists (pres. 1981), Kauai 200. Office: Kauai Med Group 3420 B Kuhio Hwy Lihue HI 96766

COUGHLIN, GEORGE FRANCIS, investment banker; b. Denver, June 4, 1938; s. Walter James and Helen (Long) C.; m. Mildred Wankum, Apr. 4,

1964; children: Mary Pat, Peggy. BA, Regis Coll., Denver, 1960. Exec. v.p. Coughlin & Co. Inc., Denver, 1961—. Bd. dirs. Cath. Community Services, Denver, 1987-88; adv. bd. Samaritan Shelter, Denver, 1986-88. Mem. Pub. Securities Assn., Mcpl. Securities Rulemaking Bd., Colo. Mcpl. Bond Dealers Assn. (pres. 1978), Valley Country Club, Optimists (pres. 1981-83), Ancient Order of Hibernians in Am.

COUGHLIN, KELLY THOMAS, investment information executive; b. Topeka, July 9, 1957; s. Eugene Joseph and Patricia Louise (O'Neil) C.; m. Cynthia McNulty, June 15, 1982. BA in History, Gonzaga U., Spokane, Wash., 1979; postgrad., Monterey Inst. Internat. Stud, 1980-81. Registered investment advisor. Registered rep. Piper Jaffray & Hopwood, Seattle, 1982-83; investment broker Merrill Lynch, Seattle, 1983-87; exec. dir. Investment Info. Svcs., Seattle, 1985—. Editor: (newsletter) Caveat Investor: Let the Investor Beware, 1986--; contbr. articles to newspapers, popular mags. Mem. Seattle Economist Club. Republican. Roman Catholic. Home: 3324 72nd Ave SE Mercer Island WA 98040 Office: 3100 Bank of Calif Ctr Seattle WA 98161

COUGHLIN, MIKE JOSEPH, banker; b. Casper, Wyo., Dec. 24, 1939; s. Pat and Teresa (Reagan) C.; m. Margo L. Nichols; children: Deborah, Stacie. BA, Casper Coll., 1960; MS in Bus. Edn., Black Hills State Coll., Spearfish, S.D., 1962. From loan officer to v.p. loans Security Bank & Trust Co., Casper, 1963-73; sr. v.p. lending div. Am. Nat. Bank, Cheyenne, Wyo., 1973-77; pres., bd. dirs. Equality State Bank, Cheyenne, 1977—, Equality Bankshares, Cheyenne, 1977—; bd. dirs. Pioneer State Bank, Evanston, Wyo., 1st State Bank of Lyman (Wyo.), Equality Bank of Evansville (Wyo.). Pres., bd. dirs. Cheyenne Indsl. Devel. Corp., 1980-86; bd. dirs. Goodwill of Wyo., 1979-82. Served as sgt. U.S. Army, 1962-64. Mem. Cheyenne C. of C. (bd. dirs. 1985—), Wyo. Bankers Assn. (bd. dirs. 1980-83). Republican. Roman Catholic. Club: Cheyenne Country. Lodge: Rotary. Home: 6814 Valley View Cheyenne WY 82009 Office: Equality State Bank 19th & Pioneer Cheyenne WY 82009

COUGHRAN, KENNETH DEAN, electronics company official; b. Pasadena, Calif., July 21, 1960; s. Herbert James and Carol Ruth (Matthews) C.; m. Suzanne Marie Sammons, Feb. 9, 1986. BS in EE, Calif. State U., Long Beach, 1985. Student engr. E & H Electronics, Signal Hill, Calif., 1981-83; research asst. TRW Systems, Redondo Beach, Calif., 1983-84; sales engr. Hewlett-Packard Co., L.A., 1984-85, Calabasas, Calif., 1985—. Mem. Kappa Sigma. Republican. Lutheran. Home: 8217 Birmingham St Bakersfield CA 93311 Office: Hewlett-Packard Co 128 S Gemstone St #E Ridgecrest CA 93555

COULOMBE, ANDRE NORMAND, financial consultant; b. N.Y.C., Oct. 7, 1953; s. Guy C. and Patricia (Collins) C.; m. Joann Marie Carpenter, May 30, 1980; children: Guy Vincent, Charles, Phillip, Nicolas. BA, Calif. State U., Northridge, 1978. Agt. K.C. Ins., New Haven, 1980-87; pres. Phoenix Group, Mission Hills, Calif., 1983—. Campaign mgr., Zerg for Congress, Hollywood, Calif., 1980, 82. Capt. USAR. Fellow Am. Inst. Cert. Fin. Planners (cert.). Republican. Roman Catholic. Office: Phoenix Group Ste 115 11565 Laurel Canyon Blvd Mission Hills CA 71340

COULSON, KINSELL LEROY, meteorologist; b. Hatfield, Mo., Oct. 7, 1916; s. Charles Samuel and Nora Madge (Swank) C.; m. Vera Vivien Vainer, Mar. 23, 1947. B.S., Northwest Mo. State Tchrs. Coll., 1942; M.A., UCLA, 1952, Ph.D., 1959. Jr. meteorologist U.S. Weather Bur., Chgo., 1942; meteorologist UN, Shanghai, China, 1946-47, Naval Civil Service, China Lake, Calif., 1950-51; assoc. research meteorologist UCLA, 1951-59; meteorologist Stanford Research Inst., Menlo Park, Calif., 1959-60; mgr. geophysics Gen. Electric Space Scis. Lab., Phila., 1960-65; prof. meteorology U. Calif., Davis, 1965-79, prof. emeritus, 1984—; dir. Mauna Loa Obs., Hilo, Hawaii, 1979-84; cons., lectr. Author: Polarization and Intensity of Light in the Atmosphere, 1988, Solar and Terrestrial Radiation: Methods and Measurements, 1975, (with J.V. Dave and Z. Sekera) Tables Related to Radiation Emerging, From a Planetary Atmosphere with Rayleigh Scattering, 1960; contbr. articles to profl. jours.; patentee atmospheric density calulator. Served with USN, 1943-46. Recipient numerous research grants. Fellow Am. Meteorol. Soc.; mem. Am. Geophys. Union, Am. Solar Energy Soc., AAAS, No. Calif. Energy Assn., Planetary Soc., Mauna Kea Astron. Soc., Sigma Xi. Home: 119 Bryce Way Vacaville CA 95688

COUNELIS, JAMES STEVE, higher education educator; b. Streator, Ill., June 26, 1927; s. Steve and Mary (Drivas) C.; m. Anna Catherine Marakas, Nov. 25, 1962; children: Steven George, George James. AA, Chgo. City Jr. Coll., 1948; AM, U. Chgo., 1951, PhD, 1961. Cert. high sch., jr. coll. tchr., pub. sch. principal, Ill. High sch. tchr. Chgo. Pub. Schs., 1951-55; asst. prof. history and social scis. Chgo. City Jr. Coll., Woodrow Wilson br., 1955-62, dir. evening program, 1962-64; asst. prof. edn. Chgo Tchrs. Coll., 1964-66; assoc. prof. edn. Pa. State U., University Park, 1966-67; sr. adminstrv. analyst U. Calif., Berkeley, 1968-70; prof. edn. U. San Francisco, 1970—, dir. instl. studies and mgmt. info. systems, 1971-75, coord. evaluation Sch. Edn., 1986—, chmn. orgn. and leadership program, 1989—. Author, editor: To Be a Phoenix: The Education Professoriate, 1969; contbr. articles, reviews and papers to profl. publs. pres., trustee Greek Orthodox Ch. of the Ascension, Oakland, Calif., 1973; pres. Hellenic Am. Profl. Soc., San Francisco, 1974, 75; trustee tenure Hellenic Coll./Holy Cross, 1951-53, trustee, 1982-86; mem. Calif. Council on Criminal Justice, 1987; bd. dirs. Paul Wattson Lecture series, 1989. Served with Signal Corps, U.S. Army, 1946-47. Recipient Archon Chartoularius (honoris causa) award Ecumenical Patriarchate of Canstantinople and New Rome, 1976, Norbert Wiener award The World Orgn. Gen. Systems and Cybernetics, 1978, Scholar U. Chgo., 1951, 52, 60-61, Pacific Sch. Religion, 1958; U. Calif., Berkeley grantee, 1962; Coolidge Research fellow Andover-Newton Theol. Sch., 1985, Wayne J. Doyle Research award, 1986. Mem. AAAS, Am. Assn. Instl. Research, Am. Ednl. Research Assn., Am. Ednl. Studies Assn., Am. Evaluation Assn., Hellenic Am. Profl. Soc. (Axion award 1982), Orthodox Theol Soc. Am., Soc. Gen. Systems Research, U. San Francisco Faculty Assn., Mensa, Gold Key, Phi Delta Kappa. Office: U San Francisco Sch Edn San Francisco CA 94117-1080

COURT, ALLEN HENRY, banker; b. Bklyn., June 15, 1942; s. Henry John and Ellen (Jack) C. BS in Bus. Adminstrn., Norwich U., 1964; MBA, Pepperdine U., 1980; grad. Pacific Coast Banking Sch. U. Wash., 1988. Sr. credit analyst Mfrs. Hanover Trust Co., N.Y.C., 1966-71; loan officer Union Bank, Los Angeles, 1971-74; v.p., mgr. Toronto Dominion Bank, Irvine, Calif., 1974-80; sr. v.p., mgr. regional office Mitsui Mfrs. Bank, Newport Beach, Calif., 1980-86; sr. v.p., divisional mgr. Calif. div. Mitsui Mfrs. Bank Corp. Hdqrs., Los Angeles, 1986-87; regional v.p. Imperial Bank, Los Angeles, 1987—. Mem. Friends of Sherman Library and Gardens, Corona Del Mar, Calif., 1980—; mem. benefactors com. South Coast Repertory, Costa Mesa, Calif., 1980-84. Served to 1st lt. U.S. Army, 1964-66. Mem. Robert Morris Assocs. Republican. Episcopalian. Clubs: Big Canyon Country, Jonathan, Balboa Bay, Pacific. Home: 163 Tangelo Irvine CA 92720

COURT, ARNOLD, climatologist; b. Seattle, June 20, 1914; s. Nathan Altshiller and Sophie (Ravitch) C.; m. Corinne H. Feibelman, May 27, 1941 (dec. Feb. 1984); children: David, Lois, Ellen; m. Mildred Futor Berry, Apr. 6, 1988. BA, U. Okla., 1934; postgrad., U. Wash., 1938, MS, 1949; PhD, U. Calif., Berkeley, 1956. Reporter and city editor Duncan (Okla.) Banner, 1935-38; observer, meteorologist U.S. Weather Bur., Albuquerque, Washington, Little Am., Los Angeles, 1938-43; chief meteorologist U.S. Antarctic Service, 1939-41; climatologist office Q.M. Gen. U.S. Army, Washington, 1946-51; research meteorologist U. Calif., Berkeley, 1951-56; meteorologist U.S. Forest Service, Berkeley, 1956-60; chief applied climatology, Cambridge Research Labs. USAF, Bedford, Mass., 1960-62; sr. scientist Lockheed-Calif. Co., Burbank, 1962-65; prof. climatology San Fernando Valley State Coll. (now Calif. State U.), Northridge, 1962-85, chmn. dept. geography, 1970-72, prof. emeritus, 1985—; part-time prof. Calif. State U., Northridge, 1986-87, UCLA, 1987-88. Editor: Eclectic Climatology, 1968; assoc. editor Jour. Applied Meteorology, 1978-88; chmn. editorial bd. Jour. Weather Modification, 1978-86; contbr. articles and revs. to profl. jours. Served to 1st lt. USAAF, 1943-46. Recipient Spl. Congl. medal, 1944. Fellow AAAS, Am. Meteorol. Soc., Royal Meteorol. Soc.; mem. Am. Geophys. Union, Am. Statis. Assn., Assn. Am. Geographers, Assn. Pacific Coast Geographers (pres. 1978-79), Calif. Geog. Soc., Weather Modification Assn. (trustee 1973-76), Western Snow Conf., Sigma Xi, Phi Beta Kappa. Home: 17168 Septo St Northridge CA 91325 Office: Calif State U Dept Geography Northridge CA 91330

COURTNEY, ROBERT LYLE, recreation director; b. Culver City, Calif., Apr. 10, 1963; s. George Clifford and Karen Ann (Curry) C. BA in Psychology, Calif. State U., Northridge, 1985; MS in Recreation Adminstrn., Calif. State U., 1986. Outpost camping dir. The Firs, Bellingham, Calif., 1983; waterfront dir. The Firs, Bellingham, 1984; sr. high program dir. Canoga Park (Calif.) Presbyn. Ch., 1984-85; recreation leader Conejo Recreation and Park Dist., Thousand Oaks, Calif., 1986-87; asst. aquatic dir. UCLA, 1987-88; aquatics dir. City of Oakland, Calif., 1988—; mem. conservation com. Calif. Park and Recreation Soc., Oakland, Calif., 1988—. Active Greenpeace, 1984-88; campus connection dir. Calvary Community Ch., Thousand Oaks. Mem. Calif. Park and Recreation Soc., Bay Area Pub. Pool Operator Assn., Wilderness Soc. (advocate 1985-88). Republican.

COURTNEY, SUSAN LYNNE, state official; b. N.Y.C., Jan. 31, 1948; d. Milton Charles and Beatrice Emily (Fritsch) Rey; m. Kenneth Harold Kasner, May 21, 1976 (div. 1985); children: Rachel Shane, Daniel Troy; m. Charles Edward Courtney, Feb. 7, 1987. BA in Social Sci., SUNY, Binghamton, 1969; MA in Counseling, Lewis & Clark Coll., Portland, 1981. Caseworker Broome County Dept. Social Svcs., Binghamton, N.Y., 1969-70, Wash. Dept. Social and Health Svcs., Colfax, 1970-74; foster care recruiter and trainer Region IV Dept. Health and Welfare, Boise, Idaho, 1975-77; intern Morrison Ctr./YWCA, Portland, Oreg., 1980-81; instr. Portland State U., 1982-84; placement support coord. Ariz. Women's Employment & Edn., Phoenix, 1984-86; tng. officer Ariz. Dept. Transp., Phoenix, 1986-88; tng. mgr. Ariz. State U., Temple, 1988—; mem. adj. faculty Rio Saludo Community Coll., Phoenix, 1988—. Mem. subcom. Phoenix Women's Commn.-Women in Transition, 1985-86; liaison and facilitator Parent Child Devel. Coun. Oreg., Portland, 1983-84. Mem. Ariz. Career Devel. Assn. (v.p. programming 1988), Am. Soc. Tng. and Devel. (v.p. mem. svcs. 1989), Ariz. Women's Initiative. Democrat. Home: 2438 W Evans Dr Phoenix AZ 85023 Office: Ariz State U Pers Dept Tng and Devel Phoenix AZ 85287-1403

COURTOT, PHILIPPE FREDERIC, service executive; b. Dax, France, Aug. 26, 1944; came to, U.S., 1980; s. Raymond Alexis and Jacqueline (Dupeyroux) C.; m. Mai Phuong Nguyen, June 9, 1969; children: Frederic, Nicolas. BS, U. Paris, 1966, M in Physics, 1968. Engr. Motorola Dee, Paris, 1970-73; gen. mgr. Modcomp France, Paris, 1973-76; sales and mktg. mgr. Modcomp Europe, London, 1977-79; gen. mgr. Modcomp Internat., Ft. Lauderdale, Fla., 1980-82; dir. mktg. Modcomp Corp., Ft. Lauderdale, Fla., 1983-84; pres., chief exec. officer Thomson CGR Med. Corp., Columbia, Md., 1985-87; exec. v.p. ADAC Lab., Milpitas, Calif., 1987-89; pres., chief exec. office CC:Mail, Inc., Palo Alta, CA, 1989—. Named to Benjamin Franklin Soc. Saturday Evening Post, 1987. Mem. Nat. Elec. Mfg. Assn. (bd. dirs. 1985—). Home: 757 Tennyson Ave Palo Alto CA 94303

COVAULT, STEPHEN GERARD, software engineer; b. Atlanta, Nov. 12, 1961; s. Donald Orville and Donna Marie (Hendrickson) C. BS in Computer Sci., So. Tech. Inst., Marietta, Ga., 1985. Product tech. mgr. CACI Products Co. (formerly CACI-Fed., Inc.), La Jolla, Calif., 1985—. Author various computer software. Mem. IEEE, Assn. for Computing Machinery. Office: CACI Products Co 3344 N Torrey Pines Ct La Jolla CA 92037

COVELL, RALPH RULUF, seminary dean, educator; b. Redondo Beach, Calif., Dec. 23, 1922; s. Ruluf Alexander and Cora (Schwarzkopf) C.; m. Ruth Frieda Laube, May 26, 1950; children: Kenneth, Ronald, Wayne. BA, Ea. Bapt. Coll., 1944; BD, Ea. Bapt. Sem., 1946; ThM, Fuller Sem., 1964; MA, U. Denver, 1970, PhD, 1975; DD (hon.), Denver Sem., 1964. Missionary Conservative Bapt. Fgn. Mission Soc., Wheaton, Ill., 1946-66; professor, dean Denver Sem., 1966—; cons. Bible Soc. Taiwan, Taipei, 1964-66. Author: W.A.P. Martin--Pioneer of Progress in China, 1978; Confucius, The Buddha and Christ, 1986; co-author: Extension Seminary Primer, 1970; transl. New Testament into Sediq, 1963. Mem. Assn. Profs. of Mission, Internat. Assn. of Mission, Am. Soc. Missiology (editor jour. 1982-88). Home: 1913 S Michigan Way Denver CO 80219 Office: Denver Sem PO Box 10000 Denver CO 80210

COWAN, ARNOLD MARTON, lawyer; b. L.A., Nov. 21, 1921; s. Samuel Sydney and Irene Edith (Kessler) C.;m. Rebecca Corona, Jan. 16, 1943; children: Thomas Benjamin, Kenneth Daniel. BA, UCLA, 1941; JD, U. So. Calif., L.A., 1948. Bar: Calif. 1948, U.S. Dist. Ct. 1948, U.S. Supreme Ct. 1977. Pvt. practice Redondo Beach, Calif., 1948—; elected city atty. Redondo Beach, 1961-65; judge pro tem Torrence, Calif., 1950-80; judge advocate King Harbor Yacht Club, Redondo Beach, 1948-55. Contbr. articles to profl. jours. Democratic organizer, candidate, Redondo Beach, 1948-80; bd. dirs. Catalina Conservancy-Marinero, Catalina Island, Calif., 1980—. With USN, 1941-45, PTO, ETO. Mem. Am. Numismatic Assn. (merit award 1987), Confederate Stamp Alliance, Paper Money Collectors, Civil War Token Soc., Long Beach Yacht Club (judge advocate 1972-74, sec., bd. dirs., port capt. 1989). Jewish. Home: 35 Vista Del Golfo Long Beach CA 90803

COWAN, BRIAN JOSEPH, naval officer; b. Rochester, N.Y., May 21, 1957; s. Joseph Patrick and Anne Marie (Fintak) C.; m. Patricia Eileen Hall, July 29, 1978; 1 child, Joseph Patrick. BS in Bus., U. Colo., 1979; postgrad. bus. adminstrn., George Washington U., 1983-85. Commd. officer USN, 1979, advanced through grades to lt., 1983; supply officer USS Knox (FF-1052), Yokosuka, Japan, 1980-82; contract negotiator Naval Sea Systems Command, Washington, 1983-85, bus. and fin. mgr., 1985-86; stock control officer USS Constellation (CV-64), San Francisco, 1986-88; inventory mgr., insp. Commd. Naval Air Forces Pacific Fleet, San Diego, 1988—. Mem. Nat. Contracts Mgmt. Assn. Republican. Roman Catholic. Home: 736 F Ave Apt 5 Coronado CA 92118 Office: Commd Naval Air Forces Pacific Fleet Naval Air Sta North Island San Diego CA 92135

COWAN, RICHARD JOHN, cattle rancher; b. Chgo., July 17, 1921; s. Percy and Jean (Feldman) C.; m. Helen Ann Cran, June 15, 1947; children: Cran, Clifford. AB, Princeton U., 1942. Freelance cattle buyer Phoenix, 1946-49; section boss Parker Ranch, Kamaela, Hawaii, 1949-50; owner, operator SunTex Ranch, Riley, Oreg., 1950—. Mem., chmn. Harney County Hosp. Bd., Burns, Oreg., 1963-74, Burns Union High Sch. Bd., 1974-83. Capt. USAF, 1942-46. Mem. Nat. Cattlemens Assn. (various coms. 1985-88, promotion and rsch. bd. 1986-89), Oreg. Cattlemens Assn. (v.p. 1977-79), Oreg. Beef Council (chmn. 1980-88). Republican. Christian Scientist. Home and Office: SunTex Ranch Riley OR 97758

COWAN, STUART MARSHALL, lawyer; b. Irvington, N.J., Mar. 20, 1932; s. Bernard Howard and Blanche (Hertz) C.; m. Marilyn R.C. Toepfer, Apr., 1961 (div. 1969); m. Jane Alison Averill, Feb. 24, 1974; children—Catherine R.L., Erika R.L., Bronwen P. B.S. in Econ., U. Pa., 1952; LL.B., Rutgers U., 1955. Bar: N.J. 1957, Hawaii 1962, U.S. Supreme Ct., 1966. Atty., Greenstein & Cowan, Honolulu, 1961-70, Cowan & Frey, Honolulu, 1970—; arbitration Fed. Mediation & Conciliation Service, Honolulu, 1972—, Am. Arbitation Assn., Honolulu, 1978—, Hawaii Pub. Employees. Relation Bd., 1972—. Served to lt. USN, 1956-61. Mem. Hawaii Bar Assn., ABA, Am. Judicature Soc., Trial Lawyers Assn. of Am. (state committeeman for Hawaii 1965-69, bd. govs. 1972-75), Hawaii Trial Lawyers Assn. (v.p. 1972-78), Japan-Hawaii Lawyers Assn., Soc. Profls. in Dispute Resolution. Jewish. Clubs: Waikiki Yacht (Honolulu), San Francisco Comml., Hawaii Scottish Assn. (chieftain 1983-88), Caledonian Soc. (vice chieftain 1983-85), St. Francis Yacht, Honolulu Club, Honolulu Pipes and Drums (sec.-treas. 1985-88). Lodges: Masons, Pearl Harbor (master 1971), Composite. Home: 47-339 Mapumapu Rd Kaneohe HI 96744 Office: Cowan & Frey 1600 Grosvenor Ctr Towers 733 Bishop St Honolulu HI 96813

COWDEN, JOANNA D(UNLAP), history educator; b. Chico, Calif., Feb. 9, 1933; d. Chesley M. and Helen C. (Cummings) Dunlap; m. George R. Cowden, Jan. 15, 1955 (div. 1972); children: Jean Cowden Moore, Sandra Cowden Johnson, Rebecca, Jennifer. AB, Radcliffe Coll., 1955; MA, Trinity Coll., Hartford, Conn., 1965; PhD, U. Conn., 1975. Lectr. in history U. Conn., Storrs, 1969-73; prof. history Calif. State U., Chico, 1973—; mem. Commn. on Bicentennial of the U.S. Constn., 1987. Contbr. articles to profl. jours. Grantee NEH, 1984. Mem. Assn. for Study of Conn. History, Orgn. Am. Historians, Western Assn. Women Historians. Home: 1455 Salem St Chico CA 95928 Office: Calif State U Dept History Chico CA 95929

COWDEN, ROBERT HAPGOOD, music educator; b. Warren, Pa., Nov. 18, 1934; s. Wallace Hapgood and Astrid Marguerite (Sundelof) C.; m. Jacqueline Vivienne Mailloux, Nov. 26, 1959; children: Jonathan, Jennifer, Marc, Adrienne. BA, Princeton U., 1956; MusB, U. Rochester, 1959, MusM, 1960, D of Mus. Arts, 1966. Prin. artist Stadttheater, Hildesheim, Fed. Republic Germany, 1963-65, Met. Opera Nat. Co., N.Y.C., 1965-66; asst. prof. music Jacksonville (Fla.) U., 1966-68; dir. Lyric Theater program Wayne State U., Detroit, 1968-71, dir. fine arts, 1970-74; chmn. dept. music U. Nebr., Omaha, 1974-76; prof. music San Jose (Calif.) State U., 1976—, chmn. dept., 1976-82; chmn. div. music Calif. State Summer Sch. for the Arts, Sacramento, 1987—; mem. adv. bd. Montalvo Ctr. for the Arts, Saratoga, Calif., 1980—. Author: (Bibliography of Biographical Materials series) Concert and Opera Singers, 1985, Concert and Opera Conductors, 1987, Instrumental Virtuosi, 1989; contbr. articles to Opera, MLA Notes, Opera Jour., NATS Bull. Grantee NEH, 1987; fellow NEH, 1985; Fulbright scholar, 1961-63. Episcopalian. Office: San Jose State U Dept Music Washington Sq San Jose CA 95192

COWELL, ERNEST SAUL, lighting designer, consultant; b. Hollywood, Calif., Jan. 27, 1927; s. Ernest S. and Bernice Michael (Waterman) C.; m. Beverly Sue Bloom, Apr. 15, 1950 (div. May 1960); children: Steven Richard, Craig Wesley, Marilyn Tobiann. BA, UCLA, 1950; student, Moorpark Coll., 1971, Cerritos Jr. Coll., 1979. Regional mgr. Prentice Hall Inc., San Francisco, 1954-59; pvt. practice indsl. and govtl. sales L.A., 1959-70; area mgr. Philips Lighting, L.A., 1970-79; v.p. Coons & Cowell Lighting Unltd., Thousand Oaks, Calif., 1979-83; pres. Lighting Designs, Thousand Oaks, 1983—; cons. City of Thousand Oaks, 1970—. Mem. Rep. Presdl. Task Force, 1978—; founder, pres. Sunset Hills Homeowners Assn., Thousand Oaks, 1968-69; pres. Conejo Valley Homeowners Assns., Thousand Oaks, 1970; chmn. City of Thousand Oaks Housing Mix Com., 1973; mem. gen. plan com. City of Thousand Oaks, 1967, gen. plan rev. com. City of Thousand Oaks, 1984, 86, 88. Sgt. U.S. Army, 1943-46, PTO; with USNR, 1950-58, 70—. Recipient Edison award Excellence in Lighting, Gen. Electric Corp., 1985, 86. Fellow Inst. Advancement Engring.; mem. Illuminating Engring. Soc. (bd. dirs. So. Calif. sect. 1977-85, nat. chmn. schs and colls. lighting standards com. 1984—, residential lighting standards com. 1985—, Internat. Illumination Design award 1983, 84, 85, 87), Internat. Assn. Lighting Designers, U.S. Nat. Com. to Internat. Commn. Illumination, Library Lighting Standards (nat. chmn. 1988—), Designers Lighting Forum (bd. dirs. 1988—), Internat. Soc. Interior Designers (design affiliate), Am. Soc. Interior Designers (allied affilate), Navy League, Roadway Lighting Forum (bd. dirs. 1988—), Kiwanis (pres. Westlake Village club 1977-79). Office: Lighting Designs PO Box 2061 Thousand Oaks CA 91360-0915

COWEN, DONALD EUGENE, physician; b. Ft. Morgan, Colo., Oct. 8, 1918; adopted s. Franklin and Mary Edith (Dalton) C.; B.A., U. Denver, 1940; M.D., U. Colo., 1943; m. Hulda Marie Helling, Dec. 24, 1942; children—David L., Marilyn Marie Cowen Dean, Theresa Kathleen Cowen Cunningham, Margaret Ann Cowen Koenigs. Intern, U.S. Naval Hosp., Oakland, Calif., 1944; gen. practice medicine, Ft. Morgan, 1947-52; resident internal medicine U. Colo. Med. Center, Denver, 1952-54; practice medicine specializing in allergy, Denver, 1954—; mem. staff Presbyn. Med. Center, Denver, Porter, Swedish hosps., Englewood, Colo.; clin. asst. prof. medicine U. Colo. Med. Center, 1964—; postgrad. faculty U. Tenn. Coll. Medicine, Memphis, 1962-82; cons. Queen of Thailand, 1973, 75, 77. Pres. Community Arts Symphony Found., 1980-82. Served to lt. M.C., USN, 1943-47. Fellow ACP, Am. Coll. Chest Physicians (vice chmn. com. on allergy 1968-72, 75-87, sec.-treas. Colo. chpt. 1971-77, pres. 1978-80), Am. Coll. Allergy and Immunology, Acad. Internat. Medicine, West Coast Allergy Soc., Southwest Allergy Forum, Am. Acad. Otolaryngic Allergy, Colo. socs. internal medicine, Colo. Allergy Soc. (past pres.), Ill. Soc. Opthalmology and Otolaryngology (hon.), Denver Med. Soc. (chmn. library and bldg. com. 1963-73), Arapahoe Med. Soc. (life emeritus mem.). Presbyterian (ruling elder 1956—). Club: Lions. Contbr. numerous articles to profl. jours. Home: 1501 E Quincy Ave Cherry Hills Village Englewood CO 80110 Office: 3510 S Marion St Englewood CO 80110

COWGER, PHYLLIS, nurse; b. San Antonio, Sept. 12, 1944; d. Russell and Mildred Marie (Hamilton) Austin; m. Robert F. Cowger, Dec. 31, 1964; children: Rhonda, Teresa, Russell, Phillip, Robert II. Diploma in Nursing, Cochise Coll., Douglas, Ariz., 1985. Lic. practical nurse, Ariz. Nurse Benson Hosp., Ariz., 1985-86; charge nurse Life Care Sierra Vista, Ariz., 1986-87; nurse Sierra Vista Care Ctr., 1987--. Com. mem. Sierra Vista council Boy Scouts Am. Nursing dept. grantee Cochise Coll., 1986. Democrat. Presbyterian. Home: 771 Tacoma Pl Sierra Vista AZ 85635

COWLES, DAVID LYLE, educator; b. Forks, Wash., Sept. 1, 1955; s. Lyle Kenneth and Cora Marjorie (Kaemmle) C.; m. Linda Ann Kreye, July 28, 1980; children: Jonathan, Joanna. BS, Walla Walla Coll., 1978, MS, 1981; PhD, U. Calif., Santa Barbara, 1987. Secondary sci. tchr. Dakota Adventist Acad., Bismarck, N.D., 1980-82; asst. rsch. biologist U. Calif., Santa Barbara, 1983-87; asst. prof. Loma Linda U., Riverside, Calif., 1987—; microcomputer cons. Loma Linda U., 1988. Earle C. Anthony fellow, 1983; Internat. Women's Fishing Assn. grantee, 1984-86. Mem. AAAS, Am. Soc. Zoologists, Am. Soc. Limnology and Oceanography, Sigma Xi. Adventist. Office: Loma Linda U Dept Biology Riverside CA 92515-8247

COWLES, WILLIAM HUTCHINSON, III, newspaper publisher; b. Spokane, Wash., Mar. 4, 1932; s. William Hutchinson and Margaret (Paine) C.; m. Allison Stacey, Mar. 28, 1959; children: William Stacey, Elizabeth Allison. BA, Yale U., 1953; JD, Harvard U., 1959. Bar: Wash. 1959. Pres., pub. Cowles Pub. Co. (pubs. The Spokesman-Rev., Spokane Chronicle), N.W. Farmer-Stockman, Inc. (pubs. Wash. Farmer-Stockman, Oreg. Farmer-Stockman, Idaho Farmer-Stockman, Utah Farmer-Stockman), Spokane, 1970—, Mont. Farmer-Stockman, Inc. (pubs. Mont. Farmer-Stockman), Billings, 1970—; v.p., dir. Inland Empire Paper Co., Millwood, Wash., 1964—; dir. AP, 1974-83, 1st vice chmn., 1982-83, dir. Am. Newspaper Publs. Assn., 1980—, chmn., 1989-90, dir. Newspaper Advt. Bur., 1968—, chmn., 1978-80, dir. Allied Daily Newspapers, 1970-71, pres., 1972-74. Bd. dirs. Inland Empire council Boy Scouts Am., 1960—, Spokane Symphony Soc., 1962-78, United Crusade Spokane County, 1963-74, pres., 1970; bd. overseers Whitman Coll., 1966—; fellow Yale Corp., 1984—. Lt. USNR, 1953-56. Mem. Am. Soc. Newspaper Editors, Spokane Club, Spokane Area C. of C. (chmn. 1987-88), Beta Theta Pi, Sigma Delta Chi. Office: The Spokesman-Rev & Spokane Chronicle W 999 Riverside Ave Spokane WA 99201

COWPER, STEPHEN CAMBRELENG, governor of Alaska, lawyer; b. Petersburg, Va., Aug. 21, 1938; s. Marion Cowper and Stephanie Smith; m. Michael Margaret Stewart; children: Katherine, Grace, Wade. BA, U. N.C., 1960, JD, 1963. Sole practice Norfolk, Va.; asst. dist. atty. State of Alaska, Fairbanks, 1968-70; ptnr. Cowper & Madson, Fairbanks, 1971-84; mem. legislature Alaska Ho. of Reps., Fairbanks and Juneau, 1974-78; Gov. State of Alaska, Juneau, 1986—. Columnist Alaska newspapers, 1979-80, 85; author: (documentary film) A Trail to Break-A History of Alaska Lands, 1979. Mem. Alaska Native Brotherhood Klawock Camp, Eielson Area Grange, Fairbanks. Served with U.S. Army, 1960. Democrat. Episcopalian. Club: Sundawgs Rugby. Office: Office of Gov PO Box A Juneau AK 99811

COX, ALBERTA LEE, communications executive; b. Palisade, Nebr., Apr. 22, 1932; d. Grover Cleveland and Fern Avis (Pratt) Kunze; m. Stanton Lytle Cox, Oct. 31, 1953. AA, Stockton Coll., 1951. Tech. writer, editor Dugway (Utah) Proving Ground, 1960-63; head project and publs. div. Naval Weapons Ctr., China Lake, Calif., 1963-82; head publs. NASA Ames Rsch. Ctr., Moffett Field, Calif., 1982—; instr. Calif. Community Colls., Kern County, Calif., 1981-83; exec. bd. Jour. of Tech. Writing and Communication (Baywood), Farmingdale, N.Y., 1978-84. Contbg. author: Handbook of Technical Writing, 1971; contbr. articles to Technical Communication jour., 1981-86. Named Fed. Woman of Yr., Naval Weapons Ctr., China Lake, 1977. Fellow, Inst. Advancement of Engring., Soc. for Tech. Communication (pres. 1980-81, past bd. dirs.). Home: 121

Promethean Way Mountain View CA 94043 Office: NASA Ames Research Ctr MS 241-13 Moffett Field CA 94035

COX, ANDREW BRIAN, mechanical engineer; b. Teague, Tex., Mar. 24, 1950; s. Jack Ray and Lillian Emily (Shutt) C.; m. Mary Ann Baker, Aug. 12, 1972; children: Emily, Julia, Katherine. BME, Rice U., 1972, MME, 1973; PhD, Stanford U., 1979. Mem. tech. staff def. and space systems group TRW Inc., Redondo Beach, Calif., 1973-75, staff engr., 1978-81; mem. tech. staff Sandia Nat. Labs., Albuquerque, 1981—. Contbr. articles to profl. jours. TRW fellow, 1975-78. Fellow AIAA (assoc., guidance and control tech. com. 1980-83, sect. chmn. 1982-83); mem. ASME (assoc.), Nat. Space Soc. Republican. Baptist. Office: Sandia Nat Labs PO Box 5800 Albuquerque NM 87185

COX, C. CHRISTOPHER, congressman, lawyer; b. St. Paul, Oct. 16, 1952; s. Charles C. and Marilyn A. (Miller) C. BA, U. So. Calif., 1973; MBA, JD, Harvard U., 1977. Bar: Calif. 1978, D.C. 1980. Law clk. to judge U.S. Ct. Appeals (9th cir.), 1977-78; assoc. Latham & Watkins, Newport Beach, Calif., 1978-85, ptnr., 1985-86; sr. assoc. counsel to the Pres. The White House, Washington, 1986-88; mem. 101st Congress from 40th Dist. Calif., Washington, DC, 1989—; prin., founder Context Corp., St. Paul, 1984-86; lectr. bus. adminstrn. Harvard U., 1982-83. Editor Harvard U. Law Rev., 1975-77. Bd. govs. Rep. Assocs. Orange County, Calif., 1985-86. Republican. Roman Catholic. Home: 4000 MacArthur Blvd E Tower Ste 403 Newport Beach CA 92660 Office: US Ho of Reps 510 Cannon Bldg Washington DC 20515

COX, CLARK BURGESS, dentist; b. St. George, Utah, Feb. 23, 1929; s. Emerald Lane and Elsie (Burgess) C.; Asso. Sci., Dixie Jr. Coll., 1949; D.D.S., U. So. Calif., 1953; PhD in Environ Sci., K.W. U., 1986; m. Donna Anderson, July 15, 1949; children—David C., Craig E., Suzanne, Dianne, Gary L., Cynthia. Practice dentistry, Delta, Utah, 1955—; v.p. Habb Corp., Delta, 1962—, Cox Trucking Inc., Delta, 1976—; farmer, livestock rancher, 1960—; dir. Del-Tex Corp., Oasis Seed Corp.; partner Fransworth-Cox Real Estate, C&D Indsl. Minerals; environ. cons. R&C Environ. Services; vice chmn. W. Millard Soil Conservation Service, 1970-76. City councilman, Delta, 1968-76, mem. bd. adjustment, 1978—. Served with Dental Corps, AUS, 1953-55. Mem. Acad. Gen. Dentistry, Am., Utah, Provo Dist. dental assns., Brigham Young U. Acad. Dentists (charter), Alpha Tau Epsilon, Psi Omega. Mem. Ch. Jesus Christ of Latter-day Saints (Delta 2d ward bishopric 1962-65, high councilor Delta West stake). Home: RFD Delta PO Box 695 Delta UT 84624 Office: Hobb Bldg Main St Delta UT 84624

COX, DARRYL, political consultant; b. San Francisco, Jan. 18, 1949; s. C. Charles and Edna Lee (Bradley) C. BA in Humanities, New Coll. Calif., 1975; M of Pub. Adminstrn., Harvard U., 1986. Program dir. La Posada House, San Francisco, 1977-78; coordinator witness services Victim Witness Assistance Program, San Francisco, 1979-80; adminstrv. aide Supr. Nancy G. Walker, San Francisco, 1980-81; dir. Boys Home div. San Francisco Senators, Inc., 1982-83; adminstrv. aide Supr. Willie B. Kennedy, San Francisco, 1984-85; budget analyst County of Santa Clara, 1986-87; prin., polit. cons. Darryl Cox Assocs., San Francisco, 1987—. Mem. Citizen's Adv. Com. on Wastewater Mgmt., 1982, Mayor's Victims of Crimes Study Task Force, San Francisco, 1983; bd. dirs. San Francisco Tomorrow, 1982-83, San Francisco Consumer Action, 1983—. Recipient cert. of honor San Francisco Bd. Suprs., 1985, True Hero award Citizens for Rep. Govt., 1985. Mem. Acad. Polit. Sci., Am. Soc. for Pub. Adminstrn., San Francisco Black Leadership Forum. Democrat. Office: 327 Highland Ave San Francisco CA 94110

COX, DENNIS CHRISTIAN, health care administrator; b. Copenhagen, Denmark, Dec. 25, 1947. BA, U. N. Mex., 1971, MA, 1975, MBA, 1979. Cert. rehab. counselor. Statistician State of N. Mex., Santa Fe, 1971-73, program mgr., 1973-75, program asst. chief, 1975-79, agy. asst. dir., 1979-81; dir. fin. Hosp. Home Health Care, Albuquerque, 1982-83; pres. Home Care Enterprises, Albuquerque, 1984-86, Vocmed Rehab. Svcs., Albuquerque, 1985—; adminstr. Internal and Family Medicine, Albuquerque, 1987—; cons. in field. Office: Internal & Family Medicine 6100 Pan Am Freeway NE #365 Albuquerque NM 87109

COX, GREGORY RICHARDSON, mayor; b. San Diego, July 2, 1948; s. Gordon Barter and Doris Margaret (Richardson) C.; m. Cheryl Sue Willett, Dec. 20, 1975; children: Elizabeth Karin, Emily Anne. BA, San Diego State U., 1970, MA, 1977. Tchr. Montgomery Jr. High Sch., San Diego, 1971-72; dean of activities Bonita Vista High Sch., Chula Vista, 1972-82; city councilman City of Chula Vista, Calif., 1976-81, mayor, 1981—. Pres. League Calif. Cities, Sacramento, 1987-88, bd. dirs. 1984—, pres. San Diego div., 1985-86; bd. dirs. Calif. Couns. Govt., 1988—; chmn. Chula Vista Parks and Recreation Commn., 1974; pres. Chula Vista Rep. Club, 1972, Chula Vista Jaycees, 1974-75; mem. San Diego Bay Cities Bd. Realtors, 1981—; bd. dirs. ARC, San Diego, 1984—, United Way, San Diego, 1983—. Named one of Five Outstanding Californians, Calif. Jaycees, 1982, Man of Yr., Chula Vista Star-News, 1983, 88; recipient Outstanding Citizen award Chula Vista C. of C., 1985, Disting. Service award Chula Vista Jaycees, 1973, 82. Mem. San Diego Assn. Govts. (bd. dirs. 1981—), Theta Chi Alumni Assn. (Disting. Service award 1982). Congregationalist. Lodges: Optimists, Elks, Rotary, Kiwanis. Home: 647 Windsor Circle Chula Vista CA 92010 Office: Office of Mayor 276 4th Ave Chula Vista CA 92010

COX, JAMES DEWITT, airline pilot; b. Farmville, Va., Feb. 16, 1940; s. James Alexander and Martha Clara (Jones) C.; m. Judith Elizabeth Carmichael, June 8, 1963; children: Kathryn Elizabeth, Kimberly Susan. BS in Civil Engring., Va. Mil. Inst., 1962. Civil engr. San Diego County, 1970-78; pilot USAIR, San Diego, 1969—; charter comml. pilot San Diego, 1978-84; check pilot USAIR, San Diego, 1978—. Capt. USAF, 1963-69. Mem. San Diego Yacht Club. Republican. Methodist.

COX, JAMES LEE, computer systems consultant; b. Knoxville, Tenn., Nov. 20, 1935; s. James Watson and Effie Pauline (Wilson) C.; m. Joan Le Marr, June 29, 1959 (div. 1968); children: Patricia Lea, Cynthia Joan; m. Elinor Ruth Emerick, Apr. 30, 1968; 1 child, John Andrew. BA, U. Tenn., 1957. Cert. data processor. Programmer, mgr. nuclear div. Union Carbide Co., Oak Ridge, Tenn., 1956-64; mgr. programming IBM, Hursley, Eng., 1964-67; mgr. computer tech. IBM, Boulder, Colo., 1967-69; prof. European Systems Rsch. Inst. IBM, Geneva, 1970-72; sr. architect IBM, Raleigh, N.C., 1972-73; mgr. architecture IBM, Boulder, 1973-81; mgr. tech. IBM, Fujisawa, Japan, 1981-85; design mgr. IBM, Boulder, 1986-87; pres., systems cons. Cox Cons. Corp., Boulder, 1987—. Home and Office: 2880 16th St Boulder CO 80304

COX, JOHN HENRY, religious organization administrator, aeronautical engineer; b. Dorking, Surrey, Eng., May 17, 1941; s. William Edward and Ethel May (Bailey) C.; m. Elizabeth Mary Iris O'Brien, June 26, 1965; children: Jared Selvoy, Rachel Sonia. Diploma, Southall Coll. Technology, Eng., 1965. Lic. airline engr.; chartered engr. Asst. chief engr. British Airways, Eng., 1965-72, chief engr., 1972-77; national dir. Latter-day Saints Ch., Eng., 1977-83; internat. dir. Latter-day Saints Ch., Salt Lake City, 1983-85, welfare dir., 1985—. Mem. Inst. Mech. Engrs., Royal Aero. Soc., Brit. Inst. Mgmt.

COX, P. THOMAS, economist, consultant; b. Jolietville, Ind., Sept. 21, 1930; s. James William and Opal May (Lytle) C.; m. Mary Louise Dietz, Sept. 16, 1949 (div. Jan. 1976); children: Mary Barbara, Bradley Thomas, Tina Rene; m. Effat Souhani, July 25, 1978. Student, DePauw U., 1948-49; BS, Purdue U., 1962; MS, U. Ariz., 1963; PhD, Okla. State U., 1967. Supervisory economist USDA, Upper Darby, Pa., 1966-70; dir. mgmt. sci. Armour Foods, Phoenix, 1971-74; assoc. prof. food industry Ariz. State U., Tempe, 1975-78; project adminstr. Iranian Ctr. Utah State U., Karaj, Iran, 1978-79; program devel. officer Treas. Office, Riyadh, Saudi Arabia, 1979-80; v.p., mng. dir. Arieb Agr., Riyadh, Saudi Arabia, 1980-84; group v.p. Arieb Devel., Ltd., Riyadh, 1985-86; team leader Ronco Cons. Corp., Jordan, 1987; agrl. economist Libya/Ariz. State U., 1976; team leader USAID, Swaziland, 1977; cons. Cudahy Foods, Phoenix, 1974-75, Nuclear Dynamics, Phoenix, 1974-76. Contbr. articles to profl. jours. Mem. Am. Soc. Agrl. Cons. Internat. (founder 1983), Council for Agrl. Sci. and Tech., Agri-Energy Roundtable (adv. com. 1985-86). Democrat. Methodist. Home: 6620 N 36th St Phoenix AZ 85018

COX, RAYMOND WHITTEN, III, political science educator, academic director; b. Cambridge, Mass., Aug. 21, 1949; s. Raymond Whitten Cox Jr. and Louise Carolyn Holmes; m. Charlene Marie Sharp, Oct. 9, 1975 (div. Jan. 1981); 1 child, Geoffrey; m. Susan Jane Buck, Feb. 5, 1982 (div. 1988). BA, Northeastern U., 1972; M in Pub. Adminstrn., Suffolk U., 1975; PhD, Va. Poly. Inst., 1983. Asst. dir. research Mass. Ho. of Reps., Boston, 1970-77; program dir. NSF, Washington, 1977-82; instr. Va. Poly. Inst., Blacksburg, 1982-83; asst. prof. Bemidji (Minn.) State U., 1983-85; dir. pub. adminstrn. programs No. Ariz. U., Flagstaff, 1985-87; assoc. prof., dir. MPA program N.Mex. State U., 1987—; cons. Beltrami County Welfare Office, Bemidji, 1984-85, Yuma (Ariz.) Econ. Devel. Corp., 1986. Contbr. articles to profl. jours. Mem. exec. com. Beltrami County Dem. Farmer Labor Party, Bemidji, 1984-85; pres. Bemidji Campus United Ministries, 1984-85; mem. Dem. precinct com. Coconino County, Flagstaff, 1985-87, vice chmn. Coconino County Dems., 1987; mem. fund-raising com. No. Ariz. U. Campus Christian Ctr., Flagstaff 1986-87. Recipient Outstanding Performance award Dept. of Def., Hartford, Conn., 1969; named one of Outstanding Young Men of Am., Jaycees, 1981. Mem. Am. Polit. Sci., Acad. Polit. Sci., Wester Polit. Sci. Assn. (chmn. membership com. 1986—), Am. Soc. Pub. Adminstrn. (nat. council 1986—, chmn. profl. devel. com.). Democrat. Episcopal. Home: 199 W Madrid Rd Apt H-1 Las Cruces NM 88005 Office: NMex State U Dept Govt Box 3BN Las Cruces NM 88003

COX, ROBERT STURGEON, JR., English educator; b. Amarillo, Tex., May 19, 1937; s. Robert Sturgeon and Ruthanna (Jackson) C.; m. Patricia Ann Ramer, Apr. 20, 1963; children: Anna, Adam, Joachim, Jesse. BA, No. Ariz. U., 1959; PhD, Indiana U., 1965. Instr. Rice U., Houston, 1964-65; asst. prof. Rice U., 1965-71; assoc. prof. U. of the Pacific, Stockton, Calif., 1971-80; prof. English U. of the Pacific, 1980—; adv. panel English, Calif. Commn. on Tchr. Credentialing, Sacramento, 1989—; U. of the Pacific team planner, mem. Project 30 at U. of the Pacific, Stockton, 1988—; chair Acad. Coun., U. of the Pacific, Stockton, 1989—. Contbr. articles to profl. jours. Vol. of the Yr. ARC, Stockton, 1988; cons., instr. Kirkwood Ski Patrol, Kirkwood, Calif., 1981—; bd. dirs. Kirkwood Meadows Assn., 1982—. Woodrow Wilson fellow Woodrow Wilson Found., Ind. U., 1959-60, Fulbright Jr. fellow Inst. Internat. Edn., London U., 1963-64, Fulbright Sr. fellow Inst. Internat. Edn., U. Tromso, Norway, 1984-85, NEH fellow, Harvard U., 1986. Mem. Liguistic Soc. Am., Medieval Acad., Modern lang. Assn., Nat. Coun. Tchrs. English. Democrat. Roman Catholic. Office: U of the Pacific Dept English Stockton CA 95211

COX, RONALD FREDERICK, electrical engineer; b. Mechanicsburg, Pa., Feb. 6, 1946; s. Frank Sterrett and Catherine Jane (Fehl) C.; m. Helen Grace Smith, July 1, 1967; children: Jennifer, Elise, Benjamin. BSEE, U. Va., 1975, MEE, 1979; MS in Engring. Mgmt., Fla. Inst. Tech., 1982. Engr. Sperry/Marine div., Charlottesville, Va., 1975-79; tech. dir. Honeywell/Mil-Av div., Clearwater, Fla., 1979-85; dir. engring. Litton/Guidance div., Woodland Hills, Calif., 1985—. Contbr. articles to profl. jours. Reg. bd. dirs. Am. Youth Soccer Orgn., Newbury Park, Calif., 1988—. With USN, 1966-71. Mem. AIAA (panel mem. navigation), Tau Beta Pi, Eta Kappa Nu, Theta Tau. Republican. Lutheran. Office: Litton Guidance MS 76 5500 Canoga Ave Woodland Hills CA 91367

COX, RONALD WAYNE, electrical engineer; b. Corning, Iowa, Dec. 29, 1942; s. Robert B. and Velma E. (Hardesty) C.; m. Janis Kay Luellen, Apr. 2, 1966; children: Raina Marie, Randall Luellen. BSEE, Iowa State U., 1964. Gen. supr. body electronics systems Delco Electronics, Kokomo, Ind., 1982-84, gen. supr. adv. body and chassis systems, 1984-87; dept. mgr. comml. vehicle electronics Delco Electronics, Goleta, Calif., 1987—. Author: Industrial Electronics, 1985; patentee in field. Mem. Soc. Automotive Engrs., Eta Kappa Nu. Republican. Presbyterian. Home: 1182 Edison St Santa Ynez CA 93460 Office: Delco Systems Ops Delco Electronics Corp 6767 Hollister Ave Goleta CA 93117

COX, WILMA BEATY, communications executive; b. Spokane, Wash., June 27, 1929; d. Robert Wilbur and Ruth Aseneth (Duran) Dudley; m. Robert S. Cox, Jr., Apr. 25, 1958 (div.); children: Charles Thomas, Leslee Ann Cox Stout, Robert Sayre, Nancy Elizabeth, Kristina Suzanne. BA, San Jose State U., 1972, MA, 1976. Cert. tchr., Calif. Asst. to dir. Crocker Art Gallery, Sacramento, 1973-74; dir. Pub. info. U. Calif.-Davis Sch. Medicine, 1974-76; dir. pub. affairs East Conn. State Coll., Willimantic, 1976-79; dir. pub. info. Bryn Mawr Coll., Pa., 1979-80; dir. pub. relations U. Puget Sound, Tacoma, Wash., 1980-83; dir. univ. communications Santa Clara U. (Calif.), 1983-85; dir. mktg. and communications Leisure Care, Inc., Bellevue, Wash., 1985-87, Village Concepts, Inc., Federal Way, Wash., 1987—; owner, operator Benchmark Communications, Redmond, Wash., 1987—; cons. Hopkins Art Ctr., Dartmouth Coll., N.H., 1978; chairperson Com. on Publs. Standards, State of Conn., 1978-79. Author art catalogs. Bd. dirs. Crocker Art Gallery Assn., Sacramento, 1974-76; charter mem. communications group No. Calif. Cancer Program, Stanford, 1974-76; charter mem. bd. dirs. Sacramento Cancer Coun., 1975-76; bd. dirs. San Jose State U. Art Alumni Assn., 1983-86. Recipient Best Mus. Pub. award, Western Assn. Museums, 1976; Disting. Service award La Sangre Latina, Hispanic Soc. ECSC, 1979. Mem. Coun. Advancement and Support of Edn. (CASE, exceptional achievement award periodicals program 1983, exceptional achievement award total publs. program 1983; chairperson publs. track 1985, Gold medal individual recruiting, Gold medal program pubs. 1985), Women in Communications (sec. Tacoma-Olympia chpt. 1980-83), Internat. Bus. Communicators, Phila. Pub. Rels. Assn. (mem. peer awards com. 1980), Phi Kappa Phi. Democrat. Home: 16727 Lake Holm Rd Auburn WA 98002 Office: Village Concepts Inc 34004 16th Ave S Ste 200 Federal Way WA 98003

COX-REIFF, CYNTHIA ELIZABETH, interior designer; b. San Diego, July 5, 1954; d. Lyle Wade and Dorothy Elizabeth (Anderson) Cox; m. Roger Stanley Bolander, Mar. 9, 1978 (div. 1980); m. Robert Allen Reiff, Jan. 15, 1984; 1 child, Ryan Andrew Morgan. BA, Ariz. State U., 1978. Mgr. J&B Home Furnishings, Manhattan Beach, Calif., 1978-81; lead designer Kellard-Baron Designs, Westwood, Calif., 1981-82; designer, mgr. Design II/L.A., West Hollywood, Calif., 1982-84; owner, designer Rebecca-Reiff Designs, L.A., 1984—; tchr. The Am. Coll., Westwood, Calif., 1985—.

COYE, BETH FRANCES, political science professor, writer; b. San Diego, Oct. 28, 1937; d. John Starr and Grace Elizabeth (Gabriel) C. BA in Polit. Sci., Wellesley (Mass.) Coll., 1959; MA in Internat. Rels., Am. U., 1968; grad., Naval War Coll., 1970. Commd. ensign USN, 1960, advanced through to comdr., 1975, ret., 1980; v.p. sales and mktg. dept., owner Coffee Inn San Diego, 1981-84; assoc. prof. polit. sci. San Diego-Mesa Coll., 1988—. Contbr. articles to profl. jours. Pres. Sane/Freeze San Diego, 1986-87. Mem. Class of 1959 Wellesley Coll. (v.p. 1985-89), Mil. Adv. Coun. Ctr. for Def. Info., Am. Polit. Sci. Assn., Wellesley Club (pres. San Diego chpt. 1982-84). Avocations: Bichon Frises (dogs), gardening, reading, camping. Home: 4557 Gesner St San Diego CA 92117 Office: San Diego Mesa Coll 7250 Mesa College Dr San Diego CA 92111-4998

COYLE, MARIE BRIDGET, microbiologist, laboratory director; b. Chgo., May 13, 1935; d. John and Bridget Veronica (Fitzpatrick) C. BA, Mundelein Coll., 1957; MS, St. Louis U., 1963; PhD, Kans. State U., 1965. Diplomate Am. Bd. Med. Microbiology. Sci. instr. Sch. Nursing Columbus Hosp., Chgo., 1957-59; research assoc. U. Chgo., 1967-70; instr. U. Ill., Chgo., 1970-71; asst. prof. U. Wash., Seattle, 1973-80, assoc. prof., 1980—; assoc. dir. microbiology labs Univ. Hosp., Seattle, 1973-76; dir. microbiology labs Harborview Med. Ctr., Univ. Wash., 1976—; co-dir. Postdoc Training Clinic Microbiology, Univ. Wash., 1978—. Contbr. articles to profl. jours. Fellow Am. Acad. Microbiology; mem. Acad. Clin. Lab. Physicians and Scientists (sec.-treas. 1980-83, exec. com. 1985—), Am. Soc. Microbiology (chmn. clin. microbiology div. 1984-85), Kappa Gamma Pi. Democrat. Roman Catholic. Office: Harborview Med Ctr 325 9th Ave Seattle WA 98104

COYLE, ROBERT EVERETT, federal judge; b. Fresno, Calif., May 6, 1930; s. Everett LaJoya and Virginia Chandler C.; m. Faye Turnbaugh, June 11, 1953; children—Robert Allen, Richard Lee, Barbara Jean. B.A., Fresno State Coll., 1953; J.D., U. Calif., 1956. Bar: Calif. Ptnr. McCormick, Barstow, Sheppard, Coyle & Wayte, 1958-82; judge U.S. Dist. Ct. (ea. dist.) Calif., 1982—. Mem. Fresno County Bar Assn. (pres. 1972), Calif. State Bar Assn. (exec. com. 1974-79, bd. govs. 1979-82, v.p. 1981). Office: US Dist Ct 5116 US Courthouse 1130 O St Fresno CA 93721

COYLE, SYLVIA HALKOUSIS, lawyer; b. Balt., Nov. 26, 1950; d. Lorentzos Demetrios and Dorothy (Blazic) Halkousis; m. Robert Richard Coyle, Oct. 8, 1988. AB in Polit. Sci., Goucher Coll., 1981; MPA, U. Balt., 1985, JD, 1985; LLM in Bus. and Taxation, U. of the Pacific, 1986. Bar: Md. 1985, D.C. 1987, Calif. 1988. Assoc. Porter, Scott, Weiberg & Delehant, Sacramento, Calif., 1987-88, Kimble, MacMichael & Upton, Fresno, Calif., 1988—. Articles editor: U. Balt. Law Forum, 1984-85. Mgr. Citizens for Kathleen Kennedy Townsend, N.W. Balt. County, Md., 1986. Mem. ABA, Calif. State Bar Assn., Md. State Bar Assn., D.C. Bar Assn., Fresno County Bar Assn., Phi Alpha Alpha. Democrat. Greek Orthodox. Office: Kimble MacMichael & Upton 5260 N Palm Ste 221 Fresno CA 93704

COYNE, CECILIA MARY, financial executive; b. Rockland, Maine, Dec. 3, 1953; d. Thomas Wolfe and Carolyn Winifred (Hanley) C.; m. Frank Schmuck III, Aug. 7, 1987. BS in Acctg., U. Utah, 1983, MBA, 1989. CPA, Utah. Sr. acct. Arthur Young & Co., Salt Lake City, 1984-87; chief fin. officer Salt Lake City Housing Authority, 1987-88; controller Assn. Univ. and Regional Pathologists, Salt Lake City, 1988—. Mem. Am. Women's Soc. CPAs, AICPA, Utah Assn. CPAs, Jr. League Salt Lake City (fin. v.p. 1982—). Democrat. Roman Catholic. Home: 2716 Louise Ave Salt Lake City UT 84109 Office: ARUP 500 Chipeta Salt Lake City UT 84108

COYNE, LISA ANN, state official; b. San Diego, Sept. 17, 1952; d. Ronald John and Rita Mae (Marrs) C. BS cum laude, Calif. State U., Long Beach, 1975, Calif. State U., Fullerton, 1976; JD, Loyola U., L.A., 1979. With State of Calif., Sacramento, 1979, mgr., 1980—; owner Spirit Path, Sacramento, 1989—. Designer (reproduction) Medieval Chain Mail Armor, 1982—, Medieval Illuminated Manuscript, 1987. Bd. dirs. Resources for Ind. Living, 1980; pub. rep. Canine Companions for Ind., 1986—; pres., founder Disabled Students Coalition, 1975-79. Mem. Inst. for Noetic Sci., Calif. Assn. Phys. Handicapped, Phi Alpha Delta. Democrat. Office: Calif Dept Rehab 830 K St Sacramento CA 95814

COYNE, RICHARD DALE, computer engineer; b. L.A., Oct. 24, 1940; s. Michael Thomas and Alma Coleen (Eagles) C.; m. Sandra Kay Humphrey Riley, Nov. 23, 1961 (div. 1968); children: Tandy, Richard, Randal; m. Jeannette Marie Tischler, Sept. 21, 1980; 1 child, Andre Michael. AS, Phoenix Coll., 1967; BS, Ariz. State U., 1970. Res. engr. Motorola Res. Labs., Phoenix, 1964-69, 73-76; lithography mgr. Semiconductor Electronic Memories, Phoenix, 1969-72; prin. engr. Electronic Memories and Magnetics, Phoenix, 1976-78, Motorola Semiconductor Sector, Mesa, Ariz., 1978-80; engring. mgr. Siliconix, Inc., Santa Clara, Calif., 1980-81; sr. scientist GCA Corp., Sunnyvale, Calif., 1981-86; res. scientist Hughes Res. Labs., Malibu, Calif., 1985-88; sr. prin. engr. Shipley Co., Inc., Tempe, Ariz., 1988—; tech. mktg. cons. Dataquest, San Jose, Calif., 1984, Sonotek, Inc., Poughkeepsie, N.Y., 1985; res. cons. Data Gen., Sunnyvale, 1984, Karl Suss, Munich, 1985. Contbr. articles to profl. jours; inventor vapor sheathed baking apparatus, phosphorus vapor deposition. Recipient IR 100 award Res. and Devel. Mag., 1985. Mem. Electrochem. Soc., Soc. Photo-Optical Instrumentation Engrs., IEEE, Scientists Interested in Growth (sec. 1965-69), Hughes/Pepperdine Recreational Club, Phoenix Chess Club, Sierra Club. Republican. Roman Catholic.

COZZI, HUGO LOUIS, psychiatrist; b. Travesio, Udine, Italy, Aug. 3, 1934; s. David NMN and Ida Domenica (Fratta) C.; m. Martha Jane Zborovan, July 2, 1966; children: Elise Ann, David John. BS, Georgetown U., Wash., 1956; MD, Georgetown U., 1960. Gen. med. officer U.S. Army, Ft. Myer, Va., 1961-63; asst. chief, then chief USPH Hosp., New Orleans, La., 1966-68; dir. inpatient psychiat. svcs. St. Luke's Med. Cntr., Phoenix, Ariz., 1969-72; dir. Good Samaritan Med. Ctr., Phoenix, 1976-78; asst. dir. Good Samaritan Med. Cntr., Phoenix, 1972-82; chief, adult psychiatry Good Smaritan Med. Cntr., Phoenix, dir., 1983-84; pvt. practice Phoenix, 1984; med. dir. Phoenix Camelback Hosp., Phoenix, 1984; psychiatric cons., Superior Ct. Maricopa County, Phoenix, 1968-69. Pres. Phoenix Psychiat. Coun. Cert. of achievement U.S. Army, Ft. Myers, Va., 1963. Fellow Am. Psychiatric Assn.; mem. Ariz. Psychiat. Soc. (pres.). Republican. Roman Catholic. Office: 3352 E Camelback Rd Ste G Phoenix AZ 85018

CRABB, WILLIAM JOHN, emergency medicine physician; b. Spokane, Wash., Nov. 6, 1950; s. Jack Husting and Jean Catherine (Carey) C. BS, Oreg. State U., 1973; MD, Oreg. Health Services U., 1978. Diplomate Am. Bd. Emergency Medicine. Intern Maricopa Med. Ctr., Phoenix, 1978-79, resident in radiology, 1979-80; emergency dept. physician Emergency Med. Systems, Phoenix, 1980-81; dir. emergency dept. Humana Hosp., Phoenix, 1981-84; regional med. dir. Emergency Med. Systems, Louisville, 1984-87; emergency dept. physician Tacoma (Wash.) Emergency Care Physicians, 1987—. Fellow Am. Coll.Emergency Physicians; mem. Pierce County Med. Soc., Washington State Med. Assn. Republican. Roman Catholic.

CRABBS, ROGER ALAN, consultant, publisher, small business owner, educator; b. Cedar Rapids, Iowa, May 9, 1928; s. Winfred Wesley and Faye (Woodard) C.; m. Marilyn Lee Westcott, June 30, 1951; children—William Douglas, Janet Lee, Ann Lee. B.A. in Sci., State U. Iowa, 1954; M.B.A., George Washington U., 1965, D.B.A., 1973; M.Christian Leadership, Western Conservative Bapt. Sem., 1978. Commd. 2d lt. USAF, 1950, advanced through grades to lt. col., 1968; Ret. U.S. Air Force, 1972; prof. mgmt. U. Portland, Oreg., 1972-79; prof. bus. George Fox Coll., Newberg, Oreg., 1979-83; pres. Judson Bapt. Coll., The Dalles, Oreg., 1983-85; pres., assoc. pub. Host Pubs. Inc. doing bus. as Travelhost of Portland, 1985—; pres., chmn. various corps., 1974-86; cons. to various orgns., corps. and agys. Author: The Storybook Primer on Managing, 1976; The Infallible Foundation for Management-The Bible, 1978; The Secret of Success in Small Business Management-Is in the Short Range, 1983. Mem. Small Bus. Adv. Council, Oreg. dist. SBA, 1983—. Decorated Air Force Commendation medal with oak leaf cluster, Meritorious Service medal Dept. Def.; rated Command Air Force Missileman; recipient regional, dist. and nat. awards SBA. Mem. Acad. Mgmt., Am. Soc. Personnal Adminstrn., Small Bus. Inst. Dirs. Assn., Am. Arbitration Assn., Service Corps. Ret. Execs./Active Corps of Execs., Air Force Assn., Alpha Kappa Psi, Delta Epsilon Sigma. Republican. Club: Portland Officers. Lodges: Rotary, Masons. Office: Host Publs Inc 13563 NW Cornell Rd Ste 173 Portland OR 97229-5892

CRAFT, ELIZABETH ANN, educator; b. Lexington, Ky., Jan. 14, 1943; d. Richard P. and Beatrice (Coles) Harris; BFA, Ohio U., 1965; MA, Ariz. State U., 1979; m. John Edward Craft, Dec. 18, 1965; children: Lauren Kelly, Jennifer Lavonia. Teaching asst. in speech Ohio U., 1964-65, in English, 1964-65; tchr. English, Steubenville (Ohio) High Sch., 1965-68; debate coach, 1966-68; teaching asst. in communication Ariz. State U., 1978-79, faculty asso. in communication, 1980-82, instructional TV coord., 1982-85, asst. dir. instructional TV, 1985—. Mem. governing bd. for cable TV Phoenix Ednl. Access, 1987—. Alumni Sesquicentennial scholar Ohio U., 1963-64, Univ. Upperclass scholar, 1964-65. Mem. AAUW, Ariz. State Button Soc. (sec. 1980-82, speaker for civic orgns.), Kappa Delta Pi. Mem. Christian Ch. (Disciples of Christ). Co-editor Ariz. State U. Faculty Wives Club newsletter, 1975-76; contbr. article to profl. jours. Home: 218 E Carter Dr Tempe AZ 85282 Office: Ariz State U Univ Media Systems Tempe AZ 85287

CRAFT, ROBBIE WRIGHT, artist; b. St. Louis, Feb. 22, 1951; d. Robert Edward and Irene (Tosch) Wright; m. Joseph Walter Epply III (div. 1978); 1 child, Joseph Walter IV; m. Raymond Wood Craft II, Feb. 14, 1987. Student, Casper Jr. Coll., 1969-71. Adminstrv. asst. U.S. Dept. Def., Andrews AFB, Md., 1974-75; illustrator, supr. U.S. Dept. Def., Cheyenne, Wyo., 1985-88, EEO counselor, 1987—, chief visual info., 1988—; pvt. practice artist Maryland, Wyo., 1974—; pvt. practice interior design Wyo., 1986—; restaurant/bar mgr. Widow Browns, Crofton, Md., 1978-84. Lutheran. Home: 5403 Hacker Ct Cheyenne WY 82009 Office: 90 MSSq/MSV FE Warren AFB WY 82005

CRAGHEAD, JAMES DOUGLAS, civil engineer; b. Petersburg, Va., Nov. 27, 1950; s. William Douglas and Edith Marcia (Smith) C.; m. Vicki Lynn Taylor, June 5, 1970; 1 child, Jeffrey Taylor. BS, N.Mex. State U., Las Cruces, 1976. Design engr. Black & Veatch Cons. Engrs., Kansas City, Mo., 1976-77; engr. Frank Henri & Assocs., Las Cruces, N.Mex., 1977-78; sr. engr. Hughes Aircraft Co., Tucson, Ariz., 1978-80; supr. engring. Hughes Aircraft Co., 1980-84, head environ. engr., 1985—. Inventor in field. Bd. dirs. Our Town Family Svcs., 1987—. Sgt. AUS, 1970-73. N.Mex. Mil. Inst. scholar, 1969. Mem. ASCE, Chi Epsilon (v.p. 1975-76). Republican. Episcopalian. Office: Hughes Aircraft Co PO Box 11337 Bldg 826 Tucson AZ 85734

CRAGIN, MICHAEL DENNIS, health care administrator; b. South Gate, Calif., Sept. 13, 1947; s. Lester James and Carmelita (Murphy) C.; m. Sheila McQuade, Oct. 17, 1981; 1 child, Kiri. BA, Calif. State U.-Northridge, 1968, MS, 1975. Staff research assoc. dept. radiol. scis. UCLA, 1968-76; adminstrv. asst. Dept. Medicine Clinics UCLA, L.A., 1976-77; adminstrv. dept. head diagnostic radiology Good Samaritan Hosp., L.A., 1977-79, dir. adminstrv. services, 1979-81; pres. ESK Investments, L.A., 1981-82; assoc. adminstr. HCMG, Hawthorne, Calif., 1982-84; regional dir. spl. services Beverly Enterprises, Austin, Tex., 1984-85; v.p., operator Ambulatory Health Systems, Santa Monica, Calif., 1985; chief exec. officer Pasadena (Calif.) Assn. Lab. Med. Svcs., 1985—. Contbr. articles to profl. publs. Mem. Health Care Execs. So. Calif. Home: 1428 12th St C Santa Monica CA 90401 Office: Pasadena Assn Lab Med Svcs 10 Congress St Ste 101 Pasadena CA 91105

CRAGUN, CALVIN, business owner; b. Salt Lake City, Nov. 14, 1940; s. Robert Wallace and Vivian (Parker) C.; m. Celestia Van Tussenbroek, Dec. 20, 1967; children: Marlayn Caroline, David Robert. BS, U. Utah, 1963, MS, 1966. Tchr. Utah Sch. for the Deaf, Ogden, 1966-72; from salesperson to mgmt. dept. Home Life of N.Y., Salt Lake City, 1972-82; with ins. sales dept. Standard of Oreg., Salt Lake City, 1982-84; owner Custom Benefits, Salt Lake City, 1984—, Rocky Mountain Beverage Brokerage, Salt Lake City, 1985-88, Ins. Designers, Salt Lake City, 1988—. Mem. Nat. Conf. for Autism, Salt Lake City, 1983; regional coord. Internat. Winter Spl. Olympics, Salt Lake City, 1985—; mem. Gov.'s Com. for Handicapped, Salt Lake City, 1983-84. Mem. Utah Coun. for Handicapped (v.p. 1982-83). Home: 2686 E Towne Dr Salt Lake City UT 84121 Office: Ins Designers 310 E 4500 S #330 Salt Lake City UT 84107

CRAIG, GAIL HEIDBREDER, architect, educator; b. Balt., Jan. 20, 1941; d. Gerald August and Ora Henderson (Longley) Heidbreder; m. Val Dean Craig, Jan. 19, 1985; children: Laura Temple Cook, John Temple. BA, Stanford U., 1966, postgrad., 1975-78. Registered architect, Calif. With various firms 1969-85; owner Gail Craig, AIA, Porterville, Calif, 1985—; instr. various construction and drafting courses Calif. Community Colls., Kern County, 1985—. Mem. AIA, Internat. Conf. Bldg. Offcls., Porterville C. of C. (bd. dirs. 1985-87), Main St. Inc. (bd. dirs. 1988—). Lodge: Zonta. Office: 639A N Main St Porterville CA 93257

CRAIG, JAMES GORDON, civil engineer; b. Schenectady, N.Y., June 12, 1951; s. Gordon Stirling Jr. and Jeanne Ann (Nicoll) C.; m. Ruth Ann Sobba Riland, Nov. 30, 1985. BS in Civil Engring., U. Wyo., 1973. Registered profl. engr., Ariz., Calif., Colo., Idaho, Nev., Oreg., Utah, Wash. Drafter Gardner Manfull, P.E., Laramie, Wyo., 1971-73; design engr. Hart, Williams & Roth, Inc., Kirkland, Wash., 1973-77; project engr. Williams, Roth & Assocs, Inc., Kirkland, 1977-82; project mgr. Hedges & Roth Engring., Inc., Kirkland, 1982—; dist. engr. Soos Creek Water and Sewer Dist., Renton, Wash., 1985—. Pres. Tiburon N. Home Owners Assn., Kirkland, 1978-80; active Big Brothers of Seattle/King County, 1981-84. Mem. Am. Soc. Testing & Materials, Constrn. Specification Inst. Office: Hedges & Roth Engring Inc 909 Kirkland Ave Kirkland WA 98033

CRAIG, LARRY EDWIN, congressman; b. Council, Idaho, July 20, 1945; s. Elvin and Dorothy Craig. B.A., U. Idaho; postgrad, George Washington U. Farmer, rancher Midvale area, Idaho; mem. Idaho Senate, 1974-80, 97th-101st Congresses from 1st Dist. Idaho, 1981—; mem. com. pub. works and transp., com. on standards ofcl. conduct, com. on interior and insular affairs, chmn. policy Rep. study com.; chmn. Idaho Republican State Senate Races, 1976-78. Pres. Young Rep. League Idaho, 1976-77; mem. Idaho Rep. Exec. Com., 1976-78; chmn. Rep. Central Com. Washington County, 1971-72; advisor vocat. edn. in public schs. HEW, 1971-73; mem. Idaho Farm Bur., 1965-79. Served with U.S. Army N.G., 1970-74. Mem. NRA (bd. dirs. 1983—), Future Farmers of Am. (v.p. 1965). Methodist. Office: US Ho of Reps 1034 Longworth House Office Bldg Washington DC 20515

CRAIG, LEXIE FERRELL, career development specialist and guidance counselor; b. Halls, Tenn., Dec. 12, 1921; d. Monroe Stancil and Hester May (Martin) Ferrell; m. Philip L. Craig, May 19, 1951; children: Douglas H., Laurie K., Barbara J. BS magna cum laude, George Peabody Coll., Vanderbilt U., 1944; MA with honors, Denver U., 1965; postgrad. Colo. U., 1972—, Colo. State U., 1964—, U. No. Colo., 1964—. Cert. local vocat. adminstr., vocat. guidance specialist, vocat. bus. specialist, vocat. home econs. specialist, reading specialist, nat. recreation dir. specialist. Danforth grad. fellow, counselor Mich. State U., East Lansing, 1944-46; nat. student counselor, field dir. univ. pastor student work dept. higher edn. Am. Bapt. Conv., summer svc. career projects dir. U.S. and Europe, 1946-51; coord. religious and career activities counselor, Colo. U., 1951-52; tchr. home econs., phys. edn., counseling, dist. 96, Riverside, Ill., 1952-54; substitute tchr., psychometrist, reading specialist part time, Deerfield, Ill., 1956-59; substitute tchr. Littleton (Colo.) Dist. VI, 1961-63, guidance and career counselor Littleton Pub. Schs., 1963-67, 68-86, career devel. specialist, guidance counselor spl. assignments state and nat., Gov.'s Youth 2000 Task Force Com., 1988—, also mem. vocat. needs and assessment com., 1988—; chmn. leadership team AARP Works, Teane, Colo.; dir., counselor YWCA Extension Program, Job Corps, Denver, 1967-68; tchr. adult edn. home econs. evenings, 1963-66; mem. Colo. State Career Task Force, 1973-77; cons. vol. home econ. cons. Colo. State U extension office, 1988-89. Lay conf. rep. Meth. Ch. Pastor/Parish Commn.; vol. sr. citizens programs United Meth. Ch., Littleton Community Ctr., mem. nominating and personnel work area com.; chmn. membership com. St. Andrew United Meth. Ch., Colo. Ch. Women United; mem. Greater Denver Frienship Force; bd. dirs. Career Awareness Council Boy Scouts Am., Metro Denver; also mem. Colo. Career Awareness Council; mem. So. Suburban Recreation, Littleton Community Arts Ctr.; adv. council Powell PTO, 1981-84; adv. council SEMBCS area vocat. schs.; mem. local caucus com. Republican Party; mem. Dist. Environ. Sci. Council. Didcott scholar, 1942; mem. AVS adv. council Early Childhood Edn., Health Occupation, Restaurant Arts and Coop Career Devel., 1970—; pres. Colo. Assn. Adult Devel. & Aging. Danforth home econs. and leadership scholar, 1943; Am. Leadership Camp Found. scholar, Shelby, Mich., 1942-45; Hildegarde Sweet Scholar, 1983; recipient Sullivan award and grant, named outstanding grad., 1944; named Littleton Mother of Year, 1977, Colo. Vocat. Counselor of Yr., 1978, Colo. Vocat. Guidance Assoc. Counselor of Yr., 1984; recipient plaque for recruiting and career guidance Navy and Air Force, 1980, Clifford G. Houston Colo. Counselor award, 1985, Outstanding award Boy Scouts of Am. Career Awareness Council, 1986, Recognition Gold Pin award United Meth. Ch. Women, 1988. Mem. NEA, AAUW, Colo. Edn. Assn., Littleton Edn. Assn., Am. Vocat. Assn., Colo. Vocat. Assn., Am. Assn. Counseling and Devel., Colo. Assn. for Counseling and Devel. (exec. bd.), Nat. Career Devel. Assn. (membership chmn.), Colo. Career Devel. Assn. (past pres., membership chmn.), Nat. Vocat. Guidance Assn. (Colo. rep.), Am. Assn. Retired Persons, Colo. Retired Sch. Employees Assn., Arapahoe County Retired Tchrs. Assn., Colo. Sch. Counselors Assn., Am. Field Service (pres. Littleton chpt.), Lit. Book Club Littleton Arts Ctr., Home Economists in Homemaking (Littleton and Bega, Australia clubs), Phi Delta Kappa, Delta Kappa Gamma Alpha Delta (past chpt. pres., Omega State DKG, state com. chmn. personal growth and svcs.), Order EAstern Star, Countryn Western Dance Club, Delta Pi Epsilon (past pres.), Pi Omega Pi (past pres.), Pi Gamma Mu (past pres.), Kappa Delta Pi (past pres.). Editor, pub. Join in a Song, 1949; editor The Church Follows Its Youth, 1950, curriculum units in consumer edn., home econs., careers, parenting classes.

CRAIG, MAYADELLE DELL, psychotherapist; b. Wildrose, N.D., June 14, 1937; d. Willie O. and Olive May (Holland) Evenson; m. John Takas, 1979 (dec.); children: Cynthia, Joni. BA, U. Nev., Las Vegas, 1978; MA, Whitworth Coll., 1982; postgrad. Saybrook Inst. Cert. relapse prevention specialist. Cert. alcoholism counselor Wash. State Profl. Staff Soc., 1982. Counselor, group therapist Ct. Referral Services, Las Vegas, 1977-79; counselor, employee assistance program facilitator Southwest Community Alcohol Ctr., Seattle, 1979-81; pres. Dell Craig Therapists Inc., Des Moines, Wash., 1981—; developer, cons. employee assistance programs; franchiser catalyst plans on alcoholism recovery, organizational enhancement. Mem. Wash. State Council on Alcoholism, Am. Personnel and Guidance Assn., Psi Chi. Club: Toastmasters (Burien, Wash.). Office: Dell Craig Therapists Inc 22030 7th Ave S Ste 204 Seattle WA 98188

CRAIG, ROBERT KENNETH, sportswear manufacturing company executive; b. Delta, Colo., Feb. 7, 1939; s. Perry and Dorothy Elenor (Ward) C.; m. Maren Louise Edlefsen, Feb. 3, 1962 (div. 1974); children: Steven Michael, Jeffrey Thomas; m. Mary Kay Thissen, July 2, 1983; stepchildren: John Charles Gibson, Kathleen Mary Gibson. BS in Math, U. Denver, 1966; MS in Computer Sci., Wash. State U., 1971. Programmer Denver Rsch. Inst., 1964-66, Bendix Aerospace Systems, Ann Arbor, Mich., 1966-68; programmer-analyst Computer Sci. Corp., Richland, Wash., 1968-69, Silver Spring, Md., 1972-73; analyst Seattle 1st Nat. Bank, 1973-77; system engr. Hewlett Packard, Bellevue, Wash., 1977-80, dist. mgr., 1980-84; cons. Craig Cons., Kirkland, Wash., 1984-85; dir. info. systems Generra Sportswear, Seattle, 1985—; cons. in field. With USAF, 1959-62. Mem. Data Processing Mgmt. Assn., ACM (pres. 1970-71). Home: 210 Boyleston Ave E #304 Seattle WA 98102 Office: Generra Sportswear 278 Broad St Seattle WA 98121

CRAIG, ROBERT WALLACE, educational administrator; b. Long Beach, Calif., Sept. 16, 1924; s. Harold Fleming and Ellen Amelia (Stagg) C.; m. Carol Williams Gallun, Nov. 5, 1957; children: Kathleen Elizabeth, Jennifer Courtney, Michael Brian. BS, BA cum laude, U. Wash., 1949; MA, Columbia U., 1951. V.p., exec. dir. Aspen (Colo.) Inst. for Humanistic Studies, 1954-64; v.p. Unimark Internat. Design Inc., Aspen and Chgo., 1965-71; prin. Robert Craig & Assocs., 1965-73; ptnr. Genesis Inc., 1971-73, Rieben & Craig, Denver, 1973-75; pres., founder The Keystone (Colo.) Ctr., 1975—; mountain and cold weather tng. cons. U.S. Army, 1951-54; hon. trustee, co-founder Aspen Ctr. for Physics. Author (with others): K-2, The Savage Mountain, 1954, Storm and Sorrow, 1978. Bd. dirs. Snake River Health Clinic, Keystone, Colo. Outward Bound, 1985, Santa Fe Inst.; mem. U.S. Antarctic Safety Rev. Panel NSF, Washington Inst. Fgn. Affairs. Served to lt. (j.g.) USNR, 1943-46, PTO. Mem. Century Assn. Democrat. Episcopalian. Clubs: Am. Alpine (pres. 1983-86), Century (N.Y.C.); Cactus (Denver); Bohemian (San Francisco). Home: 624 Montezuma Rd Keystone CO 80435 Office: The Keystone Ctr PO Box 606 Keystone CO 80435

CRAIG, ROGER LEE, professional baseball manager; b. Durham, N.C., Feb. 17, 1930; m. Carolyn Anderson, Dec. 22, 1951; children: Sherri, Roger Jr., Teresa, Vicki. Student, N.C. State U. Pitcher various minor league teams, 1950-55, 58, 59; with Bklyn. (later Los Angeles) Dodgers, 1956-58, 59-61, N.Y. Mets., 1962-63, St. Louis Cardinals, 1964, Cin. Reds, 1965, Phila. Phillies, 1966; mgr. Albuquerque, Tex. League, 1968; coach San Diego Padres, Nat. League, 1969-72; minor league pitching instr. Los Angeles Dodgers, 1973; pitching coach Houston Astros, 1974-75; pitching coach San Diego Padres, 1976-77, mgr., 1978-79; pitching coach Detroit Tigers, Am. League, 1980-84; mgr. San Francisco Giants, Nat. League, 1985—; pitcher World Series, 1955, 56, 59, 64. Author: Inside Pitch, 1984. Office: care San Francisco Giants Candlestick Park San Francisco CA 94124 *

CRAIG, ROGER TIMOTHY, professional football player; b. Preston, Miss., July 10, 1960; s. Elijah and Ernestine C.; m. Vernessia Craig; children: Damesha, Rometra, Rogdrick. Student, U. Nebr., 1978-82. Football player San Francisco 49ers, 1983—; player Pro Bowl, 1986, 88; mem. 49ers winning Super Bowl team, 1989. Holds NFL record for more than 1000 yards rushing and 1000 yards receiving in single season, 1985. Office: San Francisco 49ers 4949 Centennial Blvd Santa Clara CA 95054 *

CRAIG, STEPHEN WRIGHT, lawyer, consultant; b. N.Y.C., Aug. 28, 1932; s. Herbert Stanley and Dorothy (Simmons) C.; m. Margaret M. Baker, June 10, 1958 (div. 1984); children: Amelia Audrey, Janet Elizabeth, Peter Baker; m. Bette Piller, 1984. AB, Harvard U., 1954, JD, 1959. Reporter Daily Kennebec Jour., Augusta, Maine, 1956; mem. pub. rels. staff Am. Savoyards, 1957; atty. IRS, San Francisco, 1959-61; atty.-adviser U.S. Tax Ct., 1961-63; ptnr. Snell & Wilmer, Phoenix, 1963-78, Winston & Strawn (formerly Craig, Greenfield & Irwin), Phoenix, 1978-87, Myers, Craig & Co., Phoenix, 1987-89, Brown & Bain, Phoenix and Palo Alto, Calif., 1989—; guest lectr. Amos Tuck Sch. Bus. Dartmouth U., 1962; lectr. Ariz. and N.Mex. Tax Insts., 1966-67; guest lectr. sch. law Ariz. State U., 1984, adj. prof. law, 1985-87; sec. Edens COmmunications, Inc., 1984—. Chmn. Jane Wayland Child Guidance Ctr., 1968-70; mem. Maricopa County Health Planning Coun., chmn. mental health task force.; bd. dirs. Combined Met. Phoenix Arts, 1968, adv. bd., 1968-69; adv. bd. Ariz. State U. Tax Insts., 1968-70; bd. dirs. Phoenix Community Coun., 1970-73, Ariz. Acad. With AUS, 1954-56. Mem. state bars Ariz., Calif., Maine, Hasty Pudding Inst., Sigma Alpha Epsilon. Office: Brown & Bain 2901 N Central Ave Ste 2000 Phoenix AZ 85012

CRAIGHEAD, FRANK COOPER, JR., ecologist; b. Washington, Aug. 14, 1916; s. Frank Cooper and Carolyn (Johnson) C.; m. Esther Melvin Stevens, Nov. 9, 1943 (dec. 1980); children: Frank Lance, Charles Stevens, Jana Catherine; m. Shirley Ann Cocker, July, 1987. A.B., Pa. State U., 1939; M.S., U. Mich., 1940, Ph.D., 1950. Sr. research assoc. Atmospheric Scis. Ctr., N.Y., 1967-77; wildlife biologist, cons. U.S. Dept. Interior, Washington, 1959-66; wildlife biologist U.S. Forest Service, Washington, 1957-59; mgr. desert game range U.S. Dept. Interior, Las Vegas, 1955-57; cons. survival tng. Dept. Def., Washington, 1950-55; pres. Craighead Environ. Research Inst., Moose, Wyo., 1955—; research assoc. U. Mont., Missoula, 1959—, Nat. Geographic Soc., Washington, 1959—; lectr. in field. Author: Track of the Grizzly, 1979, A Field Guide to Rocky Mountain Wildflowers, 1963, Hawks, Owls and Wildlife, 1956, How to Survive on Land and Sea, 1943, Hawks in the Hand, 1937. Mem. Pryor Mountain Wild Horse Adv. Com., Dept. Interior, 1968; mem. Horizons adv. group Am. Revolution Bicentennial Commn., 1972. Recipient citation Sec. of Navy, 1947; recipient letter of commendation U.S. Dept. Interior, 1963, Disting. Alumnus award Pa. State U., 1970; alumni fellow Pa. State U., 1973; recipient John Oliver LaGorce Gold medal Nat. Geog. Soc., 1979; U. Mich. Sch. Natural Resources Alumni Soc. award for Disting. Service, 1984. Mem. Wilderness Soc., AAAS, Wildlife Soc., Explorers Club, Phi Beta Kappa, Sigma Xi, Phi Sigma, Phi Kappa Phi. Home: PO Box 156 Moose WY 83012 Office: Craighead Environ Rsch Inst PO Box 156 Moose WY 83012

CRAIGMILE, THOMAS KAY, neurological surgeon; b. Muncie, Ind., Dec. 28, 1924; s. William Wallace and Hallie (Metzker) C.; B.S., Northwestern U., 1946, M.B., 1948, M.D., 1949; m. Doris Wolfe, Apr. 15, 1950; children—Suzanne, Christine, Elizabeth, Marianne, Kathleen. Intern, Chgo. Wesley Meml. Hosp., 1949; resident neurol. surgery Northwestern U., 1952-54; asst. resident neurology Presbyn. Hosp., N.Y.C., 1956-57; chief resident neurol. surgery U. Colo. Med. Center, Denver, 1957-58, clin. instr. neurosurgery, 1959-61, asst. clin. prof. neurosurgery, 1961-69, assoc. clin. prof. neurol. surgery, 1969-84, clin. prof. neurol. surgery, 1984—. Served to capt., M.C., USAF, 1954-56. Diplomate Am. Bd. Neurol. Surgery. Fellow ACS; mem. Am. Assn. Neurol. Surgeons, Congress Neurol. Surgeons, Rocky Mountain Neurosurg. Soc. (sec. 1966-69, pres. 1970-71), Western Neurosurg. Soc. (v.p. 1974-75, pres. 1983-84), Colo. Neurosurg. Soc. (pres. 1978-79). Home: 4431 E 6th Ave Denver CO 80220 Office: U Colo Med Ctr 2005 Franklin St Midtown II Med Bldg Ste 440 Denver CO 80205

CRAIN, CHARLES ANTHONY, telephone company executive; b. Decatur, Ill., 1931. Grad., U. Ill., 1955. Formerly pres. Hawaiian Telephone Co., Honolulu; exec. v.p. Gen. Telephone Co. of Calif., Thousand Oaks, pres., 1989—, also bd. dirs. Office: GTE Calif Inc 1 GTE Place St Thousand Oaks CA 91362 *

CRAM, DONALD JAMES, chemistry educator; b. Chester, Vt., Apr. 22, 1919; s. William Moffet and Joanna (Shelley) C.; m. Jane Maxwell, Nov. 25, 1969. BS, Rollins Coll., 1941; MS, U. Nebr., 1942; PhD, Harvard U., 1947; PhD (hon.), U. Uppsala, 1977; DSci. (hon.), U. So. Calif., 1983, Rollins Coll., 1988, U. Nebr., 1989. Rsch. chemist Merck and Co., 1942-45; asst. prof. chemistry UCLA, 1947-50, assoc. prof., 1950-56, prof., 1956—, named S. Winstein prof., 1985—; chem. cons. Upjohn Co., 1952-88, Union Carbide Co., 1960-81, Eastman Kodak Co., 1981—, Technicon Co., 1984—, Inst. Guido Donegani, Milan, 1988—; State Dept. exchange fellow to Inst. de Quimica, Nat. U. Mex., 1956; guest prof. U. Heidelberg, Germany, 1958; guest lectr., South Africa, 1967; Centenary lectr. Chem. Soc. London, 1976. Author: (with Pine, Hendrickson and Hammond) Organic Chemistry, 1960, 4th edit., 1980, Fundamentals of Carbanion Chemistry, 1965, (with Richards and Hammond) Elements of Organic Chemistry, 1967, (with Cram) Essence of Organic Chemistry, 1977; contbr. chpts. to textbooks, articles in field of host-guest complexation chemistry, carbanions, stereochemistry, mold metabolites, large ring chemistry. Named Young Man of Yr. Calif. Jr. C. of C., 1954, Calif. Scientist of Yr., 1974, Nobel Laureate in Chemistry, 1987; recipient award for creative work in synthetic organic chemistry Am. Chem. Soc., 1965, Arthur C. Cope award, 1974, Richard Tolman medal, 1985, Willard Gibbs award, 1985, Roger Adams award, 1985; Herbert Newby McCoy award, 1965, 75; award for creative rsch. organic chemistry Synthetic Organic Chem. Mfrs. Assn., 1965; Nat. Rsch. fellow Havard U., 1947, Am. Chem. Soc. fellow, 1947-48, Guggenheim fellow, 1954-55. Mem. Am. Chem. Soc., Nat. Acad. Scis., Am. Acad. Arts and Scis., Royal Soc. Chemistry, Sigma Xi, Lambda Chi Alpha. Club: San Onofre Surfing. Home: 1250 Roscomare Rd Los Angeles CA 90077 Office: UCLA Dept Chemistry Los Angeles CA 90024

CRAMER, DALE A., manufacturing executive; b. Holland, Mich., Oct. 11, 1945; s. Norman W. and P. Esther (Poll) C.; m. Patricia M. Luikens, Oct. 6, 1978. AA, Davenport Coll., 1969; BBA, Western Internat. U., 1983, postgrad., 1984-87. Adminstrv. mgr. Mich. Dept. Hwys. and Transp., Lansing, 1966-71; warehouse mgr. All Phase Elec. Supply, Holland, 1971-76; mgr. ops. Alvan Motor Freight, Grand Rapids, Mich., 1976-79; mgr. adminstrn. Delta Calif. Industries, Phoenix, 1979-83; mgr. traffic., transp. Circle K Corp., Phoenix, 1983-86; v.p. Performance Dynamics, Phoenix, 1984—; pres. Distbn. Techs., Phoenix, 1984—; bd. dirs. I.D.E.A., Inc., Phoenix, 1985-86. Contbr. articles to profl. jour. Serving with USCG Aux., 1969—. Democrat.

CRAMER, DOUGLAS SCHOOLFIELD, broadcasting executive; b. Louisville, Aug. 22; s. Douglas Schoolfield and Pauline (Compton) C.; m. Joyce Haber, Sept. 25, 1966 (div. 1973); children: Douglas Schoolfield, III, Courtney Sanford. Student, Northwestern U., 1949-50, Sorbonne, Paris, 1951; B.A., U. Cin., 1953; M.F.A., Columbia U., 1954. Prodn. asst. Radio City Music Hall, N.Y.C., 1950-51; with script dept. Metro-Goldwyn-Mayer, 1952; mng. dir. Cin. Playhouse, 1953-54; instr. Carnegie Inst. Tech., 1955-56; TV supr. Procter & Gamble, 1956-59; broadcast supr. Ogilvy, Benson & Mather, 1959-62; v.p. program devel. ABC, 1962-66, 20th Century-Fox-TV, Los Angeles, 1966-68; exec. v.p. in charge prodn. Paramount TV, 1968-71; ind. producer, pres. Douglas S. Cramer Co., 1971—; exec. v.p. Aaron Spelling Prodns., 1976-87, vice-chmn., 1988—. Exec. producer: Bridget Loves Bernie, CBS-TV, 1972-73, QB VII, 1973-74, Dawn: Portrait of a Teenage Runaway, NBC-TV, 1976; co-exec. producer: Love Boat, ABC, 1977-86, Vegas, ABC, 1978-81, Wonder Woman, ABC, 1975-77, CBS, 1977-78; co-exec. producer: Dynasty, 1981-, Matt Houston, 1982-84, Hotel, 1983-87, Colbys, 1985-87, Nightingales, 1988-89; co-exec. producer, ABC, 1981, Nightingales, 1988—; author: plays Call of Duty, 1953, Love Is A Smoke, 1957, Whose Baby Are You, 1963. Bd. dirs., exec. v.p. Ctr. Theatre Group, Los Angeles Music Ctr.; v.p. trustee, mem. exec. com. Mus. Contemporary Art, Los Angeles; mem. internat. council Mus. Modern Art, N.Y.; pres. Douglas S. Cramer Found.; bd. dirs. Am. Ballet Theatre, Los Angeles Music Ctr. Opera. Served with U.S. Army, 1954. Mem. Beta Theta Pi. Club: Univ. (N.Y.C.). Office: Warner Hollywood Studios 1041 N Formosa Los Angeles CA 90046

CRAMER, JOHN W., psychotherapist; b. Portland, Oreg., Apr. 1, 1934; s. H. William and Martha (Linke) C.; m. Elsie R. Cramer, June 26, 1959 (div.); 1 child, Drew Saintjames; m. Joan E. Karo, Aug. 9, 1986; 1 child, Mark A. MDiv in Theology, Concordia Theol. Sem., 1959; MA in Counseling, U. San Francisco, 1976; PhD, Calif. Grad. Sch., San Rafael, 1985. Lic. marriage, family and child therapist. Pastor various churches, 1957-71, Trinity Luth. Ch., Eureka, Calif., 1971-75; chaplain, counselor Luth. Seamen's Ministry, Oakland, Calif., 1975-76; contract therapist Arcata (Calif.) Family Med. Group, 1977-78; milieu counselor various group homes 1978-83; therapist Luth. Social Svcs. Counseling Program, San Diego, 1983-85; clin. dir. Morning Star Group Home, Imperial Beach, Calif., 1985-87; contract therapist Mental Health Svcs./Child and Family Guidance Ctr., Oceanside, Calif., 1987-88; dir., therapist Luth. Counseling Ministry of Skagit County, Mt. Vernon, Wash., 1988—; dir. Luth. Counseling Svc. in San Diego County, 1985-88. Co-organizer Luth. Singles Ministry San Diego, 1983-88; cir. dean N. Coast Luth. Chs., Eureka, 1973-75; pres. Eureka Ministerial Assn., 1973-75; chpt. chmn. ARC of W. Charitan County, Brunswick, Md., 1961-65; mem. San Francisco Bach Choir and Chamer Singers, 1979-83, San Diego Luth. Choral, 1983-88. Republican. Home: 1580 Hwy 9 Mount Vernon WA 98273 Office: Luth Counseling Ministry PO Box 1714 301 S 18th Ave Mount Vernon WA 98273

CRAMER, RICHARD A., manufacturing company executive. Chmn., chief exec. officer Fisher Scientific Group Inc., La Jolla, Calif.; bd. dirs. City Nat. Bank, City Nat. Corp., Henley Group Inc. Office: Fisher Sci Group Inc 11255 N Torrey Pines Rd La Jolla CA 92037 *

CRANDALL, DAVID LYNN, mechanical engineer; b. Phila., Mar. 4, 1952; s. David Lynn and Jane (Walls) C.; m. Christine F. Borgmeier, Sept. 30, 1977. BSME, U. Utah, 1976; MSME, U. Idaho, Moscow, 1985. Registered profl. engr., Idaho. Test engr. E-Systems, Inc., Salt Lake City, 1976-77; sr. engring. specialist EG&G Idaho, Inc., Idaho Falls, 1977-87; mgr. mech. engring. EG&G Idaho, Inc., 1987—. Author: (with others) Appliications of Artificial Intelligence in Engineering Problems, 1986. Mem. ASME. Office: EG&G Idaho Inc 1955 Fremont Ave Idaho Falls ID 93415

CRANDALL, JANE LEIGH FORD, company executive; b. Ft. Wayne, Ind., Dec. 11, 1933; d. Harland Bernarde and Mary Elizabeth Anne Ford; children: Amy Leigh, Matthew Garrett. AA summa cum laude, LaSalle U., 1975, BBA summa cum laude, 1986. Sales clk. various cos., 1949-54; salesperson Snellenberg's Dept. Store, 1957-58; sales rep. Bestline Products, 1969-70, Avon Products, 1972-82, Sara Conventry Products, 1970-73; v.p. I.C. Crandall & Assocs., 1972-82, 7C's Enterprises, Concord, Calif., 1972—; with Kelley Svcs., Inc., Concord, 1978—; adminstrv. temporary Kelley Services, Inc., Concord, Ga., 1986-; bd. dirs. High Flyin Fish, Inc. Mem. Concord Child Care Task Force; past troop leader Girl Scouts U.S., past bd. mem. Concord United Meth. Ch. Choir, Diablo Valley Band Rev. Assn., Mount Diablo Unified Schs. Interested Citizens, Clayton Valley Music Boosters. Recipient Lee award Concord Women's Club, 1976; named Band Parent of Yr., Clayton Valley High Sch., 1974, 76, 77. Mem.Am. Bus. Women's Assn. (past pres. Inner Cir., Woman of Yr. 1987), Women's Network of Contra Costa County (past sec.), Nat. Assn. Female Execs., Concord C. of C. (assoc.), Concord Stitch and Chatter Soc., Dana Farms Homeowner's Assn., Nat. Travel Club, Nat. Wildlife Fedn., Smithsonian Instn., Nat. Hist. Soc., Neptune Soc., Am. Assn. Retired Persons, Alpha Alpha Pi, Beta Sigma Phi. Democrat. Home: 5747 Pepperridge Pl Concord CA 95421-4821

CRANDALL, MARGARET TAYLOR, home economics educator; b. Ames, Iowa, Mar. 18, 1918; d. Harvey Nelson and Ruby Lorraine (Britten) Taylor; m. Perry Clarence Crandall, July 5, 1941; children: Perry David, Daniel T., Linda C., Helen L. BS, Iowa State U., 1940. Cert. tchr. in home econs., sci., history. Educator Secondary Sch., Gilman, Iowa, 1940-41, 42-43; exec. bd. United Meth. Women, Pacific N.W. Conf., 1963-68; community rep. Head Start Bd., Clark County, 1967-73; leader Clark County 4-H Clubs, VAncouver, Wash., 1968-74; pres. Ch. Women United, Clark County, 1970-72, 81-83, 88-89; tchr. Bapt. Ch. Sch., Amman, Jordan, 1978; advisor St. Andrews Refugee Program, Cairo, Egypt, 1986; counselor Good Samaritan Home Aged, San Jose, Costa Rica, 1987-88. Advocate YWCA Women in Jail Program, Clark County, 1973—. Mem. Vancouver Meth. Found., AAUW. Home and Office: 201 S Devine Rd Vancouver WA 98661

CRANDALL, RICHARD PETER, foundation administrator; b. Cooperstown, N.Y., Nov. 24, 1940; s. Clarence Edward and Helen (Urban) G.; m. Marilyn Stier, Sept. 25, 1965 (div. Dec. 1980); 1 child, Michelle.; m. Gracie Helen Oliver, Apr. 22, 1984; 1 child, Michael. BABA, U. Hawaii, 1964. Purchasing agt. Hughes Aircraft, Fullerton, Calif., 1964-68; sales engr. Bell Industries, Gardenia, Calif., 1968-83, Diplomat Electronics, Costa Mesa, Calif., 1983-84; exec. Short Stature Found., Fountain Valley, Calif., 1984—. Consumer concerns dir. Dayle McIntosh Ctr., Anaheim, Calif., 1987-88; mem. Disables Citizens Com., Orange County, Calif., 1987—. Mem. Mem. Little People Am., OMNI Svc. Club, Omni Bus Club. Republican. Roman Catholic. Home: 17242 Santa Barbara Fountain Valley CA 92708 Office: Short Stature Found One Lighthouse Ln Fountain Valley CA 92708

CRANDALL, RODERICK PENDLETON, publishing executive; b. Kentfield, Calif., Oct. 18, 1948; s. R.P. and Joy (Martin) C.; m. Carolynn Quirici, Sept. 9, 1982; children: Eric,Rustin, Cara. BA in Psychology, U. Calif.-Davis, 1971; MA in Psychology, U. Mich., 1973, PhD in Psychology, 1974. Asst. prof. U. Ill., 1974-77; assoc. prof. Tex. Christian U., 1977-80; cons., tchr. San Francisco, 1981—; owner Select Press, San Rafael, Calif., 1985—, Constrn. Industry Press, San Rafael, Calif., 1986—; exec. dir. Community Entrepreneurs Orgn., San Rafael, 1982—. Author: Research Ethics, 1978; editor: Loneliness, 1987; editor: Jour. Social Behavior and Personality, 1985—. Bd. dirs. Ecumenical Housing Assn., San Rafael, 1983—; bd. dirs. San Francisco Small Bus. Network, 1987—. Named Small Bus. Advocate SBA, No. Calif., 1985. Mem. Am. Psychol. Assn., Community Entrepreneurs Orgn. (exec. dir. 1982—, founder's award 1986). Office: Select Press PO Box 9838 San Rafael CA 94912

CRANDALL, STEPHEN ARTHUR, graphic arts company executive; b. Oak Park, Ill., May 7, 1949; s. Arthur Leslie and Alice Lucille (Baker) C.; m. Cynthia Joan Agliata, Dec. 12, 1970; children: Stephen A., Vanessa, Tyler. AS, Triton Coll., 1970; BA in Communications, Ariz. State U., 1972. Founder, pres. K.C. Gutenberg, Inc., Phoenix, 1980—, K.C. Designs, Inc., Phoenix, 1978—; founder, owner Rocket Copy Ctr. I, Mesa, Ariz., 1981—, Rocket Copy Ctr. II, Mesa, 1985—, Rocket Copy Ctr. III., Mesa, 1989—; mem. graphic arts bd. Ariz. State U., Tempe, 1980-87. Mem. Plaza Club. Home: 2230 E Cinnabar St Phoenix AZ 85028 Office: KC Gutenberg Inc 2321 W Royal Palm Rd Phoenix AZ 85021

CRANDALL, VERN JAY, data processing executive, educator; b. Logan, Utah, Mar. 18, 1939; s. Bliss Hansen and Mildred (Johnson) C.; m. Linda Rae Storms, Jan. 28, 1972; children: Lance Vernon, Shane Lewis, Scott David. BA, Brigham Young U., 1963; MS, Kans. State U., 1966; PhD, U. Wash., 1972. Machine operator, systems programmer DHI Computing Svc., Provo, Utah, 1954-63, statistician, 1963-65, v.p. rsch. and devel., 1965-79; asst. prof. computer sci. and stats. Brigham Young U., Provo, 1968-72, assoc. prof., 1972-79, prof., 1979—; pres., chmn. Vern J. Crandall & Assocs. Inc., Provo, 1982—; v.p. software devel. Novell, Inc., Provo, 1988—; bd. dirs., treas. Innovation Enterprises, Inc., 1972-79; cons. Inst. Logopedics Wichita (Kans.) State U., 1963-65, IBM, Sperry Corp., IOMEGA Crop., Pacific Telesis, Novell Corp., others 1978—. Author: Problem Solving and Writing Commercial Grade Programs Using Pascal, 1986; also articles to profl. jours. Grantee NIH Kans. State U., 1963-65, U. Wash., Seattle, 1965-68, 72, NSF, 1971-72, others. 1982—. Mem. IEEE, Assn. Computing Machinery, Lions (officer Provo club 1968-74). Republican. Mormon. Home: 1224 E 700 South Provo UT 84601 Office: Brigham Young U 236 TMCB Provo UT 84602

CRANE, ADRIAN JOHN, adventurer; b. Beverley, Yorkshire, Eng., July 27, 1955; came to U.S., 1984; s. Albert Charles and Beryl Vera (Austing) C.; m. Karen Sue Menge, Aug. 22, 1983; children: Jonathan Jaro, Christopher Quito. BS in Geology, Durham U., 1977; MS in Mgmt., U. London, 1978. made trek to Lodwar, Kenya, 1977; explored Saudia Arabia, 1979, cycled in Saudi Arabia and Eng., 1980; ran up the Himalayas, Nepel, 1983, Mt. Cameroon, 1984; traversed Rift Valley on bike, 1985. Author: Running the Himalayas, 1983; contbr. numerous articles to various publs. Named Man of Yr., Royal Assn. for Disabled, 1984. Mem. Shadowchase Running Club (editor 1986-88, Runner of Yr. award 1988). Home: 2837 Levon Ave Modesto CA 95350

CRANE, DENNIS JOSEPH, information service company executive; b. Plainfield, N.J., Apr. 8, 1950; s. H. Lewis and Kathryn E. (Keenan) C.; m. Christine Surut, Sept. 29, 1973; children: Rebecca Lee, Keenan Michael. BS, U.S. Naval Acad., 1972; MBA, Stanford U., 1980. Fin. analyst Hewlett Packard, Copertino, Calif., 1979; bus. devel. mgr. Power Systems Gen. Electric, Schenectady, N.Y., 1980-82; mktg. mgr. info. services Gen. Electric, Rockville, Md., 1982-85, bus. devel. mgr. info. services, 1985-86; regional sales mgr. info. services Gen. Electric, Denver, 1987—. Lt. USN, 1972-78. Mem. Data Processing Mgrs. Assn., U.S. Naval Acad. Alumni Assn. (bd. dirs. 1986-87), Hiwan Golf Club. Episcopalian. Home: 2548 Medinah Dr Evergreen CO 80439 Office: GE Info Svcs 6300 S Syracuse Way Ste 550 Englewood CO 80111

CRANE, DOUGLAS ALLEN, communications company executive; b. Eureka, Calif., May 26, 1949; s. Clarence Jr. and Ruth (Weeks) C.; m. Katherine Ann Spangler, June 19, 1971; children: Timothy MacMillan, Benjamin McCully. AA, Coll. of Redwoods, 1969; BS, Lewis and Clark Coll., 1971; MA, Ariz. State U., 1972. Teaching asst. Ariz. State U., Tempe, 1971-72, adminstrv. asst. for audiovisual svcs., 1972-75; instr. Lewis and Clark Coll., Portland, Oreg., 1975-76; producer Odyssey Prodns., Portland, 1975-77; pres., founder Creative Media Devel., Inc., Portland, 1978--; bd. dirs. Holladay Park Plaza, Portland. Author: Producing Multi-Image Presentations, 1973. Mem. Assn. Multi-Image (pres. Oreg. chpt. 1979-81), Internat. Assn. Multi-Image (chmn. coun. of chpts. 1981-82), Internat. Assn. Bus. Communicators (chmn. electronic communication coun. 1986, Gold Quill award 1984-88), Portland C. of C. Republican. Presbyterian. Office: Creative Media Devel Inc 710 SW 9th Ave Portland OR 97205

CRANE, EILEEN GABRIELLE, winery executive; b. Mineola, N.Y., Jan. 31, 1949; d. Nicholas Edmund and Eileen (Jackson) C.; m. Eric N. Murray, June 11, 1983. AB, Regis Coll., Weston, Mass., 1971; MS, U. Conn., 1975. Enologist Domaine Chandon Winery, Yountville, Calif., 1978-84; v.p., winemaker Gloria Ferrer Winery, Sonoma, Calif., 1984-87; mng. dir. Domaine Carneros, Napa, Calif., 1987—; sec. Carneros (Calif.) Quality Alliance, 1985-87, pres., 1987; bd. dirs. Sonoma County Tech. Group, Santa Rosa, Calif., 1985-86. Mem. Am. Soc. Enology and Viticulture. Home: 1905 Brown St Napa CA 94559 Office: Domaine Carneros 1240 Duhig Rd Napa CA 94559

CRANE, FRANK MELVIN, agricultural company executive; b. Mankato, Minn., June 10, 1923; s. Lucas Melvin and Marie Regina (Lindquist) C.; m. Audrey Mae Kraus, June 26, 1948 (dec. 1985); children: Carolyn, Keith, Suzanne; m. Hildegarde S. Streufert, July 11, 1987. BS, U. Minn., 1948, MS, 1949, PhD, 1954. Instr. U. Minn., St. Paul, 1948-51; rsch. dir. Land O' Lakes, Inc., Arden Hills, Minn., 1951-70; v.p. mktg. Land O' Lakes, Inc., Ft. Dodge, Iowa, 1970-74; v.p. rsch. Land O' Lakes, Inc., Ft. Dodge, 1974-82; pres. Frank M. Crane & Assocs., Ft. Dodge and Tempe, Ariz., 1982—; chmn. bd. Am. Feed Industry Assn., Washington, 1980-82; cons., advisor Pres. Carter, Pres. Ford, Pres. Reagen, 1974-88, numerous secs. of agrl., 1952-88, Am. Soybean Assn., U.S. Feed Grains Coun., 1960-89; lectr. in field; participant in numerous seminars in confs. Contbr. numerous articles to internat. profl. jours.; inventor Land O' Lakes calf milk replacer, 1951. Chmn. United Way, Ft. Dodge, 1974-77; dir. Friendship Haven Retirement Home, Ft. Dodge, 1976-87; chmn. fin. com. Ft. Dodge Meth. Ch., 1976-80. Served with USN, 1942-46, PTO. Mem. AAAS, Am. Soc. Animal Sci., Am. Dairy Sci. Assn., Poultry Sci. Assn., World's Poultry Assn., Am. Registry of Profl. Animal Scientists (cert.), Ft. Dodge C. of C. (bd. dirs., fin. com. 1976-80), Rotary (pres. 1984-85), Alpha Zeta, Alpha Gamma Rho (pres. 1960-70, Man of the Year 1989), Gamma Alpha. Avocation: photography. Home and Office: 11239 S Tomah St Phoenix AZ 85044-1915

CRANE, REA BABCOCK, nurse; b. Oakland, Calif., June 2, 1942; d. William Joy and Adeline Hazel (Gunnufson) Babcock; m. Charles Truman Crane, Apr. 2, 1966 (div. 1977); children: Audra Joy, Elise Deborah. Diploma, Calif. Hosp. Sch. Nursing, Los Angeles, 1963. RN, Calif.; cert. ins. rehab. specialist. Emergency room nurse Kaiser Found., San Francisco, 1963-64, Santa Monica (Calif.) Hosp., 1964-65; med.-surg. floor nurse West Los Angeles VA Hosp., 1964-65; rehab. nurse Internat. Rehab. Assocs., Los Angeles, 1970-76, Fremont Compensation Ins. Co., Los Angeles, 1976-79; rehab. supr. Femont Compensation Ins. Co., Los Angeles, 1979-84; asst. dir. rehab. Fremont Compensation Ins. Co., Los Angeles, 1984—, dir., 1986—. Mem. Rehab. Nurses Soc. (pres. 1978-82), Nat. Assn. Rehab. Profls. in Pvt. Sector (founding pres. Calif. chpt. 1984-86, regional rep., chmn. constn. by-laws, 1986—, Bd. Mem. of Yr. award 1985, Lifetime Contbn. to Pvt. Sector Rehab. award 1989), Rehab. President's Council (founder), Nat. Rehab Assn. Democrat. Episcopalian. Office: Fremont Compensation Ins Co 1709 W 8th St Los Angeles CA 90017

CRANE, ROBERT MEREDITH, health care executive; b. Phila., Apr. 5, 1947; s. Frederick Barnard and Roberta Futhey (Philips) C.; m. Susan Gail Dewald, May 5, 1973; 1 child, Alexis Meredith. BA, Coll. of Wooster, 1969; M Pub. Adminstrn., Cornell U., Ithaca, N.Y., 1971. Health planning specialist U.S. Dept. Health, Edn. and Welfare, Rockville, Md., 1971-73, tech. assistance bur. chief, 1973-76, regulatory methods bur. chief, 1976-77; sr. staff assoc. U.S. Ho. of Reps., Washington, 1977-79; deputy commr. N.Y. State Health Dept., Albany, 1979-82; dir. N.Y. State Office Health Systems Mgmt., Albany, 1982-83; v.p. govt. relations Kaiser Found. Health Plan, Oakland, calif., 1983-88, sr. v.p. nat. accounts and pub. relations, 1988—. Selection judge and preceptor Coro Found., San Francisco, 1985-86. Sr. exec. fellow Harvard U., 1981. Mem. Am. Pub. Health Assn. (Community Health Planning Sect. chmn. 1983-84, bd. govs. 1979-81), Am. Health Planning Assn. (bd. dirs. 1986-88). Presbyterian. Office: Kaiser Found Health Plan 1 Kaiser Pla Oakland CA 94612

CRANE, SCOTT JAY, polymer chemist; b. Salt Lake City, Utah, Jan. 18, 1955; s. Richard Smith and Alice Bell (Cowan) C.; m. Terry Lynn Vale, Feb. 7, 1982; 1 child, Kathleen S. BS in Chemistry, San Jose (Calif.) State U., 1983. Material researcher Accurex Corp., Mountain View, Calif., 1984; polymer researcher Hewlett Packard Corp., San Jose, 1984—; cons. Hill Ceramics Co., San Jose, 1983—. Contbr. articles to profl. jours. Served with USN, 1973-78. Democrat. Roman Catholic. Office: Hewlett Packard Corp 370 W Trimble Rd MS 91BH San Jose CA 95131

CRANE, WILLIAM LEE, electronics company executive; b. Dubuque, Iowa, July 8, 1940; s. William Leonard and Ruth Martha (Weed) C.; m. Nancy Anne McKuben, Dec. 13, 1964; children: Dayna, Douglas, Daniel. BS, U. Colo., 1962; MSBA, U. Denver, 1970. Contract adminstr. Martin Co., Littleton, Colo., 1962-63; prodn. control supr. Honeywell, Inc., Littleton, 1967-72; prodn. control mgr. Beckman Instruments, Palo Alto, Calif., 1972-74; v.p. ops. Granville-Phillips, Boulder, Colo., 1974-79; materials mgr. Spectra-Physics, Inc., Eugene, Oreg., 1979-83; world wide sales mgr. Spectra-Physics, Inc., Eugene, 1983-85; v.p. sales Point of Sale Data Products, Gig Harbor, Wash., 1985-88, pres., 1988—; corp. officer Sensormatic Electronics Corp., Deerfield Beach, Fla.; bd. dirs. Micro Video Inc., Campbell, Calif. Basketball coach Youth Basketball Assn., YMCA, Eugene, 1979-81; mem. bd. rev. Boy Scouts Am., Eugene, 1979-85; pre-marriage counselor Newman Ctr., U. Oreg., Eugene, 1984-85. Lt. (j.g.) USN, 1967. Mem. Bus. Execs. for Nat. Security, Am. Electronics Assn., Optimists Club, Elks. Methodist. Home: 13109 3d Ave Ct NW Gig Harbor WA 98335

CRANSTON, ALAN, senator; b. Palo Alto, Calif., June 19, 1914; s. William MacGregor and Carol (Dixon) C.; m. Norma Weintraub, May 19, 1978; children: Robin MacGregor (dec.), Kim MacGregor. Student, Pomona Coll., 1932-33, U. Mexico, 1933; A.B., Stanford, 1936. Fgn. corr. Internat. News Service, Eng., Italy, Ethiopia, Germany, 1936-38; Washington rep. Common Council Am. Unity, Washington, 1940-41; chief fgn. lang. div. O.W.I., Washington, 1942-44; exec. sec. Council for Am.-Italian Affairs, Inc., Washington, 1945-46; partner bldg. and real estate firm Ames-Cranston Co., Palo Alto, Calif., 1947-58; controller State of Calif., 1959-67; pres. Homes for a Better America Inc., 1967-68; v.p. Carlsberg Financial Corp., Los Angeles, 1968; mem. U.S. Senate from Calif., 1969—; Democratic whip U.S. Senate, 1977—; mem. com. on banking, housing and urban affairs, chmn. subcom. housing and urban affair, mem. com. on fgn. relations, chmn. subcom. East Asia affairs, chmn. com. on vets. affairs, mem. Dem. steering com., Dem. policy com. and Select com. on Intelligence. Author: The Big Story, 1940, The Killing of the Peace, 1945. Mem. exec. com. Calif. Democratic Central Com., 1954-60; pres. Calif. Dem. Council, 1953-57. Served with AUS, 1944-45. Mem. United World Federalists (nat. pres. 1949-52). Club: Overseas Press Am. Office: US Senate 112 Hart Senate Bldg Washington DC 20510

CRANSTON, HOWARD STEPHEN, lawyer, management consultant; b. Hartford, Conn., Oct. 20, 1937; s. Howard Samuel and Agnes (Corvo) C.; m. Karen Youngman, June 16, 1962; children: Margaret, Susan. BA cum laude, Pomona Coll., 1959; LLB, Harvard U., 1962. Bar: Calif. 1963. Assoc. MacDonald & Halsted, Los Angeles, 1964-68; ptnr. MacDonald, Halsted & Laybourne, Los Angeles, 1968-82, of counsel, 1982-86; pres. Knapp Communications, Los Angeles, 1982-87; pres. S.C. Cons. Corp., 1987—; bd. dirs. Wood Knapp & Co., St. Clair & Co., Accurate, Inc. 1st lt. U.S. Army, 1962-64. Mem. Assn. Corp. Growth, Conf. Bd., San Gabriel Country Club, Harvard Club. Republican. Episcopalian. Author Handbook for Creative Managers, 1987, Management Decision Mag., 1988—. Office: SL Cons Corp 2233 Huntington Dr San Marino CA 91108

CRANTON, HAROLD, former advertising executive; b. Phila., Apr. 7, 1923; s. Jacob and Rebecca (Fineberg) Krantman; m. Rodha Lawrence Bloomstein, Dec. 30, 1947; 1 child, Nina. Student, Am. Theatre Wing, N.Y.C., 1946-49. Network radio actor CBS, NBC, ABC, N.Y.C., 1941-42, 46-49; writer, dir. Bobby Benson and His B-Bar-B Riders Sta. WOR-TV, N.Y.C., 1950-52; sales presentation writer spot sales CBS Radio, N.Y.C., 1952-53; supr. sales presentations NBC-TV Network, N.Y.C., 1954-58; dir. advt., promotion and research ABC Radio Network, N.Y.C., 1958-59; dir. advt. and promotion Met. (Metromedia) Broadcasting Corp., N.Y.C., 1959-61; broadcasting space salesman Variety Newspaper, N.Y.C., 1961-68; v.p. advt., publicity, promotion and sta. services MCA TV Syndication, N.Y.C., 1968-82; ret. 1982; instr. New Sch. for Social Research, N.Y.C., 1974-77; awards judge ind. TV sta., L.A., 1987. Writer, asst. dir., dir. radio and TV scripts, presentations in Library of Performing Arts, N.Y.C. and UCLA Library, L.A., 1948-50; dramatist Buttrio Square, 1952. Pres. Schwab House Concerned Tenants Com., N.Y.C., 1969-73, co-chair, 1979-83; trustee Nat. Hemophilia Found., 1973-78; pres., coop. bd. dirs. 11 Riverside Drive Corp., N.Y.C., 1983-84; mem. Archtl. Barriers Adv. Bd., L.A., 1986-87. Sgt. USAAF, 1942-46. Recipient award of merit Broadcast Promotion Assn. and Mich. State U., 1979, commendation Mayor of L.A., 1987. Mem. Broadcast Promotion and Mktg. Execs. (lectr. 1973, 79, Hall of Fame inductee 1986). Home: 14211 Hatteras St Van Nuys CA 91401

CRAPO, MICHAEL DEAN, laywer; b. Idaho Falls, Idaho, May 20, 1951; s. George LaVelle and Melba (Olsen) C.; m. Susan Diane Hasleton, June 22, 1974; children: Michelle, Brian, Stephanie, Lara, Paul. BA, Brigham Young U., 1973; JD, Harvard U., 1977. Bar: Calif. 1977, Idaho 1979. Law clk. to judge U.S. Ct. Appeals, San Diego, 1977-78; atty. Gibson, Dunn & Crutcher, Los Angeles, 1978-79; ptnr. Holden, Kidwell, Hahn & Crapo, Idaho Falls, 1979—. Senator Idaho State Legis., Boise, 1985—, asst. majority leader, 1987—; leader Boy Scouts Am., Calif, Idaho, 1977—. Named one of Outstanding Young Men of Am., 1985. Mem. ABA, Idaho State Bar. Republican. Mormon. Lodge: Rotary. Office: Holden Kidwell Hahn & Crapo PO Box 129 Idaho Falls ID 83402

CRARY, FRED DAILEY, data processing executive; b. Buffalo, Sept. 14, 1942; s. John Stevens and Frances Mary (Dailey) C.; m. Elizabeth Ann Deinken, Aug. 14, 1966; children: Karl Fredrick, Karen Elizabeth. BA, U. Del., 1964; MA in Math., U. Wis., 1967, PhD in Maht., 1973. Asst. prof. computer sci. dept. U. Wis., Madison, 1974-76, asst. dir. computing Math. Rsch. Ctr., 1974-77; software engr. Boeing Co., Seattle, 1977—; co-owner, mgr. Parenting Press, Inc., Seattle, 1979—. Mem. Assn. for Computing Machinery, IEEE Computer Soc. Office: Parenting Press Inc PO Box 15163 Seattle WA 98115

CRAVEN, EDWARD PATRICK, JR., accountant; b. Memphis, Dec. 22, 1952; s. Edward Patrick Sr. and Mary Ellen (Heuertz) C. BBA in Accountancy, U. Miss., 1974. CPA Tex., Nev. From staff auditor to sr. auditor Arthur Andersen & Co., Houston, 1974-78; controller Lansky Bros. Mens Stores, Memphis, 1978; sr. internal auditor, supr. internal auditing Holiday Corp., Memphis, 1979-81, mgr. consol. reporting and corp. acctg., 1981-84; dir. internal auditing Harrah's, Reno, 1984-88; contr. Harrah's Lake Tahoe, Stateline, Nev., 1989—. Mem. Nev. Soc. CPA's, Am. Inst. CPA's, Tex. Soc. CPA's, Inst. Internal Auditors (bd. govs. Nev. chpt. 1984—). Republican. Roman Catholic. Home: 3740 Timberlane Dr Carson City NV 89203 Office: Harrah's Lake Tahoe PO Box 8 Stateline NV 89449

CRAVEN, HOMER HENRY, JR., pilot, aviation consultant; b. Seattle, Jan. 31, 1925; s. Homer Henry and Juanita Normah (Briscoe) C.; student S.W. Tex. State Coll.; m. Mary Kathleen Weaver, May 3, 1945 (dec. Feb. 1985); children—James Michael, Scott Marshall, Anne Elizabeth Craven McDonald. With Boeing Airplane Co., Seattle, 1946-48, Smith Aviation, Renton, Wash., 1948-52; pilot Northwest Orient Airlines, Seattle, 1952-85, B-747 capt., 1976-85; aviation cons. Served with USAAF, 1943-45; PTO. Decorated Air medal. Mem. Am. Soc. Aerospace Edn., Nat. Aero. Assn., Exptl. Aircraft Assn., Aircraft Owners and Pilots Assn., 14th Air Force Assn., Northwest Captain's Club, Confederate Air Force. Episcopalian. Author research papers on fuel conservation. Home: 2005 180th Ct NE Redmond WA 98052 Office: Northwest Airlines Sea-Tac Airport Seattle WA 98001

CRAVENS, JAMES ELLIOT, hospital supply company executive; b. Los Angeles, June 2, 1949; s. James Elliott and Hazel Nelle (Harvey) C.; m. Janice Mary Dziekan, Nov. 29, 1974; children: Mary Nelle, James John. BS, UCLA, 1973. Med. specialist Burroughs-Wellcome Research, Triangle Park, Calif., 1974-77; parenteral specialist Travenol Labs., Deerfield, Ill., 1977-79; chmn. Dealex Hosp. Supply, Brea, Calif., 1979—; founder, pres. Packaging Techs., Brea, 1982-84; founder, v.p. Pathfinder Group, Horsham, Pa., 1984-88; v.p. sales and mktg. Implant Techs. Inc., Mpls. Bd. dirs. Diamond Bar (Calif.) Community Schs., 1985-86. Mem. Nat. Intravenous Therapy Assn. Democrat. Roman Catholic. Office: Dealex Hosp Supply 266 Viking Ave Brea CA 92621

CRAWFORD, ALLEN JAY, marketing executive; b. Schenectady, N.Y., Mar. 22, 1954; s. Allen Jay Sr. and Joan (Schmid) C.; m. Barbara L. Crawford, Oct. 20, 1978; children: Lawrence, Christine, A. Brenton. BS in Bus., N.H. U., 1979. Vice pres. mktg. Digitech Safe, Inc., Aurora, Colo., 1986—.

CRAWFORD, BARBARA TAYNTON, communications educator; b. Stockton, Calif., Apr. 25, 1937; d. Vernon Walter Taynton and Evelyn (Thomson) Jensen; m. Ian Campbell Crawford, Sep. 19, 1958 (div. 1972); children: Karen, Nancy. BA, San Francisco State U., 1968, MA, 1970; postgrad., U. Calif.-Santa Barbara, 1976-77. Instr. Santa Barbara (Calif.) City Coll., 1970-81, prof., 1985—; tchr., trainer Oreg. State U., Corvallis, 1973. Contbr. articles to profl. jours. Cons. Peace Resouce Ctr., Santa Barbara, 1986—. State Chancellors grantee, 1981. Mem. Western Speech Communications Assn. (mem. community coll. interest group 1985), Speech Communications Assn., Internat. Communications Assn. (workshop dir. 1986), Humanistic Psychology Assn. Democratic. Unitarian. Office: Santa Barbara City Coll 721 Cliff Dr Santa Barbara CA 93109

CRAWFORD, DALE L., architect; b. Raton, N. Mex., Dec. 29, 1933; s. William Pierce and Ruth Harriet (Nelson); m. Barbara Ann Mitchell Crawford, Aug. 25, 1955; children: Kelly Mitchell, Kevin Lee, Keith Nelson. BArch in Engring., U. N. Mex., 1956; student, U. Colo., 1955, USAF Inst. TEch., Wright Patterson AFB, 1957. Registered architect, N. Mex., La. Draftsman Brittle & Ginner Architects, Albuquerque, 1956-57; designer, craftsman Brittle-Ginner & Decker Architects, Albuquerque, 1960-61; designer, draftsman James Liberty Architect, Albuquerque, 1961; designer, architect Stanley & Assocs., Architects, Albuquerque, 1961-65; architect Stanley, Oravec & Crawford, Inc., Albuquerque, 1965-66, Crawford & Oravec, Architects, Albuquerque, 1966-71, Dale Crawford, Architect, Albuquerque, 1971-73, Dale Crawford & Assocs., P.C., Albuquerque, 1973—. Adminstrn. bd. Cen. United Meth. Ch., Albuquerque, 1985-88, Mil-Gracias Soc. Scholarship, N. Mex. St. U., 1981-84, Presdl. Scholarship program U. N. Mex., 1977-80. Served to capt. USAF, 1957-60. Mem. N. Mex. Soc. Architects (sec., treas. 1980, pres. elect, 1981, pres. 1982, dir. 1979-84), AIA (Albuquerque chpt. pres. 1978), N. Mex. Architects P.A.C. (pres. 1985-88), Am. Arbitration Assn. Republican. Home: 8727 Aztec Albuquerque NM 87111 Office: Dale Crawford & Assocs 117 Jefferson NE Albuquerque NM 97108

CRAWFORD, JENNIFER LYNN, interior designer; b. Portland, Oreg., May 24, 1956; d. Paul R. and Alice Evangeline (Nord) Moos; m. David Walter Crawford, Sept. 12, 1987. BS in Clothing and Textiles, Oreg. State U., 1979. Sec., clk. Freightliner, Portland, Oreg., 1980-82; salesperson Lucas Decor, West Linn, Oreg., 1981; interior designer Northwest Designers Assn., Sherwood, Oreg., 1982-84; pvt. practice Lake Oswego and West Link, Oreg., 1989—; speaker interior designer seminars for consumers, 1988—, 89—; sales mgr. Designer Powell Cabinetry & Design. Mem. Home Economists in Bus. (chmn. 1986-87, advisor, 1987-88 program advisor 1985-86, writer newsletter 1986-87), Am. Home Econs. Assn., Oreg. Home Econs. Assn. (bd. dirs. 1986-87). Republican. Home: 15140 SW 89th Pl Tigard OR 97224 Office: 3354 SE Powell Portland OR 97202

CRAWFORD, JOYCE CATHERINE HOLMES, psychologist; b. Kansas City, Mo., May 30, 1918; d. Morton Henry and Lillian Catharine (Burton) Holmes; student Kansas City Jr. Coll., 1934-36; B.S. in Edn., U. Mo., 1938; M.A. in Guidance and Counseling, No. Ariz. U., 1957; Ph.D. in Ednl. Psychology, Ariz. State U., 1976; m. Merle Eugene Crawford, Dec. 18, 1938; children—Hal Wayne, Kent Holmes. Tchr., Sedona, Ariz., 1948-49, Verde Valley Sch., 1949-51, Cottonwood, Ariz., 1952-69; sch. psychologist, child study cons., Phoenix, 1971-75, Riverside Sch. Dist., 1972-74, Avondale Sch. Dist., 1971-83. Ranger-naturalist Tuzigoot Nat. Monument, U.S. Park Service, summers 1959-66; mem. Ariz. Gov.'s Adv. Com. on Mental Health, 1964-65, Ariz. Hosp. Survey and Constrn. Adv. Council, 1965-68; head start chmn. Cottonwood Neighborhood Council, 1967-69; sec. Yavapai County Head Start Policy Adv. Com., 1968-71; bd. dirs. Yavapai County Econ. Opportunity Council, 1967-70, sec., 1968-69; bd. dirs. Ariz. Assn. Mental Health, 1955-67, sec., 1961-64, founder Verde Valley chpt., 1956, pres., 1959-61; incorporating com. Verde Valley Community Guidance Clinic, 1965, bd. dirs., 1965-70; bd. dirs. No. Ariz. Comprehensive Guidance Center, 1967-69; bd. dirs., recreation chmn. Ariz. Congress Parents and Tchrs., 1954-55; bd. dirs. Westside Mental Health Services, 1980-87, pres., 1980, v.p., 1980-81; chmn. profl. referral com. Westside Children's Mental Health Service, 1983-87; bd. dirs. Southwest Community Network, 1985-87. Cert. Ariz. Bd. Psychologist Examiners. Mem. Nat. Assn. Sch. Psychologists, Ariz. Assn. Sch. Psychologists (chmn. profl. standards com. 1980-81, pres. 1982-83, awards chmn. 1983-84, Keith Perkins Meml. award for Outstanding Achievement in Sch. Psychology 1988), Am. Psychol. Assn., Ariz. Psychol. Assn., Ariz. Edn. Assn. (mental health and spl. edn. com. 1961-67, chmn. 1964-65), Ariz. Assn. Children with Learning Disabilities, Psychologists for Social Responsibility, Planned Parenthood, Common Cause, ACLU, Delta Kappa Gamma. Democrat. Home: 6770 E Carondelet #126 Tucson AZ 85710

CRAWFORD, KELLY GRIFFITH, film editor; b. L.A., July 26, 1951; s. Broderick and Katherine (Griffith) C.; m. Marilyn Lou Williams, June 28, 1980 (div. 1986); m. Jeanne Lynn Cunningham, Jan. 10, 1988. Grad. high sch., Coronado, Calif. Asst. editor Warner Bros. TV, Hollywood, Calif., 1981-84, Warner Bros., Hollywood, 1984, 86, Paramount Pictures, Hollywood, 1985-86, Tomorrow Entertainment, Hollywood, 1986-87; editor New Star Pictures, Hollywood, 1987, MGM TV, Culver City, Calif., 1987-88; asst. editor Tisch Co., Hollywood, 1988, Stephen J. Cannell Prodns., Hollywood, 1988—. Author: (computer programs) Bytes-Dog-Man 35mm Codebook, 1983, 35mm Codebook for the Macintosh, 1988. Photographer San Diego Symphony Orchestra Assn., 1977-78, Save Our Heritage Orgn., San Diego, 1976. Recognized for Outstanding Achievement in Instrumental Music Bank of Am., 1969. Mem. Motion Picture and Videotape Editors Guild. Republican. Roman Catholic.

CRAWFORD, KENNETH VERNON, transportation company official; b. Duluth, Minn., Dec. 7, 1943; s. Kenneth Charles and Margaret Valarie

(Kenville) C.; m. Jonnie Lou Stream, July 2l, 1962; children: Kenneth William, Kyle Jon, Keri Grace. BS, U. Wis., Superior, 1968. Supr. internal audit Minn. Power & Light Co., Duluth, 1970-78; sr. auditor Arabian Am. Oil Co., Dhahran, Saudi Arabia, 1978-86, Potomac Electric Co., Washington, 1986-87; mgr. internal audit Greyhound Corp., Phoenix, 1987—. Mem. Inst. Internal Auditors (cert., pres. Dhahran chpt. 1985). Republican. Home: 5879 E Paradise Ln Scottsdale AZ 85254 Office: Greyhound Corp lll W Clarendon Phoenix AZ 85077

CRAWFORD, MARK MAXWELL, furniture manufacturing company executive; b. Seattle, May 29, 1955; s. William Maxwell and M. Gail (Hannay) C. BS, Pacific Luth. U., 1978. Sales ComMar Corp., Seattle, 1979-80; pres. Design and Archtl. Prods., Seattle, 1980-88, Ambiance Internat. Ltd., Seattle, 1981-87; owner MC Rep, Seattle, 1988—. Mem. Gideon's Internat., Seattle, 1987—; dele. Repub. Caucus, Seattle, 1988; pres. East Madison Townhomes Assn., Seattle, 1987—. Mem. Inst. of Bus. Designs (friend of the chpt. 1980—).

CRAWFORD, NATALIE WILSON, applied mathematician; b. Evansville, Ind., June 24, 1939; d. John Moore and Edna Dorothea (Huthsteiner) Wilson; BA in Math., U. Calif., Los Angeles, 1961, postgrad., 1964-67; m. Robert Charles Crawford, Mar. 1, 1969. Programmer analyst N.Am. Aviation Corp., El Segundo, Calif., 1961-64; mem. tech. staff Rand Corp., Santa Monica, Calif., 1964—, project leader, engring. tech., theater conflict and force employment programs, 1975—; dir. Theater Forces Program; mem. sci. adv. bd. USAF, 1988—; cons., joint tech. coordinating group munition effectiveness. Named YWCA Woman of Yr., 1983. Mem. Am. Def. Preparedness Assn., USAF Assn., IEEE. Republican. Home: 20940 Big Rock Dr Malibu CA 90265

CRAWFORD, PAUL GIBSON, educational administrator; b. Austin, Tex., Jan. 5, 1934; s. Neal Hayes Crawford and Willie Wanda (Woody) Carr; m. Helga Margot Rathmann, Dec. 29, 1962. AA, San Antonio Coll., 1953; BA, U. Tex., 1955; cert., Def. Postgrad. Sch., 1965. Commd. officer USN, 1956, advanced through grades to comdr., 1969; gen. line and intelligence officer USN, U.S., Far East and Rome, 1956-70; ret. 1970; stockbroker Calif. Investors, Orange, 1970-73; personnel analyst L.A. County Office Edn., Downey, Calif., 1973-76; personnel dir. Lynwood (Calif.) Unified Sch. Dist., 1976-81, Long Beach (Calif.) Unified Sch. Dist., 1981--. Choral dir. St. Barnabas Roman Cath. Ch., Long Beach. Mem. Internat. Personnel Mgmt. Assn., Calif. Assn. Sch. Bus. Ofcls., Calif. Schs. Personnel Commrs. Assn. (sec. 1986-88, Schuyler C. Joyner award 1984), So. Calif. Personnel Mgmt. Assn., Personnel Commrs. Assn. So. Calif. (sec.-treas. 1976-85, Robert Fisher Meml. award 1984), Personnel Testing Coun. So. Calif., Choral Condrs. Guild, Phoenix, Elks, Kiwanis. Republican. Home: 3734 Pacific Ave Long Beach CA 90807 Office: Long Beach Unified Sch Dist Pers Commn 701 Locust Ave Long Beach CA 90807

CRAWFORD, RICHARD EBEN, JR., investment advisor; b. Lake Forest, Ill., Dec. 24, 1930; s. Richard Eben Crawford and Alice B. (Appleton) Smith; m. Caroline Hellen Kelley, June 20, 1952 (div. 1980); children: Wes, John, J.D., Lindsay, Richard; m. Debbie Sum Chan, Feb. 1, 1985; children: Alexandra, Jessica. BA, Trinity Coll., Hartford, Conn., 1953; MBA, U. Pa., 1976. Various positions Minn. Natural Gas Co., St. Louis Park, Minn., 1957-69, pres., chief exec. officer, 1969-74; pres. Minn. Natural div. Minn. Gas Co., St. Louis Park, 1974-77; underwriter Conn. Gen. Life Ins. Co., Mpls., 1978-79; pres. Crawford Assocs., Tucson, 1980—, Crawford Meml. Cemetery, Emlenton, Pa., 1986—. Area and state judge Career Devel. Conf. Ariz. Distributive Edn. Clubs Am., 1986; vol. Mobile Meals program, Tucson, 1984—. Capt. USAF, 1955-57. Mem. Ariz. C. of C., Tucson C. of C. (com. mil. affairs 1983—), SAR (state and nat. chpts.), Pres.'s Club U. Ariz. Found., Skyline Country Club (tennis com. 1988—), Wharton Club Ariz. (pres., founder 1986—), Toastmasters (pres. Aztec club 1984, area gov. 1986-87, chmn. speechcraft com. 1987-88, Disting. Toastmaster), Rotary (bd. dirs. Catalina club internat. dist. 550, treas. 1988-89, chmn. various coms.), Alpha Delta Phi. Home: 6550 St Andrews Dr Tucson AZ 85718 Office: Crawford Assocs 5055 E Broadway Ste C 214 Tucson AZ 85711

CRAWFORD, WAYNE HALBURTON, JR., financial executive; b. Covina, Calif., Apr. 20, 1927; s. Wayne Halburton and Emogene Victoria (Crews) C.; m. Camille Lamar Tribelhorn, May 15, 1948; 1 child, Gary M. BA, U. So. Calif., 1947, MS, 1978; MS, U.S. Navy PG Sch., 1961. Commd. ensign USN, 1947, advanced through grades to capt.; chief naval ops. info. systems div. USN, Washington, 1969-72, asst. for automation orgn. joint chiefs of staff, 1972-75, staff, 1975-77; ret. USN, 1977; br. mgr. Downey Savs., LaCosta, Calif., 1978-80; v.p., br. mgr. Cen. Savs., Coronado, Calif., 1980-87, Coast Savs., Coronado, 1987-88. Active POETS, San Diego, 1982—. Mem. Phi Kappa Tau. Republican. Baptist. Clubs: Navy League (v.p. 1985-86), TROA (v.p. 1986-87) (Coronado). Lodge: Optimist (bd. dirs. 1985-87). Home: 82 Port of Spain Rd Coronado CA 92118

CRAY, ED, writer, teacher; b. Cleve., Ohio, July 3, 1933; s. Max and Sara (Negin) C.; m. Marjorie Lee, 1963 (div. 1967); 1 child, Jennifer; m. Diane Markson Kovacs, Apr. 21, 1985. BS, UCLA, 1957. Freelance writer LA, 1957-60; assoc. editor Frontier Mag., LA, 1961-64; dir pubs. ACLU of So. Calif., LA, 1965-70; dir. publicity L.A. Philharmonic, LA, 1970-71; freelance writer LA, 1971—; sr. lectr. U. So. Calif., LA, 1976-82, assoc. prof., 1982—. Author: Big Blue Line, 1967, The Erotic Muse, 1969, In Failing Health, 1970, Burden of Proof, 1973, Levis, 1979, Chrome Colossus, 1981. With U.S. Army, 1952-54. Mem. ACLU. Democrat. Jewish. Home: 10436 Kinnard Ave Los Angeles CA 90024 Office: Univ So Calif Sch Journalism Los Angeles CA 90089-1695

CREAGER, CLIFFORD RAYMOND, editor; b. N.Y.C., Oct. 8, 1937; s. Clifford Henry and Catherine (Raymond) C.; m. Dorothy Ann Carlson, Dec. 18, 1965; children: Christopher, Curtis. AB, U. Mich., 1960. Reporter, wire editor, photographer Grand Haven (Mich.) Daily Tribune, 1960-61; reporter, photographer, city editor, editor Covina (Calif.) Sentinel, weekly, 1963-72; mng. editor Car Craft mag., Los Angeles, 1972-75, Motor Trend mag., Los Angeles, 1975-81; free-lance writer, editor 1981-85; program dir. Safety Edn. Ctr., 1986-88; editor Profl. Counselor mag. and Adolescent Counselor mag., 1986—; v.p. A/D Communications Corp., 1986—. Served with AUS, 1961-63. Mem. U. Mich. Alumni Assn., Calif. Assn. Alcoholism And Drug Abuse Counselors, Calif. Assn. Drinking Driver Treatment Programs, Nat. Assn. Alcoholism and Drug Abuse Counselors.

CREAGER, JOE SCOTT, geology and oceanography educator; b. Vernon, Tex., Aug. 30, 1929; s. Earl Litton and Irene Eugenia (Keller) C.; m. Barbara Clark, Aug. 30, 1951 (dec.); children: Kenneth Clark, Vanessa Irene; m. B. J. Wren, Sept. 5, 1987. B.S., Colo. Coll., 1951; postgrad., Columbia, 1952-53; M.S., Tex. A. and M. U., 1953, Ph.D., 1958. Asst. prof. dept. oceanography U. Wash., Seattle, 1958-61; assoc. prof. U. Wash., 1962-66, prof. oceanography, 1966—, asst. chmn. dept. oceanography, 1964-65, prof. geol. scis., 1981—, assoc. dean arts and scis. for earth and planetary scis., also assoc. dean for research, 1966—; program dir. for oceanography NSF, 1965-66; chief scientist numerous oceanographic expdns. to Arctic and Sub-arctic including Leg XIX of Deep Sea Drilling project, 1959—; vis. geol. scientist Am. Geol. Inst., 1962, 63, 65; U.S. Nat. coordinator Internat. Indian Ocean Expedition, 1965-66; vis. scientist program lectr. Am. Geophys. Union, 1965-72; Battelle cons., advanced waste mgmt., 1974-75; cons. to U.S. Army C.E., 1976, U.S. Depts. Interior and Commerce, 1975; exec. sec., exec. com., chmn. planning com. Joint Oceanographic Insts. Deep Earth Sampling, 1970-72, 76-78. Editorial bd.: Internat. Jour. Marine Geology, 1964—; assoc. editor: Jour. Sedimentary Petrology, 1963-76; asst. editor: Quaternary Research, 1970-79; contbr. articles to profl. jours. Skipper Sea Scout Ship, Boy Scouts Am., Bryan, Tex., 1957; coach Little League Baseball, Seattle, 1964-71, sec., 1971; cons. sci. curriculum Northshore Sch. Dist., 1970; mem. Seattle Citizens Shoreline Com., 1973-74, King County Shoreline Com., 1980. Served with U.S. Army, 1953-55. Colo. Coll. scholar, 1949-51; NSF grantee, 1962-82; ERDA grantee, 1962-64; U.S. Army C.E. grantee, 1975-82; Office of Naval Research grantee; U.S. Dept. Commerce grantee; U.S. Geol. Survey grantee. Fellow Geol. Soc. Am., AAAS; mem. Internat. Assn. Quaternary Research, Am. Geophys. Union, Internat. Assn. Sedimentology, Internat. Assn. Math. Geologists, Soc. Econ. Paleontologists and Mineralists, Marine Tech. Soc. (sec.-treas. 1972-75), Sigma Xi, Beta Theta Pi, Delta Epsilon. Club: Explorers. Home: 6320 NE 157th St Bothell WA 98011 Office: U Wash Dept Oceanography WB-10 Seattle WA 98195

CREAN, JOHN C., housing and recreational vehicles manufacturing company executive; b. Bowden, N.D., 1925; married. Founder Fleetwood Enterprises, Inc., Riverside, Calif., 1951, pres., 1952-70, chmn., chief exec. officer, 1970—, also dir. Served with USN, 1942; with U.S. Mcht. Marines, 1944-45. Office: Fleetwood Enterprises Inc 3125 Myers St Riverside CA 92523 *

CREAN, MARK DENNIS, paper products company executive; b. Jacksonville, Fla., July 26, 1951; s. John Joseph and Helen Trude (Wolshke) C.; m. Patricia Lynn Popovac, Feb. 28, 1976. BS Pulp, Paper Sci., N.C. State U., 1973; postgrad., La. Tech. U., 1976-78. Prodn. asst. to paper mill supt. Sonoco Products Co., Hartsville, S.C., 1973-75; office mgr. asst. Sonoco Products Co., Holyoke, Mass., 1975; process engr. Continental Forest Industries, Hodge, La., 1975-78; prodn. supr. Continental Forest Industries, Hopewell, Va., 1978-84; sr. process engr. Stone Container Corp., Hopewell, 1984-88; tech. dir. Stone Container Corp., Snowflake, Ariz., 1988—. Treas., Internat. Mgmt. Coun., Hopewell, 1980-88; mem.Virginians Opposing Drunk Driving, Hopewell, 1986-88. Mem. TAPPI, Western States Tech. Dirs. Round Table, N.C. State Pulp and Paper Found., N.C. State Alumni Assn. Republican. Episcopalian. Office: Stone Container Corp PO Box 128 Snowflake AZ 85937

CREEVY, DONALD CHARLES, obstetrician/gynecologist; b. Mpls., Apr. 22, 1936; s. Charles Donald and Alice Myrtle (Youngberg) C.; m. Anne Linda Bachelder, Dec. 22, 1956 (div. 1981); children: Catherine, Kristin; m. Ginger Ann Davis, Jan. 17, 1987. BA in Anthropology, U. Minn., 1957, BS in Medicine, MD, 1961. Diplomate Am. Bd. Obstetrics and Gynecology. Intern Mpls. Gen. Hosp., 1961-62; resident in obstetrics and gynecology Stanford (Calif.) U. Med. Ctr., 1962-64, chief resident obstetrics and gynecology, 1964-66, clin. instr., 1966-68, clin. asst. prof., 1968—; pvt. practice Palo Alto and Portola, Calif., 1966—; attending physician Stanford U. Hosp., 1966—, El Camino Hosp., Mountain View, Calif., 1966—, Sequoia Hosp., Redwood City, Calif., 1985—; med. dir. The Birth Place, Menlo Park, Calif., 1979—, bd. dirs., Planetree, San Francisco, Family Planning Alternatives, Sunnyvale, Calif.; med. adv. bd. Nursing Mothers Counsel, Palo Alto, 1970—. Contbr. articles to prof. publs. Active legis. com. on birthing practices in Calif., Sacramento, 1977-78. NF fellow, 1958-59. Fellow Am. Coll. Obstetricians and Gynecologists; mem. AMA, Calif. Med. Assn., Santa Clara County Med. Soc., Nat. Perinatal Assn., Sierra Club (life). Democrat. Home: 1175 Westridge Dr Portola Valley CA 94025 Office: 4370 Alpine Rd Portola Valley CA 94025

CRENSHAW, KEVIN MILLS, software company executive; b. Libertyville, Ill., June 6, 1960; s. Mills Laurie Crenshaw and Wendy Trenker (Midgley) Salazar; m. Margaret Elizabeth Lakin, Aug. 31, 1982; children: John Benjamin, Nathan Daniel, Sarah Marie, Brian David, Jason Neal. BS summa cum laude, Brigham Young U., 1983. Software engr. WordPerfect Corp., Orem, Utah, 1984-87, dir. devel., 1988; pres. Popular Demand, Inc., Orem, 1988—. Designer computer software. Missionary, Ch. of Jesus Christ of Latter-day Saints, Brisbane, Australia, 1979-81. Republican. Office: Popular Demand Inc 11 E 200 N #202 Orem UT 84057

CREPS, PHILIP LLOYD, chemist; b. Bowling Green, Ohio, Dec. 16, 1951; s. Wayne LeRoy and Elsie Marie (Frank) C.; m. Barbara Dawn Keller, Dec. 11, 1976; children: Jesse Jean, Sarah Marie. BS, Bowling Green (Ohio) State U., 1973; BA, U. Toledo, 1980, MS, 1989; AS, Aurora (Colo.) Community Coll., 1986. Rsch. project dir. Mich. State U., East Lansing, 1984-85; instr. Lansing Community Coll., 1984-85; environ. scientist Ohio EPA, Bowling Green, 1985; rsch. chemist Fitzsimmons Med. Ctr., Aurora, 1985-86; quality assurance chemist Pine Bluff (Ark.) Army Arsenal, 1986-89; extern Coll. Osteo. Medicine Mich. State U., Okemos, 1989—. Youth dir. Assembly of God Ch., Fostoria, Ohio, 1969-71; music dir. 1st Assembly of God Ch., Toledo, 1977-79; sec. Citizen's Council #3, Lansing, 1980-83. Served with USN, 1980-83. Recipient Alfred award South Counties Council, Newport, R.I., 1981, Mayor's Commendation City of Toledo, 1980. Mem. Am. Chem. Soc., Alpha Epsilon Delta, Psi Chi, Beta Beta Beta. Libertarian.

CRESS, LUTHER MOSS, fly fishing equipment executive; b. Burning Springs, Ky., Oct. 9, 1932; s. Oliver and Martha Delona (Hacker) C.; m. Nancy Jean Rader, Oct. 30, 1953; children: Cynthia, Robert. BA, Colo. State U., 1953; MA, U. No. Colo., 1958. Sci. tchr. Ft. Lupton (Colo.) Jr. and Sr. High Sch., 1956-60; biology tchr. Fairview High Sch., Boulder, Colo., 1960-76; pres., chief exec. officer CressCraft Co., Longmont, Colo., 1986—. Served with U.S. Army, 1953-54, Korea. Mem. Nat. Sci. Tchrs. Assn., Rodcrafters of Am. Republican.

CRESTANI, ROBERT JAMES, advertising executive; b. Trentum, Pa., Sept. 9, 1954; s. Robert and Jean (Zanotti) C.; m. Marcianne Slade, Aug. 21, 1982; 1 child: John Robert. BA, Ind. U., 1976. V.p., head west coast dept. TV William Morris Agy., Beverly Hills, Calif., 1976—. Democrat. Roman Catholic. Office: William Morris Agy 151 El Camino Beverly Hills CA 90212

CRESWELL, DONALD CRESTON, management consultant, marketing specialist; b. Balt., Mar. 28, 1932; s. Carroll Creston and Verna Moore (Taylor) C.; student Johns Hopkins U., 1951-52; M.B.A., U. Dayton, 1966; postgrad. bus. Stanford U., 1975; m. Terri Sue Tidwell, Dec. 28, 1958; 1 son, Creston Lee. Cons. engr. A.D. Ring & Assocs., Washington, 1956-58; sales and mktg. mgr. Ampex Corp., Redwood City, Calif., 1959-68; dir. mktg., magnetic products div. RCA Corp., N.Y.C., 1968-71; staff v.p. sales and advt. Pan Am. World Airways, N.Y.C., 1971-74; mktg. v.p. Rocor Internat., Palo Alto, Calif., 1975; v.p., chief operating officer, gen. mgr., Am. AmBuCar Services, Inc., San Francisco, 1976; prin. mgmt. cons., dir. mktg. services Stanford Research Inst., Menlo Park, Calif., 1977-86 ; v.p. and gen. mgr. Strategic Decisions Group-Decisions Systems, 1987—; bd. dirs. Rogerson Aircraft Controls, 1981-85, Jets Cybernetics; lectr. planning and mktg. mgmt. Am. Mgmt. Assn., 1968-69; program chmn. Grad. Bus. Assn., 1965; rep. to Electronics Industries Assn., 1968-71, to Internat. Air Transport Assn., 1971-74. Bd. dirs. Peninsula Youth Soccer Club, 1981-82; nat. dir. referee assessment, mem. referee com. U.S. Soccer Fedn., 1986-88; regional chief referee San Carlos Am. Youth Soccer Orgn., 1981-85; State dir. assessment Calif. Soccer Assn., 1982-85 ; mem. Los Angeles Olympics Organizing Com., 1983-84; ofcl. N. Am. Soccer League, 1983-84. Mem. Am. Mktg. Assn. (exec. mem.), Am. Theatre Organ Assn. (bd. dirs. 1978-79), Nat. Intercollegiate Soccer Ofcls. Assn., Charles Lindbergh Found., U.S. Soccer Fedn. (cert. soccer referee). Republican. Club: Wings. Home: 8 Pyrola Ln San Carlos CA 94070 Office: SDG Decision Systems 2440 Sand Hill Rd Menlo Park CA 94025-6900

CREUTZ, EDWARD CHESTER, physicist, museum consultant; b. Beaver Dam, Wis., Jan. 23, 1913; s. Lester Raymond and Grace (Smith) C.; m. Lela Rollefson, Sept. 13, 1937 (dec. Feb. 1972); children: Michael John, Carl Eugene, Ann Jo Carmel Creutz Cosgrove; M. 2d. Elisabeth B. Cordle, Oct. 5, 1974. B.S., U. Wis., 1936, Ph.D., 1939. Research assoc. Princeton U., 1939-40, instr. physics, 1940-41; physicist NDRC, 1941-42, Metall. Lab., U. Chgo., 1942-44, Manhattan Project, Los Alamos, 1944-46; assoc. prof. Carnegie Inst. Tech., Pitts., 1946-49, prof., head dept. physics, dir. Nuclear Research Ctr., 1948-55; dir. John Jay Hopkins Lab. for Pure and Applied Sci., 1955-59; dir. research Gen. Atomic Div. Gen. Dynamics Corp., San Diego, 1955-59; v.p. research and devel. Gen. Atomic div. Gen. Dynamics Corp., San Diego, 1959-67; v.p. research and devel Gulf Gen. Atomic, San Diego, 1967-70; asst. dir. NSF, Washington, 1970-77, acting dep. dir., 1976-77; dir. Bernice Pauahi Bishop Mus., Honolulu, 1977-84; cons. Bernice Pauahi Bishop Mus., 1984—; mem. adv. council Water Resources Ctr., U. Calif.-Berkeley, 1958-65; mem. sea water conversion com. Water resources Ctr., U. Calif.-Berkeley, 1958-68; adv. com. office Sci. Personnel NRC, 1960-63; mem. exec. council Argonne Nat. Lab. (1946-51); cons. NSF, 1950-68; scientist-at-large Project Sherwood div. research AEC, 1955-56; mem. com. sr. reviewers Dept. Energy, 1972-79, fusion power coordinating com., 1971-79; cons. Oak Ridge Nat. Lab., 1946-58; adv. panel gen. scis. Dept. Def., 1959-63; research adv. com. electrophysics NASA, 1964-71, tech. adv. com., 1971-77; adj. prof. physics and astronomy U. Hawaii, 1977—; adj. prof. physics U. Calif., San Diego, 1987—. Co-editor: Handbuch der Physik, vols. 14, 15; mem. editorial bd. Ann. Rev. Nuclear Sci., 1961-66, 72-75, Handbook of Chemistry and Physics, 1961-71; mem. editorial bd.: Interdisciplinary Science Reviews, London, 1976—; editorial adv. com.: Nuclear Sci. and Engring., 1959-72. Bd. dirs. San Diego Hall Sci. and Planetarium, v.p., 1956-70; v.p. San Diego Industry-Edn. Council, 1956-65; mem. adv. council Dept. Edn. San Diego County. Fellow Am. Phys. Soc. (NRC rep. 1956-57), Am. Nuclear Soc., AAAS, Explorers Club; mem. Nat. Acad. Scis., Social Sci. Assn. Honolulu, Am. Assn. Physics Tchrs., Phys. Soc. Pitts. (pres. 1949), Am. Soc. Engring. Edn., ASME, AAUP, IEEE, Am. Inst. Physics (dir.-at-large bd. govs. 1965-68). Home: PO Box 2757 Rancho Santa Fe CA 92067

CREWDSON, JOHN MARK, journalist, author; b. San Francisco, Dec. 15, 1945; s. Mark Guy and Eva Rebecca (Doane) C.; m. Prudence Gray Tillotson, Sept. 11, 1969; children: Anders Gray, Oliver McDuff. A.B. with great distinction in Econs., U. Calif., Berkeley, 1970; postgrad. studies in politics, Oxford U., Eng., 1971-72. Reporter N.Y. Times, Washington, 1973-77; nat. corr N.Y. Times, Houston, 1977-82; nat. news editor Chgo. Tribune, 1982-83, met. news editor, 1983-84; west coast corr. Chgo. Tribune, L.A., 1984-87; corr. Chgo. Tribune, 1987—. Author: The Tarnished Door, 1983, By Silence Betrayed, 1988. Recipient Bronze medallion Sigma Delta Chi, 1974; Goldberg award N.Y. Deadline Club, 1977; Page One award N.Y. Newspaper Guild, 1977; Pulitzer prize, 1981. Office: Chgo Tribune 435 N Michigan Ave Chicago IL 60611

CREWS, JUDITH CAROL, special education educator, drug abuse consultant; b. Sanford, N.C., Apr. 30, 1948; d. Thomas Tengene and Pearl Irene (Douglas) Edwards; m. Richard Lee Crews, Oct. 12, 1967. AA in Art, Long Beach (Calif.) Community Coll., 1973; BFA in Art, Calif. State U., Long Beach, 1973-76; postgrad., U. San Francisco, 1979-80; MA in Edn., Calif. State U., Los Angeles, 1984; postgrad., U. Calif., Berkeley, 1987. Cert. elem., secondary tchr., learning disabled and resource specialist, Calif. Prof. art Compton (Calif.) Coll., Compton, Calif., 1977-80; tchr. spl. edn. Hillside Ctr., Long Beach, 1980, Hillside Devel. Learning Ctr., La Canada, Calif., 1980-82; tchr. spl. edn., coordinator dept., coordinator drug prevention, writer grants Westminster (Calif.) High Sch., 1982—; mentor sci., math., writer grants Huntington Beach (Calif.) Union Hich Sch. Dist., 1987—; prodn. mgr. Mid-Cities Assn. for the Retarded, Compton, 1978-80, tchr. ceramics, 1979-80; writer curricula Orange County Dept. Edn., Santa Ana, Calif., 1988—. Sec. Council Exceptional Children, Orange County, 1987—; patron Dollars for Scholars; active Nat. Fedn. Drug Free Youth, Washington, 1986—; exec. bd. dirs. No on Drugs in Sch., 1987—; bd. dirs. Alcohol and Substance Abuse Council, 1984—, Westminster Alcohol and Drug Abuse Council, 1984—. Named Tchr. of Yr. Orange County, Calif, 1987; recipient Compton Beautification award U.S. Dept. Rehab., Health Edn. and Welfare. Mem. Comupter Using Educator, Nat. Math. Council, Nat. Sci. Council., Calif. Math. Council, Calif. Sci. Council, Magic Castle Club. Democrat. Baptist. Home: 2040 Josie Ave Long Beach CA 90815 Office: Westminster High School 14325 Goldenwest St Westminster CA 96283

CREWS, WILLIAM ODELL, JR., seminary administrator; b. Houston, Feb. 8, 1936; s. William O. Sr. and Juanita (Pearson) C.; m. Wanda Jo Ann Cunningham; children: Ronald Wayne, Rhonda Ann Crews Patterson. BA, Hardin Simmons U., 1957, HHD, 1987; BDiv, Southwestern Bapt. Theol. Sem., 1964; DD, Calif. Bapt. Coll., 1987. Ordained to ministry Bapt. Ch., 1953. Pastor Grape Creek Bapt. Ch., San Angelo, Tex., 1952-54, Plainview Bapt. Ch., Stamford, Tex., 1955-57, 1st Bapt. Ch., Sterling City, Tex., 1957-60, 7th St. Bapt. Ch., Ballinger, Tex., 1960-65, Woodland Heights Bapt. Ch., Brownwood, Tex., 1965-67, Victory Bapt. Ch., Seattle, 1967-72, Met. Bapt. Ch., Portland, Oreg., 1972-77; dir. communications Northwest Bapt. Conv., Portland, 1977-78; pastor Magnolia Ave Bapt. Ch., Riverside, Calif., 1978-86; pres. Golden Gate Bapt. Theol. Sem., Mill Valley, Calif., 1986—; pres. NW Bapt. Conv., Portland, 1974-76, So. Bapt. Gen. Conv. Calif., Fresno, 1982-84. Trustee Fgn. Mission Bd., Richmond, Va., 1973-78, Golden Gate Bapt. Theol. Sem., 1980-85; bd. dirs. Midway-Seatac Boys Club, Des Moines, 1969-72. Mem. Marin County C. of C. (bd. dirs. 1987—), Midway C. of C. (bd. dirs. 1968-72). Lodge: Rotary (pres. Portland club 1975-76, pres-elect Riverside club 1984-85). Home: 10 Chapel Dr Mill Valley CA 94941 Office: Golden Gate Bapt Theol Sem Strawberry Point Mill Valley CA 94941

CRIBB, WAYNE WOOSLEY, JR., electrical engineer; b. Racine, Wis., June 19, 1935; s. Wayne Woosley Sr. and Mary Alice (Jenkins) C.; m. Mary Ann Neale, June 14, 1958; children: Matthew Wayne, Nancy Ann Cribb Bailey. BSEE, U. Mo., 1958. Registered profl. engr., Calif. Sr. staff specialist McDonnel Douglas, Huntington Beach, Calif., 1969—. Sustaining mem. Rep. Nat. Com., Washington, 1979—. Mem. Pi Mu Epsilon. Home: 24842 Winterwood Dr El Toro CA 92630 Office: McDonnell Douglas 5301 Bolsa Ave Huntington Beach CA 92630

CRICHTON, JOHN HAYES, investment banker; b. Minden, La., July 21, 1920; s. Thomas and Bernard Moore (Hayes) C.; m. Dale Cowgill, July 3, 1967 (dec.); children by previous marriage: Kate, Bunnie, Lili, John Hayes. BS, Davidson Coll., 1942; JD, La. State U., 1949; exec. program, Stanford U., 1970. Bar: La. 1949. Assoc. Smitherman, Smitherman & Purcell, 1949-51; mng. dir. Better Hotels of La., Shreveport, 1951-61; exec. v.p., asst. to pres. Allied Properties, San Francisco, 1961-62; pres. Guaranteed Reservations Inc., Palm Beach, Fla., 1962—, also bd. dirs.; pres., bd. dir. Computer Controls Corp., 1967-70; chmn. bd. dirs. Commonwealth Group Inc.; bd. dirs. Golden Rim Investment and Three Two Corp. Maj., inf. AUS, 1942-46. Decorated Bronze star with oak leaf cluster. Mem. ABA, La. Bar Assn., Internat. Assn. Mergers and Acquisitions Cons., Phi Delta Phi. Republican. Presbyterian. Clubs: Bankers San Francisco; Bath and Tennis (Palm Beach), The Everglades (Palm Beach), Burlingame Country (Hillsborough, Calif.). Home: 2411 Pacific Ave San Francisco CA 94115 Office: Commonwealth Inc 650 California St San Francisco CA 94108

CRICHTON, JOHN MICHAEL, author, film director; b. Chgo., Oct. 23, 1942; s. John Henderson and Zula (Miller) C. A.B. summa cum laude, Harvard U., 1964, M.D., 1969. Postdoctoral fellow Salk Inst., La Jolla, Calif., 1969-70. Writer, dir. film Westworld, 1973, Coma, 1978, The Great Train Robbery, 1979, Looker, 1980, Runaway, 1984; dir. film Physical Evidence, 1989; author: The Andromeda Strain, 1969, Five Patients, 1970, The Terminal Man, 1972, The Great Train Robbery, 1975, Eaters of the Dead, 1976, Jasper Johns, 1977, Congo, 1980, Electronic Life, 1983, Sphere, 1987, Travels, 1988. Recipient Edgar award Mystery Writers Am., 1968, 80; named med. writer of year Assn. Am. Med. Writers, 1970. Mem. Authors Guild, Writers Guild Am. West, Dirs. Guild Am., P.E.N. Am. Ctr., Acad. Motion Picture Arts and Scis., Internat. Design Conf. (bd. dirs.), Phi Beta Kappa. Club: Aesculaepian (Boston). Office: Creative Artists Agy 1888 Century Pk E Los Angeles CA 90067

CRICK, FRANCIS HARRY COMPTON, biologist, educator; b. June 8, 1916; s. Harry and Annie Elizabeth (Wilkins) C.; m. Ruth Doreen Dodd, 1940 (div. 1947); 1 son; m. Odile Speed, 1949; 2 daus. B.Sc., Univ. Coll., London; PhD, Cambridge U., Eng. Scientist Brit. Admiralty, 1940-47, Strangeways Lab., Cambridge, Eng., 1947-49; biologist Med. Rsch. Coun. Lab. of Molecular Biology, Cambridge, 1949-77; Kieckhefer Disting. prof. Salk Inst. for Biol. Studies, San Diego, 1977—, non-resident fellow, 1962-73; adj. prof. psychology and chemistry, U. Calif.-San Diego; vis. lectr. Rockefeller Inst., N.Y.C., 1959; vis. prof. chemistry dept. Harvard U., 1959, vis. prof. biophysics, 1962; fellow Churchill Coll., Cambridge, 1960-61; Korkes Meml. lectr. Duke U., 1960; Henry Sedgewick Meml. lectr. Cambridge U., 1963; Graham Young lectr., Glasgow, 1963; Robert Boyle lectr. Oxford U., 1963; Vanuxem lectr. Princeton U., 1964; William T. Sedgwick Meml. lectr. MIT, 1965; Cherwell-Simon Meml. lectr. Oxford U., 1966; Shell lectr. Stanford U., 1969; Paul Lund lectr. Northwestern U., 1977; Dupont lectr. Harvard U., 1979, numerous other invited, meml. lectrs. Author: Of Molecules and Men, 1966, Life Itself, 1981, What Mad Pursuit, 1988; contbr. papers and articles on molecular, cell biology and neurobiology to sci. jours. Recipient Prix Charles Leopold Mayer French Academies des Scis., 1961; recipient (with J.D. Watson) Rsch. Corp. award, 1961, (with J.D. Watson & Maurice Wilkins) Nobel Prize for medicine, 1962, Gairdner Found. award, 1962, Royal Medal Royal Soc., 1972, Copley Medal, 1976, Michelson-Morley award, 1981, Benjamin P. Cheney medal, Spokane, Wash., 1986,

Golden Plate award, Phoenix, 1987, Albert medal Royal Soc. of Arts, London, 1987, Wright Prize VIII Harvey Mudd Coll., Claremont, Calif., 1988, Joseph Priestly award Dickinson Coll., 1988. Fellow AAAS, Royal Soc.; mem. Am. Acad. Arts and Scis. (fgn. hon.), Am. Soc. Biol. Chemistry (hon.), U.S. Nat. Acad. Scis. (fgn. assoc.), German Acad. Sci., Am. Philos. Soc. (fgn. mem.), French Acad. Scis. (assoc. fgn. mem.), Indian Acad. Scis. (hon. fellow). Office: Salk Inst Biol Studies PO Box 85800 San Diego CA 92138

CRIDER, HOYT, health care executive; b. Arley, Ala., June 5, 1924; s. Lindsey C. and Bessie P. C.; student Ga. Sch. Tech., 1942-43; B.S. in Naval Sci. and Tactics, U. S.C., 1946; M.A. in Polit. Sci., U. Ala., 1949; D.Pub. Adminstrn., U. So. Calif., 1954; m. Judie Watkins, Nov. 2, 1951; children—Kim, Marc. Vis. asst. prof., dir. research U. So. Calif. team, Iran, 1954-56; adminstrv. analyst Chief Adminstrv. Offices Los Angeles County, 1956-59; v.p. Watkins & Watkins Constrn. Co., Hanford and Morro Bay, Calif., 1959-64; co-owner, adminstr. Kings Convalescent Hosp., Hanford, Calif., 1964-66; adminstr. Villa Capistrano Convalescent Hosp., Capistrano Beach, Calif., 1966-68; partner Hunt and Crider, San Diego Convalescent Hosp., 1968-70; pres., chief exec. officer Health Care Enterprises, Inc., San Clemente, Calif., 1970—; mem. Regional Health Planning Commn. Kings County, 1963-64. Served with USNR, 1941-46. Fellow Am. Coll. Nursing Home Adminstrs. (pres. 1976-77), Am. Coll. Health Care Adminstrs.; mem. Calif. Assn. Health Facilities (past v.p. local chpt. 1964), Gerontol. Soc., AAAS. Club: San Clemente Kiwanis (Kiwanian of Yr. 1970, pres. 1970-71). Home: 214 Calle Cortez San Clemente CA 92672 Office: 407 N El Camino Real Suite C San Clemente CA 92672 Office: 1209 W Hemlock Way Santa Ana CA 92707

CRIDER, WILLIAM GERALD, communications and publishing company executive; b. Austin, Tex., May 16, 1954; s. William Douglas and Mary Ann (Middleton) C.; m. Janet Marie Bartel, May 16, 1976. Student, Tex. A&M U., 1972-74; BA, Am. Christian Coll., 1976. Acquisitions editor Moody Press, Chgo., 1979-80; asst. prodn. mgr. Moody Press, 1980-82; prodn. mgr., acquisition editor Communication Skill Builders, Tucson, 1982-84; pres. Wordsmith Graphic Communications, Inc., Tucson, 1982--, New Type Tech., Inc., Tucson, 1987--; v.p. Rent-A-Computer, Inc., Tucson, 1985-87. Contbg. editor PC World mag., 1984-88, Publish!, 1987--; author: How to Use the Apple IIe, 1984, Business Buyer's Guide to FAX, 1987; editor: Basic Program Conversions, 1984. Mem. Tucson Computer Soc. (pres. 1986). Republican. Mem. Free Ch. America. Home: 7022 E 5th St Tucson AZ 85710

CRILLY, EUGENE RICHARD, engineering specialist; b. Phila., Oct. 30, 1923; s. Eugene John and Mary Virginia (Harvey) C.; m. Alice Royal Roth, Feb. 16, 1952; ME, Stevens Inst. Tech., 1944, MS, 1949; MS, U. Pa., 1951; postgrad. UCLA, 1955-58. Sr. research engr. N.Am. Aviation, Los Angeles, 1954-57; sr. research engr., Canoga Park and Downey, Calif., 1962-66; process engr. Northrop Aircraft Corp., Hawthorne, Calif., 1957-59; project engr., quality assurance mgr. HITCO, Gardena, Calif., 1959-62; sr. research specialist Lockheed-Calif. Co., Burbank, 1966-74; engrng. specialist N.Am. aircraft ops. Rockwell Internat., El Segundo, Calif., 1974-89. Author tech. papers. Served with USNR, 1943-46; comdr. Res. ret. Mem. Soc. for Advancement Material and Process Engrng. (chmn. Los Angeles chpt. 1978-79, gen. chmn. 1981 symposium exhbn., nat. dir. 1979-86, treas. 1982-85), Soc. Mfg. Engrs. (sr.), Naval Inst., Am. Soc. for Composites, ASM Internat., Naval Res. Assn., VFW, Mil. Order World Wars (adjutant San Fernando Valley chpt. 1985, 2d vice comdr. 1986, commdr. 1987-89, vice comdr. West, Dept Cen.Calif., 1988-89), Former Intelligence Officers Assn., Naval Intelligence Profls. Assn., Brit. United Service Club Los Angeles, Sigma Xi, Sigma Nu. Republican. Roman Catholic. Home and Business: 276 J Ave Coronado CA 92118

CRIMMIMS, JAMES CURTIS, television producer; b. Palo Alto, Calif., Jan. 13, 1935; s. Edward Curtis and Naneen (Burnap) C.; m. Marcy Tench, Feb. 23, 1962 (div. 1976); children: Ethan, Samantha, Page, Tory; m. Jennifer Leahy, Dec. 16, 1978; 1 child, Courtney. BA, Princeton (N.J.) U., 1956. With Curtis Pub. Co., Phila., 1956-59; asst. to pres. Vector Mfg. Co., Pa., 1959-61; asst. vehicle mktg. mgr. Saturday Evening Post, Phila., 1961-63; spl. projects dir. Newsweek mag., N.Y.C., 1963-68; v.p., assoc. pub. Harper's mag., N.Y.C., 1968-71; pres., chief exe. officer Playback Assocs., N.Y.C., 1971-77; pres., chief exe. officer J.C. Crimmins & Co., Inc., N.Y.C., 1977-82, Santa Barbara, Calif., 1986--; pres., chief exec. officer J.C. Crimmins & Co., Inc., Santa Barbara, 1962. Editor-in-chief Bus. Times, Inc., 1982-86; author: Nicholas, 1962, Successful Publishing, 1968, TV and Management, 1973, others; editor: Search for Solutions, 1979, Archimedes Revenge, 1988. Recipient Grand award N.Y. Film and TV Festival, 1979. Mem. Acad. TV Arts and Scis., University Club (N.Y.C.). Mem. Soc. of Friends. Home: 2721 Cuesta Rd Santa Barbara CA 93103

CRISCUOLO, WENDY LAURA, lawyer, interior design consultant; b. N.Y.C., Dec. 17, 1949; d. Joseph Andrew and Betty Jane (Jackson) C.; m. John Howard Price, Jr., Sept. 5, 1970 (div. Apr. 1981); m. Ross J. Turner, July 23, 1988. AB with honors in Design, U. Calif., Berkeley, 1973; JD, U. San Francisco, 1982. Space planner GSA, San Francisco, 1973-79; sr. interior designer E. Lew & Assocs., San Francisco, 1979-80; design dir. Beier & Gunderson, Inc., Oakland, Calif., 1980-81; sr. interior designer Environ. Planning and Research, San Francisco, 1981-82; interior design cons., Hillsborough, 1982—; law clk. to Judge Spencer Williams, U.S. Dist. Ct., San Francisco, 1983-84; atty. Ciros Investments, Hillsborough, 1985—. Author: (with others) Guide to the Laws of Charitable Giving, 3d rev. edit., 1983; mem. U. San Francisco Law Rev., 1983. Bd. dirs., v.p. and treas. Marin Citizens for Energy Planning; bd. dirs., pres. The Wildlife Ctr. Mem. ABA, State Bar Calif., Queen's Bench (San Francisco), Calif. Women Lawyers. Republican. Episcopalian. Club: Commonwealth (San Francisco). Avocation: creative writing.

CRISMAN, MARY FRANCES BORDEN, librarian; b. Tacoma, Nov. 23, 1919; d. Lindon A. and Mary Cecelia (Donnelly) Borden; m. Fredric Lee Crisman, Apr. 12, 1975 (dec. Dec. 1975). BA in History, U. Wash., 1943, BA in Librarianship, 1944. Asst. br. librarian in charge work with children Mottet br. Tacoma Pub. Library, 1944-45, br. librarian, 1945-49, br. librarian Moore br., 1950-55, asst. dir., 1955-70, dir., 1970-74, dir. emeritus, 1975—; librarian co. Frank Russell Co., 1985—; chmn. Wash. Community Library Council, 1970-72. Hostess program Your Library and You, Sta. KTPS-TV, 1969-71. Mem. Highland Homeowners League, Tacoma, 1980—, incorporating dir. 1980, sec. and registered agt., 1980-82. Mem. ALA (chmn. mem. com. Wash. 1957-60, mem. nat. library week com. 1965, chmn. library adminstrn. div. nominating com. 1971, mem. ins. for libraries com. 1970-74, vice chmn. library adminstrn. div. personnel adminstrn. sect. 1972-73, chmn. 1973-74, mem. com. policy implementation 1973-74, mem. library orgn. and mgmt. sect. budgeting acctg. and costs com. 1974-75), Am. Library Trustee Assn. (legis. com. 1975-78, conf. program com. 1978-80, action devel. com. 1978-80), Pacific N.W. (trustee div. nominating com 1976-77), Wash. Library Assn. (exec. bd. 1957-59, state exec., dir. Nat. Library Week 1965, treas., exec. bd. 1969-71, 71-73), Urban Libraries Council (editorial sec. Newsletter 1972-73, exec. com. 1974-75), Ladies Aux. to United Transp. Union (past pres. Tacoma), Friends Tacoma Pub. Library (registered agt. 1975-83, sec. 1975-78, pres. 1978-80, bd. dirs. 1980-83), Smithsonian Assocs., Nat. Railway Hist. Soc., U. Wash. Alumni Assn., U. Wash. Sch. Librarianship Alumni Assn. Roman Catholic. Club: Quota (sec. 1957-58, 1st v.p. 1960-61, pres. 1961-62, treas. 1975-76, pres. 1979-80)

CRISMOND, LINDA FRY, county librarian; b. Burbank, Calif., Mar. 1, 1943; d. Billy Chapin and Lois (Harding) Fry; m. Donald Burleigh Crismond, 1965 (div. Sept. 1980). B.S., U. Calif.-Santa Barbara, 1964; M.L.S., U. Calif.-Berkeley, 1965. Cert. county librarian, Calif. Reference librarian, EDP coordinator San Francisco Pub. Library, 1965-72, head acquisition, 1972-74; asst. univ. librarian U. So. Calif., Los Angeles, 1974-80; chief dep. county librarian Los Angeles County Pub. Library, Los Angeles, 1980-81; county librarian Los Angeles County Pub. Library, Downey, 1981-89; Western rep. quality control council Ohio Coll. Library Ctr., Columbus, 1977-80; mem. Am. Nat. Standards Inst., N.Y.C., 1978-80; bd. councillors U. So. Calif. Sch. Library and Info. Mgmt., 1980-83; adv. bd. mem. UCLA Library Sch., 1981—; chmn. bd. dirs. Los Angeles Pub. Library Found., 1982-85; mem. OCLC Users Coun., 1988—; mem. exec. com. L.A. County Mgmt. Coun., 1986-88, pres., 1988. Author: Directory of San Francisco Bay Area, 1968. Named Staff Mem. of Year San Francisco Pub. Library, 1968. Mem. ALA (chmn. Percy Jury 1976-78, chmn. Gale Jury 1982-84, exec. com. resources and tech. services div. resources sect. 1980-82), Calif. Library assn. (council 1980-82), Calif. County Librarians Assn. (pres. 1984). Home: 15985 Alcima Ave Pacific Palisades CA 90272 Office: Los Angeles County Pub Libr 7400 E Imperial Hwy PO Box 7011 Downey CA 90241-7011

CRISP, TERRY ARTHUR, professional hockey coach; b. Parry Sound, Ont., Canada, May 28, 1943; m. Sheila Crisp; children: Tony, Jeffrey, Caley. Profl. player NHL, 1965-77; with Boston, 1965-66 season, St. Louis, 1967-72, N.Y.C., 1972-73, Phila., 1973-7; formerly coach Soo Greyhounds, Ont. Hockey League; coach Calgary Flames farm club, Moncton, 1985-87, Calgary Flames, Nat. Hockey League, Calgary, Alta., 1987—. Named Coach of Yr. Ont. Hockey League, 1982-83, 84-85. Office: Calgary Flames, PO Box 1540 Sta M, Calgary, AB Canada T2P 3B9 *

CRISPIN, JAMES HEWES, engineering and construction company executive; b. Rochester, Minn., July 23, 1915; s. Egerton Lafayette and Angela (Shipman) C.; A.B. in Mech. Engrng., Stanford U., 1938; M.B.A., Harvard U., 1941; grad. Army Command and Gen. Staff Sch., 1943; m. Marjorie Holmes, Aug. 5, 1966. With C.F. Braun & Co., Alhambra, Calif., 1946-62; treas. Bechtel Corp., San Francisco, 1962-73, v.p., mem. fin. com., 1967-75, mgr. investment dept., 1973-75, ret.; personal investments, 1976—. Served to lt. col. Ordnance Corps, AUS., 1941-46. Registered profl. mech. engr., Calif. Mem. Mil. Order World Wars, S.R., Soc. Colonial Wars Calif., Baronial Order Magna Carta, Mil Order Crusades, Am. Def. Preparedness Assn., World Affairs Council No. Calif. (trustee 1968-75), Santa Barbara Mus. Art (trustee 1979—, pres. 1986-88), Calif. Hist. Soc. (trustee 1979-86), Beta Theta Pi. Republican. Clubs: Valley of Montecito (Santa Barbara) (pres. 1987—, bd. dirs. 1981—); Calif. (Los Angeles); St. Francis Yacht, San Francisco Golf, Pacific-Union, World Trade (pres. 1977-78, dir. 1971-78) (San Francisco). Home: 1340 E Mountain Dr Santa Barbara CA 93108 Office: La Arcada Bldg 1114 State St Ste 220 Santa Barbara CA 93101

CRISPO, RICHARD CHARLES, artist, ethnologist, minister; b. Bklyn., Jan. 13, 1945; s. Frank C. and Irene M. (Lamont) C. M.F.A., Trinity Hall Coll., 1975; Ph.D., Collegii Romanii, Rome, 1976, Th.D., 1977. Instr. art Monterey Peninsula Coll., 1968-69, instr. ethnic studies, 1976; instr. art history Hartwell Coll.; now coordinator Arts in Corrections, Art Project, Soledad Prison; instr. pub. sch. art, Monterey, Calif., 1967-72; counselor Intrim, Inc., Monterey, 1976; founder Mus. on Wheels, 1973-74; founder World Folk Art Collection, Monterey, 1972; 53 murals and 63 one-man shows; executed half-mile-long mural at Soledad Prison; priest N. Am. Old Roman Catholic Ch. Recipient numerous awards including 1st prize Calif. State Fair, 1964; UNESCO award, 1971-73; Calif. Arts Council grantee. Mem. Artist Equity, Found. for the Community of Artists, Carmel Art Assn., Pacific Grove Art Center. Contbr. articles to art jours.

CRISS, WILLIAM SOTELO, laser company executive; b. Akron, Ohio, Oct. 14, 1949; s. Everett Robert and Lois Marie (Gill) C.; m. Celia P. Sotelo, Sept. 15, 1973; children: Celina, David. BS, Calif. Inst. Tech., 1971; MBA, U. Chgo., 1973. Sect. supr. car product devel. Ford Motor Co., Dearborn, Mich., 1973-78; gen. supt. Consol. Rail Corp., Phila., 1978-85; pres. Automated Laser System, Inc., Danville, Calif., 1985-89, gen. mgr. data display products, 1989—. Office: Automated Laser Systems Inc PO Box 2735 Danville CA 94526-7735

CRISSEY, JOHN THORNE, dermatologist, educator; b. Tonawanda, N.Y., July 19, 1924; s. Earl Guy and Sadie Kay (Harris) C.; m. Alice Jessamine Hogue, Jul. 30, 1949; children: Jennifer, Kaye, John Jr. MD, U. Buffalo, 1946. Diplomate Am. Bd. Dermatology and Syphilology. Assoc. prof. medicine U. Buffalo, 1952-64; clin. prof. medicine U. So. Calif. Sch. Medicine, Los Angeles, 1964—. Author: Classics in Clinical Dermatology, 1952 (Garrison-Morton Classic award 1952), The Dermatology and Syphilology of the 19th Century, 1981, Syphilis, 1984. Served to capt. U.S. Army, 1943-49. Recipient Gougerot prize for med. history Société de Dermatologie Gougerot, 1985. Fellow Am. Acad. Dermatology; mem. Am. Dermatological Assn. (gold award for scientific exhibit 1988), Sigma Xi. Republican. Presbyterian. Home: 608 Sierra Madre Blvd San Marino CA 91108 Office: U So Calif Sch Medicine 960 E Green St Pasadena CA 91106

CRISTIANO, MARILYN JEAN, speech communication educator; b. New Haven, Jan. 10, 1954; d. Michael William Mary Rose (Porto) C. BA, Marquette U., 1975, MA, 1977; postgrad., Ariz. State U., 1977, Nova U., 1988-. Speech communication instr. Phoenix Coll., 1977-87, Paradise Valley Community Coll., Phoenix, 1987—; cons. IBM, various locations, Scottsdale (Ariz.) Pub. Schs., Mayo Clinic, Scottsdale, Ariz. Pub. Service, Phoenix. Published study guide on pub. speaking, 1989. Mem. Women in Higher Edn. in Ariz. (v.p., pres.), Am. Soc. Tng. and Devel., Speech Communication Assn., Western Speech Communication Assn., Ariz. Communication Assn. Office: Paradise Valley Community Coll 18401 N 32d St Phoenix AZ 85032

CRISTOL, STANLEY JEROME, chemistry educator; b. Chgo., June 14, 1916; s. Myer J. and Lillian (Young) C.; m. Barbara Wright Swingle, June 1957; children: Marjorie Jo, Jeffrey Tod. B.S., Northwestern U., 1937; M.A., UCLA, 1939, Ph.D., 1943. Research chemist Standard Oil Co., Calif., 1938-41; research fellow U. Ill., 1943-44; research chemist U.S. Dept. Agr., 1944-46; asst. prof., then asso. prof. U. Colo., 1946-55, prof., 1955—, Joseph Sewall disting. prof., 1979—, chmn. dept. chemistry, 1960-62, grad. dean, 1980-81; vis. prof. Stanford U., summer 1961, U. Geneva, 1975, U. Lausanne, Switzerland, 1981; with OSRD, 1944-46; adv. panels NSF, 1957-63, 69-73, NIH, 1969-72. Author: (with L.O. Smith, Jr.) Organic Chemistry, 1966; editorial bd., Chem. Revs., 1957-59, Jour. Organic Chemistry, 1964-68; contbr. research articles to sci. jours. Guggenheim fellow, 1955-56, 81, 82; recipient James Flack Norris award in phys.-organic chemistry, 1972, Alumni Merit award Northwestern U., 1987. Fellow AAAS (councilor 1986—), Chem. Soc. London; mem. Am. Chem. Soc. (chmn. organic chemistry div. 1961-62, adv. bd. petroleum research fund 1963-66, council policy com. 1968-73), AAUP, Colo.-Wyo. Acad. Sci., Nat. Acad. Scis., Phi Beta Kappa, Sigma Xi, Phi Lambda Upsilon. Home: 2918 3d St Boulder CO 80304 Office: U Colo Dept Chemistry CB 215 Boulder CO 80309

CRISWELL, KIMBERLY ANN, public relations executive, dancer; b. L.A., Dec. 6, 1957; d. Robert Burton and Carolyn Joyce (Semko) C. BA with honors, U. Calif.-Santa Cruz, 1980. Instr., English Lang. Services, Oakland, Calif., 1980-81; freelance writer Gambit mag., New Orleans, 1981; instr. Tulane U., New Orleans, 1981; instr., editor Haitian-English Lang. Program, New Orleans, 1981-82; instr. Delgado Coll., New Orleans, 1982-83; instr., program coord. Vietnamese Youth Ctr., San Francisco, 1984; dancer Khadra Internat. Folk Ballet, San Francisco, 1984-89; dir. mktg. communications Centram Systems West, Inc., Berkeley, Calif., 1984-87; communications coord. Safeway Stores, Inc., Oakland, 1985; dir. corp. communications TOPS, div. Sun Microsystems, Inc, 1987-88; pres. Criswell Communications, 1988—. Vol. coord. Friends of Haitians, 1981, editor, writer newsletter, 1981; dancer Komenka Ethnic Dance Ensemble, New Orleans, 1983; mem. Contemp. Art Ctr.'s Krewe of Clones, New Orleans, 1983, Americans for Nonsmokers Rights, Berkeley, 1985. Mem. Internat. Assn. Bus. Communicators, Sci. Meets the Arts Soc. (founding), NAFE, Dance Action, Bay Area Dance Coalition, Oakland Mus. Assn., Mus. Soc. Democrat. Avocations: visual arts, travel, creative writing. Office: 2560 9th St #315A Berkeley CA 94710

CRITCHLOW, B. VAUGHN, research facility administrator, researcher; b. Hotchkiss, Colo., Mar. 5, 1927; s. Arthur Burtis and Nancy Gertrude (Lynch) C.; m. Janet Lee Howell, Mar. 5, 1987; children from previous marriage: Christopher, Eric, Jan, Carey. AA, Glendale Coll., 1946-49; BA, Occidental Coll., 1951; PhD, UCLA, 1957. Instr. to prof. anatomy, acting chmn. anatomy Baylor Coll. Medicine, Houston, 1957-72; prof., chmn. anatomy Oreg. Health Scis. U., Portland, 1972-82; mem. sci. adv. com. Oreg. Regional Primate Rsch. Ctr., Beaverton, 1973-82, mem. ad hoc adv. com., 1981-82, dir., 1982—; trustee Med. Rsch. Found. Oreg., 1982—; vis. investigator Nobel Inst. Neurophysiology, Karolinska Inst., Stockholm, 1961-62; invited speaker 2d Internat. Cong. Hormonal Steroids, Milan, Italy, 1966, 3d Internt. Cong. Endocrinology, Mexico City, 1968, others; mem. NIH reproductive biology study sects., 1969-73, 75-77. Contbr. numerous articles to profl. jours. Served with USN, 1945-46. NIH rsch. career devel. awardee, 1959-69; NIH rsch. grantee, 1958—. Mem. Am. Assn. Anatomists, Endocrine Soc., Am. Physiol. Soc., Soc. for Neurosci., Internat. Soc. Neuroendocrinology, Internat. Brain Rsch. Orgn., Am. Soc. Primatologists. Office: Oreg Regional Primate Rsch Ctr 505 NW 185th Ave Beaverton OR 97006

CRITCHLOW, KENNETH ROY, biologist; b. Fresno, Calif., Aug. 31, 1943; s. Milton Thomas and Dorothy Mae (Unruh) C.; m. Janet Lynn Swett, Dec. 18, 1966; children: Kelly K., Jared Bradley. BA, Occidental Coll., 1965; MA, UCLA, 1968, PhD, 1972. Sr. biologist Marine Biol. Cons., Costa Mesa, Calif., 1972-75; sr. marine biologist, mgr. diving ops. Dames & Moore, L.A., 1975-81; sr. ecologist Woodward-Clyde Cons., San Francisco, 1981-86; sr. ecologist, office mgr. LGL Ecol. Rsch. Assn., San Ramon, Calif., 1986-87; sr. scientist, mktg. dir. Beak Cons. Inc., Sacramento, Calif., 1988—. Contbr. articles to profl. jours. NSF grantee UCLA, 1965. Mem. Ecol. Soc. Am., Am. Fisheries Soc., Am. Soc. Ichthyologists Herpetologists (Stowee award 1971). Home: 505 Hatti Ct San Ramon CA 94583 Office: Beak Cons Inc 2717 Cottage Way Ste 20 Sacramento CA 95860-0065

CRITES, RICHARD RAY, international franchising company executive; b. Rapid City, S.D., Aug. 29, 1952; s. Charles Dayton and Marcia Ann (Heil) C.; m. Randel E. Golobic, Dec. 27, 1980 (div. May 1988). B of Liberal Studies, U. Okla., 1975; MS, Stanford U., 1978. Nat. sales trainer Continental Mktg. Corp., Detroit, 1975-76, regional sales mgr., 1976-80; pres., chief exec. officer Retail Packaging Specialists, Inc., San Mateo, Calif., 1982-86; owner, chief exec. officer Miracle Method of San Mateo, Inc., 1985-87, Miracle Method of Beverly Hills, Inc., L.A., 1987—, Miracle Method of So. Calif., Inc., L.A., 1986—, Miracle Method of No. Calif., Inc., L.A., 1988—; v.p., treas., chmn. bd. Miracle Method of the U.S., Inc., L.A., 1988—; pres., chmn. Internat. Miracle Appearance Ctrs. Pacific, Inc., L.A., 1988—. Republican. Scientologist. Office: Miracle Method of the US Inc 3732 W Century Blvd #6 Inglewood CA 90303

CRITTENDEN, CINDY MARIE, small business owner; b. Denver, June 23, 1962; d. Barclay Lloyd and Leola (Thibault) C. Student, U. N.Mex., 1980-82. Sec. McCarthy & Bruson, Albuquerque, 1981-82; mgr. Rocky Mountain Spas, Albuquerque, 1982-85; owner, operator Video Visions, Albuquerque, 1985—. Mem. Video Software Dealer Assn. Republican. Roman Catholic. Home: 12200 Pine Ridge NE Albuquerque NM 87112 Office: Video Visions 9712 Candelaria Rd NE Albuquerque NM 87112

CROCKER, KENNETH FRANKLIN, data processing consultant; b. Centralia, Wash., July 29, 1950; d. Earl Thomas and Mary Jane (Hamil) C.; m. Mary Louise Underwood, June 15, 1974 (div. Dec. 1987); children: Matthew A., Benjamin F., Jonathan C.; m. Sally Marlene Gammelgard, Dec. 21, 1987. AS in Computer Programming and System Design, Control Data Inst., Long Beach, Calif., 1972. Programmer City of Greenville, S.C., 1973, Piedmont Industries, Greenville, 1975-78; computer operator Winn Dixie Stores, Greer, S.C., 1973-75; programmer, analyst Micro-Systems, Greenville, 1978; sr. programmer Reeves Bros., Lyman, S.C., 1978-80; systems analyst Cryovac div. W.R. Grace Co., Duncan, S.C., 1980-84; sr. cons. Cap Gemini Am., San Francisco, 1984-85; prin. mem. tech. staff Citicorp Savs. Calif., Oakland, 1985—. Umpire, coach South San Ramon (Calif.) Little League, 1985-86, coach, 1988—. Republican. Baptist. Home: 301 Livorna Heights Rd Alamo CA 94507

CROCKER, THOMAS NEAL, high school teacher, athletic coach; b. Mpls., June 1, 1938; s. Neal Acker Crocker and Helen Ardell (Brede) Warnecke; m. Janet Helen Christianson; children: Richard Thomas, Donald Neal, Michael Robert. BA, San Francisco State U., 1962, MA, 1972. Cert. secondary sch. tchr., Calif. Tchr., coach San Lorenzo (Calif.) Unified Sch. Dist., 1964-65; tchr., coach football, swimming and water polo Hayward (Calif.) Unified Sch. Dist., 1965—; asst. coach water polo Ohlone Coll., Fremont, Calif., 1979-80; mem. adv. com. Newark (Calif.) Swim Ctr., 1985—. Served with U.S. Army, 1956-58. Mem. Nat. Interscholastic Swimming Coaches Assn. (Calif. North Coast Swimming Honors Coach 1985, 25 Year Service award 1988). Office: Tennyson High Sch Whitman Ave Hayward CA 94544

CROCKETT, DONALD LEE, small business owner; b. Oxnard, Calif., Sept. 11, 1942; s. Burney Byron and Josephine (Genova) C.; m. Norma Lee Crabtree, Nov. 9, 1968; children: Carrie Ann, Anthony Joseph. Student, Allan Hancock Coll., 1962-63. Asst. mgr. Beneficial Fin. Co., Santa Maria, Calif., 1965-68, 70; installment loan officer Wells Fargo Bank, Santa Maria, 1971-77, asst. v.p. and mgr., 1978-82; owner, chief exec. officer The Paint Works, Inc., Santa Maria, 1982—. Bd. dirs., region chmn. March of Dimes, 1979-82. Served to sgt. U.S. Army, 1968-69. Democrat. Roman Catholic. Club: Exchange (Santa Maria) (Ventura) (charter pres. 1974, treas. 1980). Lodge: Elks. Home: 4630 Lydia Ln Santa Maria CA 93455 Office: The Paint Works Inc PO Box 5994 Santa Maria CA 93456

CROCKETT, JOEL EDWARD, printing company executive; b. Burbank, Calif., Feb. 22, 1941; s. John Harvey, Jr. and Helen Elise (Schreyer) C.; m. Susan A. Fields, Oct. 26, 1963 (div. 1984); children: Kristin Amy, Kelley Anne, Joshua John; m. Linda C. Moeller, May 11, 1985. Student, Santa Monica City Coll., 1959-63. Mgr. games div. Pacific Ocean Park, Ocean Park, Calif., 1959-63; sales rep. Los Angeles Conv. Bur., 1963-65; paper cons. Noland Paper Co., Buena Park, Calif., 1965-67; printing paper mgr. Noland Paper Co., San Diego, 1967-69; sales mgr. Frye and Smith, San Diego, 1969-75; owner The Word Shop, San Diego, 1975-77; sales mgr. Metzger Printing Co., Denver, 1977-79; pres. Nat. Press, Inc., Palo Alto, Calif., 1979-88, K/P Graphics, Sunnyvale, Calif., 1989—. Author: DM America's Fastest Growing Advertising Medium, 1979; contbr. articles, columns to profl. publs. Recipient Salesman of Yr. award Sales and Mktg. Execs., 1966, Clio award Acad. Broadcasting, 1976. Mem. Printing Industries No. Calif. (v.p. 1987-89, pres. 1989—), Rotary. Republican. Presbyterian. Home: 685 High St #2A Palo Alto CA 94301 Office: K/P Graphics 771 Vaqueros Ave Sunnyvale CA 94087

CROCKETT, MARY LOU, real estate broker, city commisioner; b. Inglewood, Calif., Oct. 2, 1938; d. Otto P. and Lorene (Mitchell) Cripps; m. Hugh Crockett, Dec. 26, 1958 (div. 1977); 1 child, Patricia Lee. BA, UCLA, 1959. Licensed Real Estate Broker. Sch. tchr. Orangedale Elementary Sch., Phoenix, 1959-62; ptnr. Cripps Crockett, Realtors, Westchester, Calif., 1963—; pres., bd. dirs. Venice-Marina del Rey Multiple Listing Svc.; bd. dirs. Venice-Marina del Rey Bd. of Realtors. Contbr. articles to community newspaper. V.p. Westchester Vitalization Corp., 1988-89; co-founder Community Plans, Inc., Westchester, Friends of the Library, Westchester and Loyola Branches; bd. dirs. L.A. Bd. Airport Commrs., 1978-84, pres., 1980-81; hon. mayor City of Westchester-Playa del Rey, 1988-89; bd. commrs. L.A. Pub. Libr. Mem. Calif. Assn. Realtors, Inglewood Bd. of Realtors, United Multiple Listing Svc. (bd. mem. 1978-87), Nat. Assn. Realtors, Calif. Assn. Library Trustees & Commrs. (bd. dirs.), Westchester C. of C. (bd. dirs.). Republican. Christian Scientist. Office: Cripps Crockett Realtors 7573 S Sepulveda Blvd Westchester CA 90045

CROCKETT, ROBERT YORK, architect; b. West Covina, Calif., Nov. 27, 1962; s. Bob York and Carolyn (McLellan) C. BArch, U. So. Calif., 1985. Registered architect, Calif. Designer TNT Architecture Internat., Malibu, Calif., 1983-85, Pace Group, Los Angeles, 1985-87; pvt. practice architecture Los Angeles, 1987—. Democrat. Roman Catholic. Home: 890 W 15th St #56 Newport Beach CA 92663 Office: 1600 S Bundy Dr 3 West Los Angeles CA 90025

CROFFORD, HELEN LOIS, accountant; b. Mesa, Ariz., Sept. 1, 1932; d. Elmer Earl and Lillian Irene (Williams) C.; grad. Lamson Bus. Coll., Phoenix, 1952. Acct., Bob Fisher Enterprises, Inc., Holbrook, Ariz., 1964-78; office mgr. for physician, Holbrook, 1978-79; office mgr. Trans Western Services, Inc., Holbrook, 1979; acct., Northland Pioneer Coll., Holbrook, 1980—. Squadron comdr. CAP, 1965-67, mission coordinator, 1970-79, group comdr., 1972-77, mem. regional staff, 1977-79, wing. historian, 1984—; mem. Navajo Fair Commn., 1966-75; mem. Navajo County Natural Resource Conservation Dist., 1970—, sec.-treas., 1971-81, chairperson, 1981-88; chmn. Navajo County Emergency Service Council, 1984-87; co-chmn. Navajo County Local Emergency Planning Com., 1987-88; troop com. sec. Boy Scouts Am., 1989. Mem. Ariz. Assn. Conservation Dists. (exec. bd. 1977-78, sec., 1979-80, v.p. 1981-82, pres. 1983-84, past pres. 1985), Nat. Assn. Conservation Dists. (past pres., edn. com. 1981-84), DAR. Democrat. Home: Box 36 Woodruff AZ 85942 Office: 1200 E Hermosa Dr Holbrook AZ 86025

CROGAN, NEVA LYNNE, nurse; b. Colfax, Wash., Feb. 22, 1957; d. George Conrad and Beverly June (Harris) Russell; m. Bill Loren Dyck, Apr. 24, 1976 (div. 1987); 1 child, David Loren; m. David Martin Crogan, June 20, 1987. AA, Big Bend Community Coll., Moses Lake, Wash., 1977, Columbia Basin Coll., Pasco, Wash., 1979; BS, Eastern Wash. U., 1983; BSN, SUNY, Albany, 1984. RN, Wash. Staff nurse Othello (Wash.) Community Hosp., 1977-80, Whitman Community Hosp., Colfax, Wash., 1980-81; charge nurse Ritzville (Wash.) Meml. Hosp., 1981; nursing instr. Big Bend Community Coll., Moses Lake, Wash., 1981-87; edn. coordinator Moses Lake Clinic, 1987-88; utilization coordinator Med. Service Corp., Spokane, Wash., 1988-89; in-svc. dir. St. Brendan Nursing Home, Spokane, 1989—; cons. Moses Lake, 1985-86; educator local ch. groups, Moses Lake, 1987--. Recipient Women of the Moose grant, 1979. Mem. Nat. League Nursing, AAUW (treas. 1986). Home: PO Box 893 Mead WA 99021 Office: Saint Brendan Nursing Home E 178th Ave Spokane WA 99220

CROKER, KENNETH SYMONDS, aerospace engineering executive; b. San Pedro, Calif., July 4, 1935; s. Richard Symonds and Annie Robertson (Gillespie) C.; m. Carolyn Jane Hagelin, June 27, 1959; children: Judith Lynn, Teri Louise, David Symonds. BSEE, Stanford U., 1958. Engr. Douglas Aircraft Co., Sacramento, Calif., 1958-63, Culver City, Calif., 1963; engring. supr. Douglas Aircraft Co., Huntington Beach, Calif., 1963-67; mgr. McDonnell-Douglas Astronautics Co., Huntington Beach, 1967—. Author: Santa Ana Mountain Trails Guide, 1976 (Orange County Author award U. Calif-Irvine 1977). Served to 2d lt. U.S. Army, 1958. Recipient Resolution award Orange County Hist. Soc., 1977, Skylab Achievement Award NASA, 1974. Mem. IEEE, Sierra Club (conservation officer Los Angeles chpt. 1970-73, nat. forest coordinator So. Calif. 1975-88). Republican. Presbyterian. Home: 2783 Mendoza Dr Costa Mesa CA 92626

CROMPTON, ARNOLD, minister, educator; b. Leeds, Yorkshire, Eng., Dec. 19, 1914; came to U.S., 1923; s. Harold and May Almyeria (Milward) C. BA, Case Western Res. U., 1936; MA, U. Chgo., 1939; BD, Meadville Theol. Sch., Chgo., 1939; ThD, Pacific Sch. of Religion, 1956; DD (hon.), Meadville-Lombard Theol. Sch., 1972. Ordained to ministry Unitarian Ch., 1939. Minister 1st Unitarian Ch. of Erie, Pa., 1939-45; minister 1st Unitarian Ch. of Erie, Oakland, Calif., 1945-82, minister emeritus, 1982—; lectr. ch. history Starr King Sch. for the Ministry, Berkeley, Calif., 1953-67; dir. Earl Morse Wilbur Library, Berkeley, 1961-67; bd. dirs., past pres. Oakland-Fukuoka Soc., Oakland, 1975—; pres. Rossmoor Religious Coun., Walnut Creek, Calif., 1989—. Author: Apostle of Liberty, 1950, Unitarianism on Pacific Coast, 1954, Aurelia H. Reinhardt, 1981; contbr. articles to profl. jours. Lectr. Ebell Soc., Oakland, 1982—; pres. Internat. Inst. of the East Bay, Oakland, 1981-82, Rossmoor Activities Coun., Walnut Creek, 1989—; chmn. Alameda County Crime Prevention Commn., Calif., 1978-80; bd. dirs. English summer sch. Bir Zeit Coll., Jordan, 1963-64, English Lang. Program-Komagane, Japan, 1967. Recipient Silver Beaver award Boy Scouts Am., 1966, Citation, Calif. State Assembly, 1970, Citation, Calif. State Senate, 1975, Disting. Alumin award Case Western Reserve U., 1989; named one of Outstanding Immigrants, Internat. Inst., 1976. Mem. Unitarian Universalist Ministers Assn. (pres. Pacific Coast chpt. 1970), Rotary (pres. Rossmoor chpt. 1986-87), Masons (grand chaplain 1979-80), Phi Alpha Theta (hon.). Home: 1449 Skycrest Dr #1 Walnut Creek CA 94595 Office: 1st Unitarian Ch 685-14th St Oakland CA 94612

CROMPTON, THOMAS CHARLES, county agency administrator; b. Springfield, Ohio, Jan. 15, 1953; s. Robert Charles and Helen Frances (Cutshall) C.; m. Linda S. Crompton, Sept. 15, 1976 (div. 1986); children: Robert William, Mark Thomas; m. Molly Lorraine Bradford, Nov. 21, 1987. AA, Hartnell Coll., 1982. Counterintelligence spl. agt. U.S. Army Intelligence and Security Command, various locations, 1972-79; dep. sheriff County of Monterey, Monterey, Calif., 1979-84; coroner's investigator County of Monterey, Salinas, Calif., 1984—; agy. rep., coord., Interpol., Tokyo and Seoul, Korea, 1976-77. Author, editor: Coroner's Division Standard Operating Procedure, 1987. Vol. March of Dimes, 1977, 85-88, Crosby Pro Am Golf Tournament, Pebble Beach, Calif., 1981-86; active Boy Scouts Am., Salinas, 1988-89, Rainbow Girls, Salinas, 1986—. Sgt. U.S. Army, 1972-79. Mem. Calif. Homicide Investigators Assn., Assn. Fed. Investigators, Peace Officers Rsch. Assn. Calif., Monterey County Peace Officers Assn., Monterey County Dep. Sheriff Assn., Mensa, Masons. Republican. Presbyterian. Office: Monterey County Coroner Div 1414 Natividad Rd Salinas CA 93906

CRONE, RICHARD ALLAN, cardiologist, educator; b. Tacoma, Nov. 26, 1947; s. Richard Irving and Alla Marguerite (Ernst) C.; m. Rita Louzetta Mitchell, June 9, 1972 (div. Oct. 1981); m. Mika Jane Hinkle, Feb. 12, 1983. BA in Chemistry, U. Wash., 1969, MD, 1973. Intern Madigan Army Med. Ctr., Tacoma, 1973-74, resident in medicine, 1974-76, fellow in cardiology, 1977-79; commd. med. officer U.S. Army, Tacoma, Denver, San Francisco, 1972; advanced through grades to lt. col. U.S. Army, 1981; dir. coronary care unit Fitzsimons Army Med. Ctr., Denver, 1979-81; practice medicine specializing in cardiology Stevens Health Clinic, Edmonds, Wash., 1981—, also dir. coronary care unit, cardiac catheter lab, 1982—; clin. asst. prof. medicine U. Wash., Seattle, 1983—. Nat. Merit scholar, 1965. Fellow Am. Coll. Angiology; mem. AMA, Am. Coll. Cardiology, Am. Heart Assn., Seattle Acad. Internal Medicine, Wash. State Soc. Internal Medicine, Wash. State Med. Assn. Republican. Roman Catholic. Home: 10325 66th Pl W Everett WA 98204 Office: Stevens Health Clinic 21700 76th Ave W #100 Edmonds WA 98020

CRONIN, TIMOTHY E(MMETT), III, sales executive; b. Chgo., Jan. 17, 1937; s. Timothy E. II and Loretta D. (Konen) C.; children: Timothy E. IV, Terrence W., Thomas E., Theodore R. BS, No. Ill. U., 1962. Mktg. cons. McKesson Drug Co., Champaign, Ill., 1962-66; pharmacy design specialist McKesson Drug Co., Chgo., 1966-69; dist. sales mgr. McKesson Drug Co., Phoenix, 1969-72, San Diego, 1972-75; zone mgr. computer services McKesson Drug Co., Orange, Calif., 1975-76; asst. to pres. Unified Pharmacies, L.A., 1976-78; nat. dir. services Valu-Rite Pharmacies, Orange, Calif., 1978-81; western regional mgr. B & E Sales Co., City of Industry, Calif., 1981—; cons. Den-Mat Corp., Santa Maria, Calif., 1986-87. Served with U.S. Army, 1955-57. Mem. Dana Point Yacht (Calif). Republican. Roman Catholic. Office: B&E Sales Co 16150 Stephen St City of Industry CA 91744

CRONK, MILDRED SCHIEFELBEIN (MILI CRONK), special education consultant; b. Waverly, Iowa, May 29, 1909; d. Emil August and Nettie Marie (Berger) Schiefelbein; m. Dale Cronk, July 20, 1930; children: Barbara Cronk Burress, Bruce, Margaret, Michael. Student, Wartburg Coll., Waverly, 1927, Tampa (Fla.) U., 1944-45, Los Angeles City Coll., 1957; BA in Psychology, Calif. State U., 1960, MA in Spl. Edn. Supervision, 1971. Aircraft communicator, weather observer CAA, Fla. and Calif., 1942-49; dir. Parkview Nursery Sch., L.A., 1956-57; tchr. trainable mentally retarded Hacienda-LaPuente United Sch. Dist., LaPuente, Calif., 1961-74; cons. spl. edn. La Mirada, Calif., 1975—; in-service trainer for tchrs.; mem. Spl. Olympics S.E. L.A. County com., 1977—; mem. Internat. Very Spl. Arts Festival Com., 1981; mem. adv. com. Very Spl. Arts Festival, Orange County, 1977-86, chmn., 1986-87; treas. Very Spl. Arts Calif., 1986—. Author: Create With Clay, 1976, Vocational Skills Taught Through Creative Arts, 1978, Attitude Change Toward Trainable Mentally Retarded Students--Mainstreaming in Reverse, 1978, Career Education for Trainable Mentally Retarded Students--It's For Life!, 1982, others. Mem. Am. Assn. on Mental Deficiency (bd. dirs. region II, editor Newsette, 1975-77, chmn. publicity com., 1977-79, presenter ann. confs.), Coun. for Exceptional Children (bd. dirs. Calif., editor Calif. State Fedn./Coun. for Exceptional Children Jour., 1977-80, past pres. San Gabriel Valley chpt. 538, mem.-at-large S. Calif. div. Mental Retardation, 1976-79, pres. Calif. div. Mental Retardation, 1980-81, chmn. com. on officers' handbook, nat. coun., div. Mental Retardation, 1977-78, sec. 1988-89, spl. recognition awards, 1976, 77, 78, 79, 89), Nat. Assn. for Retarded Citizens (rec. sec. 1980-81), Nat. Soc. Autistic Children (nat., state, local orgns.), Nat. Ret. Tchrs. Assn. (nat., state, local orgns.), Am. Ceramic Soc. (design div.), Smithsonian Instn., Wilderness Soc., Psi Chi. Democrat. Home and Office: 13116 Clearwood Ave La Mirada CA 90638

CRONKLETON, THOMAS EUGENE, physician; b. Donahue, Iowa, July 22, 1928; s. Harry L. and Ursula Alice (Halligan) C.; BA in Biology, St. Ambrose Coll., 1954; MD, Iowa Coll. Medicine, 1958; m. Wilma Agnes Potter, June 6, 1953; children: Thomas Eugene, Kevin P., Margaret A., Catherine A., Richard A., Robert A., Susan A., Phillip A. Rotating intern St. Benedict's Hosp., Ogden, Utah, 1958-59; Donahue, Iowa, 1959-61, practice family medicine, Davenport, Iowa, 1961-66, Laramie, Wyo., 1966—; asso. The Davenport Clinic, 1961-63, partner, 1963-66; active staff St. Luke's Hosp., Mercy Hosp., Davenport; staff physician U. Wyo. Student Health Service, 1966-69, 70-71, 74-75; staff physician outpatient dept. VA Hosp., Iowa City, 1969-70: staff physician outpatient dept. VA Hosp., Cheyenne, Wyo., 1971-74, chief outpatient dept., 1973-74; dir. Student Health Service Utah State U., Logan, 1975-76; physician (part-time) dept. medicine VA Hosp., Cheyenne, 1976-81; staff physician U. Wyo. Student Health Service, Laramie, 1976—. Active Long's Peak council Boy Scouts Am., 1970—, scout chaplain Diocese of Cheyenne, 1980—, mem. Diocesan Pastoral Council, 1982-85. Served with USMC, World War II, Korea. Recipient Dist. Scouter award Boy Scouts Am., 1974, St. George Emblem, Nat. Cath. Scouter award, 1981. Recipient 5-, 10-, and 15-yr. service pins Boy Scouts Am. Diplomate Am. Bd. Family Practice. Fellow Am. Acad. Family Practice; mem. Wyo. State Med. Soc., Albany County (Wyo.) Med. Soc., Iowa Med. Soc., Johnson County (Iowa) Med. Soc. Democrat. Roman Catholic. Club: K.C. (4 deg.). Home: 2444 Overland Dr Laramie WY 82070 Office: U Wyo Student Health Svc Laramie WY 82071

CROOK, KEVIN PATRICK, aerospace engineer; b. Pawtucket, R.I., July 15, 1950; s. Ralph Frederick and Rosemary Rita (Dolan) C.; m. A. Sherron Corry, Sept. 22, 1976; children: Christopher, Shana, Patrick. BS in Aerospace Engring., U.S. Naval Acad., 1972. Quality assurance mgr. Eagle-Picher Industries, Colorado Springs, 1979-81; prin. quality engr. Digital Equipment Corp., various locations, 1981—; pres. Crossmark Inc., Colorado Springs, 1978-86. Lt., aviator, USN, 1972-79. Home: 6501 Northland St NE Albuquerque NM 87109 Office: Digital Equipment Corp 5600 Kircher Blvd NE Albuquerque NM 87103

CROOK, SEAN PAUL, aerospace systems engineering manager; b. Pawtucket, R.I., July 6, 1953; s. Ralph Frederick and Rosemary Rita (Dolan) C.; m. Mary Wickman, June 10, 1978; children: Kimberly Anne, Kelly Dolan, Erin Webster, Mary Katherine. BSME, U.S. Naval Acad., 1975. Commd. ensign USN, 1975, advanced through grades to lt., 1979, resigned, 1981; sr. systems engr. space div. Gen. Electric Co., Springfield, Va., 1982-84; sr. aerospace systems engr. Martin Marietta Aero Def. Systems, Long Beach, Calif., 1984—, now sr. aerospace system engring. mgr. Served to lt. commdr. USNR, 1981-84. Mem. Am. Mgmt. Assn. Home: 23565 Via Calzada Mission Viejo CA 92691 Office: Martin Marietta Aerospace 1501 Hughes Way Ste 300 Long Beach CA 90810

CROSA, JORGE HOMERO, bacterial geneticist, educator, consultant; b. Buenos Aires, Mar. 1, 1941; came to U.S., 1972; s. Ismael and Manuela (Merino) C.; m. Lidia Marta Coscia, Sept. 1968; children: Giselle Annette, Nicholas Alexander, Paul Christopher. MS, U. Buenos Aires, 1967, PhD in Chemistry, 1974. Lectr. U. Buenos Aires, 1967-72; sr. fellow Walter Reed Army Inst. Rsch., Washington, 1972; rsch. assoc. U. Wash., Seattle, 1973-80; asst. prof. bacterial genetics Oreg. Health Scis. U., Portland, 1981-82, assoc. prof., 1983-87, prof., 1988—; mem. study sect. NIH, 1986—. Mem. editorial bd. Jour. Bacteriology, 19866, Infection and Immunity, 1986—; contbr. numerous articles to various profl. jours., chpts. to books. Mem. Am. Soc. Microbiology (lectr. div. genetics and molecular biology, 1983). Office: Oreg Health Scis U 3818 SW Sam Jackson Park Rd Portland OR 97201

CROSBY, JEFFREY WAYNE, aerospace engineer; b. Moscow, Idaho, June 4, 1958; s. James Winfield III and Betty Eileen (Lemman) C.; m. Cynthia Lynn Pierson, Aug. 29, 1987. BSEE, U. Idaho, 1981, MSEE, 1988. Elec. engr. NW Alloys, Addy, Wash., 1981-83; sr. project engr. Hughes Aircraft Co., Los Angeles, 1983—. Contbr. articles to profl. jours. Mem. AIAA (com. spl. events 1986-87), IEEE. Office: Hughes Aircraft Co PO Box 92919 Bldg 550/X346 Los Angeles CA 90009

CROSBY, JOHN O'HEA, conductor, opera manager; b. N.Y.C., July 12, 1926; s. Laurence Alden and Aileen Mary (O'Hea) C. Grad., Hotchkiss Sch., 1944; B.A., Yale U., 1950; Litt.D. (hon.), U. N.Mex., 1967; Mus. D. (hon.), Coll. of Santa Fe, 1968; Mus.D. (hon.), Cleve. Inst. Músic, 1974; L.H.D. (hon.), U. Denver, 1977. pres. Manhattan Sch. Music, 1976-86. Accompanist, opera coach, condr., N.Y.C., 1951-56, gen. dir., mem. conducting staff, Santa Fe Opera, 1957—; guest condr. various opera cos. in, U.S. and Can., 1967—; condr.: U.S. stage premiere Daphne, 1964; world premiere Wuthering Heights, 1958. Served with inf. AUS, 1945-46, ETO. Roman Catholic. Clubs: Metropolitan Opera (N.Y.C.), Century Assn. (N.Y.C.), University (N.Y.C.). Office: PO Box 2408 Santa Fe NM 87501

CROSBY, KENNETH OWEN, dentist; b. Toronto, Ont., Can., Jan. 31, 1954; came to U.S. 1956; s. John Albert and Betty Louise (Manring) C.; m. Catherine Shishmanian, Sept. 2, 1978; children: Stephen Arakel, Daniel Jordan. BA, Calif. State U., Fresno, 1976; DDS, U. Calif., San Francisco, 1985. Sys. analyst Electromagnetic Sys. Lab., Sunnyvale, Calif., 1977-79; gen. practice resident Valley Med. Ctr., Fresno, Calif., 1985-86; gen. practice dentistry Fresno, 1986--. Mem. Am. Dental Assn. Republican. Mem. Foursquare Ch. Office: 3727 N First St #101 Fresno CA 93722

CROSBY, PETER ALAN, management consultant; b. Santa Barbara, Calif., Oct. 20, 1945; s. Harold Bartley and Margaret Maida (Peterson) C.; m. Stephanie Jay Ellis, Dec. 20, 1969; children: Kelly Michelle, Michael Ellis. BS, U. Calif., Berkeley, 1967; MS in Ops. Rsch., Stanford U., 1969, postgrad., 1971. Engr. Ford Motor Co., Palo Alto, Calif., 1967-71; ops. rsch. analyst Food Machinery & Chem. Co., San Jose, Calif., 1972; assoc. A.T. Kearney, Inc., San Francisco, 1972-75; mgr. Coopers & Lybrand, Los Angeles, 1976-78; prin. Towers, Perrin, Forster & Crosby, Los Angeles, 1978-81, Crosby, Gustin, Rice & Co., 1981—; bd. dirs. Marlar Internat., L.A. Vol. YMCA, Pacific Palisades, 1976—, St. Matthew Parish Sch., Pacific Palisades, 1976—, fund raiser Stanford Bus. Sch. Alumni Assn., 1983—. Mem. Council Logistic Mgmt., Inst. Mgmt. Cons., Planning Forum, Assn. for Corp. Growth, Jonathan Club (Los Angeles). Home: 16652 Bienveneda Pl Pacific Palisades CA 90272 Office: Crosby Gustin Rice & Co 1901 Ave of the Stars Ste 542 Los Angeles CA 90067

CROSS, GLENN LABAN, development consultant, engineering executive; b. Mt. Vernon, Ill., Dec. 28, 1941; s. Kenneth Edward and Mildred Irene (Glenn) C.; m. Kim Lien Duong, Aug. 30, 1968 (div. Oct. 1975); m. Tran Tu Thach, Dec. 26, 1975; children—Cindy Sue, Cristy Luu; BA, Calif. Western U., 1981, MBA, 1982. Hosp. adminstr. pub. health div. AID, Dept. State, Washington, 1966-68; pers. mgr. Pacific Architects and Engrs., Inc., L.A., 1968-70, contract adminstr., 1970-73, mgr. mgmt. svcs., 1973-75; contracts adminstr. Internat. Svcs. div., AVCO, Cin., 1975-77; sr. contract adminstr. Bechtel Group, Inc., San Francisco, 1977-80, Arabian Bechtel Co. Ltd.; contract adminstrv. supr. Jubail Industrial City, Saudi Arabia, 1980-85; cons. Bechtel Western Power Corp., Jakarta, Indonesia, 1985—; with Pacific Engrs. & Constructors, Ltd., Jakarta, Indonesia. Author: Living With a Matrix: A Conceptual Guide to Organizational Variation, 1983. Served as sgt. 1st spl. forces group, airborne, AUS, 1962-65; Okinawa, Vietnam. Decorated Combat Infantryman's Badge. Mem. Internat. Pers. Mgmt. Assn., Assn. Human Resource Systems Profls., Human Resource Planning Soc., Assn. MBA Execs., Am. Mgmt. Assn., Am. Arbitration Assn., Internat. Records Mgmt. Council, Adminstrv. Mgmt. Soc. Republican. Avocations: swimming, reading. Home: 2841 Cottingham St Oceanside CA 92054 Office: Pacific Engrs & Constructors Ltd, PO Box 381/KBY, Jakarta 12790, Indonesia

CROSS, HAROLD EUGENE, opthalmologist; b. Goshen, Ind., Nov. 1, 1937; s. George G. and Rosa (Schmucker) C.; m. Barbara Jean Cross, Dec. 22, 1961 (div. 1976); children: Kimberly, Debbie; m. Diane Cross, Feb. 14, 1987); children: Robb, Tara, Stacie. BA, Goshen Coll., 1960; MD, Johns Hopkins U., 1964, PhD, 1967. Diplomate Am. Bd. Ophthalmology. Intern U. Wash. Hosp., Seattle, 1963-64; resident in ophthalmology Johns Hopkins U. Hosp., Balt., 1969-72, asst. prof. medicine, 1967-72, asst. prof. ophthalmology, 1972-73; assoc. prof. surgery U. Ariz. Coll. Medicine, Tucson, 1973-75, prof., 1975-80; gen. practice ophthalmology Tucson, 1980—; med. dir. low vision svcs. St. Joseph's Hosp., Tucson, 1986—. Contbr. numerous articles to profl. jours. Capt. Med. Svc. Corps., USAF, 1967-69. Fellow NIH, 1969-72. Fellow Am. Acad. Opthalmology; mem. Ariz. Opthal. Soc., AAAS. Home: 11402 E Edison Tucson AZ 85749 Office: 2375 N Wyatt Dr Ste 101 Tucson AZ 85712

CROSS, JAMES PAUL, data processing executive; b. Shreveport, La., Feb. 13, 1954; s. David Richard and Patricia Moria (Sweetman) C.; m. Gale Marie Walters, July 23, 1977; children: Derek Teton, Jared Lakota, Kiri Sioux. AA, So. Ohio Coll., 1974; BS, Nat. Coll., 1977. Project leader Westinghouse Data Score, Iowa City, 1977-81, Walt Disney Prodns., Lake Buena Vista, Fla., 1981-86; sr. systems analyst Entech, Butte, Mont., 1986—. Mem. computer com. Silver Bow Sch. Bd., Butte, 1986-87. Mem. Data Processing Mgmt. Assn. Republican. Methodist. Office: Entech 16 E Granite Butte MT 59701

CROSS, LINDA MARIE, state corrections official; b. Pasco, Wash., Feb. 14, 1950; d. Roosevelt and Vivian (Miles) Duncan; m. Lilton Cross Jr., June 22, 1972 (div. 1975); 1 child, Shawn L. AA in Sociology, San Bernardino Valley Jr. Coll., 1969; BA in Sociology, Los Angeles U., 1972; student, UCLA, 1980—. Cert. parole agt., Calif. Correctional counselor State Calif. Dept Corrections, Norco, 1980-82; women's program coordinator, equal employment analyst State Calif. Dept Corrections, Sacramento, 1982-83; parole agt. State Calif. Dept Corrections, Orange County, Calif., 1983—. Mem. Citizen's for Alternative Sentencing; adminstrv. v.p. Coalition for Women in State Service, Sacramento, 1982; com. mem. Affirmative Action, Sacramento, Calif., 1983; team mother Little League, Rialto, Calif. Recipient Dedication of Service award Chicano Pintos Inc., 1984, Dedication of Tutorer award Oak Glen Rehab. Camp, 1969-70. Mem. Friends Outside (vice chairperson 1984), Correctional Counselor Assn., Calif. Correctional Peace Officers Assn., Women's Liaison Council (head of resources 1985—), Orange County Calif. Chpt. NOW, Workers Employment Resource Council, Orange County Task Force, Women's Programs Corrections. Democrat. Baptist. Club: Toastmasters (vice chairperson 1980-82). Home: 19413 Anaconda St Rialto CA 92376 Office: Calif State Dept Corrections 9500 Norwalk Rd Santa Fe Springs CA 90670

CROSSAN, GEORDIE JOHN, financial planner; b. Rockville Centre, N.Y., Nov. 1, 1959; s. John J. and Jadoree (Oldmixon) C. AA, Wentworth Mil. Acad., 1979. Frame maintainer Gen. Telephone Calif., Santa Monica, 1979-81; project dir. Crossan Rsch. Cons., Inc., Encino, Calif., 1982-85; fin. planner NBS Fin. Svcs., Inc., West Lake Village, Calif., 1985—. Recipient Pres.'s award IDM Corp., Long Beach, Calif., 1987, 88. Mem. Internat. Assn. Fin. Planning (bd. dirs.), Inst. Cert. Fin. Planners (cert., pres.-elect), Nat. Assn. Life Underwriters, Aircrafts Owners and Pilot Assn. Republican. Baptist. Office: NBS Fin Svcs Inc 101 N Westlake Blvd Ste 201 West Lake Village CA 91362

CROSSLAND, HARRIET KENT, portrait painter; b. Cleve., Sept. 8, 1902; d. Carl and Harriet Emily (Bacon) Dueringer; pupil of Margaret McDonald Phillips; m. Paul Marion Crossland, Sept. 20, 1959. Portrait painter, 1952—; freelance editor med. papers, 1953-70; represented in permanent collection John F. Kennedy Library, Boston. Mem. Santa Rosa Symphony League; mem. art mus. com. Luther Burbank Ctr. for the Arts, Santa Rosa, 1982—. Recipient award of merit Am. Cancer Soc., 1979, 84. Mem. Sonoma County Med. Assn. Aux., Am. Med. Women's Assn. (friend), DAR, Stanford U. Alumni Assn. Clubs: Ret. Officers Wives, Sonoma County Press, Sat. Afternoon (Santa Rosa). Editor, illustrator: X-Rays and Radium in Treatment of Diseases of the Skin, 1967; included in The Fifty American Artists by Margaret McDonald Phillips, 1969. Prin. donor Crossland Lab. for Audiovisual Learning in Dermatology, Stanford U. Sch. Medicine. Address: 2247 Sunrise Dr Santa Rosa CA 95405

CROSSLAND, WILLIAM EDWARD, safety engineer; b. Detroit, July 13, 1932; s. Ernest Edward and Clara Gertrude (Davis) C.; m. Helen Charlene Thompson, July 23, 1976. B.S. in Safety Engring., U. Ala., 1960; postgrad. U. So. Calif., 1975. Registered profl. engr., Calif.; cert. safety profl., Ill.; lic. pvt. pilot; cert. police officer. Founder, chmn. bd. Internat. Safety Cons., Inc., 1969-81; dir. safety Handy Andy Corp., San Antonio, 1972-73; safety engr. Royal Globe Ins. Co., 1973-74; dir. safety U.S. Air Force, Oklahoma City, 1974-77; safety and health mgr. Dept. Labor, Kansas City, Mo., 1977-84; safety and health mgr. U.S. Air Force, Hawaii, 1984-86, San Antonio, 1986—; tchr. safety engring. Okla. State U.; cons. AF Community Coll.; mem. energy com. Fed. Exec. Bd., 1979-84. Composer: Never, 1958; Is It the Same, 1978. Contbr. articles to profl. jours. Vol. Kansas City chpt. ARC. Served with USAF, 1951-72. Decorated Commendation Medal with 3 oak leaf clusters, Meritorious Service Medal with 2 oak leaf clusters; named Top Civilian Safety Dir. in USAF, 1974; created the Safety and Health Hall of Fame, Warrensburg, Mo. Mem. Assn. Fed. Safety and Health Profls. (past pres.), Am. Soc. Safety Engrs., Vets. Safety Internat. (past pres.), Nat. Safety Mgmt. Soc., Fed. Safety and Health Council San Antonio (chmn. 1988—), System Safety Soc., Am. Legion. Baptist. Office: Rte 1 Box 295-5 Asher OK 74826

CROSSLEY, ROGER JAMES, biopharmaceutical company executive; b. England, Jan. 20, 1943; came to U.S., 1974.; s. Leslie James and Annie (Addison) C.; m. Annette Payne Crossley, Apr. 30, 1977. BS, Queens U., Belfast, No. Ireland., 1964; BM BCh, Oxford U., Eng., 1967; M Phil., U. London, Eng., 1976. Research staff Royal Air Force Inst. of Aviation Medicine, 1969-74; assoc. clin. dir. Smith Kline and French, 1974-78, dir. clin. ops., 1978, 1978-80, v.p. clin. research and devel., 1980-81; v.p. clin. research med. research div. Am. Cyanamid Co., Pearl River, N.Y., 1981-84; pres., chief exec. officer Vestar, Inc., San Dimas, Calif., 1984—. Contbr. articles to profl. jours. Served with RAF, 1966-74. Mem. Aerospace Med. Assn., Am. Gastro. Assn., Royal Soc. of Medicine, Soc. for Clin. Trials. Office: Vestar Inc 650 Cliffside Dr San Dimas CA 91773

CROSSNO, ROBERT WAYNE, civil engineer; b. Holdenville, Okla., Apr. 5, 1952; s. Joel M. Crossno and Dorotha H. (Davis) Gosling; m. Miriam Ernestine Berkman (div.); m. Patricia Joyce Smith, June 7, 1986; 1 child, Rachel Elizabeth. BSCE, U. N.Mex., 1980. Registered profl. engr., N.Mex. Engring. technician N.Mex. State Hwy. Dept., Santa Fe, 1972-78, Gary Sweenhart, P.E. Inc., Albuquerque, 1978, Roberg Hogrefe, P.E., Inc., Albuquerque, 1979; engr. Randy Holt & Assocs., Inc., Albuquerque, 1980—. Mem. ASCE (assoc.), Nat. Soc. Profl. Engrs., Tau Beta Pi. Democrat. Office: Randy Holt and Assocs Inc 7920 Mountain Rd NE Albuquerque NM 87110

CROSSON, ALBERT J., food products executive; b. 1934. With Beatrice/Hunt-Wesson (formerly Beatrice Grocery Group Inc.), 1956-69, 74—, Arden-Mayfair Inc., L.A., 1969-74, to present; exec. v.p. sales Beatrice/Hunt-Wesson Inc., from 1978, now pres., also dir. Office: Beatrice/Hunt-Wesson Foods 1645 W Valencia Dr Fullerton CA 92634 *

CROTHERS, LARRY ALAN, engineer, educator; b. Saline, Mich., June 30, 1947. Student, U. Tex., 1972. Rsch. engr. Lear-Siegler, Inc., Ann Arbor, Mich., 1968-70, Tex. Instruments, Inc., Dallas, 1970-72, U. Tex., Austin, 1972-74; chief engr. Circle Robotics/Electronics Rsch. Co., Ashland, Oreg., 1974—; tchr. Soda Mountain Sch. Computer Arts, Rural, Oreg., 1975—; cons. various scientists and industrialists throughout career. Patentee in field; inventor Mil Spec 883 Infrared Microscanner, 1971. Democrat. Home: 10500 Copco Rd Hornbrook CA 96044 Office: Circle Robotics Co PO Box 1153 Ashland OR 97520

CROTTY, HELEN KOEFOED, art history educator, researcher; b. San Francisco, Aug. 13, 1928; d. Karl Edward and Maggie Elisabeth (Wewer) K.; m. Jay Cleybourne Crotty, Sept. 27, 1947; children: Stephen Randall, Heather Dale Crotty Hegland. Student, Stanford U., 1945-47; BA in Art History, UCLA, 1976, MA in Art History, 1980, postgrad., 1985—. Coordinator Youth in Arts, San Rafael, Calif., 1972-74; research asst. dept. art UCLA, 1976-77, teaching asst., 1979-81; intern Mus. Cultural History, 1981-82; vis. lectr. art history U. N.Mex., Albuquerque, 1984, 88, Colo. Coll., Colorado Springs, 1985. Author: Honoring the Dead: Anasazi Ceramics from the Rainbow-Bridge Monument Valley Expedition, 1983; contbr. articles to various publs. Grad. div. grantee UCLA, 1978, Dickson travel grantee, 1980. Mem. Am. Rock Art Research Assn. (pres. 1986—), Archaeol. Soc. N.Mex., Soc. for Am. Archaeology, Native Am. Art Studies Assn., Albuquerque Archaeol. Soc. (v.p. 1984-85). Democrat. Home: Star Route Box 831 Sandia Park NM 87047

CROUT, ELEANOR MUECKE, civic worker; d. Berthold Muecke, Jr. and Eleanor B. Thalmann; children: Alexandra Lynn, Stephen Andrew, Charles Merrill. BA, Mt. Holyoke Coll.; MA, Columbia. Mem. Jr. Welfare Assn., Santa Fe, program chmn., treas., pres., then pub. relations chmn.; chmn. Community Christmas Store, Santa Fe; co-chmn. ticket sales Heart Fund Benefit; active March of Dimes drive, Heart Fund, Am. Cancer Soc. Drive, United Way; mem. St. Vincent Hosp. Aux., chmn. com., benefit; mem. Santa Fe Council Internat. Relations; chmn. Girl Scout Expn. Bd. dirs. Jr. Welfare Assn., Girl's Club, Shelter Care for Youth; bd. dirs., chmn. personnel services Sangre de Cristo council Girl Scouts U.S.A.; bd. dirs. St. Michael's High Sch., Santa Fe, Opera Guild; coord. City Elementary Sch. Competitive Swimming Program. Mem. AAUW (bd. dirs.), Mt. Holyoke Alumnae Assn., Delta Kappa Pi, Phi Lambda Theta. Club: Santa Fe Garden (co-chmn. house and garden tours, sec., dir., publicity chmn. 1974-76). Episcopalian. Address: 32 Old Arroya Chamisa Rd Santa Fe NM 87505

CROW, JOHN EDWARD, political science educator; b. Seattle, Sept. 17, 1934; s. Howard Ray and Grace Mildred (Schilling) C.; m. Ruth Louise Karnofsky, Nov. 4, 1959 (div. Nov. 1978); 1 child, David Alexander; m. Rebecca Lepow, Feb. 14, 1982; children: Ilana Beth, Megan Eve. BA, U. Wash., 1957; MA, U. Chgo., 1958; PhD, U. Wash., 1965. Asst. prof. polit. sci. Oreg. State U., Corvallis, 1963-64, U. Wash., Seattle, 1964-66; assoc. prof. polit. sci. U. Ariz., Tucson, 1966—; vis. asst. prof. polit. sci. Lewis and Clark Coll., Portland, Oreg., 1964; tng. cons. tng. div. Nat. Park Service, Washington, 1971-72; legis. dir. U.S. House of Reps., Washington, 1983-85; project leader Office of Arid Lands Studies U.S.-USAID, Niamey-Zinder, Niger, 1977-79; cons. Navajo Tribal Gov., Windowrock, Ariz., 1979-81, AFL-CIO, Portland, 1964, Salt River Project, Phoenix, 1977, Nat. Park Service, Grand Canyon, Ariz., 1972-74. Author: Mexican Americans in the Southwest, 1977, Blacks in Arizona, 1967; co-author: Business-Government Functions in the Gila River Indian Committee, 1971; contbr. articles to numerous profl. jours. Co-chmn. Ariz. Democrats for McCarthy, Tucson, 1968; coordinator Southern Ariz. for Fair Energy Rates, Tucson, 1981; research dir. Tucson Commn. of Human Relations Study Group, Tucson, 1968-69; polit. analyst various TV stas., Tucson, 1987. Served to sgt. U.S. Army, 1954-55, Korea. Mem. Population Reference Bur., Population Alert Network, UN Assn. of So. Ariz. (v.p. 1986—), U.S. Handball Assn., Phi Beta Kappa, Phi Alpha Theta. Club: Tucson Athletic. Home: 628 N Norton Ave Tucson AZ 85719

CROW, NEIL BYRNE, geologist; b. Chgo., July 13, 1927; s. Robert Neil and Helen (Byrne) C.; m. Fidel Schilling, Sept. 28, 1957; 1 child, Charles N. BS, Northwestern U., 1949; postgrad., Colo. Sch. Mines, 1949-50, U. Colo., 1951-52, 53-54. Registered geologist, Calif. Groundwater geologist U.S. Geol. Survey, Boise, Idaho, 1952-53; petroleum geologist Amoco Prodn. Co., Shreveport, La., 1954-61; supr. tech. library Aerospace Corp., El Segundo, Calif., 1961-66; supr. tech. library Lawrence Livermore (Calif.) Nat. Lab., 1966-74, environ. geologist, hydrogeologist, 1974—. Contbr. articles on environ. geology and hydrogeology to profl. jours. Mem. Am. Assn. Petroleum Geologists, Geol. Soc. Am., No. Calif. Geol. Soc. Republican. Roman Catholic. Home: 2341 Willet Way Pleasanton CA 94566 Office: Lawrence Livermore Nat Lab PO Box 808 L-453 Livermore CA 94550

CROWDEN, FRED THOMAS, computer auditor; b. Peru, Ind., Aug. 10, 1949; s. Thomas James and Esther Annette (Wood) C.; m. Mary Lynn Johnson (div. 1978); m. Jo Ann Miler, July 1, 1979; children: Jonas L. Ewen, Elizabeth E., Anna R. Student, Denver U., 1967-68, Ind. U., 1969-71; B in U. Studies, U. N.Mex., 1976. Cert. info. systems auditor. Jr. systems programmer Micro Instrumentation & Telemetry Systems, Albuquerque, 1976-77; EDP auditor First Nat. Bank in Albuquerque, 1977-79; sr. EDP auditor Pub. Service Co. of N.Mex, Albuquerque, 1979-84, EDP audit supr., 1984-88. Donor United Blood Services, Albuquerque, 1975-88. Mem. EDP Auditors Assn. (bd. dirs. 1987-88, Service award 1985), Inst. Internal Auditors (gov. 1983-84, Service award 1984). Office: Pub Svc Co of NMex Alvarado Sq MS 0078 Albuquerque NM 87158

CROWDER, DAVID LESTER, historian, educator; b. American Falls, Idaho, Jan. 5, 1941; s. Lester J. and E. Louise (Curtis) C.; m. JoAnne Russell, Sept. 1, 1960; children: Linda, Carolyn, Rebecca, William, Ethan, Heather, Johnathan. Student, Boise Jr. Coll., 1962-63; BA, Idaho State U., 1965, MA, 1966; PhD, U. Utah, 1972. Prof. history Ricks Coll., Rexburg, Idaho, 1966-87; dir. Idaho State Hist. Soc., Boise, Idaho, 1987—; adj. prof. history Idaho State U., Pocatello, 1967-88, Boise State U., 1987-88. Author: Tendoy: Chief of the Lemhis, 1969, James W. Webster: Upper Snake River Valley Pioneer, 1979, Tales of Eastern Idaho, 1981, Rexburg, Idaho: The First One Hundred Years, 1883-1983, 1983; contbr. articles to profl. jours. Commr. Idaho Centennial Commn., Boise; v.p. PTA, Rexburg; scoutmaster Boy Scouts Am., Rexburg. With USN, 1958-62. Research fellow U. Utah, 1971-72. Mem. Am. Assn. for State and Local History (Cert. of Commendation 1986), Nat. Hist. Adminstrs., Nat. Conf. State Hist. Preservation Officers, Idaho Geog. Names Adv. Com., Lewis and Clark Trails Com., Kiwanis (pres. Rexburg chpt. 1977-78), Phi Kappa Phi. Office: Idaho State Hist Mus 610 N Julia Davis Dr Boise ID 83702

CROWE, DOUGLAS MARTIN, wildlife management administrator, biologist; b. Arkansas City, Kans., Nov. 7, 1939; s. Richard Martin and Shirley Rose (McCumber) C.; m. Timothea Barrett, Feb. 25, 1961; children—Ardith Jeanette, Martin Gregory, Marcella Ann. B.S., U. Wyo., 1970, Ph.D., 1974. Sales mgr. Wyo. Wholesalers, Casper, 1960-68; planner Wyo. Game and Fish Dept., Cheyenne, 1974-75, planning supr., 1975-85, asst. dir., 1985—; mem. Internat. Conv. Adv. Commn., Washington, 1982-83; cons. State Wildlife Agys. (Oreg., Alaska, Ohio, Wis., Mont., others) 1980—. Author: Comprehensive Planning for Wildlife Resources, 1984, Furbearers of Wyoming, 1986. Contbr. articles to Jour. Wildlife Mgmt., Jour. Mammalogy. Mem. Govs.' Task Force on Policy and Instl. Arrangements, Cheyenne, 1977. Served with U.S. Army, 1958-60. Named Outstanding Conservationist Wyo. Wildlife Fedn., 1981; NSF research grantee, 1972. Mem. Orgn. Wildlife Planners (pres. 1980), Wildlife Soc. (bd. dirs. Wyo. chpt. 1979), Am. Soc. Mammalogists, Phi Beta Kappa, Phi Kappa Phi, Wyo. Wildlife Fedn. Office: Wyo Game & Fish Dept 5400 Bishop Blvd Cheyenne WY 82002 *

CROWE, JOHN T., lawyer; b. Cabin Cove, Calif., Aug. 14, 1938; s. J. Thomas and Wanda (Walston) C.; m. Marina Protopapa, Dec. 28, 1968; 1 dau., Erin Aleka. BA, U. Santa Clara, 1960, JD, 1962. Bar: Calif. 1962, U.S. Dist. Ct. (no. dist.) Calif. 1964, U.S. Dist. Ct. (ea. dist.) Calif. 1967. Practiced in Visalia, Calif., 1964—; ptnr. firm Crowe, Mitchell & Crowe, 1971-85; referee State Bar Ct., 1976-82; gen. counsel Sierra Wine, 1986—. Bd. dirs. Mt. Whitney Area council Boy Scouts Am., 1966-85, pres., 1971, 72; bd. dirs. Visalia Associated In-Group Donors (AID), 1973-81, pres., 1978-79; mem. Visalia Airport Commn., 1982—. Served to 1st lt. U.S. Army, 1962-64; col. Res. Decorated Meritorious Service Medal with 2 oak leaf clusters, Army Commendation Medal; named Young Man of Yr., Visalia, 1973; Senator, Jr. Chamber Internat., 1970; recipient Silver Beaver award Boy Scouts Am., 1983. Mem. ABA, Tulare County Bar Assn., Nat. Assn. R.R. Trial Counsel, State Bar Calif., Visalia C. of C. (pres. 1979-80). Republican. Roman Catholic. Clubs: Rotary (pres. 1980-81); Downtown (Fresno, Calif.). Home: 3939 W School Ave Visalia CA 93291

CROWE, JOHN WILLIAM, educator; b. Lynwood, Calif., Oct. 11, 1946; s. John J. and Margaret (Morrissey) C.; m. Mary Frances Hidalgo, Sept. 5, 1970; children: Kevin Francis, Branden Michael. BA, Calif. State U., L.A., 1969; MA, UCLA, 1975; MBA, Claremont U., 1986. Staff writer East Los Angeles Tribune, 1967-69, Daily Breeze, Torrance, Calif., 1969-72; asst. prof. communications, dir. pub. affairs Calif. State U. Dominguez Hills, Carson, 1972-77; div. devel. Harvey Mudd Coll., Claremont, Calif., 1977-85; exec. dirs. devel. U. So. Calif., Los Angeles, 1985—. Office: U So Calif 1975 Zonal Ave KAM516 Los Angeles CA 90033

CROWELL, FRANCES THATCHER, English language educator; b. Phila., Dec. 15, 1929; d. Albanus Wood and Ethel Prudentia (McConkey) Thatcher; m. Richard Bruce Crowell, Aug. 18, 1951; children: Richard Welland, Nancy Marguerite Crowell Brady. BA in English, Coll. William and Mary, 1951; MA in English Lit., U. Ariz., 1953. Instr. English U. Ariz., Tucson, 1963-66, 70-73, Mesa State Coll., Grand Junction, Colo., 1988—. Council Woman City Council, Platteville, Wis., 1977-79. MEM AAUW (pres. local chpt. 1985-87), Phi Beta Kappa, Phi Kappa Phi. Republican. Congregationalist. Club: PEO (Grand Junction, Colo.) (pres. 1982-84). Home: 2246 Tiffany Dr Grand Junction CO 81503

CROWELL, GARY DEAN, optometrist, retired military officer; b. Wykoff, Minn., Dec. 15, 1942; s. Paul Wesley and Frances Elizabeth (Wright) C.; m. Elizabeth Ann Cheslock, June 3, 1965; children: Laura Fay, Frederick Aaron. BS, Pacific U., 1965, OD, 1966. Commd. ensign USN, 1966, advanced through grades to comdr., 1981, ret., 1986; optometrist Town Ctr. Vision Clinic, McMinnville, Oreg., 1986—. Decorated Air medal. Mem. Am. Optometric Assn., Oreg. Optometric Assn., Portland Met. Optometry Assn., Early Ford Club of Am. Republican. Home: 16679 SW Peavine Rd McMinnville OR 97128 Office: Town Ctr Vision Clinic 1291 W Hwy 99W McMinnville OR 97128

CROWLEY, BRIAN SCOTT, aerospace engineering professional; b. Youngstown, Ohio, Apr. 6, 1950; s. Henry Patrick and Leone Marion (Schott) C.; m. Karen Ruth Schuh, Sept. 12, 1976; chldren: Glenn Matthew, Neil Colin. BS in Physics, History, Carnegie Mellon U., 1972; MS in Astronomy, Ohio State U., 1975. Mem. tech. staff TRW Def. and Space Systems Group, Redondo Beach, Calif., 1975-85; staff engr. TRW Def. and Space Systems Group, Redondo Beach, 1985-86, sect. head, 1986-87, subproject mgr., 1987-89, sr. staff engr., 1989—. Mem. admissions coun., Carnegie Mellon U., Pitts., 1984—. Mem. Carnegie Mellon U. Nat. Alumni Assn. (exec. bd. 1988—), L.A. Carnegie Mellon Alumni Clan (bd. dirs. 1975—, v.p. 1981-85, pres. 1985-87, corr. sec. 1987—). Republican. Roman Catholic. Home: 13918 Ocean Gate Ave Hawthorne CA 90250-6509 Office: TRW Def Systems DH5/1133 1 Space Park Dr Redondo Beach CA 90278

CROWLEY, JOHN CRANE, real estate developer; b. Detroit, June 29, 1919; s. Edward John and Lean Helen (Crane) C.; m. Barbara Wenzel Gilfillan, Jan. 12, 1945; children: F. Alexander, Leonard, Philip, Eliot, Louise, Sylvia. BA, Swarthmore Coll., 1941; MS, U. Denver, 1943. Asst. dir. Mcpl. Finance Officers Assn., Chgo., 1946-48; So. Calif. mgr. League Calif. Cities, Los Angeles, 1948-53; mgr. City of Monterey Park, Calif., 1953-56; founder, exec. v.p. Nat. Med. Enterprises, Los Angeles, 1968; pres. Ventura Towne House (Calif.), 1963—; mem. faculty U. So. Calif. Sch. Pub. Adminstrn., 1950-53; bd. dirs. Regional Inst. of So. Calif. Contbr. articles to profl. jours. Mem. State Adv. Council on Retirement Housing, 1965-68, Los Angeles County Com. on Affairs of Aging, 1966—; Mayor City of Pasadena, 1986—; city dir. Pasadena, 1979—; bd. dirs. Nat. Mcpl. League, 1986—, Pacificulture Found. and Asia Mus., 1971-76, pres., 1972-74; bd. dirs. Pasadena Area Liberal Arts Ctr., 1962-72, pres., 1965-68; trustee Pacific Oaks Friends Sch. and Coll., Pasadena, 1954-57; chmn. Pasadena Cultural Heritage Comm., 1975-78; pres. Pasadena Civic Improvement Corp., 1985—; bd. mgrs. Swarthmore Coll., 1986—. Recipient Disting. Citizen award Nat. Mcpl. League, 1984; Sloan Found. fellow, 1941-43. Mem. Internat. City Mgmt. Assn., Nat. Mcpl. League (nat. bd. 1980—), Phi Delta Theta. Democrat. Unitarian. Home: 615 Linda Vista Ave Pasadena CA 91105 Office: PO Box 93223 Pasadena CA 91109

CROWLEY, JOSEPH NEIL, university president; b. Oelwein, Iowa, July 9, 1933; s. James Bernard and Nina Mary (Neil) C.; m. Johanna Lois Reitz, Sept. 9, 1961; children: Theresa, Neil, Margaret, Timothy. BA, U. Iowa, 1959; MA, Calif. State U., Fresno, 1963; PhD (Univ. fellow), U. Wash., 1967. Reporter Fresno Bee, 1961-62; asst. prof. polit. sci. U. Nev., Reno, 1966-71, asso. prof., 1971-79, prof., 1979—, chmn. dept. polit. sci., 1976-78, pres., 1978—; bd. dirs. Citibank Nev., Channel 5 Pub. TV; policy formulation officer EPA, Washington, 1973-74; dir. instl. studies Nat. Commn. on Water Quality, Washington, 1974-75; cons. in field. Author: Democrats, Delegates and Politics in Nevada: A Grassroots Chronicle of 1972, 1976, Notes From The President's Chair, 1988; editor: (with Robert Roelofs and Donald Hardesty) Environment and Society, 1973. Mem. Commn. on Colls., 1980—, adv. commn. on mining and minerals research U.S. Dept. Interior, 1985—, NCAA council, 1987—; bd. dirs., campaign chmn. No. Nev. United Way, 1985—. Recipient Thornton Peace prize U. Nev., 1971; Nat. Assn. Schs. Public Affairs and Adminstrn. fellow, 1973-74. Mem. Am. Polit. Sci. Assn., Western Polit. Sci. Assn., No. Calif. Polit. Sci. Assn. Roman Catholic. Club: Rotary. Home: 1265 Muir Dr Reno NV 89503 Office: U Nev Reno Office of Pres Reno NV 89557-0095

CROWLEY, NICHOLAS PEARSE, nurse; b. Cork City, Ireland, Apr. 18, 1949; came to U.S., 1965; s. Cornelius and Ellen (Kelly) C.; m. Lynne Marie LeBlanc, Aug. 15, 1982; children: Jennifer Marie, Sean Michael. Staff nurse Salem Hosp., Mass., 1968-69, Peter Bent Brigham Hosp., Boston, 1970-76, Children's Hosp. Med. Ctr., Boston, 1976-83, Humana Hosp., Phoenix, 1983—. Mem. Ophthalmic Soc. RN's, Phoenix Gun club. Republican. Roman Catholic. Home: 103 E Juniper Ave Gilbert AZ 85234

CROWSON, DAN MICHAEL, electrical engineer, company executive; b. Tulsa, Aug. 1, 1953; s. Bobby Earl and Virginia Marie (Stoops) C.; m. Brenna Leigh Gentry, Oct. 16, 1982; children: Bobby Christopher, Chelsea Ann. AS in Elec. Engring. Tech., Okla. State U., 1975, BS in Engring. Tech., 1976. Engr. Xerox Corp., Oklahoma City, 1977-81, Phillips Petroleum, Dallas, 1981-82, H.P. Smith Paper Co., Chgo., 1982-83; engr., designer Stearns-Catalytic World Corp., Denver, 1984-87; electrical engr. mgr. Master Palletizer Systems, Inc., Denver, 1987-89; specialist S.W. regional automation Telemecanique Inc., Denver, 1989—; computer cons., Denver, 1985—. Office: Telemecanique Inc 6565 W Jewell Lakewood CO 80226

CRULL, TIMM F., food company executive; b. 1931; married. BA, Mich. State U., 1955. Chief operating officer Norton Simon Inc., 1977-79; with Carnation Co., Los Angeles, 1955-77, 80—, exec. v.p., 1980-83, pres., 1983—, chief exec. officer, 1985—, vice chmn., dir. Office: Carnation Co 5045 Wilshire Blvd Los Angeles CA 90036 *

CRUMMER, LARRY DEAN, music educator; b. Lake City, Iowa, July 19, 1949; s. Howard Austin and Bonnie Jean (Vinchattle) C. MusB, Morningside Coll., Sioux City, Iowa, 1971; MusM, Ind. U., 1973, MusD, 1983. cert. coll. tchr. Calif. Fellow Ind. U., Bloomington, 1971-73, assoc. instr., 1974-75; artist in residence Bay View Conservatory and Summer Music Festival, 1975; asst. prof. So. Oreg. State Coll., Ashland, 1975-81; prof. in music Evergreen Valley Coll., San Jose, Calif., 1981—; organist Trinity Presbn. Ch., San Jose, 1987—/. Organ recitalist, U.S. and Europe, 1975—. Mem. Am. Guild Organists (dean San Jose chpt., chmn. program com. 1987-88), Soc. Descendants of Mayflower, numerous genealogical and hist. soc., Phi Eta Sigma, Pi Kappa Lambda. Democrat. Episcopalain. Home: 3585 Melnikoff Dr San Jose CA 95121-1383 Office: Evergreen Valley Coll 3095 Yerba Buena Rd San Jose CA 95135

CRUMP, FREDERICK ALAN, import company executive; b. Manchester, Eng., Apr. 29, 1927; came to U.S., 1957; s. Frederick and Florence Edith (Nutter) C.; m. Joan Saunders Williams, Mar. 19, 1955; 1 child, David Alan. Ed. pub. schs., Manchester and London. Clk., then teller Lloyd's Bank of London, 1943-45; sales rep. Le Bas Tube Co., Manchester, 1948-52, Walter Slingsby Orgn., Keighley, Eng., 1952-55; sales mgr. Alco Plating Co., L.A., 1955-61; account exec. Great Western Savs. and Loan Assn., L.A., 1961-63; owner, pres. Tudor House/F.A.C. Enterprises, Santa Monica, Calif., 1962—. Lt. cpl. Royal Armed Forces, 1945-48, including CBI. Named Order of Brit. Empire Her Royal Highness the Queen of England, 1980; recipient Royal Signal Corps Brit. Armed Forces. Mem. Brit. Inst. Dirs., Brit.-Am. C. of C. (bd. dirs. L.A. 1978—). Mem. Church of England. Clubs: Toastmasters (past pres. Bell, Calif. chpt.), Brit. Athletic Soc. (past pres.). Lodge: Lions (past pres. Brentwood-Bel Air, Calif. club). Home: 15306 Bestor Blvd Pacific Palisades CA 90272 Office: FAC Enterprises Inc 824 W Hyde Park Blvd Inglewood CA 90302

CRUMP, GERALD FRANKLIN, lawyer; b. Sacramento, Feb. 16, 1935; s. John Laurin and Ida May (Banta) C.; m. Glenda Roberts Glass, Nov. 21, 1959; children—Sara Elizabeth, Juliane Kathryn, Joseph Stephen. A.B., U. Calif.-Berkeley 1956, J.D., 1959; M.A., Baylor U., 1966. Bar: Calif. 1960. Dep. county counsel Los Angeles County, 1963—, legis. rep., 1970-73; chief pub. works div. Los Angeles County Counsel, 1973-84, sr. asst. county counsel, 1984-85, chief asst. county counsel, 1985—; lectr. Pepperdine U., 1978, U. Calif., 1982. Bd. dirs. San Fernando Valley Girl Scout Coun. Served to capt. USAF, 1960-63; to col. USAFR, 1963—, staff judge advocate USAFR Systems Command. Mem. ABA, State Bar of Calif. (del.), Los Angeles County Bar Assn. (past chmn., trustee govtl. law sect., mem. exec. com. litigation sect.), Am. Judicature Soc., Am. Acad. Polit. and Social Sci., Res. Officers Assn., Air Force Assn., Phi Alpha Delta, Delta Sigma Phi. Home: 4020 Camino de la Cumbre Sherman Oaks CA 91423 Office: 648 Hall of Administrn Los Angeles CA 90012

CRUMP, JULIANNE JUANITA, quality control analyst, graphologist; b. Chgo., Jan. 25, 1950; d. Samuel and LaVergne Harriet (Bassmire) Millard; m. Richmond Alexander White, July, 1970 (div. Mar. 1975); 1 child, Zacharias Joseph; m. Lee Roy Crump Jr., Mar. 24, 1979. Cert. graphology, Inst. Graphic Sci., 1987. Office mgr. Tect Electronics Corp., Concord, Calif., 1974-75; freelance bookkeeper Santa Cruz, Calif., 1975-79; account clk. II County of Santa Cruz, 1979-84, eligibility worker, 1984-88, quality control analyst, 1988—; pvt. practice graphologist Santa Cruz, 1988—. Mem. Food Stamp Corrective Action Com., Santa Cruz, 1987. Mem. Inst. Graphological Sci., Svc. Employees Inter Union.

CRUMPTON, EVELYN, psychologist, educator; b. Ashland, Ala., Dec. 23, 1924; d. Alpheus Leland and Bernice (Fordham) Crumpton. AB, Birmingham So. Coll., 1944; MA, UCLA, 1953, PhD in Psychology, 1955. Lic. psychologist, Calif.; diplomate Am. Bd. Profl. Psychology. Research psychologist VA Hosp., Brentwood, Los Angeles, 1955-77; asst. chief, psychology service, coordinator clin. training VA Adminstrn. Med. Ctr., West Los Angeles, 1977-85; sr. assoc. chief, dir. intern training, Psychology Service VA Adminstrn. Med. Ctr., West Los Angeles, 1985-87; clin. prof. dept. psychology UCLA, assoc. research psychologist dept. psychiatry, UCLA Sch. Med., 1957—; cons. chief of staff 2d psychology services, Brentwood div., VA Adminstrn. Med. Ctr., West Los Angeles, Calif. Recipient Profl. Service award, Assn. Chief Psychologists VA, 1979. Fellow Soc. Personality Assessment; mem. Am. Psychol. Assn., Western Psychol. Assn., Sigma Xi. Contbr. numerous articles to profl. jours.

CRUSE, ALLAN BAIRD, mathematician, computer scientist, educator; b. Birmingham, Ala., Aug. 28, 1941; s. J. Clyde and Irma R. Cruse. A.B., Emory U., 1959-62, Ph.D., 1974; postgrad. (Woodrow Wilson fellow) U. Calif.-Berkeley, 1962-63, M.A., 1965; teaching fellow Dartmouth Coll., 1963-64. Instr., U. San Francisco, 1966-73, asst. prof. math., 1973-76, assoc. prof., 1976-79, prof., 1979—, chmn. math. dept. 1988—; vis. instr. Stillman Coll., summer 1967; vis. assoc. prof. Emory U., spring 1978; prof. computer sci. Sonoma State U., 1983-85; cons. math edn. NSF fellow, 1972-73. Mem. Am. Math. Soc., Math. Assn. Am., Calif. Math. Council, Computer Soc. of IEEE, Assn. Computing Machinery, U. San Francisco Faculty Assn., Sigma Xi (Dissertation award 1974). Author: (with Millianne Granberg) Lectures on Freshman Calculus, 1971; research, publs. in field. Office: U San Francisco Harney Sci Ctr San Francisco CA 94117

CRUSE, DENTON W., marketing and advertising executive, consultant; b. Washington, May 21, 1944; s. Denton W. Sr. and Frances Rankin (Moore) C.; m. Susan Costello, June 11, 1988. BS, Va. Commonwealth U., 1966; MBA, So. Ill. U., 1977. Media supr. Procter & Gamble Co., Cin., 1967-73; assoc. media dir. Ralston Purina Co., St. Louis, 1973-78; dir. advt. Armour-Dial Co., Phoenix, 1978-81; mktg. dir. Valentine Greeting Inc., Phoenix, 1981-82; dir. mktg. svcs. J. Walter Thompson/USA, L.A., 1982-83; cons. L.A., 1983-86; dir. advt. svcs. Mattel Inc., L.A., 1986-88; cons. L.A., 1988—; instr. UCLA, L.A., 1986—. Editor-in-chief: Cobblestone, 1965. Marathon monitor L.A. Olympic Organizing Com., 1984. Mem. L.A. Advt. Club, Pi Sigma Epsilon, Beta Gamma Sigma. Republican. Presbyterian. Home: 2809 Crest Dr Manhattan Beach CA 90266 Office: 4751 Wilshire Blvd Ste 203 Los Angeles CA 90010

CRUTCHER, MICHAEL EUGENE, dentist; b. Valparaiso, Ind., June 9, 1958; s. Jackie Eugene and Shirley Ann (Syler) C.; m. Sharyl Coleen McAlister, Aug. 7, 1982. BA in Psychology and Biology, Ind. U., 1980, DDS, 1984. DDS. Enlisted USPHS, 1984, advanced through grades to lt. comdr., 1988; staff dental officer USPHS, Many Farms, Ariz., 1984-85; facility dental officer USPHS, Many Farms, 1985-86; dep. chief dental officer USPHS, Chirle, Ariz., 1986-88; chief dental officer USPHS, Poplar, Mont., 1988—; Navajo Area Restorative instr. USPHS, Chirle, 1986—. Elder Trinity Presbyn. Ch., Chirle, 1987—. Mem. Am. Dental Assn., Commd. Officers Ass., New Mex. State Dental Assn. Democrat. Home: PO Box 1164 Poplar MT 59255 Office: Verne E Gibbs Health Ctr PO Box 67 Poplar MT 59255

CRUTCHFIELD, SUSAN RAMSEY, neurophysiologist; b. Pasadena, Calif., Oct. 7, 1941; d. Henry Colwell Ramsey and Rowena Ruth (Lockett) Banning; m. Ralph L. Crutchfield, Sept. 26, 1964 (div. Sept. 1973); children: Pamela Montague, Ashley Noland. AA, Pine Manor Coll., 1961; student, Sorbonne U., Paris, 1961-62; BA, George Washington U., 1964; MA, U. Calif., San Diego, 1978; PhD, Aston U., Birmingham, Eng., 1986. Research assoc. U. Calif. Med. Ctr., San Diego, 1978-80, researcher, 1986—; researcher Birmingham U., 1980-86. Mem. San Diego Jr. League. Mem. AAAS, N.Y. Acad. Scis., European Neurosci. Soc., EEG Soc., Warwick (Eng.) Boat Club, LaJolla Beach and Tennis Club. Home: 1624 Ludington Ln La Jolla CA 92037 Office: U Calif Med Ctr Dept Pediatrics H-638-A San Diego CA 92115

CRUZ, GEORGE ANTHONY, entrepreneur; b. N.Y.C., Aug. 23, 1954; s. Jorge and Rosa (Miguez) C.; m. Susan Elizabeth Shepherd, Feb. 21, 1975; children: Toni, Joseph. Grad. high sch., Bellflower, Calif. Real estate assoc. Execu Systems, Oceanside, Calif., 1978-79; pres. R&G Market, Inc., Huntington, Calif., 1979—; owner Straw Hat Restaurant, Huntington Beach, 1984-87, R&G Bakery, Huntington, 1988—. Vol. 1984 Rep. Task Force, Santa Ana, Calif., 1983-84. Sgt. USMC, 1974-78. Mem. Calif. Grocers Assn., Huntington C. of C. Republican. Roman Catholic. Office: R&G Inc 7625 California Ave Huntington CA 90255

CRUZ, L. GLORIA, volunteer; b. Nogales, Ariz., Nov. 9, 1940; d. Jess Steffani and Elvira Gowzales; m. Rev. Nicky Cruz, Nov. 4, 1961; children: Alicia Ann, Laura M., Nicole Suzanne, Elena Mia. Cert., Latin Am.-Bible Inst., LaPuente, Calif., 1961. Tchr. Zeb Pike Juvenile Detention Ctr., Colorado Springs, Colo., 1983-88. Vol. Meml. Hosp., Colorado Springs, 1988; tchr., counselor Nicky Cruz Outreach for Drug Related Problems, Calif., N.C., 1965-78. Republican. Mem. Assemblies of God Ch. Office: Nicky Cruz Outreach 1935 Dominion Way #204 Colorado Springs CO 80918

CRUZ, MICHAEL, music producer; b. Havana, Cuba, Jan. 21, 1953; came to U.S., 1960; s. Manuel Adolpho and Margarita C. BA in Music Theory and Composition, Northwestern U., 1974. Staff writer Dick Marx & Assoc.,

Chgo., 1973-75, headwriter, 1977-79; ptnr., operator StudioMedia, Evanston, Ill., 1975-77; freelance composer/arranger with Bobby Whiteside, Steve Sperry, Barry Manilow and others L.A. and Chgo., 1979-84; pres. Michael Cruz Music, L.A., 1984—. Composer: (album) Kids From Fame, 1984 (Gold Record 1984), 11 songs for TV show Fame, 1980-84, (film scores) Naked Vengeance, Basic Training, (TV theme songs) Night Tracks, Power Play, Candid Kids, Today's Bus., and others, (comml. jingles) Taco Bell, Colt 45, Coors Light, McDonald's, and others; music dir., composer 57 songs for TV show Kids, Inc., 1982-87. Recipient Clio award N.Y. Ad Club, 1988, Belding award L.A. Ad Club, 1986, 10 Addy awards Austin and Dallas Ad Leagues, 1987, 88, Award of Merit Hispanic Bus. Mag., 1988. Mem. Screen Actors Guild, Am. Fedn. Musicians, NARAS, ASCAP, AFTRA (dele. 1981—).

CRYER, RODGER EARL, educational administrator; b. Detroit, Apr. 2, 1940. AB in Fine Arts, San Diego State U., 1965; MA in Edn. Adminstrn., Stanford U., 1972; PhD in Psychol. Services Counseling, Columbia-Pacific U., 1985. Cert. tchr., N.J., Calif.; cert. gen. adminstrn., Calif. Spl. asst. to commissioner N.J. State Dept. Edn., Trenton, 1967-68; cons. N.J. Urban Sch. Devel., Trenton, 1969-70; mgmt. cons. Rodger E. Cryer, Co., Pinole, Calif., 1970-73; adminstrv. asst. Franklin McKinley Sch. Dist., San Jose, Calif., pres. Chief Exec. Tng. Corp., San Jose, 1981-82; prin. McKinley Sch., 1986—; ptnr. Guided Learning Assocs.; sec. supervisory com. Commonwealth Cen. Credit Union, 1989—. Commr. San Jose Parks & Recreation Commn., 1988—. Mem. Nat. Sch. Pub. Rels. Assn. (sec. 1975—), Calif. Sch. Pub. Rels. Assn. (pres.). Contbr. articles to profl. jours. Commr. Home: PO Box 21917 San Jose CA 95151 Office: McKinley Sch 651 Macredes Ave San Jose CA 95116

CSENDES, ERNEST, chemist, corporate and financial executive; b. Satu-Mare, Romania, Mar. 2, 1926; s. Edward O. and Sidonia (Littman) C.; came to U.S., 1951, naturalized, 1955; m. Catharine Vera Tolnai, Feb. 7, 1953; children: Audrey Carol, Robert Alexander Edward. BA, Protestant Coll., Hungary, 1944; BS, U. Heidelberg (Ger.), 1948, MS, PhD, 1951. Rsch. asst. chemistry U. Heidelberg, 1950-51; rsch. assoc. biochemistry Tulane U., New Orleans, 1952; fellow Harvard U., 1953; rsch. chemist organic chems. dept. E. I. Du Pont de Nemours and Co., Wilmington, Del., 1953-56, elastomer chems. dept., 1956-61; dir. rsch. and devel. agrl. chems. div. Armour & Co., Atlanta, 1961-63; v.p. corp. devel. Occidental Petroleum Corp., 1963-64, exec. v.p. rsch., engring. and devel., 1964-68, also mem. exec. com.; exec. v.p., dir. Occidental Rsch. and Engring. Corp., 1964-68; pres., chief exec. officer Tex. Rep. Industries, Inc., 1968-84; bd. dir. Occidental Rsch. and Emergency (U.K.) Ltd, 1964-68; pres., chief exec. officer TRI Group, 1971-74; chmn., chief exec. officer Micronic Techs., Inc., 1981-85; mng. ptnr. Inter-Consult Ltd., Pacific Palisades, Calif., 1984—. Contbr. articles to profl. jours; patentee in field. Recipient Pro Mundi Beneficio medal Brazilian Acad. Humanities. Fellow AAAS, Am. Inst. Chemists, Royal Soc. of Chemistry (London); mem. Am. Chem. Soc., German Chem. Soc., N.Y. Acad. Sci., Am. Inst. Chem. Engrs., Acad. Polit. Sci., Global Action Econ. Inst., Am. Mgmt. Assn., AIAA, Am. Def. Preparedness Assn., Sigma Xi. Rsch. in area of elastomers, rubber chemicals, dyes and intermediates, organometallics, organic and biochemistry, high polymers, phosphates, plant nutrients, pesticides, process engring. and design of fertilizer plants, sulfur, potash and phosphate ore mining and metallurgy, coal burning and acid rain, coal utilization, methods for grinding of solids, petrochemicals, also acquisitions, mergers, internat. fin. related to leasing, investment and loans, trusts and ins.; regional devel. related to agr. and energy resources. Home: 514 Marquette St Pacific Palisades CA 90272

CUDLIP, DAVID ROCKWELL, marketing executive; b. Detroit, Dec. 20, 1933; s. William Byrnes and Lynwood (Bope) C.; m. Caroline Morris Byers, June 1, 1964 (div. 1984); children: Carolina, Robert. BA, Dartmouth Coll., 1955, MBA, 1958. Asst. mgr. Brown Bros. Harriman Co., N.Y.C., 1959-65; sr. v.p., dir. Overseas Nat. Airways, N.Y.C., 1965-69; pres. Pathfinder Corp., L.A., 1970-79; v.p. Russell Reynolds Assocs., L.A., 1979-81; ptnr. Ward Howell Internat., L.A., 1981-83; chmn., dir. DataMerx, L.A., 1983—. Authro (book): Comprador, 1984, Strangers in Blood, 1987. Mem. Rep. Nat. Com., 1968—, mem. fin. com., 1968-70, vol. campaign worker, 1960, 64. Served with U.S. Army, 1954-56. Mem. Brook Club, Calif. Club (Los Angeles). Home: 8751 Sailport Dr Huntington Beach CA 92646

CUDNEY, GREG VERNE, oil field service company executive; b. Denver, June 27, 1957; s. Gerald V. and Elmira Lou (Martin) C.; m. Laurel Beamer, Feb. 17, 1985. BS in Geology, Colo. State U., 1979. Dist. engr. Dowell Div. Dow Chem. Co., various locations, 1980-84; prodn. supt. Unioil, Greeley, Colo., 1984-85; Alaska dist. engr. Dowell Schlumberger Co., Anchorage, 1985--. Mem. Soc. Petroleum Engrs. Home: 7100 Fergy Circle Anchorage AK 99507

CUDNY, HENRYK, geneticist; b. Pustelnik, Poland, Jan. 11, 1941; came to U.S., 1978; s. Jozef and Wiktoria (Czarnecka) C.; m. Jadwiga B. Grzeskowiak, Sept. 13, 1975; children: Magdalena, Witold. MS, U. Warsaw, 1967; PhD, Inst. Genetics, Poznan, Poland, 1976. Tchr. Coll. Warka, Poland, 1967-68; adj. prof. Polish Acad. Scis. Inst. Genetics, Poznan, 1969-78; postdoctoral fellow U. Conn., Farmington, 1978-87; instr. Yale U., New Haven, 1983; scientist Synergen, Boulder, Colo., 1988—. Home: 4462 Hamilton Ct Boulder CO 80303 Office: Synergen 1885 33d St Boulder CO 80301

CUFONE, GENE ANTHONY, printing company executive; b. Jersey City, Mar. 12, 1938; s. Frank Cufone and Tessie Capalbo; m. Kathleen Boyle, Apr. 15, 1960; children: Dennis, Patricia Ann. Attended Trenton State Coll. Magnetic materials research scientist RCA Labs., Princeton, N.J., 1964-71; founder Gene's Quick Copy Ctr., N.J., 1971-79; founder, pres. BCX (Business Card Express) Printing Ctrs., Inc., Phoenix, Tucson and Golden Valley, Minn., 1979—. Mem. Nat. Assn. Quick Printers, Internat. Franchise Assn. Republican. Roman Catholic. Office: BCX Printing Ctrs 613 E Indian School Rd Phoenix AZ 85012

CULBERTSON, JOHN, management consultant; b. Madison, Wis., June 23, 1937; s. John W. and Helen (Curtin) C.; m. Marrianne Peschel, Sept. 12, 1959 (div. 1979); m. Sally Maris, Oct. 10, 1981; children: John, William James, Thomas Leonard. BSA, U. Wis., 1959; MBA, U. Md., 1961; Dr. Bus., Harvard U., 1965. Asst. prof. Bentley Coll., Boston, 1963-65, U. Md., College Park, 1965-67; assoc. Allen & Hamilton, Inc., Cleve., 1967-71; mng. assoc. U.S. Office Mgmt. and Budget, Washington, 1971-73; mgr. Ernst & Whinney, Cleve., 1973-76; prin. Towers, Perrin, Foster & Crosby, Cleve., 1976-83; v.p. M&R Services, Seattle, 1983-87; pres. John Culbertson & Assocs., Inc., Seattle, 1987—; cons. in field. Contbr. articles to profl. jours. With U.S. Army, 1956-65. Mem. Harvard Bus. Sch. Alumni (pres. 1982-83), Washington Athletic Club, Cleve. Athletic Club. Home and Office: 100 W Highland Dr Seattle WA 98119

CULL, CHRIS ALAN, operations executive; b. Las Cruces, N.Mex., Jan. 3, 1947; s. William Roy Cull and Doris Jean (Compton) Morgan; m. DuAnne Elizabeth Diers King, July 26, 1967 (div. 1979); children: Joey Lynn, Jamie Ayn, Brandon Alan. BS, N.Mex. State U., 1976. Lab./field technician N.Mex. State U., Las Cruces, 1973-76; research soil scientist Mont. State U., Bozeman, 1976-77; reclamation supr. Western Energy Co., Colstrip, Mont., 1977-80; mgr. ops. permitting Western Energy Co., Billings, Mont., 1980-85; asst. project mgr. En Tech Inc., Butte, Mont., 1985-86; mgr. ops. Spl. Resource Mgmt. Inc., Billings, 1986-87; owner EnviroChek Inc., Billings, 1987-88; dir. environ. svcs. Western Techs. Inc., Tucson, 1988—. Contbr. articles to profl. jours. Mem. Assn. Environ. Scientists and Adminstrs. (charter), Am. Indsl. Hygiene Assn., Nat. Asbestos Council, Nat. Assn. Environ. Profls., Soil Conservation Soc. Am. (chmn. surface mine reclamation com. 1978-80, mem. univ. and coll. relations com. 1977-78, spl. task force surface mine reclamation div. 1977-79, pres. Mont. chpt. 1980-82), Mont. Coal Council (co-chmn. environ./tech. com. 1983-85), Mining and Reclamation Council Am. (tech. com. 1983-85), Am. Council on Sci. and Health. Home: 6651 N Campbell Ave Tucson AZ 85718 Office: Western Techs Inc 3480 S Dodge Blvd Tucson AZ 85713

CULLEY, AARON W., sales executive; b. Seattle, Wash., Jan. 29, 1951; s. Daniel B. and Dorothy Elizabeth (Smith) C.; m. Linda Lucille. ATA (Printing tech.), Olympic Com. Coll., Bremerton, 1971; BS, Western Wash. U., Bellingham, 1974. Printer Wesmar, Seattle, Wash., 1974-76; educator N.W. Tech. Inst., Seattle, 1976-77; asst. mgr. W. Internat. Hotels, Seattle, 1977-80; prodn. coordinator U. Printing Co., Seattle, 1980-81; estimator Lithocraft Printing Co., Seattle, 1981-82; brokerage sales 1st Impressions Printing, Seattle, 1982-83; printing sales Agy. N.W. Printing, Seattle, 1983-84, Printing Control, Tukwila, Wash., 1984--. Mem., Bellevue Jaycees, Bellevue, Wash., 1979, Ducks Unlimited,. Man of the year, Bellevue Jaycees, Washington, 1979; Salesman of the Year, Printing Control Inc., Tukwila, 1987. Mem., Bus. Profl. Adv. Assn., v.p special events, 1987, Seattle Ad Club,Lake Sammamish Water Ski Club, Am. Water Ski Assn., Advt. Prodns. Assn. Home: 4520 224th Pl NE Redmond WA 98053 Office: Printing Control 1011 Andover Park E Tukwila WA 98188

CULLINAN, LEOLA BARNES, educator; b. Winnipeg, Man., Can., Apr. 24, 1941; d. Leo O.H. and Ola (Solmundson) Barnes; m. Terrence Cullinan, Mar. 21, 1964 (dec. Feb. 1987); children: Tracey (dec.), Cory Patrick. BA, Stanford U., 1963. Tchr. English and French Robert E. Lee High Sch., Springfield, Va., 1964-66; acad. decathlon coach Los Altos (Calif.) High Sch., 1985—; edn. cons. Santa Clara Valley Water Dist., San Jose, Calif., 1987—; pres. Community Adv. Council, Los Altos High Sch., 1985-86. Pres. Santa Rita PTA, Los Altos, 1976-78, PTA Council of Los Altos Mountain View, 1979-81, Friends of Scholar Opera, Palo Alto, 1980-81; v.p. 6th Dist. PTA, Santa Clara County, San Jose, 1981-84. Mem. Audubon Soc. Home: 270 Santander Ct Los Altos CA 94022

CULLISON, SAMUEL WILKINSON, III, physician; b. Chgo., Jan. 14, 1948; s. Samul Wilkinson Jr. and Eleanor (Wilkins) C.; m. Beth Roberta Trussell, Dec. 21, 1971; children: Samuel Wilkinson IV, Robert John. BA, Ind. U., 1970; MD, U. Mo., 1975. Diplomate Am. Bd. Family Practice. Resident in family practice U. Wash., Seattle, 1975-78; pvt. practice specializing in family practice, Monroe, Wash., 1978—; med. dir. Evergreen Treatment Ctr., Seattle, 1978—; pres. med. staff Valley Gen. Hosp., Monroe, 1982-84; med. dir. Midvale Treatment Ctr., Seattle, 1986—, Alcohol Drug Treatment Ctr., Monroe, 1986—; asst. clin. prof. U. Wash. Sch. Medicine, 1980—; bd. dirs. Snohomish County Physicians Corp., Everett, Wash., 1985—, pres. bd., 1987-88. Contbr. articles to med. jours. Mem. AMA, Wash. State Med. Assn. (trustee 1985—, del. nat. convs. 1987—), Am. Acad. Family Physicians, Wash. Acad. Family Physicians (pres. 1987-88), Am. Med. Soc. for Alcoholism and Other Drug Dependencies. Democrat. Methodist. Office: Monroe Family Practice 14755 179th St SE Monroe WA 98272

CULMER, COLEEN ANN, special education administrator; b. Salt Lake City, Mar. 16, 1956; d. Fred Lawrence and Beverly Marie Bahr; children: Brian, Kayla. BA summa cum laude, Wash. State U., 1978, MA, 1979, postgrad., 1984-88. Communication disorders specialist Kennewick (Wash.) Sch. Dist., 1979-88, program mgr. spl. edn. dept., 1986—; pvt. practice communication disorders specialist, Kennewick, 1979-84. Mem. Am. Speech and Hearing Assn. (cert. clin. competence), Wash. Speech and Hearing Assn., Wash. Assn. Sch. Adminstrs., Council for Exceptional Children. Home: 8517 W Entiat Pl Kennewick WA 99336 Office: Spl Svcs 200 S Dayton Kennewick WA 99336

CULP, GARY, military officer, engineer; b. Columbus, Ohio, Mar. 14, 1940; s. Chester Harold and Alice May (Cole) C.; m. Caryl Ann Miller, June 7, 1962; children: Meredith Lynn, Mackinley Leigh. BS in Physics, U. Ark., 1962; MS in Engring. Space Physics, Air Force Inst. Tech., Dayton, Ohio, 1964; MS in Engring. Mgmt., Northeastern U., Boston, 1968. Commd. 2d lt. USAF, 1962, advanced through grades to col., ret., 1988; rsch. physicist Cambridge Rsch. Labs. USAF, Boston, 1964-68; program mgr. Office of Sec. of Def. USAF, Saigon, Republic of Vietnam, 1968-69; project officer Tech. Applications Ctr. USAF, Alexandria, Va., 1969-72; hdqrs staff officer USAF, Washington, 1973-77; program dir. space div. USAF, L.A., 1978-84; comdr. Systems Command Inspection Ctr. USAF, Ft. Walton Beach, Fla., 1984-86; comdr. Fgn. Tech. div. USAF, Dayton, 1986-88; lectr. U. Ark., Fayetteville, 1982-86, Air Command and Staff Coll., USAF, Montgomery, Ala., 1982-84; cons. USAF Systems Command, Washington, 1984-86. Contbr. articles, papers to physics jours. Life mem. Rep. Nat. Com., Washington, 1971—; mem. No. Va. Council Big Bros. Am., Alexandria, 1974-78. Decorated Legion of Merit; recipient Superior Mgmt. award Sec. of Def., Washington, 1982; Decorated Legion of Merit, 1985, 88. Mem. AIAA (sr.), Am. Physical Soc. (life), Armed Forces Communications and Electronics Assn. (life), Air Force Assn. (life) (Sr. Officer of Yr., Air Power chpt. 147, L.A., 1984), Nat. Mgmt. Assn., Y-Westerners Club (Anaheim, Calif.), Cypress (Calif.) Aquatics Booster Club (Calif.), Sigma Pi Sigma. Republican. Presbyterian. Home: 6106 Jeffrey Mark St Cypress CA 90630

CULTON, PAUL MELVIN, therapist, educator, interpreter; b. Council Bluffs, Iowa, Feb. 12, 1932; s. Paul Roland and Hallie Ethel Emma (Paschal) C. BA, Minn. Bible Coll., 1955; BS, U. Nebr., 1965; MA, Calif. State U., Northridge, 1970; EdD, Brigham Young U., 1981. Cert. tchr., Iowa. Tchr. Iowa Sch. for Deaf, Council Bluffs, 1956-70; ednl. specialist Golden West Coll., Huntington Beach, Calif., 1970-71, dir. disabled students, 1971-82, instr., 1982—; interpreter various state and fed. cts., Iowa, Calif., 1960—; asst. prof. Calif. State U., Northridge, Fresno, Dominguez Hills, 1973, 76, 80, 87—; vis. prof. U. Guam, Agana, 1977; allocations atsk force, task force on deafness, trainer handicapped students Calif. Community Colls., 1971-81. Editor: Region IX Conf. for Coordinating Rehab. and Edn. Svcs. for Deaf proceedings, 1970, Toward Rehab. Involvement by Parents of Deaf conf. proceedings, 1971; composer Carry the Light, 1986. Bd. dirs. Iowa NAACP, 1966-68, Gay and Lesbian Community Svcs. Ctr., Orange County, Calif., 1975-77; founding sec. Dayle McIntosh Ctr. for Disabled, Anaheim and Garden Grove, Calif., 1974-80; active Dem. Cent. Com. Pottawatomie County, Council Bluffs, 1960-70. League for Innovation in Community Coll. fellow, 1974. Mem. Registry of Interpreters for Deaf, Congress Am. Instrs. Deaf, Am. Deafness and Rehab. Assn., Calif. Assn. Postsecondary Educators Disabled, Am. Fedn. Tchrs., Nat. Assn. Deaf. Unitarian. Home and Office: 18332 Brookhurst St Fountain Valley CA 92708

CULVER, IRENE, writer; b. Sayre, Okla., Jan. 11, 1933; d. Joseph Carl and Thelma Veryl (Kirksey) C.; m. Allen L. Wray, Sept. 1, 1952 (div. 1974); children: Randall, Timothy, Christopher, Michelle. BA in English, Calif. State U., Sacramento, 1987. Freelance writer, Sacramento, 1968—; pub. relations cons. several non-profit orgns., Sacramento and Stockton, Calif., 1970-76. Contbr. numerous articles to various publs. With pub. relations dept. United Way, Sacramento, 1969-76; exec. dir. Go And Tell Everyone (G.A.T.E.) Inc., Sacramento, 1979-81.

CULVERWELL, HOWARD GLENDON, rancher; b. Concordia, Kans., May 18, 1911; s. Albert Sutcliff and Mabel Amelia (Middaugh) C.; student public schs.; m. Erma Frances Martin, Dec. 31, 1939; children: Gerald, Norman, Jon, Carolyn, Melvin, Melodie. Engaged in sheep, cattle, wheat and hay ranching, Craig, Colo., 1946—; past pres. Moffat County Farm Bur. Mem. Dist. 13 Sch. bd., also pres., 9 yrs., then mem. County Wide Bd., 16 yrs.; bd. dirs. Colo. Assn. Sch. Bds., 1965-71. Mem. Profl. Farmers Am., Farmers Union, Nat. Farmers Orgn. Republican.

CUMBERLIN, CHARLES EDGAR, auctioneer; b. Page County, Iowa, Jan. 8, 1938; s. Howard Lee and Eustatia Florence (Mendenhall) C.; m. Carolyn Joann Schmidt, Jan. 27, 1963; 1 child, Shelly Jo. Grad., Western Coll. fo Auctioneering, 1960; student, Mo. Auction Sch., 1969. Auctioneer First Ave. Furniture Auction, Greeley, Colo., 1960-66; real estate auctioneer Austin-Austin, Greeley, 1966-72; auctioneer Brush (Colo.) Livestock Comm. Co., 1972-76; auctioneer, ptnr. Odle-Cumberlin Auctioneers, Brush, 1972-86, auctioneer, owner, 1986—; instr. M. Auction Sch., Kansas City, 1972—. Mem. Nat. Auctioneers Assn. (pres. 1979-80, hall of fame, 1986), Colo. Auctioneers Assn., Nat. Assn. Realtors, Accredited Land Cons. 476 (World Champion Livestock Auctioneer 1978), Livestock Industries Inst. (trustee) Cert. Auctioneers Inst. (bd. dirs.), Bunker Hill Club, Safari Club. Republican. Methodist. Office: Odle-Cumberlin Auctioneers PO Box 248 1155 N Colo Brush CO 80723

CUMMINGS, BARTON, musician; b. Newport, N.H., July 10, 1946; s. C. Barton and Ruth (Ricard) C.; m. Florecita L. Lim, July 23, 1983;. BS in Music Edn., U. N.H., 1968; MusM, Ball State U., 1973. Dir. music Alton (N.H.) Pub. Sch., 1971-72; lectr. San Diego State U., 1974-79; instr. music Point Loma Coll., San Diego, 1976-79; instr. San Diego Community Coll. Dist., 1977-79, Delta State U., Cleve., 1979-82; supr. Clarksdale Separate Sch. Dist., 1982-84; dir. music Walnut (Calif.) Creek Concert Band, 1985--, Richmond Unified Sch. Dist., 1988—. Author: The Contemporary Tuba, 1984, The Tuba Guide, 1989. Mem. ASCAP, Am. Fedn. Musicians, Phi Mu Alpha Sinfonia. Home: 550 Cambridge Dr Benicia CA 94510

CUMMINGS, DAROLD BERNARD, designer; b. Batavia, N.Y., June 27, 1944; s. Bernard Laverne and Doris Helen (Klotzbach) C.; m. Christine Dana Lundgren, July 20, 1975 (div. Mar. 1988); children: Carla, Bret. BS in Indsl. Design, Calif. State U., Long Beach, 1967. Engr. aircraft design Rockwell Internat., Los Angeles, 1967-82; chief engr. trainer aircraft Rockwell Internat., El Segundo, Calif., 1988—; chief designer advanced design Northrop Corp., Hawthorne, Calif., 1982-88; lectr. Calif. State U., Long Beach, 1969-73; pres. Matrix Design, Hawthorne, 1967—. Author: What Not to Name Your Baby, 1982; cons., actor movie Search for Solutions, 1979. Advisor aero engring. dept. Calif. Polytech. Coll., Pomona, 1985—. Mem. Air Force Assn. Republican. Home: 5320 W 124th Pl Hawthorne CA 90250 Office: Rockwell Internat El Segundo CA 90245

CUMMINGS, GEORGE F. DAVIS, lawyer; b. Globe, Ariz., Apr. 3, 1955; s. Samuel Rowland and Dorothy (Davis) C. BA, U. Ariz., 1978, JD, 1981. Assoc. Law Offices of Daniel J. Oehler, Bullhead City, Ariz., 1982—. Mem. Ariz. State Bar Assn., Mohave County Bar Assn., Kiwanis Club, Colo. River Pioneers Hist. Soc., Bullhead Area C. of C., Phi Beta Kappa. Republican. Methodist. Office: Law Offices of Daniel J Oehler 1490 Ramar Rd Bullhead City AZ 86442

CUMMINGS, HOWARD D., quality assurance engineer; b. Idaho Falls, Idaho, Aug. 29, 1948; s. Jack Duane and Annie Laurie (Hammon) C,; m. Susan Marie Miller, July 18, 1970; children: Laura Sue, Joy Marie, Lisa Dawn, James Stuart, John Clayton, Joseph Duane, Jessie Brooke, Jason Lee. AS, Ricks Coll., Rexburg, Idaho, 1973; BS, Utah State U., 1975. Sr. quality engr. Exxon Nuclear Co., Idaho Falls, 1976-81, Consumers Power Co., Jackson, Mich., 1981-86, Battelle Pacific N.W. Labs., Richland, Wash., 1986—; Cert. quality engr. Served as sgt. U.S. Army, 1969-71, Socialist Republic Vietnam. Mem. Am. Soc. Quality Control (sr., sec. 1988-89, treas. 1987-88). Mormon. Home: 7015 W 8th St Kennewick WA 99336 Office: Battelle Pacific NW Labs PO Box 999 Richland WA 99352

CUMMINGS, MARY EISELE, clinical psychologist; b. Chgo., Oct. 3, 1939; d. Charles Wesley and Blanche Mae (Kennell) Eisele; m. David Peter Adam, 1961 (div.); m. 2d, Ronald Beavers, 1969 (div.); 1 child, John Miller Adam; m. 3d, F.L. Patrick Cummings, 1986. B.A. in History cum laude, Radcliffe Coll., 1962; M.A., U. Ariz., 1970, Ph.D. in Psychology, 1973. Cert. psychologist, Ariz. Clin. psychologist Student Counseling Service, U. Ariz., Tucson, 1972-76, asst. dir., 1976-84, acting dir., 1980, assoc. dir., 1985—, tng. dir., 1985—, dir. univ.-wide honors program, 1980-85, lectr. dept. psychology, 1973-75; Ariz. coordinator Catalyst Network for Nat. Women's Info. Co-founder Tucson Gilbert & Sullivan Theatre, 1966, bd. dirs., 1966-71; mem. Ariz. Opera Co. Chorus, 1975—; mem. adminstrv. bd. St. Francis in the Foothills Meth. Ch., 1978-81. Recipient faculty achievement award U. Ariz. Alumni Assn., 1983; NIMH fellow, 1968-69. Mem. Am. Psychol. Assn., Ariz. Psychol. Assn., So. Ariz. Psychol. Assn., Ariz. Group Psychotherapy Soc., Internat. Transactional Analysis Assn., Nat. Collegiate Honors Council. Democrat. Contbr. articles to profl. jours. Office: U Ariz Student Counseling Svc Old Main 200 Tucson AZ 85721

CUMMINGS, NICHOLAS ANDREW, psychologist; b. Salinas, Calif., July 25, 1924; s. Andrew and Urania (Sims) C.; m. Dorothy Mills, Feb. 5, 1948; children—Janet Lynn, Andrew Mark. AB, U. Calif., Berkeley, 1948; MA, Claremont Grad. Sch., 1954; PhD, Adelphi U., 1958. Chief psychologist Kaiser Permanente No. Calif., San Francisco, 1959-76; clin. dir. Biodyne Inst., San Francisco, 1976—; chmn., chief exec. officer Am. Biodyne, Inc., San Francisco, 1985—; co-dir. Golden Gate Mental Health Ctr., San Francisco, 1959-75; pres. Calif. Sch. Profl. Psychology, Los Angeles, San Francisco, San Diego, Fresno campuses, 1969-76; chmn. bd. Calif. Community Mental Health Ctrs., Inc., Los Angeles, San Diego, San Francisco, 1975-77; pres. Blue Psi, Inc., San Francisco, 1972-80, Inst. for Psychosocial Interaction, 1980-84; mem. mental health adv. bd. City and County San Francisco, 1968-75; bd. dirs. San Francisco Assn. Mental Health, 1965-75; pres., chmn. bd. Psycho-Social Inst., 1972-80; dir. Mental Research Inst., Palo Alto, Calif., 1979-80; pres. Nat. Acads. of Practice, 1981—. Served with U.S. Army, 1944-46. Fellow Am. Psychol. Assn. (dir. 1975-81, pres. 1979); mem. Calif. Psychol. Assn. (pres. 1968). Office: Am Biodyne Inc 400 Oyster Point Blvd Ste 218 South San Francisco CA 94080

CUMMINGS, SPANGLER (MELINDA JOHNSON), art dealer, artist; b. L.A., Dec. 27, 1936; d. Clyde Lewis and Lena Glyde (Spangler) Cummings; m. Richard Johnson, Nov. 25, 1955; children: Edward, Jeanne, Lisa. BA, Chatham Coll., Pitts., 1978; postgrad., Carnegie-Mellon U., Pitts., 1979-80. Founding pres., dir. Artists in Action, Pitts., 1981-82; founder, owner, operator Spangler Cummings Galleries, Columbus, Ohio, 1985-87. Community rep. Artist/Lecture Series Cypress, Calif., 1973; mem. exec. bd. Three Rivers Art Festival Pitts., 1980; docent Columbus Mus. Art, 1985-87, Mus. of Contemporary Art, L.A., 1989. Named Best of Show by Cypress Cultural Arts Assn., 1967; finalist Internat. Soc. Artists, N.Y.C., 1979. Mem. So. Calif. Community Artists (pres. 1972-73); charter mem. Internat. Soc. Artists; assoc. mem. Am. Watercolor Soc.; mem. Pitts. Soc. Artists (bd. dirs. 1980-81); Columbus Art League (bd. dirs. 1983-85). Democrat. Home and Office: 11926 White Water Ln Malibu CA 90265

CUMMINS, JOHN STEPHEN, bishop; b. Oakland, Calif., Mar. 3, 1928; s. Michael and Mary (Connolly) C. A.B., St. Patrick's Coll., 1949. Ordained priest Roman Catholic Ch., 1953; asst. pastor Mission Dolores Ch., San Francisco, 1953-57; mem. faculty Bishop O'Dowd High Sch., Oakland, 1957-62; chancellor Diocese of Oakland, 1962-71; rev. monsignor 1962, domestic prelate, 1967; exec. dir. Calif. Cath. Conf., Sacramento, 1971-77; consecrated bishop 1974; aux. bishop of Sacramento, 1974-77; bishop of Oakland, 1977—; Campus minister San Francisco State Coll., 1953-57, Mills Coll., Oakland, 1957-71; Trustee St. Mary's Coll., 1968-79. Home: 634 21st St Oakland CA 94612 Office: Oakland Diocese 2900 Lake Shore Ave Oakland CA 94610 *

CUMMINS, NEIL JOSEPH, JR., land surveyor, lawyer; b. Oxnard, Calif., Sept. 14, 1945; s. Neil Joseph and Helen Louise (Porter) C.; student Claremont Men's Coll., 1962-64, Calif. State Poly. Coll., 1965-67; JD, Mid Valley Coll. Law, 1978; Bar: Calif. 1978. m. Lynn D. Mealer, Sept. 16, 1967. Designer, Ludwig Engring., San Bernardino, Calif., 1967-69; field supr. Sikand Engring., Van Nuys, Calif., 1969-77; land surveyor, Reseda, Calif., 1977—; lectr. civil engring. Calif. Poly. Coll., Pomona, 1979-80; admitted to Calif. bar, 1978. Registered profl. engr., Ariz., Calif., Nev.; registered land surveyor, Calif., Nev., Ariz. Fellow ASCE; mem. Am. Congress Surveying and Mapping (chmn. So. Calif. sect. 1984), Am. Water Works Assn., ABA, Los Angeles County Bar Assn., Calif. Land Surveyors Assn. Died Nov. 26, 1988.

CUNDALL, LARRY DON, rancher; b. Glendo, Wyo., July 31, 1949; s. Lee Richard and Mina (Sommers) C.; m. Ruth Irene Miller, Apr. 22, 1972. Grad. high sch., Glendo, Wyo.; student, U. Wyo., 1967-68, Eastern Wyo. Coll., 1968-70. Ranch foreman Glendo, Wyo., 1972-77; draftsman Highway Dept. State of Wyo., Cheyenne, 1977-78; rancher Glendo, 1978—. Vol. fire fighter Rural Fire Dept., Platte County, Wyo., 1978—; med. tech. Wyo. Emergency Svc., Platte County, 1978; adv. bd. dirs. Platte County Extension Office, Wheatland, Wyo., 1987—; mem. county com. Agrl. Stabilization & Conservation Svc., Wheatland, 1988—. With U.S. Army, 1970-72, Vietnam. Decorated Bronze Star; recipient commendation for excellence Beef Imrpovement Fedn., 1988. Mem. Am. Angus Assn., Wyo. Beef Cattle Improvement Assn. (Wyo. Comml. Beef Producer of Yr. 1988), Am. Legion (comdr. Glendo chpt. 1983-89). Republican. Episcopalian. Home and Office: 1426 Glendo Park Rd Glendo WY 82213

CUNDICK, ROBERT, organist; b. Salt Lake City, 1926. Pvt. studies with Alexander Schreiner; PhD, U. Utah, 1955. Organist Salt Lake (City) Mormon Tabernacle, 1965—; instr. U. Utah, Brigham Young U. Performer numerous recitals U.S., Europe; composer of organ, choral, orchestral and chamber music. Fellow Am. Guild Organists (nat. councilor, recipient S. Lewis Elmer award 1970, 71). Office: 50 E North Temple St Salt Lake City UT 84150

CUNLIFFE, FREDERICK ROUTH, III, aerospace equipment company executive; b. Sayre, Pa., Dec. 31, 1946; s. Frederick Routh Jr. and Virginia Deem (Monroe) C.; m. Carol Anne Engler, July 16, 1977; children: Erica Kali, Frederick Routh IV. BA, Tulane U., 1968; Masters Internat. Mgmt. with honors, Am. Grad. Sch. Internat. Mgmt., Glendale, Ariz., 1975. Mktg. dept. Harnischfeger Internat., Milw., 1975-77; regional mgr. Africa Harnischfeger Internat., Paris and Abidjan, 1977-80; mgr., Europe, Middle East Morgan Equipment, London, 1980-81; regional mgr. Grove Internat., Singapore, 1981-84; regional dir. Clemco Internat., Singapore, 1984-86; dir. internat. Aerolyte Systems, San Francisco, 1986—. Active Am. Bus. Club, Singapore, 1981-86. Capt. USAF, 1968-73, Vietnam. Decorated Silver Star, 2 Purple Hearts, Disting. Flying Cross, Vietnamese Cross of Gallantry, 19 Air medals. Mem. Air Force Assn., Red River Valley Assn., Gathering of Eagles, Olympic Club (San Francisco), Tiburon Yacht Club. Republican. Episcopalian. Home: 123 Trinidad Dr Tiburon CA 94920 Office: Aerolyte Systems 1657 Rollins Rd Burlingame CA 94010

CUNNANE, PATRICIA S., medical facility administrator; b. Clinton, Iowa, Sept. 7, 1946; d. Cyril J. and Corinne Spain; m. Edward J. Cunnane, June 19, 1971. AA, Mt. St. Clare Coll., Clinton, Iowa, 1966. Mgr. Eye Med. Clinic of Santa Clara Valley, San Jose, Calif. Mem. Med. Adminstrs. Calif. Polit. Action Com., San Francisco, 1987. Mem. Med. Group Mgmt. Assn., Am. Coll. Med. Group Adminstrs. (nominee), Nat. Notary Assn., Resource Ctr. for Women, Nat. Assn. Female Execs., Exec. Women Internat. (v.p. 1986-87, pres. 1987—), Profl. Secs. Internat. (sec. 1979-80), Am. Soc. Ophthalmic Adminstrs., Am. Health Care Execs. Roman Catholic. Home: 232 Tolin Ct San Jose CA 95139 Office: Eye Med Clinic of Santa Clara Valley 220 Meridian Ave San Jose CA 95126

CUNNEEN, WALLACE VINCENT, JR., marketing executive; b. York, Pa., Sept. 18, 1922; student U.S. Naval Acad., 1941-44, U. Pa., 1947, Naval Aviator 1945-47; m. Joan Eleanor Frederick, Jan. 8, 1955; children: Wallace, Mary, James. Sales rep. Diebold, Inc., Canton, Ohio, 1947-49; v.p. The Cunneen Co., Phila., 1949-57, Welton Becket & Asso., L.A., 1957-64; v.p., dir. John Carl Warnecke Asso., San Francisco, 1964-69; v.p. programs devel. Daniel, Mann, Johnson & Mendenhall, Los Angeles, 1969-71; programs devel. Hoover Assos., Palo Alto, 1972-74; owner mktg.-cons. practice, Los Altos Hills, 1974—. Author Essential Element; founder San Jose Nat. Bank, 1982; mem. adv. com. AIA Rsch. Corp. Chmn. Santa Clara County, United Fund Los Altos, 1958-62; exec. bd. Stanford Area council Boy Scouts Am., 1977-78; pres. Los Altos PTA, 1961; council pres. & nat. bd. dirs. Navy League, 1979-81; chmn. Navy Moffett Field 50th Anniversary Celebration Hangar I Dinner. Republican. Roman Catholic. Mem. Fremont Hills Club, Commonwealth Club, St. Claire Club. Home and Office: 26666 Laurel Ln Los Altos Hills CA 94022

CUNNINGHAM, GARY WATSON, publishing executive; b. Denver, Jan. 15, 1943; s. Benjamin W. and Virginia M. (Lewark) C.; m. Behnaz Ghorbani-Nik, Aug. 26, 1980; children—Erin, Cameron, Kelan. B.A., U. Pacific, 1965; M.S., Eastern Wash. U., 1971. Cert. speech pathologist. Peace Corps cons. for Ministry of Ednl. TV., Medellin, Colombia, 1966-68; cons. to Ministry Spl. Edn., San Jose, Costa Rica, 1973; speech pathologist North Clakamas Sch. Dist., Milwaukie, Oreg., 1973-76; pres. C.C. Publs., Inc., Tualatin, Oreg., 1976—; dir. Oracle Computing Systems, Inc., Tualatin; cons. in field. Recipient cert. of appreciation Lyndon B. Johnson, 1968; Ednl. grantee Eastern Mont. U., 1961, Eastern Wash. U., 1969, 70, 71. Mem. Am. Speech and Hearing Assn., Oreg. Speech and Hearing Assn. Republican. Episcopalian. Club: Partners of Ams. Contbr. articles to profl. jours. Home: 08 Sudden Valley Bellingham WA 98226 Office: C C Publs Inc 19576 SW 90th Ct Tualatin OR 97062

CUNNINGHAM, GERALD GEORGE, securities company executive; b. Portland, Oreg., Aug. 23, 1942; s. George L. and Mary (Nelson) C.; m. Margaret, June 4, 1967 (div. 1985); 1 child, Christopher; m. K.C. Kane, May 9, 1986. BA, U. Mont., 1964; LLB, Harvard U., 1967. Bar: Colo. 1967. Assoc. Holland & Hart, Denver, 1967-69; ptnr. Cunningham & McLean, Denver, 1969-71; gen. counsel Shakey's, Englewood, Colo., 1971-73; regional trial counsel SEC, Seattle, 1973-81; gen. counsel GNA Corp., Seattle, 1981-87; chmn., chief exec. officer Integrated Resources Investment Ctr., San Francisco, 1987–; lectr. in field. Mem. Colo. Bar Assn., Silverado Country Club. Republican. Home: 230 Koanapoli Dr Napa CA 94558

CUNNINGHAM, PATRICK JOSEPH, lawyer; b. Denver, June 10, 1954; s. John Joseph Jr. and Doris Louise (Roper) C.; m. Mary Ellen Cavanagh, Oct. 26, 1985; children: Mary Cathleen, Meaghan Louise. BA cum laude, U. Mich., 1976; JD, Ariz. State U., 1979. Bar: Ariz. 1979, U.S. Supreme Ct. 1984. Law clk. Maricopa County Atty's Office, Phoenix, 1978-79; bailiff/law clk. Maricopa County Superior Ct., Phoenix, 1979-80; pros./command advisor 1st Armored Div. U.S. Army, Erlangen, Fed. Republic of Germany, 1980-81; sr. def. counsel Trial Def. Service U.S. Army, Nuernberg, Fed. Republic of Germany, 1981-83; appellate atty. Legal Services Agy. Supreme Ct. Practice Sect. U.S. Army, Washington, 1983-86; asst. U.S. atty. U.S. Dept. of Justice, Phoenix, 1986—; instr. U.S. Army Trial Counsel Assistance Program, Washington, 1985, U.S. Army Trial Def. Service, Nuernberg, 1981-83. Capt. U.S. Army, 1980-86; with USAR, 1986—. Mem. Judge Advocate Assn., Fed. Bar Assn., U. Mich. Alumni Club, Elks, Psi Upsilon. Office: 4000 US Courthouse Phoenix AZ 85025

CUNNINGHAM, PAUL BERNARD, strategic planner, researcher; b. San Fancisco, Jan. 10, 1943; s. Forrest Eugene and Lois Berdeen (Caster) C.; m. Patricia Lynn Jewett, Oct. 21, 1971; children: Erin, Dara. BS, Humbolt State U., 1970; MS, Calif. State U., Arcata, 1979. Research biologist Alaska Dept. Fish and Game, King Salmon, 1971-73; arctic area biologist Alaska Dept. Fish and Game, Nome, 1973-76; dep. dir. Alaska Dept. Fish and Game, Juneau, 1979-81; mgmt. biologist Quinault Indian Nation, Taholah, Wash., 1978; planner, demographer Alaska Dept. Community and Regional Affairs, Juneau, 1981—. Chmn. Luth. Ch. council, Juneau, 1983-86, mem. adv. com. City of Nome, 1974-76; mem. Iditarod Trail Race Com., Nome, 1973-76. Served with U.S. Army, 1961-64, Korea. Mem. AAAS, Alaska Assn. for Advancement of Sci. and Engring., Am. Planning Assn., Am. Fisheries Soc., Appraisers and Measures Soc. (charter). Lutheran. Office: Alaska Dept Community and Regional Affairs Box BH Juneau AK 99802

CUNNINGHAM, THOMAS EVERETT, insurance executive; b. Henderson, Nev., Dec. 31, 1943; s. Everett Merle and Barbara (Austin) C.; m. Dorothy Jean Middleton, Sept. 13, 1967; children: Jeffrey, James, Scott, Michael. AA, Phoenix Coll., 1964; BS, Ariz. State U., Tempe, 1967. Acct. Ralph Segal, CPA, Phoenix, 1961-69; mgr. fin. Seltzer Chevrolet, Yukon, Okla., 1969-71; account exec., v.p. Standard Ins. Agy., Phoenix, 1971-82; account exec. Kirke Van Orsdel, Inc., Phoenix, 1982-85; account exec., v.p. Jardine Emett and Chandler, Phoenix, 1985—. Served with USNG, 1966-70. Republican. Clubs: Thunderbirds (Outstanding Mem. 1986), Phoenix Country. Lodge: Civitan (pres. breakfast club Phoenix chpt. 1977). Home: 40 E Kaler Dr Phoenix AZ 85020 Office: Jardine Emett & Chandler Ariz 2845 E Camelback Rd #700 Phoenix AZ 85020

CUNNINGHAME-BLANK, DEBORAH, graphic designer; b. Kentfield, Calif., Oct. 28, 1961; d. Derek and Indrid Gail (Ancevich) C.-B. BA in Communications, Calif. State U., Chico, 1985. Freelance designer and illustrator 1977, San Rafael, Calif., 1982-87; graphic designer Impulse mag., Chico, 1984, 88—; illustrator, design intern Chico News and Rev., 1984; graphic designer and illustrator Armstrong Image Group, Santa Rosa, Calif., 1985-88. Vol. Marin Gen. Hosp., Kentfield, Calif., 1978. Recipient Achievement award Soc. Western Artists, 1980, Design Excellence cert. Print Mag., 1987, Art Scholarship award Fidelity Savs. and Loan, Design of Excellence award Sonoma County Advt. Club, 1988. Mem. Art Dirs. and Artists Club. Republican. Episcopalian.

CUPERY, ROBERT RINK, manufacturing executive; b. Beaver Dam, Wis., Apr. 5, 1944; s. Rink Eli and Ruby Elizabeth (Haima) C.; m. Clara N. Perez, July 17, 1970; children: Ryan Edward, Jennifer. Airframe and Powerplant, Northrop U., 1967; BSBA, U. Redlands, 1978. Aircraft mechanic Northwest Airlines, Mpls., 1968-69; corp. flight engr. Northrop Corp., Hawthorne, Calif., 1969-76, engr., 1976-79, sr. staff customer relations, 1979-82, internat. quality mgr., 1982-84; pres., chief exec. officer Aircraft Window Repairs, Torrance, Calif., 1984—, Cupery Corp, Torrance, Calif., 1986—. Contbr. articles to profl. jours. Served as staff sgt. USAF, 1962-66. Corp. mem. Profl. Aviation Maintenance Assn., Can. Aviation Mech. Engring., Nat. Bus. Aircraft Assn. Republican.

CUPP, MARY KATHERINE HYER, social worker; b. Clay, W.Va., Jan. 17, 1932; d. Oral Otis and Icie Arlene (McCracken) Hyer; divorced. BA, W.Va. State Coll. (now W.Va. Coll. Grad. Studies), 1967; MSW, W.Va. U., 1970. Lic. clin. social worker, Calif.; cert. jr. coll. tchr., Calif. Statistician W.Va. Dept. Welfare, Charleston, 1967-70; social worker Calif. Dept. Mental Hygiene, South Gate, 1970-73; adoptions worker Los Angeles County (Calif.) Dept. Adoptions, West Covina, 1973; social worker Camarillo (Calif.) State Hosp., 1973-86; parole agt. Calif. Dept. Corrections, North Hollywood, 1986—; cons. Psychiat. Residency Program, Camarillo, 1982-86. Pres. Save our Streetlights, Camarillo, 1979-81. Recipient award State Calif., 1983. Mem. Nat. Assn. Social Workers, Camarillo Bridge Club. Democrat. Methodist. Home: 1091 Dara St Camarillo CA 93010 Office: Calif Dept Corrections Parole and Community Svcs div 14058 Victory Blvd Van Nuys CA 91401

CURCIO, CHRISTOPHER FRANK, municipal agency administrator; b. Oakland, Calif., Feb. 3, 1950; s. Frank William and Virginie Theresa (Le Gris) C. BA in Speech, Drama, Calif. State U., 1971; MBA in Arts Adminstrn., UCLA, 1974; MPA in Pub. Policy, Ariz. State U., 1982. Intern John F. Kennedy Ctr. for Arts, Washington, 1973; gen. mgr. Old Eagle Theatre, Sacramento, 1974-75; cultural arts supr. Fresno (Calif.) Parks and Recreation Dept., 1975-79; supr. cultural and spl. events Phoenix Parks, Recreation and Library Dept., 1979-87, budget analyst, 1987, mgmt. svcs. adminstr., 1987—; mgmt. and budget analyst, City of Phoenix, 1985; grants panelist, Phoenix Arts Commn., 1987, Ariz. Commn. on Arts, 1987-88. Freelance theater critic, 1987—. Active, Valley Big Bros./Big Sisters, Phoenix, 1979—, Valley Leadership Program, Phoenix, 1987-88; sec. Los Olivos Townhome Assn., Phoenix, 1986—. Mem. Am. Soc. Pub. Adminstrn., Nat. Recreation and Park Assn., Ariz. Park and Recreation Assn., Herberger Theater Ctr. Assocs., Rosson House-Heritage Sq. Found. Republican. Office: Phoenix Parks Dept 2333 N Central Ave Phoenix AZ 85004

CUREAU, FRANK RAYMOND, furniture company executive; b. Tours, France, Aug. 29, 1955; came to U.S., 1981; s. Jean-Marie and Jacqueline (Marquenet) C.; m. Armelle Therese Deakin, Apr. 6, 1987; 1 child, Xavier. BA, Descartes U., Tours. Export mgr. Guinard Pumps, Paris, 1979-81; gen. mgr. Guinard Pumps, Chgo., 1981-84, T.F.G., London, 1984-85, Grosfillex, Inc., Oxnard, Calif., 1986—; physics of fluids tchr., Guinard Pumps, Paris, 1980-82. Coord. Rassemblement Pour La Republique, Paris, L.A., 1987, 88. Lt. 1976-77, France. Office: Grosfillex Inc 319 Lambert St Oxnard CA 93030

CURIEL, YORAM, inventor, product development executive; b. Hadera, Israel, May 26, 1941; came to U.S., 1981; s. Herbert and Rachel (Neiman) C.; m. Judith Adiv Yoram, June 19, 1962; children: Anat, Opher, Irit, Adi. Student, Menashe Dist. Coll., Tel Aviv, 1965-69; student, Poly. Inst., Tel Aviv, 1969-70; B.P.A., Brooks Inst. Photography, Santa Barbara, Calif., 1975. Cert. photo finishing engr. Mgr. Photographic Research Labs., Ministry of Defense Israel, Tel Aviv, 1975-78; tech. mgr. Orient Color Labs., Tel Aviv, 1978-79; chief labor adminstr. Kibbutz Ein Shemer, Israel, 1979-81; v.p. tech., founder Foto-Tek Am., Inc., Denver, 1981-84, Flexcel Internat., Inc., Denver, 1982-88; pres., founder Dynagroup Internat. Inc. and subs. companies, Aurora, Colo., 1983—; chief exec. officer, chief fin. officer TSL, Inc., Evergreen, Colo., 1988—; bd. dirs. Flexcel Internat., Inc., Denver; bd. dirs., chmn. Dynagroup Internat., Inc., Aurora, 1983—, TSL, Inc., Evergreen, 1988—; cons. tech. Dyna Safety & Rescue Products, Inc., Aurora, 1987-88. Patentee film transparency projector, building evacuation system and associated method, liquid reservoir and method of dispensing a liquid therefrom by means of a vehicle, improved escape chute, method of protecting packaging for use in food and pharm. industry; inventor method of protecting packing for use in food and pharmaceutical industries. Capt. Israeli Army, 1959-52. Mem. Photomarketing Internat., Profl. Photographers Am. Jewish. Office: Dynagroup Internat Inc 2280 S Xanadu Way Ste 202 Aurora CO 80014

CURLEY, KATHLEEN FOCKLER, librarian; b. Johnstown, Pa., May 7, 1949; d. Ernest and Dolores Maria (Roach) Fockler; m. Edward F. Curley Jr., June 5, 1971. BA with honors, U. Ariz., 1971, MA, 1973, MLS, 1976. Librarian Coolidge (Ariz.) Pub. Library, 1973-75; media specialist Pima Community Coll. Library, Tucson, 1977-85; periodicals specialist Pima Community Coll. Library, 1985—. Precinct committeeman Pima County Democratic Com., 1972-73; voter registrar Pima County, 1984–; treas. San Clemente Neighborhood Assn., Tucson, 1984-86; adv. com. Ballet Ariz. Edn. Profls. Devel. Act fellow U. Ariz., 1971-73. Mem. ALA, Ariz. Library Assn., AAUW (grantee 1975-76), Jr. League Tucson. Roman Catholic. Home: 348 S Bryant Ave Tucson AZ 85711 Office: Pima Community Coll 2202 W Anklam Rd Tucson AZ 85709

CURLEY, SARAH SHARER, bankruptcy judge; b. Oak Park, Ill.; d. Robert F. Sharer and Marian Elizabeth (White) Fitzgerald; m. Roger D. Curley; 1 child. AB, Mount Holyoke Coll., 1971; JD cum laude, N.Y. Law Sch., 1977. Bar: N.Y. 1978, Wis. 1983, Ariz. 1986, U.S. Dist. Ct. (so., ea. dists.) N.Y., U.S. Dist. Ct. Ariz., U.S. Ct. Appeals (2nd cir.). Law clk. U.S. Dist. Ct., N.Y.C., 1977; atty. Fogelson, Fogelson & Collins, N.Y.C., 1978, Otterbourg, Steindler, Houston & Rosen, N.Y.C., 1979-82; asst. counsel First Wisconsin Corp., Milw., 1982-86; atty. Ayers & Graham, Phoenix, 1986; bankruptcy judge Fed. Gov., Phoenix, 1986—. Contbr. articles to profl. jours.; exec. editor: Bankruptcy Bar Bulletin, 1978. Mem. Soroptimists Internat. of Phoenix, Inc., Nat. Conf. Bankruptcy Judges, Ariz. State Bar, Maricopa County Bar Assn., Ariz. Women's Lawyers Assn., State Bar of Wis., Am. Bar Assn., Mount Holyoke Club (v.p.). Office: US Dist Ct 230 N 1st Ave Rm 5208 Phoenix AZ 85025

CURNUTT, RONALD COLIN, teacher; b. Vallejo, Calif., Mar. 26, 1947; s. Walter Frank and Harriett Sandra (Martin) C. BA, Cen. State U., 1969, MEd summa cum laude, 1973. Cert. secondary tchr., Ariz.; Ariz. Community Coll. teaching certificate. Instr. history Parker (Ariz.) High Sch. Unified Sch. Dist. #27, 1971—; adj. prof. history Ariz. Western Coll. La Paz Ctr., Parker, 1973—; chmn. Parker High Sch. Dept. Social Studies, 1973—; chmn, adv. com. Ariz. Western Coll. La Paz County, Parker, 1985—. Chmn. Town of Parker Tras Rates Com., 1984—, Water Rates Com., 1985-87; mem. Tow of Parker Trash Appeal Bd., 1985—. Named Outstanding State Am. History Tchr. DAR, 1981, Outstanding Area Educator Parker C. of C., 1980. Mem. NEA, Ariz. Ednl. Assn., Phi Alpha Theta, Black Mountain #44, Parker York Rite Bodies, Elks, Masons. Republican. Home: PO Box 75 Parker AZ 85344 Office: Parker High Sch PO Box 1089 Parker AZ 85344

CUROTTO, RICKY JOSEPH, lawyer, corporate executive; b. Lomita Park, Calif., Dec. 22, 1931; s. Enrico and Nora M. (Giusso) C.; m. Lynne Therese Ingram, Dec. 31, 1983; children: Dina L., John F., Alexis J. BS cum laude, U. San Francisco, 1953, JD, 1958. Bar: Calif. 1959. Assoc. Peart, Baraty & Hassard, San Francisco, 1958-60; sr. counsel, asst. sec. BHP Utah Internat. Inc., San Francisco, 1960—; of counsel Curotto Law Offices, San Francisco and Sacramento, Calif., 1984—, Calif. Loan Counsel, Crossland Mortgage Corp.; counsel, sec. Ross Valley Homes, Inc., Greenbrae, Calif.; dir. Ross Valley Homes, Inc., Garden Hotels Investment Co. Trustee, U. San Francisco; pres., dir. Shorebird Homeowners Assn. Served to 1st lt. U.S. Army, 1954-56. Named to U. San Francisco Athletic Hall of Fame, 1985, Alumnus of Yr. U. San Francisco, 1989; recipient Bur. Nat. Affairs award, 1958, Disting. Service award U. San Francisco, 1981, Alumnus of Yr., U. San Francisco, 1989. Mem. ABA, State Bar Calif., San Francisco Bar Assn., Am. Arbitration Assn. (nat. panel arbitrators), Am. Corp. Counsel Assn., Commonwealth Club of Calif. Republican. Roman Catholic. Contbr. articles to law revs. Office: BHP Utah Internat Inc 550 California St Ste 800 San Francisco CA 94104

CURRAN, EDWARD MILFORD, business manager; b. Newark, Dec. 15, 1922; s. John Cleveland and Elizabeth Ellen (King) C.; m. Betty Jean Ward, Nov. 26, 1945; children: Gale Janice, Jeffery Ward, Roger Wood. BS in Journalism and Bus. Adminstn., Rider Coll., 1947; postgrad., Seton Hall U., 1947; Diploma in Contract Adjustment and Adminstrn., Toledo U., 1953; Diploma Nat. Security Mgmt., Indsl. Coll. Armed Forces, 1970; Diploma Exec. Mgmt., U. Pa., 1977; Diploma Mgmt. Devel., U. So. Calif., 1981. Asst. advt. mgr. Worthington Pump Corp., Harrison, N.J., 1947-49; real estate salesman Kammerer Real Estate, Newark, 1949-50; quality mgmt. Westinghouse Electric Corp., Newark, 1950-52; manpower specialist U.S. Govt. Army Ordnance Navy, Air Force, N.Y.C., 1952-56; bus. mgr. Rockwell Internat. Corp., Canoga Park and L.A., Calif., 1956-84; pres., dir. C & C Cons. Nat. and Internat., Canoga Park and L.A., 1984—. Author, editor: 2d Marine Divison, 1976. Candidate L.A. City Coun., State Assembly, 1959-62, U.S. Congress, 1969; com. mem. Rep. County and State Com., L.A., 1962-70; advisor Mayor's Community Adv. Bd., L.A., 1961-75; commr. Calif. Indsl. Welfare Comm., Calif. State Vets. Bd.; chmn. L.A. Mil. VIP Coordinating Coun., L.A. Toys for Tots Indian Affairs, Restoration Marine Corps Commandant's Office Residence Dept. Interior, Washington, Coordinating Coun. to Assist Returning Mil. Vets to Gain Employment; mem. Freedom Train Com., Commn. to Appoint Wage Bd, Calif., Rapid Transit Commn., L.A., Canoga Park Citizens Adv. Coun., chmn. planning and environ. concerns subcom.; bd. dirs. Boy Scouts Am., L.A., Panorama Meml. Hosp., L.A.; rep. State Dept. and USMC to 60th Anniversary Commemoration Am. Battle Monument Commn., Paris, 1978; publicity dir. High Sch. Community Adv. Coun. Sgt. USMC, 1941-44, PTO. Recipient numerous commendation and svc. awards including Meritorious Svc. award State of Mass., 1976, Commendation award USMC, 1980, Commendation Plaque Canoga Park C. of C., 1979, Congl. Meritorious Svc. award Congressman James Corman, 1976, CAlif. Golden Seal award Calif Nat. Guard and Calif Sec. State, 1982, Nautical Club award British Royal Marines, 1981, Medal Honor French Govt., 1978, Apollo Commendation NASA, 1969, Calif. Golden State Boxers award, 1986, Calif. Golden State Cade award, 1985, French Govt. Resolution Somme Pi War Meml. Commendation award, 1978, Calif. Senate and Assembly Resolution, 1973, La. City Coun. Resolution, 1967. Mem. Nat. Mgmt. Assn. (v.p. 1962-63), Navy League U.S. (v.p. 1975-88, nat. award 1985), Marine Corps Scholarship Found. (bd. dirs. 1984, pres., meritorius award 1982), So. Calif. Motion Picture Coun. (cert. appreciation 1985), Second Marine Div. Assn. (nat. pres. 1975-76, nat. exec. v.p. 1973-74, pres. Calif. chpt. 1971-72), So. Calif. Semper Fi Marine Corps Coun. (chmn. bd. trustees), L.A. Meml. Found. (pres., bd. dirs. 1982), VFW (aide-de-camp to nat. commdr. 1961-62), Marine Corps League (commandant), Canoga Park C. of C. (bd. dirs.), Nat. Mgmt. Club (chiefObooster 1962-68), West Valley Optimist Internat. (v.p. 1967-68), World Boxing Hall of Fame (bd. dirs. 1986-89), Americans against Human Suffering, Employee Support Nat. Guard and Mil. Res., Dept. Def. (pres. 1987—), L.A. Naval Meml. Found. (pres., bd. dirs. 1982—), Rider Coll. Alumni Assn. (Calif. chmn. 1980-87), Elks, Eta Upsilon Zeta, Skull and Sabres. Presbyterian. Home and Office: 20326 Stagg St Canoga Park CA 91306

CURRAN, JAMES J., banker. BA, U. San Francisco, 1961. With 1st Interstate Bank of Wash., 1977-84, sr. v.p., 1984—; also chmn. bd., pres., chief exec. officer. With USAR, 1962-69. Office: First Interstate Bank of Idaho PO Box 57 Boise ID 83702 *

CURRAN, NEIL WILLIS, state police chief; b. Raton, N.Mex., June 12, 1936; s. Cornelius R. and Buelah (Gibson) C.; m. Beatrice J. Ginther, Apr. 27, 1957; children: Kathy Jean, Robert Neil, Larry Troy. B of Agriculture and Elec. Engring., N.Mex. State U., 1959. With uniform div. N.Mex. State Police, 1965-69, with criminal investigations div., 1969-82, spl. investigations and intelligence div., 1969-70, narcotics div., 1970-74, ops. sgt. and adminstrv. asst. to bur. comdr., 1975-79, ops. lt., air detail lt., 1979-82, asst. div. comdr., adminstrv. and operational supr., 1981-82, property bur. comdr., 1982-83, asst. div. comdr. criminal investigations div., 1983-86, acting comdr. criminal investigations div., 1986-87, acting chief, 1987, chief dept. pub. safety, 1987—; instr. N.Mex. Dept. Corrections, Santa Fe, 1975-81, Criminal Investigations Div. In-Svc. Tng. Sch., 1980-81, N.Mex. State Police Recruit Sch., 1973-82; N.Mex. rep. Southwest Border Initiative, 1986—, U.S. Customs Svc. Steering Com., 1987—, Nat. Narcotics Border Interdiction System Steering Com., 1987—; testified numerous spl. hearings. Mem. Gov.'s Red Ribbon Campaign, Santa Fe, 1988, Law Enforcement Acad. Bd., 1988, Safer N.Mex. Now, 1988, Office of Med. Investigators Bd., 1988; mem. exec. bd. Turn in a Pusher, Albuquerque, 1988. Mem. Internat. Assn. Chiefs of Police, Nat. Narcotics Officers' Assn., Nat. Drug Enforcement Officers Assn. (pres. 1984-85, 85-86), N.Mex. Sheriff's and Police Assn., Fraternal Order of Police. Democrat. Home: 2026 Calle Perdiz Santa Fe NM 87505 Office: Dept Pub Safety NMex State Police Div PO Box 1628 Santa Fe NM 87504-1628

CURRAN, WILLIAM PATRICK, III, optometrist; b. St. Albans, N.Y., Apr. 15, 1953; s. William Patrick and Mary Lois (Connolly) C.; m. Teressa Jen Petersen, May 16, 1987; children: Tamara, Maressa. Student, Marist Coll., 1970-72; BA, NYU, 1975; OD, SUNY, N.Y.C., 1980; postgrad., Ariz. State U., 1981, 85-87. Supervising optometrist Indian Health Svc. USPHS, Aberdeen, S.D., 1980; pvt. practice Phoenix, 1980—; sports vision cons. major league baseball, 1982, archery team U.S. Olympics, 1983; clin. investigator U.S. FDA, 1981-83; adjunct clin. instr. So. Coll. Optometry, Memphis, 1983-85; dir. Optometric Extension Program Found., Ariz., 1982-86; founding chmn. Sun Valley Behavioral Vision Sem., 1982-84; chmn. grad. clin. seminars, 1981-82; cons. optometrist U.S. Dept of Justice, 1985-87. Bd. dirs. Pulmonary Hypertension Edn. and Rsch. Found., Phoenix, 1982-83; chmn. Forum on Learning Abilities, 1982-84; sec. St. Vincent DePaul Soc., 1983-86. Named Youth Minister of Yr. Roman Cath. Diocese of Phoenix, 1984. Mem. Am. Optometric Assn. (recognition award 1983, 84), Ariz. Optometric Assn. (chmn. edn. 1981-86), Cen. Ariz. Optometric Soc. (v.p. 1982-83, pres. 1983-84), Kiwanis (v.p. 1982-84, pres. 1984-85), Beta Gamma Sigma. Republican. Home: 6624 W Villa Rita Dr Glendale AZ 85308 Office: 9624 Metro Pkwy E Phoenix AZ 85051

CURRIE, MADELINE ASHBURN, business administration educator; b. Rankin, Tex., Sept. 28; d. Herman and Ivan G. Vinson; BS, Tex. Woman's U., 1962; MA, Calif. State U., 1967; EdD, UCLA, 1974; m. Gail G. Currie; children: Robb Ashburn, Mark Ashburn, Michael Ashburn. Tchr., Edgewood High Sch., West Covina, Calif., 1962-69; instr. Rio Hondo Coll., Whittier, Calif., 1968-69; prof., grad. dir. Coll. Bus. Adminstrn., Calif. State Poly. U., Pomona, 1969-88, prof. emerita, 1988—. Recipient award Alpha Lambda Delta; Exceptional Merit award, Meritorious Service awards Calif. State Poly. U., 1984. Mem. Grad. Sch. Edn., UCLA. Mem. Calif. Bus. Edn. Assn. (Recognition award), Tex. Woman's U. Alumnae Assn., Rotary, Delta Pi Epsilon, Pi Lambda Theta, Delta Kappa Gamma (chpt. pres.), Delta Mu Delta.

CURRIE, MALCOLM RODERICK, scientist, aerospace and automotive executive; b. Spokane, Wash., Mar. 13, 1927; s. Erwin Casper and Genevieve (Hauenstein) C.; m. Sunya Lofsky, June 24, 1951; children—Deborah, David, Diana; m. Barbara L. Dyer, Mar. 5, 1977. A.B., U. Calif. at Berkeley, 1949, M.S., 1951, Ph.D., 1954. Research engr. Microwave Lab., U. Calif. at Berkeley, 1949-52, elec. engring. faculty, 1953-54; lectr. U. Calif. at Los Angeles, 1955-57; research engr. Hughes Aircraft Co., 1954-57, v.p., 1965-66; head electron dynamics dept. Hughes Research Labs., Culver City, Calif., 1957-60; dir. physics lab. Hughes Research Labs., Malibu, Calif., 1960-61, asso. dir., 1961-63, v.p., dir. research labs., 1963-65, v.p., mgr. research and devel. div., 1965-69; v.p. research and devel. Beckman Instruments, Inc., 1969-73; undersec. research and engring. dept. Office Sec. Def., Washington, 1973-77; pres. missile systems group Hughes Aircraft Co., Canoga Park, Calif., 1977-83, exec. v.p., 1983-88, chief exec. officer, chmn. bd., 1988—, also bd. dirs.; pres., chief exec. officer Delco Electronics Corp., 1986-88, also bd. dirs.; bd. dirs. GM Hughes Electronics Co., group exec. def. ops., 1986; chmn., chief exec. officer Hughes Aircraft Co., 1988—; mem. Def. Sci. Bd. Contbr. articles to profl. jours.; patentee in field. Mem. adv. bd. U. Calif., Berkeley, UCLA, U. Tex.; trustee U. So Calif., UCLA Found. Served with USNR, 1944-47. Decorated comdr. Legion of Honor France; named nation's outstanding young elec. engr. Eta Kappa Nu, 1958, one of 5 outstanding young men of Calif. Calif. Jr. C. of C., 1960. Fellow IEEE, AIAA; mem. Nat. Acad. Engring., Am. Phys. Soc., Phi Beta Kappa, Sigma Xi, Lambda Chi Alpha. Club: Cosmos. Home: 28780 Wagon Rd Agoura CA 91301 Office: Hughes Aircraft Co 7200 Hughes Terr Los Angeles CA 90045

CURRY, DEBORAH JEAN, corporate executive; b. Safford, Ariz., Nov. 15, 1950; d. Douglas C. and Elizabeth M. (Clark) Von Gausig; 1 child, John; m. Robert W. Curry Jr., Sept. 4, 1976; children: Nicolas, Noah. AA, Palomar Coll., 1969; diploma in nursing, Maricopa Tech. Coll., 1976. Clk. Solano Lumber Co., Solano Beach, Calif., 1968-69; ward clk. Tri City Hosp., Oceanside, Calif., 1969-70; typesetter, ad layout artist Verdi Valley Ind. Co., Cottonwood, Ariz., 1971-72; phys. therapy aide Marcus Lawrence Hosp., Cottonwood, 1972-73; office mgr. Meditest, Phoenix, 1973-75; practical nurse Occupational Med. Clinic, Phoenix, 1976-78; co-owner, prin. Curry Group, Glendale, Ariz., 1982—. Co-author newsletter: The QL Report, 1986—. Mem. Glendale C. of C. Office: Curry Computer Co 15224 N 59th Ave #4 Glendale AZ 85306

CURTIN, JOE LAWRENCE, management consultant; b. Taylorville, Ill., June 7, 1950; s. William Colbrook and Margret Catherine C. BS in Edn., Eastern Ill. U., 1972, MA in Polit. Sci., 1975; PhD in Mgmt., Calif. Coast U., Santa Ana, 1986. Sales rep. Friden Alcatel, L.A., 1982-83; sales mgr. Marina del Rey (Calif.) Assocs., 1983-84, pres., mgmt. assts., 1984-85; mgmt. cons. Inst. of Mgmt. Resources, Westlake Village, Calif., 1985-86, Focus on Mgmt., Inc., Fullerton, Calif., 1986—. Author: Putting Self-Esteem First, 1986, A Reaction Theory of Leadership. Mem. Marina del Rey C. of C., L.A. Orgn. Devel. Network, Turnaround Mgmt. Assn., Forever (co-founder). Home: 702 Washington St #124 Marina Del Rey CA 90292

CURTIN, THOMAS LEE, ophthalmologist; b. Columbus, Ohio, Sept. 9, 1932; s. Leo Anthony and Mary Elizabeth (Burns) C.; B.S., Loyola U., Los Angeles, 1954; M.D., U. So. Calif., 1957; children—Michael, Gregory, Thomas, Christopher. Intern, Ohio State U. Hosp., 1957-58; resident in ophthalmology U.S. Naval Hosp., San Diego, 1961-64; practice medicine specializing in ophthalmology, Oceanside, Calif., 1967—; mem. staff Tri City, Palomar Meml., Scripps Meml. Mercy hosps.; sci. adv. bd. So. Calif. Soc. Prevention Blindness, 1973-76; cons. in field. Trustee, Carlsbad (Calif.) Unified Sch. Dist., 1975-83, pres., 1979, 82, 83. Served as officer M.C., USN, 1958-67. Diplomate Am. Bd. Ophthalmology. Mem. Am., Calif. med. assns., San Diego County Med. Soc., Am. Acad. Ophthalmology, Am. Assn. Ophthalmology, Soc. Cryobiology, Aerospace Med. Assn., Pacific Coast Ophthalmology and Otolaryngology Assn., San Diego Acad. Ophthalmology (pres. 1979), Calif. Assn. Ophthalmology (dir.), San Diego Surg. Soc. Republican. Roman Catholic. Clubs: Carlsbad Rotary, El Camino Country. Home: $S12014 Ave of Trees Carlsbad CA 92008 Office: 3231 Waring Ct Ste S Oceanside CA 92056

CURTIS, BURTON MERRILL, insurance company official; b. Kalispell, Mont., Nov. 29, 1931; s. Wintress Merrill and Mabel Victoria (Isakson) C.; m. Evelyn Aleen Smith, Apr. 16, 1960; children: Kimberly, Shelly, Dana. BS in Law, U. Oreg., 1958. Gen. agt. London Guarantee-Continental, Portland, Oreg., 1962—. Sgt. USMC, 1951-54. Home: PO Box 762 Portland OR 97207 Office: London Guarantee 111 SW Columbia St Ste 310 Portland OR 97201

CURTIS, CHARLES FLOYD, electrical engineer, academic administrator; b. Lena, La., June 4, 1936; s. Charles Floyd and Hazel Leona (Rials) C.; m. Roxie Jean Stillman, June 14, 1959; children: Keith, Gilbert, Sharon. BSEE, Mont. State U., 1964. Registered profl. engr. Mont. Design engr. Montronics Inc., Bozeman, Mont., 1962-65; relay engr. Mont. Power Co., Butte, 1965-67; research engr. Mont. State U., Bozeman, 1967-69; product line mgr. Summit Engring., Bozeman, 1969-82; exec. v.p. Tele-Tech Corp., Bozeman, 1982—; chmn. adv. council dept. agr. Mont. State U., Bozeman, 1983—. Adult leader Boy Scouts Am., Mont., 1969—; bd. dirs. United Way, Bozeman, 1983-84. Recipient Merit award Boy Scouts Am., 1982. Mem. Am. Radio Relay League, Bozeman Jaycees (bd. dirs. 1971-75). Republican. Methodist. Clubs: Bats (pres. 1969-82), Ham (v.p. 1968-70). Office: Tele-Tech Corp 2050 Fairway Dr Bozeman MT 59715

CURTIS, GEORGE DARWIN, research scientist; b. Galveston, Tex., Apr. 30, 1928; m. Jean Allen, July 23, 1988. Sr. scientist western div. LTV Rsch. Ctr., Honolulu, 1961-64, asst. dir., prin. investigator, 1965-67; staff specialist Control Data Corp., Honolulu, 1967-68, systems dir., 1969-70; systems engring. cons., lectr. U. Hawaii, Honolulu, 1970—, rsch. joint inst. for marine and atmospheric rsch., 1979—, tech. coord. Hawaii Natural Energy Inst., 1981—; cons. State of Hawaii, 1976-86, County of Honolulu, 1981-85; lectr. USN Post-Grad. Sch. Contbr. essays to books in field; pub. (jour.) Sci. of Tsunami Hazards, 1982—. Dir. ARC, Honolulu, 1978; squadron comdr. CAP, Honolulu, 1982—. Grantee IR Scanner Program, 1987. Mem. Tsunami Soc. (pres. 1985-88), Marine Tech. Soc., IEEE (program and publ. chmn. Ocean Electronics Symposium 1966, chmn. Hawaii sect. 1978-79), Acoustical Soc. Am., Am. Solar Energy Soc. Home: 2565 Laau St Honolulu HI 96826 Office: U Hawaii 1000 Pope Rd MSB 312 Honolulu HI 96822

CURTIS, JESSE WILLIAM, JR., U.S. district judge; b. San Bernardino, Calif., Dec. 26, 1905; s. Jesse William and Ida L. (Seymour) C.; m. Mildred F. Mort, Aug. 24, 1930; children: Suzanne, Jesse W., Clyde Hamliton, Christopher Cowles. A.B., U. Redlands, 1928, LL.D., 1973; J.D., Harvard U., 1931. Bar: Calif. 1931. Pvt. practice 1931-35; mem. firms Guthrie & Curtis, San Bernardino, 1935-40, Curtis & Curtis, 1946-50, Curtis, Knauf, Henry & Farrell, 1950-53; judge Superior Ct. of Calif., 1953-62, U.S. Dist. Ct. (cen. dist.) Calif., 1962—; rep. dist. ct. on Jud. Council U.S., 1972-74. Chmn. San Bernardino Sch. Bd., 1942-46, mem., 1946-49; mem. Del Rosa Bd. Edn., 1950-53; chmn. San Bernardino County Heart Fund; dir., past pres. YMCA; bd. dirs. GoodWill Industries, Crippled Children's Soc., Arrowhead United Fund; adv. bd. Community Hosp. Mem. ABA, Los Angeles County Bar Assn., Calif. State Bar, Am. Judicature Soc., Am. Law Inst., Orange County World Affairs Council, Phi Delta Phi. Democrat. Conglist. Club: Newport Harbor Yacht. Home: 305 Evening Star Ln Newport Beach CA 92660 Office: US Dist Ct 312 N Spring St Los Angeles CA 90012

CURTIS, JOHN A., dentist; b. Bertrand, Nebr., May 16, 1943; s. Albert Garfield and Mable Katherine (Larsen) C.; m. Debroah Lynn Miller, May 28, 1977; 1 child, Shannon Katherine. BA, Kearney (Nebr.) State Coll., 1965; MA, U. N.C., 1971; DDS, U. Colo., 1979. Chemist air quality Colo. Dept. Pub. Health, Denver, 1971-72; instr. scis. Englewood (Colo.) Pub. Schs., 1972-75; gen. practice dentistry Loveland, Colo., 1979—. NSF grantee 1967, 69, 70, 71. Mem. Am. Dental Soc., Colo. Dental Soc. (mem. ho. dels. 1986, 87, 88, 89), Larimer County Dental Soc. (sec. 1988-89), Colo. Dental Assn. (del. 1986-88), Delta Sigma Delta. Methodist. Lodges: Optomists, Elks. Home: 2857 Sally Ann Dr Loveland CO 80537 Office: 1703 E 18th 1A Loveland CO 80538

CURTIS, KIPP ALLEN, retail associate; b. Havre de Grace, Md., Mar. 24, 1953; s. Wesley Edmund and Janet (Austin) C.; m. Lynn Maree Mixson, Aug. 27, 1975 (div. Mar. 1982); 1 child, Kristofer. Student, U. N.Mex., 1971-73; diploma, Locksmithing Inst., Little Falls, N.J., 1980. Lot mgr. Richardson Ford, Albuquerque, 1973-76, 77-79, with maintenance, 1976-77, with data entry, warranty adminstr., 1979—. Author numerous poems. Recipient Golden Poet award, World of Poetry, 1985, Silver Poet award, 1986. Mem. NRA, Nat. Com. for Youth Suicide Prevention, Soc. for Creative Anachronism. Republican. Home: 11417 Linn NE #N-5 Albuquerque NM 87123 Office: Richardson Ford 8601 Lomas Blvd NE Albuquerque NM 87110

CURTIS, LOREN RIFTIN, chief executive officer; b. Tucson, Oct. 1, 1937; s. Loren Stanford and Josephine Versup (Rodgers) C.; m. Mary Lou STorie, Aug. 18, 1957; children: Lori Ann, Kevin Riftin. BS in Agrl. Econs., U. Ariz., 1959. Clk. Casa Grande Oil Mill, Ariz., 1959-61; bookkeeper Casa Grande Cotton Fin. Co., 1961-67, mgr., 1967-84; v.p. Chickasha Cotton Oil Co., Casa Grande, 1984—; del. Nat. Cotton Council, 1983—; dir. Elec. Dist. #1, Casa Grande, 1982—; adv. bd. Ariz. Cotton Growers Assn., Phoenix, 1984—. Councilman Casa Grande City Council, 1981—; del. Casa Grande Town Hall, 1981—, Pinal County Town Hall, 1988—, Ariz. Town Hall, Sedona, Ariz., 1988—. Mem. Ariz. Agro-Bus. Council, Casa Grande C. of C. (pres. 1986), Elks. Democrat. Presbyterian. Office: Chickasha Cotton Oil Co PO Box 959 Casa Grande AZ 85222

CURTIS, ROBERT HARLAND, mining and refining executive, consultant; b. Columbus, Ohio, Jan. 1, 1930; s. Harland Guy and Beatrice Mae (Waltermire) C.; m. Lucy Jovick, Jan. 1, 1953 (div. June 1960); m. Yolanda Ramos, Dec. 19, 1963. Comml. banking degree, Am. Inst. Banking, 1958; Metallurgy degree (hon.), Fresno State Coll., 1974. Asst. cashier and asst. sec. Bank Am. NTSA, San Francisco, 1949-60; pres. and mgr. Kaiser Aluminum Acceptance Corp., Oakland, Calif., 1960-65; v.p. Atlas Credit Corp., Oakland and Pitts., 1965-66; sales mgr. Hallman Chevrolet, Reno, Nev., 1966-70; gen. mgr. Fletcher Jones Chevrolet-Mazda, Las Vegas, Nev., 1977-87; pres. U.S. Platinum, Inc., Reno, 1970-77, Internat. Precious Metals, Las Vegas, 1987—; pres. and chmn. C&B Salvage and Investment Corp. DBA Curtis Nev. Mines, Las Vegas, 1977—. Author: Off Premisis Banking, 1959; co-editor 23 part series Exposé of Philippine Pres. Ferdinand Marcos for Philippine News, 1975-76; contbr. articles to profl. jours. Chmn. and co-founder Comstock Sertoma, Reno, 1968-72. Sgt. airborne inf. U.S. Army, 1947-49. Recipient annual sci. award Calif. Tchr. Assn., Fresno, Calif., 1974. Mem. Nat. Vehicle Lease Assn. (chmn. Las Vegas br. 1983-85), VFW. Republican. Methodist. Home: 5340 W Edna Ave Las Vegas NV 89102

CURTISS, ELDEN F., bishop; b. Baker, Oreg., June 16, 1932; s. Elden F. and Mary (Neiger) C. B.A., St. Edward Sem., Seattle, M.Div., 1958; M.A. in Ednl. Adminstrn, U. Portland, 1965; postgrad., Fordham U., U. Notre Dame. Ordained priest Roman Catholic Ch., 1958; campus chaplain 1959-64, 65-68; supt. schs. Diocese of Baker (Oreg.), 1962-70; pastor 1968-70; pres./rector Mt. Angel Sem., Benedict, Oreg., 1972-76; bishop of Helena (Mont.), 1976—; mem. priests senate Archdiocese of Portland, 1974-76; mem. ecumenical ministries State of Oreg., 1972; mem. pastoral services com. Oreg. State Hosp., Salem, 1975-76; Mem. adminstrv. bd. Nat. Conf. Cath. Bishops, 1976-80, mem. pro-life com., from 1977; bd. dirs. Cath. Mut. Relief Soc., from 1977, Mont. Cath. Conf., from 1976; mem. N.W. Assn. Bishops and Major Religious Superiors, 1976—, Mont. Assn. Chs., 1976—. Mem. Nat. Cath. Ednl. Assn. (Outstanding Educator 1973). Office: 515 N Ewing PO Box 1729 Helena MT 59624 *

CURZON, DANIEL (DANIEL R. BROWN), writer, teacher; b. Litchfield, Ill., ; s. Russell R. and Ida (Billingsley) B.; children: Zachary. B of Philosophy, U. Det., 1960; MA, Kent State U., Ohio, 1961; PhD, Wayne State U., Det., 1969. Instr. U. Detroit, 1961-64, Wayne State U., Detroit, 1964-69; lectr. U. Md., Tokyo, 1972-74, Calif. State U. -Fresno, 1974-76; instr. City Coll. San Francisco, 1980—. Author: Curzon in Love 1988, The World Can Break Your Heart 1984;. Home: 416 Dorado Terr San Francisco CA 94112 Office: City Coll San Francisco Box 196 50 Phelan San Francisco CA 94112

CUSHMAN, DEBORAH ANNE, medical record administrator; b. Reno, Sept. 5, 1952; d. James D. and Mary Jeanne (Huesgen) Rogers; m. Wendell Owen, June 26, 1976; children: Matthew James, Andrew Owen. Student, U. Nev., 1970-72, U. Md., 1974-75; BS in Med. Record Adminstrn., Colo. Women's Coll., 1980. Registered med. record adminstr. Med. records specialist Aurora (Colo.) Presbyn. Hosp., 1978-81; supr. med. records U. Colo. Health Sci. Ctr., Denver, 1981-82; mgr. med. records Carson-Tahoe Hosp., Carson City, Nev., 1982-84; assoc. dir. med. records Stanford U. Hosp., Palo Alto, Calif., 1984-88, Cushman & Assocs, Med. Info. Specialists (Cons.), Santa Clara, Calif., 1988—. Contbr. articles to profl. jours. Tchr. Confraternity of Christian Doctrine, Sunnyvale, Calif., 1987-88. Served wwith U.S. Army, 1974-76. Mem. Am. Med. Record Assn., Calif. Med. Record Assn. (publs. com. 1987-88, legis. com. 1988—). Cen. Calif. Med. Records Assn. (chmn. pub. rels. com.), Worldwide Marriage Encounter, Stanford Faculty Club. Democrat. Roman Catholic. Home and Office: Cushman & Assocs 2600 Knightsbridge Ln Santa Clara CA 95051

CUSHMAN, MICHAEL LARRY, infosystems executive, consultant; b. San Antonio, Jan. 25, 1947; s. Donald Wayne and Lorenza Olive (Calvert) C.; m. Gloria Jann Jensen, Mar. 14, 1969; children: Todd Mark, Jennifer Lynn, Heather Lori, Holly Lee, Heidi Jann, Rebecca Virginia. BA in English, Weber State Coll., 1972. Pub. relations dir. Ideal Nat. Ins. Co., Salt Lake City, 1973-74; postal clk. U.S. Post Office, Orem, Utah, 1974-76; adminstrv. asst. forest service USDA, Provo, Utah, 1975-76; writer, editor USDA, Sandpoint, Idaho, 1976-78; pub. info. officer USDA, Great Falls, Mont., 1978-83; computer specialist USDA, Gresham, Oreg., 1983-84; data base analyst Bonneville Power Adminstrn., Portland, Oreg., 1984-87; dir. computing and telecommunications U. Portland, 1987—; prin. Cushman Assocs., Gresham, 1979—. Editor column PC World mag., 1987. Served with USAF, 1964-66. Mem. Assn. Computing Machinery, Data Processing Mgmt. Assn. Republican. Mormon. Club: City (Portland). Home: 1710 SE Wendy Ct Gresham OR 97080 Office: U Portland 5000 N Willamette Blvd Portland OR 97203

CUSICK, ROBERT ERIK, advertising agency executive; b. Santa Maria, Calif., Aug. 6, 1964; s. John Clark and Eva Renee (Rosko) C. Student, UCLA, 1982-84, Moorpark Coll., 1986. Draftsman Raypak, Inc., Westlake, Calif., 1984-85; owner, mgr. Vision Quest Graphics, Thousand Oaks, Calif., 1985-86; exec. v.p., ptnr. Cusick & Klender Advt., Thousand Oaks, 1986—; pres. Happy Box, Inc., L.A., 1987—; guest lectr. Thousand Oaks High Sch., 1983—, Calif. Luth. U., Thousand Oaks, 1987—; dir. software devel. Klenco, Inc., Simi Valley, Calif., 1987—. Co-founder Internat. Day of Child, Simi Valley, 1988. Recipient proclamation Mayor City of L.A., 1988, Ventura Bd. Suprs., 1988. Mem. Creative Freelancers Assn. (co-founder, bd. dirs. 1987—), Ventura County Advt. Club (bd. dirs. 1988—, 3 awards 1988), Kiwanis (charter Westlake Village, bd. dirs. 1988—, Kiwanian of Month 1988). Republican. Home: 2191 Rosecrans Ave Simi Valley CA 93065 Office: 2320 Aldrich Circle Thousand Oaks CA 91360

CUTLER, KENNETH ROSS, pension funds investment counsel; b. Tacoma, Mar. 5, 1920; s. Clarence William and Matilda Roxanne (Ross) C.; m. Pat Virginia Reinecke, Aug. 6, 1943; children—Geoffrey William, Craig Lee, Brooke Roxanne. Student U. Chgo., 1941-42, UCLA, 1945. Broker, William R. Staats & Co., 1945-47, Dempsey-Tegeler & Co., Los Angeles, 1950-53; pres. Calif. Fund, Los Angeles, 1953-62; investment counsel, Van Nuys, Calif., 1962-66; broker Dean Witter & Co., Century City, Calif., 1966-72; mgr. spl. accounts dept. Paine Webber, Los Angeles, 1972-77; chmn. Cutler & Co., Inc., Medford, Oreg., 1977—. Bd. dirs. So. Oreg. State Coll. Found. Mem. Phi Delta Theta. Republican. Presbyterian. Clubs: Balboa Bay (Newport Beach); Rogue Valley Country; Commonwealth (San Francisco); University (Medford). Home: 4300 Livingston Rd PO Box 1411 Jacksonville OR 97530 Office: Cutler & Co Inc 503 Airport Rd Medford OR 97504

CUTLER, LORRAINE MASTERS, interior designer, facilities manager; b. Indpls., Oct. 19, 1943; d. James Mark and Dorothy Aileen (DeLawter) Masters; m. Albert B. Cutler III, June 3, 1965 (div.); children: Valina Dawn, Anthony Bret. BFA, Ariz. State U., 1973, BA, 1974; postgrad., U. Phoenix, 1989—. Intern Walsh Bros., Phoenix, 1973, jr. designer, 1973-74, staff designer, 1978-80; dir. interior design Dick & Fritsche Design Group, Phoenix, 1980-84; dir. interior design and space planning HNC Inc., Phoenix, 1984-87; mgr. advanced facilities planning PCS, Inc., Scottsdale, Ariz., 1987—. Participant Interior Designer Efforts for Ariz. Legis., Phoenix, 1986-87; bd. dirs. Southwest Builds, 1985—, chmn. fin. com., 1987-88. Recipient Presdl. Citation Am. Soc. Interior Designers, 1984. Mem. Inst. Bus. Designers (profl., pres. 1985-87, v.p. programs 1983-85, sec. 1981-83, Cert. Appreciation, 1981), Internat. Facilities Mgmt. Assn. (profl., treas.). Home: 2548 N 29th St Phoenix AZ 85008 Office: PCS Inc 9501 E Shea Blvd Scottsdale AZ 85260

CUTLER, MARY LEVIN, music educator; b. Lexington, Ky., Dec. 24, 1933; d. Jack Atticus and Mary Lee (Riddell) Medlock; m. Norman Levin, July 22, 1957 (dec. 1976); m. Gilbert Cutler, Feb. 14, 1982. BA, Calif. State U., L.A., 1955; MusM, U. So. Calif., 1959. Cert. music tchr., Calif. Ind. lectr. ethnomusicology various orgns., L.A., 1975—; preliminary judge Zachary Opera Auditions. Violinist, vocalist, performed at Dallas Summer Musicales, Ciros, Brentwood-Westwood Symphony, Hollywood Bowl Easter Svc., others. Mem. Beverly Hills (Calif.) Goals Com., 1986-87; candidate for Beverly Hills City Coun., 1988; pres. Friends of Music Calif. State U.-L.A.; sec. Am. Youth Symphony, Beverly Hills Theatre Guild (pres.); founder, mem. The Dance Gallery; bd. dirs. Opera Guild So. Calif., Beverly Hills Pops Orch., L.A. Arts Coun., Am.-Israel Cultural Found., L.A. area USO. Recipient Festival 40 award, Calif. State U.-L.A., 1987, Sybil Brand award, Bel Air chpt. Navy League, 1985. Fellow Am. Inst. Fine Arts; mem. LWV, Beverly Hills C. of C., Hillcrest C. of C., Women's Network, Soroptimist Internat., Republican Inner Circle, Sigma Alpha Iota. Republican.

CVAR, DUANE EMIL, marketing professional; b. Cleve., May 11, 1944; s. Emil Frank and Marge Evelyn (Kuehl) C.; m. Roberta Kay Kastler, Oct. 14, 1966 (div. Feb. 1974); children: David, Tamra; m. Phyllis Bernstern, Jan. 24, 1976; children: David, Brian, Scott, Michael, Jason. AA in Mktg., Cuyahoga Community Coll., 1966; BA in Mktg., Cleve. State U., 1969. Sales mktg. rep. Union Paper & Twine Co., Cleve., 1968-77; dist. sales mgr. Modern Maid, Inc., Cin., 1977-79; sales mktg. rep. Butler Paper Co., Denver, 1979-80; dist. sales mgr. Hammermill Papers Group, San Francisco, 1980-84; gen. mgr. Jim Walter Papers, Phoenix, 1984-86; regional sales mgr. Star Forms, Inc., Bellevue, Wash., 1986—; cons. Philip Kendall Indsl. Products, Denver, 1979-80, Hotel St. Claire, San Jose, Calif., 1982. Leader Indian Guides, Cleve., 1976; coach Little League, Cleve., 1976-77; mem. coun. Lyndhurst (Ohio) Luth. Ch., 1966-74; parent advisor debate team Bellevue (Ohio) High Sch., Bellevue, 1987-88. Staff sgt. U.S. Army, 1965-72. Named Mead Dynamo Winner, Mead Corp., 1972-76, most knowledgeable salesman, 1976, Beckett Paper Co., 1976, Western Div. Reg. Sales Mgr. of Yr. Beckett Paper Co., 1987. Mem. Nat. Bus. Forms Assn., Western Bus. Systems Assn., Coll. Bookstore Assn., Western Forms Caravan, Nat. Office Products Assn. Republican. Lutheran. Home: 15512 Country Club Dr Mill Creek WA 98012 Office: Star Forms Inc 1400 112th Ave SE 100 Bellevue WA 98004

CVENGROS, WILLIAM D., insurance company executive; b. Watertown, Wis., Nov. 24, 1948; m. Joan Cvengros; children: Elizabeth Anne, Christopher William, Laurie Catherine. BA in Econs., Notre Dame U., 1970; MBA in Fin. and Acctg., Northwestern U., 1972. Chartered fin. analyst. Successively investment analyst, asst. v.p., 2d v.p. fixed income securities, v.p. account mgmt., sr. v.p. pacific mut. investments Pacific Mut. Life Ins. Co., Newport Beach, Calif., 1972-86, exec. v.p. investment ops., 1986—, also bd. dirs.; chmn. bd. Pacific Fin. Asset Mgmt. Corp., Pacific Investment Mgmt. Co., PMEealty Advisors, Pacific Mut. Realty Fin., Pacific Equities Network; bd. dirs. Pacific Fin. Life Ins. Co. Chmn. investment com. United Way of Orange County North/South. Office: Pacific Mut Life Ins Co 700 Newport Ctr Dr Newport Beach CA 92663

CYR, EUGENE L., food service company executive; b. Beverly, Mass., Jan. 6, 1950; s. Eugene L. and Nancy (Femino) C.; m. Glenna S. Witham, June 25, 1967; children: Danielle J., Brenda M. Grad., Essex-Aggie Culinary, Mass., 1968; student, Northeastern U., Boston, 1971. With King's Grant, Danvers, Mass., 1965-69, Profit Foods Co., Mass. and Vt., 1969-70; food service mgr. Servomation Corp., Boston, 1970-75, with promotions dept., 1975-78; area mgr. Servomation Corp., Fullerton, Calif., 1978-83; v.p. West Coast Food Services, Los Angeles, 1983-85; pres. Total Food Mgmt., Inc., Anaheim, Calif., 1985—. Editor newspaper 4 Circles West, 1979-83. Bd. dirs. Titan Athletic Found., Fullerton, Calif., 1983-85; sponsor Titan Athletic Found., 1985-88; vol. sponsor two softball teams, Ontario, Calif., 1987-88. Recipient Key Person award United Way, Boston, 1976-78. Mem. Orange County Food Services Execs. Assn., Nat. Restaurants Assn., Orange County C. of C., Ontario C. of C. Republican. Roman Catholic. Clubs: El Prado Golf, Gold's Gym. Office: Total Food Mgmt Inc 1275 N Manassero St Anaheim CA 92807

CZARNECKI, GERALD MILTON, banker; b. Phila., Mar. 22, 1940; s. Casimir M. and Rose-Mary (Grajek) C.; m. Lois Rae DiJoseph, July 9, 1965; 1 dau., Robin Alexandra. B.S., Temple U., Phila., 1965; M.A., Mich. State U., 1967. C.P.A., Ill., Tex. With Continental Bank, Chgo., 1968-79, v.p., operating gen. mgr. trust ops. and gen. mgr. corp. services, 1971-78; pres. Fla. Computing Services, 1979; exec. v.p. Houston Nat. Bank, 1979-82; sr. v.p. fin. Republic Bank Corp., 1982-83, exec. v.p., 1983-84; pres., chief exec. officer Altus Bank, 1984-87; chmn., chief exec. officer Honfed Bank, Honolulu, 1987—; mem. faculty DePaul U., Chgo., 1975-78; adj. prof. econs. Houston Bapt. U., 1980-82; mem. faculty Bank Adminstrn. Inst., 1978-85, Grad. Sch. Banking, U. Wis., 1979-86; chmn. bd. dirs. Inroads, Inc./Chgo., 1977-79, Inroads, Inc./Houston, 1981 vis. prof. Jones Sch. Bus., Rice U., 1980; adj. prof. policy and strategy So. Methodist U., 1983-84; mem. adv. com. Banking Center, Tex. So. U., 1980-82; chmn. securities processing subcom. Am. Nat. Standards Inst., 1974-79, mem. Tuskegee Inst. State Adv. Council, 1984-87; mem . exec. com., bd. dirs. Nat. Council Savs. Instns., 1984—; pres. thrift adv. council Fed. Res. Bd. Contbr. articles to profl. publs. Bd. dirs. Hawaii Theatre Ctr., 1988—, Honolulu Econ. Devel. Corp., 1988—, Nature Conservancy Hawaii, 1988—, U. Hawaii Pres.' Coun., 1988—, Aloha United Way, 1988—. Mem. AICPA, Am. Bankers Assn. (chmn. securities processing com. 1974-77, trust ops. com. 1978, mem. exec. com. ops. and automation div. 1980-83, research com.), Am. Econ. Assn., Nat. Council Savs. Instns. (bd. dirs.), Tex. Soc. CPA's, Fin. Execs. Inst., Consumer Bankers Assn. (bd. dirs. 1986—), N. Am. Soc. Corp. Planners (bd. dirs. Dallas Chpt. 1982-83), Assn. for Corp. Growth, Hawaii C. of C. (bd. dirs. 1988—), Omicron Delta Epsilon, Alpha Delta Phi. Office: Honfed Bank 188 Merchant St Honolulu HI 96813

CZARTOLOMNY, PIOTR ANTONI, librarian; b. Kutno, Poland, June 10, 1946; came to U.S., 1984; s. Piotr Mikolai and Barbara Danuta (Galkowska) C.; m. Janina Stanislawa Janas, Feb. 16, 1971; children: Piotr Olaf, Sara Zofia. M Polish Philosophy, Poznan (Poland) U., 1970. Asst. prof. Inst. Polish Lit. Poznan U., 1970-76; mng. editor Solidarity Regional Pub. House, Poznan, 1980-81; archivist Boise (Idaho) State U., 1984-85; clk. Idaho Dept. Transp., Boise, 1985-86; lit. coord. Haynes Trane Svcs., Denver, 1987—; manuscript reader various pub. houses, Poland, 1970-84; lit. cons. City Theatre,Bielsko Biala, Poland, 1977. Lit. and art critic, Poland, 1970-80; contbr. articles to various publs. Mem. regional com. Solidarity, Poland, 1980-81. Mem. Union Solidarity Journalists (exec. pres. 1981). Roman Catholic. Home: 121590 W Virginia Ave Lakewood CO 80228 Office: Haynes Trane Svcs 5654 Greenwood Plaza Blvd Englewood CO 80111

DACKAWICH, S. JOHN, sociology educator, academic administrator; b. Loch Gelley, W.Va., Jan. 31, 1926; s. Samuel and Estelle (Jablonski) D.; m. Shirley Jean McVay, May 20, 1950; children—Robert John, Nancy Joan. B.A., U. Md., 1955; Ph.D., U. Colo., 1958. Instr. U. Colo., 1955-57; instr. Colo. State U., 1957-59; prof., chmn. sociology Calif. State U. at Long Beach, 1959-70; prof. sociology Calif. State U., Fresno, 1970—; chmn. dept. Calif. State U., 1970-75; pvt. practice survey research, 1962—. Contbr. articles and rsch. papers to profl. publs. Mem. Calif. Democratic Central Com., 1960-62; co-dir. Long Beach Central Area Study, 1962-64, Citizen Participation Study, Fresno. Served with USMCR, 1943-46; Served with AUS, 1950-53. Mem. Am., Pacific sociol. assns. Home: 1459 W Sample Ave Fresno CA 93705

DACQUISTO, JOHN FRED, electrical engineer; b. Racine, Wis., Feb. 10, 1943; s. Fred John and Rose Mary (Graceffa) D.; m. Judith Anne Walsh, Sept. 11, 1965; children: Kelli Rose, Nicole Elisabeth, John Thomas, Michael Joseph, Kathleen Anne. BSEE, Marquette U., 1965; MS in Engring., Wash. State U., 1987. Registered profl. engr., Wis. Elec. engr. Belle City Malleable Iron Co., Racine, 1965-67; project engr. Kaiser Aluminum & Chem. Co., Ravenswood, W.Va., 1967-70; design engr. Kaiser Aluminum & Chem. Co., Ravenswood, 1970-71; elec. engr. Kaiser Aluminum & Chem. Co., Portsmouth, R.I., 1971-73; quality mgr. Kaiser Aluminum & Chem. Co., Portsmouth, 1973-76; staff engr. Kaiser Aluminum & Chem. Co., Spokane, Wash., 1976-80; engring. supr. Kaiser Aluminum & Chem. Co., Spokane, 1980—; mem. Underground Utilities Commn., Barrington, R.I., 1975-76.

Contbr. articles to profl. jours. Mem. St. John Vianney Sch. Bd., Spokane, 1981-84, pres., 1982-83; mem. com. Wash. State U., Spokane, 1985—; coor. silent auction Gonzaga Preparatory Sch., Spokane, 1986. Mem. Wis. Soc. Profl. Engrs., Spokane C. of C. (mem., vice chmn. energy-environ. com.), Toastmasters (pres. local chpt. 1969-70). Roman Catholic. Home: E 10015 Holman Rd Spokane WA 99206 Office: Kaiser Aluminum & Chem Co E 15000 Euclid Ave Spokane WA 99215

DADISMAN, LYNN ELLEN, marketing executive; b. Los Angeles, Mar. 1, 1946; d. Orlan Sidney and Erna Lou (Harris) Friedman; m. Kent Dadisman, May 1973 (div. 1974). Student UCLA, 1963-65, 71-72, Willis Bus. Coll., 1965-66, Fin. Schs. Am., 1982, Viewpoints Inst., 1970-71. Office mgr. Harleigh Sandler Co., Los Angeles, 1965-67; customer svc. Investors Diversified Svcs., West Los Angeles, Calif., 1968-76; exec. sec. McCulloch Oil Corp., West Los Angeles, 1976; mgr. publs. Security 1st Group, Century City, Calif., 1976-80; office mgr. Morehead & Co., Century City, 1980-81; dir. mktg., mgr. customer svc. Ins. Mktg. Services, Santa Monica, Calif., 1981-82; v.p. Decatur Petroleum Corp., Santa Monica, 1982-83; asst. v.p., broker svcs., dir. Angeles Corp., L.A., 1984-87; asst. to pres. Pacific Ventures, Santa Monica, 1988—. Mem. Nat. Assn. Securities Dealers, Internat. Assn. Fin. Planning, NAFE, Migi Car Am. Club (sec., newsletter editor). Fin. and ins. writer; contbr. poetry to UCLA Literary Mag., 1964. Home: 3442 Centinela Ave Apt 15 Los Angeles CA 90066

DAGGETT, CHARLES EDWARD, construction company executive; b. Phoenix, Dec. 3, 1940; s. Edward and Alice (Sult) D.; m. Patricia Graham, Nov. 28, 1965; children: Anne-Marie, Gregory, Patricia. BS, Ariz. State U., 1965. Mgr. Ray Lumber Co., Glendale, Ariz., 1966-69; pres. Dagco, Inc., Glendale, 1969-75, Met. Constrn., Phoenix, 1975-82; v.p. Opus Corp., Phoenix, 1982-86; pres. Baymoor Constrn., Phoenix, 1986—. Bd. dirs. NE YMCA, Phoenix, 1980; panelist City of Phoenix Bd. Adjustment, 1978-80. Mem. Nat. Assn. Corp. Real Estate (pres. 1987-89), Nat. Assn. Office and Indsl. Pks. (pres. 1986-87), The Regal Group (pres. 1987-88), Assn. Corp. Growth (chmn. 1988), Am. Arbitration Assn. (arbitrator 1976—, mediator 1986—), Rotary (chmn. 1988-89), Pres. Club (pres. 1987-88). Republican. Roman Catholic. Home: 515 W Harmont Phoenix AZ 85021 Office: Baymoor Constrn Corp 2910 E Camelback #201 Phoenix AZ 85016

DAGGETT, ROBERT SHERMAN, lawyer; b. La Crosse, Wis., Sept. 16, 1930; s. Willard Manning and Vida Naomi (Sherman) D.; m. Lee Sullivan Burton, Sept. 16, 1961; children: Ann Sherman, John Sullivan; m. Helen Ackerman, July 20, 1976. A.B. with honors in Polit. Sci. and Journalism, U. Calif.-Berkeley, 1952, J.D., 1955. Bar: Calif. 1955, U.S. Supreme Ct. 1967. Assoc. firm Brobeck, Phleger & Harrison, San Francisco, 1958-66, ptnr., 1966—; counsel Calif. Senate Reapportionment Com., 1972-73; adj. prof. evidence and advocacy Hastings Coll. Law, 1982—; instr. No. Dist. Fed. Practice Program, 1982—, mem. teaching com., 1983—; demonstrator-instr. Nat. Inst. for Trial Advocacy, 1981—, Hastings Ctr. for Trial and Appellate Advocacy, 1981-88, mem. adv. bd., 1983-88; vol. pro tem small claims judge San Francisco Mcpl. Ct., 1981-88; arbitrator San Francisco Superior Ct., and pvt. comml. arbitration, 1984—; instr. No. Dist. Fed. Practice Program, 1982—, mem. teaching com., 1983—. Bd. editors: Calif. Law Rev., 1953-55; contbr. articles to profl. jours. Rep. Pacific Assn. AAU, 1973; bd. dirs. San Francisco Legal Aid Soc.; bd. visitors Coll. V U. Calif.-Santa Cruz. Served to 1st lt. JAGC U.S. Army, 1958-62. Walter Perry Johnson scholar, 1953. Mem. ABA, State Bar Calif. (chmn. local adminstrv. com. 1964-65), San Francisco Bar Assn. (past dir.), Am. Judicature Soc., Am. Law Inst., Order of Golden Bear, Bohemian Club, Commonwealth Club, Commercial Club (bd. dirs. 1989—), Phi Delta Phi, Theta Xi. Republican. Office: Brobeck Phleger & Harrison Spear St Tower 1 Market Pla San Francisco CA 94105

DAGHER, MOHAMAD ALI, engineer; b. Beirut, Lebanon, Dec. 15, 1957; came to U.S. 1981; s. Hussein Ali and Amine Ahmad (Kobiesy) D.; m. MaryLouise Class, May 31, 1983; 1 child, Laila Nicole. BSME, Calif. State U., 1984, MSME, 1987. Design engr., project mgr. W.G. Ingalls Co. Ltd., Montebello, Calif., 1985-88; research asst. Nuclear Space Power Inst., Long Beach, Calif., 1986-88; design engr. Rockwell Internat., Lakewood, Calif., 1988—; cons. W. G. Ingalls Co., Ltd., Montebello, Calif., 1988—. Mem. ASME. Democrat. Islamic. Home: 601 E 8th St #131 Azusa CA 91702

DAHL, DANIEL JAMES, management consultant; b. San Francisco, Oct. 20, 1944; s. Wesley Peter and Jean Claire (Dever) D. AB in Polit. Sci., U. San Francisco, 1967; 1977. cert. in mgmt. devel. and conflict mgmt. U. Calif., San Francisco, 1977. Staff program coordinator U. Calif., San Francisco, 1976-78; v.p., mgr. Bank Am. NT&SA, San Francisco, 1978-85; prin. Sykes Dahl Cons. Group, Mill Valley, Calif., 1985-86; v.p., cons. Drake Beam Morin, Inc., San Francisco, 1986-87; pres. Dolphin Circle, Mill Valley, 1987--; lectr. San Francisco State U., 1987--, New Coll. Calif., San Francisco, 1987--; monthly pub. affairs guest Sta. KFRC, San Francisco, 1987--; bus. commentator In Focus, Sta. KTSF-TV, San Francisco, 1987--. Author: Charting Your Goals, 1988. Mem. No. Calif. Human Resources Council, City Club San Francisco (founding), Pi Sigma Alpha (life).

DAHL, GARDAR GODFREY, JR., geologist, coal company executive; b. Hood River, Oreg., May 27, 1946; s. Gardar Godfrey Sr. and Margaret Jean (North) D.; m. Eva Lorraine Skolmen, Nov. 10, 1973. BS in Geol. Engring., Mont. Coll. Mineral Sci. and Tech., 1969, MS in Geol. Engring., 1971. Registered profl. geologist. Asst. geologist Burlington No., St. Paul, 1971-72; mining geologist Burlington No., Seattle, Wash. and Billings, Mont., 1972-75; mgr. coal exploration and devel. Burlington No., Billings, 1975-79; dir. resource devel. Peabody Coal Co., Flagstaff, Ariz., 1979-81; chief geologist Cyprus Coal Co., Englewood, Colo., 1981-85, mgr. geology, 1985-88; mgr. tech. services Cyprus Shoshone Coal Co., Hanna, Wyo., 1988—. Mem. AIME, Internat. Assn. Math. Geology, AAAS, Rocky Mountain Coal Inst., Am. Assn. Profl. Geologists. Lutheran. Club: Denver Coal. Home: 604 W Elm St PO Box 1453 Saratoga WY 82331 Office: Cyprus Shoshone Coal Corp PO Box 830 Hanna WY 82323

DAHL, LOREN SILVESTER, judge; b. East Fairview, N.D., Mar. 1, 1921; s. William T. and Maude (Silvester) D.; m. Luana Siler, Apr. 5, 1942 (dec.); children: Candy Dahl, Walter Ray.; m. Mary Anne Bristow, Jan. 20, 1979. AA, Coll. of Pacific, 1940; LLB, JD, U. Calif., San Francisco, 1949. Bar: Calif., 1950, U.S. Supreme Ct., 1957; lic. instrument pilot and aerial navigator. Pvt. practice Sacramento, 1950; sr. ptnr. Dahl, Hefner, Stark & Marois, Sacramento, 1950-80; judge U.S. Bankruptcy Ct. (ea. dist.) Calif., Sacramento, 1980, 86—. Pres. Golden Empire Council Boy Scouts Am., Sacramento, 1955-56, chmn. bd. trustees, 1956, exec. com. region 12, 1958, regional chmn. 1968-70, nat. exec. bd. 1968-70; Sacramento County Juvenile Justice Commn.; bd. dirs. Salvation Army, Sacramento, 1954-57; Sacramento Symphony Assn., 1958-59, Sacramento Safety Council. Served with USAAF, 1942-46. Recipient Disting. Service award Jaycees, 1957, Silver Beaver award, Boy Scouts Am., 1957, Silver Antelope award, Boy Scouts Am., 1963, Disting. Eagle Scout award, Boy Scouts Am. Mem. Univ. of Pacific Alumni Assn. (pres. 1974-78, bd. regents 1980—, Disting. Alumnus award 1963), ABA, Calif. Bar Assn. (lectr. bankruptcy, continuing edn.), Am. Judicature Soc., Phi Delta Phi. Club: Del Paso Country. Lodge: Masons, Shriners, Lions (dir. Sacramento club 1952-53). Home: 842 Lake Oak Ct Sacramento CA 95864 Office: US Bankruptcy Ct 650 Capitol Mall 8308 US Courthouse Sacramento CA 95814

DAHLE, DANIEL JOHN, electronics company executive; b. San Bernardino, Calif., Oct. 9, 1958; s. Trygve F. and Thelma V .(Finnesgard) D.; m. Ellen Jean Siebrecht, Feb. 20, 1988; children: Drew, Daniel. BSME, U. Calif., 1980, BSMSE, 1980. Registered profl. engr., Ind. Mfg. engr. consumer products div. AT&T Corp., Indpls., 1980-84, account rep. electronic components div., 1984-85; account rep. microelectronics div. AT&T Corp., North Andover, Mass., 1985-86; nat. account mgr. microelectronics div. AT&T Corp., Sunnyvale, Calif., 1986—; mktg. cons. Spectral Innovations Inc., Sunnyvale, 1987-88. Lutheran. Home: 631 W Remington Dr Sunnyvale CA 94087

DAHLE, JOHN LEE, consulting engineer, data systems executive; b. Titusville, Pa., Dec. 30, 1949; s. Wayne John and June Rose (Penick) D.; m. Helyn Margeret Horne, Aug. 27, 1970; children: Jeneane, David. BS in Aerospace Engring., U. Pitts., 1971, postgrad in Mech. Engring., 1971-75. Mech. engr. U.S. Bur. of Mines, Pitts., 1971-75, supr. mech. engr., 1975-78; dir. Mining Equipment Safety Lab., Triadelphia, W.Va., 1978-80; sr. program mgr. Woodward Assocs., Inc., San Diego, 1980-82, v.p., 1982-86; pres. JDA Sci. Enterprises, San Diego, 1986—; cons. Can. Standards Org., Montreal, Queb., 1981-86. Contbr. numerous articles to profl. jours.; patentee in field. Recipient Outstanding Achievement award U.S. Dept. Interiors, 1972, 1974, U.S. Dept. Labor, 1976. Mem. Soc. Automotive Engrs., Human Factors Soc., Nat. Forensic Ctr. Club: Southwestern Yacht. Home and Office: JDA Sci Enterprises 18 Marie St Sausalito CA 94965

DAHY, EDWARD JOHN, education specialist; b. L.A., June 21, 1930; s. Edward John Jr. and June Claudia (Thompson) D.; m. Nancy Ann Paul, Sept. 24, 1952; children: Edward John, James Patrick, Mary Elizabeth, Paul Christopher. AB, Gonzaga U., 1952; MA, Mont. State U., Missoula, 1957; EdD, Mont. State U., Bozeman, 1977. Tchr., Absarokee, Belt, Mont., 1955-57; With USMC, 1952-54, 57-71; advanced through grades to lt. col., 1970; supr. student tchrs. Coll. Gt. Falls, Mont., 1971-72; prin., Centerville, Mont., 1973-77; Navy edn. specialist State of Mont., Butte, 1977—. Decorated Bronze Star with V, others; recipient Edn. Specialist of Yr. award, 1982, 83, 88 cert. of commendation, 1983-88. Mem. NEA, Am. Assn. for Counseling and Devel., Am. Vocat. Assn., Mil. Educators and Counselors Assn., Marine Corps Assn., Phi Delta Kappa. Roman Catholic. Office: NRPS Butte Finlen Complex 100 E Broadway Butte MT 59701

DAIGLE, PAUL NELSON, lawyer; b. Valparaiso, Ind., May 5, 1938; s. Paul Joseph and Norma (MacLellan) D.; m. Judith Ann Rogers, June 24, 1961 (div. June 1981); children: Paul B., Deborah J., James M., Robert C.; m. Gretchen Nichols, Feb. 16, 1985. Student, Auburn U., 1956-57; BA, Stanford U., 1961; JD, U. Calif., San Francisco, 1968. Bar: Oreg. 1968, Wash. 1982, U.S. Supreme Ct. 1971. Assoc. Schwabe Williamson & Wyatt, Portland, Oreg., 1968-75, ptnr., 1975-82; ptnr. Schwabe Williamson & Wyatt, Seattle, 1982-89, sr. ptnr., 1989—. Editor Hastings Law Rev., 1967; contbr. articles to legal jours. 1st lt. USMC, 1961-65. Mem. ABA (chmn. marine ins. law com. 1979), Maritime Law Assn. U.S. (proctor in admiralty, exec. com. 1981-84), Thurston Soc., Order of Coif, Rainier Club, Seattle Yacht Club, Wash. Athletic Club, University Club, Multnomah Club, Whitehall Club., Propellor Club (pres. Columbia River cpt. 1979-80). Republican. Episcopalian. Office: Schwabe Williamson & Wyatt 1415 5th Ave Ste 900 Seattle WA 98171

DAIGLE, RONALD ELVIN, health science facility administrator, researcher; b. Lake Charles, La., Oct. 14, 1944; s. Elvin and Dorothy Helen (Mayo) D.; m. Ann Jean Lassman, Dec. 30, 1966; children: Janah Wryn, Jon Kim. BA in Physics, U. Calif., Santa Barbara, 1967; MSEE, Colo. State U., 1971, PhD in Physiology and Biophysics, 1974. Rsch. assoc. dept. physiology and biophysics Colo. State U., Ft. Collins, 1974; postdoctoral fellow cardiovascular tng. program Ctr. for Bioengring., U. Wash., Seattle, 1974-75; rsch. assoc. Ctr. for Bioengring., U. Wash., 1975-76; sr. engr. cen. rsch. Varian Assocs., Palo Alto, Calif., 1976-81; dir. advanced devel. Advanced Tech. Labs., Bothell, Wash., 1981-86, sr. scientist, 1986-88, chief sr. tech. staff, 1988—, lectr. Doppler physics, 1987—, tech. fellow in perpetuity, 1988—; cons. in cardiovascular instrumentation NASA, Houston, 1987—; mem. microsensor rev. bd. Wash. Tech. Ctr., Seattle, 1987—. Mem. editorial bd. Jour. Cardiovascular Ultrasonography, 1983—; contbr. articles to profl. jours., chpts. to books; patentee in field. Recipient IR-100 award Indsl. Rsch. mag., 1978; Nat. Inst. Heart and Lung grantee, 1976. Mem. Am. Inst. Ultrasound in Medicine, Amiga Users Group (pres. 1988—). Democrat. Home: 22126 NE 62d Pl Redmond WA 98053 Office: Advanced Tech Labs PO Box 3003 Bothell WA 98041-3003

DAIGNAULT, DAVID WILLIAM, insurance company executive; b. Spencerport, N.Y., Oct. 25, 1939; s. Louis Joseph and Marian Agnes (VanGeison) D.; m. Lynn Grace Crossan, Nov. 11, 1961; children: Chari Lynn, Melanie Danielle, Jacqulyn, Leigha Rene. BA, Alfred U., 1961; MS in System Mgmt., U. So. Calif., 1976. Commd. 2d lt. U.S. Army, 1961, advanced through grades to lt. col., 1978, ret., 1983; mng. dir. ERA Magnum Properties, Aiea, Hawaii, 1983-84; ops. mgr. T.I. of Hawaii Inc., Honolulu, 1984-86, exec. v.p., 1986—; pres. Communicative Pubs., Inc., 1986—; bd. dirs. ERA Beacan, Pearl City, Hawaii, 1985—; market mgmt. coll. instr. Mem. Kaneohe (Hawaii) Neighborhood Bd., 1985-87, chmn. 1986-87; mem. Small Bus. Hawaii Polit. Action Com., Honolulu, 1985-86; pres. bd. dirs. Hawaii Philharm., Honolulu, 1985-86. Decorated Bronze Star, Legion of Merit. Mem. Yacht Club Terrace Owner's Assn. (pres. 1984-87), Caledonian Soc. (vice chieftain 1988-89), Hawaiian Scottish Assn. (vice chieftain 1988-89, chmn. Scottish Heritage Week, Hawaii, 1989). Republican. Lodge: Rotary. Office: TI of Hawaii Inc 1001 Bishop Ste 700 Honolulu HI 96813

DAILEY, FRED WILLIAM, hotel executive; b. Aurora, Ill., Feb. 3, 1908; s. Louis A. and Frances (McCoy) D.; m. Elizabeth Murphy, Apr. 22, 1946; children—Michael K., Pam Sue Hinman. Builder, operator tourist resorts, 1933-42; builder, So. Calif., 1946-52; pres. Mokuleia Assos., Mokuleia Polo Farms, Inc., Waikiki Corp., A.D. Corp. Adv. bd. Hawaii, Army; past mem. Honolulu Bd. Water Supply. Served as maj. AUS, World War II. Decorated Purple Heart. Mem. U.S. Air Force Assn., C. of C., Am. Hotel Assn. (past dir.), Hawaii Hotel Assn. (past pres.), Hawaii Horse Show Assn. (past pres.), Hawaii Polo and Racing Assn. (pres.), U.S. Polo Assn. (past gov.). Clubs: Los Angeles Athletic; Hawaii Polo (Honolulu); Santa Barbara Polo; Big Bend Ranch (pres.) (Korbel). Author: Blood, Sweat and Jeers; One Man's Meat, Polo Is A Four Letter Word. Address: 2003 Kalia Rd Honolulu HI 96815 Address: Mokuleia Polo Farm Inc Gahu HI 96815

DAILEY, JACOB EDWARD, school superintendent; b. Danville, Pa., July 23, 1927; s. Jacob Lawrence and Minnie Mildred (Young) D.; m. Rose Katharine McKean, Aug. 16, 1947; children—Suzanne Marie, Jacob Edward. B.S., Bloomsburg State Coll., 1952; M.Ed., Temple U., 1956, Ed.D., 1968. Tchr. Central Bucks High Sch., Doylestown, Pa., 1952-53; prin., tchr. Doylestown Twp. Schs., 1953-56; prin., supr. Exeter Twp. Schs., Reading, Pa., 1956-61; supt. schs. Pottsgrove Schs., Pa., 1961-72, Bristol Twp., Levittown, Pa., 1972-76, No. Syracuse, N.Y., 1976-79, Natrona County Sch. Dist., Casper, Wyo., 1979—. Served with USNR, 1945-46. Pres. Daniel Boone Nat. Found., 1970-74, mem. Phila. Suburban Study Council, 1969. Mem. Am. Assn. Sch. Adminstrs., Phi Delta Kappa. Home: 2460 Allyson Pl Casper WY 82604 Office: Natrona County Sch Dist Office of Sch Supt 970 N Glenn Rd Casper WY 82601 *

DAKES-PLACENCIA, PATTY, realtor; b. Cleve., July 5, 1944; d. Edward William and Eva (Rizun) H.; m. John Dakes, Oct. 16, 1969 (div. Feb. 1984); children: Joanna Patrice, Dianna Christina; m. Robert Placencia, July 26, 1986. Student, Ariz. State Coll., U. Ariz. Resident mgr. Coldwell Banker Residential Svcs., Ventura, Calif., 1976-81, Calif. Oaks Realtors, Ventura, Calif., 1981-84; ptnr., mgr. Real Estate Unlimited/MacElhenny Levy Co., Port Hueneme, Calif., 1984-88; realtor, owner Dakes & Assocs., Ventura, Calif., 1988-89; with Wilkins & Assocs., Westlake Village, Calif., 1989—; assoc. Oceanfront Realty Internat., Kauai, Hawaii. Mem. Women's Council Realtors (pres. Oxnard, Calif. Chpt. 1983), Oxnard Harbor Bd. Realtors (bd. dirs., multiple listing svcs. com.), Ventura Bd. of Realtors (bd. dirs., multiple listing svcs. com., consumer protection com.), Oxnard C. of C., Greater Ventura C. of C. Republican. Presbyterian. Home: PO Box 1307 Kalaheo, Kauai HI 96741 Office: Wilkins & Assocs 2239 Townsgate Rd Ste 109 Westlake Village CA 91361 also: Oceanfront Realty Internat PO Box 3570 Kauai HI 96722

DALE, DENVER THOMAS, III, retired marine officer, teacher; b. Santa Barbara, Calif., July 30, 1931; s. Denver Thomas Jr. and Ethel Helen (Squire) D.; m. Elizabeth Ann Donleavy, Nov. 17, 1956 (div. Oct. 1978); children: Denver Thomas IV, Matthew J., Jeffrey N.; m. Peggy Frances Altice, Nov. 19, 1982. Student Va. Mil. Inst., 1948-52; BA, San Francisco State U., 1959; MS, Cen. Conn. State U., 1969. Cert. secondary educator, Calif. Enlisted USMC, 1952, advanced through grades to lt. col., 1975; comdg. officer Co. K., 3d Bn., 4th Marine Regt., Kaneohe Bay, Hawaii, 1961-64; manpower mgmt. officer 1st Marine Aircraft Wing, Iwakuni, Japan and Danang, Vietnam, 1964-65; exec. officer, comdg. officer 3d Bn., 5th Marine Regt., An Hoa, Vietnam, 1969-70; head officer force mgmt. unit Hdqrs. U.S. Marine Corps, Washington, 1970-73; exec. officer, comdg. officer, assoc. prof. naval sci. NROTC Unit, Rice U., Houston, 1973-75; ret., 1975; project mgr. Telemedia, Inc., Teheran, 1978; sr. marine instr. Marine Corps jr. ROTC unit, Portage High Sch., Ind., 1979-81, North High Sch., Bakersfield, Calif., 1981—, chmn. dept. mil. sci., 1981—, high sch. varsity boys tennis coach, 1983-86; prin. speaker at numerous civic, frat., vets., high sch. and coll. groups, 1965—. Asst. scoutmaster Boy Scouts Am., 1970-73. Decorated Bronze Star with V device, Comdt. U.S. Marines commendation; Vietnamese Cross of Galantry. Mem. Marine Corps Assn., VFW, Am. Legion, Republican. Lodge: Masons. Home: 5604 Logan St Bakersfield CA 93308 Office: USMC JROTC Unit North High Sch 300 Galaxy Ave Bakersfield CA 93308

DALE, FRANCIS LYKINS, foundation executive, former performing arts officer, former sports executive; b. Urbana, Ill., July 13, 1921; s. Charles Sherman and Sarah (Lykins) D.; m. Kathleen Hamlin Watkins, Mar. 20, 1947; children: Mitchell Watkins, Myron Lykins, Kathleen Hamlin, Holly Moore. A.B., Duke U., 1943; LL.B., U. Va., 1948; LL.D. (hon.), Eastern Ky. U., U. Cin., Ohio Wesleyan U., Salmon P. Chase Coll. of Law, Bloomfield Coll., Pepperdine Sch. of Bus. Bar: Ohio 1948. Assoc. Frost & Jacobs, Cin., 1948-53, ptnr., 1953-65; asst. sec. Cin. Enquirer, Inc., 1952-65, pres., pub., 1965-73; pres. The Cin. Reds, Inc., 1967-73, vice-chmn., 1973-80; pub. L.A. Herald Examiner, 1977-85; commr. Major Indoor Soccer League, 1985-86; pres. The Music Ctr. of L.A. County, 1986-88, U.S. Oil & Mining Co., Pasadena, Calif., 1988—, Maureen and Mike Mansfield Found., 1988—; cons. Meng Finseth & Co.; chmn. Nat. Council Crime and Delinquency, 1973-74, vice chmn., 1975—; chmn. Commn. White House fellows, 1973-74; U.S. ambassador and rep. to European Office of UN and other internat. orgns., Geneva, Switzerland, 1974-76; spl. asst. to asst. sec. state, 1976; spl. adviser U.S. del. 31st Gen. Assembly; bd. dirs. Viratek Inc., Beneficial Standard Life Ins. Co., New Economy Fund, Coachman, Inc. Active United Appeal, Cin.; bd. dirs. Goodwill Industries, Cin., v.p., 1968; bd. dirs., mem. exec. com. Cin. area chpt. ARC; bd. dirs. Boys Clubs' Am., Bethesda Hosp., Boys' Club Cin., Taft Inst., Natural History Museum, also symphony, opera, ballet cos.; trustee Am. U., Occidental Coll., Claremont Sch. Theology; chmn. bd. councilors U. So. Calif. Coll. Continuing Edn.; bd. councilors Sch. Internat. Relations and Sch. Bus.; bd. dirs. Los Angeles chpt. ARC, Central City Assn., 1978-84, Meth. Hosp. So. Calif., 1980-85, Huntington Meml. Research Inst., 1985—, Operating Co.-Music Center, Los Angeles World Affairs Council, Los Angeles chpt. NCCJ, Town Hall Calif., Greater Los Angeles Visitors and Conv. Bur.; bd. dirs., pres. Los Angeles County council Boy Scouts Am., 1983-84, mem. nat. adv. bd., 1984—. Served with USNR, World War II. Named Outstanding Young Man of Year Cin., 1951; recipient Gov.'s award for adding prestige Ohio, 1968; Superior Honor award State Dept., 1976; Freedoms Found. award, 1976; Silver Beaver award Boy Scouts Am., 1969. Fellow ABA; mem. Ohio Bar Assn. (pres. 1966-67), Cin. Bar Assn. (pres. 1961-62), Los Angeles C. of C. (v.p., dir.), Council Chs. Greater Cin. (pres. 1959-61), Frat. of Friends (v.p.), Order of Coif, Omicron Delta Kappa, Phi Kappa Psi, Sigma Nu Phi. Methodist (dist. lay leader 1958-64; mem. bd. publs. 1977-82). Clubs: Lincoln, Rotary; Comml. (Cin.); Annandale Golf (Los Angeles), Calif. (Los Angeles); Bohemian (San Francisco); Valley Hunt (Pasadena). also: 5604 Bridger Ct Missoula MT 59803

DALE, SHARON KAY, real estate broker, executive secretary; b. San Franciso, July 14, 1940; d. Terrill Odin and Alice Ernestine (Anthony) Glenn; divorced; 1 child, Kimberly Kay. AS, Fresno City Coll., Calif., 1982; student, Calif. State U., Fresno, 1983—. Lic. real estate broker, Calif. Sales assoc. Red Carpet Realtors, Fresno, 1974-77; broker, owner U.S. Cities Realtors, dba, Pierson & Planamento, Inc., Fresno, 1977-80; broker assoc. Easterbrook Constrn., Fresno, 1980-81, 1983-84; exec. sec. Valley Med. Ctr., Fresno, 1981—; broker Assoc. Adanalian & Jackson Real Estate, Fresno, 1981-83, 1984—; dir. div. II U.S. Cities Realtors, Inc. No. Calif, Nev., 1978-80. Vol. St. Agnes Service Guild, Fresno, 1974—, Mental Health Assn., Fresno, 1982-83, Ednl. T.V. Channel 18, Fresno,1983, Valley Med. Ctr. Aux., Fresno, 1985—. Mem. Fresno County, City C. of C. (Ambassadors Club), Calif. Assn. Realtors, Fresno Bd. Realtors, Multiple Listing Svc., Nat. Bd. Realtors. Republican. Club: Sierra Sport & Racquet (Fresno, Calif.) (charter mem.). Home: 5099 W Shields Ave Fresno CA 93722 Office: Adanalian & Jackson Real Estate 5649 N Palm Ave Fresno CA 93704

D'ALESSANDRO, JOSEPH LOUIS, state official; b. Sacramento, Calif., Feb. 6, 1956; s. Americo George and Lorraine Marie (Perry) D.; m. Kathryn Marie Olson, July 2, 1977; 1 child, Martina Lauriana Olson. Student, U. Florence, 1974; BA, Calif. State U., Sacramento, 1978. Dep. coordinator Calif. State U., Sacramento, 1975-78; cons. Bertoloni Travel Service, Sacramento, 1979-85; tourism mgr. Calif. Office Tourism, Sacramento, 1985--; research dir. Sacramento History Ctr., 1983-84; chmn. Calif. Travel Industry Commn., 1987. Contbr. articles to popular pubs. Pres. Portugese Cultural Soc., Sacramento, 1979-84, Irmandade do Divino EspiritoSanto, Sacramento, 1985; chmn. Internat. Friendship Com., Sacramemto, 1984; bd. dirs. Religious Community for Peace, Sacramento, 1987. Recipient Outstanding Achievment award, Sacramento Hist. Soc., 1982; named Person To Watch, Sacramento Bee, 1983. Mem. Luso Am. (Sacramento). Roman Catholic. Office: Calif Office Tourism 1121 L St Ste 103 Sacramento CA 95814

DALIS, IRENE, mezzo-soprano, opera company administrator, music educator; b. San Jose, Calif., Oct. 8, 1925; d. Peter Nicholas and Mamie Rose (Boitano) D.; m. George Loinaz, July 16, 1957; 1 child, Alida Mercedes. AB, San Jose State U., 1946; MA in Teaching, Columbia U., 1947; MMus (hon.), MS (hon.), San Jose State Coll., 1957; studied voice with, Edyth Walker, N.Y.C., 1947-50, Paul Althouse, 1950-51, Dr. Otto Mueller, Milan, Italy, 1952-72; MusD (hon.), Santa Clara U., 1987. Prin. artist Berlin Opera, 1955-65, Met. Opera, N.Y.C., 1957-77, San Francisco Opera, 1958-73, Hamburg (fed. Republic Germany) Staatsoper, 1966-71; prof. music San Jose State U., Calif., 1977—; founder, exec. dir. Opera San Jose, 1984-88, artistic div. opera, 1988—; dir. Met. Opera Nat. Auditions, San Jose dist., 1980—. Operatic debut as dramatic mezzo-soprano Oldenburgisches Staatstheater, 1953, Berlin Staedtische Oper, 1955; debut Met. Opera, N.Y.C., 1957, 1st Am.-born singer, Kundry Bayreuth Festival, 1961, opened, Bayreuth Festival, Parsifal, 1963; commemorative Wagner 150th Birth Anniversary; opened 1963 Met. Opera Season in Aida; premiered: Dello Joio's Blood Moon, 1961, Henderson's Medea, 1972; rec. artist Parsifal, 1964 (Grand Prix du Disque award); contbg. editor Opera Quarterly, 1983. Recipient Fulbright award for study in Italy, 1951, Woman of Achievement award Commn. on Status of Women, 1983, Pres.'s award Nat. Italian Am. Found., 1985, award of merit People of San Francisco, 1985, San Jose Renaissance award for sustained and outstanding artistic contbn., 1987, Medal of Achievement Acad. Vocal Arts, 1988; named Honored Citizen City of San Jose, 1986; inducted into Calif. Pub. Edn. Hall of Fame, 1985, others. Mem. Beethoven Soc. (mem. adv. bd. 1985—), San Jose Arts Round Table, San Jose Opera Guild, Am. Soc. Univ. Women, Arts Edn. Week Consortium, Phi Kappa Phi, Mu Phi Epsilon. Office: Opera San Jose 12 S 1st St Ste 207 San Jose CA 95113

DALLAM, TIMOTHY MICHAEL, food products company executive; b. Coral Gables, Fla., Sept. 14, 1948; s. Richard Ernest and Wilma Jean (Ball) D.; m. Patricia Marie Bridgeman, Aug. 25, 1973; children: Michele Elizabeth, Nicole Victoria. BA, San Jose State U., 1970. Asst. prodn. mgr. Blommer Chocolate, Union City, Calif., 1973-75; v.p. Shade Foods, Inc., Belmont, Calif., 1975-86; pres. Leppla Enterprises, Palo Alto, Calif., 1986-88; dir. ind. div. Carriage House Foods, San Jose, Calif., 1988—; cons. Chocolate Technologies, Palo Alto, Calif., 1986-88. Author: Flavoring Ice Cream, 1979, Confectionery Manufacturing, 1983. With U.S. Army Nat. Guard, 1971-77. Recipient Certs. of Merit Richardson Rschs., Hayward, Calif., 1978, Reofern Assocs., Raleigh, N.C., 1979. Mem. Inst. Food Technologists, Am. Assn. Candy Technologists, Calif. Dairy Industries Assn. (life, dir. 1989), Oreg. Dairy Industries, Wash. State Dairy Coun., Kiwanis (outstanding scholarship 1967). Republican. Baptist. Office: Carriage House Foods 1901 Las Plumas Ave San Jose CA 95133

DALLIN, ALEXANDER, history and political science educator; b. Berlin, Germany, May 21, 1924; came to U.S., 1940, naturalized, 1943; s. David J. and Eugenia (Bein) D.; children—Linda, Natasha, Andrew. B.S., Coll. City N.Y., 1947; M.A., Columbia, 1948, Ph.D., 1953. Assoc. dir. research program on USSR, N.Y.C., 1951-54; dir. research War Documentation Project, Washington, 1954-56; faculty Columbia U., 1956-71, prof. internat. relations, 1961-65; Adlai Stevenson prof. internat. relations Columbia, 1965-71; former dir. Russian Inst.; prof. history and polit. sci. Stanford U.,

1971—, Raymond A. Spruance prof. internat. history, 1987—, chmn. dept. internat. relations, 1980-83, dir. Ctr. Russian and East European Studies, 1985—; pres. Internat. Com. Soviet and East European Studies 1985—; cons. U.S. Govt., 1962-70; chmn. Nat. Council for Soviet and East European Research, 1978-80. Author: German Rule in Russia, 1941-1945, 1957, rev. edit., 1981, The Soviet Union at the United Nations, 1962, (with others) The Soviet Union and Disarmament, 1965, Political Terror in Communist Systems, 1970, Black Box, 1985; editor: (with others) Soviet Conduct in World Affairs, 1960, Diversity in International Communism, 1963, Politics in the Soviet Union: Seven Cases, 1966, Soviet Politics Since Khrushchev, 1968, Women in Russia, 1977, The Gorbachev Era, 1986. Served with AUS, 1943-46. Fellow Social Sci. Research Council, 1950-51; Guggenheim fellow, 1961-62; Fulbright Hays fellow, 1965-66; Wilson Center fellow, 1978-79. Mem. Am. Assn. Advancement Slavic Studies (pres. 1984-85), Council Fgn. Relations, Am. Hist. Assn. Home: 607 Cabrillo Ave Stanford CA 94305

DALLUM, GREGORY GRANT, state agency executive, artist; b. Grand Forks, N.D., Nov. 28, 1948; s. Lawerence Melvin and Myrtle Bernice (Venslund) D.; married, Sept. 11, 1977; 1 child, Kristen Elsbeth,. AA, S. Seattle Community Coll., Seattle, 1973; student, Pacific Lutheran U., 1974-76. Survey camp cook Bureau of Land Mgmt., Anchorage, 1976; realtor various companies, Tacoma/Seattle, Wash., 1977-84; right-of-way agt. Wash. State Dept. of Trans., Seattle, 1984—; artist/owner Hues by Gregory Dallum, Seattle, 1985—. Artist: Invitational Exhibit (ten paintings), Eastshore Gallery, Bellevue, Wash. 1987-88; exhibit R.A.A.S. Ink & Watercolor 1987, 1988. With USN, 1967-71, Guam, Vietnam. Republican. Home: 14810 SE Fairwood Blvd Renton WA 98058

DALRYMPLE, CHARLES ROGER, pharmacist; b. Excelsior Springs, Mo., Jan. 22, 1947; s. Robert A. and Marjorie Jeanne (Reilley) D.; m. Beth Shannon, Dec. 1, 1973. BS in Pharmacy, Southwestern Okla. State U., Weatherford, 1973; MBA, U. Phoenix, 1988. Registered pharmacist, Ariz., Colo., Okla., Tex. Mgr. Warehouse Pharmacies, Tulsa, 1973-76; staff pharmacist Okla. Osteo. Hosp., Tulsa, 1976; owner, mgr. Valley Pharmacy, Saguache, Colo., 1976-78, Crested Butte (Colo.) Drug, 1978-84; pharmacy supr. CIGNA Healthplan, Tucson, 1985—. Organizer-sponsor Crested Butte Marathon and 10-K Race, 1981-83. Served with U.S. Army, 1968-71, Vietnam. Mem. Crested Butte C. of C. (v.p. 1984). Republican. Lodge: Rotary. Home: 4605 N Paseo Pitiquito Tucson AZ 85715 Office: CIGNA Healthplan 7901 E 22d St Tucson AZ 85710

DALSHAUG, ALLAN EMORY, banker; b. Buchanan, Sask., Can., May 19, 1931; s. Ellend Johann and Cornelia (Benson) D.; m. Elva Beatrice Smith, Mar. 24, 1955; children: Ellana Beatrice, Eric Justin Charles, Errin Jon. Grad. with honors, Lutheran Bible Inst., Outlook, Sask.; student, Pacific Coast Banking Sch., 1967. With Security Pacific Bank, 1973-79; sr. v.p. strategic planning Security Pacific Bank, Los Angeles, 1977-79; chmn. bd., chief exec. officer Sterling Bank, Los Angeles, 1980—; instr. S.W. Grad. Sch. Banking. Mem. Western Ind. Bankers Assn., Calif. Bankers Assn. Methodist. Club: Wilshire Country. *

DALTON, ALAN RICK, police officer; b. Delta, Utah, June 30, 1950; s. Ted and Millie Maurine (Callister) D.; m. Carma Manon Burke, Jan. 5, 1976; children: Jason, Jessica, Erika, Helen. Student, Ariz. State U., 1969-70. Store mgr. Chess King, Scottsdale, Ariz., 1970-74; mgr. Dalton Ins. Agy. div. ITT Life Ins. Co., Mesa, Ariz., 1975-78; patrolman Mesa Police Dept., 1978—. Author: Constitrivia, Vols. 1 and 2, Analytical Index to the U.S. Constitution: A Clear and Present Danger; contbr. articles to newspapers. Com. mem. Mesa Constitution Week Com., 1980-87; founder Youth Alert, Mesa, 1981; advisor Chem. People Task Force, Mesa, 1982-83; cons. State Polit. Campaigns, 1981—; asst. dist. commr. Boy Scouts Am., 1983-85. Recipient Howard Pyle award Ariz. Safety Assn., 1985. Mem. Ariz. Crime Prevention Assn. (pres.), Am. Citizen and Lawmen Assn. (pres., chief lobbyist 1983—), Internat. Soc. Crime Prevention Practitioners, Fraternal Order of Police. Republican. Mormon. Office: Am Citizen & Lawmen Assn PO Box 135 Mesa AZ 85211

DALTON, DOUGLAS, lawyer; b. Astoria, Oreg., Sept. 1, 1929; s. Mervyn Edgar and Julia Margaret (Hitchcock) D.; m. Shirley Kirkpatrick, Aug. 29, 1953; children—Julia M., Douglas C., John D., Matthew J., Bartholomew P. B.A., UCLA, 1951; J.D., U. So. Calif., 1956. Bar: Calif. bar 1956. City prosecutor Long Beach, Calif., 1956-60; ptnr. Ball, Hunt, Hart, Brown & Baerwitz, Los Angeles, 1960-77; prin. Dalton & Godfrey, Inc., Los Angeles, 1977-89; pvt. practice Los Angeles, 1989—; adj. prof. law Pepperdine U. Sch. Law, Los Angeles, 1978-80. Counsel Pres. Nixon's Commn. on Campus Unrest, 1970. Served with USN, 1951-53. Fellow Am. Coll. Trial Lawyers; mem. ABA, Assn. State Bar Calif. (bd. govs. 1985-88), Assn. County Bar Los Angeles. Republican. Office: 4525 Wilshire Blvd 3d Fl Los Angeles CA 90010

DALTON, JAMES EDWARD, business executive, retired air force officer; b. N.Y.C., Oct. 17, 1930; s. Edward A. and Marion (Conway) D.; m. Betty Jane Irwin, Nov. 29, 1958; children: Christopher, Stephanie, Todd. B.S., U.S. Mil. Acad., 1954; M.S.E. in Instrumentation Engring, U. Mich., 1960, M.S.E. in Aero./Astronautical Engring, 1960; grad. with distinction, Air Command and Staff Coll., 1965, Indsl. Coll. Armed Forces, 1970. Commd. 2d lt. U.S. Air Force, 1954, advanced through grades to gen., 1983; served in numerous operational and research assignments 1954-73; comdr. 39th Aerospace Rescue and Recovery Wing, Eglin AFB, Fla., 1973-75, Air Res. Personnel Center, Denver, 1975-76; dep. dir. concepts Hdqrs. USAF, Washington, 1976-77; dep. dir. Force Devel. and Strategic Plans, Plans and Policy Directorate, Office Joint Chiefs of Staff, Washington, 1977-78; vice dir. Joint Staff, 1978-80; commandant Indsl. Coll. of Armed Forces, Washington, 1980-81; dir. Joint Staff, 1981-83; chief of staff SHAPE, 1983-85; pres. R & D Assocs.; corp. v.p. Logicon. Decorated Def. Disting. Service medal with two oak leaf clusters, Legion of Merit with 1 oak leaf cluster, D.F.C., Bronze Star, Air medal with 5 oak leaf clusters, Meritorious Service medal with 2 oak leaf clusters, Air Force Commendation medal. Mem. Air Force Assn., Assn. Grads. U.S. Mil. Acad., Council Fgn. Relations. Roman Catholic. Home: 61 Misty Acres Rd Rolling Hills Estates CA 90274

DALTON, PATRICK DALY, JR., biology educator; b. Salt Lake City, Oct. 11, 1922; s. Patrick Daly and Ora (Johnson) D.; m. Lela Jesperson, Dec. 20, 1948; children: Tanya, Erin Colleen, Mark Edward. BS, Ariz. State U., 1949; MS, Utah State U., 1951; PhD, U. Ariz., 1961. Reporter, printer Mesa (Ariz.) Jour. Tribune, 1939-42, L.A. Times, 1942, Sta.'s Corp., Los Angeles, 1942; lab. and teaching asst. Ariz. State U., Tempe, 1945-49; rsch. and teaching asst. Utah State U., Logan, 1949-51; range mgr., adminstrn., rsch. and instrn. Soil Conservation Svc. USDA, Tooele, Utah, 1951-52; range mgr., adminstrn. and instrn. Bur. Land Mgmt. U.S. Dept. Interior, Price, Utah, 1952; instr. math., phys. and biol. scis., agrl. and indsl. arts, supt. bldgs. and grounds, assoc. plantation mgr. Tongan Mission Liahona High Sch., Nuku'alofa, Tonga, 1953-55; pres. Tongan Mission, Nuku'alofa, Tonga, 1963-66; asst. prof., dir. farm ops. Depts. Agrl. and Phys. Sci. Ch. Coll. Hawaii, Laie, 1955-58, assoc. prof. biol. scis., 1966-70; prof. biol. scis. Ch. Coll. Hawaii now Brigham Young U. Hawaii, Laie, 1970-88; research and teaching assoc. Dept. Plant Sci. U. Ariz., Tucson, 1958-61; asst. prof. range mgmt. U. Nevada, Reno, 1961-62; dir. forest and range research and rehab. UNESCO, Soeul, Rep. of Korea, 1962-63; prof. emeritus Brigham Young U., Hawaii, 1988. Contbr. articles to profl. jours. Dist. commr. Aloha council Boy Scouts Am., Ko'olau dist., 1980-89; mem. Laie Elem. Sch. PTA, Kahuku (Hawaii) High Sch. PTA; sci. fair judge State of Hawaii High Schs., 1965-88. NSF fellow 1959-60; recipient Eagle Scout medal with Bronze, Gold and Silver palms, Silver Beaver award, Gold Service medal Boy Scouts Am., Scouter's award Boy Scouts Am., Order of Merit award Boy Scouts Am., Order of Arrow award Boy Scouts Am., Arrowhead award, Wood Badge award. Mem. AAAS, Am. Inst. Biol. Sci., Ecol. Soc. Am., Am. Soc. Range Mgmt., Nat. Geographic Soc., Hawaiian Acad. Sci., Hawaiian Bot. Soc., Blue Key, Sigma Xi, Alpha Gamma Rho, Alpha Phi Omega, Lambda Delta Sigma, Alpha Zeta, Beta Beta Beta, Xi Sigma Pi, Delta Sigma Pi. Mormon.

DALTON, THOMAS JOSEPH, sales and marketing executive; b. Kansas City, Mo., Mar. 7, 1962; s. David L. and Cecilia T. (Schweizer) D.; m. Inez M. Tinsley, Oct. 12, 1985. BSEE, U. Mo., Rolla, 1984; MBA, U. So. Calif., 1988. Mfg. engr. AT&T Microelectronics, Kansas City, Mo., 1984-86; account exec. AT&T Microelectronics, L.A., 1986-89, nat. account mgr., 1989—. Mem. IEEE. Office: AT&T 16461 Sherman Way Van Nuys CA 91406

DALY, BRIAN KEVIN, electronic engineer; b. Bay Shore, N.Y., May 6, 1960; s. William John and Grace (Greenfield) D.; m. Janice Dianne Clark, May 31, 1986; 1 child, Ashley Janaye Daly. BSE, Ariz. State U., 1983, postgrad. engring., 1984-88. Lead engr. AG Communication Systems, Phoenix, 1984—. Mem. IEEE, Nat. Soc. Profl. Engrs., Am. Radio Relay League, Ariz. State U. Radio (pres. 1983), AG 4 Wheel Drive (pres. 1988-89). Republican. Home: 8044 W Columbine Dr Peoria AZ 85345 Office: AG Communications Systems 2500 W Utopia Rd Phoenix AZ 85027

DALY, NANCY JANE, retail and manufacturing company executive; b. Mpls., May 30, 1932; d. John Vivien and Willis Faye (Parks) Crisp; m. Niler Alan Lewis, Jan. 13, 1952 (div.); children: Brenda Lynette, Brad Alan; m. Richard Alan Daly, May 11, 1967. AA in Bus., L.A. Valley Coll., 1951; student, UCLA, 1951; cert. real estate, Murphy's Bus. Coll., No. Hollywood, Calif., 1965. Admissions sec. Art Ctr. Coll. of Design, West L.A., Calif., 1965-66; v.p. Western Precision Bolt, Van Nuys, Calif., 1967-70; bonding, suretyship Agent's Bonding Service, Van Nuys, 1970-72; supr., steno pool Coachella Valley County Water Dist., Coachella, Calif., 1972-74; v.p. Slumberline Sleep Products, Inc., Phoenix, 1974-76; sec., treas. Customline, Inc., Lake Havasu City, Ariz., 1976-81, Newport Pacific, Inc., Hilo, Hawaii, 1981—, Royal Heir of Hawaii, Inc., Honolulu, 1985—; dir. Tropical Sleep Ctrs., Hawaii, 1983—; sales tng. Marsh Cos., Hawaii, 1985—. Supporter, Hilo Boy's Club, 1987-88, Hilo Exchange Club, 1987-88, Hilo Downtown Assn., 1987-88. Republican. Home: PO Box 1265 Pahoa HI 96778 Office: Tropical Sleep Ctrs 58 Kinoole St Hilo HI 96720

DALY, PAUL SYLVESTER, university chancellor; b. Belmont, Mass., Jan. 8, 1934; s. Matthew Joseph and Alice Mary (Hall) D.; m. Maureen Teresa Kenny, May 25, 1957; children: Judith Mary, Paul S. Jr., Susan Marie, John Joseph, Maureen H. BS in Engring. Sci., Naval Postgrad. Sch., 1968; MBA, U. W. Fla., 1971. Coll. dean Embry-Riddle Aero. U., Daytona Beach, Fla., 1979-81; chancellor Embry-Riddle Aero. U., 1981—; lectr. seminars, 1977-85; cons. British Aerospace, 1979-84, McDonnell Douglas, 1979-84, IBM, 1983-84; sr. faculty U. Phoenix, 1983-86. Bd. dirs. Yavapai Regional Med. Ctr., Prescott, Ariz., 1983-86, Ariz. Hosp. Fedn., Prescott C. of C., 1982-84; chmn. Ariz. State Bd. of Pvt. Postsecondary Edn., Phoenix, 1982—, Interactive Health Corp.; pres. Ind. Coll. and Univs. of Ariz., Phoenix, 1982—; pres., founder West Yvapai County Am. Heart Assn. Chpt. Capt. USN, 1953-79. Decorated Legion of Merit. Mem. Ariz. Airport Assn., Retired Officers Assn., Ariz. Town Hall, USAF Assn. Republican. Roman Catholic. Office: Embry-Riddle Aero U 3200 N Willow Creek Rd Prescott AZ 86301

D'AMBROSIO, BLANCHE FADA GRAWE, hotel executive; b. Baton Rouge, Mar. 18, 1926; d. Walter Theodore and Blanche Laura (Causey) Bozant; m. Arthur Nolan Grawe, June 5, 1949; children: Cary Nolan, Geoffrey Allan; m. Anthony Francis D'Ambrosio, Feb. 18, 1978. Student La. State U., 1943-45, U. So. Calif., 1945-47. Society editor Herald Am. newspaper, Compton, Calif., 1957-61; asst. editor Host mag., Oreg. Restaurant and Beverage Assn., Portland, 1962-66; agt. Oreg. Liquor Control Commn., Portland, 1966-69; dir. sales and catering Cosmopolitan El Mirador, Sacramento, Calif., 1969-71; mgr. Umpqua Hotel, Roseburg, Oreg., 1971-74; gen. mgr. Inn at Spanish Head, Lincoln City, Oreg., 1974—. Mem. Lincoln City Advt. Com.; mem. job service employers com. Dept. Human Resources of Lincoln County. Mem. Nat. Restaurant Assn., Oreg. Hotel and Motel Assn. (past pres., chmn. bd.), Am. Hotel and Motel Assn., Oreg. Motor Hotel Assn. (dir.), Restaurants of Oreg. Assn., Lincoln City Motel Assn. (dir.), Women's Assn. of Allied Beverage Industry (past pres. Portland chpt), Oreg. Lodging Assn. (v.p. hotels). Club: Norwalk (Calif.) Jr. Women's (life mem., past pres.). Office: Inn at Spanish Head 4009 S Hwy 101 Lincoln City OR 97367

D'AMICO, MICHAEL, architect, urban planner; b. Bklyn., Sept. 11, 1936; s. Michael and Rosalie (Vinciguerra) D.; BArch, U. Okla., 1961; postgrad. So. Meth. U. Sch. Law, 1962-63, Coll. Marin, 1988—; m. Joan Hand, Nov. 26, 1955; children: Michael III, Dion Charles. Supr. advanced planning sect. Dallas Dept. City Planning, 1961-63; designer, planner in charge Leo A. Daly Co., San Francisco, 1963-66; project planner Whisler, Patri Assos., San Francisco, 1966-67; architect, urban planner D'Amico & Assocs., San Francisco, N.Y., Guam, 1967-73, pres. D'Amico & Assocs., Inc., Mill Valley, Calif., and Guam, 1973—; pres. Jericho Alpha Inc., 1979-82; cons. architect, planner City of Seaside (Calif.), 1967-72, 79-81; cons. urban redevel. Eureka (Calif.), 1967-82; cons. planner, Lakewood, Calif.; redevel. cons. to Daly City (Calif.), 1975-77; redevel. adviser to Tamalpais Valley Bus. Assn., 1975-77; archtl. and hist. analyst to Calif. Dept. Transp., 1975-77; agt. for Eureka, Calif. Coastal Commn., 1977-79; devel. cons. City of Scotts Valley, 1988—, City of Suisun, 1988—. Mem. steering com. San Francisco Joint Com. Urban Design, 1967-72. Recipient Community Design award AIA, 1970; First prize award Port Aransas (Tex.) Master Plan Competition, 1964; Design award Karachi Mcpl. Authority, 1987. Mem. AIA (inactive), Am. Planning Assn., Calif. Assn. Planning Cons. (sec., treas. 1970-72), Am. Soc. Cons. Planners, World Future Soc., Solar Energy Soc. Am. Home and Office: 525 Midvale Way Mill Valley CA 94941

D'AMICO, NICHOLAS M., dentist; b. Dayton, Ohio, Jan. 30, 1953; s. Nicholas J. and Irma J. (Pietrantonio) D'A.; m. Jean Marie Curley, Sept. 20, 1975; 1 child, Brent. BA, Ohio Wesleyan U., 1975; DDS, Ohio State U., 1977. Dental chief Indian Health Service, Box Elder, Mont., 1977-79; assoc. dentist John Robison DDS, Canton, Mich., 1979-80, Bill Bender DDS, LaSalle, Colo., 1980-81; prin. Horiuchi & D'Amico DDS PC, Aurora, Colo., 1981—; mem. Found. for Advanced Continuing Edn. Study Club. Mem. ADA, Am. Acad. Gen. Dentistry. Republican. Roman Catholic. Home: 16537 E Berry Ln Aurora CO 80015 Office: Horiuchi & D'Amico PC 3131 S Vaughn Way Aurora CO 80014

DAMISCH, PETER WHITON, diversified technical company engineering manager; b. Chgo., Feb. 27, 1953; s. John W. and Harriet D. (Darley) D.; m. Kathleen R. Reilly, May 14, 1977. BS in Aerospace Engring., U.S. Naval Acad., 1975; MS in Nuclear Engring., NPS/NPTU, 1976; M in Mgmt. and MBA with distinction, Northwestern U., 1982. Cert. nuclear chief engr. USN. Commd. ensign USN, 1975, advanced through grades to lt. comdr., resigned, 1980, congressionl aide, 1975, elec. div. officer USS Nimitz, 1977-79, combat info. ctr. officer USS Texas, 1979-80; program mgr. No. Ordnance div. FMC, 1982-83; mgr. strategic planning and bus. devel. Def. Systems Group FMC, San Jose, Calif., 1983-84; dir. bus. devel. Def. Systems Internat. div. FMC, Santa Clara, Calif., 1985-86; mgr. system engring. Ordnance div. FMC, San Jose, 1986-87, dep. program mgr. Ground Systems div., 1987—; program dir. subs. system Naval Systems div. U.S. Naval Res., Mpls., 1988—; prodn. officer FMC, San Jose, 1988—; bd. dirs. Ideamatics, Inc., Washington; pres., v.p. Am. Inst. Aeronautics and Astronautics, USNA, 1973-75; student tchr. computer sci. U.S. Naval Acad., 1974-75. V.p. Almaden Hills Estates Homeowner's Assn., San Jose, 1984—; campaign worker Sam Young Congressional campaign, Skokie, Ill., 1970. Mem. U.S. Naval Inst. (life), U.S. Navy League (life), U.S. Naval Acad. Alumni Assn. (life), Northwestrn Univ. Alumni Assn. (life), San Jose Astron. Assn. Home: 1045 Mazzone Dr San Jose CA 95120

DAMSBO, ANN MARIE, psychologist; b. Cortland, N.Y., July 7, 1931; d. Jorgen Einer and Agatha Irene (Schenck) D. B.S., San Diego State Coll., 1952; M.A., U.S. Internat. U., 1974, Ph.D., 1975. Commd. 2d lt. U.S. Army, 1952, advanced through grades to capt., 1957; staff therapist Letterman Army Hosp., San Francisco, 1953-54, 56-58, 61-62, Ft. Devers, Mass., 1955-56, Walter Reed Army Hosp., Washington, 1958-59, Tripler Army Hosp., Hawaii, 1959-61, Ft. Benning, Ga., 1962-64; chief therapist U.S. Army Hosp., Ft. McPherson, Ga., 1964-67; ret. U.S. Army, 1967; med. missionary So. Presbyterian Ch., Taiwan, 1968-70; psychology intern Naval Regional Med. Ctr., San Diego, 1975, pre-doctoral intern, 1975-76, postdoctoral intern, 1975-76, chief, founder pain clinic, 1977-86; adj. tchr. U. Calif. Med. Sch., San Diego; lectr., U.S., Can., Eng., France, Australia, cons. forensic hypnosis to law enforcement agys. Contbr. articles to profl. publs., chpt. to book. Tchr. Sunday sch. Methodist Ch., 1945—. Fellow Am. Soc. Clin. Hypnosis; mem. AAUW, San Diego Soc. Clin. Hypnosis (pres. 1980), Am. Phys. Therapy Assn., Calif. Soc. Clin. & Hypnosis (bd. govs.), Internat. Soc. Clin. & Exptl. Hypnosis, Internat. Platform Assn., Am. Soc. Clin. Hypnosis (exec. bd.), Ret. Officers Am., Toastmasters (local pres.), Job's Daus. Club, Zonta. Republican. Home and Office: 1062 W 5th Ave Escondido CA 92025

DAMSKY, ROBERT PHILIP, communications executive; b. Boston, May 19, 1921; s. Mark and Ann (Wisser) D.; m. Rose Hollender, Jan. 18, 1955 (div. 1985); children: Marla Markley, Lori Diana. Cert., MIT, 1939, Tex. A&M U., 1944; diploma, Spartan Sch. Aero., Tulsa, 1946. Indsl. editor Spartan Aircraft Co., Tulsa, 1946-47; with Transocean Airlines, Hartford, Conn., 1947; chief pilot MIT, Beverly, Mass., 1947-48; sr. check pilot Civil Air Patrol, Beverly, 1948; airport mgr. Hartport, Inc., Bellfontaine, Ohio, 1948-49; airline pilot Slick Airlines and U.S. Overseas Airlines, Burbank, Calif. and Wildwood, N.J., 1949-55; founder Flight Edn. Assn., Santa Ana, Calif., 1955-80; pres. Aeromedia Nat. Syndicate, L.A., 1980—. With U.S. Army, 1940-45. Decorated Purple Heart, 1941. Mem. Airline Pilots Assn., Aircraft Owners and Pilots Assn., Silver Wings, VFW, Am. Legion, Pearl Harbor Survivors Assn. Home: PO Box 2704 Costa Mesa CA 92628

DANCE, FRANCIS ESBURN XAVIER, communication educator; b. Bklyn., Nov. 9, 1929; s. Clifton Louis and Catherine (Tester) D.; m. Nora Alice Rush, May 1, 1954 (div. 1974); children: Clifton Louis III, Charles Daniel, Alison Catherine, Andrea Frances, Frances Sue, Brendan Rush; m. Carol Camille Zak, July 4, 1974; children: Zachary Esburn, Gabriel Joseph, Caleb Michael, Catherine Emily. B.S., Fordham U., 1951; M.A., Northwestern U., 1953, Ph.D., 1959. Instr. speech Bklyn. Adult Labor Schs., 1951; instr. humanities, coordinator radio and TV U. Ill. at Chgo., 1953-54; instr. Univ. Coll., U. Chgo., 1958; asst. prof. St. Joseph's (Ind.) Coll., 1958-60; asst. prof., then assoc. prof. U. Kans., 1960-63; mem. faculty U. Wis.-Milw., 1963-71, prof. communication, 1965-71; dir. Speech Communication Center U. Wis-Milw., 1963-70; mem. faculty U. Denver, 1971—; partner Helix Press, Shorewood, Wis., 1970-71; cons. in field. Author: The Citizen Speaks, 1962, (with Harold P. Zelko) Business and Professional Speech Communication, 1965, 2d edit., 1978, Human Communication Theory, 1967, (with Carl E. Larson) Perspectives on Communication, 1970, Speech Communication: Concepts and Behavior, 1972, The Functions of Speech Communication: A Theoretical Approach, 1976, Human Communication Theory, 1982, (with Carol C. Zak-Dance) Public Speaking, 1986; editor: Jour. Communication, 1962-64, Speech Tchr, 1970-72; adv. bd.: Jour. Black Studies; editorial bd.: Jour. Psycholinguistic Research; Contbr. articles to profl. jours. Bd. dirs. Milw. Mental Health Assn., 1966-67. Served to 2d lt. AUS, 1954-56. Knapp Univ. scholar in communication, 1967-68; recipient Outstanding Prof. award Standard Oil Found., 1967; Master Tchr. award U. Denver, 1985, University Lectr. award U. Denver, 1986. Fellow Internat. Communication Assn. (pres. 1967); mem. Speech Communication Assn. (pres. 1982), Psi Upsilon. Office: U Denver Dept Speech Communication Denver CO 80208

DANDOY, SUZANNE EGGLESTON, physician, educator; b. Los Angeles, Jan. 2, 1935; d. Leonard Lester and Catherine (Wheelwright) Eggleston; m. Jeremiah Richard Dandoy, June 14, 1958; children: Kevin, Bret, Jolyn. BA, U. Calif., Los Angeles, 1956; MD, UCLA, 1960, MPH, 1963. Diplomate: Am. Bd. Preventive Medicine. Intern, Los Angeles Harbor Gen. Hosp., Torrance, Calif., 1960-61; resident Los Angeles Health Dept., 1961-62, 63-64; epidemiologist San Diego Dept. Pub. Health, 1967-68; bur. chief Ariz. Dept. Health Service, Phoenix, 1970-73; asst. commr. Ariz. Dept. Health Service, 1973-74, asst. dir., 1974-75, dir., 1975-80; prof. health adminstrn. Ariz. State U., Tempe, 1981-85; exec. dir. Utah Dept. Health, Salt Lake City, 1985—; adj. assoc. prof. U. Utah; bd. dirs. Pub. Health Found. Mem. editorial bd. Am. Jour. Pub. Health; contbr. articles to profl. jours. Bd. dirs. Child Crisis Ctr., Tempe St. Lukes Hosp.; chair Nat. Vaccine Adv. Com., HHS; adv. com. on immunization practices HEW; pres. Utah Women's Forum. Recipient award Ariz. Dietetic Assn., 1976; award Maricopa County Med. Soc., 1980. Fellow Am. Pub. Health Assn., Am. Coll. Preventive Medicine (pres.-elect 1989—); mem. AMA, Utah Med. Assn., Utah Pub. Health Assn., Assn. State Health Ofcls. (pres.-elect 1989—), Phi Beta Kappa, Delta Omega. Democrat. Mormon. Home: 990 S Oak Hills Way Salt Lake City UT 84108 Office: Utah Dept Health PO Box 16700 Salt Lake City UT 84116-0700

DANET, BURTON NORMAN, psychologist; b. Springfield, Mass., July 23, 1939; s. Benjamin Hyman and Lillian Rose (Sosner) D.; BA in Psychology with honors, Yale U., 1960; MA in Clin. Psychology, U. Minn., 1964, PhD in Clin. Psychology, 1967 ; cert. in psychoanalysis William Alanson White Inst. Psychiatry, Psychoanalysis and Psychology, 1973; m. Marsha Lynn Danet, Oct. 23, 1965. Rsch. asst. psychology and psychiatry depts. Yale U. Med. Sch., New Haven, 1958-60; tchr. English, Ramla-Lod High Sch., Ramla, Israel, 1960-61; clin. psychologist Mental Hygiene Clinic, U. Minn. Health Svc., Mpls., 1966-68, Hamm Meml. Psychiat. Clinic, St. Paul, 1968-69; NIMH fellow in clin. services White Inst., N.Y.C., 1969-71; chief psychologist Riverdale (N.Y.) Mental Health Ctr., 1971-82; cons. clin. psychologist Patrick J. Frawley Mental Health Clinic, Good Samaritan Hosp., Suffern, N.Y., 1980-82, Bronx Counseling Svcs., Big Sisters, Inc., Bronx (N.Y.) Family Ct., 1981-85; cons. clin. psychologist Abbott House, Irvington, N.Y., 1979-83; dir. Dept. Health and Clin. Svcs., 1983-84; supr. psychotherapy Bronx Ctr. Community Svcs., N.Y., 1985; cons. clin. psychologist The Epilepsy Inst., N.Y.C., 1985-86; pvt. practice psychoanalysis, psychotherapy, and clin. psychology, N.Y.C., White Plains, N.Y., 1969-86, Ventura and Oxnard, Calif., 1986—; pres., founder Partnerships for a Better Community , Oxnard, 1988—, pub., editor Health Examiner; editor Concerns of Disabled Persons and the Elderly. Founder, pres. Generations: An Aging Network. Mem. Nat. Register Health Svc. Providers in Psychology, Am. Psychol. Assn., Ventura County Psychol. Assn. Author: (screenplay) Journey to Say 'Good-Bye'; contbr. articles to profl. jours.

DANG, MARVIN S. C., lawyer; b. Honolulu, Feb. 11, 1954; s. Brian K.T. and Flora (Yuen) D. BA with distinction, U. Hawaii, 1974; JD, George Washington U., 1978. Bar: Hawaii 1978, U.S. Dist. Ct. Hawaii 1978, U.S. Ct. Appeals (9th cir.) 1979. Atty. Gerson, Steiner & Anderson and predecessor firms, Honolulu, 1978-81; owner, atty. Law Offices of Marvin S.C. Dang, Honolulu, 1981—; bd. dirs. Foster Equipment Co. Ltd., Honolulu; sr. v.p., bd. dirs. Rainbow Fin. Corp., Honolulu. Chmn., vice-chmn., mem. Manoa Neighborhood Bd. Honolulu, 1979-82, 84-87; pres., v.p., mem., Hawaii Coun. on Legal Edn. for Youth, Honolulu, 1979-86; state rep., asst. minority floorleader Hawaii State Legislature, Honolulu, 1982-84; mem. Hawaii Bicentennial Commn., Honolulu, 1986-88. Recipient Cert. of Appreciation award Hawaii Speech-Language-Hearing Assn., Honolulu, 1984. Mem. ABA (standing com. on law and the electoral process 1985—, spl. com. on youth edn. for citizenship 1979-85, Hawaii state membership chmn. 1983—, exec. coun. young lawyers div. 1986-88), Nat. Assn. Realtors, Hawaii State Bar Assn., Hawaii State Jaycees (one of ten Outstanding Young Persons of Hawaii 1983), Honolulu. Republican. Club: Plaza of Hawaii (Honolulu). Home: 108 Waokanaka Pl Honolulu HI 96817 Office: 220 S King St Cen Pacific Pla Ste 575 Honolulu HI 96813

DANIEL, GARY WAYNE, communications and music industry executive; b. Wendall, Idaho, June 22, 1948; s. Milan Chauncey Daniel and Ila Fay (Cox) Harkins; m. Jeanne Laurane Blandford, July 1969 (div. Aug. 1972); 1 child, Kelly Jean; m. Sandra Kay Modey, July 26, 1974; 1 child, Marcus Chauncey. AA, Boise Bus. Coll., 1969. Program dir. Sta. KSKI, Sun Valley, Idaho, 1967-68, Sta. KYME, Boise, Idaho, 1968-69; gen. mgr. Sta. KSPD, Boise, 1969-72; radio personality Sta. KBBK-FM, Boise, 1972-74; account exec. ABC-TV, Nampa, Idaho, 1974-77; nat. sales dir. Agri-Steel Corp., Boise, 1977-79; mgmt. ptnr. Agri. Devel. Corp., Caldwell, Idaho, 1979-82; owner, prin. Video Magic Amusement Co., Caldwell, 1982-85; pres., chief exec. officer Victory Media Group, Santa Rosa, Calif., 1985—; gen. mgr. Victory Record Label, 1986—, also bd. dirs.; bd. dirs. Bay City Records, San Francisco; pres. Lightforce Music Pub., Santa Rosa, 1987—; mktg. cons. Firenze Records, San Francisco, 1987—, Capital Bus. Systems, Napa, Calif., 1986—, Plum, Inc., Napa, 1985-86. Author: Concert Operations Manual, 1987. Recipient Most Humorous TV Comml. award Boise Advt. Club, 1975, Most Creative TV Comml. award Boise Advt. Club, 1976; named Top Radio Personality Idaho State Broadcasters Assn., 1971. Mem. Video Software Dealer Assn., Ind. Record Mfg. and Distbrs., ASCAP,

Gospel Music Assn. Republican. Office: Victory Media Group 1791 Marlow Rd Ste 6-347 Santa Rosa CA 95401

DANIELEWSKI, TAD ZBIGNIEW, theater, film and television director, professor; b. Radom, Poland; came to U.S., 1948; s. Teofil and Henryka (Borowska) D.; children: Christopher, Jan, Mark, Zygmunt, Anne, Decatur. Student, Royal Acad. Dramatic Art, London, 1947-48; BFA, Ohio U., 1950; postgrad., State U. of Iowa, 1950-51, John's Hopkins U., 1952-53. Mgr. program devel. Sta. NBC-TV, N.Y.C., 1953-54, 55; dir. Omnibus Sta. CBS-TV, N.Y.C., 1953-54; pres. Stratton Prodns., Inc., N.Y.C., 1955-75; prof. theatre and film Brigham Young U., Provo, Utah, 1975-89; prof. div. drama Sch. Cinema-TV, U. So. Calif., L.A., 1989—; dir. in field. Recipient The Best Acting award Berlin Film Festival, 1964, Best Picture award Barcelona (Spain) Film Festival, 1970, Dore Schary award Douglas Stone, 1984. Mem. NATAS (bd. dirs. dramatic workshop N.Y.C. chpt. 1954—, gov. 1971-75), Acad. TV, Arts and Scis. (dir. artistic repertory group 1989—), Acad. Motion Picture Arts and Scis. (bd. dirs. L.A. chpt. 1989—), Dir.'s Guild Am. Office: U So Calif Drama Ctr Los Angeles CA 90089-0791

DANIELS, CHRISTOPHER KENT, pharmacologist, researcher; b. L.A., Dec. 14, 1948; s. George Henry and Barbar Ann (Beahm) D.; m. Alice Ruth Stover, May 10, 1986. BS, Humboldt State U., 1972; MS, U. Wis., Milw., 1975; PhD, Stanford U., 1981. Lectr. U. Wis., Milw., 1974-75; USPHS fellow Stanford (Calif.) U., 1975-81; Monsanto research fellow U. Calif., San Francisco, 1981-83, asst. research anatomist, 1983-88; assoc. prof. Idaho State U., Boise, 1988--; chief immunopharmacology research VA Med. Ctr., Boise, 1988--. Contbr. articles to sci. jours. Mem. Fedn. Am. Scientists for Exptl. Biology, Am. Fedn. for Aging Research., Soc. Mucosal Immunology. Office: VA Med Ctr Boise ID 83702

DANIELS, DIANNE COMBS, social services administrator; b. Kingston, N.Y., Dec. 21, 1958; d. Alan Combs and Judy Chong Nim (Sin) Lee; m. Michael Kevin Daniels, Aug. 11, 1985. Student, U. Ariz., 1975-77; BA, Western Mich. U., 1979, MSW, 1981. pvt. practice social worker, Albuquerque, 1985—. Contractor Dianne Combs Drapes, Kalamazoo, 1977-81; social worker N.Mex. Dept. Human Services, Albuquerque, 1981-83; adoption social worker Chaparral Adoptions, Albuquerque, 1983-84, maternity supr., 1984-85; dir. Meth. Home, Albuquerque, 1985-89; with Chaparral Maternity & Adoption Svcs., Albuquerque, 1989—; bd. dirs., sec., vol. publicity com. Bright Horizons, 1986-88. Bd. dirs. adv. bd. Families for Children Adoption Agy., 1987—. Mem. Albuquerque Metro. Adoption Group, Nat. Assn. Social Workers (bd. dirs. N.Mex. chpt.), Individuals Making Positive Action for Children Today, N.Mex. Youth Work Alliance, N.Mex. Assn. Community Edn. Devel., Ultimate Players Assn. Democrat. Roman Catholic. Home: 1400 Guaymas NE Albuquerque NM 87110 Office: Chaparral Maternity & Adoption Svcs 1503 University NE Albuquerque NM 87102

DANIELS, ETHEL MARY, reading specialist; b. Phoenix, Feb. 26, 1942; d. Eddie Ernest and Alberta (Evans) D. BA in Edn., Ariz. State U., 1964; MA in Reading, U.S. Internat. U., 1976. Elem. tchr., Phoenix, 1964-67, San Diego, Calif., 1967—; demonstration tchr. reading and math., 1974-75; reading specialist San Diego City Schs., Robert E. Lee Elem. Sch., 1979—. Participant San Diego writing project, 1985. Recipient Service award PTA, 1981. Mem. San Diego Tchrs. Assn., Calif. Tchrs. Assn., NEA, Assn. Supervision and Curriculum Devel., Reading Specialists Calif., Greater San Diego Reading Assn. (Recognition of Excellence award 1987), Calif. Reading Assn., Computers and Writing Summer Inst. (mentor tchr. 1985—). Democrat. Baptist. Clubs: Mountain View Tennis (Service award 1976, 82), Balboa Tennis, Helix South Tennis. Home: 3041 Picasso Dr Bonita CA 92002 Office: Robert E Lee Elem Sch 6196 Childs Ave San Diego CA 92139

DANIELS, LYDIA M., health care administrator; b. Louisville, Dec. 21, 1932; d. Effort and Gladys T. (Turner) Williams; student Calif. State U., Hayward, 1967, 69-72, Golden Gate U., 1979, 86-87; cert. Samuel Merritt Hosp. Sch. Med. Record Adminstrs., 1959; student Cen. State Coll., Ohio, 1950-52; children by previous marriage: Danny Winston, Jeffrey Bruce, Anthony Wayne. Sec. chemistry dept. Cen. State Coll., Wilberforce, Ohio, 1950-52; co-dir. Indian Workcamp, Pala Indian Reservation, Pala, Calif., 1956-58; clk.-typist Camarillo (Calif.) State Hosp., 1956-58; student med. record adminstr. Samuel Merritt Hosp., Oakland, Calif., 1958-59, asst. med. record adminstr., 1962-63, asst. chief med. record adminstr., 1965, chief med. record adminstr., 1965-72; med. record adminstr. Albany (Calif.) Hosp., 1964-65; asst. med. record adminstr. Children's Hosp., San Francisco, 1960; co-dir. interns in community svc. Am. Friends Svc. Com., San Francisco, 1960-61; med. record adminstr. Pacific Hosp., Oakland, Calif., 1963-64; med. record cons. Tahoe Forest Hosp., Truckee, Calif., 1969-73; chief med. record adminstr. Highland Gen. Hosp., Oakland, 1972-74; dir. med. record svcs. U. Calif. San Francisco Hosps. and Clinics, 1975-82; mgr. patient appointments, reception and registration Kaiser-Permanente Med. Ctr., 1982-88; dir. ambulatory adminstrv. svcs., 1988—; adj. prof. mgmt., office automation Golden Gate U., 1978—. Leader Girl Scouts Am. Oakland area council, 1960-62; sunday sch. tchr. Soc. of Friends, Berkeley, Calif., 1961-63, mem. edn. com., 1965-68; mem. policy and adv. bd. Far West Lab. Demonstration Sch., Oakland, 1973—. Recipient Mgmt. Fellowship award U. Calif., San Francisco, 1979-80. Mem. Am. Med. Record Assn., Calif. Med. Record Assn. (editorial bd. 1976-77, pres. 1974-75), East Bay Med. Record Assn. (chmn. edn. com. 1971-72, pres. 1969-70), Assn. Systems Mgmt., Am. Mgmt. Assn., San Francisco Med. Records Assn. (pres.-elect 1982-83, pres. 1983-84). Author: Health Record Documentation: A Look at Cost, 1981; Inservice Training as a Tool in Managing the Changing Environment in the Medical Record Department, 1983; the Budget as a Management Tool, 1983. Issues editor Topics in Health Record Management, Parts I and II, 1983. Home: 545 Pierce St #1105 Albany CA 94706 Office: Kaiser-Permanente Med Ctr 280 W MacArthur Blvd Oakland CA 94611

DANIELS, RICHARD MARTIN, marketing communications company executive; b. Delano, Calif., Feb. 24, 1942; s. Edward Martin and Philida Rose (Peterson) D.; m. Kathryn Ellen Knight, Feb. 28, 1976; children: Robert Martin, Michael Edward. A.A., Foothill Coll., 1965; B.A., San Jose State U., 1967; M.A., U. Mo., 1971. News reporter Imperial Valley Press, El Centro, Calif., summers 1963-66, San Diego (Calif.) Evening Tribune, 1967-68, Columbia Daily Tribune (Mo.), 1969-70; nat. news copy editor Los Angeles Times, 1966-67; staff writer San Diego Union, 1971-74, real estate editor, 1974-77; v.p. pub. relations Hubbert Advt. & Pub. Relations, Costa Mesa, Calif., 1977-78; ptnr. Berkman & Daniels Mktg. Communications, San Diego, 1979—; lectr. various bus. groups and colls. Chmn. bd. dirs. March of Dimes San Diego County, mem. Nat. Council Vols. Served with USN, 1959-62. Recipient Excellence award Communicating Arts Group San Diego, 1981. Mem. Pub. Relations Soc. Am., Bldg. Industry Assn. San Diego County, Nat. Assn. Office and Indsl. Parks (b.d dirs. San Diego chpt., chmn. mktg. coun.), Sigma Delta Chi. Republican. Home: 9080 Oviedo St San Diego CA 92129 Office: 1501 5th Ave San Diego CA 92101

DANIELSON, GORDON DOUGLAS, dentist; b. Everett, Wash., Nov. 11, 1942; s. Marvin and Elanor (Weers) D.; m. Jamie Lynn Waters, Jan. 9, 1977. BS with honors, U. Oreg., 1968; postgrad., MIT, 1968-69; MA in Molecular Biology, U. Calif., 1974, BS in Med. Sci., DDS, 1975. DDS. Pvt. practice Larkspur, Calif., 1975—; exec. v.p. Atmospheric Rsch. Tech., Sacramento, Calif., 1984-85; cons. Freeport Fin. Svcs., Denver, 1985-87; pres. Lynmar Enterprises Inc., Rno, 1987—; bd. dirs. Freeport Venture Fund. MIT fellow, 1968-69; U. Calif., Berkeley fellow, 1969-71; U. Calif., San Francisco fellow, 1973-75, pres. fellow, 1973-75. Mem. U. Calif. Dental Alumni Assn., U. Oreg. Alumni Assn., Marin County Dental Soc. (chmn. emergency care 1975-81), St. Francis Yacht Club (mem. com. 1973—), Aircraft Owners and Pilots Assn., Assoc. Pilots Bay Area, Marin Rowing Club, Omicron Kappa Upsilon. Democrat. Office: 5 Bon Air Rd #114 Larkspur CA 94939

DANIELSON, JAMES CLAYTON, dentist; b. Seattle, Mar. 21, 1942; s. Leroy Clayton and Helen Ion (Anderson) D.; m. Cheryl Ann Casterson, Aug. 25, 1973; children: James, Sean, Kendaline, Tim, Chad, Ian, Kira. Student, U. Calif., 1960-63; DDS, Coll. Physicians and Surgeons, San Francisco, 1967; cert., Cranio-Facial Pain Ctr., Washington, 1987. Cert. gnathology, FACE. Pvt. practice Livermore, Calif., 1967—. Lt. USNR, 1966-72. Mem. Am. Dental Assn., Am. Equilibration Soc., Acad. Gen. Dentistry, Lions, Tau Kappa Omega. Democrat. Office: 1221 E Stanley Blvd Livermore CA 94550

DANIHER, JOHN M., engineer; b. LaJunta, Colo., Aug. 2, 1926; s. Gerald and Mary Isabelle (Manly) D.; m. Edna Erle Hoshall, Sept. 4, 1948; children: Lyn Mari, Suzanne Laurie, Patricia Gail, Jerome Matthew, Michael Kevin. AB, Western State Coll., Gunnison, Colo., 1948; postgrad. Idaho State U., 1957-74, U. Idaho, 1974-76. High sch. tchr., Grand Junction, Colo., 1948-52; salesman Century Metalcraft, Denver, 1952-53; chem. plant supr. U.S. Chem. Corps., Denver, 1953-56; sr. engr. instrument and controls Phillips Petroleum Co., Idaho Falls, 1956-76; project engr. E G & G Idaho, Idaho Falls, 1976-85, engrng. specialist, 1985—; adv. Eastern Idaho Vocat. Tech. Sch., 1975-80. Cubmaster, Boy Scouts Am., 1970-75, asst. scoutmaster, 1975-80. Recipient Cub Man of Yr., Boy Scouts Am., 1973. Mem. Am. Nuclear Soc. Roman Catholic. Club: K.C. (state dep. 1979-81, Supreme council 1981-84) Home: 250 12th St Idaho Falls ID 83404

DANIS, JAMES FULTON, photographer; b. Inglewood, Calif., June 14, 1953; s. John Baptist and JoyceAnn (Fulton) D. Student, Calif. Western U., 1971, Colo. Alpine Coll., 1972, U. Alaska, 1973, Art Ctr. Coll. Design, Los Angeles, 1974-76. Advt. photographer Benton and Bowles, Los Angeles, 1975-76; advt. dir. Riviera Fin., Redondo Beach, Calif., 1976-78; owner, prin. Marina Pacifica Portraits, Long Beach, Calif., 1978-81, Riviera Family Portraits, Anaheim, Calif., 1979-80; pvt. practice as photographer James F. Danis Black and White Photographs, Redondo Beach, 1981—; bd. dirs. La Empresa de la Mar de Oro, Inc., Redondo Beach. Prin. works include Yesterday's Book Shop, 1975 (Los Angeles Times award 1975), The Marriage, 1983 (Key West Art Ctr. award 1984), Star Trails, 1982, Sand Dunes, 1982. Recipient Best Photographs award City of Beverly Hills, Calif., 1986, City of Tempe, Ariz., 1985, Award of Merit Gasparilla Art Assn., 1985, Hasselblad Nat. Gold award, 1976. Mem. Alliance Photographic Arts, Palos Verdes Art Assn. Home and Office: 220 Ave I Redondo Beach CA 90277

DANKNICK, DAN ALAN, electronics engineer, physics researcher; b. Long Beach, Calif., May 31, 1967; s. Donald and Rosella (Aldducks) D. Student physics, U. Calif., Irvine, 1985—. Software engr. Off Duty mag., Santa Ana, Calif., 1986; retail div. mgr. CHA Electronics, Santa Ana, 1986-87; systems integration engr. Robotics 21, El Toro, Calif., 1987-88; electronics technician Electrodyne Techs., Santa Ana, 1988—; engrng. team leader advanced automation div. Big Corp., Santa Ana, 1988—; cons. Animation Internat., El Toro, High-Tech Recreation, Ont., Can. Mem. IEEE, Am. Electronics Assn., U.S. Naval Inst. Nat. Air & Space Mus. Republican. Office: Electrodyne Techs Box 26228 Santa Ana CA 92799

DANNA, ROBERT, consulting engineer; b. N.Y.C., June 28, 1951; s. Albert Ralph and Anna (Damiano) D.; m. Janice Sarah Agnello, Aug. 31, 1974 (div. July 1984); m. Janis Lee Wind, Dec. 23, 1984; 1 child, Elizabeth Michelle. BA in Physics, CUNY, 1973, MA in Physics, 1975; MS in Engring., U. Cen. Fla., 1979. Registered profl. mech. engr., Md., Calif. Research asst. Research Found., N.Y.C., 1974; lectr. physics dept. Hunter Coll., N.Y.C., 1973-76; dir. physics div. Naval Nuclear Power Sch., Orlando, Fla., 1976-80; project engr. Gen. Physics Corp., Columbia, Md. and San Diego, 1980-82, mgr. engring. analysis, 1982-83, dir. engring. services, 1983-88, chief engr., 1988—. Contbr. articles to profl. jours. Served to lt. comdr. USNR, 1976-87. Mem. ASME (HPS subcom. energy release protection), San Diego C. of C., Sigma Pi Sigma. Republican. Club: Physics (CUNY) (pres. 1974-76). Office: Gen Physics Corp 3990 Old Town Ave San Diego CA 92110

DANNEMAN, EDWARD CARL, bank executive; b. Fairfield, Calif., Jan. 1, 1959; s. Robert E. and Joye M. (MacDowell) D.; m. Patricia A. Gutierrez, Sept. 17, 1983; 1 child, Steven Earl. Student, Lewis and Clark Coll., 1977-79, U. Oreg., 1979-82; BS, SUNY, Albany, 1983. Office mgr. Beneficial Fin. Co., Olympia, Wash., 1982-86; 2d v.p. Capital Savs. Bank, Olympia, 1986-87; adminstrv. officer, loan trainer Gt. Am. First Bank, Federal Way, Wash., 1987—; underwriter Gt. Am. Ins. Co., San Diego, 1986—. Home: 33217 33d Ave SW Federal Way WA 98023 Office: Great Am Bank 31620 23d Ave S Federal Way WA 98063-9711

DANNEMEYER, WILLIAM EDWIN, congressman; b. South Gate, Calif., Sept. 22, 1929; s. Henry William and Charlotte Ernestine (Knapp) D.; m. Evelyn Hoemann, Aug. 27, 1955; children—Bruce, Kim, Susan. B.A., Valparaiso U., 1950; J.D., U. Calif., 1952. Bar: Calif. bar, U.S. Supreme Ct. bar. Individual practice law Fullerton, Calif., 1957-79; asst. city atty. City of Fullerton, 1959-62; mem. Calif. Assembly, 1963-66, 77-78; judge pro tem Mcpl. Ct., 1966-76, Superior Ct., 1966-76; mem. 96th-101st Congresses from 39th Calif. Dist. Author: Shadow on the Land: Homosexuality in America, 1989. Bd. dirs. Orange County Luth. High Sch., 1972-78; bd. dirs. Luth. Ch.-Mo. Synod, So. Calif. Dist.; spl. gifts chmn. Capital Fund drive Boy Scouts Am. Served with U.S. Army, 1950-52. Mem. Orange County Bar Assn. (dir.), Orange County Criminal Justice Council. Republican. Office: 2351 Rayburn Washington DC 20515

DANOFF, I. MICHAEL, museum director, writer, educator; b. Chgo., Oct. 22, 1940; s. Maurice and Matilda (Price) D.; m. Frances Evelyn Colker, May 31, 1964; children: Sharon, Brian. B.A., U. Mich., 1962; M.A., U. N.C., 1964; Ph.D., Syracuse U., 1970. Asst. prof. Dickinson Coll., Carlisle, Pa., 1970-73; curator U. Tex., Austin, 1973-74; chief curator Milw. Art Mus., 1974-80, assoc. dir., 1977-80; dir. Akron Art Mus., Ohio, 1980-84, Mus. Contemporary Art, Chgo., 1984-88, San Jose Mus. Art, 1988—; acquisitions dir. HHK Found., Milw., 1977-82; panelist Nat. Endowment for Arts, Washington, Wis. Arts Bd., Madison, Ohio Mus. Assn., Columbus, 1980. Curator: art exhibitions Jeff Koons, 1988, Robert Mangold, 1984, Robert Longo, 1984, Cindy Sherman, 1983, Emergence and Progression, 1979; co-organizer: art exhbn. Image in American Painting and Sculpture, 1981, Gerhard Richter, 1988; art juror: Milw. Conv. Ctr., 1979, Akron State Office Bldg., 1983. Active Milw. Forum, 1976-80. Syracuse U. fellow, 1968-70; NEA Mus. Prof. fellow, 1973. Mem. Intermus. Conservation (trustee 1982-84), Assn. Art Mus. Dirs., Coll. Art Assn., Am. Assn. Mus. Club: Arts of Chgo.

DANTZLER, KELLEY DIANE, nurse; b. San Diego, Nov. 1, 1959; d. Wilbert Dantzler and Phyllis Eloise Estridge. BA in Biology, Whittier Coll., 1981; diploma, Los Angeles County Med. Ctr. Sch. Nursing, 1984. RN. Nurse Los Angeles/U. So. Calif. Med. Ctr., 1986—. Democrat. Mem. AME. Home: 1928 N Marianna Ave #216 Los Angeles CA 90032 Office: Los Angeles County U So Calif Med Ctr 1200 N State St Los Angeles CA 90033

DANUPATAMPA, EKACHAI, electrical engineer; b. Bangkok, Oct. 4, 1942; s. Yok-Hoo and Uy-Ty (Ung) Dan; m. Voranart Tanehsakdi, May 26, 1973; 1 child, Irv. BEE with distinction, Feati U., Manila, 1968; MEE, Calif. State U., Long Beach, 1974; DEE, U. So. Calif., 1979. Project elec. engr. Carnation Co., L.A., 1974-78; elec. engr. Dept. Navy, Port Hueneme, Calif., 1978-79; project elec. engr. Rodriguez and Assocs., L.A., 1979-80; sr. instrument engr. C.F. Braun & Co., Alhambra, Calif., 1980-85; sr. facilities design specialist Rockwell Internat., El Segundo, Calif., 1985—; cons. Meza Engring., Inc., South Gate, Calif., 1985—. Vol. various charitable orgns., polit. orgns. Mem. IEEE, Instrument Soc. Am. Democrat. Buddhist. Home: 1136 Vera Cruz St Montebello CA 90640 Office: Rockwell Internat 100 N Sepulveda Blvd El Segundo CA 90245

DANZIGER, JERRY, broadcasting executive; b. N.Y.C., Jan. 23, 1924; s. Harry and Lillie (Lacher) D.; m. Zelda Bloom, Dec. 26, 1948; children: Sydney, Alan, Lee. Grad. high sch. With Sta. WTTV, Bloomington, Ind., 1950-53; ops. mgr. Sta. WTTV, Indpls., 1953-57; program mgr. Sta. WTSK-TV, Knoxville, Tenn., 1953; gen. mgr. Sta. KOB-TV, Albuquerque, 1957-88, v.p., 1983-88, 1988—; mem. Gov. N.Mex. Commn. for Film Entertainment, 1970-71. Bd. dirs. KIPC All Indian Pueblo Coun., 1975—, Albuquerque Little Theatre, Albuquerque Pub. Broadcast, Albuquerque Jewish Welfare Fund, v.p. for TV AP Broadcasting, 1980—, Goodwill Industries N.Mex., 1980. With USAAF, 1942-45. Recipient Compadre award Am. Women in Radio and TV, 1978, 80. Mem. N.Mex. Broadcasters Assn. (pres. 1972-73, Broadcaster of Yr. award, 1976, 78), Press Club, Advt. Club, Albuquerque Country Club. Office: Sta KOB-TV Box 1351 Albuquerque NM 87103

DARBY, JAY RODNEY, business and numismatic investment consultant; b. Valley City, N.D., Mar. 13, 1953; s. William Vincent and LaDonna Maurine (Nielson) D.; m. Mae Rose Francis Meyer, July 12, 1975; children: Kelly Katrina, Heather Christina, Ryan Christopher. Vice pres. SPG Cos., Inc., St. Cloud, Minn., 1979-80, pres., chief operating officer, 1980-81, chief exec. officer, 1981-83; pres. Jay R. Darby, Inc., St. Cloud, 1983-85; pres., chief exec. officer Jay R. Darby, Inc., Flagstaff, Ariz., 1985—; pres. AzTec, Ltd., Flagstaff, 1987—. Author: Coin Dealer Rating Guide, 1982-88; contbr. articles to profl. publs. Past treas Minn. Senate Dist. 17, St. Cloud; candidate for St. Cloud City Coun., 1983, 85. Mem. Am. Numismatic Assn., Numismatic Guaranty Corp. Am. (assoc.), Am. Soc. Bus. Cons. (v.p. 1977-79), Flagstaff C. of C. Democrat. Roman Catholic. Office: PO Box 3777 Flagstaff AZ 86003

DARBY, JEAN KEGLEY, author; b. Pomona, Calif., July 18, 1921; d. Ruth Tremaine Kegley; m. Raymond Darby, May 29, 1941; children: Diane Braden. BE, Calif. State U., Chico, 1950; PhD, City U. Los Angeles, 1976. Author: (books) What Is It? Series, 1952, Dinosaur Comes To Town, 1963, Animal Adventure Series, 1963, Time Machine Series, 1965, That's Me In Here, 1988; (biographies) Anwar el Sadat, 1989, Martin Luther King, 1989, Dwight D. Eisenhower, 1989, Douglas McArthur, 1989. Mem. Soc. Childrens Book Writers, Writers Forum (pres. 1983-85), No. Calif. Soc. Children's Book Writers, Univ. Women. Republican. Home: 363 Pearl St Redding CA 96003

DARBY, WESLEY ANDREW, clergyman, educator; b. Glendale, Ariz., Sept. 19, 1928; s. Albert Leslie and Beulah E. (Lamb) D.; student Bible Inst. L.A., 1946, No. Ariz. U., 1946-47, Rockmont Coll., Denver, 1948-50, Ariz. State U., 1965, St. Anne's Coll., Oxford (Eng.) U., 1978; m. Donna Maye Bice, May 29, 1947; children: Carolyn Darby Eymann, Lorna Dale, Elizabeth Darby Bass, Andrea Darby Perdue. Ordained minister Baptist Ch., 1950; pastor Sunnyside Bapt. Ch., Flagstaff, Ariz., 1947-48, First Bapt. Ch. of Clifton, Ariz., 1950-55, West High Bapt. Ch., Phoenix, 1955—; dep. assessor Greenlee County, 1951-55; instr. English lit. and pastoral subjects Southwestern Conservative Bapt. Bible Coll., Phoenix, 1961-87. Chmn. bd. Conservative Bapt. Found. Ariz., 1974-83, Gospel Wings, 1960-88; v.p. Ariz. Bapt. Conf., 1976-83; pres. Ariz. Alcohol-Narcotic Edn. Assn., 1968—. Recipient God, Family and Country award Freeman Inst., 1981. Mem. Evang. Philos. Soc., Greater Phoenix Assn. Evangelicals (pres. 1960-63), Ariz. Breakfast Club, (chaplain 1969—). Contbr. articles to profl. jours. Republican. Home: 5628 N 11th Dr Phoenix AZ 85013 Office: 3301 N 19th Ave Phoenix AZ 85015

DARDA, LARRY ALAN, electrical engineer; b. Chgo., May 28, 1941; s. Frank E. and Vilma (Guerrieri) D. BSEE, Ill. Inst. Tech., 1963; MSEE, Air Force Inst. Tech., 1964; MS in Polit. Sci., Auburn U., 1977. Commd. 2d lt. U.S. Air Force, 1963, advanced through grades to lt. col., 1980; dep. chief survivability dept. Space Div., L.A., 1975-80, chief command and control div., 1980-83; ret. 1983; sr. project engr. Hughes Aircraft Co., El Segundo, Calif., 1983-84, chief scientist, assoc. lab. mgr., 1984--. Decorated Meritorious Svc. medal with oak leaf cluster. Republican. Presbyterian. Office: Hughes Aircraft Co PO Box 92919 S4 X301 Los Angeles CA 90009

DARJANY, JOHN CHARLES, electrical engineer; b. San Diego, June 22, 1948; s. Whitney John and Marie Rose (Nichols) D.; m. Barbara Ann Essells, Oct. 18, 1975; children: Christopher, David. BSEE, Calif. Poly U., 1972; MS in Info. Computer Sci., U. Calif., 1982; M in Trimpotology, Bourns U., 1984. Ptnr. Amsec Co., Long Beach, Calif., 1972-74; corp. engr. Amsec div. R.D. Products, Inc., Long Beach, 1974-83; v.p. engring. Amsec div. Griffin Tech., Inc., Rancho Dominguez, Calif., 1983—. Inventor magnetic info. card, self-clocking encoder. Leader Awana Youth Assn., Long Beach Christian Service Brigade, 1982-86. Mem. IEEE. Republican. Office: Griffin Tech Inc 17621 Susana Rd Rancho Dominguez CA 90221

DARKEY, KERMIT LOUIS, association executive, lawyer; b. Berea, Ohio, Oct. 11, 1930; s. Louise Anna (Watts) D.; m. Barbara Jean Rufer, Aug. 17, 1957; children: Kathryn, Susan, Scott. AB, Ohio Wesleyan U., 1952; JD, U. Colo., 1957. Bar: Colo. 1957. Mem. labor rels. staff Mountain States Employers Coun., Denver, 1957-64, dir. labor rels., 1964-70, v.p., 1970-80, pres., 1980—; bd. dirs. United Bank Denver, Archway Cookies, Inc., Battle Creek, Mich. Chmn., Winter Park (Colo.) Recreation Assn., 1978—, St. Joseph Hosp., Denver, 1984-86. Capt. USAF, 1952-54. Mem. Colo. Bar Assn., Denver Bar Assn., Denver Met. Exec. Club (pres. 1980), Univ. Club Denver. Office: Mountain States Employers PO Box 539 Denver CO 80201

DARLING, ROBERT BRUCE, electrical engineering educator; b. Johnson City, Tenn., Mar. 15, 1958; s. Robert William and Jean Mary (Roeder) D. BSEE, Ga. Inst. Tech., 1980, MSEE, 1982, PhD, 1985. Design engr. Tex. Instruments Inc., Johnson City, Tenn., summer 1980; asst. prof. elec. engring. U. Wash., Seattle, 1985--. Named Du Pont Corp. fellow, 1981, IBM predoctoral fellow, 1984-85. Mem. IEEE, AAAS, Am. Phys. Soc., Am. Vacuum Soc., Optical Soc. Am., Sigma Xi (assoc.), Phi Kappa Phi, Tau Beta Pi, Eta Kappa Nu. Office: U Wash Dept Elec Engring FT-10 Seattle WA 98195

DARLING, SCOTT EDWARD, lawyer; b. Los Angeles, Dec. 31, 1949; s. Dick R. and Marjorie Helen (Otto) D.; m. Cynthia Diane Harrah, June 1970 (div.); 1 child, Smokie; m. Deborah Lee Cochran, Aug. 22, 1981; children: Ryan, Jacob. BA, U. Redlands, 1972; JD, U.S.C., 1975. Bar: Calif. 1976, U.S. Dist. Ct. (cen. dist.) Calif. 1976. Assoc. atty. Elver, Falsetti, Boone & Crafts, Riverside, 1976-78; ptnr. Falsetti, Crafts, Pritchard & Darling, Riverside, 1978-84; sr. ptnr. Darling, Miller & King, Riverside, 1984—; grant reviewer HHS, Washington, 1982—; judge pro tem Riverside County Mcpl. Ct., 1980, Riverside County Superior Ct., 1987-88; bd. dirs. Tel Law Nat. Legal Pub. Info. System, Riverside, 1978-80. Author, editor: Small Law Office Computer Legal System, 1984. Bd. dirs. Youth Adv. Com. to Selective Service, 1968-70, Am. Heart Assn. Riverside County, 1978-82, Survival Ministries, 1986—; atty. panel Calif. Assn. Realtors, Los Angeles, 1980—; pres. Calif. Young Reps., 1978-80; mem. GI Forum, Riverside, 1970—; presdl. del. Nat. Rep. Party, 1980-84; asst. treas. Calif. Rep. Party, 1981-83; Rep. Congl. candidate, Riverside, 1982; treas. Riverside Sickle Cell Found., 1980-82, recipient Eddie D. Smith award; pres. Calif. Rep. Youth Caucus, 1980-82; v.p. Riverside County Red Cross, 1982-84; mem. Citizen's Univ. Com., Riverside, 1978-84, World Affairs Council, 1978-82, Urban League, Riverside, 1980-82. Calif. Scholarship Fedn. (life). Named one of Outstanding Young Men in Am., U.S. Jaycees, 1979-86. Mem. ABA, Riverside County Bar Assn., Speaker's Bur. Riverside County Bar Assn., Riverside Jaycees, Riverside C. of C. Lodge: Native Sons of Golden West. Office: Darling Miller & King 7121 Magnolia Ave Riverside CA 92504

DARNALL, ROBERTA MORROW, university official; b. Kemmerer, Wyo., May 18, 1949; d. C. Dale and Eugenia Stayner (Christmas) Morrow; B.S., U. Wyo., Laramie, 1972; m. Leslie A. Darnall, Sept. 3, 1977; children: Kimberly Gene, Leslie Nicole. Tariff sec., ins. adminstr. Wyo. Trucking Assn., Casper, 1973-75; asst. clerical supr. Wyo. Legislature, Cheyenne, 1972-77; congl. campaign press aide, 1974; pub. relations dir. in Casper, Wyo. Republican Central Com., 1976-77; asst. dir. alumni relations U. Wyo., 1977-81, dir. of alumni, 1981—; exec. com. Higher Edn. Assn. Rockies. Mem. Council Advancement and Support Edn. (membership com.), Higher Edn. Assn. Rockies, Am. Soc. Assn. Execs., Laramie C. of C. (pizzazz and acad. instns. com.), PEO (courtesy com., officer), Soroptimist (com. ways and means, publicity chmn. casino night), Sigma Delta Chi. Republican. Episcopalian. Home: 1172 Frontera Dr Laramie WY 82070 Office: Box 3137 University Sta Laramie WY 82071

DARNELL, DANIEL ROE, academic administrator; b. Wyandott, Mich., Dec. 22, 1945; s. Willard Carver and Mavis Geraldine D.; m. Donna Lynn Baker, July 12, 1980; children—Raymond, Scott, Christine, Jeffery. B.A., Okla. Christian Coll., 1967; M.A., Pepperdine U., 1970; postgrad. U. So. Calif.-Los Angeles, 1972-76. Asst. registrar Pepperdine U., Los Angeles, 1967-71, asst. prof., 1972-77, asst. provost, dir., 1972-77; asst. dean Eastern Ill. U., Charleston, 1971-72; dir. instructional service Cerro Coso Community Coll., Ridgecrest, Calif., 1977-79, assoc. dean instruction, 1979-83, acad. dean, 1983—. Chmn. budget adv. com. Sierra Sands Unified Sch. Dist., Ridgecrest, 1983-84; sec. Council on Alcohol Awareness, Ridgecrest, 1979-84; founding mem. Community Youth Ctr. Orgn., Ridgecrest, 1984;

founding bd. dirs. Pepperdine Employee Fed. Credit Union, Los Angeles, 1974; youth coordinator Sunset chpt. Calif. Credit Union Assn., Santa Monica, 1975; active Kern County Rep. Cen. Com.; treas. Rep. League. Mem. Assn. Community Coll. Adminstrs., Nat. Council on Resource Devel., World Future Soc., Nat. Council of Staff, Program and Organizational Devel., Phi Alpha Theta (v.p. Eta Zeta chpt. 1970-71). Home: 700 Randall St Ridgecrest CA 93555 Office: Cerro Coso Community Coll 3000 College Heights Blvd Ridgecrest CA 93555

DARNEY, PHILIP DEMPSEY, obstetrician, gynecologist, educator; b. Granite, Okla., Feb. 27, 1943; s. Walter Preston and Corene (Barton) D.; m. Virginia Grant (div. 1981); children: Blair, Barton; m. Uta Landy, Oct 13, 1984; 1 child, Undine. AB, U. Calif., Berkeley, 1964; MD, U. Calif., San Francisco, 1968; MSc, London Sch. Hygiene, 1972. Diplomate Am. Bd. Preventive Medicine, Am. Bd. Ob-Gyn. Intern USPHS Hosp., San Francisco, 1968-69; resident in ob-gyn Brigham and Women's Hosp., Boston, 1974-77; dep. dir. div. reproductive health Ctrs. Disease Control, Atlantad, 1971-73; asst. prof. ob-gyn Harvard U. Med. Sch., Boston, 1976-78; assoc. prof. ob-gyn U. Oreg. Med. Sch., Portland, 1978-80; prof. ob-gyn U. Calif. Sch. Medicine, San Francisco, 1981--; cons. AID, Washington, 1971-74, Pathfinder Fund, Boston, 1973-83. Author: Ambulatory and Office Gynecologic Surgery, 1987; contbr. over 100 articles on contraception, abortion and sterilization to med. jours., chpts. to books. Bd. dirs. Planned Parenthood Fedn. Am., N.Y.C., 1986--. Lt. comdr. USPHS, 1968-74. Named Outstanding Young Profl. Am. Pub. Health Assn., 1984. Fellow Am. Coll. Obstetricians and Gynecologists, Am. Coll. Preventive Medicine. Democrat. Home: 15 Ashbury Terr San Francisco CA 94117 Office: San Francisco Gen Hosp Dept Ob-Gyn San Francisco CA 94110

DA ROZA, VICTORIA CECILIA, human resource administrator; b. East Orange, N.J., Aug. 30, 1945; d. Victor and Cynthia Helen (Krupa) Hawkins; m. Thomas Howard Kaminski, Aug. 28, 1971 (div. 1977); 1 child, Sarah Hawkins; m. Robert Anthony da Roza, Nov. 25, 1983. BA, U. Mich., 1967; MA, U. Mo., 1968. Contract compliance mgr. City of San Diego, 1972-75; v.p. personnel Bank of Calif., San Francisco, 1975-77; with human resources Lawrence Livermore (Calif.) Nat. Lab., 1978-86; pvt. cons. Victoria Kaminski-da Roza & Assocs., 1986—; lectr. in field; videotape workshop program on mid-career planning used by IEEE. Contbr. numerous articles to profl. jours. Mem. social policy com. City of Livermore, 1982. Mem. Am. Soc. Tng. and Devel., Western Gerontol. Soc. (planning com. Older Worker Track 1983), Gerontol. Soc. Am. Home and Office: 385 Borica Dr Danville CA 94526

DARRAH, JAMES GORE, physicist, financial executive, real estate developer; b. Milford, Mich., Nov. 28, 1928; s. Carl Williard and Marie (Rathburn) D.; m. Maud Gray, June 27, 1953; children Kimberley D., Sandra Gray Capalongan. BS in Metall. Engring., Rensselaer Poly. Inst., 1952, MS in Metall. Engring., 1953; PhD, Lehigh U., 1955. Project engr. Gen. Motors Corp., Warren, Mich., 1956-58; mgr. nuclear research and devel. United Aircraft Corp., East Hartford, Conn., 1958-64; div. mgr. Eimac-Varian, San Carlos, Calif., 1964-65; gen. mgr. Teledyne-Monolith, Mountain View, Calif., 1965-68; pres. Stratamet Corp., Sunnyvale, Calif., 1968-84; also chmn. bd. dirs. Stratamet Corp., Fremont, Calif.; pres. Darrah Capital Corp., Menlo Park, Calif., 1984—; chmn. bd. dirs. Ceramic Products Corp., Fremont, Calif., 1975—, Gold Mind of N.Y., Buffalo, 1985—, Darco Leasing Co., Menlo Park, 1984—. Patentee in field. Served as cpl. U.S. Army, 1946-47. Mem. Sigma Xi, Tau Beta Pi. Republican. Presbyterian. Home and Office: 927 Continental Dr Menlo Park CA 94025

DARVAS, ENDRE PETER, artist; b. Kisvadra, Sz-Szatmar, Hungary, July 18, 1946; came to U.S., in 1957; s. Bela and Maria (Filtczer) Darvas. BFA, U. Tex., 1969. Pres. Studio Arts and Frames, Inc., South Lake Tahoe, Calif., 1974-78; owner Darvas Studio, South Lake Tahoe, 1969—. Artist numerous paintings. Exhibited at San Angelo, Tex., 1963, Taos, N.Mex., 1971, Carmel, Calif., 1975, San Carlos, Mex., 1987. Recipient numerous awards from art exhibits. Mem. Soc. Am. Impressionists, Southwestern Watercolor Soc. Office: Darvas Studio PO Box 711 South Lake Tahoe CA 95705-0711

DASHIELL, DAVID CANNON, artist; b. Tokyo, July 4, 1952; came to U.S., 1955.; s. Samuel Curtis and Dorothy Lou (Cannon) D. BFA, Calif. Inst. the Arts, 1974, MFA, 1976. Artist San Francisco and L.A., 1976—; affiliate artist Headlands Ctr. for the Arts, Sausalito, Calif., 1989; tchr. Calif. Inst. the Arts, Valencia, Calif., 1974-76. Prin. works include Plague Journal, A Lover's Discourse, Invert Oracle. Recipient ProArts Annual award, 1988; Nat. Endowment for the Arts Fleshacker Found. fellow, 1987; Artspace Painting Support grantee, 1988. Studio: care Headlands Ctr for the Arts 400 Duboce Ave #411 Sausalito CA 94965

DASSENKO, PAMELA MARIE, dentist, violinist; b. Oxnard, Calif., Sept. 26, 1955; d. Jack and Mary Ellen (Minier) D.; m. Thomas Lloyd Miller, Sept. 4, 1977; children: Alexandra, Lauren. Student, Walla Walla Coll., 1973-76; DDS, Loma Linda U., 1980. Instr. in restorative dentistry Loma Linda (Calif.) U., 1979-80; gen. practice dentistry Upland, Calif., 1980-81, Hemet, Calif., 1980-81, Rochester, N.Y., 1981-87, San Luis Obispo, Calif., 1987—; cons. Corning Dicor Crowns, Oral B Permite Amalgam, Rochester, 1983-84. Violinist, concertmaster San Luis Obispo County Symphony, 1987—, Mozart Festival, San Luis Obispo, 1988. Mem. ADA, Calif. Dental Soc., Cen. Coast Dental Soc., Cen. Coast Med. Soc. Aux., Women's Network Cen. Coast. Home: 1320 Longview Pismo Beach CA 93499 Office: 1250 Peach St Suite #L San Luis Obispo CA 93401

DASSO, JEROME JOSEPH, real estate educator, consultant; b. Neillsville, Wis., Jan. 12, 1929; s. Henry J. and Frances (Schweickert) D.; m. Patricia Mary Conger, June 13, 1959 (div. 1978); children: James Daniel, Mary Cecilia, Nancy Ann, Wendy Jo. BS, Purdue U., 1951; MBA, U. Mich., 1952; MS, U. Wis., 1960, PhD, 1964. Ptnr. Dasso Constrn. Co., Dubuque, Iowa, 1956-58; planner Franklin County, Ohio, Columbus, 1960-61; asst. prof. U. Ill., Urbana, 1964-66; vis. chairholder U. Hawaii, Honolulu, 1982-83; mem. faculty U. Oreg., Eugene, 1966—, H.T. Miner chair in real estate, 1978—; vis. prof. U. Wis., Madison, 1984; Vivien Stewart vis. fellow Cambridge U., spring, 1987; cons. Internat. Assn. Assessing Officers, Chgo., 1972-74; ednl. cons. Hawaii Real Estate Commn., Honolulu, 1982-83. Author: S. Kahn, R. Nesslinger et. al Principle of Right of Way Acquisition, 1972; (with G. Kuhn) Real Estate Finance, 1983; (with A.A. Ring) Real Estate Principles and Practices, 8th edit., 1977, 9th edit., 1981, 10th edit., 1985, 11th edit., 1989; Computerized Assessment Administration, 1973; contbr. numerous articles to various publs. With USN, 1952-55. Fellow Am. Inst. Corp. Asset Mgmt (bd. govs. 1988-91), Homer Hoyt Inst. Adv. Studies Real Estate & Urban Land Econs.; mem. Real Estate Educators Am. (Outstanding Svc. award 1981, pres. 1980-81), Am. Real Estate and Urban Econs. Assn. (bd. dir. 1974-77, 80-83), Real Estate Ctr. Dirs. Chairholders Assn. (pres. 1987-88), Am. Real Estate Soc. (bd. dirs. 1985-86, v.p. 1989, pres. elect 1990), Am. Fin. Assn. (life mem.), Nat. Assn. Realtors (edn. com. 1970-76), Oregon Track-Masters Club, Elks, KC. Roman Catholic. Avocations: tennis, golf, racquetball, backpacking, photography. Office: U of Oreg Grad Sch Mgmt Eugene OR 97403

DATSOPOULOS, JOHN KOSTAS, business executive, consultant; b. Missoula, Mont., Feb. 28, 1939; s. Constantine and Kiki (Papainou) D. BA, U. Mont., 1962; MA, Thunderbird Sch. Internat. Mgmt., 1965. V.p. Caribbean div. Firestone Tire and Rubber Co., San Juan, P.R., 1975-76; v.p. gen. mgmt. Black & Decker Philippines, Manila, 1976-79; pres., owner Am. Diversified Products, Missoula, 1980—; bd. dirs. Athens Corp., Missoula. Mem. pub. affairs tank force Missoula Econ. Devel. Corp., 1987-88. Served to sgt. USANG, 1963-64. Recipient Plaque of Appreciation Rotary, 1977. Republican. Greek Orthodox. Club: Kapwa Ko (pres. 1977-78). Lodge: Kiwanis (pres. Manila chpt. 1978).

DATTA, ROBIN NATH, mining engineer, consultant; b. Ranaghat, India, Feb. 7, 1944; came to U.S., 1973; s. Nripendra Nath and Nilima Rani (Bose) Dutta; m. Debarati Ghosh, Nov. 24, 1969; children: Ruchira, Saheli. BS, U. Calcutta, India, 1964; PhD, U. Sheffield, Eng., 1969. Instr. Benares Hindu U., Varanasi, India, 1969-70; rock mechanics engr. Nchanga Consol. Copper Mines Ltd., Kitwe, Zambia, 1971-75; mining engr. Cleveland Cliffs Iron Co., Rifle, Colo., 1975; chief mining engr. Dravo Engrs., Inc., Denver, 1975-85; sr. project engr. Woodward Clyde Cons., Irvine, Calif., 1986-88; branch mgr. RSA Assocs., Inc., Van Nuys, Calif., 1988—. Sibeley scholar U. Calcutta, 1964. Mem. Soc. Mining Engrs. of the Am. Inst. Mining and Metallurgy. Hindu. Office: RSA Assocs Inc 15414 Cabrito Rd Ste A Van Nuys CA 91406

DAUB, GERALD JACOB, geological consulting executive; b. Bryn Mawr, Pa., Mar. 21, 1953; s. Lloyd Harrison Jr. and Ramona Isabell (Goodrich) D.; m. Joanna Marie Varieur, June 23, 1979; children: Morgan B., Graham H. BS in Geology, Colo. State U., 1975; MS in Geology, U. R.I., 1979. Cert. profl. geologist, N.C. Geol. asst. Sun Oil Co., Houghton Lake, Mich., 1974; staff geologist Atlantic Richfield Co., Paonia, Colo., 1975-76; project geologist Plateau Resources Ltd., Grand Junction, Colo., 1979-80; exec. v.p. Amedco, Grand Junction, 1980-82; staff geologist Mult Mineral Corp., Grand Junction, 1980-82; pres. Daub & Assocs. Cons. Geologists, Grand Junction, 1982—. Contbr. articles to publs. Mem. Group Study Exchange to Brazil, Rotary Internat., 1988, 89. Mem. AIME, Am. Assn. Petroleum Geologists (cert. div. profl. affairs), Grand Junction Geol. Soc. (v.p. 1987, pres. 1988), Soc. Econ. Paleontologists and Mineralogists, Rocky Mountain Assn. Geologists. Republican. Office: Daub & Assocs Cons 1980 S Broadway Grand Junction CO 81503-9593

DAUBEN, WILLIAM GARFIELD, chemist, educator; b. Columbus, Ohio, Nov. 6, 1919; s. Hyp J. and Leilah (Stump) D.; m. Carol Hyatt, Aug. 8, 1947; children: Barbara, Ann. A.B., Ohio State U., 1941; A.M., Harvard U., 1942; Ph.D., 1944; Ph.D. hon. degree, U. Bordeaux, France, 1980. Edward Austin fellow Harvard U., 1941-42, teaching fellow, 1942-43, research asst., 1943-45; instr. U. Calif. at Berkeley, 1945-47, asst. prof. chemistry, 1947-52, assoc. prof., 1952-57, prof., 1957—; lectr. Am.-Swiss Found., 1962; pres. Organic Reactions, Inc., 1967-84; mem. med. chem. study sect. USPHS, 1959-64; mem. chemistry panel NSF, 1964-67; mem. Am.-Sino Sci. Cooperation Com., 1973-76; mem. assembly math. and phys. scis. NRC, 1977-80. Mem. bd. editors: Jour. of Organic Chemistry, 1957-62; bd. editors: Organic Syntheses, 1959-67; bd. dirs., 1971—; editor-in-chief: Organic Reactions, 1967-83, bd. dirs. 1967—; contbr. articles profl. jours. Recipient award Calif. sect. Am. Chem. Soc., 1959; Guggenheim fellow, 1951, 66; sr. fellow NSF, 1957-58; Alexander von Humboldt Found. Fellow, 1980. Fellow Royal Soc. Chemistry, Swiss Chem. Soc.; mem. Am. Chem. Soc. (chmn. div. organic chemistry 1962-63, councilor organic div. 1964-70, mem. council publ. com. 1965-70, mem. adv. com. Petroleum Research Fund 1974-77, Ernest Guenther award 1973), Nat. Acad. Scis. (chmn. chemistry sect. 1977-80), Am. Acad. Arts and Scis., Pharm. Soc. Japan (hon.), Phi Beta Kappa, Sigma Xi, Phi Lambda Upsilon, Phi Eta Sigma, Sigma Chi. Club: Bohemian. Home: 20 Eagle Hill Berkeley CA 94707

DAUGHERTY, JOHN WAYNE, corporation executive; b. Dimmitt, Tex., Oct. 1, 1946; s. John Wayland and Geneva (Cooper) d.; M. Karen A. Robb, June 17, 1968 (div. Nov. 1988); children: John Earl, Laurie, Neal; m. Susan L. Holland, Apr. 14, 1989. BBED, Eastern N.Mex. U., 1968; MPA, N.Mex. State U., 1981. Tchr. Albuquerque West Mesa High Sch., 1968-72; controller N.Mex. Family Planning Coun., Albuquerque, 1972-75; exec. dir. Hospitality House Ctr., Las Cruces, N.Mex., 1981, So. Rio Grande Mental Health Found., Las Cruces, 1981; adminstr. Southwest Mental Health Ctr., Las Cruces, 1975-80; v.p. A Lee Straughan & Assocs., Albuquerque, 1981—; instr. Dale Carnegie courses, 1987. Bd. mem. Las Cruces Girls & Boys Club, Las Cruces, 1975-80, pres., 1975-80; bd. mem. Albuquerque Boys Club, 1981-82; mem. Evangelism Com., 1988, ch. stewardship com., 1989. Mem. Dona Ana Daylight Lodge. Republican. Presbyterian. Home: 909 Matador SE Albuquerque NM 87123

DAUN, LOWELL GLENN, dentist, dental insurance company executive; b. Redlands, Calif., Jan. 9, 1947; s. Glenn Shields and Audrey Lucile (Harme) D.; m. Dorothy Dooley, Feb. 1, 1969; children: Rebecca, Stacey. BA, U. Puget Sound, 1969; MA, Calif. Inst. Tech., 1970; DDS, U. Pacific, 1974. Sec. council hosp. and instnl. svcs. ADA, Chgo., 1976-79, editorial cons., 1981—; asst. dir. profl. svcs. Delta Dental Plan Calif., San Francisco, 1979-82, dir. govt. program nat. affairs, 1980-85, dir. mktg. adminstrn., 1985-86; exec. dir., chief exec. officer active duty dependents dental plan Delta Dental Plan Calif., Sacramento, Farmington Hills, Mich., Providence, 1986—; nat. dental dir. Pvt. Med. Care, Los Alimitos, CAlif., 1985-88. Contbr. articles to profl. jours. Contbr. articles to profl. jours. Mem. ADA, Am. Assn. Dental Schs., Am. Assn. Hosp. Dentists, Am. Soc. for Geriatric Dentistry, AAAS, U. Puget Sound Alumni Club, Tau Kappa Omega,. Republican. Methodist. Home: 329 Persimmon Rd Walnut Creek CA 94138 Office: Delta Dental Plan 7667 Folsom Blvd Sacramento CA 95828

DAVAULT, ELAINE JOYCE, artist; b. Hancock County, Ind., Feb. 17, 1955; d. Terry M. and Eleanor (Vining) D. Student, Indiana U., South Bend, 1975-76, So. Calif. Art Inst., Laguna Beach, 1981-85. Sales promotion James Heddons Sons, Niles, Mich., 1975-78; supr., copywriter prodn. mgr. Gick Pub. Co., Irvine, Calif., 1984-85; mem. exhibitor, Luguna Beach Festival of the Arts/Pageant of the Masters, 1985--, mem., Laguna Mus. of Art, Laguna Beach, 1982—. Illustrator Editorial Illustration, Lotus-Modern Jazz Communique mag. Exhibitor, Festival of the arts/Pageant of the Masters, Laguna Beach, 1985. Palette award City of Laguna Beach 1988; Logo award City of Milford. Methodist. Home and Office: 326 N Coast Hwy Apt H Laguna Beach CA 92651

DAVENPORT, ALFRED LARUE, JR., manufacturing company executive; b. Upland, Calif., May 6, 1921; s. Alfred Larue and Nettie (Blocker) D.; m. Darrow Ormsbee Beazlie, May 16, 1950 (div. 1953); m. Jean Ann Given, June 21, 1957; children: Lawrence, Terisa, Lisa, Nancy. Student, Chaffey Jr. Coll., Ontario, Calif., 1940; BE in Indsl. Engring., U. So. Calif., 1943. Weight engring. Lockheed Aircraft, Burbank, Calif., 1940-41; ptnr. Pacific Traders, L.A., 1946-48; founder, pres. Pactra Industries, Inc., L.A., 1947-79; owner Davenport Internat., Ltd., Van Nuys, Calif., 1979—; pres., founder Trans Container, Inc., Upland, Calif., 1970-79; pres., owner Pactra Hobby, Inc., Van Nuys, 1983—, Davenport Export-Import, Inc., Encino, Calif., 1982—; cons. Plasti-Kote, Inc., Medina, Ohio, 1985—; pres. Pactra Coatings Inc., Hobby Div., Upland, 1985—; dir. R.C. Dudek, Inc., Westlake, Calif., 1978—, Aerosol Info. Assn., L.A., 1974-79. Lt. USN, 1943-46. Recipient Blue Key, U. So. Calif., L.A., 1942. Mem. So. Calif. Hobby Industry Assn. (sec. 1959-62), Hobby Industry Assn. Am. (dir. 1961-64), Young Pres. Orgn. (L.A. chpt.), World Bus. Coun., Woodland Hills Country Club (treas. 1981-83), Sigma Phi Epsilon (v.p. 1954-81, alumni bd. dirs. 1955-75, Disting. Bro. award 1979, Alumni of Yr. award 1975). Republican. Presbyterian. Home: 4650 Hayvenhurst Ave Encino CA 91436 Office: Pactra Coatings Inc 420 S 11th Ave PO Box 280 Upland CA 91786

DAVENPORT, DAVID, university president, lawyer; b. Sheboygan, Wis., Oct. 24, 1950; s. E. Guy and Beverly J. (Snoddy) D.; m. Sally Nelson, Aug. 13, 1977; children—Katherine, Charles, Scott. B.A., Stanford U., 1972; J.D., U. Kans., Lawrence, 1977. Bar: Calif., 1977, U.S. Dist. Ct. (so. dist.) Calif.; ordained to ministry Ch. of Christ. Assoc. Gray, Cary, Ames & Frye, San Diego, 1977-78; minister Ch. of Christ, San Diego, 1979; law prof. Pepperdine U., Malibu, Calif., 1980—, gen. counsel, 1981-83, exec. v.p., 1983-85, pres., 1985—. Contbr. articles to profl. jours.; contbr. to Fed. Antitrust Law, 1985. Mem. Adminstrv. Conf. of U.S., Washington, 1984-86. Mem. ABA, Calif. Bar Assn., Am. Coun. on Edn., Nat. Assn. Colls. and Univ. Attys., Mchts. and Mfrs. Assn. Calif. (bd. dirs. 1985—), Am. Assn. Pres. of Ind. Colls. and Univs. (bd. dirs. 1985—, 1st v.p.), Young Pres. Orgn., L.A. Area C. of C. (bd. dirs.), Order of Coif. Republican. Home: 24255 Pacific Coast Hwy Malibu CA 90265 Office: Pepperdine U Office of Pres 4255 Pacific Coast Hwy Malibu CA 90265

DAVENPORT, JANET LEE, real estate saleswomen, small business owner; b. Napa, Calif., Dec. 10, 1938; d. George Perry and Stella Dolores (Ramalho) Gomez; m. Bingo George Wesner, Aug. 4, 1957 (July 1978); children: Bing George, Diane Estelle; m. Marvin Eugene Davenport, Jan. 13, 1979. Student, U. Calif., Davis, 1956-57, U. Nev., 1975-79. Co-owner, operator Bar JB Ranch, Benicia, Calif., 1960-71, Lovelock, Nev., 1971-78; owner, mgr. Wesner Bookkeeping Svc., Lovelock, 1973-78; chief tribal judge Ct. Indian Offenses, Lovelock, 1975-79; justice of peace, coroner County of Pershing, Lovelock, 1975-79; paralegal, legal sec. Samuel S. Wardle, Carson City, Nev., 1979; dep. ct. adminstr. Reno Mcpl. Ct., Reno, 1979-81; co-owner horse farm Reno, 1979—, freelance real estate investor, 1979—; real estate saleswoman Merrill Lynch Realtors, Sparks, Nev., 1981-82; realtor, farm and ranch div. mgr. Copple and Assocs., Realtors, Sparks, 1982—; co-owner, operator Lovelock (Nev.) Merc. Co., 1988—; sec. Nev. Judges Assn., 1977-78. Dir. Pershing County Drug and Alcohol Abuse Council, Lovelock, 1976-78. Mem. Reno/Spark Bd. Realtors, State and Nat. Assn. Realtors, Am. Inst. Profl. Bookkeepers, Am. Quarter House Assn., Appaloosa Horse Club Inc., Palomino Horse Breeders Am. Inc., Appaloosa Horse Club. Republican. Roman Catholic. Home: 4805 Sinelio Dr Reno NV 89502 Office: Copple & Assocs Realtors 1302 C St Sparks NV 89431

DAVEY, MILTON EDWARD (PAT DAVEY), aluminum reduction executive, consultant; b. Spokane, Wash., July 15, 1926; s. Milton Alvin and Maude Avis (Phillips) D.; m. Bobbe Lu Lytle, Jan. 14, 1950 (div. Oct. 1963); children: Theodore Edward, Michael Robert, Thomas Arthur; m. Edith May Cosby, Feb. 13, 1965; children: Barbara Dianne, David Howard, Paul Harrison, Daniel Robert. BSME, Wash. State U., 1953. Registered profl. engr., Wash. Chief engr., maintenance and prodn. mgr. Volta Aluminum Co., Tema, Ghana, West Africa, 1966-72; plant mgr. Aluminum Bahrain, Manama, 1972-74; adminstrv. mgr. Kaiser Aluminum and Chem. Corp., Oakland, Calif., 1974-75; internat. mgr. engring. maintenance Kaiser Aluminum and Chem. Corp., Oakland, 1979-82; ops. mgr. Anglesey Aluminium, Holyhead, North Wales, 1975-77; engring and tech. mgr. Mead Works Kaiser Aluminum, Spokane, 1977; plant mgr. Kaiser Aluminum, Ravenswood, W.Va., 1978-79; v.p. and gen. mgr. Energy Products Idaho, Coeur d'Alene, 1984-86; pres. Davey & Assocs., Inc., Colbert, Wash., 1984-87; v.p. and ptnr. Mgmt. and Tech. Resources Internat., Inc., Alamo, Calif., 1986—; cons. 7 Industries, Spokane, 1982, Lavalin, Montreal, Can., 1983. Vol. cons. Internat. Exec. Svc. Corps, Stamford, Conn., 1982—, Jakarta, Indonesia, 1989; profl. liaison staff Citizen Amb. Program People to People, Spokane, 1985. With USN, 1944-46, PTO. Mem. Am. Soc. Mech. Engrs. (chmn. Inland Empire 1960), Holyhead Country Club, Ravenswood Country Club, Masons, Eagles. Republican. Episcopalian. Home: 17515 Little Spokane Dr Colbert WA 99005 Office: Mgmt & Tech Resources Internat 3158 Danville Blvd Alamo CA 94507

DAVID, CHARLES EDWARD, JR., mortgage banker; b. Hammond, La., Mar. 16, 1949; s. Charles Edward and Lorraine (Miller) D.; 1 child, Robert J. Connor Jr. BS, Troy State U., Ala., 1975. V.p. Certified Svcs., Inc., Hammond, 1974-76; dir. dept. transp. & devel. Safety and Info. Systems, La., Baton Rouge, 1976-80; pres. Certified Svcs., Inc., Hammond, 1980-87; v.p. Great Am. Fin. Svcs. Corp., Tacoma, Wash., 1987—; cons. in field; bd. dirs. Certified Svcs., Inc.; advisor various commodity trading accts. Author: Hospital Heliport Development Guide, vols. 1 and 2, 1984, Hammond Airport Master Plan and Development Guide, 1986; co-author: Louisiana Heliport Systems Plan, 1985. With U.S. Army, 1970-74. Mem. C. of C., Ducks Unltd., Stearman Restorers Assn. Republican. Episcopalian. Office: Great Am Fin Svcs Corp 700 Market St Tacoma WA 98402

DAVID, GEORGE CECIL, native Indian artist; b. Port Albernie, B.C., Canada, Aug. 13, 1950; s. Hyacinth Patrick and Winifred (Hamilton) D.; m. Eileen Marie Greene, Oct. 5, 1973; 1 child, Marie Elizabeth. Exhibited in shows at Legacy Ltd., Seattle, SnowGoose Assocs., North Seattle, Indian Trader East, Pittsburg, Wildlife of the World Gallery, Aspen, Colo., Carmel, Calif.; commissions 2 large Totem Poles L.A., Seattle, Suquamich, Malibu Beach, Calif., large Panel Kobe, Japan, Norway; also numerous collections in Alaska, Calif., Ariz. Home and Office: #1 Wyattch Blvd Box 141 Neah Bay WA 98357-0141

DAVID, LEON THOMAS, judge, educator, former army officer; b. San Francisco, Aug. 25, 1901; s. Leon Kline and Ella Nancy (Thomas) D.; A.B., Stanford, 1924, J.D., 1926; M.S. in Pub. Adminstrn., U. So. Calif., 1935, Dr. Pub. Adminstrn., 1957; m. Henrietta Louise Mellin, May 22, 1927; children—Carolyn L. Eskra, Leon Colby. City editor Vallejo (Calif.) Times, 1920-21; free-lance journalist, 1921-26; admitted to Calif. bar, 1926, U.S. Supreme Ct., 1932; pvt. practice law; mem. Malcolm & David, Palo Alto, Calif., 1926-31; dep. and acting city atty. Palo Alto, 1926-31; mem. faculty Sch. Law, U. So. Calif., 1931-34, Sch. Pub. Adminstrn., 1934-41, 1947-67; sr. asst. city atty. Los Angeles, 1934-41, 46-50; spl. counsel Los Angeles Harbor Commn., 1939-41; judge Municipal Ct., Los Angeles Jud. Dist., 1950-53; judge Superior Court, 1953-67, appellate dept., 1958-60, ret., 1967; asso. justice pro tem Calif. Ct. Appeal, 1969-73. Mem. Calif. Gov.'s Adv. Com. Law Enforcement, 1959-67. Chmn. legal aid com. State Bar Calif. intermittently to 1950, chmn. state bar com. history of law, 1975-78; bd. dirs., past pres. Los Angeles Legal Aid Found. Served from 2d lt. to maj. F.A.-O.R.C., 1924-42; from lt. col. to col., AUS, 1942-61; comdt. U.S. Army Sch. for Spl. Services, 1942-43, chief Spl. Services, N. Africa and Mediterranean theaters of operation, 1943-45; col. AUS (ret.), 1961. Decorated Legion of Merit (U.S.), Hon. Officer Order Brit. Empire, Medaille d'Honneur d'Or (France), Medalha do Guerra (Brazil), Comdr. Crown of Italy; recipient Reginald Heber Smith medal for distinguished legal aid service to indigent, 1962. Mem. Los Angeles Bar Assn., Contra Costa County Bar Assn., Am. Legion (past comdr.), Calif. Judges Assn. (life), Stanford, U. Calif., U. So. Calif. Alumni assns., Calif. Hist. Soc., Mt. Diablo Amateur Radio Club, Soc. Mayflower Descendants, Gov. Alameda Cox Colony, 1989, Phi Alpha Delta, Phi Kappa Phi, Pi Sigma Alpha, Blue Key, Order of Coif. Mason (K.T., 32d degree, Shriner), DeMolay Legion of Honor (life). Presbyn. (elder, mem. laws and regulations com., social edn. and action com. Los Angeles Presbytery, 1965-69), World Affairs Council, San Francisco, 1987—. Clubs: Commonwealth, Kiwanis (pres. Palo Alto 1931, Los Angeles 1962, lt. gov. Div. 1 Calif.-Nev.-Hawaii dist. 1967). Author: Municipal Liability for Tortious Acts and Omissions, 1936; Administration of Public Tort Liability in Los Angeles, 1939; Tort Liability of Public Officers, 1940; Law and Lawyers, 1950; Role of the Lawyer in Public Administration, 1957; Law of Local Government, 1966; Old 89, My Horse, and Other Tales, Essays and Verse, 1974; History of State Bar of California, 1979; also articles in fields of municipal law, ct. procedure and practice, legal history, legal aid, pub. adminstrn. Home: 240 Kuss Rd PO Box 656 Danville CA 94526

DAVID, MARK STEVEN, personnel director; b. Chgo., July 28, 1951; s. William and Shirley (Caplin) Glickman; m. Geri Belinda Piller, Sept. 8, 1974; children: Asher, Noah, Araminta. BSBA, U. Colo., 1973. Cert. pers. cons. Pres. Roth Young Pers. Svc., Englewood, Colo., 1976—. Bd. dirs. Anti-Defamation League, Denver, 1976-79. Mem. Colo. Assn. Pers. Cons. (1st v.p. 1984, arbitration chmn. 1985—, treas. 1987). Democrat. Jewish. Office: Roth Young Pers Svc 8101 E Prentice Ave Ste M250 Englewood CO 80111

DAVIDIAN, WILLIAM DAVID, lighting and production designer; b. Bedford, Mass., Feb. 17, 1954; s. William Wood and Janice (Graeves) D.; m. Ana Cardoso, June 6, 1986; children: Maria-Mercedes, Devon Charles. Student, Emerson Coll., 1973-75. Mgr. prodn. and lights Natalie Cole, L.A., 1978-80; head electrician Journey, San Francisco, 1978, The rolling Stones, N.Y.C., 1981; lighting designer Kiss, N.Y.C., 1987, Tiffany, L.A., 1987, Santana, San Francisco, 1981, The Jacksons, L.A., 1981, Bon Jovi, N.J., 1987—, Van Halen, L.A., 1986—. Mem. Am. Soc. Lighting Dirs. Home and Office: 8060 Woodland Ln Los Angeles CA 90046

DAVIDS, DANIEL JOSEPH, flower bulb company executive; b. L.A., Dec. 21, 1955; s. Jerry Caswell and Mary Louise (Gratton) D.; m. Janet Gaines Talmadge, Jan. 14, 1978; children: Christine Marie, Michael Dean. BS, U. Ariz., 1978. Salesman Davids & Royston Bulb Co., Inc., Gardena, Calif., 1978-80; sales mgr. Davids & Royston Bulb Co., Inc., Gardena, 1980-82, v.p. sales & mktg., 1982—; panelist Sunset Mag. Garden Panel, Menlo Park, Calif., 1980—. Bd. dirs. L.A. Garden Show Com., Arcadia, Calif., 1983—, S. Coast Botanic Garden Found., Palos Verdes, Calif., 1988—. Mem. Am. Assn. Nurserymen, Calif. Assn. Nurserymen, Mailorder Assn. Nurseries (bd. dirs. 1988—), N. Am. Flowerbulb Wholesalers (bd. dirs. 1984-86)), Kappa Epsilon Alumni Assn. Republican. Roman Catholic. Home: 337 9th St Manhattan Beach CA 90266 Office: Davids & Royston Bulb Co Inc 550 W 135th St Gardena CA 90248

DAVIDSON, BILL (WILLIAM JOHN DAVIDSON), entertainment journalist, author; b. Jersey City, Mar. 4, 1918; s. Louis J. and Gertrude (Platt) D.; m. Muriel Roberts, May 21, 1960 (dec. Sept. 1983); 1 child, Carol; m. Maralynne Beth Nitz, July 27, 1986. BA, NYU, 1939. Assoc. editor Collier's mag., N.Y.C., 1946-56; contbg. editor Look mag., N.Y.C., 1956-61; editor-at-large Saturday Evening Post, N.Y.C., 1961-69; radio commentator NBC, N.Y.C., 1968-71; TV writer Universal Studios, Universal City, Calif., 1971-76; contbg. editor TV Guide, Radnor, Pa., 1971—; chmn. alumni communications com. NYU, 1959-64. Author: The Real and the Unreal, Six Brave Presidents, 1962, (with Sid Caesar) Where Have I Been?, 1982, Spencer Tracy: Tragic Idol, 1988. Mem. N.Y. County Dem. com., N.Y.C., 1948-50. Served as sgt. U.S. Army, 1941-45, ETO. Recipient Disting. Reporting award Sigma Delta Chi, 1951, 53, Albert Lasker Med. Journalism award, 1953, Disting. Journalism award Family Service Assn. Am., 1963. Mem. Writers Guild Am. West. Democrat. Home: 13225 Morrison St Sherman Oaks CA 91423 Office: TV Guide 9000 Sunset Blvd Los Angeles CA 90069

DAVIDSON, GORDON, theatrical producer, director; b. Bklyn., May 7, 1933; s. Joseph H. and Alice (Gordon) D.; m. Judith Swiller, Sept. 21, 1958; children: Adam, Rachel. B.A., Cornell U.; M.A., Case Western Res. U.; L.H.D. (hon.), Bklyn. Coll.; D. Performing Arts (hon.), Calif. Inst. Arts; D.F.A. (hon.), Claremont U. Ctr. Stage mgr. Phoenix Theatre Co., 1958-60, Am. Shakespeare Festival Theatre, 1958-60, Dallas Civic Opera, 1960-61, Martha Graham Dance Co., 1962; mng. dir. Theatre Group at UCLA, 1965-67; artistic dir., producer Center Theatre Group Mark Taper Forum, 1967—; co-founder New Theatre For Now, Mark Taper Forum, 1970; Past mem. theatre panel Nat. Endowment for Arts; past pres. Theatre Communications Group; mem. adv. council Internat. Theatre Inst.; mem. adv. com. Cornell Ctr. for Performing Arts; cons. Denver Center for the Performing Arts. Producer, dir. numerous theatrical prodns. including The Deputy, 1965, Candide, 1966, The Devils, 1967, Who's Happy Now, 1967, In the Matter of J. Robert Oppenheimer, 1968, Murderous Angels, 1970, Rosebloom, 1970, The Trial of the Catonsville Nine, 1971, Henry IV, Part I, 1972, Mass, 1973, Hamlet, 1974, Savages, 1974, Too Much Johnson, 1975, The Shadow Box, 1975, And Where She Stops Nobody Knows, 1976, Getting Out, 1977, Black Angel, 1978, Terra Nova, 1979, Children of a Lesser God, 1979, The Lady and the Clarinet, 1980, Chekhov in Yalta, 1981, Tales from Hollywood, 1982, The American Clock, 1984, The Hands of Its Enemy, 1984, Traveler in the Dark, 1985, The Real Thing, 1986, Ghetto, 1986; dir. operas including Cosi Fan Tutte, Otello, Beatrice and Benedick, Carmen, La Boheme, Il Trovatore, Harriet, A Woman Called Moses, A Midsummer Night's Dream; TV film The Trial of the Catonsville Nine, 1971; exec. producer Zoot Suit, 1981; producer for TV It's the Willingness, PBS Visions Series, 1979, Who's Happy Now?, NET Theatre in Am. Series. Trustee Ctr. for Music, Drama and Art; past pres. League Resident Theatres; past v.p. Am. Nat. Theatre Acad; advisor Fund for New Am. Plays. Recipient N.Y. Drama Desk award for direction, 1969; recipient Los Angeles Drama Critics Circle awards for direction, 1971, 74, 75, Margo Jones award New Theatre for Now, 1970, 76, Obie award, 1971, 77, Outer Critics Circle award, 1977, Tony award for direction, 1977, award John Harvard, award Nat. Acad. TV Arts and Scis., award Nosotros Golden Eagle, award N.Y. League for Hard of Hearing, award N.Y. Speech and Hearing Assn., award Am. Theatre Assn., award Los Angeles Human Relations Commn.; Guggenheim fellow, 1983. Mem. League Resident Theatres (past pres.), ANTA (v.p. 1975). Office: Ctr Theater Group 135 N Grand Ave Los Angeles CA 90012 *

DAVIDSON, HERMAN LAMONT, aerospace company executive; b. Denver, May 26, 1930; s. William Franklin and Hazel Arnetta (Lenhard) D.; Asso. Sci., Allan Hancock Coll., 1976; m. Virginia Jane Taylor, Oct. 1, 1949; children—Pamela, William, Virginia, David. Mechanic, Leeman Auto Co., Denver, 1948-51; insp. Martin Marietta Co., Denver, 1957-58, engr./supr., 1958-59, quality project chief, 1959-61, chief inspection missile site, Vandenberg, Calif., 1961-68, chief quality assurance, 1968-76, mgr. quality, 1977—, central quality mgr. programs, 1978-82, dir. mission assurance Space Transp. System, Ground Support System, mgr. quality and safety Vandenberg ops., 1982—, mgr. product assurance and safety, 1987. Served with USN, 1951-57; Korea. Registered profl. engr., Calif. Mem. Am. Soc. for Quality Control (sr.), Nat. Mgmt. Assn. (Gold Knight of Mgmt. 1983), Calif. Soc. Profl. Engrs. Air Force Assn., Am. Inst. Aeros. and Astronautics. Home: 937 Empress Circle Santa Maria CA 93454 Office: Martin Marietta Corp Vandenberg Ops PO Box 1681 Vandenberg AFB CA 93437

DAVIDSON, JAMES ARTHUR, physician assistant; b. Anaconda, Mont., Aug. 21, 1946; s. Norman B. and Emily Alice (Pechar) D.; m. Nancy Elaine Sackmann, June 27, 1970; children: Jon Eric, Jeanette Marie. AA, Big Bend Community Coll., 1966; student, Wash. State U., 1966-67, U. Wash., 1973, Cen. Wash. U., 1980. Health technician Job Corps, Moses Lake, Wash., 1971-72; physician asst. Grandview (Wash.) Med. Ctr., 1972-89, Hanford Environ. Health Found., Richland, Wash., 1989—; instr. emergency med. svc. program Yakima County, Wash., 1974-83; sports medicine adviser Grandview (Wash.) Schs., 1979—, guest lectr., 1984—; preceptor, health adv. program Yakima Valley Coll., 1986—. Assoc. editor, Physician Asst. jour., 1985—. Chmn. local bd. Selective Svc. System, 1981—; active local Boy Scouts Am., Grandview, 1982—, chmn. Chief Kamlakin Dist., 1987—; trustee, Bleyhl Community Libr., Grandview, 1982—. With USN, 1967-71. Recipient Wood Badge award of Merit Boy Scouts Am., Silver Beaver award, 1989. Fellow Wash. Acad. Physician Assts. (bd. dirs. 1975-76, v.p. 1985-86, newsletter editor 1975-86), Am. Acad. Physician Assts.; mem. Am. Legion, Phi Kappa Phi. Republican. Presbyterian. Home: PO Box 56 Grandview WA 98930 Office: Hanford Environ Health Found PO Box 100 Richland WA 99352

DAVIDSON, MELVIN GORDON, data processing executive; b. Winnipeg, Man., Can., Apr. 7, 1938; s. James Gordon and Winifred Martha (Collins) D.; m. Barbara Ann Davidson, Sept. 1, 1962; children: Iain Gordon, Diana Lynn. AB, Whitman Coll., Walla Walla, 1960; PhD, Rensselaer Poly. Inst., Troy, N.Y., 1964. Research fellow Inst. for Adv. Study, Canberra, Australia, 1964-67; asst. prof. Western Wash. U., Bellingham, 1967-69; assoc. prof. Western Wash. U., 1969-72, prof. physics, 1972—, dir. computing, 1972—; cons. Educom Cons. Group, Princeton, N.J., 1983—. Author: PL/1 Programming, 1973. Precinct committeeman Dem. Party, Bellingham, 1970-80, 85-86. Mem. ACM, IEEE, Bellingham Yacht, Whatcom County Soccer. Democrat. Episcopalian. Office: Western Wash U Computer Ctr Bellingham WA 98225

DAVIDSON, ROBERT ARNOLD, dentist; b. Denver, Oct. 5, 1929; s. Maxwell Starr and Audrey M. (Hill) D.; m. Judith Ann Snodgrass, Aug. 29, 1951; children: Jan Audrey, Robert A., Cari Ruth. Student, U. Colo., 1947-48, U. Denver, 1948-50; DDS, U. Mo., 1954. Pvt. practice dentistry Denver, 1956—. Capt. USAF, 1954-56. Mem. ADA, Colo. Dental Assn., Met. Denver Dental Assn., Kappa Sigma, Sigma Delta Sigma. Republican. Presbyterian. Home: 7182 S Silverhorn Dr Evergreen CO 80439 Office: 155 Cook St Ste 251 Denver CO 80206

DAVIDSON, SHELDON JEROME, hematologist; b. N.Y.C., Oct. 21, 1939; s. Leo and Lee (Levy) D.; m. Golda Feldman, Sept. 16, 1962; children: Larry, Debra, Sara. BA summa cum laude, NYU, 1960; MD, Albert Einstein U., 1964. Diplomate Am. Bd. Internal Medicine, Am. Bd. Hematology. Intern Maimonides Med. Ctr., Bklyn., 1964-65; fellow in hematology Mt. Sinai Med. Ctr., N.Y.C., 1967-68, resident internal medicine, 1965-67; fellow in hematology, oncology U. So. Calif. Med. Ctr., Los Angeles, 1971-72; with So. Calif. Hematol-Oncology Med. Group, Los Angeles, 1972-77, Valley Hematol-Oncology Med. Group, Los Angeles, 1977-88, Hematology-Oncology Cons., 1988—; bd. dirs. oncology Holy Cross Hosp., Mission Hills, Calif., 1978—; assoc. clin. prof. dept. medicine UCLA Sch. Medicine, 1976—; chief dept. of medicine Holy Cross Hosp., Mission Hills, 1985—, Valley Presbyn. Hosp., Van Nuys, Calif., 1986-88. Served to maj. U.S. Army, 1968-71. Cert. of Appreciation dept. medicine UCLA, 1984, 87. Mem. ACP, Am. Legion, Am. Soc. Hematology, Am. Soc. Clin. Oncology, Alpha Omega Alpha. Democrat. Jewish. Home: 14960 Dickens St Sherman Oaks CA 91403 Office: Hematol-Oncology Cons 6850 Sepulveda Van Nuys CA 91405

DAVIDSON, WILLIAM WARD, III, computer graphics company executive; b. Evanston, Ill., May 28, 1940; s. William Ward Davidson Jr. and Ann Elizabeth (Wilds) D.; m. Linda Lee Speelman, June 8, 1965 (div. Feb. 1988); children: William, Lisa, Christina. BS in Psychology, U. Md., 1966; postgrad., Am. U., 1967-68; bus. adminstrn., Northeastern U., 1981. Programmer IBM Corp., Greenbelt, Md., 1966-69; mktg. rep. IBM Corp., Roanoke, Va., 1969-72; sales group mgr. Digital Equipment Corp., San Francisco, 1972-78; dist. sales mgr. Digital Equipment Corp., Chgo., 1978-81; product line mgr. Digital Equipment Corp., Boston, 1981-84; v.p. sales & support Culler Scientific, Santa Barbara, Calif., 1984-87; v.p. ops. Wavefront Techs., Santa Barbara, 1987—, also corp. officer, 1987—. With U.S. Air Force, 1960-64. Recipient Apollo Achievment award, Manned Flight Awareness award, NASA, 1966. Republican. Presbyterian. Office: Wavefront Techs 530 E Montecito St Santa Barbara CA 93103

DAVIES, DONALD THOMAS, hospital administrator, military officer; b. Chgo., June 12, 1948; s. Brettland Lloyd and Catherine (Dobesh) D.; m. Inta Eva Delmage, Apr. 20, 1968; children: Donald Thomas, Alicia, Melissa, Sebastian. BBA, Chaminade U., 1974; MBA, Philips U., 1984. Commd. 2d lt. USAF, 1975, advanced through grades to maj., 1985; asst. adminstr. USAF Hosp., Rantoul, Ill., 1975-78; chief med. placement USAF, Chgo., 1978-81; adminstr. USAF Clinic, Enid, Okla., 1981-83, USAF Hosp., Lubbock, Tex., 1983-85, USAF Hosp., Misawa, Japan, 1985-88; staff officer Hdqrs. Pacific Air Forces Office Command Surgeon, Hickam AFB, Hawaii, 1988—. Mem. West Tex. Hosp. Assn., Am. Coll. Hosp. Adminstrs. (presiding officer 1985—, cert.), Tex. Hosp. Assn., Am. Hosp. Assn., Delta Mu Delta. Republican. Roman Catholic. Avocations: camping, golf, bowling.

DAVIES, EDWARD DAVID, architect, educator; b. Madison, Wis., Sept. 4, 1911; s. Howell D. and Julia Hosford (Merrell) D.; m. Marjorie Scheflow, Jan. 30, 1936; 1 child, Robert Huntington. Student, Ill. Inst. Tech. (formerly Armour Inst.), 1930-31, Cranbrook Acad. Art., 1933-34, U. Ill., 1934. Registered architect, Calif., Ariz., Nev. Archtl. designer J. Robert F. Swanson, Detroit, 1935; automobile designer Fisher div. Gen. Motors Corp., Detroit, 1937; plant layout engr. Bigelow-Liptak Corp., Detroit, 1937-38, Marblehead Lime Co., Chgo., 1939-40; designer new stores, warehouses Montgomery Ward & Co., Chgo., 1940—; chief coordinator Army and Navy project Convair Aircraft Corp., San Diego and Ft. Worth, 1941-45; architect Richard J. Neutra, 1945-46, Wiseman & Goldsmith, Los Angeles, 1946-47; theatre architect S. Charles Lee, 1947-50; cons. architect Hayden-Lee Devel. Corp., 1950-52; pvt. practice architecture Pasadena, Calif., 1953—; v.p., founder-dir. Pacific Architects Collaborative, Pasadena. Prin. works include layout and design Los Angeles Airport Indsl. Tract, 1950-53, Hayden-Lee Corp., 1952; designer Los Angeles County Cts., Compton, Calif., 1950; architect 25 Luth. chs. including Torrance, Calif., 1954, San Clemente, Calif., 1956, Reno, 1957, Phoenix, 1959, Pasadena, 1961. Pres. Pasadena Beautiful Found., 1961-62; vice-chmn. Citizens Urban Renewal Adv. Com., Pasadena, 1961-62; pres. Pasadena Citizens Council Planning, 1963-64; mem. Mayor's Fgn. Cities Affiliation Com.; mem. exec. com. Forward Pasadena Assn., 1961-62. Recipient Silver Cup, Pasadena Beautiful Found., 1982. Mem. AIA (pres. Pasadena chpt. 1959, mem. nat. nominating com. 1959-61), Calif. Council Architects (bd. dirs. 1958-60, sec. 1960), Planning and Conservation League (founder, v.p. 1965—), Pasadena C. of C. (bd. dirs. 1961-63), Pasadena Art Mus., Los Angeles Mus., Scarab, Mask and Bauble, 20 Club U. So. Calif. Republican. Home and Office: 45100 Brest Rd PO Box 1081 Mendocino CA 95460

DAVIES, KENNETH, research physicist; b. Merthyr Tydfil, Wales, Jan. 28, 1928; came to U.S., 1955; s. William Rees and Hannah Elizabeth (Broad) D.; m. Joyce Alice Demerchant, Feb. 20, 1958; children: Russell, Elizabeth, Kenneth. BSc, U. Wales, 1949, PhD, 1953. Physicist Defence Research Bd., Ottawa, Can., 1952-55; asst. prof. Brown U., Providence, 1956-58; physicist Dept. Commerce, Boulder, Colo., 1958-85, sr. scientist, 1985—; guest prof. Wuham U., 1988—. Author: Ionospheric Radio Propagation, 1965, Ionospheric Radio Waves, 1969, Phase and Frequency Instabilities, 1970; contbr. over 120 articles to profl. jours. Chmn. Plan Boulder County; pres. Boulder Council for Internat. Visitors. Webster fellow U. Queensland, Brisbane, Australia, 1975-76. Fellow AAAS, IEEE. Office: SEL/ERL/NOAA 325 Broadway Boulder CO 80303

DAVIES, MERTON EDWARD, planetary scientist; b. St. Paul, Sept. 13, 1917; s. Albert Daniel and Lucile (McCabe) D.; AB, Stanford, 1938, postgrad., 1938-39; m. Margaret Louise Darling, Feb. 10, 1946; children: Deidra Louise Stauff, Albert Karl, Merton Randel. Instr. math. U. Nev., 1939-40; group leader Math. Lofting, Douglas Aircraft Co., El Segundo, Calif., 1940-48; sr. staff Rand Corp., Santa Monica, Calif., 1948-59, 62—, liaison USAF, Washington, 1959-62. U.S. observer inspected stas. under terms Antarctic Treaty, 1967; TV co-investigator Mariner Mars, 1969, 71, Mariner Venus/Mercury 1973 Mission, Voyager Mission, Galileo Mission, Magellan Mission. Assoc. fellow AIAA; mem. Am. Soc. Photogrammetry, AAAS. Author: (with Bruce Murray) The View from Space, 1971; (with others) Atlas of Mercury, 1978. Patentee in field. Home: 1414 San Remo Dr Pacific Palisades CA 90272 Office: Rand Corp 1700 Main St Santa Monica CA 90406

DAVIES, PAUL LEWIS, JR., retired lawyer; b. San Jose, Calif., July 21, 1930; s. Paul Lewis and Faith (Crummey) D.; m. Barbara Bechtel, Dec. 22, 1955; children: Laura (Mrs. Segundo Mateo), Paul Lewis III. A.B., Stanford U., 1952; J.D., Harvard U., 1957. Bar: Calif. 1957. Assoc. Pillsbury, Madison & Sutro, San Francisco, 1957-63, ptnr., 1963-89; of counsel Chevron Corp., 1984-89; bd. dirs. FMC Corp., FMC Gold Co., Indsl. Indemnity Co. Hon. trustee Calif. Acad. Scis., trustee, 1970-83, chmn., 1973-80; pres. Herbert Hoover Found.; bd. overseers Hoover Instn., chmn., 1976-82; bd. regents U. of Pacific. 1st lt. U.S. Army, 1952-54. Mem. State Bar Calif., ABA, San Francisco Bar Assn., Phi Beta Kappa, Pi Sigma Alpha. Republican. Clubs: Bankers, Bohemian, Pacific-Union, Villa Taverna, World Trade (San Francisco); Claremont Country, Lakeview (Oakland, Calif.); Cypress Point (Pebble Beach, Calif.); Sainte Claire (San Jose, Calif.), Collectors, Explorers, Links (N.Y.C.); Met., 1925 F St. (Washington); Chgo., Mid-Am. (Chgo.). Office: 50 Fremont St Ste 3825 San Francisco CA 94105

DAVIES, WILLIAM WALTER, sales executive; b. Omaha, Apr. 19, 1958; s. William and Helen (Kuhn) D.; m. Linda Christine DeRosa, May 1, 1988. BS in Mktg., U. Nebraska, 1981. Salesperson Crawford Fitting Co., Solon, Ohio, 1981-84, Parker Hannifin, Cleve., 1984-86; sales mgr. Sigmaform, Santa Clara, Calif., 1986-87, Flexible Systems, Marina Del Rey, Calif., 1987-88, M.O.X., Irvine, Calif., 1988—. Home: 11 Corsica Irvine CA 92714 Office: MOX 4330 Barranca Pkwy Ste 101 Irvine CA 92774

DAVILA, WILLIAM S., supermarket chain executive; b. 1931; married. AA, Los Angeles City Coll. Produce clerk Von's Grocery Co., El Monte, Calif., 1948-56; produce mgr. Von's Grocery Co., El Monte, 1956-59, with advt. dept., 1959-65, asst. advt. mgr., 1965-67, advt. mgr., 1967-73, mgr. sales promotion, 1973-75, v.p. sales, 1975-77, group v.p. mktg. sales, 1977-80, sr. v.p. supermarkets, 1980-84, exec. v.p., from 1984, now pres., chief operating officer, also bd. dirs. Served with USAF, 1951-54. Office: Von's Co Inc 10150 Lower Azusa Rd El Monte CA 91731 *

DAVIS, ALEXANDER SCHENCK, architect; b. San Francisco, Jan. 3, 1930; s. William Schenck and Amelia (Francisco) D.; B.A. with honors in Architecture, U. Calif.-Berkeley, 1953, M.A. in Architecture (D. Zelinsky & Sons Found. Grad. scholar), 1957; m. Nancy Leah Barry, Oct. 21, 1953; children—Arthur Barry, Laurel Davis Bowden, Pamela Davis Bennett. With Hammarberg & Herman, Architects, El Cerrito, Calif., 1956-62; project architect Bonelli, Young & Wong, Architects and Engrs., San Francisco, 1962-67; chief architect Earl & Wright, Cons. Engrs., San Francisco, 1967-73; constrn. mgr. Fisher Devel., Inc., San Francisco, 1973-74; project architect Keller & Gannon, Cons. Engrs., San Francisco, 1974-77; individual practice architecture, Albany, Calif., 1977-81, El Cerrito, Calif., 1986—. Served with USCGR, 1951-56, active duty 1953-55. Registered architect, Calif., Alaska, U.K.; cert. Nat. Council Archtl. Registration Bds. Fellow Soc. Am. Registered Architects, mem. AIA, Royal Inst. Brit. Architects, Soc. Am. Mil. Engrs., Constrn. Specifications Inst. Home and Office: 928 Contra Costa Dr El Cerrito CA 94530

DAVIS, ALLEN, professional football team executive; b. Brockton, Mass., July 4, 1929; s. Louis and Rose (Kirschenbaum) D.; m. Carol Segall, July 11, 1954; 1 son, Mark. Student, Wittenberg Coll., 1947; A.B., Syracuse U., 1950. Asst. football coach Adelphi Coll., 1950-51; head football coach Ft. Belvoir, Va., 1952-53; player-personnel scout Baltimore Colts, 1954; line coach The Citadel, 1955-56, U. So. Calif., 1957-59; asst. coach San Diego Chargers, 1960-62; gen. mgr., head coach Oakland Raiders (now Los Angeles Raiders), 1963-66, owner, mng. gen. ptnr., 1966—; former mem. mgmt. council and competition com. Nat. Football League. Served with AUS, 1952-53. Named Profl. Coach of Year A.P., Profl. Coach of Year U.P.I., Profl. Coach of Year Sporting News, Profl. Coach of Year Pro-Football Illustrated, 1963; Young Man of Yr. Oakland, 1963; only individual in history to be an asst. coach, head coach, gen. mgr., league commr. and owner. Mem. Am. Football Coaches Assn. Office: Los Angeles Raiders 332 Center St El Segundo CA 90245 *

DAVIS, ANNETTE KEZER, financial analyst, educator; b. Siminole, Okla., Jan. 27, 1953; d. Alfred Dearrel and Willie Mae (Johnson) Kezer; m. Kenneth Wayne Davis, Aug. 21, 1982; children: Stephanie Michelle, Christopher Paul. AA, Valley Coll., 1977; BA, Calif. State U., San Bernardino, 1979, MBA, 1981. Instr. Skadron Coll., San Bernardino, Calif., 1979-81; adjuster Farmers Ins. Co., Riverside, Calif., 1981-82; instr. Crafton Hills Coll., Yucaipa, Calif., 1981-84; analyst San Bernardino County, 1982—. Asst. leader Girl Scouts Am., Grand Terrace, Calif., 1982-83; team mother Grand Terrace Community Soccer, 1981-82; active Am. Cancer Soc. Named Am. Bus. Women scholar, 1979-80, Am. Soc. Women Accts. scholar, 1978. Mem. Bus. and Profl. Women (treas., issues mgr., fin. chmn. San Orco dist. 1982-88, scholarship 1980-81), Inland Area Personnel Mgmt. Assn., Am. Soc. Public Adminstrn. (dir. 1987-88), Alpha Kappa Psi (fellow 1979-81). Club: Riverside (Calif.) Bicycle (treas.). Home: 30 N Buena Vista Redlands CA 92373 Office: San Bernardino County 385 N Arrowhead San Bernardino CA 92415

DAVIS, ARNOLD CARPENTER, IV, data processing administrator; b. Glendale, Calif., Aug. 18, 1944; s. Arnold Carpenter III and Beth (Davis) D.; m. Ellen Lucille Goodwin, Aug. 19, 1967; children: Laura Ellen, Rosalind Marjorie. BA, Stanford U., 1965; PhD, UCLA, 1974. Head dept. English Mt. St. Mary's Coll., L.A., 1974-78; mgr. software Unisys Corp., Irvine, Calif., 1979-84; mgr. Joseph and Cogan Assocs. Westlake Village, Calif., 1984--. Mem. IEEE, MLA. Home: 4511 Henley Ct Los Angeles CA 91361 Office: Joseph & Cogan Assocs 370 N Westlake Blvd Westlake Village CA 91362

DAVIS, ARTHUR DAVID, psychology educator, musician. s. Arthur Nichols and Lillie Mae (Connors) D.; m. Gladys Lesley Joyce, Dec. 29, 1965; children: Kimaili, Mureithi. BA suma cum laude, CUNY, 1973; MA, City Coll., N.Y.C., 1976, NYU, 1976; PhD with distinction, NYU, 1982. Lic. psychologist. Musician various worldwide tours, 1962—, NBC-TV Staff Orch., N.Y.C., 1962-63, Westinghouse TV Staff Orch., N.Y.C., 1964-68, CBS-TV Staff Orch., N.Y.C., 1969-71; prof. Manhattan Community Coll., N.Y.C., 1971-86, U. Bridgeport, Conn., 1978-82; psychologist Lincoln Med. and Mental Health Ctr., Bronx, 1982-85; psychologist, tchr. N.Y. Med. Coll., Valhalla, 1982-87; prof. Orange Coast Coll., Costa Mesa, Calif., 1987—, Calif. State U., Fullerton, 1988—; psychologist Cross Cultural Ctr., San Diego, 1986—; cons. Head Start, Bklyn., 1981-82, Orange County Minority AIDS, Santa Ana, Calif., 1987-88, Orange County Fair Housing, Costa Mesa, 1988, Sickle Cell Anemia Assn., Santa Ana, Calif., 1987-88, Human Rels. Orange County City, Costa Mesa, 1988-89, William Grant Still Mus., L.A., 1988—. Author: The Arthur Davis System for Double Bass, 1976; record composer Interplay, 1980, ARKIMU, 1985, Soulnote, 1987. Mem. coun. Dialogue, Costa Mesa, 1988; mgr. Little League of Cortlandt, N.Y., 1979-82; pack master Cub Scouts of Am., Cortlandt, Croton, N.Y., 1979-80, dist. chmn., 1980-81. NIMH grantee, 1976-77; named World's Foremost Double Bassist IBA, 1969—; recipient Lion award Black MBA Assn., 1985. Mem. N.Y. Acad. Scis., Am. Psychol. Assn., ASCAP, Orange County Psychol. Assn., Assn. of Black Psychologists, Am. Hort. Soc., Nat. Trust for Hist. Preservation Soc., Stanford U. Alumni Assn., NYU Alumni Assn., City Coll. of N.Y. Alumni Assn. Republican. Office: ARKIMU 3535 E Coast Hwy Ste 50 Corona Del Mar CA 92625

DAVIS, BETTY JEAN BOURBONIA, real estate investment executive; b. Ft. Bayard, N.Mex., Mar. 12, 1931; d. John Alexander and Ora M. (Caudill) Bourbonia; BS in Elem. Edn., U. N.Mex., 1954; children: Janice Ann Cox Plagge, Elizabeth Ora Cox. Gen. partner BJD Realty Co., Albuquerque, 1977—. Bd. dirs. Albuquerque Opera Guild, 1977-79, 81-83, 85-86, 86-87, membership co-chmn., 1977-79; mem. Friends of Art, 1978-85, Friends of Little Theatre, 1973-85, Mus. N.Mex. Found.; mem. grand exec. com. N.Mex. Internat. Order of Rainbow for Girls. Recipient Matrix award for journalism Jr. League. Mem. Albuquerque Mus. Assn., N.M. Hist. Soc., N.Mex. Symphony Guild, Jr. League Albuquerque, Alumni Assn. U. N.Mex. (dir. 1973-76), Mus. N.Mex. Found., Alpha Chi Omega (Beta Gamma Beta chpt., adv., bldg. corp. 1962-77). Republican. Methodist. Clubs: Tanoan Country. Lodges: Order Eastern Star, Order Rainbow for Girls (past grand worthy adv. N.Mex., past mother adv. Friendship Assembly 50). Home: 9505 Augusta NE Albuquerque NM 87111

DAVIS, BRIAN, marketing educator, consumer analyst; b. Ogden, Utah, Mar. 31, 1954; s. Lewis Delbert and Laverne (Gibby) D.; m. Jamie Lou Jewell, Apr. 11, 1974 (div. Dec. 1976) 1 child, Taryn Kaye; m. Debra Darline, Dec. 17, 1978. AA, Weber State Coll., 1977; BS, Utah State U., 1979, MSS, 1982; PhD, U. Ga., 1985. Fin. aid adminstr. Weber State Coll., Ogden, 1981-83, mem. faculty bus. adminstrn., 1987—; mem. faculty mktg. dept. U. No. Colo., Greeley, 1985-87. With USN, 1974-76. Fellow Acad. Mktg. Sci., Mu Kappa Tau; mem. Am. Mktg. Assn. (profl.), Am. Acad. Acvt., Gerontological Soc. Am., Psi Chi. Home: 1242 33d St Ogden UT 84403 Office: Weber State Coll Bus Sch Ogden UT 84408-3802

DAVIS, BRUCE WARREN, architect; b. Chgo., Oct. 27, 1947; s. Howard Warren and Elizabeth Florence (Barber) D. BArch., U. Ill., 1970. Registered architect, N.Mex. Jr. architect Skidmore, Owings & Merrill, Chgo., 1969-73; pvt. practice architecture Santa Fe, N.Mex., 1973—; guest instr., lectr. solar design various schs. Club: El Gancho Tennis. Home and Office: Rte 9 Box 90 BD Santa Fe NM 87505

DAVIS, CAROLYN LEIGH, psychotherapist; b. Houston, Mar. 18, 1936; d. William Harvey Speight and Veral Audra (Nunn) Speight Poole; m. John C. Rogers, June 22, 1957 (div. Nov. 1970); children: Elizabeth Leigh Porterfield, Rena Kathleen, John; m. L.B. Davis Sept. 14, 1972. Diploma in nursing, U. Houston, 1956; MSW, U. Denver, 1981; postgrad., Iliff Sch. Theology, 1987—. RN, Tex., Colo.; lic. clin. social worker, Colo.; cert. alcohol, drug counselor, Colo. Therapist Bethesda Mental Health Ctr., Denver, 1972-73; supr. emergency alcoholism services Denver Gen. Hosp., 1973-74; dir. alcoholism services Jefferson County Health Dept., Lakewood, Colo., 1974-78; pvt. practice psychotherapy Lakewood and Littleton, Colo., 1981—; adj. prof. Grad. Sch. Social Work, U. Denver, 1982—; cons. employee assistance program FAA, Longmont, Colo., 1984—; mem. adv. bd. Nurses of Colo., Denver, 1984—. Author: The Most Important Months of Your Child's Life: Fetal Alcohol Syndrome, 1976. Mem. Nat. Assn. Social Workers, Assn. Labor and Mgmt. Administrs. and Cons. on Alcoholism. Democrat. Episcopalian. Office: 6909 S Holly Circle Ste 260 Englewood CO 80112 also: 720 Kipling Lakewood CO 80215

DAVIS, CLARENCE BALDWIN, college dean, historian; b. Berwyn, Ill., Feb. 21, 1944; s. William DeOzro and Selina Grace (Morehouse) D.; m. Barbara Ann Simko, Aug. 3, 1968; children: Elizabeth, Carlton. BA, Yale U., 1966; MA, U. Wis., 1968, PhD, 1972. Instr. Madison (Wis.) Area Tech. Coll., 1970; asst. prof. Stratford Coll., Danville, Va., 1972-73; prof. Coll. Charleston, S.C., 1973-87; dean Lewis and Clark Coll., Portland, Oreg., 1987—. Author: Partners and Rivals, 1987; editor: Proceedings: 13th Consortium on Revolutionary Europe, 1985; contbr. articles to profl. jours. Grantee NEH, 1976, 77-79, Am. Philos. Soc., 1978; Am. Coun. Edn. fellow, 1984-85. Mem. Am. Hist. Assn., So. Hist. Assn., Coun. Fellows, Phi Alpha Theta. Office: Lewis & Clark Coll Coll Arts & Scis Portland OR 97219

DAVIS, COLEEN COCKERILL, teacher; b. Pampa, Tex., Sept. 20, 1930; d. Charles Clifford and Myrtle Edith (Harris) Cockerill; m. Richard Harding Davis, June 22, 1952 (div. 1984); children: David Christopher, Denis Benjamin (dec. 1979). BS, U. Okla., 1951; MS, UCLA, 1952; postgrad. U. So. Calif., Whittier Coll., UCLA. Cert. tchr., Calif. Chmn, dept. home econs., tchr. Whittier Union High Sch. Dist., Calif., 1952-85; substitute tchr., 1985—; home tchr., 1985—, cons. 1986—; co-host Am.'s Bed & Breakfast, Whittier, 1983—, also founder, pres., exec. dir. Contbr. articles to newspapers. Founder Children of Murdered Parents, Whittier, 1984, chpt. leader; founder Coalition of Orgns. and People, Whittier, 1984, Whistle, Ltd., Whittier, 1984; mem. citizens' adv. bd. Fred C. Nelles Sch. Mem. Calif. Tchrs. Assn., NEA, Internat. Tour Mgmt. Inst., Whittier C. of C. (ambassador).

Republican. Episcopalian. Avocation: volunteer worker. Office: Am's Bed & Breakfast PO Box 9302 Whittier CA 90608

DAVIS, CRAIG CARLTON, aerospace company executive; b. Gulfport, Miss., Dec. 14, 1919; s. Craig Carlton and Helen Lizette (Houppert) D.; B.S., Ga. Inst. Tech., 1941; J.D., Harvard U., 1949; children—Kimberly Patricia, Craig Carlton. Instr. aeros. Escola Tecnica de Aviacao, Sao Paulo, Brazil, 1946; contract adminstr. Convair, Fort Worth, 1949-51; mgr. contracts and pricing, atomics internat. and autonetics divs. N.Am. Aviation, Anaheim, Calif., 1954-62, asst. corp. dir. contracts and proposals, El Segundo, Calif., 1963-70; dir. contracts Aerojet Electro Systems Co., Azusa, Calif., 1971-81, v.p., 1982—. Served with AUS, 1941-45; USAF, 1951-53, to col. res., 1953-66. Mem. ABA, Fed. Bar Assn., D.C. Bar Assn., Res. Officers Assn., Harvard U. Alumni Assn., Ga. Tech. Alumni Assn. Republican. Episcopalian. Club: Harvard. Home: 10501 Wilshire Blvd Apt 1208 Los Angeles CA 90024 Office: Aerojet Electro Systems Co 1100 W Hollyvale St Azusa CA 91702

DAVIS, DANIEL EDWARD, museum director; b. Creston, Iowa, July 3, 1922; s. Fred M. and Myrtle A. D.; m. Mary Joan Kelly, July 15, 1947; children: Daniel B., Nancy, Terry, Barbara, Michelle. Student, U. Iowa, Nat. U. Mex., U. N.Mex., U. Mont. With Nat. Park Service, 1948-77; asso. regional dir. Nat. Park Service, Omaha, 1973-77; dir. Ariz.-Sonora Desert Mus., Tucson, 1977—; adv. bd. Sch. Renewable Natural Resources, U. Ariz., 1980-81; adv. Arab Center Studies Arid Zones, Kouf Nat. Park, Libya.; cons. Egyptian Wildlife Service, Nat. Parks, Netherlands West Indies, Saudi Arabia Nat. Park Service, Thumamah Nat. Park, Kuwait Inst. Sci. Research; adj. prof. Sch. Renewable Natural Resources, U. Ariz., 1986—. Author: Hikers Guide to Grand Canyon, 1956, Boatman's Guide to the Colorado River, 1957, The Little Colorado, 1958, Backcountry Travel, Sequoia National Park, 1961. Served with AUS, 1943-46. Recipient Meritorious Service award Dept. Interior, 1956, Environ. Leadership medal UN, 1982. Mem. Sierra Club, Nature Conservancy. Office: Ariz-Sonora Desert Mus 2021 N Kinney Rd Tucson AZ 85743

DAVIS, EDWARD MICHAEL, state senator; b. Los Angeles, Nov. 15, 1916; s. James Leonard and Lillian (Fox) D.; m. Aileen Bobbie Nash, Jan. 7, 1984; children: Michael, Christine Hart, Mary Ellen Burde. BS in Pub. Adminstrn. cum laude, U. So. Calif., 1961; LLD (hon.), Western Sierra Law Sch., 1972. Chief of police Los Angeles Police Dept., 1969-78; senator State of Calif., Los Angeles, 1980—; adj. prof. U. So. Calif., Los Angeles, 1967-68. Author: Staff One, 1978. Served with USN, 1942-45. Recipient George Washington Honor medal Freedom Found., Flame of Truth award Fund for Higher Edn., 1976; named Man of Yr., B'nai Brith, 1974, Outstanding Am., Los Angeles Philanthropic Found., 1977. Mem. Am. Legion (post 381 commdr. 1968-69), Internat. Assn. Chiefs of Police (pres. 1976-77). Republican. Episcopalian. Office: Calif Dist Senate Office State Capitol Rm 2048 11145 Tampa Ave 21B Northridge CA 91326

DAVIS, FRANK N., utility company executive; b. 1925. Grad., Purdue U., 1949. Pres., chief exec. officer Utah Power & Light Co., Salt Lake City. Office: Utah Power & Light Co 1407 W N Temple St Salt Lake City UT 84140 *

DAVIS, GEORGE OSMOND, communications executive; b. Seattle, July 30, 1957; s. George Osmond Sr. and Delores Lillian (Smith) D.; m. Jan Perkins; children: Felecia, Michele. Student, Portland State U., 1981-83. Technician Sta. KYYX, Seattle, 1976-77; technician, announcer Sta. KYAC, Seattle, 1977-78; radio announcer Sta. KORD, Tri-Cities, Wash., 1979-80; master control operator Sta. KNDU-TV, Tri-Cities, 1979-80; asst. editor Sta. KGW-TV, Portland, Oreg., 1980-83; remote supr. Sta. KOMO-TV, Seattle, 1983-84; transmission supr. ABC-TV, L.A., 1984-87; video ops. mgr. IDB Communications, Culver City, Calif., 1987—; telecommuncations adv. Compton Coll., Calif., 1988-89. Mem. Black Journalists Assn. (chmn. bd. L.A. chpt. 1986-88, dir. Western region). Dem. Catholic. Office: IDB Communication 10525 W Washington Blvd Culver City CA 90232

DAVIS, GERALD GLENN, sales executive; b. Natchitoches, La., Oct. 21, 1950; s. Andrew and Carrie Davis; m. Shirley Covington, Oct. 21, 1972; children: Gerald Jr., Garren Keith. BS in Agriculture, So. U., Baton Rouge, 1972. Trainee stabilization and conservation services USDA, Marksville and Lafayette, La., 1972-73; county exec. dir. USDA, Port allen, La., 1974-78; sales rep. Chevron Chem. Co., Decatur, Ga., 1978-85; product promotions specialist Chevron Chem. Co., Chgo. and Fresno, Calif., 1985-88; area sales mgr. Valent U.S.A. Corp., Fresno, Calif., 1988—. organizer Melvin Baker for Ho. of Reps., Decatur, 1984. Recipient Leadership award McDuffe County Soil and Water, Ga., 1983. Mem. Am. Agronomy Soc. (Outstanding Service award 1981), Western Agrl. Chem. Assn. Democrat. Baptist. Club: Esquire (Baton Rouge) (pres. 1975-78). Home: 8363 N Del Mar Ave Fresno CA 93711

DAVIS, GLENN MARTIN, photographer, videographer; b. Chgo., July 19, 1948; s. Alvin George and Rose (Lorber) D.; m. Shari Deener, Sept. 2, 1973; children: Erica Michelle, Daniel Mark. Student, Roosevelt U., 1966, San Fransisco State U., 1971; BS in Radio and TV, Ariz. State U., 1972. Mem. prodn. staff KOOL-TV, Phoenix, 1971-77; owner Glenn Davis Photography and Videos, Tempe, Ariz., 1977—. Mem. Profl. Photographers of Am., Wedding Photographers Internat. Democrat. Jewish. Home and Office: 3 W Dawn Dr Tempe AZ 85284

DAVIS, HIRAM LOGAN, librarian; b. St. Joseph, Mo., Apr. 10, 1943; s. Paul L. and Bertha (Turner) D.; m. Nancy Craighead, Feb. 24, 1978; 1 child, Michael. B.S., Missouri Valley Coll., Marshall, Mo., 1966; M.L.S., Emporia State U., Kans., 1969; Ph.D., U. Mich., 1984. Reference librarian Kansas City Pub. Library, Mo., summer 1967; librarian U. Kans., Lawrence, 1967-68; ref. librarian Muskingum Coll., New Concord, Ohio, 1968-69; dir. library services Kalamazoo Valley Community Coll., 1969-70; dir. com. on instl. coop. Northwestern U.-U. Mich., Ann Arbor, 1972-73; assoc. dir. Univ. libraries U. Okla., Norman, 1973-76; head undergrad. library UCLA, 1976-79; dean univ. libraries U. Pacific, Stockton, Calif., 1979-86, N.Mex. State U., Las Cruces, 1986—; mem. planning com. Calif. Conf. on Networking, Calif. State Library, Sacramento, 1984-85; mem. invitational conf. on info. economy of Calif., Grad. Sch. Library and Info. Sci., UCLA, 1984; organizer, mem. exec. council Pvt. Acad. Library Dirs. Calif., 1983-86; bd. dirs. Calif. Library Authority for Systems and Services, 1981-83; editorial adv. bd. Coll. and Research Libraries News, Chgo., 1980-84. UCLA sr. fellow, 1984; Title II-B doctoral fellow, 1970. Mem. ALA, Assn. Coll. Research Libraries (planning com. 1975-79, legis. com. 1987—), N.Mex. Library Assn., Library and Info. Tech. Assn., Beta Phi Mu. Home: 4824 Scale Ct Las Cruces NM 88001 Office: NMex State U PO Box 3475 Las Cruces NM 88003 *

DAVIS, JACK RODNEY, JR., television director; b. Dallas, Nov. 23, 1948; s. Jack Rodney Sr. and Louise (Molloy) D.; m. Susan Fleming, Apr. 8, 1983; children: Molly Beth, Austin Charles. B of Gen. Studies cum laude, U. Tex., 1977. Dir., animator Film House, Austin, Tex., 1970-72; dir., pres. Kinetic Link Inc., San Antonio, Tex., 1972-74; dir. Bill Stokes Assoc., Dallas, 1974-75, Sundance Prodns., Dallas, 1977-78, Robert Abel & Assoc., Hollywood, Calif., 1978-86, Harmony Pictures, Burbank, Calif., 1986—. Recipient CLIO award, 1983, Mobius award U.S. Festivals Assoc., 1988, Andy award Ad. Club N.Y.C., 1983, award U.S. TV Comml FEstival, 1981. Office: Harmony Pictures 2921 W Alameda Ave Burbank CA 91505

DAVIS, JAMES LUTHER, utilities executive, lawyer; b. Memphis, May 8, 1924; s. Luther and Sarah (Carter) D.; m. Natalie Young, Jan. 26, 1947; children: James Luther, Fred C., Peggy E. BBA, U. Ariz., 1946, LLB, 1949. Bar: Ariz. 1949. Sole practice Tucson, 1949-52, asst. city atty., 1952-53, city mgr., 1953-55; with Tucson Gas & Electric Co. (now Tucson Electric Power Co.), 1955—; exec. v.p. 1958-59, pres., 1959-76, chmn. bd., from 1967, now ret.; bd. dirs. El Paso br. Fed. Res. Bd., Dallas, 1974-77, chmn. 1976-77. Mem. charter rev. com. City of Tucson, 1965-71; bd. dirs. Tucson Airport Authority, 1957-62, 64-70, pres. 1965; bd. dirs. Tucson Med. Ctr., 1955-58, 59-65, pres. 1957-58; mem. Tucson Indsl. Devel. Bd., 1959-64; mem. nat. bd. advisors Coll. Bus. and Pub. Adminstrn., U. Ariz., 1985—; bd. dirs. Ariz. Acad., 1962-74, 78-82, Health Planning Council Tucson, 1964-71, Tucson Regional Plan, 1966—, United Way, 1985—; bd. dirs. Green Fields Sch., 1964-69, chmn. bd., 1964-66; bd. dirs. U. Ariz. Found., 1985—, v.p., 1987—. Mem. Tex. Bar Assn., Ariz. Bar Assn., Nat. Assn. Mfrs. (bd. dirs. 1960-62), Pacific Coast Gas Assn. (bd. dirs. 1958-60), Pacific Coast Elect. Assn. (bd. dirs. 1972-86, pres. 1978-79), Western Energy and Supply Assn. (bd. dirs. 1964-76), Tucson C. of C. (bd. dirs. 1958-60, 64-66, 80—, chmn. 1987-88), So. Ariz. Water Resources Assn. (bd. dirs. 1982—, pres. 1987), Blue Key, Phi Gamma Delta, Alpha Kappa Psi, Phi Delta Phi. Clubs: Tucson Country, Old Pueblo (bd. dirs. 1956-58, pres. 1957-58). Home: 6781 N Altos Primero Tucson AZ 85718 Office: Tucson Electric Power Co 220 W 6th St Tucson AZ 85701

DAVIS, JEREMY MATTHEW, chemist; b. Bakersfield, Calif., Aug. 5, 1953; s. Joseph Hyman and Mary (Pavetto) D.; m. Bernadette Sobkiewicz, Aug. 28, 1976; 1 child, Andrew Jeremy. BS, U. Calif., 1974; M in Pub. Adminstrn., Calif. State U., Long Beach, 1983. Salesman Camera World, San Diego, 1974-75, Gailey Photo Supply, Escondido, Calif., 1975-76; lab. technician Crosby Labs., Orange, Calif., 1976-77; chemist I, II, Orange County Water Dist., Fountain Valley, Calif., 1977-84, supervising chemist, 1984—. Papers in field. Named Lab. Person of Yr., Calif. Water Pollution Control Assn., Santa Ana River Basin, 1984. Mem. Am. Chem. Soc. (chem. health and safety sect.), Am. Water Works Assn., Am. Soc. Pub. Adminstrn., Water Pollution Control Fedn., Calif. Water Pollution Control Assn. (bd. dirs. Santa Ana River Basin chpt., Lab. Person of Yr., 1984). Office: Orange County Water Dist PO Box 8300 Fountain Valley CA 92728-8300

DAVIS, JESSE WADE, federal agency administrator; b. Fayetteville, Ark., May 10, 1953; s. John William Jr. and Betty Eudena (Hummel) D.; m. Marilyn Kay Hartung, Feb. 12, 1983. BS, Northeastern State U., Tahlequah, Okla., 1975; MBA, Northeastern State U., 1981. Internship with U.S. Postal Svc., various locations, 1981-85; mgr. delivery and collections, Mgmt. Sectional Ctr. U.S. Postal Svc., Colorado Springs, Colo., 1985-88; dir. ops. svcs. Mgmt. Sectional Ctr. U.S. Postal Svc., Colorado Springs, 1988—. Mem. Pinon Valley Neighborhodd Assn., Colorado Springs. Sgt. U.S. Army, 1975-79. Mem. Nat. Assn. Postal Suprs. (v.p. 1987-88), Am. Mgmt. Assn., Acacia Fraternity, Northeastern State U. Alumni Assn. (life mem.), Trout Unlimited (sec.-treas. Cheyenne Mountain chpt.). Mem. Disciples of Christ Ch. Home: 5429 Pinon Valley Rd Colorado Springs CO 80919-2415 Office: US Postal Svc GMF 3655 E Fountain Blvd Colorado Springs CO 80910-9993

DAVIS, JOAN, land developer, consultant, tax preparer; b. Anderson, Ind., Nov. 24, 1947; d. Harold Brewer and Alice Marie (Doll) Hall; m. L.R. Collier Sr., May 19, 1967 (div. Apr. 1980); children: Missy JoAn Collier Basham, L.R. Jr.; m. Timothy G. Davis, Oct. 10, 1982; stepchildren: Geraldine Marie Davis, Eugene Francis Davis. Grad. high sch., Riverside, Calif. Sec. Svc. Electric, Inc., Riverside, 1966-68; pres. Power Electric, Inc., Norco, Calif., 1972-76; office mgr. Cutter Electric, Inc., Rialto, Calif., 1976-77; exec. asst., controller Home & Country, Inc., Riverside, 1977—; owner, tax preparer Davis Bus. Svc., Riverside, 1978—. Mem. Rubidoux Falcon Football Boosters (sec. publicity com. Riverside chpt. 1983-89). Republican. Home: 6981 Pacheco Ct Riverside CA 92509 Office: Home & Country Inc 7265 Jurupa Ave Riverside CA 92504

DAVIS, JOHN ALBERT, lawyer; b. Seattle, July 29, 1940; s. Carl Lee and Helen Irene (Corner) D.; m. Judith Ann Colvin, June 21, 1959 (div. 1978); children: John Albert Jr., James Colvin, Jennifer Lynn; m. Michelle Ann Frkovich, June 3, 1989. Student, U. Calif., Berkeley, 1957-58; postgrad., Diablo Valley Coll., 1962; JD, Golden Gate U., 1970. Bar: Calif. 1971, U.S. Dist. Ct. (no. dist.) Calif. 1971, U.S. Ct. Appeals (9th cir.) 1971, U.S. Supreme Ct. 1986. Pres. Cal-State Distbrs., Oakland, Calif., 1959-78; pvt. practice Oakland, 1978-81, San Ramon, 1985—; v.p., chief operating officer Madre Mining, Ltd., Sacramento, 1981-85; pres., bd. dirs. O'Hara Resources, Ltd., Vancouver, B.C., Can., 1989—; bd. dirs. Troy Gold Industries, Ltd., Calgary, Alta., Can. Mem. Calif. Bar Assn., Commonwealth Club Calif. Republican. Presbyterian. Office: 100 Park Pl Ste 165 San Ramon CA 94583

DAVIS, JOHN MACDOUGALL, lawyer; b. Seattle, Feb. 20, 1914; s. David Lyle and Georgina (MacDougall) D.; m. Ruth Anne Van Arsdale, July 1, 1939; children: Jean, John, Bruce, Ann, Margaret, Elizabeth. B.A., U. Wash., 1936, LL.B., 1940. Bar: Wash. 1940. Assoc. Poe, Falknor, Emory & Howe, Seattle, 1940-45; sole practice Seattle, 1945-46; ptnr. Davis & Riese, Seattle, 1946-48, Emory, Howe, Davis & Riese, Seattle, 1948-50, Howe, Davis & Riese, Seattle, 1951-53, Howe, Davis, Riese & Aiken, Seattle, 1953-58, Howe, Davis, Riese & Jones, Seattle, 1951-68, Davis, Wright, Todd, Riese & Jones, Seattle, 1969-85; of counsel Davis, Wright & Jones, Seattle, 1985—; lectr. U. Wash. Law Sch., 1947-52. Bd. dirs. Virginia Mason Hosp., Seattle, 1952-79, pres., 1970-72; bd. dirs. Pacific Sci. Ctr., 1971—, past pres., past chmn.; trustee Whitman Coll., 1971-86, chmn., 1983-86; bd. dirs. Blue Cross Wash. and Alaska, Diabetic Trust Fund, 1954—, Wash. Student Loan Guaranty Assn., 1978-83; mem. adv. bd. Chief Seattle council Boy Scouts Am.; pres. King County Schs. Dirs., Seattle, 1958-59. Served with USNG, 1931-34. Recipient Disting. Eagle Scout award, 1982. Mem. ABA, Wash. State Bar Assn. (merit award 1965), Seattle-King County Bar Assn. (pres. 1960-61), Order of Coif, Phi Delta Phi, Alpha Delta Phi. Presbyterian. Clubs: Rainier (Seattle). Home: 7662 SE 22d St Mercer Island WA 98040 Office: Davis Wright & Jones 2600 Century Sq 1501 4th Ave Seattle WA 98101

DAVIS, KEVIN ROBERT, investor; b. Milw., Jan. 9, 1945; s. Emmett Matthew and Mary Ruth (McCarten) D.; m. Karen Susanne Veley, Nov. 9, 1963 (div. May 1979); children: Christopher, Cameron. BS, U. Wis., 1967. Computer salesperson IBM Corp., Madison, Wis., 1967-69; computer programmer and analyst Hughes Aircraft Co., Culver City, Calif., 1969-75; prin. Davis Mgmt. Corp., Los Angeles, 1975—. Screenwriter The Hoax, 1972. Mem. Mensa. Home: 456 S Spalding Dr Beverly Hills CA 90212-4104 Office: Davis Mgmt Corp 2029 Century Park E Ste 110 Los Angeles CA 90067

DAVIS, KURT REYNOLDS, political party executive; b. Hollywood, Calif., Mar. 12, 1962; s. Jack Lee and Eveline Karin (Lange) D.; m. Janet Lynn Alexander, Jan. 12, 1985; 1 child, Brittani Faith. BS in Pub. Adminstrn., No. Ariz. U., 1984, postgrad. pub. adminstrn., 1984—. Adminstrv. asst. to dir. budget and fiscal br. Coconino Nat. Forest, Flagstaff, Ariz., 1982; personal asst. to supr. Coconino County Bd. Suprs., Flagstaff, 1982; confidential asst. to dir. personnel U.S. Dept. Edn., Washington, 1984, spl. asst. to dir. intergovtl. affairs, 1985-86; adminstrv. asst. to dir. President's Commn. on White House Fellowships, Washington, 1985; spl. asst. to dir. intergovtl. and regional affairs SBA, Washington, 1986, spl. asst. to adminstr., 1986-87; exec. dir. Ariz. Rep. Party, Phoenix, 1987—. No. Ariz. coord. Campaign To Reelect Congressman Bob Stump, 1980, 82, 84, Campaign to Reelect Senator Barry Goldwater, 1980; del. Ariz. Rep. Conv., 1980; precinct committeeman, capt. Coconino Rep. Com.; exec. dir. Coconino County Rep. Hdqrs., 1984; candidate for Coconino County Bd. Suprs., 1984; bd. dirs. Ariz. Recreation Ctr. for Handicapped, 1988—, pres. bd. dirs., 1989—. Recipient cert. of appreciation League United Latin Am. Citizens, 1984. Mem. Reagan Adminstrn. Alumni Assn. Mem. Christian Ch. Office: Ariz Rep Party 3501 N 24th St Phoenix AZ 85016

DAVIS, LESLIE, aerospace engineer; b. Linden, Va., Sept. 4, 1924; s. Leslie Lo and Dora (Baliey) D.; m. Helen Claire Jansen, Apr. 4. 1959; children: Jan Marie, Robert Leslie. BGS, N.M. State U., 1981; MA in Mgmt., Webster U., 1985, MBA, 1987. Enlisted USMC, 1942, retired, 1955; Prin. engr. Raytheon Co., White Sands, N.M., 1955—; Pres., dir. Blue Sky Enterprises, El Paso, 1974-84. Adv. com. Wilderness Mus., City of El Pas, 1979. Fellow Royal Anthropol. Inst. Great Britain; mem. Tex. Archeol. Soc. (pres. 1979, v.p., dir. 1974-79, chmn. fin. com. 1988—), USMC Hist. Found. (life), U.S.Naval Inst., El Paso Archeol. Soc., N.M. Archeol. Soc., Mass. Archeol. Soc., El Paso Corral of Westerners. Democrat. Home: 9801 Gschwind El Paso TX 79924 Office: Raytheon Co PO Box B White Sands Missile Range NM 88002

DAVIS, MARY ELIZABETH, medical office administrator; b. Schenectady, May 17, 1957; d. William McColl and Phyllis Ann (Longo) Hope; m. Mark Hudson Davis, Oct. 25, 1986. Student, Idaho State U., Pocatello, 1975-80. Reg. pharmacy tech. Children's ref. librarian Pocatello Pub. Library, 1978-80; pharmacy tech. South Coast Med. Ctr., South Laguna, Calif., 1980-82; operating rm. pharmacy tech. Mission Hosp., Mission Viejo, Calif., 1982-86; office mgr. Mark H. Davis, M.D., Mission Viejo, 1987—. Author various pharmacy procedure manuals. Active various charitable orgns. Mem. Women's Hosp. Aux. (v.p. 1988-89, co-chmn. fundraiser 1988). Republican. Roman Catholic. Office: 26732 Crown Valley #443 Mission Viejo CA 92691

DAVIS, MAXINE MOLLIE, nurse; b. Salem, Oreg., July 19, 1932; d. Maxwell C. and Audrey M. (Pratt) O'Brien; m. Harold Robert Davis, July 18, 1954; children: Jackie, Julie. Cert. in Nursing, Good Samaritan Sch. Nursing, 1953. RN, Oreg. Surp. operating room Blue Mountain Gen. Hosp., Prairie City, Oreg., 1953-54; staff nurse Eugene (Oreg.) Hosp. and Clinic, 1955-56; office nurse pvt. practice, Brookings, Oreg., 1956-57; operating room staff nurse So. Oreg. Gen. Hosp., Grants Pass, 1964-67, supr. operating room, 1969-86, dir. surgical services, 1986—. Mem. Assn. Operating Room Nurses. Episcopalian. Lodge: Ea. Star. Home: 1312 NW B St Grants Pass OR 97526 Office: So Oreg Med Ctr 1505 NW Washington Blvd Grants Pass OR 97526

DAVIS, MELVIN, video engineer, producer; b. Chgo., Oct. 14, 1924; s. Henry and Elvira (Richards) D.; m. Cerie Murchison (dec. 1985). BA, Lincoln Coll., 1948. Asst. producer Playboy Prodns., L.A., 1961—. Coach, bd. dirs. Wilshire Recreational Ctr., 1985—; exec. bd. dirs., Joe Parnello Scholarship Fund, De Paul U., L.A., 1988—. Sgt. U.S. Army, 1942-45, ETO. Decorated 3 Bronze Star medals. Democrat. Baptist.

DAVIS, MICHAEL ANTHONY, computer consultant company executive, consultant; b. Detroit, May 31, 1949; s. John Henry and Jeanette (Riberdy) D.; m. Sharon Muriel Grieves, Oct. 29, 1971; children: Alison Marie, Christine Muriel, Patrick James. BBA, U. Mich., 1971. Tech. rep. Unisys Corp., Detroit, 1972-79, mgr., 1979-87; v.p. Simplified Info. Solutions, Inc., Chandler, Ariz., 1987; pres. Systems Performance Group, Inc., Puyallup, Wash., 1987-88, Resource Guidance, Inc., Glendale Ariz., 1988—. Author computer software SIMPL-ASIST RG/Modeler, 1987. Home: 5332 W Pershing Ave Glendale AZ 85304 Office: Resource Guidance Inc Glendale AZ 85304

DAVIS, MICHAEL LEO, health care administrator, consultant; b. Vancouver, Wash., June 29, 1945; s. Leo Lyle and Myrtle Beatrice (Franzen) D.; m. Patti Clarice Kurtz, July 4, 1965; children: Gregry Michael, Shonna Kay. BS, Loma Linda U., 1969; MA, U. So. Calif., 1973. Licensed physical therapist. Advisor, coord. student clinics Easter Seal Soc., San Bernardino, Calif., 1969-71; successively dir. clin. rsch., asst. dir. phys. therapy, assoc. prof. allied health Loma Linda (Calif.) U. Med. Ctr., 1969-73; adminstrv. dir. rehab. Portland (Oreg.) Adventist Med. Ctr., 1973-83, adminstrv. dir. community health and rehab., 1983-85, coord. med. staff devel., 1985—; pres. Davis Enterprises pvt. cons. firm, Portland, 1980—; cons. Portland Storm profl. football team, 1974-75, L.A. County Lung Assn., 1970-72, Edn. Svc. Dist. #112, Vancouver, 1981-83. Contbr. to manuals in field of rehabilitation. Rehab. rep. respiratory care coun., Oreg. Lung Assn., Portland, 1973-85; bd. dirs. Reins of Life, Portland, 1983, Am. Arthritis Found. of Oreg., 1975-85. Recipient Commendation Loma Linda U. Alumni Assn., 1973, Disting. Svc. award Portland Pub. Schs., 1981. Mem. Acad. Health Svcs. Mktg., Am. Physical Therapy Assn., Oreg. Physical Therapy Assn., Am. Coll. Healthcare Execs. (nominee), Kiwanis (pres. 1984-85), Gateway Boosters (Portland). Office: Portland Adventist Med Ctr 10123 SE Market St Portland OR 97216

DAVIS, PAUL WESLEY, minister of music; b. Springfield, Ill., Aug. 14, 1945; s. D. Walter and Lucy Belle (Swords) D.; m. Faith Pearl Edmonds Davis, July 14, 1973; children: Matthew, Theresa, Christina. MusB, Biola U., 1971; MA in Music, Calif. State U. at Fullerton, 1979. Ordained to ministry Bapt. Ch. Minister music Ch. of the Open Door, Los Angeles, 1972-78; Assn. pastor and music dir. Whittier Area Bapt. Fellowship, Calif., 1978—; guest lectr. and speaker for music confs. and retreats Glass Conv., Musicalifornia, 1971—. Pres. REJOICE, Inc., Walnut, Calif., 1971-87. Mem. Choral Conductors Guild (v.p. 1971-72), Am. Choral Dirs. Assn. Republican. Baptist. Home: 520 Calle Fortuna Walnut CA 91789 Office: Whittier Area Bapt Fellowship 8175 Villa Verde Dr Whittier CA 90605

DAVIS, R. W., chemical company executive; b. 1924; married. M.S., MIT, 1950; M.B.A., Northwestern U., 1966. With Chevron Chem. Co., 1951—, pres., chief exec. officer, 1982-89, also dir. Office: Chevron Chem Co 575 Market St San Francisco CA 94105 *

DAVIS, RHYSA MERYT, editor; b. Los Angeles, Jan. 7, 1948; d. Harold and Dorothy (Thomas) D. BA, Calif. State U., San Jose, 1969, MS, 1970; MA, U. So. Calif., 1978; postgrad., Cambridge (Eng.) U. Pub. relations rep. MGM Studios, Burbank, Calif., 1970-71; assoc. news writer City News Service, L.A., 1971-72; investigative news reporter KIQQ Radio Sta., L.A., 1972-75; pub. relations dir. Am. Inst. Forensic Sci., L.A., 1975-78; publ. editor Overload Publ., Inc., Canoga Park, Calif., 1978-88; mng. editor Lockheed Calif. Co., Burbank, 1980—. Mem. The Soc. Profl. Journalists, Women in Communications, Inc., AAUW (pres. 1980-82, bd. dirs. 1986-88, fellowship award, 1984-88), Kappa Tau Alpha (Scholarship award 1988). Christian Scientist.

DAVIS, RICHARD CALHOUN, dentist; b. Manhatten, Kans., Jan. 4, 1945; s. William Calhoun and Alison Rae (Wyland) D.; Danna Ruth Ritchel, June 13, 1968; 1 child, Darin Calhoun. Student, Ariz. State U., 1963-65, BA, 1978; BA, U. Ariz., 1966; DDS, U. of Pacific, 1981. Retail dept. head Walgreens, Tucson, 1965-66; mgmt. trainee Walgreens, Tucson, San Antonio, 1967-70; asst. store mgr. Walgreens, Baton Rouge, 1970-72; field rep. Am. Cancer Soc., Phoenix, 1972-74; dept. head Lucky Stores, Inc., Tempe, Ariz., 1976-78; practice dentistry specializing in gen. dentistry Tucson, 1981—. Chmn. bd. Capilla Del Sol Christian Ch., Tucson, 1984. Mem. ADA, Acad. Gen. Dentists, Am. Straight Wire Othodontic Assn., NW Dental Study Club. Republican. Mem. Diciples of Christ Ch. Lodge: Optimist (pres. NW club), Elks. Office: 2777 N Campbell Tucson AZ 85719

DAVIS, RICHARD EARL, educator; b. Memphis, Sept. 6, 1942; s. A Kennon Davis and Billie Irene (Camp) Beatty; m. Helena Lang Pfeffer, Dec. 18, 1966 (div. Aug., 1988); 1 child, Rebekah Caroline Beatty. BA with honors, San Francisco State U., 1968, MA, 1970; PhD, U. Calif., Berkeley, 1976. Mng. dir. WRAMC Little Theatre Co., Washington, 1964-67; tech. dir. Marin Shakespeare Festival, San Rafael, Calif., 1968; grad. asst. Sn Francisco State U., 1968; tech. supr. U. San Francisco, 1969-70, tech. dir, 1970-75, dept. chmn., 1975-80, dir. communication theory program, 1981-87, dir. Ctr. for Teaching Excellence, 1988—; guest expert East China Normal U., Shanghai, China, 1980-81. Lighting designer: Operas Manon LesCaut, 1986, Ernani, 1986, L'Amico Fritz, 1987; actor Ten Little Indians, 1988; designer/performer Sweet Charity, 1989. With U.S. Army, 1964-67. Mem. Profl. and Oganizational Devel. Network in Higher Edn., Golden Gate Club, Angling and Fishing Club. Democrat. Jewish. Office: Univ San Francisco Ignatian Heights San Francisco CA 94117-1080

DAVIS, RICHARD ERNEST, engineer; b. San Francisco, Nov. 20, 1936; 1 child, Richard Jr.; m. Sharon L. Buss, Aug. 26, 1961; children: Dawn, Michelle. BS in Engring., Calif. State Poly. U., San Luis Obispo, 1967. Facilities engr., energy conservation engr. Naval Weapons Ctr., China Lake, Calif., 1967-77; solar program coordinator U.S. Dept. Energy, Oakland, Calif., 1977-78; program mgr. Solar Energy Research Inst., Golden, Colo., 1978-80; engring. specialist Holmes & Narver, Mercury, Nev., 1980—. Contbr. articles to profl. jours. Served with USAF, 1954-62. Mem. Assn. Energy Engrs. (sr.). Home: SR 15 Box 495 Amargosa Valley NV 89020 Office: Holmes & Narver Inc PO Box I Mercury NV 89023

DAVIS, RICHARD HENRY, JR., chemical company executive; b. Hampton, Va., Nov. 18, 1943; s. Richard H. Davis and Dorothy L. (McCallum) Wright. AB, Temple U., 1967; MS, Georgetown U., 1972, PhD, 1974. Post doctoral fellow NIH-NIAMDD/LCB, Bethesda, Md., 1974-76; rsch. biochemist DuPont Co., Newark, Del., 1976-82; rsch. & devel. mgr. Abbott Labs., S. Pasadena, Calif., 1982-85; QA/TS mgr. Abbott Labs., S. Pasadena, 1985-88; quality assurance dir. Biotrack, Inc., Mt. View, Calif., 1988—.

Capt. Corp. Engrs., USAR, 1967-80. Office: Biotrack 1058 Huff Ave Mount View CA 94043

DAVIS, ROBERT DENNIS, advertising executive; b. Salt Lake City, Aug. 14, 1945; s. James Zimmiri and Blossom (Traver) D.; m. Jeannette Lynn Cader, Oct. 1, 1982. BS, U. Utah, 1967, postgrad., 1967. Creative dir. J. Walter Thompson, San Francisco, 1981-83; v.p., creative dir. Grey Advt., San Francisco, 1983-84; prin. Robert Davis Advt., Inc., Santa Rosa, Calif., 1984-87; mgr. mktg., new product devel. Am. Home Shield, Santa Rosa, 1987—. Contbr. articles to profl. jours. Active Big Brothers of San Francisco; v.p. North Va. Spl. Olympics, Fairfax City, Va., 1974-75. Recipient 4 Best in the West awards Am. Adv. Fedn., 1984. Mem. Ad Club San Francisco, Direct Mktg. Creative Guild, Am. Assn. Fundraising Execs, Miline Club San Francisco, Sonoma County Ad Club. Republican. Episcopalian. Home: 2359 Morningside Circle Santa Rosa CA 95405 Office: Am Home Shield 90 S E St Santa Rosa CA 95404

DAVIS, ROBERT WAYNE, broadcasting executive; b. Snohomish, Wash., May 9, 1947; s. Hugh Edward and Lorraine Mae (Tronsrud) D.; m. Joan Carol Miller, June 21, 1969; children—Emily Lyn, Alison Kay. BBA, U. Wash., 1969. sales rep. Sta. KNDO-TV, Yakima, Wash., 1969-70, ops. mgr., program mgr., 1971-73, v.p., gen. mgr., 1977; acct. exec., Simpson/Reilly & Assoc., Seattle, 1974-77, Sta. KOMO-TV, Seattle, 1977-81; pres., gen. mgr. KMTR-TV, Eugene, Oreg., 1982—, also bd. dirs. Mem. Oreg. Assn. of Broadcasters (bd. dirs. 1987—), Arbitron TV Adv. Council, Nat. Assn. Broadcasters, NBC-TV Affiliates (com. congl. rels.). Club: Wash. Athletic (Seattle); Town (Eugene). Lodge: Rotary. Office: KMTR Inc PO Box 7308 Eugene OR 97401-0208

DAVIS, ROLAND ARTHUR, laboratory scientist; b. Widen, W.Va., June 21, 1930; s. Virgil Arthur and Fanny Rebecca (Frame) D.; m. Charlotte Elaine, Apr. 8, 1961; children: Michelle, Roland Jr., Heather. BSEE, U. So. Calif., L.A., 1959. With tech. staff Hughes Aircraft Co., Culver City, Calif., 1954-72, staff engr., 1972-77, section head, 1977-79; sr. scientist Hughes Aircraft Co., El Segundo, Calif., 1979-88, lab. scientist, 1988—. Contbr. articles to profl. jours. Section dir. Pony Baseball Inc., Granada Hills, Calif., 1981-84. Sgt. USMC, 1951-54, Korea. Republican. Home: 17465 Flanders St Granada Hills CA 91344 Office: Hughes Aircraft Co 2230 Imperial Blvd El Segundo CA 90230

DAVIS, SANDRA JAMISON, educator, artist; b. Akron, Ohio, Aug. 9, 1944; m. James S. Davis, June 21, 1975. BS, Bowling Green (Ohio) State U., 1965; MA, Calif. Luth. U., Thousand Oaks, 1973; PhD, U. Santa Barbara, 1986. Lic. real estate agt. Instr. Valdosta (Ga.) State Coll., 1965-66; with spl. edn. dept. Title I, Daytona Beach, Fla., 1966-71; tchr. multi-handicapped Spl. Edn. Dept., Ventura, Calif., 1971-73; psychometrist/counselor/art therapist Juvenile Hall, Ventura, 1973-79; tchr./counselor art therapy Calabasas Woodview Psychiatric Hosp., Calabasas Park, Calif., 1979—; instr. protrait painting, to date; freelance portrait artist. Mem. Am. Art Therapy Assn., U. Santa Barbara Alunmi Assn., North Ranch Country Club, Malibu Rep. Womens Club, Calabasas Park Tennis Club, Calabasas Womens Club, Dance Gallery. Republican. Home: 4668 Park Mirasol Calabasas Park CA 91302 also: 26664 Seagull Way Malibu CA 90265

DAVIS, STANFORD MELVIN, engineering executive, publishing consultant; b. Camden, N.J., June 12, 1941; s. Winford and Rose Marie (Rich) D.; m. Pamela Davis, Nov. 25, 1967 (div. 1980); children: Peter, Shawna; m. Laura A. Rudolph, Feb. 21, 1987. AB, BSEE, Rutgers U., 1964; postgrad., UCLA, 1967; MBA, U. Portland, 1984. Elec. engr. RCA, Van Nuys, Calif., 1966-68; project engr. Tek, Wilsonville, Oreg., 1968-79; S/W mgr. Tektronix, Wilsonville, 1979-81, mgr. mktg., 1981-83; founder, v.p. engring. Concept Technologies, Portland, 1983-86; mgr. engring. program INTEL, Hillsboro, Oreg., 1986-87; product line mgr. INTEL, Hillsboro, 1987-88; engring. mgr. Graphic Printing div. Tektronix, Wilsonville, Oreg., 1989—. Patentee in field. Served to capt. U.S. Army, 1964-66. Recipient Outstanding Product award Datapro, Delran, N.J., 1985. Mem. Assn. of Computing Machinery, IEEE. Home: 7320 SW 103d Ave Beaverton OR 97005

DAVIS, THOMAS LEO, city administrator; b. Johnstown, Pa., Mar. 20, 1931; s. Thomas Leo and Leeanna (Englehart) D.; m. Carolyn Mosteller, June 5, 1954; children: Thomas Leo Jr., Christopher West, Scott Michael. BS in Econs. Acctg., Villanova U., 1953; MBA, Nova U., 1985. Mgr. distribution acctg. FMC Corp., N.Y.C., 1969-72, chief acct., organic chemical div., 1972-73, mgr. spl. studies, 1973-74, div. acctg. coordinator, 1974; plant controller FMC Corp., Green River, Wyo., 1974-83; v.p., controller FMC Wyo. Corp., Green River, 1984-85; fin., acctg. cons., pvt. practice Green River, 1985—; interim city administr. City of Green River, 1987, city administr., 1987—. Lt. USN, 1953-56, Korea. Mem. (assoc.) Internat. City Mgmt. Assn., K.C. (numerous offices Green River chpt., including Grand Knight, 1984-86; state program dir., 1986-87, state treas., 1987-89, state dep. 1989—, and others), Am. Legion, VFW. Democrat. Roman Catholic. Home: 505 Juniper St Green River WY 82935 Office: City of Green River 50 E 2nd N Green River WY 82935

DAVIS, TROY LEE, software development executive; b. Wichita, Kans., Apr. 30, 1960; s. Raymond Lee and Alene Kay (Stout) D.; m. Leisa Kay Irwin, May 29, 1987; 1 child, Aricka Dawn. Grad. high sch., Wichita. Assembler Aerospace Controls Corp., Wichita, 1978-80; master pattern maker Boeing Corp., Wichita, 1980-82; compt. Apt. Store, Wichita, 1982-84; product devel. and support mgr. ValCom Computer Ctr., Wichita, 1984-87; software devel. analyst Autodesk, Inc., Sausalito, Calif., 1987—. Mem. Nat. Computer Graphics Assn., Mensa, S.C.C.A. Republican. Office: Autodesk Inc 2320 Marinship Way Sausalito CA 94965

DAVIS, VERNE ALFRED, lawyer; b. Portland, Oreg., Feb. 8, 1935; s. Alfred Joseph and Addie Helen (Nofsinger) D.; m. Phyllis Helen Mead; children: Mark Christopher, Kent Stephen. BS, Portland State U., 1959; JD, Lewis & Clark Coll., 1969. Exec. dir. Mental Health Assn. Oreg., Portland, 1967-84; gen. counsel Tower Investment Corp., Portland, 1985; corp. sec. Power Logistics Corp., Beaverton, Oreg., 1986-87; pres. KAP, Inc., Redmond, Wash., 1988-89; pvt. practice law Portland, 1989—; cons. Multi-Power, Inc., Beaverton, Oreg., 1988; corp. sec., bd. dir. MultiPower, Inc., 1988-89; corp. sec. CitiGroup, Inc., Portland, 1987—. Pres. Hub-Cap, community action group, Portland, 1967; moderator First Bapt. Ch., Portland, 1976-82; bd. mem. Oreg. United Appeal, Salem, Oreg., 1972-73. With U.S. Army, 1954-56, Korea. Mem. Oreg. State Bar. Republican. Baptist. Home and Office: 7040 SE 35 Portland OR 97002

DAVIS, WANDA ROSE, lawyer; b. Lampasas, Tex., Oct. 4, 1937; d. Ellis DeWitt and Julia Doris (Rose) Cockrell; m. Richard Andrew Fulcher, May 9, 1959 (div. 1969); 1 child, Greg Ellis; m. Edwin Leon Davis, Jan. 14, 1973 (div. 1985). BBA, U. Tex., 1959, JD, 1971. Bar: Tex. 1971, Colo. 1981, U.S. Dist. Ct. (no. dist.) Tex. 1972, U.S. Dist. Ct. Colo. 1981, U.S. Ct. Appeals (10th cir. 1981, U.S. Supreme Ct. 1976. Atty. Atlantic Richfield Co., Dallas, 1971; assoc. firm Crocker & Murphy, Dallas, 1971-72; prin. Wanda Davis, Atty. at Law, Dallas, 1972-73; ptnr. firm Davis & Davis Inc., Dallas, 1973-75; atty. adviser HUD, Dallas, 1974-75, Air Force Acctg. and Fin. Ctr., Denver, 1976—; co-chmn. regional Profl. Devel. Inst., Am. Soc. Mil. Comptrollers, Colorado Springs, Colo., 1982; chmn. Lowry AFB Noontime Edn. Program, Exercise Program, Denver, 1977-83; mem. speakers bur. Colo. Women's Bar, 1982-83, Lowry AFB, 1981-83; mem. fed. ct. liaison com. U.S. Dist. Ct. Colo., 1983; mem. Leaders of the Fed. Bar Assn. People to People Del. to China, USSR and Finland, 1986. Contbr. numerous articles to profl. jours. Bd. dirs. Pres.'s Council Met. Denver, 1981-83; mem. Lowry AFB Alcohol Abuse Exec. Com., 1981-84. Recipient Spl. Achievement award USAF, 1978; Upward Mobility award Fed. Profl. and Adminstrv. Women, Denver, 1979. Mem. Fed. Bar Assn. (pres. Colo. 1982-83, mem. nat. council 1984—, Earl W. Kintner Disting. Service award 1983, 1st v.p. 10th cir. 1986—), Colo. Trial Lawyers Assn., Bus. and Profl. Women's Club (dist. IV East dir. 1983-84, Colo. pres. 1988-89), Am. Soc. Mil. Comptrollers (pres. 1984-85), Denver South Met. Bus. and Profl. Women's Club (pres. 1982-83), Denver Silver Spruce Am. Bus. Women's Assn. (pres. 1981-82; Woman of Yr. award 1982), Colo. Jud. Inst., Colo. Concerned Lawyers, Profl. Mgrs. Assn., Fed. Women's Program (v.p. Denver 1980), Colo. Woman News Community adv. bd., 1988—, Dallas Bar Assn., Tex. Bar Assn., Denver Bar Assn., Altrusa, Zonta, Denver Nancy Langhorn Federally Employed Women. (pres. 1979-80). Christian. Office: Air Force Acctg and Fin Ctr AFAFC/JAL Denver CO 80279

DAVIS, WILLIAM EUGENE, university administrator; b. Wamego, Kans., Feb. 15, 1929; s. Eugene Kenneth and Willa (Dickinson) D.; m. Pollyanne Peterson, Mar. 17, 1951; children: Deborah, Rebecca, Douglas, Brooke, Bonnie. BS, U. Colo., 1951, EdD, 1963; MA, U. No. Colo., 1958. Asst. to dean men U. Colo., 1951, alumni dir., head football coach, dean men, 1960-63; tchr. English, coach Loveland (Colo.) High Sch., 1954-55, Rapid City (S.D.) High Sch., 1955-59, Greeley (Colo.) High Sch., 1959-60; exec. asst. to pres. U. Wyo., 1963-65; pres. Idaho State U., Pocatello, 1965-75; commr. Western Interstate Commn. Higher Edn., Idaho, 1965-75, N.Mex., 1978-82, Oreg., 1983—; pres. U. N.Mex., Albuquerque, 1975-82; chancellor Oreg. System Higher Edn., Eugene, 1983-88; Idaho commr. Western Interstate Commn. for Higher Edn., 1965-75, vice chmn., 1973-74, chmn., 1974-75; N.Mex. commr. Western Interstate Commn. Higher Edn., 1978-82; mem. N.Mex. Selection Com. for Rhodes scholars, 1976-82, Pres.'s Coun. Western Athletic Conf., 1975-82, chmn., 1978-79; mem. N.Mex. Gov.'s Com. on Tech. Excellence, 1975-82, Nat. Collegiate Athletic Assn. Theodore Roosevelt Award Jury, 1974-79; chmn. Idaho Rhodes Scholarship Selection Com., 1971-75; mem. Gov.'s Corp. Voluntarism Com., 1982—, Am. Council Edn., 1982—, AFL-CIO Labor/Higher Edn Coun., 1982—. Author: Glory Colorado-A History of the University of Colorado, 1965, Nobody Calls Me Doctor, 1972. Capt. USMCR, 1951-54. Mem. Western Coll. Assn. (exec. com. 1981—), Assn. Western Univs. (bd. dirs. 1975-82), Oreg. Hist. Soc. (bd. dirs. 1982—), Am. Assn. State Colls. and Univs. (com. governance 1985—), Alpha Tau Omega, Phi Delta Kappa, Omicron Delta Kappa, Elks, Rotary. Methodist. Office: Oreg State System Higher Edn PO Box 3175 Eugene OR 97403

DAVISON, HELEN IRENE, teacher, counselor; b. Oskaloosa, Iowa, Dec. 19, 1926; d. Grover C. and Beulah (Williams) Hawk; m. Walter Francis Davison, June 20, 1953 (div.); 1 child, Linda Ellen. BS in Zoology, Iowa State U., 1948; MS in Biol. Sci., U. Chgo., 1951; MA in Ednl. Psychology and Counseling, Calif. State U., Northridge, 1985. Med. rsch. technician U. Chgo. Med. Sch., 1951-53; tchr. sci. Lane High Sch., Charlottesville, Va., 1953-55; med. rsch. asst. U. Va. Med. Sch., Charlottesville, 1955-56, U. Mich., Ann Arbor, 1956-60; tchr. sci. Monroe High Sch., Sepulveda, Calif., 1966—; rsch. technician Los Alamos Sci. Labs., summer 1954; part-time counselor psychotherapy Forte Found., Van Nuys, Calif., 1987—. V.p. San Fernando Valley chpt. Am. Field Svc., 1980-81; vol. counselor Planned Parenthood Am., L.A., 1982-88. NSF fellow, 1985-86. Mem. Calif. Tchrs. Assn., Calif. Assn. Marriage and Family Therapists, Iowa Acad. Sci. (assoc.), AAUW. Home: 17425 Vintage St Northridge CA 91325 Office: James Monroe High Sch 9229 Haskell Ave Sepulveda CA 91343

DAVISSON, VANESSA TERESA, graphic designer; b. Bklyn., Aug. 12, 1958; d. Vincent Peter and Elvira Elena (Ippolito) Russo; m. Danny Martin Davisson, Nov. 21, 1982; children: Elena Teresa, Daniel Lawrence. BFA, Syracuse U., 1979. Art dir. MSW Advt., N.Y.C., 1980-81; designer Best Western Internat., Phoenix, 1981-82; prodn. mgr. Mullen Advt. and Pub. Relations, Phoenix, 1982-83; pub. relations dir. North Am. Van Lines, Carson, Calif., 1983-84; owner Promotional Graphics, Long Beach, Calif., 1984-85; design coordinator Samaritan Health Systems, Phoenix, 1985-86; owner Graphic Design and Illustration, Fountain Hills, Ariz., 1986—; ptnr. Synergy III, Phoenix, 1986—; speaker in field. Mem. Fountain Hills (Ariz.) C. of C.; Profl. Bus. Assn., Long Beach, 1984. Named Young Career Woman for Ariz. Nat. Fedn. Bus. and Profl. Women, 1988. Mem. Met. Bus. and Profl. Women, U.S. Jaycees (v.p. community affairs 1988). Republican. Roman Catholic. Home and Office: 17307 E Calaveras Ave Fountain Hills AZ 85268

DAWES, DOUGLAS CHARLES, military officer; b. Detroit, Nov. 24, 1952; s. Carl Joseph and Margaret Elisabeth (Ingalls) D.; m. Belle Ann Black, May 22, 1978 (div. Feb. 1986). BBA in Mgmt., Loyola U., New Orleans, 1974. Field artillery officer U.S. Army, various locations, 1974-80; asst. fin. officer U.S. Army, Ft. Sill, Okla., 1980-82; deputy fin. and acctg. officer U.S. Army, West Germany, 1982-86, Ft. Carson, Colo., 1986-87; comdr. and fin. officer U.S. Army, Ft. Carson, 1987-88, budget officer, asst. div. comptroller, 1988—. Mem. Blazers Ski Club (treas. Colorado Springs 1988—), Pikes Peak Road Runners Club, Delta Sigma Pi (chancellor Delta Nu chpt. 1973, 1st v.p. 1974). Republican. Home: 9116 Chieftan Dr Colorado Springs CO 80925 Office: US Army HHC USAG Fort Carson CO 80913

DAWES, WILLIAM REDIN, JR., laboratory administrator; b. Charlotte, N.C., Oct. 10, 1940; s. William R. and Olive M. (Spence) D.; m. K. Jenison Klinger, Jan. 23, 1988; children: Catron, Clayton; m. Jeanne Ruth Coward, Dec. 31, 1986; children: William, Kimberly. BS, U. N.C., 1962; MS, U. Ariz., 1964, PhD, 1968. Mem. tech. staff Bell Tel. Labs, Allentown, Pa., 1968-70, supr., 1970-75; supr. Sandia Nat. Labs., Albuquerque, 1975-83, dept. mgr., 1983—. Contbr. numerous articles to profl. jours. Mem. Soc. Sigma Xi. Republican. Home: 112 White Oaks Dr NE Albuquerque NM 87122 Office: Sandia Nat Labs 2501 Box 5800 Albuquerque NM 87185

DAWSON, DAWN PAIGE, publisher; b. Paradise, Calif., Nov. 10, 1956; d. Wayne Paul and Donna Jean (Peckham) D. AB, Occidental Coll., 1979. Editorial asst. Salem Press Inc., Pasadena, Calif., 1979-80; copy editor 1980-81, sr. editor, 1982-83, mgr. editor, 1984-87, v.p. editing and prodn., 1987—. Mem. Customer's Guild West. Mem. Soc. Scholarly Pub., Nat. Assn. Female Execs. Office: Salem Press Inc 150 S Los Robles Ste 720 Pasadena CA 91101

DAWSON, JAMES PAUL, JR., commercial real estate company executive; b. Logansport, Ind., Nov. 11, 1926; s. James Paul and Gwendolyn Virginia (Benner) D.; m. Janet Marie Waters, Jan. 3, 1950; children: James P. III, Stephen Richard, Diane Sharon. BS in Mgmt., Ind. U., 1954; MBA, U. Denver, 1974. Lic. real estate broker, Colo. Pres. J.D. Assocs., Broomfield, Colo., 1975-78; mktg. dir. R.V. Lord & Assocs., Boulder, Colo., 1978-83; pres. Dawson Group, Inc., Northglenn, Colo., 1984—. Chmn. Adams County Victims Compensation Bd., Brighton, Colo., 1983-88; pres. North Metro Mobility, Inc., Thornton, Colo., 1979—. Served to staff sgt. Army Air Force, 1945-47, Korea, USAF, 1951-53. Mem. Am. Planning Assn., Am. Rifle Assn. Republican. Home and Office: 10978 Patterson Ct Northglenn CO 80234

DAWSON, LELAND BRADLEY, dentist; b. Princeton, Ill., Jan. 30, 1950; s. Harold Bradley and Frances Emilia (Strandholm) D. BA, Pacific Luth. U., 1972; DDS, U. Ill., Chgo., 1976. Dentist Group Health Dental, Burien, Wash., 1976-78; pvt. practice dentistry Kent, Wash., 1978—; clin. instr. dental asst. program Highline Community Coll., Kent, 1978-85. Deacon Kent Covenant Ch., 1983—. Mem. ADA, Pacific Luth. U. Alumni Assn., Seattle-King County Dental Soc., Q Club of Pacific Luth. U. Mem. Evang. Covenant. Home: 14224 SE 270th Pl Kent WA 98042 Office: 13210 SE 240th Blvd Ste B-1 Kent WA 98042

DAWSON, MARK H., university administrator. Chancellor U. Nev. system, 1987—. Office: U Nev System 405 Marsh Ave Reno NV 89509-0019 *

DAWSON, MICHAEL EDWARD, psychologist, educator; b. Chgo., Mar. 31, 1940; s. Peter F. and Clara (Stephens) D.; m. Lavina Thersa Caparella, June 16, 1962; children: Michael, Christopher. BS, Ariz. State U., 1963; PhD, U. So. Calif., 1967. Lic. psychologist, Calif. Asst. prof. Calif. State Coll., Los Angeles, 1967-69; research psychologist Gateways Hosp., Los Angeles, 1969-79; adj. assoc. prof. UCLA, 1979-84; assoc. prof. U. So. Calif., Los Angeles, 1984-87, prof., 1987—. Co-author: Emotions and Bodily Response, 1978; assoc. editor jour. Psychology, 1980-83; contbr. articles to profl. jours. NIMH grantee, 1969—. Mem. AAAS, Am. Psychol. Assn., Soc. Psycholphys. Research (bd. dirs. 1981-84, pres. 1988—). Office: U So Calif Dept Psychology SGM 501 Los Angeles CA 90089-1061

DAWSON, PATRICIA LUCILLE, surgeon; b. Kingston, Jamaica, W.I., Sept. 30, 1949; came to U.S., 1950.; d. Percival Gordon and Edna Claire (Overton) D.; m. Stanley James Hiserman, Sept. 6, 1980; children: Alexandria Zoe, Wesley Gordon. BA in Sociology, Allegheny Coll., 1971; MD, N.J. Med. Sch., Newark, 1977. Membership dir. N.J. ACLU, Newark, 1972; resident in surgery U. Medicine and Dentistry N.J. N.J. Med Sch., 1977-79; Virginia Mason Med. Ctr., Seattle, 1979-82; pvt. practice specializing in surgery Arlington, Wash., 1982-83, Seattle, 1983--. Bd. dirs. Beginnings Child Care, Seattle; mem. 101 Black Women, Seattle, Northwest Women's Law Ctr. Fellow: ACS, Seattle Surg. Soc.; mem. Am. Med. Womens Assn., Physicians for Social Responsibility, Wash. Black Profls. in Health Care, NOW, NARL. Office: Group Health Coop 200 15th Ave E Seattle WA 98112

DAWSON, ROBERT HAROLD, economist, researcher; b. Yakima, Wash., Aug. 28, 1935; s. William Carl and Frieda (Hein) D.; m. Blanche Elizabeth McLaughlin, Apr. 2, 1962. BA, U. Wash., Seattle, 1957; postgrad., U. Calif., Berkeley, 1964-66, Oreg. State U., 1969-72. Rsch. assoc. Food Industries Rsch. & Engring., Yakima, 1957-60; agrl. economist Chiriqui Land Co., Republic of Panama, 1960-61, Tela R.R. Co., La Lima, Honduras, 1961-63, Econ. Rsch. Svc., USDA, Corvallis, Oreg., 1963-85; cons. Experience, Inc., Mpls., 1984-85, Bonneville Power Adminstrn., Portland, Oreg., 1986; pres. Robert H. Dawson & Assoc., Inc., Corvallis, 1986—; rsch. assoc. U. Calif., Berkeley, 1963-66; instr. Oreg. State U., Corvallis, 1966-79, asst. prof., 1979-86; cons. Bur. of Reclamation, U.S. Dept. Interior, Boise, Idaho, 1985-86, U.S. Agy. for Internat. Devel., Dominica, 1984. Contbr. articles to profl. jours. Adminstr. House Com. on Agr., Forestry and Natural Resources, Salem, Oreg., 1987; economist Oreg. Dept. Revenue, Salem, 1988. Mem. Am. Assn. Agrl. Economists, Western Assn. Agrl. Economists, Oreg. Wheat Growers League, Internat. Listing Agrl. Economists, Elks. Home and Office: 3700 NW Witham Hill Dr Corvallis OR 97330

DAWSON, SETH RAY, lawyer; b. Britton, S.D., June 3, 1951; s. Leonard David and Myrtle Donna (Seth) D.; m. Lynda Marie Garman, Oct. 13, 1985. BA magna cum laude, U. Wash., 1973; JD, U. Calif., Hasting Coll., 1976; postgrad., Nat. Coll. Dist. Attys., 1979. Bar: Wash. 1976, U.S. Dist. Ct. (9th cir.) 1976, U.S. Supreme Ct. 1983. Dep. prosecutor Snohomish County, Everett, Wash., 1977-80, prosecutor, 1983—; prosecutor City of Everett, 1980-83; instr. Edmonds Community Coll., 1988; faculty adviser Nat. Coll. Dist. Attys., Houston, 1980; mem. Wash. State Criminal Justice Tng. Commn.; judge pro tem Snohomish County Dist. Ct. (so. dist.) Wash., 1981. Mem. adv. com. Office. Fin. Affairs, 1984; mem. Sen. Judiciary Com. Task Force on Child Abuse, 1985; mem. adv. com. Nat. Ctr. for Prosecution Child Abuse; chmn. adv. com. Snohomish County High Priority Infant Tracking System; bd. dirs. Open Door Theatre, numerous other orgns. for children's affairs; chmn. adv. bd., mem. exec. bd. dirs. Snohomish County Drug Enforcement Task Force; chmn. citizens adv. bd. Juvenile Awareness Program, 1979-80; coach Everett Youth Basketball, 1980, 81. Recipient Spl. Recognition award Snohomish County MAD, 1986, Human Svcs. Coun., 1987, Chem. Health Awareness Team, 1986-87, Snohomish County DWI Task Force, 1984-87, Snohomish County Alcohol and Drug Svcs., 1988. Mem. Snohomish County Bar Assn. (mem. dist. ct. com. 1981), Assn. Snohomish County City Attys. (founding pres. 1980), Snohomish County Peace Officers Assn. (pres. 1984), Wash. Assn. Prosecuting Attys. (chmn. legis. com.), Rotary, Phi Beta Kappa. Democrat. Methodist. Office: Snohomish County Prosecutor's Office 3000 Rockefeller Ave Everett WA 98201

DAWSON, STEPHEN EDWIN, magic shop and consulting service owner; b. Washington, Sept. 24, 1949; s. Edwin Gerard and Jean Elizabeth (Butler) D.; m. Julia Lynn Robinson, June 5, 1971; children: Stephen, Douglas, Travis, Amy. BA, Am. U., 1971. Dir. guest svcs. Ramada Inn Corp., San Francisco, 1971-73; mgr. magic dept. Larry's Costume and Novelty, San Jose, Calif., 1973-76; owner, operator The Magic Touch, San Jose, Milpitas, Calif., 1976—. Author: How to Be Funny Without Being Stupid, 1982, New Look at Old Magic, 1984, Foundations for Gospel Magicians, 1986. Cubmaster Boy Scouts Am., Milpitas, 1987—. Mem. Internat. Brotherhood Magicians (territorial rep. 1977—), Soc. Am. Magicians, Mystic 13 of San Jose, Magic Dealer's Assn., Oakland Magic Circle (hon.), Milpitas C. of C., Pacific Coast Assn. of Magicians (dealer coord.). Mormon. Office: The Magic Touch 144 N Milpitas Blvd Milpitas CA 95035

DAWSON, WILLIAM JAMES, JR., orthodontist; b. San Francisco, May 16, 1930; s. William James and Augusta (Rude) D.; A.B., U. Calif. at Berkeley, 1948-52; D.D.S., U. Calif. Med. Center, San Francisco, 1958; m. Judith Elizabeth Riede, Aug. 11, 1962; children—William James, Wendy, Nancy Garms, Sarah Rankin, Evelyn Elizabeth. Pvt. practice orthodontics, San Rafael, Calif., 1958—; clin. instr. oral histology, U. Calif. Med. Center, San Francisco, 1958-61; clin. instr. orofacial anomolies, 1964-75, asst. research dentist, 1968-75; mem. Calif. Bd. Dental Examiners, 1985—, sec. 1987-88. Mem. bd. adminstrn. Calif. Pub. Employees Retirement System, 1969-76. Mem. adv. om. Marin council Boy Scouts Am., 1965—; chmn. citizen's adv. com. Dominican Coll. San Rafael, 1974-76; mem. city council, Ross, Calif., 1967-69; assoc. mem. Calif. Rep. Cen. Com., 1967-68, 85-87, regular mem., 1971-73; pres. Marin County Property Owners Assn., 1980-82; bd. dirs. Marin County Coalition, 1980-86, chmn., 1983-84; mem. adv. bd. Terwilliger Nature Ctr.; trustee Marin Gen. Hosp. Found., 1985—; bd. dirs. Marian Health Care Systems, 1987—. Served with USAF, 1951-54. Recipient 1987 Disting. Vol. award Marin County United Way, certs., 1986, 88 and resolutions of commendation for pub. svc., Calif. State Assembly, 1988, resolution of commendation for publ svc., Calif. State Senate, 1988. Diplomate Am. Bd. Orthodontics (charter mem. Coll. of Diplomates). Fellow Royal Soc. Health, Am. Coll. Dentists, Internat. Coll. Dentists, Acad. Dentistry Internat. (sec., treas. No. Calif. chpt. 1987—); mem. ADA, Am. Assn. Orthodontists, Fedn. Dentaire Internationale, Pierre Fauchard Acad., Marin County C. of C. (dir. 1976—, pres. 1986-88), Am. Rifle Assn. (life), Sierra Club (life), Trout Unltd. (life), Omicron Kappa Upsilon, Chi Phi, Xi Psi Phi. Republican. Episcopalian. Rotarian (dir. San Rafael 1971-73, pres. 1978-79, Paul Harris fellow). Clubs: Lagunitas Country (pres. 1973-75), Bohemian; Meadow. Contbr. articles to profl. jours. Home: PO Box 977 Ross CA 94957 Office: 11 Greenfield Ave San Rafael CA 94901

DAWSON-HARRIS, FRANCES EMILY, poetess; b. Augsburg, Fed. Republic Germany, Dec. 7, 1952; d. Emmett C. Jr. and B. Louise (Boddie) Dawson. BS in Nursing, Pa. State U., 1974. RN, D.C. Staff nurse Howard U. Med. Ctr., Washington, 1974-75, charge nurse, 1975-77; inactive nurse, 1977—. Author: Live for Today, 1986, With You In Mind, 1987, Reflections, 1988. Active Disabled Resource Ctr., Lupus Found. Am., Calif. Assn. Physically Handicapped. Recipient Golden Poetry award, 1985, 86, 87, 88, 89, Excellence in Lit. award Pinewood Poetry, 1987, 88, 89, Merit Poet award APA, 1989. Mem. Walt Whitman Guild, Pa. State U. Alumni Assn. Democrat. Baptist. Home: 6481 Atlantic Ave N #340 Long Beach CA 90805

DAY, CECIL M., travel company executive, retired physician; b. New Brunswick, Can., Aug. 17, 1920; came to U.S., 1949; s. Stewart G. and Mary E. (Miller) D.; m. Ruth B. MacKay, Sept. 28, 1949; children: Joan A., Sandra L., Robert S. MS, Dalhousie U., Halifax, Can., 1948. Intern in internal medicine Great Falls (Mont.) Hosp., 1949-52; pvt. practice Rialto, Calif., 1955-86; chmn. bd. Travel Trails Am., Inc., Scotts Valley, Calif., 1985—; sec.-treas. John Burr Cycles, Fontana, Calif., 1969—. Capt. U.S. Army, 1953-55, Korea. Fellow Am. Coll. Angiology, Am. Geriatric Soc.; mem. Rotary Internat. (Harris fellow). Methodist. Home: 929 N Primrose Ave Rialto CA 92376

DAY, DONALD MORFOOT, mechanical engineer; b. Urbana, Ill., Aug. 16, 1954; s. Mahlon Marsh Day and Frances (Van Every) Morfoot; m. Audrey Norma Levine, July 9, 1979; 1 child, Zachary Byron. BSME, U. Ill., 1980. Registered profl. engr., Wash. Configurator Boeing Airspace Co., Seattle, 1980—. Author: N.P.B. Integrated Experiment Accelerator Configuration Description, 1987; editor, co-author: Inertial Upper Stage Acceptance, Checkout Retest and Backout Criteria, 1983. Mem. U. Ill. Mech. and Indsl. Engring. Alumni Assn. (adv. com.). Republican. Home: 5712 111th Ave SE Bellevue WA 98006 Office: Boeing Airspace Co PO Box 3999 M/S 8F-25 Seattle WA 98124

DAY, JAMES LAWRENCE, psychiatrist; b. Ft. Smith, Ark., Oct. 5, 1946; s. Diaz and Alta Pearl D.; m. Jean Marie Lundberg, Nov. 29, 1968; children: James Christopher, Catherine Teresa, Kelly Marie. Student, Tex. Tech. U.,

1964-67; MD, U. Tex., 1971. Diplomate Am. Bd. Psychiatry. Intern U. Ark. Med. Ctr., Little Rock, 1971-72; resident in psychiatry Menninger Sch. Psychiatry, Topeka, 1972-75; chief of psychiatry Malmstrom AFB Hosp., USAF, Great Falls, Mont., 1975-77; sr. staff psychiatrist Golden Triangle Mental Health Ctr., Great Falls, 1977-88, med. dir., 1988—; chmn. dept. psychiatry Mont. Deaconess Med. Ctr., Great Falls, 1981, 82, 87, 88; mem. various coms. Mont. Deaconess Med. Ctr.; cons. Meml. Hosp., Topeka, 1973-74, Quincy Elem. Sch., Topeka, 1974-75, Shawnee County Juvenile Ct., 1974-75. Served to major USAF, 1975-77. Mem. Am. Psychiat. Assn., Mont. Psychiat. Assn. (sec. 1984-85, pres. 1986-87, rep. Am. Psychiat. Assn. 1986—, newsletter editor 1988—, and various other coms.), Mont. Med. Assn., AMA, Menninger Sch. Psychiatry Alumni Assn. (disting. writing award 1975, class rep. 1977—), Audubon Soc., Wilderness Soc. Republican. Office: Golden Triangle Mental Health Ctr PO Box 3048 Great Falls MT 59405

DAY, JOHN DENTON, wholesale industrial sales company executive, cattle and horse rancher, trainer; b. Salt Lake City, Jan. 20, 1942; s. George W. and Grace (Denton) Jenkins; student U. Utah, 1964-65; BA in Econs. and Bus. Adminstrn. with high honors, Westminster Coll., 1971; m. Susan Hansen, June 20, 1971; children: Tammy Denton, Jeanett. Riding instr., rangler Uinta wilderness area, U-Ranch, Neola, Utah, 1955-58, YMCA Camp Rodger, Kans.; with Mil. Data Cons., Inc., L.A., 1961-62, Carlseon Credit Corp., Salt Lake City, 1962-65; sales mgr. sporting goods Western Enterprises, Salt Lake City, 1965-69, Western rep. PBR Co., Cleve., 1969-71; dist. sales rep. Crown Zellerbach Corp., Seattle and L.A., 1971-73; pres. Dapco paper, chem., instl. food and janitorial supplies, Salt Lake City, 1973-79; owner, pres. John D. Day, mfrs. reps., 1972—; dist. sales mgr. Surfonics Engrs., Inc., Woods Cross, Utah, 1976-78, Garland Co., Cleve., 1978-81; rancher, Heber, Utah, 1976—, Temecula, Calif., 1984—; sec. bd. Acquadyne. Group chmn. Tele-Dex fund raising project Westminster Coll. With AUS, 1963-64. Recipient grand nat. award Internat. Custom Car Show, San Diego, 1962, Key to City, Louisville, 1964, Champion Bareback Riding award, 1957, Dally team roping heading and heeling champion, 1982. Mem. Internat. Show Car Assn. (co-chmn. 1978-79), Am. Quarter Horse Assn. (high point reining champion 1981, sr. reining champion 1981, working cowhorse champion 1982), Utah Quarter Horse Assn. (champion AMAT reining 1979, 80, AMAT barrel racing 1980), Profl. Cowhorseman's Assn. (world champion team roping, heeling 1986, 88, high point rider 1985, world champion stock horse rider 1985-86, 88, world champion working cowhorse 1985, PCA finals open cutting champion, 1985-88, PCA finals 1500 novice champion 1987, PCA finals all-around champion 1985-88, inducted into Hall of Fame 1988, first on record registered Tex. longhorn cutting contest, open champion, founder, editor newsletter 1985-89, pres. 1985-89), Intermountain Quarter Horse Assn. (champion AMAT reining 1979-81), World Rodeo Assn. Profls. (v.p. Western territory 1989—). Contbr. articles to jours. Home and Office: 76 Dgts #2 PO Box 1297 Temecula CA 92390 also: Rockin D Ranch #1 Box 4 Heber City UT 84032 also: Ranch #2 John D Day Tng Ctr 39935 E Benton Rd Temecula CA 92390

DAY, JOSEPH DENNIS, librarian; b. Dayton, Ohio, Sept. 23, 1942; s. John Albert and Ruth (Pearson) D.; m. Mary Louise Herbert, Oct. 10, 1964; children: Cindy, Jeff, Chris, Steve, Tom. B.A., U. Dayton, 1966; M.L.S., Western Mich. U., 1967. Community librarian Dayton-Montgomery Pub. Library, 1967-70; dir. Troy-Miami County Pub. Library, Troy, Ohio, 1970-76, Salt Lake City Pub. Library, 1976—; chmn. Miami Valley Library Orgn., 1971-73; pres. Ohio Library Assn., 1975-76; project dir. planning and constrn. first solar powered library in world, 1973-76; exec. devel. promgram Miami Ohio libr., 1975. Pres. Troy Area Arts Coun., 1973-74 ; v.p. SLC Salvation Army Bd., 1986—. Recipient Disting. Community Service award Troy C. of C., 1974; John Cotton Dana award, 1975, 77, 83, 85; AIA-ALA architecture award, 1977. Mem. ALA (chmn. intellectual freedom com. 1981-84, exec. bd. 1987—), Utah Library Assn. (pres. 1979-80, Disting. Service award 1985), Am. Soc. Pub. Adminstrn., Mountain Plains Libr. Assn. (v.p., pres. elect). Club: Kiwanis (pres. Troy 1975-76, Disting. Service award Troy 1973, pres. Salt Lake-Foothill 1979-80). Address: 209 East 5th St S Salt Lake City UT 84111

DAY, KEVIN THOMAS, banker; b. London, Aug. 24, 1937; came to U.S., 1957; s. William Stanley and Mary Ann (Hook) D.; m. Mary Violet Scheuber, Aug. BA, Brisbane Tech. Coll., Queensland, Australia, 1957. Pres. Americana Investments, San Francisco, 1960-63; stockbroker Sutro and Co., San Francisco, 1963-66; regional v.p. Am. Express Investment Co., San Francisco, 1966-70; dir. mktg. ITT Fin. Svcs., N.Y.C., 1970-78; pres. Exec. Assocs., Reno, Nev., 1978-83, First Interstate Bank Found., Reno, 1983—; chmn. Nev. Fgn. Trade Zone, Reno 1986—, Desert Rsch. Inst., Reno. Pres. Econ. Devel. Authority, Reno, 1985; mem. exec. com. Western Indsl. Nev., Reno, 1985—; commr. Nev. Commn. on Econ. Devel., Carson City, 1987—. Named Man of Yr., Reno mag., 1988, Torch of Liberty award, 1989. Mem. U. Nev.-Reno Alumni Assn. (mem. adv. bd. 1985—). Republican. Roman Catholic. Home: 4835 Pine Springs Dr Reno NV 89509 Office: First Interstate Bank Found One E First St Reno NV 89501

DAY, L. B., management consultant; b. Walla Walla, Wash., Sept. 16, 1944; s. Frank Edmond and Geraldine Eloise (Binning) D. BS, Portland State Coll., 1966; MBA, George Washington U., 1971. Design mktg. cons. Leadership Resources Inc., Washington, 1971-76; faculty mem. USDA Grad. Sch. of Spl. Programs, Washington, 1971-76; mgr. Office of Employee Devel. Oreg. Dept. Transp., Salem, 1972-75; prin. Day-Henry Assoc. Inc., Portland, Oreg., 1975-78, Day-Floren Assocs. Inc., Portland, Oreg., 1978—; cons. Bonneville Power Adminstrn., Arthur Anderson and Co., U.S. Nat. Bank Oreg., Am. Bankers Assn., Intel Corp., Sequent Computer Systems, Allergan, Sun Micorsystems, VLSI Tech., U.S. Dept. Energy, Dept. Labor,, others; faculty mem. Am. Bankers Assn. Bank Trainers Sch., 1981-84, Grad. Personnel Sch., 1982; adj. prof. Willamette U. Grad. Sch. Adminstrn., Salem, 1978. Author: (book) The Supervisory Training Program, 1977; co-author (textbooks) Preparing for Supervision, 1979, Performance Management, 1981; contbr. articles to profl. jours. With U.S. Army, 1967-70, including S.E. Asia. Scottish Rite fellow George Washington U., 1970. Mem. Am. Soc. Tng. and Devel. (chairperson Transp. Spl. Interest Group 1978, Cert. of Appreciation 1977), The Orgn. Devel. Network, Willamette Athletic Club. Office: Day-Floren Assocs Inc 1020 SW Taylor Ste 400 Portland OR 97205-2509

DAY, LAWRENCE ELWOOD, technical manager; b. Columbus, Ohio, Sept. 17, 1947; s. Wilbur Hastings and Gloria Marie (Sega) D.; m. Joan Elizabeth Kinzley, Sept. 18, 1971; children: Katherine Ann, James Nelson, Laura Elizabeth. BSEE, Worcester (Mass.) Polytechnic Inst., 1969; MBA in Tech. and Engring. Mgmt., City U., Bellevue, Wash., 1988. Software engr. Westinghouse Electric Co., Balt., 1969-73; radar engr. Boeing Aerospace Co., Seattle, 1973-75, software engr., 1975-82, tech. subcontract mgr., 1985-86, software mgr., 1986-87, software devel. mgr., 1987, program mgr., 1987-88, system design mgr., 1988—; software mgr. Boeing Mil. Airplane Co., Seattle, 1982-85; pres. and owner Day Aircraft, Renton, Wash., 1981—. Rep. precinct commiteeman, Renton, Wash., 1988; deacon Bethel Chapel, Issaquah, Wash., 1976-77; Sunday sch. tchr. Neighborhood Ch., Bellevue, 1979—. Served with USAF, 1965-71. Recipient Speaker Recognition award Kiwanis, 1988. Mem. Boeing Employees Flying Assn. (pres. 1987-88), Boeing Mgmt. Assn., Aircraft Owners aand Pilots Assn., Full Gospel Businessmen's Fellowship Internat. (pres. Bellevue 1979-80, treas. 1975-79). Republican. Home: 11917 SE 87th Ct Renton WA 98056

DAY, LUCILLE ELIZABETH, educator, author; b. Oakland, Calif., Dec. 5, 1947; d. Richard Allen and Evelyn Marietta (Hazard) Lang; AB, U. Calif., Berkeley, 1971, MA, 1973, PhD, 1979; m. Frank Lawrence Day, Nov. 6, 1965; 1 child, Liana Sherrine; m. 2d, Theodore Herman Fleischman, June 23, 1974; 1 child, Tamarind Channah. Teaching asst. U. Calif., Berkeley, 1971-72, 75-76, research asst., 1975, 77-78; tchr. sci. Magic Mountain Sch., Berkeley, 1977; specialist math. and sci. Novato (Calif.) Unified Sch. Dist., 1979-81; instr. sci. Project Bridge, Laney Coll., Oakland, Calif., 1984-86; sci. writer and dir. edn. planning and evaluation, Lawrence Berkeley (Calif.) Lab., 1986—; author numerous poems, articles and book reviews; author: (with Joan Skolnick and Carol Langbort) How to Encourage Girls in Math and Science: Strategies for Parents and Educators, 1982; Self-Portrait with Hand Microscope (poetry collection), 1982. NSF Grad. fellow, 1972-75; recipient Joseph Henry Jackson award in lit. San Francisco Found., 1982. Mem. AAAS, No. Calif. Sci. Writers Assn., Nat. Assn. Sci. Writers, Women in Communications, Phi Beta Kappa, Iota Sigma Pi. Home: 1057 Walker Ave Oakland CA 94610

DAY, RICHARD EDWARD, casino executive; b. Bayonne, N.J., Aug. 21, 1960; s. James William and Carol Marie (Sutphen) D. BA in Econs., Rutgers U., 1982. Mktg. clk. Riviera Hotel and Casino, Las Vegas, Nev., 1983-84, casino mktg. analyst, 1984-85, casino ops. asst., 1985—. Republican. Home: 2050 Magic Way Space 88 Henderson NV 89015 Office: Riviera Inc 2901 Las Vegas Blvd S Las Vegas NV 89109

DAY, RICHARD ELLEDGE, newspaper editor; b. Denver, June 27, 1939; s. Bartle Henry and Clara Violet (Smith) D.; student Mesa Jr. Coll., 1958-60; BA, Western State Coll. Colo., 1962. Reporter, Rock Springs (Wyo.) Daily Rocket and Sunday Miner, 1962-64, Casper (Wyo.) Star-Tribune, 1964-66; reporter Montrose (Colo.) Daily Press., 1967-68, mng. editor, 1968—. Mem. accountability adv. com. Montrose County Sch. Dist.;Rep. precinct committeeman, Montrose, 1968—; mem. exec. com. Montrose County Rep. party; bd. dirs. Montrose County United Fund, 1972, Western Slope Tb and Respiratory Disease Assn., 1968-73; trustee Colo. Western Coll., 1971-72. Mem. Nat. Press Photographers Assn., AP Mng. Editors Assn., Montrose County C. of C. (dir., chmn. hwy. com.), Sigma Delta Chi. Mem. Christian Ch. Club: Denver Press. Lodges: Masons, Elks, Kiwanis. Home: PO Box 957 844 N 5th St Montrose CO 81401 Office: PO Box 850 535 S 1st St Montrose CO 81401

DAY, RICHARD SOMERS, author, editorial consultant; b. Chgo., June 14, 1928; s. Milo Frank and Ethel Mae (Somers) D.; m. Lois Patricia Beggs, July 8, 1950; children—Russell Frank, Douglas Matthew, Gail Leslie. Student, Ill. Inst. Tech., 1946, U. Miami, 1947. Promotion writer, editor Portland Cement Assn., Chgo., 1958-62, promotion writer, 1963-66; editor Am. Inst. Laundering, Joliet, Ill., 1962-63; freelance writer, Monee, Ill., 1966-69, Palomar Mountain, Calif., 1969—; cons. editor home and shop Popular Sci. mag., N.Y.C., 1966—; editorial cons. St. Remy Press, Montreal, Que., Can., 1987—. Author numerous home repair books including: Patios and Decks, 1976, Automechanics, 1982, Do-It-Yourself Plumbing--It's Easy with Genova, 1987; editor: (newspaper) Powderlines, 1958; (mag.) Concrete Hwys. and Pub. Improvements, 1958-62; (mag.) Soil-Cement News, 1960-62; (mag.) Fabric Care, 1962-63. Contbr. chpts. to books. Bd. dirs. Land Use Council, San Diego, 1977, Palomar Mountain Planning Orgn., 1984—. Mem. Nat. Assn. Home and Workshop Writers (mng. editor newsletter 1982—, bd. dirs., pres. 1984-85). Home: PO Box 10 Palomar Mountain CA 92060-0010

DAY, ROBERT WINSOR, research administrator; b. Framingham, Mass., Oct. 22, 1930; s. Raymond Albert and Mildred (Doty) D.; m. Jane Alice Boynton, Sept. 6, 1957 (div. Sept. 1977); m. Cynthia Taylor, Dec. 16, 1977; children: Christopher, Nathalia. Student, Harvard U., 1949-51; MD, U. Chgo., 1956; MPH, U. Calif., Berkeley, 1958, PhD, 1962. Intern USPHS, Balt., 1956-57; resident U. Calif., Berkeley, 1958-60; research specialist Calif. Dept. Mental Hygiene, 1960-64; asst. prof. sch. medicine UCLA, 1962-64; dep. dir. Calif. Dept. Pub. Health, Berkeley, 1965-67; prof., chmn. dept. health services Sch. Pub. Health and Community Medicine, U. Wash., Seattle, 1968-72, dean, 1972-82; dir. Fred Hutchinson Cancer Research Ctr., Seattle, 1981—; cons. in field. Pres. Seattle Planned Parenthood Ctr., 1970-72. Served with USPHS, 1956-57. Fellow Am. Pub. Health Assn., Am. Coll. Preventive Medicine; mem. Soc. Pediatric Rsch., Assn. Schs. Pub. Health (pres. 1981-82), Am. Assn. Cancer Insts. (bd. dirs. 1983—, v.p. 1984-85, pres. 1985-86, chmn. bd. dirs., 1986-87). Office: Fred Hutchinson Cancer Rsch Ctr 1124 Columbia St Seattle WA 98104

DAY, THOMAS BRENNOCK, university president; b. N.Y.C., Mar. 7, 1932; s. Frederick and Alice (Brennock) D.; m. Anne Kohlbrenner, Sept. 5, 1953; children: Erica, Monica, Mark, Kevin, Sara, Timothy, Jonathan, Patrick, Adam. B.S., U Notre Dame, 1953; Ph.D., Cornell U., 1957. Prof. U. Md., College Park, 1964-78, vice chancellor for acad. planning and policy, 1970-77, spl. asst. to pres., 1977-78, vice chancellor for acad. affairs Baltimore County, 1977-78; pres. San Diego State U., 1978—; cons. Bendix Corp., IBM Corp., Digital Equipment Corp.; vis. physicist Brookhaven Nat. Lab., 1963; cons. Argonne Nat. Lab., Ill., 1967; vice chair Nat. Sci. Bd.; bd. dirs. Scripps Clinic and Research Found. Contbr. articles to profl. jours. Mem. Am. Phys. Soc., Sigma Xi, Phi Kappa Phi. Republican. Roman Catholic. Lodge: Rotary. Office: San Diego State U Office of Pres San Diego CA 92182-0711 also: NSF Nat Sci Bd 1800 G St NW Washington DC 20550

DAY, TIMOTHY TOWNLEY, food company executive; b. Bklyn., May 9, 1937; s. David M. and Janice F. (Fowler) D.; children—Leslie, Timothy, Bryan. B.A., Wesleyan U., Middletown, Conn., 1959; M.B.A., Harvard, 1964. Fin. exec. Trans World Airlines, 1964-68; v.p., treas. Gen. Host Corp., N.Y.C., 1966-72; group v.p. Gen. Host Corp., 1972-79, exec. v.p., 1979-81; pres. Cudahy Foods Co. subs. Gen. Host Corp., 1975-81; pres., chief exec. officer Bar-S Foods Co., 1981—; Bd. dirs. Am. Meat Inst., 1976—. Coauthor: Mangement of Racial Integration in Business, 1964. Served as officer USMC, 1959-61. Mem. Young Presidents Orgn., Chi Psi. Office: Bar-S Foods 100 W Clarendon Phoenix AZ 85013

DAY, W(YNNE) GREGORY, lawyer; b. Corona, Calif., May 15, 1954; s. Wynne C. Day and Teresa Ann (Martins) Anderson; m. Roanna L. Williams, Oct. 6, 1979; children: Kristiina M., Geoffrey David-Charles. BA, U. Calif., San Diego, 1975; JD, U. Calif., Los Angeles, 1978. Bar: Calif. 1978. Assoc. Law Office of Leland H. Bray, Bishop, Calif., 1978-79; sole practice Bishop, Calif., 1979-87; assoc. Greve, Clifford, Diepenbrock and Paras, Sacramento, 1987—; special prosecuter County of Inyo, Bishop, 1980-81; judge pro tem Justice Ct. County of Inyo, Bishop, 1981-82. Active Nat. Fedn. Ind. Bus., 1985-87. Mem. Inyo-Mono Bar Assn. (pres. 1985, v.p. 1984, del. chmn. 1985-87, Commendation award 1987), Christian Legal Soc. (v.p. Sacramento chpt. 1988-89), Ctr. for Law and Religious Freedom, Sacramento County Bar Assn. (del. 1988), Calif. Orgn. Small Bar Assns. (dir. and pres. 1987—), Gideons Internat. Democrat. Home: 1210 Bunker Hill Dr Roseville CA 95661 Office: Greve Clifford Diepenbrock & Paras 1000 G St STE 400 Sacramento CA 95814

DAYALA, HAJI FAROOQ, real estate broker; b. Karachi, Pakistan, Dec. 1, 1948; s. Haji Razzak and Hamida H. (Bai) D.; m. Susanna WK. Cheung, Aug. 25, 1973; children: Sabrina R., Ryan M. BS in Indsl. Engring., Calif. Poly. State U., 1972; M in Sci. and Adminstrn., Calif. State U., Dominguez Hills, 1979. Mgr. plant Thomas & Betts Corp., L.A., 1977-82, 84-86; v.p. ops. Prime Cir. Tech., San Jose, Calif., 1982-84; real estate agt. Merrill Lynch Realty, Diamond Bar, Calif., 1987-88; broker, co-owner Ampak Realty, Diamond Bar, Calif., 1988—. Mem. Am. Inst. Indsl. Engring., Nat. Notary Assn., Diamond Bar Realtor Bd., 7 Million Dollar Club, Leading Edge Soc. Home: 24324 E Knoll Ct Diamond Bar CA 91765 Office: Ampak Realty 2040 S Brea Canyon Rd Ste 210 Diamond Bar CA 91765

DAYAN, RON, interior designer; b. Eng., Oct. 21, 1956; m. Barbara Jean Felise, Sept. 13, 1981. BA, Polytech. No. London, 1978; BS, Woodbury U., 1981. Owner, dir. interior design Piccadilly Designs, Los Angeles, 1983—. Designer Marina City Club Penthouses, Granville Hotel, 1988, Mrs. Gooch's Natural Foods Mkt., 1988, Berti Shoes, Ravissant Skin Salon, and numerous pvt. clients. Mem. Brit. Inst. Interior Design, Beverly Hills C. of C.

DAY-GOWDER, PATRICIA JOAN, association executive, consultant; b. Lansing, Mich., Apr. 9, 1936; d. Louis A. and Johanna (Feringa) Whipple; m. Duane Lee Day, Jan. 7, 1961 (div.); children—Kevin Duane, Patricia Kimberley; m. William A. Gowder, Nov. 30, 1986. B.A., Mich. State U., 1958; M.A., Lindenwood (Mo.) Coll., 1979; postgrad. U. So. Calif., 1982-83. Cert. secondary tchr., Calif. Health edn. asst. YWCA, Rochester, N.Y., 1958-59; tchr. jr. high schs., Flint, Mich., 1959-61; tchr. Brookside Acad., Montclair, N.J., 1963-68; adult program dir. YMCA, Long Beach, Calif., 1968-73; community edn. dir. Paramount (Calif.) Unified Sch. Dist., 1973-78; exec. dir. counseling ctr., Arcadia, Calif., 1978-80; sr. citizens program dir. City of Burbank (Calif.), 1981-83; div. dir. Am. Heart Assn., Los Angeles, 1983-87 ; exec. dir. Campfire Orgn., Pasadena, 1987-89; exec. dir. greater L.A. chpt. Nat. Found. of Ileitis and Colitis, 1989—; cons. community edn. State Dept. Edn., Fed. Office Community Edn., Los Angeles County Office Edn. Bd. dirs., v.p. Children's Creative Ctr., Long Beach, Calif., 1969-73, Traveler's Aid Soc., 1969-72; vice-chmn. Cerritos YMCA, 1968-73. Mott Found. fellow, 1977-78. Mem. Western Gerontology Assn., Nat. Assn. Female Execs., Calif. Community Edn. Assn. (sec.-treas., 1974-77), LWV. Democrat. Congregationalist. Club: Soroptimists. Avocations: tennis, hiking, bicycling, painting, reading. Home: 837 Silver Maple Dr Azusa CA 91702

DAYIOGLU, MURAT DAY, chef; b. Istanbul, Turkey, Aug. 22, 1939; came to U.S., 1970; s. Ali and Rukiye Zuheyre (Nazli) D.; m. Huguette D. Bertoncino, Oct. 18, 1968 (dec. 1976); m. Marge A. Lea, Nov. 28, 1987; 1 child, David Lea Cox. BS, Inst. Econs. Istanbul, 1960; diploma, Hotel Mgmt. Sch., Ankara, Turkey, 1962. Journalist, European office UN, Geneva, 1967-68; owner, chef Au Pierrot Gourmet, Montreal, Que., Can., 1968-70; mgr. Sultan's House of Kebobs, Nashville, 1970-71, Valle's Steak Houses, Inc., Warwick, R.I., 1971-73; exec. chef Villa Capri Restaurant, Wallingford, Conn., 1973-75; working chef Chez Cary Restaurant, Orange, Calif., 1975-78; exec. chef Chez Dante's Restaurant, Newport Beach, Calif., 1978-85, Chez Cary Restaurant, Orange, 1985-88, C'est la Vie, Laguna Beach, Calif., Carmelo's, Corona del Mar, Calif., Bouzy Rouge, Newport Beach; restaurant cons. Pasta Mesa Inc., Costa Mesa, Calif., 1988—; food cons., Orange County Centennial Com., 1987—; food photographer, Wstern Regional Olympic Team, Orange, 1988—. Patentee, escargot preparing device; contbr. recipes to various cookbooks. Recipient Golden Plate award, Internat. Gourmet Soc., 1978, Golden Scepter award, 1986, Gold award of merit, 1988, S.C. Restaurant Writers. Mem. Orange Empire Chefs Assn. (bd. dirs. 12987—), Les Amis d'Escoffier Soc., Am. Culinary Fedn. (bd. dirs. 1987-89), Am.-Turkish Assn. So. Calif. (pres. 1980-82). Republican. Islam. Home: 227 Monarch Bay Dr Laguna Niguel CA 92677-3436

DAYTON, HUGH KING, JR., military officer; b. Sacramento, Jan. 19, 1940; s. Hugh King Sr. and Gertrude (Newsome) D.; m. Lynda Sharon Webster, July 1, 1962; children: Geoffrey Albert, Pamela Deanna. BSEE, Calif. Poly. Tech., 1962; MSEE, U. Mo., 1972; MBA, Auburn U., 1983. Assoc. engr. Boeing, Seattle, 1962-64; commd. USAF, 1964; fighter pilot instr. USAF, Europe, Pacific, U.S., 1965-77; maintenance squadron commdr. Nellis AFB, Las Vegas, Nev., 1977-79; A-10 squadron commdr. 57 Fighter Weapons Wing, Las Vegas, 1980; comdr. 436 tactical fighter tng. squadron Hollman AFB, N.Mex., 1981-82; advanced through grades to colonel USAF, 1983; A-10 system program mgr. Sacramento Air Logistics Ctr., 1983-85; dir. material mgmt. Sacramento Air Logistics Ctr., Sacramento, 1986—; ret. USAF, 1988. Mem. Order of Dandalians. Republican. Home: 4908 Metpark Las Vegas NV 89110

DEA, MOON SUEY, telecommunications professional; b. Hong Kong, June 21, 1950; came to U.S., 1954; d. William and Jean Dea. BA summa cum laude, U. So. Calif., 1972, MLS, 1973; MBA, UCLA, 1982. Cert. tchr., Calif. Sr. librarian Los Angeles Pub. Library, 1977-80; tech. cons. AT&T Info. Systems, Los Angeles, 1983-85; product specialist Lexar div. United Techs. Communications Co., Westlake Village, Calif., 1985-86; product mgr. Security Pacific Network Services Co., Los Angeles, 1986-87, dir. planning, analysis, Jan.-June, 1987; project mgr Security Pacific Automation Co., Los Angeles, July-Nov., 1987; adv. systems engr. IBM, Los Angeles, 1987—. Mem. adv. bd. Friends of Chinatown Library, Los Angeles, 1986—, bd. dirs. 1984-85, pres., 1983-84. Calif. State scholar, 1968-72; Calif. PTA LIbrary scholar, 1972; fellow Gen. Telephone and Electronics, 1981. Mem. Asian Bus. League, Chinese Hist. Soc., Phi Beta Kappa. Home: 1409 Sycamore Ave Glendale CA 91201 Office: IBM 355 S Grand Ave Los Angeles CA 90060

DEADRICH, PAUL EDDY, lawyer, real estate associate; b. Lakeport, Calif., Jan. 30, 1925; s. John Adolph and Grace Estelle (Jackson) D.; m. Violet Ann Walls, Oct. 29, 1962 (div. Dec. 1982); children: Marjanne Robinson, Nancy Wolfer, Dianne Deadrich-Rogers, Bettianne Buck, John Fredrick, Daniel David; m. Irene Eloise Banks, Dec. 11, 1982. AA, U. Calif., Berkeley, 1946; JD, U. Calif., San Francisco, 1949. Bar: Calif. 1950. Sales assoc. Deadrich Real Estate, San Leandro, Calif., 1947-50; pvt. practice San Leandro, 1950-61; pvt. practice law, real estate and ins. Twain Harte, Calif., 1961-73; pvt. practice Loomis, Calif., 1973-75, Cameron Park, Calif., 1975-78; missionary Apostolic Alliance, Gibi, Liberia, West Africa, 1978-82; pvt. practice law and real estate San Leandro, 1982—; judge Tuolumne County Justice Ct., Calif., 1964-66; instr. phys. edn., coach Mother Lode Christian Sch., Tuolumne, 1969-73; adminstr., coach, tchr. Loomis Christian Sch., 1974-75. Bd. dirs. Alameda Contra Costa Transit Dist., Oakland, Calif., 1956-61; bd. dirs. Calif. Conservatory Theater, 1988—; sec. Clown Alley. Decorated Bronze Star, Purple Heart. Mem. So. Alameda County Bar Assn., Internat. Orgn. Real Estate Appraisers, So. Alameda County Bd. Realtors; Gospel Businessmen's Fellowship (pres. San Leandro chpt. 1988—). Republican. Home: 1808 Pearl St Alameda CA 94501 Office: 2060 Washington Ave San Leandro CA 94577

DEAGLE, EDWIN AUGUSTUS, JR., manufacturing executive; b. Boston, Oct. 29, 1937; s. Edwin Augustus and Dorothy (Campbell) D.; m. Mary Ann Grace, June 17 (div. 1976); children: Edwin A. III, Michael C.; m. Joan Banks Dunlop, Sept. 20, 1980. BEE, U.S. Mil. Acad., 1960; MPA, Harvard U., 1966, PhD in Polit. Economy and Govt., 1970. Commd. 2d lt. U.S. Army, 1960, advanced through grades to maj., 1960-72, resigned, 1972; with U.S. Army, Socialist Republic of Vietnam, 1968-69; staff analyst Nat. Security Coun., Washington, 1969-70; asst. prof. dept. social scis. U.S. Mil. Acad., West Point, N.Y., 1969-72; dir. analysis, dep. dir. cable TV info ctr. Urban Inst., Washington, 1972-75; exec. asst. to dir. Congl. Budget Office, Washington, 1975-76; def. budget coord. Carter/Mondale Transition Group, Washington, 1976-77; dir. internat. rels. Rockefeller Found., N.Y.C., 1977-86; dir. internat. bus. planning Hughes Aircraft Co., L.A., 1986—; bd. dirs. Symbol Techs., Inc., Bohemia, N.Y. Decorated 2 Silver Stars, 4 Bronze Stars, Vietnam Cross of Gallantry, Purple Heart. Mem. Coun. on Fgn. Rels., Overseas Devel. Coun., Internat. Inst. Strategic Studies, Harvard Club (N.Y.), Marina City Club (Marina del Rey, Calif.). Democrat. Office: Hughes Aircraft Co 7200 Hughes Terr Los Angeles CA 90045

DEAKMAN, MARIAN KAY, investment broker; b. Marshalltown, Iowa, July 4, 1943; d. Melvin Richard and Nellie Elizabeth (Johnston) Keigan; m. Wayne Lee Deakman, Jan. 6, 1964 (div. 1980); children: Cody, Cally. BA, Upper Iowa U., 1967; MA in Edn., Drake U., 1978. Lic. real estate appraiser. Tchr. Alden & Eagle Grove Schs., Iowa, 1967-81; ptnr. D&S Constrn. Co., Webster City, 1969-84; owner, pres. Livestock/Recreational Facility, Lehigh, 1974-82, Trophy & Awards Mfg., Webster City, 1975-77, restaurant/lounge, Tempe, Ariz., 1983; office mgr., agt. Comml. Exchange Inc., Mesa, 1984-86; v.p., broker Tri-Eagle Real Estate & Investments, Mesa, 1987—; arts cons. State of Iowa, 1977-82; v.p. Valley Bus. Exchange, Phoenix, 1986—; speaker in field; instr. Drake U., 1978-81. Author: Evaluating the Media Me3ssage, 1977, State of Iowa Arts Resource Guide, 1978; adult learning coordinator Iowa Pub. Broadcasting Network, 1979-82. Pres Mesa chpt. Network, 1988. Republican. Office: Trivest 108 E Tremaine Dr Chandler AZ 85225

DEAL, TERRY DEAN, marketing executive; b. Lyons, Kans., Sept. 27, 1948; s. Willis Clifton and Geneva G. (Gamble) D.; m. Diana Kathlene Gerstner, Feb. 14, 1970; 1 child, M. Shane. BS Agricultural Bus., Ft. Hays Kans. State U., 1971. Area sales mgr. Senvita Products Inc., Seneca, Kans., 1971-73, total sales mgr., 1973-74; unit sales mgr. Agri-Distbrs. and Leasing, Abilene, Kans., 1974-75; gen. mgr. Agri-Distbrs. and Leasing, Abilene, 1975-76; terr. mgr. Owatonna (Minn.) Mfg. Co., 1976-84, regional sales mgr., 1984-87; dir. mktg. Impulse Hydraulics Inc., San Diego, 1987-89, Olathe, Kans., 1989—; pres. Agri-Distbrs. and Leasing, 1974-85. Bd. dirs. Owatonna Swimming Assn., 1985-86; mem. Owatonna Little Theatre, 1984-88. Mem. NRA (presdl. transition com. 1989), Sertoma (bd. dirs. 1982-83), Elks, Tau Kappa Epsilon. Republican. Methodist. Home: 729 N Persimmon Olathe KS 66062 Office: Impulse Hydraulics Inc 4747 Old Cliffs Rd San Diego CA 92120

DEALY, JANETTE DIANE, retail executive; b. Phoenix, Jan. 5, 1950; d. Henry Melvin Clatterbuck and Dorothy (Eakin) Newman; m. Shannon Chris Dealy, May 7, 1983. Student World Campus Afloat, Chapman Coll., 1967-68; BA in Anthropology and Archeology, Ariz. State U., 1972. Owner, mgr., buyer Walls Galore and Bath Decor, Corvallis, Oreg., 1977-84; mgr., trainer Bloomingdales, Dallas, 1984-85; mgr. Frederick and Nelson, Seattle,

1986-87, The Bon Marché, Seattle, 1987—; intern trainer Oreg. State U., 1981-83. Writer poetry; painter portraits. Mem. Downtown Merchants Assn., Corvallis, 1977-84, Oreg. Homebuilders Assn., Corvallis, 1977-84. Mem. Am. Business Woman's Assn. (Corvallis chpt.). Republican.

DE AMICI, GIOVANNI, physicist; b. Vigevano, Italy, Aug. 9, 1954; came to U.S., 1981; s. Francesco and Maria (Ornati) De A. Maturita' Classica, Liceo Sant' Alessandro, Bergamo, Italy, 1973; Laurea in Fisica, Universita' degli Studi, Milan, Italy, 1978; Dottorato di Ricerca, Ministero Pubblica Istruzione, Rome, 1987. Research assoc. physicist Space Scis. Lab., U. Calif., Berkeley, 1983—; instr. math., various schs. in Italy; teaching asst. physics U. Calif., Berkeley, 1987, reader, 1987, vis. scientist, 1981-83; researcher CNR, Milan, 1977-79. Contbr. articles to profl. jours. Served to cpl. Italian Army, 1979-80. Consiglio Nazionale Ricerche fellow, Rome, 1981, 82. Mem. Am. Phys. Soc. Roman Catholic. Office: 50/232 LBL One Cyclotron Rd Berkeley CA 94720

DEAN, BURTON VICTOR, management educator; b. June 3, 1924. BS, Northwestern U., 1947; MS, Columbia U., 1948; PhD, U. Ill., 1952. Mathematician U.S. Dept. Def., Washington, 1952-55; rsch. mathematician Ops. Rsch., Inc., Silver Spring, Md., 1955-57; prof. ops. rsch. Case Western Res. U., Cleve., 1957-85, chmn. dept., 1965-76, 79-85; prof., chmn. dept. orgn. and mgmt. San Jose (Calif.) State U., 1985—, dir. entrepreneurial forum, 1987; program dir. Vis. Scholars in Orgn. and Mgmt., San Jose State U., 1986-87; dir. Entrepreneurial Forum, Sept., 1987; program dir. Vis. Scholars in Mfg. Mgmt., 1988-89; dir. div. experiments in mfg. Calif. Conf. Tech. Grant, 1989—; assoc. Inst. Pub. Adminstrn., N.Y.C., and Washington, 1972-79; ops. rsch. assoc. Booz, Allen and Hamilton, Cleve., 1972-79; chmn. adv. bd. Sourcenet Corp., 1986-87; vis. prof. Stanford U., 1985, Israel Inst. Tech., 1962-63, U. Louvain, Belgium, Tel-Aviv U, Ben-Gurion U., Israel, 1978; mem. sci. adv. bd. Advanced Bio-Systems, Inc., 1984-85, Applied Imaging Corp., 1987—, Telecom Inc., 1987—; cons. in field. Author: Project Management: Methods and Studies, 1985, Applications of Operations Research in Research and Development, 1963, 2d. ed., 1978, (with others) Management of Research and Innovation, 1981, Industrial Inventory Control, 1972, Mathematics of Modern Management, 3d. ed., 1967, Instructor's Manual, 1966; editor: Jour. of Bus. Venturing, 1985—, Jour. Engring. and Tech. Mgmt., 1989—, Studies in Mgmt. Sci. and Systems, 1974—, (books) Textbooks in Operations Research, 1980-84, Studies in Operations Research, 1970-73; assoc. editor, Ops. Research Letters, 1981-84, Jour. of the Ops. Research Soc. of India, 1968-74; dept. editor: IEEE Transactions on Engring. Mgmt. Dept. of Management of Technological Systems, 1985—; contbr. numerous articles to profl. jours.; contbr. numerous chpts. to books. Centennial medal scholar, Case Inst. Tech., 1981. Fellow AAAS; mem. Acad. Mgmt., Am. Prodn. and Inventory Control Soc. (Santa Clara acad. laison 1986-89), Am. Math. Soc., Inst. Mgmt. Scis. (editor Mgmt. Sci. jour. 1970—, coun. mem. 1973-85, roundtable liason panel 1983-84), Ops. Rsch. Soc. of Am., IEEE (vice chmn. seminars 1986—, founder Cleve. chpt. 1984, editorial bd. 1968—, recipient Centennial medal 1984), Beta Gamma Sigma, Sigma Xi, Omega Rho (founding mem. 1977, hon. ops. rsch., historan 1978-82, exec. com. 1977-82, 84-86, v.p. 1978-80, pres. 1980-82). Home: 161 Gabarda Way Portola Valley CA 94025 Office: San Jose State U Sch Bus Dept Orgn and Mgmt San Jose CA 95192-0070

DEAN, CAROLYNN LESLIE, health science technological administrator; b. Oak Park, Ill., Mar. 30, 1952; d. Robert Lee and Jeane Kathleen (Kenitz) D. Student, U. Hawaii, 1970-73; BS, Solano County Regional, Occupational Program, 1983. Registered vascular technologist, Calif. Cardiopulmonary and multi-phasic technologist Family Doctor Med. Group, Vallejo, Calif., 1976-78; non-invasive vascular technologist Alta Bates Hosp., Berkeley, Calif., 1979-80; cardiovascular technologist Herrick Hosp. Health Ctr., Berkeley, Calif., 1978-81; supr., dir. non-invasive vascular lab. St. Mary's Hosp., San Francisco, 1981--; ptnr. Cardiovascular Lab. Assocs., San Francisco, 1983--; sr. ptnr. Vascular Imaging Svcs., Vallejo, 1983; RVT Children's Hosp., San Francisco, 1988—; cons. in field. Contbr. articles to profl. jours. Mem. Soc. Non-Invasive Vescular Tech., Am. Registry Diagnostic Med. Sonographers, Am. Inst. Ultrasound in Medicine. Home: 113 Compas Ct Vallejo CA 94590 Office: Vascular Lab St Marys Hosp and Health Ctr 450 Stanya St San Francisco CA 94117

DEAN, HELEN HENRIETTA, volunteer; b. Pasadena, Calif., Mar. 25, 1905; d. Edward Merrill and Hannah (Damasche) Burnell; m. Frederic Percival Dean, Dec. 31, 1930 (dec. Aug. 1986); children: James Frederic, Gordon Burnell, Carolyn. Student, San Diego State Coll., 1925; BE, Cen. Wash. State U., 1960, postgrad., 1962. Instr. Chula Vista (Calif.) Grammar Sch., 1925, Lincoln Sch., Ontario, Calif., 1925-30, Broadway Elem. Sch., Yakima, Wash., 1958-70; with vocat. testing div. Detention Home, Yakima, 1970-76. Vol. Congl. Christian Ch., Yakima, 1960—, Friends in Svc. for Humanity YWCA, Yakima, 1971-74; vision examiner Wash. Soc. to Prevent Blindness, Yakima, 1969-87; chmn. UNICEF sales Ch. Women United, Yakima, 1970—; scrap book chmn. Home Base Sch. Program, Yakima, 1975—; docent Yakima Valley Mus., 1972—; lectr. Yakima Schs.and others on Beatrix Potter, 1960—. Named Wash. State Outstanding Vol., 1975, Woman of Achievement, 1977, Woman in History, 1985. Mem. AAUW (ednl. grantee 1989), Ret. Tchrs. Yakima, Allied Arts Club, Century Club (mem. 2 depts.), Agenda Club, Knife and Fork Club, Alpha Delta Kappa. Republican. Home: 214 N 33d Ave Yakima WA 98902

DEAN, MICHAEL PATRICK, government official; b. Atlantic City, July 31, 1946; s. Hercules Vincent and Estelle Gloria (Packman) Galie; m. Peggy Lee Stark, May 31, 1968; children: Jennifer Suzanne, Charles Evan. BSBA, Dakota Weslayan U., 1969; MA in Mgmt., U. Phoenix, Sierra Vista, Ariz., 1982. Contract asst. U.S. Army Ammunition Procurement and Supply Agy., Joliet, Ill., 1969; inventory mgmt. specialist intern U.S. Army Weapons Command, Rock Island, Ill., 1969-70, inventory mgmt. asst., 1970-71, supply mgmt. rep., 1971-73; contract adminstr. Def. Contract Adminstn. Svcs., Phoenix, 1973-76, property adminstr., 1978-81; contract adminstr. U.S. Army 5th Signal Command, Worms, Fed. Republic Germany, 1976-77, property adminstr., 1977-78; procurement analyst U.S. Army Info. Systems Command, Ft. Huachuca, Ariz., 1981-82, small bus. program mgr., 1982—. Contbr. articles and poems to various publs. Mem. community adv. bd., v.p. Sierra Vista (Ariz.) Care Ctr., 1986—; vol. umpire, asst. coach Sierra Vista Little League, 1987-89. Recipient cert. of appreciation Congressman McNulty, Tucson, 1984. Mem. Nat. Contract Mgmt. Assn. (founding oficer, treas. 1983-85, plaque 1984, 85), S.W. Small Bus. Coun. (past treas., pres., chmn. bd., plaque 1986), Army Small Bus. Coun. Republican. Home: PO Box 2013 Sierra Vista AZ 85636 Office: Army Info Systems Command Attn AS-PC Fort Huachuca AZ 85613-5000

DEAN, RONALD P., mechanical engineer; b. Dearborn, Mich., May 10, 1956; s. Francis P. Dean and Beverly (Fryer) Warren; m. Cynthia Smith, May 10, 1986; 1 child, Kristin M. BSME, U. Fla., 1977. Registered profl. engr., Colo. Prodn. engr. Hewlett Packard Co., Loveland, Colo., 1977-79; design and devel. engr. Hewlett Packard Co., Ft. Collins, Colo., 1979—. Contbr. articles to profl. jours. Office: Hewlett Packard Co 3404 E Harmony Rd Fort Collins CO 80525

DEAN, TREVIE CRILE, minister, educator; b. Albuquerque, Apr. 1, 1947; s. Crile Rupert and Avanelle (Timmons) D.; m. Linda Colleen England, Sept. 30, 1967; children: Glynda Sue, David Trevett. BA, Calif. Bapt. Coll., 1971, BS, 1989; MDiv, Golden Gate Bapt. Sem., 1974, MRE, 1979; EdD, Southwestern Bapt. Theol. Sem., 1985. Minister music and youth Immanuel Bapt. Ch., La Puente, Calif., 1968-71; pastor Montalvin Bapt. Ch., Pinole, Calif., 1971-74, Trinity S. Bapt. Ch., Tracy, Calif., 1978-79; adj. prof. Pacific Christian Coll., Fullerton, 1978-79; pastor Quartz Hill (Calif.) S. Bapt. Ch., 1976-79, 1st So. Bapt. Ch., Roseville, Calif., 1979-83; ch. bus. adminstr. Woods Chapel Bapt. Ch., Arlington, Tex., 1983-85; adj. prof. Southwestern Bapt. Theol. Sem., Ft. Worth, 1985; prof. religious edn. Calif. Bapt. Coll., Riverside, 1985-88; growth cons. So. Bapt. Gen. Conv., Fresno, Calif., 1974-82; pres. Calif. Bapt. Coll. Devel. Found., Riverside, 1988—. Umpire March/Moreno Valley Little League. Named Tchr. Yr. Associated Students Calif. Bapt. Coll., 1987. Fellow Nat. Assn. Ch. Bus. Adminstrs.; mem. Assn. Ministers and Coordinators Discipleship (pres. Garland, Tex. chpt. 1987—). Republican. Home: 10471 Agave St Moreno Valley CA 92387 Office: Calif Bapt Coll Devel Found 8432 Magnolia Ave Riverside CA 92504

DEAN, WARREN MICHAEL, construction company executive; b. Great Falls, Mont., Apr. 27, 1944; s. Warren Earl and Mary Amelia (Sankovich) D.; m. Pamela Carol House, June 18, 1977; children: Marc, Drew, Molly, Anna. BArch, Mont. State U., 1969; MArch in Urban Design, U. Colo., Denver, 1973; MBA, U. Denver, 1982. Registered architect, Colo. Architect Davis Partnership, Denver, 1973-74; project mgr. CRS Constructors/Mgrs., Denver, 1974-78, v.p., 1978-82, group v.p., 1982-83; pres. CRSS Constructors Inc., Denver, 1983-88; exec. v.p. CRSS Inc., Denver, 1988—. Contbr. articles to profl. jours.; speaker in field. Mem. Denver Concert Chorale, 1974-77; bd. dirs. Jr. Achievement Metro Denver, 1985-88, chmn., 1987-88; bd. dirs. Denver Opera Co., 1976-77. Served to lt. USNR, 1969-72. Advanced Acad. scholar Mont. St. U., 1967-69. Mem. AIA (com. architecture for edn. 1982—), Soc. Am. Milit. Engrs., Constrn. Industry Inst., Planning Execs. Inst., Denver C. of C. (chmn. com. econ. devel.), Colo. Soc. Architects, Rotary. Roman Catholic. Office: CRSS Constructors Inc 216 16th St Mall #1700 Denver CO 80202

DEAN, WAYNE DICKERSON, automotive executive; b. American Fork, Utah, Oct. 31, 1925; s. Owen and Amy (Dickerson) D.; m. Louise Margaret Burge, Nov. 9, 1946; children: Caron Louise Dean Shore, Scott Wayne, Mark Gordon, Kevin George. Grad. high sch., American Fork, Utah. Delivery person Shell Oil Co., Tillamook, Oreg., 1947-49; salesperson Tillamook Motor Co., 1950-51; salesperson, sales mgr. Condit Chevrolet Co., Tillamook, 1951-57; owner Dean Motors, Tillamook, 1957—; mem. Tillamook County TAC Commn., 1962—; chmn. adv. com. auto dept. Tillamook High Sch., 1987—. Pres. Tillamook Grade Sch. and Jr. High PTA; mem. Tillamook City Planning Commn., 1976-81; mem. Tillamook City Counsel, 1981-82. With USN, 1944-46. Recipient Luther Halsey Gulick award Camp Fire Girls, Inc., 1974. Mem. Nat. Small Bus. United, Nat. Bus. Assn., Nat. Automobile Dealers Assn., Am. Internat. Automobile Dealers Assn., Oreg. Automobile Dealers Assn., Tillamook County Automobile Dealers Assn., Am. Legion. Democrat. Mormon. Home: 3807 3d St Tillamook OR 97141 Office: Dean Motors 542 N Main St PO Box 334 Tillamook OR 97141

DEAN, WILLIAM SHIRLEY, poet, video production company executive, business consultant; b. Santa Ana, Calif., July 15, 1947; s. William Shirley and Mary Elizabeth (Winterborn) D. Student, El Camino Coll., 1965-67, McGill U., 1967-69, U. Toronto, 1968. Writer, designer Man and His World, Montreal, Que., Can., 1967-69; pres. Polymedia Electronics, N.Y.C., 1969-70, W.S. Dean Cons., Palos Verdes, Calif., 1979--, Head-to-Head Video Prodns., Hawthorne, Calif., 1987--; freelance writer Redondo Beach, Calif., 1971--; bus. cons. Cassman Group, Torrance, Calif., 1979--; sales-adminstrn. cons. Skyline Communications, Rollings Hills Estates, Calif., 1982-84; dir. mktg. Albert Levitt Enterprises, Torrance, 1986-87; com. dir. audio-visuals 1st Sci. Fiction and Fantasy Conv., 1973. Author: (poems) Black Swans, 1967 (Prix Medale 1972), American Poems, 1986, My Country 'Tis of Thee, 1988; producer videos Concerto for Animals in Times of Drought, 1987, Freeway Monochromes, 1988, FM TV, 1988. Recipient Light Show of Yr. Design award Deux Ex Machina Soc., 1969. Mem. Nat. Assn. Profl. Cons. (treas. L.A. chpt. 1983-84), Am. Aviation Hist. Soc. (pub. relations com. 1981-82, organizer Charles Lindbergh Day commemoration 1981). Address: 4136-B W 134th St Hawthorne CA 90250

DEANE, ELAINE, lawyer; b. Washington, Sept. 10, 1958; d. William Francis Goode and Elizabeth Anne (Downes) Deane. AB, U. Calif., Berkeley, 1980; JD, U. San Francisco, 1985. Bar: Calif. 1986. Assoc. Parkinson, Wolf, Lazar & Leo, L.A., 1985-89, Pettit & Martin, S.F., San Francisco, 1989—. Mem. Century City Bar Assn., L.A. County Bar Assn., Beverly Hills Bar Assn., Calif. Bar Assn., Sierra Club, Amnesty Internat., Wilderness Soc. Office: Pettit & Martin 101 California St 35th Fl San Francisco CA 94133

DE ANGELIS, BARBARA ANN, psychotherapist; b. Phila., Mar. 4, 1951; d. Sidney Marvin De Angelis and Phyllis (Brunstein) Garshman. BA in Communications, Lone Mountain Coll., 1975; MA in Psychology, Sierra U., 1980; PhD, Columbia Pacific U., 1982. Creative cons. Doug Henning Magic, Inc., Los Angeles, 1976-80; exec. dir. LA Personal Growth Ctr., 1980—; creator and dir. Making Love Work Seminars, Los Angeles, 1980—; counseling therapist CNN News, 1987—, ABC News, Los Angeles, 1988—. Author: How to Make Love All the Time, 1987; contbr. articles to women's mags. Mem. Assn. Humanistic Psychology, Inside Edge (bd. dirs. 1986—). Jewish. Office: LA Personal Growth Ctr 1904 Centinela Los Angeles CA 90025

DEASON-LEE, PATRICIA ANN, real estate company executive; b. N.Y.C., Nov. 28, 1950; d. Jackson Joseph and Jean Clair (Curran) Williams; m. Charles Dennis Deason, J uly 25, 1969 (div. June 1985); children: Charles D., Ryan M.; m. Jerry Lynn Lee, Feb. 14, 1988. Grad. high sch., Anaheim, Calif. Lic. real estate broker. Sec. Vet, Hanford, Calif., 1981-82; cashier, clk. Beacon Oil Co., Hanford, 1982-84; real estate agt. ERA Centurion Realtors, Hanford, 1984-86, Tony Harvey Realty, Red Bluff, Calif., 1986-87; owner, broker Able Real Estate, Red Bluff, 1987—. Publicity chmn. Lemoore (Calif.) Little League, 1982-83. Mem. Nat. Assn. Realtors, Calif. Assn. Realtors, Tehama County Bd. Realtors (bd. dirs., sec.-treas. 1989). Republican. Office: Able Real Estate 645 Antelope Blvd 15 Red Bluff CA 96080

DEASY, WILLIAM JOHN, metal processing executive; b. N.Y.C., June 22, 1937; s. Jeremiah and Margaret (Quinn) D.; m. Carol Ellyn Lemmons, Feb. 1, 1963; children: Cameron, Kimberly. B.S. in Civil Engring, Cooper Union, 1958; LL.B., U. Wash., 1963. With Morrison Knudsen Corp., Boise, Idaho, 1964-88, v.p. N.W. region, 1972-75, v.p. mining, 1975-78, group v.p. mining, 1978-83, exec. v.p. mining, shipbuilding and mfg., 1983-84, pres., chief operating officer, 1984-85, dir., pres., chief exec. officer, 1985-88; bd. dirs. Moore Fin. Group, Boise. Mem. adv. bd. Sch. Bus. Boise State U.; trustee, bd. dirs. St. Luke's Med. Ctr. Mem. Soc. Mining Engrs., Soc. Mil. Engrs., Beavers, Moles. Home: 4611 Hillcrest Dr Boise ID 83705 Office: 1st Interstate Ctr 877 W Main St Boise ID 83702

DEATS, (LEVIN) STEWART, advertising executive; b. Lynwood, Calif., May 7, 1951; s. Jack Ausbury and Sophie Pauline (Garrison) D.; m. Diane Katherine Stuart, June 7, 1979; 1 child, Dana. Student, Los Angeles Trade Tech., 1975-77, Pasadena Art Ctr., 1977-78. With George Whiteman Assocs., Los Angeles, 1970-75, Gribbit Graphic Design, Los Angeles, 1975-82; creative dir. Deats Advt., Woodland Hills, Calif., 1982—. Republican. Home and Office: 4984 Llano Dr Woodland Hills CA 91364

DEAVER, PHILLIP LESTER, lawyer; b. Long Beach, Calif., July 21, 1952; s. Albert Lester and Eva Lucille (Welton) D. Student, USCG Acad., 1970-72; BA, UCLA, 1974; JD, U. So. Calif., 1977. Bar: Hawaii 1977, U.S. Dist. Ct. Hawaii 1977, U.S. Ct. Appeals (9th cir.) 1978, U.S. Supreme Ct. 1981. Assoc. Carlsmith, Wichman, Case, Mukai & Ichiki, Honolulu, 1977-83, ptnr., 1983-86; mng. ptnr. Bays, Deaver, Hiatt, Kawachika & Lezak, Honolulu, 1986. Contbr. articles to profl. jours. Mem. ABA (forum com. on the Constrn. Industry), AIA (affiliate Hawaii chpt.). Home: 2471 Pacific Heights Honolulu HI 96813 Office: Bays Deaver Hiatt Kawachika & Lezak PO Box 1760 Honolulu HI 96806

DEAVER, RICHARD R., insurance executive; b. Flagstaff, Ariz., Nov. 11, 1931; s. Chester Franklin and Gladys Loucille (Culver) D.; m. Bonnylu Vada, June 18, 1952; children: Dana Lynn, Perri Lee, Roy Duane. Grad. high sch., Flagstaff. Mgr. Foodtocon Supermarket, Flagstaff, 1949-57; salesperson N.Y. Life Ins. Co., Phoenix, 1958--; investment mgr. Deaver Enterprises, Flagstaff, 1972--. Pres. Flagstaff C. of C., 1973, No. Ariz. Univ. Found., 1974-75; chmn. Flagstaff Med. Ctr., 1978, Flagstaff Health Mgmt. Corp., 1984-86. Master sgt. U.S. Army, 1950-59. Mem. No. Ariz. Life Underwriters (pres. 1973-75), Ariz. Assn. Life Underwriters (bd. dirs. 1974-76), Million Dollar Roundtable, Lions. Republican. Methodist. Home: 485 Oak Creek Cliffs Dr Sedona AZ 86336 Office: Deaver Fin 1785 W Highway 89A #1B Sedona AZ 86336

DE BARTOLO, EDWARD J., JR., professional football team owner, real estate developer; b. Youngstown, Ohio, Nov. 6, 1946; s. Edward J. and Marie Patricia (Montani) DeB.; m. Cynthia Ruth Papalia, Nov. 27, 1968; children: Lisa Marie, Tiffanie Lynne, Nicole Anne. Student, U. Notre Dame, 1964-68. With Edward J. DeBartolo Corp., Youngstown, Ohio, 1960—, v.p., 1972-75, exec. v.p., 1975—, pres., chief adminstrv. officer, 1979; owner, mng. ptnr. San Francisco 49ers, 1977—. Trustee Youngstown State U., 1974-77; mem. nat. adv. council St. Jude Children's Research Hosp., 1978—, local chmn., 1979-80; local chmn. fund drive Am. Cancer Soc., 1975—, City of Hope, 1977; mem. Nat. Cambodia Crisis Com., 1980—; chmn. 19th Ann. Victor awards City of Hope, 1985; apptd. adv. coun. Coll. Bus. Adminstrn. U. Notre Dame, 1988. Served with U.S. Army, 1969. Recipient Man of Yr. award St. Jude Children's Hosp., 1979, Boys' Town of Italy in San Francisco, 1985; Salvation Army Citation of Merit, 1982. Mem. Internat. Council of Shopping Ctrs. Roman Catholic. Clubs: Tippecanoe Country, Fonderlac Country, Dapper Dan (dir. 1980—). Office: Edward J DeBartolo Corp 7620 Market St Youngstown OH 44512 also: care San Francisco 49ers 4949 Centennial Blvd Santa Clara CA 95054 also: Pitts Penguins Civic Arena Gate #7 Pittsburgh PA 15219 *

DEBENEDETTI, PATRICK JOHN (P. J. DEBENEDETTI), community educator; b. San Francisco, Mar. 4, 1952; s. John Joseph and Ellen Patricia (Hession) DeB.; m. Camille Buckley, Apr. 21, 1979; children: John, Nick. BA in Sociology, Gonzaga U., 1984; BA in Recreation Adminstrn., East Wash. U., 1985. Community sch. coordinator Moses Lake (Wash.) Sch. Dist., 1976-79, dir. sch. community, 1979-88, dir. community affairs, 1988—. Pres. Community Services, Moses Lake, 1987-88, asst. to Pregnant and Parenting Teens, Moses Lake, 1987-88; cons. Washington Spl. Olympics, 1982—. Recipient Area Coordinator of Yr. award Wash. Spl. Olympics, 1978. Mem. Wash. State Community Edn. Assn. (bd. dirs. 1978-81, pres. 1982-83, treas. 1986-88, C.S. Mott award 1981, 87). Roman Catholic. Office: Moses Lake Sch Dist 1318 W Ivy Moses Lake WA 98827

DEBO, ELIZABETH LEA, futurist, accountant, financial consultant; b. Omaha, May 2, 1939; d. James Lee and Elizabeth Jane (May) Harrison; m. Richard Kent, Feb. 3, 1959 (div. 1969). BA, U. Nebr., Lincoln, 1961, MA, 1962, PhD, 1971. Instr. U Nebr., 1962-64, Simon Fraser U., Burnaby, B.C., Can., 1965-71; asst. prof. U. Nebr., Lincoln, 1971; tax technician Nebr. Dept. Revenue, Lincoln, 1972-78; instr. SE Area Community Coll., Milford, Nebr., 1978-82; owner Tucson, 1983—. Mem. Nat. Assn. Accts., IEEE (sec., treas. 1989—), AIAA, Internat. Assn. Bus. Communicators (treas. 1986), Mensa, Norseman's Fedn. Democrat. Home and Office: 1417 E Ft Lowell Tucson AZ 85719

DEBOER, KATHRYN ANNE, marketing analyst; b. Grand Rapids, Mich., Dec. 1, 1960; d. Alfred Jacob and Dora Louise (Buurma) Bloem; m. Bradley Peter DeBoer, Dec. 27, 1986. Bachelor's, Calvin Coll., 1982; Master's, Ariz. State U., 1985. Rsch. psychologist KPR Assocs., Inc., Scottsdale, Ariz., 1985-87; rsch. analyst O'Neil Assocs., Inc., Tempe, Ariz., 1988—. Contbr. articles to profl. jours. Mem. Am. Mktg. Assn. (v.p. Phoenix chpt. 1987-88, pres. 1988-89). Republican. Mem. Christian Reformed Ch. Office: O'Neil Assocs Inc 412 E Southern Ave Tempe AZ 85282

DEBON, GEORGE A., security services company executive. Chmn. Loomis Corp., Seattle, Mayne Nickless Inc., Seattle. Office: Mayne Nickless Inc 720 Olive Way Seattle WA 98101 also: Loomis Armored Inc 10 Corporated Pl S Piscataway NJ 08854 *

DEBRETTEVILLE, SHEILA LEVRANT, educator, artist; b. Bklyn., Nov. 4, 1940. Student Barnard Coll.; B.A. in Art History, Columbia U.; M.F.A., Yale U. Group shows include Am. Inst. Graphics Art, 1972, 5e Biennale des Arts Graphiques, Brno Czech, 1972, Whitney Mus., 1974; represented in permanent collections N.Y., Mus. Modern Art, N.Y.C., Community Gallery, Los Angeles; commns. include Archtl. League, N.Y., 1965, Yale Art Gallery, 1966, book design Canavese, Olivetti, Milan, Italy, 1968, poster design Calif. Inst. Arts, Valencia, 1970, spl. issue design Art Soc. Wis., 1970; typographer Yale U. Press, 1969-74; co-founder, pres. Woman's Bldg. Community Gallery, 1973—; dir. graphic design dept. Calif. Inst. Arts, 1970-74; co-founder, editor, designer Chrysalis Mag., 1977; design dir. Los Angeles Times, 1978-81; chmn. dept. communication, design and illustration Otis Art Inst., Parsons Sch. Design, Los Angeles, 1981—; judge Nat. Endowment Arts-Civil Service Commn., 1975; lectr. various colls. and univs. Recipient Grand Excellence award Soc. Pub. Designers, 1971, Communication Graphics awards Am. Inst. Graphic Arts, 1972. Mem. Am. Inst. Graphic Arts (bd. dirs nat. chpt. 1988—). Office: Otis Art Inst Parsons Sch Design 2401 Wilshire Blvd Los Angeles CA 90057

DEBREU, GERARD, economics and mathematics educator; b. Calais, France, July 4, 1921; came to U.S., 1950, naturalized, 1975; s. Camille and Fernande (Decharne) D.; m. Françoise Bled, June 14, 1945; children: Chantal, Florence. Student, Ecole Normale Supérieure, Paris, 1941-44, Agrégé de l'Université, 1946; DSc, U. Paris, 1956; Dr. Rerum Politicarum honoris causa, U. Bonn, 1977; D. Scis. Economiques (hon.), U. Lausanne, 1980; DSc (hon.), Northwestern U., 1981; Dr. honoris causa, U. des Scis. Sociales de Toulouse, 1983, Yale U., 1987, U. Bordeaux I, 1988. Research assoc. Centre Nat. De La Recherche Sci., Paris, 1946-48; Rockefeller fellow U.S., Sweden and Norway, 1948-50; research assoc. Cowles Commn., U. Chgo., 1950-55; assoc. prof. econs. Cowles Found., Yale, 1955-61; fellow Center Advanced Study Behavioral Scis., 1960-61; vis. prof. econs. Yale U., fall 1961; prof. econs. U. Calif. at Berkeley, 1962—, prof. math., 1975—, Univ. prof., 1985—; Guggenheim fellow, vis. prof. Center Ops. Research and Econometrics, U. Louvain, 1968-69, vis. prof., 1971, 72, 88; Erskine fellow U. Canterbury, Christchurch, New Zealand, 1969, 87, vis. prof., 1973; Overseas fellow Churchill Coll., Cambridge, Eng., 1972; vis. prof. Cowles Found. for Research in Econs., Yale U., 1976; vis. prof. U. Bonn, 1977; research assoc. CEPREMAP, Paris, 1980; faculty research lectr. U. Calif. Berkeley, 1984-85, univ. prof., 1985—; Class of 1958 chair U. Calif., Berkeley, 1986—; vis. prof. U. Sydney, Australia, 1987. Author: Theory of Value, 1959, Mathematical Economics: Twenty Papers of Gerard Debreu, 1983; Assoc. editor: Internat. Econ. Rev, 1959-69; mem. editorial bd.: Jour. Econ. theory, 1972—, Games and Econ. Behavior, 1989—; mem. adv. bd.: Jour. Math. Econs, 1974—. Served with French Army, 1944-45. Decorated chevalier Légion d'Honneur; recipient Nobel Prize in Econ. Scis., 1983, Commandeur de l'Ordre du Merite, 1984; sr. U.S. Scientist awardee Alexander von Humboldt Found. Fellow AAAS, Econometric Soc. (pres. 1971), Am. Econ. Assn. (disting. fellow 1982, pres.-elect 1989); mem. NAS (com. human rights 1984—), Am. Philos. Soc., French Acad. Scis. (fgn. assoc.). Office: U Calif Dept Econs Berkeley CA 94720

DEBRUHL, RICHARD R., television reporter; b. Southgate, Calif., June 22, 1955; s. H.L. and Bessie (George) Hammond; m. Patricia Kimberly White DeBruhl, June 18, 1977; children: Gregory, Kyle. BA, Calif. Poly. Inst., 1977. News dir. Sta. KAXY-AM, San Luis Obispo, Calif., 1977; anchorperson Sta. KCOY-TV, Santa Maria, Calif., 1978; reporter Sta. KPNX-TV, Phoenix, 1978—; reporter auto racing ESPN, Bristol, Conn., 1988, ESPN-Speedweek, Indpls., 1986-88; freelance writer various mags. Active Big Bros. of Phoenix, 1978-88; mem. St. Paul's Parish Coun., Phoenix, 1986-88. Named Big Bro. of Yr., 1987; recipient various 1st Pl. awards Ariz. AP, 1981-87. Mem. Ariz. Press Club (various 1st pl. awards, 1978-87), Nat. Acad. TV Arts and Scis. (recipient 2 Emmy awards 1982, 87). Democrat. Roman Catholic. Office: Sta KPNX-TV 1101 N Central Phoenix AZ 85004

DEBUS, ELEANOR VIOLA, business management company executive; b. Buffalo, May 19, 1920; d. Arthur Adam and Viola Charlotte (Pohl) D.; student Chown Bus. Sch., 1939. Sec., Buffalo Wire Works, 1939-45; home talent producer Empire Producing Co., Kansas City, Mo., sec. Owens Corning Fiberglass, Buffalo; public relations and publicity Niagara Falls Theatre, Ont., Can.; pub. relations dir. Woman's Internat. Bowling Congress, Columbus, Ohio, 1957-59; publicist, sec. Ice Capades, Hollywood, Calif., 1961-63; sec. to controller Rexall Drug Co., Los Angeles, 1963-67; bus. mgmt. acct. Samuel Berke & Co., Beverly Hills, Calif., 1967-75; Gadbois Mgmt. Co., Beverly Hills, 1975-76; sec., treas. Sasha Corp., Los Angeles, 1976—; bus. mgr. Dean Martin, Shirley MacLaine, Debbie Reynolds; pres. Tempo Co., Los Angeles, 1976—. Mem. Nat. Assn. Female Execs., Nat. Notary Assn., Nat. Film Soc., Am. Film Inst. Republican. Lodge: Order Eastern Star. Contbr. articles to various mags. Office: Tempo Co 1900 Ave of Stars #1230 Los Angeles CA 90067

DE CAMP, MARTHA LENORE, educator, nutrition consultant; b. Ann Arbor, Mich., Nov. 3, 1939; m. Samuel Tolken De Camp, July 2, 1983; 2

children. BS in Home Econ. Edn., Ea. Mich. U., 1962, occupational-vocat. cert., 1975, consumer-homemaking cert., 1973. Cert. home economist. Tchr., coord. adult edn. Ann Arbor Pub. Schs., 1962-75, tchr. jr. high sch., 1973-83; coord. for So. Calif. Cuisinarts Inc., 1985; developer, coord. sch. program for So. Calif. Cuisinarts Inc.Consumer Advisor Program, 1986—; educator Ednl. Info. Systems, Agoura, Calif., 1983—; instr. Ventura (Calif.) Coll., summers 1985—. Recipient Outstanding Home Econs. Educator award Mich. Home Econs. Educators, 1983. Mem. Am. Home Econs. Assn., Home Economists in Bus., Home Economists in Homemaking (sec. Ventura, 1985-87), Mich. Bishop Sewing Coun. (hon. life, 1st chmn. 1968-71), Kappa Delta Pi, Alpha Sigma Tau (pres. local chpts. 1965-67, 79-81, nat. svc. chmn. 1966-78, 84—, Ada A. Norton Outstanding Alumna award 1974). Roman Catholic. Office: Ednl Info Systems 27061 Esward Dr Agoura CA 91301

DE CANISY, SABINE DE CARBONNEL, cultural organization administrator; b. Saigon, Vietnam, Mar. 17, 1931; came to U.S., 1963; d. Hervé de Canisy and Henriette de Chassey; m. James Edge Faris, Sept. 15, 1961 (div. 1981); m. Constant Vauclain, Jan. 26, 1983. B., U. Alger, Algeria, 1948, Polit. Scis. Lic., 1952; student, Langues Orientales, Paris, 1957; MA, U. Hawaii, 1967. Mgr., prof. Alliance Francaise, Manila, Philippines, 1959-63; instr. Fgn. Svc. Inst., Washington, 1963-64; prof. language Tutuila High Sch., Samoa, 1964-66; prof. literature Fu Jen U., Taipei, Taiwan, 1967-75; instr. Chinese brush painting Port Oxford, Oreg., 1976-82; founder, mgr. Alliance Francaise, Portland, Oreg., 1984—; bd. dirs. French Am. Sch., Portland; speaker in field. Mem. Conf. Fgn. Language Tchrs. Republican. Roman Catholic. Home and Office: 8080 SW Canyon Dr Portland OR 97225

DECARLO, MATTHEW STEVEN, financial analyst; b. Denver, May 8, 1960; s. Matthew John and Patricia Ann (Phelan) DeC.; m. Teresa Mariana DeSimone, June 21, 1980; 1 child, Danielle Ruby. BSBA, U. Colo., 1982; MBA in Acctg. and fin., Regis Coll., 1987. Programmer, analyst Rockwell Internat., Golden, Colo., 1981-84, systems analyst, 1984-86; mgr. acctg. Landmark Pub. (name now US West), Denver, 1986-87; fin. systems analyst US West Direct (now US West Mktg. Rcsc.), Aurora, Colo., 1987—; CPA, Colo. Democrat. Roman Catholic. Home: 7626 S Ogden Way Littleton CO 80122 Office: US West Mktg Rscs 2500 S Havana St 3N Aurora CO 80014

DECHERT, PETER, photographer, writer, foundation administrator; b. Phila., Dec. 17, 1924; s. Robert and Helen Hope (Wilson) D.; m. Phoebe Jane Booth; children—Sandra, Robin Booth, Caroline. B.A., U. Pa., 1948, M.A., 1950, Ph.D., 1955. Owner, Peter Dechert Assocs., Bryn Mawr, Pa., 1956-68; asst. dir. Sch. of Am. Research, Santa Fe, 1968-71; pres. Indian Arts Fund, Santa Fe, 1971-72; pres. Southwest Found. for Audio-Visual Resources, Santa Fe, 1973-77; self-employed photographer, Santa Fe; tchr., cons. photog. communications, 1964—. Author: Canon Rangefinder Cameras, 1933-68, The Contax Connection, Olympus Pen SLR Cameras, Canon SLR Cameras, 1959-88, The Canon Collector's Guide; contbg. editor Shutterbug mag., other photographic periodicals; contbr. articles on early Canon cameras, research on history and design of miniature cameras and other photog. topics to profl. publs. Bd. dirs. St. Vincent Hosp. Found. (pres. 1981-83, v.p. 1983-84). Served with AUS, 1943-46. Mem. N.Mex. Poetry Soc. (pres. 1969-74), Am. Soc. Mag. Photographers, SAR, Southwest Assn. Indian Affairs, N.Mex. Jazz Workshop Club, Don Quixote Club, Phi Beta Kappa, Delta Psi. Address: PO Box 636 Santa Fe NM 87504

DE CHRISTOPHER, STEVEN, JR., interior designer, furniture designer, product designer; b. Wiesbaden, Federal Republic of Germany, Jan. 14, 1960; came to U.S., 1962; s. Steven and Ursula De Christopher. Student in interior and environ. design, UCLA, 1982. V.p., designer Steven De Christopher, an Interior Design Corp., Rancho Mirage, Calif., 1983—; designer Il Delfino Inc., Rancho Mirage, 1986—. Mem. Am. Mktg. Assn., Am. Soc. Interior Designers (allied). Republican. Roman Catholic. Office: 72-067 Hwy 111 Rancho Mirage CA 92270

DECIUTIIS, ALFRED CHARLES MARIA, medical oncologist, television producer; b. N.Y.C., Oct. 16, 1945; s. Alfred Ralph and Theresa Elizabeth (Manko) de C.; m. Catherine L. Gohn. B.S. summa cum laude, Fordham U., 1967; M.D., Columbia U., 1971. Diplomate Am. Bd. Internal Medicine, Am. Bd. Med. Oncology. Intern N.Y. Hosp.-Cornell Med. Ctr., N.Y.C., 1971-72, resident, 1972-74; fellow in clin. immunology Meml. Hosp.-Sloan Kettering Cancer Ctr., N.Y.C., 1974-75, fellow in clin. oncology, 1975-76, spl. fellow in immunology, 1974-76; guest investigator, asst. physician exptl. hematology Rockefeller U., N.Y.C., 1975-76; practice medicine, specializing in med. oncology Los Angeles, 1977—; host cable TV shows, 1981—; med. editor Cable Health Network, 1983—, Lifetime Network, 1984—; mem. med. adv. com. 1984 Olympics; active staff South Bay Hosp., Little Co. of Mary Hosp., Torrance Meml. Hosp., Bay Harbor Hosp.; co-founder Meditrina Med. Ctr., free out-patient surg. ctr., Torrance, Calif. Syndicated columnist Coast Media News "The Subject is Cancer", 1980's; producer numerous med. TV shows; contbr. articles to profl. jours. Founder Italian-Am. Med. Assn., 1982; co-founder Italian-Am. Med.-Legal Alliance, L.A., 1982—; mem. Italian-Am. Civic Com., L.A., 1983; mem. gov. bd. med. coun. Italian-Am. Found.; chancellor's assoc. UCLA. Served to capt. M.C., U.S. Army, 1972-74. Leukemia Soc. Am. fellow, 1974-76; N.Y. State Regents scholar, 1963-67, 67-71; recipient Physicians Recognition award AMA, 1978-80, 82-85; proclamation Senate Rules Com., State of Calif., 1982. Fellow ACP, Internat. Coll. Physicians and Surgeons; mem. AMA, Am. Union Physicians and Dentists, Am. Soc. Clin. Oncology, N.Y. Acad. Sci. (life), Calif. Med. Assn., Los Angeles County Med. Assn., Internat. Health Soc., Am. Pub. Health Assn., AAAS, Am. Geriatrics Soc., Chinese Med. Assn., Drug Info. Assn., Am. Soc. Hematology (mem. emeritus), Nat. Geog. Soc., Internat. Platform Assn., Calif. chpt. Cath. League for Civil and Religious Liberty, Nature Conservancy, Nat. Wildlife Fedn., World Affairs Coun. L.A., Am. Coll. Heraldry, Confederation Chivalry, Mensa, Phi Beta Kappa, Alpha Omega Alpha, Sigma Xi. Republican. Roman Catholic. Office: care Dr Gene Leone 4305 Torrence Blvd Ste 101 Torrance CA 90503

DE CIUTIIS, VINCENT LOUIS, hospital administrator, anesthesiology educator; b. N.Y.C., Oct. 11, 1924; s. Alfredo Ralph and Chiara Mary (Giannone) de C.; m. Claire Adele Ostuni, June 28, 1947 (div. 1976); children: Vilia, Nadine, Vincent, Mario, Elena, Michael, Elisa, Carl; m. Patricia Therese Paulson, June 3, 1976; children: James, Marianna, Michelle, Donald. BA, Columbia U., 1945; MD, N.Y. Med. Coll., 1948; grad. Med. Sch. Walter Reed Army Med. Ctr., 1954; MBA, Pepperdine U., 1976; grad. U.S. Army Command and Gen. Staff Coll., 1986. Diplomate Am. Bd. Anesthesia. Intern Met. Hosp., N.Y.C., 1948-49, resident in anesthesia, 1949-51; resident Fitzsimons Army Hosp., Denver, 1952-53; chief anesthesiology U.S. Army Hosp., Ft. Dix, N.J., 1951-52, Misericordia Hosp., Bronx, 1958-62, Torrance Meml. Hosp., Calif., 1971-79; chief anesthesiology, assoc. prof. Met. Hosp. N.Y. Med. Coll., N.Y.C., 1956-58; asst. prof. UCLA Med. Sch., Los Angeles, 1958-86, assoc. prof., 1986—; prof. surgery, anesthesiology Coll. Osteo. Medicine U. of the Pacific, Stockton, Calif., 1985; adminstr. Riviera Community Hosp., Torrance, 1963-64; adminstr., med. dir. Surg. Ctr. S. Bay, Torrance, 1979—; cons. U.S. Army Hosp., Ft. MacArthur, Calif., 1965-71; dir. med. edn. Torrance Meml. Hosp., 1972-76. Producer/dir. med. documentary with KNBC, 1972; inventor intravenous catheter laryngoscope, 1973; contbr. articles to profl. jours. Served to lt. col. U.S. Army, col. Res. Decorated World War II Victory medal, Korean Service medal, Commendation ribbon. Fellow Am. Coll. Anesthesiologists; mem. AMA, Los Angeles County Med. Assn., Calif. Med. Assn., Disabled Am. Vets., Assn. Mil. Surgeons U.S., Res. Officers Assn. (life). Republican. Roman Catholic. Home: 254 Via Linda Vista Redondo Beach CA 90277 Office: Med Care Internat Surg Ctr of S Bay 23500 Madison St Torrance CA 90505

DECKER, CARL MURRAY, entrepreneur; b. Phoenix, Oct. 11, 1955; s. Joseph Murray and Alberta (Cross) D.; m. Marla Linn Krant, Dec. 3, 1983; children: Stacy Linnette, Christy Linnel. AA in Bus. Adminstrn., Glendale (Ariz.) Community Coll., 1975; BS in Mgmt., Ariz. State U., 1977. Asst. prop mgr. Nat. Apartments, Inc., Glendale, 1975-78; v.p. Decker Vendors, Inc., Glendale, 1977-87, pres., 1988—; prin. Coffee Fountain, Glendale, 1986—. Recipient Shell Scholarship. Mem. Nat. Rifle Assn., Nat. Automatic Merchandising Assn., Glendale C. of C., Sigma Iota Epsilon. Democrat. Home: 4425 W Kristal Pl Glendale AZ 85308 Office: Decker Vendors Inc 5945 W Ocotillo Rd Glendale AZ 85301

DECKER, JAMES THOMAS, psychotherapist; b. Dayton, Ky., Jan. 16, 1944; s. Frank and Edith (Mountain) D.; m. Jane Campbell Fisher, May 6, 1972; children: Peter Campbell, James Mountain, Christina Campbell. AA, Los Angeles Pierce Coll., 1970; BA, Calif. State U., Northridge, 1972; MSW, SUNY, Stony Brook, 1974; PhD, U. Minn., 1976. Research asst. U. Minn., Mpls., 1974-76; asst. prof. San Diego State U., 1976-78; dir., assoc. prof. U. Tex., El Paso, 1978-80; dir. cons. Kern View Hosp., Bakersfield, Calif., 1980-82; exec. dir. J.T. Decker Profl. Group, Bakersfield, Calif., 1982—; adj. prof. Calif. State Coll., Bakersfield, 1981—; sch. psychotherapist Friends Sch., Bakersfield, 1983—; nursing mgmt. cons. Meml. Hosp., Bakersfield, 1983—; out placement cons. Tosco Inc., Bakersfield, 1983—; employee asst. coordinator various orgns., Bakersfield, 1982—. Contbr. articles to profl. jours. Bd. dirs. Consumer Credit Counselors, Bakersfield, 1982—; chmn. Human Resources Com., Bakersfield, 1980-85; bd. dirs. Health Care Mgmt. Adv. Council, Bakersfield, 1982—; bd. dirs. United Way., San Diego and El Paso, Tex., 1977-80. Served with U.S. Army, 1960-64. Recipient Outstanding Alumni award Sch. Social Work, SUNY. Mem. Assn. Labor Mgmt. Adminstrs. and Cons. on Alcoholism, Nat. Assn. Social Workers (cert.). Home: 231 Oleander St Bakersfield CA 93304

DECKER, JOHN ALVIN, JR., electronics company executive; b. Columbia, Mo., Oct. 25, 1935; s. John Alvin and Mildred Evaline (Harrington) D.; m. Linda Louise McCullough, Dec. 30, 1957; children: Trigg Harrington (dec.), Sarah Louise. BS in Aero. Engrng., Aero. Engrng. Profl. Degree, MIT, 1958; PhD in Plasma Physics, Cambridge U., 1965; postgrad., Boston Coll. Sch. Bus., Episcopal Theol. Sch. Rsch. physicist Sperry Rand Rsch. Lab., Bedford, Mass., 1965-67; dir. physics Comstock & Wescott, Inc., Cambridge, Mass., 1967-70; pres. Spectral Imaging, Inc., Concord, Mass., 1971-77; rsch. and tech. mgr. vacuum div. Varian Co., Lexington, Mass., 1977-79; mgr. strategic plans SPIRE, Inc., Bedford, Mass., 1979-80; mng. dir. AVCO Everett Rsch. Labs, Puunene, Hawaii, 1981-82; pres. Kuau Tech., Ltd., Puunene, 1982—; cons. John A. Decker, Jr., Cons., Puunene, 1982—. Contbr. numerous articles to profl. pubs.; patentee in field. Mem. council Episc. Diocese Hawaii, Honolulu, 1985-87; chmn. Episc. Hawaii Cursillo, 1987-88, Maui Cath. Charities, 1988—. Capt. USAF, 1962-65. Recipient IR.100 award Indsl. Rsch. mag., 1972; alumni scholar MIT, 1954;. Mem. Instrument Soc. Am. (sr.), Am. Phys. Soc., Optical Soc. Am., Catgut Acoustical Soc., Guild Am. Luthiers, Soc. Applied Spectroscopy, Am. Model Yacht Assn., Rotary (pres. Paia, Maui 1989—). Home: 307 S Alu Rd Wailuku Maui HI 96793 Office: Kuau Tech Ltd PO Box 1031 Puunene Maui HI 96784

DECKER, KENNETH CHARLES, insurance broker; b. Denver, Oct. 1, 1945; s. Charles W. and Ethel J. (Otis) D. BS, Colo. State U., 1969. Pres. Vets. Ins. Services Inc., Lakewood, Colo., 1978—; v.p. Ins. World, Denver, 1981-83. Served with U.S. Army, 1969-71, Vietnam. Republican. Lodge: Civitan (bd. dirs. Englewood, Colo. club 1983-86, pres. Englewood-South Denver 1984-85, lt. gov. Mountain/Plains Dist. 1987-88). Home: 8010 S Lamar Littleton CO 80123 Office: Vets Ins Svcs Inc 1858 S Wadsworth Ste 115 Lakewood CO 80226

DECKER, PETER RANDOLPH, state official; b. N.Y.C., Oct. 1, 1934; s. Frank Randolph and Marjorie (Marony) D.; m. Dorothy Morss, Sept. 24, 1972; children: Karen, Christopher, Hilary. BA, Middlebury Coll., Vt., 1957; MA, Syracuse U., 1961; PhD, Columbia U., 1974. Tchr. Cate Sch., Carpinteria, Calif., 1961-63; sr. writer Congl. Quar., Washington, 1963-64; asst. to pres. Middlebury (Vt.) Coll., 1964-67; staff asst. Sen. Robert Kennedy, Washington, 1967-68; instr./lectr. Columbia U., N.Y.C., 1972-74; asst. prof. Duke U., Durham, N.C., 1974-80; owner/operator Double D Ranch, Ridgeway, Colo., 1980—; commr. agr. State of Colo., Denver, 1987-89; pres. Lifeline Foods, Boulder, Colo., 1989—. Author: Fortunes and Failutres, 1978; contbr. articles to profl. jours. Trustee Middlebury Coll., 1988—; vice chmn. Colo. Commn. on Higher Edn., 1985-87; chmn. Ouray County Dem. Party, 1982-85; chmn. Ouray County Planning Commn., 1981-85, Colo. Endowment Humanities, 1982-85; mem. adv. coun. Environ. Def. Fund, 1988—. Lt. U.S. Army, 1957-60. English Speaking Union scholar, 1952-53; Nat. Endowment for Humanities fellow, 1977-78; Rockefeller Found. fellow, 1979-80. Mem. Colo. Cattlemen's Assn., Nat. Cattlemen's Assn., Am. Hist. Assn., Colo. Cattle Feeders Assn., Denver Athletic Club, Elks. Democrat. Home: Double D Ranch 6748 Hwy 62 Ridgeway CO 81432

DECKER, RICHARD KELSEY, equipment distribution company executive; b. Monrovia, Calif., Dec. 31, 1927; s. Raymond Grant and Dorothy Irene (Heady) D.; m. Barbara Carolyn Carlson, 1956; children—Richard Brian, Carolyn Ann Decker Johnson. B.S., U. So. Calif., 1952. Cost. acct. S.W. Products Co., Monrovia, 1953-55; controller Scotsman Refrigeration Inc., Monterey Park, Calif., 1955-64; with Scotsman Distbrs. of Los Angeles, Inc., La Verne, Calif., 1964—, pres., chief exec. officer, 1976—. Served with USN, 1945-47. Mem. Alpha Kappa Psi (pres.), Beta Gamma Sigma. Office: Scotsman Distbrs Los Angeles Inc 1480 Arrow Hwy La Verne CA 91750

DECKER REESE, DEBORAH, free-lance writer and photographer; b. Milw., Aug. 12, 1950; d. Ernst and Sophia (Karolewicz) Decker; m. Clyde William Reese, Oct. 22, 1983; 1 child, Robert Ernst. Student, U. Wis., Milw., 1978-82. Writer/photographer Littleton, Colo., 1982—. Author: Rutherford: The Life of a Racer, 1988; contbr. articles to profl. jours. Mem. Nat. Writers Club, Delta Gamma. Democrat. Roman Catholic. Home: 4858 S Hoyt St Littleton CO 80123

DECKER-RODRIGUEZ, PATRICIA ANNE, videotape editor; b. Blackwell, Okla., Mar. 23, 1956; d. Otto and Elfriede Maria (Schaul) Decker; m. Fabian Victor Rodriguez, July 9, 1983. BA in Communications, U. N.Mex., 1979. News intern Sta. KOB-TV, Albuquerque, 1979, news videotape editor, 1979-81; TV and news videotape editor Sta. KABC-TV, Hollywood, Calif., 1982—. Mem. NABET, Alpha Chi Omega (v.p. Albuquerque chpt. 1978-79). Republican. Lutheran. Office: Sta KABC-TV 4151 Prospect Ave Hollywood CA 90027

DECKERT, HARLAN KENNEDY, JR., manufacturing company official; b. Evanston, Ill., May 22, 1923; s. Harlan Kennedy Sr. and Lady Otey (Hutton) D.; B.S., U. Calif., Berkeley, 1949; M.B.A., U. So. Calif., 1962; m. Mary Emma Eldredge, Nov. 27, 1971; children: Mary Adrienne, Christine Ann, Daniel Gregory, Deborah Alice. Systems analyst Northrop Corp., Hawthorne, Calif., 1949-53, supr. engring. adminstrv. svcs., 1953-57, adminstrv. systems engr., 1957-59; with AiResearch Indsl. div. Garrett Corp., Torrance, Calif., 1959-88, systems svc. adminstr., 1962-72, mgr. adminstrv. svcs., 1972-75, adminstr. internat. ops., 1975-80, sr. staff advisor Garrett Automotive Group Allied-Signal, Inc., 1980-88, ret., 1988. Ret. Patron, L.A. County Mus. Art; zoo docent Greater L.A. Zoo Assn.; mem. UCLA Art Council; patron L.A. County Mus. Natural History, African Wildlife Found., Friends Cabrillo Marine Mus., Assn. Zoo & Aquarium Docents. Mem. Am. Assn. Zoo Keepers, Nat. Parks & Conservation Assn., Nat. Wildlife Fedn., San Diego Zoöl. Soc., Palm Springs Living Desert Res., World Wildlife Fund, Wilderness Soc., Nat. Audubon Soc. Nature Conservancy. With USAAF, 1943-46, CBI, capt. USAFR, 1946-57, ret., 1957. Home: 2509 20th St Santa Monica CA 90405

DE CONCINI, DENNIS, senator, lawyer; b. Tucson, May 8, 1937; s. Evo and Ora (Webster) DeC.; m. Susan Margaret Hurley, June 6, 1959; children: Denise, Christina, Patrick Evo. B.A., U. Ariz., 1959, LL.B., 1963. Bar: Ariz. 1963. Mem. firm Evo DeConcini, Tucson; ptnr. DeConcini & McDonald, Tucson, 1968-73; dep. Pima County atty. Sch. Dist. 1, 1971-72, county atty., 1972-76; U.S. Senator from Ariz. 1977—; mem. Senate Appropriations com., Judiciary com., subcom. on def., subcom. energy and water devel., subcom. on fgn. ops., subcom. on interior and related agys., subcom. on State, Justice, Commerce and Judiciary, subcom. on Constitution, subcom. on immigration, select com. on Indian Affairs, select com. on Vet.'s Affairs; chmn. subcom. on Treasury, Postal Service and gen. govt.; formerly pres., now dir. Shopping Centers, Inc.; chmn. Judiciary subcom. on Patents, Copyrights, Trademarks, Antitrust, Cts., Tech. and the Law. Chmn. legis. com. Tucson Community Council, 1966-67; mem. major gifts com., devel. fund drive St. Joseph's Hosp., 1970, mem. devel. council, 1971-73; mem. major gifts com. Tucson Mus. and Art Center Bldg. Fund, 1971; adminstr. Ariz. Drug Control Dist., 1975-76; precinct committeeman Ariz. Democratic Party, 1958—; mem. Pima County Dem. Central Com., 1958-67, Dem. State Exec. Com., 1958-68; state vice chmn. Ariz. Dem. Com., 1964-66, 70-72; vice chmn. Pima County Dem. Com., 1970-73. Served to 2d lt. JAG U.S. Army, 1959-60. Named Outstanding Ariz. County Atty., 1975. Mem. Am., Ariz., Pima County bar assns., Nat. Dist. Attys. Assn., Ariz. Sheriffs and County Attys. Assn., Am. Judicature Soc., Ariz. Pioneer Hist. Soc., NAACP, U. Ariz. Alumni Assn., Tucson Fraternal Order Police, Phi Delta Theta, Delta Sigma Rho, Phi Alpha Delta. Roman Catholic. Clubs: Nucleus (Tucson), Old Pueblo (Tucson), Pres.'s U. Ariz. (Tucson), Latin Am. (Tucson), Latin Am. Social (Tucson). Office: US Senate 328 Hart Senate Bldg Washington DC 20510

DECORE, LAURENCE GEORGE, mayor; b. Vegreville, Alta., Can., June 28, 1940; s. John N. and Myrosia Decore; m. Anne Marie Fedoruk; children: Andrea, Michael. BA, U. Alta., 1961, LLB, 1964. Prin. Decore & Co., Edmonton, Alta., Can.; alderman City of Edmonton, 1974-77, former chmn. econ. affairs com., budget com., pub. affairs com., mayor, 1983-88; ptnr. Decore and Co.; co-founder QCTV, Ltd. Former chmn. Can. Multiculturalism Council, 1980-83, mem. various coms.; mem. Edmonton Multiculturalism com., Ukrainian Community com. on multiculturalism, St. John's Ukrainian Greek Orthodox Parish, Edmonton; former vice-chmn. Devel. Appeal Bd.; bd. dirs. local Bd. Health, 1974-77, Royal Alexander Hosp., 1975-77, Greater Edmonton Found. Lt. Royal Can. Navy; res. Recipient Province of Alta. Achievement award, 1982; named to Order of Can., 1983. Mem. Elizabeth Fry Soc. (bd. dirs.), Alta. Law Soc., Can. Bar Assn., Edmonton and Dist. Soccer Assn., (past adminstrv. sec.), Alta. Soccer Assn. (past adminstrv. sec.), Ukrainian Profl. and Bus. Fedn. of Can. (past pres.), Ukrainian Can. Com. (past sec.), Can. Found. of Ukrainian Studies (past bd. dirs.), Greater Edmonton Found., Alta. Heritage Council (past 1st chmn.). Club: Ukrainian Profl. and Businessmen's (Alta.) (past pres.). Office: Office of Mayor, 1 Sir Winston Churchill Sq, Edmonton, AB Canada T5J 2R7

DECOT, DAVID, infosystems engineer; b. Beverly, Mass., Apr. 23, 1962; s. Harold Theodore and Dorothy Alma (Gaiser) D. BS in Computer Sci. and Engrng. with honors, Case Western Res. U., 1983, MS, 1984. Software quality engr. Hewlett-Packard, Cupertino, Calif., 1984-86, project mgr., 1986—. Chmn. X/Open Kernel Working Group, 1988-89. Office: Hewlett-Packard 19447 Pruneridge Ave Mail Stop 4742 Cupertino CA 95014

DECUBELLIS, ROBERT, air force official; b. Providence, Aug. 22, 1946; s. William Richard and Kathryn E. (Van Artsdalen) DeC.; m. Lourdes Alimbuyao, Aug. 26, 1983; 1 stepchild, Felisa A. BS in History-Sociology, Northland Coll., 1968; postgrad., Calif. State U., Sacramento, 1980-82; diploma, Air Command and Staff Coll., 1985. Mail carrier U.S. Postal Svc., Novato, Calif., 1973-74; security specialist USAF Res., Hamilton AFB, Calif., 1974-77; chief of security police Hdqrs. 4th Air Force, McClellan AFB, Calif., 1977—; res. patrolman Novato Police Dept., 1973-75; cons. Jr. ROTC, Del Campo High Sch., Citrus Heights, Calif., 1987-89. Contbr. articles to profl. mags. Team leader McClellan Op. Santa Claus, North Highlands, Calif., 1979-87; organizer fingerprinting grade sch. children, North Highlands, 1985. With USAF 1968-73, Vietnam, maj. USAFR. Decorated Cross of Galantry, Vietnam. Mem. Internat. Assn. Chief Police, Calif. Peace Officers Assn., Res. Officers Assn. (life), Air Force Assn. (life), Security Police Mus. Found. (life), Air Force Security Police Assn., Air Force Sgts. Assn. (life), Northland Coll. Alunni Assn. (fund raiser). Office: Hdqrs 4th Air Force Security Police McClellan AFB CA 95652-6002

DEDEAUX, PAUL J., orthodontist; b. Pass Christian, Miss., Feb. 22, 1937; s. Mack and Harriet D.; m. Thelma Murrell, Nov. 16, 1964 (div. 1969); 1 child, Michele; m. Janet Louise Harter, June 29, 1971; children: Kristen, Kelly. BA, Dillard U., 1959; DDS, Howard U., 1963; MS, Fairleigh Dickinson U., 1975. Pvt. practice, Washington, 1967-69, Santa Ana, Calif., 1976—; instr. Howard U., Washington, 1967-69; dental dir. Dr. Martin Luther King Health Ctr., Bronx, N.Y., 1969-70, dentist, 1970-76; instr. Howard U., Washington, 1967-69; cons. Hostos Community Coll., Bronx, 1971-76; mem. adv. panel Dental Econs. mag., 1976. Contbr. articles to profl. jours. Capt. U.S. Army, 1963-67, USAR, 1975—. Mem. Am. Assn. Orthodontists, Pacific Coast Soc. Orthodontists, ADA, Calif. Dental Assn., Assn. Mil. Surgeons of U.S. Democrat. Methodist. Home: 12181 Anzio St Garden Grove CA 92640 Office: 1125 E 17th St Ste 119 Santa Ana CA 92701

DEE, RALPH, JR., foundation administrator; b. Shiprock, N.Mex., Oct. 25, 1961; s. Ralph and Jennie (Mastach) D.; m. Trish Aloysius, 1981; children: Daniel, Meshack, Shadrach. Grad. high sch., Red Mesa, Ariz. Dir. Solid Rock Found., Shiprock, 1980—. Home: PO Box 2105 Shiprock NM 87420 Office: Solid Rock Found Drawer J Teec Nos Pos AZ 86514

DEERING, JOSEPH WILLIAM, manufacturing executive; b. Mpls., Apr. 7, 1940; s. Joseph W. and Helen (Forsman) D.; m. Nancy Zentner, 1963 (dec. 1972); children: Kirsten, Joseph; m. Gail Martin, Apr. 28, 1973; 1 child, Jocelyn Diane. BA, Harvard U., 1962; MBA, Stanford U., 1964. V.p. U.S. Brass, Plano, Tex., 1974-80; pres. Elijre Plumbingware, Pitts., 1980-85; exec. v.p. Philips Industries, Dayton, Ohio, 1985-87; pres. lasco products group Philips Industries, Anaheim, Calif., 1988—. Home: 20025 Paseo Louis Yorba Linda CA 92686 Office: Lasco Products Group 3255 E Miraloma Anaheim CA 92806

DEERING, ROBERT LEE, retired oil company executive; b. White Plains, N.Y., Jan. 22, 1931; s. Clarence and Muriel (Lee) D.; m. Dorothy Marie Kiessling, June 9, 1956; children: Gregg Lee, Scott Kirk. BBA, Pace U., N.Y.C., 1952; MS in Acctg., Columbia U., 1955, MBA, 1957. Various fin. positions with Exxon and affiliates Exxon Co., N.Y.C., 1955-66; controller Exxon Enterprises, N.Y.C., 1966-67; audit mgr. Exxon Co. U.S.A., Houston, 1967-69; controller Exxon Nuclear Co., Seattle, 1969-78; sr. fin. advisor Exxon Corp., N.Y.C., 1978-86. Mem. Water Utilities Coordinating Com., Island County, Wash., 1987—, Groundwater Mgmt. Com., Island County, 1987—; chmn. Sierra Club Water Com., Coupeville, Wash., 1987—. Republican. Clubs: College (Seattle), Sierra Country (Coupeville, Wash.). Home: 795 N Ft Ebey Rd Coupeville WA 98239

DEETS, DWAIN AARON, aeronautical research engineer; b. Bell, Calif., Apr. 16, 1939; s. Kenneth Robert and Mildred Evelyn (Bergman) D.; m. Catherine Elizabeth Meister, June 18, 1961; children: Dennis Allen, Danelle Alaine. AB, Occidental Coll., 1961; MS in Physics, San Diego State U., 1964; ME, UCLA, 1978. Rsch. engr. Dryden Flight Rsch. Ctr., NASA, Edwards, Calif., 62-78, 79-85; hdqrs. liaison engr. NASA, Washington, 1978-79; mgr. NASA, Edwards, 1979-85, dep. div. chief Ames-Dryden Flight Rsch. Facility, 1985-88; hdqrs. mgr. flight rsch. NASA, Washington, 1988-89. Contbr. articles to tech. publs. Recipient Exceptional Svc. medal NASA, 1988. Fellow AIAA (assoc., Wright Bros. lectr. aeronautics 1987); mem. Soc. Automotive Engrs. (chmn. aerospace control and guidance systems com. 1988—), Masons. Republican. Mem. Christian Ch. (Disciples of Christ). Office: NASA Ames-Dryden PO Box 273 Edwards CA 93523-5000

DEFAZIO, LYNETTE STEVENS, dancer, choreographer, educator, chiropractor; b. Berkeley, Calif., Sept. 29; d. Honore and Mabel J. (Estavan) Stevens; student U. Calif., Berkeley, 1950-55, San Francisco State Coll., 1950-51; D. Chiropractic, Life-West Chiropractic Coll., San Lorenzo, Calif., 1983, BA in Humanities, New Coll. Calif., 1986; children—Joey H. Panganiban, Joanna Pang. Diplomate Nat. Sci. Bd.; eminence in dance edn., Calif. Community Colls. dance specialist, standard services, childrens ctrs. credentials Calif. Dept. Edn. Contract child dancer Monogram Movie Studio, Hollywood, Calif., 1938-40; dance instr. San Francisco Ballet, 1953-64; performer San Francisco Opera Ring, 1960-67; performer, choreographer Oakland (Calif.) Civic Light Opera, 1963-70; fgn. exchange dance dir. Academie de Danses-Salle Pleyel, Paris, France, 1966; dir. Ballet Arts Studio, Oakland, 1960—; teaching specialist Oakland Unified Sch. Dist.-Childrens Ctrs., 1968-80; instr. Peralta Community Coll. Dist., Oakland, 1971—, chmn. dance dept., 1985—; cons. instr. extension courses UCLA, Dirs. and Suprs. Assn., Pittsburg Unified Sch. Dist., Tulare (Calif.) Sch. Dist., 1971-73; researcher Ednl. Testing Services, HEW, Berkeley, 1974; resident choreographer San Francisco Childrens Opera, 1970—, Oakland Civic Theater; ballet mistress Dimensions Dance Theater, Oakland, 1977-80; cons. Gianchetta Sch. Dance, San Francisco, Robicheau Boston Ballet, TV series Patchwork Family, CBS, N.Y.C.; choreographer Ravel's Valses Nobles et Sentimentales, 1976. Author: The Opera Ballets; A Choreographic Manual, Vols. I-V, 1986. Recipient Foremost Women of 20th Century, 1985, Merit award San Francisco Children's Opera, 1985. Mem. Profl. Dance Tchrs. Assn. Am. Author: Basic Music Outlines for Dance Classes, 1960, rev., 1968; Teaching Techniques and Choreography for Advanced Dancers, 1965; Basic Music Outlines for Dance Classes, 1965; Goals and Objectives in Improving Physical Capabilities, 1970; A Teacher's Guide for Ballet Techniques, 1970; Principle Procedures in Basic Curriculum, 1974; Objectives and Standards of Performance for Physical Development, 1975. Asso. music arranger Le Ballet du Cirque, 1964, Techniques of a Ballet School, 1970, rev., 1974; assoc. composer, lyricist The Ballet of Mother Goose, 1968; choreographer: Walses Nobles Et Sentimentales (Ravel); Cannon in D for Strings and Continuo (Pachelbel), 1979. Home and Office: 4923 Harbord Dr Oakland CA 94618

DEFAZIO, PETER A., congressman; b. Needham, Mass., May 27, 1947; m. Myrnie Daut. BA in Econs. and Polit. Sci., Tufts U., 1969; postgrad., U. Oreg., 1969-71, MS in Pub. Adminstrn./Gerontology, 1977. Aide to U.S. Rep. Jim Weaver, 1977-82; sr. issues specialist, caseworker, dist. field office U.S. rep. Jim Weaver, 1977-78, legis. asst. Washington office, 1978-80, dir. constituent services, 1980-82; mem. commn. representing Springfield Lane County (Oreg.) Commn., 1982-86; mem. 100th, 101st Congresses from 4th Oreg. dist., 1987—; mem. interior and insular affairs com., pub. works and transp. com., com. on small bus. U.S. Ho. Reps., mem. subcoms. on water and power, nat. parks and pub. lands, aviation, water resources, regulation and bus. opportunities, mem. Dem. study group, environ. and energy study conf., mem. arts caucus, populist caucus, arms control and fgn. policy caucus, travel and tourism caucus, human rights caucus, co-chmn. freshman task force on trade. Mem. Lane County Econ. Devel. com., Ingergovtl. Relations com.; bd. dirs. Eugene/Springfield Met. Partnership; Lane County Dem. precinct person, 1982—. Served with USAF. Mem. Assn. of Oreg. Counties (legis. com.), Nat. Assn. of Counties (tax and fin. com.). Office: US Ho of Reps Office House Mems 1729 Longworth Washington DC 20510 *

DE FELICE, SALLY ANN, foundation project executive; b. Ft. Wayne, Ind., July 2, 1947; d. Harold Maynard and Ruth Lucinda (Stratton) Sweet; m. Edward De Felice, Mar. 15, 1975 (dec. Oct. 1977). Pres. Heritage Properties Inc., Seattle, 1977-81, Sally's Bed & Breakfast, Inc., Langley, Wash., 1981—; co-dir. Project Guatemala Holyearth Found., Seattle, 1987—. Editor: (newsletter) Project Guatemala, 1987—; co-exec. producer Project Guatemala films, 1987—. Fellow Seattle Art Mus.; mem. Holyearth Found./Earthstewards Network, Presidential Roundtable, Seattle C. of C., Langley C. of C. (bd. dirs. 1981-83), Queen Anne C. of C. Republican. Avocations: world peace, travel.

DE FOREST, EDGAR LESTER, actor, poet, educator; b. Hull, Mass.; s. Edgar Leonard and Ellen Marian (Huntington) De F.; m. Beulah Mary Ingalls, Nov. 21, 1940; children: Peter, Stephen, David, Richard. Diploma, Leland Powers Sch. of Theatre, Boston, 1937; BS, Boston U., 1940; MA, U. So. Calif., 1941; EdD, Columbia U., 1954. Cert. elem. tchr., Calif. (life); cert. secondary tchr., Calif. (life); cert. sch. adminstr., Calif. Dir. reading Mich. State U. (formerly Mich. State Coll.), East Lansing, 1945-48, asst. dir. summer program, 1954-57; dir. students Suffolk U., Boston, 1948-52; assoc. survey research Columbia U., N.Y.C., 1952-53; acting dean instruction Ventura (Calif.) Coll., 1957-60; prof. Coll. Desert, Palm Desert, Calif., 1962-78, prof. emeritus continuing edn., 1979—; dean of ship U. Seven Seas, Whittier, Calif., 1964-65. Author poems. Mem. Mayor's cultural planning 2000 com., Palm Desert, 1985-86; pres. Friends of the Library Coll. of the Desert, Palm Desert, 1983-85. Named Ideal Citizen of the Age of Enlightenment, World Govt. for the Age of Enlightenment, 1971. Mem. Mich. Reading Assn. (founder, pres. 1954-55). Democrat.

DE FOREST, KELLAM, research company executive; b. Santa Barbara, Calif., Nov. 11, 1926; s. Lockwood III and Elizabeth (Kellam) de F.; m. Margaret MacCormick, July 12, 1952; children: Ann, Carmaig, Elizabeth. BA, Yale U., 1949. Pres. de Forest Research, Los Angeles, 1952—. Served with AUS, 1944-45. Mem. Acad. Motion Pictures Arts and Scis., Acad. TV Arts and Scis. Home: 2659 Todos Santos Ln Santa Barbara CA 93105 Office: De Forest Rsch Inc 1645 N Vine St Ste 701 Los Angeles CA 90028

DEGAVRE, ROBERT THOMPSON, medical electronics company executive; b. Oxford, Eng., Oct. 31, 1940; came to U.S., 1949; s. Robert Thompson and Teresa (Cameron) deG.; m. Angela Jane Hulse, Feb. 28, 1966; children: Teresa, Timothy. BA, Princeton U., 1962, MPA, 1968; Degre Moyen, Pau (France) U., 1966. Fin. analyst treas. dept. Exxon Corp., N.Y.C., 1968-69, ESSO Sekiyu K.K., Tokyo, 1970-71, Exxon Corp., Tokyo, 1970-72; sr. fin. analyst treas. dept. ESSO Chem. Co., N.Y., 1971-72; project fin. mgr. treas. dept. Inco Ltd., N.Y., 1972-77; treas. Inco Ltd., N.Y.C., 1977-82; v.p., treas. Squibb Corp., Princeton, N.J., 1982-86; sr. v.p., chief fin. officer Westmark Internat., Seattle, 1987—; bd. dirs. Schafer Value Trust, N.Y.C., 1986—, Toronto Dominion Trust Co. N.Y., 1981-86; mem. adv. coun. dept. econs., Princeton U. Trustee Wetlands Inst., Stone Harbor, N.J., trustee Hope Heart Inst., Seattle, 1989—; bd. dirs. Schafer Value Trust. Lt. USN, 1962-66. Mem. Phi Beta Kappa. Office: Westmark Internat Inc 701 5th Ave Ste 6800 Seattle WA 98104-7001

DEGERSTEDT, ROSS MAURICE, mechanical engineer; b. Portland, Oreg., June 18, 1958; s. Dean Victor and Patricia Lou (Jorgenson) D.; m. Donna Lee Day, Aug. 3, 1979 (div. Dec. 1984). BSME, U. Portland, 1980. Registered mech. engr., Alaska, Oreg., Wash. Tech. cons. Northwest Natural Gas Co., Portland, 1979-80; mech. and corrosion engr. Coffman Engrs. Inc., Anchorage, 1984—. Youth coordinator Alaska Synod Evang. Luth. Ch. in Am., Anchorage, 1988—. 1st lt. USAF, 1980-84. Decorated with oak leaf cluster; recipient Commendation medal USAF, 1984. Mem. ASME (v.p., treas., sec. 1984-86), ASHRAE, Nat. Assn. Corrosion Engrs. (Alaska chpt. bd. trustees, 1982), Soc. Am. Mil. Engrs., Air Force Assn. Republican. Lutheran. Home: 3510 E 66th Ave Anchorage AK 99507 Office: Coffman Engrs Inc 550 W 7th Ave Ste 700 Anchorage AK 99501

DE GRAAF, LAWRENCE BROOKS, history educator; b. Yonkers, N.Y., Aug. 30, 1932; s. Jacob Conrad and Kathryn (Brooks) de G.; m. Shirley Ferguson, Feb. 21, 1959; 1 child, Laurel Patricia. BA in History, Occidental Coll., 1954; MA in History, UCLA, 1956, PhD in History, 1962. Prof. in History Calif. State U., Fullerton, 1959—; vis. lectr. Howard U., Washington, 1968; coordinator MA program in soc. scis., Calif. State U., Fullerton, 1972-79, dir. oral History program, 1979-85; cons. oral history Calif. State U. Archives, Carson, 1986-88, State Archives Calif., Sacramento, 1985—; co-editor Jour. Orange County Studies, Irvine, 1987—. Contbg. editor Craft of Public History, 1983; contbr. articles to profl. jours. Chmn. Placentia Hist. Com., 1987—. Mem. Nat. Council Pub. History, Calif. Com. Promotion of History, Orgn. Am. Historians, Oral History Assn. Democrat. Methodist. Home: 1139 Naples Ave Placentia CA 92670 Office: Calif State U Fullerton CA 92634

DEGRASSI, LEONARD RENE, art historian, educator; b. East Orange, N.J., Mar. 2, 1928; s. Romulus-William and Anna Sophia (Sannicolo) DeG.; m. Dolores Marie Welgoss, June 24, 1961; children: Maria Christina, Paul. BA, U. So. Calif., 1950, BFA, 1951, MA, 1956; postgrad., Harvard U., 1953, U. Rome, 1959-60, UCLA, 1970-73. Tchr. art Redlands (Calif.) Jr. High Sch., 1951-53, Toll Jr. High Sch., Glendale, Calif., 1953-61, Wilson Jr. High Sch., Glendale, 1961; mem. faculty Glendale Coll., 1962—, prof. art history, 1974—, chmn. dept., 1972, 89. Prin. works include: (paintings) high altar at Ch. St. Mary, Cook, Minn., altar screen at Ch. St. Andrew, El Segundo, Calif., 1965-71, altar screen at Ch. of the Descent of the Holy Spirit, Glendale, 14 Stas. of the Cross at Ch. of St. Benedict, Duluth, Minn; also research, artwork and dramatic work for Spaceship Earth exhbn. at Disney World, Orlando, Fla., 1980. Decorated knight Order of Merit of Republic of Italy, 1972; knight Grand Cross Holy Sepulchre (Papal); knight St. John of Jerusalem, 1974; Cross of Merit, 1984; named First Distng. Faculty award, 1987. Mem. Art Educators Assn., Glendale Art Assn., Egypt Exploration Soc. London, Am. Research Ctr. Egypt, Tau Kappa Alpha, Kappa Pi, Delta Sigma Rho. Office: 1500 N Verdugo Rd Glendale CA 91206

DEGRAW, BETTE FEATHER, educational administrator; b. Phila., Aug. 4, 1946; d. Augustus Scott, Jr. and Margaret Garney (Moorhead) F.; m. Richard G. DeGraw, Aug. 19, 1967 (div. June 1985). BA, Thiel Coll., 1968; MSW, Rutgers U., 1971; postgrad., Ariz. State U. Social case worker N.J. Div. of Mental Retardation, Trenton, 1968-70; planner Ariz. State Legis., Phoenix, 1972-73; spl. asst. to majority leader Ariz. State Senate, Phoenix, 1973-78; project dir. Sch. of Social Work Ariz. State U., Tempe, 1978; asst. dir. for planning and policy devel. Ariz. Dept. Econ. Security, Phoenix, 1979-83, dep. dir., 1983-86; dir. Downtown Ctr. Ariz. State U., Phoenix, 1986—. Chmn. Arts Dist. Task Force, Phoenix, 1987; mem. Cen. Phoenix Com., 1986—, Phoenix Futures Forum, 1988—, subcom. chmn., 1988—; trustee Phoenix Meml. Hosp. Bd., 1987—; bd. dirs. Phoenix Community Alliance, 1987—, Phoenix Civic Plaza, 1988—. Mem. Am. Soc. Pub. Adminstrn. (Ariz. treas. 1976), Am. Pub. Welfare Assn. (bd. dirs., treas. 1989-90). Democrat. Presbyterian. Office: Ariz State U Downtown Ctr 400 N 7th St Ste 101 Phoenix AZ 85006

DEHAAS, DAVID LOUIS, real estate agent; b. Grangeville, Idaho, Dec. 13, 1957; s. Donald Louis and Myrna Bernice (Talbott) D.; m. Wendy W. Walker, June 20, 1981; 1 child, Amanda Laureen. BBA, Boise State U., 1984. Owner Satellite Tech., Boise and Twin Falls, Idaho, 1982-84; comml. real estate agt. Michener Investments, Boise, 1985-87, Quest & Co., Boise, 1987—. Mem. Boise Bd. Realtors, Rotary (v.p., pres.-elect 1987-89, pres. 1989—), Toastmasters, Boise Buckets Club (pres. 1985—).

DEHAVEN, KENNETH LE MOYNE, retired physician; b. The Dalles, Oreg., Mar. 28, 1913; s. Luther John and Dora (Beeks) DeH.; m. Ledith Mary Ewing, Jan. 11, 1937; children: Marya LeMoyne DeHaven Keeth, Lisa Marguerite DeHaven Jordan, Camille Suzanne DeHaven. BS, North Pacific Coll. Oreg., 1935; MD, U. Mich., 1946. Intern USPHS Hosp., St. Louis, 1947; intern Franklin Hosp., San Francisco, 1947-48, resident, 1949; clinician Dept. Pub. Health, City San Francisco, Dept. V.D., 1949-51; practice gen. medicine, Sunnyvale, Calif., 1955-87; mem. staff El Camino Hosp., Mt. View, Calif., San Jose (Calif.) Hosp. Pres. Los Altos Hills Assn. Served to capt., USAF, 1952-55. Fellow Am. Acad. Family Practice; mem. Calif. Med. Assn., Santa Clara Couty Med. Soc., Royal Astron. Soc. Can., Brit. Astron. Assn., Astron. Soc. Pacific, Sunnyvale C. of C. (bd. dirs. 1955-56), Alpha Kappa Kappa. Republican. Club: Book (San Francisco). Lodge: Masons. Home: 9348 E Casitas Del Rio Dr Scottsdale AZ 85255

DEIHL, RICHARD HARRY, savings and loan association executive; b. Whittier, Calif., Sept. 8, 1928; s. Victor Francis and Wilma Aileen (Thomas) D.; m. Billie Dantz Beane, Mar. 24, 1952; children: Catherine Kent, Michael, Victoria, Christine. A.B., Whittier Coll., 1949; postgrad., UCLA, 1949, U. Calif.-Berkeley, 1949-50. With Nat. Cash Register Co., Pomona, Calif., 1955-59; trainee Rio Hondo Savs. & Loan, Calif., 1959-60; loan cons. Home Savs. & Loan Assn. (now Home Savs. Am., A Fed. Savs. & Loan Assn.), Los Angeles, 1960-63; loan agt., supr., v.p. Home Savs. & Loan Assn. (now Home Savs. Am., A Fed. Savs. & Loan Assn.), 1964, loan service supr., 1964, v.p. ops., v.p. loans, 1965, exec. v.p., 1966, pres., 1967-84, chief exec. officer, 1967-84, chmn., 1984—, also dir.; chief exec. officer, dir. H.F. Ahmanson Co., 1984—, chmn., also pres., 1989—; bd. dirs. Fed. Home Loan Bank, Atlantic Richfield Good Samaritan Hosp. Contbr. articles to profl. jours. Served to 1st lt. USAF, 1951-55. Decorated D.F.C., Air medal with three clusters. Republican. Club: Fairbanks Ranch Country (Rancho Santa Fe). Office: H F Ahmanson & Co 3731 Wilshire Blvd Los Angeles CA 90010 also: Home Savs of Am 4900 Rivergrade Rd Irwindale CA 91706

DEINES, HARRY J., agricultural and livestock company executive; b. Loveland, Colo., Nov. 5, 1909; s. John and Mary (Maseka) D.; B.M.E., U. Colo.; grad. Advanced Mgmt. Program, Harvard; m. Eleanor Vrooman, 1932; children: Gretchen Deines Langston, Mark, Katrina, Stephen. Advt. mgr. Gen. Electric Co., 1930-45; v.p. Fuller & Smith & Ross, 1945-49; gen. advt. mgr. Westinghouse Electric Corp., 1949-53; v.p. J. Walter Thompson, N.Y.C., 1953-56, Fuller & Smith & Ross, N.Y.C., 1956-59; exec. v.p., dir. Campbell, Mithun, Inc., Mpls., 1959-71; mng. partner Deines Agr. & Livestock Co., Ft. Collins, Colo., 1971—; pres. Collectors' Books Ltd. Home and Office: 1852 Edna Pl Bainbridge Island WA 98110

DEIOTTE, CHARLES EDWARD, computer software company executive; b. Gary, Ind., Jan. 31, 1946; s. Raymond Louis and Dorothy Jane (Paulson) D.; A.A., Skagit Valley Jr. Coll., 1966; student Wash. State U., 1970; m. Margaret Williams Tukey, Sept. 11, 1971; children—Raymond, Karl, Ronald. Programmer, Wash. State U., Pullman, 1969-70; project dir. AGT Mgmt. Systems, Renton, Wash., sr. tech. cons., sect. mgr. McDonnell-Douglas Automation, Bellevue, Wash., 1972-73; sr. engr. Boeing Computer Services, Seattle, 1973-75, computer based instrn. specialist, Tng. div., 1975-79; mgr. microprocessor design support center Boeing Aerospace Co., Kent, Wash., 1979-80; mgr. concept research Federal Express Corp., Colorado Springs, Colo., 1980-81, mgr. microprocessor support group, 1981-82; pres. Deitron Systems, Inc., Auburn, Wash., 1976-81; pres., chmn. bd. Logical Systems Inc., Colorado Springs, 1981-87; chmn., chief exec. officer Cedsys Inc., 1987—; chmn. bd. Summit Med. Systems, Inc., 1985-86. Neighborhood commr. Chief Seattle council Boy Scouts Am., 1971-72; v.p. REACT alert, Seattle, 1974; advisor Jr. Achievement, Colorado Springs, 1980. Recipient Boeing Aerospace Co. Cert. of Achievement, 1979. Mem. Assn. Computing Machinery, IEEE, AAAS, Data Processing Mgmt. Assn., Am. Mgmt. Assn., Gamma Sigma Epsilon. Home: 2973 Fascination Circle Colorado Springs CO 80917 Office: 2973 Fascination Circle Colorado Springs CO 80917

DEISENROTH, CLINTON WILBUR, electrical engineer; b. Louisville, Aug. 9, 1941; s. Clifton Earl and Nell (Pierce) D.; B.E.E., Ga. Inst. Tech., 1965; m. Lisbeth D. Isaacs, May 10, 1974; 1 dau., Susan Michelle. With Raytheon Co., 1966-75, div. mgr. Addington Labs., Inc., solid state products div., Santa Clara, Calif., 1975-77, program mgr. electromagnetic systems div., Goleta, Calif., 1977-79, dir. surface navy electronic warfare systems, 1979-81; sr. v.p. systems div. Teledyne-MEC, 1981-84; pres. Teledyne CME, 1984—. Mem. IEEE, Am. Mgmt. Assn., Am. Def. Preparedness Assn., Navy League, Assn. Old Crows. Home: 1274 Pitman Ave Palo Alto CA 94301 Office: PO Box 58133 Santa Clara CA 95052

DEIZ, WILLIAM RONALD, video company executive, consultant; b. N.Y.C., Oct. 16, 1943; s. Carl Henry and Mercedes Frances (Lopez) D.; m. Judy Lynn Rooks, June 19, 1983; 1 child, Brendan William. BA, Portland State (Oreg.) U., 1968. Reporter Sta. KNXT-TV (now KCBS-TV), Los Angeles, 1973-75; news anchorman Sta. KCOP-TV, Los Angeles, 1976-78; ptnr. The News Team, Los Angeles, 1978-80; reporter Sta. KOIN-TV, Portland, 1980-81, Sta. KPIX-TV, San Francisco, 1981; reporter, anchor Sta. KCBS-Radio, San Francisco, 1981; commr.'s asst. City of Portland, 1981-84; pres. Corp. Video, Inc., Portland, 1985—; news cons. Boise (Idaho) Cascade Corp., 1987—, U.S. Forest Service, Portland, 1984-86. Writer, producer: (TV documentary) Eruption: St. Helens Explodes, 1980. Fellow Ford Found., Columbia U., 1968. Mem. World Affairs Council, Greater Portland Conv. and Vis. Assn., Portland C. of C. Democrat. Episcopalian. Clubs: Portland City, Willamette Athletic (Portland, Oreg.). Office: Corp Video Inc 4724 SW Macadam Ave Portland OR 97201

DE JAAGER, GERALD, management educator; b. Dumont, N.J., Jan. 13, 1946; s. Frederick John and Doris Clement (Berry) De J.; m. Ruth Linea Almquist, Apr. 23, 1973; 1 child, Laura Mary. BA in Am. Studies, Yale U., 1967. Pres. Gerald de Jaager and Assocs., Los Gatos, Calif., 1968-; pres. Seiler-Doar Books, Palo Alto, Calif., 1981—, Connections Software, Los Gatos, 1987--. Author: The Management Skills Inventory, 1981, The Best Management Resources, 1981, The Project Manager's Tool Kit, 1988. Cons. U.S. House of Reps., Washington, 1978-80, United Nations Trust Territory of the Pacific, Micronesia, 1976-77, Gov. of Jamaica, West Indies, 1975; advisor Harvard Program for Newly Elected Reps., Cambridge, Mass., 1980. Home and Office: 16625 Englewood Ave Los Gatos CA 95032

DEJARNETT, STEVEN BRADLEY, computer systems programmer; b. Dearborn, Mich., Aug. 12, 1966; s. Larry Raymond and Mary Elizabeth (Cotton) DeJ. Grad., Palos Verdes High Sch., Calif., 1984. Programmer Davidson & Assocs., Ranco Palos Verdes, Calif., 1983; engring. clk. Lear Siegler Astronics Inc., Santa Monica, Calif., 1985; engring. aide Lear Siegler Astronics Inc., 1986-87; system mgr. Calif. Poly. State U., San Luis Obispo, Calif., 1987—. Mem. IEEE, ACM. Republican. Presbyterian. Office: Calif Poly State U Dept Computer Sci San Luis Obispo CA 93407

DE JARNETTE, JAMES EDWARD, psychoanalyst, psychotherapist; b. Atlanta, Mar. 22, 1948; s. Charles Nathan and Sarah Holmes (Phillips) deJ. B.A., Shorter Coll., 1970; M.A., W. Ga. Coll., 1971; Ph.D., Sussex Coll., 1973. Exec. dir. Middle Ga. Counseling Center, Macon, 1972-80; exec. dir. Power Ferry Psychotherapy Clinic, 1976-80, deJarnette and Assocs., Beverly Hills, Calif., 1979—; chmn. bd. Leonidas Ltd., Inc.; dir. Alpha-Omega Enterprises, Inc.; chmn. bd. trustees Center for Meditative Living, Inc. Bd. dirs. Ga. Mental Health Assn., 1975, Macon/Bibb County Mental Health Assn., 1975. Fellow Am. Orthopsychiat. Assn., Am. Acad. Behavioral Sci.; mem. Am. Mental Health Couselors Assn., Nat. Psychiat. Assn., Internat. Soc. Adlerian Psychology, Mensa, Tripple Nine Soc. Pi Gamma Mu. Republican. Episcopalian. Contbr. articles to profl. jours. Home: 8260 Marmont Ln Los Angeles CA 90069

DEJONGE, DAVID EARL, financial analyst; b. Mpls., Mar. 29, 1959; s. Earl Harm and Helen Mae (Hartwick) DeJ. BA magna cum laude, Concordia Coll., 1981; postgrad., Ariz. State U., 1986—. Produce night mgr. Haugs Super Value, Minnetonka, Minn., 1976-82; parish builder Community Ch. of Joy, Glendale, Ariz., 1979-81; regional coordinator Am. Luth. Ch., 1984-85; dir. youth and edn. Prince of Peace Luth. Ch., Phoenix, 1982-85; music coordinator Concordia Coll. Outreach Teams, Moorehead, Minn., 1980-82; fin.-computer analyst Pub. Safety Personnel Retirement, Phoenix, 1985—; computer cons. Prince of Peace Luth. Ch., Phoenix, 1984-86. Troop coordinator Boy Scouts Am., Phoenix, 1983-84; pres. Explorer Scouts Am., South Bend, Ind., 1975-76; mgr. Men's Chorus, Moorhead, 1980-81; lead trumpet, student conductor Concordia Coll. Band, Moorhead, 1977-82; vice chief Order of the Arrow, Boy Scouts Am., South Bend, 1984-85. Mem. Omicron Delta Kappa. Republican. Lutheran. Home: 5123 E Pinchot Phoenix AZ 85018 Office: Pub Safety Personnel Retire 1020 E Missouri St Phoenix AZ 85014

DEKAY, DENNIS ALAN, accountant; b. Red Oak, Iowa, Aug. 2, 1952; s. Alan Carl and Audrey Jean (Stautz) DeK.; m. Barbara Ann Jones, Jan. 20, 1979; children: Adam Charles, Laura Ann. BA cum laude, Western Wash. U., 1974. CPA, Hawaii, Wash. Staff acct. Peat Marwick Mitchell, Honolulu, 1974-75; acct., mgr. Fox Corp. div. Baumgartner, Kuelkelhan & Crutcher, Seattle, 1975-83; ptnr. Smith, DeKay & Assocs., CPA's, Seattle, 1983-85, pres., 1986--. Bd. dirs. Cardiac Rehab. Inst., Seattle, 1986--. Bus. dept. scholar Western Wash. U., 1974; recipient Best Citizen award Lions (Lacey chpt.). Mem. AICPA, Nat. Soc. Pub. Accts., Wash. Soc. CPA's (mem. fin. instns. com. 1979-80). Office: Smith DeKay & Assocs CPAs 200 W Mercer St Ste 406 Seattle WA 98119-3958

DE KRUIF, JACK H., manufacturing executive; b. Grand Rapids, Mich., Mar. 5, 1921; s. Angus Alton and Lois Grace (Bailey) deK.; m. Dolores Sue Rossi; 1 child: Lisa-Nicole. AB, Mich. State U., 1948; LLB, Ind. U., 1951. Atty. Bendix Corp., South Bend, Ind., 1951-53; group atty. Bendix Corp., Teterboro, Mich., 1953-55; gen. counsel NWL, Kalamazoo, Mich., 1955-58; dir. mktg. semi-conductor div. Hughes Aircraft, Newport Beach, Calif., 1958-60; pres., chief exec. officer Aseco, Inc., Novi, Mich., 1960-68, W-K Mfg. Co., Mt. Clemens, Mich., 1968-75; sole practice cons. Newport Beach, Calif., 1975-84; chmn., chief exec. officer Wayne Corp., Richmond, Ind., 1984; chmn., chief exec. officer Richmond Transp., Newport Beach, Calif., 1984—, also bd. dirs.; bd. dirs. Wayne Corp., Richmond, Ind., Maxon Industries, City of Industry, chmn., 1982—. Pres. Big Bros./Big Sisters of Orange County, Tustin, Calif., 1987; dir., trustee Newport Harbor Art Mus., 1978-83. With USAC, 1942-45, ETO. Mem. Ind. Bar Assn., Detroit Athletic Club, Ctr. Club, Balboa Bay Club. Episcopalian. Office: Richmond Transp Corp 4931 Birch St Newport Beach CA 92660

DELANEY, MARION PATRICIA, advertising agency executive; b. Hartford, Conn., May 20, 1952; d. William Pride Delaney and Marian Patricia (Utley) Murphy. BA, Union Coll., Schenectady, N.Y., 1973. Adminstrv. asst. N.Y. State Assembly, Albany, 1973-74; account exec. Foote, Cone & Belding, N.Y.C., 1974-78; sr. account exec. Dailey & Assocs., Los Angeles, 1978-81; pub. relations cons. NOW, Washington, 1981-83; account supr. BBDO/West, Los Angeles, 1983-85; v.p. Grey Advt., Los Angeles, 1985-87, San Francisco, 1987—. Del. Dem. Nat. Conv., San Francisco, 1984; v.p. NOW, Los Angeles, 1980-83, pres. 1984, advisor 1985—. Mem. Bus. and Profl. Women Assn., Los Angeles Advt. Club. Congregationalist. Home: 3682 Fillmore St San Francisco CA 94123 Office: Grey Advt 2 Embarcadero Ctr San Francisco CA 94111

DELANEY, MATTHEW SYLVESTER, educator, academic administrator; b. Ireland, Nov. 26, 1927; s. Joseph C. and Elizabeth M. (Berrigan) D.; came to U.S., 1947, naturalized, 1952; student St. John's Coll., 1947-51; BA, Immaculate Heart Coll., L.A., 1958; MS, Notre Dame U., 1960; PhD, Ohio State U., 1971. Ordained priest Roman Cath. Ch., 1951; assoc. pastor L.A. Cath. Diocese, 1951-55; instr. math., physics Pius X High Sch., Downey, Calif., 1955-58, vice prin., 1960-62; instr. math. Immaculate Heart Coll., L.A., 1962-65, asst. prof., 1965-72, assoc. prof., 1972-76, prof., 1976—; asst. acad. dean, 1973-78; dean acad. devel. Mt. St. Mary's Coll., L.A., 1978-82, acad. dean, 1982—. NSF grantee, 1959-60, 61. Mem. Am. Math. Soc., Math. Assn. Am., Am. Conf. Acad. Deans, N.Y. Acad. Scis.. Democrat. Contbr. articles to math. publs. Home: 922 S Detroit St Los Angeles CA 90036 Office: Mt St Mary's Coll 12001 Chalon Rd Los Angeles CA 90049

DE LANGE, HANS, travel agency executive. Pres. Ask Mr. Foster, Western Area, Van Nuys, Calif. Office: Ask Mr Foster Travel Svc 7833 Haskell Ave Van Nuys CA 91406 *

DELAQUIS, NOEL, bishop; b. Notre-Dame de Lourdes, Man., Can., Dec. 25, 1934; s. Louis and Therese (Hebert) D. B.A., U. Man., 1954; B.Th., U. Laval, 1958; J.C.L., Latran, Rome, 1962. Ordained priest Roman Catholic Ch., 1958; asst. priest Christ the King Parish, St. Vital, Man., 1958-60; prof. canon law St. Boniface Sem., Man., 1962-68; chancellor Archdiocese of St. Boniface, Man., 1965-73; bishop of Gravelbourg, Sask., Can., 1974—. Address: CP 690, Gravelbourg, SK Canada S0H 1X0 *

DE LASSEN, JAN FOLMER, university administrator; b. Copenhagen, Jan. 25, 1934; came to U.S., 1980; s. Ivar Christian and Edith (Christiansen) De L.; m. Magali Florelia Cumare, Sept. 23, 1972; children—Magalita, Jan Folmer Jr., Michelle. B.S. in Math. (Gulf Oil Co. scholar), Tex. A&M U., 1959. Computer programmer Mobil Oil Co., Caracas, Venezuela, 1959-60; systems analysis, procedure supr. Gen. Electric of Venezuela, 1961-72; computer ops. mgr. Savoy Group, 1973-75; computer ops. mgr. ACO Group, Caracas, 1976-79; gen. mgr. Boulton Group, Caracas, 1980; dir. computer application services Brigham Young U., Provo, Utah, 1981-88, faculty Marriott Sch. Mgmt., 1989—; owner JDL and Assocs.; cons. in field. Mem. Assn. System Mgmt. (past pres. Venezuela), Am. Assn. Artificial Intelligence, Office Systems Research Assn., Utah Council on Computers for Edn., Tex. Aggie Former Students Assn. Mormon. Office: Brigham Young U 585 TNRB Provo UT 84602

DELEAR, RICHARD H., personnel consultant; b. Wichita, Kans., Dec. 19, 1927; s. Ernest C. Delear and Clara M. Boberg; m. Helen J. Clark, Jan. 8, 1950; children: Cherie, Cindy, Kimberly, Kirkland, Dianne, Michelle. Student, Hiedleburg U., Germany, 1946-47, San Jose St. U., 1959-60. Cert. hypnotherapist. Enlisted U.S. Army, 1944, advanced through grades to m/sgt., 1952, ret., 1959; entrepreneur Calif., 1960-74; human resources cons. Success Thru Humaneering, Scotts Valley, Calif., 1974—. Author: Leadership Strategies, 1988. Pres. Exchange club, Scotts Valley, 1978-79. Decorated two Bronze Stars, two Purple Hearts, Silver Star. Republican. Roman Catholic. Home: 202 Burlwood Dr Scotts VAlley CA 95066 Office: Success Thru Humaneering 202 Burlwood Dr Scotts Valley CA 95066

DELEIN, JUDITH ANNE, service contracting company executive; b. Auburn, N.Y., Feb. 16, 1944; d. Harry Ira and M. Virginia (James) Kintz; m. Fredric Arden Delein, Oct. 1, 1966; children: Christian, Jefferson, Melissa. Cert., Katherine Gibbs Bus. Coll., Boston, 1963; lic., Jones Real Estate Sch., Colorado Springs, Colo., 1974. Prodn. asst. Sports Network, Inc., N.Y.C., 1963-64; sec. NBC Broadcasting, N.Y.C., 1964-65, DJMC Advt., Los Angeles, 1967-68, Paul Mitchell Advt., Orange, Calif., 1968-69; prodn. asst. NET Broadcasting Network, N.Y.C., 1965-66; bookkeeper Colo. Bldg. Maintenance, Colorado Springs, 1973-76; real estate saleswoman Century 21

- The Homestead, Colorado Springs, 1976-77; v.p. Colo. Chiller Maintenacne Inc., Littleton, Colo, 1977--. Home: 995 E Briarwood Circle S Littleton CO 80122

DELGADO, GREGORY LARRABEE, investor; b. Hahn Air Base, Fed. Republic Germany, Apr. 8, 1958; came to U.S., 1959; s. Al Lopez Delgado and Ethel Larrabee; m. Lori Ann Cameron, May 28, 1988. B in Psychology, Stanford U., 1980; MBA in Fin., UCLA, 1985. Lic. securities dealer, Calif. Profl. soccer player Houston Summit, San Jose (Calif.) Earthquakes, 1980-81; analyst The Boston Cons. Group, Menlo Park, Calif., 1981-83; assoc. Salomon Bros. Inc., N.Y.C., 1984-87; v.p. Security Pacific Mergers and Acquisitions, L.A., 1987, Pratt Ptnrs., Newport Beach, Calif., 1988—. Mem. Palo Alto (Calif.) Jr. C. of C. (v.p. 1981-82). Republican. Presbyterian. Office: Pratt Ptnrs Inc 4400 MacArthur Blvd Ste 410 Newport Beach CA 92660

DELGADO, ROBERT DANIEL, protective services official; b. San Jose, Calif., July 11, 1938; s. Alex and Betty (Torres) D.; m. Lynn Williams, Nov. 18, 1982;l children: James, Daniel, Robert. Student, San Jose Community Coll., 1972, West Valley Coll., 1976; BPA, U. San Francisco, 1986. Land surveyor Santa Clara County Pub. Works, San Jose, Calif., 1958-60; dep. sheriff Santa Clara County Sheriff's Office, San Jose, 1960-64; firefighter San Jose Fire Dept., 1964-72, capt., 1972-76, batallion chief, 1976-79, dep. fire chief, 1979--; mem. Human Relations Commn., San Jose, 1985--; bd. dirs. adv. com. State Fire Marshal, Sacramento. arbitrator, Better Bus. Bur., 1988--. Recipient Life Saving award ARC, 1968. Mem. Am. Soc. Pub. Adminstrs. (issues com. 1987--), Nat. Fire Info. Council, Calif. Assn. Human Rights (sec. 1988--), San Jose Athletic Club, Los Gatos Racket Club. Office: San Jose Fire Dept 4 N 2d St 11th Fl San Jose CA 95113-1305

DELGADO, SANDRA GAYLE, finance company executive; b. Bakersfield, Calif., May 18, 1952; d. Walter Douglas Vogel and Bobbe Rhea (Davenport) Haggard; divorced; children: Melanie Renée, Stephen Charles II. AA, Coll. of the Sequoias, 1972. Ops. mgr. Santa Clarita Nat. Bank, Los Angeles, 1974-80; EDP mgr. Sequoia Community Bank, Sanger, Calif., 1980-87; mgr. membership processing Ednl. Employees Credit Union, Fresno, Calif., 1987-89; v.p. Visalia (Calif.) YMCA, 1989—. Active Sanger Perseptive Orgn. Women. Mem. Bus. and Profl. Women., Exec. Females Calif., Visalia C. of C., Women of the Y. Republican. Club: Womens Trade (Fresno). Home: 1740 N Cedar Ct Visalia CA 93291 Office: Visalia YMCA 211 W Tulare Ave Visalia CA 93277

DELL, CHRISTINE MARIE, real estate associate; b. San Diego, June 3, 1963; d. Robert Burns and Rosemarie Brigett (Mohr) Jackson; m. Samuel Bradford Dell, Oct. 30, 1983. AA, Grossmont Coll., 1983; BA, Columbia (Mo.) U., 1988. Office ops. mgr. Dell Co. Real Estate, San Diego, 1988—. With USN, 1983-88. Mem. Nature Conservancy, Wilson Ctr. Assocs., Smithsonian Assocs. Republican. Lutheran. Office: Dell Co Real Estate 6512 El Cajon Blvd San Diego CA 92115

DELL, DAVID DONALD, electrical engineer; b. Corry, Pa., Jan. 1, 1953; s. Donald David and Lucy Kathleen (Komenda) D.; m. Sheila Kay Johnson, Aug. 28, 1976 (div. 1988). BEE Tech., Ohio Inst. Tech., 1977; MSEE, U. N.Mex., 1984. Mem. tech. staff Sandia Nat. Labs., Albuquerque, 1978—. Patentee in field. Cartographer, Cave Rsch. Found., Guadalupe, 1987—. With U.S. Army, 1971-74. Mem. Am. Def. Preparedness Assn., Nature Conservancy, N.Mex. Mus. Natural History.

DELLAS, ROBERT DENNIS, investment banker; b. Detroit, July 4, 1944; s. Eugene D. and Maxine (Rudell) D.; m. Shila L. Clement, Mar. 27, 1976; children—Emily Allison, Lindsay Michelle. B.A. in Econs., U. Mich., Ann Arbor, 1966; M.B.A., Harvard U., Cambridge, 1970. Analyst Burroughs Corp., Detroit, 1966-67, Pasadena, Calif., 1967-68; mgr. U.S. Leasing, San Francisco, 1970-76; pres., dir. Energetics Mktg. & Mgmt. Assn., San Francisco, 1978-80; sr. v.p. E.F. Hutton & Co., San Francisco, 1981-85; prin. founder Capital Exchange Internat., San Francisco, 1976—; gen. ptnr. Kanland Assocs., Tex., 1982, Claremont Assocs., Calif., 1983, Lakeland Assocs., Ga., 1983, Americal Assocs., Calif., 1983, Chatsworth Assocs., Calif., 1983, Walnut Grove Assocs., Calif., 1983, Somerset Assocs., N.J., 1983, One San Diego Assocs., Calif., 1984. Bd. dirs. Found. San Francisco's Archtl. Heritage. Mem. U.S. Trotting Assn., Calif. Harness Horse Breeders Assn. (Breeders award for Filly of Yr. 1986, Aged Pacing Mare, 1987, 88), Calif. Golf Club San Francisco. Home: 1911 Sacramento St San Francisco CA 94109 Office: care Shearson Lehman Hutton Inc 580 California St San Francisco CA 94104

DELLUMS, RONALD VERNIE, congressman; b. Oakland, Calif., Nov. 24, 1935; m. Leola Roscoe Higgs; 3 children. A.A., Oakland City Coll., 1958; B.A., San Francisco State Coll., 1960; M.S.W., U. Calif., 1962. Psychiat. social worker Calif. Dept. Mental Hygiene, 1962-64; program dir. Bayview Community Ctr., San Francisco, 1964-65; from assoc. dir. to dir. Hunters Point Youth Opportunity Ctr., 1965-66; planning cons. Bay Area Social Planning Coun., 1966-67; dir. concentrated employment program San Francisco Econ. Opportunity Coun., 1967-68; sr. cons. Social Dynamics, Inc., 1968-70; mem. 92d-101st Congresses from 8th Calif. Dist.; chmn. house com. on D.C. 1979—, chmn. house armed svcs. subcom. on rsch. and devel., 1989—; lectr. San Francisco State Coll., U. Calif., Berkeley; mem. U.S. del. North Atlantic Assembly. Author: Defense Sense: The Search For A Rational Military Policy, 1983. Mem. Berkeley City Coun., 1967-71. With USMCR, 1954-56. Democrat. Office: US Ho of Reps 2136 Rayburn House Office Bldg Washington DC 20515

DELOACH, ROBERT EDGAR, corporate executive; b. Daytona Beach, Fla., Jan. 6, 1939; s. Ollie Newman and Sally Gertrude (Schrowder) DeL. Student U. Alaska-Anchorage, 1967-69, Alaska Meth. U., 1970, Pacific Luth. U., 1972. Lic. elec. engr. and adminstr., Alaska, 1979; lic. pvt. pilot; lic. real estate broker. Former chmn. bd. Alaska Stagecraft, Inc., Anchorage; pres. BG Systems Co., BG Tax & Acctg., Inc., The Electric Doctor, Inc., Apollo, Inc.; former pres. Coastal Electronics, Inc.; former owner-mgr. Bargain Towne, Anchorage. Active Anchorage Community Theatre, Anchorage Theater Guild. Mem. Assn. Ind. Accts., Internat. Assn. Theatrical Stage Employees and Moving Picture Machine Operators U.S. (pres. local 770), Ind. Elec. Contractors Assn., Internat. Assn. Elec. Insps. Home: 1207 W 47th Ave Anchorage AK 99503 Office: 7910 King St Anchorage AK 99502

DE LONG, KATHARINE ANNA PRICIE, secondary teacher; b. Germantown, Pa., Aug. 31, 1927; d. Melvin Clinton and Katherine Frances (Brunner) Barr; m. Alfred Alvin De Long, June 21, 1947; children: Renee, Claudia, Jane. AA, Mesa Jr. Coll., 1962; BA, Western State Coll., 1964; MA, Colo. State U., 1972. Grader, tutor Mesa Coll., Grand Junction, 1961-62; dorm advisor Western State Coll., Gunnison, Colo., 1962-64; tchr. Mesa County Valley Sch. Dist. #51, Grand Junction, 1964-84; substitute tchr. Mesa Coll., Grand Junction, 1986-87. Mem. Mesa County Hist. Soc.; Com. woman Dem. Precinct, Grand Junction; trustee Western Colo. Arts Ctr., Grand Junction, 1987-88; camp dir. Chipeta Girl Scouts U.S., Grand Junction, 1959-64; mem. bd. dir. Chipeta Girl Scout Coun., 1959-66. Mem. AAUW (bd. dirs. 1975-88), Mesa County Valley Edn. assn. (rep. com. 1978-84); Colo. Ret. Sch. Employees Assn., Am. Assn. Ret. Persons (state legis. com. Colo. chpt.). Home: 174 Little Park Rd Grand Junction CO 81503

DELORIA, VINE VICTOR, JR., political science educator, author; b. Martin, S.D., Mar. 26, 1933; s. Vine Victor and Barbara (Eastburn) D.; m. Barbara Jeanne Nystrom, June 1958; children: Philip, Daniel, Jeanne Ann. B.S., Iowa State U., 1958; M.Th., Lutheran Sch. Theology, 1963; J.D., U. Colo., 1970; D.H. Litt., Augustana Coll., 1971. Staff asst. United Scholarship Service, Denver, 1963-64; exec. dir. Nat. Congress Am. Indians, 1964-67; lectr. West Wash. State Coll., 1970-72; chmn. Inst. for Devel. Indian Law, Washington, 1971-76; lectr. Pacific Sch. Religion, Berkeley, Calif., Summer 1975, New Sch. Religion, Pontiac, Mich., Summer 1976, Colo. Coll., Colorado Springs, 1977, 78; vis. prof. U. Ariz., Tucson, spring 1978, prof. polit. sci., 1978—. Author: Custer Died for Your Sins, 1969, We Talk, You Listen, 1970, Of Utmost Good Faith, 1972, God Is Red, 1973, Behind the Trail of Broken Treaties, 1974, The Indian Affair, 1974, Indians of the Pacific Northwest, 1977, The Metaphysics of Modern Existence, 1979, Red Man in New World Drama, 1972, American Indians, American Justice, 1983, The Nations Within, 1984, A Sender of Words, 1984, The Aggression of Civilization, 1984, American Indian Policy in the Twentieth Century, 1985. Vice chmn. Am. Indian Resource Assocs., Oglala, S.D., 1973-75; Mem. Bd. Inquiry into Hunger and Malnutrition, 1967-68; mem. exec. council Episcopal Ch., 1969-70. Served with USMCR, 1954-56. Recipient Indian Achievement award Indian Council Fire, 1972. Mem. Am. Judicature Soc. Office: U Ariz Dept Polit Sci Tucson AZ 85721 also: care Dell Pubs One Dag Hammerskjold Pla New York NY 10017

DEL PAPA, FRANKIE SUE, state official; b. 1949. BA, U. Nev.; JD, George Washington U. Bar: Nev. 1974. Sec. of state Nev., 1987—. Democrat. Office: Office of Sec State Capitol Complex Carson City NV 89710 *

DELROSSO, DIANE, infosystems specialist, consultant; b. Teaneck, N.J., July 31, 1949; d. Angelo and Jennie (DeCarlo) DelR. AA, Lane Community Coll., 1982; BS, SUNY, 1985; MA, Antioch U., 1988. Bus. owner Eugene, Oreg., 1980-83; mem. faculty U. Oreg., Eugene, 1983-85; microcomputer dir. Loyola Marymount U., Westchester, Calif., 1987-88; program dir. Pacific Crest Outward Bound, Santa Monica, Calif., 1988—; cons. U. Oreg., Eugene, 1985. Mem. Am. Soc. Tng. and Devel., Orgn. Devel. Network. Office: Outward Bound 733 10th St Ste A Santa Monica CA 90402

DEL SANTO, LAWRENCE A., retail merchandising company executive; b. 1934; married. B.S., U. San Francisco, 1955. With Household Merchandising Inc., Des Plaines, Ill., from 1957, with advt. dept. subs. Vons Grocery Co., 1957-58, asst. advt. mgr., 1958-61, advt. mgr., 1961-68, mgr. sales and mdse., 1968-71, sr. v.p., 1971-73, pres., chief exec. officer, 1973-75, corp. sr. v.p., 1975-79, exec. v.p., from 1979, also bd. dirs.; exec. v.p. Lucky Stores Inc., Dublin, Calif., to 1986, pres., 1986—, also bd. dirs. Served with U.S. Army, 1955-57. Office: Lucky Stores Inc 6300 Clark Ave Dublin CA 94568 *

DEL SOLAR, DANIEL, broadcasting executive; b. N.Y.C., June 13, 1940; s. Daniel del Solar and Jane Louise Garcia. BA cum laude, Harvard U., 1963. Regional health care planner Health Care Research Inc., San Jose, Calif., 1974-75; community resources coordinator Open Studio Sta. KQED-TV, San Francisco, 1975-76; dir. tng. and devel. Corp. for Pub. Broadcasting, Washington, 1976-80; freelance writer NAACP, N.Y.C., 1980-82; instr. Hunter Coll., N.Y.C., 1982-84; fgn. corr. in Cen. Am. and Mexico 1984-86; gen. mgr. Sta. KALW-FM, San Francisco, 1986—. Producer: (radio feature) Introspection Towards the Future, (radio series) Readings from the Congressional Record, 1975; originating producer for radio: Music from the Pacific Basin Nations, 1987; writer, co-producer for TV: I Was Born a Chilean, 1980. Recipient Radio Meritorious Achievement award Media Alliance San Francisco, 1987. Mem. Union for Democratic Communications, Nat. Fedn. for Community Broadcasters. Office: Sta KALW-FM 2905 21st St San Francisco CA 94110

DELUCCHI, GEORGE PAUL, accountant; b. Richmond, Calif., Apr. 20, 1938; s. George Carl and Rose Caroline (Golino) D. BA, San Jose State U., 1959. Ptnr. Delucchi, Swanson & Co., Santa Clara, Calif., 1968-74, Delucchi, Swanson & Sandival, Santa Clara, 1974-76, Delucchi, Sandoval & Co., Santa Clara, 1976-77, Wolf & Co., San Jose, Calif., 1977-78; v.p. Lautze & Lautze, San Jose, 1978-82, also bd. dirs.; sr. ptnr. G.P. Delucchi & Assocs. (name changed to Delucchi, Robinson, Streit & Co., Santa Clara, 1982—. Treas. Crippled Children Soc., San Jose, 1967-71, San Jose Catholic Social Service, 1986—, F. Schmidt Found. for Youth; bd. dirs. Serra Med. Found., Mission City Community Fund; pres. Santa Clara Police Activity League, 1977-78; bd. fellows Santa Clara U., 1975—. Served to lt. U.S. Army, 1959-62. Mem. Am. Inst. CPA's, Calif. Soc. CPA's. Republican. Roman Catholic. Club: Sainte Claire (San Jose), Civic. Lodges: Elks (Santa Clara exalted ruler 1969-70). Rotary (bd. dirs. Santa Clara chpt. 1986—). Home: 774 Circle Dr Santa Clara CA 95050 Office: 2075 De La Cruz Blvd #200 Santa Clara CA 95050

DELUCHI, STEPHEN F., oral surgeon; b. Alameda, Calif., May 11, 1952; s. Frank S. and Edith M. (Liechti) DeL. BS, U. Calif., 1974, DDS, 1978. Pvt. practice, San Francisco. Fellow Am. Assn. Oral and Maxillofacial Surgery. University Club,. Republican. Roman Catholic. Office: 450 Sutter St #1525 San Francisco CA 94108

DEL VALLE, JUAN, paper company executive; b. Colon, Republic of Panama, Mar. 4, 1933; s. William A. and Vina (Saunders) del V.; m. Wendy Hobart, Sept. 4, 1954; children: Cristina Cross, Tracy Saunders. BS, Yale U., 1953; MBA, Harvard U., 1958. Engr. Weyerhauser Co., Longview, Wash., 1958-62; various positions Boise Cascade Corp., 1962-81; pres. Port Townsend Paper Corp., Bainbridge Island, Wash., 1983—. Served to lt. (j.g.) USN, 1953-56. Home: 8580 Grand Ave NE Bainbridge Island WA 98110 Office: Port Townsend Paper Corp Box 11500 Bainbridge Island WA 98110

DELVALLE, RAYMOND STEPHEN, dentist; b. El Paso, Tex., Oct. 28, 1954; s. Salvador and Irene (Davalos) D,; m. Marian Lucero, June 9, 1979. B of Univ. Studies, U. N.Mex., 1979; DDS, U. Mo., Kansas City, 1984. Staff dentist N.Mex. Corrections Dept., Grants, 1986—; gen. practice dentistry Albuquerque, 1985—. Vol. dentist Santa Fe Maternal and Child Health, 1985—, Procter and Gamble Cinco de Mayo Festival, Albuquerque, 1985. Mem. ADA, N.Mex. Dental Assn., Albuquerque Dist. Dental Soc., N.Mex. Corrections Dental Study Club (founder, pres. 1988—). Office: DelValle & DelValle DDS 9809 Candelaria NE #3-A Albuquerque NM 87112

DEMAAR, NATALIE, federal agency administrator; b. Balt., July 8, 1950; d. Paul and Vera Rebecca (Abrams) Rosenbaum; m. Verrell Leon Dethloff Jr., June 2, 1974 (div. 1987); children: Daniel, Joseph; m. Michael Henry deMaar, June 4, 1988; stepchildren: Alexander, Peter, Andrew. BA, Simmons Coll., 1972; JD with honors, U. Md., Balt., 1976. Bar: Md. 1976. With HHS, Seattle, 1976—, regional adminstr. family support adminstrn. div., 1987—; speaker in field. Contbr. articles to profl. jours. Mem. Wash. Commn. for Humanities, Alliance for Children, Youth & Families, Nat. Child Support Advocacy Coalition. Mem. Md. Bar Assn., Northwest Women's Bar Assn., Seattle-King County Bar Assn., Am. Assn. Pub. Welfare Attys., NAFE, Am. Pub. Welfare Assn., Campfire, City Club. Office: Family Support Adminstrn 2201 6th Ave M/S RX-70 Seattle WA 98121

DEMARAY, LEONARD ALLEN, military officer; b. Chgo., Aug. 23, 1946; s. Lynne Earl and Lois Loraine (Richard) D.; m. Donna Sue Foddrill, Feb. 3, 1983 (div. Feb. 1984). AAS in Police Sci., Pikes Peak Community Coll., Colorado Springs, 1981; AS in Bus. Adminstrn., Regis Coll., 1982, BS in Tech. Mgmt., 1983; BS in Aviation Mgmt., So. Ill. U., 1983. Enlisted U.S. Army, 1963—, advanced through ranks to 1st sgt., 1984; maintenance supr. 4th Aviation Battalion U.S. Army, Ft. Carson, Colo., 1979-80, ops. sergeant, 1980-82, platoon sgt. 179th Aviation Co., 1982; first sgt. 4th Aviation Battalion U.S. Army, Ft. Carson, 1982-83; personnel sgt. 19th Aviation Battalion U.S. Army, Republic of Korea, 1983, aviation logistics sgt. 17th Aviation Group, 1983-88; 1st sgt 4th squadron 3d Armored Cavalry Rgt. Ft. Bliss, Tex., 1988—. Decorated Silver Star with oak leaf cluster, D.F.C. with three oak leaf clusters, Bronze Star with oak leaf cluster, Air medal with 88 oak leaf clusters, Purple Heart with 3 oak leaf clusters, Vietnamese Cross of Gallentry with silver star, others. Mem. VFW, Nat. Geog. Soc., Nat. Rifle Assn., Fur Harvesters Tenn., Alaska Trappers Assn. Home: 540 Sharondale Dr El Paso TX 79912

DEMARAY, RONALD BENJAMIN, school system administrator; b. Billings, Mont., June 22, 1959; s. Richard Dennison and Lora Lyn (Livingston) D.; m. Carol Ann Stutterheim, Nov. 7, 1981; children: Jacob Ryan, Joshua Eric. AA, Ea. Mont. Coll., 1978, BBA, 1981; M Ednl. Adminstrn., Mont. State U., 1983. Bus. officer Dull Knife Meml. Coll., Lame Deer, Mont., 1983-86; fin. mgr. Ramah Navajo Sch. Bd., Inc., Pine Hill, N.Mex., 1986-87; dir. adminstrv. svcs. Ramah Navajo Sch. Bd., Inc., 1987—; mem. work group, Ind. Health Svc./Bur. Indian Affairs, 1988—. Native Am. grad. fellow, Mont. State U., 1982-83. Fundamentalist Evangelical Christian. Home: PO Box 489 Pine Hill NM 87357 Office: Ramah Navajo Sch Bd Inc PO Drawer C Pine Hill NM 87357

DEMARCHI, ERNEST NICHOLAS, aerospace engineering administrator; b. Lafferty, Ohio, May 31, 1939; s. Ernest Costante and Lena Marie (Cireddu) D.; B.M.E., Ohio State U., 1962; M.S. in Engring., UCLA, 1969; m. Carolyn Marie Tracz, Sept. 17, 1960; children—Daniel Ernest, John David, Deborah Marie. Registered profl. cert. mgr. With Space div. Rockwell Internat., Downey, Calif., 1962—, mem. Apollo, Skylab and Apollo-Soyuz missions design team in electronic and elec. systems, mem. mission support team for all Apollo and Skylab manned missions, 1962-74, mem. Space Shuttle design team charge elec. systems equipment, 1974-77, in charge Orbiter Data Processing System, 1977-81, in charge Orbiter Ku Band Communication and Radar System, 1981-85, in charge orbitor elec. power distbr., displays, controls, data processing, 1984-87, in charge space based interceptor flt. exper., 1987-88, kinetic energy systems, 1988—. Active, YMCA Indian Guide program, 1969-74, bd. dirs., 1971-74; vol. instr. community program of tech. tng. for high-sch. students, 1970-78; youth athletics coach, 1975-76; pres. Little League, 1976-78; bd. dirs. high sch. athletic boosters club, 1980-84. Recipient Apollo Achievement award NASA, 1969, Apollo 13 Sustained Excellent Performance award, 1970, Astronaut Personal Achievement Snoopy award, 1971; Exceptional Service award Rockwell Internat., 1972, Outstanding Contbn. award, 1976; NASA ALT award, 1979; Shuttle Astronaut Snoopy award, 1982; Pub. Service Group Achievement award NASA, 1982; Rockwell Pres.'s award, 1983, 87; registered profl. engr., Ohio. Mem. ASME, Varsity O Alumni Assn. Home: 25311 Maximus St Mission Viejo CA 92691 Office: 12214 Lakewood Blvd Downey CA 90241

DEMARCO, MICHAEL JOSEPH, petroleum educator; b. Huntington, W.Va., Jan. 1, 1939; s. Vincent L. and Ruby (Clay) DeM.; m. Beverly A. Rossman, Sept. 28, 1957 (div. May 1979); children: Cynthia, Sue Ann, Gina, Michael Jr., Gregory; m. Margaret E. Guy, Mar. 3, 1985. BS in Petroleum Engring., Marietta Coll., 1961. Prodn. engr. Conoco, various locations, Tex., La., 1961-67; reservoir engr. Tenneco, Midland, Denver, Tex., Colo, 1967-73, BTA & C&K Petroleum Co., Midland, Tex., 1973-74; prodn./reservoir engr. Stallworth O&G Co., Midland, 1974-76; dist. engr. Sabine Prodn. Co., Midland, 1977-79; cons., engr. C & D & Assocs., Midland, San Angelo, Tex., 1979-87; instr., coord. N.Mex. Jr. Coll., Hobbs, N.Mex., 1987—. Mem. Am. Petroleum Inst., Soc. Petroleum Engrs. (arrangements chmn. Hobbs Sect. 1987-88), Pi Epsilon Tau, Kappa Mu Epsilon. Democrat. Roman Catholic. Home: 1636 Marquis Hobbs NM 88240 Office: New Mexico Jr College 5317 Lovington Hwy Hobbs NM 88240

DEMARCO, RALPH JOHN, real estate developer; b. N.Y.C., Mar. 22, 1924; s. Frank and Mary (Castriota) DeM.; BA, Claremont Men's Coll., 1956; m. Arlene Gilbert, July 1, 1945; children: Sheryl DeMarco Grahn, Stephen, Laura DeMarco Wilson. Asso. John B. Kilroy Co., Riverside, Calif., 1960-64, also mgr. ops. Riverside, San Bernardino counties, 1960-64; v.p. Marcus W. Meairs Co., 1964-67; pres. Diversified Properties, Inc., Riverside, 1967-72; v.p. Downey Savs. & Loan Assn. (Calif.), 1972-75; exec. v.p. DSL Svc. Co., 1972-75; pres. Interstate Shopping Ctrs., Inc., Santa Ana, Calif., 1975-87; exec. dir. comml. devel. Lewis Homes Mgmt. Corp., Upland, Calif., 1987—. Mem. City of Riverside Planning Commn., 1955-59, Airport Commn., 1960-70; mem. Urban Land Inst. 1st lt. USAF, 1942-45. Mem. Internat. Coun. Shopping Ctrs. Home: 245 E Foothill Blvd #184 Upland CA 91786 Office: 1156 N Mountain Ave Upland CA 91786

DEMARIA, RUSEL, infosystems specialist, writer; b. San Francisco, Sept. 14, 1948; s. Donald McKinley and Marie Elizabeth (Brandeis) E.; m. Marsha Ruth Erman; 1 child, Max. Freelance musician 1976-83, freelance journalist, 1983—; columnist Maui News, Kahului, Hawaii, 1984—, Nikkei Byte, Tokyo, 1988—, Computer Play Mag., Skokie, Ill., 1988—; v.p. Andromeda Micro. Corp., Kula, Hawaii, 1988—; cons. Leading Edge Products, Needham, Mass., 1982-84. Author: (with George Fontaine) Public Domain Software and Shareware, Working with dBase Mac, (with David Altounian) PC User's Guide to the Macintosh, Quick and Easy Guide to the Macintosh for DoS Users; (with Gregory Salcedo) Elementary Paradox; editor Computar Play; contbg. editor Macazine, Austin, Tex., 1987—.

DEMARINIS, JAN, transportation company executive; b. N.Y.C., Jan. 7, 1955; d. Leopold Nicholas and Virginia Kathryn (Re) DeM.; children: Jade Saren, Leila Zaremba, Akiva DeMarinis. BFA, U. N.Mex., 1978. Owner, mgr. NohShame Ltd., San Francisco, 1978-82, Berkeley (Calif.) Local Transport, 1986—; agt. Travel W/US, Albuquerque, 1982-86. Vol. Gay Day Parade, San Francisco, 1978—, Alameda Costa Ctr. for Devel. Disabled, Berkeley, 1987, Lesbian Rights Project, San Francisco, 1988, Pledge of Resistance, San Francisco, 1988. Mem. Nat. Assn. Female Execs., Berkeley C. of C., Japan Karate Assn., Japan Sword Soc., Pacific Area Women in Martial Arts. Home and Office: 1323 Addison St Berkeley CA 94702

DEMARR, MARCIA JOY, publishing executive, management consultant; b. N.Y.C., Jan. 9, 1938; d. Louis William and Rebecca (Levine) Adler; m. Bernard M. DeMarr, Dec. 1, 1963; children: John A., Steven J. BS in Law, Irvine U., 1978; MBA, Pepperdine U., 1980. V.p. Exec. Assocs., Inc., Newport Beach, Calif., 1978-82; v.p. mktg., bd. dirs. Hide-A-Bed, Inc., Fountain Valley, Calif., 1982-85; mktg. dir. Sashiba Products, Santa Ana, Calif., 1985-86; exec. v.p. Creative Fin. Cons. Co., Newport Beach, 1986-87; pres. Creative Venture Pub. Co., Huntington Beach, Calif., 1987—; assoc. dir. Orange County Minority Bus. Devel. Ctr.; guest lectr. mktg. confs. Author: Small Business Funding, 1986, The Do-It-Yourself Business Plan, 1988, Stop Shooting Elephants with Peashooters: Sensible Small Business Marketing Strategies, 1988. Republican. Jewish. Office: Orange County Minority Bus Devel Ctr 856 N Ross Ste 250 Santa Ana CA 92701

DE MARS, CARON EMERSON, insurance manager; b. Rock Springs, Wyo., Oct. 18, 1955; d. Eugene Reynders and Mildred Evelyn (Bohmont) E.; m. Bruce David DeMars, Aug. 11, 1984. BS, U. Wyo., 1978. Chartered property and casualty underwriter, 1987; casualty claims law assoc., 1982. Claims adjuster Crawford and Co. Ins. Adjusters, Great Falls, Mont., 1978-79; adjuster-in-charge Rawlins, Wyo., 1979-80; field claim rep. State Farm Ins., Sheridan, Wyo., 1980, sr. field claim rep., 1981-82; specialist arson State Farm Ins., Casper, Wyo., 1982-85; reinsp., trainer State Farm Ins., Colorado Springs, Colo., 1985-87; property claims mgr. United Svcs. Automobile Assn., Colorado Springs, 1987—. Bd. dirs. Wyo. Girl Scout Council, Green River, 1974, Crimestoppers Cen. Wyo., Casper, 1982-85; chair publicity Sheridan County Reps., 1980-82, Jr. League El Paso County, 1988—. Mem. Western Ins. Info. Service (Wyo. coordinator level III 1987), Bus. and Profl. Women (chair young careerist com. 1985, state Outstanding Young Career Woman 1984), Nat. Assn. for Female Execs., VFW (aux.), Toastmasters (sec. dist. 26, 1988-89), Soc. of Chpt. Property Casualty Underwriters, Kappa Delta Alumnae Assn. (editor 1988-89). Republican. Mem. Unity Ch. Club: Toastmasters (pers. Casper chpt. 1984-85, ednl. v.p. Colorado Springs chpt. 1987, Competent Toastmaster 1983, pres. Colo. Springs chpt. 1988-89, sec. 1988-89). Home: 5025 Whip Tr Colorado Springs CO 80917 Office: United Svcs Automobile Assn 1855 Telstar Dr Colorado Springs CO 80920

DE MASSA, JESSIE G., media specialist. BJ, Temple U.; MLS, San Jose State U., 1967; postgrad., U. Okla., U. So. Calif. Tchr. Palo Alto (Calif.) Unified Sch. Dist., 1966; librarian Antelope Valley Joint Union High Sch. Dist., Lancaster, Calif., 1966-68, ABC Unified Sch. Dist., Artesia, Calif., 1968-72; dist. librarian Tehachapi (Calif.) Unified Sch. Dist., 1972-81; also media specialist, free lance writer, 1981—. Contbr. articles to profl. jours. Mem. Statue of Liberty Ellis Island Found., Inc. Fellow Internat. Biog. Assn.; mem. Calif. Media and Library Educators Assn., Calif. Assn. Sch. Librarians (exec. council), AAUW (bull. editor, assoc. editor state bull., chmn. publicity 1955-68), Nat. Mus. Women in Arts (charter), Hon. Fellows John F. Kennedy Library (founding mem.). Home: 9951 Garrett Circle Huntington Beach CA 92646

DEMENTIS, KATHARINE HOPKINS, interior designer; b. Indpls., Dec. 20, 1922; d. Stephen Francis and Margaret Bell (Yeager) Hopkins; m. Gilbert X. Dementis. Student, John Herron Art Sch., 1941-44; BS, U. Wis., 1971. Interior designer L.A. Ayres and Co., Indpls., 1945-51; 1st v.p. Ariz. Questers, 1988—. Mem. DAR, Lakes Club, Union Hills Country Club,

Passport Club. Republican. Presbyterian. Home: 12830 Castlebar Dr Sun City West AZ 85375 Office: Questers 210 S Quince St Philadelphia PA 19107

DEMEREE, GLORIA LENNOX, real estate executive; b. Baden, Pa., Feb. 14, 1931; d. Gilbert Leroy and Marion (Slosson) Whetson; m. William Vincel Lennox, June 19, 1954 (div. 1985); children: Cheryl Lennox Watson, Lynda Lennox Huerta, Jim; m. Philip Gilbert Demeree, July 4, 1985. BS in Edn., Kent State U., 1954; MA in Spl. Edn., Ariz. State U., 1968. Tchr. Maple Leaf Sch., Garfield Heights, Ohio, 1954-55, Madison (Ind.) Dist. Elem. Sch., 1958, Scottsdale (Ariz.) Schs., 1961-68, Devereux Sch., 1968-70, Tri-City Mental Health Sch., Mesa, Ariz., 1970-71; br. mgr. M. Leslie Hansen, Scottsdale, 1972-74; v.p., gen. mgr. John D. Noble and Assocs., Scottsdale, 1974-83; pres., broker Gloria Lennox & Assocs., Inc., Scottsdale, 1983—. Chmn. bd. Interfaith Counseling Svc., 1988-89; trustee Scottsdale Congl. United Ch.of Christ, 1986-88. Kent State U. scholar, 1950-54. Mem. Mem. Nat. Assn. Realtors, Ariz. Assn. Realtors (Realtor Assoc. of Yr. award 1975), Women's Coun. Realtors, Realtor Nat. Mktg. Inst., Scottsdale Bd. Realtors (pres. 1981-82, Realtor of Yr. 1982), Ariz. Town Halls, Ariz. Country Club. Republican. Home: 7561 Via Camello Del Sur Scottsdale AZ 85258 Office: Gloria Lennox and Assocs 4533 N Scottsdale Rd 200 Scottsdale AZ 85258

DEMET, EDWARD MICHAEL, neurochemist, educator, consultant; b. Elmhurst, Ill., July 27, 1949; s. Michael Constantine and Elvira Linnea (Franson) DeM.; m. Aleksandra Chicz, Oct. 22, 1983. Student Ill. Inst. Tech., Chgo., 1963-66, Ph.D., 1976; A.S., Harper Coll., Palatine, Ill., 1969; B.S., U. Ill., 1971. Research asst. prof. U. Chgo., 1976-80; research chemist VA Med. Ctr., West Los Angeles, Calif., 1980-83; asst. prof. dept. psychiatry UCLA, 1980-83, U. Calif., Irvine, 1983-87, assoc. prof., 1988—; cons. VA Med. Ctr., West Los Angeles, 1983—, Long Beach, Calif., 1986—, Spectra Physics Corp., 1982-84, Stuart Pharms., 1983, Vydak Inc., 1983, IBM Instruments, 1984—, Pfizer Pharms., 1985—, Fairview State Hosp., 1985—, Abbott Lab., 1986—, Kronos Inc., 1986—. Contbr. articles to profl. jours. USPHS fellow, 1976-78. Mem. Soc. Neurosci., Am. Chem. Soc., AAAS, N.Y. Acad. Sci., West Coast Coll. Biol. Psychiatry. Avocations: backpacking, rock climbing, sailing. Home: 26322 Los Alamitos Laguna Hills CA 92653 Office: U Calif Dept Psychiatry and Human Behavior Irvine CA 92717

DEMETRESCU, MIHAI CONSTANTIN, computer company executive, scientist; b. Bucharest, Romania, May 23, 1929; s. Dan and Alina (Dragosescu) D.; M.E.E., Poly. Inst. of U. Bucharest, 1954; Ph.D., Romanian Acad. Sci., 1957; m. Agnes Halas, May 25, 1969; 1 child, Stefan. Came to U.S., 1966. Prin. investigator Research Inst. Endocrinology Romanian Acad. Sci., Bucharest, 1958-66; research fellow dept. anatomy UCLA, 1966-67; faculty U. Calif.-Irvine, 1967—, asst. prof. dept. physiology, 1971-78, assoc. researcher, 1978-79, assoc. clin. prof., 1979-83; v.p. Resonance Motors, Inc., Monrovia, Calif., 1972-85; pres. Neurometrics, Inc., Irvine, Calif., 1978-82; pres. Lasergraphics Inc., Irvine, 1982-84, chmn., chief exec. officer, 1984—. Mem. com. on hon. degrees U. Calif.-Irvine, 1970-72. Postdoctoral fellow UCLA, 1966. Mem. Internat. Platform Assn., Am. Physiol. Soc., IEEE (sr.). Republican. Contbr. articles to profl. jours. Patentee in field. Home: 20 Palmento Way Irvine CA 92715 Office: 17671 Cowan Ave Irvine CA 92714

DEMGEN, KAREN DIANE KLOMHAUS, accountant; b. Chgo., Jan. 11, 1943; d. Karl William and Mary Lorraine (Lutton) Klomhaus; m. Paul Frederick Demgen, June 29, 1974; children: Erick, Drew. BS in Bus. Adminstrn., U. Colo., 1969; MS in Acctg. and Taxation, Colo. State U., 1975. CPA, Colo. Staff acct. Van Schooneveld and Co., Englewood, Colo., 1969-72, Weibel and Hendrick CPAs, Ft. Collins, Colo., 1972-73; internal auditor Farmers Union Ins. Co., Denver, 1973-74; instr. Met. State Coll., Denver, 1974-77; pres. Karen K. Demgen, CPA, P.C., Littleton, Colo., 1975—; bd. dirs. Nat. Assn. Accts., Denver. Bd. dirs. St. Mary's Sch., Littleton, 1987-88,. Mem. Colo. Assn. Commerce and Industry, Centennial Estate Planning Coun., Alliance of Profl. Women, Am. Inst. CPAs, Colo. Soc. CPAs (bd. dirs. 1987-89), Lakewood C. of C. (bd. dirs. 1982-83). Republican. Roman Catholic. Club: Pinehurst Country (Denver). Home and Office: 7800 W Phillips Ave Littleton CO 80123

DEMICHELE, LYNN BEVAN, newspaper publisher; b. Kankakee, Ill., Dec. 13, 1942; d. Franklyn Robert and Virginia (Barr) B.; m. James F. Dalton (div. 1972); 1 child, Robert Bevan Dalton; m. Mardon George DeMichele, Apr. 3, 1973; 1 child, Mardon Scott DeMichele. BA, McMurray Coll., 1964; postgrad., U. Calif., Riverside, 1967-68. Cert. secondary tchr., Calif. Instr. Kankakee Community Coll., 1964-71; chmn. communications dept. Ind. Vocat. Tech. Coll., Indpls., 1971-75; writer Muncie Star, 1975-78; creative dir. J. Allen Rent Advt., Muncie, 1978-80; freelance writer Muncie, 1975-82; editor Sr. Perspective Mag., Phoenix, 1983; exec. editor Independent Newspapers, Inc., Mesa, Ariz., 1984-87, pub., 1987—; cons. Planned Parenthood of East Cen. Ind., Muncie, 1976-78, County Arts Alliance, 1978-79; dir. Midwest Writers Workshop, 1977-79; lectr. Young Authors' Workshops, Muncie, 1978-79. Author: Business Communications, 1973, Technical Communications, 1974; editor numerous communications tech. jours.; contbr. articles to profl. jours. Mem. East Valley Partnership (edn. and arts coms.), Ariz. Nature Conservancy, Multiple Sclerosis Soc.; bd. dirs. Mesa Town Ctr. Corp. Recipient Schweiter award McMurray Coll., 1964. Mem. Mesa C. of C. (small bus. assistance council), Ariz. Newspaper Assn. (numerous Better Newspaper awards), Soc. Profl. Journalists, Women in Communications, Suburban Newspaper Assn. Republican. Methodist. Office: Independent Newspapers 101 E First Ave Mesa AZ 85210

DE MICHELE, O. MARK, utility company executive; b. Syracuse, N.Y., Mar. 23, 1934; s. Aldo and Dora (Carno) De M.; m. Faye Ann Venturin, Nov. 8, 1957; children: Mark A., Christopher C., Michele M., Julianne; m. Barbara Joan Stanley, May 22, 1982. BS, Syracuse U., 1955. Mgr. Seal Right Co., Inc., Fulton, N.Y., 1955-58; v.p., gen. mgr. L.M. Harvey Co. Inc., Syracuse, 1958-62; v.p. Niagara Mohawk Power, Syracuse, 1962-78; v.p. Ariz. Pub. Svc., Phoenix, 1978-81, exec. v.p., 1981-82, pres., chief exec. officer, 1982—, also bd. dirs.; bd. dirs. Am. West Airlines. Pres. Jr. Achievement, Syracuse, 1974-75, Phoenix, 1982-83, United Way of Central N.Y., Syracuse, 1978, Ariz. Opera Co., Phoenix, 1981-83, Phoenix Symphony, 1984-86, United Way of Phoenix, 1985-86, Ariz. Mus. of Sci. and Tech., 1988—; chmn. Valley of Sun United Way, 1984-86, Phoenix Commn. on Ednl. Excellence, 1987—, Ariz. Arts Stabilization Fund. Named Outstanding Young Man of Yr. Syracuse Jaycees, 1968. Mem. Phoenix C. of C. (chmn. bd. 1986-87). Republican. Clubs: Phoenix Country, Ariz. (Phoenix). Home: 1040 E Osborn Rd Phoenix AZ 85014 Office: Ariz Pub Svc Co 411 N Central Ave Phoenix AZ 85036

DEMITRIADES, PAUL BILL, aerospace company executive; b. Seattle, Feb. 16, 1933; s. William A. and Helen B. (Kirticos) D.; m. Anne Sharpe, Apr. 29, 1984. BA, U. Wash., 1955, MA in Pub. Adminstrn., 1975. With Boeing Aerospace Co. Kent, Wash., 1959-70, 80—; mgr. product devel. Kent, 1980-85, dir. mktg., 1985—; mgr. new bus. Boeing Computer Services, Kent, 1970-80; mgr. planning Boeing Engrng. & Constrn. Co., Kent, 1979-80. Contbr. articles to profl. jours. Lt. Col. USAFR, 1955-57. Mem. AIAA (mem. pub. policy com. 1986-88), Armed Forces Communications and Electronics Assn. (Boeing focal point 1985—), Seattle C. of C., Overlake Golf and Country, Bellevue Athletic. Republican. Greek Orthodox. Home: 2254 Evergreen Point Rd Bellevue WA 98004

DEMOFF, MARVIN ALAN, lawyer; b. Los Angeles, Oct. 28, 1942; s. Max and Mildred (Tweer) D.; m. Patricia Caryn Abelov, June 16, 1968; children: Allison Leigh, Kevin Andrew. BA, UCLA, 1964; JD, Loyola U., Los Angeles, 1967. Bar: Calif. 1969. Asst. pub. defender Los Angeles County, 1968-72; ptnr. Steinberg & Demoff, Los Angeles, 1973-83, Craighill, Fentress & Demoff, Los Angeles and Washington, 1983-86; of counsel Mitchell, Silberberg & Knupp, 1987—. Citizens adv. bd. Olympic Organizing Com., Los Angeles, 1982-84; bd. trustees Curtis Sch., Los Angeles, 1985—, chmn. bd. trustees, 1988; sports adv. bd. Constitution Rights Found., Los Angeles, 1986—; bd. dirs. 4A Found., 1988—. Mem. ABA (mem. forum com. on entertainment and sports), Calif. Bar Assn., UCLA Alumni Assn., Phi Delta Phi. Democrat. Jewish. Office: Mitchell Silberberg & Knupp 11377 W Olympic Blvd Los Angeles CA 90064

DEMORALES, MICHELLE MARIE, retail executive; b. Los Angeles, May 18, 1957; d. Lou and Mickey Margaret (Michelson) DeM. Cert. in real estate, Bill Kelley Sch. Real Estate, 1975, 78. Sec. Erickson Realty, Inc., Bullhead City, Ariz., 1975, salesperson, 1975-79; real estate assoc. Cornell Realty, Inc., Bullhead City, 1979-83, Red Carpet Realty, Vista Devel., Bullhead City, 1983-88; mgr. Sew Unique store, Bulhead City, Ariz., 1988—. Mem. Young Realty Assn., Mohave Valley Multiple Listing Service (sec. 1975-77). Republican. Home: PO Box 185 Bullhead City AZ 86430 Office: Sew Unique 1712 E Hwy 95 The Booster Village Bullhead City AZ 86442

DEMUN, TAYLOR K., military officer; b. Shreveport, La., Dec. 13, 1929; s. John Russel and Audrey May (Taylor) DeM.; m. LaVolla Mae Light, Mar. 13, 1953; children: Kory, Warren, Eric, Nancy. BS, Oreg. State U., 1952; MBA, U. Puget Sound, 1980. Commd. ensign U.S. Navy, 1952, advanced through grades to capt., 1972; comdg. officer USS Andrew Jackson U.S. Navy, Charleston, S.C., 1966-70; ret. U.S. Navy, 1978; exhbn. mgr. Seattle Trade Ctr., 1978—. Mem. King County Fair Bd., 1985-86; bd. dirs. Seattle Sea Fair, 1987.7. Mem. Navy League of U.S. (pres. Seattle Council 1986, outstanding Council award 1986, nat. bd. dirs. 1987—), Submarine League, Nat. Assn. Exhbn. Mgrs., Sigma Alpha Epsilon (pres. Oreg. State U. chpt. 1951-52).

DEMUTH, ALAN CORNELIUS, lawyer; b. Boulder, Colo., Apr. 29, 1935; s. Laurence Wheeler and Eugenia Augusta (Roach) DeM.; m. Susan McDermott; children: Scott Lewis, Evan Dale, Joel Millard. BA magna cum laude, U. Colo., 1958, LLB, 1961. Bar: Colo. 1961, U.S. Dist. Ct. Colo. 1961, U.S. Ct. Appeals (10th cir.) 1962. Assoc. Akolt, Turnquist, Shepherd & Dick, Denver, 1961-68; ptnr. DeMuth & Kemp, 1968—. Conf. atty. Rocky Mountain Conf. United Ch. of Christ, 1970—; bd. dirs. Friends of U. Colo. Library, 1978-86; bd. dirs., sec., sponsor Denver Boys Inc., 1987—; bd. advisors Metro Denver Salavation Army, 1988—. Mem. ABA, Colo. Bar Assn., Denver Bar Assn., Rotary, Phi Beta Kappa, Sigma Alpha Epsilon, Phi Delta Phi. Republican. Mem. United Ch. of Christ. Office: DeMuth & Kenp 1600 Broadway Ste 1660 Denver CO 80202

DENDO, ALBERT ULYSSES, electronics executive; b. N.Y.C., Aug. 29, 1923; s. Morris and Celia (Blittner) D.; m. Elizabeth Ann Terwillegar, June 6, 1950; children: Michael Robert, Sandra Stacy Dendo Miller. AB, Cornell U., 1949, postgrad., 1949-50; MA in Econs., Am. U., 1966, postgrad., 1967-69. From analyst to sr. inspector CIA, Washington, 1950-79; mgr. planning and requirements analysis and adminstrn. Gen. Dynamics Electronics Div., San Diego, 1979-83, dir. mktg., 1983-84, div. dir. mktg., 1984-85, div. v.p. mktg., 1985—. Mem. Tech. Mktg. Soc. Am., U.S. Strategic Inst., U.S. Naval Inst., Assn. U.S. Army, Air Force Assn., Navy League San Diego, Assn. Old Crows. Office: Gen Dynamics Electronics Div 9601 Ridgehaven Ct San Diego CA 92123

DENKE, PAUL HERMAN, aircraft engineer; b. San Francisco, Feb. 7, 1916; s. Edmund Herman and Ella Hermine (Riehl) D.; m. Beryl Ann Lincoln, Feb. 10, 1940; children—Karen Denke Mottaz, Claudia Denke Tesche, Marilyn Denke Kunert. B.C.E., U. Calif.-Berkeley, 1937, M.C.E., 1939. Registered profl. engr., Calif. Stress engr. Douglas Aircraft Co., Santa Monica, Calif., 1940-62, mgr. structural mechanics Long Beach, Calif., 1962-65, chief sci. computing, 1965-71, chief structures engr. methods and devel., 1972-78, chief scientist structural mechanics, 1979-84, staff mgr. MDC fellow, 1985—; mem. faculty dept. engrng. UCLA, 1941-50. Assoc. fellow AIAA; mem. Soc. Automotive Engrs. (Arch T. Colwell Merit award 1966, IAE Outstanding Engr. Merit award 1985), Sigma Xi, Tau Beta, Chi Epsilon. Democrat. Pioneered and developed finite element method of structural analysis; author numerous technical papers. Home: 1800 Via Estudillo Palos Verdes Estates CA 90274

DENLEA, LEO EDWARD, JR., insurance company executive; b. N.Y.C., Mar. 7, 1932; s. Leo Edward Sr. and Teresa (Carroll) D.; m. Nancy Burkley, Aug. 16, 1959; children: Leo Edward III, Thomas, Gregory, Kathryn, Nancy, Rita, Philip. B.S. in Econs., Villanova U., 1954; M.B.A., U. Pa., 1959. Group v.p. fin. services Internat. Basic Economy Corp., N.Y.C., 1966-74; v.p., treas. Pacific Lighting Corp., Los Angeles, 1974-81; sr. v.p. fin. Farmers Group, Inc., Los Angeles, 1981-85, pres., 1985—, chief operating officer, 1985-86, chief exec. officer, chmn. bd., 1986—, also bd. dirs.; Bd. dirs. Alexander and Baldwin, Inc. Served to lt. (j.g.) USN, 1954-57. Club: California; Wilshire Country. Home: 2798 McConnell Dr Los Angeles CA 90064 Office: Farmers Group Inc care Jeffrey C Beyer 4680 Wilshire Blvd Los Angeles CA 90010

DENMAN, JOHN, clarinetist; b. London, Eng., July 23, 1933; m. Paula Fan. Prin. clarinet, MGM Films, 1963-76, Guildford Philharm., 1963-7, formerly with London Symphony, English Nat. Opera, now prin. clarinet, Tucson Symphony; prof. clarinet & saxophone Trinity Coll. Music, London, 1968-76; prof. clarinet U. Ariz., 1976—; soloist and recording artist. Office: care Tucson Symphony 443 S Stone Tucson AZ 85701 *

DENNEY, AL B., JR., motion picture producer; b. Waco, Tex., Mar. 15, 1935; s. Albert B. and Mary E. (Fason) D.; m. Christine Denney; 1 son, Rick L. Student San Antonio Jr. Coll., 1953, 57-58, Tex. Chiropractic Coll., 1953, 57-58. Owner, screen writer, newsreel cameraman, location mgr., lighting dir., stunt driver Ind. Artists Prodns., Winnetka, Calif., 1965—; owner/broker DenReal Co., 1961—; owner/designer The Dennehy Touch, 1972—. Served with USMC, 1953-56. Recipient awards Brit. Broadcasting Co., Cannes Film Festival, Underwater Film Festival. Mem. Dirs. Guild Am., Internat. Photography Guild, I.A., Underwater Photographer Soc., Am. Soc. Lighting Dirs., Acad. TV Arts and Scis., Am. Film Inst., Internat. Platform Assn., VFW, Am. Legion. Republican. Lodge: Elks.

DENNEY, TALBERT L., real estate investment broker, antique and classic automobile dealer; b. Leedey, Okla., Apr. 23, 1928; s. James Harden and Myrtle Mae (Eaton) D.; student pub. schs., Stockton, Calif.; m. Barbara Pilcher, Feb. 17, 1951; children: Melanie Ann, Monica Susan. Owner cleaning co., Portland, Oreg. and Santa Barbara, Calif., 1959-67; co-founder, pres. Servpro Industries, Inc., Rancho Cordova, Calif., 1967-78, chmn. bd. 1978-84; condr. seminars on principles of success. With U.S. Army, 1950-52. Mem. Airplane Owners and Pilots Assn., Am. Bonanza Soc., Western Bonanza Soc., Internat. Platform Assn. Office: PO Box 1648 Gardnerville NV 89410

DENNING, MICHAEL MARION, computer company executive; b. Durant, Okla., Dec. 22, 1943; s. Samuel M. and Lula Mae (Waitman) D.; m. Suzette Karin Wallance, Aug. 10, 1968 (div. 1979); children—Lila Monique, Tanya Kerstin, Charlton Derek; m. Donna Jean Hamel, Sept. 28, 1985; 1 child, Caitlin Shannon. Student USAF Acad., 1963; B.S., U. Tex., 1966; B.S., Fairleigh Dickinson U., 1971; M.S., Columbia U., 1973. Mgr. systems IBM, White Plains, N.Y., 1978-79, mgr. service and mktg., San Jose, Calif., 1979-81; nat. market support mgr. Memorex Corp., Santa Clara, Calif., 1981, v.p. mktg., 1981-82; v.p. mktg. and sales Icot Corp., Mountain View, Calif., 1982-83; exec. v.p. Phase Info. Machines Corp., Scottsdale, Ariz., 1983-84; exec. v.p. Tricom Automotive Dealer Systems Inc., Hayward, Calif., 1985-87; pres. ADS Computer Services, Inc., Toronto, Ont., Can., 1985-87; pres. Denning Investments, Inc., Palo Alto, Calif., 1987—. Served with USAF, 1962-66; Vietnam. Mem. Phi Beta Kappa, Lambda Chi Alpha (pres. 1965-66). Republican. Methodist. Home: H-1030 Parkwood Way Redwood City CA 94061 Office: Denning Investments Inc O-525 University Ave Ste 203 Palo Alto CA 94301

DENNIS, CHARLES, JR., parole agent, teacher; b. Charlotte, N.C., Feb. 25, 1943; s. Charles and Christine (Jackson) D.; m. Fannie Pearl Miller, July 1967 (div. Jan. 1972); m. Jacqueline Lee Juric, Oct. 20, 1974; children: Amber, Tia, Chaz. AA, Fullerton Jr. Coll., 1968; BA, Calif. State U., Fullerton, 1971; tchrs.'s credential, Long Beach State U., 1976. Cert. life tchr., Calif. Instr. Terminal Island Fed. Prison, San Pedro, Calif., 1972-75; youth counselor Calif. Youth Authority, Whittier, Calif., 1973-77; tchr. Calif. Youth Authority, Whittier, 1977-80; tchr., dir. edn. Ben Lomond Youth Camp, Santa Cruz, Calif., 1980-84; tech., dir. edn. Oak Glen Youth Camp, Yucaipa, Calif., 1984-86; tech., evening program coord. Calif. Youth Authority, Whittier, 1986-89; parole agt. Calif. Youth Authority, Compton, Calif., 1989—; dir. Youth Against Crime, Santa Cruz, 1980-84, Yucaipa, 1984-85. Cpl. USMC, 1962-67. Mem. Youth Counselor Orgn. (v.p. 1975-77), Calif. State Employees Assn., Calif. Correctional Peace Officers Assn., Peace Officers Assn., Marine Corps Assn. Republican. Baha'i. Office: Calif Youth Authority 1315 N Bullis Rd Ste 6 Compton CA 90221

DENNIS, KAY DELOURDES, insurance agent; b. Rapid City, S.D., July 31, 1947; d. kayo and Inez (Allison) Pruitt; m. Donald Albert Dennis, Mar. 21, 1970; children: Dawn Amber, Shawn Kay. BA, Black Hills State Coll., Spearfish, S.D., 1969; MS, Calif. State U., Fullerton, 1974. Tchr. spl. edn. various Calif. sch. dists., 1969-73; salesperson Evans Furs, Woodland Hills, Calif., 1982-86; ins. agt. State Farm Ins. Co., Canoga Park, Calif., 1986—. Vol. Steve Garvey Racquet Classic, 1978-82. Mem. AAUW, LEADS, Woodland Hills C. of C., Woman's Referral Bus. Network, Warner Ctr. Racquet Club, Holiday Spa, Optimists. Republican. Lutheran. Office: State Farm Ins 22156 Sherman Way Ste G Canoga Park CA 91303

DENNIS, NORMAN DWIGHT, teacher; b. Ontario, Calif., Apr. 29, 1943; s. Wayne and Erma Lee (Neeley) D.; m. Linda Marie Glenn, Aug. 29, 1964; children: David Patrick, Michael Matthew. BA, Humboldt State U., 1966. Cert. secondary tchr., Calif. Tchr. sci. Fortuna (Calif.) Union High Sch., 1972—, mentor tchr., 1986-87, master tchr., 1974—; mem. tchr. edn. adv. com. Humboldt State U., Arcata, Calif., 1986—. Capt. USAF, 1967-71. Recipient Excellence in Teaching award Humboldt County. Mem. Cactus and Succulent Soc., British Cactus and Succulent Soc., Mesemb Study Group, South African Aloe and Succulent Soc., Calif. Tchrs. Assn. Home: 2010 Shamrock Dr Fortuna CA 95540 Office: Fortuna Union High Sch 379 12th St Fortuna CA 95540

DENNISH, GEORGE WILLIAM, III, cardiologist; b. Trenton, N.J., Feb. 14, 1945; s. George William and Mary Ann (Bodnar) D.; AB magna cum laude, Seton Hall U., 1967; MD, Jefferson Med. Coll., 1971; m. Kathleen Macchi, June 28, 1969; children: Andrew Stuart, Brian George, Michael John. Intern, Naval Hosp., Phila., 1971-72, jr. asst. resident, 1972-73, sr. asst. resident, 1973-74; fellow cardiovascular diseases Naval Regional Med. Center, San Diego, 1974-76, dir. coronary care unit, 1977-78; pvt. practice cardiology, San Diego, 1978—; v.p. Splty. Med. Clinic, La Jolla and San Diego, 1982—; staff cardiologist Naval Regional Med. Center, Faculty Medicine, San Diego, 1976—; dir. spl. care units Scripps Meml. Hosp., La Jolla, 1981—, chmn. cardiology div., 1987—; chief medicine Scripps-Encinitas Hosp., 1983—; asst. clin. prof. medicine U. Calif., San Diego, 1976—. Bd. dirs. San Diego County Heart Assn.; founder, pres., Cardiovascular Inst., La Jolla. Served to lt. comdr. USNR, 1971—. Decorated Knight of Holy Sepulchre; recipient Physician's Recognition award AMA, 1974-77; diplomate Am. Bd. Internal Medicine (sub-splty. cert. in cardiovascular diseases), Nat. Bd. Med. Examiners. Fellow ACP, Am. Coll. Cardiology, Am. Heart Assn. (clin. council), Am. Coll. Chest Physicians, Am. Coll. Angrology mem. Am. Soc. Internal Medicine, AAAS, Am. Coll. Clin. Pharmacology, N.Y. Acad. Scis., Am. Fedn. Clin. Research, N.Am. Soc. Pacing and Electrophysiology, Old Mission Players Club, K.C. Roman Catholic. Contbr. articles to med. jours. Home: 15696 El Camino Real PO Box 2302 Rancho Santa Fe CA 92067 Office: 351 Santa Fe Dr Suite 200 Encinitas CA 92024 Address: 9844 Genesee Ave Suite 400 La Jolla CA 92037

DENNISON, ANNA NASVIK, artist; b. St. Paul, June 4; d. Peter Olson and Hattie Mathilda (Swenson) Nasvik; m. Roger Bennett, Nov. 7, 1936; children: Lynne, Kristin. Student, Coll. of St. Catherine, St. Paul, 1925, St. Paul Sch. of Art, 1927, Art Student's League, 1932. Tchr. art St. Joseph's Acad., St. Paul, 1926-30; freelance fashion illustrator N.Y.C., 1930-64; artist syndicated page The Fashion Syndicate, N.Y.C., 1934-38crw. One woman shows include Colbert Galleries, Sherbrooke St., Mont., Can., 1979, Gallery Mihalis, Sherbrooke St., Mont., 1984, T. EAton Foyer des Arts, Mont., 1982, 83, 84, 85, 86, 87, Venable-Neslage Gallerie, Washington, 1979, 80, 81, 82, 83, 84, Lido Galleries, Scottsdale, Ariz., 1988. Named Woman of the Yr., Foyer des Arts-T. Eaton, 1982. Mem. Santa Cruz Valley Art Assn. (Sonora Desert br.), Lakeshore Assn. of Art, Nat. League Am. Pen Women (chmn.). Home and Office: 231 Paseo Adobe Green Valley AZ 85614

DENNISON, RONALD WALTON, engineer; b. San Francisco, Oct. 23, 1944; s. S. Mason and Elizabeth Louise (Hatcher) D.; m. Sandra Lee Johnson; children—Ronald, Frederick. B.S. in Physics and Math., San Jose State U., 1970, M.S. in Physics, 1972. Physicist, Memorex, Santa Clara, Calif., 1970-71; sr. engr. AVCO, San Jose, Calif., 1972-73; advanced devel. engr. Perkin Elmer, Palo Alto, Calif., 1973-75; staff engr. Hewlett-Packard, Santa Rosa, Calif., 1975-79; program gen. mgr. Burroughs, Westlake Village, Calif., 1979-82; dir. engring., founder EIKON, Simi Valley, Calif., 1982-85; sr. staff technologist Maxtor Corp., San Jose, 1987—; materials. Author tech. publs. Served to sgt. USAF, 1963-67. Mem. IEEE, Am. Vacuum Soc., Internat. Soc. Hybrid Microelectronics, Am. Nat. Standards Inst. (com. rigid disks), Disk Equipment and Materials Assn. Republican. Methodist. Mem. Aircraft Owners and Pilots Assn., Internat. Comanche Soc., Ventura County Aviators Assn. Home: 2764 Granvia Pl Thousand Oaks CA 91360

DENNON, GERALD BURDETTE, media executive; b. Astoria, Oreg., Sept. 18, 1938; s. Elmer Burdette and Wilma Elaine (Looney) D.; m. Anne Vining , Aug. 25, 1962; children: Elizabeth, Daniel. Pres. Jerden Music, Inc., Seattle, 1964-69, Jerden Industries, Inc., Seattle, 1969-82, First Am. Records, Inc., Seattle, 1977-82, Bainbridge Communications, Seattle, 1986—, The Montcalm Corp., Seattle, 1983—; cons. The Weyerhaeuser Co., Seattle, 1977, Union Carbide Corp., Seattle, 1976. Author: The Salmon Cookbook, 1978; editor, publ. (Newsletter) The Aquaculture, 1973-75; producer (record) Louie Louie, 1963-64. Mem. Nat. Assn. Broadcasters, Wash. State Broadcasters Assn., Oreg. Assn. Broadcasters, Nat. Assn. Media Brokers. Republican. Episcopalian. Clubs: Rainer (Seattle), Wash. Athletic (Seattle). Office: The Montcalm Corp 801 2d Ave 1410 Norton Bldg Seattle WA 98104

DENNY, BREWSTER CASTBERG, university dean; b. Seattle, Sept. 5, 1924; s. Merle Wilson and Margaraith (Castberg) D.; m. Patricia Virginia Sollitt, June 14, 1950; 1 child, Maria Janet. A.B., U. Wash., 1945; M.A., Fletcher Sch. Law and Diplomacy, 1948, Ph.D., 1959. Instr. Mass. Inst. Tech., 1948-52; with Office of Sec. of Def., 1952-60; profl. staff mem. Sub-Com. on Nat. Policy Machinery, U.S. Senate, 1960-61; asso. prof. pub. affairs U. Wash., 1961-64, prof. pub. affairs, 1964—, 1st dir. Grad. Sch. Pub. Affairs, 1962-68, 1st dean, 1968-80, dean emeritus, 1980—, chmn. marine affairs bd., 1972-79; U.S. rep. to 23d gen. assembly UN, 1968; cons. to RAND Corp., 1961-68; mem. vis. com. dept. govt. Harvard, 1967-72; mem. Presdl. Adv. Council on Intergovtl. Personnel Policy, 1971-74; chmn. Gov.'s Task Force on Exec. Orgn., 1968-72; presdl. mem. U.S.-P.R. Commn. on Status of P.R., 1964-66; mem. bd. sci. and tech. in devel. Nat. Acad. Scis., 1976-81, co-chmn. Korean com. on sci. and tech., 1977-82. Author: Seeing American Policy Whole, 1985; contbr. to Am. Polit. Sci. Rev., Sci., Pub. Adminstrn. Rev.; author, co-author, editor articles, books, chpts., and reports. Trustee 20th Century Fund, 1975—, vice chmn., 1982-86, chmn., 1986—. Served to ensign USNR, 1943-46; to lt. 1952-54. Mem. UN Assn. U.S.A. (mem. nat. policy panel on UN capabilities in the 1970's 1970-71), Nat. Acad. Pub. Adminstrn., Am. Soc. for Pub. Adminstrn., Am. Polit. Sci. Assn., Council Fgn. Relations, AAAS (com. on new directions 1975-78, charter mem. com. on sci. and pub. policy 1968-72, com. on arms control 1980—), Nat. Assn. Schs. Pub. Affairs and Adminstrn. (pres. 1968-69). Home: 2021 1st Ave Seattle WA 98121 Office: U Wash Grad Sch Pub Affairs DP-30 Seattle WA 98195

DENOFF, SAMUEL, screenwriter, producer; b. Bklyn., July 1, 1928; s. Harry and Esther (Rothbard) D.; m. Bernice Levey, Nov. 27, 1956 (div. 1964); children: Douglas, Leslie; m. Sharon Ladoris Shore, May 30, 1965; children: Melissa, Matthew. Student, Adelphi Coll., 1948-51. Writer radio program Sta. WNEW, N.Y.C., 1954-61; writer TV shows Steve Allen Show, Los Angeles, 1961-62, Andy Williams Show, Los Angeles, 1962-63; writer, producer TV shows Dick Van Dyke Show, Los Angeles, 1963-65; creator, producer TV shows That Girl, Los Angeles, 1966-71; creator, writer, producer numerous TV shows including The Don Rickles Show, Good Morning World, On Our Own, Los Angeles, 1971—. Recipient Emmy award Acad. TV Arts and Scis., 1964, 66, 67, 69. Mem. Writers Guild Am., ASCAP, Screen Actors Guild, AFTRA. Democrat. Jewish. Clubs: Friars (N.Y.C.); St. James (London). Office: 542 S Fairfax Ave Los Angeles CA 90036

DENONN, CHARLES EDWARD, retired military officer, education administrator; b. Hempstead, N.Y., June 2, 1942; s. Charles Lester and Viola Jeanette (Stiner) D.; m. Ruth Ellen Andrews, Aug. 15, 1964 (dec. 1976). ThB, Bapt. Bible Sem., Johnson City, N.Y., 1965; BA in Linguistics, SUNY, Binghamton, 1967; MS in Econs., S.D. State U., 1973. Commd. 2nd lt. USAF, 1967, advanced through grades to maj., 1979, ret., 1987; missile combat crew commdr. USAF, Ellsworth AFB, S.D., 1970-74; sr. missile codes instr. USAF, Ellsworth AFB, 1974-76; asst. prof. ROTC IIT, Chgo., 1976-79; chief recruiting div. tng. corps hdqrs. USAF, Maxwell AFB, Calif., 1979-82; dir. regional recruiting ROTC U. Calif., Berkeley, 1982-85; curriculum advisor USAF, Beale AFB, Calif., 1985-87; dir. high sch. mktg. Heald Inst. Tech., Sacramento, 1987-88; asst. prof. Chapman Coll., Sacramento, 1988—; cons., guest lectr. in field. Author tng. materials; contbr. articles to newspapers, mags. Exec. dir. mil. recreation council Chgo. USO, 1977-79; asst. to bd. dirs. Calif. Spl. Olympics, Berkeley, 1983, 84; vol. Calif. Vol. Income Tax Adviser program, 1986, 87; vol., team leader various flood and hurricane relief efforts, Ala., S.D., Calif., 1968-86. Decorated Cross of Gallantry with Palm (Republic Vietnam); recipient numerous mil. and civic awards. Mem. Air Force Assn., Res. Officer Assn., Mensa Soc., Calif. Colls. Mil. Educators Assn., Western Assn. Admissions Counselors, Shipmates Club, Sierra Club, Alpha Gamma Epsilon. Office: Heald Inst Tech 2920 Prospect Park Dr Rancho Cordova CA 95670

DENOVA, DOLORES THERESA, business educator; b. Baton Rouge, La., Jan. 1, 1931; d. Theodore Florencio and Alvina Loretta (Cassagne) Crespo; m. Charles C. Denova, Jan. 27, 1951; children: Charlene Clare, Bruce Philip, Keith Louis. AA, San Diego City Coll., 1958; BS, Calif. State U., Long Beach, 1968; MA, Calif. State U., Los Angeles, 1970. Cert. community coll. instr., Calif. Instr. bus. Cerritos (Calif.) Coll., 1971, Long Beach City Coll., 1971-77, El Camino Coll., Torrance, Calif., 1971-89, L.A. Trade Tech. Coll., 1975-76, Cypress (Calif.) Coll., 1979-80, Calif. State U., L.A., 1980-81, Santa Monica (Calif.) Coll., 1975-89, Los Angeles Harbor Coll., Wilmington, Calif., 1975—; dir. programs for unemployed Office Automation/Word Processing Program, State of Calif., Los Angeles, 1986—; cons. curriculum Los Angeles Harbor Coll., 1978-79, Long Beach City Coll., 1980; presenter workshops on mainstreaming physically handicapped student. Editor Bus. Tchrs.'s Newsletter, 1984-86. Mem. Assn. Info. Systems Profls., Internat. Bus. Edn. Assn., Nat. Bus. Edn. Assn., Western Bus. Edn. Assn., Calif. Bus. Edn. Assn. (sec. La. chpt.), Phi Kappa Phi, Delta Pi Epsilon, Theta Alpha Delta (v.p. 1979-80, pres. 1981-83, 87-88). Home: 729 N Paulina Ave Redondo Beach CA 90277 Office: Los Angeles Harbor Coll 1111 Figueroa Pl Wilmington CA 90744

DENOVE, PETER ANTHONY, account executive; b. N.Y.C., Feb. 1, 1962; s. George Thomas and Helen (Fotheringham) D. BA in Econs. & Mgmt., SUNY, Cortland, 1984. Sales rep. Evergreen Marine Corp., Dallas, 1985-86; account exec. Sea-Land Svc., Inc., Long Beach, Calif., 1986—. Mem. Airline Pilots Assn., Triathlon Fedn., Calif. City Parachute Club, Long Beach Flying. Home: 237A Newport Ave Long Beach CA 90803

DENSMORE, RANDALL REX, insurance executive; b. Alma, Mich., July 20, 1957; s. Rex R. and Barbara J. (Blair) D.; divorced. BA, Alma Coll., 1980. Office mgr. Chaparral Service and Supply Co., Denver, 1981-85; spl. agt. Northwestern Mutual Life Ins. Agy. C. Michael McKeever Gen. Agy., Denver, 1986—. Mem. Nat. Assn. Life Underwriters. Republican. Office: Northwestern Mut Life Ins 1720 S Bellaire Penthouse Denver CO 80222

DENT, CARL H., JR., information analyst, technical writer; b. San Antonio, Jan. 31, 1951; s. Carl H. and Alice (Manasseh) D.; divorced: 1 child, Christopher Williams. Student bus. adminstrn., Phoenix Coll., 1972, Glendale Coll., 1974; student land valuation, Am. Inst. Real Estate, Phoenix, 1988. Mem. task force Bubba McGee's U.S.A., Phoenix, 1970-76, Marriott Resort Corp., L.A., 1979-81; mgr. Christopher's Catering, Redlands, Calif., 1977-78; owner, mgr. La Cave Restaurant, Palm Springs, Calif., 1981-83; chief info. analyst D.R. Cons., Inc., Phoenix, 1984—; staff mem. Ariz. Gov.'s Task Force on Excellence, Efficiency and Competitiveness in Ariz. Edn., 1988. Mgr. Project Newstart, Phoenix and Las Vegas, Nev., 1988-89. Mem. Nat. Assn. Ind. Fee Appraisers, Ariz. Real Estate Sales Group (lic.), English Is the Nat. Lang. Home: 2515 N 48th St Phoenix AZ 85008 Office: DR Cons Inc 2721 E Edgemont Ave Ste 1 Phoenix AZ 85008

DENT, ERNEST DUBOSE, JR., pathologist; b. Columbia, S.C., May 3, 1927; s. E. Dubose and Grace (Lee) D.; student Presbyn. Coll., 1944-45; M.D., Med. Coll. S.C., 1949; m. Dorothy McCalman, June 16, 1949; children—Christopher, Pamela; m. 2d, Karin Frehse, Sept. 6, 1970. Intern U.S. Naval Hosp., Phila., 1949-50; resident pathology USPHS Hosp., Balt., 1950-54; chief pathology USPHS Hosp., Norfolk, Va., 1954-56; asso. pathology Columbia (S.C.) Hosp., 1956-59; pathologist Columbia Hosp., S.C. Baptist Hosp., also dir. labs., 1958-69; with Straus Clin. Labs., L.A., 1969-72; staff pathologist St. Joseph Hosp., Burbank, Calif., Hollywood (Calif.) Community Hosp., 1969-72; dir. labs. Glendale Meml. Hosp. and Health Ctr., 1972—; bd. dirs. Glendale Meml. Hosp. and Health Ctr. Diplomate clin. pathology and pathology anatomy Am. Bd. Pathology. Mem. Am. Cancer Soc., AMA, L.A. County Med. Assn. (pres. Glendale dist. 1980-81), Calif. Med. Assn. (councillor 1984—), Am. Soc. Clin. Pathology, Coll. Am. Pathologists (assemblyman S.C. 1965-67; mem. pubs. com. bull. 1968-70), L.A. Soc. Pathologists (trustee 1984-87), L.A. Acad. Medicine, S.C. Soc. Pathologists (pres. 1967-69). Lutheran. Author papers nat. med. jours. Home: 1526 Blue Jay Way Los Angeles CA 90069 Office: 1420 S Central Ave Glendale CA 91204

DEPAOLIS, POTITO UMBERTO, food company executive; b. Mignano, Italy, Aug. 28, 1925; s. Giuseppe A. and Filomena (Macchiaverna) deP.; Vet. Dr., U. Naples, 1948; Libera Docenza, Ministero Pubblica Istruzione (Rome, Italy), 1955; m. Marie A. Caronna, Apr. 10, 1965. Came to U.S., 1966, naturalized, 1970. Prof. food service Vet. Sch., U. Naples, Italy, 1948-66; retired, 1966; asst. prof. A titre Benevole Ecole Veterinaire Alfort, Paris, France, 1956; vet. inspector U.S. Dept. Agr., Omaha, 1966-67; sr. research chemist Grain Processing Corp., Muscatine, Iowa, 1967-68; v.p., dir. product devel. Reddi Wip, Inc., Los Angeles, 1968-72; with Kubro Foods, Los Angeles, 1972-73, Shade Foods, Inc., 1975—; pres. Vegetable Protein Co., Riverside, Calif., 1973—, Tima Brand Food Co., 1975—, Dr. Tima Natural Foods, 1977—. Fulbright scholar Cornell U., Ithaca, N.Y., 1954; British Council scholar, U. Reading, Eng., 1959-60; postdoctoral research fellow NIH, Cornell U., 1963-64. Mem. Inst. Food Technologists, Italian Assn. Advancement Sci., AAAS, Vet. Med. Assn., Biol. Sci. Assn. Italy, Italian Press Assn., Greater Los Angeles Press Club. Contbr. articles in field to prol. jours. Patentee in field. Home: 131 Groverton Pl Bel Air Los Angeles CA 90077 Office: 8570 Wilshire Blvd Beverly Hills CA 90211 also: 6878 Beck Ave North Hollywood CA 91605

DEPAULIS, PALMER ANTHONY, city mayor; b. Oakland, Calif., Jan. 17, 1945; s. Hugo Benjamin and Genevieve Amalia (Fontana) D.; m. Jeanne Marie Laufenberg, June 26, 1970; children—Patrick, Margaret. B.A. in English, Sacred Heart Sem., Detroit; M.A., Wayne State U., Detroit. Tchr. St. Mary's of the Wasatch, Salt Lake City, 1969-70, St. Mary of Redford, Detroit, 1970-72, Judge High Sch., Salt Lake City, 1972-74; dist. mgr. Allstate Ins. Co., Salt Lake City, 1974-83; pub. works dir. Salt Lake City Corp, 1983-85; mayor Salt Lake City, 1985—. Democrat. Roman Catholic. Home: 834 S 600 E Salt Lake City UT 84102 Office: 300 City-County Bldg Salt Lake City UT 84111 *

DEPEW, WILLIAM EARL, logistics engineer; b. Lyons, N.Y., Sept. 25, 1948; s. Bela Earl DePew and Cora (Teeter) Craine; m. Mary ELizabeth Gamino, Apr. 23, 1971 (div. June 1983); children: Carey, Anne, Miranda. Grad. high sch., Red Creek, N.Y.; student, Union Coll., Schenectady, N.Y., 1966-67. Mgr. bar and restaurant facilities Am. Legion Post 52, Sierra Vista, Ariz., 1971-75; prodn. control indsl. ops. directorate U.S. Army, Fort Huachuca, Ariz., 1975-76, quality assurance engr., 1976-83, logistics mgr., 1983-87, contracts team chief, 1987—; expert for tng. in subject matter Ft. Gordon, Ga. Signal Ctr., 1985; mem. Network Working Group Def. Communications Agy., Washington, 1988. Served with U.S. Army, 1968-71, Vietnam. Mem. Def. Contract Mgmt. Assn., Soc. Logistics Engrs., Armed Forces Communications Electronics Assn., Am. Legion (hon. life, dist. comdr. 1980-81), VFW, Mason. Democrat. Methodist. Lodges: Elks (exalted ruler Sierra Vista 1987-88), Eagles (charter mem. Sierra Vista chpt.), Moose. Home: PO Box 1751 Sierra Vista AZ 85636 Office: Hdqrs USAISC ASLO-O-M Fort Huachuca AZ 85613

DEPOLO-AYERS, HILARY ANNE, art gallery director; b. Detroit, Jan. 20, 1945; d. Bruno Alexander and Katherine Mary (Bannon) DePolo; m. James William Ayers, Sept. 10, 1977. BA, U. Detroit, 1966; MA, Wayne State U., 1971. Sales cons. Sears Roebuck Co., Denver, 1973-78; design assoc. Patty Walker Designs, Denver, 1978-79; design asst. Mason Waters and Assoc., Denver, 1979-80; dir., art cons. Alpha Gallery, Denver, 1981—; mktg. cons. Met. State Coll., 1987, Art Partnership of Denver, 1986-87, Colo. Art Edn. Assn., Denver, 1987. Pub. speaker Cultural Facilities Dist., Denver, 1988. Named Graduate fellow Wayne State U. Hillberry Classic Theatre, Detroit, 1969-70. Mem. The Theater Assn. Group (v.p. 1981-83), Denver Ctr. Alliance, Denver Art Dealers Assn. (pres. 1987—), Alliance for Contemporary Art (steering com. 1987—), Denver Art Mus. Mem. Unity Ch. Club: The Gourmet Piglets (Denver) (co-chmn. 1978—). Office: Alpha Gallery 959 Broadway Denver CO 80203

DEPP, JAMES ARTHUR, data processing executive; b. Columbia, Tenn., Mar. 6, 1949; s. John McClure and Louise (Deemer) D.; m. Priscilla G. Brock, Mar. 8, 1975; children: Alysha Nicole, Kelsen Tyler, Trevor Ramsey. BS in Indsl. Engring., Stanford U., 1971. Staff engr. Procter & Gamble Mfg. Co., Sacramento, 1971-73, dept. mgr., 1973-76, staff mgr., 1976-79, systems mgr., 1979-84; project mgr. Calif. On-Line Computer Svcs., Sacramento, 1984-85, pres., 1987-88; chief ops. officer Transdata Inc., Sacramento, 1985-87; v.p. Up Time Disaster Recovery, Inc., Sacramento, 1988—; lectr. various customer and user groups, 1985—. Republican. Club: Willowcreek Racquet (Sacramento). Office: Up Time 643 W Stadium Ln Sacramento CA 95834

DERASMO, VITO JOSEPH (BILL), marketing professional; b. Bronx, N.Y., Aug. 8, 1936; s. Anthony and Anna Errica (Errico) D.; m. Marylin F., June 11, 1960; children: Paul, Deanna, Peter, William. BSS, Fordham Coll., 1959. Cert. hotel assoc. Internat. tour mgr. Continental Trailways, N.Y.C., 1954-60; tour sales dir. Pick Hotels Corp., N.Y.C., 1960-63; mgr., agy. and tour sales N.Y. Statler Hilton, N.Y.C., 1963-66; regional dir., tour sales Hilton Hotels Corp., N.Y.C., 1966-72; pres. Garden City Tours, Boston, 1972-73; asst. v.p., sales, mktg. Marriott Sun Line Cruises, N.Y.C., 1973-78; asst. v.p., mktg. Resorts Internat., Atlantic City, 1978-82, Americana Hotels, N.Y.C., 1982-86; v.p. mktg. Best Western Internat. Hotels Corp., Phoenix, 1986—; adj. prof., New Sch. for Social Research (Hotel Mktg., Food/Beverage Dept.), N.Y.C., 1983-86. Contbg. author: Marketing Primer, 1983. With U.S. Army, NG infantry, 1959-65. Mem. Nat. Tour Assn. (1st allied chmn. 1965-68), Travel Industry Assn. of Am. (bd. dirs., mktg. council), Am. Soc. Travel Agts., Am. Bus. Assn., ASAE, AH&MA. Office: Best Western Internat Inc 6201 N 24th Pkwy Phoenix AZ 85016-2023

DER-BALIAN, GEORGES PUZANT, immunologist; b. Montmorency, France, June 22, 1943; s. Hagop and Azniv (Andelian) Der B. M in Physics, Sorbonne U., Paris, 1965, M in Biochemistry, 1969; M in Immunology, U. Calif., Berkeley, 1971, PhD in Immunology, 1976. Dir. immunology Axonics, Mountain View, Calif., 1982; v.p. research Hemogenetics, San Mateo, Calif., 1983-85; head infectious disease section SCLAVO, San Jose and Sunnyvale, Calif., 1985-87, cons., 1987—. Inventor in field; contbr. articles to profl. jours. Mem. Am. Soc. Microbiology, N.Y. Acad. Scis., Am. Chem. Soc. Home: 505 Cypress Point Dr #8 Mountain View CA 94043

DERDENGER, PATRICK, lawyer; b. Los Angeles, June 29, 1946; s. Charles Patrick and Drucilla Marguerite (Lange) D.; m. Jo Lynn Dickins, Aug. 24, 1968; children: Kristin Lynn, Bryan Patrick, Timothy Patrick. BA, Loyola U., Los Angeles, 1968; MBA, U. So. Calif., 1971, JD, 1974; LLM in Taxation, George Washington U., 1977. Bar: Calif. 1974, U.S. Ct. Claims 1975, Ariz. 1979, U.S. Ct. Appeals (9th cir.) 1979, U.S. Dist. Ct. Ariz. 1979, U.S. Tax Ct. 1979, U.S. Supreme Ct. 1979. Trial atty. honors program U.S. Dept. Justice, Washington, 1974-78; ptnr. Lewis and Roca, Phoenix, 1978—; adj. prof. taxation Golden Gate U., Phoenix, 1983—; mem. Ariz. State Tax Ct. Legis. Study Commn. Author: Arizona State and Local Taxation, Cases and Materials, 1983, Arizona Sales and Use Tax Guide, 1986, Advanced Arizona Sales and Use Tax, 1987, Arizona Sales and Use Tax Handbook, 1988; author: (with others) State and Local Taxation, Arizona Sales and Use Tax, 1989. Bd. dirs. North Scottsdale Little League. Served to capt. USAF, 1968-71. Recipient U.S. Law Week award Bur. Nat. Affairs, 1974. Mem. ABA (taxation sect., various coms.), Ariz. Bar Assn. (taxation sect., various coms., chmn. state and local tax com., chmn. continuing legal edn. com.), Maricopa County Bar Assn., Nat. Assn. Bond Lawyers, Inst. Property Taxation, Inst. Sales Taxation, Inst. Sales Taxation, Phoenix Met. C. of C., Ariz. C. of C. (tax com.), U. So. Calif. Alumni Club (bd. dirs., pres.-elect), Phi Delta Phi, Sereno Soccer (bd. dirs.). Home: 9501 N 49th Pl Paradise Valley AZ 85253 Office: Lewis & Roca 100 W Washington St 2200 1st Interstate Bank Pla Phoenix AZ 85003

DEREBERY, DANIEL PAUL, JR., accountant; b. San Antonio, Aug. 8, 1941; s. Daniel Paul Derebery and Irene (Elliott) Mockbee; m. Linda Margaret Opsahl, June 29, 1968; children: Daniel Paul III, Faith Lynn, Hope Marie. BBA, Tex. A&M U., 1963; MBA, Pepperdine U., 1976. Commd. officer U.S. Air Force, 1963, advanced through grades to lt. col., 1978; various auditing positions 1963-74; br. chief. Norton AFB, Calif., 1974-76; br. chief, office dir. Robins AFB, Calif., 1976-81; dir. svc. wide systems Norton AFB, 1981-82, program mgr., 1982-84; ret. 1984; dir. internal audit Alfred M. Lewis, Inc., Riverside, Calif., 1984—. Mem. Inst. Internal Auditors (cert. internal auditor, cert. chmn. Orange Empire chpt. 1986-87, bd. dirs. 1987—), Officers Club. Home: 1573 Gary Ln Redlands CA 92374 Office: Alfred M Lewis Inc 3021 Franklin Ave Riverside CA 92520

DER HAROOTUNIAN, DIRAN, teacher; b. San Francisco, July 12, 1929; s. Askanaz and Varsenig (Nishkian) Der H.; m. Carolyn Zari Johns, June 23, 1957;children: Candice Marie Der Harootunian Tibbetts, Kelley Michelle. BA, U. Calif., Berkeley, 1957; MS, San Francisco State U., 1972, MA, 1978. Cert. tchr., Calif. Tchr. Vallejo (Calif.) Sr. High Sch., 1964-66; tchr. Olympic Continuation High Sch., Concord, Calif., 1966—, chmn. driver edn. and tng. dept., 1970—; tchr. Juvenile Hall Ct. Schs., Martinez, Calif., 1968—, Mt. Diablo Adult Sch., Concord, 1980—; coord. drug programs Mt. Diablo Unified Sch. Dist., Concord, 1968-69. Cpl. USMC, 1951-53. Mem. Mt. Diablo Edn. Assn., Calif. Tchrs. Assn., NEA. Republican. Mem. Armenian Orthodox Ch. Home: 714 Park Hill Rd Danville CA 94526

DERMINIO, DAVID ERMAN, orthopedic implant manufacturing company executive; b. Utica, N.Y., Feb. 25, 1953; s. Dominic L. and Jane Eleanor (Caroli) D.; m. Maria Rose Scamardo, Mar. 26, 1977; children: Christina, Michael, Stephen. BS in Bus. Mgmt., Ariz. State U., 1974; post-grad. in bus., U. Portland, 1978-79. Sales rep. Am. Hosp. Supply Co., San Francisco, 1974-77; western area sales mgr. Am. Hosp. Supply Co., Santa Ana, Calif., 1977-78; regional mgr. Am. Hosp. Supply Co., Portland, Oreg., 1978-79; dir. mtkg. Carapace Inc., Tulsa, 1979-80, v.p. mktg. and sales, 1980-82; dir. mktg. Intermedics Orthopedics, Inc., Dublin, Calif., 1982-83, v.p. mktg. and sales, 1983-84; mgr. north region Med-Tech West, San Francisco, 1984-88, v.p. sales, 1988—; cons. on golf swing rsch. Kerlan-Jobe Orthopedic Group, Inglewood, Calif., 1983-86; cons. on bus. mgmt. Golf Tech. Inst., Santa Rosa, Calif., 1986-87, Golf U., San Diego, 1988—. Contbr. articles to trade jours, chpt. to book. Baseball coach San Ramon Valley Little League, Danville, Calif., 1988, mgr., 1989; coach San Ramon Valley Basketball League, 1989. Mem. Diablo County Club (Calif., greens com. 1986-88, medalist 1986-88). Republican. Home: 2320 Tree Creek Pl Danville CA 94526 Office: Med-Tech West 2364 3d St San Francisco CA 94107

DEROEST, LEON DOUGLAS, small business owner; b. Baker, Oreg., July 15, 1949; . Leon Philemon DeRoest and Toye LovDean (White) Spence; m. Lois Jean Hall Aug. 10, 1969; children: Julia, Tammera, Susan, Michael. Advt. dir. Grizzly Bear Pizza Parlors, Ont., Oreg., 1970-83; owner Klondike Pizza Parlors, La Grande, Oreg., 1983—. Mem. Am. Philatelic Soc., Oreg. Postal History Soc., Germany Philatelic Soc. Home: 482 Modelaire Dr La Grande OR 97850 Office: Klondike Pizza Parlors 2104 Island Ave La Grande OR 97850

DEROO, HENRY VALERE, dentist; b. Regina, Sask., Can., Dec. 13, 1928; came to U.S., 1964; s. Valere Cornelius and Lydia (Sapergia) D.; m. Llewella Pearl Roberts, Sept. 2, 1951; children: Carol Marie, Lynelle Fay. BSc, 1955, DDS, 1960. Med. technician Chinese Hosp., San Francisco, 1957-60; pvt. practice dentistry Williamshake, B.W.I., Can., 1960-64, Lancaster, Calif., 1964—. Mem. ADA, Calif. Dental Assn., Acad. Gen. Dentistry. Seventh-day Adventist. Office: 43823 10th St W Lancaster CA 93534

DE ROO, REMI JOSEPH, bishop; b. Swan Lake, Man., Can., Feb. 24, 1924; s. Raymond and Josephine (De Pape) De R. Student, St. Boniface (Man.) Coll.; S.T.D., Angelicum U., Rome, Italy.; LLD (hon.), U. Antigonish, N.S., 1983, U. Brandon, Man., 1987. Ordained priest Roman Catholic Ch., 1950; curate Holy Cross Parish, St. Boniface, 1952-53; sec. to archbishop of St. Boniface 1954-56; diocesan dir. Cath. action Archdiocese St. Boniface, 1953-54; exec. sec. Man. Cath. Con., 1958; pastor Holy Cross Parish, 1960-62; bishop of Victoria, B.C., Can., 1962—; Canadian Episcopal rep. Internat. Secretariat Apostleship See, 1964-78, Pontifical Commn. Culture, 1984-87; chairperson Human Rights Commn. B.C., 1974-77; mem. social affairs commn. Can. Conf. Cath. Bishops, 1973-87; pres. Western Cath. Conf. Bishops, 1984-88; mem. theology commn. Can. Conf. Cath. Bishops, 1987—. Hon. fellow Ryerson Poly. Inst., 1987. Office: 4044 Nelthorpe St #1, Victoria, BC Canada V8X 2A1

DEROSA, FRANCIS DOMINIC, chemical company executive; b. Seneca Falls, N.Y., Feb. 26, 1936; s. Frank and Frances Rose (Bruno) DeR.; m. Vivian DeRosa, Oct. 24, 1959; children: Kevin, Marc, Terri. Student, Rochester Inst. Tech., 1959-61. Cert. med. photographer. Chief exec. officer Advance Chem. & Equipment Co. Inc., Mesa, Ariz., 1984—, Pottery Plus Ltd., Mesa, 1984—, Advance Tool Supply Inc., Mesa, 1988—. Vice chmn. bd. adjustments City of Mesa, 1983—, bd. dirs. dept. parks and recreation, 1983-86; pres. Christ the King Mens Club, 1983-84; bd. dirs. Mesa C. of C., 1983-86. Mem. Ariz. Sanitary Supply Assn. (pres. 1983-84), Internat. Sanitary Supply Assn. (coordinator Ariz. chpt. 1987—, dist. dir. 1989—), Mesa Country Club, Santa Monica (Calif.) Yacht Club, Rotary (pres. Mesa Sunrise chpt. 1987-88, Paul Harris fellow 1988), Masons (pres. 1973), Sons of Italy (pres. 1983-84). Home: 3258 E Fox Mesa AZ 85213 Office: Advance Chem & Equipment Co Inc 819 E Broadway Mesa AZ 85204

DEROUIN, LAWRENCE WALTER, aerospace engineer; b. Watertown, N.Y., Mar. 29, 1948; s. Chester Leon and Ethelyn Jane (Spicer) D.; m. Marilyn Elizabeth Ballard, June 11, 1971; children: Heather Lyn, Heath Lawrence, Kevin Walter. BS in Engring. Mechanics, USAF Acad., 1971; MS in Systems Mgmt., U. So. Calif., 1976. Assoc. quality engr. Ball Aerospace Systems, Boulder, Colo., 1976-78, sr. quality engr., 1979-86, quality mgr., 1986—; systems quality engr. Martin Marietta Aerospace Co., Denver, 1978-79; instr. Met. State Coll., Denver, 1986—; chmn. Rocky Mountain Quality Tech. Seminar, Lakewood, Colo., 1979; faculty U. Phoenix, 1989—. Mem. Am. Soc. for Quality Control (sr., cert. quality and reliability engr., treas. 1979-80, edn. chmn. 1985-87, program chmn. 1988-89, Man of Yr. award Denver sect. 1979, Quality Engr. of Yr. award 1986, Quality Profl. of Yr. 1987, Quality Engr. of Yr. award No. Colo. sect. 1985). Home: 8212 Dudley Way Arvada CO 80005 Office: Ball Aerospace Systems PO Box 1062 Boulder CO 80306

DERR, JOHN FREDERICK, health care products company executive; b. Chgo., Aug. 23, 1936; s. Harry Louis and Annette Bollow D.; student Purdue U., 1954-58, Ind. U., 1970-71, Columbia U., 1972; m. Polly Laughlin Pease, Sept. 7, 1963; children: Deborah L., Jennifer. B. Projects mgr., hosp. group product mgr., dir. hosp. market planning, dir. products and systems devel. E.R. Squibb & Sons, Princeton, N.J., 1966-74; v.p. mktg. Searle Diagnostics, Des Plaines, Ill., 1974-76, v.p. imaging mktg. products group, gen. mgr. sales/service div. 1977-80; v.p., div. mgr. Nuclear and Ultrasound div. Siemens Med. Systems, Iselin, N.J., 1980; sr. v.p. mktg. internat., pres. Internat. Equipment div. Nat. Med. Enterprises, Santa Monica, Calif., 1981-82; exec. v.p., chief operating officer, dir. Internat. Remote Imaging Systems, Chatsworth, Calif., 1982-85; pres., chief exec. officer The Westlake Group, Westlake Village, Calif., 1986—; assoc. Kappa Group, Leguma, Calif.; cons. Siemens Med. systems, Iselin, N.J., Cadema, Middletown, N.J. Mem. Ind. Grad. Sch. Bus. Exec. Adv. Bd, 1970—. Dir. planning Naval Res. Region 19, San Diego, 1986—; mem. pres.'s council Purdue U. Served to capt. USN, 1959-63, USNR, 1964—. Mem. Am. Mktg. Assn., Res. Officers Assn., Naval Res. Assn., Chief Exec. Officers Club, U.S. Arab C. of C., Soc. Nuclear Medicine, Kappa Group (assoc.), Sigma Phi Epsilon (pres. alumni bd. dirs. UCLA chpt.; bd. govs. edn. found.), Purdue U. Pres. Council. Republican. Presbyterian. Clubs: Big Ten Los Angeles. Home: 1659 Larkfield Westlake Village CA 91362 Office: 2659 Townsgate Rd Ste 214 Westlake Village CA 91361

DERR, KENNETH T., oil company executive. m. Donna Mettler, Sept. 12, 1959; 3 children. BME, Cornell U., 1959, MBA, 1960. With Chevron Corp. (formerly Standard Oil Co. of Calif.), San Francisco, 1960—, v.p., 1972-85; pres. Chevron U.S.A., Inc. subs. Chevron Corp., San Francisco, 1978-84; head merger program Chevron Corp. and Gulf Oil Corp., San Francisco, 1984-85; vice-chmn. Chevron Corp., San Francisco, 1985-88, chmn., chief exec. officer, 1989—; bd. dirs. Citicorp. Trustee Cornell U., The Conf. Bd. Mem. Am. Petroleum Inst. (bd. dirs.), Bus. Roundtable, Nat. Petroleum Coun., San Francisco Golf Club, Orinda Country Club, Pacific Union Club. Office: Chevron Corp 225 Bush St San Francisco CA 94104

DERUBERTIS, PATRICIA SANDRA, software company executive; b. Bayonne, N.J., July 10, 1950; d. George Joseph and Veronica (Lukaszewich) Uhl; m. Michael DeRubertis, 1986. BS, U. Md., 1972. Account rep. Gen. Electric Co., San Francisco, 1975-77; tech. rep. Computer Scis. Corp., San Francisco, 1977-78; cons., pres. Uhl Assocs., Tiburon, Calif., 1978-81; cons. mgr. Ross Systems, Palo Alto, Calif., 1981-83; v.p. Distributed Planning Systems, Calabasas, Calif., 1983—. Troop leader San Francisco council Girl Scouts U.S., 1974; participant Women On Water, Marina Del Rey, Calif., 1983. Mem. NAFE, Delta Delta Delta. Democrat. Office: Distributed Planning Systems 23501 Park Sorrento Ste 106 Calabasas CA 91302

DE RUSSY, JOHN LANGDON, municipal government official, treasurer; b. San Francisco, May 30, 1944; s. Rene Edward and Christean Butterfield (Moore) de R.; m. Nancy Ruth Sharka, Dec. 17, 1966; children: Minda Marie, Sara Beth. AA, Citrus Coll.; AB, Calif. State U., Fullerton. Asst. to city mgr. City of Palo Alto, Calif., 1968-70; asst. city mgr. City of San Mateo, Calif., 1970-77, fin. dir., treas., 1977—. Pres. San Mateo Hist. Assn., 1978-79; bd. dirs. Peninsula Humane Soc., San Mateo, 1979-84. Mem. Calif. Mcpl. Treas. Assn. (bd. dirs. com. 1980), Calif. Soc. Mcpl. Fin. Officers (pres. state assn. 1989—), Rotary (bd. dirs. San Mateo chpt. 1979-81). Republican. Lutheran. Home: 126 W 40th Ave San Mateo CA 94403 Office: City of San Mateo 330 W 20th Ave San Mateo CA 94403

DERVAN, PETER BRENDAN, chemistry educator; b. Boston, July 28, 1945; s. Peter Brendan and Ellen (Comer) D.; m. Maria Pellegrini; children—Andrew, Peter. BS, Boston Coll., 1967; PhD, Yale U., 1972. Asst. prof. Calif. Inst. Tech., Pasadena, 1973-79, assoc. prof., 1979-82, prof. chemistry, 1982-88, Bren prof. chemistry, 1988—; adv. bd. ACS Monographs, Washington, 1979-81. Mem. adv. bd. Jour. Organic Chemistry, Washington, 1981—; mem. editorial bd. Bioorganic Chemistry, 1983—, Chem. Rev. Jour., 1984—, Nucleic Acids Res., 1986—, Jour. Am. Chem. Soc., 1986—, Acct. Chem. Res., 1988—, Bioorg Chem. Rev., 1988—; contbr. articles to profl. jours. A.P. Sloan Rsch. fellow, 1977; Camille and Henry Dreyfus scholar, 1978; Guggenheim fellow, 1983; Arthur C. Cope Scholar award 1986. Fellow Am. Acad. Arts & Scis.; mem. Am. Chem. Soc. (Nobel Laureate Signature award 1985, Harrison Howe award 1988), Nat. Acad. Scis. Office: Calif Inst Tech 1201 E California St Pasadena CA 91125

DER YEGHIAYAN, GABRIS H., academic administrator; b. Beirut, Mar. 29, 1949; s. Hagop and Lydia (Trachian) Der Y.; m. Angela Doctorian, Aug. 8, 1973; children: James Paul, Johnny Samuel. BA, BS in Polit. Sci. and Math., Am. U., Beirut, 1971, MA, 1974; PhD, U. LaVerne, 1980. Head tchr. various schs., Beirut, 1967-76; asst. dean Am. Armenian Internat. Coll., La Verne, Calif., 1976-78, dean, 1978-86, chief exec. officer, 1981-86, pres., 1986—; cons. in field. Author: Conversations in Silence, 1988; contbr. articles to profl. jours. Co-chmn. LaVerne Cultural Exch., 1987—; chmn. Armenian Olympics, L.A., 1986—, Armenia Aid Bd. Am., 1988—. Named

Outstanding Educator L.A. County Bd. Suprs., 1987, others. Mem. AAUP, Armenian Ednl. Benevolent Union (pres. 1986—), Assn. Armenian Gen. Benevolent Unions (vice-chmn. 1984-86), LaVerne C. of C. (bd. dirs. 1984-86), Rotary (pres. LaVerne chpt. 1984-86). Home: 2018 Craig Way La Verne CA 91750 Office: Am Armenian Internat Coll 1950 3d St La Verne CA 91750

DESAI, YASH DAHYABHAI, civil engineer; b. Tanga, Tanzania, Dec. 13, 1944; came to U.S., 1968; s. Dahyabhai Ranchhodji Desai and Shantagauri Naik; m. Bhanu Shankerlal Pandya, Aug. 15, 1967; children: Jitesh, Jignasa, Bhavisha, Nainesh. BCE, U. Nairobi, Kenya, 1967; MS in Engring., UCLA, 1970. Registered profl. engr., Colo., Kans., Ariz. Field engr. Hwys. Constrn. Co., Nairobi, 1967; teaching asst. U. Nairobi, 1967-68; research asst. UCLA, 1969-71; rsch. engr., teaching asst. Colo. State U., Ft. Collins, 1971-73; water resources engr. Stearns-Rogers Inc., Denver, 1974-76; drainage chief engr City of Wichita, Kans., 1976-81, sanitary chief engr., 1982-83; land devel. supr. Dooley-Jones & Assocs., Tucson, 1983-84; asst. city engr. floodplain mgmt. City of Tucson, 1984—; expert witness City of Tucson, State of Ariz., 1986—; mem. rev. com. Pima County (Ariz.) Floodplain Ordinance, 1986, City of Tucson Aviation Corridor Project, 1986—; speaker in field. Author: Probability and Statistics in Hydrology, 1973. Active Tucson Unified Sch. Dist. PTA, Cub Scouts Am., Tucson. Recipient Internat. Hydrologic Decade Assistantship Univs. Council Water Resources, L.A., 1969. Mem. Ariz. Floodplain Mgrs. Assn., India Assn., Lions. Democrat. Hindu. Home: 8101 E 4th Pl Tucson AZ 85710 Office: City of Tucson Engring Div PO Box 27210 Tucson AZ 85726

DESCH, JOHN B., petroleum engineer; b. Casper, Wyo., June 24, 1955; s. Bernard Nicholas and Louise Ann (Pugh) D.; m. Catherine Hackett, Aug. 26, 1978; children: Brian Thomas, Conrad Patrick. BSCE, U. Wyo., 1978. Field engr. Gulf Oil, Vernal, Utah, 1978-79; prodn. engr. Gulf Oil, Oklahoma City, 1979-82, Gulf Oil and Chevron USA, Casper, 1982-86; lead petroleum engr. Chevron USA, Denver, 1986—. Mem. Soc. Petroleum Engrs., KC. Roman Catholic.

DESIDERIO, FRED LEWIS, real estate broker; b. Reno, Nev., July 26, 1924; s. Luigi and Anna (Ferrari) D.; m. Lorraine Hamsa, Oct. 2, 1962; children: Denise A., Fred Lewis, John P. BSBA, U. Nev., 1949. Cert. property mgr., Nev. Pres. Fred L. Desiderio, Cert. Property Mgr., Reno, 1962-84, Sierra Nev. Ins. Inc., Reno, 1973-85; owner Desiderio Properties, Reno, 1971—. Commr. Reno Housing Authority, 1978. Mem. Reno Bd. Realtors (pres. 1966-67, named Realtor of Yr. 1968), Nev. Assn. Realtors (pres. 1970-71), Inst. Real Estate Mgmt. (pres. no. Nev. chpt. 1981), Elks, Druids, Sigma Alpha Epsilon. Republican. Roman Catholic. Office: Desiderio Properties 1750 Locust St Ste D Reno NV 89509

DESLER, LARRY ALLEN, design engineer; b. Pendleton, Oreg., Sept. 12, 1947; s. Marvin Harold and Jean (Robb) D.; m. Frances Jeanette Barker, Aug. 14, 1972; children: Jesse Allen, Rebecca Irene; 1 stepchild, Peggy Jean. ASEE, Blue Mountain Community Coll., Pendleton, 1967; student, Cogswell Coll., 1988—. Technician Battelle Northwest, Richland, Wash., 1967-69; field engr. Acoustical Mineral Exploration, Richland, 1969-71; applications engr. Holosonics, Richland, 1971-74; mgr. Singer, Richland, 1974-78; design engr. Advanced Tech. Labs., Seattle, 1978—; cons. Blue Mountain Community Coll., 1968-72. Mem. Young Republicans, Richland, 1968; Weblos leader Boy Scouts Am., Renton, Wash., 1981-83. Lutheran. Home: 1413 S 27th St Renton WA 98055 Office: Hish Performance Elec Engring PO Box 3003 Bothell WA 98041

DESMARAIS, CHARLES JOSEPH, museum director, writer, editor; b. N.Y.C., Apr. 21, 1949; s. Charles Emil and Helen Barbara (Young) D.; m. Sharon McLeod, May 1, 1970; m. Patricia Jon Carroll, June 15, 1979; m. Katherine Ann Morgan, Dec. 31, 1985. Student, Western Conn. State Coll., Danbury, 1967-71; B.S., SUNY-Rochester, 1975; M.F.A., SUNY-Buffalo, 1977. Curator Friends of Photography, Carmel, Calif., 1973-74; asst. editor Afterimage, Rochester, 1975-77; editor Exposure, Chgo., 1977-81; dir. Chgo. Ctr. Contemporary Photography, Columbia Coll., Chgo., 1977-79, Calif. Mus. Photography, U. Calif.-Riverside, 1981-88, Laguna Art Mus., Laguna Beach, Calif., 1988—; guest curator Mus. Contemporary Art, Chgo., 1980, Los Angeles Ctr. Photog. Studies, 1981; arts adv. com. Riverside County Bd. Suprs., 1981-86. Author, editor: Roger Mertin: Records 1976-78, 1978, Michael Bishop, 1979, The Portrait Extended, 1980; arts columnist Riverside Press Enterprise, 1987-88. Art Critic's fellow Nat. Endowment Arts, 1979. Mem. Soc. Photog. Edn. (dir. 1979-83), Am. Assn. Museums, Coll. Art Assn. Office: Laguna Art Mus 307 Cliff Dr Laguna Beach CA 92651-9990

DE SMIDT, FRANK JOSEPH, communications executive; b. San Francisco, Sept. 4, 1941; s. Paul Jerome and Mary Elizabeth (Ahern) D.; m. Deborah Kay Yoakum, Sept. 4, 1984; children: Michael Joseph, Jonathan Paul. Student, Peralta Coll., 1961-63. Gen. mgr. Sta. KPEN FM, Los Altos, Calif., 1978-82; pres. Los Altos Broadcasting, Inc., 1978-84, L.D.S. Enterprises, Inc., Milipitas, Calif., 1981—. Del. White House Conf. on Small Bus.; mem. Milipitas Community Task Force, 1982-83; dem. committeeman Calif., 1983-85. Mem. Milpitas C. of C. (pres. 1972-73, chmn. govt. affairs 1980, Cert. Appreciation 1977, Disting. Svc. award 1973, 78, Pres.'s award 1981), Rotary (bd. dirs. 1987, sec. 1988-89). Democrat. Roman Catholic. Office: LDS Enterprises Inc 1350 S Park Victoria #46 Milpitas CA 95035

DESMITH, LOLA MAE, educator; b. New Ulm., Minn., Aug. 18, 1946; d. Julia Olena (Brudeli) Peters; m. Edwin Joseph DeSmith, Sept. 2, 1967; children: Andrew Peter, Jennifer Lynn, Jonathan Edwin. BS in Elem. Edn., Mankato State U., 1968, MS, 1978. Cert. elem. tchr., Ariz. Tchr. Baxter Community Sch., Iowa, 1968-70, Bur. Indian Affairs Barrow Day Sch., Ala., 1970-74, Appleton Elem. Sch., Minn., 1975, Bur. of Indian Affairs Santa Rosa Bd. Sch., Ariz., 1976—; bd. dirs. Elmbrook, Inc., Mini-Convenience Stores, Inc. Chmn. Santa Rosa Bd. Sch. Banquet Com., 1988; leader Casa Grande council Girl Scouts U.S., 1980-86, 87—, Boy Scouts Am., 1987—. Home: 1123 E Brenda Dr Casa Grande AZ 85222 Office: Bur of Indian Affairs Santa Rosa Bd Sch Sells AZ 85634

DE SOLA, RALPH, author, editor, educator; b. N.Y.C., July 26, 1908; s. Solomon and Grace (von Geist) DeS.; m. Dorothy Clair, Dec. 24, 1944. Student, Columbia U., 1927, 29, 31, Swarthmore Coll., 1928. Collector N.Y. Zool. Soc., N.Y.C., 1928-29, 30-33, Am. Mus. Natural History, N.Y.C., 1930, Tropical Biology Soc., Miami, Fla., 1933-34; zool. editor Fed. Writers Project, N.Y.C., 1935-39; tech. dir. U.S. Microfilm Corp., N.Y.C., 1939-49; hist. dir. Travel U.S. 90 and Mex. Border Trails Assn., Del Rio, Tex., 1951-54; publs. editor Convair div. Gen. Dynamics Corp., San Diego, 1955-68; instr. tech. English San Diego Unified Colls., 1962—. Author: (with Fredrica De Sola) Strange Animals and Their Ways, 1933, Microstat Technicians Handbook, 1943, Microfilming, 1944, Worldwide What and Where, 1975; compiler Abbreviations Dictionary, 1958, 7th rev. edit., 1986, Crime Dictionary, 1982, rev. edit., 1988, (booklet) Great Americans Discuss Religion, 1963, (booklet) Quotations from A to Z for freethinkers and other skeptics, 1985, (with Dorothy De Sola) A Dictionary of Cooking, 1969; Great Americans Examine Religion, 1983; editor: International Conversion Tables, 1961; compiler-editor Whitman books, specializing in zool. juveniles, 1937-41; translator: Beethoven-by-Berlioz, 1975, World Wide What and Where Geographic Glossary and Traveller's guide, 1975; editor in chief The Truth Seeker, 1988—; cons. on microfilming to USN, on abbreviations to Dept. Def.; contbr. articles to Copeia, 1928-32, revs. to classical records and concerts to Freeman, Del Rio News-Herald, San Diego Engr., Downtown. Home: 1819 Puterbaugh St San Diego CA 92103

DE SOTO, SIMON, mechanical engineer; b. N.Y.C., Jan. 8, 1925; s. Albert and Esther (Eskenazi) Soto; 1 dau., Linda Jane. B.M.E., CCNY, 1945; M.M.E., Syracuse U., 1950; Ph.D., UCLA, 1965. Lic. profl. engr., Calif., N.Y. Engr. Johns-Manville Corp., N.Y.C., 1946-48; instr. in engring. Syracuse U., 1948-50; research engr. Stratos-Fairchild Corp., Farmingdale, N.Y., 1950-54; research specialist Lockheed Missile Systems div. Lockheed Corp., Van Nuys, Calif., 1954-56; sr. tech. specialist Rocketdyne Rockwell Internat., Canoga Park, Calif., 1956-69; asso. prof. mech. engring. Calif. State U., Long Beach, 1969-72; prof. Calif. State U., 1972—; lectr. UCLA, 1954-70; cons. engr.; dir., sec.-treas. Am. Engring. Devel. Co.; mem. tech. planning com. Public Policy Conf.: The Energy Crisis, Its Effect on Local Govts., 1973; founding mem. Calif. State U. and Colls.; Statewide Energy Consortium and cons. tech. assistance program. Author: Thermostatics and Thermodynamics: An Instructor's Manual, 1963; author: research publs. in field. Served with U.S. Mcht. Marine, 1945-46. Recipient Outstanding Faculty award UCLA Engring. Student Body, 1962; Outstanding Faculty award Calif. State U., Long Beach, 1971, 73, 76, 89. Mem. AAAS, Am. Soc. Engring. Edn., Tau Beta Pi, Pi Tau Sigma. Office: Calif State U Dept Mech Engring Long Beach CA 90840

DESPHY, JUPITER ARANZA, JR., merchant banker; b. Caloocan, Rizal, Philippines, Nov. 14, 1951; s. Jupiter Lindog Sr. and Adelina (Aranza) D.; m. Ameurfina Boquecosa, Mar. 1972 (div. Oct. 1979); children: Douane, Avery; m. Emily Rose Garcia, May 2, 1980; children: Jaune, Jacques-Philippe, Jireaux-Avignon. BS in Indsl. Engring., U. Philippines, 1972. Sales mgr. Prudential Property Co., Las Vegas, 1973-79; owner, mgr., broker Jupiter Ins. Mktg. Co., Las Vegas, 1979-81, Jupiter Realty, Las Vegas, 1974-81; owner Jupiter Resources Internat., Lawndale, Calif., 1982—. Office: Jupiter Resources Internat PO Box 7879 Torrance CA 90504

DESPOL, JOHN ANTON, state deputy labor commissioner; b. San Francisco, July 22, 1913; s. Anton and Bertha (Balzer) D.; m. Jeri Kaye Steep, Dec. 7, 1937, (dec. 1986); children—Christopher Paul, Anthony John. Student, U. So. Calif., 1931, Los Angeles Jr. Coll., 1929-30. Sec.-treas., council Calif. CIO, Los Angeles, 1950-58, gen. v.p. Calif. Labor Fedn. AFL-CIO, San Francisco, 1958-60; internat. rep. United Steelworkers Am., Los Angeles, 1937-68; with Dempsey-Tegeler & Co., Inc., 1968-70; rep. Bache & Co., 1970-71; commr. Fed. Mediation and Conciliation Services, Los Angeles, 1972-73; indsl. relations cons., 1971-76; dep. labor commr. State of Calif., 1976—; mem. Nat. Steel Panel Nat. War Labor Bd., 1944-45; chmn. bd. trustees Union Mgmt. Ins. Trust Fund, Los Angeles, 1948-68. Mem. Calif. Def. Council, 1939-41, 10th Regional War Manpower Commn., 1942-46; bd. dirs. So. Calif. region NCCJ, 1960-68; bd. dirs. Los Angeles Community Chest, Los Angeles World Affairs Council, 1951-80, Braille Inst. of Am., 1961—; del. Nat. Democratic Conv., 1948, 52, 56, 60; mem. Los Angeles County Dem. Com., 1942-44; mem. exec. com. Calif. Dem. Com., 1952-56; chmn. Calif. Congl. dist., 1954-56; mem. Calif. Legislative Adv. Commn. to State Legislature, 1956-59; del. Nat. Republican Conv., 1968; bd. dirs. Los Angeles World Affairs Council, 1953-81, Braille Inst. Am., 1961—; bd. govs. Town Hall, Los Angeles, 1941-44, 67-70, chmn. econ. sect., 1964-65; mem. Los Angeles Coun. Fgn. Rels., 1946—; mem. Calif. Job Tng. and Placement Coun., 1967-68. Mem. Indsl. Relations Research Assn., Inst. Indsl. Relations, Assn. Calif. State Attys. and Adminstrv. Law Judges, Soc. Profl. Dispute Resolution. Home: 4717 Willis Ave Apt 7 Sherman Oaks CA 91402 Office: 6430 Sunset Blvd Ste 301 Hollywood CA 90028

DESROCHES, DIANE BLANCHE, English language educator; b. Webster, Mass., Nov. 17, 1947; d. Victor Joseph and Rose Blanche Blouin; m. Roger John DesRoches, Aug. 27, 1966 (div. Apr. 16, 1974); 1 child, Bill. AA, Mesa Coll., 1976; BA in English magna cum laude, San Diego State U., 1979, MA, 1981. Cert. lang. arts, lit. and ESL instr., Calif. community colls. Instr. ESL, substitute Am. Lang. Inst., ESL Inst., San Diego, Calif., 1982, San Diego Community Coll., 1982—; instr. ESL Inst. Coll. English Lang., San Diego, 1982—. Author: (short story) Something Special, 1979, Cinderella of the 80s; (software) Basic MAP Reading Skills, 1981, (puzzles) The Seven Warning Signs of Cancer, 1981, Poisons Around the Home, 1980, Some Poisonous Plants, 1980, numerous other Dell Word Search Puzzles and Recipes, 1980—; contbr. (reading comprehension series) Comprehension Plus, 1982, (student assessment system) CASAS, 1982; co-author (film) Holiday Sky Show, 1988; editorial cons. (films) Dimensions, 1987, Cycles, 1987, Star Tracks, 1988, Thundering Water, 1988, Flying Blue Marble, 1988, Night on Dream Mountain, 1988, Mars, 1988, From Here to Infinity, 1989, Worlds Beyond, 1989; contbr. articles to mags.; translator: ABC of Ecology, 1982. Recipient Gregg award Gregg Inst., 1965; fellow State of Calif., 1979; DB Williams scholar San Diego State U., 1979. Mem. Phi Kappa Phi, Psi Chi, Pi Delta Phi. Democrat. Roman Catholic. Home and Office: 2029-F Cerrissa Ct San Diego CA 92154

DESSAUER, SIDNEY ROBERT, taxicab company executive; b. Chgo., Oct. 9, 1936; s. Herman and Lena (Schwab) D.; m. Sandra Kay Masters, May 12, 1963; 1 child, Helen Victoria. AA in Bus. Adminstrn., Coll. of San Mateo, 1960. Owner, mgr. Alpha Cab Co., San Jose, Calif., 1977—. Chmn. No. Calif. Vets. Employment Com., 1976. Sgt. U.S. Army, 1953-56, Korea. Mem. VFW (life, dist. 12 allstate comdr. 1980-81), AMVETS (life), Am. Legion (life), Mil. Order Cooties (life), Jewish War Vets. (life, dist. comdr. 1976-77, State Man of Yr. award 1976), United Vet. Coun. Santa Clara County (pres. 1976, Man of Yr. award 1981), Hole in One Club. Home: 2151 Old Oakland Rd Space 161 San Jose CA 95131

DESSER, KENNETH BARRY, cardiologist, educator; b. N.Y.C., Mar. 24, 1940; s. George and Sarah Ruth (Kaplan) D.; m. Carmen Yvonne Fletcher; children: Brett Karen, Lori Helene. BA, NYU, 1961; MD, N.Y. Med. Coll., 1965. Diplomate Am. Bd. Internal and Cardiovascular Disease. Intern Beth Israel Med. Ctr., N.Y.C., 1965-66, resident in medicine, 1968-70; cardiology fellow Inst. Cardiovascular Diseases, Phoenix, 1970-72, asst. dir., 1977-83; fellowship dir. cardiology Good Samaritan Med. Ctr., Phoenix, 1984—; assoc. clin. prof. medicine U. Ariz., Tucson, 1985—; editorial cons. to med. jours. Mem. emeritus Am. Jour. Cardiology, 1980-82; contbr. articles to profl. jours., chpts. to books. Capt. U.S. Army, 1966-68, Vietnam. Decorated Bronze Star with oak leaf, Purple Heart, Air medal, Cross of Gallantry; recipient Best Rsch. award Beth Israel Med. Ctr., 1966. Fellow Am. Coll. Cardiology (mem. editorial bd. 1983-85), Am. Heart Assn., Am. Coll. Physicians, Am. Coll. Chest Physicians, Am. Coll. Angiology; mem. Am. Fedn. Clin. Rsch., N.Y. Acad. Scis. Office: Cardiology Cons 1144 E McDowell Rd Phoenix AZ 85006

DETATA, JUAN CARLOS, forensic psychiatrist; b. Buenos Aires, Sept. 6, 1932; came to U.S., 1957; s. Juan Carlos and Carmen Rosa (Feola) D.; divorced; 1 child, Carmen. MD, U. Buenos Aires, 1956. Lic. MD, Calif., Wash., Hawaii. Resident psychiatry Phila. Gen. Hosp., 1957-61; consulting psychiatrist Dept. Health, Honolulu, 1961-76; chief dept. in-patient psychiatry 97th Gen. Hosp., U.S. Army, Frankfurt, Fed. Republic of Germany, 1976-80; geriatric psychiatrist Western State Hosp., Tacoma, 1980-84; chief dept. neuro-psychiatry 50th Gen. Hosp., U.S. Army Reserve Command, Seattle, 1980—; forensic psychiatrist San Quentin State Prison, San Quentin, Calif., 1985—. Contbr. articles to profl. jours. Recipient Gov. Burns' award Gov. State Hawaii, 1970. Mem. Am. Psychiat. Assn., Wash. Psychiat. Assn., King County Med. Soc., Nat. Railway Hist. Soc. Roman Catholic. Office: San Quentin State Prison Dept of Psychiatry San Quentin CA 94964

DETCH, STEVEN A., communications equipment company executive; b. Charleston, W.Va., July 21, 1951; s. Andrew and Helen Reniers (Asbury) D.; m. Kathy Fletcher (div. 1974); m. Joanne C. Farinella, Sept. 1, 1977; children: Andrew Ross, Samuel Thomas. BA, Purdue U., 1974. Engr. WXUS-FM, Lafayette, Ind., 1969-71; prodn. mgr. WLFI-TV, Lafayette, 1971-74; v.p. sales and mktg. Roscor Corp., Chgo., 1974-86; mgr., dealer govt. sales Ampex Corp., Redwood City, Calif., 1986—. Contbr. articles to profl. jours. Democrat. Methodist. Lodge: Rotary. Office: Ampex Corp 401 Broadway MS20-32 Redwood City CA 94063

DETERLINE, WILLIAM ALEXANDER, training company executive; b. Palmerton, Pa., Dec. 2, 1927; s. Harold Allen and Alexandra D.; div.; children: William A. II, Diane, Mary, Kim, Mark, Brooke, Charles. BS, U. Pitts., 1953, MS, 1955, PhD, 1958. Instr. U. Pitts., 1955-57; asst. prof. psychology Alma (Mich.) Coll., 1957-60; research scientist Am. Inst. Research, Pitts., 1960-62; research scientist, mgr. Air Force project Am. Inst. Research, San Antonio, 1962-63; cons. air tng. command Randolf AFB, Tex., 1963-64; pres. Gen. Programmed Teaching, Palo Alto, Calif., 1964-69, Deterline Corp., Palo Alto, 1969-81, W.A. Deterline & Assocs., Palo Alto, 1981—; bd. dirs. Edn. Media Council, Washington, 1964-66, Nat. Ctr. Sci. and Communications, Washington, 1985-86. Contbr. chpts. to books, articles to profl. publs.; author: Coordinated Instructional Systems, 1973. Bd. dirs. Palo Alto Crisis Intervention Ctr., 1973-74. 1st lt. U.S. Army, 1946-48, 50-51, Korea. Grantee U.S. Office Edn., 1968, 69, 71. Mem. Nat. Soc. Performance and Instrn. (pres. 1964-65, Outstanding Mem. 1972), Am. Soc. Tng. and Devel., Soc. Advanced Learning Tech. Democrat. Home: 562 Kendall Ave Palo Alto CA 94306 Office: W A Deterline & Assocs PO Box 51121 Palo Alto CA 94303

DE TORO, ANTHONY DOMINICK, lawyer; b. Jersey City, Apr. 29, 1959; s. Anthony Vincent and Angela Marie (Mastroley) D. BA in Econs., NYU, 1981; JD, U. San Francisco, 1984. Bar: Calif. 1984, U.S. Dist. Ct. (cen. dist.) Calif. 1984, U.S. Dist. Ct. (no. dist.) Calif. 1987, U.S. Ct. Appeals (9th cir.) 1987. Staff atty. U.S. Securities and Exchange Commn. Los Angeles Regional Office of Div. of Enforcement, 1984-86; assoc. Brobeck Phleger & Harrison, San Francisco, 1986—. Co-author: Securities Arbitration, 1989. Mem. ABA, San Francisco Bar Assn., Law Review. Democrat. Roman Catholic. Office: Brobeck Phleger & Harrison 1 Market Pla San Francisco CA 94105

DETTELIS, PETER FRANCIS, air force officer, space launch company executive; b. Buffalo, Sept. 30, 1963; s. Bart Francis and Judith Patricia (Syrek) D. BS in Engring., U.S. Air Force Acad., 1985. Commd. 2d lt. USAF, 1985; satellite ops. officer Air Force Satellite Control Facility, Sunnyvale, Calif., 1985-86; chief wing computer based tng. system activiation Consol. Space Test Ctr., Colorado Springs, Colo., 1986-88; dir. computer based tng. devel. 1013 Combat Crew Tng. Squadron Air Force Space Command, 1988—; owner, mgr. Aerospace Novelties Sales Co., Colorado Springs, 1987—; treas., engr. Hummingbird Launch Systems Inc., Colorado Springs, 1988—; mgr. launch track Internat. Space Devel. Conf., Denver, 1988; gen. mgr. Rocky Mountain Astrophysical Group. Editor: (books) USAF Academy Contrails Calendar, 1985, USAF Academy Basic Cadet Training Yearbook Class, 1988. Lay eucharistic minister and lector Peterson AFB Cath. Parish. Mem. Nat. Space Soc. (program dir. Pikes Peak chpt. 1988—), AIAA, U.S. Space Found., N. Am. Aerospace Def. Command Hockey League, Amateur Hockey Assn. of U.S. Referees Assn. (level 3 referee), Peterson AFB Co. Grade Officers Coun., U.S. Air Force Acad. Chess Team (pres. 1987—), Colo. Spring IBM PC User's Group (vice chmn. 1989—), Peterson AFB Officers Club. Republican. Home: 3518-D N Carefree Circle Colorado Springs CO 80917 Office: 1013 CCTS DOI Stop 34 Peterson AFB CO 80914-5000

DETTERMAN, ROBERT LINWOOD, financial planner; b. Norfolk, Va., May 1, 1931; s. George William and Jeanneille (Watson) D.; m. Virginia Armstrong; children: Janine, Patricia, William Arthur. BS in Engring., Va. Poly. Inst., 1953; PhD in Nuclear Engring., Oak Ridge Sch. Reactor Tech., 1954, postgrad., 1954; cert. in fin. planning, Coll. Fin. Planning, Denver, 1986. Registered investment advisor, Calif. Engring. test dir. Foster Wheeler Co., N.Y.C., 1954-59; sr. research engr. Atomics Internat. Co., Canoga Park, Calif., 1959-62; chief project engr. Rockwell Internat. Co., Canoga Park, Calif., 1962-68, dir. bus. devel., 1968-84, mgr. internat. program, 1984-87; pres. Bo-Gin Fin., Inc., Thousand Oaks, Calif., 1987—; owner Bo-Gin Arabians, Thousand Oaks, 1963—; nuclear cons. Danish Govt., 1960, Lawrence Livermore Lab., Calif., 1959. Trustee, mem. exec. com. Morris Animal Found., Denver, 1984—, chmn., 1984-88; treas., trustee Arabian Horse Trust, Denver, 1979—; pres. Rolling Oaks Homes Assn., Thousand Oaks, Calif., 1980-82; chmn. Cal Bred Futurity. Mem. Nat. Assn. Personal Fin. Advisers, Internat. Assn. Fin. Planners, Inst. Cert. Fin. Planners, Am. Nuclear Soc., Atomic Indsl. Forum, Acad. Magical Arts, Am. Horse Shows Assn., Am. Horse Coun., Magic Castle Club, Internat. Arabian Horse Assn. Club, Tau Beta Phi, Eta Kappa Nu, Phi Kappa Phi. Republican. Office: Bo-Gin Fin Inc 3625 Thousand Oaks Blvd Ste 220 Thousand Oaks CA 91362

DETTMANN, TERRY ROBERT, physicist; b. Milw., Oct. 3, 1947; s. Harvey Robert and Ruth Laura (Grey) D.; m. Pauline Lydia Bettin, Dec. 28, 1968; 1 child, Terry Robert Jr. BS in Physics, Marquette U., 1968; MS in Physics, Naval Post Grad. Sch., 1969; postgrad., Nuclear Power Tng. Sch., 1970, U. Wash., 1977-82. Commd. USN, 1968, advanced through grades to lt. comdr., 1977, ret., 1979; physicist applied physics lab. U. Wash., Seattle, 1979-82; chief scientist Digital Systems Internat. formerly Microperipheral Corp., Redmond, Wash., 1982—. Author: DOS Programmer's Reference, 1988; assoc. editor: Codeworks, Basic Computing, 80 US Journal; editor: NARA notes; contbr. articles to profl. publs. Mem. IEEE, Assn. Computing Machinery, Amateur Radio Relay League, Nat. Amateur Radio Assn. (bd. dirs. 1988—). Office: Digital Systems Internat 7659 178th NE Redmond WA 98052

DETTWEILER, JACK H(ENRY), JR., real estate developer; b. Washington, Nov. 21, 1945; s. John Henry Dettweiler Sr. and Mary Camilia (Calnan) Sterner. Student, St. Louis U., Mo., 1963-64; grad., U. N.Mex., 1964-68. Stockbroker Doherty & Co., Albuquerque, 1968-70; real estate broker Albuquerque, 1971-77; broker Berger-Briggs, Albuquerque, 1978-84; owner Jack Dettweiler Comml. Real Estate Interests, 1984—; pres. Equity Securities, Albuquerque, 1982—; faculty Am. Savs. and Loan Inst., Albuquerque, 1973-76; founder, chmn. Real Estate Exchangors, Albuquerque, 1981; pres. U.S. Fiduciary Svcs. Corp. Chmn. NFL Celebrity Golf tourney for Cystic Fibrosis, 1987, 88, 89. Mem. Albuquerque Bd. Realtors (bd. dirs. 1983-84, Exchangors award 1982-83), Sigma Chi, Top 100 Club (bd. dirs. 1983). Democrat. Roman Catholic. Home: PO Box 8341 Albuquerque NM 87110 Office: 4004 Carlisle #C Albuquerque NM 87107

DEUKMEJIAN, GEORGE, governor of California; b. Albany, N.Y., June 6, 1928; s. C. George and Alice (Gairdan) D.; m. Gloria M. Saatjian, 1957; children: Leslie Ann, George Krikor, Andrea Diane. BA, Siena Coll., 1949; JD, St. John's U., 1952. Bar: N.Y. 1952, Calif. 1956, U.S. Supreme Ct. 1970. Partner firm Riedman, Dalessi, Deukmejian & Woods, Long Beach, Calif., to 1979; mem. Calif. Assembly, 1963-67; mem. Calif. Senate, 1967-79, minority leader; atty. gen. State of Calif., 1979-82, gov., 1983—; former dep. county counsel Los Angeles County. Served with U.S. Army, 1953-55. Republican. Episcopalian. Office: State Capitol Office of Gov Sacramento CA 95814

DEUPREE, ROBERT MARSHALL, physician; b. Elizabeth, Colo., Dec. 26, 1912; s. Elmer Burton and Mary Ayer (Griffin) DeuP.; student Santa Ana Coll., 1930-33, L.A. City Coll., 1937-38; DO, Coll. Osteo. Physicians and Surgeons, 1942; MD, Met. U., 1948; postgrad. UCLA, 1952-53; AB, Calif. State U., Fullerton, 1962; MA, Calif. State U., Long Beach, 1963; PhD (Nat. Inst. Dental Health fellow) Purdue U., 1963-64; m. Harriett Ann Janetos, Oct. 11, 1963; children: Carol J., R. Scott. Intern, Wilshire Hosp., L.A., 1942-43, resident in neurology, 1943-44; practice medicine, L.A., 1944-57, El Monte, Calif., 1957-58, Newport Beach, Calif., 1958-59; dir. Rush-Merced Clinic, 1957-58; asso. med. dir. Aerojet Gen. Corp., Azusa, Calif., 1967-69, Am. Airlines, L.A., 1969; ships surgeon U. Calif. Scripps Inst. Oceanography, 1969; area med. officer Div. Fed. Employee Health, USPHS, L.A., 1970-85; head dept. internal medicine and radiology Hiss Orthopedic Clinic, L.A., 1953-57; instr. differential diagnosis Coll. Osteo. Physicians and Surgeons, L.A., 1945-49; instr. med. terminology N. Orange Community Coll. Dist., 1966-78; pres., Deustar Internat. Corp.; research fellow VA Hosp., Long Beach State Coll., UCLA Inst. Laryngol. Research, 1962-63. Diplomate in aerospace medicine and occupational medicine. Fellow Royal Soc. Health, N.Y. Acad. Scis., Am. Occupational Med. Assn., Am. Aerospace Med. Assn. (assoc.); mem. Royal Soc. Medicine, Aviation Hall of Fame (charter), Asclepiad. Author, editor: DeuPree International Emergency Medical Translations, 1972; co-author: Travis' Handbook of Speech Pathology and Audiology, 1972; editor Jour. Pro-Re-Nata, 1947-50; author, producer med. motion picture, U.S. Navy, 1950-51; cons. med. TV, Films, 1952—. Home: 2625 W Huckleberry Rd Santa Ana CA 92706

DEURMYER, JAMES JOSEPH, lawyer, trading company executive; b. Topeka, Feb. 28, 1946; s. James Justin and Ada Marie (Johnson) D.; m. Carol Eckert, June 17, 1971 (dec. June 1986); m. Tia Moore, Feb. 14, 1988; children: Alaina, Jared. BA in Econs., St. Michael's Coll., Eng., 1968, JD, 1971. Jr. ptnr. Albini, Braun & Conti, Zurich, Switzerland, 1971-81, 85-88; chief fin. officer, v.p. Bay Oil Co., Dallas, 1981-85; exec. dir. B&R Imports, Inc., Eugene, Oreg., 1988—. Republican. Episcopalian. Office: B&R Imports Inc PO Box 5229 Eugene OR 97405

DEUTSCH, BARRY JOSEPH, management development company executive; b. Gary, Ind., Aug. 10, 1941; s. Jack Elias and Helen Louise (La Rue) D.; B.S., U. So. Calif., 1969, M.B.A. magna cum laude, 1970; m. Gina Krispinsky, Feb. 20, 1972. Lectr. mgmt. U. So. Calif., L.A., 1967-70; pres., founder The Deutsch Group, Inc., mgmt. cons. co. tng. upper and middle mgmt., L.A., 1970—, chmn. bd., 1975—; founder, chief exec. officer, chmn. bd. Investment Planning Network, Inc., 1988—; dir. Red Carpet Corp. Am.,

1975-77, United Fin. Planners, 1984-86. Chmn. bd. govs. Am. Hist. Ctr., 1980—. With M.I., U.S. Army, 1964-66. Mem. Am. Mgmt. Assn., Am. Soc. Bus. and Mgmt. Cons.'s, Am. Soc. Tng. and Devel., Internat. Mgmt. by Objectives Inst. Author: Leadership Techniques, 1969, Recruiting Techniques, 1970, The Art of Selling, 1973, Professional Real Estate Management, 1975, Strategic Planning, 1976, Employer/Employee: Making the Transition, 1978, Managing by Objectives, 1980, Conducting Effective Performance Appraisal, 1982, Advanced Supervisory Development, 1984, Managing A Successful Financial Planning Business, 1988. Home: 4509 Candleberry Ave Seal Beach CA 90740

DEUTSCH, JUDITH SHARON, fundraising executive; b. Chgo., Dec. 27, 1953; d. Victor Henry and Ailsa Goldie (Lange) D. Student, U. Calif. San Diego, La Jolla, 1972-74; BA with honors, UCLA, 1975; MA, Coll. William and Mary, 1981. Intern decorative and ancient art conservation J. Paul Getty Mus., Malibu, Calif., 1976-78, conservation asst. decorative arts, 1978-79; asst. to dir. devel. Los Angeles County Mus. Art, 1982-83; assoc. dir. found. devel. Robert F. Kennedy Med. Ctr., Hawthorne, Calif., 1983-85; exec. dir. merchants club City of Hope Med. Ctr., Los Angeles, 1985-86, dir. western regional auxs., 1986-88; campaign dir. Jewish Fedn. Greater Long Beach and West Orange County, Long Beach, Calif., 1988—. Vol. Dem. com. campaigns, Los Angeles, 1975-77; docent Santa Monica Heritage Mus., 1987-88. Mem. Nat. Assn. for Hosp. Devel. (matching gift com.), So. Calif. Assn. for Hosp. Devel., Technion 2000 (v.p. 1982-88, social chairperson), Chautauqua Soc. (life), U. Calif. Alumni Assn. (planning com. 1985—). Jewish. Home: 3544 Centinela Ave West Los Angeles CA 90066 Office: Jewish Fedn Greater Long Beach 3801 Willow St Long Beach CA 90815

DEVANEY, DONALD EVERETT, law enforcement executive; b. Providence, Nov. 21, 1936; s. William Francis and Elizabeth Florence (Hill) D.; m. Tokiko Yoshida, May 19, 1960; 1 child, George Y. AA in Edn., El Paso Community Coll., 1973; BA, SUNY, Albany, 1979. Cert. healthcare protection adminstr. Internat. Healthcare Safety and Security Found. Sgt. maj. U.S. Army, 1954-83; customs inspector U.S. Customs Svc., Honolulu, 1983-84; provost marshal Tripler Army Med. Ctr., Honolulu, 1984—. Fin. donor Okinawa Cultural Ctr., Waipahu, Hawaii, 1987-89. Recipient Disting. Svc. award Hawaii Joint Police, 1977, 1986, George Washington Honor Medal Freedom's Found., 1973. Mem. Internat. Assn. Hosp. Security (region XIII chmn. 1989—, state chmn. 1985—), Am. Soc. Indsl. Security, Hawaii Joint Police Assn. (pres. 1985, dir. 1981-88), U.S. Army CID Command, Police Mgmt. Assn., United Okinawa Assn., Mensa, Yomitan Club, Rotary (v.p. 1989—, Paul Harris fellow), Ind. Order of Odd Fellows (noble grand 1987). Roman Catholic. Home: 98-911 Ainanui Loop Aiea HI 96701 Office: Office Provost Marshal Tripler Army Med Ctr Honolulu HI 96859

DEVENDRA, TITUS, internist; b. Ceylon, Nov. 9, 1936; came to U.S., 1970; s. Don Peter and Amabel S. (Manimendra) D.; m. Jayanthi Srima, Mar. 17, 1968; 1 child, Gehan Pushpeka. MBBS, U. Ceylon, 1965. Diplomate Am. Bd. Internal Medicine. Intern Gen. Hosp., Ratnapura, Ceylon, 1965-66; resident internal medicine Jewish Hosp., Cin., 1970-73, chief resident, 1972; pulmonary medicine VA Hosp., U. Irvine, Long Beach, Calif., 1973-76; lung cancer reseacher VA Hosps., Long Beach, 1973-76; staff internal medicine Long Beach Gen. Hosp., 1976-78; pvt. practice specializing in pulmonary and internal medicine Anaheim, Calif., 1978-79; staff Fitzsimons Army Med. Ctr., Aurora, Colo., 1979—. Mem. Am. Coll. Physicians. Buddhist.

DEVENS, JOHN SEARLE, college president, mayor; b. Shickshinny, Pa., Mar. 31, 1940; s. John Ezra and Laura (Bulkley) D.; m. Sharon I. Snyder (div. 1979); children: John, Jerilyn, James, Janis. BS, Belmont Coll., 1964; MEd, Emory U., 1966; PhD, Wichita State U., 1975. Dir. speech and hearing Columbia (S.C.) Coll., 1967-70; head dept. audiology Inst. Logopedics, Wichita, Kans., 1970-71; supr. audiology State of Alaska, Fairbanks, 1971-73; asst. prof. U. Houston, Victoria, 1975-77; pres. Prince William Sound Community Coll., Valdez, Alaska, 1977—; dir. Valdez Hearing and Speech Ctr., 1977—; mayor City of Valdez, 1985—; mem. Valdez City Council, 1980—. Producer films on hearing problems; contbr. articles to profl. jours. Nat. chmn. adv. com. Horsemanship for Handicapped, 1964-67; mem. Alaska Gov.'s Council for Handicapped, 1980-82; pres. Valdez chpt. Alaska Visitors Assn., 1980; mem. small cities adv. council Nat. League Cities, 1983-87, internat. econ. devel. task force; mem. Nat. Export Council; bd. dirs. Resource Devel. Council. Mem. Am. Speech-Lang. Hearing Assn. (cert. clin. competence in audiology and speech and lang. pathology), Am. C. of C., in Korea, Valdez C. of C., Alaska Mcpl. League (bd. dirs. 1984—), Elks, Eagles. Democrat. Methodist. Home: PO Box 730 Valdez AK 99686 Office: Prince William Sound Community Coll PO Box 590 Valdez AK 99686

DE VERE, JULIA ANNE, teacher; b. Onaga, Kans., Nov. 2, 1925; d. Goodlet Clarence and Anna (Fairbanks) Bonjour; m. Robert E. DeVere; 1 child, David E. Student Emporia State U., U. Kans., Kans. State Coll.; B.A. in Edn. and Psychology, U. Denver, 1957, M.A., 1961; postgrad. in edn. psychology and social work, U. Md., Sacramento State Coll., U. Calif., Santa Cruz, U. Denver, U. Pacific, San Jose State U. Cert. tchr. of the mentally retarded, elem. tchr.; specialist in edn., counseling. Elem. tchr. Buckeye-Jackson County, Kans., 1943-45, Bancroft (Kans.) Grade Sch., 1945-46, Belvue (Kans.) Grade Sch., 1946-53, Westmoreland Elem. Grade Sch., Kans., 1953-56; tchr. spl. edn. Stockton United Sch. Dist., Calif., 1957-64; tchr. spl. edn. Cupertino United Sch. Dist., Calif., 1964-89, ret., now specialist tchr. for learning disabilities Meyerholz Sch. Contbr. articles to profl. jours. Mem. Nat. Assn. for Retarded Citizens, Santa Clara Chpt. Assn. Retarded Citizens, NEA, Cupertino Edn. Assn., Calif. Tchrs. Assn., Assn. Retirement Credit for Out of State Svc., Coun. Exceptional Children, Delta Kappa Gamma.

DEVINE, GRANT, Canadian premier; b. Regina, Sask., Can., 1944; m. Chantal Guillaume, July 1966; children: Michelle, Monique, David, John William, Camille. BSA in Agrl. Econs., U. Sask., 1967; MSc in Agrl. Econs., U. Alta., 1969, MBA, 1970; PhD, Ohio State U., 1976. Mktg. specialist Fed. Govt. Ottawa Agr. Commodity Legislature, 1970-72; advisor to Food Prices Rev. Bd. and Provincial Govts.; assoc. prof. agr. U. Sask., 1975-79; mem. legis. assembly for Esteva; leader Progressive Conservative Party of Sask., 1979; premier Province of Sask., 1982—, re-elected 1986—. Contbr. numerous articles to U.S. and Can. jours. Recipient Vanier award, 1983. Mem. Am. Econ. Assn., Am. Mktg. Assn., Am. Assn. Consumer Research, Canadian Agr. Econ. Soc. (recipient Cert. of Merit, Vanier award 1983), Consumers Assn. Can. Office: Sask Legis Assembly, Legislative Bldg, 2405 Legislative Dr, Regina, SK Canada S4S 0B3

DEVINE, JOSEPH ANTHONY, dentist; b. Cheyenne, Wyo., Apr. 22, 1927; s. John Aloysius and Mary Elizabeth (Campbell) D.; m. Mary Margaret Lynch, Dec. 27, 1952; children: Patrick, Joseph, Martha Ann, Paul, Vincent, Luke. BA, U. Wyo., 1948; DDS, Creighton U., 1952. Pvt. practice Cheyenne, 1952—; speaker in field. Contbr. numerous articels to profl. jours. Past chmn. Cheyenne Sch. Bd., Com. for Additional Water for the City of Cheyenne; rep. Wyo. Ho. Dels., 1965-79; mem. exec. com. Health Systems Agy.; chmn. statewide Heath Coordinating Coun.; mem. Regional Med. Program. With U.S. Army, 1946-47. Named Dentist of Year State of Wyo., 1975, Creighton U., 1985. Fellow Am. Coll. Dentists, Internat. Coll. Dentists; mem. Am. Dental Assn. (trustee 14th dist. 1979-85, 2d. v.p. 1974-75, pres.-elect 1985-86, pres. 1986-87), Elks, Rotary, Serra Internat. (dist. gov.), Alpha Epsilon Delta, Sigma Alpha Epsilon. Home and Office: 219 E 20th St Cheyenne WY 82001

DEVITT, JOHN LAWRENCE, consulting engineer; b. Denver, Sept. 27, 1925; s. Oliver Hinkley and Ellen Elizabeth (McPherson) D.; children: Jane, David, Ellen. BSEE, U. Colo., 1945, MS, 1949. Registered profl. engr., Colo. Engr. U.S. Bureau of Reclamation, Denver, 1947-50; plant mgr. AMF Corp., Colorado Springs, Colo., 1951-55; v.p., gen. mgr. Whittaker Corp. Power Sources div., Denver, 1955-61; chief engr. Metron Instrument Co., Denver, 1962-65; mgr. of electrochemistry Gates Corp., Denver, 1965-71; pvt. practice as a consulting engr. Denver, 1971—; profl. jazz musician (saxophone), Denver, 1946—. Co-inventor lead-chloride battery and sealed lead battery. Lt. USNR, 1943-52, PTO. Recipient Battery Research award, The Electrochem. Soc., 1986. Mem. The Electrochem. Soc., Am. Chem. Soc., Inst. Elect. and Electronic Engrs., Colo. Mountain Club (pres. 1975), Am. Alpine Club, New York. Office: Consulting Engineer 985 S Jersey St Denver CO 80224

DE VOE, MARCIA FRISBEE, retired teacher; b. Pacific Grove, Calif., Aug. 12, 1917; d. Roy William and Viola Cecil (Smith) Frisbee; m. Aug. 7, 1944 (dec. 1947). AB with honors, San Jose (Calif.) State U., 1939, also postgrad. Cert. primary and elem. tchr., Calif. Primary tchr. Monterey (Calif.) Unified Sch. Dist., 1939-45; substitute tchr. Davis (Calif.) Sch. Dist., 1945-47; primary tchr., audio visual cons. Carmel (Calif.) Unified Sch. Dist., 1947-75, cons., 1975-80, ret., 1980; chmn. ednl. adv. com. to gov. State of Calif., 1948-50. Author, photographer: Children of the World, 1960-65, The Martins and Hattons of Carmel Valley, 1979, Entrance to the Past, 1985. Recipient Vol. of Yr. award Old Monterey Preservation Soc., 1980, Community Svc. award Vols. in Action, 1894, Spl. Commendation award State of Calif., 1984. Mem. AAUW (pres. 1988–, State Recognition award 1981), DAR (Regent 1960), Delta Phi Upsilon (pres. Monterey Peninsula 1954), Delta Kappa Gamma (pres. Monterey 1960-62), Order of Eastern Star. Republican. Episcopalian.

DE VORE, ZETH BLEVENS, teacher; b. Oakland, Calif., 1931; B.A. in Edn., San Francisco State U., 1951, M.A. in Spl. Edn., 1964; married; 3 children. Tchr. trainable mentally retarded Kailua (Hawaii) schs., 1966-69; tchr. educationally handicapped Rich-Mar Sch. Dist., San Marcos, Calif., 1969—, now dist. spl. edn. adminstr. Mem. NEA, Council Exceptional Children (pres. N. County chpt. 1980-81), Am. Assn. Mental Deficiency, Calif., Rich-Mar (pres. 1974-76) tchrs. assns., Assn. Calif. Sch. Adminstrs. Office: 270 San Marcos Blvd San Marcos CA 92069

DE VOTO, TERENCE ALAN, radio station executive; b. San Francisco, Aug. 2, 1946; s. Albert Anthony and Virginia Louise (Kohnke) De V.; m. Christine McKannay, Jan. 24, 1976; children: Tommy, Mark, Julie, Carolyn. BBA in Mktg., Gonzaga U., 1968. V.p. trading Birr, Wilson & Co., San Francisco, 1968-74; account exec. Sta. KFOG Radio, San Francisco, 1974-78, Sta. KSFO Radio, San Francisco, 1978-81; nat. sales mgr. Sta. KYUU Radio, San Francisco, 1981-83, gen. sales mgr., 1983-84, gen. mgr., 1984-88; v.p. Fuller-Jeffrey Broadcasting, San Anselmo, Calif., 1989—. Bd. dirs. Marin Assn. for Retarded Citizens, 1988—. Mem. The Olympic Club, The Guardsmen. Republican. Roman Catholic. Home: 158 Prospect Ave San Anselmo CA 94960 Office: Sta KHTT/KSRO 627 College Ave Santa Rosa CA 95402

DE VRIES, KENNETH LAWRENCE, mechanical engineer, educator; b. Ogden, Utah, Oct. 27, 1933; s. Sam and Fern (Slater) DeV.; m. Kay M. DeVries, Mar. 1, 1959; children—Kenneth, Susan. A.B., Weber State Coll., 1953; B.S., U. Utah, 1959, Ph.D., 1962. With Convair, Fort Worth, 1957; mem. faculty U. Utah, Salt Lake City, 1961—; prof. mech. engring. U. Utah, 1969-76, prof. dept. mech. and indsl. engring., 1976—, chmn. dept., 1970-81, assoc. dean research Coll. Engring., 1983—; head polymer program NSF, 1975-76; mem. Utah Council Sci. and Tech., 1973-77. Author: Analysis and Testing of Adhesive Bonds, 1977; contbr. more than 200 articles on polymers, dental materials, rock mechanics, adhesive design to profl. jours. Mem. ASME, Am. Phys. Soc., Internat. Soc. Dental Research, Am. Chem. Soc., ASTM, Material Soc. Mormon. Home: 1466 Penrose St Salt Lake City UT 84103 Office: U Utah 3008 Mech Engring Bldg Salt Lake City UT 84112

DEW, KATHI RATTIN, educator; b. Red Lodge, Mont., Dec. 20, 1950; d. Hugo and Leola Viola (Luoma) Rattin; m. Howard Byron Dew, May 24, 1986; children: Maggie, Susan. BA in Music Edn., Mont. State U., 1973, MEd, 1978; postgrad., Oreg. Coll. of Edn., 1978, 80, Portland State U., 1981-83. Cert. prin., tchr. Band dir. Butte (Mont.) Pub. Schs., 1973-77, Greater Albany (Oreg.) Pub. Schs., 1978-81; instr. windwood Linn Beton Community Coll., Albany, 1978-81; prin. Lincoln County Sch. Dist., Newport, Oreg., 1981-84, Corvallis (Oreg.) 509J Sch. Dist., 1984-87, Springfield (Oreg.) Sch. Dist., 1988—; presenter Oreg. State U. Edn. Dept., Corvallis, 1985, 87; facilitator-adminstr. Fullbright Tchr. Exchange, NW Region, 1986, 87. vol. Sweet Home Sch. Dist., Oreg., 1987-88, Dept. Human Resources Linn CIRVS, Sweet Home, 1987-88. Mem. Confederation Oreg. Sch. Adminstrs., Nat. Assn. for Elem. Prins., Oreg. Assn. for Elem. Prins., Assn. for Supervision and Curriculum Devel., NW Women in Edn. Adminstrn. Democrat. Home: 42933 Green River Dr Sweet Home OR 97386

DEW, WILLIAM WALDO, JR., bishop; b. Newport, Ky., Dec. 14, 1935; s. William Waldo and Thelma (Dittus) D.; m. Mae Marie Eggers, Jan. 5, 1958; children: Linda Dew-Hiersoux, William, Marilyn. BA, Union Coll., Barbourville, Ky., 1957; MDiv, Drew Theol. Sch., 1961. Ordained to ministry United Meth. Ch. as deacon, 1958, as elder, 1963. Pastor Springville (Calif.) United Meth. Ch., 1961-64, Lindsay (Calif.) United Meth. Ch., 1964-67, Meml. United Meth. Ch., Clovis, Calif., 1967-72, Epworth United Meth. Ch., Berkeley, Calif., 1972-79; dist. supt. Cen. Dist. Calif.-Nev. Annual Conf., Modesto, Calif., 1979-84; pastor San Ramon Valley United Meth. Ch., Alamo, Calif., 1984-88; bishop United Meth. Ch., Portland, Oreg., 1988—; lectr. Pacific Sch. Religion, Berkeley, 1976-79. Trustee Willamette U., Salem, Oreg., 1988—, Alaska Pacific U., Anchorage, 1988—. Paul Harris fellow Rotary Internat., 1988. Democrat. Office: United Meth Conf Ctr 1505 SW 18th Ave Portland OR 97201

DEWALL, KAREN MARIE, advertising executive; b. Phoenix, May 31, 1943; d. Merle C. and Agnes M. (Larson) Feller; m. Charles E. DeWall, Sept. 3, 1963 (div. Feb. 1988); 1 child, Leslie Karen. A.A., Phoenix Coll., 1969. Media buyer Wade Advt., Sacramento, 1964-66; media dir., Harwood Advt., Phoenix, 1967-71; co-owner, account exec. DeWall & Assocs. Advt. Co., 1971-87; dir. advt. Auto Media, Inc./Automotive Investment Group, Phoenix, 1987—; bd. dirs. Phoenix Festivals, Inc.; sustaining mem. Jr. League of Phoenix. Named Ad-2 Advt. Person of Yr., Phoenix, 1984. Mem. Am. Women in Radio and TV (achievement award 1986). Republican. Club: Phoenix Country. Home: 10847 N 11th St Phoenix AZ 85020 Office: Automotive Investment Group 1220 E Camelback Phoenix AZ 85014

DEWAR, JACQUELINE MICHELE, mathematics educator. d. James Martin and Dorothy Elizabeth Deveny; m. James A. Dewar; children: Jeremy, Margot. B, St. Louis U., 1968; M, U. So. Calif., 1970, PhD, 1973. Prof. math. Loyola Marymount U., Los Angeles, 1973—, chairperson dept. math, 1982-86. Co-author: Basic Mathematics for Calculus, 3d rev. edit., 1988; contbr. articles to profl. jours. Mem. Math. Sci. Interchange (co-founder), Assn. Women in Math. (council mem.), Math. Assn. Am., Nat. Council Tchrs. Math., Phi Beta Kappa. Office: Loyola Marymount U Dept Math Los Angeles CA 90045

DEWEESE, CYNTHIA MICHELLE, mineral company executive; b. St. Joseph, Mich., Dec. 7, 1943; d. Everett R. and Clarabelle L. (Metzger) Kunde; m. David L. Roter, Aug. 17, 1963 (div. Mar. 1970); m. Joe T. DeWeese, June 27, 1970; children: Michele, Matthew. BS in Geology, Mesa Coll., 1978. Reclamation specialist Nerco-Glenrock (Wyo.) Coal Co., 1981-86; permit and compliance specialist Nerco-Candelaria Mine, Hawthorne, Nev., 1986-88; compliance specialist, RMK project Meridian Minerals Co., Copperopolis, Calif., 1988—. Leader, trainer Girl Scouts Am., Casper, Wyo., 1982-86 (appeciation awards 1985, 86). Mem. Calif. Mining Assn. (environ. com.), GS Sharks Bicycling Club (race organizer 1987, 88). Home: 3510 Bow Dr Copperopolis CA 95228

DEWEESE, MALCOLM LESLIE, JR., social sciences educator; b. Moultrie, Ga., Nov. 11, 1935; s. Malcolm Leslie DeWeese Sr. and Mary Katherine (Harryman) Harper; m. Catherine Marie McGuern, Jan. 28, 1963 (div. 1984); 1 child, Abraham. AA, Valley Coll., 1957; BA cum laude, U. Ariz., 1965; PhD, U. Wash., 1973, MBA, 1979. Sr. research investigator Wash. State Hosp. Commn., Olympia, 1979-81; sci. systems programmer U. Wash., Seattle, 1981—; prin. investigator Prospective Reimbursement Program, Health and Human Services, Washington, 1979-81; cons. Geriatric Studies, Seattle, 1981—, Inst. on Aging, U. Hosp., Seattle, 1981-84; vis. faculty The Evergreen State Coll., Olympia, 1986—. Author: (software program) Electragrade, 1986; contbr. articles to profl. jours. Served with U.S. Army, 1958-60. Grantee U. Wash., 1970; Ford Found. fellow, 1965. Fellow Am. Math. Assn.; mem. Am. Econ. Assn., Nat. Assn. Bus. Economists, Nat. Econometric Assn., Medieval Acad. Am. Democrat. Roman Catholic. Home: 13739 1st Ave NW Seattle WA 98177 Office: U Wash Dept Speech Communication MS DL-15 Seattle WA 98105

DEWELL, JULIAN C., lawyer; b. San Antonio, Feb. 13, 1930; s. Julian and Hope (Correll) D.; m. Alice Jane Palmer, Aug. 28, 1954; children: Gwen A. (Dewell) Brown, Jane H., Laura M. BS, Trinity U., 1952; LLD, U. Wash., Seattle, 1957. Bar: Wash. 1957, Calif. 1958, U.S. Ct. of Appeals (9th cir.) 1958. Trial lawyer (anti trust) U.S. Dept. Justice, San Francisco, 1957-59; assoc. Howe, Davis, Riese & Jones, Seattle, 1959-63; ptnr. Anderson, Hunter, Dewell, Baker & Collins, Everett, Wash., 1963—. Freeholder City of Everett, Wash., 1966-67, mem. Growth Mgmt. Com., 1982; mem. bd. Everett (Wash.) Sch. Dist., 1966-71. Named to Law Sch. Honor Grad. Program, U.S. Dept. Justice, San Francisco, 1954. Fellow Am. Coll. Trial Lawyers; mem. ABA, Wash. Bar Assn. (disciplinary bd. 1974-77, bd. govs. 1980-83, advt. task force, 1985-86), Calif. Bar Assn. Democrat. Unitarian. Home: 609 Maulsby Ln Everett WA 98201 Office: Anderson Hunter Firm PO Box 5397 Everett WA 98206

DEWEY, DAVID LAWRENCE, banker, business consultant; b. Roswell, N.Mex., Feb. 13, 1952; s. Joseph H. Tydlaska and Dortha C. Dunlap. Student, Am. Inst. Banking, Dallas, 1973-75; BSJ Pub., Market Writing, Writers Inst. Am., Mamaroneck, N.Y., 1981; AA in Bus., N.Mex. State U., Alamogordo, 1985; cert. in computer ops., Banking Coll., Orlando, 1987. Ops. officer 1st Nat. Bank Alamogordo, 1971-77, v.p. ops., data processing officer & compliance, 1985—; bus. cons. Quik-Key Systems Inc., Alamogordo, 1978-84; chmn. bd. Quik-Key Systems Inc., Atlanta, 1978-84, Alamogordo, 1978-84; bus. mgr. Grindell & Rollins Ins. Inc., Alamogordo, 1984-85; bus. cons., 1977—; owner, mgr. 3 cos., Alamogordo, 1978-84. Freelance contbr. articles to newspapers; composer, You Walked Away with My Heart, 1978. Mem. President's Adv. Council, 1984-87. Mem. Broadcast Music Corp., Writers Guild Am. Home: 1803 Walker Rd Alamogordo NM 88310 Office: 1st Nat Bank Alamogordo 414 10th St Alamogordo NM 88310

DEWEY, MICHAEL LEE, wood technologist; b. Spokane, Wash., Nov. 9, 1944; s. Leland Sullivan and Lorraine Margaret (Kofmehl) D.; m. Beverly Jean Thompson, Dec. 30, 1967; children—Cheryl, Michelle, Marci, Monica. B.S. in Wood Tech., U. Idaho, 1968, B.S. in Chemistry, 1969; A.A. in Acctg., Mendocino Community Coll., 1980, A.A. in Bus. Adminstrn., 1980. Chemist, U.S. Plywood, Lebanon, Oreg., 1969-70; wood chemist Koppers Co., Orrville, Ohio, 1971-76; process engr. Masonite Co., Ukiah, Calif., 1976-79, sr. process engr., 1979-82, cost acct., fin. analyst, 1982-83, acctg. mgr., 1983—. Served with USNR, 1966-70. Mem. Am. Chem. Soc., Am. Mgmt. Assn., Forest Products Research Soc., Soc. Wood Sci. and Tech., Am. Legion, Alpha Phi Omega. Republican. Lodges: Elks (officer 1985—), Lions (Ukiah treas. 1986-88). Home: 650 Chablis Ct Ukiah CA 95482 Office: Masonite Co 300 Ford Rd Ukiah CA 95482

DEWHURST, WILLIAM GEORGE, psychiatrist, educator; b. Frosterley, Durham, Eng., Nov. 21, 1926; came to Can., 1969; s. William and Elspeth Leslie (Begg) D.; m. Margaret Dransfield, Sept. 17, 1960; children—Timothy Andrew, Susan Jane. B.A., Oxford U., Eng., 1947, B.M., B.Ch., 1950; MA, Oxford U., 1961; D.P.M. with distinction, London U., 1961. House physician, surgeon London Hosp., 1950-52, jr. registrar, registrar, 1954-58; registrar, sr. registrar Maudsley Hosp., London, 1958-62, cons. physician, 1965-69; lectr. Inst. Psychiatry, London, 1962-64, sr. lectr., 1965-69; assoc. prof. psychiatry U. Alta., Edmonton, Can., 1969-72, prof., 1972—, chmn. dept. psychiatry, 1975—, co-dir. Neurochem. Research Unit, 1979—, hon. prof. pharmacy and pharm. scis., 1979—, hon. prof. oncology, 1983—; cons. psychiatrist Royal Alexandra Hosp., Edmonton, Edmonton Gen. Hosp.; chmn. med. council Can. Test Com., 1977-79, Royal Coll. Test Com. in Psychiatry, 1971-80, examiner, 1975—, chmn. med. staff adv. bd., 1988—, pres. coun., 1988—, mem. hosp. planning com., 1988—, joint conf. coms. 1971, 80, 87—; mem. R.C. Rev. Com. Univ. Toronto, 1988. Co-editor: Neurobiology of Trace Amines, 1984, Pharmacotherapy of Affective Disorders, 1985; also conf. procs. Referee Nature, Can. Psychiat. Assn. Jour., Brit. Jour. Psychiatry; mem. editorial bd. Neuropsychobiology, Psychiat. Jour. U. Ottawa. Contbr. articles to profl. jours. Mem., chmn. Edmonton Psychiat. Services Steering Com., 1977-80; chmn. Edmonton Psychiat. Services Planning Com., 1985—; mem. Provincial Mental Health Adv. Council, 1973-79, Mental Health Research Com., 1973—, Edmonton Bd. Health, 1974-76, Can. Psychiat. Research Found., 1985—; bd. dirs. Friends of Schizophrenics, Ctr. Gerontology, Alta., Can. Psychiat. Research Found.; grant referee Health & Welfare Can., Med. Research Council Can., Ont. Mental Health Found., Man. Health Research Council, B.C. Health Research Found. Served to capt. Royal Army M.C., 1952-54, Hong Kong. Fellow Can. Coll. Neuropsychopharmacology (pres. 1982-84), Am. Psychopathol. Assn., Am. Coll. Psychiatrists, Am. Psychiat. Assn., Royal Coll. Psychiatrists, Royal Coll. Physicians and Surgeons Can. (nucleus speciality com. 1987—); mem. Alta. Psychiat. Assn. (pres. 1973-74), Can. Psychiat. Assn. (pres. 1983-84), Royal Coll. Physicians (clin. phamacelogy nucleus com. 1988—), Alta. Coll. Physicians and Surgeons, Alta. Med. Assn., AAAS, Am. Assn. Chmn. Depts. Psychiatry, Assn. for Acad. Psychiatry, Brit. Med. Assn., Can. Assn. Anglican. Club: Faculty (Alta.). Office: U Alberta, Dept Psychiatry, 1E7 44 Mackenzie Centre, 8440-112 St, Edmonton, AB Canada T6G 2B7

DEWITT, RICHARD JAMES, electrical engineer; b. Spokane, Wash., Nov. 20, 1946; s. Daniel Durward and Margaret Evelyn (Lane) DeW.; m. Roberta Raymond, Aug. 23, 1969; 1 child, Justin Colby. Student, Spokane Falls Community Coll., 1964-65; BSEE, Ariz. State U., 1975. Engring. aide Dynamic Sci., Phoenix, 1973-75; measurement engr. Los Alamos (N.Mex.) Nat. Lab., 1975-84, Boeing Aerospace, Seattle, 1984—. With USCG, 1966-70. Mem. Intrument Soc. Am. (scholarship 1974), Western Regional Strain Gage Com. (chmn. 1984-85, Jubilee award 1988), Sports Car Club Am. Office: Boeing Aerospace PO Box 3999 MS 86-12 Seattle WA 98124

DE WOODY, CHARLES, lawyer; b. Chgo., Oct. 18, 1914; s. Charles and Oneta (Ownby); student U. Fla., 1931-33, U. Mich., 1933-35, Columbia U., 1935-36, Western Res. U., 1936-38; m. Nancy Tremaine, June 15, 1940; children—Charles, Nancy. Office atty. Oglebay, Norton & Co., Cleve., 1939-43; ptnr. Arter, Hadden, Wykoff & Van Duzer, 1943-61; sole practice, 1961—; dir. Nat. Extruded Metal Products Co., Ferry Cap and Set Screw Co., Meteor Crater Enterprises, Inc.; gen. partner Bar-T-Bar Ranch, Mem. Am., Ohio, Cleve. bar assns., Cleve. Law Library Assn. Clubs: Rancho Santa Fe Tennis; Chagrin Valley Hunt (Gates Mills, Ohio). Home: El Mirador Box 1169 Rancho Santa Fe CA 92067

DEXHEIMER, HENRY PHILLIP, II, insurance agency executive; b. Dayton, Ohio, Sept. 16, 1925; s. Henry Phillip and Helene Francis (Veach) D.; BS in Commerce, U. So. Calif., 1952; children: James Phillip, Jana Helene; m. Maria DaGraca Fernandes, Nov. 21, 1988. Sales account exec. with various cos. and newspapers, 1946-51; broadcasting sales exec. Sta. KBIG, KTLA-TV, Los Angeles, 1952-58; broadcasting sales exec. Sta. KFXM, San Bernardino, Calif., 1956-57, pres., 1956-57; founder, owner, pres. Dexheimer Co., Los Angeles, 1958—. Served with inf. and adj. gen.'s dept. U.S. Army, 1943-46; PTO. Recipient Sammy award Los Angeles Sales Execs. Club, 1955; Silver Sales trophy Radio Advt. Bur. N.Y., 1955; named Agt. of Year, Los Angeles office Travelers Ins. Cos., 1978, 83-88, Nat. Agt. of Yr. Travelers Ins. Cos., 1983; Hal Parsons award, 1978, 83-88. C.L.U. Mem. Am. Soc. C.L.U.'s (nat. dir. Travelers chpt. 1972-73, 80-81), Am. Coll. Life Underwriters, Advt. Assn. West, Radio and TV Soc. Hollywood, Life Ins. and Trust Council Los Angeles, Los Angeles Life Underwriters Assn. (dir. 1963-65, v.p. 1967-69), Million Dollar Round Table (life, honor roll), World Affairs Council Los Angeles, Internat. Assn. Fin. Planners, Am. Art Council, Decorative Art Council of Los Angeles County Art Mus., Alpha Delta Sigma, Phi Kappa Tau. Republican. Presbyterian. Clubs: Town Hall (Los Angeles); Beverly Hills Men's (Calif.); Masons (32 degree), Shriners, Legion of Honor. Office: Dexheimer Co Marina Bus Ctr 13160 Mindanao Way Ste 222 Marina Del Rey CA 90292

DEXTER, KATHRYN LOUISE, interior designer, nutritionist; b. Sant Rosa, Calif., Nov. 6, 1949; d. Wilbur Edgar and Dorothe Dean (Haas) Hutchinson; m. James Riley Dexter, Dec. 18, 1972; children: Kimberly, Scott Riley. BS in Foods and Nutrition, Pacific Union U., 1971; MS in Nutrition, Loma Linda U., 1977; cert. interior design, U. Riverside, 1988. Pediatric dietitian Loma Linda (Calif.) U. Med. Ctr., 1972-78; cons. dietitian Inland Health Services, Riverside, Calif., 1973-75, Loma Linda, 1975-78; owner, mgr. Design by Dexter, Loma Linda, 1983—. Mem. Am. Dietetic Assn. (registered), Am. Soc. Interior Designers (allied), Loma Linda U. Nutrition Alumni Assn. (pres. 1978), Profl. Piecture Framers Assn. Republican. Adventist. Office: Design by Dexter 11185 Mountain View Ave Ste 157 Loma Linda CA 92354

DEXTER, RAYMOND ARTHUR, social services administrator; b. Hartford, Conn., Dec. 11, 1923; s. Lyman Arthur and Mona Vera (Major) D.; m. Kathleen Eleanor Ferguson, Aug. 8, 1975. BS, MS, MIT, 1947; EdD, Stanford U., 1962. Math. instr. Trinity Coll., Hartford, 1947-49; field officer Salvation Army, San Francisco, 1955-57, edn. officer, 1957-69; state commdr. Salvation Army, Honolulu, 1969-73; social svc. dir. Salvation Army, San Francisco, 1973-74; adminstr. Clitheroe Ctr. Salvation Army, Anchorage, 1977—; chaplain coord. Alyeska Pipeline Svc. Co., Fairbanks, Alaska, 1974-77; v.p. Alaska Alcohol Drug Abuse Cert. Bd., Anchorage, 1982-87; sec. State Manpower Devel. Com., Anchorage, 1979-82; active U. Alaska Annual Sch. of Addiction Studies Adv. Com., Anchorage, 1983—. Bd. dirs. Anchorage Opera, 1984—. Lt. U.S. Navy, 1942-46. Decorated Meritorious Service medal; named Administr. of Yr. Ctr. for Alcohol and Addiction Studies U. Alaska, 1987; Nat. Inst. Alcohol Abuse and Alcoholism grantee, 1988. Mem. Ret. Officers Assn., Reserve Officers Assn. (state chaplain 1985—), Substance Abuse Dirs. Assn. of Alaska (v.p. 1987—), Rotary, Sigma Xi. Democrat. Episcopalian. Home: 2440 Laird Cir Anchorage AK 99516 Office: Salvation Army Clitheroe Ctr PO Box 190567 Anchorage AK 99519-0567

DEXTER, THOMAS RAY, radio station executive; b. Denver, July 22, 1938; s. Ernest Ray and Lelia (Blevins) D.; m. Sharon Estelle Madison, Sept. 1, 1962 (div. Nov. 1976); children: Paul Thomas, John Thomas; m. Purificacion A. Mendoza, July 4, 1986. AA, Valley Coll., 1959; student, Calif. State U., Northridge, 1959-60, Don Martins, 1960-61, Bakersfield Coll., 1976-79; CPA, Becker CPA Review, 1984-85. CPA; lic. gen. operator's. Disc jockey, news reporter Sta. KZIP, Amarillo, Tex., 1966, Sta. KVOD, Albuquerque, 1966-67; various positions Wagenvoold Broadcasting Co., New Orleans, 1967-69; with news, prodn. depts. Sta. WTAN, Clearwater, Fla., 1969-71; disc jockey Sta. KVBM, Lancaster, Calif., 1971; dir. programming Sta. KCHJ, Delano, Calif., 1971—; tax preparer Benificial Fin., Delano, 1980; cons. Bloom & Co., Studio City, Calif., 1986, Melvin Crosby, Hollywood, Calif., 1987, James Lyles, Bakersfield, Calif., 1987, Brenner & Ianne, Hollywood, 1988, Stevens, Davidoo & Nenny, 1988, Hollander, Harrison, Freedman & Fine, 1988, Gross, Schlothaver & Co., 1989. Contbr. articles Contemporary Comedy mag., 1975. Bd. dir. Delano Wine and Harvest Festival, 1972; mem. Christian Outreach Ministries Inc. Mem. Filipino-Am. Soc. Tulare County (pres. 1984), Acad. Magical Arts. Home: PO Box 562 Delano CA 93216 Office: Sta KCHJ 16th and 112th Aves Delano CA 93216 also: Count on Us 13601 Ventura Blvd Sherman Oaks CA 91423

DEZA, WALTER ALEJANDRO, financial manager; b. Lima, Peru, Dec. 12, 1948; came to U.S., 1978; s. Jose Carlos and Maria Yolanda (Escobar) D.; m. Aida Lucia Salazar, Oct. 12, 1986. Student, Universidad Terenica Del Calla, Callao, Peru, 1968-72, Universidad Del Pacific, Lima, 1973-75. Mgr. rsch. dept. Quimica Del Pacifico, Lima, 1968-70; computer coord. Caracas (Venezuela) Secures La Union, 1970-71, Electro Lima, 1971-78; fin. mgr. Auto Circus, Inc., El Monte, Calif., 1978-81; gen. mgr. Baja Auto Sales, L.A., 1981-86; fin. mgr. Advance-Carnival Motors, L.A., 1986—. Roman Catholic. Home: 11012 Shaw St Alta Loma CA 91701

DHARANIPRAGADA, RAMALINGA MURTY, organic chemist; b. Vijayawada, India, Nov. 9, 1956; came to U.S., 1978; s. Late Viswanadha Sarma and Sesha Yamma Dharanipragada. BS, Andhra Loyola Coll., Vijayawada, 1975; MS, Indian Inst. Tech., Bombay, 1977; PhD in Organic Chemistry, W.Va. U., 1985. Teaching asst. W.Va. U., Morgantown, 1978-85, research assoc., 1985; postdoctoral chemist UCLA, 1985-87; research assoc. U. Ariz., Tucson, 1987—. Contbr. chpts. to books. Mem. Am. Chem. Soc. Home: 734 E Roger Rd Apt #213 Tucson AZ 85719 Office: U Ariz Dept Chemistry and Biochemistry Tucson AZ 85721

DHAWAN, GULSHAN KUMAR, chemical engineer; b. Rawalpindi, India, Oct. 30, 1944; came to Can., 1966; s. Ram Saran and Krishna (Khanna) D.; m. Rajni Kalra, Dec. 18, 1973; children: Anjli, Manisha, Sonali. BTech in Chem. Engring., India Inst. Tech., Delhi, 1966; MASc., Waterloo U., Ont., Can., 1968, PhD in Chem. Engring., 1972. Registered profl. engr. Research and devel. engr. Electrohome, Kitchener, Ont., Can., 1972-74, mgr. reverse osmosis, 1974-77; mgr. environ. systems Electrohome, Kitchener, Ont., Can., 1977-80; mktg. mgr. UOP Fluid Systems, San Diego, 1980-82, market devel. mgr., 1982-83; pres., owner Applied Membranes, Inc., San Diego, 1983—; cons. Nitto Denko, Santa Clara, Calif., 1984-85, Eastman Kodak, Rochester, N.Y., 1985—, Hydromation, Detroit, Mich., 1986—. Contbr. articles to profl. jours. Grantee Nat. Research Council, 1966, 68; postdoctoral fellow Nat. Research Council, 1972. Mem. Am. Inst. Chem. Engrs., Am. Chem. Soc., Water Quality Assn. Home: 13343 Bavarian Dr San Diego CA 92129 Office: Applied Membranes Inc 542 S Pacific St San Marcos CA 92069

DHRUV, HARISH RATILAL, textile chemist/colorist; b. Ahmedabad, India, Mar. 14, 1946; came to U.S., 1970, naturalized, 1978; s. Ratilal Chhaganial and Shantaben Hariprasad (Dave) D.; m. Kaumudini Vasudev Vyas, June 21, 1971; children: Nirav H., Niraj H. BS in Chemistry, St. Xavier's Coll., Gujarat U., India, 1966; diploma in textile chemistry, M.S. U., Baroda, India, 1967; BS in Textile Chemistry, Phila. Coll. Textiles and Sci., 1972. Trainee supr. Mafatlal Fine Mills, Ahmedabad, 1967-68; supr. Calico Mills, Ahmedabad, 1969-70; quality control and processing mgr. fashion prints U.S. Industries Co., Allentown, Pa., 1972-77; print supt., v.p. mfg. Pacific Fabric Printers, Vernon, Calif., 1977-80; owner textiles importing, converting and printing bus. South Pasadena, Calif., 1980—. Pres. India Assn. of Lehigh Valley, 1974, 75, 76. Recipient Bicentennial medal for pub. service to community City of Allentown, 1977. Mem. Am. Assn. Textile Chemists and Colorists, Am. Chem. Soc., Assn. Western Furniture Suppliers (sec.), West Coast Furniture Fabric Club (sec. 1984, treas. 1985, v.p. 1986, pres. 1987—), Bharatiya Cultural Soc. (pres. 1976). Democrat. Hindu. Home: 269 Saint Albans Ave South Pasadena CA 91030

DHUET, DAVID DARRELL, dental supply owner; b. Inglewood, Calif., Aug. 26, 1950; s. Claude Peter and Marilyn (D'arcey) D.; m. Nancy Katherine Early, Aug. 28, 1971. With Valley Dental Supply, Burbank, Calif., 1970—; ptnr. Valley Dental Supply, Burbank, 1987—. Office: Valley Dental Supply Inc 4211 W Magnolia Blvd Burbank CA 91505

DIACK, KAY, volunteer; b. L.A., July 31, 1949; d. George R. and Harriet H. (Harsh) D.; m. Joe Escamilla, June 1970 (div. 1975). Student, Ea. L.A. Jr. Coll., 1968-70; student, Cypress Community Coll., 1982-85. Vol. regional pub. relations coord. Youth For Understanding, Los Altos, Calif., 1980—; vol. Hayward (Calif.) Zucchini Festival, 1985—. Named Regional Vol. of Yr. Youth For Understanding, 1987. Democrat. Baptist. Home: 3355 Pennsylvania Ave #35 Fremont CA 94536

DIAL, EDWARD ANTHONY, educational administrator; b. San Jose, Calif., Feb. 8, 1947; s. Douglas E. and Helen (Flynn) D.; m. Taylora Jean Sullivan, Aug. 10, 1968; children: Lincoln Anthony, Wendria Jean, Toni Annette. BA, Cen. State U., Edmond, Okla., 1970; MA, Azusa Pacific U., 1975. Cert. elem. and secondary tchr., Calif. Tchr., chmn. drama dept. Western Christian High Sch., Covina, Calif., 1973-76; prin., athletic dir. Calvary Bapt. Schs., La Verne, Calif., 1976--. Deacon Bapt. Missionary Assn., 1974--. Mem. Express League (pres.), Assn. Christian Schs. (chmn. art festival). Republican. Home: 1060 Arroyo Park Dr Pomona CA 91768 Office: Calvary Bapt Ch 2990 Damien Ave La Verne CA 91750

DIAL, THOMAS FERRON, lawyer; b. Idaho Falls, Idaho, Feb. 9, 1938; s. Edwin Dial and Donna Pearl (Tyner) Eaton; m. Yvonne Mellies, June 18, 1961 (dec. Sept. 1980); children: Paul, Tamara; m. Cindy Lou Herring, Sept. 16, 1981 (div. Oct. 1988). BA, Idaho State U., 1964; JD, U. Idaho, 1967. Bar: Idaho 1967, U.S. Dist. Ct. Idaho 1967, U.S. Supreme Ct. 1967. Assoc. McDevitt & McDevitt, Pocatello, Idaho, 1967-68, Terrell, Green, Service & Gasser, Pocatello, 1968-71, 74-75; criminal magistrate 6th Dist. Bannock County, Pocatello, 1971-74; ptnr. Dial, Looze & May, Pocatello, 1975—. Contbr. articles to legal jours. County coord. Campaign Congressman Richard Stallings, 1986. Fellow Am. Acad. Family Lawyers; mem. 6th Dist. Bar Assn. (pres. 1976), Idaho Trial Lawyers Assn. (bd. govs. 1981-86), Elks. Democrat. Mormon. Office: Dial Looze & May 216 W Whitman St PO Box 370 Pocatello ID 83204

DIAMOND, JOHN ANTHONY, aeronautical engineer; b. Seattle, Mar. 12, 1964; s. Anthony John and Effie (Karavites) D. BSAA, U. Wash., 1987. Aeronautical engineer Boeing Aerospace, Kent, Wash., 1987—. Vol. worker King County Red Cross, Seattle, 1980-82. Mem. AIAA. Home: 19007 100th Ave NE #1 Bothell WA 98011

DIAMOND, JOSEF, lawyer; b. L.A., Mar. 6, 1907; s. Michael and Ruby (Shifrin) D.; m. Violett Diamond, Apr. 2, 1933 (dec. 1979); children: Joel, Diane Foreman; m. Ann Dulien, Jan. 12, 1981 (dec. 1984); m. Muriel Bach, 1986. B.B.A., U. Wash., 1929, J.D., 1931. Bar: Wash. 1931, U.S. Dist. Ct. (we. dist.) Wash. 1932, U.S. Ct. Appeals (9th cir.) 1934, U.S. Supreme Ct. 1944. Assoc. Caldwell & Lycette, Seattle, 1931-35; ptnr. Caldwell, Lycette & Diamond, 1935-45; ptnr. Lycette, Diamond & Sylvester, 1945-80, Diamond & Sylvester, 1980-82, of counsel, 1982-88; of counsel Short, Cressman & Burgess, 1988; chmn. bd. Diamond Parking Inc., Seattle, 1945-70; cons. various businesses. Bd. dirs. Am. Heart Assn., 1960; chmn. Wash. Heart Assn., 1962. Col. JAGC U.S. Army, World War II. Decorated Legion of Merit. Mem. Assn. Trial Lawyers Wash., Wash. Bar Assn., Seattle Bar Assn., The Beavers, Mil. Engrs. Soc., Wash. Athletic Club, Bellevue Athletic Club, Harbor Club, Seattle Yacht Club, Rainier Club, Columbia Tower Club.

DIAMOND, JUDY, museum administrator; b. San Francisco, Apr. 4, 1951; d. Bernard Lee and Ann (Landy) D.; m. Alan Brandon Bond, Aug. 24, 1986. BA, U. Calif., Santa Cruz, 1973; MA, U. Colo., 1976; PhD, U. Calif., Berkeley, 1980. Program dir., researcher The Exploratorium, San Francisco, 1978-86; dir. internat. environ. studies World Coll. West, Petaluma, Calif., 1982-87; dep. dir. pub. programs San Diego Nat. History Mus., 1987—; cons. exhibit design, research, evaluation Brookfield (Ill.) Zoo, 1987, Stanford Research Inst. Internat., Palo Alto, Calif., 1986-87, Calif. Acad. of Scis., San Francisco, 1986-87, Weizmann Inst., Rohovot, Israel, 1983; v.p. nat. conf. on nat. security and the environment, N.Y.C., 1982, Washington, 1984. Contbr. articles to profl. jours. Bd. trustees Dolphin Research Project, 1987—, Rainforest Action Project, 1987—, Friends of the Earth, 1984-85, Earth Island Inst., 1982—, pres., 1984-86. Regents fellow U. Calif., Berkeley, 1978-79, Smithsonian Chesapeake Bay Ctr. for Environ. Studies, 1981-82. Mem. Am. Assn. of Mus., Internat. Union for Conservation of Nature and Natural Resources (commn. on edn. 1981—). Office: San Diego Natural History Mus 1788 El Prado San Diego CA 92101

DIAMOND, MARIA SOPHIA, lawyer; b. Portland, Oreg., Aug. 29, 1958; d. Harry and Nitsa (Fotiou) D. BA in Eng. cum laude, U. Wash., 1980; JD, U. Puget Sound, 1983. Bar: Wash. 1983, U.S. Dist. Ct. (we. dist.) Wash. 1983, U.S. Ct. Appeals (9th cir.) 1985. Assoc. Levinson, Friedman, Vhugen, Duggan, Bland & Horowitz, Seattle, 1983—. Named to Nat. Order of the Barristers U. Puget Sound, 1983. Mem. ABA, Assn. Trial Lawyers Am., Wash. State Trial Lawyers Assn., Wash. Women Lawyers, Seattle-King County Bar Assn. (young lawyers sect., mem. com. legal problems disadvantaged 1984-86, legis. com. 1986—), Women's Fisheries Network, U. Wash. Alumni Assn., Alpha Gamma Delta Alumni Assn. Office: Levinson Friedman Vhugen Duggan Bland & Horowitz 1500 1 Union Sq Seattle WA 98101

DIAMOND, ROBERT FRANCIS, federal agency administrator; b. N.Y.C., Oct. 1, 1951; s. Francis Gerard and Evelyn Marie (Metz) D.; m. Evelyn Conty, Oct. 3, 1982; 1 child: Kevin Richard. BS, SUNY, Stony Brook, 1973; MBA, So. Ill. U., 1977. Personnel mgr. specialist U.S. Army Tng. Ctr., Ft. Dix, N.J., 1974-78; position classification specialist Chief Naval Ops., Washington, 1978-82; personnel mgmt. specialist European region Office Civilian Personnel Mgmt., London, 1982-86; supr. personnel mgmt. specialist Naval Aviation Depot, Alameda, Calif., 1986-88; position classification specialist Gen. Svcs. Adminstrn., San Francisco, 1988—. Mem. Classification and Compensation Soc., Beta Gamma Sigma. Democrat. Roman Catholic. Home: 2615 C San Jose Ave Alameda CA 94501

DIAMOND, ROBERT JOCKE, radiologist, real estate broker and developer; b. Passaic, N.J., Sept. 30, 1950; s. Morris and Harriet (Vogelbaum) D.; m. Aileen Frances Rankin, July 4, 1988; 1 child, Hunter Louis. BS, Tulane U., 1972; MD, SUNY, Bklyn., 1976; cert. fin. planning, UCLA, 1986. Lic. real estate broker, Calif. Radiologist, ptnr. Century City Pla. Radiology, L.A., 1984—; owner Diamond Agy. West, L.A., 1986—. Mem. Los Angeles County Med. Assn., L.A. Radiol. Soc. Office: Century City Pla Radiology 2080 Century Pk E Ste 104 Los Angeles CA 90067

DIAMOND, STEPHEN EARLE, investor, consultant, inventor; b. San Francisco, Dec. 2, 1944; s. Earl Conrad and Sally (Gonzales) D. Pvt. study music and drama, 1956-65; grad., Ft. Sam Houston (Tex.) Army Med. Sch., 1964. Exec. dir. Gondia Corp., San Francisco, 1973-76, exec. chmn., 1976-78; chief exec. officer G.C.I. C'ies, San Francisco, 1978-80, chief adminstrv. officer, 1980-85; owner S.E. Diamond Founds., San Francisco, 1985-86, S.E. Diamond Assn., San Francisco, 1986—. Patentee in field. Leader 5th Congl. dist. Strategic Def. Initiative; active Am. Inst. for Cancer Reseach, 1981—, Ronald Reagan Rep. Ctr., Washington, 1987, Stanford (Calif.) U. Library, 1987; state advisor U.S. Congl. adv. bd., Washington and San Francisco, 1983-86; hon. chmn. St. Mary's Hosp., San Francisco, 1988; friends San Francisco Symphony Orch., 1980—; founding mem. Am. Space Frontier Com., Falls Ch., 1984-86, Challenger Space Ctr., 1987—; sponser and producer Concerned Women for Am., 1984—. Recipient merit award Rep. Nat. Com., 1984, merit award Rep. Party, 1985, Achievement award United Inventors and Scientists, L.A., 1975. Mem. Nat. Small Bus. Assn., Lawyers Book Club, Nat. Taxpayers Union, Statue of Liberty and Ellis Island Found. (chartered), Presidential Task Force (pres. and chmn. 1983—), Clan Morrison Soc. (life), North Shore Animal League. Republican. Roman Catholic. Home: Oxford 248 San Francisco CA 94134 Office: Stephen Earle Diamond Assn PO Box 640238 San Francisco CA 94164-0238 also: PO Box 246 South Lake Tahoe CA 45705

DIAZ, RAMON VALERO, judge; b. Manila, Oct. 13, 1918; came to Guam, 1951; s. Vicente and Bibiana (Valero) D.; m. Josefina Dela Concepcion, July 3, 1945; children: Carlos, Marilu, Mariles, Maribel, Marilen, Maryann, Anthony, Vincent, Ramon, Maricar. PhB, U. St. Tomas, Manila, 1940, LLB, 1941; grad. U.S. Army J.A.G. Sch., 1945; Diploma Jud. Skills, Am. Acad. Jud. Edn., 1984. Bar: Philippines 1941, Guam 1956, U.S. Ct. Appeals (9th cir.) 1966, High Ct. of Trust Territories 1977, No. Marianas 1985. Assoc. Diokno Law Office, Manila, 1943-44; sole practice, Guam, 1960-80; judge Superior Ct. of Guam, Agana, 1980—; mem. U.S. Selective Service Bd. Appeals, Guam, 1950-62. Permanent deacon Roman Catholic Ch. Judge adv. Gen.'s Svc., Philippine Army, 1941-51. Mem. Am. Judges Assn., Nat. Council Juvenile and Family Ct. Judges, VFW. Survivor Bataan Death March, 1942. Home: 114 Manga Ct Dededo GU 96912 Office: Superior Ct Guam Judiciary Bldg Agana GU 96910 also: PO Box AR Agana GU 96910

DIAZ, SHARON, education administrator; b. Bakersfield, Calif., July 29, 1946; d. Karl C. and Mildred (Lunn) Clark; m. Luis F. Diaz, Oct. 19, 1968; children: Daniel, David. BS, San Jose State U., 1969; MS, U. Calif., San Francisco, 1973. Nurse Kaiser Found. Hosp., Redwood City, Calif., 1973-77; lectr. San Jose (Calif.) State Coll., 1969-70; nurse San Mateo (Calif.) County, 1971-72; instr. St. Francis Meml. Hosp., 1970-71; instr. Samuel Merritt Hosp. Sch. Nursing, Oakland, Calif., 1973-76, asst. dir., 1976-78, dir., 1978-84; founding pres. Samuel Merritt Coll., Oakland, 1984—; v.p. East Bay Area Health Edn. Ctr., Oakland, 1980-87. Mem. Nat. League for Nursing, Sigma Theta Tau. Office: Samuel Merrritt Coll 370 Hawthorne Ave Oakland CA 94609

DIAZ-AZCUY, ORLANDO, interior architectural designer; b. Pinar del Rio, Cuba, Apr. 28, 1939; came to U.S., 1962; s. Antonio Diaz-Acosta and Hortensia Azcuy-Garcia. BArch, Cath. U. Am., 1963; M Landscape Architecture, U. Calif., Berkeley, 1968; M City Planning, U. Calif., 1970; DFA (hon.), Internat. Fine Arts Coll., Miami, Fla., 1987. Designer Laurence Halprin & Assocs., San Francisco, 1969-70, Leo A. Daly Co., San Francisco, 1970-72; dir. design Environ. Planning & Rsch., San Francisco, 1972-76; design prin., v.p. Gensler & Assocs., Architects, San Francisco, 1976-87; designer, pres. Orlando Diaz-Azcuy Designs, Inc., San Francisco, 1987--; part-time instr. grad. sch. design Harvard U., Cambridge, Mass., 1986, 87, 88; lectr. various schs. and profl. orgns. Bd. dirs. U. Calif. Art Mus., Berkeley, 1977-80, Am. Conservatory Theatre, San Francisco, 1988—, Found. for Interior Design Edn. and Rsch., N.Y.C., 1987—. Recipient Star award Inst. Bus. Designers, 1987, also over 30 other design awards; named Designer of Yr. Interiors mag., 1982; inducted to Interior Design Hall of Fame Interior Design mag., 1988. Mem. San Francisco Opera Assn. (bd. dirs. 1988—). Republican. Roman Catholic. Home: 1050 Green St San Francisco CA 94133 Office: 305 Grant Ave 8th Fl San Francisco CA 94108

DIAZ BARCELONA, ISAAC ALFREDO, entertainer; b. Mexico City, June 24, 1949; came to U.S. 1966; s. Ramiro Sandoval Diaz Barcelona and Rebecca Cristina (Padilla) Garcia; divorced; children: Isaac L., Rebecca, Edward, D. Ryan-Shawn; m. Shawny Barcelona, 1988. PhD, Dr. Clark Wilkerson Inst., Los Angeles and Honolulu, 1970, D of Hypnosis, 1971, D of Metaphysics, 1972. Producer, singer, songwriter, guitarist, actor U.S., Can., Mex., S.Am., 1970—. Author: Dressings on the Sculpture, 1987, In My Words, Things We Crave, 1987, Songs fro the Gypsy, 1988, Reflection: Love is Us-You and I, 1988, Messages from the Soul, 1988, Time and Pain-Why?, 1988, The Beast, 1988. Mem. Am. Fedn. Musicians. Home and Office: 14066 Van Nuys Blvd #9 Arleta CA 91331

DIBARTOLOMEO, JOSEPH RAYMOND, otolaryngologist; b. N.Y.C., Aug. 31, 1937; s. Antoinette (Dionisio) DiB.; children: Phillip, David, Raymond. BS, St. John's U., Jamaica, N.Y., 1959; MD, Georgetown U., Washington, 1963. Diplomate Am. Bd. Otolaryngology, Nat. Bd. Med. Examiners. Intern Waterbury (Conn.) Hosp., 1963-64, resident gen. surgery, 1964-65; resident otolaryngology NYU-Bellevue Med. Ctr., 1965-68; med. dir. Ear Found., Santa Barbara, Calif., 1979—; chief of staff St. Francis Hosp., Santa Barbara, Calif., 1985, 86. Contbr. articles to profl. publs. With U.S. Army, 1955-63. Recipient Tchr.'s award UCLA, 1979, Honor award Am. Acad. Otolaryngology-Head and Neck Surgery, 1986. Fellow Triological Soc. (sec. western sect. 1982-86), Am. Coll. Surgeons. Office: 2420 Castillo St #100 Santa Barbara CA 93105-4302

DI BLASI, ROBERT JOSEPH, obstetrician, gynecologist; b. Bklyn., Mar. 8, 1939; s. Joseph and Ruth (Schnur) Di B.; m. Mariangela Gramegna, July 23, 1967; children: Joseph, Jonathan. BS, St. John's U., 1961; MD, U. Studi, Bologna, Italy, 1967. Intern Grasslands Hosp., Valhalla, N.Y., 1968-69; resident in ob-gyn Tripler Army Med. Ctr., Honolulu, 1972-75; HMO practice Santa Clara, Calif., 1978—; med. dir. Body Focus, Watsonville, Calif., 1985—. Lt. col. M.C., U.S. Army, 1969-78, col. active res., 1978—. Mem. Am. Coll. Sports Medicine, Shufelt Gynecologic Soc., Assn. Mil. Surgeons U.S. (life), Calif. Med. Assn., Santa Clara County Med. Soc., Am. Med. Athletic Assn., Res. Officers Assn. Democrat. Roman Catholic. Home: 697 Bicknell Rd Los Gatos CA 95030 Office: Permanente Med Group 900 Kiely Blvd Santa Clara CA 95051-5386

DI BONA, TONY PASQUALINO, corporate professional; b. Sydney, Australia, Nov. 15, 1961; came to U.S., 1985; s. Costanzo and Irene (Firmin) Di B.; m. Julie Ann Myers, Sept. 3, 1989. B in Econs., Sydney U., 1982. Cert. acct., Australia. Acct. Dick Smith Electronics Pty, Ltd., Sydney, 1982-84; controller Dick Smith Electronics Pty, Ltd., Auckland, New Zealand, 1984-85; chief fin. officer Dick Smith Electronics, Inc., Redwood City, Calif., 1985-87; pres. and chief exec. officer Practical Software, Inc., Redwood City, 1987-88; chief fin. officer Asset Mgmt. Co., Palo Alto, Calif., 1988—; chmn. Practical Software, Inc., Redwood City, 1988—; cons. Australian Telephone Co., Sydney, 1987—. Author: (software) BANKREC, 1987. Mem. (assoc.) Australian Soc. Accts. Home: 524 Scott Ave Redwood City CA 94063 Office: Asset Mgmt Co 2275 E Bayshore Rd 150 Palo Alto CA 94303

DICK, NANCY E., former lieutenant governor; b. Detroit, July 22, 1930; divorced; children: Margot, Timber, Justin. BA in Hotel Mgmt., Mich. State U.; law student, U. Denver. Worked in resort mgmt., interior desig; mem. Colo. Gen. Assembly, 1974-79; lt. gov. State of Colo., 1979-86; fin. chmn. Fedn. Rocky Mountain States; del. Nat. Democratic Party Conv., 1980; exec. bd. Gov's. Interstate Indian Council, 1981-83; chmn. regional selection White House Fellows, 1981, panelist, 1979-80; chmn. Colorado-Hunan (People's Republic China) Indsl. Conf. Planning Com.; del. Women's Leadership Conf. on Nat. Security. Candidate U.S. Senate, 1983; trustee Denver Symphony Assn.; hon. chmn. Friends of the Urban League; mem. rural health com. Colo. Med. Soc., 1975-76; exec. bd. U.S. Army War Coll., 1981, USAF War Coll., 1984. Recipient Disting. Alumni award Mich. State U., 1980; recipient Florence Sabin award Colo. Pub. Health Care Assn., 1980, Outstanding Alumnus award Coll. Bus., Mich. State U., 1981, Outstanding Citizen Nat. Rural Primary Care Assn., 1981, Found. scholarship Nat. Ctr. Creative Leadership, 1981, 83. Democrat.

DICK, STEPHEN LEWIS, industrial engineer; b. Denver, Mar. 17, 1951; s. Gerald Myton Dick and Martha (Fox) Bones; m. Lisbeth Diane Farlow, Aug. 19, 1972; children: Matthew Stephen, Gregory Michael, Rachael Lisbeth. BSIE, Purdue U., 1973; MBA, Mich. State U., 1979. Assoc. engr. Oldsmobile div. GM, Lansing, Mich., 1974-75, engr., 1975-77, sr. engr., 1977-79; chief engr. Automotive Tech., Madison Heights, Mich., 1979-81; indsl. mktg. cons. Auto-Trol Tech. Corp., Denver, 1981-82, mgr. tech. support, 1982-85, nat. systems engring. mgr., 1985-86, dir. R & D, 1986—. Coach Am. Youth Soccer Orgn., Sterling Heights, Mich., 1980, Northglen (Colo.) Soccer, 1984—; bd. dirs. North Area Soccer Assn., Thornton, Colo., 1983-84; jr. warden Ch. of Ascension, Denver, 1988—. Republican. Episcopalian. Home: 2636 W 119th Ave Westminster CO 80234 Office: Auto-Trol Tech Corp 12500 N Washington St Denver CO 80233

DICKENSON, ROWENA JEAN, placement coordinator; b. Butte, Mont., Aug. 25, 1949; d. Richard O. and Rowena (Gaffney) D.; m. Gerard R. Vercella, Sept. 22, 1969 (div. Oct. 1975); children: Gerard J., Christina J.; m. Gerald F. Williams, June 4, 1983 (div. Mar. 1988). AA, Mont. Coll. Mineral Sci. & Technology, 1984, BS, 1986. Gen. ledger bookkeeper First Bank Butte, 1975-85; adminstrv. asst. Office of Gov. Mont., Helena, Mont., 1985; admissions counselor Mont. Coll. of Mineral Sci. & Technology, Butte, 1986-88; placement coordinator Career Futures, Inc., Butte, 1988—. Publicist, bd. dirs. Am. Assn. Univ. Women, Butte, 1987-88;. Mem. Nat. Assn. Coll. Admissions Counselors, Butte C. of C., Am. Assn. Univ. Women. Democrat. Methodist. Home: 1117 Farrell Butte MT 59701 Office: Career Futures Inc 300 Metals Bank Bldg Butte MT 59701

DICKER, KIANA, photographer, magazine editor; b. London. Student, Salisbury Coll. Art. Owner, mgr. Kiana Photography, Phoenix, 1984—; mng. editor Ariz. Living mag., Phoenix, 1987--. Publicist Ariz. Women's Caucus for Art, 1985--. Mem. Women in Design, Ariz. Authors Assn., Women in Communications. Home and Studio: PO Box 8628 Phoenix AZ 85066

DICKERSON, BARBARA ANN RANSOM, educator, consultant; b. Jackson, Miss., Apr. 18, 1952; d. Jimmie Lee and Marie Eunice (West) Ransom; m. Mark Steven Dickerson, Dec. 30, 1978; children: Amber Tiffany, Christopher Ryan. BS, Grand Canyon Coll., 1974; MA, Ariz. State U., 1976, PhD, 1987. Tchr. Pendergast Elem. Dist., Tolleson, Ariz., 1974-76; reading clin. S. Mountain High Sch. Dist., Phoenix, 1976-80; instr. High Sch. Drop Out Program, Phoenix, 1978, Mesa (Ariz.) Community Coll., 1978; reading specialist Deer Valley Sch. Dist., Phoenix, 1980-82; asst. dir. Honors Coll. Ariz. State U., Tempe, 1984-87, asst. prof. edn., 1988—; faculty mem. Grand Canyon Coll., Phoenix, 1987-88; cons. Rising Star, Phoenix, 1987—. Pres. Valley Christian Ctrs., Phoenix, 1984—; youth instr. First Bapt. Ch., Phoenix, 1987-88; active Foster Care Review Bd., Ariz., Ariz. Adoption Spl. Kids. Greater Phoenix Area Writing Project fellow, 1979. Mem. Ariz. Tchrs. of Reading, Ariz. English Tchrs. Assn., Assn. for Curriculum and Devel., Delta Sigma Theta (sec., v.p. 1977—). Democrat. Home: 8533 N 50th Pl Paradise Valley AZ 85253 Office: Ariz State U W PO Box 37100 Phoenix AZ 85069-7100

DICKERSON, LON RICHARD, library administrator; b. Ypsilanti, Mich., Dec. 16, 1941; s. Lon E. and Maxine A. (Merryfield) D.; m. Anne Elizabeth Bryan, Aug. 24, 1968; children: Robert Lon, Sarah Elizabeth, Peter Bryan. AB, Albion Coll., 1964; MLS, U. Pitts., 1968. Dir. U. Liberia Librs., Monrovia, 1968-72, Lake Agassiz Regional Libr., Moorhead, Minn., 1972-85, Timberland Regional Libr., Olympia, Wash., 1985—; pres. Adv. Council to State Libr., Minn., 1977-78, No. Lights Libr. Network Adv. Council, Minn., 1981-82. Contbr. articles to profl. jours. Mem. planning commn. City of Lacey, Wash., 1985—; mem. various sch. dist. coms.; bd. dirs. Clay-Wilkin Opportunity Council, Moorhead, 1982-85. Mem. ALA (internat. rels. com. 1974-75), Pacific N.W. Libr. Assn., Wash. State Libr. Assn. (co-chmn. legis. planning com. 1987—; recipient Pres.'s award 1988), Tau Kappa Epsilon. Democrat. Congregationalist. Home: 5608 32d Ct SE Lacey WA 98503 Office: Timberland Regional Libr Office of Dir 415 Airdustrial Way SW Olympia WA 98501

DICKERSON, MICHAEL BRYANT, small business operator; b. Lexington, Tenn., Aug. 18, 1953; s. Dycus Bryant and Nancy F. (Fesmeyer) D.; m. Deanna Claypool, Aug. 20, 1976; 1 child, Whitney A. MA in Polit. Sci., Memphis State U., 1978. Mgr Budget Rent-A-Car Memphis, 1973-79, asst. city mgr., 1979-80; spl. projects mgr. Budget Rent-A-Car Corp., Memphis and Tulsa, 1980-81; airport operation dir. Budget Rent-A-Car Denver, 1981-82, bus. devel. dir., 1982-84; gen. mgr. Budget Rent-A-Car Tucson, 1984-85; city mgr. Thrifty Rent-A-Car, Phoenix, 1985-86; ptnr. A.I. So. Ariz., Tucson, 1986-88; owner Advantage Rent-A-Car Systems, Inc., Tucson, 1988--; mgr. RPM Rent-A-Car Systems, Tucson, 1988--; dist. mgr. Rent -a-Car System, So. Ariz., N.Mex., Colo., Utha, 1989—. Mem. Mem. SKAL Internat., Tucson Conv. and Visitors Bur., Tucson C. of C., Am. Car Rental Assn., So. Ariz. Innkeeper Assn., Tues. Morning Breakfast Club, Rotary. Democrat. Home: 7677 E Sabino Vista Dr Tucson AZ 85715 Office: RPM Rent A Car Systems 6360 S Tucson Blvd Tucson AZ 85706

DICKERSON, WILLIAM ROY, lawyer; b. Uniontown, Ky., Feb. 15, 1928; s. Banjamin Franklin and Honor Mae (Staples) D. BA in Acctg., Calif. State U., 1952; JD, UCLA, 1958. Bar: Calif. 1959. Dep. atty., ex-officio city prosecutor City of Glendale, Calif., 1959-62; assoc. James Brewer, Los Angeles, 1962-68, LaFollette, Johnson, Schroeter & DeHaas, Los Angeles, 1968-73; sole practice, Los Angeles, 1973—; arbitrator Los Angeles Superior Ct; judge pro tem Los Angeles Mcpl. Ct., Small Claims Ct., Traffic Ct.; lectr. and speaker in field. Bd. dirs. LosFeliz Improvement Assn., 1986-88, Zoning Commn.; co-chmn. Streets and Hwys. Commn. Mem. ABA, Calif. Bar Assn., Los Angeles County Bar Assn., Soc. Calif. Accts., Fed. Bar Assn., Am. Film Inst., Internat. Platform Assn. Home and Office: 813 N Doheny Dr Beverly Hills CA 90210

DICKEY, ROBERT MARVIN (RICK DICKEY), property manager; b. Charleston, S.C., Dec. 3, 1950; s. John Lincoln II and Ruth (Marvin) D.; m. Teresa Ann Curry, Dec. 19, 1969 (div. 1979); 1 child, Gena Lynette. A of Computer Sci., USMC Degree Program, Washington, 1975. Enlisted USMC, 1968, advanced through grades to staff sgt., 1968-78; shop mgr., bookkeeper Amalgamated Plant Co., Las Vegas, Nev., 1978-79; supr. constrn. Joseph Yousem Co., Las Vegas, 1979-80; apt. mgr. Robert A. McNeil Corp., Las Vegas, 1980, comml. bldg. mgr., leasing agt., 1980-82; asst. v.p., regional property mgr. Westminster Co., Las Vegas, 1982-87, Weyerhaeuser Mortgage Co., Las Vegas, 1988-89; pres., ptnr. Equinox Devel., Inc., Las Vegas, 1989—. Contbr. articles to profl. jours. Mem. Inst. of Real Estate Mgmt. (legis. chmn. 1987-88, ARM of Yr. award 1985, 86), Nev. Apt. Assn. (v.p. 1985, pres. 1988—, bd. dirs.), So. Nev. Homebuilders Assn., Las Vegas Bd. of Realtors (mgmt. legis. com. 1988). Office: Equinox Devel Inc 501 S Rancho Dr Ste D-21 Las Vegas NV 89106-4828

DICKINSON, GARY LEE, periodontist; b. Bedford, Ind., May 7, 1944; s. Robert A. and Maxine (Miller) D.; m. Laura Lynn Snyder, June 8, 1978; children: John Robert, Maria Louise. DDS, Ind. U., 1969; cert. in periodontology, U. Iowa, 1980. Diplomate Am. Bd. Periodontology. Pvt. gen. dentistry Ind., 1973-78; resident in periodontology U. Iowa, Iowa City, 1978-80; pvt. practice dentistry specializing in periodontics Albuquerque, 1980—. Maj. U.S. Army, 1979-83. Mem. ADA, Acad. Periodontology, N.Mex. Dental Assn., U.S. Chess Fedn., Tanoan Country. Republican. Roman Catholic. Office: 7123 Prospect Pl NE Albuquerque NM 87110

DICKINSON, MARION DORA, nurse, midwife; b. Shoshoni, Wyo., June 13, 1936; d. Bill H. and Pearl Loretta (Allen) Todd; m. James Allen Dickinson, Sept. 1, 1956 (div. July 1973); children: Thomas, Casey, Bill, Albert. AS, Casper Coll., 1956; A in Nursing, No. Ariz. U., 1970; cert. nurse midwife, U. Miss., 1983. Nurse Marcus Lawrence Hosp., Cottonwood, Ariz., 1970-76, Mohave Gen. Hosp., Kingman, Ariz., 1976-82; nurse midwife Planned Parenthood, Tempe, Ariz., 1983-84, Indian Health Services, Tuba City, Ariz., 1984—. Mem. Am. Coll. Nurse Midwives. Republican. Pentecostal. Home: Box 3054 Tuba City AZ 86045 Office: Indian Health Svc Tuba City AZ 86045

DICKINSON, ROBERT EARL, atmospheric scientist, administrator; b. Millersburg, Ohio, Mar. 26, 1940; s. Leonard Earl and Carmen L. (Ostby) D.; m. Nancy Mary Mielinis, Jan. 5, 1974. AB in Chemistry and Physics, Harvard U., 1961; MS in Meteorology, MIT, 1962, PhD in Meteorology, 1966. Research assoc. MIT, Cambridge, 1966-68; scientist Nat. Ctr. Atmospheric Research, Boulder, Colo., 1968-73, sr. scientist, 1973—, head climate sect., 1975-81, dep. dir. A.A.P. div., 1981-86, acting dir., 1986-87; mem. climate research com. NRC, Washington, 1985—, chmn. 1987—, com. earth sci., 1985-88, UNU steering com. Climatic, Biotic and Human Interactions in Humid Tropics, 1984—, steering com. Internat. Satellite Land Surface Climatology project, 1984-89. Editor: The Geophysiology of Amazonia, 1986; contbr. articles to profl. jours. Fellow AAAS, NAS, Am. Meteorol. Soc. (Jule Charney award 1987, chmn. com. biometeorol. and aerobiol. 1987—, Meisinger award 1973, Editors award 1976), Am. Geophys. Union (com. earth as a system 1986—); mem. AAS, Assn. Meteorol. and Atmospheric Physics (sec. climate commn. 1983-87), U.S. Nat. Acad. Scis., 1988—. Democrat. Home: 2835 Iliff St Boulder CO 80303 Office: Nat Ctr Atmospheric Rsch PO Box 3000 Boulder CO 80307

DICKINSON, ROBERT VANCE, computer company executive; b. Susanville, Calif., Nov. 16, 1941; s. Fred Eugene and Doris Elida (Vance) D.; m. Janet Lucy Mayfield, July 17, 1965 (div. Apr. 1975); m. Sylvia Olivia Avenente, May 17, 1975; 1 child Lauren Elissa. AB in Physics, U. Calif., Berkeley, 1963; MS in Physics, U. Wash., 1964. Dir. engring. Singer Co., San Leandro, Calif., 1964-75; dir. product mgmt. TRW Inc., L.A., 1976-78; v.p. engring. Systems Devel. Corp., L.A., 1978-80; v.p., gen. mgr. Burroughs Corp., Danbury, Conn., 1981-83, Zilog Inc., Campbell, Calif., 1983; pres., chief exec. officer Mouse Systems Corp., Santa Clara, Calif., 1984-86, Verticom Inc., Sunnyvale, Calif., 1987-88; v.p., gen. mgr. Computer Graphics, Western Digital Corp., Mountain View, Calif., 1989—. Contbr. articles to profl. jours.; inventor in field. Sloan Found. fellow Stanford (Calif.) U. Sch. Bus., 1972-73. Mem. IEEE, AAAS, Stanford Bus. Sch. Alumni Assn. Republican. Club: Ladera Oaks Country, Ladera Oaks Swim and Tennis. Office: Western Digital Corp 800 E Middlefield Rd Mountain View CA 94303

DICKINSON, THOMAS EDWARD, university dean, agriculture educator; b. Madison, Wis., Dec. 19, 1943; s. Fred Eugene and Doris Elida (Vance) D.; m. Roberta Ann Peery, Aug. 22, 1965; children: Sasha Ann, Georgia Peach. BS, U. Calif., Davis, 1966; PhD, Mich. State U., 1971. Asst. prof. U. Calif., Davis, 1970-75; assoc. prof. Calif. State U., Chico, 1975-80, prof. agr., 1980-88, assoc. dean Coll. Agr. and Home Econs., 1988—; vis. prof. Lincoln Coll., New Zealand, 1985; project dir. spl. study Calif. Coastal Zone Commn., Santa Barbara, 1976; project leader soils program Calif. Dept. Conservation, Sacramento, 1979; exec. dir. Bolivian Project U.S. AID, 1988. Co-author several chpts. in books including Social Impact Analysis, 1977; contbr. articles, monographs to profl. jours.; editor 2 conf. proceedings. Mem. Am. Agrl. Econs. Assn., Western Agrl. Econs. Assn. (Calif. rep. 1986-89), Chico Aqua Jets Orgn. (treas. 1982-84). Office: Calif State U Coll Agrl and Home Econs Chico CA 95929-0440

DICKS, HAL TRENT, architect; b. Billings, Mont., June 27, 1952; s. Emet L. and Pearl C. (Webb) D. BArch Engring., U. Wyo., 1974. Registered architect, Wyo. Archtl. apprentice George W. Tresler & Assocs., Cody, Wyo., 1974-80, architect, 1980-82; architect, ptnr. Tresler & Dicks Architects, Cody, 1982-85, architect, owner, 1985-86; architect, owner Tresler & Dicks Architects, Powell, Wyo., 1986—. Recipient Human Relations award Dale Carnegie & Assocs., 1988. Mem. AIA, Powell Valley C. of C. (bd. dirs., econ. devel. com. mem. 1988), Cody County C. of C. Clubs: Big Horn Foxtrotter Assn., Foxy Trotters 4-H, Big Horn Basin Singles Assn. Office: Tresler & Dicks Architects PO Box 1299 Powell WY 82435

DICKS, JOYCE CAROLEE, adult education administrator; b. Centerville, Iowa, Mar. 21, 1936; d. Max Arlee and Laura Jean (Oehler) Martin; m. Donald Dean Dicks, May 5, 1955; children: Stephanie Lynn Dicks Hall, Dawn Michelle. AA in Social Sci., Ohlone Coll., Fremont, Calif., 1978; BA in History, Calif. State U., Hayward, 1980, MA, 1984; Adminstrv. credential, San Jose State U., 1987. Instrnl. aide GATE program Fremont Unified Schs., 1972-77; instr. social scis. Fremont Adult Edn., 1980-88; instr. history Ohlone Coll., 1982—, DeAnza Coll., Cupertino, Calif., 1986-88; asst. dir. East Side Adult Edn. Program, San Jose, Calif., 1988—; lectr. Ottawa (Kans.) U., 1979-80; cons. Calif. Adult Schs. Assessment System Task Force, Sacramento, 1987—. Founding editor The Student Historian, Calif. State U., 1981; reviewer The Pacific Historian mag., Stockton, Calif., 1984—; author, narrator several video study programs. Active Fremont PTA, 1970-76; founding pres. Parents of Gifted Children, Fremont, 1975; charter mem. Ohlone Coll. Mus. Com., 1978—. Mem. Assn. Calif. Sch. Adminstrs., Calif. Council for Adult Edn., Orgn. Am. Historians, Inst. Hist. Study, Washington Twp. (Calif.) Hist. Soc. Home: 4641 Boone Dr Fremont CA 94538 Office: East Side Adult Edn Program 625 Educational Park Dr San Jose CA 95133

DICKS, NORMAN DE VALOIS, congressman; b. Bremerton, Wash., Dec. 16, 1940; s. Horace D. and Eileen Cora D.; m. Suzanne Callison, Aug. 25, 1967; children: David, Ryan. BA, U. Wash., 1963, JD, 1968; LLD (hon.), Gonzaga U., 1987. Bar: Wash. 1968, D.C. Salesman, Boise Cascade Corp., Seattle, 1963; labor negotiator Kaiser Aluminum Co., Seattle, 1964; legis. asst. to Senator Warren Magnuson of Wash., 1968-73, adminstrv. asst., 1973-76; mem. 95th-101st Congresses from 6th Wash. Dist., mem. appropriations com., interior, mil. constrn., def. subcoms., House appointed observer to U.S.-Soviet arms control talks, 1985-89. Mem. U. Wash. Alumni Assn., Sigma Nu. Democrat. Lutheran. Office: US Ho Reps 2429 Rayburn House Office Bldg Washington DC 20515

DICKSON, PAUL WESLEY, JR., physicist; b. Sharon, Pa., Sept. 14, 1931; s. Paul Wesley and Elizabeth Ella (Trevethan) D.; m. Eleanor Ann Dunning, Nov. 17, 1952; children: Gretchen Ann, Heather Elizabeth, Paul Wesley. BS in Metall. Engring., U. Ariz., 1954, MS, 1954; PhD in Physics, N.C. State U., 1962. With Westinghouse Electric Corp., Large, Pa., 1963-84, mgr. weapon systems, 1965-68, mgr. advanced projects, 1969-72, mgr. reactor analysis and core design, Madison, Pa., 1972-79, tech. dir., Oak Ridge, 1979-84; with EG & G Idaho, Idaho Falls, 1984—, mgr. new tech. devel., 1984-87, reactor projects and programs, 1987—; mem. adv. com. on advanced propulsion systems NASA, Washington, 1970-72; mem. adv. com. reactor physics AEC/Dept. Energy, 1974-79; mem. rev. com. applied physics Argonne (Ill.) Nat. Lab., 1978-83, chmn., 1980; mem. rev. com. engring. physics Oak Ridge Nat. Lab., 1982-86, chmn. 1986; mem. sci. and tech. adv. com. Argonne Nat. Lab., 1985—. Contbr. numerous sci. articles to profl. publs. Capt. USAF, 1955-63. Fellow Am. Nuclear Soc.; mem. Am. Phys. Soc., N.Y. Acad. Scis., AIME , AAAS, Scabbord and Blade, Sigma Xi, Phi Kappa Phi, Tau Beta Pi, Phi Lambda Upsilon, Sigma Pi Sigma. Republican. Methodist. Subspecialties: Nuclear fission; Nuclear engineering. Current work: Nuclear reactor development.

DICKSTEIN, SIMONE ANDREA, commercial and industrial practice consultant; b. Washington, Jan. 9, 1957; d. Aaron Gilbert and Ruth Gladys (Berman) Saidman; m. Matthew Howard Dickstein, Oct. 17, 1987. BSBA cum laude, Tulane U., 1979; MBA, N.Y. U., 1984. Mgr. gobal investment bank Citicorp, Inc., N.Y.C., 1979-84; sr. cons. fin. insts. group Deloitte Haskins & Sells, N.Y.C., 1984-86; sr. cons. ops. group Peat, Marwick, Main & Co., Seattle, Wash., 1986-87; cons. mgr. comml. and indsl. practice Peat, Marwick, Main & Co., San Francisco, 1987—; fin. planner Advanced Image Tech., N.Y.C., 1983-84; cons. Apple Computers, Hitachi, Merrill Lynch, U. Calif., numerous others. Mem. Mensa, Tulane U. Alumni Assn., Beta Gamma Sigma. Republican. Jewish. Home: 221 Commons Ln Foster City CA 94404 Office: Peat Marwick Main & Co 3 Embarcadero Ctr San Francisco CA 94111

DICTEROW, HAROLD J., violinist; b. Waterbury, Conn., Oct. 19, 1919; s. Morris and Zina (Bailin) D.; m. Irina L. Lourie, July 7, 1945; children: Maurice L., Glenn E., Marina L. Student, CCNY. Violinist San Francisco Symphony, 1938-42; prin. violin Los Angeles Philharm., 1945—; violinist for all maj. studios in Hollywood 1946—. Served with U.S. Army, 1942-45. Jewish. Office: Los Angeles Philharm Orch 135 N Grand Ave Los Angeles CA 90012 *

DIDIER, JULIE, songwriter; b. Marksville, La.; d. Kenneth Edward and Emanuelino Virginia (Moreau) D.; m. Daniel Cohen (div. Mar. 1985); 1 child, Danielle Cohen. Staff writer House of Gold Music, Nashville, 1975-77, Screen Gems/Colo. Gems Music, Nashville, 1977-80, Larry Butler Music, Nashville, 1984—. songwriter Anyone Who Isn't Me Tonight (Kenny Rogers), varoius others by America, Helen Reddy, Tanya Tucker and others. Mem. ASCAP, Broadcast Music, Inc. Democrat. Roman Catholic. Home: 6706 Hesperia Ave Reseda CA 91335

DIDION, JAMES J., real estate company executive; b. Sacramento; s. Frank R. D. and Eduene J. Didion. AB in Polit. Sci., U. Calif., Berkeley, 1961. With Coldwell Banker Co., 1962—; v.p., resident mgr. Coldwell Banker Co., Sacramento, 1969-71; sr. v.p., regional mgr. Coldwell Banker Co., Houston, from 1971; now chmn., chief exec. officer Coldwell Banker Comml. Group, L.A. Office: Coldwell Banker Comml Group 533 Fremont Ave Los Angeles CA 90071 *

DIDOMENICO, ERIC DAVID, electrical and aeronautical engineer, military; b. Seattle, July 7, 1958; s. Louis Joseph and Ruth Lois (Clements) D.; m. Debra Kim Johnson, July 5, 1958; children: Rachel Ann, Sarah Joy. BSEE, Wahhington State U., 1980; MSEE, Air Force Inst. Tech., 1984; Student, Test Pilot Sch., 1987. Design engr. Boeing, Kent, Washington, 1980-81; adv., staff spl. Sec. of Defense (OSD), Arlington, Va., 1981-83; lead avionics engr. Advanced Fighter Tech. Integration F-16, Edwards AFB, Calif., 1985-87; test program mgr. Air Force Wright Advanced Labs, Dayton, Ohio, 1988--. Youth group leader, Ch. of Christian Fellowship, Federal Way, Wash., 1980; youth group asst. Christ Bible Fellowship, Del Rio, Tex., 1981, Emanuel Baptist Ch., Springfdield, Va., 1982-83; Sunday sch. tchr. Edwards AFB, Calif., 1985. Servingwith USAF, 1981--. Republican. Born again Christian/Baptist. Home: 10 B St Edwards AFB CA 93523 Office: USAF Edwards AFB CA 93523-5000

DIDOMIZIO, VINCENT JAMES, financial and strategic planner; b. Waterbury, Conn., Mar. 5, 1939; s. James V. and Carmella M. (Cipriano) DiD.; B.S., Post Coll., 1961; LL.B., LaSalle U., 1965; M.B.A., Calif. Western U., 1974; m. Alexandria Ramanauskas, Oct. 27, 1962; children—Kim, Vincent, Robert. Group controller Timex Corp., 1976-78, dir. planning and control, 1980; dir. planning and control Timex Clock Co., 1978-80; dir. govt. fin. Talley Industries, Mesa, Ariz., 1980-82; pres. VJ Assocs., 1983—; v.p. fin. Dynamic Science, Inc.; chief fin. officer Stencel Aero. Engring. Corp., 1985—; dir. Lasting Impressions, Inc. Budget com. United Fund, recipient award. Served with AUS, 1957, 61-62. Recipient Outstanding Fin. Achievement award Timex Corp., 1978. Mem. Nat. Assn. Accts., Nat. Contract Mgmt. Assn., Nat. Indsl. Security Assn. Republican. Roman Catholic. Clubs: KC, Civitan (award). Contbr. articles on acctg., govt. contracting and strategic planning to profl. jours. Home: 11093 E Mercer Ln Scottsdale AZ 85259 Office: PO Box 1140 Phoenix AZ 85029

DIEDRICK, GERALDINE ROSE, nurse; b. Chgo.; d. Milton Edward and Rose Agnes (Michalski) Goodman; R.N., Mt. San Antonio Coll., Walnut, Calif., 1963; BS, Calif. State U., L.A., 1966; MS, UCLA, 1968; divorced; 1 son, Scott Wesley. Nurse, State of Calif., 1960-83, dir. nursing Met. State Hosp., Norwalk, 1977-83; cons. in mental health, devel. disabilities. Recipient Letter of Commendation, State of Calif., 1974-77. Mem. Am. Nurses Assn., Nat. League Nursing, Am. Assn. Devel. Disabilities, Calif. Nurses Assn. (svc. awards), Am. Hosp. Assn., World Future Soc., Town Hall Calif. Democrat. Lutheran. Contbr. to profl. jours.

DIEFFENBACH, JON MICHAEL, film maker, playwright; b. Washington, Sept. 29, 1948; s. Albert Woodson and Margaret Virginia (Wood) D. BA in Sociology, Princeton U., 1970; MA in Journalism, U. Mo., 1973. Film producer Princeton U., N.J., 1968-70; film editor Shelby Storck, St. Louis, 1970; news writer Sta. WJLA-TV, Washington, 1973-74; reporter/camera Sta. KUSA, Denver, 1974-75, Sta. KTVI, St. Louis, 1975-80; cameraman Sta. WNBC News/NBC Sports, N.Y.C., 1983-84, Eye on L.A., 1985-86; freelance cameraman L.A., 1987; cameraman USA Today - The TV Show, L.A., 1988—. Author plays: The Exile of Ezra Pound, 1987, The Genuine Georgia O'Keeffe, 1988; dir./producer tv documentaries: The Ozarks, 1978, Isaac Stern at the Acropolis, 1979. Princeton Creative Arts fellow, 1968. Mem. Dramatists Guild, Amnesty Internat. Home: 238A E Elmwood Ave Burbank CA 91502 Office: Deepbrook Prodns 238A E Elmwood Ave Burbank CA 91502

DIEGEL, DONALD WAYNE, banker; b. Glendive, Mont., Dec. 2, 1953; s. Christian and Betty Marjorie (Hansen) D.; m. Patricia Lee Morasko, Sept. 1, 1973; children: Christian Joel, Erin Lane. Student, Bozeman (Mont.) Vo-Tech., 1974; BS in Agri-business, Mont. State U., 1977. V.p./sec. Western Mont. Production Credit Assn., Missoula, 1977-84; v.p. Norwest Corp. Region VIII, Billings, 1984-85, Norwest Bank Billings, N.A., 1985--. Alumni/grad. Leadership Billings, 1988. Mem. Hamilton C. of C. (bd. dirs.). Republican. Lutheran. Home: 4505 Toyon Dr Billings MT 59106 Office: Norwest Bank Billings NA Billings MT 59117

DIEHL, DIGBY ROBERT, journalist; b. Boonton, N.J., Nov. 14, 1940; s. Edwin Samuel and Mary Jane Shirley (Ellsworth) D.; m. Kay Beyer, June 6, 1981; 1 dau., Dylan Elizabeth. A.B. in Am. Studies (Henry Rutgers scholar), Rutgers U., 1962; M.A. in Theatre Arts, UCLA, 1966, postgrad., 1969—. Editor Learning Center, Inc., Princeton, N.J., 1962-64; dir. research Creative Playthings, Los Angeles, 1964-66; editor Coast mag., Los Angeles, 1966-68, Show mag., Los Angeles, 1968-69; book editor Los Angeles Times, 1969-78; v.p., editor-in-chief Harry N. Abrams, Inc., N.Y.C., 1978-80; book editor Los Angeles Herald Examiner, 1981-86; movie critic, entertainment editor Sta. KCBS TV, Los Angeles, 1986-88; book columnist Playboy mag., 1988—; instr. journalism UCLA, 1969-78; jurist Nat. Book Awards, 1972; mem. nominating com. Nat. Medal for Lit., 1972-75; v.p. Nat. Book Critics Circle, 1975-78, bd. dirs., 1981-87; jurist Am. Book Awards, 1981-85, v.p. programming, 1984-86. Author: Supertalk: Extraordinary Conversations, 1974, Front Page, 1981. Trustee KPFK-Pacifica Found. Recipient; Irita Van Doren award, 1977. Mem. Am. Soc. Journalists and Authors, AAUP, PEN (pres. Los Angeles Ctr. 1987), AFTRA, Writers Guild Am., Phi Beta Kappa, Phi Sigma Delta. Home: 788 S Lake Ave Pasadena CA 91106

DIEHL, MARK EMORY, dentist, consultant; b. Upland, Calif., Feb. 7, 1951; s. John Earl and Patricia Eileen (Stell) D.; m. Lee Ann Collins, July 17, 1976; children: Erin Lee, Brynn Elyse, Megan Eileen. BS, U. So. Calif., 1973; DMD, Washington U., St. Louis, 1978. Resident gen. dentistry VA Hosp., Palo Alto, Calif., 1978-79, staff dentist, 1979-87, asst. chief dental service, 1987—; cons. Dental Ins. Cons. Inc., Saratoga, Calif., 1985—. Fellow Acad. Gen. Dentists; mem. ADA, Omicron Kappa Upsilon. Republican. Mem. Christian Ch. Home: 6880 Chiala Ln San Jose CA 95129 Office: Dental Svc 3801 Miranda Ave Palo Alto CA 94304

DIEKMANN, JAMES EDWARD, civil engineering educator; b. St. Louis, Nov. 6, 1945; s. Edward B. and Margaret (Feld) D.; divorced; children: Joshua, Jessica, Jacob; m. Barbara B. Fowler, June 1, 1984; children: Megan, Molly. BSME, U. Mo., Rolla, 1967, MS in engring. mgmt., 1971; PhD civil engring., U. Wash., Seattle, 1979. Design engr. GE, Cin., 1967-68; sr. cost engr. Bechtel Power Corp., San Francisco, 1971-75; ptnr. Symtic Corp., St. Louis, 1974-75; cost/sch. mgr. Ebasco Svcs. Inc., Elma, Wash., 1975-77; lectr. civil engring. U. Wash., Seattle, 1977-79; prof. civil engring. U. Colo., Boulder, 1979—; prin. Diekmann & Assocs., Lafayette, Colo., 1980—; cons. in field. Reviewer for McGraw-Hill, Harper & Row, Addison-Wesley, 1979—. Rsch. grantee NSF, U.S. Army Corps Engrs., Constrn. Industry Inst., Associated Gen. Contractors Am. Mem. ASCE (chair cost control 1979), Constrn. Industry Inst. (cost/sch. task force), Project Mgmt. Inst., Am. Assn. Cost. Engr., Tau Beta Pi. Office: U of Colo Box 428 Boulder CO 80309

DIEM, MARY ANN, cosmetic company sales executive; b. Madison, Wis., Mar. 31, 1951; d. John and Juliana Gertrude (Zander) D.; m. Thomas Robert Paape, Dec. 31, 1979 (div. 1988). Student, U. Wis., Madison, 1969-70; cert., Madison Tech. Coll., 1972. Recreation dir. Pleasant View Nursing Home, Monroe, Wis., 1972-73; recreation dir. Manor House Nursing Home, Madison, 1973-75; sales cons. Mary Kay Cosmetics, Madison, 1976-77, sales dir., 1977-79, exec. sr. dir., 1979—. Roman Catholic. Home: 17506 Seventh Ave W Bothell WA 98012

DIENER, ROYCE, health care services company executive; b. Balt., Mar. 27, 1918; s. Louis and Lillian (Goodman) D.; m. Jennifer S. Flinton; children: Robert, Joan, Michael. BA, Harvard U.; LLD, Pepperdine U. Comml. lending officer, investment banker various locations to 1972; pres. Am. Med. Internat., Inc., Beverly Hills, Calif., 1972-75, pres., chief exec. officer, 1975-78, chmn., chief exec. officer, 1978-85, chmn. bd., 1986-88, chmn. exec. com., 1986—; bd. dirs. Calif. Econ. Devel. Corp., Advanced Tech. Venture Funds, Am. Health Properties, AMI Healthcare Group, plc. Author: Financing a Growing Business, 1966, 3d edit., 1978. Bd. visitors Grad. Sch. Mgmt., UCLA; mem. governing bd., UCLA Med. Ctr.; mem. vis. com. Med. Sch. and Sch. Dental Medicine, Harvard U.; trustee Andrus Gerontol. Inst., U. So. Calif.; bd. dirs. L.A. Philharm. Assn., L.A. chpt. ARC, Heritage Sq. Mus., Santa Monica. Served to capt. USAF, 1942-46, PTO. Decorated D.F.C. with oak leaf cluster. Mem. L.A. C. of C. (bd. dirs.), Calif. C. of C. (bd. dirs.), Calif. Bus. Round Table (bd. dirs.), Harvard Club, Regency Club, Calif. Yacht Club, Riviera Country Club (L.A.), Marks Club (London). Office: Am Med Internat Inc 414 N Camden Dr Beverly Hills CA 90210

DIENNER, DAVID WALLY, rental company executive; b. Evanston, Ill., Nov. 1, 1951; s. John Astor and Betty (Wally) D.; m. Alison Lee Cartwright, July 14, 1979; children: Jesse Cartwright, Rebecca Justice. BA, Princeton U., 1974; MBA, U. Chgo., 1979. Account exec. HDO Prodns., Inc., Highland Park, Ill., 1975-79; v.p., gen. mgr. HDO Prodns., Inc., Glendale and Burlingame, Calif., 1984—; also. bd. dirs. HDO Prodns., Inc., Northbrook, Ill. gen. mgr. Numisco, Inc., Chgo., 1979-82; credit mgr. Giftco, Inc., Northbrook, 1982-84. Libertarian. Presbyterian. Office: HDO Prodns Inc 1465 N Carolan Ave Burlingame CA 94010

DIEPHOLZ, DAVID LESTER, chemical company executive; b. Hemet, Calif., Nov. 14, 1962; s. Eugene Lester and Ruby Jeanette (Forsch) D. BS in Chemistry, Valparaiso U., 1984; Grad., Claremont Coll., 1987—. Prodn. technician electronic materials div. Johnson Matthey, Inc., San Diego, 1984; research chemist Olin Hunt Conductive Materials, Temple City, Calif., 1985-87; prodn. mgr. Olin Hunt Conductive Materials, Ontario, Calif., 1987—. Republican. Lutheran. Office: Olin Hunt Conductive Materials 1496 E Francis Ontario CA 91761

DIETSCH, STEVEN WILLIAM, insurance executive; b. Milw., Mar. 19, 1956; s. William L. and Barbra Ann (Algrem) D. BS, U. N.D., 1979. Sr. underwriter Wausau Ins. Co., L.A., 1979-82; v.p. sales Automobile Rental Ins. and Svc., Long Beach, Calif., 1982-86; pres., chief exec. officer Dietsch Ins. Svcs., Long Beach, 1986—; v.p. underwriting and sales Rental Industry Svcs., San Clemente, Calif., 1987—. Author: Profitability in Rental Operations, 1986. Mem. Long Beach C. of C., Com. 500 Grand Prix (security com. 1983-87), Pacific Club, L.A. Athletic Club. Republican. Methodist. Office: Rental Industry Svcs 634 Camino de Los Mares San Clemente CA 92672

DIETZ, VIDA LEE, utility company executive; b. Brawley, Calif., July 2, 1952. BSBA, U. Nev., 1975. Spl. asst. Sierra Pacific Co., Reno, 1976-78, asst. analyst, 1978-79, adminstr. extension agreement, 1979-83, adminstr. speaker's bur. and sch. programs, 1983-85, rep. community info., 1985-87, dir. spl. events, adminstr. charitable foundation, 1988—. 1st v.p. Sierra Nev. coun. Girl Scouts U.S.A., Reno, 1984—; chmn. pub. rels. com. Jr. League Reno, 1986, asst. chmn. ways and means, bd. trustees, 1989—; chmn. meetings and events com. United Way No. Reno, 1987, mem. pub. rels. com., 1988;, Nev. Gov's. Conf. Women, Individual Sessions Com.,1989—, Sierra Arts Found. Mem. AAUW (program v.p. 1986), Reno Women in Advt. (ednl. chmn. 1986), Western Indsl. Nev., Reno-Sparks C. of C. (mem. edn. com. 1986-87, Leadership Reno award 1987), U. Nev. Alumni Assn.(bd. dirs. 1989—). Home: 5460 Goldenrod Dr Reno NV 89511 Office: Sierra Pacific Power Co 6100 Neil Rd PO Box 10100 Reno NV 89520

DIEZ-LUCKIE, JEFFREY THOMAS, electrical engineer; b. Toronto, Ont., Can., Oct. 10, 1954; s. Jorge Thomas and Nancy (Ashcroft) Diez-L. BSEE, Bucknell U., Lewisburg, Pa., 1976. Elec. designer Topps Chewing Gum, Inc., Duryea, Pa., 1977-80; elec. engr. Raychem Corp., Menlo Park, Calif., 1980—. Mem. Ironhorsemen Motorcyclist Club (pres. 1987-88). Office: Raychem Corp 300 Constitution Dr Menlo Park CA 94025

DIGGS, NATALIE VIRGINA, director, headmaster; b. Imperial, Calif., May 18, 1918; d. Jerome Richard and Callie Leovia (Hammond) Collins; m. Orville Singleton Diggs, Dec. 14, 1940; children: Janet Diane, Richard Allen, Denise Gayle. Student, San Bernadino Jr. Coll., 1935-36, Tuskegee Inst., 1937-39; AA, San Bernardino Jr. Coll., 1956; BA, U. Redlands, 1969. Sec. Rialto (Calif.) Edn. Assn., 1972-73; dir. elem. St. Paul A.M.E. Ch., San Bernardino, Calif., 1977-79; bd. dirs. Rolling Start for the Deaf, San Bernardino, Calif. Access Com. for the Disabled, San Bernardino. Dir. elem. segment Rialto Edn. Assn.; active Girl Scouts Am., 1977-78, mayor's Adv. Council for Sr. Affairs, San Bernardino, 1978-79; bd. dirs. Goodwill Industries Inland County, San Bernardino, 1979-85; mem. Dept. Hwy. Patrol, Sacramento, Calif., 1984-85. Mem. Calif. Tchrs. Assn., AAUW (sec. 1981-83; community awareness chmn. 1985-87; program v.p. 1987-88), nat. Council Negro Women (membership v.p. 1978-80), Cosmos Club (treas. 1981-82). Democrat. African Methodist.

DIGIORGIO, ROBERT MICHAEL, dentist; b. Bklyn., Sept. 14, 1952; s. Oronzio Antonio and Jean Grace (Fiorenzo) DiG.; m. Linda Catherine Wynne, June 15, 1974; children: Nancy Rose, Katelyn Lauren. BA, CUNY, 1974; DDS, Georgetown U., 1978. Staff dentist USPHS-Indian Health Service, White Earth, Minn., 1979-80, Colo. Family Dental Ctr., Aurora, 1980-82; gen. practice dentistry Denver, 1982—. Pres. Resolve of Colo., Denver, 1985-86. Mem. ADA (bd. dirs. 1986-87, membership com. 1982-87), Met. Denver Dental Soc. (treas. 1985, v.p. 1986, pres. 1988—, del. to ADA conv.), Colo. Dental Assn. (membership services com. 1982-87, bd. dirs. 1986-87), Acad. Gen. Dentistry. Club: Contacts (Denver) (recorder 1987-88). Office: 3773 Cherry Creek N Dr #120 Denver CO 80209

DIGNAM, ROBERT JOSEPH, orthopaedic surgeon; b. Manchester, N.H., July 8, 1925; s. Walter Joseph and Margaret Veronica (Lowe) D.; m. Evelyn Pettitt, Aug. 4, 1961; children—Stephen Mark, Lyn Shore, Margaret Gale. B.S., Bates Coll., 1945; M.D., Tufts U., 1949. Intern Boston City Hosp., 1949-50, resident in orthopedic surgery, 1954-57; resident in orthopedic surgery Lahey Clinic, Boston, 1953-54; practice medicine specializing in orthopedic surgery Santa Monica, Calif., 1960—; mem. staff St. Johns Hosp. UCLA Med. Center; clin. prof. orthopedic surgery UCLA. Served to lt., M.C. USN, 1951-54. Fellow A.C.S.; mem. AMA, Mass. Med. Soc., Calif. Med. Assn., Am. Acad. Orthopedic Surgeons. Club: Jonathan. Home: 821 Alma Real Pacific Palisades CA 90272 Office: 2021 Santa Monica Blvd Santa Monica CA 90404

DIKE, JEANINE, nurse; b. Prescott, Ariz., Dec. 7, 1945; d. N. Boyd and Rachel (Teeples) Tenney; m. Ronald C. Naegle, June 30, 1967 (dec. 1968); 1 child, Rachelle; m. Roy W. Dike, June 4, 1970 (div. 1983); children: Chad, Jason, Janae, Nathan, Adam; m. James A. Montgomery, Apr. 7, 1989. AA in Nursing, Phoenix Coll., 1967; BA, Prescott Coll., 1987. RN, Ariz. Staff nurse Dr.'s Hosp., Phoenix, 1967-68, 70-71; ob. nurse Yavapai Regional Med. Ctr., Prescott, 1968-70; pediatric nurse Crippled Children's Hosp., Tempe, Ariz., 1972-74; childbirth educator Tempe, 1974-77; geriatric nurse Ariz. Pioneers Home, Prescott, 1980-84, geriatric nursing dir., 1987--; nurse Yavapai County Health Dept., 1984-87; childbirth educator Yavapai Regional Med. Ctr., 1984--. Home: HC 32 Box 25 Prescott AZ 86303 Office: Ariz Pioneers Home Prescott AZ 86303

DILBECK, CHARLES STEVENS, JR., real estate company executive; b. Dallas, Dec. 2, 1944; s. Charles Stevens Sr. and Betty Doris (Owens) D.; m. Lennie Jean Routledge, Apr. 29, 1964 (div. Aug. 1970); 1 child, Stephen Douglas. BS, Wichita State U., 1968; MS, Stanford U., 1969, postgrad., 1970-71. Engr. United Tech. Ctr., Sunnyvale, Calif., 1971-72; cons. Diversicom, Inc., Santa Clara, Calif., 1972-73; engr. Anamet Labs., San Carlos, Calif., 1973-75; cons. real estate investment Cert. Capital Corp., San Jose, Calif., 1975-82; pvt. practice in real estate, San Jose, 1981—; prin. Am. Equity Investments, San Jose, 1982—; mem. Los Gatos (Calif.) Rent Adv. Com., 1988. Mem. Nat. Apt. Assn., San Jose Real Estate Bd., Tri-County Apt. Assn., Gold Key Club, Tau Beta Pi (pres. 1968), Sigma Gamma Tau. Republican. Home: 301 Alta Loma Ln Santa Cruz CA 95062 Office: Am Equity Investments 650 Saratoga Ave #200 San Jose CA 95129

DILBECK, HAROLD ROY, finance educator; b. Taft, Calif., May 28, 1932; s. Roy E. and Osalee E. (Swafford) D.; divorced; 1 child: Russell. BS, Fresno State U., 1956; MBA, UCLA, 1958, PhD, 1961. CPA, Calif. Assoc. prof. fin. U. So. Calif., Los Angeles, 1961-66; vis. assoc. prof. Escuela de Administracion de Negocios Para Graduados, Lima, Peru, 1966-69; prof. fin. Calif. State U., Long Beach, 1969—; Pres. Harold Dilbeck Accts., Inc., Tustin, Calif., 1977—. Contbr. articles to profl. jours. Served with USMC, 1952-54. Mem. Am. Inst. CPA's, Calif. State Soc. CPA's, Am. Fin. Assn., Fin. Mgmt. Assn. Home: 18722 Vanderlip Ave Santa Ana CA 92705 Office: Harold Dilbeck Accts Inc 1442 Irvine Blvd Tustin CA 92680

DILDINE, DANA EDRIE THIRY, teacher; b. Kansas City, Mo., Feb. 10, 1956; d. Herbert Leroy and Dorthy Fay (Killion) Thiry; m. David John Dildine, Dec. 20, 1981; stepchildren: Denise Joy Dildine Diede, Tami Lynn. BS in Elem. Edn., Southwestern Adventist Coll., 1978. Tchr. Enterprise (Kans.) Acad., 1979-80, Keene (Tex.) Adventist Elem. Sch., 1984-86; tchr., prin. Tempe (Ariz.) Adventist Christian Sch., 1980-83, Kingman (Ariz.) Seventh-day Adventist Sch., 1983-84, El Cajon (Calif.) Seventh-day Adventist Christian Sch., 1986-89, Glenview Adventist Elem. Sch., Phoenix, 1989—; del. Pacific Union Ednl. Coun., Glendale, Calif., 1980-83; mem. Ariz. Conf. Edn. Mgmt. Team, Scottsdale, Ariz., 1980-83, Southeastern Calif. Conf. Seventh-day Adventist Ednl. Mgmt. Team, Riverside, 1986—. Columnist, Paycheck jour., 1988. Chair, Witnessing and Svc. Com., Keene, 1985-86; active, ARC. Mem. Southeastern Calif. Adventist Tchrs. Home: 8903 W Butler Dr Peoria AZ 85345 Office: Glenview Adventist Elem Sch 6801 N 43rd Ave Phoenix AZ 85019

DILL, MARY CORNELIA, sales executive; b. Wynnewood, Okla., Mar. 10, 1923; d. Garland Deward and Lillian Beatrice (Parette) Conatser; widowed; children: Betty Hamilton, Particia Sexton, Michael Dill. Student, U. Cen. Ark., 1941-42. Key distbr. Nutrilite Products, Inc., Buena Park, Calif., 1970-73; dir. Amway Corp., Ada, Mich., 1973—, ruby dir., 1976—; nutrition cons., Dill Internat., Riverside Calif., 1970—, color cons., 1980—, network mktg. cons., 1984—. Sustaning mem. Rep. Nat. Com., Washington, 1979—; mem. Nat. Rep. Senatorial Com., Washington, 1988-89, Calif. Rep. Com., 1983—. Mem. Nat. Direct Distbr. Leadership (travel award 1988), Ctr. for Growth (lectr.), Riverside C. of C., Police Officers Wives, 2% Club. Baptist. Home: 7868 Dufferin Ave Riverside CA 92504

DILLARD, JOHN MARTIN, lawyer, pilot; b. Long Beach, Calif., Dec. 25, 1945; s. John Warren and Clara Leora (Livermore) D.; student U. Calif., Berkeley, 1963-67; B.A., UCLA, 1968; J.D., Pepperdine U., 1976; m. Patricia Anne Yeager, Aug. 10, 1968; 1 child, Jason Robert. Instr. pilot Norton AFB, Calif., 1973-77. Bar: Calif., 1976. Assoc. Magana, Cathcart & McCarthy, L.A., 1977-80, Lord, Bissell & Brook, L.A., 1980-85, Finley, Kumble, Wagner, 1985-86, Law Office s of John M. Dillard, 1986—, v.p., gen. counsel, dir. Resort Aviation Svcs, Inc., Calif., 1988—. Capt. USAF, 1968-73, Vietnam. Mem. Am. Trial Lawyers Assn. (aviation litigation com.), Am. Bar Assn. (aviation com.), Orange County Bar Assn., Fed. Bar Assn., L.A. County Bar Assn. (aviation com.), Century City Bar Assn., Internat. Platform Assn., Res. Officers Assn., Sigma Nu. Home: 19621 Verona Ln Yorba Linda CA 92686 Office: 333 N Birch St Santa Ana CA 92702

DILLARD, MARILYN DIANNE, property manager; b. Norfolk, Va., July 7, 1940; d. Thomas Ortman and Sally Ruth (Wallerich) D.; m. James Conner Coons, Nov. 6, 1965 (div. June 1988); 1 child, Adrienne Alexandra Coons (dec.). Student, UCLA, 1958-59; BA in Bus. Adminstrn., U. Wash., 1962. Modeling-print work Harry Conover, N.Y.C., 1945; model Elizabeth Leonard Agy., Seattle, 1955-68; retail worker Frederick & Nelson, Seattle, 1962, I. Magnin & Co., Seattle, 1963-64; property mgr. Seattle, 1961—; antique and interior design John J. Cunningham Antiques, Seattle, 1968-73. Author: (poem) Flutterby, 1951; asst. chmn.: Seattle Classic Cookbook, 1980-83. Charter mem., pres. Children's Med. Ctr., Maude Fox Guild, Seattle, 1965—; organizer teen groups Episcopal Ch. of the Epiphany, Seattle, 1965-67; bd. dirs. Patrons of Northwest Civic, Cultural and Charitable Orgns., Seattle, 1976—, prodn. chmn., 1977-78, 1984-85, auction party chmn., 1983-84, exec. com., 1984-85; mem. U. Wash. Arboretum Found. Unit, 1966-73, pres., 1969; provisional class pres. Jr. League Seattle, 1971-72, next to new shop asst. chmn., 1972-73, bd. dirs., admissions chmn., 1976-77, exec. first v.p., exec. com., bd. dirs., 1978-79; mem. Coun. for the Prevention of Child Abuse and Neglect, Seattle, 1974-75. Mem. Seattle Tennis Club. Republican. Episcopalian. Home and Office: 201 Galer Ste 428 Seattle WA 98109

DILLE, BRIAN CHARLES, real estate broker; b. Denver, Sept. 15, 1962; s. Alan Charles Francis and Jacquita (Gilbreth) D. BS in Econs., U. Colo., 1985. Lic. real estate broker. Leasing agt. Cardon Glenn Meadows, Englewood, Colo., 1986-87; real estate broker Grubb & Ellis, Denver, 1988—. Mem. Denver Execs. Assn. (treas. 1986—), Denver Bd. Realtors. Office: Grubb & Ellis 1200 17th St Ste 2000 Denver CO 80228

DILLER, BARRY, entertainment company executive; b. San Francisco, Feb. 2, 1942; s. Michael and Reva (Addison) D. Vice pres. feature films and movies of week ABC, 1971-73, ABC (prime time TV), 1973-74; chmn. bd. Paramount Pictures Corp., 1974-84; pres. Gulf & Western Entertainment Group, 1983-84; chmn., chief exec. officer Twentieth Century Fox Film Corp., Los Angeles, 1984—, Fox, Inc., 1985—. Office: Fox Inc PO Box 900 Beverly Hills CA 90213 *

DILLON, FRANCIS PATRICK, human resources executive, management consultant; b. Long Beach, Calif., Mar. 15, 1937; s. Wallace Myron and Mary Elizabeth (Land) D.; B.A., U. Va., 1959; M.S., Def. Fgn. Affairs Sch., 1962; M.B.A., Pepperdine U., 1976; m. Vicki Lee Dillon, Oct. 1980; children: Cary Randolph, Francis Patrick Jr., Randee, Rick. Traffic mgr., mgr. personnel svcs. Pacific Telephone Co., Sacramento and Lakeport, Calif., 1966-69; asst. mgr. manpower planning and devel. Pan-Am. World Airways, N.Y.C., 1969-71; mgr. personnel and orgn. devel. Continental Airlines, Los Angeles, 1971-74; dir. personnel Farwest Svcs., Inc., Irvine, Calif., 1974; dir. human resources Bourns, Inc., Riverside, Calif., 1974-80; dir. employee and community relations MSI Data Corp., 1980-83; pres. Pavi Enterprises, 1983—; mgmt. cons., 1983—; pres., chief exec. officer Personnel Products & Svcs., Inc., 1984—; pres. Meditrans Inc. Bd. dirs. Health Svcs. Maintenance Orgn., Inc., Youth Svcs. Ctr., Inc.; vol. precinct worker. Served to lt. comdr. USN, 1959-66; asst. naval attaché, Brazil, 1963-65. Recipient Disting. Svc. award Jaycees, 1969; Jack Cates Meml. Vol. of Year award Youth Svc. Ctr., 1977. Mem. Assn. Internal Mgmt. Cons.'s, Am. Soc. Personnel Adminstrn., Personnel Indsl. Relations Assn., Am. Soc. Tng. and Devel., Am. Electronics Assn. (human resources com., chmn. human resources symposium). Republican. Episcopalian. Clubs: Mission Viejo Sailing, YMCA Bike, Mission Viejo Ski, Caving, Toastmasters (pres. 1966-67), Have Dirt Will Travel. Office: Pers Products & Svcs Inc 27331 Via Amistoso Mission Viejo CA 92692

DILLON, GEORGE CHAFFEE, manufacturing company executive; b. Kansas City, Mo., Oct. 29, 1922; s. Edward J. and Mary (Coon) D.; m. Joan Alamo Kent, Sept. 11, 1948; children: Kent, Courtney, Emily. BS, Harvard U., 1944, MBA, 1948. Adminstrv. asst. J. A. Bruening Co., Kansas City, Mo., 1948-51; with Butler Mfg. Co., Kansas City, Mo., 1951-86, treas., from 1960, v.p., 1961-63, exec. v.p., 1963-67, pres., 1967-78, chmn. bd., chief exec. officer, 1978-86; chmn. Manville Corp., Denver, 1986—; bd. dirs. Johns Manville Corp., Phelps Dodge Corp., Newhall Land and Farming Co., Astec Industries, Chattanooga. Past. chmn. bd. trustees Midwest Research Inst., Kansas City, Mo.; trustee Mayo Found., Rochester, Minn., Children's Mercy Hosp., Kansas City, Mo.; bd. overseers Harvard U., 1980-86. Lt. USNR, 1943-46. Home: 5049 Wornall Rd Kansas City MO 64112 Office: Manville Corp 5045 Wornall Rd PO Box 5108 Denver CO 80127

DILLON, J. PAT, telecommunications engineer; b. Long Beach, Calif., Sept. 10, 1945; s. Joseph C. and Mary (Friend) D.; m. Kathleen Doffing, Sept. 14, 1974; children: Shondra L., Jeffrey J. Student U. Colo., 1963-67. Chemist, Longmont Foundry (Colo.), 1965-67; metallurgist Dow Chem. Co., Rocky Flats, Colo., 1967-68; chemist Great Western Sugar Co., Longmont, Colo., 1968-70; engr. Mountain Bell Co., Boulder, Colo., 1970-72; cons. engr. Henkels & McCoy, Blue Bell, Pa., 1972-80; staff engr. Northwestern Bell Co., Mpls., 1980-85; sr. communications specialist Burnup and Sims, Camarillo, Calif., 1985-88; project mgr., engr. supr. northwest regional mgr. Henkels & McCoy, Portland, Oreg., 1988—; owner, mgr. Papillon Enterprises, Apple Valley, Minn., 1982-85, Camarillo, Calif., 1985-89, Hillsboro, Oreg., 1989—; co-owner Butterfly Boutique, Apple Valley, 1981-85; owner Country Craftworks, Camarillo, 1986-88, TelCom Tech, Port Hueneme, Calif., 1987, Camarillo, 1987-88. Author: (pamphlet) How to Save Money Building Your Own House. Mem. Minn. Ind. Businessmen, Innovators Council (award 1982). Roman Catholic. Home: 25805 Ridgeview Dr Hillsboro OR 97123 Office: Henkels & McCoy 5031 NE 148th St Portland OR 97230

DILLON, KRISTINE ELAINE, university official; b. Orange, Calif., May 10, 1951; d. Juan and Elizabeth Sue Ann (Ducommun) D.; m. John Reeder Curry, Nov. 21, 1982; 1 child, Patrick Dillon Curry; 1 stepchild, Christopher Rule Curry. BA, Whittier Coll., 1973; MA, Claremont Grad. Sch., 1977, PhD, 1980. Asst. to dean faculty Harvey Mudd Coll., Claremont, Calif., 1976-77; instnl. researcher U. So. Calif., L.A., 1978-81, budget analyst, 1981-83, asst. v.p., 1983-85, assoc. v.p. for student affairs, 1985--. Contbr. articles to profl. jours., chpts. to books. Founding pres. Pacific Wind Ensemble, Long Beach, Calif., 1980--; mem. alumni council Claremont Grad. Sch., 1986--; mem. South Park task force L.A. Cen. Bus. Dist. Redevel., 1987--. Signal Oil & Gas Co. merit scholar, 1969; merit fellow Claremont Grad. Sch., 1974-75. Mem. Nat. Assn. Student Personnel Adminstrs., Assn. for Study Higher Edn., Sigma Xi. Republican. Methodist. Office: U So Calif STU 201 Los Angeles CA 90015-4891

DILORETO, ANN MARIE, legal information systems consultant; b. Detroit, July 4, 1953; d. Gilbert Remo and Nathalie Marie (Gouine) DiL. BGS, U. Mich., 1975; MLS, Simmons Coll., 1976. Law librarian Widett, Slater & Goldman, Boston, 1978-83, Herrick & Smith, Boston, 1983-84; prin. Legal Info. Mgmt., Menlo Park, Calif., 1984—. Mem. Am. Assn. Law Libraries (profl. standards com. 1984), Spl. Libraries Assn. (sec., treas. legis. reference sect. 1984-85, chair-elect of sect., 1986-88, coordinator law and pub. policy roundtable 1986—), Assn. Boston Law Libraries (chmn. profl. standards com. 1979-84, consulting com., nominating com.), No. Calif. Assn. Law Libraries (editor NOCALL News 1985-86, liaison to Assn. Legal Administrs. 1986-87). Home and Office: Legal Info Mgmt 444 University Dr Menlo Park CA 94025

DIMAIO, VIRGINIA SUE, gallery owner; b. Houston, July 6, 1921; d. Jesse Lee and Gabriella Sue (Norris) Chambers; AB, U. Redlands, 1943; student U. So. Calif., 1943-45, Scripps Coll., 1943, Pomona Coll., 1945; m. James V. DiMaio, 1955 (div. 1968); children: Victoria, James V. Owner, dir. Galeria Capistrano, San Juan Capistrano and Santa Fe, N.Mex., 1979—; founder Mus. Women in Arts, Washington; cons., appraiser Southwestern and Am. Indian Handcrafts; lectr. Calif. State U., Long Beach; established ann. Helen Hardin meml. scholarship for woman artist grad. Inst. Am. Indian Art, Santa Fe, also ann. Helen Hardin award for outstanding artist at Indian Market, S.W. Assn. on Indian Affairs, Santa Fe; bd. dirs. Mus. Man, San Diego, 1989. Author: (forward to exhibit catalogue) Paths Beyond Tradition. Recipient Bronze Plaque Recognition award Navajo Tribal Mus., 1977. Mem. Indian Arts and Crafts Assn., S.W. Assn. Indian Affairs, Heard Mus., San Juan Capistano C. of C. Republican. Roman Catholic. Office: 31681 Camino Capistrano San Juan Capistrano CA 92675 also: 409 Canyon Rd Santa Fe NM 87501

DIMARIA, VINCENT ANTHONY, pediatrician, educator; b. Waterbury, Conn., Nov. 18, 1948; s. Vincent and Vincenza Florence (Denorfia) DiM.; m. Joan Elizabeth Wilson, May ll, 1974; children: Michael Vincent, Cristina Elizabeth. BA magna cum laude, Seton Hall U., 1970; MD, Yale U., 1974. Diplomate Am. Bd. Pediatrics. Intern in pediatrics U. Colo. Med. Sch., Denver, 1974-75, resident in pediatrics, 1975-77, chief resident, 1979-80, assoc. clin. prof. pediatrics, 1988—; pediatrician USPHS Hosp., Tuba City, Ariz., 1977-79; pvt. practice Littleton, Colo., 1980—. Lt. comdr. USPHS, 1977-79. Fellow Am. Acad. Pediatrics. Office: 7720 S Broadway Ste 330 Littleton CO 80122

DI MASSA, ERNANI VINCENZO, JR., broadcast executive, television producer, writer; b. Phila., Sept. 12, 1947; s. Ernani Vincenzo and Rita C. (Iacovoni) Di M.; m. Karen Sue Bryant, July 10, 1976; 1 child, Michael Colin. BS, La Salle Coll., 1970; MS, Temple U., 1972. Producer, writer Mike Douglas Show, Phila. and L.A., 1969-81, Regis Philbin Show, L.A., 1981, Fantasy NBC-TV, L.A., 1981-83; exec. producer, writer Thicke of the Night, L.A., 1983-84, Tony Orlando Show, L.A., 1985-86; supervising producer Hollywood Squares, L.A., 1987-89; v.p. programming and devel. King World Prodns., L.A., 1989—. Recipient Emmy award NATAS, 1982. Mem. Producers Guild Am., Writers Guild Am. Roman Catholic. Office: King World Inc 12400 Wilshire Blvd Ste 1200 Los Angeles CA 90025

DIMEFF, JOHN, physicist, educator; b. Detroit, July 2, 1921; s. Stephen and Olga (Nickoloff) D.; m. Virginia Mae Gorrell, May 25, 1944; children: John Craig, Carol Lynn. BS, Harvard U., 1942. Vacuum tube devel. engr. Naval Research Lab., Anacostia, D.C., 1943-46; physicist NACA-NASA, Moffett Field, Calif., 1946-75, Dimeff Assocs., San Jose, Calif., 1975—; prof. stomatology U. Calif. Med. Ctr., San Francisco, 1978—; cons. various firms, Calif., Tex., Utah, 1975—. Author 30 patents; contbr. articles to sci. publs. Served as ensign, USN, 1944-45. Republican. Home: 2346 Greenside Dr San Jose CA 95127 Office: 5346 Greenside Dr San Jose CA 95127

DIMMICK, CAROLYN REABER, federal judge; b. Seattle, Oct. 24, 1929; d. Maurice C. and Margaret T. (Taylor) Reaber; m. Cyrus Allen Dimmick, Sept. 10, 1955; children: Taylor, Dana. BA, U. Wash., 1951, JD, 1963; LLD, Gonzaga U., 1982, CUNY, 1987. Bar: Wash. Asst. atty. gen. State of Wash., Seattle, 1953-55; pros. atty. King County, Wash., 1955-59, 60-62; sole practice Seattle, 1959-60, 62-65; judge N.E. Dist. Ct. Wash., 1965-75, King County Superior Ct., 1976-80; justice Wash. Supreme Ct., 1981-85; judge U.S. Dist. Ct. (we. dist.) Wash., Seattle, 1985—. Recipient Matrix Table award, 1981, World Plan Execs. Council award, 1981, others. Mem. Am. Judges Assn. (gov.), Nat. Assn. Women Judges, World Assn. Judges, ABA, Wash. Bar Assn., Am. Judicature Soc. Clubs: Wash. Athletic, Wingpoint Golf and Country, Harbor. Office: US Dist Ct 911 US Courthouse 1010 5th Ave Seattle WA 98104

DIMOTAKIS, PAUL EMMANUEL, aeronautics and physics educator; b. Athens, Apr. 21, 1945; came to U.S., 1964; s. Emmanuel Paul Dimotakis and Euterpe (Kandarakis) Delipetros; m. Susan Lynn Kolden, Mar. 30, 1979; children: Manolis, Yannis. BS in Physics (George Green Honor), Calif. Inst. Tech., 1968, MS in Nuclear Engring., 1969, PhD in Applied Physics, 1973. Research fellow in aeronautics Calif. Inst. Tech., Pasadena, 1973-75, asst. prof. aeronautics and applied physics, 1975-81, assoc. prof., 1981-85, prof., 1986—; vis. research scientist Democritos Research Ctr., Athens, 1975-76; mem. adv. com. on sci. and tech. Govt. of Greece, 1976-81. Contbr. articles to profl. jours. Fellow AIAA (Citation for survey paper 1987), Am. Phys. Soc. Home: 3962 Alzada Rd Altadena CA 91001 Office: Calif Inst Tech Grad Aero Labs Pasadena CA 91125

DINARDO, LUELLA KAY, bookkeeper; b. Montrose, Colo., May 3, 1948; d. William Edgar and Evelyn Ruth (Carlson) Bray; m. Monte Talbot, Aug. 22, 1970 (div. May 1972); m. John Nicholas Di Nardo, Sept. 25, 1976 (div. July 1989); 1 child, Nicholas John. BS, Colo. State U., 1970. With accounts payable and receivable dept. Beaver Mesa Exploration, Denver, 1976-79; pres. Ind. Bookkeeping Svcs., Denver, 1986—. Charter mem. Rep. Presdl. Task Force, 1981—. 2d lt. USAF, 1973-75. Mem. NAFE, Women Bus. Owners Assn., Beta Epsilon. Congregationalist. Avocations: reading, aerobic dance. Home and Office: 4927 S Eagle Circle Aurora CO 80015

DINEL, RICHARD HENRY, lawyer; b. L.A., Sept. 16, 1942; s. Edward Price and Edith Elizabeth (Rheinstein) D.; m. Joyce Ann Korsmeyer, Dec. 26, 1970; children: Edward, Alison. BA, Pomona Coll., 1964; JD, Stanford U., 1967. Bar: Calif. Owner Richard H. Dinel, A Profl. Law Corp., L.A., 1971-79; ptnr. Richards, Watson & Gershon, L.A., 1979—. Chmn. bd. Pomona Coll. Assocs., 1987-89; ex-officio trustee Pomona Coll., 1987-89; arbitrator Chgo. Bd. Options Exch., 1978—, Pacific Stock Exch., 1979—. Mem. Securities Industry Assn. (speaker compliance and legal div. 1978—), Pomona Coll. Alumni Assn. (chmn. alumni fund, continuing edn. com. 1972-73), Nat. Assn. Securities Dealers (mem. nat. bd. arbitrators, 1978—), City Club on Bunker Hill, Bond Club L.A. Office: 333 S Hope St 38th Fl Los Angeles CA 90071

DINER, RALPH GORDON, psychologist; b. Oceanside, N.Y., Mar. 11, 1951; s. Harry and Miriam (Greenberg) D. BA, NYU, 1973; MA, Calif. Sch. Profl. Psychology, Berkeley, 1978, PhD, 1980. Lic. psychologist, Calif. Dir. vols. psychol. svcs. Haight-Ashbury Free Clinics, San Francisco, 1981; pvt. practice San Francisco and Walnut Creek, Calif., 1982—; cons. psychologist Metabolic Nutrition Program, 1984—, chief psychologist, 1985—. Author: Patient Lectures and Psychological Training, 1984. Regents scholar N.Y. Bd. Regents, 1969-73. Mem. Am. Psychol. Assn. Office: Metabolic Nutrition Program 112 La Casa Via Ste 120 Walnut Creek CA 94598

DINGES, RICHARD ALLEN, entrepreneur; b. Englewood, N.J., June 17, 1945; m. Kathie A. Headley; children: Kelly, Courtney. Grad., Jersey City State Coll., 1967; MEd, U. Hawaii, 1972; postgrad., William Peterson Coll., 1974-79. Cert. sch. adminstr.; cert. sch. spl. services dir., N.J., Ariz., Hawaii. Pres. Def. Industry Assocs., Sierra Vista, Ariz., 1979—, Fed. Career Cons., Sierra Vista, Ariz., 1985; dir. Nat. Scholarship Locators, Sierra Vista, 1985—. Editor: Guide to U.S. Defense Contractors, 1985, 87, 10 Step Guide to College Selection, Salary Negotiations for Military, How to Survive the Job Interview. Mem. Cochise County Merit Commn. (vice-chmn.). Home: 75 Ellison R Somerset NJ 08873 Office: 2160 E Fry Blvd Ste 400 Sierra Vista AZ 85635

DINGMAN, MICHAEL BRUCE, dentist; b. Rupert, Idaho, Sept. 11, 1950; s. David Robert and DeVaun (Gruwell) D.; m. Sharon Patricia Malone, Aug. 29, 1970 (div. Apr. 1989); children: Benjamin, David. BS, Coll. Idaho, 1972; DDS, Emory U., 1976. Pvt. practice dentistry Twin Falls, Idaho, 1976—; pres. Delta Dental Plan Idaho, Boise, 1984-85, chmn. 1988-89, bd. dirs.; cons. Magic Valley Rehab. Svcs., Twin Falls, 1981—. Mem. ADA, South Cen. Idaho Dental Assn. (pres. 1979-80), Idaho Dental Assn., Kiwanis (bd. dirs. Twin Falls chpt. 1988). Office: 800 Falls Ave Suite 8 Twin Falls ID 83301

DINGMAN, MICHAEL DAVID, industrial company executive; b. New Haven, Sept. 29, 1931; s. James Everett and Amelia (Williamson) D.; m. Jean Hazlewood, May 16, 1953 (div.); children: Michael David, Linda Channing (Mrs. Michael S. Cady), James Clifford; m. Elizabeth G. Tharp, Apr. 13, 1984; children: James Tharp, David Ross. Student, U. Md. Various mgmt. positions Sigma Instruments, Inc., Braintree, Mass., 1954-64; gen. and ltd. ptnr. Drexel Burnham Lambert, Inc. (formerly Burnham & Co.), N.Y.C., 1964-70; pres., chief exec. officer, bd. dirs. Wheelabrator-Frye, Inc., Hampton, N.H., 1970-83; chmn. bd. Wheelabrator-Frye Inc., Hampton, N.H., 1977-83; pres., bd. dirs. The Signal Cos., Inc., La Jolla, Calif., 1983-85, Allied-Signal Inc., Morristown, N.J., 1985-86; chmn. bd., chief exec. officer

The Henley Group, Inc., La Jolla, 1986—; bd. dirs. Ford Motor Co., Time Inc. Trustee John A. Hartford Found. Mem. IEEE (mem. adv. bd.). Clubs: Links, Bd. Room, N.Y. Yacht (N.Y.C.); Union (Boston); Cruising of Am. (Conn.); Bohemian (San Francisco), Fairbanks Ranch Country; Lyford Cay (Nassau); La Jolla Country, San Diego Yacht. Office: Henley Group Inc Liberty Ln Hampton NH 03842

DINKELSPIEL, PAUL GAINES, investment banking and public financial consultant; b. San Francisco, Feb. 12, 1935; s. Edward Gaines and Pauline (Watson) D.; A.B., U. Calif.-Berkeley, 1959. Gen. ptnr. Stone & Youngberg, San Francisco, 1961-71; 1st v.p. Shearson/Lehman and predecessor firms, San Francisco, 1971-79; pres., chmn. bd. dirs. Dinkelspiel, Belmont & Co., Inc., investment banking and pub. fin. cons., San Francisco, 1979—. With AUS, 1959-60. Mem. Govt. Fin. Officers Assn., Am. Water Works Assn., San Francisco Mcpl. Forum, Pub. Securities Assn. (public fin. com.), San Francisco Comml. Club, Commonwealth Club of Calif., Mcpl. Bond Club, N.Y. World Trade Club, Calif. Waterfowl Assn., Ducks Unltd., Sigma Chi. Home: PO Box 727 Stinson Beach CA 94970 Office: 101 California St 37th Fl San Francisco CA 94111

DINSMORE, PHILIP WADE, architect; b. Gilroy, Calif., Nov. 4, 1942; s. Wilbur Allen and Elizabeth Eleanor (Hill) D.; m. Mary Kathryn Mead; children—Robert Allen, Kerry Philip. B.Arch., U. Ariz., 1965. Registered architect, Ariz., Calif. Designer, William L. Pereira & Assocs., Los Angeles, 1965-67; assoc. CNWC Architects, Tucson, 1967-69; prin., ptnr. Architecture One Ltd., Tucson, 1979—. Mem., chmn. Archtl. Approval Bd., City of Tucson, 1974-75, 77. Fellow AIA (nat. bd. dirs. 1981-84, nat. sec. 1984—, Ariz. Architects Medal 1985, Western Mountain Region Citation award 1973, 76, 78, Award of Honor 1983); mem. Constrn. Specifications Inst., Ariz Soc. Architects (Citation award 1977, 78, 79, 80), Bldg. Stone Inst. (nat. sec. 1984-88, Tucker award 1986). Republican. Presbyterian. Office: Architecture One Ltd 6303 E Tanque Verde Rd Ste S200 Tucson AZ 85715

DION, PHILIP JOSEPH, consumer products and services, real estate and construction company executive; b. Chgo., Nov. 30, 1944; s. Philip J. and Loretta (Loftus) D.; B.A., St. Ambrose Coll., 1966; M.B.A., Loyola U., Chgo., 1968; m. Patricia Ann Reichert, June 24, 1967; children—Philip Joseph, David, Jaime. Cons. Booz, Allen & Hamilton, Chgo., 1966-68; pres., gen. mgr. Cocrema Inc., Lorenzo DeMexico, Chgo., 1968-70; with Armour-Dial Inc., Phoenix, 1970-82, pres. subs., 1970-82; sr. v.p. fin. Del Webb Corp., Phoenix, 1982-83, exec. v.p., 1983-87, pres., 1987; chmn. bd., chief exec. officer, 1987—; mem. Allendale Adv. Bd. Phoenix 40; bd. dirs. Boy's Hope. Mem. Assn. Corp. Growth, Paradise Valley Country Club. Office: Del Webb Corp 2231 E Camelback Rd Phoenix AZ 85038

DIPALMA, JOYCELYN ENGLE, talent consultant; b. Jersey City, Aug. 10, 1948; d. Raymond Joseph and Joan Jennie (Lupo) Engle; m. Joseph A. DiPalma; children: Joycelyn, Julianne. Student, H-B Studio, N.Y.C., 1964-67, N.J. Cen. State Tchrs.' Coll., 1966-69, N.J. Cen. State Tchrs.' Coll., 1966-69. Actress N.Y.C. and N.J., 1968-78; tchr. The J-E Sch. Dwight-Englewood (N.J) Sch., 1986-87; talent mgr. Beverly Hills, Calif., 1986—; image and speech cons., N.Y., N.J., 1982—. Narrator: (album) So You Want To Improve Your Speech, 1979; dir. (off-Broadway play) Plaza Suite, 1978, (film) Say Yes--You Die; author screenplays. Dir. Community Theatre, Ft. Lee, 1976-78. Mem. Screen Actors Guild, AFTRA. Roman Catholic. Home: 3111 Bel Air Dr Ste 21-B Las Vegas NV 89109 also: 1590 Anderson Ave Apt 10-D Fort Lee NJ 07024 Office: Engle Prodns 320 N La Peer Dr Ste 309 Beverly Hills CA 90211

DIPIETRO, CAROL ANN, real estate broker; b. Edinburgh, Scotland, July 2, 1956; d. Joseph Arthur and Pamela Jean (Bragger) Schlaepfer; m. Frank Richard DiPietro, June 18, 1983. Student, U. Calif., Irvine, 1973-76. Fantasyland hostess Disneyland, Anaheim, Calif., 1974-78; owner Creative Prodns., W. Hollywood, Calif., 1978-80, Baseball Fever, San Jose, Calif., 1987—, FunProdns., San Jose, 1987—; real estate broker Countywide Realty, San Jose, 1983—; instr., trainer San Jose Real Estate Bd., 1986—. Campaign mgr., mayor, councilman City of W. Hollywood, 1984; membership chmn. Human Rights Coalition, L.A., 1977; mem. adv. bd. L.A. Gay Community Ctr., Hollywood, 1977, 78, 79; bd. dirs. Orange County Community Svc. Ctr., Garden Grove, Calif., 1974, 75, 76, 77, 78. Mem. Nat. Assn. Realtors, Calif. Assn. Realtors, Nat. Assn. Real Estate Appraisers. Office: Countywide Realty 7055 Martwood Way San Jose CA 95120

D'IPPOLITO, ANTHONY, chemical engineer; b. Yonkers, N.Y., Nov. 27, 1962; s. Ralph Edmondo and Agnes (Marchetti) D'I. BSChemE, Ariz. State U., 1985. Asst. engr. Ariz. State U., Tempe, 1980-81; serviceman Blaine Ingram Inc., Phoenix, 1983; chem. engr. Ariz. Pub. Svc. Co., Phoenix, 1986—. Lector St. James Cath. Ch., Glendale, Ariz., 1982—, supervising vol. carpenter, 1988—. Mem. Am. Inst. Chem. Engrs. Office: Ariz Pub Svc Co PO Box 53999 Phoenix AZ 85072-3999

DIREEN, HARRY GEORGE, JR., electrical engineer; b. Rochester, N.Y., Jan. 19, 1955; s. Harry George and Carolyn (Bechtold) D.; m. Susan Elizabeth Knox, Aug. 2, 1980; children: Randal Hugh, James Edward. BSEE, U. Calif., Irvine, 1982. Elec. engr. Cubic Corp., San Diego, 1982-84, E.F. Johnson Co., Twin Falls, Idaho, 1984-85, Ehrhorn Tech. Ops., Canon City, Colo., 1985—. Served with USAFR, 1973-79. Mem. Eta Kappa Nu, Tau Beta Pi. Baptist. Office: Ehrhorn Tech Ops 4975 N 30th St Colorado Springs CO 80919

DIRKS, LOLITA ANN, interior designer; b. Washington, Feb. 14, 1944; d. America Matthew and Lucille Francis (Neznanski) Borzello; m. Algimantas J. Rutelionis, May 6, 1967 (div.); 1 child, Ari A.; m. Joseph Edward Dirks, Nov. 7, 1981. BS, U. Md., 1966. Interior display designer Hecht Co., Washington, 1966-69, May D&F, Denver, 1969-70; mgr. C.J. Welch Co., Denver, 1970-72; owner, operator Wall Art, Denver, 1972-74; v.p., owner Possibilities for Design, Inc., Denver, 1974—; tchr. retailing and merchandising Barbazon Schs., Englewood, Colo., 1976-80; lectr. bldg. industry, 1985—. Illustrator (book) Historic Costume, 1977; contbr. articles to profl. jours. Chmn. com. Colo. Folk Life Festival, Denver, 1972, 73. Mem. Nat. Assn. Home Builders, Home Builders Assn. Colorado Springs, Inst. Residential Mktg. (trustee), Nat. Sales and Mktg. Coun. (Mame award 1985, 86), Colo. Assn. of Home Builders, Home Builders Assn. Denver, Lithuanian Orgn. Colo. (officer 1970-71). Roman Catholic. Office: Possibilities for Design Inc 600 Elati Denver CO 80204

DIRRING, WILLIAM ANDREW, military officer; b. Miami, Fla., Dec. 22, 1946; s. Eugene and Rosamond (Eisenhaur) D.; m. Joanne Elizabeth Carlton, June 22, 1974; children: Stephanie, David. BS in Indsl. Engring., Ga. Tech., 1969; M. in Bus. Mgmt. and Supervision, Cen. Mich. U., 1974. Commd. 2d lt. USAF, 1969, advanced through grades to lt. col., 1985; mgmt. engring. officer Detachment 9 1600 mgmt. engr. squardon USAF, McChord AFB, Wash., 1969-71; mgmt. engring. officer Detachment 3 3025 mgmt. engr. squardon USAF, Hill AFB, Utah, 1971-73; computer systems analyst Hqtr. AF Logistics Commd., Wright-Patterson AFB, Ohio, 1973-76; division chief contingency plans Hqtr. USAF in Europe, Ramstein Air Base, Fed. Republic Germany, 1976-79; division chief rsch. and modeling Hqtr. AF Mgmt. Engring. Agy., Randolph AFB, Tex., 1979-83; chief wartime manpower plans Hqtr. USAF, Pentagon, Washington, 1983-87; commdr. Detachment 5 3025 mgmt. engr. squardon USAF, McClellan AFB, Calif., 1987—; cons. Pa. Fin.Group, State College, Pa., 1986—; chmn. Sports Council, McClellan AFB, 1989—. Mem. Boy Scouts Am., Folsom, Calif., 1987—, Rona Village Homeowners Assn., Fairborn, Ohio, 1974-76, Fairfax (Va.) Club Homeowners Assn., 1983-87, Sundahl PTA, Folsom, 1987—. Decorated Meritorious Svc. medal with 2 Oak Leaf Clusters, Air Force Commendation medal with 2 Oak Leaf Clusters. Mem. Inst. Indsl. Engrs., Air Force Assn., The Ret. Officers Assn., Ga. Inst. Tech. Alumni Assn., Folsom Soccer Club (coach). Republican. Roman Catholic. Home: 130 River Ridge Way Folsom CA 95630 Office: USAF Det 5 3025 Mgmt Eng Squadron McClellan AFB CA 95652

DIRUSCIO, LAWRENCE WILLIAM, business executive; b. Buffalo, Jan. 2, 1941; s. Guido Carmen and Mabel Ella (Bach) DiR.; m. Gloria J. Edney, Aug. 19, 1972; children—Lawrence M., Lorie P., Darryl C., Teresa M., Jack D. With various broadcast stas. and instr., adminstr. Bill Wade Sch. Radio and TV, San Diego, San Francisco, Los Angeles, 1961-69; account exec. Sta. KGB Radio, San Diego, 1969, gen. sales mgr., 1970-72; pres. Free Apple Advt., San Diego, 1972—, Fin. Mgmt. Assocs., Inc., San Diego, 1979-84, Self-Pub. Ptnrs., San Diego, 1981—, Media Mix Assocs. Enterprises, Inc., 1984-86; pres. Press-Courier Pub. Co., Inc., 1985-86; pres. Media Mix Advt. and Pub. Relations, 1985—; lectr., writer on problems of small bus. survival. Served with USN, 1958-60. Five Emmy nominations for T.V. commercial writing and prodn. Mem. Nat. Acad. TV Arts and Scis. Democrat. Roman Catholic. Office: Free Apple Advt 726 W Kalmia St San Diego CA 92101

DISNEY, KEVIN ALAN, power company official, consultant; b. Berkeley, Calif., May 20, 1953; s. Ralph Alan and Emma Gertrude (Honer) D.; m. Pamela Ann Rodriquez, Nov. 9, 1985; children: Christina, Jason. BS in Engring., Century U., Beverly Hills, Calif., 1986. Cert. welding insp., mech. insp., Calif. Insp. Hartford Steam Boiler Co., San Francisco, 1978-79; mech. technician Air Products & Chems. Inc., Santa Clara, Calif., 1979-82; sr. field constrn. specialist Saudi Consol. Electric Co., Damman, Saudi Arabia, 1983-84; quality control engr. Dravo Constructors Inc., San Jose, Calif., 1984-85; quality control supr. Reactor Controls Inc., San Jose, 1985; inspection coord. Sohio, Dallas, 1985-86; project mgr. Quality Mgmt. Inc., Santa Clara, 1986-87; field rep. Pacific Gas & Electric Co., San Francisco, 1987-88; mgr. quality surveillance and inspection Combustion Power Co., Menlo Park, Calif., 1988—. Mem. East Hills Sch. Bd., San Jose, 1986-87. With USN, 1972-78. Mem. Am. Welding Soc. (pub. rels. subcom. 1986—), Am. Soc. for Quality Control, Am. Soc. for Non Destructive Testing, ASTM (com. on stats. and quality 1987—), Nat. Hot Rod Assn., Smithsonian Assocs. Republican. Presbyterian. Office: Combustion Power Co 1020 Marsh Rd Ste 100 Menlo Park CA 94025

DISNEY, MICHAEL GEORGE, financial service firm executive; b. Harvey, Ill., Nov. 30, 1955. Grad. high sch., Harvey, Ill. Sales mgr. Met. Life Ins. Co., Naperville, Ill., 1979-84; regional dir. Firemens Fund Ins. Co., San Diego, 1984-85; owner, mgr. Disney Fin., Inc., El Cajon, Calif., 1985—. Mem. Nat. Assn. Life Underwriters, Life Underwriters Tng. Council (moderator-cons. 1986-87), Million Dollar Round Table (coordinator, chmn. San Diego chpt. 1987), La Mesa (Calif.) C. of C., San Diego C. of C., Toastmasters. Home: 3910 Dorsie Ln La Mesa CA 92041 Office: Disney Fin Inc 1333 E Madison Ave El Cajon CA 92021

DISTEFANO, PETER ANDREW, insurance executive; b. N.Y.C., Nov. 26, 1939; s. Peter Julian and Marie Antoinette (Onorato) D.; student City Coll. San Francisco, 1965, Costa Mesa (Calif.)-Orange Coast Coll., 1975; cert. enrolled employee benefits, Wharton Sch., U. Pa., 1980; cert. profl. ins. agt., 1987; children: Diane, Daniel, Donald. Agt., Mut. N.Y., San Francisco, 1971-73; regional mgr. Hartford Ins. Group, Santa Ana, Calif., 1972-77; v.p. Lachman & Assos., Inc., ins., Lafayette, Calif., 1977-80; pres., owner Distefano Ins. Svcs., Benicia, Calif., 1980—; lectr., cons. risk mgmt., employee benefits. Pres. Contra Costa/Solano County Easter Seal Soc. Served with USNR, 1957-62. Recipient various ins. sales awards, Cert. Profl. Ins. Agt. Designation award, 1987; registered profl. disability and health ins. underwriter. Fellow Acad. Producer Ins. Studies; mem. Nat. Assn. Health Underwriters, Nat. Assn. Life Underwriters, Soc. Registered Profl. Health Underwriters, Nat. Assn. Security Dealers, Internat. Found. Employee Benefit Plans, Profl. Ins. Agts. Calif./Nev. Soc. (cert.), Oakland/East Bay Assn. Life Underwriters. Greek Orthodox. Office: Distefano Ins Svcs Inc 827 First St Benicia CA 94510

DITHRIDGE, BETTY (MRS. ANDREW MORRISON DITHRIDGE), civic worker; b. L.A., Sept. 11, 1920; d. Thomas Edward and Louise (Miles) Mitchell; m. Andrew Morrison Dithridge, May 11, 1940; 1 child, Andrew Morrison Jr. Student, UCLA, 1937-39. Boy scout and cub scout leader L.A. Orphan's Home Soc., 1952-69, sec. extension com., 1959-61, chmn., 1966-68; vol. worker USO; mem. L.A. Jr. Philharmonic Com., 1949—; active Symphonies for Youth Concerts, 1958-59; founder, chmn. San Marino Protection Com., 1971-72; sec. L.A. County Grand Jury, 1974-75; bd. dirs. Pasadena chpt. ARC, 1961-62, Vol. Service Bur. Pasadena; bd. dirs., treas. Wilshire Community Police Coun., 1979-81; mem. citizens adv. com. L.A. Olympics Organizing Com., 1982-84; dir. Capistrano Bay Community Svcs. Dist., 1987—. Recipient awards for work with local youth groups. Mem. Wilshire C. of C. (chmn. women's bur. 1957-59), L.A.C. of C. Assocs. L.A. City Coll., Orange County Marine Inst., Friends of Huntington Libr., D.A.R., Friends of San Juan Capistrano Libr., San Juan Capistrano Hist. Soc., L.A. Grand Jurors Assn., Alpha Phi, Sigma Alpha Iota. Home: 35411 Beach Rd Capistrano Beach CA 92624

DITMORE, MICHAEL CONRAD, medical company executive; b. Mpls., May 14, 1943; s. Conrad William and June Carol (VanNest) D.; student U.S. Air Force Acad., 1961-64; B.A., U. Wash., 1966; M.B.A., Stanford U., 1970; m. Rebecca Patterson Ditmore; children—Brooke, Nathan, Nicholas, Caitlin. With IBM, Portland, Oreg., 1966-68; dir. European ops. Canberra Industries GmbH, Wiesbaden, Germany, 1970-72; regional sales mgr. Rolm Corp., Santa Barbara, Calif., 1972-73; cons. to NASA-Gen. Research Corp., Santa Barbara, 1973-74; divisional mgr. Gyrex Corp., Santa Barbara, 1974-75; v.p. mktg. and fin. Browne Corp., Santa Barbara, 1975-78; pres. Endotek Corp., Santa Barbara, 1979-84; chmn., chief exec. officer Vistek Corp., Santa Barbara, 1984—. Mem. Montecito Sch. Bd., 1975-79; mem. Santa Barbara alumni bd. Stanford U., 1976-78, 86—; Santa Barbara Symphony bd., 1986-88. Served with USAF, 1961-64. Mem. IEEE, Fgn. Relations Com. Episcopalian. Clubs: Birnam Wood Golf, Channel City. Home: 211 Rametto Rd Santa Barbara CA 93108 Office: PO Box 50839 Santa Barbara CA 93150

DITORRICE, GUY LOUIS, marketing consultant, small business owner; b. Rockford, Ill., Aug. 26, 1952; s. Enrico and Lucia (Orazi) D.; m. Nancy Jean Hunter, July 22, 1974 (div. 1980); 1 child, Matthew. AA, Rangely Coll., 1972; BA, Colo. State U., Ft. Collins, 1974. Radio newman KCOL, Fort Collins, Colo., 1974-76; newsman Sta. KASH, Eugene, Oreg., 1976-77; dir. pub. rels. Green Assocs., Eugene, Oreg., 1978-80; mktg. dir. Citizens Bank of Oreg., Eugene, 1980-82; dir. pub. rels. Cappelli, Miles & Wiltz, Eugene, 1982-84; cons., owner Mktg. Communications Techniques, Eugene, 1984—, MCT, Inc., Eugene, 1984—. Recipient Pres. award, Jr. Achievement, Eugene, 1984. Mem. Am. Mktg. Assn. (bd.dirs. Southwest Oreg. chpt.), Pub. Soc. Am., Internat. Assn. Bus. Communications, LWV (adv. bd. 1984), Newport C. of C., Eugene C. of C. (named outstanding greeter, 1985), Rotary, Lane Leaders (named leader of the year, 1986, 87, 88). Democrat. Office: Mktg Communications Techniq 309 W Fourth Ste 200 Eugene OR 97401

DITTMAN, DEBORAH RUTH, real estate broker; b. Sacramento, Apr. 15, 1932; d. Charles Harwood and Ruth Boice (Potter) Kinsley; m. John Alvin Cardoza, Sept. 1950 (div. 1964); children: Harold, Nancy Jongeward, John Allan, Gregory, Janice Boswell; m. Edgar Marshall Dittman, Jan. 22, 1967 (dec. Jan. 6 1982). Student Humprey's Coll., Stockton, Calif., 1966; grad. real estate sales Anthony Schs., 1974, cert. real estate broker, 1978; cert. in real estate San Joaquin Delta Coll., 1977; diploma Grad Real Estate Inst., 1987. Lic. real estate broker, Calif., real estate salesperson; cert. residential specialist. Sec. Calif. Dept. Water Resources, Patterson and Tracy, 1966-72; hostess Welcome Wagon, Tracy, 1973-74; assoc. realtor Reeve Assocs., Tracy, 1975-80; broker Allied Brokers, Tracy, 1980-83; ptnr. real estate Putt, Fallavena, Willbanks & Dittman, Tracy, 1983—; mem. adv. bd. Tracy Savs. and Loan, 1987—. Mem. Tracy Bd. Realtors (pres. 1981, 85, dir. 1976, 77, 80-83, 85-86), Calif. Assn. Realtors (dir. 1980-81, 85), Tracy C. of C. (bd. dirs. 1988—). Presbyterian. Home: 12134 Midway Dr Tracy CA 95376 Office: 1300 W 11th St Tracy CA 95376

DIVINE, THEODORE EMRY, electrical engineer; b. Hailey, Idaho, May 27, 1943; s. Theodore Clyde and Muriel Juanita (Kirtley) D.; BSEE, U. Wash., Seattle, 1966, MBA, 1970; m. Roberta Louise Erickson, Mar. 19, 1966; children: Timothy Shannon, Brianna Kristine, Rachel Melissa. Engr., Gen. Telephone Co. of N.W., 1968-69; mem. tech. saff NW ops. Computer Scis. Corp., 1970-72; research engr. Battelle Pacific N.W. Labs., Richland, Wash., 1973—, research sect. mgr., 1978, staff engr. def. programs, 1980—. Pres., Mid-Columbia Sci. Fair Assn., 1975-76; ruling elder First Presbyn. Ch., Prosser, Wash., 1982-84. Served as officer Signal Corps, USAR, 1966-84; Vietnam, 1967. Decorated Bronze Star. Mem. IEEE, Am. Def. Preparedness Assn., Assn. of U.S. Army, Am. Soc. Agrl. Engrs. (com. chmn. 1977-78, 82-83, chmn. nat. conf. on electronics in agr. 1983), Beta Gamma Sigma. Mem. editorial adv. bd. Internat. Jours. Computers & Electronics in Agr., Elsevier, The Netherlands, 1983—.

DIXEN, PATRICIA ANN, home cleaning company executive; b. Owatonna, Minn., Mar. 8, 1952; d. Jens Alfred and Mary Ann (Johnson) D. BA in Bus., U. Minn., 1974; postgrad. in fin., U. Colo., 1988. Account exec. Campbell Mithun Advt. Agy., Mpls., 1974-78; sales mgr. Procter & Gamble Co., Cin., 1978-81; owner, mgr. Basisk Home Cleaning, Denver, 1981—. Vol. illiteracy program Share Our Strength Program, Denver, chmn. corp. sponsors. Mem. Colo. Homecleaners Assn. (founder, pres.), NAFE, Denver C. of C., Denver Art Mus., Colo. Ballet. Republican. Lutheran. Home and Office: Basisk Home Cleaning 3120 Xenia St Denver CO 80231

DIXON, DOUGLAS STEPHEN, forensic pathologist; b. East Orange, N.J., Aug. 28, 1945; s. William Robert and Angela Marguarite (Genoese) D. MA in English, U. Va., 1967, MD, 1971. Diplomate Am. Bd. Pathology. Resident in anatomic pathology George Washington U., Washington, 1971-74; resident in forensic pathology Office Chief Med. Examiner, Washington, 1974-75, dep. med. examiner, 1979-84, acting chief med. examiner, 1984; dep. med. examiner Office Chief Med. Examiner, Boston, 1984-87, assoc. chief med. examiner, 1985-87; dep. med. examiner Office of Coroner San Diego County, San Diego, 1987—; cons. in field, 1979—. Author: Management of Gunshot Wounds, 1988; contbr. articles to med. jours. Maj. M.C., U.S. Army, 1975-79. Fellow Am. Acad. Forensic Scis.; mem. Nat. Assn. Med. Examiners. Democrat. Episcopalian. Office: Office Coroner San Diego Co 5555 Oakland Ave Bldg A San Diego CA 92123-4219

DIXON, FRANK JAMES, medical scientist, educator; b. St. Paul, Mar. 9, 1920; s. Frank James and Rose Augusta (Kuhfeld) D.; m. Marion Edwards, Mar. 14, 1946; children: Janet Wynne, Frank, Michael. B.S., U. Minn., 1941, M.B., 1943, M.D., 1944. Diplomate: Am. Bd. Pathology. Intern U.S. Naval Hosp., Great Lakes, Ill., 1943-44; research asst. dept. pathology Harvard, 1946-48; instr. dept. pathology Washington U., 1948-50, asst. prof., 1950-51; prof., chmn. dept. pathology U. Pitts. Med. Sch., 1951-60; chmn. dept. exptl. pathology Scripps Clinic and Research Found., La Jolla, Calif., 1961-74; chmn. biomed. research depts. Scripps Clinic and Research Found., 1970-74, dir. research inst., 1974-86, dir. emeritus, 1986—; research assoc. dept. biology U. Calif. at San Diego, 1961-64, prof. in residence in dept. biology, 1965-68, adj. prof. dept. pathology, 1968—; sci. adviser NIH, Nat. Found., Helen Hay Whitney Found., St. Jude's Med. Center, Christ Hosp. Inst., Cin.; mem. expert adv. panel on immunology WHO; sci. adv. bd. Nat. Kidney Found.; Pahlavi lectr. Ministry of Sci. and Higher Tech., Iran, 1976. Co-editor: Advances in Immunology; Editorial bd.: Excerpta Medica, Jour. Exptl. Medicine, Am. Jour. Pathology, Cellular Immunology, Kidney Hosp. Practice, Perspectives in Biology and Medicine; Contbr. articles to profl. jours. Served with M.C. USNR, 1943-46. Recipient Theobald Smith award, 1952; Parke-Davis award in exptl. pathology, 1957; Disting. Achievement award Modern Medicine, 1961; Martin E. Rehfuss award in internal medicine, 1966; Von Pirquet medal Ann. Forum on Allergy, 1967; Bunim medal Am. Rheumatism Assn., 1968; Internat. award Gairdner Found., 1969; Mayo Soley award Western Soc. Clin. Research, 1969; Albert Lasker Basic Med. Research award, 1975; Dickson prize U. Pitts., 1975; Homer Smith award N.Y. Heart Assn., 1976; Rous-Whipple award Am. Assn. Pathologists, 1979, Gold-Headed Cane award, 1987; Regents award U. Minn., 1985; H.P. Smith award Am. Soc. Clin. Pathologists, 1985; Distinguished Service award Lupus Found. Am., 1987. Mem. Nat. Acad. Scis., N.Y. Acad. Scis. Western Assn. Physicians, Western Soc. Clin. Research, Soc. Exptl. Biology and Medicine, Transplantation Soc., AAAS, Am. Soc. Clin. Investigation, Am. Acad. Allergists, Interurban Path. Soc., Harvey Soc. (lectr. 1962), Am. Soc. Exptl. Pathology (pres. 1966), Am. Assn. Immunologists (pres. 1972), Am. Assn. for Cancer Research, Assn. Am. Physicians, Am. Acad. Arts and Scis., Sigma Xi, Nu Sigma Nu, Alpha Omega Alpha. Office: Scripps Clinic & Rsch Found 10666 N Torrey Pines Rd La Jolla CA 92037

DIXON, FRANK JAMES, lawyer; b. Ft. Belvoir, Va., Feb. 20, 1951; s. Frank Jerome and Anne (Marincel) D. BA, U. Notre Dame, 1973; JD, Lewis and Clark Law Sch., 1979. Bar: Oreg. 1979, U.S. Dist. Ct. Oreg. 1980, U.S. Ct. Appeals (9th cir.) 1981, U.S. Tax Ct. 1988. Legal intern Multnomah County Legal Aid Svc., Portland, Oreg., 1977-79; ptnr. Dixon and Friedman, Portland, 1979—. Chmn. Neighborhood West/Northwest Rev. Bd. Dirs., Portland, 1987—. 2nd lt. U.S. Army, 1973-75. Mem. Oreg. State Bar Assn., Oreg. Trial Lawyers Assn., Multnomah Athletic Club. Office: Dixon and Friedman 1020 SW Taylor 430 Portland OR 97205

DIXON, GEORGE LANE, JR., orthopaedic surgeon; b. Burlington, Iowa, Oct. 10, 1928; s. George Lane Dixon and Ellen Christina (Swanson) Payson; m. Margery Jane Myers, Mar. 29, 1953; children: Frank Wesley, Martha Jane, Jennifer Lynn, Amy Carol. BA, State U. Iowa, 1950, MD, 1954. Diplomate Am. Bd. Orthopaedic Surgery. Intern gen. surgery U.S. Army Hosp., Ft. Benning, Ga., 1957-58; resident orthopaedic gen. surgery Letterman Gen. Hosp., San Francisco, 1958-60; resident orthopaedic surgery Childern's-Shriner's Hosp., San Francisco, 1960-61; orthopaedic surgeon Lovelace Clinic, Albuquerque, 1966-72; pvt. practice Albuquerque, 1972—; med. dir. St. Joseph Rehabilitation Ctr., Albuquerque, 1988—; clin. prof. dept. orthopaedic surgery sch. medicine U. N.Mex., Albuquerque, 1966—; med. adv. bd. Carrie Tingley Hosp., Albuquerque, 1980-88; pres. Cycle Vision Tours, Inc., Albuquerque, 1983—; bd. dirs. N.Mex. Physicians Mut. Ins. Co., Albuquerque, 1988—. Contbr. articles med. jours. Lt. col. U.S. Army, 1955-66. Mem. Western Orthopaedic Assn. (bd. dirs. 1985-88), Greater Albuquerque Med. Assn. (pres. 1975), Am. Acad. Orthopaedic Surgeons (bd. councilors 1983-89), Hibbs Soc. (co-pres. 1985), N.Mex. Orthopaedic Assn. (pres. 1971-72, sec. 1978-83). Home: 1020 Green Valley Rd NW Albuquerque NM 87107 Office: 1101 Med Arts Ave NE Albuquerque NM 87102

DIXON, HAROLD WESLEY, JR., drama educator; b. Buffalo, June 14, 1948; s. Harold Wesley and Isabelle Delores (Carriero) D.; m. Maedell Ann Hallbeck, Aug. 28, 1971; children: Shannon Maedell, Wesley Powell. BA, U. Redlands, 1970; MA, U. Minn., 1972, PhD, 1976. Asst. prof. U. Wis. Dept. Theatre, Madison, 1974-79; asst. prof. U. Ariz. Dept. Drama, Tucson, 1979-83, assoc. prof., 1983-89, prof., 1989—. Actor in various plays. Dir. various plays and operas. Nat. bd. mem. Am. Coll. Theatre Festival, Washington, 1984-87; chmn. Ariz. Coll. Theatre Festival, 1981-84. Mem. Actors' Equity Assn., Screen Actors' Guild, Ariz. Theatre Educators' Assn., So. Calif. Ednl. Theatre Assn. Democrat. Home: 3555 E Ventana Canyon Dr Tucson AZ 85718 Office: U Ariz Dept Drama Tucson AZ 85721

DIXON, JULIAN CAREY, congressman; b. Washington, Aug. 8, 1934; m. Betty Lee; 1 son, Cary Gordon. B.S., Calif. State U., Los Angeles, 1962; LL.B., Southwestern U., Los Angeles, 1967. Mem. Calif. State Assembly, 1972-78; mem. 96th-101st Congresses from Calif. 28th Dist., mem. House Appropriations Com., chmn. Com. on Standards Ofcl. Conduct, mem. Congl. Black Caucus; pres., bd. dirs. CBC Found., Inc. Served with U.S. Army, 1957-60. Mem. NAACP, Urban League, Calif. Arts Commn. Democrat. Office: 2400 Rayburn Bldg Washington DC 20515

DIXON, MICHAEL WAYNE, designer, writer; b. Honolulu, May 3, 1942; s. Gordon Alvin and Terry (Mendes) D.; m. Janis Marie Travis, Jan. 4, 1963 (div. 1977); children: Kimberlee Ann, Gregory Page, Morgan Ashley. Tech. illustrator Rockwell Internat., Anaheim, Calif., 1962-66, Western Gear Corp., Lynwood, Calif., 1966-69; owner Unisex Clothing Store, Norwalk, Calif., 1969-71; mgr. Am. Health Industries, Downey, Calif., 1971-72; police officer Vernon (Calif.) Police Dept., L.A. Police Dept., 1972-81; designer, pres. Dornaus and Dixon Enterprises, inc., Huntington Beach, Calif., 1979-88; freelance writer Huntington Beach, 1986—. Author: Bren Ten Owner's Manual, 1982, Bodyshaping, 1986; inventor firearm safety devices, 10 millimeter auto cartridge. With USN, 1959-62. Mem. Am. Film Inst.

DIXON, ROBERT MORTON, soil scientist; b. Leon, Kans., May 30, 1929; s. William Gill and Vivian (Mendes) D.; BS, Kans. State U., 1959, MS, 1960; PhD, U. Wis., 1966; children: James, Curtis, Donna, Gregory. Instr., Kans. State U., Manhattan, 1959-60; irrigation specialist Ford Found., Cairo, 1967; research soil scientist U.S. Dept. Agr., 1960-85, Tucson, 1973-85; agrl. cons. U.S. Agy. Internat. Devel., Haiti, 1977; People-to-People Irrigation del. People's Republic of China, 1982. Served with U.S. Army,

1954-56. Mem. Internat. Soc. Soil Sci., Am. Soc. Agronomy, Am. Geophys. Union, Am. Soc. Agrl. Engrs., Soil Sci. Soc. Am., Soil Conservation Soc. Am., Internat. Platform Assn., Soc. Range Mgmt., Ariz.-Nev. Acad. Sci., Land Imprinting Found. (organizer 1986, chmn. 1986—). Democrat. Unitarian. Contbr. articles to profl. jours. Patentee land imprinter. Home and Office: 1231 E Big Rock Rd Tucson AZ 85718

DJERASSI, CARL, chemist, educator, writer; b. Vienna, Austria, Oct. 29, 1923; s. Samuel and Alice (Friedmann) D.; m. Norma Lundholm (div. 1976); children: Dale, Pamela (dec.); m. Diane W. Middlebrook, 1985. A.B. summa cum laude, Kenyon Coll., 1942, D.Sc. (hon.), 1958; Ph.D., U. Wis., 1945; D.Sc. (hon.), Nat. U. Mex., 1953, Fed. U., Rio de Janeiro, 1969, Worcester Poly. Inst., 1972, Wayne State U., 1974, Columbia, 1975, Uppsala U., 1977, Coe Coll., 1978, U. Geneva, 1978, U. Ghent, 1985, U. Man., 1985. Research chemist Ciba Pharm. Products, Inc., Summit, N.J., 1942-43, 45-49; asso. dir. research Syntex, Mexico City, 1949-52; research v.p. Syntex, 1957-60; v.p. Syntex Labs., Palo Alto, Calif., 1960-62; v.p. Syntex Research, 1962-68, pres., 1968-72; pres. of Zoecon Corp., 1968-83, chmn. bd., 1968-86; prof. chemistry Wayne State U., 1952-59, Stanford, 1959—; bd. dirs. Cetus Corp., Monoclonal Antibodies, Inc., Affymax, Vitaphore Inc.; pres. Djerassi Found. Resident Artists Program. Mem. editorial bd. Jour. Organic Chemistry, 1955-59, Tetrahedron, 1958—, Steroids, 1963—, Proc. of Nat. Acad. Scis, 1964-70, Jour. Am. Chem. Soc, 1966-75, Organic Mass Spectrometry, 1968—, Chemica Scripta, 1985—; author 9 books; contbr. numerous articles to profl. jours., poems and short stories to lit. publs. Recipient Intrasci. Research Found. award, 1969; Freedman Patent award Am. Inst. Chemists, 1970; Chem. Pioneer award, 1973; Nat. Medal Sci., 1973; Perkin medal, 1975; Wolf prize in chemistry, 1978; John and Samuel Bard award in Sci. and Medicine, 1983, Roussel prize, 1988, Discoverers award Pharm. Manual Assn., 1988, Esselen award ACS, 1988; named to Nat. Inventors Hall of Fame, 1978. Mem. Nat. Acad. Scis. (Inst. Medicine), Am. Chem. Soc. (award pure chemistry 1958, Baekeland medal 1959, Fritzsche award 1960, award for creative invention 1973, award in chemistry of contemporary tech. problems 1983), Royal Soc. Chemistry (hon. fellow, Centenary lectr. 1964), Am. Acad. Arts and Scis., German Acad. (Leopoldina), Royal Swedish Acad. Scis. (fgn.), Royal Swedish Acad. Engring. Scis. (fgn.), Am. Acad. Pharm. Scis. (hon.), Brazilian Acad. Scis. (fgn.), Mexican Acad. Sci. Investigation, Bulgarian Acad. Scis. (fgn.), Phi Beta Kappa, Sigma Xi, Phi Lambda Upsilon (hon.). Office: Stanford U Dept Chemistry Stanford CA 94305

DO AMARAL, LUIZ HENRIQUE DE FILIPPIS DE STEFANO REZENDE, architect, interior designer, construction company executive; b. Rio De Janeiro, Oct. 18, 1952; came to U.S., 1964; s. Jefferson R. and Erminia D. Do Amaral. BArch, U. Calif., Berkeley, 1975. Lic. gen. contractor. Sr. ptnr. Do Amaral, Brower & Stewart, Santa Clara, Calif., 1976-77, Do Amaral & Stewart, Santa Clara, 1977-78; prin. Do Amaral Assocs., Santa Clara, 1978-80, Do Amaral Assocs. Definitive Environments & Arch-West Constrn. Co., Los Gatos, Calif., 1980-82; pres., chief exec. officer Amalgamated Devel. Enterprises, Inc., Los Gatos, 1982—. Charles M. Marshall Found. scholar, 1972. Mem. Am. Inst. Bldg. Design (cert. bldg. designer, bd. dirs. 1978-79, chpt. v.p. 1979-80), Internat. Conf. Bldg. Officials, Constrn. Specifications Inst., Pi Lambda Phi, Alpha Mu Gamma. Roman Catholic. Office: Amalgamated Devel Enterprises 61 E Main St Ste C Los Gatos CA 95030

DOAN, TUAN ANH, electronic engineer; b. Saigon, Vietnam, Nov. 6, 1961; came to U.S., 1975; s. Van Khanh Doan and Thanh Thi Ngoc Nguyen. BEE, Calif. Polytechnic U., Pomona, 1982; MEE, West Coast U., 1984. Electronic engr. Amistar Corp., Torrance, Calif., 1983-85; sr. electronic engr. Aerojet Electrosystems, Azusa, Calif., 1985—. Named outstanding grad. student award, West Coast U., 1984. Mem. Tau Beta Pi, Eta Kappa Nu. Home: 22045 E La Puente Rd Walnut CA 91789 Office: Aerojet Electrosystems 1100 W Hollyvale St Azusa CA 91702

DOANE, DAVID ALLEN, computer industry sales manager, consultant; b. Escondido, Calif., Nov. 9, 1951; s. Eric David and Arlene Betty (Helfand) D.; m. Gail Barbara Davidson, Dec. 17, 1977; children: Erin, Megan, Lauren. AA, Orange Coast Coll., Costa Mesa, 1974; BS, BA, Brigham Young U., 1980, MA, 1981. Firefighter, emergency med. technician Provo City Fire Dept., Utah, 1979-82; sales rep. Monsanto Corp., St. Louis, 1982-83; product mktg. mgr. Mountain Computer, Scotts Valley, Calif., 1983-84; dist. sales mgr. Archive Corp., Costa Mesa, Calif., 1984-86; western regional sales mgr. Univation, Freemont, Calif., 1986-87; cons. mktg. and sales Los Gatos, Calif., 1987; sales dir. Nara Technologe, Sunnyvale, Calif., 1987; dist. sales mgr. Systech Corp., San Diego, 1987; dir. OIM Mktg. Novell, Inc., 1988—. Local campaign mgr., Utah, 1980. Served to cpl. USAF, 1970-72. Republican. Mormon. Home: 2081 E 10225 South Sandy UT 84092

DOANE, ROSEANNE MARIE, medical technologist, educator; b. Flint, Mich., Mar. 18, 1950; d. Robert LeRoy and Maxine Lucille (Vincent) Wood; m. Steven Chandler Doane, June 6, 1981; 1 child, Nathaniel Luce. BS in Biology, U. Oreg., 1972, cert. in med. tech., 1972; MA in Internat. Affairs, Ohio U., 1978. Med. technologist St. James Hosp., Butte, Mont., 1972-73; instr., med. technologist U. Abidjan, Ivory Coast, 1973-75; chief hematology St. Elizabeth's Hosp., Yakima, Wash., 1975-76; med. technologist staff Willamette Falls Hosp., Oregon City, Oreg., 1976-77, O'Bleness Hosp., Athens, Ohio, 1977; med. technologist hematology USPHS-Indian Hosp., Crownpoint, N.Mex., 1978-79; chief lab. services USPHS-Indian Health Service Clinic, Bellingham, Wash. and Salem, Oreg., 1979-81; pvt. practice Lewiston, Idaho, 1981-88; med. technologist Indian Health Svcs., Crownpoint, N.Mex., 1988—; instr., med. technologist Cen. Wash. U., Ellensburg, 1975-76; instr., coordinator Rio Grande Coll., 1977-78; instr. English as a Second Lang. Lewis Clark State Coll., Lewiston, 1982-85. Mem. Am. Soc. Clin. Pathologists. Republican. Lutheran. Club: Twin River Cyclists (Lewiston). Home: PO Box 1756 Crownpoint NM 87313

DOBBEL, RODGER FRANCIS, interior designer; b. Hayward, Calif., Mar. 11, 1934; s. John Leo and Edna Frances (Young) D.; m. Joyce Elaine Schnoor, Aug. 1, 1959; 1ž child, Carrie Lynn. Student, San Jose State U., 1952-55, Chouinard Art Inst., L.A., 1955-57. Asst. designer Monroe Interiors, Oakland, Calif., 1957-66; owner, designer Rodger Dobbel Interiors, Piedmont, Calif., 1966—. Contbr. articles to mags and newspapers. Decorations chmn. Trans Pacific Ctr. Bldg. Opening, benifit Oakland Ballet, and various other benifits and openings, 1982—; chmn. Symphonic Magic, Lake Marritt Plz., Opening of Oaklnd Symphony Orchestra Season and various others, 1985—; cons. An Eving of Magic, Oaklnd Hilton Hotel, benig=fit Providence Hosp. Found. Recipient Cert. of Svc., Nat. Soc. of Interior Designers, 1972, 74, Outstanding Artistic Contbn., Oakland Symphony, 1986. Mem. Nat. Soc. Interior Designers (profl. mem. 1960-75, v.p. Calif. chpt. 1965, edn. found. mem. 1966—, nat. conf. chmn. 1966), Am. Soc. Interior Designers , Claremont Country, Diabetic Youth Found. Democrat. Roman Catholic.

DOBBERPUHL, WAYNE BRIAN, senior energy engineer; b. Port Washington, Wis., Sept. 30, 1955; s. Chester Arthur and Verna Evelyn (Merzdorf) D. BS in Energy Engring., U. Wis., Milw., 1978; MBA, Ariz. State U., 1987. Registered profl. engr., Ariz., Wis. Mech. design engr. APS Generation Engring., Phoenix, 1979-83, 1979-83; nuclear engr. APS Nuclear Engring., Phoenix, 1983-87; sr. energy engr. APS Comml. & Indsl. Mktg., Phoenix, 1987—. Coordinator Grapefruit Pick for Westside Food Bank, Phoenix, 1988. Mem. Am. Soc. of Mech. Engrs. Republican. United Church of Christ. Home: 3231 Ellis St Chandler AZ 85224

DOBBS, WARREN CRAIG, community organization executive; b. Atlanta, Apr. 15, 1928; s. Samuel C. and Marjorie D. (Frampton) D.; student Yale U., 1945-47, various mil. schs., 1950-53, San Francisco State Coll., 1956-57, Coll. Notre Dame, 1966, Wash. State U., 1976; grad. United Community Funds and Councils Inst., 1969; m. Mary Anne Karish, Sept. 27, 1950; children—Marjorie Stanish, Catherine Candler, Warren Craig. Ind. sales contractor, San Francisco, 1957-62; exec. dir. United Cerebral Palsy, Oakland, Calif., 1962-65; area dir. United Crusade, San Francisco, 1965-69, asso. exec. dir., Sacramento, 1969-72; exec. dir. United Way of Benton and Franklin Counties, Kennewick, Wash., 1972-82, United Way Spokane County, 1982—; community orgn. cons. Office Community Devel., State of Wash., 1977-79. Bd. dirs. Benton Franklin Opportunities Industrialization Center, 1978-79; trustee Mid-Columbia Symphony Soc., 1977-79; pres. Mid-Columbia Arts Council, 1975-76; regional adv. com. Wash. State Dept. Social and Health Services, 1982—; mem. Spokane Human Services Adv. Bd., 1983—; mem. SSS Bd., 1984—. Served with Transp. Corps, U.S. Army, 1950-56; Korea. Republican. Presbyterian. Club: Rotary (pres. Pasco-Kennewick 1981-82). Contbr. articles to profl. jours.; founder of Counterpart, an interracial orgn. Home: W 403 21st Ave Spokane WA 99203 Office: PO Box 326 Spokane WA 99210

DOBELIS, GEORGE, manufacturing company executive; b. July 31, 1940; s. John and Dorothy (Arins) D.; m. Dolores Ann Nagle, Dec. 2, 1972; children: Sally Ann Berg, Christian Eric Berg, Kurt Conrad Berg. AA in Engring., Santa Monica Coll., 1963; student, Control Data Inst., 1970. Engring. Masterite Ind., Torrance, Calif., 1969-70; engring. mgr. Elco Corp., El Segundo, Calif., 1964-76, mgr. new products, 1976-77; pres. Connector Tech. Inc., Anaheim, Calif., 1977—; V.p. Guide Services, Calif., 1982—. Patentee in field; contbr. articles to profl. jours. Served as sgt. N.G., 1963-69. Mem. IEEE. Republican. Lutheran. Club: Palm Valley.

DOBRY, SYLVIA HEARN, writer, consultant historian; b. L.A., Aug. 16, 1938; d. Joseph Charles Hearn and Leona May (Crocker) DuBay; m. Ernest John McMichael, Jr., Aug. 13, 1956 (div. 1962); children: Patricia May, Pamela Frances, Debra Stacy, Ernest John III; m. George Maynard Dobry, Oct. 12, 1985. Student, U. Hawaii, 1971-73; BA, U. Calif., Santa Barbara, 1963. Singer concerts, opera, TV, commls., 1948-63; real estate developer various firms, 1960—; writer Hawaii Tribune Herald, Hilo, 1965-68; pres. European Castle Restorations, Lurcy-Levis, France, 1973-83; writer, producer Hawaii Actors & Musicians Soc., Kailua-Kona, 1983-85; exec. dir. West Kauai Main St., Waimea, Hawaii, 1986-89; gen. mgr. Kauai Heritage Found., Lihue, Hawaii, 1988—; dir. numerous U.S. and British corps., 1969-83; sec. Valueur Pub. Ltd., London, 1975—. Editor: Living in Kona, 1985; author: (plays) Voyage of Destiny, 1988, Island Love Song, 1989, (book) Historical Sites and Sights of Kauai, 1989; contbr. articles numerous pubs. Commr. Kauai Historical Preservation Rev. Commn., Lihue, Hawaii, 1986—; dir. Kauai Economic Devel. Bd., Lihue, 1986-89; coord., mgr. Captain Cook Celebration, Waimea, Hawaii, 1987-88; mem. Mayor's Beautification Com., Lihue, 1986-88; pub. relations Island of Kauai, 1985—; goodwill ambassador of County of Kauai to Whitby, Eng., Cooktown, Australia, 1987, 88; mem. Kauai Historical Soc., Friends of the Kauai Musuem, Kauai Community Players. Mem. Inst. Outdoor Drama, Nat. Trust for Historic Preservation, Quota Club (dir. 1989—, pres.-elect), Sister Cities Internat. (state dir. 1989—). Home and Office: 3-3400 Kuhio Hwy #A207 Lihue HI 96766

DOBSON, BRIDGET MCCOLL HURSLEY, television executive and writer; b. Milw., Sept. 1, 1938; d. Franklin McColl and Doris (Berger) Hursley; m. Jerome John Dobson, June 16, 1961; children: Mary McColl, Andrew Carmichael. BA, Stanford U., 1960, MA, 1964; CBA, Harvard U., 1961. Assoc. writer General Hospital ABC-TV, 1965-73, headwriter General Hospital, 1973-75; producer Friendly Road Sta. KIXE-TV, Redding, Calif., 1972; headwriter Guiding Light CBS-TV, 1975-80, headwriter As the World Turns, 1980-83; creator, co-owner Santa Barbara NBC-TV, 1983—, headwriter Santa Barbara, 1983-86, exec. producer Santa Barbara, 1986-87. Recipient Emmy award Nat. Acad. TV Arts and Scis., 1988. Mem. Acad. TV Arts and Scis. (mem. com. on substance abuse 1986-88, Emmy nomination 1986), Writers Guild Am., Am. Film Inst. (mem. TV com. 1986-88). Office: 2121 Ave of the Stars Ste 656 Century City CA 90067

DOBSON, KATHI A., insurance company manager; b. Northridge, Calif., Oct. 10, 1958; d. James Everett McCarthy and Lillian Theresa (Jaquier) McCarthy Caldwell; m. Christopher Francis Crawford, Dec. 12, 1982 (div. 1988); m. Mark James Dobson, Mar. 11, 1989. Grad. high sch., Van Nuys, Calif. Sr. cashier Avco Fin., Van Nuys, Calif., 1976-78; asst. mgr. Pacific Plan Calif., Van Nuys, 1978-79; real estate loan mgr. Imperial Thrift & Loan, Panorama City, Calif., 1979-82; account exec. Lincoln Savs. & Loan, Portland, Oreg., 1982-83, Anderson Fin. Group, Portland, 1983-84; account mgr. Ticor Title Ins., Beaverton, Oreg., 1984—. Writer, arranger music record, 1988; author poem. Exec. chair lst Citizen Award Banquet, Tigard, 1986-87. Mem. Tigard C. of C. (bd. dirs. 1985—), I-5 Corridor Assn. (com. chair. 1987—), Tualatin Valley Econ Devel. Corp., Sunset Corridor Assn., Inst. Mgmt. and Profl. Women, Home Builders Assn., Washington County Bd. Realtors, Portland Music Assn. Repubican. Home: 4210 SE Drake St Milwaukie OR 97222 Office: Ticor Title Ins 4450 SW Lombard St Beaverton OR 97005

DOBSON, MARGARET JUNE, educational administrator, health and physical fitness educator; b. Seattle, June 20, 1931; d. James Walter and Frances May (Howard) D. BS in Health and Physical Edn., U. Oreg., 1954, MS in Physical Edn., 1959; EdD, U. Wis./U. Oreg., 1965; postgrad., Brigham Young U., 1966. Instr. health and physical edn. Portland State U., 1955-65, Lincoln High Sch., Portland, 1954-55; assoc. prof. health and physical edn. Portland State U., 1965-68, prof. health and physical edn., 1968—, various adminstrv. positions, 1972-87, exec. v.p. emeritus, 1988—; instr. Portland Bur. Parks and Recreation, Eugene Bur. Parks, 1951-54; vis. prof. Mt. Hood Community Coll., Gresham, Oreg., 1969-70; instr. U.S. Mil. Spl. Services, Okinawa, Japan, 1959. Recipient numerous athletic and softball awards. Fellow Royal Soc. Promotion Health, Am. Alliance Health, Physical Edn. Recreation and Dance; mem. Am. Assn. Higher Edn., Am. Assn. State Colls. and U., AAUW, Nat. Mus. Women Arts (charter), Japan/Am. Soc. Oreg., Pacific Ballet Co., Am. coll. Sports Medicine and Sci. and numerous other memberships. Home: 4404 SW Primrose Portland OR 97219 Office: Portland State U. PO Box 751 Portland OR 97207

DOBSON, TERRANCE JAMES, banker; b. Odessa, Wash., Aug. 16, 1940; s. Leon C. and Dorothy (Armstrong) D.; m. Judith Kaye Blaesi, June 12, 1965; children: Terrance James Jr., Tad Jeremy. BA, Wash. State U., 1964; MBA, Mich. State U., 1969. Venture analyst Gen. Mills, Mpls., 1969-71; v.p., mgr. First Nat. Bank of Mpls., 1971-77; v.p. First Bank System, Inc., Mpls., 1977-78; exec. v.p. Old Nat. Bank of Wash., Spokane, 1978-87; sr. v.p. U.S. Bancorp, Portland, Oreg., 1987, exec. v.p., 1987—. Chmn. YMCA Inland Empire, Spokane, 1979-86; mem. bus. adv. council Wash. State U., 1980—; bd. dirs. Sisters of Holy Names, 1983-87. Capt. USAF, 1964-68. Mem. Am. Automobile Assn. (bd. dirs. 1978-88), Hayden Lake Country Club (bd. dirs. 1986-87), Oswego Lake Country Club, Rotary. Home: 17960 Ridge Lake Dr Lake Oswego OR 97034 Office: US Bancorp 111 SW 5th Ave PO Box 8837 Portland OR 97208

DOBYNS, THEODORE ARTHUR, artist; b. Medford, Oreg., July 7, 1950; s. Arthur William and Lillian (Bernstrom) D. BFA cum laude, U. Wash., 1984; post grad., Cen. Wash. U., 1989. Freelance bronze casting Seattle, 1984—; owner Equity Broze & Burl, Seattle, 1986-88; pres. Filter Works, Seattle, 1986—; metal casting pres. Art Production Inc., 1984-89. Pres. Evans Creek Christian Retreat, Ellensberg, 1988—. Baptist. Home and Office: PO Box 916 Ellensburg WA 98926

DOCKSON, ROBERT RAY, savings and loan executive; b. Quincy, Ill., Oct. 6, 1917; s. Marshall Ray and Letah (Edmondson) D.; m. Katheryn Virginia Allison, Mar. 4, 1944; 1 child, Kathy Kimberlee. A.B., Springfield Jr. Coll., 1937; B.S., U. Ill., 1939; M.S. in Fgn. Service, U. So. Calif., 1940, Ph.D., 1946. Lectr. U. So. Calif., 1940-41, 45-46, prof., head dept. mktg., 1953-59; dean U. So. Calif. (Sch. Bus. Adminstrn.); and prof. bus. econs. 1959-69; vice chmn. bd. Calif. Fed. Savs. & Loan Assn., Los Angeles, 1969-70; pres. Calif. Fed. Savs. & Loan Assn., 1970-77, chmn., 1977-88, chief exec. officer, 1973-83; chmn. CalFed Inc., 1984-88, chief exec. officer, 1984-85, also dir.; instr. Rutgers U., 1946-47, asst. prof., 1947-48; dir. Bur. Bus. and Econ. Research, 1947-48; economist Western home office Prudential Ins. Co., 1948-52, Bank of Am., San Francisco, 1952-53; econ. cons., 1953-57; dir. McKesson Corp., IT Corp., Pacific Enterprises Corp., Transam. Capital Fund, Inc., Transam. Income Shares, Inc., Internat. Lease Fin. Corp., Computer Scis. Corp. Am. specialist for U.S. Dept. State; mem. Town Hall, 1954—, bd. govs., 1963-65, hon. bd. govs., 1965—, pres., 1961-62; Trustee John Randolph Haynes and Dora Haynes Found., Rose Hills Meml. Park Assn., Com. for Econ. Devel., Calif. Council for Econ. Edn.; trustee, pres. Orthopedic Hosp.; bd. councilors Grad. Sch. Bus. Adminstrn., U. So. Calif.; bd. regents, chmn. univ. bd. Pepperdine U.; chmn. housing task force Calif. Roundtable. Served from ensign to lt. USNR, 1942-44. Decorated Star of Solidarity Govt. of Italy.; Recipient Asa V. Call Achievement award; Distinguished Community Service award Brandeis U.; Whitney M. Young Jr. award Urban League, 1981, Albert Schweitzer Leadership award; Man of Yr. award Nat. Housing Conf., 1981; Industrialist of Yr. award Calif. Mus. Sci. and Industry, 1984. Mem. Calif. C. of C. (pres. 1980, dir. 1981-86), Los Angeles C. of C. (dir.), Am. Arbitration Assn., Newcomen Soc. North Am., Hugh O'Brian Youth Found., Phi Kappa Phi (Diploma of Honor award 1984), Beta Gamma Sigma. Clubs: Bohemian, California, Los Angeles Country, One Hundred, Silver Dollar, Birnam Wood Golf, Thunderbird Country. Office: CalFed Inc 5670 Wilshire Blvd Los Angeles CA 90036

DOCKSTADER, JACK LEE, electronics executive; b. Los Angeles, Dec. 14, 1936; s. George Earl and Grace Orine (Travers) D.;m. Kerry Jo King, Oct. 24, 1987; children: Travis Adam Mayer, Bridget Olivia Mayer. student UCLA, 1960-70. Rate analyst Rate Bur., So. Pacific Co., Los Angeles, 1954-57; traffic analyst traffic dept. Hughes Aircraft Co., Fullerton, Calif., 1957-58, Culver City, Calif., 1958-59, traffic mgr. Hughes Research Labs., Malibu, Calif., 1959-70, materiel mgr., 1970-75; materiel mgr. Hughes Aircraft Co., Culver City, 1975-80, prodn. materiel mgr. Electro-Optical and Data Systems Group, El Segundo, Calif., 1980-84, mgr. materiel total quality 1984-85, mgr. cen. materiel ops. and property mgmt. 1987—. Mem. adv. council transp. mgmt. profl. designation program UCLA, 1966-80, mem. Design for Sharing Com., 1977-82; adv. com. transp. program Los Angeles Trade Tech. Coll., 1970-80. Served with USNR, 1954-76. Mem. UCLA Alumni Assn., Nat. Contracts Mgmt. Assn., Naval Enlisted Res. Assn., Hughes Aircraft Co. Mgmt. Club, Delta Nu Alpha (pres. San Fernando Valley chpt. 1965-66, v.p. Pacific S.W. region 1969-71, region man of year 1971). Republican. Presbyn. Home: PO Box 3156 Redondo Beach CA 90277 Office: PO Box 902 El Segundo CA 90245

DODD, DEBORAH JANE, military contracting officer; b. Longmont, Colo., Oct. 11, 1947; d. John Jerome and Margaret Cora (Slee) D. BA, U. Colo., 1969; cert. teaching, Keane Coll., 1971; MS, San Jose State U., 1975. Vista vol. Palatka, Fla., 1969-70; tchr. N.J. Urban Edn. Corp., Newark, 1971-72, English Conversation Circle, Tokyo, Japan, 1972-73; camp dir. Baker Beach Golden Gate Nat. Recreation Area, San Francisco, 1975; recreation therapist Casa Grande (Ariz.) Rehab. Ctr., 1975-76; office mgr., counselor Tucson Rape Crisis Ctr., 1976-78; customs inspector U.S. Customs Service, Nogales, Ariz., 1978-81; elem. edn. tchr. Salome Show-Low Schs., Ariz., 1981-82; contract negotiator and contracting officer USAF, McClellan AFB, Calif., 1982—; gen. ptnr. Wymer and Assocs., Citrus Heights, Calif., 1986—. Mem. Calif. Native Plant Soc., Sacramento Minerology Soc., Fossils for Fun, Phi Beta Kappa. Democrat. Home: 8100 oak Ave Citrus Heights CA 95610

DODD, JOE DAVID, safety engineer, consultant, administrator; b. Walnut Grove, Mo., Jan. 22, 1920; s. Marshall Hill and Pearl (Combs) D.; m. Nona Bell Junkins, Sept. 17, 1939; 1 dau. Linda Kay Dodd Helmick. Student SW Mo. State U., 1937-39, Wash. U., 1947-55. Cert. profl. safety engr. Calif. Office asst. retail credit co., Kansas City, Mo., 1939-42; bus driver City of Springfield (Mo.), 1945-47; ops., engring., and personnel positions Shell Oil Co., Wood River (Ill.) Refinery, 1947-66; health and safety dept. mgr. Martinez Mfg. Complex, Calif., 1966-83, retired 1983; exec. dir. Fire Protection Tng. Acad., U. Nev.-Reno; rep. Shell Oil Co., Western Oil and Gas Assn., 1970-81. Mem. Republican Presdl. Task Force. Served with USMC, 1942-45. Decorated Presdl. Citation. Mem. Western Oil and Gas Assn. (Hose Handler award 1972-81, Outstanding mem. award), Am. Soc. Safety Engrs., Veterans Safety, State and County Fire Chiefs Assn., Peace Officers Assn., Nat. Fire Protection Assn. Presbyterian (elder). Established Fire Protection Tng. Acad., U. Nev.-Reno, Stead Campus.

DODDS, DALE IRVIN, chemical executive; b. Los Angeles, May 3, 1915; s. Nathan Thomas and Mary Amanda (Latham) D.; m. Phyllis Doreen Kirchmayer, Dec. 20, 1941; children: Nathan E., Allan I., Dale I. Jr., Charles A. AB in Chemistry, Stanford U., 1937. Chem. engr. trainee The Texas Co., Long Beach, Calif., 1937-39; chemist Standard Oil of Calif., Richmond, 1939-41; chief chemist Scriver and Quinn Interchem., L.A., 1941-46; salesman E.B. Taylor and Co. Mfg. Rep., L.A., 1947-53, Burbank (Calif.) Chem. Co., 1953-57, Chem. Mfg. Co./ICI, L.A., 1957-68; pres., gen. mgr. J.J. Mauget Co., L.A., 1969—. Inventor: Systemic Fungicide, 1976; patentee in field; contributed to devel. Microinjection for Trees. Mem. Am. Inst. Chemists, Am. Chem. Soc., Sigma Alpha Epsilon Alumni (pres. Pasadena (Calif.) chpt. 1973), L.A. Athletic Club. Republican. Christian Scientist. Office: JJ Mauget Co 2810 N Figueroa St Los Angeles CA 90065

DODDS, WILLIAM FARRELL, writer, columnist, author; b. Des Moines, July 24, 1952; s. John Joseph and Margaret Evelyn (Farrell) D.; m. Monica Lynn Faudree, Mar. 23, 1974; children: Thomas, Carolyn, Andrew. Student, St. Thomas Sem., Kenmore, Wash., 1970-72; BA, U. Wash., 1974. Reporter The Progress, Seattle, 1978-82, asst. editor, 1982-84, editor, 1984-88; pvt. practice Mountlake Terr, Wash., 1988—. Co-author: Speaking Out, Fighting Back, 1985, paperback edit., 1987; syndicated columnist Dad Knows Best; columnist On the Home Front, Columbia mag.; contbr. articles to Our Sunday Visitor, Cath. Digest, Critic, Liguorian, Nat. Cath. News Svcs., St. Anthony Messenger. Mem. Pacific Northwest Writers Conf., Cath. Press Assn. (journalism awards 1981, 82, 83, 85-87), Wash. Press Assn., Soc. Profl. Jours.-Sigma Delta Chi (journalism awards 1979, 81-84, 86,88).

DODGE, THEODORE AYRAULT, geological mining consultant, drilling company executive; b. Chgo., Jan. 17, 1911; s. Robert Elkin Neil and Katherine Eleanor (Staley) D.; m. Isabelle Stebbins, June 15, 1935; children—Eleanor Dodge Gray, Janet, Richard Neil, Thomas Marshall. A.B. in Geology, Harvard Coll., 1932; A.M. in Geology, Harvard U., 1935, Ph.D. in Geology, 1936; M.A. in Geology, U. Wis., 1933. Registered geologist, Ariz. Geologist, sr. geologist Cerro de Pasco Copper Corp., Morococha, Peru, 1935-38; geologist, petroleum engr. various cos., 1939-41; geologist Anaconda Copper Mining Co., Las Cruces, N.Mex., 1941-42; geologist, acting chief geologist Cananea Consol. Copper Co., Cananea, Mexico, 1942-45; cons. geologist various companies, Ariz. and Mex. 1946-70; mgr. Christmas div. Inspiration Consol. Copper Co., Christmas, Ariz., 1971-75; pres. Hoagland & Dodge Drilling Co., Inc., Tucson, 1976—; instr. geology U. So. Calif., Los Angeles, 1940. Contbr. articles to profl. jours. Fellow Geol. Soc. Am., Mineral. Soc. Am.; mem. Ariz. Geol. Soc. (pres. 1955), Soc. Econ. Geologists, Am. Inst. Mining Engrs., Phi Beta Kappa, Sigma Xi. Baha'i. Club: Mining of the Southwest (Tucson). Home and Office: 1770 N Potter Pl Tucson AZ 85719

DODSON, CHARLES LEON, JR., chemist; b. Knoxville, Tenn., Mar. 15, 1935; s. Charles L. Sr. and Margaret Glenn (Berry) D; m. Vicki L., Sept. 6, 1958; children: Alyssa, Bronwyn. BS, Emory and Henry Coll., 1957; MS, U. Tenn., 1962, PhD, 1963. Asst. prof. U. Ala., Huntsville, 1966-67, assoc. prof., 1967-81; tech. specialist Beckman Instruments Inc., Atlanta, 1981-83, principal applications chemist, 1983-87, sr. staff scientist, 1988—; vis. prof. Oxford, Eng., 1972-73. Contbr. articles to profl. jours. Postdoctoral fellow European office of U.S. Aerospace Agy., Birmingham, Eng., 1963, Na.t Research Council, Ottawa, Can., 1964. Mem. AAAS, Am. Chem. Soc., Am. Physical Soc. Office: Beckman Instruments Inc 2500 Harbor Blvd Fullerton CA 92634

DODSON, FRANK ROBERT, hotelier, real estate investor; b. Albuquerque, Dec. 15, 1946; s. Conrad C. and Martha (Ellen) D. Student, UCLA, 1965-66, San Diego State U., 1966-68, U. N.Mex., 1970-71. Bus. cons. Dodson & Assocs., Albuquerque, 1970-84, real estate developer, 1980—; hotelier, owner Royal Inn of Albuquerque, 1971—; pres., founder Albuquerque Innkeepers Assn., 1972-73, Albuquerque Conv. & Visitors Bur., 1981-82, Cen. Ave. Assn. Albuquerque, 1982-84; lobbyist N.Mex. Legis., 1985—. Publisher: New Mexico TravelTrends, 1988—; founder, pub. New Mex. Travel Trends. Mgr. Econ. Adv. Council to Mayor, Albuquerque, 1977-83. Served with USN, 1968-69. Named Educator of Yr. award Am. Hotel-Motel Assn.,1976 1st person cert. as Hotel Adminstr. in N.Mex., 1977; recipient Cen. Ave. Assn. Beautification Program City Honor, 1984. Mem. Albuquerque C. of C. (conv. and tourism div. 1975-80), Rotary. Republican. Roman Catholic. Office: 4119 Central Ave NE Albuquerque NM 87108

DODSON, MICHAEL VERNE, animal sciences educator; b. Caldwell, Idaho, Jan. 27, 1954; s. Vernon E. and Zola (Owings) D.; m. Jean Rene

Norris, June 25, 1988; children : Jaclyn Marie, Alicia Nanette, Steven Michael. BS, U. Idaho, 1980, MS, 1982; PhD in Animal Physiology, U. Ariz., 1985. Vet asst. Lewiston (Idaho) Vet Clinic, 1977-78; grad. research asst. U. Idaho, Moscow, 1980-82, U. Ariz., Tucson, 1982-83; asst. prof. animal scis. Wash. State U., Pullman, 1985--. Contbr. articles to sci. jours. With USN, 1972-76, Vietnam. Named Moormans Mfg. Co. Calif. scholar, 1977, grad. acad. scholar U. Ariz., 1982-85, E. Ray Cowden grad. scholar U. Ariz., 1983-85; grantee USDA, 1986-87, Am. Diabetes Assn., 1986-88. Mem. Am. Soc. Animal Sci., Endocrine Soc., AAAS, In Vitro, N.Y. Acad. of Scis., Am. Diabetes Assn., Sigma XI, Alpha Zeta, Phi Eta Sigma, Phi Sigma, Gamma Sigma Delta. Office: Wash State U Dept Animal Scis Clark 207 Pullman WA 99164-6320

DODSON-EDGARS, JEANNIE ELIZABETH, marketing and management consultant; b. El Paso, Tex., July 12, 1950; d. Minot Boyd and Florence Elizabeth (Smith) Dodson; m. Darryl Eugene Edgars, Sept. 18, 1973; 1 child, Ginja Rachel. BS, UCLA, 1972. Freelance writer, editor, producter Portland, Oreg., 1978-83; founder, prin. Chandler & Assocs., Portland, 1984—; prin. DynaMetrix Corp., Portland, 1986—, v.p. mktg., 1989—; bd. advisors Portland Smal Bus. Devel. Ctrs. Mem. steering com. Women in Yr. 2000, Portland, 1985-86; active Citizens for Sch. Support, 1987—; bd. dirs. Meet the Leaders, 1986-87. NEH grantee, 1978-79. Mem. Women in Communications (v.p. fin. adminstrn. 1987-88, chmn. honors com. 1988-89), Network of Bus and Profl. Women. Club: The City Club of Portland.

DOENGES, DEBRA LYNNE, interior design consultant; b. Waukegan, Ill., July 15, 1956; d. Milan S. and Lila M. (Leppanen) Pelouch; m. Mark C. Doenges, Aug. 18, 1979. BA in Fine Arts, Design and Mgmt., So. Ill. U., 1979; postgrad., Western Ill. U., 1979. Contract mgr. Design Resources, Seattle, 1980-82; sr. interior design buyer Design Internat., Seattle, 1982-85, interior design project coordinator, 1983-85; textile designer Debra Doenges, Seattle, 1985—; interior design cons. Doenges Cons., Seattle, 1986—; instr. U. Wash. Extension, Seattle, 1987—. Author course handbook Commercial Textiles, 1987.

DOERFLING, HANK, aerospace engineer; b. San Pedro, Calif., Nov. 3, 1936; s. Laurence Howard and Julia Margret (Rusbarsky) D.; B.S. in Physics, Oreg. State U., 1958, M.S., 1963; M.Pub. Adminstrn., Pepperdine U., 1975; m. Elaine Carole; children—Howard, Carrie, Cassie, Tony, Evon. Analyst, No. Am. Aviation Co., Downey, Calif., 1963-64; mem. tech. staff TRW Systems Redondo Beach, Calif., 1964-66, adminstrv. and project mgr. Logicon, San Pedro, Calif., 1966-77; mgr. data processing mgmt. info. div., space and communications group Hughes Aircraft Co., El Segundo, Calif., 1977—. Mem. Hermosa Beach Improvement Commn., 1970-72, chmn., 1971-72; mem. City of Hermosa Beach City Council, 1972-80, mayor, 1973-74, 79-80; pres. South Bay Cities Assn., 1975-76; commr. South Coast (Calif.) Regional Coastal Commn., 1977-80, Calif. Coastal Commn., 1978-80. Served with USN, 1958-61. Mem. Hermosa Beach C. of C. (bd. dirs. 1970-71), League Calif. Cities, Sigma Pi Sigma. Home: 1011 2d St Hermosa Beach CA 90254 Office: Hughes Aircraft Co 650 N Sepulveda Blvd El Segundo CA 90245

DOERING, RICHARD, sociologist, educator; b. Cleve., May 17, 1939; s. Roy A. and Gertrude (Koubek) D.; m. Clara Mae Weber, Aug. 1, 1969; children: Bart Lee, Karl Curtis, Marlena Rae, Mark Richard. BA, Ohio Wesleyan U., 1960; MA, Columbia U., 1962; BSEd, Kent State U., 1967; MA, U. Calif., Riverside, 1974, PhD, 1975. Instr. Cen. Wyo. Coll., Riverton, 1968-70; research sociologist U. Calif., Riverside, 1972-74; instr. Orange Coast Coll., Costa Mesa, Calif., 1975-76, Golden West Coll., Huntington Beach, Calif., 1975-76; asst. prof. sociology and statistics Calif. State U., Los Angeles, 1977—; evening instr. Chaffey Coll., Alta Loma, Calif., 1976—. Contbr. articles to profl. jours. Recipient Leland Publs. award, 1960. Mem. Am. Sociol. Assn., Am. Psychol. Assn., Calif. Assn. for Gifted, Mensa, Psi Chi, Kappa Delta Pi, Tau Kappa Epsilon. Home: 7286 Nixon Dr Riverside CA 92504 Office: Calif State U Dept Sociology and Social Work Los Angeles CA 90032

DOERPER, JOHN ERWIN, food writer; b. Wuerzburg, Fed. Republic of Germany, Sept. 17, 1943; came to U.S., 1963; s. Werner and Theresia (Wolf) D.; m. Victoria McCulloch, Jan. 14, 1971. BA, Calif. State U., Fullerton, 1968; MA/ABD, U. Calif., Davis, 1972. Food writer/author Seattle, 1984—; food columnist Washington, Seattle, 1985-88, Seattle Times, 1985-88; food editor Wash.-The Evergreen State Mag., Seattle, 1988—; pub., editor, founder Pacific Epicure, Quarterly Jour. Gastronomy, Bellingham, Wash., 1988—; columnist Bellingham Herald, 1983—; dir. Annual Washington Invitational Chef's Symposium. Author: Eating Well: A Guide to Foods of the Pacific Northwest, 1984, The Eating Well Cookbook, 1984, Shellfish Cookery: Absolutely Delicious Recipes from the West Coast, 1985; contbr. articles to profl. jours. Bd. dirs. Bellingham/Whatcom County Visitors & Conv. Bur., Bellingham, 1984-86. Mem. Wash. Food & Wine Symposiu (founder, bd. dirs.), Internat. Riesling Soc. (founder, trustee), Oxford Symposium Food and Cookery (speaker 1988, 89). Home: 111 Old Mill Village Bellingham WA 98226 Office: Wash Evergreen State Mag 200 W Thomas Seattle WA 98119

DOGLIONE, ARTHUR GEORGE, data processing executive; b. Bklyn., May 24, 1938; s. Francis and Georgia (Smith) D.; m. Maryann Laurette Bonfanti, Sept. 3, 1960; children: Dana Ann, Arthur Todd, Lora Michele. AA, Scottsdale (Ariz.) Community, 1978; AAS, Maricopa Tech. Coll., Phoenix, 1984; BS, Ariz. State U., 1985. Salesman Columbus Realty Co., Trenton, N.J., 1962-65; appraiser J.H. Martin Appraisal Co., Trenton, 1965-68; office mgr. Mcpl. Revaluations, Avon-by-the-Sea, N.J., 1968-69; pres., broker Area Real Estate Agy., Wall, N.J., 1969-76; property appraiser Ariz. Dept. Revenue, Phoenix, 1976-78; investment appraiser Continental Bank, Phoenix, 1978-79; appraisal systems specialist Ariz. Dept. Revenue, Phoenix, 1979-80; project dir. Ariz. Dept. Adminstrn., 1980-83; pres. Logical Models, Scottsdale, Ariz., 1983—; tax assessor Upper Freehold Twp., N.J., 1974-75, Borough of Bradley Beach, N.J., 1975; lectr. in field. Author various software. Counselor SCORE, SBA, Mesa, Ariz., 1986—. Mem. Phi Theta Kappa. Republican. Roman Catholic. Office: Logical Models 2828 N 74th Pl Scottsdale AZ 85257

DOHERTY, ALFRED EDWARD, engineer, consultant; b. Shaker Heights, Ohio, Nov. 11, 1929; s. Alfred Edward and Florence (Pylick) D.; m. Jeannette Smith, Dec. 31, 1931 (dec. Feb. 1981); children: James Edward, Thomas Vincent, George Michael; m. Virginia Dolores Meza. BS, Calif. Coast U., 1987. Registered profl. engr.; cert. mech. engr. Methods devel. Douglas Aircraft Co., Torrance, Calif., 1954-59; mgr. advanced materials Aerojet Gen. Corp., Downey, Calif., 1959-69; v.p. Electro-Form, Inc., Ft. Worth, 1969-78; pres. A&T Engring., A&T Mfg., Ft. Worth, 1978-84; plant mgr. Leland Southwest, Ft. Worth, 1984-87; v.p. and gen. mgr. formed products Explosive Fabricators, Inc., Louisville, Colo., 1987—. Contbr. technical papers to profl. jours.; patentee in field. Sgt. U.S. Army, 1948-54, Korea. Mem. Soc. Mech. Engrs., Elks. Lutheran. Home: 4955 Cornwall Dr Boulder CO 80301

DOHERTY, GEORGE WILLIAM, psychologist; b. N.Y.C., Oct. 18, 1941; s. William George and Catherine Marguerite (Nierenhausen) D.; BS, Pa. State U., 1964; MS, Miss. State U., 1977; postgrad. Baylor U., 1972, North Tex. State U., 1979. Cert. Nat. Acad. Cert. Clin. Mental Health Counselors. Program coord., dir. youth devel. program Econ. Opportunities Advancement Corp., Waco, Texas, 1968-71; psychol. counselor, parent tng. Counseling or Referral Assistance Svcs., Phila., 1973-75; psychologist III, Rural Clinics Community Counseling Ctr., Ely, Nev., 1980-85; counselor, rsch.er, Ely, 1985-86; evaluator San Luis Valley Comprehensive Community Mental Health Ctr., 1987-88; therapist adolescent spl. program. Cen. Wyo. Counseling Ctr., Casper, 1989—; mem. faculty No. Nev. Community Coll., Ely, 1980-85; co-chmn. human rights com. Blue Peaks Devel. Ctr., Alamosa, Colo., 1988—; mem. Wyo. CAP. Capt. U.S. Air Force, 1964-68. Mem. Am. Psychol. Assn. (assoc.), Western Psychol. Assn., Inter-Am. Soc. Psychology, Internat. Assn. Applied Psychology, Assn. Behavior Analysis, Am. Assn. Counseling and Devel., Assn. Counselor Edn. and Supervision (chmn. task force and interest group community counseling 1984-85), Western Assn. Counselor Edn. and Supervision, Assn. Measurement Edn. and Guidance, Am. Mental Health Counselors Assn., Air Force Assn., World Future Soc., AAAS, Pa. State U. Alumni Assn., Smithsonian Assn., Irish-Am. Cultural Inst., O'Dochartaigh Family Rsch. Assn., Am. Legion, Wilderness Soc., Nat. Audubon Soc. Democrat. Home: PO Box 194 Casper WY 82602 Office: 1200 E 3rd St 3rd Fl Casper WY 82601 also: Monte Vista CO 81144

DOHERTY, RICHARD MICHAEL, law firm administrator; b. San Francisco, Mar. 29, 1943; s. George Daniel and Alice Elizabeth (Kehl) D.; BS in Biochemistry, U. Santa Clara, 1965, MBA, 1968; m. Karen Lynn Kinney, Aug. 18, 1980; children: Shannon Elizabeth, Matthew John. Mgr. data processing Pacific Telephone Co., San Jose, Calif., 1966-69; mgr. internat. fin. Memorex Corp., Santa Clara, Calif., 1969-73; group controller Rohr Industries, San Diego, 1973-76; v.p. fin. and adminstrn. Photosonics, Inc., L.A., 1976-79; v.p. fin. and adminstrn. Korn/Ferry Internat., L.A., 1979-81; mng. dir., partner Cox, Castle, Nicholson, L.A., 1981—; vis. prof. UCLA, U. Calif., Berkeley. Lt. U.S. Army, 1965-66. Mem. Nat. Assn. Accts., Am. Inst. Corp. Controllers, Century West Club, Beverly Hills Gun Club. Republican.

DOHN, GEORGE THOMAS, lawyer; b. Chillicothe, Mo., Nov. 6, 1935; s. George Eckel and Lula Mae (Handley) D.; m. Nancy Lorraine Moore, Oct. 29, 1961 (div. 1971); children: Kari L., Katrina S., Derek S., Kristin K.; m. Rita Rae Gardner, June 2, 1972. AAS, Yakima Valley Coll., 1959; BBA, U. Wash., 1961, LLB, JD, 1963. Bar: Wash. 1963. Assoc. Tunstall & Hettinger, Yakima, Wash., 1963-65; ptnr. Tunstall, Hettinger & Dohn, 1965-72; prin. McArdle, Dohn, Talbott, Simpson & Gibson, P.S., 1973—, pres., 1982-83; city atty. Ellensburg, Wash., 1964-84, Union Gap, Wash., 1976, Goldendale, Wash., 1979—, Kittitas, Wash., 1985-86; bd. dirs. Mut. of Enumclaw (Wash.) and Enumclaw Life Ins. Cos., 1985—; instr. legal rsch. techniques U. Wash., 1963. Bd. dirs., legal counsel Spring Acres Group Homes, Inc., 1969-76; bd. dirs. Planned Parenthood Assn., Yakima, 1965-75, Yakima County Young Republicans, 1963-65; mem. adv. bd., Wash. Criminal Justice Edn. and Tng. Ctr., 1973-74; mem. legal adv. bd., Wash. Found. Handicapped, 1975-76; mem. YMCA, Yakima; deacon Presbyn. Ch. With USAF, 1953-57. Mem. ABA, Wash. State Bar Assn., Yakima County Bar Assn., U.S. Supreme Ct. Bar Assn., Wash. Assn. Mcpl. Attys. (pres. 1972-73), Am. Arbitration Assn. (arbitrator 1973—), Nat. Inst. Mcpl. Law Officers, Wash. Govtl. Lawyers Assn., Wash. Def. Trial Attys., Wash. Trial Lawyers Assn., Rep. Nat. Lawyers Assn., U.S. Supreme Ct. Bar Assn., Def. Rsch. Inst., Phi Theta Kappa, Phi Delta Phi, Yakima Ski, Cascadians Mountaineering Club, Nordic Nautilus, Yakima Tennis, Washington Athletic Club. Office: PO Box 590 308 N 2d St Yakima WA 98907

DOHNER, BARRY CRAIG, veterinarian, biochemical research executive; b. Omaha, May 9, 1952; s. Edson Royal and Marcella Louise (Wolfe) D.; m. Debby Ann McClain, Sept. 3, 1983. BS, U. Calif., Davis, 1976, DVM, 1978. Intern Grand Ave. Pet. Hosp., Santa Ana, Calif., 1978-79; staff veterinarian Mangrove Vet. Hosp., Chico, Calif., 1980-83; clin. practice vet. medicine, Chico, 1983—; owner, pres. Butte Biochemicals, Chico, 1986—. Author: (with others) Methods in Bio-inorganic Chemistry, 1977. Mem. No. Valley Vet. Med. Assn. (pres. 1984), Calif. Vet. Med. Assn., AVMA, Am. Animal Hosp. Assn. Home and Office: 135 W 9th Ave Chico CA 95926

DOI, LOIS KIKUMI, psychiatric social worker; b. Honolulu, Oct. 24, 1951; d. James Masato and Thelma Kimiko Miyamoto; m. Brian Kenji Doi, May 26, 1972; children: Michael Leslie, Lorian Naomi. BS, U. Hawaii, 1974, MSW, 1978. Lic. clin. social worker, Calif. Psychiat. social worker, child specialist Desert Community Mental Health Ctr., Indio, Calif., 1979—, coordinator children's day treatment program, 1982—; pvt. practice psychiat. social worker Indio, 1983—; counselor Los Angeles Urban League, 1975-76; commr. Bd. Behavioral Sci. Examiners for Licensed Clin. Social Workers in Calif., 1987—. Vol. advisor Community Recreation Ctr. Youth Group, Hawaii, 1967-69; vol. interviewer ARC Food Stamp Program, Hawaii, 1973; vol. asst. YWCA Programs Young Mothers and Teens, Hawaii, 1973; vol. group leader YWCA Juvenile Delinquent Program, Hawaii, 1973; placement counselor Vols. In Service to Am., Los Angeles, 1975. Mem. Nat. Assn. Social Workers. Office: Desert Community Mental Health Ctr 82-485 Miles Ave Indio CA 92201

DOI, MARY ELLEN, research chemist, laboratory administrator; b. Memphis, Mo., Jan. 15, 1933; d. Earl Edward and Beulah Mae (Leach) Tucker; m. Minoru Doi, June 16, 1962; 1 child, Paul Edward. BS, Northeast Mo. State U., 1953. Cert. med. technologist, 1957. Tchr. chemisty, biology Princeton (Mo.) High Sch., 1953-54; tchr. sci. Evans Jr. High Sch., Ottumwa, Iowa, 1954-56; lab. technician Shelby County Hosp., Shelbyville, Ill., 1957-58; med. chemist Barnes Hosp., St. Louis, 1958-60; research chemist Monsanto Chem. Co., St. Louis, 1960-63; chief chemist, dir. lab. E.S. Erwin and Assocs., Tolleson, Ariz., 1963—. Active Rep. campaign, 1976. Mem. Am. Chem. Soc., Assn. Official Analytical Chemists, Ariz. Assn. Cert. Labs. Republican. Methodist. Club: Bus. and Profl. Women (Maryvale, Glendale, Ariz.) (past sec.-treas., v.p., pres., Woman of Yr. 1974, 79). Home: 5963 W Hazelwood Phoenix AZ 85033 Office: Nutrition-Lab Svcs PO Box 237 Tolleson AZ 85353

DOIDA, STANLEY Y., dentist; b. Kalamath Falls, Calif., Dec. 15, 1944; s. Sam S. and Mae M. (Nakao) D.; m. Eileen M. Crilly; children: Stanley Jr., Scott Samuel. Student, Knox Coll., 1965-67; DDS, Northwestern U., 1970. Asst. prof. Sch. Dentistry Northwestern U., Chgo., 1970-71; pres. Midtown Dental, Denver, 1971—; instr. U. Colo. Dental Sch., Denver, 1972-74. Mem. ADA, Acad. Operative Dentistry, Acad. Gold Foil Operators, Glenmoor Country Club. Home: 4700 E 6th Ave Denver CO 80220 Office: Midtown Dental 1800 Vine St Denver CO 80206

DOIG, IVAN, writer; b. White Sulphur Springs, Mont., June 27, 1939; s. Charles Campbell and Berneta (Ringer) D.; m. Carol Dean Muller, Apr. 17, 1965. BJ, Northwestern U., 1961, MS in Journalism, 1962; PhD in History, U. Wash., 1969; LittD (hon.), Montana State U., 1984, Lewis and Clark Coll., 1987. Editorial writer Lindsay-Schaub Newspapers, Decatur, Ill., 1963-64; asst. editor The Rotarian, Evanston, Ill., 1964-66. Author: (memoir) This House of Sky, 1978; (non-fiction) Winter Brothers, 1980; (novels) The Sea Runners, 1982, English Creek, 1984, Dancing at the Rascal Fair, 1987. Sgt. USAFR, 1962-69. NEA fellow, 1985; recipient Gov.'s Writers Day award, 1979, 81, 85, 88, Pacific N.W. Booksellers award for Lit. Excellence, 1979, 81, 83, 85, 88. Mem. Authors Guild, PEN Am. Ctr., Forest History Soc.

DOKTER, PATRICIA ANN, interior design executive; b. Downey, Calif., Jan. 19, 1956; d. Garrett Henry and Katherine Marie (Schleael) D. Student, Cerritos Coll., 1974-76; BA, Long Beach State U., 1979. Interior designer Haus & Home Interiors, Big Bear Lake, Calif., 1979-86; owner Interiors, Big Bear Lake, 1986--. Mem. Am. Soc. Interior Designers. Office: Interiors Box 348 Big Bear Lake CA 92315

DOLAN, G. KEITH, educator; b. L.A., June 14, 1927; s. George Kline and Ruth (Brookhart) D.; m. Florence Ellen Campbell, Apr. 5, 1952; children: Diana Evans, Clarice, Daniel, Carole. BA, George Pepperdine U., 1950; MEd, UCLA, 1952, EdD, 1961. Tchr. La Mesa (Calif.) Jr. High Sch., 1951-52, vice prin., 1954-56; tchr. Lemon Grove (Calif.) Jr. High Sch., 1952-54; prin. Spring Valley Jr. High Sch., La Mesa, 1956-60, San Bernardino (Calif.) High Sch., 1960-67; prof., coord. secondary edn. Calif. State U., San Bernardino, 1967-75, dir. tchr. corps, 1975-79, prof., coord. adminstrv. svcs., 1979—; cons. various Calif. sch. dists., 1967—, MGM TV show Mr. Novak, Culver City, Calif., 1964-65, Govt. Brazil, Brazilia, 1974; expert witness sch. bd., San Bernardino, Indio, Calif., 1984—. Author: Sports Almanac USA, 1984; pres., editor Footprint Pub. Co., 1984—, Acad. Tapes, 1964—; contbr. articles to profl. jours. Pres. San Bernardino Uptown YMCA, 1963-65; mem. Human Rels. Commn., City of San Bernardino, 1964-66; mem. bd. alumni George Pepperdine U., L.A., 1981. Served with USN, 1945-46, PTO. Named to Athletic Hall of Fame, George Pepperdine U., 1986; recipient Community Svc. award San Bernardino YMCA, 1988. Mem. Calif. Faculty Assn., Kiwanis (bd. dirs. 1963-65), Phi Delta Kappa (v.p. 1978-79). Democrat. Home: 3946 Ironwood St San Bernardino CA 92404 Office: Calif State U 5500 State University Pkwy San Bernardino CA 92407

DOLAN, MARYANNE MCLORN, writer, educator, lecturer; b. N.Y.C., July 14, 1924; d. Frederick Joseph and Kathryn Cecilia (Carroll) McLorn; m. John Francis Dolan, Oct. 6, 1951; children: John Carroll, James Francis McLorn, William Brennan. B.A., San Francisco State U., 1978, M.A., 1981. Tchr. classes and seminars in antiques and collectibles U. Calif.-Berkeley, U. Calif.-Davis, U. Calif.-Santa Cruz, Coll. of Marin, Kentfield, Calif., Mills Coll., Oakland, Calif., St. Mary's Coll., Moraga, Calif., 1969—; tchr. writing Dolan Sch., 1978—; owner antique shop, Benicia, Calif., 1970—. Author: Vintage Clothing, 1880-1960, 1983; Collecting Rhinestone Jewelry, 1984, Old Lace & Linens, 1989; weekly columnist The Collector, 1979-88; contbr. articles to profl. jours. Mem. AAUW, Internat. Soc. Appraisers, Calif. Writers Club, Internat. Platform Assn. Republican. Roman Catholic. Home: 138 Belle Ave Pleasant Hill CA 94523 Office: 191 West J St Benicia CA 94510

DOLENCE, DEANN JOAN, oil company executive; b. Rock Springs, Wyo., Sept. 9, 1962; d. Eric Victor and Joan Margaret (Ripperger) D. BS in Polit. Sci., U. Wyo., 1984; BS in Fin., Ariz. State U., 1988. Asst. mgr. Trans Am. Fin. Services, Scottsdale, Ariz., 1985-87; assoc. analyst Conoco Inc., Casper, Wyo., 1988--. Republican. Roman Catholic. Office: Conoco Inc 851 Werner Ct Casper WY 82601

DOLEZAL, PETER, mining company executive; b. Czechoslovakia, Apr. 13, 1943; arrived in Can., 1957; m. Gaye Beverley, May 16, 1965; children: Katherine, Kimberley, Mark, Peter Jr. BA, Queen's U., Kingston, Ont., Can., 1965, MBA, 1967. Mem. labor relations staff Chrysler Can., Windsor, Ont., 1967-69; successively materials mgr., indsl. relations rep., mine adminstr. Great Can. Oil Sands (now SUNCOR Corp.), Ft. McMurray, Alta., 1970-77; pres., chief exec. officer BC Bldgs. Corp., Victoria, B.C., 1977-87; pres. Westar Mining, Ltd., Vancouver, B.C., 1987—.

DOLGOW, ALLAN BENTLEY, consultant; b. N.Y.C.; BIE, NYU, 1959, MBA, 1972; m. Nina Kim; children: Nicole, Marc, Ginger, Kimbie. with, Republic Aviation Corp., Farmingdale, N.Y., 1959-60; mgr. Internat. Paper Co., N.Y.C., 1960-73; project mgr. J.C. Penney Co. Inc., N.Y.C., 1973-76; dir. mfg. and planning Morse Electro Products, N.Y.C., 1976-77, exec. mgr. Morse Electrophonic Hong Kong Ltd., 1976-77; internat. project mgr. Revlon Inc., Edison, N.J., 1977-79; mgmt. cons. SRI Internat., Menlo Park, Calif., 1979—. With U.S. Army, Germany. Office: 333 Ravenswood Ave Menlo Park CA 94025

DOLIBER, DARREL LEE, design engineer, consultant; b. Mpls., June 19, 1940; s. Russell Clifford Doliber and Helen Carol (Homa) Price; m. Ethel Lorraine Dzivi, June 17, 1962; children: Wendy Lorraine, Heather Leigh; m. Helga Renate Miggo, Oct. 31, 1986. AA, Palomar Coll., 1973. Prodn. engr. Hughes Aircraft Co., Carlsbad, Calif., 1969-74; sr. engr. I.T.T., Roanoke, Va., 1974-77; dir. mfg. Gainsboro Elec. Mfg. Co., Inc., Roanoke, Va., 1977-78; mfg. engr. Litton Industries, Tempe, Ariz., 1978-82; sr. engr. Datagraphix, Inc., San Diego, 1982-84; lab. mgr. S.A.I.C., San Diego, 1984—. Contbr. articles in field; patentee in field. Mem. Soc. Info. Display, Soaring Soc. Am. Roman Catholic. Home: 3625 128 Avocado Village Ct La Mesa CA 92041 Office: Sci Applications Internat Corp 11526 Sorrento Valley Rd San Diego CA 92121

DOLIM, DENNIS WILLET, distribution company executive; b. Honolulu, Apr. 5, 1947; s. Lorrin Willet and Evelyn (Holmberg) D.; m. Andrea Leinaala Wilson, July 4, 1974; children: Traciann Lei, Douglas Pekelo. BS, St. Mary's Coll., Moraga, Calif., 1969. Sales mgr. Holsum/Oroweat, Honolulu, 1969-80; owner D.D. Brokerage, Honolulu, 1980—; pres. T.A.P. Dists., Honolulu, 1980—. Bd. dirs. United Cerebral Palsy Assn. Hawaii, Honolulu, 1985—. Mem. Hawaii Food Industry Assn., Food Industry Assn. (bd. dirs.). Democrat. Roman Catholic. Club: Oahu Country (Honolulu). Home: PO Box 29447 Honolulu HI 96820 Office: TAP Distbrs Inc 3207 N Nimitz Hwy Honolulu HI 96819

DOLINAY, THOMAS V., bishop; b. Uniontown, Pa., July 24, 1923. Student, St. Procopius Coll., Ill. Ordained priest Roman Catholic Ch., 1948. Ordained titular bishop Tiatira and aux. bishop Byzantine rite Diocese of Passaic, 1976-81; aux. bishop Byzantine rite Diocese of Van Nuys Calif., 1981; installed 1982—. Editor: Eastern Cath. Life, 1966-82. Office: Chancery Office 5335 Sepulveda Blvd Van Nuys CA 91411 *

DOLL, LINDA A., artist, teacher; b. Bklyn., May 5, 1942; d. William James Harrington and Ann B. (Casey) Cook; m. William John Doll, Feb. 4, 1962; children: Patricia, William Jr. AA, Palomar Coll., 1974; BA, San Diego State U., 1976. chairperson Arts Adv. Com. to Congressman Jim Bates, 1983-84; U.S. Coast Guard Artist, 1985—. Exhibited in group shows with Am. Watercolor Soc., 1985-88 (selected for one yr. nat. travel show, Elsie and David Ject-key award 1988) N.Y.C., 1986, 87, 88, Canton, Ohio, 1985, Nat. Watercolor Soc., Brea, Calif., 1984-85, Watercolor West Annual, Riverside, Calif., 1982, 84-88 (E. Gene Crain Purchase Selection award 1985, Second Place Jurors award 1982), Rocky Mountain Nat., Golden, Colo., 1984-85, Midwest Annual, Davenport, Iowa, 1983, 85, Nat. Watercolor Soc., Riverside, 1985 (selected for one yr. nat. travel show) 88, Canton Ohio, 1985, Watercolor Internat., San Diego, 1978-79, 82-88 (selected for one yr. nat. travel show 1983-84), Watercolor Okla., 1982-84 (Harry Hulett Jr. award 1984), Pa. Soc. Watercolor Painters, Harrisburg, 1988, 1982 (hon. mention); represented in permanent collections including E. Gene Crain Collection, Scripps Hosp., La Jolla, Calif., Redlands Community Hosp., Riverside, Campbell River Community Art Council, Can., Simpact Assocs. Inc., San Diego. Mem. San Diego Watercolor Soc. (past pres., life), Nat. Watercolor Soc., Watercolor West, Knickerbocker Artists, Am. Watercolor Soc. (chmn. of assocs. 1985—), Midwest Watercolor Soc. (assoc. mem., ann. show chmn. 1985). Office: 17490 Matinal Dr Rancho Bernardo CA 92127-1238

DOLLAR, DEBRA LOUISE, city official; b. Globe, Ariz., July 28, 1953; d. Robert Paul and Frances (Bertoglio) D.; m. William Eugene Vins, Feb. 18, 1978. BFA, Ariz. State U., 1975. Tech. illustrator Ariz. State U., Tempe, 1973-76; graphic artist Callan Assocs. Inc., San Francisco, 1976-79; tech. illustrator Simula Inc., Tempe, 1979-80; publs. asst. City of Scottsdale, Ariz., 1980-82; pub. info. asst. City of Scottsdale, 1982-83, mgr. pub. affairs, 1983-86, dir. communications and pub. affairs, 1986—. Editor Scottsdale Citizen, 1985-88 (Grand award City Hall Digest 1985, award of merit 1987). Mem. Pub. Rels. Soc. Am., Internat. Assn. Bus. Communicators, Nat. Assn. Govt. Communicators, Assn. Film Commrs., Nat. Mgmt. Assn., Scottsdale Mgmt. Club. Republican. Lutheran. Office: City of Scottsdale 3939 Civic Ctr Blvd Scottsdale AZ 85251

DOLLIVER, JAMES MORGAN, state supreme court justice; b. Ft. Dodge, Iowa, Oct. 13, 1924; s. James Isaac and Margaret Elizabeth (Morgan) D.; m. Barbara Babcock, Dec. 18, 1948; children: Elizabeth, James, Peter, Keith, Jennifer, Nancy. BA in Polit. Sci. with high honors, Swarthmore Coll., 1949; LLB, U. Wash., 1952; D in Liberal Arts (hon.), U. Puget Sound, 1981. Bar: Wash. 1952. Clk. to presiding justice Wash. Supreme Ct., 1952-53; sole practice Port Angeles, Wash., 1953-54, Everett, Wash., 1961-64; adminstrv. asst. to Congressman Jack Westland, 1955-61, Gov. Daniel J. Evans, 1965-76; justice Supreme Ct. State of Wash., 1976—, chief justice, 1985-86; 2d v.p. conf. Chief Justices, 1985-86. Chmn. United Way Campaign Thurston County, 1975, pres., 1976, mem. exec. bd., 1977—; chmn. Wash. chpt. Nature Conservancy, 1981—; pres. exec. bd. Tumwater Area council Boy Scouts Am., 1972-73, Wash. chpt. The Nature Conservancy, 1981-83, mem. 1979—, Wash. State Capital Hist. Assn., 1976-80, 85—, also trustee, 1983-84 ; trustee Deaconess Children's Home, Everett, 1963-65, U. Puget Sound, 1970—, Wash. 4-H Found., 1977-84, also v.p., 1983—, Claremont (Calif.) Theol. Sem., assoc. mem., Community Mental Health Ctr., 1977-84; bd. mgrs. Swarthmore Coll., 1980-84; bd. dirs. Thurston Mason Community Health Ctr., 1977-84, Thurston Youth Services Soc., 1969-84, also pres., 1983, mem. exec. com., 1970-84, Safety Tng. and Research Assn. Wash., 1979—, Wash. Women's Employment and Edn., 1982-84; mem. jud. council United Meth. Ch., 1984—, gen. conf., 1970-72, 80—, gen. bd. ch. and society, 1976-84; adv. council Retired Senior Vol. program, 1979-83; mem. bd. visitors Cen. Wash. U. Coll. of Letters, Arts and Scis., 1983—; pres. Washington Ctr. Law-related Edn., 1987—; bd. dirs. Western Assn. Concerned Adoptive Parents, 1987—, South Sound Samaritan Counseling Ctr., 1988—; trustee U. Washington Law Sch. Found., 1982—, Olympic Park Inst., 1988—; mem. bd. visitors U. Washington Sch. Social Work, 1987—; chair bd. visitors U. Puget Sound Sch. Law, 1988—. Served as ensign USCG, 1945-46. Recipient award Nat. Council Japanese Am. Citizens

League, 1976; Silver Beaver award, 1971; Silver Antelope award, 1976. Mem. Am., Wash. bar assns., Am. Judges Assn., Am. Judicature Soc., Pub. Broadcast Found. (bd. dirs. 1982—), Am. Acad. Youth Exchange (adv. council 1983-86). Clubs: Masons, Rotary. Office: Wash Supreme Ct Temple of Justice AV11 Olympia WA 98504-0511

DOLLY, JOHN PATRICK, university dean, educational psychologist; b. N.Y.C., May 16, 1942; s. Thomas Joseph and Anna Maria (Barron) D.; m. Carol Ann Dolly, Oct. 23, 1966; children: Sheila, Erin. B.S., Manhattan Coll., 1964; M.S., SUNY, 1966; Ed.D., U. Ga., 1973. Area dir. Founds. of Edn. U. S.C., Columbia, 1975-78, asst. dean acad. affairs Coll. Edn., 1978-79, acting dean, 1979-80, asst. dean research and devel., 1980; dean Coll. Edn. U. Wyo., Laramie, 1981-86, U. Hawaii, Manoa, 1986—; cons., lectr. in field. Co-author: Learning to Teach: A Decision Making System. Contbr. articles to profl. jours. Served to capt. USAF, 1966-70. Vocat. Rehab. Adminstrn. trainee, 1964-66. Mem. Am. Psychol. Assn., Am. Ednl. Research Assn., Phi Delta Kappa, Phi Kappa Phi, Kappa Delta Pi. Office: U Hawaii Coll Edn 1776 University Ave Manoa HI 96822

DOLOWITZ, DAVID AUGUSTUS, otolaryngologist, educator; b. N.Y.C., Nov. 3, 1913; s. Alexander and Florence Reda (Levine) D.; m. Frances Marie Fleisher, May 6, 1937 (dec. 1967); children: David S., Julia Louise, Wilma Florence, Susan Reda, Fridolyn Gimble; m. Emma Ruth Halvorsen, June 11, 1968. AB, Johns Hopkins U., 1933; MD, Yale U., 1937; MA, U. Utah, 1951, ScD (hon.), 1978.Intern, Morristown (N.J.) Meml. Hosp., 1937-38, Albany (N.Y.) Hosp., 1938-39; resident Johns Hopkins Hosp., Balt., 1939-43; practice medicine, specializing in otolaryngology, Salt Lake City, 1946-78; asst. otolaryngology Johns Hopkins U., Balt., 1938-39, instr., 1942-43; instr. U. Utah, Salt Lake City, 1943-48, assoc. clin. prof., 1948-58, assoc. prof., chief otolaryngology, 1958-67, clin. prof. otolaryngology, 1967—; instr. biology Dixie Coll., St. George, Utah, 1987—; staff Holy Cross Hosp., VA Hosp., Salt Lake City, U. Utah Med. Hosp., Primary Children's Hosp., Salt Lake City, all 1946-78; councilman, treas. Town of Toquerville (Utah), 1982-87, mayor, 1987—. Chmn. bd. Pioneer Craft House, Salt Lake City, 1965-84; mem. gov.'s com. study exceptional children, Utah, 1967; mem. Com. for Endowment of the Humanities, 1988—; mem. otolaryngologic del. to China, People to People, 1986. Served with M.C., U.S. Army, 1943-46. NIH fellow, U. Lund, Sweden, 1959-60. Fellow ACS; mem. AMA, Utah Med. Assn., Am. Bd. Otolaryngology, Am. Acad. Otolaryngology, Am. Bd. Clin. Allergy, Am. Otol. Soc., Deafness Research Found., Soc. Univ. Otolaryngologists (adv. com. pulmonary-allergy drugs 1973-78), Am. Laryngology, Rhinology and Otolaryngology Soc., Barany Soc., C. of C. Democrat. Jewish. Author: Basic Otolaryngology, 1964; editor: Allergy in Otolaryngologic Practice: The Otolaryngologic Clinics of North America, 1971; Transactions of Am. Soc. Ophthalmologic and Otolaryngologic Allergy, 1973-78; contbr. articles to profl. jours. Home: PO Box 189 Toquerville UT 84774

DOLSEN, DAVID HORTON, mortician; b. Durango, Colo., Feb. 27, 1940; s. Donald B. and Florence I. (Maxey) D.; BA, Southwestern Coll., 1962; Mortuary Sci. Degree, Dallas-Jones Coll. Mortuary Sci., 1963; m. Jo Patricia Johnson, Dec. 23, 1962; children: Wendy, Douglas. Apprentice, Davis Mortuary, Pueblo, Colo., 1963-64; bus. mgr. George F. McCarty Funeral Home, Pueblo, 1964-65; owner Dolsen Mortuary, Lamar, Colo., 1965-72; pres., gen. mgr., dir. Almont, Inc., Lamar, 1972—; sec. Dolsen, Inc., 1967—; pres. Wilson Funeral Dirs. Inc.; gen. ptnr. Let's Talk Travel, Ltd. Mem. Lamar City Council, 1969-73; mayor City of Lamar, 1971-73. Bd. dirs. Lamar Community Coll., 1967-73, Prowers County Hist. Soc., 1966—, San De Cristo Arts and Conf. Center, 1979-85; bd. dirs., sec. Pueblo Met. Mus. Assn., 1975-79; chmn. council on fin. and adminstrn. Rocky Mountain Conf. United Meth. Ch., 1976—, del. Gen. Conf., 1979, 80, 84, 88; mem. Pres.'s Council Nat. Meth. Found., 1978—, Iliff Sch. Theology, 1986-88; trustee, mem. exec. com. Southwestern Coll., Winfield, Kans., 1979—; dist. chmn. Boy Scouts Am., 1981-88; treas., mem. exec. com. Girl Scouts USA, 1981-88; mem. council on fin. and adminstrn. Western Jurisdiction, United Meth. Ch., 1980-88; trustee, gen. council on fin. and adminstrn. United Meth. Ch., 1980-88, gen. coun. on ministries, mem. gen. bd. of higher edn. and ministries; trustee Meth. Corp., 1980-88, United Meth. Ch. Ins. Trust, 1982-88; mem. World Service Commn., Meth. Episcopal Ch., 1980-88; mem. gen. council on adminstrn., bd. adminstrn. Ch. of United Brethren in Christ, 1980-88; trustee Sunny Acres Retirement Community, 1986, bd. dirs. Mem. Nat. Funeral Dirs. Assn., Nat. Selected Morticians, Cremation Assn. Am., Monument Builders N.Am., Colo. Funeral Dirs. Assn. Pi Sigma Eta, Pi Kappa Delta, Pi Gamma Mu, Masons, Shriners, Elks, Rotary (bd. dirs., Paul Harris fellow). Home: 3503 Morris Ave Pueblo CO 81008 Office: 401 Broadway Pueblo CO 81004

DOMAGALSKI, TAMMY JO, newspaper advertising executive; b. San Jose, Calif., Jan. 26, 1965; d. Gerald Stephen Domagalski and Kathryn Nina (Baldue) Harris. Grad. high sch., Kelseyville, Calif. Head clk. Bruno's Foods Inc., Lakeport, Calif., 1983-87; asst. agt. State Farm Ins. Co., Lakeport, 1987-88; classified newspaper mgr. Lakeport Pub. Inc., 1988—. Republican. Home: PO Box 1662 Lakeport CA 95453 Office: Lakeport Pub Inc 2150 S Main St Lakeport CA 95453

DOMENICI, PETE (VICHI DOMENICI), senator; b. Albuquerque, May 7, 1932; s. Cherubino and Alda (Vichi) D.; m. Nancy Burk, Jan. 15, 1958; children: Lisa, Peter, Nella, Clare, David, Nanette, Helen, Paula. Student, U. Albuquerque, 1950-52; BS, U. N.Mex., 1954, LLD (hon.); LLB, Denver U., 1958; LLD (hon.), Georgetown U. Sch. Medicine; HHD (hon.), N.Mex. State U. Bar: N.Mex. 1958. Tchr. math. pub. schs. Albuquerque, 1954-55; ptnr. firm Domenici & Bonham, Albuquerque, 1958-72; mem. U.S. Senate from N.Mex. 1972—; mem. energy and natural resources com., chmn. subcom. on energy research and devel.; mem. com. on environ. and public works; chmn. budget com.; mem. spl. com. on aging; mem. Presdl. Adv. Com. on Federalism. Mem. Gov.'s Policy Bd. for Law Enforcement, 1967-68; chmn. Model Cities Joint Adv. Com., 1967-68; mem. Albuquerque City Commn., 1966-68, chmn. and ex-officio mayor, 1967. Mem. Nat. League Cities, Middle Rio Grande Council Govts. Home: 120 3rd St NE Washington DC 20002 also: 135 E 50th St #5L New York NY 10022-7515 Office: US Senate 434 Dirksen Senate Office Bldg Washington DC 20510 *

DOMINIC, ANDREA LYNNE, pharmacist; b. Newark, Jan. 8, 1954; d. Thomas J. and Susan Anne (DiMartino) D. BS in Pharmacy, Rutgers U., 1978. Pharmacist Easton Pharmacy, New Brunswick, N.J., 1978-79, Rossmore Drugs, Belleville, N.J., 1980-81, UCLA Med. Ctr., 1981-85; dir. outpatient pharmacy St. Francis Hosp., Santa Barbara, Calif., 1985-88; owner, pharmacist Riviera Profl. Pharmacy, Santa Barbara, 1988—; clin. instr., Morris Cody & Assocs., L.A., 1982-84; dir. seminars, Werner Erhard & Assocs. Organizer, contbr. Holiday Project, San Francisco, 1984—, Hunger Project, San Francisco, 1984—, Youth At Risk, San Francisco, 1984—. Mem. Am. Pharm. Assn., Calif. Pharmacists Assn. Roman Catholic. Home: 2780 Torito Rd Santa Barbara CA 93108 Office: Riviera Profl Pharmacy 525 E Micheltorena St Santa Barbara CA 93103

DOMMER, DONALD DUANE, architect; b. Fargo, N.D., Dec. 6, 1938; d. Carl Otto and Margret Catherine (Innes) D.; m. Judith Frazer, June 12, 1962 (div. Sept. 1977); children: Jason, Toby; m. Shelley Hayden, June 15, 1986; 1 child, Andrea. Student, Concordia Coll., Moorhead, Minn., 1960-61; BArch, U. Minn., 1963, MArch, 1965. Registered architect, Calif. Planner urban Nason, Law, Wehrman & Knight, Mpls., 1961-62; archtl. designer Cerny Assocs., Mpls., 1963-65, Gruen Assocs., L.A., 1965-67; architect, urban planner Lawrence Halprin Assocs., San Francisco, 1967-72, 74-77; architect, owner Don Dommer Environ. Design, Berkeley, Calif., 1972-74, Don Dommer Assocs., Oakland, Calif., 1977—; lectr. architecture and landscape depts. Sch. Environ. U. Calif., Berkeley, 1968-89. Active World Wildlife Fund, Nat. Foud. Hist. Perservation, Oakland Design Advocates; speaker conv. Western Mus. Conf. 1988. Recipient Restoration award Berkeley Archtl. Heritage Assn., 1984, Merit award Calif. Dept. Rehab., 1987; grantee HUD, 1976. Mem. AIA (chmn. program 1983-84, bd. dirs. 1985-86, design award 1986, Merit award 1986), Urban Land Inst., Oakland C. of C., Audubon Soc. Democrat. Club: Berkeley Yacht. Office: Don Dommer Assocs 580 2d St Oakland CA 94607

DOMNIKOV, LARISSA, engineer; b. Odessa, Russia, Mar. 27, 1933; came to U.S., 1946; d. Boris A. and Galina (Dobrowolsky) Konstantinovsky; m. Alexis M. Domnikov, Jan. 22, 1956; children: Alexander, Vera, Victor. BS in Chemistry, CCNY, 1955. Process engr. Northrop Corp., L.A., 1955-63, McDonnell Douglas, L.A., 1963; process engr. Hughes Aircraft Co., L.A., 1963-79, staff engr., 1979-81, sr. staff engr., 1981-87, sr. scientist/engr., 1987—. Patentee in field. Recipient Creative Devel. award NASA, 1986. Mem. Soc. Advancement Materials and Process Engring., Am. Electroplaters and Surface Finishers Soc. Home: 8108 Creighton Ave Los Angeles CA 90045 Office: Hughes Aircraft Co Space and Communications Gp Bldg S33/C33 PO Box 92919 Los Angeles CA 90009

DOMONDON, OSCAR, dentist; b. Cebu City, Philippines, July 4, 1924; s. Antero B. and Ursula (Maglasang) D.; D.M.D., Philippine Dental Coll., 1951; D.D.S., Loma Linda U., 1964; m. Vicky Domondon. children—Reinelda, Carolyn, Catherine, Oscar. Came to U.S., 1954, naturalized, 1956. Dentist, Manila. (Philippines) Sanitarium and Hosp., 1952, U.S. embassy, Manila, 1952-54; pvt. practice dentistry, Long Beach, Calif., 1964—. Dentist, Children's Dental Health Center, Long Beach, part-time, 1964-68; past mem. Calif. State Bd. Dental Examiners. Past pres., Filipino Community Action Services, Inc. Served with AUS, 1946-49, 54-60. Fellow Acad. Dentistry International, Acad. Gen. Dentistry, Internat. Inst. Community Service, Acad. Internat. Dental Studies, Internat. Coll. Dentists, Am. Coll. Dentists (Acad. Continuing Edn.); mem. Am. Soc. Dentistry Children, ADA, Am. Acad. Oral Radiology (award 1964), Internat. Acad. Orthodontists, Am. Soc. Clin. Hypnosis, Am. Endodontic Soc., Western Conf. Dental Examiners and Dental Sch. Deans, Fedn. of Assns. of Health Regulatory Bds., Calif. Assn. Fgn. Dental Grads. (past pres.), Filipino Dental Soc. (past pres.), Philippine Tech. and Profl. Soc. (v.p.), Am. Acad. Dentistry for Handicapped, Am. Assn. Dental Examiners, Nat. Assn. Filipino Practicing Dentists in Am. (pres.), Pierre Fauchard Acad., Lions (past pres.), Elks (past chmn. rangers), Masons. Republican. Home: 3570 Aster St Seal Beach CA 90740 Office: 3714 Atlantic Ave Long Beach CA 90807

DONAHOO, STANLEY ELLSWORTH, orthopaedic surgeon; b. St. Joseph, Mo., Dec. 3, 1933; s. Charles Ellsworth and Opal (Cole) D.; m. Cheryl R. Donahoo; children—Shan Maureen, Brian Patrick, Mary Kathleen, Jane Eileen; stepchildren: Trina Person, Kevin Person. MD, U. Wash., 1963. Resident, Duke U., Durham, N.C., 1967-68, U.S. Naval Hosp., Oakland, Calif., 1963-67; commd. lt., U.S. Navy, 1963 advanced through grades to lt. comdr. (orthopaedic surgeon), 1971, ret. 1971; practice medicine, specializing in orthopaedic surgery, Roseburg, Oreg., 1971—; chief surgery Mercy Hosp., Roseburg, 1973-74; chief surgery Douglas Community Hosp., Roseburg, 1973, chief of staff, 1974—; cons. Guam Meml. Hosp., codir. rehab. unit, 1970-71; cons. orthopaedic surgery VA Hosp., Roseburg, 1971—; chmn. Douglas County (Oreg.) Emergency Med. Services Com., 1973-74. Trustee Douglas Community Hosp., 1975. Served with AUS, 1952-55. Diplomate Am. Bd. Orthopaedic Surgery. Fellow Am. Acad. Orthopaedic Surgeons (admissions com. region 14), North Pacific Orthopaedic Assn. (v.p. 1984-85); mem. Piedmont Orthopaedic Soc., AMA, Oreg. Med. Assn. (mem. sports medicine com., ins. and fee rev. com. 1981), Guam Med. Soc. (pres. 1970), Am. Trauma Soc. (founding mem.), Roseburg C. of C. (bd. govs. 1978—). Home: 205 Wildfern Dr Winchester OR 97495 Office: 1813 W Harvard St Ste 100 Roseburg OR 97470

DONAHUE, DENNIS DONALD, foreign service officer; b. Indpls., May 31, 1940; s. George Robert and Lucille Kathryn (Tannrath) D.; m. Gretchen Jane Siedling, Sept. 21, 1963 (dec. 1987); children: Mauree Denise, Megan Jane, Benjamin Josef. BA, Marian Coll., 1962; student, Ind. U., 1962-63; MA, Am. U., 1980, postgrad., 1981—. With USIA, 1967—; asst. cultural officer Am. Consultate Gen., Calcutta, India, 1969-70; asst. publs. officer Am. Embassy, New Delhi, 1970-72; publs. officer Am. Embassy, Saigon, Republic of Vietnam, 1973-75; cultural affairs officer Am. Embassy, Wellington, New Zealand, 1975-78; country/program officer East Asia/Pacific Office, Washington, 1979-81, 83-84; East Asia policy officer Voice of Am., Washington, 1982-83; program chief Am. Embassy, Tokyo, 1984-88; advisor U.S. Pacific Command, Honolulu, 1988—; adj. lectr. polit. sci. Temple U. Japan, Tokyo, 1986. Mem. Am. Fgn. Svc. Assn., Internat. Communicatin Assn., Internat. House Japan, Phi Kappa Phi. Roman Catholic. Office: US Pacific Command Hdqrs Bldg Room 212 Camp Smith HI 96861

DONAHUE, MARY KATHERINE, librarian; b. Dallas, Jan. 14, 1942; d. Joseph W. and Ellen (Onan) D.; m. John Patrick Hooker, July 29, 1976. BA, Our Lady of the Lake U., 1963; MLS, U. Calif., Berkeley, 1965; MA, Tex. Agrl. and Mech. U., 1983. Librarian Dallas Pub. Library, 1963-64, 65; 1st asst. Lubbock (Tex.) City-County Libraries, 1965-69, asst. dir., 1966-68; librarian U. Tex., Arlington, 1969; corp. librarian Univ. Computing Co., Dallas, 1969-72; sr. librarian Corpus Christi (Tex.) Pub. Libraries, 1973-75, adminstrv. coord., 1975-76; coord. Hidalgo County (Tex.) Library System, McAllen, 1976-80; asst. prof. Tex. Agrl. and Mech. U., College Station, 1981-84; cons. Stone Child Coll. Library, Box Elder, Mont., 1988—. cons. in field. Recipient Disting. Svc. award Tex. Hist. Commn. Mem. ALA, Tex. Library Assn., Alpha Chi.

DONAHUE, MICHELLE MAY, marine corps officer; b. Riverside, Calif., Dec. 17, 1958; d. Norman Dudley and Nomah Lee (Johnson) Trachsel; m. James Edward Donahue, Oct. 12, 1985. BS in Psychology, U. Utah, 1981; MA in Personnel Mgmt., Cen. Mich. U., 1984. Commd. 2d lt. USMC, 1981, advanced through grades to capt., 1982; personel officer Hdqrs. and Svc. Bn., 3d Force Support Group, Okinawa, Japan, 1982; budget officer Fleet Marine Force Pacific Hdqrs., Camp H.M. Smith, Hawaii, 1983-84; awards officer, officer-in-charge adminstrv. mgmt. unit Exec. Officer Hdqrs. and Svc. Bn., 1984-85; sta. adj. Marine Corps Air Sta., Tustin, Calif., 1986—. Mem. Officer's Wives Club. Home: 25802 Sycamore Ln Laguna Hills CA 92653 Office: Marine Corps Air Sta Tustin CA 92710-5001

DONALD, IAN, wood products company executive. Formerly pres. Crown Forest Industries Ltd, Vancouver, B.C., Can.; pres. Brit. Col. Forest Products Ltd, Vancouver, B.C., Can., 1987—. Office: BC Forest Products Ltd, 1050 W Pender St, Vancouver, BC Canada V6E 2X3 *

DONALDSON, GEORGE BURNEY, chemical company executive; b. Oakland, Calif., Mar. 16, 1945; s. George T. and L.M. (Burney) D.; m. Jennifer L. Bishop, Feb. 16, 1974; children: Dawn Marie, Paul Matthew. AS in Criminology, Porterville Coll., 1972. Police officer City of Lindsay (Calif.), 1966-67; distbn. mgr. Ortho div. Chevron Chem. Co., Lindsay, 1967-73; safety specialist Wilbur-Ellis Co. Fresno, Calif., 1973-77, safety dir., 1977-79, dir. regulatory affairs, 1979—; industry rep. to White House Intergovtl. Sci. Engring., and Tech. Adv. Panel, Task Force on Transp. of Non-Nuclear Hazardous Materials, 1980; industry rep. Transp. Rsch. Bd.'s Nat. Strategies Conf. on Transp. of Hazardous Materials and Wastes in the 1980's, NAS, 1981, Hazardous Materials Transp. Conf., Nat. Conf. of State Legislatures, 1982. speaker and moderator in field; dir. Western Fertilizer and Pesticide Safety seminar, Sacramento, 1979; speaker Southeastern Agrl. Chem. Safety seminar, Winston-Salem, N.C., 1986; moderator spring conf. Nat. Agrl. Chems. Assn., Washington, 1989. Chmn. industry/govt. task force for unique on-site hazardous waste recycling, devel. task force for computerized regulatory software and data base system, devel. task force modifying high expansion foam tech. for fire suppression; hazardous materials adviser, motor carrier rating com. Calif. Hwy. Patrol, 1978-79. With U.S. Army, 1962-65. Mem. Western Agrl. Chems. Assn. (past chmn. transp., distbn. and safety com., outstanding mem. of year 1981, govtl. affairs com., trustee polit. action com.), Nat. Agrl. Chems. Assn. (past chmn. transp. and distbn. com., occupational safety and health com., environ. mgmt. com., state affairs com.), Am. Soc. Safety Engrs., Calif. Fertilizer Assn. (transp. and distbn. com., environ. com.), Fresno City and County C. of C. (agrl. steering com., govt. affairs com.), Calif. C. of C. (environ. policy com.), Am. Legion, Elks. Republican. Office: 191 W Shaw Ave Ste 107 Fresno CA 93704

DONALDSON, JAMES ADRIAN, otolaryngology educator; b. St. Cloud, Minn., Jan. 22, 1930; s. Charles Scott and Catharine Agnes (Ritchie) D.; m. Merrilyn Dorothy Ward, June 17, 1950; children: Deborah, Susan, James, Scott, Anne. BA, U. Minn., 1950, BS, 1952, MD, 1954; MS in Otolaryngology, 1961. Diplomate Am. Bd. Otolaryngology. Intern Mpls. Gen. Hosp., 1954-55; sr. asst. surgeon USPHS, 1955-57; resident U. Minn., 1957-60; fellow Otologic Med. Group, L.A., 1960-61; clin. instr. otolaryngology U. So. Calif., L.A., 1960-61; asst. prof. otolaryngology U. Iowa, Iowa City, 1961-63, assoc. prof., 1963-65; prof. otolaryngology U. Wash., Seattle, 1965—, dept. chmn., 1965-75. Author (with Barry Anson) Surgical Anatomy of the Temporal Bone, 1967, 3rd edit.1981. Fellow: ACS, Am. Otol. Soc., Am. Neurotology Soc., Triological Soc. Office: U Wash RL-30 Seattle WA 98195

DONALDSON, MARY KENDRICK, nurse; b. Tifton, Ga., June 25, 1937; d. Howard Story and Trudy (Donalson) Marlin; m. Harvey Kendrick Sr., Apr. 13, 1953 (dec. 1965); children: Jerome, Micheal, Harvey Jr., Merry, Sheila, Larry; m. Isaac Hargett, Feb. 16, 1985. AA, Compton (Calif.) Coll., 1969; BS, Pepperdine U., 1972, MA, 1976; diploma in nursing, SW Coll., Los Angeles, 1984. Staff nurse St. Francis Hosp., Lynwood, Calif., 1965-67; pvt. duty nurse Profl. Nurse's Registry, Los Angeles, 1967-82; elem. tchr. Compton Sch. Dist., Calif., 1975-80; caseworker, clk. Los Angeles County Probation Dept., 1980—; pediatric, nurse companion Personal Care Health Service, Torrance, Calif., 1984—; home economist Dept. Welfare, Compton, 1970-72; asst. dir. Century Plaza Hotel, Century City, Calif., 1971-72. Chairperson Com. To Elect Garland Hardeman For Councilman, Inglewood, Calif., 1987. Exec. Housekeeping scholarship Century Plaza Hotel, Los Angeles, 1971. Mem. Fellow Am. Home Econs. Assn., Pepperdine Alumni Assn., Pepperdine's Kappa-Kappa Sorority, Am. Nurse's Assn. Democrat. Home: 802 W 228th St Torrance CA 90502 Office: Los Angeles County Probation Dept 1601 Eastlake Ave Los Angeles CA 90033

DONALDSON, W. LESTER, mortgage broker, real estate consultant; b. St. Augustine, Fla., Mar. 2, 1928; s. Chester Campbell and Dovie (Pratt) D.; m. Patricia Lilias Babcock Hareson, Sept. 11, 1946; children: John Randolph, David Chester, James Robert. BA, San Francisco State U., 1968, MA, 1971. Transp. clk. Armour Food Co., San Francisco, 1955-60, transp. mgr., 1960-65, product mgr., 1965-70; So. Calif. sales mgr. Armour Food Co., L.A., 1970-73; tng. mgr. Armour Food Co., Phoenix, 1973-77, nat. mktg. mgr., 1977-80; region sales mgr. Armour Food Co., Pitts., 1980-83; nat. tng. mgr. Armour Food Co., Phoenix, 1983-84; mortgage broker Brokers Fin. Group, Phoenix, 1984—. Author: How To Use Psychological Leverage, 1978, Conversational Magic, 1978, Behavioral Supervision, 1980, Human Resource Development, 1986. Sgt. U.S. Army, 1948-52, Korea. Mem. Nat. Real Estate Assn. Republican. Home: 350 E Deepdale Phoenix AZ 85022 Office: Brokers Fin Group 1121 E Missouri S-123 Phoenix AZ 85014

DONKER, RICHARD BRUCE, health association administrator; b. Modesto, Calif., Sept. 29, 1950; s. Laverne Peter and Ruth Bernice (Hoekenga) D.; m. Susan Gail Content, May 3, 1986. AA, Modesto Jr. Coll., 1970; BS, Calvin Coll., Grand Rapids, Mich., 1972; MA, Calif. State Coll., Turlock, 1978; EdD, U. Pacific, 1980. Grant dir. Yosemite Community Coll. Dist., Modesto, 1975-77; dir. flight ops. Meml. Hosps. Assn., Modesto, 1980-85, adminstrv. coord., 1985-87, v.p. bus. systems, 1987—; exec. dir. MediPLUS Health Plans, Inc., Modesto, 1986—; pres. Calif. Aeromed. Rescue and Evacuation, Inc., Modesto, 1985—; lectr. Am. Hosp. Assn., Chgo., 1984—; cons. in field, 1984—. Author: Emergency Medical Technician Outreach Training, 1977, (with others) The Hospital Emergency Department: Returning to Financial Viability, 1987. Bd. dirs. Stanislaus Paramedic Assn., Modesto, 1978-82, Head Rest, Inc., Modesto, 1980; bd. dirs. regional occupational program Stanislau County Dept. Edn., 1980; del. People-to-People Citizen Amb. Program, People's Republic of China, 1988. Mem. Am. Acad. Med. Adminstrs., Phi Delta Kappa, Commonwealth Club. Presbyterian. Home: 1322 Edgebrook Dr Modesto CA 95354 Office: Meml Hosps Assn 1700 Coffee Rd Modesto CA 95355

DONLEY, DAVID ALLEN, aerospace engineer; b. Thermopolis, Wyo., Sept. 11, 1958; s. Howard Frank and Carole Jillian (Jones) D.; m. Jill Charlaine Seivert, Nov. 26, 1977; children: Christina Charlaine, Thomas Howard. BS in Aero. Engring., Calif. Poly. State U., 1981. Pyrotechnic engr., program mgr. Teledyne-McCormick/Selph, Hollister, Calif., 1981-83; tech. contract adminstr. Martin Marietta Corp., Denver, 1983--, Vandenberg AFB, Calif., 1983--. Troop cookie dir. Girl Scouts U.S.A., Castle Rock, Colo., 1987--. Mem. AIAA, Space Studies Inst. (assoc.). Republican. Mem. Evangelical Christian Ch. Office: Martin Marietta Corp 6050 Greenwood Plaza Blvd Englewood CO 80111

DONLEY, RUSSELL LEE, III, engineer, former state representative; b. Salt Lake City, Feb. 3, 1939; s. R. Lee and Leona (Sherwood) D.; m. Karen Kocherhans, June 4, 1960; children: Tammera Sue, Tonya Kay, Christina Lynn. B.S. in Civil Engring. with honors, U. Wyo., 1961; M.S. in Engring., U. Fla., 1962. Registered profl. engr., Wyo., Mont., Colo., N.Y. land surveyor, Wyo. Mem. Wyo. Ho. of Reps., 1969-84, chmn. appropriations com., 1975-78, mem. rules com., 1973-84; chmn. rules com. Wyo. Ho. Reps., 1983-84; majority floor leader Wyo. Ho. of Reps., 1979-80, speaker pro tem, 1981-82, chmn. legis. mgmt. council, 1983-84, speaker of house, 1983-84; chmn. bd. Nat. Ctr. Constl. Studies, Wyo. region 1983-87; exec. dir. Constn. Schs., Inc., 1988—. Chmn. Western Region Council State Govts., 1982-83; Republican candidate for gov. Wyo., 1986; precinct committeeman Rep. Party, 1967; chmn. Wyo. Young. Reps., 1968; fin. chmn. Natrona County Rep. Party, 1970; pres. bd. dirs. YMCA, Casper, 1976-77. Recipient award for engring. excellence Am. Cons. Engrs. Council; recipient Legislator of Yr. award Nat. Republican Legislators Assn., 1981; named Wyo. Outstanding Young Engr. Sigma Tau, 1974, Disting. Wyo. Engr. Tau Beta Pi., 1976. Former mem. Am. Water Works Assn., Nat. Soc. Profl. Engrs., Wyo. Soc. Profl. Engrs., Wyo. Engring. Soc., Wyo. Assn. Cons. Engrs. and Surveyors. LDS Church. Home: 1140 Ivy Ln Casper WY 82609 Office: 240 S Wolcott St Casper WY 82601

DONLON, WILLIAM CHRISTOPHER, oral surgeon; b. N.Y.C., Oct. 17, 1952; s. William Aloyisius and Margaret Mary (O'Donovan) D.; m. Marianne Patricia Truta, May 28, 1983. BA, Hofstra U., 1974, MA, 1975; DMD, Tufts U., 1979. Diplomate Am. Bd. Oral Maxillofacial Surgery. Resident Mt. Sinai Med. Ctr., N.Y.C., 1979-81, chief resident, 1981-82; asst. clin. prof. U. Pacific, San Francisco, 1982-88, assoc. clin. prof., 1988—; prin. surgeon Peninsula Maxillofacial Surgery, South San Francisco, Calif., 1982—, Burlingham, Calif., 1988—; dir. Facial Pain Rsch. Ctr., San Francisco, 1986—. Fellow Am. Dental Soc. Anesthesiology, Am. Assn. Oral Maxillofacial Surgeons, Am. Bd. Oral Maxillofacial Surgery, Am. Coll. Oral Maxillofacial Surgeons; mem. AMA, ADA, Western Soc. Oral Maxillofacial Surgeons, European Assn. Craniomaxillofacial Surgery, Internat. Assn. Maxillofacial Surgery, Calif. Dental Assn., No. Calif. Soc. Oral Maxillofacial Surgeons (bd. dirs. 1986-88). Office: Peninsula Maxillofacial Surgery 1860 El Camino Real Ste 300 Burlingame CA 94010

DONNALLY, PATRICIA BRODERICK, fashion editor; b. Cheverly, Md., Mar. 11, 1955; d. James Duane and Olga Frances (Duenas) Broderick; m. Robert Andrew Donnally, Dec. 30, 1977. B.S., U. Md., 1977. Fashion editor The Washington Times (D.C.), 1983-85, The San Francisco Chronicle, 1985—. Recipient Atrium award, 1984, 87, Lulu award, 1985, 87. Mem. San Francisco Fashion Group, Inc. Avocation: travel. Home: 1 Lansdale San Francisco CA 94127-1608 Office: San Francisco Chronicle 901 Mission St San Francisco CA 94103

DONNAN, GREGORY DOUGLAS, safety/standards executive; b. Long Beach, Calif., May 23, 1952; s. Douglas W. and Jane E. (Johnson) D. BA, UCLA, 1974, postgrad., 1982; MA, Am. Grad. Sch. Internat. Mgmt., 1975. Salesman Automatic Sprinkler Corp. Am. L.A., 1975-79; salesman, mgr. spl. hazards div. Cosco Fire Protection Div. Zurn Constructors, Inc., Gardena, Calif., 1979—; bd. dirs. AFM, Inc., L.A.; lectr., instr. UCLA Extension, 1981. Mem. Soc. Fire Protection Engrs., Nat. Fire Protection Assn., Internat. Conf. Bldg. Ofcls., Sports Connection. Republican. Home: 1346 Oakheath Dr Harbor City CA 90710 Office: Zurn Constructors Inc Cosco Fire Protection Div 321 E Gardena Blvd Gardena CA 90247

DONNELLY, GARY MICHAEL, marketing educator; b. Wendell, Idaho, Feb. 22, 1950; s. Paul E. Donnelly and Marjorie (Brown) Ehresman; m. Julie Halseth, June 30, 1978; children: Stephanie Lynn, Katie Lynn, Gary Michael Jr. AA, Coll. So. Idaho, 1970; BS in Bus. Edn., U. Idaho, 1974, MEd, 1978; postgrad., U. Wyoming, 1983. Tchr. bus. Globe (Ariz.) High Sch., 1974-76; salesman Hudsons Shoes, Twin Falls, Idaho, 1976-79; tchr. bus. Boise (Idaho) High Sch., 1979-80, Emmett (Idaho) High Sch., 1980-81; instr. mktg. and retail Casper (Wyo.) Coll., 1981—; mktg. cons. Donnelly & Assocs., Casper, 1981—; counselor Small Bus. Adminstrn., Casper, 1982—. Mem. vertical bus. curriculum com., Casper, 1985—; mem. subcom. Wyo. Bus.

Devel. Ctr., 1985—. Named to Distributive Edn. Hall of Fame, Mktg. and Distributive Edn. div. Am. Vocat. Assn., 1975. Mem. Western Mktg. Educators Assn. Home: 5221 S Oak Casper WY 82601

DONNELLY, JUDITH ANDREA, development executive; b. Kingston, Jamaica, Oct. 25, 1945; came to U.S., 1952; d. Kenneth Alfred and Ethel Monica (Matthews) Campbell; m. Craig Allen Donnelly, Apr. 8, 1972 (div. 1984). BA, St. Joseph's Coll., N.Y.C., 1967. Sales rep. REA-Rwy. Express, N.Y.C., 1967-69; travel dir. Nat. Student Travel Assn., N.Y.C., 1969-70; nat. coord. Nat. Acad. Svcs., N.Y.C., 1969-70; dept. mgr. Mervyn's Dept. Store, San Jose, Calif., 1972-74; real estate assoc. Devor Realty, Portola Valley, Calif., 1975-77, Wright & Co., Menlo Park, Calif., 1977-79; assoc. dir. office of devel. Stanford (Calif.) U., 1979—; cons. in field; fashion model, Calif. and N.Y. Bd. dirs. Children's Health Coun., Palo Alto, Calif., 1979-88, assoc., 1988—, De Anza Foothill Coll. Foun., Palo Alto YMCA, Interplast Fund Devel., Palo Alto, 1989—, KARA, Palo Alto, 1988; mem. exec. bd. Friend's of Stanford Meml. Ch., 1982-84; chairperson Calif. Profl. Engrs. Ednl. Found. Recipient Community award Calif. Soc. Profl. Engrs. Mem. Nat. soc. Fundraising Execs.. Home: 437 Homer Ave Palo Alto CA 94301 Office: Stanford U Office Devel 301 Encina Hall Stanford CA 94305

DONNELLY, MICHAEL TIMOTHY, counselor; b. Alhambra, Calif., Mar. 30, 1950; s. Patrick John and Mary Allanette (MacAller) D.; m. Joanie Ledger, Sept. 2, 1978; 1 child, Morgan Alexandra. BA, San Francisco State U., 1973; MA, Point Loma Coll., San Diego, 1981; postgrad., Hayward State U., 1978. Cert. tchr., counselor, adminstr. Tchr. Oakland (Calif.) Cath. Schs., 1974-77, Colegio Americano de Quito (Ecuador), 1978-79, Alhambra (Calif.) Schs., 1979-80; tchr. San Gabriel (Calif.) High Sch., 1980-81, counselor, 1981—; cons. Peer Counseling Cons., Pasadena, Calif., 1984-89; exec. v.p. Peer Concepts, Pasadena, 1988—. Co-author: Advanced Peer Counseling, 1988; assoc. editor Nat. Peer Helper Assn., 1988—; contbr. articles to profl. jours. Fulbright scholar, India, 1976; Fulbright exchange, Eng., 1986, Can., 1987; recipient Senate Commendation, Senate of State of Calif., Sacramento, 1988. Mem. Nat. Peer Helper Assn., Calif. Peer Counseling Assn. (pres. 1988). Home: 545 N Catalina Ave Pasadena CA 91106-1007 Office: San Gabriel High Sch 801 Ramona St San Gabriel CA 91776

DONNER, PAUL CHRISTOPHER, baby products manufacturing company executive; b. Chgo., Sept. 24, 1959; s. Frank Donald and Dorothy (Kanabay) D.; m. Christy Lynn Irwin, Feb. 28, 1980 (div. June 1988); children: Jason Christopher, Sean Michael; m. Tamsen Elizabeth Strong, Sept. 10, 1988. Asst. mgr. Wild West Clothing Stores, Northridge, Calif., 1977-79; svc. coord. Ladds Trucking Co., Northridge, 1979-82; prodn. mgr. Reddi Brake, Canoga Park, Calif., 1982-83; svc. mgr. Guy Martin Oldsmobile, Woodland Hills, Calif., 1983-87, Nesen Motor Car Inc., Thousand Oaks, Calif., 1987-88; sr. v.p. Degree Baby Products, Thousand Oaks, 1988--. Democrat. Unitarian Universalist. Home: 1726 Alhambra Rd South Pasadena CA 91030 Office: Degree Baby Products 1726 Alhambra Rd South Pasadena CA 91030

DONOHOE, GREGORY WOOD, electrical engineer; b. Detroit, Jan. 20, 1948; s. Robert Walter and Katherine Leone (Wood) D.; m. Mary Geraldine Wertman, Aug. 21, 1971; children: James Robert, Brian Patrick. BS, Lake Superior State U., 1976; MSEE, U. N.Mex., 1982, PhD in Elec. Engring., 1989. Engring. & sci. asst. Sandia Nat. Labs., Albuquerque, 1976-82, mem. tech. staff, 1982—; cons. Ctr. for Research and Technol. Assistance, Chihuahua, Mex., 1984. Contbr. articles to profl. jours.; inventor computer vision method. Pres. St. Jude Express Inc., Albuquerque, 1978—; dir. Internat. Med. Assistance Program. With USN, 1967-71, Vietnam. Decorated Navy Achievement medal. Mem. IEEE, AAAS. Democrat. Methodist. Home: 1320 Truman SE Albuquerque NM 87108

DONOHUGH, DONALD LEE, physician; b. Los Angeles, Apr. 12, 1924; s. William Noble and Virginia (Shelton) D.; m. Virginia McGregor, June 21, 1950 (div. 1971); children: Ruth, Laurel, Marilee, Carol, Greg; m. Beatrice Ivany, Dec. 3, 1976. BS, U.S. Naval Acad., 1946; MD, U. Calif., San Francisco, 1956; MPH, Tulane U., 1961. Diplomate AM. Bd. Internal Medicine. Intern U. Hosp., San Diego, 1956-57; resident Monterey County Hosp., 1957-58; dir. of med. svcs. U.S. Depart. Interior, Am. Samoa, 1958-60; instr. Tulane U. Med. Sch., New Orleans, 1960-63; resident Tulane Svcs. V.A. and Charity Hosp., New Orleans, 1961-63; asst. prof. Med. Sch. La. State U.; assoc. prof. epidemiology Internat. Ctr. for Rsch and Tng., Costa Rica, 1961-63; assoc. prof. La. State U. Sch. Med., 1963-65; vis. prof. U. Costa Rica, 1963-65; founder 1st med. sch. in Costa Rica, faculty advisor U.S. State Dept.; dir. med. svcs. Med. Ctr. U. Calif. (formerly Orange County Hosp.), Irvine, 1967-69; assoc. clin. prof. U. Calif., Irvine, 1967-79, clin. prof., 1980; pvt. practice Tustin, Calif., 1970-80; with Joint Commn. on Accreditation of Hosps., 1981; cons. Kauai, Hawaii, 1981—. Author (book): The Middle Years, 1981, Practice Management, 1986, Kauai, 1988; contbr. articles to profl. jours. Served to capt. USNR, 1971-84. Fellow Am. Coll. Physicians (life). Republican. Episcopalian. Home: 4890 Lawai Rd Koloa HI 96756

DONOVAN, JOHN JOSEPH, JR., real estate broker and developer; b. Oakland, Calif., Mar. 10, 1916; s. John Joseph and May Ella (Coogan) D.; Ph.B., Santa Clara U., 1938; postgrad. Stanford U., 1938-40, Harvard U., 1942; m. Margaret Mary Abel, June 7, 1941; children—John Joseph III, Mary Margaret Donovan Szarnicki, Patricia Anne Donovan Jelley, Eileen Marie, Marian Gertrude Corrigan, George Edwin, Michael Sean. Sales mgr. Universal Window Co., Berkeley, Calif., 1940-41, v.p., 1946-49, pres., chmn. bd., 1949-66; real estate broker and developer, 1966—. Mem. aluminum window mfrs. adv. com. NPA, 1951-52; chmn. pace setters com., commerce and industry div. Alameda County United Crusade, 1961. Mem. Republican small businessmen's com., Alameda County, Calif., 1946. Bd. dirs. Providence Hosp., 1970-80, also Found., 1980-82; bd. dirs. Apostleship of the Sea Center, 1968-85, Hanna Boy's Center, Sonoma County, 1976-79; mem. Oakland Mayor's Internat. Welcoming Center, 1972-77; trustee, treas. Serra Internat. Found., 1980-87, pres., 1981-82; mem. Serra Bicentennial Commn., 1983-86; mem. membership enrollment maj. div. San Francisco Bay Area council Boy Scouts Am., 1984—; mem. bd. Jesuit Sch. Theology, Berkeley, 1982-85, Grad. Theol. Union, Berkeley, 1982-85. Served from ensign to lt. Supply Corps, USNR, 1940-46; in U.S.S. General Ballou; capt. Res. Named knight St. Gregory the Gt., Pope John XXIII, 1962 (pres. Oakland diocese 1970—); Knights of Malta, (decorated Cross of Comdr. Merit, 1978, Cross of Comdr. of Merit with swords Order of Malta, Rome, 1981; named grand officer of merit, Order of Malta with swords, 1983, Knight Grace and Devotion, Order of Malta, 1987, Knight of Obedience, Order of Malta, 1988); invested and decorated Knight of Grace, Sacred Mil. Constantinian Order of St. George, 1988. Mem. Western Archtl. Metal Mfrs. Assn. San Francisco (dir. 1956-65, exec. com. 1958-65, pres. 1959-60), Aluminum Window Mfrs. Assn. N.Y.C. (dir. 1950-58, 1st v.p. 1955-56), Newcomen Soc. N.Am., Naval Order U.S., Navy Supply Corps Assn. San Francisco Bay Area (2d v.p. 1970—), Father Junipero Serra 250th Anniversary Assn. (v.p., sec.), Internat. Council Shopping Centers, AIM (pres.'s council), Naval Res. Assn., VFW. Roman Catholic. Clubs: Berkeley Serra (charter mem.); Comml., Commonwealth, Pacific-Union (San Francisco); Monterey Peninsula Country (Pebble Beach, Calif.); Claremont Country (Oakland, Calif., bd. dirs. 1988—); Army-Navy (Washington). Home: 2 Lincolnshire Dr Oakland CA 94618 Office: PO Box 11100 Oakland CA 94611

DONZE, JERRY LYNN, electrical engineer; b. Wauneta, Nebr., June 12, 1943; s. John Henry and Virgina May (Francis) D.; m. Marilyn Grace Bascue, Feb. 22, 1964 (div. May. 1980); children: Scott. L., Michele A.; m. Sandra Kay Morris, July 25, 1981. Cert. technician, Denver Inst. Tech., 1964; BSEE, U. Colo., 1972; postgrad., Advanced Metaphysics Inst. Religios Sci., 1986. Electronic technician A.B.M. Co., Lakewood, Colo., 1964-71; computer programmer Nat. Bur. Standards, Boulder, Colo., 1971-72; electronic engr. Autometrics Co., Boulder, Colo., 1972-76, Gates Research and Devel., Denver, 1976-77; devel. engr. Emerson Electric Co., Lakewood, 1977; engring. mgr. Storage Tech., Louisville, Colo., 1977—; cons. Sun Co., Arvada, Colo., 1974-75. Patentee in field. Mem. IEEE Student Soc. (treas. 1971-72), Eta Kappa Nu. Republican. Religious Scientist. Home: 12021 W 54th Ave Arvada CO 80002 Office: Storage Tech 2270 S 88th Louisville CO 80028-4257

DOOLAN, MARILYNE M., writer; b. New London, Wis.; m. Michael L. Doolan. BS, U. Wis., Oshkosh, 1975. Freelance Burbank, Calif., 1988—. Recipient Award for Excellence Bus./Profl. Advt. Assn., 1982, 1st Pl. Cable Advt. and Promo Awards, 1984.

DOOLEY, HELEN BERTHA, artist, art gallery owner; b. San Jose, Calif., July 27, 1907; s. George W. and Frances (Arwine) Macrae D. AB, San Jose State Coll., 1928; MA, Claremont Grad. Sch., 1939; postgrad. Douglas Donaldson Sch. of Design, Hollywood, 1933, Calif. Sch. Fine Arts, 1933-34, Chouinard Art Inst., Los Angeles, 1935, U. Calif., Berkeley, 1937-39, Columbia U., 1948. Tchr. Scripps Coll., 1937-39, San Jose State Coll., 1940-55, 56; art supr. Kern County Schs., 1939-48; prof. U. Pacific Stockton, 1948-68; owner Dooley Gallery, Carmel, Calif., 1965—. One man shows include U. of the Pacific, 1961, 63, 68, San Jose Art League Gallery, 1962, Artists' Guild, Carmel, 1962, Haggin Mus. and Art Gallery, Stockton, 1962, Seven Arts Gallery, Bakersfield, 1963, Lord and Taylor Galleries, N.Y.C., 1969, Carmel Art Assn. Galleries, 1965, 71, 73, 77, 79, Art Works Gallery, Fair Oaks, Calif., 1978, 80, Stary-Sheets Gallery, Gualala, Calif., 1983, Farnsworth Gallery, San Francisco, 1986; exhibited in group shows at Am. Watercolor Soc., Nat. Acad. Galleries, N.Y.C., Pa. Acad. Fine Arts, Oakland Art Mus., Laguna Beach Art Festival, Los Angeles County Art Exhbn., Mission Galleries, Taos, N.Mex., West Coast Watercolor Soc., San Francisco traveling shows, Royal Watercolor Soc., London, Atley Gallery, Sacramento, Watercolor Gallery, Berkeley, Noroton Gallery, Darien, Conn., Ackley Galleries, Sacramento, 1988, The Calif. Style (1925-55), The N.Y. Art Rev., 1988, Belle Annex Co., Omiya City, Japan, 1987-88; represented in permanent collections: Shimizu Art Mus., Japan, U. Pacific, Stockton, Monterey Peninsula Mus. Art, Irving Coleman Library, U. of the Pacific, Stockton; also pvt. collections. Teaching fellow Scripps Coll.; recipient First and Third awards Soc. Western Artists, DeYoung Mus., San Francisco, 1951, 54, Stockton Art League, Haggin Mus., 1956, 1st and 2d awards Monterey County Fair, 1955, Grumbacher award Crocker Gallery, Sacramento, 1954, Mother Lode Art Assn., Sonora, 1971, 1st Prize watercolor Lodi Art Assn., Top award 6th Ann. Exhibit Contemporary Religious Art, Carmel, 1967, award in contemporary oil painting Calif. State Fair, 1965, award Monterey Peninsula Mus. Art, 1967. Mem. Carmel Art Assn., West Coast Water Color Soc. Republican. Methodist. Office: Dooley Gallery Box 5577 Carmel CA 93921

DOOLITTLE, WILLIAM HOTCHKISS, internist; b. Cheshire, Conn., June 20, 1929; s. Joseph Delos and Geraldine (Lincoln) D.; B.S., U. Vt., 1956, M.D., 1960; m. Marla M. Rescott; 1 son, William Lawrence. Commd. lt. M.C., U.S. Army, 1959, advanced through grades to lt. col., 1971; intern U.S. Army Hosp., Fort Bragg, N.C., 1959-60; resident in internal medicine Walter Reed Gen. Hosp., Washington, 1961-64, ret., 1973; practice medicine specializing in internal medicine, Fairbanks, Alaska, 1973—; dir. Arctic Med. Research Lab. Alaska, Ft. Wainwright; pres. Fairbanks Internal Medicine and Diagnostic Center; staff Fairbanks Meml. Hosp., chief of staff, 1974-76. Bd. dirs. Fairbanks Meml. Hosp. Found. Served with USAF, 1947-53. Decorated Army Commendation medal, Legion of Merit. Diplomate Am. Bd. Internal Medicine. Fellow A.C.P.; mem. AAAS, AMA, Alaska Med. Assn., Fairbanks Med. Soc., Assn. Mil. Surgeons, Alpha Omega Alpha. Republican. Episcopalian. Club: Rotary. Contbr. articles in field to profl. jours. Home: 666 11th Ave Apt 207 Fairbanks AK 99701 Office: 1919 Lathrop St Fairbanks AK 99701

DOOM, DON NEIL, electrical engineer; b. Phoenix, Nov. 14, 1949; s. Sam and Esther (Deck) D.; m. Maria Mercedes Tapia, Dec. 30, 1977; children: Milka, Ana. BA, Murray State U., 1971, MACT, 1973; BS, Ariz. State U., 1984. Asst. prof. Paducah (Ky.) Community Coll., 1974-81; product engr. Intel Corp., Chandler, Ariz., 1983—. Democrat. Pentecostal. Home: 4923 W Chicago Chandler AZ 85226

DOPP, ALICE FLORENCE, librarian; b. Detroit, Oct. 28, 1931; d. Kenneth Wilton and Florence Caroline (Gabriel) Marsh; m. James Wellington Dopp, Jr., Aug. 1, 1969; m. Harold Lewis Allen, Aug. 1, 1953 (div. July 1960); 1 child, Laurie Jeanne. B.A., Wayne State U., 1965; M.L.S., U. Mich., 1967. Reference librarian Detroit Pub. Library, 1967-69; cataloger San Luis Obispo (Calif.) City Library, 1970-73; head tech. services San Luis Obispo City/County Library, 1973-78; head tech. services Las Vegas-Clark County Library Dist., 1981—; cons. San Luis Obispo Friends of Library, 1975-78; organizer, cons. Second Edit. Book Store, Las Vegas, 1982-83. Art tchr. local 500, United Auto Workers, Detroit, 1964; bd. mem. Detroit Pub. Library Staff Credit Union, Detroit, 1968; chmn. Internat. Inst. Supper Club, Detroit, 1967. Mem. ALA, Mich. Library Assn., Calif. Library Assn., Nev. Library Assn. (chmn. S.O.U.P. 1983-84), Black Gold Tech. Services Com. (chmn. 1977-78), AAUW. Democrat. Lutheran. Club: Silver Queens Investment (acctg. ptnr. 1981-83) (Las Vegas). Office: Las Vegas-Clark County Libr Dist 1401 E Flamingo Rd Las Vegas NV 89119

DOR, YORAM, accountant, health care executive; b. Tel Aviv, Apr. 17, 1945; came to U.S., 1974; s. Simon and Shulamit (Remple) D.; m. Ofra Lipshitz, Apr. 9, 1967; children: Gil, Ron. Diploma in Acctg., Hebrew U. Jerusalem, 1969; BA in Econs., Tel Aviv U., 1971; MBA, UCLA, 1977. CPA, Calif. Sr. auditor Somekh Chaikin, CPA, Tel Aviv, 1969-72; chief fin. officer East African Hotels, Dar-es-Salaam, Tanzania, 1972-74; staff acct. Hyatt Med. Enterprises, Inc. (name now Nu Med, Inc.), Encino, Calif., 1974-75, controller, 1977-79, v.p. fin., 1979-82, sr. v.p. fin., chief fin. officer, 1982-87, exec. v.p. fin., chief fin. officer, 1987—; also bd. dirs. Mem. AICPA, Calif. Soc. CPA's. Office: NU Med Inc 16633 Ventura Blvd Encino CA 91436

DORAN, DOROTHY FITZ, business educator; b. Nekoosa, Wis., Feb. 27, 1934; d. Edwin E. and Ruby E. (Burch) Larson; m. John David Doran; children—Jean Marie Fitz Harkey, Kenneth Lee Fitz, Cynthia Ann Fitz Whitney. B.S. with high distinction in Bus. and English, No. Ariz. U., 1969; M.A. in English, 1971; Ed.D. in Bus., Ariz. State U., 1980. Tchr. English, Cottonwood (Ariz.) Oak Creek Elem. Sch., 1969-70; tchr. bus. and English, Mingus Union High Sch., Cottonwood, 1970-79, dir. vocat. edn., 1976-79; mem. faculty dept. office adminstrn. Yavapai Coll., 1979—, chairperson Bus. div., 1981—; cons. Ariz. Dept. Edn. Mem. Ariz. Bus. Edn. Assn. (pres. 1980-81), Nat. Bus. Edn. Assn., Am. Vocat. Assn., Ariz. Edn. Assn., NEA, Internat. Word/Info. Processing Assn., Pi Omega Pi, Delta Pi Epsilon, Phi Kappa Phi, Alpha Delta Kappa, Phi Delta Kappa. Republican. Club: Soroptimists Internat. Editor Ariz. Bus. Edn. Newsletter, 1972-74. Home: 1195 Solar Heights Dr Prescott AZ 86301 Office: 1100 E Sheldon Prescott AZ 86301

DORAN, THOMAS FREDERICK, manufacturing executive; b. Framingham, Mass., July 11, 1949; s. Thomas F. and Jean S. (Tucker) D.; m. Patricia Ann, May —, 1967 (div. July 1983); m. Cyndi Ann Lloyd, Aug. 30, 1986; children: Robert, Elizabeth. Cert., Harper Jr. Coll., Elgin, Ill., 1977. Western regional sales mgr. Wlison Sporting Goods Co., River Grove, Ill., 1968-85; v.p., gen. mgr. Bell Helmet, Inc., Norwalk, Calif., 1985—. Fellow Nat. Fire Protection Assn. Home: 425 Seville Ave Balboa CA 92661

DORAN, VINCENT JAMES, steel fabricating company consultant; b. Ephrata, Wash., June 13, 1917; s. Samuel Vincent and Sarah Anastasia (Fitzpatrick) D.; B. Phil., Gonzaga U., Spokane, 1946; m. Jean Arlene Birrer, Jan. 15, 1949; children: Vincent James, Mollie Jean, Michele Lee, Patrick Michael. Mgr., Flying Service, Coulee Dam, Wash., 1947-58; mgr. constrn. Morrison-Knudsen Co., Wash. and Alaska, 1959-60; co-owner C.R. Foss Inc., constrn., Anchorage, 1961-64; mgr. Steel Fabricators, Anchorage, 1965-86. Inventor method of reducing and dewatering sewage sludge. Active Boy Scouts Am.; co-founder, pres. Chugach Rehab. Assn., 1962; mem. Alaska Gov.'s Rehab. Adv. Bd., 1962-63; mem. CAP. Served with USAAF, 1943-45, USAF, 1949-50. Decorated Air medal with 4 clusters. Mem. Anchorage C. of C., Welding Inst. Alaska (co-organizer, dir. 1977-78), 34th Bomb Group Assn., Am. Arbitration Assn. Roman Catholic. Club: Toastmasters. Compiler, pub. home owners' and builders' guide to sun's positions in N.Am. during solstices and equinoxes, designer packaged water, sewage treatment plants and water collection systems Arctic communities. Home: 3811 Knik Ave Anchorage AK 99517 Office: Steel Fabricators 2131 Railroad Ave Anchorage AK 99501

DORAY, ANDREA WESLEY, corporate communications director, writer; b. Monte Vista, Colo., Oct. 4, 1956; d. Dant Bell and Rosemary Ann (Kassap) D.; m. Paul Dean Doray, Nov. 25, 1978. BA, U. No. Colo., 1977. Cert. post secondary tchr. Asst. advt. mgr. San Luis Valley Publ. Co., Monte Vista, 1977-78; mktg. dir. Stuart Scott & Assocs. (formerly Philip Winn & Assocs.), Colorado Springs, Colo., 1978-80; sr. v.p. Heisley Design & Advt., Colorado Springs, Colo., 1980-85; pres., creative dir. Doray Doray, Monument, Colo., 1985—; account svcs. dir. Praco Ltd., Advt., Colorado Springs, 1987-88; dir. corp. community rels. Current, Inc., Colorado Springs, 1988—; instr. part time Pikes Peak Community Coll., Colorado Springs, 1983-86, mem. mktg. adv. coun. 1985-89; guest lectr. Colo. Mountain Coll., 1982-84, U. So. Colo., 1983, Pikes Peak Community Coll, 1983—, U. Colo., Colorado Springs, 1988—. Author: The Other Fish, 1976, Oil Painting Lessons, 1986, Coming to Terms, 1986, Roger Douglas, 1987; editor: Current Impressions; contbg. editor Colorado Springs Bus. Mag., 1984-86; creative writer World Cycling Fedn. Championships, 1986; speaker in field. Chmn. Colorado Springs Local Advt. Review Program, 1985; chmn., advt. pub. rels. task force exec. com. U.S. Olympic Hall of Fame, 1986; mem. State Legis. Alert & Action Coalition, 1985-87, project bus. cons. Jr. Achievement, Colorado Springs, 1985-86, trustee Citizen's Goals Colorado Springs, 1988-89; speaker Nat. Coun. Community Rels. , Orlando, Fla., 1988. Named One of Colorado Springs Leading Women Colorado Springs Gazette Telegraph, 1984, Outstanding Young Women of Am. State of Colo., 1987, Outstanding Young Alumna U. No. Colo., 1987. Mem. Am. Advt. Fedn. (chmn. dist. 12 legis com. 1985—, pub. rels. com. 1986, Silver medal award 1986), Pikes Peak Advt. Fedn. (pres. 1984-86, Advt. Person of Yr. award), Colorado Springs C. of C. (advt. roundtable, speaker small bus. coun. 1986—). Office: Current Inc PO Box 2559 Colorado Springs CO 80901

DORE, FRED HUDSON, state supreme court justice; b. Seattle, July 31, 1925; s. Fred Hudson and Ruby T. (Kelly) D.; m. Mary S. Shuham, Nov. 26, 1956; children: Margaret, Fred Hudson, Teresa, Tim, Jane. BS in Fgn. Service, Georgetown U., 1946, JD, 1949. Bar: Wash. 1949. Pvt. practice Seattle, 1949-77; mem. Wash. Ho. of Reps., 1953-59; U.S. senator from Wash. 1959-74; judge Wash. State Ct. Appeals, 1977-80; justice Wash. State Supreme Ct., Olympia, 1981—. Office: Wash Supreme Ct Temple of Justice Olympia WA 98504

DOREN, NEALL EVAN, electrical engineer; b. Denver, Jan. 21, 1961; s. Carl and Hortense Rafaella (Gitlin) D.; m. Maribeth Crandall, Mar. 21, 1987. AAS, Arapahoe Community Coll., Littleton, Colo., 1981; BS in Elec. Tech., U. So. Colo., 1983; postgrad., U. N.Mex., 1984—. Sr. tech. aide Sandia Nat. Labs., Albuquerque, 1984—. Inventor in field. Sci. fair judge N.W. Reg. Sci. Fair, U. N.Mex., 1985—. Colo. state scholar, 1979, others. Mem. IEEE, Am. Modelling Assn., Tau Alpha Pi, Tau Beta Pi, Kappa Mu Epsilon, Eta Kappa Nu. Republican. Home: 6221 Coppice Dr NW Albuquerque NM 87120 Office: Sandia National Labs PO Box 5800 Div 5265 Albuquerque NM 87185

DORLAND, FRANK NORTON, art conservator; b. Peru, Nebr., Oct. 11, 1914; s. Frank Norton and Marion Hope (Abbot) D.; student Calif. Christian Coll., 1931-33; San Diego State Coll., 1933-38; m. Mabel Vyvyan Jolliffe, July 29, 1938. Artist preliminary design engring. Convair Co., San Diego, Calif., 1938-49; pvt. practice as art conservator, La Jolla, Calif., 1949-59, San Francisco, 1959-63, Mill Valley, Calif., 1963-73, Santa Barbara, Calif., 1973-85; engaged in authentication and classification art objects; cons. art assns. galleries, museums, collectors, churches. Mem. Internat. Inst. for Conservation, Internat. Council Museums, Am. Mus. Assn. Pioneer in use of spl. waxes in painting; inventor oil and water mix wax mediums; engaged in research and devel. waxes and resins and properties and usage of electronic quartz crystals, also pioneer biocrystallographer, researcher on crystals and the human mind. Address: PO Box 6233 Los Osos CA 93412-6233

DORMAN, REX LEE, forest products executive; b. Wendell, Idaho, Jan. 13, 1934; s. Lee Roy and Leona Rose (Dillie) D.; m. Marilyn Jane Frazier, May 6, 1956; children; Donald, Michael, Diane. AA, Boise Jr. Coll., 1954; BS in Acctg./Econs., U. Idaho, 1961; postgrad., Stanford U., 1975. CPA, Idaho. Acct. Low, Viehweg, Hill and Grow, Boise, Idaho, 1961-66; supr., internal auditor Boise Cascade Corp., 1966-69, mgr. internal audit, 1969-73, asst. controller, 1973-75, controller, 1975-84, v.p. planning and control, 1984-86, v.p. control and info. services, 1986—; bd. dirs. Boise Cascade Can., Ltd., Toronto, Ont. Mem. adv. bd. U. Idaho, Moscow, 1968—; treas. Boise Philharm. Assn., 1969-72, Boise Civic Opera, Inc., 1977-80; chmn. Associated Taxpayers Idaho, Boise, 1982. Lt. (j.g.) USN, 1954-58. Mem. AICPA (internal control com. 1978-79), Idaho Soc. CPA's (pres. 1976-77), Am. Paper Inst., Fin. Acctg. Standards Bd. (task force 1979-86, cert. internal auditor 1962—). Republican. Clubs: Arid (Boise), Crane Creek Country. Office: Boise Cascade Corp PO Box 50 Boise ID 83728

DORN, DAPHNE NICHOLE, photographer; b. Hawthorne, Calif., June 10, 1962; d. Nico and Ilse J. (Bornemann) Martin; m. Clifford George Dorn, June 9, 1982. Freelance photographer, Mountain Ctr., Calif., 1982—; outfitter, Mountain Ctr., 1982—. Home: Box 25 Trails End Mountain Center CA 92361

DORN, MARIAN MARGARET, educator, sports management administrator; b. North Chicago, Ill., Sept. 25, 1931; d. John and Marian (Petkovsek) Jelovsek; m. Eugene G. Dorn, Aug. 2, 1952 (div. 1975); 1 child, Bradford Jay. B.S., U. Ill., 1953; M.S., U. So. Calif., 1961. Tchr., North Chicago Community High Sch., 1954-56; tchr., advisor activities, high sch., Pico-Rivera, Calif., 1956-62; tchr., coach Calif. High Sch., Whittier, 1962-65; prof. phys. edn., chmn. dept., coach, asst. chmn. div. women's athletic dir. Cypress (Calif.) Coll., 1966—; mgr. Billie Jean King Tennis Ctr., Long Beach, Calif., 1982-86; founder King-Dorn Golf Schs., Long Beach, 1984; pres. So. Calif. Athletic Conf., 1981; curriculum cons. Calif. Dept. Edn., 1989—. Recipient cert. of merit Cypress Elem. Sch. Dist., 1976; Outstanding Service award Cypress Coll., 1986. Mem. Calif. (v.p. So. dist.), San Gabriel Valley (pres.) assns. health, phys. edn. and recreation, So. Calif. Community Coll. Athletic Council (sec., dir. pub. relations), NEA, Calif. Tchrs. Assn., AAHPERD, Ladies Profl. Golf Assn. Republican. Conglist. Author: Bowling Manual, 1974. Office: 9200 Valley View Cypress CA 90630

DORN, NATALIE REID, consultant; b. N.Y.C.; d. John A. and Marianna (Tresenberg) Borokhovich; m. Ed Reid, July 31, 1938 (div. Apr. 1963); children: Michael John, Douglas Paul; m. Robert M. Dorn, Nov. 28, 1964. Student, Bklyn. Coll., 1937-40, Pepperdine Coll., 1969-70. Model Conover Agy., N.Y.C., 1950-54; columnist Westchester (N.Y.) Recorder, 1954-59; mgr., buyer Joseph Magnin, Los Vegas, Nev., 1961-62; ptnr., cons. Personnel Placement Employment Agy. and Conv. Coords., Los Vegas, Nev., 1961-63; account exec. John A. Tetley Co., L.A., 1963-65; cons. Sport Ct. Am., Salt Lake City, 1975--; realtor, Va., Calif., 1974--. Exec. v.p., Clark County (Nev.) Mental Health Assn., 1961-63; ednl. chmn. Hollywood Wing, Greek Theatre Assn., 1965, mem. hospitality com., 1969, LWV; co-founder Child Abuse Listening Line, 1973—; sponsor Ashland (Oreg.) Sheakesperean Festival, 1984; patron Sacramento Opera, Davis Art Ctr., Internat. House. Mem. AMA Aux., Los Angeles County Med. Assn. Aux. (chmn. publs. dist. 5, 1970-72, program chmn. 1972), Nat. Trust for Historic Preservation, Nat. Mus., Women in Arts, Crocker Art Mus., Crocker Art Mus. Assocs. Corps, Crocker Soc., El Macero Country Club.

DORN, ROBERT MURRAY, psychiatrist, educator; b. Cleve., May 1, 1921; s. Karl and Frieda (Cohan) D.; m. Natalia Ivanavna Borokhovich Reid, Nov. 28, 1964; children: Nancy Osterman Kotler, Robert Murray Jr., Mary, Anthony J. BS, Western Res. U., 1941, MS, 1944, MD, 1945. Intern Strong Meml. Hosp., U. Rochester (N.Y.), 1945-46; tng. U. London, 1948-49; clin. clk. Nat. Hosp. Queens Sq. Inst. Neurology, 1948-49; psychoanalytic trainee Brit. Inst. Psychoanalysis, 1948-51; pvt. practice psychoanalysis Beverly Hills, Calif., 1953—; pvt. practice psychiatry Davis, Calif., 1986—, Sacramento, 1986--; prof. psychiatry U. Calif., Davis, 1981-86, clin. prof., 1986—; attending psychiatrist L.A. Psychiat. Svc., 1955-59, instr. Davis Clinic Child Guidance, L.A., 1955-59; lectr. L.A. Inst. Psychoanalysis, 1958-65, mem. sr. faculty, 1965-68, tng. analyst, 1968-75, analyst supr., 1969—; cons. Whittier (Calif.) Family Svc. Agy., 1960-68, Reiss Davis Child Study Ctr., 1960—; asst. clin. prof. Sch. Medicine, UCLA, 1962-69, assoc. clin. prof., 1969—; prof. Med. Sch., Ea. Va. U., Norfolk, 1975-81. Contbr. articles to profl. jours. Chmn. psychiat. div. Community Chest, L.A., 1959-60; tchr.

Beverly Hills YMCA, 1964—; mem. Town Hall, L.A., 1964—; founding patron Huntington Hartford Theatre Wing, Greek Theatre; sustaining mem. Community TV, Los Angeles County Mus. Art;mem. Tidewater Assembly on Family Life, 1977-8l, Task Force on Sch. Age Parents, 1977-8l; mem. profl. adv. bd. Parents with Heart, 1982-86; mem. Yolo County Mental Health Adv. Bd., 1986-88, Crocker Art Mus.; patron, mem. Sacramento Opera; concertmaster, mem. Sacramento Symphony, 1986—; donor Internat. House Davis. Capt. USAF, 1946-47, U.S. Army, 1953-55. Recipient Disting. Svc. award YMCA, 1966. Fellow Am. Psychiat. Assn., Am. Geriatric Soc., Am. Orthopsychiat. Assn., Royal Soc. Health, Am. Coll. Psychiatrists, Am. Coll. Psychoanalysts, Am. Acad. Child and Adolescent Psychology; mem. AMA, CMA, So. Calif. Med. Assn. (coun. 1964-68), Yolo County Med. Soc. (exec. com. 1986—), Brit. Psychoanalytical Soc., Internat. Psychoanalytical Soc., Am. Psychoanalytical Soc., Am. Psychoanalytical Assn., Calif Psychoanalytical Assn. (del. 1960-63, 68—), Crocker Soc., El Macero Country Club, Sigma Xi. Office: 79 Scripps Dr Ste 2l2 Sacramento CA 95825

DORNAN, ROBERT KENNETH, congressman; b. N.Y.C., Apr. 3, 1933; s. Harry Joseph and Gertrude Consuelo (McFadden) D.; m. Sallie Hansen, Apr. 16, 1955; children: Robin Marie, Robert Kenneth II, Theresa Ann, Mark Douglas, Kathleen Regina. Student, Loyola U., Westchester, Calif., 1950-53. Nat. spokesman Citizens for Decency Through Law, 1973-76; mem. 95th-97th Congresses from 27th Calif. Dist., 1977-83, 99th-101st Congresses from 38th Calif. Dist., 1985—. Host TV polit. talk shows in Los Angeles, 1965-73; host, producer: Robert K. Dornan Show, Los Angeles, 1970-73; combat photographer/broadcast journalist assigned 8 times to Laos-Cambodia-Vietnam, 1965-74; originator POW/MIA bracelet. Served to capt. as fighter pilot USAF, 1953-58, as fighter pilot and amphibian rescue pilot USAFR, 1958-75. Mem. Am. Legion, Navy League, Air Force Assn., Assn. Former Intelligence Officers, AFTRA. Republican. Roman Catholic. Lodge: K.C. Office: Cannon House Office Bldg Rm 301 Washington DC 20515

DORNBUSH, VICKY JEAN, medical billing systems executive; b. Willowick, Ohio, Aug. 12, 1951; d. Charles W. and Josephine H. (Palumbo) Rader; m. Eric D. Erickson, Oct. 22, 1972 (div. June 1974); m. Thomas Dornbush, Dec. 29, 1979 (div. 1987); 1 child, Dana. Student, Kent State U., 1969-72, San Jose State U., 1982-84. Accounts receivable clk. MV Nursery, Richmond, Calif., 1975-76; accounts receivable and computer supr. Ga. Pacific, Richmond, 1976-78; acct. Ga. Pacific, Tracy, Calif., 1978-79, Crown-Zellerbach, Anaheim, Calif., 1979-80; acct. Interstate Pharmacy Corp., San Jose, Calif., 1981-83, contr., 1983-85; gen. ptnr. Med. Billing Systems, San Jose, 1984—; seminar trainer Systems Plus, Mountain View, Calif., 1987—. Mem. San Jose Civic Light Opera, 1987—, San Jose Repertory Co., 1986—. Mem. Women in Bus. Republican. Methodist. Office: Med Billing Systems 255 W Julian St #403 San Jose CA 95110

DORNEMAN, ROBERT WAYNE, manufacturing engineer; b. Oaklawn, Ill., Nov. 13, 1949; s. Robert John and Julia (Vorchenia) D.; M. Katrina Holland, July 30, 1977; children: Tamara, Tiana. BA in Biol. Sci., Calif. State U., Fullerton, 1974. Mfg. engr. Gen. Telephone Co., Anaheim, Calif., 1974-77, Xerox/Century Data, Anaheim, 1977-80; advance mfg. engr. MSI Data, Costa Mesa, Calif., 1980-83; sr. mfg. engr. Parker Hannifin, Irvine, Calif., 1983-86; sr. advanced mfr. engr. Western Digital, Irvine, 1986-89, mgr. advanced mfg. engring., 1989—; specialist automated assembly of circuits; cons. Base 2, Fullerton, 1980; developer surface mount tech. for computer mfg. industry; set up computer assemble plants internat. Innovator in field; contbr. articles in 3M-Alert to profl. jours. Mem. Nat. Assn. Realtors (broker), N. Orange County Bd. Realtors (broker), Calif. Assn. Realtors, Internat. Platform Assn., Internat. Soc. Hybrid Mfg., Phillips Ranch Assn., Tau Kappa Epsilon. Republican. Home: 56 Meadow View Dr Phillips Ranch Pomona CA 91766 Office: Western Digital 2802 Kelvin St Irvine CA 92714

DORRANCE, STURGES DICK, III, broadcasting executive; b. N.Y.C., Jan. 1, 1942; s. Sturges Dick and Marjorie Colt (Wooster) D; m. Pamela Winters, Sept. 21, 1963; children—Elizabeth, Sarah, Meredith, Jennifer. B.A. in English, Dartmouth Coll., 1963. With King Broadcasting, Seattle, 1966—, gen. sales mgr., 1976-82, v.p., gen. mgr. King-TV, 1982—. Past pres. Northwest Chamber Orch., trustee United Way, Pacific Med. Ctr., TV Acad. Arts and Scis., Wash. State Broadcasters, Seattle Chamber Festival. Served to 1st lt. U.S. Army, 1964-66. Com. Anglican. Clubs: Wash. Athletic, Columbia Tower (Seattle). Office: King-TV 333 Dexter N Seattle WA 98109

DORSEY, DEAN, management executive; b. Santa Monica, Calif., Aug. 15, 1951; s. George and Carmen (Hamilton) D.; m. Lyn Leonard, July 11, 1981 (div. Dec. 1985); 1 child, Janelle. BS, U.S. Air Force Acad., 1974. Sales Newport Motortown, Newport, Oreg., 1979-80; sales mgr. All Am. Dodge, Napa, Calif., 1980-83; fin. mgr. Good Chevrolet, Sacramento, 1983-84; sales mgr. Vintage Chevrolet/Toyota, Napa, 1984-85; sales Ron Goode Toyota, Alameda, Calif., 1985-86; fleet mgr. Val Strough Toyota, Antioch, Calif, 1987; sales Concord BMW, Concord, Calif., 1988; sales and fin. mgr. Barber Bros. Lotus, Walnut Creek, Calif., 1988--. Capt. USAF, 1974-79. Republican. Home: 2403 Heatherleaf Ln Martinez CA 94553 Office: Barber Bros Lotus 2244 N Main St Walnut Creek CA 94553

DORSEY, HELEN DANNER (JOHNA BLINN), writer, author, educator; b. Tarentum, Pa., Jan. 18, 1928; d. Frederick William and Harriet (Wiggins) Danner; m. Thomas Brookshier Dorsey, June 30, 1951 (dec.); children: Diana, F. Blinn. BA, U. Iowa, 1949; postgrad., U. Wis., 1950. Food columnist Herald Tribune News Service, N.Y.C., 1956-58; remedial edn. educator U.S. Army, Hoechst, Fed. Republic of Germany, 1954-56; food editor Am. Weekend, Frankfurt, Federal Republic of Germany, 1954-56; with elec. drafting dept. Newport News (Va.) Shipbuilding and Dry Dock Co., 1952-54; tchr. George Wythe Jr. High Sch., Hampton, Va., 1951-52; home econs. tchr. Keokuk (Iowa) High Sch., 1949-51; tchr. Thomas Jefferson Jr. High Sch., Arlington, Va., 1956-57; tchr. home econs. Sr. High Sch., Massapequa, N.Y., 1958-59; contbg. editor Forecast Mag., N.Y.C., 1958-59, 50 Mag., N.Y.C., 1958-60; asst. food editor LOOK mag., N.Y.C., 1962-64; celebrity cookbook columnist Newsday Spls. (syndicated), Garden City, N.Y.C., 1964-69, Chgo. Tribune-N.Y. News Syndicate, N.Y.C., 1969-75, Los Angeles Times Syndicate, 1975-87; celebrity foodstyles producer, writer Family Circle mag., N.Y.C., 1985—; contbg. correspondent USA Today & USA Weekend, Arlington, Va., 1985—; contbg. editor The Phila. Inquirer Mag., 1985—; celebrity cookbook columnist Celebrity Foodstyle Syndicate, Los Angeles, 1987-88; contract writer for N.Am. The Times of London Syndicates, 1988—; columnist Editors Press Service, Inc., N.Y.C., 1987-88; 1 cons. in field. Author: Great performances in the Kitchen, 1988, and 38 cookbooks, 1974-88; contbr. articles to mags. and newspapers. Home and Office: 9239 Doheny Rd Los Angeles CA 90069

DOSS, DIANA LYNN, executive search consultant; b. Wheeling, W.Va., Nov. 26, 1957; d. Jack Curtis and Genevieve (Groch) Birkhimer; m. Bill R. Doss, Jr., Aug. 1, 1981; 1 child, Billy Rogers Doss, III. BA, W.Va. U., 1980; student, U. Nev., Las Vegas, 1980-81, Ariz. State U., 1981. Pers. adminstr. Bank of Scottsdale, Ariz., 1982-83; asst. dir. pers. Loew's P.V. Resort, Scottsdale, 1983-85; dir. pers. Scottsdale Hilton Safari Resort, 1985-86, Sheraton Tempe (Ariz.) Mission Palms, 1986-88; pres. Human Resource Network, Scottsdale, 1988—. Mem. task force Valley of the Sun United Way, Tempe, 1987; active Am. Heart Assn., Tempe, 1987. Mem. Scottsdale C. of C. Republican. Office: Human Resource Network 4141 N Scottsdale Rd Ste 304 Scottsdale AZ 85251

DOSSETT, LAWRENCE SHERMAN, professional services company official; b. Santa Ana, Calif., May 11, 1936; s. Wheeler Sherman and Eunice Elizabeth (Bright) D.; student U. Ariz., 1957-58, U. Calif., Irvine, 1973-75, Loyola Marymount Coll., 1974; m. Joanne Kallisch; children—Todd Sherman, Garrick Robert (dec.), Dana Shelene, Ryan William. Engring. draftsman Hughes Aircraft Co., Tucson, 1955-57, John J. Foster Mfg. Co., Costa Mesa, Calif., 1958, Standard Elec. Products, Costa Mesa, 1959; engring. mgr. Electronic Engring. Co., Santa Ana, 1959-79; product quality mgr. Farwest Data Systems, Irvine, Calif., 1979-82; dist. mgr. profl. services, nat. cons. mgr. Comserv/MSA, 1982—, Western Electronic Mfrs. Assn., Am. Prodn. and Inventory Control Soc., 1976-82, Computer Mfrs. Conf., 1980. Cert. in mgmt. Am. Mgmt. Assn., 1968. Mem. Am. Prodn. and Inventory Control Soc. Co-author patent reel spindle, 1972.

DOTO, IRENE LOUISE, statistician; b. Wilmington, Del., May 7, 1922; d. Antonio and Teresa (Tabasso) D. BA, U. Pa., 1943; MA, Temple U., 1948, Columbia U., 1954. Engring. asst. RCA-Victor, 1943-44; research asst. U. Pa., 1944; actuarial clk. Penn Mut. Life Ins. Co., 1944-46; instr. math. Temple U., 1946-53; commd. sr. asst. health services officer USPHS, 1954, advanced through grades to dir., 1963; statistician Communicable Disease Ctr., Atlanta, 1954-55, Kansas City, Kans., 1955-67; chief statis. and publ. services, ecol. investigations program Ctr. for Disease Control, Kansas City, 1967-73, chief statis. services, div. hepatitis and viral enteritis, Phoenix, 1973-83; statis. cons., 1984—; mem. adj. faculty Phoenix Ctr., Ottawa U., 1982—. Mem. Am. Statis. Assn., Biometrics Soc., Am. Pub. Health Assn., Ariz. Pub. Health Assn., Ariz. Council Engring. and Sci. Assn. (officer 1982—, pres. 1988—), Primate Found. Ariz. (mem. animal care and use com. 1986—), Bus. and Profl. Women's Club Phoenix, Sigma Xi, Pi Mu Epsilon. Office: PO Box 22197 Phoenix AZ 85028

DOTTS, DONALD VERN, education educator; b. Covina, Calif., Nov. 7, 1935; s. John Ward and Lela Mae (Folsom) D.; m. F. Annis Jones, June 7, 1958; children: Deborah Annis, John David. BA, Ariz. State U., 1958. Asst. exec. dir., editor Ariz. State U. Alumni Assn., Tempe, 1958-67, exec. dir., 1967—. Active Maricopa County Air Pollution Hearing Bd., Phoenix, 1968-74; chmn. bd. dirs. YMCA, Tempe, 1984-86. Served to capt. USAR, 1958-66. Mem. Am. Alumni Council (mem. nat. bd. 1968-70), Council for Advancement and Support of Edn. (memb. nat. bd. 1980-83, dist. chmn. 1980-83, Dist. VII Tribute award 1986), Coun. Alumni Assn. Execs. (founding), Phi Sigma Kappa (editor 1974-79, dist. gov. 1958-88). Democrat. Methodist. Home: 1206 E Harbor View Dr Tempe AZ 85283 Office: Ariz State U Alumni Ctr Tempe AZ 85287

DOTY, CHARLES WILLIAM, electrical engineer; b. Zanesville, Ohio, Aug. 1, 1947; s. Charles W. Sr. and Elizabeth (Head) D.; m. Lesa Adair, Sept. 3, 1982; children: Kathryn, Jennifer. BSEE, Stanton U., Orlando, Fla., 1968. Prin. Applied Control Tech., Orlando, 1967-72; facilities engr. Ramada Inns, Phoenix, 1972-76; distbr. engr. Reliance Electric, Cleve., 1976-79; prin. Electronic Analyzing Sys., Indpls., 1979-86, Automated Control Tech., Phoenix., 1986--. lst lt. USAF, 1965-67. Mem. ASHRAE (advisor 1987-88), Assn. Energy Engrs. (sr. mem.). Democrat. Lutheran. Home: 9133 S Alder Tempe AZ 85284 Office: Automated Control Tech 55 W Hoover #12 Mesa AZ 85210

DOTY, DOUGLAS HOWARD, chemical company executive; b. Ames, Iowa, July 20, 1948; s. William Joseph and Inza Lorae (Halterman) D.; m. Kelly Ann Reed, May 28, 1978; children: Jerri Lynn, Melissa Kay, Anna Lorae, William Reed. BA, Calif. State U., Stanislaus, 1971; MBA, U. So. Calif., 1973. Cert. tchr., Calif.; lic. pest control adv. Account exec. Dean Witter and Co., Inc., Scottsdale, Ariz., 1973-75; br. mgr. Interlink Agrl. Chems., Inc., Modesto, Calif., 1975-77; v.p. Winton (Calif.) Agrl. Chem. Co., Inc., 1977-82; dist. mgr. Puregro Co., Pixley, Calif., 1982-87; regional mgr. Stoller Chem. Co., Inc., Fresno, Calif., 1987—. Mem. Dow Bus. Roundtable (adv. bd. 1985-86), Calif. Agrl. Prodn. Cons. Assn., Calif. Fertilizer Assn. Republican. Home: 3310 N Arthur Ave Fresno CA 93705 Office: Stoller Chem Co Inc 2641 S Maple Ave Fresno CA 93725

DOTY, GORDON LEROY, hematologist-oncologist; b. Belding, Mich., Apr. 3, 1931; s. George Henry and Frances Louie (Witt) D.; m. Joanne Ranell, June 20, 1953 (div. 1984); m. Nancy Joyce Moorman, Nov. 20, 1983. BS, Mich. State U., 1952; MD, Wayne State U., 1956. Diplomate Am. Bd. Internal Medicine. Rotating intern Detroit Receiving Hosp., 1956-57, asst. resident, then chief resident internal medicine, 1961-64; USPHS trainee in hematology Tufts U., Boston, 1964-65; rsch. fellow hematology Boston City Hosp., 1964-65; pvt. practice Suburban Med. Clinic, Portland, Oreg., 1965-67, Hematology Clinic, Portland, 1967--; clin. instr. medicine U. Oreg. Health Scis. U., 1967-72, clin. asst. prof., 1972—; attending physician hematology-oncology, Portland VA Hosp., 1967—; cons. Providence Med. Ctr., 1965—, med. dir. cancer program, 1985—, chmn. cancer com., 1985—; clin. prof. medicine Oreg. Health Scis. U., 1987—; co-founder, co-chmn. Futures Rsch. Group, Providence Med. Ctr., 1987—; prin. investigator Columbia River CCUP, 1987—. Capt. MC, U.S. Army, 1957-61. Mem. ACP, Am. Soc. Internal Medicine, Am. Soc. Hematology, Am. Acad. Med. Dirs.,Oreg. Med. Assn., Oreg. Soc. Clin. Oncology, Multnomah County Med. Soc., World Future Soc.d, City Club Portland, Am. Alpine Club (chmn. Oreg. sect. 1980), Mazamas (climbing leader 1971--), Phi Kappa Phi, Alpha Omega Alpha. Office: Hematology Clinic 510 NE 49th Ave Portland OR 97213

DOTY, HORACE JAY, JR., theater administrator, arts consultant; b. St. Petersburg, Fla., May 25, 1924; s. Horace Herndon and Mabel (Bruce) D.; student Sherwood Music Sch., Chgo., 1942-43; BA in Music, Pomona Coll., 1950; cert. La Verne Coll., 1969; MA in Edn., Claremont Grad. Sch., 1972; cert. in Bus. Adminstrn., 1984; m. Wanda L. Flory, Dec. 27, 1947; 1 child, Janet. Propr. Jay Doty's Inc., Claremont, 1960-68; concert mgr. Claremont Colls., 1968-73, supr. Garrison Theater, U. Ctr. Box Office, dir. Auditorium, theater events, coordinator programs, 1973-79, 81—; exec. dir. Flint Ctr. for Performing Arts, Cupertino, Calif., 1979-81. Mem. blue ribbon com. Fox Theater Restoration, Pomona, Calif., 1982; mem. Claremont Bicentennial Com. for Performing Arts, 1975—; mem. touring adv. panel, cons. and site visitor Calif. Arts Council; mem. exec. bd., Calif. Presenters. Served with inf. AUS, 1943-46. NEA fellow, 1986. Mem. Assn. Coll., Univ. and Community Arts Adminstrs. (dir. 1983-86), Western Alliance Arts Adminstrs. (pres. 1975-77), Internat. Assn. Auditorium Mgrs., Claremont C. of C. (pres. 1965-66). Home: 4145 Oak Hollow Rd Claremont CA 91711 Office: Claremont Colls Ctr Performing Arts Bridges Auditorium Claremont CA 91711

DOTY, MARJORIE LU, real estate broker; b. Boulder, Colo., Feb. 23, 1927; d. Henry Heywood and Ella Chandler (Jones) Donnelley; m. Harold Franklin Doty, June 14, 1944 (div. 1956); children: Judith Ann Doty Flesher, James Arthur, Frederick Lee; m. Russell Andrew McGilvery, 1968. Student, Met. State Coll., 1966-70. Dir. hosp. admissions dept. health Denver Gen. Hosp., 1950-84; real estate assoc. Home Sweet Home Realty, Denver, 1984—; cons. in field; bd. dirs. Genlink, Inc. Trustee Denver Employees Retirement Plan, 1985, adv. bd., 1968-88; chmn. Met. Action Com., Inc., 1987—. Mem. Colo. Bd. Realtors, Denver Bd. Realtors, Colo. Genealogic Soc., H&H. Republican. Presbyterian. Home and Office: 10 S Lincoln St Denver CO 80209

DOTY, MATTHEW EMERSON, engineering company executive; b. Long Beach, Calif., Sept. 10, 1959; s. Jack Emerson and Grace Edith (Westberg) D. BS, U. Calif., Berkeley, 1984. Chemist Fairchild Semiconductor, San Rafael, Calif., 1984-85, lab. supr., 1985-86; device engr. Internat. Rectifier, El Segundo, Calif., 1986-87, quality and reliability mgr., 1987-88, reliability engring. mgr., 1988—. Home: 228 31st Pl Manhattan Beach CA 90266 Office: Internat Rectifier 233 Kansas St El Segundo CA 90245

DOTY, PHILIP EDWARD, accountant; b. Red Oak, Iowa, Dec. 9, 1943; s. Wade Bryan and Vera Mae (Dodd) D.; m. Della Corrine Mack, Dec. 23, 1967; children: Sarah, Anne. BSBA, Drake U., 1967. CPA, Colo. Ptnr. Arthur Andersen & Co., Denver, 1967—, dir. energy practice, litigation support svcs. and worldwide oil and gas tng., 1987—. Treas. Mile High United Way, Denver, 1984—, Girl Scouts U.S., Denver, 1987—, Leadership Denver Assn., 1987—; bd. dirs. Artreach, Inc., Denver, 1986—; bd. fellows U. Denver, 1986—. Served with USAR, 1967-73. Mem. Am. Inst. CPA's, Am. Petroleum Inst., Rocky Mountain Oil and Gas Assn., Petroeum Accts. Soc. (v.p. 1988—), Colo. Soc. CPA's (bd. dirs. 1987—), Ind. Petroleum Assn. Mountain States (bd. dirs. 1987—), Columbine Country Club, Flatirons Club, Petroleum Club (sec., treas. 1988—), Beta Gamma Sigma. Republican. Baptist. Clubs: Columbine Country (Littleton, Colo.); Flatirons (Boulder, Colo.), Petroleum (Denver).

DOUGHERTY, CELIA BERNIECE, educator; b. Toronto, Ohio, Aug. 7, 1935; d. Ernest Merle and Dorthy Grace (Erwin) Putnam; student Ohio U., 1953-54; BA, Calif. State U., Fullerton, 1971, MS, 1974; postgrad. U. So. Calif., 1981-83; m. William Vincent Dougherty, May 14, 1955; children: Marie Collette, Michael Charles. Reading specialist Anaheim (Calif.) Union High Sch. Dist., 1972-78, asst. prin. jr. high, 1978-80; asst. prin. jr. high Orange (Calif.) Unified Sch. Dist., 1980-88, prin., 1988—; trustee Anaheim City Sch. Dist., 1985—. Leader, Girl Scouts, 1968-71; mem. alumni council Calif. State U., Fullerton. Scholar Ohio U., 1953-54. Mem. Orange County Reading Assn. (bd. dir. 1986, pres. 1982-83), Calif. Reading Assn., Internat. Reading Assn., Assn. Calif. Sch. Adminstrs., Calif. Sch. Bd. Assn., Assn. Supervision and Curriculum Devel., Educare. Phi Kappa Phi, AAUW, Phi Alpha Theta, Phi Delta Gamma. Democrat. Home: 860 S Cardiff St Anaheim CA 92806 Office: 370 N Glassell St Orange CA 92666

DOUGHERTY, HOWARD WILLIAM, oil and gas producer; b. Kansas City, Mo., Jan. 5, 1915; s. Frank C. and Elsie (Braecklein) D.; m. Violeta van Ronzelen, Sept. 15, 1984; children: William, Robert, Patrick, Michael, Mary, Peter. BS in Earth Sci., Stanford U., 1938. Oil and gas producer, Pasadena, Calif., 1947—; dir. Santa Anita Consol., Inc.; pres. Pioneer Kettleman Co., Book Cliffs Oil & Gas Co. Mem. Conservation Com. Calif.; trustee Neuro Scis. Inst. Mem. Ind. Petroleum Assn. Am., Beta Theta Pi. Clubs: L.A. Country, California, Bohemian; Valley Hunt (Pasadena); Birnham Wood Golf (Santa Barbara); Mil. Order of St. Lazarus (comdr.). Office: 2234 E Colorado Blvd 2d Fl Pasadena CA 91107-3608

DOUGHERTY, MATTHEW, business executive; b. Louisville, Ky., Aug. 14, 1959; s. John Thomas and Katherine Elizabeth (Terstegge) D.; m. Suzanne Provencio Enriquez, Sept. 3, 1988. BBA, Loyola U., New Orleans, 1982; MBA, Ind. U., 1985. Fin. analyst Louisville Paving Co., 1980-85; pres. N.Mex. Discount Office Supply, Santa Fe, 1986—. Mem. Jaycees. Republican. Home: 325 E Buena Vista #2 Santa Fe NM 87501

DOUGHERTY, RALEIGH GORDON, manufacturer's representative; b. Saginaw, Mich., Aug. 19, 1928; s. Raleigh Gordon and Helen Jean (McCrum) D.; 1 child, Karen Kealani. Salesman, H.D. Hudson Mfg. Co., Chgo., 1946-48; field sales rep. Jensen Mfg. Co., Chgo., 1948-50; field sales mgr. Regency Idea, Indpls., 1950-54; mgr. Brenna & Browne, Honolulu, 1954-56; owner, pres. Dougherty Enterprises, Honolulu, 1956—. With U.S. Army, 1950-52. Mem. Hawaii Hotel Assn., Internat. Home Furnishings Reps. Assn., Air Force Assn., D.A.V. (life), Am. Soc. Interior Designers (industry found.), Navy League U.S., Am. Legion, Hawaii Restaurant Assn., Nat. Fedn. Ind. Bus., Korean Vet. Small Bus. of Hawaii, Historic Hawaii Found., Hawaii Visitors Bur., Elks (past trustee Hawaii), Kani Ka Pila Golf Club. Republican. Methodist. Home: 1466 Kamole St Honolulu HI 96821 Office: PO Box 10446 Honolulu HI 96821

DOUGHTY, RICHARD G., telecommunications consultant; b. Sulphur, Okla., Oct. 12, 1945. BSEE, Northwestern U., 1968; MS in Engring., Econs., U. Colo., 1973. Registered profl. engr., Wash. Engr. Magnaflux Corp., Chgo., 1965-66, Lockheed Missiles & Space Co., Sunnyvale, Calif., 1966-68, Martin Marietta Corp., Denver, 1968-78; mgr. Boeing Computer Svcs. Co., Seattle, 1985-86; cons. Touche Ross & Co., Seattle, 1986-88, Tech. Mgmt. Group, Seattle, 1989—. Contbr. articles to profl. publs. Chmn. Sch. Dist. Com., Issaquah, Wash., 1980-83. Recipient Skylab Achievement award NASA, 1974, cert. of achievement, 1976. Mem. AIAA, Ops. Research Soc. Am. Office: Touche Ross & Co 1111 3d Ave Seattle WA 98101

DOUGLAS, DAN RAYMOND, systems management specialist; b. Toronto, Ontario, Can., Feb. 27, 1951; s. Robert Alan and Marilyn Day (Ellis) D.; m. Gail Elizabeth Burton, Apr. 28, 1973; children: Scott, Erica. Diploma bus. adminstrn., St. Clair Coll., Can., 1973. Computer ops. mgr. Can. Packers, Toronto, 1973-75; mgr., mgr. info. products Bank of Montreal, Toronto, 1975-88; sr. cons. Diederich & Assocs., South Pasadena, Calif., 1988—; systems mgmt. group mgr. Guide Internat. Corp., Chgo., 1984—; speaker European Info. Mgmt. Users Conf., London, 1987-89. Mem. Systems Mgmt. Users Group (pres. 1984-86), Calif. Systems Mgmt. Orgn. (exec. bd. 1989—). Home: 1201 S Washington Ave Glendora CA 91740 Office: Diederich & Assocs 1445 Huntington Dr Ste 320 South Pasadena CA 91030

DOUGLAS, GARY MICHAEL, mechanical design engineer; b. Spokane, Wash., Dec. 27, 1954; s. Stephen Nick and Shirley Mae (Eansor) Krenytzky; m. Janice Ann Hart, Oct. 4, 1979 (div. 1985); children: Pascale Mae, Nicholas Scott; m. Joan Alice Fulmer, Oct. 27, 1987; children: Jacqueline Marie, Robert Joseph. Student, Cen. Mich. U., 1978-79; BSME, U. N.Mex., 1984. Mem. tech. staff III, Rockwell power systems div., contracted to Sandia Nat. Labs. Rockwell Internat., Albuquerque, 1985—; engring. rsch. support Dept. Energy . Contbr. articles to profl. jours. Pres. Engrs. for Social Responsibility, Alburquerque, 1983—. Served with USN, 1974-77. Home: Box 45 Rincon Loop Tijeras NM 87059 Office: Sandia Nat Labs PO Box 5800 Div 1243-1 Albuquerque NM 87185

DOUGLAS, GEOFFREY PAGE, insurance claims manager; b. Berkeley, Calif., Mar. 31, 1951; s. William Whitton and Rowena (Anna) D.; m. Susan Helen Boarman, Dec. 26, 1976. AA in Gen. Edn., Diablo Valley Jr. Coll., Pleasant Hill, Calif., 1971; BA in Psychology, Sonoma State U., 1978; postgrad., Boston U., Bremerhaven, Fed. Republic of Germany, 1978-80, J.F. Kennedy U., Orinda, Calif., 1980-81. Detention svc. counselor All County Resource Ctr., Martinez, Calif., 1980; social worker mental health Contra Costa County, Martinez, 1980-81; pvt. investigator Group Five DBA Calif. Internat. Investigation, San Francisco, 1981-82; claims rep. Allstate Ins. Co., San Ramon, Calif., 1982-84; recovery specialist CIGNA Recovery Svc., San Francisco, 1984-86; claims rep. toxic tort claims Cravens Dargan Pacific Coast CIGNA, San Francisco, 1986; claims recovery mgr. CIGNA Recovery Svcs. Internat., San Francisco, 1986, Rancho Cordova, Calif., 1986—; arbitrator Nat. Arbitration Forum, N.Y.C., 1984-87; mgr. no. Calif. region CIGNA Recovery Svc. Internat., Rancho Cordova, 1986—. Imagery interpreter and behavioral sci. specialist Community Detention Svcs. Com., Contra Costa County, 1980-81. Staff sgt. U.S. Army, 1974-80. Decorated U.S. Army Commendation medals. Mem. Claims Assn. Sacramento, Civil Affairs Assn.-U.S. Army Reserve. Republican. Office: CIGNA Recovery Svcs 11050 Olson Dr Rancho Cordova CA 95670

DOUGLAS, HUGH, mining executive; b. Harare, Zimbabwe, Oct. 28, 1927; s. James Douglas and Marguerite Eleanor (Carter) Carter; m. Anita Margereta Hedberg, Jan. 3, 1953 (div. 1975); m. Marie Ann Billante, Mar. 21, 1987; children: Hugh Jr., Ian H., Craig H., Ann M. BA, Amherst (Mass.) Coll., 1949; MA, Columbia U., N.Y.C., 1951; M in Philosophy, U. London, 1985. Geologist U.S. Atomic Energy Commn., Denver, 1951; sr. geologist Texasgulf, Inc., N.Y.C., 1951-55; asst. mgr. geol. ops. Am. Overseas Petroleum, Turkey and Libya, 1955-62; sec., treas. Thermonetics, Inc., Canoga Park, Calif., 1962-64; mgr. mineral econs. SRI Internat., Menlo Park, Calif., 1964-71; mgr. mineral planning div. Utah Internat., Inc., San Francisco, 1971-77; dir. mineral econs. dept. Dames & Moore, Inc., San Francisco, 1977-78; pres. Hugh Douglas & Co., Ltd., San Francisco, 1978—; mng. dir. DMB Rsch., Ltd., London, 1985-87; adj. prof. minerals econs. Stanford (Calif.) U., 1979-82. Contbr. articles to profl. jours. Trustee Mechanics Inst., San Francisco, 1988—. Mem. Mining and Metall. Soc. Am. (former trustee), Soc. Mining Engrs. chpt. Am. Inst. Mining Engrs., Soc. Econ. Geologists, Soc. Econ. Geologist Found. (trustee DeKalb, Ill. chpt. 1985—), St. Andrews Soc. Republican. Episcopalian. Office: 124 16th Ave San Francisco CA 94118

DOUGLAS, JOHN DAVID, pharmacist; b. Salt Lake City, Oct. 7, 1949; s. Raymond T. and U. Dean (Warner) D.; m. Cindy Sue Entress, Sept. 3, 1983. BS in Pharmacy, U. Utah, 1979. Lic. pharmacist, CAlif. Pharmacy mgr. Sav On Drugs, San Diego, 1976-86; owner, prin. Ind. Phar. Svcs., San Diego, 1986-87, Douglas Drug Store, Lakeside, Calif., 1988—; owner Douglas Feed Store and Douglas Grocery, Lakeside, 1988—. Contbr. articles to profl. jours. With U.S. Army, 1968-70. Mem. Humane Soc., Calif. Pharmacist Assn., Kiwanis. Home: 11529 Rocosa Rd Lakeside CA 92040 Office: Douglas Drugs 12346 A Woodside Ave Lakeside CA 92040

DOUGLAS, JOHN HENRY, writer, science; b. Chgo., May 22, 1941; s. Henry Pickett and Goldie May (Johnson) D.; m. Marilyn Ann Kuhel, May 24, 1974; children: Heather, Benjamin. BA magna cum laude, Vanderbilt U., 1963; MS, Cornell U., 1966; MJ, U. Calif., 1972. Physicist Knolls Atomic Power Lab, Schnectady, N.Y., 1966-67; sci., soc. editor Sci. News

Mag., Washington, 1973-77; rsch. journalist Fulbright Found., Tokyo, 1977-78; west coast editor Sci. News Mag., San Francisco, 1978-79; sci. writer Palo Alto, Calif., 1979-83; west coast editor High Tech. Mag., Palo Alto, Calif., 1982-83; sci. writer Palo Alto, Calif., 1983—; sci. columnist Union-Star newspaper, Schnectady, 1967, stringer Time Mag., Berkeley, Calif., 1971-73, correspondent (part-time) Nature Mag., San Francisco, 1978-79, cons. Electric Power Rsch. Inst., Palo Alto, 1979—. Author: The Future World of Energy, 1984, Parent Power, 1977; contbr. articles to profl. jours. U.S. Peace Corps vol., Muar, Malaysia, 1967-69. Recipient Sci. in Soc. award Coun. for the Advancement of Sci Writing, 1977; fellow Fulbright for working journalists, 1977-78, Nate Haseltine, U. Calif., 1971, Woodrow Wilson, Cornell U., 1964-65; scholar Vanderbilt U., 1959-63. Mem. No. Calif. Sci. Writers Assn. (pres. 1980-81), Nat. Assn. of Sci. Writers. Home and Office: 360 Maclane St Palo Alto CA 94306

DOUGLAS, LARRY J., chemistry consultant; b. Oklahoma City, Okla., Mar. 3, 1937; s. Harry Edward Douglas Jr. and Joan L. (Gamble) Croomes; m. Kathleen S. Brandes, Sept. 18, 1978; children: James Stuart, Joanna Kristine. BS in Chemistry, U. Denver, 1958, PhD, 1970. Research engr. Nat. Cash Register Co., Inglewood, Calif., 1958-64; research scientist Marathon Oil Co., Littleton, Colo., 1970-76; owner Photography Unlimited Studios, Denver, 1976-78; sr. program mgr. Solar Energy Research Inst., Golden, Colo., 1978-87; pres. Entropy Assocs., Lakewood, Colo., 1987—; cons. U. Colo. Med. Ctr., Denver, 1968-78, Hydratron Energy Systems, Farmingdale, N.Y., 1984—, Starmark Energy Systems, Memphis, Tenn., 1987—. Chmn. Vocat. Electronic Review Com., Denver Pub. Sch., 1972-75; mem. Math/Sci. program review, Denver Pub. Sch., 1982, United Way-Soc Planning Group, Denver, 1980; advisor Explorer Scout Sci. Post, Golden, Colo., 1986-87. Research grantee NASA, Denver, 1966-69. Mem. AAAS, Electro Chem. Soc. (v.p. 1973-74), Rocky Mountain Region (pres. 1974-75), Sigma Xi (v.p. 1974-75). Club: North Denver Camera, Lakewood, Colo. (pres. 1983-85). Home: 1747 S Field Ct Lakewood CO 80226

DOUGLAS, MARION JOAN, labor negotiator; b. Jersey City, May 29, 1940; d. Walter Stanley and Sophie Frances (Zysk) Binaski; children: Jane Dee, Alex Jay. BA, Mich. State U., 1962; MSW, Sacramento State Coll., 1971; MPA, Calif. State U.-Sacramento, 1981. Owner, mgr. Linkletter-Totten Dance Studios, Sacramento, 1962-68, Young World of Discovery, Sacramento, 1965-68; welfare worker Sacramento County, 1964-67, welfare supr., 1968-72, child welfare supr., 1972-75, sr. personnel analyst, 1976-78, personnel program mgr., 1978-81, labor relations rep., 1981—; cons. State Dept. Health, Sacramento, 1975-76; cons. in field. Author/editor: (newsletter) Thursday's Child, 1972-74. Presiding officer Community Resource Orgn., Fair Oaks, Calif., 1970-72; exec. bd. Foster Parent's Assn., Sacramento, 1972-75; organizer Foster Care Sch. Dist. liaison programs, 1973-75; active Am. Lung Assn., 1983-87; rep. Calif. Welfare Dirs. Assn., 1975-76; county staff advisor Joint Powers Authority, Sacramento, 1978-81; mem. Mgmt. Devel. Com., Sacramento, 1979-80; vol., auctioneer sta. KVIE Pub. TV, Sacramento, 1970-84, 88—; adv. bd. Job and Info. Resource Ctr., 1976-77; spl. adv. task force coordinator Sacramento Employment and Tng. Adv. Council, 1980-81; vol. leader Am. Lung Assn., Sacramento, 1983-86 Calif. Dept. Social Welfare ednl. stipend, 1967-68, County of Sacramento ednl. stipend, 1969-70. Recipient Achievement award Nat. Assn. Counties, 1981. Mem. Mgmt. Women's Forum, Indsl. Relations Assn. No. Calif., Indsl. Relations Research Assn., Nat. Assn. Female Execs., Mensa. Republican. Avocations: real estate, nutrition. Home: 7812 Palmyra Dr Fair Oaks CA 95628 Office: Sacramento County Dept Pers Mgmt 700 H St Sacramento CA 95814

DOUGLASS, DONALD ROBERT, banker; b. Evanston, Ill., Oct. 7, 1934; s. Robert William and Dorothy (Gibson) D.; B.B.A., U. N.Mex., 1959, M.B.A., 1966; m. Susan Douglass. With Security Pacific Nat. Bank, Los Angeles, 1961—, mgmt. trainee, 1962-63, asst. mgr. Vernon (Calif.) br., 1963-64, asst. mgr. Whittier (Calif.), 1964, asst. v.p., 1965, asst. v.p., credit officer regional adminstrn., Los Angeles, 1966-69, v.p., San Francisco, 1969-74, mgr. corp. accounts credit adminstrn. No. Calif. Corp. Banking, 1974-77; group v.p. Annco Properties, Burlingame, Calif., 1977-79; v.p., sr. loan officer Borel Bank and Trust Co., San Mateo, Calif., 1979-83, sr. v.p., 1983-84, exec. v.p. mortgage banking div. comml. property sales, Los Altos, 1984-87; ptnr. Key Equities, Inc., San Mateo, 1987—; ptnr., broker Centre Fin. Group, Inc., San Mateo; instr. Am. Inst. Banking, 1963, Coll. San Mateo, 1982—. Served with AUS, 1954-56. Mem. U. N.Mex. Alumni Assn., Sigma Alpha Epsilon, Delta Sigma Phi. Republican. Presbyn. Home: 745 Celestial Ln Foster City CA 94404

DOUGLASS, ENID HART, educational director; b. L.A., Oct. 23, 1926; d. Frank Roland and Enid Yandell (Lewis) Hart; m. Malcolm P. Douglass, Aug. 28, 1948; children: Malcolm Paul Jr., John Aubrey, Susan Enid. BA, Pomona Coll., 1948; MA, Claremont (Calif.) Grad. Sch., 1959. Research asst. World Book Ency., Palo Alto, Calif., 1953-54; exec. sec., asst. dir. oral history program Claremont Grad. Sch., 1963-71, dir. oral history program, 1971—, history lectr., 1977—; mem. Calif. Heritage Preservation Commn., 1977-85, chmn. 1983-85. Contbr. articles to hist. jours. Mayor pro tem City of Claremont, 1980-82, Mayor, 1982-86; mem. planning and research adv. council State of Calif., mem. city council, Claremont, 1978-86; founder Claremont Heritage, Inc., 1977-80, bd. dirs., 1986—; bd. dirs. Pilgrim Pla., Claremont; founder steering com. Claremont Community Fedn. Mem. Oral History Assn. (pres. 1979-80), Southwest Oral History Assn. (founding steering com. 1981, J.V. Mink award 1984), Nat. Council Pub. History, LWV (bd. dirs. 1957-59, Outstanding Svc. to Community award, 1986). Democrat. Home: 1195 Berkeley Ave Claremont CA 91711 Office: Claremont Grad Sch Oral History Program 150 E 10th St Claremont CA 91711-6160

DOUGLASS, JOHN MICHAEL, internist; b. Takoma Park, Md., Apr. 13, 1939; s. Jones All and Helen Louise D.; BA, Columbia Union Coll., Takoma Park, 1959; MD (Salerni Collegium scholar), U. So. Calif., 1964; DPh Pacific West U., 1986; PhD Clayton U., 1987. m. Sue Nan Peters, May 15, 1962; children: Dina Lynn, Lisa Michele. Rotating intern Los Angeles County, U. So. Calif. Med. Ctr., 1964-65, resident internal medicine, 1965-67, home care physician, 1965-68; practice medicine specializing in internal medicine, Cin., 1968-70, Los Angeles, 1970—; physician Pasadena Emergency Center, 1965-68, Deaconess Hosp., 1968-70; postdoctoral fellow automobile safety and trauma research U. Calif., Los Angeles, 1967-68, med. cons. Emergency Med. Services Project, 1970-71; commd. med. officer USPHS, 1968-70; asst. sci. adviser, injury control program ECA, USPHS, Cin., 1968-69, med. specialities cons. Office Product Safety, FDA, USPHS, 1969-70; internal medicine cons. East End Neighborhood Community Health Center, Cin., 1968-70; lt. comdr.-04, USPHS Res. officer, 1970-82; internal medicine cons. Hollywood Sunset Free Clinic, 1971-72; sr. med. cons. multidisciplinary hwy. accident investigation unit U. So. Calif., 1971-73; staff internist, coordinator health improvement service Kaiser Found. Hosp., Los Angeles, 1970—; instr. biomedical engring. course U. Calif., Los Angeles, 1968, instr. internal medicine, 1971-74; instr. internal medicine U. Cin. Sch. Medicine, 1968-70; instr. kinesthesiology, traumatic anatomy and head injury U. So. Calif., 1971-74, instr. foodstyle and lifestyle, 1977—; mem. med. adv. bd. Dominican Sisters of Sick Poor, 1969; traffic safety cons. Countywide Conf. on Emergency Med. Services, 1972; mem. nutrition council Las Virgenes Sch. Dist., 1977. Active mgmt. devel. program Boy Scouts Am. Execs., 1966; bd. dirs. Calif. Assn. Pvt. Schs. and Colls., 1967, Coronary Club (adult jogging program), 1967-68; co-organizer Oriental rug exhibit Pacificulture Mus., Pasadena, Calif., 1973; v.p. Los Angeles Med. Milk Commn. Diplomate Nat. Bd. Med. Examiners, Am. Bd. Internal Medicine. Comdr. USPHS Officers Res. Corps. Fellow ACP; mem. AMA, Calif. Med. Assn., Los Angeles County Med. Assn., Am., Calif., Los Angeles socs. internal medicine, Am. Assn. Automotive Medicine (exec. com. Western chpt. 1977-82), Nutrition Today Soc., Internat. Hajji Baba Soc., Decorative Arts Council, Los Angeles Mus. Art, Sierra Club, Phi Delta Epsilon, Alpha Omega Alpha, Phi Kappa Phi. Author: The Lost Language; contbr. articles to profl. jours. Home: 99 Buckskin Rd Bell Canyon CA 91307 Office: 1510 N Edgemont St Los Angeles CA 90027

DOUGLASS, RICHARD H., teacher, reserve police officer, retired naval reserve officer; b. Dubuque, Iowa, Nov. 13, 1933; s. Millard Horace and Olive Lola (Smith) D.; m. Kathleen Naoma Lilley, July 14, 1964; children: Michael Derald, Kathleen Elizabeth. AA, John Muir Jr. Coll., 1953; BA, U. Calif., Santa Barbara, 1955; MA, U. So. Calif., 1965; gen. secondary credential, U. Calif., Santa Barbara, 1956; post cert., Pasadena Police Acad., 1972. Tchr. Duarte (Calif.) Unified Sch. Dist., 1959—; foreign language dept. chairperson Duarte (Calif.) High Sch., 1966-78; tchr. Citrus Community Coll., Glendora, Calif., 1983—. Advisor yearbook Halconado, 1962; advisor, editor yearbooks Upward Bound III, Upward Bound IV, 1980-81. Instr. Boy Scouts Am., 1972-83. Served to sr. chief USNR, 1952-87, sr. chief petty officer ret. NDEA scholar U. So. Calif., 1965; scholar Nat. Endowment Humanities, 1973; recipient Cert. of Appreciation, City of Pasadena, 1975—, City of Duarte Community Svc. award, Svc to Youth, 1988, Calif. Assemblyman Richard Mountjoy Svc. Youth award, 1988, Calif State Senate Svc. award, 1988, PTSA Golden Apple award Svc. to Youth, 1989; named Hon. Counselor U.S. Military Acad., West Point, N.Y., 1983. Mem. Lang. Tchrs. Assn. (Calif. forum), Naval Enlisted Res. Assn. (lifetime mem.), U. So. Calif. Alumni Assn. (lifetime alumnus), Duarte Unified Edn. Assn. (pres. 1964-65, negotiator 1969-79, Appreciation cert. 1979), Duarte High Sch. Key Club (advisor 1985—), Lambda Chi Alpha. Democrat. Home: 347 Fairview Ave Arcadia CA 91006 Office: Duarte Unified Sch Dist 1427 Buena Vista Ave Duarte CA 91010

DOUTHETT, DOLORES ANN, anesthetist; b. Mich., Mar. 23, 1931; d. Francis William and Eleanor (Hibbard) Glade; children: Peggy, Kathleen, William. Mem. Am. Assn. Nurse Anesthetist. Home: 374 Chateau La Salle Dr San Jose CA 95111

DOUTT, JEFFREY (THOMAS), marketing and management specialist, university dean; b. Oakland, Calif., Mar. 30, 1947; s. Richard L. and Lucinda M. (Killian) D.; B.S., U. Calif.-Berkeley, 1968, M.S., 1970, Ph.D., 1976. Assoc. in bus. adminstrn. U. Calif.-Berkeley, 1974; asst. prof. mgmt. Sonoma (Calif.) State U., 1974-78, assoc. prof., 1978-83, prof., 1983—, chmn. dept. mgmt. studies, 1976-80, dean Sch. Social Scis., 1980-86, dean Sch. Bus. and Econs., 1986—; prin. assoc. Mgmt. Devel. Internat.; cons. mktg. and mgmt. Recipient Internat. Exchange award Rotary Found., 1979; Giannini Found. fellow, 1968-70. Mem. Am. Mktg. Assn., Am. Agrl. Econs. Assn., Am. Econ. Assn., Am. Inst. Decision Scis., Acad. Mktg. Sci., Acad. Internat. Bus., Am. Soc. Tng. and Devel., Internat. Communication Assn., Soc. Intercultural Edn. Tng. and Research, Am. Bus. Communication Assn., Western Mktg. Educators Assn., Phi Beta Kappa. Democrat. Club: Rotary. Contbr. articles to profl. jours. Home: 5130 Gilchrist Rd Sebastopol CA 95472 Office: 1801 E Cotati Ave Rohnert Park CA 94928

DOVE, DONALD AUGUSTINE, city planner, educator; b. Waco, Tex., Aug. 7, 1930; s. Sebert Constantine and Amy Delmena (Stern) D.; m. Cecelia Mae White, Feb. 9, 1957; children—Angela Dove Gaddy, Donald, Monica, Celine, Austin, Cathlyn, Dianna, Jennifer. B.A., Calif. State U.-Los Angeles, 1951; M.A. in Pub. Adminstrn., U. So. Calif., 1966. Planning and devel. cons. D. Dove Assocs., Los Angeles, 1959-60; supr. demographic research Calif. Dept. Pub. Works, Los Angeles, 1960-66, environ. coordinator, Sacramento, 1971-75; dir. transp. employment project State of Calif., Los Angeles, 1966-71, chief Los Angeles Region transp. study, 1975-84; chief environ. planning Calif. Dept. Transp., Los Angeles, 1972-75; dir. U. So. Calif. Praetors, Los Angeles, 1984-87; panelist, advisor Pres. Conf. on Aging, Washington, 1970—, Internat. Conf. on Energy Use Mgmt., 1981; guest lectr. univs. western U.S., 1969—. Author: Preserving Urban Environment, 1976; Small Area Population Forecasts, 1966. Chmn. Lynwood City Planning Commn., Calif., 1982—; pres. Area Pastoral Council, Los Angeles, 1982-83; mem., del. Archdiocesan Pastoral Council, Los Angeles, 1979-86, Compton Community Devel. Bd., Calif., 1967-71. Served to cpl. U.S. Army, 1952-54. Mem. Am. Planning Assn., Am. Inst. Planners (transp. chmn. 1972-73), Calif. Assn. of Mgmt. (pres. 1987-88), Am. Inst. Cert. Planners, Assn. Environ. Profls. (co-founder 1973), Optimists (sec. 1978-79), K.C., Knights of Peter Claver. Democrat. Roman Catholic. Home: 11356 Ernestine Ave Lynwood CA 90262 Office: Calif Dept Transp 120 S Spring St Los Angeles CA 90012

DOW, MARY ALEXIS, financial executive; b. South Amboy, N.J., Feb. 19, 1949; d. Alexander and Elizabeth Anne (Reilly) Pawlowski; m. Russell Alfred Dow, June 19, 1971. BS with honors, U. R.I., 1971. CPA, Oreg. Staff acct. Deloitte, Haskins & Sells, Boston, 1971-74; sr. acct. Price Waterhouse, Portland, Oreg., 1974-77, mgr., 1977-81, sr. mgr., 1981-84; chief fin. officer Copeland Lumber Yards Inc., Portland, 1984-86; ind. cons. in field, 1986—; bd. dirs. Longview Fibre Co. Mem. council and fin. com. Oreg. Mus. Sci. and Industry; bd. dirs., exec. com., chair budget com. Oreg. Trails chpt. ARC, chmn. bd. N.W. Regional Blood Svcs.; mem. budget rev. com. Multnomah County. Mem. AICPA, Oreg. Soc. CPAs, Fin. Execs. Inst. Roman Catholic. Clubs: City (bd. govs.), University (Portland), Multnomah Athletic. Contbr. articles to profl. publs.

DOW, TONY FARES, healthcare company administrator; b. Amman, Jordan, Apr. 1, 1947; came to U.S., 1975; s. Fares A. and Farha (Haddad) D.; m. May I. Mudarry, Dec. 25, 1976. BA in Bus. Adminstrn., Middle East Coll., Beirut, 1972; GCE advanced level, U. London, 1973-74. Sr. tech. rep. Scheing A.G. Berlin, Middle East, 1964-73; mgr. Ferrer Internat., 1973-76; cons. internat. bus. Whittier, Calif., 1976-81; chief exec. officer, pres. Lifecare Internat., Inc., Whittier, 1981—; cons. in field. Author: Damascus for the Tourist, 1965; translator: Round the World in Eighty Days, 1968; contbr. articles to profl. jours. Mem. Am. Cons. Assn., Am. Lebanese League (pres. 1982), Export Mgmt. Assn. Office: Lifecare Internat Inc 14831 E Whittier Blvd 103 Whittier CA 90605

DOWD, DIANE, communications executive, lawyer; b. San Francisco, Mar. 11, 1953; d. Harry John and Dorothy Bridget (Taylor) D.; m. Scott Allen Spiro, Aug. 8, 1984; children: Ashley, Weston. BS, Ariz. State U., 1976; JD, Pepperdine U., 1984. Bar: Pa. 1985, D.C. 1986. News dir. Sta. KPRW-TV Ralph Guil Co., Bakersfield, Calif., 1977; asst. editor Sta. KFWB-AM Westinghouse Broadcasting Co., L.A., 1977; producer Sta. KPNX-TV Combined Communications Corp., Phoenix, 1977-79; producer WPVI-TV ABC/Capital Cities Communications, Phila., 1979; producer Cable News Network, L.A., 1980; law clk. Times-Mirror Corp., L.A., 1982, Fed. Communications Commn., Washington, 1983; pvt. practice Washington, 1986—; chmn., chief exec. officer Pharos Communications Corp., Beverly Hills, Calif., 1984—; cons. Coun. for Technol. Growth, Washington, 1982, NASA Private Funding, L.A., 1981. Contbg. editor ABA Securities Glossary, 1987. Law clk. Calif. Dem. Party, L.A., 1984. Recipient Cert. of Appreciation, Spl. Olympics, 1979. Mem. NATAS, ABA, D.C. Bar Assn., Ariz. Press Club. Home: 4110 Vanetta Pl Studio City CA 91604 Office: 9025 Wilshire Blvd Ste 309 Beverly Hills CA 90211

DOWD, MICHAEL BURKE, architect; b. Alexandria, Va., Dec. 1, 1958; s. Thomas John and Catherine Jean (Burke) D.; m. Hilary Mackenzie, Aug. 16, 1986. BA, U. Wash., 1980, MArch, 1983. Registered architect Nat. Coun. Archtl. Registration Bds., Wash., Oreg. Designer Charles Bergmann, Architect, Seattle, 1983, Ibsen Nelsen & Assocs., Seattle, 1983-84, GBD Architects, Portland, Oreg., 1984—. Corr. ARCADE Jour., 1983— (Blue ribbon 1985); contbr. archtl. drawing to mags. and profl. jours. 1st prize Arts N.W., 1982, Portland Landmarks Commn. award 1986; recipient Design award City of Beaverton, 1987. Mem. AIA (exhbn. Portland Oreg. chpt. 1988, chmn. design com. 1989). Home: 2722 SW Rutland Terr Portland OR 97201 Office: GBD Architects 920 SW 3rd Ave Ste 4000 Portland OR 97204

DOWDLE, PATRICK DENNIS, lawyer; b. Denver, Dec. 8, 1948; s. William Robert and Helen (Schraeder) D.; m. Eleanor Pryor, Mar. 8, 1975; children: Jeffery William, Andrew Peter. BA, Cornell Coll., Mt. Vernon, Iowa, 1971; JD, Boston U., 1975. Bar: Colo. 1975, U.S. Dist. Ct. Colo. 1975, U.S. Ct. Appeals (10th cir.) 1976, U.S. Supreme Ct. 1978. Acad. dir. in Japan Sch. Internat. Tng., Putney, Vt., 1974; assoc. Decker & Miller, Denver, 1975-77; ptnr. Miller, Makkai & Dowdle, Denver, 1977—; designated counsel criminal appeals Colo. Atty. Gens. Office, Denver, 1980-81; guardian ad litem Adams County Dist. Ct., Brighton, Colo., 1980-83; affiliated counsel ACLU, Denver, 1980—. Mem. ABA, Colo. Bar. Assn., Denver Bar Assn. (various coms.), Assn. Trial Lawyers Am., Sierra Club, Boston U. Sch. Alumni Assn. (regional rep. 1977—). Democrat. Clubs: Porsche of Am.(Rocky Mountain region 1983—). Home: 11825 W 30th Pl Lakewood CO 80215 Office: Miller Makkai & Dowdle 2325 W 72d Ave Denver CO 80221

DOWELL, SHIRLEY MARIE, nurse, educator; b. La Porte, Ind., Mar. 8, 1940; d. Stephen Edward and Dollafa (Kammerer) Bolinger; m. Ralph Eugene Dowell, Sept. 16, 1961 (div. 1978); children: Michael, Bradford Kevin, Gregory Matthew. Nursing degree, Meml. Hosp., South Bend, Ind., 1961; AS, Chaffey Coll., 1976; BS in Nursing, U. Phoenix, 1986; postgrad. in nursing edn., Calif. State U., Dominguez Hills, 1988—. RN, Calif. Staff nurse Porter Meml. Hosp., Valparaiso, Ind., 1961-63, Elkhart (Ind.) Gen. Hosp., 1963-66; staff nurse Pomona (Calif) Valley Community Hosp., 1966-75, head surg. nurse, 1975-78, instr. surgery, 1983-85, tchr. surg. nursing, 1985—; head surg. nurse La Porte Hosp., 1978-81; sec.-treas. hosp. credit union Pomona Valley Community Hosp., 1983—; head nurse surgery La Porte Hosp., 1978-81, instr. surgery, 1981-83; instr. adult edn. Mt. San Antonio Coll., Walnut, Calif., 1988-89; cons. in field. Den mother Ontario coun. Cub Scouts Am., 1971-75, La Porte coun., 1982-83. Mem. Assn. Operating Rm. Nurses (pres. 1986—), Nat. Assn. Orthopedic Nurses, Am. Urol. Assn. (allied), Laser Inst. Am., Order Ea. Star, White Shrine. Democrat. Methodist. Home: 1105 Golden Rain Upland CA 91786 Office: Pomona Valley Community Hosp 1798 N Garey Ave Pomona CA 91767

DOWLIN, KENNETH EVERETT, librarian; b. Wray, Colo., Mar. 11, 1941; s. Ross Everett and Fern Mae (Peterson) D.; m. Janice Marie Simmons, Mar. 11, 1961; children: Kevin Everett, Kristopher Everett. B.A., U. Colo., 1963, M.P.A., 1981; M.A., U. Denver, 1966. Bookmobile librarian, library asst. Adams County Public Library, Westminster, Colo., 1961-63; library asst. II Denver Public Library, 1962-64; head librarian Arvada Public Library, Colo., 1964-68; adminstrv. asst. Jefferson County Public Library, Colo., 1969; dir. Natrona County Public Library, Casper, Wyo., 1969-75, Pikes Peak Regional Library Dist., Colorado Springs, Colo., 1975-87; city librarian San Francisco Pub. Library, 1987—; instr. Casper Coll., 1971-73; chmn. Colo. Libraries in Coop., 1975-76, Colo. Ad-hoc Com. Networking, 1976; city librarian, San Francisco, 1987; mem. Western Interstate Commn. Higher Edn. Library Network Task Force; past trustee Wyo. Dept. Library, Archives and History; mem. Library of Congress Commn. on Book of Future; bd. dirs. Satellite Library Info. Network; vis. instr. U. Denver, 1980, 81; cons. in cable TV. Editorial bd. Microcomputers for Info. Mgmt., Library Hi Tech., Elec. Library. Mem. adv. bd. for series on tech. WNET, N.Y.C., 1981—; active San Francisco Mayor's com. on Juveniles in Detention; bd. dirs. Citizens Goals for Colorado Springs, 1981—; bd. govs. Colo. Tech. Coll., 1982-85. With USMCR, 1959-65. Recipient Disting. Alumni award U. Denver Grad. Sch. for Library and Info. Mgmt. Mem. ALA (council 1985—, commn. on equality and freedom access to info. 1984-85, chmn. awards com. 1985-86, Hammond Inc. Library Award Jury 1968), ALA Library and Info. Tech. Assn. (long range planning com. 1981-82, pres. 1983-84), Mountain Plains Library Assn., Colo. Library Assn. (pres. 1968-69), Denver Council Govts. (chmn. librarians com. 1966), Colo. Mcpl. League (chmn. librarians sect. 1967), Bibliog. Ctr. Rocky Mountains (pres. 1972-74), Pikes Peak Area C. of C. (chmn. cultural affairs com. 1976-77). Home: 359 Melrose Ave San Francisco CA 94127 Office: San Francisco Pub Libr Civic Ctr San Francisco CA 94102

DOWNER, HUGH CAMERON, JR., judge; b. Cleve., Apr. 27, 1946; s. Hugh C. and Marian W. (Wearth) D.; m. Lynn C. Chamberlain, June 21, 1969; children: Megan E., Shannon L. BS Naval Architecture, U. Mich., 1968; JD, Stanford U., 1971. Bar: Oreg. 1972. Assoc. Lillick, McHose, Wheat & Charles, San Francisco, 1971-72; 1st Lt. U.S. Army Corps Engrs., Ft. Belvoir, Va., 1972; asst. dist. atty. Coos County, Coquille, Oreg., 1972-75; assoc. Miller, Anderson, Nash, Yerke & Wiener, Portland, Oreg., 1975-78; ptnr. Spicer and Downer, Gold Beach, Oreg., 1978-81; dist. judge Curry County (Oreg.), Gold Beach, 1981-85; cir. judge State of Oreg., Gold Beach, 1985—. Mem. Oreg. Cir. Ct. Judges Assn., Oreg. Juvenile Ct. Judges Assn. (exec. com. 1986-88), Rotary. Office: Circuit Ct PO Box H Gold Beach OR 97491

DOWNES, DAVID ANTHONY, English educator; b. Victor, Colo., Aug. 17, 1927; s. David Michael and Julia (Zitnik) D.; m. Audrey Romaine Ernst, Sept. 7, 1949; children: Mary Kathryn, Jane Frances, Daniel Ross, Michelle Marie. BA cum laude, Regis Coll., 1949; MA, Marquette U., 1950; PhD, U. Wash., 1956. Instr. English Gonzaga U., Spokane, Wash., 1950-53; asst. prof., then prof., chmn. dept. Seattle U., 1953-68; prof. English, dean humanities and fine arts Calif. State U., Chico, 1968—, dir. ednl. devel. projects, 1972—, chmn. English dept., 1978—. Author: Gerard Manley Hopkins: A Study of His Ignatian Spirit, 1959, Victorian Portraits: Hopkins and Pater, 1965, Pater, Kingsley and Newman, 1972, Ruskin's Landscape of Beatitude, 2d edit. 1984, The Great Sacrifice: Studies in Hopkins, 1983, Hopkins: Sanctifying Imagination, 1985, other studies on Hopkins; editor Univ. Journal, 1974-78; contbr. articles to Thought, Victorian Poetry, other jours. Grantee Western Gear Found., 1960, Seattle U., 1961, 62, 67, Andrew Mellon Found., Stanford U., 1982; Pres. Merit award, 1984, 88, Profl. Achievement award, 1984. Office: Calif State U Dept English Chico CA 95926

DOWNEY, D'ANN BARBARA, science administrator; b. Medford, Oreg., Feb. 16, 1940; d. Myron Marcus and Marianna (Koepsell) D. BA in Econs., Calif. State U., Hayward, 1979; postgrad., UCLA, 1980-81, Golden Gate U., 1986—. Proposal analyst Stanford (Calif.) U., 1969-73, asst. research adminstr., 1973-75, contracts officer, 1975-80; sr. contracts adminstr. Jet Propulsion Lab., Pasadena, Calif., 1980-81; sr. subcontract buyer GTE-Govt. Systems Corp., Mountain View, Calif., 1981-85, procurement specialist, 1985—; cons. NCI, Bethesda, Md., 1973-79. Mem. Nat. Contract Mgmt. Assn., Soc. Research Adminstrs. Republican. Mormon.

DOWNING, CHRISTINE ROSENBLATT, theology educator; b. Leipzig, Germany, Mar. 21, 1931; came to U.S., 1935; d. Edgar Fritz and Herta (Fischer) Rosenblatt; m. George Downing, June 9, 1951, (div. Jan. 1978); children: Peter, Eric, Scott, Christopher, Sandra; m. River Malcolm, Sept. 2, 1984. BA, Swarthmore Coll., 1948; PhD, Drew U., 1966; MA, U.S. Internat. U., 1982. From instr. to assoc. prof. religion and psychology Rutgers U., New Brunswick, N.J., 1963-75; prof., chmn. dept. religious studies San Diego State U., 1974—; mem. core faculty Calif. Sch. Profl. Psychology, Pomona, 1974—. Author: The Goddess, 1981, Journey Through Menopause, 1987, Psyche's Sisters, 1988; co-author: Face to Face to Face, 1975; contbr. articles to profl. jours. Fellow NEH, 1982-83. Fellow Soc. Values in Higher Edn. (bd. dirs. 1966-81); mem. AAUP, Am. Acad. Religion (pres. 1973-74). Office: San Diego State U Dept Religious Studies San Diego CA 92182

DOWNING, DAVID JOHN, sales company executive, air filter consultant; b. Phoenix, Dec. 16, 1950; s. John Wesley and Isabelle Beatrice (Renkiewicz) D.; m. Linda Lee Bechtel, Jan. 5, 1973; children: Jason David, Kristi Nicole, Jeron Brett. Student, Ariz. State U., 1968-71. Account exec. Sta. KHEP-FM, Phoenix, 1972-73; sales engr. Chem-Serv, Inc., Phoenix, 1973-77; br. mgr. Farr Co., Phoenix, 1977-80; pres. D.L. Sales Corp., Phoenix, 1981—. Bd dirs. Calvary Temple, Phoenix, 1984-89. Mem. ASHRAE (assoc., past sec., treas., pres. Phoenix chpt., cert. of appreciation 1985), S.W. Maintenance Inst. (pres. 1976-77). Republican. Mem. Assembly of God Ch. Office: Dave Downing & Assocs 3615 N 34th Ave Phoenix AZ 85017

DOWNING, HAROLD SEARS, III, software engineering executive; b. Pitts., July 9, 1951; s. Harold Sears Jr. and Jane (McCall) D.; m. Barbara Ann Tallberg, May 2, 1981. BS in Math and Biology, U. Alaska, 1974; cert., Inst. Cert. of Computer Profls. Mgr. data processing Skyline Labs., Inc., Wheat Ridge, Colo., 1980-82; pres. Chiptech, Inc., Mpls., 1982-89, Half Moon Bay, Calif., 1989—; tech. mgr. Asia-Pacific sales Ready Systems Corp., Sunnyvale, Calif., 1989—.

DOWNS, WILLIAM FREDRICK, geochemist; b. Santa Maria, Calif., Aug. 4, 1942; s. William Nielson and Lotus (Mankins) D.; m. Karen Mona Farnsworth, July 15, 1967; 1 child, William Ross. BA, U. Colo., 1965, MS, 1974; PhD, Pa. State U., 1977. Registered geologist, Calif., Idaho. Reseach assoc. Pa. State U., University Park, Pa., 1974-77; scientist Idaho nat. Engring. Lab., Idaho Falls, Idaho, 1977-88; geochemist Jacobs Engring. Group, Albuquerque, 1988—; adj. prof. U. Idaho, Idaho Falls, 1979—, Idaho State U., Idaho Falls, 1984—. Governing body Albuquerque Waldorf Sch., 1988. Lt. USNR, 1966-69, Vietnam. Mem. Geochem. Soc., Geol. Soc. Am., Civitan (pres. Idaho Falls chpt. 1986-87), Am. Legion (commander Idaho Falls 1980-81). Home: 5309 Noreen Dr NE Albuquerque NM 87111

DOYLE, MARK RANDALL, manufacturing executive; b. Erie, Pa., Jan. 29, 1954; s. James Randall and Betty Eilleen (Litz) D.; m. Deborah Ann Avping, Nov. 29, 1974 (dikv. Oct. 1985); children: Stephanie Jane, Sean Randall; m. Carol Christine Longwell, Aug. 8, 1986; children: Jennifer Jacqueline, Benjamin Shaw (adopted). Restaurant mgr. Far West Svcs., Irvine, Calif., 1975-77; gen. mgr. BioAcoustical Engring. Corp., Santa Ana, Calif., 1976—. Republican. Office: BioAcoustical Engring Corp 1833 E 17th St Suite 103 Santa Ana CA 92701

DOYLE, MICHAEL JAMES, educational administrator, organist; b. Bell, Calif., Aug. 24, 1939; s. Joseph Edward and Irma Louise (Smith) D.; m. Mina Katherine Martensen, Feb. 8, 1964; children: Michael James II, Mary Katherine, Matthew John. BA, Whittier Coll., 196l, MEd, 197l. Tchr. El Rancho Unified Sch. Dist., Pico Rivera, Calif., 196l-79, dept. chmn., 1967-74, acting prin., 1979; tchr., asst. prin. Alta Loma (Calif.) Sch. Dist., 1979-86, summer sch. prin., 1985, prin., 1986—; organist, dir. various Luth. chs. in So. Calif., 1955-86; organist St. Paul's Luth. Ch., Pomona, Calif., 1986—; mem. Calif. State Program Rev., 1982-83; assoc. mem. Calif. Sch. Leadership Acad., Ontario, 1986—; v.p. So. Calif. Luth. Music Clinic, 1978-8l. Clk. Zion. Luth. Sch. Bd. Edn., Maywood, Calif., 1962-64, chmn., 1966-67; mem. Downey (Calif.) City Water Bd., 1977-78; mem. Luth. High Personnel Commn., La Verne, Calif., 1988—. Named Outstanding Tchr. of Yr., Burke Jr. High Sch. PTA, Pico Rivera, 1973; recipient hon. svc. award Jasper Sch. PTA, Alta Loma, 1983, continuing svc. award, 1988; employee recognition award Alta Loma Sch. Dist., 1985. Mem. Assn. Calif. Sch. Adminstrs., Assn. West End Sch. Adminstrs., Calif. Tchrs. Assn., Am. Guild Organists, Downey Hist. Soc., Cucamonga Hist. Soc., Casa de Rancho (Cucamonga, Calif.), Phi Delta Kappa. Democrat. Home: 2085 N Palm Ave Upland CA 91786 Office: Alta Loma Sch Dist 688l Jasper St Alta Loma CA 91701

DOYLE, MICHAEL SCOTT, Spanish literature and language educator, translator; b. Lynchburg, Va., Jan. 1, 1953; s. William Allen and Elizabeth (Nesbit) D.; m. Kenni Elaine Hilton, Aug. 9, 1980; 1 child, Sean Patrick. BA, U. VA., 1975, PHD, 1981; MA, U. Salamanca, Spain, 1976; certificat, Sorbonne, Paris, 1977. Asst. prof. U. Notre Dame, South Bend, Ind., 1981-84; asst. prof. U. New Orleans, 1984-87, assoc. prof., 1987-88; assoc. prof. San Diego State U., 1988—; mem. coun. for Devel. Spanish in La., New Orleans, 1987; proposal reviewer Nat. Endowment for Humanities Translations Category, 1987. Contbr. articles and interviews to Spanish publs.; translator of The Heliotrope Wall, 1989, and many stories. Bd. dirs. Coun. Internat. Visitors, New Orleans, 1985-88. Mem. MLA, Am. Translators Assn. (accerited), Am. Lit. Translators Assn., Am. Coun. on Teaching Fgn. Langs. (cert. oral proficiency tester), Sigma Delta Pi. Office: San Diego State U Dept Spanish and Portuguese San Diego CA 92182

DOYLE, PATRICIA KATHERINE, music therapist; b. South Bend, Indiana, Apr. 9, 1946; d. Bernard Louis and Katherine Susan (Lehner) D. MusB, St. Mary's Coll., Notre Dame, Ind., 1969; B in Music Therapy, U. Kans., 1973. Registered music therapist. Ednl. supr. No. Ind. Children's Hosp., So. Bend, 1968-71; teaching asst., coord. Music Therapy Clinic, U. Kans., Lawrence, 1973-75; clinic ptnr. Rehab. Activity Services, Inc., Lawrence, 1974-76; supr. music therapy Golden Valley Helath Ctr., Minn., 1976-81; exec. dir. Nat. Assn. Music therapy, Inc., Lawrence, 1981-82; clin. therapist No. Pines Mental Health Ctr., Brainerd, Minn., 1982-84; asst. dir., aftercare counselor Focus Unit, St. Joseph's Med. Ctr., Brainerd, 1984-86; sr. counselor The Cedu Sch., Running Springs, Calif., 1987—; mem. faculty The Cedu Sch., Running Springs, 1987-88; task force mem. Sexual Assault Program, Brainerd, 1984-86; mem. Minn. Women's Network, Mpls., 1984-86. Bd. dirs. Tri-County Sexual Assault, Bemidji, Minn., 1982-84. Mem. Nat. Assn. Music Therapy Inc. (exec. bd. 1981-85, pres. award 1982), Nat. Assn. Female Execs., Arrowhead Arts Assn. Democrat. Roman Catholic. Home: PO Box 1426 Lake Arrowhead CA 92352 Office: The Cedu Sch PO Box 1176 Running Springs CA 92382

DOYLE, RICHARD, building executive; b. Oneonta, N.Y., Apr. 10, 1947; s. Irving Doyle and Helen Barcus; m. Katherine Cole, May 11, 1984 (div.). Student, U.S. Naval Acad., 1965-66; BS, U. Miami, 1969; MBA, Harvard U., 1974. Pres., owner Doyle Constrn., Miami, Fla., 1968-73, RV Enterprises, Las Vegas, Nev., 1974—; bd. mem. Fla. St. Home Builders Assn., Miami, 1971-73, Assn. of Gen. Vice chmn. econ. adv. coun. City of Miami, 1968-69; pres. Young Reps. Mem. Nat. Assn. Gen. Contract AGC, Nat. Assn. Home Builders (Builder of Yr.). Office: RV Enterprises 21 N Arlington Las Vegas NV 89110

DOYLE, THOMAS PATRICK, mechanical engineer; b. Doylestown, Ohio, Jan. 6, 1962; s. Patrick Joseph and Ruth Eileen (Durbin) D.; m. Betsy Sue Vyskocil, Mar. 16, 1985; children: Taryn, Aubrey. BSME, U. Ariz., 1985; MAM, U. Phoenix, 1988. Registered profl. engr., Ariz. Results engr., constrn. mgr., mech. engr. Tucson Electric Power, 1985—. Precinct committeeman Pima County. Mem. ASME (membership chmn. 1985-86, vice chmn. Tucson chpt. 1986-87, systems and power generating facilities design com.). Republican. Episcopalian. Home: 5212 W Montuoso Tucson AZ 85745 Office: Tucson Electric Power 3950 E Irvington Tucson AZ 85702

DOYLE, WILFRED EMMETT, bishop; b. Calgary, Alta., Can., Feb. 18, 1913; s. John Joseph and Mary (O'Neill) D. B.A., U. Alta, 1935; D.C.L., U. Ottawa, Ont., Can., 1949. Ordained priest Roman Cath. Ch., 1938; chancellor Archdiocese Edmonton, Alta., Can., 1949-58; bishop Nelson, B.C., Can., 1958—; Chmn. bd. govs. Notre Dame U., Nelson, 1963-74. Address: 813 Ward St, Nelson, BC Canada V1L 1T4

DOYLE, WILLIAM BURROUGHS JR., investment banker; b. Peoria, Ill., May 11, 1959; s. William Burroughs and Nancy (Siegle) D. BSE magna cum laude, Princeton U., 1981; MBA, Stanford U., 1985. Analyst McKinsey & Co., Dallas, 1981-83; prodn. mgr. Rover S.A., Allied-Signal subs., Paris, 1985-87; assoc. Alex Brown & Sons, San Francisco, 1987—. Office: Alex Brown & Sons 345 California St 24th Fl San Francisco CA 94104

DOYON, ANDRE JEWELL, educator; b. Glendale, Calif., Mar. 25, 1943; s. Walter William and Kathryn Elizabeth (Brewer) D.; m. Karen Elaine Pike, Dec. 22, 1967; (div. Sept. 1980); m. Linda Lee Saferite, July 16, 1985. AA, Citrus Coll., 1963; BA, Ariz. State U., 1966, MA, 1974; Ariz. peace officer cert., Glendale Community Coll., 1979. Cert. secondary tchr., Ariz.; cert. peace officer, Ariz. Tchr., biology, photography Agua Fria Union High Sch., Avondale, Ariz., 1967-78; tchr., TV prodn., photography Agua Fria Union High Sch., Avondale, 1978-79, media dir., 1979—; officer (on call) City of Avondale, Avondale Police, 1973—; pres. SoftLynx, an Ariz. Corp., Scottsdale, Ariz., 1988—. Contbr. articles to profl. jours. Chmn. edn. com. Am. Cancer Soc., Western Gateway, Goodyear, Ariz., 1988, mem. exec. bd., 1987. Sgt. USAFR, 1966-72. Named Ariz. State Tchr. of Yr., Ariz. State Sch. Bd., 1978. Mem. Ariz. Ednl. Media Assn. (pres. 1986-87, Spl. Service award 1986), Nat. State Tchrs., Phi Delta Kappa (pres. Phoenix chpt. 1976-77). Republican. Episcopalian. Office: Aqua Fria Union High Sch 530 E Riley Dr Avondale AZ 85323

DOZIER, THOMAS JEFFERSON, mortgage company executive; b. Lynnwood, Calif., July 4, 1954; s. Tommie John and Marilyn Louise (Woods) D. Mgr. High Country Ranch Mgmt., Longmont, Colo., 1980-86; appraiser, cons., real estate specialist Woodinville, Wash., 1986-88; ind. real estate appraiser Phoenix, 1988—; loan officer Eagle Mortgage Co., Phoenix, 1988—; real estate appraiser Simms and Assocs., Phoenix, 1988—. Mem. Internat. Real Estate Inst. (sr. cert. valuer), Nat. Assn. Real Estate Appraisers (cert.), NRA. Republican. Roman Catholic. Office: Eagle Mortgage Co 1130 E Missouri St Ste 300 Phoenix AZ 85014

DOZORETZ, JERRY, communications professional; b. L.A., Jan. 11, 1947; s. Leo and Elaine (Bomicino)D.; m. Jacquelyn Sue Schneider, June 21, 1969 (div. 1981); children: Paul Gabriel, Amy Beth, Jessica Ann; m. Ann Marie Vestecka, Nov. 3, 1985; 1 child, Leah. BA, U. Calif., Santa Barbara, 1969, MA, 1975, CPhil, 1975, PhD, 1977. Lifetime cert. tchr., Calif. Instr. Moorpark (Calif.) Community Coll., 1972-73; lectr. Santa Maria (Calif.) Community Coll., 1973-75; assoc. prof. U. Calif., Santa Barbara, 1975-76; prof. philosophy U. Denver, 1976-83; mgr. competitive markets Mountain Bell Co., Denver, 1983-84, policy witness, lobbyist, 1984-86; spectrum mgmt. staff U.S. West Communications, Denver, 1986-87, spl. projects mgr., 1987—; cons. So. Bell Co., Tallahassee, Fla., 1985-86; regulatory advisor New Vector Group, Bellevue, Wash., 19867—; speaker Peirce on Wittgenstein, Regensburg, West Germany, 1979. Contbr. articles to profl. publs. Bd. dirs. Project PAVE, Denver, 1988. Mem. AAAS, Colo. Alliance for Sci., Info. Industry Assn., Charles S. Peirce Soc., Am. Mgmt. Assn., Am. Philos. Assn., Greenpeace, Scientists for Nuclear Disarmament. Democrat. Jewish. Office: US West Communications 1801 California St Ste 2230 Denver CO 80202

DRABEK, DANIEL JAMES, graphic designer; b. Chgo., May 30, 1948; s. Edward John and Marjory June (Tolan) D.; m. Nancy Barbara Nelson, Oct. 12, 1974. AA, Pasadena City Coll., 1968; postgrad., Long Beach State Coll., 1968-70. Graphic artist Acme Cello Converting Corp., Brooklyn Ctr., Calif., 1970, Zenith Engraving, Vancouver, B.C., 1971, United Way, St. Louis Pk., Minn., 1972-73; designer Kloster Advt., Mpls., 1974-75; pvt. practice graphic art 1975-76; art dir. G.S. Graphics, Mpls., 1976-84; graphic designer in pvt. practice Santa Cruz, Calif., 1984—. Home: 115 Avalon Ave Santa Cruz CA 95060

DRACH, GEORGE WISSE, urology educator; b. Trenton, N.J., Aug. 24, 1935; s. John D. and Johanna (Opthof) D.; m. Paula Thomas, June 15, 1957; children: Diane, David, Cora. BA, U. Ariz., 1957; MD, Case Western Res. U., 1961. Diplomate Am. Bd. Urology (trustee 1986—). Intern in surgery U. Hosps., Cleve., 1961-62, resident in surgery, 1962-63; research fellow in urology Bowman-Gray Sch. Medicine Wake Forest U. and N.C. Bapt. Hosp., Winston-Salem, 1965-66, asst. resident in urology, 1965-68, chief resident in urology, 1968-69; fellow in immunology U. N.Mex. Sch. Medicine, 1969-70; instr. surgery U. N.Mex., Albuquerque, 1969-70; asst. prof., chief urology U. Ariz., Tucson, 1970-74, assoc. prof., chief urology, 1974-77, acting assoc. dean acad. affairs, 1977-79, prof., chief urology, 1977—; cons. urology VA Hosp., Tucson, 1970—; mem. NIH site visit teams, 1979-82; trustee Am. Bd. Urology, 1985—; chmn. com. of 9 U. Ariz. Coll. Medicine, 1972-74, mem. curriculum com., 1974-80; sci. coordinator FDA Clin. Study Extracorporeal Shock Wave Lithotripsy, 1982—; v.p. Am. Bd. Urology, chmn. residency rev. com. Asst. editor Jour. Urology, 1972-78, ad hoc reviewer, 1972—; mem. editorial bd. Investigative Urology, 1972-78, ad hoc reviewer, 1972—; ad hoc reviewer Sci.; ad hoc reviewer Urol. Research; contbr. numerous articles to profl. jours.; numerous chpts. to books. Served to lt. comdr. USNR, 1963-65. Fogarty Sr. Internat. Research fellow Gen. Infirmary, Leeds, Eng., 1980; recipient Resident Essay award Cleve. Surgical Soc., 1963; Am. Geriatrics Soc. Resident Research fellow, 1966-68; Nat. Inst. Arthritis and Metabolic Disease spl. fellow, 1969-70. Fellow ACS (pres. Ariz. chpt. 1981); mem. AMA, Am. Urol. Assn. (research com. 1978-81, pubs. com. 1981—, chmn. pubs. com. 1985-86, pres. 1988-89, 1st award sci. exhibit S.E. sect. 1968, 2d award sci. exhibit Nat. Conv., 1975, Hugh Hampton Young award 1986), Clin. Soc. Genitourinary Surgeons (sec.-treas. 1988—), Am. Assn. Genitourinary Surgeons, Soc. Univ. Surgeons, Ariz. Med. Assn., Western Urol. Forum, So. Ariz. Urol. Soc. (pres. 1980-81), Tucson Urol. Soc. (pres. 1982-83), Am. Assn. Med. Colls., Soc. Univ. Urologists, Internat. Soc. Nephrology, Soc. Internat. de Urologie, Sigma Xi, Phi Beta Kappa, Phi Kappa Phi. Home: 2681 E Calle Los Altos Tucson AZ 85718-2060 Office: U Ariz Health Scis Ctr 1501 N Campbell Ave Tucson AZ 85724

DRACHNIK, CATHERINE MELDYN, art therapist; b. Kansas City, Mo., June 7, 1924; d. Gerald Willis and Edith (Gray) Weston; m. Joseph Brennan Drachnik, Oct. 6, 1946; children: Denise Elaine, Kenneth John. BS, U. Md., 1945; MA, Calif. State U., Sacramento, 1975. Lic. family and child counselor; registered art therapist. Art therapist Vincent Hall Retirement Home, McLean, Va., Fairfax Mental Health Day Treatment Ctr., McLean, Arlington (Va.) Mental Health Day Treatment Ctr., 1971-72, Hope for Retarded, San Jose, Calif., Sequoia Hosp., Redwood City, Calif., 1972-73; supervising tchr. adult edn. Sacramento Soc. Blind, 1975-77; ptnr. Sacramento Div. Mediation Svcs., 1981-82; instr. Calif. State U., Sacramento, 1975-82, Coll. Notre Dame, Belmont, Calif., 1975—; art therapist, mental health counselor Psych West Counseling Ctr. (formerly Eskaton Am. River Mental Health Clinic), Carmichael, Calif., 1975—; instr. U. Utah, Salt Lake City, 1988—; lectr. in field. One woman shows throughout Calif., East Coast and abroad; group juried shows in Calif. and Orient. Active various charitable orgns. Mem. Am. Art Therapy Assn. (pres. 1987-89), No. Calif. Art Therapy Assn., Calif. Coalition of Rehab. Therapists, Nat. Art Edn. Assn., Am. Assn. Marriage and Family Therapists, Alpha Psi Omega, Omicron Nu, Kappa Kappa Gamma. Republican. Home: 4124 American River Dr Sacramento CA 95864 Office: Psych West Counseling Ctr 6127 Fair Oaks Blvd Carmichael CA 95608

DRACK, PAUL E., aluminum company executive; b. Chgo., Nov. 18, 1928; s. Paul and Alice (Baumann) D.; m. Elaine Cheli, June 20, 1953; children: Kathleen, Lisa. BA, St. Mary's Coll., Winona, Minn., 1950. Purchasing agt. Kawneer Inc., Niles, Mich., 1955-63; plant mgr. Kawneer Inc., Norcross, Ga., 1965-67, gen. mgr., 1967-72, group v.p., 1973-78, exec. v.p., 1978-79, pres., 1979-86; asst. gen. mgr. South Bend (Ind.) Screw Products, 1963-65; pres., chief exec. officer Alumax Inc., San Mateo, Calif., 1986—. Served to lt. (j.g.) USNR, 1951-55, Korea. Republican. Roman Catholic. Office: Alumax Inc 400 S El Camino Real San Mateo CA 94402 *

DRAKE, BRIAN WILLIAM, photography company executive; b. Elkhart, Ind., Sept. 22, 1954; s. George M. and Virginia (Krukowski) D. BS in Broadcasting, Ariz. State U., 1978. Staff, photo editor Longview Daily News, Longview, Wash., 1978-84; pres. N.W. Imagination Photography, Vancouver, Wash., 1984—, Portland, Oreg., 1984—; chmn. region II Nat. Press Photography, Longview, 1980-83. Recipient Pulitzer prize news (team), 1981. Mem. N.P.P.A., Sigma Nu (pres., pledge chmn. Tempe chpt. 1977). Roman Catholic. Home: 1209 NE 126th St Vancouver WA 98685 Office: NW Imagination Photography 401 SW 11th Ave Portland OR 97205

DRAKE, DEBORAH ELLEN, patient accounts manager; b. Cooperstown, N.Y., Jan. 13, 1948; d. David C. Drake and Florence Estelle (Camp) Harais; m. Harry L. Empie, Oct. 22, 1966 (div. 1982). Student, Carnegie Tech. Inst., 1965, SUNY, Brockport, 1974-76, U. Phoenix, Colo., 1987-88. Patient fin. supr. Rochester (N.Y.) Gen. Hosp., 1974-76; various positions in claims and HMO mgmt. Rochester Blue Cross/Blue Shield, 1970-74, 76-82; patient accounts mgr. Phoenix Bapt. Hosp., 1984-88; dir. patient accounts Denver Health and Hosps., 1988—. Recipient Outstanding Achievement award Healthcare Fin. Mgmt. Assn., Phoenix, 1987; mem. of New Elite of Hosp. Receivable Mgrs. in U.S., Zimmerman & Assocs, 1988. Mem. Healthcare Fin. Mgmt. Assn. (publs. com., patient services com.), Am. Guild of Patient Account Mgrs. (bd. sec. 1982-84), Ariz. Hosp. Assn. (accounts receivable com.). Home: 1503 S Ivy St Denver CO 80224 Office: 777 Bannock St Denver CO 80204-4507

DRAKE, E. MAYLON, academic administrator; b. Nampa, Idaho, Feb. 8, 1920; s. Austin Henry and Daisy Naomi (Smith) D.; m. Lois Elloise Noble, Oct. 12, 1940; children: E. Christopher, Cameron Lee. BS, U. So. Calif., Los Angeles, 1951, MS, 1954, EdD, 1963. Mgr. Frederick Post Co., San Francisco, 1943-47; asst. supt. Baldwin Park (Calif.) Schs., 1947-51; supt. Duarte (Calif.) Schs., 1951-64, Alhambra (Calif.) City Schs., 1964-70; dep. supt. Los Angeles County Schs., 1970-78; prof. U. So. Calif., Los Angeles, 1978-80; dir. Acad. Ednl. Mgmt., Los Angeles, 1978-80; pres. Los Angeles Coll. Chiropractic, Whittier, 1980—. Author Attaining Accountability in Schools, 1972; contbr. articles to profl. jours. Pres. Industry-Ednl. Council So. Calif., 1978; dir. United Way 1970; dir. Greater Los Angeles Zoo Bd., 1970. Recipient Am. Educator's medal Freedom Found.; named Educator of Yr. Los Angeles Chiropratic Soc., 1981. Mem. Council on Chiropratic Edn. (pres. 1988—). Republican. Presbyterian. Club: Rotary (Duarte) (pres. 1954-56) (Alhambra) (dir. 1964-70). Office: Los Angeles Coll Chiropractic 16200 E Amber Valley Dr Whittier CA 90609

DRAKE, FRANK DONALD, astronomy educator; b. Chgo., May 28, 1930; s. Richard Carvel and Winifred (Thompson) D.; m. Elizabeth Bell, Mar. 7, 1953 (div. 1979); children: Stephen, Richard, Paul; m. Amahl Zekin Shakhashiri, Mar. 4, 1978; children: Nadia, Leila. B in Engring. Physics, Cornell U., 1952; MA in Astronomy, Harvard U., 1956, PhD in Astronomy, 1958. Astronomer Nat. Radio Astron. Obs., Green Bank, W.Va., 1958-63; sect. chief Jet Propulsion Lab., Pasadena, Calif., 1963-64; prof. Cornell U., Ithaca, N.Y., 1964-84; dir. Nat. Astron. and Ionospace Ctr., Ithaca, 1971-81; dean natural sci. dept. U. Calif., Santa Cruz, 1984-88, prof., 1984—. Author: Intelligent Life in Space, 1962, Murmurs of Earth, 1978. Lt. USN, 1947-55. Fellow AAAS, Am. Acad. Arts and Scis.; mem. Nat. Acad. Scis., Internat. Astron. Union (chair U.S. nat. com.), Astron. Soc. Pacific (pres. 1988—), Seti Inst. (pres. chpt. 1984—). Office: U Calif Santa Cruz CA 95064

DRAKE, LUCIUS C., JR., school administrator, university consultant; b. Tacloban, Philippines, June 29, 1946; s. Lucius Charles and Victoria (Badiles) D. BA, Fisk U., 1968; EdM, Temple U., 1970. Cert. sch. adminstr.; cert. guidance counselor. Math. tchr. Sch. Dist. of Phila., 1968-70, Gary (Ind.) City Schs., 1970-72, Dept. Defense Dependents Sch., Fed. Republic Germany and Okinawa, 1972-77; elemtary tchr. Dept. Defense Dependents Sch., Philippines, 1977-79; guidance counselor Dept. Defense Dependents Sch., Japan and Korea, 1979-83; asst. prin. Dept. Defense Dependents Sch., Seoul and Taegu, Korea, 1983—; chmn. math dept. Sayre Jr. High Sch., Phila., 1969-70; math. curriculum rev. com., Dept. Defense Dependents Schs., Karlsruhe, Fed. Republic Germany, 1972-73; dir. Far East Basketball Tourney, Taegu, Korea, 1984-86; mem. regional mgmt. council, Dept. Defense Dependents Schs., Okinawa, 1985-86. Mem. human rels. commn. Ft. Collins City Coun. Recipient Disting. Educator award IDEA Acad. Fellows, Denver, 1985. Fellow Am. Bd. Master Educators (disting.); mem. Nat. Assn. Secondary Sch. Prins., Nat. Assn. Elem. Sch. Prins., Internat. Educator's Inst., Phi Delta Kappa, Alpha Phi Alpha (edn. sec. Seoul chp. 1984-85). Democrat. Baptist. Home: 3318 Hickok Dr Unit B Fort Collins CO 80526 Office: U No Colo Tchr Edn Ctr Greeley CO 80639

DRAKE, RICHARD LEE, food service company executive; b. Ithaca, N.Y., Aug. 30, 1942; s. Marshall Landon and Elizabeth (Blauvelt) D.; m. Dianne Leslee McBride, Nov. 28, 1969; children: Adam C., Colleen E. BS, Cornell U., 1965. Dir. food services U. Chgo. Hosps. and Clinics, 1969-73; dir. regional ops. Service Direction Inc., Mpls., 1973-76; pres. Crothall Food Services Inc., Newark, Del., 1976-84, Drake Mgmt. Services, Inc., Scottsdale, Ariz., 1984—; lectr. in field. Author: (manual) The Determination and Allocation of Food Service Costs; contbr. articles to profl. jours. Served to 1st lt. U.S. Army, 1965-67. Mem. Am. Soc. for Food Service Adminstrs. (bd. dirs. 1974-75), Cornell Soc. Hotelmen. Office: Drake Mgmt Svcs Inc 7373 E Doubletree Ranch Rd Ste 170 Scottsdale AZ 85258

DRANGSTVEIT, MELODY CAROLYNN, health care administrator; b. Williston, N.D., Oct. 15, 1959; d. Orvin Arnold and Janet Carol (Solem) D.; 1 child, Tara Janelle. BS, Concordia Coll., Portland, Oreg., 1987. Receptionist Ontario (Oreg.) Optical, 1972-74, Precision Cosmet, Portland, 1977; receptionist Drangstveit Optical Co., Portland, 1974-81, office mgr., 1981-87; exec. dir. Silent Victims of Innocence, Portland, 1988; case mgr., program dir. Luke-Dorf, Tigard, Oreg., 1988—. Mem. choir St. Luke Luth. Ch., Portland, 1974—, Sunday sch. tchr., 1984—, chmn. parish edn., 1988—, mem. ch. coun., 1987—; tutor Maplewood Sch., Portland, 1986-87; v.p. Pilgrim Luth. Sch. PTA, 1988—. Mem. Sex Abuse Treatment Providers, Order Eastern Star. Democrat. Home: 4645 SW Flower Pl Portland OR 97221 Office: Luke-Dorf l03l3 SW 69th St Tigard OR 97223

DRAPER, GARY JAMES, contract negotiator, lawyer; b. Portsmouth, Va., Aug. 29, 1957; s. C. William and Jennie May (Lavender) D.; m. Doreen Kay Lange, June 1, 1979; l child. BS, USAF Acad., 1979; MBA, U. Fla., 1982; JD, U. Denver, 1986. Commd. 2d lt. USAF, 1979, advanced through grades to capt., 1983; personal fin. counselor USAF, Denver, 1985-86; resigned USAF, 1986; contract adminstr., negotiator Martin Marietta Corp., Denver, 1986—; pres. Draper Labels, Inc., Aurora, Colo., 1987—; real estate salesman ERA Questor, Aurora, 1985-87; owner Jake's Jigs, Aurora, 1986—; mem. credit com. Eglin Fed. Credit Union, Ft. Walton Beach, Fla., 1982. Mem. ABA, Colo. Bar Assn., Aurora Bar Assn., Arapahoe County Bar Assn., Nat. Contract Mgmt. Assn., Bass Anglers Sportsman Soc., U.S. Bass Club, U.S. Bass Fishing Assn. Home: 17938 E Amherst Ave Aurora CO 80013 Office: Martin Marietta Corp PO Box 179 Denver CO 80201

DRASEN, RICHARD FRANK, public relations executive; b. Chgo., Jan. 16, 1930; s. Frank Bernard and Margaret Louise (Lindsteadt) D.; student Mich. State U., 1948-49, Northwestern U., 1954-55, UCLA, 1956-58, 1960-61, Calif. State U., Northridge, 1961-63. Teacher, dir. The Acad., L.A., 1959-61; mgr. communications United Parcel Service, L.A.and N.Y.C., 1961-68; mgr. pub. rels. and communications Signal Oil & Gas Co., L.A. and Houston, 1968-74; mgr. pub. affairs Burmah Oil, Inc., N.Y., 1974-75, Burmah Oil & Gas Co., Houston, 1975-77; mgr. pub. rels.and energy R.J. Reynolds Industries, Inc., Winston-Salem, N.C., 1977-78; v.p. corp. affairs Howell Corp., Houston, 1978-80; mgr. pub. rels. MAPCO, Inc., Tulsa, 1980-81; v.p. corp. rels. Geosource Inc., Houston, 1981-84; corp. rels. cons., 1984-87; v.p. communication Amyotrophic Lateral Sclerosis Assn., L.A., 1987—. With AUS, 1951-53. Mem. Internat. Assn. Bus. Communicators, Pub. Rels. Soc. Am., Houston Club, Warwick Club. Home: 11908 Montana Ave #103 Los Angeles CA 90049

DRASNER, ROBERT JOSEPH, marketing executive; b. N.Y.C., Sept. 10, 1949; s. Jack and Renee (Dollar) D.; m. Donna Donan. Student, St. John's U., N.Y.C., 1974. Regional sales mgr. Snap on Tools, Jacksonville, Fla., 1974-78; dir. sales Esbenson Co., Denver, 1978-82; nat. svc. mgr. Packaging Systems Internat., Denver, 1982-85; v.p., dir. mktg. W. G. Durant Corp, Brea, Calif., 1985—. Mem. Packaging Inst. Internat., Soc. Mfg. Engrs. Home: 14121 Browning Ave Tustin CA 92680 Office: W G Durant Corp 2980A Enterprise Brea CA 92621

DRAZNIN, JULIUS NATHAN, arbitrator, mediator; b. Chgo., Sept. 14, 1920; s. Max and Ida (Kramen) D.; m. Yaffa Bernstein, Dec. 29, 1942; children: Anne Louise, Michael Ernest. Student, Wright Jr. Coll., 1938-39, U. Chgo., 1942-44. Field examiner Region 18, NLRB, Mpls., 1944-47, Region 19, NLRB, Seattle, 1947-54; Field examiner Region 13, NLRB, Chgo., 1954-60, supervisory examiner, 1980-85; asst. regional dir. Region 31, NLRB, L.A., 1965-75; pvt. practice L.A., 1975—. Contbg. editor Personnel Jour., 1978-88; contbr. articles to profl. jours., labor rels. and newspapers. Mem. Inst. Indsl. Rels. Assn. (pres. 1987--), Indsl. Rels. Rsch. Assn., Am. Arbitration Assn., Soc. Profls. in Dispute Resolution. Jewish. Office: 5410 Wilshire Blvd Ste 400 Los Angeles CA 90036

DRECHSLER, RANDALL RICHARD, real estate development company executive; b. Red Bank, N.J., Dec. 17, 1945; s. John Henry and Maura (Turner) D.; m. Joyce D. Hansen, Dec. 1976 (div. 1980); m. Roxanne Pinkerton, Dec. 22, 1984; children: Courtney Autumn, Whitney Anne. Student, UCLA, 1963-64, Calif. State U., Northridge, 1964-68, San Fernando Coll. Law, 1968-69. Asst. v.p. Gt. Western Cities, Inc., L.A., 1968-72; pres., owner Internat. Registration Svc., Denver, 1972-73, R.D. Whitcor, Inc., Reno, 1984—; exec. v.p. R.J.B. Devel. Co., Reno, 1973—; pres. Plaza Resort Club, Inc., Reno, 1980-83; chief exec. officer, owner Bosley/Turner/Finch Advt., Reno, 1984—; pres., bd. dirs. Plaza Resort Club Assocs., Reno, 1980—, Rye Patch Ranch Assocs., Reno, 1986—; expert witness various bankruptcy cases, Las Vegas, Nev., 1988—; cons. Vacation Resorts Internat., Laguna Hills, Calif., 1988—. Staff mem. Robert F. Kennedy Presdl. Campaign Com., Washington, 1968. Mem. Am. Resort and Residential Devel. Assn., Resort Condominiums Internat., Aircraft Owners and Pilots Assn., Greater Reno C. of C., Reno Flying Club. Democrat. Home: 2470 Sagittarius Dr Reno NV 89509 Office: RJB Devel Co l00 N Arlington Ave Reno NV 89501

DREES, ROBERT GAITHER, judge; b. L.A., Jan. 11, 1927; s. Herbert William and Gertrude (Reavis) D.; m. Gloria Jacqueline McCoy, Apr. 3, 1950; children: Debbie Lynn Drees Gordon, Barry McCoy. BA in Bus. Adminstrn., Woodbury Coll., L.A., 1949; JD, Southwestern U., 1969. Bar: Calif. 1969. Sgt. L.A. Police Dept., 1949-70; dep. dist. atty. County of Orange, Santa Ana, Calif., 1970-71; ptnr. Harriman, Nelson and Drees, Fullerton, Calif., 1971-74; pvt. practice Downey, Calif., 1974-85; judge mcpl. ct. County of Los Angeles, Downey, 1985—. With AUS, 1945-46. Mem. Calif. State Bar Assn., Southeast Dist. Bar Assn. (pres. 1985). Republican. Home: 9709 Pomering Rd Downey CA 90240 Office: Downey Mcpl Ct 8206 E Third St Downey CA 90241

DREIER, DAVID TIMOTHY, congressman; b. Kansas City, Mo., July 5, 1952; s. H. Edward and Joyce (Yeomans) D. BA cum laude, Claremont McKenna Coll., 1975; MA in Am. Govt., Claremont Grad. Sch., 1976. Dir. corp. relations Claremont McKenna Coll., 1975-78; dir. mktg. and govt. relations Indsl. Hydrocarbons, San Dimas, Calif., 1978-80; mem. 97th Congress from 35th Calif. Dist., 98th-101st Congresses from 33d Calif. Dist.; v.p. Dreier Devel. Co. 1986—; mem. banking com., small bus. com.; vice-chmn. Anti-trust, Impact of Deregulation and Privatization subcom.; POW/MIA Task Force, Afghanistan Task Force; mem. Calif. Rep. Party; chmn. Task Force on Hunger and the Homeless, Rep. Task Force on Fgn. Policy; co-chmn. Task Force on Housing. Office: 411 Cannon House Office Bldg Washington DC 20515

DREISBACH, JOHN GUSTAVE, investment banker; b. Paterson, N.J., Apr. 24, 1939; s. Gustave John and Rose Catherine (Koehler) D.; BA, NYU, 1963; m. Janice Lynn Petitjean; 1 child, John Gustave Jr. With Shields & Co., Inc., 1965-68, Model, Roland & Co., Inc., N.Y.C., 1968-72, F. Eberstadt & Co., Inc., N.Y.C., 1972-74; v.p. Bessemer Trust Co., 1974-78; pres. Community Housing Capital, Inc., 1978-80; chmn., pres. John G. Dreisbach, Inc., Santa Fe, N.Mex., 1980—; JGD Housing Corp., 1982—; bd. dirs., pres. The Santa Fe Investment Conf., 1986—; assoc. KNME-TV; active U. N.Mex. Anderson Schs. Mgmt. Affiliate Program. Mem. Santa Fe Community Devel. Commn. Served with USAFR, 1964. Mem. Internat. Assn. for Fin. Planning, NYU Alumni Assn., Venture Capital Club N.Mex., N.Mex. First, NYU Alumni Assn., Mensa, Santa Fe C. of C. Republican. Episcopalian. Clubs: St. Bartholomew's Community, Essex, Hartford, Amigos del Alcalde. Office: 730 Camino Cabra Santa Fe NM 87501-1596

DREMIN, LEONARD LONNIE ALEXANDER, risk analyst, insurance agency executive; b. Winnipeg, Manitoba, Can., June 3, 1953; s. Leonard Authur D. and Rose Evelyn (Chorlton) Stuart; m. Virginia Dell Brown Dremin, June 16, 1973 (div. Feb. 1978); m. Charlene Alexandra Smith Dremin, March 20, 1981. Cert., U.S. Army Mil. Police Sch., Fort Gordon, Ga., 1972; AA, Mt. San Antonio Coll., Walnut, Calif., 1978. Auditor ins. Century Nat. Ins. Co., N. Hollywood, Calif., 1976-78; v.p. and bd. dir. Pennant Fin. Ins. Services, Glendora, Calif., 1978-79; Mgr. corp. brokerage CMCI-Cuna Mutual Ins. Group, Pomona, Calif., 1980-81; v.p. mktg. Insureco Ins. Agy., Inc., S. Pasadena, Calif., 1981-83, Crown Valley-A Transam. Co., Orange, Calif., 1983-84; pres., chief exec. officer, founder, and owner Borrowers and Creditors Ins. Services, Inc., Loma Linda, Calif., 1984-88. Author: (book) Risk Aware, On-Premise System Manual; inventor on-premise computer tracking system. Sr. plans non-commd. officer Calif. State Mil. Reserve, Norco, 1988; sponsoring mem. 720th Mil. Police Bn. Reunion Assn., Kenosha, Wis., 1988. Served with U.S. Army, 1972-74. Recipient Merit award Boys Scouts Am., Claremont, Calif., 1978, Achievement Ribbon award Calif. State Mil. Reserve, Sacramento, 1986. Mem. Profl. Ins. Agts of Calif. and Nev., Am. Legion, Sierra Club (Chmn. and vice-chmn., 1978-82). Republican. Methodist. Office: Borrowers and Creditors Ins Svcs Inc 11165 Mt View Ave Ste 143 Loma Linda CA 92354

DRENNAN, MICHAEL ELDON, bank executive; b. Yakima, Wash., June 24, 1946; s. George Eldon and Jane (Nilsson) D.; m. Alice Marie Seabolt, May 13, 1972; children: Brian, David. BS in Fin., U. Oreg., 1968; grad., Pacific Coast Banking Sch. U. Wash., 1981. Ops. officer First State Bank, Aloha, Oreg., 1972-73; ops., loan officer First State Bank, Portland, Oreg., 1973-74; asst. mgr. First State Bank, Milwaukie, Oreg., 1974-76; asst. v.p. Citizens Bank, Corvallis, Oreg., 1976-80, v.p., 1980-81; pres., chief exec. officer Bank of Corvallis, 1981-87; v.p. dist. mgr. U.S. Bank, Corvallis, Oreg., 1987; sr. v.p. market area mgr. U.S. Bank, Bend, Oreg., 1988—; bd. dirs. Cascades W. Fin. Svcs. Bd. dirs. United Way Benton County, 1984-88; trustee Good Samaritan Hosp. Found., 1984-88; bd. dirs. Jr. Achievement of Benton County, 1983-85, treas. 1984-85, mem. exec. bd., 1984-85; mem. budget comm. Corvallis Sch. Dist., 1987; bd. dirs. Benton County Family YMCA, 1978-80, sec. 1979, mem. fin. com., 1978-80, mem. personnel com. 1979, active sustaining membership dr.; bd. dirs. Community Club, 1978-83, pres., 1978, treas. 1979-80; active Corvallis Ambassadors, 1976-88; mem. mgmt. com. Corvallis Conv. and Vis. Bur., 1982-85; fund. raising chmn. Com. City Improvemnt Levy, 1980; mem. exec. com. Pack 17 Boy Scouts Am., 1984-87, treas. 1984-87; mem. adv. bd. Cen. Oreg. Econ. Devel. Corp., 1988—; bd. dirs. Regional Arts Coun. of Cen. Oreg., treas. 1989—; mem. Bend Bus. Assistance Team, 1989—. Lt. USN, 1968-71. Named Jr. First Citizen, Corvallis, Oreg., 1980, one of Outstanding Young Men of Am., 1979. Mem. Bend C. of C. (chmn. mem. dir. task force 1988, chmn. mem. svcs. council 1989), Corvallis C. of C. (v.p. fin. 1980-83, pres. 1985-86, chmn. bd. dirs. 1986-87, Econ. Devel. award 1978, Chmn. of Bd. award, 1979, George award 1980-81, Devel. award 1983), Am. Inst. Banking (cert.), Rotary (bd. dirs. Corvallis club 1981-87, Bend 1988—), Chi Phi, Alpha Kappa Psi, Beta Gamma Sigma. Home: 21725 Eastmont Dr Bend OR 97701 Office: US Bank PO Box 911 Bend OR 97709

DRESANG, RICHARD WAYNE, social services administrator; b. Kimberly, Wis., May 11, 1947; s. Norbert E. and Margie (Tracy) D.; m. Barbara Ann Rooyakkers, Sept. 7, 1967 (div. Feb. 1979); children: Jill Renee, Vicki Ann; m. JoEllen Jorgensen, Mar. 7, 1980; children: Christopher Richard, Nicklaus Norbert. BSSW, U. Wis., Oshkosh, 1971; student, U. Wis., Madison, 1971-73, U. Wyo., 1981—. Co-dir. La Rasa, Fond du Lac, Wis., 1970-71; social worker Brown County Dept. Social Services, Green Bay, Wis., 1971-74; adminstr. Green Bay Free Clinic, 1974-80; asst. mgr. Homax Oil Co., Glenrock, Wyo., 1980-82; dir. Youth Crisis Ctr., Casper, Wyo., 1982—; cons. Wyo. Dept. Health and Social Services, Cheyenne, 1984—, Converse County Group Home, Douglas, Wyo., 1985—; pres. Wyo. Youth Services Assn., 1985—; pres. elect. Wyo. Human Resource Conf., 1986—. Community organizer Brown County Youth Resource Council, Green Bay, 1972, Oneida Tribe Youth Resource Council, Green Bay, 1972, Green Bay Street Worker Program, 1972, Women, Infants, and Children's Program, Casper, Wyo., 1981. Recipient President's award Wis. Med. Assn., 1979. Mem. Nat. Assn. Social Workers, Am. Pub. Welfare Assn., Natrona County Child Protection Team. Democrat. Roman Catholic. Home: 6658 Sharrock Rd NBU 9 Casper WY 82604 Office: Youth Crisis Ctr Inc 242 S Jefferson Casper WY 82601

DRESNER, THOMAS LELAND, engineer; b. Washington, Aug. 29, 1948; s. Allan Rosedale and Barbara Ann (Harrison) D. BE, Stevens Inst. Tech., 1970; MSME, U. Pa., 1973; PhD ME, Stanford U., 1988. Engr. Westinghouse Electric Corp., Lester, Pa., 1970-79, Ford Aerospace & Communications Corp., Palo Alto, Calif., 1980; sr. engr. Communications Satellite Corp., Palo Alto, 1981; staff engr. Hughes Aircraft Co., El Segundo, Calif., 1985; prin. engr. Westinghouse Electric Corp., Sunnyvale, Calif., 1988—. Patentee, throttle valve pilot operator; contbr. papers to profl. publs. Vol. cons., Stanford U., 1984-88. Mem. ASME, Soc. Automotive Engrs. Home: 1285 Montecito Ave Mountain View CA 94043 Office: Westinghouse Electric Corp PO Box 3499 Sunnyvale CA 94088-3499

DRESSER, JESSE DALE, real estate investor; b. San Diego, May 5, 1906; s. Charlwood Fessenden and Ora (Evans) D.; m. Mary A. Goldsworthy, June 9, 1934; children—Dennis T., Brian D., Linda A. Ed. pub. schs. Trainee Union Title Ins. Co., San Diego, 1926; sr. title examiner, chief title officer, v.p. So. Title & Trust Co., San Diego, 1927-51; v.p., chief title officer Security Title Ins. Co., San Diego, 1951-54; asst. to pres. San Diego Fed. Savs. & Loan Assn., 1954-55, v.p., sec., 1955-56, exec. v.p., dir., 1956-70; v.p., dir. Calif. Gen. Mortgage Service, Inc., 1967-70, San Diego Federated Ins. Agy., Inc., 1967-70; real estate investments La Mesa, Calif., 1970—. Home: 3833 Acacia St Bonita CA 92002

DRESSER, ROBLYN LAFFERTY, accountant, tax practitioner; b. Grants Pass, Oreg., Mar. 6, 1957; d. Ray Nicholas Wiebe and Roberta Carol Lafferty; m. Michael R. Dresser, Aug. 25, 1985. Owner, mgr. Alaskan Coop. Tax Svc., Fairbanks, 1976—. Mem. Nat. Soc. Pub. Accts., Alaska Soc. Ind. Accts., Nat. Assn. Tax Practitioners, Nat. Notary Assn., Tanana Valley Sportsmen's Assn., Interior Horseman's Assn. Democrat. Office: Alaskan Coop Tax Svc PO Box 83809 Fairbanks AK 99708

DRESSER, TAMRA ADAMS, personnel analyst; b. Indpls., Sept. 25, 1962; d. Robert Henry and Carmona (McClanahan) Adams; m. Daniel Godard Dresser, Mar. 26, 1988. BS, Brigham Young U., 1984; MPA, Ariz. State U., 1987. Cert. spl., elem. edn. tchr., Utah, Ariz. Teaching intern Alpine (Utah) Sch. Dist., 1984, Provo (Utah) City Sch. Dist., 1984; intern performance audit Ariz. Auditor Gen., Phoenix, 1986; rsch. asst. Ariz. State U., Tempe, 1986-87; adminstrv. intern Police Dept. City of Tempe, 1987; personnel analyst City of Phoenix, 1988—. Mem. adv. bd. Maricopa County Skills Ctr., Phoenix, 1988—. Regents Academic scholar, Ariz. State U. Bd. Regents, Tempe, 1986-87; recipient Humanitarian award City of Phoenix, 1989. Mem. Am. Soc. Pub. Adminstrs. (sect. on personnel mgmt and labor relations), Internat. Personnel Mgmt. Assn., Personnel Testing Council Ariz. Republican. Mormon. Office: City of Phoenix Pers Dept 135 N 2nd Ave Phoenix AZ 85003

DRESSLER, ALAN MICHAEL, astronomer; b. Cin., Mar. 23, 1948; s. Charles and Gay (Stein) Dressler. BA in Physics, U. Calif., Berkeley, 1970; PhD in Astronomy, U. Calif., Santa Cruz, 1976. Carnegie Instn. of Washington fellow Hale Obs., Pasadena, Calif., 1976-78, Las Campanas fellow, 1978-81; mem. sci. staff Mt. Wilson and Las Campanas Obs. (formerly Hale Obs.), Pasadena, 1981—; acting assoc. dir. The Obs. of Carnegie Instn. of Washington (formerly Mt. Wilson and Las Campanas Obs.), Pasadena, 1988—. Contbr. to sci. jours. Mem. Am. Astron. Soc. (councilor 1989—; Pierce prize 1983), Internat. Astron. Union. Office: The Obs of Carnegie Instn of Washington 813 Santa Barbara St Pasadena CA 91101

DREW, CHARLES MILTON, chemist; b. McKinney, Tex., Feb. 13, 1921; s. Andrew Everett and Lutie Lella (Weger) D.; divorced; children: Darrell Everett, Donna Lee, Carl Allen. BS, U. N. Tex., 1943. Supr. chemist Columbia Southern, Corpus Christi, Tex., 1943-47; research scientist Naval Weapons Ctr., China Lake, Calif., 1947-70; cons. U. Ariz., Tucson, 1980—. Author: Principles of Gas Chromatography, 1959; contbr. articles to profl. jours.; patentee in field. Mem. Rsch. Soc. Am., Soaring Soc. Am., Colo. West Soaring Club, Glider Club (pres. China Lake, Calif. chpt. 1967-70), Rockhounds Club (pres. local chpt. 1949-50), Sigma Xi. Home: 0187 Sagemont Circle Parachute CO 81635 Office: Glass By Charles Parachute CO 81635

DREW, GENE RICHARD, aerospace engineer, consultant, artist; b. Eudora, Mo., Aug. 3, 1928; s. Charles Watson and Esther Rebecca (Barclay) D.; m. Helen Rae Carlson, Oct. 22, 1955; children: Nancy, Catherine, Laura. BS in Aero. Engring., Northrop U., 1962. Engr. Coleman Engring. Corp., L.A., 1957-58, Lockheed Propulsion Corp., Redlands, Calif., 1958-60, Wyle Labs., El Segundo, Calif., 1960-62, Naval Weapons Ctr., China Lake, Calif., 1962—; sec.-treas. Imperial Mining Corp., Reno, 1975-80. Contbr. numerous articles to profl. jours.; patentee in field; represented in numerous pvt. collections. With USMC, 1946-47. Recipient internat. award Safety and Flight Equipment Assn., 1979. Republican. Baptist. Home: 725 Mamie St Ridgecrest CA 93555 Office: Naval Weapons Ctr Code 62C2 SNORT China Lake CA 93555

DREWEL, ROBERT JOSEPH, college president; b. Seattle, June 21, 1946; s. Kenneth Lee and Charlotte Elizabeth Drewel; m. Cheryl Rae Olson, June. Student, U. Wash., 1970. Dir. pers. Wash. Community Coll. Dist. V, Everett, 1964-81; interim, pres. Everett Community Coll., 1981; labor and pers. rels. cons. Conner, Gravrock & Treverton, Bellevue, Wash., 1981-84; interim pres. Everett Community Coll., 1984, pres., 1984—. Bd. dirs. Boy Scouts Am., Everett, Japan-Am. Soc., Big Bros./Big Sisters. Mem. Rotary. Office: Everett Community Coll 801 Wetmore Ave Everett WA 98201

DREXLER, CLYDE, professional basketball player; b. New Orleans, June 22, 1962. Student, U. Houston, 1980-83. Basketball player Portland (Oreg.) Trailblazers, 1983—. Named to NBA All-Star Team, 1986, 88. Office: Portland Trailblazers Lloyd Bldg 700 NE Multnomah St Ste 950 Portland OR 97232 *

DREXLER, KENNETH, lawyer; b. San Francisco, Aug. 2, 1941; s. Fred and Martha Jane (Cunningham) D.; BA, Stanford U., 1963; JD, UCLA, 1969. Bar: Calif. 1970. Assoc., David S. Smith, Beverly Hills, Calif., 1970, McCutchen, Doyle, Brown and Enersen, San Francisco, 1970-77; assoc. Chickering & Gregory, San Francisco, 1977-80, ptnr., 1980-82; ptnr. Drexler & Leach, San Rafael, Calif., 1982—. Served with AUS, 1964-66. Mem. ABA, Calif. State Bar (resolutions com. conf. of dels. 1979-83, chmn. 1982-83, adminstrn. justice com. 1983—, chmn. 1987-88), Marin County Bar Assn. (bd. dirs. 1985-87), Bar Assn. San Francisco (dir. 1980-81), San Francisco Barristers Club (pres. 1976, dir. 1975-76), Marin Conservation League (bd. dirs. 1985—). Office: 1330 Lincoln Ave Ste 300 San Rafael CA 94901

DREYER, KENNETH ALLEN, air force officer; b. Cape Girardeau, Mo., Apr. 17, 1946; s. Alfred Henry and Myrl Louise (Barber) D.; m. Joyce Cecilia Moore (div. 1987); children: Rebecca Lynn, Brian Matthew, Michael Paul; m. Edna Mary Didwall, Jan. 22, 1988. BSc in Physics, Southeast Mo. State U., 1968; MSc in Nuclear Engring., Air Force Inst. Tech., 1974, PhD in Nuclear Engring., 1979. Commd. 2d lt. USAF, 1969, advanced through grades to maj., 1982; duty weather forecaster, Forbes AFB USAF, Topeka, 1969-72; chief weather forecaster USAF, Osan Air Base, Republic Korea, 1972-73; officer, Endo-Atmospheric Group Air Force Weapons Lab. USAF, Kirtland AFB, N.Mex., 1976-79; tech. area mgr. Tech. Applications Ctr. USAF, Patrick AFB, Fla., 1979-84; spl. asst. to dir. advanced weapons concepts USAF, Livermore, Calif., 1984-89; staff physicist Lawrence Livermore (Calif.) Nat. Lab, 1989—. Contbr. physics rsch. papers to various publs. Mem. Tau Beta Pi. Home: 937 Hazel St Livermore CA 94550 Office: Lawrence Livermore Nat Lab PO Box 808 Livermore CA 94550

DRIEBERG, KEITH LAMBERT, educational psychologist; b. Bombay, Oct. 19, 1952; came to U.S., 1970; s. Justin and Ivy (Nicholas) D. MA in Instrnl. Media, Calif. State U., Long Beach, 1977; MA in Counseling, Loma Linda U., 1979; MLS, Calif. State U., San Jose, 1981; MA in Sch. Psychology, U.S. Internat. U., 1985, postgrad. Freelance audiovisual producer 1973-80; tchr. Mesa Grande Sch., Calimesa, Calif., 1978-80; guidance dir., media specialist Auburn (Wash.) Acad., 1980-84; sch. psychologist San Bernardino (Calif.) City Schs., 1985—; rehabilitation psychologist, psychologist asst. San Bernardino Community Hosp., 1988—; psychol. asst. Counseling Ctr., Loma Linda (Calif.) U., 1985-88; cons., workshop leader in computer edn.; seminar leader, trainer audiovisual prodn.; owner, ptnr. ins. agy., computer software co., sporting goods mfg. co. Mem. Am. Psychol. Assn., Calif. Assn. Marriage and Family Therapists, Assn. Seventh-day Adventist Librarians (pres. 1984-85). Office: San Bernardino City Schs 777 North F St San Bernardino CA 92407

DRIESEL, TIMOTHY MICHAELS See OBERHEIM, THE BARON

DRIESSEN, STEVE EDWARD, aerospace engineer; b. Appleton, Wis., Dec. 12, 1951; s. Norbert Edward and Anna Marie (Van Wymerren) D. BSEE, U. Wis., 1974; cert. in mgmt., U. Denver, 1984. Design engr. IBM, Rochester, Minn., 1975-76; test engr. IBM, Boulder, Colo., 1976-79; programmer, owner, mgr. Creative Program Design, Boulder, 1979-80; programmer Creative Aplications, Denver, 1980-81; programmer Martin Marietta Co., Denver, 1981-84, mgr., 1984-86; cons. Martin Marietta Co., Colorado Springs, Colo., 1987—. Home: 6547 N Academy Colorado Springs CO 80918 Office: Martin Marietta Co Falcon AFB Colorado Springs CO 80921

DRIGGS, GARY HARMON, financial executive; b. Phoenix, July 13, 1934; s. Douglas H. and Effie (Killian) D.; m. Kay Taylor, June 9, 1959; children: Rebecca Driggs-Campbell, Kimberly, Taylor, Benjamin. Student, Stanford U., 1952-54; BA, Brigham Young U., 1959; MBA, Ind. U., 1960, DBA, 1962. Economist Western Savs. and Loan Assn., Phoenix, 1962—, v.p., 1969-73, pres., chief exec. officer, 1973-88, vice chmn., 1988-89, cons., 1989—; faculty lectr. real estate dept. Ind. U. Grad. Sch. Bus., 1960-62, vis. lectr. urban econs., 1962-76; lectr. econs. Ariz. State U., 1963-67; pres. Ariz. Tomorrow, Inc., chmn. Visions of Future; div. dir. Nat. Council Savs. Instns.; mem. dean's adv. council Ind. U. Sch. Bus.; bd. dirs. Newell Cos., Weidner Communications Inc.; v.p. Valley Leadership; mem. corp. adv. bd. Karl Eller Ctr.; chmn. nat. task force Gov.'s Com. Nat. and Internat. Commerce; fin. chmn. Gov.'s Transportation Task Force; mem. Maricopa Ctrs. Commn. Author: How to Reduce Risk in Apartment Lending, 1966. Mem. exec. bd. Phoenix Community Alliance; bd. dirs. Phoenix Together; adv. bd. Morrison Inst. Pub. Policy, Ariz. Rep. Caucus; mem. Ariz. State U. Centennial Bus. Support Com., dean's council of 100 Ariz. State U. Coll. Bus.; bd. advisors, exec. com. U. Ariz.; chmn. Phoenix Streets Adv. Com., Gov.'s State Urban Lands Task Force; bd. dirs. Silent Witness Program; served ch. mission Mormon Ch., Finland. Named Outstanding Young Man of Yr., Ariz. Jr. C. of C., 1968, named Outstanding Young Man of Yr., Phoenix Jr. C. of C., 1968-69; recipient Disting. Citizen award U. Ariz. Alumni Assn., 1982, Disting. Citizen award Ind. U. Sch. Bus. Acad. Alumni Fellows, 1983. Mem. Nat. Assn. State Savs. and Loan Suprs. (future planning com.), Internat. Union Bldg. Socs. and Savs. Assns., U.S. League (legis. policy com., spl. task force on deficit reduction, com. econ. affairs, com. capital stock and holding cos., mem. home ownership task force), Savs. and Loan League Ariz. (past pres.), Phoenix 40, Assn. for Corp. Growth, Chief Execs. Orgn., World Bus. Council, Inc. (chief exec. officer), U.S. C. of C. (banking, monetary and fiscal affairs com.). Republican. Lodge: Rotary. Office: Western Savs & Loan Assn 6001 N 24th St Phoenix AZ 85016 *

DRIGGS, JOHN D., bank executive; b. 1927. AB, Stanford U., 1952, MBA, 1954. Former chmn. Western Savs. and Loan Assn., Phoenix. Office: Western Savs & Loan Assn 6001 N 24th St Phoenix AZ 85016 *

DRISCOLL, JOSEPH EDWARD, lawyer, retired air force officer; b. Bklyn., June 18, 1941; s. John Edward and Mary Rose (Laurer) D.; m. Patricia Ann Tezuka, July 31, 1982 (div. 1984); 1 child, Crystal. BS in Mil. Sci., USAF Acad., 1964; MS in Engring. Adminstrn., So. Methodist U., 1973; JD, McGeorge Sch. Law, 1982. Bar: Calif. 1986, U.S. Dist. Ct. (cen. and so. dist.) Calif. 1986, U.S. Ct. Appeals (9th cir.) 1986. Commd. 2d lt. USAF, 1964, advanced through grades to lt. col., 1980; dir. tech. planning Hdqrs. Space Div. USAF, L.A. AFB, 1964—; with systems acquisition hdqrs., electronic systems div. USAF, Hanscom AFB, Mass., 1973-77; with long range planning Hdqrs. Aero. Systems Div. USAF, Wright-Patterson AFB, Ohio, 1982-85; dir. Strategic Def. Initiative Planning, Hqdrs. Space Div. USAF, L.A. AFB, 1985-88; ret. USAF, 1988; pvt. practice lawyer San Diego. Mem. USN League, Air Force Assn., Am. Def. Preparedness Assn., ABA, Calif. Bar Assn., L.A. County Bar Assn., San Diego County Bar Assn., Lawyer-Pilots Bar Assn., Order of Daedalians. Office: PO Box 210406 San Diego CA 92121-0406

DROSDICK, JOHN GIRARD, oil company executive; b. Hazelton, Pa., Aug. 9, 1943; m. Gloria J. Shenosky, May 10, 1944; children: Scott E., Candice M., Courtney J., Brooke K. BSChemE, Villanova U., 1965; MSChemE, U. Mass., 1968. Crude oil coordinator Exxon USA, Houston, 1973-74, marine planning mgr., 1974-76, corp. analysis mgr., 1978-81; facilities devel. dept. head Exxon USA, Baton Rouge, 1976-78, refinery ops mgr., 1981-83; v.p. refining Tosco Corp., Santa Monica, Calif., 1983-85, sr. v.p. refining, 1985-86, exec. v.p., 1986-87, pres., chief ops. officer, 1987—, also bd. dirs. Mem. Nat. Petroleum Refiners Assn. (bd. dirs. 1985—), Am. Petroleum Refiners Assn. (bd. dirs. 1985-87). Roman Catholic. Club: Jonathan. Office: Tosco Corp 2401 Colorado Ave Box 2401 Santa Monica CA 90406

DROSOS, ARGYRIS (ART DROSOS), small business owner; b. Angona, Kefallinia, Greece, Dec. 18, 1936; came to U.S., 1951; s. Demosthenes N. and Angelica (Kalaviti) D.; m. Lynn S. Dente, Aug. 7, 1963; children: Alexander, Kristina, Dean. BS, Ariz. State U., 1965. Owner, mgr. Motel & Rentals, Chandler, Ariz., 1962—; gen. contractor Bravo Constrn. co., Chandler, 1972—. Mem. St. Katherine Greek Orthodox Ch., Chandler, pres., 1985-86. Served with U.S. Army, 1956-58. Mem. Am. Hellenic Edn. Program Orgn., Am. Hellenic Ednl. Progressive Assn. (pres. local chpt. 1976-77, treas. 1980—), Chandler C. of C. Republican. Office: Bravo Constrn Co 401 N Alma Sch Rd #6 Chandler AZ 85224

DROST, KATHLEEN ANDERSON, speech pathologist, small business owner; b. Jamestown, N.Y., Apr. 8, 1957; d. Robert James and Joyce Mary (Palm) Anderson; m. Russell Charles Drost, June 29, 1985; 1 child, Russell Charles Jr. AA, Orange Coast Community Coll., 1978; BA, Calif. State U., Long Beach, 1980; MA, Calif. State U., Fullerton, 1983. Lic. speech pathologist, Calif.; cert. clin. rehab. services and competency, Calif., nursery sch. edn., Calif. Speech, lang. pathologist La Habra (Calif.) City Schs., 1983, Jurupa Unified Sch. Dist., Riverside, Calif., 1983—. Mem. Am. Speech Lang. Hearing Assn., Calif. Speech Lang. Hearing Assn., Nat. Tchrs. Assn., Calif. Tchrs. Assn., Yorba Linda C. of C., Phi Kappa Phi. Democrat. Roman Catholic. Home: 21850 Feather Ave Yorba Linda CA 92686 Office: Jurupa Unified Sch Dist 3924 Riverview Dr Riverside CA 92509

DROWN, EUGENE ARDENT, national park service official; b. Ellenburg, N.Y., Apr. 25, 1915; s. Frank Arthur and Jessie Kate D.; BS, Utah State U., 1938; postgrad. Mont. State U., 1939-40; PhD in Pub. Adminstrn., U. Beverly Hills, 1979; m. Florence Marian Munroe, Mar. 5, 1938; children: Linda Harriett Oneto, Margaret Ruth Lunn. Park ranger Nat. Park Svc., Yosemite Nat. Park, 1940-47; forest ranger U.S. Forest Svc., Calif. Region, 1948-56; forest mgr. and devel. specialist U.S. Bur. Land Mgmt., Calif., 1956—; forest engring. cons., 1970—; R&D coord. U.S. Army at U. Calif., Davis., 1961-65. Mem. adv. bd. Sierra Coll., Rocklin, Calif., 1962—; active Boy Scouts Am.; instr. ARC, 1954—. With AUS, 1941-45. Decorated Bronze Star, Silver Star; registered profl. engr., profl. land surveyor, profl. forester, Calif. Recipient Nat. Svc. medal ARC, 1964. Mem. Nat. Soc. Profl. Engrs., Soc. Am. Foresters, Am. Inst. Biol. Scientists, Ecol. Soc. Am., Res. Officers Assn. U.S., NRA, Internat. Rescue and First Aid Assn., Internat. Platform Assn., Bulldog Sentinels of Superior Calif, Masons, Shriners. Methodist. Home: 5624 Bonniemae Way Sacramento CA 95824

DROZD, LEON FRANK, JR., lawyer; b. Victoria, Tex., Sept. 11, 1948; s. Leon Frank and Dorothy Lucille (Smith) D.; BBA, Tex. A&M U., 1971; J.D., U. Denver, 1979. Bar: Colo., U.S. Dist. Ct. Colo. U.S. Dist. Ct. (no. dist.) Calif., U.S. Ct. Appeals (10th cir.). Legis. asst. U.S. Ho. of Reps., also Dem. Caucus, Washington, 1971-74, chief clk. com. on sci. and tech., 1974-75; asst. to dean for devel. Coll. Law, U. Denver, 1975-79; v.p. Braddock Publs., Inc., Washington, 1975-79; land and legal counsel Chevron Shale Oil Co.; land and legal counsel Chevron Resources Co., 1980-87, land and legal counsel ins. div., 1987—; atty. Chevron Real Estate Mgmt. Co., 1989—, Chevron Corp. Law Dept. 1987-89, corp. div., 1989—, Chevron Overseas Petroleum and White Nile Petroleum Co. Ltd. (Sudan), 1983, Chevron Real Estate Mgmt. Co., 1989— Colo. elector Anderson/Lucey Nat. Unity Campaign, 1980. Mem. ABA, Fed. Bar Assn., Am. Trial Lawyers Assn., Denver C. of C. (steering com. 1981-82), Nat. Lawyers Club, Commonwealth Club of San Francisco. Home: 255 Red Rock Way #H-204 San Francisco CA 94131 Office: Chevron Corp Law Dept 225 Bush St San Francisco CA 94104-4287

DROZIN, GARTH MATTHEW, deputy district attorney; b. Albany, N.Y., Dec. 10, 1953; s. Harold and Harriet D.; m. Renee Marie McMurray, May 24, 1987. BA, SUNY, Plattsburgh, 1975; MM, N. Tex. State U., 1977; D of Mcpl. Adminstrn., Cornell U., 1981; JD, Southwestern U. Sch. Law, 1987. Bar: Calif. 1987, U.S. Dist. Ct. Calif. 1987. Instr. N. Tex. State U., Denton, Tex., 1975-77; dir. Auralisms Ensemble, Ithaca, N.Y., 1978-84; editor, musicologist Calouste Gulbenkian Found., Lisbon, Portugal, 1981-82; faculty composer, lectr. SUNY, Binghamton, N.Y., 1982-83; Fulbright prof. U.F.R.J. Nat. Sch. Music, Rio de Janeiro, Brazil, 1983; atty. Yusim, Stein & Hanger, Encino, Calif., 1987-88; dep. dist. atty. Los Angeles County, 1988—. Composer Parabolics, 1980, Systemics, 1978, Sacred Service, 1979. Recipient Fulbright Sr. Scholar award Fulbright Commn., 1983, Darmstadt City Ring Fellowship award Internationales Music Institut, 1982, Cornell U. Western Soc. Dissertation Grant Cornell U., 1981. Mem. Percussive Arts Soc. (chpt. pres. 1981-82), ASCAP, State Bar Calif., ABA, Phi Mu Alpha Sinfonia. Democrat. Jewish. Home: 7924 Woodman Ave #37 Van Nuys CA 91402 Office: Los Angeles Dist Atty 210 W Temple St Rm 18000 Los Angeles CA 90012

DRUCKER, PETER FERDINAND, writer, consultant, educator; b. Vienna, Austria, Nov. 19, 1909; came to U.S., 1937, naturalized, 1943; s. Adolph Bertram and Caroline D.; m. Doris Schmitz, Jan. 16, 1937; children: Kathleen Romola, J. Vincent, Cecily Anne, Joan Agatha. Grad., Gymnasium, Vienna, 1927; LL.D., U. Frankfurt, 1931; 16 hon. doctorates, U.S. and fgn. univs. Economist London Banking House, 1933-37; Am. adviser for Brit. banks, Am. corr. Brit. newspapers 1937-42; cons. maj. bus. corps. U.S., 1940—; prof. philosophy, politics Bennington Coll., 1942-49;

prof. mgmt. NYU, 1950-72, chmn. mgmt. area, 1957-62, disting. univ. lectr., 1972—; Clarke prof. social sci. Claremont Grad. Sch. (Calif.), 1971—; prof. dept. art Pomona Coll., Calif., 1979-85. Author: The End of Economic Man, 1939, The Future of Industrial Man, 1941, Concept of the Corporation, 1946, The New Society, 1950, Practice of Management, 1954, America's Next Twenty Years, 1957, The Landmarks of Tomorrow, 1959, Managing for Results, 1964, The Effective Executive, 1966, The Age of Discontinuity, 1969, Technology; Management and Society, 1970, Men, Ideas and Politics, 1971, Management: Tasks, Responsibilities, Practices, 1974, The Unseen Revolution: How Pension Fund Socialism Came to America, 1976, People and Performance, 1977, Management, An Overview, 1978, Adventures of a Bystander, 1979, Managing in Turbulent Times, 1980, Toward the Next Economics and Other Essays, 1981, The Changing World of the Executive, 1982, Innovation and Entrepreneurship, 1985, The Frontiers of Management, 1986, The New Realities, 1989; (fiction) The Last of All Possible Worlds, 1982, The Temptation to Do Good, 1984; producer: movie series The Effective Executive, 1969, Managing Discontinuity, 1971, The Manager and the Organization, 1977, Managing for Tomorrow, 1981; producer 25 audiocassette series The Non-Profit Drucker, 1988. Recipient gold medal Internat. U. Social Studies, Rome, 1957; Wallace Clark Internat. Mgmt. medal, 1963; Taylor Key Soc. for Advancement Mgmt., 1967; Presdl. citation NYU, 1969; CIOS Internat. Mgmt. gold medal, 1972; Chancellor's medal Internat. Acad. Mgmt., 1987. Fellow AAAS (council), Internat., Am., Irish Acads. Mgmt., Brit. Inst. Mgmt. (hon.), Am. Acad. Arts and Scis.; mem. Soc. for History Tech. (pres. 1965-66), Nat. Acad. Pub. Adminstrn. (hon.).

DRUCKMAN, MICHAEL MARK, financial planner; b. Amityville, N.Y., Apr. 17, 1952; s. Daniel D. and Lauretta (Burdman) D.; m. Patricia Ann Smith, Jan. 8, 1977. Student, New Eng. Coll., 1970-72; BS, U. N.H., 1975; postgrad., Ariz. State U., 1975. Advisor, planner Am. Gen. Life Ins. Co., Phoenix, 1977-78, Home Life Ins. Co. N.Y., Phoenix, 1978-82, Physicians Fin. Svcs., Ltd., Phoenix, 1982—. Treas. Found. Burns and Trauma, Inc., Phoenix, 1986—. Mem. Internat. Assn. Fin. Planning. Home: 10166 N 96th Pl Scottsdale AZ 85258 Office: Physicians Fin Svcs Ltd 4520 N 12th St #100 Phoenix AZ 85014

DRUMHELLER, GEORGE JESSE, motel and hotel chain owner; b. Walla Walla, Wash., Jan. 30, 1933; s. Allen and Ila Margaret (Croxdale) D.; student Wash. State U., 1951-52, Whittier Coll., 1955-58; m. Carla Rene Cunha, May 4, 1965 (div. 1985). Asst. mgr. Olympic Hotel, Seattle, 1959; jr. exec. Westin Hotels, Seattle, 1959-63; founder, pres. George Drumheller Properties, Inc., motel holding co., Pendleton, Oreg., 1963—; founder, chmn. bd. Dalles Tapadera, Inc., motel and hotel holding co., The Dalles, Oreg., 1964-77; founder, pres. Lewiston Tapadera, Inc. (Idaho), motel holding co., 1970-77; founder, pres. Yakima Tapadera, Inc. (Wash.), 1971-77; founding ptnr. Drumheller & Titcomb (Tapadera Motor Inn), Ontario, Oreg., 1972-84; merger with Tapadera motel holding cos. and George Drumheller Properties, Inc., 1978—, founder Tapadera Budget Inns, Kennewick and Walla Walla, Wash., 1981-85, also merged with George Drumheller Properties, Inc., 1986; engaged in farming, eastern Wash., 1958-80. With USCG, 1952-55. Mem. Am. Hotel and Motel Assn. (nat. dir. 1980-84, pres.'s exec. com. 1983-84), Oreg. Hotel Motel Assn. (dir. 1974-78), Wash. State Lodging Assn. (dir., v.p. 1976-84), Spokane Club, Walla Walla Country Club, Washington Athletic Club, J.D. Shea Club, LaJolla Beach and Tennis Club, Kona Kai Club, San Diego Club. Home: 3132 Morning Way La Jolla CA 92037 Office: George Drumheller Properties Inc PO Box 1234 Walla Walla WA 99362

DRUMMER, DONALD RAYMOND, banker; b. Binghamton, N.Y., Oct. 10, 1941; s. Donald Joseph and Louise Frances (Campbell) D.; AS, Broome Community Coll., 1962; BS, U. Colo., 1972; MBA, Regis Coll., 1981; m. Rita Kovac, May 22, 1965; children: Shelley Rita, Adam Donn. With, Lincoln First Bank, Binghamton, N.Y., 1962-69; asst. comptroller Adams & Horne, Denver, 1969; with Colo. State Bank, Denver, 1969-87, v.p., 1972-81, comptroller, 1972-87, sr. v.p., 1981-87; sr. v.p., chief fin. officer Wyo. Nat. Bancorp. (formerly Affiliated Bank Corp. of Wyo.), Casper, 1987—; sr. v.p., chief fin. officer Wyo. Nat. Bank, Casper, Cheyenne; bd. dirs. Wyo. Nat. Bank, Lovell and Kemmerer; corp. sec. Wyo. Nat. Bancorp. (formerly Affiliated Bank Corp. of Wyo.), 1987—; adj. faculty Regis Coll., mem. grad. edn. task force, 1986-87. Bd. dirs. Girl's Club of Casper, 1988. Mem. Nat. Assn. Accts. (dir. 1975-79, v.p. 1977-79), Am. Acctg. Assn., Am. Taxation Assn. Clubs: Denver Sertoma (past pres.), City (v.p., dir. 1979-83). Editor: Chronicle, 1980-81. Office: Wyo Nat Bancorp 152 N Durbin Casper WY 82601

DRUMMOND, GERARD KASPER, resource development company executive, lawyer; b. N.Y.C., Oct. 9, 1937; s. John Landells and Margaret Louise (Kasper) D.; m. Donna J. Mason, Sept. 14, 1957 (div. 1976); children: Alexander, Jane, Edmund; m. Sandra Hamilton, Aug. 31, 1985. B.S., Cornell U., 1959, LL.B. with distinction, 1963. Bar: Oreg. 1963. Assoc. Davies, Biggs, Strayer, Stoel & Boley, Portland, Oreg., 1963-64; assoc., ptnr. Rives, Bonyhadi, Drummond & Smith, Portland, 1964-77; pres. Nerco, Inc., Portland, from 1977, chmn. bd. dirs., 1987—; mem. corp. policy group PacifiCorp, 1979—, exec. v.p., 1987—; bd. dirs. Pacific Telecom. Pres. Tri-County Met. Transit Dist., Portland, 1974-86, bd. dirs., 1974-86; mem. Oreg.-Korea Econ. Coop. Com., Portland, 1981-85, Oreg. Investment Council, 1987—; trustee Reed Coll., 1982—; bd. dirs. Oreg. Contemporary Theatre, 1983-85, Oreg. Symphony, 1987—; community bd. dirs. Providence Hosp., 1986—. Served to 1st lt. USAR, 1959-67. Mem. ABA, Oreg. Bar Assn., Am. Mining Congress (bd. dirs. 1986—), Silver Inst. (bd. dirs. 1987—). Clubs: Arlington, Univ. Home: 28815 S Needy Rd Canby OR 97013 Office: Nerco Inc 111 SW Columbia St Ste 800 Portland OR 97201

DRUMMOND, OLIVER LEE, protective services official; b. Van Nuys, Calif., Oct. 7, 1947; s. Joseph Lester and Ollie Lee (Rodabaugh) D.; m. Deborah Louise Clark, Oct. 14, 1970; 1 child, Deborah Lee. BS in Criminology, Calif. State U.-Long Beach, 1974; advanced grad. cert. in exec. mgmt. Pacific Christian Coll., 1979; postgrad. in human behavior Newport U., 1979—; LHD (hon.) Newport Internat. U., 1979; LLD (hon.) Van Norman U., 1980. Community coll. lifetime tchr. credential, Calif.; basic, intermediate, advanced and mgmt. certs., exec. cert. Calif. Dept. Justice. Police officer Santa Ana (Calif.) Police Dept., 1970-75, sgt., 1975-78, lt., 1978-82; chief of police Hanford (Calif.) Police Dept., 1982-89, Oceanside (Calif.), 1989— ; instr. Advanced Investigators Acad., Saddleback Coll., 1981-83. Mem. sch. site coun. Kings River-Hardwick Sch., 1982-89; bd. dirs. Kings County Vol. Bur., 1982-89 , chmn., 1985. Served with Army N.G., 1969-75; served to lt., Mil. Police Corps, USAR, 1972-76. Recipient Profl. Svc. award Santa Ana Police Dept., 1982; Meritorious Svc./Valor award Santa Ana Police Benevolent Assn., 1973; named Chief of Yr., Calif. Law Enforcement Mgmt. Ctr., 1982. Mem. Internat. Assn. Chiefs of Police, Internat. Police Assn., ABA (criminal justice sect.), Calif. Peace Officers Assn. (law and legis. com.), Calif. Chiefs Assn., Calif. Police Chiefs Assn. (standards and ethics com., tng. com.), Calif. Assn. Police Tng. Officers, Calif. Assn. Adminstrn. of Justice Educators, Calif. League of Calif. Cities (1st v.p. police chiefs sect., pres. police chiefs sect.), Oceanside C. of C., Hanford C. of C. (dir. 1983, pres. 1985, mem. ambassador corps, City Employee of Yr. award 1982, President's award 1984), SAR (Law Enforcement Commendation medal), Rotary (sgt.-at-arms 1983-84). Office: 1617 Mission Ave Oceanside CA 92054

DRUMMONDS, VONITA MARIE, chiropractor; b. Independence, Mo., Feb. 18, 1950; d. Hobart Garland Arms and Violet May (Graham) Arms Adkins; m. William George Drummonds, Nov. 1, 1969; children: Jennifer Hannelore, Christina Nicole. BS, Cen. Mo. State U., 1972; D in Chiropractic, Logan Chiropractic Coll., 1982. Lic. chiropractor, Ariz., Calif., Colo., Mo., Ill., Va. Med. technician Trinity Luth. Hosp., Kansas City, Mo., 1972-73, Pathology Assn., Spokane, Wash., 1973-76, Mo. Bapt. Hosp., St. Louis, 1976-83; chiropractor Assoc. Le Baron Chiropractic, Ariz., 1983-86; chiropractor, owner Fountain Hills (Ariz.) Chiropractic, 1986—. Mem. Chiropractic Assn. Ariz., Am. Chiropractic Assn., Fountain Hills C. of C. (fair com. 1987), Am. Bus. Women's Assn. (v.p. 1986), Internat. Arabian Horse Assn., Am. Horse Shows Assn. Republican. Roman Catholic. Home: 17231 E Baca St Fountain Hills AZ 85268 Office: Fountain Hills Chiropractic 12035 N Saguaro Blvd #202 Fountain Hills AZ 85268

DRUTCHAS, GERRICK GILBERT, publisher; b. Detroit, Sept. 23, 1953; s. Gilbert Henry and Elaine Marie (Rutkowski) D.; m. Martha Eugenia Hernandez, DEc. 23, 1984; 1 child, Gilbert Henry II. BA, Mich. State U., 1975; postgrad., U. Redlands, 1983-85. Pres. Argentum Publs., Los Angeles, 1986—. Dir. Childrens Welfare Found. Sgt. USAR, 1981-85. Mem. KP, Delta Sigma Phi. Unitarian. Home: 601 E California Blvd Pasadena CA 91106 Office: Argentum Publs Inc 3610 W 6th St Ste 645 Los Angeles CA 90020

DRUZIK, CECILY MELISANDE GRZYWACZ, chemist, researcher; b. Inglewood, Calif., Jan. 16, 1960; d. John Michael and Anita Louise (Nalli) Grzywacz. BS, Calif. State U., Northridge, 1984; postgrad., Calif. State U., 1985—. Technician corp. tech. dept. ARCO, Chatsworth, Calif., 1984-85; teaching asst. Calif. State U., Northridge, 1985; asst. scientist Getty Conservation Inst., Marina Del Rey, Calif., 1985—. Mem. Am. Chem. Soc., Western Assn. Art Conservation (inst. mem.). Democrat. Home: 6616 Springpark Ave Los Angeles CA 90056 Office: Getty Conservation Inst 4503 Glencoe Ave Marina Del Rey CA 90292

DRYDEN, ROBERT EUGENE, lawyer; b. Chanute, Kans., Aug. 20, 1927; s. Calvin William and Mary Alfreda (Foley) D.; m. Jetta Rae Burger, Dec. 19, 1953; children: Lynn Marie, Thomas Calvin. A.A., City Coll., San Francisco, 1947; B.S., U. San Francisco, 1951, J.D., 1954. Bar: Calif. 1955; diplomate: Am. Bd. Trial Advocates. Assoc. Barfield, Dryden & Ruane (and predecessor firm), San Francisco, 1954-60, jr. ptnr., 1960-65, gen. ptnr., 1965-89; sr. ptnr. Dryden, Margoles, Schimaneck, Hartman & Kelly, San Francisco, 1989—; lectr. continuing edn. of the bar, 1971-77. Served with USMCR, 1945-46. Fellow Am. Coll. Trial Lawyers, Am. Bar Found.; mem. ABA, San Francisco Bar Assn., State Bar Calif., Am. Judicature Soc., Assn. Def. Counsel (dir. 1968-71), Def. Research Inst., Internat. Assn. Ins. Counsel, Fedn. Ins. Counsel, Am. Arbitration Assn., U. San Francisco Law Soc. (mem. exec. com. 1970-72), U. San Francisco Alumni Assn. (bd. govs. 1977), Phi Alpha Delta. Home: 1320 Lasuen Dr Millbrae CA 94030 Office: Dryden Margoles Schimaneck Hartman & Kelly 1 California St Ste 3125 San Francisco CA 94111

DRYSDALE, THOMAS TOWNSEND, education educator; b. Alamosa, Colo., May 4, 1921; s. Thomas Townsend Drysdale and Oneta Moore (Kirkpatrick) Walton; m. Norma Fay Hall, Mar. 8, 1943; children: Lianne, Peter, Connie, Dale, Brian, Karl. BA, Whittier Coll., 1952, MEd, 1956; EdD, George Washington U., 1974. Asst. dist. supt. Dept. Def., Overseas Dependents Sch., throughout Mediterranean and Middle East region, 1959-60, London, 1960-62; dist. supt. Dept. Def., Overseas Dependents Sch., Wiesbaden, Fed. Republic of Germany and Paris, 1962-64; asst. area supt. Dept. Def., Overseas Dependents Sch., Honolulu and Far East, 1964-66; dep. dir. Dept. Def., Overseas Dependents Sch., Washington, 1966-73; dir. Atlantic region Dept. Def., Overseas Dependents Sch., London, 1973-81; assoc. prof. No. Ariz. U., Flagstaff, 1986—; adj. prof. U. West Fla., Pensacola, 1976-85; tchr. Whittier City (Calif.) Sch., 1952-54, prin., 1954-56, 58-59; prin. Dept. Def. Overseas Dependents Sch., Wiesbaden, 1956-57, London, 1957-58. Author: Millions of People, 1965; patentee in field. Served to lt. col. USAF, 1942-46. Named Outstanding Civilian Dept. Navy, Pensacola, 1976. Mem. Comparative and Internat. Edn. Soc., NEA, Phi Delta Kappa. Home: 4015 Lugano Way Flagstaff AZ 86004

DUARTE, RAMON GONZALEZ, nurse; b. San Fernando, Calif., Jan. 5, 1948; s. Salvador Revelez and Juanita (Gonzalez) D.; m. Sophia Constant Garabedian, Apr. 17, 1983; children: David Ramon, John Robert. AA in Nursing, Los Angeles Valley Coll., 1972; student, Calif. State U., Los Angeles, 1972-76. RN; Cert. Bd. Nephrology Examiners. Staff nurse hemodialysis unit U. So. Calif. Med. Ctr., Los Angeles, 1971-75; charge nurse self care hemodialysis unit Kaiser Found. Hosp., Los Angeles, 1976, Culver City (Calif.) Dialysis Services, Inc., 1981-82; adminstrv. head nurse hemodialysis unit Valley Prebyn. Hosp., Van Nuys, Calif., 1976-78; adminstrv. head nurse Kidney Dialysis Care Units, Lynwood, Calif., 1980-81; ind. nursing contractor Nursing Services in Nephrology, Van Nuys, 1982—, clin. instr., researcher, 1980—, dir. research, 1988—; coordinator clin. research Valley Dialysis Assocs., Inc., Van Nuys, 1978-80; mem. research com. Valley Presbyn. Hosp. Research; founder, pres. Dialysis Mus. Council, chmn. So. Calif. Dialysis Earthquake Preparedness Commn.; mem. council nephrology nurses and technicians, mem. allied profl. adv. com., chmn. allied health profl research grant com. Nat. Kidney Found. Inc.; mem. sci. adv. council Nat. Kidney Found. So. Calif. Mem. editorial bd. Dialysis and Transplantation mag.; contbr. articles to med. publs.; patentee biologicals. Founder Mus. Hope, Van Nuys. Recipient Dedicated Service award Hemodialysis Found., 1976; named Allied Health Profl. of Yr. Nat. Kidney Found. So. Calif., 1986; scholar Am. G.I. Forum, 1966, Am. Legion Forty and Eight Coll., Los Angeles Valley Coll. Associated Students. Mem. Am. Assn. Artificial Internal Organs, Am. Assn. Nephrology Nurses and Technicians, Kidney Found. So. Calif., Am. Assn. Critical Care Nurses, Ind. Nurses' Assn., Nat. Assn. Patients on Hemodialysis and Transplantation Inc., Am. Soc. Nephrology, N.Y. Acad. Scis. Democrat. Roman Catholic. Home and Office: 383 Mesa Ln Santa Barbara CA 93109

DUBA, STEPHEN CHARLES, naval officer; b. St. Louis, July 13, 1953; s. Charles Edward and Anna Maria (Daugherty) D.; m. Marcella Maxwell, June 11, 1977; children: Stephen Charles, Timothy G., Marcella A., Katherine M. BS in Ocean Engring., U.S. Naval Acad., 1975; ME in Ocean Engring., Fla. Atlantic U., 1982. Registered profl. engr., Calif. Commd. USN, 1975, advanced through grades to lt. comdr.; exec. officer, salvage diving officer USS Escape (AR5-6), Mayport, Fla., 1976-78; program mgr. R & D Naval Civil Engring. Lab., Port Hueneme, Calif., 1978-81; engring. officer Navy Exptl. Diving Unit, Panama City, Fla., 1983-85; dep. resident officer-in-charge constrn. Western div. Naval Facilities Engring. Command Contracts Office, Point Mugn, Calif., 1985-87; comdg. officer Underwater Constrn. Team Two, Port Hueneme, 1987—. Decorated Nave Commendation medal. Mem. ASME, Soc. Am. Mil. Engrs., Naval Acad. Alumni Assn., Lincoln Continental Club, Shelby Am. Automobile Assn. Republican. Mem. Christian Ch. Office: Comdg Officer Underwater Constrn Team Bldg 524 NCBC Port Hueneme CA 93043

DUBIN, GARY VICTOR, lawyer; b. Phila., Aug. 27, 1938; s. Jacob and Iris Dubin; 1 child, Robert Scott Adams. AB summa cum laude, U. So. Calif., L.A., 1960; JD magna cum laude, NYU, 1963. Bar: Calif. 1964, Hawaii 1982, U.S. Supreme Ct. 1973. Faculty law sch. Stanford U., Palo Alto, Calif., 1963-64; rsch. faculty U. Calif., Berkeley, 1964-66; faculty law sch. U. Denver, 1966-69; rsch. faculty law sch. Harvard U., Cambridge, Mass., 1969-70; resident cons. Rand Corp., Santa Monica, Calif., 1970-71; pvt. practice law Honolulu, 1964—. With USAF, 1956-62. Home: Dubin Plantation 46 403 Haiku Plantation Dr Kaneohe HI 96744 Office: 733 Bishop St 1915 Honolulu HI 96813

DUBOFF, LEONARD DAVID, legal educator; b. Bklyn., Oct. 3, 1941; s. Rubin Robert and Millicent Barbara (Pollach) DuB.; m. Mary Ann Crawford, June 4, 1967; children—Colleen Rose, Robert Courtney, Sabrina Ashley. J.D. summa cum laude, Bklyn. Law Sch., 1971. Bars: N.Y. 1974, U.S. Dist. Cts. (so. and ea. dists.) N.Y. 1974, U.S. Ct. Appeals (2d cir.) 1974, U.S. Customs Ct. 1975, U.S. Supreme Ct. 1977, Oreg. 1977. Teaching fellow Stanford (Calif.) U. Law Sch., 1971-72; mem. faculty Lewis & Clark Coll. Northwestern Sch. Law, Portland, Oreg., 1972—, prof. law, 1977—; instr. Hastings Coll. Law Coll. Civil Advocacy, San Francisco, summers 1978, 79. Founder, past pres. Oreg. Vol. Lawyers for Arts; mem. lawyers' com. ACLU, 1973-78, bd. dirs. Oreg., 1974-76; mem. Mayor's Adv. Com. Security and Privacy, 1974; bd. dirs. Portland Art Mus. Asian Art Council, 1976-77, Internat. Assn. Art Security, N.Y.C., 1976-80; Gov. Oreg. Com. Employment of Handicapped, 1978-81; cons., panelist spl. projects Nat. Endowment for Arts, 1978-79; mem. Mayor's Adv. Com. on Handicapped, 1979-81; mem. Wash. State Atty. Gen's. Com. to Reorganize Mayhill Mus.; Oreg. Commn. for Blind; Oreg. Com. for Humanities, 1981-87. Recipient Bklyn. Law Sch. Stuart Hirschman Property, Jerome Prince Evidence, Donald W. Matheson Meml. awards, 1st scholarship prize; Hofstra U. Lighthouse scholar 1965-71; recipient Hauser award, 1967, Howard Brown Pickard award, 1967-69. Mem. Am. Soc. Internat. Law, Assn. Alumni and Attenders of Hague Acad. Internat. Law, Assn. Am. Law Schs. (chmn. sect. law and arts 1974-80, standing com. sect. activities 1975), ABA, N.Y. State Bar Assn., Oreg. Bar Assn., Delta Kappa Phi, Sigma Pi Sigma, Sigma Alpha. Spl. columnist on craft law, The Crafts Report; editor, contbr. materials to legal and art textbooks; author textbooks and articles for legal and art jours. Office: Lewis & Clark Law Sch 10015 SW Terwilliger Portland OR 97219

DUBOFSKY, JEAN EBERHART, lawyer, retired justice Colorado Supreme Court; b. 1942; B.A., Stanford U., 1964; LL.B., Harvard U., 1967; m. Frank N. Dubofsky; children: Joshua, Matthew. Admitted to Colo. bar, 1967; legis. asst. to U.S. Senator Walter F. Mondale, 1967-69; atty. Colo. Rural Legal Services, Boulder, 1969-72, Legal Aid Soc. Met. Denver, 1972-73; ptnr. Kelly, Dubofsky, Haglund & Garnsey, Denver, 1973-75; dep. atty. gen. Colo., 1975-77; counsel Kelly, Haglund, Garnsey & Kahn, 1977-79, 88—; justice Colo. Supreme Ct., Denver, 1979-87; vis. prof. U. Colo. Law Sch., Boulder, 1987-88. Office: Kelly Haglund Garnsey & Kahn 1441 18th St Denver CO 80202 *

DUBOIS, FRANK A., III, state agency official, agriculturist; b. Lynwood, Calif., May 29, 1947; s. Frank A. and Wanda Eileen (McCarey) DuB.; m. Sharon Rose Chesher, May 24, 1973; children: Frank Austin, Sevon Nicole. BA in Agri. and Extn. Edn., N.M. State U., 1973, MA in Agri. and Extn. Edn., 1987. Insp. N.Mex. Dept. Agriculture, Albuquerque, 1973-74; agrl. programs specialist N.Mex. Dept. Agri., Las Cruces, 1979-81, asst. dir., 1983-87, dir., sec., 1988—; legis. asst. U.S. Senator Pete V. Domenici, Washington, 1974-76; spl. asst. field office U.S. Senator Pete V. Domenici, Las Cruces, 1976-79; dep. asst. sec. land and water resources U.S. Dept. Interior, 1981-83; mem. Water Quality Control Commn., N.M., 1988—, Western States Water Council, 1987—, Interstate Oil Compact Commn., 1987—. Contbr. articles to profl. jours. Mem. Soc. Range Mgmt., Soc. Am. Foresters, N.Mex. Cattle Growers Assn., N.Mex. Wool Growers Assn., Nat. Assn. State Depts. Agriculture, Western Assn. State Depts. Agriculture, Western U.S. Agrl. Trade Assn., Mil Gracias Assn. (pres. 1986-88), Riff Raff Roping, Las Cruces C. of C. Republican. Methodist. Office: NMex Dept Agr Box 30005 Dept 3189 Las Cruces NM 88003

DU BOIS, REYNOLD COOPER, international marketing consultant; b. Troy, N.Y., Apr. 16, 1940; s. Eugene Herman and Vivian (Cooper) D.; m. Margaret Ann Snodgrass, Apr. 26, 1980. BS in Geography, Ariz. State U., 1974, MA in Geography, 1975. Engr. USS Maury, Pearl Harbor, Hawaii, 1964-68; gen. mgr. Hawaii Tape Tours, Honolulu, 1969; mgmt. trainee Kona Village Resort, Kailua-Kona, Hawaii, 1970-72; radio announcer KKON Radio, Kealekekua, Hawaii, 1971-72; cons. Mountain West Research, Tempe, Ariz., 1974-76; v.p. Vanguard Properties, Scottsdale, Ariz., 1977-82, Real Estate Profls., Scottsdale, 1983-87; pres. Du Bois Internat., Inc., Phoenix, 1987—; pres. FIABCI-Ariz., Phoenix, 1989—; internat. advisor Ariz. Assn. Ind. Devel., Phoenix, 1988; instr. in field. Mem. Gov.'s Ariz.-Mexico Commn., Phoenix, 1986—; internat. advisor Phoenix Sister Cities Commn., 1988-89; mem. Ariz. World Affairs Council, Phoenix, 1986-89. Fellow Royal Geog. Soc.; mem. Internat. Real Estate Fedn. (pres. 1989-90), Internat. Real Estate Inst., Nat. Assn. Realtors, Am. Assn. Geographers, Ariz. World Trade Assn., Optimists, Toastmasters. Republican. Home: 8016 E Earll Dr Scottsdale AZ 85251 Office: Du Bois Internat Inc 2141 E Highland Suite 138 Phoenix AZ 85016

DUBOSE, FRANCIS MARQUIS, clergyman; b. Elba, Ala., Feb. 27, 1922; s. Hansford Arthur and Mayde Frances (Owen) DuB.; BA cum laude, Baylor U., 1947; MA, U. Houston, 1958; BD, Southwestern Bapt. Sem., 1957, ThD, 1961; postgrad. Oxford (Eng.) U., 1972; m. Dorothy Anne Sessums, Aug. 28, 1940; children: Elizabeth Anne Parnell, Frances Jeannine Stevens, Jonathan Michael, Celia Danielle Carmichael. Pastor, Bapt. chs., Tex., Ark., 1939-61; supt. missions. So. Bapt. Conv., Detroit, 1961-66; prof. missions Golden Gate Bapt. Sem., 1966—, dir. World Mission Ctr., 1979—; lectr., cons. in 115 cities outside U.S., 1969-82; v.p. Conf. City Mission Supts., So. Bapt. Conv., 1964-66; trustee Mich. Bapt. Inst., 1963-66; mem. exec. bd. San Francisco Conf. Religion, Race and Social Concern. Mem. Internat. Assn. Mission Study, Am. Soc. Missiology, Assn. Mission Profs. Co-editor: The Mission of the Church in the Racially Changing Community, 1969; author: How Churches Grow in an Urban World, 1978, Classics of Christian Missions, 1979, God Who Sends: A Fresh Quest for Biblical Mission, 1983, Home Cell Groups and House Churches, 1987; contbr. to Toward Creative Urban Strategy; Vol. III Ency. of So. Baptists, also articles to profl. jours. Home: 21 Platt Ct Mill Valley CA 94941 Office: Golden Gate Bapt Sem Mill Valley CA 94941

DUBOW, SUSAN DIANE, investment broker; b. Phila., June 13, 1948; d. Milton and Esther (Kalish) D.; m. Thomas J. Volgy, Feb. 8, 1987. BArch with distinction, U. Ariz., 1974-78, postgrad., 1988--. Architect in tng. Macneil Riedel Architects,, Tucson, 1977-79; constrn. coordinator Empire West Cos., Tucson, 1979-81; investment broker A.G. Edwards, Tucson, 1982-85, Merrill Lynch, Tucson, 1985-86, Rauscher Pierce Refsnes, Inc., Tucson, 1986--; investment broker Womens' Investment Network, Tucson, 1983—, Red Herring, Tucson, 1986-88, Health Investment Profile, Tucson, 1987—, Gt. Expectations, Tucson, 1988. Mem. Tucson Womens' Commn., 1983-84; coordinator Cigna/Michael Landon Celebrity Tennis Classic, Tucson, 1987-88; bd. dirs. Comstock Children's Found., 1985-88; mem. steering com., chmn. speakers bd. Tucson First, 1987—. Mem. Nat. Assn. Security Dealers. Democrat. Office: Rauscher Pierce Refsnes Inc 3561 E Sunrise Ste 125 Tucson AZ 85718

DUCHAC, LAWRENCE ALLEN, services industry executive; b. Cleve., Sept. 2, 1935; s. Edwin L. and Christine E. (Durk) D.; m. Roberta A. Ray, Sept. 29, 1961; children: Bruce A., Christopher A. BBA, Ohio State U., 1957. Contract negotiator USAF, Ohio, 1959-62; sr. contract adminstr. Garrett Turbine Engine Co., Phoenix, 1962-66, sr. buyer, procurement specialist, 1966-74, supv. purchasing dept., 1974-80, gen. supv., 1980-84; mgr. purchasing dept. Garrett Controls Div. Garrett Turbine Engine Co., Tucson, 1984-87; exec. v.p. Servicon Systems, Inc., Culver City, Calif., 1987-- . Bd. dirs. Scottsdale (Ariz.) YMCA, 1976-77. With USAR, 1957-62. Mem. Purchasing Mgmt. Assn. Los Angeles, Purchasing Mgmt. Assn. Ariz. (bd. dirs. 1982-84), Scottsdale Aquatic Club (pres., chmn. bd. dirs. 1974-76). Republican. Home: 11801 Clonlee Ave Granada Hills CA 91344 Office: Servicon Systems Inc 3965 Landmark St Culver City CA 90232

DUCHAK, GEORGE DEMETRIUS, naval officer; b. Evergreen Park, Ill., Oct. 28, 1955; s. Daniel George and Felice Diane (Revak) D.; m. Sonya Marie Milley, June 19, 1977; 1 child, Alexander George. BSME, U.S. Naval Acad., 1977; MBA, The Ohio State U., 1985; MSAE, Naval Postgrad. Sch., 1989, postgrad., 1989—. Commd. ensign USN, 1977, advanced through ranks to lt. commdr., 1986; aeronautical engr. duty officer Naval Postgrad. Sch., Monterey, Calif., 1988—. Named one of Outstanding Young Men Am., 1983. Mem. U.S. Naval Acad. Alumni Assn., The Ohio State U. Alumni Assn., Am. Soc. Mech. Engrs. (assoc., nat. newsletter editor 1986—). Republican. Home: 1802 McAdam Rd Darien IL 60559

DUCKETT, ANN LORRAINE, lawyer; b. San Francisco, Jan. 20, 1951; d. O.C. and Sara (Lockman) D. BA in English, Recreation, Western State Coll. Colo., 1973; JD, U. Denver, 1983. Bar: Colo. 1983, U.S. Dist. Ct. Colo. 1983, U.S. Ct. Appeals (10th cir.) 1983, U.S. Supreme Ct. 1988. Co-founder, pub., advt. dir. Callett Pub. Co., 1974-80; legis. asst. to rep. State of Colo., Denver, 1979-80, legis. asst. to senator, 1983-84; of counsel Bader & Villanueva, P.C., Denver, 1983—; co-founder Callihan Broadcasting Group, Inc., 1982-88; mem. faculty Women's Leadership Tng. Inst., 1987—; lectr. Colo. Law Related Edn. Confs., 1986-87, tchrs. workshop, 1987; mem. adv. com. Colo. Securities Commr., 1989. Editor: Law in Colo., 1986-87, Adminstrv. Law Rev., 1983; pub. Capitol Reporter, 1989—; asst. dir., legis. advisor Statehouse to Schoolhouse video series, 1987-88. Hearing officer, mem. Colo. State Bd. Optometric Examiners, 1984—; mem. adv. bd. Colo. Civic and Legal Edn. Program, 1986-87; co-chmn. inauguration com. Gov. of Colo., 1986-87; campaign mgr., fin. dir., media and advt. cons. to various state and local polit. campaigns, 1974-89; instr., coach Gunnison Jr. Tennis Program, 1972-76; mem. Univ. Park Community coun., Denver; treas., bd. dirs. Gunnison Community Concert Assn., 1977-79; sec. RE1J Sch. Bd. Accountability Com., Gunnison, 1977-78; exec. bd. Denver Downtown Dem. Forum, 1987—. Mem. ABA, Colo. Bar Assn. (law edn. com. 1983—), Denver Bar Assn., Colo. Women's Bar Assn., Phi Alpha Delta. Home: 2075 S Saint Paul St Denver CO 80210

DUCKWORTH, ROBERT H., banker. Student, Ind. U., Rutgers U., Stonier Grad. Sch. Banking. Asst. v.p. 1st Interstate Bank of Ariz. (formerly

1st Nat. Bank of Ariz.), 1966-67, v.p., mgr., 1967-70, div. v.p., then sr. v.p. home office lending div., 1970-75, exec. v.p. comml. banking group, 1975-85, chmn. bd., pres., chief exec. officer, from 1985, now chmn. bd., chief exec. officer; also bd. dirs. Office: 1st Interstate Bank Ariz 100 W Washington PO Box 53456 Phoenix AZ 85072 *

DUCKWORTH, WALTER DONALD, museum executive, entomologist; b. Athens, Tenn., July 19, 1935; s. James Clifford and Vesta Katherine (Walker) D.; m. Sandra Lee Smith, June 17, 1955; children: Clifford Monroe, Laura Lee, Brent Cullen. Student, U. Tenn., 1953-55; BS, Middle Tenn. State U., 1955-57; MS, N.C. State U., 1957-60, PhD, 1962. Entomology intern Nat. Mus. Nat. History, Washington, 1960-62, asst. curator, 1962-64, assoc. curator, 1964-75, entomology curator, 1975-78, spl.asst. to dir., 1975-78; spl. asst. to asst. sec. Smithsonian Inst., Washington, 1978-84; dir. Bishop Mus., Honolulu, 1984-86, pres., dir., 1986—; trustee Sci. Mus. Va., Richmond, 1982-86, bd. dirs. 1982-84; bd. dirs. Hawaii Maritime Mus., Honolulu, 1984—; mem. Sci. Manpower Commn., Washington, 1982-84. Co-editor: Amazonian Ecosystems, 1973; Am. editor: Dictionary of Butterflies and Moths, 1976; author, co-author numerous monographs and jour. articles in systematic biology. Pres. Social Ctr. for Psychosocial Rehab., Fairfax, Va., 1975. N.C. State U. research fellow, 1957-62; recipient numerous grants NSF, Am. Philos. Soc., Smithsonian Research Found. Assn., Exceptional Service awards Smithsonian Inst., 1973, 77, 80, 82, 84, Disting. Alumnus award Middle Tenn. State U., 1984. Mem. Am. Inst. Biol. Scis. (pres. 1985-86, sec. treas. 1978-84), Entomol. Soc. Am. (pres. 1982-83, governing bd. 1976-85, Disting. Service award 1981), Assn. Tropical Biology (exec. dir. 1971-84, sec. treas. 1976-71), Hawaii Acad. Sci. (council 1985—), Arts Council Hawaii (legis. com. 1986-87), Assn. Sci. Mus. Dirs., Social Sci. Assn., Assn. Systematic Collections (v.p. 1988-89), Pacific Sci. Assn. (pres. 1987-91, pres. Pacific Sci. Congress, Honolulu 1991). Democrat. Presbyterian. Lodges: Rotary, Masons, Order Eastern Star. Office: Bishop Mus PO Box 19000-A Honolulu HI 96817-0916

DUDDY, GERALD JOSEPH, process and assembly systems designer; b. Wilkes Barre, Pa., June 26, 1927; s. Gerald Joseph and Tryphena (Hobson) D.; m. Irene Trauner, Oct. 23, 1963; children: Kevin, Brain, Erin, Loren. Student, Newark Coll. Engring., 1949. Cert. robotics engr. Design engr. Unio Carbine, Newark, 1944-62, Tampa Bay (Fla.) Engring., 1963-68; mgr. mfg. engring. I.R.C. div. TRW, St. Petersburg, Fla., 1968-72; chief engr. Solatron, Inglewood, Calif., 1972-77; pres. Design Duddy & Mercien, Inglewood, 1977-87; owner Design & Duddy, Thousands Oaks, Calif., 1987—; cons. AMP, Harrisburg, Pa., 1984-86, Westinghouse, Columbia, Md., 1983-85, Miigata Engring., Tokyo, 1986-87, MTS Vecktronics, Carlsbad, Calif., 1988. Commetteeman Dem. Party, Newark, 1958-59. With USN, 1945-47. Fellow Soc. Mfg. Engr., Robotics Internat., Machine Vision Assn., Am. Welding Soc. Republican. Roman Catholic. Office: Design & Duddy 50 W Hillcrest Dr Ste 210 Thousand Oaks CA 91360

DUDEK, ANTHONY EDWARD, telecommunications executive; b. Torrington, Conn., July 5, 1953; s. Edward Anthony and Josephine Dudek; m. Laura Battersby, May 3, 1986. BS in Biology, MIT, 1975; MS in Telecommunications, Colo. U., 1985. V.p. telecommunications Hatfield Assocs., Boulder, Colo., 1985-89; v.p. cellular solutions Hatfield Assocs., Boulder, 1989—; cons. in field. Office: Hatfield Assoc Inc 4840 Riverbend Rd Boulder CO 80301

DUDLEY, MICHAEL JAMES, safety specialist; b. Newport News, Va., Nov. 9, 1960; s. Henry Franklin and Dorthy Ann (Morrow) D.; m. Robin Louise Soma, Oct. 14, 1984. BA, U. Va., 1981; diploma, U.S. Army Def. Ammo Sch., Savanna, Ill., 1983. Specialized safety cert. Def. Logistics Agy. Quality assurance specialist Sierra Army Depot, Herlong, Calif., 1983-85, Navajo Army Depot, Flagstaff, Ariz., 1985-86; safety specialist Def. Logistics Agy., San Bruno, Calif., 1986—; advisor Bay Area Explosive Safety Com., San Ramon, Calif., 1987—. Mem. Indsl. Emergency Coun., Nat. Safety Coun., San Francisco Bay Area Fed. Safety Coun. (exec. bd. 1987—), Kappa Alpha Psi. Republican. Baptist. Home: 2310 Rock St #12 Mountain View CA 94046 Office: Def Logistics Agy DCASMA-SF 1250 Bayhill Dr San Bruno CA 94006

DUENSING, CAROL JANET, corporate professional; b. Bellflower, Mo., Apr. 14, 1937; d. Charles Donald and Mary Lois (Drewer) Buermann; m. George Herman Duensing, Aug. 26, 1967; children: Mary Theresa, Julie Ann. Student, Suburba Sch. Music. Office mgr. Dempsey Tegeler, Corpus Christi, Tex., 1960-62; sec. Goldman Sachs Investment Co., Los Angeles, 1962-63; sec., treas. Music Systems Enterprises Inc., Orange, Calif., 1966—. Recipient Community Service award Tustin (Calif.) Schs., 1976. Mem. Pacific Coast Buckskin Horse Assn. (sec. 1980-88). Republican. Home: 18901 Valley Dr Villa Park CA 92667 Office: Music Systems Enterprises Inc PO Box 1744 935 N Main Orange CA 92668

DUESBERG, PETER HEINZ HERMANN, molecular biology educator; b. Münster, Fed. Republic Germany, Dec. 2, 1936; s. Richard and Hilde Maria (Saettele) D.; m. Astrid Datzer, 1961; children: Nicola, Sibyl, Susi. Grad., U. Würzburg, 1958, U. Basel, Switzerland, 1959; diploma in chemistry, U. Munich, Fed. Republic Germany, 1961; PhD in Chemistry, U. Frankfurt, Fed. Republic Germany, 1963. Postdoctoral fellow Max-Planck Inst. Virus Research, Tübingen, Fed. Republic Germany, 1963; asst. research virologist Virus Lab., U. Calif., Berkeley, 1964-66, postdoctoral fellow, 1966-68, asst. prof. in residence, asst. research biochemist, dept. molecular biology, 1968-70; asst. prof. molecular biology U. Calif., Berkeley, 1970-71, assoc. prof., 1971-73, prof., 1973—. Recipient Merck award, 1969, Calif. Scientist of Yr. award, 1971, 1st Ann. Am. Med. Ctr. Oncology award, 1981, Outstanding Investigator award NIH, 1985, Fogarty Scholar-in-Residence award NIH, Bethesda, Md., 1986-87, Johann-Georg-Zimmerman prize, 1988. Mem. Nat. Acad. Scis. Home: 414 Beloit Ave Kensington CA 94708 Office: U Calif Berkeley Dept Molecular Biology Berkeley CA 94720

DUFAULT, CHRISTOPHER JOHN, soft drink company executive and founder; b. Long Beach, Calif., Apr. 17, 1957; s. James E. and Carol (Hoehne) D.; m. Beth Anne Leavenworth, Nov. 24, 1986; children: Joshua, Alexandra. BSBA, Calif. State U., Long Beach, 1981, MBA, 1987. Shipping mgr. L&R Mfg., Anaheim, Calif., 1976-78; shipping mgr. Ernie Ball Inc., Newport Beach, Calif., 1978-80; acct. Mobil Oil Corp., L.A., 1980-82, Thums Long Beach Co., Long Beach, 1982-86; founder, chmn. CJ Spice Soft Drink Co., Newport Beach, 1987. Mem. Am. Entrepreneurs Soc. Republican. Roman Catholic. Office: CJ Spice Soft Drink Co 3901 MacArthur Blvd Newport Beach CA 92660

DUFF, ANGUS MACLEAN, pilot; b. Raleigh, N.C., Mar. 25, 1939; s. William Erskine and Martha Lawrence (MacLean) D.; stepson of Louisa Rankin MacIlwinen; m. Harriet Ethel Fielder, Aug. 24, 1964 (div. Oct. 1980); children: Angus MacLean Jr., Ian Lawrence, Duart Sinclair. BA in English, U. N.C., 1961; student, Oxford (Eng.) U., 1961, NYU, 1961-62; MSA in Mgmt., U. Ga., Milledgeville, 1975; postgrad., U. Kans., 1976-78. Lic. comml. pilot, instr. Comml. pilot Trans World Airlines, Kansas City, Mo., 1968-75, Chgo., 1978-80, St. Louis, 1980—. Capt. USAF, 1964-68, 75-77, Vietnam; lt. col. USAFR. Decorated D.F.C.; named Morehead (N.C.) Fedn. U. scholar, 1957, Root-Tilden Fedn. scholar, N.Y.C., 1961. Mem. Airline Pilots Assn., Air Force Assn., Res. Officers Assn. (pres. 1983-85), NRA, Rocky Mountain Elk Fedn., Rocky Mountain Bighorn Soc., St. Andrew Soc., Pikes Peak Scottish Soc., Colo. Hunting Club, N.Am. Hunting Club, Air force Acad. Quarterback Club, Sigma Alpha Epsilon. Republican. Episcopalian. Home: 958D Fontmore Rd Colorado Springs CO 80904 Office: Trans World Airlines Lambert Internat Airport Saint Louis MO 63145

DUFF, DAVID POTTER, lawyer; b. Chgo., Apr. 4, 1947; s. Elmer Potter and Helen Cecelia (Bolger) D. AB in Polit. Sci., U. Ill., 1969; MS in Adminstrn. Justice, So. Ill U., 1972; JD, Washington U., 1975. Bar: Ill. 1975. Prin. David Potter Duff and Assocs., Ltd., Westchester, Ill., 1975—; prof. law DePaul U., Chgo., 1975-82; vis. asst. prof. Northwestern U., Chgo., 1976-77; vis. asst. prof. bus. law and adminstrn. of justice U. Ill., Chgo. 1975—; vis. asst. prof. Loyola U., Chgo., 1976-77. Mem. Am. Trial Lawyers Assn., Ill. Trial Lawyers Assn., ABA, Ill. State Bar Assn.

DUFFY, HARRY ARTHUR, violin expert and dealer; b. Eureka, Calif., Nov. 29, 1915; s. Harry Arthur and Caroline Mary (Reason) D.; m. Clara Nell Cromwell, Oct. 15, 1941 (div. 1971); children: Duane Arthur, Glenn Ellis. AB, BS, U. Calif., Berkeley, 1939; postgrad., San Jose State U., 1939-40. Archivist, appraiser Rembert Wurlitzer, N.Y.C., 1946-70; pres. Harry A. Duffy Violins, Inc., Miami, Fla., 1970-86. 1st lt. U. S. Army, 1941-46. Mem. Westshore Music Club (L.A.), Classical Music Club (San Diego). Episcopalian.

DUFRESNE, ARMAND FREDERICK, management and engineering consultant; b. Manila, Aug. 10, 1917; s. Ernest Faustine and Maude (McClellan) DuF.; m. Theo Rutledge Schaefer, Aug. 24, 1940 (dec. Oct. 1986); children: Lorna DuFresne Turnier, Peter, m. Lois Burrell Klosterman, Feb. 21, 1987. BS, Calif. Inst. Tech., 1938. Dir. quality control, chief product engr. Consol. Electrodynamics Corp., Pasadena, Calif., 1945-61; pres., dir. DUPACO, Inc., Arcadia, Calif., 1961-68; v.p., dir. ORMCO Corp., Glendora, Calif., 1966-68; mgmt., engring. cons., Duarte and Cambria, Calif., 1968—; dir., v.p., sec. Tavis Corp., Mariposa, Calif., 1968-79; dir. Denram Corp., Monrovia, Calif., 1968-70, interim pres., 1970; dir., chmn. bd. RCV Corp., El Monte, Calif., 1968-70; owner DUFCO, Cambria, 1971-82; pres. DUFCO Electronics, Inc., Cambria, Calif., 1982-86, chmn. bd. 1982—; pres. Freedom Designs, Inc., Northridge, Calif., 1982-86, chmn. bd. dirs., 1982—. Patentee in field. Bd. dirs. Arcadia Bus. Assn., 1965-69; bd. dirs. Cambria Community Services Dist., 1976, pres., 1977-80; mem., chmn. San Luis Obispo County Airport Land Use Commn., 1972-75. Served to capt. Signal Corps, AUS, 1942-45. Decorated Bronze Star. Mem. Instrument Soc. Am. (life), Arcadia (dir. 1965-69), Cambria (dir. 1974-75) C. of C., Tau Beta Pi. Home: 901 Iva Ct Cambria CA 93428

DUGAN, DANIEL CARLISLE, aerospace engineer; b. Manila, Phillipines, Oct. 28, 1931; s. Augustine Davis and Dorothy (Carlisle) D.; m. Margaret Ann Muller, Dec. 17, 1955 9div. 1988); children: Jenifer, Daniel, Suzanne, Jessica. BS, U.S. Mil. Acad., 1955; MS, Va. Polytechnic Inst., 1963. Commd. 2nd lt. U.S. Army, 1955; advanced through grades to lt. col. 1955-76, army aviator, 1958-76; experimental test pilot Edwards Air Force Base, 1965-68; unit comdr. Vietnam, 1968-69; ret. 1976; rsch. pilot, aero engr. XV-15 Tiltrotor project NASA, Moffett Field, Calif., 1970-83; asst. br. chief flight ops. NASA, Moffett Field, 1983-86, airworthiness engr., 1986-88, mem. V-22 multisvc. test team, 1988—. Decorated Bronze Star, Air medals, Cross of Gallantry. Fellow Soc. Experimental Test Pilots (assoc.); mem. Am. Helicopter Soc. Republican. Baptist. Home: 4761 La Pinta Way San Jose CA 95129 Office: NASA Ames Rsch Ctr Rotorcraft Tech 237-5 Moffett Field CA 94035

DUGGAN, JOHN PATRICK, aerospace industry security specialist; b. Ann Arbor, Mich., Apr. 30, 1952; s. John Robert and JoAnn Maureen (Thomas) D.; m. Sherrill Lyn Fitzpatrick, Mar. 25, 1972; 1 child, Timothy John. Student, U. Calif., Riverside, 1970-71; BS in Engring. Mgmt., U. Mo., Rolla, 1976. Enlisted USAF, 1972, advanced through grades to capt., 1981; electronic systems br. mgr. USAF, Vandenberg AFB, Calif., 1977-80; ground communications systems mgr. USAF, Vandenberg AFB, 1980-81; resigned USAF, 1981; systems engr. Martin Marietta Corp./Denver Aerospace, Denver, 1981-82; payload integration engr. Martin Marietta Corp./Denver Aerospace, Vandenberg AFB, 1982-85; security engr. The Aerospace Corp., Vandenberg AFB, 1985—; dir. security group, Space Test Range Working Group, Vandenberg AFB, 1987-88; permanent mgr. Titan Security Working Group, Vandenberg AFB, 1987—. Scout leader, Santa Maria (Calif.) area Boy Scouts Am., 1982—; coach, Santa Maria Valley Soccer Assn., 1983-88. Office: Aerospace Corp Bldg 8500 Vandenberg AFB CA 93437

DUHNKE, ROBERT EMMET, JR., aerospace engineer; b. Manitowoc, Wis., Jan. 28, 1935; s. Robert Emmet and Vivian Dorothy (Abel) D.; m. Patricia R. Ebben, 1956 (div. 1972); children: Kim Marie, Lori Ann, Dawn Diane, Robert III, Mary Lynn; m. Judy Anne Lind, Feb. 14, 1978. B of Aero. Engring., Purdue U., 1957. Engr. Convair/Aerodyns. Group, Pomona, Calif., 1957-58; engr., instr. Boeing Co., Seattle, 1964-66, 72-84, engr., analyst mil. div., 1984—; flight navigator Flying Tigers, San Francisco, 1966-68; salesman various real estate and ins. cos., Seattle, 1968-72. Author poems. Mem. Rep. Nat. Com., Washington, Am. Conservative Union, Washington; sponsor World Vision, Pasadena, Calif. Capt. USAF, 1958-64. Recipient Hon. Freedom Fighter award Afghan Mercy Fund, 1987. Mem. AIAA, Mem. Inst. Navigation, Air Force Assn., Wild Goose Assn. Home: 1219 30th St NE Auburn WA 98002

DUKE, GARY PHILIP, architect, developer, broker; b. Chgo., July 25, 1957; s. Godfrey Lawrence and Audrey Louise (Huey) D.; m. Jan Alison Mosteller, May 14, 1983. BS in Architecture, Calif. Polytechnic U., 1979, MBA, 1980. Licensed architect, real estate broker, Calif. Architect Godfrey L. Duke A.I.A., San Diego, 1980-83; facility planner Hotel del Coronado, San Diego, 1983-85; architect, developer Duke Ptnrs., Deerfield, Ill., 1985-88; comml. real estate broker Cushman & Wakefield, L.A., 1988—. Mem. Big Brothers Am., San Luis Obispo, Calif., 1977-80. Recipient First Place award So. Calif. Art Exposition, San Diego, 1975. Mem. Am. Inst. of Architects (pres. assoc. student chpt. San Luis Obispo, Calif., 1979), Calif. Scholarship Found. (life mem.), Culver City C. of C., Toastmasters Club Internat., Kiwanis Club (v.p. Coronado, Calif. 1982-83). Home: 10747 Wilshire Blvd #1205 Los Angeles CA 90024 Office: Cushman & Wakefield 1801 Century Park E Ste 120 Los Angeles CA 90067

DUKE, WILLIAM EDWARD, petroleum company executive; b. Bklyn., July 18, 1932; m. Leilani Kamp Lattin, May 7, 1977; children by previous marriage, William Edward, Jeffrey W., Michael R. BS, Fordham U., 1954. City editor Middletown (N.Y.) Record, 1956-60; asst. state editor Washington Star, 1961-63; exec. asst. to U.S. Senator from N.Y. State, Jacob K. Javits, Washington, 1963-69; dir. pub. affairs Corp. Pub. Broadcasting, Washington, 1969-72; dir. fed. govt. relations Atlantic Richfield Co., Washington, 1973-78, mgr. pub. affairs, Los Angeles, 1978—; lectr. U. So. Calif. Grad. Sch. Journalism, 1988—; cons. in field. Community trustee Greater Washington Ednl. Telecommunications Assn., WETA-TV-FM, chmn. radio com., exec. com., 1976-78; assoc. Ctr. Strategic and Internat. Studies, 1975—. Mem. Pub. Relations Soc. Am. (accredited, bd. dirs. pub. affairs sec., Los Angeles chpt.), Am. Petroleum Inst. Clubs: Nat. Press, Internat., Capitol Hill, Los Angeles Athletic. Office: Atlantic Richfield Co 515 S Flower St Los Angeles CA 90071

DUKES, DAVID (COLEMAN), actor; b. San Francisco, June 6, 1945; s. James Coleman and Keldora (Maples) D.; m. Carolyn Lee McKenzie, Oct. 9, 1965 (div. Feb. 1981); 1 child, Shawn David; m. Carol Anne Muske, Jan. 31, 1983; 1 child, Anne Cameron Muske-Dukes. AA, Coll. of Marin, 1963-66. Appeared with Am. Conservatory Theater, San Francisco, Calif.'s Shakespeare Festival, Los Gatos, Walnut St. Playhouse, Phila., N. Shore Music Theatre, Beverly, Mass., New Phoenix Repertory Co., N.Y.C., Alley Theater, Houston, San Diego Shakespeare Festival, Charles St. Playhouse, Boston, Phila. Drama Guild, Williamstown Summer Theater, Center Theater Group, L.A. (L.A. Drama Critics award), Goodman Theatre, Chgo. (Joseph Jefferson award nomination), Westwood Playhouse (Dramalogue award), others; appeared in Broadway plays including Madam Butterfly, Bent (Tony and Drama Desk nomination), Amadeus, Frankenstein, Dracula, Rebel Women, Rules of the Game, Travesties, Love for Love, Holiday, Chemin de Fer, The Visit, Great God Brown, Don Juan, The Play's the Thing, School for Wives, 1971 (also nat. tour); films include Bullit, 1968, Call Me Mister Tibbs with Sidney Poitier, The Wild Party, A Little Romance with Laurence Olivier, First Deadly Sin with Frank Sinatra, Only When I Laugh, Without A Trace, The Men's Club, Rawhead Rex, Catch the Heat, Date with an Angel, Deadly Intent, 1988, See You in the Morning, 1988; TV appearances include Beacon Hill, Cat on a Hot Tin Roof, Strange Interlude, A Fire in the Sky, Triangle Factory Fire, Some Kind of Miracle, Margaret Sanger - Portrait of a Rebel, Mayflower - Pilgrim Advneture, 79 Park Avenue, The Winds of War, George Washington, Kane and Abel, Space, War and Remembrance, also episodes in series including The Virginian, Police Story, The Jeffersons, Barney Miller, Three's Company, One Day at a Time, All in the Family, others. Mem. Actors Equity Assn., SAG, AFTRA, Acad. Motion Picture Arts and Scis. Office: care Internat Creative Mgmt 8899 Beverly Blvd Los Angeles CA 90048

DUKES, FREDERICK RICE, principal, lecturer; b. Santa Maria, Calif., July 1, 1920; s. Fred Richard and Marie Harriet (Rice) D.; m. Beverly Anne Davis, Dec. 21, 1963. AA, Fullerton (Calif.) Jr. Coll., 1942; BA, Whittier (Calif.) Coll., 1947; MS in Edn., U. So. Calif., L.A., 1958. Cert. elem. tchr., Calif. Jr. high math. tchr. Bakersfield (Calif.) City Schs., 1949-51, tchr. elem., 1952-54, counselor, 1954-56, elem. sch. prin., 1956-80; tchr. elem. L.A. Unified Sch., 1951-52; adj. lectr. in elem. edn. Calif. State U., Bakersfield, 1981—. Mem. Kern County Grand Jury, Bakersfield, 1980, foreman, 1981-82; chmn. Kern County Emergency Food and Shelter Bd., Bakersfield, 1983—, Citizens Adv. Coun. on Enterprise Zone, Bakersfield, 1988—. Named Layman of the Yr., Coun. of Chs., 1967, Vol. Estraordinaire, Salvation Army, 1988; recipient Alfred Harrell-Man of the Yr. award Bakersfield Californian & Vol. Ctr., 1986. Mem. Kern chpt. Calif. Ret. Tchrs. (pres. 1983-85), Sixty Plus (sec. Bakersfield chpt. 1986-88, v.p. 1988—), Phi Delta Kappa (pres. 1962-63, Kappan of the Yr. 1980), Kappa Delta Pi. Republican. Home: 733 Del Mar Dr Bakersfield CA 93307 Office: Calif State U 9001 Stockdale Hwy Bakersfield CA 93311

DULANY, JAY NORMAN, state official; b. Minden, La., Sept. 2, 1944; s. Norman Albertus and Jewel Amazone (Wood) D.; m. Nancy Ann Daugherty, Aug. 30, 1975; children: Mary Ann, Eric Daniel, Shannon Kathleen Elizabeth. BS, La. State U., 1970. Microfilmer La. Dept. Pub. Safety, Baton Rouge, 1966-70; photocopy machine operator Alaska Dept. Pub. Safety, Juneau, 1970-71, statis. clk., 1971-72, rsch. analyst, 1972-75; chief driver improvment Alaska Div. Motor Vehicles, Anchorage, 1975-87, dir., 1987—. Pres. Sand Lake Community Coun., Anchorage, 1984-89. Sgt. USMC, 1962-66. Mem. Am. Soc. for Pub. Adminstrn. (bd. dirs. Alaska chpt. 1987-89, 89-91), Nat. Assn. Adminstrv. Law Judges, Alaska Peace Officers Assn., Am. Assn. Motor Vehicle Adminstrs. (1st v.p. region IV). Home: 3240 W 71st Ave Anchorage AK 99502 Office: Alaska Div Motor Vehicles 5700 E Tudor Rd Anchorage AK 99507

DULBECCO, RENATO, biologist, educator; b. Catanzaro, Italy, Feb. 22, 1914; came to U.S., 1947, naturalized, 1953; s. Leonardo and Maria (Virdia) D.; m. Gulseppina Salvo, June 1, 1940 (div. 1963); children: Peter Leonard (dec.), Maria Vittoria; m. Maureen Muir; 1 dau., Fiona Linsey. M.D., U. Torino, Italy, 1936; D.Sc. (hon.), Yale U., 1968, Vrije Universiteit, Brussels, 1978; LL.D., U. Glasgow, Scotland, 1970. Asst. U. Torino, 1940-47; research asso. Ind. U., 1947-49; sr. research fellow Calif. Inst. Tech., 1949-52, asso. prof., then prof. biology, 1952-63; sr. fellow Salk Inst. Biol. Studies, San Diego, 1963-71; asst. dir. research Imperial Cancer Research Fund, London, 1971-74; dep. dir. research Imperial Cancer Research Fund, 1974-77; disting. research prof. Salk Inst., La Jolla, Calif., 1977—; prof. pathology and medicine U. Calif. at San Diego Med. Sch., La Jolla, 1977-81, mem. Cancer Ctr.,; vis. prof. Royal Soc. Great Britain, 1963-64, Leeuwenhoek lectr., 1974; Clowes Meml. lectr., Atlantic City, 1961; Harvey lectr. Harvey Soc., 1967; Dunham lectr. Harvard U., 1972; 11th Marjory Stephenson Meml. lectr., London, 1973, Harden lectr., Wye, Eng., 1973, Am. Soc. for Microbiology lectr., Los Angeles, 1979; Mem. Calif. Cancer Adv. Council, 1963-67; adv. bd. Roche Inst., N.J., 1968-71, Inst. Immunology, Basel, Switzerland, 1969-84; chmn. sr. council Internat. Assn. Breast Cancer Research, 1980-84; pres., trustee Am.-Italian Found. for Cancer Research. Trustee LaJolla Country Day Sch. Recipient John Scott award City Phila., 1958; Kimball award Conf. Pub. Health Lab. Dirs., 1959; Albert and Mary Lasker Basic Med. Research award, 1964; Howard Taylor Ricketts award, 1965; Paul Ehrlich-Ludwig Darmstaedter prize, 1967; Horwitz prize Columbia U., 1973; (with David Baltimore and Howard Martin Temin) Nobel prize in medicine, 1975; Targa d'oro Villa San Giovanni, 1978; Mandel Gold medal Czechoslovak Acad. Scis., 1982; named Man of Yr. London, 1975; Italian Am. of Yr. San Diego County, Calif., 1978; hon. citizen City of Imperia (Italy), 1983; Guggenheim and Fulbright fellow, 1957-58; decorated grand ufficiale Italian Republic, 1981; hon. founder Hebrew U., 1981. Mem. Nat. Acad. Scis. (Selman A. Waksman award 1974), Am. Acad. Arts and Scis., Am. Assn. Cancer Research, Internat. Physicians for Prevention Nuclear War, Accademia Nazionale dei Lincei (fgn.), Accademia Ligure di Scienze e Lettre (hon.), Royal Soc. (fgn. mem.). Club: Athenaeum. (London). Home: 7525 Hillside Dr La Jolla CA 92037

DULEY, CHARLOTTE DUDLEY, vocational counselor; b. Lincoln, Nebr., Oct. 2, 1920; d. Millard Eugene and Inez Kathryn (Miller) Dudley; student U. Nebr., 1938-41; M.A. in Guidance Counseling, U. Idaho, 1977; B.S., Lewis and Clark State Coll., 1973; m. Phillip D. Duley, Mar. 28, 1942; (dec. Sept. 1984); children: Michael Dudley (dec.), Patricia Kaye. Tchr., Nebr. schs., 1951-56; with Dept. of Employment, Lewiston, Idaho, 1958-81, local office counselor handling fed. tng. programs, 1958-81; ind. job cons.; counselor; rep. Avon, Lewiston; part-time counselor, tester, 1981—. Pres., bd. dirs. Civic Arts, Inc., 1972-81; mem. women's service league Wash.-Idaho Symphony Orch., 1972—; bd. dirs. YWCA, 1980-88, treas., 1981-88; dir. artist series Lewis and Clark State Coll., 1984—. Mem. Am., Idaho personnel guidance Assns., Idaho State Employees Assn., Internat. Assn. Employees in Employment Security, Am. Assn. Counseling & Devel., Idaho State Employment Counselors Assn. (pres. 1979-80), Stateline Guidance and Counseling Assn. (sec.-treas. 1964, 76-77), Lewiston Community Concert Assn. (bd. dirs., pres. 1980—), Greater Lewiston C. of C. (chmn. conv. and tourism com. 1984-87), Altrusa (bd. dirs.), Elks (pres. 1986-87, exec. bd. 1985-88, election bd. chmn. 1986—). Presbyterian. Home: 1819 Ridgeway Dr Lewiston ID 83501

DULGAR, PAM, realtor; b. Glendale, Calif., May 15, 1945; d. John W. Heath and Helen E. (Ruddock) Meusell; m. Thomas G. Dulgar, June 7, 1965 (div. Apr. 1985); 1 child, Brian T. Student, U. Nev., 1963-66; grad., Realtors Inst. Cert. residential specialist. Realtor Lane Ltd., Reno, 1978-80, Dickson Realty, Reno, 1980—; project coordinator Caughlin Ranch Devel., Reno, 1985—, Multiple Listing Service Fairs, 1987; instr. Reno Bd. Realtors, 1985—. Dir. Nev. Self Help Found., Reno, 1987. Named Outstanding Woman Profl. Reno Woman in Bus., 1987. Mem. Reno Bd. Realtors (edn. com. 1984, co-chmn. bldg. com. 1985-87, dir. 1986-88, chmn. strategic planning 1988, awards). Office: Dickson Realty Caughlin Ranch Office 1010 Caughlin Crossing Reno NV 89509

DULIN, PATRICIA ANN, accountant; b. Muleshoe, Tex., Mar. 24, 1952; d. Woodroe G. and Donna (Radosevich) D. BSBA, U. Nev., Las Vegas, 1985. CPA, Nev. Staff acct. Alex Logan & Co., Las Vegas, 1975; staff acct. Goussak & Raben, Ltd., Las Vegas, 1976-84, acct., owner, ptnr., 1980-84; acct., owner, ptnr. Goussak, Raben & Co., Las Vegas, 1984-88, Dulin & Raben, Ltd., Las Vegas, 1988—. Bd. dirs., officer Frontier coun. Girl Scouts U.S.A., 1980—; bd. dirs. Jr. League Las Vegas, 1983—, Clark County chpt. ARC, 1987-89, So. Nev. div. Desert Southwest chpt. Multiple Sclerosis Soc., 1989—. Recipient appreciation pin Frontier coun. Girl Scouts U.S.A., 1986. Mem. AICPA, Nev. Soc. CPA's, Am. Soc. Women Accts. (bd. dirs. officer 1976-79). Office: 1785 E Sahara Ste 245 Las Vegas NV 89104

DULLA, STEVEN GLENN, psychiatrist; b. Chgo., Jan. 6, 1947; s. Steven Joseph and Maureen (Ayers) D.; m. Joan Henley Duhamel, Aug. 14, 1971; children: Christopher, Emily. BS in Pharmacy with honors, Drake U., 1971; MD, U. Central del Este San Pedro de Macoris, Dominican Republic, 1982. Diplomate Am. Bd. Psychiatry and Neurology; registered pharmacist. Pharmacist, asst. mgr. Walgreen Drug Co., Champaign, Ill., 1971-72; pharmacist, mgr. Skelton Pharmacy Inc., Champaign, 1972-75; staff pharmacist, pharmacist in charge of outpatient counseling Northwestern Meml. Hosp., Chgo., 1976-77; rep. med. sales Roche Labs., Rochester, Mich., 1977-78; intern in internal medicine Oakwood Hosp., Dearborn, Mich., 1982-83; resident in psychiat. Maricopa Med. Ctr., Phoenix, 1983-86; staff. psychiatrist C.H.A.P.S., Phoenix, 1984-86, Tri-City Community Mental Health Ctr., Mesa, Ariz., 1985—, Maricopa Med. Ctr., Phoenix, 1986—; pvt. practice Chandler, Ariz., 1988—; lectr. in addiction field; pres. med. staff East Valley Charter Hosp. of Chandler; chmn. pharmacy and therapeutics com. East Valley St. Luke's. Mem. AMA, Am. Acad. Psychiatrist in Alcohol and Addiction, Am. Psychiatric Assn., Ariz. Psychiatric Soc., Phoenix Psychiatric Council. Office: 3200 N Dobson Ste B-3 Chandler AZ 85224

DULLY, FRANK EDWARD, JR., physician, educator; b. Hartford, Conn., Jan. 19, 1932; s. Frank Edward and Monica Theresa (Cooney) D.; m. Rebecca Sue Akers, Apr. 23, 1982; children: Kathleen, Ann, Margaret, David, Nancy, Tammy. BS, Coll. of Holy Cross, 1954; MD, Georgetown U., 1958; MPH, U. Calif., Berkeley, 1970. Diplomate Am. Bd. Preventive

Medicine. Intern D.C. Gen. Hosp., Washington, 1958-59; resident Bridgeport (Conn.) Hosp., 1959-60; pvt. practice Shelton, Conn., 1960-64; commd. lt. USN, 1964, advanced through grades to capt., 1972; served with Destroyer Squadron 14, 1964-65; USN student flight surgeon 1965-66; sr. med. officer USS Hornet, 1966-68, Naval Air Sta., Glynco, Ga., 1968-69; aerospace medicine resident USN, Pensacola, Fla., 1970-72; sr. med. officer USS Enterprise, 1972-74; dir. tng. Naval Aerospace Med. Inst., Pensacola, 1974-77, commdg. officer, 1982-85; sr. med. officer First Marine Aircraft Wing, 1977-78, Pacific Fleet Naval Air Force, 1978-82; aviation safety tchr. U.S. Naval Postgrad. Sch., Monterey, Calif., 1985-87; ret. 1986; assoc. prof. Inst. Safety and Systems Mgmt. U. So. Calif., L.A., 1987—; lectr. aviation safety worldwide, 1978—; tchr. safety N.W. Airlines, Mpls., 1988—. Co-editor: U.S. Navy Flight Surgeon Manual, 1976; contbr. articles on aviation medicine to med. jours. Decorated Legion of Merit, Air medal with oak leaf cluster, Meritorious Svc. medal. Fellow ACP, Am. Coll. Preventive Medicine, Aerospace Med. Assn.; mem. Internat. Acad. Aviation and Space Medicine, Soc. U.S. Naval Flight Surgeons (pres. 1980, 81, 83), Am. Helicopter Soc., Acad. Model Aeros. Republican. Roman Catholic. Home: 854 Anderson Ct Redlands CA 92374

DULMAGE, DONALD WRIGHT, audio-visual producer; b. San Francisco, July 31, 1936; s. Claude Samuel and Archylene Bernice (Wright) D.; m. Bonnie Lillian Goodrich, Nov. 24, 1957; children—Debora Dawn Dulmage Moore, Christopher Wright. B.A., Stanford U., 1958. Dir. photography Sta. KNTV, San Jose, Calif., 1962-69; free lance audio-visual producer, 1964-69; founder Panorama Prodns., Santa Clara, Calif., 1969, pres., owner, 1972—; advisor De Anza Coll., Foothill Coll. Ford Found. fellow, 1957-58; recipient IFPA Cindy awards, SJAC Murphy awards, SFAC awards, AMI awards, others. Mem. Profl. Photographers Am., Info. Film Producers Am., San Jose Ad Club, San Francisco Ad Club, Profl. Photographers Greater Bay Area, Profl. Photographers Calif., others. Republican. Methodist. Club: Decathlon. Office: 2353 De La Cruz Blvd Santa Clara CA 95050

DUMAINE, R. PIERRE, bishop; b. Paducah, Ky., Aug. 2, 1931; student St. Joseph Coll., Mountain View, Calif., 1945-51, St. Patrick Sem., Menlo Park, Calif., 1951-57; Ph.D., Cath. U. Am., 1962. Ordained priest Roman Cath. Ch., 1957; asst. pastor Immaculate Heart Ch., Belmont, Calif., 1957-58; mem. faculty dept. edn. Cath. U. Am., 1961-63; tchr. Serra High Sch., San Mateo, Calif., 1963-65; asst. supt. Cath. schs., Archdiocese of San Francisco, 1965-74, supt., 1974-78; ordained bishop, 1978, bishop of San Jose, Calif., 1981—; dir. Archdiocesan Ednl. TV Ctr., Menlo Park, Calif., 1968-81. Mem. Pres.'s Nat. Adv. Council on Edn. of Disadvantaged Children, 1970-72; bd. dirs. Cath. TV Network, 1968-81, pres., 1975-77; bd. dirs. Pub. Service Satellite Consortium, 1975-81. Mem. Nat. Cath. Edn. Assn., Assn. Cath. Broadcasters and Allied Communicators, Internat. Inst. Communications, Assn. Calif. Sch. Adminstrs. Office: St Patrick Cathedral 389 E Santa Clara St San Jose CA 95113 *

DUMBRILL, RICHARD SPENCER, lawyer; b. Traverse City, Mich., Mar. 26, 1926; s. Harold Ray and Frances Fern (Spencer) D.; m. Lucille Clarke; children: Deborah Jane McLeland, Richard Douglas, John Clarke. BA, U. Wyo., 1951, JD, 1951. Bar: Wyo. 1952. Dep. county atty. Newcastle, Wyo., 1952-60; atty. City of Newcastle, 1960-68, Town of Upton (Wyo.), 1976-87; sch. dist. atty. Dist. #1, Newcastle, 1966-87, Dist. #7, Upton, 1966-87. Chmn. Alan Simpson for Senate, Weston County, Wyo., 1979, 85, Newcastle Pageant Com., 1974; pres. Anna Miller Mus. Bd., Weston County, 1965-72. Served as T-5, U.S. Army, 1944-46. Recipient Community Service award, City of Newcastle, 1974. Mem. ABA, Wyo. State Bar Assn. (bar commr. 1957-59, mem. several bar coms.), Wyoming State Hist. Soc. (pres. 1975-76, L.C. Bishop award 1974), Am. Family Forum (pres. 1982-83). Republican. Methodist. Lodge: Lions (pres. 1965-66).

DUMINY, MARTIAL ANDREW, physician assistant; b. New Orleans, Mar. 29, 1947; d. Manuel Andrew Duminy and Ethel Gloria (Dedeaux) Hammond; m. Karen Laurent, Oct. 1966 (div. 1972); 1 child, Kimberly Ann; m. Kalliope G. Chrissikis, Nov. 21, 1980; children: Anthony G.W., Adrienne G. AA, Sacramento City Coll., 1972; physician asst., Charles R. Drew Med. Sch., 1981. Cert. physician asst. Physician asst. primary care Santa Clara County Health Dept., San Jose, Calif., 1981-87, San Joaquin County Local Health Dept., Stockton, Calif., 1987-88, San Joaquin Gen. Hosp., Stockton, 1988—; cons. drug abuse State of Calif. Bd. Med. Quality Assurance, Sacramento, Calif., 1988—. Served to sgt. U.S. Air Force, 1965-69. Fellow Am. Acad. Physician Assts., Calif. Acad. Physician Assts.; mem. Am. Pub. Health Assn. Democrat. Roman Catholic. Home: 2114 Atchenson St Stockton CA 95210

DUNAWAY, DAVID R., construction executive, business owner; b. Kansas City, Kans., Apr. 20, 1939; s. Raymond John and Martha Cathryn (Whittelsey) D. BA in Sociology, Duke U., 1971; postgrad., U. Nev., 1979-81. Tight end receiver Green Bay (Wis.) Packers, 1966-68, Atlanta Falcons, 1969, N.Y. Giants, N.Y.C., 1969-72; owner, gen. contractor Custom Home Builder, L.A., 1973-79, Las Vegas, Nev., 1979—. Mem. spl. events com. Am. Cancer Soc., Las Vegas, 1980-82; counselor nutrition and weight tng. Child SuperStar Program, L.A., 1977—; with spl. events com. Muscular Dystrophy Assn., Las Vegas, 1989—, Make-A-Wish Found., Las Vegas, 1989—; mem. Rep. Senatorial Inner Circle, 1988. Mem. NFL (bd. dirs. Las Vegas chpt. 1989—), Nat. Football League Alumni Assn. (bd. dirs. Las Vegas chpt. 1986), Nat. Football League Players Assn., Nat. Home Builders Assn., Am. Golf Assn. Presbyterian. Home: 6136 Oakhaven Ln Las Vegas NV 89108

DUNAWAY, MARGARET ANN (MAGGIE DUNAWAY), consultant; b. Fresno, Calif., Feb. 10, 1943; d. Joseph John and Anna Frances (Dice) Cumero; children from previous marriage Christian Anthony Freitag, Erika Lynn Freitag. Student, U. Calif., Davis, 1960-62, U. Calif., Berkeley, 1962-63. Supr. Gov's Office, Sacramento, 1969-72; office mgr. State Health and Welfare Agy., Sacramento, 1972-73; analyst regulations devel. Calif. State Depts. Health and Social Services, Sacramento, 1974-84, cons. adult and children's services, 1984—, rep. adult svcs., 1986-87, with food drive com., 1987-88, rep. ind. living program com., 1989—. Active Southpark Homeowner's Assn., Sacramento, 1974-78; presenter Adult Svcs. Ann. Asilomar Conf., 1987. Office: Calif Dept Social Svcs 744 P St MS 6-532 Sacramento CA 95814

DUNAWAY, SUZANNE SHIMEK, entrepreneur; b. Dallas, July 20, 1940; d. E. Joe and Evelyn E. S.; m. Winston Brock Chappell; (div.); m. Don Carlos Dunaway Jr.; 2 step children. Student, Sweet Briar U. Tex., Berkeley, 1981. Illustrator L.A. Times Gourmet Mag., L.A. West, The New Yorker. Episcopalian. Home: 10333 Chrysanthemum Ln Los Angeles CA 90077

DUNAWAY, TRUDY VINCENT, medical service executive; b. Detroit, Sept. 29, 1951; d. Clarence Eugene and Hilda Anne (Hearn) Vincent; m. Michael Wicks Dunaway, June 21, 1980; children: E. Kelly, Ginny Anne, Rebecca Anne, Patrick Michael. BS in Biology, U. Detroit, 1973. Cert. clin. perfusionist. Respiratory therapist Shadyside Hosp., Pitts., 1973-74; v.p. ops., asst. sec. PSICOR, San Diego, 1974-88, also bd. dirs. Mem. Am. soc. Extracorporeal Technologists. Roman Catholic. Home: 18075 Polvera Way San Diego CA 92128 Office: PSICOR 16818 Via Del Campo Ct San Diego CA 92127

DUNBAR, PATRICIA LYNN, new product development consultant; b. St. Louis, Feb. 11, 1953; d. William R. and Beryl Ione Noland (Ferrand) Dunbar; m. Michael R. Jeffrey, Oct. 2, 1950. BS, Northwestern U., 1973, MFA, 1975. With NBC-TV, Chgo., 1975-79; regional sales/mktg. mgr. Home Box Office, Chgo., 1979-81; sr. product mgr. Bank of Am., San Francisco, 1981-82, v.p., 1982-84; interactive communications services cons., 1984—. Mem. Women in Cable (1st pres. Chgo. chpt. 1981), Jr. League Seattle. Episcopalian. Patentee on child's chair, 1973.

DUNBAR, RICHARD PAUL, sales representative; b. Watertown, S.D., Aug. 28, 1951; s. Earl Paul and Leona Matilda (Clausen) D. Student, S.D. State U., 1969-71; BSBA, U. Ariz., 1981. Account mgr. bus. forms and supplies div. Nat. Cash Register, Phoenix, 1981-83; sales cons. Compugraphic Corp., Phoenix, 1983-84; sales rep. constrn. products div. W.R. Grace and Co., Phoenix and Tucson, 1985-87; sales rep. constrn. products div. for Ariz. and so. Nev. region Pleko Southwest, Inc., Tempe, Ariz., 1987—. Mem. Jaycees (treas. 1977-78, recipient Outstanding Jaycee award, Pres.'s award and Jaycee of the Month award), Constrn. Specifications Inst. (program chmn. Phoenix chpt. 1987—, chmn.tech. documents com. 1986-87, bd. dirs. Phoenix chpt. 1988—recipient pres.'s award 1987-88), Constrn. Products Mfrs. Council (treas. 1985-86), Alpha Mu Alpha. Republican. Congregational. Office: Pleko Southwest Inc 1824 E 6th St Tempe AZ 85281

DUNBAR, ROBERT GEORGE, historian, educator; b. LaGrange, Wis., Apr. 30, 1907; s. Charles Sales and Johannah (Van de Vrede) D.; B.A., Miltoh Coll., 1929; M.A., U. Wis., 1933, Ph.D., 1935; m. Mary Snell Albertson, June 19, 1937; children—Ann Marie, George Roger. High sch. tchr., Colby, Wis., 1929-31; asst. prof. history U. S.D., 1935-37; faculty Colo. State U., 1937-47, asso. prof., 1943-47; faculty Mont. State U., Bozeman, 1947—, prof. history, 1950-72, emeritus prof., 1972—, dir. Center for Intercultural Programs, 1966-72. Served with USNR, 1944-45. Mem. Orgn. Am. Historians, Agrl. History Soc. (pres. 1966-67), Western History Assn. (award of honor 1978), Phi Kappa Phi, Phi Alpha Theta. Author: Farmer and the American Way, 1952; Forging New Rights in Western Waters, 1983; editorial bd. Agrl. History, 1943-77. Home: 715 S Grand Ave Bozeman MT 59715

DUNCAN, ANSLEY MCKINLEY, aerospace company manager; b. Homer City, Pa., Jan. 25, 1932; s. William McKinley and Marion Melissa (Davis) D.; student U. Denver, 1955-57, Pa. State U., 1957-59. Engring. adminstr. RCA, Van Nuys, Calif., 1959-61; program evaluation coordinator N.Am. Aviation, Anaheim, Calif., 1961-66; mfg. supr., Rockwell Internat., Anaheim Calif., 1966-70, program adminstr., 1970-76, program controls mgr., 1976-81, plans/schedule advisor, 1981—. Served with USN, 1951-55. Home: 12600 Willowood Ave Garden Grove CA 92640 Office: 3370 Miraloma Ave Anaheim CA 92803

DUNCAN, DONALD KEITH, educator; b. Nashua, Mont., Oct. 26, 1926; s. Merle Dewey and Pearl Irene (Sha) D.; m. Irene Florence Lando, June 25, 1950; children: Gary Brian, Diane Susan. BS in Edn., U. So. Calif., 1950, MS in Edn., 1957, EdD, 1964. Tchr. L.A. City Unified Sch. Dist., 1950-54; prin. Torrance (Calif.) Unified Sch. Dist., 1954-60, curriculum cons., 1960-69; asst. dir. L.A. County Office Edn., Downey, Calif., 1969-83, dir. curriculum and instructional programs, 1983--. Bd. dirs. Torrance YMCA, 1954-69. With USN, 1944-46, PTO. Recipient Golden Apple award Torrance Adminstrs. Assn., 1969. Mem. Constl. Rights Found. (chmn. edn. adv. com. 1984--), U. So. Calif. Edn. Alumni Assn. (pres. 1980), Calif. Assn. for Gifted (past pres.), Assn. Calif. Sch. Adminstrs. (chmn. curriculum and instrn. leaders com. 1986-89), Region 14 Assn. Calif. Sch. Adminstrs. (pres. 1980-81), Toastmasters (pres. 1960-61). Home: 2785 Vista Mesa Dr Rancho Palos Verdes CA 90274 Office: Los Angeles County Office Edn 9300 E Imperial Hwy Downey CA 90242

DUNCAN, JOHN WILEY, air force officer, educator; b. San Francisco, Aug. 8, 1947; s. Vernon Alexander and Nellie May (Shaw) D.; m. Trudy Rae Hirsch, Feb. 25, 1967; children: Amber Rose, John Anthony. BS in Math. and Physics, N.W. Mo. State U., 1969; MBA, So. Ill. U., 1973; MS in Computer Sci., U. Tex., San Antonio, 1982. Tchr. Savannah (Mo.) High Sch., 1969; enlisted USAF, 1969, advanced through grades to maj.; aeromed. ops. officer UTSA, Clark Air Base, The Philippines, 1978-80, Clark Air Base, 1981-82; chief implementation team Sch. Health Care Scis./Med. Systems Div., Sheppard AFB, Tex., 1982-83; asst. chief med. systems Hdqrs. Air Tng. Command, Randolph AFB, Tex., 1983-86; chief med. systems Hdqrs. Pacific AF, Hickham AFB, Hawaii, 1986-89, 15 Med. Group, Hickham AFB, Hawaii, 1989—; computer cons., 1983—; instr. Tex. Luth Coll., Seguin, 1984-86, Hawaii Pacific Coll., Honolulu, 1987—, Leeword Community Coll, 1989. Cons. Ronald McDonald House, San Antonio, 1986. Presbyterian. Office: 15 Medical Group Hickam AFB HI 96853-5300

DUNCAN, JOHNNY LEE, electrical engineer; b. Adair, Okla., Feb. 2, 1939; s. Lloyd Talbot Duncan and Ruby Adelia Jeans; m. Kerin Dale Boston, June 17, 1961; children: Glenn Keith, David Lloyd (dec.), Melinda Elizabeth. AA, Northeastern Okla. A&M U., 1959; BSEE, Okla. State U., 1962; MSEE, U. N.Mex., 1964. Mem. staff Sandia Labs., Albuquerque, 1962—, div. supr., 1969—, test mgr. cruise missile warhead, 1978-82, test and evaluation mgr. Trident II fuze, 1982-88; mem. Trident II Blue Ribbon Com., 1986-87; mgr. stockpile evaluation All Nuclear Bombs, 1989—. With U.S. Army, 1957. Mem. IEEE (sr.). Republican. Baptist. Home: 10820 Nelle St Albuquerque NM 87111 Office: Kirtland AFB Sandia Labs Albuquerque NM 87185

DUNCAN, LINDA HELEN, elementary school teacher; b. Fitchburg, Mass., Sept. 10, 1947; d. Arvo Theodore and Helen (Kukkula) Heikkila; m. William David Duncan, Dec. 22, 1971; stepchildren: Joye Brady, Glen Scot, Jill Becksted, Jana Brinkman. AA, Palm Beach Jr. Coll., 1967; BA, Fla. Atlantic U., 1970; MEd, Utah State U., 1978. Cert. tchr., Wyo. Elem. sch. tchr. Rock Springs (Wyo.) Sch. Dist. 1, 1970-72; elem. sch. tchr. Green River (Wyo.) Sch. Dist. 2, 1972—, local young author program coordinator, 1981—. Recipient State K-3 1st Place award Wyo. Ednl. Media Assn., 1984, 2d Place, 1985, 3d Place, 1987, 2d Place, 1988. Mem. NEA, Green River Edn. Assn., Wyoming Edn. Assn., Beta Sigma Phi. Democrat. Congregationalist. Office: Wilson Elem Sch 351 Monroe Ave Green River WY 82934

DUNCAN, RALPH EDGAR, military officer; b. Memphis, Nov. 18, 1943; s. Ralph Hugh and Mary Virginia (Crowder) D.; m. Sandra Jeanne Lay, June 25, 1967; children: Susan Kimberly, Matthew Allen. BS, Georgetown (Ky.) Coll., 1965; MA, Webster U., 1976. Commd. 2d lt. USAF, 1966, advanced through grades to col., 1988, various assignments as fighter pilot, 1968-80; dir. F-16 flight test USAF, Wright Patterson AFB, Ohio, 1980-84; chief of safety USAF, George AFB, Calif., 1984-86, squadron ops. officer, 1985-86, squadron comdr., 1986-88, base comdr., 1988—. Decorated DFC, Air medals. Mem. Air Force Assn., Rotary, Foot Printers, Victorville C. of C., Order of Daedalians. Home: 1 Nevada George AFB CA 92354 Office: USAF 831CSG/CC George AFB CA 92394

DUNCAN, RICHARD FREDRICK, JR., educator, travel consultant; b. Millry, Ala., July 12, 1947; s. Richard F. and Claire Louise (Wood) D.; m. Rebecca Susan Davis, July 14, 1973. AA, Okaloosa-Walton Jr. Coll., 1967; BS, Fla. State U., 1969, MS, 1971; postgrad., Ore. State U., 1981-82. Tchr. Gadsden County Sch. Bd., Quincy, Fla., 1970-71, Leon County Sch. Bd., Tallahassee, Fla., 1972-73, Beaverton (Ore.) Sch. Dist. No. 48, Ore., 1973--; microbiologist Washington County, Hillsboro, Ore., 1971-72; cons. on sci. edn. Northwest Regional Ednl. Lab., Portland, Ore., 1978-79; cons. on marine edn. Ore. Dept. Edn., Salem, 1980-81. Recipient award for excellence in sci. teaching Ore. Mus. Sci. and Industry, Portland, 1984, Psdl. award, 1984. Mem. Assn. Presdl. Awardees in Sci. Teaching (nat. pres. 1987-88), Nat. Assn.Biology Tchrs. (Ore. Biology Tchr. of Year award 1981), Nat. Sci. Tchrs. Assn. (Presdl. award for excellence in sci. teaching, 1983), Ore. Sci. Tchrs. Assn. (pres. 1980-81, Ore. Jr. High Tchr. of Yr. award 1982), North Assn. Marine Educators (state dir. 1978-80), Masons, Shriners. Democrat. Home: 13240 SW Juanita Pl Beaverton OR 97005 Office: Beaverton Sch Dist #48 PO Box 200 Beaverton OR 97075

DUNCAN, TIMOTHY HAROLD, computer systems specialist; b. Washington, Sept. 20, 1959; s. Burris Richard and Nancy Lee (Poos) D.; m. Maria Thelma Alves, Dec. 27, 1980; children: David, Benjamin. BArch, U. Ariz., 1984. Cert. Starlan network adminstr., system mgr., novel network adminstr. Asst. systems mgr. Haver, Nunn and Coll, Phoenix, 1984-86; mgr. computer systems Anderson, DeBartolo Pan, Inc., Tucson, 1986—. Mem. Ariz. Intergraph Users Assn. (sec. 1988—), Nat. Computer Graphics Assn., Autocad User Group. Republican. Home: 5574 E Glenn St Apt D Tucson AZ 85712 Office: Anderson DeBartolo Pan Inc 2480 N Arcadia Ave Tucson AZ 85712

DUNCAN, VERNE ALLEN, state education official; b. McMinnville, Oreg., Apr. 6, 1934; s. Charles Kenneth and S. La Verne (Robbins) D.; m. Donna Rose Nichols, July 11, 1964; children—Annette Marie Kirk, Christine Lauree. B.A., Idaho State U., 1960, M.Ed., 1964; Ph.D., U. Oreg., 1968; M.B.A., U. Portland, 1976. Tchr. Butte County (Idaho) Pub. Schs., 1954-56, prin., 1958-63, supt. schs., 1963-66; research asst. U. Oreg., 1966-68, asst. prof. ednl. adminstrn., 1968-70; supt. Clackamas County (Oreg.) Intermediate Edn. Dist., 1970-75; supt. pub. instruction State of Oreg., 1975—; chmn. commn. on ednl. credits and credentials Am. Council on Edn.; commr. Gov's Commn. on Futures Research; mem. Edn. Commn. of States. Author numerous articles on ednl. adminstrn. Trustee Marylurst Coll.; bd. dirs. Oreg. Hist. Soc.; mem. Gov's. State Job Tng. Coordinating Council; mem. Idaho Ho. of Reps., 1962-65, chmn. econ. affairs com.; mem. interim com. Oreg. Legis. Assembly Improvements Com. Served with U.S. Army, 1956-58. Mem. Am. Assn. Sch. Adminstrs., Council Chief State Sch. Officers (pres. 1988), Res. Officers Assn., Nat. Forum Edn. Leaders, Phi Delta Kappa (Educator-Statesman of Yr. award 1977). Republican. Presbyterian. Home: 16911 SE River Rd Milwaukie OR 97267 Office: Oreg Dept Edn 700 Pringle Pkwy SE Salem OR 97310

DUNCAN, WILLIAM LOUIS, photographer, educator; b. Salt Lake City, Nov. 17, 1945; s. Louis William and Mae U. (Jeppsen) D.; m. Marilyn Bardsley, Apr. 1, 1968; children: Cindy Kay, Gay Linn, LeAnn Dawn. Student, U. Utah, 1964-68; grad., Famous Artists Sch., Westport, Conn., 1969; M Photography, Profl. Photographers Am., New Orleans, 1989. Advt. artist Ross Jurney Advt. Agy., Salt Lake City, 1967-71; artist, prodn. lithographer Blaine Hudson Printing Co., Salt Lake City, 1971-73; artist, prodn. camerman Rocky Mountain Bank Note Co., Salt Lake City, 1973-74; artist, photographer Skaggs Cos. Inc., Salt Lake City, 1974-76; owner, mgr. Duncan Photography Studio, Salt Lake City, 1976—; tech. and pub. affairs photographer, technician Hercules Aerospace Co., Magna, Utah, 1984—; tchr. photography high schs., Salt Lake City, 1976, 77, 78, profl. photog. orgns., Miss., Salt Lake City, Wash., Denver, Idaho, 1985—, bus. and comml. orgns., Salt Lake City, 1987, 88. Contbr. illustrated articles to profl. publs. Photog. judge Utah Fair Expns., 1978-88. Recipient award Hallmark Color Labs., 1982, award of excellence Kodak Gallery, 1988, 89, Best of Show award Utah Div. Expns., 1981, 82, Salt Lake County Fair Assn., 1982, 88, also numerous awards from photog. assns. Mem. Profl. Photographers Am. (cert., nat. photog. judge 1982—, numerous awards), Wedding Photographers Internat. (life, awards 1973—, award of excellence 1989), Rocky Mountain Profl. Photographers Assn. (conv. bd. 1987), Intermountain Profl. Photographers Assn. (bd. dirs. 1980-86, program dir., conv. dir. 1985-86), Photog. Soc. Am. (instr. 1986—). Republican. Mormon. Office: 4915 S 3200 West Salt Lake City UT 84118

DUNCOMBE, PATRICIA WARBURTON, social worker; b. London, Jan. 30, 1925; came to U.S., 1940.; d. P.G. Eliot and Mary Louise (Thompson) Warburton; m. David S. Duncombe, July 11, 1947 (dec. Apr. 1976); children: Elizabeth, Mari, Edward, David, Peter. BA, Barnard Coll., 1944; MS in Social Work, Columbia U., 1947. Cert. social worker. Social worker YWCA, Chgo., Evanston, Ill., 1947-50, B.I.A., Elko, Nev., 1966-67, Nev. State Welfare Div., Elko, Nev., 1967-69; dir. St. Michael's Youth Residence, Ethete, Wyo., 1970-76; asst. prof. U. Wyo., Laramie, 1976-83; program dir. St. Jude's Ranch, Boulder City, Nev., 1983-85; med. social worker home health agys., Las Vegas, Nev., 1985—. Author: Within the Circle, 1981; contbr. articles to profl. jours. Mem. Wyo. Commn. for Women, 1971-83, chmn., 1975-77; bd. dirs. SE Wyo. Mental Health, 1980-83. Named Mother of Yr., Clark County, Nev., 1985. Mem. AAUW (nat. bd. 1983-85), Nat. Assn. Social Workers (chpt. pres. 1979, 81, commn. on women 1977-79, exec. dir. Nev. chpt. 1985—, Social Worker of Yr. Wyo. chpt. 1980), Phi Theta Kappa. Democrat. Episcopalian. Club: Mesquite (Las Vegas) (treas. 1987-88).

DUNFORD, CRAIG RUSSELL, optician; b. Provo, Utah, Sept. 11, 1948; s. A. Rex and Beverly (Duckett) D.; m. Sherrie Lynn Farr, May 27, 1970; children: Nathan, Bonnie, Amy, Lynsie, Steven. Student, Brigham Young U., 1967-70. Rd. mgr. The Lettermen, Beverly Hills, Calif., 1966-67; mgr. Vista Optical, Provo, 1975-78, Benson Optical, Provo, 1978-88, Cottontree Optical, Provo, 1988—. 1st tenor Payson Civic Chorale, World Fair, New Orleans, 1984, Mexico City tour, 1988. Mem. steering com. 1st Internat. Latter-day Saints Explorado, 1964; asst. to pres. Latter-day Saints Mission, Uruguay, Paraguay, 1969; pres. Payson (Utah) Community Theatre, 1988. Named Top Nat. Performer, Am. Optical, 1986, Benson Optical, 1986. Fellow Am. Bd. Opticianry, Opticians Assn. Am.; mem. Timp Lions, Sertoma Club, Kiwanis. Republican. Mormon. Home: 355 S 300W Payson UT 84651 Office: Cottontree Optical 2230 N University Pkwy Provo UT 84604

DUNIGAN, PAUL FRANCIS XAVIER, JR., federal agency administrator; b. Richland, Wash., June 22, 1948; s. Paul Frances Xavier Sr. and Eva Lucille (Reckley) D.; m. Elizabeth Anne Henricks, Apr. 8, 1978; children: Katherine Anne, Theresa Anne. BS in Biology, Gonzaga U., 1970; MS in Environ. Sci., Washington State U., 1973. Tech. program mgr. ERDA, AEC, Richland, 1972-75; environ. biologist U.S. Dept. Energy, ERDA, Richland, 1975-81; waste mgmt. engr. U.S. Dept. Energy Waste Mgmt., Richland, 1981-84; civilian program mgr. Surplus Facilities Mgmt. Program U.S. Dept. Energy, Richland, 1984-87, environ. biologist, 1987—. Contbr. articles to profl. jours. Named Eagle Scout Boy Scouts Am., 1962. Mem. AAAS, Water Pollution Control Fedn., Pacific Northwest Pollution Control Fedn. Roman Catholic. Home: 1612 Judson Richland WA 99352 Office: US Dept Energy PO Box 550 Richland WA 99352

DUNIN, ELSIE IVANCICH, dance educator; b. Chgo., July 19, 1935; d. Frank and Ilona (Pazman) Ivancich; m. Stanley Dunin, June 14, 1958; children: Elonka, Teresa. BA, UCLA, 1957, MA, 1966. From lectr. to prof. dept. dance UCLA, 1968—. Contbr. articles to profl. jours. Mem. Congress on Rsch. in Dance (treas.1980-82), Gypsy Lore Soc. (exec. bd. dirs. North Am. chpt. 1982-85), Dance Notation Be. (profl. bd. 1984-86). Office: UCLA Dept Dance 124 Dance Bldg Los Angeles CA 90024

DUNIPACE, IAN DOUGLAS, lawyer; b. Tucson, Dec. 18, 1939; s. William Smith and Esther Morvyth (McGeorge) D.; B.A. magna cum laude, U. Ariz., 1961; J.D. cum laude, 1966; m. Janet Mae Dailey, June 9, 1963; children: Kenneth Mark, Leslie Amanda. Reporter, critic Long Branch (N.J.) Daily Record, 1963; admitted to Ariz. bar, 1966, U.S. Supreme Ct. bar, 1972; assoc. firm Jennings, Strouss, Salmon & Trask, Phoenix, 1966-69, Jennings, Strouss & Salmon, 1969-70, ptnr., 1971—. Reporter, Phoenix Forward Edn. Com., 1969-70; bd. mgmt. Downtown Phoenix YMCA, 1973-80, chmn., 1977-78; bd. dirs. Phoenix Met. YMCA, 1976-87, 89—, chmn., 1984-85; bd. mgmt. Paradise Valley YMCA, 1979-82, chmn., 1980-81; bd. mgmt. Scottsdale/Paradise Valley YMCA, 1983, mem. legal affairs com. Pacific Region YMCA, 1978-81; bd. dirs. Beaver Valley Improvement Assn., 1977-79, Pi Kappa Alpha Holding Corp., 1968-72; trustee Paradise Valley Unified Sch. Dist. Employee Benefit Trust, 1980—, chmn., 1987—; trustee First Meth. Found. of Phoenix, 1984—; mem. Greater Paradise Valley Community Council, 1985-87. Served to capt. AUS, 1961-63. Mem. State Bar Ariz. (securities regulation sect. 1970—, sect. council 1983—, sec. 1987-88, budget officer 1988-89, vice chmn. 1989—, mem. sect. unauthorized practice of law 1972-84, chmn. 1975-83, mem. corp. law sect. 1981—, chmn., 1984-85), Am., Fed. (sec. Ariz. chpt. 1978-79, pres. 1980-81), Maricopa County bar assns., Ariz. Zool. Soc., U. Ariz. Law Coll. Assn. (bd. dirs. 1983—, pres. 1985-86), Heard Mus. Mens Coun., Smithsonian Assn., U. Ariz. Alumni Assn. (bd. dirs. 1985-86), Phi Beta Kappa, Phi Kappa Phi, Phi Delta Phi, Phi Alpha Theta, Sigma Delta Pi, Phi Eta Sigma, Pi Kappa Alpha (nat. counsel 1968-72). Democrat. Methodist (mem. met. Phoenix commn. 1968-71, lay leader 1975-78, trustee 1979-81, pres. 1981; mem. Pacific S.W. ann. conf. 1969-79, lawyer commn. 1980-85, chancellor Desert S.W. ann. conf. 1985—). Clubs: Mansion, Renaissance. Lodges: Masons, Kiwanis (pres. Phoenix 1984-85, lt. gov. 1986-87, SW dist. community service chmn. 1987-88, mem. internat. com. on Project 39, 1988-89, trustee SW dist. found. 1987—). Comments editor Ariz. Law Rev., 1965-66. Home: 3601 E Mountain View Phoenix AZ 85028 Office: Jennings Strouss & Salmon 2 N Central 1 Renaissance Sq Phoenix AZ 85004-2393

DUNLAP, CHARLES LEE, oil and refining company executive; b. Milw., May 3, 1943; s. Charles Ewing and Helen Florence (Chelminiak) D.; m. Carol Elise Jones, Feb. 3, 1968; children: Kristin, Megan, Charles. AB with honors, Rockhurst Coll., 1965; LLB, St. Louis U., 1968. Bar: Wis. 1968, Mo. 1968. Assoc. corp. counsel Clark Oil & Refining Corp., Milw., 1969-75, corp. sec., sr. corp. counsel, 1975-79; v.p. crude oil supply and transp. Clark

Oil & Refining Corp., Dallas, 1979-82; mgr. crude oil acquisition and sales Atlantic Richfield Co., Los Angeles, 1982-84, mgr. refining supply and crude oil trading, 1984-85; exec. v.p. Pacific Resources, Inc., Honolulu, 1985—, also bd. dirs. Regent Chaminade U., Honolulu, 1986—; trustee Hist. Hawaii Found., Honolulu, 1987, Palama Settlement, Honolulu, 1987, PRI Found., Honolulu, 1987; bd. dirs. Econ. Devel. Coun. Honolulu, 1987, Hawaii Food Bank, 1988—, Boys and Girls Club Honolulu, 1989—; mem. exec. coun. Aloha coun. Boy Scouts Am., 1988—. Thomas More fellow St. Louis U. Law Sch., 1965-68. Mem. Am. Petroleum Inst., Wis. Bar Assn., Mo. Bar Assn., Nat. Petroleum Refiners Assn. (bd. dirs. 1985—), Navy League, Wailae Country Club, Jonathan Club, Pacific Club, Plaza Club. Office: Pacific Resources Inc 733 Bishop St Honolulu HI 96813

DUNLAP, JAMES RILEY, SR., financial executive, credit manager; b. Portland, Oreg., May 21, 1925; s. William Gates and Laura (Riley) D.; m. Betty Towe; children: James R. Jr., Brian Jay, William David. BSBA, U. Oreg., 1950; postgrad., Portland State Coll., 1963-65. Sales rep. Hyster Co., Portland, 1950-61; br. asst. mgr. Reynolds Metals Co., Portland, 1961-71; corp. credit mgr. Burns Bros. Inc., Portland, 1971-79, sec.-treas., 1979—. Contbr. articles on credit and fin. mgmt. to profl. jours. With USAAF, 1943-46. Mem. Nat. Assn. Credit Mgmt. (past pres., bd. dirs.), Internat. Assn. Credit Mgmt. (past pres., bd. dirs., Disting. Svc. award 1985, Herb Barnes Meml. award 1987), Portland Retail Credit Assn. (past pres., bd. dirs.), Oreg. State Cons. Credit Assn. (past pres., lifetime bd. dirs.), Portland J. C. of C., Oreg. Motor Supply Credit Assn. (past pres., bd. dirs.), Consumer Counseling Svc. Oreg. (exec. com. 1979—), Am. Contract Bridge League (past pres. Portland chpt., life master), Lions (past pres. local club), Masons, Elks, Delta Tau Delta Alumni Assn. (past pres.). Office: Burns Bros Inc 511 SE Morrison St Ste 1200 Portland OR 97214

DUNLAP, RON, investment securities branch manager; b. South Bend, Ind., Oct. 31, 1937; s. Claude Delbert and Thelma Marie (Sanner) D.; m. Allison Marie Dale, Oct. 12, 1966; children: Marcia Marie, Lynne Marie. BS, Purdue U., 1959, MS, 1961. Engr. Boeing Co., Seattle, 1962-74, fin. analyst, 1974-80; exec. King Co., Seattle, 1981-82; resident mgr. Dain Bosworth, Bellevue, Wash., 1982--. State rep. U.S. Ho. of Reps., Olympia, 1974-80; candidate U.S. Congress, Washington, 1980. Mem. Rotary. Republican. Office: Dain Bosworth 10900 NE 4th St Ste 1400 Seattle WA 98004

DUNLEVIE, ERNIE G., realtor; b. N.Y.C., Aug. 3, 1917; s. George B. and Adelaide (Thompson) D.; children: Jon Taylor, Scott George, Michael Raymond, Geoffrey Kyle Dunlevie; m. Joy R. Nicholson, Nov. 8, 1982. Ptnr., Desert Bermuda Devel. Co., Bermuda Dunes, Calif., 1957—; pres. Dunray Land Co., Inc., 1957—, Ernie Dunlevie Assos., Palm Springs, Calif., 1946—. Past pres. Bob Hope Desert Classic. With USAAF, 1942-45. Decorated Air medal with 3 oak leaf clusters, D.F.C. Mem. Palm Springs C. of C. (dir. 1958), Calif. Real Estate Assn. (v.p. 1959, dir.), Palm Springs Bd. Realtors (past pres.), Bermuda Dunes Country Club, Bermuda Dunes Racquet Club, Balboa Bay Club, Mt. Kenya Safari Club, Catalina Island Yacht Club. Home: 79-050 Ave 42 Bermuda Dunes CA 92201

DUNN, GLORIA TUK-NAM, lawyer; b. Hong Kong; came to U.S. 1965; d. Tsing Liang and Helen (Chen) D. BA, Iowa Wesleyan Coll., Mt. Pleasant, 1968; MEd, Springfield (Mass.) Coll., 1970; JD, U. Calif., San Francisco, 1975. Bar: Calif. 1977, U.S. Dist. Ct. (no. and cen. dists.) Calif. 1977, U.S. Supreme Ct. 1977. Trust tax officer Wells Fargo Bank, San Francisco, 1976; atty. Title Ins. & Trust, Rosemead, Calif., 1978-79; pvt. practice law Arcadia, Calif., 1980-82, Monterey Park, Calif., 1985—; lectr. Chinese U. of Hong Kong, 1982-84; asst. prof. Calif. State U., L.A., 1985-87; judge pro-tempore L.A. County Mcpl. Ct., Alhambra br., 1987—. Commr. Housing & Urban Devel. Commn., Alhambra, 1985-87; adv. bd. Salvation Army, L.A., 1986—, sec., 1986—. Mem. L.A. County Bar Assn., So. Calif. Chinese Lawyers Assn. (bd. govs. 1988—), Kiwanianne Club (v.p. 1985-86, pres.-elect San Gabriel Valley East chpt. 1989—). Office: 108 N Ynez Ave #206 Monterey Park CA 91754

DUNN, HARRIET DAWN, telephone company representative; b. Big Spring, Tex., Nov. 24, 1958; d. Lt. Col. James and Anne Lucky (Armstrong) Hayes; m. Stephen A. Dunn, Oct. 10, 1977; 1 child (dec.) Matthew. Supr. Rocky Mountain Bank Note, Phoenix, 1978-80; instr., model Bobby Ball Talent Agy., Phoenix, 1981-82; telephone service rep. Am. Express, Salt Lake City, 1987—. State chmn. Pilot Parents Orgn. of Utah, Salt Lake City, 1984-85. Roman Catholic.

DUNN, INGEBORG CAROLINE, theatrical designer; b. Munich, Nov. 5, 1948; came to U.S., 1955; d. Josef and Theresa Maria (Erlwein) Wolf; m. Gregory Hugh Dunn, Sept. 25, 1971; children: Alexander Fitzpatrick, Fiona Erlwein. BA, Rutgers U., 1971. Art dir., pub. rels. staff Rutgers U., New Brunswick, N.J., 1971-73; set designer Candlewood Theatre, New Fairfield, Conn., 1973, El Paso (Tex.) Civic Opera and Ballet, 1974-76, Cohoes (N.Y.) Music Hall, 1976-77; designer Wavelength Systems Design, El Segundo, Calif., 1978—; freelance designer, set and sketch artist, art dir., Coast Prodns., Walt Disney Prodns., Paramount Pictures, others, Hollywood, Calif., 1977-84; design cons., Royal Viking Cruise Lines, Admiral Cruises, Princess Cruise Line, Carnival Cruise Line, 1986—. Democrat. Roman Catholic. Home: 2102 Ernest Ave Redondo Beach CA 90278 Office: Wavelength Systems Design 214 A Standard St El Segundo CA 90245

DUNN, JACK HIBBARD, neurological surgeon; b. Clayton, N.Y., Apr. 5, 1944; s. Jack K. and Helen (Hibbard) D.; m. Rosemary Moroney, May 1, 1980; children: Erica Rose, Allison Marie. BA, Yale U., 1967; MD, Wayne State U., 1971. Diplomate Am. Bd. Med. Examiners, Am. Bd. Neurol. Surgery. Clin. instr. surgery NYU, N.Y.C., 1971-72, clin. instr. neurosurgery, 1974-79; asst. chief physiol. neurosurgery West Chester County Med. Ctr., N.Y.C., 1980; asst. prof. surgery, neurosurgery U. Ariz., Tucson, 1980-82; v.p. Western Neurosurgery, Tucson, 1982—; chief of neurosurgery El Dorado Med. Ctr., St. Joseph's Med. Ctr., 1988—. Lt. M.C., USN, 1972-74. Mem. Pima County Med. Soc. (sec.-treas.). Home and Office: 2100 N Rosemont Tucson AZ 85712

DUNN, JERRY CAMARILLO, JR., writer; b. L.A., Mar. 30, 1947; s. Gerold Camarillo and Margaret (Eastman) D.; m. Merry Vaughan, Apr. 24, 1976; children: Graham Camarillo, Lachlan Vaughan. AB, Stanford U., 1968; postgrad., U. So. Calif., 1968-69. Editor Santa Barbara (Calif.) Mag., 1977-80; free-lance feature writer Santa Barbara, 1980-84; editor, writer Nat. Geog. Soc., Washington, 1984-87; writer Nat. Geog. Traveler mag., Washington, 1987—. Author: Smithsonian Guide to Historic America: The Rocky Mountain States, 1989. Recipient Maggie award, 1978, 79, 80. Mem. Soc. Am. Travel Writers (Best Article U.S. runner up 1986). Home: 816 El Paseo Rd Ojai CA 93023

DUNN, JESSIE JOYCE, psychotherapist, consultant; b. Pineville, Mo., July 16, 1930; d. Silas and Lucretia (Packwood) Clark; m. Robert E. Dunn, Dec. 13, 1958 (div. 1970); 1 child, Jonathan. BA in Soc. and Justice magna cum laude, U. Wash., 1974, MSW, 1977. Counselor Salvation Army, Seattle, 1977-78; therapist Divorce Lifeline, Seattle, 1977-84; pvt. practice specializing in psychotherapy Seattle, 1980—; practicum instr. U. Wash. Sch. Social Work, 1980-81. Screen clients Mcpl. Probations and Parole, Seattle, 1974; bd. dirs. Seattle Counseling, 1973-74, v.p.; coordinator of adult single programs Univ. Unitarian Ch., Seattle, 1979-83. Mem. Nat. Assn. Social Workers, Phi Beta Kappa. Democrat.

DUNN, JOSEPH MCELROY, manufacturing company executive; b. Toledo, Aug. 9, 1926; s. Robert C. and Myrtle (Bridgeman) D.; m. Martha Louise Nutt, Dec. 29, 1950; children: Christopher, Kathryn, Barbara, David. BBA, Ohio State U., 1949. Jr. acct. Arthur Young & Co., Toledo, 1949-50; ptnr. Bob Dunn Automobile, Seattle, 1950-58; v.p., then pres. Moline (Ill.) Corp., 1958-64; sales trainee to pres. PACCAR Inc., Bellevue, Wash., 1964—, also bd. dirs. Bd. dirs. Seattle First Nat. Bank, Seafirst Corp. Served with Q.M.C. USN, 1944-45, PTO. Mem. Western Hwy. Inst. (v.p. at large 1987-88). Republican. Presbyterian. Clubs: Seattle Golf; Desert Island Golf (Rancho Mirage, Calif.). Lodge: Masons. Home: 1556 77th Pl NE Bellevue WA 98004 Office: PACCAR Inc 777 106th Ave NE Bellevue WA 98004

DUNN, KATHLEEN LESLIE, nurse; b. San Diego, Oct. 13, 1952; d. Charles Ervin and Lois Lenore (Knutson) D.; m. David Bruce Lynch, July 5, 1975 (div. 1981). BSN summa cum laude, Humboldt State U., 1974; MSN, Rush U., 1982. RN, Calif. Staff nurse U. Calif. Med. Ctr., San Diego, 1974-76; staff nurse Sharp Rehab. Ctr., San Diego, 1976-80, nurse clinician, 1981, clin. nurse specialist, coord. spinal cord injury svcs., 1982-89; clin. nurse specialist spinal cord injury VA Med. Ctr., San Diego, 1989—; lectr. Am. Spinal Injury Assn., 1986; cons. in field. Mem. Assn. Rehab. Nurses, Am. Congress Rehab. Medicine, Am. Assn. Spinal Cord Injury Nurses, Nurses Orgn. of VA, Assn. Relief Nurses (cert. rehab. RN), Sigma Theta Tau (pres. Gamma Gamma chpt. 1983-84). Democrat. Office: VAMC Sci Unit #128 3350 La Jolla Village Dr San Diego CA 92161

DUNN, MICHAEL DAVID, hotel company president; b. Chgo., Oct. 28, 1944; s. Phillip Samual and Joan Mamie (Osten) D.; m. Ronna Rochelle Kravitz, June 14, 1964; children: Brian, Rhoda, Jennifer. BS, Ill. Inst. Tech., 1964; cert. of completion, Marquette U., 1965. Corp. staff Allis-Chalmers, Inc., West Allis, Wis., 1964-65; plant supt. Essex Wire Corp., Lafayette, Ind., 1965-66; mfg. mgr. Elect. Parts Corp., Georgetown, Ky., 1966-67; project mgr. Gauger & Diehl, CPA's, Peoria, Ill., 1967-68; pres., chief exec. officer, co-founder Advanced Health Systems, Inc., Irvine, Calif., 1969-82; chmn., chief exec. officer, founder Westworld Community Health Care, Inc., Lake Forest, Calif., 1982-86; pres., chief exec. officer Wadco Svcs. Inns, Inc., Santa Ana, Calif., 1987—; bd. dirs. Pharma Kinetics Labs., Inc., Judicial Arbitration & Mediation Svcs., Inc., First Western Healthcare, Inc., Inst. of Health Mgmt., Inc., Profl. Examination Svc. Contbg. author: Standards of Nursing Care, 1972, How To Select A Computerized Hospital Information System, 1973; contbr. articles to profl. jours.; editor in chief Listenings Mag., 1962-64. Dir. Ctr. for Acholism Studies, Rutgers U., 1980-86, Hosp. Info. Systems Sharing Group, 1969-80 (also v.p.), Raleigh Hills Found., 1973-82, HMO Task Force, Orange County (Calif.) Health Planning Council, 1976-78. Republican. Jewish. Home: 28411 La Pradera Laguna Niguel CA 92677 Office: Wadco Svcs Inc 2921 S Damler Santa Ana CA 92705

DUNN, PATRICE MARIE, graphic arts executive; b. Scott AFB, Ill., Aug. 19, 1956; d. Norman Edward and Patricia Marie (Baker) Wagner; m. Stuart Thomas Dunn, Oct. 28, 1986. BS, U. Wis., LaCrosse, 1978; MA, San Francisco State U., 1983; postgrad., MIT, 1983. Prodn. mgr. The Film Unit, La Crosse, 1977-78; freelance writer, photographer Inverness, Calif., 1978-79; prodn. editor Med. Self-Care Jour., Inverness, 1979-80; sr. editor Computer Graphics World, San Francisco, 1981-85; v.p. Dunn Tech., Inc., Vista, Calif., 1985—. Author short stories; contbr. articles to profl. jours. Mem. Art Dirs. Club, Assn. Computing Machinery, Am. Inst. Graphic Arts, IEEE, Tech. Assn. Graphic Arts (bd. dirs.), Bay Area Spl. Interest Group in Computer Graphics, Computers in Art, Design, Rsch. and Edn., Am. Nat. Standards Inst. (founder local chpt.). Office: Dunn Tech Inc 1855 E Vista Way Vista CA 92084

DUNNE, THOMAS, geology educator; b. Prestbury, U.K., Apr. 21, 1943; came to U.S., 1964; s. Thomas and Monica Mary (Whitter) D. BA with honors, Cambridge (Eng.) U., 1964; PhD, Johns Hopkins U., 1969. Research assoc. USDA-Agrl. Research Service, Danville, Vt., 1966-68; research hydrologist U.S. Geol. Survey, Washington, 1969; asst. prof. McGill U., Montreal, Que., Can., 1969-73; from asst. prof. to prof. U. Wash., Seattle, 1973—, chmn. dept., 1984—; vis. prof. U. Nairobi, Kenya, 1969-71; cons. in field, 1970—. Author (with L.B. Leopold) Water in Environmental Planning. Fulbright scholar, 1964; grantee NSF, NASA, Rockefeller Found., 1969—; recipient Horton award Am. Geophysics Union, 1987; named to Nat. Acad. Scis., 1988; Guggenheim fellow, 1989—. Fellow Am. Geophys. Union; mem. AAAS, NAS, Geol. Soc. Am., Brit. Geomorphol. Research Group, Sigma Xi. Office: U Wash Dept Geol Scis AJ-20 Seattle WA 98195

DUNNETT, DENNIS GEORGE, state official; b. Auburn, Calif., Aug. 5, 1939; s. George DeHaven and Elizabeth Grace (Sullivan) D. AA in Elec. Engring., Sierra Coll., 1959; AB in Econs., Sacramento State Coll., 1966. Engring. technician State of Calif., Marysville, 1961-62; data processing technician State of Calif., Sacramento, 1962-67, EDP programmer and analyst, 1967-74, staff services mgr. and contract adminstr., 1974-76, hardware acquisition mgr., 1976-86, support services br. mgr., information security officer, 1986—; instr. Am. River Coll., 1972; cons. to state personnel bd. on data processing testing, 1983. Mem. Data Processing Mgmt. Assn. (certs.), Calif. State U. Sacramento Alumni Assn. (life), Assn. Computing Machinery, IEEE Computer Soc., Assn. Inst Cert. of Computer Profls., Intergovtl. Council on Tech. of Info. Processing, The Mus. Soc., San Francisco Opera Guild. Home: 729 Blackmer Circle Sacramento CA 95825-4704 Office: Box 13436 Sacramento CA 95813-4436

DUNNIGAN, MARY ANN, former educational administrator; b. St. Maries, Idaho, Sept. 7, 1915; d. William Henry and Mary Ellen (Kelly) D.; BA, Holy Names Coll., Spokane, 1942; MA, Gonzaga U., Spokane, 1957; postgrad. U. Idaho, UCLA. Tchr. rural schs. Bonner County, 1936-41, elem. schs., 1941, 45-59, high sch., 1942, 45, coordinator elem. edn., 1959-78; prin. kindergarten Sch. Dist. 271, Coeur d'Alene, Idaho, 1978-81; tchr. extension classes U. Idaho; curriculum chmn. Gov.'s Conf. on Edn.; adv. council Head Start. Adv. council Council for Aging; mem. N. Idaho Mus., Community Council, Community Concerts, Community Theater, N. Idaho Booster Club, Mayor's Com. on Handicapped; mem. task force and diocesan bd. Catholic Edn. of Idaho, 1969-74. Bd. dirs. Coeur d'Alene Tchrs. Credit Union, 1958-87, pres., treas., 1976—; hist. chmn. Coeur d'Alenecentennial, 1986—. Named Citizen of Yr. N. Idaho Coll., 1974, Idaho Cath. Dau. of Year, 1968; named to Idaho Retired Tchr.'s Hall of Fame, 1987; recipient Hon. Alumnus award N. Idaho Coll., 1987, Nat. Community Svc. award AARP/NRTA, 1989. Mem. Idaho Edn. Assn., NEA, Idaho Ret. Tchrs. Assn. (state chmn. pre-retirement 1985—), Kootenai County Ret. Tchrs. Assn. (pres. 1983-87), Delta Kappa Gamma. Club: Cath. Daus. Am. (state regent 1956-62). Home: 720 9th St Coeur d'Alene ID 83814

DUNOYER, PHILIPPE, petroleum industry executive; b. Paris, May 3, 1930; came to U.S., 1975; s. Bernard and Suzanne (De Mones) D.; m. Cynthia Troxell, Apr. 4, 1956; children: Cecilia, Louis, François, Jean. G-rad. Engr., École Polytechnique, Paris, 1951; Certificate of Geology, U. Montpellier, France, 1952; postgrad. in geophysics, Colo. Sch. Mines, 1952-53, U. Calif., Los Angeles, 1953-54; postgrad. exec. program, Stanford U., 1970. With Total Compagnie Française des Petroles and Affiliates, 1954—; chmn. bd., pres., chief exec. officer Total Petroleum (N.Am.) Ltd., 1975. Trustee Alma Coll., 1976; mem. Rocky Mountain regional bd. Inst. Internat. Edn., 1984. With French Army, 1953-54. Mem. Am. Petroleum Inst. (dir.), French Assn. Oil Industry Profls. (chmn. econ. com. 1968-71), Denver Club (pres. 1986), Chevaliers du Tastevin Club. Roman Catholic. Office: Total Petroleum N Am Ltd 999 18th St Box 500 Denver CO 80201

DUNSTAN, LARRY KENNETH, insurance company executive; b. Payson, Utah, May 26, 1948; s. Kenneth Leroy Dunstan and Verna Matilda (Carter) Taylor; m. Betty K. Limb, Sept. 23, 1966 (div. June 1975); children: Tamara, Thane; m. Jacqueline Lee Darron, Oct. 7, 1975; children: Tessa, Matthew, Bennett, Spencer, Adam. CLU, CPCU, chartered fin. cons., registered health underwriter, life underwriter tng. council fellow. Mgr. Diamond Bar Inn Ranch, Jackson, Mont., 1972-73; agt. Prudential Ins. Co., Missoula, Mont., 1973-77; devel. mgr. Prudential Ins. Co., Billings, Mont., 1977-78; div. mgr. Prudential Ins. Co., Gt. Falls, Mont., 1978-83; pres. Multi-Tech Ins. Services, Inc., Oswego, Oreg., 1983—; agy. mgr. Beneficial Life Ins. Co., Portland, Oreg., 1983-88. Mem. planning commn. City of West Linn, Oreg., 1986; mem. bishopric Ch. Jesus Christ of Latter Day Sts., West Linn, 1984-86, exec. sec. Lake Oswego Oreg. Stake, 1987—; scouting coordinator Boy Scouts Am., West Linn, 1984-86, scoutmaster various troops. Named Eagle Scout Boy Scouts Am., 1965, recipient Heroism award 1965. Fellow Life Underwriter Tng. Coun. (bd. dirs. 1980-81); mem. Gen. Agts. and Mgrs. Assn. (bd. dirs. 1981-82), Am. Soc. CLU (pres. 1982-83). Republican. Home: 19443 Wilderness Dr West Linn OR 97068 Office: Multi-Tech Ins Svcs Inc 1 Centerpointe Dr #330A Lake Oswego OR 97035

DUPAR, ROBERT W., hotel executive; b. Seattle, Feb. 14, 1926; s. Francis Augustus and Ethel Leona (Gilbert) D.; m. Jessie Jane Gladys. Student, U. Wash., Cornell U., Seattle U., Harvard U. Clk, asst. mgr. Westin St. Francis Hotel, San Francisco, 1949-53; asst. mgr., mgr. Westin Cascadian Hotel, Wenatchee, Wash., 1953-57; resident mgr. Westin Davenport Hotel, Spokane, Wash., 1957; redident mgr. Westin Multnomah Hotel, Portland, Oreg., 1957-59; adm. asst. v.p. Westin Exec. Office, Seattle, 1959-69; owner Bellevue (Wash.) Holiday Inn, Wash., 1969—; dir. Palmer Supply Co., Seattle 1961-75; dir., chmn. Orca Secured Environment Systems, 1984—; trustee Mission Ivestment Trust, San Diego 1969-80; dir. Seattle Conv. and Tourist Bur., Seattle 1970-85. Dir., past pres. Presbyn. Ministries, Inc. Seattle 1964-74; trustee, past pres. Swedish Hosp. Med. Ctr., Seattle. Mem. Cornel Soc. Hotelmen. Home: 1899-123 Rd SE Bellevue WA 98005

DUPONT, COLYER LEE, television and film producer, video and film distributing company executive; b. Golden, Colo., Oct. 23, 1957; s. Alfred Lee and Frances Dudley (Smith) D. BA, More U., 1980. Advt. mgr. Magical Blend mag., San Francisco, 1981-83; owner, mgr. Newave Co., San Francisco, 1983; mktg. dir. Venture Rsch., Inc., San Francisco, 1983-84; assoc. producer Left Coast Prodns., San Francisco, 1984-86; owner, mgr. Cinemagic Prodns., San Francisco, 1986—. Author: Inventor's Guidebook, 1984; writer, producer, dir. TV spl. Computer Magic, 1987; videoworks exhibited Mus. Modern Art, N.Y.C., Nat. Mus. Natural History, Smithsonian Inst., Washington, N.Y. Hall of Sci., Corona, Fine Arts Mus. L.I., Hempstead, N.Y.; inventor belt-attached carrier. Recipient Chris award 34th Columbus (Ohio) Internat. Film and Video Festival, 1986, Silver medal Internat. Film and TV Festival N.Y., 1986, Joey award of merit Profl. Media Network, 1986, Golden Eagle award Coun. for Internat. Non-theatrical Events, 1987, Gold Electra award Birmingham (Ala.) Internat. Edn. Film Fetival, 1987, Silver plaque Chgo. Internat. Film Festival, 1987. Mem. Bay Area Video Coalition, Ind. Filmmakers No. Calif. (founder), Film Arts Found., Visual Communicators Calif., San Francisco Advt. Club (Excellence award 1987). Office: Cinemagic Prodns 537 Jones St Ste 898 San Francisco CA 94102

DUPRÉ, HEIDI H(ILDEGARD), accountant, consultant; b. Berlin, Germany, Dec. 5, 1942; came to U.S., 1961; d. Otto F. H. and Hildegard L.H. Berndt; m. Franz Dupré, Sept. 10, 1962; children: Nicole, René, Désirée. Student, Sch. Commerce, Berlin, 1956-57, Bus. Mgmt. Sch., Berlin, 1957-60. Prin. European Imports, San Francisco, 1970-73; agt. life and disability ins. N.Y. Life, San Mateo, Calif., 1974; ins. broker Ind. Order Foresters, San Mateo, 1975-78; acct. Accountemps, San Mateo, 1984-88, Mgmt. Solutions, San Jose, Calif., 1988; cons. Dupré Bookkeeping Service, Brisbane, Calif., 1985—. Contbr. articles to profl. jours. Mem. Brisbane Planning Commn., 1977-80, chairwoman, 1978-79; mem. San Mateo County Regional Planning Commn., 1979, Brisbane City Council; adv. com. Neighborhood Services Ctr., Brisbane, 1979-80; bd. dirs., tour dir., chmn. audience promotion Calif. Youth Symphony, Palo Alto, 1982-84. Mem. Am. Bus. Woman's Assn. Republican. Lutheran. Club: Federated Women's (Brisbane) (treas. 1979-80). Lodge: Eagles. Office: PO Box 456 Brisbane CA 94005

DUPREE, ANDREW LANE, SR., teacher, writer, actor; b. Hattisburg, Miss., May 15, 1956; s. Donald Nolan and Joy Katherine (Carter) D.; m. Vanessa Estrelita Tano, July 27, 1979; children: Andrew Lane Jr., Jeremy Mark, Jason Neil. Student bus. and psychology, Ricks Coll., Rexburg, Idaho, 1974, 76-77; student bus. and drama, Brigham Young U., Laie, Hawaii, 1978-80; BBS, Calif. Coast U., 1989, postgrad. Tchr. Barbizon Modeling Sch., Honolulu, 1982; wholesaler, distbr. A.L. Dupree Internat., Honolulu, 1983-84; tchr. English, reading and scis. Hawaii Dept. Edn., Honolulu, 1985—; pvt. tutor, 1986—. Actor, prodn. asst., stuntman: (TV series) Hawaiian Heat, 1984; appeared in: (TV series) Tour of Duty, 1988, Magnum P.I., 1980-88, (film) Blood and Orchids, also various TV commls.; co-author: (screenplay) The Mobius Man, 1987; producer, dir., actor: (film) The Mobius Man, 1987; writer, producer, dir., actor Joy Entertainment, 1988. Chair pub. rels. com. Pauoa PTA, Honolulu, 1987-88; mem. Hawaii Alliance for Arts Edn., Honolulu, 1987—. Mem. Am. Film Inst., Screen Actors Guild, Writer's Group. Home: 330 Kawaena Pl Honolulu HI 96813-1611

DUPREY, HARRY ERNEST, electrical engineer; b. Denver, Mar. 31, 1940; s. Carroll Griffin and Harriet (Moxham) D. BSEE, U. Colo., 1970. R & D technician A.R.F. Products, Inc., Boulder, Colo., 1966-70, engr., 1970-80, sr. engr., 1980--. With USN, 1959-63. Mem. IEEE, Range Comdrs. Coun., Flight Safety Group. Home: 9141 Judson St Westminster CO 80030 Office: ARF Products Inc 2559 N 75th St Boulder CO 80301

DUPREY, THOMAS DONALD, pharmacist; b. Wyandotte, Mich., July 7, 1951; s. Donald Arthur and Laura Irene (White) D.; m. Cahtryn Patricia Bell, June 29, 1974; children: Kimberly Christine, Stephen Thomas. BS in Pharmacy, Wayne State U., 1976; M in Pub. Adminstrn., U. San Francisco, 1985. Pharmacist West Outer Drive Med. Ctr., Lincoln Park, Mich., 1974-77; chief pharmacist CGM Enterprises, San Francisco, 1977-79; pharmacist Kaiser Permanente, Santa Clara, Calif., 1979-80; adminstrv. assoc. Oakland, Calif., 1980-81; asst. chief pharmacist Santa Clara, 1981; chief pharmacist Redwood City, Calif., 1981—. Mem. Calif. Soc. Hosp. Pharmacists. Republican. Roman Catholic. Office: Kaiser Permanente 1150 Veterans Blvd Redwood City CA 94063

DUPUY, HOWARD MOORE, JR., lawyer; b. Portland, Oreg., Mar. 15, 1929; s. Howard Moore and Lola (Dunham) D.; m. Anne Irene Hanna, Aug. 26, 1950; children: Loanne Kay, Brent Moore. BA, U. Portland, 1951; postgrad., Willamette U., 1951; LLB, Lewis and Clark Coll., 1956. Bar: Oreg. 1956. Since practiced in Portland; assoc. Green, Richardson, Green & Griswold, 1956; ptnr. Morton & Dupuy, 1957-67, Black & Dupuy (and predecessor firm), 1968—. Mem. fin. com. Oreg. Rep. Cen. Com., 1962. Served with AUS, 1946-47. Mem. Am., Oreg., Multnomah County Bar Assns., Am. Arbitration Assn. (nat. panel arbitrators), World Trade Club, Oregon Trial Lawyers Assn., Am. Judicature Soc. Club: World Trade (Portland). Home: 16116 NE Stanton St Portland OR 97230 Office: Black & Dupuy 1515 SW 5th Ave Ste 515 Portland OR 97201

DUQUETTE, DIANE RHEA, library director; b. Springfield, Mass., Dec. 15, 1951; d. Gerard Lawrence and Helen Yvette (St. Marie) Morneau; m. Thomas Frederick Duquette Jr., Mar. 17, 1973. BS in Sociology, Springfield Coll., 1975; MLS, Simmons Coll., 1978. Library asst. Springfield City Library, 1975-78; reference librarian U. Mass., Amherst, 1978-81; head librarian Hopkins Acad., Hadley, Mass., 1980; instr. Colo. Mountain Coll., Steamboat Springs, 1981-83; library dir. East Routt Library Dist., Steamboat Springs, 1981-84; agy. head Solono County Library, Vallejo, Calif., 1984; dir. library svcs. Shasta County Library, Redding, Calif., 1984-87; dir. libraries Kern County Library, Bakersfield, Calif., 1987—. Contbr. articles to profl. jours. Mem. ALA, Calif. Library Assn. (council 1987—), Calif. County Librarians Assn. (v.p. 1988-89), San Joaquin Valley Library System (chmn. 1988), AAUW, Soroptimists. Democrat. Roman Catholic. Home: PO Box 6595 Pine Mountain Club Frazier Park CA 93222 Office: Kern County Libr 701 Truxtun Ave Bakersfield CA 93301

DURAN, JUNE CLARK, legal research company executive; b. Los Angeles, June 10, 1919; d. Willis W. and Ethel M. (King) Clark; m. Frank M. Duran, Apr. 26, 1940; children—Timothy Clark, Patricia Ellen. Student Santa Monica Jr. Coll., 1936-37, UCLA, 1937-38; B.A., U. So. Calif., 1949; postgrad. U. Calif.-Berkeley, 1951-53; LL.B., LaSalle U. Personnel mgr., dir. ops. Calif. Test Bur., Los Angeles, 1950-65, asst. to gen. mgr., Monterey, Calif., 1965-66, asst. v.p., managing editor, 1966-68; asst. v.p. CTB/McGraw-Hill, Monterey, 1968-84; pres. Legal Research and Services Ctr., Monterey, 1985—; dir. First Nat. Bank Monterey County. Pres. Clark Found.; trustee Community Hosp. Monterey Peninsula; bd. dirs. Alliance on Aging, 1971-82; mem. Monterey County Republican Central Com., 1963-78; mem. governing bd. Monterey Peninsula Coll. Mem. Copyright Soc. U.S.A., Monterey Peninsula C. of C. (dir. 1973-75). Office: Legal Rsch & Svcs Ctr 810 Airport Rd Monterey CA 93940

DURAN, MICHAEL CARL, bank executive; b. Colorado Springs, Colo., Aug. 27, 1953; s. Lawrence Herman and Jacqueline Carol (Ward) D. BS magna cum laude, Ariz. State U., 1980. With Valley Nat. Bank Ariz., Phoenix, 1976—, corp. credit trainee, 1984-85, comml. loan officer, 1985-86, br. mgr., asst. v.p., 1986—; cons. various schs. and orgns., 1986—; incorporator Avondale Neighborhood Housing Svcs., 1988. Mem. Cen. Bus. Dist. Revitalization Com., Avondale, Ariz., 1987—, Ad-Hoc Econ. Devel.

Com., 1988; coord. Avondale Litter Lifters, 1987—; vol. United Way, Phoenix, 1984. Mem. Robert Morris Assocs., Ariz. State U. Alumni Assn. (life), Toastmasters, Kiwanis (local bd. dirs. 1986—), Beta Gamma Sigma, Phi Kappa Phi, Phi Theta Kappa, Sigma Iota Epsilon. Democrat. Home: 5430 E Charter Oak Rd Scottsdale AZ 85254

DURAN, MIGUEL, electronic engineer; b. Ysleta, Tex., Sept. 30, 1934; s. Matilde and Feliciana (Herrera) D.; m. Emma Luna, Aug. 3, 1955; children: Edsel, Wyatt, Mary, Michael. AS in Elec. Engring., Capitol Radio Engring. Inst., Washington, 1970; BA in Bus. Adminstrn., Upper Iowa U., 1974; BS in Engring. Tech., Southwestern U., Tucson, 1984. Lic. mfg. engring. technologist. Field engr. RCA Svc. Co., Camden, N.J., 1959-67; telemetry systems engr. Lockheed Electronics Co., Houston, 1967-72; systems engr. E-Systems, Inc., Dallas, 1972-84; sr. test engr. Tech. Devel. Corp., Arlington, Tex., 1984-87; sr. mem. tech. staff Electronic Warfare Assocs., White Sands Missile Range, N.Mex., 1987—; instr. electronic engring. DeVry Inst. Tech., Dallas, 1979-80, Nat. Inst. Tech., Dallas, 1980-87. With USAF, 1955-59. Mem. Am. Soc. for Engring. Edn. Democrat. Roman Catholic. Home: 5249 Chiricahua Trail Las Cruces NM 88001 Office: GWA Inc 7500 Viscount Blvd Ste 233 El Paso TX 79925

DURAN, PETER, fire chief; b. Espanola, N.Mex., July 2, 1957; s. Pedro F. and Lillian C. (Roybal) D.; divorced; children: Nathan, Jacob, Darlene. Grad. high sch., Pojoaque, N.Mex. Heavy equipment operator Espanola Transit Mix, 1975; carpenter's asst. Espanola Mercantile, 1975-76; partsman Johnny's Auto Supply, Espanola, 1977-78; firefighter Santa Fe (N.Mex.) Fire Dept., 1978-84, firefighter lt., 1984-86, firefighter capt., 1986-87, fire chief, 1987—. Vol. firefighter Pojoaque (N.Mex.) Vol. Fire Dept., 1974-88, Pueblo De San Ildefonso (N.Mex.), 1985—. Named Instr. of Yr. Fire Dept. Instrs. Conf., Cin., 1987. Mem. Internat. Soc. Fire Svc. Instrs. (instr. of yr. 1987), Internat. Fire Chief's Assn., N.Mex. State Fire Chief's Assn. (bd. dirs. 1987, chmn. legis. com. 1988). Democrat. Home: Rt 5 Box 293A Santa Fe NM 87501 Office: Sante Fe Fire Dept PO Box 909 Santa Fe NM 87501

DURAZO, GUILLERMO, JR., protective services company executive; b. Chula Vista, Calif., Jan. 17, 1952; s. Guillermo Bustamante Durazo and Alicia (Niebla) Hernandez; m. Joy Eva Estrada, May 25, 1974; children: Monique Andrea, Natacha Monet, Guillermo III. Student, U. Utah, 1971-72, Mesa Jr. Coll., 1973, Nat. U., 1980-81. Editor newsletter Naval Supply Ctr., San Diego, 1980-83; corrections officer Met. Correctional Ctr., San Diego, 1975-78; insp. U.S. Customs, San Diego, 1978-79; owner, mgr. Precision Investigations, San Diego, 1981-83, Durazo Security Patrol, Calexico, 1983-84; pres., chief exec. officer Dugazo, Inc., Chula Vista, 1980—; mem. San Diego Equal Employment Coun., 1980-83, Hispanic Employment Com., San Diego, 1980-83. Co-chmn. Padre Hidalgo Community Ctr., 1973-78; active Mex. and Am. Found., San Diego, 1979—; v.p. Chula Vista Pop-Warner Football League, 1986; founder, pres. Southbay Young Republicans, 1986, pres. San Diego County Nat. Rep. Hispanic Assembly, 1988, nat. committeeman. Served with U.S. Army, 1969-72, Vietnam. Named Caballero of Distinction Mex. and Am. Found., 1981, Entrepreneur of Month U.S. SBA, 1986, 89, One of Outstanding Young Men of Am., 1985. Mem. VFW. Roman Catholic. Office: Dugazo Inc 815 3d Ave Ste 321 Chula Vista CA 92011

DURBETAKI, N. JOHN, computer company executive; b. Rochester, N.Y., Oct. 7, 1955; s. Pandeli and Elisabeth (Megerle) D.; m. Jeanne Feng, June 16, 1984; 1 child, Lee Daniel. BEE, Ga. Inst. Tech., 1977. Product engr. Nat. Semiconductor, Santa Clara, Calif., 1977-78; product engr. Intel, Aloha, Oreg., 1978-80, test engr., 1980-83; cons. Intel, Hillsboro, Oreg., 1983-84; chmn. bd., pres. OrCAD Systems Corp., Hillsboro, 1984-86, chmn. bd., chief exec. officer, 1986—. Mem. ACM, IEEE. Republican. Lutheran. Office: OrCAD Systems Corp 1049 SW Baseline St Ste 500 Hillsboro OR 97123

DURBIN, PETER, Lawyer; b. Denver, Apr. 9, 1931; s. Edgar Durbin and Ann (Pate) Durbin LeFevre; m. Emily Andrews, June 26, 1954; children: Peter Jr., John, Ann. AB cum laude, Harvard Coll., 1953; JD, U. San Diego, 1986, LLM cum laude, 1987. Bar: Calif. 1986, U.S. Dist. Ct. Calif. (so. dist.) 1986. Commd. ensign USN, 1953, advanced through ranks to capt., 1967; commdg. officer USS James K. Polk, New London, Conn., 1967-71, submarine divs. 42 and 43, Charleston, S.C., 1971-73; head submarine combat systems staff of chief of naval ops., Washington, 1973-75; commdg. officer USS Sperry, San Diego, 1975-76, Submarine Squadron Three, San Diego, 1976-78; dep. dir. RDT&E, Washington, 1978-79; head ocean policy br. staff of chief of naval ops., Washington, 1979-80; commdg. officer, dir. Naval Tactical Interoperability Support Activity and Joint Interoperability Test Force, San Diego, 1980-83; ret. USN, 1983; dep. counsel County of San Diego, 1987—; bd. dirs. U. San Diego Law Alumni. Decorated Legion of Merit; recipient Alumni Achievement award U. San Diego Law Alumni, 1985. Mem. San Diego County Bar Assn., Calif. Bar Assn., ABA, US Naval Inst., Navy League, Submarine League, Curtain Raisers, La Jolla 100. Republican. Clubs: University (San Diego), Hasty Pudding (Cambridge, Mass.). Home: 852 Cordova St San Diego CA 92107 Office: San Diego County Counsel's Office 1600 Pacific Hwy San Diego CA 92101

DURCK, CRAIG HAROLD, physiologist; b. Navy Base, Philippines, Oct. 5, 1953; s. Harold Loy and Sylvia Joan (Bowles) D.; m. Linda Sharon Hayes, May 7, 1983; 1 child, Brianna Leigh. BA with high honors, Calif. State U., Long Beach, 1978, MA, 1983. Tchr., coach Calif. State U., Los Angeles, 1984-87; aerospace physiologist McDonnell Douglas, Long Beach, 1987—; lectr. sport physiology People's Republic of China, summer 1986; exercise physiologist Trisphere Sports Medicine, Fountain Valley, Calif., 1987—. Vol. ARC, Santa Monica, Calif., 1985-87; athletes rep. U.S. Olympic Com., Lake Placid, N.Y., 1987-88. Served with U.S. Army, 1973-75, Germany. Mem. Coll. Sports Medicine.

DURDY, JAMES DIRK, marketing professional; b. Denver, Nov. 24, 1957; s. James G. and Elizabeth (Collins) D. BA in Biol., Colo. State U., 1980. Cert. emergency med. technician, in CPR. and as a CPR instr. Founder, mgr. firewood service 1974-75; owner/operator DD and Y Springling System, 1978-81, summers; pres., dir., chief ops. officer Mt. Experience Inc., Littleton, Colo., 1982—; cons. Roo Mark, Victoria, Australia, 1986—. Tchr. CPR and emergency first aid Red Cross throughout Colo., mem. Idaho Mt. Search and Rescue Team. Named Outstanding Young Man in Am., 1985. Republican. Roman Catholic. Home: 6010 S Detroit St Littleton CO 80121 Office: Roo Mark, 16 Wooten Cres, Longwarrin Victoria Australia 3910

DUREMDES, LARARD ONAGA, trade company executive; b. Naha, Japan, Mar. 13, 1956; came to U.S., 1975; s. Ressureccion Doronilla and Hatsuko (Onaga) D.; m. Nancy Diane Beacham, June 18, 1988; 1 child, Ramon Alex. AA, Orange Coast Coll., Costa Mesa, Calif., 1979. Exec. dir., founder Rodes Internat., Huntington Beach, Calif., 1983-87; distbn. dir. Incom Group Inc., Carson, Calif., 1987-88; chief adminstrv. officer Nat. Peripherals, Costa Mesa, 1988—; v.p. Pass Inc., Carson, Calif., 1987—. Republican. Home: 8122 Foxhall Dr Huntington Beach CA 92646

DURFEE, GLENN RUSSELL, lawyer; b. Quincy, Mass., Apr. 15, 1947; s. Laurence and Flora (Kenworthy) D. AB, Tufts U., Medford, Mass., 1969; JD, U. Chgo., 1972. Rsch. atty. Calif. Ct. Appeal, L.A., 1972-74; dist. atty. County of Sierra, Downieville, Calif., 1974-75, of counsel, 1975-77; pvt. practice Nevada City, Calif., 1977-83, Santa Barbara, Calif., 1983-88, Fair Oaks, Calif., 1988—. Mem. bd. trustees. Sacramento Waldorf Sch. Fair Oaks, Calif., 1988—. Mem. ABA, Calif. State Bar Assn., State Bar Commn. Appellate Cts. Office: 8125 Sunset Ave Ste 200 Fair Oaks CA 95628

DURHAM, BARBARA, state justice; b. 1942. BSBA, Georgetown U.; JD, Stanford U. Bar: Wash. 1968. Former judge Wash. Superior Ct., King County; judge Wash. Ct. Appeals; assoc. justice Wash. Supreme Ct., 1985—. Office: Wash Supreme Ct Temple of Justice Olympia WA 98504

DURHAM, HARRY BLAINE, III, lawyer; b. Denver, Sept. 16, 1946; s. Harry Blaine and Mary Frances (Oliver) D.; m. Lynda L. Durham, Aug. 4, 1973; children: Christopher B., Laurel A. BA cum laude, Colo. Coll., 1969; JD, U. Colo., 1973. Bar: Wyo. 1973, U.S. Tax Ct. 1974, U.S. Ct. Appeals (10th cir.) 1976. Assoc., Brown, Drew, Apostolos, Massey & Sullivan, Casper, Wyo., 1973-77, ptnr., 1977—. Permanent class pres. Class of 1969, Colo. Coll.; bd. dirs. Casper Symphony Assn., 1974-88, v.p., 1979-82, pres., 1983-87; bd. dirs., sec. Wyo. Amateur Hockey Assn., 1974-85, pres., 1985-88; bd. dirs. Natrona County United Way, 1974-76, pres., 1975-76; mem. City of Casper Parks and Recreation Commn., 1985—, vice chmn., 1987—. Mem. Wyo. Bar Assn., Natrona County Bar Assn., ABA, Phi Beta Kappa. Republican. Articles editor U. Colo. Law Rev., 1972-73. Home: 3101 Hawthorne Casper WY 82601 Office: 111 W 2d 500 Petroleum Bldg Casper WY 82601

DURHAM, RICHARD L., management consultant; b. Portland, Ore., Mar. 20, 1929; s. Walter Albert and Vesta (Broughton) D.; m. Shirley Schuab, June 3,. BS in Engring., U.S. Military Acad., W. Point, 1953; Diploma, Nat. War Coll., Wash., 1970. Supr. Sandia Nat. Lab., Livermoroe, Calif., 1958-64; dir. classification U.S. Arms Control & Disarm Agy., Washington, 1964-65; civilian asst. to asst. sec. defense (atomic energy) Washington, 1965-67; intelligence advisor U.S. Arms Control & Disarmament Agy., Washington, 1967-74; asst. dir. intelligence U.S. A.E.C., Washington, 1974-76; spl. projects officer U.S. Dept. Energy, Richland, Wash., 1976-79; spl. asst. to dir. Oregan Dept. Energy, Salem, 1979-84; city council pres. City of Lake Oswego, Ore., 1986—; pres. R.L. Durham's Asssoc., Lake Oswego, Ore., 1984—; founder, past pres., bd. mem. Nat. Classification Mgmt. Soc., Inc., Washington, 1964-76. Contbr. articles to profl. jours. Chmn. Wood Energy Coordination Group, Portland Ore., 1978-88. Mem. Assn. Graduates W. Point, Assn. Graduates Nat. War Coll. Republican. Presbyterian. Home: 3413 Royce Way Lake Oswego OR 97034 Office: R L Durham & Assocs 3413 Royce Way Lake Oswego OR 97034

DURHAM, ROBERT EARL, video specialist; b. Eureka, Calif., Jan. 5, 1930; s. Ernest Earl Durham and Velma Olive (Rhoads) Hopkins; m. Rosslyn Jeanne Sloss, Feb. 21, 1954; children: Robyn Eileen, Pamela Helene. BA, Coll. of Pacific, 1952; MA, UCLA, 1957. Film editor Rocketdyne div. Rockwell Internat., Canoga Park, Calif., 1957-58, writer, dir., 1958-86, adminstr. video prodn., 1986—; music editor for competitive figure skaters, Tarzana, Calif., 1969—. Recipient citation Aviation Space Writers Assn., 1981, Golden Eagle award Coun. for Non-Theatrical Events, 1981. Mem. Internat. TV Assn. Republican. Home: 18236 Weddington St Tarzana CA 91356 Office: Rocketdyne Dept 057-AB-26 6633 Canoga Ave Canoga Park CA 91303

DURICK, MICHAEL DENNIS, labor relations executive; b. Council Bluffs, Iowa, Mar. 11, 1942; s. Dewey Theodore and Lorene (Davison) D.; m. Martha Claire Ashmore, Aug. 24, 1962 (div.); children: Kyle, Judi, Janice; m. Diana Lynn Lowrance, Dec. 12, 1978. BBA, U. Iowa, 1967. Sales rep. The Dow Chem. Co., Cin., 1967-69; credit rep. The Dow Chem. Co., Midland, Mich., 1969-70; credit mgr. AMSPEC, Inc., Columbus, Ohio, 1970-72; dir. activities S.D. Bldg. Contractors Assn., San Diego, 1972-73, exec. v.p., 1973-78; pres. Profl. Labor Relations, La Mesa, Calif., 1978-88; adv. bd. Mesa Coll., San Diego, 1972-78. Contbr. articles to profl. pubs. Trustee Roofers Benefit Funds, San Diego, 1985—. With USN, 1960-64. Recipient Seldon Hale award Nat. Assn. Home Builders, 1974, 75, 76, 77; named Spike of Yr. Bldg. Industry Assn., San Diego, 1983. Mem. Indsl. Relations Research Assn. Republican. Presbyterian. Club: Sertoma (San Diego) (pres. 1972-73). Office: Profl Labor Rels Inc 8278 University Ave La Mesa CA 92041

DURKIN, LISA MARIE, cosmetics company executive; b. Elkhart, Ind., Apr. 25, 1957; d. John Frank and Pamela Kay (Pauley) Sweazy; m. John Thomas Durkin, Apr. 23, 1979; children: Danielle Marie, Derilynn Kay. BS in Phys. Edn., Calif. State U., Fullerton, 1980. Sr. sales dir. Mary Kay Cosmetics, Texas, Calif., 1981-86; asst. store mgr. Buffums, Santa Ana, Calif., 1986-87; asst. buyer Robinsons, L.A., 1987-88; buyer J.C. Penney Co., City of Industry, Calif., 1988-89; bus. mgr. Lancome Cosmetics, Costa Mesa, Calif., 1988-89; account exec. Lancome Cosmetics, L.A., 1989—. Republican.

DURLING, JAMES RICHARD, electrical engineer; b. Pitts., Sept. 4, 1959; s. Richard James and Mary Magdalene (Auman) D. BSEE, Point Park Coll., 1984; AS in Spl. Elec. Tech., Pa. Tech. Inst., 1979; postgrad., Pa. State U., 1983, UCLA, 1988. Electronics tech. Electro Optics div. Tex. Instruments, Inc., Dallas, 1979-80; electromech. componenting engring. specialist Ford Aerospace & Communications Corp., Newport Beach, Calif., 1984-86; system effectiveness engr., scientist McDonnell-Douglas Astronautics Co., Huntington Beach, Calif., 1986-88; design assurance specialist Satellite and Space Electronics Rockwell Internat., Seal Beach, Calif., 1988-. Mem. IEEE, ASME, Huntington Beach Mgmt. Assn. Republican. Roman Catholic.

DURON, ERIC RAYMOND, air force officer; b. Aurora, Ill., May 18, 1960; s. Raymond and Elizabeth Elanora (Batt) D. BS in Aerospace Engring., Va. Poly. Inst. and State U., 1982. Commd. 2d lt. USAF, 1982, advanced through grades to capt.; instr. 494th Tactical Fighter Squadron USAF, RAF Lakenheath, Eng., 1984-87; chief, radar strike, 522d Tactical Fighter Squadron USAF, Cannon AFB, N.Mex., 1987. Mem. Air Force Assn., AIAA. Roman Catholic. Office: Captain Eric R Duron 522 TFS/DOR Cannon AFB NM 88103

DURON, SUSAN BUDDE, research corporation executive; b. Chgo., Mar. 17, 1947; d. Earl Leslie and Ivy May (Smith) Budde; m. Guillermo Duron, June 27, 1981. BA, Ill. State U., 1969; MEd, No. Ill. U., 1975; PhD, So. Ill. U., 1978. Cert. tchr., ednl. adminstr. Tchr. West Aurora (Ill.) Pub. Schs., 1969-72, coord. bilingual program, 1972-76; instr. So. Ill. U., Carbondale, 1976-78; evaluations cons. Ill. State Bd. Edn., Chgo., 1978-81; sr. program analyst Advanced Tech., Inc., Indpls., 1982-83; rsch. assoc. N.W. Regional Ednl. Lab., Denver, 1983-85; owner, pres. META Assocs., Littleton, Colo., 1985—; v.p., regional officer dir. RMC Rsch. Corp., Denver, 1988—. Author: Student Study Skills, 1987; contbr. articles to profl. pubs.; editor cons. handbook. Grantee World Congress Spl. Edn., 1978, Bur. Edn. of Handicapped, 1988. Mem. Am. Edn. Rsch. Assn., Nat. Assn. Bilingual Edn., Coun. Computer Users Edn., Coun. Exceptional Children, Greenpeace Club, Valley Racquet Club, Kappa Delta Pi. Democrat. Congregationalist. Home: 4904 S Routt St Littleton CO 80127 Office: RMC Rsch Corp 1512 Larimer Ste 540 Denver CO 80202

DURRANT, DEAN OBORN, podiatrist; b. Tooele, Utah, Dec. 1, 1929; s. Rendell Porter and Emily (Oborn) D.; BA, City Coll. San Francisco, 1955; BS, Calif. Coll. Podiatric Medicine, 1956-57; D.Podiatric Medicine, 1960; m. Dian Overson, Apr. 10, 1953; children: Kathrine, Calleen, Russell Dean, Joyce, Suzanne, Ronda, LaDean. Gen. practice podiatry, Napa, Calif., 1960—; chief podiatry staff Broadway Hosp., Vallejo, 1978-81. Mem., sec. Solano County Comprehensive Health Planning Council, 1974-75; trustee Calif. Coll. Podiatric Medicine, 1974-75; councilor Boy Scouts Am., 1963-64; bd. dirs. Vallejo Symphony Assn., 1968-72. Served with USN, 1953-55. Mem. Calif. Podiatric Assn. (pres. 1974-75), Am. Podiatry Assn. (commr. Region 12 1970-79), Redwood Empire Soc., Sons Utah Pioneers. Democrat. Mem. Ch. Jesus Christ Latter-day Saints. Club: Toastmasters. Lodges: Masons, Shriners, Elks. Home: 1950 Jefferson St Napa CA 94558 Office: 609 Georgia St Vallejo CA 94590

DURRETT, JOHN CHARLES, aerospace corporation executive; b. Fort Worth, Feb. 5, 1939; s. John H. and H. Beatrice (Burkhart) D.; B.S., U. Kans., 1962; M.S., Air Force Inst. Tech., 1963; Ph.D., U. Colo., 1970; m. Leilani Mary Gresham, July 31, 1976; children by previous marriage: Michelle Rene, John Edward. Commd. 2d lt. USAF, 1962, advanced through grades to lt. col., 1978; flight test engr. Edwards AFB, Calif., 1963-67; supervising engr. Air Force Flight Dynamics Lab., Wright-Paterson AFB, Ohio, 1970-73; assoc. prof. astronautics USAF Acad., Colo., 1973-77; space test program spacecraft program mgr. Space and Missile Systems Orgn., Los Angeles, 1977-79, dep. dir. space test program office, space div., Los Angeles, 1979-80, dir. space sensor test directorate, space div., 1980-82, ret., 1982; dep. program mgr. Def. Systems, Martin Marietta Aerospace Corp., Denver, 1983, program mgr. def. systems, 1984-85, spacecraft design mgr., 1985—. Decorated Meritorious Service medal with oak leaf cluster, Air Force Commendation medal with 2 oak leaf clusters. NASA summer faculty fellow Stanford U., 1975. Mem. AIAA, Am. Astron. Soc. Club: Toastmasters (Calif. area gov. 1966-67). Office: Martin Marietta Aerospace Mail Stop 8030 PO Box 179 Denver CO 80201

DURST, WILLIAM BRUCE, comedian; b. Milw., Mar. 18, 1954; s. William Duerst Sr. and Gloria Ann (Strauss) Perkins; m. Debi Ann Pickell, Nov. 4, 1981. Intra-arts degree, U. Wis., Milw., 1978. Columnist numerous newspaper articles. Mayoral candidate, San Francisco, 1987. Recipient Best Male Comedian award, San Francisco Coun. on Entertainment, 1986-87, Entertainer of Yr. award, 1987. Mem. AFTRA, SAG. Democrat. Office: Worst of Durst Comedy 2107 Van Ness Ave #303 San Francisco CA 94109

DURSTENFELD, ROBERT M., marketing executive; b. Bklyn., Apr. 2, 1955; s. Richard and Ligia (Matallana) D.; m. Becky Susan Carlson, Aug. 20, 1983; 1 child, Matthew Stephen. BS in Engring., U. Calif., L.A., 1978; MS in Engring. Mgmt., Santa Clara U., 1984. Engring mgr. Nat. Semiconductor Corp., Santa Clara, Calif., 1978-84; sr. applications engr. Tektronix, Inc., Beaverton, Oreg., 1985-86; applications mgr. EPRO Corp., San Jose, Calif., 1986; sr. applicatons engr. AOT Corp., Milpitas, Calif., 1987-89; mgt. tch. mktg. AOT Corp., Milpitas, 1989—; Bd. dirs. Santa Teresa Community Ch. San Jose, Calif., 1985-88, deacon, 1986-88. Mem. IEEE. Democrat. Home: 1013 Drexel Way San Jose CA 95121 Office: AOT Corp 801 Buckeye Ct Milpitas CA 95035

DURUSAU, JOSEPH AUGUSTUS, electrical engineer; b. Natchitoches, La., May 1, 1943; s. Clarence X. and Sherman (Dumas) D. BSEE, La. State U., 1966. Customer engr. Control Data Corp., Mpls., 1968-76; field engr. Northrop Corp., Anaheim, Calif., 1976—. 1st lt. U.S. Army, 1966-68, Vietnam. Decorated Bronze Star. Mem. IEEE, Assn. of U.S. Army, KC. Republican. Catholic. Home: 107 Washington St Saint Mary's GA 31558 Office: Northrop Corp Dept 7610 500 E Orangethorpe Anaheim CA 92801

DURYÉE, CARYL JO, interior designer; b. Plymouth, Ind., Nov. 14, 1942; d. Carl Joseph Thompson and Mary Irene (Woodbury) Rush; m. William Albert Duryee, June 19, 1965 (div. June 1978); children: Carin Candace, Cadre Christine; m. Thomas Jay Lindell, Nov. 29, 1985. BFA in Interior Design, Moore Coll. of Art, Phila., 1964. Interior designer Dorothy Lerners, Phila., 1964-66, Herndon (Va.) House, 1976-78, Barrows Furniture, Tucson, Ariz., 1978-79, Apollo Carpet and Furniture, Tucson, 1979-81; prin. Caryl Duryee Interiors, Tucson, 1981—. Designed rooms in Tucson Mus. of Art showcases 1983, 84, 86. Mem. Tucson Mus. of Art. Mem. Am. Soc. Interior Design. Republican. Episcopalian. Home and Office: 3440 N Millard Dr Tucson AZ 85715

DUSARD, CHRISTOPHER RIME, electronics company executive; b. St. Louis, June 5, 1955; s. Leo Francis and Beatrice (Popoon) D. BSEE magna cum laude, Tex. A&M U., 1977. Technician remote sensing ctr. Tex. A&M U., College Station, 1976-77; design engr. advanced systems Garland div. E-Systems, Dallas, 1977-79; project engr. Sperry Flight Systems, Phoenix, 1979-80, sr. project engr., 1980-83, mktg. rep., 1983-85, sr. mktg. rep., 1985-87; internat. mktg. mgr. Sperry Flight Systems Group, Honeywell, Inc., Phoenix, 1987—. Patentee dynamic convergence control, moire reduction in CRT/S. Mem. Tau Beta Pi, Eta Kappa Nu. Office: Honeywell Inc Comml Flight Systems PO Box 21111 Phoenix AZ 85036

DUSENBURY, DAVID ALLAN, police officer; b. Alhambra, Calif., Mar. 20, 1940; s. Jack Hamlin and Mildred Leigh (Galloway) D.; A.A., Compton Coll., 1967; BS, Calif. State U., Los Angeles, 1970, MS, 1976; m. Nancy Nugent Dusenbury, July 16, 1966; children—Debra Ann, David Alan. With Lynwood (Calif.) Police Dept., 1961-68; with Long Beach (Calif.) Police Dept., 1968—, police sgt., 1976, police lt., 1981, police comdr., 1985, dep. chief police, 1986—; instr. Long Beach City Coll. Served with U.S. Army, 1963-65. Mem. Am. Soc. Pub. Adminstrn., Mensa. Republican. Office: 400 W Broadway Long Beach CA 90802

DUSHANE, PHYLLIS MAXINE, nurse; b. Portland, Oreg., June 3, 1924; d. Joseph Anton and Josephine Florence (Eicholtz) Miller; m. Frank Maurice Jacobson, Mar. 13, 1945 (dec. 1975); children: Karl, Kathleen, Kraig, Kirk, Karen, Kent, Krista, Kandis, Kris, Karlyn; m. Donald McLelland DuShane, July 21, 1979; stepchildren: Diane DuShane Bishop, Donald III. BS in Biology, U. Oreg., 1948; BS in Nursing, Oreg. Health Scis. U., 1968. R.N., Oreg. Pub. health nurse Marion County Health Dept., Salem, Oreg., 1968-77; pediatric nurse practitioner Marion County Health Dept., Salem, 1977—, Allergy Assocs., Eugene, Oreg., 1979—; mem. allied profl. staff Sacred Heart Gen. Hosp., Eugene, 1979—. Mem. Oreg. Pediatric Nurse Practitioners Assn. (v.p. Salem chpt. 1977-78), Am. Nurses Assn., Oreg. Nurses Assn., Nat. Assn. Pediatric Nurse Assocs. and Practitioners, Nurse Practitioners Spl. Interest Group, Salem Med. Aux. (sec. 1968), Oreg. Republican Women, Delta Gamma Alumni (v.p. 1979). Presbyterian. Home: 965 E 23d Ave Eugene OR 97405-3074 Office: Marion County Health Dept 3180 Center St NE Salem OR 97301

DUSHKIND, DONALD STANFORD, forensic psychologist; b. N.Y.C., Jan. 24, 1926; s. Michael Herbert and Hannah (Gordon) D.; m. Winifred Joan Saphir, Sept. 6, 1953 (div. 1974); children: Paul Richard, James Alan, Laura Susan; m. Louise Friedman Bennett, July 6, 1975 (div. 1988). BS, CCNY, 1945; MA, Iowa State U., 1946; PhD, NYU, 1959. Diplomate Am. Bd. Adminstrv. Psychology, Am. Bd. Psychotherapy, Am. Bd. Family Psychology; cert. supr. of mediators Am. Assn. Family Counselors and Mediators. Youth parole worker N.Y. State Tng. Sch. for Boys, N.Y.C., 1948-49, 50-56; pvt. practice N.Y.C. and San Francisco, 1956-86; pres. Litigation Behavioral Scientists, Inc., San Francisco, 1986—; Peer and hosp. utilization reviewer Psychology Systems, Inc., Milpitas, Calif., 1981—; cons. in psychol. malpractice Am. Bd. Med.-Legal Cons., 1984—; pscyhiat. social worker South Bay Guidance Clinic, Chula Vista, Calif., 1966-67; psychologist Calif. Parole Out-Patient Clinic, San Francisco, 1972-77; from psychologist to acting clinic dir. dept. pub. health, San Francisco, 1967-88; Bay area adv. bd. Nat. Ctr. on Instns. and Alternatives, 1988—; prof. sociology and psychology LIU, 1957-65. Author: Relation of Status to Attitudes and Perception of Attitudes Toward Probation, 1960; columnist: Marriage Counseling Quarterly, 1969-71. Active Dem. Cen. Com. of Marin San Rafael, Calif., 1978-80, 88—. Recipient Cert. Appreciation Marin Civic Ctr. Lions Club, 1971, Marin County Community Mental Health Services, 1978. Fellow Calif. Assn. Marriage and Family Therapists (bd. dirs. 1968-74, cert. appreciation 1969-72), Am. Coll. Forensic Psychology (adv. bd. 1983—); mem. Am. Psychol. Assn., Sociol. Practice Assn., Am. Soc. Trial Cons. (profl. standards com. 1988—). Office: Litigation Behavioral Scis 1255 Post St Ste 482 San Francisco CA 94109

DUTOIT, PATRICIA KAY, insurance executive; b. Ft. Worth, Oct. 10, 1958; d. Charles Russell Corns and Bonnie Ann (Hamilton) Hunsicker; m. Fred James Perry, Apr. 23, 1978 (div. 1982); m. James Ralph Dutoit, May 21, 1983. Student, Linfield Coll., McMinnville, Oreg., 1987—. Claims adjuster, supr. Viking Ins. Co., Salem, Oreg., 1979-87; claims adjuster, legal asst. Haugh Dean & Powell, Portland, Oreg., 1987—. Mem. Nat. Assn. Ins. Women (v.p. Salem chpt. 1986-87, pres. 1987-88). Republican. Home: 20553 SW Colville Ct Tualatin OR 97062 Office: Haugh Dean & Powell 1200 SW Main Portland OR 97205

DUTTON, JOHN EDGAR, librarian; b. Lethbridge, Alta., Can., Aug. 30, 1924; s. Edgar Evans and Hannah Eleanor (Turner) D.; m. Helen Irene, Nov. 28, 1945; children: Corinne Eleanor, Carolyn Ann, Dianne Lillian. B.A. with honors in History, U. Alta., Can., 1950; B.L.Sc., U. Toronto, Ont., Can., 1951. Librarian U. Alta. Library, Edmonton, Can., 1951-53; chief librarian Lethbridge Pub. Library, Alta., 1953-63, North York Pub. Library, Toronto, Ont., Can., 1963-77; city librarian Winnipeg Pub. Library, Man., Can., 1977-79; dir., sec.-treas. Calgary Pub. Library, Can., 1979—. Contbr. articles to profl. jours. and encys. Served with RCAF, 1943-46. Mem. Library Assn. Alta. (pres. 1962), Can. Library Assn. (2d v.p.), Ont. Library Assn. (pres. 1969-70), Nat. Library Adv. Bd. Progressive Conservative. Mem. United Ch. of Canada. Office: Calgary Pub Library, 616 MacLeod Terr SE, Calgary, AB Canada T2G 2M2 *

DUTTON, PAULINE MAE, fine arts librarian; b. Detroit, July 15; d. Thoralf Andreas and Esther Ruth (Clyde) Tandberg; B.A. in Art, Calif. State U., Fullerton, 1967; M.S. in Library Sci., U. So. Calif., 1971; m. Richard Hawkins Dutton, June 21, 1969. Elem. tchr., Anaheim, Calif., 1967-68, Corona, Calif., 1968-69; fine arts librarian Pasadena (Calif.) Public Library, 1971-80; art cons., researcher, 1981—. Mem. Pasadena Librarians

Assn. (sec. 1978, treas. 1979-80), Calif. Library Assn., Calif. Soc. Librarians, Art Librarians N.Am., Nat. Assn. Female Execs., Am. Film Inst., Am. Entrepreneurs Assn., Gilbert and Sullivan Soc., Alpha Sigma Phi. Club: Toastmistress (local pres. 1974).

DVORAK, RAY PETER, insurance company official; b. Center, N.D., Sept. 24, 1931; s. Stanley Joseph and Katherine (Schimpf) D.; m. Deanna Ellen Kern, June 1961 (div. 1974); children: Mitchell Scott, Lara Suzanne; m. Delores Marie Davis, Mar. 12, 1975. BS, U. Oreg., 1953; LLB, LaSalle Extension U., Chgo., 1964. CLU; CPCU; charter fin. cons. Claim rep. State Farm Ins. Co., Salem, Oreg., 1957-67; claim supt. State Farm Ins. Co., Oregon and Medford, Oreg., 1967—. With USAF, 1953-55, lt. col. Res. ret. Mem. Soc. CPCU, Am. Soc. CLU's. Republican. Methodist. Home: PO Box 188 840 S Oregon St Jacksonville OR 97530 Office: State Farm Ins Co PO Box 757 940 Ellendale Medford OR 97504

DWORSKY, DANIEL LEONARD, architect; b. Mpls., Oct. 4, 1927; s. Lewis and Ida (Fineberg) D.; m. Sylvia Ann Taylor, Aug. 10, 1957; children: Douglas, Laurie, Nancy. B.Arch., U. Mich., 1950. Practice architecture as Dworsky Assocs., Los Angeles, 1953—; design critic, lectr. arch. UCLA, 1983-84. Recipient Design citation Progressive Arch. mag. 1967, Gov. Calif. award 1966, 3 Los Angeles Grand Prix awards So. Calif. AIA and City of Los Angeles 1967; prin. works include Angelus Plaza Elderly Housing, Los Angeles, 1981, Ontario (Calif.) City Hall, 1980, CBS Exec. Office Bldg, North Hollywood, Calif., 1970, U. Calif. at Los Angeles Stadium, 1969, Fed. Res. Bank Bldg., Los Angeles, 1987—; U. Mich. Crisler Arena at Ann Arbor, 1968, Dominguez Hills State U. Theatre, 1977, Ventura County Govt. Center, 1979, Lloyds Bank Ops. Ctr., Los Angeles, 1980, The Park Office Bldgs., Los Angeles, 1980, Skyline Condominiums, Los Angeles, 1982, Northrop Electronics Hdqrs., Los Angeles, 1983, Hewlett-Packard Region Office, North Hollywood, 1984, Los Angeles County Mcpl. Cts. Bldg., 1985. Fellow AIA (20 awards So. Calif. chpt., including 11 honor awards; Nat. honor award 1974, 1968-69, merit award Calif. chpt. 1985, Firm award Calif. chpt. 1985). Home: 9225 Nightingale Dr Los Angeles CA 90069 Office: Dworsky Assocs 3530 Wilshire Blvd Ste 1000 Los Angeles CA 90010-2300

DWYER, JAMES RICHARD, librarian, consultant; b. Seattle, July 21, 1949; s. William Carroll and Ellen Dagmar (Carlson) D. BA in English, U. Wash., 1971, MLS, 1973. Cataloger SUNY, Albany, 1973-76, U. Oreg., Eugene, 1976-82; cataloging coordinator No. Ariz. U., Flagstaff, 1982-86; head bibliographic services Calif. State U., Chico, 1986—; vis. asst. prof. U. Wash., Seattle, 1978; library cons. Maricopa County Library, Phoenix, 1985-86. Contbg. editor (jour.) Technicalities, 1980—, cons. editor Library Hi Tech, 1986—; contbr. articles to profl. jours. Canvassing coordinator Friends of Flagstaff Pub. Library, 1985-86; mem. Bus. and Profl. for Sane Energy, Eugene, 1980-82, Earth First, Flagstaff, 1985-86, Future Options Com., Friends of Chico Pub. Library, 1987—. Named Poet Laureate, Olde Dexter (Oreg.) Theatre, 1978. Mem. ALA (councilor 1981-85, Disting. Service award 1985, Shirley Olofson Novia award 1974), Libr. Info. Tech. Assn., Ariz. State Libr. Assn. (chmn. IFC 1985-86), Calif. Libr. Assn. (head cataloging discussion group 1987-88, pres. tech. svcs. chpt. 1989—), Serials Online Ariz. (steering com. 1984-86), Social Responsibilities Round Table (action coun. 1979-81). Democrat. Home: 464 E 3d Ave Chico CA 95926 Office: Calif State U Meriam Libr Chico CA 95929-0295

DWYER, KATHI LOUISE, insurance company executive; b. Tucson, Oct. 25, 1955; d. Walter and Jane Arline (Opdyke) Dzuban; m. John Patrick Dwyer, May 15, 1977; 1 child, John Michael. BS in Distributive Edn., U. Ariz., 1977. Asst. br. mgr. County Fed. Savs. & Loan, Rockville, Md., 1977-79; benefits coordinator La. Bank and Trust, Shreveport, La., 1979-82; account exec. CIGNA Health Plan, Tucson, 1982-87; sr. account exec. Ptnrs. Nat. Healthplans, Tucson, 1987-89. Mem. Jr. League Tucson, 1987—. Mem. Nat. Assn. Health Underwriters (leading producers roundtable, 1987, 88, 89), So. Ariz. Assn. Health Underwriters (treas. 1988—, bd. dirs. 1987), Greater Tucson Assn. Life Underwriters, U. Ariz. Alumni Assn. Republican. Presbyterian. Club: Therapeutic Riding (Tucson). Office: Tucson Ins Svcs Inc 2625 E 22d St Tucson AZ 85713

DWYER, TIMOTHY EDWARD, social services administrator; b. Albany, N.Y., Dec. 29, 1951; s. Edward Joseph and Eleanor Lucille (Cote) D. AA, Hudson Valley Community Coll., 1976; BA in Psychology, SUNY, Stony Brook, 1978; MSW, U. Hawaii, 1983. Asst. office mgr. All Lifts, Inc., Albany, 1974-76; intake coord. Community Mediation Ctr., Coram, N.Y., 1978-81; social services coordinator Castle Med. Ctr., Kailua, Hawaii, 1984—. Mem. Nat. Assn. Social Workers, Acad. Cert. Social Workers. Office: Castle Med Ctr Human Svcs 640 Ulukaniki St Kailua HI 96813

DWYER, WILLIAM WARREN, radio station executive; b. Perth Amboy, N.J., Aug. 18, 1935; s. Joseph and Eva (Slosberg) D.; BA, Johns Hopkins U., 1957; LLB, N.Y. Law Sch., 1960; m. Jane Stankovich, June 30, 1961; children: Debra, Joseph, John. Account exec. Henry I. Christal Co., Los Angeles, 1965-66; mgr. Blair Radio, San Francisco, 1966-70; v.p., gen. mgr. Sta. KNBR, San Francisco, 1970—; v.p. NBC Radio, San Francisco, 1977—; founder Borel Bank. Bd. dirs. Joe Morgan Youth Found., Save High Sch. Sports. Served with U.S. Army, 1960. Recipient cert. for 10 yrs. pub. service San Francisco Bd. Suprs., 1985; William W. Dwyer Day proclaimed in his honor City of San Francisco, 1985. Mem. Nat. Assn. Broadcasters, Calif. Assn. Broadcasters, San Francisco C. of C., San Francisco Press Club, Moraga Country Club, San Leandro Boys Club, Olympic Club. Office: KNBR 1700 Montgomery St San Francisco CA 94111

DYE, LARRY WAYNE, political consultant; b. Louisville, July 20, 1948; s. Howard Charles and Rouie Mae (Lykins) D. AB, Centre Coll. of Ky., 1970; postgrad., Rutgers U., 1970-71. Various positions Rep. Nat. Com., Washington, 1971-75; rsch. asst. Sen. William V. Roth, Washington, 1975-77; mem. profl. staff U.S. Senate Subcom. for Intergovtl. Relations, Washington, 1977-78; rsch. cons. Armstrong for Senate, Englewood, Colo., 1978; legis. asst. U.S. Senator Bill Armstrong, Washington, 1979; rsch. asst. U.S. Representative Steve Symms, Washington, 1979-80; various positions various polit. candidates, Denver and Washington, 1980-87; asst. exec. dir. Morris Animal Found., Englewood, 1987; campaign mgr. Hefley for Congress, Colorado Springs, Colo., 1988; exec. dir. Colo. Rep. Party, Denver, 1988—. Home: 775 S Granby Circle Aurora CO 80012

DYER, ALICE MILDRED, psychologist; b. San Diego, July 4, 1929; d. William Silas Cann and Louise Lair (Addenbrooke) Vaile; divorced; children: Alexis Dyer Guagano, Bryan, Christine Dyer Murphy; m. James Vawter, Dec. 26, 1972. BA, Calif. State U., Fullerton, 1965, MA, 1967; PhD, U.S. Internat. U., 1980. Coord., counselor Brea (Calif.)-Olinda High Sch., 1968-72; sch. psychologist Cypress (Calif.) Sch. Dist., 1972-86; instr. North Orange County Community Coll., Fullerton, 1975-77; pvt. practice ednl. psychology Long Beach and Fountain Valley, Calif., 1978—; pvt. practice marriage and family therapy Fullerton and Brea, Calif., 1979—; psychologist, cons. Multiple Sclerosis Soc. Orange County, 1986—; facilitator adult mental health La Habra (Calif.) Community Hosp., 1988—. Bd. dirs., officer Friends of Fullerton Arboretum, 1974—; bd. dirs. Fullerton Beautiful, 1987-88, Brea Ednl. Found., 1988—; therapist Orange County Juvenile Connection Project, 1988. Recipient Appreciation award Gary Ctr., La Habra, 1975, Multiple Sclerosis Soc. Orange County, 1987. Mem. Am. Psychol. Assn., Calif. Psychol. Assn., Calif. Assn. Marriage and Family Therapists, Assn. for Children and Adults with Learning Disabilities (cons. 1970—, bd. dirs., facilitator), AAUW, Am. Bus. Women Am., Soroptomists (health chmn. Brea chpt. 1987-88). Republican. Unitarian. Office: Brea Mental Health Assocs 1203 W Imperial Hwy Ste 102 Brea CA 92621

DYER, THOMAS ALLAN, teacher, author; b. Newberg, Oreg., Aug. 19, 1947; s. Fredrick Calvin and Eldoris Pauline (Morter) D.; m. Elizabeth Ann Easley, Dec. 22, 1968. BA in English, Portland State U., 1970, MA in English, 1972; BA in Elem. Edn., Ea. Oreg. State Coll., 1975; MA in Linguistics, U. Ariz., 1978. Cert. elem. tchr., Oreg. Teaching asst. Portland (Oreg.) State U., 1970-72, instr. English, 1971-72; tchr. Simnasho Elem. Sch., Warm Springs, Oreg., 1975-77, Klamath County Sch. Dist., Klamath Falls, Oreg., 1978-80; instr. English Oreg. Inst. Tech., Klamath Falls, 1981; chmn. dept. English Internat. Sch. Islamabad, Pakistan, 1981-82; kindergarten team leader Internat. Sch. Kuala Lumpur, Malaysia, 1983-86; tchr. Gearhart Elem. Sch., Bly., Oreg., 1987—; cons. N.W. Regional Ednl. Lab., Portland, 1976-77; speaker, workshop leader Conf. on Lit. for Children & Youth Ft. Hays (Kans.) State U., 1981; workshop organizer S.E. Asia Tchr.-Counselor Conf., Kuala Lumpur, 1985; coach Interscholastic Assn. S.E. Asian Schs. Debate Champions, Kuala Lumpur, 1985-86. Author: The Whipman is Watching, 1979 (Children's Book award Bank St. Coll.), A Way of His Own, 1981 (ALA Notable Book award). Oreg. Tchr. Incentive Program grantee, 1980. Mem. Authors League, Soc. Children's Book Writers, Phi Delta Kappa.

DYER, WALTER SULLIVAN, III, computer hardware field engineer; b. Indpls., June 30, 1957; s. Walter Sullivan and Eleanor Ridonia (Potts) D.; m. Sun Hui Yun, Nov. 3, 1978; children: Walter Sullivan, William Sullivan. BS, U. Md., 1987; AS, DeKalb Community Coll., Augusta, Ga., 1979; Cert. Info. Sys., U. So. Calif., Seoul, S. Korea, 1988. Field engr./computer hardware Contel Fed. Systems, Data Systems Svcs. Div., Marina Del Rey, Calif., 1987—. With U.S. Army, 1975-87. AME Ch. Home: GDS Box 399 APO San Francisco CA 96301 Office: Contel Fed Systems 13274 Fiji Way Box 9961 Marina Del Rey CA 90295-2361

DYE-SWANEY, LISA KAY, educator; b. Sacramento, Dec. 5, 1960; d. Brian Chester Dye and Linda Kay (Switter) Sherman; m. James W. Swaney, Aug. 18, 1984; 1 child, Christina Nicole Swaney. AA in ECE, Pacific Christian Coll., Fullerton, Calif., 1984; BA in Edn., Pacific Christian Coll., 1984, BA Children's Ministries, 1984. Tchr. PCC Early Childhood Devel. Ctr., Fullerton, 1981-82; tchr. Town and Country Pre-Sch., Anaheim Hills, Calif., 1982-84, Eastside Christian Sch., Fullerton, 1984—. Dir. Fun in the Sun Summer Camp for Kids, Chandler, Ariz., 1982, Chino, Calif., 1987-88; camp counselor Prescott (Ariz.) Christian Camp, 1981-82. Mem. Pacific Christian Women's Assn. (v.p. 1988-89), Christian Women's Assn. (team leader 1987-89). Republican. Home: 2225 E Nutwood Fullerton CA 92631

DYETT, MICHAEL VANVEBER, city planning consultant; b. Buffalo, June 30, 1946; s. James Granger and Irene (Soyka) D.; m. Hildegard Anna Richardson, Sept. 21, 1980; one child, James Granger. AB, Harvard U., 1968, MRP, 1972. Vol. U.S. Peace Corps, Dakar, Senegal, 1968-72; Planner Livingston & Blayney, San Francisco, 1972-75; v.p. and chief fin. officer, prin. Blayney-Dyett, Urban and Reg. Planners, San Francisco, 1976--; Chief fin. officer Richardson-Butler Architects, San Francisco, 1988--. Contbr. articles to profl. jours. Pres. Econ. Roundtable, San Francisco, 1979. Mem Am. Planning Assn. (Outstanding Planning Award 1987), Am. Inst. Cert. Planners, U. Club (house com. 1986-88). Democrat. Episcopalian. Office: Blayney-Dyett 70 Zoe St Ste 100 San Francisco CA 94107

DYGERT, HAROLD PAUL, JR., cardiologist; b. Rochester, N.Y., June 21, 1919; s. Harold Paul and Elsie Viola (Howe) D.; m. Helen Adelaine Nelson, Apr. 22, 1944; children: Harold Paul III, William Nelson, Peter Howe. BA, U. Rochester, 1941; postgrad., Alfred U., 1942-43; MD, Syracuse U., 1950. Diplomate Am. Bd. Internal Medicine. Intern Receiving Hosp., Detroit, 1950-51, resident internal medicine, 1951-53, chief resident, 1953-54; instr. medicine Wayne State U., Detroit, 1954-55; mem. staff VA Hosp., Vancouver, Wash., 1955-59; practice medicine specializing in cardiology and internal medicine Vancouver, 1959—; chmn. Health Care Consortium, 1974-87. Pres. Wash. State Med., Ednl. and Research Found., 1971-73; bd. dirs. Wash.-Alaska Regional Med. Program, 1966-72; participant Manhattan Project, 1943-46. Served with AUS, 1943. Fellow ACP, Am. Coll. Cardiology; mem. AMA (del. 1976-77), Am. Fedn. Clin. Research, Wash. State Med. Assn. (pres. 1973-74), Portland Heart Club (pres. 1975-77), Wash. State Soc. Internal Medicine (trustee 1976-80). Home: 8407 SE Evergreen Hwy Vancouver WA 98664 Office: 2101 E McLoughlin Blvd Vancouver WA 98661

DYKSTRA, DAVID CHARLES, accountant, management consultant, author, educator; b. Des Moines, July 10, 1941; s. Orville Linden and Ermina (Dunn) D.; BSChemE, U. Calif., Berkeley, 1963; MBA, Harvard U., 1966; m. Ello Paimre, Nov. 20, 1971; children—Suzanne, Karin, David S. Corp. contr. Recreation Environs., Newport Beach, Calif., 1970-71, Hydro Conduit Corp., Newport Beach., 1971-78; v.p. fin. and adminstrn. Tree-Sweet Products, Santa Ana, Calif., 1978-80; pres., owner Dykstra Cons., Irvine, Calif., 1980-88; pres. Easy Data Corp., 1981-88; pub. Easy Data Computer Comparisons, 1982—; prin. Touche Ross Internat., Irvine, Calif., 1988—; prof. mgmt. info. systems Nat. U., Irvine, 1984—; pub. Dykstra's Computer Digest, 1984-88. Chmn. 40th Congl. Dist. Tax Reform Immediately, 1977-80; mem. nat. com. Rep. Com.; vice-chmn. Orange County Calif. Rep. Assembly, 1979-80; bd. dir. Corona Del Mar Rep. Assembly, 1980—, v.p., 1980-87, pres. 1987—. CPA, Calif. Mem. Am. Inst. CPA's, Am. Mgmt. Assn., Calif. Soc. CPA's, Data Processing Mgmt. Assn., Ind. Computer Cons. Assn., Internat. Platform Assn., Data Processing Mgmt. Assn., Orange County C. of C., Newport Beach C. of C., Harvard U. Bus. Sch. Assn. Orange County (bd. dir. 1984—, v.p 1984-86, 87—, pres. 1986-87), Harvard U. Bus. Sch. Assn. So. Calif. (bd. dirs. 1986-87), Town Hall. Clubs: John Wayne Tennis, Lido Sailing. Lodge: Rotary (bd. dir. 1984-86). Author: Manager's Guide to Business Computer Terms, 1981, Computers for Profit, 1983; contbr. articles to profl. jours. Home: 1724 Port Ashley Pl Newport Beach CA 92660 Office: 2201 Dupont Dr Irvine CA 92715

DYKSTRA, DENNIS PETER, educator, forestry scientist; b. Roseburg, Oreg., June 27, 1944; s. Albert Peter and Lois Margaret (Canaga) D.; BS in Forestry, Oreg. State U., 1966, PhD in Indsl. Engring., 1976; MBA, U. Oreg., 1971; m. Petronella Clara Spit, Mar. 28, 1968; children: Alexander Ian, Mason Lewis. Ops. research analyst Pope & Talbot, Inc., Portland, Oreg., 1969-71; mgmt.-sci. analyst Fibreboard Corp., San Francisco, 1971-72; instr., then asst. prof. Sch. Forestry, Oreg. State U., Corvallis, 1972-78; assoc. prof. Sch. Forestry and Environ. Studies, Yale U., New Haven, 1978-81; assoc. prof. div. forestry U. Dar es Salaam, Morogoro, Tanzania, 1981-82, prof., 1982-83; prof. forest sector project Internat. Inst. for Applied Systems Analysis, Laxenburg, Austria, from 1983; prof. forestry No. Ariz. U., Flagstaff, 1986-87, prof. 1988—; cons. UN, 1985-86. Author: Mathematical Programming for Natural Resource Management, 1984; editor, co-author: The Global Forest Sector: An Analytical Perspective, 1987; contbg. editor PC World mag., 1988—; contbr. 100 articles to profl. jours. Served to 1st lt. U.S. Army, 1966-69, Vietnam. Decorated Bronze Star, Air medal; recipient Nat. Doctoral Dissertation award Am. Inst. Decision Scis., 1977; numerous research grants; registered profl. engr., Oreg., Calif. Mem. Soc. Am. Foresters, Am. Forestry Assn., Internat. Soc. Tropical Foresters, Tanzanian Assn. Foresters, Ops. Research Soc. Am., Am. Inst. Indsl. Engrs., Inst. Mgmt. Sci., Sigma Xi, Phi Kappa Phi, Alpha Pi Mu, Omega Rho. Democrat. Avocations: photography, writing. Home: 3260 W Wilson Dr Flagstaff AZ 86001 Office: No Ariz U Sch Forestry Flagstaff AZ 86011

DYMALLY, MERVYN MALCOLM, congressman; b. Trinidad, W.I., May 12, 1926; s. Hamid A. and Andreid S. (Richardson) D.; m. Alice M. Gueno; children: Mark, Lynn. BA, Calif. State U., 1954; MA, Calif. State U., Sacramento, 1970; LLD (hon.), U. W. L.A., 1970; PhD in Human Behavior, U.S. Internat. U., 1978; JD (hon.), Lincoln U., Sacramento, 1975; PhD (hon.), Shaw U., N.C., 1981. Lectr. Whittier and Claremont Colls.; mem. Calif. Assembly, 1962-66, Calif. Senate, 1967-74; lt. gov. Calif., 1975-79; mem. 97th-101st Congresses from 31st Calif. Dist., 1981—; mem. Fgn. Affairs Com., Com. on Post Office and Civil Svc.; mem. Com. on D.C., chmn. subcom. on judiciary and edn. and subcom. on internat. ops.; chmn. Congl. Caucus for Sci. and Tech., Caribbean Task Force on Congl.; chmn. bd., pres. Caribbean Am. Rsch. Inst.; founder Congl. Inst. for Space, Sci. and Tech. Author: Black Politician-His Struggle for Power. Chmn. Congl. Caucus on Sci. and Technology; chmn. bd. Caribbean Action Lobby; bd. govs. Joint Ctr. Polit. Studies. Mem. AAUP, Am. Acad. Polit. Sci., Am. Polit. Acad., Phi Kappa Phi Honor Soc. Office: 1717 Longworth House Office Bldg Washington DC 20515

DZYGRYNIUK, LEE, senior buyer nuclear power plant; b. Lancashire, Eng., Sept. 13, 1951; s. David and Particia (Harris) D.; m. Sonia Janine Price, Apr. 30, 1972; children: Crystal Yvonne, Heidi Lynn. Purchasing agt. Guy F. Atkinson Co., San Francisco, 1976-77; purchasing agt. Guy F. Atkinson Co., Dateland, Ariz., 1977-78, Atkinson-Wright Schuckart & Harbor, Richland, Wash., 1978-80, Guy F. Atkinson Co., Ramon, Israel, 1980-81; material supr. Bechtel Power Corp., Palo Verde, Ariz., 1981-84; sr. buyer Ariz. Nuclear Power Project, Palo Verde, 1985—. Staff sgt. U.S. Army, 1970-76, Vietnam. Decorated Army Commendation medal. Mem. Ariz. Nuclear Soc. Office: Ariz Pub Svc PVNGS PO Box 52034 Sta 6400 Phoenix AZ 85072-2034

EACHUS, JAMES, software development executive; b. Canastota, N.Y., July 18, 1942; s. Joseph J. and Ruth M. (Porter) E.; m. Ann L. Hallstrand, May 28, 1966; children: Laura, Linda, Susan. BS cum laude, Yale U., 1964; PhD, Syracuse U., 1970. Programmer Avco Everett, Everett, Mass., 1965; programmer St. Joseph Hosp., Milw., 1970-73; systems rep. Burroughs Corp., Milw., 1973-76, systems supr., 1976-78; systems analyst Port of Seattle, 1978-80, systems mgr., 1980-81; pres. EDP System Svcs., Inc., Lynnwood, Wash., 1981—; cons. Bapt. Hosp., Nashville, 1972, U. Calif., Davis, 1972; instr. AC Spark Plug, Detroit, 1976, Joseph & Cogan, San Francisco, 1983. Programmer Pcbar computer program; designer CheckMate computer program, ScanLink computer program. Republican precinct chmn., Syracuse, N.Y., 1968, Snohomish County, Wash., 1988; chmn. bd. deacons Summit Baptist Ch., Milw., 1977; vice chmn. bd. trustees United Baptist Ch., Syracuse, 1969; treas. Bethany Baptist Ch., Seattle, 1986-89. Mem. North Star Club (treas. 1982-83). Home: 1620 Locust Way Alderwood Manor WA 98036 Office: EDP System Services Inc 19905 Scriber Lake Rd Ste 201 Lynnwood WA 98036

EADS, DEBORAH ROGERS, educator; b. Balt., July 30, 1958; d. Robert Gordon Cooper and Jeanne Rogers (Krauk) E. BS, Towson State U., 1980; MA, U. Colo., 1982. Cert. sci. tchr., outdoor educator, Md., N.Mex., Colo. Wilderness instr. Towson State U., Balt., 1978-84, S.W. Outward Sch., Santa Fe, 1980, Colo. Outward Bound Sch., Denver, 1986—; tchr. sci. and health; coord. PASSAGES Nederland (Colo.) Jr.-Sr. High Sch., 1981—. Vol. Nederland Elem. Sch., 1985-86, Colo. Freeze Voters, Boulder, 1988. Mem. NEA, Colo. Edn. Assn., Nat. Sci. Tchrs. Assn., Assn. for Experiential Edn. (chmn. profl. interest group, workshop presenter 1986, steering com. for regional conf. 1989), Greenpeace, Sierra Club. Democrat. Episcopalian. Office: Nederland Jr-Sr High Sch PO Box 714 Nederland CO 80466

EAGER, RICHARD ALVIN, television executive; b. Pasadena, Calif., July 6, 1945; s. William Henry and Helen (Hoblit) E.; m. Linda Carol Callaway, Dec., 1973 (div. 1978); children: Claire C., Colleen C.; m. Alana Rae Cecchini, June 16, 1984. BA, U. N.Mex., 1970. Dir. pub. affairs Sta. KUNM-FM Radio, Albuquerque, 1964-69; disk jockey Sta. KMYR-FM Radio, Albuquerque, 1970-71; band leader, musician Albuquerque and Taos, N.Mex., 1972-80; comml. dir., ABC affiliate Sta. KOAT-TV, Albuquerque, 1974-81; gen. mgr., dir. Sta. CCA TV 30, Albuquerque, 1981—; communications task force, Albuquerque, 1986-87; adv. bd. cable TV, Albuquerque, 1984—. Producer Eager Image, 1981-87; dir. numerous comml. prodns. and TV advt. campaigns. Active Albuquerque Arts Alliance, 1989—, youth 2000 promotional com. Am. Cancer Soc., Albuquerque, 1988—; camp counselor Sandia Prep. Sch., Albuquerque and Mountainaire, N.Mex., 1987-88, career day rep., 1988; citizen adv. com. latchkey campaign for kids Sta. KOB-TV, Albuquerque, 1986. Recipient Cert. of Appreciation Mayor of Albuquerque, 1987, 88, Award of Appreciation Albuquerque Environ. Health Dept., 1988. Mem. Internat. TV Assn. (treas. Zia chpt. 1985—), N.Mex. Jazz Soc., Acoustic Music Soc. Mem. Christian Ch. Home: 1409 Los Arboles NW Albuquerque NM 87107 Office: Sta CCA TV30 One Civic Pla NW Albuquerque NM 87102

EAMER, RICHARD KEITH, health care company executive, lawyer; b. Long Beach, Calif., Feb. 13, 1928; s. George Pierce and Lillian (Newell) E.; m. Eileen Laughlin, Sept. 1, 1951; children: Brian Keith, Erin Maureen. B.S. in Acctg., U. So. Calif., 1955, LL.B., 1959. Bar: Calif. 1960; C.P.A., Calif. Acct. L. H. Penney & Co. (C.P.A.s), 1956-59; asso. firm Ervin, Cohen & Jessup, Beverly Hills, Calif., 1959-63; partner firm Eamer, Bell and Bedrosian, Beverly Hills, 1963-69; chmn. bd., chief exec. officer Nat. Med. Enterprises, Inc., Los Angeles, 1969—; also dir. Nat. Med. Enterprises, Inc.; dir. Union Oil Co. Calif., Imperial Bank. Mem. Am. Bar Assn., Am. Inst. C.P.A.s, Calif. Bar Assn., Los Angeles County Bar Assn. Republican. Clubs: Bel Air Country, Bel Air Bay; California. Office: Nat Med Enterprises Inc 11620 Wilshire Blvd Los Angeles CA 90025 *

EARHART, J. PATRICK, layout designer; b. Arcana, Calif., Apr. 30, 1947; s. James Kenneth and Jacqueline Mavis (Ortinier) E.; m. Linda Ann Wilson, Sept. 21, 1968; children: Zachary Atsa, Zina Melanie. AA, DeAnza Coll., Cupertino, Calif., 1972; postgrad., Oreg. State U., 1981-86. Integrated circle layout designer Fairchild Semiconductor Co., Mountain View, Calif., 1968-69; Integrated cir. layout designer Intel Corp., Santa Clara, Calif., 1969-76; sr. integrated layout designer Advanced Memory Systems, Santa Clara, 1976-77, Advanced Micro Devices, Sunnyvale, Calif., 1977-79, Hewlett-Packard, Corvallis, Oreg., 1979--; pvt. practice computer cons., Corvallis, 1986--; instr. Linn-Benton Community Coll., Corvallis, 1980-82, Foothill Community Coll., Los Altos, Calif., 1978-79. Author: Integrated Circuit Layout Design, 1984. Mem. Model A (v.p. Albany, Oreg. chpt. 1983-84), Bonsai. Democrat. Home: 6205 NW Fair Oaks Dr Corvallis OR 97330-3126

EARL, EDWARD DENNIS, small business owner; b. Combs, Ark., July 21, 1937; s. Irving Dennis Earl and Melva Pearl (Eckles) Provencher; m. Joanne Marie DiTolla, Aug. 29, 1959; children: Maryann, Edward Dennis Jr. BS in Mktg., Calif. State U., Long Beach, 1971. Salesman, mgr. Indsl. Filtration, Long Beach, Calif., 1960-80; pres., owner Aqua-Tec Filter Co., Santa Fe Springs, Calif., 1975—. Vice pres. Downey (Calif.) Community Hosp. Meml. Trust Found., 1983—; chmn. bd. Downey Family YMCA, 1968—. Recipient Red Triangle award, Downey Family YMCA, Downy, 1988, Disting. Svc. award, Downey Family YMCA, Downey, 1980. Mem. L.A. Soc. of Coatings Technology, Kiwanis (pres. Downey Los Amigos 1986-87). Republican. Roman Catholic. Home and Office: Aqua-Tec Filter Co 12410 Clark Ave Santa Fe Springs CA 90670

EARL, WILLIAM LEE, research chemist; b. Chgo., June 13, 1945; s. Lewis Harold and Patricia (Miller) E.; m. Elaine Kaye Mehollin, 1969 (div. 1976); m. Jary Jacklin Sheppard, Jan. 30, 1988. BA, Beloit Coll., 1967; MS, U. Calif., Berkeley, 1969, PhD, 1975. Postdoctoral fellow U. Lausanne (Switzerland), 1975-79; NRC postdoctoral fellow Nat. Bur. Standards, Gaithersburg, Md., 1977-79, rsch. chemist, 1979-81; staff mem. Los Alamos Nat. Lab., 1981—; cons. Philip Morris Co., Richmond, Va., 1981-85. Contbr. articles to profl. jours. With U.S. Army, 1969-71. Mem. Phi Beta Kappa, Phi Eta Sigma. Democrat. Office: Los Alamos Nat Lab Mail Stop G740 Los Alamos NM 87545

EARLE, DEBRA KNOTT, teacher; b. Glendale, Calif., May 26, 1952; d. Clifton Bryant and Hazel Jean (Smithwick) Lawson; m. David D. Earle. BA in History, U.C. Santa Barbara, 1983, postgrad., 1983-84. Tchr. Westminster Ctr., L.A., 1972-77; asst. purchasing dir. Otologic Med. Group, L.A., 1977-79; tchr. Antelope Valley Union High Sch. Dist., Palmdale, Calif., 1983—. Advisor Keywanettes-Kiwanis Girl's Club Palmdale 1984--, Social Studiess. Fellow NEH. Mem. Phi Alpha Theta. Democrat. Presbyterian. Home: 3335 E Ave Q-6 Palmdale CA 93550 Office: Palmdale High Sch 2137 E Ave R Palmdale CA 93550

EARLE, ROBERT ALFRED, computer infosystems engineer; b. Concord, N.H., July 1, 1937; s. Charles Edwin and Lois Maude (Merril) E.; m. Anne Patrice Johnson, June 20, 1964 (div. Apr. 1988); children: Elizabeth Anne, Charles Lewis. BS in Math., Calif. Poly., 1964, MS in Math., 1982. Research engr. Gen. Dynamics, Pomona, Calif., 1964-69, sr. research engr., 1969-76, design specialist, 1976-79, group engr., 1979-83, engr. specialist, 1983-87, engr. staff specialist, 1987—. Author, editor: Trail Construction Maintenance, 1984, Where to Go Camping Book, 1985. Scoutmaster Old Baldy council Boy Scouts Am., Ontario, Calif., 1981-88, commr., 1988—, mem. high adventure team, 1983—, adviser Order of the Arrow, 1983—. Served to cpl. USMC, 1956-60. Recipient Vigil Honor award Old Baldy council Boy Scouts Am., 1988; named Arrowman of Yr., Old Baldy council Boy Scouts Am., 1985. Republican. Home: PO Box 415 Mount Baldy CA 91759 Office: Gen Dynamics PO Box 2507 Pomona CA 91766

EARLE, SYLVIA ALICE, research biologist, oceanographer; b. Gibbstown, N.J., Aug. 30, 1935; d. Lewis Reade and Alice Freas (Richie) E. B.S., Fla. State U., 1955; M.A., Duke U., 1956, Ph.D., 1966. Resident dir. Cape Haze Marine Lab., Sarasota, Fla., 1966-67; research scholar Radcliffe Inst., 1967-

69; research fellow Farlow Herbarium, Harvard U., 1967-75, researcher, 1975—; research assoc. in botany Natural History Mus. Los Angeles County, 1970-75; research biologist, curator Calif. Acad. Scis., San Francisco, from 1976; research assoc. U. Calif., Berkeley, 1969-75; founder, v.p., sec.-treas., bd. dirs. Deep Ocean Tech., Inc., Oakland, Calif.; founder, v.p., sec.-treas. Deep Ocean Engring., Oakland, 1981-88, chief exec. officer, 1988—, also bd. dirs. Author: Exploring the Deep Frontier, 1980. Editor: Scientific Results of the Tektite II Project, 1972-75. Contbr. 60 articles to profl. jours. Trustee World Wildlife Fund U.S., 1976-82, council mem., 1984—; trustee World Wildlife Fund Internat., 1979-81, council mem., 1981—; trustee Charles A. Lindbergh Fund., Ocean Trust Found.; council mem. Internat. Union Conservation Nature, 1979-81; corp. mem. Woods Hole Oceanographic Inst.; mem. Nat. Adv. Com. Oceans and Atmosphere, 1980-84. Recipient Conservation Service award U.S. Dept. Interior, 1970, Boston Sea Rovers award, 1972, 79, Nogi award Underwater Soc. Am., 1976, Conservation service award Calif. Acad. Sci., 1979, Lowell Thomas award Explorer's Club, 1980, Order of Golden Ark Prince Netherlands, 1980; named Woman of Yr. Los Angeles Times, 1970, Scientist of Yr., Calif. Mus. Sci. and Industry, 1981. Fellow AAAS, Marine Tech. Soc., Calif. Acad. Scis., Explorers Club, Calif. Acad. Sci.; mem. Internat. Phycological Soc. (sec. 1974-80), Phycological Soc. Am., Am. Soc. Ichthyologists and Herpetologists, Am. Inst. Biol. Scis., Brit. Phycological Soc., Ecol. Soc. Am., Internat. Soc. Plant Taxonomists. Club: Explorers (fellow). Home: 12812 Skyline Blvd Oakland CA 94619 Office: Calif Acad Scis Golden Gate Pk San Francisco CA 94118

EARLY, JAMES MICHAEL, electronics research consultant; b. Syracuse, N.Y., July 25, 1922; s. Frank J. and Rhoda Gray E.; m. Mary Agnes Valentine, Dec. 28, 1948; children—Mary, Kathleen, Joan Early Farrell, Rhoda Early Alexander, Maureen Early Mathews, Rosemary Early North, James, Margaret Mary. B.S., N.Y. Coll. Forestry, Syracuse, N.Y., 1943; M.S., Ohio State U., 1948, Ph.D., 1951. Instr., research assoc. Ohio State U., Columbus, 1946-51; dir. lab. Bell Telephone Labs., Murray Hill, N.J., 1951-64, Allentown, Pa., 1964-69; dir. research and devel. Fairchild Semicondr. Corp., Palo Alto, Calif., 1969-83, sci. advisor, 1983-86; research cons. 1986—. Served with U.S. Army, 1943-45. Fellow IEEE (recipient J.J. Ebers award IEEE Electron Device Soc. 1979); mem. AAAS, Am. Phys. Soc., Internat. Platform Assn. Roman Catholic. Home and Office: 740 Center Dr Palo Alto CA 94301

EARP, KENNETH ROLAND, psychology educator; b. Denver, Oct. 30, 1929; s. John Rosslyn and Kathleen May (Goodliffe) E.; m. Sherrie McGillivray, Oct. 1, 1961 (div. 1983); children: Dwight David Vandegrift, Valorie Victoria, Susan Marie, Timothy A.; m. Dorothy Louise Palmer, Nov. 26, 1983. BS, U. N.Mex., 1956, MS, 1959. Cert. secondary tchr., Calif.(life). Research assoc. U. N.Mex., Albuquerque, 1958-59; ednl. psychologist Human Resources Inst., Albuquerque, 1959-60; tchr. high sch. dist. El Cantro, Calif., 1960-63, Salinas, Calif., 1983-86; coordinator testing, high sch. dist. Salinas, 1984—. Pres. Unitarian Universalist Fellowship Salinas, 1976-88. Served as cpl. U.S. Army, 1947-51. Mem. Am. Psychol. Assn. (assoc.), Calif. Tchrs. Assn. (v.p., pres. local chpt.), Sigma Xi, Phi Delta Kappa. Democrat. Unitarian. Home: 644 University Ave Salinas CA 93901 Office: Salinas Union High Sch Dist 431 W Alisal St Salinas CA 93901

EASLEY, GEORGE WASHINGTON, construction executive; b. Williamson, W.Va., Mar. 14, 1933; s. George Washington and Isabel Ritchie (Saville) E.; student U. Richmond, 1952-56; children—Bridget Bland, Kathy Clark, Saville Woodson, Marie Alexis, Isabell Roxanne, George Washington, Laura Dean. Hwy. engr. Va. Dept. Hwys., Richmond, 1956-62; dep. city mgr. City of Anchorage, 1962-68; prin. assoc. Wilbur Smith & Assos., Los Angeles, 1969-70; commr. pub. works State of Alaska, Juneau, 1971-74; exec. v.p. Burgess Internat. Constrn. Co., Anchorage, 1974, pres., 1975; pres., chmn. bd. George W. Easley Co., Anchorage, 1976-86 ; pres. Alaska Aggregate Corp., Fairbanks Sand & Gravel Co., 1986—; bd. dirs. Totem Ocean Trailer Express, Inc., Life Ins. Co. Alaska. Mem. New Capital Site Planning Commn. State of Alaska, 1981—; bd. dirs. Anchorage YMCA. Recipient commendations City of Anchorage, 1966, Greater Anchorage, Inc., 1969, Ketchikan C. of C., 1973, Alaska State Legis., 1974, Gov. of Alaska, 1974; named one of Outstanding Young Men, Anchorage Jaycees, 1964. Registered profl. engr., Calif. Mem. U.S. C. of C. (nat. com. on small bus.), Alaska C. of C. (dir. 1978—, chmn. 1982-83), Anchorage C. of C. (sec.-treas. 1976, v.p. 1977, pres.-elect 1978, pres. 1979-80, dir. 1982-88, Gold Pan award 1969, 77), Hwy. Users Fedn. Alaska (dir. 1972—, treas. 1974—), Orgn. Mgmt. of Alaska's Resources (past dir.), Am. Pub. Works Assn., Anchorage Transp. Commn. (past chmn.), Associated Gen. Contractors (dir. Alaska chpt. 1978—, chpt. treas. 1980-81, sec. 1981, pres. 1984, nat. com. labor relations, Hard Hat award, 1985), Am. Mil. Engrs. (v.p. Alaska chpt. 1978), Ak. Trucking Assn. (bd. dirs. 1986—), Inst. Mcpl. Engrs., Inst. Traffic Engrs., Internat. Orgn. Masters, Mates and Pilots (hon.), Common Sense for Alaska (past pres.), Commonwealth North (charter). Democrat. Presbyterian. Club: San Francisco Tennis. Lodge: Rotary. Home: 333 M St #210 Anchorage AK 99501 Office: 240 E 68th Ave Anchorage AK 99518

EASLEY, LOYCE ANNA, painter; b. Weatherford, Okla., June 28, 1918; d. Thomas Webster and Anna Laura (Sanders) Rogers; m. Mack Easley, Nov. 17, 1939; children: June Elizabeth, Roger. BFA, U. Okla., 1943; postgrad., Art Students League, N.Y.C., 1947-49, Santa Fe Inst. Fine Arts, 1985. Tchr. Pub. Sch., Okmulgee, Okla., 1946-47, Hobbs, N.Mex., 1947-49; tchr. painting N.Mex. Jr. Coll., Hobbs, 1965-80; tchr. Art Workshops in N.Mex., Okla., Wyoming. Numerous one-woman and multiple painting exhibitions in mus., univs., galleries, including: Gov.'s Gallery, Santa Fe, Selected Artists, N.Y.C., Roswell, N.Mex. Mus., N.Mex. State U., Las Cruces, Tex., West Tex. Mus., Tex. Tech. Coll., Lubbock and many others; paintings in permnent collections include: USAF Acad., Colo. Springs, Colo., Roswell Mus., Carlsbad, N.Mex. Mus.. Coll. of Santa Fe and others in private and pub. collections; featured in S.W. and Art and Santa Fe Mag., 1981, '82. Named Disting. Former Student, U. Okla. Art Sch., 1963; nominated for Gov's. award in Art, N.Mex., 1988. Mem. N.Mex. Artists Equity (lifetime mem. 1963). Democrat. Presbyterian.

EASON, PETER LAWRENCE, mortgage company executive; b. N.Y.C., May 2, 1955; s. Leroy and Gloria Ruth (Abrams) E.; m. Irene Jessie Seager, Nov. 17, 1984. BA, Ohio State U., 1977; MPA, U. So. Calif., L.A., 1982. Merchandiser Bloomingdale's, N.Y.C., 1977-78; adminstrv. asst. McVail Ltd. div. McDonald's, Vail, Colo., 1978-79; rsch. analyst Mayor Tom Bradley, L.A., 1982; asst. mgr. Toys "R" Us, Compton, Calif., 1983; ops. supr. Great Western Bank, Northridge, Calif., 1983-85; ops. mgr. Sears Savs. Bank, Northridge, 1985-86; systems and ops. coord. Empire of Am., FSB, Woodland Hills, Calif., 1986-88; adminstrv. mgr., compliance officer Presdl. Mortgage Co. & Pacific Thrift Loan Co., Woodland Hills, 1988—. Producer 24K golf plated "Bush 88", 1988. Coord. March of Dimes Walk Am., Woodland Hills, 1988, 89; pres. P.I.E. Mgmt. Svcs. Republican. Avocations: photography, skiing, tennis, collecting baseball cards, political memorabilia. Office: Presdl Mortgage Co 21031 Ventura Blvd Woodland Hills CA 91364

EAST, ERNEST EARL, lawyer; b. Vallejo, Calif., Oct. 17, 1942; s. Ernest Earl East Sr. and Evelyn E. (Pendergrass) Walworth. BA, U. Tulsa, 1965; JD, U. Ark., 1969. Bar: Ark. 1969, Tex. 1973, U.S. Supreme Ct. 1973. Atty. SEC, Washington, 1969-73; assoc. Ritchie, Ritchie & Crosland, Dallas, 1973-74; assoc. gen. counsel Boise (Idaho) Cascade Corp., 1974-80, Ga. Pacific Corp., Atlanta, 1980-84; assoc. gen. counsel, asst. sec. Del Webb Corp., Phoenix, 1984-85, v.p., sec., gen. counsel, 1985—. Pres. Idaho Human Rights Commn., Boise, 1976-80; bd. dirs. Ariz. Hist. Soc., Phoenix, 1987—. Mem. ABA, Am. Soc. Corp. Secs., Am. Corp. Counsel Assn., State Bar Tex. Clubs: Plaza, Mansion (Phoenix). Home: 6817 N 4th Pl Phoenix AZ 85012 Office: Del Webb Corp 2231 E Camelback Rd Phoenix AZ 85016

EASTLAKE, CARLETON CHESMORE, screenwriter, producer; b. N.Y.C., Dec. 23, 1947; s. Alfred Chesmore and Marion Hilda Eastlake; m. Loraine Depsres, Nov. 24, 1985; 1 stepson, David Mulholland. Student, Columbia U., 1965-66; AB, UCLA, 1969; JD, Harvard U., 1972. Bar: Calif. 1973, U.S. Dist. Ct. (cen. dist.) Calif. 1982. Atty. FTC, Washington, 1972-74, atty., advisor Office of Comm. Nye, 1974-76; atty. Los Angeles Regional Office FTC, 1977-79, acting regional dir., asst. dir., 1979-83; assoc. Lawler, Felix & Hall, Los Angeles, 1976-77; screenwriter, pres. The Eastlake-Despres Co., Los Angeles, 1983—; producer Warner Bros. TV. Writer (TV movies, series) Murder She Wrote, The Equalizer, Airwolf, V, A Man Called Hawk. Recipient Edgar Allan Poe award, 1986. Mem. Writers Guild Am., Calif. Bar Assn., ABA, Zuma Beach Protective Assn. Democrat.

EASTMAN, CAROLYN BERTHA, drug and alcohol counselor; b. Madison, Wis., Feb. 12, 1933; d. Edward William and Lillian (Rude) Rogers; m. Donald Duane Eastman, Aug. 28, 1954 (dec. 1980); children: Debra Riches, Donald, Mary, Cathy, Roger. AAS, Glendale Community Coll., 1984; BEd, Ariz. State U., 1985; postgrad., No. Ariz. U., 1986, St. Francis, 1988. Cert. addiction counselor, Ariz. Sec. drug and alcohol unit Valley View Hosp, Youngtown, Ariz., 1982-85, drug and alcohol counselor, 1985-86; drug and alcohol counselor New Beginnings, North Las Vegas, Nev., 1987—. Mem. NAFE, Am. Bus. Women's Assn., Assn. for Death Edn. and Counseling. Roman Catholic. Home: 1750 E Karen Apt 184 Las Vegas NV 89109 Office: New Beginnings 1409 E Lake Mead Blvd North Las Vegas NV 89114

EASTMAN, SUSAN ELIZABETH, probation officer; b. San Jose, Calif., Jan. 24, 1948; d. David Clyde Gray and LaVelle Jeroline (Sandau) Hughes; m. William Edward Eastman, Feb. 14, 1976; children: Kimberley Lynn, James Michael. AA, Fresno City Coll., 1975; BS, Calif. State U., Fresno, 1977, postgrad., 1982—. Crisis counselor Mariposa County Mental Health, Yosemite, Calif., 1975-77; dep. probation officer Fresno County Probation Dept., Fresno, 1977—; instr., Model Treatment Program, Fresno, 1976. Mem. Cen. Calif. Juvenile Officers Assn. (treas., bd. dirs. 1982—), Womens Criminal Justice Assn., Greater Fresno Soccer League (pres. 1987—). Democrat. Office: Fresno County Probation PO Box 453 Fresno CA 93709

EASTON, ROBERT (OLNEY), author, environmentalist; b. July 4, 1915; s. Robert Eastman and Ethel (Olney) E.; m. Jane Faust, Sept. 24, 1940; children: Joan Easton Lentz, Katherine Easton Renga (dec.), Ellen Easton Brumfiel, Jane. Student, Stanford U., 1933-34, postgrad., 1938-39; B.S., Harvard U., 1938; M.A., U. Calif.-Santa Barbara, 1960. Ranch hand, day laborer, mag. editor 1939-42; co-pub., editor Lampasas (Tex.) Dispatch, 1946-50; instr. English Santa Barbara City Coll., 1959-65; writing and pub. cons. U.S. Naval Civil Engring. Lab., Port Hueneme, Calif., 1961-69; co-founder Sisquoc Sanctuary for Calif. condor, 1937; responsible for first wilderness area established under Nat. Wilderness Act, Los Padres Nat. Forest, Calif., 1968. Author: The Happy Man, 1943; (with Mackenzie Brown) Lord of Beasts, 1961; (with Jay Monaghan and others) The Book of the American West, 1963; The Hearing, 1964; (with Dick Smith) California Condor: Vanishing American, 1964; Max Brand: The Big Westerner, 1970; Black Tide: The Santa Barbara Oil Spill and Its Consequences, 1972; Guns, Gold and Caravans, 1978; China Caravans: An American Adventurer in Old China, 1982; This Promised Land, 1982; Life and Work, 1988, Power and Glory, 1989; editor: Max Brand's Best Stories, 1967; co-editor: Bullying the Moqui (Charles F. Lummis), 1968; contbr. to numerous mags. including Atlantic and N.Y. Times mag.; also anthologies, including Great Tales of the American West. Co-chmn. Com. for Santa Barbara; trustee Santa Barbara Mus. Natural History and Santa Barbara Community Environ. Coun. 1st lt. inf. U.S. Army, 1942-46, ETO. Recipient Honor award Calif. Conservation Coun. Home: 2222 Las Canoas Rd Santa Barbara CA 93105

EASTON-HAFKENSCHIEL, CYNTHIA RUTH, architect; b. San Francisco, Mar. 27, 1949; d. Ellis Herbert and Mary Alice (Scott) Easton; m. Joseph Henry Hafkenschiel, Sept. 28, 1972; children: Erin Thomas, Alexander Scott. BA in Environ. Design, U. Calif., Berkeley, 1972; BArch with honors, U. Md., 1975. Lic. architect, Calif. Intern architecture Leo A. Daly, Washington, 1972-75, Living Systems, Inc., Winters, Calif., 1975, Alan Oshima, Sacramento, 1976-80; pvt. practice architecture Sacramento, 1980—; writer Calif. Architect's Lic. Exam, 1987-88. Recipient Spl. Achievement award Legal Services, Washington, 1986. Mem. AIA (bd. dirs. 1981-82), Soc. for Mktg. Profls. (bd. dirs. 1980-81), Constrn. Specifications Inst. (co-editor 1980-81), Nat. Coun. Archtl. Registration Bds. (com. mem. 1989—). Lodge: Soroptimist. Office: 2122 J St Sacramento CA 95816

EATHERTON, LARRY EUGENE, pharmacist, consultant; b. Burwell, Nebr., Mar. 8, 1932; s. William W. and Fern M. (Shafer) E.; m. Shirley J. Lysinger, Aug. 23, 1953 (div. July 1981); children: Jeffry A., Melinda S. (dec.), Sarah Jane (dec.); m. Nelrita J. Lydia, Aug. 1, 1981. BS in Pharmacy, U. Nebr., 1954. Cert. emergency med. technician. Pharmacist Warren Drug Co., Beatrice, Nebr., 1956-58, Macy Drug, Ft. Morgan, Colo., 1958-60; pharmacist, owner, mgr. Akron (Colo.) Drug, 1960—; cons. pharmacist Washington County Pub. Hosp., Akron, 1962—. Vol. Washington County Ambulance Svc., 1982-89. 1st lt. U.S. Army, 1954-56, Korea. Mem. Colo. Pharmacal Assn. (bd. dirs. 1984—, pres. 1989—), Akron C. of C. (pres. 1962-65, 88), Masons, Elks. Republican. Home: 155 E 8th Ave Akron CO 80720 Office: Akron Drug 141 Main St Akron CO 80720

EATON, THOMAS CLARK, insurance company executive; b. Fresno, Calif., Nov. 24, 1952; s. Robert Louis and Polly (Gregory) E.; m. Deborah Thomason, Nov. 19, 1983; children: Jonathan, Elisabeth. BA, Pacific U., 1976. Salesman Fred S. James & Co., Portland, Oreg., 1974-75; v.p., treas. Eaton & Eaton Ins. Brokers, Fresno, 1976-84; mgr. truck ins. div. Marsh & McLennan, San Francisco, 1984-85; chmn., pres. Wyndham Ins. Services Ltd., Burlingame, Calif., 1985—; chmn. bd. dirs. Wyndham cons. Services, Burlingame, Calif. Dir. San Mateo (Calif.) County Vol. Ctr., 1987—. Mem. Ind. Ins. Agts. and Brokers, Fedn. Afro Asian Insurors and Reinsurors, Sunnyside Country Club, Green Hills Country Club. Republican. Office: Wyndham Ins Svcs Ltd 1213 Donnelly Ave Burlingame CA 94010

EATOUGH, DELBERT JAY, chemistry educator; b. Provo, Utah, Sept. 15, 1940; s. Richard George and Thelma Elizabeth (Burr) E.; m. Judith Mae Pursley, Mar. 5, 1964; children: Michael, Michele, David, Rebecca, Melinda, Jennifer, Elizabeth. BS, Brigham Young U., 1964, PhD, 1967. Chemist Shell Devel. Co., Emeryville, Calif., 1967-70; dir. Thermochem. Inst. Brigham Young U., Provo, 1970-85, prof. chemistry, 1985—. Author: Heats of Metal Ligand Interactions, 1978; editor, author: Titration Calorimetry, 1977, 3d rev. edit. 1985; contbr. numerous articles to sci. jours. Scoutmaster Boy Scouts Am., Provo, 1975-86. mem. Calorimetry Conf. (sec., treas. 1976-85, chmn. 1985—), Am. Chem. Soc., Air Pollution Control Assn., Am. Assn. Aerosol Research. Mormon. Home: 1252 N Uinta Dr Provo UT 84604 Office: Brigham Young U 276 FB Provo UT 84602

EAVES, ALLEN CHARLES EDWARD, hematologist, medical agency administrator; b. Ottawa, Ont., Can., Feb. 19, 1941; s. Charles Albert and Margaret Vernon (Smith) E.; m. Connie Jean Halperin, July 1, 1975; children—Neil, Rene, David, Sara. B.Sc., Acadia U., Wolfville, N.S., Can., 1962; M.Sc., Dalhousie U., Halifax, N.S., 1964, M.D., 1969; Ph.D., U. Toronto, Ont., Can., 1974. Intern Dalhousie U., Halifax, N.S., Can., 1968-69; resident in internal medicine Sunnybrook Hosp., Toronto, 1974-75, Vancouver Gen. Hosp., 1975-79; dir. Terry Fox Lab., Cancer Control Agy. B.C., Vancouver, Can., 1981—; asst. prof. medicine U. B.C., 1979-83, assoc. prof., 1983-88, head div. hematology, 1985—, prof., 1988—; bd. dirs. B.C. Cancer Found., Vancouver, Can., 1984—. Fellow Royal Coll. Physicians (Can.), ACP. Home: 2705 W 31st Ave, Vancouver, BC Canada V6L 1Z9 Office: Terry Fox Lab, BC Cancer Rsch Ctr, 601 W 10th Ave, Vancouver, BC Canada V5Z 1L3

EBBESEN, LAURITS BEN, supermarket chain executive; b. Copenhagen, Nov. 12, 1938; came to U S, 1949; s Ole Edwin and Helga Elna (Pedersen) E; m.Sharon Kay Tavenner, Feb. 14, 1980; children Douglas, Pamala, Jeffrey, Randall, James. Student, U. Oreg., 1962. Dir. perishables Mayfair Markets, Seattle, 1965-75; gen. mgr. Thriftway Stores, Seattle, 1975-85; pres. RBI Major League Baseball Support, Seattle, 1987-88. Co-editor Am. Investments, 1980-85. Mem. Northwest Produce Assn. (pres. 1975--), Twin Lakes Country Club Federal Way, Wash.). Republican. Lutheran. Office: Thriftway Stores PO Box 3763 Seattle WA 98124

EBELL, CECIL WALTER, lawyer; b. Baker, Oreg., June 26, 1947; s. Cecil John and Sylvia Jean (Malone) E.; m. Dianna Rae Gentry, June 2, 1980; children: Erik, Anne, Michael. BS, Oreg. State U., 1970; MS, U. No. Colo., 1973; JD, Lewis & Clark Coll., 1977. Bar: Oreg. 1977, Alaska 1978, U.S. Ct. Appeals (9th cir.) 1981, U.S. Supreme Ct. 1985. Pvt. practice Portland, Oreg., 1977-78; ptnr. Hartig, Rhodes, Norman & Mahoney, Anchorage, 1978-84, Jamin, Ebell, Bolger & Gentry, Kodiak, Alaska, 1984—. Press sec., Clay Myers for Gov. campaign, Oreg., 1974. Capt. USMC, 1970-73. Mem. ABA, Assn. Trial Lawyers Am., Rotary. Democrat. Office: Jamin Ebell Bolger Gentry 323 Carolyn St Kodiak AK 99615

EBERLE, RICHARD MICHAEL, divorce mediator and business consultant; b. Everett, Wash., Oct. 21, 1942; s. Michael and Cecile Eugenie (Clement) E.; m. Christina Ersteniuk, Apr. 20, 1975. BA, St. Thomas Sem., 1964, MDiv., 1968. Roman Cath. priest Archdiocese of Seattle, 1968-74; mgr. St. Vincent de Paul, Seattle, 1974; dir. sales. devel. The Pacific Inst., Seattle, 1975-80; v.p. Human Devel. Tng. Inst., Bellevue, Wash., 1980-82, Human Resources Assocs., Seattle, 1982-83; owner Eberle & Assocs., Bellevue, 1983—; bd. dirs. Wash. Women Employment and Edn., Seattle, Divorce Lifeline; owner G.B.E. Pubs., Inc. Author: Divorce with Dignity, 1988. Mem. Mediation Consortium of Wash. State (v.p., sec. 1986-88), Indsl. Rels. Rsch. Assn., Nat. Coun. Childrens Rights (Northwest chpt.), Nat. Speakers Assn., Assn. Labor Mgmt. Adminstrn. and Cons. on Alcoholism, Acad. Family Mediators, Kiwanis. Republican. Home: 4720 154th Pl SE Bellevue WA 98006 Office: Eberle & Assocs 10900 NE 8th St Ste 900 Bellevue WA 98004

EBERWEIN, BARTON DOUGLAS, construction company executive, consultant; b. Balt., Aug. 19, 1951; s. Bruce George and Thelma Joyce (Cox) E.; m. Marci R. Eberwein.,. BS, U. Oreg., 1974, MBA, 1988. Sales mgr. Teleprompter of Oreg., Eugene, 1974-75; pres., owner Oreg. Images, Eugene, 1975-80; mktg. mgr. Clearwater Prodns., Eugene, 1980-82; sales mgr. Western Wood Structures, Portland, Oreg., 1982-84, mktg. coordinator, 1984-85, mktg. dir., 1985-89; dir. bus. devel. Hoffman Constrn. Co., Portland, 1989—; chmn. Forest Products Com., Portland, 1984—, Am. Inst. Timber Constrn., Denver, 1985—; cons. Dept. Econ. Devel., Oregon City, 1984—, Oreg. Forest Industry, Salem, 1985—. Editor: (jour.) Why Wood, 1984; prod. video Vault of Man, 1984. Bd. Dirs. N.W. Youth Corps, Eugene, 1984—; vol. Portland Marathon Com., 1984—, Portland Festival Arts, 1986—; vol. Clackamas County (Oreg.) Econ. Devel., 1985—. Recipient Johnny Horizen award U.S. Dept. Interior Bur. Land Mgmt., 1978; named Mktg. Firm of Yr., Portland C. of C., 1984. Mem. Soc. Mktg. Profl. Services, Am. Mktg. Assn., Constrn. Specifications Inst., Nat. League Cities, Internat. Assn. Bus. Communication, Univ. Club, Founders Club, Riverside Athletic Club, Oreg. Road Runners Club. Democrat. Methodist. Home: 263 Cervantes Lake Oswego OR 97035 Office: Hoffman Constrn Co 1300 SW Sixth Ave Portland OR 97207

EBIE, WILLIAM D., museum director; b. Akron, Ohio, Feb. 7, 1942; s. William P. and Mary Louise (Karam) E.; m. Gwyn Anne Schumacher, Apr. 11, 1968 (div. Jan. 1988); children: Jason William, Alexandra Anne. BFA, Akron Art Inst., 1964; MFA, Calif. Coll. of Arts and Crafts, 1968. Graphic artist Alameda County Health Dept., Oakland, Calif., 1967-68; instr. painting Fla. A&M U., Tallahassee, 1968-69; instr. photography Lawrence (Kans.) Adult Edn. Program, 1969-70; asst. dir. Roswell (N.Mex.) Mus. & Art Ctr., 1971-87, dir., 1987—; juror various art exhbns., 1971—; panelist N.Mex. Arts Div., Santa Fe, 1983—; field reviewer Inst. for Mus. Svcs., 1988. Chmn. Roswell Cultural Arts Com., 1981-82, Roswell Cultural Affairs Com., 1983-85; mem. Roswell Conv. and Vis. Bur., 1983. Mem. Am. Assn. of Mus., Mountain Plains Mus. Assn., N.Mex. Assn. of Mus. Democrat. Office: Roswell Mus & Art Ctr 100 W 11th St Roswell NM 88201

EBNER, GAIL SHIRLEY, pharmaceutical company executive; b. Chgo., Apr. 22, 1953; d. Richard Theodore and Shirley Helen (Smith) E.; m. Thomas Paul Stockfisch, July 9, 1977. BA, Trinity Coll., Deerfield, Ill., 1979. Clin. research coord. Feighner Research Inst., La Mesa, Calif., 1982-84; clinic dir. PharmaKinetics, Inc., San Diego, 1984-85; clinic mgr. GeneralMed, San Diego, 1986; sr. clin. research assoc. Parexel Internat. Corp., San Diego, 1986--. Mem. Assocs. of Clin. Pharmacology. Office: Parexel Internat Corp 5465 Morehouse Dr Ste 145 San Diego CA 92121

EBY, DAVID EUGENE, geologist; b. Harrisburg, Pa., Sept. 26, 1947; s. Eugene Elwood and Ruth Dunkleberger (Crozier) E.; m. I. Marie Cooper, Aug. 17, 1968; children: Rebecca L., Matthew A. AB, Franklin and Marshall Coll., 1969; MS, Brown U., 1972; PhD, SUNY, Stony Brook, 1977. Teaching asst. Brown U., Providence, 1969-71, SUNY, Stony Brook, N.Y., 1971-73; asst. prof. geology prof. L.I.U., Southampton, N.Y., 1973, Franklin and Marshall Coll., Lancaster, Pa., 1973-74, U. Tex., Dallas, 1975-79; adj. asst. prof. U. Tex., Arlington, Dallas, 1979-83; sr. research geologist Mobil Oil R&D Co., Dallas, 1979-83; geologic advisor Union Pacific Resources Co., Englewood, Colo., 1983—; speaker in field. Contbr. articles to profl. jours. Dir. Lookout Preschool Richardson, Tex., 1977-78; ch. coucil mem. Community Luth. Ch., Richardson, 1977-78; mem. Geology Adv. Com., U. Colo., Denver, 1986—. Recipient Yeakel Sedimentology award, Franklin and Marshall Coll., 1969; U. Tex. Research grantee, 1975-77. Mem. Am. Assn. Petroleum Geologist (standing com. 1979-87, chmn. 1979-87, editor, 1986-88, cert. of Merit, 1987), Soc. Econ. Minerologists and Paleontologists, Geol. Soc. Am., Internat. Assn. Sedimentologists, AAAS, Nat. Assn. Geol. Tchrs., Dallas Geol. Soc. (v.p. 1980-81), Rocky Mountain Assn. Geologists. Republican. Mem. United Church of Christ. Home: 1324 E Easter Circle Littleton CO 80122

ECCLES, SPENCER FOX, banker; b. Ogden, Utah, Aug. 24, 1934; s. Spencer Stoddard and Hope (Fox) E.; m. Cleone Emily Peterson, July 21, 1958; children: Clista Hope, Lisa Ellen, Katherine Ann, Spencer Peterson. B.S., U. Utah, 1956; M.A., Columbia U., 1959; degree in Bus. (hon.), So. Utah State Coll., 1982; LLB (hon.), Westminster Coll., Salt Lake City, 1986. Trainee First Nat. City Bank, N.Y.C., 1959-60; with First Security Bank of Utah, Salt Lake City, 1960-61, First Security Bank of Idaho, Boise, 1961-70; exec. v.p. First Security Corp. Salt Lake City, 1970-75, pres., 1975—, chief operating officer, 1980-82, chmn. bd. dirs., chief exec. officer, 1982—; dir. Union Pacific Corp., Amalgamated Sugar Co., Anderson Lumber Co., Zions Corp., Merc. Instn., Aubrey G. Lanston & Co., Inc.; mem. adv. council U. Utah Bus. Coll. Served to 1st lt. U.S. Army. Recipient Pres.'s Circle award Presdl. Commn., 1984, Minuteman award Utah N.G., 1988; Named Disting. Alumni U. Utah, 1988. Mem. Am. Bankers Assn., Assn. Bank Holding Co., Assn. Res. City Bankers, Young Pres. Orgn. Clubs: Salt Lake Country, Alta, Arid. Office: 1st Security Corp 79 S Main St PO Box 30006 Salt Lake City UT 84130 *

ECHOLS, RICHARD LEE, accountant; b. Tucson, Sept. 26, 1947; s. Malon Reed and Elna (Nelson) E.; m. Sandra Lee Tippets, June 5, 1970; children: Brett, Karlee, Devon, Justin, Alex. BS, U. Ariz., 1973. CPA, Ariz. Staff mem. Wayne M. Tippets, CPA, Phoenix, 1971-74; mng. ptnr. Tippets and Echols, P.C., Phoenix, 1975-88, Stoker and Echols, P.C., Phoenix, 1988—; keynote speaker various orgns., 1980—. Author acctg. software. Youth counselor LDS Ch., Phoenix, 1973—; youth counselor Boy Scouts Am., Phoenix, 1973—, dist. exploring chmn., 1983-87; bd. dirs. Thunderbird Little League, Phoenix, 1986-88. Recipient award of merit Boy Scouts Am., 1984, Woodbadge, 1986. Mem. AICPA, Ariz. Soc. CPA's. Home: 16210 N 33d Ln Phoenix AZ 85023 Office: 3877 N 7th St Phoenix AZ 85014

ECK, ANNE ELIZABETH, utilities executive; b. Pasadena, Calif., Mar. 28, 1930; d. John Charles and Rachel (Genung) Downey; m. Richard C. Eck, Feb. 24, 1952; children: Elizabeth, Patricia, Mary Jane. Student, San Diego State U., 1952. V.p. Ecklectics Resource, Inc., Grass Valley, Calif., 1987—. Mem. Republic Women's Club, Kappa Alpha Theta. Home and Office: 205 Sharon Way Grass Valley CA 95949

ECKELBERRY, ALEXANDER CARRILLO, sales executive; b. Paris, Oct. 22, 1962; came to U.S., 1974; s. Tener Riggs Eckelberry and Renee Duke; m. Marisa Eckelberry, Dec. 21, 1986; 1 child, Cameron. Student, Calif. Inst. Tech., 1980-82. Sales mgr. Picture Source, Inc., L.A., 1982-84; v.p. sales High Tech. Mktg., L.A., 1984-85; corp. sales mgr. TCS div. Compustar, L.A., 1985-87; channel account mgr. Borland Internat., Santa Cruz, Calif., 1987-88; dir. U.S. sales Aegis Devel. Inc., L.A., 1988—; pres. Westside Computing Devel. Orgn., L.A., 1985-86, Creative Fin. Inst., 1985—. Mem. Internat. Hubbard Ecclesiastical Found., 1985—. Home: 410 S Hauser #5

Los Angeles CA 90036 Office: Aegis Devel Inc 2115 Pico Los Angeles CA 90405

ECKELMAN, RICHARD JOEL, quality engineer; b. Bklyn., Mar. 25, 1951; s. Leon and Muriel (Brietbart) E.; m. Janet Louise Fenton, Mar. 21, 1978; children: Christie, Melanie, Erin Leigh. Student in Indsl. Tech., Ariz. State U., 1987—. Sr. engr., group leader nondestructive testing Engring. Fluor Corp., Irvine, Calif., 1979-83; sr. engr. nondestructive testing McDonnell Douglas, Mesa, Ariz., 1983—. Mem. Am. Soc. Nondestructive Testing (nat. aerospace com. 1987—, sec. Ariz. chpt. 1987-88, treas. 1988—, sect. chmn. 1989—), Am. Soc. Quality Control, Am. Soc. Mfg. Engrs., Porsche Owners Club Am., Val Vista Lakes Club. Home: 2150 E Nantuckett Dr Gilbert AZ 85234 Office: McDonnell-Douglas 5000 McDowell Ave Mesa AZ 85205

ECKER, DONALD NESS, accountant; b. Gettysburg, Pa.; m. Dianne Haskell; children: Kristi, Scott. BSBA, Calif. State Poly. Inst., 1986. CPA, Calif. Mng. ptnr. Ernst & Whinney, Riverside, Calif., 1982—; chmn. physician rsch. project Ernst & Whinney, Riverside, 1985-87; bd. dirs. Security Pacific Nat. Bank Inland Empire. Pres., bd. dirs. Econ. Devel. Coun.; mem. Estate Planning Coun., Riverside County, 1978—; chmn. edn. com. Inland Empire Young Pres.'s Orgn., pres., 1987; bd. dirs. Riverside Area United Way, 1978-85, assoc. chmn., 1981, campaign chmn., 1982, v.p., 1983-84, pres., 1984-85; co-founder Riverside County 2% and 5% Club, chmn. bd. dirs. 1985-86; original organizer Keep Riverside Ahead, gen. campaign chmn.; mem. World Affairs Coun., Monday Morning Group, Riverside Athletic Bd., 1978-83, YMCA, 1980—; mem. Riverside Community Hosp. Found., 1982—, asst. campaign chmn. capital, 1986-87; mem. adv. bd. sch. bus. adminstrn. U. Calif., Riverside, Calif. State Poly. U., mem. U. Calif. at Riverside Athletic Booster Club, 1978-85, Casa Colina Hosp. Found., 1982; pres., bd. dirs. Econ. Devel. Coun., Riverside Downtown Assn., 1982, Riverside Visitor Conv. Bur., City Riverside Yr. 2000 Strategic Planning Com.; mem. chancellor's com. Calif. Mus. Photography, 1987; mem. Chancellor's Blue Ribbon Com.; coach Riverside Youth Sports, 1978-84; treas. Efficient Transp. for Riverside County, 1988—; chmn. task force Bus. Vols. for the Arts, 1988—. Named United Way Vol. of Yr. award, 1985, Chamber Vol. of Yr. award United Way, 1985, Vol. of Yr. award Greater Riverside C. of C., 1985, Citizen of Yr. City of Riverside. Mem. AICPA, Calif. Soc. CPA's (state bd. dirs., mem. quality control of audit reports com.), Citrus Belt Chpt. CPA's (bd. dirs. 1980-85, chmn. credit grantors com. 1980, 82, pres. 1985), Med. Group Mgmt. Assn., Am. Group Practice Assn., Greater Riverside C. of C. (pres.-elect 1985, pres. 1986), L.A. C. of C. (bd. dirs.), Raincross Club of Riverside (founder 1987—). Office: Ernst & Whinney 3750 University Ave Ste 600 PO Box 1270 Riverside CA 92502-1270

ECKERLINE, WILLIAM JAMES, electronic engineer; b. Poughkeepsie, N.Y., Feb. 17, 1936; s. William J. and Katharine (Austin) E.; m. Betty L. Hunt, Sept. 16, 1956; 1 child, Diane. BSEE, Union Coll., Schenectady, N.Y., 1958; postgrad., Stanford U., 1979. Project engr. U.S. Army Electronic Command, Ft. Monmouth, N.J., 1958-67; systems engr. GTE Sylvania Systems, Mountain View, Calif., 1967-73; dept. mgr. GTE Sylvania Systems, Mountain View, 1973-77, asst. mgr. shipboard systems, 1978-79, mgr. AN/WLQ-4 program, 1980-83, dir. engring., 1984-88; dir. engring. tactical electronic def. div. GTE Govt. Systems, Mountain View, 1988—. Advisor Jr. Achievement, Santa Clara County, 1977-79. Mem. Assn. Old Crows, GTE Mgmt. Assn. (Mountain View chpt. v.p. 1978-79), Montgomery Jaycees (Outstanding Young Man in Am. 1965). Republican. Club: Los Gato's Caravaners (San Jose) (pres.,treas.). Home: 410 Ives Terr Sunnyvale CA 94087

ECKERMANN, GERALD CARLTON, writer, management consultant; b. Covina, Calif., Feb. 10, 1934; s. Carlton Herman and Ethel Marie (Argue) E.; m. Jeri Lynn Anderson, Dec. 3, 1960 (div. 1978); children: G. Kevin, Darci Lee Crotty, Darin Allen. BBA, UCLA, 1956. Personnel specialist Gen. Dynamics/Astronautics, San Diego, Calif., 1960-65; dir. personnel Computer Scis. Corp., El Segundo, Calif., 1965-66; internal cons. ITT, N.Y.C., 1966-71; v.p. personnel Kaiser Industries, Oakland, Calif., 1971-75; cons. prin. Exec. Mgmt. Cons., Walnut Creek, Calif., 1975-77; dir. personnel Lawrence Livermore Labs., Walnut Creek, 1977; dir. regional practice compensation A.S. Hansen, L.A., 1978-81; gen. mgr. Security Corp. of Am., West Lake Village, Calif., 1981-82; mgmt. cons. Coopers & Lybrand CPAs, L.A., 1982-83, Grant-Thorton CPAs, L.A., 1983-86, Versys Legal Svcs., L.A., 1986—; dir. Transp. Scis. Corp., L.A., 1979—. Author: Price of Ambition, 1986, Forgotten Man, 1988, Amethyst Idol, 1988. Vice chmn. bd. trustees, West Coast U., L.A., 1979—; nat. rep. Boy Scouts Am., 1972; v.p. Mt. Diablo Council, 1974-75; bd. dirs. Mt. Diablo Rehab. Ctr., Alameda County Counseling Ctr., 1973-76. With USN, 1956-62; commdr. res. Mem. Am. Compensation Assn., Am. Soc. Personnel Adminstrs., Res. Officers Assn., Naval Res. Assn. (v.p. Jack London chpt. 1976), Jonathan Club, Calif. Yacht Club (chmn. yachting luncheons 1989—). Republican. Home: 8828 Pershing Dr Unit 321 Playa del Rey CA 90293 Office: Legal Info Tech Group 12121 Wilshire Blvd Ste 920 Los Angeles CA 90025

ECKERSLEY, NORMAN CHADWICK, banker; b. Glasgow, Scotland, June 18, 1924; came to U.S., 1969; s. James Norman and Beatrice (Chadwick) E.; m. Rosemary J. Peters, May 25, 1986, 1 child, Anne. D Laws Strathclyde U., Scotland. With Chartered Bank, London and Manchester, 1947-48; acct., Bombay, 1948-52, Singapore, 1952-54, Sarawak, 1954-56, Pakistan, 1956-58, Calcutta, 1958-59, Hong Kong, 1959-60, asst. mgr. Hamburg, 1960-62, mgr. Calcutta, 1962-67, Thailand, 1967-69; pres. Chartered Bank London, San Francisco, 1964-74, chmn., chief exec., 1974-79; chmn. Standard Chartered Bancorp, San Francisco, 1978-81; dep. chmn. Union Bank, L.A., 1979-82; chmn., chief exec. officer The Pacific Bank, San Francisco, 1982—; chmn. Scottish Am. Investment Com., U. Strathclyde Found. With RAF, 1940-46. Decorated D.F.C.; comdr. Order Brit. Empire. Mem. Overseas Banks Assn. Calif. (chmn. 1972-74), Calif. Coun. Internat. Trade, San Francisco C. of C., World Trade Assn., World Trade Club, Royal and Ancient Club, Royal Troon Golf Club (Scotland), World Trade Club, San Francisco Golf Club, Pacific Union Club (San Francisco). Mem. Ch. of Scotland. Home: 401 El Cerrito Hillsborough CA 94010 Office: Pacific Bank 351 California St San Francisco CA 94104

ECKERT, GERALDINE GONZALES, language professional, educator; b. N.Y.C., Aug. 5, 1948; d. Albert and Mercedes (Martinez) Gonzales; m. Robert Alan Eckert, Apr. 1, 1972; children: Lauren Elaine, Alison Elizabeth. BA, Ladycliff Coll., Highland Falls, N.Y., 1970; student, U. Valencia, Spain, 1968; MA, N.Y.U., 1971; student, Instituto de Cultura Hispanica, Madrid, 1970-71. Tchr. Spanish Clarkstown High Sch. N. (N.Y.), 1971-73, Rambam Torah Inst., Beverly Hills, Calif., 1973-75; translator election materials City of Beverly Hills, 1976-83; edn. cons. Los Angeles County of Calif. Dept. Forestry, Capistrano Beach, 1982-84; lang. services and protocol Los Angeles Olympic Organizing Com., 1983-84; pension adminstr. Pension Architects, Inc., Los Angeles, 1984-87; instr. El Camino Coll., Torrance, Calif., 1987-88, Santa Monica(Calif.) Coll., 1975—; owner, pres. Bilingual Pension Cons., Los Angeles, 1987—; bd. dirs. Institute for Hispanic Cultural Studies, Los Angeles; spl. asst. to Internat. Olympic Com., Lausanne, Switzerland, 1983—. V.p. Notre Dame Acad. Assoc., West Los Angeles, 1987—; mem. Los Angeles March of Dimes Ambassadors Group, 1987. Democrat. Roman Catholic. Clubs: Five Ring, Los Angeles, Friends of Sport, Amateur Athletic Found., Los Angeles. Office: Bilingual Pension Cons 10573 W Pico Blvd Ste 235 Los Angeles CA 90064

ECKERT, WILLIAM TERRY, aerospace researcher; b. Seattle, Aug. 11, 1948; s. Walter Ethelbert Jr. and Gracejean (Quintin) E.; children: Lisa Kristine, Wendy Michelle. BS in Aeronautics, U. Wash., 1970; MS in Applied Math., U. Santa Clara (Calif.), 1977; postgrad., U. Pa., 1981, San Jose State U., 1982. Rsch. aide Aerospace Rsch. Lab., U.Wash., Seattle, 1969-70; aerospace rsch. engr. U.S. Army Aeromechanics Lab., NASA Ames Rsch. Ctr., Moffett Field, Calif., 1970-79; chief rsch. support div. U.S. Army Aeroflightdynamics Dir., NASA Ames Rsch. Ctr., Moffett Field, 1979-84, 1985—, asst. dir., 1988—; dep. chief AH-64 Apache acquisition team U.S. Army Aviation Systems Command, St. Louis, 1984-85; speaker, lectr., tech. cons. in field; mem. steering com. NASA-Army Rotorcraft Tech. Conf., Washington, 1986-87. Contbr. articles to profl. publs.; editor: DoD Major System Procurement, 1984. Mem. U. Wash. Alumni Assn., Subsonic Aerodynamic Testing Assn., Phi Eta Sigma. Office: US Army Aeroflightdynamics Dir NASA Ames Rsch Ctr M/S 215-1 Moffett Field CA 94035-1099

ECKHARDT, WILLIAM BOYDEN, credit union executive; b. Bellefonte, Pa., Aug. 31, 1949; s. Boyden and Maxine Alice (Young) E.; BBA, Oreg. State U., 1971. Adminstrv. officer Alaska U.S.A. Fed. Credit Union, Anchorage, 1971-72, ops. mgr., 1972-74, asst. gen. mgr., 1974-79, pres., 1979—; chmn. bd. Alaska USA Ins., Inc., 1986—; chmn. Alaska Option Services Corp.; dir. Alaska League Services Corp. Mem. Credit Union Execs. Soc. (pres. Alaska council 1975-88), Alaska Credit Union League (pres. Anchorage chpt. 1979-81), Credit Union Nat. Assn. (dir.). Club: Elks, Commonwealth North. Home: 12850 Ben Ct Anchorage AK 99515 Office: Mail Pouch 6613 4000 Credit Union Dr Anchorage AK 99502

ECKLE, JULIE KAY, nurse; b. Seattle, June 6, 1962; d. John James and Joan Delores (Armstrong) E.; m. Michael Stachowiak, July 29, 1989. BS in Nursing, Biolia U., 1984. RN, Calif. Nurse U. So. Calif. Med. Ctr., L.A., 1984-85, Anaheim (Calif.) Meml. Hosp., 1985-86, Orange County Health Dept., Anaheim, 1987—. Mem. Am. Heart Assn. (CPR instr.). Home: 821 N Chestnut Rd La Habra CA 90631

ECKLEY, WILTON EARL, JR., humanities educator; b. Alliance, Ohio, June 25, 1929; s. Wilton Earl and Louise (Bert) E.; m. Grace Ester Williamson, Sept. 12, 1954; children: Douglas, Stephen, Timothy. B.A., Mt. Union Coll., 1952; M.A., Pa. State U., 1955; Ph.D., Case Western Reserve U., 1965; John Hay fellow, Yale U., 1961-62. Chmn. English Euclid (Ohio) Sr. High Sch., 1955-63; dir. tchr. tng. Hollins Coll., 1963-65; prof. English Drake U., 1965-84, chmn. dept. English, 1965-80; head dept. humanities and social scis. Colo. Sch. Mines, 1984—; Fulbright prof. Am. lit. U., Ljubljana, Yugoslavia, 1972-73, U. Veliko, Turnovo, Bulgaria, 1981-82. Author: A Guide to E.E. Cummings, 1970, A Checklist of E.E. Cummings, 1970, Harriette Arnow, 1974, T.S. Stribling, 1975, Herbert Hoover, 1980, The American Circus, 1983. chmn. bd. dirs., Colo. Endowment for the Humanities, 1989. Coe fellow Am. Studies, 1957—. Mem. MLA, Circus Hist. Soc., AAUP, Phi Kappa Tau. Home: 744 Chimney Creek Dr Golden CO 80401

ECKSTEIN, HARRY, political science educator; b. Schotten, Germany, Jan. 26, 1924; came to U.S., 1936; s. Moritz and Bella (Bachenheimer) E.; divorced; 1 child, Jonathan; m. Silvia Frankenthal. AB summa cum laude, Harvard Coll., 1948; MA, Harvard U., 1950, PhD, 1951; postgrad., U. London Sch. Econs., 1950-51, 52-53. Instr. govt. Harvard U., Cambridge, 1954-56, asst. prof. govt., 1956-58; assoc. prof. politics Princeton (N.J.) U., 1959-61, prof., 1961-69, IBM prof. internat. studies, 1969-80; disting. prof. polit. sci. U. Calif., Irvine, 1980—; mem. interuniv. seminar on comparative politics Social Sci. Rsch. Coun., 1952, com. social change, 1961-63; cons. rsch. group psychology, social scis. Smithsonian Instn., 1961-62; faculty assoc. Ctr. Internat. Studies Princeton U., 1959-80, mem. coun. human rels., 1962-65, dir. rsch program in authority studies, 1981-84, chair acad. senate com. rsch., 1981-83, senate com. overhead costs, 1981-82, 3, dean sch. com. sch. social scis., 1981-82, com. program in comparative culture, 1981-82, dept. politics and soc. 1986-88; mem. (ex officio) senate exec. com., 1981-85, (ex officio) grad. coun. 1981-82; mem. dean's faculty adv. coun., 1982-85; mem. dean's adv. com. departmentalization 1985-86; mem. disting. professorship nomination com. 1985—. Auhtor: The English Health Service, 1958, Pressure Group Politics, 1960, A Theory of Stable Democracy, 1961, Internal War: Problems and Approaches, 1964, Division and Cohesion in Democracy, 1966, The Evaluation of Political Performance, 1971, Natural History of Congruence Theory, 1980; (with others) Patterns of Government, 1958, Comparative Politics: A Reader, 1963, Patterns of Authority, 1975; contbr. articles to profl. jours.; editor: Sage Professional Papers in Comparative Politics, 1966-72; cons. editor Rand-McNally, Inc. 1964-79. With U.S. Army 1943-46. Teaching fellow in Govt. Harvard U. 1951-52, 53-54, Ctr. for Advanced Study of Behavirol Scis. fellow Princeton U., 1958-59. Fellow AAAS; mem. Am. Polit. Sci. Assn. (v.p. 1981-82, various coms.). Home: 31 Mann St Irvine CA 92715

ECONOMY, JAMES, polymer researcher, consultant; b. Detroit, Mar. 28, 1929; s. Peter George and Bessie (Lalousie) E.; m. Stacy Zapantis, Nov. 25, 1961; children—Elizabeth, Peter, Katherine, Melissa. B.S. in Chemistry, Wayne State U., 1950; Ph.D., U. Md., 1954. Research assoc. U. Ill., Urbana, 1954-56; gen. research leader Allied Chem. Co., Tonawanda, N.Y., 1956-60; mgr. research Carborundum Co., Niagara Falls, N.Y., 1960-75; mgr. polymer sci. and tech. IBM, San Jose, Calif., from 1975; cons. Army Research Orgn., 1976-80, Air Force Res., 1979-83, Dept. Energy, 1979-84, Nat. Materials Adv. Bd., 1984—. Inventor various types of fibers and plastics. Recipient 14 I-R 100 awards Indsl. Research, 1965-75; award for devel. of Kynol (flame resistant fibers) So. Research Burn Inst., 1976. Fellow Am. Inst. Chemistry (Chem. Pioneer award 1987); mem. Nat. Acad. Engring., Am. Chem. Soc. (chmn. elect West N.Y. sect. 1975, chmn. polymer div. 1985, Schoelkopf medal 1972, Phillips medal, 1985), Internat. Union of Pure and Applied Chemistry. Home: 6694 Heathfield Dr San Jose CA 95120 *

EDAM, CLAUDIA RUTH, sales representative; b. Salt Lake City, May 22, 1947; d. Owen Browning and Beverly (Ostler) Pearson; m. Richard W. Anderson, June 15, 1966 (div. May 1986); children: Jill, Christopher, Travis, Blake, Cary, Debra; m. Donald Merle Edam. Student, Brigham Young U., 1965-66, U. Utah, 1966-67, 86-88; AS in Bus., LDS Bus. Coll., 1986. Coowner Salt Lake Ceramics, Salt Lake City, 1966-84; mfg. rep. Tech. Mktg. Assn., Salt Lake City and Denver, 1984-88, Sunbird Industries, Monument, Colo., 1988—; also bd. dirs. Sunbird Industries. Author poetry. Voting judge Rep. Party, Salt Lake City, 1968, 72. Mem. Electronic Reps. Assn. (sec. 1988). Home: 475 Scrub Oak Circle Monument CO 80132 Office: Sunbird Industries 475 Scrub Oak Circle Monument CO 80132

EDDY, GLADYS LOUISE, educational administrator; b. Castle Rock, Colo., Dec. 25, 1915; d. William Adam and Jessie Louise (Cozens) Shellabarger; m. Willard Oscar Eddy, Aug. 21, 1938; children: Sandra Carol, William Radford. BSBA, U. Denver, 1937. Asst. Colo. State U., Ft. Collins, 1937-42, sect. to pres., 1945-46, instr., 1957-62, 67-79, asst. prof. bus., 1979-84, asst. to dean, Coll. Bus., 1984—; instr. U.S. Army Air Force, Ft. Collins, 1942-43; tchr. Poudre R-1 Sch. Dist., Ft. Collins, 1957-62; cons. in field; pres., bd. dirs. Colo. Assn. Sch. Bds., Denver, 1973-83; mem. Nat. Adv. Coun. on Vocat. Edn., Washington, 1982-84. Mem. Poudre R-1 Bd. Edn., Ft. Collins, 1971-83, Colo. State Bd. Edn., Denver, 1987—; bd. dirs. Colo. Parks and Recreation Found., 1984—. Mem. PEO, Mortar Bd. (nat. program dir. 1982), Ft. Collins Country Club, Order Eastern Star, Delta Kappa Gamma, Sigma Kappa. Republican. Episcopalian. Home: 509 Remington St Fort Collins CO 80542 Office: Colo State Univ Fort Collins CO 80524

EDEL, (JOSEPH) LEON, biographer, educator; b. Pitts., Sept. 9, 1907; s. Simon and Fannie (Malamud) E.; m. Roberta Roberts, Dec. 2, 1950 (div. 1979); m. Marjorie P. Sinclair, May 30, 1980. M.A., McGill U., 1928, Litt.D., 1963; D.ès.L., U. Paris, 1932; D.Litt., Union Coll., 1963, U. Sask., 1982, Mauna Loa Coll., 1988. Writer, journalist 1932-43; vis. prof. N.Y. U., 1950-52, assoc. prof. English, 1953-54, prof. English, 1955-66, Henry James prof. English and Am. letters, 1966-73, emeritus, 1973; citizens prof. humanities U. Hawaii, 1971-78, emeritus, 1978—; mem. faculty Harvard U., summer 1952, vis. prof., 1959-60; Centenary vis. prof. U. Toronto, 1967; Gauss seminar lectr. Princeton U., 1952-53; vis. prof. Ind. U., 1954-55, U. Hawaii, summer 1955, 69-70; Alexander lectr. U. Toronto, 1956; Westminster Abbey address Henry James Meml., 1976; vis. prof. Center Advanced Study, Wesleyan U., 1965; vis. fellow Humanities Rsch. Ctr., 1976; Vernon prof. biography Dartmouth Coll., 1977; Bollingen Found. fellow, 1958-61. Author: Henry James: Les années dramatiques, 1932, The Prefaces of Henry James, 1932, James Joyce: The Last Journey, 1947, The Life of Henry James, 5 vols. (The Untried Years, 1953, The Conquest of London and The Middle Years, 1962, The Treacherous Years, 1969, The Master, 1972), Henry James, A Life, 1985; (with E.K. Brown) Willa Cather, A Critical Biography, 1953; The Psychological Novel, 1955, revised, 1959, Literary Biography, 1957; (with Dan H. Laurence) A Bibliography of Henry James, 1957; Henry D. Thoreau, 1970, Henry James in The Abbey, The Address, 1976, Bloomsbury, A House of Lions, 1979, Stuff and Sleep of Dreams, Experiments in Literary Psychology, 1982, Writing Lives, Principia Biographica, 1984. Editor: (writings of Henry James) The Complete Plays, 1949, Ghostly Tales (reissued as Tales of the Supernatural, 1970), Selected Fiction, 1954, Selected Letters, 1955, American Essays, 1956, The Future of the Novel: Critical Papers, 1956; (with Gordon N. Ray) James and H.G. Wells, Letters, 1958; Complete Tales, 12 vols., 1962-64, HJ: Letters, 4 vols., 1974-84; (with Mark Wilson) Complete Criticism, 2 vols., 1984; (with Lyall H. Powers) The Complete Notebooks, 1987; Henry James Reader, 1965, Selected Letters, 1987. Editor (other authors) Edmund Wilson Papers, 4 vols., 1972-86, Literary History and Literary Criticism, 1965, The Diary of Alice James, 1964. Mem. adv. com. edn. Met. Mus. Centenary, 1969-70; mem. ednl. adv. com. Guggenheim Found., 1967-80. Served as lt. AUS, World War II; dir. Press Agy. 1945-47, U.S. zone Germany. Decorated Bronze Star; recipient Pulitzer prize in biography, 1963; Nat. Book award for non-fiction, 1963; Nat. Book Critics Circle award for biography, 1985; medal of lit. Nat. Arts Club, 1981; Nat. Inst. Arts and Letters grantee, 1959; elected to Am. Acad. Arts and Letters, 1972; Gold medal for biography Acad.-Inst., 1976; Hawaii Writers award, 1977; Guggenheim fellow, 1936-38, 65-66; Nat. Endowment for Humanities grantee, 1974-77. Fellow Am. Acad. Arts and Scis., Royal Soc. Lit. (Eng.); mem. Nat. Inst. Arts and Letters (sec. 1965-67), W.A. White Psychoanalytic Soc. (hon.), Am. Acad. Psychoanalysis (hon.), Soc. Authors (Eng.), Authors Guild (mem. council, pres. 1969-71), P.E.N. (pres. Am. Center 1957-59), Hawaii Lit. Arts Council (pres. 1978-79), Modern Humanities Research Assn., Soc. Am. Historians. Clubs: Century (N.Y.C.); Athenaeum (London). Address: 3817 Lurline Dr Honolulu HI 96816

EDELMAN, LAWRENCE, electrical engineer; b. Bklyn., Aug. 6, 1928; s. Abe and Florence (Bernstein) E.; m. Betty Edelman, Sept. 26, 1954; children: Jeffrey, Andrew. BSEE, Poly. Inst. Bklyn., 1959. Sr. engr. Radio Receptor Co., Bklyn., 1956-58; engr. Melpar Corp., Falls Church, Va., 1958-59; EMC cons. Eaton Corp., Deer Park, N.Y., 1959-85; sr. tech. specialist Northrop Corp., Pico Rivera, Calif., 1985-86; engring. staff specialist Gen. Dynamics, Pomona, Calif., 1986—; ptnr. L & B Co., E. Islip, N.Y., 1972-85. With AUG, 1946-49. Mem. IEEE (sr. mem., chpt. sec. 1973-74, treas. 1978-79, chmn. 1982-84).

EDELMAN, SAMUEL MARTIN, communication educator; b. Altoona, Pa., May 13, 1948; s. Jack and Helen (Cazen) E.; m. Carol F. Stern, Sept. 6, 1970. BA, Pa. State U., 1969, MA, 1975; PhD, U. Ariz., 1981. Prof. Calif. State U., Chico, 1979—; dir. Applied Communication Inst., Chico, 1986—; cons. Israel Fgn. Ministry, Israel Ministry Edn., 1986. Producer radio documentaries include Cultural Resistance to Genocide, 1984 (award Corp. for Pub. Broadcasting, 1985), Underground Without Bullets, 1985. Bd. dirs. No. Calif. Am. Israel Pub. Affairs Com., 1982—, Univ. Found. Calif. State U., Chico. Recipient award San Francisco State Broadcast Industry; grantee Calif. Council for the Humanities, 1983-87, Nat. Endowment for the Arts, 1984. Mem. Speech Communication Assn., Western Speech Communication Assn. Democrat. Jewish. Office: Calif State U Coll Communication Dept Human Communication Studies Chico CA 95929-0502

EDELSTEIN, DAVID ALLEN, financial executive; b. San Antonio, Aug. 25, 1956; s. Edward Gene and Marcia (Fleisfeder) E.; m. Julie Olinda Pratt, Dec. 24, 1978. BS summa cum laude, Santa Clara U., 1978; cert. in Mgmt., Northwestern U., 1985. CPA, Calif. Sr. mgr. Deloitte Haskins & Sells, San Jose and Sacramento, Calif., 1978-87, instr. for staff tng., 1983-87; chief fin. officer Occupational-Urgent Care, Sacramento, 1987—; mem. newsletter com. Sacramento Valley Venture Capital Forum. Contbr. articles to fin. mags. Office coordinator Sacramento Area United Way, 1985-87; mem. Sta. KVIE Pub. TV. Mem. Am. Inst. CPAs, Calif. State Soc. CPAs, Beta Gamma Sigma. Office: Occupational-Urgent Care Health Systems Inc 2400 Venture Oaks Way Sacramento CA 95833

EDENFIELD, T(HOMAS) KEEN, JR., real estate developer; b. Chattanooga, May 8, 1943; s. Thomas Keen Sr. and Francis (Love) E.; m. Ann Louise Goodney, Jan. 24, 1976; children: Thomas Keen III, Andrew Ward, Stuart Douglas, Curtis Arthur. BS in Econs., Emory U., 1967; MBA, London Sch. Econs., 1969. Capt. Saudi Arabian Airlines, 1976-78, Air Jamaica, 1978-80; owner, pres. Lamb Realty & Investment, Albuquerque, 1980—, Seeganex Internat., Ltd. (formerly Littletree, Inc.), Albuquerque, 1984—; CIA aviation operative, Washington, 1974-85. Contbr. articles to profl. jours. Decorated Turkish Civilian Wings award; recipient Nicaraguan Civilian Humanitarian award, 1984. Mem. Albuquerque Country Club, Wings Club of Arabia (pres. 1978-79). Office: Lamb Realty & Investment PO Box 26026 Albuquerque NM 87125

EDENS, GARY DENTON, banker; b. Asheville, N.C., Jan. 6, 1942; s. James Edwin and Pauline Amanda (New) E.; m. Hannah Suellen Walter, Aug. 21, 1965; children: Ashley Elizabeth, Emily Blair. BS, U. N.C., 1964. Account exec. PAMS Prodns., Dallas, 1965-67; account exec. Sta. WKIX, Raleigh, N.C., 1967-69; gen. mgr. Sta. KOY, Phoenix, 1970-81; sr. v.p. Harte-Hanks Radio, Inc., Phoenix, 1978-81, pres., chief exec. officer, 1981-84; chmn., chief exec. officer Edens Broadcasting, Inc.; dir. Gt. Western Bank & Trust Ariz., 1975-86, Citibank Ariz., 1986—. Bd. dirs. Valley Big Bros., 1972-80, Ariz. State U. Found., 1979—, COMPAS, 1979—, Men's Arts Coun., 1975-78. Named One of Three Outstanding Young Men, Phoenix Jaycees, 1973; entrepreneurial fellow U. Ariz., 1989. Mem. Phoenix Execs. Club (pres. 1976), Nat. Radio Broadcasters Assn. (dir. 1981—), Radio Advt. Bur. (dir. 1981—), Young Pres.'s Orgn. (chmn. Ariz. chpt. 1989—), Phoenix Country Club, Univ. Phoenix Club. Republican. Methodist. Office: 840 N Central Ave Phoenix AZ 85004

EDENS, PATRICK CLINTON, tax accountant; b. El Paso, Tex., Feb. 28, 1947; s. Roger Russell and Dorthy Jean (Pierce) E.; m. Leanna Dee Givens, Aug. 6, 1966; children: Carrie Ann, Leslie Renee. BS in Acctg., San Francisco State U., 1970. Staff acct. Bruce Fielding and Co., Mountain View, Calif., 1971, Craig Bertorelli and Asiano CPAs, San Francisco, 1972-76; controller Bell Industries Graphic Arts div., Sunnyvale, Calif., 1977; realtor Bosetti Properties, Redwood City, Calif., 1987-88; tax acct. Redwood City, Calif., 1978—; pntr. Wholesale Connection, Redwood City, 1988—. Mem. Foster City Rod and Gun Club, St. Pius Men's Club. Democrat. Roman Catholic. Home: 1020 Lakeview Way Redwood City CA 94052 Office: 234 Marshall St #8 Redwood City CA 94063

EDER, RICHARD GRAY, newspaper critic; b. Washington, Aug. 16, 1932; s. George Jackson and Marceline (Gray) E.; m. Esther Garcia Aguirre, Apr. 21, 1955; children: Maria, Ann, Claire, Michael, Luke, Benjamin, James. BA, Harvard U., 1954. Fgn. corr. N.Y. Times, various countries in Europe and Latin Am., 1962-77, 80-82; theater critic N.Y. Times, 1977-79; book critic Los Angeles Times, 1982—. Recipient Pulitzer prize for criticism, 1987. Mem. Nat. Book Critics Circle (citation for reviewing 1987). Roman Catholic. Office: Los Angeles Times 86 Charles St Boston MA 02114

EDGAR, ALVIS, JR. See OWENS, BUCK

EDGAR, JAMES MACMILLAN, JR., management consultant; b. N.Y.C., Nov. 7, 1936; s. James Macmillan Edgar and Lilyan (McCann) E.; B. Chem. Engring., Cornell U., 1959, M.B.A. with distinction, 1960; m. Judith Frances Storey, June 28, 1958; children—Suzanne Lynn, James Macmillan, Gordon Stuart. New product rep. E.I. duPont Nemours, Wilmington, Del., 1960-63, mktg. services rep., 1963-64; with Touche Ross & Co., 1964-78, mgr., Detroit, 1966-68, partner, 1968-71, partner in charge, mgmt. services ops. for No. Calif. and Hawaii, San Francisco, 1971-78, partner Western regional mgmt. services, 1978; prin. Edgar, Dunn & Conover, Inc., San Francisco, 1978—; mem. San Francisco Mayor's Fin. Adv. Com., 1976—, mem. exec. com., 1978—, Blue Ribbon com. for Bus., 1987—; mem. Alumnae Resources adv. bd., 1986—, mem. San Francisco Planning and Urban Research Bd., 1986—; mem. alumni exec. council Johnson Grad. Sch. Mgmt. Cornell U., 1985—, Cornell Council, 1970-73. Recipient Award of Merit for outstanding pub. service City and County of San Francisco, 1978; Honor award for outstanding contbns. to profl. mgmt. Johnson Grad. Sch. Mgmt., Cornell U., 1978. CPA, cert. mgmt. cons. Mem. Assn. Corp. Growth (v.p. membership San Francisco chpt. 1979-81, v.p. programs 1981-82, pres. 1982-83, nat. bd. dirs. 1983-86), AICPA, Calif. Soc. CPAs, Am. Mktg. Assn., Inst. Mgmt. Cons. (regional v.p. 1973-80, dir. 1975-77, bd. v.p. 1977-80), Profl. Services Mgmt. Assn., San Francisco C. of C. (bd. dirs. 1987—, v.p. econ. affairs 1988-89, mem. exec. com. 1988-89), New Main Library Found. (chmn.

1989—), Tau Beta Pi. Clubs: Univ., Pacific Union, Commonwealth of San Francisco, Marin Rod and Gun. Patentee nonwoven fabrics. Home: 10 Buckeye Way Kentfield CA 94904 Office: Edgar Dunn & Conover Inc 847 Sansome St San Francisco CA 94111

EDGAR, JAMES ROBERT, aerospace company official; b. San Francisco, Nov. 24, 1949; s. Robert Claren and Naomi Genevieve (Sackett) E.; m. Martha Alice Atkinson, June 12, 1976; children: Peter James, Julie Alice. BA in Econs., Rutgers U., 1971; MBA in Internat. Bus., U. Wash., 1979. Asst. gen. mgr. Columbia Pacific Airlines, Richland, Wash., 1976-79; asst. dir. Columbia Pacific Found., Richland, 1979-85; program planner Boeing Aerospace Co., Seattle, 1985—. Bd. dirs. Northwest Bapt. Sem., Tacoma, 1985-86, Tacoma Bapt. Schs., 1985-86, Western Bapt. Coll. Found., Salem, Oreg., 1985—. Capt. USAF, 1971-76. Republican. Home: 1309 Aqua Vista Dr Gig Harbor WA 98335 Office: Boeing Aerospace Co PO Box 3999 Seattle WA 98124

EDGE, GARY MICHAEL, aerospace engineer, consultant; b. Danville, Va., Jan. 12, 1959; s. Paul Alexander and Sadie Ann (Gossett) E. BS, Grand Canyon Coll., Phoenix, 1982. Dir. computer svcs. Grand Canyon Coll., 1984-85; staff engr. Loral Def. Systems, Litchfield Park, Ariz., 1985--; pres., chief exec. officer Profl. Solutions, Peoria, Ariz., 1985--. Active Evan Mecham Reelection campaign, Phoenix, 1988. Mem. Assn. for Computing Machinery, Data Processing Mgmt. Assn. Republican. Baptist. Home: 7142 W Paradise Dr Peoria AZ 85306-8941 Office: Loral Def Systems PO Box 85 Litchfield Park AZ 85340-0085

EDGE, JERRY T., manufacturing company executive; b. Roseboro, N.C., Jan. 17, 1941; s. Shelton B. and Ella (Bunnel) E.; m. Ulrike Macy, Sept. 10, 1966; children: Russell, Melissa, Christina. BS, U. N.C., Chapel Hill, 1966; MBA, Ga. State U., 1969; student, George Washington U., 1971-75. Cert. compensation profl. Track supr. Southern Railway, Gordon, Ga., 1968; recruiter Southern Railway, Washington, 1969-70, compensation analyst, 1971-73, mgr. salary adminstr., 1973-76; dir., compensation Morrison Inc., Mobile, Ala., 1976-79; mgr. salaried personnel Solar Turbines Inc., San Diego, Calif., 1979-82; mgr. employee relations Solar Turbines Inc., San Diego, 1982-85, dir. human resources, 1985—; adj. prof. San Diego State U., 1980—; dir. Tele-Sec Temporaries, Inc., Washington, 1976—. Bd. trustees, mem. San Diego Repertory Theatre, 1986—, treas., 1987-88, v.p. corp. devel., 1989. With USAF, 1958-62. Mem. Am. Compensation Assn. (chmn. 1981-82, pres. 1982-83, instr. 1977—). Republican. Presbyterian. Home: 2210 Levante St Carlsbad CA 92009 Office: Solar Turbines Inc 2200 Pacific Hwy San Diego CA 92138-5376

EDGE, ROBERTA MARIE, technologist; b. Ft. Dix, N.J., Apr. 17, 1955; d. Benjamin John and Maria (Tuono) Spain; m. Kristopher Daniel Edge; children: Kristopher, Jaclyn. Postgrad., Calif. State U., Northridge, 1988—. Staff radiology technician St. Mary's Desert Valley Hosp., Apple Valley, Calif., 1975-77, Holy Cross Hosp., Mission Hill, 1977-80, 84-86; asst. chief technician 1986-88; radiology technician Shepard & Yazdi MD's, 1980-84; mammography technician Humana Hosp., West Hills, Calif., 1985; chief technician Holy Cross Med. Ctr., 1988—. Mem. Am. Soc. Radiologic Technologists, Am. Healthcare Radiology Adminstrs., Am. Registry Radiologic Technologists. Home: 14360 Germain St Mission Hills CA 91345 Office: Holy Cross Med Ctr 15031 Rinaldi St Mission Hills CA 91345-1285

EDGERLY, CHARLES ESTES, veterinarian; b. Selma, Calif., Nov. 12, 1940; s. Alvin Crowell and Maurine (Estes) E.; m. Lee Adella Groves, June 15, 1963; children: Linda Lee, Debra Kay. BS, U. Calif., Davis, 1962, DVM, 1964. Owner, veterinarian Reedley (Calif.) Veterinary Hosp., 1967—. Mem. Reedley High Sch. Band Boosters, 1985—. Mem. Am. Veterinary Med. Assn., Am. Veterinary Dental Soc., Calif. Veterinary Dental Soc., Am. Animal Hosp. Assn., Calif. Acad. Veterinary Medicine, Calif. Veterinary Med. Assn. (continuing edn. com. 1988—, ad hoc com. practice standards 1986—, ad hoc com. licensure 1989—), Tulare Kings Veterinary Med. Assn. (pres. 1972, sec. 1985—), Reedley C. of C., Fresno (Calif.) Bonsai Soc. (pres. 1981-83, treas. 1984-87), Rotary, Phi Kappa Phi, Phi Zeta. Republican. Home: 695 Ann Dr Reedley CA 93654 Office: 21311 E Dinuba Ave Reedley CA 93654

EDGETT, STEVEN DENNIS, transportation consultant; b. Indpls., June 3, 1948; s. Robert Neil and Elizabeth Catherine (Hatch) E.; m. Catherine Ann Bartel, June 19, 1971; children: Jeffrey Steven, Christopher Steven. Student, N.Mex. State U., 1965-68, U. Cin., 1968-69, Grossmont Coll., 1972-74, San Diego State U., 1974-75. Lead designer U.S. Elevator Corp., Spring Valley, Calif., 1970-76; safety engr. State of Calif., San Diego, 1976-78; assoc. Skidmore, Owings & Merrill, San Francisco, 1978-86; pres. Edgett Williams Cons. Group Inc., Mill Valley, Calif., 1986—. Mem. Constrn. Specifications Inst. Home: 541 Shasta Way Mill Valley CA 94941 Office: Edgett Williams Cons Group Inc 100 Shoreline Hwy Mill Valley CA 94941

EDMISTON, JOSEPH TASKER, state official; b. Monterey Park, Calif., Oct. 27, 1948; s. Tasker Lee and Beula Viola (Bates) E.; m. Pepper Salter Abrams, 1985; children: William Tasker, Charles Henry. A.A., East Los Angeles Coll., 1968; A.B., U. So. Calif., 1970. Mgr. of ct. process Roy Rottner & Associates, Hollywood, Calif., 1970-73; So. Calif Coastal coordinator Sierra Club, Los Angeles, 1973-76, energy coordinator, Sacramento, Calif., 1976-77; dir. State of Calif. Santa Monica Mountains Land Acquisition Program, 1979-80; exec. dir. Santa Monica Mountains Comprehensive Planning Commn., Los Angeles, 1977-79; exec. dir. Santa Monica Mountains Conservancy, State of Calif., 1980—. Pres. Associated Students, East Los Angeles Coll., 1968. Recipient Weldon Heald Conservation award Sierra Club, 1970; Hollywood Heritage, Inc. (bd. dirs.). Mem. Marine Tech. Soc. (dir. Los Angeles region sect. 1975-77), Coastal Soc., Phi Rho Pi, Delta Sigma Rho, Tau Kappa Alpha. Democrat. Office: 3700 Solstice Canyon Rd Malibu CA 90265

EDMONDS, CHARLES HENRY, publisher; b. Lakewood, Ohio, Sept. 4, 1919; s. Howard H. and Mary Frances (Galena) E.; student Woodbury Bus. Coll., 1939-40; m. Ruth Audrey Windfelder, Nov. 4, 1938; children—Joan Dickey, Charles Henry, Carolyn Anne, Dianne Marie. Owner, Shoreline Transp. Co., Los Angeles, 1946-58; mgr. transp. Purity Food Stores, Burlingame, Calif., 1958-61; supr. Calif. Motor Express, San Jose, 1961-64; account exec. Don Wright Assos., Oakland, Calif., 1964-65; sales mgr. Western U.S., Shippers Guide Co., Chgo., 1965-70; pub. No. Calif. Retailer, San Jose, 1970-83; v.p. Kasmar Publs., 1983—. Recipient journalism awards various orgns. Republican. Roman Catholic. Contbr. articles to profl. jours. Home: 1442 Sierra Creek Way San Jose CA 95132

EDMONDS, IVY GORDON, author; b. Frost, Tex., Feb. 15, 1917; s. Ivy Gordon and Delia Louella (Shumate) E.; student pub. schs.; m. Reiko Mimura, July 12, 1956; 1 dau., Annette. Freelance writer; author books including: Ooka the Wise, 1961; The Bounty's Boy, 1963; Joel of the Hanging Gardens, 1966; Trickster Tales, 1966; Taiwan—the Other China, 1971; The Magic Man, 1972; Mao's Long March, 1973; Motorcycling for Beginners, 1973; Microness, 1974; Pakistan, Land of Mystery, Tragedy and Courage, 1974; Automotive Tuneups for Beginners, 1974; Ethiopia, 1975; The Magic Makers, 1976; The Shah of Iran, 1976; Allah's Oil: Mid-East Petroleum, 1976; Second Sight, 1977; Motorcycle Racing for Beginners, 1977; Islam, 1977; Buddhism, 1978; The Mysteries of Troy, 1977; Big U Universal in the Silent Days, 1977; D.D. Home, 1978; Bicycle Motocross, 1979; Girls Who Talked to Ghosts, 1979; The Magic Brothers, 1979; (with William H. Gebhardt) Broadcasting for Beginners, 1980; (with Reiko Mimura) The Oscar Directors, 1980; The Mysteries of Homer's Greeks, 1981; The Kings of Black Magic, 1981; Funny Car Racing for Beginners, 1982; The Magic Dog, 1982; author textbooks: (with Ronald Gonzales) Understanding Your Car, 1975, Introduction to Welding, 1975; also author pulp and soft cover fiction and nonfiction under names of Gene Cross and Gary Gordon and publishers house names; pub. relations mgr. Northrop Corp., Anaheim, Calif., 1968-79, indsl. editor, Hawthorne, Calif., 1979-86. Served with USAAF, 1940-45, USAF, 1946-63. Decorated D.F.C., Air medals, Bronze Star. Mem. Authors' Guild, Authors' League Am. Home: 5801 Shirl St Cypress CA 90630

EDWARDS, BARRY ALBERT, manufacturing executive; b. San Mateo, Calif., Oct. 24, 1945; s. Norman W. and Marian E. (Gallaway) E.; m. Jean Ellen Haile, Nov. 27, 1968 (div. Nov. 1984); m. Janet W. Cleary, May 4, 1985; 1 child, Christopher Garth. BA, Wesleyan U., 1968; MS, U. Nebr., Omaha, 1970; MBA, Stanford U., 1976. Investment mgr. Prudential Ins. Co. Am., San Francisco, 1976-80; treas. McCall Oil and Chem. Corp., Portland, Oreg., 1980-84; v.p. fin. Arnav Systems, Salem, Oreg., 1984-85; v.p., chief fin. officer Peerless Corp., Tualatin, Oreg., 1986—. Office: Peerless Corp PO Box 447 Tualatin OR 97062

EDWARDS, BRUCE GEORGE, ophthalmologist, naval officer; b. Idaho Springs, Colo., Apr. 6, 1942; s. Bruce Norwood and Evelyn Alice (Kohut) Edwards. BA, U. Colo., 1964; MD, U. Colo., Denver, 1968. Diplomate Am. Acad. Ophthalmology. Commd. 2d lt. USN, 1964; advanced through grades to capt. U.S. Naval Hosp., 1980; intern U.S. Naval Hosp., San Diego, 1968-69; USN med. officer USS Long Beach (CGN-9), 1969-70; gen. med. officer U.S. Naval Hosp., Taipei, Taiwan, 1970-72, U.S. Naval Dispensary Treasure Island, San Francisco, 1972-73; resident in ophthalmology U.S. Naval Hosp., Oakland, Calif., 1973-76, U. Calif., San Francisco, 1973-76; mem. opthalmologist staff Naval Hosp., Camp Pendleton, Calif., 1976-83; ophthalmologist, chief of med. staff Naval Hosp., Naples, Italy, 1983-85; ophthalmology head Naval Hosp., Camp Pendleton, 1985—; credential chmn. Camp Pendleton Naval Hosp., 1986—; bd. dirs. Physician Advisor Quality Assurance, Camp Pendleton Naval Hosp., 1985-86; vol. Internat. Eye Found., Harar, Ethiopia, 1975. Fellow. Am. Acad. Ophthalmology; mem. AMA, Calif. Med. Assn., Calif. Assn. Ophthalmologists, Am. Soc. Comtemporary Ophthalmologists, Assn. U.S. Mil. Surgeons, Pan Am. Assn. Opthalmology. Republican. Methodist. Lodge: Order of DeMolay (Colo. DeMolay of Yr. 1961, Idaho Springs Chevalier, Colo. State sec. 1961-62), Elks. Office: US Naval Hosp Ophthalmology Dept Camp Pendleton CA 92055

EDWARDS, CECIL LEROY, historian; b. Salem, Oreg., Nov. 20, 1906; s. Arthur James and Mary Jane (Greene) E. Grad., Salem Sr. High Sch., 1925; D Pub. Svc. (hon.), Wilamette U., 1988. Legis. sec. Oreg. State Senate, Salem, 1935-37, sec., 1965-75; pvt. sec. Gov. Charles A. Sprague, Salem, 1939-41; mem. Oreg. State Parole Bd., 1939-41; state supr. Pari Mutuel Racing Bd., State of Oreg., Portland, 1947-58; sec. Oreg. Cattlemen's Assn., Prineville, 1959-60; exec. sec. Oreg. Legis. Com., Salem, 1960-61; chief clk. Oreg. Ho. Reps., Salem, 1961-63; legis. historian Oreg. State Legislature, Salem, 1976—; mem. Hist. Landmarks Commn., Salem, 1981—, Hist. Records Commn., Salem, 1983—; steward Hist. Preservation, Salem, 1982—; vice chmn. Hist. Properties Commn., Salem, 1977—; chmn. Oreg. State Marine Bd., Salem, 1979-80; researcher in field. Author: Historical Oregon's Submerged and Submersible Lands, 1970-72. Mem. boating safety com. U.S. Power Squadron, Salem, 1965—; mem. ednl. history com. Mission Mill Mus., Salem, 1975—, trustee, 1982—; bd. dirs. Pioneer Cemetery, Salem, 1983—; commr. City Hist. Landmarks, 1982. Lt. col. cav. U.S. Army, 1944-46. Cecil L. Edwards' Day, Oreg. State Legislature, 1988. Mem. Marion County Hist. Soc. (award 1985), Oreg. Hist. Soc. (Spl. Recognition 1987), Nat. Hist. Preservation Soc., Isaac Walton League (pres. 1978—), Am. Legion, Thoroughbred Breeder Assn. (pres. 1939), NRA, Embarcadero Yacht Club, Elks. Democrat. Home: 2375 High St SE Salem OR 97301 Office: Oreg State Legislature State Capitol S431 Salem OR 97310

EDWARDS, CHARLES BENTON, JR., director, writer; b. Dallas, Sept. 19, 1944; s. Charles Benton Sr. and Margaret Lee (Dickhout) E. Student, Tyler Jr. Coll., 1963-65, No. Tex. State, 1965-66. Dir. Pyramid Prodns., various locations, 1970-80; actor, asst. stage mgr. Theatre Under the Stars, Houston, 1983-86; dir., choreographer Actor's Workshop, Houston, 1986; owner Pacific Overtures Photography, San Francisco, 1986—; dir., writer Keep Your Day Job Prodns., San Francisco, 1986—. Author, lyricist: Streets, 1988. Mem. Actor's Equity Assn. Democrat.

EDWARDS, CHARLES CORNELL, physician, research administrator; b. Overton, Nebr., Sept. 16, 1923; s. Charles Busby and Lillian Margaret (Arendt) E.; m. Sue Cowles Kruidenier, June 24, 1945; children: Timothy, Charles Cornell, Nancy, David. Student, Princeton U., 1941-43; B.A., U. Colo., 1945, M.D., 1948; M.S., U. Minn., 1956; L.L.D. (hon.), Phila. Coll. Pharmacy and Sci.; L.H.D. (hon.), Pa. Coll. Podiatry. Diplomate: Am. Bd. Surgery. Intern St. Mary's Hosp., Mpls., 1948-49; resident surgery Mayo Found., 1950-56; pvt. practice medicine specializing in surgery Des Moines, 1956-61; mem. surg. staff Georgetown U., Washington, 1961-62; also cons. USPHS; dir. div. socio-econ. activities A.M.A., Chgo., 1963-67; v.p., mng. officer health and sci. affairs Booz, Allen & Hamilton, 1967-69; commr. FDA, Washington, 1969-73; asst. sec. for health HEW, Washington, 1973-75; sr. v.p., dir. Becton, Dickinson & Co., 1975-77; pres. Scripps Clinic and Research Found., La Jolla, Calif., 1977—; bd. regents Nat. Library Medicine, 1981-85; bd. dirs. Bergen Brunswig Corp., Biomagnetic Techs., Inc., Coordinated Health Care Systems, Nova Pharm. Corp.; mem. Nat. Leadership Commn. on Health Care, 1986—; bd. govs. Hosp. Corp. Am., 1986—. Served to lt. M.C. USNR, 1942-46. Mem. Inst. Medicine, Nat. Acad. Scis. Clubs: Chevy Chase, Princeton; La Jolla Country, La Jolla Beach and Tennis; Fairbanks Ranch Country. Office: Scripps Clinic Keeney Park 10666 N Torrey Pines Rd La Jolla CA 92037 *

EDWARDS, CHARLES RICHARD, printing equipment and supplies company executive; b. South Bend, Ind., July 16, 1931; s. Bernard Stuart and Mary Irene (Chamberlaine) E.; student pub. schs.; m. Joanne Wood, Dec. 15, 1950; children—Timothy Stuart, Terry Lynne, David Bryan. Pressman, Toastmasters Internat., Santa Ana, Calif., 1954-60; with 3M Co., 1960-69, Salesman, Western U.S. tech. service and nat. market mgr., St. Paul, 1966-69; chief exec. officer, sec., chief fin. officer, co-owner Graphic Arts Supplies, Inc., Orange, Calif., 1969-86; owner, operator Edwards Bus. Services, 1987—; bus. and trade cons., 1986—; instr., cons. in field. Bd. dirs., treas. #1 Network, Inc., Chgo., 1982-86. Served with USAF, 1950-54; Korea. Mem. Nat. Assn. Lithographic Clubs (chpt. co-founder, officer, dir.), Nat. Assn. Printing House Craftsmen (past chpt. pres., regional officer), Toastmasters, Hobo Golf Assn. (pres. 1985—). Republican. Home: 7221 Judson Ave Westminster CA 92683

EDWARDS, DANIEL WALDEN, lawyer; b. Vancouver, Wash., Aug. 7, 1950; s. Chester W. Edwards and Marilyn E. Russell; m. Joan S. Heller, Oct. 18, 1987; children: Nathaniel, Matthew. BA in Psychology magna cum laude, Met. State Coll., Denver, 1973, BA in Philosophy, 1974; JD, U. Colo., 1976. Bar: Colo. 1977, U.S. Dist. Ct. Colo. 1977. Dep. pub. defender State of Colo., Denver, 1977-79, Littleton, 1979-81, Pueblo, 1981-86; head office pub. defender State of Colo., Brighton, 1987-88, mem. jud. faculty, 1988—; moot ct. judge, advocacy natural resources, appellate sch. of law U. Denver, 1987—; intsr., 1988. Named Pub. Defender of Yr., Colo. State Pub. Defender's Office, 1985. Mem. ABA, Assn. Trial Lawyers Am., Colo. Bar Assn., Adams County Bar Asss., Denver Bar Assn. Home: 2335 Clermont St Denver CO 80207 Office: Colo State Pub Defender 2426 E Bridge St Brighton CO 80601

EDWARDS, DARREL, psychologist; b. San Francisco, July 9, 1943; s. Darrus and Rose Pearl (Sannar) E.; m. Christine Hatton-Ward, Sept. 3, 1965; children: Alexander Hugh, Peter David, James Royce. BS in Psychology and Philosophy, Brigham Young U., 1965, MS in Psychology and Philosophy, 1967, PhD in Clin. Psychology, 1968; postgrad., Penn. State U., 1969. Commd. lt. (j.g.) USN, 1970, advanced through grades to lt. comdr., 1978; dir. psychologist Tri Community Svc. Systems, San Diego, 1973-78; prof. Calif. Sch. Profl. Psychology, San Diego, 1971-78; dir. Grid Rsch., San Diego, 1978-83; pres. The Edwards Assoc., San Diego, 1983—; co-founder Summus Cons. Strategies, Darien, Conn., 1989—, Strategic Solutions, Washington and London; consulting strategist for govt. and pvt. sector, U.S. and Eng., 1978—. Co-inventor in field; contbr. articles to profl. jours. Mem. Am. Psychol. Assn. Office: The Edwards Assoc PO Box 24429 San Diego CA 92124

EDWARDS, DON, congressman; b. San Jose, Calif., Jan. 6, 1915; s. Leonard P. and Clara (Donlon) E.; m. Edith B. Wilkie; children—Leonard P., Samuel D., Bruce H., Thomas C., William D. A.B., Stanford, 1936; student, Law Sch., 1936-38. Agt. FBI, 1940-41; mem. 88th-93d Congresses from 9th Calif. Dist., 94th-101st Congresses from 10th Calif. Dist.; Nat. chmn. Americans for Democratic Action, from 1965. Served to lt. USNR, 1941-45. Democrat. Unitarian. Office: US Ho of Reps 2307 Rayburn House Office Bldg Washington DC 20515

EDWARDS, ELIZABETH T., realtor; b. Fullerton, Calif., June 12, 1953; d. James Martin and Patricia Keaton (McCullough) E. BA in Drama, U. Calif., Irvine, 1978. Owner Headlines Salon, Breckenridge, Colo., 1978-87; realtor Tarbell Realtors, San Clemente, Calif., 1987—. Mem. South Orange County Bd. Realtors. Office: Tarbell Realtors 616 S El Camino Real #A San Clemente CA 92672

EDWARDS, HARRY, sociology educator, activist; b. St. Louis, Nov. 22, 1942; m. Sandra Y. Boze; children: Tazamisha, Fatima, Changa. BA, San Jose State U., 1964, MA, 1966; PhD, Cornell U., 1972; hon. doctorate, Columbia Coll., 1981. Instr. San Jose State U., 1966-68, U. Santa Clara, Calif., 1967-68; asst. prof. U. Calif., Berkeley, 1970-77, assoc. prof., 1977—; disting. vis. scholar Ind. State U., 1984; author, lectr., cons. on sports and soc. Disting scholar in rsch. Oreg. State U., 1980, Norwegian Coll. Phys. Edn. and Sports, Oslo, 1983. Office: U Calif Dept Sociology Berkeley CA 94720 *

EDWARDS, IAN KENNETH, electronics manufacturing executive; b. Melbourne, Australia, July 12, 1953; came to U.S., 1980; s. William Alexander and Mavis Maud (Turner) E.; m. Rita Jane Williams, Dec. 12, 1982. Tutor math. U. Melbourne, 1978-80; project engr. CLS Industries, Hawthorne, Calif., 1980-83; dir. instrument ops. United Detector Tech., Hawthorne, 1983—. Contbr. articles to profl. jours. Mem. Australian Inst. Physics, Optical Soc. Am., Laser Inst. Am., Soc. Photo-Optical Instrumentation Engrs. Office: United Detector Tech 12525 Chadron Ave Hawthorne CA 90250

EDWARDS, JACK A., state agency professional; b. Riverside, Calif., Nov. 17, 1948; s. Douglas Eugene and Billie Sue (Pruitt) E.; m. Donna Lee Klahr, Dec. 20, 1968 (div. Mar. 1973); m. Carolyn Ann Strause, May 7, 1983. Student, Riverside City Coll.; BS in Zoology, U. Calif., Davis, 1975; postgrad., Calif. State U., Sacramento. Horseshoer Riverside, Calif., 1972-75; park ranger asst. Sacramento Parks and Recreation, 1975-77; game warden Calif. Dept. Fish and Game, Half Moon Bay, Calif., 1977-81; game warden Calif. Dept. Fish and Game, Sacramento, 1981-86, patrol capt., statewide hunter edn. coordinator, 1986—. Co-author, editor: Defense Tactics and Arrest Techniques, 1985; author: Wildlife Protection Computer Database for California Fish and Game. Mem. South Sacramento Planning Com., 1985-86. Served to staff sgt. USAF, 1968-72. Mem. Calif. Fish and Game Warden's Protective Assn. (treas. 1981-86, pres. 1986—), N.Am. Wildlife Officers Assn. Republican. Home: 7288 Gardner Ave Sacramento CA 95828

EDWARDS, JOHN HENRY, manufacturing company executive; b. Washington, Mar. 14, 1930; s. George Allan and Carole Marie (Boots) E.; m. Joanne Marcsisak, Jan. 13, 1952; 1 child, Jay Marc. BBA, Calif. Western U., 1962. Logistics rep. Gen. Dynamics Convair, San Diego, 1956; contract analyst Gen. Dynamics Astronautics, San Diego, 1957, contract rep., 1958, contract adminstr., 1959-61, chief of contracts, 1962-66; chief of contracts Gen. Dynamics Convair Div., San Diego, 1967-80; mgr. contracts Gen. Dynamics Svc. Co., San Diego, 1981-83, Gen. Dynamics Space System, San Diego, 1984—; adj. prof. Nat. U., San Diego, 1981-83. Drafter/negotiator numerous govt. contracts. Pres. Little League, San Diego, 1977. With USN, 1950-53, Korea. Mem. Nat. Mgmt. Assn., Nat. Contract Mgmt. Assn. (pres. San Diego chpt. 1969-70). Republican. Home: 7921 Blue Jay Pl San Diego CA 92123

EDWARDS, JOHN WOMER, aerospace systems engineer; b. Sharon, Pa., Aug. 12, 1958; s. John Roy and Doris Ellen (Womer) E.; m. Elise Anne Mock, Aug. 26, 1985. AA in Math, Cochise Community Coll., 1977; BS in Physics, Math., U. Ariz., 1979, MS in Systems Engring., 1982. Cons. Computerland, Tucson, 1980-82; systems engr. Rockwell Internat., Anaheim, Calif., 1982-85, Tex. Instruments, Dallas, 1985-87; sr. engr. Garrett Controls, Tucson, 1987-88; supr. engring. computing and computer network div. Garrett Controls (name changed to AiReارch Tucson div. Allied-Signal Aerospace Co.), Tucson, 1988—; cons. Starfyre Software, Brea, Calif., 1982-87, Arnell Audio/Visual Prodns., Tucson, 1980—. Author: (with others) The Rock Record, 1987; contbr. articles to profl. jours. Mem. Crime Watch of Tucson, 1988. Mem. Nat. Card Collectors Assn., Am. Assn. of Recording Arts and Sciences, Ariz. Engring. Alumni, Soc. of Personal Computers Software Developers, Plantary Soc. Republican. Presbyterian. Home: 5060 W Albatross Tucson AZ 85741 Office: Allied-Signal Aerospace Co AiResearch Tuson Div Tucson AZ 85740

EDWARDS, JONATHAN HAYES, insurance claims representative; b. Wrentham, Mass., May 15, 1949; s. Wilfred Carl and Cecile Marie-Ann (Pepin) Hyatt E.; m. Susan Gail Dumas, May 27, 1967; children: Dawn Marie, Jonathan Hayes. Grad., Mass. State Police Acad., Framingham, 1972; student, Bryant Coll., 1982. Police officer Civil Svc. Mass., 1970-80; claims special investigator Nationwide Ins. Co., Randolph, Mass., 1980-85; supr. Burns Internat., Honlulu, 1985-86; claims rep. Hawaiian Ins., Honolulu, 1986—; speaker in field; owner, proprietor KeyNote performances, Hon, Hawaii, 1987—. Coach YMCA, N. Attleboro, Mass., 1981-85; mem. Plainville (Mass.) Hist. Soc., 1974-75; pres. Police Assn., Plainville, 1971-80. Mem. Internat. Auto Theft Investigators, Hawaii Claims Orgn. Home: 94-182 Anania Dr Mililani Town HI 96789 Office: KeyNote Performances Box 3401 Mililani Town HI 96789

EDWARDS, (FLOYD) KENNETH, journalist, educator, management consultant, marketing executive; b. Salina, Kans., Sept. 29, 1917; s. Floyd Altamus and Grace Frances (Miller) E.; AB, Fort Hays State U., 1940; MS, 1970; m. Virginia Marie Lewark, Sept. 10, 1970; children: Elaine Patricia, Diana, Kenneth, John Michael, Melody, Daniel J. Ins. sales exec., Denver, 1947-50; reporter Sterling (Colo.) Daily Jour., 1950, editor, 1950-52; editor Waverly (Iowa) Newspapers, 1953-55; editor, pub. Edina (Minn.) Courier Newspapers, 1955-56; v.p., editor Mpls. Suburban Newspapers, Hopkins, Minn., 1956-65; editor, gen. mgr. Valley of the Sun Newspapers, Tempe, Ariz., 1968; instr. Mankato (Minn.) State U., 1970-72, asst. prof., 1972-73; assoc. prof. U. Ala., 1973-80, prof., 1980; vis. prof. communications U. Portland (Oreg.), 1981-83, Western Wash. U., 1987-88; mktg. and sales dir. C.C. Publs., Tualatin, Oreg., 1983-86; pres. GoodLife Publs., Bellingham, Wash., 1988—; cons. on newspaper mgmt.,mktg., videotex ops. Pres. Calhoun-Harriet Home Owners Assn., Mpls., 1958-60; bd. dirs. Hennepin County Assn. for Mental Health, 1959-60, S.W. Activities Council, 1960-61, S.W. High Sch. PTA, Mpls., 1960-61. Served with USN, World War II. Grantee Ford Found., 1976, U. Ala., 1977. Recipient awards for community service and editorial writing. Mem. Am. Mgmt. Assn., Nat. Conf. of Editorial Writers. Republican. Contbr. articles to profl. jours., chpts. to books; author newspaper profit planning and management manual. Home: 8 Sudden Valley Bellingham WA 98226

EDWARDS, KENNETH BERNARD, technician; b. Valdosta, Ga., Apr. 9, 1961; s. Jonas III and Willie Ruth (Lucas) Mitchell E. Student, U. Alaska, 1988—. Salesman Nordstrom, Inc., Fairbanks, Alaska, 1979-81; broadcast announcer Midnight Sun Broadcasters, Fairbanks, 1979-80; salesman Fred Meyer Corp., Fairbanks, 1981-82; radio technician Bur. Land Mgmt., Ft. Wainwright, Alaska, 1980-81; technician Mcpl. Utilities Telephone, Fairbanks, 1983—. Office: PO Box 2215 645 5th Ave Fairbanks AK 99707

EDWARDS, L. WILLIAM, international management consultant, oil executive; b. Chgo., Nov. 28, 1946; s. Lewis William and Lucy (Chapdelaine) E.; m. Nancy Imlay, June 8, 1968; children: Heather Anne, Amy Rebecca. BS in Geology, St. Louis U., 1969. Geophys. trainee Arco Oil & Gas Co., Denver, 1969, 69-61; geophysicist Arco Alaska & Arco Internat., Anchorage and L.A., 1971-74; sr. geophysicist Arco Indonesia & Arco Oil & Gas, Jakora and Houston, Indonesia, 1974-77; dist. geophysicist Arco Alaska, Anchorage, 1977-81; sr. corp. planning cons. Arco Corp., L.A., 1981-82, corp. cons., 1987-88; chief geophysicist Arco China, Inc., Zhanjiang, People's Republic of China, 1982-84, exploration mgr., 1984-85; resident mgr. Arco Turkey, Inc., Ankara, 1985-87; pres. Edvest Mgmt. Ltd., L.A., 1988—; pres., chief exec. officer Edvest Mgmt. Ltd., Brea, Calif., 1988—; pres. Overseas Exploration Corp., Brea, 1988—. Mem. Am. Assn.

Petroleum Geologists, Am. Inst. Profl. Geologists, Soc. Exploration Geophysicists, Soc. Petroleum Engrs., Computer Oriented Geol. Soc., Jaycees (pres. Anchorage chpt. 1973). Republican. Roman Catholic. Office: Edvest Mgmt Ltd 1033 E Imperial Hwy Ste E Brea CA 92621

EDWARDS, LYDIA JUSTICE, state official; b. Carter County, Ky., July 9, 1937; d. Chead and Velva (Kinney) Justice; m. Frank B. Edwards, 1968; children: Mark, Alexandra, Margot. Student, San Francisco State U. Began career as acct, then Idaho state rep., 1982-86; treas. State of Idaho, 1987—; legis. asst. to Gov. Hickel, Alaska, 1967; conf. planner Rep. Gov.'s Assn., 1970-73; mem. Rep. Nat. Commn., 1972, del. to nat. conv., 1980. Mem. Rep. Womens Fedn. Congregationalist. Office: State Treas's Office State Capitol Bldg Rm 102 Boise ID 83720 *

EDWARDS, MARIE BABARE, psychologist; b. Tacoma; d. Nick and Mary (Mardesich) Babare; B.A., Stanford, 1948, M.A., 1949; m. Tilden Hampton Edwards (div.); 1 son, Tilden Hampton Edwards III. Counselor guidance center U. So. Calif., Los Angeles, 1950-52; project coordinator So. Calif. Soc. Mental Hygiene, 1952-54; pub. speaker Welfare Fedn. Los Angeles, 1953-57; field rep. Los Angeles County Assn. Mental Health, 1957-58; intern psychologist UCLA, 1958-60; pvt. practice, human relations tng., counselor tng. Mem. Calif., Am., Western, Los Angeles psychol. assns., AAAS, So. Calif. Soc. Clin. Hypnosis, Internat. Platform Assn. Author: (with Eleanor Hoover) The Challenge of Being Single, 1974, paperback edit., 1975. Office: 6100 Buckingham Pkwy Culver City CA 90230

EDWARDS, MICHAEL DAVID, business executive; b. Iromagawa, Japan, Aug. 19, 1955; came to U.S., 1957.; s. John Robert and Virginia (Pemberton) E.; 1 child, Kimberly C. BBA, U. Miami, 1976, MBA, 1977. Stock broker AG Edwards & Sons, Denver, 1979-81; v.p. of investment Drexel Burnham Lambert, Denver, 1981-86; pres., chief exec. officer Pure Bred Co. Inc., Denver and Los Angeles, 1986—; fin. advisor City of Denver, 1986. Vol. Am. Cancer Soc., 1985, Big Brothers, Miami, 1976. Republican. Presbyterian. Office: Purebred Co Inc PO Box 37122 Denver CO 80237

EDWARDS, MICHAEL RUSS, sales consultant; b. Duncan, Okla., July 24, 1935; s. Marshall James Edwards and Emma Elizabeth Persson; A.A., Casper Coll. (Wyo.), 1969; B.S., U. Wyo., 1974, postgrad., 1984. With Mid-Continent Supply Co., Ft. Worth, 1974-82, expeditor, Ft. Worth 1974-77, mktg. systems analyst, Ft. Worth and Houston, 1977-79, pricing and inventory control specialist, Farmington, N.Mex., 1979-82; mktg. mgmt. analyst, 1983-85; ind. sales cons., Casper, 1985—. Casper, Wyo. Served with USAF, 1957-60. Mem. U. Wyo. Alumni Assn. Republican. Episcopalian. Address: 1724 N Grass Creek Rd Casper WY 82604

EDWARDS, RALPH M., librarian; b. Shelley, Idaho, Apr. 17, 1933; s. Edward William and Maude Estella (Munsee) E.; m. Winifred Wylie, Dec. 25, 1969; children: Dylan, Nathan, Stephen. B.A., U. Wash., 1957, M.Library, 1960; D.L.S., U. Calif.-Berkeley, 1971. Librarian N.Y. Pub. Library, N.Y.C., 1960-61; catalog librarian U. Ill. Library, Urbana, 1961-62; br. librarian Multnomah County Library, Portland, Oreg., 1964-67; asst. prof. Western Mich. U., Kalamazoo, 1970-74; chief of the Central Library Dallas Pub. Library, 1975-81; city librarian Phoenix Pub. Library, 1981—. Author: Role of the Beginning Librarian in University Libraries, 1975. U. Calif. doctoral fellow, 1967-70; library mgmt. internship Council on Library Resources, 1974-75. Mem. ALA, Ariz. Library Assn., Pub. Library Assn. Democrat. Home: 4839 E Mulberry Dr Phoenix AZ 85018 Office: Phoenix Pub Libr 12 E McDowell Rd Phoenix AZ 85004

EDWARDS, RICHARD CHARLES, financial analyst; b. Jacksonville, Fla., Feb. 7, 1948; s. Robert David and Jean Alice (Bauer) E.; m. Robin Mary Morse, Aug. 30, 1970; children: Michael, Jonathan. BSEE, Princeton U., 1969; MBA, Stanford U., 1976. Mktg. mgr. Hewlett Packard Co., Cupertino, Calif., 1976-83; prin. Robertson, Stephens & Co., San Francisco, 1983—. Editor photography, Bric-a-Brac, 1968; author: Using Edit2, 1981. Bd. dirs. Oakland (Calif.)-Piedmont Jewish Community Ctr., 1983-87. Served to lt. USN, 1970-74. Recipient NSF award, 1964. Mem. IEEE, San Francisco Soc. Security Analysts. Club: Lakeview (Oakland). Home: 2661 Mountain Gate Way Oakland CA 94611 Office: Robertson Stephens & Co 1 Embarcadero Ctr Ste 3100 San Francisco CA 94111

EDWARDS, RONALD LEE, data processing executive; b. Oklahoma City, June 7, 1952; s. Velman Duane Edwards and Faye Louise (Garver) Perry; m. Carol Jean Caplinger, Oct. 15, 1971; children: Christopher Lee, Matthew Lee, Melissa Lee. BBA, Cen. State U., Edmond, Okla., 1980. Mgr. data processing Hahn Truck Lines, Oklahoma City, 1976-80; programmer analyst Adams Affiliated, Bartlesville, Okla., 1980-81; mgr. data processing Am. Truck Lines, Oklahoma City, 1981-82, Melton Truck Lines, Shreveport, La., 1982-85, Lindsey & Newsom, Tyler, Tex., 1985-86; dir. MIS Wingate Taylor Maid, Albany, Ga., 1986-87; dir. adminstrn. systems Burlington No. Motor Carriers, Joplin, Mo., 1987-88; dir. info. systems Country Wide Trucking, Pomona, Calif., 1988—. With USAF, 1970-74. Republican. Baptist. Office: Country Wide Truck Svc 1110 S Reservoir Pomona CA 91766

EDWARDS, SÈBASTIAN, economist, educator; b. Santiago, Chile, Aug. 16, 1953; came to U.S., 1977; s. Hernan Edwards and Magdalena Figueroa; m. Alejandra Cox, Aug. 27, 1976; children: Magdalena, Benjamin, Victoria. Licenciado, Cath. U. Chile, 1975; MA, U. Chgo., 1978, PhD, 1981. Rsch. fellow Cath. U., Santiago, 1975-77; sr. economist Empresas BHC, Santiago, 1976-77; cons. World Bank, Washington, 1982—; assoc. Nat. Bur. Econ. Rsch., Cambridge, Mass., 1983—; prof. UCLA, 1981—; cons. World Bank, Washington, 1982—, IMF, 1984, 87, 88, OECD, Paris, 1989. Co-author: The Chilean Experiment, 1987; editor: Exchange Rates in LDC's, 1986, Econ. Adjustment and Exchange Rates in Developing Countries, 1986; co-editor Debt Adjustment and Recovery, 1989; author: Exchange Rate Misalignment, 1989, Real Exchange Rates and Devaluation, 1989; numerous articles. Mem. Am. Econ. Assn., Can. Econ. Assn. Office: UCLA Dept Econs 405 Hilgard Ave Los Angeles CA 90024

EDWARDS, WARD, educator, psychologist; b. Morristown, N.J., Apr. 5, 1927; s. Corwin D. and Janet W. (Ferriss) E.; m. Silvia Callegari, Dec. 12, 1970; children: Tara, Page. B.A., Swarthmore Coll., 1947; M.A., Harvard U., 1950, Ph.D., 1952. Instr. Johns Hopkins U., 1951-54; with Personnel and Tng. Research Center, USAF, Denver, 1954-56, San Antonio, 1956-58; research psychologist U. Mich., 1958-63, prof. psychology, 1963-73, head Engring. Psychology Lab., 1963-73; asso. dir. Hwy. Safety Research Inst., 1970-73; prof. psychology and indsl. engring., dir. Social Sci. Research Inst., U. So. Calif., 1973—; cons. in field. Author: (with J. Robert Newman) Multiattribute Evaluation, 1982, (with D.v. Winterfeldt) Decision Analysis and Behavioral Research, 1986; editor (with A. Tversky) Decision Making: Selected Reading, 1967; contbr. Ency Social Scis, 1968. Served with USNR, 1945-46. Recipient Franklin V. Taylor award Soc. Engring. Psychologists, 1978. Fellow Am. Psychol. Assn., Decision Scis. Inst.; mem. Western Psychol. Assn., Psychonomic Soc., Soc. Med. Decision-Making, Ops. Research Soc. Am. (Frank P. Ramsey medal 1988), Inst. Mgmt. Scis. (pres. Coll. Managerial Problem Solving 1987-88). Address: U So Calif Social Sci Rsch Inst Los Angeles CA 90089-1111

EFNOR, RICHARD MERRILL, data processing executive; b. Newton, Iowa, Aug. 6, 1949; s. Guy m. Efnor and Emagene (Reid) Pettit. BS in Math., No. Ill. U., 1971; MBA in Mgmt., Golden Gate U., 1987. Cert. data processing, Calif. Computer specialist data svcs. ctr. USAF, Washington, 1973-83; chief info. systems hdqtrs. audit agy. USAF, Norton AFB, Calif., 1983--. With USAF, 1971-75. Mem. Inst. Cert. Computer Profls.

EFRON, BRADLEY, mathematics educator; b. St. Paul, May 24, 1938; s. Miles Jack and Esther (Kaufman) E.; m. Gael Guerin, July 1969 (div.); 1 son, Miles James; m. Nancy Troup, June 1986 (div.). B.S. in Math., Calif. Inst. Tech., 1960; Ph.D., Stanford U., 1964. Asst. and assoc. prof. stats. Stanford (Calif.) U., 1965-72, chmn. dept. stats., 1976-79, chmn. math. scis., 1981—, prof. stats., 1974—, assoc. dean humanities and scis., 1987—, endowed chair Max H. Stein prof. humanities and scis., 1987—; statis. cons. Alza Corp., 1971—, Rand Corp., 1962—, Aprex Corp., 1986. Author: Bootstrap Methods, 1979, Biostatistics Casebook, 1980. MacArthur Found. fellow, 1983; named Outstanding Statistician of the Yr. Chgo. Statis. Assn., 1981; Wald and Rietz Lectr. Inst. Math. Stats., 1977, 81. Fellow Inst. Math. Stats. (pres. 1987), Am. Statis. Assn.; mem. Internat. Statis. Assn., Nat. Acad. Scis. Democrat. Office: Stanford U Dept Stats Sequoia Hall Stanford CA 94305

EGAN, JOHN TINNERMAN, rancher; b. Cleve., May 18, 1948; s. Robert Brooks and Elisabeth Neubauer (Tinnerman) E.; children: Joseph Clinton, Elisabeth Lindsay Jane; m. Deborah Anne Montoya, Oct. 12, 1986. BA, Loretto Heights Coll., 1973; BA (hon.), Coll. Santa Fe, 1982. Gen. mgr. Rancho Encantado, Santa Fe, 1968-83, owner, mgr., 1983—; chmn. Encantado Mgmt., Santa Fe, 1985—. Author: The Present, 1973. Bd. dirs. Symphony Santa Fe, 1986—; pres. N.Mex. North, Santa Fe, 1982; mem. Council Dist. 2, 375th Anniversary Commn. City Santa Fe, 1986—. Named one of Outstanding Young Men Am., U.S. Jaycees, 1984, Outstanding New Mex. N.Mex. Jaycees, 1988. Mem. Santa Fe Lodgers Assn. (pres. 1981), N.Mex. Amigos, Santa Fe C. of C. (pres. 1986—, Dir. Yr. award 1982). Republican. Methodist. Club: Santa Fe Country. Lodge: Eagles. Office: Rancho Encantado Inc Rte 4 Box 57-C Santa Fe NM 87501

EGER, DENISE LEESE, rabbi; b. New Kensington, Pa., Mar. 14, 1960; d. Bernard D. and Estelle (Leese) E. BA in Religion, U. So. Calif., 1982; MA in Hebrew Lit., Hebrew Union Coll., L.A., 1985; Rabbi, Hebrew Union Coll., N.Y.C., 1988. Ordained rabbi, 1988. Rabbi Temple Beth Ora, Edmonton, Alta., Can., 1983-85; chaplain Isabella Geriatric Ctr., N.Y.C., 1986-88; rabbi Beth Chayim Chadashim, L.A., 1988—. Contbr. articles to religious publs., chpt. to anthology. Bd. dirs. Nechama: A Jewish Response to AIDS; mem. AIDS task force S.W. coun. Union Am. Hebrew Congregations; mem. spiritual adv. com. AIDS Project L.A. Mem. Cen. Conf. Am. Rabbis. Office: Beth Chayim Chadashim 6000 W Pico Blvd Los Angeles CA 90035

EGER, JOHN GAYLORD, military officer; b. San Diego, Oct. 25, 1948; s. Frank Anton and Dorothy Louise (Abbaduska) E. BA in History, Geog., U. Hawaii, 1970, MA in U.S. History, 1971, PhD in U.S. History, 1977. Enlisted U.S. Navy; tng. officer Patrol Squadron 24, Jacksonville, Fla., 1972-75; instr. Air Anti-Submarine Squadron 41, San Diego, 1975-78; maintenance officer Commandor Patrol Wings Pacific, Adak, Ala., 1978-79; exec. officer Naval Facility, Lewes, Dele., 1979-81; staff, planning officer Commander Fleet Air Keflavik, Iceland, 1981-83; tactics officer Patrol Squadron 22, Barber's Point, Hawaii, 1983-86; asst. officer in charge Forward Area Support Team, Norwalk, Va., 1986-88; instr. Weapons Tng. Group, San Diego, 1988—. Counsellor, Boy Scout Am. Mem. Nat. Geog. Soc., Smithsonian Assocs., U. S. Naval Inst., Am. Mus. Home: 2825 3rd Ave #306 San Diego CA 92103

EGGE, RICHARD CHENOWETH, construction company executive; b. Seattle, Mar. 24, 1941; s. Richard Dexter and Louise (Chenoweth) E.; m. Sharron G. Anderson, June 9, 1962 (div. Nov. 1976); 1 child, Jordan Elisha; m. Jeanette Reiser, Dec. 2, 1976; children: Laura Brownlee, John Benjamin. BSCE, Gonzaga U., 1964. Project engr. Norcoast-B.E.C.K., Anchorage, 1964-65; material engr., supt. Morrison-Knudsen Co., Melbourne, Australia, 1965-66; supt., engr. Austin Co., Renton, Wash., 1966-68; head estimator J.E. Work, Inc., Redmond, Wash., 1968-71; pres. Dyad Constrn., Inc., Woodinville, Wash., 1971—; ptnr. Shemya Constructors, Seattle, 1984—. Bd. dirs. Little Bit Spl. Riders, Inc., Woodinville, 1986—. Mem. Nat. Utility Contractors Assn. (bd. dirs. 1978—, pres. 1988, contbr. pres.'s message Industry Outlook mag. 1988— Ditch Digger of Yr. award 1980), Utility Contractors Assn. Wash. (founder, pres. 1979-81, bd. dirs. 1978—, Ditch Digger of Yr. award 1979, 80), Assoc. Gen. Contractors Assn., Wash. State Horse Breeders Assn., Useless Bay Golf and Country Club (Whidbey Island, Wash.). Republican. Roman Catholic. Office: Dyad Constrn Inc PO Box 1188 Woodinville WA 98072

EGGERS, JOHANNES L., electrical engineer; b. Scribner, Nebr., Mar. 20, 1934; s. Emil Henry and Emma Lena (Hillen) E.; m. LaVella Carol Eggers, Nov. 29, 1952; children: Deanna Carol, John Harold, Matthew Eric. BSEE, Oreg. State U., 1960, MSEE, 1965. Registered profl. engr., Oreg., Wash., Utah, Calif., Alaska, B.C. With Hyster Co., Portland, Oreg., 1951-58, Mater Machine Works, Corvallis, Oreg., 1958-60; elec. engr. U.S. Army Corps of Engrs., 1960-63; elec. devel. engr. IBM, San Jose, Calif., 1969-70; elec. mktg. rep. IBM, Vancouver, B.C., 1970-73; elec. engr. Flomatcher Controls, Corvallis, 1973-78, CH2M Hill Engring., Corvallis, 1978-87, USCG, Juneau, Alaska, 1987—; cons. in field. Inventor in field; contbr. articles to profl. jours. With USCG, 1953-55. Omark Industries rsch. fellow Oreg. State U., 1963-64. Mem. IEEE, Profl. Engrs. of Oreg., Profl. Engrs. of B.C., Indsl. Apparatus Soc., Nat. Soc. Profl. Engrs., Juneau Officers Assn. Republican. Lutheran. Home: PO Box 22335 Juneau AK 99802 Office: USCG PO Box 3-5000 Juneau AK 99802

EGGERS, LARRY ALAN, tax and financial planning company executive; b. Maryville, Tenn., Oct. 15, 1941; s. Robert Carroll and Pearl Etta Glen (Jenkins) E.; A.S. in Edn. (High Scholastic scholar), Ricks Coll., 1965; B.S. in Bus. Adminstrn., U. Redlands, 1979; m. Ruth Ann Pearson, Apr. 4, 1963; children—Laurie Ann, Mark, David, Robert, Amber, April, Jason, Michelle. Cert. Fin. Planner. With toll transmission dept. Am. Telephone Co., Long Lines, Pocatello, Idaho, 1965-66; operations engr. Lockheed Co., Sunnyvale, Calif., 1966-72; owner, gen. mgr. Eggers Tax Service, San Jose, Calif., 1968-78, editor The ETS Taxpayer, 1972-78; v.p. Mighty-Mite Computer Systems, Inc., San Jose, 1975-87, chmn. bd., 1975-87; gen. partner E.T.S. Real Estate Partnership, San Jose, 1978—; pres. E.T.S. & Assocs., Inc., San Jose, 1978—; tax and fin. cons. Active Better Bus. Bur. Lic. real estate broker, life and disability agt., securities rep. and prin. Mem. Nat. Assn. Tax Cons., Calif. Assn. Realtors, Nat. Assn. Realtors, Internat. Assn. Fin. Planners, San Jose Real Estate Bd. Mormon. Author: Basic Federal Income Tax Training Course, 1971, 72, 73; Copyrighted Tax Questionaire Booklet, 1974, 80, 82, 83, 84; programming cons. income tax software for mini-computers, acctg. software for mini-computers. Home: 700 Dartmouth Pl Gilroy CA 95020 Office: 6920 Santa Teresa Blvd Ste 208 San Jose CA 95119

EGGERTSEN, FRANK THOMAS, research chemist; b. Provo, Utah, Mar. 26, 1913; s. Burton Simon and Anne (Thomas) E.; m. Beth Marie Krueger, Dec. 29, 1939; children: Karl F., Thomas K., Grace Ann. BA, U. Utah, 1934; PhD, U. Minn., 1939. Research chemist Sherwin-Williams Co., Chgo., 1939-43, Shell Devel. Co., Emeryville, Calif., 1943-72; prin. research scientist Calif. Ink Co. div. Flint Ink Corp., Berkeley, Calif., 1973—. Contbr. articles to profl. jours.; patentee in field. Shevlin fellow U. Minn., 1938-39. Mem. Am. Chem. Soc., Sigma Xi, Phi Lambda Upsilon, Phi Kappa Phi. Democrat. Mormon. Home: 21 Daryl Dr Orinda CA 94563 Office: Calif Ink Co div Flint Ink Corp 711 Camelia St Berkeley CA 94710

EGGETT, DOUGLAS BURNINGHAM, financial investment counselor; b. Salt Lake City, Mar. 5, 1942; s. Lloyd E. and Lucile (Burningham); m. Linda Ellen Ricks, Dec. 13, 1963; children: Glade, Brandon, Deanne, Debra, Teresa. BS, Weber State Coll., 1967; MBA, U. Utah, 1968; Cert. fin. planner, Calif. Luth. U., 1988. Ins. license, Life and Casualty, Calif., NASD Securities License Series 7, Calif.; Tax Preparation License, Calif. Trust adminstr. Walker Bank and Trust, Salt Lake City, 1968-70; gen. mgr., owner Eggett's Inc., Preston/Smithfield, Idaho/Utah, 1970-85; sales mgr. Orange County, Deseret Industries, Ft. Valley, Calif., 1985-87; fin. investment counselor Republic Fed. Savs., Woodland Hills, Calif., 1987--. Served with Utah Air Nat. Guard, 1960-65. Republican. Mormon. Home: 1250 S Brookhurst 2027 Anaheim CA 92804 Office: Republic Fed Savs 6320 Canoga Ave Woodland Hills CA 92804

EGLAND, ERIC GLEN ALAN, sales executive; b. Portland, Oreg., Nov. 17, 1950; s. Glen Alan and Esther Alvina (Janz) E.; m. Sally O. Swinford, Dec. 18, 1970; children: Aaron, Adam, Benjamin, Abagail. BA, Portland State U., 1972. Mgmt. trainee J.K. Gill Co., Portland, 1972; underwriter United Pacific Ins. Co., Portland, 1972-73; area exec. Boy Scouts Am., Portland, 1973-76; sales rep. Gen. Foods Corp., Portland, 1976-79; account mgr. Gen. Foods Corp., L.A., 1979-81; ter. mgr. Gen. Foods Corp., Cin., 1981-84; region mgr. Gen. Foods Corp., White Plains, N.Y., 1984-85, product mgr., 1985-87; area sales mgr. Gold Bond Ice Cream, Portland, 1987—. Bd. dirs. Prepared Childbirth Assn., Portland, 1976-79, Skyline Ridge Neighborhood Assn., West Linn, Oreg., 1987—; active Boy Scouts Am., Portland, Cin., Conn., 1979—. Mem. Optimists. Democrat. Roman Catholic. Home and Office: 1491 Braemar Dr West Linn OR 97068

EGLEY, THOMAS ARTHUR, computer services executive, accountant; b. Aberdeen, S.D., June 23, 1945; s. Ralph Joseph and Cora Ellen (Wade) E.; m. Cecelia K. Kuskie, Feb. 22, 1984. BBA, U. Mont., 1967, postgrad., 1973-75. CPA, Mont. Programmer, analyst Comml. Data, Missoula, Mont., 1973-77; data processing mgr. John R. Daily, Inc., Missoula, 1977-78; ptnr. Egley & White CPA's, Missoula, 1978-84, Egley & White Computer Services, Missoula, 1978-85; pres. Able Fin., Inc., Missoula, 1984—, PC Software, Inc., 1987—, E & W Computer Services, Inc., 1983—; lectr., Missoula, 1973—. Bd. dirs. Missoula Children's Theater, 1975-82. Served to sgt. U.S. Army, 1968-71. Mem. Am. Inst. CPA's, Mont. Soc. CPA's, Nat. Assn. Accts., EDP Auditors Assn., Mont. Data Processing Assn., Phi Sigma Kappa Alumni Club (pres. 1973—). Republican. Lutheran. Lodge: Elks. Home and Office: E&W Computer Svcs Inc PO Drawer 2729 Missoula MT 59806-2729

EGLINTON, WILLIAM MATTHEW, utility company executive. m. Paula Eglinton; children: Amy, Carrie. BSME, U. N.Mex., 1970. Various positions Pub. Svc. Co. N.Mex., Albuquerque, 1970-1983, v.p. planning and regulation, 1983-84, sr. v.p. retail customer svc. sector, 1988, exec. v.p., chief operating officer, 1988—. Trustee U. Albuquerque; bd. dirs., mem. fin. com. St. Joseph Health Care Corp., Greater Albuquerque C. of C. Exec. Com., vice chairperson ednl. affairs div.; bd. dirs. United Way Exec. Com., vice chairperson resource devel. com.; chairperson Albuquerque Bus. Edn. Compact. Office: Pub Svc Co NMex Alvarado Sq Albuquerque NM 87158

EGNER, JOHN DAVID, electrical engineer; b. New Castle, Pa., June 30, 1957; s. John David Egner Sr. and Ann Irene (Nevin) Parta; m. Margaret Virginia Winecoff, Feb. 14, 1985. BS in Elec. Engring., U. Vt., 1979. Devel. engr. Hewlett-Packard Co., Sunnyvale, Calif., 1979-82, Apple Computer, INc., Cupertino, Calif., 1982-86; analog engr. NEXT, Inc., Palo Alto, Calif., 1986—. Mem. IEEE, Tau Beta Pi. Office: NEXT Inc 3475 Deer Creek Rd Palo Alto CA 94304

EGUCHI, MICHAEL STEVEN, television station sales executive; b. Chgo., Nov. 26, 1947; s. Hiroshi and Emma (Iguchi) E.; m. Linda Diane Robins, July 1, 1973; 1 child, Lauren Brooke. BA, U. Wash., 1970, BA in Bus. Adminstrn., 1972; MBA, Seattle U., 1978; cert. mgt. devel. seminar, Harvard U., 1980. Film editor Sta. KOMO-TV, Seattle, 1969-73; TV sales coord. Sta. KOMO-TV, 1973-75, mgr. TV traffic systems, 1975-78, nat. sales mgr., 1984-; ; mgr. traffic systems, Fisher Broadcasting Inc., Seattle, 1978-79; mgr. info. systems, 1979-82; v.p., gen. mgr. Fisher Communications Inc., 1982-84.; instr. Alpine Ski Acad. Inc., Crystal Mountain, Wash.; part-time, 1970-73. Contbr. articles to mags. Mem. Seattle Advt. Fedn., NATAS. Methodist. Home: 20103 24th Ave NW Seattle WA 98177 Office: Sta KOMO-TV 100 4th Ave N Seattle WA 98109

EHLERS, ELEANOR MAY COLLIER (MRS. FREDERICK BURTON EHLERS), civic worker; b. Klamath Falls, Oreg., Apr. 23, 1920; d. Alfred Douglas and Ethel (Foster) Collier; BA, U. Oreg., 1941; secondary tchrs. credentials Stanford, 1942; m. Frederick Burton Ehlers, June 26, 1943; children—Frederick Douglas, Charles Collier. Tchr., Salinas Union High Sch., 1942-43; piano tchr. pvt. lessons, Klamath Falls, 1958—. Mem. Child Guidance Adv. Coun., 1956-60; mem. adv. com. Boys and Girls Aid Soc., 1965-67 ; mem. Gov.'s Adv. Com. Arts and Humanities, 1966-67; bd. mem. PBS TV Sta. KSYS, 1988—, Friends of Mus. U. Oreg., 1966-69, Arts in Oreg., 1966-68, Klamath County Colls. for Oreg.'s Future, 1968— ; co-chmn. Friends of Collier Park, Collier Park Logging Mus., 1986-88, sec. 1988—; chpt. pres. Am. Field Svc., 1962-63; mem. Gov.'s Com. Governance of Community Colls., 1967; bd. dirs. Favell Mus. Western Art and Artifacts, 1971—, Community Concert Assn., 1950— , pres., 1966-74; established Women's Guild at Merle West Med. Ctr., 1965, sec. bd. dirs, 1962-65, 76—, bd. dirs., 1962—, mem. bldg. com. 1962-67, mem. planning com., chmn. edn. and rsch. com. hosp. bd., 1967—. Named Woman of Month Klamath Herald News, 1965; named grant to Oreg. Endowed Fellowship Fund, AAUW, 1971; recipient greatest Svc. award Oreg. Tech. Inst., 1970-71, Internat. Woman of Achievement award Quota Club, 1981, U. Oreg. Pioneer award, 1981. Mem. AAUW (local pres. 1955-56), Oreg. Music Tchrs. Assn. (pres. Klamath Basin dist. 1979-81), P.E.O. (Oreg. dir. 1968-75, state pres. 1974-75, trustee internat. Continuing Edn. Fund 1977-83, chmn. 1981-83), Friends of Collier State Park Logging Mus. (sec. 1988—), Pi Beta Phi, Mu Phi Epsilon, Pi Lambda Theta. Presbyterian. Address: 1338 Pacific Terr Klamath Falls OR 97601

EHMANN, NORMAN ROBERT, chemical executive; b. Long Beach, Calif., Sept. 24, 1924; s. Carl Eugene and Julia Eugenia (Loesch) E.; m. Fay Skipwith, Dec. 21, 1947; children: Robert, Margaret, Carl, John, Janet. BA, Occidental Coll., 1947; MPH, U. MIch., 1952. Entomologist Tulare (Calif.) Mosquito Abatement Dist., 1947-48, L.A. City Health Dept., 1949-52; with Neil A. MacLean Co., Inc., 1953-68; sales mgr. Neil A. MacLean Co., Inc., Belmont, Calif., 1962-65, v.p. mktg. dept., 1966-68; v.p. mktg. dept. Namco, Inc., Milpitas, Calif., 1968-71, pres., 1972-74; mktg. mgr. Van Waters & Rogers, San Mateo, Calif., 1974-84; v.p. Van Waters & Rogers, Seattle, 1984—. Author: Urban Pest Control, vols. 1-12, 1974-80. Mem. troop com. Boy Scouts Am., Sunnyvale, Calif., 1962-72, scoutmaster, 1972—; bd. dirs. Internat. Order Rainbow for Girls, Los Altos, Calif., 1977-87. With U.S. Army, 1945-46. Named Citizen of the Month, Mayor of Kailua, Hawaii, 1975, Hon. Citizen Gov. State of Tex., 1980, Gov. State of La., 1985; recipient Silver Beaver award Boy Scouts Am., 1984. Mem. Am. Pub. Health Assn., Am. Registry Profl. Entomologists, Entomol. Soc. Am., Soc. Vector Ecologists, Nat. Pest Control Assn. (Man of the Yr. Calif. chpt. 1973), Pest Control Operators (hon.), Calif. Mosquito Control Assn. (bd. dirs. Berkeley, Calif. chpt. 1948-49), United Product Formulators and Distbrs. (pres. Atlanta chpt. 1975-76), Sertoma Internat. (pres. 1954), Masons, Pi Chi Omega (pres. W. Lafayette, Ind. chpt. 1964-65). Republican. Presbyterian. Home: 1453 Kyle Ct Sunnyvale CA 94087 Office: Van Waters & Rogers Inc 2256 Junction Ave San Jose CA 95131

EHRETH, JENIFER LEE, nurse, educator; b. Bakersfield, Calif., May 10, 1946; d. Jerry Edward Herndon and Helen Irene (Lamb) King; m. William Walter Ehreth, Sept. 8, 1973; children: Donya, Kimberly, Dylan, Hugh. AA, Bakersfield Coll., 1965; BS cum laude, U. Puget Sound, 1974; MHA, U. Wash., 1983, PhD, 1987. RN. Psychiat. supr. Jackson Hosp., Montgomery, Ala., 1966-67; ICU nurse U.S. Air Force, Philippines, 1967-68; open heart nurse San Joaquin Community Hosp., Bakersfield, Calif., 1970-72; nurse St. Peter's Hosp., Olympia, Wash., 1972-73; clin. supr. St. Joseph Hosp., Tacoma, Wash., 1974-75; head drug and alcohol sect. state of Mont., Missoula, 1975-78; nurse supr. Island Manor Nursing Home, Vashon Island, Wash., 1980-81; researcher U. Wash., Seattle, 1982-87, prof., 1987—; bd. dirs. Community Home Health Care; cons. N.W. Oncology Found, 1983-87; trainee USPHS, 1982. Author: A Case Study of United Healthcare, 1986; editor HMO Report newsletter, 1984-86. Vol. ARC, Philippines, 1968, Am. Diabetic Assn., 1980. Fellow V.A., 1987, Edna Benson, 1987. Mem. Acad. of Mgmt. (editor newsletter 1988—), Am. Pub. Health Assn., Healthcare Fin. Mgmt. Assn. Jewish. Club: Brandeis Women's Orgn. (Seattle) (bd. dirs. 1987-88). Home: 8409 East Mercer Way Mercer Island WA 98040 Office: U Wash Health Svcs Dept Seattle WA 98195

EHRHARDT, THOMAS ANDREW, marketing executive; b. St. Louis, Dec. 27, 1961; s. Joseph Edward and Carole Ann (Overbee) E.; m. Linda Marie Andrews, Nov. 14, 1987. AA, Glendale Community Coll., 1982; BSBA, No. Ariz. U., 1985. Computer trainer No. Ariz. U., Flagstaff, 1983-85; sr. mtkg. analyst Gen. Dynamics Corp., San Diego, 1985—; pub., author Airline Reporter newsletter, 1988. Vol. 78th Assembly Dist. Election Campaign, San Diego, 1988. Mem. So. Calif. Demographers, Tng. Assn. So. Calif., Beta Gamma Sigma. Republican. Home: 4670 Arizona St Apt 4 San Diego CA 92116 Office: Gen Dynamics Corp 9089 Claremont Mesa Blvd Ste 300 San Diego CA 92123

EHRLICH, PAUL RALPH, biology educator; b. Phila., May 29, 1932; s. William and Ruth (Rosenberg) E.; m. Anne Fitzhugh Howland, Dec. 18, 1954; 1 dau., Lisa Marie. A.B., U. Pa., 1953; A.M., U. Kans., 1955, Ph.D., 1957. Research assoc. U. Kans., Lawrence, 1958-59; asst. prof. biol. scis. Stanford U., 1959-62, assoc. prof., 1962-66, prof., 1966—, Bing prof. population studies, 1976—, dir. grad. study dept. biol. scis., 1966-69, 1974-76, dir. Ctr. for Conservation Biology, 1988—; cons. Behavioral Research Labs., 1963-67. Author: How to Know the Butterflies, 1961, Process of Evolution, 1963, Principles of Modern Biology, 1968, Population Bomb, 1968, 2d edit., 1971, Population, Resources, Environment: Issues In Human Ecology, 1970, 2d edit., 1972, How to Be a Survivor, 1971, Global Ecology: Readings Toward a Rational Strategy for Man, 1971, Man and the Ecosphere, 1971, Introductory Biology, 1973, Human Ecology: Problems and Solutions, 1973, Ark II: Social Response to Environmental Imperatives, 1974, The End of Affluence: A Blueprint for the Future, 1974, Biology and Society, 1976, Race Bomb, 1977, Ecoscience: Population, Resources, Environment, 1977, Insect Biology, 1978, The Golden Door: International Migration, Mexico, and the U.S., 1979, Extinction: The Causes and Consequences of the Disappearance of Species, 1981, The Machinery of Nature, 1986, Earth, 1987, The Science of Ecology, 1987, The Birder's Handbook, 1988, New World/New Mind, 1989; contbr. articles to profl. jours. Recipient World Wildlife Fedn. medal, 1987. Fellow Calif. Acad. Scis., Am. Acad. Arts and Scis., Am. Assn. Advt. Sci.; mem. Nat. Acad. Scis., Entomological Soc. Am., Soc. for Study Evolution, Soc. Systematic Zoology, Am. Soc. Naturalists, Lepidopterists Soc., Am. Mus. Natural History (hon. life mem.). Office: Stanford U Dept Biol Scis Stanford CA 94305

EHRLICH, PETER, lawyer; b. Denver, Dec. 12, 1952; s. Maxim Ellis and Carol (Hansen) E.; m. Jo Ann Marilyn Loeffel, May 24, 1975; children: Jodie R., Nina C., Brianne L. BA, Western State Coll., 1975; JD, Wake Forest U., 1978. Bar: Colo. 1978, U.S. Dist. Ct. 1978. Assoc. Cen. Devel. Group, Denver, 1978-81; mgr. real estate Manville Corp., Denver, 1981-82; regional mgr. World Savs. and Loan Assn., Oakland, Calif., 1982-84; of counsel mountain region Wood Bros. Homes, Inc., Denver, 1984-86; sole practice Denver, 1986—; mem. attys. com. Community Assns. Inst., Denver, 1985—; panelist Am. Arbitration Assn., Denver, 1987—; hearing officer City and County of Denver, 1987-88; adminstrv. hearings officer Jefferson County, Golden, Colo., 1987-88; apptd. adminstrv. property tax appeals arbitrator, Routt County, Douglas County, El Paso County, Adams County. Mem. ABA, Colo. Bar Assn. (legal admissions 1988—, real estate and titles sect., author jour. 1988), Denver Bar Assn., Phi Alpha Delta. Republican. Office: 1580 Lioncoln St #635 Denver CO 80203

EICHELBERGER, FRANK, JR., investment manager; b. Piedmont, Calif., Jan. 24, 1931; s. Frank and Constance (Allen) E.; m. Dianne Patterson, July 16, 1952; children: Peggy Ann McConnochie, Kristy Eichelberger Langbehn, Frank III. BA in Chemistry, Williams Coll., 1952; BSc in Metall. Engring., Wash. State U., 1956. Cons. mining and metall. engr. Eichelberger & Assocs., Engrs., Spokane, Wash., 1954-56; gen. mgr. Conjecture Mines, Inc., Lakeview, Idaho, 1954-56; metall. engr. Kaiser Aluminum and Chem. Corp., Mead, Wash., 1956-58; mem. sales staff Mut. of N.Y., Spokane, 1958-69; pres., dealer Center Ford, Inc., Spokane, 1970-86; sec., treas., ptnr. H & E Investment Co., Double F Ltd. Ptnrs., Spokane, 1970—; v.p., dir. Roff Ford-Mercury, Inc., Moscow, Idaho, 1978—; bd. dirs. Conjecture Mines, Inc. Bd. dirs. Exec. Women Internat., Spokane, 1980-84, chmn. bd. dirs., 1984-85; chmn. Spokane March of Dimes, 1988. 1st lt. USAF, 1952-54. Mem. Inland Empire Automobile Dealers, Sigma Tau, Tau Beta Pi, Spokane Country Club, Masons, Shriners. Republican. Episcopalian. Office: H&E Investment Co Inc PO Box 108 Spokane WA 99210

EICHLER, EDWARD PHILIP, mortgage company executive, writer; b. San Francisco, July 1, 1930; s. Joseph and Lillian (Moncharsh) E.; m. Doris Eichler, Sept. 4, 1956 (div. 1968); children: David, Stephen; m. Audrey Tomaselli, Feb. 5, 1974; 1 child, Gina. BA in econs., Dartmouth Coll. V.p. Eichler Homes, Inc., Palo Alto, Calif., 1951-52, 54-63; research mgr. and lectr. U. Calif., Berkeley, 1964-66, vis. prof., 1980-81; v.p. Reston, Reston, Va., 1967, Klingbeil Co., San Francisco, 1968-72; mgr. prin. Palmieri Co., Wash. D.C., N.Y.C., 1973-74; pres. Levitt Corp., Lake Success, N.Y., 1975-79; chmn. Ned Eichler Assocs., Inc., San Francisco, 1982--. Author: The Community Builders, 1966, The Merchant Builders, 1982; contbr. articles to Stanford Law Review. U.S. rep. UN Conf. on New Towns, USSR, 1964; chmn. Gov.'s ad. com. on Housing Problems, Calif., 1961-63; mem. Coordination Council on Urban Policy, Calif., 1962, HUD spl. adv. com. on Demonstration Cities, Wash. D.C., 1964. With U.S. Army, 1952-54. Democrat. Jewish. Office: Ned Eichler Assocs Inc 1632 Union St San Francisco CA 94123

EICHMEIER, KURT JAMES, consumer product company executive; b. Fargo, N.D., Jan. 1, 1950; s. Herman Christian and Doris Margaret (Jensen) E.; m. Marla Kay Wilson, Aug. 25, 1973; children: Jennifer Ann, Megan Nicole. BS, N.D. State U., 1975. Registered profl. engr. Mont., Colo., Wash. Industrial engr. Bemis Co. Inc., Willmington, Calif., 1975-77; plant mgr. Bldg. Specialties, Billings, Mont., 1977-78; project engr. Morrison Knudson Co. Inc., Boise, Idaho, 1978-81, Anaconda Minerals Div. of ARCO, Denver, 1981-82; project mgr. ARCO Solar Div., Camarillo, Calif., 1982-87; pres. Sonne, Inc., Everett, Wash., 1987—. Scoutmaster Boy Scouts of Am., Fargo, 1973-75, Huntington Beach, Calif., 1975-77. Recipient Research scholarship, Nat. Sci. Found., U. N.D., 1966, U. Ga., 1967. Mem. Nat. Soc. Profl. Engrs., Inst. Industrial Engrs., Soc. Mfg. Engrs., Am. Soc. Cost Engrs., Project Mgmt. Inst., Masonic Lodge. Republican. Lutheran. Office: Sonne Inc 3101 J 111th St S W Everett WA 98204

EICHNER, JOHN THOMAS, military officer, aeronautical engineer; b. Coolumbus, Ohio, July 4, 1964; s. Thomas Anthony and Carol Ann (Staib) E. BS in Aero and Auto Engring., Ohio State U., 1987. Commd. 2nd lt. USAFR, 1987; tech. writer AT&T Nat. Prod. Tng. Ctr., Dublin, Ohio, 1987-88; project engr., human factors/system safety engr., data processing officer HQ USAF Space Systems div., El Segundo, Calif., 1988—. Recipient AFROTC Silver Valor award, Ohio State U., 1986. Mem. AIAA, Nat. Soc. Profl. Engrs., Soc. Am. Military Engrs., Air Force Assn., U.S. Naval Inst., Sports Connection Club. Republican. Roman Catholic. Office: HQ Space Systems Div USAF 2400 E El Segundo Blvd El Segundo CA 90009

EIFERT, GERALD HOWARD, nurse, farmer; b. Roseburg, Oreg., May 12, 1945; s. Justin William Sr. and Ruth Alyne (Neal) E.; m. Marilyn Faye Albertson, Sept. 18, 1968; children: Kurt Wayne, Edward Scott, Lisa Rene. BSN cum laude, So. Oreg. State Coll., 1988. Nursing asst. VA Med. Ctr., Roseburg, 1964-69, operating rm. technician, 1969-78, nurse, 1982—; operating rm. technician Douglas Community Hosp., Roseburg, 1979-82. With U.S. Army N.G., 1965-71. Mem. Assn. Oper. Rm. Nurses, Elks (esquire 1988-89, lecturing knight 1989—). Democrat. Home: 7528 Buckhorn Rd Roseburg OR 97470

EIFLER, CARL FREDERICK, retired psychologist; b. Los Angeles, June 27, 1906; s. Carl Frederick and Pauline (Engelbert) E.; Ph.D., Ill. Inst. Tech., 1962; B.D., Jackson Coll.; m. Margaret Christine Aaberg, June 30, 1963; 1 son, Carl Henry; 1 adopted son, Byron Hisey. Insp., U.S. Bur. Customs, 1928-35, chief insp., 1936-37, dep. collector, 1937-56; bus. mgr. Jackson Coll., Honolulu, 1954-56, instr., 1955-56; grad. asst. instr., research asst. Ill. Inst. Tech., Chgo., 1959-62; psychologist Monterey County Mental Health Services, Salinas, Calif., 1964-73; ret., 1973. Served with U.S. Army, 1922-23, 40-47; col. ret. Decorated Combat Infantryman's Badge, Legion of Merit with 2 oak leaf clusters, Bronze Star medal, Air medal, Purple Heart; recipient Military Intelligence Corps Hall of Fame, 1988. Mem. Am., Western States, Calif., Monterey County psychol. assns., AAUP, Res. Officers Assn. (Hawaii pres. 1947), Assn. Former Intelligence Officers (bd. govs., Western coordinator), Pearl Harbor Survivors, 101 Assn., Assn. U.S. Army, Vets. of OSS (western v.p.), Am. Law Enforcement Officers Assn., Nat. Intelligence Study Center, Security and Intelligence Fund, Ret. Officers Assn., Psi Chi. Clubs: Masons, KT, Shriners, Elks, Nat. Sojourners. Contbg. author Psychon. Sci., vol. 20, 1970; co-author: The Deadliest Colonel; author, pub.: Jesus Said. Home: 22700 Picador Dr Salinas CA 93908

EIKENBERRY, ARTHUR RAYMOND, service executive, researcher, writer; b. Sebring, Fla., June 5, 1920; s. Leroy Albertus and Vernie Cordelia (Griffin) E.; m. Carol Jean Parrott, June 10, 1955; children: Robin Rene, Shari LaVon, Jan Rochelle, Karyn LaRae, Kelli Yvette. Student, Pasadena (Calif.) Jr. Coll., 1939, Kunming U., China, 1944-45. Enlisted USAF, 1947; retired 1973, mgmt., pers., adminstrv. and security insp.; mgr. inventory control TR Devel. Co., Englewood, Colo., 1973-74; real estate agt. The Pinery, Parker, Colo., 1974-75; mgr., patient acctg. dept. U. Colo. Health Scis. Ctr., Denver, 1975—. Author: Investment Strategies for the Clever Investor, 1989, Lotto Strategy, How To Win Megabucks Repeatedly, 1989. Charter mem. U.S. Congl. Adv. Bd. Sgt. U.S. Army, 1941-45. Fellow Internat. Biog. Ctr. (life); mem. Am. Biog. Inst. (dep. gov., nat. adviser), U.S. Senatorial Club, Masons. Republican. Office: The Strategic & Precious Metals Researcer PO Box 31754 Aurora CO 80041

EIKENBERRY, KENNETH OTTO, state attorney general; b. Wenatchee, Wash., June 29, 1932; s. Otto Kenneth and Florence Estelle E.; m. Beverly Jane Hall, Dec. 21, 1963. BA in Polit. Sci., Wash. State U., 1954; LLB, U. Wash., 1959. Bar: Wash. 1959. Spl. agt. FBI, 1960-62; dep. pros. atty. King County (Wash.), Seattle, 1962-67; with firm Richey & Eikenberry, 1967-68, Clinton, Andersen, Fleck & Glein, Seattle, 1968-73; legal counsel King County Council, 1974-76; chmn. Wash. Republican party, 1977-80; atty. gen. State of Wash., 1981—; judge pro tem Seattle Mcpl. Ct., 1979-80; mem. Pres.'s Task Force on Victims of Crime, 1982, Pres.'s Child Safety Partnership, 1986, state Criminal Justice Training Commn. 1980, state Corrections Standards Bd. 1980-85; mem. Legis. Exchange Council, 1986. Chmn., King County Rep. Conv., 1974, 78; mem. Wash. Ho. of Reps., 1970-76. Served with AUS, 1954-56. Named Legislator of Year, Young Americans for Freedom/Wash. Conservative Union, 1974, Rep. Man of Year, Young Men's Rep. Club King County, 1979. Mem. Wash. Bar Assn., Western Conf. Attys.-Gen. (chmn. 1983-84), Soc. Former Spl. Agts. FBI, Nat. Assn. Attys.-Gen. (chmn. energy com. 1983-84, sub-com. on RICO issues, 1984-86, criminal law com. 1987-89, crime victims adv. com. 1984-86, working group on model patient abuse legis. 1986-87, mem. consumer protection com. 1986—, environ. control com. 1988—, asbestos coordination com. 1988—, Indian affairs working group 1988—), Internat. Footprint Assn., Delta Theta Phi, Alpha Tau Omega. Clubs: Kiwanis, Rainrunners. Office: State of Wash Atty Gen Hwys Lics Bldg 7th Fl MS-PB 71 Olympia WA 98504

EIKER, BECKY ANN, sculptor, potter; b. Valley City, N.D., May 22, 1942; d. R. Kenneth and Ann (Foley) Raveling; m. William L. Eiker, June 10, 1967. BS, U. N.D., 1964; postgrad., U. S.C., 1968-69. Elem. art tchr. Flint (Mich.) Community Schs., 1964-65, jr. high art. tchr., 1965-67; jr. high art. tchr. Center (Mich.) Line Schs., 1967-68; jr. high art. tchr. Helena (Mont.) Sch. Dist. #1, 1969-72, high sch. art. tchr., 1973-75; studio potter 1975—, sculptor, 1980—. Ceramic sculpture exhibited group shows at various mus., 1984—. Mem. Mont. League of Profl. Women Artists, Helena Art Ctr., Monday Night Drawing Group (co-chmn 1980—). Home and Office: 708 Hillsdale Helena MT 59601

EILER, LINDA, marketing specialist; b. Neenah, Wis., Oct. 28, 1951; d. Elwood M. and June M. (Eiler) Holtz. Student, Pa. State U., 1970, U. Colo., 1980. Lic. in real estate, Colo. Paralegal tax/pension law C. Bryant Rever, P.C., Colorado Springs, Colo., 1977-82; paralegal investor relationa and syndication Craddock Fin. Corp., Colorado Springs, 1982-84; paralegal securities Holland & Hart, Colorado Springs, 1984-86; mktg. specialist McGinnis/Better Homes & Gardens, Colorado Springs, 1986-88; real estate mktg. specialist RE/MAX Properties, Inc., Colorado Springs, 1988—. Vol. Girl Scouts Am., Colorado Springs, 1980, Second Horizon Ctr. for Srs., Colorado Springs., 1988; mem. adv. com. Channel 9 Health Fair, Denver, 1986. Mem. Colo. Bd. Realtors, Colorado Springs Bd. Realtors (arbitration com. 1988—), Colo. Bar Assn. (legal asst. com. 1985-87), Colo. Exchangers, Colo. Mountain Club (head social com. 1987—). Office: RE/MAX Properties Inc 1465 Kelly Johnson Blvd Colorado Springs CO 80920

EILS, RICHARD GEORGE, retail company executive; b. Milw., 1937; married. Grad., U. Wis., 1960. With Thrifty Corp., Los Angeles, 1965—; treas. Thrifty Corp., 1972-74, v.p., 1974-76, sr. v.p., 1976-77, exec. v.p., 1977-79, pres., 1979—, also chief operating officer, chief fin. officer, dir.; pres., dir. Thrifty Realty Co., Pay n Save Drug Stores Inc., Seattle, 1988; bd. dirs. United Merchandising Corp., Newman Importing Co. Inc., FTM Sports, Thrifty Wilshire Inc., MC Sporting Goods, Gart Bros. Sporting Goods. Office: Thrifty Corp 3424 Wilshire Blvd Los Angeles CA 90010

EINES, IVAR GUNNAR, credit company executive; b. Ketchikan, Alaska, Nov. 18, 1926; s. Ingebrigt Olsen Eines and Gertrude (Sather) Michalsen; m. Donna Charmaine Hanson, Sept. 9, 1950; children: Trina Eines, Eric Conrad. BA in Bus. Administrn., Pacific Lutheran U., 1951. Lic. real estate escrow officer, Wash. Dist. credit supr. Texaco Inc., Seattle, 1951-68; ops. mgr. Wendell-West Co., Seattle, 1969-70; pres. Tellus Fin. Services, Inc., Seattle, 1970-81; div. mgr. SAFECO Credit Co., Inc., Redmond, Wash., 1981-88, asst. v.p., 1988--. Bd. dirs. Shamrock Plaza Condo Assn., Edmonds, Wash., 1984-86; pres. Beverly Beach Improvement Club, Inc., Freeland, Wash., 1986-88. Lt. comdr. USNR, 1944-46. Mem. Seattle C. of C., Norwegian Comml. Club (pres. 1987). Lutheran. Home: 10530 Nottingham Rd Edmonds WA 98020 Office: SAFECO Credit Co Inc 4909 156th Ave NE Redmond WA 98082

EINSTEIN, CLIFFORD JAY, advertising executive; b. L.A., May 4, 1939; s. Harry and Thelma (Bernstein) E.; m. Madeline Mandel, Jan. 28, 1962; children: Harold Jay, Karen Holly. BA in English, UCLA, 1961. Writer Norman, Craig and Kummel, N.Y.C., 1961-62, Foote, Cone and Belding, L.A., 1962-64; ptnr. Silverman and Einstein, L.A., 1965-67; pres., creative dir. Dailey and Assos., L.A., 1968—, also bd dirs.; dir. Campaign '80, advt. agy. Reagan for Pres., 1980; lectr. various colls.; dir. El Segundo First Nat. Bank. Contbr. articles to Advertising Age; producer (play) Whatever Happened to Georgie Tapps, L.A. and San Francisco, 1980. Bd. dirs. Rape Treatment Ctr., Santa Monica Med. Ctr., Mus. Contemporary Art, L.A., 1989—. With U.S. Army, 1957. Recipient Am. Advt. award 1968, 73, 79, Clio award, 1973, Internat. Broadcast Pub. Svc. award, 1970, 85, Nat. Addy award, 1979, Gov.'s award, 1987; named Creative Dir. of the West, Adweek Poll, 1982, Exec. of West, 1986. Mem. AFTRA, ASCAP, Screen Actors Guild., Dirs. Guild Am., Western States Advt. Agys. Assn., L.A. Advt. Club (Sweepstakes award 1974, 78). Office: Dailey & Assocs 3055 Wilshire Blvd Los Angeles CA 90010

EINSTEIN, STEPHEN JAN, rabbi; b. L.A., Nov. 15, 1945; s. Syd C. and Selma (Rothenberg) E.; m. Robin Susan Kessler, Sept. 9, 1967; children: Rebecca Yael, Jennifer Melissa, Heath Isaac, Zachary Shane. AB, UCLA, 1967; B.H.L., Hebrew Union Coll., L.A., 1968; M.A.H.L., Hebrew Union Coll., Cin., 1971. Ordained rabbi. Rabbi Temple Beth Am, Parsippany, N.J., 1971-74; rabbi Temple Beth David, Westminster, Calif., 1974-76, Congregation B'nai Tzedek, Fountain Valley, Calif., 1976—. Co-author: Every Person's Guide to Judaism, 1989; co-editor: Introduction to Judaism, 1983. Pres., trustee Fountain Valley Sch. Bd., Fountain Valley, Calif., 1984—. Honored for Maj. Contributions to Jewish Learning, Orange County (Calif.) Bur. Jewish Edn., 1986; recipient Micah Award for Interfaith Activities, Am. Jewish Com., 1988. Mem. Cen. Conf. Am. Rabbis (exec. bd. 1989—), Pacific Assn. Reform Rabbis (exec. bd. 1987—), Orange County Bd. Rabbis (pres., sec.-treas. 1974-79), Jewish Educators Assn. Orange County (pres. 1979-81), Orange County Bur. Jewish Edn. (v.p. 1982-84). Democrat. Office: Congregation Bnai Tzedek 9669 Talbert Ave Fountain Valley CA 92708

EISELE, MILTON DOUGLAS, viticulturist; b. N.Y.C., Apr. 2, 1910; s. Charles Francis and Helen Agnes (Dolan) E.; B.A., U. Calif.-Berkeley, 1933; grad. San Francisco Stock Exchange Inst., 1938; m. Barbara Lois Morgan, July 26, 1941; children—Helen Frances Eisele Osthimer, Barbara Glennis, William Douglas. Investment cashier Wells Fargo Bank, San Francisco, 1934-39; coordinator cement sales Permanente Corp., 1940-41, constrn. supt., 1941-43; mgr. refractory div. Kaiser Aluminum, 1943-47, mgr. regional sales, Chgo., 1947-50, mgr. foil div., 1950-55, mgr. prodn., 1955-60, mgr. market and prodn. devel., 1960-65, mgr. investments, 1966-71; ret., 1971; owner, operator Eisele Vineyards, Napa Valley, Calif., 1969—. Dir., former pres. Napa Valley Found., 1981—; bd. dirs., past chmn. Vintage Hall, Inc., 1973—; bd. dirs., pres. Napa Valley Heritage Fund, 1973—; past pres., bd. dirs. Upper Napa Valley Assocs., 1976-80; mem. adv. council Napa County Land Trust, 1976-79; mem. Napa County Grand Jury, 1988-89. Mem. Am. Soc. Enologists, Napa Valley Grape Growers Assn. (dir.), Calif. Assn. Wine Grape Growers (dir., former sec., chmn. 1986—), Calif. Vintage Wine Soc., Agri. Council of Napa County, Wine and Winegrape Mktg. Order State of Calif. (dir. 1984), Napa Valley Vinter/Grower (chmn. bd. dirs.), Kappa Alpha Order. Republican. Episcopalian (vestryman, sr. warden 1966-69). Home and Office: 2155 Pickett Rd Calistoga CA 94515

EISENBERG, MORRIS, management executive; b. Poland, Aug. 26, 1921; came to U.S., 1947; s. Solomon Z. Eisenberg and Haya Henna Troppe; m. Esther Eisenberg, June 20, 1950; children: Zachary, Abigail, David; m. Edith Boxer, Aug. 26, 1981. BS, U. Calif., Berkeley, 1950, MS, 1951, PhD, 1953. Reg. Profl. Engr., Calif. Dir. electron-chemistry lab. Lockheed MSD, Sunnyvale, Calif., 1957-62; pres. Ela Battery Co., Sunnyvale, 1971-75, Electrochimica Corp., Menlo Park, Calif., 1962—; lectr. Stanford U., 1953-57; asst. prof., U. Calif., Berkeley, 1951-53. Patentee in field; contbr. articles to profl. jours. Mem. Electochem Soc., Internat. El-chem. Soc., Technion Soc., Rsch. Soc. Am., Sigma Xi. Democrat. Jewish.

EISENBERGER, ROBERT ALAN, astronautical engineer; b. Newark, N.J., Aug. 23, 1958; s. Bernard Eisenberger and Miriam (Hamburger) Parnes; m. Karen Bonnie Wertheim, Mar. 21, 1987; children: Mitchell Bradly. BS Astronautical Engring., U.S. Air Force Acad., 1980; MBA in Aviation, Embry Riddle Aero U., 1983; Student, Squardon Officer Sch, Montgomery, Ala., 1984; M.E. in Controls, Calif. State Poly. U., 1985. Commd. 2d lt. USAF, 1980; advanced strategic missile project officer Ballistic Missile Office, San Bernardino, Calif., 1980-85; B-1B flight test engr. B-1B FOT & E Test Team, Abilene, Tex., 1985-88; hypersonic vehicle program engineer Lockheed Missiles & Space Comp., Sunnyvale, Calif., 1988—; capt. USAFR, 1988—. Author: B-1B Navigation Drift Testing. Mgr. Little League, Calif., Tex., 1980-88. Mem. Soc. Flight Test Engrs., AIAA. Democrat. Jewish. Home: 5428 Twilight Common Fremont CA 94555 Office: Lockheed Missiles & Space Comp 1111 Lockheed Way Sunnyvale CA 94088

EISENHARDT, (EMIL) ROY, professional baseball team executive; b. 1939; m. Auban Slay, 1965 (div. 1976); m. Elizabeth Haas, 1978; children: Sarah, Jesse. BA, Dartmouth Coll., 1960; LLB, U. Calif., Berkeley, 1965. Bar: Calif. 1966. With firm Farella, Braun and Martel, San Francisco; vis. prof. U. Calif. Boalt Hall Sch. Law, Berkeley, from 1974; pres. Oakland A's, Am. League, Calif., 1980-88; exec. v.p. Oakland A's, Am. League, 1988—; former coach U. Calif. rowing crew. Served with USMC, 1960-62. Address: Oakland A's Oakland-Alameda County Coliseum Oakland CA 94621 *

EISENZIMMER, BETTY WENNER, insurance agency executive; b. Twisp, Wash., July 25, 1939; d. Bren William and Julia Emogene (Salmon) Wenner; m. Erwin LeRoy Cook, June 19, 1955 (div. 1960); 1 child, Richard Jeffrey; m. Jerome Anthony Eisenzimmer, Feb. 18, 1966. Cert. in gen. ins. Ins. Inst. Am., 1981; cert. profl. ins. woman. Clk. typist MR Ins., Seattle, 1957-59; records clk. Assigned Risk Plan, Seattle, 1959-61; acct. asst. Robinson Jenner, Inc., Seattle, 1961-66; sec., acct. asst. Falkenberg & Co., Seattle, 1966-75, adminstrv. asst., 1975-77; ins. agt., corp. officer Service Ins. Inc., Seattle, 1975—; mem. adv. bd. Sch. Ins., Wash. State U. Coll. Bus., 1981—. Asst. editor Today's Ins. Woman, 1980-81. Exec. bd. Wash. chpt. Cystic Fibrosis Found., 1978-86, pres., 1983-85; mem. Wash. State Centennial Speakers' Bur., 1987—; mem. long range planning com. Cedar Cross United Meth. Ch., 1986-87, mem. worship com., 1988—. Recipient Disting. Service award Cystic Fibrosis Found., 1984; named Vol. of Yr., Wash. chpt. Cystic Fibrosis Found., 1980. Mem. Seattle C. of C., Ins. Women Puget Sound (pres. 1970-72, Ins. Woman of Yr. 1978, 81, Industry award 1984 Wash. State Communicate with confidence speakoff winner), Ins. Women's Assn. Seattle (chmn. 1992 conf., Ins. Woman of Yr. 1981), Nat. Assn. Ins. Women (nat. sec. 1976-77, regional dir. 1981-82, mem. exec. bd. 1976-77, 81-82, You Make the Difference award 1977, Regional IX Lace Speakoff winner 1983), Ind. Ins. Agts. and Brokers Wash. (edn. com. 1982-83), Ind. Ins. Agts. and Brokers King County (chmn. bylaws 1984-85), Profl. Ins. Agts. Wash. (edn. com. 1982-86, chmn. 1983-86), Wash. Ins. Council (mem. speakers bur. 1980—), Women's Bus. Exchange, Women's Profl. and Managerial Women's Network, Nat. Assn. Life Underwriters, Women Life Underwriters Conf. (nat. bd. dirs., region I dir. 1987-88), Acad. Producer Ins. Studies (fellow of acad.), Network of Exec. Women, Seattle Assn. Life Underwriters, Nat. Assn. Female Execs. Club: Toastmasters (pres. Wallingford chpt. 1986-87, ednl. v.p. 1987-88, dist. 2 area 5 gov. 1987-88, Gov.'s Honor Roll dist. 2 1987, NC div. Lt. Gov. 1988-89, dist. 2 area Gov. of Yr, 1988, able toastmaster silver 1988 and other awards and positions). Home: 8932 240th St SW Edmonds WA 98020 Office: Svc Ins Inc 332 Securities Bldg Seattle WA 98101

EISLER, ANN OLMSTED, social worker; b. Whittier, Calif., Jan. 17, 1954; d. Alvin Herman and Joane Winette (Free) Olmsted; m. Gerald Richard Eisler, Sept. 11, 1976; 1 child, Brandon Richard. BJ, Iowa State U., 1976; MSSW, U. Tex., Austin, 1985. Cert. social worker. Copy editor and feature writer The Albuquerque Tribune, 1976-79; home visitor and social worker Ctr. Devel. Non-formal Edn., Austin, 1983-84; social worker neonatal ICU dept. Darnall Army Hosp., Ft. Hood, Tex., 1985; investigator sexual abuse Tex. Dept. Human Services, Austin, 1985-86; therapist Albuquerque Rape Crisis Ctr., U. N.Mex., 1986-87, clinical dir., 1987—. Pres. Temple Albert Sisterhood, Albuquerque, 1982-83; bd. trustees Temple Albert, 1978-83; active Albuquerque chpt. Operation Identity. Mem. Nat. Assn. Social Workers, LWV (bd. dirs. 1978-79), Phi Beta Kappa, Phi Kappa Phi. Democrat. Jewish. Home: 9713 Admiral Emerson NE Albuquerque NM 87111

EISNER, HARVEY BRIAN, controller, tax consultant; b. L.A., May 7, 1958; s. Donald Laurence and Lillian (Israel) E. BS, U. Nev., Las Vegas, 198l. CPA, Nev. Staff acct. Laventhol & Horwath, Las Vegas, Nev., 198l-83; sr. acct. Laventhol & Horwath, Tucson, 1983; acctg. and reporting supr. Holiday Casino, Holiday Corp., Las Vegas, 1983-87; tax and acctg. mgr. Harrah's Holiday Corp., Reno, 1987; contr. Desert Radiologists, Las Vegas, 1987—. Treas. Jewish Family Svc. Agy., Las Vegas, 1988—. Mem. Nat. Acctg. Assn., Nev. Soc. CPA's. Democrat. Office: Desert Radiologists 2020 Palomino Ln Ste l00 Las Vegas NV 89106

EISNER, MICHAEL DAMMANN, motion picture company executive; b. N.Y.C., Mar. 7, 1942; s. Lester and Margaret (Dammann) E.; m. Jane Breckenridge; children: Michael, Eric, Anders. BA, Denison U., 1964. Began career in programming dept. CBS; asst. to nat. programming dir. ABC, 1966-68, mgr. spls. and talent, dir. program devel.-East Coast, 1968-71, v.p. daytime programming, 1971-75, v.p. program planning and devel., 1975-76, sr. v.p. prime time prodn. and devel., 1976; pres., chief operating officer Paramount Pictures, 1976-84; chmn., chief exec. officer Walt Disney Co., Burbank, Calif., 1984—. Bd. dirs. Denison U., Calif. Inst. Arts, Am. Film Inst., Performing Arts Council Los Angeles Music Ctr. Office: Walt Disney Co 500 S Buena Vista St Burbank CA 91521

EITNER, LORENZ EDWIN ALFRED, art historian, educator; b. Brunn, Czechoslovakia, Aug. 27, 1919; came to U.S., 1935, naturalized, 1943; s. Wilhelm and Katherina (Thonet) E.; m. Trudi von Kathrein, Oct. 26, 1946; children: Christy, Kathy, Claudia. A.B., Duke U., 1940; M.F.A., Princeton U., 1948, Ph.D., 1952. Research unit head Nuremberg War Crimes Trial, 1946-47; from instr. to prof. art U. Minn., Mpls., 1949-63; chmn. dept. art, dir. mus. Stanford U., Calif., 1963—; organizer exhbn. works of Gericault for museums of Los Angeles, Detroit and Phila., 1971-72. Author: The Flabellum of Tournus, 1944, Gericault Sketchbooks in the Chicago Art Institute, 1960, Introduction to Art, 1951, Neo-Classicism and Romanticism, 1969, Gericault's Raft of the Medusa, 1972, Gericault, His Life and Work, 1983 (Mitchell prize 1984, C.R. Morey award 1985), An Outline of 19th Century European Painting from David through Cezanne, 1987; (with others) The Arts in Higher Education; contbr. articles to profl. jours. Mem. Regional Arts Council San Francisco Bay Area. Served as officer OSS, AUS, 1943-46. Fulbright grantee, Belgium, 1952-53; Guggenheim fellow, Munich, Federal Republic Germany, 1956-57. Mem. AAAS, Coll. Art Assn. Am. (bd. dirs., past v.p.), Phi Beta Kappa. Home: 684 Mirada Stanford CA 94305 Office: Stanford U Mus Art Gallery Lomita Dr and Museum Way Stanford CA 94305

EKINS, ROGER ROBIN, academic administrator; b. Salt Lake City, Oct. 10, 1945; s. Vern Ross and Sonoma (Orme) E.; m. Helen Kaye Leonard, Aug. 16, 1971; children: Sarah Robin, Adam Elias, Rachael Eliza. BA in English with honors, U. Utah, 1970, MA in Creative Writing, 1972; PhD, Union Grad. Sch., 1976. Asst. prof. English, dir. Open Community Learning Ctr. CUNY, N.Y.C., 1972-76; counselor SEEK program CUNY, Staten Island, N.Y., 1977; faculty fellow in English/edn., dean student life Johnston Coll., U. Redlands, Calif., 1977-79; dean student devel., dir. honors program U. Maine, Augusta, 1979-86; dean instrn. Butte Coll., Oroville, Calif., 1986—; cons. various colls. and univs. Author poetry, short stories and essays. Mem. Calif. Humanities Assn. (mem.-at-large bd. govs. 1988—), Am. Assn. Higher Edn., Community Coll. Humanities Assn., Phi Beta Kappa (no. Calif. chpt.), Phi Kappa Phi, Phi Theta Kappa (hon.). Democrat. Mormon. Home: 908 Wagstaff Paradise CA 95969

EKLUND, PAUL JOSEPH, operations management specialist; b. Phoenix, Feb. 27, 1963; s. Melvin Harry and JoAnn (Sturek) E.; m. Susan Danley Terhune. BS in Gen. Bus., U. Ariz., 1984, MBA, 1986. Expediter IBM GPD, Tucson, 1983; prodn. mgr. Mfg. and Rsch., Inc., Tucson, 1986-88; mgmt. analyst Climax Portable Machine Tools, Inc., Newberg, Oreg., 1988—. Mem. Am. Prodn. and Inventory Control Soc. (v.p. fin. 1988—). Home: 17462 SW Bryant Rd Lake Oswego OR 97035 Office: Climax Portable Machine Tools Inc 2712 E 2nd St Newberg OR 97132

EKROM, ROY H., electronic equipment company executive; b. 1929. AB, U. Wash., 1951. With Boeing Airplane Co., Seattle, 1952-59, AiResearch Mfg. Co. Ariz., Phoenix, 1959-81; v.p., mgr. Pneumatic Systems div. Garrett Corp., 1981-83; pres., chief exec. officer Ampex Corp., Redwood City, Calif., 1983-86, Garrett Corp., L.A., 1986-87; pres. Aircraft Equipment Co., Torrance, Calif., 1987—, Allied-Signal Aerospace Co., Morristown, N.J., 1987—. Office: Allied-Signal Aerospace Co 2525 W 190th St Torrance CA 90509 *

EKTARE, ARUN, computer science educator; b. Indore, India, Oct. 31, 1945; came to U.S., 1986; s. Bhalchandra and Sushila (Apte) E.; m. Bharati Manerikar, Oct. 28, 1973; children: Abhay, Mallika. BSc in Engring., G.S. Technol. Inst., India, 1967; ME, U. Roorke, India, 1969; PhD, U. Roorke, 1981. Asst. lectr. Mil. Coll. Telecommunications Engring., Mhow, India, 1970-72; rsch. fellow, asst. prof., then assoc. prof. U. Roorke, 1972-82; assoc. prof. computer sci. U. Technology, Baghdad, Iraq, 1982-86, Mesa State Coll., Grand Junction, Colo., 1986—. Contbr. papers to tech. publs. Judge local sch. sci. fair, Grand Junction, 1987. Mem. IEEE (reviewer 1987—), Assn. Computing Machinery (reviewer 1988), Am. Assn. Artificail Intelligence. Office: ComputerSci Mesa State Coll PO Box 2647 Grand Junction CO 81502

EKWALL, STEPHEN WARD, fast food chain executive; b. Sheridan, Wyo., Jan. 21, 1965; s. Roy Duane and Charlotte Kathern (Burgmen) E.; 1 child, Robert Lynn Rythen. Student, Central Community Coll., Hastings, Nebr., 1988, Internat. Corr. Schs., 1985--. Laborer Custon Energy Constrn. Co., Casper, Wyo., 1983-84; head security Tower West Lodge, Gillette, Wyo., 1984-86; custodian Energy Downs div. Cam-Plex, Gillette, Wyo., 1986-87; asst. mgr. Arby's, Gillette, Wyo., 1986-88, Wendy's, Gillette, Wyo., 1988--; cook Deckers Food Ctr., Gillette, Wyo., 1988; owner, mgr. Custom Cakes & Catering, Gillette, Wyo., 1988--. Mem. Am. Culinary Fedn. Presbyterian. Home: 909 Camel Dr Apt 215 Gillette WY 82716 Office: Wendy's of Gilette 913 S Hwy 59 Gillette WY 82716

ELDER, JAMES FRANCIS, transportation consultant; b. Joliet, Ill., May 13, 1926; s. Chester Bernard and Marie (Gibbons) E.; m. Patricia Darlene Kinney, Dec. 20, 1953; children: Richard James, David Patrick, Eric Thomas. Student, Chillicothe (Mo.) Bus. Coll., 1947, Mellon U., Pitts., 1971. Asst. supt. transp. Milw. R.R., Chgo., 1945-68; asst. gen. mgr. transp. Port Authority Transit Corp., Lindenwold, N.J., 1968-88; ind. transp. cons. San Diego, 1988—. With USN, 1944-46, PTO. Mem. Am. Pub. Transit Assn. (chmn. rails ops. com. 1985-87), Antique Auto Club Am. Republican. Methodist. Home and Office: 16068 Caminito Aire Puro San Diego CA 92128

ELDER, RICHARD DANIEL, small business owner; b. Cleve., Apr. 7, 1927; s. E.M. and Edna E. (Lee) E.; m. Mary F. Jeffery, June 15, 1947 (div. 1966); m. Virginia E. Chase, June 4, 1977; children, Nancy, Mark, Lauren, Bradley. BS, Ohio State U., 1949. Cert. riding instr., Colo. V.p. production Joseph M. Stern Co., Cleve., 1950-59; adminstr. N.E. Ohio Equine Inst., Novelty, Ohio, 1958-60; gen. ptnr., chief exec. officer Colo. Trails Ranch, Durango, Colo., 1960—; dir. edn. Nat. Horse Abuse Investigation Sch. Am. Humane Assn. Exec. producer Colorado Ridin High, 1985, (outstand acheivement 1986); composer: We're Having Fun Now, 1982; contbr. articles to profl. jours. Pres., chmn. LaPlata County Hosp. Dist., Durango; chmn. LaPlata County Lodgers Tax Panel, Durango, 1988—. With USN, 1945-46. Mem. Colo. Dude and Guest Ranch Assn. (dir., pres 1985), The Dude Ranchers Assn. (dir. v.p. 1975), Durango C. of C. (dir. 1974-76). Republican. Office: Colo Trails Ranch Box 848 Durango CO 81302

ELDREDGE, BONNIE JO, insurance broker, beauty supply company executive; b. Fargo, N.D., Mar. 25, 1936; d. Clifford Charles and Gladys (Harvey) Blackburn; m. Thomas H. Eldredge, Aug. 20, 1960; children: Monica Lyn, Rachelle Lea. BS in Comml. Edn. and English, Mont. State U., 1958; postgrad., U. Mont. Bus. edn. tchr. Bayard (Nebr.) High Sch.; tchr. Alberton (Mont.) High Sch.; adult edn. tchr. Sentinel High Sch., Missoula, Mont.; instr. Billings (Mont.) Bus. Coll., Stevens-Henager Bus. Coll., Salt Lake City; ins. agt. Farmers Ins. Group, Billings, 1978-82; agt., broker The Bankers Life of Des Moines, Billings, 1982—; v.p. Paris Beauty Supply, Billings, 1986—. Campaign mgr. for Howard Porter, Billings, 1968; dir. childrens' theatre prodns. Billings Jr. League; bd. dirs. Billings Studio Theatre, pres. 1986-87, sec. 1969-71), Billings United Way, mem. several coms. Named one of Outstanding Young Women of Am., 1969. Mem. Beauty and Barber Supply Inst. Republican. Roman Catholic. Office: Paris Beauty Supply 2015 2d Ave N Billings MT 59101

ELDREDGE, EDDA ROGERS, securities transfer company executive; b. Deseret, Utah, Feb. 15, 1915; d. James Noah and Alice (Critchley) Rogers; student Henager Bus. Coll., 1930-31, U. Utah, 1932-35; m. Frank Aubrey Eldredge, Sept. 5, 1936; children—Frank A., Noah R., Alice Lou, Julie, Joseph U. With Gen. Petroleum Corp., 1945-55; mgr. land dept. Utah So. Oil Co., 1955-62, asst. sec., 1956-62; pres., dir. Edda R. Eldredge & Co., Inc., Salt Lake City, 1967—; pres., dir. Bonneville Petroleum Corp., 1974—. Republican. Mormon. Office: 315 Newhouse Bldg 10 Exchange Pl Salt Lake City UT 84111

ELDREDGE, FRANK AUBREY, II, geneticist; b. Salt Lake City, Jan. 8, 1940; s. Frank Aubrey and Esther Edda (Rogers) E.; m. Birgitta Veronica Osterberg, Dec. 19, 1963; children: John William, Jennifer, Christine, Emilie Birgitta. Student, U. Utah, 1958-60, BA, 1965, MS, 1969, PhD, 1972. Teaching assoc. U. Utah, Salt Lake City, 1971; assoc. prof. biology Cen. Mich. U., Mt. Pleasant, 1972—. Contbr. research articles on plant cytogenetics and evolution to profl. jours. Active troop com. Lake Huron council Boy Scouts Am., 1973—. NIH genetics tng. fellow, 1967-72; faculty research and creative endeavors grantee, 1973-75, 77-79. Mem. AAAS, Am. Genetic Assn., Bot. Soc. Am., Smithsonian Assn., Amateur Radio Club, Sigma Xi, Beta Beta Beta, Phi Sigma, Phi Eta Sigma. Republican. Mormon. Office: Eldredge Resources Inc 6124 Stratler St Salt Lake City UT 84107

ELECCION, MARCELINO, computer corporate executive, writer, lecturer, artist; b. N.Y.C., Aug. 22, 1936; s. Marcelino G. and Margaret J. (Krcha) E.; B.A., NYU, 1961; postgrad. Courant Inst. Math. Scis., 1962-64; m. Naomi E. Kor, Jan. 5, 1978; children—Mark Eaton, Jordan Kai. Electromech. draftsman Coll. Engring., NYU, Bronx, 1954-57, chief designer dept. elec. engring., 1957-60, tech. editor lab. for electrosci. research, 1960-62, editor publs. Sch. Engring. and Scis., 1962-67; asst. editor IEEE Spectrum, N.Y.C., 1967-69, assoc. editor, 1969-70, staff writer, 1970-76, contbg. editor, 1976—; dir. adminstrn. Internat. Bur. Protection and Investigation, Ltd., N.Y.C., 1976-78; account exec. Paul Purdom & Co., pub. relations, San Francisco, 1978-81, creative dir., 1981-83; dir. mktg. communications Am. Info. Systems, Palo Alto, 1983-85; dir. engring. Tech. Cons., Palo Alto, 1986—; cons. tech. artist, 1953—; music orchestration cons., 1956-70; cons. Ency. Britannica, 1969-70, Time-Life Books, 1973; spl. guest lectr. Napa Coll., 1979—. Recipient Mayor's commendation award N.Y.C., 1971. Mem. IEEE (sr.), N.Y. Acad. Scis., Am. Math. Soc., AAAS, Optical Soc. Am., Smithsonian Assocs., Am. Numis. Assn., Nat. Geog. Soc., U.S. Judo Fedn., Athletic Congress, AAU. Fedn. Home: 3790 El Camino Real #2004 Palo Alto CA 94306

ELFLEIN, KENNETH JOHN, military officer; b. Mineola, N.Y., June 25, 1952; s. Paul Peter and Louise Barbara (Rebhan) E.; m. Tawin Saamsaad, Jan. 24, 1986. BA in Polit. Sci., Duquesne U., Pitts., 1974. Commd. 2d lt. U.S. Army, 1980, advanced through grades to capt., 1983; intelligence analyst CIA, Washington, 1974-77; intelligence officer U.S. Army, Ft. Huachuca, Ariz., 1977—; chief officer devel. U.S. Army Intelligence Ctr. and Sch., Ft. Huachuca, 1986—. Author: High Technology Testing, 1980. Mem. Intelligence Mus. Found. Republican. Roman Catholic. Office: US Army Intelligence Ctr Fort Huachuca AZ 85613-7000

ELGIN, GITA, psychologist; b. Santiago, Chile; came to U.S., 1968, naturalized 1987; d. Serafin and Regina (Urízar) Elguin; BS in biology summa cum laude, U. Chile, Santiago, PsyD, 1964; PhD in Counseling Psychology, U. Calif., Berkeley, 1976; m. Bart Bödy, Oct. 23, 1971; 1 child, Dio Christopher Kíroy Elgin-Bödy. Clin. psychologist Barros Luco-Trudeau Gen. Hosp., Santiago, 1964-65; co-founder, co-dir. Lab. for Parapsychol. Rsch., Psychiat. Clinic, U. Chile, Santiago, 1965-68; rsch. fellow Found. Rsch. on Nature of Man, Durham, N.C., 1968; researcher psychol. correlates of EEG-Alpha waves U. Calif., Berkeley, 1972-76; originator holistic method of psychotherapy Psychotherapy for a Crowd of One, 1978; co-founder, clin. dir. Holistic Health Assos., Oakland, Calif., 1979—; lectr. holistic health Piedmont (Calif.) Adult Sch., 1979-80; hostess Holistic Perspective, Sta. KALW-FM, Nat. Public Radio, 1980. Lic. psychologist, Chile, Calif. Chancellor's fellow U. Calif., 1976, NIMH fellow, 1976. Mem. Am. Psychol. Assn., Am. Holistic Psychol. Assn. (founder 1985—), Alameda County Psychol. Assn., Calif. State Psychol. Assn., No. Calif. Group Psychotherapy Soc., Assn. for Transpersonal Psychology, Montclair Health Profls. Assn. (co-founder, pres. 1983-85), No. Calif. Soc. for Clin. Hypnosis, Sierra Club, U. Calif. Alumni Assn., Assn. Cognitive Behavior Therapy. Contbr. articles in clin. psychology and holistic health to profl. jours. and local periodicals. Presenter Whole Life Expo, 1986. Office: Montclair Profl Bldg 2080 Mountain Blvd Ste 203 Oakland CA 94611

ELIAMSTAM, MICHAEL, physician; b. Springs, Republic of South Africa, Jan. 3, 1944; came to U.S., 1967; s. Theodore and Isa Eliastam; m. Suzanne Maynard, Dec. 31, 1983; children: Taylor, Jordan. MB B.Ch., U. Witwatersrand, Johannesburg, Republic of South Africa, 1966; MPA, Harvard U., 1972, MPP, 1973. Diplomate Am. Bd. Emergency Medicine, Am. Bd. Internal Medicine. Intern Rush Presbyn. St. Lukes Hosp., Chgo., 1967-68, resident, 1968-71; asst. prof. Stanford U., Stanford, Calif., 1974-83; dir. emergency svcs. Stanford U. Hosp., Palo Alto, Calif., 1974—; assoc. prof. emergency medicine Stanford U., Palo Alto, 1983—. Editor: Manual of Emergency Medicine, 1983; contbr. articles to profl. jours. Fellow Am. Coll. Emergency Physicians; mem. Am. Coll. Physicians, Univ. Assn. for Emergency Medicine. Jewish. Office: Stanford U Hosp 300 Pasteur Dr Palo Alto CA 94305

ELIAS, EDMOND, mechanical engineer; b. Beirut, May 1, 1957; came to U.S., 1977; s. Toni and Mary (Helou) E. BSEE, U. Dayton, 1980, MS in Mech. Engring., 1981. Grad. rsch. asst. U. Dayton (Ohio), 1980-81; design engr. Heapy Engring. Co., Dayton, 1982-83; sr. mech. engr. Signetics, Albuquerque, 1983—. Mem. ASHRAE (edn. chmn. Albuquerque chpt. 1985-87). Home: 5309 Overlook Dr Albuquerque NM 87100 Office: Signetics 9201 Pan American Frwy Albuquerque NM 87111

ELIAS, JERRY CARLOS, construction company executive; b. Pomona, Calif., June 29, 1959; s. Carlos and Anita (Salazar) E. BA in Econs., Claremont (Calif.) Men's Coll., 1981; MBA, Pepperdine U., 1985. Registered profl. engr., Calif. Mktg. rep. Xerox Corp., El Monte, Calif., 1980-82; mgr. Elias Bros. Contractors, Pomona, 1982-87; v.p. Elisa Bros. Contractors, Pomona, 1987—. Mem. Calif. Builder and Engr. Assn., Engring. Contractors Assn. Republican. Roman Catholic. Home: 11445 Norton Ave Chino CA 91710 Office: Elias Bros Contractors 1535 E Phillips Blvd Pomona CA 91766

ELIAS, RUSSELL JOSEPH, aerospace engineer; b. Cleve., Jan. 19, 1960; s. Richard Joseph and Marie Teresa (Seivers) E. BS in Chem. Engring., Georgia Tech., 1982; MS in Stats., Ariz. State U., 1989. Process design engr. Kinetics Consulting Group, Atlanta, 1982-83; prodn. engr. Milliken and Co., Greenville, S.C., 1983-84; reliability engr. Motorola, Inc., Phoenix, 1984-88; com. rep. Inst. Printed Circuits, Lincolnwood, Ill., 1987-88; process cons. Elias and Assoc., Phoenix, 1987—. Contbr. articles to profl. jours. Mem. Inst. Printed Circuits, Am. Soc. of Quality Control, Phoenix Water Skiers, Sports Car Club. Republican. Home: 30 E Brown Rd Mesa AZ 85201

ELIAS, THOMAS DAVID, newspaper correspondent and columnist; b. Waltham, Mass., Feb. 8, 1944; s. M. Hans and Anneliese J. (Buchthal) E.; m. Marilyn Koral, June 15, 1968; 1 child, Jordan S. BA in History, Stanford U., 1966, MA in Communications, 1967. Newsman AP, Detroit, 1968-69; reporter Outlook, Santa Monica, Calif., 1969-72; so. Calif. corr. McClatchy Newspapers, Los Angeles, 1975-81; syndicated columnist So. Calif. Focus, Santa Monica, 1972—; west coast corr. Scripps Howard News Svc., Santa Monica, 1980—. Recipient Greater Los Angeles Press Club Journalism award, 1974, Cal-Tax Media award, 1979, Nat. Headliner award, 1987.

ELIAS, THOMAS S., botanist, author; b. Cairo, Ill., Dec. 30, 1942; s. George Sam and Anna (Clanton) E.; m. Barbara Ana Elias; children: Stephen, Brian. BA in Botany, So. Ill. U., 1964, MA in Botany, 1966; PhD in Biology, St. Louis U., 1969. Asst. curator Arnold Arboretum of Harvard U., Cambridge, Mass., 1969-71; adminstr., dendrologist Cary Arboretum, N.Y. Botanical Garden, Millbrook, 1971-73, asst. dir., 1973-84; dir., chief exec. officer Rancho Santa Ana Botanic Garden, Claremont, Calif., 1984—; chmn., prof. dept. botany Claremont Grad. Sch., 1984—; lectr. in extension Harvard U., 1971; adj. prof. Coll. Environ. Science and Forestry, Syracuse, N.Y., 1977-80; coord. U.S.A/U.S.S.R. Botanical Exch., Program for U.S. Dept. of Interior, Washington, 1976—, U.S.A./China Botanical Exch., Program for U.S. Dept. of Interior, 1988—. Editor: Extinction is Forever, 1977 (one of 100 Best Books in Sci. and Tech. ALA 1977), Conservation and Management of Rare and Endangered Plants, 1987; author: Complete Trees of North America, 1980 (one of 100 Best Books in Sci. and Tech. ALA 1980), Field Guide to Edible Wild Plants of North America (one of 100 Best Books in Sci. and Tech. ALA 1983). Recipient Cooley award Am. Soc. Plant Taxonomist, 1970, Disting. Alumni award So. Ill. U., 1989. Home: 2447 San Mateo Ct Claremont CA 91711 Office: Rancho Santa Ana Botanic Garden 1500 N College Ave Claremont CA 91711

ELIAS-BAKER, BARBARA ANN, chemist; b. Oakland, Calif., June 28, 1946; d. Albert and Helen (Elias) Baker; m. Armando Peraza, Jan. 15, 1970 (div. Mar. 1978). BA in Biology, San Francisco State U., 1971; postgrad., U. Calif., Berkeley, 1971-75, cert. in alcohol counseling, 1982. Outpatient clin. mgr. U. Calif., Berkeley, 1974-77; alcohol and drug counselor Centerpoint, San Rafael, Calif., 1984—; rsch. chemist U. Calif., San Francisco, 1977—; cons. alcohol abuse, San Francisco, 1984—. Mem. AAAS, Calif. Acad. Sci., Am. Chem. Soc., Am. Inst. Chemists, Commonwealth Club Calif. Office: U Calif Langley Porter Inst 401 Parnassus San Francisco CA 94143

ELINSON, HENRY DAVID, artist, language educator; b. Leningrad, USSR, Dec. 14, 1935; came to U.S., 1973; s. David Moses and Fraida Zelma (Ufa) E.; m. Ludmila Nicholas Tepina, Oct. 7, 1955; 1 child, Maria Henry. Student, Herzen State Pedagogical U., Leningrad, 1954-57; BA, Pedagogical Inst., Novgorod, USSR, 1958; MA, Pedagogical Inst., Moscow, 1963. Cert. educator. Spl. edn. tchr. Leningrad Sch. Spl. Edn., 1961-64; supr. dept. speech therapy Psychoneurological Dispensary, Leningrad, 1964-73; instr. Russian lang. Yale U., New Haven, Conn., 1975-76, Def. Lang. Inst., Presidio of Monterey, Calif., 1976—. One-man shows include The Light and Motion Transmutation Galleries, N.Y.C., 1974, Thor Gallery, Louisville, 1974, Monterey (Calif.) Peninsula Art Mus., 1977, U. Calif. Nelson Gallery, Davis, 1978, Nahamkin Gallery, N.Y.C., 1978, Nahamkin Fine Arts, N.Y.C., 1980, Gallery Paule Anglim, 1981, 85, 87; exhibited in group shows at Bklyn. Coll. Art Ctr., 1974, CUNY, 1974, Galleria II Punto, Genoa, Italy, 1975, New Art From the Soviet Union, Washington, 1977, Gallery Hardy, Paris, 1978, Mus. of Fine Art, San Francisco, 1979, and numerous others; represented in permanent collections Mus. Fine Arts, San Francisco, Yale U. Art Gallery, Monterey Mus. Art, U. Calif. Art Mus., Berkeley, Bochum Mus., West Germany, Check Point Charlie Mus., West Berlin; participant Nonconformist Art Exhbns., Leningrad, 1960; contbr. articles to profl. jours. Mem. Underground Anti-Soviet Govt. Students' Orgn., 1957. Recipient Gold medal Art Achievement City of Milan, 1975. Home: 997 Benito Ct Pacific Grove CA 93950

ELKINS, GLEN RAY, service company executive; b. Winnsboro, La., May 23, 1933; s. Ceicel Herbert and Edna Mae (Luallen) E.; m. Irene Kay Hildebrand, Aug. 25, 1951; children: Steven Breen, Douglas Charles, Karen Anne, Michael Glen. AA in Indsl. Mgmt, Coll. San Mateo, 1958. Successively mgr. production control, mgr. logistics, plant mgr., asst. v.p. ops. Aircraft Engring. and Maintenance Co. (Aemco), 1957-64; successively mgr. field ops., v.p. ops., exec. v.p., pres. Internat. Atlas Svcs. Co., Princeton, N.J., 1964-85; sr. v.p. Atlas Corp., Princeton; chmn., chief exec. officer, dir. Global Assocs.; pres. Global Assocs. Internat. Ltd., 1973-85; pres., chief exec. officer Triad Am. Svcs. Corp., 1985—; pres. Pacific Mgmt. Services Corp. Area chmn. Easter Seals drive, 1974; bd. dirs. Utah Children's Mus. With USN, 1950-54. Mem. Nat. Mgmt. Assn., Electronic Industries Assn. Clubs: Lakeview, Willow Creek Country (Salt Lake City). Home: 1904 E Lakewood Dr Salt Lake City UT 84117 Office: 57 W 200 S Ste 101 Salt Lake City UT 84101

ELKINS, THOMAS RICHARD, broadcasting executive; b. Davenport, Iowa, Apr. 25, 1931; s. Richard M. and Nadienne C. (Blemker) E.; m. Joan E. Winters, Aug. 28, 1955 (div. Mar. 1972); children: Richard H., Geoffrey A., Wendy J., Marjorie N.; m. Prentice Brannan, Apr. 10, 1972 (dec. Apr. 1985). AB cum laude, Wabash Coll., 1953. Lic. FCC. Announcer, reporter Sta. WKJG, Ft. Wayne, Ind., 1953-56; announcer Sta. WOC, Davenport, 1956-58; disc jockey Sta. KSTT, Davenport, 1958-59; owner, mgr. Sta. KBUS, Mexia, Tex., 1959-63, Sta. KKJO, Saint Joseph, Mo., 1963-71, Stas. KNUI and KHUI, Kahului, Hawaii, 1973—; bd. dirs. 1st Amendment Congress; commentator Voice of Am., 1982-83. Over 240 broadcast editorials per yr., 1961—. Pres. Maui chpt. Hawaii Heart Assn., 1978. Mem. Nat. Broadcast Editorial Assn. (bd. dirs. 1981—, pres. 1986-87, nat. excellence award 1981, regional excellence award 1981, 84, Mgmt. award 1989), Nat. Assn. Broadcasters (1st Amendment com.), Nat. Conf. Editorial Writers (bd. dirs. 1986-87), Soc. Profl. Journalists (bd. dirs. 1986-87), Radio-TV News Dirs. Assn. (bd. dirs. 1986-87), Hawaiin Assn. Broadcasters (bd. dirs. 1978-82, pres. 1980-81), Maui C. of C. (bd. dirs. 1987—). Office: Stas KNUI/KHUI 311 Ano St Kahului HI 96732

ELLAHIE, JAVED INAM, lawyer; b. Karachi, Sind, Pakistan, Mar. 31, 1949; came to U.S., 1967; s. Inam Ellahie and Rasila Begum (Yusaf) Shaikh; m. Naveeda Ahmed, June 15, 1980. BSEE, Calif. State U., 1970; JD, Santa Clara U., 1974. Bar: Calif. 1974, U.S. Dist Ct. 1975, Sind-Baluchistan High Ct. 1973. Sole practice San Jose, Calif., 1977—. Bd. dirs. San Jose Ctr. for Poetry and Lit., 1988; pres. Am. Muslims-Friends Dem. Club, 1988; mem. Calif. Dem. Cen. Com., 1989. Mem. Pakistan Engrs. and Scis. Assn.

ELLAM, GUNNAR, architect, planner; b. Tallinn, Estonia, July 25, 1929; came to U.S., 1950; s. Hanno and Erika (Siirak) E.; m. Renate Sternberg, June 7, 1959 (div. 1984); 1 child, Inger. BA in Architecture, U. Calif., Berkeley, 1955, MA in Architecture, 1963. Registered architect, Calif. Head. archtl. dept. Soule Steel Co., San Francisco, 1959-63; chief architect CSB Constrn., Inc., Oakland, Calif., 1963-83; prin. Gunnar Ellam Architect, Oakland, 1983—. Prin. works include Pacific Gas and Electric Co. Offices, Merced, Calif. (City of Merced archtl. commendation award 1969), March Metalfab Co. Facility, Hayward, Calif., 1971 (Hayward C. of C. 1st award for archtl. design), Milne Trucking Co. Facility, San Leandro, Calif., 1975 (City of San Leandro archtl. design award), DiSalvo Trucking Co. Facility, Oakland, 1969, South San Francisco, Calif., 1978 (award Archtl. Record and Fleet Owner mag.), Centennial Bank Bldg., San Leandro, 1981 (City of San Leandro comml. devel. design award), Yellow Cab Office and Maintenance Facility, San Francisco (Calif. Systems Builders Assn. 1st honor award 1987, Systems Builders Assn. nat. honor award 1988). Capt. with USAF, 1956-59, Korea. Mem. AIA, Estonian Soc. San Francisco (v.p. 1986-87, pres. 1988—). Democrat. Office: 1700 Broadway Oakland CA 94612

ELLENSON, GORDON EUGENE, service executive; b. St. Paul, Aug. 24, 1950; s. Gerald Martin and Gaynell Maxine (Halterman) E.; m. Mary Cynthia Grisafi, July 14, 1973 (div. Feb. 1989); children: Cory Philip, Joseph Gordon. Student, Cerritos Coll., 1972-75. With WeldRing Co., Huntington Park, Calif., 1972-73; radiographer Aircraft X-Ray Labs., Inc., Huntington Park, 1973-75; insp. Lamco Industries, Inc., El Cajon, Calif., 1975-82; supr. Chem-Tronics, Inc., El Cajon, 1982-88; mgr. Comml. Inspection Svcs., San Diego, 1988—. Soccer coach Boys Club Am., El Cajon, 1983-87; asst. cubmaster Cub Scouts Am., El Cajon, 1986-87. With U.S. Army, 1969-71. Mem. Am. Soc. for Nondestructive Testing (sec. San Diego chpt. 1988—). Republican. Methodist. Office: Comml Inspection Svcs 1995 Bayfront Blvd #1A San Diego CA 92113

ELLER, JAMES MILTON, business owner; b. North Wilkesboro, N.C., Feb. 5, 1942; s. Isaac Milton and Frances (Crawford) E.; m. Linda Barton, June 27, 1970. BA, U. N.C., 1964; MBA, San Francisco State U., 1972. Cost acct. Itek Corp., Sunnyvale, Calif., 1972-75; fin. analyst Amdahl Corp., Sunnyvale, 1975-80; mgr. capital investments Crown Zellerbach, San Francisco, 1980-85; v.p., gen. mgr. Frederic Bruns Showrooms, San Francisco, 1985—; owner, operator Concorde, Inc., San Francisco, 1983—. Bd. dirs. Condo Assn. San Francisco, 1987—; Show Place Sq. Complex, San Francisco, 1987—. Served to lt. USNR, 1966-70. Republican. Office: Frederic Bruns Showrooms 2 Henry Adams San Francisco CA 94103

ELLER, KARL, holding company executive; b. 1928; married. BBA, U. Ariz, 1952. Founder Eller Outdoor Advt., 1968; founder, pres., chief exec. officer Combined Communication Corp., 1968-79; pres. Columbia Pictures Communications, 1980-83; chmn., chief exec. officer, Circle K Corp., Phoenix, 1983—, dir.; chmn. Swensen's, Inc., Phoenix. Office: The Circle K Corp 1601 N 7th St PO Box 52084 Phoenix AZ 85006 *

ELLER, LESLIE ROBERT, lawyer; b. Denver, Aug. 30, 1949; s. Burton and Eileen E. BA cum laude, Claremont (Calif.) Men's Coll., 1971; JD, U. Denver, 1975. Bar: Colo. 1976, U.S. Dist. Ct. Colo. 1976, U.S. Ct. Appeals (10th cir.) 1976. Assoc. Neil C. King, Atty. at Law, Boulder, Colo., 1976-80; v.p., ptnr. King & Eller, P.C., Boulder, 1980—, also bd. dirs.; v.p. First Colo. Title Corp., Boulder, 1987—; v.p. Mesa Moving and Storage Co., Grand Junction, Colo., 1981—. Mem. ABA, Boulder County Bar Assn., Colo. Bar Assn. Home: 515 Valley View Dr Boulder CO 80302 Office: King and Eller PC 1919 14th St Suite 300 Boulder CO 80302

ELLERSICK, STEVEN DONALD, electromagnetic effects engineer, scientist; b. Pullman, Wash., Apr. 20, 1961; s. Donald Kay and Sandra Lee (Dyke) E. Student, Pacific Luth. U., 1979-81; BSEE, Wash. State U., 1983; MS in Applications of Physics, U. Wash., 1987. Elec. engr. Boeing Advanced Systems Co., Seattle, 1983—; change engr. Boeing Co., Seattle, 1983-84, electromagnetic compatability engr., 1984-86, infra-red scientist, engr., 1986—. Recipient Eagle Scout award Boy Scouts Am., 1976. Lutheran. Home: 7333 47th Ave SW #1 Seattle WA 98136

ELLETT, HENRY, design engineer; b. Buffalo, Dec. 20, 1938; s. Henry Drake and Murial (Bishop) E.; m. Ann Whitt, Dec. 7, 1973; children: Carl, Lora, Christopher, Sean. BA in Indsl. Design, Art Ctr.Coll. Profl. Design, L.A., 1962. Cert. transp. designer. Sr. indsl. designer Gulfstream Aerospace Co. (formerly Rockwell Internat.), Oklahoma City, 1963-85; dir. interior design Dee Howard Co., San Antonio, 1985-86; interior design engr., cons. CDI, Little Rock, 1986, Volt Tech. Co., Long Beach, Calif., 1987; sr. design engr., scientist McDonnell Douglas Co., Long Beach, 1987—; freelance designer, Oklahoma City, 1963-85. With U.S. Army, 1956-64. Mem. So. Calif. Profl. Engring. Soc., Art Ctr. Alumni Assn., SCCA (regional exec. Oklahoma City 1970-71, editor Gaskett Gazette 1973, Most Outstanding Mem. award 1969, 71). Republican. Office: McDonnell Douglas Co 3855 Lakewood Blvd M/C 75-21 Long Beach CA 90846

ELLGAS, ROBERT ALAN, environmental engineering consultant; b. Albany, Calif., Aug. 23, 1952; s. William Morley and Dorothy Elizabeth (Brown) E. BS with distinction, Stanford U., 1974; MS, Harvard U., 1979,

PhD, 1986. Student rels. rep. Bank of Am., Stanford, Calif., 1972-74; rural works engr. Peace Corps, Fiji Islands, 1974-75; environ. planner Peace Corps, Honduras, 1975-77; staff analyst Meta Systems Inc., Cambridge, Mass., 1978-81; head teaching fellow Harvard U., Cambridge, 1982; sr. environ. engr. The Mark Group, Pleasant Hill, Calif., 1986—; predoctoral rsch. fellow U.S. Dept. of Energy, Washington, 1980-81. Mem. Nat. Water Well Assn., Tau Beta Pi. Office: The Mark Group Inc 3450 Burkirk Ave Ste 120 Pleasant Hill CA 94523

ELLINGBOE, KAREN LEE, nurse; b. Fresno, Calif., Nov. 18, 1957; d. James Merrill and Phyllis Ruth (Hanson) Hersey; m. Bradley Ross Ellingboe, July 18, 1981; children: Peter James, Alexander. BS in Nursing, St. Olaf Coll., 1980; cert., U. Oslo, Norway, 1984; postgrad., U. N.Mex. RN, N.Y., Minn., N.Mex. Nurse oncology staff Mpls. Med. Ctr., 1980-81, Highland Hosp., Rochester, N.Y., 1981-83; home health nurse Lincoln County Bd. Health, Hazlehurst, Miss., 1983-85; ICU nurse U. N.Mex. Hosp., Albuquerque, 1985—. Democrat. Lutheran. Home: 4621 Robin Ave NE Albuquerque NM 87110

ELLINGTON, JOHN STEPHEN, psychotherapist; b. Moses Lake, Wash., July 7, 1950; s. John Wiley and Lydia Maria (Antognini) E.; m. Melanie Thiele, August 8, 1987; children: Holly Valdez, Simonie Kralj, Mia Thiele. Student, Merced Coll., 1968-70; BA in Biology, U. Calif., Santa Barbara, 1973; MSW, Calif. State U., Fresno, 1978; postgrad., Profl. Sch. Psychology, San Francisco. Lic. clin. social worker. Psychiat. social worker Therapeutic Day Sch., Merced (Calif.) County Mental Health, 1974-76, Family-Adolescent Intervention, Merced County Mental Health, 1978-80, Turlock (Calif.) Inpatient Ctr., Stan County Mental Health, 1980-81; clinician mental health Turlock Counseling Ctr., 1981-83; prog. dir. Psychiat. Health Facility, Modesto, Calif., 1983-85; clinician mental health Adolescent Day Treatment program, Stanislaus County Mental Health, Hughson, Calif., 1985-87; pvt. practice psychotherapy Modesto, 1987—; psychotherapist Psychiatric Med. Group, 1987—; program dir. Pain Mgmt. Systems, Modesto, 1985-87; part-time social worker Modesto Psychiat. Ctr., 1987—; psychotherapist Psychiat. Med. Group, Modesto, 1987—. Actor Loose Assn., 1982-83; bd. dirs. Friends of the Sunshine Place, Modesto. Mem. Nat. Assn. Social Workers. Home: 537 Castle Modesto CA 95350 Office: 3501 Coffee Rd Ste 1 Modesto CA 95355

ELLIOTT, CHARLES HAROLD, clinical psychologist; b. Kansas City, Mo., Dec. 30, 1948; s. Joseph Bond and Suzanne (Wider) E.; 1 child, Brian Douglas. BA, U. Kans., 1971, MA, 1974, PhD, 1976. Cert. clin. psychologist, N. Mex. Asst. prof. E. Cen. Univ., Ada, Okla., 1976-79, U. Okla. Health Sciences, 1979-85; assoc. prof. Dept. Psychiatry U. Okla., 1983-85; assoc. prof. Dept. Psychiatry U. N. Mex. Sch. Medicine, Albuquerque, 1985-87, adj. assoc. prof., 1986—; faculty full appointment Fielding Inst., Santa Barbara, Calif., 1987—; consulting editor Jour. of Child Clinical Psychology, 1987—; ad hoc reviewer to profl. jours., 1983—; cognitive therapist NIMH Collaborative Study of Depression, Okla. City, 1980-85. Contbr. numerous articles to profl. jours. Mem. Biofeedback and Behavioral Medicine Soc. N. Mex. (pres. 1988), S.W. Psychol. Assn., APA, Assn. for Advancement of Behavior Therapy, Assn. For Advancement of Psychology. Home: 403 Dartmouth Dr SE Albuquerque NM 87106 Office: Health Psychology Assn 801 Encino Pl NE B10 Albuquerque NM 87102

ELLIOTT, CONNIE LOU, nurse; b. Belvedere, Ill., July 14, 1950; d. Bernhart William Carl and Marion Elizabeth (Ciertz) Rahn; m. Robert Russell Elliott, Mar. 22, 1968; children: Chad Robert, Mickey Ryan, Bryan Reese. AS, Victor Valley Coll., 1985, AS in Nursing, 1986. RN definitve observation unit Lancaster (Calif.) Community Hosp., 1986--. CPR instr. Am. Heart kAssn., 1988; vol. ARC, 1985. Democrat. Lutheran. Home: 37834 N Cardiff St Palmdale CA 93550

ELLIOTT, DARRELL KENNETH, legal researcher; b. Inglewood, Calif., Apr. 19, 1952; s. Lloyd Kenneth and Marjorie (Myers) E. BA, Biola Coll., La Mirada, Calif., 1975; M Div., Talbot Theol. Sem., La Mirada, 1980; cert. in legal assistantship, U. Calif., Irvine, 1986; MS in Taxation, Northrop U., L.A., 1988; postgrad., Western State U., Fullerton, Calif., 1988—, U. Strasbourg, France, summer 1979. Ind. legal researcher, businessman Buena Park, Calif., 1970—. Calif. State scholar, 1970-75, fellow 1975-80. Mem. Christian Legal Soc., Concerned Women for Am. Republican. Baptist. Home: 7839 Western Ave #B Buena Park CA 90620

ELLIOTT, ERICA MERRIAM, physician; b. Ft. Leavenworth, Kans., June 14, 1948; d. Wheeler Godfrey and Erica (Bauer) Merriam; m. Jeff Elliott, Dec. 27, 1967 (div. 1970); m. Thomas Dwyer, Dec. 13, 1988; 1 child, Barrett Wheeler. BA, Antioch Coll., Yellow Springs, Ohio, 1970; MA in Teaching, U. Colo., 1977, MD, 1983. Tchr. 4th grade Bur. of Indian Affairs, Chinle, Ariz., 1971-73; tchr. Peace Corps, Ecuador, 1974-76; camp counselor Boston U., 1976; wilderness leader Antioch Coll., Smokey Mt., Tenn., 1976; instr. rock and ice climbing Colo. Mt. Club, Boulder, 1977; mountaineer instr. Colo. Outward Bound, Denver, 1977-79; leader all-women's expedition to summit of Mt. McKinley, 1980; resident in family practice Mercy Med. Ctr., Denver, 1983-86; physician, med. dir. Checkerboard Area Health Svcs., 1986-88; pvt. practice Pecos, N.Mex., 1988-89; with La Families Clinic, San Fe, 1989—. Contbr. articles to profl. jours.; reached Summity Aconcaqua 23,000 feet in Argentina, 1976. Recipient Boettcher Found. grantee, 1981, F. William Barron award, 1986, others. Mem. Am. Acad. Family Practitioners, N.Mex. Med. Soc., AMA. Democrat. Presbyterian. Office: 14 Enebro Rd Santa Fe NM 87505

ELLIOTT, GORDON JEFFERSON, educator; b. Aberdeen, Wash., Nov. 13, 1928; s. Harry Cecil and Helga May (Kennedy) E.; m. Suzanne Tsugiko Urakawa, Apr. 2, 1957; children: Meiko Ann, Kenneth Gordon, Nancy Lee, Matthew Kennedy. AA, Grays Harbor Coll., 1948; BA, U. Wash., 1950; Cert. Russian, Army Lang. Sch., Monterey, Calif., 1952; MA, U. Hawaii, 1968. Lifetime credential, Calif. Community Coll. System. English prof. Buddhist U., Ministry of Cults, The Asian Found., Phnom Penh, Cambodia, 1956-62; English instr. U. Hawaii, Honolulu, 1962-68; dir., orientation English Coll. Petroleum and Minerals, Dhahran, Saudi Arabia, 1968-70; asst. prof., English/linguistics U. Guam, Mangilao, 1970-76; tchr., French/English Medford (Oreg.) Mid High Sch., 1976-77; instr., English Merced (Calif.) Coll., 1977—; cons. on Buddhist Edn., The Asia Found., San Francisco, Phnom Penh, Cambodia, 1956-62; cons. on English Edn., Hawaii State Adult Edn. Dept., Honolulu, 1966-68; conf. on English Edn. in Middle East, Am. U., Cairo, Egypt, 1969; vis. prof. of English, Shandong Tchrs. U., Jinan, China, 1984-85. Co-author: (textbooks, bilingual Cambodia) English Composition, 1962, Writing English, 1966, (test) Standard English Recognition Test, 1976; contbr. articles to profl. jours. Mem. Statue of Liberty Centennial Commn., Washington, 1983, Rep. Presidential Task Force, Washington, 1980-86, Heritage Found., Washington, Lincoln Inst., Am Near East Refugee Aid, Washington. Sgt. U.S. Army Security Agy., 1951-55, Japan. Tchr. Fellowship, U. Mich., Ann Arbor, 1956; recipient summer seminar stipend, Nat. Endowment For Humanities, U. Wash., Seattle, 1976, travel grants, People's Rep. of China, Beijing, 1984-85. Mem. Nat. Council Tchrs. of English, Collegiate Press (editorial adv. bd.), Merced Coll. Found., Am. Assn. Woodturners, NRA, BPOE. Republican. Home: 680 Dennis Ct Merced CA 95340 Office: Merced Coll 3600 M St Merced CA 95340

ELLIOTT, JACK RAYMOND, government official, hospital executive; b. Winchester, Ind., July 15, 1953; s. Robert and Winifred (Powell) Elliot Cox. BS, Ind. State U., 1975; postgrad., San Francisco State U., 1980-85, U. Calif., San Francisco, 1980-85. Mgr. Gen. Cinema Corp., Terre Haute, Ind., 1974-76; customs specialist Arvin Industries, Franklin, Ind., 1976-78; personnel asst. Calif. 1st Bank, San Francisco, 1978-80; personnel specialist Toronto Dominion Bank, San Francisco, 1980-82; human resources cons. Elliott Cons. Co., San Francisco, 1982-84; job placement dir. Southwestern Coll., San Francisco, 1984-86; minister Fellowship in Light Ministry, San Francisco, 1985--; program dir. vocat. rehab. workshops, counselor VA, Palo Alto, Calif., 1986--; exec. dir. human rels., cons. Hillhaven Hosps., San Francisco, 1987--. Author: 30-Days to a New Career, My Diet Book. Office: VA Med Ctr 380l Miranda Ave ll7 Bldg 22 Palo Alto CA 94523

ELLIOTT, JAMES HEYER, museum consultant; b. Medford, Oreg., Feb. 19, 1924; s. Bert R. and Marguerite E. (Heyer) E.; m. Judith Ann Algar, Apr. 23, 1966 (div.); children—Arabel Joan, Jakob Maxwell. B.A., Willamette U., Salem, Oreg., 1947, D.F.A. (hon.), 1978; A.M., Harvard U., 1949. James Rogers Rich fellow Harvard U., 1949-50; Fulbright grantee Paris, 1951-52; art critic European edit. N.Y. Herald-Tribune, 1952-53; curator, acting dir. Walker Art Center, Mpls., 1953-56; asst. chief curator, curator modern art Los Angeles County Mus. Art, 1956-63, chief curator, 1964-66; dir. Wadsworth Atheneum, Hartford, Conn., 1966-76; dir. Univ. Art Mus., Berkeley, Calif., 1976-88, spl. cons., 1989—; adj. prof. Hunter Coll., N.Y.C., 1968, U. Calif., Berkeley, 1976—; commr. Conn. Commn. Arts, 1970-76; fellow Trumbull Coll., Yale U., 1971-75; mem. museum arts panel Nat. Endowment Arts, 1974-77; bd. dirs. San Francisco Art Inst., 1980—; art adv. com. Exploratorium, 1982—; adv. com. Artists TV Access, 1987—. Author: Bonnard and His Environment, 1964. Served with USNR, 1943-46. Mem. Internat. Council Mus., Am. Assn. Mus., Coll. Art Assn., Assn. Art Mus. Dirs. (sec., trustee 1980-81), Artists Space N.Y. (dir. 1980-84). Club: Arts (Berkeley). Home: PO Box 4840 Berkeley CA 94704 Office: Univ Art Mus 2625 Durant Ave Berkeley CA 94720

ELLIOTT, JEANNE MARIE KORELTZ, transportation executive; b. Virginia, Minn., Mar. 9, 1943; d. John Andrew and Johanna Mae (Tehovnik) Koreltz; m. David Michael Elliott, Apr. 30, 1983. Student, Ariz. State U., 1967, U. So. Calif. Cert. aviation safety inspector. Tech. asst. Ariz. State U., Tempe, 1966-68; from supr. to mgr. inflight tng./in-svc. programs Northwest Airlines Inc. (formerly Republic Airlines, Hughes Airwest, Air West Inc.), Mpls., 1968—; air carrier cabin safety specialist Flight Standards Service, FAA, Washington, 1975-76; cons. Interaction Research Corp., Olympia, Wash., 1982—. Contbg. editor Cabin Crew Safety Bull., Flight Safety Fedn., 1978—. Recipient Annual Air Safety award Air Line Pilots Assn., Washington, 1971, Annual Safety award Ariz. Safety Council, Phoenix, 1972; first female to receive FAA cabin, 1976. Mem. Soc. Air Safety Investigators Internat., Survival and flight equipment Assn., Assn. Flight Attendants (tech. chmn. 1968-85), Internat. Brotherhood Teamsters Airline Div., Soc. Automotive Engrs. (assoc.) (chmn. cabin safety provisions com. 1971—). Republican. Roman Catholic. Home: 16215 SE 31st St Bellevue WA 98008 Office: Northwest Airlines Inc Inflight Services Dept Minneapolis-St Paul Internat Airport Saint Paul MN 55111

ELLIOTT, JENNIFER LYNN, lawyer; b. Ann Arbor, Mich., Oct. 18, 1957; d. Thomas E. and Suzanne E. (Sinclair) E.; children: Tyler Jensen, Kasey Suzanne. BA, Calif. State U., Chico, 1980; postgrad., Calif. State U., Sacramento, 1982-83; JD, U. of the Pacific, 1985. Bar: Nev. 1986. Jud. law clk. Clark County Dist. Ct., Las Vegas, Nev., 1985-86; assoc. B. Mahlon Brown, Chartered, Las Vegas, 1986-87; pvt. practice Las Vegas, 1987—. Mem. ABA, Nev. Bar Assn., Las Vegas C. of C. Office: 4012 S Rainbow Blvd Ste K 451 Las Vegas NV 89103

ELLIOTT, JOHN GREGORY, aerospace design engineer; b. Surabaya, Dutch East Indies, Nov. 9, 1948; came to U.S., 1956; s. Frans Jan and Charlotte Clara (Rosel) E.; m. Jennifer Lee Austin, May 7, 1988. AA, Cerritos Coll., 1974; BS, Calif. State U., Long Beach, 1978. Design engr. Douglas Aircraft Co., Long Beach, 1978-82, lead engr., 1983-87, lead engr. elec. installations group, 1987—. With USN, 1969-73. Mem. So. Calif.Profl. Engring. Assn., Douglas Aircraft Co. Tennis Club, Douglas Aircraft Co. Surf Club, Douglas Aircraft Co. Mgmt. Club. Republican. Presbyterian. Office: Douglas Aircraft Co Internal Mail Code 203-10 3855 Lakewood Blvd Long Beach CA 90846

ELLIS, BONNIE KATHLEEN, biologist; b. Louisiana, Mo., Mar. 31, 1953; d. Charles William and Corinne Lillian (McKenzie) E. BS in Biology, Lamar U., 1975; MS in Biology, N. Tex. State U., 1980. Supr. electron microscope lab. N. Tex. State U., Denton, 1978-79, rsch. biologist grad. asst. dept. biol. scis., 1977-79; analytical water quality technician Flathead Lake Biol. Sta., U. Mont., Polson, 1980-82, rsch. specialist II, 1982—. Contbr. articles to profl. jours. Mem. Mont. Wilderness Assn., Kalispell, 1984—, Nature Conservancy, Helena, Mont., 1986—; linmology tchr. Elderhostel, Kalispell, 1986, 88. Grantee EPA, 1977-80, 84-86, Nat. Park Svc., 1985—. Mem. Internat. Assn. Theoretical and Applied Limnology, Am. Soc. Limnology and Oceanography, Phycological Soc. Am., Mont. Acad. Sci., Phi Kappa Phi. Office: U Mont Flathead Lake Sta Polson MT 59860

ELLIS, ELDON EUGENE, surgeon; b. Washington, Ind., July 2, 1922; s. Osman Polson and Ina Lucretia (Cochran) E.; BA, U. Rochester, 1946, MD, 1949; m. Irene Clay, June 26, 1948 (dec. 1968); m. 2d, Priscilla Dean Strong, Sept. 20, 1969; children: Paul Addison, Kathe Lynn, Jonathan Clay, Sharon Anne, Eldon Eugene, Rebecca Deborah. Intern in surgery Stanford U. Hosp., San Francisco, 1949-50, resident and fellow in surgery, 1950-52, 55; Schilling fellow in pathology San Francisco Gen. Hosp., 1955; partner Redwood Med. Clinic, Redwood City, Calif., 1955—, med. dir., 1984-87; dir. Sequoia Hosp., Redwood City, 1974-82; asst. clin. prof. surgery Stanford U., 1970-80. Pres. Sequoia Hosp. Found., 1983—; pres., chmn. bd. dirs. Bay Chamber Symphony Orch., San Mateo, Calif., 1988—; mem. Nat. Bd. of Benevolence Evang. Covenent Ch., Chgo., 1988—. Served with USNR, 1942-46, 50-52. Named Outstanding Citizen of Yr., Redwood City, 1987. Mem. San Mateo County (pres. 1961-63), Calif. (pres. 1965-66), Am. (v.p. 1974-75) heart assns., San Mateo Med. Soc. (pres. 1969-70), San Mateo County Comprehensive Health Planning Coun. (v.p. 1969-70), Calif., Am. med. assns., San Mateo, Stanford surg. socs., Am. Coll. Chest Physicians, Calif. Thoracic Soc., Cardiovascular Council. Republican. Mem. Peninsula Covenant Ch. Club: Commonwealth. Home: 3621 Farm Hill Blvd Redwood City CA 94061 Office: Redwood Med Clinic 2900 Whipple Ave Redwood City CA 94062

ELLIS, EVA LILLIAN, artist; b. Seattle, June 4, 1920; d. Carl Martin and Hilda (Persson) Johnson; B.A., U. Wash., 1941; M.A., U. Idaho, 1950; M. in Painting (h.c.), U. delle Arti, 1983; m. Everett Lincoln Ellis, May 1, 1943; children: Karin, Kristy, Hildy, Erik. Assoc. dir. art Best & Co., Seattle, 1943; dir. Am. Art Week, Idaho, 1949-55; mem. faculty dept. art U. Idaho, 1946-48; dir., tchr. Children's Art Oreg., 1966-71; mem. faculty aux. bd. U. Wash., Seattle, 1987—; works include : Profilo d'Artisti Contemporanei Premio Centauro D'Oro, 1982; exhbns. include: Henry Gallery, U. Wash., 1941, Immanuel Gallery, N.Y.C., 1943-46, U. Mich., 1956-65, Detroit Inst. Art, 1959, Kresge Gallery, 1959-64, Portland Art Mus., 1967, Corvallis Art Center, Oreg., 1966, U. Idaho, 1946-56, U. Canterbury, N.Z., 1979, Boise Mus., 1949-55, CSA, 1972, 79, Survey of New Zealand Art, 1979, Shoreline Mus., Seattle, 1981, N.Z. Embassy, London, 1979, Karlshamn Art Soc., Sweden, 1979, Italian Acad. Art, 1982, Palos Verdes (Calif.) Art Ctr., 1982, Aigantighe Gallery, N.Z., 1983; represented in permanent collections: U. Calif.-Berkeley, U. Wash.; guest appearances on NBC-TV, N.Y.C. Counselor Cancer Soc.; active Girl Scouts U.S.A. Recipient awards Acad. Art and Sci., 1958-66, Ann Arbor Women Painters, diploma with gold medal, Italian Acad. Art, 1980, hon. diploma fine art, 3 Nat. awards Nat. League Profl. Artists, N.Y.C.; World Culture prize, 1984; Internat. Peace award in Art, 1984; Internat. Art Promotion award, 1986, others. Fellow I.B.C. (Cambridge, Eng. chpt.); mem. Mich. Acad. Art and Sci., Nat. League Am. Pen Women, Nat. Mus. Women in Arts (charter mem.), Royal Overseas League, Fine Arts Soc. Idaho, Canterbury Soc. Art New Zealand, Copley Soc. Fine Arts (Boston), Inst. D'Atre Contemporanea Di Milano (Italy), Alpha Omicron Pi. (featured in nat. mag.). Clubs: Scandinavian (pres. 1977—), Faculty Wives (pres. 1979). Address: 19614 24th Ave NW Seattle WA 98177

ELLIS, GEORGE EDWIN, JR., chemical engineer; b. Beaumont, Tex., Apr. 14, 1921; s. George Edwin and Julia (Ryan) E.; B.S. in Chem. Engring., U. Tex., 1948; M.S., U. So. Calif., 1958, M.B.A., 1965, M.S. in Mech. Engring., 1968, M.S. in Mgmt. Sci., 1971, Engr. in Indsl. and Systems Engring., 1979. Research chem. engr. Tex. Co., Port Arthur, Tex., 1948-51, Long Beach, Calif., Houston, 1952-53, Space and Information div. N.Am. Aviation Co., Downey, Calif., 1959-61, Magna Corp., Anaheim, Calif., 1961-62; chem. process engr. AiResearch Mfg. Co., Los Angeles, 1953-57, 57-59; chem. engr. Petroleum Combustion & Engring. Co., Santa Monica, Calif., 1957, Jacobs Engring. Co., Pasadena, Calif., 1957, Sesler & Assos., Los Angeles, 1959; research specialist Marquardt Corp., Van Nuys, Calif., 1962-67; sr. project engr. Conductron Corp., Northridge, 1967-68; information systems asst. Los Angeles Dept. Water and Power, 1969—. Instr. thermodynamics U. So. Calif., Los Angeles, 1957. Served with USAAF, 1943-45. Mem. Am. Chem. Soc., Am. Soc. for Metals, Am. Inst. Chem. Engrs., ASME, Am. Electroplaters Soc., Am. Inst. Indsl. Engrs., Am. Mktg. Assn., Ops. Research Soc. Am., Am. Prodn. and Inventory Control Soc., Am. Assn. Cost Engrs., Nat. Assn. Accts., Soc. Mfg. Engrs., Pi Tau Sigma, Phi Lambda Upsilon, Alpha Pi Mu. Home: 1344 W 20th St San Pedro CA 90731 Office: LA Dept Water and Power Los Angeles CA 90012

ELLIS, GEORGE RICHARD, museum administrator; b. Birmingham, Ala., Dec. 9, 1937; s. Richard Paul and Dorsie (Gibbs) E.; m. Sherroll Edwards, June 20, 1961 (dec. 1973); m. Nancy Enderson, Aug. 27, 1975; 1 son, Joshua. BA, U. Chgo., 1959, MFA, 1961; postgrad., UCLA, 1971. Art supr. Jefferson County Schs., Birmingham, 1962-64; asst. dir. Birmingham Mus. Art, 1964-66; asst. dir. UCLA Mus. Cultural History, 1971-81, assoc. dir., 1981-82; dir. Honolulu Acad. Arts, 1981—. Author various works on non-western art, 1971—. Recipient Ralph Altman award UCLA, 1968; recipient Outstanding Achievement award UCLA, 1980; fellow Kress Found., 1971. Mem. Pacific Arts Assn. (v.p. 1985—), Hawaii Mus. Assn. (v.p. 1986-87, pres. 1987-88), Assn. Art Mus. Dirs., Am. Assn. Mus., L.A. Ethnic Arts Coun. (hon.), Pacific Club (Honolulu). Club: Pacific (Honolulu). Office: Honolulu Acad Arts 900 S Beretania St Honolulu HI 96814

ELLIS, HENRY CARLTON, psychologist, educator; b. Bern New, N.C., Oct. 23, 1927; s. Henry Alford and Frances Lee (Mays) E.; m. Florence Pettyjohn, Aug. 24, 1957; children: Joan, Diane Elizabeth, John Weldon. B.S., Coll. William and Mary, 1951; M.A., Emory U., 1952; Ph.D. (Van Blarcom fellow), Washington U., 1958. Asst. prof. psychology U. N.Mex., Albuquerque, 1957-62, assoc. prof., 1962-67, prof. psychology, 1967-87, distinguished prof. psychology, 1987—, chmn. dept., 1975-84; v.p. Gen. Programmed Teaching Corp., 1960-62; mem. vis. faculty Washington U., St. Louis, 1963-67; vis. prof. psychology U. Calif.-Berkeley, 1971, U. Hawaii, 1977; disting. vis. prof. U.S. Air Force Med. Ctr., Lackland AFB, Tex., 1978; chmn. Nat. Council Grad. Depts. Psychology, 1977-79, bd. dirs., 1976-81; vis. scholar Learning Research and Devel. Ctr., U. Pitts., 1985; cons. Fla. State Bd. Regents, U. Fla. System. Author: The Transfer of Learning, 1965, Fundamentals of Human Learning and Cognition, 1972, Fundamentals of Human Learning, Memory and Cognition, 1978, (with Bennett, Daniels and Rickert) Psychology of Learning and Memory, 1979, (with Hunt) Fundamentals of Human Memory and Cognition, 1983; editorial bd. Jour. Exptl. Psychology, 1967-74, Jour. Exptl Psychology: Human Learning and Memory, 1974-76, Perception and Psychophysics, 1971-78; co-editor Cognition and Emotion, 1986—; cons. Motivation and Emotion, 1986—; contbr. articles to profl. jours. Mem. Gov.'s Coun. for N.Mex. Disting. Pub. Svc. Awards, 1989. Served with USAAF, 1946-47. Fellow Am. Psychol. Assn. (council reps. 1980-81, 83—, edn. and tng. bd. 1981-84, chmn. 1984, bd. dirs. 1986-89, pres. div. exptl. psychology 1983-86, policy and planning bd. 1989—; chmn. edn. and tng. oversigt com. 1989, G. Stanley Hall lectr. 1986, SWIM Disting. lectr. 1987); mem. Psychonomic Soc., AAAS, Sigma Xi, Phi Kappa Phi. Methodist. Clubs: Albuquerque Tennis, Twenty-One; Cosmos (Washington). Home: 1905 Amherst Dr Albuquerque NM 87106 Office: U NMex Dept Psychology Albuquerque NM 87131

ELLIS, JOHN W., utility company executive; b. Seattle, Sept. 14, 1928; s. Floyd E. and Hazel (Reed) R.; m. Doris Stearns, Sept. 1, 1953; children: Thomas R., John, Barbara, Jim. B.S., U. Wash., 1952, J.D., 1953. Bar: Wash. State bar 1953. With firm Perkins, Coie, Stone, Olsen & Williams, Seattle, 1953-70; with Puget Sound Power & Light Co., Bellevue, Wash., 1970—, exec. v.p., 1973-76, pres., chief exec. officer, 1976-87, also dir., chmn., chief exec. officer, 1987—; dir., chmn. Seattle br. Fed. Res. Bank of San Francisco, 1982-88; mem. Wash. Gov's Spl. Com. Energy Curtailment, 1973-74; chmn. Pacific N.W. Utilities Coordinating Com., 1976-82; bd. dirs. Wash. Mut. Savs. Bank, Seattle, SAFECO Corp., Electric Power Research Inst., 1984-89, Nat. Energy Found., 1985-87, FlowMole corp., Associated Electric & Gas ins. Svcs. Ltd. Pres. Bellevue Boys and Girls Club, 1969-71, Seattle/King County Econ. Devel. Council, 1984—; mem. exec. dirs. Seattle/King County Boys and Girls Club, 1972-75; bd. dirs. Overlake Hosp., Bellevue, 1974—, United Way King County, 1977—, Seattle Sci. Found., 1977—, Seattle Sailing Found., Evergreen Safety Council, 1981, Assn. Wash. Bus., 1980-81, Govs. Adv. Council on Econ. Devel., 1984—; chmn. bd. Wash. State Bus. Round Table, 1983; pres. United for Washington; adv. bd. Grad. Sch. Bus. Adminstrn. U. Wash., 1982—, Wash. State Econ. Ptnrship., 1984—; chmn. Seattle Regional Panel White Ho. Fellows, 1985—; trustee Seattle U., 1986—. Mem. ABA, Wash. Bar Assn., King County Bar Assn., Nat. Assn. Elec. Cos. (dir. 1977-79), Edison Electric Inst. (dir. 1978-80, exec. com. 1982, 2d vice chmn. 1987, 1st vice chmn. 1988), Assn. Edison Illuminating Cos. (exec. com. 1979-81), Seattle C. of C. (dir. 1980—, 1st vice chmn. 1987-88, chmn. 1988—), Phi Gamma Delta, Phi Delta Phi. Clubs: Rainier (Seattle) (sec. 1972, v.p. 1984, pres. 1985), Seattle Yacht (Seattle), Corinthian Yacht (Seattle); Meydenbauer Bay Yacht (Bellevue), Bellevue Athletic. Lodge: Rotary (Seattle). Home: 901 SE Shoreland Dr Bellevue WA 98004 Office: Puget Sound Power & Light Co PO Box 97034 OBC-15 Bellevue WA 98009-9734 *

ELLIS, JOY CEOLIA, human resource and development company official; b. Detroit, June 1, 1945; d. King Ferando and Constance Ethel (Johnson) E.; widow; children: Willie Maples, Ryan Smith. AA, Miramar Coll, 1981; BA, Nat. U., 1985, Ma in Human Behavior, 1988. Drug-alcohol specialist U.S. Army, Monterrey, Calif., 1981; marriage and family counselor U.S. Navy, San Diego, 1981-83; with employee assistance dept. 1985-87; asst. officer social actions USAF, Sacramento, 1983-84; program coordinator USAF, Lompoc, Calif., 1986-87; chief family support programs USAF, Fairfield, Calif., 1987-88; owner, mgr. Human Dimensions, Fairfield, 1988—; cons. Credo, San Diego, 1976-86, Women's Ctr., San Diego, 1982-83, Sacramento State Coll., 1986, Proctor and Gamble Co., Albany Ga., 1988. Author: Music and Personal Growth, 1981, Family Separations, 1983, Family Dynamics of Alcoholism, 1985, Moving through Grief, 1987. With USN, 1974-80. Mem. Nat. Assn. Alcoholism Counselors, Calif. Assn. Marriage and Family therapists, Child Haven Children Network (bd. dirs. 1988—), Nat. Assn. Female Execs., Negro Bus. and Profl. Women. Home and Office: 4859 Cork Pl San Diego CA 92117

ELLIS, LEE, publisher, editor; b. Medford, Mass., Mar. 12, 1924; s. Lewis Leeds and Charlotte Frances (Brough) E.; m. Sharon Kay Barnhouse, Aug. 19, 1972. Child actor, dancer, stage, radio, movies, Keith-Albee Cir., Ea. U.S., 1927-37; announcer, producer, writer, various radio stas. and CBS, Boston and Miami, Fla., 1946-50; TV dir. ABC; mem. TV faculty Sch. Journalism U. Mo., Columbia, 1950-55; mgr. Sta. KFSD/KFSD-TV, San Diego, 1955-60, GM Imperial Broadcasting System, 1960-62; v.p., dir. advt., Media-Agencies-Clients, Los Angeles, 1962-66; v.p., dir. newspaper relations Family Weekly (name now USA Weekend), N.Y.C., 1966-89; pres., owner, editor Sharlee Publs., 1989—; lectr. gen. semantics and communications Idaho State U., Utah State U., San Diego State U. Served with USN, 1941-44, PTO. Mem. San Diego Press Club. Republican. Methodist. Home and Office: 47-800 Madison St #53 Indio CA 92201

ELLIS, MICHAEL DAVID, aerospace company executive; b. Sacramento, July 13, 1952; s. John David and Priscilla Agnes (Tupper) E.; m. Virginia Katherine Hanlon, Mar. 27, 1976; children: Gwendolyn Dawn, January Marie, Jennifer Noel. BS in Space Sci., Fla. Inst. Tech., 1975. With satellite ops., orbit analyst Western Union, Sussex, N.J., 1976-77; with satellite ops., 3 axis RCA Americom, Sussex, N.J., 1977-78; with satellite ops., Land Sat ATS-6 Goddard Space Flight Ctr., Greenbelt, Md., 1978-79; with Voyager System Lead Jet Propulsion Lab., Pasadena, Calif., 1979-82; STS ground ops. analyst Applied Rsch. Inc., El Segundo, Calif., 1982-83; mission ops. Aerospace Corp., El Segundo, Calif., 1983-88, Johnson Spaceflight Ctr., Houston, 1988—. Mem. troop asst. Tres Condados Girl Scouts, Moorpark, Calif., 1983—; Confraternity Christian Doctrine tchr. Holy Cross Ch., Moorpark, 1988. Mem. Soc. Automotive Engrs. (chmn. spacecraft com. 1986-87), Am. Inst. Aeronautics and Astronautics (chmn. 1972-75).

ELLIS, ROBERT HARRY, television executive, university administrator; b. Cleve., Mar. 2, 1928; s. John George Ellis and Grace Bernice (Lewis) Kline; m. Frankie Jo Lanter, Aug. 7, 1954; children: Robert Harry Jr., Kimberley Kay Murphy, Shana Lee. BA, Ariz. State U., 1953; MA, Case Western Res. U., 1962. Newswriter, announcer Sta. KOY, Phoenix, 1953-55, continuity dir., 1955-61; dir., radio ops. Ariz. State U., Tempe, 1959-61; gen. mgr. Sta. KAET-TV, Tempe, 1961-87; assoc. v.p. Ariz. State U., Tempe, 1986—; exec. com. bd. dirs. Pub. Broadcasting Service, Washington, 1973-77, 80-86;

founder Pacific Mountain Network, Denver, 1972, pres. 1973-75; mem. ednl. telecommunications com. Nat. Assn. State Univs. and Land Grant, Washington, 1973-77, 80-86. Mem. Sister City, Tempe, 1986, Tempe Ctr. for the Handicapped, East Valley Mental Health Alliance, Mesa, Ariz., Ariz. Acad. Bd. Govs. award Pacific Mountain Network, 1987. Mem. Nat. Assn. TV Arts and Scis. (life, v.p. bd. trustees 1969-70, bd. dirs. Phoenix chpt. 1986), Nat. Assn. Pub. TV Stas. (bd. dirs. 1988—), PBS Interconnection Com., Ariz. Broadcasters, Phoenix Met. Broadcasters, Tempe C. of C. (diplomate, bd. dirs.), Sundome Performing Arts Assn. (bd. dirs. 1986—), Ariz. Zoological Soc. (bd. dirs., sec. 1984—), Ariz. State U. Alumni Assn. (life), Tempe Conv. and Visitors Bur. (bd. sec./treas.), Tempe Sports Authority. Methodist. Office: Ariz State U Univ Rels Tempe AZ 85287-2503

ELLIS, ROGER STEPHEN, physician; b. Knoxville, Tenn., Dec. 31, 1952; s. Joseph Roberts Ellis and Betty (Wininger) Raman. BS, U. Ill., 1974; MD, U. Ill., Chgo., 1978. Diplomate Am. Bd. Emergency Medicine. Intern U. Louisville, Ky., 1978-79; pvt. practice San Francisco, 1979—. Home and Office: 456 Missouri St San Francisco CA 94107

ELLIS, STEPHEN, physician; b. Knoxville, Tenn., Dec. 31, 1952; s. Joseph Roberts Ellis and Betty (Wininger) Raman. BS, U. Ill., 1974, MD, 1978. Diplomate Am. Bd. Emergency Medicine. Intern in internal medicine U. Louisville, 1978-79; pvt. practice emergency medicine San Francisco, 1980-87. Home: 456 Missouri St San Francisco CA 94107

ELLIS, STEPHEN D., physics educator; b. Detroit; s. Myron P. and Violetta C. (Bowmaster) E.; m. Penny Molander, June 28, 1981; 1 child, Meme. BSE in Physics and Math., U. Mich., 1965; PhD, Caltech., 1971. Research physicist Fermilab, Batavia, Ill., 1971-73, 1974-75; vis. physicist Cern, Geneva, 1973-74; research asst. prof. U. Wash. Dept. Physics, Seattle, 1975-80, assoc. prof., 1980-85, prof., 1985—. Fellow Am. Physics Soc.; mem. Sigma Xi, Tau Beta Pi. Office: U Wash Dept Physics FM-15 Seattle WA 98145

ELLIS, TAMRA ANN, company executive; b. Colorado Springs, Dec. 4, 1958; d. Harold Gene Roth and Barbara Kay (Lord) Ware; m. George Randal Ellis, Dec. 11, 1976 (div. Jan. 1989). Student, Community Coll., Canon City, Colo., 1987-88. With Coast to Coast, Canon City, 1975-85, U.S. Post Office, Canon City, 1985-86, 1989—; asst. to pres. Coast to Coast, 1986-88; owner Deeper Shade Tanning Salon, Canon City, 1988—. Instr. Women's Self Def., Law Enforcement, Probation and Parole Survival, Canon City, 1988--, Canon City Kenpo Karate, 1987--. Home: 700 Yale #2 Canon City CO 81212

ELLISON, DIANE MARIE, timber company executive; b. Aberdeen, Wash., June 18, 1941; d. Russell M. and Syster (Edlund) E.; m. Thomas C. Rowe, Apr. 12, 1963 (div. 1969); children: Dawn Marie, Robert Ellison. BA in Sociology cum laude, U. Wash., 1963; teaching credential in social scis., U. Calif., Irvine, 1970; MS in Human Resource Mgmt. and Devel., Chapman Coll., 1984; cert. alcohol/drug studies, Seattle U., 1987-88. Counselor Seattle (Wash.) Detention Ctr., 1963; adolescent counselor Oakland (Calif.) YMCA, 1964; youth leader St. Andrews Ch., Newport Beach, Calif., 1971-75; tennis coach Tustin Hills Racquet Club, Tustin, Calif., 1977-80; tennis instr. Utt Currie Jr. High Sch., Tustin, 1978-80; sales and mktg. exec. Don Caster Fashions, Aberdeeen, Wash., 1980-82; prin. Ellison Timber, Aberdeen, Wash., 1982—, Ellison Truffles Corp., Aberdeen, 1984—; speaker Chapman Coll. Enterprise Inst., 1986-87. Co-author: Reach for the Sky, 1986; video producer log rolling history The Contest Logger, White Water Man, 1988. Vol. dir. Tall Ships Restoration, Aberdeen, 1986, Pacific Rim Cultural Ctr., Aberdeen, 1987; bd. govs. Evergreen State Coll., 1987—; pres., mem. steering com. Wash. State Folk Life Council, 1988—; bd. dirs. Aberdeen chpt. Am. Heart Assn., 1988—. Mem. N.Am. Truffling Soc., Pacific N.W. Writers Conf., Internat. Log Rolling Orgn., Women in Timber, Aberdeen C. of C. (bd. dirs. 1985—), U. Wash. Alumni Assn., Alumni Assn. Chapman Coll., Polson Mus., Mus. Aberdeen, Aberdeen Lions, Alpha Chi Omega. Republican. Home and Office: Rte 1 Box 142 Aberdeen WA 98520

ELLIS-VANT, KAREN MCGEE, special education teacher, consultant; b. La Grande, Oreg., May 10, 1950; d. Ellis Eddington and Gladys Vera (Smith) McGee; m. Lynn F. Ellis, June 14, 1975 (div. Sept. 1983); children—Megan Marie, Matthew David; m. Jack Scott Vant, Sept. 6, 1986; children: Kathleen Erin, Kelli Christine (dec.). BA in Elem. Edn., Boise State U., 1972, MA in Spl. Edn., 1979; postgrad. studies in curriculum and instruction, U. Minn., 1985—. Tchr. learning disabilities resource room New Plymouth Joint Sch. Dist., 1972-73; tchr. learning disabilities resource room Payette Joint Sch. Dist., 1973, diagnostician project SELECT, 1974-75; cons. tchr. in spl. edn. Boise Sch. Dist., 1975—; mem. profl. Standards Commn., 1983-86. Active Hotline, Inc.; mem. Idaho Coop. Manpower Commn., 1984-85. Recipient Disting. Young Woman of Yr. award Boise Jaycettes, 1982, Idaho Jaycettes, 1983; Coffman Alumni scholar U. Minn., 1985-86. Mem. NEA (mem. civil rights com. 1983-85, state contact for peace caucus 1981-85, del. assembly rep., 1981-85), Idaho Edn. Assn. (bd. dirs. region VII 1981-85, pres. region VII 1981-82), Boise Edn. Assn. (v.p. 1981-82, 84-85, pres. 1982-83), Nat. Council Urban Edn. Assn., World Future Soc., Council for Exceptional Children (pres. chpt. 1978-79), Assn. Supervision and Curriculum Devel., Minn. Council for Social Studies, Calif. Assn. for Gifted, Assn. for Grad. Edn. Students. Unitarian. Contbr. articles to profl. jours.; editor, author ednl. texts and communiques; conductor of workshops. Office: Boise Sch Dist Lincoln Annex Pupil Pers 1207 Fort St Boise ID 83702

ELLS, ROBERT HARE, pharmaceutical company executive; b. Thibodaux, La., Nov. 9, 1936; s. Clarence Carter Ells, Sr. and Rose Jane (Landry) Walsh; m. Barbara Jeanne Tutschek, Aug. 25, 1962; children: Steven, David, Christina, Lisa. BS in Chem. Engring. magna cum laude, La. State U., 1959; student, U. Md., 1960-61, MIT, 1962-63; MBA with honors, Ind. U., 1968. Cert. profl. engr., Ind. Sr. design assoc. Eli Lilly and Co., Indpls., 1963-65; project mgr. Puerto Rican Chem. Plant Eli Lilly and Co., Mayaguez, 1965-68; sr. project mgr. Clinton Labs. Eli Lilly and Co., Indpls., 1968-70; mgr., plant engr. Clinton Labs Eli Lilly and Co., Clinton, Ind., 1970-73; project dir. EEC Chem. Plant Eli Lilly and Co., Landsberg, Fed. Republic Germany, 1973-75; mfg. dir. Tippecanoe Labs. Eli Lilly and Co., Lafayette, Ind., 1975-79; div. pres. Arapahoe Chems. Inc., Boulder, Colo., 1980-83; subs. v.p. chem. manufacturing Syntex USA, Palo Alto, Calif., 1983-86; pres. Syntex Chems. and corp. group v.p. worldwide chem. ops. and engr. services Syntex Corp., Palo Alto, Calif., 1986—; bd. dirs. Syntex Chems., Inc., Syntex SA, Mex., Syntex Ireland.; co. officer Syntex USA, Syntex Agri-Bus., Syntex Internat., Syntex Corp. Contbr. articles to profl. jours. Pres., founder Coalition to Stop Highway By-Pass Through Western Side of W. Lafayette, 1978-79. Served as 1st lt. U.S. Army, 1960-62. Mem. Pharmaceutical Mfgrs. Assn. (bd. dirs. Prodn./Engring/Materials Mgmt. Steering Section 1987—, chmn. Bulk Pharmaceutical Chems. Section Com 1986-87, mem., sec., vice-chair 1981-86), Am. Inst. Chem. Engrs. Republican. Episcopalian. Lodge: Rotary (Boulder). Home: 17 Sandstone Portola Valley CA 94025 Office: Syntex Corp 3401 Hillview Ave Palo Alto CA 94303

ELLSWORTH, EDWARD IZUMI, publisher; b. Sasebo, Japan, July 20, 1954; s. Donald Ray and Michiki (Izumi) E. BA in Psychology, Calif. State U., Long Beach, 1979. Dir. pub. rels. Passport Designs, Half Moon Bay, Calif., 1980-82; mgr. Computerland, Belmont, Calif., 1982-83; communications researcher Human/Dolphin Found., Redwood City, Calif., 1980-84; communications cons. Network Nexus, Belmont, 1984-86; mktg. cons. Grapevine Communications, Redwood City, 1986; tech. support staff H.S. Dakin Co., San Francisco, 1987; founder, pub. The Dolphin Network, San Francisco, 1987—; adminstr. Pinnacle Type, San Francisco, 1987—. Mem. Printing Industries No. Calif. Home and Office: Dolphin Network 3220 Sacramento St San Francisco CA 94115

ELLSWORTH, KENNETH WAYNE, detention officer, inmate canteen manager; b. Mesa, Ariz., Apr. 8, 1957; s. Dennis Reid and Ataloah (Lewis) E.; m. Carma Lynn Epps, Apr. 13, 1985; 1 child, Amanda Marie. Office mgr. Custom Farm Svcs., Queen Creek, Ariz., 1980-83; asst. office mgr. Sunworth Packing Co., Queen Creek, 1986, Pinto Creek Mgmt., Queen Creek, 1987; office mgr. McKeon & Sons, Bakersfield, Calif., 1987; detention officer Maricopa County Sheriff's Office, Phoenix, 1983-86, 87—; mem. sheriff's wage & benefit com., 1988—; mem. automated security system com. Detention Bur., 1988—. Candidate for constable Chandler Justice Precinct, 1986. Republican. Mormon. Office: Maricopa Sheriff's Office 225 W Madison St Phoenix AZ 85003

ELLSWORTH, PETER KENNEDY, health care executive; b. L.A., June 19, 1931; s. J. Phil and Virginia Ruth (Eastman) E.; m. Doris A. Anderson, Aug. 14, 1955; children: Michael P., Thomas B. BA, Stanford U., 1953, JD, 1956. Bar: Calif. 1957. Assoc., pres. Ellsworth, Corbett, Seitman, McLeod Law Firms, San Diego, 1958-86; pres., chief exec. officer Sharp HealthCare, San Diego, 1986—. Pres. San Diego Blood Bank, 1975, Combined Arts of San Diego, 1984. Fellow ABA; mem. Calif. Bar Assn., Rotary. Republican. Presbyterian. Office: Sharp HealthCare 3131 Berger Ave San Diego CA 92123

ELLSWORTH, RICHARD GERMAN, psychologist; b. Provo, Utah, June 23, 1950; s. Richard Grant and Betty Lola (Midgley) E.; BS, Brigham Young U., 1974, MA, 1975; PhD, U. Rochester (N.Y.), 1979; postgrad. UCLA, 1980-84; PhD, Internat. Coll., 1983; m. Carol Emily Osborne, May 23, 1970; children: Rebecca Ruth, Spencer German, Rachel Priscilla, Melanie Star, Richard Grant. Cert. Am. Bd. Med. Psychotherapy, 1986 (fellow). Instr. U. Rochester, 1976-77; rsch. assoc. Nat. Tech. Inst. for Deaf, Rochester, 1977; instr. West Valley Coll., Saratoga, Calif., 1979-80, San Jose (Calif.) City Coll., 1980; psycholinquist UCLA, 1980-81; rsch. assoc. UCLA, 1982-85; psychologist Daniel Freeman Meml. Hosp., Inglewood, Calif., 1981-84, Broderick, Langlois & Assocs., San Gabriel, Calif., 1982-86, Beck Psychiat. Med. Group, Lancaster, Calif., 1984-87, Angeles Counseling Ctr., Arcadia, Calif., 1986—, Assoc. Med. Psychotherapists, Palmdale, Calif., 1988—; cons. LDS Social Svcs. Calif. Agy., 1981—, Antelope Valley Hosp. Med. Ctr., 1984—, Palmdale Hosp. Med. Ctr., 1984—, Treatment Ctrs. of Am. Psychiat. Hosps., 1985—. Scoutmaster, Boy Scouts Am., 1976-79. UCLA Med. Sch. fellow in psychiatry, 1980-81. Mem. Am. Psychol. Assn., Am. Assn. Sex Educators, Counselors and Therapists, Assn. Mormon Counselors and Psychotherapists, Am. Soc. Clin. Hypnosis, Psi Chi. Contbr. articles to profl. jours. Office: 1220 East Ave S Ste A Palmdale CA 93550

ELMER, CARLOS HALL, publisher, photographer; b. Washington, July 22, 1920; s. Charles Percival and Dorothy Winslow (Hall) E.; m. Wilma Virginia Hudson, Jan. 29, 1943; children: Frank Hudson, Elizabeth Anne. BA, UCLA, 1947. Sect. head, asst. div. head, div. head U.S. Naval Ordnance Test Sta. (now U.S. Naval Weapons Ctr.), China Lake, Calif., 1947-57; instrumentation salesman Traid Corp., Encino and Glendale, Calif., 1957-72; instrumentation salesman L-W Internat., Inc., Woodland Hills, and Simi Valley, Calif., 1972—; travel photographer, Kingman, Ariz., China lake, Scottsdale, Ariz., 1940—; owner, mgr. pub. co., Scottsdale and Kingman, 1967—; chmn. 9th Internat. Congress on High-Speed Photography, Denver, 1970. Author: Carlos Elmer's Arizona, 1967, The Glorious Seasons of Arizona, 197l, London Bridge in Pictures, 197l, Arizona in Color, 1973, Mohave County, Arizona, U.S.A., 1974, Grand Canyon Country, 1975, Colorful Northern Arizona, 1977, Hoover Dam, Lake Mead and Lake Mohave, 1978, Laughlin in Color, 1989; contbg. editor Ariz. Hwys. mag., 1984—. Capt. AUS, 1942-46, PTO. Fellow Soc. Motion Picture and TV Engrs., Soc. Photo-Optical Instrumentation Engrs., Am. Soc. Mag. Photographers. Republican. Presbyterian. Office: PO Box 6608 Kingman AZ 86402

ELMORE, KATHLEEN ANN MARIE, food company executive; b. Indpls., Sept. 9, 1952; s. Martin Alfred and Florence Cecilia (Miara) E. BS, Purdue U., 1974; MBA in Mktg., Cen. State U., Okla., 1978. Regional merchandiser Castle & Cooke Foods, Inc., Indpls., 1975, divisional merchandiser, New Orleans, 1975-76, asst. dist. sales mgr., Dallas, 1976, dist. sales mgr., Oklahoma City, 1976-77; mgr. field mktg. projects Pizza Hut div. PepsiCo, Inc., Wichita, Kans., mgr. market rsch., 1978; mgr. sales planning Stokely-Van Camp Inc., Indpls., 1981-83; asst. product mgr. Star-Kist Foods Inc. (named changed to Heinz Pet Products), Long Beach, Calif., 1983-84, product mgr. dog snacks, 1984-89; product mgr. cat food, 1989—. Ind. State scholar, 1970-74, Am. Bus. Women's Assn. scholar, 1971-73; Purdue U. Centennial grantee, 1974. Mem. Assn. MBA Execs. Office: Heniz Pet Products 180 E Ocean Blvd Long Beach CA 90802

ELMS, RICHARD ALDEN, transportation executive; b. Oklahoma City, July 4, 1931; s. William Grady and Merle Helen (Jones) E.; m. Emelita Faraon, June 5, 1986; children: Sander, Alexander. BSEE, U. Okla., 1954; MS, UCLA, 1965. Customer svcs. mgr. Beckman Instruments, Inc., Fullerton, Calif., 1958-67; exec. v.p., pres. Containerfreight Corp., Wilmington, Calif., 1968-86; pres., chief exec. officer Universal Warehouse Co., Carson, Calif., 1987—; pres., chief exec. officer Universal Logistics System, Inc., Carson, 1986—, also bd. dirs.; pres., chief exec. officer ULS Express, Inc., Carson, 1987—, also bd. dirs. Author handbook: Container Freight Station Operation, 1968; contbr. articles to profl. publs. Capt. USMC, 1954-57. Recipient Svc. award Am. 1st Day Cover Soc., 1972, Grand award, 1981, 88. Mem. Calif. Trucking Assn., Collectors Club (N.Y.C.). Democrat. Methodist. Office: Universal Warehouse Co PO Box 4308 Carson CA 90749

ELMSTROM, GEORGE P., optometrist, writer; b. Salem, Mass., Dec. 11, 1925; s. George and Emily Irene (Wedgwood) E.; grad. So. Calif. Coll. Optometry, 1951; m. Nancy DePaul, Apr. 29, 1973; children—Pamela, Beverly, Robert. Pvt. practice optometry, El Segundo, Calif., 1951—; mem. staff So. Calif. Coll. Optometry, 1951—; book cons. Med. Econs. Books, 1970—; instrument and forensic editor Jour. Am. Optical Assn.; comml. airplane and balloon pilot, 1968—. Served with U.S. Army, World War II. Decorated Bronze Star; named Writer of Year, Calif. Optometric Assn., 1957, Man of Year, El Segundo, 1956; recipient spl. citation Nat. Eye Found., 1955. Fellow Am. Acad. Optometry, AAAS, Southwest Contact Lens Soc., Disting. Service Found. of Optometry, Internat. Acad. Preventive Medicine; mem. Am. Optometric Assn., Assn. for Research in Vision, Am. Soc. Ultrasonography, Am. Pub. Health Assn., Optometric Editors Assn., Assn. Research in Vision, Internat. Soc. Ophthalmic Ultrasound, Profl. Airshow Pilots Assn., Flying Optometrists Assn. Am., Beta Sigma Kappa, So. Calif. Coll. Optometry Alumni (pres. 1955-56). Author: Optometric Practice Management, 1963; Legal Aspects of Contact Lens Practice, 1966; Advanced Management for Optometrists, 1974; Modernized Management, 1982; mgmt. editor Optometric Monthly, 1973. Home: 484-B Washington St Monterey CA 93940 Office: Box S-3061 Carmel-by-the-Sea CA 93921

ELROD, JERRY DAVID, clergyman; b. Palestine, Tex., Dec. 31, 1938; s. Joe Regester and Hazel Louise (Fitzgerald) E.; m. Jerry Jo McNeely, Aug. 4, 1963 (div. 1979); 1 child, Joel David; m. Sharon Ann Shaw, Aug. 31, 1975. BA, Southwestern U., 1960; MDiv, So. Meth. U., 1963; DD (hon.), Nebr. Wesleyan U., 1984. Ordained to ministry Meth. Ch., 1963. Assoc. editor Tex. Meth., Dallas, 1960-62; pastor Lake June Meth. Ch., Dallas, 1961-63; exec. dir. United Meth. Ministries, Omaha, 1966-82; dist. supt. Omaha Dist. United Meth. Ch., 1982-85; exec. dir. Tucson Met. Ministry, 1985-88; sr. pastor Desert Skies United Meth. Ch., Tucson, 1988—; cons. nat. div. United Meth. Ch., N.Y.C., 1970-85, Ch. World Svc., N.Y.C., 1975-85; del. South Cen. Jurisdictional Conf., 1972, 80, 84; vice chmn. Conf. Coun. on Ministries Desert SW Conf., 1988—; chmn. Bd. of Communications Desert SW Conf., 1988—. Producer, host TV talk show Point of View, Omaha and Tucson, 1975-82; co-editor Borderline, 1987-89. Bd. dirs. Joint Action in Community Svcs., Washington, 1971—, Nebr. Meth. Hosp., 1982-85. Named Outstanding Citizen City of Omaha, 1976. Democrat. Home: 6573 E Via Cavalier Tucson AZ 85715 Office: Desert Skies United Meth Ch 3255 N Houghton Rd Tucson AZ 85749

EL SAYED, HATEM M., greeting card company executive, artist; b. Cairo, Apr. 10, 1954; came to U.S., 1978; s. Mohamed Mostafa El Sayed and Samira Ragib; m. Iris F. Stallworth, Dec. 8, 1978 (div. Nov. 1980); m. Rosemary Hallacy, Oct. 16, 1982. BS in Engring., Alexandria (Arab Republic Egypt) U., 1974; MFA, Egypt Coll. Fine Arts, Alexandria, 1976; PhD in Visual Arts, Helwan U., Alexandria, 1978. Founder, pres. Arabian Greetings, Ltd., San Francisco, 1980—; design cons. various firms; lectr. in field. Author: Marriage Invitation, 1976, Monk of the Violet, 1977, Posing for Red, 1978, Graphics of Pharaohs, 1979; lithography includes Beardless Jars series; designed scenery and costumes several Cairo theatre prodns.; numerous exhbns. include the Alexandria Mus., 1972, traveling sculpture show Denmark, Sweden, Greece, Fed. Republic Germany, 1973, Kerckhoff Gallery at UCLA, 1979, "Treasures of Tutankhamen", San Francisco, 1979, Involution Gallery, San Francisco, 1979, Maelstrom Gallery, San Francisco, 1980; represented in many pvt. collections. Mem. Am.-Arab Anti-Discrimination Com., Washington, 1987. Served as lt. Egyptian Commando Forces, 1973-74. Recipient Cert. Excellence in the Fine Arts Nat. Com. of the Arts, Cairo, 1977, Gold Medal Salon Annuel, Alexandria, 1977, Cert. Excellence Pres. Anwar Sadat and Presdl. Commn. on the Arts, 1978, Award of Merit Toronto (Ont.) Art Dirs. Club, 1983. Mem. Am.-Egyptian Cooperation Found., Pacific U.S.-Arab C. of C. Inc., Egyptian Culture Club of San Francisco. Republican. Office: Arabian Greetings Ltd 2215-R Market St Ste 112 San Francisco CA 94114

ELSBERRY, SUSAN DAVISE, computer-aided manufacturing engineer; b. Lincoln, Nebr., Oct. 27, 1953; d. Leo Herbert and Genevieve (Richards) Bischof; m. Terence Ray Elsberry, Aug. 9, 1986. BS, Brigham Young U., 1985, postgrad., 1985. CAM engr. Northrop, Hawthorne, Calif., 1986—. Mem. Westec Adv. Com., 1987—. named Whirlpool Corp. fellow, 1984-86. Fellow Inst. for Advancement of Engring.; mem. Soc. Mfg. Engr., Computer and Automated Systems Assn. Republican. Roman Catholic. Home: 1129 W Sepulveda Blvd M102 Torrance CA 90502 Office: Northrop 1 Northrop Ave 5984/AV Hawthorne CA 90250

ELSE, CAROLYN JOAN, library system administrator; b. Mpls., Jan. 31, 1934; d. Elmer Oscar and Irma Carolyn (Seibert) Wahlberg; m. Floyd Warren Else, 1962 (div. 1968); children—Stephen Alexander, Catherine Elizabeth. B.S. Stanford U., 1956; M.L.S., U. Wash., 1957. Cert. profl. librarian, Wash. Librarian Queens Borough Pub. Library, N.Y.C., 1957-59, U.S. Army Special Services, France, Germany, 1959-62; info. librarian Bennett Martin Library, Lincoln, Neb., 1962-63; br. librarian Pierce County Library, Tacoma, Wash., 1963-65, dir., 1965—. Bd. dirs. Campfire, Tacoma, 1984. Mem. South Sound Women's Network (bd. dirs.), Wash. Library Assn. (v.p. 1969-71), Pacific Northwest Library Assn. (sec. 1969-71), ALA. Club: City (Tacoma). Office: Pierce County Rural Library Dist 2356 Tacoma Ave S Tacoma WA 98402 *

ELSER, DAN RAY, financial planner; b. Butte, Mont., June 22, 1953; s. Duane Donald and Edith N.H. (Tam) E.; m. Janet L. Bottom, Dec. 1, 1974; children: Sara E., Katie V., Andrew J., Patrick M. BS, Colo. St. U., 1976. CLU. Mgr. Coll. Life, Bloomington, Ind., 1976-82, Prin. Fin. Group, Bloomington, 1982-86; prin. Fin. Strategies Corp., Bloomington, 1986-88; mgr. No. Colo. Prin. Fin. Group, 1988-89, Prin. Fin. Group, Billings, Mont., 1989—. Bd. dirs. Community Svc. Coun., Bloomington, 1982-85; mem. Young Reps., Bloomington, 1982-86; mission chmn. Evang. Community Ch., Bloomington, Ind., 1985-86; missions com. Faith Evang. Ch., Ft. Collins, Colo., 1987-88. Mem. Nat. Assn. Life Underwriters (Nat. Quality and Sales Achievement award 1980-88, Outstanding Young Man of Am. 1983-85), Ind. State Assn. Life Underwriters (Bloomington chpt. bd. dirs. 1980-84, state bd. dirs. 1985-86), Internat. Assn. Fin. Planning, Nat. Assn. Security Dealers (registered rep.), So. Ind. Estate Planning Forum, Million Dollar Round Table, Bloomington C. of C. (chmn. leadership Bloomington 1982-86), Ft. Collins C. of C. (bus., excellence com.), No. Rocky Mountain Chpt. CLU (sec., treas. 1988, bd. dirs. ChFC 1988), Bloomington Jaycees (pres. 1982-86), ECC Club (misson chmn. 1985-86). Republican. Office: Prin Fin Group 2720 3rd Ave N Ste 200 Billings MT 59101

ELSNER, ROBERT HOLMES, medical association administrator; b. Orange, Calif., June 2, 1933; s. Ernest Edgar Elsner and Geneva Florence (Holmes) Van Zant; m. Nancy Lee Robison, June 14, 1958; 1 child, Alison. AB in Journalism, U. So. Calif., 1955. Staff Daily News Tribune, Fullerton, Calif., 1955-56; northwest mgr. Allen's Press Clipping Bureau, San Francisco and Portland (Oreg.), 1957-60; pub. relations account exec. Pacific Nat. Advt. Agy., Portland, 1960-61; pub. relations dir. Assoc. Oreg. Industries, Portland, 1961-63; exec. dir. Multhomah County Med. Soc., Portland, 1963-77; exec. v.p., chief exec. officer Los Angeles County Med. Assn., 1977-85; chief exec. officer Calif. Med. Assn., San Francisco, 1985—; pres. Northwest Oreg. Health systems, 1976-77; mem. Nat. Council on Health Planning and Resource Devel., Washington, 1976-77. Bd. dirs. Calif. Med. Polit. Action Com., San Francisco, 1979-85; pres. Oregon Rep. Club, 1964, sustaining mem. Rep. Nat. Com., 1975—. Served with USN, 1956-57. Mem. AMA (adv. com. to exec. v.p. 1974-82), Am. Assn. Med. Soc. Execs. (pres. 1975-76), Calif. Med. Execs. Conf. (chmn. 1983-84), Nat. Council Against Health Fraud, Los Angeles County Med. Assn. (hon.), Multhomah County Med. Soc. (hon.), Am. Soc. Assn. Execs. (bd. dirs. 1986-88, vice chmn. 1988-89), Profl. Conv. Mgmt. Assn. (bd. dirs. 1986—), Soc. Profl. Journalists, Portland C. of C. (forum chmn. 1972-73), Delta Tau Delta. Clubs: Portland Pub. Relations Roundtable (pres. 1968), Cardinal and Gold. Home: 105 Golden Gate Ave Belvedere CA 94920 Office: Calif Med Assn 221 Main St 2d Fl PO Box 7690 San Francisco CA 94120

ELSOM, CLINT GARY, credit union executive; b. Spokane, Wash., May 7, 1946; s. Joseph Logan and Louise Catherine (Worster) E.; m. Teresa Ellen Coe, Sept. 2, 1967; children: Tonya, Travis. AA in Data Processing, Seattle Community Coll., 1971; BA in Bus., U. Wash., 1973. Mgmt. trainee Sears Roebuck & Co., Seattle, 1967-68; data processing clk. King County, Seattle, 1969-70, EDP coordinator, 1970-71, programmer analyst, 1972-73, asst. supr. data processing, 1974-75, mgr. elections, 1976-80; pres., chief exec. officer King County Credit Union, Seattle, 1981—; mem. bd. Fed. Election Com., Washington, D.C., 1977-80. Northwest chmn. Nat. Inhancement-Citi Corp., San Diego, 1983—. Served with USN, 1964-66. Recipient Disting. Svc. award Fed. Election Com., 1978. Mem. Wash. Share Guarantee Assn. (bd. dirs. 1984—, v.p.), Wash. Assn. County Ofcls. (pres. 1977-80, Disting. Svc. award 1980). Republican. Christian Scientist. Office: King County Credit Union 2265 1st Ave S Seattle WA 98134

ELSTNER, RICHARD CHESNEY, structural engineer; b. Pitts., Jan. 23, 1924; s. Richard Alfred and Marguerite (Chesney) E.; m. Elizabeth Ann Smith, Sept. 19, 1947; children—Richard Graham, Dwight Smith, Charles William. B.S. in Civil Engring., Rose Poly. Inst., 1947; M.S. in Theoretical and Applied Mechanics, U. Ill., 1953. Registered profl. engr., Ill., Iowa, Ind., Miss., Calif., Hawaii, Wash. Instr. Rose Poly., Terre Haute, Ind., 1947-48, U. Hawaii, Honolulu, 1948-50; research assoc. U. Ill., Urbana, 1950-53; devel. engr. Portland Cement Assn., Skokie, Ill., 1953-59; prin. Wiss, Janney, Elstner, Northbrook, Ill., 1960-78, br. mgr., Honolulu, 1979—, Bd. dirs. Insulating Glass Certification Council, Chgo., 1975—. Served with U.S. Army, 1943-46; PTO. Fellow Am. Concrete Inst. (bd. dirs., Wason medal 1955); mem. ASCE (sect. pres. 1983), Cons. Engrs. Council Hawaii, Structural Engrs. Assn. Hawaii, Structural Engrs. Assn. Ill. (life). Office: Wiss Janney Elstner Assocs 1210 Auahi St Suite 108 Honolulu HI 96814 *

ELSTON, LESTER CHARLES, aerospace executive; b. Flint, Mich., Sept. 22, 1929; s. Alfred Samuel and Elizabeth Catherine (Nankervis) E.; m. Marilyn Joyce Anderson, July 12, 1952; children: David, Arthur, Nancy, Karen. Student, U. Mich., Flint, 1947-48, So. Ill. U., 1948-49; profl. cert., Ariz. State U., 1972, degree in mgmt., 1976. Cert. profl. contract mgr. Design engr. Bendix Aviation, South Bend, Ind., 1949-55; sr. design engr. Electric Boat div. Gen. Dynamics, Groton, Conn., 1955-59; sr. devel. engr. AiResearch Mfg. Co. of Ariz., Phoenix, 1959-68; mgr. of contracts Garrett Turbine Engine co., Phoenix, 1968-88; dir. contracts and quotations Allied Signal Aerospace Co., Phoenix, 1988—. Cpl. U.S. Army, 1951-53. Mem. Machinery and Allied Products Inst., Nat. Contract Mgmt. Assn., Masons, Vasa (master Ariz. dist. 1988—). Republican. Lutheran. Home: 7423 N 62d St Paradise Valley AZ 85253 Office: Garrett Aux Power Div 2739 E Washington St Phoenix AZ 85010

ELVERUM, GERARD WILLIAM, JR., electronic and diversified company executive; b. Mpls., Sept. 29, 1927; m. Mary Jean Proverbs, Dec. 28, 1948. Student, U. Nebr., 1945, S.D. State U., 1945; B in Physics, U. Minn., 1949. Engr. Jet Propulsion Lab., Pasadena, Calif., 1949-59; sect. head, mgr. dept. Space Tech. Lab., El Segundo, Calif., 1959-62; dir. lab. Systems Group TRW, Redondo Beach, Calif., 1963-66, mgr. ops. Def. and Space Systems Group, 1969-81, v.p., gen. mgr. Applied Tech. Div./Space and Tech. Group, 1981—; mem. adv. panel NASA/Aerospace Safety Bd., Washington, 1982—. Contbr. articles to profl. jours.; patentee in field. Served with USAF, 1944-46. Recipient Spl. Achievement award ASME, 1971; named Outstanding Engr. Inst. Advancement Engring., 1972. Fellow AIAA (James H. Wyld Propulsion award 1973); mem. Am. Def. Preparedness Assn., Nat. Acad. Engring. Office: TRW ATD/STG Bldg R 1 Space Pk Rm 2094 Redondo Beach CA 90278

ELVIN, DENNIS CHARLES, military officer; b. Elgin, Ill., Mar. 16, 1949; s. LeRoy Charles and Janet Marion (Marsh) E.; m. Becky Ellen Jensen, June 7, 1969; 1 child, Heather Lynn. AS, Southern Ill. U., 1974; BA, Sangamon State U., 1977; postgrad., Oreg. State U., 1987. Lic. pvt. pilot and aircraft mechanic. Aircraft mechanic Ill. Air Nat. Guard, Springfield, 1974-77; mgr. major maintenance Republic Airlines, Mpls., 1977-85; aircraft maintenance staff officer Oreg. Nat. Guard, Klamath Falls, 1985--; aircraft maintenance conversion officer 114 Tactical Fighter Tng. Squadron, Kingsley Field, Oreg., 1987--; staff advisor 114 Tactical Fighter Tng. Squadron, 1985--. Chmn. Sacred Heart Auction, Klamath Falls, 1986; sponsor Boy Scouts Am., Kingsley Field, 1987; safety chmn. Internat. Assn. Machinists, Mpls., 1982-83. Served as NCO USAF, 1968-72. Recipient Spl. Achievement Commendation, Adj. Gen. State of Ill., 1977, Air Force Commendation medal, 1987. Mem. Air Force Assn., Nat. Guard Assn. of the U.S., AMVETS. Methodist. Office: 114 TFTS/MAX Kingsley Field Klamath Falls OR 97603

ELWAY, JOHN ALBERT, professional football player; b. Port Angeles, Wash., June 28, 1960; s. Jack Elway; m. Janet Elway; 2 daughters: Jessica Gwen, Jordan Marie. BA in Econs., Stanford U., 1983. Quarterback, Denver Broncos, 1983—. Mem. Mayor's Council on Phys. Fitness, City of Denver; chmn. Rocky Mountain region Nat. Kidney Found. Played in NFL Pro Bowl, 1987, Super Bowl XXII, 1988. Office: Denver Broncos 5700 Logan St Denver CO 80216 *

ELWIN, ALICIA ANDUZE, teacher; b. St. Thomas, U.S. V.I., July 27, 1940; d. Aubrey Alfred and Arminthia (Lee) Anduze; m. Bernard David Elwin, Sept. 3, 1970; children: Bernadette, Jeanine. BA, Interam. U., P.R., 1962; postgrad., U. Calif., Riverside. Sec. Internat. Orgn., Leiden, Netherlands, 1964-67; social worker Govt. of V.I., Christiansted, St. Croix, 1967-68; tchr. Govt. of V.I., 1968-70, St. Dunstan's Episc. Sch., 1970-71, 83-84, Emakaala Sch., Hilo, Hawaii, 1976-78; sec. U. Calif., Berkeley, 1980-83; teaching asst. U. Calif., Riverside, 1986-89. Mem. AAUW, Am. Council on Teaching Fgn. Lang., Am. Assn. Tchrs. Spanish and Portuguese, Lambda Iota Tau, Sigma Delta Pi, Newcomers Club. Democrat. Episcopalian. Home: 8110 Orchard St Alta Loma CA 91701

ELY, BETTY JO, school system administrator, educational consultant; b. Oakland, Calif., June 28, 1947; d. Levi and Betty (Turner) E.; m. Joseph Dettling, July 15, 1967 (div.); 1 child, Aiyana A. BA, San Diego State U., 1969; postgrad., U. Calif.-San Diego, La Jolla, 1971-74, U. Hawaii, 1973; MA in Psychology, Coll. Devel. Studies, L.A., 1989; postgrad., Cambridge U., England, 1989—. Cert. tchr., learning handicapped tchr., spl. edn. tchr., Calif. Tchr. Carlsbad (Calif.) Unified Sch. Dist., 1970-74; spl. edn. tchr. Teton County Sch. Dist. 1, Jackson, Wyo., 1975-76; resource specialist The Learning Ctr., Jackson, 1977-78; dir. Carlsbad Montessori Sch., 1979-81; learning handicapped specialist Del Amo Hosp., Torrance, Calif., 1982-87; owner, dir. Ely Edn., San Pedro, Calif., 1983—; resource specialist Torrance Unified Sch. Dist., 1987—; speaker, cons. in field; instr. U. Wyo., Laramie, 1978, Loyola Marymount U., L.A., 1985. Author: Interface, 1987; interviewee TV, radio and profl. publs. Democrat. Office: Ely Edn 322 Miraleste Dr Suite 179 San Pedro CA 90732

ELY, JACK BROWN, freelance rock musician; b. Portland, Oreg., Sept. 11, 1943; s. Kenneth Ely and Helen Cherie (Brown) Nelson, stepfather: Robley W. Nelson; divorced; children: Robert Sterling, Sean Nelson; m. Dawn D. Ely. Lead singer The Kingsmen, Portland, 1957-63. Singer popular song "Louie Louie". Home and Office: RR 7 20220 Nichols Market Rd Bend OR 97701

ELY, MARICA MCCANN, interior designer; b. Pachuca, Mex., May 2, 1907 (parents Am. citizens); d. Warner and Mary Evans (Cook) McCann; m. Northcutt Ely, Dec. 2, 1931; children—Michael and Craig (twins), Parry Haines. B.A., U. Calif.-Berkeley, 1929; diploma Pratt Inst. of Art, N.Y.C., 1931. Free-lance interior designer, Washington and Redlands, Calif., 1931—; lectr. on flower arranging and fgn. travel, 1931—; prof. Sogetsu Ikebana Sch., Tokyo, 1972. Art editor (calendar) Nat. Capital Garden Club League, 1957-58. Pres. Kenwood Garden Club, Md.; bd. dirs. Nat. Library Blind, Washington; v.p. bd. dirs. Washington Hearing and Speech Soc., 1969; cofounder Delta Gamma Found. Pre-Sch. Blind Children, Washington. Finalist Nat. Silver Bowl Competition, Jackson-Perkins Co., 1966; garden shown on nat. tour Am. Hort. Soc., 1985. Mem. Calif. Arboretum Found., Redlands Hort. and Improvement Soc. (bd. dirs. 1982—), Yucaipa Valley Garden Club, Town and Country African Violet Soc., Redlands Country Club, Washington Club, Chevy Chase Club, Berkeley Tennis Club, Order of Delta Gamma Rose.

ELY, PAUL C., JR., electronics company executive; b. McKeesport, Pa., Feb. 18, 1932; s. Paul C. and Jean C. E.; m. Barbara Sheiry, Apr. 3, 1953; children: Paul C., Glenn E. B.S. in Engring. Physics, Lehigh U., 1953; M.S. in Elec. Engring, Stanford U., 1964. Research and devel. engr. Sperry Rand Corp., Great Neck, N.Y. and Clearwater, Fla., 1953-62; research and devel. sect. mgr., engring. mgr. microwave div. Hewlett-Packard Co., Palo Alto, Calif., 1962-73; gen. mgr. data systems div. Hewlett-Packard Co., 1973-74, gen. mgr. computer group, 1974-76, v.p., 1976-80, exec. v.p., 1980-85, also bd. dirs.; chmn., chief exec. officer Convergent Technologies (name now Unisys Convergent), San Jose, Calif., from 1985; now also exec. v.p. Unisys Corp., San Jose. Chmn. Cupertino United Fund, 1976, Bay Area Sci. Fair, 1969; regent U. Santa Clara; mem. Calif. Econ. Devel. Commn., 1976. Mem. IEEE, Am. Electronics Assn. (bd. dirs., exec. com. 1985—). Office: Unisys Convergent PO Box 6685 San Jose CA 95150 *

ELY, ROBERT THOMAS, manufacturing company executive; b. Joplin, Mo., Apr. 5, 1946; s. Joseph Connolly and Ava Trois (Edmundson) E.; m. Linda Jean Jacobs, June 6, 1970. BS, U. Mont., 1969. Quality assurance specialist U.S. Army, Seneca Falls, N.Y., 1976-79; quality engr. Gen. Instrument Co., Port Falls, Idaho, 1979-81; prodn. control mgr. Advanced Input Devices, Coeur d'Alene, Idaho, 1981-87; agt. Allstate Ins. Co., Post Falls, Idaho, 1987-88; quality engr. Boroloy Industries, Post Falls, 1988; ops. mgr. Deming Industriess, Coeur d'Alene, 1988--. Chmn. bd. trustees N. Idaho Coll., Coeur d'Alene, 1982-88, pres. Booster Club, 1986-88; vol. Juvenile Diversion Project, Coeur d'Alene, 1983-86. Mem. Am. Mensa, Sigma Phi Epsilon. Home: 3315 S Vista Rd Coeur d'Alene ID 83814 Office: Deming Industries 2945 Government Way Coeur d'Alene ID 83814

EMAL, JANET ANN, home economist; b. Spokane, Wash., May 3, 1944; d. John Michael and Mary Louise (Black) Kilzer; m. Christopher Renton Oberg, Aug. 12, 1967 (div. Dec. 1979); children: Michael, Gretchen; m. Ronald Leroy Emal, May 10, 1980. BA in Home Econs., Sacramento State U., 1967. Dir. Children's Day Care Ctr., Poway, Calif., 1971-72; instr. Maricopa County Community Coll., Phoenix, 1977-86; owner, coordinator Easy Elegance Microwave Cooking Schs., Phoenix, 1979—; spokesperson Pillsbury Co., various locations, 1986-88; speaker Phi U Home Econ. Hon. Soc., Phoenix, 1987—. Author: Kids Cook Microwave, 1983, Light and Healthy Microwave Cooking, 1986; publisher (quarterly newsletter) Sun Waves, 1983—. Mem. Women in Food and Wine. Republican. Roman Catholic. Home and Office: 6138 N 8th Ave Phoenix AZ 85013

EMAMJOMEH, ALI, mechanical engineer; b. Tehran, Iran, Oct. 16, 1960; came to U.S., 1977; s. Jalal and Khadijeh (Jazayeri) E.; m. Elizabeth Camarena, June 1, 1983. BSME, Calif. State U., Fresno, 1983; MS, Santa Clara U., 1988. Sect. head Nat. Semiconductor Corp., Santa Clara, Calif., 1983-88; engring. mgr. NARA Technologies, Santa Clara, 1988—. patentee in field. Mem. ASME, ASCE, Am. Soc. Testing and Materials, Am. Soc. Metals (assoc.). Home: 1436 Carnot Dr San Jose CA 95126 Office: Nara Techs 3333 Octavius Dr Santa Clara CA 95054

EMBRY, DIANNE C., psychologist; b. Portland, Maine, Apr. 22, 1932; d. Daniel Wheeler and Dorella Marie (Viel) Nudd; m. Richard E. Pierce, Nov. 30, 1950 (div. 1958); children: Richard, Patricia Pearce Wilder (dec.), Pamela Pearce Miller, Linda M. Pearce Prestley; m. Jay Creston Embry, June 17, 1959; children: Joel Patrick, Barbara Leigh, Susan Ellen; stepchild, Stephen C. BA in Psychology, Conn. Coll., 1977; EdM, Harvard U., 1978; PhD in Psychology, U.S. Internat. U., 1983. Lic. psychologist, Wis. Postdoctorate fellow Tex. A&M U., College Station, 1984; counselor U.S. Naval Base, New London, Conn., 1973, Norwich (Conn.) State Hosp., 1974; psychotherapist, counselor Tex. A&M U., 1984; lectr. Nat. U., San Diego, 1985; clin. coordinator, postdoctoral fellow Camarillo (Calif.) State Hosp., 1987; staff psychologist Calif. Instn. for Men, Chino, 1987-89. Dir. dist. campaign State Rep. Conn., Groton, 1972-74; mem. Charter Revision Commn., Groton, 1974-76; mem. Groton Govtl. Study Commn., 1975; vol. therapist Conn. Valley Hosp., Middleton, 1972. Mem. Tex. Psychol. Assn., Ventura County Psychol. Assn., Am. Psychol. Assn., Phi Delta Kappa, Psi Chi. Democrat. Roman Catholic.

EMERINE, STEPHEN EDWARD, communications executive; b. Scottsbluff, Nebr., May 4, 1935; s. Edward and Mary Lou (Stephenson) E.; m. Carolyn Ruth Swaim, July 11,1959. BA, U. Idaho, 1956; postgrad., U. Ariz., 1973. Reporter, editor Twin Falls Times-News, Idaho, 1956-57; info. officer USAF, Little Rock, 1957-60; reporter, editor Tucson Daily Citizen, 1960-67; asst. prof. journalism Univ. Ariz., 1967-70; pres., editor, pub. The Green Valley News, Ariz., 1967-71; pres. Steve Emerine & Assocs., Tucson, 1971-73; county assessor Pima County, Tucson, 1973-80; editor, columnist The Ariz. Daily Star, Tucson, 1980-87; asst. dir. for. publs. The U. Ariz., 1987—. Co-Author, Editor: Book, Jack Sheaffer's Tucson, 1985; Editor: Mag. The U. Ariz. Report on Research 1987— (awarded 2 Nat. Sch. Pub. Relations Assn.). Vice chmn. Tucson Commn. Human Rels., 1968-71; bd. dirs. Ariz. Families Children, Tucson, 1986—, Tucson Jazz Soc. Named Newspaper Reporter of the Year Tucson Press Club 1967. Mem. Soc. Profl. Journalists, Tucson Press Club (Pres. 1965). Democrat. Home: 2741 S Gwain Pl Tucson AZ 85713 Office: U Ariz Office Pub Info Tucson AZ 85721

EMERSON, ADELE GILLETTE, catering company owner; b. Detroit, Sept. 8, 1928; d. John Dudley and Agnes (Gibson) Gillette; m. John C. Emerson, June 12, 1950 (div. 1973); children: Sara, Lisa, Nina, John, Matthew. BA, Rockford (Ill.) Coll., 1950. Owner Nutcracker Sweet Co., Inc., Lakewood, Colo., 1968—. Mem. Nat. Caterers Roundtable, Am. Inst. Wine and Food, Rotary. Office: Nutcracker Sweet Co Inc 2484 Kipling St Lakewood CO 80215

EMERSON, ALTON CALVIN, physical therapist; b. Webster, N.Y., Sept. 29, 1934; s. Homer Douglas and Pluma (Babcock) E.; m. Nancy Ann Poarch, Dec. 20, 1955 (div. 1972); children: Marcia Ann, Mark Alton; m. Barbara Irene Stewart, Oct. 6, 1972. BS in Vertibrate Zoology, U. Utah, 1957; cert. phys. therapy, U. So. Calif., 1959. Staff phys. therapist Los Angeles County Crippled Children's Services, 1958-65; pvt. practice phys. therapy Los Angeles, 1966—; cons. City of Hope, Duarte, Calif., 1962-72; trustee Wolcott Found. Inc., St. Louis, 1972-86, chmn. bd. trustees, 1980-85. Recipient Cert. of Achievement, George Washington U., Washington, 1986. Mem. Temple City High Twelve Club (pres. 1971), Calif. Assn. High Twelve Clubs (pres. 1986), Aston Martin Owners Club, Milestone Car Soc. Lodges: Masons (master Camellia 1973, v.p. High Twelve Internat. Pasadena Scottish Rite Bodics), Royal Order Scotland, Al Malaikah Temple, Ancient Arabic Order Nobles Mystic Shrine. Home and Office: 287 W Ave de Las Flores Thousand Oaks CA 91360

EMERSON, BEVERLY MARIE, molecular biologist; b. Eugene, Oreg., Jan. 18, 1952; d. James Homer and Marie (Farley) E. BA, U. Calif., San Diego, 1975; PhD, Wash. U., St. Louis, 1981. Staff fellow NIH, Bethesda, Md., 1981-86; asst. prof. Salk Inst. for Biol. Studies, La Jolla, Calif., 1986—. Contbr. articles to profl. jours. Grantee HHS, 1987, Mathers Found., 1988; PEW Scholar, 1988. Democrat. Office: The Salk Inst 10010 N Torrey Pines Rd La Jolla CA 92037

EMERY, ALYSON DEAN, dentist; b. Santa Ana, Calif., Sept. 15, 1960; d. Dean Jr. and Jacquelyn Mae (Duffy) Edgerton; m. Douglas Vernon Emery, June 26, 1983. BS in Psychobiology, UCLA, 1982; DDS, U. Pacific, 1985. Gen. practice dentistry Long Beach, Calif., 1985--. V.p. Long Beach Women's Council, 1987--. Mem. ADA, Calif. Dental Assn., Harbor Dental Soc. (mktg. chmn. 1987-88, bd. dirs. 1988, Outstanding New Mem. Award 1987), Am. Assn. Women Dentists, Long Beach Area C. of C. (Ann Small Bus. award 1988, Bus. Person of Month award 1988), Leads Unltd. (pres. 1987--). Republican. Office: 3318 E Anaheim St Long Beach CA 90804

EMERY, CHARLES CHRISTIAN, JR., health care and information systems executive; b. Pitts., Oct. 11, 1946; s. Charles C. and Gloria V. (Nutridge) E.; m. Marcia A. Balestrino, May 7, 1988; children: Charles C. III, Sandra J. BSME in Aero. Engring., U. Pitts., 1968, MS, 1972, MBA, 1982. Engr. AVCO Lycoming, Bridgeport, Conn., 1968-69, Westinghouse Co., Pitts., 1969-71; systems mgr. U. Pitts., 1971-72; v.p. hosp. info. systems Monsour Hosp. and Clinic, Jeannette, Pa., 1972-73; assoc. exec. dir., chief fin. officer St. Elizabeth Hosp. Med. Ctr., Youngstown, Ohio, 1973-85; v.p. info. svcs. Samaritan Health Svc., Phoenix, 1985--. Bd. dirs. Yw-YMCA, Phoenix, 1987. Mem. Am. Coll. Healthcare Execs., Healthcare Fin. Mgmt. Assn. (adv. mem.), Moon Valley Country Club. Methodist. Office: Samaritan Health Svc 1441 N 12th St Phoenix AZ 85006

EMERY, DOUGLAS VERNON, dentist; b. Conrad, Mont., June 15, 1960; s. Edward W. and Genevieve M. (Stucky) E.; m. Alyson D. Edgerton, June 26, 1983. BA in Biology, Carroll Coll., Helena, Mont., 1982; DDS, U. Pacific, 1985. Gen. practice dentistry Drs. Douglas and Alyson Emery, DDS, Long Beach, Calif., 1985—. Mem. ADA, Calif. Dental Assn., Harbor Dental Soc. (chair profl. relations 1988—, mktg. com. 1986-87), Tau Kappa Omega. Republican. Presbyterian. Club: Le Tip of Seal Beach (Calif.). Lodge: Elks. Office: 3318 E Anaheim St Long Beach CA 90804

EMERY, EDWARD J., JR., banker; b. Bklyn., Jan. 11, 1944; s. Edward J. and Mary (Galazka) E.; m. Marriann Kelty, Mar. 12, 1966; children: Karen, Edward, Matthew, Christopher. BA, St. Joseph Coll., Rensselaer, Ind., 1966; postgrad., NYU, 1967-68. Asst. mgr. Chem. Bank, N.Y.C., 1967-72; asst. v.p. Nat. Westminster, Brentwood, N.Y., 1972-77; v.p. Ariz. Bank, Phoenix, 1977-84; group v.p. Citibank Ariz., Phoenix, 1984—. Community chmn. Boy Scouts Am., Port Jefferson, N.Y., 1977; bd. dirs. Suffolk City (N.Y.) Girl Scouts U.S.A., Hauppauge, 1977. Named one of Outstanding Young Men of Am. U.S. Jaycees, 1977. Mem. Ariz. Mortgage Bankers (edn. com. 1987-88), Robert Morris Assn., Ariz. Bankers Assn. Club: Mansion (Phoenix). Office: Citibank Ariz 4041 N Central Ave Phoenix AZ 85012

EMERY, HENRY ALFRED, engineer; b. Northfield, N.H., Feb. 9, 1926; s. Henry A. and Ruth (Trask) E.; B.A., U. Maine, 1950; M.B.A., U. Denver, 1966; Petroleum Engr., Colo. Sch. Mines, 1956; m. Barbara Sadwith, June 10, 1971; children—Trask, Timothy, Ptarmigan. With Mobil Pipeline Co., 1950-53, Portland Montreal Pipeline Co., 1956-59; maintenance design engr., planning supr., engring. supt., project mgr. Pub. Service Co. Colo., 1959-72; pres. Computer Graphics Co., Denver, 1972-78; div. mgr. Kellogg Corp., Littleton, Colo., 1978-82; chmn., chief exec. officer Emery DataGraphic Inc., 1982-86; chmn., chief exec. officer Emery DataGraphic II Inc., Englewood, 1986-87; pres. Emery DataGraphic div. Harris-McBurney Co., 1987—. Registered profl. engr., Colo. Mem. Assn. Systems Mgmt., Rocky Mountain Ski Instrs. Assn., Profl. Ski Instrs. Am., Tau Beta Pi. Democrat. Home: 5680 S Big Canyon Dr Englewood CO 80111 Office: 6767 S Spruce Ste #140 Englewood CO 80112

EMERY, VINCE, advertising writer and designer, record producer; b. Mpls., Oct. 29, 1951. BA in English, Ariz. State U. Advt. dir. Harkins Amusement Enterprises, Scottsdale, Ariz., 1972-75; mng. editor CableVision Guide, San Francisco, 1976; west coast creative dir. World Wide Advt. and J. Walter Thompson, Los Angeles, 1978-80; dir. advt. and publicity Jerry Gross Orgn., Inc., Los Angeles, 1980-81; advt. dir. PBL Assocs., Point Richmond, Calif., 1983—; pres. Vince Emery Prodns., San Francisco, 1985—; editorial cons. Magical Bend mag., San Francisco, 1982-84; guest lectr. Film Arts Found., San Francisco, 1982, Media Alliance, San Francisco, 1983; bd. dirs. SPAVCO, Inc., Richmond, Calif. Author: (books) The Linnington Building, 1971, Selling Movies, 1978, Guide to Non-Stop Fun at Walt Disney World, 1984; producer record albums The Boogeyman, 1980, Star Trek Comedy-The Unofficial Album, 1986, Jim Samuels: Dean of Comedy, 1988, The Funniest Computer Songs, 1989. Recipient Best Poster award Creative Concepts, 1979-80, Best Mag. Campaign award Creative Concepts, 1980. Mem. Nat. Assn. of Ind. Record Distbrs., Film Arts Found., Internat. Tandem Users Group. Office: Vince Emery Prodns PO Box 460279 San Francisco CA 94146

EMETERIO, THOMAS MILFORD, dentist; b. Brea, Calif., Nov. 2, 1958; s. Frank and Sally (Chapman) E. BS, U. So. Calif., 1981; DDS, Georgetown U., 1986. Gen. practice dentistry Western Dental Ctr., Santa Ana, Calif., 1986—. Republican. Episcopalian. Home: 120 St Crispen Ave Brea CA 92621

EMISON, SIDNEY THARP, insurance company executive; b. Burbank, Calif., July 30, 1931; s. Harold Rice and Velva Marie (Chamberlain) E.; m. Joyce Elaine Kahn, Jan. 26, 1952; children: Sharon, Susan, Lori, Todd. Student, Coll. of Marin, 1950-52; BA, San Francisco State U., 1952-54. V.p. Calif. Casualty Group, San Mateo, Calif., 1957—. Pres., San Mateo County Safety Coun., 1976-77; comdr., U.S. Power and Sail Squadron, Marin County, 1983-84; chmn. bd. dirs. San Francisco/San Mateo Counties Safety Coun., Foster City, 1986-89; bd. dirs. Nat. Safety Coun., Chgo., 1986—. Capt. USAF, 1954-57. Mem. Profl. Photographers Am., Loch Lomand Yacht Club. Republican. Presbyterian. Home: 16 Montevideo Way San Rafael CA 94903 Office: Calif Casualty Group PO Box M San Mateo CA 94402

EMMEL, EDWARD, aviation and transportation consultant; b. Washington, Aug. 22, 1948; s. Francis and Clara Mae (Bowman) E.; m. Leigh Whitten, Feb. 15,1969 (div. 1985); 1 child, Heather Leigh. MBA, NYU, 1968. V.p. sales Pepsico Mgmt. Systems, Purchase, N.Y., 1970-75; pres. Corp. Svcs. Internat., San Francisco, 1976—; mem. adv. bd., U.S. Dept. Transp., 1988; mem. Pres.'s Commn. Transp. Devel. Contbr. articles to various profl. and gen. interest publs. Recipient Presdl. Humanitarian award for contbns. to aviation industry, 1988. Mem. Am. Soc. Travel Agts., World Aviation Coun. Office: Corp Svcs Internat 1199 Broadway Burlingame CA 94010

EMMELUTH, BRUCE PALMER, investment banker; venture capitalist; b. Los Angeles, Nov. 30, 1940; s. William J. and Elizabeth L. (Palmer) E.; children: William J. II (dec.), Bruce Palmer Jr., Carrie E.; m. Canda E. Samuels, Mar. 29, 1987. Sr. investment analyst, corp. fin. dept. Prudential Ins. Co. Am., Los Angeles, 1965-70; with Seidler, Amdec Securities, Inc., Los Angeles, 1970—, sr. v.p., mgr. corp. fin. dept., 1976—, bd. dirs., 1974—; pres., bd. dirs. SAS Captial Corp., Venture capital subs. Seidler Amdec Securities; bd. dirs. Denar Corp.; allied mem. N.Y. Stock Exchange, Inc. Past. bd. dirs. UCLA Grad. Sch. Mgmt. Served with Army NG, 1965-71. Mem. Assn. for Corp. Growth (pres. Los Angeles chpt. 1979-80), Beta Gamma Sigma. Republican. Presbyterian. Club: Jonathan. Home: 17146 Palisades Circle Pacific Palisades CA 90272 Office: Seidler Amdec Securities Inc 515 S Figueroa St Los Angeles CA 90071

EMMET, THOMAS ADDIS, JR., college administrator, consultant; b. Detroit, July 26, 1930; s. Thomas Addis and Leona Margaret (Schneider) E.; m. Anne Marie Baker, Mar. 3, 1972; children: Lynn, Anthony, William Novitsky. PhB, U. Detroit, 1952, ME, 1954; EdS, EdD, U. Mich., 1963. Asst. dean U. Detroit, 1953-57, dean men, 1957-64, dean evening coll. arts and scis., 1964-66, asst. prof. higher edn., 1964-67; asst. exec. v.p. Marquette U., 1966-67, adj. prof. higher edn. Wayne State U., Detroit, 1968-70; spl. asst. to pres., prof. edn. Regis Coll., Denver, 1972—; pres. higher edn. exec. assocs., 1967-72, 84-86; chmn. bd. Higher Edn. Group, 1986—; pres. Thomas A. Emmet & Assos., 1972-84. Cons. collective negotiations in higher edn. Edn. Commn. of States, 1971—; cons. higher edn. Opinion Research Corp.; dir. leadership seminars, sr. adviser Am. Council on Edn., 1979-85. Staff dir. Mich. State Senate Student Unrest Com., 1968-69; exec. sec. Conf. Jesuit Student Personnel Adminstrs., 1956-64; sec. Council Student Personnel Assns. in Higher Edn., 1966-69. Recipient Bernard Webster Reed award, 1963, John P. McNichols award U. Detroit, 1986. Mem. Adult Student Personnel Assn. (v.p. 1961-64), Nat. Assn. Student Personnel Adminstrs. (editor Jour. 1962-63), Phi Kappa Phi, Alpha Sigma Nu, Alpha Sigma Lambda, Phi Delta Kappa, Phi Eta Sigma. Editor: The Academic Department and Division Chairman, 1972; Collective Bargaining in Postsecondary Institutions: The Impact on the Campus and the State, 1974; asso. editor Coll. and Univ. Bus., 1969-71; pub. The Department Advisor, 1985—. Home: 14687 Madison Brighton CO 80601 Office: Regis Coll 50th St and Lowell Blvd Denver CO 80221

EMMONS, CHARLES EDWARD, retired foreign service officer, travel agency owner; b. Downey, Calif., Dec. 27, 1935; s. Lawrence Edward Emmons and Hester Luvena (Partain) Sonne; m. Carol Ann Bottarini; children: Mark Edward, Jessica Ann. AA, Coll. Marin, 1959; Cert., U. Mainz, Germersheim, Ger., 1960; BA in World Bus., San Francisco State U., 1964; MS in Polit. Sci., MIT, 1972. Asst. controller Rietz Mfg. Co., Santa Rosa, Calif., 1962-64; chmn. liaison Spl. Projects Office, USN, Washington, 1964-66; 3d sec., vice counsel Am. Embassy, Bogota, Columbia, 1966-69; 2d sec. Am. Embassy, Bujumbra, 1969-71; chief manpower planning div. Dept. State, Washington, 1972-74; counselor U.S. Embassy, Abidjan, Ivory Coast, 1974-75, Buenos Aires, 1975-78, Warsaw, Poland, 1978-81; minister counselor U.S. Embassy, Paris, 1981-85; owner, prin. travel agy. San Rafael, Calif., 1986-87; ret. With U.S. Army, 1954-57. Mem. Airplane Owners and Pilots Assn., World Affairs Council N. Calif., Lions. Home: 100 Surrey Ln San Rafael CA 94903

EMMONS, ROBERT JOHN, corporate executive; b. Trenton, N.J., Sept. 18, 1934; s. Charles John and Ruth Marie (Heilhecker) E.; m. Christine Young Bebb, July 13, 1980; children: Bradley Thomas, Cathy Lynne, Christopher Robert. A.B. in Econs, U. Mich., 1956, M.B.A., 1960, J.D., 1964. V.p. Baskin-Robbins Co., Burbank, Calif., 1964-68; pres. United Rent-All, Los Angeles, 1968-69, Master Host Internat., Los Angeles, 1969-71; prof. Grad. Sch. Bus., U. So. Calif., 1971-82; pres. LTI Corp., Monterey, Calif., 1982-84; chmn., chief exec. officer, dir. Casino USA/SFI Corp., from 1984; now pres., chief exec. officer Smart & Final Iris Corp., Los Angeles. Author: The American Franchise Revolution, 1970; poetry Other Places, Other Times, 1974, Love and Other Minor Tragedies, 1980. Mem. Am. Mktg. Assn., European Mktg. Assn., Am. Econ. Assn., AAUP, Beta Gamma Sigma, Pi Kappa Alpha. Clubs: Calif. Yacht (Los Angeles); Hawaii Yacht (Honolulu); Montecito Country (Santa Barbara, Calif.); Useppa Island (Fla.). Office: Smart & Final Iris Corp 400 S Boyle Ave Los Angeles CA 90058 *

EMPEY, CHARLES HOWARD, small business owner; b. Ogden, Utah, May 19, 1931; s. Charles Henry and Elnora (South) E.; m. Linda Gayle Ottley, June 8, 1970; children: Matthew, Cara, Megan, Lindsey. BSEE, U. Utah, 1953, MEA, 1968. Engr. sales Nat. Carbon Co., San Francisco, 1953; engr. Westinghouse Corp., Sunnyvale, Calif., 1958; engr., v.p. mktg. GTE Corp., Mt. View, Calif., 1958-83; owner Interface Internat., Saratoga, Calif., 1983—; pres. Lintec, Inc., Saratoga, 1986—. Capt. USAF, 1953-57. Mem. IEEE. Republican. Mormon. Office: Lintec Inc PO Box 2728 Saratoga CA 95070

EMPEY, DONALD WARNE, educational administrator; b. McMinnville, Oreg., Feb. 8, 1932; s. Earnest Warne and Anna May (Alsman) E.; m. Mary Catherine Reeh, July 14, 1956; children: Elizabeth, Margaret, Jennifer. BA, Willamette U., 1954; MA, Stanford U., 1955; EdD, U. Oreg., 1964. Tchr. history South Salem High Sch., Salem, Oreg., 1955-58; asst. prin. Bend Sr. High Sch., Oreg., 1958-61; prin. Bend Sr. High Sch., 1961-63; grad. asst. U. Oreg., Eugene, 1963-64; dir. instrn. Arcadia Sch. Dist., Calif., 1964-68; dep.supt. Lake Washington Sch. Dist., Kirkland, Wash., 1968-69; supt. Lake Washington Sch. Dist., 1969-76; dep. supt. Glendale Unified Sch. Dist., Calif., 1976—; vis. lectr. Claremont (Calif.) Grad. Sch., 1966-68, Calif. State U., Northridge, 1986—; mem. adv. com. on profl. growth Calif. Commn. on Tchr. Credentialing, 1985. Contbr. articles to profl. jours. Co-chmn. Glendale Youth Leadership Conf., 1986—; mem. exec. bd. Glendale Child Care Council, 1987—; pres. Glendale Community Coordinating Council, 1987. Recipient Golden Acorn award Lake Washington PTA Council, 1975, hon. service award Glendale PTA Council, 1980, spl. recognition award L.A. Co. Schs., 1985. Danforth Found. fellow, 1975. Mem. Assn. Supervision and Curriculum Devel., Am. Assn. Sch. Adminstrs., Kiwanis (v.p. Glendale 1984—), Phi Delta Kappa. Republican. Presbyterian. home: 5334 Ramsdell Ave LaCrescenta CA 91214 office: Glendale Unified Sch Dist 223 N Jackson St Glendale CA 91206

EMPEY, GENE F., real estate executive; b. Hood River, Oreg., July 13, 1923; BS in Animal Husbandry, Oreg. State U., 1949; M. of Tech. Journalism Iowa State U., 1950; m. Janet Halladay, Dec. 27, 1950; children: Stephen Bruce, Michael Guy. Publs. dir. U. Nev., Reno, 1950-55; mgr. Zephyr Cove Lodge Hotel, Lake Tahoe, Nev., 1955-65; owner Empey Co., real estate agy., Carson City and Tahoe, Nev., 1964—; land developer, owner investment and brokerage firm. Mem. Nev. Planning Bd., 1959-72, chmn., 1961-66; mem. Nev. Tax Commn., 1982—. Capt., inf. U.S. Army, 1943-47; PTO. Grad. Realtors Inst. Mem. Nat. Assn. Realtors, (cert. comml. investment mem.; pres. Nev. chpt. 3 terms), Tahoe Douglas C. of C. (pres. 1962, dir.), Carson City C. of C., Carson-Tahoe-Douglas Bd. Realtors, Capital City Club, Rotary, Heavenly Valley Ski (pres. 1968) Club, The Prospector's Club. Republican. Home: PO Box 707 Zephyr Cove NV 89448 Office: 512 S Curry St Carson City NV 89701

EMURA, EDWARD TAKEICHI, dermatologist; b. Lahaina, Hawaii, May 1, 1922; s. Kinichi and Takeno (Nakamoto) E.; m. Jean Sumiko Oho, June 19, 1950; children: Steven T., Ann S. BS, U. Hawaii, 1945; MD, Washington U., St. Louis, 1950. Diplomate Am. Bd. of Dermatology. Pres. Edward T. Emura, MD, Inc., Honolulu, 1957—. 1st lt. U.S. Army, 1953-55. Mem. Am. Acad. Dermatology, Hawaii Med. Assn., Hawaii Dermatol. Assn., Pacific Dermatol. Assn., Waialae Country Club. Office: Edward T Emura MD Inc 1010 S King St Honolulu HI 96814

ENCISO, J. RAUL, data processing company executive; b. Saginaw, Mich., Aug. 7, 1954; s. Jose Nieves and Eladia (Almanza) E.; m. Guillermina Salgado, June 30, 1979; children: Martha, Kari, Megan. AA, Delta Coll., 1974; BBA, Cen. Mich. U., 1976; MBA, U. So. Calif., 1977. Info. systems analyst Burroughs Corp., Guadalajara, Mex., 1977-81; MIS mgr. Burroughs Corp., 1982-85; mfg. resource planning tng. mgr. Burroughs Corp., Mission Viejo, Calif., 1985-86; cons. mgr. Unisys Corp., Mission Viejo, 1986-87; tng. implementation mgr. Unisys Corp., Dallas and Guadalajara, 1987-88; mgr. customer svc. Bus. & Mfg. Control System div. Unisys Corp., Santa Ana, Calif., 1988--. Mem. Am. Prodn. and Inventory Control Soc., Am. Soc. Tng. and Devel., Assn. for Devel. of Computer Based Instrnl. Systems. Office: Unisys Corp 5 Hutton Centre Dr Santa Ana CA 92707

ENDACOTT, DREW MICHAEL, microcomputer systems and software engineer; b. Pomona, Calif., May 2, 1956; s. James Harrisson and Rita Agnes (Melia) E. Student, U. Tex., 1978-82; BS, Tex. Tech. U., 1984. Mech. engr. Naval Sea Systems Command, Phila., 1985-86; owner, mgr., computer systems engr. Endacott Micro Services, Anaheim, Calif., 1987—. With USMC, 1974-78. Mem. ASME (assoc.; exec. com. Orange County sect. 1987—, editor newsletter 1987), Soc. Automotive Engrs. (assoc.), Internat. Brotherhood Magicians. Republican. Office: Endacott Micro Services 211 S State College Ste 283 Anaheim CA 92816

ENDERUD, WILBUR DONALD, JR., data processing executive; b. Pueblo, Colo., Nov. 4, 1945; s. Wilbur Donald and Loretta Faye (Jackson) E.; BA in Math., San Diego State U., 1967; MBA, Calif. State U., Long Beach, 1972; children: Cynthia. From programmer to project leader Mattel, Inc., Hawthorne, Calif., 1967-72; dir. mgmt. info. systems Audio-Magnetics Corp., Gardena, Calif., 1972-75; founder, 1975, since owner, prin. cons. Don Enderud & Assocs. (now Mgmt. Info. Solutions, Inc.), Diamond Bar, Calif.; founding ptnr. New Century Leasing, Diamond Bar, 1978—. Served with USAR, 1968-69; Vietnam. Decorated Army Commendation medal. Mem. Assn. Computing Machinery, Aircraft Owners and Pilots Assn. Republican. Lutheran. Office: PO Box 4237 Diamond Bar CA 91765

ENDICOTT, GENE THOMAS, public relations executive; b. Louisville, June 27, 1959; s. William F. and Mary Frances (Thomas) E. BA, U. Calif., Davis, 1981. Pub. affairs rep. Bechtel Group, Inc., San Francisco, 1982-85; mgr. product press rels. Hewlett-Packard Co., Palo Alto, Calif., 1985—. Democrat. Episcopalian. Home: 2850 Middlefield Palo Alto CA 94306 Office: Hewlett-Packard Co 3000 Hanover St Palo Alto CA 94304

ENDORE, GITA, small business owner; b. L.A., Oct. 16, 1944; d. Guy Sam and Henrietta (Portugal) E.; 1 child, Guy Endore-Kaiser. BA, U. Calif., 1966. Art dir. Kaiser & Father, Santa Monica, Calif., 1969-81; owner/operator Endore, Ink, L.A., 1981-83, Scottsdale, Ariz., 1983—. Mem. MADD. Mem. NOW, 602-Ariz. (film group), Phoenix Soc. Communicating Artists. Democrat. Jewish.

ENDS, RICHARD MERWIN, restaurant owner; b. Sacramento, Calif., Sept. 28, 1946; s. Joseph F. and Celestie A. (Fox) E.; m. Nancy D. McCoy; children: Jeff, Scott, Lauren. BS in Finance, Santa Clara U., 1968. Dir. ops. Victoria Sta., Inc., Larkspur, Calif., 1973-79; sole proprietor RM Enterprises, San Rafael, Calif., 1979-83; gen. ptnr. Pan Pacific Ptnrs., Honolulu, 1983—. Capt. U. S. Army, 1968-71. Named Humanitarian of Yr. Pacific Cancer Rsch. Found., 1987. Mem. The Guardsmen, Olympic Club. Republican. Roman Catholic. Home: 266 Bret Harte Rd San Rafael CA 94901 Office: Pan Pacific Ptnrs 2003 Kalia Rd #17K Honolulu HI 96815

ENG, ROSEMARY TOY, freelance writer; b. Chgo., July 30, 1943; d. Walter Toy and Rose Leong (Hong) E.; div.; 1 child, Peter. BA, Syracuse U., 1965; postgrad., Boston U., 1966-67. Reporter Star Gazette, Elmira, N.Y., 1965-66, Quincy (Mass.) Patriot Ledger, 1967-68, San Diego Tribune, 1968-72; chair publs. dept. Sch. of Art Inst. Chgo., 1973-76; freelance writer North Vancouver, B.C., Can., 1976—. Contbr. articles to Vancouver Mag., B.C. Bus. Mag., Can. Living Mag., Asiam mag., Rice mag., various newspapers and other mags. Vol. tchr. English as 2d lang., United Chinese Community Enrichment Svcs. Soc., Vancouver, 1977—. Recipient writing awards. Home and Office: 323 E 24th St, North Vancouver, BC Canada V7L 3E9

ENGDAHL, TODD PHILIP, newspaper editor; b. Jamestown, N.Y., Feb. 8, 1950; s. George Philip and Janice Marie (Wallin) E.; m. Caroline C.N. Schomp, Dec. 29, 1973; 1 child, Anders Justus Schomp. BA, Pomona Coll., 1971; MS, Northwestern U., 1972. Reporter Oregonian, Portland, 1972-75; reporter Denver Post, 1975-80, asst. city editor, 1980-83, night city editor, 1983-85, Sunday editor, 1985-86, city editor, 1986—; lectr. journalism Portland State U., 1974. Mem. Soc. Profl. Journalists, Denver Press Club. Democrat. Lutheran. Office: Denver Post Box 1709 Denver CO 80201

ENGEL, LINDA JEANNE, mining executive; b. Denver, Aug. 24, 1949; d. Thomas Mintor and Irene Evelyn (Esbenson) Kelley; m. William Stephen Engel, May 6, 1972; children: Kacey, Ryan. BA in Polit. Sci. and Econs., U. Colo., 1975. Statis. researcher Martin Marietta, Waterton, Colo., 1971; asst. dir. Fed. Drug Abuse Program, Denver, 1972-74; corp. sec./treas. Grayhill Exploration Co., Arvada, Colo., 1981-84; controller Western Internat. Gold-Silver, Westminster, Colo., 1985-86; investor rels. dir. and corp. sec. Canyon Resources Corp., Golden, Colo., 1986—. Dem. campaign mgr., Mayor of Boulder, Colo., 1970. Mem. Nat. Assn. Exec. Women, Am. Mgmt. Assn., Am. Soc. Corp. Secs., Nat. Investor Rels. Inst., Women in Mining, Fellowship Christian Athletes, Delta Delta Delta. Republican.

ENGEL, MARVIN LEROY, dermatologist; b. Kansas City, Mo., May 12, 1936; s. David M. and Sadye (Shaffer) E.; m. Sara Mizrachi, July 24, 1967; children: Renat, Dan, Soshana, Tamar. BA, Stanford U., 1956, MD, 1959. Diplomate Am. Bd. Dermatology, Am. Bd. Dermatology and Pathology. Intern Phila. Gen. Hosp., 1959-60; post-doctoral fellow in genetics Stanford U., Palo Alto, Calif., 1960-61, resident in dermatology, 1960-63; sr. investigator Nat. Cancer Inst., Bethesda, Md., 1963; pvt. practice dermatology Walnut Creek, Calif., 1968—; assoc. clin. prof. dermatology U. Calif. Med. Ctr., San Francisco, 1968—. With USPHS, 1963. Mem. AMA, San Francisco Dermatol. Soc. (pres. 1985), Am. Soc. Dermatol. Surgery, Am. Soc. Dermatol. Pathology. Jewish. Office: 130 La Cas Via Bldg 2 Ste 110 Walnut Creek CA 94611

ENGELMAN, DONALD BERTAM, engineering manager; b. Long Beach, Calif., Feb. 26, 1948; s. John Leslie and Theresa M. (Briar) E.; m. Linda Gail Price, June 9, 1973 (div. Jan. 1988); children: Catherine, Patrick. BS, Calif. Tech., 1970; MBA, Calif. State U., L.A., 1976. Prodn. coord. Signet Scientific, Burbank, Calif., 1973-74; prodn. mgr. Kennedy Co., Altadena, Calif., 1974-76; owner Idaho Solar, Idaho Falls, 1976-77; program mgr. EG&G Idaho, Idaho Falls, 1977-82; engring. mgr., dir. EG&G Fla., Cocoa, Fla., 1983-85; engring mgr. UNC Nuclear Industries, Richland, Wash., 1985-87; mgr. quality improvement Westinghouse Hanford, Richland, 1987—; cons. in field. Bd. dirs. Mountain View Sch., Idaho Falls, 1981-82; mem. Fla. State Sci. & Engring. Fair, Melbourne, 1984. Mem. Am. Productivity Mgmt. Assn. Roman Catholic. Office: Westinghouse Hanford PO Box 1970 XI-76 Richland WA 99352

ENGELMEIER, ROBERT LEO, prosthodontist, military officer; b. Pitts., June 19, 1944; s. Leo Julius and Ruth Margaret (Milton) E.; m. Nancy Beth Hope, June 25, 1972; children: Tanya Hope, Lee Stephen, Robert Leo II. BS, U. Pitts., 1966, DMD, 1970; MS, U. Tex., 1978. Diplomate Am. Bd. Prosthodontics; cer. maxillofacial prosthodontist. Commd. USAF, 1970, advanced through grades to col., 1985; gen. dentist 483d div. USAF Hosp., Cam Rahn bay, Vietnam, 1970-71; gen. dentist USAF Hosp., Otis AFB, Mass., 1971-72; gen. practice dentistry Provincetown, Mass., 1972-74; resident in prosthodontics USAF, San Antonio and Houston, 1974-80; maxillofacial prosthodontist USAF Regional Hosp., Elgin AFB, Fla., 1980-84, USAF Med. Ctr., Travis AFB, Calif., 1984—; spl. cons. to Surgeon Gen., USAF, 1984—; instr. USAF hosps., San Antonio, Elgin AFB and Travis AFB, 1978—; lectr. various nat. and state profl. meetings. Contbr. numerous articles to profl. jours. Active Boy Scouts Am., Tex. and Fla., 1978-80; mem. sch. adv. bd. Elgin AFB, 1983-84. Decorated over 13 medals, USAF, 1970-84; recipient Eagle Scout award Boy Scouts Am. Fellow Am. Coll. Prosthodontics, Acad. Gen. Dentistry; mem. ADA, Fedn. Prosthodontic Orgns., Assn. Military Surgeons of U.S., Phi Gamma Delta Frat. Alumni Assn., No. Calif. Kyudo Assn., M.D. Anderson Hosp. Assocs., Smithsonian Soc., Nat. Rifle Assn. (All-U.S.A.F. Nat. Pistol team). Roman Catholic. Clubs: Buick Am., Yolo Sportsman's, USAF Nat. Pistol Team. Office: PSC#4 Box 9418 Travis AFB CA 94535

ENGELSTAD, JEFFREY LYALL, real estate executive; b. Denver, Feb. 28, 1961; s. Lyall Duwayne and Gladys Irene (Donovan) E.; m. Susan Kittrell, Aug. 10, 1985; 1 child, Jeffrey Lyall II. BBA, U. Denver, 1983. V.p. Thunderbird Cos. Colo., Inc., Aurora, 1981—. Mem. Nat. Assn. Realtors, Denver Jaycees (dir. 1985). Republican. Episcopalian. Lodge: Rotary (bd. dirs. Smoky Hill chpt. 1987-88). Office: Thunderbird Cos Colo Inc 13731 E Mississippi Ave Aurora CO 80012

ENGENE, GENE LEONARD, theater educator, small business owner; b. Compton, Calif., June 23, 1942; s. Leonard and Helen Lucille (Ode) E. AA, Everett (Wash.) Community Coll., 1966; BA, Whitman Co., 1968; MFA, Stanford U., 1970. Teaching fellow Stanford (Calif.) U., 1969-70; vis. instr. Ea. Wash. State Coll., Cheney, 1970-71; prof. of theatre Ea. Wash. U., Cheney, 1973—; instr. Dartmouth Coll., Hanover, N.H., summer 1969; acting instr. U. Mo., Kansas City, summer 1971; faculty senator Ea. Wash. U., Cheney, 1986—; dept. chmn. Dept. of Theatre, Cheney, 1988—. Co-dir. The Spokane Story, 1979-81; dir., actor, designer, numerous theatre prodns., 1977—; artistic cons. over 30 prodns., 1982—. Served as cpl. USMC, 1960-64. Recipient Wheeler Grant award Wheeler Found., Stanford U., 1968-69. Mem. Centre Theatre Group (chmn. bd. dirs., pres., co-founder). Office: Ea Wash U Dept Theatre Cheney WA 99004

ENGER, LINDA MAY, photographer; b. St. Louis, May 22, 1955; d. Morris and Clara (Binder) E. Student, U. Mo., 1973-75; BFA in Photography, So. Ill. U., 1978. Freelance photographer Boulder, Colo., 1979-80, Phoenix, 1983-87, Tempe, Ariz., 1987—. Exhibited in group shows at Durango Photographic Salon, 1987, Phoenix Sky Harbor Airport, 1988, Ratliff Williams Gallery, Sedona, Ariz., 1988, Ariz. Mus. for Youth, 1989, Phoenix Little Theater, 1989, and many others. Photography coordinator Expo 2: Caring for Our Children, Scottsdale, Ariz., 1987. Named one of Outstanding Young Women of Am., 1988. Mem. Women in Design (pres. 1988-89, sec. 1986-88), Phoenix Soc. Communicating Arts. Jewish. Office: Linda Enger Photography 915 S 52d St Ste 5 Tempe AZ 85281

ENGLE, BENJAMIN J., lawyer; b. Erie, Pa., Oct. 1, 1941; s. Paul T. and Jane F. (Joyce) e.; children from previous marriage: Julie Ann, Wendy S.; m. Martha M. Hancock, Feb. 17, 1983. BA, Gonzaga U., 1963; JD, U. San Fernando Valley, 1974. Bar: Calif. 1974, U.S. Dist. Ct. (cen. dists.) Calif. 1974, U.S. Dist. Ct. (so. dists.) Calif. 1978. Claims supr., staff atty. Travelers Ins. Co., 1968-74; assoc. Law Offices Robert Bolton, 1975, Ross, Feinberg and Wolf, 1976, Miller and Folse, 1977-79; ptnr. McGahan and Engle, Ventura, Calif., 1979-88, Engle and Bride, Ventura, 1988—; judge pro tem Ventura County Superior Ct.; examiner State Bar Calif.; arbitrator Ventura County Superior Ct. Panel. Capt. U.S. Army, 1963-67. Mem. ABA, Calif. Bar Assn., Ventura County Bar Assn. (arbitrator), Am. Arbitration Assn. (arbitrator), Am. Soc. of Law and Medicine, Assn. of So. Calif. Def. Consel. Republican. Roman Catholic. Office: Engle and Bride 2125 Knoll Dr Ventura CA 93003

ENGLE, KENNETH WILLIAM, information management executive; b. Hazleton, Pa., Feb. 1, 1937; s. Ishmael Charles and Margaret Elizabeth (Bond) E.; m. Jeanne Mae Davis, June 3, 1961; children: Kenneth Richard, Jonathan Edward. BA, George Washington U., 1964; MA, Am. U., 1970; MS, Colo. State U., 1984—. Intelligence officer USAF, 1955-59, 64-82; research analyst Sci. Applications Internat., Denver, 1982-85, cons., 1985—; dir. mgmt. infosystems Hosp. Service, Inc., Ft. Collins, Colo., 1985—. Contbr. articles to profl. jours. Named Outstanding Colo. State U. Mgmt. Infosystems Grad., Denver Bus. Mag., 1984-85. Mem. Ret. Officers Assn. (2d v.p. 1986-88, pres 1988—), World Future Soc. Republican. Presbyterian. Home: 2018 Rollingwood Dr Fort Collins CO 80525 Office:.Hosp Svc Inc PO Box 2367 200 S Coll Ave Fort Collins CO 80522

ENGLEHART, HARRY A., communications executive; b. Johnstown, Pa., Apr. 8, 1947; s. Harry A. Jr. and Mercedes (Parsons) E.; m. Elizabeth Bennett, Sept. 4, 1988. BA in English, U. Mich., 1969. V.p. corp. communications Mellon Bank, Pitts., 1969-80; communications/mktg. cons. JG Communications, Pitts., 1980-82; unit mgr. Pitts. office Hill & Knowlton, 1982-85; sr. v.p., mng. dir. Hill & Knowlton, Chgo., 1985-88; v.p. corp. communications Lockeed Corp., Woodland Hills, Calif., 1989—. Bd. dirs. Leukemia Soc. Mem. Aerospace Industries Assn. (mem. communications coun.), Calif. Mfrs. Assn. (bd. dirs.), Am. V.P.'s Forum, Bel-Air Country Club. Democrat. Roman Catholic. Office: Lockheed Corp 4500 Park Granada Blvd Calabasas CA 91399

ENGLER, RANDALL KEITH, sales executive; b. Tucson, Nov. 16, 1954; s. Irwin Ira and Eloise Dorothea (Oakes) E. BS, Ariz. State U., 1977. Plant mgr., sales mgr. Microbio Products, Inc., Phoenix, 1977-81; mfg. rep. Tegal Sci., Phoenix, 1981-83; tech. sales rep. Am. Microscan, San Diego, 1983-84; dist. mgr. Pandex Labs., San Francisco, 1985—. Mem. AAAS. Home: 2945 Webster St San Francisco CA 94123 Office: 909 Orchard St Mundelein IL 60060

ENGLISH, ALEXANDER, professional basketball player; b. Columbia, S.C., Jan. 5, 1954; m. Vanessa English; 3 children. Ed., U. S.C. Forward Milw. Bucks, NBA, 1976-78, Indiana Pacers, NBA, 1978-80, Denver Nuggets, NBA, 1980—; player NBA All-Star Game, 1982-86; leading NBA scorer, 1985-86 season. Author poetry; co-author (autobiography) The English Language. Office: care Denver Nuggets PO Box 4658 Denver CO 80204-0658 *

ENGLISH, DONALD MARVIN, insurance inspector; b. Raleigh, N.C., July 31, 1951; s. Marvin Lee and Lois (Woodard) E.; m. Rebecca Pritchard, Sept. 3, 1970 (div. 1977). Student, Miami U., Oxford, Ohio, 1969-70, 73-74, U. Cin., 1977-78, Calif. State U., Fresno, 1980—. Ins. inspector Comml. Services, Cin., 1974-78, Ohio Casualty Ins. Co., Fresno, 1978—. Served with U.S. Army, 1970-73. Mem. Am. Soc. Safety Engrs. Club: E. Fresno Exchange (pres. 1984-85). Home: 4417 N Teilman Fresno CA 93705-1053 Office: The Ohio Casualty Ins Co 4420 N First St Ste 106 Fresno CA 93755

ENGMANN, DOUGLAS JOE, securities trader; b. Shanghai, China, Aug. 3, 1947; s. Julius Otto and Masha (Klatchko) E.; m. Barbara Jo Mikesell, June 20,. AB in Econs., U. Calif., 1969; MS in Econs., Mass. Inst. Tech., 1970. Asst. dir., dir. White House Conf. on Youth, Washington, 1970-72; cons. Urban Mgmt. Cons., San Francisco, 1972-76; pres. Engemann & Assocs., San Francisco, 1976-86, Engemann Options Inc., San Francisco, 1978—, Sage Clearing Corp., San Francisco, 1982—; gov. Pacific Stock Exchange, San Francisco, 1982-88, vice chmn., chrmn. Commr. Bd. of Permit Appeals, San Francisco, 1977-88; pres. City Planning Commn., San Francisco, 1988—. Mem. Phi Beta Kappa, Delta Phi Epsilon (pres. 1967-68), Silverado Country Club. Home: 2724 Pacific Ave San Francisco CA 94115

ENGORON, EDWARD DAVID, food service consultant; b. Los Angeles, Feb. 19, 1946; s. Leo and Claire (Gray) E.; m. Charlene Scott, Oct. 7, 1970 (div. July 1982). BArch., U. So. Calif., 1969, MBA, 1973, PhD, 1974; MA, Cordon Bleu, Paris, 1975. Art dir. ABC, Los Angeles, 1964-67, Paramount Pictures, Los Angeles, 1967-68, Warner Bros. Pictures, Burbank, Calif., 1968-69; mktg. dir. Lawry's Foods Inc., Los Angeles, 1969-74; v.p. Warehouse Restaurants, Marina del Rey, Calif., 1968-72; pres. Perspectives, San Francisco, 1974-82, Los Angeles, 1986—; pres. China Rose Inc., Dallas, 1982-86; exec. v.p. T.G.I. Fridays Inc., Dallas, 1986-87; pres., chief exec. officer, bd. dirs. Guilt Free Goodies, Ltd., Vancouver, B.C., Can., 1986—, Sugarless Co., L.A., 1987—; cons. The Southland Corp., Dallas, 1982-86, Pizza Hut Inc., Wichita, Kans., 1975-87, Frank L. Carney Enterprises, Wichita, 1982-87; pres. Sweet Deceit, Inc., Guilt-Free Goodies Ltd.; host radio show Perspectives On Food Radio Stas. KIEV, KNRY. Author cookbook Stolen Secreats, 1980; patentee Pasta Cooking Station, 1981, micro-wave controller, 1982. Bd. govs. Los Angeles Parks, 1971-74; mem. Fine Arts Commn., Tiburon, Calif., 1974-76. Mem. Foodservice Cons. Soc. Internat., Soc. Motion Picture Art Dirs., Food, Wine & Travel Writers Assn., Masons. Republican. Office: Perspectives/The Cons Group 11444 W Olympic Blvd Los Angeles CA 90064

ENGSTROM, DONALD JAMES, printing company executive; b. Sheridan, Mich., Aug. 18, 1948; s. Theodore Wilhelm and Dorothy Elizabeth (Weaver) E.; m. Laurel Lynn Dawson, Nov. 2, 1974; children: Theodore James, Megan Elizabeth. AA, Pasadena (Calif.) City Coll., 1975. Printer World Vision, Monrovia, Calif., 1972-77, mgr. printing, 1977-79; pres., chief exec. officer Engstrom-Smith Lithography, The Workshop, Arcadia, Calif., 1979—. Staff sgt. USAF, 1968-72. Mem. Monrovia C. of C., Nat. Assn. Printers and Lithographers, Arcadia C. of C., Rocky Mountain Mastiff Fanciers. Republican. Mem. Evangelical Free Ch. Home: 61 W Las Flores Arcadia CA 91007 Office: The Workshop 407 N 2d Ave Arcadia CA 91006

ENGSTROM, ROGER ALLEN, real estate development executive; b. Bloomer, Wis., Nov. 19, 1944; s. Carl Clifford and Alice C. (Christianson) E.; m. Marlene Karen Kostuchik, June 2, 1973; 1 child, Seth Michael. BSME, U. Wis., 1967; MBA, San Jose State U., 1986. Registered profl. engr., Calif.; lic. real estate broker, Calif., Nev. Project engr. Syntex, Palo Alto, Calif., 1976-78; sr. facilities engr. Signetics Corp., Sunnyvale, Calif., 1978-79; projects mgr. Intel Corp., Santa Clara, Calif., 1979-80; facilities mgr. Triad Systems Corp., Sunnyvale, 1980-81; sr. project mgr. GTE Sprint, Burlingame, Calif., 1981-84; v.p. engring. Security & Facility Engring., Inc., Los Altos, Calif., 1984-86; v.p. The Holding Co., Cupertino, Calif., 1986—; engring. cons., Mountainview, Calif., 1980—. Served as capt. USAF, 1967-71. Mem. Nat. Assn. Realtors, Mountainview Bd. Realtors, Reserve Officers Assn. Republican. Lutheran.

ENNIS, C. BRADY, guidebook editor; b. Alton, Ill., Mar. 19, 1954; s. Calvin Franklin and Virginia Jo (Moody) E. BA in Journalism with high honors, Tex. Christian U., 1978. Copywriter Concordia Pub. House, St. Louis, 1978; display ad rep. Ft. Worth Star-Telegram, 1979; proofreader LeWay Composing, Ft. Worth, 1979-80, Deloitte Haskins & Sells, San Francisco, 1980-83; assoc. editor Airline Svcs. Unltd. Travel Guide, San Francisco, 1983-86; mng. editor ASU Travel Guide, San Francisco, 1986—; writer, cons. pub. relations Different Spokes Bicycling Club of San Francisco, 1982-83. Contbr. articles to profl. publications. Mem. Airline Svcs. Unltd., San Francisco Advt. Club, Soc. Profl. Journalists, Sigma Delta Chi (Best News Story 1975), Golden Gate Bus. Assn., Internat. Platform Assn., Tex. Christian Univ. Alumni Assn. Office: Airline Svcs Unltd Travel Guide 1325 Columbus Ave San Francisco CA 94133

ENNIS, THOMAS MICHAEL, health foundation executive; b. Morgantown, W.Va., Mar. 7, 1931; s. Thomas Edson and Violet Ruth (Nugent) E.; m. Julia Marie Dorety, June 30, 1956; children—Thomas John, Robert Griswold (dec.). Student, W.Va. U., 1949-52; A.B., George Washington U., 1954; J.D., Georgetown U, 1960. Dir. ann. support program George Washington U., 1960-63; nat. dir. devel. Project HOPE, People to People Health Found., Inc., Washington, 1963-66; nat. exec. dir. Epilepsy Found. Am., Washington, 1966-74; exec. dir. Clinton, Eaton, Ingham Community Mental Health Bd., 1974-83; nat. exec. dir. Alzheimer's Disease and Related Disorders Assn., Inc., Chgo., 1983-86; exec. dir., pres. French Found. for Alzheimer Rsch., Los Angeles, 1986—; clin. inst. dept. community medicine and internat. health Georgetown U., 1967-74; adj. assoc. prof. dept. psychiatry Mich. State U., 1975-84; lectr. Univ. Ctr. for Internat. Rehab., 1977; cons. health and med. founds., related orgns.; cons. Am. Health Found., 1967-69, Reston, Va.-Georgetown U. Health Planning Project, 1967-70;. Contbr. articles on devel. disabilities, mental health and health care to profl. jours. Mem. adv. bd. Nat. Center for Law and Handicapped, 1971-74; advisor Nat. Reye's Syndrome Found.; mem. Internat. Bur. Epilepsy, Nat. Com. for Research in Neurol. Disorders, 1967-72; mem. nat. adv. bd. Developmental Disabilities/Tech. Assistance System, U. N.C., 1971-78, Handicapped Organized Women, Charlotte, N.C., 1984—; Nat. del. trustee, v.p. Nat. Capitol Area chpt., bd. dirs., exec. com. Nat. Kidney Found., 1969-74, Nat. trustee, 1970-74, pres., 1972—; bd. dirs. Nat. Assn. Pvt. Residential Facilities for Mentally Retarded, 1970-74; bd. dirs., mem. exec. com. Epilepsy Found. Am., 1977-84, Epilepsy Center Mich., 1974-83; nat. bd. dirs. Western Inst. on Epilepsy, 1969-72; bd. dirs., pres. Mich. Mid-South Health Systems Agy., 1975-78; sec. gen. Internat. Fedn. Alzheimer's Disease and Related Disorders, 1984-86. World Rehab. Fund fellow Norway, 1980. Mem. Nat. Rehab. Assn., Am. Pub. Health Assn., Nat. Epilepsy League (bd. dirs. 1977-78), Mich. Assn. Community Mental Health Bd. Dirs. (pres. 1977-79), AAAS, Phi Alpha Theta, Phi Kappa Psi.

ENO, ESTHER RENA, investment company executive, educator; b. Sterling, Colo., Nov. 21, 1942; d. Tiberio and Angela (Vidale) Rizzolo; m. Richard H. Eno, Feb. 18, 1961; children: Debora, Gregory, Dana. BS in Edn., U. Oreg., 1974; MA in Edn., Oreg. State U., 1976. Sec. Sterling Credit Union, 1960-61, Mountain States Telephone, Greeley, Colo., 1962-64; owner, operator Holiday Abroad, Eugene, Oreg., 1968-75; co-owner Eno Investments, Eugene, 1965; prof. bus. Lane Community Coll., Eugene, 1974—; bd. dirs. SELCO Credit Union, Eugene, Mems. Service Ins. Agy., Eugene; treas. Women's Missionary Fellowship, Eugene, 1970-83; dist. rep. Oreg. Bus. Edn. Assn., Eugene. Author: (textbook) Briefwriting by Eno, 1987. Rep. CU Polit. Action Group, Eugene, 1986-87; leader Girl Scouts, Eugene, 1968-70. Mem. Oreg. Bus. Edn. Assn. (dist. rep. Eugene chpt.), Assn. of Records Mgrs. and Adminstrs., Phi Kappa Phi. Republican. Lutheran. Home: 4485 Larkwood Eugene OR 97405 Office: Lane Community Coll 4000 E 30th Ave Eugene OR 97405

ENRIGHT, CYNTHIA LEE, illustrator; b. Denver, July 6, 1950; d. Darrel Lee and Iris Arlene (Flodquist) E. BA in Elem. Edn., U. No. Colo., 1972; student, Minn. Sch. Art and Design, Mpls., 1975-76. Tchr. 3d grade Littleton (Colo.) Sch. Dist., 1972-75; graphics artist Sta. KCNC TV, Denver, 1978-79; illustrator No Coast Graphics, Denver, 1979-87; editorial artist The Denver Post, 1987—. Illustrator (brochure) Northrop-King Seeds, 1985, (poster) Nat. Pork Coun., 1987, (mag.) Sesame St., 1984, 85. Recipient Print mag. Regional Design Ann. awards, 1984, 85, 87, Phoenix Art Mus. Biannual award, 1979. Mem. Mensa. Democrat. Home: 5722 E 14th Ave Denver CO 80220 Office: The Denver Post 650 15th St Denver CO 80202

ENRIGHT, WILLIAM BENNER, judge; b. N.Y.C., July 12, 1925; s. Arthur Joseph and Anna Beatrice (Plante) E.; m. Bette Lou Card, Apr. 13, 1951; children—Kevin A., Kimberly A., Kerry K. A.B., Dartmouth, 1947; LL.B., Loyola U. at Los Angeles, 1950. Bar: Calif. 1951; diplomate: Am. Bd. Trial Advs. Dep. dist. atty. San Diego County, 1951-54; ptnr. Enright, Levitt, Knutson & Tobin, San Diego, 1954-72; judge U.S. Dist. Ct. So. Dist. Calif., San Diego, 1972—; Mem. adv. bd. Joint Legis. Com. for Revision Penal Code, 1970-72, Calif. Bd. Legal Specialization, 1970-72; mem. Jud. Council, 1972; Bd. dirs. Defenders, 1965-72, pres., 1972. Served as ensign

USNR, 1943-46. Recipient Honor award San Diego County Bar, 1970; Extraordinary Service to Legal Professions award Mcpl. Ct. San Diego Jud. Dist., 1971. Fellow Am. Coll. Trial Lawyers, Am. Bar Found.; mem. ABA, San Diego County Bar Assn. (dir. 1963-65, pres. 1965), State Bar Calif. (gov. 1967-70, v.p. 1970, exec. com. law in a free soc. 1970—), Dartmouth Club San Diego, Am. Judicature Soc., Alpha Sigma Nu, Phi Delta Phi. Club: Rotarian. Office: US Dist Ct 940 Front St San Diego CA 92189

ENRIQUEZ, JIMMY A., insurance and real estate executive; b. Las Cruces, N.M., July 11, 1963; s. Gonzalo Holquin Sr. and Mary (Arzabal) E.; m. Nora Campos, July 14, 1984 (div.); 1 child, Vincent. Student, Colo. Inst. Art, 1981-82; BS in fin., real estate, N. Mex. State U., 1987. Agt. Northwestern Mut. Ins. Co., Las Cruces, 1987; dist. mgr., supr., registered rep. Prudential Ins., Las Cruces, 1987; real estate salesman Century 21, Las Cruces, 1987. Candidate for county commr. Dona Ana County, N.M., 1988. Mem. Nat. Assn. Life Underwriters, Toastmasters assoc.), Kiwanis (Sun County chpt.), N.Mex. State U. Ruby Club (Las Cruces, treas. 1984-87). Democrat. Roman Catholic. Home: 2521 Enriquez Ln Las Cruces NM 88005 Office: Prudential Fin Svcs 500 S Main #311 Las Cruces NM 88001

ENSIGN, DOUGLAS HARMON, electronic manufacturing engineer; b. Springfield, Ohio, Feb. 8, 1951; s. James Harmon and Norma Jo (Flannery) E.; m. Cheryl Irene Thompson, June 19, 1976; 1 child, Ashley Lynne. BS in Elec. Engring., Ohio State U., 1974; postgrad., IBM Robotic Inst., 1983. Mem. tech. staff missile systems div. Rockwell Internat., Columbus, Ohio, 1974; sr. test equipment engr. Litton Guidance and Controls, Grants Pass, Oreg., 1975-80, sr. advanced mfg. engr., 1980-85, group leader advanced mfg. systems, 1985—; cons. engr., Grants Pass, 1987—; mem. Solder Joint Reliability and Inspection Task Force Industry com. Mem. Assn. Laser Inspection Tech. Republican. Lutheran. Home: 3150 Southside Rd Grants Pass OR 97527 Office: Litton Guidance & Control Systems 1001 Redwood Hwy Spur Grants Pass OR 97526

ENSLEY, MARY LOUISE, secondary education counselor; b. Moscow, Idaho, July 28, 1938; d. Hugo and Dorothy (Blood) Walser; m. Thomas R. Ensley, Dec. 19, 1959; 1 child, Shelton. BS in Home Econs., U. Idaho, 1960; MA, Coll. of Idaho, 1973. Cert. in sec. edn. and pupil personnel svcs., Idaho, sch. counselor, Idaho; lic. profl. counselor, Idaho. Tchr. White Pine Sch. Dist., Troy, Idaho, 1960-61; tchr. home econs. Caldwell (Idaho) Sch. Dist. #132, 1961-74, sch. counselor, 1974—; lectr. Boise (Idaho) State U., 1983—, Coll. of Idaho, 1986-88; adj. faculty U. Idaho, 1988; mem. guidance adv. com. Idaho State Dept. Edn., Boise, 1985—, mem. evaluation team, 1988; mem. crisis team Caldwell Sch. Dist. #132, 1987—. Mem. adv. bd. Canyon Vocat. Ctr., Nampa, Idaho, 1988—, Dist. Mental Health Adv. Bd., Caldwell, 1982-83; Am. Sch. counselor Assn. Leadership Devel. Conf., Milw., 1987; bd. dirs. Conservative Bapt. Assn. Am., Wheaton, Ill., 1988—. Recipient Cert. of Merit COSSA Sch. Counselors, 1987, Outstanding Service award Idaho Assn. Vocat. Home Econs. Tchrs., 1973. Mem. Idaho Sch. Counselor Assn. (pres. 1988—, counselor of yr. 1987), Am. Sch. Counselor Assn., Am. Assn. for Counseling and Devel., Idaho Assn. for Counseling and Devel., Idaho Assn. for Career Devel., NEA, Idaho Edn. Assn., Caldwell Edn. Assn., AAUW (pres. Caldwell br. 1967-69). Home: 2505 Terrace Dr Caldwell ID 83605 Office: Jefferson Jr High Sch 3311 S 10th Ave Caldwell ID 83605

ENSTROM, JAMES EUGENE, cancer epidemiologist; b. Alhambra, Calif., June 20, 1943; s. Elmer Melvin, Jr. and Klea Elizabeth (Bissell) E.; B.S., Harvey Mudd Coll., Claremont, Calif., 1965; M.S., Stanford U., 1967, Ph.D. in Physics, 1970; M.P.H., UCLA, 1976; m. Marta Eugenia Villanea, Sept. 3, 1978. Research asso. Stanford Linear Accelerator Center, 1970-71; research physicist, cons. Lawrence Berkeley Lab., U. Calif., 1971-75; Celeste Durand Rogers cancer research fellow Sch. Pub. Health, UCLA, 1973-75, Nat. Cancer Inst. postdoctoral trainee, 1975-76, cancer epidemiology researcher, 1976-81, assoc. research prof., 1981—; program dir. for cancer control epidemiology Jonsson Comprehensive Cancer Center, 1978—, sci. dir. tumor registry, 1984-87, mem. dean's council, 1976—; cons. epidemiologist Linus Pauling Inst. Sci. and Medicine, 1976—; cons. physicist Rand Corp., 1969-73, R&D Assos., 1971-75; mem. sci. bd. Am. Council on Sci. and Health, 1984—. NSF predoctoral trainee, 1965-66; grantee Am. Cancer Soc., 1973—, Nat. Cancer Inst., 1979—; Preventive Oncology Acad. award, 1981-87. Fellow Am. Coll. Epidemiology; mem. Soc. Epidemiologic Research, Am. Heart Assn., Am. Pub. Health Assn., Am. Phys. Soc., AAAS, N.Y. Acad. Scis., Galileo Soc. Author papers in field. Office: U Calif Sch Pub Health Los Angeles CA 90024

ENTREMONT, PHILIPPE, conductor, pianist; b. Rheims, France, June 7, 1934; s. Jean and Renée (Monchamps) E.; m. Andree Ragot, Dec. 21, 1955; children: Félicia, Alexandre. Student, Conservatoire National Superieur de Musique, Paris, Jean Doyen. Profl. debut at 17, in Barcelona, Spain, Am. debut at 19, at Nat. Gallery, Washington, 1953, performs throughout world; pianist-condr. debut at, Mostly Mozart Festival, Lincoln Center, N.Y.C., 1971; rec. artist, CBS, Teldec, EMI, Schwann and ProArte records, guest condr. Pitts. Symphony, Royal Philharm., Orch. Nat. de France, Montreal Symphony, San Francisco Symphony, Phila. Orch., Detroit Symphony, numerous others; lifetime mus. dir. Vienna Chamber Orch., 1975—; mus. dir. New Orleans Symphony Orch., 1981-85, Denver Symphony, 1986—, l'Orchestre Colonne de Paris, 1988—. Decorated Knight, Legion of Honor, Officer de l'Ordre National du Merite; Austrian First Class Cross of Honor for the Arts and Scis.; A finalist Queen Elizabeth of Belgium Internat. Concours, 1952; Grand Prix Marguerite Long-Jacques Thibaud Competition, 1953; Harriet Cohen Piano medal, 1953; 1st prize Jeunesses Musicales; Grand Prix du Disque, 1967, 68, 69, 70; Edison award, 1968; Nominee Grammy award, 1972. Former mem. Academie Internationale de Musique Maurice Ravel (pres. 1975-80). Office: ICM Artists Ltd 40 W 57th St New York NY 10019 also: Amara-Chantaco, 64500 Sain-Jean-de-Lux France

ENTRIKEN, ROBERT KERSEY, management educator; b. McPherson, Kans., Jan. 15, 1913; s. Frederick Kersey and Opal (Birch) E.; m. Elizabeth Freeman, May 26, 1940 (div. Nov. 1951); children—Robert Kersey, Jr., Edward Livingston Freeman, Richard Davis; m. Jean Finch, June 5, 1954; 1 child, Birch Nelson. B.A., U. Kans. 1934; M.B.A., Golden Gate U., 1961; postgrad. City Univ. Grad. Bus. Sch., London, 1971-73. C.P.C.U. Ins. broker, Houston, Tex. and McPherson, Kans., 1935-39; asst. mgr. Cravens, Dargan & Co., Houston, 1939-42; br. mgr. Nat. Surety Corp., Memphis and San Francisco, 1942-54; v.p. Fireman's Fund Ins. Co., San Francisco. 1954-73; adj. prof. Golden Gate U., San Francisco, 1953-73, prof. mgmt., 1974—; resident dean Asia Programs, Singapore, 1987-88; prof. emeritus 1989—, underwriting mem. Lloyd's of London, 1985—. Contbr. articles to trade and profl. jours. Bd. dirs., sec., treas. Northstar Property Owners Assn., Calif., 1982-86. Served to capt. USNR, 1944-73, ret., 1973. Mem. Ins. Forum San Francisco (pres. 1965, trustee 1975-78, 84-88), Surety Underwriters Assn. No. Calif. (pres. 1956), CPCU Soc. (pres. No. Calif. chpt. 1957, named Ins. Profl. of Yr., San Francisco chpt. 1981, bd. dirs., 1989—), Chartered Ins. Inst., Ins. Inst. London, Musicians' Union Local No. 6 life), Acad. Polit. Sci., U.S. Naval Inst., Phi Delta Theta. Republican. Episcopalian. Clubs: University, Marines' Meml. (San Francisco); Commonwealth. Lodge: Naval Order U.S. Office: Golden Gate U 536 Mission St San Francisco CA 94105

ENTSMINGER, TERRYLEA, nursing home administrator; b. Brush, Colo., Mar. 11, 1948; d. Joseph Walter and Evelyn Marie (Reich) Daniels; m. John Ardys Entsminger, Jan. 6, 1968; children: Daphne Eve, John Joseph. Student of spl. edn., U. No. Colo., 1966-67. Lic. nursing home adminstr., Colo. From nursing asst. to adminstr. in tng. Eventide North, Ft. Collins, Colo., 1973-77; asst. to purchasing dir. Geriatrics, Inc., Greeley, Colo., 1977; asst. adminstr. Centennial Health Care, Greeley, 1977; adminstr. Eventide of Longmont (Colo.) Living Ctr., 1977, Alpine Manor Living Ctr., Thorton, Colo., 1977-86, Foothills Care Ctr., Longmont, 1986, Western Hills Health Care Ctr., Lakewood, Colo., 1986-88, Briarwood Health Care Ctr., Denver, 1988—; exec. dir. Denver Health Group, 1988—. Mem. Am. Coll. Health Care Adminstrs., Colo. Health Care Assn. (2d v.p. 1988—, vol. legis. contact com. 1986—), Nat. Assn. Female Execs. Republican. Office: Briarwood Health Care Ctr 1440 Vine St Denver CO 80206

ENZENAUER, ROBERT WILLIAM, ophthalmologist; b. St. Louis, Nov. 25, 1953; s. Robert Aloys and Dorothy Vera (Oberkfell) E.; m. Jill S. Montrey, Mar. 30, 1979; 1 child, Katherine Elizabeth. BS, U.S. Mil. Acad., 1975; MD, U. Mo., 1979; MPH, U. Hawaii, 1984. Diplomate Am. Bd. Pediatrics, Am. Bd. Preventive Medicine. Commd. 2d lt. U.S. Army, 1975, advanced through grades to maj., 1984; intern, resident in pediatrics Tripler Army Hosp., Honolulu, 1979-82; staff pediatrician U.S. Army Health Clinic, Schofield Barracks, Hawaii, 1982-84; flight surgeon 101st Airborne div., Fort Campbell, Ky., 1984-86; resident in ophthalmology Fitzsimons Army Hosp., Aurora, Colo., 1986-89; fellow pediatric ophthalmology Hosp. for Sick Children, Toronto, Ont., Can., 1989—. Contbr. articles to profl. jours. Fellow Am. Acad. of Pediatrics, Am. Coll. Preventive Medicine; mem. Assn. of Mil. Surgeons of the U.S., Am. Acad. of Ophthalmology, Aerospace Med. Assn., Assn. of U.S. Army Flight Surgeons. Republican. Methodist. Home: 774 Locust St Denver CO 80220 Office: Fitzsimmons Army Hosp Dept Ophthalmology Aurora CO 80045

ENZER, SELWYN, academic researcher, planning consultant; b. N.Y.C., July 23, 1928; s. Morris J. and Helen (Woloski) E.; m. Sandra Rose Palius, Apr. 9, 1950 (div. 1973); children: Bruce L., Barbara S.; m. Adrienne Hinds Adan, May 30, 1976. BCE, CCNY, 1951; PhD, U. So. Calif., 1980. Structures engr. Buell Engring. Co., N.Y.C., 1950-52, Design Svcs. Co., N.Y.C., 1952-53; prin. structures engr. Ramseyer & Miller Co., N.Y.C., 1953-55, Rep. Aviation Corp., Farmingdale, N.Y., 1955-62; project mgr. No. Am. Aviation Co., Downey, Calif., 1962-67; br. mgr. McDonnell Douglas Co., Huntington Park, Calif., 1967-69; sr. rsch. fellow Inst. for the Future, Menlo Park, Calif., 1969-75; rsch. dir. U. So. Calif., L.A., 1975—; cons. UN Devel. Program, Santiago, Chile, 1986-88; visiting scholar Western Australia Inst. of Tech., Perth, Australia, 1981; nat. materials adv. bd. Nat. Rsch. Coun., Washington, 1970-80; cons. Soc. Univ. Urologists, L.A., 1976. Author: Neither Feast Nor Famine, 1978; contbr. articles profl. jours.; inventor (computer program) Interax, 1979. Cons. United Way, L.A., 1984-86. With USN, 1946-48. Mem. World Future Soc., Chi Epsilon, Omega Rho. Jewish. Home: 1751 S Barrington Ave #2 Los Angeles CA 90025 Office: U So Calif GSBA-IBEAR Los Angeles CA 90089-1421

EOFF, KIMBERLY JEAN, entrepreneur; b. Prescott, Ariz., June 2, 1957; d. William Robert and Wilma Loretta (Baker) E. Student, Yavapai Coll., Prescott, 1976-79, Rochester Inst. Tech., 1982. Mgr. 4 Color Works, Phoenix, 1986-87; v.p. Am. Zela Inc., Norwalk, Conn., 1987-88; ptnr. B & B Landscaping, Prescott, 1987—; pres. Colonwave House Lifts, Prescott, 1987—, Flagdeco Furniture Designs, Phoenix, 1988—, In Photo, Phoenix, 1988—; cons. Colorific, Virginia Beach, Va., 1987-88, Express Color Printing, San Francisco, 1988-89. Vol. Spl. Olympics, Pensacola, Fla., 1979-86. With USN, 1979-86. Mem. Am. Health Care Assn. (mem. adv. com. 1989—). Republican. Home and Office: PO Box 186 Prescott AZ 86302 also: 9618 1st Ave Phoenix AZ 85021

EPLING, RALPH E., utilities administrator; b. Guam, Mariannis, July 26, 1955; came to U.S., 1955; s. Robert C. and Marjorie A. (Bean) E.; m. Lisa A. Harstedt, July 16, 1988. BS in Mech. Engr., Oregon State U., 1977. Reg. profl. engr., Oreg. Plant engr. Esco Corp., Portland, Oreg., 1977-78; weatherization engr. NW Natural Gas, Portland, 1978-80; owner Sunspot Energy Co., Portland, 1980-81; sales engr. Cascade Nat. Gas, Seattle, 1981-84; tech. svc. rep. Wash. Nat. Gas, Seattle, 1984-89; oil & gas adminstr. Thermal Exploration Inc., Seattle, 1989—. Contbr. articles to profl. jours. Republican. Office: Thermal Exploration Inc 815 Mercer St Seattle WA 98111

EPPERSON, ERIC ROBERT, financial executive; b. Oregon City, Oreg., Dec. 10, 1949; s. Robert Max and Margaret Joan (Crawford) E.; B.S., Brigham Young U., 1973, M.Acctg., 1974; M.B.A., Golden Gate U., 1977, J.D., 1981; m. Lyla Gene Harris, Aug. 21, 1969; 1 dau., Marcie. Instr. acctg. Brigham Young U., Provo, Utah, 1973-74; supr. domestic taxation Bechtel Corp., San Francisco, 1974-78; supr. internat. taxation Bechtel Power Corp., San Francisco, 1978-80; mgr. internat. tax planning Del Monte Corp., San Francisco, 1980-82, mgr. internat. taxes, 1982-85; internat. tax specialist Touche Ross & Co., San Francisco, 1985-87; dir. internat. tax Coopers & Lybrand, Portland, 1987-89; exec. v.p., chief fin. officer Dawntreader Internat., Inc., Salt LAke City, 1989—. Eagle Scout, 1965; scoutmaster, Boy Scouts Am., Provo, 1971-73, troop committeeman, 1973-74, 83—; mem. IRS Vol. Income Tax Assistance Program, 1972-75; pres. Mut. Improvement Assn., Ch. Jesus Christ of Latter-day Saints, 1972-74, pres. Sunday sch., 1977-79, tchr., 1974-80, ward clk., 1980-83, bishopric, 1983-87; ; bd. dirs. Oreg. Art Inst. Film Ctr.; Hist. Preservation League of Oreg. Mem. Am. Acctg. Assn., Tax Assn. Am., World Affairs Council, Japan/Am. Soc., Internat. Tax Planning Assn., Internat. Fiscal Assn., U.S. Rowing Assn., Beta Alpha Psi. Republican. Clubs: Riverplace Athletic Club, Commonwealth, Masters of Accountancy Brigham Young U. Author: (with T. Gilbert) Interfacing of the Securities and Exchange Commission with the Accounting Profession: 1968 to 1973, 1974. Office: Dawntreader Internat Inc 340 Whitney Ave Salt Lake City UT 84115

EPPERSON, VAUGHN ELMO, civil engineer; b. Provo, Utah, July 20, 1917; s. Lawrence Theophilus and Mary Loretta (Pritchett) E.; m. Margaret Ann Stewart Hewlett, Mar. 4, 1946; children: Margaret Ann (Mrs. Eric V.K. Hill), Vaughn Hewlett, David Hewlett, Katherine (Mrs. Franz S. Amussen), Lawrence Stewart. BS, U. Utah, 1953. With Pritchett Bros. Constrn. Co., Provo, 1949-50; road design engr. Utah State Road Commn., Salt Lake City, 1951-53, bridge design engr., 1953-54; design engr. Kennecott Copper Corp., Salt Lake City, 1954-60, office engr., 1960-62, sr. engr., 1962, assigned concentrator plant engr., 1969-73, assigned concentrator project engr., 1973-78; cons. engr. Vaughn Epperson Engring. Service, Salt Lake City, 1978-87; project engr. Newbery-State Inc., Salt Lake City, 1980, geneal. computerized research programs, 1983-88, ancestral file programs family history dept. Ch. Jesus Christ of Latter-Day Saints, 1989—. Scoutmaster Troop 190, Salt Lake City, 1949-51. Served to capt. AUS, 1941-45; maj. N.G., 1951; col. Utah State Guard, 1952-70. Decorated Army Commendation medal; recipient Service award Boy Scouts Am., 1949, Community Service award United Fund, 1961, Service award VA Hosp., Salt Lake City, 1977. Mem. ASCE, Am. Soc. Mil. Engrs., Sons of Utah Pioneers. Republican. Mormon. Home: 1537 E Laird Ave Salt Lake City UT 84105 Office: PO Box 8769 Salt Lake City UT 84108

EPPINK, JEFFREY FRANCIS, oil industry executive, petroleum explorationist; b. Whittier, Calif., Jan. 31, 1955; s. Reno Paul and Bertina (Gilje) I.; m. Sheryl Ann Baumberger, Aug. 27, 1977; children: Christina Michelle, Michael Jeffrey. BS, Calif. State Poly. U., 1978; MS, U. So. Calif., 1981. Planetary scientist Jet Propulsion Lab., Pasadena, Calif., 1979-81; earth scientist Chevron Overseas Petroleum Inc., San Ramon, Calif., 1981—. Hotline vol. Contra Costa County Crisis & Suicide Intervention, Pleasant Hill, Calif., 1987—; mem. World Affairs Council, San Francisco, 1988—. Mem. Am. Assn. Petroleum Geologists, Soc. Exploration Geophysicists, No. Calif. Geol. Soc. (treas. 1984, v.p. 1985), Toastmasters (pres. San Ramon chpt. 1989). Republican. Roman Catholic. Home: 756 Cheryl Dr Benicia CA 94510 Office: Chevron Overseas Petroleum 6001 Bollinger Canyon Rd San Ramon CA 94583

ERBACHER, KATHRYN ANNE, corporate editor; b. Kansas City, Mo., Dec. 11, 1947; d. Philip Joseph and Thelma Lillian (Hines) E. BS in English Edn., U. Kans., 1970; BA magna cum laude in Art, Metro State Coll., Denver, 1983. Reporter, Kansas City Star (Mo.), 1970-71; newswriter Washington U., St. Louis, 1972-76; copy editor Kansas City Star-Times (Mo.), 1976-79; editor Petro-Lewis Corp., Denver, 1979-82; assoc. Artours, Inc., Denver, 1983-84; assoc. editor arts and travel editor Denver Mag., 1984-86; freelance arts writer, editor, mktg. cons., 1986—; internat. editor Gates Rubber Co., Denver, 1987—. Creative dir. TV shorts for contemporary art collection Denver Art Mus., 1983. Mem. Metro State Coll. Alumni Bd. Dirs., 1986-87, co-chair 1987 Metro State Coll. Alumni Awards Dinner, Denver; bd. govs. Metro State Coll. Found., 1986-87. Recipient award for arts writing Denver Partnership, 1986, award for Artbeat column in Denver mag. Colo. MAC News, 1986, also award for spl. fashion sect. Dressing the Part; co-recipient award for Gates Rubber Co. Global Communications Bus./Profl. Advt. Assn., 1988 Mem. Denver Art Mus., Am. Assn. Mus., Am. Assn. Travel Editors, Colorado Springs Fine Arts Ctr. Avocations: visual art, theater, films, travel, Spanish language. Home: 1539 Platte St Denver CO 80202 Office: Gates Corp 900 S Broadway Denver CO 80209

ERBST, LAWRENCE ARNOLD, lawyer, consultant; b. N.Y.C., Oct. 5, 1930; s. Ben Erbst and Rose (Farbish) Levy; m. Eileen Sheila Frohman, July 29, 1956; children: Leslie Charles, Allison Carol, Jonathan Stuart. ABcum laude, Harvard Coll., 1952, LLB, 1955. Bar: N.Y. 1956. Assoc. Sylvester and Harris, N.Y.C., 1958-59; atty. NBC, N.Y.C., 1959-62, Screen Gems, Inc., N.Y.C., 1962-65; assoc. Regan, Goldfarb, Powell and Quinn, N.Y.C., 1965-69; assoc. to ptnr. Krause, Hirsch and Gross, N.Y.C., 1969-72; ptnr. Pryor, Cashman, Sherman and Flynn, N.Y.C., 1972-80; v.p. United Artists Corp., Culver City, Calif., 1980-82, Lorimar, Culver City, 1982-84; pvt. practice L.A., 1984—; bd. dirs., v.p. L.A. Venture Assn. With U.S. Army, 1955-57. Mem. ABA, L.A. Copyright Soc. Democrat. Jewish. Home: 4818 Mary Ellen Ave Sherman Oaks CA 91423

ERBURU, ROBERT F., newspaper publishing company executive; b. Ventura, Calif., Sept. 27, 1930. BA, U. So. Calif., 1952; LLB, Harvard U. Law Sch., 1955. Chmn. bd., chief exec. officer Times-Mirror Co., Los Angeles, also bd. dirs.; bd. dirs. Tejon Ranch Co.; bd. dirs., chmn. Fed. Res. Bank San Francisco. Trustee Huntington Library, Art Collections and Bot. Gardens, 1981—, Flora and William Hewlett Found., 1980—, Brookings Instn., 1983—, Tomas Rivera Ctr., 1985—, Carrie Estelle Doheny Found., Fletcher Jones Found., 1982—, Pfaffinger Found., 1974—, J. Paul Getty Trust; mem. exec. panel on future of welfare state Ford. Found., 1985—; bd. dirs., chmn. Times Mirror Found., 1962—; bd. dirs. Los Angeles Festival, 1985—, Ralph M. Parsons Found., 1985—; mem. Nat. Gallery of Art Trustees Council. Mem. Am. Newspaper Pubs. Assn. (treas., bd. dirs. 1980—), Council on Fgn. Relations (bd. dirs.), Bus. Roundtable, Bus. Council. Home: 1518 Blue Jay Way Los Angeles CA 90069 Office: Times Mirror Co Times Mirror Sq Los Angeles CA 90053

ERDMAN, BARBARA, visual artist; b. N.Y.C., Jan. 30, 1936; d. Isidore and Julia (Burstein) E. Student, Chinese Inst., 1959-60; BFA, Cornell U., 1956. Visual artist Santa Fe, 1977—; guest critic Studio Arte Centro Internat., Florence, Italy, 1986; guest lectr. Austin Coll. Sherman, Tex., 1986; mem. Oracle Conf. Polaroid Corp., nationwide, 1986—. Exhibited in numerous group shows, 1959—; one man shows include Aspen Inst., Baca, Colo., 1981, Scottsdale (Ariz.) Ctr. for the Arts, 1988; author: New Mexico, USA, 1985. Bd. dirs. N.Mex. Right to Choose, Santa Fe, 1981-87; mem. N.Mex. Mus. Found., Aluquerque Mus. Found. Mem. Art Student's League, Soc. for Photographic Edn. (guest lectr. 1987), Santa Fe Ctr. for Photography (pres., bd. dirs. 1984-89). Home: 1080 Calle Largo Santa Fe NM 87501

ERDMANN, JOACHIM CHRISTIAN, physicist; b. Danzig, June 5, 1928; s. Franz Werner and Maria Magdalena (Schreiber) E.; doctorate Tech. U. Braunschweig (Germany), 1958; m. Ursula Maria Wedemeyer, Aug. 24, 1957; children—Michael Andreas, Thomas Christian, Maria Martha Dorothea. Physicist, Osram Labs., Augsburg, Germany, 1954-60; sr. research scientist Boeing Sci. Research Labs., Seattle, 1960-72; sr. research scientist Boeing Aerospace Co., Seattle, 1972-73; prin. engr. Boeing Comml. Airplane Co., Seattle, 1973-81, sr. prin. engr., 1981-84; sr. prin. engr. Boeing Aerospace, Seattle, 1984—; vis. prof. Max Planck Inst. for Metals Research, Stuttgart, Germany, 1968-69; lectr. Tech. U. Stuttgart, 1968-69; pres. Optologics Inc., Seattle, 1973—. Mem. Am. Phys. Soc., Optical Soc. Am., Soc. Photo Optical Instrumentation Engrs. Author: Heat Conduction in Crystals, 1969. Contbr. articles to profl. jours. Research in cryogenics, statis. physics and opto electronics. Home: 14300 Trillium Blvd SE #8 Mill Creek WA 98012 Office: Boeing Aerospace PO Box 3999 Seattle WA 98124

ERDMANN, ROBERT JOSEPH, publisher; b. Chgo., Oct. 11, 1937; s. William E.A. and Florence (Enault) E.; m. Dorothy Mary Hermance, Aug. 16, 1958; children: Kathleen, Karen, Jennifer, Julia, Mary Ellen. AA, Kendall Coll., 1959; student, Northern Ill. U., 1960; LA, Loyola U., Chgo., 1962. Trainee Bell & Howell, Chgo., 1962-65; dist. mgr. Avery Products, L.A., 1965-68; regional mgr. Macmillan Pub. Co., L.A., 1968-74; v.p. Petersen Pub., L.A., 1974-76, World Pubs., San Francisco, 1976-78; pres., publisher Robert Erdmann Pub., L.A., 1978—; cons. to numerous publishers. Publisher: (mag.) Colorado Sportstyles, 1980-86, (book) Love and Power: Parent and Child, 1988. Mem. Am. Booksellers Assn., Pubs. Mktg. Assn. (bd. dirs. 1989—), Internat. Assn. Ind. Pubs. Roman Catholic. Home: 25 Cypress Way Rolling Hills Estates CA 90274 Office: Robert Erdmann Pub 28441 Highridge Rd Ste 101 Rolling Hills Estates CA 90274

ERICKSON, ALICE REBECCA, nurse; b. Pineville, La., Aug. 14, 1959; d. Arlington Lee and Mary Marie (Bush) McKee; m. Curt Joseph Erickson, Apr. 6,1979. AS in Nursing, Grayson County Coll., 1986. R.N., Tex., Calif., La. Staff nurse Dominican Hosp., Santa Cruz, Calif., 1987, Salinas (Calif.) Valley Meml. Hosp., 1987—. Mem. Am. Nurses Assn., Calif. Nurses Assn. Democrat. Home: 3117 Fredericksburg Ct Fort Ord CA 93941 Office: Salinas Valley Meml Hosp 450 E Romie Ln Salinas CA 93901

ERICKSON, ARTHUR CHARLES, architect; b. Vancouver, B.C., Can., June 14, 1924; s. Oscar and Myrtle (Chatterson) E. Student, U. B.C., Vancouver, 1942-44; B.Arch., McGill U., Montreal, Que., Can., 1950; LL.D. (hon.), Simon Fraser U., Vancouver, 1973, U. Man., Winnipeg, Can., 1978, Lethbridge U., 1981; D.Eng. (hon.), Novia Scotia Tech. Coll., McGill U., 1971; Litt.D. (hon.), U. B.C., 1985. Asst. prof. U. Oreg., Eugene, 1955-56; assoc. prof. U. B.C., 1956-63; ptnr. Erickson-Massey Architects, Vancouver, 1963-72; prin. Arthur Erickson Architects, Vancouver and Toronto, 1972—, Los Angeles, 1981—; dir. Campus Planning Assocs., Toronto. Prin. works include Can. Pavilion at Expo '70, Osaka (recipient first prize in nat. competition, Archtl. Inst. of Japan award for best pavilion), Robson Square/The Law Courts (honor award), Mus. of Anthropology (honor award), Eppich Residence (honor award), Habitat Pavilion (honor award), Sikh Temple (award of merit), Champlain Heights Community Sch. (award of merit); subject of Time mag. cover article and New Yorker profile; contbr. articles to profl. publs. Mem. com. on urban devel. Council of Can., 1971; bd. dirs. Can. Conf. of Arts, 1972; mem. design adv. council Portland Devel. Commn., Can. Council Urban Research; trustee Inst. Research on Pub. Policy. Served to capt. Can. Intelligence Corps, 1945-46. Recipient Molson prize Can. Council for Arts, 1967, Triangle award Nat. Soc. Interior Design, Royal Bank of Can. award, 1971, Gold medal Tau Sigma Delta, 1973, residential design award Can. Housing Council, 1975, August Perret award Internat. Union of Architects' Congress, 1975, Chgo. Architecture award, 1984, Gold medal French Acad. Architecture, 1984, Pres.' award Excellence, Am. Soc. Landscape Architects, 1979; named Officer, Order of Can., 1973, Companion, Order of Can., 1981; McLennan Travelling scholar; Can. Council fellow, 1961. Fellow AIA (hon., Pan Pacific citation Hawaiian chpt. 1963, Gold medal 1986), Royal Archtl. Inst. Can. (recipient award 1980, Gold medal 1984); mem. Archtl. Inst. B.C., Ont. Assn. Architects, Royal Can. Acad. Arts (academician), Am. Soc. Interior Designers, Ordre des Architectes du Quebec, Am. Soc. Planning Officials, Community Planning Assn. Can., Heritage Can., Planning Inst. B.C., Urban Land Inst. Clubs: Vancouver, U. B.C. Faculty, Univ. Office: Arthur Erickson Architects Inc, 80 Bloor St W 16th Fl, Toronto, ON Canada M5S 2V1 also: 2412 Laurel St, Vancouver, BC Canada V5Z 3T2 also: 125 N Robertson Los Angeles CA 90048 *

ERICKSON, CALVIN HOWARD, computer systems engineer; b. Worcester, Mass., June 18, 1946; s. Stanley Howard and Mae Harriet (Wivagg) E.; m. Radmila Frencic, June 5, 1970; children: Jennifer Joy, Melissa Mae. Student, Clark U., 1975-77; ABS in Computer Sci., Quinsagumord Community Coll., Worcester, 1971. Sr. systems programmer Datatrol Inc., Hudson, Mass., 1972-76; tech. support mgr. Keane Inc., Wellesley, Mass., 1976-81; software support specialist Data Gen. Corp., Westboro, Mass., 1981-87; computer systems engr. Loral Rolm-Mil Spec Computers, San Jose, Calif., 1987—. Author: AOS/VS Internal RWS, 1986. With USN, 1965-71. Mem. Nat. Geog. Soc., San Francisco Zool. Soc., Golden Gate Nat. Park Assn., The Friends of Photography (sustaining), Smithsonian (assoc.), Alpha Nu Omega. Home: 34786 Comstock Common Fremont CA 94555 Office: Loral Rolm Mil Spec Computers 1 River Oaks Pl San Jose CA 95134

ERICKSON, CAROL ANN, psychotherapist; b. Worcester, Mass., Dec. 26, 1933; d. Milton Hyland and Helen (Hutton) E.; m. Jean LaRue Barnes, Mar. 20, 1952 (div. Sept. 1962); children: Stephanie Free, Suzanne Hackett, Paul, Sandra Smith, Larry, Cynthia Baker. BS, Ariz. State U., 1964; MSW, Calif.

State U., Fresno, 1977. Social worker Los Angeles County, 1964-83; pvt. practice psychotherapy Berkeley, Calif., 1977—; exec. dir. Erickson Inst., Berkeley, 1981—; adj. faculty U. Calif., Berkeley; adj. faculty Vermont Coll. San Francisco, 1986—. Co-writer, composer Deep Self Appreciation, 1983, Self-Hypnosis, A Relaxing Time Out, 1984, Natural Self Confidence, 1985, Deep Sleep and Sweet Dreams, 1989, Rapid Pain Control, 1989, Easy Enhanced Learning, 1989. Bd. dirs. YWCA, Torrance, Calif., 1981-83. Mem. Internat. Soc. Hypnosis, No. Calif. Soc. Clin. Hypnosis, So. Calif. Soc. Clin. Hypnosis, Calif. Assn. Marriage and Family Therapists (cert.), Soc. Clin. and Exptl. Hypnosis, Soc. Clin. Social Workers, Nat. Assn. Social Workers (cert.), AAUW, NOW, Phi Kappa Phi. Democrat. Office: Erickson Inst PO Box 739 Berkeley CA 94701

ERICKSON, DAVID ERICK, banker; b. Portland, Oreg., Sept. 12, 1950; s. Erick Helge and Hope (Bishop) E.; m. Linda Eileen Bryant, Sept. 30, 1978; ch ildren: Peter, Thomas. BS, Portland State U., 1975. Letter of credit officer U.S. Nat. Bank Oreg., Portland, 1977-80, letters of credit mgr., 1980--, asst. v.p., 1983-85, v.p., 1987--; guest lectr. Pacific Northwest Internat. Trade Assn., Portland, 1980--. Hom. bd. dirs. Portland Rose Festival Assn., 1986-88. Mem. Portland Rose Soc. (bd. dirs.), Alpha Kappa Psi. Republican. Anglo Catholic. Office: US Nat Bank Oreg 309 SW 6th Ave Portland OR 97208

ERICKSON, LARRY RAY, dermatologist; b. Rapid City, S.D., July 17, 1937; s. Lawrence Ervin and Doris G. (Nelsen) E.; m. Valerie J. Wagner, Aug. 23, 1980; children: Melanie, Timothy, Jonathan, Lisa, Sarah, Daniel. BA, St. Olaf Coll., 1959; MD, U. Minn., 1963. Flight surgeon dermatologist USAF, 1964-73; practice medicine specializing in dermatology Lakewood, Colo., 1974—; asst. clin. prof. dermatology, Health Scis. Ctr. U. Colo., Denver, 1978—. Contbr. articles to profl. jours. Fellow Am. Acad. Dermatology; mem. Colo. Dermatol. Soc., Colo. Med. Soc., Clear Creek Valley Med. Soc., Colo. Soc. for Dermatol. Surgery. Repulican. Lutheran. Office: 255 Union Blvd Suite 440 Lakewood CO 80228

ERICKSON, LELAND JOHN, manufacturing executive; b. Milw., Oct. 26, 1951; s. Orland Jerald and Shirley Eudean (Thornsen) E.; m. Lynn Margaret Wright, June 25, 1977 (div. 1987). Student, U. Wis., 1970-72. Mfg. engr. Component Parts Inc., Waukesha, Wis., 1971-73; mgr. engr. Indsl. Concepts Corp., Albuquerque, 1973-74, Noor Mfg. Co., Albuquerque, 1975-77; gen. mgr. Gruber Co., Albuquerque, 1977-80; plant mgr. Seeley Enterprises, Inc., Albuquerque, 1980-86, mgr. mfg. engring., 1986—. Spl. mgr. Carruthers for Gov. Campaign, Albuquerque, 1986. Mem. Precision Machining Assn. (v.p. 1987-89, bd. dirs. 1985-89), Nat. Geographic Soc., Tech. Vocat. Inst., NRA. Republican. Lutheran.

ERICKSON, RALPH HULL, judge; b. Egg Harbor, Wis., Dec. 19, 1931; s. Alric and Bess Maxwell (Miller) E.; m. Barbara Bond, Oct. 1, 1955 (dec.); children: Lynn, Julia, Robert; m. Suzanne Liebers, Feb. 14, 1978 (dec.). BS, Lawrence U., 1954; JD, U. Mich., 1957. Bar: Colo. 1958, Calif. 1977. Staff atty. SEC, Denver, 1957-59, spl. counsel, 1960-70; regional counsel, asst. gen. counsel SEC, L.A., 1972-82; pvt. practice Denver, 1959-60; adminstrv. law judge Social Security Adminstrn., L.A., 1982—; guest lectr. Loyola U. Law Sch., L.A., 1976, 77, Pepperdine U. Law Sch., 1980. Recipient Achievement award SEC, 1963, 78. Mem. ABA, Calif. Bar Assn., Colo. Bar Assn., L.A. Bar Assn., Fed. Bar Assn., L.A. Opera League, L.A. World Affairs Coun. Presbyterian. Home: 18434 Clifftop Way Malibu CA 90265 Office: Social Security Adminstrn 11000 Wilshire Blvd Ste 8200 Los Angeles CA 90024

ERICKSON, RICHARD BEAU, life insurance company executive; b. Chgo., May 14, 1952; s. Charles Arthur and Carole Annette (Beaumont) E.; m. Pamela J. Sievers, Aug. 20, 1977. BS, U. Ky., 1974, MBA, 1975. CLU. Sales rep. Met. Life and affiliated cos., Chgo. Hgts., Ill., 1975-78; sales mgr. Met. Life and affiliated cos., Flossmoor, Ill., 1978-80; mktg. specialist Met. Life and affiliated cos., Aurora, Ill., 1980-81; branch mgr. Met. Life and affiliated cos., Orland Park, Ill., 1981-84; corp. dir. Met. Life Gen. Ins. Agy. Inc., N.Y.C., 1984-86; regional sales mgr. Met. Life Gen. Ins. Agy. Inc., L.A., 1986—, regional exec., sr. mktg. and sales exec., 1986—, agy. v.p., 1989; rep. (Midwest) Sales Mgr. Adv., N.Y.C., 1979; dir. South Cook County Assn. Life Underwriters, Chgo., 1983. Author: Met. Manpower Development, 1981, Met. Manpower Development: A Guideline for Success, 1986. Sponsor L.A. Lazers Indoor Soccer, 1986—, UCLA Soccer, 1986—, L.A. Kings Ice Hockey, 1988—. Mem. Nat. Assn. Securities Dealers, Life Underwriters Tng. Counsel, Chartered Life Underwriters, U. Ky. Alumni Assn., Sigma Nu. Republican. Office: Met Life 15910 Ventura Blvd #1729 Encino CA 91436

ERICKSON, ROBERT ANDREW, franchise sales executive, consultant; b. Hartford, Conn., Apr. 2, 1940; s. Oscar Emanuel and Madeline Augusta (Pickering) E. BS, U. Hartford, 1962. Mgr. maintenance for various services cos. 1962-69; owner, pres. Service Keepers, Inc., Ft. Lauderdale, Fla., 1969-76; owner, operator Erickson Bldg. Services, Phoenix, 1976, Modern Maintenance Corp., St. Petersburg, Fla., 1979, Sunrise Maintenance Systems, Phoenix, 1979-85; pres. Januz Internat. Ltd., El Cajon, Calif., 1986—; cons. in field. Contbr. articles to profl. jours. Former mem. Fla. legis., 1966-67. Mem. Internat. Franchise Assn., Bldg. Service Contractors Assn. Internat. Republican. Roman Catholic. Office: Januz Internat Ltd 356 N Marshall Ave Suite B El Cajon CA 92020

ERICKSON, ROBERT GREGORY, defence writer; b. Mpls., Apr. 20, 1944; s. Robert Charles and Margie (Gibson) E.; m. Gloria Jane Blake, Apr. 1, 1983. AA, U. Minn., 1974; student, Mpls. Sch. Bus., 1975. Commd. 2d lt. USMC, 1961, advanced through grades to capt., 1965; various combat assignments USMC, Vietnam, 1961-71; resigned USMC, 1972; petroleum engr. Brit. Petroleum Co., N. Slope, Alaska, 1976-78; security advisor P.S.S. Security, 1978-86; engr. Petredat, Inc., Anchorage, 1983-89, Internat. Strategic Studies Def. and Fgn. Affairs, Anchorage, 1989—. Decorated Purple Heart with silver oak leaf cluster, Silver Star, Bronze Star with oak leaf cluster. Mem. NRA, Masons. Republican. Lutheran. Home: 8440 Stacey Circle Anchorage AK 99507 Office: Internat Strategic Studies Def and Fgn Affairs 8440 Stacey Circle Anchorage AK 99507

ERICKSON, RUSSELL CARL, III, dentist; b. Chgo., Dec. 9, 1955; s. Russell Irving Jr. and Dorothy Lee (White) E.; m. Kathy Fernanne Piper, Sept. 7, 1980; children: Russell Carl IV, Avery Karyn. BS, Pacific Union Coll., 1978; DDS, Loma Linda U., 1983. Pvt. practice cosmetic and reconstructive dentistry Portland, Oreg., 1983—; mem. med. and dental staff Portland Adventist Med. Ctr., 1988—; mem. dental research group Saul Robinson, Portland, 1986—; lectr. corps., service clubs and health clubs. Mem. ADA, Oreg. Dental Assn., Multnomah Dental Soc. Republican. Lodge: Rotary (program com., student guest com.). Office: 511 SW 10th Ave Ste 1202 Portland OR 97205-2792

ERICKSON, VIRGINIA BEMMELS, chemical engineer; b. Sleepy Eye, Minn., June 19, 1948; d. Gordon Boothe and Marion Mae (Rieke) Bemmels; m. Larry Douglas Erickson, Sept. 6, 1969; children: Kirsten Danielle, Dean Michael. Diploma in Nursing, Swedish Hosp. Sch. Nursing, 1969; BSChemE, U. Wash., 1983, MChemE, 1985. RN. Asst. head nurse N. Meml. Hosp., Mpls., 1970-73; intensive care RN Swedish Med. Ctr., Seattle, 1973-83; research asst. U. Wash., Seattle, 1983-85; instrumentation and control engr. CH2M Hill, Bellevue, Wash., 1985—, mgr. dept., 1988—; cons. instrumentation and control engr. Leader Girl Scouts U.S., Seattle, 1985; supt. Seattle Ch. Sch., 1983; rep. United Way, 1986—. Recipient Cert. Achievement, Soc. Women Engrs., 1983. Mem. Am. Inst. Chem. Engrs., Instrument Soc. Am., Tau Beta Pi. Democrat. Mem. United Methodist Ch. Home: 6026 24th NE Seattle WA 98115 Office: CH2M Hill 777 108th Ave NE PO Box 91500 Bellevue WA 98009-2050

ERICKSON, WILLIAM HURT, judge; b. Denver, May 11, 1924; s. Arthur Xavier and Virginia (Hurt) E.; m. Doris Rogers, Dec. 24, 1953; children: Barbara Ann, Virginia Lee, Stephen Arthur, William Taylor. Student, Colo. Sch. Mines, 1947, U. Mich., 1949; LLB, U. Va., 1950. Bar: Colo. 1951. Pvt. practiced law Denver; justice Colo. Supreme Ct., 1971—, chief justice, 1983-85; faculty NYU Appellate Judges Sch., 1972-85; mem. exec. com. Commn. on Accreditation of Law Enforcement Agys., 1980-83. With USAAF, 1943. Recipient award of merit Colo. Com. Continuing Legal Edn., 1968. Fellow Internat. Acad. Trial Lawyers (former sec.), Am. Coll. Trial Lawyers, Am. Bar Found. (state chmn. 1971), Internat. Soc. Barristers (pres. 1971); mem. ABA, (bd. govs. 1975-79, former chmn. ocm. on standards criminal justice, fomer chmn. coun. criminal law sect., former chmn. com. to implement standards criminal justice, mem. long-range planning com., action com. to reduce ct. cost and delay),Am. Law Inst. (coun.), Practising Law Inst. (nat. adv. coun., bd. govs. Colo.), Denver Bar Assn. (past pres., trustee), Freedoms Found. at Valley Forge (nat. coun. trustees, 1986—), Order of Coif, Scribes (pres. 1978). Home: 10 Martin Ln Englewood CO 80110 Office: Colo Supreme Ct 2 E 14th Ave Denver CO 80203 also: Colorado Supreme Ct Denver CO 80203

ERICSSON, ERIC OSCAR, consultant; b. Coos Bay, Oreg., Dec. 10, 1912; s. Oscar S. and Agnes (Nyquist) E.; m. Clara Maude Newton, Aug. ll, 1934; children: Mark S., Heidi M. BSChemE, U. wash., 1937. Registered profl. engr., Wash. Vice pres. ops. Puget Sound Pulp & Timber Co., Bellingham, Wash., 1934-65; gen. mgr. chem. Ga.-Pacific Co., Portland, Oreg., 1965-67; gen. mgr. pulp Ga.-Pacific Co., Samoa, Calif., 1967-69; gen. mgr. paper Ga.-Pacific Co., Toledo, Oreg., 1969-7l; mgr. pulp div. Ga.-Pacific Co., Bellingham, 197l-77; cons. Pulp, Paper & Chems. Mgmt. Svcs., Bellingham, 1977--. Patentee in field. Fellow TAPPI. Home and Office: 222 S Garden St Bellingham WA 98225

ERIKSON, GLENN ROBERT, real estate developer, architect; b. Indpls., Feb. 12, 1951; s. Erik Gunnar and Mabel Elizabeth (Anderson) E.; m. Lorie Lloyd, Aug. 30, 1977; children: Annika, Sören. BArch, U. Ariz., 1974, MS in Real Estate and Fin., 1981. Registered architect, Calif.; lic. real estate broker and contractor, Calif.; cert. community coll. tchr., Calif. Prin. Erikson Design Group, Tucson, San Diego, L.A., 1975-85; project designer, mgr. Deems/Lewis & Ptnr.s, San Diego, 1977-80; v.p. design and devel. Subbiondo & Assocs., Fountain Valley, Calif., 1981-82; v.p. Ctr. Fin. Group, Century City, Calif., 1982-85; gen. ptnr., exec. v.p. L.A. Land Co., 1985—; mng. ptnr. The Erikson Partnership, L.A., 1988—; seminar tchr. UCLA, U. Calif., San Diego, Santa Barbara, Berkeley, 1982-85. Prin. works include NCR Office Bldg., San Diego, 1978, Orangegate Pla., Westminster, Calif., 1980-85, Morton Pk. Apts., L.A., 1985, Exposition Plaza, L.A., 1985, Sherman Pla., L.A., 1986, Tustin Ctr. Pla., Orange, Calif., 1986, 10401 Bldg., L.A., 1986, New York Lake Pla., L.A., 1986, Marina Fashion Pla., Long Beach, Calif., 1987, Magnolia Pla., Westminster, Calif., 1987, Chaparrel Lanes, San Dimas, Calif., 1987, Sawtelle Pla., West L.A., 1988, Newport/El Camino Pla., Tustin, Calif., 1988, North Venice Artist Studios, 1989, 520 San Julien SRO Housing, 1989. Young Mens Pres. Ch. Jesus Christ of Latter-day Sts., San Diego, 1978, elders quorum pres., La Jolla, Calif., 1979-80; scoutmaster Boy Scouts Am., Van Nuys, Calif., 1986-87. Mem. AIA, Urban Land Inst., Internat. Coun. Shopping Ctrs. Office: The Erikson Ptnrship 10401 Venice Blvd Ste 201 Los Angeles CA 90034

ERISMAN, TERRANCE LEE, research and development engineer; b. Sterling, Colo., Feb. 15, 1964; s. Edwin Chris. Jr. and Barbara Jean (Dickson) E. BA in Chemistry cum laude, Harvard U., 1986; postgrad., Stanford U., 1988—. Research mgr. First Omega Group Inc., Golden, Colo., 1987; research and devel. engr. Adolph Coors Co., Golden, 1987-88; vis. scientist Colo. Alliance for Sci., Westminster, Colo., 1987—; co. advisor Colo. Bus. Week, Greeley, 1987. Mem. Leadership Devel. program, Golden, 1987—. Mem. Am. Chem. Soc., Internat. Soc. for Optical Engring., Zeta Psi (social dir. 1985-86). Home: Rains Houses Box 735 Stanford CA 94305 Office: Adolph Coors 17755 W 32d Ave #CC152 Golden CO 80401

ERLITZ, PETE R., business school director; b. Bklyn., Apr. 21, 1949; s. Sidney and Alice M. (Malm) E.; 1 child, Alicia Ellen. Advt. dir. UBI Ltd. doing bus. as United Coll., St. Louis, 1981-83; nat. advt. dir. UBI Ltd. doing bus. as Price, Rubin & Assocs., St. Louis, 1983-84; agy. dir. UBI Ltd. doing bus. as USA Advt. Inc., St. Louis, 1984-86; dir. admissions Career Com Corp. doing bus. as Mansfield Bus. Coll., St. Louis, 1986; dir. Career Com. Corp. doing bus. as Mansfield Bus. Sch., Denver, 1986—. Active St. Louis Ambassadors, 1985-86. Served with USAF, 1967-71, Vietnam. Mem. Colo. Pvt. Sch. Assn. (polit. action com. 1987—, pub. rels. com. 1989—, bd. trustees 1989—). Home: 4369 S Quebec St #6308 Denver CO 80237 Office: Mansfield Bus Sch 2200 W Alameda Ave Denver CO 80223

ERNST, ED WILLIAM, technical educator, furniture designer; b. Huntington Park, Calif., July 21, 1950; s. Carl Conrad and Ruth (Hilmer) E.; m. Virginia Loretta Oates, March 26, 1988. AA, Fullerton Jr. Coll., 1968-70; BA, Calif. State U., Long Beach, 1970-72; MA, Pepperdine U., 1984-85. Instr. Canyon High Sch., Anaheim, Calif., 1972—; instr. Fullerton (Calif.) Jr. Coll., 1976-85, Adult Edn. Classes, Orange, Calif., 1974-84; cabinetmaker Ganahl Lumber Co., Anaheim, 1985-88; private class instr. Ganahl Lumber Co., 1980-88; wood finishing tech. cons. Ganahl Lumber Co., 1982-83; owner and mgr. Ed Ernst Fine Furniture, Orange, 1980-82. Roman Catholic. Home: 509 Avenida Faro Anaheim CA 92807 Office: Canyon High Sch 220 Imperial Hwy Anaheim CA 92807

EROKAN, DENNIS WILLIAM, magazine publisher; b. Istanbul, Turkey, Aug. 20, 1950; came to U.S., 1955; s. Don H. and Athena (Caragianis) E.; m. Lori Engelfried, Dec. 18, 1976; children: Lane Katharine, Darcy Beth, William Bruce. Grad. high sch., San Jose, Calif., 1968. Bassist Green Catherine band, San Francisco and N.Y.C., 1973-74; mgr. Peter's Plum Restaurant, Boston, 1974-75; nat. sales mgr. Dean Markley Strings, Santa Clara, Calif., 1975; chief exec. officer Bam Publs., Oakland and Los Angeles, Calif., 1976—; Exec. producer, founder Bay Area Music awards, San Francisco, 1978-; pres., founder Bay Area Music Archives, San Francisco, 1979-86; concert producer, Hollywood, 1983, San Francisco, 1978-83; bd. dirs. San Francisco Rock and Roll Mus., 1986—. Editor, publisher (mag.) The Mix, 1977-78, BAM, 1976— (Maggie award 1984, 86, 87, 89), MicroTimes, 1984— (2 Maggie awards 1986); exec. producer (TV show) The 1981 Bammies, 1981, A San Fransisco Celebration, 1986; contbr. articles to mags. Auctioneer KQED Fundraiser, San Francisco, 1978—. Mem. Nat. Acad. Songwriters (bd. dirs. 1983-88), Freedom Found. (bd. dirs. 1980-83). Episcopalian. Office: BAM Pubs The BAM Network/MicroTimes 5941 Canning St Oakland CA 94609

EROS, JAMES MICHAEL, sales executive; b. Detroit, June 12, 1942; s. Louis and Ellen Taylor (Beauvais) E.; m. Beverly Jean Leitgeb, Feb. 18, 1964 (div. 1982); children: James Albert, Jennifer Michelle. BS, Madonna Coll., Livonia, Mich., 1975; BS in Criminology, Madonna Coll., 1975; grad., Metro Police Acad., Livonia, 1970. Producer WKBD-TV, Southfield, Mich., 1968-70; patrolman Livonia Police Dept., 1970-77; owner Eros Ent., Las Vegas, Nev., 1978-83; sales mgr. Thousand Trails, Cleve., 1983-85, NACO, Yosemite Lakes, Calif., 1985-88, Sta. KSBQ Radio, Santa Maria, Calif., 1988—. With U.S. Army, 1959-62. Named Policeman of the Year, VFW, 1975.

ERPELDING, CURTIS MICHAEL, furniture designer; b. Ft. Dodge, Iowa, Nov. 29, 1950; s. Clarence Peter and Catherine Angela (Swirzcynski) E. BS in English Edn., U. Colo., 1972. Designer, prin. Curtis Erpelding Furniture Design, Seattle, 1977—; bd. dirs. Northwest Gallery Fine Woodworking, Seattle. Subject (videotape): Radial Arm Saw Joinery, 1985; contbr. articles to profl. publs.; one man shows at Oreg. Sch. Arts and Crafts, 1982, North West Gallery Fine Woodworking, 1983; exhibited in group show at Am. Craft Mus., 1986-88. NEA grantee, 1980-81. Mem. Am. Craft Coun. Office: Curtis Erpelding Furniture Design 1300 Post Alley Seattle WA 98101

ERSKINE, CHRISTOPHER FORBES, geologist; b. Worcester, Mass., Apr. 30, 1927; s. Linwood Mandeville and Katharine Maria (Forbes) E.; m. Joanne Lewis, Sept. 5, 1952; children: Christopher L., William T. (dec.); 1 stepchild, Dennis W. AB, Harvard U., 1949; postgrad., Colo. Sch. Mines., Golden, 1949-50. Cert. profl. geologist, profl. hydrogeologist. Geologist U.S. Geol. Survey, Denver, 1950-57, Eugene B. Waggoner, Cons. Engring. Geologists, Denver, 1957-60; project geologist Woodward-Clyde-Sherard & Assocs., Denver, 1960-62; water geologist Kennecott Copper Corp., Salt Lake City, 1962-70; groundwater geologist AMAX Exploraiton, Inc., Denver, 1970-82; cons. groundwater geologist Christopher F. Erskine, Cons. Groundwater Geologist, Littleton, Colo., 1982-85; hydrologist Pinto Valley Copper Co., Miami, Ariz., 1985-87, Magma Copper Co., Pinto Valley div., Miami, 1987—. Bd. mgrs. Littleton YMCA, 1975-85. With U.S. Army, 1945-46. Mem. AIME, Am. Inst. Hydrology, Am. Inst. Profl. Geologists, Geol. Soc. Am., Nat. Water Well Assn. (tech. div.). Home: PO Box 97 Claypool AZ 85532 Office: Magma Copper Co PO Box 100 Miami AZ 85539

ERSKINE, JOHN MORSE, surgeon; b. San Francisco, Sept. 10, 1920; s. Morse and Dorothy (Ward) E. Diplomate Am. Bd. Surgery. Surg. intern U. Calif. Hosp., San Francisco, 1945-46; surg. researcher Mass. Gen. Hosp., Boston, 1948; resident in surgery Peter Bent Brigham Hosp., Boston, 1948-53; George Gorham Peters fellow St. Mary's Hosp., London, 1952; pvt. practice in medicine specializing in surgery San Francisco, 1954—; asst. clin. prof. Stanford Med. Sch., San Francisco, 1956-59; asst., assoc. clin. prof. U. Calif. Med. Sch., San Francisco, 1959—; surg. cons. San Francisco Vets. Hosp., 1959-73. Contbr. articles to profl. jours., chpts. to books. Founder No. Calif. Artery Bank, 1954-58, Irwin Meml. Blood Bank, San Francisco, commr., pres., 1969-74; bd. dirs. People for Open Space-Greenbelt Alliance, 1984—; chmn. adv. coun. Dorothy Enskine Open Space Fund. Capt. with U.S. Army, 1946-48. Fellow ACS; mem. San Francisco Med. Soc. (dir. 1968-72), Am. Cancer Sco. (bd. dirs. San Francisco br. 1965-75), San Francisco Surg. Soc. (v.p. 1984), Pacific Coast Surg. Soc., Calif. Med. Assn., Olympic Club. Democrat. Unitarian. Home: 233 Chestnut St San Francisco CA 94133 Office: 2340 Clay St San Francisco CA 94120

ERSKINE, JOHN WARD, electrical engineer, consultant; b. Huntington, W.Va., Oct. 7, 1941; s. Charles Thomas and Marcella May (Ward) E.; m. Jan Morris, Sept. 7, 1967; children: David Morris, Deborah Foster. BSEE, Mich. State U., 1969. Staff engr. Sperry Gyroscope Co., Gt. Neck, N.Y., 1969-73; program mgr. Kaman Scis. Corp., Colorado Springs, Colo., 1973-84; v.p. Energy Billing Systems, Colorado Springs, 1984—; dep. program mgr. Kaman Aerospace Corp., Colorado Springs, 1986—. With USAF, 1960-64. Home: 1070 Hidden Valley Rd Colorado Springs CO 80919 Office: Kaman Aerospace Corp 1500 Garden of Gods Rd Colorado Springs CO 80907

ERVEN, ERIC LYNN, construction company executive; b. Grand Junction, Colo., Sept. 2, 1965; s. Homer Lee and Wilma Edwina (Stewart) E.; m. Janelle Lynn Brehm, Nov. 14, 1987. BA in Bus. Adminstrn., Mesa Coll., 1987. Owner Silver "E" Tng. Stables, Delta, Colo., 1979-83; loan officer AVCO Fin. Services, Grand Junction, Colo., 1987—; office mgr. Hansen Bldg. Specialties, Grand Junction; owner ERven's Fin., Fruita, Colo., 1987—. Youth dir. Midwest/Northwest ApHC, Grand Junction, 1986-88; state del. Colo. Reps., Grand Junction, 1986-88. Mem. Future Farmers Am. (dist. pres. 1982-83, state winner pub. speaking, Denver 1982, 83). Methodist. Club: Appaloosa Horse (20th in World show). Home: 2022 Hwy 6 Fruita CO 81521

ERVIN, PATRICK FRANKLIN, nuclear engineer; b. Kansas City, Kans., Aug. 4, 1946; s. James Franklin and Irma Lee (Arnett) E.; m. Rita Jeanne Kimsey, Aug. 12, 1967; children: James, Kevin, Amber. BS in Nuclear Engring., Kans. State U., 1969, MS in Nuclear Engring., 1971. Registered profl. engr., Ill., Colo., Calif. Reactor health physicist Kans. State U. Dept. Nuclear Engring., Manhattan, 1968-69, research asst., 1969-72, sr. reactor operator, temp. facility dir., 1970-72; system test engr. Commonwealth Edison Co., Zion, Ill., 1972-73, 73-74, shift foreman, 1973, shift foreman with sr. reactor operator lic., 1974-76, prin. engr., 1976-77, acting operating engr., 1977; tech. staff supr. Commonwealth Edison Co., Byron, Ill., 1977-81; lead test engr. Stone & Webster Engring. Corp., Denver, 1982-83, project mgr., 1982—, ops. services supr., 1982-86, asst. engring. mgr., 1986—. Contbr. articles to profl. jours. Served with U.S. Army N.G., 1971-77. Mem. Am. Nuclear Soc. (Nat. and Colo. chpts., treas. exec. bd. reactor ops. div.), Am. Nat. Standards Inst. (working group on containment leakage testing). Republican. Roman Catholic. Home: 2978 S Bahama St Aurora CO 80013 Office: Stone & Webster Engring Corp PO Box 5406 Denver CO 80217

ERVIN, ROBERT I., technical engineer; b. Coeur D'Alene, Idaho, Feb. 1, 1954; s, Lawrence D. and Charlotte M. (Crane) E.; m. Barbara A. Bentley, July 27, 1984; 1 child, Natalie A. AAS in Mech. Engring. Tech., Spokane (Wash.) Community Coll., 1983; student in design graphics, Gonzaga U., 1984, student in autocad, 1985, student in autolisp lang., 1988. Surgery porter Kootenai Meml. Hosp., Couer D'Alene, 1976-78; shop foreman Krishian Bros. Carpet, Inc., Spokane, 1978-79; ind. carpet installer Spokane, Seattle, 1979-81, Meier's Carpet Service, Inc., Olympia, Wash., 1981-82; draftsman Wanless-Cook Asscos., Spokane, 1983-85; cad operator Bovay NW, Inc., Spokane, 1985-87, CAD ops. dir., sr. system designer, prodn. mgr., autolisp programmer, 1989—; tech. engr. Spokane County Engrs., 1987-88. Lutheran. Office: Bovay Northwest Inc N 4904 Adams Spokane WA 99205

ESCHENBURG, EMIL PAUL, real estate broker; b. Mt. Clemens, Mich., Dec. 26, 1915; s. Paul Frederick and Ella Sophia (Weise) E.; m. Betty G., June 5, 1943 (div. July 1975); children: Paula, Emil P., Erich G., Lise Ann. BS with high honors, Mich. State U., 1939; grad., Nat. War Coll., Washington, 1957; postgrad., Harvard U., 1960; MA in Internat. Rels., George Washington U., 1971. Cert. real estate residential specialist, real estate investment specialist. With U.S. Army, 1939-70, 2d lt., 1940-60, brig. gen., 1960-63, asst. comdr. 101st Airborne div., 1963-65, chief joint mil. asst., 1965-67, comdg. gen. 1st inf. div., 1967-70; salesman Crows Nest Harbor, Washington, 1971-72, Sandy McPherson Realty, Helena, Mont., 1973-80; broker, mgr. Century-21/Heritage Realty, Helena, 1980—; pres. Century-21 Broker's Coun. for Mont., 1988—. Pres. Helena Bd. Realtors, 1976-77, YMCA, 1988, Helena MLS, 1986; elder Luth. ch., 1981-83; bd. dirs. Mont. State Bd. Realtors, 1977-80, Model Cities Devel. Corp., 1976-80; chmn. Nat. Fund Drive Mont. Vietnam Vets., Washington, 1983-85. Named Top C-21 Real Estate Salesperson State of Mont., 1987, 88. Mem. Nat. Assn. Realtors, Century-21 Investment Soc., Million Dollar Sales Club, Nat. Mktg. Assn., Helena C. of C., DAV, Purple Heart, VFW, Helena Navy League (pres. 1985-86), Kiwanis (pres. Helena chpt. 1980-81, bd. govs. 1983-87), Green Meadow Country Club, Mont. Club (pres. 1981). Republican. Lutheran. Home: 2108 8th Ave Helena MT 59601 Office: Century 21/Heritage Realty 1744 N Montana Ave Helena MT 59601

ESHERICK, JOSEPH, architect, emeritus educator; b. Phila., Dec. 28, 1914; s. Josep and Helen (Gangwisch) E.; m. Rebecca Wood, 1939; children—Lisa, Joseph, Peter; m. Ann Rowe, 1953; children—Maria, Julia; m. Norma Nashida, 1981. B.Arch., U. Pa., Phila., 1937. Registered architect, Mo., Idaho, Ariz., Oreg., Colo., N.Y., Utah, Nev., U.K. Sole practice in architecture San Francisco, 1946-53; pres. Joseph Esherick & Assocs., San Francisco, 1953-72, Esherick Homsey Dodge & Davis, San Francisco, 1972—; instr. dept. architecture U. Calif., Berkeley, 1952-56, assoc. prof., 1956-58, prof., 1958-85, chmn. dept. architecture, 1977-82, prof. emeritus, 1985—; cons. and lectr. in field. Contbr. chpts. to books, articles to profl. jours.; subject of numerous books; archtl. works include: New Exhibits, San Francisco Zool. Gardens, 1977, Gallo House, Modesto, Calif., 1977. Recipient numerous awards, fellowships and grants for excellence in architecture including: Graham Found. fellow for Advanced Studies in Fine Arts, 1962; Bay Area Honor award, 1967; fellow Adlai E. Stevenson Coll., U. Calif.-Santa Cruz, 1968. Fellow AIA (numerous coms., Gold medal 1989); mem. NAD, Lambda Alpha. Democrat. Office: Esherick Homsey Dodge & Davis 2789-25th St San Francisco CA 94110 *

ESKEW, CATHLEEN CHEEK, organization administrator; b. Oklahoma City, Oct. 20, 1953; d. John Dasherman and Nancy Lucile (Gray) Cheek; m. Bruce Lynn Eskew, Aug. 23, 1986; children (twins): William Michael, Matthew James. BA in Math., Whitworth Coll., 1976; MST, Fuller Sem., Pasadena, Calif., 1984; postgrad., U. Colo., Colorado Springs. Cert. secondary tchr., Colo. Tchr., adminstrv. asst. The Colorado Springs Sch., 1976-78; recruiter, trainer Young Life, Colorado Springs, 1978-82; researcher Young Life Internat., Port-au-Prince, Haiti, 1982-83; documentation specialist Compassion Internat., Colorado Springs, 1984-85, program adminstr., 1986—. Named an Outstanding Young Woman in Am., 1981. Mem. Assn. Evang. Relief and Devel. Orgn., Whitworth Coll. Alumni Assn. (councilperson 1978-81). Democrat. Presbyterian. Home: 6215 Moorfield Ave Colorado Springs CO 80919 Office: Compassion Internat 3955 Cragwood Dr Colorado Springs CO 80918

ESKIND, NORMAN JO ANDREW, statistical analyst; b. Manhattan, N.Y., Aug. 11, 1955; s. Sigmund Harold and Jean Grace (Hepner) E. BA in History, McGill U., Montreal, Can., 1980; M in Internat. Rels., U. Paris, 1982, M in Internat. Econs., 1982. Statistician Anders, Aktiebolaget, Stockholm, 1980-83; estate appraiser Scandphil Assocs., Mountain View, Calif., 1983-84; v.p. Scandphil Assocs., Mountain View, 1985—; chief investment officer Norman-James Assocs., San Jose, Calif., 1985; pres., chief exec. officer Norman-Anders, Inc., Mountain View, 1985—. Author: Anzac Participation in World War I, 1982, European Economic Community and Member Nations' Stock Markets: Winners and Losers in International Trading, 1973-1983, 1983; contbr. articles newspapers. Mem. Nat. Assn. Securities Dealers, Soc. Israel Philatelists, Royal Philatelic Soc. Can., McGill Grads. Soc. No. Calif., Sino-Judaic Inst., Can. Cutural Orgn. Republican. Jewish. Home: 3412 Churin Dr Mountain View CA 94040-4533

ESPALDON, ERNESTO MERCADER, senator, plastic surgeon; b. Sulu, Philippines, Nov. 11, 1926; s. Cipriano Acuna Espaldon and Claudia (Cadag) Mercader); m. Leticia Legaspi Virata, May 31, 1952; children: Arlene Espaldon Ramos, Vivian Espaldon Wolff, James, Diane, Karl, Ernesto Jr. AA, U. Philippines, Manila, 1949; MD, U. Santo tomas, Manila, 1954; postgrad., Washington U., St. Louis, 1961. Diplomate Am. Bd. Plastic Surgery. Resident in gen. surgery U. Okla. Med. Ctr., Oklahoma City, 1959; gen. and plastic surgeon Guam Meml. Hosp., Agana, 1963—, chief surgery, 1965-69; pres., plastic surgeon Espaldon Clinic, Agana, 1969—; mem. Guam Legislature, Agana, 1974-80, 86—, chmn. Com. on Health, Welfare and Ecology and Com. on Ethics and Standards, 1986—; vis. prof. Bicol Med. and Edn. Ctr., Legaspi City, The Philippines, 1980—. Pres., founder Guam Balikbayan Med. Mission, Agana, 1974—; organizer, co-founder Aloha Med., Mission, Honolulu, 1982—; pres. PTA Acad. Our Lady Guam, Agana, 1969-71; bd. dirs. Am. Cancer Soc., Agana, 1969-82, ARC, Agana, 1969-82, Vocat. Rehab., Agana, 1969-82, Guam Meml. Hosp., 1969-82. Guerrilla comdr. Sulu (Philippines) Area Command, 1943-46, 2d lt. Philippine Army, 1946-47. Recipient Thomas Jefferson award for pub. svc., Washington, 1983; named Outstanding Filipino Overseas Philippine Govt. and Philippine Jaycees, 1982, Most Outstanding Alumni U. Santo Tomas, 1981, Outstanding Community Leader of Guam Philippine-Am. Community, 1979, Outstanding Community Leader of Guam Jaycees, 1982. Fellow Am. Coll. Surgeons, Philippine Coll. Surgeons; mem. AMA, Guam Med. Soc. (pres. 1970-72, chief del. to AMA 1973-76), KC. Republican. Roman Catholic. Home: PO Box CE Agana GU 96910 Office: Guam Legislature Capitol Bldg Agana GU 96910

ESPINEIRA, ANDY, IV, manufacturing executive; b. Guatemala, Dec. 14, 1949; came to U.S., 1962; s. Andy III and Amalia (Barbosa) E.; m. Barbara Louise Daniels, July 14, 1967 (div. 1973); m. Francine A. Boschetti, Oct. 12, 1974; children: Veronica Lynn, Andy V. AA, Santa Rosa (Calif.) Jr. Coll., 1970; BS, Sonoma State U., 1972; postgrad., Calif. State U., Berkeley, 1973. Divisional sales mgr. Alcoa Aluminum, Inc., Columbus, Ohio, 1972-76; regional sales mgr. GF Bus. Equipment, San Francisco, 1976-80; West Coast sales mgr. Hufcor, Inc., Janesville, Wis., 1980-87; pres., gen. mgr. Hufcor-Airwall, Paramount, Calif., 1987—. Mem. Constrn. Specifications Inst. (bd. dirs., bull. editor 1986-87), Santa Rosa C. of C., Lions (v.p., treas., pres., zone chmn. Santa Rosa chpt. 1971—, N. Calif. Lion of the Yr. 1982). Roman Catholic. Office: Hufcor Airwall 8140 E Rosecrans Ave Paramount CA 90723

ESPINOSA, SAMUEL, occupational safety health professional, consultant; b. Matanzas, Cuba, Dec. 5, 1930; came to U.S., 1953; s. Antonio and Blanca (Arencibia) E.; m. Eva Esther Hernandez, Sept. 4, 1953; children: Victor Samuel, David Samuel. BA, Columbia Union Coll., Takoma Park, Md., 1961; MA, Loma Linda U., 1966; MS, U. Tenn., 1974, EdD, 1978. Registered profl. safety engr., Calif.. Bus. mgr. Antillian Coll., 1961-65, chmn. bus. dept., 1966-68; dir. safety dept. Loma Linda U., Riverside, Calif., 1968-76; safety engr. Teledyne, Redlands, Calif., 1979-80, Kwikset, Anaheim, Calif., 1980-81; safety, security mgr. Western Wheel Corp., La Mirada, Calif., 1981—. Author: (manual) Occupational Safety Health Manual, 1974, (handbook) Supervisors Safety Handbook, 1983, 86, Emergency Handbook, 1985, Doctoral Dissertation, 1978. Instr. Rehab. Ctr. for Drug Addicts, Norco, Calif. 1972-73; coach La Sierra Little League and Pony League, Riverside, 1978-82; instr. ARC, Riverside, 1979—; vice chmn. Environ. Protections Com., Riverside, 1980-84; mem. Rep. Senatorial Inner Circle. Recipient Cert. Merit NSC, 1973, Merit award NSC, 1974, Honor award NSC, 1975. Mem. Acad. Accreditation Team, Am. Soc. Safety Engrs., San. Diego Zool. Soc., Campus Safety Assn., Internat. Platform Assn. Home: 11262 Gramercy Pl Riverside CA 92503 Office: PO Box 2385 Buena Park CA 90621

ESPINOZA, ARMIDA MARIE, human resources executive; b. Los Angeles, Feb. 27; d. Francisco and Francisca (Robles) E. AA, East Los Angeles Coll., 1965; BA, Calif. State U., Los Angeles, 1971. Asst. dist. customer service mgr. Montgomery Ward Stores, Rosemead, Calif., 1963-71; tng. coordinator Singer Co., Parmount, Calif., 1971-73; personnel mgr. Carter Hawley Hale Stores, Los Angeles, 1973-79; personnel dir. May Dept. Stores, Los Angeles, 1979-80; regional dir. human resources Westinghouse Broadcasting Co., Encino, Calif., 1980-84, Dorotronics, San Gabriel, Calif., 1984—; cons. Career Recruitment in Telecommunications Industries Inc., 1980-86; hon. lectr. Calif. Assn. Latinos in Broadcasting, 1980-83. Mem. West San Gabriel Valley Mayor's Com. for Employment of Handicapped, 1980-83, budget com. Los Angeles Bd. Edn. Bus., United Way, Congl. Hispanic Caucus, mem. panel on edn. Nat. Council of La Raza, 1980-84. Recipient Disting. Leadership award Am. Broadcast Inst., 1988. Mem. Acad. Mgmt., Am. Compensation Assn., Am. Soc. Personnel Administrn., Am. Soc. Tng. and Devel., Personnel Indsl. Relations Assn., Personnel Women Am., Am. Women in Radio and TV, Am. Film Inst. (assoc.), Found. Community Service Cable TV, Minorities in Telecommunications, Hispanic Women's Council, Latin Small Bus. Assn., Nat. Hispanic Council for High Tech Careers. Home: 9913 Candia Cr Whittier CA 90603 Office: Dorotronic Data Systems & Equipment Inc 260 W Ralph St San Gabriel CA 91776

ESPLIN, FREDERICK CHARLES, public television executive; b. Cedar City, Utah, Apr. 16, 1947; s. Charles Cutler and Leah (Crofts) E.; m. Martha Dickey, Nov. 29, 1972; children: Eric, Jason, Grant, Erin. BA, So. Utah State Coll., 1971; MA, U. Utah, 1974. Writer Pub. Broadcasting Service, Washington, 1973-75; dir. devel. and pub. relations Pa. Pub. TV Network, Hershey, 1975-78; dir. devel. and planning Sta. WITF-TV FM, Hershey, 1978-79; dir. mktg. Sta. KUED-TV, Salt Lake City, 1979-81, gen. mgr., 1981—; bd. dirs. Pacific Mountain Network, Denver, 1981—, chmn. bd., 1988—; cons. Carnegie Com. on The Future of Pub. Broadcasting, 1978. Editor: Forum, 1985-86; mem. editorial bd. Pub. Telecommunications Rev., 1974-80. Bd. dirs. Utah Shakespearean Festival. Mem. Utah Hist. Soc., Sigma Delta Chi. Lodge: Kiwanis. Home: 2839 Glenmare St Salt Lake City UT 84106 Office: Sta KUED U Utah 101 Gardner Hall Salt Lake City UT 84112

ESPOSITO, STEPHEN MICHAEL, social organization executive; b. Bklyn, Dec. 23, 1949; s. Michael Fiore and Agnes Louise (Kirschenheiter) E.; m. Loretta Jean Rollason, Oct. 6, 1979; children: Michael Robert, John Stephen. BA in English, Mass Media, SUNY, 1972. Club mgr. Plaza Club, Phoenix, 1985; mktg. cons. Braemar Country Club, Tarzana, Calif., 1985; gen. mgr. Lakes Club, Sun City, Ariz., 1986—. Chmn. Bd. Search Com., Am. Cancer Soc., 1987. Mem. Club Mgrs. Assn. of Am., Rotary Club (dir. 1986, 88, Paul Harris Fellow 1988), Pres. Club., Nat. Club Assn. Home: 4321 W Bobbie Terr Glendale AZ 85306 Office: Lakes Club 10484 Thunderbird Blvd Sun City AZ 85351

ESSA, LISA BETH, teacher; b. Modesto, Calif., Nov. 19, 1955; d. Mark Newyia and Elizabeth (Warda) Essa. B.A., U. Pacific-Stockton, 1977, M.A. in Curriculum and Instrn. Reading, 1980. Cert. tchr. elem., multiple subject and reading specialist, Calif. Tchr. primary grades Delhi (Calif.) Elem. Sch. Dist., 1978-80; reading clinic tutor San Joaquin Delta Community Coll., Stockton, Calif., 1980; tchr. primary grades Hayward (Calif.) Unified Sch. Dist., Supr., San Francisco host com. Dem. Nat. Conv., 1984. Femmes Club scholar, 1973; U. Calif. Optometry Alumni Assn. scholar, 1973; Jobs Daughters scholar, 1974. Mem. Internat. Reading Assn., Calif. Tchrs. Assn., Hayward Unified Tchrs. Assn., San Francisco Jr. C. of C., Jr. League San Francisco. Democrat. Episcopalian. Home: 1960 Clay Apt 109 San Francisco CA 94109

ES-SAID, OMAR SALIM, metallurgist, professor; b. Cairo, Egypt, Apr. 3, 1952; came to U.S., 1981; s. Salim Asim and Haifa Aref (El-Imam) E. BS, Am. U., Cairo, 1976, MS, 1979; PhD, U. Ky., 1985. Bilingual tng. tchr Arabian Am. Oil Co., Dharan, Saudi Arabia, 1979-81; grad. rsch. asst. U. Ky., Lexington, 1981-85; asst. prof. mech. engring. Loyola Marymont U., L.A., 1985—, dir. mech. engring. grad. program, 1986—. Contbr. articles to profl. jours. Mem. Islamic Catholic Com., L.A., 1986—. Grantee NSF, 1986, Soc. Mech. Engrs., 1987, Dept. of Engery, 1988. Mem. AAUP, ASME, AIME, Am. Soc. Metals, Internat. Assn. Sci. and Tech. for Devel., Am. Soc. Engring. Edn., Alpha Sigma Mu. Home: 7051 Manchester Ave Los Angeles CA 90045 Office: Loyola Marymont U Loyola Blvd at W 80th St Los Angeles CA 90045

ESSICK, EDWARD LOUIS, data processing executive, consultant; b. Barstow, Calif., Oct. 8, 1940; s. John Robert and Ruth Irene (Kiethley) E.; m. Aug. 29, 1962 (div.); children: Mark, Kristi. BA, San Jose (Calif.) State U., 1963, MA, 1965. Prof. data processing Marin Community Coll., Kentfield, Calif., 1968--. Author: Principles of Business Data Processing, 5th edit., 1985, RPG II Programming, 2d edit., 1988. 1st lt. U.S. Army, 1965-67. Named Prof. of Yr., Marin Community Coll., 1987. Republican. Office: Marin Community Coll Kentfield CA 94904

ESSICK, RAYMOND BROOKE, III, amateur sports administrator; b. Murphysboro, Ill., Sept. 18, 1933; s. Raymond Brooke Jr. and Ida Mae (Bailey) E.; m. Frances Antoinette Stewart, June 14, 1958; children: Raymond Brooke IV, Anne, Bradley, Katherine. BS in Phys. Edn., U. Ill., 1955, MS in Phys. Edn., 1958. Swimming tchr., coach New Trier Twp. High Sch., Winnetka, Ill., 1958-66, So. Ill. U., Carbondale, 1966-73; swimming coach Harvard U., Cambridge, Mass., 1973-76; swimming adminstr. Nat. Amateur Athletics Union, Indpls., 1976-80; exec. dir. U.S. Swimming, Inc., Colorado Springs, Colo., 1980—. Contbr. articles to profl. jours. Sgt. USN, 1955-57. John Newman award Ill. Swimming Assn., 1977; named Coach of Yr., Coll. Swimming Coaches Assn., 1971. Mem. Am. Swimming Coaches Assn., Nat. Interscholastic Swim Coach Assn., U. Ill. Lettermans Club, Colo. Amateur Sports Corp., Ind. Amateur Sports Corp., Country Club of Colo., U.S. Officials Club (chmn. coaches edn. com., substance abuse com., TV com.). Office: US Swimming Inc 1750 E Boulder St Colorado Springs CO 80909

ESSINGER, STEPHEN WILLIAM, property management executive; b. Santa Ana, Calif., Nov. 4, 1962; s. Paul Richard and Beverly Marie (Price) E.; m. Amy Maria Johnson, Apr. 4, 1987. BA, U.Calif., Berkeley, 1986. Pres. Esslinger Mgmt. Co., Laguna Beach, Calif., 1987—. Mem. housing com., City of Laguna Beach, 1988; exec. bd. Orange County Mobilehome Edn. Trust, 1988—. Office: Esslinger Mgmt Co 30802 S Coast Hwy Laguna Beach CA 92051

ESSLINGER, HARTMUT HEINRICH, industrial designer, artist; b. Beuren, Germany, June 5, 1944; s. Heinrich and Ottilie (Albers) E.; children: Marc, Nico. Student, Tech. U., Stuttgart, Fed. Republic Germany, 1966-67, Coll. Design, Schw. Gmund, Fed. Republic Germany, 1968-70. Pres., owner frogdesign, Fed. Republic Germany, 1969--, San Jose, Calif., 1983--, Japan, 1987--; pres., founder FROX Inc., San Jose, 1988--.

ESTABROOK, EVELYN MARIE BASOM, musician, educator; b. nr. Farmer City, Ill., Jan. 7, 1908; d. Samuel Jay and Lura Frances (Hillman) Basom; m. Dale Russell Reeser, Oct. 20, 1929 (dec. July 1962); children: William Jay, Carolyn Jane Waugh; m. Kenneth Charlie Estabrook, Oct. 3, 1966 (dec. Jan. 1984). Diploma in Pub. Sch. Music Methods, Millikin Conservatory, 1928, degree as collegue, 1954, degree as Child Specialist, 1955. Pianist for silent movies Farmer City, 1925-26; pvt. tchr. piano 1928—; music tchr. pub. schs. Farmer City, Mansfield, Ill., 1928-39; accompanist, asst. Grossmont High Sch., La Mesa, Calif., 1941-45; freelance dir., pianist Evelyn's Serenaders, San Diego, 1945-62; dir., accompanist various choral prodns. San Diego, La Mesa, 1945—; ballet pianist Grossmont (Calif.) Coll., 1980-85; freelance performer, choreographer various fashion shows San Diego County, 1962—; chartered accompanist Woman's Club Choral Pro Musica, La Mesa, 1947—, Community Concert and Women's Com., Grossmont, 1957—. Composer: (gospel music) Those Who Love and Care, 1962, (club song) Our Club, 1963, others, occasion pieces for Air Streams All Am. Girl, 1977, also teaching material; participant Super Bowl '88 Piano Extravaganza, San Diego; pianist, writer, dir. numerous local mus. prodns. Entertainer, accompanist various pub. and ch. activities, Ill., Calif., 1923—; pianist La Mesa C. of C., 1987—. Mem. Am. Fedn. Musicians, Soroptimist Internat. (pres. 1959-60), Ladies Philanthropic Ednl. Orgn., Music Tchrs. Assn. (cert. 1948, 55, pres. 1960-61), Delta Omicron (pres. 1927-28). Republican. Methodist. Clubs: P.E.O. (pres. 1980-81), Toastmaster (toastmistress) (La Mesa). Home and Office: 7730 Homewood Pl La Mesa CA 92041

ESTRADA, JACQUELYN ANN, freelance writer and editor; b. Bainbridge, Md., Sept. 10, 1946; d. John Walter and Ruth Eileen (Coleman) Harper; m. Davey Leon Estrada, Aug. 17, 1968 (div. 1980). BA, San Diego State U., 1968. Editor CRM Books, Del Mar, Calif., 1969-75; editor, writer coll. textbooks San Diego, 1975--; editorial cons. Del Mar Assocs., 1981--, San Diego State U. Press, 1987; sr. devel. editor Bovee Books/Collegiate Press, San Diego, 1987--; bd. dirs. San Diego Comic Conv., Inc. Co-author: The Future of Being Human, 1977, Psychology Today and Tomorrow, 1978; contbr. photographs and articles to various publs. Recipient Inkpot award San Diego Comic Conv., 1977. Mem. San Diego Profl. Editors Network (cofounder, chmn. 1987--, newsletter editor 1987--), Save Our Heritage Orgn., Art Deco Soc. San Diego, San Diego Hist. Soc. Libertarian. Home: 4657 Cajon Way San Diego CA 92115

ESTRIN, THELMA AUSTERN, electrical engineer; b. N.Y.C., Feb. 21, 1924; d. I. Billy and Mary (Ginsburg) Austern; m. Gerald Estrin, Dec. 21, 1941; children: Margo, Judith, Deborah. BSEE, U. Wis., Madison, 1947, MSEE, 1948, PhD, 1951. Cert. clin. engr. Research engr. UCLA Brain Research Inst., 1960-70, dir. data processing, 1970-80; prof. UCLA Sch. Engring. and Applied Sci., 1980—; dir. div. electronics, computer and systems engring. NSF, Washington, 1982-84; dir. dept. engring., asst. dean Sch. Engring. and Applied Sci. UCLA, 1984—; trustee Aerospace Corp., 1979-82; mem. biomed. tech. resources com. NIH, 1981-86; mem. U.S. Army Sci. Bd., 1982-83; mem. energy engring. bd. NRC, 1985—. Contbr. articles to tech. jours. Mem. Los Angeles Women in Bus. Recipient Disting. Contbn. to Engring. Edn. award NSPE, 1985, Achievement award Soc. Women Engrs. 1981, Disting. Service citation U. Wis., 1976. Fellow IEEE (bd. dirs. 1979-80, exec. v.p. 1982, recipient Centennial medal 1984, pres. Engring. in Medicine and Biology Soc. 1977), AAAS (chair Engring. sect. 1989). Jewish. Office: UCLA Sch Engring & Applied Sci Boelter Hall Rm 7620 Los Angeles CA 90024

ETESSAMI, RAMBOD, endonontist; b. Tehran, Iran, Mar. 20, 1960; came to U.S., 1977; s. Abdollah and Mahin E. BA in Math., Ind. U., 1980; DDS, Georgetown U., 1984; cert. in advanced endodontics, U. So. Calif., 1986. Head research & devel., chief sci. researcher, bd. dirs. Laseronics, Inc., Torrance, Calif., 1983—; assoc. clin. prof. endodontics U. So. Calif., Los Angeles, 1986—; pvt. practice, Los Angeles and Beverly Hills, Calif., 1986—; assoc. clin. prof. Sch. of Dentistry UCLA, 1989—. Chmn. Ind. U. chpt. United Jewish Appeal, 1978-79, chmn. Georgetown U. chpt., 1982-83; bd. dirs. dental cabinet Los Angeles chpt., 1987—; bd. dirs. Iranian Jews Am., Washington, 1980-83, Am.-Israel Pub. Affairs Com., Washington, 1982-84; bd. dirs., chmn. Iranian immigration sect. Jewish Vocat. Svc., Los Angeles, 1987—. NIH grantee, 1978-79; B. Baj Bhussry fellow George U., 1981; Alpha Omega scholar, 1984. Mem. ADA (cert. Recognition and Appreciation 1984, 86), Am. Assn. Endodontists, Am. Dental Profls. Israel, Calif. Dental Assn., Study Club for Oral Facial Research. Jewish. Home: 200 N Foothill Beverly Hills CA 90210 Office: 9201 Sunset Blvd #908 Los Angeles CA 90069

ETTER, RICHARD ARTHUR, marketing executive; b. Groveland, Mass., Nov. 8, 1944; s. Walter Benjamin and Hazel Irene (Snow) E.; m. Margaret Anne Dawson, June 17, 1972; children: Nathan Arthur, Rebecca Anne, Kristin Arlene. AS in Electronics, Northern Essex Community Coll., 1966; BEd, U. Mass., 1971; MA in Spl. Edn., Assumtion Coll., 1974; PhD in Ednl. Adminstrn., Boston Coll., 1982. Cert. elem. and spl. edn. tchr., adminstr., Mass. Guidance counselor Eagle Hill Sch., Hardwick, Mass., 1969-71, asst. headmaster, 1971-74; prin. Devereaux Found., Devon, Pa., 1974-76, v.p. mktg., 1985-87; coordinator field experience, then rsch. assoc. Boston Coll., Chestnut Hill, Mass., 1976-78; asst. adminstr. Devereaux Ctr., Victoria, Tex., 1978-79; adminstr. Devereaux Ctr., Scottsdale, Ariz., 1979-85, Western Inst. Neuropsychiatry, Salt Lake City, 1987-88; tech. coordinator Assoc. Regional and Univ. Pathologists, Salt Lake City, 1988—; pres. Etter Enterprises Cons., Sandy, Utah, 1988—. Author tng. program, 1980. Mem. Ariz. Coun. Child Care Agys., 1982-85. Vol. Peace Corps, Madhya Pradesh, India, 1966-68. Mem. Assn. Mental Health Adminstrn. (cert.), Am. Coll. Health Care Execs. (cert.), Nat. Assn. Pvt. Schs. for Exceptional Children (bd. dirs. 1985-87), Ariz. Assn. Pvt. Spl. Edn. (pres. 1981-83, Svc. award 1983), Rotary (pres. local chpt. 1984-85). Home: 8948 Summer Mesa Circle Sandy UT 84093 Office: Assoc Regional & Univ Path 500 Chipeta Way Salt Lake City UT 84108

ETTL, DOROTHY ANNE, home economist, educator; b. Marysville, Calif., Apr. 19, 1943; d. Walter Joseph and Celia Marie (Hill) E. BS, U. Calif., Davis, 1964; MS in Home Econs., Tex. Tech. U., 1969; postgrad., U. Hawaii, summer 1970; PhD in Home Econs., U. Minn., 1976. Cert. spl. vocat. tchr., Tex., standard secondary tchr., Calif. County extension home economist Agrl. Extension Service, U. Wyo., Lusk, Wyo., 1964-67; teaching and rsch. asst. Tex. Tech. U., Lubbock, 1968-69; asst. prof. home econs. Calif. State U., Chico, 1969-73; rsch. asst. U. Minn., St. Paul, 1973-76; assoc. prof. Wash. State U., Pullman, 1976—, mem. faculty senate, 1980-84. Contbr. numerous articles to extension publs.; author audio-visual ednl. materials; columnist Info. Kettle, 1964-67. Bd. dirs. Friends Mus. Art, Wash. State U., 1985-88. Mem. Am. Home Econs. Assn. (life; cert.), Assn. Coll. Profls. Textiles and Clothing (exec. bd. 1979-82), Nat. Assn. Extension Home Economists, Coop. Extension Assembly (v.p. 1985-88), Assn. Faculty Women Wash. State U. (treas. 1987-89), Whitman County Hist. Soc. (life), Epsilon Sigma Phi (sec. Beta chpt. 1987-89). Home: NW 340 North St Pullman WA 99163 Office: Wash State U Coop Extension 104 F White Hall Pullman WA 99164-2020

ETULAIN, DAN ROY, communications executive; b. Wapato, Wash., July 6, 1937; s. Sebastian and Mary (Gillard) E.; m. Kathie Santo, Aug. 17, 1962; children: Todd, Troy. BA, NW Nazarene Coll., 1960; MEd, U. Oreg., 1962; PhD, U. North Colo., 1971. Tchr. sci. North Jr. High, Boise, Idaho, 1960-61, Hamlin Jr. High, Springfield, Oreg., 1962-64; asst. dean of men U. Oreg., Eugene, 1964-66; dean of men NW Nazarene Coll., Nampa, Idaho, 1966-69; resident dir. U. North Colo., Greeley, 1969-71; dean students Sheldon Jackson Coll., Sitka, Alaska, 1971-73; dir. Alaska Christian TV Services, Sitka, 1977—; pres. North Star TV Network, Sitka, 1988—. Exec. producer (video program): Sitka, Wrangel, Native New Life Musicales, 1980—. Bd. dirs. Ch. of Nazarene, Sitka, 1971-88, Raven Radio KCAW-FM, Sitka, 1979-88; mem. adv. com. community schs., 1977—. Named Outstanding Alumni NW Nazarene Coll., 1982, Outstanding Community Educator State of Alaska, 1987. Republican. Home: 301 Charteris Sitka AK 99835 Office: KTNL-TV 520 Lake St Sitka AK 99835

EU, MARCH KONG FONG, state official; b. Oakdale, Calif., Mar. 29, 1922; d. Yuen and Shiu (Shee) Kong; children by previous marriage—Matthew Kipling Fong, Marchesa Suyin Fong You; m. Henry Eu, July 30, 1973; stepchildren—Henry, Adeline, Yvonne, Conroy, Alaric. Student, Salinas Jr. Coll.; B.S., U. Calif.-Berkeley; M.Ed., Mills Coll., 1951; Ed.D., Stanford U., 1956; postgrad., Columbia U., Calif. State Coll.-Hayward; LL.D., Lincoln U., 1984. Chmn. div. dental hygiene U. Calif. Med. Center, San Francisco; dental hygienist Oakland (Calif.) Pub. Schs.; supr. dental health edn. Alameda County (Calif.) Schs.; lectr. health edn. Mills Coll., Oakland; mem. Calif. Legislature, 1966-74, chmn. select com. on agr., foods and nutrition, 1973-74; mem. com. natural resources and conservation, com. commerce and pub. utilities, select com. med. malpractice; sec. state State of Calif., 1975—, chief of protocol, 1975-83, sec. of state; chmn. Calif. State World Trade Commn., 1982-87; spl. cons. Bur. Intergroup Relations, Calif. Dept. Edn.; ednl., legis. cons. Sausalito (Calif.) Pub. Schs., Santa Clara County Office Edn., Jefferson Elementary Union Sch. Dist., Santa Clara High Sch. Dist., Santa Clara Elementary Sch. Dist., Live Oak Union High Sch. Dist.; mem. Alameda County Bd. Edn., 1956-66, pres., 1961-62, legis. adv., 1963. Mem. budget panel Bay Area United Fund Crusade; mem. Oakland Econ. Devel. Council; mem. tourism devel. com. Calif. Econ. Devel. Commn.; mem. citizens com. on housing Council Social Planning; mem. Calif. Interagy. Council Family Planning; edn. chmn., mem. council social planning, dir. Oakland Area Baymont Dist. Community Council; charter pres., hon. life mem. Howard Elementary Sch. PTA; charter pres. Chinese Young Ladies Soc., Oakland; mem., vice chmn. adv. com. Youth Study Centers and Ford Found. Interagy. Project, 1962-63; chmn. Alameda County Mothers' March, 1971-72; bd. councillors U. So. Calif. Sch. Dentistry, 1976; mem. exec. com. Calif. Democratic Central Com., mem. central com., 1963-70, asst. sec.; del. Dem. Nat. Conv., 1968; dir. 8th Congl. Dist. Dem. Council, 1963; v.p. Dems. of 8th Congl. Dist., 1963; dir. Key Women for Kennedy, 1963; women's vice chmn. No. Calif. Johnson for Pres., 1964; bd. dirs. Oakland YWCA, 1965. Recipient ann. award for outstanding achievement Eastbay Intercultural Fellowship, 1959; Phoebe Apperson Hearst Disting. Bay Area Woman of Yr. award; Woman of Yr. award Calif. Retail Liquor Dealers Inst., 1969; Merit citation Calif. Assn. Adult Edn. Adminstrs., 1970; Art Edn. award; Outstanding Woman award Nat. Women's Polit. Caucus, 1980; Person of Yr. award Miracle Mile Lions Club, 1980; Humanitarian award Milton Strong Hall of Fame, 1981; Outstanding Leadership award Ventura Young Dems., 1983; Woman of Achievement award Los Angeles Hadassah, 1983. Mem. Am. Dental Hygienists Assn. (pres. 1956-57), No. Calif. Dental Hygienists Assn., Oakland LWV, AAUW (area rep. in edn. Oakland br.), Calif. Tchrs. Assn., Calif. Sch. Bd. Assn., Alameda County Sch. Bd. Assn. (pres. 1965), Alameda County Mental Health Assn., So. Calif. Dental Assn. (hon.), Bus. and Profl. Women's Club, Chinese Retail Food Markets Assn. (hon.), Delta Kappa Gamma. Office: Sec of State State of Calif 1230 J St Sacramento CA 95814 *

EUCKER, WILLIAM, III, geologist; b. Pompton Plains, N.J., Oct. 17, 1955; s. William and Janet Irene (Miller) E.; m. Penelope Josephine Hudson, Feb. 16, 1985; 1 child, William. BA in Geology, Temple U., 1977. Geologist Kerr McGee Corp., Casper, Wyo., 1978-79, Fugro Inc., Long Beach, Calif., 1979-80; mud logger, geologist H.H. Cate Logging, Park City, Utah, 1980-81; cons. geologist Decollement Cons., Denver, 1981-82; pres., geologist Subsurface Inc., Denver, 1982—; chief geologist Dune Oil Enterprises, 1986—. Mem. Am. Assn. Petroleum Geologists, Petroleum Club, Oxford Club, Masons. Home: 1777 Larimer St Apt 1502 Denver CO 80202

EVANKOVICH, GEORGE JOSEPH, labor union administrator; b. Butte, Mont., Jan. 27, 1930; s. Joseph and Lubja (Broze) E.; m. Nevada Murray, Aug. 16, 1969; children: Karen, Lucy, Joseph, Janna. Student, U. Mont., 1954-57; BA, U. San Francisco, 1958. Miner Anaconda Co., Butte, 1946-50, Ind. Lease Mining, Helena, Mont., 1957-60; sec., treas. local 261 Laborers Internat. Union, San Francisco, 1960-68, bus. mgr., 1968-87, pres., 1987—; pres. No. Dist. Council of Laborers, 1977—; bd. dirs., trustee Laborers' Trust Funds, Inc., San Francisco. Dir. labor studies program San Francisco City Coll., 1978—; chmn. San Francisco Housing Authority, 1972-76; advisor various senatorial, congl. and mayoral campaigns, 1966—; sustained mem. Rep. Nat. Com., 1980—. With inf. U.S. Army, 1951-54, Korea. Mem. Laborers Polit. Action Com. (bd. dirs.), Commonwealth Club of San Francisco. Roman Catholic. Office: Laborers Union Local #261 3271 18th St San Francisco CA 94110

EVANS, A. MICHAEL, JR., broadcasting executive; b. Washington, May 19, 1948; s. Alvin Michael Sr. and Marie Athelstein (Pickens) E.; m. Angela Marie Price, Feb. 28, 1976; children: Alan Michael, Adrian Marie. AA, West Los Angeles Coll., 1975. Classified document sorter TRW, Inc., Redondo Beach, Calif., 1966-69; asst. chief train dispatcher So. Pacific Transp. Co., Los Angeles, 1971-85; dir. media Crenshaw Christian Ctr., Los Angeles, 1985—; dir. crusades and promotions Ever Increasing Faith Ministries, Los Angeles, 1985—; media buyer Faith One Advt., Los Angeles, 1988—. Pres. Heights at Ladera Homeowners Assn., Los Angeles, 1988.

asst. coach Ladera Heights Rangers, 1988. Served with U.S. Army, 1969-71. Mem. Religious Conf. Mgmt. Assn., Nat. Religious Broadcasters, Full Gospel Businessmen's Fellowship Internat. (pres. Carson, Calif. chpt. 1985). Republican. Home: 6516 Bradley Pl Los Angeles CA 90056 Office: Faith One Advt 7901 S Vermont Ste 124 Los Angeles CA 90044

EVANS, BRYANT ROBERT, title agency executive; b. Steubenville, Ohio, Feb. 20, 1945; s. Thomas Edgar and Sarah Ellen (Bauer) E.; m. Sharon Marie Kocal, June 4, 1966; children: Bryant, Brittany. BA in Psychology, Bowling Green State U., 1967. Tchr. Los Angeles Unified Sch. Dist., 1968-80; pres. Cochise Title Agy., 1980—; v.p. Bayshore Inc.; cons. Sierra Vista Diagnostics; v.p., bd. dirs. Fidelity Nat. Title of Pinal, Casa Grand, Ariz., 1986—. Pres. Am. Heart Assn., Sierra Vista, Ariz., 1988-89, state bd. dirs., 1988—; mem. adv. bd. U. Ariz., Tucson, Chapman Coll., Sierra Vista; bd. dirs. Cochise Coll. Found. Bd., v.p. 1988-89, pres. 1989—, Douglas, Ariz., Cochise Pvt. Industry Council, Bisbee, Ariz., 1985-87. Mem. Mensa, Sierra Vista Exec. Assn. (pres. 1985-86), Sierra Vista C. of C. (pres. 1987-88, nominee Citizen of Yr. 1985), U.S. Army Assn. (bd. dirs. 1988—). Republican. Club: Rotary (Sierra Vista). Office: Cochise Title Agy Inc 333 W Wilcox Sierra Vista AZ 85635

EVANS, D. N., fashion designer; b. Chgo., Aug. 6, 1944; d. Sydney and Cyrna (Glickman) Shaw; m. Michael R. Evans, July 7, 1977; children: Ronald, Leesa, Christopher, Damen. Student, Art Inst. Chgo., 1956-66. Weaver Chgo., 1966-70, designer jewelery, 1970-74; designer fashion Laguna Beach, Calif., 1974—. Author: (newsletter) Traveler, 1987. Recipient Outstanding Achievement Design award Bowers Mus., Santa Ana, Calif., 1987, Career Archievent award Saddle Back Coll., Mission Vieso, Calif., 1988, award Merit Beautification Council Laguna Beach, 1985. Mem. Designing Women Art Inst. So. Calif., Jr. Art Council Laguna Beach Art Mus., Chariot Champions. Home: 1970 S Coast Hwy Laguna Beach CA 92651 Office: 1970 S Coast Hwy Laguna Beach CA 92651

EVANS, DALE ELDON, computer engineer, consultant; b. Blackfoot, Idaho, Jan. 17, 1951; s. Homer R. and Ruby L. Evans; m. Cindy Lee Rudd, Dec. 2, 1972; children: Ellisa, Justin, Lynzee, Cody. AS in Design Tech., Ricks Coll., Rexburg, Idaho, 1973; BS in Engring. Tech., Brigham Young U., 1975. Engring. designer Position Control Systems Inc., Provo, Utah, 1973-75; computer-aided-design rsch. and devel. engr. Sandia Nat. Labs., Albuquerque, 1976-78; computer-aided-design systems supr. EG&G Idaho Inc., Idaho Falls, 1978-82, engring. specialist, 1983-88; regional mgr. Cascade Graphics Devel., Santa Ana, Calif., 1982-83; sr. engring. specialist Cascade Graphics Devel., Santa Ana, 1988—; prin. D.E. Evans and Assocs., Idaho Falls, 1986—; adj. faculty mem. U. Idaho, Idaho Falls, 1978—; adv. com. Idaho State U. Vocat. Coll., Pocatello, 1983—, Ricks Coll., 1983—. Columnist CADENCE mag., 1986—; contbr. articles to profl. jours. Mem. Computer Press Assn. Republican. Mormon. Home and Office: 1463 N 1190 East Shelley ID 83274

EVANS, DANIEL JACKSON, former U.S. senator; b. Seattle, Oct. 16, 1925; s. Daniel Lester and Irma (Ide) E.; m. Nancy Ann Bell, June 6, 1959; children: Daniel Jackson, Mark L., Bruce M. B.S. in Civil Engring. U. Wash., 1948, M.S., 1949. Registered profl. engr., Wash. With Assoc. Gen. Contractors, Seattle, 1953-59; cons. civil engr. Seattle, 1949-51; partner Gray & Evans, structural and civil engrs., Seattle, 1959-65; mem. Wash. Ho. of Reps. from, King County, 1956-65; Republican floor leader Wash. Ho. of Reps. from, 1961-65; gov. State of Wash., 1964-77; pres. Evergreen State Coll., Olympia, 1977-83; mem. U.S. Senate from Wash. State 1983-89; mem. Adv. Council on Intergovernmental Relations, 1972-77, Fed. Adv. Commn. Project Independence, 1974, Nat. Commn. on Productivity and Work Quality, 1975, President's Vietnamese Refugee Adv. Com., 1975; chmn. Pacific NW Electric Power and Conservation Planning Council, 1981-83. Keynote speaker Rep. Nat. Conv., 1968; mem. Nat. Gov.'s Conf., chmn., 1973-74; chmn. Western Gov.'s Conf., 1968-69; trustee Carnegie Found. for Advancement of Teaching, Nature Conservancy, 20th Century Fund. Served to lt. USNR, 1943-46, 51-53. Recipient Human Rights award Pacific N.W. chpt. Nat. Assn. Intergroup Relations Ofcls., 1967; Service to the Profession award Cons. Engrs. Council, 1969; Scales of Justice award Nat. Council Crime and Delinquency, 1968; Pub. Ofcl. of Year award Wash. Environmental Council, 1970; Distinguished Eagle, Silver Beaver, Silver Antelope awards Boy Scouts Am.; Distinguished Citizen award Nat. Municipal League, 1977. Congregationalist. Address: US Senate 702 Hart Senate Bldg Washington DC 20510

EVANS, DAVID C., computer company executive; b. Salt Lake City, Feb. 24, 1924; s. David W. and Beatrice (Cannon) E.; m. Joy Frewin, Mar. 21, 1947; children: Gayle Evans Scheidel, Susan Evans Foote, David F., Ann Evans Brown, Peter F., Douglas F., Katherine Evans Orchard. BS, U. Utah, 1949, PhD in Physics, 1953, DSc (hon.), 1987. Dir. engring. computer div. Bendix Corp., Los Angeles, 1953-62; prof. elec. engring. and computer sci. U. Calif.-Berkeley, 1962-66; prof. elec. engring. and computer sci., chmn. dept. U. Utah, Salt Lake City, 1965-73; chmn. bd., pres. Evans & Sutherland Computer Corp., Salt Lake City, 1968—. Served in U.S. Army, 1942-45. Recipient Silver Beaver award Boy Scouts Am., Emmanual Piore award, 1986, Nat. Computer Graphics Assn. award, 1986; named to Computer Hall of Fame. Fellow IEEE; mem. Nat. Acad. Engring. Republican. Mem. Ch. of Jesus Christ of Latter-day Saints. Office: Evans & Sutherland 600 Komas Dr Salt Lake City UT 84108

EVANS, HAROLD G., construction executive; b. Marshfield, Mo., Aug. 21, 1944; s. John Raymond and Wilma Lee (Graham) E.; m. Jane Carol Francis, June 22, 1967; children: Britta May, John Derek. BSCE, U. Mo., 1967, MSCE, 1968. Registered profl. engr., Mo., Colo. Commd. officer U.S. Pub. Health Svc., Whiteriver, Ariz., 1968-70; project engr. Irvin Bilt Constrn. Co., Chillicothe, Mo., 1970-71; superintendent Hensel Phelps Constrn. Co., Greeley, Colo., 1971-73; project mgr. Hensel Phelps Constrn. Co., Greeley, 1973-78, mgr. of corp. services, 1978-80, v.p., 1980-85; pres. Clearwater Constrn. Inc., Greeley, 1985—; bd. dirs. IntraWest Bank of Greeley. Active Bldg. Inspection Adv. Bd., Greeley, 1980—; alternate mem. Colo. Forum, Denver, 1988; bd. dirs. United Way of Weld County; mem. exec. com., Longs Peak Council Boy Scouts Am. Mem. ASCE, Associated Gen. Contractors Am. (exec. com. mem. 1987—), Associated Gen. Contractors Colo., Rotary. Republican. Methodist. Office: Clearwater Constrn Inc 420 6th Ave Greeley CO 80631

EVANS, JAMES LOUIS, mathmatics and science teacher; b. Washington, June 29, 1935; s. Felton Jasper and Nellie (Brown) E.; m. Ada Earley, Aug. 10, 1957; children: Kevin, Kyle, Cheryl, Shawna. BEE, Cath. U. Am., 1957; MEE, Air Force Inst. Tech., Dayton, Ohio, 1968; MS in Secondary Edn., Eastern N.Mex. U., 1984. Enlisted USAF, 1958, advanced through grades to maj., navigator, 1958-80, ret., 1980; tech. instr. Eastern N.Mex. U., Pontales, 1980—; tchr. Muleshoe (Tex.) Ind. Sch. Dist., 1987—. Mem. NEA, Masons (dep. grand master N.Mex. dist.). Home: 1708 Courtland Clovis NM 88101 Office: Muleshoe Sch Dist 514 W Ave G Muleshoe TX 79347

EVANS, JUNIUS ANTHONY, physician; b. Festus, Mo., Aug. 13, 1911; s. George James and Daisy (Keiser) E.; AB in Chemistry, U. Tex., 1937, BS in Pharmacy, 1939, MD, 1943; m. Josephine Van Zandt, Nov. 28, 1936 (dec. Apr, 1986); children: Martha Ellen Metarelis, Mary Daisy Everhart, Junius Anthony Jr. Intern U.S. Marine Hosp., New Orleans, 1943-44; resident No. Mich. Tb San., Gaylord, Mich., USPHS, Washington, 1945-46, U. Ark., VA Hosps. Little Rock and North Little Rock, 1960-62; career officer USPHS, 1943-47; pvt. practice, Las Vegas, N.Mex., 1947-60; specializing in dermatology, Roswell, N.Mex., 1962—; formerly chief of staff Las Vegas, St. Anthony hosps. (both Las Vegas); staff mem. St. Mary's Hosp.; chief of staff Eastern N.Mex. Med. Center, Roswell, 1968-69; clin. assoc. dermatology U. N.Mex., 1974—. Lt. USCG, 1943-46; capt. Res. Recipient A.H. Robins award for Outstanding Pub. Svc., 1985. Mem. Chaves County, N.Mex. (councillor 1956-59, mem. pub. relations com. 1963-73, chmn. pub. relations com. 1963-64, ho. of dels. 1969—, mem. liaison com. to allied professions 1972-74) med. socs., Am., N.Mex. (pres. 1958) thoracic socs., Am. Acad. Dermatology, N.Mex. Tb Assn. (dir. 1950-62), Am. Acad. Tb Physicians, Am. Cancer Soc. (v.p. 1970, chmn. svc. com. N.Mex. div. 1965-70), Chaves County Cancer Soc. (dir. 1965-79), Am. Council Med. Staffs (regional dir. S.W. area 1972—, pres. N.Mex. council 1972-74), Assn. Am. Physicians and Surgeons, N.Mex. (dir.), Chaves County (pres. 1970-71) heart assns., S.W. Dermatol Soc. (pres. 1966-67), N.Mex. Dermatol. Soc., Rho Chi, Theta Kappa Psi. Mason (Shriner), Rotarian. Home: 2200 Palomar Dr Roswell NM 88201 Office: 207 N Union St PO Box 1226 Roswell NM 88201

EVANS, LAWRENCE JACK, JR., lawyer; b. Oakland, Calif., Apr. 4, 1921; s. Lawrence Jack and Eva May (Dickinson) E.; m. Marjorie Hisken, Dec. 23, 1944; children: Daryl S. Kleweno, Richard L., Shirley J. Coursey, Donald B. Diplomate Near East Sch. Theology, Beirut, 1951; MA, Am. U. Beirut, 1951; PhD, Brantridge Forest Sch., Sussex, Eng., 1968; JD, Ariz. State U., 1971; grad. Nat. Jud. Coll., 1974. Bar: Ariz. 1971, U.S. Dist. Ct. Ariz. 1971, U.S. Ct. Claims 1972, U.S. Customs Ct., 1972, U.S. Tax Ct. 1972, U.S. Ct. Customs and Patent Appeals 1972, U.S. Ct. Appeals (9th cir.) 1972, U.S. Supreme Ct. 1975. Served as enlisted man U.S. Navy, 1938-41; enlisted man U.S. Army, 1942-44, commd. 2d lt., 1944, advanced through ranks to lt. col., 1962; war plans officer, G-3 Seventh Army, 1960-62, chief, field ops. and tactics div., U.S. Army Spl. Forces, 1963, chief spl. techniques div., U.S. Army Spl. Forces, 1964, unconventional warfare monitor, U.S. Army Spl. Forces, 1964-65; assigned to Command and Gen. Staff Coll., 1960; ops. staff officer J-3 USEUCOM, 1965-68; mem. Airborne Command Post Study Group, Joint Chiefs of Staff, 1967; ret., 1968; sole practice law, cons. on Near and Middle Eastern affairs, Tempe, Ariz., 1971-72, 76—; v.p., dir. Trojan Investment & Devel. Co., Inc., 1972-75; active Ariz. Tax Conf., 1971-75; mem. adminstrv. law com., labor mgmt. relations com., unauthorized practice of law com. Ariz. State Bar. Author: Legal Aspects of Land Tenure in the Republic of Lebanon, 1951; (with Helen Miller Davis) International Constitutional Law, Electoral Laws and Treaties of the Near and Middle East, 1951. Contbr. articles to mags., chpts. to books. Chmn. legal and legis. com. Phoenix Mayor's Com. To Employ Handicapped, 1971-75; active Tempe Leadership Conf., 1971-75; chmn. Citizens Against Corruption in Govt.; mem. Princeton Council on Fgn. and Internat. Studies. Decorated Silver Star, Legion of Merit, Bronze Star, Purple Heart; named Outstanding Adminstrv. Law Judge for State Service for U.S., 1974; named to U.S. Army Ranger Hall of Fame, 1981. Mem. Ranger Bns. Assn. World War II (life), Tempe Rep. Mens Club (v.p., bd. dirs. 1971-72, U.S. Army Airborne Ranger Assn. (life), Mil. Order Purple Heart (life), Nat. Rifle Assn. (official referee), Phi Delta Phi, Delta Theta Phi. Episcopalian. Lodges: Masons, SL (past master), YR (past high priest, past thrice illustrious master, past comdr.), SR (32, ritual dir.). Home: 539 E Erie Dr Tempe AZ 85282

EVANS, LOUISE, psychologist; b. San Antonio; d. Henry Daniel and Adela (Pariser) E.; m. Thomas Ross Gambrell, Feb. 23, 1960; B.S., Northwestern U., 1949; M.S. in Psychology, Purdue U., 1952, Ph.D. in Clin. Psychology, 1955; Lic. Marriage, Family and Child Counselor Nat. Register of Health Service Providers in Psychology; lic. psychologist N.Y. (inactive), Calif.; diplomate Clin. Psychology, Am. Bd. Profl. Psychology. Intern clin. psychology Menninger Found., Topeka (Kans.) State Hosp., 1952-53, USPHS-Menninger Found. fellow clin. child psychology, 1955-56; staff psychologist Kankakee (Ill.) State Hosp., 1954; head staff psychologist child guidance clinic Kings County Hosp., Bklyn., 1957-58; dir. psychology clinic, instr. med. psychology Washington U. Sch. Medicine, 1959; clin. research cons. Episcopal City Diocese, St. Louis, 1959; pvt. practice clin. psychology, 1960—; approved fellow Internat. Council Sex Edn. and Parenthood, 1984; hon. Research Bd. Advs. nat. div. Am. Biog. Inst., 1985; hon. adv. coun. Internat. Biog. Ctr., 1989; psychol. cons. Fullerton (Calif.) Community Hosp., 1961-81; staff cons. clin. psychology Martin Luther Hosp., Anaheim, Calif., 1963-70; lectr. clin. psychology schs. and profl. groups, 1950—; participant psychol. symposiums, 1956—; guest speaker clin. psychology civic and community orgns., 1950—. Elected to Hall of Fame, Central High Sch., Ind., 1966; recipient Service award Yuma County Head Start Program, 1972, Statue of Victory Personality of the Yr. award Centro Studi E. Ricerche Delle Nazioni, 1985; named Miss Heritage, Heritage Publs., 1965. Fellow Am. Psychol. Soc., Royal Soc. Health of England, Internat. Council of Psychologists (dir. 1977-79, sec. 1962-64, 73-76), AAAS, Am. Orthopsychiat. Assn., World Wide Acad. of Scholars of N.Z., Am. Psychol. Soc.; mem. AAUP, Nat. Register Health Svc. Providers in Psychology, Los Angeles Soc. Clin. Psychologists (exec. bd. 1966-67), Calif. State Psychol. Assn., Los Angeles County Psychol. Assn., Orange County Psychol. Assn. (exec. bd. 1961-62), Orange County Soc. Clin. Psychologists (exec. bd. 1963-65, pres. 1964-65), Am. Public Health Assn., Internat. Platform Assn., Am. Acad. Polit. and Social Scis., N.Y. Acad. Scis., Purdue U. Alumni Assn. (Citizenship award 1975), Center for Study of Presidency, Alumni Assn. Menninger Sch. Psychiatry, Sigma Xi, Pi Sigma Pi. Contbr. articles on clin. psychology to profl. publs. Office: 905-907 W Wilshire Ave Fullerton CA 92632

EVANS, MAX JAY, historical society director; b. Lehi, Utah, May 11, 1943; s. Karl Robinson and Lucile (Johnson) E.; m. Mary Wheatley, June 16, 1967; children: David Max, Joseph Michael, Katherine Anne, Laura, Emily. BS, U. Utah, 1968; MS, Utah State U., 1971. Archivist Mormon Ch. Hist. Dept., Salt Lake City, 1971-75, asst. ch. librarian, archivist, 1975-77; dep. state archivist State Hist. Soc. Wis., Madison, 1977-86, library dir., 1986; dir. Utah State Hist. Soc., Salt Lake City, 1986-88; acting dir. Utah State Archives, Salt Lake City, 1986—; archival cons. N.Y. State Archives, Albany, 1981, Wyo. Dept. Archives and Hist., Cheyenne, 1982. Co-author: MARC for Archives and Manuscripts: A Compedium of Practice, 1985 (SAA Coker award 1986); articles in field. Trustee Middleton (Wis.) Pub. Library, 1974-86. Fellow Soc. Am. Archivists; mem. Utah State Hist. Soc. Mormon. Office: Utah State Hist Soc 300 Rio Grande St Salt Lake City UT 84101

EVANS, OWEN CARLYLE, dentist; b. Bevier, Mo., Mar. 20, 1920; s. Owen Thomas and Beatrice Victoria (Williams) E.; m. Elizabeth Elena Cass, Apr. 17, 1987; children: David Brooks, Abbey Lynn Evans Hughmanick, Deborah Dale Dowd Cherez, Denise DeLaine Dowd. AS, Moberly (Mo.) Jr. Coll., 1939; BS, Washington U., St. Louis, Mo., 1944; DDS, Washington U., 1950; postgrad., U. of the Pacific, 1953-54. Oral surgeon Throndson and Schmitz DDS, San Francisco, 1953-55; staff oral surgeon Sequoia Hosp., Redwood City, Calif., 1954-70, chief dental sect., 1965-68; gen. practice dentistry Redwood City, 1955-69, Palo Alto, Calif., 1969-72, Reno, Nev., 1972—; staff Reno Med. Plaza Outpatient Service; instr. oral surgery Univ. Pacific, Stockton, Calif., 1954-66. Hon. mem. San Mateo County Sheriff's Mounted Patrol, 1958. Served with USN, 1941-44, PTO, to capt. U.S. Army, 1949-52. Mem. ADA, Northern Nev. Dental Soc., Omicron Kappa Epsilon. Republican. Congregationalist. Club: Sequoia. Lodges: Elks, Kiwanis. Office: 3700 Grant Dr Ste E Reno NV 89509

EVANS, PAUL M., retail executive; b. Kansas City, Dec. 10, 1954; s. John Paul and Mary H. (Sackuvich) E.; m. Pamela Ann Porter, Oct. 6, 1979; children: Paige Marie, John Paul. Student, Kansas City Community Coll., 1972-74. Printing apprentice Raden-C Auto Step Photography, Kansas City, 1972-73; freelance landscape designer Kansas City, 1973-74, freence display artist, cons., 1974-75; city display mgr. K-G Men's Stores, Kansas City, 1975-77, advtg./visual regional supr., 1977-82; dir., store planning K-G Retail Stores Inc., Engelwood, Colo., 1983—; design cons. NB Assocs., Engelwood, 1985—, Dover Elevator Co., Denver, 1985-86; store planning cons. Underworld Ltd., Boulder, Colo., 1986. Designer Barrel-B-Que Grill, 1985. T-ball coach, Littleton (Colo.) YMCA, 1986; bd. dirs. design control com. Dakota Sta. Subdivision, Littleton, 1985-86. Republican. Roman Catholic. Home: 9409 W Nichols Dr Littleton CO 80123 Office: K-G Retail Stores Inc 2 Denver Highlands 10065 E Harvard Ave Denver CO 80231

EVANS, PENNEY, realtor; b. Denver, Oct. 10, 1941; Children: Thos, Kara. AA, Colby Jr. Coll., 1961; BA, Wellesley Coll., 1963. Lic. broker. Broker assoc. Carol Ann Jacobson Realty, Aspen, Colo., 1976-83; broker assoc. Mason & Morse, Inc., Aspen, 1983—, also bd. dirs. Active Aspen Valley Hosp. Assisted Living Program, 1988; candidate for mayor City of Aspen, 1987; mem. Pitkin County Fin. Adv. Bd., Pitkin County Code Task Force, Aspen Valley Improvement Assn. Mem. Aspen Bd. Realtors (pres. 1986-87, sec., treas. 1984, v.p. 1985), Aspen Women Forum, Aspen Ski Club (bd. dirs. 1985-87). Office: Mason & Morse Inc 514 E Hyman Aspen CO 81611

EVANS, RICHARD LLOYD, financial services company executive; b. Seattle, Oct. 16, 1935; s. Lloyd Herman and Dorleska L. (Rotta) E.; m. Judith Anne Sahlberg, Dec. 20, 1958; children: Dallas J., Douglas L., Daniel A., Marjorie A., Rebecca M. BA in Bus. Adminstrn., U. Wash., 1957. CLU; chartered fin. cons. Agt. Phoenix Mut. Life Ins. Co., Seattle, 1960-69; pres. R.L. Evans Co. Inc., Seattle, 1969—; speaker on ins. and fin. planning to numerous orgns., 1975—. Mem. exec. bd. Chief Seattle coun. Boy Scouts Am., 1976—; chmn. N.W. Theol. Union, Seattle, 1984-88. Lt. USN, 1957-59. Recipient award of merit Chief Seattle coun. Boy Scouts Am., 1984. Mem. Am. Soc. CLU, Am. Soc. Chartered Fin. Cons., Nat. Assn. Life Underwriters, Wash. State Assn. Life Underwriters (bd. dirs. 1973-79, pres. 1977-78), Seattle Assn. Life Underwriters (v.p. 1972-73), Assn. Advanced Underwriting, Million Dollar Round Table, Estate Planning Coun. Seattle, Rainier Club, Masons, Rotary. Republican. Presbyterian. Home: 4001 Hunts Point Rd Bellevue WA 98004 Office: 1210 Plaza 600 Bldg Seattle WA 98101

EVANS, STEPHEN DOUGLAS, physician; b. Port Arthur, Tex., Aug. 18, 1947; s. Adrian David and Gloria Ann (Byrns) E.; m. Terry Lynn Daniel, May 23, 1975; children: Daniel Adrian, Douglas Andrew. BBA, Tex. A&M U., 1972; BS, U. Tex., Dallas, 1978; MD, Am. U. Caribbean, Plymouth, Montserrat, 1984. Diplomate Am. Bd. Family Practice. Physician asst. Bob Herrin, M.D., Marshall, Tex., 1978-81; resident in family practice Oakwood Hosp., Dearborn, Mich., 1984-87; pvt. practice Tucumcari, N.Mex., 1987—. Named Ky. Col., Commonwealth of Ky., 1983. Mem. AMA, Am. Acad. Family Practice, N.Mex Acad. Family Practice. Mem. Ch. of Christ. Office: Family Med Ctr 310 S 2d St Tucumcari NM 88401

EVANS, STUART ANTHONY, marketing consultant; b. Phoenix, Apr. 11, 1951; s. Stuart and Patricia (Heuloth) E.; m. Leslie Lynne Anderson, Apr. 25, 1981; children: Megan Lorimer, Stuart Alexander. BS in Psychology, Ariz. State U., 1973. Exec. mktg. rep. Armstrong World Ind., Lancaster, Pa., 1973-84; product mgr. Am. Fence Corp., Phoenix, 184-87; pres. Lanton Assocs., Tempe, Ariz., 1987—; chief exec. officer P & MG, Inc., Phoenix, 1988—; bd. dirs. P & MG, Inc., Phoenix, PSKA, Inc., Phoenix. Co-inventor modular steel barn. Com. mem. YMCA, Tempe, 1988; campaign com. mem. DeConcini Campaign, Phoenix, 1978. Mem. Mfrs. Agt. Nat. Assn., Archons Honor Fraternity (life). Democrat. Episcopalian. Office: Lanton Assocs 1840 E Warner Rd A-105-167 Tempe AZ 85284

EVANS, THOMAS EDGAR, JR., title insurance agency executive; b. Toronto, Ohio, Apr. 17, 1940; s. Thomas Edgar and Sarah Ellen (Bauer) E.; BA, Mt. Union Coll., 1963; m. Cynthia Lee Johnson, Feb. 23; children: Thomas Edgar, Douglas, Melinda, Jennifer. Tchr. Lodi, Ohio, 1963-64; salesman Simpson-Evans Realty, Steubenville, Ohio, 1964-65, Shadron Realty, Tucson, 1965-67; real estate broker, co-owner Double E Realty, Tucson, 1967-69; escrow officer, br. mgr., asst. county mgr., v.p. Ariz. Title Ins., Tucson, 1969-80; pres. Commonwealth Land Title Agy., Tucson, 1980-82, also dir.; pres. Fidelity Nat. Title Agy., 1982—; v.p. Fidelity Nat. Corp.; bd. dirs. Western Fin. Trust Co., Fidelity Nat. Fin. Inc., Fidelity Nat. Title Ins. Co., Fidelity Nat. Title Agy. Pinal, The Griffin Co.; bd. dirs., chmn. bd. Cochise Title Agy., TIPCO; v.p., dir. A.P.C. Corp. Named Boss of Year, El Chaparral chpt. Am. Bus. Women's Assn., 1977. Mem. So. Ariz. Escrow Assn., So. Ariz. Mortgage Bankers Assn. (bd. dirs. 1982-85), Ariz. Mktg. Bankers Assn., Old Pueblo Businessmen's Assn. Tucson, Tucson Bd. Realtors, Ariz. Assn. Real Estate Exchangors (bd. dirs. 1968-69), Land Title Assn. Ariz. (pres. 1984), So. Ariz. Homebuilders Assn., Blue Key, Sigma Nu. Republican. Methodist. Clubs: Old Pueblo Courthouse, La Paloma, Ventana Country, Centre Court, Elks, Pima Jaycees (dir. 1966), Sertoma (charter pres., chmn. bd. Midtown sect. 1968-70); Tucson Real Estate Exchangors (pres. 1968); Sunrise Rotary; Old Pueblo. Home: 5316 E Vista Rica Paradise Valley AZ 85253 Office: 2390 E Camelback Rd #140 Phoenix AZ 85016

EVANS, WILLIAM THOMAS, physician; b. Denver, Aug. 21, 1941; s. Alfred Lincoln and Marian Audrey (Biggs) E.; BA, U. Colo., 1963; MD, Baylor U., 1967; grad. Chinese Coll. U.K.; Licentiate Acupuncture, Oxford, Eng., 1976; m. Lucy Fales. Intern, Mary Fletcher Hosp., Burlington, Vt.; physician Villages of Kodiak Island and Lake Iliamna, 1968-70; founder, dir. emergency dept. St. Elizabeth Hosp., Yakima, Wash., 1970-75; practice medicine specializing prevention and conservative treatment of spine injuries, Denver; founder, dir. Colo. Back Sch., Denver, 1979-89; assoc. med. dir. Ctr. for Spine Rehab., 1989—. Friends of Earth del. Limits to Medicine Congress, 1975. Initiated Colo. Sun Day, 1978. Lt. comdr. Indian Health Service, USPHS, 1968-70. Mem. Rocky Mountain Traumatological Soc. (exec. sec., treas.), Denver County Med. Soc., Colo. Med. Soc. (workmen's compensation com.), No. Am. Spine Soc., Am. Coll. Occupational Medicine Assn., Rocky Mountain Acad. Occupational Medicine (pres.), AMA, Am. Coll. Sports Medicine, Traditional Acupuncture Soc. Home: Box 174 Littleton CO 80120 Office: 125 E Hampden Ave Englewood CO 80110

EVELAND, LOU ELLEN, retail salesperson, decorating consultant; b. Woodfairie, Idaho, Mar. 31, 1943; d. Carl Arthur and Arbutus Mae (Mercer) Hulquist; m. Glen Eugene Eveland, Aug. 20, 1960 (div. Sept. 1968); m. Jim Arthur Johnson, Nov. 23, 1968 (div. June 1972); m. Glen Eugene Eveland, Nov. 26, 1973; children: Colin Eugene, Bonita Jean. Student, Spokane Community Coll., Spokane, Wash., 1966, U. Mont., 1972-73. Produce dept. mgr. McGowans-Mercantile Stobies IGA, Plains, Mont., 1968-72; ways and means chmn. Army Community Svc., Ft. Riley, Kans., 1974-75; mgr. Derby Oil Co., Manhattan, Kans., 1975-76; asst. mgr. Hy-Fy Self-Service Gas Co., Woodbridge, Va., 1976; mgr. Mademoiselle Fashions, Inc., 1976; asst. mgr. Phillipsborn, Inc., Springfield, Va., 1978-79; with Town Pump, Inc., Butte, Mont., 1979-84; asst. mgr./credit mgr. Sherwin Williams Co., Butte, Mont., 1984-87; outside sales rep. Office Products, Inc., Butte, Mont., 1987--. Cub scout leader, Missoula, 1969-70. Mem. Knowledge Network of Women, Copper City Radio Club. Republican. Methodist. Home: Rte 3 Box 259 Rocker MT 59701 Office: Office Products Inc 55 E Galena Butte MT 59701

EVEREST, CHARLES EUGENE, electronics manufacturing company executive; b. Tenino, Wash., May 20, 1933; s. Charles Sydney and Lucille (Inman) E.; m. Nancy Arlene Shey, Sept. 5, 1959 (div. 1968); 1 child, Geni Arlene Fisher; m. Marilyn Murfield, May 14, 1976. BSEE, MIT, 1957. Engr. Bell & Howell, Pasadena, Calif., 1957-62, Rockwell Internat., Anaheim, Calif., 1962-67; pvt. inventor Wahl Corp., Culver City, Calif., 1967-70, Telatemp Corp., Fullerton, Calif., 1970-80; pres. Everest Intersci., Inc., Fullerton, Calif., 1980—; cons. E2 Tech., Santa Barbara, Calif., 1969; speaker in field. Contbr. articles to profl. jours.; patentee in field. Recipient Tech. award Am. Soc. Agrl. Engrs., 1985, 50 award Am. Soc. Engrs., 1986, 87. Mem. Instrument Soc. Am. (Kermit Fischer award 1984), Am. Soc. Agrl. Engrs. (Tech. award, Salute award 1985, award for one of top 50 agrl. products 1986-88), IEEE (sr.), Am. Soc. Engrs. (50 awards 1986, 87). Republican. Home: 11662 Pincian Way Santa Ana CA 92705 Office: Everest Intersci Inc 1120 S Raymond Unit D Fullerton CA 92631

EVERETT, JACK WILCOX, financial planner; b. Nyack, N.Y., Aug. 30, 1942; s. Jack W. and Mabel Claire (Jones) E.; m. Glennis A. Fraser, June 13, 1964 (dec. Oct. 1979); children: Sherri, Jack; m. Patricia P. Olmstead, Jan. 21, 1984. BS, US Naval Acad., 1964; MBA, Golden Gate U., 1970. Cert. fin. planner. Sales rep. Burroughs Corp., Sacramento, Calif., 1972-74; real estate broker Sacramento, 1974-80; account exec., tax mgr. TMI Equities Inc., Sacramento, 1976-80; pres. The Fin. and Tax Planning Ctr., Sacramento, 1980—; pres. Credit Union Fin. Services, 1982-87. Author, pub.: A. Fin. Planning Newsletter, 1980—, Bus. Planning Letter, 1985—, (book) Winning Money Psychology, 1989. Treas. Sacramento Seapower, 1980—; treas. Delta King Mus. Assocs., 1985—. Lt. U.S. Navy, 1964-72. Mem. Sacramento Brokerage and Loan Assn. (bd. dirs.), Hidden Valley Community Assn. (treas. 1987—), Internat. Assn. Fin. Planners (chpt. pres. 1984-85, chpt. service award 1987), Inst. Cert. Fin. PLanners (chpt. treas. 1984-85), Nat. Ctr. Fin. Edn., Navy League US (v.p., treas. 1980-85), No. Calif. Ofcls. Assn. (wrestling chmn. 1985-86). Republican. Home: 8125 Morningside Dr Looms CA 95850 Office: The Fin & Tax Planning Ctr 2277 Fair Oaks Blvd Ste 205 Sacramento CA 95825

EVERETTE, SHARON ESTHER MCLEOD, state official; b. Detroit, Sept. 4, 1949; d. Bruce Burns and Myrtle Ruth (Zerran) McLeod; m. Michael Warren Everette, Mar. 29, 1986. BEd, U. Alaska, 1971. Clk., typist Alaska Dept. Hwys., Glenallen and Fairbanks, 1966-72; right of way asst. II Alaska Dept. Hwys., Fairbanks, 1972-74, right of way agt. I, 1974-76; right of way agt. II Alaska Dept. Transp., Fairbanks, 1976-80, planner IV, 1980-84, right of way agt. IV, 1984—. Vol. Tanana Valley Spl. Olympics, Fairbanks, 1987. Mem. Internat. Right of Way Assn. (sec.-treas.

Fairbanks chpt. 1979-80, v.p. 1981, newsletter editor 1982-85, pres. 1984-86, publicity chmn. 1987-88, internat. bd. dirs. 1984-86, internat. nominations and elections com. 1988-89), Alaska Outdoor Coun., Alaska Profl. Hunters Assn., Nat. Rifle Assn., Pioneers of Alaska, U. Alaska-Fairbanks Alumni Assn., Faribanks Women's Basketball Assn. (pres. 1980). Office: Alaska Dept Transp ROW 600 University Ave Ste F Fairbanks AK 99709

EVERHART, THOMAS EUGENE, physicist, educator; b. Kansas City, Mo., Feb. 15, 1932; s. William Elliott and Elizabeth Ann (West) E.; m. Doris Arleen Wentz, June 21, 1953; children—Janet Sue, Nancy Jean, David William, John Thomas. A.B. in Physics magna cum laude, Harvard, 1953; M.Sc., UCLA, 1955; Ph.D. in Engring., Cambridge U., Eng., 1958. Mem. tech. staff Hughes Research Labs., Culver City, Calif., 1953-55; mem. faculty U. Calif., Berkeley, 1958-78, prof. elec. engring. and computer scis., 1967-78, Miller research prof., 1969-70, chmn. dept., 1972-77; prof. elec. engring., Joseph Silbert dean engring. Cornell U., Ithaca, N.Y., 1979-84; prof. elec. and computer engring., chancellor U. Ill., Champaign-Urbana, 1984-87; pres., prof. electrical engring. Calif. Inst. Tech., Pasadena, 1987—; fellow scientist Westinghouse Research Labs., Pitts., 1962-63; guest prof. Inst. für Angewandte Physik, U. Tuebingen, Fed. Republic Germany, 1966-67, Waseda U., Tokyo, Osaka U., Japan, fall 1974; vis. fellow Clare Hall, Cambridge U., 1975; chmn. Electron, Ion and Photon Beam Symposium, 1977; cons. to industry; mem. sci. and ednl. adv. com. Lawrence Berkeley Lab., 1978-85, chmn., 1980-85; mem. sci. adv. com. Gen. Motors Corp., 1980—, chmn. 1984—; mem. tech. adv. com. R.R. Donnelley & Sons, 1981—. NSF sr. postdoctoral fellow, 1966-67; Guggenheim fellow, 1974-75. Fellow IEEE; mem. AAAS, Nat. Acad. Engring. (ednl. adv. bd. 1984—, membership com. 1984—, chmn. membership com. 1988—), Electron Microscopy Soc. Am. (council 1970-72, pres. 1977), Microbeam Analysis Soc. Am., Deutsche Gesellschaft für Elektronenmikroskopie, Assn. Marshall Scholars and Alumni (pres. 1965-68), Nat. Assn. State Univs. and Land Grant Colls. (chmn. higher edn. and tech. com. 1986-87), Sigma Xi, Eta Kappa Nu. Clubs: Athenaeum, Chgo. Home: 415 S Hill Ave Pasadena CA 91106 Office: Calif Inst Tech Office of Pres 1201 E California Blvd Pasadena CA 91125

EVERTS, CONNOR, artist; b. Bellingham, Wash., Jan. 24, 1926; s. William Edward and Sophia (Mehan) E.; m. Chizuko Sugita, Mar. 15, 1953; children—Anon Connor, Meigan Mariko, Geoffrey, Tamura. A.A., El Camino Coll., 1950; B.A., U. Wash., 1952. Mem. faculty dept. art Calif. State U., Northridge, 1960-62, Calif. Inst. Arts, 1962-65, Calif. State U., Long Beach, 1965, San Francisco Art Inst., 1966, U. So. Calif., 1967-69, U. Calif., Riverside, 1972-76; graphics chmn. Cranbrook Acad. Art, Bloomfield Hills, Mich., 1976-81; exchange prof. Prahran Coll. Advanced Studies, Melbourne, Australia; artist in residence Calif. Inst. Tech., 1970-71. One man shows include Pasadena Art Mus., 1960, Michael Walls Gallery, San Francisco, 1967-69, Los Angeles Mcpl. Gallery, 1971, Meckler Gallery, Los Angeles, 1979, World Print Council, 1982, retrospective exhibit, Los Angeles Mus., 1983, Orange County Ctr. for Contemporary Art, 1986, Whatcom Mus. Art, 1987, Print Works Gallery, Chgo., 1988, Ruth Bachofner, L.A., 1986, 89, Dominguez Hills State U., 1989; exhibited in group shows at Tokyo Biann. Painting Exhbn, 1967, Homage to Lithography, Mus. Modern Art, N.Y.C., 1969, Printmaking, Oskokunst Forening, Oslo, Norway, 1974, Mint Mus., 1987, Kunstsamm-Luggen Der Veste Coburg, 1988; represented in permanent collections, Chgo. Art Inst., Long Beach Mus. Art, Los Angeles County Mus. Art, Milw. Art Mus., Mus. Modern Art, N.Y.C., Pasadena Art Mus., San Francisco Mus. Modern Art, Washington Gallery Modern Art, others. Pres. adv. bd. Los Angeles Mcpl. Gallery, 1968. With USCG, 1946. Mem. AAUP, L.A. Printmaking Soc., Mich. Assn. Printmakers, Artists Equity. Studio: 2351 Sonoma St Torrance CA 90501

EWALD, TOR, power corporation executive; b. Santa Barbara, Calif., July 18, 1965; s. A. Timothy and Delphine (DeGrazia) E. BA in Econs., U. Calif., San Diego, 1987. Pres. United Power Corp., San Diego, 1987—; owner Del Mar (Calif.) Farms, 1987—; bd. dirs. gen. Rancho Del Mar Del Rosarito (Mex.), 1988—. Republican. Home and Office: PO Box G Del Mar CA 92014

EWELL, A(USTIN) B(ERT), JR., lawyer; b. Elyria, Ohio, Sept. 10, 1941; s. Austin Bert and Mary Rebecca (Thompson) E.; children: Austin Bert III, Brice Ballantyne. BA, Miami U., Oxford, Ohio, 1963; JD, Hasting Coll. Law, U. Calif.-San Francisco, 1966. Bar: Calif. 1966, U.S. Dist. Ct. (ea. dist.) Calif. 1967, U.S. Supreme Ct. 1982, U.S. Ct. Appeals (9th cir.) 1967. Pres. A. B. Ewell, Jr., A. Profl. Corp., Fresno, 1984—; formerly gen. counsel to various water dists. and assn.; gen. counsel, chmn. San Joaquin River Flood Control Assn., 1984-88; chief oper. officer Millerton New Town Devel. Co., 1988—; mem. task force on prosecution, cts. and law reform Calif. Coun. Criminal Justice, 1971-74; mem. Fresno Bulldog Found., Calif. State U. Mem. affiliated San Joaquin Valley Agrl. Water Com. 1979—; co-chmn. nat. adv. coun. SBA, 1981, 82, mem. 1981-87; bd. dirs. Fresno East Community Ctr., 1971-73; mem. Fresno County Water Adv. Com., Fresno Community Council, 1972-73; chmn. various polit. campaigns and orgns., including Reagan/Bush, 1984, Deukmejian for Gov., 1986; mem. adv. com. St. Agnes Med. Ctr. Found., 1983—; trustee U. Calif. Med. Edn. Found., Fresno Met. Mus. Art, History and Sci. Mem. ABA (water resources com. of natural resources sect., real property probate and trust law sect.), Internat. Platform Assn., Phi Alpha Delta, Assn. Calif. Water Agys. (affiliate), U.S. Supreme Ct. Hist. Soc., Sigma Nu. Clubs: Downtown, Racquet (Fresno), Commonwealth (San Francisco), President's. Congregationalist. Office: 83 E Shaw Ave Ste 201 Fresno CA 93710

EWER, WILLIAM HANSON, graphics specialist; b. Bklyn., Dec. 3, 1942; s. Robert Curtis and Agneta Irene (Hanson) E.; m. Carol Ann Petersen, June 22, 1968; 1 child, Jennifer Irene. BFA, U. Bridgeport, 1965. Account exec. Young & Rubicam, N.Y.C., 1969-72; v.p. Wells, Rich, Greene, Inc., N.Y.C., Los Angeles, 1972-78; pres., chief exec. officer Fuel Conservation Systems, Inc., Laguna Beach, Calif., 1978-81; v.p. Lasergraphics, Inc., Irvine, Calif., 1981-86; prin. Graphics Resource Group, Laguna Beach, 1986—; ptnr., dir. Quasar Tech. Mgmt., New Canaan, Conn., 1988—. Contbr. articles to profl. jours. Served to lt. comdr. USNR, 1965-69. Mem. Nat. Computer Graphics Assn.

EWING, COLEMAN CLAY, architect; b. San Antonio, Oct. 11, 1944; s. William Thomas and Ina Fay (Talley) E.; student San Antonio Jr. Coll., 1963-65; B.S., U. Houston, 1970; m. Marjorie Glennda Sewell, Aug. 28, 1965; children—Christopher Coleman, Michelle InaMarie. Customer engr. IBM Co, Houston, Tex., 1965-67; draftsman Morton Levy, Houston, 1967-71, Roland Johnson, Denver, 1971-72, DMJM Phillips, Denver, 1972-73, Wheeler/Lewis, Denver, 1973-75, Frank Lundquist, Denver, 1975-76, Oliver, Hellegren, Denver, 1976-77; prin. Coleman C. Ewing Architect & Assocs., Denver, 1977-80, 86—; pres. Ewing Gorman Archtl. Group, Denver, 1980-81, also dir.; pres. Ewing Archtl. Group, P.C., 1981-86; CAD/CAM specialist archtl. dept. Martin Marietta Co., Denver, 1981-86. Republican. Mem. Ch. of Christ. Office: Ewing Architect & Assocs 6634 S Clarkson St Littleton CO 80221

EWING, FREDERICK JAMES, real estate broker; b. San Pedro, Calif., June 15, 1938; s. Frederick Burton Ewing and Veda Grace (Maddox) Cassells; m. Betty Lou Miller, Mar. 10, 1957 (dec.); children: Ricky Lynn, Denise Elizabeth. AA, Santa Rosa Jr. Coll., 1981. Enlisted USCG, 1957, retired, 1982; prin. Ewing Real Estate Svcs., Santa Rosa, Calif., 1982—. Republican. Methodist. Home: 1739 W 3d St Santa Rosa CA 95401 Office: 320 W 3d St C Santa Rosa CA 95401

EWING, MICHAEL DELVIN, artist, teacher; b. Detroit, Dec. 5, 1951; s. Harold Francis and Juanita Ann (Klingensmith) E.; m. Nancy Hyde Ewing, July 17, 1976; children: Lindsay Michelle, Tyler William. BA magnum cum laude, Mercy Coll., Detroit, 1974. Cert. tchr., Ariz. Tchr. Grand Blanc (Mich.) Communigy Sch. Dist., 1975-80; artist Rosequist Gallery, Tucson, 1979-84; field rep. WBC Cons. Engrs., Tucson, 1980-82; tchr. Tucson Unified Sch. Dist., Tucson, 1982—; artist El Prado Galleries, Sedona, Ariz. and Santa Fe, 1984—; illustrator McGraw/Hill Pub. Co., 1985. One-man show in El Prado Gallery, 1987—; exhibited individual shows 1986, 87. Mem. Tucson Edn. Assn., Kappa Delta Phi Honors Soc. Republican. Home and Office: 5132 E Camino Bosque Tucson AZ 85718

EWING, RICHARD EDWARD, mathematics, petroleum, engineering educator; b. Kingsville, Tex., Nov. 24, 1946; s. Floyd Ford and Olivia Clara (Henrichson) E.; m. Rita Louise Williams, Aug. 8, 1970; children: John Edward, Lawrence Alan, Bradley William. BA, U. Tex., 1969, MA, 1972, PhD, 1974. Asst. prof. Oakland U., Rochester, Mich., 1974-77; asst. prof. Ohio State U., Columbus, 1977-80, assoc. prof., 1980-81; sr. research matematician Mobile Research and Devel. Corp., Dallas, 1980-82, assoc. mathematician, 1982-83; prof. math., petroleum and chem. engring. U. Wyo., Laramie, 1983--, J E Warren dist. prof. energy and environ., 1984--; dir. Enhanced Oil Recovery Inst., 1984--, Inst. for Sci. Computation, 1986--, Ctr. for Math. Modeling, 1986--; adj. prof. Rice U., Houston, 1980-84; cons. oil cos., Norway, Wyo., Tex., Calif., Colo., 1982--; advisor Res. Inst. for Petroleum, Beijing, 1987--; mem. steering com. Ctr. for Fluid Dynamics and Geoscis., Columbia, S.C., 1987--; hon. prof. Shandong (People's Republic China) U., 1987. Author: The Mathematics of Reservoir Simulation, 1983, Mathematical Modeling in Energy and Environmental Sciences, 1988; contbr. articles to sci. jours., chpts. to books. Cubmaster Boy Scouts Am., Dallas, 1981, Webelos leader, 1982, asst. scoutleader,Laramie, 1984. Recipient Halliburton award for excellence U. Wyo., 1986, Burlington No. Faculty award, 1986; recipient numerous research grants NSF, Dept. Energy, NRC, oil cos., others, 1978--. Mem. Soc. Petroleum Engrs., Soc. Indsl. and Applied Math. (trustee 1986--), Am. Math. Soc., Math. Assn. Am., Internat. Assn. for Maths. and Computers in Simulation, Inst. for Advancement Sci. Computing (trustee 1987--), Geoscis. Inst. (bd. dirs. 1988--). Democrat. Home: 1055 Grasnito St Laramie WY 82070 Office: U Wyo Dept Math Laramie WY 82071

EWING, RONNIE RUE, sales executive; b. St. Francis, Kans., Aug. 22, 1942; s. Arvid Nelson and Barbara Ruth (Anderson) E.; m. Patricia Ann Hoffman. BBA, U. N.Mex., 1965. Mgr. internat. benefits Internat. Paper Co, N.Y.C., 1973-76; dir., benefits Envirotech Corp., Menlo Park, Calif., 1979-81; pres. Exec. Resource Group, Denver, 1981-84; v.p. Frank B. Hall Cons. Co., Denver, 1984-87; nat. sales exec. GE Capital, Denver, 1988—; speaker IBIS Conf. N.Y.C., 1972. Author: Trade Publ., Benefits Internat. 1974. Mem. Curtis Park. Mem. U. N.Mex. Alumni Assn., Sigma Phi Epsilon, Elks. Republican.

EWING, RUSSELL CHARLES, II, physician; b. Tucson, Aug. 16, 1941; s. Russell Charles and Sue M. (Sawyer) E.; m. Louise Anne Wendt, Jan. 29, 1977; children: John Charles, Susan Lenore. BS, U. Ariz., 1963; MD, George Washington U., 1967. Intern, Los Angeles County-U. So. Calif. Med. Ctr., Los Angeles, 1967-68; gen practice medicine and surgery, Yorba Linda, Calif. and Placentia, Calif., 1970—; mem. staff St. Judes Hosp., Fullerton, Calif., 1970—; mem. staff Placentia Linda Community Hosp., 1972—, vice chief staff, 1977-78, chief staff, 1978-80; sec., dir. Yorba Linda Med. Group, Inc., 1974—; dir. Western Empire Savs. & Loan Assn. (Calif.). Bd. dirs. Yorba Linda YMCA, 1973-88, pres., 1973-74, 81; bd. dirs. Placentia Linda Community Hosp., 1974-81. Served with USN, 1968-70. Diplomate Am. Bd. Family Practice. Fellow Am. Acad. Family Practice; mem. AMA, Calif. Med. Assn. (house of del. 1978—), Orange County Med. Assn. (dir. 1983—, pres. 1988—). Republican. Episcopalian. Home: 9212 Smoketree Ln Villa Park CA 92667 Office: 4900 Prospect Yorba Linda CA 92686

EWING, SHERMAN, rancher; b. Mpls., July 5, 1926; s. Sherman and Mary Peavey (Heffelfinger) E.; m. Clarissa R. Clement, Aug. 12, 1950; children: Wanina J., Charles M., Leslie C. BA, Yale U., 1949. Mgr., foreman 3 C Bar Ranch, Browning, Mont., 1952-54; pres., gen. mgr. SN Ranch, Ltd., Claresholm, Alta., Can., 1955-82; chmn. bd. SN Ranch, Ltd.; pres. MTX Genetics, Inc., Great Falls, Mont., 1981—; sec., treas. Beefbooster Cattle Mont, Inc., Great Falls, 1983—; bd. dirs. LK Ranches, Ltd., Beefbooster Mgmt., Ltd. Editor IMS-SRM newsletter, 1982-86; contbr. articles to profl. jours. Pres. Progressive Conservative Assn., Macleod, Alta., 1975-80; founder 1st v.p. N.Am. Limousin Found., Denver, 1968-74, Can. Limousin Assn., 1969-73. Served with USAF, 1944-45. Recipient Outstanding Achievement award Soc. Range Mgmt., 1987-88. Mem. Soc. Range Mgmt. (dir. 1967), Western Stock Growers Assn. (pres. 1977-79), Stockmen's Meml. Found. (pres., chmn. 1979-82), Mont. Stock Growers Assn., Nat. Cattlemen's Assn., Meadow Lark Club, Masons. Republican. Episcopalian. Home and Office: 482 Flood Rd Great Falls MT 59404

EXLINE, BRENDA KAY, advertising agency executive; b. Wichita, Kans., Sept. 12, 1960; d. John Paul and Mary Jean (Von Furstenburg) Bauer; m. Robert William Exline, Jan. 2, 1982. BS in Journalism, Kans. State U., 1981. Account exec. Sta. KDEN, Denver, 1982; copywriter May D & F, Denver, 1982-83; account exec. Barnhart Advt., Denver, 1983-84; pub., editor Women's Yellow Pages, Denver, 1984-85; pres. Exline Agy., Inc., Denver, 1985—; pub. speaker, 1985—; cons., com. mem. ArtReach Found., Denver, 1987—. Bd. dirs. Denver Ctr. for Performing Arts, 1987-88. Recipient design award Profl. Personnel Assn., 1985, award Silver Microphone Award Com., 1986. Mem. Am. Mktg. Assn. (profl.), Am./Australian C. of C., Denver Advt. Fedn. (profl.), Denver C. of C., Young Entrepreneurs Assn., Colo. Racquetball Assn., U.S. Sr. Soccer Assn., Denver Athletic Club (com. 1988-89). Republican. Roman Catholic. Office: 1543 Champa St Ste 300 Denver CO 80202

EYNI, ELIAHU ELLIOT (EDDIE EYNI), international trade consultant; b. Jerusalem, Jan. 31, 1932; came to U.S., 1977; s. Yaacov Nissim and Shoshana (Tarabulus) E.; m. Sheila Mehager, Dec. 27, 1957; children: Amos, Dorit, Doron. With Israeli Police Forces, Jerusalem, 1950-51, Israeli Commando Officers Army-Sch., 1951-52, Israeli Def. Forces, 1952-54; with parliament Gov. of Israel, Jerusalem, 1955-56; with Sinai Frontier, 1956; with fgn. affairs Israeli Embassy, Teheran, Iran, 1958-64, Athens, 1965-68, Kampala, Uganda, 1969-72, Bonn, Fed. Republic Germany, 1975-76; cons. import/export Global Internat. Trading, Anaheim, Calif., 1977—; coordinator Italian-Chino Group Florence and Beijing, 1983-84. Served to lt. Israeli Commando, 1947-49. Mem. Anaheim C. of C. Republican. Lodge: B'nai-B'rith. Home: PO Box 4527 Anaheim CA 92803

EYRING, HENRY BENNION, bishop; b. Princeton, N.J., May 31, 1933; s. Henry and Mildred (Bennion) E.; m. Kathleen Johnson, July 27, 1962; children: Henry J., Stuart J., Matthew J., John B., Elizabeth, Mary Kathleen. BS, U. Utah, 1955; MBA, Harvard U., 1959, PhD, 1963; D of Humanities (hon.), Brigham Young U., 1985. Asst., then assoc. prof. Stanford U., Palo Alto, Calif., 1962-71; pres. Ricks Coll., Rexburg, Idaho, 1972-77; dep. commr. edn., then commr. LDS Ch., Salt Lake City, 1977-85, presiding bishopric, 1985—; mem. adv. bd. Bonneville Telecommunications Co., Salt Lake City, 1984—. Co-author: The Organizational World, 1973. With USAF, 1955-57. Sloan faculty fellow MIT, 1963-64. Office: LDS Ch Presiding Bishopric 50 E N Temple St 18th Fl Salt Lake City UT 84150

FABER, EDWARD EARL, computer retail executive; b. Buffalo, Mar. 19, 1933. BS in Indsl. and Labor Relations, Cornell U., 1955. Data processing salesman IBM Corp., Miami, Fla., 1957-62; instr. Customer Exec. Sch. IBM Corp., Endicott, N.Y., 1963; instr. European Edn. Ctr. IBM Corp., Blaricum, The Netherlands, 1964; program adminstr. New Bus. Mktg. Dept. IBM Corp., White Plains, N.Y., 1965-66; mgr. devel. info mktg. IBM Corp., San Jose, Calif., 1967-68; v.p., dir. mktg. services Memorex Sales and Services Corp., 1969-72; dir. mktg. services Four-Phase Systems Inc., 1972-75; mgr. nat. sales Omron Corp. Am., 1975, Im Sai Mfg., 1975-76; pres. Computerland Corp., Hayward, Calif., 1976-83, vice chmn., 1983-85, pres., chief exec. officer, 1985-86, chmn., chief exec. officer, 1986—. Served to capt. USMC, 1955-57. Office: Computerland Corp 2901 Peralta Oaks Ct Oakland CA 94605 *

FABRIS, NEDA SARAVANJA, mechanical engineer, educator; b. Sarajevo, Yugoslavia, Aug. 2, 1942; came to U.S., 1970; d. Zarko and Olga (Majstorovic) Saravanja; m. Gracio Fabris, Nov. 4, 1967; children: Drazen, Nicole. Diploma in Engring., U. Sarajevo, 1965; MS in Mech. Engring., Ill. Inst. Tech., 1972, PhD in Mech. Engring., 1976. Asst. prof. U. Sarajevo, 1965-70; lectr. U. Ill., Chgo., 1974-75; mem. tech. staff Bell Telephone Lab., Naperville, Ill., 1976-79; asst. prof. mech. engring. Calif. State U., L.A., 1979-83, assoc. prof., 1983-87, prof., 1987—, assoc. dept. chmn., 1987-88, dept. chmn., 1989—; assoc. researcher Technische Hoschschule, Aachen. Fed. Republic Germany, 1966-67. Deutsche Academische Austautdienst fellow, 1966-67, Amelia Earhart fellow, 1973, 75. Mem. Soc. Women Engrs. (sr.), soc. Mfg. Engrs. (sr.), AAUW. Home: 2039 Dublin Dr Glendale CA 91206 Office: Calif State U 5151 State University Dr Los Angeles CA 90032

FACCINI, ERNEST CARLO, mechanical engineer; b. Livo, Trento, Italy, May 28, 1949; s. Carlo and Elena Agnes (Pancheri) F.; parents Am. citizens; AA, Western Wyo. Community Coll., 1969; BS, U. Wyo., 1972, MS, 1976. Engring. technician Laramie (Wyo.) Energy Research Center, 1968-71; field engr. Mountain Fuel Supply Co., Rock Springs, Wyo., 1972; research engr. Aberdeen (Md.) Proving Grounds, 1972-73; research asst. mech. engring. U. Wyo., Laramie, 1973-76; engring. asst. Bridger Coal Co., Rock Springs, Wyo., 1973; mech. engr. Naval Explosive Ordnance Disposal Facility, Indian Head, Md., 1976-85; sr. scientist TERA/NMIMT, Socorro, N. Mex., 1986—. Registered profl. engr., Wyo., Md. Mem. ASME (chmn. student sect. 1971-72), Am. Phys. Soc., AAAS, Am. Soc. Metals. Roman Catholic. Contbr. articles to profl. jours.; patentee in field. Researcher rapid explosive excavation techniques, underwater non-explosive excavation, surface/subsurface ordnance clearance vehicle design, remote fuse disassembly, multi-fuel combuster design, internal ballistics, blast effects design of shaped charges and of grenades for spl. applications, explosive mine countermeasures. Home: 1211 Hilton Pl Socorro NM 87801 Office: TERA/NMIMT Socorro NM 87801

FACKLER, MARTIN L(UTHER), surgeon; b. York, Pa., Apr. 8, 1933; s. Martin Luther and Naomi Dorcas (Gibbs) F.; m. Nancy Aleen Gray, Sept. 29, 1964. AB magna cum laude, Gettysburg Coll., 1955; MD, Yale U., 1959. Diplomate Am. Bd. Surgery. Enlisted USN, 1960, advanced through grades to col.; intern U. Oreg. Med. Sch. Hosp., 1959-60; resident in gen. surgery U.S. Naval Hosp., Boston, 1961-65; resident in plastic surgery U.S. Naval Hosp., Bethesda, Md., 1966-67; staff surgeon NSA Hosp., DaNang, Socialist Republic of Vietnam, 1967-68, USN Hosp., Yokosuka, Japan, 1969-71; chief dept. surgery USN Hosp., Memphis, 1972-74; intersvc. transfer U.S. Army chief dept. surgery 2d Gen. Hosp., Landstuhl, Republic of Germany, 1975-80; chief dept. surgery U.S. Army Hosp., Ft. Carson, Colo., 1980-81; dir. wound ballistics lab. Presidio, San Francisco, 1981—; tech. adv. Assn. Firearm and Toolmark Examiners, 1984—; adv. forensic sci. grad. sch. U. Calif., Berkeley, 1985—; speaker on war surgery, wound ballistics, weapons effects; expert witness, cons. to various state, city and nat. law enforcement agys. and criminalistics labs.; appointed steering com. on devel. less-than-lethal weapons for law enforcement use Nat. Inst. Justice, 1986—; mem. of Can. Gen. Standards Bd. Com. on Police Ammunition, 1989—. Contbr. articles to profl. jours.; patentee in field. Recipient Commendation 2d Gen. Hosp., Landstuhl, 1981. Fellow ACS (com. on trauma); mem. Phi Beta Kappa, Nat. Rifle Assn. (life). Home: 1809 Wyman Ave Presidio San Francisco CA 94129 Office: The Presido Letterman Army Inst Rsch San Francisco CA 94129

FACTOR, MAX, III, lawyer, investment advisor; b. Los Angeles, Sept. 25, 1945; s. Sidney B. and Dorothy (Levinson) F.; BA in Econs. magna cum laude, Harvard Coll., 1966; JD, Yale U., 1969. Bar: Calif. 1970, U.S. Ct. Appeals (6th cir.) 1971, U.S. Dist. Ct. (cen. dist.) Calif. 1971. Law clk. U.S. Ct. Appeals (6th cir.), 1969-71; exec. dir. Calif. Law Ctr., Los Angeles, 1973-74; dir. Consumer Protection Sect., Los Angeles City Atty., 1974-77; pres. MF Capital Ltd., Beverly Hills, Calif., 1978-86; ptnr. Cooper, Epstein & Hurewitz, Beverly Hills, Calif., 1986—; expert witness numerous state and fed. bds., 1974-78; guest lectr. UCLA, U. So. Calif., Los Angeles County Bar Assn., Calif. Dept. Consumer Affairs, 1974-76; hearing examiner City of Los Angeles, 1975. Contbr. articles to profl. jours. Bd. dirs. Western Law Ctr. for the Handicapped, Los Angeles, 1977-79, Beverly Hills Unified Sch. Dist., 1979-83; pres. Beverly Hills Bd. Edn., 1983; bd. councilors U. So. Calif. Law Ctr., Los Angeles, 1983—. Recipient scholarship award Harvard Coll., 1965; Max Factor III Day proclaimed in his honor Beverly Hills City Council, 1979; recipient Disting. Service to Pub. Edn. award Beverly Hills Bd. Edn., 1979. Mem. Los Angeles County Bar Assn. (chmn. various coms. 1976-78), Beverly Hills C. of C. (pres. 1987-88), Beverly Hills Edn. Found. (pres. 1977-79). Democrat. Jewish. Office: Cooper Epstein & Hurewitz 345 N Maple Dr Ste 200 Beverly Hills CA 90210

FADALLA, MICHAEL ANDREW, automotive executive; b. Mobile, Ala., Jan. 1, 1966; s. George Aziz and Eloise Theresa (Naman) F. Student, Valley Coll., 1989—. Purchase agent Auto Air of Ala., Mobile, 1984-85, customer svc. mgr., 1985-86; gen. operations mgr. Filters Inc., N. Hollywood, Calif., 1987—. Republican. Roman Catholic. Home: 4320 Van Nuys Blvd Sherman Oaks CA 91403 Office: Filters Inc 11846 Sherman Way North Hollywood CA 91605

FADDICK, ROBERT RAYMOND, civil engineering educator; b. Sudbury, Ont., Can., May 18, 1938. BSCE, Queen's U., 1961, MSCE, 1963; PhD, Mont. State U., 1970. Hydraulic engr. Alden Research Lab. Worcester (Mass.) Polytech Inst., 1963-66; research asst. Mont. State U., Bozeman, 1966-69; prof. Colo. Sch. Mines, Golden, 1969—; pres. Slurry Pipeline Corp., Golden, 1970—. Contbr. articles to profl. jours. Mem. Assn. Profl. Engrs. Ont., ASCE, Slurry Transport and Tech. Assn., Soc. Rheology, Brit. Hydromechanics Rsch. Assn. (hon. mem.). Home: 2373 Coors Dr Golden CO 80401 Office: Colo Sch Mines Engring Dept Golden CO 80401

FADELEY, EDWARD NORMAN, state supreme court justice; b. Williamsville, Mo., Dec. 13, 1929. A.B., U. Mo., 1951; J.D., U. Oreg., 1957. Bar: Oreg. 1957. Practice law Eugene, Oreg., 1957—; mem. Oreg. Ho. of Reps., 1961-63; mem. Oreg. Senate, 1963-89, pres., 1983-89; judge Oregon Supreme Ct., 1989—. Chmn. Oreg. Dem. Party, 1966-68; chmn. law and justice com. Nat. conf. Legislators, 1977-78; mem. adv. com. to State and Local Law Ctr., Washington; mem. participants com. Wash. Pub. Power Supply System; candidate for nomination for gov., 1986. Lt. USNR, 1951-54. Recipient Pioneer award U. Oreg., 1980, Assn. Oreg. Counties award, 1982. Mem. ABA, Oreg. State Bar Assn. (chmn. uniform laws com. 1962-64), Order of Coif, Alpha Pi Zeta, Phi Alpha Delta. Democrat. Methodist. Office: Supreme Ct Salem OR 97310

FADEN, ALAN IRA, neurology educator; b. Phila., Jan. 11, 1945. BA in Physics, U. Pa., 1966; postgrad., Ind. U., 1966-67; MD, U. Chgo., 1971. Resident in neurology U. Calif., San Francisco, 1972-75; research neurologist Walter Reed Army Inst. Research, Washington, 1975-80; assoc. prof. neurology and medicine Uniformed Services U. of Health Scis., Bethesda, Md., 1978-81, prof. neurology and physiology, 1981-84, vice chmn. neurology, 1980-82; chief neurobiol. research unit Uniformed Serviced U. of Health Scis., Bethesda, Md., 1982-84; prof. neurology, vice chmn. dept. U. Calif., San Francisco, 1984—; chief neurology VA Med. Ctr., San Francisco, 1984—; dir. Ctr. for Neural Injury, San Francisco, 1984—; sci. dir. Nat. Research Inst. for Neural Injury, Washington, 1983—. Assoc. editor J. Neurotrauma; mem. editorial bd. Arch Neurol and CNS Trauma; contbr. articles to profl. jours.; patentee in field. Named one of 100 Top Leaders of Washington, Washington mag., 1982. Fellow ACP, Am. Acad. Neurology; mem. Am. Soc. Pharmacology and Exptl. Therapeutics, Am. Soc. Clin. Investigation, Am. Physiol. Soc., Am. Neurol. Assn., Neurotrauma Soc. (pres.), San Francisco Neurol. Soc. (sec., treas.). Office: VA Med Ctr Neurology Svc 127 4150 Clement St San Francisco CA 94121

FAGAL, HAROLD EDWARD, minister; b. Ilion, N.Y., May 5, 1923; s. William and Anna Mary (Fritschler) F.; m. Ruth Ellen Smith, Oct. 15, 1944; children: Carolyn, Marilyn. BTh, Atlantic Union Coll., 1944; MDiv, Andrews U., 1964; ThM, Fuller Theol. Sem., 1969, PhD, 1975. Assoc. pastor Seventh-day Adventist Ch., Springfield, Mass., 1944-46, Pittsfield, Mass., 1946-47, New Haven, Conn., 1947-51; pastor Prospect Ave. Ch., Hartford, Conn., 1951-53, Cleve. First Seventh-day Adventist Ch., 1953-55; dept. dir. Ohio Conf. Seventh-day Adventists, Mount Vernon, 1955-56; pastor Balt. First Seventh-day Adventist Ch., 1956-58, Miami (Fla.) Temple Seventh-day Adventist Ch., 1958-63; prof. Loma Linda U., Riverside, Calif., 1964-88; assoc. dean Coll. Arts and Sci., Riverside, Calif., 1977-86. Author (with others): Scripture, Tradition and Interpretation, 1978, The Advent Hope in Scripture and History, 1987; contbr. articles to New International Bible Encyclopedia, 1985. Mem. Soc. of Bibl. Lit., Evang. Theol. Soc., Palomar Nature Club (pres. 1983-86). Republican. Home: 11845 Claycroft Ln Riverside CA 92505

FAGAN, MICHAEL GLENNON, aerospace engineer; b. Lemay, Mo., Sept. 1, 1949; s. L. Glennon and Clare Isabel (Essex) F.; m. Mary Elizabeth

Finder, Oct. 13, 1973; children: Kathryn Elizabeth, Elizabeth Ann. BS in Aerospace Engring., St. Louis U., 1970. Mem. tech. staff Space Transp. System div. Rockwell Internat., Downey, Calif., 1973-79, project engr., 1979-85, project mgr., 1985-86, 1988—; engring. mgr. Space Sta. System div. Rockwell Internat., Downey, 1986-87. 1st Lt. USAF, 1970-73. Mem. Planetary Soc., YMCA (Huntington Beach, Calif.). Republican. Roman Catholic. Home: 19962 Weems Ln Huntington Beach CA 92646 Office: Rockwell Internat Space Transpn Systems Div 12214 Lakewood Blvd Downey CA 90241

FAGEN, SHELDON B., art dealer, gallery owner; b. N.Y.C., July 12, 1933; s. Isadore and Celia (Lane) F.; m. Eleanor Kuznetzoff, May 2, 1953. Student, Sch. Art. & Design, N.Y.C., 1947-51, Pratt Inst., N.Y.C., 1951-52. Art dealer Fagen-Peterson Fine Art, Scottsdale, Ariz., 1970—; sr. designer Honeywell Bull, Phoenix, 1960-88. Staff sgt. USAF, 1952-60, Korea. Mem. Friends Mexican Art, Leader in Design and Art, Variety Club. Office: Fagen Peterson Fine Art Inc 7077 Main St Scottsdale AZ 85251

FAGLIANO, DENISE ROTHMAN, cartoonist, graphic designer; b. Oakland, Calif., Nov. 22, 1951; d. Albert Joel and Jeannette (Jacot) Rothman; m. Robert James Fagliano, Feb. 10, 1979. BFA in Graphic Design, Calif. Coll. Arts & Crafts, Oakland, 1974. Art dir. U. San Francisco, 1975-76; asst. art dir. Pritkin & Gibbons, San Francisco, 1976-77; freelance graphic artist San Francisco, 1977-83, cartoonist of Darf cartoons, 1983-85; cartoonist of Darf cartoons Bozeman, Mont., 1985--; cartoonist Profiles mag., 1984-85, Wyo. Tribune, 1986-87, High Country Ind. Press, 1987--; graphic artist Intermountain Opera, Bozeman, 1988. Mem. Cartoon Art Mus., The Conservancy, Mus. of the Rockies, Mont. Ad Club SW (2d v.p., treas. 1988). Democrat. Home: PO Box 3061 Bozeman MT 59772 Office: Darf Cartoons 321 E Main St Ste 210 Bozeman MT 59715

FAHEY, JUDELL SPOERING, infosystems specialist; b. Springfield, Mo., June 11, 1955; d. Clell Norman and June Catherine (Stimson) Spoering; m. Mark Joseph Fahey, Aug., 1983. BS in Geology, U. Mo., Columbia, 1977. Cartographer Def. Mapping Agy., Dept. Def., St. Louis, 1978-82, Nat. Mapping Div. U.S. Geol. Survey, Denver, 1982-85; computer specialist nat. mapping div. U.S. Geol. Survey, Denver, 1985-87, supr. computer specialist, 1987—. Mem. Nat. Assn. Female Execs., Assn. Computing Machinery. Office: US Geol Survey DFC Bldg 25 MS 502 Lakewood CO 80225

FAHLENKAMP, LANNY ELMER, astronautics company executive; b. Ft. Dodge, Iowa, July 10, 1945; s. Donald Henry and Lela Yvonne (Collins) F.; m. Carolyn Joan Martinez, Aug. 12, 1967; children: Heather, Chad, Kindle, Jeremiah. BS, U. Colo., 1978. Pres., owner House of TV Repair, Inc., Aurora, Colo., 1971-82; svc. mgr., cons. House of TV Repair, Inc., 1982-84; sr. logistics engring. specialist Martin Marietta Astronautics Group, Denver, 1984-87; chief tng. devel. Martin Marietta Astronautics Group, 1987—. Choir dir. St. Mark's Ch., Westminster, Colo., 1980-82; pres. St. Pius X Parish Council, Aurora, 1984-85; instr. Jr. Achievement, Denver, 1987--. Mem. Am. Soc. Tng. Devel. Republican. Roman Catholic. Home: 3280 Tucson St Aurora CO 80011 Office: Martin Marietta Astronautics Group Box 179 DC 1825 Denver CO 80201

FAHRENKAMP, BETTYE M., state legislator; b. Wilder, Tenn.; m. Gilbert H. Fahrenkamp, 1952 (dec.). BS, U. Tenn., 1949; MA, U. Alaska, 1962. Formerly sch. music tchr.; mem. Alaska Senate, 1978—. Served with WAC, 1944-46. Chmn. dist. Democratic com., 1968-72; nat. Dem. committeewoman, 1972-78; pres. Western Legis. Conf., Coun. State Govts., 1988. Office: Alaska State Senate PO Box V Juneau AK 99811

FAHRNEY, BYRON WELTIE, computer software development company executive; b. Nashville, Dec. 16, 1932; s. Byron Weltie and Margaret Louise (Soles) F.; m. Elsie Marie Vasey, May 7, 1957 (div. Oct. 1970); children: Marie Elaina, Richard Byron; m. Karen Roney Johnson, Sept. 22, 1984. Student, U. Fla., 1952-54, 59, Rollins Coll., 1955. Store mgr. W.T. Grant Co., N.Y.C., 1957-69; owner, mgr. Merchandising Methods, Denver, 1969-76; ptnr. Vail (Colo.) Book & Poster, 1976-80; mgr. Cloth World, Amarillo, Tex., 1980-82, Cunningham Drug, Detroit, 1982-85; pres. Etek Labs., Boulder, Colo., 1987—; cons. Pitkin Country Dry Goods, Aspen, 1968-78, Aspen Leaf, Denver, 1970-74. Inventor luminaire reflector and diffuser. Del. Colo. Dem. Conv., 1974. Republican. Office: Etek Labs 2888 Bluff St Ste 387 Boulder CO 80301

FAIKS, JAN OGOZALEK, state senator, real estate developer; b. Hempstead, N.Y., Nov. 17, 1945; d. Edmund Frank and Anna Marie (Chupella) Ogozalek. B.A., Florida State U., 1967. Tchr. Anchorage Sch. Dist., 1968-76, counselor, 1976-78; owner, mgr. Green Connection, Anchorage, 1978-81; mem. Alaska State Senate, Juneau, 1982—, pres. Author: Llama Training-Who's In Charge, 1981. Editor course devel. in career math., 1976. Bd. dirs. People Against State Income Tax, 1979—, Common Sense for Alaska, bd. dirs. Common Sense for Alaska, 1980—, research chmn., v.p., 1980-82; bd. dirs. Anchorage Symphony, 1984, Alaska Spl. Olympics; Recipient First Lady vol. award Gov. of Alaska, 1981; President's award Common Sense for Alaska, 1981; named Outstanding Secondary Tchr., Anchorage Sch. Dist., 1977. Mem. Nat. Council State Legislators, Anchorage C. of C. (bd. dirs. 1981-86, legis. chmn. 1980-82), Gen. Fedn. Women's Club (legis chmn. 1979-82), Anchorage Symphony Women's League (pres. 1980-81), Anchorage C. of C. (bd. dirs. 1987—, exec. com. 1981-82), Phi Beta Phi (pres. 1974-76). Republican. Presbyterian. Avocations: backpacking, fishing, llamas.

FAIN, KAREN KELLOGG, history and geography educator; b. Pueblo, Colo., Oct. 10, 1940; d. Howard Davis and Mary Lucille (Cole) Kellogg; m. Sept. 1, 1961; divorced; 1 child, Kristopher. Student, U. Ariz., 1958-61; BA, U. So. Colo., 1967; MA, U. No. Colo., 1977. Cert. secondary tchr., Colo. Tchr. history and geography Denver Pub. Schs., 1967—; area adminstr., tchr. coordinator Close Up program, Washington, 1982-84. Vol., chmn. young profls. Inst. Internat. Edn. and World Affairs Council, Denver, 1980—; mem. state selection com. U.S. Senate and Japan Scholarship Com., Denver, 1981—, Youth for Understanding, Denver. Fulbright scholar Chadron St. Coll., Pakistan, 1975; Geographic Soc. grantee U. Colo., 1986. Mem. Colo. Council Social Studies (sec. 1984-86), Nat. Council Social Studies (del. 1984), World History Assn., Nat. Geog. Soc., Rocky Mountain Regional World History Assn. (steering com. 1984-87), Colo. Geographic Alliance (steering com. 1986), Gamma Phi Beta. Democrat. Episcopalian. Home: 12643 E Bates Cir Aurora CO 80014 Office: Montbello High Sch 5000 Crown Blvd Denver CO 80239

FAIN, MICKEY ALLEN, data processing executive; b. Dallas, Mar. 4, 1956; s. Allen Maurice and Lourene (Strain) F.; 1 child, Brandon. BEE, U. Tex.-Austin, 1978; M Bus. and Pub. Mgmt., Rice U., 1981. CPA, Tex. Elec. engr., project mgr. I.A. Naman & Assocs., Houston, 1978-79; mgmt. adv. svcs. cons. Price Waterhouse, Houston, 1980; mgmt. adv. svcs. mgr. Ferguson, Camp & Co., Houston, 1980-81; v.p. E.I. Corp., Boulder, Colo., 1981-86; pres. Smartscan, Inc., Boulder, 1986—; bd. dirs. Rocky Mountain Export Council. Contbr. articles to tech. publs. Bd. dirs. Pvt. Industry Ptnrship., Boulder, 1986-87; mem. Boulder Econ. Devel. Cuncil, 1987. Mem. Am. Inst. CPAs, Nat. Computer Graphics Assn., Automated Mapping and Facilities Mgmt. Assn., Urban and Regional Info. Systems Assn. Home: 7275 Siena Way Boulder CO 80301

FAIR, RICH ALLEN, lighting company executive; b. Panama C.Z., Nov. 13, 1951; s. George Harvey and Marie Hilda (Tallent) F.; m. Donna Carol McFall, Dec. 5, 1970 (div. July 1981); children: Rebecca Ann, Christina Dianne; m. Vicky Dianne Allen, Feb. 28, 1987. Grad., high school, Colorado Springs, Colo. Warehouseman Cen. Electric Supply Co., Denver, 1969-71, inside salesman, 1971-74, outside salesman, 1974-79, sales mgr., 1979-84; v.p., regional mgr. Cummins Lighting, Denver, 1984—. Democrat. Home: 988 Northridge Ct Golden CO 80401 Office: Cummins Lighting 2626 N Speer Blvd Denver CO 80401

FAIRCHILD, ARVID PERSHING, travel agency executive; b. Turlock, Calif., Jan. 6, 1925; s. Clarence Frank and Maybelle (Dunagan) F.; B.S. in Civil Engring., U. Miami (Fla.), 1955; m. Grace M. Stewart, June 20, 1943; children—Jack W., Jean A. Fairchild Gartner. Dir. ops. Interocean Airways, Luxembourg, 1961-63; flight instr. United Airlines, 1963-64; check pilot Japan Air Lines, 1964-74; pres., chmn. bd. Island Air Tours, Kilohana World Travel (formerly Scenic Island Travel), Honolulu, 1974-85; v.p. Horizon Airlines/Trans Nat. Airlines; v.p. Pacific Air Express, 1982-87; v.p., dir. Care-All Aviation, 1987—; dir. ops. UN airlift for Congo, 1962; capt. Seaboard Western Airlines, 1955-62. Served with USN, 1940-53, USNR 1953-62. Decorated Air medal (3), Purple Heart, Army Disting. Service medal with oak leaf clusters. Mem. Nat. Assn. Businessmen. Republican. Presbyterian. Clubs: Masons, Shriners, Order Eastern Star. Author: Instrument Flight Technique; also articles in aviation publs. Office: 3031 Aolele Honolulu HI 96819

FAIRCHILD, THOMAS NEWMAN, psychologist, educator; b. Burley, Idaho, Nov. 21, 1947; s. Loyal Bryant and Bernyce Elizabeth (Rudolph) F.; m. Carolyn Ardria Yoder, Oct. 1, 1966 (div.); children: David Brian, Brandi Michelle, Nicole Kathryn; m. Ellen Lorett Bodkin; children: Joshua Thomas, Megan Lorett. BS in Psychology, U. Idaho, 1969, MEd in Guidance and Counseling, 1971, Specialist D. in Sch. Psychology, 1972; PhD in Sch. Psychology, U. Iowa, 1974. Cert. sch. counselor, psychologist, Idaho; nat. cert. counselor; lic. profl. counselor, Idaho. Counselor, sch. psychologist Walla Walla Community Sch. Dist. (Wash.), 1971; sch. psychologist Cedar Rapids Community Schs. (Iowa), 1971-74; counselor educator, sch. psychologist trainer Coll. Edn., U. Idaho, Moscow, 1974—, chmn. dept. counseling and human services, 1978-86, coordinator sch. psychology tng. program, 1974—; cons. Kendrick, Genesee, Craigmont, Lapwai Culdesac Sch. Dists., Idaho. Mem. Rocky Mountain Assn. for Counselor Edn. Supervision (sec. treas. 1981-82), Nat. Assn. Sch. Psychologists (state del. 1984-86, 88—, Cert. Appreciation 1985,86), Am. Assn. Counseling and Devel., Am. Psychology Assn., Council Exceptional Children, Assn. for Counselor Edn. and Supervision (resources and rsch. com. 1982-86), Idaho Assn. for Counselor Edn. and Supervision, Idaho Assn. Counseling and Devel., Idaho Sch. Psychologists Assn. (pres. 1976, 86-87, historian 1984-87, chmn. awards com. 1983-85, licensure com. 1975-82, Disting. Service award 1985, Leadership award 1987), Idaho Stateline Guidance Assn., Phi Delta Kappa. Co-author: (with A. Lee Parks) How to Survive Educator Burnout, 1981, (with D. Fairchild, E. Woolums, D. Starr) Everything You Always Wanted to Know About Drinking Problems and a Few Things You Didn't Want to Know, 1978, (with A. Iriarte, M. Yutzy) The Kindergarten Primer: A Guide for Professionals and Parents, 1975; editor: Accountability for School Psychologists: Selected Readings, 1977, Crisis Intervention Strategies for School-Based Helpers, 1985; editor, author: Mainstreaming Series, 1975-77; mem. editorial bd. Psychology in the Schools, 1976-83, Sch. Psychology Rev., 1978-81; contbr. to profl. jours. and filmstrips. Home: 2201 Westview Dr Moscow ID 83843 Office: U Idaho Coll Edn Moscow ID 83843

FAIRLY-GREEN, SUZANNE PHIPPS, interior designer, educator; b. Carroll, Iowa, May 5, 1935; d. Joseph Montgomery and Mary Elizabeth (Grems) P.; m. Harold Paul Fairly, Mar. 21, 1955 (div.); children: Suzan Lyn, Steven Paul, David Carl; m. Harlan Russell Green, June 4, 1983. Student, U. Denver, 1958-60, UCLA, 1974-79; BA in Communications, Antioch West U., 1986; postgrad., U. Calif., Santa Barbara. Profl. cert. interior design. Design apprentice Cornell & Chaffin, Santa Barbara, 1968-71; with pub. rels. dept., radio and copy writer Furniture Guild, Santa Barbara, 1972-74; instr., curriculum developer, coord. interior design program Santa Barbara City Coll., 1974-81; instr. environ. and interior design, mem. adv. bd., student advisor U. Calif., Santa Barbara, 1986—; owner, designer Inside-Out Design Assocs., Santa Barbara, 1981—; docent Santa Barbara Mus. Art, 1968-71. Contbr. to Creative Ideas for Your Kitchen, 1984. Founder Santa Barbara Woman's Support Group; v.p. Semana Natica Sports Festival, Santa Barbara; mem. adv. bd. Children's Creative Project, Santa Barbara; fund raiser youth programs YMCA, Santa Barbara; Santa Barbara coordinator, 1st Earth Run of the UN, 1983. Recipient appreciation and recognition award Planned Parenthood, 1978-81, Santa Barbara City Coll. Found., 1981. Mem. Interior Design Networking Guild, Internat. Soc. Interior Designers (2d v.p.), Am. Assn. Interior Designers (edn. com. L.A. br.), AIA, Nat. Mus. Women in Arts (charter), Edn. Am. Soc. Interior Designers. Democrat. Unitarian. Home: 952 Miramonte Dr Apt 5 Santa Barbara CA 93109 Office: U Calif Extension Santa Barbara CA 93016

FAIRWEATHER, EDWIN ARTHUR, electronics company executive; b. London, July 21, 1916; came to U.S., 1967; s. Arthur Henry and Elizabeth (Dawson) F.; m. Joan Barbara Branson, Sept. 14, 1946; children: David Martin, Janet Elizabeth Fairweather Nelson. BSME, London Poly., 1940. Quality engr. Lucas-Rotex, Toronto (Ont., Can.) and Birmingham (Eng.), 1951-58; mfg. engr. Flight Refuelling Co., Dorset, Eng., 1958-62, Spar Aerospace, Toronto, 1962-67, Sperry Flight Systems, Phoenix, 1967-71; engr. research and devel. Ford Aerospace Co., Palo Alto, Calif., 1971-85; founder, pres., chief engr. Fairweather & Co., Sunnyvale, Calif., 1980—. Patentee in field. Served with RAF, 1940-46. Home and Office: 1442 Wolfe Rd Sunnyvale CA 94087

FAISON, DELORES, government accountant; b. Atlanta, Aug. 28, 1945; d. Harry and Ella Maud (Hunter) Campbell; 1 child, Harold Ernest Campbell. Student CUNY, Helene Fuld Sch. Nursing, N.Y.C., U. Ariz.; grad. with high honors, Pima Coll., 1984; postgrad., Columbia Pacific U., 1987—. In various positions U.S. Govt., N.Y.C., 1965-74; health unit coordinator Polyclinic Med. Ctr., Harrisburg, Pa., 1978-81, St. Joseph's Hosp., Tucson, 1981-86; acctg. technician Agrl. Research Service, Dept. Agr., Tucson, 1984—; v.p. Tucson Employees Benefit Assn., 1984-85. Recipient Woman On The Move award YWCA, Tucson, 1985. Mem. Nat. Assn. Health Unit Coordinators, Nat. Assn. Female Execs., Federally Employed Women, Fed. Women's Program (alt. rep.), Phi Theta Kappa. Democrat. Baptist. Club: Federally Employed Women (com. chairperson 1985—) (Tucson). Avocations: writing; singing; public speaking.

FAJARDO, SARAH ELIZABETH JOHNSON, financial planner; b. Montgomery, Ala., July 27, 1956; d. Robert Kellogg and Mary Loretta (Franks) Johnson; m. Thomas Ronald Fajardo, Sept. 5, 1987. BA in Anthropology, U. Ariz., 1979; postgrad., Inst. Fin. Edn., Tucson, 1985-87. Resident advisor Tucson Job Corps, 1980-81; felony release specialist Pretrial Release of Pima County, Tucson, 1981-82; dir. retention counseling Tucson Coll. Bus., 1982-84; teller, new account rep. Western Savs., Tucson, 1984-86; stockbroker Western Savs./Invest, Tucson, 1986-87; fin. planner Boucher, Oehmke & Quinn, Tucson, 1987—; mgr. telemarketing dept. Ariz. Theatre Co, Tucson, 1988—. Contbr. articles to profl. jours. Mem. com. Tucson Tomorrow, 1988; founding mem. Brewster Ctr. for Victims of Family Violence, Tucson, 1982-86; vol. Peace Corps, Senegal, Africa, 1979. Mem. Resources for Women, NAFE, Successful Bus. Referral Club, Indsl. Recreation Coun. (treas. 1986-87), Am. Bus. Women's Assn., the Profl. Aux. Assistance League. Democrat. Home: 1313 N Rook Tucson AZ 85712 Office: Diversified Fin Planning 1141 N El Dorado Pl Ste 300 Tucson AZ 85712

FAKHOURY, SAYEL SALEH, marble company executive; b. Salt, Jordan, Aug. 5, 1961; came to U.S., 1975; s. Saleh and Victoria (Adwani) F.; m. Loredana Diona, Feb. 14, 1981; children: Ivano, Natasha. Student respiratory therapy tech., Valley Coll., North Hollywood, Calif., 1984; AA, West Coast U., 1985; BS, Cleveland Chiropractic U., L.A., 1987, postgrad., 1988—. Office mgr. Diona Marble Co., North Hollywood, 1983-85; sec., treas. Diona & Sons Marble Inc., North Hollywood, 1985-86, v.p., 1987—. With U.S. Army, 1981-82. Mem. Am. Pub. Health Assn.

FALATER, SCOTT LOUIS, electrical engineer; b. Miami Beach, Fla., Sept. 14, 1955; s. Frederick Lawrence and Lois Rita (Gyure) F.; m. Tyrmila Marie Klesken, June 26, 1976; children: Megan Ann, Michael David. BS in Elec. Engring., Ill. Inst. Tech., 1977. Engr. Zenith Radio Corp., Glenview, Ill., 1977-80; sr. engr. Harris Semicondr., Melbourne, Fla., 1980-84; prin. engr. div. solid state electronics div. Honeywell, Plymouth, Minn., 1984-87; design mgr. SGS-Thompson Microelectronics, Phoenix, 1987—. Holder 6 patents in field. Mem. IEEE. Republican. Mormon. Home: 3922 E Tierra Buena Ln Phoenix AZ 85032 Office: SGS-Thomson Microelectronics 1000 E Bell Rd Phoenix AZ 85022

FALCO, JOHN ANTHONY, real estate development company executive; b. N.Y.C., Aug. 27, 1946; s. John Anthony and Irene (Gileski) F.; m. Marlene Ilana Alhadaf, May 3, 1975; children: Micole Rachal, Michael Solomon. AS in Civil Engring., Westchester Community Coll., Valhalla, N.Y., 1971; BS in Constrn. Mgmt., Pratt Inst., 1973. Project mgr. HRH Constrn. Co., N.Y.C., 1973-77, Kraus Anderson, Mpls., 1978-79; product mgr. Flour City Archtl. Metals, Mpls., 1977-78; sr. constrn. mgr. Gerald D. Hines Interests, Seattle, 1979-86; owner's rep. Lincoln Property Co., San Jose, Calif., 1986-87; v.p. VMS Realty Ptnrs., Beverly Hills, Calif., 1987—. With USN, 1966-68. Republican. Jewish. Home: 2662 Yellowwood Dr Westlake Village CA 91361 Office: VMS Realty Ptnrs 9465 Wilshire Blvd Beverly Hills CA 90212

FALCONE, PHILIP FRANCIS, computer engineer; b. Bethlehem, Pa., Jan. 20, 1929; s. Dominic Thomas and Mary Elizabeth (Beresh) F.; m. Kathryn Frances Buck, Sept. 9, 1950; children: Teresa Marie Holley, Philip Thomas. Student, Lehigh U., 1948-50, U. Cin., 1957-59, Ariz. State U., 1968, 70, 72. With Roller-Smith Corp., Bethlehem, 1950-55; nuclear engring. designer Gen. Electric. Co., Cin., 1955-60; supr. engring., drafting Honeywell, Phoenix, 1960-67, computer systems analyst, 1967-82, mgr. computer aided engring., 1982—; mem. steering com. Honeywell Computer Aided Design, 1982—. Rep. Sunburst Farms Home Owners Assn., Phoenix and Glendale, Ariz., 1969-75; leader horses Maricopa County 4-H Program, Phoenix, 1970-77; eucharistic minister Our Lady of the Valley parish, Phoenix, 1984—. Served with U.S. Army, 1946-48. Mem. Italian-Am. Wine Promoters Assn. (pres. Phoenix chpt. 1985—), Mensa. Democrat. Roman Catholic. Lodge: Moose (mem. exec. com. 1954-55). Home: 4701 W Country Gables Glendale AZ 85306 Office: Honeywell Inc IASD 16404 N Black Canyon Hwy Phoenix AZ 85023

FALEOMAVAEGA, ENI F. H., territorial delegate to U.S. Congress; b. Vailoatai Village, Am. Samoa, Aug. 15, 1943; m. Hinanui Bambridge Cave; children: Temanuata Tuilua'ai, Taualai, Nifae, Vaimoana, Leonne. BA in Polit. Sci. and History, Brigham Young U., 1966; JD, U. Houston, 1972; LLM, U. Calif., Berkeley, 1973. Bar: Am. Samoa, U.S. Supreme Ct. Adminstrv. asst. Am. Samoa del. to Washington, 1973-75; staff counsel to house com. on interior and insular affairs U.S. House of Reps., Washington, 1975-81; dep. atty. gen. Am. Samoa, 1981-84, lt. gov., 1984—; chmn. Gov.'s Task Force for Reorgn. of the Adminstrn., Am. Samoa Adv. Fisheries Council, 1985—, Gov.'s Adv. Com. on Grants Programs, 1985—; mem. nat. lt. gov.'s mission to Egypt, Jordan and Saudi Arabia, South Pacific Leaders Orientation Mission to Paris, 1987; leader Am. Samoa's del. to South Pacific Conf., Noumea New Caledonia, 1987; keynote speaker and leader Am. Samoa's del. to Pacific Trade/Omvestment Conf., 1986. With U.S. Army, 1966-69, including Vietnam, USAR, 1985—. Recipient Alumni Svc. award Brigham Young U., 1979; named Chieftain Faleomavaega, leone Village. Mem. Nat. Conf. of Lt. Govs., Nat. Assn. Secs. of State, Navy League of U.S., VFW, Nat. Am. Indian Prayer Breakfast Group, Lions (charter mem. Pago Pago chpt.), Go for Broke Assn. (life; pres. Samoa chpt.). Office: US Ho of Reps Office House Mems Washington DC 20515

FALICK, ABRAHAM JOHNSON, printing company executive; b. Chgo., Oct. 11, 1920; s. Simon Falick and Ellen Martina (Johnson) Sherwood; m. Carolyn Weber, Dec. 11, 1947; 1 child, Leslie Carol Falick Koplof. BA, Ind. U., 1947; MBA, U. Chgo., 1951; MA, UCLA, 1967, PhD, 1970. Cert. pub. planner. Commd. ensign USNR, 1941; advanced through grades to lt. comdr. USN, 1941-46, ret., 1967; mgr. sales/mktg. Webb-Linn Printing Co., Chgo., 1948-56; pres., chief exec. officer Murray and Gee, Inc., Culver City, Calif., 1956-60; planning economist City of Los Angeles, 1967-75; pres., chief exec. officer AJ Falick Assocs., Los Angeles, 1960-67, Navigator Press, Inc., Los Angeles, 1975—. Contbr. transp. research articles to profl. jours. Chmn. Coalition Rapid Transit, Los Angeles, 1978—; bd. dirs. Los Angeles County Dem. Cen. Com., 1984—. Mem. Am. Econ. Assn., Am. Planning Assn., Am. Inst. Cert. Planners (counselor 1972-74). Democrat. Jewish. Office: Navigator Press Inc 1636 W 8th St Los Angeles CA 90017

FALKENBERG, WILLIAM STEVENS, architect, contractor; b. Kansas City, Mo., July 21, 1927; s. John Joseph and Maraba Elizabeth (Stevens) F.; m. Janis Patton Hubner, Apr. 13, 1951; children: Ruth Elizabeth, Christopher Joseph, Charles Stevens. BS in Archtl. Engring., U. Colo., 1949. Pres. Falkenberg Constrn. Co., Denver, 1951-71, 74-84, devel. cons., 1984—; broker Hogan & Stevenson Realty, Denver, 1971-74. Chmn. constrn. Archdiocesan Housing Com., Inc.; chmn. restoration 9th St. Hist. Park; chmn. bldg. com. Four Mile House Hist. Park; chmn. Housing Trust Coun., Denver, 1986—; chmn. Rocky Mountain Better Bus. Bur., 1965-67; pres. Denver Friends of Folk Music, 1966. Served to lt. (j.g.) USNR, 1945-51. Mem. AIA (bd. dirs. Denver chpt. 1978-81, treas. 1981), Home Builder Assn. Met. Denver, Colo. Hist. Soc. Found. (bd. trustees, sec. 1987—), Serra Internat. (pres. 1971, dist. gov. 1973), Delta Tau Delta. Clubs: Denver Athletic, Cactus, Equestrian Order of Holy Sepulchre. Home and Office: 430 Marion St Denver CO 80218

FALLON, JOAN DOLORES, teacher; b. Purcell, Okla., July 2, 1937; d. Walter Lawrence and Rubye Maye (Webb) Simser; m. Thomas James Fallon, June 16, 1973; 1 child, Heather Lynn. BA in Edn., Ariz. State U., 1959, MA in Adminstrn., 1964. Cert. sch. supt., elem. tchr. and prin. Tchr. Isaac Sch. Dist., Phoenix, 1959-63, devel. reading program tchr., 1964-65, drama/English tchr., 1966-73, dist. curriculum specialist, 1974-79, tchr., 1980—; mem. curriculum council Isaac Sch. Dist., Phoenix, 1985—. Mem. strategic planning com. City of Glendale, 1985, civic ctr. bond com. City of Glendale, 1986, bd. of adjustment City of Glendale, 1987—; active Phoenix Art Mus., Friends of the Glendale Pub. Libr. Named Outstanding Young Educator Phoenix Jaycees, 1966. Mem. NEA, Delta Kappa Gamma. Republican. Baptist. Office: Mitchell Sch 1702 N 35th Ave Phoenix AZ 85009

FALLOWS, JAMES ALBERT, cardiologist; b. Abington, Pa., May 18, 1925; s. Lloyd Howard and Marion Elizabeth (Hoerr) F.; m. Mary Jeannette Mackenzie, Aug. 7, 1948; children: James Mackenzie, Susan Fallows Tierney, Thomas Stuart, Katharine Fallows Neider. Student, Ursinus Coll., 1943-45; MD, Harvard U., 1949. Diplomate Am. Bd. Med. Examiners. Intern and resident Phila. Gen. Hosp., 1949-51; resident in neurology and psychiatry U.S. Naval Hosp., Bethesda, 1952; resident in internal medicine and cardiology V.A. Hosp., Phila., 1954; mem. staff Beaver Med. Clinic, Redlands, Calif., 1955—; also bd. dirs. Beaver Med. Clinic, pres., 1960-62, chief exec. officer, 1982-88; mem. staff Redlands Community Hosp., chief of staff, 1968-69, chmn. intensive care unit, 1967-82. Sr. Warden Trinity Episcopal Ch., 1967; pres. Redlands Community Scholarship Found., 1969-70; mem. Ecology Task Force, Redlands, 1970-72, San Bernardino County Heart Assn., Redlands Art Assn., Redlands Mounted Police (1st pres. 1978), Long Beach Mounted Police; pres. bd. YMCA, Redlands, 1965; trustee A.K. Smiley Pub. Library, 1969-80, Redlands Unified Sch. Dist., 1971-75. Fellow Univ. Redlands. Fellow Am. Coll. Physicians, Am. Coll. Cardiology; mem. AMA, Calif. Med. Assn., San Bernardino County Med. Soc., Am. Soc. Internal Medicine, L.A. Acad. Medicine, Inland Soc. Internal Medicine, Arabian Horse Assn., Redlands Swim and Tennis Club, Redlands Racquet Club (1st pres. 1963), Rim of the World Riders (pres. 1984-85), Redlands Country Club. Home: 728 W Crescent Ave Redlands CA 92373 Office: The Beaver Med clinic Inc 2 W Fern Redlands CA 92373

FALSETTI, CHRISTINE MARIE, space research engineer; b. Burlington, Vt., Apr. 8, 1961; d. Herman Leo Falsetti and Sandra Jean Gruver. BA in Chemistry, Cen. Coll., 1983. Data systems engr. NASA Ames Rsch. Ctr., Moffett Field, Calif., 1984-86, computer and communications systems engr., 1986-88; space flight planning engr. NASA Ames Rsch. Ctr., Moffett Field, 1988—. Mem. Nat. Assn. System Programmers, SHARE. Office: NASA Ames Rsch Ctr 240A-3 Moffett Field CA 94035

FALTIN, BRUCE CHARLES, hotel executive; b. Cin., Mar. 7, 1947; s. Charles F. and Meryl (Gunther) F.; m. H. Ann Walker: children: Sharon, Laura, John. BS, Cornell U., 1969. Mgr. Winegardner & Hamarons Inc., Cin., 1969-78; ptnr. Idahotels Ltd., Boise, Idaho, 1978—; pres. Mountain States Mgmt. Inc., Boise, 1978—, also bd. dirs; trustee Rodeway Inns Advt. Fund, Phoenix, 1985—; chmn. Rodeway Inns Owner's Council, Phoenix, 1986-88. Mem. Am. Hotel and Motel Assn. (state dir. 1983-84), Nat. Restaurant Assn., Idaho Innkeepers Assn. (bd. dirs. 1974-86, pres. 1979), Greater Boise C. of C. (bd. dirs. 1987). Home: 2423 Hillway Dr Boise ID 83702 Office: Rodeway Inn of Boise 1115 N Curtis Rd Boise ID 83706

FANKHAUSER, JAMES CHRISTIAN, meteorologist; b. Humboldt, Nebr., June 2, 1930; s. Christian Raymond and Rose Wilhelmina (Rexroth)

F.; m. Jo Ann Dvoracek, Aug. 31, 1957; children: Julie Christine Fankhauser Kennedy, Jeri Ann. BA, Nebr. Wesleyan U., 1951; postgrad., U. Chgo., 1957-61. Pub. svc. meteorologist U.S. Weather Bur., Chgo. and Casper, Wyo., 1956-61; rsch. meteorologist NOAA, Kansas City, Mo., 1962-67, Nat. Ctr. Atmospheric Rsch., Boulder, Colo., 1967—; vis. assoc. prof., Fla. State U., Tallahassee, 1976. Editor, Monthly Weather Rev., 1978-81; contbr. articles to sci. publs. Sgt., weather observer USAF, 1951-55. Mem. Am. Meteorol. Soc. Democrat. Mem. United Ch. of Christ. Office: Nat Ctr Atmospheric Rsch PO Box 3000 Boulder CO 80307

FANNIN, DANIEL PAUL CLARK, information systems executive; b. Tallahassee, Dec. 17, 1942; s. Harvey Fayette and Kathryn Alice Fannin; m. Kerry Kathleen Barbour, July 14, 1980; children: Daniel Paul Clark, Kourtney Kathleen, Katie Rose. BS in Psychology, Loyola U., Los Angeles, 1965; MBA in Mgmt. with honors, U. N.D., 1974; MS in Computer Sci. with honors, North Tex. State U., 1976. Commd. USAF, 1967, advanced through grades to lt. col., 1983; mgr. computer ctr. Strategic Air Command, Beale, Calif., 1970-72, Minot, N.D., 1972-74; program mgr. Dept. of Def. Computer Inst., Washington, 1976-79; mgr. edn. with industry Boeing Aerospace Co., Seattle, 1979-80; dir. software and data base mgmt. USAF Data Systems Evaluation Ctr., Montgomery, Ala., 1980-83; dir. info. systems 25th air div. USAF, Tacoma, 1983-87; ret. USAF, 1987; chief info. systems Wash. Dept. Social and Health Svcs, Olympia, 1987—; tech. advisor Space Transp. System, El Segundo, Calif., 1980-83; cons. Computer Security Program Office, Montgomery, 1980-83, Brit. Parliament, England, 1978, N.Y. Police Dept., N.Y.C., 1978, Maritime Adminstrn., Washington, 1978, Comptroller of the Currency, Washington, 1978, FBI, Washington, 1977-79; mem. staff Pres. Carter's Nat. Com. on Electronic Fund, Washington, 1976-79. Editor: Nat. Bur. of Standards Inst. for Computer Sci. and Tech., 1980; contbr. articles to profl. jours. Bd. dirs. Fed. Credit Union, Minot, 1973-74, Washington, 1977-79; coach Little League, Washington, 1978-79. Fellow Office of Mgmt. Budget. Republican. Roman Catholic. Home: 48 Hewitt Dr Steilacoom WA 98388 Office: Wash Dept Social and Health Svcs Office Infosystems Olympia WA 98504

FANNY-DELL (FANNY HENDRICKS), artist, sculptor, educator; b. Trinidad, Colo., May 30, 1939; d. Troy Stephen and Madelene Leona (Ball) Swift; div. first husband; children: Dennis Howard, Kim Renee, Terry Don, Laura Beth Wigley; m. Cecil Gene Hendricks, Dec. 10, 1979; stepchildren: Richard, Elizabeth Russell, K. Renee, Beverly. Student, South Oklahoma City Jr. Coll., 1978, Highline Community Coll., Seattle, 1980, Bellevue Community Coll., 1982-84. Freelance illustrator, 1978—; owner, artist Fannytastics, Seattle, 1983—; asst. instr. Bellevue (Wash.) Community Coll., 1984—; vol. archaeol. field excavations, Okla., 1977-80; sec. to Okla. state archaeologist, Norman, 1977-78; exhibit preparer and coord. Spiro Mounds, Okla. State Park Visitor Ctr. Exhibits, 1978; asst. art lab. South Okla. City Jr. Coll., 1979; docent Cowboy Hall of Fame, Oklahoma City, 1979; artist, craftsman Bringloe Hist. Figures, Seattle, 1980-81. One-woman shows include Bellevue (Wash.) Community Coll. Art Faculty Shows, 1986, 87, 88, St. David Religious and Fine Art Show, Lynwood, Wash., 1986, 87, Mercer Island Visual Arts League Summer Arts Festival, Mercer Island, Wash., 1982, 83, 85, 86; represented in permanent collections Pacific Northwest Mus. of Flight, Seattle, Okla. SPIRO Archaeol. State Park Interpretive Ctr., Stoval Mus. Okla. U., Norman; producer (videotapes) Wax Sculpture, 1988, Lost Wax Sculpture, 1988, How to Make Molds, 1988; commd. bronze trophy Exptl. Aircraft Assn., bronze bust Seattle 99's, Woman Entrepreneur Network. Recipient 2d place award Art X 5 Show, Oklahoma City, 1979, 1st place medal SeaTac Visual Arts Olympics, 1984. Mem. Internat. Sculpture Ctr., Women in Arts, Sculpture Source and Artist Trust, Western Art Assn., Pacific Resources in Major Arts, Women's Entrepreneur Network, Exptl. Aircraft Assn. (historian 1982-88), 99's, Aircraft Owners and Pilots Assn. Office: Fannytastics 4735 S 158th St Seattle WA 98188

FANTE, JAMES PETER, business executive; b. L.A., Nov. 15, 1950; s. John Thomas and Joyce Hild (Smart) F.; m. Jennifer Haru Kato, June 20, 1977; 1 child, Damian. BS in Bus. Mgmt., Calif. State U., Northridge, 1976; cert. in exec. mgmt., UCLA, Westwid, 1981. Supr. prodn. control G&H Tech., Santa Monica, Calif., 1979-81, mgr. prodn. control, 1981-84, mgr. group program, 1983-85, asst. mgr. ops., 1985-88; mgr. prodn. and inventory control Everest & Jennings, Camarillo, Calif., 1988-89; dir. ops. Spatz Labs., Oxnard, Calif., 1989—. With USAR, 1968-74. Mem. Am. Prodn. and Inventory Control Soc. (cert.), Camarillo Springs Men's Golf Club. Republican. Roman Catholic. Home: 217 Longfellow St Thousand Oaks CA 91360

FARAH, ELIE GEORGE, civil engineer; b. Beirut, Achrafieh, Lebanon, June 8, 1962; came to U.S., 1978; s. George Amin and Jeanette (Chaiban) F. Assoc. Sci., Southeastern La. U., 1981; BSCE, La. State U., 1983; MSCE, U. New Orleans, 1985. Registered profl engr., Calif. Project engr. J. J. Krebs & Assocs. Inc., Metairie, La., 1984-86; project mgr. Tait & Assocs., Anaheim, Calif., 1986-88, Willdan Assocs. Inc., Anaheim, 1988—; cons. Registered Profl. Civil Engr., Anaheim, 1987-89. Republican. Home: 314 S Prospectors Ave Diamond Bar CA 91765 Office: Wildan Assocs 290 S Anaheim Blvd Ste 100 Anaheim CA 92805-3896

FARAH, TAWFIC ELIAS, political scientist; b. Nazareth, Palestine, Aug. 12, 1946; came to U.S., 1965; s. Elias Tawfic and Itaf Fahim F.; BA, Calif. State U., Fresno, 1970, MA, 1971; PhD, U. Nebr., 1975; m. Linda Maxwell, Apr. 24, 1969; children—Omar Lee, Aliya Jane. Market researcher Xerox Corp., Lincoln, Nebr., 1974-75; asst. prof. polit. sci. Kuwait U., 1975-79; pres. Merg Analityca, 1979—; vis. asso. prof. UCLA, summers 1978-83, fellow Center for Internat. and Strategic Affairs, 1980-81, Ctr. for Near Eastern Studies, 1986; Fulbright scholar, 1983. Toyota Found. grantee, 1985. Mem. Am. Polit. Sci. Assn., Middle East Studies Assn. Greek Orthodox. Coauthor: Research Methods in the Social Sciences, 1977; A Dictionary of Social Analysis, 1980; author: Aspects of Modernization and Consociationalism: Lebanon as an Exploratory Test Case, 1975, 77; co-editor: Palestinians Without Palestine: Socialization of Palestinian Children, 1979; Learning to Become Palestinians, 1985; editor Political Behavior in the Arab States, 1983; Pan Arabism and Arab Nationalism: The Continuing Debate, 1986, Political Socialization in the Arab States, 1987, Survey Research in the Arab World, 1987; editor Jour. Arab Affairs, 1981—. Office: 2611 N Fresno St Fresno CA 93703

FARANDA, JOHN PAUL, college administrator; b. Orange, Calif., Feb. 21, 1957; s. Paul L. and Kay S. (Wilson) F. BA cum laude, Claremont McKenna Coll., 1979. Staff liaison L.A. County Bar Assn., 1979-80; spl. programs adminstr. L.A. County Med. Assn., 1980-85; dir. corp. rels. Claremont (Calif.) McKenna Coll., 1985-87, dir. campaign and devel. svcs., 1987-89, dir. devel., 1989—. Contbr. articles to profl. jours. Campaign chmn. United Way, Mt. Baldy Region, Ontario, Calif., 1987-88. Recipient Gold award United Way Mt. Baldy Region, Ontario, 1988. Mem. Coun. for Advancement and Support of Edn. (USX award 1986). Club: Univ. (L.A.). Home: 728 N Laurel Ave Upland CA 91786

FARBEROW, NORMAN LOUIS, psychologist; b. Pitts., Feb. 12, 1918; s. Louis and Minnie (Cohen) F.; m. Pearl Ross, Mar. 16, 1947; children: L. David, Hilary. BA, U. Pitts., 1938, MSc, 1940; PhD, UCLA, 1950. Cert. Am. Bd. Examiners in Profl. Psycholoyg. Psychologist VA, L.A., 1949-81; co-dir. L.A. Suicide Prevention Ctr., 1958—; emeritus adj. prof. U. So. Calif. Sch. Medicine, L.A., 1960—. Author: (with David Reynolds) Suicide Inside and Out, 1961, (with Glen Evans) The Encyclopedia of Suicide, 1988; editor: Family Shadow, 1980, Many Faces of Suicide, 1981. Capt. USAAF, 1941-45, ETO. Fellow Am. Psychol. Assn. (Harold M. Hildreth award div. 18, 1972, Disting. Sci. Contbn. award 1977); mem. Internat. Assn. Suicidology (past pres.), Am. Assn. Suicidology (past pres., Louis I. Dublin award 1973), Soc. for Personality Assessment, So. Calif. Psychol. Assn. (Disting. Sci. Contbn. award 1974, Disting. Humanitarian award 1981). Jewish. Office: Suicide Prevention Ctr 1041 S Menlo Ave Los Angeles CA 90006

FARD, HASSAN, real estate developer, jeweler, insurance broker; b. Tehran, Iran, June 11, 1952; came to U.S., 1976; s. Ali Khaksar and Tahereh (Sangestanian) F.; m. Nov. 15, 1980; children: Jennifer, Christopher. Assoc. degree, Tehran Inst. Architecture, 1976; BA, So. Calif. Inst. Architecture, 1981. Lic. realtor, life and disability ins. broker. Furniture designer Monterey Park, Calif., 1976-80; photographer Pasadena, Calif., 1985-86; real estate agt. Coldwell Banker Co., San Marino, Calif., 1985-86; jeweler Jennifer's Jewelry, Pasadena, 1985-89; real estate investor San Clemente, Calif., 1982—; ins. broker Transamerica Life, L.A., 1982—; jeweler Pier Gifts & Fine Jewelry, San Clemente, 1987—; owner Precious Gems, San Clemente, 1989—; fin. planner Transamerica Life, L.A., 1983-87; jewelry appraiser, Pasadena, San Clemente, 1985—; loan officer Spectrum Fin. Corp, Laguna Niguel, Calif., 1989. Republican. Home: 2139 Via Aguila San Clemente CA 92672

FARE, CHARLEY EUGENE, entrepreneur; b. Sheridan, Mich., June 1, 1948; s. Charles Fred and Geraldine Dorothey (Thompson) F.; student Montcalm Community Coll., 1967-68, grad. basic psychiatric tech. program Lansing Community Coll., 1984; children: Mark John, Steven Matthew. Owner, pres. Gene Fare Inc., Stanton, Mich., 1973-84, Fare Investment Co., 1975-84; mentor, advocate Mentally Ill and Crises Intervention Dwelling Pl., Inc., 1985; adv. supr. trainer Govt. Am. Samoa Pub. Works, 1986-87; cons. concrete and head injury case litigation, Honolulu, 1988—. With AUS, 1968-69. Home: 1211 Kamaile Rd Ste 6 Honolulu HI 96814 Address: PO Box 17813 Honolulu HI 96817

FARINA, GLORIA, small business owner; b. Raton, N.Mex., Dec. 28, 1939; d. Roman and Emma (Valdez) Solano; m. Anthony Joseph Farina, Dec. 17, 1960; children: Joseph Jerome, Helena Deanna Farina Miller. Grad. high sch., Albuquerque. Prin. Style Rite Hair Styling Salon, Albuquerque, 1960-67; successively receptionist, cosmetologist, instr., mgr. Hollywood Beauty Sch., Albuquerque, 1959—, prin., 1978—; com. chmn. Teachers Edn. Council., 1st v.p., 1977—. Mem. Nat. Cosmetology Assn. (pres. 1975), N.Mex. Coiffeur Guild, N.Mex. Cosmetology Sch. Owners (sect. v.p. 1975-77, pres. 1986-88). Republican. Roman Catholic. Office: Hollywood Beauty Schs 7915 Menaul Blvd NE Albuquerque NM 87110

FARISS, BRUCE LINDSAY, endocrinologist, educator; b. Allisonia, Va., July 22, 1934; s. Alven Pierce and Hetty Jo (Lindsay) F.; BS, Roanoke Coll., 1957; MD, U. Va., 1961; m. Cheryl Louise Tomasie, Jan. 18, 1975; children—Bruce Lindsay, Melissa, Margaret, Susan, Henry, Sarah Jane, Caroline, Adam. Diplomate Am. Bd. Internal Medicine and Am. Bd. Endocrinology. Intern in medicine U. Va. Hosp., 1961-62; commd. capt. M.C. U.S. Army, 1962, advanced through grades to col., 1976; gen. med. officer, Ft. Monroe, Va., 1962-63; resident in internal medicine Brooke Gen. Hosp., Ft. Sam Houston, Tex., 1963-66; fellow in endocrinology U. Calif.-San Francisco, 1966-68; chief, endocrine service Madigan Gen. Hosp., Tacoma, Wash., 1968-71, chief clin. research service, 1968-76, asst. chief dept. medicine, 1972-73, dir. endocrine fellowship program, 1971-76, chief dept. clin. investigation, 1979-85, dir. endocrine-metabolism fellowship tng. program, 1979-85; cons. internal medicine MEDCOM Europe, 1976-79; cons. endocrinology to surgeon gen. U.S. Army, 1979-85; prof. biology dept. Va. Poly. Inst., Blackburg, 1987—. Mem. bd. suprs. Pulaski County, Va., 1988-92. Decorated Legion of Merit with oak leaf cluster; recipient Meritorious Service award Office of Surgeon Gen. Army, 1977, Roanoke Coll. medal, 1982. Fellow ACP; mem. Southwest Va. Med. Soc. (trustee 1986-89), Am. Fedn. Clin. Research, Endocrine Soc. (ednl. com. 1980-83), Am. Diabetes Assn. (trustee 1986—), Alpha Omega Alpha. Contbr. articles to med. jours.

FARKAS, PAULA LYNETTE, librarian; b. Roswell, N.Mex., Feb. 20, 1958; d. Idolia Mary Cox Hawkins; m. Todd Ellis Farkas, Jan. 22, 1983. BA in Psychology, U.N.Mex., 1987. Librarian Arthur Andersen & Co., Albuquerque, 1984—; rsch. asst. human learning lab. U. N.Mex., 1987—. Mem. adv. bd., v.p. Albuquerque Rape Crisis Ctr., 1988—; active Children's Ct., Albuquerque, 1986. Recipient Appreciation award Channel 4 News, Albuquerque, 1985, Albuquerque Rape Crisis Ctr., 1985. Mem. Assn. for Behavioral Analysis. Democrat. Home: 10209 San Gabriel NE Albuquerque NM 87111

FARLEY, CHRISOPHER JAMES, solar energy company executive; b. N.Y.C., Nov. 17, 1952; s. John David and Margret (Kingston) F. BA, U. Wis., 1976. Salesman El Camino Solar Systems, Santa Barbara, Calif., 1977-79; mgr. solar sales Pool Supply and Patio Ctr., Santa Barbara, 1980-82; mgr. solar sales The Solar Energy Co. Inc., Santa Barbara, 1982-84, owner, 1984—. Office: Solar Energy Co Inc 1216 State St Ste 602 Santa Barbara CA 93101

FARLEY, RUSSELL CLIFFORD, business development and financial executive; b. Eugene, Oreg., May 8, 1957; s. Russell William and Myrtle Ellene Farley; m. Cathy Joanne Jones, Sept. 4, 1981; children: Andrew Russell, Bryan Michael. BBA, Oral Roberts U., 1979; postgrad., Portland State U., 1979-80. CPA, Oreg. Staff acct. Davis Dunn & Co., Portland, Oreg., 1979-80; interim mgr. Arthur Anderson & Co., Portland, 1980-85; supr. fin. reporting Nerco, Inc., Portland, 1985-86; pres. Tri-Con, Inc., Portland, 1986—, CDS, Inc., Portland, 1988; chief fin. officer Williams Controls, Inc., Portland, 1989—; cons. Plaid Pantries, Inc., Portland, 1986-87. Bd. dirs. Youth for Christ, Portland, 1987; active Jr. Achievement, Portland, 1984-85. Mem. Planning Forum (bd. dirs. Portland chpt. 1986—), Oreg. State Soc. CPA's (v.p. legis. policy com. 1987-88), Am. Inst. CPA's. Republican. Office: Williams Controls Inc 14100 SW 72nd Ave Portland OR 97224

FARMER, JANENE ELIZABETH, artist, educator; b. Albuquerque, Oct. 16, 1946; d. Charles John Watt and Regina M. (Brown) Kruger; m. Michael Hugh Bolton, Apr. 1965 (div.); m. Frank Urban Farmer, May, 1972 (div.). B.A. in Art, San Diego State U., 1969. Owner, operator Iron Walrus Pottery, 1972-79; designer ceramic and fabric murals, Coronado, Calif., 1979-82; executed commns. for clients in U.S.A., Can., Japan and Mex., 1972—; pvt. tchr. pottery; mem. faculty U. Calif.-San Diego; substitute tchr. Calif. community colls.; designer fabric murals and bldg. interiors, Coronado and La Jolla, Calif., 1982—; tchr. Blessed Sacrament Sch., San Diego, 1982-85, San Diego Unified Sch. Dist., 1985-87. Mem. Coronado Arts and Humanities Council; resident artist U. Calif.-San Diego. Recipient grant Calif. Arts Council, 1980-81; U. San Diego grad. fellow dept. edn., 1984. Mem. Am. Soc. Interior Designers (affiliate). Roman Catholic. Home: 4435 Nobel Dr #35 San Diego CA 92122

FARMER, JEROME RICHARDSON, systems engineer; b. Cleve., Feb. 23, 1941; s. Maxwell Jerome Farmer and Frances Patricia (McGraw) West; m. Mary Elizabeth Lachman, Oct. 1, 1966 (div. 1976). BA, Loyola U., L.A., 1970; MA, Calif. State U., Northridge, 1976. Asst. mgr. Crocker-Citizens Nat. Bank, San Francisco, 1963-67; staff psychologist Hughes Aircraft Co., Culver City, Calif., 1972-74; scientist Northrop Corp., Hawthorne, Calif., 1974-80; engring. specialist Northrop Corp., Hawthorne, 1980—; chief operating officer, The Med. Ctr., Gardena, Calif., 1988—. With U.S. Army, 1959-62. Mem. San Pedro Bridge Club, Psi Chi. Republican. Home: 1937 Mt Shasta Dr San Pedro CA 90732

FARMER, JOHN DAVID, museum administrator; b. Washington, Ga., Jan. 25, 1939; s. John Lloyd and Frances Heard (Woolley) F.; m. Patricia Phelps Dow, Aug. 21, 1965; children: Emily Dow, Rachel Aldrich. B.A., Columbia U., 1960; M.A., U. N.C., 1963; M.F.A., Princeton U., 1965, Ph.D., 1981. Curatorial asst. Worcester (Mass.) Art Mus., 1967-69; curator Busch-Reisinger Mus. Germanic Art, Harvard, 1969-72; curator earlier painting Art Inst. Chgo., 1972-75; dir. Birmingham (Ala.) Mus. Art, 1975-78; lectr. fine arts Clark U., Worcester, 1968-69; lectr. art Harvard U., 1970; lectr. U. Ala., Birmingham, 1976-78; exec. dir. Commn. for Ednl. Exchange between U.S.A., Belgium and Luxembourg, Brussels, 1979-80; dir. U. Calif.-Santa Barbara Art Mus., 1981—; adj. prof. art history U. Calif.-Santa Barbara, 1981—. Author: The Virtuoso Craftsman: Northern European Design in the 16th Century, 1969, Concepts of the Bauhaus, 1971, German Master Drawings of the 19th Century, 1972, James Ensor, 1976, Rubens and Humanism, 1978, Rowing/Olympics, 1984, also articles. Bd. dirs. Boston Musica Viva, 1971-72, Santa Barbara Rowing Found., 1984—. Albert M. Friend fellow, 1963-64, 65-66; Fulbright-Hayes fellow Belgium, 1966-67. Mem. Coll. Art Assn., Assn. Am. Museums, Assn. Art Mus. Dirs., U.S. Rowing Assn. Club: Odd Volumes (Boston). Office: U Calif Univ Art Mus Santa Barbara CA 93106

FARMER, LESLEY SUZANNE JOHNSON, library director; b. Spokane, Wash., June 15, 1949; d. Leslie Harlan and Emma Cecelia (Johnson) Johnson; m. Mark Lesley Farmer; 1 child, Christopher. BS in English, Whitman Coll., 1971; MLS, U. N.C., 1972; EdD, Temple U., 1981. Cert. tchr., Calif. Info. specialist Balt. County Pub. Library, Randallstown, Md., 1972-73; tech. librarian Singer Bus. Machines, San Leandro, Calif., 1974-75; instr., librarian Peace Corps, Tunis, Tunisia, 1975-77; media specialist Archdiocese Phila., 1977-81; asst. prof. Va. Commonwealth U., Richmond, 1981-82; young adult librarian Meml. Library Radnor Twp., Wayne, Pa., 1982-83; library dir. San Domenico Sch., San Anselmo, Calif., 1984—; adj. prof. Villanova (Pa.) U., 1982-83, San Jose State U., 1988—; speaker Calif. Library Assn., 1987; cons. Va. Dept. Edn., 1981-82, Marin County (Calif.) Office Edn., 1984-87. Editor: Media and the Young Adult, 1985; contbr. articles on library sci. to profl. jours. Chair Marin County Council Girl Scouts USA, 1986-88. Grantee NEH, 1986, Marin County Computer Edn. Consortium, 1984-86. Mem. ALA (chair young adult svcs. div. rsch. com. 1985-88, chair young adult svcs. div. computer applications com. 1985-88), Calif. Library Assn., Calif. Media and Library Educators Assn., Cath. Library Assn. (sect. pres. 1989—), Marin County Reference Network (chair 1987-88). Democrat. Roman Catholic. Home: 135 Golden Hind Passage Corte Madera CA 94925 Office: San Domenico Sch 1500 Butterfield Rd San Anselmo CA 94960

FARMER, WILLIAM ROBERT, comedian, impressionist; b. Pratt, Kans., Nov. 14, 1952; s. Robert Vernon and Mary Frances (Jones) F.; m. Sherry Ann Fanning, Feb. 1, 1980 (div. 1981); m. Jennifer Wynne Shadbolt, June 2, 1984. BS in Journalism, U. Kans., 1975. Ofcl. voice of Goofy and Pluto Walt Disney Prodns. Featured actor: America, You're Too Young to Die, Robocop, 1986, Dallas; guest: Showtime's Funniest Person in America, PM Mag.; featured voice artist, Who Framed Roger Rabbit, 1988, Skedaddle; narrator TV and radio commls. (Bronze award Film & TV Festival N.Y. 1984, Gold ADDY award Advt. Club Ft. Worth 1986); performer comedy routines at various clubs, Calif., Tex., La., Wash., Ariz., Oreg. Mem. Screen Actors Guild, AFTRA, Sigma Chi. Republican. Methodist. Home: 3716 Barham Blvd Los Angeles CA 90068

FARNES, GARY WILLIAM, hospital administrator; b. Feb. 20, 1940; m. Mary Orton; 7 children. BS, Brigham Young U., 1966, postgrad., 1967; MBA, George Washington U., 1970. Resident Johns Hopkins Hosp. and Sch. Medicine, 1968-70; asst. adminstr. Holy Cross Hosp., Salt Lake City, 1970-74, assoc. adminstr., 1974-77; assoc. adminstr., chief exec. officer ops. Latter Day Saints Hosp., Salt Lake City, 1977-79; adminstr. Cottonwood Hosp. Med. Ctr., Murray, Utah, 1979-82; exec. v.p. Profl. Services Inc. subs. Intermountain Health Care Co., Salt Lake City, 1982-85; adminstr. Latter Day Saints Hosp., Salt Lake City, 1985—. Mem. Am. Coll. Hosp. Adminstrs., Utah Hosp. Assn. (bd. dirs. 1986—), Utah Profl. Rev. Orgn. (bd. dirs. 1986—). Home: 2174 Pinecrest Ln Sandy UT 84092 Office: Latter Day Saints Hosp 8th Ave and C St Salt Lake City UT 84143

FARNEY, THOMAS PATRICK, corporate professional; b. Springfield, Ill., Nov. 3, 1948; s. James J. and Margaret Ellen (Ballard); m. Cheryl. L. Knox (div. June 1986). Student, Ark. Tech. U., 1966-68, Lasalle U., 1970-72, NYU, 1987—. Sr. field rep. GTR Gov. Systems, Mt. View, Calif., 1978—. With USN, 1968-78. Mem. U.S. Powerlifting Fedn., Am. Drug Free Power Lifting Assn. Republican. Roman Catholic. Home: 6191 Ranco Mission Rd #308 San Diego CA 92108 Office: GTR Gov Systems Corp PO Box 7188 Mountain View CA 94039

FARNHAM, MARY GLADE SIEMER, women's sportswear manufacturing executive; b. Ross, Calif., Nov. 1, 1924; d. Albert Henry and Mabel Meta (Jones) Siemer; children—Thomas Ross, Evan Neil, Gwen Marie, William Blair, Hugh Porter. Student Marin Jr. Coll., 1942-43, Goucher Coll., 1943-44; B.A., U. Calif.-Berkeley, 1947. Profl. athlete, Curry Co., Yosemite, Calif., 1945; advt. prodn. mgr. City of Paris/Hale's, San Francisco, 1947; advt. artist Lipman Wolfe, Portland, Oreg., 1947-48; advt. layout artist Meier & Frank, Portland, 1948; art dir. Olds & King, Portland, 1948-50; free lance comml. artist, Portland, 1950-56; pres. Marin County Devel. Co., San Anselmo, Calif., 1963-78; pres., designer Mary Farnham Designs, Inc., Portland, 1983—. Exhibited in numerous West Coast one woman and nat. group shows, 1960-83. Mem. pub. art selection panel II, Met. Arts Commn., Portland, 1982-83; bd. dirs. N.W. Artists Workshop, Portland, 1977-78; sec. Artist Membership, Portland Art Assn., 1973-74. Episcopalian. Club: Multnomah Athletic. Avocations: swimming; diving.

FARNHAM, PEGGY JO, truck line company executive; b. Denver, Sept. 9, 1955; d. Lyle Earl and Marcelle (McKay) F. BS, Carroll Coll., Waukesha, Wis., 1977. Svc. rep. Mt. Bell, Denver, 1977-80; account rep. Colo. Nat. Bank, Denver, 1980-81; sales sec. Electromedics, Inc., Englewood, Colo., 1981-84; customer svc. supr. Blue Bird Internat., Englewood, 1984-86; office mgr. Churchill Truck Lines, Denver, 1986—. Mem. Nat. Assn. Female Execs., Alpha Kappa Delta, Carroll Coll. Sociology Club. Republican. Home: 12368 W Nevada Pl #106 Lakewood CO 80228 Office: Churchill Truck Lines Inc 4201 E 52nd Ave Commerce City CO 80228

FARNHAM, RICHARD EUGENE, educator; b. San Diego, Dec. 6, 1944; s. Eugene Boyer and June (Cook) F.; m. Sally Lynn Dunn, Apr. 13, 1976. AA, Pierce Coll., 1964; BA, San Jose State U., 1967; MA, Pepperdine U., 1978. Cert. tchr., Calif. Tchr. Foothill High Sch., San Jose, Calif., 1968-74, Piedmont High Sch., San Jose, 1974-76, Independence High Sch., San Jose, 1976—. Mem. Eastside Union High Sch. Dist. Tchrs. Assn., Seahawk Rugby Club (v.p. 1974-79). Republican. Presbyterian.

FARNHAM, STEVEN JOHN, instrument manufacturing executive; b. Loveland, Colo., Jan. 23, 1938; s. William Henry and Geneva Rose (Mothershed) F.;m. Patricia Ann Trethewey, Dec. 16, 1959; childen: David Wayne, Douglas Alan. BA, U. No. Colo., 1960, MA, 1961. Tchr. Corcoran Pub. Schs., Corcoran, Calif., 1961-62; vol. Peace Corps, Jimma, Ethiopia, 1962-64; tchr. Aurora Pub. Schs., Aurora, Colo., 1964-65; mgmt. instr. Western Electric Co., Aurora, 1965-67; personnel adminstr. Western Electric Co., 1967-68; buyer Western Electric Co., Salt Lake City, 1968-70, Westminster, Colo., 1970-78; purchasing agt. Hach Co., Loveland, Colo., 1978-81; dir. purchasing & materials Hach Co., Loveland, 1981—. Rep. precinct. committeeman, Aurora, Loveland, 1966-89; del. Rep. Nat. Conv., Kansas City, Mo., 1976; chmn. Reagan for Pres., Aurora, 1976; sec. Loveland-Berthoud United Way, Loveland, 1988-89, pres., 1989—; team mem. Thompson Sch. Dist. Strategic Planning Team, Loveland, 1988; treas. "We Care" Anti-Recall Campaign of City Counselors, Loveland, 1987; bd. dirs. YMCA, Loveland, 1984-85; asst. chmn. U.S. Savs. Bond Drive, Salt Lake City, 1969. Named Vol. Yr. Loveland-Berthoud United Way, 1989. Mem. Loveland C. of C. (bd. dirs. 1986-89), Rotary (bd. dirs. Loveland chpt. 1985-87). Home: 2550 Farisita Dr Loveland CO 80538 Office: Hach Co 5600 Lindbergh Dr Loveland CO 80537

FARON, JOHN FRANK, engineering executive; b Chgo., Aug. 27, 1933; s. John Theodore and Mary Rose (Szczecina) F.; m. Martha Darling, Nov. 2, 1957; children—Kathleen, Susan, Sandra, Edward. Student Ohio State U., 1951-53, U. So. Calif., 1962, Fresno State U., 1967-69; AB, U.S. Naval Postgrad. Sch., 1971; postgrad. George Washington U., 1972; MA, Calif. State U.-Dominguez Hills, 1982. Commd. ensign U.S. Navy, 1955; advanced through grades to comdr., 1968; pilot, 1953-78; intelligence officer, 1955-59; flight instr., 1959-61; combat pilot, Vietnam, 1962-64; aviation maintenance officer USS Hancock, 1964-66; dept. head tech. tng. Attack Squadron 125, 1966-69; exec. sec. to chief naval ops. sub-com. command, control and communication, 1971-73; chmn. ops. sub-group R-2508 enhancement program, mgr. USN portion 56M radar enhancement program, test pilot, 1973-78; ret. 1978. sr. engring. tech. writer, Comarco Engring. Inc., Ridgecrest, Calif., 1978-80; head systems effectiveness engring. group, sr. staff cons. PRC Ridgecrest Engring. Co., 1980-83; staff engr. Vitro Corp., Oxnard, Calif., 1984-87; advanced programs mgr. Computer Tech. Assocs., 1988—. Decorated Navy Commendation medal, 1973. Mem. AIAA (chmn. China Lake sect. 1986-87), Nat. Air Racing Group, U.S. Air Racing Assn. (hon.), Assn. Naval Aviation, Tailhook Assn., Assn. Old Crows, Soc. Flight Test Engrs. (pres. China Lake chpt. 1986-88), Delta Chi. Republican. Roman Catholic. Clubs: China Lake Men's Golf, So. Calif. Golf Assn., Calif. Golf Assn. Home: 618 Scott St Ridgecrest CA 93555 Office: 900 Heritage Dr Ridgecrest CA 93555

FARR, LEE EDWARD, physician; b. Albuquerque, Oct. 13, 1907; s. Edward and Mabel (Heyn) F.; m. Anne Ritter, Dec. 28, 1936 (dec.); children: Charles E., Susan E., Susan A., Frances A.; m. Miriam Kirk, Jan. 22, 1985. BS, Yale U., 1929, MD, 1933. Asst. pediatrics Sch. Medicine, Yale U., 1933-34; asst. medicine Hosp. of Rockefeller Inst. Med. Research, 1934-37, assoc. medicine, 1937-40; dir. research Alfred I. duPont Inst. of Nemours Found., Wilmington, Del., 1940-49; vis. assoc. prof. pediatrics Sch. Medicine, U. Pa., 1940-49; med. dir. Brookhaven Nat. Lab., 1948-62; prof. nuclear medicine U. Tex. Postgrad. Med. Sch., 1962-64, prof. nuclear and environ. medicine Grad. Sch. Bio-Med. Scis., U. Tex. at Houston, 1965-68; chief sect. nuclear medicine U. Tex.-M.D. Anderson Hosp. and Tumor Inst., 1962-67, prof. environ. health U. Tex. Sch. Pub. Health, Houston, 1967-68; head disaster health services Calif. Dept. Health, 1968, chief emergency health services unit, 1968-70, 1st chief bur. emergency med. services, 1970-73; Lippitt lectr. Marquette U., 1941; Sommers Meml. lectr. U. Oreg. Sch. Med., Portland, 1960; Gordon Wilson lectr. Am. Clin. and Climatol. Assn., 1956; Sigma Xi nat. lectr., 1952-53. Mem. NRC adv. com. Naval Med. Res., 1953-68; chmn. NRC adv. com. Atomic Bomb Casualty Commn., 195-76; mem. adv. com. Naval Res. to Sec. of Navy and CNO, 1968-78; adv. com. on medicine and surgery, 1955-56, exec. com., 1962-65; Naval Research Mission to Formosa, 1953; tech. adviser U.S. delegation to Geneva Internat. Conf. for Peaceful Uses Atomic Energy, 1955; mem. N.Y. Adv. Com. Atomic Energy, 1956-59; mem. AMA Com. Nuclear Medicine, 1963-66; mem. com. med. isotopes NASA Manned Spacecraft Ctr., 1966-68; mem. expert adv. panel radiation WHO, 1957-79; mem. Calif. Gov.'s Ad Hoc Com. Emergency Health Service, 1968-69; mem. sci. adv. bd. Gorgas Meml. Inst., 1967-72; mem. Naval Res. Adv. Com., numerous other sci. adv. bds., panels; cons. TRW Systems, Inc., 1966-70, Consol. Petroleum Co., Beverly Hills, Calif., 1946-70. Mem. alumni bd. Yale, 1962-65, mem. alumni fund, 1966-76. Served as lt. comdr. M.C., USNR, 1942-46; capt. (M.C.) USNR, ret. Recipient Mead Johnson award for pediatric research, 1940; decorated Gold Cross Order of Phoenix, Greece; Order of Merit, West Germany, 1963; named Community Leader in Am., 1969, Disting. Alumni Yale U. Med. Sch., 1989. Diplomate Nat. Bd. Med. Examiners, Am. Bd. Pediatrics. Fellow AAAS, Royal Soc. Arts, Am. Acad. Pediatrics, N.Y. Acad. Scis., Royal Soc. Health, Am. Coll. Nuclear Medicine (disting. fellow); mem. Soc. Pediatric Research, Soc. Exptl. Biology and Medicine (chmn. adv. com. atom bomb casualties 1954-76, naval research adv. com. 1970-78), Harvey Soc., Am. Pediatric Soc., Soc. Exptl. Pathology, Am. Soc. Clin. Investigation, Radiation Research Soc., A.M.A. (mem. council on sci. assembly 1960-70, chmn. 1968-70), Houston C. of C. (chmn. subcom. on quality in living 1966-68), Med. Soc. Athens (Greece) (hon., Order of Phoenix award 1956), Alameda County Med. Assn., Sigma Xi, Alpha Omega Alpha, Phi Sigma Kappa, Nu Sigma Nu, Alpha Chi Sigma. Club: Commonwealth (San Francisco). Author articles on nuclear medicine, protein metabolism, emergency med. services, radioactive and chem. environ. contaminants, environ. noise. Home: 2502 Saklan Indian Dr Apt 2 Walnut Creek CA 94595

FARRAF, DAVIS SUTCLIFFE, town manager; b. Mt. Kisco, N.Y., Oct. 31, 1952; s. Louis Vollers and Emily (Earp) F.; m. Cathie F. Feulner, Nov. 18, 1978; children: Matthew Davis, Hanna Emily. BA, U. Vt., 1975; MA, Ariz. State U., 1978. Field engr. City of Scottsdale, Ariz., 1976-79; county planner Garfield County Planning, Glenwood Springs, Colo., 1980-82; town mgr. Carbondale, Colo., 1982—. Pres. Panorama Ranches Homeowners Assn., Garfield County, Colo., 1985—; v.p. Mo. Heights Community League, Garfield County, 1985, Crystal River Trails Assn., Carbondale, Colo., 1984—. Mem. Internat. City Mgrs. Assn., Colo. City Mgrs. Assn. Democrat. Episcopalian. Office: Town of Carbondale 76 S 2nd St Carbondale CO 81623

FARRAR, ELAINE WILLARDSON, artist; b. Los Angeles, Feb. 27, 1929; d. Eldon and Gladys Elsie (Larsen) Willardson; BA, Ariz. State U., 1967, MA, 1969, now doctoral candidate; children: Steve, Mark, Gregory, Leslie Jean, Monty, Susan. Tchr., Camelback Desert Sch., Paradise Valley, Ariz., 1966-69; mem. faculty Yavapai Coll., Prescott, Ariz., 1970—, chmn. dept. art, 1973-78, instr. art in watercolor and oil and acrylic painting, intaglio, relief and monoprints, 1971—; one-man shows include: R.P. Moffat's, Scottsdale, Ariz., 1969, Art Center, Battle Creek, Mich., 1969, The Woodpeddler, Costa Mesa, Calif., 1979; group show Prescott (Ariz.) Fine Arts Assn., 1982, 84, 86, 89, N.Y. Nat. Am. Watercolorists, 1982; Ariz. State U. Women Images Now, 1986, 87, 89; works rep. local and state exhibits; supt. fine arts dept. County Fair; com. mem., hanging chmn. Scholastic Art Awards; owner studio/gallery Willis Street Artists, Prescott. Mem. Mountain Artists Guild (past pres.), Nat. League Am. Pen Women (Prescott br.), NAEA, Ariz. Art Edn. Assn., Nat. Art Edn. Assn., Ariz. Coll. and Univ. Faculty Assn., AAUW, Verde Valley Art Assn., Ariz. Women's Caucus for Art, Kappa Delta Pi, Phi Delta Kappa. Republican. Mormon. Home: 635 Copper Basin Rd Prescott AZ 86303 Office: Yavapai Coll Art Dept 1100 E Sheldon Rd Prescott AZ 86301

FARRELL, FELIX JEFFERY, real estate associate; b. Detroit, Feb. 28, 1937; s. Felix Martin and Eleanore (Pettee) F.; m. Gabrielle Marie Tollie, Nov. 8, 1969; children: Felix Marco, Caroline Marie. BBA, U. Okla., 1958; MA, Yale U., 1963; postgrad., U. Sorbonne, 1960-61. Mng. dir. Siam Fabrics Co., Ltd., Bangkok, Thailand, 1968-80; sales cons. Merrill Lynch Realty, Santa Barbara, Calif., 1981—. V.p. Semana Nautica Assn., Santa Barbara, 1987-88, pres. 1989-90; dir. Cornerstone House; co-capt. U.S. Olympic Swim Team, 1960. Lt. j.g. USN, 1958-60, PTO. Recipient Gold Medal award Pan Am. Games, 1959, Olympic Games, 1960. Mem. Santa Barbara Bd. Realtors, Calif. Assn. Realtors, Am C. of C. Thailand. Republican. Mem. Christian Ch. Clubs: Royal Bangkok (chmn. swimming 1974-76), Thailand Sub Aqua (v.p. 1976-77), Fgn. Corr. (mem. com.); Coral Casino (Montecito) (bd. dirs. 1985-87). Home: 127 Olive Mill Rd Santa Barbara CA 93108 Office: Merrill Lynch Realty 1290 Coast Village Rd Santa Barbara CA 93108

FARRELL, THOMAS GEORGE, lawyer, educator; b. Pitts., Aug. 6, 1931; s. Thomas Joseph Farrell and Christine Geddes (Burnett) Litz; m. Suzanne Marion Kellogg, Feb. 18, 1967; children: Colleen Suzanne, Sean Thomas. BA, Pa. State U., 1954; JD, Southwestern U., Los Angeles, 1970. Bar: Calif. 1971. Commd. ensign USNR, 1954, advanced through grades to lt. comdr., 1964, ret., 1976; staff asst. Congressman James G. Fulton, Washington, 1957-58; contract negotiator Dept. of the Navy, Washington, 1959-62; contract adminstr. Rockwell Internat., Los Angeles, 1962-64; radio announcer Sta. KFMU-FM, Los Angeles, 1964-65; contracting officer, asst. counsel Def. Logistics Agy., Los Angeles, 1966-72; resident counsel The RAND Corp., Santa Monica, 1973-75; atty., spl. counsel for acquisition policy USAF Space div., Los Angeles AFB, El Segundo, Calif., 1975--; adj. prof. Woodbury U., Los Angeles, 1974-79, Northrop U., Los Angeles, 1983--; instr. UCLA Extension Govt. Contracts, Westwood, Calif., 1986--; lctr. Def. Sys tems Mgmt. Coll., 1985--. Mem. Irish Am. Bar Assn. Calif., Am. Legion, Nat. Contract Mgmt. Assn. (cert.profl. contract mgr.), The Classical Assn., U.S. Tennis Assn., U.S. Golf Assn., Phi Alpha Delta, Chi Phi (chapt. pres. 1954).

FARRELL, THOMAS JOSEPH, insurance company executive; b. Butte, Mont., June 10, 1926; s. Bartholomew J. and Lavina H. (Collins) F.; m. Evelyn Irene Southam, July 29, 1951; children: Brien J., Susan M., Leslie A., Jerome T. Student U. San Francisco, 1949. CLU. Ptnr. Affiliated-Gen. Ins. Adjusters, Santa Rosa, Calif., 1949-54; agt. Lincoln Nat. Life Ins. Co., Santa Rosa, 1954-57, supr., 1957-59, gen. agt., 1959-74; pres. Thomas J. Farrell & Assos., 1974-76, 7 Flags Ins. Mktg. Corp., 1976-81, Farrell-Dranginis & Assocs., 1981—; pres., bd. dirs. Lincoln Nat. Bank, Santa Rosa, San Rafael. Pres. Redwood Empire Estate Planning Council, 1981-82, Sonoma County Council for Retarded Children, 1956—, City Santa Rosa Traffic and Parking Commn., 1963; del. Calif. State Conf. Small Bus., 1980; mem. Santa Rosa City Schs. Compensatory Edn. Adv. Bd.; bd. dirs. Santa Rosa City Schs. Consumer Edn. Adv. Bd.; pres., nat. dir. United Cerebral Palsy Assn., 1954-55; nat. coordinator C. of C.-Rotary Symposia on Employment of People with Disabilities, 1985—; v.p. Vigil Light, Inc.; chmn. bd. dirs. Nat. Barrier Awareness for People with Disabilities Found.;ound., Inc.; mem. Pres.'s Com. on Mental Retardation, 1982-86; chmn. Santa Rosa Community Relations Com., 1973-76; pres. Sonoma County Young Reps., 1953; past bd. dirs. Sonoma County Fair and Expn., Inc.; bd. dirs. Sonoma County Family Service Agy., Eldridge Found., North Bay Regional Ctr. for Developmentally Disabled; trustee Sonoma State Hosp. for Mentally Retarded. Recipient cert. Nat. Assn. Retarded Children, 1962, Region 9 U.S. HHS Community Service award, 1985, Sonoma County Vendor's Human Service award, 1986, Individual Achievement award Community Affirmative Action Forum of Sonoma County, 1986. Mem. Nat. Assn. Life Underwriters, Redwood Empire Assn. CLU's (pres. 1974—), Japanese-Am. Citizens League, Jaycees (Outstanding Young Man of Year 1961, v.p. 1955), Santa Rosa C. of C. (bd. dirs. 1974-75), Calif. PTA (hon. life). Lodge: Rotary. Home: 963 Wyoming Dr Santa Rosa CA 95405 Office: Farrell Dranginis & Assoc 1160 N Dutton Ave Ste 160 Santa Rosa CA 95401

FARRELL, WILLIAM EDGAR, sales executive, infosystems specialist; b. Jeanette, Pa.; Mar. 13, 1937; s. Arthur Richard and Lelia (Ryder) F.; m. Sara Lynnette Swing, Aug. 20, 1960; children: Wendy J., Tracy L., Rebecca J. BS in Edn., Pa. State U., 1959. Location mgr. IBM Corp., Dover, Del., 1969-72; corp. lobbyist IBM Corp., Washington, 1972-74, planning cons., 1974-78, nat. mktg. mgr., 1978-80, exec. asst., 1980-81; account exec. IBM Corp., Denver, 1981-87, policy exec., 1987—; chief fin. officer Wide Horizon, Inc., Denver, 1987—; pres. Exec. Mgmt. Cons., 1987—. Founding mem. River Falls Community Assn., Potomac, Md., 1975; first reader First Ch. of Christ Scientist Chevy Chase, Md., 1976-80. Recipient Outstanding Contbn. award IBM Corp., 1968. Republican. Home: 6063 S Beeler St Englewood CO 80111 Office: IBM Corp 4700 S Syracuse Pkwy Denver CO 80237

FARRER, JOHN, orchestra conductor; b. Detroit, July 1, 1941; s. John and Beulah (Finley) F.; m. Bonnie Bogle, June 3, 1967; children: Matthew, Joanna. B in Music Theory, U. Mich., 1964, M in Music Theory, 1966; diploma, Mozarteum, Salzburg, Austria, 1969. Music dir. Roswell (N.Mex) Symphony Orch., 1972—, Bakersfield (Calif.) Symphony Orch., 1975—; bd. dirs. N.H. Youth Orch. Mem. Am. Symphony Orch. League (mem. standing com. on artistic affairs 1981—, condr. workshops, 1986—), Assn. Calif. Symphony Orchs. (bd. dirs. 1977-81). Lodge: Rotary. Office: Bakersfield Symphony Orch 400 Truxtun Ave Ste 201 Bakersfield CA 93301

FARRIMOND, GEORGE FRANCIS, JR., business educator; b. Peerless, Utah, Sept. 23, 1932; s. George Francis Sr. and Ruth (Howard) F.; m. Polly Ann Fowler, Mar. 21, 1988; children: George Kenneth, Ronald Kay, Carrie Frances, Holly Jean. BS, U. Utah, 1955; MBA, U. Mo., 1968; postgrad., Portland State U., 1979—. Cert. profl. contracts mgr. Enlisted USAF, 1955, advanced through grades to lt. col., 1971; master navigator USAF, various locations, 1955-71; flight commdr. 360th tactical elec. war squadron USAF, Saigon, Socialist Republic of Vietnam, 1971-72; chief procurement ops. USAF, Wright-Patterson AFB, Ohio, 1972-73, chief pricing ops. div., 1973-76; retired USAF, 1976; asst. prof. bus. So. Oreg. State Coll., Ashland, 1976-82, assoc. prof., 1982—; cons. small bus., Jackson County, Oreg., 1976-88; cons. Japanese mgmt., Jackson County, 1981-88. Author: (computer program) Spanish Verb Conjugation, 1980, (workbook) Pricing Techniques, 1983. Chmn. Wright-Patterson AFB div United Fund, 1973-76; little league coach various teams, Ark. and Mo., 1963-71; Sunday Sch. tchr. Ch. of Latter-day Saints, various states. Decorated Disting. Flying Cross, 5 Air medals; Minuteman Ednl. scholar Air Force Inst. Tech., 1964, Education with Industry scholar Air Force Inst. Tech., 1970. Mem. Am. Prodn. and Inventory Control Soc. (v.p. edn. com. 1982-84), Cascade Systems Soc., Air Force Soc., Soc. Japanese Studies, Beta Gamma Sigma. Republican. Home: PO Box 805 Ashland OR 97520-0027 Office: So Oreg State Coll Sch Bus 1250 Siskiyou Blvd Ashland OR 97520

FARRINGTON, ROBERT BOIS, mechanical engineer; b. Tripoli, Libya, July 24, 1957; (parents Am. citizens); s. Arthur Bois and Marile (Ansbacher) F.; m. Cathleen Camacho, May 22, 1982. BSME, Columbia U., 1978, MSME with acad. distinction, 1979. Registered profl. engr., Colo. Mech. engr. Solar Energy Rsch. Inst., Golden, Colo., 1979—; instr. Red Rocks Community Coll., Denver, 1980-81; cons. in field. Inventor Solar System Fault Detector, 1986; contbr. more than 40 articles and reports to periodicals. Elder Covenant Presbyn. Ch., Wheatridge, Colo., 1982—. Mem. ASME, Instrument Soc. Am., Am. Solar Energy Soc. Republican. Presbyterian. Office: Solar Energy Rsch Inst 1617 Cole Blvd Golden CO 80401

FARRIS, ANN, producer; b. Vancouver, B.C., Can., Jan. 15, 1937; d. John Lauchlan and Dorothy (Colledge) F.; m. Robert E. Darling, Aug. 22, 1970 (div.). BA, U. B.C., Vancouver, 1959; MFA, Yale U., 1963; cert., Columbia U., 1979. Head theater prodn. 1967 World Expn., Montreal, Que., Can., 1965-67; adminstrv. asst. San Francisco Opera, 1969-71; mgmt. assoc. Lyric Opera Theater Kansas City, Mo., 1973; prodn. adminstr. Wolf Trap Found., Vienna, Va., 1974; exec. dir. OPERA Am., Washington, 1974-79; mng. dir. Cen. City Opera House Assn., Denver, 1981; dir. opera mus. theater program Nat. Endowment of Arts, Washington, 1982-84; producer World Festival, 1986 World Expn., Vancouver, 1984-86; pres. Global Art and Bus., Honolulu, 1987—; cons. San Francisco Opera, 1987, 1982 World Expn., Knoxville, Tenn., 1980. Home and Office: 3674 Hilo Pl Honolulu HI 96816

FARRIS, LARRY DEAN, management consultant; b. Eugene, Oreg., Sept. 29, 1964; s. Grady Washington Jr. and Ardell Anna (Towne) F.; m. Brenda Lee Robison, Dec. 7, 1985. BS in Mgmt., Linfield Coll., 1989. Co-owner, mgr. G & A Trucking, Springfield, Oreg., 1985-87; exec. v.p. Ardell, Inc., Springfield, 1987; exchange officer Banco Continental, Guayaquile, Ecuador, 1987; ind. mgmt. cons. Springfield, 1987—; spl. agt., registered rep. Prudential-Bache, Eugene, Oreg., 1988--. Missionary Ch. of Jesus Christ of the Latter Day Saints, Recife, Brazil, 1984-85; Republican candidate for Oreg. Ho. of Reps., 1988; precinct person Lane County Rep. Cen. Com., 1987-88; del. to Rep. Nat. Conv., 1988; chmn. Oregonians Against Crime for Lane County. Home: 536 S 42nd St Springfield OR 97478

FARRIS, MARTIN THEODORE, economist, educator; b. Spokane, Wash., Nov. 5, 1925; s. Jacob B. and Edith S. (Gunderson) F.; m. Rhoda H. Harrington, Aug. 20, 1948; children—Christine A. Farris Zenobi, Diana Lynn, Elizabeth Farris-Fisher, M. Theodore II. BA, U. Mont., 1949, MA, 1950; PhD, Ohio State U., 1957. Grad. asst. U. Mont., 1949-50; asst. in econs. Ohio State U., Columbus, 1950-51, asst. instr., 1953-55, instr., 1955-57; asst. prof. Ariz. State U., Tempe, 1957-59, assoc. prof., 1959-62, chmn. dept. econs., 1967-69, prof. transp. and pub. utility econs., 1962-72, prof. transp., 1972-88, Regents' prof., 1988—; vis. prof. U. Hawaii, 1969-70, vis. scholar, 1979. Author: (with Roy Sampson and David Shrock) Domestic Transportation: Practice, Theory and Policy, 1985; (with Roy Sampson) Public Utilities: Regulation, Management and Ownership, 1973; (with Paul McElhiney) Modern Transportation, 1973; (with Grant Davis and Jack Holder) Management of Transportation Carriers, 1975; (with Forrest Harding) Passenger Transportation, 1976; (with Dave Bess) U.S. Maritime: History and Prospects, 1981, (with Stephen Happel) Modern Managerial Economics, 1987; contbr. articles to profl. jours. Served with U.S. Army, 1944-46, PTO. Decorated Philippine Liberation medal, with bronze star; recipient Transp. Man of Yr. award, 1972, Outstanding Faculty Achievement award Ariz. State U. Alumni Assn., 1978, Outstanding Faculty Researcher award Coll. Bus., Ariz. State U., 1982. Mem. Am. Econ. Assn. (Outstanding Contbn. to Scholarship in Transp. and Pub. Utilities award 1984), Western Econ. Assn. (bd. dirs. 1966-67), Assn. Transp. Practitioners, Transp. Research Forum, Am. Soc. Transp. and Logistics (chief examiner 1961-73, Joseph C. Schleen award 1988), Coun. of Logistics Mgmt., Traffic Clubs Internat., Phi Kappa Phi, Omicron Delta Epsilon, Sigma Phi Epsilon, Delta Nu Alpha, Beta Gamma Sigma. Episcopalian. Club: Traffic (Phoenix) (pres. 1960). Home: 6108 E Vernon Scottsdale AZ 85257 Office: Ariz State U Coll Bus Adminstrn Tempe AZ 85287-4706

FARROKH, REZA, architecture planner, consultant; b. Tehran, Iran, Apr. 21, 1943; came to U.S., 1984; s. Mozafar and Irandokht (Moini) F.; m. Homera Amirsanai, Aug. 19, 1973; 1 child, Alireza. Cert. in archtl. engring., T.H. Universitat Aachen, Fed. Republic Germany, 1963; D in Architecture, U. Rome, 1970, cert. in urbanistic architecture, 1974. Registered architect, Calif., lic. architect Italy, Iran, lic. contractor, Calif. Asst. prof. architecture U. Rome, 1969-71; prof. Nat. U. Iran, Tehran, 1971; mng. dir. JOCAJ, Tehran, 1973-86; prin. Navona Inc., Newport Beach, Calif., 1986; pres. Farrokh and Assocs., Torrance, Calif., 1987-88, Creative Am. Builders, Inc., West Los Angeles, Calif., 1988—. Contbr. articles to profl. jours. Served to 1st lt. Iranian Armed Forces, 1971-73. Italian govt. scholar 1965-69.an Novin Party, 1972, first place prize Iranian Govt., 1973;. Mem. AIA, Iranian and Am. Soc., Iranian Mgmt. Soc., Iranian and Am. C.of C., Am. Planning Assoc., Iranian Inst. Architects (bd. dirs. 1975-77), Italian Inst. Architects, Iranian Cons. Engrs. Republican. Moslem. Home: 2800 Plaza Del Amo #207 Torrance CA 90503 also: PO Box 13342 Torrance CA 90503

FARROW, BERNARD EDWARD, psychologist, educator; b. Monticello, N.Y., July 6, 1936; s. Saul and Ruth (Finkelstein) F.; BS, SUNY, Oswego, 1961; MA, No. Ariz. U., Flagstaff, 1971; PhD Columbia Pacific U., 1988; m. Arlene Mendelson, May 30, 1960; children: Scott Andrew, Randy Mark. Tchr., Brentwood (N.Y.) Pub. Schs., 1961-62, Roslyn (N.Y.) Pub. Schs., 1962-66, Half Hollow Hills Pub. Schs., Huntington, N.Y., 1966-67; tchr. Clark County Schs., Las Vegas, Nev., 1968-72, counselor, 1978-79; adj. prof. Nova U., Fort Lauderdale, Fla., 1978—; instr. Park Coll., Nellis AFB, Las Vegas, Nev., 1979—; prof. Embry Riddle Aero. U., Nellis AFB, Las Vegas, 1978—; pvt. practice psychology, Las Vegas, 1979—; prof. Nat. U., Las Vegas; psychologist State Nev., Nev. Indsl. Commn., State Indsl. Ins. System, 1979-84; sr. tng. rep. Reynolds Elec. & Engring. Co., Inc., employee assistance program dir.; spl. investigator child custody div. 8th Jud. Dist. Ct., 1979-80. Mem. Town Bd., Mount Charleston, Nev., 1980—, chmn., 1981—; team couple World Wide Marriage Encounter, 1982—; precinct chmn. Nev. Dem. Com., 1982; active fitness for duty and drug free work place com. U.S. Dept. Energy; mem. Nev. Speakers Bur., 1983—. With USN, 1954-57. Cert. clin. neuropsychologist; cert. counselor. Mem. Assn. Humanistic Edn. and Devel. (pub. INFOCHANGE, employee asst. jour.), Am. Personnel and Guidance Assn., Am. Fedn. Tchrs., Rehab. Counselors Assn., Am. Psychol. Assn., Soc. Behavioral Medicine, Nev. Adlerian Soc., Nev. State Counselors Assn., Nev. Mental Health Counselors Assn. (county rep.), Nev. Psychol. Assn., Am. Soc. Quality Control, Am. Soc. Tng. and Devel., Nat. Property Mgmt. Assn., Nat. Assn. of Alcoholism and Drug Abuse Counselors.

FARSDAHL, DONA MARY, public relations director; b. Sandpoint, Idaho, May 13, 1947; d. Joseph Alfred and Mary Donson (Bradetich) Bouchard; m. Mark Allen Farsdahl, Dec. 6, 1980. BS in Home Econs. Edn., U. Idaho, 1969; MBA, City U., Yakima, Wash., 1984. Tchr. Clarkston (Wash.) Middle Sch., 1969-70; sr. citizens nutritionist County Coop. Extension, Yakima, 1977-79; poison ctr.supr. Meml. Hosp., Yakima, 1979-82; program mgr. YWCA, Yakima, 1982-84; mktg. dir. New Valley Osteo. Hosp., Yakima, 1984—; cons. Yakima County Osteoporosis Ctr., 1986-87. Pres. Yakima County Div. Am. Heart Assn., 1988-89. Mem. Wash. Chpt. Am. Soc. for Hosp. Mktg. and Pub. Relations (sec. 1987-88, treas. 1988-89) Yakima Advt. Fedn. (bd. dirs. 1986-88), Yakima Home Econs. Assn. (pres. 1980-81, v.p. 1988-89). Republican. Methodist. Home: 6002 Douglas Dr Yakima WA 98908 Office: New Valley Osteo Hosp 3003 Tieton Dr Yakima WA 98902

FARTHING, GREGORY GEORGE, periodontist; b. Sullivan, Ind., Apr. 29, 1955; s. Charles Leroy and Beverly Ann (Miller) F.; m. Melanie Kay Mayberry, July 15, 1978; children: Amy Elizabeth, John Gregory. BS, Colo. State U., 1977; DDS, Ind. U., Indpls., 1982; MS in Dentistry, Baylor U., 1984. Cert. periodontics, 1984. Pvt. practice periodontics Denver, 1984--; assoc. prof. U. Colo. Health Sci. Ctr., Denver, 1984-88. Recipient award Am. Coll. Stomatologic Surgeons, 1982, Mosby award Mosby Book Co., Indpls., 1982. Mem. ADA, Am. Acad. Periodontics, Rocky Mountain Soc. Periodontists, Colo. Dental Assn., Met. Denver Dental Soc., Omicron Kappa Upsilon, Rotary. Home: 5769 S Geneva St Englewood CO 80111

FARWELL, HERMON WALDO, JR., parliamentarian, educator, speech communicator; b. Englewood, N.J., Oct. 24, 1918; s. Hermon Waldo and Elizabeth (Whitcomb) F.; A.B., Columbia, 1940; M.A., Pa. State U., 1964; m. Martha Carey Matthews, Jan. 3, 1942; children—Gardner Whitcomb, Linda Margaret (Mrs. Richard Hammer). Mil. service, 1940-66, advanced through grades to maj. U.S. Air Force; ret., 1966; instr. aerial photography Escola Tecnica de Aviação, Brazil, 1946-48; faculty U. So. Colo., Pueblo, 1966-84, prof. emeritus speech communication; cons., tchr. parliamentary procedure. Mem. Am. Inst. Parliamentarians (nat. dir. 1977-87), Commn. on Am. Parliamentary Practice (chmn. 1976), Ret. Officers Assn., Nat. Assn. Parliamentarians, Am. Legion. Author: The Majority Rules-A Manual of Procedure for Most Groups; Parliamentary Motions; Majority Motions; editor The Parliamentary Jour., 1981-87. Home and Office: 65 MacAlester Rd Pueblo CO 81001

FARWELL, IRENE, retired educator; b. Decatur, Tex., Apr. 30, 1916; d. Samuel Corless and Mary Ida (Erwin) Applewhite; m. William A. Farwell, June 20, 1950. Student, Decatur Bapt. Coll., 1934-36; BS, No. Tex. State Tchrs. Coll., 1939. Tchr. Westbrook Pub. Sch., Westbrook, Tex., 1940-42; tchr. Loraine Pub. Sch., Loraine, Tex., 1942-43; bookkeeper Montgomery Ward, Ft. Worth, 1943; tchr. Boyd Pub. Sch., Boyd, Tex., 1943-44, Southwestern Bible Inst., Waxahachie, Tex., 1944-49, Paul Elem. Sch., Paul, Idaho, 1955-58; sponsor jr. class Southwestern Bible Inst., Waxahachie, 1947-48. Author poems. Elections registrar Cassia County, Idaho, 1955-88; county extension club pres. Cassia County, 1976-78; sec.-treas. Assembly of God Ch., 1958-68, Sunday sch. sec., 1974-80, Women's Ministries Club, Adult Class Club. Home: 1040 E 17th St Burley ID 83318

FASCIANA, GUY S., health publication executive, consultant; b. Pittston, Pa., Sept. 8, 1943; s. Samuel M. and Salvatrice (Augello) F. BS, King's Coll., Wilkes-Barre, Pa., 1965; D of Dental Medicine, U. Pitts., 1971; MEd, U. Ariz., 1987, MS, 1988. Pvt. practice dentistry Wyoming, Pa., 1973-81; columnist The Human Ecologist, Chgo., 1983-85; pres. Health Challenge Press, Tucson, 1985—. Author: Are Your Dental Fillings Poisoning You?, 1986, You Can't Lose: Getting the Mental Advantage in Sport, 1989; (booklet) Dental Materials: Guide for Allergics, 1985. Served to lt. USN, 1971-73. Mem. ADA, Am. Acad. Environ. Medicine, Nat. Wellness Assn., Assn. for Advancement of Sports Psychology. Home and Office: 7721 E 39th St Tucson AZ 85730

FASI, FRANK F., mayor of Honolulu; b. Hartford, Conn., Aug. 27, 1920. B.S., Trinity Coll., Hartford, 1942. Mem. Hawaii Senate, from 1958; Dem. mayor City and County of Honolulu, 1969-81, Rep. mayor, 1985—. Mem. Dem. Nat. Com. for Hawaii, 1952-56; del. 2d Constl. Conv., 1968; mem.-at-large Honolulu City Council, from 1965. Served to capt. USMCR. Mem. VFW (former comdr. Hawaii dept.), AFTRA (past v.p.). Office: City Hall 530 S King Honolulu HI 96813

FASS, BARBARA, city official. Mayor, Stockton, Calif., 1985—. Address: City of Stockton 425 N El Dorado St Stockton CA 95202 *

FASSEL, WILLIAM FRANK, forging die manufacturer; b. Downey, Calif., June 23, 1955; s. John Joseph and Theresa Mary (Vorwerk) F.; m. Erma Marie Wilhelm, Jan. 12, 1985. BS in Biol. Sci., U. So. Calif., 1977; MBA, Pepperdine U., 1983. Chemist Lever Brothers Co., Los Angeles, 1978-80, Best Foods, Santa Fe Springs, Calif., 1980-81; pres. FASDICO, Inc., Fullerton, Calif., 1981—. Republican. Roman Catholic. Home: 22260 Rolling Hills Ln Yorba Linda CA 92686 Office: FASDICO Inc 606 S State College Blvd Fullerton CA 92631

FASSIO, VIRGIL, newspaper publishing company executive; b. Pitts., Aug. 10, 1927; s. Domenico and Carolina (Pia) F.; m. Shirley DeVirgilis; children: Richard, David, Michael. BA with honors, U. Pitts., 1949. Founder, editor, pub. Beechview News, Pitts., 1947-51; reporter Valley Daily News, Tarentum, Pa., 1950, circulation mgr., 1951-58; circulation dir. Morning News and Evening Jour., Wilmington, Del., 1958-65; circulation dir. Detroit Free Press, 1965-71, v.p., bus. mgr., 1971; v.p., circulation dir. Chgo. Tribune, 1972-76; v.p., gen. mgr. Seattle Post-Intelligencer, 1976, pub., 1978—; lectr. Am. Press Inst.; cons., lectr. in field. Contbr. articles to profl. jours. Del. White House Conf. on Children, 1960, 70; bd. dirs. Pacific Mus. Flight, Mus. History & Industry, Pacific Sci. Ctr. Found., Maritime Ctr, Region V State Tourism Bd.; bd. regents Seattle U., Washington Coun. on Internat. Trade; pres. Seattle-King County Conv. and Visitors Bur., 1982-84; bd. dirs. Seattle Goodwill Industries, Hope Heart Inst., Medic I Emergency Med. Svcs. Found., Boys and Girls Clubs of King County (1987 Svc. to Youth award), Wash. Coun. of Internat. Trade; mem. adv. bd. Seattle Mariners. Served with USNR, 1945-46, comdr. USNR (ret.). Recipient Frank Thayer award U. Wis., 1972, Varsity Letterman of Distinction award U. Pitts. 1974, Bicentennial Medallion of Distinction U. Pitts., 1989. Mem. Internat. Circulation Mgrs. Assn. (Man of Yr. award 1964), Inter-State

Circulation Mgrs. Assn. (sec.-treas. 1954-65, Outstanding Achievement award 1967), Seattle C. of C. (bd. dirs.), Downtown Seattle Devel. Assn. (vice-chmn.), Am. Newspaper Pubs. Assn. (vice-chmn. industry affairs com. 1982-86), Rainier Club, Columbia Tower Club, Wash. Athletic Club (bd. dirs.), Rotary. Office: Seattle Post-Intelligencer 101 Elliott Ave W Seattle WA 98111

FASTRING, RICHARD ARTHUR, engineering executive, consultant; b. New Orleans, Oct. 25, 1938; s. Wernex Theodore and Evelyn Lucille (Bondurant) F.; m. Glenda Marie Hintz, July 13, 1960; children: Rhonda, Gregg, Roger. BSEE, Tulane U., 1959; postgrad., U. Pa., 1960-61. Engr. RCA, Camden, N.J., 1959-65; engring. mgr. Sci. Mgmt. Assocs., Haddonfield, N.J., 1965-71, Semcor Inc., Moorestown, N.J., 1971-85, Synetics Corp., San Diego, 1985—; rep. Indsl. Adv. Group, NATO,. 1975-80; mem. local area network standards com., USN, 1985—, A2K com. mem. Soc. Automotive Engrs., 1971-73. Adult Bapt. Sunday sch. tchr., San Diego, 1983—. Mem. Am. Soc. Naval Engrs. (Speakers award 1986). Republican. Office: Synetics Corp 810 Jamacha Rd Ste 206 El Cajon CA 92019

FATHAUER, THEODORE FREDERICK, meteorologist; b. Oak Park, Ill., June 5, 1946; s. Arthur Theodore and Helen Ann (Mashek) F.; m. Mary Ann Neesan, Aug. 8, 1981. BA, U. Chgo., 1968. Cert. cons. meteorologist. Research aide USDA No. Dev. Labs., Peoria, Ill., 1966, Cloud Physics Lab., Chgo., 1967; meteorologist Sta. WLW radio/TV, Cin., 1967-68, Nat. Meteorol. Ctr., Washington, 1968-70, Nat. Weather Service, Anchorage, 1970-80; meteorologist-in-charge Nat. Weather Service, Fairbanks, Alaska, 1980—; instr. U. Alaska, Fairbanks, 1975-76, USCG aux., Fairbanks and Anchorage, 1974—. Contbr. articles to weather mags. Bd. dirs. Fairbanks Concert Assn., 1988—. Recipient Outstanding Performance award Nat. Weather Service, 1972, 76, 83, 85, 86, Fed. Employee of Yr. award, Fed. Exec. Assn., Anchorage, 1978. Mem. Am. Meteorol. Soc. (TV seal of approval), Am. Geophys. Union, AAAS, Royal Meteorol. Soc., Western Snow Conf. Republican. Lutheran. Office: Nat Weather Svc Forecast Office 101 12th Ave Box 21 Fairbanks AK 99701

FAULCONER, KAY ANNE, communications executive; b. Shelbyville, Ind., Aug. 19, 1945; d. Clark Jacks and Charlotte (Tindall) Keenan; B.A. in English, Calif. State U., Northridge, 1968; M.B.A., Pepperdine U., 1975, M.A. in Communications, 1976; m. James Faulconer; children—Kevin Lee, Melissa Lynne. Pres., Kay Faulconer & Assos., Oxnard, Calif., 1977—; instr. Oxnard Coll., U. LaVerne. Dir. bus. adminstrn of justice programs, Ventura (Calif.) Coll.; former pres., founder Oxnard Friends of Library; former exec. bd. Ventura County March of Dimes; mem. PTA; officer, bd. dirs. Oxnard Girls Club. Named Businesswoman of Yr., Ventura Bus. and Profl. Women's Club, 1976; Woman of Achievement, Oxnard Bus. and Profl. Women's Club, 1973, recipient Career Woman award, 1974; Mark Hopkins award for excellence in teaching Oxnard Coll., 1982. Mem. Am. Soc. Tng. and Devel., Am. Assn. Women in Community and Jr. Colls. (Leaders for 80's program), Ventura County Profl. Women's Network. Club: Oxnard Jr. Monday (past pres., hon. life). Home and Office: 601 Janetwood Dr Oxnard CA 93030

FAULCONER, MICHAEL GRANT, architect; b. Indpls., Nov. 29, 1954; s. Hal Marvin and Mary Joanne (Joyce) F.; m. Sharon Kay Leary, Dec. 29, 1973 (div. 1984); children: Christina, Jennifer, Michael, Katheryn; m. Cecile Evanthia Gurrola, Sept. 1, 1985; children: Chemayne, Marissa. BArch, Calif. Polytech. St. U., 1977. Registered architect, Calif. Intern planner City of Grover, Calif., 1976-77; intern architect Hunter, Shute, Martin Architects, Medford, Oreg., 1977-78; designer Rasmussen & Ellinwood Architects, Ventura, Calif., 1978-79; plan-checker City of Oxnard, Calif., 1979-83; owner, ptnr. Mainstreet Architects and Planners, Ventura, 1983—, Coastal Profl. Code Services, Oxnard, 1987—; preservation architect San Buenaventura Heritage, Inc., Ventura, 1985—, Heritage Sq. Commn., Oxnard, 1987—, Victorian Row Group, Ventura, 1987—. Architect on numerous preservation projects. Active, Gen. Plan Com. City of Oxnard, 1986—; mem. Redevel. Agy. Com. City of Ventura, 1986. Mem. AIA (v.p. 1984, pres. 1985), Ventura C. of C., Internat. Conf. of Bldg. Officials (v.p. 1983). Democrat. Roman Catholic. Office: Mainstreet Architects 468 E Main St Ventura CA 93001

FAULKNER, DEXTER HAROLD, magazine publishing executive, editor; b. Grand Island, Nebr., Sept. 10, 1937; s. Jack L. and Wanetta May (Howland) F.; student U. Calif.-Fresno, 1956-58, Ambassador Coll., 1958-60; m. Shirley Ann Hume, Jan. 11, 1959; children—Nathan Timothy, Matthew Benjamin. Ordained minister Worldwide Ch. of God. Exec. editor Plain Truth Mag; editor Good News mag., Youth/89 mag. and Worldwide News-Tabloid internat. div. Ambassador Coll., Sydney, Australia, 1960-66, news research asst. dir. Ambassador Coll. Editorial, Pasadena, Calif., 1966-71, regional editor Plain Truth mag., Washington, 1971-75, asst. mng. editor, Pasadena, 1975-78, mng. editor, 1980-82, exec. editor, 1982—, mng. editor Good News mag., Worldwide News-Tabloid, 1978-85, editor, 1986—; mng. editor Youth/89 mag., 1981-85, editor, 1986—; instr. mass communications Ambassador Coll., 1980—; columnist Just One More Thing . . ., By the Way, Just Between Friends. Mem. Inst. Journalists (London), Profl. Photographers Am. Inc., Bur. Freelance Photographers (London), Nat. Press Club, World Affairs Council (Los Angeles), Internat. Assn. Bus. Communicators, Nat. Press Photographers Assn., Am. Mgmt. Assn., Sigma Delta Chi. Mem. Worldwide Ch. God. Contbr. articles, photos on internat. relations, social issues to Plain Truth mag., Good News mag., Worldwide News Publs. Club: Commonwealth of Calif. Home: 7859 Wentworth St Sunland CA 91040 Office: Plain Truth Mag 300 W Green St Pasadena CA 91129

FAULKNER, GERALD DALE, ophthalmologist; b. Fairfield, Ala., Aug. 14, 1932; s. Drennen Dewitt and Edna Earle (Eastis) F.; m. Paula Eugenia Binion, June 18, 1954; children: Alan Richard, Kelly Bryan, Steven Jackson. BS, U. Ala., 1953; MD, Med. Coll. Ala., 1956. Diplomate Am. Bd. Ophthalmology. Intern U.S. Naval Hosp., Jacksonville, Fla., 1956-57; resident U.S. Naval Hosp., Bethesda, Md., 1957-60; lt. comdr. USN, 1956-64; pvt. practice Honolulu, 1964—; pres. Faulkner Inst. for Eye Care and Surgery, Honolulu, 1985—. Contbr. articles to profl. jours. Fellow ACS, Am. Acad. Opthalmology; mem. AMA, Hawaii Med. Assn., Honolulu County Med. Soc., Hawaii Ophthal. Soc., Internat. Assn. Ocular Surgeons, Outpatient Ophthalmic Surgery Soc., Am. Soc. Cataract and Refractive Surgeons, Pan Pacific Surg. Assn. (chmn. 1978-80), Outrigger Canoe, Pacific Club. Office: 1100 Ward Ave Ste 1000 Honolulu HI 96814

FAULKNER, MAURICE ERVIN, educator, conductor; b. Fort Scott, Kans., Feb. 2, 1912; s. Ervin Phyletus and Minnie Mae (Munday) F.; m. Ellen Stradal, May 24, 1934 (div. 1951); children: Katherine Sydney, Barbara Ellen; m. Suzanne Somerville, Oct. 18, 1958. BS in Music, Fort Hays State Coll., 1932; postgrad. Interlochen U., 1933; MA in Music, Tchrs. Coll., N.Y.C., 1936; PhD, Stanford U., 1956. Instr. music pub. schs., Kans., 1932-37; assoc. prof. instrumental music Columbia U., summers 1934-40; asst. prof. San Jose (Calif.) State Coll., 1937-40; from asst. prof. to assoc. prof. to prof. emeritus U. Calif., Santa Barbara, 1940—, also chmn. dept.; rsch. papers on Bronze Age musical instruments presented Biennial Archeol. Musicology Symposiums, Congress of Traditional Music of UNESCO, Stockholm, 1984, Hanover, Fed. Republic Germany, 1986, Royal Acad. Music, 1986, Hanover, Fed. Republic of Germany, 1988, bronze age musical instruments; vis. prof. U. Tex., summer 1947; music critic Salzburg (Austria) Festival, 1951— (Reinhardt award 1969, Golden Svc. award 1981), Santa Barbara Star, 1951-56, Santa Barbara News-Press, 1956-82; rsch. musicologist Inst. for Environ. Stress, U. Calif., Santa Barbara, 1979—; condr. Santa Barbara Symphony Orch., 1941-44, All-Calif. High Sch. Symphony Orch., 1941-73, Kern County Honor Band of Calif.; guest condr. Seoul (Korea) Symphony Orch., 1945-46, officer in charge Seoul Nat. U., 1945-46; mus. dir. Santa Barbara Fiesta Bowl Mus. Show, 1951-53. Contbg. editor The Instrumentalist, 1964-86; contbr. articles and criticisms to Mus. Courier, Sat. Rev., Christian Sci. Monitor. Chmn. Santa Barbara Mayor's Adv. Com. on Arts, 1966-69. Lt. (j.g.) to lt. USNR, 1944-46. Fellow Internat. Inst. Arts and Letters (life); mem. Music Acad. West (pres. 1949-85, pres. emeritus 1954—, sustaining dir. 1985—), So. Calif. Sch. Band and Orch. Assn. (hon. life, v.p. 1955), Am. Fedn. Musicians (hon. life), Nat. Music Educators Conf., Internat. Congress Traditional Music (lectr. Stockholm 1984, Hanover 1986), Archeol. Musicol. Work Study Group UNESCO's Congress of Traditional Music, Internat. Trumpet Guild, U. Calif. Emeriti Assn., Masons, Phi Mu Alpha (life), Phi Delta Kappa. Republican. Presbyterian. Avocation: world traveling. Home and Office: PO Box 572 Goleta CA 93116

FAULKNER, SEWELL FORD, realtor; b. Keene, N.H., Sept. 25, 1924; s. John Charles and Hazel Helen (Ford) F.; A.B., Harvard, 1949; M.B.A., 1951; m. June Dayton Finn, Jan. 10, 1951 (div.); children—Patricia Anne, Bradford William, Sandra Ford, Jonathan Dayton, Winthrop Sewell; m. 2d, Constance Mae Durvin, Mar. 15, 1969 (div.); children—Sarah Elizabeth, Elizabeth Jane. Product mgr. Congoleum Nairn, Inc., Kearny, N.J., 1951-55; salesman, broker, chmn., pres. Jack White Co. real estate, Anchorage, 1956-86 ; dir. Life Ins. Co. Alaska. Mem. Anchorage City Council, 1962-65, Greater Anchorage Area Borough Assembly, 1964-65, Anchorage Area Charter Commn., 1969-70. Pres., Alaska World Affairs Council, 1967-68; treas. Alyeska Property Owners, Inc., 1973-75, pres., 1977-78; pres. Downtown Anchorage Assn., 1974-75; mem. Girdwood Bd. Suprs. Served with USAAF, 1943-45. Mem. Anchorage Area C. of C. (dir. 1973-74), Urban Land Inst., Bldg. Owners and Mgrs. Assn., Nat. Inst. Real Estate Brokers. Clubs: Alaska Notch, Anchorage Petroleum. Office: Jack White Co 3201 C St Anchorage AK 99503

FAULL, JAMES EDWARD, civil engineer, construction manager; b. Berkeley, Calif., June 20, 1945; s. Richard Francis and Margaret Helen (Traganza) F.; m. Bernadette Claire Molenaar, Nov. 5, 1975. BS, Stanford U., 1968, MS, 1978. Registered profl. engr., Calif., Hawaii, Australia. Structural engr. Cameron Chisholm & Nicol, Perth, Australia, 1971-72; civil engr. Hughes-Trueman-Ludlow, Sydney, Australia, 1973-75, Camp Scott Furphy, Sydney, 1975-76, Bissell & Karn, Inc., Burlingame, Calif., 1977; project engr. Charles Pankow Assocs., Honolulu, 1978-85; constrn. mgr. Calif. Assn. for Research in Astronomy, Pasadena and Hilo, Hawaii, 1985-89; dir. constrn. Waikoloa (Hawaii) Land Co., 1989—; constrn. mgr. W.M. Keck Observatory. Mem. ASCE, NSPE (pres. local chpt. 1989—). Republican. Club: Hilo Yacht. Lodge: Rotary (bd. dirs. 1988—). Office: Waikoloa Land Co PO Box 3028 Waikoloa Village HI 96743

FAUST, GEORGE RAYMOND, tax consultant, accountant; b. Phila., Apr. 20, 1938; s. Charles William and Cecelia Teresa (Ardiff) F.; m. Mittie Lee Hawkins, Nov. 21, 1981; children: James A., George L., Marsha Spaulding, John Russell. BS in Mgmt., Park Coll., 1985; AS in Acctg. and Taxation, Grossmont Coll., 1988. With USN 1956-85; owner, mgr. George Faust-Tax Cons., San Diego, 1985--; mng. ptnr. Am. Bookkeeping Svc., San Diego, 1987--; tax cons. Am. Tax & Law Ctr., San Diego, 1987--; instr. various tax orgns., Calif., N.Y., 1985--. Treas. Carlton Hills Luth. Ch., Santee, Calif., 1985-87; mem. Santee Curriculum Adv. Council, 1985, San Diego County Rep. Com., 1987--. Mem. Calif. Assn. Ind. Accts., Inland Soc. Tax Cons. (state sec. 1987-88, 2nd v.p. San Diego, 1988). Nat. Soc. Pub. Accts., Am. Inst. Profl. Bookkeepers, Fleet Reserve Assn. (Arlington, Va.) (pres. 1983-84). Home: 10333 Ridgewater Ln San Diego CA 92131

FAUST, MARGARET SILER, psychology educator; b. Tientsin, China, Feb. 22, 1926; came to U.S., 1928; d. Charles Arthur and Marion Louise (Pierce) Siler; m. William Langdon Faust, Aug. 26, 1950; children—Katherine, Ann, Marion. B.A., Pomona Coll., 1948; M.A., Stanford U., 1951, Ph.D., 1957. Lic. psychologist, Calif. From asst. prof. to prof. Scripps Coll., Claremont, Calif., 1960-70, prof. psychology, 1970—. Author: Somatic Development of Adolescent Girls, 1977; contbr. articles to profl. jours. Bur. for Edn. of Handicapped Postdoctoral fellow UCLA, 1980; Grant Found. grantee, 1970-72. Mem. Am. Psychol. Assn., Soc. for Research in Child Devel., Sigma Xi. Office: Scripps Coll Dept Psychology Claremont CA 91711

FAUST, THOMAS GREGORY, software development executive; b. Elmhurst, Ill., May 16, 1956; s. Ralph Michael and Margaret Mabel (Schweisthal) F.; m. Sherry Lynn Danks, Sept. 1, 1979; children: Christopher, Stefanie, Trevor. AS in Data Processing, Coll. of Marin, Kentfield, Calif., 1981. Software devel. engr. Sequoia Med. Group, Inc., Larkspur, Calif., 1981-82; programmer Stephens-Nelsen Computer Ctr., Spokane, Wash., 1983; software cons. Software Designs, Spokane, 1984-87; programming mgr. Seattle Tech., Inc., Bothell, Wash., 1988—; cons. Software Designs, Woodville, Wash., 1988—. Sgt. U.S. Army, 1975-78. Mem. Alpha Micro User Soc. Republican. Office: Seattle Tech Inc 17928 Bothell Way SE Bothell WA 98012

FAUTSKO, TIMOTHY FRANK, state agency administrator; b. Canton, Ohio, Dec. 27, 1945; s. Frank F. and Helen E. (Gozdan) F.; children: T. Matthew, David F. BA in English, BBA, Walsh Coll., 1967; MA in Human Services Adminstrn., U. Colo., 1972. Dir. tng. Vista Programs, Washington, 1967-70, Nat. Info. Ctr., Boulder, Colo., 1972-76; ct. adminstr. State of Colo., Boulder, 1976-80; jud. adminstr. State of Colo., Aspen, 1980—; instr. Colo. Mountain Coll., Glenwood Springs, Aspen, Colo., 1980—; co-dir. T/SDA & Assocs., Denver, 1975—. Co-author: Volunteer Programs in Prevention/Diversion, 1973, 2d rev. edit., 1975, Solving Problems in Meetings, 1981, QUID-How You Can Make the Best Decisions of Your Life, 1978, Como Tomar las Mejores Deciones de Su Vida, 1985; contbr. articles to profl. jours. Mem. Centennial Com., Glenwood Springs, 1983-85; mem. Mayor's com., Denver, 1977-78. HEW scholar, U. Colo., Boulder, 1971-72; recipient Cert. Appreciation Office of Mayor, Denver, 1978, Colo. Mountain Coll., Glenwood Springs, 1985-86, Outstanding Alumni award Walsh Coll., 1987. Mem. Nat. Assn. Trial Ct. Adminstrs., Nat. Orgn. Victims Assistance. Home: PO Box 603 Glenwood Springs CO 81602 Office: State of Colo Jud Dept PO Box 1486 Aspen CO 81612

FAVERO, JANET LOUISE, psychologist, educator; b. Pomona, Calif., June 24, 1959; d. Louis Robert and Jane Carol (Rathwell) F. BA magna cum laude, Colo. Coll., 1981; MS, Purdue U., 1983, PhD in Indsl. and Organizational Psychology, 1985. Teaching asst. Purdue U., West Lafayette, Ind., 1981-85, rsch. asst., 1982-84; rsch. cons. Ctr. for Creative Leadership, Greensboro, N.C., 1984-85, CTS Corp., West Lafayette, 1984-85; indsl. and organizational psychologist US West, Inc., Englewood, Colo., 1985—; guest lectr. U. Hawaii, U. Colo., U. Denver, Colo. Coll., 1981—; hon. prof. U. Colo., 1988—; presenter in field. David Ross fellow Purdue U., 1984. Mem. Am. Psychol. Assn., Colo. Coll. Alumni Group (chmn. 1986—). Office: US West Inc 6300 S Syracuse Ste 300-N Englewood CO 80111

FAY, ABBOTT EASTMAN, history educator; b. Scottsbluff, Nebr., July 19, 1926; s. Abbott Eastman and Ethel (Lambert) F.; m. Joan D. Richardson, Nov. 26, 1953; children: Rand, Diana, Collin. BA, Colo. State Coll., 1949, MA, 1953; postgrad., U. Denver, 1961-63, Western State U., 1963. Tchr. Leadville (Colo.) Pub. Schs., 1950-52, elem. prin., 1952-54; prin. Leadville Jr. High Sch., 1954-55; pub. info. dir., instr. history Mesa Coll., Grand Junction, Colo., 1955-64; asst. prof. history Western State Coll. of Colo., Gunnison, 1964-76, assoc. prof. history, 1976-82, assoc. prof. emeritus, 1982—; propr. Mountaintop Books, Paonia, Colo.; bd. dirs Colo. Assoc. Univ. Press; profl. speaker in field; dir. hist. tours. Author: Mountain Academia, 1968, Writing Good History Research Papers, 1980, Ski Tracks in the Rockies, 1984; playwright: Thunder Mountain Lives Tonight!; contbr. articles to profl. jours.; freelance writer popular mags. Founder, coordinator Nat. Energy Conservation Challenge; project reviewer NEH, Colo. Hist. Soc. Served with AUS, 1944-46. Named Top Prof. Western State Coll., 1969, 70, 71; fellow Hamline U. Inst. Asian Studies, 1975, 79. Mem. Western Writers Am., Rocky Mountain Social Sci. Assn. (sec. 1961-63), Am. Hist. Assn., Assn. Asian Studies, Western History Assn., Western State Coll. Alumni Assn. (pres. 1971-73), Internat. Platform Assn., Am. Legion (Outstanding Historian award 1981), Phi Alpha Theta, Phi Kappa Delta, Delta Kappa Pi. Home: 1750 Hwy 133 Paonia CO 81428

FAY, JAMES WINFIELD, engineer; b. Somerset, Pa., Dec. 22, 1938; s. John Emmett Fay and Rosalie Ruth (Mostoller) Gamble; m. Ann Hellion, Nov. 12, 1962 (div. 1970); 1 child, Michael; m. Joan Babson, May 15, 1971; children: J.D., Laura Jean. BS in Engring., Ariz. State U., 1967, MS in Engring., 1969. Registered profl. engr., Calif. Commd. 2d lt. USAF, 1967, advanced through grades to capt., 1970, electronics technician, 1956-67, civil engring. officer, 1967-78, ret., 1978; sr. staff engr. TRW Corp., Redondo Beach, Calif., 1978-80, San Bernadino, Calif., 1980-84, Springfield, Va., 1984-86, Colorado Springs, Colo., 1986—. Mem. pub. works com. City of redlands, Calif., 1982-84; del. County Rep. Cov., Colorado Springs, 1988, 5th Dist. Rep. Conv., Denver, 1988. Decorated Commendation medal with oak leaf cluster. Mem ASCE, NSPE, Am. Legion, Armed Forces Communications and Electronics Assn. Republican. Presbyterian. Lodge: Elks. Home: 7095 Switchback Tr Colorado Springs CO 80919

FAY, MICHAEL JAMES, orthopedic surgeon, military officer; b. Denver, Nov. 12, 1946; s. John William and Gladys Vivian (Kassel) F.; m. Samar Sandra Margaret Freemon, June 14, 1970; children: Jason Andrew, Britten Hunter. BS, U.S. Mil. Acad., 1968; MD, Georgetown U., 1977. Commd. 2d lt. U.S. Army, 1968, advanced through grades to col., 1987; orthopedic surgeon 130th Sta. Hosp., Heidelberg, Baden-Wüttemberg, Fed. Republic Germany, 1981-82, chief of orthopedic service, 1982, chief dept. surgery, 1982-84; div. surgeon, bn. comdr. 7th med. bn., Ft. Ord, Calif., 1985-87; chief sports medicine sect., asst. chief orthopedic surgery service Tripler Army Med. Ctr., Honolulu, 1987—. Fellow Am. Acad. Orthopedic Surgeons; mem. Soc. Mil. Orthopedic Surgeons, Nat. Wildlife Assn., Assn. Mil. Surgeons of U.S., Order Mil. Med. Merit, Sierra Club. Episcopalian. Home: 1350 Parks Dr Honolulu HI 96819 Office: Tripler Army Med Ctr Orthopedic Surgery Svc Honolulu HI 96859

FAY, RICHARD JAMES, mechanical engineer, executive, educator; b. St. Joseph, Mo., Apr. 26, 1935; s. Frank James and Marie Jewell (Senger) F.; m. Marilyn Louise Kelsey, Dec. 22, 1962; B.S.M.E., U. Denver, 1959, M.S.M.E., 1970; Registered profl. engr., Colo., Nebr. Design engr. Denver Fire Clay Co., 1957-60; design, project engr. Silver Engring. Works, 1960-63; research engr., lectr. mech. engring. U. Denver, 1963-74, asst. prof. Colo. Sch. of Mines, 1974-75, founder, pres. Fay Engring. Corp., 1971—. Served with Colo. N.G., 1962. Mem. Soc. Automotive Engrs. (past chmn. Colo. sect.), ASME (past chmn. Colo. sect., regional v.p.). Contbr. articles to profl. jours.; patentee in field. Office: 5201 E 48th Ave Denver CO 80216

FAYE, LINDSAY ANTON, JR., sugar company executive; b. Waimea, Hawaii, Dec. 26, 1932; s. Lindsay Anton Faye and Leilani (Scott) Humphreys; m. Barbara Cleghorn, Aug. 25, 1955 (div. July 1973); children: Laura, Callie, Carrie; m. Diane Guslander, Apr. 20, 1974; children: Diane, Lindsay. Student, Stanford U., 1951-53; BS, U. Calif., Davis, 1958. Agrl. trainee Hawaiian Sugar Planter's Assn., Honolulu, 1958-60; agriculturist Kekaha (Hawaii) Sugar Co., Ltd. subs. Amfac, Inc., 1960-63, exec. v.p., mgr., 1973-77; agriculturist, harvest supt. Oahu Sugar Co., Ltd. subs. Amfac, Inc., Waipahu, Hawaii, 1963-68; irrigation-mech. ops. supt. Lihue (Hawaii) Plantation Co., Ltd. subs. Amfac, Inc., 1968-73, pres., mgr., 1977-80; pres., mgr. Kekaha Sugar Co., Ltd. 1980—; pres., bd. dirs. Kikiaola Land Co., Ltd., Waimea, Hawaii, 1963—. Bd. dirs. United Way Kauai, Lihue, 1969—; v.p., trustee G.N. Wilcox Meml. Hosp., Lihue, 1977-80; pres., trustee Waimea Dispensary, 1980—; v.p., bd. dirs. Kauai Econ. Devel. Bd., Puhi, Hawaii, 1985—. With U.S. Army, 1953-55. Mem. Hawaiian Sugar Planter's Assn., Internat. Soc. Sugar Cane Tech., Kauai Sugar Planter's Assn. (pres., bd. dirs. 1973—). Republican. Episcopalian. Home: 4461 Kaumualii Hwy Kekaha HI 96752 Office: Kekaha Sugar Co Ltd 8315 Kekaha Rd Kekaha HI 96752

FAZIO, VIC, congressman; b. Winchester, Mass., Oct. 11, 1942; m. Judy Kern; children: Dana, Anne. BA, Union Coll., Schenectady, 1965; postgrad., Calif. State U., Sacramento. Congl. and legis. cons. 1966-75; mem. Calif. State Assembly, 1975-78; mem. 96th-101th Congresses from Calif. 4th Dist., 1979—, mem. appropriations, budget and standards of ofcl. conduct coms., chmn. legis. br. appropriations com., majority whip-at-large, mem. exec. com. Democratic Study Group, also co-chmn. Fed. Govt. Services Task Force, mem. appropriations subcom. energy and water, appropriations subcom. milt. constrn., mem. Select Com. on Hunger, chmn. budget com. task force on Defense, chmn. bipartisan com. on ethics; Former mem. Sacramento County Charter and Planning Commns. Founder: Calif. Jour. Bd. dirs. Asthma Allergy Found., Jr. Statesman; chmn. Project 500; co-chmn. USA Votes. Coro Found. fellow; named Environmentalist of Yr. Calif. Planning and Conservation League; named Solar Congressman of Yr. Mem. Air Force Assn., Navy League, UNICO. Democrat. Office: Rayburn House Office Bldg Rm 2113 Washington DC 20515 *

FECHTEL, EDWARD RAY, lawyer, educator; b. Pocatello, Idaho, Apr. 20, 1926; s. Edward Joseph and Frances Lucille (Myers) F.; m. Jewell Reagan, Apr. 7, 1950 (div.); children—Scot Gerald, Mark Edward, Kim; m. 2d Mary K. Milligan, Dec. 1983. B.A. in Bus., Idaho State U., 1949; J.D., U. Oreg., 1967; M.B.A. in Fin., 1968. Bar: Oreg. 1967, U.S. Dist. Ct. Oreg. 1967, U.S. Tax Ct. 1967, U.S. Ct. Appeals (9th cir.) 1968, U.S. Ct. Appeals (11th cir.) 1985, U.S. Ct. Appeals (10th cir.) 1986, U.S. Ct. Appeals (8th cir.) 1987. Sales rep. Genesco, 1950-59; gen. mdse. mgr. Fargo Wilson Wells Co., Pocatello, 1960-64; ptnr. Husband, Johnson & Fechtel, Eugene, Oreg., 1967-83, Ray Fechtel, P.C., 1984—; prof. bus. law U. Oreg.; lectr. Oreg. State Bar. Bd. dirs. Legal Aid Soc., Lane County, Oreg., Oreg. Citizens for Fair Land Planning. Served with USN, 1944-46. Mem. ABA, Oreg. State Bar Assn., Assn. Trial Lawyers Am., Phi Alpha Delta. Republican. Home: 1498 Quaker St Eugene OR 97402 Office: 132 E Broadway Ste 431 Eugene OR 97401-3127

FEDER, HAROLD ABRAM, lawyer; b. Denver, Aug. 22, 1932; s. Harry A. and Surriee A. (Aarons) F.; m. Flora Sue Dunn, June 6, 1954; children: Harlan M., Sharon J., Janet B. BA, U. Colo., 1954, LLB, 1959, J.D., 1968. Bar: Colo. 1959, U.S. Dist. Ct. Colo. 1959, U.S. Ct. Appeals (10th cir.) 1969, U.S. Supreme Ct. 1971. Pres. Feder, Morris, Tamblyn and Goldstein, Denver, 1959—; spl. asst. atty. gen. Colo., 1960-71; adj. prof. law U. Denver, 1963; arbitrator Am. Arbitration Assn.; co-founder, dir. Pub. Justice Found. Author more than 70 lectures and 10 papers on trial technique and law practice mgmt. Mem. Gov.'s coordinating com. on implementation of mental health and retardation planning State Colo., 1966-69; mem. adv. coun. Cert. Profl. Sec. Program, 1967-70; hon. mem. bd. dirs. Spl. Olympics, 1978-83; co-founder, dir. Summit Acad. for Culture and Values; bd. dirs., treas. Colo. Alzheimers Disease Found.; founder Pub. Justice Found. With USNR, 1954-56. Law Alumni scholar, 1956-59. Fellow Internat. Soc. Barristers, Am. Acad. Forensic Scis., Colo. Bar Found.; mem. Fed. Bar Assn., ABA (litigation and local govt. sect., coun. econs. of law practice sect. 1980-86), Colo. Bar Assn. (bd. govs. 1972-74), Denver Bar Assn., Continental Divide Bar Assn., Assn. Trial Lawyers Am. (sustaining mem.), Colo. Trial Lawyers Assn. (pres. 1971-72), Denver Tennis Club, Phi Delta Phi, Sigma Nu. Jewish. Home: 460 S Marion Pkwy 1556 B Denver CO 80209 also: PO Box 238 Eagle CO 81631 Office: Feder Morris Tamblyn & Goldstein PC 1441 18th St Ste 150 Denver CO 80202

FEDERHAR, DAVID BERNARD, psychologist, educator; b. Tucson, Apr. 4, 1951; s. Richard Harvey and Doris (Lakritz) F.; m. Kristin Pedersen, Aug. 3, 1974; children: Peter Alexander, Lars Andreas. BA, U. Ariz, 1972, MA, 1975, PhD, 1983. Lic. psychologist, SABPE, sch. psychologist, Ariz., tchr. psychology Ariz. and Calif. Program cons. Autism Program Tucson Unifed Sch. Dist., 1975-77; sch. psychologist Tucson Unified Sch. Dist., 1977—; adj. faculty Pima Community Coll., Tucson, 1979—; prof. Embry-Riddle Aero. U., Tucson, 1982—, Park Coll., Tucson, 1983—; instr. Chapman Coll., Tucson, 1988—; participant Pediatric Task Force U. Med. Ctr., Tucson, 1987—, Tucson Sudden Infant Death Syndrome Group, 1977-86, Tucson Nat. Soc. Autistic Children Group, 1975-80. Author (reports to U.S. Gov. for Autism Program) P.A.C.T. programs, 1975-77. Pres. Van Horne PTA, Tucson, 1984-85; coach Am. Youth Soccer Assn., 1985-87; bd. dirs. Jewish Family Service, Tucson, 1984-87, Tanque Verde Ednl. Enrichment Fund, 1989—. Mem. Am. Psychol. Assn., Ariz. State Psychol. Assn. (editor 1979-80, meritorious achievement award 1980), So. Ariz. Psychol. Assn. (v.p., sec., chmn. membership 1977-82), Nat. Assn. Sch. Psychologists. Democrat. Home: 12355 E Barbary Coast Tucson AZ 85749 Office: Tucson Unifed Sch Dist #1 1010 E 10th St Tucson AZ 85710

FEDORA, THOMAS JOSEPH JAMES, manufacturing engineer. AS in Mech. Tech., St. Don Bosco Tech. Inst., 1972; BS in Indsl. Tech., Calif. State U., 1979. Asst. engr. Jet Propulsion Lab., Pasadena, Calif., 1971-73; data technician Lockheed Aircraft Svc. Co., Ontario, Calif., 1973-75; mil. jr. mfg. engr. Sargent Industries, Burbank, Calif., 1976-78; asst. prodn. control and purchasing mgr. Bardwell & McAlister Inc., Burbank, Calif., 1978-79; mil. mfr. engr. Infrared Industries Inc., Santa Barbara, Calif., 1980; comml. indsl. project engr. Ajax Hardware Corp., City of Industry, Calif., 1980; manual n/c programmer, mfg. engr. Houdaille Industries Inc., L.A., 1980-81; mil. numerical control-MDSI programmer The Singer Co. div. Librascope,

Glendale, Calif., 1981-87. Mem. Soc. Mfg. Engrs., Am. Soc. Indsl. Tech., The Planetary Soc. Home: 1437 East I St Ontario CA 91764-3028 Office: The Singer Co div Librascope 811 Sonora Ave Glendale CA 91201

FEDORUK, SYLVIA O., Canadian provincial official, educator; b. Canora, Sask., Can., May 5, 1927; d. Theodore and Annie (Romaniuk) F. BA, U. Sask., 1949, MA, 1951; DSc, U. Windsor, Ont., Can., 1987. Asst. physicist Saskatoon (Sask.) Cancer Clinic, 1951-57, sr. physicist, 1957; asst. prof. U. Sask., Saskatoon, 1956-89, chancellor, 1986—, prof. emeritus, 1989—; dir. physics svcs. Sask. Cancer Found., 1966-86; lt. gov. Province of Sask., 1988—; cons. in nuclear medicine. Recipient Queen's Jubilee medal, 1977, Century Saskatoon medal, 1982. Fellow Can. Coll. Physicists in Medicine; mem. Can. Ladies Curling Assn. (past pres.), Sports Fedn. Can. (past bd. dirs.). Ukrainian Greek Orthodox. Office: Govt House, 4607 Dewdney Ave, Regina, SK Canada S4T 3B7 also: U Sask, Office of Chancellor, Saskatoon, SK Canada S7N 0W0 *

FEENEY, CHARLES STONEHAM, professional baseball executive; b. Orange, N.J., Aug. 31, 1921; s. Thaddeus and Mary Alice (Stoneham) F.; m. Margaret Ann Hoppock, July 10, 1948; children: Katharine Willard, Charles Stoneham, John Hoppock, William McDonald, Mary Patrick. B.A., Dartmouth Coll., 1943; LL.B., Fordham U., 1949. Vice pres. San Francisco Giants, 1946-69; pres. Nat. League Profl. Baseball Clubs, San Francisco, 1970-77, N.Y.C., 1977-87, San Diego Padres, 1987-89. Served to lt. USNR, 1943-46. Mem. Casque and Gauntlet, Phi Kappa Psi. Clubs: Pacific Union, Burlingame (Calif.) Country. Home: 1998 Broadway San Francisco CA 94109

FEENEY, ROBERT EARL, research biochemist; b. Oak Park, Ill., Aug. 30, 1913; s. Bernard Cyril and Loreda (McKee) F.; m. Mary Alice Waller, Dec. 3, 1954; children: Jane, Elizabeth. Student, Rochester (Minn.) Jr. Coll., 1932-33; BS in Chemistry, Northwestern U., 1938; MS in Biochemistry, U. Wis., 1939, PhD in Biochemistry, 1942. Diplomate Am. Bd. Nutrition. Rsch. assoc. Harvard U. Med. Sch., Boston, 1942-43; rsch. biochemist USDA Lab., Albany, Calif., 1946-53; prof. chemistry U. Nebr., Lincoln, 1953-60; prof. dept. food sci. and tech. U. Calif., Davis, 1960-84, prof. emeritus, rsch. biochemist, 1984—; bd. dirs. Creative Chemistry Cons., Davis. Author: (with Richard Allison) Evolutionary Biochemistry of Proteins, 1969, (with Gary Means) Chemical Modification of Proteins, 1971, Professor On the Ice, 1974; editor: (with John Whitaker) Protein Tailoring for Food and Medical Uses, 1986; editor jour. Comments on Agr. and Food Chemistry, 1985—. Capt. wound rsch. team M.C., U.S. Army, 1943-46. Recipient Superior Svc. award USDA, 1953, ; Feeney Peak, Antarctica named in his honor U.S. Bd. on Geog. Names, 1968. Mem. Am. Chem. Soc. (chmn. div. agrl. and food chemistry, 1978-79, award for disting. svc. in agrl. and food chemistry, 1978), Am. Soc. for Biochemistry and Molecular Biology, Inst. of Food Technologists, Explorers Club. Democrat. Home: 780 Elmwood Dr Davis CA 95616 Office: U Calif Dept Food Sci and Tech 1480 Chemistry Annex Davis CA 95616

FEENEY, ROBERT HICKMAN, public relations executive; b. Beacon, N.Y., Oct. 8, 1930; s. John Patrick and Francis Winifred (Flynn) F.; m. Ann Philippa Feeney, Oct. 6, 1956; children: Michael, Kathryn, Matthew and Roberta. BA, Siena Coll., 1953. Reporter Poughkeepsie (N.Y.) Jour., 1953-55; dir. publicity Prentice-Hall, Inc., N.Y.C., 1955-57; asst. dir. pub. rels. H.K. Porter Co., Inc., N.Y.C., 1958-59; v.p. G.M. Basford Co., N.Y.C., 1959-62; ptnr. Turner and Feeney, Inc., N.Y.C., 1962-70; dir. corp. advt. Manville Corp., Colo., 1971-86; sec. communications Archdiocese of Denver, 1986—; exec. editor, Denver Catholic Register, 1986--. Contbr. articles to profl. jours. Bd. Mem. Denver Advt. Fedn., 1974-76; Colo. Hearing and Speech Cntr. Denver, 1974-80; Bd. Chmn., Mt. Airy Psychiatric Cntr. Denver, 1984-88; Denver Catholic Register, 1979-83. Named Communicator Yr., Bus./Profl. Advt. Assn., 1985. Mem. Pub. Rels. Assn. (chmn.), Asphalt Roofing Mfrs. Assn., Mineral Insulation Mfrs. Assn. Roman Catholic. Home: 5812 Laurel Pl Littleton CO 80123 Office: Archdiocese of Denver 200 Josephine Denver CO 80206

FEES, NANCY FARDELIUS, special education educator; b. Santa Monica, Calif., Mar. 25, 1950; d. Carl August and Dodi Emma (Hedenschau) Fardelius; m. Paul Rodger Fees, June 4, 1971; children: Evelyn Wyoming, Nelson August. BS, Mills Coll., 1971; MA in Edn., Idaho State U., 1975. Cert. tchr., Calif., Idaho, Wyo., R.I. Specialist curriculum mgmt. Barrington (R.I.) High Sch., 1975-81; coordinator learning skills ctr. Northwest Community Coll., Powell, Wyo., 1982-84, instr., 1985—; pres. Children's Resource Ctr., 1985—, bd. dirs., 1983—. Editor (with others) The Great Entertainer, 1984. Vol. Buffalo Bill Hist. Ctr., Cody, Wyo., 1981—; mem. Centennial Com., Cody, 1983. Mem. Council Exceptional Children, Assn. Children with Learning Disabilities, Council Adminstrs. of Spl. Edn. Democrat. Episcopalian. Home: 1201 Sunset Blvd Cody WY 82414

FEHER, STEVE JOSEPH KENT, design engineer, research developer; b. Honolulu, Mar. 29, 1950; s. Joseph and Lillian Elizabeth (Waller) F. Ptnr., chief engr. Charger Hawaii, Honolulu, 1975-77, Transitron, Honolulu, 1977-84, EVR, Inc., Honolulu, 1985-88, Feher Design, Inc., Honolulu, 1985—. Inventor in field. Mem. Soc. Automotive Engrs. (treas. Honolulu chpt. 1977-78). Republican. Home and Office: Feher Design 1909 Aleo Pl Honolulu HI 96822

FEHR, J. WILL, newspaper editor; b. Long Beach, Calif., Mar. 8, 1926; s. John and Evelyn (James) F.; m. Cynthia Moore, Sept. 4, 1951; children—Michael John, Martha Ann. B.A. in English, U. Utah, 1951. City editor Salt Lake City Tribune, 1964-80, mng. editor, 1980-81, editor, 1981—. Served to 1st lt. USAF, 1951-53. Mem. Am. Soc. Newspaper Editors, Sigma Chi. Clubs: Hidden Valley, Fort Douglas (Salt Lake City). Home: 468 13th Ave Salt Lake City UT 84103 Office: Salt Lake City Tribune 143 S Main St Salt Lake City UT 84110

FEHRING, WILLIAM PAUL, athletic coach; b. Columbus, Ind., May 31, 1912; s. Lynn Clifford and Iva Rae (Thompson) F.; m. Edna Rose Suverkrup, June 7, 1939; children: Susan Lee Hanson, Mary Ann Larkin, Carol Jane Irvin. BS, Purdue U., 1934, BPE, 1935, MPE, 1936; postgrad., NYU, summer 1937; EdD, Stanford U., 1952. Football, basketball, baseball coach Purdue U., West Lafayette, Ind., 1934-43; football coach U. Okla., Norman, 1946-48, UCLA, 1948-49; football and baseball coach Stanford (Calif.) U., 1949-67, dir. intramural and club sports, 1967-77; dir. sports tours Cardoza Travel Services, Palo Alto, Calif., 1977—; mem. exec. bd. U.S. Olympic Com., N.Y.C., 1963-79. 1st lt. USNR, 1943-46, PTO. Named to Ind. Basetball Hall of Fame, 1977; named Sangamore of Wabash, State of Ind., 1984; honored during Home Town Day City of Columbus, 1977. Mem. U.S. Baseball Fedn. (pres. 1963-77, hon. pres.), World Amateur Baseball Fedn. (pres. 1972-75, hon. pres.), Am. Baseball Coaches Assn. (pres. 1974-75, Hall of Fame 1972). Republican. Lutheran. Club: Stanford U. Faculty. Home: 1735 Poppy Ave Menlo Park CA 94025-5737 Office: Cardoza Travel Svcs 550 Hamilton Ave Ste 125 Palo Alto CA 94301

FEIBLEMAN, GILBERT BRUCE, lawyer; b. Portland, Oreg., Jan. 29, 1951; s. Herbert Frank and Bernice (Kaplan) F.; m. Ellen M. Hobson, June 20, 1981; 1 child, Benjamin David. BS, U. Oreg., 1972; JD, U. Pacific, 1976. Bar: Oreg. 1976, U.S. Dist. Ct. Oreg. 1976, U.S. Ct. Appeals (9th cir.). Assoc. Goodenough & Pierson, Salem, Oreg., 1976-78; mng. ptnr. Ramsay, Stein, Feibleman & Myers PC, Salem, 1978—; adj. prof. trial law and negotiation skills Willamette U., bus. law Chemeketa Community Coll., Marion County, Oreg., 1977; arbitrator Marion County Ct., Salem, 1985—; referee juvenile ct., 1985; pro-tem judge Oreg. Dist. Cts., 1982—, Oreg. Cir. Cts., 1987—. Mem. Assn. Trial Lawyers Am., Oreg. Trial Lawyers Assn., Oreg. Bar Assn. (arbitrator), Oreg. State Bar Assn. (counsel 1989—). Democrat. Home: 552 Stagecoach Way SE Salem OR 97302 Office: Ramsay Stein Feibleman & Myers 960 Liberty St SE Ste 110 Salem OR 97302

FEIGENBAUM, EDWARD ALBERT, computer science educator; b. Weehawken, N.J., Jan. 20, 1936; s. Fred J. and Sara Rachman; m. H. Penny Nii, 1975; children: Janet Denise, Carol Leonora, Sheri Bryant, Karin Bryant. BEE, Carnegie Inst. Tech., 1956, Ph.D. in Indsl. Adminstrn., 1960. Asst., then assoc. prof. bus. adminstrn. U. Calif. at Berkeley, 1960-64; assoc. prof. computer sci., then prof. Stanford U., 1965—; prin. investigator heuristic programming project 1965—; dir. Computation Ctr. Stanford U., 1965-68, chmn. dept. computer sci., 1976-81; pres. Intelli Genetics Inc., 1980-81; chmn., dir. Teknowledge, Inc., 1981-82; mem. tech. adv. bd. Intelli Genetics Inc., 1983-86; dir. IntelliCorp, 1984—; cons. to industry, 1957—; dir. Sperry Corp., 1983-86; mem. computer and biomath. scis. study sect. NIH, 1968-72, mem. adv. com. on artificial intelligence in medicine, 1974—; mem. adv. com. Health Care Tech. Center, U. Mo., Columbia; mem. Math. Social Sci. Bd., 1975-78; computer sci. adv. com. NSF, 1977-80; mem. Internat. Joint Council on Artificial Intelligence, 1973-83. Author: (with others) Information Processing Language V Manual, 1961, (with P. McCorduck) The Fifth Generation; author: (with R. Lindsay, B. Buchanan, J. Lederberg) Applications of Artificial Intelligence to Organic Chemistry: the Dendral Program; Editor: (with J. Feldman) Computers and Thought, 1963, (with A. Barr and P. Cohen) Handbook of Artificial Intelligence, 1981, 82, (with Pamela McCorduck and H. Penny Nii) The Rise of the Expert Company: How Visionary Companies are using Artificial Intelligence to Achieve Higher Productivity and Profits; mem. editorial bd.: Jour. Artificial Intelligence, 1970—. Fulbright scholar Gt. Britain, 1959-60. Fellow AAAS, Am. Coll. Med. Informatics; mem. Nat. Acad. Engring., Assn. Computing Machinery (nat. council 1966-68, chmn. spl. interest group on biol. applications 1973-76), Am. Assn. Artificial Intelligence (pres. 1980-81), Cognitive Sci. Soc. (council 1979-82), AAAS, Sigma Xi, Tau Beta Pi, Eta Kappa Nu, Pi Delta Epsilon. Home: 1017 Cathcart Way Stanford CA 94305 Office: Stanford U Dept Computer Sci Stanford CA 94305

FEIGENBERG, MITCHELL H., human resource management and training specialist; b. Oakland, Calif., Dec. 15, 1951; s. Maurice Solomon and Frances Shirley (Grutman) F.; m. Agnes Gertrude Garcia, Aug. 30, 1980; 1 child, Alicia Nicole. AB in Politics, U. Calif., Santa Cruz, 1973; M Pub. Policy, U. Calif., Berkeley, 1977. Cert. coll. instr., Calif. Sci. policy analyst Environ. Def. Fund, Berkeley, 1976-77; devel. economist, mayor's office City of L.A., 1978-80; fgn. svc. officer Dept. State, Washington, 1980; consular officer U.S. Embassy, Kingston, Jamaica, 1981-82; econ. officer Bur. Econ. and Bus. Affairs Dept. State, Washington, 1982-83; gen. svcs. officer U.S. Embassy, Bujumbura, Burundi, 1983-85; trainer Lifespring, Inc., San Rafael, Calif., 1986—; mem. exec. com. Lifespring, Inc., San Rafael, 1989—; area dir. Lifespring, Inc., L.A., 1988, regional dir. SW region, 1989—. Democrat. Jewish. Office: Lifespring Inc 161 Mitchell Blvd San Rafael CA 94903

FEIN, WILLIAM, ophthalmologist; b. N.Y.C., Nov. 27, 1933; s. Samuel and Beatrice (Lipschitz) F.; BS, CCNY, 1954; MD, U. Calif., Irvine, 1962; m. Bonnie Fern Aaronson, Dec. 15, 1963; children: Stephanie Paula, Adam Irving, Gregory Andrew. Intern, Los Angeles County Gen. Hosp., 1962-63, resident in ophthalmology, 1963-66; instr. U. Calif. Med. Sch., Irvine, 1966-69; mem. faculty U. So. Calif. Med. Sch., 1969—, asso. prof. ophthalmology, 1979—; attending physician Cedars-Sinai Med. Center, Los Angeles, 1966—, chief ophthalmology clinic service, 1979—, chmn. div. ophthalmology, 1981-85; attending physician Los Angeles County-U. So. Calif. Med. Center, 1969—; chmn. dept. ophthalmology Midway Hosp., 1975-78; dir. Ellis Eye Ctr., Los Angeles, 1984—. Diplomate Am. Bd. Ophthalmology. Fellow Internat. Coll. Surgeons, Am. Coll. Surgeons; mem. Am. Acad. Ophthalmology, Am. Soc. Ophthalmic Plastic and Reconstructive Surgery, AMA, Calif. Med. Assn., Los Angeles Med. Soc. Contbr. articles to med. publs. Home: 718 N Camden Beverly Hills CA 90210 Office: 415 N Crescent Dr Beverly Hills CA 90210

FEINHANDLER, EDWARD SANFORD, art gallery owner; b. Elko, Nev., Jan. 13, 1948; s. Samuel and Sylvia (Manus) F. BA, U. Nev., Reno, 1972. Supr. underpriveledged Washoe County Extension Program, Reno, 1970-71; sports editor, writer Sagebrush Campus newspaper, Reno, 1971-72; internal salesman, mgr. Trigon Corp., Sparks, Nev., 1973-88; owner, operator Art Internat. Gallery Extraordinaire, Reno, 1981—; with nat. news, Top Ten radio interviews, U.S. and Can., 1978-79. Contbr. articles to newspapaers; extra in various movies; TV interviewee AM Chgo., AM Los Angeles, 1979, Afternoon Exchange, Cleve., 1979, To Tell the Truth, 1975, Reno Tonight TV show, 1989, Fox Across America TV show, 1989. Player, coach Summer Volleyball League, Reno, 1982-85; tennis coach Community Service Ctr., Reno, 1986-88; participant Make-A-Wish Found., Reno, 1985-88, U. Nev. Journalism Dept., 1985-88, UNR Children's Services, Reno, 1986-88; coach Cath. Basketball, 1987-89 (2d place). Sgt. U.S. Army, 1968-69, Vietnam. Winner U. Reno Ugly Man Contest, 1967, 70-72, Ugly Bartender Contest Multiple Sclerosis, 1989. Mem. Sierra Arts Found., Disabled Am. Vets., Orthodox Jewish Union. Democrat. Office: Art Internat Gallery Extraordinaire PO Box 13405 Reno NV 89507

FEINSTEIN, DIANNE, former mayor; b. San Francisco, June 22, 1933; d. Leon and Betty (Rosenburg) Goldman; m. Bertram Feinstein, Nov. 11, 1962 (dec.); 1 child, Katherine Anne; m. Richard C. Blum, Jan. 20, 1980. BS, Stanford U., 1955; LLB (hon.), Golden Gate U., 1977; D Pub. Adminstrn. (hon.), U. Manila, 1981; D Pub. Service (hon.), U. Santa Clara, 1981; JD (hon.), Antioch U., 1983, Mills Coll., 1985; LHD (hon.), U. San Francisco, 1988. Fellow Coro Found., San Francisco, 1955-56; mem. Mayor's com. on crime, chmn. adv. com. Audit Detention, L.A. and San Francisco, 1967-69; mem. Bd. of Suprs., San Francisco, 1970-79, pres., 1970-72, 74-76, 78; mayor of San Francisco 1979-88; Mem. exec. com. U.S. Conf. of Mayors, 1983-88. Mem. Bay Area Conservation and Devel. Commn., 1973-78. Recipient Women of Achievement award Bus. and Profl. Women's Clubs of San Francisco, 1970, Disting. Woman award San Francisco Examiner, 1970, Coro Found. award, 1979, Scopus award Am. Friends Hebrew U., Jerusalem, 1981, Brotherhood/Sisterhood award NCCJ, 1986, Comdr.'s award U.S. Army, 1986, French Legion of Honor award Pres. Mitterand, 1984, Disting. Civilian award, USN, 1987, Fiscal Leadership award City & State Mag., 1987; named Team Number One Mayor All-Pro City Mgmt. Team City and State Mag., 1987. Mem. Trilateral Commn., Japan Soc. of No. Calif. (pres. 1988). Office: 909 Montgomery St Ste 400 San Francisco CA 94133

FEINSTEIN, JAMES RONALD, construction company executive; b. Cleve., Apr. 25, 1944; s. Edward and Billie (Reeves) F.; m. Gayle Millie Smith, Oct. 27, 1962; children: Cindy Lee, James Edward, Geneen Allynn. Student, Los Angeles Valley Coll. V.p. All Valley Washer Service, Inc., Van Nuys, Calif., 1968-72, pres., 1972—; pres. Smoke Detectors, Inc., Van Nuys, 1980—, Feinstein-Minas Constrn. Co., Inc., Van Nuys, 1986—. Named Business Man of Yr. Calif. State Assembly, Van Nuys, 1987, Rotary, Van Nuys, 1988. Mem. Calif. Multi-Housing Laundry Assn., So. Calif. Multi-Housing Laundry Assn., Multi-Housing Laundry Assn., San Fernando/Ventura Apt. Assn., Calif. Apt. Assn., Mid Valley Police Council (pres. com. 1988), Greater Van Nuys C. of C. (pres. elect 1988—). Office: All Valley Washer Svc Inc 15008 Delano St Van Nuys CA 91411

FEIR, MARVIN LEONARD, school system administrator; b. Phila., Aug. 6, 1940; s. Harvey and Reba (Miller) F.; m. Betty Jean Taub, Mar., 1966 (div. 1972); 1 child, Tammy Gayle; m. Kathryn Royrene Brill, Mar. 27, 1976. BS, Pa. State U., 1962; MA, U. Okla., 1971; MHA, Loma Linda U., 1982. Cert. internal auditor. Commd. 2nd lt. USAF, 1962, advanced through grades to major, ret., 1982; bus. cons. Riverside County (Calif.) Office Edn., 1982-85, personnel adminstr., 1985-86; dir. bus. services Jurupa Unified Sch. Dist., Riverside, 1986-87; bus. mgr. Moreno Valley (Calif.) Unified Sch. Dist., 1987-89; asst. supt. bus. services Hemet (Calif.) Unified Sch. Dist., 1989—. Mem. Calif. Assn. Sch. Bus. Officials (budget research and devel. com. so. sect. 1988—), Assn. Sch. Bus. Officials Internat. Republican. Jewish. Office: Hemet Unified Sch Dist 2350 W Latham Ave Hemet CA 92343

FEKARIS, DINO GEORGE, songwriter, record producer, music publisher; b. Pitts., Jan. 24, 1945; s. George N. and Irene A. (Madias) F.; m. Barbara Leanna Chase, June 28, 1980; children: George D., Dino G., Jr. BA in Philosophy, Wayne State U., 1968. Recording artist, songwriter Impact Records, Gomba Music, Highland Park, Mich., 1967-69; songwriter, record producer, recording artist Motown Records, Jobete Music, Detroit and Hollywood, 1969-75; songwriter, record producer Sidney A. Seidenberg, Inc., N.Y.C., 1975-76, Perren-Vibes Music, Grand Slam Prodns., Studio City, Calif., 1977-81, Fekaris Music, Regina Prodns., Sherman Oaks, Calif., 1981—; chief executive officer Fekaris Enterprises, Inc., Sherman Oaks, 1981—; instr. UCLA, 1988. Writer, composer: I Will Survive, 1978 (Grammy 1979), Reunited, 1978, Two Hot, 1978, I Just Want to Celebrate, 1971, Hey, Big Brother, 1971, Makin' It, 1979. Recipient Citizen and Scholarship medal, Am. Legion, Pitts., 1958, Citizenship medal, Order of AHEPA, Pitts., 1958, Sons and Daus. Am. Revolution, Pitts., 1958, Grammy award, Best Disco Recording, Nat. Acad. Recording Arts and Scis., Burbank, Calif., 1979; Billboard Mag. Composer of the Yr. award, 1979, Songwriter of the Yr. award, Songwriter Mag., 1980. Mem. ASCAP (Top Song awards 1971, 79, 80; West Coast Songwriter's adv. 1984—, dir. West Coast Songwriter's workshop, 1982), Mr. and Mrs. Club of L.A. (copres. 1989). Greek Orthodox. Home: 3505 Vista Haven Rd Sherman Oaks CA 91403 Office: Fekaris Enterprises Inc 3505 Vista Haven Rd Sherman Oaks CA 91403

FELBER, BRYAN COLEMAN, aerospace company official; b. Augsburg, Fed. Republic Germany, Dec. 1, 1958; (parents Am. citizens); s. Theodore Dotzler and Barbara Jane (Fenton) F.; m. Denee Trudell Holm, June 21 1981; children: Jeremy Bryan, Christian Joseph, Bryn Denee. BSBA, San Diego State U., 1982, postgrad., 1985—; Cert. in Cost Analysis, U. San Diego, 1988. Mfg. control specialist Convair div. Gen. Dynamics Co., San Diego, 1983-85; sr. estimator Convair div. Gen. Dynamics Co., 1985-87, estimating specialist Space Systems, 1988—; prog. cost analyst Rohr Industries, Chula Vista, Calif., 1987-88. Dist. coord. Freedom Coun., Virginia Beach, Va., 1984-87; deacon Chula Vista (Calif.) Community Ch., 1984-87, treas., 1987; troop com. mem. Boy Scouts Am., 1984-86; prison visitor M2, San Quentin, Calif., 1988. Mem. Inst. Cost Analysis, Toastmasters (treas. 1987-88). Mem. Evangelical Free Ch. Home: 102 Halsey St Chula Vista CA 92010

FELD, MYRON XANE, urban planner; b. Bklyn., Apr. 29, 1915; s. Abraham Louis and Helen (Taub) F.; m. Sylvia B., Aug. 13, 1938; children: April Marina, Jason Mendy. BS in Engring., CCNY, 1936, MCE, 1937. Registered profl. engr., Calif. Civil engr. U.S. Army Corps of Engrs., N.Y.C., 1937-42; dir. pub. works Boro of Rossevelt, N.J., 1946-49; dir. devel. Israel Inst. Tech., Haifa, Israel, 1949-53; dir. pub. works Twp. of Hamilton, Trenton, N.J., 1953-59; regional engr. air base constrn. U.S. Army, Turkey, Israel, 1959-62; transp. engr. N.J. Motor Vehicle Dept., Trenton, 1962-69; reconstrn. planner, city engr. Jerusalem, 1969-72; regional planner City of Los Angeles, 1974—; asst. prof. gen. engring. Rutgers U., New Brunswick, N.J., 1956-59; guest lectr. Tel Aviv U., Jerusalem, 1970-72. Contbr. articles to profl. jours. Councilman Borough of Roosevelt, 1964-70; mem. planning bd. Twp. of Hamilton, 1953-59. Served as chief warrant officer U.S. Army, 1942-46, PTO. Mem. Assn. Mcpl. Engrs. (sec.-treas. to pres. 1953-59). Home: 609 S Burnside Ave Los Angeles CA 90036 Office: LA Dept Regional Planning Los Angeles County 320 W Temple St Los Angeles CA 90012

FELDMAN, ANNETTE YOUNG, civic worker; b. Hoopeston, Ill., July 23, 1916; d. Reuben and Ida (Horvitz) Yonkelowitz; m. Jerome Feldman, Oct. 19, 1941 (dec. 1986); children: Jill Feldman Crane, Robert. Student, Northwestern U., 1934-36; BS, U. Chgo., 1938, MS, 1940. Nutritionist ARC, Chgo., 1940-41; nutrition cons. Med. Coll. Va., Richmond, 1941-42; specialist food and nutrition U. Ill. Extension Svc., Champaign, 1943-45. Editor cookbooks for philanthropic orgns. Chmn. fund drives and disaster food ARC, Hayward, Calif., 1948, bd. dirs., 1954-58; chmn. bldg. fund St. Rose Hosp., Hayward, 1956; chmn. heart fund drive Am. Heart Assn., Hayward, 1958; mem. adult edn. com. Temple Sinai, Oakland, Calif., 1965; chmn. fund-raising events Scholarships, Inc., Hayward, 1969; pres. Alameda-Contra Costa Med. Aux., 1961-62, condr. nutritional symposium, 1975; charter assoc. Children's Hosp. Found. Circle of Friends, 1985—; life mem. Hayward Sch. Dist. PTA, Hayward Forum Arts; mem. Friends of Hayward Edn. Fund, World Affairs Coun., Women's Am. Orgn. for Rehab. Through Tng., Judah Magnes Mus.; mem. Tamarack br. Children's Med. Ctr. No. Calif. Recipient Appreciation award Alameda-Contra Costa Med. Aux., 1962. Mem. Am. Dietetic Assn. (life; registered), Bay Area Dietetic Assn., Eden Hosp. Found., AAUW, Chgo. Alumni Assn., Hill and Valley Club, Order of Ea. Star, Hadassah (life mem. Eden chpt., Svc. award 1960). Home: 22119 Prospect St Hayward CA 94541

FELDMAN, BURTON LEON, insurance executive; b. Bklyn., Sept. 9, 1946; s. Samuel and Dorothy F.; m. Noanna Loyce Dix, Nov. 8, 1969; 1 dau., Andrea Eden. BS in Psychology, Bklyn. Coll., 1966. Rehab. adminstr. Occidental Life Ins. Co., L.A., 1969-78; asst. sec., dir. rehab. Mission Ins. Co., L.A., 1978—; asst. v.p., dir. rehab. svcs. Mission Am. Ins. Co., L.A., 1978-86; chief operating officer, v.p. case mgmt. svcs., Cost Care Inc., Huntington Beach, 1986-88; pres. Burt Feldman & Assocs., Hacienda Heights, Calif., 1988—; cons. Neurol. Learning Ctr., South Pasadena, Calif., Neurol. Rehab., Inc., Glendale, Calif., Chart Corp., Honolulu, Synergas Neurological Ctr., Newport Beach, Calif.; tng. programs in ins. rehab. Casa Colina Hosp., Pomona, Calif., Craig Rehab. Hosp., Englewood, Colo. Mem. Mayor's Com. for Employment Handicapped, L.A., 1976-80; mem. blue ribbon ins. com. Nat. Head Injury Found., 1981—. Mem. Nat. Rehab. Assn. (pres. Pacific region and a So. Calif. chpt. 1979-80), Nat. Rehab. Counselors Assn., Calif. Assn. Rehab. Profls., Nat. Assn. Rehab. Profls. in the Pvt. Sector, Nat. Rehab. Adminstrs. Assn., Ins. Rehab. Study Group, Indian Palms Country Club, Channel Island Shores Marina Club. Office: 15865 B Gale Ave Ste 809 Hacienda Heights CA 91745

FELDMAN, IRWIN, librarian; b. L.A., Oct. 11, 1946; s. Boris and Anne (Willner) F.; m. Penny Walker, Nov. 22, 1977; children: Benjamin Walker. Student Pomona Coll., 1964-66; BA, Simon Fraser U., 1972; MLS, U. Calif.-Berkeley, 1975. Librarian, Salinas Pub. Libr. (Calif.), 1975-77; libr. Mendocino Coll., Ukiah, Calif., 1977-84; pres. Shelfmark Cataloging, Ukiah, 1981—. Author: Monterey Bay Area Community Resource Directory, 1977, Library Handbook, 1980. Recipient Jennings Meml. prize in English lit. NSF grantee, 1966. Mem. ALA, No. Calif. Tech. Services Group, In Defense of Animals, Humane Soc. Inland Mendocino County (bd. dirs.). Democrat. Jewish. Office: Shelfmark Cataloging 277 Valley View Rd Ukiah CA 95482

FELDMAN, STANLEY GEORGE, judge; b. N.Y.C., Mar. 9, 1933; s. Meyer and Esther Betty (Golden) F.; m. Norma Arambula; 1 dau., Elizabeth L. Student, U. Calif., Los Angeles, 1950-51; LL.B., U. Ariz., 1956. Bar: Ariz. 1956. Practiced in Tucson, 1956-81; partner firm Miller, Pitt & Feldman, 1968-81; justice Ariz. Supreme Ct., Phoenix, from 1982, now vice chief justice; lectr. Coll. Law, U. Ariz., 1965-76, adj. prof., 1976-81. Bd. dirs. Tucson Jewish Community Council. Mem. Am. Bd. Trial Advocates (past pres. So. Ariz. chpt.), ABA, Ariz. Bar Assn. (pres. 1974-75, bd. govs. 1967-76), Pima County Bar Assn. (past pres.), Am. Trial Lawyers Assn. (dir. chpt. 1967-76). Democrat. Jewish. Office: Ariz Supreme Ct 201 West Wing State Capitol Phoenix AZ 85007

FELDMANN, PETER, electronics engineer; b. Bleicherode, Germany, Mar. 2, 1945; came to U.S., 1949; s. Hans and Julia (Vaga) F.; m. Faye McGrew, June 1, 1975. BSEE, Monmouth Coll., Long Branch, N.J., 1969. Elec. engr. U.S. Army Electronics Command, Fort Monmouth, N.J., 1969-77, U.S. Army ERADCOM, Fort Monmouth, N.J., 1977-84, U.S. Army Missile Command, Fort Monmouth, N.J., 1984-86, U.S. Army Electronic Proving Ground, Fort Huachuca, Ariz., 1986—; R & D mgr. Electronic Warfare Testing, 1988. Mem. Old Crows, Sigma Pi Sigma. Office: US Army Proving Ground Mail Stop STEEP-CT-E Fort Huachuca AZ 85613

FELDSTEIN, LISA ZOLA, art dealer, consultant; b. Santa Monica, Calif., Dec. 9, 1958; d. Donald James and Dorothy Naomi (Kahn) Zola; m. Alan H. Feldstein, Oct. 19, 1980; 1 child, Sasha Leigh. BA in History, UCLA, 1980; MBA, Pepperdine U., 1986. Theater, community svc. mgr. L.A. Trade-Tech. Coll., 1980; corp. art dir. Louis Newman Galleries, Beverly Hills, Calif., 1980-84; dir., v.p. Toluca Lake Galleries, Burbank, Calif., 1984-86; owner Zola Fine Art, L.A., 1986—; speaker, panelist Art Expo N.Y. and Art Expo Dallas, N.Y.C., 1983; project art cons. Litton Industries, Beverly Hills, 1984-86, Union Bank, Los Angeles, 1986—, Bateman Eichler, Hill Richards, 1988—. Contbr. articles to mag. Canvasser Dem. Party, L.A., 1972; mem. Campaign for Econ. Democracy, L.A., 1986—. Carnation Found. scholar, 1985, 86. Mem. Amnesty Internat., NAFE, Century City Rotary, Alpha Epsilon Phi. Democrat. Jewish. Office: 8730 W Third St Los Angeles CA 90048

FELICETTA, JAMES VINCENT, endocrinologist, educator; b. Seattle, Mar. 1, 1949; s. Vincent Frank and Alice Marie (Felton) F.; m. Susan Marie

Roman, Aug. 3, 1985. BS, U. Wash., 1970, MD, 1974, postgrad., 1977-80. Intern U. Utah, Salt Lake City, 1974-75, resident, 1975-77; asst. prof. medicine U. Mich., Ann Arbor, 1980-84; chief endocrinology Wayne County Gen. Hosp., Westland, Mich., 1980-84; from asst. prof. medicine to vice chief endocrinology Wayne State U., Detroit, 1984-87; chief endocrinology VA Med. Ctr., Allen Park, Mich., 1985-87; chief medicine VA Med. Ctr., Phoenix, 1987—; assoc. clin. prof. medicine U. Ariz., Tucson, 1988—. Contbr. many articles and abstracts to profl. jours. Fellow Am. Coll. Physicians; mem. Am. Fed. for Clin. Research, Am. Diabetes Assn., Am. Soc. Hypertension, The Endocrine Soc. Roman Catholic. Home: 7701 E Turquoise Ave Scottsdale AZ 85258 Office: VA Med Ctr 7th St and Indian Sch Phoenix AZ 85012

FELICITA, JAMES THOMAS, aerospace company executive; b. Syracuse, N.Y., May 21, 1947; s. Anthony Nicholas and Ada (Beech) F.; AB, Cornell U., 1969; postgrad. Harvard U., 1969, U. So. Calif., 1970, UCLA, 1975-77. Contracting officer U.S. Naval Regional Contracting Office, Long Beach, Calif., 1974-80; sr. contract negotiator space and communications group Hughes Aircraft Co., El Segundo, Calif., 1980-81, head NASA contracts, 1981-84, mgr. maj. program contracts, 1984—. Recipient cost savs. commendation Pres. Gerald R. Ford, 1976. Mem. Cape Canaveral Missile Space Range Pioneer, Nat. Contract Mgmt. Assn., Cornell Alumni Assn. So. Calif., Planetary Soc. Republican. Club: Nat. Space, Hughes Mgmt. Home: 8541 Kelso Dr Huntington Beach CA 92646 Office: 909 N Sepulveda Blvd Los Angeles CA 90245

FELIX, RICHARD JAMES, engineering executive, consultant; b. Sacramento, Apr. 21, 1944; s. Joseph James and Faye Lola (Thornburg) F.; m. Nancy Tucker Thompson, 1970 (div. 1972). Cert., Electronics Tech. A Sch., Treasure Island, Calif., 1963; student, Am. River Coll., 1968-72, Calif. State U., 1972-74. Ptnr. ADRA, Sacramento, 1971-73, Doggie Domes, Sacramento, 1971-72, Fong and Co., Sacramento, 1976-79; project dir. Dynascan Project, Sacramento, 1976-88; dir. research Omni Gen. Corp., Sacramento, 1988—; ptnr. Am. Omnigraph, Sacramento, 1985—; instr. Calif. State U., Sacramento, 1973-74; cons. KDM Design, 1985—. Creator documentary film American River College Rat Decathlon, 1974; editor publicity manual, 1978; inventor omnigraph, 1967, Multiplex Video Display System, 1976, Multiplex Video Display System II, 1984. Vol. Leukemia Soc., Sacramento, 1984; artist Camellia City Ctr., Sacramento, 1983. Served with USN, 1962-66. Mem. Sacramento chpt. Mental Health Assn. (bd. dirs. 1980, Clifford Beers award 1983), Mensa. Republican. Episcopalian. Club: New Horizons (Sacramento) (editor 1977-79).

FELLIN, OCTAVIA ANTOINETTE, librarian; b. Santa Monica, Calif.; d. Otto P. and Librada (Montoya) F.; student U. N.Mex., 1937-39; B.A., U. Denver, 1941; B.A. in L.S., Rosary Coll., 1942. Asst. librarian, instr. library sci. St. Mary-of-Woods Coll., Terre Haute, Ind., 1942-44; librarian U.S. Army, Bruns Gen. Hosp., Santa Fe, 1944-46, Gallup (N.Mex.) Public Library, 1947—; post librarian Camp McQuaide, Calif., 1947; free lance writer mags., newspapers, 1950—; library cons.; N.Mex. del. White House Pre-Conf. on Libraries and Info. Services, 1978; dir. Nat. Library Week for N.Mex., 1959. Vice-pres., publicity dir. Gallup Community Concerts Assn., 1957-78, 85—; organizer Gt. Decision Discussion groups, 1963-85; mem. Gallup St. Naming Com., 1958-59, Aging Com., 1964-68; chmn. Gallup Mus. Indian Arts and Crafts, 1964-78; mem. publicity com. Gallup Inter-Tribal Indian Ceremonial Assn., 1966-68; mem. Gov's Com. 100 on Aging, 1967-70; N.Mex. Humanities Council, 1979; mem. U. N.Mex.-Gallup Campus Community Edn. Adv. Council, 1981-82; N.Mex. organizing chmn. McKinley Hosp. Aux., pres., 1983; mem. N.Mex. Library Adv. Council, 1971-75, vice chmn., 1974-75; chmn. adv. com. Gallup Sr. Citizens, 1971-73; mem. steering com. Gallup Diocese Bicentennial, 1975-78, chmn. hist. com., 1975; chmn. Trick or Treat for UNICEF, Gallup, 1972-77; chmn. pledge campaign Rancho del Nino San Huberto, Empalme, Mexico; bd. dirs. Gallup Opera Guild, 1970-74; bd. dirs., sec., organizer Gallup Area Arts Council, 1970-78; mem. N.Mex. Humanities Council, 1979, Gallup Centennial Com., 1980-81; mem. Cathedral Parish Council, 1980-83, v.p., 1981, century com. Western Health Found., 1988—. Recipient Dorothy Canfield Fisher $1,000 Library award, 1961; Outstanding Community Service award for mus. service Gallup C. of C., 1969, 70, Outstanding Citizen award, 1974, Benemerenti medal Pope Paul VI, 1977, Celebrate Literary award Gallup Internat. Reading Assn., 1983-84, N.Mex. Disting. Pub. Svc. award, 1987. Mem. ALA, N.Mex. Library Assn. (v.p., sec., chmn. hist. materials com. 1964-66, salary and tenure com., nat. coordinator N.Mex. legislative com., chmn. com. to extend library services 1969-73, Librarian of Yr. award 1975, chmn. local and regional history roundtable 1978, Community Achievement award 1983), AAUW (v.p., co-organizer Gallup br., N.Mex. nominating com. 1967—, chmn. fellowships and centennial fund Gallup br., chmn. com. on women), Plateau Scis. Soc., N.Mex. Folklore Soc. (v.p. 1964-65, pres. 1965-66), N.Mex. Hist. Soc. (dir. 1979-85), Gallup Hist. Soc., Gallup Film Soc. (co-organizer, v.p. 1950-58), LWV (v.p. 1953-56), NAACP, Gallup C. of C. (organizing chmn. women's div. 1972, v.p. 1972-73), N.Mex. Women's Polit. Caucus, N.Mex. Mcpl. League (pres. librarian's div. 1979—), Dictionary Soc. N. Am., Alpha Delta Kappa (hon.). Roman Catholic (Cathedral Guild, Confraternity Christian Doctrine Bd. 1962-64, Cursillo in Christianity Movement, mem. of U.S. Cath. Bishop's Adv. Council 1969-74; corr. sec. Latin Am. Mission Program 1972-75, sec. Diocese of Gallup Pastoral Council 1972-73, corr. sec. liturgical commn. Diocese of Gallup 1977);chmn. Artists Coop., 1985—; mem. N.Mex. Diamond Jubilee/U.S. Constitution Bicentennial Gallup Com., 1986—. Author: Yahweh the Voice that Beautifies the Land. Home: 513 E Mesa Ave Gallup NM 87301 Office: 115 W Hill St Gallup NM 87301

FELLNER, BERNARD SAMUEL, medical center financial executive; b. Boston, Aug. 11, 1947; s. Theodore and Harriet (Kulvin) F.; m. Janice Weiner, June 15, 1969; children: Brian Scott, Anna Rose. BA with highest honors, Bentley Coll., 1968; MS in Acctg., U. Mass., 1969. CPA, Colo. Staff acct. Price Waterhouse, Boston, 1969; internal auditor, fin. analyst Beth Israel Hosp., Boston, 1969-73, mgr. cost acctg. and fin. analysis, 1973-74; asst. contr. U. Mass. Med. Ctr., Worcester, 1974-76, adminstr. physicians group practice plan, 1976, dir. Office Budget, 1976-78, dir. Office Reimbursement and Spl. Studies, 1978-79, asst. dir. fiscal affairs, 1979-80; dir. fin. Nat. Jewish Ctr. for Immunology and Respiratory Medicine, Denver, 1980—; lectr. bus. adminstrn. and continuing edn. Clark U., Worcester, 1975-79. Mem. fin. com. Marlboro-Westboro (Mass.) Community Mental Health Clinic, 1979; bd. dirs. Greater Framingham (Mass.) Jewish Fedn., 1979-80; v.p. Jewish Family Svc. Greater Framingham, 1979; dedication chmn. Congregation Bais Chabad, Framingham, 1979, pres. 1980; treas. East Denver Orthodox Synagogue, 1986-88. Fellow Healthcare Fin. Mgmt. Assn. (cert. mgr. patient accounts, bd. dirs. Mass. chpt. 1976-77, William G. Follmer merit award 1979), Colo. Soc. CPA's, Beta Tau Alpha. Home: 295 S Jasmine St Denver CO 80224 Office: Nat Jewish Ctr 1400 Jackson St Denver CO 80206

FELT, DOUGLAS CARLYLE, retired educator; b. Ogden, Utah, Apr. 23, 1932; s. William Carlyle and Mae (Douglas) F.; m. Jane Dalton, 1953 (div. 1963); children: Douglas, Janet, Bruce; m. Karin Raabe, 1981. BA in Lit. and English,, San Francisco State U., 1956; MA in Edn., U. San Francisco, 1977. Tchr. English for adults USIS, Munich, 1959; tchr. English, San Rafael (Calif.) High Sch., 1960-61; tchr. San Francisco Pub. High Schs., 1962-68; tchr. English, Washington High Sch., San Francisco, 1968-87; ret. 1987; photographer Mood Photography and Artography, 1985—. With U.S. Army, 1961-62. Democrat. Christian Buddhist. Home: 2355 Leavenworth St San Francisco CA 94133

FELTER, PAUL, educator; b. Dobbs Ferry, N.Y., July 4, 1947; s. Clarence Everett and Catherine Eleanor (Batten) F.; m. Donna Mae VanLuchene, July 24, 1975 (div. Apr. 16, 1987); 1 child, Andrew Paul. BA, Marietta Coll., 1969; MA, U. N.D., 1972; postgrad., Mont. State U., 1973-78, U. Alaska, 1984—. Cert. supt., prin., secondary tchr., Alaska; supt., prin., secondary social studies, Mont.; K-12 prin., history & polit. science, Wyo. Secondary sch. tchr. Busby (Mont.) Tribal Sch., 1972-74; prin., tchr. Plenty Coups High Sch., Pryor, Mont., 1974-76; asst. supt. Bering Strait Sch. dist., Nome, Alaska, 1976-77; prin., athletic dir. Lodge Grass (Mont.) High Sch., 1978-81; asst. prin. Green River (Wyo.) High Sch., 1981-83; dir. fed. programs Yukon Flats Sch. Dist., Fort Yukon, Alaska, 1984-89. Co-editor Indian Education: Management, Operations, Evaluation Handbook, 1988. Mem. Assn. Supervision & Curriculum Devel., Nat. Staff Devel. Council, Alaska Sch. Leadership Acad., Lions. Roman Catholic. Home: PO Box 341 Fort Yukon AK 99740 Office: Yukon Flats Sch Dist PO Box 359 Fort Yukon AK 99740

FELTON, GARY SPENCER, clinical psychologist; b. San Francisco, Mar. 8, 1940; s. Jean Spencer and Janet Elizabeth (Birnbaum) F.; m. Lynn Ellen Sandell, Mar. 21, 1970; children: Colin Spencer, Megan Ariana. BA, Grinnell Coll., 1961; MS in Clin. Psycholoty, Calif. State U., 1966; PhD in Clin. Psychology, U. So. Calif., 1970. Lic. clin. psychologist, Calif. Coord. counseling svcs., co-dir. rsch. programs Student Devel. Ctr. Mount St. Mary's Coll., 1969-71; coord. human svcs. worker tng. program Brentwood VA Hosp., L.A., 1971-72; dir. allied health, coord. child health care worker tng. program U. Affiliated Program Childrens Hosp., L.A., 1972-75; dir. spl. edn. programs, assoc. prof. psychology L.A. City Coll., 1972-81; ptnr. Spectrum Psychol. Resources, L.A., 1986—; cons. Adult Back Clinic Orthopaedic Hosp., L.A., 1967-69; researcher, writer, Am. Heart Assn. program Calif. State U., San Francisco, 1965-66. Author: Up from Underachievement, 1977, The Record Collector's International Directory, 1980; mem. ed. bd. Coll. Student Jour., Journ. Ednl. Psychology; contbr. articles to profl. jours. Bd. dirs. Pub. Advt. Council, L.A. Fellow UCLA, 1963. Mem. Am. Psychol. Assn., Western Psychol. Assn., Calif. State Psychol. Assn., L.A. County Psychol. Assn., L.A. Soc. Clin. Psychologists, Assn. Humanistic Psychology, Am. Humanist Assn., Am. Name Soc. Democrat. Office: Spectrum 10780 Santa Monica Blvd Ste 450 Los Angeles CA 90025

FELTON, SAMUEL PAGE, biochemist; b. Petersburg, Va., Sept. 7, 1919; s. Samuel S. and Pearl (Williams) F.; m. Helen Florence Martin, Dec. 31, 1955; 1 child, Samuel Page. Degree in pharmacy, U.S. Army, San Francisco, 1942; BS in Chemistry, U. Wash., 1951, postgrad., 1954. Chief technician U. Wash., Seattle, 1952-59, research assoc., 1959-62, sr. research assoc., 1976—, dir. cen. facilities lab. anesthesiology, 1969-73, dir. water quality lab., 1976-83, dir. biochem. lab. sch. of Fisheries, 1983—; asst. mem., asst. to dir. div. biochemistry Scripps Clinic and Research Found., La Jolla, Calif., 1962-66; asst. biochemist Children's Orthopedic Hosp., Seattle, 1966-68; vis. scientist Va. Inst. Marine Scis. at Coll. William and Mary, Williamsburg, 1985. Mem. bd. of adjustments City of Edmonds, Wash. Served to sgt. MC, U.S. Army 1941-45. Fellow Am. Inst. Chemists; mem. Am. Chem. Soc., Am. Inst. Fishery Research Biologists, N.Y. Acad. of Scis., Soc. Exptl. Biology and Medicine. Office: U Wash Fisheries Rsch Inst Seattle WA 98195

FENKER, DANIEL EUGENE, insurance executive; b. Ft. Wayne, Ind., Oct. 19, 1935; s. Frank L. and Mary E. (Alberding) F.; m. Judith Ann Eggen, Nov. 28, 1964; children: Katherine, Stephen, Julia, Deborah. BS, St. Joseph's Coll., Rensselaer, Ind., 1957. CLU. Group sales mgr. Lincoln Nat. Life Ins. Co., Ft. Wayne, Ind., 1957-58, Portland, Oreg., 1959-71; western div. mgr. Lincoln Nat. Life Ins. Co., Denver, 1971-73; v.p. Lincoln Nat. Life Ins. Co., Ft. Wayne, 1973-75; pres. Lincoln Cascades, Inc., Portland, Oreg., 1975—; mem. Adv. Coun. Lincoln Nat. Life, 1985—. With U.S. Army, 1958-64. Mem. Arlington Club, Multnomah Athletic Club (trustee 1985-88, treas. 1987). Republican. Roman Catholic. Home: 4600 NW Malhuer Portland OR 97229 Office: Lincoln Cascades Inc 1221 SW Yamhill Ste 100 Portland OR 97205

FENLASON, JAMES JAY, accountant, consultant, business owner; b. Mpls., Sept. 18, 1959; s. Edward James and Delpha Lorraine (Wittrup) F.; m. Debra Lynn Koontz, June 11, 1983. BS in Acctg., Liberty U., 1981. Cons. Va. Credit Union League, Lynchburg, 1982; v.p. fin. and ops. CWA, Washington, 1982-86; pres., owner J.D. Enterprises, Bozeman, Mont., 1983-87, Montana Nat. Fin., Inc., Bozeman, 1987—; pres., owner Rocky Mtn. Chrysler, Inc., 1988—; chmn. Anchor Plating Co., Inc., 1988—; treas. CWA, 1984-88. Fin. chmn. Gallatin Rep. Cen. Com., Bozeman, 1987, 89—; treas. Concerned Americans Polit. Action Com., Washington, 1986-87, Deaf Community Svcs., San Diego, 1983-85; chmn. Rep. Lincoln Day Dinner, 1989. Mem. Rotary. Republican. Baptist. Office: Mont Nat Fin Inc 309 W Mendenhall Bozeman MT 59715

FENNELL, CHRISTINE ELIZABETH, lodge administrator; b. Providence, July 14, 1948; d. Edmond John and Geraldine Mary (Goodenough) F. BS cum laude, Nat. Coll, Denver, 1983. Activity dir. Turtle Creek Convalescent Centre, Ft. Wayne, Ind., 1974-76; co-owner, operator Trail Ridge Welding, Estes Park, Colo., 1976-77; accounts mgr. Mayfair Women's Clinic, Denver, 1977-80; asst. adminstr. OB-Gyn Assocs., Aurora, Colo., 1980-82; admissions supr. St. Anthony Hosp. Sys., Denver, 1982-86; adminstr. Parkside Lodge of Colo., Thornton, 1986—; part-time instr. Nat. Coll., Denver, 1983-84. Contbr. articles to profl. jours. Bd. dirs. S.W. Denver Community Mental Health Svcs., 1986. Mem. Denver Bus. Women's Network (pres. 1986-87), Colo. Council Hosp. Admitting Mgrs. (v.p. 1985-86). Home: 9765 Orangewood Dr Denver CO 80221 Office: Parkside Lodge Colo 8801 Lipan St Thornton CO 80221

FENNING, LISA HILL, federal judge; b. Chgo., Feb. 22, 1952; d. Ivan Byron and Joan (Hennigar) Hill; m. Alan Mark Fenning, Apr. 3, 1977; children: Rachel May, Danielle Rebecca, David Paige. BA with honors, Wellesley Coll., 1971; JD, Yale U., 1974. Bar: Ill. 1975, Calif. 1979, U.S. Dist. Ct. (no. dist.) Ill., U.S. Dist. Ct. (no., ea., so., cen. dists.) Calif., U.S. Ct. Appeals (6th, 7th, 9th cir. cts.). Law clk. U.S. Ct. Appeals 7th cir., Chgo., 1974-75; assoc. Jenner and Block, Chgo., 1975-77, O'Melveny and Myers, Los Angeles, 1977-85; judge U.S. Bankruptcy Ct. Cen. Dist. Calif., Los Angeles, 1985—; pres. Nat. Conf. on Women's Bar Assns., Balt., 1987-88, pres.-elect, 1996-87, v.p., 1985-86, bd. dirs., 1984—; lectr., program coordinator in field. Mem., bd. advisors: Lawyer Hiring & Training Report, 1985-87; contbr. articles to profl. jours. Durant scholar Wellesley Coll., 1971. Mem. ABA (mem. commn. on women in the profession 1987—, Women's Caucus 1987—, Individual Rights and Responsibilities sect. 1984—, Bus. and Banking Law sect. 1986—, Bankruptcy com., Rules and Trust subcom.), Nat. Assn. Women Judges (Nat. Task Force Gender Bias in the Cts. 1986-87), Nat. Conf. Bankruptcy Judges (com. on adminstrv. office of the cts. 1986—), Calif. State Bar Assn. (chair com. on women in law 1986-87), Women Lawyers' Assn. of Los Angeles (ex officio mem., bd. dirs., chmn, founder com. on status of women lawyers 1984-85, officer nominating com. 1986, founder, mem. Do-it Yourself Mentor Network 1986—), Phi Beta Kappa. Democrat. Office: US Bankruptcy Ct 312 N Spring St Rm 831 Los Angeles CA 90012

FENSTERMAKER, PERRY MOLAN, retired teacher; b. Burley, Idaho, Nov. 10, 1926; s. Francis Molan and Jessie Eileen (Fuller) F.; BA, Idaho State Coll., 1959, MA in Edn., 1965; postgrad. U. Idaho, 1962-63, Calif. State U., San Bernardino, 1969, U. Calif., Riverside, 1969-70, Calif. State U., L.A., 1971, Whittier Coll., 1971; m. Neta McLean, May 28, 1949; children: Teresa Rae, Francis Mark, Scott McLean, Jared Luke, Connie Eileen, Bryan Edward. Tchr., Aberdeen, Idaho, 1953-56, Pocatello, Idaho, 1957-63, Thomas Jefferson Sch., Indio, Calif., 1963-71; asst. prin. Palm Desert Middle Sch., Indio, 1971-78, tchr. math., 1978-88, tchr. computer literacy, 1982-88; Calif. textbook evaluator, 1970-88; owner, operator Perry M. Fenstermaker & Assocs., Tax Preparers, Fence's Swap Shop, The Yarn Barn. Merit badge counselor Boy Scouts Am., 1950-76, camp dir., 1960-61, Eagle bd. chmn., 1968-71. With USMCR, 1944-46, 50-51, 67. Decorated Purple Heart. Mem. Nat. Tchrs. Assn. (life), Calif. Tchrs. Assn., Nat. Tchrs. Math., Calif. Tchrs. Math., Assn. for Supervision and Curriculum Devel., Am. Philatelic Soc., Coachella Valley Mineral Soc. (past pres.), Ye Olde Timers Mineral Soc., Prineville Rockhound Pow-Wow (pres.), Indio C. of C. Republican. Mormon. Editor: Mathematics Game Book, 1970; Mathematics Curriculum Guide, 1982. Co-discoverer of Crystal Ice Cave, 1956. Home: 82 357 Oleander St Indio CA 92201

FENWICK, JERRY LEE, city safety inspector, risk manager; b. Exeter, Calif., Sept. 20, 1936; s. Omar Thomas and Erma Mae (Weaser) F.; m. Patricia C. Reynolds, June 1, 1958 (div. Oct. 1979); children: Daniel L., Raymond H. BA, U. Nev., 1958. Asst. mgr. Fenwick's, Reno, 1958-76; supply officer Reno Police Dept., 1976-81; revenue officer City of Reno, 1981, safety inspector, risk mgr., 1982—. Active Adv. Bd. Community Coll., Reno, 1976-81; mem. cen. com. Wahoe County Rep. Party, 1984—; chmn. City of Reno Employees United Fund, 1984, 86, Local Bd. 7 Selective Service, Sparks, Nev., 1982-87. Mem. Am. Soc. Safety Engrs, Reno Coin Club (pres.), Reno Colorfoto Club (pres.), Nev. Stamp Study Soc. (bd. dirs.). Republican. Methodist. Lodge: Masons. Home: 2061 Tangerine St Sparks NV 89434 Office: City of Reno 450 S Center Reno NV 89502

FERBER, ROBERT RUDOLF, physics researcher, educator; b. New Eagle, Pa., June 11, 1935; s. Rudolf F. and Elizabeth J. (Robertson) F.; m. Eileen Merhaut, July 25, 1964; children: Robert Rudolf, Lynne C. BSEE, U. Pitts., 1958; MSEE, Carnegie-Mellon U., 1966, Ph.D. in Semiconductor Physics, 1967. Registered profl. engr., Pa. Mgr. engring. dept. WRS Motion Picture Labs., Pitts., 1954-58, sec., 1959-76, v.p., 1976-79; sr. engr. Westinghouse Rsch. Labs., Pitts., 1956-67; mgr. nuclear effects group Westinghouse Elec. Corp., Pitts., 1967-71, mgr. adv. engr. energy projects, East Pittsburgh, 1971-77; photovoltaic materials and collector rsch. mgr. Jet Propulsion Lab., Pasadena, Calif. 1977-85, SP100 Project contract tech. mgr., 1985—; v.p. Executaire Inc., Pitts., 1960-64; pres. Tele-Cam Inc., Pitts., 1960-78. Editor: Transactions of the 9th World Energy Conf. 1974, Digest of the 9th World Energy Conf., 1974. Contbr. articles to profl. jours. Patentee in field. Mem. Franklin Regional Sch. Dist. Bd., Murrysville, Pa., 1975-77. Fellow Buhl Found., 1965-66, NDEA, 1976-77. Mem. IEEE (sr.), Am. Solar Energy Soc., ASME (chmn. 1986 Solar Energy Div. Conf.). Republican. Lutheran. Home: 5314 Alta Canyada Rd La Canada CA 91011 Office: Jet Propulsion Lab 4800 Oak Grove Dr Pasadena CA 91109

FERDEN, BRUCE, conductor; b. Fosston, Minn., Aug. 19, 1949; s. Maurice Raymond and Irene Geneva (Torgerson) F. Student, Moorhead State U., 1967-70; B Music summa cum laude, U. Miami, Coral Gables, Fla., 1971; M Music summa cum laude, U. So. Calif., 1973. Asst. condr. N.Y. Philharmonic, N.Y.C., 1975-76; guest condr. Santa Fe Opera, 1977-81, San Francisco, Detroit, St. Louis Symphony Orchs., 1981-85, Scottish Chamber Orch., Edinburgh, 1983, Opera Theatre of St. Louis, 1978-86, Netherlands Opera Co., Amsterdam, 1980-86, Brabants (The Netherlands) Symphony Orch., 1987, 88, Pacific Symphony Orch., 1988, Seattle Opera, 1988-92, Cin. Opera Debut, 1989, Pitts. Symphony Orch., San Diego Symphony Orch., 1989; music dir. Nebraska Chamber Orch., Lincoln, 1983—, Spokane (Wash.) Symphony Orch., 1985—. Debut appearance with San Francisco Opera, 1987, also appeared 1989; condr. European debut of Philip Glass' The Making of the Representation for the Planet 8, Amsterdam, 1989. Mem. artistic adv. com. Olga Forrai Found., N.Y.C., 1987—; adv. com. Cathedral and the Arts Assn., Spokane, 1985—. Recipient Outstanding Young Alumnus award Moorhead State U., 1983, Outstanding Alumnus award U. So. Calif., 1985. Office: Spokane Symphony Orch W 621 Mallon Ste 203 Spokane WA 99201

FERDIG, SUE HARFORD, financial consultant; b. South Gate, Calif., Feb. 2, 1940; d. Norman Morgan and Evelyn Emma (Booth) Harford; m. Myron Edward, Oct. 18, 1963 (div. 1980); children: Jonathan, Rebecca, Lorinda, Elliott; m. Robert J. Sarvis, May 14, 1983. AA, Chabot Coll., 1976; BA, Calif. State U., Hayward, 1978, M Pub. Adminstrn., 1980. Owner, mgr. Sue's Resume and Secretarial Service, Hayward and Castro Valley, Calif., 1970-80; owner, pres. Associated Career Cons., Castro Valley and San Jose, 1978-82; regional sales mgr. Wang Labs, No. Calif., 1982-83; fin. cons. Merrill Lynch, San Jose, 1984—. Author: How to Start Your Own Word Processing Service, 1982. Mem. Univ. Women Am., Calif. State U. Alumni, San Jose C. of C. Republican. Office: Merrill Lynch 50 W San Fernando 16th Fl San Jose CA 95113

FERDMAN, RICHARD ALEXANDER, business systems analyst; b. Glen Cove, N.Y., Apr. 26, 1961; s. Joanne (Deneau) F. BSE in Chem. Engring., U. Pa., 1983; BBA, SUNY, Albany, 1985. Systems analyst Chevron Corp., San Ramon, Calif., 1985-86; bus. systems analyst James River Corp., Oakland, Calif., 1986—. N.Y. State Regents scholar, 1979. Mem. Am. Inst. Chem. Engrs., Nat. Honor Soc., Beta Gamma Sigma. Democrat. Home: 645 El Dorado Apt 302 Oakland CA 94611 Office: James River Corp 300 Lakeside Dr Oakland CA 94612

FERDUN, GARETH STANLEY, social service executive; b. Modesto, Calif., Nov. 17, 1937; s. Stanley and Jean (Van Buskirk) F.; m. Georgenne Marie Brann, Feb. 19, 1961; children: Severn, Muir, Destin. Student, UCLA, 1958; BA, U. Calif., Berkeley, 1961; MA, San Francisco State U., 1962. Sr. social research analyst Calif. Youth Authority, Sacramento, 1970-76, project dir. PMES, 1976-83, chief program planning and evaluation, 1983-85, chief mgmt. and policy analysis, 1985—. Contbr. numerous articles to profl. jours. Office: Calif Youth Authority Mgmt and Policy Analysis 4241 Williamsborough Dr Sacramento CA 95823

FERGUSON, DEE ANN, academic director; b. Columbus, Ohio, July 13, 1947; d. Walter Lewis and Rachel Dixon (Stone) Lucas; m. David Elton Ferguson (dec. June 1969); 1 child, Patrick Antonio. B cum laude, Ohio State U., 1966; MBA, U. Exeter, Eng., 1975. Mng. dir. Lori of London, Internat. London, 1973-80; bus. mgr., cons. Los Angeles, 1978-80; adminstr. Gussi Watches, Los Angeles, 1979-82; dir. facilities Marlborough Sch., Los Angeles, 1983—; mem. steering com. Earthquake Preparedness Marlborough Sch., 1984—. Inventor roll-r-shoe, load stabilizer, chem. formulae. Mem. Assn. Phys. Plant Admistrs. of Colls. and Univs., Am. Inst. Plant Engrs. (treas.-elect 1988, bd. dirs.). Roman Catholic. Home: 1147 N Wilcox Pl Los Angeles CA 90038 Office: Marlborough Sch 250 S Rossmore Ave Los Angeles CA 90004

FERGUSON, ISAAC CLYDE, religious organization administrator; b. Rock Springs, Wyoming, May 16, 1943; s. Isaac Jr. and Helen Marie (Youngbird) F.; m. Gloria Rae Bateman, Mar. 19, 1965; children: Shawn, Kiera, Devin. BS in Prephys. Therapy, Brigham Young U., 1967, MS in Health Edn., 1968; MS in Preventative Medicine, Ohio State U., 1973, PhD in Preventative Medicine, 1974. Instr. Brigham Young U., Provo, Utah, 1968-69, Ea. Ill. U., Charleston, 1969-71; asst. prof. So. Ill. U., Carbondale, 1974; mgr. health svcs. Church of Jesus Christ of LDS, Salt Lake City, 1975-77; exec. dir. Thrasher Rsch. Fund, Salt Lake City, 1977-82; adj. asst. prof. Brigham Young U., U. Utah, Provo., Salt Lake City, 1975-82; area dir. Church of Jesus Christ of LDS, Indpls., 1982-86; adj. prof. health adm. Ind. U., Purdue U., Indpls., 1985-86; exec. sec. humanitarian svcs. Church of Jesus Christ of LDS, Salt Lake City, 1986—. Author, editor: Personal and Family Preparedness, 1978, Mission Pres. Health Guide, 1979; contbr. author: Edn. Alcohol Intervention, Resource Study Guide & Family Discussion Plans. Chmn. bd. Utah State Task Force on Prevention of Alcohol Problems, 1976-79; bd. dirs. Intermountain Area Cystic Fibrosis Summer Camp, Salt Lake City, 1978-80. Office: LDS Welfare Svcs 50 East North Temple 7th Fl Salt Lake City UT 84150

FERGUSON, JAY EDWARD, pilot; b. Glenbar, Ariz., Dec. 17, 1925; s. Meredith and Rose Evelyn (Snyder) F.; m. Vergie Rae Vest, June 11, 1947; children: Pamela Jane, Steven Jay, Melissa Ann. BS, U. Ariz., 1949. Owner, mgr. Ferguson's Firestone Store, Safford, Ariz., 1950-67; charter pilot Wright Flight Service, Flagstaff, Ariz., 1967-70; corp. pilot Gleason Roman's Pipe Patrol, Tulsa, 1970-77, Black Mesa Pipeline, Flagstaff, 1977-87; pilot Northern Ariz. U., Flagstaff, 1987—; cons. Black Mesa Pipeline, 1987—. Commr. Flagstaff Airport Adv. Commn., 1983-87. Served as cpl. USAAF, 1942-45. Republican. Episcopalian. Lodges: Elks, Kiwanis (Safford, Ariz.) (pres. 1960), (Flagstaff) (treas. 1978). Home: 1160 U Heights Dr S Flagstaff AZ 86001 Office: No Ariz U PO Box 4115 Flagstaff AZ 86011

FERGUSON, JULIE ANN, corporate professional; b. Washington, Sept. 26, 1959; d. Carl Frederick Banks and Diette Agnes (Porter) Hissey; m. Joseph Pierre Ferguson, Mar. 16, 1978 (div. 1985). Student, Montgomery Coll., 1980-86; BBA with Distinction, U. Redlands, 1988. Asst. dept. mgr. Montgomery Ward Co., Gaithersburg, Md., 1978-80; sec., pubs. asst. U.S. Dept. Justice, Washington, 1979-83; project asst. Aero. and Space Engring. bd., NRC, Washington, 1983-86; adminstrv. sec. Lockheed Corp., Calabasas, Calif., 1986-88; staff asst. Lockheed Aero. Systems Co., Burbank, Calif., 1988—. Recipient Citizenship award KC, 1977. Mem. Lockheed Mgmt. Assn., NAFE, Nat. Wildlife Fedn. Democrat. Home: 1714-B Grismer Ave Burbank CA 91504 Office: Lockheed Aero Systems Co PO Box 550 Burbank CA 91520-1020

FERGUSON, KATHARINE ADELE, librarian; b. Tulare, Calif., Apr. 6, 1941; d. Paul Andrew and Dora Gladys (Skidmore) Hancock; m. Lonnie L. Ferguson, May 15, 1966 (div. Aug. 1982); children: Tonya, Keith. AA, Bakersfield Coll., 1960; BA, Lewis and Clark Coll., 1962; MLS, U. Calif., Berkeley, 1963. Reference librarian U.S. Army, Korea, 1963-64; catalog librarian Calif. Poly. U., San Luis Obispo, 1964-66, Colorado Coll., Colorado Springs, 1970-72; pub. services librarian Mary Hardin Baylor Coll., Belton,

Tex., 1972-77; acquisitions librarian U.S. Army, Ft. Huachuca, Ariz., 1981-87; chief librarian U.S. Army, Yuma, Ariz., 1987—. Pub. relations vol. Parents Without Ptnrs., Sierra Vista, Ariz., 1984-87. Mem. ALA, Ariz. State Library Assn. Office: Post Libr STEYP-IM-LC Yuma Proving Ground AZ 85365

FERGUSON, LLOYD ELBERT, manufacturing engineer; b. Denver, Mar. 5, 1942; s. Lloyd Elbert Ferguson and Ellen Jane (Schneider) Romero; m. Patricia Valine Hughes, May 25, 1963; children: Theresa Renee, Edwin Bateman. BS in Engring., Nova Internat. Coll., 1983. Hypnotherapist. Crew leader FTS Corp., Denver, 1968-72; program engr. Sundstrand Corp., Denver, 1972—. Team captain, March of Dimes Team Walk, Denver, 1987. Mem. Soc. Mfg. Engrs. (chmn. 1988—; recognition award, 1986), Nat. Mgmt. Assn. (program instr. 1982—, honor, 1987), Am. Indian Sci. & Engring. Soc. Republican. Religious Science. Home: 10983 W 76th Dr Arvada CO 80005 Office: Sundstrand Corp 2480 W 70th Ave Denver CO 80221

FERGUSON, WARREN JOHN, federal judge; b. Eureka, Nev., Oct. 31, 1920; s. Ralph and Marian (Damele) F.; m. E. Laura Keyes, June 5, 1948; children: Faye F., Warren John, Teresa M., Peter J. B.A., U. Nev., 1942; LL.B., U. So. Calif., 1949; LL.D. (hon.), Western State U., San Fernando Valley Coll. Law. Bar: Calif. 1950. Mem. firm Ferguson & Judge, Fullerton, Calif., 1950-59; city atty. for cities of Buena Park, Placentia, La Puente, Baldwin Park, Santa Fe Springs, Walnut and Rosemead, Calif., 1953-59; mcpl. ct. judge Anaheim, Calif., 1959-60; judge Superior Ct., Santa Ana, Calif., 1961-66, Juvenile Ct., 1963-64, Appellate Dept., 1965-66; U.S. dist. judge Los Angeles, 1966-79; judge U.S. Circuit Ct. (9th cir.), Los Angeles, 1979-86; sr. judge U.S. Circuit Ct. (9th cir.), Santa Ana, 1986—; faculty Fed. Jud. Ctr., Practising Law Inst., U. Iowa Coll. Law, N.Y. Law Jour.; assoc. prof. psychiatry (law) Sch. Medicine, U. So. Calif.; assoc. prof. Loyola Law Sch. Served with AUS, 1942-46. Decorated Bronze Star. Mem. Phi Kappa Phi, Theta Chi. Democrat. Roman Catholic. Office: US Ct Appeals 500 Federal Bldg 34 Civic Center Pla Santa Ana CA 92701

FERGUSON, WAYNE SANDER, retired superintendent; b. Ogden, Utah, Apr. 26, 1926; s. George Cochran and Charlotte (Sander) F.; BS, Brigham Young U., 1950, MEd, 1953; EdD, U. So. Calif., 1960; m. Dorothy Jean Curtis, Dec. 19, 1952; children—George Ray, April Lynne, Susan Gaye. Math. tchrs. Tooele County Sch. Dist., Utah, 1950-53; prin. Dugway (Utah) Elem. and High Schs., 1953-55; asst. supt. bus. services Mt. Eden Sch. Dist., Hayward, Calif., 1956-61, asst. supt. instructional services, 1961-63; supt. Orland (Calif.) public schs., 1963-72, Palmdale (Calif.) Sch. Dist., 1972-75, Fremont (Calif.) Unified Sch. Dist., 1975-87, ret., 1987; instr. San Jose State U., part-time, 1978-80. Served with USN, 1944-46. Mem. Am. Assn. Sch. Adminstrs., Assn. Calif. Sch. Adminstr., Phi Kappa Phi, Phi Delta Kappa, Delta Epsilon. Republican. Mormon. Lodge: Kiwanis (pres. 1980-81, lt. gov. div. 40 Calif.-Nev.-Hawaii 1983-84). Home: 2620 Forrest Ct Fremont CA 94536

FERGUSSON, ROBERT GEORGE, retired army officer; b. Chgo., May 20, 1911; s. Archibald Campbell and Anne (Sheehan) F.; m. Charlotte Lawrence, Nov. 18, 1937; 1 son, Robert Lawrence (dec.). Student, Beloit Coll., 1929-32; B.S., U.S. Mil. Acad., 1936; M.A. in Internat. Relations, Boston U., 1959. Commd. 2d lt. U.S. Army, 1936, advanced through grades to maj. gen., 1962; comdg. officer 14th Inf. Regt., Hawaii, 1955-57; chief army adv. group Naval War Coll., Newport, R.I., 1957-61; asst. div. comdr. 24th Inf. Div., Augsburg, Ger., 1961-62; chief staff Hdqrs. Central Army Group (NATO), Heidelberg, Ger., 1962-65; comdg. gen. U.S. Army Tng. Center, Inf., Ft. Ord, 1965-67; comdr. U.S. Forces, Berlin, 1967-70; ret. 1970; corp. group v.p. manpower planning Dart Industries, Inc., Los Angeles, 1970-78; cons., 1978-82, ret., 1982. Decorated D.S.M., Legion of Merit with oak leaf cluster, Bronze Star with 3 oak leaf clusters, Purple Heart (U.S.); knight comdr. Cross with badge and star Order of Merit (W.Ger.); officer Legion of Honor (France). Mem. Clan Fergusson Soc. (Scotland), Beta Theta Pi. Clubs: Cypress Point (Pebble Beach); Old Capitol (Monterey, Calif.). Home: Box 1515 Pebble Beach CA 93953

FERNWALT, DARRON LEE, investment broker; b. Niles, Mich., Nov. 3, 1966; s. Donald Lee and Kaylene Jo (Shreve) F. Cert. in Italian, U. Degli Studi Di Firenze, Florence, Italy, 1985; BA in Econs., Ariz. State U., 1988. Mktg. rep. Comml. Lease Guide, Inc., Mesa, Ariz., 1986-87; account exec. Blinder, Robinson & Co., Inc., Scottsdale, Ariz., 1987-88; investment broker The Equitable, Phoenix, 1988—. Coordinator Young Reps., Phoenix, 1987-88; fund raiser Mar. Dimes, Phoenix, 1988. Mem. Nat. Assn. Securities Dealers. Home: 9020 E Jomax Scottsdale AZ 85255 Office: 2231 E Camelback Rd Phoenix AZ 85260

FERRANG, EDWARD GEORGE, library director, school system administrator; b. Pitts., Nov. 8, 1950; s. Joseph Emerald and Mary Catherine (Stuthers) F.; m. Carole Ann Russell, Apr. 16, 1988. BS in Edn., U. Pa., 1972; MLS, U. Pitts., 1976; postgrad., Keller Grad. Sch. Bus., 1988—. Cert. tchr., Pa., S.C., N.Mex. Library dir., AV coord. E. Lebanon County High Sch., Myerstown, Pa., 1972-73; asst. mgr. S.S. Kresge-K-Mart Div., Dover, N.J., 1973-74; librarian, film coord. Hilltop Cath. High Sch., Pitts., 1974-76; instr. media svc. Newberry (S.C.) Coll., 1976-78; asst. prof., library dir. U. N.Mex., Gallup, 1978; regional mktg. rep. Prentice-Hall, Inc. GBM div., Englewood Cliffs, N.J., 1979-85; library dir., dept. head City of Tolleson, Ariz., 1985—; mem. editorial bd. Cath. Library Assn., Phila., 1975-77; sec. Maricopa County Library Coun., Phoenix, 1986—; dirs. Tolleson Summer Food Program. Mem. Ariz. Library Friends, Phoenix, 1986—; mem. Tolleson Community Pride Steering Com., 1987—, Manitas de Armistad-Tolleson Elem. Sch., 1987—; active publicity Tolleson Whoopee Daze Steering Com., 1987—. Named Jaycee of the Month, Myerstown Jaycees, 1973. Mem. ALA, Ariz. State Library Assn. (publicity com. 1989—), Mountain Plains Library Assn., Kappa Delta Pi, Alpha Beta Alpha, Mu Kappa Gamma. Democrat. Roman Catholic. Home: 10623 N 63d Dr Glendale AZ 85304 Office: City of Tolleson 9555 W Van Buren Tolleson AZ 85353

FERRANTO, MICHAEL DONALD, education educator; b. Kane, Pa., May 10, 1937; s. Rocco and Emiddia (Minolfe) F.; children: Michael David, Matthew Douglas. BA, U. Md., 1969; MBA, La. Tech. U., 1980; postgrad., U. Ariz., 1980-88. Enlisted USAF, 1956, advanced through grades to capt., ret., 1980; instr. Pima Community Coll., Tucson, 1980-84; dir. research dept. Cochise Coll., Douglas, Ariz., 1984—. Decorated Bronze Star. Mem. Data Processing Mgmt. Assn., Assn. for Instl. Research, Ednl. Research Assn., Am. Assn. for Higher Edn. Roman Catholic. Office: Cochise Coll Douglas AZ 85607

FERRARI, DOMENICO, computer science educator; b. Gragnano, Piacenza, Italy, Aug. 31, 1940; came to U.S., 1970; s. Giacomo and Erina (Fracchioni) F.; m. Alessandra Ferrari Cella-Malugani, Apr. 16, 1966; children: Giuliarachele, Ludovica. Dr. Ing., Politecnico di Milan, Italy, 1963. Asst. Politecnico di Milano, 1964-67, asst. prof. computer sci., 1967-70, prof., 1976-77; asst. prof. U. Calif., Berkeley, 1970-75, assoc. prof., 1975-79, prof. dept. elec. engring. and computer sci., 1979—, dep. vice chmn. dept. elec. engring. and computer sci., 1977-79, assoc. chmn. computer sci., 1983-87; dep. dir. Internat. Computer Sci. Inst., 1988—; cons. in field. Author: Computer Systems Performance Evaluation, 1978; (with Serazzi and Zeigner) Measurement and Tuning of Computer Systems, 1983; Editor: Performance of Computer Installations, 1978; Experimental Computer Performance Evaluation, 1981; Theory and Practice of Software Technology, 1983; Performance Evaluation, 1979—. Contbr. articles to profl. jours. Recipient Libera Docenza, Italian Govt., 1969; O. Bonazzi award Associaz Elettrotecnica Italiana, 1970. Grantee NSF, 1974—, Univ. Calif., 1982—, Def. Advanced Research Projects Agy., 1983—. Fellow IEEE (editor Transactions on Software Engring. 1984-87); mem. Computer Measurement Group (A.A. Michelson award 1987), Assn. Computing Machinery. Clubs: U. Calif. Faculty, Kosmos (Berkeley); Croara Country (Italy). Office: U Calif Computer Sci Div Dept EECS Berkeley CA 94720

FERRARIO, JOSEPH A., bishop. Educ. St. Charles Coll., Catonsville, Md., St. Mary's Sem., Baltimore, Catholic U., Washington, D.C., U. of Scranton, Pa. Ordained Roman Catholic priest, 1951; ord. aux. bishop of Honolulu, titular bishop of Cuse, 1978, bishop of Honolulu, 1982-. Office: Diocese of Honolulu 1184 Bishop St Honolulu HI 96813 *

FERRARO, ARTHUR KEVIN, broadcasting executive; b. Bronx, Sept. 25, 1934; s. Gaspero and Mary (Unk) F.; m. Jodi J.L. Ferraro, Sept. 1, 1968; children: Guy, Ross, Dena. Student, St. Francis U. Mgr. west coast UPI-Audio div., Los Angeles; news dir. KHJ Radio, Los Angeles; investigative reporter KMPG Radio, Los Angeles; ptnr., mgr. KRRI-FM Radio, Boulder City, Nev., 1982—. Mem. Nev. Broadcasters Assn. (v.p. Las Vegas 1988—), RTV News Assn. (recipient various awards), Calif. State Exposition (Best Radio Newscast award 1974), Golden Miro Found. (Best Radio Comml. award 1985), Sigma Delta Chi (Best Radio Commentary award 1978). Office: KRRI Box 97 Boulder City NV 89005

FERREIRA, DEIRDRE CHARLYN, corporate executive; b. Salinas, Calif., June 2, 1958; d. Mervyn Malcolm Ferreira and Eva Charlene (Gustaveson) Pascal. BS in Polit. Sci., Calif. State U., 1985. Service mgr. Ralphs Grocery Co., Canoga Park, Calif., 1975-85; account mgr. Lever Bros., Santa Ana, Calif., 1985-88, dist. field sales mgr., 1988—. Women's Profl. Racquetball Assn. (65 awards, Calif. State champion, reanked 24th nationally). Republican. Reorganized Ch. of Jesus Christ of Latter-day Saints.

FERRELL, TIMOTHY E., financial executive; b. Cin., June 4, 1963; s. James Edward and Leona Marie (Elliott) F.; m. Leslye Susan Stanbro, July 29, 1983; 1 child, Valynn Brooke. Student, Okla. Bapt. U., 1980-81; student fin. mgmt., Community Coll. of the Air Force, 1987; BBA Assoc. Fin. Mgmt., U. of the Philippines, 1988. Office mgr. Mid-West Enterprises Inc., Midwest City, Okla., 1981-83, jr. v.p., 1986; office mgr. McGhee Enterprises, Inc., Shawnee, Okla., 1983-85; tax acct. Met. Mgmt. Co. Inc., Mustang, Okla., 1985-86; enlisted USAF, 1986; fin. services specialist USAF, The Philippines, 1986—. Republican. Baptist. Home: 7-1B Sta Maria Ave, Angeles City The Philippines Office: USAF Box 14299 APO San Francisco CA 96311-0006

FERRERI, JOSEPH RONALD, business executive; b. Youngstown, Ohio, Oct. 29, 1933; s. Domonic Marino an Estella Margaret (mazzochi) F.; divorce; 1 child; Candyce Laurice; m. Donna Jean Anderson, Jan. 1, 1983; 1 child, Ronald Stephen. BS in Civil Engring., U. N.Mex., 1956. Field engr. Robert E. Mckee Constrn. Co., Colorado Springs, Colo., 1956-58; plant and design engr. Am. Marietta Concrete, Albuquerque, 1958-61; pres. Prestressed Concrete Products, Inc., Albuquerque, 1961-72; v.p. Stanley Structures, Inc., Denver, 1972-87; pres. Ferreri Concrete Structures, Inc., Albuquerque, 1987—. Bd. dirs. Goodwill Industries of N.Mex., Albuquerque, 1969-75. Mem. Greater Albuquerque C. of C. (bd. dirs. 1968-73), Exec. Assn. Greater Albuquerque (pres. 1971). Republican. Methodist. Lodge: Shriners. Office: Ferreri Concrete Structures Inc 3411 Candelaria Rd NE PO Box 30310 Albuquerque NM 87190-0310

FERREY, JEFFREY BAKER, computer research scientist, educator; b. Altadena, Calif., Oct. 31, 1943; s. Lloyd Baker and Helen (Burrows) F.; Donna Ferrey, Mar. 17, 1971; children: Scott Jeffrey, Robert, Steven. BA, Whittier (Calif.) Coll., 1966; MBA, Calif. Western U., San Diego, 1969; D in Bus. Adminstrn., U.S. Internat. U., 1983. CPA; cert. info. systems auditor. Mem. pres.'s staff Vector Electronics Inc., Sylmar, Calif., 1969-72; info. technologist Lockheed Aircraft Corp., Burbank, Calif., 1972-77; corp. audit supr. Gen. Dynamics Corp., San Diego, 1977-83, mgr. systems devel., 1983-85, mgr. comml. integrating mfg., 1985—; prof. U. San Diego, 1983-87, Nat. U., San Diego, 1987—; cons. Security Pacific Corp., Glendale, Calif.,1985-86, CanAudit Inc., Toronto, 1986—, EDP Auditors Assn., Chgo., 1983-87; pres. Ferrey Enterprises, Rancho Mirage, Calif., 1985—; mem. SHARE; internat. speaker in field. Contbr. articles to profl. jours. Appointee exec. com. Calif. State Developmental Disabilities Bd., San Diego, 1987—. Republican. Office: Ferrey Enterprises PO Box 435 Solana Beach CA 92075

FERRIGNO, DANIEL JOSEPH, JR., internist; b. Bronx, N.Y., Jan. 23, 1933; s. Daniel J. and Serena (Natarelli) F.; m. Patricia Bettencourt, Feb. 14, 1975; children: Shireen, Janine. AB, NYU, 1954; MD, SUNY, Downstate Bronx, 1960. Intern Bklyn. VA Hosp., 1961-62; resident in internal medicine Bklyn. Jewish Hosp., 1962-64; gen. practice internal medicine Sacramento, Calif., 1966—; med. dir. CAREUnit (adult and adolescent), Starting Point Adolescent, Smokenders Internat., Sacramento; assoc. corp. med. dir. CompCare, Irvine; assoc. clin. prof. med., U. Calif. Med. Sch., Davis, 1975—. Bd. advisors Mercy Hosp. Found., Sacramento, 1975—. Served to capt. USAF, 1964-66. Mem. AMA, Calif. Med. Assn., Am. Soc. Internal Medicine, AMA for Alcoholism and Other Drug Dependencies, Nat. Council Alcoholism. Republican. Home: Box 178 Clarksburg CA 95612

FERRIS, EVELYN SCOTT, lawyer; b. Detroit, d. Ross Ansel and Irene Mabel (Bowser) Nafus; m. Roy Shorey Ferris, May 21, 1969 (div. Sept. 1982); children—Judith Ilene, Roy Sidney, Lorene Marjorie. J.D., Willamette U., 1961. Bar: Oreg. 1962, Fed. Dist. Ct. 1962. Law clk. Oreg. Tax Ct., Salem, 1961-62; dep. dist. atty. Marion County, Salem, 1962-65; judge Mcpl. Ct., Stayton, Oreg., 1965-76; ptnr. Brand, Lee, Ferris & Embick, Salem, 1965-82; chmn. Oreg. Workers' Compensation Bd., Salem, 1982—. Bd. dirs. Friends of Deepwood, Salem, 1979-82, Salem City Club, 1972-75; bd. dirs. Marion County Civil Svc. Commn., 1970-75; com. mem. Polk County Hist. Commn., Dallas, Oreg., 1976-79; mem. Oreg. legis. com. Bus. Climate, 1967-69, Govs. Task Force on Liability, 1986. Recipient Outstanding Hist. Restoration of Comml. Property award Marion County Hist. Soc., 1982. Mem. Oreg. Mcpl. Judges Assn. (pres. 1967-69), Altrusa, Internat., Mary Leonard Law Soc., Western Assn. Workers Compensation Bds. (pres. 1987—), Capitol Club (pres. 1977-79), Internat. Assn. Indsl. Accident Bds. and Commns. (exec. com.), Phi Delta Delta. Republican. Episcopalian. Home: 747 Church St SE Salem OR 97301 Office: Oreg Workers' Compensation Bd Bd 480 Church St SE Salem OR 97310

FERRIS, RANDALL PRESTON, airline pilot; b. Bloomington, Ill., Jan. 28, 1953; s. Harry Jr. and Dorothy Jean (Wieklinski) F.; m. Janet Kay Ihde, Dec. 8, 1984. BSBA, Colo. State U., 1975. Pres. Ferris Industries, Denver, 1976-79; bus. mgr. Lawrenceville (N.J.) Bd. Edn., 1979-87; commd. 2d lt. USAF, 1979, advanced through grades to capt., 1983; resigned Lawrenceville (N.J.) Bd. Edn., 1987; flight officer Am. Airlines, N.Y.C., 1988—. Episcopalian. Home: 15985 Wintun Rd Apple Valley CA 92307 also: 1233 York Ave Apt 2-I New York NY 10021

FERRIS, RONALD CURRY, bishop; b. Toronto, Ont., Can., July 2, 1945; s. Harold Bland and Marjorie May (Curry) F.; m. Janetm Agnes Waller, Aug. 14, 1965; children: Elisa, Jill, Matthew, Jenny, Rani, Jonathon. Grad., Toronto Tchrs. Coll., 1965; B.A., U. Western Ont., London, 1970; M.Div., Huron Coll., London, 1973, D.D. hon., 1982. Ordained to ministry Anglican Ch., 1970. Tchr. Pape Ave. Sch., Toronto, 1965-66; prin. Carcross Elem. Sch., Y.T., 1966-68; incumbent St. Luke's Ch., Old Crow, Y.T., 1970-72; rector St. Stephen's Ch., London, Ont., 1973-81; bishop Diocese of Yukon, Whitehorse, 1981—. Home: 41 Firth Rd, Whitehorse, YK Canada Y1A 4R5 Office: Diocese of Yukon, PO Box 4247, Whitehorse, YK Canada Y1A 3T3

FERRIS, YVONNE MARIE, manufacturing company executive, statistician; b. East St. Louis, Ill., June 6, 1934; d. Clarence Raymond and Frankye Elizabeth (Bradberry) Clark; m. Livingston Polk Ferris II, July 5, 1967. BS, Iowa State U., 1956; postgrad. Rochester Inst. Tech., 1962, U. Colo., 1964-66. Statistician, Rockwell Internat., Golden, Colo., 1956-63, sr. statistician, 1963-73, mgr. stats. lab., 1973-75, mgr. stats. and nuclear material control, 1975-77, mgr. stats. and systems analysis, 1977-79; group leader safeguards IAEA, Vienna, Austria, 1977-79; chmn. Measurement Control Task Force; mem. speakers bur.; chmn. Standard N15.46, Measurement Control. com. Am. Nat. Standards Inst. Counselor Rocky Flats Personal Assistance Program; mem. Expts. in Friendship; active local programs emotionally disturbed and mentally retarded adults. Recipient Cost Improvement Suggestion awards Rockwell Internat., 1971-73, named Engr. of Yr., 1982. Mem. Inst. Nuclear Materials Mgmt. (chmn., cert. safeguards specialist), Am. Statis. Assn. (adv. com. nuclear regulatory research), Am. Soc. Quality Control, Nat. Mgmt. Assn., LWV, Altrusa Internat. (past pres.). Contbr. articles to profl. jours. Office: Rockwell Internat PO Box 464 Golden CO 80401

FERRO, JUDITH GAY, teacher; b. Nampa, Idaho, Mar. 23, 1943; d. Frank Marion and Beulah Elzora (Payne) Willmorth; m. William Lanny Ferro, Jan. 30, 1986; 1 child, Toni D. BA, Stanford U., 1964; MEd, U. Wash., 1974. Cert. secondary tchr., Idaho. Polit. intern to Congressman Compton I. White, Jr. U.S. Ho. of Reps., Washington, 1964; rsch. asst. Time Mag., N.Y.C., 1965; secondary tchr. Pub Schs., Middleton, Idaho, 1966-68, Seattle, 1969-76, Meridian, Idaho, 1976-79; lifestyle writer, editor Idaho Press-Tribune, Nampa, 1980-82; grant writer Coll. of Idaho, Caldwell, 1982-85, 87-88, dir. pub rels., 1985-87, bull. editor, 1985-88; secondary tchr. Pub. Schs., Caldwell, Idaho, 1988—; co-owner Ferro's Appliance Svc., Caldwell, Idaho, 1980—. Dir.: Snake Basin Drama, Caldwell, Idaho, 1979-82; contbr. articles on history and edn. to profl. jours. Mem. AAUW (state pub. info. officer 1980-82, br. v.p. 1985-87). Democrat. Office: Wilson Middle Sch 1004 E Linden Caldwell ID 83605

FERTIG, TED BRIAN O'DAY, producer, public relations and association executive; b. Miami, May 18, 1937; s. Peter John and Frances Marie (Aswell) F.; A.B., 1960; M.B.A., 1969. Mem. profl. staff Congress U.S., Washington, 1965; dir. mem. relations Nat. Bellas Hess, Inc., Kansas City, 1963-69; mgr. employment/manpower planning Capitol Industries, Inc., 1969-70; pres. Mgmt. Cons. Group, Hollywood, Calif., 1970—, Fertig, Toler & Dumond, Hollywood, 1973; sr. partner Nascency Prodns., Hollywood and Sacramento, 1971—; exec. dir. Soc. Calif. Accts., 1974-83, Ednl. Found., Inc., 1975-80. Pres., Hollywood Community Concert Assn., 1971-72; exec. dir. Hollywood Walk of Fame, 1971-74; sec.-treas. Save the Sign, 1972-73; producer, Santa Claus Lane Parade of Stars, Hollywood, 1971-73; dir. Old Eagle Theatre, Sacramento, Sacramento Film Festival. Trustee, finance chmn. Los Angeles Free Clinics, 1970-71; mem. Calif. Commn. on Personal Privacy. Served with AUS, 1960-62. Cert. assn. exec. Mem. Pub. Relations Soc. Am., Am. C. of C. Execs., Am. Soc. Assn. Execs., Sacramento Soc. Assn. Execs. (pres. 1980). Author: A Family Night to Remember, 1971; Los Ninos Cantores de Mendoza, 1972; (with Paul Yoder) Salute to Milwaukee, 1965. Office: 715 Regatta Dr Sacramento CA 95833-1715

FERY, JOHN BRUCE, forest products company executive; b. Bellingham, Wash., Feb. 16, 1930; s. Carl Salvatore and Margaret Emily (Hauck) F.; m. Delores Lorraine Carlo, Aug. 22, 1953; children: John Brent, Bruce Todd, Michael Nicholas. BA, U. Wash., 1953; MBA, Stanford U., 1955; D of Nat. Resources (hon.), Gonzaga U., 1982, D of Law (hon.), 1982; D of Nat. Resources (hon.), U. Idaho, 1983. Asst. to pres. Western Kraft Corp., 1955-56; prodn. mgr. 1956-57; with Boise Cascade Corp., Idaho, 1957—, pres., chief exec. officer, 1972-78, chmn. bd., chief exec. officer, 1978—; bd. dirs. Albertsons, Inc., Hewlett-Packard Co., West One Fin. Group, Inc., Nat. Park Found., Union Pacific Corp., The Boeing Co.; mem. Bus. Coun.; sr. mem. Conf. Bd.; mem. adv. coun. Chase Internat. Mem. adv. coun. sch. bus. Stanford U.; chmn. bd. Idaho Community Found. With USN, 1950-51. Named Most Outstanding Chief Exec. Officer Fin. World, 1977, 78, 79, 80. Mem. Am. Paper Inst. (bd. dirs., past chmn., mem. exec. com.), Bus. Roundtable (policy com.). Clubs: Arid, Hillcrest Country, Link's, Arlington. Office: Boise Cascade Corp 1 Jefferson Sq Boise ID 83728

FESHBACH, NORMA DEITCH, education educator, department chairman; b. N.Y.C., Sept. 5, 1926; m. Seymour Feshbach; children: Jonathan Stephan, Laura Elizabeth, Andrew David. BS in Psychology, CCNY, 1947, MS in Ednl. Psychology, 1949; PhD in Clin. Psychology, U. Pa., 1956. Diplomate Am. Bd. Prof. Psychology; cert. in clin. psychology, Phila.; lic. clin. and ednl. psychologist, Calif. Tchr. Betsy Ross Nursery Sch., Yale U., 1947-48; clin. psychologist Yale U. Med. Sch., 1948; teaching asst. dept. psychology Yale U., 1948-51; research asst. human resources research office George Washington U., Washington, 1951-52; psychology intern Phila. Gen. Hosp., 1955-56; research assoc. dept. psychology U. Pa., 1959-61; research assoc. Inst. Behavioral Sci. U. Colo., 1963-64; assoc. research psychologist dept. psychology UCLA, 1964-65; clin. psychologist II UCLA Neuropsychiat. Inst., 1965; prof. Grad. Sch. Edn. UCLA, 1965—, prof. psychology dept., 1975—, chmn. dept. edn., 1985—; lectr. Jr. Coll. Phys. Therapy, New Haven, Conn., 1948-49, dept. psychology, U. Pa., 1956-57, UCLA Neuropsychiat. Inst., Calif. Dept. Mental Hygiene, Los Angeles, 1966-69; vis. asst. prof. Stanford U. dept. psychology, 1961-62, U. Calif. Berkeley, 1962-63; vis. scholar dept. exptl. psychology Oxford U., 1980-81; co-prin. investigator various projects and programs; co-prin. dir. and investigator NIMH Tng. Program in Applied Human Devel., 1986-91; clin. and research cons. Youth Services, Inc., Phila., 1955-61; also cons. various media orgns.; head program in Early Childhood and Devel. Studies, 1968-80; dir. NIMH Tng. Prog. in Early Childhood and Devel. Studies, 1972-82; prog. dir. Ctr. for Study of Evaluation, UCLA Grad. Sch. Edn., 1966-69; co-dir. UCLA Bush Found. Tng. Prog. in Child Devel. and Social Policy, 1978-82; chair grad. faculty UCLA Grad. Sch. Edn., 1979-80. Editorial cons., mem. editorial bd. psychology and ednl. research revs., contbr. numerous articles on child psychology to profl. jours. Mem. adv. council of Women's Clinic, Los Angeles, 1974-76; mem. adv. bd. Nat. Com. to Abolish Corporal Punishment in Schs., 1972-80, Nat. Ctr. for Study of Corporal Punishment and Alternatives in the Schs., 1976—; mem. profl. adv. com. on Child Care, Los Angeles Unified Sch. Dist., 1978-80; trustee EVAN-G Com. to End Violence Against the Next Generation, 1972-80; exec. bd. Internat. Soc. for Research in Agression, 1982-84. Recipient James McKeen Cattell Fund Sabbatical award, 1980, 81, Townsend Harris Medal, Disting. Alumnus award CCNY, 1982, Disting. Sci. Achievement in Psychology award Calif. Psychol. Assn., 1983; named Faculty Mem. Woman of Yr. Nat. Acad. Profl. Psychologists, Los Angeles, 1973; U.S. Pub. Health Tng. Fellow, 1953-56; research grantee NIMH, 1972-77 (co-principal with D. Stipek), 77-82, 1986—, Hilton Found., 1985-86, Spencer Found. 1984-85; Child Help, USA, 1982-84 (co-principal with C. Howes), UCLA Acad. Senate, 1981—, Bush Found., 1978-83, 79-80, 80-81, 81-82, 82-83 (co-dir. with J.I. Goodlad), Adminstrn. for Children, Youth and Families, 1981-82 (co-dir. with J.I. Goodlad), NSF, 1976-77, 77-78, 78-80 (co-prin. with S. Feshbach), Com. on Internat. and Comparative Studies, 1973-74, 77-78. Fellow Am. Psychol. Assn. (officer var. coms.); mem. Assn. Advancement Psychology, AAAS, AAUP, Am. Bd. Profl. Psychologists, Am. Ednl. Research Assn., Calif. Assn. for Edn. Young Children, Nat. Assn for Edn. Young Children, Internat. Assn. Applied Psychology, Internat. Soc. for Research on Aggression, Internat. Soc. Study of Behavioral Devel., Internat. Soc. Prevention Child Abuse and Neglect, Nat. Register of Health Services Providers in Psychology, Soc. for Research in Child Devel., Western Psychol. Assn.; Sigma Xi, Delta Phi Upsilon. *

FESSENDEN, JUNE SHIRLEY, credit union official; b. Pitts., Nov. 10, 1951; d. Stanley Howard and Lillian Bertha (Weyman) Barton; m. Mel L. Fessenden, Oct. 26, 1984; children: Amy Sue, Todd Olen. AS in Data Processing, Community Coll. Allegheny, Pitts., 197l; BS in Tng. and Devel., Grand Canyon U., 1987; postgrad., Ottawa U., Phoenix, 1987—. Payroll clk. Graybar Electric Co., Inc., Pitts., 1972-75; bd. dirs. Fessenden Prosthetic-Orthotic Svc., Toledo, 1975-83; tng. and devel. intern City of Phoenix, 1986-87; tng. asst. Motorola Employees Credit Union-West, Phoenix, 1987—; adj. instr., course developer Grand Canyon U., Phoenix, 1986—; graphics generator operator for TV sta., Phoenix, 1987. Bd. dirs. Midwest Med. Missions, Inc., Toledo, 1980-82. Mem. Nat. Soc. for Performance and Instrn. (sec. Ariz. chpt. 1987, pres. 1989), Am. Soc. for Tng. and Devel., Am. Psychol. Assn. Republican. Baptist. Home: 4220 W Frier Dr Phoenix AZ 85051 Office: Motorola Employees Credit 8250 E Roosevelt Scottsdale AZ 85271

FETHEROLF, JOYCE WILSON, production company executive; b. Richlands, Va., July 28, 1952; d. Cecil Wilson and Betty (Martin) Woods; m. William Floyd Fetherolf (div. Apr. 1975); 1 child, William. Student, Ohio State U., 1970-7l. Exec. asst. Don-Don, Inc., N.Y.C., 1979—, chief exec. officer, 1985-88; with prodn. and devel. dept. Harding Prodns. Inc., Beverly Hills, Calif., 1989—. Office: care John G Avildsen 2423 Briarcrest Rd Beverly Hills CA 90210

FETTERLY, JEANINE DUMAS, real estate development executive, writer; b. Milw., Aug. 23, 1938; d. Henry Alfred and Gerda Frances (Egloff) Dumas; m. Larry Leon Fetterly, Dec. 22, 1956; children: Sean, Kendall, Sara, Kerrye. BA in Social Sci., San Francisco State U., 1963. Lic. comml. pilot. Mng. ptnr. Fetterly Constrn. Co., Oakland, Calif., 1969—; aeronaut, owner, mgr. Fetterly's Hot Air Flying Machine Co., Oakland, 1972—; freelance writer, photographer Oakland, 1986—; flyer exptl. balloons, 1971-78. Active Camron-Stanford House Preservation Bd., 1976—, Oakland Heritage Alliance, 1988—. Mem. Media Alliance, Balloon Fedn. Am., AAUW. Democrat. Presbyterian. Home and Office: 1793 Northwood Ct Oakland CA 94611

FETTGATHER, ROBERT, counselor, special education educator; b. Seattle, May 3, 1951; s. Robert Paul and June Marie (Christensen) F.; m. Louise Elaine Rebello, Aug. 18, 1979; children: Aaron, David. AS in Psychiat. Tech., West Valley Coll., Saratoga, Calif., 1976; BA in Psychology, San Jose U., 1979; MA in Edn., U. Santa Clara, 1981; PhD in Psychology, Calif. Coast U., 1985. Lic. learning handicapped specialist, psychiat. technician, Calif; cert. stress mgmt. instr. Instr. psychology and spl. edn. Mission Coll., Santa Clara, Clif., 1979—; instr. psychology Mission Coll., Santa Clara, Calif., 1983—; counselor Alexian Assocs., San Jose, Calif., 1987—; program cons. Santa Clara Unified Adult Handicapped Program, 1984—; spl. cons. Comprehensive Adult Student Assessment System Project, Calif. Dept. Edn., 1983-84. Mem. Agnews Community Library Grant Adv. Bd., 1988. Mem. Am. Mental Health Counselors Assn., Am. Psychol. Assn., Am. Assn. for Counseling and Devel., Calif. Psychol. Assn., No. Calif. Assn. Behavior Analysis, San Jose State U. Alumni Assn., Calif. Coast U. Alumni Assn. Democrat. Roman Catholic. Home: 14899 Payton Ave San Jose CA 95124 Office: Alexian Assocs 750 N Capitol Ave Ste C-6 San Jose CA 95133

FEUERSTEIN, MARCY BERRY, dental health service organization executive; b. Wellsville, N.Y., June 18, 1950; d. Marshall Newton and Miriam May (Lingle) Jones; m. Ronald Glenn Berry, Aug. 7, 1967 (div.) 1 dau., Angelia Lynn; m. Richard Alan Feuerstein, Jan. 8, 1984. Student Chaffey Jr. Coll., Alta Loma, Calif. Jr. clk. N.Y. Life Ins., Los Angeles, 1970-73; jr. acct. FMC Corp., Pomona, Calif., 1973-78; sec. Gen. Med. Ctrs., Anaheim, Calif., 1978-79, service rep., 1979-80; dir. mktg. services Protective Health Providers, San Diego, 1980-81, Dental Health Services, Long Beach, Calif., 1981—; owner Mar-Rich Enterprises, 1985—; v.p. So. Calif. chpt. Healthdent of Calif., 1987-88; account exec. Oral Health Svcs., Inc., 1988—. Mem. Nat. Assn. Female Execs. Republican. Home: 9582 Golden St Alta Loma CA 91701 Office: Oral Health Svcs 15720 Ventura Blvd #222 Encino CA 91436

FEUSNER, RANDY BRUCE, insurance executive; b. Lovell, Wyo., Sept. 13, 1960; s. R. Dale and Virginia (Bruce) F.; m. Angela Jones, May 16, 1981; children: Chelsey, Amberly. AS, Ricks Coll., 1982; BS, Brigham Young U., 1984. Spl. agt. Prudential Life Ins. Co., Billings, Mont., 1984-85, mgr., 1985—. Mem. South Ea. Assn. Life Underwriters. Republican. Mormon. Office: The Prudential PO Box 2520 Billings MT 59103

FIALA, TERRY ALAN, publishing company owner; b. Berwyn, Ill., Dec. 10, 1946; s. Edward August and Dorothy Ann (Savage) F.; m. C.L. Osborn, Apr. 28, 1983. BA in Journalism, Bowling Green U., 1969. Broadcast journalist CBS News, Chgo., 1970-76, Sta. KDEN, Denver, 1976-78; freelance author various, 1978-84; nat. rep. Spectrum, Inc., Arvada, Colo., 1984-86; gen. mgr. Cable Ready, Inc., Denver, 1986-88; owner, pres. The Publishing Works and Image Systems, Inc., Boulder, Colo., 1987—; v.p. Partnership, Inc., Boulder, 1987—; bd. dirs. Small Bus. Resource Ctr., Boulder. Home and Office: 4644 MacArthur Ln Boulder CO 80303

FIALER, PHILIP ANTHONY, research scientist, electronics company executive; b. San Francisco, Nov. 6, 1938; s. Harry A. and Elyse E. (Palin) F.; m. Dianne M. Hater, Mar. 4, 1967 (div. 1982); children: Michele S., Melissa L.; m. Sue Eble, Dec. 14, 1985; 1 stepdaughter, Shannon T. Leinbach. BS, Stanford U., 1960, MS, 1964, PhD, 1970. Engr. Lockheed Corp., Sunnyvale, Calif., 1961-67; research assoc. Stanford (Calif.) U., 1967-70; dep. lab. dir., staff scientist SRI Internat., Menlo Park, Calif., 1970—; pres. Mirage Systems, Sunnyvale, Calif., 1984—; research scientist in ionospheric radiosci. and electromagnetic scattering. Contbr. articles to profl. jours. Mem. IEEE. Democrat. Episcopalian. Home: 742 Torreya Ct Palo Alto CA 94303 Office: Mirage Systems 537 Lakeside Dr Sunnyvale CA 94086

FIALKOW, PHILIP JACK, medical educator; b. N.Y.C., Aug. 20, 1934; s. Aaron and Sarah (Ratner) F.; m. Helen C. Dimitrakis, June 14, 1960; children: Michael, Deborah. B.A., U. Pa., 1956; M.D., Tufts U., 1960. Diplomate: Am. Bd. Internal Medicine, Am. Bd. Med. Genetics. Intern U. Calif., San Francisco, 1960-61, resident, 1961-62; resident U. Wash., Seattle, 1962-63, instr. medicine, 1965-66, asst. prof., 1966-69, assoc. prof., 1969-73, prof. medicine, 1973—, chmn. dept. medicine, 1980—; chief med. svc. Seattle VA Ctr., 1974-81; physician-in-chief U. Wash. Med. Ctr., Seattle, 1980—; attending physician Harborview Med. Ctr., Seattle, 1965; cons. Children's Orthopedic Hosp., Seattle, 1964—. Contbr. articles to profl. jours. Trustee Fred Hutchinson Cancer Research Ctr., Seattle, 1982—. NIH fellow, 1963-65; NIH grantee, 1965—. Fellow ACP; mem. Am. Soc. Clin. Investigation, Assn. Am. Physicians, Assn. Profs. Medicine, Am. Soc. Human Genetics (dir. 1974-77), Alpha Omega Alpha. Office: U Wash Dept Medicine RG 20 Seattle WA 98195

FIANDACA, MARIANO CHIP, corporate professional; b. Chgo., June 6, 1950; s. Anthony John and Dorothy Jeanette (Hogan) F.; m. Joanne MacAulay, July 1970 (div. 1975); 1 child, Chrissy; m. Winifred Sylvia Sumner, July 8, 1978; children: Royal Jay, Andrea Joy. AA, Elgin (Ill.) Community Coll., 1970. Adminstrv. mgr. Goodhost Foods Internat., Elk Grove, Ill., 1975-77; rt. salesman MJB Coffee Co., Phoenix, 1977-80; sales supr. Hills Bros. Coffee Co., Phoenix, 1980-84, dist. mgr., 1984-87, mgr. pvt. label distbn. groups, 1987-88; v.p. The Upper Deck Co., Anaheim, Calif., 1988—. Sponsor, adv. Youth of Unity Ch., Mesa, Ariz., 1983. With USAF, 1970-74. Home: 1908 E Ranch Rd Tempe AZ 85284 Office: The Upper Deck 1174 B N Grove St Anaheim CA 92806-2198

FIEDLER, LOIS JEAN, psychologist; b. Park Falls, Wis., July 4, 1938; d. Herbert W. and Ethel (Newman) F.; m. Harold John LeVesconte, Jan. 31, 1986. BS, U. Wis., 1960; MS, Purdue U., 1963; PhD, Mich. State U., 1970. Lic. Cons. Psychologist, Minn. Tchr. Wausau (Wis.) Bd. of Edn., 1960-62; counselor Wis. State U. Counseling Ctr., Oshkosh, 1963-66; advisor, asst. dir. Mich. State U., E. Lansing, 1966-69, instr., asst., 1968-70; psychologist, asst. prof., asst. dir. student counseling bur. U. Minn., Mpls., 1970-86, prof. emeritus, 1986—; assoc. dir. counseling services San Jose (Calif.) State U., 1986-88. Contbr. numerous profl. articles. Co-founder and officer New Communities, Mpls., 1971-75, Psyche, Inc., Mpls., 1973-80; bd. dirs. Alcohol and Other Drug Abuse Programming, Minn., 1980-83. Mem. Am. Psychol. Assn., Am. Coll. Personnel Assn. (exec. council 1978-81, pres. 1974-75). Home: 577 Millpond Dr San Jose CA 95125-1418

FIELD, CHARLES W., small business owner, consultant; b. Kankakee, Ill., Feb. 4, 1934; s. Euell Charles and Genevieve Thelma (Fletcher) F.; m. Barbara Sue Bird, Sept. 20, 1957; children: Charles Scott, Lynda Lois. BS in Metall. Engring., U. Ariz., 1960. Lic. real estate broker, Ariz. Research metallurgist Titanium Metals Corp. Am., Henderson, Nev., 1960-62; mgr. tech. service Titanium Metals Corp. Am., N.Y.C., 1962-67; with research and mktg. dept. Large Jet Engine div. Gen. Electric Co., Cin., 1967-69; sr. engr. specialist Garrett Corp., Phoenix, 1969-76; realtor Realty Execs., Scottsdale, Ariz., 1976-85; prin. C.W. Field Field & Co., Scottsdale, 1985—; cons. armor titanium specialties U.S. Secret Service. Contbr. articles to profl. jours. Active local Boy Scouts Am., Youth Scottsdale. Recipient commendation U.S. Govt., 1964, Pres's. Round Table award Phoenix Bd. Realtors, 1981, 84. Mem. Nat. Assn. Realtors, Scottsdale Bd. Realtors (Million Dollar club), Scottsdale C. of C.. Club: Camelback Country. Lodge: Rotary (treas. Scottsdale club). Office: CW Field & Co 6560 N Scottsdale Rd Scottsdale AZ 85253

FIELD, CLAYTON SCOTT, insurance company executive; b. Spokane, Wash., July 7, 1945; s. Stephen W. and Mabel (Jackson) F.; m. Sandra Knerr, Feb. 5, 1971 (div. 1987); 1 child, Julie A. BA, Walla Walla Coll., 1970. V.p. Blue Shield, Seattle, 1972-85; sr. mgr., Peat, Marwick, Main, 1985-88; pres. 1st Choice Health Network Inc., Seattle, 1988—. Contbr. articles to profl. jours. Mem. Wash. Profl. Rev. Orgn., 1976-83; hon. bd. dirs. Bellevue Wash. Philharmonic Orch., Inc., 1976—; candidate Wash. State Bd. Edn., 1984; adv. bd. U. Wash. Extension Program. With U.S. Army, 1966-68. Mem. Health Care Fin. Mgmt., Assn. Patient Acct. Mgrs., Group Health Assn. Am., Am. Med. Care Rev. Assn., Am. Assn. Prefered Provider Organs., Wash. Basic Health Plan (adv. coun.), Rotary. Home: 2134 Waverly Pl N Seattle WA 98109 Office: 1st Choice Health Plan 1100 Olive Way #1480 Seattle WA 98101-1838

FIELD, DOUGLAS SCOTT, dentist; b. Cleve., Dec. 4, 1955; s. Charles Alexander and Janice Thompson (Walker) F.; m. Miyoung Linda Lee, Mar. 28, 1979; children: Paul Timothy, Sarah Anne. AA in Bus., Saddleback Coll., 1979; BA in Biology, Calif. State U., 1979; DDS, UCLA, 1983. Lic. dentist, Calif. Gen. practice resident dentistry Dept. Med. and Surgery, VA Hosp., West L.A., 1983-84; assoc. dentist Village Dental Ctr., Long Beach, Calif., 1984-85; pvt. practice San Clemente, Calif., 1985—. Vol. Children's Clinic, Santa Ana, Calif., 1985—, Daffy Dental Care Program, San Juan Capistrano, Calif., 1987—, San Juan Community Clinic, San Juan Capistranto, 1986—; vol. greeter Holt Childrens' Services, L.A., 1980-85; Sunday sch. tchr. St. John's Presbyn. Ch., West L.A., 1980-85, Ocean Hills Community Ch., San Juan Capistrano, 1986—. Mem. ADA, Calif. Dental Assn., Orange County Dental Soc., Am. Philatelic Soc., Omicron Kappa Upsilon. Republican. Home: 253 Calle Cuervo San Clemente CA 92672 Office: 110 W Escalones Ste B San Clemente CA 92672

FIELD, JEFFREY FREDERIC, designer; b. Los Angeles, July 6, 1954; s. Norman and Gertrude Clara (Ellman) F.; m. Susan Marie Merrin, Jan. 8, 1978. BA in Art, Calif. State U., Northridge, 1977, MA in Art, 1980. Cert. indsl. plastics tchr., Calif. Designer Fundamental Products Co., N. Hollywood, Calif., 1972-82; designer/model maker The Stansbury Co., Beverly Hills, Calif., 1982-84; mech. engr. Vector Electronic Co., Sylmar, Calif., 1984-87; pres., prin. Jeffrey Field Design Assocs., Sepulveda, Calif., 1987—; cons. MiniMed Techs., Sylmar, 1987—, Best Time Inc., Leander, Tex., 1987—, Spectrum Design, Granada Hills, Calif., 1987—, Raycom Systems Inc., Boulder, Colo., 1988-89, Alfred E. Mann Found. for Sci. Rsch., Sylmar, 1988—, Atomic Elements, L.A., E-O Products, Laguna Hills, Calif. Democrat. Jewish. Home and Office: 16715 Vincennes St Sepulveda CA 91343

FIELD, JOHN AUSTIN, orthopedic surgeon; b. San Francisco, May 6, 1935; s. John and Sally (Miller) F.; m. Wilma Buursma, Dec. 24, 1966; children: John Clark, Cara Lisa, David Buursma. BS in Engring., UCLA, 1957, MD, 1961. Diplomate Am. Bd. Orthopedic Surgery. Intern then resident Los Angeles County Hosp., 1962-66; orthopedic surgeon Dominican Hosp., Santa Cruz, Calif., 1968-76, Kaiser Hosp., Santa Cruz, 1976—. Served to capt. U.S. Army, 1966-68. Mem. Am. Acad. Orthopedic Surgeons, ACS, AMA, Tau Beta Pi. Presbyterian. Office: Kaiser Found Hosp 900 Kiely Blvd Santa Clara CA 95051

FIELD, JOHN LOUIS, architect; b. Mpls., Jan. 18, 1930; s. Harold David and Gladys Ruth (Jacobs) F.; m. Carol Helen Hart, July 23, 1961; children: Matthew Hart, Alison Ellen. B.A., Yale, 1952; M. Arch., 1955. Individual practice architecture San Francisco, 1959-68; v.p. firm Bull, Field, Volkmann, Stockwell, Architects, San Francisco, 1968-83; ptnr. Field/Gruzen, Architects, San Francisco, 1983-86, Field Paoli Architects, San Francisco, 1986—; guest lectr. Stanford, 1970; chmn. archtl. council San Francisco Mus. Art, 1969-71; mem. San Francisco Bay Conservation and Devel. Commn., Design Rev. Bd., 1980-84; founding chmn. San Francisco Bay Architects Review, 1977-80. Co-author, producer, dir.: film Cities for People (Broadcast Media award 1975, Golden Gate award San Francisco Internat. Film Festival 1975, Ohio State award 1976); documentary film maker: film The Urban Preserve (Calif. Council AIA Commendation of excellence 1982); co-design architect: design for New Alaska Capital City (winner design competition). Recipient Archtl. Record award, 1961, 1972; AIA, Sunset mag. awards, 1962, 64, 69; No Calif. AIA awards, 1967, 82, Calif. council AIA award, 1982, certificate excellence Calif. Gov.'s Design awards, 1966, Homes for Better Living awards, 1962, 66, 69, 71, 77, Albert J. Evers award, 1974, Best Bldg. award Napa (Calif.) C. of C., 1987, Ann. Design award Internat. Coun. Shopping Ctrs., 1988, Excellence award Nat. Mall Monitor Ctr. and Stores, 1989; co-design architect winner Santa Barbara retail redevel. competition, 1985; NEH grantee, 1972; Nat. Endowment for Arts fellow, 1975. Fellow AIA (mem. com. on design); mem. Nat. Council Archtl. Registration Bds., Lambda Alpha. Club: Yale (San Francisco). Address: 222 Sutter St San Francisco CA 94108

FIELD, THOMAS GORDON, animal sciences educator; b. Gunnison, Colo., Aug. 20, 1957; s. Frederick Roblee and Mary Esther (McIllwee) F.; m. Lisa Susan Bard, Jan. 4, 1986. BS, Colo. State U., 1980, MS, 1987, postgrad. Mgr. purebred div. Field Land & Cattle Co., Gunnison, 1980-82; owner, mgr. Quartz Creek Cattle Co., Parlin, Colo., 1982-84; rsch. teaching asst. in animal sci. Colo. State U., Ft. Collins, 1984—; dir. Extension Adv. Bd., Gunnison, 1982-84; cons. Agri-West Mgmt., Ft. Collins, 1988. Contbr. articles to profl. jours. Coach 4-H Livestock Judging Team, Gunnison, 1983-84, Youth Basketball League, Ft. Collins, 1984-85; sr. high sch. tchr. 1st Meth. Ch., Ft. Collins, 1986-88. Recipient Shepardson Teaching award Coll. Agr., Colo. State U., 1985; ShepardsonFound. agrl. teaching grantee, 1988. Mem. Am. Soc. Animal Scientists, Nat. Cattlemen's Assn., Colo. Cattlemen's Assn., Am. Angus Assn., Am. Hereford Assn., Colo. Hereford Assn. (v.p. 1986-88), Gunnison County Stockgrowers Assn. (bd. dirs. 1983-84), Colo. State U. Alumni Assn.,Ram Boosters Club. Republican. Office: Colo State U Dept Animal Sci Fort Collins CO 80523

FIELD, THOMAS WALTER, JR., drugstore chain executive; b. Alhambra, Calif., Nov. 2, 1933; s. Thomas Walter and Pietje (Slagveld) F.; m. Ruth Inez Oxley, Apr. 10, 1959; children: Julie, Sherry, Cynthia, Thomas Walter, III, James. Student, Stanford U., 1951-53. V.p. retail ops. Alpha Beta Co., La Habra, Calif., 1972-73, sr. v.p., 1973-75, exec. v.p., 1975-76, pres., chief exec. officer, 1976-81; pres. Am. Stores Co., 1981-85; pres., chief exec. officer McKesson Corp., San Francisco, 1986—, also chmn. bd. Bd. dirs. La Habra Boys' Club. Mem. Calif. Retailers Assn. (dir.), Automobile Club So. Calif. (adv. bd.). Republican. Office: McKesson Corp 1 Post St San Francisco CA 94104 *

FIELDEN, C. FRANKLIN, III, teacher; b. Gulfport, Miss., Aug. 4, 1946; s. C. Franklin and Georgia Freeman F.; children: Christopher Michaux (dec.), Robert Michaux, Jonathan Dutton. Student Claremont Men's Coll., 1964-65; AB, Colo. Coll., 1970; MS, George Peabody Coll. Tchrs., 1976, EdS, 1979. Tutor Proyecto El Guacio, San Sebastian, P.R., 1967-68; asst. tchr. GET-SET Project, Colorado Springs, Colo., 1969-70, co-tchr., 1970-75, asst. dir., 1972-75; tutor Early Childhood Edn. Project, Nashville, 1975-76; public policy intern Donner-Belmont Child Care Ctr., Nashville, 1976-77; asst. to urban minister Nashville Presbytery, 1977; intern to prin. Steele Elem. Sch., Colorado Springs, 1977-78, tchr., 1978-86; resource person Office Gifted and Talented Edn. El Paso County Sch. Dist. #11, 1986-87; tchr. Columbia Elem. Sch., 1987—; lectr. Arapahoe Community Coll., Littleton, Colo., 1981-82; instr. Met. State Coll., Denver, 1981; cons. Jubail Human Resources Devel. Inst., Saudi Arabia, 1982. Mem. governing bd. GET-SET Project, 1969-79; mem. Nashville Children's Issues Task Force, 1976-77; mem. Tenn. United Meth. Task Force on Children and Youth, 1976-77; mem. ad hoc bd. trustees Tenn. United Meth. Agy. on Children and Youth, 1976-77; mem. So. Regional Edn. Bd. Task Force on Parent-Caregiver Relationships, 1976-77; mem. day care com. Colo. Commn. Children and their Families, 1981-82; mem. El Paso County Sch. Dist. #11 Staff Devel. Coordinating Coun., 1982-84; mem. Citizens' Goals Leadership Tng., 1986-87, Child Abuse Task Force, 4th Judicial Dist., 1986-87; mem. task force FIRST IMPRESSIONS, 1987-88. Recipient Arts/Bus./Edn. award, 1983; Innovative Teaching award, 1984; NIMH fellow, 1976. Mem. Assn. Supervision and Curriculum Devel., Nat. Assn. Edn. Young Children, Colo. Assn. Edn. Young Children (legis. com. 1979-84, governing bd. 1980-84, 85-86, exec. com. 1980-84, sec. 1980-84, rsch. conf. chmn. 1982, tuitions awards com. 1983-86, chmn. tuition awards com. 1985-86), Pikes Peak Assn. Edn. Young Children, Am. Film Inst., Colorado Springs Fine Arts Ctr., Huguenot Soc. Great Britain and Ireland, Nat. Trust Historic Preservation, Country Club of Colo., Phi Delta Kappa. Presbyterian. Home: PO Box 7766 Colorado Springs CO 80933 Office: 835 E St Vrain Colorado Springs CO 80903

FIELDEN, GEORGIA FREEMAN, interior designer, residential and commercial consultant. m. Clarence Franklin Fielden, Jr., July 16, 1942; children: Clarence Franklin III, Landis Michaux. Student fine arts, Ward-Belmont Coll., 1932-37, Blue Mountain Coll., 1937-38; BS, Vanderbilt U., 1941; postgrad., N.Y. Sch. Interior Design, 1953. Head dept. arts and crafts Camp Bon Air, Sparta, Tenn., 1939-42; asst. instr. fin arts Demonstration Sch. Peabody Coll. Vanderbilt U., Nashville, 1940-41; instr. fine arts Jackson (Miss.) Pub. Schs., 1939-42; free-lance interior designer 1942-52; designer, assoc. Marshall Morin Interiors, 1952-56; pvt. practice interior designing Colorado Springs, Colo., 1956-64; owner, designer Georgia Fielden Interiors, Colorado Springs, Colo., 1964-67, Denver, 1967-86, Aurora, Colo., 1986—; lectr. in field. Contbr. articles to profl. jours. Pres. local PTA 1954-56. Mem. Am. Soc. Interior Designers (cert., bd. dir. Colo. chpt.), Constrn. Specifications Inst., Nat. Soc. Colonial Dames of Am., Illuminating Engring. Soc. (assoc.), DAR, Young Life Aux. (local pres. 1960-61), Huguenot Soc. Founders of Manakintown in the Colony of Va., Nat. Geneal. Soc., PEO, St. Andrews Soc., The Denver Exec. Club. Presbyterian. Home: PO Box 441083 Aurora CO 80014 Office: 2417 S Victor St Aurora CO 80044

FIELDER, BARBARA LEE, human resources consultant; b. Long Beach, Calif., Dec. 6, 1942; d. Thomas G. Coultrup and Elizabeth L. (Doran) Cox; m. Alford W. Fielder, Apr. 14, 1970; children: Kris, Kimberly, Brian. BBA, Redlands U., 1979. Cert. tchr., Calif. Sr. compensation analyst Shiley div. Pfizer Co., Newport Beach, Calif., 1973-76; pers. adminstr. Shiley div. Pfizer Co., Irvine, Calif., 1976-78; asst. dir. human resources BASF-Video Corp., Fountain Valley, Calif., 1978-79; prin. Barbara L. Fielder & Assocs., Roseville, Calif., 1979—; instr. U. Calif., Davis, 1985—. Contbr. articles to profl. jours. Pres. Calif. Employers Coun., 1983-86; past mem. Pvt. Industry Coun., Orange County, Calif., 1983-84; mem. Foothill Adv. Bd., 1987—; bd. dirs. Industry Edn. Coun. Calif., 1987—. Recipient Outstanding Svc. award Interstate Conf. Employment Security Agys., Indpls., 1984. Mem. Am. Compensation Assn., Sierra Foothills Employers Assn. (founder, pres. 1985—), Roseville C. of C., Nevada County C. of C., Nevada City C. of C., Soroptimists. Presbyterian. Office: Barbara L Fielder & Assocs 801 Riverside Ave #J-5 Roseville CA 95678

FIELDS, JAMES RALPH, lawyer, lobbyist, arbitrator, consultant; b. Los Angeles, Mar. 14, 1943; s. Paul Raymond Fields and Della Louise (Brabb) Klebe; m. Barbara Smith Knudson, May 18, 1985. BS in Bus. Adminstrn., U. Idaho, 1965, JD, 1973. Bar: Idaho 1973, U.S. Dist. Ct. Idaho 1973. Staff counsel U.S. Sen. James McClure, Washington, 1973-76; gen. counsel Idaho Assn. Commerce and Industry, Boise, 1976-83, v.p., gen. counsel, 1983-87; assoc. Penland & Munther, Boise, 1987—; cons. Knudson-Fields Human Devel. Cons., Boise, 1985—. Organizer, pres. Idaho Liability Reform Coalition, 1986; mem. Gov.'s Adv. Com. on Workers' Compensation, Idaho, 1978-87; active US Peace Corps, Philippines, 1965-67; bd. dirs. Idaho Jr. Achievement, 1988—. Served to 1st lt. U.S. Army, 1968-71, Vietnam. Mem. ABA, Idaho Bar Assn., Am. Soc. Personnel Adminstrn., Human Resources Assn. Treasure Valley (bd. dirs. 1986, 88—), Am. Arbitration Assn. (comml. arbitrator, 1988—). Republican. Baptist. Lodge: Kiwanis (pres. Boise chpt. 1985-86). Home: 1183 Wild Phlox Way Boise ID 83709

FIELDS, LEE ARTHUR, manufacturing company executive; b. Greenwood, La., May 27, 1932; s. George and Mary (Birdsong) F.; student Long Beach City Coll., 1966-68; m. Velma Myles, Aug. 5, 1953 (div.); children: Patricia, Gwendolyn, Brenda, Geanell, Lee Arthur, Belinda, DeAndria, Leah Megan; m. 2d, Syvilla Armstrong Pettiford, May 4, 1982. Nurses aide VA, Shreveport, La., 1956-60; urol. asst. VA, Long Beach, Calif., 1960-75, hemodialysis technician, 1975-78; owner, mgr. craft products mfg. bus., Long Beach, 1979—; owner, dir. nursing facility for handicapped; owner, mgr. Bar-B-Que Restaurant, Long Beach; pvt. practice importer/exporter spl. gifts, Los Angeles. Active Nat. Republican Congressional Com., Norman Rockwell Mus. Soc., PTA, NAACP; mem. Rep. Presdl. Task Force. Served with U.S. Army, 1951-54. Decorated Purple Heart. Recipient cert. of recognition Nat. Rep. Congressional Com., 1980; various service awards VA. Mem. Nat. Fedn. Ind. Bus., Nat. Urol. Assn., Long Beach Area C. of C., Calhoun Collectors' Soc. Home: 2041 Caspian Ave Long Beach CA 90810 Office: 1819 W Anaheim St Long Beach CA 90813

FIELDS, TERRI SUSAN, freelance writer. BA, U. Ariz., 1970; MA, Ariz. State U., 1975; LHD (hon.), No. Ariz. U., 1986. Tchr. Sunnyslope High Sch., Phoenix; featured speaker Ariz. Press Women Freelance Writer Seminar, 1982, 86, Ariz. Sch. Bds. Assn., 1985, Ariz. Interscholastic Journalism Assn., 1985, Reader's Digest Writing Seminar, 1986, Ariz. Prin.'s Acad., 1986. Author: Help Your Child Make the Most of School, 1987; also articles. Named one of twelve Outstanding Women in Communication, 1985, Ariz. Tchr. of Yr., 1986; recipient 1st Place U.S. Ednl. Writing award Nat. Fedn. Press Women, 1982, 3d Place U.S. Mag. Editorial Writing award Nat. Fedn. Press Women, 1983, Outstanding Writing award Ariz. Press Women, 1982, 84, Golden Bell award Ariz. Sch. Bds. Assn., 1984, 88, Achievement Above All award Glendale Union High Sch. Dist. Bd. Edn., 1985 and others. Home: 8228 N 15th Ave Phoenix AZ 85021

FIERRO, SAMUEL ARTHUR, real estate executive; b. Phoenix, June 22, 1949; s. Angelo S. and Wilma A. (Suggs) F.; m. Christine E. D'Arcangelo, Oct. 6, 1972; children: Daniel, Kathyrn, James. BS, Ariz. State U., 1972. Lic. real estate broker, Ariz. With new home sales dept. Suggs Homes div. U.S. Home, Phoenix, 1972-74; with new home sales dept. Cavalier Homes div. Richmond Am., Phoenix, 1975-84, sales mgr., 1979-82, v.p. sales and mktg., 1982-83, pres., 1983-84; v.p. sales and mktg. Marlborough Devel. Corp., Phoenix, 1984—. Staff sgt. USNG, 1966-72. Mem. Ariz. Sales and Mktg. Coun. (chmn. 1982, Million Dollar Roundtable award 1972-79), Ariz. Young Mortage Bankers, Cen. Ariz. Homebuilders Assn. Republican. Office: Marlborough Devel Corp 300 W Clarendon Ste 140 Phoenix AZ 85013

FIFE, DENNIS JENSEN, military officer, chemistry educator; b. Brigham City, Utah, Feb. 10, 1945; s. Glen Shumway and June (Jenson) F.; m. Metta Marie Gunther, June 22, 1972; children: Kimball, Kellie, Keith, Kurt, Katie, Kenton. BS in Chemistry, Weber State U., Ogden, Utah, 1969; MBA, Inter-Am. U., San German, P.R., 1973; MS in Chemistry, Utah State U., 1978, PhD in Phsy. Chemistry, 1983. Assoc. chemist Thiokol Chem. Corp., Brigham City, 1969; commd. 2d lt. USAF, 1969, advanced through grades to lt. col.; pilot, instr., flight examiner Hurricane Hunters, Ramey AFB, P.R. and Keesler AFB, Miss., 1971-76; test project pilot 6514th Test Squadron, Ogden, Utah, 1979-81; instr. chemistry USAF Acad., Colorado Springs, Colo., 1977-79, asst. prof., 1983-85, assoc. prof., 1985—; pres. Select Pubs., Inc., Colorado Springs, 1985—, also chmn. bd. dirs. Author: How to Form a Colorado Corporation, 1986; contbr. articles to profl. jours. Active Boy Scouts Am., Colorado Springs, 1981—, varsity scout coach, Colorado Springs, 1986; sustaining mem. Rep. Nat. Com., Washington, 1983—. Decorated Air medal with oak leaf cluster: NSF research grantee, 1967-68. Mem. Internat. Union Pure and Applied Chemistry (affiliate), Am. Chem. Soc., Phi Kappa Phi. Republican. Mormon. Office: USAF Acad Dept Chemistry Colorado Springs CO 80840

FIFER, KELLY RAY, real estate officer; b. Lincoln, Nebr., Nov. 28, 1955; s. Duane Norman and Bonnie Jolene (Johnson) F.; m. Patricia Baldwin, June 28, 1977 (div.); m. Nancy Marie Richardson, Aug. 21, 1982; children: Ryan, Matthew, Natalie. Grad., high sch., Scottsdale, Ariz. Lic. real estate broker, Ariz. Salesman Los Arcos Realty, Scottsdale, Ariz., 1972-75; v.p., office mgr. Los Arcos Realty, Gilbert, 1979-83; pres. Los Arcos Realty, Scottsdale, 1983—; pres., v.p. Gilbert Econs. Devel., 1980-84; bd. dirs. Chandler Airpark Econ. Devel. Corp. Pres., bd. dirs. Gilbert C. of C., 1979-85. Mem. Rotary. Republican. Methodist. Office: Los Arcos Realty & Investments Inc 9449 N 90th St 207 Scottsdale AZ 85258

FIGHTS, MICHAEL LEWIS, manufacturing company executive; b. Muncie, Ind., Mar. 31, 1954; s. Gerald Lewis and Naomi Ruth (Gasper) F.; m. Cydney Terese Haynes, Feb. 23, 1974; children: Michael Lewis II, Matthew Kirk, Mitchell Alex. Lab. supr. and tech. Ball Meml. Hosp., Muncie, 1972-74; advt. devel. lab. supr. Ball Corp., Muncie, 1974-85; supr. packing maintenance Ball Corp., El Monte, Calif., 1985—. Patentee in field. Mem. Internat. Platform Assn. Republican. Home: 3235 Merrifield Ave Pomona CA 91767 Office: Ball-InCon Glass Packaging Corp 4000 N Arden Dr El Monte CA 91734

FIGLIOZZI, JOHN PHILIP, banker, consultant, teacher; b. N.Y.C., Aug. 31, 1946; s. John Joseph and Ida Theresa (Liva) F.; m. Rosalinda Cintron, Jan. 21, 1978; children: John, Gabriella. BA in Edn., Montclair (N.J.) State U., 1972; MBA, cert. internat. mgmt, NYU, 1974. Cert. English tchr., N.J. Mng. dir. Citicorp Leasing P.R., San Juan, 1978-80; regional supr. Citibank Audit Div., Caracas, Venezuela, 1980-82; dir. credit adminstrn. Citibank Spain, Madrid, 1982-87; dir. credit policy Citibank Ariz., Phoenix, 1987—; cons. in field; speaker Remer Reporting Svcs., Cleve., 1988, Am. Grad. Sch. Internat. Mgmt., Phoenix, 1988—. Sgt. U.S. Army, 1968-72. Mem. Robert

Morris Assocs., NYU Alumni Assn. Republican. Roman Catholic. Home: 608 W Straford Dr Chandler AZ 85224 Office: Citibank Ariz 16010 N 28th Ave Phoenix AZ 85023

FIGUEIREDO, HUBERT FERNANDES, aerospace engineer; b. Elizabeth, N.J., Nov. 21, 1958; s. Fernando and Maria Alexandria Figueiredo; m. Donna Maybee, Mar 26, 1988. BS in Aerospace Engring., Polytech. Inst. N.Y., 1980; postgrad. in systems mgmt., U. So. Calif., 1986—. Prodn. inspector Amax, Inc., Carteret, N.J., 1978; analytical engr. Pratt and Whitney Aircraft Corp., East Hartford, Conn., 1979; space shuttle mech. systems test engr. Rockwell Internat. Space Div., Palmdale, Calif., 1980-84, pub. relations speaker, 1981-84; space shuttle mechanisms/structures engr. Lockheed Space Ops. Co., Vandenberg AFB, Calif. and Kennedy Space Ctr., Fla., 1984-87; engring. specialist, design engr. B-2 div. Northrop Corp., Palmdale, Calif., 1987—. Recipient Superior Achievement award Rockwell Internat. Space Div. Mem. AIAA. Republican. Roman Catholic. Office: Northrop B-2 Div D/E971-4D AF Plant 42 Site 4 Palmdale CA 93550

FIGUEROA, MICHAEL OTTO, law enforcement official; b. Los Angeles, Dec. 26, 1943; s. Jesse Albert and Elsie (Lea) F.; m. Andrea L. Ashcraft; children: Jeffrey Michael, Noelle Kathryn. AA in Bus. Adminstrn., East Los Angeles Coll., 1965; BA, in Adminstrn., Calif. State Coll.-San Bernardino, 1974; grad. U. So. Calif. Delinquency Control Inst., 1978, Calif. Peace Officers Standards and Tng. Commn. Command Coll., 1985. Cert. peace officer, supr., Calif. Dep. Los Angeles County Sheriff's Dept., 1970-72; patrolman Riverside, Police Dept., Calif., 1972-74, agt., 1974, spl. agt., investigator, 1974-76, sgt., 1976-80, lt. adj. to chief of police, 1980-83, capt., 1983-88, dep. chief, 1988—; cons. on street gangs and graffiti. Bd. dirs. Riverside Area Child Abuse Council, 1980, Riverside Area Rape Crisis, 1977-80; Cub master local Cub Scouts, 1975-77; active local Y-Indian Guides. 1st. lt. AUS, 1966-68. Decorated Bronze Star with oak leaf cluster; named Supr. of Yr., Riverside Police Officers Assn., 1984. Mem. Internat. Police Assn., Hispanic-Am. Police Command Assn., Latino Peace Officers Assn., Calif. Gang Investigators Assn., Peace Officer Research Assn. Calif., Nat. Police Athletic Fedn., Vietnam Vets. of Am., Riverside Athletic Assn., Am. Legion, VFW (Law Enforcement Officer of Yr. 1986), Command Coll. Alumni Assn. (bd. dirs.), U. Calif.-Riverside Athletic Assn., Athletic Express Track Club (Male Athlete of Yr. 1985, 87) (Riverside), Athletic Congress (Masters All-Am. for 5,000- and 10,000-meter run 1988, Masters Nat. Champion 3000 meters indoor track and field 1989). Republican. Roman Catholic. Office: 4102 Orange St Riverside CA 92501

FIKE, GARY EDWARD, real estate appraiser; b. Las Vegas, Jan. 7, 1951; s. M. Edward and Doris Alene (Stewart) Taylor F.; m. Dee Jane Campbell, July 24, 1980 (div. May 21, 1986); children: Jason, Orion, Paul. BA, U.S. Internat. U., 1973. Title officer Lawyers Title, Las Vegas, 1973-84; real estate licenses Nev. Properties, Las Vegas, 1976-79; mortgage broker Priority Mortgage & Investment, Las Vegas, 1983-84; real estate appraiser R. Scott Dugan Appraisal Co., Las Vegas, 1985-88, Gary E. Fike Appraisal Co., Las Vegas, 1988—. Mem. Soc. Real Estate Appraisers, Recovery Road, Inc. (sec. treas. 1987—). Home: 213 Veeder Dr Las Vegas NV 89128 Office: Real Estate Appraisal 50 S Jones Suite 201 Las Vegas NV 89107

FILES, GORDON LOUIS, lawyer, judge; b. Ft. Dodge, Iowa, Mar. 5, 1912; s. James Ray and Anna (Louis) F.; m. Kathryn Thrift, Nov. 24, 1942; children: Kathryn Lacey, James Gordon. A.B. in Polit. Sci. with honors, UCLA, 1934; LL.B., Yale U., 1937. Bar: Calif., U.S. Supreme Ct. Law clk. U.S. Ct. Appeals (8th cir.), 1937-38; enforcement atty. Office Price Adminstrn., 1942; ptnr. Freston & Files, Los Angeles, 1938-59; judge Los Angeles Superior Ct., 1959-62; assoc. justice 2d dist., div. 4 Calif. Ct. Appeal, 1962-64, presiding justice, 1964-82, adminstrv. presiding justice, 1970-82; arbitrator, referee and mediator, 1982-86; mem. Jud. Council Calif., 1964-71, 73-77; mem. governing com. Ctr. for Jud. Edn. and Research, 1981-82; mem. bd. govs. State Bar Calif., 1957-59. Mem. bd. editors Yale Law Jour., 1935-37. Served to lt. USN, 1942-45. Fellow Am. Bar Found.; mem. ABA, Am. Judicature Soc., Inst. Jud. Adminstrn., Los Angeles County Bar Assn. (trustee 1952-56), Calif. Judges Assn. (exec. com. 1971-72), Am. Legion, Order of Coif, Phi Beta Kappa, Phi Delta Phi. Democrat. Clubs: Chancery (pres. 1972-73) (Los Angeles); Valley Hunt (Pasadena). Home: 154 S Arroyo Blvd Pasadena CA 91105

FILES, JAMES LINCOLN, editor; b. Barnhill, Ill., Sept. 18, 1946; s. James Vernon and Dorothy May (Atteberry) F.; m. Margaret Kay Bryan, Nov. 22, 1971; 1 child, Steven. BS, U. Ill., 1972. Editor Village Publ., Bourbonnais, Ill., 1975-76, The Weekly Newspaper, Glenwood Springs, Colo., 1976-83; gen. mgr. TV Guam Mag., Tamuning, Guam, 1983-86; news editor Mobridge (S.D.) Tribune, 1987; editor Apache Junction (Ariz.) Ind., 1987—. Contbr. articles, book revs., poems to numerous publs. Cpl. USMC, 1966-69. Recipient Fiction Writing award Nat. Endowment for Arts, 1983, Rocky Mountain Writers Forum, 1977, Mary Roberts Rinehart Found., 1972. Mem. Ariz. Press Club, Ariz. Press Assn., Colo. Press Assn. (chmn. ethics com. 1983), Nat. Newspaper Assn. Home: 210 W Apache Trail Ste 708 Apache Junction AZ 85220 Office: Apache Junction Ind 2066 W Apache Tr Ste 109 Apache Junction AZ 85220

FILEVICH, BASIL, bishop; b. Jan. 13, 1918. Ord. priest, Roman Catholic church, 1942. Consecrated bishop Ukrainian Eparchy of Saskatoon, Sask., Can., 1984. Office: Bishop's Residence, 866 Saskatchewan Crescent E, Saskatoon, SK Canada S7N 0L4 *

FILIPELLO, DAVID VERN, acupuncturist, researcher; b. Lodi, Calif., May 15, 1952; s. Ferrer and Mildred Filipello; m. Geraldine Joan De Stefano, June 6, 1973; children: Ananda Cessina, Alexeis Mikel. BS, Paideia U., Berkeley, Calif., 1980; cert. acupuncture and Oriental medicine, San Francisco Coll., 1986. Cert. acupuncturist. Tchr. San Francisco Coll. Acupuncture and Oriental Medicine, 1986; pvt. practice Santa Rosa, Calif., 1986—; acupuncture assoc. Dr. Mason Shen, Livermore and Danville, Calif., 1988—; researcher San Francisco AIDS Initiative, 1987—. Mem. Am. Assn. Acupuncture and Oriental Medicine, Calif. Acupuncture Assn., Sonoma Oriental Medicine Assn. Democrat. Home: 1017 Benton St Santa Rosa CA 95404 Office: Pain and Stress Clinic 919 San Ramon Valley Blvd Danville CA 94550

FILIZETTI, GARY JOHN, construction executive; b. Neguanee, Mich., June 22, 1945; s. John and Edna (Jandron) F. BS, Santa Clara U., 1967, MBA in Commerce, 1969. Project mgr., estimator Carl N. Swenson Co. Inc., San Jose, Calif., 1976-80; v.p. Devcon Constrn. Inc., Milpitas, Calif., 1980-86, pres., 1986—. Served to 1st lt. U.S. Army, 1970-71.

FILLET, ROBERT E., investment banker, research psychologist; b. N.Y.C., Nov. 29, 1921; s. Maxwell Edward and Fan (Palley) F.; m. Barbara Auerbach (div. 1969); children: Mitchell H, Andrea Sara. MetD, 1976; BBA cum laude, Nat. U., San Diego, 1978; MA, U. Humanistic Study, 1979, PhD, 1981; ThD in Metaphysics, Fathers of St. Thomas, Imperial Beach, Calif., 1981; student, Columbia U., NYU. Fin. and mgmt. cons. numerous orgns. and govts., N.J., Ill., N.Y.C., Haiti, Republic of Korea, Pakistan, 1948—; pres., founder U.S. China C. of C., Washington, 1972-79; also cons. U.S. Congress and Senate regarding China's comml. and econ. relations., Washington, 1972-76; pres. Fillet Capital Corp., Los Angeles, 1976—; instr. San Diego State U.; prof. U. Humanistic Studies; bd. dirs. Fillet Livestock Corp., Middleton, Idaho, Alverca Aerotek Internat., Lisbon, Portugal; joint venture ptnr. Nat. Housing Ptnrs.; chmn. bd. dirs. Am. Renewal Co.; asst. chmn. Heartland Energy Corp.; chmn. bd. dirs. Insulock Mfg. Corp. So. Calif.; real estate developer. Mem. acad. adv. bd. Nat. U., San Diego; com. mem. Tarrytown chpt. Boy Scouts Am. Decorated D.F.C., Air medal, Purple Heart; recipient Silver Star award Am. Legion. Mem. Mental Health Assn. (chmn. speakers bur. San Diego chpt.), Am. Mgmt. Inst. Home: 23 Northampton Ct Newport Beach CA 92660 Office: 24 Balboa Coves Newport Beach CA 92663

FILLEY, BETTE ELAINE, computer software manufacturing executive; b. Phila., June 4, 1933; d. Russell S. and Martha (Spayd) Riley; m. Laurence D. Filley, Oct. 23, 1954; children: Richard David, Barbara Nan Filley Hamilton, Patricia Lynn Filley Messenger, Kathryn Gwyn, Thomas John. Columnist, editor Johnstown (Ohio) Independent, 1957-60; illustrator, columnist Chgo. Sun-Times, 1959-60; publs. editor Sicks Rainier Brewing Co., Seattle, 1962-66; pub. Silent Majority Voice, Seattle, 1971-73; pres. The Name People, Issaquah, Wash., 1985—; freelance writer, editor Seattle, 1966—; caricature artist, various events, 1972—. Mem. Wash. Press Women, Pacific Northwest Indsl. Editors, Am. Name Soc., Can. Soc. for Study of Names, Wash. Software Assn. Republican. Home and Office: The Name People 19801 SE 123d St Issaquah WA 98027

FILLMORE, WILLIAM L., lawyer. m. Mary Rawson; six children. BA in English Lit. magna cum laude, Brigham Young U., 1972; JD, U. Chgo., 1976. Bar: Colo., Utah, U.S. Ct. Appeals (10th cir.), U.S. Supreme Ct. Assoc. Holland & Hart, Denver, 1976-78; ptnr. Southam & Fillmore P.C., Colorado Springs, 1978-80, Olson & Hoggan, Logan, Utah, 1980-86; assoc. gen. counsel, asst. corp. sec. Brigham Young U., Provo, Utah, 1986—; instr. honors program Utah State U., 1982-84. Mem. platform com. Utah Reps., 1984; vice chmn. for Cache County (Utah) Rep. Com., 1983-86; intern White House, 1973. Hinckley scholar Brigham Young U., U. Chgo. Law Sch. scholar. Mem. ABA, Colo. Bar. Assn., Assn. Trial Lawyers Am., Nat. Assn. of Coll. and Univ. Lawyers, Legal Aid Soc., Brigham Young U. Alumni Assn. (bd. dirs. 1986—), Phi Kappa Phi. Home: 4105 N Devonshire Dr Provo UT 84604 Office: Brigham Young U Gen Counsel's Office A-357 ASB Provo UT 84602

FILOSA, GARY FAIRMONT RANDOLPH DE VIANA, II, private investor; b. Wilder, Vt., Feb. 22, 1931; s. Gary F.R. de Marco de Viana and Rosaline M. (Falzarano) Filosa; divorced; children: Marc Christian Bazire de Villadon, III, Gary Fairmont Randolph de Viana, III. Grad., Mt. Hermon Sch., 1950; PhB, U. Chgo., 1954; BA, U. Americas, Mex., 1967; MA, Calif. Western U., 1968; PhD, U.S. Internat. U., 1970. Sports reporter Claremont Daily Eagle, Rutland Herald, Vt. Informer, 1947-52; pub. The Chicagoan, 1952-54; account exec., editor house publs. Robertson, Buckley & Gotsch, Inc., Chgo., 1953-54; account exec. Fuller, Smith & Ross, Inc., N.Y.C., 1955; editor Apparel Arts mag. (now Gentlemen's Quar.), Esquire, Inc., N.Y.C., 1955-56; pres., chmn. bd. Teenarama Records, Inc., N.Y.C., 1956-62; pres., chmn. bd. Filosa Publs. Internat., N.Y.C., 1956-61, Los Angeles, 1974-83, Palm Beach, Fla., 1983-88; pres. Montclair Sch., 1958-60, Pacific Registry, Inc., Los Angeles, 1959-61, Banana Chip Corp. Am., N.Y.C., 1964-67; producer Desilu Studios, Inc., Hollywood, 1960-61; exec. asst. to Benjamin A. Javits, 1961-62; dean adminstrn. Postgrad. Ctr. for Mental Health, N.Y.C., 1962-64; chmn. bd., pres. Producciones Mexicanes Internationales (S.A.), Mexico City, 1957-68; chmn. bd., pres. Filosa Films Internat., Beverly Hills, 1962-83, Palm Beach, Fla., 1984—; pres. Casa Filosa Corp., Palm Beach, Fla., 1982-87; dir. tng. Community Savings, North Palm Beach, Fla., 1983-87; chmn. bd., pres. Cinematografica Americana Internationale (S.A.), Mexico City, 1964-74; pub. Teenage, Rustic Rhythm, Teen Life, Talent, Rock & Roll Roundup, Celebrities, Stardust, Personalities, Campus monthly mags., N.Y.C., 1955-61; v.p. acad. affairs World Acad., San Francisco, 1967-68; asst. to provost Calif. Western U., San Diego, 1968-69; assoc. prof. philosophy Art Coll., San Francisco, 1969-70; v.p. acad. affairs, dean of faculty Internat. Inst., Phoenix, 1968-73; chmn. bd., pres. Universite Universelle, 1970-73; bd. dirs., v.p. acad. affairs, dean Summer Sch., Internat. Community Coll., Los Angeles, 1970-72; chmn. bd., pres. Social Directory Calif., 1967-75, Am. Assn. Social Registries, Los Angeles, 1970-76; pres. Social Directory U.S., N.Y.C., 1974-76; chmn. bd. Internat. Assn. Social Registers, Paris, 1974—; surfing coach U. Calif. at Irvine, 1975-77; instr. history Coastline Community Coll., Fountain Valley, Calif., 1976-77; v.p. Xerox-Systemic, 1979-80; pres., chief exec. officer Internat. Surfing League, Palm Beach, 1987—; pres., chief exec. officer Filosa Harrop Internat., Phoenix, 1987-89. Editor: Sci. Digest, 1961-62. Author: (stage play) Let Me Call Ethel, 1955, Technology Enters 21st Century, 1966, musical Feather Light, 1966, No Public Funds for Nonpublic Schools, 1968, Creative Function of the College President, 1969, The Surfers Almanac, 1977, Payne of Florida (TV series), 1985, The Filosa Newsletter, 1986—, Conversations With America (TV series), 1989—. Contbr. numerous articles to mags., and profl. jours. and encys. including Sci. Digest, World Book Ency., Ency. of Sports. Trustee Univ. of the Ams., 1986—; candidate for Los Angeles City Council, 1959; chmn. Educators for Reelection of Ivy Baker Priest, 1970; mem. So. Calif. Com. for Olympic Games, 1977-84. Served with AUS, 1954-55. Recipient DAR Citizenship award, 1959; Silver Conquistador award Am. Assn. Social Registers, 1970; Ambassador's Cup U. Ams., 1967; resolution Calif. Legislature, 1977; Duke Kahanamoku Classic surfing trophy, 1977; gold pendant Japan Surfing Assn., 1978. Mem. Am. Surfing Assn. (founder, pres. 1960—), Internat. Surfing Com. (founder, pres. 1960—), U.S. Surfing Com. (founder, pres. 1960—), Am. Walking Soc. (founder, pres. 1980—), Internat. Walking Soc. (founder, pres. 1987—), Am. Assn. UN, Authors League, Alumni Assn. U. Americas (pres. 1967-70), Sierra Club, NAACP, NCAA (bd. dels. 1977-82), AAU (gov. 1978-82), Sigma Omicron Lambda (founder, pres. 1965—). Democrat. Episcopalian. Clubs: Embajadores (U. of Americas,.); Palm Beach Surf (Fla); Coral Reef Soc. (Palm Beach). Home: PO Box 3432 Palm Beach FL 33480 also: PO Box 1315 Beverly Hills CA 90213 also: PO Box 1315 Beverly Hills CA 90213

FILUK, ROBERT BRUCE, physician; b. Winnipeg, Man., Can., Sept. 17, 1955; s. Bruce Filuk and Orysia (Melnychuk) F. MD, U. Ottawa, Ont., 1980. Diplomate Am. Bd. Internal Medicine; cert. Royal Coll. of Can. Internal Medicine, Respiratory Medicine. Intern U. Toronto, Ont., 1980-81, medical resident, 1981-83; pulmonary fellow U. Man., Winnipeg, 1983-85, med. researcher, 1985-87; lectr. Dept. Medicine Stanford U., Palo Alto, Calif., 1987—; chest cons. San Jose (Calif.) Med. Group, 1987—; chief pulmonary medicine and intensive care San Jose Med. Group, 1988—. Contbr. articles to profl. jours. Fellow Am. Coll. Chest Physicians, Royal Coll. Physicians Can.; mem. ACP, Am. Thoracic Soc., Calif. Thoracic Soc, Ont. Med. Assn., Can. Med. Assn., Alpha Omega alpha (pres. 1978-79). Home: 18400 OverlooK Rd #32 Los Gatos CA 95030 Office: San Jose Med Group 45 S 17th St San Jose CA 95112

FINAN, ELLEN CRANSTON, English language educator, consultant; b. Worcester, Mass., June 26, 1951; d. Thomas Matthew and Maureen Ann (Moulton) F. BA, U. San Francisco, 1973; MA, U. Calif., Riverside, 1978. ESL specialist U.S. Peace Corps, Finote Selam, Ethiopia, 1974-75; English instr. U. Redlands, Calif., 1977-79; mentor tchr. Jurupa Unified Sch. Dist., Riverside, 1979—; tech. writer Callan Assocs., San Francisco, 1973-74, Wilshire Assocs., Santa Monica, Calif., 1976-77; English instr. U. Pa., Phila., 1979; writing cons. Inland Area Writing Project U. Calif., Riverside, 1980—; tchr., coordinator U. Calif., Riverside, 1982. Author: Prickley Pear, 1981, CAP Attack Handbook, 1987. NEH fellow, 1985; Squaw Valley Community of Writers scholar, 1981, Carnegie Mellon fellow, 1987, NEH Inst. fellow, 1988. Mem. Nat. Council English Tchrs., Assn. Supervision and Curriculum Devel., Alpha Sigma Nu, Phi Delta Kappa. Democrat. Mem. Unitarian Ch. Home: 23607 Whispering Winds Moreno Valley CA 92388 Office: Jurupa Unified Schs 4250 Opal Riverside CA 92509

FINCH, SAMUEL PRESTLEY, III, systems engineer; b. Pitts., Mar. 31, 1942; s. Samuel Prestley Jr. and Mary Elizabeth (Booth) F.; m. Sarah Weidner, June 3, 1964 (div. Aug. 1974); children: Lucy Garnett, Sarah Elizabeth; m. Andrea Gudahl, Aug. 29, 1975; 1 child, Nicole Samantha. BS in Engring., USAF Acad., 1964; MS in Chemistry, U. Calif., Riverside, 1973. Commd. 2d lt. USAF, 1964, advanced through grades to lt. col., 1980, ret., 1985; asst. prof. chemistry USAF Acad., 1973-77; asst. chief tng. div. 43d Strategic Wing, Anderson AFB, Guam, 1977-79; chief mission devel. 319 Bomb Wing, Grand Forks AFB, N.D., 1979-81; research assoc. Air Power Research Inst., Maxwell AFB, Ala., 1981-83; comdr. det. 3 Field Command Def. Nuclear Agy., Los Alamos, N.Mex., 1983-85; systems engr., ops. research scientist, dep. dept. mgr. Lockheed Aero. Systems Co., Burbank, 1985—. Mem. Air Force Assn., Ret. Officers Assn., Assn. USAF Acad. Graduates, Air War Coll. Grads.

FINCH, THOMAS WESLEY, corrosion engineer; b. Alhambra, Calif., Dec. 17, 1946; s. Charles Phillip and Marian Louisa (Bushey) F.; m. Jinx L. Heath, Apr. 1979. Student Colo. Sch. Mines, 1964-68. Assayer, prospector Raymond P. Heon, Inc., Idaho Springs, Colo., 1968; corrosion engr. Cathodic Protection Service, Denver, 1973-80, area mgr., Lafayette, La., 1980-81; area mgr. Corrintec/USA, Farmington, N.Mex., 1981-83; dist. mgr. Cathodic Protection Services Co., Farmington, 1983—. Served with C.E., U.S. Army, 1968-72. Mem. Nat. Assn. Corrosion Engrs., Soc. Am. Mil. Engrs., U.S. Ski Assn., Am. Security Council (nat. adv. bd. 1978—), Kappa Sigma. Republican. Lutheran. Home: 1710 E 22d St Farmington NM 87401 Office: PO Box 388 Farmington NM 87499

FINCHER, ARVEL LAWRENCE, university official; b. Chattanooga, Aug. 14, 1934; s. Arvel Luther and Lois Genevieve (Smith) F.; m. Marian Louise Moulton, June 16, 1957; children: Katherine Anne, David Lawrence. BS, U. Tenn., 1956; MS, Vanderbilt U., 1958; PhD, U. Mich., 1969. Asst. prof. physics U. Tenn., Chattanooga, 1961-66; asst. v.p. state relations and planning U. Mich., Ann Arbor, Mich., 1969-78, assoc. v.p. acad. affairs, 1978-80; vice chancellor U. N.C., Greensboro, N.C., 1980-86; vice provost U. Oreg., Eugene, Oreg., 1986--. 1st lt. U.S. Army, 1958-60. Mem. AAAS, AAUP, Am. Assn. Higher Edu., Soc. Coll. and U. Planning, Assn. Instl. Research. Home: 2585 Charnelton St Eugene OR 97405 Office: U Oreg 103 Johnson Hall Eugene OR 97403

FINCK, PETER KEVIN, lawyer; b. Portsmouth, N.H., Apr. 27, 1951; s. Curt Reinhardt and Marie-Margaret (Lunt) F.; m. Karin Elizabeth Pettersson, June 20, 1986. BA, U. Calif., Berkeley, 1973; JD, U. San Diego, 1978; postgrad., Inst. Air and Space Law, McGill U., 1983—. Bar: Calif. 1978. Dep. atty. City of Oakland, Calif., 1979-83; pvt. practice Oakland, 1983--; asst. to pres. on environ. concerns Grange Debris Box & Wrecking Co., Inc., San Rafael, Calif., 1986--. Mem. Nat. Space Soc., Calif. Bar Assn. Home: 922 Everett Ave Oakland CA 94602 Office: 2021 Francisco Blvd San Rafael CA 94901

FINDLEY, JAMES E., corporate executive; b. Capulin, N.Mex., Apr. 11, 1923; s. Thomas Lee and Gladys Marion (Childress) F.; m. Neva Joy Hansen (dec.); children: Sharon, Susan, Peggy, James Jr.; m. Ginger Marie Taylor, 1969. BS, Wash. State U., 1949; postgrad., UCLA, 1956-58. Missile test conductor Gen. Dynamics, San Diego, 1952-54, chief ops. control, 1960-61; supr. missile div. Firestone Tire & Rubber Co., Southgate, Calif., 1954-56; chief new bus. Northrop Corp., Hawthorne, Calif., 1956-60; pres., chief exec. officer Tex. Tech. Products, Lubbock, 1961-67; mgr. Boeing Co., Seattle, 1967-78, Power Systems, Inc., Schaumburg, Ill., 1978-83; pres., chief exec. officer Global Tech. Internat., Inc., Mukilteo, Wash., 1985—, Maverick Microsystems Internat., Inc., Mukilteo, 1984—. Author: A New Way to Schedule Production, 1956. Served to comdr. USN, 1941-52, Korea. Decorated Purple Heart, Navy Cross. Mem. Am. Inst. Indsl. Engrs. (sr.), Am. Soc. Quality Control (sr.), Wash. State Software Bd. (exec. bd. 1987—), Am. Mgmt. Assn. Republican. Baptist. Club: Wash. State Athletic. Lodge: Elks (Newport). Home: 13521 103rd Ave NE Arlington WA 98223

FINE, DANIEL MATTHEW, advertising executive; b. Detroit, Jan. 28, 1959; s. Herbert Leslie Fine and Constance Marilyn Gonek; m. Kim Marie Hadam, Aug. 8, 1987. BA, Wash. State U., 1982; grad., Inst. Advanced Advt. Studies, 1985. Sr. planner Scali, McCabe, Sloves, N.Y.C., 1982-84; media supr. Levine, Huntley, Schmidt & Beaver, N.Y.C., 1984-86; dir. mktg. services WBA, Inc., Seattle, 1986-88; owner, mgr. Fine Advt., Seattle, 1988—; chmn. pub. services AD 2, N.Y.C., 1984-85. Mem. Am. Mktg. Assn., Am. Advt. Fedn., Advt. Club Seattle. Democrat. Jewish. Home: 1221 Queen Anne Ave N Apt #201 Seattle WA 98109 Office: Fine Advt 1904 3d Ave Seattle WA 98101

FINE, RICHARD ISAAC, lawyer; b. Milw., Jan. 22, 1940; s. Jack and Frieda F.; m. Maryellen Olman, Nov. 25, 1982; 1 child, Victoria Elizabeth. B.S., U. Wis., 1961; J.D., U. Chgo., 1964; Ph.D. in Internat. Law, U. London, 1967; cert., Hague (Netherlands) Acad. Internat. Law, 1965, 66; cert. comparative law, Internat. U. Comparative Sci., Luxembourg, 1966; diplome superiere, Faculte Internat. pour l'Ensignment du Droit Compare, Strasbourg, France, 1967. Bar: Ill. 1964, D.C. 1972, Calif. 1973. Trial atty. fgn. commerce sect. antitrust div. U.S. Dept. Justice, 1968-72; chief antitrust div. Los Angeles City Atty.'s Office, also spl. counsel gov. efficiency com., 1973-74; prof. internat., comparative and EEC antitrust law U. Syracuse (N.Y.) Law Sch. (overseas program), summers 1970-72; individual practice Richard I. Fine and Assocs., Los Angeles, 1974; mem. antitrust adv. bd. Bur. Nat. Affairs, 1981—. Contbr. articles to legal publs. Mem. ABA (chmn. subcom. internat. antitrust and trade regulations, internat. law sect. 1972-77, co-chmn. com. internat. econ. orgn. 1977-79), Am. Soc. Internat. Law (co-chmn. com. corp. membership 1978-83, mem. exec. council 1984-87, devel. com. 1988—), Am. Fgn. Law Assn., Fed. Bar Assn., Internat. Law Assn., Brit. Inst. Internat. and Comparative Law, State Bar Calif. (chmn. antitrust and trade regulation law sect. 1981-84, exec. com. 1981-87), Retinitis Pigmentosa Internat. (bd. dirs. 1985—), Los Angeles County Bar Assn. (chmn. antitrust sect. 1977-78), Ill. Bar Assn., Am. Friends London Sch. Econs. (bd. dirs. 1984—, co-chmn. So. Calif. chpt. 1984—), Phi Delta Phi. Office: 10100 Santa Monica Blvd Ste 1000 Los Angeles CA 90067

FINEGAN, JACK, humanities educator; b. Des Moines, July 11, 1908; s. Henry Mentor and Clarissa Artemisia (Chestnut) F.; m. Mildred Catherine Meader, Sept. 4, 1934; 1 child, Jack Richard. BA, Drake U., 1928, MA, 1929, BD, 1930; BD, Colgate Rochester Div. Sch., 1931, MTh, 1932; lic. theol., U. Berlin, 1934; LLD (hon.), Drake U., 1953; LittD (hon.), Chapman Coll., 1964. Pastor First Christian Ch., Ames, Iowa, 1934-39, U. Christian Ch., Berkeley, Calif., 1949-74; prof. religious edn. Iowa State U., Ames, 1939-46; prof. New Testament Hist., Archeology Pacific Sch. of Religion, Berkeley, Calif., 1946-75; humanities instr. Sierra Nev. Coll., Incline Village, 1987—. Author: The Archeology of the New Testament, The Mediterranean World of Early Christian Apostles, 1981, Discovering Israel, An Archeological Guide to the Holy Land, 1981, Tibet--A Dreamt of Image, 1986, and others. Retreat leader Army, Navy, Marine and Air Force Chaplains, Korea, Okinawa, Japan, 1962. Recipient Fulbright Research Scholarship, Indian Museum, Calcutta, India. Republican. Mem. Christian Ch. Office: Pacific Sch of Religion 1798 Scenic Ave Berkeley CA 94709

FINERTY, JAMES PATRICK, telecommunications network designer; b. Long Beach, Calif., June 3, 1945; s. James Winfred and Juanita (Denton) F. BA in Biophysics, Amherst Coll., 1967; MA in Biology, Yale U., 1969, PhD in Biology, 1972. Tech. specialist communications network design AT&T, San Francisco, L.A., Cin. and Boston, 1979—. Author: Population Ecology of Cycles in Small Mammals, 1981; contbr. articles to profl. jours. Fellow chaos studies Santa Fe Inst., N.Mex., 1988, sci., tech. and soc. Andrew Mellon Found., MIT, 1988-89. Office: AT&T 795 Folsom Rm 310 San Francisco CA 94107

FINESILVER, SHERMAN GLENN, judge; b. Denver, Oct. 1, 1927; s. Harry M. and Rebecca M. (Balaban) F.; m. Annette Warren, July 23, 1954; children: Jay Mark, Steven Brad, Susan Lynn. B.A., U. Colo., 1949; LL.B., U. Denver, 1952; certificate, Northwestern U. Traffic Inst., 1956; LL.D. (hon.), Gallaudet Coll., Washington, 1970. Bar: Colo. 1952, U.S. Supreme Ct 1952, U.S. Ct. of Appeals 1952, 10th Circuit, U.S. Dist. Ct. Legal asst. Denver City Atty.'s Office, 1949-52; asst. Denver city atty. 1952-55; judge Denver County Ct., 1955-62; judge Denver Dist. Ct., 2d Jud. Dist., 1962-71, presiding judge domestic relations div., 1963, 67, 68; judge U.S. Dist. Ct., Denver, from 1971, now chief judge; Faculty Denver Opportunity Sch., 1949-54, U. Denver Coll. Law and Arts and Sci. Sch., 1955—; Faculty Westminster Law Sch., 1955-61, Nat. Coll. Judiciary, Reno, 1967—, Atty. Gen.'s Advocacy Inst., Washington, 1974—, seminars for new fed. judges, 1974—; cons. HEW, 1958-62. Author: Model Law for Interpreters in Court Proceedings, 1968, Protect Your Life-Wise Words for Women, 1969, Timely Tips When Disaster Strikes-No Second Chance, 1970; Contbr.: chpt. to Epilepsy Rehabilitation, 1974; Editor: chpt. to Proceedings Nat. Symposium on the Deaf, Driving and Employability, 1964; Contbg. editor: chpt. to Lawyers Coop. Pub. Co, Rochester, N.Y., 1958-60, Teaching Driver and Traffic Safety Education, 1965; Contbr. articles to profl. jours. Founder Denver Driver Improvement Sch., 1959, dir., 1959-71; chmn. Denver Citizenship Day, 1967; organizer Denver Youth Council, 1968; dir. leadership conf. Neighborhood Youth Corps, 1969; mem. Pres.'s Task Force on Hwy. Safety, 1969-71; mem. advisory com. Nat. Hwy. Traffic Safety Adminstrn., Dept. Transp., 1969-72; mem. task force White House Conf. on Aging, 1972; chmn. Gov.'s Adv. Com. on Hwy. Safety, 1960-71; commr. Gov.'s Commn. on Aging, 1967-71; mem. nat. youth commn. B'nai B'rith, 1970-74; Pres. Jewish Family and Childrens Service of Colo., 1962-64; bd. dirs. Nat. Council Orgns. Serving Deaf, Washington, 1968-71; trustee Am. Med. Center, Denver, 1960-72. Decorated Knight Comdr. Ct. of Honor K.C.,

Rocky Mountain Consistory, 1967; recipient numerous awards including citation Nat. Safety Council, 1958, Paul Gray Hoffman award Automotive Safety Found., 1960, spl. award N.Am. Judges Assn., merit award Colo. Assn. Deaf and Nat. Soc. Deaf, 1966, Service to Mankind award Denver Sertoma Club, 1969, Freedoms Found. award, 1969, medallion for outstanding service by a non-handicapped person to physically disabled Nat. Paraplegia Found., 1972, certificate of commendation Sec. Transp., 1974, numerous others. Mem. ABA (nat. chmn. Am. citizenship com. 1968, award of merit Law Day 1968), Colo. Bar Assn. (chmn. Law Day 1964, chmn. Am. citizenship com. 1963), Denver Bar Assn. (chmn. Law Day 1964), Am. Judicature Soc., Hebrew Ednl. Alliance, Allied Jewish Community Council, Phi Sigma Delta (trustee 1960-66); mem. B'nai B'rith. Clubs: Mason (Shriner), Am. Amateur Radio. Office: US Dist Ct 1929 Stout St Rm C-236 Denver CO 80294 *

FINGARETTE, HERBERT, philosopher, educator; b. Bklyn., Jan. 20, 1921; m. Leslie J. Swabacker, Jan. 23, 1945; 1 dau., Ann Hasse. B.A., UCLA, 1947, Ph.D., 1949. Mem. faculty U. Calif.-Santa Barbara, 1948—, Phi Beta Kappa Romanell prof. philosophy, 1983—; William James lectr. religion Harvard U., 1971; W.T. Jones lectr. philosophy Pomona Coll., 1974; Evans-Wentz lectr. Oriental religions Stanford U., 1977; Gramlich lectr. human nature Dartmouth Coll., 1978; cons. NEH; Raphael Demos lectr. Vanderbilt U., 1985; Disting. tchr. U. Calif.-Santa Barbara, 1985, faculty research lectr., 1977. Author: The Self in Transformation, 1963, On Responsibility, 1967, Self Deception, 1969, Confucius: The Secular as Sacred, 1972, The Meaning of Criminal Insanity, 1972, Mental Disabilities and Criminals Responsibility, 1979, Heavy Drinking: The Myth of Alcoholism as a Disease, 1988. Washington and Lee U. Lewis law scholar, 1980; fellow NEH, NIMH, Walter Meyer Law Research Inst., Battelle Research Ctr., Addiction Research Ctr., Inst. Psychiatry, London; fellow Ctr. for Advanced Studies in Behavioral Sci., Stanford, 1985-86. Mem. Am. Philos. Assn. (pres. Pacific div. 1977-78). Home: 1507 APS Santa Barbara CA 93103 Office: U Calif Dept Philosophy Santa Barbara CA 93106

FINGER, DIAMON LEE, mining company executive; b. Lakeland, Fla., Aug. 14, 1927; s. Diamon L. and Elsie Marie (Reynolds) F.; m. Mafrie Louise Higgins, May 27, 1946; children: Ronald, Robert, Susan, Richard. Student, Fla. So. Coll., 1960. Gen. mgr. Theiss Peabody Mitsui, Australia, 1967-73; v.p., gen. mgr. Fla. Crushed Stone, Brooksville, Fla., 1973-74; dir. mine ops. Morrison-Knudsen Co., Inc., Boise, Idaho, 1974-77, gen. mgr. region/div., 1977-79, v.p. ops., mining, 1979-82, v.p. mine devel., ops., 1982-83, group v.p. mining, 1983-85, sr. v.p. mining, 1985—; pres. Kanawha Mining Co., Cannelton, W.Va., Atascosa Mining Co., Jourdanton, Tex., Navasota Mining Co., Carlos, Tex., Limecrest Mining Co., Newton, N.J.; bd. dirs. Westmoreland Resources, Billings, Mont. Mem. Am. Inst. Mining Engrs. Office: Morrison-Knudsen Co Inc 720 Park Blvd Boise ID 83712

FINGER, JOHN HOLDEN, lawyer; b. Oakland, Calif., June 29, 1913; s. Clyde P. and Jennie (Miller) F.; m. Dorothy C. Riley, Dec. 30, 1950; children: Catherine, John Jr., David, Carol. A.B., U. Calif., 1933. Bar: Calif. 1937. Pvt. practice of law San Francisco, 1937-42; chief mil. commn. sect. Far East Hdqrs. War Dept., Tokyo, 1946-47; mem. firm Hoberg Finger Brown Cox & Molligan, San Francisco, 1947—; trustee Pacific Sch. Religion, bd. chmn., 1969-78; bd. dirs. Calif. Maritime Acad., San Francisco Legal Aid Soc., 1955-70; bd. visitors Judge Adv. Gen. Sch., Charlottesville, Va., 1964-76, Stanford U. Law Sch., 1969-71. Pres. Laymen's Fellowship, No. Calif. Conf. Congl. Chs., 1951-53, moderator, 1954-55. Served to maj. JAGC AUS, 1942-46; col. Res. ret.; comdg. officer 5th Judge Adv. Gen. Detachment, 1962-64; U.S. Army Judiciary, 1967-68. Decorated Legion of Merit. Fellow Am. Bar Found., Am. Coll. Trial Lawyers; mem. Am. Judicature Soc., Am. Bar Assn. (ho. of dels. 1970-78, council jud. adminstrn. div. 1972-77, standing com. assn. communications), Bar Assn. San Francisco (dir. 1960-62, recipient John A. Sutro award for legal excellence 1980), Judge Adv. Assn. (dir. 1957—, pres. 1964-65), Lawyers Club San Francisco (pres. 1953, dir. 1950—), State Bar Calif. (bd. govs. 1965-68, pres. 1967-68), Sierra Club (exec. com. legal def. fund), Phi Alpha Delta, Sigma Phi Epsilon, Alpha Kappa Phi. Home: 12675 Skyline Blvd Oakland CA 94619 Office: Hoberg Finger Brown Cox & Milligan 703 Market St San Francisco CA 94103

FINGER, PHILLIP REID, college administrator; b. St. Joseph, Mo., Feb. 9, 1941; s. Henry Reid and Norma Laura (Van Buskirk) F.; BA, U. Wash., 1963; MBA, Central Mo. U., 1974; m. Dorothy Ann Lund, Sept. 4, 1977; children: Derek Reid, Kevin Donald, James Edward. Sr. personnel asst. Seattle City Light, 1969-72; media technician III, Bellevue (Wash.) Community Coll., 1976-77, fin. aid supr., 1977-78, asst. dir.-fin. aid, 1978-79; asst. dir. fin. aid N. Seattle Community Coll., 1979-81; dir. fin. aid Yakima Valley Community Coll., 1981-87, Shoreline Community Coll., 1987—. Served in USAF, 1964-68; Vietnam. Mem. Wash. Fin. Aid Assn. (exec. com.), Nat. Assn. Student Fin. Aid Adminstrs., Western Assn. Student Fin. Aid Adminstrs., Wash. Assn. Community Coll. Fin. Aid Adminstrs., Assn. Wash. Community Coll. Adminstrs., Wash. Council High Sch. and Coll. Relations. Office: 16101 Greenwood Ave N Seattle WA 98133

FINK, ALAN MARK, security company executive; b. L.A., Sept. 17, 1958; s. Eugene David and Barbara Felice (Atlas) F. Student, Humboldt State U., 1978; AS, Pierce Coll., 1979. Salesman Tandy Corp., Sherman Oaks, Calif., 1980-81; mgr. Tandy Corp., Woodland Hills, Calif., 1981-83; regional mgr. Tandy Corp., Seattle, 1983-85, Thermal Topp, Phoenix, 1985-86; dir. ops. Pactel Infosystems, Walnut Creek, Calif., 1986-88; v.p. ops. Just Security, Walnut Creek, 1988—. Fellow Internat. Franchise Assn.; mem. Am. Radio Relay League, Silicon Valley Entrepreneurs Club. Republican. Home: 105 Reflections Dr Apt 11 San Ramon CA 94583 Office: Just Security 3566 Investment Blvd Hayward CA 94545

FINK, JAMES BREWSTER, consulting geophysicist; b. Los Angeles, Jan. 12, 1943. BS in Geophysics and Geochemistry, U. Ariz., 1969; MS in Geophysics cum laude, U. Witwatersrand, Johannesburg, Transvaal, Republic of South Africa, 1980; PhD in Geol. Engring., Geohydrology, U. Ariz, 1989. Registered profl. engr., Ariz.; registered land surveyor. Geophysicist Geo-Comp Exploration, Inc., Tucson, 1969-70; geophys. cons. IFEX-Geotechnica, S.A., Hermosillo, Sonora, Mex., 1970; chief geophysicist Mining Geophys. Surveys, Tucson, 1971-72; research asst. U. Ariz., Tucson, 1973; cons. geophysics Tucson, 1974-76; sr. minerals geophysicist Esso Minerals Africa, Inc., Johannesburg, 1976-79; sr. research geophysicist Exxon Prodn. Research Co., Houston, 1979-80; pres. Geophynque Internat., Tucson, 1980—; cons. on NSF research U. Ariz., 1984-85, adj. lectr. geol. engring., 1985-86, assoc. instr. geophysics, 1986—, supr. geophysicist, geohydrologist, 1986—, bd. dirs. Lab. Advanced Subsurface Imaging, 1986; lectr. South African Atomic Energy Bd., Pelindaba, 1979. Contbr. articles to profl. jours. Served as sgt. U.S. Air NG, 1965-70. Named Airman of Yr., U.S. Air NG, 1967. Mem. Soc. Exploration Geophysicists (co-chmn. Houston chpt. 1980, Dallas chpt. 1981, co-editor IP monograph), Am. Geophys. Union, European Assn. Exploration Geophysicists, South African Geophys. Assn., Assn. Ground Water Scientists, Nat. Water Well Assn. (reviewer), Mineral and Geotech. Logging Soc., Assn. Petroleum Geochem. Explorationists, Ariz. Geol. Soc., Ariz. Computer Oriented Geol. Soc. (bd. dirs., v.p.), Mining Geophysicists Denver, Mensa, Intertel, Internat. Platform Assn. Republican. Home: 5865 S Old Spanish Tr Tucson AZ 85747 Office: Geophynque Internat 5865 S Old Spanish Trail Tucson AZ 85747

FINK, JOEL CHARLES, dermatologist; b. Lebanon, Pa., June 29, 1922; s. Isadore Harry and Rose (Cohn) F.; m. Selma Florence Fink, Dec. 28, 1946 (dec. Dec. 1979); children: Ellen, Myles, Janet, Bruce, Paul; m. Carol Kaplan, Aug. 31, 1980. BS, U. Ala., 1943; MD, U. Md., 1947. Diplomate Am. Bd. Dermatology. Commd. 1st lt. U.S. Army, 1950, advanced through grades to maj., 1954, resigned, 1954; intern Walter Reed Army Hosp., Washington, 1947-48, resident, 1948-50; resident Brooke Army Hosp., San Antonio, 1952-53; pvt. practice Smithtown, N.Y., 1955-82, Phoenix, 1982--. Fellow Am. Acad. Dermatology; mem. Phoenix Dermatology Soc. (pres. 1987--), Southwestern Dermatology Soc., Sonoran Dermatology Soc. Republican. Home: 9760 E San Salvador Dr Scottsdale AZ 85258 Office: 4232 E Cactus Rd Ste 205 Phoenix AZ 85032

FINK, JOSEPH RICHARDSON, college president; b. Newark, Mar. 20, 1940; s. Joseph Richard and Jean (Chorznay) F.; children: Michael, Taryn. AB, Rider Coll., 1961; PhD, Rutgers U., 1971; DLitt (hon.), Rider Coll., 1982. Asst. then assoc. prof history Immaculata (Pa.) Coll., 1964-72, adminstrv. asst. to pres., 1969-72; dean of Arts & Scis. City Colls. Chgo., 1972-74; pres. Somerset County Coll., Somerville, N.J., 1974-79, Coll. Misericordia, Dallas, 1979-88, Dominican Coll. of San Rafael, Calif., 1988—; cons., evaluator Commn. Higher Edn. Middle States Assn., 1975—; mem. nat. bd. cons. NEH; mem. Gov. Pa.'s adv. com. on block grants to edn., 1981-83; pres. Regional Planning Coun. Higher Edn., Region Three/Northeastern Pa., 1986-88. Pres. Greater Wilkes-Barre (Pa.) Coun. of Pres., 1982-87; exec. com. Philharmonic Soc. Northeastern Pa., 1986-89; bd. dirs. Marin Symphony, 1989—. Mem. Nat. Assn. Ind. Colls. and Univs. (secretariat mem. 1986), Nat. Assn. Intercollegiate Athletics (pres.'s adv. coun. 1986), Am. Coun. on Higher Edn. (acad. adminstrn. fellow 1974-75, commn. leadership devel. higher edn. 1978-82), Assn. Mercy Colls. (pres. 1985-87, exec. com. 1981—), Coun. for Ind. Colls., Found. Ind. Colls. of Pa. (exec. com. 1980-86), Northeastern Pa. Ind. Colls. Assn. (pres. 1981-82), Pa. Assn. Colls. and Univs. (govt. rels. com. 1980-84), Am. Hist. Assn., Westmoreland Club (Wilkes-Barre). Roman Catholic. Home: 2 Falmouth Cove San Rafael CA 94901 Office: Dominican Coll of San Rafael Grand Ave San Rafael CA 94901

FINK, ROBERT JAMES, newspaper editor; b. Tacoma, Mar. 13, 1948; s. Robert J. and Verla Mae (Bates) F.; m. Carol J. Silbernagel, Sept. 2, 1967; children—Melissa, Michael, Stephen. B.S. in Social Sci., St. Cloud State U., 1970. Sports editor Morning Pioneer, Mandan, N.D., 1967-68; Daily Times, St. Cloud, Minn., 1968-70; news editor Gazette-times, Corvallis, Oreg., 1970-73; news editor Press Democrat, Santa Rosa, Calif., 1973-82, mng. editor, 1982—. Office: The Press Democrat PO Box 569 Santa Rosa CA 95402 *

FINK, STEVEN B., public relations executive; b. Phila., Mar. 3, 1948; s. Samuel and Beatrice (Cooperman) F.; m. Harriet B. Braiker, Dec. 27, 1984; 1 child, Stuart. BA in Polit. Sci., Pa. State U., 1968; postgrad., Temple U., 1968-70. Pres. Fink & Assocs., Inc., Phila., 1975-79; dep. press sec. to Gov. of Pa., Harrisburg, 1979-81; v.p. Carl Terzian Assocs., Los Angeles, 1982-83; pres., chief exec. officer Lexicon Communications Corp., Los Angeles, 1983—. Author: Crisis Management: Planning for the Inevitable, 1986, The Hailing Sign, 1987; contbr. articles to profl. jours. Mem. Masons, Mac Sanders Brotherhood Lodge. Office: Lexicon Communications Corp 1880 Century Park E Ste 810 Los Angeles CA 90067

FINK, TERI ANN, librarian; b. Torrance, Calif., Oct. 10, 1955; d. Charles Leo and Ethel May (Krockenberger) Bellisine; m. Donald Edward Fink, Mar. 29, 1980. AA, Wenatchee (Wash.) Valley Coll., 1976; BA in Edn., Cen. Wash. U., 1978, MA in Edn., 1985. Cert. tchr., Wash. Tchr. English Quincy (Wash.) Sch. Dist., 1979-80; rsch. asst. tree and fruit rsch. Wash. State U., Wenatchee, 1980-81; circulation supr. Wenatchee Valley Coll., 1982-83, tech. svcs. coord., 1983-85, part-time instr. data processing, 1984-85; librarian Eastmont Sch. Dist., E. Wenatchee, Wash., 1985—; workshop instr. Seattle Pacific U., 1985; speaker Supt. of Pub. Instrn. Edn. Forum, Seattle, 1988. Contbg. author: Innovative Applications of Optical Disc Technology, 1989. Mem. N.W. Coun. for Computer Edn., Wash. Library Media Assn., Wash. Edn. Assn., NEA. Republican. Home: 215 39th NW East Wenatchee WA 98802 Office: Eastmont Sch Dist 460 NE 9th St East Wenatchee WA 98803

FINK, TOM, mayor. m. Pat Fink; 11 children. JD. Mem. Alaska Ho. of Reps., speaker, mem. fin. com.; mayor City of Anchorage, 1987—; owner ins. agy. Anchorage. Office: Office of Mayor PO Box 196650 Anchorage AK 99519

FINKELMAN, JAY MATTHEW, personnel, financial services executive; b. N.Y.C., Nov. 3, 1945; s. Milton and Florence (Sokolov) F.; m. Carin Lesley Wong, June 29, 1985. BA, CUNY, 1966, MBA, 1968; PhD, NYU, 1970. Lic. psychologist, N.Y., Calif.; diplomate Am. Bd. Profl. Psychology, Am. Bd. Forensic Psychology. Prof. industrial psychology Baruch Coll. CUNY, 1967-79, mem. bus. doctoral faculty, 1974-79, dean, 1976-79; exec. v.p. Lenox, Inc., N.Y.C., 1980; mgr. Sta. KTVU-TV, San Francisco, 1981-84; pres. TV Mktg. Co., Seattle, 1984-85; v.p. mktg. Walt Disney Co., Burbank, Calif., 1985-87; exec. v.p. United Pers. Systems, L.A., 1988—; bd. dirs. Oakland Regency Hotel; mgmt. cons. BFS Assocs., N.Y.C., 1967-80. Editor: The Role Human Factors in Computers, 1977; contbr. to profl. publs. Bd. dirs. New Oakland (Calif.) Com., 1982; speaker in field. Mem. Am. Bd. Forensic Psychology, Am. Bd. Profl. Psychology, Beta Gamma Sigma, Delta Sigma Rho, Psi Chi, Tau Kappa Alpha. Home: 1735 Crisler Way Los Angeles CA 90069 Office: United Personnel Systems 555 Pointe Dr Ste 300 Brea CA 92621

FINKELSTEIN, JAMES ARTHUR, management consultant; b. N.Y.C., Dec. 6, 1952; s. Harold Nathan and Lilyan (Crystal) F.; m. Lynn Marie Gould, Mar. 24, 1984; 1 child, Matthew. BA, Trinity Coll., Hartford, Conn., 1974; MBA, U. Pa., 1976. Cons. Towers, Perrin, Forster & Crosby, Boston, 1976-78; mgr. compensation Pepsi-Cola Co., Purchase, N.Y., 1978-80; mgr. employee info. systems Am. Can. Co., Greenwich, Conn., 1980; mgr. bus. analysis Emery Airfreight, Wilton, Conn., 1980-81; v.p. Meidinger, Inc., Balt., 1981-83; prin. The Wyatt Co., San Diego, 1983-88; pres., chief exec. officer C & B Cons. Group, San Franciso, 1988—; mem. regional adv. bd. Mchts. and Mfrs. Assn., San Diego, 1986-88; instr. U. Calif., San Diego, 1984-88. Mem. Camp com. State YMCA of Mass. and R.I., Framingham, 1982—; pres. Torrey Pines Child Care Consortium, La Jolla, Calif., 1987-88; vice-chmn. La Jolla YMCA, 1986-88; chmn. Y-camping svcs. com., bd. dirs. YMCA, San Francisco. Mem. Am. Camping Assn., Am. Compensation Assn., Am. soc. Personnel Adminstrn., Marin Yacht Club, Rotary. Home: 17 Bracken Ct San Rafael CA 94901 Office: C&B Cons Group 550 California St San Francisco CA 94104

FINLAYSON, BRUCE ALAN, chemical engineering educator; b. Waterloo, Iowa, July 18, 1939; s. Rodney Alan and Donna Elizabeth (Gilbert) F.; m. Patricia Lynn Hills, June 9, 1961; children—Mark, Catherine, Christine. B.A., Rice U., 1961, M.S., 1963; Ph.D., U. Minn., 1965. Asst. prof. to assoc. prof. U. Wash., Seattle, 1967-77, prof. dept. chem. engring. and applied math., 1977-85, Rehnberg prof. dept. chem. engring., 1985—; vis. prof. Univ. Coll., Swansea, Wales, U.K., 1975-76, Denmark Tekniske Hojskole, Lyngby, 1976, Universidad Nacional del Sur, Bahia Blanca, Argentina, 1980; Gulf vis. prof. Carnegie Mellon U., 1986; trustee Computer Aids to Chem. Engring. Edn., Salt Lake City, 1980—. Mem. editorial bds. Internat. Jour. Numerical Methods Engring., Swansea, 1974-86, Internat. Jour. Numerical Methods in Fluids, Swansea, 1980—, Numerical Heat Transfer, 1981—, Numerical Methods for Partial Differential Equations, 1984—. Author: The Method of Weighted Residuals and Variational Principles, 1972; Nonlinear Analysis in Chemical Engineering, 1980. Served to lt. USNR, 1965-67. Mem. Am. Inst. Chem. Engrs. (CAST div. programming 1981-85, dir. 1984-86, vice chmn. 1987-88, chmn. 1989), William H. Walker award 1983), Am. Chem. Soc., Soc. Indsl. & Applied Math., Soc. Rheology. Home: 6315 22d Ave NE Seattle WA 98115 Office: U Wash Dept Chem Engring Benson Hall 105 BF-10 Seattle WA 98195

FINLEY, DAVID DEWEES, college dean, political science educator; b. Indpls., Nov. 4, 1933; s. Thomas Dewees and Constance Bonner (Bissell) F.; m. Judith Ann Reid, Dec. 28, 1959; children: Bruce Bissell, Karen Killian, Laura Margaret. BS, U.S. Mil. Acad., 1955; AM, Stanford U., 1961, PhD, 1966. Instr. polit. sci. Colo. Coll., Colorado Springs, 1963-65, from asst. prof. to assoc. prof., 1965-76, prof., 1976—, chmn. dept. polit. sci., 1980-84, dean polit. sci., mem. faculty, 1987—; vis. asst. prof. Stanford (Calif.) U., 1966-67; assoc. faculty U. Denver, 1978. Co-author: Soviet Foreign Policy, 1968; contbr. articles to profl. jours. Bd. dirs. World Affairs Council, Colorado Springs, 1982—. 1st lt. U.S. Army, 1955-58. Carnegie Endowment Internat. Peace grantee, 1972. Mem. Internat. Studies Assn. (Soviet-Am. sect., mem. exec. com.), Am. Polit. Sci. Assn., Am. Assn. Advancement Slavic Studies. Democrat. Home: 1503 Culebra Ave Colorado Springs CO 80907 Office: Colo Coll Office of Dean Colorado Springs CO 80903

FINLEY, JAMES DAVID, government official; b. Clearwater, Fla., Oct. 4, 1946; s. Arnold Rudolph and Sylvia (Francis) F.; m. Barbara Elizabeth King, Dec. 17, 1967; children: Jeffrey King, Douglas Jason, Christopher Micheal. BS in Engring., U. Ala., 1970; MS in Engring., Tex. A&M U., 1972. Mgr. liaison div. 7260 USN Sandia Nat. Labs., Albuquerque, 1977-80; sr. program engr. ops. office U.S. Energy Dept., Albuquerque, 1980-84; chief systems evaluation U.S. Energy Dept., 1984-86, mgr. programs, 1986—. Bd. dirs. Albuquerque Internat. Balloon Fiesta, 1988—, N.Mex. Arts and Crafts Fair, Albuquerque, 1987; ofcl. Tucson Balloon Festival, 1986-89. Republican. Home: 3708 Parsifal St NE Albuquerque NM 87111

FINN, BRADLEY BRYAN, shoe company sales executive; b. Pasadena, Calif., Dec. 4, 1953; s. Gerald Leo Finn and Esther Carmen (Rheinheimer) Pierce; m. Mary Cecilia Newton, July 29, 1973 (div. 1987); children: Julie, Natalie; m. Kitty Joan House, Aug. 28, 1987; 1 child, Kaitlyn. BA, UCLA, 1976. Account exec. U.S. Shoe Corp., Cin., 1981-87; nat. sales mgr. Maxwell Shoe Co., Valencia, Calif., 1987—. Bd. dirs. 210 Shoe Charity, Boston, 1988—. Mem. Western Shoe Assn. (bd. dirs. 1978-85, v.p. 1984). Democrat.

FINNANE, DANIEL F., professional basketball team executive. m. Carol F.; 3 sons, 2 daughters. Grad. Univ. Wis., 1958. CPA. Registered rep. Robert W. Baird and Co., Wis., 1965-68; sr. v.p. Dain Bosworth and Co., Mpls.; pres. First Financial Group, 1975-82; exec. v.p. TOTAL-TV Inc. cable television system, Janesville, Wis., 1980-85; co-owner, now also pres. Golden State Warriors (Nat. Basketball Assn.), Oakland, Calif.; mem. bd. dirs., Milwaukee Bucks (Nat. Basketball Assn.), 1978-85. Office: Golden State Warriors Oakland Coliseum Arena Oakland CA 94621

FINNELL, DALLAS GRANT, fundraising executive; b. Scott, Sask., Can., Jan. 10, 1931; s. Grant and Della (Loadman) F.; m. Shirley Mae Sproule, Nov. 25, 1954 (div. 1977); children: Kenneth Wayne, Karlyn Sue Finnell Cieslinski, Darryl Dallas; m. Patricia Frances Irving Lewis, Mar. 20, 1982; stepchildren: Stephen Joseph Lewis, Janine Lewis Watts. BSBA, Lewis Clark Coll., 1954. Trust adminstr. U.S. Bank Oreg., Portland, 1955-60; alumni dir. Lewis & Clark Coll., Portland, 1960-62; dir. annual fund Austin Coll., Sherman, Tex., 1962-65; corp. relations officer Duke U., Durham, N.C., 1965-69; exec. dir. U. Oreg. Med. Sch. Found., Portland, 1969-73; dir. devel. Salk Inst., San Diego, 1973-74; western area dir. Cystic Fibrosis Found., San Diego, 1974-78; pres. Gen. Hosp. Found., Everett, Wash., 1978-89; prin. counsel for philanthropic devel. Dallas Finnell & Co., Everett, 1989—; cons. Finnell Assocs., Portland and San Diego, 1971-78. Pres. Bishop Sch. of Everett, 1983. With USAF, 1950-52. Mem. Nat. Assn. Hosp. Devel. (bd. dirs. 1985-86), Northwest Devel. Officers Assn. (pres. 1982), Nat. Soc. Fundraising Execs. (bd. dirs. Wash. state chpt. 1988-89), Planned Giving Officers Puget Sound, Everett Area C. of C. (v.p. 1988), Cascade Club, Rotary. Republican. Presbyterian. Home: 11238 75th Ave NE Kirkland WA 98034-3459 Office: Dallas Finnell & Co 3224 Wetmore Ave Ste 201 Everett WA 98201

FINNEY, BRIAN HUBERT, literature educator; b. London, Oct. 1, 1935; s. Hugh Arthur and Nita Pattie (Hayes) F.; m. Marlene Trott, Aug. 25, 1958 (div. Apr. 1988); m. Jacqueline Kay Lavin, Sept. 12, 1988. BA in English, Philosophy, U. Reading, England, 1956; PhD in English, U. London, 1973. Tutor U. London, 1964-81, lectr., 1981-84, sr. lectr., 1984-87; vis. lit. prof. U. Calif., Riverside, 1987-89; with dept. English U. Calif., L.A., 1989—; part-time vis. lit. prof. U. So. Calif.; lectr. at various univs. Author: Since How It Is, 1972, Christopher Isherwood, 1979 (Tait Black Award), The Inner I, 1985; editor: D.H. Lawrence, Selected Short Stories, 1982, St. Mawr and Other Stories, 1983. Mgmt. com. mem. Consortium for Drama and Media, London, 1979-81. Recipient Writer's award Arts Council of Great Britain, 1976, Research Grant British Acad., 1980. Mem. MLA. Office: U So Calif Dept English Los Angeles CA 90089

FINNEY, JOHN EDGAR, III, food products executive; b. Hominy, Okla., Oct. 13, 1943; s. John Edgar and Ella Frances (Beckett) F.; m. Claudia Maddalena, Aug. 29, 1965 (div. Nov. 1979); children: Kristen, Eric; m. Tiare Richert, Oct. 18, 1980; 1 child, Thomas Beckett. BA, Okla. State U., 1965; JD, Stanford U., 1968. Bar: Colo. 1969, Hawaii 1969, U.S. Dist. Ct., Hawaii 1970, U.S. Ct. Appeals (ninth cir.) 1970, Calif. 1974. Assoc. law Carlsmith, Carlsmith, Wichman Case, Honolulu, 1970-73; ptnr. law Augustine & Delafield, San Diego, 1973-75; pres., chief exec. officer Pentagram Corp., Honolulu, 1976—; bd. dirs. Competitive Foods Ltd., Sidney, Australia, Perth, Australia, Pentagram Corp., Honolulu. Bd. dirs. bd. visitors Stanford U. Law Sch., Stanford, Calif., 1986—, USAF Pacific Adv. Bd., Hickam Air Force Base, Honolulu, 1987—, Hawaii Maritime Ctr., Honolulu, 1988—. Capt. USMC, 1968-75. Named Okla. Ambassador, State of Okla., 1989; recipient Community Svc. award Aloha United Way, Honolulu, 1988, Community Svc. award Burger King Corp., San Francisco, 1987. Mem. Young Presidents' Orgn. (chmn. 1983-84), Okla. Cattlemen's Assn., Hawaii Cattlemen's Assn., Outrigger Canoe Club. Home: 2949 Hibiscus Pl Honolulu HI 96815 Office: Pentagram Corp 81 S Hotel St Honolulu HI 96813

FINNIE, C(LARENCE) HERB(ERT), aerospace company executive; b. San Marcos, Tex., Feb. 22, 1930; s. Clarence Herbert and Robbie Mary (Hinkle) F.; B.S., S.W. Tex. State U., 1951; M.A., U. Calif.-Berkeley, 1955; M.B.A., U. Santa Clara, 1968; m. Bruna Rebecchi, June 28, 1955; children—Elisa Gene, John Herbert, Mary Lea, Ann Catherine. Bur. chief, disk jockey KCNY, 1950; with Lockheed Missiles & Space Co., Inc., Sunnyvale, Calif., 1958—, supr. computer programming, systems analyst, mgr. software design and devel., advanced system staff engr. sr; free-lance writer, photographer; pres. Creative Imagineering, Sunnyvale, 1984—; cons. in field. Mem. adv. bd. KRON-TV. Served to capt. USAF, 1951-58. Mem. Assn. Computing Machinery, Nat. Mgmt. Assn., Pentagon Players (charter), Photog. Soc. Am., Air Force Assn., Assn. Old Crows, Alpha Chi, Beta Gamma Sigma, Phi Mu Alpha Sinfonia. Roman Catholic. Club: Marquis. Designed and developed first generally used compiler prepared for a digital electronic computer, computer game package, 1952. Home: 1582 Lewiston Dr Sunnyvale CA 94087-4148 Office: 1111 Lockheed Way Sunnyvale CA 94088-3504

FINNIE, PHILLIP POWELL, aerospace engineer; b. Memphis, Dec. 21, 1933; s. Phillip and Daisy L. (Green) F.; B.S.C.E., Howard U., 1956; postgrad. U. Calif., Los Angeles, U. So. Calif.; M.B.A., Pepperdine U., 1979; m. Mary Bebe Clark, Sept. 14, 1968. Stress analyst N.Am. Aviation Corp., Los Angeles, 1956-59; dynamicist RCA, Van Nuys, Calif., 1959-62, Aerojet Gen. Corp., Azusa, Calif., 1962-64, Philco-Ford Corp., Newport Beach, Calif., 1964-67; dynamicist, analyst of radar observables, TRW Inc., Redondo Beach, Calif., 1967—. Mem. Republican Nat. Com. Mem. AIAA, Air Force Assn. Baptist. Home: 20102 Dalfsen Ave Carson CA 90746

FINOCCHIARO, MAURICE ANTHONY, philosophy educator; b. Floridia, Italy, June 13, 1942; s. Biagio and Jane (Mudano) F.; came to U.S., 1957; m. Ramona K. Thomason, Dec. 11, 1966. B.S., MIT, 1964; Ph.D., U. Calif.-Berkeley, 1969. Asst. prof. philosophy U. Nev., Las Vegas, 1970-74, assoc. prof., 1974-77, prof., 1977—. Recipient Barrick Disting. Scholar award U. Nev., 1981-82, 86-87; NEH fellow, 1983-84; NSF grantee, 1976-77. Mem. Am. Philos. Assn., Philosophy of Sci. Assn., History of Sci. Soc., Soc. for Social Study Sci., Am. Hist. Assn. Author: History of Science as Explanation, 1973, Galileo and the Art of Reasoning, 1980, Gramsci and the History of Dialectical Thought, 1988, The Galileo Affair, 1989. Office: U Nev Dept Philosophy Las Vegas NV 89154

FINTON, MICHAEL JAMES, nurse; b. Helena, Mont., June 23, 1958; s. James Fredrick and Marian Adele (Reynolds) F.; m. Jacqueline Marie Montgomery, June 27, 1987. Cert. emergency med. technician, Rancho Santiago Coll., Santa Ana, Calif., 1974. Lic. vocat. nurse; cert. paramedic. Nurse, emergency med. technician Westminster (Calif.) Hosp., 1974-80; nurse Good Samaritan Hosp., Anaheim, Calif., 1978-80, U. Calif., Irvine, 1980-82, U. Ariz., Tucson, 1982-83, Costa Mesa (Calif.) Med. Ctr. Hosp., 1983-87; paramedic Santa Ana (Calif.) Fire Dept., 1987-88; emergency room nurse Humana Hosp., Huntington Beach, Calif., 1989—; chief instr. emergency technician program Orange Coast Coll., 1983-87; cons. in field. Contbr. articles to profl. jours. Dir. planning Orange County Dept. Emergency Mgmt., Santa Ana, 1985. Mem. Calif. State Nurses Assn., Nat. Registry of Emergency Med. Technicians, Orange County Nurses Assn., Calif. Assn. Emergency Nurses. Republican.

FIORANTE, ROSALIE FRANCES, sales representative; b. Long Beach, Calif., Mar. 29, 1943; d. Joe and Ruby (Marcotrigiano) F.; m. Alfred

Canino, Apr. 30, 1965 (div. 1978); children: Cynthia, Celeste, Cory, Chrissie. AA in psychology, Golden West Coll., Huntington Beach, Calif., 1978. Sec. Chem. Milling Internat. Corp., El Segundo, Calif., 1961-65; sales rep. El Segundo C. of C., 1983-85, Hollywood (Calif.) C. of C., 1985-89; dir. membership devel. L.A. Bus. Coun., 1989—. Named Miss El Segundo, 1961-62. Mem. Bus. and Profl. Womens Club (minute taker 1984-85), Rotary, Inglewood Club. Home: 310 West Imperial Ave #1 El Segundo CA 90245 Office: LA Bus Coun 6255 Sunset Blvd Hollywood CA 90028

FIORE, FRANK FRED, computer company owner; b. Bklyn., Oct. 16, 1946; s. Vincent James and Anella (Esposito) F.; m. Lynne Alexis Peacock, Nov. 17, 1979; 1 child, Christopher James. BA, Stockton State Coll., 1975. Store mgr. Micro-Age, Phoenix, 1976-77, mail order mgr., 1977-78, service ctr. mgr., 1978-79; precious metal broker North Am. Coin, Phoenix, 1980-81, Nat. Bullion & Coin, Phoenix, 1981-82; conf. mgr. Vectors Unlimited, Phoenix, 1982-83; owner Lobby Letters of Am., Phoenix, 1982-83; buyer Software Land, Scottsdale, Ariz., 1983; owner, mgr. Computer Warehouse, Phoenix, 1984—. Bd. dirs. Phoenix Urban League; mem. policy com. Phoenix Futures Forum, 1989. 1st lt. U.S. Army, 1966-69. Mem. Microcomputer Mktg. Coun. of DMA (operating com. mem. 1987—). Office: Computer Warehouse 8804 N 23rd Ave Phoenix AZ 85021

FIORINO, JOHN WAYNE, podiatrist; b. Charleroi, Pa., Sept. 30, 1946; s. Anthony Raymond and Mary Louise (Caramela) F.; m. Susan K. Bonnett, May 2, 1984; children—Jennifer, Jessica, Lauren, Michael; student Nassau Coll., 1969-70; B.A. in Biology, U. Buffalo, 1972; Dr. Podiatric Medicine, Ohio Coll. Podiatric Medicine, 1978. Salesman, E. J. Korvettes, Carle Place, N.Y., 1962-65; orderly Nassau Hosp., Mineola, N.Y., 1965-66; operating room technician-trainee heart-lung machine L.I. Jewish-Hillside Med. Center, New Hyde Park, N.Y., 1967-69; pharmacy technician Feinmel's Pharmacy, Roslyn Heights, N.Y., 1969-70; mgr., asst. buyer Fortunoffs, Westbury, N.Y., 1972-73; bd. certified perfusionist L.I. Jewish-Hillside Med. Center, New Hyde Park, N.Y., 1973-74; clin. instr. cardiopulmonary tech. Stony Brook (N.Y.) Univ., 1973-74; operating room technician Cleve. Met. Hosp., 1975; lab. technician Univ. Hosp., Cleve., 1976-78; surg. resident Mesa Gen. Hosp., 1978-79; staff podiatrist, 1979—; pvt. practice podiatry, Mesa, 1979—; staff podiatrist Sacaton (Ariz.) Hosp., 1979—, Mesa Gen. Hosp., 1979, Valley Luth. Hosp., Mesa, 1985, Chandler Community Hosp., 1985, Desert Samaritan Hosp., Mesa, 1986, podiatrist U.S. Govt. Nat. Inst., Sacaton, 1980-87, Indian Health Services, Sacaton, 1980-87; cons. staff Phoenix Indian Med. Ctr., 1985. Served with USN, 1966-67. Mem. Am. Podiatry Assn., Ariz. Podiatry Assn. (treas. 1984-86), Acad. Ambulatory Foot Surgery, Am. Coll. Foot Surgeons (assoc.), Mut. Assn. Profls., Pi Delta, Alpha Gamma Kappa. Home: 2624 W Upland Dr Chandler AZ 85224 Office: 5520 E Main St Mesa AZ 85205

FIRDMAN, HENRY ERIC, infosystems specialist, consultant; b. Leningrad, USSR, Oct. 24, 1936; came to U.S., 1981; s. Roman and Mina (Loytsanskaya) F.; m. Larissa Zhogova, May 27, 1975; children: Philip, Polina, Natasha, Tanya, Henry Eric Jr. MSEE, Polytechnic Inst., Leningrad, 1959; PhD in Microelectronics, Ctr. for Microelectronics, Moscow, 1966; PhD in Computer Sci., Inst. for Electronic Design, Moscow, 1969. Staff mem. Leningrad Design Bur., 1959-64, lab dir., 1964-71, v.p., 1971-73; prof. computer sci. Vladivostok State U., Vladivostok, USSR, 1975-77; dir. lab. Inst. for Automation and Control Processes, Vladivostok, 1974-77; "refusenick" (was refused emigration and job) Leningrad, 1978-81; research scientist Hewlett-Packard Corp., Palo Alto, Calif., 1981-83; dir., advanced product devel. Access Technologies, Inc., South Natick, Mass., 1983-84; pres. Henry Firdman & Assocs., Fallbrook, Calif., 1984—; cons. McDonnell Douglas Corp., St. Louis, 1987—, IBM, White Plains, N.Y., Long Beach, Calif., 1987. Author: Putting AI to Work (2 vols.), 1988, Knowledge Representation Theory, 1977; co-author: Theoretical Foundations of Artificial Intelligence, 1976; newsletter editor: AI Through the Looking Glass, Lexington, Mass., 1986-88, Information Technology and You, Fallbrook, Calif., 1988—. Recipient numerous Certs. of Appreciation, Soc. Mfg. Engrs., 1985-88. Mem. IEEE Computer Soc., Assn. for Computing Machinery, Am. Assn. for Artificial Intelligence, Computer and Automated Systems Assn., N.Y. Acad. of Scis. Republican. Office: Henry Firdman & Assocs 2954 Alta Vista Dr Fallbrook CA 92028

FIRESTONE, CHARLES MORTON, lawyer, educator; b. St. Louis, Oct. 16, 1944; s. Victor and Betty (Solomon) F.; m. Pattie Winston Porter, Apr. 19, 1975; children: Laurel, Asa. BA, Amherst Coll., 1966; JD, Duke U., 1969. Bar: D.C. 1969, U.S. Ct. Appeals (D.C. cir.) 1970, U.S. Ct. Appeals (5th cir.) 1972, U.S. Ct. Appeals (9th cir.) 1973, U.S. Ct. Appeals (2d cir.) 1975, U.S. Ct. Appeals (3d cir.) 1976, U.S. Ct. Appeals (8th cir.) 1977, U.S. Supreme Ct. 1977, Calif. 1983. Litigation atty. FCC, Washington, 1969-73; dir. litigation Citizens Communications Ctr., Washington, 1973-77; adj. prof. law, dir. communications law program, UCLA, 1977-86; vis. lectr. UCLA Sch. Law, 1986—; counsel firm Mitchell, Silberberg & Knupp, L.A., 1983—; faculty adviser Fed. Communications Law Jour., L.A., 1977-86; cons. FTC, Washington, Pub. Agenda Found., N.Y.C., 1978; counsel statewide television debates LWV, Calif. 1978—, counsel Calif. media Dukakis/Bentsen Com.; co-chmn. LWV, Calif., Adv. com. Speak Out 1988, Election Project; pres. Bd. Telecommunications Commrs., City of L.A., 1984-86. Editor case materials, symposia resource manuals on communications; contbr. articles to profl. jours. Bd. dirs. Corp. for Disabilities and Telecommunications, L.A., 1980-82, KCRW Found., Santa Monica, Calif., 1982— (vice chmn. 1987—); trustee Ctr. for Law in Pub. Interest, 1988-89, adv. com. campaign Mondale for Pres., Los Angeles, 1984. Recipient Am. Jurisprudence award, 1968, 69; Cert. Commendation award Mayor L.A., 1986; Resolution Commendation award City Council L.A., 1986; Recognition award NOW, Nat. Black Media Coalition, Nat. Latino Media Coalition, Nat. Citizens Com. for Broadcasting, Washington, 1977; Luther Ely Smith scholar and Andrew Laurie scholar Amherst Coll., 1965-66. Mem. ABA (chmn. broadcast and spectrum use com., sect. sci. and tech. 1981-83, chmn. electronic campaigning com. 1984-86), Fed. Communications Bar Assn., Soc. Satellite Profls. (sec. bd. dirs. So. Calif. chpt. 1984-87), So. Calif. Cable Assn. Democrat. Jewish. Office: Mitchell Silberberg & Knupp 11377 W Olympic Blvd Los Angeles CA 90064

FIROOZMAND, FARZIN, electrical engineer; b. Tehran, Iran, May 12, 1955; s. Ardeshir and Simin (Rowshan) F. BSEE, Arya Mehr U., Tehran, 1977; MSEE, Ohio State U., 1979. Engr., sr. engr. Toledo Scale/Relaince Electric, Columbus, Ohio, 1980-83; sr. design engr. Alkon Corp., Columbus, 1983-84; sr. product planning engr. Advanced Micro Devices, Sunnyvale, Calif., 1984-87, strategic devel. sect. mgr. high speed networking div., 1987—. Contbr. articles to profl. jours. Mem. IEEE, Soc. Iranian Profls., LSA (chmn. 1981-84, 86-88). Baha'i. Home: 3760 Tamarack #36 Santa Clara CA 95051 Office: Advanced Micro Devices 901 Thompson Pl M/S 70 Sunnyvale CA 94088

FIRTH, BARRY THOMAS, food service management executive; b. Coldsprings, N.Y., Jan. 24, 1947; s. William Victor and Katherine Louise (LeBdck) F.; m. Vicki Firth; children: David, Sean, Tamara. BS in Hotel/Restaurant, Fla. State U., 1969. Various positions, then dist. mgr. Ara Svcs., Seattle, 1970-80; regional mgr. Food Mgmt. Control, Seattle, 1980—. Home: PO Box 59026 Renton WA 98058

FISCH, FREDRICK LEE, lawyer; b. Evanston, Ill., Nov. 5, 1955; s. William Sennen and lucie (Zalik) F. BA in Philosophy, U. Colo., 1981; JD, U. Wyo., 1987. Bar: Wyo. 1987, Colo. 1988, U.S. Tax Ct. 1987. Assoc. Dennis K. Ridley and Assocs., Cheyenee, Wh=yo., 1987; sr. assoc. Law Offices J.E. Losavio Jr., Pueblo, Colo., 1987-88; in-house counsel Fed Deposit Ins Corp, Denver, 1988—. Bd. editors Land and Water Law Review, 1986-87. Thurman Arnold scholar, 1985. Mem. ABA, Wyo. Bar Assn., Colo. Bar Assn., Pueblo County Bar Assn., Laramie County Bar Assn. Roman Catholic. Home: 8173 Vance Dr Arvada CO 80003 Office: FDIC 1125 17th St Ste 1700 Denver CO 80202

FISCHER, BRUCE ELWOOD, consultant for hospitals, community mental health fields, and holistic medical field; b. Wahpeton, N.D., June 10, 1930. BA in Bus., Econs., and Edn., 1955; M in Hosp. Adminstrn., 1957. Adminstrv. residency Syracuse Meml. Hosp., N.Y., 1956; hosp. adminstr. Onodaga County Hosp., Syracuse, N.Y., 1957-63, Anoka State Hosp., Mpls. and St. Paul, 1963-68; dir. community mental health programs Hennepin County, Minn., 1968-70; cons. hosps., community mental health fields and holistic med. field, Scottsdale, Ariz., 1970—; pres. Bruce Fischer Assocs. and Health for People, Scottsdale, 1971—. Author: The National Directory of Holistic Professionals. With N.D. State Guard, 1948-54. Mem. State of Minn. Hosp. Administrs. (chmn.), Am. Holistic Med. Assn. (hon.), Am. Hosp. Assn. Office: Scottsdale AZ

FISCHER, EDMOND HENRI, biochemistry educator; b. Shanghai, Republic of China, Apr. 20, 1920; came to U.S., 1953; s. Oscar and Renée (Tapernoux) F.; m. Beverley B. Bullock. Lic. es Sciences Chimiques et Biologiques, U. Geneva, 1943, Diplome d'Ingenieur Chimiste, 1944, PhD, 1947; D (hon.), U. Montpellier, France, 1985, U. Basel, Switzerland, 1988. Pvt. docent biochemistry U. Geneva, 1950-53; research assoc. biology Calif. Inst. Tech., Pasadena, 1953; asst. prof. biochemistry U. Wash., Seattle, 1953-56, assoc. prof., 1956-61, prof., 1961—; mem. exec. com. Pacific Slope Biochem. Conf., 1958-59, pres. 1975; mem. biochemistry study sect. NIH, 1959-64; symposium co-chmn. Battelle Seattle Research Ctr., 1970, 73, 78; mem. sci. adv. bd. Biozentrum, U. Basel, Switzerland, 1982-86; sci. adv. bd. Friedrich Miescher Inst., Ciba-Geigy, Basel, 1976-84, chmn. 1981-84. Contbr. numerous articles to sci. jours. Mem. sci. council on basic sci. Am. Heart Assn., 1977-80, sci. adv. com. Muscular Dystrophy Assn., 1980—, sci. adv. bd. Friedrich Miescher Inst. CIBA-GEIGY, Basel, 1976-84, chmn., 1981-84. Recipient Lederle Med. Faculty award, 1956-59, Guggenheim Found. award, 1963-64, Disting. Lectr. award U. Wash., 1983, Laureate Passano Found. award, 1988; Spl. fellow NIH, 1963-64. Mem. AAAS, AAUP, Am. Soc. Biol. Chemists (council mem. 1980-83), Am. Chem. Soc. (biochemistry div., mem. adv. bd. 1962, exec. com. div. biology 1969-72, monography adv. bd. 1971-73, editorial adv. bd. Biochemistry Jour., 1961-66, assoc. editor 1966—), Swiss Chem. Soc. (Werner medal), Brit. Biochem. Soc., Am. Acad. Arts and Scis., Nat. Acad. Scis., Sigma Xi. Office: U Wash Dept Biochemistry SJ70 Seattle WA 98195

FISCHER, IMRE ANDREW, biochemist; b. Budapest, Hungary, Apr. 12, 1935; came to U.S., 1965; naturalized, 1970; s. Jeno and Julianna (Varga) F.; m. Eugenie M. Martin, Dec. 28, 1961. MS in Biol. Chemistry, U. Louvain (Belgium), 1962, PhD in Microbial Biochemistry, 1965. Diplomate Am. Bd. Bioanalysis. Postdoctoral biochemist U. Calif., Davis, 1965-67, U. Calif. Med. Sch., Los Angeles, 1967-69; sr. chemist Xerox Corp., Pasadena, Calif., 1969-70; tech. dir. Bio-Technics Labs., Inc., Los Angeles, 1970-72; clin. biochemist Los Angeles County Long Beach (Calif.) Gen. Hosp., 1972-78; head emergency lab. services Los Angeles County Harbor-UCLA Med. Ctr., 1978-82; dir. program QualiMedTech, Inc., Long Beach, 1982—; asst. prof. Calif. State U., Dominguez Hills, 1974-79, U. Calif. Med. Sch., Los Angeles, 1978-82; lectr. Calif. State U., Fullerton, 1982—; mem. lab. standards com. Dept. Health Services County of Los Angeles, 1973-82; clin. lab. tech. adv. com., Calif., 1982—; dir. QMT Lab. Svcs., Long Beach, 1984—. editor-in-chief Scientific Newsletters Inc., Anaheim, Calif., 1982-86; contbr. articles to profl. publs. Cons. planned and organized doping program XXIII Olympiad, Los Angeles, 1983; past bd. dirs. La Clinica Familiar Del Barrio, East Los Angeles; mem. Festival of Arts, Laguna Beach, Calif. Fellow Inst. Advancement Engring, Nat. Acad. Clin. Scientists, Am. Soc. Quality Control (chmn. Los Angeles chpt., Testimonial award 1978); mem. AAAS, Am. chem. Soc., Am. Assn. Clin. Chemistry (chmn. So. Calif. chpt. 1983, nominating com. 1986-87, govt. relations com. 1988—), Acad. Clin. Lab. Physicians and Scientists. Home: PO Box 712 Cypress CA 90630 Office: PO Box 15331 Long Beach CA 90815

FISCHER, LYNN SUZANNE, computer engineer; b. Buffalo, Sept. 16, 1951; d. Alfred Norman and Jane Louise (Wagner) F. Student, So. Ill. U., 1970-74; BS in Physics, U. Ariz., 1977; postgrad., Calif. Inst. Tech., 1982-83, 86. Radio telescope operator Nat. Radio Astronomy Obs., Tucson, 1975-76; optical engr. Hughes Aircraft Co., Culver City, Calif., 1978-79; engr. radio astronomy project Jet Propulsion Lab., Pasadena, Calif., 1979-81, engr. meteorol. microwave, 1981, data analyst IRAS, 1981-84, author Galileo software component, 1984-85, sci. coord. Galileo software, 1985-87, astrometry asst., 1987; engring. mgr. L-Com Ltd. Aircraft Intercoms, Pasadena, 1982-84; pvt. practice engring. and computer cons., tech. writing Altadena and Glendale, Calif., 1987—; astrometry asst. UCLA, 1978; pub. speaker Jet Propulsion Lab., 1982—. Author: Galileo MAGPAC User's Guide, 1988. Precinct officer L.A. County Registrar-Recorder, Altadena, 1988; pres. Caltech's Amnesty Internat. Group, Pasadena, 1981-83; tchr. Sunday sch. St. Elizabeth Ch., Altadena, 1984; sponsoring mem. Com. Concerned Scientists. Recipient Group Achievement award NASA, 1984; named Outstanding Toastmaster of Yr., 1983. Mem. Acad. Applied Sci., Aircraft Owners and Pilots Assn.,, Planetary Soc., Soc. Physics Students. Home: 1113 Boynton St Glendale CA 91205

FISCHER, NEIL JEFFREY, mortgage banking executive; b. Portsmouth, Va., Jan. 19, 1955; s. Samuel and Rosalie (Woolf) F.; m. Denise Louise Rymer, Feb. 5, 1983 (div. Nov. 1986); 1 child, Sarah Louise. BS in Commerce, U. Louisville, 1978. Internal auditor Humana Inc., Louisville, 1978-81; asst. adminstr. Humana Hosp. West Hills, Canoga Park, Calif., 1981-82, Panorama (City) Community Hosp., Calif., 1982-83, Humana Hosp., Phoenix, 1983-84; controller Serra Hosp.-Am. Health Group, Sun Valley, Calif., 1984; asst. adminstr. Palmdale Hosp.-Am. Health Group, Palmdale, Calif., 1984-85; pres., treas. Investor's Mortgage Service Co., Burbank, Calif., 1985-88; v.p. Lowell Smith & Evers, Inc., Van Nuys, Calif., 1988—. Mem. U. Louisville Alumni Club of So. Calif. (pres. 1986—). Home: 849 Country Club Dr #8 Simi Valley CA 93065 Office: Lowell Smith & Evers Inc 16600 Sherman Way #165 Van Nuys CA 91406

FISCHER, RONALD STEVEN, executive search consultant; b. Chgo., Nov. 4, 1944; s. Gordon Ray and Sylvia (Deutch) F.; m. Judith Lynn Riman, Aug. 21, 1966; children: Geoffrey Todd, Jody Beth. BS in Accountancy, U. Ill., 1966; MBA in Info. Systems, Loyola U., 1968. Asst. controller Stone Container Corp., Chgo., 1966-68; mgr., cons. Arthur Andersen & Co., Chgo., 1968-75; sr. cons. Touche Ross, Los Angeles, 1975-76; mgr. cons. BDO Seidman, Beverly Hills, Calif., 1976-77; cons. L.A., 1977-79; mgr. cons. Peat Marwick Main, L.A., 1979-81; v.p., owner R.J. Assocs., Woodland Hills, Calif., 1981—; Guest lect. MBA program Pepperdine U., Calif. Arbitrator Coun. of Better Bus. Burs., L.A.; bd. dirs. Jewish Vocat. Svcs., L.A.; adv. com. The Bus. Industry Sch., L.A. Democrat. Office: RJ Assoc 21550 Oxnard Woodland Hills CA 91367

FISCHER, ZOE ANN, real estate and property marketing company executive, real estate consultant; b. Los Angeles, Aug. 26, 1939; d. George and Marguerite (Carrasco) Routsos; m. Douglas Clare Fischer, Aug. 6, 1960 (div. 1970); children—Brent Sean Cecil, Tahlia Georgienne Marguerite Bianca. B.F.A. in Design, UCLA, 1964. Pres. Zoe Antiques, Beverly Hills, Calif., 1973—; v.p. Harleigh Sandler Real Estate Corp. (now Merrill Lynch), 1980-81; exec. v.p. Coast to Coast Real Estate & Land Devel. Corp., Century City, Calif., 1981-83; pres. New Market Devel., Inc., Beverly Hills, 1983—; dir. mktg. Mirabella, Los Angeles, 1983, Autumn Pointe, Los Angeles, 1983-84, Desert Hills, Antelope Valley, Calif., 1984-85; cons. Lowe Corp., Los Angeles, 1985. Designer album cover for Clare Fischer Orch. (Grammy award nomination 1962). Soprano Roger Wagner Choir, UCLA, 1963-64. Mem. UCLA Alumni Assn. Democrat. Roman Catholic. Avocations: skiing, designing jewelry, interior design, antique collecting, photography.

FISCHL, CHARLES FREDERICK, ballet company executive; b. N.Y.C., Mar. 15, 1950; s. Harry and Theresa (Weidengher) F.; m. Linda Carmella Marrone, Jan. 2, 1971; children: Katrina Theresa, Tanya Ann. Student, Carnegie Tech. Coll. Mgr. stage and prodn. Miniola (N.Y.) Theatre, 1965-68, Theatre of the Stars, Atlanta, 1968-73; pres., gen. mgr. Atlanta Ballet, 1974-78; ops. mgr. Dallas Ballet, 1978-79; pres., gen. mgr. Balt. Ballet, 1980-85; gen. mgr. Ballet Ariz., Phoenix, 1985—; Vice-chmn. Am. Assn. Dance Cos., N.Y.C., 1977-79; mem. arts mgmt. bd. Loyola Coll., Balt., 1980-81; dance chmn. Artscape, Balt., 1982-85; coun. mgr. Dance U.S.A., Washington, 1982—. Mem. Phoenix Commn. Arts, Ariz. Arts Commn. Mem. Ind. Assn. Theater Employees, Actors Equity Assn. Office: Ballet Ariz 3645 E Indian School Rd Phoenix AZ 85018

FISCHLER, BRYANT, venture capital executive; b. Bklyn., Nov. 15, 1928; s. Alfred Louis and Fannie (Kluger) F.; m. Joyce Pepose (div. 1976); children: Diane, Scott, Deborah, Lisa, Aimee. BA, L.I. U., 1951; LLB, Bklyn. Law Sch., 1954. Bar: U.S. Dist. Ct. (so. and ea. dists.) N.Y. 1959, U.S. Tax Ct. Ins. agt. Occidental TransAm. Ins. Co., Phoenix, 1981, IHA Life Ins. Co., Phoenix, 1981, State Mut. Life Ins. Co., Phoenix, 1981-82; prof. bus. law, mgmt., and bus. adminstrn. Western Internat. U., Phoenix, 1981—, Ottawa U., Phoenix, 1986—; chmn. bd. Omni Fin. and Ins. Services Ltd., 1982-86; chmn., bd. dirs., pres. U.S. Capital Corp., Phoenix, 1983—; sec. treas., owner White Eagle Travel, Inc., Peoria, Ariz., 1986—; chief exec. officer U.S. Venture Capital Fund, Inc., Phoenix, 1988—; mediator Ariz. Atty. Gen. Office, 1987—. Author: (poems) Feelings, 1980. Chmn. N.Y. State Selective Service Draft Bd., 1973-75; bd. dirs. Widow's Guild, Phoenix, 1980-84. Served as seaman 1st class USN, 1946-48. Recipient Robert Roesler de Villier's decoration Leukemia Soc. of Am., 1968, Community Leader of Am. award, 1969, Cert. Appreciation former U.S. Pres. Richard Nixon, 1973. Mem. Am. Arbitration Assn. Home: 1441 E Maryland #7 Phoenix AZ 85014 Office: US Venture Capital Fund Inc 600 E Baseline Tempe AZ 85282 also: 5227 7th St Phoenix AZ 85014

FISH, DAVID GROVER, real estate appraiser; b. Ashtabula, Ohio, June 23, 1930; s. David Livingston Fish and Dorotha (Grover) Bailey; m. Sarah Baker Murphy, June 10, 1961 (div.) children: David Joseph, Mary Kathryn, Robert Norman; m. Monica Margaret Moore, Jan. 8, 1977. AA, Pasadena City Coll., 1950; BA, Stanford U., 1952; MBE, in Bus. Econs., Claremont Grad. Sch., 1966. Commd. USNR, 1947, advanced through grades to comdr., 1966, retired, 1968; Mgmt. systems analyst Aerojet-Gen. Corp., Azusa, Calif., 1956-67; dept. head Douglas Aircraft, Long Beach, Calif., 1967-73; real estate appraiser Fish & Moore Appraisers Inc., Corona del Mar, Calif., 1973—. Mem. Soc. Real Estate Appraisers (chmn. research com. 1980—), Newport Harbor-Costa Mesa Bd. Realtors, Sigma Zeta Psi, Alpha Gamma Sigma. Republican. Presbyterian. Home: 429 Marigold Ave Corona Del Mar CA 92625 Office: Fish & Moore Appraisers Inc 429 Marigold Ave Corona Del Mar CA 92625

FISH, RUBY MAE BERTRAM (MRS. FREDERICK GOODRICH FISH), civic worker; b. Sheridan, Wyo., July 24, 1918; d. Ryan Lawrence and Ruby (Beckwith) Bertram; R.N., St. Luke's Hosp., 1936; postgrad. Washington U., St. Louis, 1941; m. Frederick Goodrich Fish, Apr. 12, 1942; children—Bertram Frederick, Lisbeth Ann Fish Kalstein. Staff nurse Huntington Meml. Hosp., Pasadena, Calif., 1941-42; dr.'s office nurse, Denver, 1943-44; travel cons. Buckingham Travel Agy., Aurora, Colo., 1976—. Bd. dirs. Jefferson County Easter Seal Soc., 1949—, pres., 1952-53, 56-57, 66-67; pres. Colo. Easter Seal Soc., 1960-61; bd. dirs. Nat. Easter Seal Soc., 1968-69, sec. ho. of dels., 1976-77; bd. dirs. Assistance League Denver, 1968-70, 75-76, People to People for Handicapped; mem. Pres.'s Com. on Employing Handicapped, 1976—; active Rehab. Internat. of U.S.A., 1972—, Rehab. Internat., 1960—. Mem. Dau. Nile-El Mejedel. Home: 4646 Bow Mar Dr Littleton CO 80123 Office: 13741 E Mississippi Ave Aurora CO 80012

FISHBEIN, JUSTIN MANTEL, public relations executive; b. Chgo., Apr. 7, 1927; s. Morris and Anna (Mantel) F.; m. Marianne Demereckis, July 21, 1951;. BA, Harvard U., 1949; postgrad., U. Chgo., 1958-60, Richland Coll., 1978-80, U. Tex., Dallas, 1980-81. APR, Ill., Calif. Reporter Chicago Sun-Times, 1949-60; editor to sr. edit. mgr. Sci. Research Assocs., Chgo., 1960-76; with communications dept. IBM Corp., Chgo., Dallas, Houston and Boulder, Colo., 1976—; with area communications dept. IBM Corp., L.A., 1987—; stringer Time Inc., Springfield, Ill., 1953-55, Newsweek, Chgo. 1957-60. Co-editor: (books) A Successful Marriage 1971, A Question of Competence. Chmn. communications com. So. Calif. chpt. March of Dimes; bd. dirs. Stevenson High Sch., Prairie View, Ill., 1967-72. Named Outstanding Citizen, Highland Park (Ill.) Jr. C. of C., 1963. Mem. Pub. Rels. Soc. Am. (accredited, dir. L.A. chpt. 1989), Soc. Profl. Journalists, Publicity Club L.A. Home: 9901 Wystone Ave Northridge CA 91324 Office: IBM Corp 355 S Grand Ave Los Angeles CA 90071

FISHER, BETH FRY, investment management sales executive, consultant; b. Portland, Oreg., Jan. 29, 1958; d. Wayne Rolland and Betty Marie (McCloskey) Fry; m. Anthony H. Fisher, June 27, 1987. Student, Scripps Coll., 1975-77; BA, Yale U., 1979. Portfolio asst. Mitchell Hutchins Asset Mgmt., N.Y.C., 1980-81, mktg. assoc., 1981-83, asst. v.p., inst. clients, 1983-86; v.p., mgr. Paine Webber Cons., N.Y.C., 1986-87, L.A., 1987—. Mem. Yale Alumni Assn. of Met. N.Y. (founder), Assn. of Investment Mgmt. Sales Execs., Investment Mgmt. Cons. Assn. Democrat. Presbyterian.

FISHER, CARL A., bishop; b. Pascagoula, Miss., Nov. 24, 1945. Student, Epiphany Apostolic Coll., Newburgh, N.Y., St. Joseph's Sem., Oblate Coll., Am. U. Ordained priest Roman Cath. Ch., 1973. Titular bishop of Tlos, aux. bishop of L.A. 1987—. Office: Archdiocese of Los Angeles 3555 St Pancratius Pl Lakewood CA 90712 *

FISHER, CINDY LOU, biophysics researcher; b. Iruma, Japan, Sept. 17, 1958; came to U.S. 1958; d. Marvin Arthur and Chieko (Isobe) Franz; m. William Charles Fisher, Aug. 16, 1981. BS, UCLA, 1981; PhD, U. Calif., Irvine, 1986. Lab asst. UCLA, Los Angeles, 1978-81; teaching asst. U. Calif., Irvine, Calif., 1981-83, research asst., 1983-84, 85, mass spectroscoptist, 1984-85; research fellow Agouron Inst., La Jolla, Calif., 1985-87; postdoc. fellow Scripps Clinic and Research Found., La Jolla, Calif., 1988--. Univ. fellow U. Calif., Irvine, 1981, 84, minority fellow, 1985, Control Data Corp. Pacer fellow, 1986, postdoc. fellow, NIH, 1987—, rsch. fellow Scripps Clinic, LaJolla, Calif., 1987—. Fellow Am. Chem. Soc. Presbyterian. Home: 8 Cattail Irvine CA 92714 Office: Scripps Clinic & Rsch 10666 N Torrey Pines Rd La Jolla CA 92037

FISHER, DELBERT ARTHUR, physician, educator; b. Placerville, Calif., Aug. 12, 1928; s. Arthur Lloyd and Thelma (Johnson) F.; m. Beverly Carne Fisher, Jan. 28, 1951; children: David Arthur, Thomas Martin, Mary Kathryn. B.A., U. Calif., Berkeley, 1950; M.D., U. Calif., San Francisco, 1953. Diplomate: Am. Bd. Pediatrics (examiner 1971-80, mem. subcom. pediatric endocrinology 1976-79). Intern, then resident in pediatrics U. Calif. Med. Center, San Francisco, 1953-55; resident in pediatrics U. Oreg. Hosp., Portland, 1957-58; Irwin Meml. fellow pediatric endocrinology U. Oreg. Hosp., 1958-60; from asst. prof. to prof. pediatrics U. Ark. Med. Sch., Little Rock, 1960-68; prof. pediatrics UCLA Med. Sch., 1968-73; prof. pediatrics and medicine 1973—; research prof. devel. and perinatal biology Harbor-UCLA Med. Ctr., 1975-85, chmn. pediatrics, 1985-89; cons. genetic disease sect. Calif. Dept. Health Services, 1978—; mem. organizing com. Internat. Conf. Newborn Thyroid Screening, 1977-88; dir. Walter P. Martin Rsch. Ctr., 1987—. Co-editor: 5 books including Pediatric Thyroidology, 1985; editor-in-chief: Jour. Clin. Endocrinology and Metabolism, 1978-83; Pediatric Research, 1984-89; contbr. 350 articles profl. jours., chpts. to 80 books. Served to capt. M.C. USAF, 1955-57. Recipient Career Devel. award NIH, 1964-68. Mem. Am. Acad. Pediatrics (Borden award 1981), Soc. Pediatric Research (v.p. 1973-74), Am. Pediatric Soc., Endocrine Soc. (pres. 1983-84), Am. Thyroid Assn. (pres. 1988-89), Am. Soc. Clin. Investigation, Assn. Am. Physicians, Lawson Wilkins Pediatric Endocrine Soc. (pres. 1982-83), Western Soc. Pediatric Research (pres. 1983-84), Inst. Medicine Nat. Acad. Sci., Phi Beta Kappa, Alpha Omega Alpha. Home: 4 Pear Tree Ln Rolling Hills Estates CA 90274 Office: Harbor-UCLA Med Ctr Dept Pediatrics 1000 W Carson St Torrance CA 90509

FISHER, DONALD G., casual apparel chain stores executive; b. 1928; married. B.S., U. Calif., 1950. With M. Fisher & Son, 1950-57; former ptnr. Fisher Property Investment Co.; co-founder, pres. The Gap Stores Inc., San Bruno, Calif., dir., now chmn., chief exec. officer. Office: The Gap Stores Inc 900 Cherry Ave Box 60 San Bruno CA 94066 *

FISHER, EARL MONTY, utilities executive; b. Chgo., June 26, 1938; s. Harry George and Fannie (Feinberg) F.; m. Joyce Leah Bender, Mar. 14, 1969 (div. Dec. 1978); children: Jan Carol, Wendy Robbin; m. Teri Jean Jannsen, Jan. 27, 1979. Student, La. Trade Tech. Coll., 1961. Apprentice and journeyman Comfort Air Refrigeration Corp., L.A., 1955-64; contractor Bonanza Air Conditioning and Refrigeration Corp., Van Nuys, Calif., 1964—. Bd. dirs. Hidden Hills (Calif.) Homeowners Assn., 1982-84; chmn. Hidden Hills Rds. Com., 1984-85, Hidden Hills Gate Ops. Commn., 1988; vice chmn. Hidden Hills Security Com., 1987—; commr. emergency svcs. City of Hidden Hills, 1986—. Cpl. USMCR, 1955-64. Democrat. Office: Bonanza Air Conditioning Heating & Refrigeration Corp 7653 Burnet Ave Van Nuys CA 91405

FISHER, EVALYN JEAN, interior designer; b. Roswell, N.Mex., Aug. 27, 1943; d. Newel Edward and Genevieve (Kester) Porter; m. Robert Earl Fisher, Apr. 3, 1966. BA in Art and Design, Calif. State U., Los Angeles, 1968. Cert. tchr., Calif.; cert. interior and environ., designer, Calif. Art instr. pub. schs. Baldwin Park and Rialto, Calif., 1969-74; visual arts specialist pub. schs. Riverside, Calif., 1975-79; assoc. designer Maryanne Levine Interior Designs, Los Angeles, 1982-85; prin. Evalyn Fisher, ASID & Assocs., Redlands, Calif., 1985—; adj. instr. U. Calif., Riverside, Fashion Inst. Design and Merchandising, Los Angeles and Santa Ana, Calif., 1985—. Recipient numerous design awards from area hist. socs. and civic groups. Mem. Am. Soc. Interior Designers (cert., chmn. significant interiors survey com. 1987—, chmn. com. 1987—), Nat. Trust Hist. Preservation (design assoc.). Democrat. Office: Evalyn Fisher ASID & Assocs 300 E State St Ste 503 Redlands CA 92373

FISHER, FREDERICK HENDRICK, oceanographer; b. Aberdeen, Wash., Dec. 30, 1926; s. Sverre and Astrid (Kristofferson) F.; midshipman U.S. Naval Acad., 1945-47; B.S., U. Wash., 1949, Ph.D., 1957; m. Julie Gay Saund, June 17, 1955; children—Bruce Allen, Mark Edward, Keith Russell, Glen Michael. Research fellow acoustics Harvard, 1957-58; research physicist, research oceanographer Marine Phys. Lab., Scripps Instn. Oceanography, La Jolla, Calif., 1958—, assoc. dir., 1975-87, dep. dir., 1987—; dir. research Havens Industries, San Diego, 1963-64; prof., chmn. dept. physics U. R.I., Kingston, 1970-71; mem. environ. sci. panel Naval Research Adv. Com., 1984—; mem. governing bd. Am. Inst. Physics, 1984—; cons., 1964—; lectr. Nat. Acad. Scis., NRC.; Editor: Jour. Oceanic Engineering, 1988; contbr. numerous articles to profl. jours.; patentee in field. Mem. San Diego County Dem. Cen. Com., 1956-57, 60-62; NCAA nat. tennis doubles champion, 1949. Served with USNR, 1945. Fellow Acoustical Soc. Am. (assoc. editor jour. 1969-76, v.p. 1980-81, pres. 1983-84, lectr.), Am. Inst. Chemists, Explorers Club; mem. IEEE (sr.), Am. Chem. Soc., U.S. Naval Inst., Am. Phys. Soc., Am. Meteorol. Soc., Navy Submarine League, Marine Tech. Soc., Am. Geophys. Union, U.S. Naval Inst., Am. Def. Preparedness Assn., Sigma Xi, AAAS, Pi Mu Epsilon. Club: Seattle Tennis. Co-designer research platform FLIP, 1960-62, chief scientist numerous seatrips. Home: 3726 Charles St San Diego CA 92106 Office: U Calif Marine Phys Lab Scripps Inst Oceanography La Jolla CA 92093

FISHER, GEORGE H., insurance company official; b. N.Y.C., July 22, 1952; s. George and Patricia (Semple) F.; m. Christine Wilson, Dec. 21, 1975; children: Jennifer, Beth. BS, Manhattan Coll., 1974; MA, U. Denver, 1975. Head basketball coach St. John's High Sch., West Islip, N.Y., 1972-74, Northland Coll., Ashland, Wis., 1976-78, U. Minn., Duluth, 1978-84, Calif. Poly. U., Pomona, 1984-87; grad. asst. U. Denver, 1974-75; athletic dir. Nat. Coll., Rapid City, S.D., 1975-76; agt. State Farm Ins. Co., Ontario, Calif., 1987—. Named Coach of Yr. Wis. Ind. Collegiate Assn., 1978-80, No. Intercollegiate Conf., 1980-83, Nat. Assn. Intercollegiate Athletics, 1981-83. Mem. Ontario C. of C. (amb. 1988—, bd. dirs.), Lions (bd. dirs. 1984—, v.p.). Lutheran. Office: State Farm Ins Co 853 N Mountain Ave Ontario CA 91762

FISHER, JAN BRADDOCK, gallery executive; b. Ithaca, N.Y., May 27, 1951; d. C. Coleman and Mary Elizabeth (Braddock) F. BA in Liberal Arts, Sarah Lawrence Coll., 1974; postgrad., Cooper Union, N.Y.C., 1974-75, Ariz. State U., 1988. Asst. editor Inst. Archtl.-Urban Studies, N.Y.C., 1973-74; planning asst. Implementation, Inc., Balt., 1976; drafter R.T.K.L. Assocs., Balt., 1977; gallery asst. 1708 E. Main St. Gallery, Richmond, Va., 1979-80; tchr. arts and crafts Mesa (Ariz.) Park System, 1984; office mgr. Applied Arts Pottery, Tempe, Ariz., 1984—. Vol. various arts orgns., Eugene, Oreg., 1980-83. Mem. Woman Image Now, Women in Design, Ariz. Women's Caucus for Art, Tempe Fine Arts Ctr., Shemer Art Ctr. Democrat. Home: 1215 Vista del Cerro Dr #1111 Tempe AZ 85281 Office: Applied Arts Pottery 1004 E Vista Del Cerro Dr Tempe AZ 85281

FISHER, JOHN RICHARD, engineering consultant, former naval officer; b. Columbus, Ohio, Dec. 28, 1924; s. Don Alfred and Katherine Buchanan (Galigher) F.; m. Kitson Overmyer, Oct. 2, 1946; children—Scott Owen, Lani Kitson. B.S., U.S. Naval Acad., 1946; B.Civil Engring., Rensselaer Poly. Inst., Troy, N.Y., 1950, M.Civil Engring., 1950; grad. Advanced Mgmt. Program, Harvard, 1971. Registered profl. engr., S.C. Commd. ensign U.S. Navy, 1946, advanced through grades to rear adm., 1972; service in N.Africa, Cuba, Philippines, Antarctica, Vietnam; dep. comdr. Naval Facilities Engring. Command; also comdr. Chesapeake div. constrn. facilities U.S. Naval Acad. and Omega Nav. System, 1969-73; comdr. Pacific div. Naval Facilities Engring. Command, 1973-77; ret. 1977; v.p. Raymond Internat., Inc., 1977-81, sr. group v.p., 1981-83, exec. v.p., 1983-86. Pres. Community Hosp. Assn. Mid-Am., Scottsdale, Ariz., 1985—; nat. dir. Teke Edn. Found., Inc. Decorated DSM, Legion of Merit with combat V (2). Fellow Soc. Am. Mil. Engrs., ASCE; mem. Navy League of U.S. (nat. dir.), Am. Legion, Mil. Order Carabao, Sigma Xi, Tau Beta Pi. Clubs: Outrigger Canoe (Honolulu); Army-Navy Country (Arlington, Va.); Scottsdale (Ariz.) Country. Home: 10615 E Arabian Park Dr Scottsdale AZ 85258 Office: PO Box 5585 Scottsdale AZ 85261

FISHER, JOHN SERGIO, architect, educator; b. Milano, Italy, May 7, 1934; s. Albert Darius and Elsa Maria (Weinstock) F.; came to U.S., 1939, naturalized, 1952; BArch, Carnegie Inst. Tech., 1958; Finnish Inst. Tech., 1959; MArch, Carnegie Inst. Tech., 1961; m. Bonnie Jean McIntosh, Jan. 28, 1962; children—Ava, Carina, Matt. Asst. prof. dept. architecture U. Calif., Berkeley, 1963-69; partner Fisher/Jackson Assos., Architects/Urban Designers, Berkeley, N.Y.C., 1964-67; pres. Fisher/Jackson Assos., Inc., Architecture/Systems Development/Urban Planning, Berkeley, Calif., 1967-72; dean Sch. Architecture, Syracuse (N.Y.) U., 1972-75; pres. John Sergio Fisher AIA & Assos., Inc., Tarzana and Palo Alto, Calif., 1976—; adj. lectr. dept. architecture Calif. Poly. Inst., Pomona, fall 1975, Sch. Architecture & Urban Planning, UCLA, 1979, 80, 82; hearing examiner Calif. Bd. Archtl. Examiners. Shelter analyst, instr. Office of CD, 1962. Mem. Com. on Aging, Berkeley, 1966-69; chmn. Fisher Housing Systems, 1977-79; trustee Los Angeles Actors Theatre, 1979—; bd. dirs. Back Alley Theatre, 1986—. Fulbright grantee, 1958; HUD Urban Devel. Action grantee, 1979, 82. Mem. AIA (San Fernando Valley chpt. Spl. Design award 1969, Grand award, 1986, Honor award, 1986, Merit award 1987, Citation award 1988), Design Methods Group, Internat. Solar Energy Soc., Inst. Urban Planning, Nat. Trust Historic Preservation. Democrat. Patentee in industrialized housing. Office: 5567 Reseda Blvd #209 Tarzana CA 91356

FISHER, JOSEPH STEWART, management consultant; b. Athens, Pa., Mar. 3, 1933; s. Samuel Royer and Agnes Corinne (Smith) F.; m. Anita Ann Coyle, May 15, 1954; 1 child, Samuel Royer. BS in Tech. Mgmt., Regis Coll., 1981; postgrad., U. Colo., 1986-87, Iliff Sch. Theology, 1988-89. Field engr. IBM Corp., Syracuse, N.Y., 1956-60; qualtiy analyst, engr. IBM Corp., Endicott, N.Y., 1960-68; systems support adminstr. IBM Corp., Boulder, Colo., 1968-72, field support adminstr., 1972-78, systems assurance adminstr., 1978-79, security adminstr., 1979-87; sec. cons. Fisher Enterprises, Boulder, 1980—; bd. dirs. Vervcraft Inc., Loveland, Colo. Leadership devel. Boy Scouts Am., Boulder, 1975—, chmn. long range planning, 1982-86; bd. dirs. Longs Peak Council 1983-87, Colo. Crime Stoppers, 1983-88. Served with USN, 1952-56, Korea. Recipient Silver Beaver award Boy Scouts Am., Boulder, 1978. Mem. Am. Soc. Indsl. Security (cert. CPP 1984, treas. 1985), Colo. Crime Prevention Assn., Elks, Masons (treas. Columbia chpt 1969-85), Optimists. Republican. Methodist. Home and Office: 4645 Bedford Ct Boulder CO 80301

FISHER, KATHLEEN MARY, biology educator; b. Long Branch, Aug. 4, 1938; d. James F. and Katherine E. Flynn; m. L. Karl Fisher, Dec. 4, 1959 (div. 1980); children: Tawn, Dore. BS, Rugers U., 1960; PhD, U. Calif., Davis, 1969. Professorial series U. Calif., Davis, 1971-88; prof. dept. natural scis. San Diego State U., 1988—; postdoctoral fellow Atomic Energy Commn., Davis, 1970; dir. teaching resources ctr., U. Calif., Davis, 1974-79; program assoc. NSF, Washington, 1980-81; Fulbright lectr., Universiti Sains, Penang, Malaysia, 1980. Contbr. articles to profl. jours.; editor, producer tv programs on genetics and sci. writing. Mem. AAAS, Am. Ednl. Research Assn., Nat. Assn. Research in Sci. Teaching, Sigma Xi. Office: San Diego State U Dept Nat Scis San Diego CA 92182

FISHER, KENNETH L., sculptor; b. Tacoma, Apr. 28, 1944; s. Henry John and Anna Mary (Trafford) F. B.S., U. Oreg., 1968, B.F.A., 1969, M.F.A., 1971. Cert. univ. level tchr., Calif. One-man shows include Thelma Pearson Gallery, Lincoln City, Oreg., 1971, Internat. Art Gallery, Pitts., 1971, Jewish Community Ctr., Portland, Oreg., 1971, Howell Street Gallery, Seattle, 1981, Lakewood Ctr. Gallery, Lake Oswego, Oreg., 1983, William Temple House, Portland, 1984, Grants Pass Art Mus., Oreg., 1984, 86, Benton County Hist. Mus., Philomath, Oreg., 1984, Pacific U., Forest Grove, Oreg., 1985, Mondak Hist. & Art Soc., Sidney, Mont., 1986, Umpqua Community Coll., Roseburg, Oreg., 1986, Lower Columbia Coll., Longview, Wash., 1987, Pacific Northwest Art Expo., Seattle, 1987; group shows include Coos Art Mus., Oreg., 1981 (hon. mention), 82, Ga. Inst. Tech., 1982, 83 (cert. of recognition), Painters and Sculptors Soc., N.J., 1982, La. Arts Guild, 1982, Galerie Triangle, Washington, 1982, 83, Alexandria Mus. Arts, La., 1982, Terrance Gallery, N.Y.C., 1982 (hon. mention), Cooperstown Art Assn., N.Y., 1982, Knickerbocker Artists, N.Y.C., 1982, 83, 84, Idaho State U. (1st place award), 1982, Del Mar Coll., (Joseph A. Cain Meml. Purchase award in sculpture), Corpus Christi, Tex., 1982, 83, Goldsboro's 3d Ann. Juried Exhbn., N.C., 1982, Fine Arts League 14th Nat. Show (1st place award), Colo., 1982, Franklin Sq. Gallery (M. Grumbacher Inc. Bronze medallion), N.C., 1982, J.K. Ralston Mus. (1st and 2d Place awards), Mont., 1982, Oreg. State U. (honor award), 1983, Hill Country Arts Found., 11th Ann. Exhbn. (1st place award in sculpture), Tex., 1983, Hill Country Arts Found., Tex., 1983, Art Ann. Four, Okla., 1983, Audubon Artists, N.Y.C., 1983, 86, Salmagundi Club, N.Y.C., 1983, Las Vegas Art Mus., 1984, Nat. Art Appreciation Soc., 1984 (hon. mention), Palm Beach Galleries, La. (grand prize), 1984, NAD, N.Y.C., 1984, Allied Artists Am., N.Y.C., 1984, N.Am. Sculpture Exhbn., Colo., 1986, Audobon Artists Nat. exhbn., 1986, 87; represented in permanent collections Grants Pass Art Mus., Coos Art Mus., U. Oreg. Mus. Art, Oreg. State U., Del Mar Coll., Pacific U., Umpqua Community Coll., U. Portland, also numerous pvt. collections. Mem. Portland Art Assn.

FISHER, RICHARD FORREST, soils educator, academic administrator; b. Champaign, Ill., May 15, 1941; s. Richard Forrest Fisher and Hannah Elizabeth (Ponath) Kistler; m. Karen Dangerfield Fisher, Sept. 4, 1959; children: William Forrest, Marilu, Kevin Royden. BS, U. Ill., 1963; MS, Cornell U., 1967, PhD, 1968. Research scientist Can. Forestry Service, Sault Sainte Marie, Ont., 1968-69; asst. prof. forestry U. Ill., Urbana, 1969-72; assoc. prof. U. Toronto, Ont., 1972-77; prof. U. Fla., Gainesville, 1977-82; prof. and head dept. forest resources Utah State U., Logan, 1982—. Author: (with others) Properties and Management of Forest Soil, 2d edit.; contbr. articles to profl. jours. Fellow Soc. Am. Foresters, Soil Sci. Soc. Am. (assoc. editor journal); mem. Assn. Tropical Biology, Internat. Soc. Tropical foresters, AAAS, Ecol. Soc. Am. Democrat. Home: 1573 E 1260N Logan UT 84321 Office: Utah State U Forest Resources Dept Logan UT 84322-5215

FISHER, RICHARD J., SR., staff applications engineer; b. Shelby, Ohio, Apr. 26, 1946; s. Francis A. and Margaret (Buckmaster) F.; m. Lynn Norris, Feb. 17, 1972; children: Monica Lynn, Robert Justin, Curtis Richard. AA, Glendale Community Coll., Ariz., 1976; BS in Math. and Environ. Sci., Grand Canyon Coll., 1978. Computer tech. Honeywell Info. Systems, Phoenix, 1971-78, logic engr., 1978-81; prin. engr. A.B. Dick, Scottsdale, Ariz., 1982-83; sr. design engr. Genrad SPD, Phoenix, 1983-85; sr. applications engr. Fairchild Semiconductor, Phoenix, 1985-87, Nat. Semiconductor, Tempe, Ariz., 1987--. Patentee in field. With USAF, 1966-69. Democrat. Roman Catholic. Home: 3361 N Kings Ave Phoenix AZ 85023 Office: Nat Semiconductor 1575 W University Dr Tempe AZ 85821

FISHER, ROBERT HENRY, newspaper publisher; b. Newark, May 2, 1954; s. Edwin and Marilyn (Bauer) F.; m. Penny Lee Poole, Aug. 14, 1982; children: Max, Joanna. BA, Northwestern U., 1976. Reporter Corpus Christi (Tex.) Caller-Times, 1976-77, Macon (Ga.) Telegraph, 1977-79, Kansas City (Mo.) Times, 1979, Wichita (Kans.) Eagle-Beacon, 1980-84; assoc. editor Kansas City (Mo.) Bus. Jour., 1985-86, editor, 1986; pub. Portland (Oreg.) Bus. Jour., 1986—. Bd. dirs. Jr. Achievement, Portland, Portland Jewish Acad. Mem. Area Assn. Bus. Publs., Assn. for Portland Progress. Club: Northwestern U. Alumni (pres. 1988). Office: Bus Jour 10 NW 10th Ave Portland OR 97209

FISHER, WESTON JOSEPH, land developer; b. Glendale, Calif., Aug. 29, 1942; s. Edward Weston and Rosalie Eloise (Bailey) F. BS, U. So. Calif., 1962, MA, 1965, MS, 1971. Sr. mgr. Naval Undersea Ctr., Pasadena, Calif., 1964-69; chief exec. officer, prin. Ventura County, Ventura, Calif., 1969-73; So. Calif. dir. County Suprs. Assn., L.A., 1974-75; coord. govtl. rels. So. Calif. Assn. Govts., L.A., 1975-78; devel. dir. Walter H. Leimert Co., L.A., 1979—; bd. dirs. Gray Energy Corp., L.A., Mission Inn Group, Riverside, Calif. Mem. Calif. Gov.'s Task Force on Women's Rights, 1975-78; bd. dirs. Pvt. Library Coun., Boston, 1980-86, So. Calif. Arts Coun., 1985-89; trustee Los Hermanos Drug Prevention, San Gabriel, Calif., 1984-89. Mem. Univ. Club, South Coast Yacht Club, Lambda Alpha. Republican. Episcopalian. Home: 1410 Holly Ave Arcadia CA 91006 Office: Walter H Leimert Co 606 N Larchmont Blvd Los Angeles CA 90004

FISHER, WILLIAM COURTNEY, dentist, military officer; b. Tucson, Mar. 7, 1952; s. Bernard Francis and Realla Jane (Johnson) F.; m. Paula Wilson, Aug. 28, 1975; children: Adam Courtney, Matthew Scott, Jonathan Bernard, Rebekka Jane, Lisa Sarah, Benjamin, Wilson. BS, Brigham Young U., 1976; DDS, Creighton U., 1980. Commd. 2d lt. USAF, 1976, advanced through grades to maj., 1986; dental officer David-Monthan AFB, Tucson, 1980-81, USAF Clinic, Semback Air Base, Fed. Republic Germany, 1981-84, USAF Hosp., Mountain Home, Idaho, 1984—; base dental health officer Mountain Home AFB, 1984-86, infection control officer, 1986-. Coach Youth Soccer, Mountain Home Recreation, 1984--; mem. dist. com., chmn. troop com. troop 59, Boy Scouts Am., Mountain Home, 1986-87, scoutmaster, 1987--; pres. West Elem. Sch. PTO, Mountain Home, 1988. Mem. Air Force Assn., Arnold Air Soc. Mormon. Home: 1060 S Haskett St Mountain Home ID 83647-3313 Office: 366th Med Group (TAC)/SGD Mountain Home ID 83648-5300

FISHMAN, JOAN R., health associate; b. Cambridge, Mass., Sept. 1, 1945; d. Joseph and Tilla (Gerson) F.; m. Stephan S. Abramson, June 8, 1969 (div. 1983). BA, Wheaton Coll., Norton, Mass., 1967; MS, U. So. Calif., 1978. Research asst. Harvard U. Med. Sch., Boston, 1967-69; pulmonary technologist Peter Bent Brigham Hosps., Boston, 1969-71, Framingham (Mass.) Union Hosp., 1971-74; chief pulmonary physiol. lab. Los Angeles County-U. So. Calif. Med. Ctr., 1975-79; dir. pulmonary diagnostic lab. White Meml. Med. Ctr., Los Angeles, 1979-84; asst. dir. respiratory care Pacific Med. Ctr., San Francisco, 1984-85; asst. product mgr. Gould Med. Products, Dayton, Ohio, 1985-86; installation specialist Health Data Scis., San Bernardino, Calif., 1987—; health profl. educator Am. Lung Assn., N.Y.C., 1977-78. Author: Programmed Gas Law for Cardiopulmonary Technology, 1979, Blood Gas Electrodes, 1984, (with others) Standards and Controversies in Pulmonary Function Testing, 1982. Mem. Nat. Soc. Cardiopulmonary Technology (regional dir. 1978-83), Nat. Bd. Respiratory Care (bd. dirs. 1983—), Calif. Soc. Respiratory Care. Office: Health Data Scis 268 W Hospitality Ln San Bernardino CA 92408

FISHMAN, SHERMAN SARA, ultrasonicologist, pharmacologist, toxicologist; b. Miami, Fla., Feb. 20, 1926; s. Maurice and Gertrude (Segal) F. AB, Tufts U., 1948; MS, U. Chgo., 1952. cert. in med. adminstrn., Calif. Sci. investigator U.S. Naval Radiol. Def. Lab., San Francisco, 1956-59; pres., dir. research and devel. Sara Sci. Co., San Francisco, 1960--. Contbr. articles on biol. effects of ultrasound to profl. jours.; patentee in ultrasound machines field. Lt. comdr. USNR, 1944-46, 56-59. Mem. Am. Chem. Soc. (chmn. profl. relations com. No. Calif. chpt. 1980-86), Am. Assn. for Advancement Med. Instrumentation (nat. standards com.), AAAS, Western Pharmacology Soc. (charter). Office: SaraSci Co PO Box 321 San Francisco CA 94101

FISHMAN, WILLIAM HAROLD, cancer research foundation executive, biochemist; b. Winnipeg, Man., Can., Mar. 2, 1914; s. Abraham and Goldie (Chmelnitsky) F.; m. Lillian Waterman, Aug. 6, 1939; children—Joel, Nina, Daniel. B.S., U. Sask., Can., Saskatoon, 1935; Ph.D., U. Toronto, Ont., Can., 1939; MDhc U. Umea, Sweden, 1983; Dir. cancer research New Eng. Med. Ctr. Hosp., Boston, 1958-72; research prof. pathology Tufts U. Sch. Medicine, 1961-70, prof. pathology, 1970-77, dir. Cancer Research Ctr., 1972-76, dir., 1981; pres. La Jolla Cancer Research Found., Calif., 1976—; mem. basic sci. programs merit rev. bd. com. VA, 1971-75; mem. pathobiol. chemistry sect. NIH, Bethesda, Md., 1977-81. Author in field. Research Career award NIH, 1962-77; Royal Soc. Can. research fellow, 1939, 17th Internat. Physiol. Congress-U.K. Fedn. fellow, 1947. Fellow AIC; mem. Am. Assn. Cancer Research, Am. Soc. Biol. Chemists, Am. Soc. Cell Biology, Am. Soc. Exptl. Pathology, Histochem. Soc. (pres. 1983-84), Internat. Soc. Clin. Enzymology (hon.). Jewish. Club: University (San Diego). Current work: Basic research on expression of placental genes by cancer cells; monoclonal antibodies; oncodevelopmental markers; immunocytochemistry. Home: 715 Muirlands Vista Way La Jolla CA 92037 Office: La Jolla Cancer Rsch Found 10901 N Torrey Pines Rd La Jolla CA 92037

FISK, EDWARD RAY, civil engineer, author; b. Oshkosh, Wis., July 19, 1924; s. Ray Edward and Grace O. (Meyer) Barnes; student Marquette U., 1945-49, Fresno (Calif.) State Coll., 1954, UCLA, 1957-58; B.S., M.B.A., Calif.-Western U.; m. Oct. 28, 1950; children—Jacqueline Mary (Fisk) Stamp, Edward Ray II, William John, Robert Paul. Engr., Calif. Div. Hwys., 1952-55; engr. Bechtel Corp., Vernon, Calif., 1955-59; project mgr. Toups Engring Co., Santa Ana, Calif., 1959-61; dept. head Perliter & Soring, Los Angeles, 1961-64; Western rep. Wire Reinforcement Inst., Washington, 1964-65; cons. engr., Anaheim, Calif., 1965; asso. engr. Met. Water Dist. So. Calif., 1966-68; chief specification engr. Koebig & Koebig, Inc., Los Angeles, 1968-71; mgr. constrn. services VTN Consol., Inc., Irvine, Calif., 1971-78; pres. E.R. Fisk Constrn., Orange, Calif., 1978-81; corp. dir. constrn. mgmt. James M. Montgomery Cons. Engrs., Inc., Pasadena, Calif., 1981-83; v.p. Lawrance, Fisk & McFarland, Inc., Santa Barbara and Orange, 1983—; pres. E.R. Fisk & Assocs., Orange, 1983—; pres. Gleason, Peacock & Fisk, Inc., 1987—; adj. prof. engring., constrn. Calif. State U., Long Beach U., Orange Coast Coll., Costa Mesa, Calif., 1957-78, Calif. Poly. State U., Pomona, 1974; lectr. U. Calif., Berkeley, ITS extension, internationally for ASCE Continuing Edn.; former mem. Calif. Bd. Registered Constrn. Insps. Served with USN, 1942-43, USAF, 1951-52. Registered profl. engr., Ariz., Calif., Colo., Fla., Idaho, La., Mont., Nev., Oreg., Utah, Wash., Wyo.; lic. land surveyor, Oreg., Idaho; lic. gen. engring. contractor, Calif.; cert. abritator Calif. Constrn. Contract Arbitration Com. Fellow ASCE (past chmn. exec. com. constrn. div.; former chmn. nat. com. inspection 1978—); mem. Nat. Acad. Forensic Engrs. (diplomate), Orange County Engring. Council (former pres.), Calif. Soc. Profl. Engrs. (past pres. Orange County), Am. Arbitration Assn. (nat. panel), U.S. Com. Large Dams, Order Founders and Patriots Am. (past gov. Calif.), Soc. Colonial Wars (gov.), S.R. (past dir.), Engring. Edn. Found. (trustee), Tau Beta Pi. Republican. Author: Machine Methods of Survey Computing, 1958, Construction Project Administration, 1978, 82, 88, Construction Engineers Form Book, 1981, Contractor's Project Guide, 1988. Home: PO Box 6448 Orange CA 92613-6448 Office: Three Pointe Dr Ste 103 Brea CA 92621

FISKE, SHIRLEY ANN, radiologist; b. Viroqua, Wis., May 15, 1951; d. Keith Wilson and Magdalene A. (Langve) F. BS in Zoology, U. Wis., 1972; DO, Kans. City Coll. Osteopathic Medicine, 1978. Diplomate Am. Bd. Radiology; cert. Am. Osteopathic Bd. Radiology. Staff radiologist Algoma (Wis.) Meml. Hosp., 1982-84, Lakeview Hosp., Milw., 1984-85, Phoenix Gen. Hosp., 1985—. Nat. Osteopathic Found. grantee, 1981. Mem. Am. Osteo. Assn., Ariz. Osteo. Assn., Radiol. Soc. N.Am., Am. Assn. Women Radiologists, Phoenix Radiol. Soc., Mineral. Soc. Methodist.

FITCH, DAVID BRODERICK, stockbroker, financial consultant; b. Wenatchee, Wash., Aug. 31, 1952; s. William Louis and Alice May (Broderick) F.; m. Molly Ann McIntyre, Sept. 13, 1986. AA, Montreat-Anderson Coll., 1972; BA in Econs. and Urban Planning, U. Wash., 1976. Project mgr. Olympic Assocs., Seattle, 1977-78; asst. mgr. Paul Nels Carlson Co., Seattle, 1978-79; project mgr. Koll Co., Newport Beach, Calif., 1979-82; fin. cons. Merrill Lynch, Bellevue, Wash., 1982—. Mem. Bellevue Athletic Club, Lakes Club, Seattle Tennis Club. Home: 1823 40th Ave E Seattle WA 98112 Office: Merrill Lynch 10900 NE 4th St Suite 2100 Bellevue WA 98004

FITCH, JOHN RICHARD, newspaper executive; b. Newark, Ohio, June 1, 1938; s. John Clyde and Mildred Josephine (Nethers) F.; m. Peggy Spencer, Apr. 17, 1959 (div. Jan. 1983); children: Joanne, Troy, Victoria, Valerie; m. Carol Critchlow, Mar. 24, 1984; 1 child, Megan Nicole. Student, Baylor U., 1958-59, Imperial Valley Coll., 1962. Newspaper advt. salesperson Associated Desert News, El Centro, Calif., 1960-64, advt. mgr., 1964-65, bus. mgr., 1965-66, gen. mgr., 1966-69, pub., 1969—, pres., editor, 1978—; chmn. govt. affairs Calif. Newspaper Pubs., Sacramento, 1982—, bd. dirs., former mem. exec. bd. Former mem. advt. bd. El Centro Community Hosp.; charter pres. Regional Econ. Devel. Corp., El Centro. With USAF, 1956-60. El Centro C. of C. (past pres.). Republican. Lodge: Kiwanis (past pres. and lt. gov., bd. dirs.). Home: 903 W McCabe Rd El Centro CA 92243 Office: Imperial Valley Press 205 N 8th St El Centro CA 92243

FITSCHEN, GARY THOMAS, architect; b. San Mateo, Calif., July 4, 1945; s. Stanley Adolph and Bessie Winifred (Bennett) F.; m. Susan Barbara Sborov, Sept. 16, 1967 (div. 1974); children: Leah Eve, Erica Alyce; m. Ophelia Barron Basgal, Oct. 6, 1984. BArch, U. Calif., Berkeley, 1968. Designer Welton Becket and Asscs., San Francisco, 1971-73; project mgr. Gensler and Assocs., San Francisco, 1974-79; pres. Fitschen and Assocs. Inc., San Francisco, 1979—. Prin. works include Shelter Project, Acameda County, remodelled Commercial Pier 33, San Francisco, project Bank of Am. Interiors; design team mem. So. Pacific office bldg., San Francisco. Mem. Pvt. Ind. Council (mem. Chair Planning Com. 1987—). Democrat. Club: City (San Francisco). Office: Fitschen & Assocs 448 Bryant St San Francisco CA 94107

FITZ, HERBERT HENRY, lawyer; b. San Francisco, June 21, 1934; s. Earl Moore and Alice Miller (MacCornack) Ellingson; m. Mary Powers. AB, Stanford U., 1956; JD, U. Calif., 1963. Atty. Spray, Gould & Powers, L.A., 1964-70; prof. Southwestern U. Sch. Law, L.A., 1970-74.

FITZGERALD, GLENN LESLIE, petroleum engineering company executive, consultant; b. Pottsville, Pa., Dec. 12, 1954; s. John Earl and Ethel Louise (Frantz) F. BS with high distinction, U. Ariz., 1976. Tchr., coach Lincoln High Sch., San Jose, Calif., 1976-77; sales rep. Century Pipe and Supply Co., Midland, Tex., 1977-79; engring. technician Amoco Prodn. Co. subs. Standard Oil Ind., Andrews, Tex., 1979-81; engring. mgr. Nabla Corp., Bakersfield, Calif., 1981—. Developer oil-related software programs, 1980—. Mem. Am. Petroleum Inst. Republican. Baptist. Home: 3605 Sonoita Dr Bakersfield CA 93309 Office: Nabla Corp PO Box 9275 Bakersfield CA 93389

FITZGERALD, JAMES MARTIN, judge; b. Portland, Oreg., Oct. 7, 1920; s. Thomas and Florence (Linderman) F.; m. Karin Rose Benton, Jan. 19, 1950; children: Dennis James, Denise Lyn, Debra Jo, Kevin Thomas. BA, Willamette U., 1950, LLB, 1951; postgrad., U. Wash., 1952. Bar: Alaska 1953. Asst. U.S. atty. Ketchikan and Anchorage, Alaska, 1952-56; city atty. City of Anchorage, 1956-59; legal counsel to Gov. Alaska, Anchorage, 1959; commr. pub. safety State of Alaska, 1959; judge Alaska Superior Ct., 3d Jud. Dist., 1959-69, presiding judge, 1969-72; assoc. justice Alaska Supreme Ct., Anchorage, 1972-75; judge U.S. Dist. Ct. for Alaska, Anchorage, from 1975, now chief judge. Mem. advisory bd. Salvation Army, Anchorage, 1962—, chmn., 1965-66; mem. Anchorage Parks and Recreation Bd., 1965-77, chmn., 1966. Served with AUS, 1940-41; Served with USMCR, 1942-46. Office: US Dist Ct 701 C St Box 50 Anchorage AK 99513 *

FITZGERALD, MARK CHARLES, publisher; b. Greenville, Miss., Oct. 9, 1955; s. James Charles and Alice Catherine (French) F. BA in Biology, U. Ariz., 1977; MA in Energy and Environ. Planning, Gov.'s State U., 1980. Community energy mgmt. specialist Nat. Ctr. Appropriate Tech., Butte, Mont., 1979-81; dir. mktg. RES Photovoltaic Engring., Scottsdale, Ariz., 1981-82; publisher PV Internat. mag. PVI Pub. Co., Denver, 1983—; co-founder Stone Soup and Salad, Inc., 1988—; bd. dirs. Sunwize Energy Systems, Inc. PV Info. Edn. Assn. (bd. dirs., chmn. 1985—). Roman Catholic. Home: PO Box 4168 Highlands Ranch CO 80126 Office: Photovoltaics Info Edn Assn PO Box 4169 Highlands Ranch CO 80126

FITZGERALD, MICHAEL THOMAS, administration executive; b. Beaumont, Tex., Mar. 12, 1948; s. Vincent Thomas and Elizabeth (Wilson) F.; m. Jonna Whalen, June 19, 1971; children: Sarah Laycock, Hilary Whalen. BA in Polit. Sci., Carroll Coll., Helena, Mont., 1970. Adminstrv. asst. to gov. State of Mont., Helena, 1971-73, 73-76, dep. dir. gov.'s office of commerce and trade, 1976-78; pres. and mng. dir. Mont. Internat. Trade Commn., Helena, 1978-86; dir. econ. devel. bd. State of Wash., Seattle, 1986-89; v.p., mng. dir. The Pacific Inst., Seattle, 1989—; mem. exec. com. Fedn. of Rocky Mountain States, 1971-75, Mont. Adv. Council on Children and Youth, 1972-74, U.S. Senator Max Baucus' Econ. Adv. Com. for the GATT and U.S. Trade bill, 1978-80, Dist. Export Council U.S. Dept. Commerce, 1978-87, We. Gov.'s Policy Office, 1979, We. Gov.'s Policy Office Internat. Trade Adv. Com., 1980-83, Learning Services Adv. Com. Mont. State U. System, 1980-81. Adv. Com. on Fgn. Language Skills and Internat. Studies Mont. State Bd. Edn., 1980-81; bd. dirs. and first v.p. Pvt. Industry Council Mont., Inc.; mem. and trustee Helena Learners Exchange, Inc., 1979-81, (founding) Mont. Ambassadors, 1984-86; Gov.'s Adv. Council on Econ. Devel., 1984-86; mem. and coordinator Gov.'s Fgn. Trade Expansion Com., 1973-74, Gov.'s Task Force on the Future Role of State Govt. in Econ. Planning and Devel., 1976, Gov.'s Coal Gasification Task Force, 1976-77; chmn. Indsl. Devel. Com. Old West Regional Commn., 1976-77, Internat. Trade Seminar We. Gov.'s Conf./Vail Symposium, 1980; vice-chmn. and project dir. Mont. Econ. Devel. Project, 1981-83; co-chmn. and project coordinator Gov. Schwinden's Trade and Investment Briefing for Japanese Cos., 1983; pres. and co-founder Mont. Internat. Friendship Service, Inc., 1982-86; del. White House Conf. on Internat. Trade, 1980, U.S.A./Taiwan Trade and Econ. Council Meetings, 1979, 80, 83, We. Gov.'s Roundtable on Internat. Trade, 1983, Japan Media Relations Forum com. for Humanities and The Wilson Ctr., 1984; Gov.'s rep. Indian Affairs Adv. Council Office of Indian Affairs, 1973-75; organized and conceptualized "Public Forum on the Future of Montana's Economy" Mont. Com. for the Humanities, 1977; organized and chaired first USSR/Mont. Trade Meeting USSR/USA Trade and Econ. Council, 1985; Mont. liaison White House Conf. on Balanced Growth and Econ. Devel., 1977; selected to attend Long Term Credit Bank of Japan's Internat. Trade and Banking Seminar, 1984; selected by Gov. Booth Gardner to attend exec. sem. Kennedy Sch., 1988; speaker Mont. Constl. Conv. Reunion, 1982; organized trade missions to Can., Asia, Europe and North Africa for Gov.'s Judge and Schwinden, 1975-86; bd. dirs., trustee New Milwaukee Lines Corp. New Milw. Found., 1980-82; bd. dirs. Mike Mansfield Ctr. for Pacific Affairs, 1984-87, Mountain States Energy Co., 1983-86. Club: The Montana (Helena),(bd. govs. 1983-86). Home: 19215 SE 46th S Cove Issaquah WA 98027 Office: The Pacific Inst 1201 Western Ave Seattle WA 98101

FITZGERALD, ROBERT EMMET, architect; b. Derby, Conn., Sept. 22, 1954; s. Robert William and Katherine (Welser) F.; m. Jessie Marie Brunner, Sept. 3, 1983; 1 child, Robert Lewis. BS, Cen. Conn. St. U., 1976; MArch, Ohio State U., 1980. Registered architect, Colo. Sr. designer Skidmore, Owings & Merrill, Denver, 1981-87; project designer The Mulhern Group, Denver, 1987—; furniture designer STC, Inc., Denver, 1987—. Mem. Historic Denver. Mem. AIA (com. mem. Colo. Design Conf. 1986), Nat. Trust for Historic Preservation. Democrat. Roman Catholic. Office: The Mulhern Group 1900 Wazee St Denver CO 80202

FITZGERALD, ROBERT LYNN, small business owner; b. Indiana, Pa., Oct. 1, 1939; s. Joseph and Jean (Smith) F.; m. Ellen J. Turner, July 17, 1971 (div. Aug. 1974); 1 child, Robert Lynn Jr. Student, Orange Coast Coll., 1985-86. Dist. mgr. Napco Sci., Portland, Oreg., 1981-88; prin., pub. Fitzgerald's Real Esate Yellow Pages, Santa Ana, Calif., 1987—. Hospice vol. Orange County (Calif.), Vis. Nurses Assn., 1980; founder Orange County HELP chpt., Santa Ana, 1982. Home: 330E W Carriage Dr Santa Ana CA 92707 Home: Fitzgerald's Real Estate Yellow Pages 1420 E Edinger Ave Santa Ana CA 92705

FITZGERALD, WILLIAM BRENDAN, lawyer; b. Waterbury, Conn., May 4, 1936; s. William Brendan Sr. and Margaret (Cunning) F.; m. Teresa Vannini, Oct. 12, 1963 (div. Oct. 1980); children: W. Brendan III, Nicholas S., Francesca V. BA cum laude, Yale U., 1958; JD, Harvard U., 1961; cert. in higher European Studies, Coll. Europe, Bruges, Belgium, 1962. Bar: Conn. 1961, Calif. 1985. Ptnr. Fitzgerald & Fitzgerald, Waterbury, Conn., 1961-72, Carmody & Torrance, Waterbury, 1972-85, Haight, Dickson, Brown & Bonesteel, Santa Monica, Calif., 1985-88, Dickson, Carlson & Campillo, Santa Monica, 1988—. Rotary Internat. fellow, 1961. Fellow Am. Coll. Trial Lawyers, Roscoe Pound Found; mem. ABA (litigation, torts and ins. sects.), Calif. Bar Assn., Conn. Bar Assn. (acad. continuing profl. devel. 1982, judiciary com. 1982-85, jud. liason com. 1985), Def. Rsch. inst., Assn. So. Calif. Def. Counsel, Am. Arbitrations Assn. (panelist), Conn. Trial Lawyers Assn. (pres. 1985), Am. Bd. Trial Advs., Nat. Bd. Trial Advocacy (diplomate). Democrat. Club: Yale (N.Y.C.). Office: Dickson Carlson & Campillo 1401 Ocean Ave 2nd Fl Santa Monica CA 90401

FITZGIBBONS, JOSEPH GARRET, data processing executive; b. Cordeele, Ga., Mar. 10, 1929; s. Eleanor (Dekle) F.; divorced; children: Janet, Greg; m. Betty Chandler. BS in Math, U. N.C., 1951. System engr. IBM Corp., Atlanta, 1955-56, Washington, 1956-57; salesman IBM Corp., Miami, Fla., 1957-59, West Palm Beach, Fla., 1959-60; dept. mgr. IBM Corp., Cambridge, Mass., 1960-64; system mgr. IBM Corp., White Plains, N.Y., 1964-66; ops. mgr. IBM Corp., San Jose, Calif., 1966-69; system mgr. IBM Corp., Raleigh, N.C., 1969; pres. sales and svc. corp. Memorex Corp., Santa Clara, Calif., 1970-72, v.p., gen. mgr., 1972-73; v.p. mktg. and ops. TRW, Los Angeles, 1975-80; v.p., gen. mgr. TRW-Fujitsu, Los Angeles, 1980-82; pres. Baron Data Systems, San Learcho, Calif., 1982—; chief exec. officer MSC Technologies, Santa Clara, 1988—; bd. dirs. Wave Tek Corp., San Orego, Calif., MSC Technologies, Santa Clara. Served to Lt. j.g. USN, 1951-55. Republican. Episcopalian. Home: 229 Oyster Pond Rd Alameda CA 94501 Office: MSC Techs Inc 47505 Seabridge Dr Fremont CA 94538

FITZ-HENLEY, NORMAN HOWARD, physician; b. Port-au-Prince, Haiti, Sept. 25, 1931; came to U.S., 1961, naturalized, 1968; s. Randolph and Doris (Campbell) Fitz-Henley; children: Onyl Grace, Garnell Dean, John Aldwyn, Orville Jay. Student CCNY, 1967; M.D., George Washington U., 1971. Ofcl. verbatim ct. reporter Supreme Ct. Kingston, Jamaica, 1951-61; freelance ct. reporter Beekman's Reporting Service, N.Y.C., 1962-67; intern D.C. Gen. Hosp., George Washington U. Service, Washington, 1971-72; resident in internal medicine, U. Calif., San Diego, 1972-75; practice medicine specializing in internal medicine, El Centro, Calif., 1975—; chmn. dept. medicine El Centro Community Hosp., 1977, 85, chief-of-staff, 1987—; chmn. dept. medicine Pioneers Meml. Hosp., Brawley, 1986, vice chief-of-staff, 1987—; bd. dirs. Valley Ind. Bank, El Centro, John M. Perkins Found. Active non-denominational religious evang. affairs. Life fellow Royal Soc. Arts (London); mem. AMA, Calif. Med. Assn., Am. Heart Assn., Imperial County Med. Soc., Calif. Heart Assn., Imperial Valley Heart Assn. (bd. dirs.), Alpha Sigma Lambda. Co-inventor Fitz-Henley's All-Curve System of Shorthand, 1962. Home: PO Box 479 El Centro CA 92244 Office: 1745 S Imperial Ave El Centro CA 92243 Office: 126 Main St Brawley CA 92227

FITZMAURICE, LEONA CLAIRE, biotechnology researcher; b. Grand Rapids, Minn., Apr. 25, 1945; d. Clair Carlton and Norma Annetta (Behm) Phillips. BA in Biology, U. Chgo., 1967; PhD in Cellular and Molecular Biology, U. So. Calif., 1973. Postdoctoral fellow Nat. Inst. Med. Research, London, 1973-74, U. Glasgow, Scotland, 1974-77, U. Calif., Los Angeles, 1977-79; research expert NIH, Bethesda, Md., 1979-82; research scientist Phytogen, Inc., Pasadena, Calif., 1982-83; staff scientist SIBIA, Inc., La Jolla, Calif., 1983—. Contbr. articles to profl. jours. Bd. dirs. Timberlane Homeowners' Assn., San Diego, 1985—. Scholar Nat. Merit, 1963-67, U. Chgo., 1963-67; fellow NATO postdoctoral, 1973-74, Nat. Cancer Inst., 1973-78; recipient traineeship NSF, 1970-73, Nat. Cancer Inst., 1978-79. Mem. AAAS, ACS, N.Y. Acad. Scis., Internat. Soc. Plant Molecular Biology, Sierra Club. Democrat. Episcopalian. Office: SIBIA Inc 505 Coast Blvd S San Diego CA 92037

FITZPATRICK, ROBERT WILLIAM, service executive; b. Omaha, Sept. 1, 1929; s. James J. and Gladys (Reece) F.; m. Patricia Ann Cunningham, June 25, 1946; children: Linda A., Robert P., James J., Michaela M., Matthew S. Student, Omaha Tech., 1947-52. Cert. engring. ops. exec., 1988; lic. elect. contractor, Nev., Nebr., Iowa. Various positions Met. Utilities Dist., Omaha, 1946-51; founder, pres. Fitzpatrick Constrn. Co., Fitzpatrick Electric Inc., Sun Ray Lighting Co. of Nebr., Omaha, 1951-78; project mgr., cons. supt. Scott Corp., Tonopah/Las Vegas, 1978-80; project mgr. Union Plaza Hotel and Casino, Las Vegas, 1980-83; asst. facilities mgr. Caesars Palace, Las Vegas, 1983-85; dir. facilities MGM Desert Inn, Inc., Las Vegas, 1985—; v.p. Desert Inn Improvement, Las Vegas. Charter mem. Daniel Gross High Sch. Bd., 1974-77. Mem. Nev. Resort Assn., KC, Edn. Inst. Am. Hotel and Motel Assn. (chief exec. officer), Cosmopolitan Internat. Club. Democrat. Roman Catholic. Office: MGM Desert Inn Inc 3145 Las Vegas Blvd S Las Vegas NV 89109

FITZSIMMONS, CHRISTOPHER, electrical engineer; b. San Antonio, Oct. 20, 1960; s. James Martin and Joan Barbara (Deisenroth) F. BS, U. Ariz., 1984. Engring. technician NASA/Johnson Space Ctr., Houston, 1983; elec. engr. govt. electronics group Motorola, Scottsdale, Ariz., 1984-87; mktg. engr. semiconductor products sector Motorola, Phoenix, 1987—. Republican. Roman Catholic. Office: Motorola 5005 E McDowell A125 Phoenix AZ 85008

FITZSIMMONS, KEVIN MICHAEL, biologist, consultant; b. Tucson, Apr. 9, 1956; s. James Martin and Joan Barbara (Deisenroth) F.; m. Linda Anne Almond, Dec. 30., 1978; children: Michael, Patrick. BS, U. Ariz., 1978; MS, U. W. Fla., 1988. Biologist Nat. Marine Fisheries Svc., Destin, Fla., 1979-81; rsch. asst. environ. rsch. lab. U. Ariz., Tucson, 1981-84, program coord., 1984—; cons. Fusades, U.S. Aid, El Salvador, 1985, Ptnrs. of the Americas, Washington, 1985, Biosphere II Project, Tucson, 1985-87, Alfico, Houston, 1987—. Contbr. articles to profl. jours. U. W. Fla. fellow, 1979. Mem. Ariz. Aquaculture Assn. (bd. dirs. 1987—, v.p. 1989—), World Aquaculture Soc., Am. Fisheries Soc., Nat. Geographic Soc. Office: U Ariz Environ Rsch Lab 2601 E Airport Dr Tucson AZ 85706

FITZSIMMONS, LOWELL COTTON, professional basketball coach; b. Hannibal, Mo., Oct. 7, 1931; s. Clancy and Zelda Curry (Gibbs) F.; m. JoAnn D'Andrea, Sept. 2, 1978 (div.); 1 child, Gary. B.S., Midwestern Univ., Wichita Falls, Tex., M.A. Head coach, athletic dir. Moberly Jr. Coll, Moberly, Mo., 1958-67; head coach Kans. State U., Manhattan, 1967-70; head coach NBA Phoenix Suns, 1970-72, 1988—, dir. player personnel, 1987-88; head coach NBA Atlanta Hawks, 1972-76; dir. player personnel NBA Golden State Warriors, Oakland, Calif., 1976-77; head coach NBA Buffalo Braves, 1977-78, NBA Kansas City Kings, Mo., 1978-84, NBA San Antonio Spurs, 1984-87. Recipient Coach of the Yr. award Nat. Jr. Coll. Athletic Assn., 1966, 67, Coach of the Yr. award Big 8 Conf., 1970, Coach of the Yr. award NBA, 1979, 89, Coach of the Yr. award Sporting News, St. Louis, 1979, 89; inducted into Mo. Sports Hall of Fame, Jefferson City, 1981, Nat. Jr. Coll. Basketball Hall of Fame, Hutchinson, 1985. Fellow Nat. Assn. Basketball Coaches. Office: Phoenix Suns 2910 N Central Ave Phoenix AZ 85012 *

FJORDBOTTEN, EDWIN LEROY, Canadian provincial official; b. Claresholm, Alta., Can., Nov. 4, 1938; s. Artun Edwin and Belinda Janet (Enbysk) F.; m. Deanne Marie Perchinsky, Nov. 16, 1962; children—Tracy, Karine. Grad. Camrose Luth. Coll., 1956. Farmer, nr. Granum, Alta., Can., 1960-83; mem. Alta. Legis. Assembly, Edmonton, 1979—, minister of agr., 1982-86, minister of tourism, 1986-87, minister of forestry, Lands and Wildlife, 1987—. Progressive Conservative. Lutheran. Office: Alta Legis Assembly, Legislature Bldg, Rm 403, Edmonton, AB Canada T5K 2B7

FLAGG, NORMAN L., retired advertising executive; b. Detroit, Jan. 21, 1932; s. Frank and Harriet (Brown) F.; m. Carolanne; 1 child, James. BFA, U. Miami, Fla., 1958. advt. supr. Smithkline Beckman, Phila., 1970-75, creative dir., 1975-80; owner Illusions Restaurante, Bryn Maur, Pa., 1979-87, Tucson, Ariz., 1984-88. With USMCR 1954-56. Recipient Diana awards Whlse Druggest Assn. 1977, Aesculapius award Modern Medicine 1978. Mem. Acad. Magical Arts. Republican.

FLAGLER, WILLIAM LAWRENCE, publisher, purchasing consultant; b. Oakland, Calif., June 13, 1922; s. Albert William and Violet Dorthy (Marris) F.; B.A., San Francisco State U., 1951; degree in Library Sci., San Jose State U., 1963; m. Ruth Greiner Gilbert, Aug. 23, 1970; children by previous marriage—Vickie, David, Michael; stepchildren—Denise Gilbert La Hay, Ethan Gilbert. Pres., LaRu Enterprises, San Jose, Calif., 1975—. Active Boy Scouts Am. Served with U.S. Army, World War II, ETO. Republican. Club: Masons. Office: PO Box 10460 San Jose CA 95157

FLAHAVIN, MARIAN JOAN, artist; b. Colton, Wash., Nov. 19, 1937; d. Herbert Joseph and Margaret Thersa (McGinn) Druffel; m. G. Thomas Flahavin, Aug. 6, 1960; 1 child, John Thomas. BA in Art, Holy Names Coll., 1959; studied with, John Howard and Daniel Green. With pub. rels. Holy Names Coll., Spokane, Wash., 1959-70; artist-in-residence Spokane, 1974—; tchr. and speaker in field. Prin. work represented in galleries and shows, nation wide; prin. work includes collectible plate series. Mem. Pastel Soc. Am., Am. Portrait Soc., Pastel Soc. Spokane, Pastel Soc. West Coast. Roman Catholic. Home and Office: RR 7 Schafer Rd Spokane WA 99206

FLAIM, SILVIO JOSEPH, economist, consultant; b. Augusta, Ga., Feb. 19, 1952; s. Rudolph Alfred and Bernice Marie (Haddock) F.; m. Mary Louise Prosser, May 25, 1974; children—Amanda Leigh, Michael Joseph. B.S. in Agrl. Econs., U. Mo., Columbia, 1973, M.S., 1974; Ph.D. in Resource Econs., Cornell U., 1978. Teaching and research asst., U. Mo., Cornell U., 1970-77; econ. cons., AID, Nicaragua, 1973; sr. economist Solar Energy Research Inst., Golden, Colo., 1977-81; sr. economist, Amoco Prodn. Co., Denver, 1981-83, Argonne Nat. Labs., Chgo., 1985—; cons. on valuation of mineral properties, tax, fin. for litigation and renewable energy applications in agr., environ. econ., tax law. Mem. Am. Agrl. Econs. Assn., Am. Econs. Assn., Western Econs. Assn. Contbr. articles to profl. jours. Home: 31808 Quarterhorse Rd Evergreen CO 80439 Office: PO Box 879 Evergreen CO 80439

FLAKE, DONALD OWENS, automation manufacturing company executive; b. Boise, Idaho, Apr. 12, 1957; s. Robert Kenneth and Mae (Thomas) F.; m. Bridget Kem Driggs, May 18, 1979; children: Amanda, Kemberlyn, Benjamin, Thomas, Moroni. BS, Ariz. State U., 1984. Pres., chief exec. officer Ammon Corp., Mesa, Ariz., 1982--. Trustee Internat. Biomechanics Found., Mesa, 1985--. Republican. Mormon. Office: Ammon Corp 2150 S Country Club Dr 16 Mesa AZ 85210

FLAMSON, RICHARD JOSEPH, III, banker; b. Los Angeles, Feb. 2, 1929; s. Richard J. and Mildred (Jones) F.; m. Arden Black, Oct. 5, 1951; children: Richard Joseph IV, Scott Arthur, Michael Jon, Leslie Arden. B.A., Claremont Men's Coll., 1951; cert. Pacific Coast Banking Sch., U. Wash., 1962. With Security Pacific Nat. Bank, Los Angeles, 1955—, v.p., 1962-69, sr. v.p., 1969-70, exec. v.p. corp. banking dept., 1970-73, vice-chmn., 1973-78, pres., chief exec. officer, 1978-81, chmn., chief exec. officer, 1981—, dir., 1981-85; also dir. Security Pacific Corp., Los Angeles; vice-chmn. Security Pacific Corp., 1973-78, pres., 1978-81, chief exec. officer 1978—, chmn., 1981—; bd. dirs. Northrop Corp., Kaufman and Broad, GTE Calif. Inc. Trustee Claremont Men's Coll. 1st lt. AUS, 1951-53. Mem. Res. City Bankers, Robert Morris Assocs., Town Hall, Stock Exchange Club. Clubs: Caif. Los Angeles Country; Balboa Bay (Newport Beach, Calif.), Balboa Yacht (Newport Beach, Calif.). Office: Security Pacific Corp 333 S Hope St Los Angeles CA 90071 *

FLANDERS, GEORGE JAMES, mechanical engineer, engineering development manager; b. Bunker Hill, Ind., June 3, 1960; s. Melvin S. and Edith J. (Mason) F. BSME, Bradley U., 1982, MBA, 1984. Lab. engr. Materials Testing & Rsch. Lab., Peoria, Ill., 1982; rsch. design engr. Caterpillar Tractor Co., Peoria, 1982-85; staff engr. Bristol Myers Co., Englewood, Colo., 1985-86, sr. engr., bus. unit mgr. arthoscopy and reconstructive surgery products, 1986-87; sr. engr., Titan project bus. proposal coordinator Titan Space Launch Systems, Martin Marietta Astronautics Group, Denver, 1987-88; co-founder, chief exec. officer ILCO Mgmt. and Holding Group, Denver, 1988—; cons. in field. Area coordinator Neighborhood Watch Program, 1988—; mem. fin. com. Littleton United Meth. Ch., 1987—. Mem. NSPE, ASME, Soc. Automotive Engrs., Sigma Phi Delta (grand pres. 1988—, v.p. 1985-87, trustee chmn. 1988—), Tau Beta Pi, Pi Tau Sigma, Omicron Delta Kappa. Home: 15095 E Louisiana Dr Aurora CO 80012 Office: Martin Marietta Astronautics Group PO Box 179 Denver CO 80201

FLANTER, JILL SELEVAN, TV hostess; b. Miami Beach, Fla., July 8, 1950; d. Bernard E. and Phyllis Anita (Gordon) Selevan; m. Neil Flanter, Dec. 30, 1972 (div. Feb. 1974). BA, U. Tex., 1972. TV hostess Palm Springs, Calif., 1985—; neurolinguistic programming expert Advanced Community Techs., Glendale, Calif., 1986—. Mem. Internat. Brotherhood Magicians, SAG, AFTRA. Republican. Office: PO Box 46381 Los Angeles CA 90046

FLATT, MICHAEL OLIVER, manufacturing company executive; b. Glen Rogers, W.Va., Aug. 14, 1938; s. Reuben Edgar and Margaret Elenor (Gansor) F.; m. Judie Arlene Carroll, Aug. 12, 1961 (div. Oct. 1970); m. Joanie Louise Smith, Nov. 26, 1970; children: Rachel, Joshua. BS in Mech. Engring., U. Ill., 1961. Mfg. engr. Gen. Electric Co., Bloomington, Ill., 1961-63; process engr. Gen. Electric Co., Detroit, 1963-64; quality control mgr. Gen. Electric Co., Daytona Beach, Fla., 1964-65; advance planner Gen. Electric Co., Phoenix, 1965-68; mgr. quality control Computer Memory Devices, Glendale, Ariz., 1968-71; gen. mgr. Continental Cirs. Corp., Phoenix, 1971-75, pres., 1975-83, chmn. bd., 1983--. Mem. editorial rev. bd. Printed Cir. Fabrication, 1985--; contbr. articles to tech. mags. Active various state, local and nat. polit. campaigns, Mesa, 1974--; bd. dirs. Prehab Ariz., Mesa, 1981--. Mem. IPC (bd. dirs. 1989), Inst. for Packaging and Interconnecting Electronic Cirs., Tech. and Mktg. Rsch. Coun., Ariz. Printed Cir. Assn. (founding bd. dirs. 1975), Western Cirs. Assn. (pres. Phoenix chpt. 1972-73), Lions (pres. Phoenix chpt. 1975-76, mem. pres.'s coun. Ariz. chpt. 1975-76), Phi Eta Sigma, Pi Mu Epsilon. Republican. Office: Continental Cirs Corp 3502 E Roeser st Phoenix AZ 85040

FLATTERY, DAVID KEVIN, technology corporation executive; b. South Ruislip, Middlesex, Eng., July 10, 1960; s. Thomas Wilson and Annette (La Brucherie) F. BS, Harvard U., 1980; postgrad., U. Pa., 1983-85. Research, applications engr. Radiant Tech. Corp., Cerritos, Calif., 1980-83, dir. research, 1985-88, also bd. dirs., 1986—, v.p., 1988—; pres. Spectrum Cons. Group, Phila., 1983-85. Contbr. articles to profl. jours.; holder 2 patents in field. Mem. Internat. Soc. for Hybrid Microelectronics (Tech. Achievement award 1986), IEEE, Semicondr. Equipment and Materials Inst. Office: Radiant Tech Corp 13856 Bettencourt St Cerritos CA 90701

FLAX, MICHAEL GREG, obstetrician, gynecologist, educator; b. Salt Lake City, Oct. 27, 1945; s. Leo Jay and Bernice (Goldberg) F.; m. Jane Vogan, Aug. 8, 1971; children: Rebecca Dara, Rachel Michel. BA, U. Colo., 1967, postgrad., 1967-69; Medico-Cirujano, Autonomous U. Guadalajara, 1973; MD, Dalhousie U., Halifax, N.S., Can., 1975. Diplomate Am. Bd. Ob-Gyn. Resident in ob-gyn U. Western Ont. (Can.), London, 1975-78; chief resident W.Va. U., Morgantown, 1978-79; pvt. practice Newport, Oreg., 1979-80, Albuquerque, 1980—; instr. ob-gyn U. N.Mex. Med. Sch., Albuquerque, 1981—. Fellow Am. Coll. Obstetricians and Gynecologists, Cen. Assn. Obstetricians and Gynecologists; mem. AMA, Internat. Soc. for Advancement Humanistic Studies in Gynecology, Am. Med. Athletic Assn., S.W. Ob-Gyn Soc. Democrat. Jewish. Office: 8401 Constitution NE Albuquerque NM 87110

FLECK, PAUL DUNCAN, continuing education center administrator; b. Montreal, Que., Can., Apr. 17, 1934; s. Robert Douglas and Norma Marie (Byrnes) F.; m. Margaret Louise Pollard, Sept. 1, 1956; children—John, Christopher, Franklin Conor. B.A., U. Western Ont., 1955, M.A., 1958; Ph.D., Queen's U., Northern Ireland, 1961. Chmn. dept. English, U. Western Ont., London, Can., 1967-70, prof. English, 1970, chmn. dept. English, 1970-74; pres. Ont. Coll. Art, Toronto, Can., 1975-82, The Banff Centre, Alta., Can., 1982—; dir. The Ency. of Music in Can., The Banff Television Found.; pres., chmn. bd. dirs. NDWT Theatre Co., Toronto, 1979-82; bd. dirs. Art mag., Toronto, 1980-82, Toronto Consort, 1981-82; mem. exec. bd. Council for Bus. and Arts in Can., 1982-88; mem. OCO '88 Arts Festival com.; lectr. in field. Contbr. articles to profl. jours. Imperial Oil fellow, 1958-61; Can. Council grantee, 1964, 75. Mem. Assn. Can. Univ. Tchrs. of English (pres. 1974-76), Byron Soc. (chmn. Can. com. 1974—), Can. Assn. Fine Arts Deans (chmn. 1980-82), Internat. Council Fine Arts Deans (Can. exec. bd. 1980-83), Can. Soc. Decorative Arts (v.p. 1985—). United Ch. of Can. Clubs: University, Arts and Letters (v.p. 1980-82) (Toronto). Home: 101 St Julian Rd, Banff, AB Canada T0L 0C0 Office: The Banff Centre, Box 1020, Banff, AB Canada T0L 0C0

FLECKNER, ALAN NORMAN, obstetrician, gynecologist; b. N.Y.C., May 3, 1934; s. Paul Richard and Martha (Feldman) F.; m. Marlyn Heckel, Dec. 17, 1955 (div. 1974); children: David, Marcia, Brett; m. Ann Marie McGranachan, March 29, 1976; stepchildren: Patricia Minard, Charles Minard, Donna Minard. BS in Pharm., Forham U., 1956; MD, Jefferson Med. Coll., Phila., 1960; MPH, Harvard U., 1969. Diplomate Am. Bd. Ob-Gyn., Am. Bd. Emergency Obstetricians and Gynocologists (cert.), Am. Bd. Emergency Medicine. Intern Fitznam Gen. Hosp., Denver, 1960-61; resident in ob-gyn. Boston City Hosp., 1964-67; fellow in demography and human ecology Harvard U. Sch. Pub. Health, Cambridge, 1967-69; med. dir. Maternal Infant Care Project, Boston, 1967-69; physician, v.p. Middlesex GYN-OB, Inc., Billerica, Mass., 1969-80; assoc. chief ob. St. Joseph's Hosp., Lowell, 1972-78; chief emergency svcs. San Bernadino (Calif.) County Med. Ctr., 1980-83; pvt. practice Hemet, Calif., 1982-87; emergency room physician Desert Hosp., Palm Springs, Calif., 1983—; dir. ambulatory care dept. St. Joseph Hosp., Lowell, Mass., 1977-80; instr. ob-gyn. Boston U. Sch. Medicine, 1967-70; clin. instr. ob-gyn. Tufts U. Med. Sch., Boston, 1975-80; adj. assoc. profl. health services Lowell U., 1973-80; instr. health sci. Calif. Community Coll., 1982—; cons. in field. Editor: Programmed Guide to Sex Education, 1969; contbr. articles to profl. jours. Mem. Nashoba Assn. Bd. Health, 1973-74, Westford Bd. Health, 1973-74 ; chmn. Lowell Emergency Med. Services com., 1978-80; dist. med. officer, Lowell Council Boy Scouts Am., 1970-80, asst. scout master, 1970-77; advisor med. assts. program, Middlesex Community Coll. Served to col. USAF, 1959-64, Vietnam; with reserves, 1964-87; with U.S. Army, 40th inf. div. CAARNG, 1987—. Decorated Meritorious Service medal, Air Force Commendation medal, and others; recipient Outstanding Aerospace Medicine Physician USAFR, 1975. Fellow Am. Coll. Emergency Physicians, Am. Coll. Obstetricians and Gynocologists, Coll. Physicians of Phila. (assoc.), Am. Coll. Preventative Medicine; mem. Soc. Air Force Flight Surgeons (Flight Surgeon of the Year 1976), AMA, Am. Occupational Medicine Assn., Assn. Mil. Surgeons, Air Force Assn., Res. Officers Assn., Calif. Med. Assn., Am. Acad. Family Physicians, Aerospace Med. Assn., Riverside County Med. Assn., Am. Soc. Colposcopy and Cervical Pathology, Am. Coll. Med., Nat. Guard Assn. Office: Desert Hosp 1150 Indian Ave Palm Springs CA 92262

FLEDDERJOHN, KARL ROSS, manufacturing executive; b. Indpls., Aug. 28, 1935; s. Riley Bartel and Virginia Louise (Saalmiller) F.; m. Mary Ann Hilligoss, Apr. 5, 1953; children: Deborah Westley, Diane Luke, Dan, Laura. BSME, Gen. Motors Inst., Flint, Mich., 1958; MBA, Butler U., 1966. Engr. Allison div. Gen. Motors, Indpls., 1957-69; devel. specialist Garrett Turbine Engine Co., Phoenix, Ariz., 1970-71; asst. project. engr. Garrett Turbine Engine Co., Phoenix, 1971-74, chief project engr., 1974-83; engring. dir. Garrett Pneumatic Systems Div., Tempe, 1983, asst. div. mgr., 1983-86, v.p., div. mgr., 1986-88; pres. AiResearch Group, Allied Signal Aerospace Co., Torrance, Calif., 1988—. Office: AiResearch Group Allied-Signal Aerospace Co 2525 W 190th St Torrance CA 90509

FLEGENHEIMER, DIANA VAUGHN, fundraiser; b. Denver, Jan. 26, 1945; d. Michael and Virginia Rose (Barnes) Grega; m. Michael Lee, Dec., 1967 (div. Dec. 1973); m. Roy Alan Flegenheimer, July 28, 1974; children: Elon Michael, Rachel Anne. AA, Hutchinson (Kans.) Jr. Coll., 1965; BS, Kans. U., 1967; MA, Ariz. State U., 1972. Cert. high sch. tchr., Ariz. Math tchr. various high schs., Ariz. and Mo., 1967-75; devel. officer Ariz. Mus. Sci. and Tech., Phoenix, 1986-88, Desert Botanical Garden, Phoenix, 1988—. Mem. Samaritans, 1987—; adv. mem. Actors Theater, 1987—; Women's campaign chmn. United Jewish campaign, 1984-86; mem. Valley Leadership, 1986-87. Recipient Lee Amada Young Leadership award Jewish Fedn. Greater Phoenix, 1981. Mem. Nat. Soc. Fund Raising Execs. (bd. dirs. Greater Ariz. chpt.), Jewish Bus. and Profl. Women's Nat. Coun., Beta Gamma Sigma, Phi Lambda Theta, Phi Theta Kappa. Democrat. Jewish. Home: 11626 N 50th Pl Scottsdale AZ 85254

FLEISCHMANN, ERNEST MARTIN, music association administrator; b. Frankfurt, Germany, Dec. 7, 1924; came to U.S., 1969; s. Gustav and Antonia (Koch) F.; children: Stephanie, Martin, Jessica. B of Commerce, U. Cape Town, Republic of South Africa, 1950, MusB, 1954; postgrad., South African Coll. Music, 1954-56; MusD (hon.), Cleve. Inst. Music, 1987. Gen mgr. London Symphony Orch., 1959-67; dir. European div. CBS Records, 1967-69; exec. dir. L.A. Philharm. Orch., 1969-88; gen. dir.. Hollywood Bowl, 1969-88; exec. v.p., mng. dir. L.A. Philharm. Assn., 1988—; bd. dirs. Am. Music Music Ctr., Inc.; mem. French Govt. Commn. Reform of Paris Opera, 1967-68; steering com. U.S. nat. commn. UNESCO Conf. Future of Arts, 1975. Debut as condr. Johannesburg (Republic of South Africa) Symphony Orch., 1942; asst. condr. South African Nat. Opera, 1948-51, Cape Town U. Opera, 1950-54; condr. South African Coll. Music Choir, 1950-52, Labia Grand Opera Co., Cape Town, 1953-55; music organizer Van Riebeeck Festival Cape Town, 1952; dir. music and drama Johannesburg Festival, 1956; contbr. to music publs. Bd. dirs. Calif. Confedn. of Arts. Recipient award of merit Los Angeles Jr. C. of C., John Steinway award, Friends of Music award Disting. Arts Leadership Univ. So. Calif., 1989. Mem. Assn. Calif. Symphony Orchs. (bd. dirs., Pres.'s Spl. award), Major Orch. Mgrs. Conf., Am. Symphony Orch. League (vice chmn. bd. dirs.). Office: Los Angeles Philharm Orch 135 N Grand Ave Los Angeles CA 90012

FLEMING, ELIZABETH JOYCE, dentist; b. Phoenix, Aug. 27, 1959; d. George Lawrence and Margaret Clare (Clark) F. BS cum laude, Ariz. State U., 1981; DDS with honors, U. Pacific, 1984. Gen practice dentistry Phoenix, 1984—; dentist Sunshine Dental Clinic, Phoenix, 1984-86; staff mem. dental dept. St. Joe's Hosp., Phoenix, 1985—. Mem. Cen. Ariz. Dental Assn. (mem. study club 1985—). Democrat. Roman Catholic. Office: 10240 N 31st Ave Suite 100 Phoenix AZ 85051

FLEMING, KATHLEEN GAIL, computer operations specialist; b. Staten Island, N.Y., Nov. 21, 1944; d. Fulton Lamont and Edna (Geist) Reid; m. Terry Lowell Fleming, Sept. 27, 1969; children: Heather Kathleen, Kevin Reid, Shannon Joy, Colin Martin. BS in Nursing, Wagner Coll., 1966. R.N., Oreg. Office nurse pvt. practice physician, Reno, Nev., 1972-73; staff nurse Green Valley Care Ctr., Eugene, Oreg., 1973-74, Good Samaritan Hosp., Portland, Oreg., 1974-75, Vet.'s Hosp., Portland, 1975, Woodland Park Hosp., Portland, 1975-78; office nurse pvt. practice physician, Beaverton, Oreg., 1978; staff nurse Forest Grove (Oreg.) Community Hosp., 1978-79; head maternity dept. Tuality Community Hosp., Hillsboro, Oreg., 1979-82; computer operator Transaction Recording Systems, Inc., Portland, 1982—. Bd. dirs. Washington County Assn. Retarded Citizens, Beaverton, 1984-86; parent contact, Pilot Parents, Washington County, 1986—. Lt. USN, 1964-69. Mem. Oreg. Apt. Assn. Republican. Presbyterian. Home: HCR61 Box 78K Banks OR 97106

FLEMING, MARILYN BROKERING, nurse, educator; b. Hart, Mich., Sept. 21, 1941; d. Harry Bernard and Miriam Irene (Slanker) Brokering; m. Thomas Charles Fleming, Aug. 24, 1963; children: Jon, Janine Allen, Juliana, Charley, Skye, Rainbow. BS in Nursing, U. Pitts., 1963; MS in Nursing, U. N.Mex., 1981. Cert. Lamaze Prepared Childbirth instr., vocat. tchr., N.Mex. Staff head, head nurse Columbia Presbyn. Hosp., N.Y.C., 1963-67; staff nurse Univ. Heights Hosp., Albuquerque, 1968-69; recovery room nurse Sinai Hosp. of Detroit, 1969-71; instr. Lamaze Prepared Childbirth, Childbirth Without Pain Ednl. Assn., various cities, 1972-85; coordinator edn. and infection control S.W. Meml. Hosp., Cortez, Colo., 1986-87; orthopedic nurse clinician Four Corners Orthopedics, Cortez, 1987—; mem. faculty U. Albuquerque, 1981; asst. prof. U. N.Mex., Gallup, 1976-86; curriculum cons. San Juan Coll., Farmington, N.Mex., 1986-87, mem. faculty, 1987—; preceptor at various colls. and univs.; speaker on health issues to civic orgns. Contbr. articles to profl. journals. Mem. Am. Nurses Assn., Nat. League Nursing, N.Mex. League Nursing (bd. dirs. 1983-85), Nat. Assn. Orthopedic Nurses, Sigma Theta Tau.

FLETCHER, ARTHUR JAMES, engineer, consultant; b. South Pasadena, Calif., July 23, 1928; s. Arthur and Dorothy (Clements) F.; m. Alma Kahrs, Aug. 21, 1960; children: Mark, Austri. AA in Mech. Tech., San Francisco City Coll., 1957; BA in Design and Industry, San Francisco State U., 1975. Engrng. draftsman San Francisco Naval Shipyard, 1951-55; draftsman GTE Sylvania, Mountain View, Calif., 1955-59; designer Microwave Engrng. Labs, Palo Alto, Calif., 1959-61; mfg. engr. GTE Lenkurt, San Carlos, Calif., 1961-84; standards engr. Ampex Corp., Redwood City, Calif., 1985-88; cons. Woodside, Calif., 1988—. Trustee 4-H scholarship, San Mateo County, 1985—. With USCG, 1953-54. Home and Office: 13568 Skyline Blvd Woodside CA 94062

FLETCHER, HON. BETTY B., judge; b. Tacoma, Mar. 29, 1923. B.A., Stanford U., 1943; LL.B., U. Wash., 1956. Bar: Wash. 1956. Mem. firm Preston, Thorgrimson, Ellis, Holman & Fletcher, Seattle, 1956-1979; judge U.S. Ct. Appeals (9th cir.), Seattle, 1979—. Mem. ABA, Wash. Bar Assn., Order of Coif, Phi Beta Kappa. Office: US Ct Appeals 1010 5th Ave Seattle WA 98104

FLETCHER, CHARLES ELMO, II, lawyer, real estate developer, broker; b. Wenatchee, Wash., Apr. 14, 1948; s. Charles Elmo and Edwarda Joyce (Harmon) F.; m. Olive Vivian Grasham, Oct. 30, 1969; 1 child, Charlene Eleanor. STB, Bear Valley Sch. of Preaching, 1969; BA in Humanities, Grand Canyon Coll., 1973; JD, Ariz. State U., 1976. Bar: Ariz. 1977; lic. realty broker. Minister Payson (Ariz.) Ch. of Christ, 1969-75; realty salesman Roy Brunner - Strout Realty, Payson, 1973-78; pvt. practice Law Office C.E. Fletcher, Payson, 1977-85; realty broker Timberline Realty, Payson, 1978-88; pub. defender Gila County, Payson, 1984-85; dep county atty. Graham County, Safford, Ariz., 1986-87; pvt. practice Law Offices of C.E. Fletcher, Clifton, Ariz., 1987-88; town atty. Town of Duncan (Ariz.), 1987-88; realty broker Greenlee Realty Sales, Clifton, 1988—; county atty. Greenlee County, Clifton, 1989—; mem. Ariz. Pros. Attys. Adv. Coun., Phoenix, 1989—. Leader Boy Scouts Am., Morenci, Ariz., 1987; mem. So. Greenlee County Econ. Devel. Assn., Duncan, 1987. Recipient Disting. Svc. award Town of Duncan, 1988. Mem. Graham - Greenlee Bar Assn., Greenlee County C. of C. (bd. dirs. 1987—), Lions (tailtwister Payson club 1971), Elks. Democrat. Mem Ch. of Christ. Home: 247 Chase Creek Clifton AZ 85533 Office: Greenlee County Atty PO Box 1387 Clifton AZ 85533

FLETCHER, CLIFF, professional hockey executive; b. 1935; m. Donna Owens; 2 children. With Montreal Canadien Orgn., 1956-66; mgr. Verdun Jr. B team; later mgr. Jr. Canadiens; chief scout St. Louis Blues, 1966-69, asst. gen. mgr., 1969-72; v.p., gen. mgr. Atlanta Flames, Nat. Hockey League, 1972-80; v.p., gen. mgr. Calgary (Alta., Can.) Flames, from 1980, now pres., gen. mgr. Office: Calgary Flames, PO Box 1540 Sta M, Calgary, AB Canada T2P 3B9 *

FLETCHER, HOMER LEE, librarian; b. Salem, Ind., May 11, 1928; s. Floyd M. and Hazel (Barnett) F.; m. Jacquelyn Ann Blanton, Feb. 7, 1950; children—Deborah Lynn, Randall Brian, David Lee. B.A., Ind. U., 1953; M.S. in L.S, U. Ill., 1954. Librarian Milw. Pub. Library, 1954-56; head librarian Ashland (Ohio) Pub. Library, 1956-59; city librarian Arcadia (Cal.) Pub. Library, 1959-65, Vallejo (Calif.) Pub. Library, 1965-70, San Jose, Calif., 1970—. Contbr. articles to profl. jours. Pres. S. Solano chpt. Calif. Assn. Neurol. Handicapped Children, 1968-69. Served with USAF, 1946-49. Mem. ALA (intellectual freedom com. 1967-72), Calif. Library Assn. (pres. pub. libraries sect. 1967), Phi Beta Kappa. Democrat. Mem. Christian Ch. Disciples of Christ (elder, chmn. congregation 1978-79). Club: Rotarian. Home: 7921 Belknap Dr Cupertino CA 95014 Office: San Jose Pub Libr 180 W San Carlos St San Jose CA 95113-2096

FLETCHER, JAMES ALLEN, video company executive; b. Toledo, Sept. 18, 1947; s. Allen Rae and Ruth Helen (Scharf) F.; m. Kathy Jane Barrett, Jan. 25, 1975. AS, West Coast U., 1977, BSEE, 1979. Electronic technician Hughes Aircraft Co., El Segundo, Calif., 1970-72; engrng. technician Altec Corp., Anaheim, Calif., 1972-75, Magna Corp., Santa Fe Springs, Calif., 1975-76; engrng. technician Odetics Inc., Anaheim, 1976-79, electronic engr., 1979-86; pres., founder Gaslight Video, Orange, Calif., 1986—. Served as sgt. U.S. Army, 1967-69. Mem. Soc. Motion Picture and TV Engrs., Internat. TV Assn., Mensa. Libertarian. Club: Bikecentennial. Office: Gaslight Video 479 N Tustin St Ste #8 Orange CA 92667

FLETCHER, JUDITH ANN, finance company executive; b. Youngstown, Ohio, Aug. 8, 1851; d. Robert Albert and Caroline Marie (Kukula) Merrick; m. Bruce Donald Fletcher, Sept. 5, 1987. BS, Wright State U., 1973; MS, U. Redlands, Calif., 1983. CPA, Calif. Staff acct. Elmer Fox & Co., Denver and Los Angeles, 1973-78; acctg. mgr. Allstate Savings & Loan, Glendale, Calif., 1978-83; asst. to treas. Summit Orgn., Inc., Redwood City, Calif., 1983—. Republican. Roman Catholic. Office: The Summit Orgn Inc 386 Main St Redwood City CA 94063

FLETCHER, KARLY ANN, management consultant; b. McKeesport, Pa., Nov. 24, 1951; s. Carl and E. Elaine (McCombs) F. Grad. data processing, Steel Valley Tech., West Mifflin, Pa., 1969. Sr. programmer Union Nat. Bank, Pitts., 1969-74; sr. systems analyst Pitts. Nat. Bank, 1974-76, Equibank, N.A., Pitts., 1976; lead systems analyst Valley Nat. Bank, Phoenix, 1977-87; cons., owner Cactus Cons., Sun City West, Ariz., 1988—. Mem. Am. Home Bus. Assn., Pep User Com. (chmn. 1981-82), Calif. Automated Clearing House Systems and Program Ops. (chmn. 1982-83). Democrat. Roman Catholic. Home and Office: 13138 Castlebar Dr Sun City West AZ 85375

FLETCHER, KIM, savings and loan executive; b. Los Angeles, 1927; married. Grad., Stanford U., 1950. Chmn. bd., chief exec. officer Home Fed. Savs. & Loan Assn., San Diego. Office: Home Fed Savs & Loan Assn 625 Broadway San Diego CA 92101

FLETCHER, LELAND VERNON, artist; b. Cumberland, Md., Sept. 18, 1946; s. Kenneth L. and Marjorie L. (Benecke) F.; m. Janis Traub, July 19, 1978; children—Nathan Fletcher, Joshua Traub. BS, U. Minn., 1972. One man shows include, U. Minn. Exptl. Gallery, 1972, La Mamelle Art Ctr., San Francisco, 1976, San Jose State U. Union Gallery, 1978, Place des Nations, Maubeuge, France, 1987; group exhbns. include, Mus. Contemporary Art, Sao Paulo, Brazil, 1977, Urbanart '77, Vancouver, Can., 1977, Los Angeles Inst. Contemporary Art, 1978, Inst. Modern Art, Brisbane, 1978, Hansen Gallery, N.Y.C., 1978, Fendrick Gallery, Washington, 1979, 8th Internat. Print Bienale, Cracow, Poland, 1980, Cooper-Hewitt Mus., N.Y.C., 1980 Sch. Art Inst. Chgo., 1981, Metronome Gallery, Barcelona, 1981, 16th Bienal de Sao Paulo, 1981, Neue galerie der Stadt Linz, 1982, Bienal de Pontevedra, Spain, 1983, Lyng by Kunstbibliotek, Denmark, 1984, Otis Art Inst./Parsons Sch. Design, Los Angeles, 1984, 10th Internat. Print Bienale, Cracow, Poland, 1984, Mus. Arte da Univ. Fed. de Mato Grosso, Brazil, 1984, 11th Biennal Internat., Mus. Art Contemporani d'Eivissa, Spain, 1984, Intergrafik '84 Triennale, Berlin, Fiatel Muveszek Klubja Budapest, 1985, Intersection Gallery, San Francisco, 1985, Mus. Petit Format, Couvin, Belgium, 1985, 9th British Internat. Print Biennale, Bradford, Eng., 1986, Victoria and Albert Mus., London, 1986, Sculpt 87/3, Maubeuge, 1987, Fundacio la Caixa, Valencia, Spain, 1987, Acad. Belles Arts Sabadell, Barcelona, 1987, Taliesin Ctr. for Arts, Swansea, Eng., 1987, Worcester (Eng.) City Art Gallery, 1987, Symposium Sculpture en Plein Air, Maubeuge, France, 1987, Richards Gallery, Northwestern U., Boston, 1987, Montserrat Coll. Art, Beverly, Mass., 1987; 11 Internat. Print Biennale, Krakow, 1986, Skulptur Biennale '88 Royal Gardens, Copenhagen, Internat. Biennale Palais des Roi de Majorque, Peripignan, France, 1988, Fine Art Mus., Budapest, Hungary, 1988, Works gallery, San Jose Calif., 1988, numerous others; represented in permanent collection at Mus. Contemporary Art, Sao Paulo, Mpls. Inst. Arts, Art Mus. of Calif. State U., Long Beach, deSaisset Mus., U. Santa Clara (Calif.), Art Inst. Chgo., Victoria and Albert Mus., London, Museen der Stadt Koln, Ludwig Mus., Cologne, Mus. Plantin-Moretus, Antwerp, Mus. de Arte Moderno, Barcelona, Bradford Mus., Eng., Kunsthalle, Hamburg, Galleria D'Arte Moderna, Trieste, Ecole des Beaux-Arts, Mus. Maubeuge, Musee de la Sculpture en plein Air, Maubeuge, Musee de Maubeuge, FMK Galeria, Budapest, Bur. for Artistic Exhibitions, Cracow, Poland, Kunsthalle Bremen, West Germany, Museu de Arte da Universidad Federal de Mato Grosso, Brazil, others. Address: PO Box 335 San Geronimo CA 94963

FLETCHER, MARY REBECCA, sales executive; b. Seattle, July 28, 1948; d. Myron Jay and Leona Marie (Kirwin) Stevens; m. James L. Fletcher, July 31, 1971 (div. 1984). BA in English Lit., U. Wash., 1970. Editorial asst. Med. Soc. of D.C., Washington, 1971-73; editor Nat. Council Catholic Laity, Washington, 1973; exec. editor Puget Sound Living Mag., Seattle, 1973-74; assoc. editor Seattle Bus. Mag., 1974-78; spl. sections editor Seattle Post-Intelligencer, 1978-82; mgr. corp. communications Energy Scis. Corp., Seattle, 1982-84; v.p. Hebert Research Corp., Bellevue, Wash., 1984-88; v.p. sales N.W. region Outbound Calling Corp., Seattle, 1988; sr. account mgr. The Calling Co., Seattle, 1988—; bd. dirs., sec. Fashion Group, Inc., Seattle, 1984-87. Mem. com. Private Initiatives in Pub. Edn., 1985—; mem., vice chmn. Seattle Milk Fund, 1978—; mem. mktg. com. Pacific Northwest Ballet, 1987; bd. dirs. World Affairs Council, 1982-85. Mem. Seattle Advt. Fedn. (bd. dirs., treas. 1980-84), Sales and Mktg. Execs., Jr. League Seattle (bd. dirs. 1989), Seattle C. of C., Bellevue C. of C., Seattle Direct Mktg. Assnn. Club: Womens Univ. (Seattle). Office: The Calling Co 83 S King St Ste 106 Seattle WA 98104

FLETCHER-SMITH, CLAUDIA ANN, commercial artist; b. Madera, Calif., June 24, 1948; d. William Edwin and Marie Clara (Maricich) F.; m. Robert Edward Smith, May 14, 1988. Student, Immaculate Heart Coll., L.A., 1966-68. Commercial artist Certified Ad Co., Fresno, Calif.; illustrator Valley Decorating Co., Fresno; pres. Artwork by Claudia, Clovis and Madera, Calif., 1970—; tchr. PACES Program for Arts, Madera, 1989—. Address: PO Box 876 Madera CA 93639

FLICK, ROBBERT, fine arts photography educator; b. Amersfoort, The Netherlands, Nov. 15, 1939; naturalized, 1986; s. Pieter and Jurdina (Materman) F; m. Susan A. Rankaitis, June 5, 1976. BA, U. B.C., Vancouver, Can., 1967; MA, UCLA, 1970, MFA, 1971. Asst. prof. U. Ill. art dept., Champaign-Urbana, 1971-76; prof. U. So. Calif. art dept., Los Angeles, 1976—. Listed works: (photography) MIN Gallery of Photography, 1987, Facets of Modernism, 1987, Radical Rational Space Time, 1983, Photographer's Choice, 1976. Recipient Photographer's fellowship Can. Council, Los Angeles, 1967, 69, Nat. Endowment for the Arts, Los Angeles, 1982, 84. Mem. Coll. Art Assn., Soc. for Photographic Edn., Interactive Communication Soc. Office: U So Calif Sch Fine Arts WAH 104 Los Angeles CA 90089-0292

FLICKINGER, JOE ARDEN, telecommunications educator; b. Cadillac, Mich., Feb. 4, 1949; s. Arden Henry and Stella Frances (Hurst) F.; m. Judith Marie Gardner, Sept. 17, 1971; children: JAn Elsa, Jill Kimberly. BA, Kalamazoo Coll., Mich., 1971; MA, U. So. Calif., 1975; AS, Clatsop Community Coll., 1985; postgrad., U. Oreg. Asst. chief engr. Sta. KUSC-FM, L.A., 1972-74; sta. engr. Sta. KAST-AM-FM, Astoria, Oreg., 1974-75; studio operator, instr. Clatsop Community Coll., Astoria, 1975-88; grad. teaching fellow in telecommunications U. Oreg., Eugene, 1988—. Dir. TV muscular dystrophy telethon Astoria Jaycees, 1980, 81; canvasser Friends of Coll., Astoria, 1982; pres. bd. dirs. Sta. KMUN-FM Tillicum Found., Astoria, 1983-84. Mem. IEEE, IEEE Computer Soc., IEEE Communications Soc., IEEE Broadcasting Soc., Am. Radio Relay League (life), Nat. Model R.R. Assn., Sunset Empire Amateur Radio Club (sec. 1978-81). Democrat. Presbyterian. Avocations: amateur radio, golf, fishing, astronomy, cooking. Office: U Oreg Eugene OR 97403-1231

FLINN, PAUL ANTHONY, materials scientist; b. N.Y.C., Mar. 25, 1926; s. Richard A. and Anna M. (Weber) F.; m. Mary Ellen Hoffman, Aug. 20, 1949; children: Juliana, Margaret, Donald, Anthony, Patrick. AB, Columbia Coll., 1948, MA, 1949; ScD, MIT, 1952. Asst. prof. Wayne U., Detroit, 1953-54; research staff Westinghouse Research Lab., Pitts., 1954-63; prof. Carnegie-Mellon U., Pitts., 1964-78; sr. staff scientist Intel Corp., Santa Clara, Calif., 1978—; vis. prof. U. Wancy, France, 1967-68, U. Fed. Do Rio Grand du Sol, Porto Allegro, Brazil, 1975, Argonne (Ill.) Nat. Lab., 1977-78, Stanford (Calif.) U., 1984-85, cons. prof., 1985—. Contbr. sci. articles to profl. jours. Served with USN, 1944-46, PTO. Fellow Am. Phys. Soc.; mem. AAAS, The Metall. Soc., Phi Beta Kappa, Tau Beta Pi. Office: Intel Corp SC1-2 3065 Bowers Ave Santa Clara CA 95052-8126

FLINT, LOU JEAN, state education official; b. Ogden, Utah, July 11, 1934; d. Elmer Blood and Ella D. (Adams) F.; children—Dirk Kershaw Brown, Kristie Susan Brown Felix, Flint Kershaw Brown. B.S., Weber State Coll., 1968; M.Ed., U. Utah, 1974, Ed.S, 1981. Cert. early childhood and elem. edn., Utah Bd. Edn., 1968, edn. adminstrn., 1981. Master tchr. Muir Elem., Davis Sch. Dist., Farmington, Utah, 1968-77; edn. specialist Dist. I, Dept. Def., Eng., Scotland, Norway, Denmark, Holland, Belgium, 1977-79; ednl. cons. Office Higher Edn. State of Utah, Utah System Approach to Individualized Learning, Tex., S.C., Fla., Utah, 1979-81; acad. affairs officerCommr. Higher Edn. Office State of Utah, Salt Lake City, 1982—; mem. Equity Vocat. Edn. Bd.; mem. review com. United Way, 1989; adv. bd. Women and Bus. Conf.; State bd. dirs. Am. Coun. Edn. Named Exemplary Tchr., Utah State Bd. Edn., 1970-77, Outstanding Educator, London Central High Sch., 1979; recipient Appreciation award, Gov. of Utah, 1983, 84, 85, Woman of Achievement award Utah Bus. and Profl. Women, 1985, Pathfinder award C. of C., 1988. Mem. AAUW (Edn. Found. award given in her honor, 1986), Nat. Assn. Women's Work/Women's Worth (com. mem., Disting. Woman award 1987), Am. Council Edn. (Nat. Identification Program 1982, Susa Young Gates award 1987), Nat. Assn. Edn. Young Children, Utah Assn. Edn. Young Children (past pres.), Women Concerned About Nuclear War, Utah Jaycee Aux. (past pres. Centerville), Phi Delta Kappa, Delta Kappa Gamma. Mormon. Author: The Comprehensive Community College, 1980; others. Office: State of Utah Office Commr Higher Edn 355 W North Temple #3 Triad Salt Lake City UT 84180-1205

FLINT, RANDELL SHERMAN, computer software executive; b. Lynwood, Calif., Sept. 17, 1955; s. Harold James and Elenor Gamble (Bornemann) F.; m. Martin Carla Hanzlik, Sept. 2, 1978. BS, U. Calif., Irvine, 1976, MS, 1979, PhD, 1984. Asst. prof. computer sci. Calif. State U., Fullerton, 1979-82; dir. software devel. Ordain Inc., Torrance, Calif., 1982-84; v.p. Dahlia Assocs. Inc., Seal Beach, Calif., 1985-88; pres. Sundial Systems Corp., Seal Beach, 1988—; book reviewer Addison-Wesley Pub., Reading, Mass., 1980—; cons. Jet Propulsion Lab., Pasadena, Calif., 1985—. Contbr. articles to profl. jours. Mem. IEEE Computer Soc., Assn. for Computing Machinery. Home: 215 17th St PO Box 521 Seal Beach CA 90740 Office: Sundial Systems Corp 909 Electric Ave Ste 204 Seal Beach CA 90740

FLINT, WENDY JO, business owner, consultant, freelance writer; b. Cleve., Oct. 20, 1949; d. John Erwin Leach and Ruth Helen (Twitchell) Kelly; m. Terry Joe Flint, Nov. 1, 1969; children: Scott Ryan, Todd Andrew, Tracy Jo. Student, Bowling Green (Ohio) State U., 1967-68; AA in Adminstrn. Justice, Clark Coll., 1975. Cert. early childhood edn., Wash. Owner Kings Kids Daycare, Vancouver, Wash., 1979-80; PBX installer AT&T Telephone, Portland, Oreg., 1980-82; dir. New Creations Presch., Vancouver, 1982-84; pvt. practice polit. activist and edn. lobbyist Vancouver, 1984-87; owner Word Unltd., Vancouver, 1987—; nat. dir. Nat. Edn. Task Force, Washington; christian edn. dir. Trinity Life Ctr., Vancouver, 1983-84. Author: School Boards-A Call to Action, 1988; pub: (video) Our Children - Our Future, 1989; contbr. articles to profl. jours. Scout leader Girl Scouts US, Vancouver, 1980-85; instr. CPR, ARC, Vancouver, 1982-86; pres., sch. bd. dirs. Evergreen Sch. Dist., Vancouver, 1985—. With USN, 1968-70. Mem. Nat. Sch. Bd. Assn., Am. Legion, DAR. Republican. Home and Office: 9612 NE 91st Ave Vancouver WA 98662

FLINTON, SUZANNE HOLT, manufacturing executive; b. North Adams, Mass., Mar. 6, 1933; d. Edgar William and Doris Saunders (Holt) F. Student, Radcliff Coll., 1951-53. Asst. to dir. N.Y. Coun. on Arts, 1963-68; assoc. Coun. the Arts, N.Y.C., 1969-72; spl. projects dir. N.Y. Coun. Architecture, N.Y.C., 1972-75; asst. to mayor City of Louisville, 1975-77; exec. dir. Hollywood Revitalization Com., Calif., 1977-81; art cons. Gen. Svcs. Adminstrn., Santa Monica, Calif., 1981-82; assoc. Community Devel. Dept., Santa Monica, 1983-85; owner, pres. L.A. Settings, 1985—; cons. in field. Trustee L.A. Conservancy, 1978-83, Craft and Folk Art Mus., 1982—, Verde Vally Sch., 1982-87, 89—. Democrat. Office: LA Settings 923 E 3rd St Ste 108 Los Angeles CA 90013

FLIPPO, CHARLES WAYNE, federal hazardous waste management specialist; b. Tulsa, July 10, 1952; s. Doren Gene and Lorna Jo (Johnson) F.; m. Karen Francine Feuerstadt, Aug. 6, 1978; 1 child, Ian David. BA, U. Calif., Berkeley, 1976; MPA, Calif. State U., 1978. Organizer United Farm Workers, AFL-CIO, Chgo., 1972-74; dist. intern to mem. Calif. Assembly, Oakland, 1977-78; pub. info. specialist U.S. EPA, San Francisco, 1978-80, noise control specialist, 1980-81, hazardous waste specialist, 1981—. Office: US EPA 215 Fremont St San Francisco CA 94105

FLOCK, GAIL CURRY, realtor; b. San Jose, Calif., Apr. 21, 1917; d. Harry Frank and Roxie Gail (Orr) Curry; m. Claude Ernest Flock, Aug. 25, 1938 (dec. Aug. 1985); children: Carl, David, Claudia, Harry, Elizabeth, Robert. BA in History and Sci., San Jose State U., 1939, MA, 1961; postgrad. in edn., Leland Stanford Jr. U., 1940. Cert. life elem., secondary tchr., secondary adminstr., Calif. Tchr., counselor Campbell (Calif.) Union High Sch., 1957-80; realtor assoc. Century 21-Wollam, San Luis Obispo, 1981-83; realtor Red Carpet Co., San Luis Obispo, 1985-86, Newby Realty, San Luis Obispo, 1986—. Author: California and Elections of 1916, 1961. Mem. Nat. Assn. Realtors, Calif. Assn. Realtors, Calif. Assn. Tchrs. (life), Lady Lions, Phi Lambda Theta, Phi Epsilon Phi. Republican. Congregationalist. Home: 402 Buckley Rd San Luis Obispo CA 93401 Office: Newby Realty 2241 Broad St San Luis Obispo CA 93401

FLOEGEL, JACK EDWARD, electronics executive, real estate broker; b. Albuquerque, May 4, 1944; s. Richard Edward and Aileen V. (Costello) F.; m. Sharon Elaine Barnes, Aug. 29, 1969; children: Richard, Suzanne. BSEE, UCLA, 1966. Dir. engrng. Centralab Electronics, L.A., 1967-75; mgr. microelectronics GTE, Albuquerque, 1976-85; plant mgr. Siemens, Albuquerque, 1986—. Mem. Internat. Soc. Hybrid Microelectronics, Am. Ceramic Soc., Lamda Chi Alpha (pres. 1964), Kiwanis (pres. Los Altos chpt. 1984). Home: 7801 Spain Rd Albuquerque NM 87109 Office: Siemens 1 Camino De Lenkurt Albuquerque NM 87109

FLOOD, JAMES TYRRELL, broadcasting executive, public relations consultant; b. Los Angeles, Oct. 5, 1934; s. James Joseph and Teresa (Rielly) F.; m. Bonnie Carolyn Lutz, Mar. 25, 1966; children: Hilary C., Sean L. BA in Sociology, U. Calif., Santa Barbara, 1956; MA in Communications, Calif. State U., Chico, 1981. Publicist Rogers & Cowan, 1959-60, Jim Mahoney & Assocs., 1960-61, ABC-TV, San Francisco and Hollywood, Calif., 1961-64; cons. pub. relations, Beverly Hills, Calif., 1964-72; pub. relations, advt. dir. Jerry Lewis Films, 1964-72; dir. pub. rels. MTM Prodns., 1970-72; pub. relations cons. Medic Alert Found. Internat., 1976-83; owner, mgr. Sta. KRIJ-FM, Paradise, 1983-88; instr. Calif. State U. Sch. Communications, Chico, 1982, 89; worked with numerous artists including Pearl Bailey, Gary Owens, Ruth Buzzi, Allen Ludden, Betty White, Celeste Holm, others. Calif. media cons. Carter/Mondale campaign, 1976; mem. Calif. Dem. Fin. Com., 1982-83. Served with USNR, 1956-58. Mem. Calif. Broadcasters Assn. (bd. dirs. 1986-88), Pub. Rels. Soc. Am., Rotary.

FLOR, LOY LORENZ, chemist, corrosion engineer, consultant; b. Luther, Okla., Apr. 25, 1919; s. Alfred Charles and Nellie M. (Wilkinson) F.; BA in Chemistry, San Diego State Coll., 1941; m. Virginia Louise Pace, Oct. 1, 1946; children: Charles R., Scott R., Gerald C., Donna Jeanne, Cynthia Gail. With Helix Water Dist., La Mesa, Calif., 1947-84, chief chemist, 1963—, supr. water quality, 1963—, supr. corrosion control dept., 1956—. 1st. lt. USAAF, 1941-45. Registered profl. engr., Calif. Mem. Am. Chem. Soc. (chmn. San Diego sect. 1965—), Am. Water Works Assn. (chmn. water quality div. Calif. sect. 1965—), Nat. Assn. Corrosion Engrs. (chmn. western region 1970), Masons. Republican. Presbyterian. Office: 11315 Manzanita Rd Lakeside CA 92040

FLORA, EDWARD BENJAMIN, research and development company executive, mechanical engineer; b. Phillipsburg, Ohio, June 23, 1929; s. Russell Thomas and Elizabeth Lucille (Hollinger) F.; m. Dolores Genevieve Havrilla, May 3, 1952; children: Christopher Dennis, Stephanie Ann, Christine Marie. BS, Carnegie Mellon U., 1951, MS, 1953. Registered profl. engr., Calif., Ohio. Project engr. Nevis Cyclotron Lab. Columbia U., Irvington, N.Y., 1953-58; sr. engr. Dalmo Victor Co., Belmont, Calif., 1958-63; ptnr. PYRCO Co., San Carlos, Calif., 1960-63; v.p., mgr. Anamet Labs., Inc., San

Carlos, 1963-68, v.p., mgr. applied mechanics div., 1968-82; pres., treas. Anamet Labs., Inc., Hayward, Calif., 1982—. Mem. St. Gregory's Cath. Sch. Bd. Edn., San Mateo, Calif., 1971-72. Mem. ASME, AIAA, Soc. Automotive Engrs., Soc. for Exptl. Mechanics (chpt. treas. 1981-84), ASTM, Sequoia Club (Redwood City, Calif.). Home: 1292 Laurel Hill Dr San Mateo CA 94402 Office: Anamet Labs Inc 3400 Investment Blvd Hayward CA 94545

FLORENCE, KENNETH JAMES, lawyer; b. Hanford, Calif., July 31, 1943; s. Ivy Owen and Louella (Dobson) F.; m. Verena Magdalena Demuth, Dec. 10, 1967. BA, Whittier Coll., 1965; JD, Hastings Coll. Law, U. Calif.-San Francisco, 1974. Bar: Calif. 1974, U.S. Dist. Ct. (cen. dist.) Calif. 1974, U.S. Dist. Ct. (ea. and so. dists.) Calif., 1976, U.S. Dist. Ct. (no. dist.) Calif. 1980, U.S. Ct. Appeals (9th cir.) 1975, U.S. Supreme Ct. 1984. Dist. mgr. Pacific T&T, Calif., 1969-71; assoc. Parker, Milliken, et al, Los Angeles, 1974-78; ptnr. Dern, Mason, et al, 1978-84, Swerdlow & Florence, A Law Corp., Beverly Hills, 1984—; pres. Westside Legal Services, Inc., Santa Monica, Calif., 1982-83. Served to lt. USNR, 1966-69, Vietnam. Col. J.G. Boswell scholar, 1961. Mem. ABA (co-chmn. state labor law com. 1988—). Democrat. Home: 1063 Stradella Rd Los Angeles CA 90077 Office: Swerdlow & Florence 9401 Wilshire Blvd Ste 828 Beverly Hills CA 90212

FLORENCE, VERENA MAGDALENA, legal administrator; b. Interlaken, Switzerland, Nov. 4, 1946; came to U.S., 1967; d. Paul Robert and Marie (Raess) Demuth; m. Kenneth James Florence, Dec. 10, 1967. BA, U. Calif., Berkeley, 1974; MS, UCLA, 1979, PhD, 1982. Research scientist Procter & Gamble, Cin., 1983; adminstr. Swerdlow & Florence, Beverly Hills, Calif., 1984—. Contbr. articles to profl. jours. Democrat. Home: 1063 Stradella Rd Los Angeles CA 90077 Office: Swerdlow & Florence 9401 Wilshire Blvd Ste 828 Beverly Hills CA 90212

FLORES, ADELSO SALOME, real estate company executive; b. Chalatenango, El Salvador, Oct. 22, 1957; came to U.S., 1981; s. Guillermo and Lucia (Flores) Torres; m. Alga Flores, Sept. 30, 1983; children: Adrian, Nathalie, Adelso Jr. Student, Nat. U., San Salvador, 1979-81. Acct. asst. PROGRESA, San Salvador, 1979-81; paralegal asst. El Rescate, L.A., 1981-83, Imperial Valley Immigration Project, L.A., 1983-85; real estate cons. Galindo Realty, Huntington Park, Calif., 1986-87, U.S. Homes Real Estate, Lynwood, Calif., 1987—. Fund raiser, Refugee Com., L.A., 1983-85. Mem. Nat. Assn. Notaries. Democrat. Roman Catholic. Home: 1750 E 84th Los Angeles CA 90001

FLORES, FRANK CORTEZ, dentist educator; b. L.A., Mar. 13, 1930; s. Frank Chaves and Jane (Cortez) F.; m. Juliette Carmen Sotelo, Nov. 24, 1951; children: Patricia, Marie, Frank Anthony, Gregory, Mark Adam, Jon Eric, Aaron. AA, E. L.A. Coll., 1951; BS, U. So. Calif., L.A., 1955, DDS, 1957, MSEd, 1988. Pvt. practice of dentistry L.A., 1957-69, owner group practice of dentistry, 1969-78; dental care implementor Specialist Ctr. For Dental Therapy, Riyadh, Saudi Arabia, 1984-86; asst. clin. prof. Univ. So. Calif. Sch. Dentistry, L.A., 1987—; dentist vol., Mexico, 1964-87; dentist Am. Dental Vols. For Israel, Jerudalem, 1987—. Fundraiser for various colls. and univs., 1988; 2nd v.p. Project Hosp. Ship Oceanic, Upland, Calif. 1986. Served in USNR, 1947-52. Mem. Fedn. Spl. Care Orgns. In Dentistry, Am. Assn. Dental Schs., Am. Assn. Dental Examiners, Am. Dental Assn., Am. Coll. Healthcare Execs., AAUP. Democrat. Roman Catholic.

FLORES, M. BETSI, banker; b. Newton, N.J., July 22, 1955; d. Richardson and Jean (Mackerly) Buist; m. Jose Y. Flores Jr., Apr. 1, 1983; 1 child, Sheila Jean. BA, U. Ariz., 1979, MBA in Fin., 1986. Cert. fin. planner. Admissions counselor Chaparral Career Coll., Tucson, 1980-84; fin. planner Freeman Fin. Services, Tucson, 1984-86; corp. officer Valley Nat. Bank of Ariz., Tucson, 1986—. Vol. counselor YWCA Women Helping Women, 1987—; fundraiser Tucson Mus. of Art, 1988. Mem. Internat. Assn. Fin. Planning (v.p. membership 1988-89), Ariz. Bus. Edn. Assn. (dir. 1982-85), Soroptimist (treas. Tucson chpt. 1987-89, pres. 1988-89), Casas Adobes Bus. Club. Home: 4634 W Condor Dr Tucson AZ 85741 Office: Valley Nat Bank 2 E Congress Dept K-240 Tucson AZ 85702

FLORES, RENE L., electronics company executive; b. Lynwood, Calif., May 20, 1956; s. Lee Joseph Shamaley and Esperanza Flores. BBA, U. Tex., 1981. Sr. fin. analyst Nat. Econ. Devel. Assn., El Paso, Tex., 1977-80; mgr. fin. planning and acctg. Samsonite Corp., El Paso, 1980-82; contr. Tonka Toys, El Paso, 1982-84; area contr. Texscan Corp., El Paso, 1984-85; corp. contr. Texscan Corp., Scottsdale, Ariz., 1985-86; v.p. fin., chief fin. officer, corp. sec. Texscan Corp., Scottsdale, 1986—; instr. El Paso Community Coll., 1978-83; bd. dirs. Texscan Instruments Ltd., London, Texscan S.A., Paris, Texscan de Mexico, Texscan, Cd Juarez, Chih, Mex.; Texscan MSI, Salt Lake City, Texscan Trading Co., Inc., El Paso. Author: (courses) Starting a New Business, 1978, Strategic Planning and Budgeting, 1978. Bd. dirs., chmn.-mem. drive com. Pan Am. C. of C., El Paso, 1979-80; speaker El Paso Mech. Contractors Assn., 1979, SER Jobs for Progress Ann. Conv., Washington, 1980; speaker KEYS Small Bus. Workshops, El Paso, 1979-80, Amalgamated Clothing Workers Union, El Paso, 1980. Named Men of Mines U. Tex., 1980. Mem. Nat. Assn. Accts., Am. Soc. Corp. Secs. Inc., Delta Sigma Pi, Gamma Phi (pres. 1977). Democrat. Home: 1728 E Turquoise Ave Phoenix AZ 85020 Office: Texscan Corp 7320 E Butherus Dr #200 Scottsdale AZ 85260

FLOREY, JERRY JAY, aerospace company executive, consultant; b. Geddes, S.D., Apr. 3, 1932; s. Henry Clifford Florey and Lizzie M. Rabie; m. Mary E. Richey, Sept. 17, 1955; children: Glenn David, Janet Renee. BS in Chem. Engring., Oreg. State U., 1955. Cert. in electronics. From research engr. to engring. supr. Rockwell Internat., Canoga Park, Calif., 1955-66; sr. project engr. Rockwell Internat., Downey, Calif., 1966-67; successively engring. mgr., engring. dir., chief engr. Rockwell Internat., Seal Beach, Calif., 1967-85, dir. advanced systems, rsch. and tech., 1985-89; sr. staff mgr. strategic devel. McDonnell Douglas Space Co., Huntington Beach, Calif., 1989—. Scoutmaster Boy Scouts Am., Costa Mesa, Calif., 1970. Recipient NASA Cert. Appreciation Marshall Space Flight Ctr., Huntsville, Ala., 1972, Astronaut Person Achievement award NASA, 1969, Skylab Achievement award NASA, 1973. Fellow AIAA (assoc.); mem. Nat. Mgmt. Assn., Nat. Mktg. Soc. Am. Republican. Home: 2085 Goldeneye Pl Costa Mesa CA 92626

FLORIE, TERRY LYNN, naval flight officer; b. NAS Sangley Pt., Philippines, May 18, 1956; s. Julian and Hazel Savannah (Byrd) F.; m. Deborah Louise Murchison, Aug. 31, 1985. BBA, Augusta Coll., 1977. Cost acct. BE&K Inc., Augusta, Ga., 1977; naval officer USN, Aviation Schs. Command, Pensacola, Fla., 1978, USN, Patrol Squadron Five, Jacksonville, Fla., 1979-82, USN, Naval Air Tng. Unit, Sacramento, Calif., 1982-85, USN, USS Constellation, San Diego, Calif., 1985-88; lt. cmmdr. USN, 1987—; naval officer Fleet Tng. Group, San Diego, 1988—. Mem. Civil Air Patrol, Sacramento, 1984-85. Mem. U.S. Naval Inst., Aircraft Owners and Pilots Assn., Cessna Pilots Assn. Republican. Methodist. Home: 601 Telegraph Canyon Rd Chula Vista CA 92010 Office: Fleet Tng Group Code N623 San Diego CA 92147

FLORSHEIM, STEWART JAY, management computer software company; b. N.Y.C., Nov. 14, 1952; s. Max and Flora (Falk) F.; m. Judith Rosloff, May 24, 1987: 1 child,. BA in Journalism, Syracuse U., 1974; MA in English, San Francisco State U., 1978. Asst. editor Excerpta Medica, Amsterdam, Netherland, 1974-76; dir., tech. communications Ask Computer Systems, Mt. View, Calif., 1978--. Editor: Ghosts of the Holocaust, 1989; contbr. articles to profl. jours. Mem. Amhesty Internat., San Francisco, 1987--. Mem. Society Tech. Communications (pres. 1980—).

FLORY, ABRAM, III, personnel manager; b. Newark, July 21, 1945; s. Louis Abram and June Eileen (Pierce) F. BA, Denison U., 1967; MS, W.Va. U., 1969; MPA, Ariz. State U., 1974. Staff asst. N.Am. Rockwell Internat., Newark, 1963-67; rsch. asst. W.Va. Inst. Labor Studies, Morgantown, 1968-69; cons. Am. Pub., Inc., Phoenix, 1971-72; personnel mgr. Ariz. State Personnel, Phoenix, 1972—; cons. Flory and Assocs., Phoenix, 1987—; pres., owner Aspen Forest Homes, Inc., Pinetop, Ariz., 1982-85. Author: (with others) Training/Experience Evaluation, 1976; contbr. articles to profl. jours. Organizer Neighborhood Action Com., Phoenix, 1987-88. Mem. Personnel Mgmt. Orgn. (v.p. 1976-77). Republican. Home: 1705 N Laurel Ave Phoenix AZ 85007 Office: Ariz State Pers 1831 W Jefferson Phoenix AZ 85007

FLOURNOY, JOHN CHARLES, SR., training specialist, retired military officer; b. Florala, Ala., Nov. 30, 1936; s. Q.P. and Alice Ruby (Cope) F.; m. Charlene Renee Lett, June 7, 1957; children: Jamie Lynn, John Charles Jr., Jeffrey Allan. BS, Auburn (Ala.) U., 1959. Commd. 2d lt. USAF, 1959, advanced through grades to col., asst. dep. chief of staff for ops. 23rd; USAF, Scott AFB, 1983-86, dir. ops.; dep. chief of staff for ops. 23d Air Foce, Hurlburt Field, Fla., 1985-88; site mgr. Link Tng. Svcs., C-130 Simulator, Kirkland AFB, N.Mex., 1988—. Recipient German Gratitude medal Fed. Republic of Germany, 1962; decorated Leigon of Merit, 1988. Mem. Jolly Green Assn. (1st v.p. 1983-84, pres. 1985-86), Order of Daedalians, Airlift Assn., Auburn U. Alumni Assn. Republican. Home: Box 5672 Albuquerque NM 87185

FLOWER, BRETT PHILLIP, dentist; b. Lamar, Colo., Aug. 8, 1962; s. Glenn Alvin and Deloris Jean (Hull) F.; m. Vicki Lynette , Aug. 4, 1984; 1 child, Zachary Michael. BS, U. Colo., 1983, DDS, 1987. Pvt. practice Lamar, Colo., 1987—; Bd. dirs. Lamar Area Hospice Assn. Active Boulder County (Colo.) Dental Aid, 1988. Recipient Kenneth Groves Meml. award, U. Colo. Sch. Dentistry, 1987. Mem. ADA, Acad. Gen. Dentistry. Home: 4227 Moore St Wheat Ridge CO 80033

FLOYD, ELLIS RAY, communications specialist; b. Ozan, Ark., Oct. 25, 1952; s. Tyree and Claudia Mae (Atkins) F. A in General Studies, Community Coll. Denver, 1988, AAS, 1989. Computer specialist U.S. West Communications, Denver, 1980-87, asst. staff supr., 1987—. Pres. Community Coll. of Denver Black Students Alliance, 1984. Democrat. Protestant. Home: 2836 Madison St Denver CO 80205

FLOYD, JONATHAN CURRAN, communications educator; b. San Luis Obispo, Calif., Oct. 1, 1954; s. Gerald Leroy and Mary Alice (Palmer) F.; m. Dawn Marie Hayes. BA in Psychology, U. Calif., Santa Barbara, 1976; MA in Communications, Calif. State U., Northridge, 1989. Tech. writer Mike Burns & Assocs., Tempe, Ariz., 1988; audio-visual producer Focal Point Prodns., Long Beach, Calif., 1988—; prof. communications Calif. State U., Northridge, 1988—. Mem. Assn. for Multi-Image, Assn. Visual Communicators (bd. dirs.). Democrat. Unitarian. Home: 1140 Junipero Ave Long Beach CA 90804 Office: Calif State U RTUF Dept 18111 Nordhoff St Northridge CA 91330

FLUHARTY, JESSE ERNEST, lawyer, judge; b. San Antonio, Tex., July 25, 1916; s. Jesse Ernest and Gwendolyn (Elder) F.; m. Ernestine Gertrude Corlies, Oct. 25, 1945; 1 son, Stephen Robert. Student Calif. State U.-San Diego, 1935-36, Art Ctr. Sch. Design Los Angeles, 1938-39; J.D. with distinction, U. Pacific, 1951; grad. Nat. Jud. Coll. Adminstrv. Law 1982. Bar: Calif. 1952, U.S. Dist. Ct. (no. dist.) Calif. 1952, U.S. Ct. appeals (9th cir.) 1952, U.S. Dist. Ct. (cen. dist.) Calif. 1979, U.S. Supreme Ct. 1983. Sole practice, Sacramento, 1952-60; referee in charge Indsl. Accident Commn., Stockton, Calif., 1960-67; presiding referee so. Calif. Workers Compensation Appeals Bd., Los Angeles, 1967-71, workers compensation Judge, Los Angeles, 1971-79; presiding judge, Los Angeles, 1979-81, Long Beach, 1981-83; of counsel Law Office of Stephen Fluharty, Glendale, Calif., 1984-87; workers compensation judge., Van Nuys, Calif., 1987—. Pres. Family Service Agy., Sacramento, 1958, 59, Community Council Stockton and San Joaquin County, 1965, Service Club Council Los Angeles, 1973-74, Glendale Hills Coordinating Council, 1976-78, Chevy Chase Estates Assn., 1971-77; chmn. San Joaquin County Recreation and Park Commn., 1963-67. Served with U.S. Army, 1943-45. Decorated Bronze Star, Philippine Liberation medal; recipient Meritorious citation Calif. Recreation Soc., 1967. Mem. Calif. State Bar, Los Angeles County Bar Assn., Glendale Bar Assn., Lawyers Club Los Angeles (pres. 1980, Judge of Yr. 1982). Republican. Congregationalist. Clubs: Chevy Chase Country, Verdugo. Lodges: Lions (pres. Los Angeles 1971-72), Masons. Home: 3330 Emerald Isle Dr Glendale CA 91206

FLUKE, JOHN MAURICE, JR., electrical equipment manufacturing company executive; b. 1942; s. John Maurice Sr. and Lyla (Schram) F. BS in elec. engring., Univ. of Wash., 1964; MS in elec. engring., Stanford Univ., 1966. With John Fluke Mfg. Co. Inc., 1966—, gen. mgr. Central Products Group, 1978-82, gen. mgr. Indsl. Measurement & Control Div., 1982, vice-chmn., 1982-84, chief exec. officer, 1983-88, chmn., 1984—; chmn. Fluke Capital & Mgmt. Services Co. Office: John Fluke Mfg Co Inc 6920 Seaway Blvd Box C 9090 Everett WA 98206 *

FLUKE, LYLA SCHRAM, publisher; b. Maddock, N.D.; d. Olaf John and Anne Marie (Rodberg) Schram; m. John M. Fluke, June 5, 1937; children: Virginia Fluke Gabelein, John M. Jr., David Lynd. BS in Zoology and Physiology, U. Wash., Seattle, 1934, diploma teaching, 1935. High sch. tchr., 1935-37; tutor Seattle schs., 1974-75; pub. Portage Quar. mag., Hist. Soc. Seattle and King County, 1980—. Author articles on history. Founder N.W. chpt. Myasthenia Gravis Found., 1953, pres., 60-63; obtained N.W. artifacts for destroyer Tender Puget Sound, 1966; mem. Seattle Mayor's Com. for Seattle Beautiful, 1968-69; sponsor Seattle World's Fair, 1962; charter mem. Seattle Youth Symphony Aux., 1974; bd. dirs. Cascade Symphony, Salvation Army, 1985-87; mem. U.S. Congl. Adv. Bd.; benefactor U. Wash., 1982—, nat. chmn. ann. giving campaign, 1983-84; benefactor Sterling Circle Stanford U., 1984, Wash. State Hist. Soc., Pacific Arts Ctr.; mem. condr.'s club Seattle Symphony, 1978—. Fellow Seattle Pacific U., 1972—; mem. Wash. Trust for Hist. Preservation, Nat. Trust for Hist. Preservation, N.W. Ornamental Hort. Soc. (life, hon.), Smithsonian Assocs., Nat. Assn. Parliamentarians (charter mem., pres. N.W. unit 1961), Wash. Parliamentarians Assn. (charter), IEEE Aux. (chpt. charter mem., pres. 1970-73), Seattle C. of C. (women's div.), Seattle Symphony Women's Assn. (life, sec. 1982-84, pres. 1985-87), Hist. Soc. Seattle and King County (exec. com. 1975-78, pres. women's mus. league 1975-78, pres. Moritz Thomsen Guild of Hist. Soc., 1978-80, 84-87), Highlands Orthopedic Guild (life), Wash. State Hist. Soc., Antiquarian Soc. (v.p. 1986-88, pres. 1988—), Women's U. Club, Rainier Club, Seattle Golf Club, Seattle Tennis Club, U. Wash. Pres.'s Club. Republican. Lutheran. Address: 1206 NW Culbertson Dr Vendovi Island WA 98177

FLYGARE, RICHARD WATTS, mechanical engineer; b. Altadena, Calif., June 2, 1955; s. Richard Wilson and Jane Ellen (Watts) F.; m. Roberta Anne Young, June 16, 1978. BSME, U. Utah, 1977. Engr. Mountain Fuel Resources, Inc., Salt Lake City, 1977-82, supr., system design, 1982-86; B-727 pilot Western Airlines, Inc., L.A., 1986-87; engr. Mountain Fuel Supply Co., Salt Lake City, 1987-88; sr. planner, dir. planning Questar Pipeline Co., Salt Lake City, 1988—. Mem. ASME, U.S. Naval Inst. Democrat. Mormon. Home: 2493 Pioneer Circle Salt Lake City UT 84109

FLYNN, ELIZABETH ANNE, advertising and public relations company executive; b. Washington, Aug. 21, 1951; d. John William and Elizabeth Goodwin (Mahoney) F. A.A., Montgomery Coll., Rockville, Md., 1972; B.S. in Journalism, U. Md., 1976; postgrad. San Diego State U., 1976. Writer, researcher, Sea World, Inc., San Diego, 1977-79; sr. writer Lane & Huff Advt., San Diego, 1979-80; account exec. Kaufman, Lansky, Baker Advt., San Diego, 1980-82; mng. dir. Excelsior Enterprises, Beverly Hills, Calif., 1983-84; sr. account exec. Berkhemer & Kline, Inc., Los Angeles, 1985; pres. Flynn Advt. & Pub. Relations, Los Angeles, 1985—; cons. Coca-Cola Bottling Co. Los Angeles, 1982-84. Bd. dirs. Friends of Reconstructive Surgery, Beverly Hills, 1983—. Recipient Cert. of Distinction, Art Direction Mag., 1982. Mem. Nat. Assn. Female Execs., Beverly Hills C. of C., Republican. Roman Catholic. Avocations: screenwriting; short stories; painting; horseback riding. Office: Flynn Advt & Pub Rels 1440 Reeves St Ste 104 Los Angeles CA 90035

FLYNN, GERRI LEIGH, writer; b. Chgo., Apr. 22, 1939; d. Milton and Sylvia (Reinitz) Guren; m. Raymond Verr, June 5, 1960 (div. 1976); children: Andrea, Richard; m. Donald James Flynn, Jan. 24, 1978; children: Julia, Matthew, Susan. BA in Music, Calif. State U., Carson, 1983, MA, 1984. Cert. tchr., Calif. Sr. copywriter Aldens, Chgo., 1960-65; continuity dir. Sta. KTUK-TV, Phoenix, 1965-66; direct account writer Sta. KTAR-TV and Radio, Phoenix, 1966-76; sr. copywriter Direct Mktg. Corp., Los Angeles, 1976-77; writer, editor McAuto, Long Beach, Calif., 1977-79; owner, operator The Printery, Huntington Beach, Calif., 1979-82; writer, editor Douglas Aircraft, Long Beach, 1982-84; journalism tchr., band and chorus dir. St. Anthony High Sch., Long Beach, 1984-86; freelance writer Los Angeles, 1986—. Editor Music Assn. Calif. Community Colls. Newsletter, 1981-83. Bd. dirs. Baroque Consortium Chamber Orch., Rancho Palos Verdes, Calif., 1983-84. Mem. Mu Phi Epsilon (collegiate pres. 1982-83, dist. dir. 1986-87, internat. editor 1987—), Phi Kappa Phi. Republican. Roman Catholic. Home: 4271 N First St #116 San Jose CA 95134

FLYNN, RALPH MELVIN, JR., sales executive, marketing consultant; b. Winchester, Mass., May 2, 1944; s. Ralph Melvin and Mary Agnus (Giuliani) F.; m. Rose Marie Petrock; children: John Patrick, Marc Jeffery. Engr. Bell Telephone Labs., Holmdel, N.J., 1966-68; tech. coord. Expts. in Art and Tech., N.Y.C., 1968-69; exec. v.p. Bestline Products, San Jose, Calif., 1969-73; pres. Internat. Inst. for Personal Achievement, Palo Alto, Calif., 1975-76, Diamite Corp., Milpitas, Calif., 1977-84; dir. mktg. IMMI, Campbell, Calif., 1973-77; v.p. internat. Neo-Life Co., Fremont, Calif., 1984—; pres. Ultra Promotions, Los Gatos, Calif., 1988—; tech. cons. Robert Rauschenberg, N.Y.C., 1968; cons. Standard Oil Co., San Francisco, 1975, I.B.C., Geneva, 1984—, 1st Interstate Bank, L.A., 1985. Author: The Only Variable, 1985, Navigating towards Success, 1986; contbr. articles to profl. publs. Named adm. State of Nebr., 1987; Joseph Kaplan Trust scholar, 1961. Mem. Direct Selling Assn., Rolls Royce Owners Club. Republican. Office: Ultra Promotions 20 S Santa Cruz Ave Los Gatos CA 95031

FOCH, NINA, actress, educator; b. Leyden, Netherlands, Apr. 20, 1924; came to U.S. 1927; d. Dirk and Consuelo (Flowerton) F.; m. James Lipton, June 6, 1954; m. Dennis de Brito, Nov. 27, 1959; 1 child, Dirk de Brito; m. Michael Dewell, Oct. 31, 1967. Grad., Lincoln Sch., 1939; studies with Stella Adler. Adj. prof. drama U. So. Calif., 1966-68, 78-80, adj. prof. film, 1987—; artist-in-residence U. N.C., 1966, Ohio State U., 1967, Calif. Inst. Tech., 1969-70; mem. sr. faculty Am. Film Inst., 1974-77; founder, tchr. Nina Foch Studio, Hollywood, Calif., 1973—; founder, actress Los Angeles Theatre Group, 1960-65; bd. dirs. Nat. Repertory Theatre, 1967-75; creative cons. to dirs., writers, producers of all media. Appeared in motion pictures Nine Girls, 1944, Return of the Vampire, 1944, Shadows in the Night, 1944, Cry of the Werewolf, 1944, Escape in the Fog, 1945, A Song to Remember, 1945, My Name Is Julia Ross, 1945, I Love a Mystery, 1945, Johnny O'Clock, 1947, The Guilt of Janet Ames, 1947, The Dark Past, 1948, The Undercover Man, 1949, Johnny Allegro, 1949, An American in Paris, 1951, Scaramouche, 1952, Young Man with Ideas, 1952, Sombrero, 1953, Fast Company, 1953, Executive Suite, 1954 (Oscar award nominee), Four Guns to the Border, 1954, You're Never Too Young, 1955, Illegal, 1955, The Ten Commandments, 1956, Three Brave Men, 1957, Cash McCall, 1959, Spartacus, 1960, Such Good Friends, 1971, Salty, 1973, Mahogany, 1976, Jennifer, 1978, Rich and Famous, 1981, Skin Deep, 1988; appeared in Broadway plays including John Loves Mary, 1947, Twelfth Night, 1949, A Phoenix Too Frequent, 1950, King Lear, 1950, Second String, 1960; appeared with Am. Shakespeare Festival in Taming of the Shrew, Measure for Measure, 1956, San Francisco Ballet and Opera in The Seven Deadly Sins, 1966; also many regional theater appearances including Seattle Repertory Theatre (All Over, 1972 and The Seagull, 1973); actress on TV, 1947—, including Playhouse 90, Studio One, Pulitzer Playhouse, Playwrights 56, Producers Showcase, Lou Grant (Emmy nominee 1980), Mike Hammer; series star: Shadow Chasers, 1985, War and Remembrance, 1988; many other series, network spls. and TV films; TV panelist and guest on The Dinah Shore Show, Merve Griffin Show, The Today Show, Dick Cavett, The Tonight Show; TV moderator: Let's Take Sides, 1957-59; assoc. dir. (film) The Diary of Ann Frank, 1959; dir. (nat. tour and on-Broadway) Tonight at 8:30, 1966-67; assoc. producer re-opening of Ford's Theatre, Washington, 1968. Hon. chmn. Los Angeles chpt. Am. Cancer Soc., 1970. Recipient Film Daily award, 1949, 53. Mem. Acad. Motion Pictures Arts and Scis. (co-chmn. exec. com. fgn. film award, exec. com. student film award, com. mem. spl. projects), Hollywood Acad. TV Arts and Scis. (gov. 1976-77). Office: PO Box 1884 Beverly Hills CA 90213

FOELLER, KLARA LORRAIN, art consultant; b. N.Y.C., Nov. 18, 1957; d. Peter Van Tassell and Eleanor (Malm) F. Student, U. Redlands (Calif.), 1975-77; BA in Art History, UCLA, 1979. Adminstrv. asst. Riverside Art & Cultural Assn., Cherry Valley, Calif., 1980-81; prodn. asst. rsch. DoD Motion Media Records Ctr., Norton AFB, Calif., 1981-87; pvt. practice rsch. cons. Yucaipa, Calif., 1987—. Democrat. Lutheran. Home and Office: 34934 Cedar Ave B Yucaipa CA 92399

FOERCH, BRUCE FREDERICK, school system adminstrator; b. St. Johns, Mich., Mar. 20, 1949; s. Berl L. and Doris Foerch; m. Elena Wassillie, May 22, 1982; children: Frederick Bruce, John Berl, Eugene Frederick. BA, Western Mich. U., 1972; MA, Mich. State U., 1976. Cert. elem. tchr. Tchr. St. Johns Pub. Schs., 1972-78; prin., tchr. Southwest Region Schs., Dillingham, Alaska, 1978—; cons. Bristol Bay curriculum project U. Alaska, Dillingham, 1983—. Advisor: (newspaper) Togiak Times, 1984—; producer, dir. (video) Togiak Village Profile, Togiak At the Cross Roads. Mem. exec. bd. East Olive PTO, St. Johns, 1976; chmn. Sjea Profl. Rights and Responsibility Com., St. Johns, 1977 (editor newsletter, 1973-75), SRS Social Studies Com., Dillingham, 1984; mem. exec. com. Togiak (Alaska) Com. on Future Edn., 1986. Mem. NEA, Social Studies Educators of Alaska, Nat. Alaska Assn. Curriculum Devel. and Supervision, Internat. Platform Assn., Southwest Region Edn. Assn. (pres.). Home: 454 Bayview Dr Togiak AK 99678 Office: Togiak Sch Togiak AK 99678

FOERST, DENIS LEE, chemist; b. Pipestone, Minn., Sept. 11, 1946; s. Louis Lee and Rosemary Louise (Duer) F.; m. Barbara Jean Heer, July 7, 1973; children: Benjamin, Stephanie, Matthew, Renata. BS, U. Notre Dame, 1968; PhD, Miami U., Oxford, Ohio, 1975. Postdoctoral fellow U. Wis., Milw., 1975-76; chemist Nat. Inst. for Occupational Safety and Health, Cin., 1976-78, EPA, Cin., 1978-85; mktg. engr. Sci. Instruments div. Hewlett-Packard Co., Palo Alto, Calif., 1985-87, product mgr., 1987--. Contbr. articles to profl. jours., chpts. to books. Asst. cubmaster Boy Scouts Am., Fremont, Calif., 1987, cubmaster, mem. roundtable staff, 1988--. Recipient Sci. and Tech. Achievement award EPA, 1983, Spl. Achievement award, 1984. Mem. Am. Chem. Soc., Am. Soc. for Mass Spectrometry, Bay Area Mass Spectrometry Soc. Methodist. Home: 38500 Athy Ct Fremont CA 94536 Office: Hewlett-Packard Co Sci Instruments Div 1601 California Ave Palo Alto CA 94308

FOFLYGEN, RONALD WAYNE, manufacturing executive; b. Washington, Pa., Oct. 14, 1944; s. James Wayne and Elma Grace (Dunfee) F.; m. Yvonne Emma Sinnett, Nov. 20, 1965; children: Jeffrey Wayne, Kara Leigh. BSEE, Pa. State U., 1973. Design engr. Midland-Ross Corp., Pitts., 1973-75; chief elec. engr. Crucible Steel, Inc., Midland, Pa., 1975-83; sales mgr. Advanced Tech. Sales, Inc., Pitts., 1983-84; sr. staff BDM Corp., Albuquerque, 1984-87; engring. mgr. Plasmatronics, Inc., Albuquerque, 1987-88; v.p. ops. Indsl. Lasers, Inc., Albuquerque, 1988—; pres. Advanced Tech. Cons., Albuquerque, 1987—. Inventor bar hanger box fastener for elec. constrn. products, patentee in field. Elder Ambridge United Presbyn. Ch., Pa., 1984; deacon Covenant Presbyn. Ch., Albuquerque, 1988. With USAF, 1966-70. Mem. Phi Kappa Phi, Tau Beta Pi, Sigma Tau, Eta Kappa Nu, Phi Eta Sigma, Pa. State Alumni Assn. Republican. Home: 11720 Molly Brown NE Albuquerque NM 87111 Office: Indsl Lasers Inc 2460 Alamo SE Albuquerque NM 87106

FOIANINI, LARRY DEAN, dentist; b. Rock Springs, Wyo., Apr. 13, 1949; s. Sasto and Mable (Covolo) F.; m. Mary Melinkovich, Jan. 29, 1971; children: Anthony, Christopher, Gina. BS, U. Wyo., 1974; DDS, Creighton U., 1978. Ptnr. Laramie (Wyo.) Family Dental Clinic, 1978—. Bd. dirs. Laramie Bd. Health, 1981—; coach Laramie Soccer League, 1985-87, Little League Baseball, 1988; trustee Albany County Sch. Dist. #1, 1988—. With U.S. Army, 1969-70. Fellow Wyo. Acad. Gen. Dentistry (pres. 1982-85); mem. ADA, Wyo. Dental Soc. (peer rev. com. 1986—), South Cen. Wyo. Dental Soc. (pres. 1984-85), Am. Orthodontic Soc., Am. Straight Wire Orthodontic Assn., Am. Acad. Functional Orthodontists, Alpha Epsilon Delta. Home: 2336 Skyview Ln Laramie WY 82070 Office: Laramie Family Dental Clinic 3529 Grand Ave Laramie WY 82070

FOIST, EVE LYNN, travel consultant; b. N.Y.C., Jan. 5, 1934; d. Monroe Henry and Beatrice (Koppel) Green; m. William Fillmore Foist, Mar. 25, 1956; children: Elisabeth, Laura, Dana. BA in English Lit., UCLA, 1955. Tchr. Milikan High Sch., Long Beach, Calif., 1960-65; real estate agt. Russ Lyon, Phoenix, 1970-79; travel agt. Savage Travel, Long Beach, 1982-84; asst. mgr. Clark Ave. Travel, Long Beach, 1984-86; travel cons. Lineberger Travel, Long Beach, 1986—. Mem. Health Edn. Com., Homeowners Assn., Dem. Nat. Com. Unitarian. Club: Plaza. Home: 6223 Seaside Walk Long Beach CA 90803 Office: Lineberger 4611 E Anaheim St Long Beach CA 90804

FOIST, WILLIAM FILLMORE, management consultant; b. Muncie, Ind., July 26, 1937; s. Millard Fillmore and Mildred (Bell) F.; m. Eve Lynn Green, Mar. 25, 1956; children: Elisabeth, Laura Ann, Dana. BS, Calif. State U., Long Beach, 1958. Chief program control space div. Rockwell, Downey, Calif., 1959-68; mgr. cons. Arthur Young & Co., Phoenix, 1968-72; dir. cons. Laventhol & Horvath, Phoenix, 1972-74; chief exec. Behavior Research Ctr., Phoenix, 1974-76; dir. planning Scottsdale (Ariz.) Meml. Ctr., 1976-79; dir. cons. Coopers & Lybrand, Los Angeles, 1979-82; freelance mgmt. cons. Seal Beach, Calif., 1982—; bd. dirs. Behavior Research Ctr., Phoenix, 1970-76, PRS Corp., Chatsworth, Calif., 1987-88, DPI Labs., Inc., Pasadena, Calif., 1987-88. Author: Program Evaluation and Review, 1967; co-author: Measurement and Planning, 1966. Chmn. Urban Planning Council, Phoenix, 1970-75, Environ. Planning Commn., Phoenix, 1973-79; pres. Madison Sch. Bd., Phoenix, 1974-78. Served with USAF, 1950-54. Behavior Study grantee Ctr. for Disease Control, 1975. Republican. Unitarian. Clubs: Jonathan (Los Angeles); Plaza (Phoenix). Lodge: Rotary (Los Angeles). Home: 6223 Seaside Walk Long Beach CA 90803 Office: Box 3214 Seal Beach CA 90740

FOLEY, CRAY LYMAN, mechanical engineer; b. Tulsa, Apr. 15, 1927; s. Lyndon Lyman and Margaret Clark (Cray) F.; student U. Tulsa, 1945-48; BS, Okla. State U., 1951, MS, 1957; children: Kelly Ann, Jill, Cray, Seth. Jr. Rsch. engr. Lockheed Aircraft Corp., Burbank, Calif., 1951-52; engr. Sperry Gyroscope Co., Great Neck, N.Y., 1953-57; advanced systems staff engr. Lockheed Missile & Space Co., Sunnyvale, Calif., 1957-82, sr. staff engr., 1982—. Pres. Homeowners Assn., 1964-66; Cub Scout com. chmn. Santa Clara County council Boy Scouts Am., 1971-72. Mem. Nat. Soc. Profl. Engrs., Okla. Soc. Profl. Engr., Soc. Automotive Engrs., Am. Def. Preparedness Assn., Lockheed Mgmt. Assn., Okla. State U. Alumni Assn., Lambda Chi Alpha. Republican. Home: 7090 Galli Dr San Jose CA 95129 Office: Lockheed Missile & Space Co 7090 Galli Dr San Jose CA 95129

FOLEY, DANIEL EDMUND, real estate develelopment executive; b. St. Paul, Mar. 1, 1926; s. Edward and Gerry (Fitzgarld) F.; student U. Minn., 1941-43; m. Paula Evans, Apr. 1, 1946. Chmn. bd. Realty Ptnrs. Ltd., Los Angeles; pres. Alpha Property Mgmt. Served with AUS, 1943-46.

FOLEY, THOMAS STEPHEN, speaker of the U.S. House of Representatives; b. Spokane, Wash., Mar. 6, 1929; s. Ralph E. and Helen Marie (Higgins) F.; m. Heather Strachan, Dec. 1968. B.A., U. Wash., 1951, LL.B., 1957. Bar: Wash. Partner Higgins & Foley, 1957-58; dep. pros. atty. Spokane County, Spokane, 1958-60; asst. atty. gen. State of Wash., Olympia, 1960-61; spl. counsel interior and insular affairs com. U.S. Senate, Washington, 1961-64; with 89th-101st Congresses from 5th Dist. Wash.; mem. interior com. 1965-75, mem. com. on standards of official conduct, 1973-77, chmn. agr. com. subcom. on livestock and feedgrains, 1973-75, chmn. agr. com., 1975-80, vice chmn. agr. com., 1981-86, chmn. House Dem. Caucus, 1976-80, House majority whip, 1981-86, House majority leader, 1987-89; speaker U.S. Ho. of Reps., 1989—; instr. law Gonzaga U., 1958-60; mem. bd. advisors Ctr. Strategic and Internat. Studies; mem. adv. council Am. Ditchley Found. Bd. overseers Whitman Coll.; bd. advisors Yale U. council; bd. dirs. Council on Fgn. Relations. Mem. Phi Delta Phi. Democrat. Office: 1201 Longworth Bldg Washington DC 20515

FOLLETTE, WILLIAM ALBERT, electronics company executive; b. Tampa, Fla., Dec. 29, 1946; s. Harold Albert and Louise Olga (Mehm) F.; m. Barbara Ann Cunneen, June 8, 1968; children: Kelly, James, William T. BBA, U. Notre Dame, 1968; MBA, Ariz. State U., 1978. Prodn. control analyst Motorola, Mesa, Ariz., 1974-77; successively bus. planner, bus. planning mgr., dir. strategic planning Sperry Corp., Phoenix, 1977-87; dir. bus. and strategic planning Honeywell Inc., Phoenix, 1987—; bd. dirs. Phoenix chpt. Planning Forum. Maj. USAFR, 1968—. Republican. Roman Catholic. Home: 5041 E Cortez Scottsdale AZ 85254 Office: Honeywell Inc Comml Flight Systems Group 21111 N 19th Ave Phoenix AZ 85027

FOLLICK, EDWIN DUANE, chiropractor, law educator; b. Glendale, Calif., Feb. 4, 1935; s. Edwin Fulfford and Esther Agnes (Catherwood) F.; m. Marilyn K. Sherk, Mar. 24, 1986. BA Calif. State U., L.A., 1956, MA, 1961; MA Pepperdine U., 1957, MPA, 1977; PhD, ThD St. Andrews Theol. Coll., Sem. of the Free Protestant Episc. Ch., London, 1958; MLS, U. So. Calif., 1963, MEd in Instructional Materials, 1964, AdvMEd in Edn. Adminstrn., 1969; Calif. Coll. Law, 1965; LLB Blackstone Law Sch., 1966, JD, 1967; DC Cleve. Chiropractic Coll., L.A., 1972; PhD, Academia Theatina, Pescara, 1978. Tchr., library adminstr. L.A. City Schs., 1957-68; law librarian Glendale U. Coll. Law, 1968-69; coll. librarian Cleve. Chiropractic Coll., L.A., 1969-74, dir. edn. and admissions, 1974-84, prof. jurisprudence, 1975—, dean student affairs, 1976—, chaplain, 1985—; assoc. prof. Newport U., 1982—; extern prof. St. Andrews Theol. Coll., London, 1961; dir. West Valley Chiropractic Health Ctr., 1972—. Contbr. articles to profl. jours. Served as chaplain's asst. U.S. Army, 1958-60. Decorated Cavaliere Internat. Order legion of Honor of Immacolata (Italy); knight of Malta, Sovereign Order of St. John of Jerusalem; chevalier Ordre Militaire et Hospitalier de St. Lazare de Jerusalem, numerous others. Mem. ALA, NEA, Am. Assn. Sch. Librarians, L.A. Sch. Library Assn., Calif. Media and Library Educators Assn., Assn. Coll and Rsch. Librarians, Am. Assn. Law Librarians, Am. Chiropractic Assn., Internat. Chiropractors Assn., Nat. Geog. Soc., Internat. Platform Assn., Phi Delta Kappa, Sigma Chi Psi, Delta Tau Alpha. Democrat. Episcopalian. Home: 6435 Jumilla Ave Woodland Hills CA 91367 Office: 590 N Vermont Ave Los Angeles CA 90004 also: 7022 Owensmouth Ave Canoga Park CA 91303

FOLLINGSTAD, CAROL ANN, nurse; b. Oak Park, Ill., June 1, 1945; d. Raymond Donald and Iris Eleane (Hofmann) F. RN with honors, Swedish Hosp. Sch. of Nursing, Mpls., 1968; student, U. Minn., 1968-70, L.A. City Coll., 1971-73, 77-79; BS in Health Sci. with di, U. Redlands, 1983. Cert. Lactation Cons. Sr. staff nurse UCLA Ctr. for the Health Scis., Westwood Village, L.A., 1970-71; labor and delivery staff nurse Queen of Angels Hosp., L.A., 1971-74; nursing cons. Trainex Corp., Garden Grove, Calif., 1973; operating room staff nurse Queen of Angels Hosp., L.A., 1974-75; operating room team leader St. Vincent Med. Ctr., L.A., 1975-78; night supr. Beverly Manor Convalescent Hosp., Burbank, Calif., 1978; OB staff nurse, perinatal nurse educator Memorial Hosp. of Glendale, Glendale, Calif., 1978-80; physician's rep. Medela, Inc., Crystal Lake, Ill., 1985-88; infant devel. specialist Calif. State U., L.A., 1984—; prenatal breastfeeding instr. St. Joseph Med. Ctr., Burbank, Calif., 1985—; mem. internat. immunication Team to Uganda (African Enterprise), 1988, 89. Outreach coord. Emmanuel Evang. Free Ch., Burbank, 1987—. Mem. Calif. Perinatal Assn., Internat. Lactation Cons. Assn., La Leche League Internat., Nurses Assn. Am. Coll. Ob-Gyn., UCLA Lactation Alumni Assn. Republican. Home and Office: 2021 Grismer #38 Burbank CA 91504

FOLWICK, DANIEL A., JR., convention center manager; b. San Antonio, Aug. 1, 1953; s. Daniel A. and Imogene (Sousley) F.; m. Suzanne Lynn Witmer, Nov. 13, 1975; 1 child, Zachary. Mgr. Sterling Recreation Orgn., Longview, Wash., 1974-79, Wometro-Lathrop Theatres, Anchorage, 1980-82; sales rep. Asplund Supply, Inc., Anchorage, 1982-84; mgr. Egan Conv. Ctr., Anchorage, 1984—. Bd. chmn. Vols. of Am. of Alaska, 1986—; assoc. dir. Greater Anchorage, Inc., 1987—; mem. Anchorage Sea Services Com., 1986—; bd. dirs. Armed Services YMCA of Anchorage, 1987—. Mem. Internat. Assn. Auditorium Mgrs. Democrat. Lodge: Mason (master 1987). Club: Navy League. Home: 801 Airport Heights #314 Anchorage AK 99508 Office: Egan Civic and Conv Ctr 555 W 5th Ave Anchorage AK 99501

FONDI, MICHAEL EUGENE, district judge; b. Ely, Nev., Apr. 4, 1937; s. Mike and Clara (Orueta) F.; children: Michael David, Anthony Paul, Jonathan. BA, Stanford U., 1959; JD, Hastings Coll., 1962. Bar: Calif. 1963, Nev. 1964. Adminstrv. asst. to gov. of Nev. Carson City, Nev., 1963-65; dep. atty. gen. St. of Nev., Carson CIty, 1965-67; chief dep. dist. atty. of Carson City 1967-70, dist. atty. of Carson City, 1971-77; dist. judge First Jud. Dist. Ct., Carson City, 1977—; mem. com. for establishing suggested sentences for felonies State of Nev., Carson City, 1985-88; chmn. Com. on Cameras in the Courtroom, 1979-85; attendee Nat. Inst. of Justice, Phoenix, Ariz., 1987, Nat. Conf. of the Judiciary on Rights of Victims of Crime, 1983. Mem. Nat. Judicial Coll. Task Force to study Nev.'s Correctional Insts. and Felony Sentencing, 1989. Mem. Nev. Dist. Judges Assn., State Bar of Nev., Washoe County Bar Assn., First Jud. Dist. Bar Assn. Democrat. Office: Dist Ct 198 N Carson Ste 101 Carson City NV 89701

FONDREN, CECILIA DIANN, real estate executive; b. Louisville, Mar. 22, 1943; d. Leland Dean and Gilda Ross (Rowe) Hall; m. Harry Edmond Fondren, Sept. 28, 1963. AA in Computer Programming, Casper (Wyo.) Coll., 1977; cert., Wyo. Real Estate Inst., 1987. Clk. Jefferson Standard Life, Corpus Christi, Tex., 1963, Ark. Power and Light, Wynne, 1964; records analyst Colony Shop Inc., Wynne, 1965-70; loan clk. FHA, Wynne, 1971-72; owner, operator Koop Restaurant, Douglas, Wyo., 1976; legal sec. Frank Peasley Law Offices, Douglas, 1976-79; owner, mgr. Kwik Print Shop, Douglas, 1979-87; real estate agt. My Realty Co., Douglas, 1987—. Dir. non-career games Wyo. Spl. Olympics, Douglas, 1986; asst. county chmn. Gov.'s Campaign Converse County Rep. Com., 1979; trustee 1st United Meth. Ch. Douglas. Mem. Nat. Assn. Realtors, Wyo. Assn. Realtors, Douglas C. of C., Beta Sigma Phi (sec. 1985-86). Club: Toastmasters (edn. v.p. 1987—). Office: My Realty 102 N 2nd St Douglas WY 82633

FONG, BERNARD W.D., physician educator; b. Honolulu, May 18, 1926; s. Leonard K. and Francis C. Fong; m. Roberta Wat, Aug. 13, 1950; children: Phyllis K., Jeffrey S., Camille K., Allison K. BS, Bucknell U., 1948; MD, Jefferson Med. Coll., 1952. Diplomate Am. Bd. Internal Medicine. Intern Germantown Hosp., Phila., 1952-53; chief med. resident Germantown Hosp., 1953-55; teaching fellow cardiology Jefferson Med. Coll. Hosp., Phila., 1955-56; attending physician Queen's Med. Coll., Honolulu, 1956-89, St. Francis Hosp., Honolulu, 1956-89; clin. prof. medicine U. Hawaii, Honolulu, 1982—; mem. adv. coun. Nat. Heart Lung & Blood Inst., NIH, Bethesda, Md., 1976-80, chairperson third forum on cardiovascular risk factors, 1985; mem. adv. com. cardiovascular risk factors in minorities NIH, 1976—. Pres. Hawaii Heart Assn., Honolulu, 1962-63; bd. dirs. Am. Heart. Assn., N.Y.C., 1963-66; pres. Chung Shan Assn., Honolulu, 1969-70, United Chinese Soc. Hawaii, Honolulu, 1973-74; 1st v.p. Wong Leong Doo Benevolent Soc., Honolulu, 1973—; 1st v.p. Ocean View Cemetery, Honolulu, 1973—. With USNR, 1944-46, PTO. Fellow Am. Coll. Physicians (gov. 1972-76, inaugural laureate internal medicine Hawaii chpt. 1986), Am. Coll. Cardiology, Am. Coll. Chest Physicians; mem. Am. Soc. Internal Medicine (pres. Hawaii chpt. 1980-82). Republican. Roman Catholic. Home: 97 Dowsett Ave Honolulu HI 96817 Office: 1380 Lusitana St 706 Honolulu HI 96813

FONG, HAROLD MICHAEL, federal judge; b. Honolulu, Apr. 28, 1938; m. Judith Tom, 1966; children—Harold Michael, Terrence Matthew. A.B. cum laude, U. So. Calif., 1960; J.D., U. Mich., 1964. Bar: Hawaii 1965. Dep. pros. atty. City and County of Honolulu, 1965-68; assoc. Mizuha and Kim, Honolulu, 1968-69; asst. U.S. atty. Dist. Hawaii, 1969-73; U.S. atty. 1973-78; ptnr. Fong and Miho, Honolulu, 1978-82; judge U.S. Dist. Ct. Hawaii, 1982-84, chief judge, 1984—. Office: US Dist Ct PO Box 50128 Honolulu HI 96850

FONG, PETER C. K., lawyer; b. Honolulu, Oct. 28, 1955; s. Arthur S.K. and Victoria K.Y. (Chun) F. BBA with honors, U. Hawaii, 1977; JD, Boston Coll., 1980. Bar: Hawaii 1980, U.S. Dist. Ct. Hawaii 1980, U.S. Ct. Appeals (9th cir.) 1980, U.S. Supreme Ct. 1983. Law clk. Honolulu Atty. Gen's Office, 1979, Supreme Ct. Hawaii, Honolulu, 1980-81; dep. pros. atty. Pros. Atty.'s Office, Honolulu, 1981-84; with Davis, Reid & Richards, Honolulu, 1984—; chief legal counsel, chief clk. Senate jud. com. Hawaii State Legislature, 1989—; gen. legal counsel Hawaii Jr. C. of C., 1983-84; pres., bd. dirs. Legal Aid Soc. Hawaii, 1984—; pres., 1986-87; arbitrator Hawaiian Cir. Ct., 1986—; chief legal counsel, chief clk. Senate Juiciary com. Hawaii State Legislature, 1989—. Mem. City and County Honolulu Neighborhood Bd., 1981-83; campaign treas. for Hawaii state senator, 1981—, Boston Coll. Internat. Law Review; mem. aux. admissions com. Boston Coll. Law Sch., 1982—, Internat. & Comp. Law Rev., major gifts com. and sustaining membership fundraising drive com. YMCA, 1988; del. Gov.'s Congress on Hawaii's internat. role, 1988. Recipient Pres.'s award Hawaii Jr. C. of C., 1984. Mem. ABA, Hawaii Bar Assn., Assn. Trial Lawyers Am., Nat. Assn. Dist. Attys., U.S. Supreme Ct. Hist. Soc., Mortar Bd., Tu Chiang Sheh (past pres.). Home: 5255 Makalena St Honolulu HI 96821 Office: Davis Reid & Richards 1200 Pauahi Tower 1001 Bishop St Honolulu HI 96813

FONKALSRUD, ERIC WALTER, pediatric surgeon, educator; b. Balt., Aug. 31, 1932; s. George and Ella (Fricke) F.; m. Margaret Ann Zimmermann, June 6, 1959; children: Eric Walter Jr., Margaret Lynn, David Loren, Robert Warren. B.A., U. Wash., 1953; M.D., Johns Hopkins U., 1957. Diplomate Am. Bd. Surgery, Am. Bd. Thoracic Surgery, Am. Bd. Pediatric Surgery. Intern Johns Hopkins Hosp., Balt., 1957-58, asst. resident, 1958-59; asst. resident U. Calif. Med. Ctr., Los Angeles, 1959-62, chief resident surgery, 1962-63, asst. prof. surgery, chief pediatric surgery, 1965-68, assoc. prof., 1968-71, prof., 1971—, vice chmn. dept. surgery, 1982—; resident pediatric surgery Columbus (Ohio) Childrens Hosp. and Ohio State U., 1963-65; practice medicine specializing in pediatric surgery Los Angeles, 1965—; Mem. surg. study sect. NIH; James IV surg. traveller to, Gt. Britain, 1971. Mem. editorial bd. Jour. Surg. Research, Archives of Surgery, Annals of Surgery, Surgery, Current Problems in Surgery, Am. Jour. Surgery, Current Surgery; author book, chpts. in textbooks; contbr. over 350 articles to med. jours. Recipient Mead Johnson award for grad. tng. surgery A.C.S., 1963; Golden Apple award for teaching UCLA Sch. Medicine, 1968; John and Mary R. Markle scholar in acad. medicine, 1963-68. Fellow ACS (surg. forum com., bd. govs. 1978-84), Am. Acad. Pediatrics (exec. bd., chmn. surgical sect. 1986-87); mem. Soc. Univ. Surgeons (sec. 1973-76, pres. 1976-77), Assn. Acad. Surgeons (pres. 1972), AMA, Calif. Med. Assn., Los Angeles County Med. Assn., Am. Surg. Assn., Pan Pacific Surg. Assn., Pacific Coast Surg. Assn. (recorder 1979-85, pres. 1989), Am. Pediatric Surg. Assn. (gov. 1975-78, pres.-elect 1988), Pacific Assn. Pediatric Surgeons (pres. 1983-84), S.W. Pediatric Soc., Los Angeles Pediatric Soc., Soc. for Clin. Surgery, Transplantation Soc., Pediatric Surgery Biology Club, Am. Thoracic Surg. Assn., Bay Surg. Soc., Los Angeles Surg. Soc. (sec. 1988—), Am. Acad. Sci., Sigma Xi, Alpha Omega Alpha. Methodist. Club: Pithotomy (pres.). Home: 428 24th St Santa Monica CA 90402 Office: U Calif Med Ctr Dept Surgery Los Angeles CA 90024

FONTAINE, VALERIE ANNE, lawyer; b. Honolulu, May 17, 1955; d. Warren Tremlett Chaffey and Dorine Marks Foster; m. Michael Fontaine, . JD, Hastings Coll., San Francisco, 1979; AB, UCLA, 1976. Assoc. O'Melveny & Myers, L.A., 1979-81; cons. Lee, Jackson & Bowe, Beverly Hills, Calif., 1981-83; v.p. Bench Ltd., L.A., 1983-88; ptnr. Seltzer-Fontaine Group, L.A., 1988—. Co-author: Nat. Law Jour., 1988-89. Area coord. Jewish Marriage Enhancement, L.A., 1981-84. Mem. State Bar Calif., L.A. Bar Assn., Hastings Alumni Assn. (bd. dirs. 1988), Phi Beta Kappa. Democrat. Jewish. Office: Seltzer-Fontaine Group 5657 Wilshire Blvd #220 Los Angeles CA 90036

FONTANA, PERRY HOWARD, environmental consultant; b. Grass Valley, Calif., Jan. 31, 1955; s. Alfred Eugene and Janice Joyce (Crispin) F.; m. Deborah Ann Wilson, June 24, 1984; 1 child, Evan James. BS in Meteorology, San Jose State U., 1977, MS in Meteorology, 1979. Rsch. fellow NSF, San Jose, Calif., 1977-79; hydrometeorologist U.S. Army C.E., Sacramento, 1978-79; v.p. Woodward-Clyde Cons., Santa Barbara, Calif., 1979-. Contbr. numerous articles on air pollution meteorology to profl. jours. Dean's scholar, 1973-77, President's scholar, 1977-79. Mem. Am. Meteorol. Soc., Air Pollution Control Assn., Santa Barbara C. of C. (bd. dirs. 1987), Phi Kappa Phi. Republican. Office: Woodward-Clyde Cons 121 Gray Ave Ste 201 Santa Barbara CA 93101

FOOSHE, DAVID SELF, digital systems engineer; b. McCormick, S.C., Sept. 8, 1954; s. John William and Mary Kathryn (Self) F. BS in EE, U. S.C., 1975. Design engr. Westinghouse Elec. Corp., Balt., 1976-78; test engr. Burr-Brown Research Corp., Tucson, 1978-79; mem. tech. staff div. electronic systems TRW, Redondo Beach, Calif., 1979-81, head sect. digital processing lab., 1982-85, project mgr. digital processing lab., 1985-86, mgr. digital systems dept., 1986—. Mem. Tau Beta Pi. Office: TRW Div Electronic Tech One Space Park Redondo Beach CA 90278

FOOTE, ANDREA DAVETTE, financial executive; b. Chgo., Aug. 2, 1946; d. Merrill E. Skilling and Norma W. (Mansfield) Nunes;m. David Scott Foote, Dec. 15, 1969. BS in Acctg., Nat. U., San Diego, 1979, MS in Fin., 1981. Controller Univ. Club San Diego, 1975-81; Controller Action Instruments, Inc., San Diego, 1981-86, chief fin. officer, corp. sec., 1986--. Bd. dirs. San Diego Community Coll. Dist., 1988. Mem. Nat. Assn. Accts. (dir. San Diego chpt. 1985-88, Mem. of Yr. 1986), Mensa, Toastmasters (asst. area gov. dist. 5 1986-87, pres. Fireside 1985). Home: 9869 Park Crest Ln San Diego CA 92124 Office: Action Instruments Inc 8601 Aero Dr San Diego CA 92123

FOOTE, KAY REBBER, artist; b. Long Beach, Calif., Mar. 3, 1923; d. Leland Lester Rebber and Mary Alice Thomas; m. John Taintor Foote, Dec. 24, 1943; children: Carol Ann, John Taintor Jr., Ellen Jackson. BA, U. So. Calif., Los Angeles, 1943; postgrad., Art Ctr. Coll., Los Angeles, 1943-45, Chouinard Art Inst., Los Angeles, 1943-45. Co-owner Gallery Xyst, Laguna Beach, Calif., 1975-84; juror Calif. State Fair, 1979, Laguna Hills Art Assn. Works exhibited Laguna Beach Art Mus., 1976-79, City of Newport Beach (Calif.) Ann. Juried Show, 1976-77, Dafca Show, Disney Studios, Los Angeles, 1977, Laguna Beach Festival Art, 1976-89, Brea (Calif.) Mcpl. Art Gallery, 1987, Designs Recycled Gallery, Brea, 1984, San Bernardino County (Calif.) Mus. Art, 1983, Laguna Beach Art. Mus. Invitational, 1983. Donated works to Laguna Beach Boys' Club, Our Lady of Angels, Junior League, Children's Home Soc. Recipient Past Pres. award Nat. Watercolor Soc., Los Angeles, 1987, Spl. award Laguna Beach Art Mus., 1983. Mem. Nat. Watercolor Soc. (Past Pres. award 1987). Home: 74 Emerald Bay Laguna Beach CA 92651

FOOTMAN, GORDON ELLIOTT, educational administrator; b. Los Angeles, Oct. 10, 1927; s. Arthur Leland and Meta Fay (Neal) F.; m. Virginia Rose Footman, Aug. 7, 1954; children: Virginia, Patricia, John. BA, Occidental Coll., 1951, MA, 1954; EdD, U. So. Calif., 1972. Tchr., Arcadia, Calif., 1952, Glendale, Calif., 1954-56; psychologist Burbank (Calif.) Schs., 1956-64, supr., 1964-70, dir. pupil personnel services, 1970-72; dir. div. evaluation, attendance and pupil svcs. L.A. County Office Edn., Downey, Calif., 1972—. Lectr. ednl. psychology U. So. Calif., 1972-75, asst. prof. ednl. psychology, 1976—. Pres. Council for Exceptional Children, 1969-70; pres. Burbank Coordinating Council, 1969-70; mem. Burbank Family Service Bd., 1971-72. Served with AUS, 1945-47. Mem. Am. Edn. Research Assn., Am. Assn. for Counseling and Devel. (senator 1983—, western region br. assembly publs. editor 1985-87), Calif. Personnel and Guidance Assn. (pres., chair 1988—), Calif. Assn. Sch. Psychologists and Psychometrists, Nat., Calif. (monograph editor 1977—) assns. pupil personnel adminstrs., Calif. Assn. Counselor Educators and Suprs. (trustee), Calif. Assn. Sch. Adminstrs., Calif. Soc. Ednl. Program Auditors and Evaluators (sec. 1975-76, v.p. 1976-77, pres.), Calif. Assn. Measurement and Evaluation in Guidance (sec. 1976, pres.), Council Exceptional Children (pres. Foothill chpt. 1969-70), Phi Beta Kappa, Phi Alpha Theta, Psi Chi. Republican. Presbyn. Home: 1259 Sherwood Rd San Marino CA 91108 Office: 9300 E Imperial Hwy Downey CA 90242

FORAKER, DAVID ALAN, lawyer; b. Mpls., Feb. 22, 1956; s. Crawford Jackson and Norma Jane (Settlemoir) F.; m. Nancy Jean Howard, May 9, 1987. MS, St. Cloud State U., 1978; JD, U. Oreg., 1981. Bar: Oreg. 1981. Assoc. McMenamin, Joseph, Babener, Greene & Perris, Portland, Oreg., 1981-83, Greene & Perris, Portland, 1983-84; ptnr. Greene & Markley, P.C., Portland, 1984—; mem. Blue Ribbon Com. for Local Bankruptcy Rules, 1987-88; speaker Oreg. Trial Lawyers Assn., 1987. Editor: Oreg. Debtor-Creditor News, 1987-89, editor-in-chief, 1988. Mem. ABA, Oreg. Bar Assn., Multnomah County Bar Assn., Am. Bankruptcy Inst. Democrat. Episcopalian. Office: Greene & Markley PC 1515 SW 5th St Ste 600 Portland OR 97201

FORBES, ALFRED A., III, military officer; b. Greenville, N.C., May 20, 1940; s. Alfred A. and Virginia C. (Evans) F.; m. Diane S. Bertrand, July 4, 1964; children: Allison, Christopher. BS in Aerospace Engring., N.C. State U., 1963. Commd. 2d lt. USAF, 1964, advanced through grades to col., 1985; missile combat crew comdr. 71st Tac Missile Squadron, Bitburg, Fed. Republic Germany, 1964-67; pilot 317 Tactical Airlift Wing, Lockbourne AFB, Ohio, 1968-70; C-7 aircraft comdr. 483 Tactical Airlift Wing, Cam Rahn Bay, Republic Vietnam, 1970-71; C-130 E aircraft comdr. 316 Tactical Airlift Wing, Langley AFB, Va., 1971-73; civil engring. staff officer Air Force Communications Command, Richards Gebaur AFB, Mo., 1973-76; satellite ops. and plans officer 6594th Test Group, Hickam AFB, Hawaii, 1976-79; dir. Aircraft Ops. and Engring. Air Force Satellite Control Facility, Sunnyvale AFS, Calif., 1979-83; chief Satellite Control Div. Air Force Space Command, Colorado Springs, Colo., 1983-85; dep. comdr. ops. 2d Space Wing, Falcon Air Force Sta., Colo., 1985-88; sr. adv. engr. IBM Corp., Colorado Springs, 1988—. Decorated Legion of Merit, Air medal, Vietnamese Cross of Gallantry, and others. Mem. Air Force Assn. Home: 1285 Deer Creek Rd Monument CO 80132

FORBES, JUDIE, aeronautical engineer; b. Fullerton, Calif., Sept. 27, 1942; d. James Franklin and Lois Virginia (Couse) F.; children: Laurel Alice Schader, James Joseph Resha, Edward John Resha III. BA in Physics, Calif. State U., Fullerton, 1974; MS in Engring., Calif. State U., 1979; MBA, U. So. Calif., 1983; postgrad., Claremont Grad. Sch. Engr. electromech. div. Northrop, Anaheim, Calif., 1975-80; project engr., mgr. electronic div. Northrop, Hawthorne, Calif., 1981-87; tech. staff TRW, San Bernadino, Calif., 1981; project mgr. Gen. Research Corp., El Segundo, Calif., 1987—; v.p. D.C. Caldwell & Co., Inc., Buena Park, Calif., 1987—. Active Town Hall Calif., Los Angeles, 1983—. Calif. State U. Found. grantee, 1974; named Disting. Alumni Calif. State U., 1986; recipient Engring. Merit award Orange County Engring. Council, 1985. Fellow Inst. for Advancement Engring., AIAA (assoc., pres. Orange County 1986-87), Soc. Women Engrs. (pres. Los Angeles chpt. 1981-82, nat. v.p. 1983-84). Democrat. Home: 8650 Gulana #L3174 Playa del Rey CA 90293 Office: Gen Rsch Corp 240 N Nash El Segundo CA 90245

FORBES, KENNETH ALBERT FAUCHER, urological surgeon; b. Waterford, N.Y., Apr. 28, 1922; s. Joseph Frederick and Adelle Frances (Robitaille) F.; m. Eileen Ruth Gibbons, Aug. 4, 1956; children: Michael, Diane, Kenneth E., Thomas, Maureen, Daniel. BS cum laude, U. Notre Dame, 1943; MD, St. Louis U., 1947. Diplomate Am. Bd. Urology. Intern St. Louis U. Hosp., 1947-48; resident in urol. surgery Barnes Hosp., VA Hosp., Washington U., St. Louis. U. schs. medicine, St. Louis, 1948-52; fellow West Roxbury (Harvard) VA Hosp., Boston, 1955; asst. chief urology VA Hosp., East Orange, N.J., 1955-58; practice medicine specializing in urology Green Bay, Wis., 1958-78, Long Beach, Calif., 1978-85; mem. cons. staff Fairview State Hosp. U. Calif. Med. Ctr., Irvine, VA Hosp., Long Beach; asst. clin. prof. surgery U. Calif., Irvine, 1978-85; cons. Vols. in Tech. Assistance, 1986—. Contbr. articles to profl. jours. Served with USNR, 1944-46; capt. U.S. Army, 1952-54. Named Outstanding Faculty Mem. by students, 1981. Fellow ACS, Internat. Coll. Surgeons; mem. AAAS, AMA, Calif. Med. Assn., Am. Urol. Assn. (exec. com. North Cen. sect. 1972-75, western sect. 1980—), Royal Soc. Medicine (London), N.Y. Acad. Scis., Santa Barbara County Med. Soc., Surg. Alumni Assn. U. Calif. Irvine, Justin J. Cordonnier Soc. of Washington U., Confedn. Americana de Urologia, Urologists Corr. Club, Notre Dame Club (Man of Yr. 1965), Great Lakes Cruising Club, Retired Officers Club, Channel City Club, Cosmopolitan Club of Santa Barbara, Phi Beta Pi. Republican. Roman Catholic. Home and Office: 15 Langlo Terr Santa Barbara CA 93105

FORBES, LEONARD, engineering educator; b. Grande Prairie, Alta., Can., Feb. 21, 1940; came to U.S., 1966; s. Frank and Katie (Tschetter) F.; B.Sc. with distinction in Engring. Physics, U. Alta., 1962; M.S. in E.E., U. Ill., 1963, Ph.D., 1970. Staff engr. IBM, Fishkill, N.Y. and Manassas, Va., 1970-

72; IBM vis. prof. Howard U., Washington, 1972; asst. prof. U. Ark., Fayetteville, 1972-75; assoc. prof. U. Calif.-Davis, 1976-82; prof. Oreg. State U., Corvallis, 1983—; with Hewlett-Packard Labs., Palo Alto, Calif., 1978; cons. to Telex Computer Products, D.H. Baldwin, Hewlett-Packard, Fairchild, United Epitaxial Tech.; organizer Portland Internat. Conf. and Exposition on Silicon Materials and Tech., 1985-87. Served with Royal Can. Air Force, 1963-66. Mem. IEEE. Contbr. articles to profl. jours. Home: 537 Mountain View Ave Santa Rosa CA 95407 Office: Oreg State U Dept Elec Engring Corvallis OR 97331

FORD, BETTY BLOOMER (ELIZABETH FORD), wife of former President of U.S.; b. Chgo., Apr. 8, 1918; d. William Stephenson and Hortence (Neahr) Bloomer; m. Gerald R. Ford (38th Pres. U.S.), Oct. 15, 1948; children: Michael Gerald, John Gardner, Steven Meigs, Susan Elizabeth. Student, Sch. Dance Bennington Coll., 1936, 37; LL.D. hon., U. Mich., 1976. Dancer Martha Graham Concert Group, N.Y.C., 1939-41; model John Powers Agy., N.Y.C., 1939-41; fashion dir. Herpolscheimer's Dept. Store, Grand Rapids, Mich., 1943-48; dance instr. Grand Rapids, 1932-48; pres., bd. dirs. The Betty Ford Ctr., Rancho Mirage, Calif. Author: autobiography The Times of My Life, 1979, Betty: A Glad Awakening, 1987. Bd. dirs. Nat. Arthritis Found. (hon.); trustee Martha Graham Dance Ctr.; mem. theatre mgmt. com. Bob Hope Cultural Ctr.; trustee Eisenhower Med. Ctr., Rancho Mirage; hon. chmn. Palm Springs Desert Mus.; nat. trustee Nat. Symphony Orch.; trustee Nursing Home Adv. and Research Council Inc.; mem. Golden Circle Patrons Ctr. Theatre Performing Arts; bd. dirs. The Lambs, Libertyville, Ill. Episcopalian (tchr. Sunday sch. 1961-64). Home: PO Box 927 Rancho Mirage CA 92270 *

FORD, DAVID K., quality assurance manager; b. Indpls., Aug. 9, 1948; s. William F. and Alta R. (Keeler) F.; m. Earlene Finney, May 16, 1981. BS, U. Phoenix, 1987. Programmer Civil Engring. Firm, Indpls., 1966-68; process tech. CBS Tape Facility, Terre Haute, Ind., 1968-70; owner, operator Ford's Audio Svc. Ctr., Terre Haute, 1970-73; electronics shop supr. Rose-Hulman Inst. Tech., Terre Haute, 1973-77; design engr. Applied Computing Devices, Terre Haute, 1977-78, prodn. supr., 1978-79, ops. mgr., 1979-82; customer support mgr. Gen Rad, Inc., Phoenix, 1982-86, quality assurance mgr., 1986—; ptnr. Desert Art Product, Phoenix, 1985—. Patentee in field. Fund raiser Easter Seals, Heart Fund, Phoenix, 1984—. Mem. Scottsdale Artists League Club, Valley Artists League Club. Office: Gen Rad Inc 14841 N Blk Canyon Hwy Phoenix AZ 85023

FORD, DAVID THURMAN, water resources engineer; b. Alice, Tex., Oct. 1, 1950; s. Thurman Stanford and Elsie Christine (Corder) F.; m. Lynne Parnell Cannady, Oct. 5, 1986. AA, Schreiner Coll., 1971; BS, U. Tex., Austin, 1973; MS, U. Tex., 1976, PhD, 1978. Registered profl. engr., Calif., Tex. Ind. engring. cons. Sacramento, 1978—; engr. U.S. Army C.E., Davis, Calif., 1978—; lectr., U. Calif.-Davis, 1980-84, Calif. State U.-Sacramento, 1980—; tech. expert UN Devel. Program, New Delhi, India, 1983, 84, 85. Author: Catchment Runoff Analysis, 1988; contbr. articles to profl. jours. Fulbright grantee, USIA, Portugal, 1988-89. Mem. ASCE (assoc. editor Water Resource Planning jour. 1988-90), Am. Geophys. Union (assoc. editor Water Resource jour. 1988-89), Am. Water Resources Assn. Republican. Home: 3237 Cutter Way Sacramento CA 95818 Office: Hydrologic Engring Ctr 609 2d St Davis CA 95616

FORD, DAWN CALLISON, pharmacist, educator; b. Tonasket, Wash., Feb. 7, 1958; d. Keith Wayne and Joyce Louella (Fletcher) Callison; m. Charles Davis Ford, Oct. 23, 1982; children: Katherine Anne, William Jesse. BS in Pharm., Wash. State U., 1981; PharmD, U. Utah, 1983. Licensed pharmacist. Poison info. pharmacist Intermt. Regional Poison Control Ctr., Salt Lake City, 1981-84; clin. pharmacy supr. Cook County Hosp., Chgo., 1984-87; asst. prof. clin. pharmacy U. Wyoming, Laramie, 1987—. Mem. Wyoming Pharm. Assn., Am. Soc. of Hosp. Pharmacists, Am. Assn. of Colls. of Pharmacy. Home: 1503 W Wrangler Rd Cheyenne WY 82009 Office: U Wyo Sch Pharmacy Box 3375 CS Laramie WY 82071

FORD, GERALD RUDOLPH, JR., former President of United States; b. Omaha, July 14, 1913; s. Gerald R. and Dorothy (Gardner) F.; m. Elizabeth Bloomer, Oct. 15, 1948; children: Michael, John, Steven, Susan. A.B., U. Mich., 1935; LL.B., Yale U., 1941; LL.D., Mich. State U., Albion Coll., Aquinas Coll., Spring Arbor Coll. Bar: Mich. 1941. Practiced law at Grand Rapids, 1941-49; mem. law firm Buchen and Ford; mem. 81st-93d Congresses from 5th Mich. Dist., 1949-74, elected minority leader, 1965; v.p. U.S., 1973-74, pres., 1974-77; del. Interparliamentary Union, Warsaw, Poland, 1959, Belgium, 1961; del. Bilderberg Group Conf., 1962; dir. Santa Fe Internat., GK Technologies, Shearson Loeb Rhoades, Pebble Beach Corp., Tiger Internat. Served as lt. comdr. USNR, 1942-46. Recipient Grand Rapids Jr. C. of C. Distinguished Service award, 1948; Distinguished Service Award as one of ten outstanding young men in U.S. by U.S. Jr. C. of C., 1950; Silver Anniversary All-Am. Sports Illustrated, 1959; Distinguished Congressional Service award Am. Polit. Sci. Assn., 1961. Mem. Am., Mich. State, Grand Rapids bar assns., Delta Kappa Epsilon, Phi Delta Phi. Republican. Episcopalian. Clubs: University (Kent County), Peninsular (Kent County). Lodge: Masons. Home: PO Box 927 Rancho Mirage CA 92262 *

FORD, J. DOUG, state administrator; b. Columbus, Ohio, July 3, 1943; s. Samuel Edwin and Margaret A. (Puskar) F.; m. Michelle A. Wood, Dec. 11, 1985. AA, Orlando Jr. Coll., 1964; BA, Fla. StateU., 1966; MS, U. No. Colo., 1973. Instr. Lake Tahoe Community Coll., South Lake Tahoe, Calif., 1983-87; sr. counselordept. rehab. State of Calif., San Jose, San Francisco and South Lake Tahoe, 1973-88; program supr. State of Calif., Sacramento, 1988—; mem. distng. tng. com., 1986—. Mem. affirmative action com. City of South Lake Tahoe, 1986-87; founder Lake Tahoe Bi-State AIDS Task Force, South Lake Tahoe, 1986—, vol. Sacramento AIDS Found., 1987—. Capt. USAF, 1967-71. Democrat. Home: 6940 10th St Rio Linda CA 95673 Office: Calif Dept Rehab 5777 Madison Ave Ste 1050 Sacramento CA 95841

FORD, JOHN T., JR., art, film and video educator; b. Rotan, Tex., Feb. 17, 1953; s. John T. and Lala Fern (Shipley) F.; m. Betty Jean Crawford; children: Casey, Craig, Kirk. BA, U. Redlands, 1975. Cert. tchr., Calif. Tchr. art, film, video Yucaipa (Calif.) Joint Unified Sch. Dist., 1976-88; cons. Dist. Fine Arts Inservice, Yucaipa, 1987. Creator, coordinator (conceptual art) Whole School Environments, Caves, Tubes and Streamers, Forest Edge, 1980-84; creator (comml. art prints) Toy Horse Series, 1982-83. Mem. Yeoman Service Orgn., U. Redlands, 1972, Dist. Fine Arts Task Force, Yucaipa, 1984-87; interim dir. Hosanna House, Redlands, Calif., 1975; liaison Sch. Community Service/San Bernardino County (Calif.) Fire Dept., 1980-81. Recipient Golden Bell award Calif. Sch. Bd. Research Found., 1987, Ednl. Service award Mason's, 1987-88; named one of Outstanding Young Men of Am., 1987, Tchr. of Yr. Calif. Continuation Edn. Assn., 1987-88; grantee Calif. Tchrs. Instructional Improvement Program, 1985; scholar U. Redlands, 1975. Mem. NEA, Calif. Tchrs. Assn., Calif. Continual Edn. Assn., Yucaipa Edn. Assn., Am. Film Inst. Office: Green Valley High Sch 35912 Ave H Yucaipa CA 92399

FORD, JUDITH ANN, retired natural gas distribution company executive; b. Martinsville, Ind., May 11, 1935; d. Glenn Leyburn and Dorotha Mae (Parks) Tudor; m. Walter L. Ford, July 25, 1954 (dec. 1962); children—John Corbin, Christi Sue. Student, Wichita State U., 1953-55; student, U. Nev.-Las Vegas. Legal sec. Southwest Gas Corp., Las Vegas, 1963-69, adminstrn. sec., 1968-79, asst. corp. sec., 1969-72, corp. sec., 1972-82, v.p., 1977-82, sr. v.p., 1982-88, also bd. dirs., dir. 7 subs. Trustee Nev. Sch. Arts, Las Vegas, 1979—, chmn. bd. dirs., 1985-86; trustee Disciples Sem. Found., Claremont Sch. Theology, Calif., 1985—; mem. Ariz. Acad., Ariz. Town Halls, 1986—. Mem. Am. Soc. Corp. Secs., Greater Las Vegas C. of C. (bd. dirs. 1979-85), Pacific Coast Gas Assn. (bd. dirs. 1984-88), Ariz. Bus. Women Owners (exec. com. 1985-88). Democrat. Mem. Christian Ch. (Disciples of Christ). Office: SW Gas Corp PO Box 98510 Las Vegas NV 89193-8510

FORD, ROBERT LEE, insurance executive; b. Primghar, Iowa, July 4, 1950; s. Robert Lee and Mary Jean (Pohlman) F.; m. Julie Diane Soland, Sept. 12, 1970; 1 child, Stacy. AA, Iowa Tech. Sch., 1970. Sr. programmer Network Data Processing, Cedar Rapids, Iowa, 1970-71; supr. programming Seaboard Life Ins. Co., Chgo., 1971-73; mgr. programming United Fire & Casualty Co., Cedar Rapids, 1973-77; systems analyst Iowa Mut. Ins. Co., DeWitt, 1977-78; asst. v.p. systems Midland Nat. Life, Sioux Falls, S.D., 1978-80; v.p. data processing Minn. Protective Life, Mpls., 1980-83; sr. v.p. MIS Am. Founders Life, Phoenix, 1983—. Mem. Data Processing Mgmt. Assn. (bd. dirs. Southeastern Iowa chpt. 1975-77, Phoenix chpt. 1987). Republican. Methodist. Office: Am Founders Life 2720 E Camelback Phoenix AZ 85072

FORD, VICTORIA, public relations executive; b. Carroll, Iowa, Nov. 1, 1946; d. Victor Sargent and Gertrude Francis (Headlee) F.; m. John K. Frans, July 4, 1965 (div. Aug. 1975); m. David W. Keller, May 2, 1981 (div. Nov. 1985). AA, Iowa Lakes Community Coll., 1973; BA summa cum laude, Buena Vista Coll., 1974; MA in Journalism, U. Nev., Reno, 1988. Juvenile parole officer Iowa Dept. Social Services, Sioux City, 1974-78; staff reporter Feather Pub. Co., Quincy, Calif., 1978-80; tng. counselor CETA, Quincy, 1980; library pub. info. officer U. Nev., Reno, 1982-84; pub. relations exec. Brodeur/Martin Pub. Relations, Reno, 1984-87; pub. relations dir. Internat. Winter Spl. Olympics, Lake Tahoe (Calif.) and Reno, 1987—. Contbr. articles to profl. jours. Mem. adv. bd. Reno Philharm., 1985-87, Reno-Sparks Conv. and Visitors Authority, 1985—. Mem. ALA, Reno Women in Advt., Pub. Relations Soc. Am. (charter v.p. Sierra Nevada chpt. 1986-87, pres. 1987-88), NOW, Sigma Delta Chi. Democrat. Home: 380 Mogul Mountain Dr Reno NV 89523 Office: 1989 IWSOG 135 N Sierra St Reno NV 89501

FORD, WALLACE ROY, clergyman, religious organization executive; b. Walnut, Ill., Apr. 7, 1937; s. Roy Wallace and Evelyn Mary (Hand) F.; m. Valerie Laine Brown, Aug. 18, 1961; children: Tara Chantille, Christopher Wallace. BA, Tex. Christian U., 1959; BD, Brite Divinity Sch., Ft. Worth, 1962; Cert. Theologie, U. Geneva, 1963; D of Ministry, Iliff Sch. Theology, Denver, 1978. Ordained to minstry Disciples of Christ, 1962. Pastor La Porte (Tex.) Community Ch., 1964-67, 1st Christian Ch., Boulder, Colo., 1967-83; pres. Colo. Council Chs., Denver, 1981-82; exec. sec. N.Mex. Conf. Chs., Albuquerque, 1983—; chmn. Ch. Fin. Council, Indpls., 1984-86. Author: Wise Up O Men Of God, 1981, Worship and Evangelism, 1981, Snow Melts, 1983. Mem. Nat. Assn. Ecumenical Staff, Theta Phi. Democrat. Office: NMex Conf of Chs 124 Hermosa SE Albuquerque NM 87108

FORD, WILLIAM FRANCIS, bank holding company executive; b. Albany, N.Y., Mar. 11, 1925; s. Patrick J. and Ellen M. F.; m. Marcia J. Whalen, Jan. 7, 1956; children: William Francis, Michael P., Timothy K., Daniel J., Cathleen A. B.A. in Acctg. with honors, St. Michaels Coll., 1950. V.p. Equitable Credit Corp., Albany, 1950-60, Am. Fin. Systems Inc., Silver Spring, Md., 1960-65, Gen. Electric Credit Corp., Stamford, Conn., 1965-74; chmn., chief exec. officer Security Pacific Fin. Corp., San Diego, 1974-81; exec. v.p., adminstr. specialized fin. services group Security Pacific Corp., Los Angeles, 1981-84; vice chmn. Security Pacific Corp., 1984—. Served with USN, 1943-46. Mem. Am. Fin. Services Assn. (chmn., dir. exec. com.). Club: Stone Ridge Country.

FORDYCE, JAMES FORREST, psycholinguist; b. July 11, 1953; s. Joseph Warder and Grace (Sommerville) F. BA summa cum laude, U. Fla., Gainesville, 1976, MA in Linguistics, cert., 1978; C. Phil. Linguistics, UCLA, 1984, PhD in Linguistics, 1988. Teaching asst. Ctr. for African Studies, U. Fla., Gainesville, 1977-78; teaching, rsch. assoc. dept. linguistics UCLA, 1979-82; asst. prof. Glendale (Calif.) Community Coll., 1982—; dir. Life Formation Cons. Group, Santa Monica, Calif., 1988—. Contbr. articles on linguistics to profl. jours. Nat. Def. Fgn. Lang. fellow U. Fla., U.S. Dept. Edn., 1977-78; NDEA fellow UCLA, U.S. Dept. Edn., 1979-80. Mem. Linguistic Soc. Am., Nat. Coun. Geocosmic Rsch. Office: Glendale Coll 1500 N Verdugo Rd Glendale CA 91208

FORE, RICHARD LEWIS, real estate development company executive; b. Lynchburg, Va., Apr. 9, 1945; s. James Cleveland Fore and Catherine (Staton) Hobbs; children: Jonathan, Jessica, Rebecca, Richard. BS in Criminology, Fla. State U., 1968; MPA, Ariz. State U., 1971. Adminstrv. asst. to sec. HUD, Washington, 1973-74; dep. adminstr. new communities adminstrn. HUD, 1974-75; v.p. Huber Devel. Co., Dayton, Ohio, 1975-77; pres. CANV, Inc., Reno and Las Vegas, Nev., and Foster City, Calif., 1977—; ptnr. Lincoln Property Co., Westlake Village, Calif., 1977—; energy cons. FEA, Washington, 1976-77; lectr. Stanford U., Ohio State U., So. Meth. U.; speaker on housing and regulation, numerous nat. orgns.; guest, Phil Donahue Show, Today Show, McNeil-Lehrer Report. Mem. bd. editorial advisers Housing Devel. Reporter, 1980-82. Vice-chmn. Com. on Govt. Regulation, 1980-81; chmn. Tax Force on Use Govtl. Lan ds for Housing, 1980-81; mem. Pres. Reagan's Transition Team, Washington, 1980-81, Nat. Reagan Housing Task Force, 1982; chmn. Nev. Republican Com., 1980-82; mem. Presdl. Housing Commn., 1982; mem. central com. Calif. Rep. Com., 1987-88, Pres. Bush's Nat. Campaign Housing Task Force; co-chmn. Calif. Commn. on Drugs, 1989, Calif. Com. on Drugs, 1989. Recipient Rose award, Council Competitive Economy, 1981. Mem. Nat. Multi Housing Council (founder, bd. dirs., pres. 1978—), Bldg. Industry Assn. Orange County (bd. dirs. 1987-88-88, pres.'s coun.), Nat. Assn. Homebuilders (speaker, multi-family com.), Young Pres.'s Orgn. (forum officer South Bay chpt. 1987-88,chmn. spl. project 1989—). Roman Catholic. Office: Lincoln Property Co 310 N Westlake Blvd Ste 200 Westlake Village CA 91362

FORENTI, JOHN HENRY, teacher, physical fitness specialist; b. Stockton, Calif., Sept. 20, 1946; s. John Anthony and Alma Josephine (Belluzzi) F.; m. Barbara Elizabeth Keller; 1 child, Angela Mary. BA, Calif. State U., Fresno, 1972. Speech therapist North Country Ednl. Svcs., North Conway, N.H., 1972-73, Tulare County Dept. Edn., Visalia, Calif., 1973-87; sci. and civics tchr. Tulare County Court Sch., Visalia, 1987-88, lead tchr., 1988—; fitness specialist, Cooper Clinic, Dallas, 1985; physical edn. tchr. Porterville Jr. Coll., Calif., 1986—. Coach Spl. Olympics, Internat. Games, South Bend, Ind., 1987. With USAF, 1967-69. Named Tulare County Teacher of the Yr., 1989. Mem. Calif. Tchr.'s Assn. Democrat. Roman Catholic. Home: 333 N Indiana #108A Porterville CA 93257 Office: Tulare County Edn Bldg County Civic Ctr Visalia CA 93291

FORGE, JONI ANDERIA, dentist; b. Birmingham, Ala., Jan. 16, 1957; d. Willie James and Lizzie Pearl (Lee) F. BS, U. Calif., Irvine, 1979; DDS, U. Calif., San Francisco, 1985. Adminstrv. asst. U. Calif., Irvine, 1979-80, UCLA, 1980-82; pvt. practice dentistry Los Angeles, 1985—; bd. dirs. ABC Dental Health Ctr., Hawaiian Gardens. Cons. Nat. Black Child Devel. Inst., Compton, Calif., 1988—. Named one of Outstanding Young Women in Am., 1979; Fleming scholar U. Calif., 1983; Recipeint No. Calif. Black Med. Dental Pharmacy scholar, 1984, Community Service and Preventive Dentistry award U. Calif., 1985. Mem. ADA, Calif. Dental Soc., Los Angeles Dental Soc., Nat. Dental Soc., Delta Sigma Theta. Democrat. Roman Catholic. Home: 1999 Stanley Ave #1 Signal Hill CA 90806 Office: 2756 Santa Rosalia #204 Los Angeles CA 90008

FORKERT, CLIFFORD ARTHUR, civil engineer; b. Verona, N.D., Oct. 16, 1916; s. Arthur Louis and Bessie (Delamater) F.; grad. N.D. State Coll., 1940; postgrad. M.I.T.; m. Betty Jo Erickson, July 1, 1940; children: Terry Lynn Forkert Williamson, Michael, Debra. Hwy. engr., N.D., Tex., 1937-40; hydraulic engr. Internat. Boundary Commn. Tex. on Rio Grande and Tributaries, 1940-43; constrn., topographic and cons. engr., Calif. 1946—; now civil engr., prin. Clifford A. Forkert, Civil Engr.; pres. Calif. Poly. Pomona Assos. Capt. USMCR, 1943-46. Registered civil engr. Calif., Oreg., Ariz., profl. engr., Nev.; lic. land surveyor, Nev. Fellow Am. Congress and Mapping (life); mem. ASCE (life), Land Surveyors Assn. Calif. (dir.), Alumni Assn. N.D. State Coll. Home: 20821 Skimmer Ln Huntington Beach CA 92646 Office: 22311 Brookhurst St Huntington Beach CA 92646

FORLAND, JOHN STABILE, real estate development specialist; b. Rochester, Minn., Feb. 11, 1948; s. Arthur Eugene and Louise (Moore) F. BA in Econs., U. Idaho, 1971, MS in Econs., 1975. Intern Western Interstate Commn., Boulder, Colo., 1972; asst. dir. Clearwater Econ. Devel. Assn., Moscow, Idaho, 1973-74; exec. dir. Mid Columbia Econ. Dist., The Dalles, Oreg., 1974-80; pvt. practice Wash. and Oreg., 1980-87, Calif., 1988—. Author: Regional Labor Markets, rev., 1975, Barriers to Progress, 1979 (HUD award 1980). Pres. Big Bend Econ. Devel. Coun., Ephrata, Wash., 1983-88; mem. Gov.'s exec. com. Superconducting Super Collider; chmn. econ. devel. subcom., Spokane, Wash., 1988; chmn. Japan Am. Soc. Wash., Seattle, 1988; assoc. Grant County Indsl. Devel. Coun., Moses Lake, Wash., 1987. Mem. Econ. Devel. Execs. Wash., Nat. Assn. Devel. Orgns. (exec. bd. 1979-80), Am. Econ. Devel. Coun., Wash. Pub. Ports Assn. (assoc.). Home: 3100 E Palm Dr #1 Fullerton CA 92631 Office: PO Box 773 Fullerton CA 92632

FORMAN, RONALD CRAIG, lawyer; b. Cleve., July 16, 1947; s. Jack P. and Marian J. (Justice) F.; m. Lois C. Richman, May 18, 1974; 1 child, Alexander Bradford; m. Jeanne S. Sloman, May 1971 (div. May 1973). BA, U. Miami, Coral Gables, Fla., 1969, JD, 1974. Bar: Fla., 1974, Colo., 1977, U.S. Dist. Ct., Colo., 1978, U.S. Ct. Appeals (10th cir.), 1978. Acct. adminstr. Gulf Am. Corp., Miami, 1969-70; registration dept. dir. Cavanagh Communities Corp., Miami, 1970-71; asst. state atty. Dade County State Atty. Office, Miami, 1974-76; assoc. atty. Alperstein, Plaut & Snead, Lakewood, Colo., 1977-78; assoc. Law Offices of Arnold Alperstein, Denver, 1978-80; atty., shareholder Alperstein, Alperstein & Forman, P.C., Denver, 1980-83; pvt. practice attorney Denver, 1983—. Mem. Colo. Bar Assn., Aurora Bar Assn. Democrat.

FORMWALT, WILLIAM ALEXANDER, military officer, civil engineering educator; b. Balt., June 24, 1951; s. William Swan and Florence Tait (Dornin) F.; m. Incha Pak, May 8, 1982; children: Cynthia Florence, Lucie Dornin, Alice Tait. BS in Architecture, U. Va., 1974; diploma in Russian, Def. Lang. Inst., 1976; MS in Archtl. Engring., Pa. State U., 1982. Commd. 2d lt. USAF, 1976, advanced through grades to maj., 1987; chief of programs USAF, Pope AFB, N.C., 1976-79; project engr. Pacific Air Forces USAF, Taegu AFB, Republic of Korea, 1979-80; mgr. commd. facility energy program USAF, Europe, 1982-85; asst. prof. archtl. computer-aided design and civil engring. USAF Acad., Colorado Springs, Colo., 1985—; mem. energy conservation task group U.S. Air Force Acad., 1985—, personnel officer dept. civil engring., 1986-88, researcher air base combat capabilities, 1987—, software devel. engr., 1987—. Mem. ASHRAE, Soc. Am. Mil. Engrs., Am. Solar Energy Soc., AutoCAD user's group, Phi Kappa Phi, Theta Tau. Republican. Episcopalian. Office: HQ USAF Acad/DFCE Colorado Springs CO 80840

FOROUZAN, BEHROUZ A., computer programming educator; b. Arak, Iran, Oct. 15, 1944; came to U.S., 1981; s. Ahmad A. Forouzan and Soror Mina; m. Faezeh Golboo, June 4, 1971; one child, Setareh. BS in Elec., Tehran (Iran) U., 1967; MS in Elec., U. Calif., Irvine, 1984. Chmn. bd. dirs. Techno Frigo, Tehran, 1969-79; project engr. Memco, Zurich, Switzerland, 1979-81; computer instr. Navajo Community Coll., Shiprock, N.Mex., 1984—. Served to lt. Army of Iran, 1967-69. Mem. IEEE, BYTE. Home: 2800 N Dustin Apt #205 Farmington NM 87401 Office: Navajo Community Coll Dept Sci Shiprock NM 87420

FORREST, BILLY JOE, federal agency investigator; b. Martinez, Calif., Mar. 1, 1950; s. Clarence and Corrine E. (Robinson) F.; m. Judith Ann Scott, Nov. 27, 1971; children: Billy, Regina, Gerald, Kenya, Tanzania. AA, Diablo Valley Coll., 1972; student, Los Medanos Coll., Pittsburg, Calif., 1975-76; BA, San Francisco State U., 1980; postgrad., Hayward (Calif.) State U., 1983-84. Counselor, workshop supr. Phoenix Programs, Corcord, Calif., 1984; substitute tchr. pub. schs., Concord and Pittsburg, 1984; personnel mgmt. specialist USN Engring. Command, Alexandria, Va., 1984-86; employee devel. specialist USN Engring. Command, Alexandria, 1986-87; investigator U.S. EEOC, San Francisco, 1987—. Minister, Churches of God in Christ, Pittsburg, 1972—; fin. sec. No. Calif. jurisdiction, Churches of God in Christ, 1985—. Mem. Bay Area Urban League, Black Polit. Assn. Democrat. Home: 4201 Heights Ave Pittsburg CA 94565

FORREST, KENTON HARVEY, science educator, historian; b. Fort Lauderdale, Fla., Oct. 3, 1944; s. Harvey William and Marjorie A. (Boxrud) F. B.A., Colo. State Coll., 1968; M.A., U. No. Colo., 1981. Science tchr. Dunstan Jr. High, Jefferson County Pub. Schs., Lakewood, Colo., 1968—; pres. Tramway Press, Inc., 1983—. Author: Denver's Railroads, 1981; (with William C. Jones) Denver-A Pictorial History, 1973; (with others) The Moffat Tunnel, 1978; Rio Grande Ski Train, 1984, History of the Public Schools of Denver, 1989. Trustee Colo. Railroad Hist. Found., Golden, 1975—; mem., 1st pres. Lakewood Hist. Soc. (Colo.), 1976. Mem. NEA (life) Rocky Mountain Assn. Geologists, Colo. Sci. Soc., Nat. Railway Hist. Soc. (Intermountain chpt. pres. 1980-83), Mobile Post Office Soc., Mile High Ry. Club. Home: PO Box 15607 Lakewood CO 80215 Office: Dunstan Jr High Sch 1855 S Wright St Lakewood CO 80226

FORREST, THOMAS EUGENE, food wholesale company executive; b. Chgo., Apr. 22, 1937; s. Glenn Knowlton and Frances H. (Smith) F. m. Carol Ann O'Neal, Sept. 30, 1962 (div. 1982); children: Nancy Joann, Sally Ann, Susan Eileen; m. Nova Earline Smith, Aug. 14, 1982; children: Mary Louise Smith, Ralph A. Smith, Stuart F. Smith. Student, Ind. Cen. U., 1963, Ind. U., Indpls., 1970-74, Glendale Community Coll., Ariz., 1985-88, No. Ariz. U., 1988—. Advanced cert. credit adminstr. Credit supr. Electric Credit Corp., Indpls., 1962-65; salesman Gt. West Life Assurance Co., Indpls., 1965-67; group account supr. Blue Cross-Blue Shield, Indpls., 1967-72; acctg. supr. Indpls. Life Ins. Co., Indpls., 1972-75; project analyst Larry Heine & Assocs. Inc., Dallas, 1975-80; nat. market mgr. Cado Systems Corp., Torrance, Calif., 1980-83; collection supr. Continental Foods Inc., Phoenix and Los Angeles, 1983-84; credit mgr. Arrowhead Drinking Water Co., Phoenix, 1984-88; div. credit mgr. Southwest Hardware Co., Phoenix, 1988-88; asst. contr. Taylor Bros. Wholesale, Phoenix, 1988—. Mem. Internat. Credit Assn. (bd. dirs. Phoenix chpt. 1988—, treas. 1989), Nat. Assn. Credit Mgmt. (treas., bd. dirs. 1988-89, pres., state bd. dirs. 1989—), Soc. Credit Execs., Exec. Athletic Club. Republican. Home: 20620 N 4th Ave Phoenix AZ 85027

FORRESTER, GEORGE THEODORE, educator; b. Paterson, N.J., Mar. 31, 1931; s. Morris and Blanche (Stutz) Feigelman; m. Gilda Newman, Dec. 30, 1954; children: Richard Alan, Tracy Leigh, Kimberly Amie. BS, CCNY, 1953; MA, U. So. Calif., 1957, postgrad., 1958—. Tchr. drama Pomona Coll., Claremont, Calif., 1956-60, Claremont Grad. Sch., 1960; dir. entertainment Dept. Def., Mainz, Fed. Republic Germany, 1960-62; tchr. drama St. Paul's Sch., Walla Walla, Wash., 1962-63, Blue Mountain Coll., Pendleton, Oreg., 1963-66; mem. faculty San Jose (Calif.) City Coll., 1963—, prof. drama, 1965—; recorder Shakespearean readings, Recording for the Blind, Inc., 1956-60; exec. com. Western region, Am. Coll. Theatre Festival, 1978—, regional chmn., 1986—. Dir. theatrical prodns. various orgns., Fed. Republic Germany, Calif., Wash., Oreg., 1956-66. With AUS, 1953-55, Korea. Recipient Kennedy Medallion for Outstanding Svc. to Arts, Kennedy Ctr. Performing Arts, 1984. Mem. Am. Theatre in Higher Edn., Calif. Ednl. Theatre Assn., Am. Theatre Assn., Am. Community Theatre Assn., Am. Nat. Theatre Assn., European Community Theatre Coun., Northwest Drama Assn., Film Soc. San Jose (pres. 1974-76), Phi Delta Kappa. Home: 98 Central Ct Los Gatos CA 95032 Office: San Jose City Coll 2100 Moorpark Ave San Jose CA 95128

FORRESTER, MARY GORE, nurse; b. Norfolk, Va., Dec. 9, 1940; d. William Arthur and mary Foster (Cannaday) Gore; m. James William Forrester, June 14, 1965; children: James, Sarah. BA in Chemistry, Randolph Macon Women's Coll., 1962; PhD, Johns Hopkins U., 1969; BS in Nursing, U. Wyo., 1984, postgrad., 1985--. Tchr. Chatham Hall, Va., 1962-64; instr. Newark Coll., Rutgers U., 1970-71; lectr. philosophy Herbert Lehman Coll., CUNY, 1972; tutor Inst. Liberal Edn., St. John's Coll., Santa Fe, 1979; lectr. U. Wyo., Laramie, 1975, 82-83, 86; staff nurse Carbon County Meml. Hosp., Rawlins, Wyo., 1984-86, Ivinson Meml. Hosp., Laramie, Wyo., 1986, High Country Home Health, Laramie, 1986-87, Bethesda Care Ctr., Laramie, 1987--. Author: Moral Language, 1982; contbg. author: Reflecting on Values, 1983; contbr. articles to philos. jours. Mem. Phi Beta Kappa, Sigma Theta Tau (treas. 1982-84). Democrat. Office: Bethesda Care Ctr 503 S 18th St Laramie WY 82070

FORRESTER, TERRENCE JOHN, medical association administrator; b. Hagerstown, MD, Mar. 30, 1950; s. James Randolph and Margaret Mary (Kurrent) F.; m. Janet Marie Valmassoi, Apr. 16, 1983. BA in Psychology, U. Conn., 1972; MSW, U. Louisville, 1979. Lic. ind. social worker, Ohio. Protective caseworker Children's Protective Svcs., Cin., 1973-82; probation officer Hamilton Co. Juvenile Ct., Cin., 1982-85; program coord. Beech Acres, Cin., 1985-87; program dir. Canyon Acres Residential Treatment Ctr., Anaheim Hills, Calif., 1988—. Mem. Pleasant Ridge Community Coun., 1986, adv. com. of Aring Inst., 1985-87, Greater Cin Youth Svcs. Network, 1985-87. Mem. Calif. Svcs. for Children. Roman Catholic. Home: 1307 Milburn Redlands CA 92373

FORSBACH, JACK ALAN, lawyer; b. Oklahoma City, Sept. 3, 1932; s. Jacob Allen and Mary Louise (Morton) F. BA, Okla. State U., 1955; JD, U. Okla., 1957. Bar: Okla. 1959, U.S. Supreme Ct. 1965. Pvt. practice Bartlesville, Okla., 1959-65; claims cons. CIGNA, Toplis & Harding, Inc., L.A., 1965-78; freelance arbitrator L.A., 1978—. Judge Mcpl. Ct., Bartlesville, 1959; vol. Traveler's Aid Soc., L.A., 1986—; appointee Okla. Ambassador by Gov. Henry Bellmon, 1989—. Mem. Amnesty Internat. (legal support 1986—), Soc. Profls. in Dispute Resolution, ABA (internat. comml. arbitration com., internat. torts and ins. practice com.), Union Internat. des Avocats (entertainment and sports law com.), Okla. Bar Assn., Tulsa County Bar Assn. (exec. dir. 1964), Am. Arbitration Assn. (arbitrator 1978—), Southwestern Legal Found. (rep. 1962—), Okla. State U. Bar Assn. (life), U. Okla. Coll. Law Assn. (life), Delta Theta Phi (tribune). Republican. Home and Office: 8306 Wilshire Blvd Ste 1232 Beverly Hills CA 90211-2382

FORSBERG, CHARLES ALTON, computer/infosystems engineer; b. Willamette, Ill., Mar. 6, 1944; s. Delbert Alton and Mareelu (McCleary) F. Student, Rensselaer Polytechnic Inst.; BEE, U. Wis., 1966, MSEE, 1968; postgrad., various univs. and colls. From design engineer to project leader Tektronix, Portland, Oreg., 1968-74; research and devel. mgr. Sidereal, Portland, 1974-80; chief engr. Computer Devel. Inc., Portland, 1980-84; pres. Omen Tech. Inc., Portland, 1984—. Recognized for outstanding contribution to field IBM-PC Users Group, Madison, Wis., 1988, Alamo PC Orgn., San Antonio, 1988. Home and Office: 17505-V NW Sauvie Island Rd Portland OR 97231

FORSBERG, KEVIN JOHN, consulting company executive; b. Oakland, Calif., July 20, 1934; s. Ted Otto and Gladys (Reid) F.; m. Glenda Jones, June 1955 (div. Dec. 1964) m. Edna Dorles, Apr., 1966 (div. Nov. 1979); m. Cindy Jane Beason, Jan. 1, 1981; children: Ian, Chenoa. BSCE, MIT, 1956; MS in Engring. Mechanics, Stanford U., 1958, PhD in Engring. Mechanics, 1961, postgrad., 1979. Mem. tech. staff Lockheed Missiles & Space Co., Sunnyvale, Calif., 1956-61; mgr. solid mech. Lockheed Missiles & Space Co., Palo Alto, Calif., 1963-71, asst. dir., 1971-73; program mgr. Lockheed Missiles & Space Co., Sunnyvale, 1973-84; v.p. Consulting Resources, Inc., Santa Clara, Calif., 1984—; lectr. grad. sch. Santa Clara U., 1984—, U. Calif. Santa Cruz, 1985—. Co-author: (handbook) Project Management and Project Leadership, 1985; regional editor Jour. Computers and Structures, Washington, 1970-80; contbr. articles to profl. jours. Chmn. Citizens' Com. on High Sch. Edn., Redwood City, Calif., 1969-70. Served to capt. U.S. Army, 1961-63. Recipient Pub. Service medal NASA, 1981. Fellow ASME; assoc. fellow AIAA. Home: 1225 Vienna Dr #584 Sunnyvale CA 94089 Office: Cons Resources Inc 5333 Betsy Ross Santa Clara CA 95052

FORSBERG, SUSAN MARIE, occupational therapist; b. Milw., Jan. 6, 1953; d. Richard Anton and June Christine (Graff) Mutsch; m. Lawrence Stanley Forsberg, July 23, 1977; 1 child, Angela Marie. BS in Occupational Therapy, Mt. Mary Coll., Milw., 1975. Registered and lic. occupational therapist. Occupational therapist VA Med. Ctr., Walla Walla, Wash., 1976—; cons. occupational therapy Blue Mountain Convalescent Ctr., College Place, Wash., 1978-87; pvt. practice Walla Walla, 1978—; chief occupational therapy VA Med. Ctr., Walla Walla, 1981—; contract occupational therapist Inst. for Functional and Occupational Restoration, Walla Walla, 1987—; guest lectr. Multiple Sclerosis Soc., Walla Walla, 1984—, Parkinsons Soc., Milton-Freewater, Oreg., 1988; chmn. student program Am. Occupational Therapy Assn. Nat. Conv., Milw., 1974. V.p. Wa-Two Fed. Credit Union, Walla Walla, 1978, pres. 1979, chmn. supervisory com., 1981-84; chmn. religious edn. adv. bd. St. Patrick's Roman Cath. Ch., Walla Walla, 1987-88; bd. dirs. Walla Walla Dance Found, 1989. Named Walla Walla's Young Career Woman Bus. and Profl. Women's Club, 1980, Fed. Employee of Yr. in Profl. and Sci. category Blue Mountain Fed. Exec. Assn., Wash. and Oreg., 1982; recipient Voluntary Service award Vols., VA, Walla Walla, 1982. Mem. Am. Occupational Therapy Assn. (phys. disabilities and work capacity spl. interest groups), Wash. Occupational Therapy Assn., Fed. Employed Women Club. Home: 1829 Leonard Dr Walla Walla WA 99362 Office: VA Med Ctr 77 Wainwright Dr Walla Walla WA 99362

FORSELIUS, RANDALL A., marketing professional; b. Ely, Minn., Nov. 8, 1924; s. Arth Robert and Lily (Niemi) F.; m. Ruth Valentine Hans, June 8, 1948; children: Valerie Ruth Miller, Wendy Lou, Randilyn Stroh. Student, Hope Coll., Holland, Mich.; BA, St. Olaf Coll., 1948; postgrad., U. Denver. Founder, chief exec. officer, chmn. bd. Randall's Formalwear, Denver, 1949-68; founder, chief exec. officer Tie Village, Littleton, Colo., 1969; gen. ptnr. Crestmoor Downs Townhouse, Denver, 1966-72; owner, chief exec. officer Igotathingabout ANTIQUES Denver, 1973; founder, chief exec. officer Trifles, Denver, 1987; ptnr. Red Door Gallery, Denver, 1988; founder, chmn. bd. RAF, Inc., Denver, 1972—; consul of Finland, 1962-86, emeritus, 1986—; trustee, bd. of trustee Suomi Coll., Hancock, Mich., 1964—. One-man shows include painter and sculptor, 1960, 65, 72. Pres. Jr. Knights of Kaleva, Ely, Minn., 1936-41, Club 16 Businessman's Organ., Denver, 1955, Nat. Franchisors Coun., Chgo., 1964-65; mem. Messiah Luth. Ch., Denver, 1961, Augustana Luth. Ch., Denver, 1972—; founding mem. Diplomatic Ball, Denver, 1979—; chmn., founder Scandinavian Symphony Orchestra, Denver, 1967-68; vice pres. Am. Scandinavian Found., 1966-68, Leif Ericson Soc. Internat., Media, Penn., 1979— 1st lt. U.S. Army, 1942-46. Named Exec. Advertiser of the Yr., Rocky Mountain News, Denver, 1954-56, Brand Name Retailer of the Yr., Brand Names, Inc., New York, 1955, First Regional Cons., Formalwear Inst. of Am., New York, 1962; recipient Republica Finlandia L Annos Liberia, 1976-82, Finnish Student League medal, 1985. Mem. Suomi Seura, Denver C. of C., Am. Field Svcs. (charter mem. 1979—), Sanua Soc. of Am., Knighted Order of the White Rose, Denver Athletic Club, Petroleum Club. Republican. Home and Office: 2315 E 7th Ave Pkwy Denver CO 80206

FORSEN, HAROLD KAY, engineering executive; b. Sept. 19, 1932; s. Allen Kay and Mabel Evelyn (Buehler) F.; m. Betty Ann Webb, May 25, 1952; children: John Allen, Ronald Karl, Sandra Kay. AA, Compton Jr. Coll., 1956; BS, Calif. Inst. Tech., 1958, MS, 1959; PhD, U. Calif., Berkeley, 1965. Research assoc. Gen. Atomic, San Diego, 1959-62; research assoc., elec. engr. U. Calif., Berkeley, 1962-65; assoc. prof. nuclear engring. U. Wis., Madison, 1965-69, prof., 1969-73, dir. Phys. Sci. Lab., 1970-72; mgr. engring. Exxon Nuclear Co., Bellevue, Wash., 1973-75, v.p., dir., 1975-80, exec. in charge laser enrichment, 1981; exec. v.p. Jersey-Avco Isotopes, Inc., 1975-80, pres., 1981, dir., 1975-81; mgr. engring. and materials Bechtel Group, Inc., San Francisco, 1981-83, dep. mgr. research and engring., 1983-84, mgr. advanced systems, 1984-85, mgr. research and devel., 1986-89; sr. v.p. Bechtel Nat. Inc., 1989—; mem. fusion power reactor sr. rev. com. Dept. Energy, 1977, magnetic fusion adv. com., 1982-86; chmn. U.S. del. of AEC on Ion Sources to Soviet Union, 1972; cons. Oak Ridge Nat. Lab., Tenn., 1969-72, Argonne Nat. Lab., Ill., 1970-72, Exxon Nuclear Co., 1970-73, Battelle N.W. Lab., 1971-72; mem. sci. and tech. adv. com. Argonne Nat. Lab., 1983-85; mem. fusion energy adv. com. Oak Ridge Nat. Lab., 1977-84. Contbr. articles to tech. jours. Patentee fusion and laser isotope separation. Vice pres., trustee Pacific Sci. Ctr. Found., 1977, pres., 1978-80, chmn., 1981; mem. dean's vis. com. Coll. Engring., U. Wash., 1981—; chmn. dept. nuclear engring. and engring. physics relations council U. Wis., 1987—; mem. com. magnetic fusion in energy policy Nat. Research Council, 1987; pres. bd. dirs. Bay Area Sci. Fair, Inc., 1988-89; bd. dirs. Plasma and Materials Techs., Inc., 1988—. Served with USAF, 1951-55. Fellow Am. Phys. Soc.; mem. Am. Nuclear Soc. (Arthur H. Compton award 1972, chmn. tech. group controlled nuclear fusion 1973), IEEE (sr.), Nat. Acad. Engring., Sigma Xi. Home: 255 Tim Ct Danville CA 94526 Office: Bechtel Nat Inc PO Box 3965 San Francisco CA 94119

FORSHEY, J. PATRICK, transportation executive; b. Albuquerque, Mar. 9, 1959; s. John Samuel and Teola Mae (Wood) F.; m. Carolyn Jane Richardson, Jan. 12, 1980 (div. 1987); 1 child, Bethany Hope. BBA, Hardin-Simmons U., 1982. Sales rep. Lever Bros., Wichita Falls, Tex., 1983-84; asst. city mgr., city ops. mgr. Avis Car Rental, Albuquerque, 1984—. Chmn. packaging task force Albuquerque Conv. and Vis. Bur., 1988, active tourism task force, 1988. Mem. Alburquerque C. of C. (mem. to mem. com.), Duke City Civitan, Masons (jr. deacon 1988). Home: 3415 Aspen Ave NE Albuquerque NM 87106

FORSIAK, WALTER WILLIAM, publishers' representative; b. Detroit, Apr. 30, 1935; s. John J. and Patricia (Jurek) F.; m. Ella Eggers, July 27, 1963; children—Erica, Christa. B.S. in Bus. Adminstrn., Wayne State U., 1957. Advt. sales McGraw-Hill Pub. Co., various locations, 1957-83; v.p. Bus. Times, Inc., TV show, 1983-85; pres. Forsiak & Assocs., Inc., 1985—. Bd. dirs. Switzer Ctr. Ednl. Therapy, 1979-81, Timber Cove Homes Assn. Served in USAFR, 1958-64. Mem. San Francisco Advt. Club, Los Angeles Advt. Club. Roman Catholic. Clubs: Trail Ride of N.Mex.; The Guardsmen (San Francisco). Office: PO Box 2649 San Anselmo CA 94960

FORSTE, KARL ANDREW, flight engineer; b. Sacramento, Calif., July 6, 1964; s. Norman Lee and Catherine Jean (Culver) F. Student, Embry-Riddle Aero. U., Prescott, Ariz., 1987—. Aircraft mechanic USAFR McClellan AFB, Calif., 1982-84; flight engr. Travis AFB, Calif., 1984--. Pell grantee, 1987-88. Fellow Airline Pilots Assn. Democrat. Home: 5401 Valhalla Dr Carmichael CA 95608

FORSTE, NORMAN LEE, management consultant; b. Carthage, Mo., Aug. 18, 1935; s. John Edward and Lula Mae (Martin) F.; m. Catherine Jean Culver, July 20, 1958; children: Patricia, Diana, John II, Karl. AA, Am. River coll., 1961; BA, Calif. State U., 1964, MA, 1971; MBA, Golden Gate U., 1973; PhD in Higher Edn., U. Wash., 1984. Adminstrv. analyst State of Calif., Sacramento, 1962-64, sr. data processing systems analyst, 1966-67, supr. info. systems devel., 1967-68; sr. adminstrv. analyst County of Sacramento (Calif.), 1964-66, dir. systems and data processing dept., 1968-74; dir. adminstrv. data processing div. U. Wash., Seattle, 1974-76; mgr. mgmt. adv. services Deloitte Haskins & Sells, 1976-81, dir. mgmt. adv. services, 1981-85; pvt. practice mgmt. cons., Carmichael, Calif., 1985—; instr. mgmt. scis. program U. Calif. at Davis, 1968; professorial lectr. mgmt. info. systems Golden Gate U., Sacramento, 1971-74, 79—; instr. info. systems Calif. State U.-Sacramento, 1982-83; instr. systems analysis and introduction to data processing Am. River Coll., Sacramento, 1968-71. Mem. curriculum adv. com. for data processing Am. River Coll., Sacramento, 1969-74, mem. com. to evaluate vocational and tech. edn. program for accreditation, 1972-73. Served with USAF, 1954-57, 62, maj. USAFR, Ret. Mem. Am. Soc. Pub. Adminstrn. (dir. 1969-71, 84-85), Data Processing Mgmt. Assn. (chpt. pres. 1968-69), Methods and Procedure Assn. (pres. 1969), Calif. Assn. County Data Processors (1st v.p. 1973-74), Air Force Res. Officers Assn. (chpt. v.p. 1971-74, 79-82), Air Force Calif. Dept. Res. Officers Assn. (jr. v.p. 1971). Home and Office: 5401 Valhalla Dr Carmichael CA 95608

FORSYTH, RAYMOND ARTHUR, civil engineer; b. Reno, Mar. 13, 1928; s. Harold Raymond and Fay Exona (Highfill) F.; B.S., Calif. State U., San Jose, 1952; M.C.E., Auburn U., 1958; m. Mary Ellen Wagner, July 9, 1950; children—Lynne, Gail, Alison, Ellen. Jr. engr., asst. engr. Calif. Div. Hwys., San Francisco, 1952-54; assoc. engr., sr. supervising, prin. engr. Calif. Dept. Transp., Sacramento, 1961-83, chief geotech. br., 1972-79, chief soil mechanics and pavement br., 1979-83, chief Transp. Lab., 1983—; cons., lectr. in field. Served with USAF, 1954-56. Fellow ASCE (pres. Sacramento sect., chmn. Calif. council 1980-81); mem. Transp. Research Bd. (chmn. embankments and earth slopes com. 1976-82, chmn. soil mechanics sect. 1982-88, chmn. group 2 council 1988—), ASTM. Contbr. articles to profl. publs. Home: 5017 Pasadena Ave Sacramento CA 95841

FORT, LARRY WALLACE, electronics executive consultant, small business owner; b. Joplin, Mo., Feb. 16, 1938; s. Wallace Delbert and Sylvia Lorene (Russell) F. Grad. high sch., Tulsa. Engr. Motorola Corp., Phoenix, 1962-69, Telex Corp., Tulsa, 1969-70, Barnum Ind., Gilbert, Ariz., 1970-72; co-founder Progressive Electronics, Inc., Mesa, Ariz., 1972-82; owner Phase II, Prescott, Ariz., 1982—. Inventor of electronic circuits, 2 U.S. patents, 1969. Home and Office: Phase II 174 View Point Rd Prescott AZ 86303

FORT, LEE EARTHMON, financial services representative; b. Detroit, Sept. 15, 1950; s. Esmar Earthmon and Leona Mary Ann (Lucky) F.; m. Mary Elizabeth Thomas, Aug. 26, 1972. BA in Psychology, U. Notre Dame, 1972; EdM in Clin. Psychology, Harvard U., 1973; postgrad., Ind. U., 1973-75. Donor cons. ARC, Louisville, 1975-77; asst. dir. donor resources ARC, San Jose, Calif., 1977-78; dir. donor resources ARC, San Jose, 1978-88; rep. BMA Fin. Group, San Jose, 1988—. Rotary sponsor Silver Creek High Sch. Interact Club, San Jose, 1986—; fundraiser East Valley YMCA, San Jose, 1987-88. Named co-winner Donor Recruiter of Yr. Am. Assn. Donor Recruitment Profls. Mem. San Jose Life Underwriters, Nat. Assn. Securities Dealers, Pres.'s Club (Penn Mut.), Interact Club, Rotary (trea. 1987-88, bd. dir. community svc. 198-89 San Jose chpt., area rep. dist. 517 Youth Leadership Camp 1989-90). Democrat. Roman Catholic. Home: 1720 Quimby Rd San Jose CA 95122

FORTE, CRAIG ANTHONY, amusement park, motion picture location executive; b. Phila., Feb. 9, 1958. BS in Bus., U. Ariz., 1980; MBA, U. So. Calif., 1985. Asst. v.p. mktg. Gates Learjet Corp., Tucson, 1980-83; pres. Old Tucson Co., Tucson, 1985--. Bd. dirs. Tucson Lighthouse YMCA, 1986-88; pacesetter United Way Tucson, 1987-88; fund raiser Am. Cancer Soc., Tucson, 1988, pres. Tucson Active 20/30, 1988. First Interstate Bank Calif. John King scholar, 1984, U. So. Calif. etrepeneurship scholar, 1988.

FORTH, KEVIN BERNARD, beverage distributing executive; b. Adams, Mass., Dec. 4, 1949; s. Michael Charles and Catherine Cecilia (McAndrews) F.; m. Alice Jane Farnum, Sept. 14, 1974; children: Melissa, Brian. AB, Holy Cross Coll., 1971; MBA, NYU, 1973. Div. rep. Anheuser-Busch, Inc., Boston, 1973-74, dist. sales mgr., L.A., 1974-76, asst. to dir. mktg. staff, St. Louis, 1976-77; v.p. Straub Distbg. Co., Ltd., Orange, Calif., 1977-81, pres., 1981—, chmn., chief exec. officer, 1986—, also bd. dirs. Commr. Orange County Sheriff's Adv. Coun., 1988—; mem. adv. bd. Rancho Santiago Community Coll. Dist. 1978-80; bd. dirs. Children's Hosp. of Orange County, 1983-85, St. Joseph's Hosp. Found., Orange County Sports Hall of Fame, 1980—; exec. com., bd. dirs. Nat. Coun. on Alcoholism, 1980-83; mem. pres.' coun. Holy Cross Coll., 1987—; mem. Orange County Trauma Soc.; pres. Calif. State Fullerton Titan Athletic Found., 1983-85, bd. dir. 1983-85, v.p. Freedom Bowl 1984-85, pres., 1986, chmn., 1986-87, Anaheim Vis. & Conv. Bur., 1989—; mem. Rep. Silver Circle; bd. dirs. Orangewood Children's Home, 1988; mem. Calif. Rep. State Cen. Com. Benjamin Levy fellow, 1971-73. Mem. Nat. Beer Wholesalers Assn. (bd. dirs., asst. sec. 1989—), Calif. Beer and Wine Wholesalers Assn. (bd. dirs., exec. com., pres. 1985, asst. sec. 1980—), Industry Environ. Coun., Holy Cross Alumni Assn., NYU Alumni Assn., Nat. Assn. Stock Car Auto Racing, Small Bus. Inst., Sports Car Club Am. (Ariz. state champion 1982), Beta Gamma Sigma. Roman Catholic. Club: Lincoln, Holy Cross (Southern Calif.). Home: 4333 Mahagony Circle Yorba Linda CA 92686 Office: Straub Distbg Co Ltd 410 W Grove Ave Box 3165 Orange CA 92665

FORTIER, QUINCY ERNEST, obstetrician, gynecologist; b. Auburn, Mass., Sept. 16, 1912; s. Edgar Quincy and Nina (Chase) F.; divorced, 1967; children: Carlene, Renee, Kathleen, Annette, Quincy, Dana, Sonia, Nannette, Dorothy. BS, U. S.D., 1941; MS, U. Minn., 1944. Diplomate Am. Bd. Ob-Gyn. Intern Wichita Falls (Tex.) Clinic Hosp., 1945; surgeon Combined Metals Reductions Co., Proche, Nev., 1945-50; teaching fellow dept. ob-gyn U. Minn., Mpls., 1951-55; adj. clin. prof. ob-gyn U. Nev. Med. Sch., Las Vegas and Reno, 1984—, resident ob-gyn, 1955-57; owner, chief physician Women's Hosp., Las Vegas, 1958-70; owner hosp., Proche, 1945-50, univ. physician, instr. hygiene U. Nev., Reno, 1950-51; adj. clin. prof. ob.-gyn. U. Nev. Med. Sch., Reno, 1982—. Trustee So. Nev. Meml. Hosp., Las Vegas, 1960-62; candidate Nev. Legislature, 1962; fund raiser, donor of shc. bldg. and property Luth. Jr. and Sr. High Schs., Las Vegas. Fellow Am. Coll. Ob-Gyn; mem. AMA, VFW, Am. Fertility Soc., Pacific Coast Fertility Soc., Res. Officers Assn., Armed Forces Med. Soc., Aerospace Med. Assn., Nev. State Med. Assn., Clark County Med. Assn., Masons, Shriners. Republican. Episcopalian. Home and Office: 1431 Wengert Ave Las Vegas NV 89104

FORTIN, MARTIN EMERSON, JR., educator; b. Tacoma, Dec. 7, 1952; s. William Marvin and Jeannette Elaine (Rosier) Healy; m. Susan Lynn Fulkerson, Aug. 18, 1984. BS, Wash. State U., 1975; postgrad., Cen. Wash. U., 1980. Cert. tchr., Wash. Tchr. Yelm (Wash.) Middle Sch., 1975-79; dir. activities and athletics Yelm High Sch., 1979—; cons. in leadership devel., 1980—. Mem. staff, seminar dir., Am. Legion Boys State, Cheney, Wash., 1980—; city councilman, Town of Yelm, 1982-84; cemetery commr., Thurston County, Yelm, 1985—; com. mem. Wash. State Centennial Commn., Olympia, 1988—. Mem. Wash. Activities Coord. Assn. (pres.1983-85), Wash. Assn. Secondary Sch. Prins. (asst. camp dir. 1985—), Nat. Assn. Workshop Dirs., Wash. State Coaches Assn., Future Farmers Am. Alumni Assn., Nat. Assn. Activity Advisers, Pierce County Athletic League (chmn. 1987-88), Tornado Booster Club (adviser 1982—). Methodist. Home: PO Box 7 Yelm WA 98597 Office: Yelm High Sch PO Box 476 Yelm WA 98597

FORTNEY, SHIRLEY ANN, mathematics educator; b. Matheson, Colo., Aug. 3, 1934; d. Clyde Leroy and Mabel Florence (Wilson) Peck; m. David S. Fortney, Apr. 10, 1955; children: Rick David, Paul Brian. BA, Colo. State Coll., 1955, MA, 1963. With civil svc. USAF, FE Warren AFB, Wyo., 1955-56, acct., 1956-57; teller No. Colo. Savs. & Loan, Greeley, Colo., 1957-59; part-time tchr. Laramie County Community Coll., Cheyenne, 1973-74, math. instr., 1975—. Pres. PTA, Cheyenne, 1971-72; active youth baseball 1969-85. State of Colo. scholar, 1951; recipient Faculty award for Teaching Excellence Physical Sci. Div., 1986. Mem. Am. Math. Assn. of Two Yr. Colls., Wyo. Math. Assn. of Two Yr. Colls. Republican. Mormon. Home: 621 Ridgeland St Cheyenne WY 82009-3251 Office: Laramie County Comm Coll 1400 E College Dr Cheyenne WY 82007

FORTUNA, ANTHONY FRANK, teacher, consultant; b. Thomas, W.Va., Apr. 8, 1914; s. Anton and Rose (Secna) F.; m. Ann Marie Barthel, Sept. 27, 1938; children: Richard, Eugene. Student, L.A. Trade Tech. Coll., Pierce Coll., Valley Coll.; grad. Warren Sch. Astronautics, L.A. Coll.; student, U.S. Aviation Cadets. Registered profl. engr., Calif. Leadman Vultee Aircraft, Downy, Calif., 1939-40; gen. supr. Hindustan Aircraft, Bangalore, India, 1942-44; supr., inspector U.S. Air Corp., Long Beach, Calif., 1945-46; tng. supr. Douglas Aircraft Co., El Segundo, Calif., 1946-55; mgr. Northrop Ventura Div., Newberry Park, Calif., 1955-79; devel. engr. Hughes Space, El Segundo, 1981-86; dir. Talley Corp., Newberry, 1980-81; tchr., instr. Pierce Coll., Canoga Park, 1962—. Mem. Am. Inst. Astronautic/Aeronautic. Republican. Morman. Home: 3415 Loadstone Dr Sherman Oaks CA 91403

FORTUNE, FREDERIC ANDRE, writer, producer; b. Columbia, S.C., Feb. 9, 1952; s. Freddie Cecil and Gwendolyn (Young) F. Student, NYU, 1970-74. Owner, product devel. and sales Jass, N.Y.C. and Chgo., 1975-80; sales and mktg. rep. Direct Press-Modern Litho, 1981-82; product devel., mktg. and sales exec. Product Devel. and Mktg., 1982-83; dir. mktg. Integrated Cellular Techs. Inc., 1984-85; personal apprentice to 1st asst. dir. Leslie Jackson (Fame), 1985-86; trainee film and tape prodn. various film and TV cos., 1986-88; assoc. producer Sands of Time Prodn., 1988; free-lance writer, packaging exec. 1988—. Office: 24 Brooks Ave #3 Venice CA 90291

FORTUNE, JAMES MICHAEL, marketing executive; b. Providence, Sept. 6, 1947; s. Thomas Henry and Olive Elizabeth (Duby) F.; m. G. Suzanne Hein, July 14, 1973. Student, Pikes Peak Community Coll., Colorado Springs, Colo., 1981-83, Regis Coll., 1987—. Owner Fortune Fin. Services, Colorado Springs, Colo., 1975-79; ptnr. Robert James and Assocs., Colorado Springs, 1979-81; pres. Fortune & Co., Colorado Springs, 1981-88; v.p. mktg. and editorial Phoenix Communications Group, Ltd., Colorado Springs, 1988—, also bd. dirs.; bd. dirs. Colorado Springs Computer Systems, Perfect Printer Inc., Colorado Springs, Am. Discount Securities, Inc.; radio talk show host Sta. KRCC; fin. commentator Wall St. Report Sta. KKHT, 1983-84. Editor Fortune newsletter, 1981-85, The Can. Market News, 1981-83; editor, pub. Penny Fortune newsletter, 1981—, The Low Priced Investment newsletter, 1986-87, Women's Investment Newsletter, 1987—; editor, pub. Can. Market Confidential, 1988—, Spl. Option Situations, 1988—; contbr. articles to profl. jours. Cons. Jr. Achievement bus. project, Colorado Springs, 1985. Sgt. U.S. Army, 1968-70, Vietnam. Mem. Direct Mktg. Assn., Newsletter Assn., Colorado Springs C. of C. Lodge: Elks. Office: Phoenix Communications Group PO Box 670 Ste 2B Colorado Springs CO 80901-0670

FOSBURG, RICHARD GARRISON, cardiothoracic surgeon; b. Jamestown, N.Y., Dec. 22, 1930; s. Richard James and Ruth Adele (Garrison) F.; m. Catherine Louise Miller, June 16, 1955; children: Richard Scott, Kimberly Ann, Tracy Lynn, Jeffrey Craig. BA, Wash. & Jefferson U., 1952; MC, Temple U., 1955. Diplomate Am. Bd. Surgery, Am. Bd. Thoracic Surgery. Intern Nat. Naval Med. Ctr., Bethesda, Md., 1955-56; student flight surgeon Naval Sch. Aviation Medicine, Pensacola, Fla., 1956; flight surgeon Utility Wing Pacific, Chula Vista, Calif., 1956-58; resident gen. surgery Naval Hosp., Phila., 1958-62; sr. med. officer USS Independence (CVA-62), Norfolk, Va., 1962-64; resident thoracic surgery Naval Hosp., St. Albans, N.Y., 1964-66; asst. chief thoracic surgery Naval Hosp., San Diego, 1966-70, chmn. dept. cardiothoracic surgery, 1970-75; pvt. practice cardiothoracic surgery La Jolla, Calif., 1975—; chmn. dept. surgery Scripps Meml. Hosp., La Jolle, Calif., 1986—; sec. Western Thoracic Surgical Assn., Manchester, Mass., 1984—; bd. dirs. Calif. Med. Rev. Inc., San Francisco, 1985—; mem. health adv. com. Calif. Dept. Health Services, Sacramento, 1987—. Contbr. articles to profl. jours. Mem. adv. com. Am. Cancer Soc., San Diego chpt., 1980—, com. on Standards & Ethics The Soc. Thoracic Surgeons, Chgo., 1987—. Served to capt. U.S. Navy, 1955-75. Decorated Nat. Defense medal, Naval Reserve medal, Meritorius Service medal. Fellow Am. Coll. Surgeons, Am. Coll. Cardiology, Am. Coll. Chest Physicians (gov. 1972-75); mem. Am. Assn. for Thoracic Surgery, Pacific Coast Surgical Assn. Republican. Home: 2170 Pinar Pl Del Mar CA 92014 Office: 9834 Genesee Ave Ste 105 La Jolla CA 92037

FOSMIRE, FRED RANDALL, forest products company executive; b. Mission, Tex., June 23, 1926; s. Frank David and Marjorie Pauline (Davis) F.; m. Barbara Helen Schunk, Oct. 24, 1953; children: Helen, David, Lee, Emily. BA, U. Tex., 1948, MA, 1949, PhD, 1952. Cert. Am. Bd. Examiners in Profl. Psychology. Instr. to asst. prof. psychology U. Mont., Missoula, 1950-54; postdoctoral fellow U. Pa., Phila., 1954-56; clin. psychologist VA Hosp., Sheridan, Wyo., 1956-58; assoc. to full prof. U. Oreg., Eugene, 1958-81; v.p. Weyerhaeuser Co., Tacoma, 1981-83, sr. v.p., 1983—. Dir. Seattle Symphony, 1986-88, Forest History Soc., 1988—, St. Joseph Hosp., Tacoma, 1989—; mem. Can.-Am. Com., 1987—. With USN, 1944-46, PTO. Republican. Home: 505 S Marine Hills Way Federal Way WA 98003 Office: Weyerhaeuser Co Tacoma WA 98477

FOSS, FRANK WILLIAM, electronics executive; b. St. Louis, Oct. 4, 1947; s. Frank Willaim Foss Jr. and Betty Lee (Ammon) Elliot; m. Helga Karoline Mayer, May 15, 1968 (div. Oct. 1973); m. Nancy Elaine Marshall, June 2, 1979; children: Frank William IV, Bridget Lee. BSEE, Jackson State U., 1985. Prodn. engr. Electronic Processors, Englewood, Colo., 1973-76; v.p. engring. Solar Electric, Westminster, Colo., 1978-79; test design engr. Ampex, Wheatridge, Colo., 1981-83; systems engr. Custom Engring., Englewood, 1983-87; assoc. CMR & Assocs., Englewood, 1988—; ptnr. Applied Solar Engring., Englewood, 1985—; pres. Foss Engring., 1988—; assoc. CMR & Assocs., 1988—. Contbr. articles to profl. jours.; inventor line operated switcher supply (design award 1981), 5W CW krypton laser, room temperature heat camera, computer axis tracker for solar collectors, low cost tracking solar collector. Served as sgt. USAF, 1965-69. Dept. Energy and Clearance grantee, Sandia, N.Mex., 1983. Home: 2877 S Clarkson Englewood CO 80110

FOSS, PAULETTE D., information specialist; b. Cheyenne, Wyo., Oct. 3, 1952; d. Paul H. and Leona F. (Ronnecker) F. BA cum laude, U. Colo., 1973; MA in Library Sci., San Jose State U., 1974; postgrad., U. Idaho, 1988—. Reader's adv. librarian Svcs. for the Blind of Colo., Denver, 1974-75; sr. cons. Colo. State Library Refs., Denver, 1975-81; info. specialist Postharvet Inst. for Perishables U. Idaho, Moscow, 1981-88; fellow tropical agrl. info. svcs. U. Hawaii, U. South Pacific, 1988—; library cons. U.S. Agy. for Internat. Development, Washington, 1982—. Author (bibliographies): Roots and Tubers, 1981, Export Mktg., 1982, Exotic Fruits, 1982, EDB Alternatives, 1984; editor: Caerthan Cookery, 1978. Dir. religious edn., Unitarian Ch. of Palouse, Idaho, 1984-88; leader Brownie Troop, Girl Scouts U.S.A., Moscow, 1986-87. Mem. Spl. Libraries Assn., Internat. Assn. Agrl. Librarian and Documentalists, Am. Hist. Assn., Phi Beta Kappa, Beta Phi

Mu, Phi Alpha Theta, Delta Phi Alpha. Home and Office: Univ S Pacific Alafua Campus, Pvt Bag Apia, Apia Western Samoa Office: U Idaho Library Postharvest Inst for Perishables Moscow ID 83843

FOSSLAND, JOEANN JONES, advertising executive; b. Balt., Mar. 21, 1948; d. Milton Francis and Clementine (Bowen) Jones; m. Richard E. Yellott III, 1966 (div. 1970); children: Richard E. IV, Dawn Joeann; m. Robert Gerard Fossland Jr., Nov. 25, 1982. Student, Johns Hopkins U., 1966-67; cert. in real estate, Hogan's Sch. Real Estate, 1982. Owner Kobble Shop, Indiatlantic, Fla., 1968-70, Downstairs, Atlanta, 1971; seamstress Aspen (Colo.) Leather, 1972-75; owner Backporch Feather & Leather, Aspen and Tucson, 1975-81; regional mgr. Welcome Wagon, Tucson, 1982; realtor assoc. Tucson Realty & Trust, 1983-85; sales mgr. Home Illustrated mag., Tucson, 1985-87, gen. mgr., 1988-89; asst. to pub. Phoenix/Scottsdale, Tricities, Tucson Homes Illustrated, Tucson, 1989—; speaker continuing edn. Lindquist Seminars, Tucson, 1987—; cons. Albuquerque Homes Illustrated, 1987—. Designer leather goods (Tucson Mus. Art award 1978, Crested Butte Art Fair Best of Show award 1980). Mem. Tucson Met. Conv. and Visitors Bur.; vol. Warner for Ariz. Gov., 1986-87; notary pub. State of Ariz., 1984-88; voter registrar Recorder's Office City of Tucson, 1985—; bd. dirs. Hearth Found., Tucson, 1987—. Mem. Women's Coun. Realtors (treas. Tucson chpt. 1987, sec. 1988, Affiliate of Quarter 1986), Tucson Bd. Realtors (chmn. realtors of Ariz. polit. action Com. 1985, multiple listing svc. mktg. session chmn. 1987—, Affiliate of Yr. 1986), Tucson C. of C. Democrat. Presbyterian. Office: Homes Illustrated 426 E 7th St Tucson AZ 85705

FOSTER, DUDLEY EDWARDS, JR., musician, educator; b. Orange, N.J., Oct. 5, 1935; s. Dudley Edwards and Margaret (DePoy) F.; student Occidental Coll., 1953-56; AB, UCLA, 1957, MA, 1958; postgrad. U. So. Calif., 1961-73. Lectr. music Immaculate Heart Coll., Los Angeles, 1960-63; dir. music Holy Faith Episcopal Ch., Inglewood, Calif., 1964-67; lectr. music Calif. State U., Los Angeles, 1968-71; assoc. prof. music Los Angeles Mission Coll., 1975-83, prof., 1983—, also chmn. dept. music, 1977—; dir. music First Lutheran Ch., Los Angeles, 1968-72; organist, pianist, harpsichordist; numerous recitals; composer O Sacrum Convivium for Trumpet and Organ, 1973, Passacaglia for Brass Instruments, 1969, Introduction, Arioso & Fugue for Cello and Piano, 1974. Fellow Trinity Coll. Music, London, 1960. Recipient Associated Students Faculty award, 1988. Mem. Am. Guild Organists, Am. Musicol. Soc., Town Hall Calif., Los Angeles Coll. Tchrs. Assn. (pres. Mission Coll. chpt. 1976-77, v.p., exec. com. 1982-84), Mediaeval Acad. Am. Republican. Anglican. Office: Los Angeles Mission Coll Dept Music 1212 San Fernando Dr San Fernando CA 91340

FOSTER, JEANETTE YVONNE, journalist; b. Bethesda, Md., Apr. 28, 1951; d. Mark Coleman and Christina (Silveria) F. BA, U. Calif., Berkeley, 1972. Writer for various publs. 1972--; media coord. Ironman Triathlon World Championship, Kona, Hawaii, 1981-88. Publicity chmn. West Hawaii chpt. Am. Cancer Soc., Kona, 1986--. Recipient Young Career Woman award Maui Bus. and Profl. Women, 1979; Rotary scholar, 1969; holder internat. world fishing record Internat. Game Fishing Fedn., 1985, 87. Home: 73-1062 Ahikawa St Kailua-Kona HI 96740

FOSTER, JERRY ROBERT, transportation educator; b. Wichita, Kans., Feb. 2, 1942; s. Leo Mark and Lydia Rose (Federer) F.; m. Karen L. Kelly, Dec. 27, 1964; children: Damon, Kellie. BA, U. Wyo., 1968; M in Pub. Adminstrn., U. Colo., 1969; PhD, Syracuse U., 1973. Transp. analyst Atchison, Topeka & Santa Fe R.R., Houston, 1969-70; from asst. prof. to assoc. prof. transp. U. Colo., Boulder, 1973—, assoc. dean, 1978-85; assoc. dir. Colo. Grad. Sch. Bank, Boulder, 1979—; cons. Burlington North R.R., Ft. Worth, 1985, Baxter Healthcare, 1988, Anheuser-Busch, St. Louis, 1982-83, Tiger Internat. Air, Los Angeles, 1982, Tex. Internat. Air, Houston, 1979; participant Chinese Assn. Sci. and Tech., U.S. Dept. Transp. Urban Systems, Bejing, 1987. Author: Small Business Administration, 1981, Journal of Transportation Management, co-editor; editorial bd. Nat. Def. Transp. Jour. contbr. numerous articles to profl jours. Chmn. transp. com. Colo. Outlook Forum, Denver, 1980-84; mem. edn. adv. com. E. Griffith, Denver, 1981—; examiner Dept. Regulatory Agys., Denver, 1983, Law and Econs. Am. Soc. of Transp. Logistics; dir. transp. council Boulder C. of C., 1976-84. Served with U.S. Army, 1961-63. Recipient C. of C. Service award Boulder, 1977, Pvt. Sector Initiative Commendation Office of U.S. Pres., 1987. Mem. Nat. Def. Transp. Assn. (editorial rev. com.), Am. Soc. Transp. and Logistics (examiner, 1981—), Council of Logistics Mgmt., Colo. Dist. Export Council, Assn. Transp. Practioners, Dinner Transp. Club (bd. dirs.), Delta Nu Alpha (chmn. coll. liason, editorial review bd. Jour. Transp. Mgmt., transp. leadership award 1983, nat. edn. com. 1979-81). Republican. Office: U Colo Coll Bus Adminstrn Office of Assoc Dean Boulder CO 80309

FOSTER, MARY FRAZER (MARY FRAZER LECRON), anthropologist; b. Des Moines, Feb. 1, 1914; d. James and Helen (Cowles) LeCron; B.A., Northwestern U., 1936; Ph.D., U. Calif., Berkeley, 1965; m. George McClelland Foster, Jan. 6, 1938; children—Jeremy, Melissa Foster Bowerman. Research asso. dept. anthropology U. Calif., Berkeley, 1955-57, 75—; lectr. in anthropology Calif. State U., Hayward, 1966-75; mem. faculty Fromm Inst. Lifelong Learning, U. San Francisco, 1980. Fellow Am. Anthropol. Assn.; mem. Linguistic Soc. Am., Internat. Linguistic Assn., Southwestern Anthrop. Assn., AAAS, Soc. Woman Geographers. Democrat. Author: (with George M. Foster) Sierra Popoluca Speech, 1948; The Tarascan Language, 1969; editor: (with Stanley H. Brandes) Symbol As Sense: New Approaches to the Analysis of Meaning, 1980, (with Robert A. Rubinstein) Peace and War=Cross-Cultural Perspectives, 1986, (with Robert A. Rubinstein) The Social Dynamics of Peace, 1988. Home: 790 San Luis Rd Berkeley CA 94707

FOSTER, MICHAEL WILLIAM, librarian; b. Astoria, Oreg., June 29, 1940; s. William Michael and Margaret Vivian (Carlson) F. BA in History, Willamette U., 1962; MA, U. Oreg., 1965; postgrad., So. Oreg. Coll., 1976. Tchr. Astoria High Sch., 1963-66, librarian, 1970—; tchr. Am. Internat. Sch. of Kabul (Afghanistan), 1966-70; bd. dirs. Astoria High Sch. Scholarships, Inc., 1976—. Commr. Oreg. Arts Commn., Salem, 1983—; bd. dirs. Am. Cancer Soc., Clatsop County, Oreg., 1980-87; bd. dirs., treas. Astoria Community Concert Assn., 1964-88, pres., 1989—; bd. dirs., treas. Ed and Eda Ross scholarship trust. Mem. NEA, Oreg. Edn. Assn., Oreg. Edn. Media Assn., Clatsop County Hist. Soc. (bd. dirs., pres. 1983-87), Ft. Clatsop Hist. Assn. (treas. 1974—, bd. dirs.), Astoria C. of C. (bd. dirs. 1982-88, George award 1985, pres. 1987), Lewis and Clark Trails Heritage Found., Rotary (pres. Astoria Club 1986), Beta Theta Pi. Republican. Roman Catholic. Home: 1636 Irving Ave Astoria OR 97103 Office: Astoria High Sch Libr 1001 W Marine Dr Astoria OR 97103

FOSTER, RICHARD LAYNE, marketing executive; b. Temple, Tex., Apr. 3, 1955; s. Lloyd Leroy and Vera Dorothy (Osborn) F.; m. Nancy Marie Balleck, May 28, 1988. BS in Bus., U. Colo., Denver, 1989. With Kroger Inc., Temple, Tex., 1972-75, McLane Co., Inc., Temple, 1975-77; musician Mondo Romo, P.C., Denver, 1977; with PremMark, Inc., Denver, 1988—. Mem. NOW (chpt. sec.), Beta Gamma Sigma, Phi Chi Theta. Home: 1265 Garfield Denver CO 80206

FOSTER, RUTH MARY, business administrator; b. Little Rock, Jan. 11, 1927; d. William Crosby and Frances Louise (Doering) Shaw; m. Luther A. Foster, Sept. 3, 1946 (dec. Dec. 1980); children: William Lee, Robert Lynn. Grad. high sch., Long Beach, Calif. Sr. hostess Mon's Food Host of Coast, Long Beach, 1945-46; dental asst., office mgr. Dr. Wilfred H. Allen, Opportunity, Wash., 1946-47; dental asst., bus. asst. Dr. H. Erdahl, Long Beach, 1948-50; office mgr. Dr. B.B. Blough, Spokane, Wash., 1950-52; bus. mgr. Henry G. Kolsrud, D.D.S., P.S., Spokane, 1958—, Garland Dental Bldg., Spokane, 1958—. Sustaining mem. Spokane Symphony Orch. Mem. Nat. Assn. Dental Assts., Disabled Am. Vets. Aux., Spokane Club, Credit Women's Breakfast Club, Spokane Bus. and Profl. Women's Club, Nat. Alliance Mentally Ill, Wash. State Alliance Mentally Ill (sustaining mem.). Republican. Mem. First Christian Ch. Office: Henry G. Kolsrud DDS 3718 N Monroe St Spokane WA 99205

FOSTER, STEPHEN GLEN, nuclear engineering educator; b. Memphis, Feb. 12, 1952; s. Laurence Brock and Bertie Mae (Hale) F.; m. Sally Irene Snode, May 9, 1970 (div. Apr. 1981); children: Sarah Irene, Stephen Brock; m. Elda Marie Bender; 1 child, Elda Marie Smith. Assoc. in Nuclear Engring., Saddleback Community Coll., 1984. Enlisted USN, 1969, advanced through grades to interior communications chief electrician, 1979, resigned, 1978; freelance constrn. worker various locations, Calif., 1979-81; maintenance planner So. Calif. Edison Co., Rosemead, 1981-83; instr. nuclear engring. dept. So. Calif. Edison, San Clemente, Calif., 1983—; peer evaluator Inst. Nuclear Power Ops., Atlanta, 1986—. Mem. Rep. Nat. Com., Washington, 1978; com. chmn. Boy Scouts Am., San Juan Capistrano, Calif., 1985. Mem. Am. Nuclear Soc., VFW. Home: 29333 Edgewood Rd San Juan Capistrano CA 92675 Office: So Calif Edison PO Box 128 San Clemente CA 92672

FOSTER, TERESA MARIA, sales executive; b. New Orleans, July 23, 1960; d. Walter Paul and Beverly May (Soublet) F. Grad. high sch., Sun Valley, Calif. With Applause Inc., Woodland Hills, Calif., 1981—, order entry supr., 1982-83, sales adminstr., 1983-84, mgr. sales adminstrn., 1984—. Mem. Nat. Assn. Meeting Planners, NAFE. Office: Applause Inc 6101 Variel Ave Woodland Hills CA 91364

FOSTER, VIRGINIA LEE See REEDER, VIRGINIA LEE

FOSTER, WANELL BAIZE, oncology social worker; b. Hartford, Ky., May 7, 1928; d. Charles Ellis and Viola (Simpson) Baize; children: Charles Keaton, Don Franklin, Susan Kay. AA, U. Ky., 1975; MS in Social Work, U. Louisville, 1977. Tchr. Jefferson County Pub. Schs., Louisville, 1978-79; social worker Dept. Human Services, Louisville, 1979-80, VA Med. Ctr., Long Beach, Calif., 1980—; adj. prof. Calif. State U., Long Beach, 1986—; cons. at large, 1981—. Author: Health & Social Work Jour., 1981. Named to Hon. Order of Ky. Cols. Mem. Nat. Assn. Social Workers, Nat. Assn. Oncology Social Workers. Home: PO Box 90031 Long Beach CA 90809 Office: VA Med Ctr 5901 E 7th St Long Beach CA 90822

FOSTER, WILLIAM JAMES, III, jeweler, gemologist; b. Princeton, N.J., Dec. 9, 1953; s. William James and Frances Alberta (Savidge) F.; m. Lynn Marie McDonald, Sept.6, 1975; children: Trevor James, Tracy Lynn. BA in Geology, Carleton Coll., 1976. Mgr. installations David Beatty Stereo, Kansas City, Mo., 1976-79; programmer U. Mo., Kansas City, 1979-81; staff cons. DST Systems, Inc., Kansas City, 1981-86; owner, mgr. Carats and Crystals, Pismo Beach, Calif., 1986—. Founder, dir., officer Facts About Tomorrow's Energy, Westwood, Kans., 1981-84; councilman City of Westwood, Kans., 1980-86; City of Pismo Beach, Calif., 1988—. Mem. Gemmological Assn. Grt. Britain, Pismo Beach C. of C. (bd. dirs. 1986-88, pres. 1988), Cen. Coast Mktg. Coun. (treas., dir. 1988—), Kiwanis. Republican. Presbyterian. Home: 241 Elaine Way Pismo Beach CA 93449 Office: Carats and Crystals 580 Cypress #N4 Pismo Beach CA 93449

FOTSCH, DAN ROBERT, physical education educator; b. St. Louis, May 17, 1947; s. Robert Jarrel and Margaret Louise (Zimmermann) F.; m. Jacquelyn Sue Rotter, June 12, 1971; children: Kyla Michelle, Jeffrey Scott, Michael David. BS in Edn. cum laude, U. Mo., 1970; MS in Edn., Colo. State U., 1973. Cert. tchr. Tchr. phys. edn., coach North Callaway Schs., Auxvasse, Mo., 1970-71; grad. teaching asst., asst. track coach Colo. State U., Ft. Collins, 1971-73; tchr. elem. phys. edn., coach Poudre R-1 Sch. Dist., Ft. Collins, 1973—; co-dir. Colo. State U. Handicapped Clinic, Ft. Collins, 1973—; dir. Moore Elem. Lab. Sch., Ft. Collins, 1979—, Colo. State U. Super Day Camp, 1979—; presenter for conf. in field. Contbr. articles to profl. jours. State dir. Jump Rope for Heart Project, Denver, 1981. Recipient Scott Key Acad. award, Sigma Phi Epsilon, 1969, Honor Alumni award, Coll. of Profl. Studies of Colo. State U., 1983; grantee Colo. Heart Assn., 1985. Mem. NEA, Poudre Edn. Assn., Colo. Edn. Assn., Colo. Assn. of Health, Phys. Edn., Recreation and Dance (pres. 1979-82, Tchr. award 1977, Honor award 1985), Am. Alliance for Health, Phys. Edn., Recreation and Dance (exec. bd. mem. council on phys. edn. for children 1983-85, fitness chairperson, convention planner 1986), Internat. Platform Assn., Assn. for Supervision and Curriculum Devel., Cen. Dist. Alliance for Health, Phys. Edn., Recreation and Dance (elem. div. chairperson for phys. edn. 1989—), Phi Delta Kappa (found. rep. 1985), Phi Epsilon Kappa (v.p. 1969, pres. 1970). Republican. Home: 3042 Appaloosa Ct Fort Collins CO 80526 Office: Moore Elem Sch 1905 Orchard Pl Fort Collins CO 80521

FOUGHT, SHERYL KRISTINE, environmental scientist, engineer; b. Washington, Mo., Oct. 17, 1949; d. James Paul and Alice Marie (Kasper) McSpadden; m. Randy Bruce Stucki, Nov. 23, 1968 (div. 1973); children: Randy Bruce, Sherylynne Sue; m. Larry Donald Fought, July 31, 1980 (div. 1982); 1 child, Erin Marie. BS, N.Mex. State U., 1976, postgrad., 1977-79. Tchr. N.Mex. State U., Las Cruces, 1977-78; hydrologist U.S. Dept. Interior, Las Cruces, 1978-81; environ. scientist U.S. EPA, Dallas, 1981-84; hazardous waste inspector Ariz. Dept. Health Svc., Phoenix, 1984-85; environ. engr., technician Yuma Proving Ground U.S. Army, 1985-87, chief phys. scientist environment div. Yuma Proving Gound, 1987-88, chief hazardous waste mgmt br. Aberdeen Proving Ground, 1988—. Co-author: The Ghost Town Marcia, 1975, tng. manuals. With USMC, 1968-69. Recipient 2 Quality awards U.S. Army, 1986, Army Materiel Command, 1986. Mem. NAFE, Internat. Platform Assn., Nat. Environ. Tng. Assn., Federally Employed Women, Fed. Women Engrs. and Scientists, The Wildlife Soc., Air Pollution Control Assn., Dept. Def. Excellent Installations. Democrat. Office: Aberdeen Proving Ground STEAP-SA-DSHE-E Aberdeen MD 21001

FOULK, DOROTHY JEAN, electronic publishing specialist; b. Kingsport, Tenn., July 7, 1943; d. Lee Roy and Mabel Jean (Rodgers) Hickman; m. Thomas John McDonald, July 10 (div. 1971); children: Spencer T., Elizabeth R.; m. John Willis Foulk, Aug. 24, 1985. AA, Cypress Community Coll., 1980; BSBA, La Verne U., 1983. Adminstr. Rockwell Internat., L.A., 1979-83, adminstr. automated systems, electronic pub. systems, 1983—. Artist: Prin. works include Snow Scene, 1982, Country Dust, 1982, Duck in Flight, 1984. Election judge, San Bernardino, Calif., 1987, 88. Recipient Gold Seal award, Calif. Scholarship Assn., Paramount, 1961. Mem. Nat. Mgmt. Assn., Nat. Assn. Suggestion Systems (sec. 1981), Nat. Assn. Exec. Females, South Calif. Beagle Club (sec. 1988-90), Blossom Valley Beagle Club. Democrat. Mormon. Office: Rockwell Internat Info Systems Ctr PO Box 2315 D/451 110-SG34 2201 Seal Beach Blvd Seal Beach CA 90741

FOULKROD, MARC JONATHAN, small business owner; b. Red Wing, Minn., Jan. 18, 1955; s. Charles Samuel and Ella Bertha (Raether) F. BS in Aerospace Engring., Calif. State Poly. U., 1977. Performance engr. Boeing, Seattle, 1977-78; assoc. engr. and contracts adminstrn. McDonnell Douglas, Long Beach, Calif., 1978-80; performance engr., sales engr. and flight test Tiger Air, L.A., 1980-81; mktg. cons. Avjet Corp., Burbank, Calif., 1982-86, pres., owner, 1986—. Recipient ROTC scholarship, USAF, 1973. Mem. Nat.Bus.Aircraft Assn., Nat. Air Transp. Assn. Republican. Office: Avjet Corp 4409 Empire Ave Burbank CA 91505

FOURNIER, WALTER FRANK, real estate executive; b. Northampton, Mass., Feb. 26, 1912; s. Frank Napoleon and Marie Ann F.; m. Ella Mae Karrey, May 16, 1938; children: Margaret Irene, Walter Karrey. BS in Mktg., Boston U., 1939; postgrad., Anchorage Community Coll., 1963-64, Alaska Pacific U., 1964-65. Coin sales supt. Coca Cola Co., Springfield, Mass., 1939-43; electrician foreman Collins Electric Co., Springfield, 1946-48; sales coord. for pre-fabricated homes Sears Roebuck & Co., Western Mass., 1948-49; wholesale sales rep. Carl Wiseman Steel and Aluminum Co., Great Falls, Mont., 1949-51; supt. City Electric Co., Anchorage, 1951-52; owner, adminstr. Acme Electric Co., Anchorage, 1953-64; appraiser Gebhart & Peterson, Anchorage, 1964-68; broker, owner Walter F. Fournier & Assocs., Anchorage, 1968—; pres. Alaska Mortgage Cons., Anchorage, 1968-69. Pres. Fairview Community Council, Anchorage, 1980-81. Served with U.S. Army, 1928-31, with USN, 1944-45, PTO. Recipient Spl. Recognition award HUD, 1967. Mem. Review Mortgage Underwriters, Inst. Bus. Appraisers, Internat. Soc. Financiers, Soc. Exchange Counselors (rep. 1970), Alaska Creative Real Estate Assn. (pres. 1978, Gold Pan award 1988), Alaska Million Plus Soc. (pres. 1983). Roman Catholic. Lodge: KC. Office: Walter F Fournier & Assocs 613 E 22d Ave Anchorage AK 99503

FOUST, MARIA NIKI, real estate broker; b. Youngstown, Ohio, Mar. 3, 1948; d. Nicholas George and Sophia N. (Pamfilis) Loijos; 1 child, Michael Nicholas Loijos. Student bus. mgmt., Calif. State U., Sacramento, 1966-67, Calif. State U., Sonoma, 1983-84. Lic. real estate salesman and broker, Calif. Mem. sales staff MacElhenny Levy & Co., Inc., 1975-79; sales and tng. supr. MacElhenny Levy & Co., Inc., Merrill Lynch Realty, 1979-83, subdiv. sales mgr., 1980-83; owner, broker Foust & Co., Santa Rosa, Calif., 1983—; bd. dirs. Golden Pacific Fin. Co. Fin. devel. chmn. Redwood Empire chpt. ARC, 1987-88, chmn. bd. dirs., 1988—. Recipient Virginia Kline Meml. Bd. Mem. of Yr. award ARC, 1987. Mem. Women's Council Realtors, Sonoma County Multiple Listing Svc. (life), Sonoma County Bd. Realtors (instr. ethics 1982-83, bd. dirs. 1983-84), Ducks Unltd (charter women's chpt.), Internat. Platform Assn., Soroptimists. Republican. Eastern Orthodox. Home: 1626 Kelley St Santa Rosa CA 95401 Office: Foust & Co 1410 Neotomas Ave Santa Rosa CA 95405

FOUST, RICHARD DUANE, JR., academic administrator; b. Windber, Pa., Dec. 3, 1945; s. Richard Duane and Edna Larue (Pebley) F.; m. Lorriane Beverly Felt, June 24, 1967 (div. Oct. 1983); children: Richard Duane III, Barbara Anne, Cynthia Marie; m. Glenda Earle Swanner, Oct. 29, 1983. BS, Pa. State U., 1967; PhD, U. Calif., Santa Barbara, 1971. Chemist Westvaco, Luke, Md., 1966-67; asst. prof. No. Ariz. U., Flagstaff, 1972-75, assoc. prof., 1975-87, prof., 1987—, dir. Bilby Research Ctr., 1981—; state dir. Am. Energy Week, Washington, 1982. Author: Arizona Energy Education Activities, 1982; mem. edit. bd. Jour. Coll. Sci. Teaching, 1983—; contbr. articles to profl. jours. Bd. dirs. Arizonans for Jobs and Energy, Phoenix, 1977-82; mem. Ariz. Adv. Council on Energy Edn., Phoenix, 1977-86; mem. The Ariz. Acad., 1981—. Recipient Excellence in Coll. Teaching award Danforth Found., St. Louis, 1980. Mem. Internat. Soc. Chem. Ecology, Soc. Archaeolo. Scis., Soc. Applied Spectroscopy, NSF (peer rev. psnel 1977—), Nat. Sci. Teachers Assn. (Search for Excellence in Sci. Edn. award 1984), Am. Chem. Soc., Ariz. Sci. Teachers Assn. (pres. 1982-83), Sigma Xi (pres. 1982-83). Democrat. Methodist. Home: 4805 E Hightimber Ln Flagstaff AZ 86004 Office: No Ariz U Ralph M Bilby Rsch Ctr Flagstaff AZ 86011

FOUT, GEORGE DOUGLAS, lawyer; b. Findlay, Ohio, Dec. 15, 1950; s. Westley Dean and Catherine Diane (Fisher) F.; m. April Joy Rodewald, July 31, 1981; children: Adam Wayne, Marshall Eugene. BA, U. Calif., San Diego, 1978, MS in Tax Law, 1986; JD, U. Calif., Davis, 1981. Pvt. practice law Law Office George D. Fout, Woodland, 1981-83; assoc. Siegel & Borovitz, San Diego, 1983-86, Rose & Munns, Coronado, Calif., 1986-87; sr. ptnr. Rose, Munns & Fout, Coronado, 1987—. With USN, 1969-73, Vietnam. Mem. State Bar Calif., San Diego County Bar Assn., Optimist Club Coronado (chmn. 1987—), NRA. Republican. Office: Rose Munns & Fout 1014 Park Pl Coronado CA 92118

FOUTS, DANIEL FRANCIS, former professional football player; b. San Francisco, June 10, 1951; s. Robert Oliver and Carolyn Doris (Morgan) F.; m. Juliane Mehl, Apr. 16, 1977; children: Dominic Daniel, Suzanne Marie. B.S., U. Oreg., 1973. Quarterback San Diego Chargers, 1973-88. Named to NFL Pro Bowl, 1980-84. Address: San Diego Chargers San Diego Stadium PO Box 20666 San Diego CA 92120 *

FOWLE, DENNIS ROBERT, retailing executive; b. Locust Valley, N.Y., Aug. 14, 1943; s. Robert William and Christi Anna (Schween) F.; m. Constance Klier, Oct. 24, 1982; children: Christopher, Andrew, Timothy, Jessica. AAS, Paul Smiths Coll., 1963; BBA, U. Denver, 1966; MBA, Inter Am. U., San Juan, P.R., 1969. Asst. gen. mgr. Denver Country Club, 1964-65, Creek Country Club, Locust Valley, N.Y., 1966; dir. mgmt. svcs. Hotel Corp. Am., Washington, 1969-70; food svc. dir. Woodward Lothrop Dept. Store, Washington, 1970-85, Irvine Ranch Farmers Mkt., Newport Beach, Calif., 1985-88, The Price Club, San Diego, 1988--. Bd. dirs. U. Denver, 1980--; vestryman The Falls Ch., Falls Church, Va., 1982-85. Mem. Nat. Retail Mchts. Assn. (bd. dirs. 1980-88), So. Calif. Deli Council, Nat. Assn. Fancy Food Trade (bd. dirs. 1984-88), Food Mktg. Inst., Nat. Deli Assn. (cert. mgr.). Episcopalian.

FOWLER, AUDRIAN HUFF, principal; b. Grangeville, Idaho, Oct. 28, 1940; d. Earl W. and Eleanor Genevieve (Gunter) Huff; m. Dwight L Folwer (div. Dec., 1987); children: Mitchell Lyn, Heather Audrian. BS, U. Idaho, Moscow, 1962; MEd, U. Wash., Seattle, 1970; PhD, Wash. State U., 1983. Cert. Prin. Tchr. Kiona Benton City (Wash.) Sch. Dist., 1962-63, Prosser (Wash.) Sch. Dist., 1963-65; tchr., counselor Highline Sch. Dist., Seattle, Wash., 1966-74; from tchr., counselor to prin. Endicott (Wash.) Sch. Dist.; prin. Othelfo (Wash.) Sch. Dist., 1985-88, Kent (Wash.) Sch. Dist., 1988—. co-founder Othello Literacy Program, 1988, mother adv. bd. mem. Rainbow for Girls, St. John, Benton City, Othello. Mem. Assn. of Wash. Schs. Principals (co-chair legis. com. 1986-88), Wash. Interscholastic Activities Assn., Altrusa, Alpha Chi Omega. Home: 20912 114th Pl SE #22 Kent WA 98031 Office: Fairwood Elem Sch 1660-148th Ave SE Benton WA 98058

FOWLER, JAIME MICHAEL, television editor; b. Montgomery, Ala., Feb. 5, 1959; s. David Howard and Bettie Jane (Allen) F.; m. Peggy Jo Bowes, Sept. 7, 1985. BS in Communication, U. Tex., 1981. Intern Sta. KERA-TV, Dallas, 1980; cameraman Sta. KTVT-TV, Fort Worth, 1981; editor Sta. KTXA-TV, Dallas, 1981-83, Sta. KOCE-TV, Huntington Beach, Calif., 1983-86; pres. Broadcat Group, Ltd., Huntington Beach, 1986—; instr. Rancho Santiago Coll., Santa Ana, Calif., 1988—; cons. McDonnell Douglas Corp., Long Beach, Calif., 1985—. Editor: (TV program) Inside Orange County 1983 (Emmy award 1983, 84), (TV game show) Jeopardy!, 1988—. Sec. bd. dirs. Mariners Cove Inc., Huntington Beach, 1987—. Recipient Emmy award NATAS, 1983, 84, 85. Mem. Acad. TV Arts and Scis.

FOWLER, JON FREDERICK, marketing executive; b. Seattle, Dec. 17, 1943; s. Homer Trawl and Isabel Marie (Caverly) F.; m. Catherine Elizabeth, Sept. 1962 (div. 1965); m. Beverley Sue Miller, Oct. 11, 1980; 1 child, Michele Danise Koslofsky. Student, Foothill Coll., Los Altos Hills, Calif., 1962-63; B. in Gen. Studies, Stanford U., 1981. Computer operator Lockheed Corp., Sunnyvale, Calif., 1962-64; computer programmer Philco-Ford Corp., Palo Alto, Calif., 1964-66; program mgr. Litton Corp., Sunnyvale, 1966-74; v.p. Ramtek Co., Santa Clara, 1974-81; pres. Graphic Strategies Co., San Jose, Calif., 1981-84; v.p. Recognition Concepts Co., Incline Village, Nev., 1984—; bd. dirs. Graphic Strategies Inc., Sunnyvale; dir. steering com. Electronic Imaging Inc., Boston, 1988—. Mem. Soc. Optical Engrs. Republican. Home: 966 Caddy Ct PO Box 5099 Incline Village NV 89450 Office: Recognition Concepts 341 Ski Way PO Box 8510 Incline Village NV 89450

FOWLER, MARY MARSHALL, nuclear applications analyst; b. L.A., June 14, 1937; d. Albert Bonnell and Edith Mary (Kelsea) Marshall; m. Graham Eugene Frye, Apr. 27, 1957 (div. 1972); 1 child, K. Lambda Frye Clausen. BA in Applied Math., U. Calif.-Berkeley, 1976. Systems analyst Control Data Corp., Sunnyvale, Calif., 1976-78; tech. mktg. rep. Boeing Computer Svcs., San Francisco, 1978-81, U. So. Calif., Sunnyvale, 1980-82; user cons. Tech. Devel. Calif. NASA Ames Rsch. Ctr., Moffett Field, Calif., 1982-85; nuclear applications analyst, local area network adminstr. Pacific Gas & Electric Co., San Francisco, 1985—. Mem. IEEE, AAAS, Assn. Computing Machinery (chpt. pres. 1980-81), Assn. for Persons with Severe Handicaps, Toastmasters. Democrat. Home: 424 Staten Ave Apt 207 Oakland CA 94610-4903 Office: Pacific Gas & Electric Co 77 Beale St Ste 1456 San Francisco CA 94106

FOWLER, NANCY CROWLEY, government economist; b. Newton, Mass., Aug. 8, 1922; d. Ralph Elmer and Margaret Bright (Tinkham) Crowley; m. Gordon Robert Fowler, Sept. 11, 1949; children—Gordon R., Nancy Pualani, Betty Kainani, Diane Kuulei. A.B. cum laude, Radcliffe Coll., 1943; Cert., Harvard-Radcliffe, 1946; postgrad. U. Hawaii, 1971-76. Econ. rsch. analyst Dept. Planning & Econ. Devel., Honolulu, 1963-69; assoc. chief rsch. Regional Med. Program, Honolulu, 1969-70; economist V and VI, Dept. Planning and Econ. Devel., Honolulu, 1970-78, chief policy analysis br., 1978-85, tech. info. services officer, 1985-87, energy cons., 1988—; staff rep. State Energy Functional Plan Adv. Com., Honolulu, 1983—, Hawaii Integrated Energy Assessment, 1978-81; energy resources report coord., 1988. Contbr. articles to profl. jours. Com. mem. Kailua Com. to Re-elect Mayor Eileen Anderson, 1984. Recipient Employee of Yr. award Dept. Planning and Econ. Devel., Honolulu, 1977, others. Mem. Hawaii Econs. Assn. (various offices). Democrat. Clubs: Radcliffe of Hawaii, Propeller of Port of

Honolulu (past pres.), Honolulu (pres.). Avocations: gardening, surfing. Home and Office: 203 Aumoe Rd Kailua HI 96734

FOWLER, NATHANIEL EUGENE, ophthalmologist; b. Rochester, N.Y., Dec. 19, 1922; s. John Denison and Lettie (Oliver) F.; student U. Wis., summers 1940, 41, U. Mich., 1940-43; M.D., U. Rochester, 1946; postgrad. Northwestern U., 1947-48; m. Norma Pammenter, Dec. 27, 1944; children—Leigh Pammenter, James Nathaniel, Richard Edward. Intern Genesee Hosp., Rochester, N.Y., 1946-47; commd. lt. (j.g.), M.C., USN, 1946, advanced through grades to lt. comdr., 1956; chief eye, ear, nose throat dept. U.S. Naval Hosp., Key West, Fla., 1948-51, 54-56; resident in ophthalmology U.S. Naval Hosp., Bethesda, Md., 1951-53; sr. med. officer in U.S.S. Baltimore, 1953-54; practice medicine specializing in ophthalmology, Casper, Wyo., 1956-88; chief of staff Natrona County (Wyo.) Meml. Hosp., 1964-66. Trustee Natrona County Sch. Bd., 1963-70, pres., 1967-68; mem. Natrona County Commn., 1971-82, chmn., 1980; bd. dirs. Natrona County Parks and Pleasure Grounds. Diplomate Am. Bd. Ophthalmology. Fellow ACS, Am. Acad. Ophthalmology; mem. Casper C. of C. (dir. 1962-64), Natrona County Med. Soc. (pres. 1959), AMA, Pan Am. Med. Assn., Pan Am. Assn. Ophthalmology, Wyo. Sch. Bds. Assn., N.Am. Yacht Racing Union. Clubs: Elks, Lions (dir. 1961-64), Masons, Shriners, Casper Mountain Ski, Casper Boat (commodore 1960-62), Nat. Ski Patrol, U.S. Navy League. Home: 2957 Kalakaua Ave #516 Honolulu HI 96815

FOWLER, THOMAS GEOFFREY, data consultant; b. Denver, June 4, 1924; s. Willard Breck and Norma Louise (Spacey) Longshore; m. Kathleen Ann Knutson, Feb. 14, 1949; children: Julie Ann, Randall Breck, Kevin Spacey. BBA, Woodbury U., 1950; postgrad., Maren Elwood Coll., 1952, Pierce & Valley Colls., 1976-78; postgrad. in bus. adminstrn., Kennedy-Western U., 1988—. Reporter, editor various newspapers 1951-63; with Rockwell Corp., Chatsworth, Calif., 1969, Parsons, Pasadena, Calif., 1971, 76, Xerox Corp., El Segundo, Calif., 1978, Litton GCS, Canoga Park, Calif., 1979; engr. and quality control writer Arco-Solar, Chatsworth, 1980-81; with Bechtel Corp., Norwalk, Calif., 1982; pvt. practice cons. Renton, Wash., 1985—; pvt. practice cons. live data; owner Listen Ink, 1985. Contbr. articles to profl. jours. Scoutmaster, various offices Boy Scouts Am., Wyo., Colo. and L.A., 1946-72. Mem. Am. Assn. Profl. Cons., Brit. Theatre Assn., Internat. Soc. for Gen. Semantics, Valorian Soc., SAR. Republican.

FOWLER, WILLIAM ALFRED, physicist, educator; b. Pitts., Aug. 9, 1911; s. John McLeod and Jennie Summers (Watson) F.; m. Ardiane Olmsted, Aug. 24, 1940; children: Mary Emily, Martha Summers Fowler Schoenemann. B of Engring. Physics, Ohio State U., 1933, DSc (hon.), 1978; PhD, Calif. Inst. Tech., 1936; DSc (hon.), U. Chgo., 1976, Denison U., 1982, Ariz. State U., 1985, Georgetown U., 1986, U. Mass., 1987, Williams Coll., 1988; Doctorat honoris causa, U. Liège (Belgium), 1981, Observatoire de Paris, 1981. Research fellow Calif. Inst. Tech., Pasadena, 1936-39; asst. prof. physics Calif. Inst. Tech., 1939-42, asso. prof., 1942-46, prof. physics, 1946-70, Inst. prof. physics, 1970—; condr. research on nuclear forces and reaction rates, nuclear spectroscopy, structure of light nuclei, thermonuclear sources of stellar energy and element synthesis in stars and supernovae and the early universe; study of gen. relativistic effects in quasar and pulsar models, nuclear cosmochronology; Fulbright lectr. Cavendish lab. U. Cambridge, 1954-55; Guggenheim fellow, 1954-55; Guggenheim fellow St. John's Coll. and dept. applied math. and theoretical physics U. Cambridge, 1961-62; vis. fellow Inst. Theoretical Astronomy, summers 1967-72; vis. scholar program Phi Beta Kappa, 1980-81; asst. dir. research, sect. L Nat. Defense Rsch. Com., 1941-45; tech. observer, office of field service OSRD, South Pacific Theatre, 1944; sci. dir., project VISTA, Dept. Def., 1951-52; mem. nat. sci. bd. NSF, 1968-74; mem. space sci. bd. Nat. Acad. Scis., 1970-73, 77-80; chmn. Office of Phys. Scis., 1981-84; mem. space program adv. council NASA, 1971-73; mem. nuclear sci. adv. com. Dept. Energy/Nat. Sci. Found., 1977-80; Phi Beta Kappa Vis. scholar, 1980-81; E.A. Milne Lectr. Milne Soc., 1986; named lectr. univs., colls. Contbr. numerous articles to profl. jours. Bd. dirs. Am. Friends of Cambridge U., 1970-78. Recipient Naval Ordnance Devel. award U.S. Navy, 1945, Medal of Merit, 1948; Lammé medal Ohio State U., 1952; Liège medal U. Liège, 1955; Calif. Co-Scientist of Yr. award, 1958; Barnard medal for contbn. to sci. Columbia, 1965; Apollo Achievement award NASA, 1969; Vetlesen prize, 1973; Nat. medal of Sci., 1974; Bruce gold medal Astron. Soc. Pacific, 1979; Nobel prize for physics, 1983; Benjamin Franklin fellow Royal Soc. Arts; Sullivant medal Ohio State U., 1985. Fellow Am. Phys. Soc. (Tom W. Bonner prize 1970, pres. 1976, 1st recipient William A. Fowler award for excellence in physics So. Ohio sect. 1986), Am. Acad. Arts and Scis., Royal Astron. Soc. (assoc., Eddington medal 1978); mem. Nat. Acad. Scis. (council 1974-77), AAAS, Am. Astron. Soc., Am. Inst. Physics (governing bd. 1974-80), AAUP, Am. Philos. Soc., Soc. Royal Sci. Liège (corr. mem.), Brit. Assn. Advancement Sci., Soc. Am. Baseball Research, Mark Twain Soc. (hon.), Naturvetenskapliga Foreiningen (hon.), Sigma Xi, Tau Beta Pi, Tau Kappa Epsilon. Democrat. Clubs: Athenaeum (Pasadena); Cosmos (Washington). Office: Calif Inst Tech Kellogg 106-38 Pasadena CA 91125

FOWLES, ROY RONALD, psychotherapist; b. Chgo., Mar. 30, 1944; s. James A. and Agnes M. (Bruha) F.; m. Sally Anne Hammon, Dec. 18, 1980; children: Amy, Matthew, Jonathan. BS, U. Oreg., 1968; MSW, U. Denver, 1970, PhD, 1978. Lic. social worker Colo. Bd. Social Work Examiners. Program dir. Western Inst. Human Resources, Denver, 1973-75; adminstrv. social worker Suburban Community Tng. and Services, Englewood, Colo., 1975-76; asst. prof. Metro State Coll., Denver, 1977-81; pvt. practice psychotherapy Denver, 1973—; clin. adminstr. Ft. Logan Mental Health Ctr., Denver, 1981-87; exec. dir. Mo. Girls Town, Kingdom City, 1987—; cons. dept. gerontology Denver U., 1979-81. Mem. Nat. Assn. Social Workers.

FOX, CARL ALAN, biological sciences company executive; b. Waukesha, Wis., Nov. 24, 1950; s. Frank Edwin and Margaret Alvilda (Rasmussen) F.; m. Susan Jane Smith, June 18, 1977; children: Thomas Gordon, James David, Joseph Carl. BS, U. Wis., River Falls, 1973; MS, U. Minn., 1975; PhD, Ariz. State U., 1980. Lab. asst. dept. biology U. Wis., River Falls, 1971-73; rsch. asst. dept. agronomy and plant genetics U. Minn., St. Paul, 1973-75; tchr. high sch. Le Center (Minn.) Pub. Schs., 1975-76; rsch. fellow dept. botany Ariz. State U., Tempe, 1976-79; rsch. asst. Lab. Tree-Ring Rsch. U. Ariz., Tucson, 1978-79; rsch. scientist, then sr. rsch. scientist So. Calif. Edison Co., Rosemead, 1979-87; rsch. assoc. agrl. experiment sta. U. Calif., Riverside, 1986—; exec. dir. Desert Rsch. Inst., Reno, 1987—; cons., Lawrence Livermore (Calif.) Lab., 1981-82; rsch. adviser, Electric Power Rsch. Inst., Palo Alto, Calif., 1983-87; liaison, Utility Air Regulatory Group, Washington, 1983-87, cons., 1989; mem. peer rev. panel, EPA, Corvallis, Oreg., 1986; invited reviewer air quality rsch. div. Nat. Park Svc., Denver, 1989. Contbr. numerous papers to profl. publs. Asst. troop leader, Newport Beach, Calif. area Boy Scouts Am., 1981-82; Deacon vocenant Presbyn. Ch., 1989—; Judge State of Nev. Odyssey of the Mind. NSF fellow, 1976-79, grantee NSF, 1987—, So. Calif. Edison Co., Rosemead, 1987-88, Nat. Sci. Found., 1987, Dept. Def. and Energy, 1987. Mem. AAAS, Air Pollution Control Assn., Ecol. Soc. Am., Am. Soc. Agronomy, Greentree Gators Swim Team (pres. 1986-87), Beta Beta Beta. Republican. Presbyterian. Office: Desert Rsch Inst 7010 Dandini Blvd Reno NV 89512

FOX, CHARLES ATKINSON, advertising executive and author; b. Chgo., Sept. 13, 1940; s. Charles Henry and Ethel Marie (Grubel) F.; m. Ursula Maria Kammer, Dec. 17, 1967. BA, Colgate U., 1964. Copywriter Compton Advt., N.Y. and Fed. Republic of Germany, 1968-70; creative dir. McCann-Erickson, Guatelmala and Fed. Republic of Germany, 1973; co-creative dir. Grey Advt., Los Angeles, N.Y. and Japan, 1973-76; creative dir. and v.p. J.R. Navarro, Los Angeles, 1977-83; pres. Rabuck & Fox, Los Angeles, 1986—. Author: Lanquin, 1985. Served to sgt. U.S. Army, 1964-67, Germany. Home: 1114 Euclid St Santa Monica CA 90403 Office: Rabuck & Fox 1513 6th St Santa Monica CA 90401

FOX, DERRICK SEAN, marketing executive; b. Eugene, Oreg., Oct. 25, 1964; s. James Arthur and Helen Veronica (O'Neill) F. BA in Polit. Sci., Duke U., 1986. Dir. mktg. Fiesta Bowl, Scottsdale, Ariz., 1987—; cons. RacePlace, Eventures, Phoenix, 1986—. Republican. Roman Catholic. Home: 7928 E Joshua Tree Ln Scottsdale AZ 85253 Office: Fiesta Bowl PO Box 9847 Scottsdale AZ 85252

FOX, DORIS KENT, journalist; b. LaGrange, Ill., Jan. 28, 1917; d. William Ralph and Litta May (Scott) Kent; m. Grover Harvey Fox, July 26, 1941; children: Michael Kent, Duncan Scott. BA, U. Kans., 1937; MS in Journalism, Northwestern U., 1940. Columnist Iola (Kans.) Daily Register, 1933-35; advt. copywriter Marshall Field & Co., Chgo., 1937-39; fashion/feature story writer UP, Paris, 1939; free lance writer N.Y. Herald Tribune and Paris Herald Tribune, 1939; advt. copywriter Carson Pirie Scott & Co., Chgo., 1939-40, Russeks Fifth Ave., Chgo., 1940-41; pub. relations writer Northwestern U., Evanston, Ill., 1963-66; free lance travel writer Lake San Marcos, Calif., 1988—. Contbr. articles to profl. jours. U. Kans. scholar, 1935-37. Mem. AAUW (br. pres. 1984-86), U. Kans. Alumni Assn. Methodist. Home: 920 Knoll Vista Dr Lake San Marcos CA 92069

FOX, JACK, financial service executive; b. Bklyn., Mar. 8, 1940; s. Benjamin and Rebecca (Shure) F.; m. Carolyn Gleimer, Apr. 16, 1967 (div. Dec. 1975); m. Carole Olafson, July 8, 1987; children: Neal, Stuart. BBA, CCNY, 1961; MBA, CUNY, 1969. Sales specialist Am. Can Corp., N.Y.C., 1962-63; talent agt. Gen. Artists Corp., N.Y.C., 1963-66; bus. specialist N.Y. Times, 1966-70; pres. Ednl. Learning Systems, Inc., Washington, 1971-78; budget dir. Nat. Alliance of Bus., Washington, 1979-80; pres. Computerized Fin. Services, Rockville, Md., 1980-87; regional v.p. Govt. Funding Corp., Los Angeles, 1987—; adj. prof. Am. U., Washington, 1983-85; tchr. fin. Montgomery Coll., Rockville, 1978-86. Author: How to Obtain Your Own SBA Loan, 1983, Starting and Building Your Own Accounting Business, 1984. Mem. Nat. Assn. Accts. Republican. Jewish. Home: 766 S Nardo Ave Apt A-5 Solana Beach CA 92075

FOX, JEAN DEWITT, medical director, neurosurgeon; b. Santa Ana, Calif., July 25, 1918; s. Mark I.D. and Ruth Pace (Carmichael) F.; m. Evelyn Winifred Snider, July 21, 1940; children: Jean DeWitt Jr., Evelyn Jeanne, Jere Lamont. BA, Columbia Union Coll., 1944; Dr.med., Loma Lina U., 1946; MS in Surgery, U. Mich., Ann Arbor, 1954; LLD (hon.), Far Eastern Theol. Sem., Hong Kong, 1952. Diplomate Am. Bd. Neurol. Surgery. Intern the resident Henry Ford Hosp., Detroit, 1945-58; pvt. practice Silver Spring, Md., 1949-53, Glendale, Calif., 1958-68; med. dir. Neurol. Ctr., L.A., 1968—. Author: Why Not Smoke, 1968, Best of Life and health, 1972; inventor in field; tech. adv. TV show Ben Casey, 1959. Chmn., Rep. Buck & Ballot, Glendale, Calif., 1960. Capt. AUS M.C., 1946-48. M.&R. award G.P. Mag., 1951. Fellow ACS; mem. Rep. Senatorial Inner Cir. (life), Congress of Neurosurgenos, Am. Assn. Neurol. Surgeons, Rotary, Masons, Shriners. Home: 1894 Carla Ridge Beverly Hills CA 90210 Office: Neurologic Ctr 7080 Hollywood Blvd Los Angeles CA 90028

FOX, M. BRADFORD, sales executive; b. Hartford, July 13, 1961; s. Arthur Stephen Fox Jr. and Bette (Pugh) Risedorf. BS, Elmira Coll., 1983; 1983. Account exec. Group W. Satellite Communications, Stamford, Conn., 1983-84, ESPN, Bristol, Conn., 1985; sr. account exec. ESPN, Bristol, 1986-87, nat. accounts dir., 1986-87; v.p. Movietime Channel Inc., Hollywood, Calif., 1987—. Mem. Zoning Bd. Appeals, Simsbury, Conn.; mem. Hist. Soc., Simsbury, 1987, Town Com., Simsbury, 1987, Hartford Whalers Oldtimers Youth Hockey, 1985--. Mem. Nat. Cable TV, Cable TV Mktg. Assn., Fla. Cable TV Assn. (adv. bd.), Washington Cable Club. Roman Catholic. Office: Movietime Channel Inc 1800 N Vine St Hollywood CA 90028

FOX, MICHAEL ROBERT, nuclear scientist; b. Olympia, Wash., Dec. 31, 1936; s. Earnest R. and Helene M. (Omeara) F.; m. Linda Ruth Lamborn, Aug. 7, 1959 (div. May 1973); children: Marianne, Michelle, Brian; m. Jennifer Lee Espey, June 19, 1976; 1 child, Ryan. BS, St. Martin's coll., Olympia, 1959; PhD, U. Wash., 1965. Sr. scientist Phillips Petroleum, Idaho Falls, Idaho, 1965-73; sr. engr. Rockwell Hanford, Richland, Wash., 1973-77; program mgr. Rockwell Hanford, 1977-87; prin. engr. Westinghouse Hanford, 1987—; cons. Sandlin and Assocs., Richland, 1985-87; speaker Sci. and Energy, 1980-88. Contbr. articles to profl. jours.; inventor, patentee desalination of sea water invention. Mem. Low-Level Waste Adv. Bd., Olympia, 1987, Kadlec Hosp. Found., Richland, 1987—, Legis. Coun., Kennewick, Wash., 1987, Energy Coun., Richland, 1987. Named one of Outstanding 100 City of Richland, 1988. Mem. Am. Nuclear Soc. (bd. dirs. 1985-88, pub. communications award 1985), Am. Assn. Engring. Societies, Pacific Basin Nuclear Com., Rotary (bd. dirs. Richland 1986-89). Republican. Roman Catholic. Home: 348 Broadmoor Richland WA 99352 Office: Westinghouse Hanford 450 Hills H4-51 Richland WA 99352

FOX, RONALD LEE, public affairs company executive; b. Inglewood, Calif., July 26, 1952; s. Robert Edward and Ruby Inez (Raw) F.; m. Linda P. Johnson, Jan. 10, 1976; children: Jennifer Jamie, Elizabeth Anne. Student, El Camino Coll., 1971-73; BS, Calif. State U., Fullerton, 1976. Senate minority cons. to fin. com. Calif. State Senate, Sacramento, 1979-81, asst. to minority whip, 1981-82, con. commn. on Constl. amendments, 1982-84; dir. pub. affairs Am. Med. Internat., Beverly Hills, Calif., 1984-86; pres. Fox & Co., Brea, Calif., 1987; ptnr. Weinberger Fox & Easum, Laguna Niguel, Calif., 1987—. Bill mgr., Calif. State Senate, 1980, 81; elected to Orange County Rep. Com., Santa Ana, Calif., 1976; advance man for Pres. Nixon, Ford, Reagan, Bush, Washington, 1972—, for U.S. Dept. State, Washington, 1982—. Mem. Rep. Assocs., Von Strobel Soc., El Camino Coll. Alumni Assn. (pres. 1977-79). Mormon. Office: Weinberger Fox & Easum Ste O115 30100 Town Center Dr Laguna Niguel CA 92677

FOX, STUART IRA, physiologist; b. Bklyn., June 21, 1945; s. Sam and Bess Fox; m. Ellen Diane Fox; 1 dau., Laura Elizabeth. BA, UCLA, 1967; MA, Calif. State U., Los Angeles, 1967; postgrad., U. Calif., Santa Barbara, 1969; PhD, U. So. Calif., 1978. Research assoc. Children's Hosp., Los Angeles, 1972; prof. physiology Los Angeles City Coll., 1972-85, Calif. State U., Northridge, 1979-84, Pierce Coll., 1986—; cons. William C. Brown Co. Pubs., 1976—; project dir. NSF. Author: Computer-Assisted Instruction in Human Physiology, 1979, Laboratory Guide to Human Physiology, 2d edit., 1980, 3d edit., 1984, 4th edit., 1987, Textbook of Human Physiology, 1984, 2d edit., 1987, Concepts of Human Anatomy and Physiology, 1986, 2d edit., 1989, Laboratory Guide to Human Anatomy and Physiology, 1986. Named Outstanding Tchr. Los Angeles City Coll., 1978. Mem. AAAS, So. Calif. Acad. Sci., Am. Physiol. Soc., Sigma Xi. Home: 5556 Forest Cove Ln Agoura Hills CA 91301 Office: Pierce Coll 6201 Winnetka Ave Woodland Hills CA 91371

FOX, SUNNY JESSICA, marketing professional; b. Palo Alto, Calif., Jan. 27, 1946; d. Jose Mateus Lucas and N.L. Sawyer; div.; 1 child, Shelli Marie. Student, Calif. Coll. Arts and Crafts, 1963-64; BA, BS, U. Calif., Berkeley, 1968, MBA, 1976; postgrad., U. Calif., San Francisco, 1968-70, 71-72. Pres. Sunshine Enterprises, San Francisco, 1972-87, Seattle, 1976-82, L.A., 1976-82; chief exec. officer Avenues (formerly Sunshine Enterprises), San Francisco, 1972—; new product coord. ACOF Div. Determined Prodns., San Francisco, 1980-82; founder, owner Metro Mktg. Cons., Lafayette, Calif., 1986—. Author: The Busy Gourmet, 1986, Follow Your Heart, 1988. Mem. NAFE, Am. Assn. Individual Investors, Commonwealth Club San Francisco. Republican. Mailing Address: PO Box 964 Lafayette CA 94549

FOX, SUSAN STUART, sales executive; b. L.A., Apr. 9, 1943; d. Stuart Edwin and Elizabeth Clayson; m. Nicholas Lynn Fox, Aug. 19, 1979; stepchildren: Jesse, Anna. AA, Pasadena City Coll., 1963; BA, UCLA, 1966. Corp. sales adminstr. Penn Phillips Properties, Pasadena, Calif., 1971-76; co-owner Internat. Wholesale Supply, Pasadena, 1975-78; exec. v.p. Realty Register, Pasadena, 1978-80; dir. regional sales Armstrong Nurseries, Ontario, Calif., 1980-84; dir. sales 1984 Summer Olympics, L.A., 1983-84; pres., chief exec. officer, chmn. bd. McFox Floral Design, Inc., Huntington Beach, Calif., 1984—; vocat. instr. high sch. and Community Coll. Vol. tchr. literacy to adults. Mem. Women in Bus., NAFE, Am. Soc. Tng. and Devel., Sales and Mktg. Exec. Assn., Newport Harbor C. of C., Toastmasters. Republican. Presbyterian. Club: Toastmasters. Office: McFox Floral Design Inc PO Box 1757 Huntington Beach CA 92647

FOX, TERRY JAMES, architect, remodeling contractor; b. Olympia, Wash., June 30, 1946; s. Earnest Robert and Helene Marie (O'Meara) F. BA in Econs., U. Wash., 1968, MArch summa cum laude, 1978. Registered architect, Oreg. Foreman Hawaiian Improvement Corp., Honolulu, 1975-78; architect Skidmore Owings & Merrill, Portland, Oreg., 1979, Army Corps Engrs., Portland, 1979-88, engr.-in-charge Navy Pub. Works Ctr., Oakland, Calif, 1988—. With U.S. Army, 1968-71. Mem. AIA, Am. Soc. Mil. Engrs., San Francisco Opera Assn., Phi Kappa Psi. Republican. Roman Catholic. Clubs: U. Wash. Alumni.

FOXHOVEN, MICHAEL JOHN, retail/wholesale company executive, retail merchant; b. Sterling, Colo., Mar. 2, 1949; s. Mark John and Mary Kathryn (Hagerty) F.; m. Catherine Marie Carricaburu, Feb. 16, 1980; children—Patrick Michael, Rachel Marie. Student U. Colo., 1967-70, U. San Francisco, 1971-72, postgrad. Columbia Pacific U., 1987—. Comml. sales mgr. Goodyear Tire & Rubber Co., Denver, 1978-80, area sales mgr., 1980-81, store mgr., 1981-83, wholesale mgr., 1983-84, appeared in TV commls., 1972; v.p. Foxhovens, Inc., Sterling, 1984—; cons. Foxhoven Bros., Inc., Sterling, 1984—; participant dealer mgmt. seminar, Akron, Ohio, 1973, 85. Mem. mgmt. adv. com. Northeastern Jr. Coll., Sterling, 1976-78; sec. Highland Park Sanitation Dist., Sterling, 1984—. Mem. Logan County C. of C. Republican. Roman Catholic. Club: Sterling Country. Lodges: Elks, Kiwanis. Home: 107 Highland Ave Sterling CO 80751 Office: Foxhovens Inc 1100 W Main St Sterling CO 80751

FOXLEY, MATTHEW C., art gallery administrator; b. Omaha, May 14, 1965; s. William C. Foxley and Paula C. Washburn. Adminstr. Mus. Western Art, Denver, 1985-87; pres. Frontier Spirit Gallery Inc., Denver, 1987—, 1st Nat. Communications, Denver, 1987—. Office: Frontier Spirit Gallery 1727 Tremont Pl Denver CO 80202

FOXLEY, WILLIAM NOALL, obstetrician, gynecologist; b. Salt Lake City, Oct. 14, 1949; s. William and Norma LaVon (Noall) F.; m. Janet Lynn Kersley (div. Aug. 1987); children: Nathan Edward, Sarah DeAnne, William Noall, Corinne. BS, Boise State U., 1976; MD, U. Utah, 1983. Resident in ob-gyn Hurley Med. Ctr.-Mich. State U., Flint, 1983-86, chief resident, 1986-87; pvt. practice Winslow, Ariz., 1987—; chief ob-gyn Winslow Meml. Hosp., 1987—, Community Gen. Hosp., Holbrook, Ariz., 1987—. Fellow Am. Coll. Obstetricians and Gynecologists (jr.); mem. AMA, Ariz. Med. Assn., Am. Assn. Gynecologic Laparascopists, Winslow C. of C. Republican. Office: 116 1/2 E Hillview Winslow AZ 86047

FOXX, CHARLES LAWERENCE, chemist; b. Caldwell, Idaho, Dec. 19, 1937; s. Charles Lawerence and Georgia Isabella (Van Curen) F.; m. Teralene Stevens, Sept. 10, 1961; children: Alison Foxx Carlisi, Erin Foxx Huss, Kerri Elizabeth. BS, Coll. of Idaho, 1960; PhD, Kans. State U., 1969. Staff mem. Los Alamos Nat. Lab., 1969-85, acting section leader for waste mgmt., 1985-86, project leader for transuranic waste, 1986-88, sect. leader for wast mgmt., 1988—; mem. Reduced Waste Generation Working Group, 1988—; presenter in field. Contbr. articles to profl. publs. Vol. Big Bros., Los Alamos, 1970-80; challenge leader Girl Scouts U.S.A., Los Alamos, 1979; trustee White Rock United Meth. Ch., Los Alamos, 1983—. Mem. Am. Chem. Soc., Am. Inst. Chemists, Soc. Vertebrate Paleontology (assoc.), Los Alamos Geol. Soc. Democrat. Home: 412 Rover Blvd Los Alamos NM 87544 Office: Los Alamos Nat Lab MS E 524 Los Alamos NM 87545

FRAKER, MARK ARNOTT, environmental scientist; b. Columbus, Ind., Dec. 13, 1944; s. Ralph Waldo and Carol (Arnott) F.; m. Pamela Norton, May 27, 1967 (div. Feb. 1985); 1 child, Russell; m. Donice Horton, Aug. 23, 1986. BA with honors, Ind. U., 1967, MA, 1969. Biologist, project mgr. F.F. Slaney and Co., Vancouver, Can., 1972-78; biologist, project dir. LGL Ltd., Sidney, B.C., Can., 1978-82; sr. environ. scientist Standard Alaska Prodn. Co., Anchorage, 1982—; broadcaster CBC, Vancouver, 1970-72; mem. sci. com. Internat. Whaling Com., Cambridge, Eng., 1982—; adj. prof. U. Alaska Anchorage, 1985—; mem. NAS panel, 1987—; mem. N.Am./USSR scientific exchange, 1989-90. Author: Balaena mysticetus, 1984; also articles; mem. editorial bd. Biol. Papers of the U. of Alaska. Ambassador to Peru, Anchorage Olympic Organizing Com., 1986—. Woodrow Wilson fellow, Princeton, N.J., 1967. Mem. AAAS, NSF (adv. com. on polar programs 1988—), Am. Soc. Mammalogists, Arctic Inst. N.Am., Ottawa Field Naturalists' Club, Can. Soc. Zoologists, Soc. for Marine Mammalogy, The Wildlife Soc., Sigma Xi. Office: BP Exploration (Alaska) Inc PO Box 196612 Anchorage AK 99519

FRAKES, DENNIS CLYDE, port official; b. Memphis, Nov. 5, 1953; s. Eldred Clyde and Opal Mae (Young) F.; m. Cynthia Belle Munoz, Dec. 30, 1978; children: Shelby Colbere, Whitney Morgan, Austin Clyde. BS in Engring., Tex. A&M U., 1978. Project engr. Santa Fe Engring. & Constrn. Co., Houma, La., 1978-79; project mgr. Am. Natrtural Resources Co., Houston, 1979-82, Sohio Petroleum Co., San Francisco, 1982-85; spl. project mgr. Port of Portland, Oreg., 1985—. Named Employee of Yr., Port of Portland, 1987. Mem. Am. Def. Preparedness Assn. (bd. dirs. Oreg. chpt. 1986—), Oreg. Ports Group (chmn. 1986—), Arrowhead Club. Republican. Mem. Ch. of Christ. Home: 21641 S Molalia Ave Oregon City OR 97045 Office: Port of Portland 700 Multinomah St Portland OR 97208

FRAKES, LEE WAYNE, business consultant; b. Lyman, Nebr., Jan. 5, 1930; s. Fred M. and Mable G. F.; m. Anna J. Holmes,July 14, 1970; children: Kimie, Mark, Sam, Sue. BSBA, Pepperdine U., 1977. Enlisted USMC, 1950, advanced through grades to maj., 1976, ret., 1976; prin. Frakes Industries, Internat., Grants Pass, Oreg., 1976—. Mem. Oreg. Marine Corp. League (comdt. 1979-80), Rogue Valley Marine Corps League (comdt. 1988), Rogue Valley Detachment (comdt. 1978, 88). Home: 1311 Shady Ln Grants Pass OR 97527 Office: Frakes Industries Internat 815 SW 4th St Grants Pass OR 97526

FRAKES, ROD VANCE, plant geneticist, educator; b. Ontario, Oreg., July 20, 1930; s. Wylie and Pearl (Richardson) F.; m. Ruby L. Morey, Nov. 27, 1952; children:Laura Ann, Cody Joe. BS, Oreg. State U., 1956, MS, 1957; PhD, Purdue U., 1960. Instr. dept. agronomy Purdue U., West Lafayette, Ind., 1959-60; asst. prof. dept. crop sci. Oreg. State U., Corvallis, 1960-64, assoc. prof., 1964-69, prof., 1969—, assoc. dean research, 1981-88,, emeritus dean of rsch., prof. emeritus crop sci., 1989—. Author numerous papers and abstracts; contbr. to books in field. Served with USCG, 1950-53. Named Man of Yr., Pacific Seedsmen's Assn., 1972; recipient Elizabeth P. Ritchie Disting. Prof. award Oreg. State U., 1980. Fellow Am. Soc. Agronomy, Crop Sci. Soc. Am.; mem. AAAS, Soc. Research Adminstrs., Nat. Council Univ. Research Adminstrs., Western Soc. Crop Sci. (pres. 1978). Club: Corvallis Historic Auto. Lodge: Rotary. Home: 2625 NW Linnan Circle Corvallis OR 97330 Office: Oreg State U Rsch Office Corvallis OR 97331

FRAKNOI, ANDREW, astronomical society executive, educator; b. Budapest, Hungary, Aug. 24, 1948; came to U.S., 1959; naturalized; s. Emery I. and Katherine H. (Schmidt) F.; m. Beverly Carol McMillan, Apr. 23, 1983. B.A. in Astronomy, Harvard U., 1970; M.A. in Astrophysics, U. Calif.-Berkeley, 1972. Instr. astronomy and physics Cañada Coll., Redwood City, Calif., 1972-78; exec. officer Astron. Soc. of Pacific, San Francisco, 1978—; part-time prof. San Francisco State U., 1980—; fellow Com. for Sci. Investigation of Claims of Paranormal, Buffalo, 1984—; bd. dir. Search for Extra Terrestrial Intelligence Inst., Palo Alto, Calif., 1984—; host radio program Exploring the Universe Sta. KGO-FM, San Francisco, 1983-84; rev. panelist NSF, 1989-91. Author: Resource Book for the Teaching of Astronomy, 1978, Universe in the Classroom, 1985, (with others) Effective Astronomy Teaching and Student REasoning Ability, 1978, The Planets, 1985, (with R. Robert Robbins) The Universe at Your Fingertips, 1985, (with others) Interdisciplinary Approaches to Astronomy, 1985, (with others) Universe, 1987; editor: Mercury Mag., 1978—, The Universe in the Classroom Newsletter, 1985—; assoc. editor: The Planetarian, 1986—; columnist monthly column on astronomy San Francisco Examiner, 1986-87 and others. Bd. dirs. Bay Area Skeptics, San Francisco, 1982—. Recipient award of merit Astron. Assn. No. Calif., 1980. Mem. AAAS (astronomy sect. com. 1988—), Am. Astron. Soc., Astron. Soc. Pacific, Am. Assn. Physics Tchrs., Nat. Assn. Sci. Writers, No. Calif. Sci. Writers Assn. (program chmn. 1983-85), Nat. Sci. Found. (mem. rev. panel informal sci edn. 1989—). Office: Astron Soc Pacific 390 Ashton Ave San Francisco CA 94112

FRAME, TED RONALD, lawyer; b. Milw., June 27, 1929; s. Morris and Jean (Lee) F.; student UCLA, 1946-49; AB, Stanford U., 1950, LLB, 1952; m. Lois Elaine Pilgrim, Aug. 15, 1954; children: Kent, Lori, Nancy, Owen. Bar: Calif. 1953. Gen. agri-bus. practice, Coalinga, Calif., 1953—; sr. ptnr. Frame & Courtney, 1965— . Trustee, Baker Mus. Mem. ABA, Calif. Bar Assn., Fresno County Bar Assn., Coalinga C. of C. (past pres.), Masons,

Shriners, Elks. Home: 1222 Nevada St Coalinga CA 93210 Office: 201 Washington St Coalinga CA 93210

FRAMPTON, THOMAS C., ceiling fan manufacturing company executive; b. Hawthorn, Calif., Apr. 17, 1956; s. Marvin C. and Cynthia A. (Kelsey) F.; m. Rachel R. Rushing, May 15, 1975; children: Nathan Thomas, Jennifer Colleen. Dir. spl. prods. Casablanca Fan Co., Pasadena, Calif., 1973-84; pres. Fanimation Design and Mfg. Co., Monrovia, Calif., 1984—. Inventor in field. Mem. Pasadena C. of C. Office: Fanimation Design & Mfg Co 150 W Pomona Ave Monrovia CA 91016

FRANCESCHI, ERNEST JOSEPH, JR., lawyer; b. Los Angeles, Feb. 1, 1957; s. Ernest Joseph and Doris Cecilia (Beluche) F. BS, U. So. Calif., 1978; JD, Southwestern U., Los Angeles, 1980. Bar: Calif. 1984, U.S. Dist. Ct. (cen. dist.) Calif. 1984, U.S. Dist. Ct. (ea. dist.) Calif. 1986, U.S. Dist. Ct. (no. and so. dists.) Calif. 1987, U.S. Ct. Appeals (9th cir.) 1984, U.S. Supreme Ct. 1989. Sole practice Seal Beach, Calif., 1984—. Mem. Assn. Trial Lawyers Am., Calif. Trial Lawyers Assn., Los Angeles Trial Lawyers Assn. Republican. Roman Catholic. Office: 500 Pacific Coast Hwy Ste 212 Seal Beach CA 90740

FRANCIA, FLORENCIO VASQUEZ, real estate investment counselor; b. Nabua, Camarines Sur, Philippines, Oct. 19, 1933; came to U.S., 1972; s. Nicolas Ramos Francia and Juana (Hallare) Vasquez; m. Maria Colico Beltrano Francia, Oct. 19, 1958; children: Deborah, Jessica, Rockefeller, Murphy, Kimberl . LLB, Philippines Law Sch., Manila, 1972. Bar: Calif. 1975. Elocutionist Ateneo de Naga U., Manila, Philippines, 1952-54; editor Philippine Law Sch News Organ, 1966-72; v.p. Francia Internat. Corp., Calif., current; legal adviser Bicol Assn. Greater Los Angeles. 1972—. Lodges: Mason, Bixby Knolls. Home: 4481 Marion Ave Cypress CA 90630

FRANCIS, JAMES ROBERT, systems engineer; b. Blue Rapids, Kans., June 2, 1933; s. Ernest and Ruth Lucile (Vail) F.; m. Joyce Elaine Daily, Apr. 8, 1956; children: Mark James, Wayne Robert, Carol Lynn. BA, SUNY, Plattsburgh, 1973; diploma, Ind. Coll. Armed Forces, 1972; MS in Systems Mgmt., U. So. Calif., 1975, MS in Systems Engring., 1986. Command pilot. Carpenter Francis Constrn., Rose Hill, Kans., 1950-52; jig builder Boeing Airplane Co., Wichita, Kans., 1952-53; enlisted USAF, 1953; aircraft mechanic USAF, Hunter AFB, Ga., 1953-55; commd. 2d lt. USAF, 1956, advanced through grades to col., 1976; pilot USAF, Forbes AFB, Kans. and Little Rock AFB, Ark., 1955-71; comdr. 529th Bomb Squadron USAF, Plattsburgh AFB, N.Y., 1971-74; inspector Inspector Gen. USAF, Norton AFB, Calif., 1974-76; dir. ops. 379th Bomb Wing USAF, Wurtsmith AFB, Mich., 1976-79; chief aircrew tng. Hqtrs. SAC USAF, Offutt AFB, Nebr., 1979-81, dep. dir. tng., 1981-82; ret. USAF, 1982; sr. tech. specialist Northrop Corp., Pico Rivera, Calif., 1982—. Decorated Air medal with 1 oak leaf cluster, D.F.C., Legion of Merit. Mem. Human Factors Soc., Order Daedalions, Pathfinder Homeowners Assn. Republican. Home: 20759 Missionary Ridge Walnut CA 91789 Office: Northrop Corp Div Advanced Systems 8900 E Washington Blvd Pico Rivera CA 90660

FRANCIS, LOIS DAHLIN, french educator; b. St. Paul, Dec. 31, 1945; d. Clifford Erick and Nora J. (Davidson) Dahlin; m. Mark Elgin Francis, May 23, 1981; 1 child, Laura Elizabeth-K. BA in French, Gustavus Adolphus Coll., 1967; MA, U. Iowa, 1969, PhD, 1977; Lic-es-Lettres, U. Poitiers, 1970. Tchr. Barrington (Ill.) High Sch., 1967-68; teaching asst. U. Iowa, Iowa City, 1968-69, teaching and rsch. fellow, 1970-74, instr. French, 1974-75; lectr. in English U. Poitiers, France, 1969-70; instr., asst. prof. French N.C. State U., Raleigh, 1975-81; mem. faculty Diablo Valley Coll., Pleasant Hill, Calif., 1981—; teaching assoc. U. Calif., Berkeley, 1982-84; lectr. Stanford (Calif.) U., 1983; text cons. Rand McNally Co., 1978. Contbr. poetry, revs. and articles to various publs. V.p. Fremont (Calif.) br. New-in-Town, 1985-86. NEH fellow U. N.C., 1978; N.C. State faculty rsch. grantee, 1979. Mem. MLA, Am. Assn. Tchrs. French, Philol. Assn. Pacific Coast, AAUW (bd. dirs. Fremont br. 1986-87). Office: Diablo Valley Coll 321 Gold Club Rd Pleasant Hill CA 94523

FRANCIS, MARC BARUCH, pediatrician; b. Rochester, N.Y., Mar. 3, 1934; s. Nathan and Beverly (Salsburg) F.; A.B., U. Rochester, 1955; M.D., N.Y. U., 1959; m. Janet Irene Harding, Sept. 21, 1960; children—Josephine, Teresa, Jacqueline, Wallace. Intern, Los Angeles County Harbor Gen. Hosp., 1959-60; resident in pediatrics Children's Hosp. of Los Angeles, 1960-62; practice medicine specializing in pediatrics, Salt Lake City, 1962-65; clin. instr. pediatrics U. Utah Med. Sch., 1962-70; chief dept. pediatrics Cottonwood Hosp., 1963-65; partner dept. pediatrics Permanente Med. Group Inc., Napa, Calif., 1971—, chief dept., 1982-86. Served to capt. M.C., USAF, 1966-68. Diplomate Am. Bd. Pediatrics. Fellow Am. Acad. Pediatrics; mem. Calif. Med. Assn., Napa County Med. Soc. Clubs: NYU, U. Rochester Alumni. Office: Permanente Med Group Inc 3284 Jefferson St Napa CA 94558

FRANCIS, ROBERT JAMES, aerospace company executive; b. Everett, Wash., Mar. 23, 1940; s. James Henry and Emma Sophia (Bryce) F.; m. Judie Wood, May, 1959 (div. 1974); m. Barbara Joanne Fitzgerald, Nov. 1, 1975; children: Andrea, Tricia, Jeannie. BS in Physics, U. Tex., 1962; MBA, U. So. Calif., 1971. Assoc. engr. Douglas Aircraft Co., Santa Monica, Calif., 1962-63; mem. tech. staff Hughes Aircraft Co., L.A., 1963-77, head mgmt. devel., 1977-80, bus. mgr. F/A-18 Radar, 1980-82, bus. mgr. spl. programs, 1982-86, bus. mgr. Gen. Motors programs, 1986—; bus. instr. Biola U., La Mirada, Calif., 1986—; cons. in field. Mem. Christian Ministries Mgmt. Assn. Democrat. Office: Hughes Aircraft Co 7200 Hughes Terr PO Box 45066 Los Angeles CA 90045

FRANCIS, STEVEN CABOT, business owner; b. Phoenix, Oct. 8, 1954; s. Gesford Herbert Francis and Marilyn (Griffin) Quidry; m. Gayle Ann Marchinko, June 25, 1983. BS in Hotel Adminstrn., U. Nev., Las Vegas, 1978. Asst. to v.p. Caesars Palace Hotel, Las Vegas, 1978-85; owner Am. Mobile Nurses, Inc., San Diego, 1985—. Bd. dirs. Nev. Spl. Olympics, Reno, 1986; state assemblyman Nev. Legislature, Carson, City, 1983-84, assembly major leader, 1985-86; mem. community planning council United Way, Las Vegas, 1985-86, San Diego Boys & Girls Club, 1988—. Mem. Nat. Rep. Legislators Assn. Lutheran. Office: Am Mobile Nurses Inc 12520 High Bluff Dr Ste 260 San Diego CA 92130

FRANCIS, TIMOTHY DUANE, chiropractor; b. Chgo., Mar. 1, 1956; s. Joseph Duane and Barbara Jane (Sigwalt) F. BS, L.A. Coll. Chiropractic, 1982, Dr. of Chiropractic magna cum laude, 1984; postgrad., Clark County Community Coll., 1986—. Bd. qualified team physician; cert. kinesiologist; lic. chiropractor, Calif., Nev. Instr. dept. recreation and phys. edn. U. Nev., Reno, 1976-80; from tchng. asst. to lead instr. dept. principles & practice L.A. Coll. Chiropractic, 1983-85; pvt. practice Las Vegas, 1985—. Mem. Am. Chiropractic Assn., Nev. State Chiropractic Assn., Nat. Strength and Conditioning Assn., Internat. Coll. Applied Kinesiology. Republican. Roman Catholic. Home: PO Box 43465 Las Vegas NV 89116 Office: 1st Chiropractic 1111 Las Vegas Blvd S #A Las Vegas NV 89104

FRANCIS, WALTER MOSER, criminologist; b. Greeley, Colo., Nov. 23, 1947; s. Everett Earl and Evelyn P. (Moser) F.; m. Barbara L. Quick, Aug., 1975. BA, U. No. Colo., 1971, MA, 1973; MA, SUNY, Albany, 1979. Criminal investigator 19th Jud. Dist., Greeley, 1974-75; exec. v.p. Greeley Fin. Co., 1975-76; chmn. criminal justice dept. McCook (Nebr.) Community Coll., 1979-80, Linn-Benton Community Coll., Albany, Oreg., 1980-81; div. comdr. Greeley Police Dept., 1981-83; pres., chief exec. officer, chmn. bd. Bank of Greeley, 1983-85; pvt. practice legal investigative cons. Greeley, 1986-89; prof. criminal justice Cen. Wyoming Coll., Riverton, 1989—. Commr. human rels. commn. City of Greeley. SUNY fellow, 1978. Mem. Acad. Criminal Justice Scis., Am. Sociol. Assn., Am. Judicature Soc., Kappa Delta Pi. Democrat. Home and Office: 2053-17th Ave Greeley CO 80631

FRANCISCO, WAYNE M(ARKLAND), automotive executive; b. Cin., June 14, 1943; s. George Lewis and Helen M. (Markland) F.; student Ohio State U., 1962-63; BS in Mktg. and Acctg., U. Cin., 1967; m. Susan Francisco; children: Diana Lynn, W. Michael. Unit sales mgr. Procter & Gamble, Cin., 1967-69; mktg. mgr. Nat. Mktg. Inc., Cin., 1969-70; pres. Retail Petroleum Marketers, Inc., Cin., 1970-72, chmn. bd., chief exec. officer, Phoenix, 1972-85; chmn. bd., chief exec. officer DMC Industries, Inc., 1985-88; pres., chief exec. officer Cassia Petroleum Corp., Vancouver, B.C., Can., 1980-84; bd. dirs. P.F.K. Enterprises, F.I.C. Inc., Internat. Investment and Fin. Enterprises, Inc., Alpha Realty, Inc. Mem. Ednl. Found. Superintendent's Club, Eugene C. Exxley Club, Phoenix Bd. Appeals, 1978-80; v.p. Cuervanaca Homeowners Assn., 1982, pres., 1983-86. Recipient Image Maker award Shell Oil Co., 1979; Top Performer award Phoenix dist. Shell Oil Co., 1979, 80. Mem. Petroleum Retailers Ariz. (pres. 1977-79), Nat. Congress Petroleum Retailers (adv. bd.), Nat. Inst. Automotive Service Excellence (cert.), Culver Legion (life), Studebaker Drivers Club (zone coord. Pacific S.W. 1983, 84, 85, 86; nat. v.p. 1986-89; Grand Canyon chpt. pres. 1986), Avanti Owners Assn. (nat. bd. dirs. 1975-88, internat. pres. 1986-90). Republican. Lodge: Optimists (bd. dirs. Paradise Valley club 1984, sec.-treas. 1984). Office: 21824 N 19th Ave Phoenix AZ 85027

FRANCO, DOUGLAS EUGENE, financial executive; b. Evanston, Ill., Feb. 20, 1948; s. Daniel Jr. and Marjorie Jane (Peterson) F.; m. Betsy Lou Verne, Dec. 21, 1969; children: James, Thomas, David. BS in Math., Stanford U., 1971; MBA, Harvard U., 1975. Fin. analyst Hewlett-Packard Co., Palo Alto, Calif., 1971-73, fin. mgr., 1977-80; fin. analyst Xerox Corp., Rochester, N.Y., 1975-77; fin. mgr. Memorex Co., Santa Clara, Calif., 1980, Raychem Co., Menlo Park, Calif., 1981-83; div. controller Signetics Co., Sunnyvale, Calif., 1983-85; fin. mgr. Rolm Inc., Santa Clara, 1985—. Vol., speaker, organizer local and regional svc. groups, 1983—. Jewel Co. scholar, 1966-70, Stanford U. scholar, 1966-70. Home: 2921 Ramona St Palo Alto CA 94306 Office: Rolm Systems Inc 4900 Old Ironsides Dr Santa Clara CA 95054

FRANCO, FRANK, desert marshal; b. Indio, Calif., May 6, 1945; s. Antonio Verdugo and Josefa (Ramirez) F.; m. Rose Balderrama, Jan. 14, 1967; children: Renée, Frank Anthony. AA in Police Sci., Coll. of the Desert, Palm Desert, Calif., 1973; BS in Pub. Mgmt., Pepperdine U., 1975. Field rep. Western Exterminator, Rancho Mirage, Calif., 1969-70; mem. growers relations staff Tenneco West, Inc., Thermal, Calif., 1978-80; dep. marshal Riverside County Desert Marshal's Office, Palm Springs, Calif., 1970-78, 80-84, marshal, 1985—. Bd. dirs. Hayman Ctr. Treatment, Palm Springs, 1986—, Desert Blind and Handicap, Palm Springs, 1987, v.p.; adv. bd. Coachella Valley Girls Club, Indio, 1987. Served with USAF, 1965-66. Mem. State Marshals Assn. (exec. bd. mem. 1985—), Riverside County Law Enforcement Adminstrs. Assn., Peace Officers Rsch. Assn. Calif. Democrat. Roman Catholic. Home: 81-911 Victoria St Indio CA 92201 Office: 3255 E Tahquitz McCallum Way Palm Springs CA 92262

FRANCO, JORGE, pathologist; b. Ica, Peru, June 9, 1929; s. Fortunato and Sabina (Cabrera) F.; B.S., San Marcos U., 1947, M.D., 1955; m. Mary Loretta Jones, Sept. 19, 1957; children—Mary Pat, Lori, Ann Marie, Raymond Joseph, Stephen Michael. Came to U.S., 1955. Intern, Bon Secours Hosp., Balt., 1955-56; fellow medicine Stanford Med. Sch., 1956-58, asst. clin. prof. nuclear medicine, 1969-76, assoc. clin. prof., 1976—; resident pathology O'Connor Hosp., San Jose, Calif., 1958-62, assoc. pathologist, 1963—, chief clin. pathology, dir. nuclear medicine, 1968—. Diplomate Am. Bd. Pathology, Am. Bd. Nuclear Medicine. Mem. Am. Fedn. Clin. Research, Am. Soc. Clin. Pathologists, Am. Soc. Hematology, Am. Assn. Blood Banks, Soc. Nuclear Medicine, Am. Inst. Ultrasonics in Medicine, AMA, Calif. Med. Assn., Calif. Soc. Pathologists, Am. Thermographic Soc., Calif. Acad. Medicine, N.Y. Acad. Scis. Contbr. articles to profl. jours.; also clin. and lab. research. Home: 1259 Central Ave San Jose CA 95128 Office: O'Connor Hosp Tumor Ctr San Jose CA 95128

FRANCOIS, DEBORAH JOAN, medical transcriptionist; b. El Paso, Tex., Sept. 26, 1959; d. Paul Jacques Mathieu and Sandra Lee (Dombrow) Dobson; m. Steven Robert Francois, Oct. 10, 1987. AA, Pima Community Coll., 1980, emergency med. technician cert., 1983. Med. transcriptionist Health Am./Maxicare, Tucson, 1980-85, Tucson Med. Ctr., 1985-86; med. transcriptionist/supr. Dictation West, Phoenix, 1986-88; med. transcriptionist PDW, Phoenix, 1988—, Healthfocus, Casa Grande, Ariz., 1988—, Sierra Orthopedics, Casa Grande, 1988—; med. transcriptionist self employed Tucson, 1985-86. Home: 1732 E Shasta Casa Grande AZ 85222

FRANCUSKI, GEORGE EMIL, real estate developer; b. Akron, Ohio, July 16, 1952; s. Emil and Margaret Louise (Schneckenberger) F. AA, Kent State U., 1978, BS, 1979; postgrad., U. Phoenix, 1988. Cert. tchr., Ariz. Switchman GTE-Ohio, Medina, 1970-76; tchr. El Rito (N.Mex.) Elem. Sch. Dist., 1979-80, Kingman (Ariz.) Elem. Sch. Dist., 1980-86; project mgr. Francuski Enterprises, Inc., Kingman, 1986—. Commr. Kingman Planning and Zoning Commn., 1983—; bd. dirs. Main St. Kingman, 1985-87; sec. Kingman in Action, 1987—. Mem. Internat. Coun. Shopping Ctrs., Am. Planning Assn. Home: 3045 Louise Ave Kingman AZ 86401 Office: Francuski Enterprises Inc Hualapai Village Marketplace Kingman AZ 86401

FRANK, ALFRED LOUIS, endodontist; b. Cleve., July 17, 1922; s. Jacob and Yetta (Bergman) F.; m. Teri Frank, Dec. 16, 1951; children: Clifford, Robert, Bradley, Jeffrey, David. Student, Case Western Res. U., 1940-42, Ohio State U., 1942; DDS, U. So. Calif., 1945. Clin. prof. U. So. Calif., L.A., 1956-88; prof. endodontics Loma Linda (Calif.) U., 1988—; cons. Long Beach (Calif.) Vets. Hosp., Hudson comprehensive Health Ctr., L.A., ADA Council on Dental Edn.; lectr. Loma Linda (Calif.) U., UCLA. Author: Clinical and Surgical Endodontics, 1983; contbr. articles to profl. jours., chpts. to books. Bd. dirs. U. West L.A., 1980-85, Jewish Big Bros., L.A., 1960-70. Capt. U.S. Army, 1946-48. Internat. Coll. Dentistry fellow, 1968. Fellow Am. Coll. Dentistry; mem. Am. Assn. Endodontics (pres. 1974-75, Edgar A. collidge award 1981, Ralph Sommer award 1985), Internat. Assn. Dental Rsch., Am. Bd. Endodontists (pres. 1972), So. Calif. Acad. Endodontists (pres. 1962), Alpha Omega (pres. L.A. chpt. 1969, internat. trustee 1970). Alpha Tau Epsilon, Omicron Kappa Epsilon, Sigma Xi. Democrat. Home: 1570 Brookhollow Dr Apt 116 Santa Ana CA 92705 Office: Loma Linda U Sch Dentistry Loma Linda CA 92350

FRANK, CHARLES ALEXANDER, restaurateur; b. Portland, Oreg., Feb. 24, 1948; s. Marvin Conrad and Jacqueline (Cohn) F.; m. Barbara Laibly, May 16, 1971; children: Amanda, Meredith, Rebecca. BS in Econs., U. Pa., 1970. Acct. Laventhol & Horwath, Pa., 1970-73; controller Spectrum Foods, Inc., L.A., 1973-74, v.p., 1974-78, exec. v.p., chief fin. officer, 1978-85; pres. Spectrum Foods, Inc., San Francisco, 1985—; bd. dirs. Marquel, Ltd., Burlingame, Calif. Bd. dirs. Cen. City Hospitality House, San Francisco, 1987—. Mem. Calif. Restaurant Assn. (bd. dirs. 1980—), AICPAs, Pa. Soc. CPAs, Calif. Soc. CPAs. Office: Spectrum Foods Inc 617 Front St San Francisco CA 94111

FRANK, CHRISTOPHER LYND, mechanical engineer; b. Chesterton, Ind., Dec. 26, 1949; s. Clarence Edward and Marie Caroline (Saylor) F.; m. Deborah Lynn Tanner, July 3, 1971; 1 child, Erin Marie. BS in Engring., Calif. State U., Sacramento, 1983; cert. injection molding, U. Lowell, 1986. Plant mgr. Redelco Plastics, Clouis, Calif., 1975-79; owner, designer The Energy Factory, Fresno, Calif., 1977-79, Solar Utility Network, Yuba City, Calif., 1979-81; engr., designer Houston Fearless 76, Carson, Calif., 1983-86; engr., designer Air Force Advanced Composites Program, Sacramento, 1986—, head thermoplastics devel. Served as sgt. USAF, 1970-74. Mem. Soc. Automotive Engrs., ASME, Soc. Mfg. Engrs., Soc. Plastics Engrs. Office: SM-ALC/MMEP Bldg 243-E McClellan AFB CA 95652

FRANK, KAREN ELAINE, teacher; b. Detroit, Aug. 27, 1942; d. Edward Peter and Dorothea June (Ludwig) Malew; m. Glenn Marvin Frank, Dec. 15, 1962; children: Pamela, Julie. BA, Mich. State U., 1963; MA, U. Colo., Colorado Springs, 1985. Tchr. Mich. Sch. for Blind, Lansing, Mich., 1964-66, Woods Consol. Schs., Warren, Mich., 1967-68; tchr., dir. Am. Kindergarten and Nursery Sch., Izmir, Turkey, 1968-70, Raggedy Ann & Andy Nursery Sch., Columbia, Mo., 1971-72; vet. asst. Yorkshire Vet. Clinic, Colorado Springs, Colo., 1973—; tchr. asst. Acad. Sch. Dist., Colorado Springs, 1982-83, tchr., 1983—. Mem. NEA, Colo. Edn. Assn., AVMA Aux., Colo. Vet. Med. Assn. Aux., Colorado Springs Vet. Med. Aux. (organizer), Delta Gamma (chmn. vision screening Colorado Springs 1975, 76, organizer glaucoma screening with Nat. Soc. Prevention Blindness 1980). Republican. Lutheran. Home: 540 Hidden Valley Rd Colorado Springs CO 80919 Office: Acad Sch Dist Pine Valley Sch USAF Acad Colorado Springs CO 80840

FRANK, MICHAEL VICTOR, risk assessment engineer; b. N.Y.C., Sept. 22, 1947; s. David and Bernice (Abrams) F.; m. Jane Griminger, Dec. 21, 1969; children: Jeffrey, Heidi, Heather. BS, UCLA, 1969; MS, Carnegie-Mellon U., 1972; PhD, UCLA, 1978. Registered profl. engr., Calif. Engr. Westinghouse Electric Corp., Pitts., 1970-72, Southern Calif. Edison, Los Angeles, 1972-74; lectr. U. Calif., Santa Barbara, 1976-77; sr. exec. engr. NUS Corp., San Diego, 1981-85; sr. cons. Pickard, Lowe & Garrick, Newport Beach, Calif., 1986—; various research and cons. jobs in Calif., 1974-76; mgr. or participant major quantitative risk assessment studies world-wide. Contbr. articles to profl. jours. Mem. Soc. for Risk Analysis, Am. Assn. for Artificial Intelligence.

FRANK, SANDERS THALHEIMER, physician, educator; b. Middletown, Conn., May 11, 1938; s. Harry S. and Pauline (Thalheimer) F.; B.A., Amherst Coll., 1959; M.D., N.Y. Med. Coll., 1963; m. Marta Santoyo, Jan. 7, 1981; children by previous marriage—Geoffrey Brooks, Susan Kimberly, Jonathan Blair, Adam. Intern, Sinai Hosp., Balt., 1963-64; resident Wilford Hall Med. Center, San Antonio, 1965-68; practice medicine, specializing in pulmonary disease, Monterey Park, Calif., 1971—; dir. respiratory care Garfield Hosp., Monterey Park, 1974—, Beverly Hosp., Montebello, Calif., 1975-78; assoc. prof. medicine U. So. Calif., Los Angeles, 1972—. Served to maj. USAF, 1964-71. Decorated USAF Commendation medal; recipient Philip Hench award for demonstrating relationship of rheumatoid arthritis to lung disease, 1968; award of merit Los Angeles County Heart Assn., 1974. Fellow Royal Soc. Medicine (London), Am. Coll. Chest Physicians, A.C.P.; mem. Am. Thoracic Soc., Calif. Thoracic Soc., Nat. Assn. Dirs. Respiratory Care, Respiratory Care Assembly Calif., Alpha Omega Alpha. Contbr. articles in field to med. jours. Recorded relationship of ear-lobe crease to coronary artery disease, 1973. Home: 891 E Grandview Sierra Madre CA 91024 Office: 500 N Garfield Ave Monterey Park CA 91754

FRANK, STEPHEN RICHARD, lawyer; b. Portland, Oreg., Dec. 13, 1942; s. Richard Sigmund Frank and Paula Anne (Latz) Lewis; divorced; children: Richard Sigmund II, Theresa Anne; m. Patricia Lynn Graves, Aug. 20, 1988. AB in Econs., U. Calif., Berkeley, 1964; JD, Willamette U., 1967. Bar: Oreg., U.S. Ct. Appeals (9th cir.), U.S. Supreme Ct. Assoc. Tooze, Marshall, Shenker, Holloway & Duden, Portland, 1967-72, ptnr., 1972—; mem. audit com. Seligman & Latz NYSE, 1981-85, bd. dirs. 1976-85. Editor Willamette Law Jour., 1967. Trustee, sec. Oreg. High Desert Mus., 1977-86; sec., bd. dirs. Palatine Hill Water Dist., 1973-77; bd. dirs. Emanuel Hosp. Found., 1980-83, Portland Ctr. for Visual Arts, 1977-82. Mem. ABA, Assn. Trial Lawyers Am., Oreg. Trial Lawyers Assn., Oreg. State Bar Assn. (dir., sec. minority scholarship program 1981—, sec.-chmn. com. worker's compensation 1974-77), Oreg.Assn. Ins. Def. Counsel, Oreg. Assn. Workers Compensation Def. Counsel. Clubs: Multnomah Athletic; City (Portland). Home: 3103 SW Cascade Dr Portland OR 97201 Office: Tooze Marshall Shenker Holloway & Duden 333 SW Taylor St Portland OR 97204

FRANKE, WILLIAM AUGUSTUS, corporate executive; b. Bryan, Tex., Apr. 15, 1937; s. Louis John and Frances (Hanna) F.; m. Carolyn D. Walker, July 16, 1977; children: Catherine Anne, Paige Estelle, Brian Hanna, David Parker, Rebecca Ann Walker. BA, Stanford U., 1959, LLB, 1961. Bar: Wash. 1961. Assoc. MacGillivray, Jones, Clark & Schiffner, Spokane, 1962-67, ptnr., 1967-70; v.p., sec., corp. counsel S.W. Forest Industries, Phoenix, 1970-72, sr. v.p., sec., 1972-73, exec. v.p., asst. chief exec. officer, 1973-75, pres., 1975—, chief oper. officer, 1977-78, chief exec. officer, 1978; chmn. bd. dirs. S.W. Forest Industries (merged with Stone Container Corp.), Phoenix, 1986—; pres., owner WAFCO Capital, Inc., Scottsdale, Ariz., 1987—; prin. Sterling Prodn. Co.; bd. dirs. Phelps Dodge Corp.; chmn. exec. com. Circle K Corp., Valley Nat. Bank. Mem. dean's council Stanford U. Law Sch., Ariz. State U. Sch. Bus. Served to capt. U.S. Army, 1961-62. Mem. ABA, Wash. Bar Assn., Spokane County Bar Assn., Young Pres.'s Orgn. Episcopalian. Clubs: Stanford, Paradise Valley Country, Phoenix Country, Mansion (Phoenix); Plaza. Home: 7701 N Saguaro Dr Paradise Valley AZ 85253 Office: 7373 N Scottsdale Rd Ste D-102 Scottsdale AZ 85253

FRANKEL, PAUL ROBERT, management consultant; b. N.Y.C., July 29, 1957; s. Robert Alan and Evelyn Dawn (Hickman) F. BS in Indsl. Engring., N.C. State U., 1979; MBA, U. Va., 1983. Indsl. engr. Westinghouse Aerospace, Balt., 1979-81; gen. mgr. Montdomaine Cellars, Charlottesville, S.C., 1983-86; v.p. data processing Unitel Corp., San Diego, 1986-87; mgr. fin. and ops. Electronic Compassy, San Diego, 1987-88; founder, owner Paul Frankel Mgmt. Cons., San Diego, 1988—. Republican. Home: 3145 Galloway Dr San Diego CA 92122

FRANKENSTEIN, JOHN, international management educator, consultant; b. San Francisco, Jan. 27, 1940; s. Alfred Victor and Sylvia (Lent) F.; m. Veronica M.C. Li, July 1, 1967; children: Karen, Paul, William. BA, Stanford U., 1961; MA, San Francisco State U., 1967; Diploma, Johns Hopkins S.A.I.S., Bologna, Italy, 1975; PhD, MIT, 1983. Lectr. U. Hawaii, Honolulu, 1967-68; U.S. fgn. service officer USIA, Senegal, Belgium, Taiwan, Hong Kong, Italy, France, 1968-77; lectr. U. Mass., Boston, 1980-81; assoc. prof. Am. Grad. Sch. Internat. Mgmt., Glendale, Ariz., 1982—; vis. prof. Inst. for Internat. Studies and Tng., Japan, 1987, U. Internat. Bus. and Econs., Beijing, 1984, 88. Contbr. articles to profl. jours. Mem. Phoenix Com. on Fgn. Relations, 1982—, Phoenix Sister Cities Commn. (China com.), 1986—. With USN, 1961-64, Philippines, Vietnam. Office: Am Grad Sch Internat Mgmt Thunderbird Campus Glendale AZ 85306

FRANKISH, BRIAN EDWARD, film producer, director; b. Columbus, Ohio, July 28, 1943; s. John (Jack) Fletcher Frankish and Barbara Aileen (Tondro) Gray; m. Tannis Rae Benedict, Oct. 13, 1985; children: Merlin L. Reed III, Michelle Lynn Reed. AA, Chaffey Coll., 1964; BA, San Francisco State U., 1967. Freelance producer L.A.; prin. Frankish Inc., L.A. Producer (film) Vice Squad, 1981, (TV series) Max Headroom, 1987; assoc. producer: (films) Elephant Parts, 1981, Strange Brew, 1982, The Boy Who Could Fly, 1985, In the Mood, 1986; exec. producer, unit prodn. mgr. (film) Field of Dreams, 1989; 1st asst. dir.: (TV shows) Big Shamus, 1979, Skag, 1979, Why Me?, 1983, Making Out, 1984, Berrengers, 1984, (films) Strange Brew, 1982, Uncle Joe Shannon, 1978, Savage Harvest, 1980, Dead and Buried, 1980, Spring Break, 1982, Brainstorm, 1982-83, The Last Starfighter, 1983, The New Kids, 1983, Aloha Summer, 1984, The Best of Times, 1985, Odd Jobs, 1985; unit prodn. mgr. Second Serve, 1986; distbr.'s rep. and completion bond rep. Made in Heaven, 1986; other prodn. credits include: Play it Again, Sam, 1971, Everything You Always Wanted to Know About Sex..., 1972, Time to Run, 1972, Haunts, 1975, Mahogany (Montage), 1975, King Kong, 1976, The Betsy, 1977. Mem. Dirs. Guild Am., Nat. Acad. Cable Programming, Calif. Yacht Club. Republican. Home: 8162 Kirkwood Dr Los Angeles CA 90046

FRANKLIN, CHESTER ARTHUR, JR., mechanical engineer, executive; b. Baxter Springs, Kans., Sept. 17, 1934; s. Chester Arthur and Vera Zelma (Smith) F.; m. Sharon Kay Williams, Jan. 28, 1956 (div. Jan. 1961); 1 child, Elizabeth Ann; m. Sherill Helena Smith, Aug. 26, 1978; children: Bradley James, Christine Noelle, Courtenay Andrew. Student, L.A. Valley Coll., UCLA, Calif. State U., L.A., Calif. State U., Dominguez Hills, U. San Francisco. Prodn. leadman Janco Corp., Burbank, Calif., 1952-56; designer Bendix Aviation, North Hollywood, Calif., 1956-58; chief draftsman Telecomputing Corp., North Hollywood, 1958-60; prin. Work Ctr. Employment Agy., Van Nuys, Calif., 1960; mem. tech. staff indsl. products div. ITT, Sylmar, Calif., 1960-65; supr. design sect. Gilfillan div. ITT, L.A., 1965-66; project engr. advanced mech. labs. ITT, Chatsworth, Calif., 1966-68; mgr. engring. adminstrn., asst. dir. R&D Barton Instrument div. ITT, Monterey Park, Calif., 1968-71; prin. Cashea Enterprises, Inc., Torrance, Calif., 1971-85; design engr. Hughes Aircraft, El Segundo, Calif., 1985, 86, head mech. engring., 1986—; mgr. mech. engring. Satellite Tech. Mgmt., Torrance, 1985. Author: (play) Coming of the Zebra, 1969; patentee in field. Lay minister St. Andrew's Episc. Ch., Torrance, 1987-88. Mem. ASME, Soc. Mfg. Engrs., Nat. Assn. Watch and Clock Collectors, Lions. Home: 27999 Kalmia Ave Moreno Valley CA 92360

FRANKLIN, DAVID JANSEN, teacher; b. Des Moines, Dec. 29, 1951; s. Wesley Ernest and Phyllis Jean (Jansen) F.; m. Helen Irene Sherman. BS in Geology, Engring. Sci., Iowa State U., 1974, MS in Material Sci., 1976; cert. tchr., Boise (Idaho) State U., 1984. Cert. secondary tchr., Idaho; registered engr.-in-tng., Idaho. Supr. Bunker Hill Co., Kellogg, Idaho, 1976-82; tchr. Weiser (Idaho) High Sch., 1984—. Mem. Nat. Sci. Tchrs. Assn., Phi Beta Kappa. Home: 830 Pringle Rd Weiser ID 83672 Office: Weiser High Sch Rt 1 Box 22 Weiser ID 83672

FRANKLIN, DELANCE FLOURNOY, horticulture educator; b. Yakima County, Wash., Apr. 9, 1909; s. Watson Miller Taylor and Hattie Belle (Flournoy) F.; m. Florence Rebecca Kooser, Sept. 3, 1935; children: De-Lance Flournoy Jr., Eleanor Gay. BS in Agriculture, U. Idaho, 1942, MS in Agriculture, 1955. Food products inspector Idaho State Dept. Agriculture, 1928-39; asst. horticulturist U. Idaho, Parma, 1942-45, assoc. horticulturist, 1945-50; supr. Agricultural Research and Extension Ctr., Parma, 1942-74; research prof. horticulture U. Idaho, Parma, 1950-74, research prof. emeritus, 1974—; collaborator USDA, 1942-74, cons. 1974—; cons. to U.N., Cairo, 1974; chmn., co-founder Nat. Carrot and Onion Improvement Program, 1960; originator numerous F, hybrid onions and carrots; sec. Idaho Seed Council, 1955-73; cons. Vegetable Seed Prodn. and Breeding, 1974—. Contbr. numerous articles to profl. jours. Trustee Parma Devel. Corp., 1955-60, Sch. Bd., Parma, 1945-50, Idaho State Redevel. Bd., Boise, 1968-74. Named Disting. Citizen, Idaho Statesman Newspaper, 1968, Man-of-Yr., Pacific Seedsmen's Assn., 1968; recipient Disting. Service award Idaho-Eastern Oreg. Seed Assn., 1971, U. Idaho Gold and Silver award, 1985. Mem. Idaho Seed Council (hon.), Idaho Seed Assn. (hon.), Parma C. of C. (pres. 1943-45), Nat. Carrot and Onion Confs., SW Idaho-Eastern Oreg. Onion Assn. (Hall of Fame 1987), Am. Hort. Sci., Nat. Soc. Horticulturists, Entomologists and Plant Pathologists (pres. 1958-59), Shriners, Lions (pres. Parma club 1949—), Sigma Xi, Alpha Zeta (Chancellor 1941—), Phi Gamma Delta, Gamma Sigma Delta. Republican. Home: 227 N 10th St Parma ID 83660

FRANKLIN, SAMUEL DAVID, communications executive; b. Cin., May 25, 1957; s. Ralph and Leah Ann (Billingsley) F. BA in Psychology, Stanford U., 1979. Office svc. technician Dictaphone, Mountain View, Calif., 1981-83; facility coord. 3 Com Corp., Mountain View, 1984-86; telecom coord. 3 Com Corp., Santa Clara, Calif., 1986—. Democrat. Jewish. Office: 3 Com Corp 3165 Kifer Rd Santa Clara CA 95052

FRANKS, GARY LEE, engineering and construction company executive; b. Spokane, Wash., Sept. 9, 1950; m. Aleta G. Franks, June 14, 1975; children: Benjamin, Marissa. BA in Bus. Adminstrn., BS in Engring. and Constrn. Mgmt., Wash. State U., 1973. Project control mgr. Fluor Corp., Irvine, Calif., London and South Africa, 1973-79; project engr. Stearns-Roger Corp., Denver, 1979-80, Rust Internat. Corp., Portland, Oreg., 1980—. Mem. Project Mgmt. Inst., Tau Beta Pi. Office: Rust Internat PO Box 25374 Portland OR 97225

FRANSON, PAUL OSCAR, III, public relations executive; b. Tampa, Fla., Jan. 22, 1941; s. Paul O. and Kathleen (Collins) F.; m. Theodora L. Nelson, Dec. 29, 1959 (div. 1986); children—Chris Soden, Wendy. B.S., Davidson Coll., 1961. Editor 73 Mag., Peterborough, N.H., 1964-67; bur. mgr. Electronics mag., Dallas, Los Angeles, 1970-75, EDN mag., San Jose, Calif., 1975-77; editor Electronic Bus. mag., Boston, 1977; pres. Franson & Assocs., Inc., San Jose, 1980—. Contbr. articles to profl. jours. Bd. dirs. Children's Discovery Mus., San Jose, 1975—. Office: Franson & Assocs Inc 181 Metro Dr Suite 300 San Jose CA 95110

FRANTZ, JEANNETTE LOUISE, nurse; b. Pueblo, Colo., Dec. 4, 1959; d. Robert O. and Barbara Anne (Stavast) F. AA, U. Southern Colo., 1981, BS in Nursing, 1985. RN, Colo. Nurse St. Mary-Corwin Hosp., Pueblo, 1981—. Violinist Peublo Symphony Assn., 1978-85; soprano Pueblo Symphony Chorale, 1978-86. Republican. Methodist. Home: 449 Westwood Ln Pueblo CO 81005 Office: St Mary-Corwin Hosp 1008 Minnequa Ave Pueblo CO 81005

FRANTZ, SHARON PATRICIA, transport coordinator; b. Toronto, Ontario, Can., Nov. 10, 1953; came to U.S., 1966; d. John R. and Patricia J. (Payne) Hammond; 1 child, Christopher Shawn. BSN, U. Ariz, 1981; MBA, U. Phoenix, 1988. RN, Ariz.; cert. emergency nurse. Lab asst. U. Ariz., Tucson, 1976-81; staff nurse, surgical intensive care U. Health Sci. Ctr., Tucson, 1981-82, staff nurse, emergency svcs., 1982-87; flight nurse Medtran, Tucson, 1985-87; surgery biller U. Physicians, Inc., Tucson, 1987-88; transport coord. U. Med. Ctr., Tucson, 1988—; instr. advanced cardiac life support, U. Med. Ctr., Tucson, 1984-87. Contbr. articles profl. jours. Active, Boy Scouts Am., Tucson, 1985-88; vol. Therapeutic Riding of Tucson, 1988—. Recipient Cert. Appreciation, Pima County Sheriff's Dept., Tucson, 1983. Mem. Emergency Nurses Assn., Nat. Flight Nurses Assn. (Ariz. chpt. found. com. 1988—), Assn. Aero Med. Svcs., So. Ariz. Rescue Assn. Roman Catholic. Office: Univ Med Ctr 1501 N Campbell Ave Tucson AZ 85724

FRANTZ, THEODORE CLAUDE, fisheries biologist; b. Reno, Jan. 27, 1922; s. Theodore and Alma Natalia (Swanson) F.; B.S. in Biology, U. Nev., 1951. Researcher stream and lake surveys Nev. Dept. Wildlife, 1951-58, mgr. fisheries Eastern Nev., 1958-60, researcher interstate fisheries study, Lake Tahoe, Nev., 1960-65, mgr. fisheries Western Nev., Smith, 1965—. Mem. Lake Tahoe Basin Environ; Coms., 1970-72; mem. tech. resource team Lake Tahoe Regional Planning Agy., 1982-85. With USNR, 1942-45. Recipient Nev. Fish and Game Fisheries Project, 1964, Shikar Safari Internat. award, 1981; commended by Lake Tahoe Area Council, 1972. Mem. Am. Fisheries Soc., Wildlife Soc. Contbr. articles on fisheries research to tech. jours. Home and Office: PO Box 50 Smith NV 89430

FRANZ, JENNIFER DANTON, public opinion and marketing researcher; b. Oakland, Calif., Oct. 31, 1949; d. Joseph Periam and Lois (King) Danton; m. William Edwin Behnk, July 30, 1978. BA, Antioch Coll. West, 1973; MA, Stanford U., 1974. Cert. Community Coll. Student Personnel Worker, Calif., Community Coll. Supr., Calif. Cons. Alum Rock Union Elem. Sch. Dist., San Jose, Calif., 1973-75; rsch. asst. Far West Lab. for Ednl. Rsch. and Devel., San Francisco, 1974-75; project dir. Hartnell Coll., Salinas, Calif., 1975-77; project dir. Chancellor's Office Calif. Community Colls., Sacramento, 1978-80; pres., owner J.D. Franz Rsch., Sacramento, 1981—. Contbr. numerous articles to profl. jours. Mem. small bus. adv. com. Calif. State Sen., Sacramento, 1986—. Recipient various rsch., svc. awards. Mem. Am. Mktg. Assn., Am. Assn. Pub. Opinion Rsch., Am. Ednl. Rsch. Assn. (editor 1984-86, mem. Div. H Evaluation Steering Com. 1984-85, pol. edn. spl. interest group, survey rsch. spl. interest group, judge Div. H Awards Competition 1984, program reviewer 1982—), Mktg. Rsch. Assn., Calif. Ednl. Rsch. Assn., Calif. State Senate Select Com., Sacramento Met. C. of C. (state govt. affairs, local govt. affairs, small bus. advocacy coms. 1985—), Sacramento Valley Mktg. Assn. Democrat. Episcopalian. Office: JD Franz Rsch 2100 Northrop Ave Ste A-200 Sacramento CA 95815

FRANZ, JOHN JOSEPH, manufacturing and consulting engineer; b. Chgo., July 22, 1927; s. John Joseph and Anna May (Sholtz) F.; m. Ethel Kalas, July 14, 1951; children: Gail, Andrew, Thomas, Elaina. BA, Calif. State U.-Fullerton, 1975. Registered profl. engr., Calif. Project engr. Beckman Instruments Co., Fullerton, 1964-70; tooling mgr. Weiser Co., South Gate, Calif., 1970-74; mfg. engr. Clemar Corp., Azusa, Calif., 1976-79, Keyboard Co., Garden Grove, Calif., 1980-82; sr. mech. engr. Optical Radiation Corp., Azusa, 1979-80; sr. mfg. engr. Weslock Corp., L.A., 1980—. Patentee rotor and shaft assembly for variable resistor. With USN, 1945-48, PTO. Fellow Nat. Soc. Profl. Engrs., Calif. Soc. Profl. Engrs.; mem. Soc. Mfg. Engrs. (2d vice chmn. 1979-80), Am. Soc. for Metals, Melody Rounders Dance Club. Republican. Roman Catholic. Home: 15505 E Rojas St Hacienda Heights CA 91745 Office: Weslock Corp 13344 S Main St Los Angeles CA 90061

FRANZETTI, TONY RAYMOND, restaurant and hotel executive; b. Berne, Switzerland, Mar. 18, 1950; came to U.S., 1983; s. Raymondo and Helen Elisabeth (Muehlemann) F.; m. Anita M. Kuebler, July 14, 1978 (div. Jan. 1988); 1 child, Sandro R. Grad. summa cum laude, Lausanne Sch. Hotel Mgmt., 1971. Food and beverage mgr. Intercontinental Hotels, Rio de Janeiro, 1977-81; exec. asst. mgr. Intercontinental Hotels, London, 1981-82; resident mgr. Intercontinental Hotels, Paris, 1982-83; mgr., gen. mgr. Intercontinental Hotels, San Diego, 1983-88; owner, pres. Carmel Valley Ptnrs., Inc., Carmel, Calif., 1988—; interior designer Lon Yatman, L.A., 1987-88. Mem. mktg. com. Conv. and Visitors Bur., San Diego, 1988. Capt. Swiss Army, 1969-77. Office: Carmel Valley Ptnrs Inc 3626 The Barnyard Carmel CA 93923

FRAPPIA, LINDA ANN, management executive; b. St. Paul, May 14, 1946; d. Orville Keith Ferguson and Marilyn Ardis (Morris) Bidwell; 1 child, Jennifer. Grad. high sch., Seattle. Cert. claims adminstr. Claims rep. Fireman's Fund Ins., L.A., 1965-68; adminstrv. asst. to v.p. Employee Benefits Ins., Santa Ana, Calif., 1969-72; claims specialist Indsl. Indemnity Ins., Orange, Calif., 1972-83; claims supr. CNA Ins., Brea, Calif., 1983-86; claims mgr. EBI Ins. Svcs., Tustin, Calif., 1986; v.p. United Med. Specialists, Santa Ana, 1986—; chief executive officer United Chiropractic Specialists, Santa Ana, 1988—; instr. Ins. Edn. Assn., Brea, 1988—; speaker Western Info. Service, Orange, 1976-83. Mem. Calif. Mfrs. Assn., Pub. Agencies Risk Mgmt. Assn., Calif. Self-Insured Assn., Toastmasters Internat. (v.p. Orange chpt. 1978). Republican.

FRASCO, DAVID LEE, chemistry educator; b. Brush, Colo., Apr. 8, 1931; s. Anthony Eric and Elma Arlene (Bartram) F.; m. Nancy Ann Morrison, Aug. 29, 1954 (dec. Oct. 1975); children: Michael, Eric; m. Emilie Gwyn Williams, Oct. 8, 1976; stepchildren: Bradley, Barry. BA, No. Colo. U., 1953; MS, Wash. State U., 1955, PhD, 1958. Teaching asst. Wash. State U., Pullman, 1953-56, research asst., 1956-58; cons. Battelle Northwestern Labs., Richland, Wash., 1966-75; prof. chemistry Whitman Coll., Walla Walla, Wash., 1958—, chmn. dept. chemistry, 1984—. Contbr. articles to profl. jours. Mem. Sigma Xi.

FRASER, CLAYTON BOYD, architect; b. St. Paul, July 4, 1952; s. Ronald Chester and Lorraine Marie (Nadon) F.; m. Susan Lynn Cason, July 2, 1977; 1 child, Cody Laurel. BArch, U. Tenn., 1974. Historical architect Hist. Am. Bldgs. Survey, Washington, 1974-75, Wyo. Hist. Preservation Office, Cheyenne, 1975-77, 80; archtl. designer Thomas Muths & Assoc., Jackson, Wyo., 1977-78, Terrestria Design and Planning, Loveland, Colo., 1978-80; project supr. Hist. Am. Bldgs. Survey, Loveland, 1978; prin. Fraserdesign, Loveland, 1980--; cons. in field. Author, photographer: Historic Bridges of Colorado, 1986, Behemoths, 1989; co-author, photographer: Promised Land on the Solomon, 1986, Beyond the Wasatch, 1989. Mem. Wyo. Gov.'s Cons. Com. on Hist. Preservation, Cheyenne, 1980--; mem. Colo. Pub. Interest Research Group, Denver, 1986--. Mem. Soc. Indsl. Archeology, Nat. Trust for Hist. Preservation, Assn. for Preservation Tech., Colo. Hist. Soc., Friends of Photography, Camera Club. Home: 2868 Sally Ann Dr Loveland CO 85037

FRASER, KATHRYN LUCILLE, psychotherapist; b. Swea City, Iowa, Oct. 16, 1925; d. Albert B. and Annette Lillian (Anderson) Tweeten; m. Robert H. Fraser, Apr. 19, 1952 (div. 1968); children: Susan Elizabeth, Nancy Jane. BA cum laude, St. Olaf Coll., 1947; postgrad., U. Colo., 1949; MA, U. Iowa, 1953; postgrad., UCLA, 1961, Calif. State U., Long Beach, 1964-70, Chapman Coll., 1974, Calif. State U., Los Angeles, 1973; PhD, Calif. Grad. Inst., 1979. Cert. counselor, instr.; lic. counselor, secondary tchr., sch. psychologist, pupil personnel services, Calif. Tchr. St. James (Minn.) High Sch., 1947-50; counselor Davenport (Iowa) High Sch., 1951-52; tchr. high sch. Pasedena (Calif.) Sch. Dist., 1953-54; tchr. high sch. Downey Unified Sch. Dist., 1965-68, counselor, 1968-75; psychotherapist, prin. AID In Developing Counseling Service, Downey, 1976—; assoc. staff Rio Hondo Hosp., Downey, 1984—, Charter Hosp. Long Beach, 1984—, Los Altos Hosp. and Mental Health Ctr., Long Beach, 1987—. Bd. dirs. Downey Symphonic Soc., 1965-83, women's com., 1965—; pres. Choral Soc. So. Calif., Beverly Hills, 1985—; active First Presbyn. Ch., Downey, 1958—. Mem. Am. Assn. Counseling and Devel., Am. Mental Health Counselors Assn., AAUW, Calif. Assn. Marriage and Family Therapists, Calif. State Psychol. Assn. Democrat. Office: AID In Developing Counseling Svcs 8207 3d St Ste 202 Downey CA 90241

FRASIER, WILLIAM MARSHALL, insurance company executive; b. McKook, Nebr., Oct. 14, 1946; s. Burnell Emerick and Jeanette Mae (Jorgensen) F.; m. Gail Jane Hudgins, Sept. 18, 1971; children: Jill Beth, Becky Anne, Timothy Ray. BS in Math., Colo. State U., 1969. Math tchr. Cen. High Sch., St. Louis, 1969-70; actuarial student Nelson & Warren, Inc., St. Louis, 1970-74; actuarial asst. Security Life of Denver, 1974-79, mgr. reins. tech. services, 1979-82, asst. v.p., 1982-85, 2nd v.p., 1986--. Area rep. West Jefferson Recreation Assn., Evergreen, Colo., 1987-88; bd. dirs. Girls' Softball League Jefferson County, 1986--. Mem. Kiwanis (local bd. dirs. 1988). Democrat. Home: 5086 Greenwood Ct Evergreen CO 80439 Office: Security Life of Denver 1290 Broadway Denver CO 80203

FRAY, MARTHA JANE, investment banker; b. Frankfurt, Fed. Republic of Germany, June 2, 1952; d. John Aaron and Joann (Isaacson) F.; m. Karl Garthwaite Smith, Aug. 1, 1981. BA cum laude, Smith Coll., 1974; MArch, Yale U., 1981, M. Pub. and Pvt. Mgmt., 1981. Henry Luce fellow Sun Hung Kai & Co., Hong Kong, 1981-82; officer Hong Kong and Shanghai Banking Corp., Hong Kong, 1982-83; mng. dir. Fray & Co. Ltd., Hong Kong, 1983-86, Leach McMicking & Co., San Francisco, 1986—; bd. dirs. Frye Copysystems, Inc. Des Moines, Hunter-Melnor, Inc., Memphis. Trustee Fourwinds Camp, Deer Harbor, Wash., 1987—; chair Smith Coll. Fundraising for No. Calif., 1988; active The Jr. League, San Francisco, 1986—; fundraiser Victory '88, Republican Party, San Francisco, 1988. Republican. Episcopalian.

FRAYSER, SUZANNE GARNETT, anthropologist, educator; b. Richmond, Va., July 11, 1943; d. Franklin Aubrey and Susan (Garnett) F.; m. George McGahey Wilson, Jan. 28, 1968 (div. 1974); m. Gary Lee Kaake, July 24, 1982. BA, Coll. William and Mary, 1965; MA, Cornell U., 1968, PhD, 1976. Researcher Cross-Cultural Cumulative Coding Ctr., Pitts., 1968-74; asst. prof. anthropology SUNY, Potsdam, 1974-79, George Washington U., Washington, 1980; vis. asst. prof. Colo. Coll., Colorado Springs, 1981-83; sr. rsch. analyst Sundel Rsch., Inc., Denver, 1983—; mem. faculty Univ. Coll., U. Denver, 1983-; cons. and lectr. in field. Contbr. numerous articles to profl. jours. Vol. Paramount Theater, Denver, 1982—; mem. exec. com. Colo. Com. for Women's History, Denver, 1983-85. Recipient Profl. Assoc. award East-West Ctr., 1977; Cornell U. fellow, 1968-69. Fellow Am. Anthrop Assn.; mem. Soc. for Sci. Study Sex (bd. dirs. 1987—, long-range planning com. 1988—, personnel com. 1988—, co-chmn. spl. interest group on cross-cultural rsch. on sexuality 1988—, chmn. Soc. for Sci. Study Sex/AAAS liaison com. 1988—), Soc. for Cross-Cultural Rsch. (sec.-treas. 1985-88), Colo. Assn. Sex Therapy (bd. dirs. 1988—), Soc. for Med. Anthropology, Soc. for Psychol. Anthropology, Nat. Assn. for Practice Anthropology, AAAS (rep.), Pi Beta Phi. Democrat. Presbyterian. Office: Box 1093 Conifer CO 80433

FRAZEE, RICHARD ORVILLE, SR., judge; b. Newark, Mar. 19, 1938; s. Walter Melvin and Alyce (Thomesen) F.; m. Elaine Wincek, Aug. 24, 1957; children: Richard O. Jr., Jill Suzanne. BSBA, UCLA, 1961; JD, U. Calif.-San Francisco, 1966. Bar: Calif. 1967. Pvt. practice Laguna Niguel, Calif., 1967-87; judge Orange County Superior Ct., Santa Ana, Calif., 1987—. 1st lt. U.S. Army, 1961-63. Mem. Calif. Judges Assn., Laguna Niguel C. of C. (bd. dirs. 1982-83) , Laguna Niguel Bus. Club (bd. dirs. 1981-82), Rotary (pres. 1986-87). Republican. Office: Orange County Superior Ct 700 Civic Center Dr W Santa Ana CA 92701

FRAZER, CLOYCE CLEMON, retired teacher; b. Warren, Ark., Jan. 2, 1919; s. Charles Columbus and Maude Mae (Jones) F.; m. Beverley Jane Mundorff, Apr. 10, 1942. BA, Calif. State U.-San Jose, 1952, MA, Calif. State U.-Sacramento, 1961. Cert. spl. secondary life diploma in indsl. arts, 1959, gen. secondary life diploma, 1960, standard teaching credentials life, 1971, services, 1971 (all Calif.); FAA comml. pilot lic. with flight instr. cert., 1949, aircraft and power plant lic., 1948. Aircraft mechanic, flight instr., Oakland, Calif., 1946-50; tchr. Folsom (Calif.) Unified Sch. Dist., 1953-54, Sacramento City Unified Sch. Dist., 1954-63; tchr. San Mateo (Calif.) Union High Sch. Dist., 1963-83, dept. head, 1963-73, program evaluator, 1976-77. Pres., Crestmoor High Sch. Faculty Assn., 1965-66; treas. Calif. Aerospace Edn. Assn., 1983—, pres. No. sect., 1978-79; mem. advocacy com. San Mateo County Commn. on Aging. Served to major USAF, 1941-79. Recipient honorable mention for sculpture San Mateo County Fair and Floral Fiesta, 1967. Mem. NEA, Calif. Tchrs. Assn., Calif. Ret. Tchrs. Assn. (pres. San Mateo County div. 1986—), Air Force Assn., Calif. Indsl. Edn. Assn., Vocat. Edn. Assn., Am. Craft Council, Aircraft Owners and Pilots Assn., Exptl. Aircraft Assn. (Individual Achievement award 1982), Res. Officers Assn. U.S., Epsilon Pi Tau. Democrat. Club: Caterpillar. Contbr. articles to profl. jours.; co-author curriculum materials. Home: 620 Alameda Belmont CA 94002

FRAZER, IRA, lawyer; b. Jersey City, June 22, 1954; s. Jesse and Rita Belle (Malofsky) F.; m. Judy Ann Prell, Dec. 28, 1986. BS in Econs., U. Pa., 1975; MBA in Fin., U. Chgo., 1977; JD, U. Mich., 1980. Bar: Calif. 1980, U.S. Tax. Ct. 1980, U.S. Ct. Appeals (9th cir.) 1980, U.S. Dist. Ct. (cen. dist.) Calif. 1981, U.S. Dist. Ct. (so. dist.) Calif. 1984. Bus. assoc. Kindel & Anderson, L.A., 1980-83; sr. assoc. McKenna, Conner & Cuneo, Costa Mesa, Calif., 1983-86; v.p. First Alliance Fin. Group, Santa Ana, Calif., 1986-87; counsel Exec. Life Ins. Co., L.A., 1987-88; co-counsel PMC, Inc., Sun Valley, Calif., 1988—; adj. prof. Nat. U., Irvine, Calif., 1988—; cert. inst. Calif. Dept. Real Estate, 1987—. Bd. dirs. Am. Jewish Com., 1985—; active Town Hall, World Affairs Coun. Named Outstanding Young Leader, Am. Jewish Com. Orange County, 1987. Mem. ABA, Assn. Am. Corp. Counsels, Western Pension Conf., Mortgage Inst. Calif. (bd. dirs.) Orange County Bar Assn., L.A. County Bar Assn. Home: 26 Orangegrove Irvine CA 92714 Office: PMC Inc 12243 Branford St PO Box 1367 Sun Valley CA 91353-1367

FRAZIER, DEAN SPALDING, mathematics educator; b. Honolulu, Apr. 13, 1939; s. Dale Ira and Myra Spalding (Gray) F.; m. Nancy Amelia Staron, Mar. 8, 1973; children: April Joyce, Amelia Jan, Natalie Ann. BS in Engring., U.S. Mil. Acad., 1961; MS in Maths., U. Hawaii, 1972, MS in Physics, Astronomy and Edn., 1973. Cert. maths. educator, Hawaii. Commd. 2d lt. U.S. Army, 1961, advanced through grades to capt., 1964; served as unit comdr. U.S. Army, various locations including Korea and Vietnam; resigned U.S. Army, 1969; prof. physics U. Hawaii, Honolulu, 1969-73, tchr. maths., 1973; tchr. maths. Hawaii Dept. Edn., Honolulu, 1973—; fin. cons. Futures, Inc., Honolulu, 1977—. Author: The '80s Bull Market, 1981, Profit Compounding, 1982, Risk/Reward, 1983, The Mathematics of Winning, 1985. Group leader Neighborhood Bd., Honolulu, 1974-86. Mem. NEA, U.S. Parachute Assn., Nat. Assn. Maths. Tchrs., Hawaii State Tchrs. Assn., Citizens for Sound Economy, Greenpeace, Cousteau Soc., NAUI, Masons. Home: 94-567 Kuaie St Mililani Town HI 96789 Office: Aiea Intermediate Sch 99-600 Kulawea St Aiea HI 96701

FRAZIER, J(OHN) PHILLIP, manufacturing company executive; b. Beech Grove, Ind., Mar. 2, 1939; s. Stanley C. and Dorothy E. Frazier; m. Carole Gilbert, Aug. 15, 1964; children: Gregory and Bradley (twins), Natalie. BS, Butler U., 1965; MBA, Harvard U., 1969. Acct. Wolf & Co., Indpls., 1962-65; acct. Cummins Engine Co., Inc., Columbus, Ind., 1965-73, controller, 1970-73; pres., chief exec. officer Hyster Co., Portland, Oreg., 1973—, also bd. dirs.; bd. dirs. Guy F. Atkinson Co. Calif. Bd. dirs. United Way-Columbia Willamette. Served with USAR, 1957-61. Mem. Harvard U. Bus. Sch. Assn. (past pres., chmn. Oreg. chpt), Portland Golf Club, Arlington Club. Republican. Presbyterian. Home: 722 NW Albemarle Terr Portland OR 97210 Office: Hyster Co 2701 NW Vaughn Ste 900 Portland OR 97210

FRAZIER, ROBERT WOOD, stock market technician; b. Seattle, Sept. 19, 1941; s. James Wood and Ali-Lou (Jamison) F. BA in Bus. Adminstrn., U. Wash., 1967. Lending officer Peoples Nat Bank, Bremerton, Wash., 1971-72; ind. stock market technician Seattle, 1973--. Treas. Assn. King County Hist. Orgns., 1984--. Mem. Am. Assn. Ind. Investors, Coll. Club, Phi Kappa Psi. Home: 2406 Bigelow Ave N Seattle WA 98109

FREAS, GEORGE CRAIG, civil engineer; b. New Brunswick, N.J., Mar. 23, 1947; s. George Edwin and Virginia Grace (Woolnough) F.; m. Carol Louise Lease, June 22, 1969 (div. 1980); children: Miriam Rebekah, Virginia Elizabeth; m. Nancy Jean Cliff, May 21, 1983. BSCE, Pa. State U., 1969. Registered profl. engr., Alaska, Alta., Guam. Project engr. Wince-Corthell & Assocs., Kenai, Alaska, 1972-78; prin. Wince-Corthell-Bryson-Freas, Kenai, 1978-80; mgr. civil engring. Tryck Nyman & Hayes, Anchorage, 1980-84, ptnr., 1984-88; sr. project mgr. R&M Cons., Anchorage, 1988—. Served with USN, 1970-72. Mem. ASCE, Am. Concrete Inst., Soc. Am. Mil. Engrs., Prestressed Concrete Inst., Assn. Profl. Engrs., Geologists and Geophysicists of Alta. Home: 1004 Potlatch Circle Anchorage AK 99503 Office: R&M Cons Inc 5024 Cordova St Anchorage AK 99503

FRECCIA, MICHAEL D., insurance executive; b. N.Y.C., Apr. 1, 1941; s. Sal R. and Lona (Urovsky) F.; m. Sirpa S. Kaloninen; children: Susan Tara, David Michael. BS, Cornell U., 1962. CLU. Owner, prin. Internat. Transp. Tariffs, N.Y.C., 1969-73; co-owner Alans Apparel for Men, Albuquerque, 1973-81; agt. Aetna Life Ins. Co., Albuquerque, 1981-83; dir. employee benefits Ins. Ctr., Albuquerque, 1983—. Pres. N.Mex. Symphony Orch., Albuquerque, 1989. Mem. Assn. Life Underwriters (Million Dollar Round Table, 1981-89). Office: Ins Ctr PO Box 90278 Albuquerque NM 87199

FREDERIC, ROBERT EUSTICE, printing company executive; b. Denver, Oct. 12, 1926; s. Homer Joseph and Agnes Josephine F.; m. Norma Lee Rogers, Jan. 27, 1951; children: Linda, Gail, Rand, Doug, Matt. BS in Bus., U. Colo., 1947. Pres., chief exec. officer Frederic Printing Co., Aurora, Colo., 1947—; bd. dirs. Mountain States Bank, Denver, Independence Inst., Denver, Colo. Uplift Program, Denver; NFL referee, 1967-87. Mem. Nat. Assn. Printers and Lithographers, Printing Industries Am., Graphic Arts Tech. Found. (bd. dirs. 1987—). Republican. Roman Catholic. Office: Frederic Printing 14701 E 38th Ave Aurora CO 80011

FREDERICKS, WARD ARTHUR, technology executive; b. Tarrytown, N.Y., Dec. 24, 1939; s. Arthur George and Evelyn (Smith) F.; BS cum laude, Mich. State U., 1962, MBA, 1963; m. Patricia A. Sexton, June 12, 1960; children: Corrine E., Lorrine L., Ward A. Assoc. dir. Technics Group, Grand Rapids, Mich., 1964-68; gen. mgr. logistics systems Massey-Ferguson Inc., Toronto, 1968-69, v.p. mgmt. services, comptroller, 1969-73, sr. v.p. fin., dir. fin. Americas, 1975—; comptroller Massey-Ferguson Ltd., Toronto, Ont., Can., 1973-75; cons. W.B. Saunders & Co., Washington, 1962—; sr. v.p. mktg. Massey/Ferguson, Inc., 1975-80, also sr. v.p., gen. mgr. Tractor div., 1978-80; v.p. ops., Rockwell Internat., Pitts., 1980-84; v.p. Fed. MOG., 1983-84; pres. MIXTEC Corp., 1984—, also dir., chmn.; dir. Badger Northland Inc., Tech-Mark Group Inc., SPECTRA Tech., Inc., MIXTEC Corp., Compu-Kore Ltd., Unicorn Corp., Harry Ferguson Inc., M.F. Credit Corp., M.F. Credit Co. Can. Ltd. Bd. dirs., mem. exec. com. Des Moines Symphony, 1975-79; exec. com. Conejo Symphony, pres. 1988-90; mem. exec. com. Alliance for Arts.; mem. Constn. Bicentennial Com., 1987-88, v.p. Com. Leaders Club, 1988, pres., 1989, Gov.'s Task Force on Tech., Am. Transp. Assn. fellow, 1962-63; Ramlose fellow, 1962-63. Mem. Am. Mktg. Assn., Nat. Council Phys. Distbn. Mgmt. (exec. com. 1974), IEEE, Soc. Automotive Engrs., U.S. Strategic Inst., Tech. Execs. Forum, Toronto Bd. Trade, Westlake Village C. of C. (chmn.), Old Crows, Assn. for Advanced Tech. Edn., Community Leaders Club, Pres.'s Club Mich. State U., Rotary, Beta Gamma Sigma. Author: (with Edward W. Smykay) Physical Distribution Management, 1974, Management Vision, 1988; contbr. articles to profl. jours. Office: 32123 Lindero Canyon Rd Westlake Village CA 91361 also: 625 I St Washington DC 20001

FREDERICKSON, ARMAN FREDERICK, minerals company executive; b. Glenbore, Man., Can., May 5, 1918; came to U.S., 1923, naturalized, 1940; s. Albert F. and Ethel M. (Wilton) F.; m. Mary Maxine Stubblefield, Sept. 23, 1943; children—Mary Christene, Clover Diane, Penny Kathlene, Kimberly Mei, Sigrid, Janice. B.S. in Mining Engring, U. Wash., 1940; M.S. in Metall. Engring, Mont. Sch. Mines, 1942; Sc.D. in Geology, Mass. Inst. Tech., 1947. Registered profl. engr., Tex., Colo., Nev., Mo.; cert. petroleum geologist. Mining engr., chief geologist Cornucopia Gold Mines, Oreg., 1939-40; instr. mineral dressing Mont. Sch. Mines, 1941-42; research asst. Mass. Inst. Tech., 1942-43; prof. geology and geol. engring. Washington U., St. Louis, 1947-56; organizer, supr. geol. research Standard (Amoco) Oil and Gas Co., Tulsa, 1955-60; prof. geology, chmn. dept. earth and planetary sci., dir. oceanography U. Pitts., 1960-65; sr. v.p., dir. research, mgr. petroleum prospecting and mineral programs in U.S., Middle East, Africa, Latin Am., 1965-71; pres., chief engr. Sorbotec, Inc., Houston, 1971-74; pres. Global Survey, 1972—; v.p. Samoco (Panama), Challenger Desert Oil Corp., 1977-81; cons. in mining and petroleum exploration, 1971—; v.p. SAMOCO, Del.,

1977-81, Panama, 1977-81; v.p. ops. CHADOIL, 1978-81, Crown Gens, Inc., Thailand; Organizer, past chmn. clay minerals com. Nat. Acad. Sci.-NRC; organizer, econ. analyst of land and real estate projects, Calif.; negotiator oil, gemstone and mining programs, U.S., Africa, Thailand, Middle and Far East, Latin Am., Africa; specialist in on-shore and off-shore exploration in S. Africa, Egypt, Syria. Author papers in field; patentee fertilizer, oil and water pollution processes and products. Served with USNR, 1943-45. Fulbright prof. Norway, 1955. Fellow Geol. Soc. Am., Mineral Soc. Am.; mem. Am. Inst. Mining, Metall. and Petroleum Engrs., Am. Assn. Petroleum Geologists, Soc. Econ. Geologists, Geochem. Soc. Am., Underwater Soc. Am. Republican. Lutheran. numerous clubs. Office: Global Survey Inc 25221 Perch Dana Point CA 92629

FREDERIKSEN, PAUL ASGER, lawyer; b. Copenhagen, June 1, 1946; came to U.S., 1954; s. George A. and Valborg (Andersen) F.; m. Brenda Jane Pazaricky; children: Cassandra, Anders. BA, U. Kans., 1970; postgrad., So. Bapt. Sem., Louisville, 1971; JD, U. Colo., 1976. Bar: Colo. 1976. Pvt. practice Boulder and Denver, Colo., 1976-81; assoc. Hemminger & Frederiksen, Englewood, Colo., 1981-82; ptnr. Hemminger & Frederiksen, Englewood, 1982-86, mng. ptnr., 1986--. Chmn. tnr. com. Longs Park council Boy Scouts Am., Greeley, 1975-77; founder, chmn. bd. Christian Conciliation Svc. Denver, 1980--; com. mem. Douglas County Dem. Com., 1986--. Mem. ABA, Colo. Bar Assn. (vice chmn. tech. com. 1988--), Douglas County Bar Assn. (sec. 1988--), Am. Arbitration assn., Christian Legal Soc. (conciliation com. 1980-86). Office: Hemminger & Frederiksen 13111 E Briarwood Ave Ste 250 Englewood CO 80112 also: 11479 S Pine Dr Parker CO 80134

FREDMAN, DANIEL JOSEPH, psychiatrist; b. La Salle, Ill., July 9, 1949; s. Avery Leon and Henrietta (Anderman) F.; m. Susan Arenson, Dec. 1981 (div. July 1983); m. Jill Melanie Sosin, Feb. 19, 1989. Student, U. Wis., 1967-69, Hebrew U., Jerusalem, 1969-70; BA in Biology, U. Mo., St. Louis, 1971; MD, U. Autonoma Guadalajara, 1975. Diplomate Am. Bd. Psychiatry and Neurology. Intern in surgery Michael Reese Hosp. and Med. Ctr., Chgo., 1976-77, resident in psychiatry, 1977-81; pvt. practice Tucson, 1981—; psychiat. cons. U.S. Fed. Prison, Tucson, 1982—; clin. dir. adult svcs. Charter Hosp., Tucson, 1988-89. Contbr. chpts. to med. books. Mem. Am. Psychiat. Assn. Office: 2695 N Craycroft Rdr Ste 260 Tucson AZ 85712

FREDRICKSON, ROXANNA LYNN, program development specialist, college professor; b. Princeton, Minn., Nov. 2, 1952; d. Robert Wayne and Shirley Maye (Hovland) F; m. Nicholas J. Emslander, Aug. 26, 1978 (div. 1984). BA in English and Recreat, St. Cloud State U., 1975; MA in Health Adminstrn., U. Colo., Denver, 1988. Asst. community edn. dir. Buffalo Sch. Dist., Buffalo, Minn., 1979-77; mgr., real estate Westside Rental Advisors, Edina, Minn., 1978-79; asst. health dir. Mont. United Indian Assoc., Helena, Mont., 1981-83; coordinator of edn. programs St. Vincent Hosp., Billings, Mont., 1983-86, program devel. spl., 1986—; Grantsmanship, Mont., 1984-89; cons. No. Rockies Cancer Ctr., Billings, 1987-89; coll. prof. Ea. Mont. Coll., 1986-89. Mem. Nat. Review Com. Indian. Named Outstanding Young Woman, Outstanding Young Ams., 1986; scholar Health Svc. Rockville, Md., 1987-89. Mem. Am. Coll. Healthcare Exec., Am. Soc. Training and Devel. (state pres. 1987-88), Toastmasters Internat. (chpt. pres. 1987-88, dist. sec. 1988-89), Nat. Com. Prevention of Child Abuse (pres. 1989), Mont. and Billings JC's (outstanding 1st year 1986, State Speakup contest winner 1986, state and chpt. sec. 1986-88). Democrat. Lutheran. Home: 3567 Cambridge Billings MT 59101 Office: St Vincent Hosp 1241 N 30th St Billings MT 59101

FREEBY, WAYNE ALFRED, chemical engineer; b. Elkhart, Ind., Aug. 21, 1929; s. Wayne Leo and Luella Jane (Fishley) F.; m. Delores Jane Noffsinger, July 1, 1951; children: Steven Wayne, Linda Sue. BSChemE, Tri-State U., 1959; MSChemE, U. Idaho, 1966. Rsch. engr. Miles Labs., Elkhart, 1959-60; sr. reactor engr. Phillips Petroleum Co., Idaho Falls, Idaho, 1960-66; sr. engr. Idaho Nuclear Corp., Idaho Falls, 1966-70; supr., mgr. Allied Chem. Corp., ICP, Idaho Falls, 1970-79; mgr. Exxon Nuclear Idaho Co., Idaho Falls, 1979-80, Ford, Bacon & Davis Utah, Salt Lake City, 1980-81; mgr., supr. Bechtel Nat. Inc., San Francisco, 1981-87; staff engr. Westinghouse Idaho Nuclear Co., Idaho Falls, 1987—. Author of reports for profl. publs.; reviewer Nuclear Technology Journal, Am. Nuclear Soc., LaGrange Park, Ill., 1987-88; patentee in field. Troop leader Boy Scouts of Am., Idaho Falls, 1967-69. Corp. U.S. Army, 1952-54, Korea. Mem. Am. Nuclear Soc., Am. Inst. Chem. Engrs. (div. dir. 1984-86, div. vice chmn. 1987, div. chmn. 1988), Tam Twirlers Square Dance Club, Calif. (publicity chmn. 1984). Republican. Methodist. Home: 2147 Enell St Idaho Falls ID 83402 Office: Westinghouse Idaho Nuclear PO Box 4000 Idaho Falls ID 83403

FREED, LEWIS VAUGHAN, department head, teacher; b. Des Moines, Dec. 12, 1928; s. Lewis C. and Thelma (Vaughan) F.; m. June Ann Allenson, Nov. 21, 1951; children: Stephen L., Elizabeth L. BA, San Diego State U., 1951, MA, 1963. Cert. tchr., Calif. Tchr. math. Helix High Sch., La Mesa, Calif., 1955—, chair dept. math., 1972—; numerous presentations at workshops and math. confs., dist. and county of Calif. Lt. comdr. USNR, 1951-54, 61-62, Korea. Recipient Calif. award Calif. Sch. Adminstrs. Assn., 1985, Recognition award Calif. Assn. for Supervision and Curriculum Devel., 1984; named Tchr. of the Yr., San Diego County Dept. Edn., 1985, Math. Tchr. of the Yr., San Diego County Industry Edn. Coun., 1984. Mem. Grossmont Edn. Assn., Calif. Tchr.'s Assn., NEA, Nat. Coun. Tchrs. of Math. Office: Helix High Sch 7323 University Ave La Mesa CA 92041

FREEDMAN, DANIEL X., psychiatrist, educator; b. Lafayette, Ind., Aug. 17, 1921; s. Harry and Sophia (Feinstein) F.; m. Mary C. Neidigh, Mar. 20, 1945. B.A., Harvard U., 1947; M.D., Yale U., 1951; grad., Western New Eng. Inst. Psychoanalysis, 1966; D.Sc. (hon.), Wabash Coll., 1974, Indiana U., 1982. Intern pediatrics Yale Hosp., 1951-52, resident psychiatry, 1952-55; from instr. to prof. psychiatry Yale U., 1955-66; chmn. dept. U. Chgo., 1966-83, Louis Block prof. biol. scis., 1969-83; Judson Braun prof. psychiatry and pharmacology UCLA, 1983—; career investigator USPHS, 1957-66; dir. psychiatry and biol. sci. tng. program Yale U., 1960-66; cons. NIMH, 1960—, U.S. Army Chem. Center, Edgewood, Md., 1965-66; chmn. panel psychiat. drug efficacy study NAS-NRC, 1966; mem. adv. com. FDA, 1967-78; rep. to div. med. scis. NRC, 1971-82, mem. com. on brain scis., 1971-73, mem. com. on problems of drug dependence, 1971-83; mem. com. problems drug dependence Nat. Inst. Medicine, 1971-76, com. substance abuse, and habitual behavior, 1976-84; advisor Pres.'s Biomed. Research Panel, 1975-76; mem. selection com., coordinator research task panel Pres.'s Commn. Mental Health, 1977-78; mem. Joint Commn. Prescription Drug Use, Inc., 1977-80. Author: (with N.J. Giarman) Biochemical Pharmacology of Psychotomimetic Drugs, 1965, What Is Drug Abuse?, 1970, (with F.C. Redlich) The Theory and Practice of Psychiatry, 1966, (with D. Offer) Modern Psychiatry and Clinical Research, 1972; editor: (with J. Dyrud) American Handbook of Psychiatry, Vol. V, 1975, The Biology of the Major Psychoses: A Comparative Analysis, 1975; chief editor: Archives Gen. Psychiatry, 1970—. Bd. dirs. Founds. Fund for Research in Psychiatry, 1969-72, Drug Abuse Council, 1972-80; vice chmn. Drug Abuse Council Ill., 1972-82. Served with AUS, 1942-46. Recipient Distinguished Achievement award Modern Medicine, 1973; William C. Menninger award ACP, 1975; McAlpin medal for research achievement, 1979; Vestermark award for edn., 1981. Fellow Am. Acad. Arts and Scis., Am. Psychiat. Assn. (chmn. commn. on drug abuse 1971-78), Am. Coll. Neuropsychopharmacology (pres. 1970-71); mem. Inst. Medicine Nat. Acad. Scis., ACP (William C. Menninger award 1975), Ill. Psychiat. Soc. (pres. 1971-72), Social Sci. Research Council (dir. 1968-74), Chgo. Psychoanalytic Soc., Western New Eng. Psychoanalytic Inst., Am. Soc. Pharmacology and Exptl. Therapeutics, AAAS, Am. Assn. Chairmen Depts. Psychiatry (pres. 1972-73), Am. Psychiat. Assn. (v.p. 1975-77, pres.-elect 1980-81, pres. 1981-82), Group Advancement Psychiatry, Psychiat. Research Soc., Am. Psychosomatic Soc. (councillor 1970-73), Assn. Research in Nervous and Mental Disease (pres. 1974), Soc. Biol. Psychiatry (pres. 1985-86), Sigma Xi, Alpha Omega Alpha. Home: 806 Leonard Rd Los Angeles CA 90049 Office: UCLA Sch Medicine 760 Westwood Pla Los Angeles CA 90024

FREEDMAN, JAY MICHAEL, automobile care company executive, lawyer; b. Chgo., Aug. 25, 1939; s. Nathan and Adele (Klong) F.; m. Barbara Picker, Jan. 17, 1963 (div. 1972); children: Joel L., Lee, Keith, Mark; m. Nancy J. Biddick, Nov. 12, 1972. BA, Mich. State U., 1960; JD, U. Wis., 1963; DJP, U. Johannesburg, 1969. Bar: Ill. 1963. Assoc. Freeman, Liebling & Adelman, Chgo., 1963-65; ptnr. McCarty, Watson, Hootman & Freedman, Chgo., 1965-69, Freedman & Michaels, Chgo., 1969-74; sole practice Chgo., 1974-80; chief exec. officer Broken Bow Corp., Chgo., 1980-8l, L.G.I.C., Inc., L.A., 1981-87, Infotech Mgmt. Svcs., Inc., Long Island City, N.Y., 1983, Autocare Am., Inc., Denver, 1988—; cons., bd. dirs. Guarantee Ins. Agy. Inc., Skokie, 1967—; cons. Cogenco Corp., Denver, 1986-87, BPS Corp., New Orleans, 1987-88, Anchor Fin., L.A., 1988—; chmn. bd. Fuji Electrocell Corp., 1989—. Author: (novel) Fever of Violence, 1971. Kapp Found. fellow, 1962. Home: 1206 Grant St Santa Monica CA 90067 Office: Autocare Am Inc 4260 E Evans St Ste l Denver CO 80222 also: Fuji Electrocell Corp 9911 W Pico Blvd Ste 67253 Los Angeles CA 90035

FREEDMAN, JONATHAN BORWICK, journalist, columnist; b. Rochester, N.Y., Apr. 11, 1950; s. Marshall Arthur and Betty (Borwick) F.; m. Maggie Locke, May 4, 1979; children: Madigan, Nicholas. AB in Lit. cum laude, Columbia Coll., N.Y.C., 1972. Reporter AP of Brazil, Sao Paulo and Rio de Janeiro, 1974-75; editorial writer The Tribune, San Diego, 1981—; syndicated columnist Copley News Service, San Diego, 1987—; mem. U.S.-Japan Journalists Exchange Program, Internat. Press Inst., 1985. Author, illustrator: The Man Who'd Bounce the World, 1979; author: The Editorials and Essays of Jonathan Freedman, 1988; contbg. author: Best Newspaper Writing, 1986, The Pulitzer Prize Vol. 1, 1988; freelance columnist; contbr. articles to N.Y. Times, Chgo. Tribune, San Francisco Examiner, Oakland Tribune, others. Moderator PBS, San Diego, 1988; bd. dirs. Schs. of the Future Commn., San Diego, 1987. Cornell Woolrich Writing fellow Columbia U., 1972, Eugene C. Pulliam Editorial Writing fellow, Sigma Delta Chi Found., 1986; recipient Copley Ring of Truth award, 1983, Sigma Delta Chi award, 1983, San Diego Press Club award, 1984, Spl. Citation, Columbia Grad. Sch. Journalism, 1985, Disting. Writing award Am. Soc. Newspaper Editors, 1986, Pulitzer Prize in Editing. Editorial Writing, 1987. Mem. Soc. Profl. Journalists (Disting. Service award 1985), Nat. Conf. Editorial Writers, Phi Beta Kappa. Jewish. Office: The Tribune 350 Camino de la Reina San Diego CA 92112-4106

FREEDMAN, MERVIN BURTON, psychologist, educator; b. N.Y.C., Mar. 6, 1920; s. Eli and Rose (Weithorn) F.; m. Marjorie Ellingson, Feb. 16, 1952; children: Eric, Kristin, Rolf, Anne Marie. B.S., Coll. City N.Y., 1940; Ph.D., U. Calif. at Berkeley, 1950. Lectr. dept. psychology U. Calif. at Berkeley, 1950-53; research asso. Mellon Found. for Advancement Edn., Vassar Coll., 1953-58; dir. Mellon Found., 1958-60; research assoc. Inst. for Study Human Problems Stanford U., 1962-63, asst. dean undergrad. edn. Stanford U., 1963-65; chmn. dept. psychology San Francisco State U., 1965-68, prof. psychology, 1968—; dean grad. sch. Wright Inst., Berkeley, 1969-79; sr. Fulbright research scholar U. Oslo, 1961-62; fellow Center for Advanced Study Behavioral Sci., 1960-61. Author: The College Experience, 1967; (with others) Search for Relevance, 1969, Academic Culture and Faculty Development, 1978, Human Development in Social Settings, 1983, Personality and Social Change, 1986, Americans and the Irrational, 1988; Assoc. editor: Polit. Psychology. Vice pres. San Francisco Am.-Scandinavian Found. Served with AUS, 1941-45. Decorated Bronze Star. Fellow Am. Psychol. Assn.; mem. Western Psychol. Assn., Internat. Soc. Polit. Psychology. Home: 866 Spruce St Berkeley CA 94707 Office: San Francisco State U Dept Psychology San Francisco CA 94132

FREEDMAN, MICHAEL HARTLEY, mathematician, educator; b. Los Angeles, Apr. 21, 1951; s. Benedict and Nancy (Mars) F.; 1 child by previous marriage, Benedict C.; m. Leslie Blair Howland, Sept. 18, 1983; children: Hartley, Whitney. Ph.D., Princeton U., 1973. Lectr. U. Calif., 1973-75; mem. Inst. Advanced Study, Princeton, N.J., 1975-76; prof. U. Calif., San Diego, 1976—; Charles Lee Powell chair math. U. Calif., 1985—. Author: Classification of Four Dimensional Spaces, 1982; assoc. editor Jour. Differential Geometry, 1982—, Annals of Math., 1984—, Jour. Am. Math. Soc., 1987—. MacArthur Found. fellow, 1984-89; named Calif. Scientist of Yr., Calif. Mus. Assn., 1984; recipient Veblen prize Am. Math. Soc., 1986, Fields medal Internat. Congress of Mathematicians, 1986, Nat. Medal of Sci., 1987, Humboldt award, 1988. Mem. Nat. Acad. Scis., Am. Assn. Arts and Scis. Office: U Calif Dept Math La Jolla CA 92093-0112

FREEL, MARLIN JAMES, manufacturing executive; b. Glendive, Mont., Feb. 27, 1924; s. Amos F. and Beatrice (Polen) F.; children—Michael, Cynthia. B.S., U. So. Calif., 1948; postgrad. Woodbury Coll., 1955, UCLA, 1973, LaVerne U. Law, 1974. Pres., Sproco Mfg. Inc., 1949-58; v.p. Tasker Instruments, 1958-63, mgr. contracts TRW Systems Group, 1964-68, Litton Data Systems, 1968-72; legal asst. Ingram, Baker & Griffiths Law Office, Covina, Calif., 1972-78; pres. Ricon Corp., Ricon Internat., Inc. and Ricon Sales, Sun Valley, Calif., 1978—, Freel Enterprizes, Inc., 1984—, M. Freel and Assocs., 1968—. Chmn. Park and Recreation Dept. City of San Dimas (Calif.), 1979—; PTA sch. bd. rep. Bonita Sch. Dist.; scoutmaster Boy Scouts Am., Troop 106, Pomona, Calif. Served with USN, 1942-46. Mem. U. So. Calif. Assocs. Co-inventor wheelchair lift, 1982. Office: Ricon Corp 11684 Tuxford St Sun Valley CA 91352

FREELAND, ARTHUR GLENN, physician; b. Corpus Christi, Tex., Apr. 16, 1956; d. Max Quentin F. and Jeanette Elaine (Kidd) Hartje; m. Kelly Ann McDermott, Aug. 5, 1985. BS, NE Mo. State U., 1978; MD, U. Mo., 1982. Diplomate Am. Bd. Family Practice. Intern Family Practice Program U. Mo. Kansas City Truman Med. Ctr. East, 1982-83, resident Family Practice Program, 1983-85; physician Klamath Med. Clin., Klamath Falls, Oreg., 1985—; chmn. dept. obstetrics Merle West Med. Ctr., Klamath Falls, 1988—. Fellow Am. Acad. Family Physicians; mem. Aerospace Med. Assn., Klamath Acad. Family Physicians (pres. 1988—), Klamath County Med. Soc. (sec. 1987-88), Oreg. Med. Assn. Republican. Presbyterian. Office: Klamath Med Clin 1905 Main St Klamath Falls OR 97601

FREELAND, DARRYL CREIGHTON, psychologist, educator; b. Omaha, Feb. 22, 1939; s. Elverson Lafayette and Lauretta Joyce (Coffelt) F.; m. Tina Anne Richmond, July 21, 1979; children—Adam Daniel, Noah Nathan, Sarah Eileen. B.S., U. Nebr., 1961; S.T.B., Fuller Theol. Sem., 1965; M.A., Calif. State U.-Fullerton, 1966; Ph.D., U. So. Calif., 1972. Lic. psychologist, Calif.; lic. marriage, family and child therapist, Calif. Tchr. elem. schs., Calif., 1961-66; instr. Glendale Community Coll., Calif., 1966-67, Citrus Community Coll., Glendora, Calif., 1967-79; pvt. practice psychology, Laguna Niguel, Calif., 1969—; field faculty and vis. prof. Calif. State U.-Los Angeles, 1970, San Marino Community Presbyterian Ch., 1972, Calif. Sch. Profl. Psychology, Los Angeles, 1972-73, U. Calif.-Riverside, 1973, Humanistic Psychology Inst., San Francisco, 1976-79, Prof. U. Humanistic Studies, San Diego, 1983—; asst. dir. clin., M.F.T. tng. U.S. Internat. U., 1986—, assoc. prof. psychology, 1986-87; mem. pvt. post-secondary com. for qualitative rev. and assessment of licensure Calif. Dept. Edn., 1989—. Finisher, Newport Beach-Irvine Marathon, 1981, San Francisco Marathon, 1982, Long Beach Marathon, 1988. Office: 30131 Town Center Dr Ste 298 Laguna Niguel CA 92677

FREELAND, ROBERT FREDERICK, librarian; b. Flint, Mich., Dec. 20, 1919; s. Ralph V. and Susan Barbara (Goetz) F.; m. June Voshel, June 18, 1948; children: Susan Beth Visser, Kent Richard. BS, Eastern Mich. U., 1942; postgrad., Washington & Lee U., 1945; MS, U. So. Calif., 1948, postgrad., 1949; postgrad., U. Mich., 1950-52, Calif. State U., 1956-58, UCLA, 1960; LittD (hon.), Linda Vista Bible Coll., 1973. Music supr. Consol. Schs. Warren, Mich., 1946-47; music dir. Carson City (Mich.) Pub. Schs., 1948-49; librarian, audio-visual coord. Ford Found., Edison Inst., Greenfield Village, Dearborn, Mich., 1950-52, Helix High Sch. Library, 1952-77; librarian, prof. library sci. Linda Vista Bible Coll., 1976—; guest prof. Calif. State U., San Diego, 1963-66, U. Calif., San Diego, 1969-71, Linda Vista Bible Coll., 1970-72; lectr. San Diego City Coll., 1954-65, Grossmont Coll., El Cajon, 1966-68; librarian San Diego City Coll., 1953-54, San Diego County Library, 1955-56, San Diego Pub. Library, 1968—; cons. in edn., library and multi-media. Editor book and audio-visual aids review, Sch. Musician, Dir. and Teacher, 1950—. Former deacon and elder Christian Reform Ch., librarian, 1969-72; pub. affairs officer Calif. wing CAP. Served with USAAF, 1942-46. Named Scholar Freedoms Found., Valley Forge, Pa., 1976-80. Mem. NEA (life), ALA, Assn. for Ednl. Communication and Tech., Western Ednl. Soc. for Telecommunications, Calif. Tchrs. Assn., Music Library Assn. So. Calif. (adviser exec. bd.), Calif. Library Assn. (pres. Palomar chpt. 1972-73), Sch. Library Assn. Calif. (treas. 1956-58), Calif. Media and Library Educators (charter mem.), Am. Legion (Americanism chmn. 22d dist. San Diego County, chmn. oratorical contest com. La Mesa post), Ret. Officers Assn., San Diego Aero Space Mus., San Diego Mus. Art. Home: 4800 Williamsburg Ln Apt 223 La Mesa CA 92041 Office: Coll Library 2075 E Madison Ave El Cajon CA 92021

FREELAND, THOMAS BREEN, electronics manufacturing executive; b. Ft. Benning, Ga., Aug. 29, 1936; s. William H. and Louise (Breen) F.; m. Carole A. Sothmann, 1965; children: Amy, Anne, Michele, Kevin. Student, San Jose City Coll., 1959-60; grad., Duncan Sch. Flying, 1960. Materials mgr. TRW, Inc., San Luis Obispo, Calif., 1967-72; mgr. ops. Hewlett-Packard, Palo Alto, Calif., 1972-74; dir. mfg. General, Inc., Santa Clara, Calif., 1975-86; v.p. ops. Diasonics, Inc., Milpitas, Calif., 1988—; co-founder Pacific Electronic Mfg., Inc., 1980—. With USAF, 1954-58. Mem. Sunnyvale Svc. Athletic Club (pres.). Home: 1176 Sesame Dr Sunnyvale CA 94087 Office: Diasonics Inc 1565 Barber Ln Milpitas CA 95035

FREEMAN, BRUCE L., JR., physicist, researcher; b. Wharton, Tex., Apr. 2, 1949; s. Bruce L. Sr. and Audrey May (Wear) F.; m. Susan Hope Balog, Jan. 9, 1982. BS, Tex. A&M U., 1970; MS, U. Calif.-Davis, Livermore, 1971, PhD, 1974. Staff physicist Los Alamos (N.Mex.) Nat. Lab., 1974—. Contbr. articles to profl. jours. Mem. IEEE, N.Y. Acad. Sci., Pajarito Astronomers. Republican. Home: 1431 11th St Los Alamos NM 87544-2904 Office: Los Alamos Nat Lab PO Box 1663 Los Alamos NM 87545

FREEMAN, DICK, professional baseball executive. m. Judi Freeman; 1 child, Heather. Grad. in Bus. Adminstrn., U. Iowa. CPA. Acct. Peat, Marwick, Mitchell & Co., San Diego and L.A.; with San Diego Padres, 1981—, chief fin. officer, from 1981, exec. v.p., 1986-89, pres., 1989—. Lt. (j.g.) USN. Office: San Diego Padres PO Box 2000 San Diego CA 92120 *

FREEMAN, DONNA COOK, small business owner; b. Waldron, Ark., Apr. 18, 1937; d. Oliver Raymond and Lura Edna (Doyle) Cook; m. Clarence Lee Freeman, Jan. 24, 1954; children: Scott, Kevin, Steven, Melissa, Melinda. Student, Humphrey's Bus. Coll., Tracy, Calif., U. So. Calif., Bodega Bay (Calif.) Sch., 1973-75. Staff dept. aquaculture U. Calif. Bodega Marine Lab., 1976-77; real estate assoc., 1978-82; ptnr. Freeman's Union 76 Service, Bodega Bay, 1983—; co-owner fishing vessel Noyo Belle, 1981-84. Vice chmn. Shoreline Trust Ednl. Program Services, 1981—; bd. dirs. Bodega Bay Area Rescue, 1973-74; chmn. Bodega Bay Fisherman's Festival, 1973-74, 83; alt. mem. Dem. Cen. Com., 1982; mem. local bd. SSS, 1982—; chmn. Spud Point Adv. Bd., 1985—; bd. dirs. Sonoma County Fair, 1985—, Coastal Fisheries Found., 1986—; Sonoma County (Calif.) grand juror; 1983-84; mgr. polit. campaign, 1984. Mem. Bodega Bay Fisherman's Aux., Bodega Bay C. of C. (pres. 1979-81, bd. dirs. 1982-86), Bodega Bay Community Assn., Bodega Bay Grange. Home: 1409 Hwy One Bodega Bay CA 94923

FREEMAN, FRANCIS EDWIN (FRANK FREEMAN), construction company executive; b. Pasadena, Calif., Dec. 25, 1942; s. Edwin Carl and Rose Margaret (Bruns) F.; m. Sandra Hargrave, Nov. 1, 1962 (div. 1964); 1 child: Janice Lyn; m. Kathleen Lee Eisenman, Feb. 15, 1965 (div. 1970); 1 child: Robert Brent; m. Cheryl Rae McKeand, Dec. 18, 1972; 1 child, Brandee Lee. AA in Constrn., Pasadena City Coll., 1974. Registered inspector, Calif. Sr. resident engr. James M. Montgomery Cons. Engrs. Inc., Pasadena, 1963-78; resident engr. CH2M Hill, San Francisco, 1978-79; sr. coordinator technical sci. U. Calif., Berkeley, 1979-81; owner Dayspring Constrn. Inspection Services, Martinez, Calif., 1981—. Mem. North Bay chpt. Constrn. Insps. Assn. (pres. 1988, bd. dirs. 1986-88), Full Gospel Bus. Men's Fellowship Internat. (sec. 1980-84, treas. 1977-80). Republican. Mem. Assembly God Ch. Office: Dayspring Constrn Inspection PO Box 2562 Martinez CA 94553

FREEMAN, HERBERT JAMES, educational administrator; b. Raleigh, N.C., May 14, 1941; s. Hurley Lee and Annie Lee (Upchurch) F.; m. Ollie Faye Mack, Aug. 23, 1965 (div.). BA, Shaw U., 1963; MA, U. Nev., 1978. Cert. elem. tchr., spl. edn. tchr., elem. prin. Elem. tchr., 1963-65, 70-72; spl. edn. tchr. emotionally disturbed, 1965-70; program specialist Clark County Sch. Dist., Las Vegas, Nev., 1972-79, adminstrv. asst., 1979-80, coordinator basic adult edn. program, 1984—; prin. Rex Bell Elem. Sch., Las Vegas, 1980—, Parson Elem. Sch., 1989—; mem. Nev. State Bd. for Child Care, NAACP; choir dir. Zion United Methodist Ch., 1977—, So. Nev. Mass Meth. Chs.; registrar voter registration. Named Boss of Yr., Clark County Assn. Office Personnel, 1982. Mem. Assn. Supervision & Curriculum Devel., Nat. Alliance Black Sch. Educators, Clark County Elem. Prins. Assn., Clark County Assn. Sch. Adminstrs., NAACP, Phi Delta Kappa, Kappa Alpha Psi. Democrat. Home: 1101 Sharon Rd Las Vegas NV 89106 Office: 2900 Wilmington Way Las Vegas NV 89102

FREEMAN, HOWARD EDGAR, sociology educator; b. N.Y.C., May 28, 1929; s. Herbert M. and Rose H. (Herman) F.; m. Sharon W. Kleban, Apr. 20, 1952 (div. 1977); children—Seth R., Lisa J.; m. Marian A. Solomon, Feb. 2, 1979. BA, NYU, 1948, MA, 1950, PhD, 1956. Asst. social scientist Rand Corp., Santa Monica, Calif., 1955-56; rsch. assoc. sch. pub. health Harvard U., Boston, 1956-62; Morse prof. urban studies Brandeis U., Waltham, Mass., 1960-72; social sci. advisor Ford Found., Mexico City, Mex., 1972-74; prof. sociology UCLA, 1974—, chmn. dept. sociology, 1986—; sociologist Russell Sage Found., N.Y.C., 1967-77; rsch. advisor Robert Wood Johnson Found., Princeton, N.J., 1976—; advisor Inst. Nutrition C.Am. and Panama, 1965—, U.S.-Mex. Border Health Assn., San Antonio, 1981-82; cons. NIMH, Washington, 1971-76; mem. panel on social indicators HEW, Washington, 1966-69. Author: (with others) The Mental Patient Comes Home, 1963 (Hofheimer prize, 1967), The Middle Income Negro Family Faces Urban Renewal, 1965, The Clinic Habit, 1967, Social Problems, 1957, 3rd edit., 1967, Academic and Entrepreneurial Research, 1975, Evaluation Research, 1971, 4th edit, 1989; editor Evaluation Review, Los Angeles, 1976—, Health and Social Behavior, Washington, 1969-72, Policy Studies Review Annual, 1987; (with others) Handbook of Medical Sociology, 1963, 4th edit., 1989, The Social Scene, 1972, America's Troubles, 1973, The Dying Patient, 1982, Applied Sociology, 1983, Collecting Evaluation Data, 1985, others; contbr. articles to profl. jours. Capt. USAF, 1952-53. Mem. Am. Sociol. Assn., Am. Psychol. Assn., Am. Assn. Pub. Opinion Rsch., Am. Pub. Health Assn., Nat. Acad. Scis. (Inst. Medicine). Home: 7911 Hillside Ave Los Angeles CA 90046

FREEMAN, HUGH JAMES, gastroenterology educator; b. Edmonton, Alta., Can., June 9, 1947; s. James Gale and Kathryn Christina (MacIsaac) F.; m. Sally Jean Spanier, May 18, 1968; children: Marcus James, Katy Jean. BSc magna cum laude, Loyola U. of Montreal, Que., Can., 1968; MD, CM, McGill U., Montreal, 1972. Resident U. Alta. Hosp., Edmonton, 1972-74, gastroenterology fellow, 1974-76, MRC research fellow, 1974-75; MRC research fellow U. Calif., San Francisco, 1976-79; asst. prof. medicine U. B.C., Vancouver, 1979-81, assoc. prof. medicine, 1981-86, BCHRCF research fellow, 1979-83, head gastroenterology, 1981—, prof. medicine, 1986—. Editor (book) Inflammatory Bowel Disease, 1988; contbr. articles to profl. jours. Med. Research Council Research fellow, Edmonton and San Francisco, 1974-75, 76-79; Queen Elizabeth scholar Province of Alta., 1965-72, B.C. Health Care Research Found. Research scholar, 1979-83. Fellow Royal Coll. Physicians and Surgeons Can., ACP; mem. Am. Soc. for Clin. Investigation, Can. Soc. Clin. Investigation, Am. Gasteroenterology Assn., Can. Assn. Gasteroenterology. Office: U BC Hosp, 2211 Wesbrook Mall, Vancouver, BC Canada V6T 1W5

FREEMAN, JAMES JOSEPH, engineering educator; b. Erie, Pa., Mar. 11, 1940; s. James Patrick and Laura (Bundy) F.; m. Nancy Sitter, June 20, 1962; children: James, Mark, Peter. BEE, Gannon U., 1962; MSEE, U. Detroit, 1964, MS, 1967, PhD, 1968. Registered profl. engr., Calif. Prof. elec. engring. U. Detroit, 1968-82, prof., chmn., 1978-82; prof., chmn. San Jose State U., 1982—. Contbr. articles to profl. jours. Mem. IEEE (sr., dir. student 1980—), Tau Beta Phi (advisor 1978—), Eta Kappa Nu (advisor 1980-86). Office: San Jose State U Dept Elec Engring San Jose CA 95192

FREEMAN, JOEL, movie producer; b. Newark, N.J., June 12, 1922; s. Louis and Frances Miriam (Schary) F.; m. Betty Ann Kinley, June 16, 1968; children: Josh, Jeff, Martin, Kurina. Student, Upsala Coll., 1939-41. Various positions MGM Studios, Hollywood, Calif., 1941-42; asst. dir., assoc. producer MGM Studios, Hollywood, 1948-56; asst. dir. RKO Studios, Hollywood, 1946-48; freelance asst. dir, production mgr. Hollywood, 1957-59; production mgr., assoc. producer Warner Bros., Hollywood, 1959-63; producer exec. Warner Bros./7 Arts, N.Y., 1964-69; producer CBS, Hollywood, 1963-64; assoc. producer, producer, exec. Joel Freeman Productions, Inc., Sherman Oaks, Calif., 1968—; sr. v.p. production New Century Entertainment Corp., Sherman Oaks, 1987-88. Asst. dir.: Bad Day at Black Rock, 1954 (Dirs. Guild award 1954); producer: Shaft, 1971 (NAACP Image award 1971), The Heart is a Lonely Hunter, Love at First Bite, Octagon, and numerous others. Bd. dirs. Permanent Charities Com., L.A. With USAF, 1942-46. Mem. Producers Guild of Am. (bd. dirs.), Dirs. Guild of Am., Acad. Motion Pictures, Arts and Scis., TV Acad. Democrat. Jewish. Office: 4641 Halbrent Ave Sherman Oaks CA 91403

FREEMAN, JOSH, graphic design company executive; b. Santa Monica, Calif., Dec. 4, 1949; s. Joel David Freeman and Jo (Stack) Napoleon; m. Nicki Ellen Huggins, July 5, 1980; 1 child, Noah John. BFA, UCLA, 1972. Assoc. designer Anthony Goldschmidt Graphic Design, Ltd., Los Angeles, 1972-73; prin. Josh Freeman Design, Los Angeles, 1973-75; ptnr., pres. Freeman: Blitzer Assocs., Los Angeles, 1975-80, Interrobang Inc., Los Angeles, 1980-83; pres. Josh Freeman/Assocs., Los Angeles, 1983—. Coauthor, illustrator (children's book) The Thing Nobody Could See, 1972 (Best Western Book Show 1973, Rounce and Coffin Club 1973). Mem. Mayor's Council for the Arts, Los Angeles, 1983-84. Recipient Gold award Typographers Internat. Assn., 1983, Project of the Yr. award Nat. Assn. Home Builders, 1987, Project of the Yr. award Sales and Mktg. Council of Bldg. Industry Assn., 1987, Project of the Yr. award Builder mag., 1987., Maxi award Internat. Council Shopping Ctrs., 1988, numerous awards from various advt. clubs, mags. and insts. Mem. Am. Inst. Graphic Arts (v.p. 1987—, awards), Art Dirs. Club Los Angeles (awards). Office: Josh Freeman/Assocs 8019 1/2 Melrose Ave Ste 1 Los Angeles CA 90046

FREEMAN, KURT MELVILLE, health facility administrator; b. Oakland, Calif., Nov. 2, 1938; s. Melville George and Hazel (Robertson) F.; m. Peggy Jeanette Collins, Sept. 11, 1960; children: Celisa Freeman Edwards, Erich W. BS, Calif. State U., Hayward, 1964; MS, Columbia U., 1967; MPA, U. So. Calif., 1972. Cert. tchr., Calif. Rehab. therapist VA Hosp., Palo Alto, Calif., 1964-65; recreation therapist Inst. Physical Medicine & Rehab., NYU, 1966-67; asst. to chief of rehab. svcs. Action Rehab. Ctr., 1967; adminstr. Warm Springs Rehab. Ctr., 1978-84; dir. Rehab. Ctrs., L.A. County, 1974—; Numerous lectrs. in various countries on mgmt., alcohol and drug abuse, and recreation. Contbr. articles profl. publs.; author: From Skid Row to the Olympics, 1977. Vol. Chaplain for Christian Chaplaincy Svcs., Inc.; founder Al-impics Internat., Inc., L.A. 1973—; dir. Santa Clarita Valley Rep. Assembly, Calif., 1984-89; active First Bapt. Ch., Castaic, Calif., 1980-89; planning coun. Castaic Planning Coun., 1987-88. Fellowship, Columbia U., 1965; numerous award and resolutions for Alcoholic Olympics Internat., L.A., 1980, 82, 83, 86, 87, 88; Merit award, L.A. Publicity Soc., 1984, Supr. Michael Antonovich, 5th Dist., L.A. County, 1985, 86; Health and Wellness award, Mayor of Massoins, France, 1984, Edn. and Community Service award, Alcohol Commn., L.A. County, 1981, Senate Resolution, State of Calif., 1976, Assembly Resolution, State of Calif., 1974. Mem. Calif. Park and Recreation Soc., L.A. Mgmt. Coun., Toastmasters Internat. Republican. Baptist. Home: 31500 Karena Ave Castaic CA 91384

FREEMAN, MILTON MALCOLM ROLAND, anthropology educator; b. London, Apr. 23, 1934; came to Can., 1958; s. Louis and Fay (Bomberg) F.; m. Mini Christina Aodla; children: Graham, Elaine, Malcolm. BS, Reading U., Eng., 1958; postgrad., U. Coll., London, 1962-64; PhD, McGill U., 1965. Research scientist No. Affairs Dept., Ottawa, Ont., Can., 1965-67; asst. prof. Meml. U., St. John's, Nfld., Can., 1967-71, assoc. prof., 1971-72; dir. Inuit Land Use Study, Hamilton, Ont., 1973-75; prof. anthropology McMaster U., Hamilton, 1976-81; Henry Marshall Tory prof. U. Alta., Edmonton, Can., 1982—; adj. prof. environmental studies U. Waterloo, Ont., 1977-81; sr. sci. advisor Indian and No. Affairs, Ottawa, 1979-81. Author: People Pollution, 1974; editor: Inuit Land Use and Occupancy Report, 1976, Proceedings International Symposium on Renewable Resources and the Economy of the North, 1981. Bd. dirs. Sci. Inst. N.W.T., 1985-87. Sr. Research scholar Boreal Inst. No. Studies, U. Alta., 1984—. Fellow Am. Anthrop. Assn., Arctic Inst. N.Am., Soc. Applied Anthropology; mem. Soc. Applied Anthropology Can. (pres. 1984-85), Can. Ethnology Soc. Home: 10650-11 Ave, Edmonton, AB Canada T6J 6H5 Office: U Alta, Dept Anthropology, Edmonton, AB Canada T6G 2H4

FREEMAN, NEIL, accounting and computer consulting firm executive; b. Reading, Pa., Dec. 27, 1948; s. Leroy Harold and Audrey Todd (Dornhecker) F.; m. Janice Lum, Nov. 20, 1981. BS, Albright Coll., 1979; MS, Kennedy-Western U., 1987, PhD, 1988. Cert. systems profl.; cert. data processing specialist. Acct. Jack W. Long & Co., Mt. Penn, Pa., 1977-78; comptroller G.P.C., Inc., Bowmansville, Pa., 1978-79; owner Neil Freeman Cons., Bowmansville, 1980-81; program mgr., systems cons. Application Systems, Honolulu, 1981-82; instr. Chaminade U., Honolulu, 1983—; owner Neil Freeman Cons., Kaneohe, Hawaii, 1982—. Author: (computer software) NFC Property Management, 1984, NFC Mailing List, 1984; (book) Learning Dibol, 1984. Served with USN, 1966-68, Vietnam. Mem. Nat. Assn. Accts., Am. Inst. Cert. Computer Profs., Data Processing Mgmt. Assn., Assn. Systems Mgmt. Office: 45-449 Hoene Pl Kaneohe HI 96744

FREEMAN, PATRICIA ELIZABETH, library and education specialist; b. El Dorado, Ark., Nov. 30, 1924; d. Herbert A. and M. Elizabeth (Pryor) Harper; m. Jack Freeman, June 15, 1949; 3 children. B.A., Centenary Coll., 1943; postgrad. Fine Arts Ctr., 1942-46, Art Students League, 1944-45; B.S.L.S., La. State U., 1946; postgrad. Calif. State U., 1959-61, U. N.Mex., 1964-74; Ed.S., Peabody Coll., Vanderbilt U., 1975. Librarian, U. Calif.-Berkeley, 1946-47, U.S. Air Force, Barksdale AFB, 1948-49, Albuquerque Pub. Schs., 1964-67; ind. sch. library media ctr. cons., 1967—. Painter lithographer; one-person show La. State Exhibit Bldg., 1948; author: Pathfinder: An Operational Guide for the School Librarian, 1975; compiler, editor: Elizabeth Pryor Harper's Twenty-One Southern Families, 1985. Mem. task force Goals for Dallas-Environ., 1977-82; pres. Friends of Sch. Libraries, Dallas, 1979-83. Honoree AAUW Ednl. Found., 1979; vol. award for outstanding service Dallas Ind. Sch. Dist., 1978; AAUW Pub. Service grantee 1980. Mem. ALA, AAUW (dir. Dallas 1976-82, Albuquerque 1983-85), LWV (sec. Dallas 1982-83, editor Albuquerque 1984—), Nat. Trust Historic Preservation, Friends of Albuquerque Pub. Library, N.Mex. Symphony Guild, Alpha Xi Delta. Home: 3016 Santa Clara SE Albuquerque NM 87106

FREEMAN, PAUL DOUGLAS, symphony conductor; b. Richmond, Va., Jan. 2, 1936; s. Louis H. and Louise (Willis) F.; m. Cornelia Perry; 1 son, Douglas Cornel. MusB, Eastman Sch. Music, 1956, MusM, 1957; PhD, 1963; PhD Fulbright scholar, Hochshule für Musik, Berlin, Germany, 1957-59. Dir. Hochstein Music Sch., Rochester, N.Y., 1960-66; music dir., condr. Chgo. Sinfonietta, 1987—; First v.p. Nat. Guild Community Music Schs., 1964-66; bd. dirs. N.Y. State Opera League, 1963-66, Detroit Community Music Sch.; music adv. com. San Francisco chpt. Young Audiences, 1966—; mem. Calif. Framework Com. for Arts and Humanities, 1967-68. Founder, conductor, Faculty-Community Orch., also music dir., Opera Theatre, Rochester, 1961-66, dir., San Francisco Community Music Center, 1966-68, conductor, San Francisco Conservatory Orch., 1966-67, music dir., San Francisco Little Symphony, 1967-68, asso. conductor, Dallas Symphony, 1968-69, 69-70, conductor-in-residence, Detroit Symphony Orch., 1970-79, condr., music dir., Victoria (B.C., Can.) Symphony, 1979—, music dir., Saginaw Symphony, 1979-88, music. dir. emeritus, 1988—; artistic dir. Delta Fstival Music and Art, 1977-79, Can. Music Educator's Arist Rec. Services; numerous guest appearances with maj. orchs. in, U.S. and Europe; recording artist, Columbia Records, Vox Records, Orion Records, music dir., conductor Chgo. Sinfonetta, 1987—. Recipient prize Dimitri Mitropolous Internat. Conductor's competition, 1967—; Spoleto award Festival of Two Worlds, 1968. Office: Chgo Sinfonietta 7900 W Division 631 Superior St River Forest IL 60305

FREEMAN, RICHARD DWAINE, minister; b. Stockton, Calif., May 6, 1945; s. Milford Dwaine and Shirley Jean (Bourn) F.; m. Vicki Ann Jarvis, May 23, 1970; 1 child, Christina Lynn. AA, McCook Jr. Coll., 1965; BA, Hastings Coll., 1967; MDiv, United Theol. Sem., St. Paul, 1971; Doctor of Ministry, McCormick Theol. Sem., 1985. Ordained to ministry United Ch. of Christ, 1971; lic. instr. Parent Effectiveness Tng. Assoc. pastor Bath Community Ch., Akron, Ohio, 1971-72, 1st Congl. Ch., Grand Junction, Colo., 1972-73; sr. minister 1st Congl. Ch. Forest Glen, Chgo., 1974-80, St. Peter's United Ch. of Christ, Champaign, Ill., 1980-87, St. Paul's United Ch. of Christ, Rio Rancho, N.Mex., 1987—; cons. Christian Edn. Shared Approaches Ch. Sch. Curriculum; exec. sec. Chgo. Met. Assn. Ill. Conf. United Ch. of Christ, Chgo., 1978-80; on-site coord. Nat. Gathering United Ch. of Christ Clergy, 1978-81. Pres. Ill. Consortium on Govtl. Concerns, Springfield, 1982-84; mem. long-range planning com. Ill. Conf. Chs., 1985-87, ann. meeting planning com. Ill. Conf. of United Ch. Christ., 1984-86; dean Prairie Mission Coun. Ill. Conf. of United Ch. Christ, 1986-87. Recipient Alfred and Catherine Cook Meml. award United Theol. Sem., 1971. Mem. Profl. Assn. Clergy Ill. Conf. of United Ch. of Christ (sec. 1975-79), Champaign-Urbana Ministerial Assn. (pres. 1985-87, bd. dirs. SW Conf. 1988—), Kiwanis (lt. gov. Ea. Iowa Dist. 1978-79, dist. conv. chmn. 1979-80, dist. interclub chmn. 1981-82, dist. maj. emphasis chmn. 1982-83, dist. bull. editor 1983-84, pres. Forest Glen-Mayfair, Chgo. 1975-76, NW Albuquerque). Home: 4250 Pirone Ct NE Rio Rancho NM 87124 Office: St Paul's United Ch of Christ 3801 Rio Rancho Blvd NW PO Box 15154 Rio Rancho NM 87174

FREEMAN, RUSSELL ADAMS, banker; b. Albany, N.Y., July 22, 1932; s. Russell Marvin and Edith (Adams) F.; m. Elizabeth Frances McHale, June 30, 1956; children: Lynn, James. B.A., Amherst Coll., 1954; J.D., Albany (N.Y.) Law Sch., 1957; LL.M., U. So. Calif., 1966. Bar: N.Y. 1957, Calif. 1960. Practiced in Albany, 1957-59; with Security Pacific Nat. Bank, Los Angeles, 1959—; v.p. Security Pacific Nat. Bank, 1968-72, counsel, 1968-74, head legal dept., 1968-74, sr. v.p., 1972-81, exec. v.p., 1981-87, gen. counsel, 1984-87; gen. counsel Security Pacific Corp., 1973—, exec. v.p., 1981—; bd. govs. Fin. Lawyers Conf., 1972-74; faculty Pacific Coast Banking Sch., 1980-81; lectr. in field, 1965—. Contbr. articles to profl. publns. Trustee Flintridge Prep. Sch., La Canada, Calif., 1978-80. Mem. ABA, Am. Bankers Assn. (mem. govt. relations com. 1981-84, del. to Leadership Conf. 1984-86), Assn. Banking Holding Cos., Calif. Bankers Assn. (dir., chmn. govt. relations group 1979-81, 86-88, dir. and chmn. fed. govt. relations 1985-86), Calif. Bankers Clearing House Assn. (chmn. public policy adv. com. 1980-81, 88-89), Calif. State Bar, Los Angeles County Bar Assn. (past chmn. comml. law and bankruptcy sect.), Constl. Rights Found. (bd. dirs. 1986—). Office: Security Pacific Corp 333 S Hope St 54th Fl Los Angeles CA 90071

FREEMAN, VAL LEROY, geologist; b. Long Beach, Calif., June 25, 1926; s. Cecil LeRoy and Marjorie (Austin) F.; BS, U. Calif., Berkeley, 1949, MS, 1952; m. June Ione Ashlock, Sept. 26, 1959 (div. June 1962); 1 child, Jill Annette Freeman Michener; m. Elizabeth Joann Sabia, Sept. 4, 1964 (div. Oct. 1972); 1 child, Rebecca Sue; 1 stepchild, Jeffrey David. Geologist, U.S. Geol. Survey, 1949-85, Fairbanks, Alaska, 1955-57, Denver, 1957-70, 74-85, Flagstaff, Ariz., 1970-74, dep. chief coal resources br., until 1985. With USNR, 1943-45. Fellow Geol. Soc. Am. Contbr. articles to profl. jours. Home: 65 Clarkson St Apt 508 Denver CO 80218

FREEMAN, WILLIAM TAFT, JR., clergyman; b. L.A., Aug. 28, 1937; s. William Taft and Virginia (Sabella) F.; m. Patricia Ann Moomjean, Feb. 25, 1956; children: Renee, Jennifer, William Taft III, Desiree, Jonathan. BA, Asuza Pacific U., 1960; MA, Fuller Theol. Sem., 1979. Min. Evang. Tabernacle Ch., 1957; asst. min. Alamitos Friends Ch., Garden Grove, Calif., 1957-60; co-pastor Yorba Linda Friends Ch., 1960-64; min. Evang. Ch., Yorba Linda, Calif., 1964-70, Seattle, 1970-87, Scottsdale, Ariz., 1987—; conf. speaker Ministry of Word Inc., Scottsdale, 1969—, pres., 1981—; instr. ch. history Ariz. State U., Tempe, 1988; radio Bible instr, Seattle, Scottsdale, 1981—. Author: The Testimony of Church History Regarding the Mystery of the Triune God, 1976, The Testimony of Church History Regarding the Mystery of the Mingling of God with Man, 1977, In Defense of Truth, 1981, The Dividing of Soul and Spirit, 1984, The Triune God in Experience, 1984, also booklets; editor: How They Found Christ: In Their Own Words, 1983. Mem. Am. Soc. Ch. History. Republican. Home: 7561 E Sweetwater Ave Scottsdale AZ 85260 Office: Ministry of Word Inc 7125 E Paradise Dr Scottsdale AZ 85254

FREEMAN-LONGO, ROBERT EARL, psychotherapist; b. Harrison, N.Y., Sept. 26, 1951; s. Angelo Earl Longo and Shirley Mae (Shavenaugh) DeWalt; m. Patricial Lynn, Sept. 17, 1983. BA in Psychology, U. Fla., 1974, MA in Rehab. Counseling, 1976. Unit dir. North Fla. Evaluation and Treatment Ctr., Gainesville, 1979-81; mental health analyst Health and Rehabilitative Svcs., Gainesville, 1981-83; dir. Correctional Sex Offender Treatment Program, Salem, Oreg., 1983—; counselor The Human Ctr. Gainesville, Fla., 1978-79, The Gestalt Ctr., Gainesville, 1979-81; founder, pres. The Sexual Assault Rsch. Assn., Gainesville, 1981-83; adj. faculty Forensic Mental Healt Assn., Webster, Mass., 1982-88; part time faculty Santa Fe Community Coll., Fla. Police Acad., Gainesville, Eustis, Lake County Vocational-Tech. Community Coll., 1982; cert. Law Enforcement Instr. Fla., 1983-87, Oreg., 1983—; cons., lectr. and conductor of seminars nationwide. Co-author: (with L. Bays) Who Am I and Why Am I in Treatment, 1988; author: (with others) The Sexual Agressor: Current Perspectives on Treatment, 1983; contbr. numerous articles to profl. jours. Mem. Gov's. Task Force on Rape Prevention, Kans. City, Mo., 1980; bd. dirs. Oreg. Crime Victims Assistance Network, Salem, 1984-86; adv. staff Nat. Task Force on Adolescent Sex Offenders, Denver, 1987—; adv. bd. Office of Atty. Gen. Victims of Crime Act, Salem, 1989—. Assn. for the Behavioral Treatment of Sexual Abusers (founder and pres. 1984-86, bd. dirs. 1986-87), Am. Mental Health Counselors Assn., Pub. Offenders Counselor Assn., Am. Assn. for Counseling and Devel. Democrat. Presbyterian. Home: 2627 SW Anchor Ave Lincoln City OR 97367 Office: Robert E Freeman-Longo Cons PO Box 12951 Salem OR 97309

FREESE, RALPH, trust company executive; b. Dyersburg, Tenn., Dec. 12, 1943; s. Ralph Earl and Dorothy Marie (Sheridan) F.; m Susan Lee Kramer; 1 child, Johnny. AA, Riverside Community Coll., 1967. Title searcher Security Title, Riverside, Calif., 1967-69, title officer, 1969-70; title officer Transam. Title, Riverside, 1970-72, br. mgr., 1972-76; loan officer Calif. Morgage Svc., Riverside, 1976-78; loan officer Dirs. Mortgage Loan Corp., Riverside, 1978-80, asst. v.p., 1980-86; v.p. Courtesy Mortgage Svc., Riverside, 1986—. Served in U.S. Army, 1961-64, Germany. Mem. Assn. Profl. Mktg. Women (v.p. 1983-84), Calif. Trustee's Assn., Ind. Trustees Assn., Riverside County Escrow Assn., Greater Riverside C. of C., Gamma Iota Alpha (life). Republican. Office: Courtesy Mortgage Svc 1595 Spruce St Riverside CA 92507

FREI, DAVID LEE, enterpreneur; b. Portland, Oreg., Apr. 4, 1949; s. Gerald Lee and Marian Elizabeth (Benson) F.; m. Sandra Lee Withington, Mar. 17, 1979. BS, Oreg. State U., 1976. Dir. of promotions Denver Broncos, Denver, Colo., 1976-78; dir. of pub. rels. San Francisco 49ers, San Francisco, Calif., 1978-79; account exec. Cole Weber Adv., Seattle, 1979-80; publicist ABC-TV Sports, N.Y.C., 1981; ptnr. Pacific Pub. Rels., Seattle, 1982-85; private investor Seattle, 1985—; owner Stormhill Kennels. Mem. Morris Animal Found. (trustee 1987—), Afghan Hound Club Am. (pres. 1987-88, dir. 1988—). Home and Office: PO Box 1245 Woodinville WA 98072

FREILICH, JEFF, television producer, writer, director; b. N.Y.C., June 29, 1948; s. Seymour David and Natalie Freilich; m. Marguerite Hester Copp, Nov. 17, 1979; children: Nicholas Brandon, Molly Alyssa. BA, Antioch Coll., 1969; postgrad., U. So. Calif., Los Angeles, 1969-71. Freelance writer New World Pictures, Am. Internat. Pictures, Los Angeles, 1972-75; creative cons. Baretta Universal Studios, Universal City, Calif., 1976, exec. story cons. Quincy, 1979, producer, writer The Incredible Hulk, 1980, producer, writer Galactica 1980, 1980; exec. story editor Flamingo Road Lorimar Telepictures, Culver City, Calif., 1980-82, supervising producer Boone, 1983, exec. producer, creator Better Days, 1986, exec. producer, writer, dir. Falcon Crest, 1986—, exec. producer, writer dir. A Nightmare on Elm Street: The Series, 1988—. Mem. Writers Guild Am. West, Dirs. Guild Am. Office: Lorimar Telepictures 3970 Overland Dr Culver City CA 90230

FREIMANN, JOHN RAYMOND, theater educator; b. Yakima, Wash., Nov. 10, 1926; s. Raymond Christopher and Elsie Mary (Doyle) F. BS, NYU, 1951; MFA, Fordham U., 1955. Tchr. drama NYU, 1954-59; tchr. Whitman Coll., Walla Walla, Wash., 1962—, chmn. drama dept., 1967—; actor, designer, dir. Forestburgh (N.Y.) Playhouse, 1982-85, Berkeley (Calif.) Repertory Theatre, 1974-82. Mem. United Scenic Artists, Scenic and Title Artists, Actors Equity Assn., Soc. Stage Dirs. and Choreographers, Dramatists Guild, Screen Actors Guild. Office: Whitman Coll Harper Joy Theatre Walla Walla WA 99362

FREISMUTH, THOMAS PATRICK, financial consulting company executive; b. Grosse Pointe, Mich., Jan. 8, 1948; s. William Thomas and Margaret Ann (McLaughlin) F.; m. Carolyn Kay Petre, Feb. 19, 1954; children: Thomas Patrick II, Joy Hailey, Maxx Skylar. BA, Mich. State U., 1970. CLU; chartered fin. cons.; registered investment advisor SEC. Sales rep. Aetna Life & Casualty Co., Southfield, Mich., 1971-75; pres. Fin. Adv. Svcs. Aetna Life & Casualty Co., Southfield, 1975-86, chief exec. officer, 1986--; chief exec. officer Fin Adv. Svcs., San Diego, 1986—; bd. dirs. Haas Fin., Southfield, Levin Assocs., Southfield. Contbr. articles to profl. publs. Asst. treas. Am. Kidney Found., Detroit, 1976; active Big Bros. Orgn., Detroit, 1978; mem. fund program Am. Cancer Found., Detroit, 1982--. Mem. Internat. Assn. Fin. Planners, San Diego Assn. Life Underwriters, Detroit Assn. Life Underwriters, Registered Investment Advisors Assn., Million Dollar Round Table, Eagles, Rotary. Republican. Mem. Unity Ch. Office: Fin Adv Svcs 450 A St Ste 500 San Diego CA 92101 Also: 12555 High Bluff Dr Ste 333 San Diego CA 92130

FREITAS, BEATRICE B(OTTY), artistic director, musician, educator; b. Youngstown, Ohio, Aug. 28, 1938; d. John and Pauline (Esterhay) Botty; m. Lewis P. Freitas, Nov. 30, 1963; children—Roslyn K., John B. B.A., Oberlin Coll., 1958; M.Mus., Boston U., 1959; spl. student Juilliard Sch. Music, 1959-62. Artistic dir. Hawaii Opera Theatre, Honolulu; pianist, organist, harpsichordist, tchr. Recipient Outstanding Achievement in Area of Arts award YMCA, 1983.

FRENCH, ALAN DOUGLAS, lawyer; b. Berkeley, Calif., Jan. 8, 1947; s. Eldred French. AB, U. Calif., Berkeley, 1968; JD, Golden Gate U., 1979. Admitted to the Calif. Supreme Ct., 1979. Mem. Bay Area Lawyers for Individual Freedom, San Francisco, 1983. Mem. Chinese-Am. Dem. Club, Golden Gate Men's Chorus. Roman Catholic. Home and Office: 460 Noe San Francisco CA 94114

FRENCH, CLARENCE LEVI, JR., retired shipbuilding company executive; b. New Haven, Oct. 13, 1925; s. Clarence L. Sr. and Eleanor (Curry) F.; m. Jean Sprague, June 29, 1946; children: Craig Thomas, Brian Keith, Alan Scott. B.S. in Naval Sci., Tufts U., 1945, B.S. in Mech. Engring., 1947. Registered profl. engr., Calif. Foundry engr. Bethlehem Steel Corp., 1947-56; staff engr., asst. supt. Kaiser Steel Corp., 1956-64; supervisory engr. Bechtel Corp., 1964-67; with Nat. Steel & Shipbldg. Co., San Diego, 1967-86; exec. v.p., gen. mgr. Nat. Steel & Shipbldg. Co., to 1977, pres., chief operating officer, 1977-84, chmn., chief exec. officer, 1984-86; mem. maritime transp. rsch. bd. NRC. Bd. dirs. United Way, San Diego, YMCA, San Diego; past chmn., bd. dirs. Pres. Roundtable; chmn. emeritus bd. trustees Webb Inst. Lt. USN, 1943-53. Fellow Soc. Naval Architects and Marine Engrs. (hon., past pres.), Shipbuilders Council Am. (past chmn. exec. com.), ASTM, Am. Bur. Shipping; mem. Am. Soc. Naval Engrs., U.S. Naval Inst., Navy League U.S., Propeller Club U.S.

FRENCH, DAWN ELIZABETH, stock broker; b. Rocky Mount, N.C., July 21, 1964; d. Richard James and Mary Beatrice (Yonka) F. BA in Econs., U. Calif., Santa Barbara, 1986; postgrad., U. San Francisco, 1987—. Options computer clk. Goldberg Securities, San Francisco, 1986-87; stock options broker Coast Options, San Francisco, 1987—; research asst. U. San Fransisco, 1987—. Fellow U. San Francisco, 1987. Mem. Pacific Stock Exchange. Office: 1st Options Chgo 220 Bush St 5th Fl San Francisco CA 94104

FRENCH, GEORGINE LOUISE, guidance counselor; b. Lancaster, Pa., May 15, 1934; d. Richard Franklin and Elizabeth Georgine (Driesbach) Beacham; B.A., Calif. State U., San Bernardino, 1967; M.S., No. Ill. U., 1973; D.D., Am. Ministerial Assn., 1978; m. Barrie J. French, Feb. 4, 1956; children—Joel B., John D., James D., Jeffrey D. Ordained minister Am. Ministerial Assn., 1979; Personnel counselor Sages Dept. Store, San Bernardino, 1965-66; asst. bookkeeper Bank Calif., San Bernardino, 1964-65; tchr. Livermore (Calif.) Sch. Dist., 1968-69; guidance counselor Bur. Indian Affairs, Tuba City, Ariz., 1974-80, Sherman Indian High Sch., Riverside, Calif., 1980-82, Ft. Douglas Edn. Ctr., U.S. Army, Salt. Lake City, 1982-86; guidance counselor L.A. Air Force Sta., USAF, 1986-87, edn. svcs. officer, Comiso AFB, Italy, 1987-88; pvt. practice cert. counselor, 1985—; extension tchr. Navajo Community Coll., Yavapai Jr. Coll.; personnel counselor USNR, 1976-86. Served with USAF, 1954-56. Cert. guidance counselor, secondary tchr. Mem. Am. Assn. for Counselor Devel., Am. Assn. Retired Persons. Office: 1721 Aviation Blvd #53 Redondo Beach CA 90278-2960

FRENSLEY, WILLIAM FITZHUGH, public relations executive, consultant; b. Houston, Aug. 1, 1938; s. Frank W. and Maida (Parr) F.; m. Martha Rose Taylor, Apr. 22, 1967; children: Ann Elizabeth, Robert Banks. BA in Journalism, U. Okal., 1960; postgrad., Boston U., 1965. Pub. relations officer USAF, various locations, 1962-83; communications coordinator U. Hawaii Cancer Research Ctr., Honolulu, 1984-86; pub. relations coordinator Bishop Mus., Honolulu, 1986-87; v.p. Profl. Communications, Inc., Honolulu, 1987-88—; chmn. crisis communications com. Hawaii Visitors Bur., Honolulu, 1987-88. Mme. Honolulu Community Media Council, 1981-88. Mem. Hawaii C. of C. (visitor industry com. 1987-88), Pub. Relations Soc. Am. (bd. mem. Hawaii chpt. 1984-85), Honolulu Press Club (sec. 1986), Lamda Chi Alpha. Republican. Presbyterian. Club: Honolulu. Lodge: Elks. Home: 4385 Halupa St Honolulu HI 96818-1855 Office: Profl Communications Inc 1001 Bishop St Pauahi Tower Ste 490 Honolulu HI 96813-3404

FRESE, VERNE, concrete company executive; b. Spokane, Wash., May 26, 1915; s. Julius and Rose (Materne) F.; m. Clare Laverne Phillips, June 26, 1939 (div. 1952); children: Julianne, Marilyn, Dennis; m. Evelyn E. Mitchell, June 11, 1953 (dec. 1977). BS in Physics, Wash. State U., 1939. Ptnr. J. Frese & Son, Spokane, 1932-40, J. Frese & Son Concrete Block Co., Richland, Wash., 1943-44; instrumentation engr. Boeing Aircraft Co., Seattle, 1940-43; pres. Layrite Concrete Prods. of Seattle (now JLF, Inc.), 1943—; pres. Belre, We. Investments, Seattle, Shalex, Inc., Briliantyle, Inc., Highland Properties, inc., Seattle, Mainroads, Inc., 1963-87, chmn. bd., 1987—; v.p. Layrite Concrete Products of Kennewick (Wash.), 1949-86, dir., Spokane, 1958—, chmn. bd. 1987—; dir. Brookside Concrete Products, Vancouver, Wash., 1957-70; researcher in field. Patentee in field. Bd. dirs. Georgetown Boys Club, 1947-57, pres., 1948-49; field advisor Small Bus. Adminstrn., 1954-55; People-to-People Goodwill Tour Iron Curtain countries, 1961. Mem. AAAS, Nat. Concrete Masonry Assn. (dir. 1957-63, v.p. 1960-61), Nat. Assn. Mfgrs., Seattle Structural Engrs., Assn. Am. Phys. Soc., Am. Concrete Inst., Seattle Engrs. Club, Lions. Home and Office: 17021 1st Ave S Seattle WA 98148

FRETER, MARK ALLEN, marketing and public relations executive, consultant; b. Chgo., Oct. 31, 1947; s. John Maher and Christopher Patricia (Allen) F. BA, U. Calif., Santa Barbara, 1969; MBA, U. Calif., Berkeley, 1971. Regional dir. House Box Office Svcs., Inc., L.A. and Denver, 1979-84; v.p. affiliate relations X-Press Info. Services, Denver, 1984-85; v.p. mktg. Telecrafter Corp., Denver, 1985-86; mktg. dir. Computer Services Corp., Boulder, Colo., 1986-87; v.p. pub. relations services MultiMedia, Inc., Denver, 1987-88; dir. documentation and corp. communications, product specialist Data Select Systems Inc., Woodland Hills, Calif., 1988—; lectr. Internat. Council Shopping Ctrs., N.Y.C., 1977; conf. planner ICSC-West, San Francisco, 1978-79; training program devel. HBO, N.Y.C., 1982. Youth coach South Suburban YMCA, Littleton, Colo., 1984-86. Recipient First Place cert. for Retail Ad Campaign San Diego Advt. Assn., 1980. Mem. Calif. Cable TV Assn., No. Calif. Promotion Mgrs. Assn. (v.p. 1977-78), So. Calif. Promotion Mgrs. Assn. (sec., treas. 1976-77). Democrat. Mem. Soc. Friends.

FRETTE, DONALD EUGENE, insurance company executive; b. Ames, Iowa, Mar. 24, 1947; s. Dale Marvin and Erma Mae (Barkema) Flygstad F.; m. DeAnne Kae Jansen, June 7, 1969 (div.); 1 child, Jay David; m. Minerva Menchaca, Apr. 4, 1981. AA, Webster Jr. Coll., 1967; BBA, U. Iowa, 1969. CPCU. Claim adjuster AID Ins., Des Moines, 1969-70, underwriter, 1970-72, mktg. rep., 1972-73, mgr., 1973-74, underwriting mgr., 1974-77; resident v.p. AID Ins., Denver, 1977-79, Santa Rosa, Calif., 1979-81; regional v.p. Allied Group, Aurora, Colo, 1981—; bd. dirs. Colo. Guarantee Fund Assn., Golden; chmn. Colo. Adv. Com. on Arson Prevention, Denver. Chmn. United Way, Denver, 1986-88. Mem. CPCU Soc. Republican. Office: Allied Group Ins 350 Blackhawk Aurora CO 80011

FREUND, IRV J., manufacturing executive; b. N.Y.C., Apr. 23, 1953; s. Nathan and Fanny (Hittman F.; m. Elizabeth Julie Frotiner, Sept. 20, 1981. BS, Columbia U., 1974; MSc., McGill U., Montreal, 1976; MBA, NYU, 1980. Tech. service rep. Stange Co., Paterson, N.J., 1976-79; market specialist Drew Chem. Co., Boonton, N.J., 1979-81; sr. market analyst Great LAkes Carbon Corp., N.Y.C., 1981-83; dir. mktg. Hitco Materials div. U.S. Polymeric, Santa Ana, Calif., 1983—; mgmt. cons. various cos., Los Angeles, 1981-83. Recipient research grant Canadian Ctr. for No. Affairs, 1974-76. Mem. Am. Chem. Soc., Soc. for the Advancement of Material and Process Engring. Home: PO Box 24476 Los Angeles CA 90024 Office: US Polymeric 700 E Dyer Rd Santa Ana CA 92707

FREY, JULIA BLOCH, French language educator; b. Louisville, July 25, 1943; d. Oscar Edgeworth and Jean Goldthwaite (Russell) B.; m. Roger G. Frey, Dec. 27, 1968 (div. Mar. 1976). BA, Antioch Coll., 1966; MA, U. Tex., 1968; MPhil, Yale U., 1970, PhD, 1977. Instr. Brown U., Providence, 1972-73; chargé de cours U. de Paris, 1974-75; lectr. Yale U., New Haven, 1975-76; prof. French, Inst. Internat. Comparative Law U. San Diego, Paris, 1979—, adminstrv. dir., 1989—; assoc. prof. U. Colo., Boulder, 1976—; guest prof. Sarah Lawrence Coll., Bronxville, N.Y., 1983. Editor: Gustave Flaubert's La Lutte du Sacerdoce et de L'Empire (1837), 1981; contbr. articles and monographs to profl. publs., chpts. to books; translator: Réné. Recipient Conn. Grad. Study award, 1970-73; grantee NDEA, 1967, Brown U. Research and Travel, 1973, Boulder Arts Com., 1979, 80, Ctr. for Applied Humanities, 1985, S.W. Inst. for Research on Women, 1985-86, NEH, 1986; fellow NDEA, 1966-68, Yale U., 1968-72, Gilbert Chinard, Inst. Français de Washington, 1977. Mem. Mod. Lang. Assn. Mem. Unitarian Ch. Club: Yale (Denver). Home: 1505 Bluebell Ave Boulder CO 80302 Office: U Colo Dept French and Italian Campus Box 238 Boulder CO 80309

FREY, WILLIAM CARL, bishop; b. Waco, Tex., Feb. 26, 1930; s. Harry Frederick and Ethel (Oliver) F.; m. Barbara Louise Martin, June 12, 1952; children: Paul, Mark, Matthew, Peter, Susannah. B.A., U. Colo., 1952; Th.M., Phila. Div. Sch., 1955, D.D. (hon.), 1970. Ordained to ministry Episcopal Ch.; vicar Timberline Circuit (Colo.) Missions, 1955-58; rector Trinity-on-the-Hill Ch., Los Alamos, 1958-62; missionary priest Episcopal Ch., Costa Rica, 1962-67; bishop Episcopal Ch., 1967, Diocese of Guatemala, 1967-72; chaplain U. Ark., Fayetteville, 1972; bishop Diocese of Colo., Denver, 1972—; chmn. Episcopal Ch.'s Joint Commn. on Peace, 1979-85. Contbr. articles to religious mags. Office: PO Box 18-M Denver CO 80218

FRIBERG, GEORGE JOSEPH, electronics company executive. m. Mary Seymour; children: Fane George, Felicia Lynn Friberg Clark. BSME, U. N.Mex., 1962, MBA, 1982, postgrad. Sales engr. Honeywell, L.A., 1962-64; laiason engr. ACF Industries, Albuquerque, 1964-66; quality assurance mgr. data systems div. Gulton Industries Inc., Albuquerque, 1966-72; mgr. mfg. Femco div. Gulton Industries Inc., Irwin (Pa.), High Point (N.C.), 1972-77; v.p. mfg. data systems div. Gulton Industries Inc., Albuquerque, 1977-86; pres., chief exec. officer Tetra Corp., Albuquerque, 1986—, also bd. dirs. Mem. Mayor's hazardous waste adv. task force, 1986—, ground water protection adv. task force, 1988, N.Mex. Rsch. and Devel. Gross Receipts Task Force, 1988-89; mem. Econ. Forum of Albuquerque; bd. dirs. Technet, 1983—, pres., 1983-84, 88-89, RioTech, 1984—, treas. 1984-87, Lovelace Sci. Resources subs. Lovelace Med. Found., 1988—, Bus.-Industry Polit. Action Com., 1988—. Mem. Am. Soc. Quality Control, Am. Prodn. and Inventory Control Soc., Albuquerque C. of C. (bd. dirs. 1985—, polit. action com. 1983-84, chair buy N.Mex. chpt. 1986-87, vice chmn. econ. affairs planning coun. 1987—), U. N.Mex. Alumni Lettermen's Club, Rotary. Home: 13234 Sunset Canyon NE Albuquerque NM 87111

FRICKER, JOHN ARTHUR, pediatrician, educator; b. Detroit, Nov. 11, 1931; s. Franklin and Elizabeth Jane (Cossitt) F.; m. Patricia Alice Bedford, Sept. 10, 1955; children: Elizabeth Janet, Karen Paula. BA, Wayne U., 1956; MD, Western Res. U., 1961. Diplomate Am. Bd. Pediatrics. Intern Yale-New Haven Med. Ctr., New Haven, 1961-62; asst. resident in pediatrics Yale-New Haven Med. Ctr., 1962-64, resident, 1964-65; pvt. practice specializing in pediatrics L.A., 1965—; pediatrician, ptnr. So. Calif. Permanente Med. Group, L.A., 1965—; pediatrician, physician-in-charge Woodland Hills (Calif.) Hosp., 1977-83; instr. pediatrics Yale U. Sch. Medicine, 1964-65; clin. instr. pediatrics UCLA, 1968-72, asst. prof., 1972-80, clin. assoc. prof., 1980-86, clin. prof., 1986—. Mem. diocesan council Episcopal Diocese L.A., 1976-84, mem. standing com., 1980-84; dep. Gen. Conv. Episcopal Ch., New Orleans, 1982, L.A., 1985, Detroit, 1988.With USN, 1951-53. Recipient clin. teaching award dept. pediatrics UCLA, 1974, 78, 83, 84, 85. Fellow Am. Acad. Pediatrics; mem. Nat. Bd. Examiners (cert.), L.A. Pediatric Soc., Am. Bd. Pediatrics. Democrat. Office: Permanente Med Group 5601 De Soto Ave Woodland Hills CA 91365

FRIDLEY, SAUNDRA LYNN, internal audit executive; b. Columbus, Ohio, June 14, 1948; d. Jerry Dean and Esther Eliza (Bluhm) Fridley. BS, Franklin U., 1976; MBA, Golden Gate U., 1980. Accounts receivable supr. Internat. Harvester, Columbus, Ohio, San Leandro, Calif., 1972-80; sr. internal auditor Western Union, San Francisco, 1980; internal auditor II, County of Santa Clara, San Jose, Calif., 1980-82; sr. internal auditor Tymshare, Inc., Cupertino, Calif., 1982-84, div. contr., 1984; internal audit mgr. VWR Scientific, Brisbane, Calif., 1984-88, audit dir., 1988—; internal audit mgr. Pacific IBM Employees Fed. Credit Union, 1989—. Mem. Friends of the Vineyards. Mem. Internal Auditors Speakers Bur., Inst. Internal Auditors (pres., founder Tri-Valley chpt.), Internal Auditor's Internat. Seminar Com., NAFE. Avocations: woodworking, gardening, golfing. Home: 862 Bellflower St Livermore CA 94550 Office: VWR Scientific 3745 Bayshore Blvd Brisbane CA 94005

FRIED, ELAINE JUNE, business executive; b. Los Angeles, Oct. 19, 1943; grad. Pasadena (Calif.) High Sch., 1963; various coll. courses; m. Howard I. Fried, Aug. 7, 1966; children: Donna Marie, Randall Jay. Agt., office mgr. Howard I. Fried Agy., Alhambra, Calif., 1975—; v.p. Sea Hill, Inc., Pasadena, Calif., 1973—. Publicity chmn., unit telephone chmn. San Gabriel Valley unit; past chmn. recipient certificate appreciation, 1987, Am. Diabetes Assn.; past publicity chmn. San Gabriel Valley region Women's Am. Orgn. for Rehab. Tng. (ORT); chmn. spl. events publicity, past v.p. membership Temple Beth Torah, Alhambra; former mem. bd. dirs., pub. relations com., personnel com. Vis. Nurses Assn., Pasadena and San Gabriel Valley, Recipient Vol. award So. Calif. affiliate Am. Diabetes Assn., 1974-77; co-recipient Ner Tamid award Temple Beth Torah. Contbr. articles to profl. jours. Clubs: B'nai B'rith Women, Hadassah, Temple Beth Torah Sisterhood. Speaker on psycho-social aspects of diabetes, insurance and the diabetic, ins. medicine. Home: 404 N Hidalgo Ave Alhambra CA 91801

FRIED, LOUIS LESTER, information systems, artificial intelligence and management consultant; b. N.Y.C., Jan. 18, 1930; s. Albert and Tessie (Klein) F.; m. Haya Greenberg, Aug. 15, 1960; children: Ron Chaim, Eliana Ahuva, Gil Ben. BA in Pub. Adminstrn., Calif. State U., Los Angeles, 1962; MS in Mgmt. Theory, Calif. State U., Northridge, 1965. Mgr. br. plant data processing Litton systems, Inc., Woodland Hills, Calif., 1960-65; dir. mgmt. info. systems Bourns, Inc., Riverside, Calif., 1965-68, Weber Aircraft Co., Burbank, Calif., 1968-69; v.p. mgmt. services T.I. Corp. of Calif., Los Angeles, 1969-75; dir. advanced computer systems dept. Stanford Research Inst., Menlo Park, Calif., 1976-85, dir. ctr. for info. tech., 1985-86, dir. worldwide info. tech. practice, 1986—; cons. editor Auerbach Pubs., 1978—, Reston Pubs., 1979—; lectr. U. Calif., Riverside, 1965-69, lectr. mgmt. and EDP. Contbr. numerous articles to profl. jours., textbooks. Mem. Assn. Systems Mgmt. Home: 788 Loma Verde Ave Palo Alto CA 94303 Office: Stanford Rsch Inst Menlo Park CA 94025

FRIEDBERG, NATHAN GEORGE, marketing executive; b. Boston, June 28, 1916; s. Alexander Nicolas and Fania (Solosko) F.; m. Elsie Korn, Mar. 17, 1945; 1 child, Jordan Seth. BA, Franklin and Marshall Coll., 1939; engring. cert., U. So. Calif., 1942. Sales rep. Purofied Down Products, Burbank, Calif., 1946-50, Fashion Furniture Mfg. Co., L.A., 1950-58; owner, pres. Unique Furniture Mfg. Co., L.A., 1958-68, Friedberg Assocs., L.A., 1968—. Pres. Zool. Soc. L.A., 1957-59; organizing mem. L.A. Mayor's Adv. Com. for New Zoo, 1963, 73; commr. Boy Scouts Am., L.A., 1969. 1st lt. AUS, 1942-46, PTO. Mem. Home Furnishing Reps. Guild (pres. L.A. 1959-61, pres. Fed. Credit Union 1970—), Masons, Shriners. Democrat. Jewish. Home: 15559 Briarwood Dr Sherman Oaks CA 91403

FRIEDL, RICK, former college president, lawyer; b. Berwyn, Ill., Aug. 31, 1947; s. Raymond J. and Ione L. (Anderson) F.; m. Diane Marie Guillies, Sept. 2, 1977; children: Richard, Angela, Ryan. BA, Calif. State U., Northridge, 1969; MA, UCLA, 1976; postgrad. UCLA, 1984; JD Western State U., 1987. Bar: Calif. 1988. Dept. mgr. Calif. Dept. Indsl. Relations, 1973-78; mem. faculty dept. polit. sci. U. So. Calif., 1978-80; pres. Pacific Coll. Law, 1981-86; staff counsel state fund, Calif. State U., Northridge, 1988—. Author: The Political Economy of Cuban Dependency, 1982; tech. editor Glendale Law Rev., 1984; contbr. articles to profl. jours. Calif. State Grad. fellow, 1970-72. Mem. Calif. State Bar Assn., Los Angeles County Bar Assn., Am. Polit. Sci. Assn., Latin Am. Studies Assn., Acad. Polit. Sci., Pacific Coast Council Latin Am. Studies, L.A. County Bar Assn., Calif. Trial Lawyers Assn. Home: 13068 Sundown Ct Victorville CA 92392

FRIEDLANDER, CHARLES DOUGLAS, investment company executive, consultant; b. N.Y.C., Oct. 5, 1928; s. Murray L. and Jeane (Sottosanti) F.; m. Diane Mary Hutchins, May 12, 1951; children: Karen Diane, Lauren Patrice, Joan Elyse. BS, U.S. Mil. Acad., 1950; exec. mgmt. program, NASA, 1965; grad., Command and Staff Coll. USAF, 1965, Air War Coll. USAF, 1966. Commd. 2d lt. U.S. Army, 1950, advanced through grades to 1st lt.; officer inf. U.S. Army, Korea, 1950-51; resigned U.S. Army, 1954; mem. staff UN Forces, Trieste, Italy, 1953-54; chief astronaut support office NASA, Cape Canaveral, Fla., 1963-67; space cons. CBS News, N.Y.C., 1967-69; exec. asst. The White House, Washington, 1969-71; pres. Western Ranchlands Inc., Scottsdale, Ariz., 1971-74; pres. Fairland Co. Inc., Scottsdale, 1974—, also bd. dirs.; bd. dirs. Internat. Aerospace Hall of Fame, San Diego; space program cons., various cos., Boca Raton, Fla., 1967-69; mem. staff First Postwar Fgn. Ministers Conf., Berlin, 1954; radio/TV cons. space program. Author: Buying & Selling Land for Profit, 1961, Last Man at Hungnam Beach, 1952. V.p. West Point Soc., Cape Canaveral, Fla., 1964. Served to lt. col. USAFR, maj. USAR. Decorated Bronze Star, Combat Inf. badge; co-recipient Emmy award CBS TV Apollo Moon Landing, 1969. Mem. Nat. Space Club, Nat. Exec. Service Corps, Explorer's Club, West Point Soc., Chosin Few Survivors Korea.

FRIEDLEY, DAVID P., electronics manufacturing company executive; b. 1939; married. BSEE, Cornell U., 1962. With Genrad Inc., 1962-74, Tektronix Inc., Beaverton, Oreg., 1974—; mktg. mgr. Tektronix Inc., 1974-78, bus. unit mgr., 1978, exec. v.p., gen. mgr. Grass Valley group, 1978-83, v.p., gen. mgr. communications, then v.p., mgr. communications group, 1983-88, pres., chief exec. officer, dir., 1988—; bd. dirs. MIT Ctr. Advanced TV Studies. With U.S. Army, 1963-65. Office: Tektronix Inc PO Box 500 Delivery Sta 50 409 Beaverton OR 97077 *

FRIEDMAN, BRUCE A., lawyer; b. Los Angeles, June 6, 1935; s. Samuel L. and Irene L. (Oreck) F.; children—David, Julie, Stephen. B.A., UCLA, 1957; J.D., U. Calif.-Berkeley, 1960. Bar: Calif. 1961, U.S. Supreme Ct. 1976. Research atty. Calif. Ct. Apl. 4th App. Dist., 1960-61; sole practice, Los Angeles, 1961—; instr. Southwestern U., Los Angeles, 1965; arbitrator Los Angeles Superior Ct., 1980—. Mem. Assn. Trial Lawyers Am., Calif. Trial Lawyers Assn., Los Angeles Trial Lawyers Assn., ABA, Los Angeles County Bar Assn. Office: 2029 Century Park E Ste 2610 Los Angeles CA 90067-3012

FRIEDMAN, GLORIA A., tennis coach. d. Nicholas Alexander and Ethel Agnes (Kalionzes) Pananides; m. Gary Thomas Friedman; children: Lori Nicole, Gary Thomas. AA, Bakersfield (Calif.) Jr. Coll., 1971; BA, U. Calif., Santa Barbara, 1973; Secondary Teaching Credential, Calif. State U., 1975, MA, 1977. Head coach women's tennis, assoc. athletic dir. Calif. State U., Bakersfield; tennis rep. So. Calif. Women's Intercollegiate Athletic Conf., 1974, 75, 76, Pacific Coast Theltic Conf., 1979, 80, 81, Calif. Collegiate Athletic Assn., 1985; tournament official Jr. Coll. and Div. II divs. Ojai Tennis Championships, 1980—; tournament dir. Roadrunner Tennis Classic, 1979-85; organizer NCAA Nat. Div. II Women's Tennis Championships, 1985—; camp dir. instr. Roadrunner Summer Tennis Camps, 1986—. Faculty rep. dean's adv. com. Calif. State U., 1983, 83, mem. substance abuse com., 1986—, chairperson Student's Athletic Assistance Program, 1987—. Named NCAA Nat. Coach of Yr. for Div. II Women's Tennis, 1987, Calif. Collegiate Athletic Assn. Coach of Yr., 1983. Mem. Bakersfield Tennis Patrons (ex-officio bd. dirs. 1978—), Kern County Tennis Council (bd. dirs. 1985—). Greek Orthodox. Office: Calif State U 912 Vista Verde Way Bakersfield CA 93309

FRIEDMAN, HERBERT SHELDON, urologist; b. Chgo., Dec. 30, 1928; s. Harry and Rose (Brown) F.; m. Miriam Gabel Kranz, Dec. 27, 1953; children: Saul B., Daniel B., Naomi G. Student, Wright Coll., 1946-47; AB, U. Ill., 1950, MD, 1952. Diplomate Am. Bd. Urology. Intern, Indpls. Gen. Hosp., 1952-53; resident in urology Michael Reese Hosp., Chgo., 1953-55, Sinai Hosp., Balt., 1957-58; pvt. practice Albuquerque, 1958—; mem. exec. com. med. staff St. Joseph Hosp., Albuquerque, 1975-84, pres., 1981-82; bd. dirs. Lectronsonics Corp., Albuquerque. Mem. N.Mex. Gov.'s Adv. Coun. on Vocat. Rehab., 1967; trustee Congregation Albert, Albuquerque; bd. dirs. Albuquerque Dance Theater, 1979-84; pres. Jewish Fedn. Greater albuquerque, 1983-84. Mem. N.Mex. Med. Soc. (pres. 1988—). Republican. Home: 347 Paint Brush Dr NE Albuquerque NM 87122 Office: 6100 Pan American Frwy NE Albuquerque NM 87109

FRIEDMAN, HOWARD SCOTT, information systems specialist; b. Seattle, June 11, 1952; s. Frank Louis and Nancy Ceciel (Berliner) F.; m. Kathleen Ann McNutt, Oct. 18, 1986; children: Howard Max, Nicholas Jerome, Matthew Craig Mazanti, Aaron Douglas, Mark Andrew. Computer operator Safeco Ins. Co., Seattle, 1976-78, People's Nat. Bank, Seattle, 1978-80; shift supr. Citicorp Data Resources, Bellevue, Wash., 1980-82; recovery analyst Airborne Freight Corp., Seattle, 1982-83; supr. computer ops. Wash. Mut. Savs. Bank, Seattle, 1983-85; mgr. computer ops. Olympic Bank, Everett, Wash., 1985-86, Blue Shield Ins. Co., Tacoma, Wash., 1986-87, 1st Interstate Services Co., Tukwila, Wash., 1987--; owner, mgr. Premier Pools & Spas, Federal Way, Wash., 1987--. Republican. Jewish. Office: 1st Interstate Svcs Co 6801 S 180th St Tukwila WA 98188

FRIEDMAN, JEANIE JOYCE, interior designer, educator; b. Clinton, Iowa, Oct. 10, 1947; d. Walter Vernon and Esther Elizabeth (Sorensen) Rickertsen; m. Philip Joseph Friedman, Aug. ll, 1984; 1 child, Ronda Rene Hennings. AA, Scott Coll., 1980. Interior designer Equipment Planners, Rock Island, Ill., 1979-81, Sandstrom Products, Port Byron, Ill., 1982-83, Tri City Equipment, Davenport, Iowa, 1983-84; owner, mgr. Interiors By Jeanie, Moline, Ill., 1980-85, Kaleidoscope Interiors, Moline and Portland, Oreg., 1985--; instr. interior decorating Blackhawk Community Coll., Moline, 1983-84, Portland Community Coll., 1985-87; organizer Quad City Interior Designers, Bettendorf, Iowa, 1984-85. Newspaper columnist Kaleidoscope Interiors, 1985. Mem. edn. com. Historic Preservation League, Portland, 1987--. Mem. Home Builders Assn., Nat. Trust for Historic Preservation. Democrat. Lutheran. Home: 01225 SW Mary Failing Dr Portland OR 97219 Office: Kaleidoscope Interiors PO Box l05 Lake Oswego OR 97034

FRIEDMAN, JOHN LEE, physician, consultant; b. Cin., Aug. 23, 1930; s. Leo Samuel and Janet (Meiss) F.; m. Carolyn Jacobson, Aug 15, 1954; children: Lisa K., Daniel H., Ellen C. BA, U. Mich., 1952; MD, U. Cin., 1956. Cert. Am. Bd. Internal Medicine, subspecialty bd. in pulmonary disease. Intern Cin. Gen. Hosp., 1956-57; resident internal medicine U. Iowa Hosps., Iow City, 1957-59; fellow pulmonary disease Gen. Hosp., Cin., 1961-62; asst. prof. internal medicine U. Cin, 1962-68; pvt. practice specializing in pulmonary medicine Cin., 1962-68, Phoenix, 1968—; dir. dept. medicine Synergos Neurol. Ctr., Phoenix, 1987—; cons. pulmonary diseases VA Hosp., Phoenix, 1969—; tech. advisor to attys., Phoenix, 1982—. Contbr. papers to profl. jours. V. p., program chmn., Phoenix Chamber Music Soc., 1982—; bd. dirs. Phoenix Symphony Assn., 1975-78; mem. Phoenix Symphony Council, 1971. Capt. U.S. Army, 1959-61. Named Fellow Pulmonary Diseases, U. Cin. Hosps., 1961-62. Fellow Am. Coll. Physicians, Am. Coll. Chest Physicians (pres. Ohio chapt. 1967-8); mem. Ariz Thoracic Soc. (pres. 1973-74). Home: 135 E Winter Dr Phoenix AZ 85020 Office: 375 E Virginia Ave Ste B Phoenix AZ 85004

FRIEDMAN, KENNICIA CORINNE, civic worker; b. Los Angeles, Aug. 21, 1939; d. Kenneth Edwin and Forestine Patricia (Wilson) Gillett; m. Louis Friedman, May 28, 1964; children: Cary, Stacey. BS, UCLA, 1963, MBA, 1964. Staff acct. Price Waterhouse & Co., Los Angeles, 1964-65. Mem. Local Agy. Formation Commn. Stanislaus County, 1984; chmn. selection com. for outstanding women Stanislaus County Commn. for Women; fund raiser United Way, Modesto, 1986, account mgr., 1987, mem. allocation comn., 1988—; mem. adv. com. for ocmmunity leadership Internat. City Mgrs. Assn.; chief fin. officer Ed Source (formerly calif. Coalition for Fair Sch. Fin.), 1983-85, pres., 1985-87, devel. chmn., 1987—; bd. dirs., mem. long range planning com., planned giving com. Meml. Hosp. Assn. Recipient Outstanding Woman award Stanislaus Commn. for Women, 1982, community service award UCLA Alumni Assn., 1983. Mem. League of Women Voters of U.S. (pres. Modesto 1975-77; dir. publs. Calif. League 1977-79, v.p. mgmt. tng. 1979-81, pres. 1981-83; nat. league budget chmn. 1981-82, dir. devel. 1984-86, sec.-treas. 1986-88, mem. Edn. Fund). Home: 508 Andover Ln Modesto CA 95350

FRIEDMAN, LEONARD HOWARD, university official, educator; b. Culver City, Calif., Jan. 24, 1953; s. Phil and Annette (Friedman) F.; m. Patti Lynn Heyward, Aug. 14, 1977 (div. Dec. 1986); children: Lynn Anne, Allison Rose. BA, Calif. State U., Northridge, 1977, MPH, 1982; cert., UCLA, 1985. Cert. health edn. specialist, Calif. Dialysis technician UCLA Med. Ctr., 1973; sr. dialysis technician Bio Med. Community Dialysis Ctr., Beverly Hills, Calif., 1973-77; chmn. sci. dept. Lycee Francais L.A., 1977-79; tchr. sci. Abraham Joshua Heschel Day Sch., Northridge, 1979-82; staff assoc. High Blood Pressure Coun., L.A., 1982; asst. dir. Area Health Edn. Ctr., Northridge, 1982-83; exec. dir. Area Health Edn. Ctr., L.A., 1983-85; exec. asst. U. So. Calif., L.A., 1985—, lectr. health edn., 1986-88; lectr. health edn. So. Calif. Coll. Optometry, Fullerton, 1986—, Calif. State U., Northridge, 1987—, U. La Verne (Calif.), 1988—. Contbr. articles to profl. publs. Mem. Am. Soc. for Pub. Adminstrn., Am. Pub. Health Assn., Calif. State U.-Northridge Gen. Alumni Assn. (pres. health edn. chpt. 1986-88, mem. gen. bd. 1988, sr. v.p. 1989). Office: U So Calif University Park ADM-201 Los Angeles CA 90089-4012

FRIEDMAN, LONNIE R., nursing agency administrator; b. Hartford, Conn., Aug. 20, 1947; d. Herman and Betty (Shrobe) F. BS in Nursing, U. Conn., 1969; PhD in Transpersonal Psy., Internat. Coll., 1985. Nurse Yale New Haven (Conn.) Hosp., 1969-70; with med. surg. Mt. Sinai Hosp., N.Y.C., 1970-71; rsch. nurse LAC-USC Med. Ctr., L.A., 1973-77, acupressurist, health counselling, 1977-86; utilization review coord. Hollywood Presbyn. Med. Ctr., L.A., 1982-86; co-owner Vital Signs, L.A., 1987-88; prin. Quality Review Assocs., L.A., 1988—. Mem. Calif. Assn. Quality Assocs. Profl., Calif. Nurses Assn.,. Democrat. Jewish. Home: 11818 Gateway Blvd #7 Los Angeles CA 90064

FRIEDMAN, LOUIS, food products executive; b. St. Louis, Sept. 24, 1939; s. Al and Elinor (Rubin) F.; m. Kennicia Gillett; children: Cary, Stacey. BS with honors, Ariz. State U., 1960; LLB, Loyola U., Los Angeles, 1964; LLM in Taxation, NYU, 1967. CPA; Bar: N.Y., Calif. Tax mgr. Price Waterhouse, Los Angeles and N.Y.C., 1961-73; v.p., treas. E. & J. Gallo Winery, Modesto, Calif., 1973—. Jewish. Lodge: Rotary. Home: 508 Andover Ln Modesto CA 95350 Office: E&J Gallo Winery 600 Yosemite Blvd Modesto CA 95354

FRIEDMAN, MARK, physician; b. Chgo., Aug. 15, 1948. BA in Psychology, UCLA, 1975; MD, U. Autonoma de Guadalajara, 1981. Diplomate Am. Bd. Family Practice. Physician, owner Bilingual Family Practice Office, Phoenix, 1988—. Mem. Am. Med. Assn., So. Med. Assn., Ariz. Acad. Family Physicians, Am. Acad. Family Physicians. Office: Westridge Family Physicians 2330 N 75th Ave Ste 108 Phoenix AZ 85035

FRIEDMAN, MARK ALLAN, organization executive; b. Youngstown, Ohio, May 2, 1945; s. Sam and Pearl (Schermer) F.; m. Leslie Levit, June 16, 1968; children: Daniel S., Ellen B. BS in Math., Ohio State U., 1966, MBA, 1968. Bus. analyst Owens-Ill., Inc., Toledo, 1969-7l, dir. environ. affairs, 1972-75, dir. pub. and environ. affairs, 1976-80, dir. compensation, 198l-83, dir. personnel planning, 198l-85; dir. personnel Jewish Fedn. Coun., L.A., 1985-86, dir. fin. and adminstrn., 1986—. Mem. U.S. C. of C., Sphinx, Pacesetters, Phi Eta Sigma. Democrat. Home: 17426 Flanders St Granada Hills CA 91344 Office: Jewish Fedn Coun 6505 Wilshire Blvd Los Angeles CA 90048

FRIEDMAN, MAURICE STANLEY, religion educator; b. Tulsa, Dec. 29, 1921; s. Samuel Herman and Fanny (Smirin) F.; m. Eugenia Chifos, Jan. 1947 (div. 1974); children: David Michael, Dvora Lisa; m. Aleene Marie Wright Dorn, Sept. 29, 1986. SB in Econs. magna cum laude, Harvard U., 1943; MA in English, Ohio State U., 1947; PhD in History of Culture, U. Chgo., 1950; LLD (hon.), U. Vt., 1961; MA in Psychology, Internat. Coll., 1983; LHD (hon.), Profl. Sch. Psychol. Studies, San Diego, 1986. Prof. philosophy and lit. Sarah Lawrence Coll., 1951-54, prof. philosophy, 1954-64; prof. philosophy and religion Manhattanville Coll. of the Sacred Heart, Purchase, N.Y., 1966-67, Vassar Coll., Poughkeepsie, N.Y., 1967; prof. religion Temple U., Phila., 1966-73, also dir. PhD programs in religion and psychology and religion and lit.; prof. religious studies, philosophy and comparative lit. San Diego State U., 1973—; tutor Internat. Coll., Los Angeles, 1976-86, William Lyon U., 1986—; vis. prof. religious philosophy Hebrew Union Coll.-Jewish Inst. Religion, Cin., 1956, Union Theol. Sem., N.Y.C., 1965, 67; mem. faculty New Sch. for Social Research, N.Y.C., 1954-66, Pendle Hill, Quaker Ctr. for Study, Wallingford, Pa., 1959-60, 64-65, 67-73; univ. lectr. research San Diego State U., 1984-85; sr. Fulbright lectr. Hebrew U., Jerusalem, 1987-88; fellow com. on the history of culture U. Chgo., 1947-49; co-dir. Inst. for Dialogical Psychotherapy, San Diego. Author: Martin Buber: The Life of Dialogue, 1955, Problematic Rebel: Melville, Dostoievsky, Kafka, Camus, 1963, rev. edit. 1970, The Worlds of Existentialism, 1964, To Deny Our Nothingness: Contemporary Images of Man, 1967, Touchstones of Reality: Existential Trust and the Community of Peace, 1972, The Hidden Human Image, 1974, The Human Way: A Dialogical Approach to Religion and Human Experience, 1982, The Confirmation of Otherness: In Family, Community and Society, 1983, Martin Buber's Life and Work: The Early Years 1878-1923, 1982, The Middle Years, 1923-45, 1983, The Later Years 1945-65, 1984 (Nat. Jewish Book award for biography 1985), Contemporary Psychology: Revealing and Obscuring the Human, 1984, The Healing Dialogue In Psychotherapy, 1985 (main selection of Psychotherapy and Social Sci. Book Club, Mar. 1985), Martin Buber and The Eternal, 1986, Abraham Joshua Heschel and Elie Wiesel: "You are my Witnesses", 1987, A Dialogue with Hasidic Tales: Hallowing the Everyday, 1988; contbr. numerous articles to profl. jours. Recipient Outstanding Faculty award San Diego State U., 1980. Mem. Religious Edn. Assn. (past bd. dirs., past edit. bd.), Am. Philol. Assn., Am. Acad. Religion, Am. Soc. Study Religion, Fellowship of Reconciliation, Jewish Peace Fellowship, Assn. Humanistic Psychology (edit. bd. Jour. Humanistic Psychology and Person-Centered Rev.), Inst. Dialogical Psychotherapy (co-dir.). Home: 421 Hilmen Pl Solana Beach CA 92075 Office: San Diego State U Dept Religious Studies San Diego CA 92182-0304 *

FRIEDMAN, MILTON, economist, educator emeritus, author; b. Bklyn., July 31, 1912; s. Jeno Saul and Sarah Ethel (Landau) F.; m. Rose Director, June 25, 1938; children: Janet, David. AB, Rutgers U., 1932, LLD, 1968; AM, U. Chgo., 1933; PhD, Columbia U., 1946; LLD, St. Paul's (Rikkyo) U., 1963; LLD (hon.), Kalamazoo Coll., 1968, Lehigh U., 1969, Loyola U., 1971, U. N.H., 1975, Harvard U., 1979, Brigham Young U., 1980,

Dartmouth Coll., 1980, Gonzaga U., 1981; DSc (hon.), Rochester U., 1971; LHD (hon.), Rockford Coll., 1969, Roosevelt U., 1975, Hebrew Union Coll., Los Angeles, 1981; LittD (hon.), Bethany Coll., 1971; PhD (hon.), Hebrew U., Jerusalem, 1977; DCS (hon.), Francisco Marroquín U., Guatemala, 1978. Assoc. economist Nat. Resources Com., Washington, 1935-37; mem. research staff Nat. Bur. Econ. Research, N.Y.C., 1937-45, 1948-81; vis. prof. econs. U. Wis., Madison, 1940-41; prin. economist, tax research div. U.S. Treasury Dept., Washington, 1941-43; assoc. dir. research, statis. research group, War Research div. Columbia U., N.Y.C., 1943-45; assoc. prof. econs. and statistics U. Minn., Mpls., 1945-46; assoc. prof. econs. U. Chgo., 1946-48, prof. econs., 1948-62, Paul Snowden Russell disting. service prof. econs., 1962-82, prof. emeritus, 1983—; Fulbright lectr. Cambridge U., 1953-54; vis. Wesley Clair Mitchell research prof. econs. Columbia U., N.Y.C., 1964-65; fellow Ctr. for Advanced Study in Behavioral Sci., 1957-58; sr. research fellow Stanford U., 1977—; mem. Pres.'s Commn. All-Vol. Army, 1969-70, Pres.'s Commn. on White House Fellows, 1971-74, Pres.'s Econ. Policy Adv. Bd., 1981-88; vis. scholar Fed. Res. Bank, San Francisco, 1977. Author: (with Carl Shoup and Ruth P. Mack) Taxing to Prevent Inflation, 1943, (with Simon S. Kuznets) Income from Independent Professional Practice, 1946, (with Harold A. Freeman, Frederic Mosteller, W. Allen Wallis) Sampling Inspection, 1948, Essays in Positive Economics, 1953, A Theory of the Consumption Function, 1957, A Program for Monetary Stability, 1960, Price Theory: A Provisional Text, 1962, (with Rose D. Friedman) Capitalism and Freedom, 1962, (with R.D. Friedman) Free To Choose, 1980, Tyranny of the Status Quo, 1984, (with Anna J. Schwartz) A Monetary History of the United States, 1867-1960, 1963, (with Schwartz) Monetary Statistics of the United States, 1970, (with Schwartz) Monetary Trends in the U.S. and the United Kingdom, 1982, Inflation: Causes and Consequences, 1963, (with Robert Roosa) The Balance of Payments: Free vs. Fixed Exchange Rates, 1967, Dollars and Deficits, 1968, The Optimum Quantity of Money and Other Essays, 1969, (with Walter W. Heller) Monetary vs. Fiscal Policy, 1969, A Theoretical Framework for Monetary Analysis, 1972, (with Wilbur J. Cohen) Social Security, 1972, An Economist's Protest, 1972, There's No Such Thing As A Free Lunch, 1975, Price Theory, 1976, (with Robert J. Gordon et al.) Milton Friedman's Monetary Framework, 1974, Tax Limitation, Inflation and the Role of Government, 1978, Bright Promises, Dismal Performance, 1983; editor: Studies in the Quantity Theory of Money, 1956; bd. editors Am. Econ. Rev, 1951-53, Econometrica, 1957-69; adv. bd. Jour. Money, Credit and Banking, 1968—; columnist Newsweek mag, 1966-84, contbg. editor, 1971-84; contbr. articles to profl. jours. Recipient Nobel prize in econs., 1976, Pvt. Enterprise Exemplar medal Freedoms Found., 1978, Grand Cordon of the Sacred Treasure Japanese Govt., 1986, Presdl. medal of Freedom, 1988, Nat. medal of Sci., 1988; named Chicagoan of Yr. Chgo. Press Club, 1972, Educator of Yr. Chgo. United Jewish Fund, 1973. Fellow Inst. Math. Stats., Am. Statis. Assn., Econometric Soc.; mem. Nat. Acad. Scis., Am. Econ. Assn. (mem. exec. com. 1955-57, pres. 1967; John Bates Clark medal 1951), Am. Enterprise Inst. (adv. bd. 1956-79), Western Econ. Assn. (pres. 1984-85), Royal Economic Soc., Am. Philos. Soc., Mont Pelerin Soc. (bd. dirs. 1958-61, pres. 1970-72). Club: Quadrangle. Office: Stanford U Hoover Instn Stanford CA 94305-6010

FRIEDMAN, RON, television and performing arts producer; b. Pitts., Aug. 1, 1932; s. Louis and Mina (Hirschfield) F.; divorced; children: Ian C., Liza P.; m. Valerie Clare Fidgeon, Aug. 15, 1973; 1 child, Ashley R. BArch, Carnegie-Mellon U., 1955. Registered architect, Pa., Ohio, W.Va. Writer (TV series) The Odd Couple, Fantasy Island, Starsky and Hutch, The Fall Guy, Chico and the Man, Bewitched, All in the Family, others; writer, producer (TV dramas, comedies, animated spls.) The Jonathan Winters Show, Danny Kaye Show, Betty Boop-CBS, Marathon, Murder Can Hurt You, GI Joe, Bionic 6, Transformers, Sledgehammer. Mem. AFTRA, Writers Guild Am. West, Dramatists Guild. Office: ILI Prodns Inc 9171 Wilshire Blvd Suite 627 Beverly Hills CA 90210

FRIEDMAN, SHELLY ARNOLD, cosmetic surgeon; b. Providence, Jan. 1, 1949; s. Saul and Estelle (Moverman) F.; m. Andrea Leslie Falchook, Aug. 30, 1975; children: Bethany Erin, Kimberly Rebecca. BA, Providence Coll., 1971; DO, Mich. State U., 1982. Diplomate Nat. Bd. Med. Examiners. Intern Pontiac (Mich.) Hosp., 1982-83, resident in dermatology, 1983-86; assoc. clin. prof. dept. internal med. Mich. State U., 1984—; med. dir. Inst. Cosmetic Dermatology, Scottsdale, Ariz., 1986—. Contbr. aritcles to profl. jours. Mem. B'nai B'rith Men's Council, 1973, Jewish Welfare Fund, 1973. Am. Physicians fellow for medicine, 1982. Mem. AMA, Am. Osteopathic Assn., Am. Assn. Cosmetic Surgeons, Am. Acad. Cosmetic Surgery, Internat. Soc. Dermatologic Surgery, Internat. Acad. Cosmetic Surgery, Am. Acad. Dermatology, Am. Soc. Dermatol. Surgery, Frat. Order Police, Sigma Sigma Phi. Jewish. Office: Scottsdale Inst Cosmetic Dermatology 10603 N Hayden Rd Ste 112 Scottsdale AZ 85260

FRIEDMAN, STUART HOWARD, manufacturer's agent; b. St. Louis, Mar. 16, 1954; s. Melvin and Geri (Loomstein) F. BS, Washington U., St. Louis, 1978; M. Hotel, Mich. State U., 1988; JD, St. Louis U., 1986. Law clk. Friedman & Fredericks, St. Louis, 1978-80; owner The Factory Rep Group, St. Louis, 1980—, Denver, 1985—; cons. Trandewinds Outdoor Funiture, Miami, Fla., 1981—, Victor Stanley, Inc., Dunkirk, Md., 1982—, Flexsteel Industries, Inc., Dubuque, Iowa, 1986—, Am. Textile Co., 1989—. Mem. Am. Hotel & Motel Assn., Denver Apt. Assn., Rocky Mountain Restaurant Assn., Sporting Club. Jewish. Office: The Factory Rep Group 1801 Wynkoop St C-30 Denver CO 80202

FRIEDMANN, PERETZ PETER, aerospace engineer, educator; b. Timisoara, Romania, Nov. 18, 1938; came to U.S., 1969; s. Mauritius and Elisabeth F.; m. Esther Sarfati, Dec. 8, 1964. DSc, MIT, 1972. Engring. officer Israel Def. Force, 1961-65; sr. engr. Israel Aircraft Industries, Ben Gurion Airport, Israel, 1965-69; research asst. dept. aeronautics and astronautics MIT, Cambridge, 1969-72; asst. prof. mech., aerospace and nuclear engring. dept. UCLA, 1972-77, assoc. prof., 1977-80, prof., 1980—; chmn. Dept. Mech Aerospace Nuclear Engring., Los Angeles, 1988—. Editor-in-chief Vertica-Internat. Jour. Rotorcraft and Powered Lift Aircraft; contbr. numerous articles to profl. jours. Grantee NASA, U.S. Army Research Office, NSF. Fellow AIAA (assoc.); mem. ASME (Structures and Materials award 1983), Am. Helicopter Soc., Sigma Xi. Jewish. Office: UCLA Dept Mech Aerospace and Nuclear Engring 5732 Boelter Hall Los Angeles CA 90024

FRIEMAN, EDWARD ALLAN, university administrator, educator; b. N.Y.C., Jan. 19, 1926; s. Joseph and Belle (Davidson) F.; m. Ruth Paula Rodman, June 19, 1949 (dec. May 1966); children: Jonathan, Michael, Joshua; m. Joy Fields, Sept. 17, 1967; children: Linda Gatchell, Wendy. B.S., Columbia U., 1945, M.S. in Physics, 1948; Ph.D. in Physics, Poly. Inst. Bklyn., 1951. Prof. astrophys. scis., dep. dir. Plasma Physics Lab. Princeton U., N.J., 1952-79; dir. energy research Dept. Energy, Washington, 1979-81; exec. v.p. Sci. Applications Internat. Corp., La Jolla, Calif., 1981-86; dir. Scripps Instn. Oceanography, La Jolla, 1986—; vice chancellor marine scis. U. Calif., San Diego, 1986—; vice chmn. White House Sci. Council, 1981—, Def. Sci. Bd., Washington, 1984—; chmn. supercollider site evaluation com. NRC, 1987-88. Contbr. articles to profl. jours. Served with USN, 1943-46, PTO. Recipient Disting. Service medal Dept. Energy; Disting. Alumni award Poly. Inst. Bklyn.; NSF sr. postdoctoral fellow; Guggenheim fellow. Fellow Am. Phys. Soc. (Richtmyer award); mem. AAAS, Nat. Acad. Scis. Club: Cosmos (Washington). Home: 6425 Muirlands Dr La Jolla CA 92037 Office: Scripps Instn Oceanography Dirs Office A-010 La Jolla CA 92093

FRIEND, DAVID ROBERT, chemist; b. Vallejo, Calif., Aug. 10, 1956; s. Carl Gilbert and Roberta (Schwarzrock) F.; m. Carol Esther Warren, Dec. 17, 1983; 1 child, Ian, Michael. BS in Food Biochemistry, U. Calif., Davis, 1979; PhD in Agrl. Chemistry, U. Calif., Berkeley, 1983. Polymer chemist SRI Internat., Menlo Park, Calif., 1984-87, sr. polymer chemist controlled release and biomed. polymers dept., 1987—. Asst. editor Jour. Controlled Release; contbr. articles to scholarly jours.; patentee in field. Mem. Am. Chem. Soc., N.Y. Acad. Scis., Controlled Release Soc., Am. Assn. Pharm. Sci., Sigma Xi. Democrat. Jewish. Home: 301 Gilbert Ave Menlo Park CA 94025 Office: SRI Internat 333 Ravenswood Ave Menlo Park CA 94025

FRIES, MICHAEL THOMAS, architect; b. Norwalk, Ohio, Jan. 25, 1959; s. Thomas George and Nancy Elizabeth (Neuberger) F.; m. Margaret Herre, Sept. 4, 1983. Student, San Francisco Ctr. for Architecture and Urban Studies, 1980; B. in Environ. Design, Miami U., Oxford, Ohio, 1981; MArch., U. Tex., 1984. Archtl. draftsman Kolb Assocs., Austin, Tex., 1981-82; archtl. apprentice Wukasch and Assocs., Austin, 1982; market researcher Horne Co., Austin, 1982; design capt. Villalva-Cotera-Kolak, Austin, 1982-83; constrn. office mgr. Tao-Ono Inc., Austin, 1983-84; pres. Urban Concern Inc., Austin, 1984-86; project mgr. Black and Veatch Engrs. and Architects, Phoenix and Austin, 1986-87, Nelson-Kubicek Architects, Phoenix, 1987-88; project architect Architecture One Ltd., Phoenix, 1988—; part-time instr. archtl. drafting Phoenix Inst. Tech., 1988—. Dir. programming svcs. Jaycees, Austin, 1985-86; pres. Quadrangle Homeowners Assn., Austin, 1984-87; mem. Coronado Neighborhood Assn., Phoenix, 1988, Phoenix Art Mus. Recipient 2nd place award Affordable Housing Competition City of Austin, 1986. Mem. AIA (assoc.), Phoenix City Club, Laguna Gloria Club. Democrat. Roman Catholic.

FRIESE, ROBERT CHARLES, lawyer; b. Chgo., Apr. 29, 1943; s. Earl Matthew and Laura Barbara (Mayer) F.; m. Chandra Ullom; 1 child, Matthew Robert. A.B. in Internat. Relations, Stanford U., 1964; J.D., Northwestern U., 1970. Admitted to Calif. bar, 1972; dir. Tutor Applied Linguistics Center, Geneva, Switzerland, 1964-66; atty. Bronson, Bronson & McKinnon, San Francisco, 1970-71, SEC, San Francisco, 1971-75; atty., partner Shartsis, Friese & Ginsburg, San Francisco, 1975—; dir., co-founder Internat. Plant Research Inst., Inc., San Carlos, Calif., 1978-86. Chmn. Bd. Suprs. Task Force on Noise Control, 1972-78; chmn. San Franciscans for Cleaner City, 1977; exec. dir. Nob Hill Neighbors, 1972-81; bd. dirs. Nob Hill Assn., 1976-78, Inst. of Range and the Am. Mustang, Calif. Heritage Council, 1977-78, San Francisco Beautiful, 1986— (pres. 1988—); mem. major gifts com. Stanford U. Mem. Am. Bar Assn., Calif. Bar Assn., Bar Assn. San Francisco, (bd. dirs. 1982-85, chmn. bus. litigation com., 1978-79, chmn. state ct. civil litigation com. 1983—), Lawyers Club of San Francisco, Mensa, Calif. Hist. Soc. Clubs: Commonwealth; Swiss-American Friendship League (chmn. 1971-79). Office: Shartsis Friese & Ginsburg 1 Maritime Pla 18th Fl San Francisco CA 94111-2204

FRIESECKE, RAYMOND FRANCIS, management consultant; b. N.Y.C., Mar. 12, 1937; s. Bernhard P. K. and Josephine (De Tomi) F.; BS in Chemistry, Boston Coll., 1959; MS in Civil Engring., MIT, 1961. Product specialist Dewey & Almy Chem. div. W. R. Grace & Co., Inc., Cambridge, Mass., 1963-66; market planning specialist USM Corp., Boston, 1966-71; mgmt. cons., Boston, 1971-74; dir. planning and devel. Schweitzer div. Kimberly-Clark Corp., Lee, Mass., 1974-78; v.p. corp. planning Butler Automatic, Inc., Canton, Mass., 1978-80; pres. Butler-Europe Inc., Greenwich, Conn. and Munich, Fed. Republic Germany, 1980; v.p. mktg. and planning Butler Greenwich Inc., 1980-81; pres. Strategic Mgmt. Assocs., San Rafael, Calif., 1981—; corp. clk., v.p. Bldg. Research & Devel., Inc., Cambridge, 1966-68. State chmn. Citizens for Fair Taxation, 1972-73; state co-chmn. Mass. Young Reps., 1967-69; chmn. Ward 7 Rep. Com., Cambridge, 1968-70; vice chmn. Cambridge Rep. City Com., 1966-68; vice-chmn. Kentfield Rehab. Hosp. Found., 1986-88, chmn., 1988—; Rep. candidate Mass. Ho. of Reps., 1964, 66; pres. Marin Rep. Council, 1986—; chmn. Calif. Acad., 1986-88; sec. Navy League Marin Council, 1984—. Served to 1st lt. U.S. Army, 1961-63. Mem. Am. Chem. Soc., World Affairs Coun., The Planning Forum , Am. Mktg. Assn., The World Affairs Coun., Am. Rifle Assn. Author: Management by Relative Product Quality; contbr. articles to profl. jours. Home and Office: 141 Convent Ct San Rafael CA 94901

FRIGON, JUDITH ANN, electronics executive, office systems consultant; b. Wisconsin Rapids, Wis., Feb. 11, 1945; d. Harold Leslie and Muriel Alice (Berard) Neufeld; m. Gene Roland Frigon, June 17, 1967; children: Shane P., Shannon M., Sean M. Sec., office mgr. George Chapman D.D.S., Fairfax, Va., 1971-75; owner, operator Sunset Motel, Havre, Mont., 1976-78; sec. Wash. State U. Social Research Ctr., Pullman, 1978-80; adminstrv. sec. Wash. State U. Systems and Computing, Pullman, 1980-85, office automation cons., word processing trainer, IBM profl. office system adminstr., 1983—; systems analyst, programmer Wash. State U. Computing Ctr., Pullman, 1985—. Pres. Pullman Svc. Unit Girl Scouts U.S., 1983-89; v.p. Inland Empire coun. Girl Scouts U.S., Spokane, Wash., 1985-89, pres., 1989—; mem. Pullman Civic Trust, 1986—; mem.-at-large Pullman United Way, 1988—. Mem. Profl. Secs. Internat., Jaycees (Jayceen of Yr. 1978). Roman Catholic. Home: NW 1235 Davis Way Pullman WA 99163 Office: Wash State U $S1Computing Ctr $S22072 Computer Sci Bldg Pullman WA 99164-1220

FRINGS-KEYES, MARGARET PATRICIA, social worker; b. Butte, Mont., Aug. 8, 1929; d. John Matthew and Mary Ellen (Dyer) F. BA, U. Calif., 1951; MSW, Nat. Cath. U., 1953; postgrad., U. Chgo., 1961. Lic. clin. social worker. Med. social worker U. Calif. Med. Sch., San Francisco, 1955-61; postgrad. fellow U. Chgo. Sch. Social Sci. Adminstrn., 1961-62; dir. profl. services Cath. Social Services, Marin County, Calif., 1962-69; pvt. practice psychotherapy San Francisco, 1969—; assoc. prof. psychology Lone Mountain Coll., San Francisco, 1972-78; cons. to psychotherapists, 1969—. Author: Inward Journey, 1974, revised edit., 1984, Staying Married, 1975, Out of the Shadows, 1988, Emotions and the Enneagrown, 1989. Mem. San Francisco Organizing Project, 1985—; pres. bd. dirs. Berkeley Ctr. Human Interaction, Calif., 1978-79. Fellow Soc. Clin. Soc. Workers (founding mem.); mem. Am. Soc. Group Psychotherapists and Psychodramatists, Am. Group Psychotherapists Assn., Nat. Assn. Social Workers, No. Calif. Group Psychotherapy Soc. (coun. mem. 1987—). Democrat. Roman Catholic. Home: 203 Star Route Muir Beach CA 94965 Office: 613 Wisconsin St San Francisco CA 94107

FRINK, EUGENE HUDSON, JR., business and real estate consultant; b. Denver, Feb. 6, 1927; s. Eugene Hudson and Maxine Louella (Ingle) F.; m. Catherine Claire Heath, Dec. 27, 1947; children: Douglas Martin, Bryan Clifford, Daniel Neal. BA, Denver U., 1947. Mgr. Frink Creamery Co., Ft. Collins, Colo., 1948-64; co-founder, mgr. ops Aqua-Tec Corp. (Water Pik), Ft. Collins, 1964-66; archtl. designer Gene Frink Designers, Ft. Collins, 1967-84; ptnr. Wakaya Island, Ltd., Fiji, 1968-71; chmn. Beehive Internat., Salt Lake City, 1969-85; prin. Architecture Plus, P.C., Ft. Collins, 1985-88; ptnr. Naindi Plantation, Fiji, 1969—; gen. ptnr. Elk River Assocs., Steamboat Springs, Colo., 1978—; pres., Assocs. Corp., Nantucket, Mass.; cons. Architecture Plus, Charles Bowling Real Estate, both Ft. Collins, 1988—. Councilman, City of Ft. Collins, 1959-63, mayor, 1961-63; mem. Ft. Collins Regional Planning Bd., 1962-64. Mem. Rotary Club, Pres.'s Seminar. Republican. Episcopalian. Home: 1212 Morgan St Fort Collins CO 80524 Office: 2120 S College Ave Fort Collins CO 80525

FRIPP, RAYMOND RALPH, pediatric cardiologist; b. Pinetown, Natal, Republic of South Africa, Sept. 22, 1946; came to U.S., 1977; s. Alfred Downing and Jessie (Purves) F.; m. Lynette Doveton, Aug. 29, 1970; children: Nicolette, Matthew, Jessica. MB, BCh, U. Witwatersrand, Johannesburg, Republic of South Africa, 1971. Diplomate Am. Bd. Pediatrics. Intern Grey's Hosp., Pietermaritzberg, Natal, Republic of South Africa, 1972-73, Hosp. St. Raphael, New Haven, 1973-74; resident Red Cross Children's Hosp., Cape Town, Republic of South Africa, 1975-77; resident Milton S. Hershey Med. Ctr., Hershey, Pa., 1977-78, asst. prof., 1980-85; fellow pediatric cardiology Yale U. Hosp., New Haven, 1978-80; asst. prof. U. N.Mex., Albuquerque, 1985; practice medicine specializing in pediatric cardiology Albuquerque, 1986—. Author: Techniques, Diagnostics and Advances in Nuclear Medicine, 1983, Managemnt of the Cardiac Patient Requiring Non-Cardiac Surgery, 1983. Am. Heart Assn. grantee, 1983-86. Fellow Coll. Physicians South Africa (pediatrics), Am. Bd. Pediatrics (bd. pediatric cardiology). Office: Pediatric Cardiology Assocs 715 Grand Ave NE Ste 207 Albuquerque NM 87102

FRISBEE, DON CALVIN, retired utilities executive; b. San Francisco, Dec. 13, 1923; s. Ira Nobles and Helen (Sheets) F.; m. Emilie Ford, Feb. 5, 1947; children: Ann, Robert, Peter, Dean. BA, Pomona Coll., 1947; MBA, Harvard U., 1949. Sr. investment analyst, asst. cashier investment analysis dept. 1st Interstate Bank Oreg., N.A., Portland, 1949-52, now dir.; with PacifiCorp, Portland, 1953—, treas., 1958-60, then v.p., exec. v.p., pres., 1966-73, chief exec. officer, chmn., 1973-89, chmn., 1989—; bd. dirs. First Interstate Bancorp, Weyerhaeuser Co., Standard Ins. Co., Portland., Precision Castparts Corp., Portland, First Interstate Bank of Oreg., Portland, Pacificorp Fin. Svcs. Trustee Reed Coll., Com. for Econ. Devel., Safari Game Search Found.; chmn. assn. coun. YMCA; pres., bd. dirs. Oreg. Community Found., Oreg. Bus. Coun., Oreg. Wildlife Heritage Found., Oreg. Indep. Coll. Found.; cabinet mem. Columbia Pacific Coun. Boy Scouts Am. 1st lt. AUS, 1943-46. Mem. Japan-Western U.S. Assn. (exec. coun.). Clubs: Arlington, University, Multnomah Athletic. Office: PacifiCorp 825 NE Multnomah Lloyd Tower Ste 1055 Portland OR 97232

FRITCHER, EARL EDWIN, civil engineer, consultant; b. St. Ansgar, Iowa, Nov. 24, 1923; s. Lee and Mamie Marie (Ogden) F.; m. Dorsille Ellen Simpson, Aug. 24, 1946; 1 child, Teresa. BS, Iowa State U., 1950. Registered civil engr., Calif. Project devel. engr. dept. transp. State of Calif., Los Angeles, 1950-74, traffic engr. dept. transp., 1974-87; pvt. practice cons. engr. Sunland, Calif., 1987—. Patentee in field. Mem. Profl. Engrs. Calif. Govt. Served to 2d lt. USAF, 1942-46, 50-51. Mem. Iowa State Alumni Assn. Republican. Methodist. Clubs: Verdugo Hills Numismatic (Sunland), Glendale Numismatic.

FRITSCH, COLIN MICHAEL, aerospace engineer; b. Milw., May 5, 1948; s. Colin Benard and Mary Ann (Volkmann) F. BSEE, Marquette U., Milw., 1970. Jr. engr. Naval Avionics Facility, Indpls., 1971-72; engr. Honeywell Aerospace, Clearwater, Fla., 1972-75, Gen. Dynamics, Orlando, Fla., 1975-77; staff engr. Martin Marietta Corp., Denver, 1977—. Club: Denver Ski. Home: 1491 W Long Ave Littleton CO 80120

FRITSCH, FREDERICK NORMAN, research numerical mathematician, consultant; b. Portland, Oreg., Mar. 12, 1939; s. Robert William and Dorothy Marie (Hansen) F.; m. Nancy Ann Newkirk, Sept. 14, 1958; children: Michael, Eric, Lisa. BS in Chemistry and Math., Oreg. State U., Corvallis, 1961; MA in Math., U. Calif., Berkeley, 1965, PhD in Applied Math., 1969. Teaching asst. U. Calif., Berkeley, 1961-62; computer programmer Standard Oil Co., San Francisco, 1962; computer programmer Lawrence Radiation Lab., Livermore, Calif., 1963, math programmer, tech. writer, 1964-69; mathematician Lawrence Livermore Nat. Lab., 1969-82 83—; vis. prof. Drexel U., Phila., 1982-83; tech. cons. C. Abaci, Inc., Raleigh, N.C., 1984—; assoc. editor ACM Transactions on Math. Software, 1984—, Communications of the ACM, 1978-81. Contbr. articles to profl. jours. Fellow NSF, Berkeley, 1963. Mem. Soc. for Indsl. and Applied Math. (nominating com. No. Calif. Sect. 1988), Assn. Computing Machinery and Spl. Interest Group on Numerical Math. (vice chmn. 1981-83). Democrat. Presbyterian. Office: Lawrence Livermore Nat Lab PO Box 808 L-316 Livermore CA 94550

FRITSCHE, RONALD D., rehabilitation counselor; b. Denver, Oct. 27, 1948; s. Louis Paul and Margaret Lorraine (Miller) F.; m. Louise Ruth Good, Aug. 15, 1970; children: Dan, Johanna, Holly, Jeremy. BA, Rockmont Coll., 1970; MA, U. Colo., 1976. Cert. rehab. cons., ins. rehab. counselor, nat. cert. counselor, qualified rehab. cons. Tchr. All Saints Sch., Denver, 1971-72; dir. of admissions Rockmont Coll., Lakewood, Colo., 1972-77; dir. admissions Sioux Falls (S.D.) Coll., 1977-78; pvt. vocat. rehab. counselor Nat. Rehab. Cons., St. Paul, 1978-82, Am. Rehab. Cons., Maple Grove, Minn., 1982; prin., pvt. vocat. rehab. counselor Midwest Cons. Rehab. Service, St. Paul, 1982-87; pvt. vocat. rehab. counselor Crawford Rehab. Services, Englewood, Colo., 1987-88; rehab. counselor Colo. Rehab. and Clin. Consultants, Englewood, 1988—. Republican. Home: 7751 Inns Brook Dr Evergreen CO 80439

FRITTS, HAROLD CLARK, dendrochronology educator, researcher; b. Rochester, N.Y., Dec. 17, 1928; s. Edwin Coulthard and Ava Lee (Washburn) F.; m. Barbara Smith, June 11, 1955 (dec.); children: Marcia L., Paul T.; m. Miriam Colson, July 19, 1982. AB, Oberlin Coll., 1951; MS, Ohio State U., 1953, PhD in Botany, 1956. Asst. prof. botany Eastern Ill. U., Charleston, 1956-60; asst. prof. dendrochronology U. Ariz., Tucson, 1960-64, assoc., 1964-69, prof., 1969—; dir., founder Internat. Tree-Ring Data Bank, 1975—; NSF faculty, mem. Task Group 3 adv. com. on paleoclimatology, Climate Dynamics Program, 1978—; lectr. NATO Advanced Study Inst. on Climatic Variability, Sicily, 1980; vis. dr. U. Wyo. Summer Sci. Camp, summer 1956; mem. U. Ariz. del. to People's Republic of China, 1976; participant Nat. Def. Univ., 1978—; mem. organizing group internat. conf. on dendroclimatology, England, 1980. Author: Tree Rings and Climate, 1976; edit. adv. bd. Quaternary Research, 1977-82; contbr. articles to profl. jours. Mem. local sch. bd., 1971-72. Grad. fellow Ohio State U., 1954-56, NSF fellow Oreg. Inst. Marine Biology, summer 1957, Guggenheim fellow, 1968-69; grantee NSF 1971-87, U. Calif. Lawrence Livermore Lab., 1978-79, State of Calif., 1979-80, 85-86. Mem. Am. Assn. Quaternary Environment (council 1978-82, adv. com. paleonclimatology), Ecol. Soc. Am. (edit. bd. 1964-66, council rep., chmn. paleoecology sect 1984), AAAS, Am. Inst. Biol. Scis., Tree-Ring Soc., Am. Meteorol. Soc. (Oustanding Achievement in Bioclimatology award 1982), Am. Quaternary Assn. (mem. council 1978—), Internat. Assn. for Ecology, Internat. Soc. Ecol. Modeling, Internat. Union Quaternary Research, Sigma Xi. Home: 5703 N Lady Ln Tucson AZ 85704 Office: U Ariz Lab of Tree-Ring Rsch Bldg 58 Tucson AZ 85721

FRITZ, ETHEL MAE HENDRICKSON, writer; b. Gibbon, Nebr., Feb. 4, 1925; d. Walter Earl and Alice Hazel (Mickish) Hendrickson; BS, Iowa State U., 1949; m. C. Wayne Fritz, Feb. 25, 1950; children—Linda Sue, Krista Jane. Dist. home economist Internat. Harvester Co., Des Moines, 1949-50; writer Wallace's Farmer mag., Des Moines, 1960-64; free-lance writer, 1960—. Chmn. Ariz. Council Flower Show Judges, 1983-85. Accredited master flower show judge. Mem. Women in Communications (pres. Phoenix profl. chpt.; nat. task force com. 1980—), Am. Soc. Profl. and Exec. Women, Am. Home Econs. Assn., SW Writers' Conf., Ariz. Authors Assn., Phi Upsilon Omicron, Kappa Delta. Republican. Methodist. Club: PEO. Author: The Story of an Amana Winemaker, 1984, Prairie Kitchen Sampler, 1988.

FRITZ, GREGORY ROBERT, public warehouse company official; b. Seattle, July 9, 1948; s. Robert Gordon and Elizabeth Jane (Weil) F.; m. Karla Kay Copeland, July 26, 1975. BA in Edn., Western Wash. U., 1976. Ops. supr. Assoc. Warehouses, Seattle, 1977--. Office: Assos Thavehouses 770 S Michigan St Seattle WA 98108

FRIZZELL, THOMAS WILLIAM, lawyer; b. Long Beach, Calif., June 3, 1953; s. William Benjamen and Charlotte Mae (Smith) F.; m. Janice Lee Merdink, Sept. 23, 1978; children: William Benjamen, Andrew Thomas. BA, Mont. State U., 1975; JD, U. Mont., 1978; student, Am. U., Washington, 1973, Carroll Coll., Helena, Mont., 1974. Exec. asst. Environ. Quality Council, Helena, 1974-75; research assoc. Environ. Quality Council, 1976; assoc. Tipp & Hoven, Missoula, Mont., 1978-80; ptnr. Tipp, Hoven, Skjelset & Frizzell, Missoula, 1980-87, Tipp, Frizzell & Buley, Missoula, 1987—. Co-author: Primer On The Theory And Proof Of Discovery Of Valuable Mineral Deposits Under the 1872 Mining Law Public Land Law Rev., 1985, Montana Energy Policy Study EQC, 1975, Montana's Natural Gas Crisis, EQC, 1976. Mem. Mont. Bar Assn. (trustee natural resources sect. 1987—), Soc. Mining Engrs. Presbyterian. Office: Tipp Frizzell & Buley 2200 Brooks Missoula MT 59806

FROBEL, RONALD KENNETH, geosynthetic engineer, consultant; b. Middletown, Conn., Oct. 10, 1946; s. Kenneth LeRoy and Hazel (Austin) F. AS in Archtl. Engring., Wentworth Inst. Tech., 1966; BS in Civil Engring., U. Ariz., 1969, MS in Geotech. Civil Engring., 1975. Registered profl. engr., Colo., Ariz. Civil engr. NE Utilities, Hartford, Conn., 1969-70; research engr. Engring. Experiment Sta. U. Ariz., Tucson, 1974-75, Water Resources Research Ctr., Tucson, 1975-77; materials engring. specialist U.S. Bur. Reclamation, Denver, 1978-85; tech. mgr. geosynthetics Polyfelt Ges. M.B.H., Denver and Linz, Austria, 1985-88; prin., cons. GeoSynthetics Cons. Inc., Evergreen, Colo., 1988—; cons. Woodward-Clyde Cons., Chgo., 1982-85. Author: Geosynthetics Terminology, 1987, (with others) Polyfelt Design and Practice, 1987; co-editor: Hydraulic Barriers in Soil and Rock, 1985; editor spl. edit. jour. Geomembrane Quality Assurance, 1986; mem. editorial bd. Internat. Jour. Geotextiles and Geomembranes, 1986—, Geotech. Fabrics Report Mag., 1985—; contbr. over 40 articles to profl. jours. Lt. USN, 1970-73. Mem. ASCE, Internat. Standards Orgn. (U.S. rep.), Internat. Geosynthetics Soc., ASTM (com. chmn.), NSPE, ISSMFE. Republican. Home: 115 Cedar Way Evergreen CO 80439

FROCKT, RICHARD JAY, telecommunications company executive; b. Louisville, Oct. 20, 1944; s. Robert J. Frockt and Johanna (Fleischaker) Shomer; m. Janet Clark, Aug. 10, 1972; 1 child, Ryan. BS, Western Ky. U., 1967; JD, U. Louisville, 1972. Bar: Ky. 1972. Ptnr. Frockt & Klingman, Louisville, 1973-78, Miller, Frockt & Pundzak, Louisville, 1978-80, Barnett & Alagia, Louisville, 1980-86; exec. v.p., chief operating officer TMC Communicaitons, Santa Barbara, Calif., 1986—. Bd. dirs., officer The Temple, Louisville, 1978-84, pres. 1984-86. Lt USNR, 1968-71. Mem. Ky. Bar Assn., Calif. Assn. Long Distance Tel. Cos. (pres. 1988). Republican. Office: TMC Communications 1528 Chapala St Santa Barbara CA 93101

FROHLICH, ALI CAN, career military officer; b. Wright-Patterson AFB, Ohio, Aug. 30, 1958; s. Donald Ralph and Leyla (Yalcin) F.; m. Serra Gül Giray, June 7, 1980; 1 child, Danyal Sibel. BS, USAF Acad., 1980. Commd. 2d. lt. USAF, 1976, advanced through grades to capt., 1984; student pilot 82d flying tng. wing, Williams AFB, Ariz., 1980-81; liason officer and 0-2A forward air controller 24th composite wing, Howard AFB, Republic of Panama, 1981-84; flight commdr. 24th composite wing, Republic of Panama, 1983-84; F-16 instr. pilot 56th tactical tng. wing, Macdill AFB, Fla., 1984-85; F-16 pilot, mobility and plans officer 4th tactical fighter squadron, 388 tactical fighter wing, Hill AFB, Utah, 1985-88, chief readiness div., 1985-88; F-16C instr. pilot liaison for Turkish Air Force USAF, 1988—. Mem. Air Force Assn., Ankara AFB Officers Club, Order of Daedalions. Republican. Mem. Moslem Ch. Office: USAF Joint US Mil Mission for, Aid to Turkey, Ankara AFB Turkey

FROHNEN, RICHARD GENE, educator; b. Omaha, Mar. 26, 1930; s. William P. and Florence E. (Rogers) F.; student U. Nebr., Omaha, Mo. Valley Coll., 1948-52; BA, Calif. State U., 1954; MS, UCLA 1961; EdD, Brigham Young U., 1976; grad. Army War Coll., 1982 m. Harlene Grace LeTourneau, July 4, 1958; children: Karl Edward, Eric Eugene. Bus. mgr. athletics and sports publicity dir. U. Nebr., Omaha, 1951-52; pub. rels. dir. First Congl. Ch. Los Angeles, 1953-54, 58-59; writer Los Angeles Mirror News, 1959; gen. assignment reporter, religion editor Los Angeles Times, 1959-61; prof. journalism, dean men Eastern Mont. Coll., Billings, 1961-65; N.W. editor, editorial writer Spokesman-Review, Spokane, 1965-67, also editor Sunday mag.; prof. journalism U. Nev., Reno, 1967-79; exec. dir. devel. Coll. of Desert/Copper Mountain, 1982-85, Ariz. Health Scis. Ctr., Tucson, 1986—; pub. relations devel. officer Sch. Med. Scis. U. Nev., 1969-75; adj. prof. mgmt., dir. grad. pros. in Mgmt. U. Redlands (Calif.), 1979-85; cons. pub. rels. and develop. Mem. exec. bd. Nev. area council Boy Scouts Am., 1968-76, council commr., 1973-74, v.p., 1975-76; mem. exec. bd. Yellowstone Valley council Boy Scouts Am., 1961-65, council pres. 1963-64; v.p. Catalina council Boy Scouts Am., 1987—; founder, mng. dir. Gt. Western Expdns., 1958—; adminstrv. asst. to Gov. of Nev., 1985. Served to 1st lt. USMC, 1954-58; now col. Res. Recipient Silver Beaver award Boy Scouts Am., 1974, Pres.' Vol. Action award Coll. Desert/Copper Mountain, 1984, Outstanding Faculty award U. Redlands, 1984; named to Benson High Sch. Hall of Fame, Omaha, 1988. Mem. Assn. Edn. Journalism, Am. Legion, Res. Officers Assn. U.S., Marine Corps Assn., Marine Corps Res. Officers Assn., Am. Humanics Found., Internat. Platform Assn., Nat. Soc. Fund Raising Execs., Planning Execs. Inst., Internat. Communication Assn., Religion Newswriters Assn., Navy League, Semper Fidelis Soc., Am. Mgmt. Assn., Assn. Am. Med. Colls. Group on Pub. Affairs, Counc. for Advancement and Support Edn., Res. Officers Assn. U.S., Nat. Assn. Hosp. Devel., Kappa Tau Alpha, Alpha Phi Omega, Sigma Delta Chi (sec.-treas. chpt.). Episcopalian. Kiwanian, Lion, Rotarian. Home: 6631 N Cibola Ave Tucson AZ 85718 Office: U Ariz 1501 N Campbell Ave Tucson AZ 85724

FROHNMAYER, DAVID BRADEN, state attorney general; b. Medford, Oreg., July 9, 1940; s. Otto J. and Marabel (Fisher) B.; m. Lynn Diane Johnson, Dec. 30, 1970; children: Kirsten, Mark, Kathryn, Jonathan, Amy. AB magna cum laude, Harvard U., 1962; BA, Oxford (Eng.) U., 1964, MA (Rhodes scholar), 1971; JD, U. Calif., Berkeley, 1967; LLD (hon.), Willamette U., 1988. Bar: Calif. 1967, U.S. Dist. Ct. (no. dist.) Calif. 1967, Oreg. 1971, U.S. Dist. Ct. Oreg. 1971, U.S. Supreme Ct. 1981. Assoc. Pillsbury, Madison & Sutro, San Francisco, 1967-69; asst. to sec. Dept. HEW, 1969-70; prof. law sch. U. Oreg., 1971-81, spl. asst. to pres. law sch., 1971-79; atty. gen. State of Oreg., 1981—; chmn. Conf. Western Attys. Gen., 1985-86; pres. Nat. Assn. Attys. Gen., 1987-88. Mem. Oreg. Ho. of Reps, 1975-81. Recipient awards Weaver Constl. Law Essay competition Am. Bar Found., 1972, 74; Rhodes scholar, 1962. Mem. ABA (Ross essay winner 1980), Oreg. Bar Assn., Calif. Bar Assn., Assn. Attys. Gen. (pres. 1987-88), Nat. Assn. Attys. Gen. (Wyman award 1987), Round Table Eugene, Order of Coif, Phi Beta Kappa, Rotary. Republican. Presbyterian. Home: 2875 Baker St Eugene OR 97403 Office: Office of Atty Gen 100 Justice Bldg Salem OR 97310

FROMHOLTZ, PAUL CHARLES, physical therapist; b. Eng., May 29, 1959; came to U.S., 1960; s. Paul Henry Hugo Jr. and Amy Alice (Estall) F.; m. Rebecca Lynn Herlacher, Nov. 5, 1982 (div.). Student, Ariz. State U., 1977-80; BS in Phys. Therapy, No. Ariz. U., 1982. Registered phys. therapist, Ariz. Phys. therapist Desert Samaritan Hosp., Mesa, Ariz., 1981-89; staff specialist orthopedics Good Samaritan Hosp., Phoenix, 1989—. Mem. Am. Phys. Therapy Assn., Nat. Strength and Conditioning Assn. Home: 2408 W Stottler Dr Chandler AZ 85224 Office: Good Samaritan Hosp 1111 E McDowell Rd Phoenix AZ 85006

FRONK, RHONDA BETH, accountant; b. Liberal, Kans., Sept. 8, 1956; d. Ronald Solomon and Margaret Belle (Williams) F. BEd magna cum laude, Oral Roberts U., 1979. Trust officer First Nat. Bank, Liberal, 1978-79; tchr. Tyrone (Okla.) Pub. Schs., 1979-80; staff acct. Leming and Thomas, CPA's, Tulsa, 1981-85, Sparks & Chancey, CPA's, Fort Smith, Ark., 1985-87; asst. controller Kennedy & Noel Devel., Phoenix, Ariz., 1987; internal auditor North Phoenix Bapt. Ch., 1987-88; acct. Laventhol & Horwath, Phoenix, 1988—. Contbr. articles to profl. jours. Exec. dir. Big Bros./Big Sisters, Inc., Liberal, 1980; activities chmn. 1st United Meth. Singles Club, L.I.V.E. Singles Club, Fort Smith, 1982-87; lighting supr. Theatre Tulsa, 1984-85; vol. ch. youth worker, 1987-88, church pianist, 1988—. Mem. Gospel Music Assn., U.S. Golf Assn., Phoenix Art Mus., NAFE, North Phoenix Bapt. Ch. Sanctuary Choir. Republican. Baptist. Home: 15402 N 28th St Ste 129 Phoenix AZ 85032 Office: Laventhol & Horwath 3200 N Central Ave Ste 1600 Phoenix AZ 85012

FRONTIERE, GEORGIA, professional football team executive. m. Carroll Rosenblum, July 7, 1966 (dec.); children: Dale Carroll, Lucia; m. Dominic Frontiere. Pres., owner L.A. Rams, NFL, 1979—. Bd. dirs. L.A. Boys and Girls Club, L.A. Orphanage Guild, L.A. Blind Youth Found. Named Headliner of Yr., L.A. Press Club, 1981. Office: Los Angeles Rams 2327 W Lincoln Ave Anaheim CA 92801 *

FROST, DONALD IRVINE, paper company executive; b. San Jose, Calif., Jan. 21, 1925; s. Audley Leo and Clara G. (Wagner) F.; m. Lois Barry, June 14, 1951; children: John Christopher, Robin Elizabeth. BBA, Golden Gate U., 1953. Mgr. prodn. Coast Envelope, South San Francisco, 1953-74; mgr. mfg. Precision Rotary Forms, Santa Clara, Calif., 1975-77; mgr. ops. Papercone Corp., San Francisco, 1978—; instr. Golden Gate U., 1955-56. Served to sgt. U.S. Army, 1943-46. Mem. Soc. Advancement Mgmt. (v.p. univ. relations 1956-57), Am. Vet. Com. (chmn.1947-48), Purchasing Mgmt. Assn. No. Calif. (chair pub. com. 1982—). Democrat. Home: 4946 Santa Rita Rd Richmond CA 94803 Office: Papercone Corp 672 Toland Pl San Francisco CA 94124

FROST, JAMES MICHAEL, entrepreneur; b. Encino, Calif., Apr. 15, 1964; s. Mack McCabe and Julia (Malesic) F. BS, U. Southern Calif., 1987. Owner, pres. J. Michael Frost Fine Flowers, 1983-85, Western Direct Mktg., 1986, Mesa Research Inst., 1987, Perfect Images Automotive Detailing, Los Angeles, 1983--, South Bay Comml. Real Estate Services, 1987-88; v.p. fin. Wilshire Constrn., Los Angeles, 1988--. Calif. State scholar. Mem. Am. Fin. Assn., Alpha Gamma Sigma. Home: 1611 N Formosa Ave #311 Los Angeles CA 90048

FROST, JOSEPH ROY, electrical materials engineer; b. Flushing, Mich., Sept. 6, 1931; s. John Frederick Dederick Frost and Theo (Manchester) Traubenkraut; ; Betty Sue Sprague, Jan. 15, 1955; children: Karen Sue Grant, Joseph R. Jr., John William, Michael T. Student, Lowell Tech., 1965-68, Worcester Jr. Coll., 1969-72. Machine operator Buick Motor Co., Flint, Mich., 1950; TV serviceman Hasselback TV, Corunna, Mich., 1951-52, 54; pvt. practice TV repair Lennon, Mich., 1954-57, 58.

FROST, RICHARD RAY, manufacturing executive, consultant; b. Stockton, Calif., Jan. 2, 1942; s. George Raymond and Violet Pearl (Yabsley) F.; m. Jean Tunnel, Auge. 8, 1965 (div. Aug. 1979); children: Raymond Dennis, Robert Douglas, Rakhel Denine, Renae Dennice. Student electronics tech., Stockton Coll., 1957. Ordained to ministry, 1975. Bapt. ch. checker Centr-O-Mart Grocers, Stockton, 1962065; dist. mgr. Gold Rush Potato Chip Co., Central Point, Oreg., 1965-67; mgr. Jeld-Wen, Inc., Klamath Falls, Oreg., 1967—; owner, mgr. Woodworking Cons., Everett, Wash., 1982—; owner, editor Spl. Effects mag., Everett, 1988—. Founder, pres. Ford Fedn., Klamath Fall, 1982. With USAF, 1958-62. Democrat. Home: 4027 C Rucker Ste 714 Everett WA 98201 Office: Jeld-Wen Inc 3303 Lakeport Blvd Klamath Falls OR 97601

FROST, S. NEWELL, computer company executive; b. Oklahoma City, Dec. 21, 1935; s. Sterling Johnson and Eula Dove (Whitford) F.; m. Patricia Joyce Rose, Aug. 18, 1957; children: Patricia Diane Wiscarson, Richard Sterling, Lindy Layne Wasilko. BS Indsl. Engring., U. Okla., Norman, 1957; MS Indsl. Engring., Okla. State U., 1966. Registered profl. engr., Okla. Calif. Asst. mgr. acctg. Western Electric, Balt., 1972-73, mgr. indsl. engring., Chgo., 1973-75, mgr. devel. engring., 1975-76, mgr. acct. mgmt., San Francisco, 1976-78, dir. staff, Morristown, N.J., 1978-79; gen. mgr. distbn. & repair AT&T Techs., Sunnyvale, Calif., 1979-85, area v.p. material mgt. svcs. AT&T Info. Systems, Oakland, Calif., 1985-87, ops. v.p. material mgmt. svcs., San Francisco, 1988-89; dir. configuration ops. Businessland, Inc., San Jose, Calif., 1989—; bd. dirs. Contract Office Group, San Jose, 1983—, chmn., 1984—; Bd. dirs. Santa Clara County YMCA, San Jose, Calif., 1981-84, Imedia, L.A., 1987—. Recipient Man of Day citation Sta. WAIT Radio, Chgo. Mem. Nat. Soc. Prof. Engrs. (chmn. edn. com. 1969-70), Am. Inst. Indsl. Engrs. (pres. bd. dirs. 1966-68), Okla. Soc. Profl. Engrs. (v.p. 1968-69). Republican. Baptist. Home: 4144 Paradise Dr Tiburon CA 94920 Office: Businessland Inc 1001 Ridder Park Dr San Jose CA 95131

FROST, WILLIAM, English educator; b. N.Y.C., June 8, 1917; s. John William and Christina (Gurlitz) F.; m. Marjorie Hayes Pangburn, Aug. 5, 1942; children—Marjorie Augusta Frost McCracken, Christina Emily, Clifford William. A.B., Bowdoin Coll., 1938, D.Litt. (hon.), 1980; M.A., Columbia U., 1942; Ph.D., Yale U., 1946. Instr., Carnegie Inst. Tech., 1942-44; instr. Yale U., 1946-47, vis. assoc. prof., 1958-59; asst. prof. Wesleyan U., 1947-51; asst. prof. U. Calif., Santa Barbara, 1951-55, assoc. prof., 1955-58, 59-61, acting chmn. dept. English, 1965-66, chmn., 1974-79, prof. English, 1961—, co-editor Works of John Dryden, Vol. IV, 1974. Guggenheim fellow, 1959, 79-80, Am. Council Learned Socs. fellow, 1966-67, Nat. Endowment for Humanities fellow, 1972-73; Am. Philos. soc. grantee, 1982-83. Mem. MLA, Philol. Assn. of Pacific Coast, Medieval Acad. Am., Calif. State Employees Assn., Phi Beta Kappa. Club: Elizabethan (Yale U.). Author: Fulke Greville's Caelica: An Evaluation, 1942; Dryden and the Art of Translation, 1955, 69; Dryden and Future Shock, 1976; editor, co-editor, assoc. editor: English Masterpieces, 1950, 61; Selected Works of Dryden, 1953, 71; Pope's Homer, 1967; Dryden's Juvenal and Persius and Other Poems, 1974, Dryden's Virgil, 1987; contbr. articles on Chaucer, Shakespeare, Pope, Persius, others to publs. Office: U Calif Dept English Santa Barbara CA 93106

FRUCHTER, JONATHAN SEWELL, research scientist, geochemist; b. San Antonio, June 5, 1945; s. Benjamin and Dorothy Ann (Sewell) F.; m. Cecelia Ann Smith, Mar. 31, 1973; children: Diane, Daniel. BS in Chemistry, U. Tex., 1966; PhD in Geochemistry, U. Calif., San Diego, 1971. Research assoc. U. Oreg., Eugene, 1971-74; research scientist Battelle Northwest, Richland, Wash., 1974-79, mgr. research and devel., 1979-87, staff scientist, 1987—. Contbr. numerous articles to profl. jours. Mem. AAAS, Am. Chem. Soc., Phi Beta Kappa, Phi Kappa Phi. Office: Battelle Northwest PO Box 999 Richland WA 99352

FRUCHTHENDLER, FRED BARRY, insurance executive, consultant, business owner; b. Tucson, July 19, 1951; s. Jacob Carl and Jean (Abend) F. BA, U. Calif., San Diego, 1973. With mgmt. personnel Foodmaker, Inc., San Diego, 1970-73; legal intern Ctr. for Legal & Social Change, San Diego, 1971-73; ins. exec. J.C. Fruchthendler & Co., Tucson, 1973-80, pres., owner, 1980—. Adv. youth group Yonaton AZA-B'nai B'rith Youth, Tucson, 1980—. Recipient Merit award Tucson Fire Dept., 1977; named Outstanding Young Man of Am., 1978, Young Man of Yr., Tucson Jewish Community Coun., 1978. Mem. Ind. Ins. Agts. Am. (bd. dirs. Phoenix chpt. 1987—, 83-86, pres. Tucson chpt. 1987), Profl. Ins. Agts. Am., ISU Internat. (presdl. adv. bd. Hartford, Conn. chpt. 1984-87), Ariz. Acad. Sci. (life), PIA, Kiwanis (chartered). Democrat.

FRUEAUF, WENDY HOLLY, oil trade association executive; b. Greenville, Pa., Dec. 26, 1953; d. Robert Paul and Shirley Jane (Kerr) Lowe; m. David John, Nov. 15, 1980; 1 child, Allyson Jean. BA in Polit. Sci., Coll. of Wooster, Ohio, 1976. Legis. aid Senator Aronoff Ohio Senate, Columbus, 1978-80; asst. buyer Rike's Dept. Store, Dayton, Ohio, 1980-81; research asst. Wyo. Heritage Soc., Casper, 1982; assoc. dir. Petroleum Assn. Wyo., Casper, 1982--. Named one of Outstanding Young Woman of Am., 1980. Mem. Wyo. Assn. Trade Execs., Casper Area C. of C. (minerals com. 1982--). Mem. Disciples of Christ. Office: Petroleum Assn Wyo 951 Werner Ct Ste 100 Casper WY 82601

FRUEH, DONALD LAWRENCE, aeronautical engineer; b. Lima, Ohio, Nov. 12, 1960; s. Jerome Louis and Elizabeth Eileen (Devlin) F. BS, U. Dayton, 1983, MS, 1985. Design engr. aircraft engine group Gen. Electric, Lynn, Mass., 1985-87; engr., scientist Douglas Aircraft div. McDonnell Douglas Corp., Long Beach, Calif., 1987—. Mem. Peace and Freedom Party. Zen Buddhist. Home: 601 Santa Fe Ave #6 Placentia CA 92670

FRUEHLING, JOHN WILLIAM, commercial real estate banker; b. Seattle, Feb. 20, 1947; s. William Clifford and Juanita Alfreda (Eckert) F.; m. Sharon Lee Johnson, Sept. 8, 1967; 1 child, Jacob Elliot. BA in Econs., Seattle Pacific U., 1969. Mgr. Household Finance, Seattle, 1969-73; mgr., asst. v.p. Rainier Nat. Bancorp, Seattle, 1973-80; mgr., v.p. Old Nat. Bancorp, Seattle, 1980-84; sr. credit officer, v.p. Seafirst Bank, Seattle, 1984-87; sr. loan officer, v.p. Bank of Calif., Seattle, 1987—. Master sgt. U.S. Army, 1969-75. Mem. Mortgage Bankers Am., Urban Land Inst., Internat. Coun. Shopping Ctrs., Tam O'Shanter Country Club (dir. 1980-83), College Club, Harbor Club. Republican. Methodist. Home: 17616 NE 15 Pl Bellevue WA 98008 Office: Bank of Calif 910 4th Ave Seattle WA 98164

FRUMKIN, GENE, author, educator; b. N.Y.C., Jan. 29, 1928; s. Samuel and Sarah (Blackman) F.; B.A. in English, UCLA, 1951; m. Lydia Samuels, July 3, 1955 (dec.); children—Celena, Paul. Exec. editor Calif. Apparel News, Los Angeles, 1952-66; asst. prof. English, U. N.Mex., Albuquerque, 1967-71, assoc. prof., 1971-88, prof. 1988—. Mem. Rio Grande Writers Assn., Associated Writing Programs, Hawaii Literary Arts Council. Author: The Hawk and the Lizard, 1963; The Orange Tree, 1965; The Rainbow-Walker, 1968; Dostoevsky and Other Nature Poems, 1972; Locust Cry: Poems 1958-65, 1973; The Mystic Writing-Pad, 1977; Loops, 1979; Clouds and Red Earth, 1982, A Sweetness in the Air, 1987; mem. editorial bd. Blue Mesa Rev.; co-editor San Marcos Rev., 1976-83; The Indian Rio Grande: Recent Poems from 3 Cultures (anthology), 1977; editor: Coastlines Lit. Mag., 1958-62, N.Mex. Quar., 1969. Home: 3721 Mesa Verde NE Albuquerque NM 87110

FRUMKIN, SIMON, political activist and columnist; b. Kaunas, USSR, Nov. 5, 1930; came to U.S., 1949; s. NIcholas and Zila (Oster) F.; m. Rhoda Hirsch, June 1953 (div. 1978); children: Michael Alan, Larry Martin; m. Kathy Elizabeth Hoopes, June 22, 1981. BA, NYU, 1953; MA in History, Calif. State U., Northridge, 1964. Pres., chief exec. officer Universal Drapery Fabrics, Inc., Los Angeles, 1953-87; chmn. Southern Calif. Council for Soviet Jews, Studio City, 1969—; lectr. Simon Wiesenthal Ctr. for Holocaust Studies, Los Angeles, 1980—; chmn. Union of Councils for Soviet Jews, 1972-73. Columnist Los Angeles Messenger, numerous other So. Calif. newspapers, 1980—; corr., columnist Panorama, U.S.A Russian Lang., 1985—; editor-in-chief Them mag.; contbr. articles to newspapers. Pres. Media Analysis Found., Los Angeles, 1988; chmn. Ams. for Peace and Justice, 1972-74; mem. Pres.' Senatorial Inner Circle, U.S. Senatorial Club. Honored by Calif. Govt., Los Angeles City Council, Los Angeles Office of City Atty., numerous Jewish orgns. Mem. Assn. Soviet Jewish Emigrants (pres. 1987—), Zionist Orgn. Am., Am. Israel Polit. Action Com., Russian Republican Club, Mensa. Home and Office: 3755 Goodland Ave Studio City CA 91604

FRUSH, JAMES CARROLL, JR., health services consulant; b. San Francisco, Oct. 18, 1930; s. James Carroll and Edna Mae (Perry) F.; BA, Stanford, 1953; postgrad. U. Calif. at San Francisco, 1957-58; MA, Saybrook Inst., 1981; PhD, 1985; m. Patricia Anne Blake, Oct. 29, 1960 (div. 1977); children: Michael, Gloria; m. Carolyn Fetter Bell, Aug. 23, 1978; 1 child, Stephen. Partner, James C. Frush Co. San Francisco, 1960-70; v.p., bd. dir. Gwynedd, Inc., Blue Bell, Pa., Retirement Residence, Inc., San Francisco, 1964-70, pres., 1970—; pres. Nat. Retirement Residence, San Francisco, 1971-89, Casa Dorinda Corp., 1971-89; lectr. Pres., Marin Shakespeare Festival, 1971-73, James C. Frush Found., 1972-78; prof. gerontology, psychology Spring Hill Coll., Mobile, Ala., 1988—. Bd. dirs. San Francisco Sr. Ctr., 1973-78, Found. to Assist Calif. Tchrs. Devel. Inc., 1987—. Mem. Gerontol. Soc., Southeastern Psychol. Assn., Assn. for Anthropology and Gerontology, Stanford Alumni Assn, RSVP (adv. bd., Mobile, Ala., chpt.), Christus Theol. Inst. (adv. bd.). Author (with Benson Eschenbach): The Retirement Residence: An Analysis of the Architecture and Management of Life Care Housing, 1968, Self-Esteem in Older Persons Following a Heart Attack: An Exploration of Contributing Factors, 1985. Contbr. articles to profl. jours.; producer ednl. films. Office: care T Pimsleur 2155 Union St San Francisco CA 94123

FRUTCHEY, ROBERT WARREN, civil engineer; b. Ravenna, Ohio, Aug. 28, 1960; s. Robert C. and Suzanne (Warren) F.; m. Heidi M. Bichsel, July 5, 1986. BSCE, U. Akron, 1982. Registered profl. engr., Ohio, Calif. Project engr. W.E. Quicksall & Assoc., Inc., New Philadelphia, Ohio, 1982-86; project mgr. Brown and Caldwell, Pleasant Hill, Calif., 1986--; cons. in field. Contbr. articles to profl. publs. Mem. Nat. Soc. Profl. Engrs., Tuscarawas Valley Soc. Profl. Engrs. (sec. 1984-85), Water Pollution Control Fedn. (San Francisco Bay sect.), Calif. Water Pollution Control Fedn. Republican. Methodist. Home: 2525 Saratoga Ave Concord CA 94519 Office: Brown & Caldwell 3480 Buskirk Ave Pleasant Hill CA 94523

FRY, JAMES LAWRENCE, artist; b. Parryton, Tex., Jan. 2, 1957; s. James Leroy and Betty Adell (Anderson) F. Pvt. practice Denver, 1978-82; art dir. Profl. At Your Svc., Tulsa, 1983-84; tube bender Star Signs, Kans. City, Mo., 1984, Paris Neon, Kans. City, 1984-85; pres. Nite Writers Enterprise, Denver, 1985—, Nite Sriters Neon Clocks, Denver, 1986—, Elipse, Inc., Denver, 1987—, Blue Moon, Denver, 1988—. Office: Nite Writers Enterprise 1930 S Broadway Denver CO 80210

FRY, MICHAEL EUGENE, biologist; b. Denver, Apr. 20, 1951; s. Donald Mills and Hazel Lucile (Hartzler) F.; Katherine May Dow, July 29, 1979. AA, Feather River Coll., 1971; BS, U. Calif., 1974, MS, 1983. Cert. wildlife biologist. Biologist cons. Multi-Tech Labs., Ukiah, Calif., 1976-77; biologist Pacific Gas & Electric Co., San Ramon, Calif., 1978—. Contbr. articles to profl. jours. Mem. The Wildlife Soc., The Soc. Range Mgmt., Assn. Power Biologists, Assn. Power Industry Biologists. Office: Pacific Gas & Electric Co 3400 Crow Canyon Rd San Ramon CA 94583

FRY, ROBERT LLOYD, audiovisual specialist; b. Findlay, Ohio, Aug. 24, 1952; s. Max Mearl and Julia Margaret (Shoemaker) F.; m. Jennifer Jean Davis, Oct. 16, 1982; children: Elizabeth A., E. Robert, Dennis V. Student, No. Mich. U., 1976-77; AA, Cosumnes River Coll., Sacramento, Calif., 1986. Enlisted USAF, 1970, advanced through grades to staff sgt., 1976, resigned, 1978; security guard Vanguard Security Systems, North Highlands, Calif., 1978-79; night auditor Sacramento Inn, 1979-80; audio-visual repair technician USAF, McClellan AFB, Calif., 1980—; bd. dirs. Sacramento Community Council, 1987—. Vol. Jean Moorehead Duffy Re-election Campaign, 1986; mem. facilities com. Synergy II, Sacramento, 1987. With USNG, 1978-82, 88—. Mem. Assn. for Multi-Image (pres. 1987—), Photo Mktg. Assn. Office: USAF 2852 ABG/DAVL McClellan AFB CA 95652

FRY, WILLIAM FINLEY, JR., psychiatrist, educator; b. Cin., Mar. 25, 1924; s. William Finley and Sylvia (Luebbert) F.; m. Elizabeth Stockett, June 3, 1951; children: Peter F., Stephen S., Susan E. Fry Van Rheenen. Student, Bowdoin, then Grinnell colls., 1942-44, U. Oreg., then U. So. Calif., 1945-47, U. Oslo, 1948; MD, U. Cin., 1949. Diplomate Am.Bd. Psychiatry and Neurology. Intern Queen's Hosp., Honolulu, 1949-50; resident in psychiatry VA Hosp., Palo Alto, Calif., 1950-53; pvt. practice Menlo Park, Calif., 1953-88; clin. asst. U. Calif.-San Francisco, 1953-56, Langley Porter Clinic, 1953-56; clin. instr. psychiatry Stanford (Calif.) U., 1959-63, asst. clin. prof., 1963-70, assoc. clin. prof., 1970-88, prof. emeritus, 1988—, dir. Gelotology Inst., 1985—; mem. staff Agnews (Calif.) State Hosp., 1953-54, Stanford Hosp., 1959-85; adv. editor press series Wayne State U., Detroit; lectr. in field. Author: Sweet Madness, 1963, (with Melanie Allen) Make 'Em Laugh, 1978; (with Waleed A. Salameh) The Handbook of Humor and Psychotherapy, 1987; mem. cons. editorial bd. Internat. Jour. Humor Research; contbr. numerous articles to profl. jours. and popular publs., also chpts. to books. With AUS, 1943-46; lt. USN, 1954-56. Fellow Am. Psychiat. Assn. (life, emeritus); mem. AAAS, N.Y. Acad. Scis., Calif. Acad. Scis., No. Calif. Psychiat. Soc., Mid-Peninsula Psychiat. Soc. (pres. 1965), Stanford U. Clin. Faculty Assn., Calif. Hist. Soc., Order Mil. Wine Tasters, Stanford U. Faculty Club, Calif. Book Club, Sierra Club, Audubon Soc. Home and Office: 156 Grove St Nevada City CA 95959

FRYDENBERG, ERLING, service executive; b. Alta, Norway, Apr. 11, 1953; came to U.S., 1983.; s. John and Marit (Olstad) F. Diploma, Oslo (Norway) Handelsgymnasium. Hotel purser Royal Viking Line, Oslo, 1979-80, crew purser, chief purser, 1980, chief steward, 1981-82, hotel mgr., 1982-83; hotel supr. Royal Viking Line, San Francisco, 1983-85, v.p., 1985-88; sr. v.p. Crystal Cruises Inc., L.A., 1988—. Served with Norwegian Army, 1972-73. Recipient Marine Hotel Catering & Duty Free award, 1987. Mem. La Chaine des Rotisseurs, Assn. des Anciens Eleves de l'Ecole Hoteliere, La Commanderie du Bontemps de Medoc et des Graves. Office: Crystal Cruises Inc 2121 Ave of the Stars Los Angeles CA 90067

FRYE, FREDRIC L., veterinarian; b. Los Angeles, May 21, 1934; s. Benjamin and Ann (Wilson) F.; m. Brucye B. Klein; children: Lorraine M., Erik C. AA, Santa Monica Community Coll., 1958; BS, U. Calif., Davis, 1960, DVM, 1964, MS, 1978. Account exec. ADSCO, Los Angeles, 1955-57; cancer epidemiologist Calif. Cancer Field Research Program, Berkeley, Calif., 1964-65; pvt. practice, chief of staff Berkeley Dog & Cat Hosp., Calif., 1966-76; clin. prof. medicine U. Calif., Davis, 1976—; attending staff clinician Davis Animal Hosp., Davis, Calif., 1986—, Sacramento Animal Med. Group, 1987—; assoc. prof. Calif. State U., Sacaramento, 1989—; cons. Aphton Corp., Woodland, Calif., 1984—; cons. in surgery USPHS Hosp., San Francisco, 1966-76, VA Hosp., San Francisco, 1966-75, San Francisco Gen. Hosp., 1966-74. Author: Husbandry, Medicine and Surgery, 1973, Biomedical and Surgical Aspects, 1981, Phyllis, Phallus, Genghis, Cohen..and Other Creatures I Have Known, 1984, First Aid for Your Cat, 1987, First Aid for Your Dog, 1987, Schnauzers: An Owner's Guide, 1988, Mutts, 1989. Served in USN, 1952-60. Recipient Practitioner Research award Am. Veterinary Med. Assn., 1969, Kodak Internat. Newspaper Snapshot award, 1971, Nat. Wildlife Fedn. Photo award, 1986. Mem. AAAS, Am. Veterinary Med. Assn., Fedn. Am. Scientists, Calif. Veterinary Med. Assn., Soc. Study Amphibians and Reptiles, Alpha Gamma Sigma, Phi Zeta. Home: 741 Plum Ln Davis CA 95616-3237 Office: Davis Animal Hosp 1617 Russell Blvd Davis CA 95616

FRYE, HELEN JACKSON, federal judge; b. Klamath Falls, Oreg., Dec. 10, 1930; d. Earl and Elizabeth (Kirkpatrick) Jackson; m. William Frye, Sept. 7, 1952; children: Eric, Karen, Heidi; m. Perry Holloman, July 10, 1980. B.A. in English, B.A. with honors, U. Oreg., 1953, M.A., 1960, J.D., 1966. Bar: Oreg. 1966. Public sch. tchr. Oreg., 1956-63; pvt. practice Eugene, 1966-71; circuit ct. judge State of Oreg., 1971-80; U.S. dist. judge Dist. Oreg. Portland, 1980—. Office: US Dist Ct 118 US Courthouse 620 SW Main St Portland OR 97205

FRYE, JUDITH ELEEN MINOR, editor; b. Seattle; d. George Edward and Eleen G. (Hartelius) Minor; student UCLA, 1947-48, U. So. Calif., 1948-53; m. Vernon Lester Frye, Apr. 1, 1954. Acct., office mgr. Colony Wholesale Liquor, Culver City, Calif., 1947-48; credit mgr. Western Distbg. Co., Culver City, 1948-53; ptnr. in restaurants, Palm Springs, L.A., 1948, ptnr. in date ranch, La Quinta, Calif., 1949-53; ptnr., owner Imperial Printing, Huntington Beach, Calif., 1955—; editor, pub. New Era Laundry and Cleaning Lines, Huntington Beach, 1962—; registered lobbyist, Calif., 1975-84. Mem. Laundry & Cleaning Allied Trades Assn., Laundry & Dry Cleaning Suppliers Assn., Calif. Coin-op Assn. (exec. dir. 1975-84), Cooperation award 1971, Dedicated Svc.award 1976), Nat. Automatic Laundry & Cleaning Coun. (Leadership award 1972), Women Laundry & Drycleaning (past pres., Outstanding Svc. award 1977), Printing Industries Assn., Master Printers Am., Nat. Assn. Printers & Lithographers, Huntington Beach C. of C. Office: 22031 Bushard St Huntington Beach CA 92646

FRYE, MARTIN CLIFFORD, dentist; b. Del Norte, Colo., Oct. 5, 1946; s. Kenneth Woodrow and Ruth Jean (Martin) F.; m. Susan Linda Spangenberg, June 20, 1970; children: Nathaniel Martin, Thaddeus Justin, Susannah Bronwynn. BA, U. Colo., 1968; DDS, U. Wash., 1972. Gen. practice dentistry Boulder, Colo., 1974—; asst. prof. U. Colo., Denver, 1975-81. Coach Boulder Jr. Soccer, 1982-88; host Colo. Music Festival Fundraiser, Boulder, 1987-88. Served to capt. USAF, 1972-74. Fellow Acad. Gen. Dentistry; mem. Boulder County Dental Assn. (pres. 1986-87). Lodge: Optimists (Boulder). Office: 3400 Table Mesa Dr Boulder CO 80303

FRYER, GLADYS CONSTANCE, nursing home medical director, educator; b. London, Mar. 28, 1923; came to U.S., 1967; d. William John and Florence Annie (Dockett) Mercer; m. Donald Wilfred Fryer, Jan. 20, 1944; children: Peter Vivian, Gerard John, Gillian Celia. MB, BS, U. Melbourne, Victoria, Australia, 1956. Resident Box Hill Hosp., 1956-57; cardiologist Assunta Found., Petaling Jaya, Malaysia, 1961-64; clin. research physician U.S. Army Clin. Research Unit, Malaysia, 1964-66; internist Hawaii Permanente Kaiser Found., Honolulu, 1968-73; practice medicine specializing in internal medicine Honolulu, 1973-88; med. dir. Hale Nani Health Ctr., Honolulu, 1975—, Beverly Manor Convalescent Ctr., Honolulu, 1975—; asst. clin. profl. medicine John Burns Sch. Medicine U. Hawaii, 1968—; med. cons. Salvation Army Alcohol Treatment Facility, Honolulu, 1975-81; physician to skilled nursing patients VA, Honolulu, 1984-88; preceptor to geriatric nurse practitioner program U. Colo., Honolulu, 1984-85; lectr. on geriatrics, Alzheimer's disease, gen. medicine, profl. women's problems, and neurosci., 1961—; mem. ad hoc due process bd. Med. Care Evaluation Com., 1982—, Hospice Adv. Com., 1982—; mem. pharmacy com. St. Francis Hosp. Clin. Staff, 1983—, chmn. 1983-84. Contbr. articles to profl. jours. Mem. adv. com. Honolulu Home Care St. Francis Hosp., Honolulu, 1974-87; mem. adv. bd. Honolulu Gerontology Program, 1983—, Straub Home Health Program, Honolulu, 1984-87; mem. sci. adv. bd. Alzheimers Disease and Related Disorders Assn., Honolulu, 1984—; mem. long term care task force Health and Community Services Council Hawaii, 1978-84. Recipient Edgar Rouse Prize in Indsl. Medicine, U. Melbourne, 1955, Outstanding Supporter award Hawaii Assn. Activity Coordinators, 1987. Mem. AAAS, ACP, Hawaii Med. Assn. (councillor 1984—), Honolulu County Med. Soc. (chmn., mem. utilisation rev. com. 1973—), World Med. Assn., Am. Geriatrics Soc., Gerontol. Soc. Am., N.Y. Acad. Scis. Episcopalian. Office: Hale Nani Health Ctr 1677 Pensacola St Honolulu HI 96822-2699

FRYER, JAMES FINLEY, county official; b. San Francisco, May 21, 1929; s. John Cornelius and Lillian (Finley) F.; m. Leona Ruth Van Stone; children: David James, Mary Suzanne, Christopher Jon, Melissa Gayle. BA, Fresno State U., 1953, MA, 1962; EdD, U. So. Calif., 1972. Tchr. Fresno (Calif.) Unified Sch. Dist., 1956-69, counselor, 1969-70, media dir., 1971-72; media dir. office of edn. Alameda County, Hayward, Calif., 1972—; instr. health edn. Fresno State U., 1962-66; cons. in field, 1978—. Produced ednl. films, including California's Heritage, 1979, California's Challenge, 1980. Pres. YMCA, Hayward, 1978-81. Lt. Col. ANG, 1956-80. Mem. Assn. for Ednl. Communications and Tech., Calif. Media and Library Edn. Assn. (pres. 1989—), Phi Delta Kappa. Democrat. Methodist. Home: 3287 Oakes Dr Hayward CA 94542 Office: Alameda County Office Edn 313 W Winton Ave Hayward CA 94544-1198

FRYER, ROBERT SHERWOOD, theatrical producer; b. Washington, Nov. 18, 1920; s. Harold and Ruth (Reade) F. B.A., Western Res. U., 1943. Asst. to mng. dir. Theatre Inc., 1946, casting dir., 1946-48; asst. to exec. CBS, 1949-51, casting dir., 1951-52; producer: (Broadway plays) (with others) A Tree Grows in Brooklyn, 1951, (with others) By the Beautiful Sea, 1954, Wonderful Town, 1953, The Desk Set, Shangri-La, Auntie Mame, Redhead, There Was a Little Girl, Advise and Consent, A Passage To India, Hot Spot, Roar Like a Dove, Sweet Charity, Chicago, 1975, The Norman Conquests, 1976, California Suite, 1976, On the Twentieth Century, 1977, Sweeney Todd, 1978, Merrily We Roll Along, The West Side Waltz, 1981, Brighton Beach Memoirs, Noises Off, 1983, Benefactors, 1985, Wild Honey, 1987, Hapgood, 1989, (films) The Boston Strangler, 1963, Abdication, 1973, Mame, 1973, Great Expectations, 1974, Voyage of the Damned, 1976, The Boys from Brazil, 1978, Prime of Miss Jean Brodie 1969, Travels with My Aunt, 1973, The Shining 1979 ; artistic dir.: Ahmanson Theatre, Ctr. Theatre Group, L.A.; author: Professional Theatrical Management New York City, 1947. Bd. dirs. Kennedy Ctr., Ctr. Theatre Group, Music Ctr., Los Angeles; trustee, exec. com. John F. Kennedy Ctr., Washington. Served as capt. AUS, 1941-46; maj. Res. Decorated Legion of Merit.; Rockefeller Found. fellow. Mem. Episcopal Actors Guild (v.p.), League of N.Y. Theatres (bd. govs.). Office: 135 N Grand Ave Los Angeles CA 90012

FRYMER, MURRY, theater critic, columnist; b. Toronto, Ont., Can., Apr. 24, 1934; came to U.S., 1945; s. Dave and Sylvia (Spinrod) F.; m. Barbara Lois Grown, Sept. 4, 1966; children: Paul, Benjamin, Carrie. BA, U. Mich., 1956; MA, NYU, 1964. Editor Town Crier, Westport, Conn., 1962-63, Tribune, Levittown, N.Y., 1963-64; viewpoints editor, critic Newsday, L.I., N.Y., 1964-72; asst. mng. editor Rochester Democrat & Chronicle, N.Y., 1972-75; Sunday and feature editor Cleve. Plain Dealer, 1975-77; editor Sunday Mag., Boston Herald Am., 1977-79; film and TV critic San Jose Mercury News, Calif., 1979-83, theater critic, 1983—, columnist, 1983—; instr. San Jose State U., Cleve. State U., judge Emmy awards Nat. Acad. TV Arts and Scis., 1968. Author, dir. musical revue Four by Night, N.Y.C., 1963; author (play) Danse Marriage, 1955 (Hopwood prize 1955). Served with U.S. Army, 1956-58. Mem. Bay Area Theater Critics Assn. Jewish. Home: 1060 Moongate Pl San Jose CA 95120 Office: San Jose Mercury News 750 Ridder Park Dr San Jose CA 95190

FTOREK, ROBBIE BRIAN (ROBERT BRIAN FTOREK), professional hockey coach; b. Boston, Jan. 2, 1952; s. Stephen Joseph and A. Ruth (Barton) F.; m. Wendy Joan Bray, May 20, 1972; children: Sam, Lucie, Casey, Anna. Grad. high sch., Needham, Mass. Hockey player U.S. Olympic Team, Sapporo, Japan, 1972; profl. hockey player various teams, 1972-81, N.Y. Rangers, N.Y.C., 1982-85; coach New Haven Nighthawks, 1985-87, L.A. Kings, 1987-89. Recipient Silver medal U.S. Olympic Com., 1972. Office: care Los Angeles Kings 3900 W Manchester Blvd PO Box 17013 Inglewood CA 90306

FUCHS, GAYNELL MCAULIFFE, teacher; b. Hartford, Conn., Feb. 5, 1935; d. Norman Stanley and Carolyn Leffingwell (Palmer) McAuliffe; m. Roland J. Fuchs, June 15, 1957; children: Peter K., Christopher K., Andrew K. AA, Hartford Coll., 1954; AB, Clark U., 1956, MA in Edn., 1964. Tchr. English Mid-Pacific Inst., Honolulu, 1962-63; substitute tchr. Iolani Sch., Honolulu, 1975-79, Kamehameha Schs., Honolulu, 1979-81; tchr. Iolani Sch., Honolulu, 1981-82; English tchr. English Tchr., 1982—; tchr. high sch. Iolani Sch., Honolulu, 1982-87, 88—; Englishtchr. Kamehameha Schs., Honolulu, 1982—. Author: (with others) Five Treasures of Chinese Cuisine, 1975, Mona Lisa Writes a Letter, 1987. Chairperson Candlelight Concert Series, Honolulu, 1985-87. Hawaii Writing Project fellow U. Hawaii, 1981. Mem. Nat. Council Tchrs. of English, Hawaii Council Tchrs. of English. Democrat. Mem. United Ch. of Christ. Home: 5136 Maunalani Circle Honolulu HI 96816 Office: Kamehameha Schs Kapalama Heights Honolulu HI 96817

FUCHS, MARTHA ROSE, information systems manager; b. Milw., Mar. 28, 1952; d. Harold Victor and Mary Elizabeth (McCollow) F. BS, Marquette U., 1974. Cert. info. systems auditor. Systems analyst Johnson Controls, Inc., Milw., 1974-76; auditor NN Corp., Milw., 1976-78; with Security Pacific Nat. Bank, Glendale, Calif., 1978; EDP audit mgr. Continental Airlines, Inc., L.A., 1978-81, H.J. Heinz Co., L.A., 1981-88; info. systems mgr. Medtronic, Inc., Anaheim, Calif., 1988—. Am. Soc. Women Accts. scholar, 1973. Mem. EDP Auditors Assn., Beta Alpha Psi. Home: 21052 Poolside Ln Huntington Beach CA 92648 Office: Medtronic Inc 4633 E LaPalma AVe Anaheim CA 92807

FUCHS, ROBERT LOUIS, investment banker; b. Bay Shore, N.Y., Dec. 7, 1929; s. Carl Ludwig and Edith May (Nye) F.; m. Josephine Servello, Dec. 26, 1953 (div. Aug. 1986); children: Edward Thomas, Robert Brian; m. Jeanne Carol Fee, Sept. 20, 1986. BA with distinction, Cornell U., Ithaca, N.Y., 1951; MS, U. Ill., 1952. Cert. petroleum geologist. Geologist, supr. analyst Mobil Oil Corp., N.Y., La., Venezuela, Libya, 1952-65; asst. to pres. Flow Labs., Rockville, Md., 1965-66; pres. and dir. Automation Inst. and Con-Serv Corp., Wheaton, Md., 1966-69; sr. v.p. Intercontinental Energy Corp., N.Y.C. and Greenwich, Conn., 1969-71; pres. and dir. Geosystems Corp., Westport, Conn. and Denver, 1971-84, Caland Petroleum Corp., Denver, 1984-86; mng. dir. First Fairfield Investment Co., Denver, 1987—; bd. dirs. Canyon Resources Corp., Golden, Colo., 1980—, Sheffield Exploration Co., Inc., Denver, 1981—; chmn. bd. dirs. Sundance Oil Co., Denver, 1982-84. Active bd. fin. Town of Westport, Conn., 1977-83, Genesee Fire Protection Dist., Golden, 1988—, Denver Symphony Orchestra Chorus, 1984—. Lt. USN, 1955-58. Fellow Geol. Soc. Am. (treas. 1983—, found. pres. 1987—); mem. Am. Assn. Petroleum Geologists (EMD div. pres. 1981-82, Dist. Svc. award 1982), Am. Inst. Mining and Metall. Engrs. Republican. Episcopalian. Office: First Fairfield Investment Co 1675 Larimer St Ste 720 Denver CO 80202

FUCHS, ROLAND JOHN, geography educator; b. Yonkers, N.Y., Jan. 15, 1933; s. Alois L. and Elizabeth (Weigand) F.; m. Gaynell Ruth McAuliffe, June 15, 1957; children: Peter K., Christopher K., Andrew K. BA., Columbia U., 1954, postgrad., 1956-57; postgrad., Moscow State U., 1960-61; MA, Clark U., 1957, PhD, 1959. Asst. prof. to prof. U. Hawaii, Honolulu, 1958—; chmn. dept. geography U. Hawaii, 1964-86, asst. dean to assoc. dean coll. arts and scis., 1965-67, dir. Asian Studies Lang. and Area Ctr., 1965-67, adj. rsch. assoc. East West Ctr., 1980—, spl. asst. to pres., 1986; vice rector UN U., 1987—; vis. prof. Clark U., 1963-64, Nat. Taiwan U., 1974; mem. bd. internat. orgns. and programs Nat. Acad. Scis., 1976—, chmn., 1980—, mem. bd. sci. and tech. in devel., 1980-85; mem. U.S. Nat. Commn. for Pacific Basin Econ. Coop., 1985—; sr. advisor United Nations U., 1986. Author, editor: Geographical Perspectives on the Soviet Union, 1974, Theoretical Problems of Geography, 1977, Population Distribution Policies in Development Planning, 1981, Urbanization and The Urban Policies in the Pacific-Asia Region, 1987; assoc. editor Econ. Geography, 1963-64; mem. editorial adv. com. Soviet Geography: Review and Translation, 1966—, Geoforum, 1988—, African Urban Quar., 1987, Geoforum, 1988—. Ford Found. fellow, 1956-57; Fulbright Rsch. scholar, 1966-67. Mem. Internat. Geog. Union (v.p. 1980-84, 1st v.p. 1984-88, pres. 1988—), AAAS, Assn. Am. Geographers, (honors award 1982), Am. Assn. Advancement Slavic Studies (bd. dir. 1976-81), Pacific Sci. Assn. (coun. 1978—, mem. exec. com. 1986—). Home: 5136 Maunalani Circle Honolulu HI 96816

FUDULI, ROBIN, insurance sales executive; b. Seattle; d. Anthony R. and Dorothy (Tatarka) Chapetta; divorced; children: Francesca, Allessander; m. Alfredo Fuduli, Dec. 7, 1980; 1 child, Gianluca. Account adminstr. Frank B. Hall, L.A., 1978-80; underwriter Mission Ins. Co., L.A., 1980-82; mktg. rep. Ins. Co. of the West, Encino, Calif., 1982-85; account mgr., supr., account exec. Sullivan Kelly & Assocs., L.A., 1985—. Active L.A. county Mus. Mem. Am. Mgmt. Assn., Am. Soc. Profl. Exec. Women, Calif. Assn. of Risk Mgrs., So. Calif. Risk Mgrs., L.A. Athletic Club, Toastmasters (pres.). Office: Sullivan Kelly & Assocs 800 W 6th ST Los Angeles CA 90017

FUERST, NICKIE JACOB, military pilot; b. Yreka, Calif., July 12, 1955; s. Fred Furot and Audrey Julia (Lethtomaki) F. BS in Engring. Mechanics, USAF Acad., 1978. Commd. 2d lt. USAF, 1978, advanced through grades to maj., 1988; pilot USAF, Vance AFB, Okla., 1978-79, Macdill AFB, Fla., 1979-80, Seymour Johnson AFB, N.C., 1981-84, Nellis AFB, Nev., 1980-81, 84—. Mem. Daedalians. Home: 5982 Applegate Ln Las Vegas NV 89110 Office: USAF 65 Aggressor Squadron Nellis AFB NV 89191

FUERSTENAU, DOUGLAS WINSTON, mineral engineering educator; b. Hazel, S.D., Dec. 6, 1928; s. Erwin Arnold and Hazel Pauline (Karterud) F.; m. Margaret Ann Pellett, Aug. 29, 1953; children: Lucy, Sarah, Stephen. BS, S.D. Sch. Mines and Tech., 1949; MS, Mont. Sch. Mines, 1950; ScD, MIT, 1953; Mineral Engr., Mont. Coll. Mineral Sci. and Tech., 1968; D honoris causa, U. Liege, Belgium, 1989. Asst. prof. mineral engring. MIT, 1953-56; sect. leader, metals research lab. Union Carbide Metals Co., Niagara Falls, N.Y., 1956-58; mgr. mineral engring. lab Kaiser Aluminum & Chem. Corp., Permanente, Calif., 1958-59; asso. prof. metallurgy U. Calif.-Berkeley, 1959-62, prof. metallurgy, 1962-86, P. Malozemoff prof. of mineral engring., 1987—, Miller research prof., 1969-70, chmn. dept. materials sci. and mineral engring., 1970-78; dir. Homestake Mining Co.; chmn. Engring. Found. Research Conf. on Comminution, 1963; mem. adv. bd. Sch. Earth Scis., Stanford, 1970-73; mem. Nat. Mineral Bd., 1975-78; Am. rep. Internat. Mineral Processing Congress Com., 1978—. Editor: Froth Flotation-50th Anniversary Vol, 1962; co-editor-in-chief: Internat. Jour. of Mineral Processing, 1972—; Mem. editorial adv. bd.: Jour. of Colloid and Interface Sci, 1968-72, Colloids and Surfaces, 1980—; Contbr. articles to profl. jours. Recipient Disting. Teaching award U. Calif., 1974; Alexander von Humboldt Sr. Am. Scientist award Fed. Republic Germany, 1984. Fellow Instn. Mining and Metallurgy, London. Mem. Nat. Acad. Engring., Am. Inst. Mining and Metall. Engrs. (chmn. mineral processing div. 1967, Robert Lansing Hardy Gold medal 1957, Rossiter W. Raymond award 1961, Robert H. Richards award 1975, Antoine M. Gaudin award 1978, Mineral Industry Edn. award 1983, Henry Krumb disting. lectr. 1989, hon. 1989), Soc. Mining Engrs. (dir. 1968-71, Distinguished mem.), Am. Chem. Soc., Am. Inst. Chem. Engrs., Sigma Xi, Theta Tau. Congregationalist. Home: 1440 LeRoy Ave Berkeley CA 94708

FUGATE, DONALD JAMES, minister, teacher; b. Oakland, Calif., May 8, 1953; s. James Duke and Doris Colleen (Norris) F.; m. Diann Georgette De Graaf, Jan. 26, 1974; children: Donald Thomas, David James. BA in Music, Calif. Bapt. Coll., Riverside, 1976; M in Ch. Music, Golden Gatge Sem., 1978. Minister of music 1st Bapt. Ch., Arlington, Calif., 1974-75, Calvary Bapt. Ch., Modesto, Calif., 1975-76; assoc. pastor Western Hills Bapt. Ch., San Mateo, Calif., 1976-83, Foxworthy Bapt. Ch., San Jose, Calif., 1983—; dir. choral music dept. Valley Chrisitan Schs., San Jose, 1988—; asst. conductor Golden Gate Sem., Mill Valley, Calif., 1977-78; bd. dirs. Destiny-Vocal Ensemble, San Jose; cons. Sound Svcs., San Jose, 1983—. Contbr. articles to profl. jours. Recipient 1st Pl. award Crescendo Music Corp., 1979; named one of Outstanding Young Men in Am., 1981, 83. Republican. Baptist. Home: 1493 Ilikai Ave San Jose CA 95118

FUHRMAN, ROBERT ALEXANDER, aerospace company executive; b. Detroit, Feb. 23, 1925; s. Alexander A. and Elva (Brown) F. B.S., U. Mich., 1945; M.S., U. Md., 1952; postgrad., U. Calif., San Diego, 1958; Exec. Mgmt. Program, Stanford Bus. Sch., 1964. Project engr. Naval Air Test Center, Patuxent River, Md., 1946-53; chief tech. engring. Ryan Aero. Co., San Diego, 1953-58; mgr. Polaris 1958-64, chief engr. MSD, 1964-66; v.p., asst. gen. mgr. missile systems div. Lockheed Missiles & Space Co., Sunnyvale, Calif., 1966-68; v.p., gen. mgr. Lockheed Missiles & Space Co., 1969, v.p., 1973-76, pres., 1976-83, chmn., 1979—; v.p Lockheed Corp., Burbank, Calif., 1969-76; group pres. Missiles, Space & Electronics System Lockheed Corp., 1983-85; pres., chief operating officer Lockheed Corp., Calabasas, Calif., 1986-88; vice chmn. bd., chief operating officer Lockheed Corp., 1988—; also dir., pres. Lockheed Ga. Co., Marietta, 1970-71; pres. Lockheed Calif. Co., Burbank, 1971-73; bd. dirs. Bank of the West, Charles Stark Draper Lab, Inc.; mem. FBM Steering Task Group, 1966-70. Mem. adv. coun. Sch. Engring., Stanford U.; mem. adv. bd. Coll. Engring., U. Mich., 1981—. Ensign USNR, 1944-46. Recipient Silver Knight award Nat. Mgmt. Assn., 1969, John J. Montgomery award, 1964; award Soc. Mfg. Engrs., 1973; Disting. Citizen award Boy Scouts Am., 1983; Donald C. Burnham award Soc. Mfg. Engrs., 1983; Recipient Eminent Engr. award Tau Beta Pi, 1983. Fellow AIAA (hon., dir.-at-large, Von Karman 1978), Soc. Mfg. Engrs.; mem. Nat. Acad. Engring., Am. Astron. Soc. (sr.), Nat. Aero. Assn., Ga. C. of C. (dir.), Am. Def. Preparedness Assn. (dir., exec. com.), Navy League U.S. (life), Air Force Assn., Assn. U.S. Army, Soc. Am. Value Engrs. (hon.), Santa Clara County Mfrs. Group (past chmn.), Beta Gamma Sigma. Clubs: Los Altos Country (Calif.),Burning Tree (Bethesda, Md.), N. Ranch Country (Westlake Village). Office: Lockheed Corp 4500 Park Granada Blvd Calabasas CA 91399

FUHS, ALLEN EUGENE, engineer, physicist, educator; b. Laramie, Wyo., Aug. 11, 1927; s. Michael Allen and Grace Emeline (Terrill) F.; m. Emily Ann Large, Dec. 22, 1951; 1 child, Susan Elizabeth. B.S.M.E., U. N.Mex., 1951; M.S.M.E., Calif. Inst. Tech., 1955, Ph.D., 1958. Owner service sta. Gallup, N.Mex., 1944-46; asst. prof. Northwestern U., Evanston, Ill., 1958-59; mem. tech. staff TRW Systems, El Sequndo, Calif., 1959-60; staff scientist Aerospace Corp., El Segundo, 1960-66; prof., chmn. aeros. Naval Postgrad. Sch., Monterey, Calif., 1966-68, disting prof., 1970-87, chmn. dept. mech. engring., 1975-78, chmn. space systems, 1982-87; chief scientist Air Force Aeropropulsion Lab., Dayton, Ohio, 1968-70, Orbital Scis. Corp., 1987—; cons. TRW Systems, Aerospace Corp., others. Author: Instrumentation for High Speed Plasma Flow, 1965; editor 4 books; editor-in-chief: Jour. of Aircraft, 1974-79; contbr. articles to profl. jours.; patentee in field. Served with USN, 1951-54, Korea. Recipient SAE Ralph R. Teetor award, Superior Civilian Service award Dept. Navy, 1987; named Disting. Alumnus, U. N.Mex. Coll. Engring., 1985; Guggenheim fellow, 1957-58. Fellow AIAA (v.p. publs. 1979-81, dir. 1982-85, pres. 1986-87), ASME; mem. Soc. Automotive Engrs., Am. Phys. Soc., Am. Soc. Naval Engrs., Soc. Naval Architects and Marine Engrs., Am. Optical Soc., Sigma Xi. Office: Monterey Cons Svcs PO Box 222040 Carmel CA 93922

FUJII, KIYO, pharmacist; b. Portland, Oreg., July 1, 1921; s. Kanji and Mitoyo (Kurata) F.; student U. Wash., 1939-42; B.S., St. Louis Coll. Pharmacy, 1943. Pharmacist, C.F. Knight Drug, St. Louis, 1943-48, Sargent Drug, Chgo., 1950-52, Mt. Sinai Hosp., Chgo., 1953-54, Campus Pharmacy, Los Angeles, 1973—; chief pharmacist Evang. Hosp., Chgo., 1948-49, Am. Hosp. Clinic, Los Angeles, 1958-60. Mem. Am., Calif. Pharm. Assns., St. Louis Coll. Pharmacy Alumni Assn., Rho Chi, Sigma Epsilon Sigma. Democrat. Presbyterian. Home: 7913 Kentwood Ave Los Angeles CA 90045

FUJIKAMI, RAYMOND HAJIME, surgeon; b. Honolulu, Jan. 2, 1932; s. Harry K. and Ruth S. (Murashige) F.; m. Diane Y. Yanagisako, May 24, 1970. BS in Medicine, Northwestern U., 1954, MD, 1957. Diplomate, Am. Bd. Surgery. Intern Ind. U. Med. Ctr., Indpls., 1957-58; resident in gen. surgery Hartford (Conn.) Hosp., 1958-62; practice medicine specializing in surgery Honolulu, 1964-76, 84—; surgeon Med. Specialty Clinic, Honolulu, 1976-84. Capt. U.S. Army, 1962-64. Fellow ACS; mem. AMA, Hawaiian Surg. Soc., Hawaii Med. Assn., Honolulu Club. Republican. Office: 1481 S King St Ste 543 Honolulu HI 96814

FUJIKAWA, JOHN HIROSHI, dentist; b. Lodi, Calif., May 27, 1961; s. Hiroshi and Masako (Hiramoto) F. BS in Biology, U. Pacific, 1983; BS in Dental Sci., DDS, U. Calif., San Francisco, 1987. Lic. dentist, Calif. Assoc. dentist Diablo Dental Group, San Ramon, Calif., 1987—. Mem. ADA, Calif. Dental Assn., Japanese Am. Citizen League.

FUJIKAWA, SAMUEL TOORU, plumbing and mechanical company executive; b. Honolulu, Nov. 8, 1948; s. Kaoru and Kiyoko Fujikawa; m. Patricia Ann Birringer, July 10, 1971; children: Robert Kaoru, Tricia Kishino, Michael Tooru, David Hiroshi. BSME, Milw. Sch. Engring., 1970. Project engr. Continental Mech. of the Pacific, Honolulu, 1970-71; contract mgr. Continental Mech. of the Pacific, 1971-77, sr. contract mgr., 1977-82, v.p., 1982—. Judo instr. Salt Lake Judo Hawaii. With U.S. Army, 1970-76. Mem. ASHRAE, ASME. Home: 1864 Ala Noe Pl Honolulu HI 96819 Office: Continental Mech of Pacific 2146 Puuhale Pl Honolulu HI 96819

FUJIMOTO, REBECCA YAE, microbiologist; b. Wailuku, Hawaii, Jan. 9, 1958; d. Masakazu Robert and Takako (Oka) F. Student, U. Hawaii, Manoa, 1976-77; BS, Colo. State U., 1980. Lab. asst. Colo. State U., Ft. Collins, 1979-80; microbiologist Foster Farms, Livingston, Calif., 1980-81; microbiologist Hawaii Dept. Health, Lihue, 1981-86, Honolulu, 1986—. Mem. AAAS, Am. Soc. Microbiology (Hawaii chpt.), Nat. Registry of Microbiologists, Hawaii Pub. Health Assn. Clubs: Brown Bag (Lihue) (pres. 1985-86); Golden Ripples (4-H leader). Home: 1503 Emerson St Apt 5 Honolulu HI 96813 Office: Hawaii Dept Health Lab 1250 Punchbowl St Honolulu HI 96813

FUJITANI, KIRSTEN B., marketing and advertising executive; b. Stuttgart, Fed. Republic of Germany, June 27, 1961; (parents Am. citizens); d. Donald Sadao and Lillian Sumiko (Kaya) F. BS in Bus. Adminstn. and Mktg., San Diego State U., 1984. Mktg. and mgmt. info. systems trainee Toyota Hawaii Servco Pacific, Honolulu, 1986-87, mktg. mgr. Bridgestone Hawaii, 1987-88; assoc. Bus. Cons. Resources, Honolulu, 1989—. Republican. Office: Bus Cons Resources 1164 Bishop St Honolulu HI 96813

FUKUDA, MICHAEL K., aeronautical engineer; b. Honolulu, Dec. 19, 1949; s. Tsuruichi and Ethel S. (Kobayashi) F. BS, Case Inst. Tech., 1971; MS, Case Western Res. U., 1975, PhD, 1977. Mem. tech. staff Aerospace Corp., L.A., 1977-84, sect. mgr., 1984-89, dept. dir., 1989—. Recipient Achievement awards Aerospace Corp., 1983, 85, 88. Mem. AIAA, Sigma Xi. Office: The Aerospace Corp MS M4/967 PO Box 92957 2350 E El Segundo Blvd El Segundo CA 90245

FUKUHARA, PAUL HISASHI, data processing executive; b. Honolulu, Dec. 9, 1957; s. Paul Akira and Catherine (Harries) F.; m. Ruth Larita Cabudol, Dec. 26, 1980; children: Saesha Davina, Natasha Penelope, Paula Heather. Computer systems analyst USDA Soil Conservation Svc., Honolulu, 1984—; pres. Fukuhara Sys., Honolulu, 1983—. Named Fed. Employee of the Yr., Honolulu-Pacific Fed. Exec. Bd., 1986. Mem. Am. Soc. Photogrammetry and Remote Sensing, Hawaii Fed. Computer Users Group (pres. 1986-88). Office: Fukuhara Systems PO Box 30626 Honolulu HI 96820

FUKUMOTO, BENJAMIN I., telecommunications executive; b. Honolulu, Dec. 18, 1938; s. Edward K. and Tsuruko (Kawamoto) F.; m. Elmira E. Kojima, July 27, 1961; children: Reid, Teri Ann, Lori Ann, Eric. BA, U. Hawaii, 1961. Mktg. mgr. IBM Corp., Honolulu, 1967-81; dep. dir. City and County of Honolulu, 1981-83; sales dir. GTE Hawaiian Telephone, Honolulu, 1983—. Served to capt. AUS, 1961-67, Vietnam. Mem. Armed Forces Communications and Electronics Assn. (pres. 1987-88, meritorious service award 1987), Hawaii C. of C., Honolulu Japanese C. of C. (bd. dirs. 1976-88, treas. 1988). Democrat. Clubs: Honolulu, Waikiki Athletic. Lodge: Masons. Home: 6852 Niumalu Loop Honolulu HI 96825 Office: GTE-Hawaiian Tel PO Box 2200 Honolulu HI 96841

FUKUNAGA, GEORGE JOJI, finance company executive; b. Waialua, Oahu, Hawaii, Apr. 13, 1924; s. Peter H. and Ruth (Hamamura) F.; BA, U. Hawaii, 1948; cert. Advanced Mgmt. Program Harvard U./U. Hawaii, 1955; HHD (hon.) U. Hawaii, 1985; m. Alice M. Tagawa, Aug. 5, 1950; 1 son, Mark H. Adminstrv. asst., dir. Svc. Motor Co., Ltd. (named changed to Servco Pacific Inc. 1969), Honolulu, 1948-52, v.p., 1952-60, pres., 1960-81; chmn., 1981—, also chmn., bd. dirs. 15 subs. and affiliates, Svc. Fin., Ltd. (name now Servco Fin. Corp.), Servco Svcs. Corp., Am. Ins. Agy. Inc., Servco Ins. Agy. Inc., Servco Securities Corp., Servco Investment Corp., Servco Calif. Inc., Servco Japan, Inc., Servco Fgn. Sales Corp. (Guam), Hawaiiana Advt. Agy., Pacific Internat. Co. Inc. (Guam), Pacific Fin. Corp. (Guam), Pacific Motors Corp. (Guam), Pacific Internat. Marianas Inc., (Saipan), Pacific Marshalls Inc., (Majuro); dir. Am. Fin. Svcs. Hawaii Inc., Am. Trust Co. of Hawaii Inc., Island Ins. Co. Ltd., Hawaiian Pacific Resorts, Inc. Bd. govs. Iolani Sch.; mem. Japan-Hawaii Econ. Coun.; trustee Fukunaga Scholarship Found., Servco Found., Contemporary Arts Ctr., Oceanic Inst., U.S. Army Mus.; bd. govs. Pub. Schs. Found., East-West Ctr. Found., Hawaii Pacific Coll., Hawaiin Japanese Cultural Ctr. Found. 2d lt. AUS, 1945-47, to 1st lt., 1950-52. Mem. C. of C. Hawaii (v.p. 1970, 83-84, bd. dirs. 1970-75, 82-84), Honolulu Japanese (pres. 1969, bd. dir. 1963—) C. of C., Bus. Roundtable Hawaii (bd. dirs.), Hawaii Econ. Study Club (pres. 1962), U.S.-Japan Soc. (dir. 1983—, v.p. 1986—), Plaza Club (bd. dirs.), Club 200, Deputies Club, Oahu Country Club, Rotary. Methodist. Office: Servco Pacific Inc 900 Fort Street Mall Honolulu HI 96813

FUKUSHIMA, BARBARA NAOMI, accountant; b. Honolulu, Apr. 5, 1948; d. Harry Kazuo and Misayo (Kawasaki) Murakoshi; B.A. with high honors, U. Hawaii, 1970; postgrad. Oreg. State U., 1971, 73, U. Oreg., 1972; m. Dennis Hiroshi Fukushima, Mar. 23, 1974; 1 son, Dennis Hiroshi Jr. Intern, Coopers & Lybrand, Honolulu, 1974; auditor Haskins & Sells, Kahului, Hawaii, 1974-77; pres. Book Doors, Inc., Pukalani, 1977—; pres. Barbara N. Fukushima C.P.A., Inc., Wailuku. 1979—; sec. treas. Target Pest Control, Inc., Wailuku, 1979—; internal auditor, acct. Maui Land & Pineapple Co., Inc., Kahului, 1977-80; auditor Hyatt Regency Maui, Kaanapali, 1980-81; ptnr. D & B Internat., Pukalani, 1980—; instr. Maui Community Coll., Kahului, 1982-85; fin. cons. Merrill Lynch, Pierce, Fenner & Smith, Inc., 1986—. Recipient Phi Beta Kappa Book award, 1969. Mem. Am. Inst. C.P.A.s, Hawaii Soc. C.P.A.s, Nat. Assn. Accts., Hawaii Assn. Public Accts., Bus. and Profl. Women's Club. Tenrikyo. Home: 200 Aliiolani St Pukalani HI 96768 Office: 270 Hookahi St Suite 210 Wailuku HI 96793

FULCHER, GLEN DALE, natural resources manager; b. Meridian, Idaho, Mar. 20, 1925; s. Earl Cyrus and Ethel Anna (Spurgeon) F.; m. Ardevee Fay Copenhaver, July 30, 1945 (dec. July 1987); children: Deleice, Neil, Glenna, Bryan; m. Shirley Lee Volk McColloch, June 5, 1988; children: Dan, Colleen, Aaron. BS in Range Mgmt., U. Idaho, 1951; MS in Resource Econs., U. Wis., 1954, PhD in Resource Econs., 1957. Range mgr. Bur. of Land Mgmt., Shoshone, Boise, Idaho, 1951-53; chief, div. of range mgmt. Bur. of Land Mgmt., Washington, 1964-68; chief, div. of standards and tech. Bur. of Land Mgmt., Denver, 1971-81; asst. prof. U. Nev., Reno, 1957-61, chmn. dept. of agrl. Econ., 1963-64; assoc. prof. Mont. State U., Asuncion, Paraguay, 1961-63; water resources scientist Office of Water Resources and Research, Washington, 1968-71; prof. and project leader Colo. State U., Banjul, The Gambia, 1981-86; cons. Third World, 1986—; cons. Nigerian Consortium for Econ. Devel., 1970-71; instr. FAO Latin Am. Watershed Devel., 1972; dept. of interior rep. Joint Iran U.S.A. Devel. Team, 1975; rep. bur. land mgmt., 1977-80. Contbr. articles to various publs. With USN, 1943-45. Recipient Meritorious Svc. award Dept. of the Interior, 1976, Disting. Svc. award U.S. Ambassador the The Gambia, 1986. Mem. Soc. of Range Mgmt. (pres. Washington chpt. 1967-68), Taylor/Hibbard Agrl. Econ. Club (pres. 1956-57), Rotary, Xi Sigma Phi. Democrat. Congregationalist. Home and Office: Rt 1 Box 115-B Mc Call ID 83638

FULCHER, MICHAEL CHARLES, sales and marketing professional; b. St. Louis, Apr. 2, 1954; s. Charles Orris and Ruth Helen (Haerting) F.; m. Judy Melinda Pope, June 25, 1988. BS, Ariz. State U., 1976; MBA, U. Phoenix, 1986. Escrow mgr. Am. Equity Corp., Salt Lake City, 1976-78; ter. sales mgr. Carnation Co., Salt Lake City, 1978-80, Phoenix, 1981-84; med. sales rep. Mead Johnson & Co., Phoenix, 1981-84, govt. area mgr., 1984-87; nat. sales mgr. Zila Pharma., Phoenix, 1987--; pres. Franchise Store, Phoenix, 1985-88. Mem. Am. Public Health Assn., Sales and Mktg. Execs., Am. Logistics Assn., Central Ariz. Club, Dx Assn. (pres. 1987-88), Am. Radio Relay League. Republican. Roman Catholic. Home: H C 02 Box 363 6648 E Milton Rd Cave Creek AZ 85331 Office: 777 E Thomas Rd Phoenix AZ 85331

FULCO, ARMAND JOHN, biochemist; b. Los Angeles, Apr. 3, 1932; s. Herman J. and Clelia Marie (DeFeo) F.; m. Virginia Loy Hungerford, June 18, 1955 (div. July 1985); children: William James, Lisa Marie, Linda Susan, Suzanne Yvonne; m. Doris V.N. Goodman, Nov. 29, 1987. B.S. in Chemistry, UCLA, 1957, Ph.D. in Physiol. Chemistry, 1960. NIH postdoctoral fellow Lipid Labs. UCLA, 1960-61; NIH research fellow dept. chemistry Harvard U., Cambridge, Mass., 1961-63; biochemist, prin. investigator Lab. Nuclear Medicine and Radiation Biology, UCLA, 1963-80; asst. prof. dept. biol. chemistry UCLA (Med. Sch.), 1965-70, assoc. prof., 1970-76, prof., 1976—, prin. investigator, lab. biomed. and environ. scis., 1981—; cons. biochemist VA, Los Angeles, 1968—. Author: (with J.F. Mead) The Unsaturated and Polyunsaturated Fatty Acids in Health and Disease, 1976; contbr. over 80 articles to sci. jours. Served with U.S. Army, 1952-54. Mem. Am. Chem. Soc., Am. Soc. Biochem. and Molecular Biology, Am. Oil Chemists Soc., AAAS, Am. Soc. Microbiology, Harvard Chemists Assn., Sigma Xi. Office: U Calif Lab Biomed and Environ Scis 900 Veteran Ave Los Angeles CA 90024

FULKERSON, WILLIAM MEASEY, JR., college president; b. Moberly, Mo., Oct. 18, 1940; s. William M. and Edna Frances (Pendleton) F.; m. Grace Carolyn Wisdom, May 26, 1962; children: Carl Franklin, Carolyn Sue. B.A., William Jewell Coll., 1962; M.A., Temple U., 1964; Ph.D., Mich. State U., 1969. Asst. to assoc. prof. Calif. State U.-Fresno, 1966-73, asst. to pres., 1971-73; assoc. exec. dir. Am. Assn. State Colls., Washington, 1973-77; acad. v.p. Phillips U., Enid, Okla., 1977-81; pres. Adams State Coll., Alamosa, Colo., 1981-87, 1988—; interim pres. Met. State Coll., Denver, 1987-88. Author: Planning for Financial Exigency, 1973; contbr. articles to profl. jours. Commr. North Central Assn., Chgo., 1980—; bd. dirs. Acad. Collective Bargaining Info. Service, Washington, 1976, Office for Advancemnet Pub. Negro Colls., Atlanta, 1973-77, Colo. Endowment for Humanities, 1988—. Named Disting. Alumni William Jewell Coll., 1982. Mem. Am. Assn. State Colls. and Univs. (parliamentarian), Am. Council on Edn. (bd. dirs.), Alamosa C. of C. (dir., pres 1984 Citizen of Yr. award). Lodge: Rotary. Office: Adams State Coll Office of Pres Alamosa CO 81102

FULLER, EDWIN DANIEL, hotel executive; b. Richmond, Va., Mar. 15, 1945; s. Ben Swint and Evelyn (Beal) F.; m. Denise Kay Fuller, July 17, 1969. Student, Wake Forest U., 1965; BSBA, Boston U., 1968; postgrad., Harvard Sch. Bus., 1987. Security officer Pinkerton Inc., Boston, 1965-68; with sales dept. Twin Marriott Hotel, Arlington, Va., 1972-73; nat. sales mgr. Marriott Hotels & Resorts, N.Y.C.; dir. nat. and internat. sales Marriott Hotels & Resorts, Washington, 1976-78; v.p. mktg. Marriott Hotels & Resorts, 1978-82; gen. mgr. Marriott Hotels & Resorts, Hempstead, N.Y., 1982-83, Marriott Copley Place, Boston, 1983-85; v.p. ops. Midwest region Marriott Corp., Rosemont, Ill., 1985-89; v.p. ops. Western and Pacific regions Marriott Corp., Costa Mesa, Calif., 1989—; chmn. bd. SNR Reservation System, Zurich, Switzerland 1979-81; com. chmn. Boston U. Hotel Sch., 1984—; bd. dirs. Mgmt. Engrs. Inc., Reston, Va.; treas. MEI Pacific, Honolulu 1985—. Capt. U.S. Army, 1968-72, Vietnam. Decorated Bronze Star. Mem. Boston U. Alumni Coun., Harvard Sch. Bus. AMP (fund agt.), Sigma Alpha Epsilon, Delta Sigma Pi. Republican. Home: 25362 Derby Hill Dr Laguna Hills CA 92653

FULLER, GLENN R., park ranger; b. Van Nuys, Calif., Sept. 1, 1946; s. Earl D. and Virginia (Allen) F. Masters, Calif. State U., Sacramento, 1972. Park ranger Grand Canyon (Ariz.) Nat. Park, 1975-80, Cape Cod Nat. Park, Wellfleet, Mass., 1980-81, Rocky Mountain Nat. Park, Estes Park, Colo., 1981-82, Golden Gate NRA, San Francisco, 1982-83; park supt. Muia Woods Nat. Monument, Mill Valley, Calif., 1983—. Sgt. U.S. Army, 1970-68. Mem. Friends of the River, Assn. Nat. Park Rangers. Office: Muir Woods Nat Monument Mill Valley CA 94941

FULLER, KENNETH ROLLER, architect; b. Denver, Mar. 7, 1913; s. Robert Kenneth and Nelle Grace (Roller) F.; m. Gertrude Alene Heid, June 16, 1938; children: Robert K. II, Richard H. Student in archtl. engring., U. Colo., 1932-35; student in engring., U. Denver, 1935-36; student in architecture, U. Ill., 1936-37. Registered architect, Colo. Archtl. draftsman Robert K. Fuller, Denver, 1937-40, chief draftsman, 1941-42; architect, engr. U.S. Engrs., Denver and Nebr., 1942-46, architect, 1947-48; ptnr., architect Fuller Fuller & Fuller, Denver, 1949-64; prin. Fuller & Fuller, Denver, 1965-70; pres., owner Fuller Fuller & Assocs., Denver, 1971-81, semi-retired, 1982—; archtl. cons., 1973-76; instr. in architecture U. Colo., Denver, 1947-48. Author: 100 Years of Architecture Roeschlaub-Fuller, 1873-1973, 1973; co-author: Life and Work of Roeschlaub, 1873-1923, 1987. Bd. dirs. Park Hill Improvement Assn., Denver, 1966-80. Recipient Honor award U. Colo. Coll. of Design and Planning, 1983. Fellow AIA (chmn. membership com. Colo. chpt. 1951-60, bd. dirs. Colo. chpt. 1960-63, author history Colo. chpt. 1985-86, Combined Service award with Colo. Soc. Architects and Denver, North, South and West chpts. 1980, honored with nat. fellowship 1984); mem. Colo. Soc. Architects-AIA (fellow emeritus 1985, permanent corp. trustee and sec./treas. ednl. fund 1966—, Disting. Service award 1970, Outstanding Service Cert. 1974), Am. Arbitration Assn. (adv. council Rocky Mountain area 1968-86), Colo. Hist. Soc. (hon. curator 1981), Nat. Trust for Hist. Preservation, Colo. Wildlife Fedn., Grand County Hist. Soc., Nat. Rifle Assn., Sigma Chi. Republican. Presbyterian. Lodge: Lions (bd. dirs. Denver 1964-66, 76-77, 30 Yr. Old Monarch award 1987). Home: 1932 Hudson St Denver CO 80220 Office: Fuller Fuller & Assocs 1615 California St #508 Denver CO 80202

FULLER, MARC STUART, educator, consultant; b. Greenville, S.C., Apr. 2, 1950; s. Robert and Mildred (Gluck) F.; m. Deborah Anne Paul, Aug. 18, 1974; 1 child, Lisa Heather. BSEE, MIT, 1972; MSEE, U. Pa., 1974; MS in Computer Engring., U. Mich., 1977, PhD in Elec. Engring., 1979. Mem. tech. staff AT&T Bell Labs, North Andover, Mass., 1979-81; asst. prof. Worcester Polytechnic Inst., Worcester, Mass., 1981-87; asst. research prof. U. Utah, Salt Lake City, 1987—. Contbr. articles to profl. jours. Recipient initiation grant, Nat. Sci. Found., 1982-84, research grant, Nat. Inst. Health, 1987-92. Mem. IEEE, Am. Heart Assn., Eta Kappa Nu. Jewish.

FULLER, ROBERT KENNETH, architect, urban designer; b. Denver, Oct. 6, 1942; s. Kenneth Roller and Gertrude Ailene (Heid) F.; m. Virginia Louise Elkin, Aug. 23, 1969; children: Kimberly Kirsten, Kelsey Christa. BArch, U. Colo., 1967; MArch and Urban Design, Washington U., St. Louis, 1974. Archtl. designer Fuller & Fuller, Denver; architect, planner Urban Research and Design Ctr., St. Louis, 1970-72; pres. Fuller & Fuller Assocs., Denver, 1972—. prin. works include Pattonsburg New Town, Mo., 1972. del. Aspen Design Conf., 1966, bd. dirs. Cherry Creek Improvement Assn., Greater Cherry Creek Steering com., Colo. Arlberg Club, Horizons, Inc.; past pres. Denver East Cen. Civic Assn. Served with USMCR, 1964-70. Mem. AIA (past pres. Denver chpt. 1987, traveling scholar to Gt. Britain, Colo. 1972), Phi Gamma Delta, Delta Phi Delta. Home: 2244 E 4th Ave Denver CO 80206 Office: 3320 E 2d Ave Denver CO 80206

FULLERTON, CHARLES MICHAEL, physics educator, dean; b. Oklahoma City, Mar. 10, 1932; s. Joseph Austin and Rose Marsh (Ingraham) F.; m. Jane Jo Wyatt, Dec. 27, 1954; children: Stephanie Malia, Christopher Damien, Amy Juliet. BS in Math., U. Okla., 1954; postgrad., U. N.Mex., 1957-61; MS in Physics, N.Mex. Inst. Mining and Technology, 1964, PhD, 1966. Instr. math, physics Coll. St. Joseph, Albuquerque, 1957-61; from asst. prof. to full prof. U. Hawaii, Hilo, 1966—, dean arts and scis., 1984—; dir. Cloud Physics Obs., Hilo, 1966-84; dir. mgmt. services State Dept. Health and Social Services, Santa Fe, 1972, dir. personnel services, 1975. Contbr. articles to profl. jours. Served to 1st lt. U.S. Army, 1954-57. Grantee NSF, 1964-66, U.S. Dept. Interior, 1971-77. Mem. Am. Meteorol. Soc., Am. Geophys. Union, Hawaiian Acad. Sci., N.Mex. Acad. Sci., Sigma Xi (local pres. 1975-76). Republican. Roman Catholic. Lodge: Rotary. Office: U Hawaii Coll Arts and Scis Hilo HI 96720-4091

FULLERTON, GAIL JACKSON, university president; b. Lincoln, Nebr., Apr. 29, 1927; d. Earl Warren and Gladys Bernice (Marshall) Jackson; m. Stanley James Fullerton, Mar. 27, 1967; children by previous marriage—Gregory Snell Putney, Cynde Gail Putney. B.A., U. Nebr., 1949, M.A., 1950; Ph.D., U. Oreg., 1954. Lectr. sociology Drake U., Des Moines, 1955-57; asst. prof. sociology Fla. State U., Tallahassee, 1957-60; asst. prof. sociology San Jose (Calif.) State U., 1963-67, asso. prof., 1968-71, prof., 1972—, dean grad. studies and research, 1972-76, exec. v.p. univ., 1976-78, pres., 1978—; bd. dirs. Assoc. Western Univs., Inc., 1980—; mem. sr. accrediting commn. Western Assn. Schs. and Colls., 1982-88, chmn., 1985-86. Author: Survival in Marriage, 2d edit, 1977, (with Snell Putney) Normal Neurosis: The Adjusted American, 2d edit, 1966. Carnegie fellow, 1950-51, 52-53; Doherty Found. fellow, 1951-52. Mem. Am. Sociol. Assn., Western Coll. Assn. (exec. com., past pres.), Nat. Collegiate Athletic Assn. (pres.'s commn.), San Jose C. of C. (bd. dirs.), Phi Beta Kappa. Home: 97 E St James St #58 San Jose CA 95112 Office: San Jose State U Washington Sq San Jose CA 95192-0001

FULLMER, STEVEN MARK, banker; b. San Francisco, Mar. 15, 1956; s. Thomas Patrick and Patricia Ann (Carroll-Boyd) F. BA in Chemistry, Willamette U., 1978, BA in Biology, 1978; postgrad., Ariz. State U., 1988—. Sr. engr., project leader Honeywell Large Computer Products, Phoenix, 1981-86; analyst First Interstate Bank Ariz., Phoenix, 1987—; cons. J.A. Boyd & Assoc., San Francisco, 1985—, ImaginInc. Consulting, Phoenix, 1985—, Resources Internat., Scottsdale, 1986. Contbr. articles to profl. jours. Mem. exec. bd. Theodore Roosevelt council, Boy Scouts Am., scoutmaster, 1983—; founder, lt. comdr. Maricopa County Sheriff's Adj. Posse, 1982-86. Named Eagle Scout Boy Scouts Am., Phoenix, 1974; Recipient Order of Merit Boy Scouts Am., 1988. Mem. Data Processing Mgmt. Assn., Am. Inst. for Certification Computer Profls. (cert. data processor 1985), Mensa, Phi Lambda Upsilon, Phi Eta Sigma, Kappa Sigma (v.p. 1973-74), Alpha Chi Sigma. Republican. Roman Catholic. Lodge: KC (membership dir. 1988). Office: First Interstate Bank Ariz 114 W Adams Phoenix AZ 85003

FULMER, RUSSELL FRANCIS, librarian; b. Birmingham, Ala., Nov. 28, 1946; s. John A. and Agnes E. (Parker) F. AB, Dickinson Coll., 1968; MLS, U. Ala., 1972. Cataloger, U. Ala., Tuscaloosa, 1971-74; coordinator tech. services Jackson Met. Library System, Miss., 1974-83; asst. dir. tech. services Colo. Sch. Mines, Golden, 1983—; mem. data base quality adv. com. Southeastern Library Network, 1979-81; cons. Miss. Library Assn., 1983. Asst. editor Miss. Libraries, 1980-81. Vol., Easter Seals Miss., 1975-76; mem. mission com. St. Christopher's Episcopal Ch., Jackson, 1981-83. Mem. ALA, Library Sch. Alumni Assn. (pres. 1972), Miss. Library Assn. (resolution 1983), Southeastern Library Assn., Colo. Library Assn. (chmn. tech. services and automation div. 1987-88), Beta Phi Mu. Episcopalian. Home: 1612 Secrest St Golden CO 80401 Office: Colo Sch Mines Libr Golden CO 80401

FULTON, GEOFFREY LYLE, sales and marketing professional; b. Westover, Mass., Nov. 20, 1952; s. Printiss Jr. and Willadean (Landrum) F.; m. Sherry Suzanne Stuntz, Aug. 20. 1974; children: Angela Marie, Stephanie Ann. BS in Aerospace Engring., Mid. Tenn. State U., 1974. Cert. flight instr. Mgr. Smyrna (Tenn.) Drug Co., 1966-72; flight instr. Mid. Tenn., Murfreesboro, 1972-75; salesman Rexall Drug Co., St. Louis, 1975-81; mktg. specialists Fox-Stanley Photo, San Antonio, 1982; sales rep. Goldline Labs., Cin., 1983-84, regional mgr. key accounts, 1985-86; regional mgr. retail Goldline Labs., City of Industry, Calif., 1986-87; regional sales dir. Goldline Labs., Rancho Cucamonga, Calif., 1987-88; mgr. sales and mktg. Tyson & Assocs., Santa Monica, Calif., 1989—. Res. officer Upland Police Dept., Calif., 1987—. Mem. am. Pharmacist Assn., Am. Soc. Pharmacists, Calif. Soc. Hosp. Pharmacists, Calif. Pharmacist Assn., Calif. Rifle and Pistol Assn., Aircraft Owners and Pilots Assn., NRA. Home: 211 Deborah Ct Upland CA 91786 Office: Tyson & Assocs 1661 Lincoln Blvd Santa Monica CA 90404

FULTON, NORMAN ROBERT, home entertainment company executive; b. Los Angeles, Dec. 16, 1935; s. Robert John and Fritzi Marie (Wacker) F.; A.A., Santa Monica Coll., 1958; B.S., U. So. Calif., 1960; m. Nancy Butler, July 6, 1966; children—Robert B., Patricia M. Asst. v.p. Raphael Glass Co., Los Angeles, 1960-65; credit adminstr. Zellerbach Paper Co., Los Angeles, 1966-68; gen. credit mgr. Carrier Transicold Co., Montebello, Calif., 1968-70, Virco Mfg. Co., Los Angeles, 1970-72, Superscope, Inc., Chatsworth, Calif., 1972-79; asst. v.p. credit and adminstrn. Inkel Corp., Carson, Calif., 1980-82; corp. credit mgr. Gen. Consumer Electronics, Santa Monica, Calif., 1982-83; br. credit mgr. Sharp Electronics Corp., Carson, Calif., 1983—. Served with AUS, 1955-57. Fellow Nat. Inst. Credit; mem. Credit Mgrs. So. Calif., Nat. Notary Assn. Home: 3801 Seamoor Dr Malibu CA 90265

FULTZ, PHILIP NATHANIEL, transportation analyst; b. N.Y.C., Jan. 29, 1943; s. Otis and Sara Love (Gibbs) F.; m. Bessie Learleane McCoy, Mar. 11, 1972. AA in Bus., Coll. of the Desert, 1980; BA in Mgmt., U. Redlands, 1980, MA in Mgmt., 1982. Enlisted USMC, 1967, advanced through grades to capt., 1972, served in various locations, 1964-78, resigned commn., 1978; CETA coord. County of San Bernardino, Yucca Valley, Calif., 1978-85; contract analyst Advanced Technology, Inc., Twentynine Palms, Calif., 1985-88; spl. transit analyst Omnitrans, San Bernardino, Calif., 1988—. Founding dir., Unity Home Battered Women's Shelter, Joshua Tree, Calif., 1982, Morongo Basin Adult Literacy, Twentynine Palms, 1984. Mem. Rotary (sec. Joshua Tree chpt. 1983-85). Republican. Home: 73477 Desert Trail Dr Twentynine Palms CA 92277 Office: Omnitrans 1700 W 5th St San Bernardino CA 92411

FUNDABURK, ALBERT LAMAR, JR., company executive, former air force officer; b. Jacksonville, Fla., Oct. 6, 1947; s. Albert Lamar and Cathryn Lee (Gregson) F.; m. Linda Lee Mueller (div. Sept. 1983); children: Stacey Lynn, Christopher Rye. BS in Edn., So. Ill. U., 1979; MPA, Golden Gate U., 1987. Commd. 2d lt. USAF, 1967, advanced through grades to capt., 1983; chief base mgmt. team USAF, Kusan, Republic of Korea, 1984-85; chief ops. and maintenance USAF, Nellis AFB, Nev., 1985-87; ret. 1987; chief exec. officer Orgn. Systems Devel., Las Vegas, Nev., 1987—; mem. adj. faculty Embry-Riddle Aero. U., Las Vegas, 1987—. Author: Stress and You, 1988, Business Expansion, 1988; editor: Position Descriptions, 1988. Mem. Air Force Assn. Home: 3827 Steinbeck Dr Las Vegas NV 89115 Office: Orgn Systems Devel 6400 S Eastern Ave Las Vegas NV 89119

FUNK, BEVERLEY MAE, retired community college instructor, writer, magazine or journal articles/features; b. Tacoma, Mar. 6, 1925; d. Harry William and Loretta Mary (Foye) Naubert; m. Roy I. Funk, April 17, 1951; children: Christopher R., Catherine A. BS, OregonState U., 1948; postgrad., U. Wash., 1950. Bus. instr. Mountlake Terrace High Sch., Wash., 1964-70; instr. bus. adminstrn. div. Everett Community Coll., Wash., 1970-82; research asst. vocat. office block program Mich. State U., E. Lansing, 1966-69. Author: (audio tape, workbook) Transcription Skills for Information Processing, 1981-82; contbr. articles to profl. jours. Active Stanwood Juvenile Diversion Com., 1983—; library task force Stanwood Community Library, 1984-86; pres. Sunrise Inn, Inc., Stanwood, Wash., 1987—; publicity chmn. Stanwood Hist. Assn., 1988; mem. found. bd. Skagit Valley Hosp., Mt. Vernon, Wash., 1988—. Recipient Outstanding Achievement award Wash. State Bus. Edn. Assn., 1974. Mem. Motar Bd. Soc. (hon.), Camano Island C. of C., Am. Assn. U. Women (pres. 1985-87). Republican. Roman Catholic. Home: 1279 S Beach Dr Camano Island WA 98292

FUNK, CHRISTOPHER ROY, contracting company executive; b. Lakewood, Ohio, Oct. 5, 1952; s. Roy Irving and Beverly Mae (Naubert) F. BS in Bldg. Constrn., U. Wash., 1974. Estimator J.R. Keyes Co., Inc., Tukwila, Wash., 1974-76; mem. quality control staff Santa Fe Engrs., Inc. (Trident Submarine Base), Bangor, Wash., 1976-78; project mgr., ptnr., gen. contractor M.D. Moore Co., Inc., Renton, Wash., 1978--. Mem. Profl. Ski Instrs. Am. Republican. Roman Catholic. Office: Md Moore Co Inc 12226 142nd Ave SE Renton WA 98056

FUNK, JOHN CALVIN, service organization executive; b. Olympia, Wash., Oct. 21, 1941; s. Orlo Vernon and Geneva (Dowdy) F.; m. Barbara Ann Hutcherson, July 12, 1963; children: Maria, Bobby, Timmy, Angela. AA, Phoenix Coll., Ariz., 1961; BS, Portland (Oreg.) State U., 1965. Sales Standard Ins. Co., Portland (Oreg.) and Phoenix, 1965-69; various positions Dow Chem. Co., Phoenix and L.A., 1969-85; v.p. health care bus. devel. Penn Corp. Fin., 1985-87; pres., chief exec. officer PPO Alliance, Cypress, Calif., 1987—. Chmn. trustees Calif. Bapt. Coll., Riverside, 1986; local com. chmn. Gideons Internat., Thousand Oaks, Calif., 1986—; chmn. ch. council, chmn. deacons First So. Bapt. Ch., Canoga Park, Calif., 1987, deacon, chmn. , 1988. Mem. The Healtcare Forum, Am. Mktg. Assn., AAPPO (sec. 1988—). Office: PPO Alliance 21800 Oxnard St PO Box 4203 Woodland Hills CA 91367-4203

FUNK, MILTON ALBERT, real estate broker; b. Cantonement, Okla., Oct. 12, 1918; s. John Anton and Cornelia Elizabeth (Schwake) F.; m. Earline Myrtle Burkholder, Feb. 15, 1937; children: DeAnne Funk Kiralla, Gary Milton. Cert. in real estate, UCLA, 1960. Owner Realty Sales & Exchange Co., South Gate, Calif., 1961—; sec.-treas. Apt. Investments, Inc., South Gate, 1961—; dir. Apple Valley View Water Assn., cons. to Los Angeles Apartment Assn. Directory, 1987. Served with arty. AUS, 1944-46, PTO. Mem. Calif. Assn. Realtors (regional v.p. 1969, dir.), S.E. Bd. Realtors (pres. 1966, dir. 1980), Los Angeles County Apt. Assn. (dir., sec.), Laguna Shores Owners Assn. (pres.), VFW, Downey and South Gate C. of C's. Home: 11714 Bellflower Blvd Downey CA 90242 Office: 3947 Tweedy Blvd South Gate CA 90280

FUNK, WILLIAM HENRY, environmental engineering educator; b. Ephraim, Utah, June 10, 1933; s. William George and Henrietta (Hackwell) F.; m. Ruth Sherry Mellor, Sept. 19, 1964 (dec.); 1 dau., Cynthia Lynn. B.S. in Biol. Sci, U. Utah, 1955, M.S. in Zoology (USPHS trainee), 1963, M.S. in Zoology, 1963, Ph.D. in Limnology, 1966. Tchr. sci., math. Salt Lake City Schs., 1957-60; research asst. U. Utah, Salt Lake City, 1961-63; head sci. dept. N.W. Jr. High Sch., Salt Lake City, 1961-63; mem. faculty Wash. State U., Pullman, 1966—; assoc. prof. environ. engring. Wash. State U., 1971-75, prof., 1975—, chmn. environ. sci./regional planning program, 1979-81; dir. Environ. Research Center, 1980-83, State of Wash. Water Research Ctr., 1981—; cons. Harstad Engrs., Seattle, 1971-72, Boise Cascade Corp., Seattle, 1971-72, U.S. Army C.E., Walla Walla, Wash., 1970-74, ORB Corp., Renton, Wash., 1972-73, State Wash. Dept. Ecology, Olympia, 1971-72, U.S. Civil Service, Seattle, Chgo., 1972-74; mem. High Level Nuclear Waste Bd., State of Wash.; apptd. by Gov. to Wash. state 2010 Com. to rev. state environment and natural resources, 1989. Author publs. on water pollution control and lake restoration. Mem. Gov.'s 2010 Com. to review condition of state's water and natural resources. Served with USNR, 1955-57. Recipient President's Disting. Faculty award Wash. State U., 1984. Grantee NSF Summer Inst., 1961, Office Water Resources Research, 1971-72, 73-76, EPA, 1980-83, U.S. Geol. Survey, 1983-88, Nat. Parks Service, 1985-87. Mem. Naval Res. Officers Assn. (chpt. pres. 1969), Res Officers Assn. (U.S. Naval Acad. info. officer 1973-76), N.Am. Lake Mgmt. Soc. (pres. 1984-85, Secchi Disk award 1988), Pacific N.W. Pollution Control Assn. (editor 1969-77, pres.-elect 1982-83, pres. 1983-84), Water Pollution Control Fedn. (Arthur S. Bedell award Pacific N.W. assn. 1976, nat. dir. 1978-81), Nat. Assn. Water Inst. Dirs. (chair 1985-87, bd. dirs. Universities council on water resources 1986-89), Wash. Lakes Protection Assn. (co-founder 1986), Am. Water Resources Assn. (v.p. Wash. sect. 1988), Am. Soc. Limnology and Oceanography, Am. Micros. Soc., N.W. Sci. Assn., Sigma Xi, Phi Sigma. Home: SW 330 Kimball Ct Pullman WA 99163

FUNKEY, GEORGE EDWARD, data processing executive; b. Hancock, Mich., Aug. 10, 1951; s. Frances and Ethel Mae (LaFave) F. BS, Mich. Tech. U., 1972, MS, 1974. Systems analyst Mich. Tech. U., Houghton, 1974-77, dir. acad. computing, 1977-82; dir. computing U. Colo., Denver, 1982—; cons. in field. Mem. Denver Profl. Men's Club. Office: U Colo 1200 Larimer St Denver CO 80204

FUNKHOUSER, BRUCE BEDFORD, music business executive; b. Memphis, Apr. 28, 1949; s. Richard Edgar and Phyllis (Parkin) F.; m. Christine Herrick, 1971 (div. 1973); m. Michelle Friars, July 3, 1982. BA, Princeton U., 1970. Program dir. King Broadcasting Co., Portland, Oreg., 1970-74; group program dir. Glo-Lee Broadcasting, Portland and Seattle, 1975-76; mgr. KTM Music, Inc., Bellevue, Wash., 1976-79; prodn. dir. Sandusky Broadcasting/KZAM-FM, Bellevue, 1979-81; instr. in communications Bellevue Community Coll., 1978-83; dir. programming Yesco Foreground Music, Inc., Seattle, 1983-87; v.p. programming Muzak Ltd. Partnership, Seattle, 1987—; cons., Funkhouser Prodns., Bellevue, 1977-84; owner, pres., chief exec. officer, Etoile Records, Seattle, 1986—. Producer album: Peggy Stern: A Christmas Album, 1986. Mem. Nat. Acad. Recording Arts and Sics., Nat. Assn. Broadcasters, AFTRA, Corp. Coun. for Arts, Northwest Area Musicians' Assn., World Affairs Coun., Washington Athletic Club. Office: Muzak Ltd Partnership 200 400 N 34th St Ste 200 Seattle WA 98103

FUNKHOUSER, MORTON LITTELL, JR., clergyman; b. Charlotte, N.C., Apr. 20, 1943; s. Morton Littell and Helen (Jones) F.; m. Mary Hope Moore, Sept. 6, 1969; children: Margaret Helen, Meredith Hope. BA, Asbury Coll., Wilmore, Ky., 1970; MDiv, Asbury Theol. Sem., 1973; postgrad., Chapman Coll., Orange, Calif., 1979-82. Ordained to ministry, United Meth. Ch., 1975. Minister Meth. Ch., N.C., 1973-79; commd. U.S. Air Force, 1979; advanced through grades to maj. to date chaplain Malstrom Air Force Base Chapel, Mont., 1979—. Democrat. Home: 4440B Gumwood Great Falls MT 59405-6623 Office: Malmstrom Air Force Base Chapel 341 CSG/HC Malmstrom AFB MT 59402-5000

FURLOW, MARY BEVERLEY, English educator; b. Shreveport, La., Oct. 14, 1933; d. Prentiss Edward and Mary Thelma (Hasty) F.; children: Mary Findley Johnson, William Prentiss, Samuel Christopher; m. William P. Cleary, 1988. BA, U. Tenn., 1955; MEd, Governors State U., 1972, MA, 1974; cert., U. Chgo., 1988. Mem. faculty Chattanooga State Community Coll., 1969-73, Moraine Valley Community Coll., Palos Hills, Ill., 1974-78; English faculty Pima Community Coll., Tucson, 1978—; cons. in field. Contbr. articles to profl. jours. Named one of Outstanding Educators of Am., 1973; grantee various found. Mem. Internat. Soc. Philosophical Enquiry, Ariz. Antiquarian Guild, Pi Beta Phi, Cincinatus Soc., Jr. League, Mensa, Holmes Socs., Clan Chattan Soc., DAR, Daughters of the Confederacy, Alpha Phi Omega (Tchr. of Yr. 1973). Democrat. Episcopalian. Home: 1555 N Arcadia Tucson AZ 85712 Office: Pima Community Coll 8202 E Poinciana Dr Tucson AZ 85730

FURMANSKI, PHILIP, cancer research scientist; b. Fed. Republic Germany, July 26, 1946; came to U.S., 1947, naturalized, 1954; s. Ed and Rose (Warsawski) F.; m. Elizabeth Ann Fremer, Oct. 5, 1968; children: Lisa Anne, Jonathan David. BA, Temple U., 1966, PhD, 1969. Research assoc. Albert Einstein Med. Ctr., Phila., 1970; research assoc., instr. Dartmouth Coll. Med. Sch., Hanover, N.H., 1970-72; chmn., asst. dir. Mich. Cancer Found., Detroit, 1974-81; asst. prof., then assoc. prof. Wayne State U. Sch. Med., Detroit, 1974-81; assoc. dir., sci. dir. AMC Cancer Research Ctr., Denver, 1981—; mem. virus working group WHO/Food and Agriculture Orgn., 1977-80; mem. rev. com. Nat. Cancer Inst., Bethesda, Md., 1981—; cons. numerous indsl. and acad. concerns, 1975—. Editor: Biological Carcinogenesis, 1982, Understanding Breast Cancer, 1983, RNA Tumor Viruses, Oncogenes, Human Cancer, and AIDS, 1985; mem. editorial bd. Leukemia Revs. Internat., 1980—; also articles. Damon Runyon Meml. fellow NIH, 1967-72; Nat. Cancer Inst. grantee, 1969—. Mem. Internat. Soc. Exptl. Hematology, Internat. Assn. Breast Cancer Research, Am. Soc. Cell. Biology, AAAS, Am. Assn. Cancer Research. Office: AMC Cancer Rsch Ctr 1600 Pierce St Denver CO 80214

FURNAS, DAVID WILLIAM, plastic surgeon; b. Caldwell, Idaho, Apr. 1, 1931; s. John Doan and Esther Bradbury (Hare) F.; m. Mary Lou Heatherly, Feb. 11, 1956; children: Heather Jean, Brent David, Craig Jonathan. AB, U. Calif.-Berkeley, 1952, MS, 1957, MD, 1955. Diplomate: Am. Bd. Surgery, Am. Bd. Plastic Surgery (dir. 1979-85). Intern, U. Calif. Hosp., San Francisco, 1955-56; asst. resident in surgery U. Calif. Hosp., 1956-57; capt., chief surgery 6580th USAF Hosp., Holloman AFB, N.Mex., 1957-59; asst. resident in psychiatry, NIMH fellow Langley Porter Neuropsychiat. Inst., U. Calif., San Francisco, 1959-60; resident in gen. surgery Gorgas Hosp., C.Z., 1960-61; asst. resident in plastic surgery N.Y. Hosp., Cornell Med. Center, N.Y.C., 1961-62; chief resident in plastic surgery VA Hosp., Bronx, N.Y., 1962-63; registrar Royal Infirmary and Affiliated Hosps., Glasgow, Scotland, 1963-64; asso. in hand surgery U. Iowa, 1965-68, asst. prof. surgery, 1966-68, asso. prof., 1968-69; asso. prof. surgery, chief div. plastic surgery U. Calif., Irvine, 1969-74; prof., chief div. plastic surgery U. Calif., 1974-80, clin. prof., chief div. plastic surgery, 1980—; surgeon East Africa Flying Doctors Service, African Med. and Research Found., Nairobi, Kenya, 1972-87; plastic surgeon S.S. Hope, Nicaragua, 1966, Ceylon, 1968, Sri Lanka, 1969; mem. Balakbayan med. mission, Mindanao and Sulu, Philippines, 1980, 81, 82. Contbr. chpts. to textbooks, articles to med. jours.; author/editor 4 textbooks; assoc. editor Jour. Hand Surgery, Annals of Plastic Surgery. Expedition leader Explorer's Club Flag 171 Skull Surgeons of the Kisii Tribe, Kenya, 1987. Served to capt. M.C., USAF, 1957-59. Recipient Golden Apple award for teaching excellence U. Calif.-Irvine Sch. Medicine, 1980, Kaiser-Permanente award U. Calif.-Irvine Sch. Medicine, 1981, Humanitarian Service award Black Med. Students, U. Calif. Irvine, 1987, Sr. Research award (Basic Sci.) Plastic Surgery Ednl. Found., 1987; named Orange County Press Club Headliner of Yr., 1982. Fellow ACS, Royal Coll. Surgeons Can., Royal Soc. Medicine, Explorers Club, Royal Geog. Soc.; mem. AMA, Calif., Orange County med. assns., Am. Soc. Plastic and Reconstructive Surgeons, Am. Soc. Reconstructive Microsurgery, Soc. Head and Neck Surgeons, Am. Cleft Palate Assn., Am. Soc. Surgery of Hand, Soc. Univ. Surgeons, Am. Assn. Plastic Surgeons (trustee 1983-86, treas. 1988—), Am. Soc. Aesthetic Plastic Surgery, Am. Soc. Maxillofacial Surgeons, Assn. Acad. Chmn. Plastic Surgery (bd. dirs. 1986—), Assn. Surgeons East Africa, Pacific Coast Surg. Assn., Internat. Soc. Aesthetic Plastic Surgery, Internat. Soc. Reconstructive Microsurgery, Pan African Assn. Neurol. Scis., African Med. and Research Found. (bd. dirs. N.Y. 1987), Phi Beta Kappa, Alpha Omega Alpha. Clubs: Muthaiga, Center, Club 33. Office: U Calif Div Plastic Surgery Irvine Med Ctr 101 City Dr S Orange CA 92625

FURNISH, RAYMOND DOUGLAS, controller; b. Hollywood, Calif., Nov. 11, 1949; s. Richard Douglas and Margaret Ann (Karns) F.; children: Ray Anne, Sandra Marie, Gregory. BA, Calif. State U., L.A., 1981; postgrad., Calif. State U., 1982. Leader mus. group Spectrum, L.A., 1970-75; legal rep. Met. News, L.A., 1975-78; music dir. St. Francis (Maryknoll), L.A., 1975-81, St. Philip Neri Ch., Lynwood, Calif., 1979—; controller Deems & Carpenter, LA., 1982—. Fellow Assn. Choral Dirs. of Am.; mem. L.A. C. of C., Griffith Park Men's Club. Democrat. Roman Catholic.

FURNIVAL, GEORGE MITCHELL, petroleum and mining consultant; b. Winnipeg, Man., Can., July 25, 1908; s. William George and Grace Una (Rothwell) F.; B.Sc., U. Man., 1929; M.A., Queens U., 1933; Ph.D., MIT, 1935; m. Marion Marguerite Fraser, Mar. 8, 1937; children—William George, Sharon (Mrs. John M. Roscoe), Patricia M., Bruce A. Field geologist in Man., Ont., N.W.T., and Que., 1928-36; asst. mine supt. Cline Lake Gold Mines, Ltd., 1936-39; geologist Geol. Survey Can., No. and Southwestern Sask., 1939-42; from 1942-70 employed by the Standard Oil Co. Calif. (Chevron) subs. including following positions: sr. geologist Standard Oil Co. of Calif. (Chevron Standard, Ltd.), Calgary, Alta., 1942-44, asst. to chief geologist, 1944-45, field supt. So. Alta., 1945-46, mgr. land and legal dept., 1948-50, v.p. land and legal, dir., 1950-52, v.p. legal, crude oil sales, govt. relations, dir., 1952-55; pres., dir. Dominion Oil, Ltd., Trinidad and Tobago, 1952-60; v.p. exploration, dir. Calif. Exploration Co. (Chevron Overseas Petroleum, Inc.), San Francisco, 1955-63; staff asst. land to v.p. exploration and land Standard Oil Co. of Calif., 1961-63; chmn. bd., mng. dir. West Australian Petroleum Pty., Ltd. (Chevron operated), Perth, 1963-70; dir. mines Dept. Mines and Natural Resources, Man., 1946-48; v.p., dir. Newport Ventures, Ltd., Calgary, 1971-72; v.p. ops., dir., mem. exec. com. Brascan Resources, Ltd., Calgary, 1973-75, sr. v.p., dir., 1975-77, sr. cons., 1977-78; pres., chief exec. officer, dir. Western Mines Ltd., 1978-80, exec. v.p., gen. mgr. mining div. Westmin Resources Ltd., also dir., mem. exec. com., 1981-82; dir. Western Mines Inc., 1978-82; pres., acting gen. mgr. Coalition Mining, Ltd.; pres., chief operating officer, dir. Lathwell Resources Ltd., 1983-84; cons. petroleum and mining, 1985—; founder Man. Geol. Survey, 1947; dir. Cretaceous Pipe Line Co., Ltd., Austen & Butta Pty., Ltd., Western Coal Holdings, Inc., Quest Explorations Ltd., San Antonio Resources Inc.; del. Interprovincial Mines Ministers Conf., several years; sec. Winnipeg Conf., 1947. Elected to Order of Can., 1982. Fellow Royal Soc. Can., Geol. Soc. Am., Geol. Soc. Can.; mem. Am. Assn. Petroleum Geologists, Engring. Inst. Can. (hon. life), Canadian Inst. Mining and Metallurgy (hon. life mem., past br. chmn., dist. councillor, v.p., chmn. petroleum div., Distinguished Service award 1974, Selwyn G. Blaylock gold medal 1979), Australian Petroleum Exploration Assn. (hon. life mem., chmn. com. West Australian petroleum legislation, councillor, state chmn. for Western Australia), Australian Am. Assn. in Western Australia (councillor), Australian Geol. Soc., Soc. Econ. Geologists, Assn. Profl. Engrs., Geologists and Geophysicists of Alta. (hon. life mem., Centennial award 1985), Coal Assn. of Can. (bd.dirs.). Clubs: Calgary Golf and Country, Calgary Petroleum, Ranchmen's. Author numerous govt. and co. papers, reports, reference texts, also sci. articles to profl. jours. Home: 1315 Baldwin Crescent SW, Calgary, AB Canada T2V 2B7

FURPHY, DANIEL RICHARD, soft drink company executive; b. Salida, Colo., Sept. 2, 1950; s. Charles Emmit and Evelyn May (Egan) F.; m. Beverly Lynn Crosby, Fec. 3, 1974; children: Brenton Daniel, Jason Charles. BS, So. Colo. State Coll., 1972. Asst. mgr. Town House Restaurant, Pueblo, Colo., 1968-72; asst. mgr. Alamosa (Colo.) Coca-Cola Bottling Co., 1972-78, v.p., gen. mgr., 1978089; v.p., ops. mgr. Albuquerque Coca-Cola Bottling Co., 1989—. Bd. dirs. Adams State Coll. Athletic Found., Alamosa, 1987, v.p., 1988. Recipient svc. award athletic dept. Alamosa High Sch., 1984, 85. Mem. Colo. Soft Drink Assn. (bd. dirs. 1983-87, v.p. 1988), Alamosa C. of C. Ambs. (bd. dirs. 1987, pres. 1988), Kiwanis, Elks. Democrat. Roman Catholic. Home: 8605 Brandywine Rd NE Albuquerque NM 87111 Office: Coca-Cola Bottling Co 205 Marquette Ave NE Albuquerque NM 87125

FURR, COLEMAN, college president; b. Lincoln, Nebr., Feb. 22, 1925; s. Archie and Mattie (Houghton) F.; B.S., U. Nebr., 1950; Ed.D., U.S. Internat. U.; m. Lois Stewart, July, 1952; children—Jean Elizabeth, Lisa Martin, Kevin Clark, Colette Marie, Martina. Buyer, Archie Furr Co., Lincoln, 1946-51; dir. ops. S&W Foods, San Francisco, 1951-59; computer cons. Govt. of P.R., 1959-61; pres. Union Distbg. Co., San Diego, 1961-62; founder, pres. Coleman Coll., San Diego, 1963—. Served with AUS, 1943-46. Mem. Assn. Ind. Colls. and Schs. (chmn. accrediting commn. 1977), Inst. Certification Computer Profls. (founder, chmn. 1979-86), Data Processing Mgmt. Assn., Automation I Assn. Republican. Unitarian. Home: 6014 Sierra View Way San Diego CA 92120 Office: 7380 Parkway Dr La Mesa CA 92041

FURTADO, DANIEL EDWARD, pharmacist; b. San Jose, Calif., Nov. 11, 1943; s. Daniel Edward Sr. and Ann Marie (Yerkovich) F. Student, U. Calif., Berkeley, 1961-62; BA, San Jose State U., 1965; PharmD, U. Calif., San Francisco, 1969; MPA, U. San Francisco, 1982. Registered pharmacist, Calif. Chief pharmacology Acad. Health Sci. U.S. Army, San Antonio, Tex., 1969-71; clin. coordinator VA Med. Ctr., Palo Alto, Calif., 1971-79; clin. pharmacist O'Connor Hosp., Campbell, Calif., 1979-80; assoc. dir. Primary Care Assoc. Program Stanford U., Palo Alto, 1980—; asst. clin. prof. U. Calif., San Francisco, 1971—; instr. DeAnza Coll., Cupertino, Calif., 1973—, Modesto (Calif.) Jr. Coll., 1981-83; adj. prof. U. Pacific, Stockton, Calif., 1977-85. Author: Curr Concepts P'Col, 1987. Sec. Santa Clara County Heart Assn., San Jose, Calif., 1986-88, chmn. emergency care, 1987—; mem. Civic Improvement commn., Campbell, Calif., 1985—. Served as col. USAR, 1965—. Mem. Am. Pharm. Assn. (Service award 1969), Am. Soc. Hosp. Pharmacists, Am. heart Assn. (life mem.), Am. Soc. Parenteral Nutrition, Am. Coll. Healthcare Execs. Democrat. Roman Catholic. Office: Stanford U Primary Care 703 Welch Rd Ste F-1 Palo Alto CA 94304

FURTH, ALAN COWAN, corporate director, lawyer; b. Oakland, Calif., Sept. 16, 1922; s. Victor L. and Valance (Cowan) F.; m. Virginia Robinson, Aug. 18, 1946; children: Andrew Robinson, Alison Anne. A.B., U. Calif., Berkeley, 1944, LL.B., 1949; grad., Advanced Mgmt. Program, Harvard U., 1959. Bar: Calif., U.S. Supreme Ct. With So. Pacific Co., San Franciso, 1950-87, gen. counsel, from 1963, v.p., 1966, exec. v.p. law, 1976-79, pres., 1979-87, also dir. and mem. exec. com.; bd. dirs. Indsl. Indemnity Co., Bank of Calif., Am. Home Shield Corp., Flecto Corp., Oreg. Steel Mills. Trustee Merritt Hosp., Oakland, Calif.; trustee Pacific Legal Found. Capt. USMCR, 1944-46, 51-52. Mem. Calif. State Bar Assn. Clubs: Bohemian (San Francisco), Pacific-Union (San Francisco), San Francisco Golf (San Francisco). Home: 244 Lakeside Dr Oakland CA 94612 Office: So Pacific Co 1 Market Pla Stewart St Tower San Francisco CA 94105 *

FUSCO, SAL M., small business owner; b. Bronx, N.Y., July 18, 1932; s. Joseph and Anna (Calvi) F.; m. Catherine Therese Muetze, Apr. 8, 1961; children: Marc, Lisa, William, Giannine, Suzanne, Michelle. Pres., founder Old Roman Inc., Hicksville, N.Y., 1953-73; pres., co-founder Numismatic Funding Corp., Jericho, N.Y., 1970-73; pres. Numismatic Corp. Am., Port Jefferson, N.Y., 1975-85; pres., founder T. Fox, Inc., Port Jefferson, 1973-80, Shoreham Enterprises, Ltd., Phoenix, Ariz., 1980—; bd. dirs. numismatic and philatelic dept. Adelphi U.; money mus. advisor 1st Nat. Bank P.R., San Juan, 1970-73. Contbr. to book, periodicals. N.Y. state chmn. Nat. Com. Social Justice, 1975-79. With U.S. Army, 1952-54. Mem. Am. Numismatic Soc. (life), Internat. Soc. Appraisers (assoc.), Cen. State Numismatic Soc. (assoc.), Calif. State Numismatic Assn. (assoc.), Sons of Italy. Republican. Roman Catholic. Avocations: jogging, basketball, softball, reading.

FUSINATI, ROBERT PAUL, project engineer; b. Tucson, July 21, 1959; s. Robert Dominique and Janet June (Kerkmeyer) F.; m. Sigrid Deem Nelson, Dec. 31, 1982 (div. 1987). BS in Elec. Engring., U. Ariz., 1982; MBA, George Washington U., 1986. With Hughes Aircraft, Tucson, 1980-83; group leader Hughes Aircraft, Torrance, Calif., 1986-87; systems engr. Hughes Aircraft, Washington, 1983-86; project engr. TRW, Redondo Beach, Calif., 1987—. Home: 1517 Steinhart Redondo Beach CA 90278

FUTAS, GEORGE PAUL, management executive, consultant; b. Tulare, Calif., Sept. 11, 1934; s. Joseph Paul and Cora E. (Wells) F.; m. Eileen M. Scott, June 6, 1959 (div. Dec. 1982); children: Scott J., Shari L., Leanne M. BS in Engring., Calif. State U., San Luis Obispo, 1956; MS in Engring., U. Wash., 1962; MBA, Nat. U., 1980. Registered profl. engr., Ariz., Calif. Controls engr. Westinghouse Electric Co., Pitts., 1956-63; product mgr. Gen. Electric Co., Inc., Phoenix, 1963-67; advanced devel. and mktg. mgr. Logicon, Inc., San Diego, 1967-77; gen. and ops. mgr. Johnson Controls, Inc., San Diego, 1977-83; v.p. product devel. Microrim, Inc., Bellevue, Wash., 1983-84; pres., chief exec. officer Expert Systems, Inc., Bellevue, 1986-87; v.p. mktg. Telecalc, Inc., Bellevue, 1987-88; pres. Corus Co., Inc., Bellevue, 1984—; pres., chief exec. officer Internat. Telecommunications Network Ltd., Bellevue, 1988—; bd. dirs. Zao Med., Inc., Kirkland, Wash., N.W. Venture Group, Seattle. Contbr. articles to profl. jours.; patentee disk storage technology, 1969. Home: PO Box 591 Kirkland WA 98083 Office: Corus Co Inc PO Box 4201 Bellevue WA 98009

FUTCH, TOMMY RAY, health service corporation executive; b. Jacksonville, Fla., Dec. 8, 1951; s. Charleton Harris and Barbara Ann (Whidden) F.; m. Virginia Ann Thweatt, Sept. 11, 1976; children: Bradley Allen, Branden Wesley. BS, Fla. Tech. U., 1974; MBA, Nova U., 1981. Registered respiratory therapist, physician asst.; lic. lab. technologist. Dir. cardiopulmonary Fla. Med. Ctr., Ft. Lauderdale, 1976-77, adminstr. profl. svcs., 1977-82, Southeastern Med. Ctr., North Miami Beach, Fla., 1982; regional adminstr. Rehab. Hosp. Svcs., Ft. Lauderdale, 1982-85, v.p., 1985-86, sr. v.p., 1986-87; sr. v.p. Continental Med. Systems, Mechanicsburg, Pa., 1987-88; sr. v.p. Continental Med. Systems, Roseville, Calif., 1988—; chmn. bd. N. La. Rehab. Ctr., Ruston, 1987-88, Baton Rouge Rehab. Inst., 1988, Rocky Mountain Rehab. Hosp., Denver, 1988, Kansas Rehab. Hosp., Topeka, 1987-88, Midwest Rehab. Hosp., Kansas City, Kans., 1988, Kentfield (Calif.) Rehab. Hosp., 1987-88, Lakeview Rehab. Hosp., Elizabethtown, Ky., Braintree (Mass.) Hosp., Coral Gables Rehab. Hosp., Miami, Fla., Sunrise Hosp., Ft. Lauderdale, 1984-86, Pinecrest Hosp., Delray Beach, Fla., 1986, Rehab. Inst. Sarasota (Fla.), 1986-87, Edison Rehab. Hosp., Ft. Myers, Fla., 1986-87, Seacrest Health Corp., Melbourne, Fla., 1987, Montgomery (Ala.) Health Corp., 1987, Kentfield (Ca.) Hosp., 1987; dir. Fla. Assn. Rehab. Facilities, Tallahassee; del. Fla. Renal Adminstrs., Tampa, 1981. Contbr. articles to profl. jours. Trustee Am. Lung Assn., Ft. Lauderdale, 1977-80; mem. adv. council Broward Community Coll., Ft. Lauderdale, 1976-82; mem. Southeast Air Quality Council, Ft. Lauderdale, 1978. Mem. Am. Coll. Hosp. Adminstrs., Am. Health Planning Assn., Am. Hosp. Assn., Internat. Assn. Rehab. Facilities, Nat. Assn. Rehab. Facilities, Broward County C. of C. Democrat. Presbyterian.

FUTTERMAN, JACOB, physicist, consultant; b. N.Y.C., Aug. 19, 1928; s. Benjamin and Helen (Sheinbaum) F.; m. Marian Fay Miller, June 17, 1975; children: Bonnie, Kathleen. BS in Physics, U. So. Calif., 1951; MS in Physics, NYU, 1954; PhD in Physics, Pacific Western U., 1988. Instr. physics Maritime Coll. SUNY, 1954-57; rsch. engr., scientist Grumman Aerospace Corp., N.Y.C., 1957-67; sr. engr., scientist Douglas Aircraft Co., Long Beach, Calif., 1967-75; sr. analyst Interstate Electronics Co., Anaheim, Calif., 1975-78; sr. scientist, engr. McDonnell Douglas Co., Long Beach, Calif., 1978-84, cons., 1987—; cons. Rockwell Internat., Seal Beach, Calif., 1984-87; pres., chief exec. officer Gravitorium Devel. Co., Inc., L.A., 1987—. Inventor structure of astronaut tng. Mem. IEEE, Am. Inst. Physics. Office: Gravitorium Devel Co Inc PO Box 10934 Beverly Hills CA 90213

FYE, RODNEY WAYNE, real estate company executive, writer; b. Sutherland, Nebr., Aug. 3, 1928; s. Elmer Theodore and Pearl Gertrude (Combs) F. Grad., Chillicothe Bus. Coll., 1948; BS, Brigham Young U., 1959; secondary teaching cert., U. Utah, 1962; MA, San Francisco State U., 1964. Clk. Union Pacific R.R. Co., Salt Lake City, 1948-57; sec. to pres., sr. staff asst. Hughes Tool Co., L.A., 1958-59; instr. English, Brigham Young U., Provo, Utah, 1959-60; high sch. tchr. Granite Sch. Dist., Salt Lake City, 1960-63; adminstr. Millcreek Terrace Nursing Home, Salt Lake City, 1962-63; instr., dir. instrn. REading Dynamics No. Calif., 1967-75; owner, mgr. Keycount Properties, San Francisco, 1975-79; pres. Casa Loma Properties, Inc., San Francisco, 1979—, Pan Am. Investments, Inc., San Francisco, 1980—. Author: (musical comdey) Gandy, 1959, (drama) Absinthe and Wormwood, 1964, (mystery) To Catch a Falling Saint, 1989. Missionary LDS Ch., Colo., Nebr., 1949-51, mem. San Francisco stake high coun., 1986—, dir. pub. communication San Francisco region, 1989—; pres. San Francisco Safety Coun., 1980-84. With U.S. Army and USMC, 1953-56, Korea. Republican. Office: Casa Loma Properties Inc PO Box 15308 San Francisco CA 94115

GABERSON, HOWARD AXEL, mechanical engineer; b. Detroit, Apr. 11, 1931; s. Axel Rudolph and Lillian (Quatherine) G.; BSME, U. Mich., 1955; MS, MIT, 1957, PhD, 1967; m. Dale Virginia Maitland, Apr. 27, 1969. Stress analysis engr. Raytheon Co., Wayland, Mass., 1957-59; asst. prof. mech. engring. Lowell (Mass.) Tech. Inst., 1959-60; asst. prof. Boston U., 1960-64; assoc. prof. mech. engring. U. Hawaii, 1967-68; shock and vibration rsch. mech. engr. Naval Civil Engring. Lab., Port Hueneme, Calif., 1968-82, div. dir. mech. systems, 1982-87, sr. technologist dynamics, 1987—. Contbr. articles to profl. jours.; inventor vibratory locomotion; patentee in field. NSF fellow, 1964; Wilfred Lewis fellow, 1966. Mem. Am. Acad. Mechanics, ASME (chpt. pres. 1973, 80, region IX operating bd., nat. mem. interests com. 1985-88), Soc. Exptl. Mechanics , Soc. Automotive Engrs. (G-5 shock and vibration com.), Inst. Noise Control Engrs. Vibration Inst., U. Mich. Alumni Assn., MIT Alumni Assn., UCLA Alumni Assn., Rare Bird Preservation Soc. (pres. 1980-81), West Valley Bird Soc., Ventura County Bird Soc., Am. Fedn. Aviculture, Aviculture Soc. Am., Bromeliad Soc., Alpha Sigma Phi, Sigma Xi, Tau Beta Pi, Pi Tau Sigma. Home: 234 Corsicana Dr Oxnard CA 93030 Office: US Naval Civil Engring Lab Port Hueneme CA 93043

GABLEHOUSE, TIMOTHY REUBEN, lawyer; b. Boulder, Colo., May 13, 1951; s. Reuben H. and Genevieve M. (Willburn) G.; m. Barbara Lynn DoRough, June 23, 1973; children: Brian, Kristin, Andrew. BA, U. Colo., 1973; JD, U. Denver, 1975, MBA, 1981. Bar: Colo. 1976, U.S. Dist. Ct. Colo. 1983. Assoc. Gedder, McDougal & McHugh, Colorado Springs, Colo., 1976-77; regulatory affairs analyst Adolph Coors Co., Golden, Colo., 1977-79; mgr. new product devel. Adolph Coors Co., 1979-82, mgr. regulatory affairs, 1982-84, mng. atty. regulatory affairs, 1984-87; dir. regulatory affairs Thortec Internat., Englewood, Colo., 1987-88; pres. Timothy R. Gablehouse, P.C., Arvada, Colo., 1988—; chmn. Hwy. 36 landfill monitoring com. Colo. Dept. Health, Denver, 1986—; water quality task force chmn. EPA Denver Integrated Environ. Mgmt. Project, 1987—. Commr. Arvada Commn. for Prevention of Sexual Assault, 1982-85; arbitrator Better Bus. Bur., Denver, 1984—. Mem. ABA, Environ. Law Inst., Am. Corp. Counsel Assn., Colo. Hazardous Waste Mgmt Soc. (pres. 1985-86, bd. dirs. 1986-88), Jefferson County Local Emergency Planning Com. (sub-com. chair 1986—). Republican. Office: 1515 Arapahoe St Ste 1100 Denver CO 80202

GABRIELI, CHRISTOPHER FRATER OSCAR, venture capitalist; b. Buffalo, Feb. 5, 1960; s. Elemer Rudolph and Lilla Elizabeth (Eross) G. BA, Harvard U., 1981; postgrad., Columbia U., 1981-83. Pres. GMIS, Inc., Phila., 1981—; vice-chmn. GMIS, Inc., 1984—; gen. ptnr. Praxis Ptnrs., N.Y.C., 1983-86, St. Mark Biomed., N.Y.C., 1983—; assoc. Bessemer Venture Ptnrs., Menlo Park, Calif., 1986-88; ptnr. Bessemer Venture Ptnrs., 1989—; chmn. Enzytech, Inc., Cambridge, Mass.; bd. dirs. U.S. Behavioral Health, Emeryville, Calif., Allscrips, Inc., Vernon Hills, Ill., Focus, Inc., Brentwood, Tenn., August Internat., Orange, Calif., Isis Pharms., San Diego. Contbr. articles to profl. publs. Mem. Harvard Club. N.Y.C. Presbyterian. Office: Bessemer Venture Ptnrs 3000 Sand Hill Rd Ste 3-225 Menlo Park CA 94025

GABRIELSON, SHIRLEY GAIL, nurse; b. San Francisco, Mar. 17, 1934; d. Arthur Obert and Lois Ruth (Lanterman) Ellison; m. I. Grant Gabrielson, Sept. ll, 1955; children: James Grant, Kari Gay. BS in Nursing, Mont. State U., 1955. RN, Mont. Staff and operating room nurse Bozeman (Mont.) Deaconess Hosp., 1954-55, 55-56; staff nurse Warm Springs State Hosp., 1955; office nurse, operating room asst. Dr. Craft, Bozeman, 1956-57; office nurse Dr. Bush, Beach, N.D., 1957-58; pub. health nurse Wibaux County, 1958-59; staff and charge nurse Teton Meml. Hosp., Choteau, Mont., 1964-65; staff pediatric and float nurse St. Patrick Hosp., Missoula, Mont., 1965-70; nurse, insvc. dir. Trinity Hosp., Wolf Point, Mont., 1970-79; ednl. coord. Community Hosp. and Nursing Home, Poplar, Mont., 1979—; insvc. dir. Faith Luth. Home, Wolf Point, 1980-81; office nurse Dr. Listerud, 1983—; CPR instr. ARC, Am. Heart Assn., Gt. Falls, Mont., 1979—; condr. workshops and seminars. AuthorP Independent Study for Nurse Assistants, 1977. Former asst. camp leader Girl Scouts U.S.A.; former mother advisor, bd. dirs. Rainbow Girls; pres. Demolay Mothers's Club, 1977; bd. dirs. Mont. div. Am. Cancer Soc., 1984—, mem. awards com., 1986-88; founder Tri-County Parkinson's Support Group, N.E. Mont. Recipient Lifesaver award Am. Cancer Soc., 1987. Mem. Am. Nurses Assn., Mont. Nurses Assn. (chmn. commn. on continuing edn. 1984-86), Order Eastern Star, Alpha Tau Delta (alumni pres. 1956). Presbyterian. Home: 428 Hill St Wolf Point MT 59201 Office: Community Hosp-Nursing Home PO Box 38 Poplar MT 59255

GAC, FRANK DAVID, materials engineer; b. Granite City, Ill., Mar. 26, 1951; s. Frank John and Betty Marie (Kasprovich) G.; m. Christina Lynn McMullen, Aug. 12, 1973; children: Jessie Lynn, Benjamin Thomas. BS in Ceramic Engring., U. Ill., 1973; MS in Ceramic Engring., U. Mo., Rolla, 1975; postgrad., U. N.Mex., 1982-83; PhD in Materials Sci. and Engring., U. Wash., 1989. Registered profl. engr., N.Mex. Mem. staff Los Alamos (N.Mex) Nat. Lab., 1975-78, sect. leader, 1980-83, staff mem., 1983-84, advanced study candidate, 1984-85; research engr. U. Wash., Seattle, 1979-80; project leader Los Alamos (N.Mex) Nat. Lab., 1986-88, group leader, 1988—; mem. steering com. Advanced Composites Working Group, Cocoa Beach, Fla., 1981—. Contbr. articles to profl. jours. Father helper Aspen Elem. Sch., Los Alamos, 1983-84; Sunday sch. supt. Trinity Bible Ch., Los Alamos, 1986, elder, 1987—; deacon, youth leader Sangre de Cristo Covenant Ch., Los Alamos, 1975-79; scoutmaster Boy Scouts Am., Granite City, 1967-69; com. mem. Young Life, Los Alamos, 1988—. Fellow A.P. Green Refractories Co., 1973-74; named Knight of St. Pat 100 Club, U. Ill., Champaign, 1973, one of Outstanding Young Men Am., 1986. Fellow: Am. Ceramic Soc. (div. chmn. 1985-86, Cert. 1986, Karl Schwartzwalder Profl. Achievement Ceramic Engring. award 1988, chmn. programs and meetings ocm. 1987-88); mem. Nat. Inst. Ceramic Engrs. (coordinator 1979-80), Gideons Internat. (pres. 1976), Young Life (leader 1975-79). Democrat. Home: 901 Tewa Loop Los Alamos NM 87544 Office: Los Alamos Nat Lab MST 4 MS G771 Los Alamos NM 87545

GADBOIS, RICHARD A., JR., judge; b. Omaha, June 18, 1932; s. Richard Alphonse Gadbois and Margaret Ann (Donahue) Bartlett; m. Jeanne E. Roach, Dec. 15, 1956; children: Richard, Gregory, Guy, Geoffrey, Thomas. A.B., St. John's Coll., Camarillo, Calif., 1955; J.D., Loyola U., Los Angeles, 1958; postgrad. in law, U. So. Calif., 1958-60. Bar: Calif. 1959, U.S. Dist. Ct. (cen. dist.) Calif. 1959, U.S. Supreme Ct. 1966. Ptnr. Musick, Peeler & Garrett, Los Angeles, 1962-68; v.p. Denny's Inc., La Mirada, Calif., 1968-71; judge Mcpl. Ct., Los Angeles, 1971-72, Superior Ct., Los Angeles, 1972-82, U.S. Dist. Ct. (cen. dist.) Calif., Los Angeles, 1982—. Decorated knight Order of Holy Sepulchre (Pope John Paul II). Mem. ABA, Los Angeles County Bar Assn. (trustee 1966-67), State Bar Calif. (profl. ethics com. 1965-70). Republican. Roman Catholic. Home: 2155 El Molino Ave San Marino CA 91108 Office: US Dist Ct 312 N Spring St Los Angeles CA 90012

GADDY, GARY LYNN, quality assurance engineer; b. Phoenix, Aug. 28, 1942; s. Buster Brown Gaddy and Jackie Marie (Osburn) Gaddy Cumiford; m. Kathryn Suzanne Nash, May 28, 1966; children: Michelle Lynn, Stephanie Kay. BA, Augsburg Coll., Mpls., 1972; MS in Systems Mgmt., U. So. Calif., 1982. Quality engr. Sperry-Univac, Roseville, Minn., 1968-77; sr. quality engr., mgr. indsl. technology Amdahl Corp., Sunnyvale, Calif., 1977-80; sr. adv. quality engr. Shugart Assocs., Sunnyvale, 1980-82; mgr. quality assurance Trimax Controls, Sunnyvale, 1982-84, Pyramid Technology, Mountain View, Calif., 1984-86, Rugged Digital Systems, Mountain View, 1987—. With USN, 1963-65. Mem. Am. Soc. Quality Control. Democrat. Lutheran. Home: 1708 Grand Teton Dr Milpitas CA 95035

GAFFNEY, MYRICK WILLIAM (RICK GAFFNEY), photojournalist, marine consultant; b. Honolulu, Sept. 24, 1947; s. Robert Theodore and Constance Stewart (Herbert) G. BS, Oreg. State U., 1970. Lic. capt. USCG. Beach capt. Kona Village Resort Hawaii, 1972-74; marine adv. specialist Sea Grant Marine Adv. Program, Maui, Hawaii, 1974-76; pres. Hawaii Marine Cons. Ltd., Maui, 1976-86; ptnr. Foster-Gaffney Assoc., Kona, 1983—; pres. Rick Gaffney & Assoc. Inc., Kona, 1986—; press coord. Ironman Triathlon Champ, Kona, 1982-88; dir. Hawaii Light Tackle Tournament Kona, 1986—, Chuck Machado Luau Jackpots, 1978-85, Fiji Internat. Game Fish Assn., Suva, 1981—. Contbr. articles to numerous jours. Bd. dirs. Maui County Marine Mammal Com., 1983; exec. dir. Pacific Ocean Def. Fund, Kona, 1987—. Ensign U.S. Navy, 1970-72, Vietnam. Mem. Internat. Game Fish Assn., Hawaii Big Game Fishing Club (bd. dirs. 1986—), Outdoor Writers Assn. Am. Office: PO Box 4010 Kailua-Kona HI 96745

GAGAR, ELEUTERIO CASTRO, accountant; b. La Paz, Tarlac, Philippines, May 26, 1935; came to U.S., 1969; s. Arsenio Driz and Julieta (Castro) G.; m. Virginia J. Calderon, Oct. 8, 1960; children: Marievel, Juliet, Jonathan, Emmanuel. BS in Commerce, Far Eastern U., Manila, 1957; postgrad., UCLA, 1972-86; cert. in real estate, Anthony Schs., Los Angeles, 1983. CPA, Philippines, Calif. Acct. Unitours Inc.-Club Universe, L.A., 1969-72; internal auditor So. Calif. UFWC Employer's Joint Trust Funds, Cypress, Calif., 1972-88; owner Fund Investment Research and Fin. Svcs., L.A., 1983—; bd. dirs., corp. sec. Gold Label Corp., Carson, Calif., 1988—. Mem. Glendale (Calif.) YMCA. Mem. AICPA, Calif. Soc. CPAs, Philippine Am. Soc. CPAs, Nat. Assn. Real Estate Appraisers, Nat. Notary Assn., UCLA Alumni Assn. Democrat. Home: 3937 Revere Ave Los Angeles CA 90039 Office: Terry C Gagar CPA 2330 Beverly Blvd Ste 105 Los Angeles CA 90057

GAGE, ANGELA WALEETA, financial executive; b. St. Louis, June 27, 1959; d. Frank Sullivan and Phyllis (Davison) Greene; m. Henry Gage, July 17, 1982; 1 child, Henry Joe III. BSc in Fin., U. Santa Clara, 1980. Acct. Hewlett-Packard Co., Santa Clara, Calif., 1980-81; sr. acct. Hewlett-Packard Co., Santa Clara, 1981, cost acctg. supr., 1981-82, gen. acctg. supr., 1982-84, acctg. info. systems mgr., 1984-85; sr. group analyst Hewlett-Packard Co., Palo Alto, Calif., 1985-88; acctg. supr. Hewlett-Packard Co., Palo Alto, 1988; controller Synernet Corp., Fremont, Calif., 1985. Mem. Santa Clara County Urban League, 1985-88; active City Team Ministries, San Jose, Calif., 1986—, Focus On The Family, Arcadia, Calif., 1985—. Mem. NAACP. Democrat.

GAGE, MARTIN, talent agency executive; b. N.Y.C., May 4, 1934; s. Herman F. and Sylvia (Wolff) Gutchoen. Student, CCNY, 1951-55. Talent agt. Oscard/Gage, Ltd., N.Y.C., 1966-73; agt., owner Gage Group, Inc., N.Y.C., 1973—, L.A., 1975—; bd. dirs. Cast Theatre, L.A. Home: 9255 Sunset Blvd Los Angeles CA 90069 Office: Gage Group Inc 1650 Broadway New York NY 10019

GAGLIANO, VINCENT, diversified consumer products manufacturing company executive; b. Chgo., Jan. 17, 1931; s. Salvatore and Phyllis Rose (Monaco) G.; m. Janet Rose Terrafino, Sept. 25, 1954; children: Phyllis Marie, Madeline Rose. Student, U. Ill., Chgo., 1948-49, Wright Jr. Coll., 1950-51; BS in Indsl. Engring., Indls. Engring. Coll., Chgo., 1956. Indsl. engr. U.S. Steel Corp. (now called USX Corp.), Chgo., 1954-56, Motorola Corp., Chgo., 1956-58; dir. procurement Webcor Dormeyer Corp., Chgo., 1958-62; div. v.p. Thomas Div. Whirlpool, Sepulveda, Calif., 1962-81; v.p. ops. Forecast Lighting Co., Inglewood, Calif., 1982-85; group v.p. Kidde Consumer Durables Corp., Compton, Calif., 1985-87; pres. Vigon Lighting Co. subs. Kidde Corp., 1987-, Dalme, Inc. Automobile Security Systems Mfg., Canoga Park, Calif., 1987—. Chmn. Elk Grove (Ill.) Cancer Soc., 1970; pres. Jaycees, Elk Grove, 1959-60. Lifetime bd. mem. (hon.) Elk Grove Boys Baseball, 1968. Republican. Roman Catholic. Club: Porter Valley Country. Home: 9403 Vanalden Ave Northridge CA 91324 Office: Dalme Inc 7234 Eton Ave Canoga Park CA 91303

GAGNON, DONALD JOSEPH, telecommunications executive; b. Chicopee Falls, Mass., Feb. 3, 1939; s. Joseph and Rose (Goyette) G. Postgrad., U. So. Calif., 1977. Air intelligence officer USAF, 1962-72; dist. mgr. Cumberland Farms, Inc., Canton, Mass., 1972-74; account exec. Pacific Telephone, Alhambra, Calif., 1979-82; mgr. telecom planning Northrop Corp. Aircraft Div., Hawthorne, Calif., 1982—; systems cons. Apple Computers, Inc., Cupertino, Calif., 1987--. Contbr. articles to profl. jours. Mem. Rep. Nat. Com., Washington, 1982—, Gov. Edn. Ctr., L.A. Mem. Western Govtl. Rsch. Assn., Res. Officers Assn., Amnesty Internat. Roman Catholic. Office: Northrop Aircraft Div 1 Northrop Ave 1333/12 Hawthorne CA 90250

GAILE, GARY LEE, geographer; b. Cleve., Aug. 3, 1945; s. Stanley V. and Helen A. (Wawrzyniak) G.; m. Susan E. Clarke, June 26, 1983; 1 child by previous marriage, Jeffrey V. BA, UCLA, 1971, MA, 1972, CPhil, 1973, PhD, 1976. Asst. prof. geography Northwestern U., Evanston, Ill., 1975-82; assoc. prof. geography U. Conn., Storrs, 1982-84, U. Colo., Boulder, 1984—; regional planning adv. Harvard Inst. for Internat. Devel., Harvard U., Cambridge, Mass., 1986-87; cons. Internat. Devel. and Energy Assocs., Washington, 1987—; bd. dirs. Global Technology Found., Boulder, 1988—. Co-author: Spatial Diffusion, 1988; co-editor: Spatial Statistics and Models, 1984, Geography in America, 1989. Fulbright fellow, Kenya, 1974, NSF fellow, 1974. Mem. Assn. Am. Geographers, Assn. Third World Studies, Sigma Xi, Phi Beta Kappa. Office: U Colo Dept Geography Boulder CO 80309-0260

GAILLARD, MARY KATHARINE, physics educator; b. New Brunswick, N.J., Apr. 1, 1939; d. Philip Lee and Marion Catharine (Wiedemayer) Ralph; children: Alain, Dominique, Bruno. BA, Hollins (Va.) Coll., 1960; MA, Columbia U., 1961; Dr du Troiseme Cycle, U. Paris, Orsay, France, 1964, Dr-es-Sciences d'Etat, 1968. With Centre National de Recherche Scientifique, Orsay and Annecy-le-Vieux, France, 1964-84; maitre de recherches Centre National de Recherche Scientifique, Orsay, 1973-80; maitre de recherches Centre National de Recherche Scientifique, Annecy-le-Vieux, 1979-80, dir. research, 1980-84; prof. physics U. Calif., Berkeley, 1981—; Morris Loeb lectr. Harvard U., Cambridge, Mass., 1980; Chancellor's Disting. lectr., U. Calif., Berkeley, 1981; Warner-Lambert lectr. U. Mich., Ann Arbor, 1984; vis. scientist Fermi Nat. Accelerator Lab., Batavia, Ill., 1973-74, Inst. for Advanced Studies, Santa Barbara, Calif., 1984; group leader L.A.P.P., Theory Group, France, 1979-81, Theory Physics div. LBL, Berkeley, 1985-87; sci. dir. Les Houches (France) Summer Sch., 1981; cons., mem. adv. panels U.S. Dept. Energy, Washington, and various nat. labs. Co-editor: Weak Interactions, 1977, Gauge Theories in High Energy Physics, 1983; author or co-author 120 articles, papers to profl jours., books, conf. proceedings. Recipient Thibaux prize U. Lyons (France) Acad. Art & Sci., 1977, E.O. Lawrence award, 1988. Fellow Am. Phys. Soc. (mem. various coms., chair com. on women), AAAS. Office: U Calif Dept Physics Berkeley CA 94720

GAIN, JONATHAN WESLEY, electrical engineer; b. Portland, Oreg., Dec. 7, 1945; s. Wesley Howard and Faith Elizabeth G.; m. Jenetta Ellen Gray, May 10, 1967; children: Angelina, Luke, Daniel, Christiana. BS in Elec. Tech., LeTourneau Coll., Longview, Texas, 1968. With TransWorld Radio, 1970-80; transmitter engr. Bonaire, Netherlands, 1970-73, Manzini, Swaziland, 1973-79; chief engr. Colombo, Sri Lanka, 1979-80; elec. engr. TCI Internat., Inc., Mountain View, Calif., 1981--. Mem. Calling Club. Republican. Home: 1407 Bouret Dr San Jose CA 95118 Office: TCI Internat Inc 1625 N Shoreline Blvd Mountain View CA 94043

GAINES, HAYDON DECATUR, data processing executive; b. Moline, Ill., Jan. 19, 1943; s. Jay Haydon and Betty Louise (McDannell) G.; m. Suzanne Taylor Lee, Oct. 13, 1979 (div. Aug. 1983); m. Kendra Jeanne Roby, Feb. 11, 1984; stepchildren: Jeffery Hagedorn, Jennifer Hagedorn. BS, U. Ariz., 1965, postgrad., 1967-68. Programmer Wallgreen's Inc., Chgo., 1965-67; sr. programmer So. Ariz. Bank, Tucson, 1967-69; systems div. mgr. Computer Scis. Corp., San Francisco, 1970-76; dir. program devel. Electronic Data Systems, San Diego, 1978-81; systems devel. mgr. San Diego City Schs., 1981-83; data adminstrn. mgr. Equitable Life Leasing, San Diego, 1983-86; pres. The Delphi Group, San Diego, 1986—; cons. A.G. Aguilar, Mexico city, 1977-78, Coast Community Coll., Costa Mesa, Calif., 1985-86; chmn. IDEAL CADRE User Group, Princeton, N.J., 1985-86. Contbr. articles to profl. jours. Mem. Zoolog. Soc. San Diego, LaJolla Mus. Contemporary Art, San Diego Hall of Sci., 1986. Recipient SPOKE award Tucson Jaycees, 1968. Mem. Data Processing Mgmt. Assn., Soc. Info. Mgmt. REpublican. Methodist. Club: Berkeley (Calif.) Yacht. Home: 15467 Avenida Rorras San Diego CA 92128 Office: The Delphi Group 12355 Fernando Dr San Diego CA 92128

GAINES, MARC A., technician; b. Ft. Lee, Va., Sept. 15, 1963; s. Arthur Lee Gaines and Ruth Helen Hollemon. AAS, P.P. Community Coll., Colo. Springs, Colo., 1984; student, Chapman Coll., Denver, 1988—. Q.a. operator to production engring. technician Inmos Corp., Colorado Springs, Colo., 1983-86; elecronic technician Digital Equipment Corp., Colorado Springs, 1986-87; technician quality engring. lab. Martin Marietta Astronautics, Denver, 1987—. Mem. Phi Theta Kappa. Baptist. Office: Martin Marietta Corp Dept 0959 MS 9659 PO Box 179 Denver CO 80201

GAJDORUS, CARL, II, architect; b. Endicott, N.Y., May 17, 1952; s. Carl and Katherine (Constantinou) G. BArch, U. Ariz., 1976. Registered architect, Ariz. Programmer Studio 3, Ltd., Tucson, 1977-78; project architect R.M. Reif Assocs., Tucson, 1978-82, 83-88; job capt. CNWC Architects, Tucson, 1983; architect U. Ariz Facilities Design and Constrn., 1989—; mem. adv. com. City of Tucson Floodplain, 1981-82. Pres. So. Ariz. Environ. Council, Tucson, 1981. Mem. AIA (exec. com. Ariz. Soc. 1985-86). Home: 4467 E Dianthus Pl Tucson AZ 85712 Office: U Ariz Facilities Design and Constrn Bldg 49 Tucson AZ 85721

GAJEWSKI, WIESLAW PETER, electronics company executive; b. Guisburough, England, Sept. 26, 1946; came to U.S., 1956; s. Witold and Irena (Bialoblocki) G.; m. Mary Heller, Aug. 22, 1970; children: Katherine Lorene, Nicholas Heller. BEE, Northwestern U., Evanston, Ill, 1968; MBA, U. Chgo., 1975. Project engr. Vapor Corp., Niles, Ill., 1965-71; account supr. NW Ayer Internat., Chgo., 1971-75; corp. mktg. mgr. Gould Inc., Rolling Meadows, Ill., 1975-76; product mktg. mgr. power conversion div. Gould Inc., Bishops Stortford, England, 1976-79; ops. mgr. power conversion div. Gould Inc., El Monte, Calif., 1979-81; plant mgr. med. products div. Gould Inc., Oxnard, Calif., 1981-83; v.p. sales and mktg. Calif. D.C., Newbury Park, 1983-85, v.p. and gen. mgr., 1985-86; v.p. sales and mktg. Shindengen Am., Inc., Westlake Village, Calif., 1986—; cons., Thousand Oaks, Calif., 1986-87. Contbr. articles to profl. jours. Patentee dew point hygrometer. Office: Shindengen Am Inc 2649 Townsgate Rd Westlake Village CA 91361

GALANE, MORTON ROBERT, lawyer; b. N.Y.C., Mar. 15, 1926; s. Harry J. and Sylvia (Schenkelbach) G.; m. Rosalind Feldman, Dec. 22, 1957; children: Suzanne Galane Duvall, Jonathan A. B.E.E., CCNY, 1946; LL.B., George Washington U., 1950. Bar: D.C. 1950, Nev. 1955, Calif. 1975. Patent examiner U.S. Patent Office, Washington, 1948-50; spl. partner firm Roberts & McInnis, Washington, 1950-54; practice as Morton R. Galane, P.C., Las Vegas, Nev., 1955—; spl. counsel to Gov. Nev., 1967-70. Contbr. articles to profl. jours. Chmn. Gov.'s Com. on Future of Nev., 1979-80. Fellow Am. Coll. Trial Lawyers; mem. Am. Law Inst., IEEE, Am. Bar Assn. (council litigation sect. 1977-83), State Bar Nev., State Bar Calif., D.C. Bar. Home: 2019 Bannies Ln Las Vegas NV 89102 Office: 302 E Carson Ave Ste 1100 Las Vegas NV 89101

GALBREATH, JACQUELYN RODGERS, marriage and family counselor; b. Paris, Tex., Apr. 30, 1958; d. Ralph and Gaynell Olean (Reese) Rodgers; m. Tony DeWayne Galbreath, Aug. 7, 1982. AA, Paris Jr. Coll., 1978; BA, N. Tex. State U., 1980, MS, 1982. Lic. marriage, family, child counselor. Pvt. practice therapy Orange, Tex., 1984-85; therapist Daybreak Youth Ctr., Orange, 1982-85; counselor San Andreas Regional Ctr., Campbell, Calif., 1985—; pres. Svc. Employees Internat. Union, San Jose, Calif., 1989—. Co-chair Delta Sigma Theta Sorority Social Action Com., Orange, 1984-85. Mem. NAFE, SARC (San Jose chpt.), Calif. Assn. Marriage and Family Therapists. Democrat. Baptist. Office: San Andreas Regional Ctr PO Box 50002 San Jose CA 95150-0002

GALBREATH, TERRY STEPHEN, military officer; b. DeKalb, Ill., Oct. 6, 1950; s. Hal Shoot and Donna Gene (Rich) G.; m. Sarah Light Morgan, Aug. 20, 1978 (div. June 1983); m. Heather Virginia Waldie, Apr. 27, 1984. AS in Aviation Mgmt., U. Ill, 1970, BS in Edn., 1973; postgrad., DeVry Inst. Tech., Chgo., 1975-77; MS in Systems Mgmt., U. So. Calif. Commd. USAF, 1973, advanced through grades to maj.; missle combat crew 319th Strategic Missle Squad, Warren AFB, Wyo., 1973-76; airborne missle ops. 4th Airborne Command and Control Squad, Ellsworth AFB, S.D., 1976-78; mfg. engr. Space and Missile Systems Orgn., Los Angeles AFS, 1978-79; dep. dir. policy planning space div. Command Staff, Los Angeles AFS, 1979-81; plans and requirements officer space div. Dep. Chief Staff Space Ops., Los Angeles AFS, 1981-83; chief standardization 12 Missile Warning Squadron, Thule AB, Greenland, 1983-84; chief test and evaluation div. Consol. Space Ops. Ctr. Site Activation Task Force, Falcon AFS, Colo., 1984-86; chief manned spaceflight div. 2d Space Wing, Falcon AFS, 1986-87; dep. command competition advocate hdqurs. Air Force Space Command, Peterson AFB, Colo., 1987—; adj. prof. Webster U., Colorado Springs, Colo., 1988—. Maj. Civil Air Patrol, Colo. wing. Mem. Air Force Assn. (life), Experimental Aircraft Assn., Airplane Owners and Pilots Assn., Smithsonian Air and Space Found., Clan Galbraith Assn. N.Am. Republican. Mem. Anglican Ch. Home: 14125 Citation Ln Falcon CO 80831 Office: AFSPACECOM/C Stop 7 Peterson AFB CO 80914-5001

GALBRETH, WILLIAM EDWARD, dentist; b. Albuquerque, Nov. 10, 1952; s. Wilmer Edward and Peggy Marie (Moore) G.; 1 child, William Scott. BS, U. N.Mex., 1974; DMD, Tufts U., 1977. Physician sports medicine Albuquerque Pub. Sch. System, 1983—. Mem. ADA, N.Mex. Dental Soc., Albuquerque Dental Soc. Demcrat. Baptist. Office: 11005 Spain NE Albuquerque NM 87111

GALE, DANIEL BAILEY, architect; b. St. Louis, Nov. 6, 1933; s. Leone Caryll and Gladys (Wotowa) G.; student Brown U., 1951-53, Ecole Des Beaux Arts, Paris, 1954-55; BArch., Washington U., 1957; m. Nancy Susan Miller, June 15, 1957; children: Caroline Hamilton, Rebecca Fletcher, Daniel Bailey With Gale & Cannon, Architects and Planners, Hellmuth, Obata & Kassabaum, Inc., Architects, St. Louis, and exec. v.p. corp. devel., dir. HOK, Inc., St. Louis, 1961-79; ptnr. Heneghan and Gale, architects and planners, Aspen, Colo., 1967-69; pres., chief exec. officer Gale Kober Associates, San Francisco, 1979-83; pvt. practice architecture, Belvedere, Calif., 1984—; pres. Program Mgmt. Inc., Belvedere, 1984—. Recipient Henry Adams prize Washington U., 1957. Mem. AIA, Singapore Inst. Architects. Home and Office: 280 Belvedere Ave Belvedere CA 94920

GALE, G. DONALD, broadcast company executive; b. Salt Lake City, Aug. 23, 1933; s. Glen Franklin and Doris Alma G.; m. Doris Jean Chipman, June 24, 1954; children: Michael Glen, Pamela Dawn, Christine Lynne. BA in Journalism, U. Utah, 1958, MA in Journalism, 1960, PhD in Communication, 1986. Pubs. edito Utah Power & Light Co., Salt Lake City, 1958-61, U. Utah, Salt Lake City, 1961-64; instr. journalism Weber State Coll., Ogden, Utah, 1964-65, U. Utah, 1965-70; mng. editor Olympus Pub. Co., Salt Lake City, 1970-75; editorial writer KSL Radio/TV, Salt Lake City, 1977-80; dir. pub. affairs KSL Radio/TV, 1980-85; v.p. Bonneville Internat. Corp., Salt Lake City, 1985—. Co-author: Your Child's Career, 1977, Career Education, 1977; editor numerous books; author numerous editorials. Bd. dirs. Nat. Kidney Found. Utah, Salt Lake City, 1988—, Freedoms Found., Salt Lake City, 1988—. With U.S. Army, 1954-56. Recipient Service to Journalism award, U. Utah, Dept. Communications, 1982, Editorial/Commentary award, Radio/TV News Dirs. Assn., 1979, 80, Communication Leadership award, Toastmasters, 1983, Light of Learning award, Utah Bd. Edn., 1988. Mem. Nat. Broadcast Editorial Assn. (pres. 1984-85), Radio/TV News Dirs. Assn., Soc. Profl. Journalists (Disting. Svc. award 1989). Mem. Ch. of Jesus Christ of Latter Day Saints. Office: Bonneville Internat Corp Broadcast House Salt Lake City UT 84110-1160

GALE, JEFFREY H., publisher, public relations professional, writer; b. Chgo., Sept. 10, 1940. Student, Menlo Jr. Coll., Menlo Park, Calif., 1958-59, U. Calif., Berkeley, 1959-60, NYU, 1960-62, John Marshall Law Sch., 1962-63, U. Calif., Santa Cruz, 1980-81. Reporter City News Bur. Chgo., 1964; asst. sports editor Elgin (Ill.) Daily Courier-News, 1965; reporter San Francisco Chronicle, 1966; dir. pub. rels. Golden Gate Gales Soccer Club, San Francisco, 1967; dir. publicity Dallas Tornado Soccer Club, 1968; reporter L.A. bur. AP, 1969; asst. editor San Francisco Jewish Bull., 1970-74; free-lance journalist various organizations, 1975-76; corr. Nat. Pub. Radio, San Francisco, 1977; editor morning drive Sta. KFRC Radio, San Francisco, 1977; mem. staff resource ctr. Marin (Calif.) Community Video, 1978; moderator, commentator Marin II, 1979-80; media cons. Jeremy P. Tarcher Pub., 1983-84; nat. press sec. Media Liaison for Promoting Enduring Peace Inc., Woodmont, Conn., 1984-85; media cons. Sonia Johnson Ltd., 1985-86; film producer 1986-87; publicity cons. Crossing Press, Freedom, Calif., 1987; pub. Bold Hawk Press, Palm Springs, Calif., 1988—. Author: Bullshi—!...The Media As Power Brokers in Presidential Elections, 1988. Vol. reader Newspapers for Blind KQED-FM; bd. dirs. Am. Jewish Congress, 1973-74. Pvt. USAR, 1963-69. Grantee U. Calif. Santa Cruz, 1980-83. Mem. ACLU, Media Alliance, Amnesty Internat., Alliance for Survival. Office: PO Box 588 Palm Springs CA 92263

GALE, ROBERT PETER, physician, medical educator, scientist, researcher; b. N.Y.C., Oct. 11, 1945; s. Harvey Thomas and Evelyn (Klein) G.; m. Tamar Tishler, June 2, 1976; children—Tal, Shir, Elan. B.A., Hobart Coll., 1966; M.D., SUNY, Buffalo, 1970; Ph.D., UCLA, 1976. Diplomate Am. Bd. Internal Medicine, Am. Bd. Med. Oncology. Intern, then resident dept. medicine UCLA, 1970-72, resident I and II in hematology and oncology, 1972-74; Postdoctral studies UCLA Med Ctr.; assoc. prof. medicine UCLA, 1974—; chmn. Internat. Bone Marrow Transplant Registry, Milw., 1982—; Meyerhoff vis. prof. Weizmann Inst. Sci., Israel, 1983; vis. prof. Excerpta Medica Found., Amsterdam, 1979; pres. Armand Hammer Ctr. for Advanced Studies in Nuclear Energy and Health. Author 13 books, numerous articles on hematology, oncology and transplantation. Recipient Presdl. award N.Y. Acad. Sci., 1986, Olender Peace Prize, 1986; Leukemia Soc. Am. scholar, 1976-81. Fellow ACP; mem. Transplantation Soc., Am. Soc. Hematology, Am. Assn. Immunologists, Internat. Soc. Hematology, Internat. Soc. Exptl. Hematology, Am. Soc. Clin. Oncology, Am. Assn. Cancer Research. Home: 2316 Donella Circle Bel Air CA 90077 Office: UCLA Sch Medicine Los Angeles CA 90024 *

GALE, VALERIE CHAPMAN, psychotherapist; b. Jersey City, Sept. 2, 1932; d. Norman Nathan and Gertrude (Aronson) Chapman; m. Alan B. Handler; children: Nancy, Carolyn, Julia; m. Roger S. Gale, Jan. 17, 1971. AB, Finch Coll., 1954; EdM, Tufts U., 1956; PhD, Columbia PacificU., 1983. Lic. sch. social worker, marriage and family counselor. Dir. Kent Pl. Nursery Sch., Tucson, 1966-80; social worker Bow Sch., Morris Plains, N.J., 1978-80; pvt. practice psychotherapy Tucson, 1980--; exec. dir. Roots & Wings, Inc., Tucson, 1985--; lectr. Overlook Hosp., Summit, N.J., 1986, 87. Contbr. articles to profl. jours. Miller Found. grantee, 1986-88. Mem. Am. Assn. Counseling and Devel., Am. Mental Health Counselors, Am. Assn. Marriage and Family Therapy (clin.), Am. Group Psychotherapy Assn., Ariz. Group Psychotherapy Soc. Democrat. Jewish. Home: 5861 Via Andada Tucson AZ 85715 Office: 5447 E 5th St Suite 203 Tucson AZ 85711

GALEF, ANDREW GEOFFREY, investment and management corporations executive; b. Yonkers, N.Y., Nov. 3, 1932; s. Gabriel and Anne (Fruchter) G.; m. Suzanne Jane Cohen, June 26, 1954 (div. Feb. 1963); children: Stephanie Anne Galef Streeter, Marjorie Lynn Galef England, Michael Lewis; m. Billie Ruth Medlin, Nov. 7, 1964 (div. May 1988); children: Phyllis Anne Galef Bulmer, Catherine Marie; m. Bronya Kester, Dec. 18, 1988. B.A., Amherst Coll., 1954; M.B.A., Harvard U., 1958. Vice pres. Kamkap, Inc., N.Y.C., 1958-60; pres. Kemline Calif., San Jose, 1960-61, Zeigler Harris Corp., San Fernando, Calif., 1961-63; v.p. Fullview Industries, Glendale, Calif., 1963-65; cons. Mordy & Co., Los Angeles, 1965-68; prin. Grisanti & Galef, Inc., Los Angeles, 1968-84; pres. Spectrum Group, Inc., Los Angeles, 1978—; chmn., chief exec. officer MagneTek, Inc., Los Angeles, 1984—; chmn. bd. dirs. Midland Color, Inc. (formerly Roberts & Porter, Inc.), Chgo., Exide Corp., Horsham, Pa., Warnaco Inc., Los Angeles, Grantree Corp., Portland, Petco, Inc., San Diego; bd. dirs. Post Group, Inc., Hollywood, Calif. Mem. nat. adv. bd. Childhelp, USA, Woodland Hills, Calif., 1984—; bd. dirs. Pacific Homes, Encino, Calif. Served to capt. USAF, 1956-58. Office: Spectrum Group Inc 11111 Santa Monica Blvd Los Angeles CA 90025

GALES, SAMUEL JOEL, army logistics specialist; b. Dublin, Miss., June 14, 1930; s. James McNary McNeil and Alice Francis (Smith) Broadus-Gales; m. Martha Ann Jackson; children: Samuel II, Martha Diane, Katherine Roselein, Karlmann Von, Carolyn B., Elizabeth Angelica. BA, Chapman Coll., 1981, MS, 1987. Ordained Eucharistic minister. Enlisted U.S. Army, 1948, advanced through grades to master 1st sgt., 1969, ret., 1976; tchr. Monterey (Calif.) Unified Sch. Dist., 1981-82; civilian U.S. Army Directorate of Logistics, Ft. Ord, Calif., 1982—. Active Family Service Agy., Monterey, 1979-85; rep. Episc. Soc. for Ministry on Aging, Carmel, Calif., 1980-86, Task Force on Aging, Carmel 1983-87. Decorated Air medal. Mem. Am. Legion (post comdr. 1973-74), Forty and Eight (chef-de-gare 1979, 80), Monterey Chess Club, Comdr's. Club Calif. (past pres. Outpost 28th 1981-82). Republican. Home: 1617 Lowell St PO Box 919 Seaside CA 93955-0919 Office: Self-Service Supply Ctr 2080 Quartermaster Ave Fort Ord CA 93941

GALICIAN, MARY-LOU, broadcasting educator; b. New Bedford, Mass., Apr. 5, 1946; d. Benn and Evelyn Nancy (Scott) G. BA magna cum laude, L.I. U., 1966; MS, Syracuse U., 1969; EdD, Memphis State U., 1978. Writer, N.Y. corr. Standard Times, New Bedford, 1961-66; producer, dir., talk show host Sta. WCMU-TV, Mt. Pleasant, Mich., 1967-70, dir. programming, 1968-70; v.p., dir. Evelyn-Nancy Cosmetiques, Inc., New Bedford, 1970-73; nat. advt. mgr. Maybelline Co./Schering-Plough, Memphis, 1973-75; pres., creator FUN-dynamics!, Memphis, Little Rock, Phoenix, 1976—; prof. journalism Memphis State U., 1978-80; nat. mktg. mgr. Fedn. Am. Hosps., Little Rock and Washington, 1980-82; prof. broadcasting Ariz. State U., Tempe, 1983—; motivation, communication cons. various nat. pub. and pvt. orgns., 1966—; speaker, performer nat. convs. and co., 1966—; mem. broadcast services subcom. FCC Industry Adv. Com., Grand Rapids, Mich., 1967-70; mem. adv. bd. Cen. Mich. Ednl. Resources Council, Mich., 1967-70; anchor nat. TV fund drives, 1984—. Author: Medical Education and the Physician-Patient Relationship, 1978, The Dr. Galician Prescription for Healthy Media Relations, 1980; writer, producer No Miracles Here, 1967, Witch is it?, 1969-70, Saturday's Child: 20 Years of Network TV Children's Programs, 1969; editor: The Coming Victory, 1980; radio host To Broadway with Love, 1967, TV host Interview with Mary-Lou Galician, 1967-70; scriptwriter, songwriter, presenter FUN-dynamics! The FUN-damentals of DYNAMIC Living, 1976—; writer, performer FUN-dynamics! FUN-notes, 1982; contbr. articles to profl. pubs. Charter mem. Symphony League of Cape Cod, Mass., 1972-73; adviser Boy Scout Explorer Post, Cape Cod, 1972-73; mem. exec. bd. Tenn.-Ark.-Miss. Girl Scouts U.S., Memphis, 1973-75; patron Memphis Ballet Co., 1974-75; mem. steering com. Make Today Count, Memphis, 1976; Health Systems Agy. Council mem. MidSouth Med. Ctr. Council, Memphis, 1976-78; chair campaign kick-off Valley of the Sun United Way, Phoenix, 1987; co-chair Ariz. State U. United Way Campaign, 1988-90. Recipient Cert. Achievement, S.W. Edn. Council for Journalism, 1985, 86, 87, Walter Cronkite Sch. Service award, 1988; named Mich.'s Woman of Yr., Outstanding Ams. Found., 1969; Conolly Coll. scholar L.I. U., 1963-66; grantee Ariz. State U., 1984, 85, 87; Syracuse U. fellow, 1966-67. Mem. AAUW (bd. dirs. Mich. and Mass. chpts. 1967-73), Am. Advt. Fedn. (pyramid awards com. 1980), Am. Women in Radio and TV (com. chair Tenn. chpt. 1979), Ariz. State U. Faculty Women's Assn., Assn. Edn. in Journalism and Mass Communication, Broadcast Edn. Assn. (promotion com. 1985, leadership challenge com. 1988—), Pub. Relations Soc. Am. (faculty adviser Ariz. State U. 1983-84), Sales and Mktg. Execs. Internat. (com. chair Ark. chpt. 1981-83), Women in Communications Inc. (founding faculty adviser Cen. Mich. U. 1969-70, Memphis State U. 1979-80, Ariz. State U. 1985—, bd. dirs. Phoenix Profl. chpt., 1985—, mem. Nat. bd. dirs. and v.p. Far West region, 1987-88, nat. editorial bd. 1987—(Outstanding Adv. award 1985-86, 87-88), Zeta Tau Alpha (gen. faculty adviser 1968-70, membership adviser 1974-75). Club: Univ. of Ariz. State U. Home: 614 E Diamond Dr Tempe AZ 85283 Office: Ariz State U Walter Cronkite Sch Journalism Tempe AZ 85287-1305

GALINDO, HECTOR ELOY, teacher; b. Mexicali, Baja, Mexico, Sept. 3, 1949; s. Jesus Galindo and Margaret (Ramirez) G. BA, UCLA, Westwood, Calif., 1972. Acct., program specialist SER-Jobs For Progress, Inc., L.A., 1972-75, regional coord. nat. ops., 1975-78, regional adminstr., 1978-79; program devel. adminstr. SER-Jobs For Progress, Inc., Carson, Calif., 1980-81; self-employed Senor's G's Mexican Restuarant, Playa Del Rey, Calif., 1981—; classroom advisor United Way Harbor Area Gang Alternatives Program, San Pedro, Calif., 1986—. Mem. Playa Del Ray (Calif.) Bus. Assn., 1986-87, League of United Latin Am. Citizens, 1980. Recipient Tchr. Aprreciation award San Pedro Pen. C. of C., 1988. Republican. Roman Catholic. Home: 6650 Vista Del Mar #3 Playa Del Rey CA 90293

GALL, DONALD ALAN, data processing executive; b. Reddick, Ill., Sept. 13, 1934; s. Clarence Oliver and Evelyn Louise (McCumber) G.; m. Elizabeth Olmstead, June 25, 1960 (div. 1972); children: Christopher, Keith, Elizabeth; m. Kathleen Marie Insognia, Oct. 13, 1973; 1 child, Kelly Marie. BSME, U. Ill., 1956; SM, MIT, 1958, ME, 1960, ScD, 1964. Research engr. Gen. Motors, Detroit, 1956-57; staff engr. Dynatech Corp., Cambridge, Mass., 1959-60; mgr. ctr. systems Dynatech Corp., Cambridge, 1962-63; asst., assoc. prof. Carnegie-Mellon U., Pitts., 1964-69; assoc. prof. surgery and anesthesiology U. Pitts. Sch. Medicine, 1969-73; vis. fellow IBM Research Lab., Ruesch/Kon, Switzerland, 1970-71; pres. Omega Computer Systems, Inc., Scottsdale, Ariz., 1973—. Contbr. articles to profl. jours.; inventor fuel injection system. Bd. dirs. Scottsdale Boys Club, 1982—; mem. Scottsdale Head Honchos, 1978-87. Mem. AAAS, Am. Soc. Mech. Engrs. Home: 12223 N 85th St Scottsdale AZ 85260 Office: Omega Computer Systems Inc 4300 N Miller Rd Suite 136 Scottsdale AZ 85251

GALL, ERIC PAPINEAU, physician educator; b. Boston, May 24, 1940; s. Edward Alfred and Phyllis Hortense (Rivard) G.; m. Katherine Theiss, Apr. 20, 1968; children: Gretchen, Michael Edward. AB, U. Pa., 1962, MD, 1966, fellowship, 1973. Asst. instr. U. Pa., Phila., 1970-71, post doctoral trainee, 1971-73; asst. prof. U. Ariz., Tucscon, 1973-78, assoc. prof., 1978-83, prof. internal medicine, 1983—, prof. surgery, 1983—, prof. family/community medicine, 1983—, chief rheumatology and allergy immunology, 1983—, med. dir. arthritis ctr., 1986—; chair Ednl. Materials Com. Am. Coll. Rheumatology, Atlanta, 1986—; vice-chmn. Arthritis Found., Atlanta, 1982-83; pres. Arthritis Health Professions Assn., Atlanta, 1982-83. Author, editor: Illustrated Guide to Path DX & Management, 1988, Rheumatic Disease: Rehab & Management, 1984, Primary Care, 1984; contbr. numerous articles to profl. jours. Chmn. Arthritis Found., Tucson, 1979-81. Recipient Addie Thomas Nat. Svc. award Arthritis Found., 1988. Fellow Am. Coll. Physicians, Am. Coll. Rheumatology; mem. Arthritis Health Professions Assn. (pres. 1982-83), Am. Assn. Med. Colls. Am. Fedn. Clin. Rsch. Office: U Ariz Arthritis Ctr 1501 N Campbell Ave Tucson AZ 85724

GALL, MEREDITH DAMIEN, education educator, author; b. New Britain, Conn., Feb. 18, 1942; s. Theodore A. and Ray (Ehrlich) G.; m. Joyce Pershing, June 12, 1968; 1 child, Jonathan. AB, Harvard U., 1963, EdM, 1963; PhD, U. Calif., Berkeley, 1968. Sr. research assoc. Far West Lab. for Ednl. Research and Devel., San Francisco, 1968-75; assoc. prof. edn. U. Oreg., 1975-79, prof., 1980—. Author: (with J.P. Gall) Making the Grade, 1988, (with K.A. Acheson) Techniques in the Clinical Supervision of Teachers, 1980, 2d rev. edit., 1987; Handbook for Evaluating and Selecting Curriculum Materials, 1981; (with Borg) Educational Research: An Introduction, 4th edit., 1983; co-author: Study for Success: the Most Essential Study Skills for School and College, 1985; editor: (with B.A. Ward) Critical Issues in Educational Psychology, 1974; cons. editor Jour. Ednl. Research, Jour. Experimental Edn. U.S. Pub. Health fellow, 1963-64. Fellow Am. Psychol. Assn.; mem. Am. Ednl. Research Assn., Assn. Supervision and Curriculum Devel., Nat. Soc. Performance and Instrn., Oreg. Ednl. Research Assn. (pres. 1985-86), Nat. Soc. for Study of Edn., Phi Delta Kappa (Dist. I Meritorious award 1978). Home: 4810 Mahalo Dr Eugene OR 97405 Office: U Oreg Coll Edn Eugene OR 97403

GALLAGHER, DENNIS JOSEPH, state senator, educator; b. Denver, July 1, 1939; s. William Joseph and Ellen Philomena (Flaherty) G.; B.A., Regis Coll., 1961; M.A., Cath. U. Am., 1968; postgrad. (Eagleton fellow) Rutgers U., 1972, 86; m. Joanne Ruth Froling, July 8, 1973; children—Meaghan Kathleen, Daniel Patrick. With locals of Internat. Assn. Theatrical and Stage Employees, Denver and Washington, 1956-63; tchr. St. John's Coll. High Sch., Washington, 1964-66, Heights Study Center, Washington, 1965-67, Regis Coll., 1967; mem. Colo. Ho. of Reps from 4th Dist., 1970-74; mem. Colo. Senate, 1974—, chmn. Dem. Caucus, 1982-84, Dem. Whip, 1985—. Mem. Platte Area Reclamation Com., 1973—; mem. Denver Anti-Crime Council, 1976-77; trustee Denver Art Mus.; bd. dirs. Cath. Community Services; mem. Colo. Commn. on Aging; mem. Colo. State Adv. Council on Career Edn.; mem. Victim Assistance Law Enforcement Bd., Denver, 1984—; Named Gates Found. fellow Harvard U. Mem. Colo. Fedn. Tchrs. (pres. local 1333, 1972-74), Colo. Calligrapher's Guild, James Joyce Reading Soc. Democrat. Roman Catholic. Home: 2511 W 32d Ave Denver CO 80211 Office: Regis Coll Dept Communication W 50th Ave and Lowell Blvd Denver CO 80221

GALLAGHER, MARIAN GOULD, librarian, educator; b. Everett, Wash., Aug. 29, 1914; d. John H. and Grace (Smith) Gould; m. D. Wayne Gallagher, Oct. 1, 1942 (dec. 1953). Student, Whitman Coll., 1931-32; A.B., U. Wash., 1935, LL.B., 1937, M.L.S., 1939. Law librarian, instr. law U. Utah, Salt Lake City, 1939-44; law librarian U. Wash., Seattle, 1944-81; asst. prof. law U. Wash., 1944-48, asso. prof., 1948-53, prof., 1953-81, prof. emeritus, 1981—, adj. prof., 1944-84; vis. prof. law and disting. law librarian, Hastings Law Sch., San Francisco, 1982; cons. various law schs. and govt. law libraries. Mem. Gov.'s Commn. on Status of Women, 1964-71, Pres.'s Nat. Adv. Com. on Libraries, 1967-68; mem. adv. com. White House Conf. on Library and Info. Services, 1976-80; mem. council sect. on legal edn. and admissions to bar Am. Bar Assn., 1979-83. Named Disting. Alumna U. Wash. Sch. of Librarianship, 1970, Disting. Alumna U. Wash. Sch. Law, 1980, Disting. Alumna Whitman Coll., 1981. Fellow Am. Bar Found.; mem. Am. Bar Assn., Am. Assn. Law Libraries (pres. 1954-55, Disting. Service award 1966, 84), Wash. State Bar Assn., Seattle-King County Bar Assn., PEO, Mortar Bd., Order of Coif, Delta Delta Delta, Phi Alpha Delta. Presbyterian. Office: 900 University St Seattle WA 98101-2765

GALLAHER, CHARLES MORRIS, realtor; b. Upper Darby, Pa., June 29, 1944; s. Howard S. and Glenys (Morris) G.; m. Jenny O. Garcia, June 1, 1969; children: Veronica, Charles Jr. BA, San Francisco State, 1971. Lic. real estate broker. Mgr. Esquire Rm., San Francisco, 1968-73; owner Brian Thomas, Inc., Portland, Oreg., 1973-82; assoc. Coldwell Banker, Port Townsend, Wash., 1983-86; owner Keystone Real Estate, Inc. (now Century 21 Keystone Real Estate, Inc.), Bellingham, Wash., 1987—. With USN, 1964-68. Mem. French-USA Internat. Real Estate Fedn., Nat. Assn. Realtors, Realtors Nat. Mktg. Inst., Comml. Investment Real Estate Coun., Whatcom County Assn. Realtors. Office: Century 21 Keystone Real Estate 1211 Cornwall Ave Bellingham WA 98225

GALLAR, JOHN JOSEPH, mechanical engineer, educator; b. Poland, July 3, 1936; came to U.S., 1981; s. Joseph and Sophie (Gallar) Filipecki; m. Christina B. Wilczynski, June 30, 1962; 1 child, Darek A. BSME, State U. Poland, 1957, MSME, 1958; PhD in Tech. Scis., M & M Acad., 1966; professorship, Ahmadu Bello U., Zaria, Nigeria, 1980. Dir., prof. engring. Acad. State U., Poland, 1957-72; dir., prof. engring. Ahmadu Bello U., 1973-81, dir. postgrad. studies, 1976-81; with module design Timex Co., Cupertino, Calif., 1981-82; mgr. mfg. Computer Research Co., Santa Clara, Calif., 1982-84; mgr. hardware devel. Nat. Semiconductor Co., Santa Clara, 1984-85; chief robotics engr. Varian Corp., Palo Alto, Calif., 1986—; dep. vice-chancellor State U., Poland, 1970-71; cons. Enplan Corp., Kaduna, Nigeria, 1980-81, Criticare Tech., Sparks, Nev., 1985-86, also bd. dirs.; mgr. mfg. engring. Retro-Tek Co., Santa Clara, 1986. Contbr. articles to profl. jours.; patentee in field. Trustee, charter mem. Presdl. Task Force, Washington, 1984; mem. Nat. Conservative Polit. Action Com., Washington, 1981. Recipient U.S. Ceremonial Flag Presdl. Task Force; Medal Merit from Pres. Ronald Reagan, Washington, 1985. Mem. Calif. State Sheriff's Assn., Nat. Rifle Assn. Roman Catholic. Home: 5459 Entrada Cedros San Jose CA 95123 Office: Varian Corp 611 Hansen Way Palo Alto CA 95051

GALLEGLY, ELTON WILLIAM, congressman; b. Huntington Park, Calif., Mar. 7, 1944; married; four children. Student, Calif. State U., L.A., 1962-63. Businessman, real estate broker Simi Valley, Calif., from 1968; mem. Simi Valley City Coun., 1979; mayor City of Simi Valley, 1980-86; mem. Congress from the 21st dist. of Calif., 1986—; mem. fgn. affairs and interior & insular affairs coms. U.S. Ho. of Reps.; exec. mem. Rep. Study com.; formerly vice-chmn., chmn. Ventura County Assn. Govts., Calif. Bd. dirs. Moorpark Coll. Found.

GALLEGO, JOSE MIGUEL, research chemist; b. Mexicali Baja, Mex., Nov. 5, 1955; came to U.S. 1981.; s. Waldemar and Josefina (Garcia) G.; m. Leticia Osuna, Jan. 10, 1981; children: Kimberly L., Stephanie M. BS in Chemistry, U. Autonoma, Guadalajara, 1977; postgrad. inorganic chem., U. Autonoma, 1977-78. Supr. ops. State Water Commn., Tijuana, Mex., 1978-79; research chemist Quimica Organica Mex., S.A., Mexicali, 1979-81, Caspian, Inc., San Diego, 1984-88; v.p., chief chemist, co-owner Laboratorios Industriales y Servicios Internacionales, S.A., Tijuana, 1981-84; owner, mgr. G.C. Systems, Chula Vista, Calif., 1983-85; founder, gen. mgr., ptnr. Innovative Computer Accessories, Imperial Beach, Calif., 1985-88, Vega Techs., San Ysidro, Calif., 1988—; with Indsl. Monitoring Lab., San Diego, 1989—; microcomputer maint. man U. Autonoma Baja Calif., Tijuana, 1982-84, instr. instrumental analysis, 1981-84; instr. chemistry U. Autonoma Guadalajara, 1976, instr. gen. chemistry and physics, 1978; presenter at confs. in field. Author: Programacion BASIC en Quimica, 1981, CP/M Kit for the Commodore 128, An Introduction to CP/M, 1987, AmKit for the Amiga, An Introduction to the Workbench and CLI, 1988; contbr. articles to profl. jours.; patentee recycling process for spent caustic etchants. Served with Mexican Army, 1973-74. Mem. South Bay Commodore Users Group (v.p. 1983-85), San Diego Computer Soc., Toronto Users Group. Roman Catholic. Home: 1844 D St $S2PO Box 2746 National City CA 92050 Office: Vega Techs 3171 Iris St San Ysidro CA 92073

GALLEGOS, ALPHONSE, bishop; b. Albuquerque, Feb. 20, 1931; s. Jose Angel and Caseana (Apodaca) G. B.S., St. Thomas Aquinas Coll., 1971; M.S., St. John's U., Jamaica, N.Y., 1972; M.E., Loyola U., Los Angeles, 1979. Ordained priest Roman Catholic Ch., 1958. Pastor San Miguel Ch., Los Angeles, Our Lady of Guadalupe Ch., Sacramento; vicar Hispanics in Sacramento area; first hispanic bishop Sacramento; Aux. bishop of Sacramento 1981—; pastor Guadalupe Ch., Sacramento; Vicar gen. Roman Catholic Ch., Sacramento, vicar for Hispanics; active campaign for human devel. U.S. Catholic Conf., Washington. Mem. Calif. Govs. Com.; bd. dirs. Sacramento Concilio, Boy Scouts Am.; mem. Sacramento Mayor's Hispanic Adv. Com., County of Sacramento Multi-Cultural Park Com.; mem. adv. bd. Calif. Hispanic Cath. Inst.; mem. supt. of edn.'s adv. council on Hispanic affairs State of Calif. Recipient Silver Beaver award. Home: 1119 K St Sacramento CA 95808 Office: PO Box 1706 Sacramento CA 95808 *

GALLEGOS, GERALDINE MARIE, teacher; b. Long Beach, Calif., Aug. 16, 1953; d. John Andrew and Dolores Rita (St. John) G.; m. Edward Alan Stang, Aug. 12, 1978; children: Michael Jon, Amanda Michelle. BA, U. N.Mex., 1977, MA, 1986. Sec. U. N.Mex., Albuquerque, 1972-74; leader Camp KYSOC, Carrollton, Ky., 1976; elem. tchr. Weaver Pub. Schs., Merced, Calif., 1978, St. Mary's Elem. Sch., Sacramento, 1978-79; ednl. resource tchr. Columbia (Mo.) Pub. Schs., 1979-81; tchr. learning disabilities Albuquerque Pub. Schs., 1981—; tchr. trainer Monterey Reading Program, Albuquerque, 1982—. Vol. campaign Gary Hoocever for Ho. of Reps., Albuquerque, 1986. Democrat. Roman Catholic. Home: 4471 Robinwood Ctr Irvine CA 92714

GALLEGOS, LISA ANGELINA, social worker; b. Albuquerque, Aug. 28, 1963; d. Gilbert R. and Rita (Lucero) G. BSW, N.Mex. State U., 1985; MSW, N.Mex. Highlands U., 1987. Social work intern N.Mex. Div. Vocat. Rehab., Las Cruces, 1984, Los Lunas (N.Mex.) Hosp. and Tng. Sch., 1984, Adolescent Family Life Program, Las Cruces, 1985; counselor LULAC Ednl. Ctr., Albuquerque, 1985-86; social work intern Las Vegas (Nev.) Med. Ctr., 1986-87; social worker U. N.Mex. Maternity and Infant Care Project, Albuquerque, 1987-. Mem. Albuquerque Youth Force Coalition, 1986. Mem. Nat. Assn. Social Workers. Republican. Roman Catholic. Home: PO Box 307 Ribera NM 87560 Office: U NM Maternity & Infant Care Project Med Bldg #3 Albuquerque NM 87131

GALLENSKY, NEIL ELLIS, electrical engineer; b. Cheyenne, Wyo., Nov. 26, 1959; s. Howard D. and Lila A. (Helfand) G. BSEE, U. Wyo., 1982; MSEE, Calif. Inst. Tech., Pasadena, 1983. Mem. tech. staff AT&T Bell Labs., Denver, 1982-89. Mem. Tau Beta Pi (chpt. pres. 1981-82), Phi Kappa Phi. Office: AT&T 12110 N Pecos St 9Z113 Denver CO 80234

GALLETTA, JOSEPH LEO, physician; b. Bessemer, Pa., Dec. 21, 1935; s. John and Grace (Galletta) G.; student U. Pitts., 1953-56; MD, U. Santo Tomas, Manila, Philippines, 1962; m. Teresita Suarez Soler, Feb. 19, 1961; children: John II, Angela, Eric, Christopher, Robert Francis, Michael Angelo. Intern, St. Elizabeth Hosp., Youngstown, Ohio, 1963-64; family practice medicine, 29 Palms, Calif., 1967-77, Hemet, Calif., 1977—; chief of staff 29 Palms Community Hosp., 1970-71, 73-76; vice chief of staff Hi-Desert Med. Center, Joshua Tree, Calif., 1976-77; chmn. dept. family practice Hemet Valley Hosp., 1981-83, med. dir. chem. dependency dept., 1985-88; pres. Flexisplint, Inc.; founding mem. Hemet Hospice; former cons. Morongo Basin Mental Health Assn. Hon. mem. 29 Palms Sheriff's Search and Rescue, 1971-77. Bd. dirs. 29 Palms Community Hosp. Dist., Morongo Unified Sch. Dist. Served with M.C. USN, 1964-67. Diplomate Am. Bd. Family Practice. Founding fellow West Coast div. Am. Geriatric Soc.; fellow Am. Acad. Family Practice; mem. AMA, Calif. Med. Assn., Riverside County Med. Assn., Am. Holistic Med. Assn. (charter), Am. Med. Soc. on Alcoholism and Other Drug Dependencies, Calif. Soc. Treatment Alcoholism and Drug Dependencies, Am. Acad. Family Practice, Calif. Acad. Family Practice. Roman Catholic. Established St. Anthonys Charity Clinic, Philippines, 1965; inventor Flexisplint armboards. Home: 27691 Pochea Trail Hemet CA 92344 Office: 850 E Latham Ave Ste B Hemet CA 92343

GALLIVAN, JOHN WILLIAM, publisher; b. Salt Lake City, June 28, 1915; s. Daniel and Frances (Wilson) G.; m. Grace Mary Ivers, June 30, 1938; children—Gay, John, William, Michael D., Timothy. B.A., U. Notre Dame, 1937. With Salt Lake Tribune, 1937—, promotion mgr., 1942-48, asst. pub., 1948-60, pub., 1960—; pres. Kearns-Tribune Corp., 1960—; v.p., dir. Telemation, Inc., 1963—; v.p. Tele-Communications, Inc., from 1965, dir.; pres. Silver King Mining Co., 1960—. Pres. Utah Symphony, 1964-65; exec. com. Pro-Utah, 1964—. Mem. Sigma Delta Chi. Clubs: Nat. Press (Washington); Alta (Salt Lake City), Salt Lake Country (Salt Lake City), Rotary (Salt Lake City). Home: 17 S 12th E Salt Lake City UT 84102 Office: Kearns-Tribune Corp 143 S Main St Salt Lake City UT 84110 *

GALLIVAN, MAUREEN ANN, real estate salesperson; b. Buffalo, N.Y., Nov. 6, 1944; d. Bernard Joseph and Veronica (McPhee) McKernan; m. John Francis Gallivan, Sept. 4, 1965; children: Timothy John, Dawn Marie. A in Applied Sci., Erie County Community Coll., 1964. Realtor assoc. Century 21 Jack Carter Realty, Inc., San Diego, 1985—. Mem. High Country West Property Owners Assn., San Diego. Recipient Centurian award. Mem. San Diego Bd. Realtors, Rancho Bernardo Bd. Realtors. Republican. Roman Catholic. Office: Century 21 Jack Carter Realty Inc 12405 Rancho Bernardo Rd San Diego CA 92128

GALLO, ERNEST, vintner. Co-owner E & J Gallo Winery, Modesto, Calif. Office: E & J Gallo Winery PO Box 1130 Modesto CA 95353 *

GALLO, JULIO, vintner. m. Aileen Gallo; 1 child, Bob. Co-owner E & J Gallo Winery, Modesto, Calif. Office: E & J Gallo Winery 600 Yosemite Blvd Modesto CA 95354 *

GALLOWAY, DONALD WALL, florist; b. San Francisco, Sept. 29, 1927; s. Riley Elbert and Laila Eleanor (Wall) G.; m. Rose Marie Fowler, Aug. 27, 1949 (div. Jan. 1983); children: Karen Eileen Galloway Snelson, John Michael; m. Barbara Lynn Forney, Jan. 9, 1987; children: Brian N. Cox, Leona R. Fouts, Bradley A. Cox. Grad. high sch., Concord, Calif. Designer, driver Laila's Concord (Calif.) Florist, 1945-58, ptnr., mgr., 1958-83, owner, mgr., 1983—. Inventor fiberglass delivery van. Cub master Boy Scouts Am., 1959-61. Staff sgt. Calif. NG, 1947-58. Named Man of Yr. Soroptimist Club, 1974. Mem. Florists Transworld Delivery Assn. (dist. chmn. 1969-72, dist. rep. 1947—, bd. dirs. 1958—, 94 Gt. People award 1974), Teleflora, Am. Floral Svc., Redbook, Master Florist Assn. (pres. San Francisco chpt. 1969-72, flower chmn., bd. dirs. 1958-72, master florist appreciation award 1970, 72), Concord C. of C., Odd Fellows. Democrat. Office: Laila's Concord Florist 1910 Concord Ave Concord CA 94520

GALLOWAY, KENNETH FRANKLIN, engineering educator; b. Columbia, Tenn., Apr. 11, 1941; s. Benjamin F. and Carrie (Dowell) G.; m. Dorothy Elise Lamar; children: Kenneth Jr., Carole A. BA, Vanderbilt U., 1962; PhD, U. S.C., 1966. Rsch. assoc. Ind. U., Bloomington, 1966-67, asst. prof., 1967-72, assoc. prof., 1972; rsch. physicist Naval Weapons Support Ctr., Crane, Ind., 1972-74; tech. staff Nat. Bur. Standards, Gaithersurg, Md., 1974-77; chief sect. Nat. Bur. Standards, Gaithersurg, 1977-79, chief div., 1980-86; prof. elect. engring. U. Md., 1980-86; prof., dept. head elect. and computer engring. U. Ariz., Tucson, 1986—. Contbr. articles to profl. jours. Sci. and Tech. fellow U.S. Dept. Commerce, 1979-80. Fellow IEEE (gen. chmn. Nuclear and Space Radiation Effect Conf. 1985); mem. Electrochem. Soc., Am. Physical Soc., Am. Soc. Engring. Edn., AAAS, Sigma Xi, Eta Kappa Nu. Office: U Ariz Dept Elec & Computer Engring Tucson AZ 85721

GALLOWAY, LEE, music educator; b. San Diego, Dec. 23, 1945; s. Robert Lee Galloway and Mary Josephine (Funk) Myers; m. Carol Jean Dreher (div. 1983). BA with honors, San Diego State U., 1977. Engring. technician Calif. Dept. Transp., San Diego, 1966-71; pvt. piano tchr. San Diego, 1971—; wine cons., salesman J.B.N. Imports, San Diego, 1983—; wine judge, cons., San Diego, 1983—; jazz pianist local clubs, San Diego, 1985—; wine taster Calif. Grapevine Newsletter, 1985—; wine judge San Diego Nat. Wine Competition, 1987—, Riverside (Calif.) Farmer's Fair, 1989—; music dir. Vanguard Theatre, San Diego, 1983. Author: The Contemporary Pianist, Book 1 and 2, 1978, Teacher's Guide for The Contemporary Pianist, 1988. Pres. Pacifica Homeowners Assn., San Diego, 1982—; v.p. San Diego Park and Recreation Com., 1982-84; co-chmn. wine auction com. Sta. KPBS, San Diego, 1987—. With USMC, 1966-68, Vietnam. Mem. Music Tchrs. Assn. Calif. (state v.p. 1983-85, state treas. 1985-87, chmn. bylaws revision com. 1983-85), San Diego Music Tchrs. Assn. (pres. 1980-82), Les Amis du Vin. Home and Office: 4588-A W Point Loma Rd San Diego CA 92107

GALLUP, BONNIE LEE, small business owner, training consultant; b. Reed City, Mich., Nov. 12, 1948; d. Robert K. Bobo and Nancy M. McCracken; m. Joseph G. Gallup,May 30, 1980; 1 child, Megan Nicole. BS in Edn., Cen. Mich. U., 1970; MA in Edn., San Francisco State U., 1980. Tchr., art cons. Kenowa Hills Sch. Dist., Grand Rapids, Mich., 1970-74; rate analyst, acct. rep. 333 Ins. Brokers, San Francisco, 1974-76; trainer, cons. Presidio, San Francisco, 1976-78; tng. designer Deterline Corp., Palo Alto, Calif., 1978-80, Louis Allen Mgmt. Cons., Palo Alto, 1980-81; pres., tng. cons. Bonnie Gallup & Assocs., Fremont, Calif., 1981—; lectr. San Francisco State U., 1983—; instr. U. Calif., Berkeley, 1984—; mem. adv. bd. for human resource devel. and tng. U. Calif., Berkeley, 1984—. Mem. Nat. Soc. Performance and Instrn., Am. Soc. Tng. and Devel. Home and Office: Bonnie Gallup & Assocs 491 Lowell Pl Fremont CA 94536

GALLUP, GEORGE KEENE, floroculturist; b. L.A., Dec. 21, 1947; s. Emmett Robert and Miriam Hope (Baile) G.; m. Rebecca Joy Lawrence, July 25, 1973; children: Jennifer Joy, Heather Christine, Jeffrey Keene, Timothy Keene, Matthew Keene. AA, Santa Barbara City Coll., 1969. Owner/grower Gallup Carpinteria (Calif.) Co., 1970—. With USCG, 1967-71. Republican. Presbyterian. Home: Serafin Way Carpinteria CA 93013 Office: Gallup Carpinteria Co 3896 Via Real Carpinteria CA 93013

GALNICK, MITCHELL NEIL, real estate developer, lawyer; b. Chgo., Oct. 5, 1953; s, Asher Harold and Helen (Karel) G.; m. Marta Jean Bromschwig, May 17, 1980. BS in Bus. magna cum laude, U. Colo., 1975, JD, 1978. Bar: Colo. 1978; lic. real estate salesman, Colo. Staff acct. Arthur Anersen & Co., Denver, 1978-79; prin. Dupler, Hult & Galnick. P.C., Boulder, Colo., 1979—; pres. Venture Group Cos., Boulder, 1980—; mgr. Lake Valley Golf Club, Boulder, 1987—. Mem. U. Colo. Law Rev., 1976; contbr. articles to legal jours. Mem. Colo. Bar Assn., Boulder Bar Assn. (co. chmn. real estate com. 1987-88), Urban Land Inst., Nat. Golf Found., Boulder C. of C. (resource ctr. task force 1988), Boulder Country Club, U. Colo. Dirs. Club, Beta Alpha Psi, Beta Gamma Sigma. Office: Venture Group 2338 Broadway Ste 100 Boulder CO 80302

GALT, JOHN KIRTLAND, physicist, laboratory administrator; b. Portland, Oreg., Sept. 1, 1920; s. Martin Happer and Elsie (Lee) G.; m. Marguerite VanNest, Dec. 30, 1949; children: James Michael (dec.), Lloyd Anthony. A.B., Reed Coll., 1941; Ph.D., MIT, 1947. Mem. tech. staff Bell Labs., Murray Hill, N.J., 1948-57; head solid state and plasma physics dept. Bell Labs., 1957-61, dir. solid state electronics lab., 1961-74; dir. solid state scis. research orgn. Sandia Nat. Labs., Albuquerque, 1974-78; v.p. Sandia Nat. Labs., 1978-85; prin. scientist Aerospace Corp., 1985—; mem. Air Force Studies Bd., Nat. Acad. Sci., 1971-76, Air Force Sci. Adv. Bd., 1975-82. Cons. editor: McGraw-Hill Ency. Sci. and Tech., 1965-86. NRC fellow Bristol, Eng., 1947-48. Fellow Am. Phys. Soc., IEEE, AAAS, Nat. Acad. Engring. Office: Aerospace Corp PO Box 92957 Los Angeles CA 90009

GALUTEN, ALBHY, record producer; b. N.Y.C., Dec. 27, 1947; s. Jacob Morris and Iris (Gieter) G.; m. Nancy Lyons, Aug. 25, 1978 (div.); children: Jason, Noah. Producer records by recording artists including Eric Clapton, Andy Gibb, Barbra Streisand, Kenny Rogers, Diana Ross. Recipient Grammy awards. Home and Office: 125 Palisades #105 Santa Monica CA 90402

GALVAN, SABINO, public school business officer; b. Kyle, Tex., Oct. 27, 1934; s. Paul R. and Mary A. Galvan; student Trinity U., 1954; AA, Sacramento Community Coll., 1960; BS, Sacramento State U., 1967; m. Jo Ana K., June 12, 1981; children by previous marriage: Gregory P., Jeanette K.; stepchildren: Jimmy, Peggy, Donna, Steve, Todd. Auditor trainee dept. fin. State of Calif., Sacramento, 1962; tax examiner IRS, Sacramento, 1962-63; auditor-appraiser Sacramento County Assessor's Office, 1963-64; acct. Sacramento County Office Edn., 1965-67, adminstrv. asst., 1967-68; chief acct. San Juan Unified Sch. Dist., Carmichael, Calif., 1968-76, sr. fin. analyst, 1976-78, asst. dir. fin., 1978-80, dir. acctg. services, 1980—, San Juan United Dir. Compensation and Benefits, 1983-87, dir. support services, 1988—; chmn. payroll task force, 1977-78. Troop treas. Golden Empire council Boy Scouts Am., 1968-69, chmn. membership com., 1969-70; bd. dirs. Superior Calif. Sch. Employees Credit Union, 1977—, chmn. nominating com., 1979, chmn. planning com., 1979-80; mem. Sacramento County Acad. Decathalon Scholarship com., 1986-87. Served with USAF, 1954-58. Mem. Calif. Assn. Sch. Bus. Ofcls. (dir. 1972-73, 75-76, pres. 1976-77, chmn. acctg. research and devel. com. 1980—), Assn. Calif. Sch. Adminstrs. (dir. 1982-83), San Juan Adminstrs. Assn. (dir. 1979—, pres. 1982-83), Assn. Calif. Sch. Adminstrs. Region III (v.p. programs, pres. 1985-86), Calif. Assn. Purchasing Officers. Democrat. Home: 8215 Scarlet Oak Circle Citrus Heights CA 95610 Office: San Juan Unified Sch Dist 3738 Walnut Ave Carmichael CA 95608

GALVIN, EILEEN TERESA, credit manager; b. Spalding, Nebr., July 6, 1949; d. Ambrose and Eileen (Wray) G. BA in Polit. Sci., U. Nebr., Omaha, 1971; MBA in Mktg., U. Colo., 1983. Credit mgr. Calandra Photo, Omaha, 1968-73; dir. adminstrn. Samsonite Corp., Denver, 1973-87; credit mgr. U.S. Recycling Industries, Denver, 1988—. Mem. Denver Art Museum, 1988—; vol. Museum After Dark, Denver, 1988. Mem. Bus. and Profl. Women's Assn. (treas. 1988—). Home: 1423 S Salem Way Aurora CO 80012

GAMBAN, DENNIS LAURINARIA, mechanical engineer; b. San Francisco, July 2, 1963; s. Daniel Caroche and Helen (Laurinaria) G. BSME, U. Calif., Berkeley, 1985; postgrad., Santa Clara U., 1987—. Registered profl. engr., Calif. Assoc. design engr. Westinghouse Electric Corp., Sunnyvale, Calif., 1986-88, design engr., 1988—. Mem. Ohlone Coll. Wind Symphony, Fremont, Calif.; trumpet player Claif. Repercussions. Chancellor's scholar, 1981. Mem. ASME, Calif. Engring. Alumni Assn., Calif. Bank Alumni Assn., Nat. Soc. Profl. Engrs. Roman Catholic. Office:

Westinghouse Electric Corp 401 E Hendy Ave MS EV-12 Sunnyvale CA 94088

GAMBARO, ERNEST UMBERTO, lawyer, consultant; b. Niagara Falls, N.Y., July 6, 1938; s. Ralph and Teresa (Nigro) G.; m. Winifred Sonya Gambaro, June 3, 1961. B.A. in Aero. Engring. with honors, Purdue U., 1960, M.S. with honors, 1961; Fulbright scholar, Rome U., 1961-62; J.D. with honors, Loyola U., Los Angeles, 1975. Bar: Calif. 1975, U.S. Tax Ct. 1976, U.S. Supreme Ct. 1979, U.S. Ct. Appeals (9th cir.). With Aerospace Corp., El Segundo, Calif., 1962-80, counsel, 1975-80; asst. gen. counsel, asst. sec. Computer Scis. Corp., El Segundo, 1980-88; v.p., gen. counsel, sec. INFONET Svcs. Corp., El Sequndo, 1988—; cons. bus. fin. and mgmt., 1968—. Recipient U.S. Air Force Commendation for contbns. to U.S. manned space program, 1969; Purdue U. Pres.'s scholar, 1959-60. Mem. ABA (internat., taxation sects.), Los Angeles Bar Assn. (exec. com. 1976—, founder chmn. sect. law and tech. 1976-78, chmn. bar reorgn. com. 1981-82), Am. Arbitration Assn. Los Angeles Ctr. Internat. Comml. Arbitration (founder, bd. dirs.), Internat. Law Inst. (faculty), St. Thomas More Law Soc., Phi Alpha Delta, Omicron Delta Kappa (past pres.), Tau Beta Pi, Sigma Gamma Tau (past pres.), Phi Eta Sigma. Republican. Newspaper columnist Europe Alfresco; contbr. articles to profl. publs. Home: 6542 Ocean Crest Palos Verdes CA 90274 Office: 2100 E Grand Ave El Segundo CA 90245

GAMBILL, ROBERT POWELL, real estate executive; b. Oak Park, Ill., May 6, 1927; s. Denman Powell and Helen Elizabeth (Clithero) G.; m. Jane Alexander Bimmerman (div. 1971); 1 child, Dana Elizabeth; m. Janice Brecklein. BS in Bus. Adminstrn., Northwestern U., 1950; postgrad., Stanford U. Law Sch., 1950-51. With Gen. Electric Co., Schenectady, N.Y., 1951-54; asst. v.p. Security Pacific Nat. Bank, Los Angeles, 1954-61; v.p. new bus. Electronics Capital Corp., San Diego, 1961-70; asst. v.p. Union Bank, Los Angeles, 1970-72; v.p. corp. div. Crocker Nat. Bank, Los Angeles, 1972-76; v.p. mktg. Devlin Pharms., Inc., El Segundo, Calif., 1976-78; pres. JBD Properties, Inc., Scottsdale, Ariz., 1978—, JB Devel. Co., Scottsdale, 1979—; pres. Price Rd. Indsl. Park, Chandler, Ariz., 1979—; mem. adv. council Phoenix Metrogroup, 1987—. Pres. Men's League Scottsdale Ctr. for the Arts, 1984-85. Served with Merchant Marine Cadet Corps, 1945-46. Northwestern U. scholar, 1948. Mem. Ariz. Assn. Indsl. Devel., Chandler C. of C. (pres. 1988-89). Republican. Clubs: Valley Hunt (Pasadena, Calif.); Fairfield Continental Country (Flagstaff, Ariz.).

GAMBINO, JEROME JAMES, nuclear medicine educator; b. N.Y.C., Sept. 13, 1925; m. Jacquelyn Ann Mazzola, Mar. 27, 1948; children: Charles, John, Mary Ellen, Jacquelyn. BA, U. Conn., 1950, MS, 1952; PhD, U. Calif., 1957. Asst. prof. natural scis. SUNY, New Paltz, 1957-59; research radiobiologist UCLA, 1959-61; mem. research staff Northrop Corp., Hawthorne, Calif., 1961-69; dir. edn. nuclear medicine dept. VA Med. Ctr., Los Angeles, 1969—; lectr. anatomy U. So. Calif., Los Angeles, 1963—, radiol. scis. UCLA, 1978—. Mem. Radiation Research Soc., Soc. Nuclear Medicine (pres. So. Calif. chpt. 1981-82). Office: VA Med Ctr W Los Angeles Wadsworth Div Nuclear Med W115 Wilshire and Sawtelle Blvds Los Angeles CA 90073

GAMBLE, DOUGLAS SCHIBSBY, food company executive; b. Waterloo, Iowa, 1925; married. BA Williams Coll., 1947, MBA Stanford U., 1949. With Pacific Gamble Robinson Co., Inc., Kirkland, Wash., 1949—, v.p. distbn. brs. from 1965, pres., chief exec. officer, 1974-86, also dir. Served to lt. (j.g.) USN. Office: 4227 E Madison Seattle WA 98112 *

GAMBLE, MICHAEL IRVING, aerospace company executive; b. Everett, Wash., Dec. 19, 1935; s. Paul I. and Margaret (Isacson) G.; m. Charlotte A. Albrecht, Dec. 20, 1957; children: Michael Scott, Paula Michel. BS in Physics, U. Wash., 1957. Assoc. engr. applied physics staff Boeing Co., Seattle, 1956-59, rsch. engr. physics tech. dept., 1959-62; mgr. environ. physics dept. AVCO Corp., Tulsa, 1962-65, mgr. engring. instrument div., 1965-66, mgr. program devel., 1966-69; area mktg. mgr. space applications, govt. products group AVCO Corp., Los Angeles, 1970-72; area mktg. mgr., govt. products group AVCO Corp., Albuquerque, 1972-73; laser systems mgr. Boeing Aerospace Co., Seattle, 1974-80, dir. strategic def. programs, 1980-89, dir. advanced systems preliminary design, 1989—. Capt. AUS, 1953-62. Fellow AIAA (assoc.); mem. Nat. Space Club, Phi Kappa Psi. Home: 13915 SE 241st St Kent WA 98042 Office: Boeing Aerospace and Electronics PO Box 3999 Seattle WA 98124

GAMBOA, GEORGE CHARLES, oral surgeon, educator; b. King City, Calif., Dec. 17, 1923; s. George Angel and Martha Ann (Baker) G.; predental certificate Pacific Union Coll., 1943; DDS, U. Pacific, 1946; MS, U. Minn., 1953; AB, U. So. Calif., 1958; EdD, U. So. Calif., 1976; m. Winona Mae Collins, July 16, 1946; children: Cheryl Jan Gamboa Williams, Jon Charles, Judith Merlene Gamboa Hiscox. Fellow oral surgery Mayo Found., 1950-53; assoc. prof. grad. program oral surgery U. So. Calif., Los Angeles, 1954—; assoc. prof. Loma Linda (Calif.) U., 1958—, chmn. dept. oral surgery, 1960-63; pvt. practice oral surgery, San Gabriel, Calif., 1955—. chmn. first aid com. West San Gabriel chpt. ARC; Diplomate Am. Bd. Oral and Maxillofacial Surgery. Fellow Am. Coll. Dentists, Am. Coll. Oral and Maxillofacial Surgeons, Am. Assn. Oral and Maxillofacial Surgeons; mem. Internat. Assn. Oral Surgeons, So. Calif. Soc. Oral and Maxillofacial Surgeons, Western Soc. Oral and Maxillofacial Surgeons, Am. Acad. Dental Radiology, Marsh Robinson Acad. Oral Surgeons, So. Calif. Acad. Oral Pathology, Profl. Staff Assn. Los Angeles County-U. So. Calif. Med. Ctr. (exec. com. 1976—), Am. Cancer Soc. (Calif. div., profl. edn. subcom. 1977—), Calif. Dental Soc. Anesthesiology (bd dirs.), San Gabriel Valley Dental Soc. (past pres.), Xi Psi Phi, Omicron Kappa Upsilon, Delta Epsilon. Seventh-day Adventist. Home: 1102 Loganrita Ave Arcadia CA 91006 Office: 132 S Mission Dr San Gabriel CA 91776

GAMBOA, RONALD MANUEL, packaging manufacturing executive; b. L.A., July 14, 1935; s. Manuel and Viola H. (Herrera) G.; m. Sarah J. Gamboa, July 28, 1957; children: Lora, Brian, Kevin, Aaron. AA, Pasadena Coll., 1955; BA, UCLA, Westwood, Calif., 1958. Accounts supr. R.T. French Co., Fullerton, Calif., 1960-67; reg. scs. mgr. St. Regis Paper Co., L.A., 1967-80; territory scs. mgr. Mobil Chem. Co., Woodland, Calif., 1981-83; scs & mktg. mgr. Diamond Straw, Inc., L.A., 1984-87; nat. scs mgr. Aelco Corp., Van Nuys, Calif., 1987—. Republican. Methodist. Home: 9526 Reverie Rd Tujunga CA 91042 Office: Aelco Corp 16010 Strathern St Van Nuys CA 91406

GAMMAGE, GRADY, JR., lawyer; b. Phoenix, Oct. 1, 1951; s. Grady and Kathryn (Klink) G.; m. Karen Marie Quick, Aug. 7, 1976; children: Mathew Taylor, Christopher Alan, Andrew Grady. BA magna cum laude, Occidental Coll., 1973; JD, Stanford U., 1976. Bar: Ariz. 1976, U.S. Ct. Claims, 1978, U.S. Ct. Appeals (9th cir.) 1979. Assoc. Jennings, Strouss & Salmon, Phoenix, 1976-80, ptnr., 1980-83; ptnr. Gammage & Burnham, Phoenix, 1983—; teaching asst. for legal writing Ariz. State u. Coll. Law, 1980; speaker to profl. assns. and civic orgns. Vice chmn. Phoenix Historic Preservation Commn.; mem. exec. bd. Phoenix Community Alliance; mem. visual arts improvement awards com. City of Phoenix, also mem. zoning ordinance revision com.; bd. dirs. Ariz. Parklands Found., Ariz. Hist. Soc., Tucson; mem. Phoenix Mayor's Ad Hoc Adv. Com. on Square One Grad. Mem. Ariz. Bar Assn., Maricopa County Bar Assn., Urban Land Inst., Ariz. Planning Assn., Ariz. Acad., Valley Forward Assn., Phoenix Met. C. of C. (devel. services com., mid-rise subcom.), Phoenix City Club, Order of Coif, Phi Beta Kappa, Lambda Alpha (v.p. Phoenix chpt.). Office: Gammage & Burnham 2 N Central Ave 18th Fl Phoenix AZ 85004

GAMMELL, GLORIA RUFFNER, sales executive; b. St. Louis, June 19, 1948; d. Robert Nelson and Antonia Ruffner; m. Doyle M. Gammell, Dec. 11, 1973. AA in Art, Harbor Coll., Harbor City, Calif., 1969; BA in Sociology, Calif. State U., Long Beach, 1971. Cert. fin. planner. Bus. analyst Dun & Bradstreet Inc., Los Angeles, 1971-81; rep. sales Van Nuys, Calif., 1981-86; v.p., sec. bd. dirs. Gammell Industries, Paramount, Calif., 1986—. Mem. Anne Banning Assistance League, Hollywood, Calif., 1981-82; counselor YWCA, San Pedro, Calif., 1983-84; fundraiser YMCA, San Pedro, 1984-85; mem. womens adv. com. Calif. State Assembly, 1984-86. Recipient Best in the West Presdl. Citation, 1981-86. Home: 991 Channel St San Pedro CA 90731

GAMMILL, DARRYL CURTIS, business executive; b. Milw., Jan. 20, 1950; s. Lawrence H. and Eunice G. (Birkett) G.; BS, U. Colo., 1973; m. Maureen Mulcahy, Sept. 16, 1972; children: Rebecca, Bridgett, Maureen, Bryann. Lic. Gen. Prin., Fin. Prin., Registered Options Prin., Sr. Compliance Officer, Registered Rep., SEC, registerd investment advisor, broker dealer, SEC. Stockbroker, Douglas, Stanat, Inc., Denver, 1974; dir. research Pittman Co., Denver, 1975; option specialist B.J. Leonard & Co., Denver, 1976; v.p. research, corp. fin. Neidiger, Tucker Bruner, Denver, 1977; chmn., pres., chief exec. officer G.S. Omni Corp., 1979-82; chmn., chief exec. officer Gammill and Co., 1981—; mng. broker ESI Ltd., 1988—; mng. ptnr. G.S. Oil, G.S. Leasing; dir. Valudyne, Inc., 1973-79; pres. Chalton Investment Services; chmn., pres. Fusion Mgmt. Corp., 1981-83; chmn. Applied Fusion Research & Tech. Corp., 1982, Pres. Research Mgmt., 1984; gen. partner Fusion Ltd. Trustee Gammill Found.; pres. Platinium Club Inc., 1985—; founder AudioOptics. Founder Nicholas R. Massano Ednl. Scholarship, 1985; co-founder Opera Colo. Mem. Fin. Analysts Fedn., Nat. Assn. Security Dealers, Denver Soc. Security Analysts, IEEE, Am. Nuclear Soc., Nat. Energy Assn. (nat. chmn.), U.S. Ski Assn. Clubs: Optimists, Elks. Contbr. articles to profl. jours. Home: 28 Red Fox Ln Littleton CO 80127

GANAKIS, E. JOHN, psychiatrist; b. Hopewell, Va., July 17, 1937; s. John George and Katherine (Andrews) G.; m. Catharine Wilson, Dec. 30, 1987; 1 child, Jon. BS, Va. Poly. Inst. and State U., Blacksburg, 1954; MD, U. Innsbruck, Austria, 1964. Intern Providence Hosp., Seattle, 1964-65; resident in internal medicine VA Hosp., Oakland, Calif., 1965-66; resident in surgery St. Mary's Hosp., San Francisco, 1966-67; resident in psychiatry U. Utah Med. Ctr., Salt Lake City, 1967-70; med. dir. day hosps. Santa Barbara County Health Svcs., Santa Barbara, Calif., 1970-82; sr. psychiatrist San Diego County Health Svcs., 1982—; med. dir. Addition Rsch. Ctr., Santa Barbara, 1972-75. Mem. parish council Santa Barbara Greek Orthodox Ch., 1976-80. 2nd Lt. U.S. Army, 1954-56. Mem. Calif. Med. Assn. Home: 3754 Scenic Way Carlsbad CA 92056 Office: San Diego County Health 1700 Pacific Hwy San Diego CA 92101-2417

GANAPOL, CAROL LYNN, insurance company executive; b. San Francisco, Oct. 28, 1951; d. Irving and Claire Ann (Wallace) Jarkovsky; m. David L. Ganapol, Aug. 15, 1971(div. 1977). Student, San Francisco State U., 1969-70, Golden Gate U., 1987, U. Calif., San Francisco, 1987—. Surety trainee Indsl. Indemnity Co., San Francisco, 1970-71; surety asst. Alexander & Alexander, San Jose, 1971-79; sr. surety underwriter Employers of Wausau, San Francisco, 1979; surety mgr., account exec. Curtis Day & Co., San Francisco, 1979-86; account exec. Corroon & Black, San Francisco, 1986—. Presenter of seminars and workshops in field. Vol. Sta. KQED-TV, San Francisco, 1986—. Mem. Nat. Assn. Women in Constrn. (pres. San Francisco chpt. 1984-85, regional com. chair edn. sect. 1985-86, nat. coordinator edn. found. 1986-88, nat. dir. 1988—, mem. of yr. award 1988), Surety Forum, Common Cause, San Francisco Mus. Soc. Democrat. Jewish. Club: Commonwealth (San Francisco). Office: Corroon & Black 50 California St San Francisco CA 94111

GANDHI, OM PARKASH, electrical engineer; b. Multan, Pakistan, Sept. 23, 1934; came to U.S., 1967, naturalized, 1975; s. Gopal Das and Devi Bai (Patney) G.; m. Santosh Nayar, Oct. 28, 1963; children: Rajesh Timmy, Monica, Lena. BS with honors, Delhi U., India, 1952; MSE, U. Mich., 1957, Sc.D., 1961. Rsch. specialist Philco Corp., Blue Bell, Pa., 1960-62; asst. dir. Cen. Electronics Engring. Rsch. Inst., Pilani, Rajasthan, India, 1962-65, dep. dir., 1965-67; prof. elec. engring., rsch. prof. bioengring. U. Utah, Salt Lake City, 1967—; cons. U.S. Army Med. Rsch. and Devel. Command, Washington, 1973-77; cons. to industry and govtl. orgns.; mem. Internat. URSI Commn. B, 1976—; mem. study sect. on diagnostic radiology NIH, 1978-81; co-chmn. ANSI C 95.4 Com. on RF Safety Standards, 1988—. Author: Microwave Engineering and Applications, 1981; editor Engineering in Medicine and Biology mag., Mar., 1987; contbr. over 200 articles on biol. effects and med. applications of electromagnetic energy, microwave semicondr. devices and microwave tubes to profl. jours. Recipient Disting. Rsch. award U. Utah, 1979-80; grantee NSF, NIH, EPA, USAF, U.S. Army, USN, N.Y. State Dept. Health, others. Fellow IEEE (editor Procs. of IEEE Spl. Issue, 1980; Tech. Achievement award Utah sect. 1975); mem. Bioelectromagnetics Soc. (dir. 1979-82, 87—). Office: U Utah Elec Engring Dept 4516 Merrill Engring Salt Lake City UT 84112

GANGI, ROBERT CURTIS, lawyer; b. Glendale, Calif., Apr. 8, 1962; s. Salvatore Frank and Roberta Ann (Shanklin) G. BA, UCLA, 1984; JD, Loyola U., L.A., 1987. Bar: Calif. 1987. Legal counsel Gangi Bldrs., Inc., Glendale, 1987—, v.p., 1984—, also bd. dirs.; legal cons. 1987. Recipient Am. Jurisprudence award, 1987. Mem. ABA, L.A. County Bar Assn., Glendale Bar Assn., Ducks Unltd., Golden Key, Phi Eta Sigma, Pi Gamma Mu, Theta Xi. Republican. Presbyterian. Home: 3225 Beaudry Terr Glendale CA 91208 Office: Gangi Bldrs Inc 1000 N Central Ae #204 Glendale CA 92102

GANGITANO, ERNESTO SEBASTIAN, neonatologist; b. San Juan, Argentina, Oct. 30, 1948; came to U.S., 1973; s. Sebastian and Ramona Gabriela (Palacio) G.; m. Susana Maria Virgolini, May 11, 1973; children: Gabriela, Michelle, Andre, David. MD, U. Cordoba, Argentina, 1972. Am. Bd. Med. Examiners. Surg. intern Washington Hosp. Ctr., 1973-74; resident in pediatrics Bronx Lebanon Hosp., N.Y.C., 1974-77, pediatrician, 1977-78; neonatology fellow Cedars Sinai Hosp., L.A., 1978-80; neonatologist Huntington Meml. Hosp., Pasadena, Calif., 1980—; bd. dirs. extra corporeal membrane orgn. svc. Huntington Meml. Hosp. Fellow Am. Acad. Pediatrics; mem. L.A. Pediatric Soc., Calif. Perinatal Assn. Home: 1341 Descanso Dr La Canada CA 91011 Office: Huntington Meml Hosp 100 Congress St Pasadena CA 91105

GANNATAL, JOSEPH PAUL, electronics engineer; b. Ventura, Calif., Sept. 9, 1955; s. Paul and Janet Mae (Carpenter) G.; m. Sandy Jean Lincoln, Jan. 14, 1984; children: Leonard Troy Garcia, Jennfier Lynn Garcia, Sarah Jean Gannatal, Smantha Leigh. BSME, Calif. Polytech. Inst., San Luis Opisbo, 1979; M in Space Systems Tech., Naval Postgrad. Sch., 1987. Indsl. engr. Nat. Semiconductor, Santa Clara, Calif., 1979-81; spl. projects engr. Pacific Missile Test Ctr., Point Mugu, Calif., 1981—, mgr. devel. program, 1986-88. Mem. bldg. com. Camarillo Bapt. Ch., 1984-86. Recipient Spl. Achievement award USN, 1982, 84, Letter of Commendation USN, 1983, Outstanding Service award USN, 1985, 86. Mem. AIAA, ASME. Republican.

GANNON, FRANCES VIRGINIA, marketing and sales professional; b. Washington, May 10, 1929; d. Philip and Ruth Pomona (Garvin) Chaffin; m. Vincent DePaul Gannon, Feb. 4, 1974 (div. 1978). BS in Speech, U. So. Miss., 1951; cert., U.S. Army War Coll., 1969. Commd. 2d lt. U.S. Army, 1951, advanced through grades to col.; WAC recruiting officer Wilkes-Barre, Pa., 1952-55; comdg. officer WAC Co., Ft. MacArthur, Calif., 1955-57, Camp Zama, Japan, 1957-59, Ft. Huachuca, Ariz., 1962-63; personnel officer Ft. Meyers, Va., 1959-61; sec. gen. staff Ft. Huachuca, 1963-64; budget officer Office of Dep. Chief of Staff, Washington, 1964-66; with personnel, dept. of Army Pentagon, Washington, 1964-66; sr. advisor Vietnamese Womens Armed Forces, Saigon, 1967-68; chief WAC Recruiting, Hampton, Va., 1969-72; sr. WAC advisor Hdqrs. U.S. Army, Europe, Heidelberg, Fed. Republic. Germany, 1972-73, dir. Office Equal Opportunity, 1973-74, exec. officer for Dep. Chief of Staff, Intelligence, 1974-75; dir. evaluation U.S. Army Intelligence Ctr. & Sch., Ft. Huachuca, Az., 1975-77; retired U.S. Army, 1977; co-owner, operator Charron House Restaurant, Sierra Vista, Ariz., 1975-79; co-owner Fiesta Fabrics, Sierra Vista, Ariz., 1981-84; dir. mktg. and sales Mountain View Inn, Sierra Vista, Ariz., 1987; resident mgr. InnSuites Hotel, 1988-89, resigned, 1989. Bd. dirs. Forgash House for Abused Wifes, 1987—; pres. Huachuca Art Assn., 1986—; precinct committeewoman Cochise County Rep. Com., 1976—; leader 4-H Club, 1979; council mem. City of Sierra Vista, 1983-87. Decorated Legion of Merit, Bronze Star. Mem. The Ret. Officer Assn. (pres. 1979-80), Ariz. Council of Chpts. (sec. 1980-81), WAC Veterans Assn. Republican. Club: 1200 (pres. 1984-85). Home: 947 Cardinal Dr Sierra Vista AZ 85635

GANONG, WILLIAM F(RANCIS), physician, physiologist; b. Northampton, Mass., July 6, 1924; s. William Francis and Anna (Hobbet) G.; m. Ruth Jackson, Feb. 22, 1948; children: William Francis III, Susan B., Anna H., James E. A.B. cum laude, Harvard U., 1945, M.D. magna cum laude, 1949. Intern, jr. asst. resident in medicine Peter Bent Brigham Hosp., Boston, 1949-51; asst. in medicine and surgery Peter Bent Brigham Hosp., 1952-55; research fellow medicine and surgery Harvard U., 1952-55; asst. prof. physiology U. Calif., San Francisco, 1955-60; asso. prof. U. Calif., 1960-64, prof., 1964-82, Jack D. and Deloris Lange prof., 1982—, faculty research lectr., 1968, vice chmn. dept., 1963-68, chmn., 1970-87; cons. Calif. Dept. Mental Hygiene. Author: Review of Medical Physiology, 14th edit., 1989; editor: (with L. Martini) Neuroendocrinology, vol. I, 1966, vol. II, 1967, Frontiers in Neuroendocrinology, 1969, 71, 73, 76, 78, 80, 82, 84, 86, 88; editor-in-chief: Neuroendocrinology, 1979-84. Served with U.S. Army, 1943-46; served to capt. M.C. 1951-52. Recipient Boylston Med. Soc. prize Harvard U., 1949, A.A. Berthold medal, 1985; named Disting. Svc. mem. Assn. Med. Coll., 1988. Fellow AAAS; mem. Am. Physiol. Soc. (pres. 1977-78), Assn. Chairmen Depts. Physiology (pres. 1976-77), Am. Soc. for Gravitational and Space Biology, Soc. Exptl. Biology and Medicine (councillor 1989), Endocrine Soc., Chilean Endocrine Soc. (corr.), Internat. Brain Research Orgn., Nat. Soc. Med. Research, Soc. for Neurosci., Internat. Soc. Neuroendocrinology (v.p. 1976-80). Home: 710 Hillside Ave Albany CA 94706 Office: U Calif Dept Physiology San Francisco CA 94143

GANT, JOSEPH ERWIN, former state senator, chemist; b. Altamahaw, N.C., Feb. 4, 1912; s. Joseph Erwin and Mary (Banner) G.; B.S., U. N.C., 1934; m. Opal Martin, Feb. 11, 1938 (dec. June 1982); children—Joseph Erwin III, Mary Martin; m. Margaret Minter Doss, Dec. 28, 1985. With U.S. Potash Co., Carlsbad, N.Mex., 1934-56, U.S. Borax & Chem. Co., Carlsbad, 1956-67; chmn. N.Mex. Bd. Eddy Commrs., 1967-68; mem. N.Mex. Senate, 1969-84, mem. judiciary com., 1969-72, rules com., 1973-84, chmn. conservation com., 1973-84, chmn. majority caucus, 1973-84, also vice chmn. legis. univ. study com., 1971-75, mem. local govt. com., 1974-75, chmn. legis. higher edn. admissions standards com., 1976-77, legis. energy com., 1976-77, mem. legis. council, 1978-84, chmn. joint interim radioactive waste consultation com., 1979-84, vice chmn. com. on coms.; cons. govtl. affairs, 1985—; dir. Glen Raven Mills, Inc. (N.C.). Pub. mem. N.Mex. State Investment Council, 1959-60; v.p. N.M. Assn. Counties, 1969; dir. Southeastern N.Mex. Econ. Devel. Dist.; mem. Southwestern Regional Energy Council, 1975-84; mem. nat. resources task force intergovtl. com. Nat. Conf. State Legislatures, 1973-77; mem. state-fed. relations energy com., 1977-84; mem. Roswell Dist. Land Use Com., Bur. Land Mgmt., 1978-82, N.Mex. Water Resources Adv. Com., 1982-84; chmn., Eddy County Democratic Com., 1948-60; mem. N.Mex. Dem. Exec. Com., 1953-54. Mem. Am. Chem. Soc., Alpha Tau Omega. Episcopalian. Elk. Home: 1204 W Orchard Ln PO Box 909 Carlsbad NM 88220 Office: 111 W Menmod PO Drawer DD Carlsbad NM 88220

GANTZ, NANCY ROLLINS, nurse; b. Buffalo Center, Iowa, Mar. 7, 1949; d. Troy Gaylord and Mary (Emerson) Rollins; diploma in Nursing, Good Samaritan Hosp. and Med. Center, Portland, Oreg., 1973; BSBA, City Univ., 1986; MBA, Kennedy-Western U., 1987, postgrad., 1988—; m. Aug. 1981. Nurse ICU, Good Samaritan Hosp., 1973-75; charge nurse Crestview Convalescent Hosp., Portland, 1975; dir. nursing services Roderick Enterprises, Inc., Portland, 1976-78, Holgate Center, Portland, 1978-80; nursing cons. in field of adminstrn., 1980-84; coordinator CCU; mgr. ICU/CCU Tuality Community Hosp., Hillsboro, Oreg., 1984-86; head nurse intensive care unit, cardiac surgery unit, coronary care unit, Good Samaritan Hosp. & Med. Ctr., Portland, 1986-88, nurse mgr. critical care units, 1988—; mem. task force Oreg. State Health Div. Rules and Regulations Revision for Long Term Health Facilities and Hosps., 1978-79. Mem. Am. Nurses Assn. (cert.), Oreg. Nurses Assn., Nat. League Nursing, Am. Assn. Critical Care Nurses (regional cons., pres. elect greater Portland chpt. 1985-86, pres. 1986-87), Am. Heart Assn., Oreg. Heart Assn., Geriatric Nurses Assn. Oreg. (founder, charter pres.), Clackamus Assn. Retarded Citizens, AACN (chpt. cons. for reg. 18). Adventist. Home: 2670 NW Eastway Ct Beaverton OR 97006

GANULIN, ELADIA MARGARITA, real estate executive; b. San Francisco, Oct. 16, 1949; d. Raul and Helen (Palmon) Laines; m. Marty Ganulin, Sept. 27, 1970 (div. June 1988). Student, Chabot College, San Lorenzo, Calif., 1968-69; Diploma in Real Estate, San Francisco City Coll., 1974. V.p. Unique Homes, San Francisco, 1974-80, pres., 1980—. Active Mus. Soc. San Francisco; bd. dirs. Diamond Heights Neighborhood Assn., San Francisco, 1972-73. Mem. Nat. Assn. Realtors, Calif. Assn. Realtors, San Francisco Bd. Realtors. Republican. Club: Commonwealth of Calif. Office: Unique Homes 1774 Union St San Francisco CA 94123

GARAMENDI, JOHN R., state legislator; m. Patricia Garamendi; 6 children. Grad., U. Calif.-Berkeley; M.B.A., Harvard U. Rancher nr. Sacramento County, Calif.; former mem. Calif. Assembly, now mem. Calif. Senate, chmn. revenue and taxation Joint Com. on Sci. and Tech., mem. energy and pub. utilities com., govt. orgn. com., natural resources com., wildlife com. Served with Peace Corps. Office: Office of State Senate State Capitol Sacramento CA 95814

GARAT, GERALD MIGUEL, citrus grower; b. Riverside, Calif., Aug. 14, 1935; s. Miguel John and Mary Evelyn (Young) G.; m. Elizabeth James (div. 1964); children: Paula, Jack, Michael; m. Mary Elizabeth Diederich, Feb. 14, 1976; stepchildren: Michael P. Scott, John D. Scott. Student, Riverside City Coll., 1954, 85. Foreman Miguel J. Garat Farm, Riverside, 1955-57; foreman. supt. H.M. Robertson Inc., Riverside, 1958-69; area gen. mgr. John R. Davis Inc., LaHabra, Calif., 1970-72; project engr. Dorfman Constrn., Los Angeles, 1973-78; fruit grower B&G Ranch, Riverside, 1979—; vice chmn. Blue Banner Fruit Exchange, Riverside, 1987—; bd. dirs. Sunkist, Inc., Los Angeles, 1987—. Vice-chmn. Riverside Bd. Pub. Utilities, 1984—; chmn. Lake Matthews Community Plan Com., Riverside, 1984-87; captain Riverside County Sheriffs Posse, 1974-78. Mem. Elks. Home and Office: B&G Ranch 2991 Tyler St Riverside CA 92503

GARBARINO, JOSEPH WILLIAM, economics and business educator; b. Medina, N.Y., Dec. 7, 1919; s. Joseph Francis and Savina M. (Volpone) G.; m. Mary Jane Godward, Sept. 18, 1948; children: Ann, Joan, Susan, Ellen. B.A., Duquesne U., 1942; M.A., Harvard U., 1947, Ph.D., 1949. Faculty U. Calif., Berkeley, 1949—; prof. U. Calif., 1960-88, dir. Inst. Bus. and Econ. Research, 1962-88, prof. emeritus, 1988—; vis. lectr. Cornell U., 1959-60, UCLA, 1949, SUNY, Buffalo, 1972; Fulbright lectr. U. Glasgow, Scotland, 1969; vis. scholar U. Warwick; mem. staff Brookings Instn., 1959-60; vis. lectr. U. Minn., 1978; labor arbitrator. Author: Health Plans and Collective Bargaining, 1960, Wage Policy and Long Term Contracts, 1962, Faculty Bargaining: Change and Conflict, 1975, Faculty Bargaining in Unions in Transition. Served with U.S. Army, 1942-45, 51-53. Decorated Bronze Star. Mem. Indsl. Relations Research Assn. Democrat. Roman Catholic. Home: 7708 Ricardo Ct El Cerrito CA 94530

GARBELL, GEORGE GREGORY, marketing executive; b. Menominee, Mich., May 26, 1935; s. George Harold and Aldia (Sharon) G.; m. Ruth Joanne Lacoursiere, June 4, 1960; children: Carrie J., Ann S., Jeanne E. BS in Fin., Marquette U., Milw., 1961; MBA, Ariz. State U., 1967, postgrad., 1969-71. With Salt River Project, Phoenix, 1961-69; asst. v.p., dept. head First Interstate Bank of Ariz., Phoenix, 1969-74; asst. v.p., mgr. planning First Interstate Svcs. Co., Mesa, Ariz., 1974-77; asst. v.p., planning officer Valley Nat. Bank of Ariz., Phoenix, 1978-83; v.p., mktg. planner Valley Nat. Bank of Ariz., 1983—; prin. Primavera Strategies, Mesa, 1985—; vis. faculty Scottsdale Community Coll., 1971—, mem. curriculum adv. com., 1983—. Mem. Phoenix Forward Com., 1970; active various charitable orgns.; pres. Planning Forum Phoenix, 1985-86. Recipient Svc. award, Maricopa County Community Coll. Dist., 1986. Mem. Assn. for Systems Mgmt. (pres. 1971-72), S.W. Systems Conf. Office: Valley Nat Bank Ariz 241 N Central Ave Phoenix AZ 85001

GARBER, JANICE WINTER, advertising executive; b. N.Y.C., July 25, 1950; d. Irving and Frances (Edelman) Winter; stepdau. of Daniel Friedman; m. Dale Wayne Garber, Nov. 30, 1978. B.A., Queens Coll., 1979. Prodn. asst. P & F Graphics, N.Y.C., 1969-73; guest service mgr. Sheraton Corp., N.Y.C., 1973-76; advt. mgr. Am. Specialty Corp., N.Y.C., 1976-79; mng. editor VPO Industry News, 1979; advt. mgr. B & M Automotive Products, 1980-81; advt. mgr. Toyota Indsl. Equipment div. Toyota Motor Sales, U.S.A., Inc., Torrance, Calif., 1981-87, .et. 1987 . Mem. Bus./Profl. Advt. Assn. (dir. Los Angeles chpt. 1981), Am. Mktg. Assn. (Marsy award So. Calif. chpt. 1983).

GARBER, JEROLD ALLAN, broadcasting executive; b. Peoria, Ill., Aug. 10, 1942; s. Allan Edward and Mary Maxine (King) G.; m. Judith Jane Clause, June 18, 1966 (div. 1977); 1 child, Timothy; m. Susan Annette Colonese, May 21, 1982; stepchildren: Sara, Seth, Jason. BSE, No. Ill. U., 1964; MA, U. Mich., 1969. tchr., mgr. Sta. WHFH-FM, Homewood-Flossmoor High Sch., Flossmoor, Ill., 1964-79; tchr. Prairie State Coll., Chicago Heights, Ill., 1970-79; dir. telecommunications Central Wyo. Coll., Riverton, 1979—; gen. mgr. Sta. KCWC-FM-TV, Riverton, 1979-85; gen. mgr. Idaho Ednl. Pub. Broadcasting System, 1985—; bd. dirs. Rocky Mountain Corp. for Pub. Broadcasting, 1980-88, pres., 1987-88; cons. in pub. radio and T.V. NDEA fellow, 1969. Writer recreational computer programs, 1985—. Staff officer USCGR, 1985—. Mem. Western Ednl. Soc. Telecommunications (bd. dirs. 1979-86, pres. 1986-87), Alpha Psi Omega, Pi Kappa Delta. Democrat. Methodist. Avocations: boating, computer programming, acting and directing. Home: 1515 Shenendoah Dr Boise ID 83712 Office: Sta KAID-TV 1910 University Dr Boise ID 83725

GARBY, CLAUDINE MERLE, educational administrator; b. Jackson, Mich., July 19, 1929; d. Roy L. and Effie A. (Wright) Pier; m. Louis Charles Gerby, June 22, 1957 (dec. 1986); children: Gage L., C. Leigh Garby Meinig, Craig C., Eric Wright. BA in English, Western Mich. U., 1954; MA in Adminstrn. and Edn., U. Mich., 1957; PhD in Adminstrn., U. Colo., 1974. Cert. tchr., adminstr., Colo. Tchr. Richardson Sch. Dist., Jackson County, Mich., 1947-48, Clement Sch. Dist., Jackson County, 1948-52, Pittsfield Sch. Dist., Ann Arbor, Mich., 1954-58; teaching assoc. U. Colo., Boulder, 1969-73, asst. dir. student tchng., 1972-73, asst. dir. ind. studies, 1974-75; prin. St. Vrain Valley Sch. Dist., Longmont, Colo., 1975-84; supr. elem. edn. St. Vrain Valley Sch. Dist., Longmont, 1984-85, dir. elem. edn., 1985--. Mem. Nat. Assn. Elem. Prins., Colo. Assn. Sch. Execs., Colo. Internat. Reading Assn., Phi Delta Kappa, Kappa Delta Pi. Democrat. Methodist. Office: Saint Vrain Sch Dist RE-1J 395 S Pratt Pkwy Longmont CO 80501

GARCELON, CHARLOTTE MARIE, sales executive; b. L.A., July 22, 1942; d. Charles Jack and Helen Marie (Likens) Alric; children: Eric Steven, Daniel Arthur, David Andrew. AA, Cerritos Coll., 1977; BA, Calif. State U., 1981. Mgmt. trainee First Interstate Bank, Orange County, Calif., 1982-83; pub. rels. asst. Dean Davisson, Fullerton, Calif., 1983-84; br. mgr. Wiko Ltd., Anaheim, Calif., 1985-87; western sales rep. Wiko Ltd., Fullerton, 1987—. Mem. Profl. Women's Network, Sierra Club. Home: 1000 S Coast Dr Costa Mesa CA 92626

GARCIA, ALFRED ROBERT, small business owner; b. L.A., Oct. 15, 1957; s. Alfred Daniel and Amelia (Sandoval) G; m. Margaret Rodriguez; children: Nicole Marie, Natalie Michelle. BS, Loyola Marymount U., L.A., 1979. Salesman Roadway Express, Inc., L.A., 1979-83; owner, pres. Alto Systems, Inc., Commerce, Calif., 1983—; pres. Angel's Bay Trading Co., Inc., 1985—. Sustaining mem. Rep. Nat. Com. Mem. Phi Kappa Theta. Republican. Roman Catholic. Office: Alto Systems Inc 5650 E Olympic Blvd Commerce CA 90022

GARCIA, F. CHRIS, academic administrator, political science educator, public opinion researcher; b. Albuquerque, Apr. 15, 1940; s. Flaviano P. and Crucita A. Garcia; m. Sandra D. Garcia; children—Elaine L., Tanya C. B.A., U. N.Mex., 1961, M.A. in Govt., 1964; Ph.D. in Polit. Sci., U. Calif.-Davis, 1972. Asst. prof. polit. sci. U. N.Mex., Albuquerque, 1970-74, assoc. prof., 1974-78, prof., 1978—, asst. dir. div. govt. research, 1970-72, assoc. dean Coll. Arts and Scis., 1975-80, dean Coll. Arts and Scis., 1980-86, v.p. acad. affairs, 1987—; founder, chmn. bd. Zia Research Assocs., Inc., Albuquerque, 1973—. Author: Political Socialization of Chicano Children, 1973, La Causa Politica: A Chicano Politics Reader, 1974, The Chicano Political Experience, 1977, State and Local Government in New Mexico, 1979, New Mexico Government, 1976, 1981, Latinos and the Political System, 1988. Served with N.Mex. Air N.G., 1957-63. Mem. Western Polit. Sci. Assn. (pres. 1977-78), Am. Polit. Sci. Assn. (exec. council 1984-86), Am. Assn. Pub. Opinion Research, Council of Colls. of Arts and Sci. (bd. dirs. 1982-85), Nat. Assn. State Univs. and Land Grant Colls. (mem. coun. acad. affairs 1987—, exec. com. 1989), Western Social Sci. Assn. (exec. council 1973-76), Phi Kappa Phi, Phi Beta Kappa. Democrat. Roman Catholic. Home: 1409 Snowdrop Pl NE Albuquerque NM 87112 Office: U NMex Scholes Hall 226 Albuquerque NM 87131

GARCIA, HECTOR THOMAS, accountant; b. San Juan Bautista, Calif., Oct. 28, 1926; s. Tomás Jose Garcia y Espinosa and Aurelia María Esparza y Terrazas; m. Leah Adele Mumm, Nov. 3, 1951; children: Thomas R., Carolyn A., Daniel C., Susan L. BS, U. Calif.-Berkeley, 1950; MBA, Santa Clara U., 1966; MS, Golden Gate U., San Francisco, 1978. Cost acct. Bethlehem Steel Corp., South San Francisco, 1951-54; supr. cost acctg. Western Gear Corp., Belmont, Calif., 1954-56; supr. microwave cost acctg. Varian Assos., Palo Alto, Calif., 1956-62; sr. budget analyst Lockheed Missiles & Space Co., Sunnyvale, Calif., 1962-66; supr. auditing Calif. Dept. Finance, Sacramento, 1966-70; chief acct. San Jose State U., 1971-72; prin. acct., Office of Pres., U. Calif., Berkeley, 1972-80; dir. Internal audit U. Calif., Davis, 1980—. Tech. sgt. inf., U.S. Army, 1944-46; PTO, ETO. CPA, Calif. Mem. AICPA, Calif. Soc. CPA's, Inst. Internal Auditors (cert.). Home: 630 Cleveland St Davis CA 95616 Office: U Calif Internal Audit Office Orchard Park Dr Davis CA 95616

GARCIA, MARTI, interior designer; b. Marrakech, French Morocco, Sept. 28, 1942; d. Meyer and Sabine (Corcos) Sabbah; children—Anthony Martin, Mark Othon. B.P.A. cum laude in Interior Design, Woodbury U., L.A., 1965. Interior designer Robinsons, Los Angeles, 1972-74, Bullocks, Santa Ana, 1975-77; prin. Interiors By Marti, Huntington Beach, Calif., 1977-85; sr. adminstr. design and facilities Pacific Mut., Newport Beach, Calif., 1985-89; project designer Reel/Grobman & Assocs., Santa Ana, Calif., 1989—. Recipient Most Outstanding Nat. Corry Hiebert Contract Installation award, Calif. Collaborations of Westweek, 1987/88. Mem. Am. Soc. Interior Designers (dir.). Home: 59 Claret Irvine CA 92714 Office: Reel/Grobman & Assocs 3720 S Susan St Santa Ana CA 92704

GARCIA, NICOLAS ANTONIO, III, radiologist; b. N.Y.C., May 27, 1932; s. Nicolas Antonio Jr. and Rosa Emma (Rodriguez) G.; m. Mary Katherine Evans, July 30, 1955; children: Kimberly, Pamela, Gillian. BA, Johns Hopkins U., 1953; MD, U. Md., 1957. Diplomate Am. Bd. Radiology. Intern, resident in radiology U.S. Naval Hosp., St. Albans, N.Y.; pvt. practice Fresno, Calif., 1965-66; mem. med. staff St. Agnes Med. Ctr., Fresno, 1966—, dir. dept. radiology, 1977—. Contbr. articles to med. jours. Lt. comdr. M.C., USN, 1957-65. Mem. AMA, Radiol. Soc. N.Am., Am. Coll. Radiology, Fresno-Madera Med. Soc., Cen. Valley Radiol. Soc. (pres. 1977). Republican. Roman Catholic. Office: St Agnes Med Ctr 1303 E Herndon Ave Fresno CA 93710

GARCIA-BORRAS, THOMAS, oil company executive; b. Barcelona, Spain, Feb. 2, 1926; came to U.S., 1955, naturalized, 1961; s. Thomas and Teresa (Borras-Jarque) Garcia-Julian; M.S., Nat. U. Mex., 1950; postgrad. Rice U., 1955-56; m. Alia Castellanos Lima, Apr. 30, 1952; children—Erik, Angelica, Laureen, Cliff. Chief chemist Petroleos Mexicanos, Veracruz, Mex., 1950-55; research engr. Monsanto, Texas City, Tex., 1956-60; pilot plant mgr. Cabot and Foster Grant Co., 1960-69; engring. mgr. Signal Chem. Co., Houston, 1969-71; mgmt. and engring. cons., Covina, Calif., 1971-73; project mgr. Occidental Petroleum Co., Irvine, Calif., 1973-79; fleet and indsl. mgr. internat. ops. Wynn Oil Co., Fullerton, Calif., 1979-87; dir. export Sta-Lube, Inc., Rancho Dominguez, Calif., 1987—. Mem. Internat. Mktg. Assn., Am. Inst. Chem. Engrs., Am. Chem. Soc. Author: Manual for Improving Boiler and Furnace Performance, 1983; contbr. articles to profl. jours. Home: 1430 E Adams Park Dr Covina CA 91724 Office: 3039 Ana St Rancho Dominguez CA 90224

GARCIA-BUNUEL, LUIS, neurologist; b. Madrid, Spain, Feb. 24, 1931; s. Pedro Garcia and Concepcion Bunuel; came to U.S., 1956, naturalized, 1965; B.A., Universidad de Zaragoza, 1949, B.S., 1949, M.D., 1955; m. Virginia M. Hile, June 30, 1960. Intern, Universidad De Zaragoza Hosp. Clinico, 1955-56 resident in neurology Georgetown U., Washington, 1956-59; NIH fellow in neurochemistry dept. pharmacology, Washington U., St. Louis, 1959-61; practice medicine specializing in neurology St. Louis, 1959-61; instr. neurology Jefferson Med. Coll., Phila., 1961-64, asst. prof. neurology, 1964-67; asst. prof. neurology U. N.Mex., Albuquerque, 1967-72; chief neurology service VA Hosp. Portland, Oreg., 1972; asso. prof. neurology, U. Oreg. Health Center, 1972-84; chief staff Phoenix VA Med. Ctr., 1984—. Diplomate Am. Bd. Neurology and Psychiatry. Fellow Am. Acad. Neurology; mem. AAAS, Am. Soc. Neurochemistry, Oreg. Neuropsychiat. Soc., Portland Myasthenia Gravis Assn. (med. adv. bd.), Sigma Xi, Phi Kappa Phi. Contbr. articles to profl jours. Office: VA Med Ctr 7th St & Indian School Rd Phoenix AZ 85012

GARDESKI, THOMAS FRANK, chemical research executive, consultant; b. Milw., June 1, 1945; s. Frank Dominic and Joyce Marie (Fedrizzi) G.; m. Carole Ann Champion, June 18, 1966; children: Dawn Marie, Shawn Thomas. BS ChemE, U. N.D., 1964; BS in Chemistry, U. Minn., 1966. Chemist Sheldahl Inc., Northfield, Minn., 1964-67; dir. Sheldahl Inc., Northfield, 1979-84; polymer chemist 3M Co., St. Paul, 1967-69, advanced chemist, 1969-73, sr. chemist, 1973-79; v.p. Gila River Products, Chandler, Ariz., 1984—. Adv. bd., Chemical Week mag.; patentee in field. Fellow Am. Inst. Chemistry; mem. AAAS, Soc. Advancement Materials and Process Engring., Am. Mgmt. Assn., N.Y. Acad. Scis., Am. Taekwondo Assn. Republican. Roman Catholic. Home: 1259 E Louis Way Tempe AZ 85284 Office: Gila River Products 6615 W Boston St Chandler AZ 85226

GARDINER, PETER ALEXANDER JACK, agribusiness executive; b. Edinburgh, Scotland, Nov. 22, 1935; came to U.S., 1976; s. Peter G.W. and Nancy (Aitkin) G.; m. Jill Mackenzie, Sept. 7, 1968; 1 son, Holt. Diploma brewing and indsl. fermentation, Heriot Watt U., Edinburgh, 1956. With Arthur Guinness Son & Co. Ltd., London, 1959-61; project mgr. Caribbean Devel. Corp., Trinidad, 1961; prodn. mgr. Munton & Fison Ltd. Stowmarket, 1962, PE Cons. Group, 1962-67, Unilever Ltd., 1967-70; mng. dir. Atcherley & Co., Liverpool, Eng., 1970-72, Goldwell Ltd., Kent, Eng., 1972-73, Assoc. Brit. Maltsters Ltd., Newark, Eng., 1973-76; pres., chief exec. officer Dalgety, Inc., San Mateo, Calif., 1976—, also bd. dirs.; mem. U.S. adv. com. to Scottish Devel. Agy.; dir. Dalgety PLC, London, 1982—. Mem. adv. coun. Sch. Bus. San Francisco State U. Served as lt. Royal Navy, 1956-59. Mem. World Bus. Forum, World Bus. Coun., Brit.-Am. C. of C. (pres., dir.), World Trade Club, San Francisco Golf Club, Caledonian Club, Oriental Club of U.K., The Family Club. Mem. Ch. of Scotland. Clubs: San Francisco Golf; Caledonian, Oriental (U.K.). Home: PO Box 5919 San Mateo CA 94402 Office: Dalgety Inc 901 Mariner Island Blvd Ste 700 San Mateo CA 94404

GARDIS, GILDA J., quality analyst; b. Jersey City, Jan. 16, 1944; d. William Patrick and Gilda Esther (Weber) Cornett; m. David Richard Gardis, Oct. 8, 1966 (div. 1981). Student, Oceanside-Carlsbad Jr. Coll., Santa Monica City Coll. Prin. typist clk. UCLA, 1966-69, adminstrv. asst., 1969-73, acctg. asst., 1973-75, mgmt. services officer, UCLA, 1975-79; mgmt. services officer U. Calif., San Diego, La Jolla, 1979-85; quality analyst Teledyne Kinetics, Solana Beach, Calif., 1986—; part-time sales rep. Mervyn's, Oceanside, Calif., 1986—. Active Oceanside High Sch. Booster Club, 1980-83. Recipient Tiffany award Manpower, Inc., Carlsbad, Calif., 1985. Mem. Am. Mgmt. Assn. (assoc.), Nat. Assn. Female Execs., Network Exec. Women, Am. Soc. Profl. and Exec. Women, Nat. Assn. Profl. and Exec. Women, Teledyne Kinetics Recreation Assn. (sec. 1987, chairperson 1988). Roman Catholic. Avocations: tennis, bicycling, art, bowling. Home: 3559 Guava Way Oceanside CA 92054 Office: Teledyne Kinetics 410 S Cedros Solana Beach CA 92075 also: PO Box 1401 Oceanside CA 92054

GARDNER, A. BARCLAY, state employment services executive; b. Spanish Fork, Utah, Jan. 25, 1930; s. Archibald Barclay and Virginia (Williams) G.; m. Renee Wilkey, Feb. 16, 1951; children—Kristie Gardner Mikstas, Gregory Barclay, Janeanne Smith. B.S., Brigham Young U., 1954, M.S., 1956. Supr., mgr. Utah Dept. Employment Security, Provo, Vernal, and Salt Lake City, 1954-75, dir. adminstr. svcs., Salt Lake City, 1975-78, adminstr., 1978-86, gov.'s adminstrv. asst., 1986-87, gov.'s exec. asst., 1987-88, gov.'s compaign staff, 1988-89. Pres. Interstate Conf. Employment Security Agencies, 1982-83, bd. dirs., 1979-84. Mem. Utah Job Tng. Coordinating Coun., 1983-86, Utah Gov.'s Coun. Econ. Advisers, 1981-84, Nat. Vets. Planning and Coordinating Com., 1984-86, Utah Commn. on Efficiency and Effectiveness in Govt., 1985-86, Practitioners Task Force Nat. Commn. Employment Policy, 1984-86; bd. dirs. Utah br. Nat. Alliance Bus., 1979-80. With U.S. Army, 1950-52, Korea. Mem. Am. Legion. Mormon. Home: 2805 Marcus Rd Salt Lake City UT 84119 Office: 6290 State Office Bldg Salt Lake City UT 84114

GARDNER, AUTREY THADDEUS, JR., industrial technology educator; b. Scottsboro, Ala., Aug. 5, 1939; s. Autrey Thaddeus and Faye Louise (Kennamer) G.; m. Joyce Elva Keel; children: Tracey Anne, Autrey Thaddeus III. BSBA, U. Ala., 1962; postgrad., U. N.D., 1967-70; MA in Communications, U. No. Colo., 1983; postgrad., U. Wy., 1987—. Commd. 2d lt. USAF, Amarillo AFB, Tex., 1962; advanced through grades to major USAF, various locations, 1972; chief of plans 351st Strategic Missile Wing, Whiteman AFB, Mo., 1973-74, supr. maintenance, 1974-76; maintenance staff officer 3901st Strategic Missile Squadron, Vandenberg AFB, Calif., 1976-80; dir. tng. 90th Strategic Missile Wing, F.E. Warren AFB, Wyo., 1980-83; ret. USAF, 1983; asst. prof. So. Ill. U., F.E. Warren AFB, Wyo., 1983—, faculty rep., 1983—. Contbr. articles to profl. jours. Mem. Nat. Assn. Indsl. Technologists, Inst. Indsl. Engrs., Am. Soc. Safety Engrs., Speech Communications Assn., Western Speech Assn., Air Force Assn., Ret. Officers Assn., Phi Kappa Phi (honor soc.). Republican. Mem. Ch. Christ. Clubs: Warren AFB Officers (bd. dirs. 1982-83), Rocky Mountain Health. Home: 3300 Carey Ave Cheyenne WY 82001 Office: So Ill U 90 CSG/DPE F E Warren AFB WY 82005

GARDNER, BOOTH, governor of Washington; b. Tacoma, Aug. 21, 1936; m. Jean Gardner; children—Doug, Gail. B.A. in Bus., U. Wash., 1958; M.B.A., Harvard U., 1963. Asst. to dean Sch. Bus. Adminstrn., Harvard U., Cambridge, Mass., 1966; dir. Sch. Bus. and Econs., U. Puget Sound, Tacoma, 1967-72; pres. Laird Norton County, 1972-80; mem. Wash. Senate, 1970-73; county exec. Pierce County, Tacoma, 1981-84; gov. State of Wash., 1985-89, 89—. Co-founder Central Area Youth Assn. Seattle; trustee U. Puget Sound. Office: Office of Gov Legislature Bldg AS-13 Olympia WA 98504

GARDNER, DAVID PIERPONT, university president; b. Berkeley, Calif., Mar. 24, 1933; s. Reed S. and Margaret (Pierpont) G.; m. Elizabeth Fuhriman, June 27, 1958; children: Karen, Shari, Lisa, Marci. BS, Brigham Young U., 1955, DH (hon.), 1981; MA, U. Calif., Berkeley, 1959, PhD, 1966; DLitt (hon.), U. Utah, 1983; LLD (hon.), U. of the Pacific, 1983, U. Nev., Las Vegas, 1984, Westminster Coll., 1987; HHD (hon.), Utah State U., 1987; Docteur Honoris Causa, de l' Universite de Bordeaux, 1988. Dir. Calif. Alumni Found., U. Calif. at Berkeley, 1962-64; asst. to the chancellor, asst. prof. higher edn. U. Calif. at Santa Barbara, 1964-67, asst. chancellor, asst. prof. higher edn., 1967-69, vice chancellor, exec. asst., assoc. prof. higher edn., 1969-70; v.p. U. Calif. System, Berkeley, 1971-73, pres., 1983—; prof. higher edn. U. Calif., Berkeley, 1983—; pres., prof. higher edn. U. Utah, Salt Lake City, 1973-83, pres. emeritus, 1985; vis. fellow Clare Hall, Cambridge U., 1979, assoc., 1979—. Author: The California Oath Controversy, 1967; mem. editorial bd. Higher Edn. Quarterly; contbr. articles to profl. jours. Bd. dirs. First Security Corp., Fluor Corp., George S. and Dolores Dore Eccles Found., The Nature Conservancy, Calif. C. of C., Calif. Econ. Devel. Corp.; trustee Tanner Lectures on Human Values; chmn. Southwestern Dist. Rhodes Scholarship Selection Com.; mem. Hong Kong U. Sci. and Tech. Coun. Decorated Legion d'Honneur (France), 1985; recipient Benjamin P. Cheney medal East Wash. U., 1984, James Bryant Conant award Edn. Commn. of the States, 1985, Calif. Sch. Bds. Rsch. Found. Hall of Fame award, 1988; 40th Anniversary Disting. Fellow, Fulbright Found., 1987. Fellow Am. Acad. Arts and Scis.; mem. Nat. Assn. State Univs. and Land Grant Colls., Nat. Acad. Pub. Adminstrn., Assn. Am. Univs., Higher Edn. Forum (mem. exec. com. bus.), Phi Beta Kappa (hon.), Phi Kappa Phi (hon.). Home: 70 Rincon Rd Kensington CA 94707 Office: U Calif Office of Pres 300 Lakeside Dr Oakland CA 94612-3550

GARDNER, DAVID ROBERT, architect; b. Macon, Ga., Jan. 13, 1954; s. Robert Granville and Sara Anne (Fargason) G.; m. Judy Kemp, June 27, 1987. BS, Ga. Tech., 1975, M in Architecture, 1977. Reg. architect, Ga., Calif. Health lab. design cons. Ctrs. for Disease Control, Atlanta, 1976-77; apprentice architect Thompson, Ventulett, Stainback Architects, Atlanta, 1977-81; pvt. practice Atlanta, 1981-86; project architect Gerson/Overstreet Architects, San Francisco, 1986—; lectr. Ctrs. for Disease Control, Atlanta, 1978, Ga. State U., Atlanta, 1978-79. Chmn. art auction facilities com. Atlanta Arts Festival, 1985. Democrat. Office: Gerson/Overstreet Architects 57 Post St Ste 804 San Francisco CA 94104

GARDNER, DUNCAN PHILIP KENNETH, data processing executive; b. Encino, Calif., Dec. 22, 1955; s. Derek Frank and Helen Marion (Ransom) G.; m. Susan Georgina Ward, Aug. 20, 1977; children: Helen Louise, Thomas Derek Paul. AS in Chemistry, Redrice, U.K., 1974; BS in Computer Sci., Nat. U., Sacramento, 1987. Lab. adminstrv. supr. Acurex Corp., Mountain View, Calif., 1978-80; research engr. Exxon Corp., Sunnyvale, Calif., 1980-84; sr. programmer analyst Teledyne/MEC, Rancho Cordova, Calif., 1984-88; sr. scientific programmer Lockheed Missles & Space Co., Sunnyvale, Calif., 1988—; cons. Hetherington Inc., Goleta, Calif., 1982-84, Source Tech. Corp., Los Gatos, Calif., 1982-84, TLI, Hayward, Calif., 1984; system mgr. River City Delirium Bull. Bd. System, Orangevale, Calif., 1987. Mem. C Users Group, Nat. Geographic Soc., Smithsonian Instn. Democrat. Office: Lockheed Middles & Space Co PO Box 504 Sunnyvale CA 94086

GARDNER, E. MARIE, court clerk; b. Colorado Spring, Colo., Mar. 26, 1930; d. Edgar Gilman and Evelyn Mayme (Gasaway) Bevens; m. Robert R. Gardner, Feb. 9, 1950; children: Carol L. Gardner Sperlik, Russell W., Reggie B., Connie M. Gardner Condie. BS in Behavioral Sci., U. Southern Colo., 1975; fellow, Inst. Ct. Mgmt. Dep. clk. El Paso County Dist. Ct., Colorado Springs, Colo., 1966-70; chief dep. clk. El Paso County Dist. Ct., 1970-75, clk. to dist. ct., 1976—. Adv. bd. child support enforcement Nat. Ctr. for State Cts and Inst., Denver, 1986-88; mem. com. Colo. Judicial Dept. and Dept. Social Svcs., 1977—. Mem. Legal Secs. Assn. (pres. 1981-82), Colo. Trial Ct. Adminstrs. (pres. 1980-81), nat. Assn. Trial Ct. Adminstrs. (treas., sec., v.p. 1982-85), Colo. Springs Choral Soc. (chmn. bd. 1960's, 1979-80), Nat. Assn. Ct. Mgrs. (past officer), Colo. Assn. ct. Employees, Nat. Ctr. State Cts.; fellow Inst. Ct. Mgmt. Republican. Methodist. Home: 4605 Brady Rd Colorado Springs CO 80915 Office: El Paso County Dist Ct 20 E Vermijo St Colorado Springs CO 80903

GARDNER, EDWARD ARTHUR, home health care executive; b. Los Angeles, Sept. 22, 1953; s. Leonard Eugene and Anita Shirley (Barkin) G. AA in Nursing, Golden West Community Coll., 1976; BS in Human Svcs., Calif. State U., Fullerton, 1981. RN, Calif.; community coll. tchr., Calif. Staff nurse Tustin Community Hosp., Riverside, Calif., 1974-78; drug abuse nurse specialist Orange County, Riverside, 1978-81; nurse St. Joseph Hosp., Riverside, 1978-81; coord. discharge planning, field nurse Visiting Nurse Assn.-Orange County, Riverside, 1981-85; supr. discharge planning and utilization rev. Fountain Valley Regional Hosp., Riverside, 1985-87; dir. profl. svcs., adminstr. Total Home Health Care Loma Linda, Riverside, 1987-88; owner, pres. Home Care Network, Riverside, Calif., 1988—. Mem. profl. adv. bd. Riverside County Pvt. Industry Coun., 1989; bd. dirs. Riverside chpt., Am. Heart Assn. Mem. Calif. Assn. Health Svcs. Home (pub. relations com.), Inland Home Care Council, Nat. Assn. Home Care, Riverside C. of C. Republican. Jewish. Home: 12279 Heritage Dr Moreno Valley CA 92387 Office: Home Care Network 4009 Brockton Ave Riverside CA 92501

GARDNER, ERIC, film and television producer, entertainment personal manager; b. Tampa, Fla., Nov. 20, 1949; s. Ray and Claire (Citrin) G.; m. Janis Gardner, Sept. 12, 1981. BA, Rollins Coll., Winter Park, Fla., 1970; MFA, Columbia U., 1972. Pres., chief exec. officer Panacea Entertainment Mgmt., L.A., 1972—. Recipient Shubert award for playwriting, Shubert Found., 1971. Office: Panacea Entertainment 2705 Glendower Ave Los Angeles CA 90027

GARDNER, EVELYN AMEL, realtor; b. Jerusalem, Palestine, July 31, 1943; came to U.S., 1951, naturalized, 1957; d. Jerry S. and Adele (Nasrawi Assad; (div.); children: Troy Kevin Spears, Kenneth Eric Gardner. Grad., high sch., Modesto, Calif.; Student, U. Calif, Berkeley, San Diego State U. Legal sec. LaCoste, Keller, Reid, Azevedo and Rose, Modesto, 1967-75, LaForce and Dunn, Modesto, 1977-75; adminstrv. sec. The Modesto Bee, 1975-77; free-lance legal sec. Modesto, 1985-87; realtor Matel Realtors, 1987-88, Paul M. Zagaris Inc., 1988—. Mem. Calif. Assn. Realtors, Modesto Bd. Realtors. Home: 3617 Val Verde Ln Modesto CA 95356 Office: Paul M Zagaris Inc 1230 E Orangeburg Ave Modesto CA 95350

GARDNER, FREDERICK BOYCE, library director; b. Hopkinsville, Ky., Mar. 12, 1942; s. Boyce and Alleen Louise (Brown) G. BA, U. Ky., 1964; MA, Ind. U., Bloomington, 1966. Head librarian U. Ky. Hopkinsville Community Coll., Hopkinsville, 1966-69; head, readers service CUNY, Manhattan Community Coll., N.Y.C., 1969-71; reference librarian Calif. Inst. of the Arts, Valencia, Calif., 1971-74; head, pub. svcs. Calif. Inst. of the Arts, Valencia, 1974-87, dir. computer svcs., 1984-87, acting dir., 1987-88, dean of the library, 1988—; del. Calif. Conf. on Networking, Pomona, Calif., 1985. Sec. Sequoia String Quartet Found., L.A., 1977-87. Capt. USAF, 1968-69. Mem. ALA, Santa Clarita Interlibrary Network (pres. 1989—), Calif. Pvt. Acad. Libraries (exec. bd. 1988-90), Total Interlibrary Exchange (v.p. 1980-81, pres. 1981-82, chmn. 1983-86, cons. 1983-85), Calif. Library Assn. Office: Calif Inst of the Arts 24700 McBean Pkwy Valencia CA 91355

GARDNER, JAMES ELDEN, lumber company executive; b. Mesa, Ariz., Oct. 11, 1922; s. Lucius Levier and Winnie Estelle (Le Baron) G.; m. Ellen Christin Henry Gardner; children: James E. Jr., Douglas K., Christene E., Sharon E., Michael H., Stephen D., David L., Irene S. Grad., high sch., Mesa. Supr. Lockheed Aircraft, Burbank, Calif., 1940-41; shift foreman Goodyear Aircraft, Avondale, Ariz., 1941-45; mgr. Capital Auto Supply, Mesa, 1945-47; owner Jim Gardner Contractor, Mesa, 1947—, Mesa Lumber & Supply, 1953-72; pres., chmn. Mesa Lumber & Supply, Inc., 1972-86, chmn. bd., 1986—; ptnr. Gardner Investment & Devel., Mesa, 1976—, Ind. Investments, Mesa, 1982—; dir. Camp LoMia, Pine, Ariz., 1981—, A Basket of Flowers, Inc., Tempe, Ariz., 1974—. Appeals bd. mem. City Mesa, 1984-85. Mem. Sertoma Club (pres. 1954). Republican. Mormon. Home: 520 N Emerson St Mesa AZ 85201 Office: Mesa Lumber & Supply Inc 320 S Alma School Rd Mesa AZ 85210

GARDNER, JOEDY EARL, real estate corporation officer, educator; b. Ellwood City, Pa., June 23, 1935; s. Joseph Henry and Alberta Elizabeth (Allison) G.; m. Ruth Ann Ash, Sept. 12, 1958; children: Deborah Sue, Joedy Paul, Tamlynn Ann Villiapondo Gardener. B, W.Va. U., 1959; M, Ariz. State U., 1972. Lic. realtor, Ariz.; cert. real estate appraiser. Commd. 2nd lt. USMC, 1958, advanced through ranks to major, 1967, various pilot, Blue Angel assignments, 1958-69; asst. to head basketball coach, edn. dept. Ariz. Western Coll., 1969-74; head basketball coach, prof. physical edn. W.Va. U., 1974-78; head basketball coach No. Ariz. U., 1978-81; asst. basketball coach U. Iowa, 1983-85; head basketball coach Murray Intrnat., United Kingdom, 1985-88; pres., owner Top-Line Appraisal Svcs., Tempe, Ariz., 1988—; with Television Basketball Commentary, PAC-10, Tempe, 1982-83. Named NJCAA Coach of Yr., 1974, Big-Sky coach of Yr., 1979, Coach of Yr./Champs of Great Britain, 1988. Mem. Optimist Club, Nat. Assn. Basketball Coaches. Republican. Methodist/Presbyterian. Home: 7807 S Heather Dr Tempe AZ 85284

GARDNER, LEONARD BURTON, II, industrial automation engineer; b. Lansing, Mich., Feb. 16, 1927; s. Leonard Burton and Lillian Marvin (Frost) G.; m. Barbara Jean Zivi, June 23, 1950; children: Karen Sue, Jeffrey Frank. B.Sc. in Physics, UCLA, 1951; M.Sc., Golden State U., 1953, Sc.D. in Engring., 1954; M.Sc. in Computer Sci, Augustana Coll., Rock Island, Ill., 1977. Registered profl. engr.; cert. mfg. engr. Instrumentation engr. govt. and pvt. industry 1951—; prin. engr. computerized systems Naval Electronic Systems Engring. Center, San Diego, 1980-82; founder, dir. Automated Integrated Mfg., San Diego, 1982—; prof. and dir. Center for Automated Integrated Mfg.; cons. govt. agys. and industry, lectr., adj. prof. vaious univs. and colls., sci. advisor state and nat. legislators, 1980—, speaker in field. Author: Computer Aided Robotics Center; editor: Automated Manufacturing. Contbg. author: Instrumentation Handbook, 1981; contbr. numerous articles to tech. jours. Recipient award U.S. Army. Fellow IEEE; sr. mem. Soc. Mfg. Engrs. (Pres.'s award 1984); mem. ASTM, Nat. Soc. Profl. Engrs., Calif. Soc. Profl. Engrs., Sigma Xi. Office: PO Box 1523 Spring Valley CA 92077

GARDNER, MARJORIE HYER, science administrator; b. Logan, Utah, Apr. 25, 1923; d. Saul Edward and Gladys Ledingham (Christiansen) Hyer; B.S., Utah State U., 1946, Ph.D. (hon.), 1975; M.A., Ohio State U., 1958, Ph.D., 1960; cert. Ednl. Mgmt. Inst., Harvard U., 1975; m. Paul Leon Gardner, June 6, 1947; children—Pamela Jean, Mary Elizabeth. Tchr. sci., journalism and English high schs., Utah, Nev., Ohio, 1947-56; instr. Ohio State U., Columbus, 1957-60; asst. exec. dir. Nat. Sci. Tchrs. Assn., 1961-64; vis. prof. Australia, India, Yugoslavia, Nigeria, Thailand, Peoples Republic of China, 1965-82; assoc. dean, dir. Bur. Ednl. Research and Field Service, College Park, Md., 1975-76; dir. Sci. Teaching Center, U. Md., College Park, 1976-77, prof. chemistry, 1964-84; dir. Lawrence Hall Sci., U. Calif.-Berkeley, 1984—; div. dir. NSF, 1979-81; cons. UNESCO, 1970—; NSF grantee, 1964—; recipient Catalyst medal Chem. Mfrs. Assn., 1980, Nyholm medal Royal Soc. Can., 1987, U.S.U. Centennial award, 1987, ACS Chemical Edn. award, 1988. Fellow AAAS (council), Am. Inst. Chemistry; mem. Am. Chem. Soc., Chemistry Assn. Md. (pres.), Internat. Union of Pure and Applied Chemistry (exec. com.), Internat. Orgn. Chemistry in Devel. (edn. panel), Assn. Edn. of Tchrs. of Sci., Nat. Assn. Research in Sci. Teaching, Nat. Sci. Tchrs. Assn., Am. Assn. Higher Edn., Soc. Coll. Sci. Tchrs. (pres.), Fulbright Alumni Assn. (pres., dir.), Phi Delta Kappa, Phi Kappa Phi. Author: Chemistry in the Space Age, 1965; editor: Theory in Action, 1964, Vistas of Sci. Series, 1961-63; Investigating the Earth, 1968, Interdisciplinary Approaches to Chemistry, 1973, 1978-79; Under Roof, Dome and Sky, 1974, Toward Continuous Professional Development: Designs and Directions, 1976; contbr. articles in on chemistry and sci. edn. to profl. jours. Home: 517 Vista Height Rd Richmond CA 94805 Office: U Calif Lawrence Hall Sci Centennial Dr Berkeley CA 94720

GARDNER, NORD ARLING, management consultant; b. Afton, Wyo., Aug. 10, 1923; s. Arling A. and Ruth (Lee) G.; BA, U. Wyo., 1945; MS, Calif. State U., Hayward, 1972, MPA, 1975; postgrad. U. Chgo., U. Mich., U. Calif.-Berkeley; m. Thora Marie Stephen, Mar. 24, 1945; children—Randall Nord, Scott Stephen, Craig Robert, Laurie Lee. Commd. 2d lt. U.S. Army, 1945, advanced through grades to lt. col., 1964; ret., 1966; personnel analyst Univ. Hosp., U. Calif.-San Diego, 1966-68; coordinator manpower devel. U. Calif.-Berkeley, 1968-75; univ. tng. officer San Francisco State U., 1975-80, personnel mgr., 1976-80; exec. dir. CRDC Maintenance Tng. Corp., non-profit community effort, San Francisco, 1980-85; pres., dir. Sandor Assos. Mgmt. Cons., Pleasant Hill, Calif., 1974-86; gen. mgr. Vericlean Janitorial Service, Inc.; in-charge bus. devel. East Bay Local Devel. Corp., Oakland, Calif., 1980-85; incorporator and pres. Indochinese Community Enterprises, USA, Ltd., Pleasant Hill, Calif., 1985-87; freelance writer, grantsmanship cons., 1987—; ptnr. Oi Kit Bldg. Maint. Svc., 1988—; cons. Phimmasone Internat. Import-Export, Richmond, Calif., Lao Lanx-Xang Assn., Oakland Refugee Assn., 1988—; instr. Japanese, psychology, supervisory courses, 1977-78. Adv. council San Francisco Community Coll. Dist. Decorated Army Commendation medal. Mem. Ret. Officers Assn., Am. Soc. Tng. and Devel., No. Calif. Human Resources Council. Am. Assn. Univ. Adminstrs., Internat. Personnel Mgrs. Assn., Internat. Platform Assn., Coll. and Univ. Personnel Assn. Republican. Clubs: Commonwealth of Calif., U. Calif.-Berkeley Faculty, Univ. (San Francisco). Author: To Gather Stones, 1978. Home and Office: 2995 Bonnie Ln Pleasant Hill CA 94523

GARDNER, SUSAN MARIE, foundation administrator; b. Mpls., Dec. 2, 1955; d. George James and Janice Marie (Erickson) G. BS cum laude, Harvard U., 1987. Founder, then mgr. non-profit food distbn. svc. Plaza Coop., San Diego, 1978-79; researcher, survey designer Calif. Coop. Law Revision, San Diego, 1982-84; founder, mag. editor Appaloosa Sport Horse Assn., Cambridge, Mass., 1986-87; founder, mgr. High Meadows Retreat for Environmentally Ill, Steamboat Springs, Colo., 1988—; cons., Packaging, Inc., Minnetonka, Minn., 1986-88. Vol., Oxfam Am., Boston, 1985; bd. dirs., v.p. adminstrn. The Janice Gardner Found., 1987—. Democrat.

GARDNER, THOMAS MICHAEL, county official, educator, consultant; b. Salinas, Calif., Mar. 11, 1952; s. John Howard and Alice (Von Christierson) G.; m. Lee S. Stewart, June 25, 1977; 1 child, Steward Logan. BA, U. Calif., Berkeley, 1977; M. Pub. Adminstrn., San Jose State U., 1979; postgrad., U. So. Calif. Planning commr. City of Hollister, Calif., 1977-79; adminstrn. analyst County of Fresno, Calif., 1979-86, asst. budget dir., 1984-86; asst. county adminstr. Yolo County, Woodland, Calif., 1987—; Advisor State Controller's Adv. Com., Sacramento, 1987-88; lectr. San Jose State U., 1983-87; cons. County Suprs. Assn. Calif. 1986-87. Designer fin. data base for Calif. counties containing more than 52,000 records. Commr. Hist. Landmark Comm., Fresno, Calif., 1980-84. With USN, 1970-73. Mem. Am. Soc. Pub. Adminstrs. (sec. Fresno chpt. 1984). Home: 1301 Columbia Dr Woodland CA 95695

GARDNER, WILFORD ROBERT, physicist, educator; b. Logan, Utah, Oct. 19, 1925; s. Robert and Nellie (Barker) G.; m. Marjorie Louise Cole, June 9, 1949; children: Patricia, Robert, Caroline. B.S., Utah State U., 1949; M.S., Iowa State U., 1951, Ph.D., 1953. Physicist U.S. Salinity Lab., Riverside, Calif., 1953-66; prof. U. Wis., Madison, 1966-80; physicist, prof., head dept. soil and water sci. U. Ariz., Tucson, 1980-87; dean coll. natural resources U. Calif., Berkeley, 1987—. Author: Soil Physics, 1972. Served with U.S. Army, 1943-46. NSF sr. fellow, 1959; Fulbright fellow, 1971-72; Soil Sci. Soc. Am. Research awardee, 1962. Fellow AAAS, Am. Soc. Agronomy; mem. Internat. Soil Sci. Soc. (pres. physics commn. 1968-74), Nat. Acad. Scis. Office: U Calif Coll Natural Resources Berkeley CA 94720

GARDNER-MAYFIELD, CINDÉ KAE, advertising agency executive; b. Portland, Oreg., Mar. 27, 1962; d. Terry Newman and Judith Wilma (Neil) Gardner; m. Charles Keith Mayfield, July 7, 1979 (div. Aug. 1984); 1 child, Justin Keith. Student, Pub. schs., Spanaway, Wash. Sec. Spanaway Multi-Service Ctr., 1979-80; Janitor Am. Bldg., Tacoma, 1983-85; account exec. Sea Tac Foods, Tacoma, 1985-86, Regional Telephone Directories, Tacoma, 1986, TV Facts, Tacoma, 1987--; owner, mgr. Gardner/Hicks Agy., Tacoma, 1988, Cinde's TV Mag., Inc., Kent, Wash., 1988--. Mem. Bonney Lake Profl. Women's Assn., Tacoma Jaycees (past bd. dirs. and v.p. individual devel. Jaycee of Month of Yr. award 1987, Outstanding Officer of Yr. award 1987). Republican. Home: 11044 SE 252nd Pl CC-303 Kent WA 98031

GAREY, DONALD LEE, oil company executive; b. Ft. Worth, Sept. 9, 1931; s. Leo James and Jessie (McNatt) G.; BS in Geol. Engring., Tex. A&M U., 1953; m. Elizabeth Patricia Martin, Aug. 1, 1953; children: Deborah Anne, Elizabeth Laird. Reservoir geologist Gulf Oil Corp., 1953-54, sr. geologist, 1956-65; v.p., mng. dir. Indsl. Devel. Corp. Lea County, Hobbs, N.Mex., 1965-72, dir., 1972-86, pres., 1978-86; v.p., dir. Minerals, Inc., Hobbs, 1966-72, pres., dir., 1972-86, chief exec. officer, 1978-82; mng. dir. Hobbs Indsl. Found. Corp., 1965-72, dir., 1965-76; v.p. Llano, Inc., 1972-74, exec. v.p., chief operating officer, 1974-75, pres., 1975-86, chief exec. officer, 1978-82, also dir.; pres., chief exec. officer, Pollution Control, Inc., 1969-81; pres. NMESCO Fuels, Inc., 1982-86; chmn., pres., chief exec. officer Estacado Inc., 1986—; pres. Llano Co2, Inc., 1984-86; cons. geologist, geol. engr., Hobbs, 1965-72. Chmn., Hobbs Manpower Devel. Tng. Adv. Com., 1965-72; mem. Hobbs Adv. Com. for Mental Health, 1965-67; chmn. N.Mex. Mapping Adv. Com., 1968-69; mem. Hobbs adv. bd. Salvation Army, 1967-78, chmn., 1970-72; mem. exec. bd. Conquistador coun. Boy Scouts Am., Hobbs, 1965-75; vice chmn. N.Mex. Gov.'s Com. for Econ. Devel., 1968-70; bd. regents Coll. Southwest, 1982-85. Capt. USAF, 1954-56. Registered profl. engr., Tex. Mem. Am. Inst. Profl. Geologists, Am. Assn. Petroleum Geologists, AIME, N.Mex. Geol. Soc., Roswell Geol. Soc., N.Mex. Amigos Club, Rotary. Home: 315 E Alto Dr Hobbs NM 88240 Office: Broadmoor Bldg PO Box 5587 Hobbs NM 88241

GAREY, H. DEXTER, real estate consultant; b. Lewiston, Mont., July 13, 1932; s. John Hubert and Letha (Gladys) G.; m. Beatrice Ann Marriott, Dec. 27, 1956 (div. 1983); children: Kevin Mark, Timothy David. BS, Oreg. State U., 1960; MBA, Pepperdine U., 1974. Real estate mgr. Shell Oil Co., Seattle, 1960-70; sr. v.p. Hillman Properties Northwest, Portland, Oreg., 1970-88; pres. Dex. Ltd., Portland, 1988—; bd. dirs. Columbia Corridor Assn., Portland, Jubitz Truck Stops, Portland; supv. Peninsula Drainage Dist., Portland, 1982-88. Trustee, Oreg. State U. Found., Corvallis, 1984, Multnomah Athletic Club, Portland; bd. dirs. City of Portland Task Force, 1986; pres. Clark County Community Found, Vancouver, Wash., 1984. With USAF, 1952-56, Korea. Mem. Am. Arbitration Assn. Republican. Episcopalian. Home: 2300 SE Balboa Dr Vancouver WA 98684

GARFIELD, ERNEST, bank consultant; b. Colorado River, Ariz., July 14, 1932; s. Emil and Carmen (Ybarra) G.; m. Betty Ann Redden, Apr. 18, 1953; children: Laural, Jeffery Alan. BS, U. Ariz., 1975; B of Internat. Mgmt., Am. Grad. Sch., Phoenix, 1975, M of Internat. Mgmt., 1976. Owner Garfield Ins. Agy., Tucson, 1962-70; senator State of Ariz., Phoenix, 1967-68, dep. treas., 1970-71, treas., 1971-74; commr. Ariz. Corp. Commn., Phoenix, 1974-79; chmn. Allied Bancorp, Inc., Phoenix, 1979—; chmn. The White House Conf. on Energy, Com. on Energy Policy of Nat. Assn. Regulatory Utility Commn.; pres. Western Conf. Pub. Svc. Commns.; mem. Ad Hoc Com. on Regulatory Reform, Electric and Nuclear Energy Com. Mem. Ariz. Kidney Found., Ariz. Mexican C. of C., Multiple Sclerosis Soc., Rep. Senatorial Inner Circle, 1989, Pres. Bush Task Force, 1989; adv. bd. mem. St. Joseph's Hosp., Phoenix; mem. Establishment Com. of Pima County JHr. Coll., Tucson, Orgn. Com. of Pima County Halfway House, Tucson. Recipient Outstanding Young Men Ariz. award, Press Club award. Republican. Roman Catholic. Home: 8426 N 32nd Ave Phoenix AZ 85051 Office: Allied Bancorp Inc 555 W University Mesa AZ 85201

GARGAN, THOMAS JOSEPH, plastic surgeon; b. Denver, Sept. 28, 1952; s. Thomas Joseph and Maria Augusta (Casagranda) G.; m. Nancy Lee Hall, Jan. 20, 1979; children: Daniel Thomas, John William. BA summa cum laude, Colo. Coll., 1974; MD, U. Colo., 1978. Diplomate Am. Bd. Plastic Surgery. Intern Presbyn. Med. Ctr., Denver, 1978-79, resident in surgery, 1978-79; resident in surgery Beth Israel Hosp., Boston, 1979-81, instr. gen. surgery, 1979-82, sr. resident in surgery, 1981-82, chief resident in plastic surgery, 1983-84; sr. resident in plastic surgery Cambridge (Mass.) City Hosp., 1982-83; resident in plastic surgery Children's Hosp. and Brigham and Women's Hosp., Boston, 1983, Newton-Wellesley Hosp., Mass., 1983; clin. fellow in surgery Harvard U. Med. Sch., Boston, 1979-84; clin. instr. plastic surgery U. Colo. Sch. Med., Denver, 1984; chief plastic surgery div. Rose Med. Ctr., 1987—; instr. plastic surgery Cambridge Hosp., Children's Hosp., and Beth Israel Hosp., Boston, 1982-84, Harvard Med. Sch., Boston, 1984. Contbr. articles to profl. jours. Bd. dirs. Rocky Mt. Adoption Exchange. Recipient George B. Packard award for excellence in surgery U. Colo. Med. Ctr., 1978; Eagle Scout; Barnes Chemistry scholar Colo. Coll. Fellow ACS; mem. AMA, Denver Med. Soc. (Pres. Gold Star award), Colo. Med. Soc., Am. Soc. Plastic and Reconstructive Surgeons, Colo. State Soc. Plastic and Reconstructive Surgeons, Rocky Mountain Hand Surgery Soc., Rocky Mountain Soc. of Reconstructive Plastic Surgeons. Lodge: Ancient Order Hibernians in Am. Home: 10 Blackmer Rd Englewood CO 80110 Office: 4545 E 9th Ave Denver CO 80220

GARGUILO, JOSEPH CHRISTOPHER, communications executive; b. Bklyn., June 23, 1952; s. Joseph Patrick and Kathleen (Armstrong) G.; m. Jean Mangin (dec. May 1982); m. Karrie Skonier, Aug. 23, 1986. BA in Econs. cum laude, SUNY, New Paltz, 1974; degee in TV prodn., Colo. State U., 1976. Tchr. speech, film criticism Colo. State U., Ft. Collins, 1974-76; owner, mgr. Frontier Fence Co., Boulder, Colo., 1976-81; mgr. facilities Visual Communications Group, Boulder, 1985-86; ptnr., mgr., cons. Media, Inc., Ft. Collins, 1979—; chief fin. officer, corp. sec. New West Tech., Boulder, 1983-84. Scriptwriter TV and radio commls., med. and indsl. tng. videos, 1979—; editor, pub. R.M.F.A. Newsletter, 1988—; contbr. articles to profl. jours. Cons. Office City Mgr., Ft. Collins, 1981. Mem. Nat. Assn. Broadcasters, Internat. TV Assn., Internat. Platform Assn., Rocky Mountain Fabricare Assn. (bd. dirs. 1988—), BMW Car Club. Democrat. Roman Catholic. Home and Office: Media Svcs 2612 Blue Mountain Ave Berthoud CO 80513

GARLAND, ROBERT LEE, educator, writer; b. Chgo., Feb. 26, 1932. BA, UCLA, 1953; MA, Calif. State U., 1962; postgrad., U. Calif., Berkeley, Nat. U. Mex., Mexico City, Stanford U., Singapore U., U. N.C., Charlotte. Educator L.A. Sch. Dist., 1957—; mem. various coms. Los Angeles Schs., 1970—. Contbr. articles on travel and edn. to jours. Served with U.S. Army, 1955-57. Nat. Def. Edn. Act scholar U.S. Govt., 1966, Fulbright scholar, U.S. Govt., 1967, Freedoms Found. scholar, 1982, 86; Robert Taft fellow, 1977, 81, 86, 88. Mem. NEA, Nat. Council Social Studies (com. chmn. 1980—), Fulbright Alumni Assn., Navy League of U.S., Steamship Hist. Soc., Am. Film Inst., Naval Inst., Big Band Soc. Am., Calif. Hist. Soc. Club: Travelers Century. Office: Los Angeles Unified Sch Dist 13000 Oxnard St Van Nuys CA 91401

GARLOUGH, WILLIAM GLENN, marketing executive; b. Syracuse, N.Y., Mar. 27, 1924; s. Henry James and Gladys (Killam) G.; m. Charlotte M. Tanzer, June 15, 1947; children: Jennifer, William, Robert. BEE, Clarkson U., 1949. With Knowlton Bros., Watertown, N.Y., 1949-67, mgr. mfg. services, 1966-67; v.p. planning, equipment systems div. Vare Corp., Englewood Cliffs, N.J., 1967-69; mgr. mktg. Valley Mould div. Microdot Inc., Hubbard, Ohio, 1969-70; dir. corp. devel. Microdot Inc., Greenwich, Conn., 1970-73, v.p. corp. devel., 1973-76, v.p. adminstrn., 1976-77, v.p. corp. devel., 1977-78; v.p. corp. devel. Am. Bldg. Maintenance Industries, San Francisco, 1979-83; pres. The Change Agts., Inc., Walnut Creek, Calif., 1983—; bd. dirs. Gourmet To Go Inc.; mem. citizens adv. com. to Watertown Bd. Edn., 1957. Bd. dirs. Watertown Community Chest, 1958-61; ruling elder Presbyn. ch. Served with USMCR, 1942-46. Mem. Am. Mgmt. Assn., Bldg. Service Contractors Assn., Internat. Sanitary Supply Assn., Mensa, Am. Mktg. Assn., TAPPI, Assn. Corp. Growth (pres. San Francisco chpt. 1984-85, v.p. chpts. west 1985-88), Lincoln League (pres. 1958), Am. Contract Bridge League (life master), Clarkson Alumni Assn. (Watertown sect. pres. 1955), Tau Beta Pi. Clubs: Olympic; No. N.Y. Contract (pres. 1959), No. N.Y. Transp. Home: 2557 Via Verde Walnut Creek CA 94598 Office: The Change Agts Inc 1990 N California Blvd Walnut Creek CA 94596

GARN, EDWIN JACOB (JAKE GARN), senator; b. Richfield, Utah, Oct. 12, 1932; s. Jacob Edwin and Fern (Christensen) G.; m. Hazel Rhae Thompson, Feb. 2, 1957 (dec. 1976); children: Jacob Wayne, Susan Rhae, Ellen Marie, Jeffrey Paul; m. Kathleen Brewerton, Apr. 8, 1977; children: Matthew Spencer, Christopher Brook, Jennifer Kathleen. B.S., U. Utah, 1955. Spl. agt. John Hancock Mut. Life Ins. Co., Salt Lake City, 1960-61; asst. mgr. Home Life Ins. Co. N.Y., Salt Lake City, 1961-66; gen. agt. Mut. Trust Life Ins. Co., Salt Lake City, 1966-68; city commr. Salt Lake City, 1968-72, mayor, 1972-74; dir. Met. Water Dist., 1968-72; mem. U.S. Senate from Utah, 1974—. Chmn. joint bd. commrs. Salt Lake Model Cities Agy., 1973—; Bd. dirs. Salt Lake Community Action Program, 1968—; pres. Salt Lake County unit Am. Cancer Soc., 1970-72, chmn. county crusade, 1967, bd. dirs. Utah div., 1968—; mem. advisory bd. Salvation Army; bd. dirs. Utahns for Effective Govt., Columbus Community Center; Mem. Utah Republican party fin. com., 1965-68; chmn. Rep. voting dist., 1960-64, Rep. legis. dist., 1962-66; bd. dirs. Salt Lake County Young Reps., 1960-66; co-chmn. Coalition Peace Through Strength. Served to lt. (s.g.) USNR, 1956-60; brig. gen. Utah Air N.G., 1963-79; payload specialist, space shuttle mission 51D, 1985. Recipient Tom McCoy award Utah League Cities and Towns, 1972. Mem. Utah League Cities and Towns (pres. 1971-72, dir. 1968—), Nat. League Cities (1st v.p. 1973-74, hon. pres. 1975), Sigma Chi. Mormon. Club: Kiwanian. Office: US Senate 505 Dirksen Senate Bldg Washington DC 20510

GARNER, CARLENE ANN, orchestra administrator; b. Dec. 17, 1945; d. Carl A. and Ruth E. (Mathison) Timblin; m. Adelbert L. Garner, Feb. 17, 1964; children: Bruce A., Brent A. BA, U. Puget Sound, 1983. Adminstrv. dir. Balletacoma, 1984-87; exec. dir. Tacoma Symphony, 1987—; cons. Wash. PAVE, Tacoma, 1983-84. Pres. Wilson High Sch. PTA, Tacoma, 1983-85; chmn. Tacoma Sch. Vol. Adv. Bd., 1985-87; pres. Emmanuel Luth. Ch., Tacoma, 1984-86; sec.-treas. Tacoma-Narrows Conf., 1987-89. Mem. Northwest Devel. Officers Assn., Am. Symphony Orch. League, Jr. Women's Club Tacoma (pres. 1975-76), Wash. State Fedn. Women's Clubs (pres. Peninsula Dist. 1984-86, treas. 1988—, Clubwoman of Yr. 1977, Outstanding FREE chmn. Gen. Fedn.). Lutheran. Home: 1115 N Cheyenne Tacoma WA 98406 Office: Tacoma Symphony PO Box 19 Tacoma WA 98401

GARNER, CHESTER ALEXANDER, agriculturist, consultant; b. Lebanon, Ind., Sept. 25, 1897; s. Abner Anderson and Effie Almyra (Alexander) G.; m. Frances Johanna Schotthoeffer, Sept. 21, 1923 (dec.); children: Edmund Gale, Joan Lenore. Diploma in violin, Music Conservatory, Indpls., 1916; BSA, Purdue U., 1921; MS, Iowa State U., 1924; postgrad., U. Ill., 1925-26, U. So. Calif., 1928. Mgr. muck soil exploration stas. U.S. Dept. Agr., Washington and N.Y., 1922-25; prof. olericulture U. Ill., Champaign, 1925-26; fed. and state plant quarantine guardian L.A., 1926-29; involved with domestic and fgn. commerce El Centro, Fullerton, L.A., Calif., 1928-33; contractor-cons. agrl. industries U.S. and abroad, 1933-40; agronomist engr. U.S. Dept. Def., L.A., Ariz., Puerto Rico, 1940-43; civilian chief to Adm. Ingram Region 6, Bahia, Brazil, 1943; coord. Inter-American Affairs, Brazil, 1944; contractor-cons. Biol. Controls, Stamd. Oil, Colombia, L.A., Ventura, 1944-73; bd. dir.-entomogist Rotenone Chem. Co., L.A., 1930-40; chmn. Inst. Tropical Rsch. Harvard U., Barro, Colo., Panama, 1939-40; raw products explorer Am. Colombian Corp., Lands O'Loba, Colombia 1940; exec. cons. Canengco Ltd. Engrs., Montreal, Can., 1955-56; mgr. Muck Soil Exptl. Sta., Williamson, N.Y., South Bend, Ind. Author: Aborigines' Medicinal Plants (Pioneer and Indian Sourcebook),1974-75, Biomedical Manual: Emollients from Plants, 1975-77; contbr. articles to profl. jours; patentee in field. Sponsor fgn. grad. student exch. program, L.A., 1973-74; explorerfor antitumor plants Nat. Cancer Inst., Ind., Fiji, Australia and West Indies, 1977-86, Colo., Mojave Desert, West Indies; musical vol. Motion Picture Country House, Calabasas, Calif., 1986-88, Beverly Hosp., Canoga Park, Calif., 1980—; ch. organist. With U.S. Army, 1917-18. Named Grad. scholar Purdue U., 1921-22, Outstanding Vol. Beverly Enterprises, Canoga Park; recipient Disting. Svc. to Fgn. Com. award L.A. C. of C., 1942, Motion Picture TV Fund 500-Hours award, 1988-89. Mem. Earthwatch, World Wildlife Fund, Smithsonian Inst. (assoc.), Platinum Club , Biomedical Found. (pres., chief exec. officer 1977—), Humana Hosp. Srs. (Woodland Hills chpt.), Motion Picture Guild Arts and Crafts, Alpha Gamma Rho (Delta chpt.), Aborist Woodland Hills Country Club, Taipan Passport Club. Mem. Ecumenical Ch. Home: Lynn Ranch 1007 Camino Magenta Thousand Oaks CA 91360 Office: Harmony Found PO Box 1746 Thousand Oaks CA 91360

GARNER, LEE ELTON, executive assessment and development executive; b. Ivan, Ark., Aug. 24, 1931; s. Iverson Lee and Cynthia Elizabeth (Mc Allister) G.; m. Billie Joyce Barr, Apr. 17, 1953; children: Steven Lee, Cynthia Joyce, Craig Andrew. BS in Edn., So. State U., Magnolia, Ark., 1952, MRE, 1958, DRE, 1966; EdD, Southwestern Sem., Ft. Worth, 1975; postgrad., U. Tenn., Nashville, 1973-74, Vanderbilt U., 1970, Orange Coast Coll., 1988. Various positions So. Bapt. Chs., Ft. Worth, 1956-61; vocat. guidance counselor Tex. Bapt. Conv., Dallas, 1961-65; mktg. coord. Sunday sch. bd. So. Bapt. Conv., Nashville, 1965-79; tchr. Tenn. State U., Nashville, 1977-80; cons. Webster's Internat., Brentwood, Tenn., 1979-81; trainer Human Devel. Seminars, St. Petersburg, Fla., 1980-83; pres. Humanagement, Inc., Santa Ana, Calif., 1983—; conf. dir. RACF User Conf. Vanguard Integrity Profl., Brea, Calif., 1987-89; faculty assoc. Mgmt. Svcs. Group, Concord, Calif., 1987—. With U.S. Army, 1952-54. Republican. Office: Humanagement Inc 3941-B S Bristol Ste 61 Santa Ana CA 92704

GARNER, RONALD WAYNE, transportation executive; b. Seattle, July 27, 1947; s. Mervyn LeRoy and Mildred Dean (Woods) G.; m. Cynthia Ann Ablott, 1968 (div. 1976); children: John, Jeff; m. Marilyn Louise Dodge, Dec. 18, 1976; children: Amy, Timmy, Candice. Owner, operator Ron Garner Trucking, Renton, Wash., 1965-72, Buckley, Wash., 1976—; driver All Service Heavy Transport, Kirkland, Wash., 1972-74, Tamarade Enterprises, Maple Valley, Wash., 1974-76; owner, operator Quality Hwy. Co., Buckley, 1976—; v.p., mgr. B&B Transport Inc., Maple Valley, 1976-78; pres., mgr. Garner Transp. Inc., Milton, Wash., 1981—. Republican. Office: Garner Transp Inc 407A Porter Way Milton WA 98354

GARRETSON, STEVEN MICHAEL, teacher; b. L.A., Nov. 2, 1950; s. Fredrick Harmon and Mildred (Mason) G.; m. Candice Kay Clouse, Sept. 23, 1972; children: Joshua Steven, Amanda Jeanine. BA, U. Calif., Irvine, 1972, tchr. credential, 1974; postgrad., U. Calif., Santa Barbara, 1973; MA, U. San Francisco, 1980. Cert. tchr., adminstr., Calif. Tchr. Irvine Unified Sch. Dist., 1974—; energy conservation cons. Irvine Unified Sch. Dist., 1981-85, grant writer, 1983—, archtl. design cons., 1975—, mentor tchr., 1984-86; presenter state social studies conf., 1980. Mem. Irvine Tchrs. Assn. (grievance chmn. 1980-82, treas., 1977-78, v.p., 1978-79, contract negotiator, 1976-84, 89—), Phi Delta Kappa. Roman Catholic. Office: Northwood Elem Sch 28 Carson Irvine CA 92720

GARRETT, ARTHUR RICHARD, II, oil company executive; b. Needles, Calif., Apr. 24, 1942; s. Arthur Richard and Nancy Elizabeth (Stewart) G.; m. Debby Cruit, Jan. 27, 1968 (div, 1977); children: Gina, Skye; m. Heather Galloway, Mar. 1, 1980. BSEE, U. Ariz., 1966, MBA, 1969. Registered profl. engr., La. Petroleum engr. Amoco Prodn. Co., Odessa, Tex., 1966-67, Midland, Tex., 1979; acct. exec. Security Pacific Bank, L.A., 1969-72; sr. reservoir engr. Conoco, Inc., Lake Charles, La., 1972-76; supervising reservoir engr. Conoco, Inc., Corpus Christi, Tex., 1976; mgr. engring. planning Conoco, Inc., London, 1977-80; coord. engring. Conoco, Inc., Houston, 1980-81; chief ops. planning engr. Occidental Petroleum Co., Lima, Peru, 1981-87; ops. planning mgr. Occidental Petroleum Co., Aberdeen, Scotland, 1987--. Mem. Soc. Petroleum Engrs., Beta Gamma Sigma, Sigma Iota Epsilon. Home: Lakeside House, Tillycorthie Udny, Aberdeenshire AB4 OSD, Scotland Office: Occidental Aberdeen PO Box 11174 Bakersfield CA 93389

GARRETT, DENNIS ANDREW, police official; b. Phoenix, Feb. 9, 1940; s. Lynn Patrick and Louise A. (Yates) G.; m. Joan Marie Braun, June 12, 1980. AA, Glendale Community Coll., 1975; BS magna cum laude, No. Ariz. U., 1980; MPA, Ariz. State U., 1985. Officer Phoenix Police Dept., 1963-69, sgt., 1969-72, lt., 1972-75, capt., 1975-80, maj., 1980, asst. police chief, 1980—; chmn. Ariz. Comprehensive Data System Adv. Com., 1978. Chmn. St. Jerome's Sch. Bd., Phoenix, 1978-79; mem. Phoenix Together, 1983—, Valley Leadership, Phoenix, 1985—. Mem. Am. Soc. Pub. Adminstrn. (pres. Ariz. chpt. 1988-89), Internat. Assn. Chiefs Police, Am. Mgmt. Assn., Ariz. Assn. Chiefs Police, Maricopa Assn. Govts. (chmn. 911 com. 1977-78), Fraternal Order Police, Phi Kappa Phi. Republican. Roman Catholic. Office: Phoenix Police Dept 620 W Washington St Phoenix AZ 85003

GARRETT, DUANE DAVID, hospitality executive; b. N.Y.C., Mar. 28, 1952; s. Gloria Lynne (Magliana) G.; m. Chahla Zarinzad, Nov. 10, 1977 (div. Feb. 1987). BBA, SUNY, Albany, 1989; postgrad., West Coast U. Gen. mgr. Reise Orgn., N.Y.C., 1974-77, Burger King Corp., L.A., 1977-83; staff acct. Baar Accountancy Corp., Encino, Calif., 1983-85; comptroller The Playboy Club of Hollywood, L.A., 1985-86, The Mayfair Hotel, L.A., 1986-87; administr. employees stock purchase plan Litton Industries, Inc., Beverly Hills, Calif., 1987—; cons. No. Star Prodn. Co., Beverly Hills, 1985-89, Video Butler Enterprises, Van Nuys, Calif., 1984-86; cons., auditor Bank of Am., L.A., 1987; adv. bd. Restaurant Bus. Mag., L.A., 1985-89. Fund raiser Rep. Party, Calif., 1986-88; publicity chmn. Calif. State Women's Ctr., Northridge, 1985. Mem. NAFE (site coord. 1988-89), Internat. Student Orgn. Republican. Episcopalian. Home: 15353 Weddington St #C102 Van Nuys CA 91411 Office: Litton Industries Inc 360 N Crescent Dr Beverly Hills CA 90210

GARRETT, KENNETH JAMES, marketing executive; b. Casper, Wyo., Jan. 21, 1953; s. James Robert and Mary Agnes (Colby) G.; m. Kristin Hatlen, Sept. 21, 1985. AS, Casper Coll., 1973; BS with honors, U. Wyo., 1975, M Computer Sci., 1977, MBA, 1979. Mktg. rep. IBM Corp., Denver, 1978-79; account exec. Mountain Bell, Boulder, Colo., 1979-81; tng. mgr. AT&T, Denver, 1981-83; dir. product mktg. U.S. West, Denver, 1983-85; dir. bus. planning U.S. West Info. Systems, Englewood, Colo., 1985-86; dir. planning Norand Corp., Boulder, 1986-87; dir. mktg. EI Corp., Boulder, 1987—; pres. K. Garrett and Assocs., 1982—. Contbr. articles to profl. jours. Named to Achievers Club, Mountain Bell, 1981. Mem. Phi Beta Kappa, Phi Kappa Psi. Roman Catholic. Home: 4232 Quince Ct Boulder CO 80302 Office: XEL Communications Inc 17600 E Exposition Dr Aurora CO 80017

GARRETT, KRISTINE REED, real estate executive; b. Titusville, Pa., Sept. 8, 1958; d. David Andrew and Virginia Anne (Rogers) Reed; m. Jonathan Miles Garrett, Nov. 21, 1987. BA in History, Allegheny Coll., 1982. Loan processor, closer Sun State Savs. & Loan Assn., Phoenix, 1983-84, loan officer, 1984-85, asst. v.p., asst. mgr., 1985-87, v.p., dept. mgr., 1987—. Mem. allocations panel Valley of the Sun United Way, Phoenix, 1987—; mem. Sun State Polit. Action Com., 1987—; mem. Valley Partnership, Phoenix, 1987—. Mem. Women in Comml. Real Estate, Assn. Profl. Mortgage Women, Young Mortgage Bankers Assn. Republican. Presbyterian. Office: Sun State Savs & Loan Assn 4250 E Camelback Rd #200 K Phoenix AZ 85018

GARRETT, LAWRENCE TAIT, infosystem specialist, corporate executive; b. Astoria, Oreg., Sept. 29, 1931; s. George and Ethel (Tait) G.; m. Lydia Frieda Lipp, Aug. 10, 1957; children: Philip Arthur, Katherine Lydia, Yvonne Celia. Student, Syracuse U., 1953-54; BS in Indsl. Adminstrn., Yale U., 1959; postgrad., U. Wash., 1965-67; MBA, U. Puget Sound, 1982. Sr. supr., systems analyst The Boeing Co., Seattle, 1959-68; mgr. product service dept. Computer Scis. Corp., Richland, Washington, 1968-73; project mgr. Computer Scis. Europe, Ltd., Wuppertal, Fed. Rep. of Germany, 1969; tech. services mgr. Data Processing Ctr. State of Wash., Olympia, 1973-81; asst. dir. Office Fin. Mgmt. State of Wash., 1980-81, mgr. systems devel. Data Processing Service Ctr., 1981-87, mgr. systems devel. Dept. Info. Services, 1987-88, mgr. computer ctr. Dept. Info. Services, 1988—; v.p., sec./treas. Garrett-Lipp and Assocs., Inc., Olympia, 1982—. Del. Thurston County Dem. Party, Olympia, 1988. Served with USAF, 1952-56, United Kingdom. Fellow Yale Sci. and Engring. Assn.; mem. Yale Alumni Club. Lodge: Rotary. Home: 1500 Lake Park Dr 24 Tumwater WA 98502 Office: Garrett-Lipp & Assocs Inc PO Box 401 Olympia WA 98507

GARRETT, MALCOLM G., agriculturist; b. Lubbock, Tex., Apr. 21, 1940; s. John J. and V. Irene (Stockstill) G.; m. Donna Jean Decker, Aug. 27, 1957; children: Dudley L., D'Ann Irene. From asst. gen. mgr. to gen. mgr. Garrett Farms, Clovis, N.Mex.; v.p. bd. regents N.Mex. State U.; mem. county agr. and stabilization com. USDA; del. western states meeting U.S. Agr.; trustee High Plains Research Found.; adv. com. U.S. Sec. Agr.; chmn. N.Mex. Govs. Agrl. Task Force; mem. N.Mex. State Bd. Econ. Devel. Contbr. articles to profl. jours. Tchr. Sunday Sch. Cen. Christian Ch.; active United Fund. Mem. N.Mex. Seedsman Assn. (pres.), Internat. Crop Improvement Assn. (del.), Am. Soc. Agronomy, Am. Soil Sci. Soc., Internat. Crop Scientist Soc., Internat. Soil Sci. Soc., Future Farmers Am., 4-H Club, N.Mex. State U. Found. Democrat. Office: GARCO Ltd 229 Innsdale Terr PO Box 219 Clovis NM 88101

GARRETT, ROBERT STEPHENS, public relations executive; b. Bell, Calif., July 12, 1937; s. Sammie Jacob and Martha Ethelwynn (Dench) G.; m. Mary Lynn Harris, Sept. 9, 1955 (div. July 1972); children: Lisa, Julie, Kim; m. Camille Ann Priestley, Feb. 15, 1975; children: Lee Ann, Nikki, Grant. Grad. high sch., Downey, Calif. From machinist to head shipping dept. Axelson Mfg. Co., Vernon, Calif., 1955-60; prodn. control planner, methods analyst autonetics div. Rockwell Internat., Downey, Compton and Anaheim, Calif., 1960-70; pub. relations mgr., property mgr., clinic coordinator, investigator, property researcher and chief adminstr. bd. UMEDCO Inc., Long Beach, Calif., 1970-77; dir. ops. Regency Mgmt. Service, Anaheim, 1977-78; cons. med. pub. relations Garden Grove, Calif., 1978—. Bd. dirs. Boys Club of Garden Grove, 1978—, Girls Club of Garden Grove, 1980—,treas. 1983-84, v.p. 1984-86, pres. 1986; traffic commr. City of Garden Grove, 1981—; vice chmn. traffic commn., 1988-89, chmn. 1989—. Republican. Lodges: Rotary (bd. dirs. Paramount 1975-76, Garden Grove club 1978-79), Elks. Office: PO Box 1221 Garden Grove CA 92642

GARRETT, STEPHEN GEORGE, architect, museum director; b. Ashtead, Eng., Dec. 26, 1922; s. Howard George and Ida (King-Harman) G.; m. Petronella Jones, 1952; children: Carey, Georgia; m. Jean Mackintosh, 1964; children: Rebecca, Jason. M.A., Trinity Coll., Cambridge (Eng.) U., 1950. Pvt. archtl. practice London, 1952-73; dep. dir. J. Paul Getty Mus., Malibu, Calif., 1973-77; dir., trustee J. Paul Getty Mus., 1977-82; dir. Long Beach (Calif.) Mus. Art, 1984-88; lectr. architecture Poly. Central London. Author booklets, articles arch. and design projects. Assoc. Royal Inst. Brit. Architects. Served with Brit. Navy, 1941-46. Mem. Assn. Art Mus. Dirs. Office: Long Beach Mus Art 2300 E Ocean Blvd Long Beach CA 90803

GARRETT, WILLIAM FLOYD, JR., physician, consultant; b. Greensboro, N.C., Jan. 17, 1947; s. William Floyd and Louise (Thornbro) G.; m. Pamela Campbell, Feb. 11, 1984; 1 child, Katherine Campbell. BS, Tulane U., 1969; MD, U. Miami, Fla., 1973. Intern, then resident in emergency medicine Med. Coll. Pa., Phila., 1973-76; emergency physician West Reading (Pa.) Med. Ctr., 1976-78; dir. emergency med., dept. chmn. Del County Meml. Hosp., Drexel Hill, Pa., 1978-81, Humana Hosp. Aurora, Colo., 1981—; sr. cons. Emergency Med. Services Assns., Plantation, Fla., 1984-87, regional med. dir., 1987—; sr. v.p. Telemed, Inc., Denver, 1985-87; med. dir. Adolph Coors Co., Golden, Colo., 1986—; emergency med. cons. Luth. Med. Ctr., St. Louis, 1987—; med. dir., cons. Human Hosp. Aurora and Paramedic Sch., 1987—; mem. adv. bd. home care service Norrell, Inc., 1984-87, Quality Connector, 1987—; cons., physician Lifespring, Inc. Provider, instr. advanced life support system Am. Heart Assn., 1980; med. dir. Cunningham Fire Dept., Aurora, 1985—, Cherry Creek State Recreational Area, Aurora, 1983-86. Mem. Am. Occupational Med. Assn., Undersea Med. Soc., Internat. Physicians for Prevention Nuclear War, Physicians for Social Responsibility, Internat. Wildlife Fedn., Dumb Friends League, Am. Coll. Emergency Physicians (bd. dirs. 1986-88), AMA, Aurora-Adams County Med. Soc. Office: Emergency Med Svcs Assocs 100 NW 70th Ave Plantation FL 33317

GARRIDO, JOHN MARCO HANIU, pediatrician; b. Agana, Guam, Mar. 8, 1954; s. Francisco Borja and Serafina (Haniu) G.; m. Josephine Ann L. Mallo, Feb. 16, 1980; 1 child, Josiah Michael. BS in Phys. Therapy, St. Louis U., 1976; MD, U. Hawaii, 1985. Diplomate Am. Bd. Pediatrics. Chief phys. therapist Med. Ctr. Marianas, Tamuning, Guam, 1977-78; staff phys. therapist Guam Meml. Hosp., Tamuning, 1978-79; pediatrics intern Loma Linda (Calif.) U. Med. Ctr., 1985-86; resident in pediatrics Mt. Zion Hosp. and Med. Ctr., San Francisco, 1986-87, chief resident, 1987-88; med. staff St. Luke's Hosp., San Francisco, 1987-88; pvt. practice Tracy Community Meml. Hosp., Tracy, Calif., 1988—. Co-author: Cross-Cultural Caring, 1980. Vol. St. Louis Coun. for Exceptional Children, 1974-76, Spl. Olympics, Agana, 1976-78, Engaged Encounter, Honolulu, 1980-84. Mem. AMA, Am. Med. Student Assn. Roman Catholic. Office: Tracy Pediatrics 1425 Tracy Blvd Tracy CA 95376

GARRIGUES, GAYLE LYNNE, lawyer; b. Anchorage, Aug. 7, 1955; s. James Martin and Julia Ann (Harris) G. B.A. in Polit.Sci., U. Alaska, 1977; J.D., U. Idaho, 1980. Bar: Alaska 1981, U.S. Dist. Ct. Alaska 1982. Atty. Alaska Legal Services Corp., Kotzebue, 1980-82; assoc. Settles, Kalamarides & Assocs., P.C., Anchorage, 1982; sole practice, Kotzebue, 1982-84; asst. dist. atty. Dept. of Law 2d Jud. Dist., Kotzebue, 1984-87, Fairbanks, 1987—; instr. criminal justice Chuckchi Community Coll., 1985-86. Bd. dirs. Kotzebue Womens Crisis Project, 1982-84; del. Alaska State Dem. Conv., 1974, 84, 88; bd. dirs. Women in Crisis, Counseling and Assistance, 1988—, v.p., 1989—; leader Girl Scouts U.S., 1981-83, 86-87. Mem. ABA, Assn. Trial Lawyers Am., Alaska Bar Assn., Anchorage Women Lawyers, Phi Alpha Delta.

GARRIGUS, CHARLES BYFORD, retired literature educator; b. Benton, Ill., June 13, 1914; s. Charles Byford and Ailene Marie (Fowler) G.; m. Ferne Marie Fetters, Dec. 28, 1936 (dec.); children: Marmarie (dec.), Charles, Richmond, Karis, Rose Ann. AB, U. Ill., 1936, MA, 1937. Prof. humanities King's River Coll., Reedley, Calif., 1949-73; Calif. poet laureate for life, 1966—. Author: California Poems, 1955, (poems) Echoes of Being, 1975, (novel) Brief Candel, 1987; editor: Modern Hamlet, 1950. Mem. Calif. Assembly, 1958-86. Democrat. Methodist. Home: 8030 E Conejo St Selma CA 93662

GARRISON, DOUGLAS RICHARD, English educator, educational testing consultant, writer; b. San Diego, Jan. 21, 1950; s. Richard Hamilton and Carol Louise (Grady) G.; m. Renee Danielle Rutan-Garrison, Dec. 21, 1986; children: Ian H., Nathan D., Nicholas R. BA, U. Calif., San Barbara, 1972; MA, San Francisco State U., 1974; postgrad., U. So. Calif., 1979-80. Cert. English prof., Calif. Instr. English San Francisco State U., 1973-74; prof. English Coll. of Desert, Palm Desert, Calif., 1974—; chmn. communications div. coordinator academic skill ctr. Coll. of the Desert, Palm Desert, Calif., 1981—; exchange prof. Childwall Hall Coll., Liverpool, Eng., 1981-82; adj. prof. Calif. State U. , San Bernardino, Calif., 1984—; cons. Ednl. Testing Service, Princeton, N.J., 1987—. Author: Natural and Native, 1987; editor variety of textbooks and audio tapes; contbr. articles to Friend World Travel. Mem. Nat. Council Tchrs. English, Community Coll. Humanties Assn., Fulbright Alumni Assn., Learning, Assessment, Retention Consortium (state steering com. 1987-88), EDUCOM Nat. Consortium (bd. dirs. 1988—). Democrat. Presyterian. Office: Coll of the Desert 43-500 Monterey Ave Palm Desert CA 92260

GARRISON, LESTER BOYD, chemist; b. Eureka, Calif., May 7, 1948; s. Lester Boyd and Marian (Weamer) G.; m. Sandra Marie Ryan, June 21, 1980; children: Jay Patrick, Kaye Camille, Brian Lee. AA in Gen. Edn., Coll. of the Redwoods, 1971-73; BA in Chemistry, Humboldt State U., 1973-76; postgrad. in chemistry, Portland State U., 1978-79; student in sales and mktg., Portland Community Coll., 1983-84; postgrad., City U., 1988—. Rsch. asst. Oreg. Health Scis. U., Portland, 1976-78, sr. rsch. asst., 1978-79; systems engr. Alpkem Corp, Clackamas, Oreg., 1979-81; sr. lab. technician Qatar Gen. Petroleum Corp., Doha, 1981-82; diagnostics prodn. mgr. Alpkem Corp., Clackamas, 1982-85; plant mgr. Alpkem Corp., Orchards, Wash., 1985-86; chief operating officer Intersect, Inc., Longview, Wash., 1987—. Co-author, contbr. articles to profl. jours. With USMC, 1967-71. Decorated Nat. Def. Svc. medal. Mem. AAAS, Am. Chem. Soc., Am. Assn. Clin. Chemists, Alexander von Humboldt Marine Scis. Assn. (life) (chmn. marine lab and open house com. 1975), Humboldt State U. Oceanographic Soc. (chmn., co-founder). Home: 504 E C St Rainier OR 97048 Office: Intersect Inc 1606 E Kessler Blvd #100 Longview WA 98632

GARROP, BARBARA ANN, reading specialist; b. Chgo., Sept. 2, 1941; d. Marshall and Esther (Barbakoff) Stickles; widowed; children: Alana Beth, Stacy Lynn. AA with honors, Wright Jr. Coll., Chgo., 1961; BA with honors, Roosevelt U., 1963; MS with honors, Calif. State U., Hayward, 1982. Cert. elem. tchr., reading specialist, Calif. Tchr. Von Humboldt Sch., Chgo., 1963-64, Haugan Sch., Chgo., 1964-67; primary grades reading specialist Mt. Diablo Sch. Dist., Concord, Calif., 1979-80, Mills Elem. Sch., Benicia, Calif., 1980-87; primary grades reading specialist Mary Farmar Sch., Benicia, 1987—, mentor tchr., 1989-90. Author phonics manual, 1982; featured in article Woman's Day mag., 1982; contbg. author Celebating The National Reading Initiative, 1988. Bd. dirs. Sisterhood of Congregation B'nai Shalom, Walnut Creek, Calif., 1987-88. Grantee Reading Is Fundamental, 1979-80. Mem. NEA, Internat. Reading Assn., Calif. Reading Assn. (Achievement award 1984), Contra Costa Reading Assn., Calif. Tchrs. Assn., Pi Lambda Theta. Jewish. Lodge: B'nai Brith Women (v.p. Columbus, Ohio 1971-72, pres. Walnut Creek 1973-74). Office: Mary Farmar Sch 901 Military W Benicia CA 94510

GARRUTO, JOHN ANTHONY, cosmetics executive; b. Johnson City, N.Y., June 18, 1952; s. Paul Anthony and Katherine Helen (DiMartino) G.; m. Denise Kitty Conlon, Feb. 19, 1971 (div. May 1978); 1 child, James Joseph; m. Anita Louise, May 12, 1979 (div. Sept. 1984); 1 child, Christopher Russell; m. Debra Lynn Brady (div. Dec. 1986); m. Michelle Bartok, Apr. 2, 1988. BS in Chemistry, SUNY, Binghamton, 1974; AAS in Bus. Adminstrn., Broome Coll., 1976. Rsch. chemist Lander Co. Inc., Binghamton, 1974-77; rsch. dir. Lander Co. Inc., St. Louis, 1977-79, Olde Worlde Products, High Point, N.C., 1979-81; v.p. rsch. and devel. LaCosta Products Internat., Carlsbad, Calif., 1981—; cons. Trans-Atlantic Mktg., Binghamton, 1975-78. Mem. AAAS, Am. Chem. Soc., Soc. Cosmetic Chemists (newsletter editor 1980-81, publicity chmn. 1984—, edn. chmn. 1987), Fedn. Am. Scientists, Internat. Platform Assn., N.Y. Acad. Scis. Democrat. Roman Catholic. Home: PO Box 793 Carlsbad CA 92008 Office: La Costa Products 2251 Las Palmas Dr Carlsbad CA 92008

GARRY, JACQUELYNN LEE, holding corporation executive; b. Salem, N.J., Mar. 11, 1957; d. Henry Edward Klingler and Josephine Sarah (Poulson) Parker. Student, Delcastle Vocat. Tech. Inst., 1975; AA, AS, Fort Steilacoom Community Coll., AS in Bus., AS in Broadcasting; student, L.H. Bates Vocat. Tech. Inst., 1979-80. Mgr. inventory control, pub. relations McDonalds of Wilmington, Del., 1974-77; sales account rep. Rainbow of Tacoma/Auburn, Wash., 1977-80; mgmt. trainee Agy. Rent-A-Car, Wash., 1980; sales mgr. Puget (Wash.) Mobilex Inc., 1980-82; planning specialist Bus. Ins. Assocs., 1982, Target Ins. Bus. Service, 1982-84; chief exec. officer Just Like Gold, Inc., San Diego, 1983—. Dir. TV including The Music Hour, Meet the Candidates; co-dir. film The Great Am. Masacare; producer TV The Fashinable Female, (co-producer) Condomania; author newspaper columns The Fashionable Female, 1984-85. Served with USAF, 1974-77. Mem. Ch. Religious Sci.

GARRY, JAMES B., storyteller, researcher; b. Taylor, Tex., Apr. 28, 1947; s. Mahon Barker and Grace (Dellinger) G. BS, U. Mich., 1970, MS, 1975. Part-time wilderness guide, naturalist Triangle X Ranch, Moose, Wyo., 1969-75; community organizer, media cons., tchr. Hobart St. Project, Detroit, 1974-75; media specialist, lobbyist Powder River Basin Resource Coun., Sheridan, Wyo., 1975-76; pvt. practice media and polit. cons. Big Horn, Wyo., 1976-78; video and film artist-in-residence Wyo. Coun. on the Arts/Sheridan Coll., Sheridan, 1978-80; mem. staff Great Plains Lore and Natural History, Big Horn, 1980—; storyteller part-time Buffalo Bill Hist. Ctr., Cody, Wyo., 1980—; tchr. Yellowstone (Wyo.) Inst., summers 1986—; tour study leader, rsch. collaborator Smithsonian Instn., Washington, part-time 1984—. Co-author: Writing About Wildlife, 1974; author, editor: Buck: Stories by Lloyd Buck Bender, 1984; storyteller in field. 2d lt. U.S. Army, 1970. Recipient Spl. Heritage award Old West Trail Found., 1983; named one of Individual Humanist of Yr., Wyo. Coun. for Humanities, 1986. Democrat. Roman Catholic. Home: Box 204 Big Horn WY 82833 Office: Great Plains Lore & History Box 204 Big Horn WY 82833

GARSTANG, ROY HENRY, astrophysicist, educator; b. Southport, Eng., Sept. 18, 1925; came to U.S., 1964; s. Percy Brocklehurst and Eunice (Gledhill) G.; m. Ann Clemence Hawk, Aug. 11, 1959; children—Jennifer Katherine, Susan Veronica. B.A., U. Cambridge, 1946, M.A., 1950, Ph.D., 1954, Sc.D., 1983. Research assoc. U. Chgo., 1951-52; lectr. astronomy U. Coll., London, 1952-60; reader astronomy U. London, 1960-64, asst. dir. Obs., 1959-64; prof. astrophysics U. Colo., Boulder, 1964—; chmn. Joint Inst. for Lab. Astrophysics, 1966-67; researcher on atomic physics and astrophys. applications; cons. Nat. Bur. Standards, 1964-73; v.p. commn. 14 Internat. Astron. Union, 1970-73, pres., 1973-76; Erskine vis. fellow U. Canterbury, New Zealand, 1971; vis. prof. U. Calif., Santa Cruz, 1971, chmn. Boulder Faculty Assembly, 1988. Editor: Observatory, 1953-60; Contbr. numerous articles to tech. jours. Fellow Am. Phys. Soc., AAAS, Optical Soc. Am., Brit. Inst. Physics, Royal Astron. Soc.; mem. Am. Astron. Soc., Royal Soc. Scis. Liege (Belgium). Home: 830 8th St Boulder CO 80302 Office: U Colo Joint Inst for Lab Astrophysics Boulder CO 80309

GARTLER, STANLEY MICHAEL, geneticist, educator; b. Los Angeles, June 9, 1923; s. George David and Delvira (Cupferberg) G.; m. Marion Ruth Mitchelson, Nov. 7, 1948. B.S., UCLA, 1948; Ph.D., U. Calif.-Berkeley, 1952. Research assoc. Columbia U., N.Y.C., 1952-57; research asst. prof. U. Wash., Seattle, 1957-60, assoc. prof., 1960-64, prof. genetics, 1964—; dir. NATO meeting on mosaicism, Venice, Italy, 1972. Author: (with R.E. Cole) Inactivation Sexual Differentiation, 1978. Grantee NIH and NSF, 1956—; merit scholar NIH. Mem. Am. Soc. Human Genetics (dir. 1970, pres.-elect 1986, pres. 1987), Genetics Soc. Am., Soc. Cell Biology, Am. Soc. Naturalists. Home: 9009 42d St NE Seattle WA 98115 Office: Dept Genetics U Wash Seattle WA 98195

GARTNER, WILLIAM J., product development consultant; b. Sterling, Ill., Mar. 2, 1942; s. Leonard P. and Dorothy L. Gartner; m. Susan Louise Nicol, Aug. 22, 1964; children: Kathryn, Kimberly, Andrea. BS, Lewis U., 1963; postgrad., Northwestern U., 1972-74. Rsch. chemist Burgess Battery Co., Freeport, Ill., 1963-64, U.S. Gypsum Co., Des Plaines, Ill., 1963-68; project mgr. DeSoto Chem., Des Plaines, 1966-69; pres. Aqualab, Inc., Bartlett, Ill., 1970-86, Halex, Inc., Bartlett, 1981—, Reflex, Inc., Scottsdale, Ariz., 1986—; cons. Aqualab, Inc., Bartlett, 1986—, Nat. Environ. Test, London, 1986—, Associated Mills, Inc., Chgo., 1984—, Westrend, Inc., Phoenix, 1987—. Author: Toxin, 1988; patentee in field. Leader Girl Scouts USA, Elgin, Ill, 1976-82. Mem. Am. Council of Ind. Labs., Elgin Country Club, Desert Highlands Golf Club, Rotary. Office: Reflex Inc 14435 N Scottsdale Rd Scottsdale AZ 85254

GARTON, ROY LEWIS, video production executive; b. Grand Rapids, Mich., Sept. 1, 1953; s. Carl J. and Patrica L. (Beals) G.; m. Chris Anne Garton, April 1, 1988; 3 children. AAS in Broadcasting and Mktg., Cen. Wyo. Coll., 1973. Announcer Sta. KVOW, Riverton, Wyo., 1972-73, Sta. KOVE, Lander, Wyo., 1973-74; announcer, news asst. Sta. KSGT, Jackson, Wyo., 1974-75; tech. dir. Sta. KID-TV, Idaho Falls, Idaho, 1975-76, Jackson (Wyo.) Hole Cable TV, 1976; asst. mgr. Healt Mart Drugs, Jackson, 1976-86; owner R.A.P. Prodns., Jackson, 1986—; adv. co-founder Old West Days Pageant, Jackson, 1981—; bd. dirs. Jackson Hole Film Commn., 1986—. Past pres. Jackson Jaycees, 1978, Jackson Hole Howdy Pardners Ambassadors, 1985-86; bd. dirs. Teton County Republican Party, 1986—; mem. com. Republican Party, Jackson, 1986—; chmn. Red Cross, 1984-85. Mem. Jackson Hole C. of C. (bd. dirs. 1986-87), Jackson Hole Film Commn., Am. Film Inst. Republican. Baptist. Lodge: Rotary.

GARTZ, WILLIAM FREDERICK, architect; b. Chgo., Nov. 12, 1953; s. Frederick Samuel and Lillian Louise (Korschet) G. B in Archtl. Edn., U. Wash., 1976; MArch, U. Wis., Milw., 1983. Registered architect, Wash. Project architect McCool McDonald Architect, Seattle, 1976-77, Morse Stafford Architects, Seattle, 1977-80, Davis & Fatica, Milw., 1982-83, Callison Partnership, Seattle, 1984--; prin. Gartz Architects, Seattle, 1983-84. Prin. works include Baranof Hotel, Juneau, Alaska, 1984, Inn at Semi-Ah-Moo, Blaine, Wash., 1987, Carillon Point-Woodmark Hotel, Kirkland, Wash., 1988. Chmn. crime com. Capitol Hill Community Coun., 1978-79. Mem. AIA (Colo. honor award 1987, Seattle Charter Honor award 1988). Home: 6748 1st Ave NW Seattle WA 98117 Office: Callison Partnership Ltd 1423 3d Ave Seattle WA 98104

GARVER, OLIVER BAILEY, JR., bishop; b. L.A., July 19, 1925. BSBA, UCLA, 1945; MBA, Harvard U., 1948; STB, Episc. Theol. Sch., Cambridge, Mass., 1962. Ordained to ministry Episcopal Ch. as deacon, 1962, as priest, 1963. With Lockheed Aircraft Corp., 1948-59; curate St. Alban's, L.A., 1966-72; urban assoc. Ch. of the Epiphany, L.A., 1966-72; canon to the ordinary Staff Bishop Rusack, 1973-85; consecrated bishop suffragan Diocese of L.A., from 1985. With USNR. Mem. Phi Beta Kappa, Beta Gamma Sigma. Office: Diocese of Los Angeles PO Box 2164 Los Angeles CA 90051 *

GARVEY, DANIEL CYRIL, mechanical engineer; b. Chgo., Nov. 25, 1940; s. Cyril and Genei Marie (McCarthy) G; children: Michael Daniel, Erin T. BSME, Marquette U., Milw., 1963; MS in Mech. Engring., IIT, Chgo., 1965. With Kearney & Trecker Corp., Milw., 1960-63, A C Electronics div. Gen. Mtrs. Corp., Milw., 1965-68; vibration and control sys. engr. Woodward Governor Co., Ft. Collins, Colo., 1970—. Reviewer tech. papers IEEE, 1980—; contbr. articles to profl. jours.; patentee in field. Recipient Arch T. Colwell Merit award, SAE, 1984; Speakers award, ASME, 1982; NASA fellow, 1967-69, others. Mem. IEEE, SAE. Home: 5205 Mail Creek Ln Fort Collins CO 80525 Office: Woodward Governor Co 1000 E Drake Rd Fort Collins CO 80521

GARVEY, DORIS BURMESTER, environmental administrator; b. N.Y.C., Oct. 3, 1936; d. William Henry and Florence Elizabeth (Sauerteig) Burmester; m. Gerald Thomas John Garvey, June 6, 1959; children: Deirdre Anne, Gerald Thomas John Jr., Victoria Elizabeth. BA with honors, Wilson Coll., 1959; MA with honors, Yale U., 1959. Rsch. assoc. Princeton U., N.J., 1967-76; environ. scientist Argonne (Ill.) Nat. Lab., 1976-84; staff mem. Los Alamos (N.Mex.) Nat. Lab., 1984-86, regulatory compliance officer, 1986—. Contbr. articles to profl. jours. Bd. dirs. N.Mex. Repertory Theater, Santa Fe, 1987-88; mem. Environ. Improvement Bd., Glen Ellyn, Ill., 1980-82. Mem. Air Pollution Control Assn., N.Mex. Hazardous Waste Soc., Women in Sci., Gov.'s Task Force Emergency Response, Phi Beta Kappa. Democratic. Roman Catholic. Home: 368 Calle Loma Norte Santa Fe NM 87501 Office: Los Alamos Nat Lab PO Box 1663 MS K491 Los Alamos NM 87545

GARVEY, STEVEN PATRICK, professional baseball player; b. Tampa, Fla., Dec. 22, 1948; s. Joseph Patrick and Mildred Emma (Winkler) G.; m. Cynthia Ann, Oct. 29, 1971 (div.), m. Candace Thomas, Feb. 18, 1989; children: Krisha Lee, Whitney Alyse. BS, Mich. State U., 1971. First baseman Los Angeles Dodgers; later with San Diego Padre, asst. player rep., 1972-76; mem. Nat. League All-Star Team, 1974-81, 84-85; operator Garvey Mktg. Group, San Diego; pub. relations for Pepsi-Cola Bottling Co., Los Angeles, 1974—, Allegretti Co., 1976—, Head Shampoo Co., 1977—. Trustee U. San Diego, Cath. U. Am., Scripps Clinic and Research Inst.; bd. dirs. Profl. Athletes Career Enterprises. Named Most Valuable Player Nat. League, 1974, Most Valuable Player, All Star Game, 1974, 78, Outstanding Young Man of Calif., 1976. Mem. Baseball Players Assn. Am., North Hills Jr. C. of C. Democrat. Roman Catholic. Office: Garvey Mktg Group 4320 La Jolla Village Dr San Diego CA 92122 *

GARVIN, SAM SCOTT, marketing executive; b. Pitts., Aug. 16, 1964; s. Sam Landis and Mary Ann (Conn) G. BA, U. Pitts., 1983; M of Internat. Mgmt., Am. Graduate Sch., 1988. Sales rep. Heinz U.S.A., Pitts., 1983-85; dir. bus. devel. ACS Mktg., Portland, Oreg., 1988—; advisor North Allegheny German Exchange, 1983—; cons. FAI, Pitts., 1983—; bd. dirs. Trois Assocs., Pitts. Mem. Rep. Nat. Com., 1988—. Recipient Cert. of Commendation U.S.-Western German Govts., 1983. Mem. Am. Mktg. Assn., Promo Mktg. Assn. Am. Clubs: ASGIM German (Phoenix) (pres. 1987-88); German (Pitts.) (pres. 1982-84). Home: 13421 N 43rd Ave #3043 Phoenix AZ 85029 Office: ACS Mktg Svcs Inc 11811 N Tatum Phoenix AZ 85028

GARVIN, THOMAS WILLIAM, systems analyst; b. Dover, N.H., July 23, 1957; s. William Norse and Dorothy (Kathios) G.; m. Kristina Joanne Wilkinson, Mar. 15, 1983. BM in Music Theory, U. Ariz., 1980, MS in Mgmt. Info. Systems, 1985. Programmer, analyst Hamilton Test System div. United Techs, Tucson, 1983-85; systems analyst Chevron Info. Tech. Co., San Ramon, Calif., 1986—; cons. Weather Publs., Petaluma, Calif., 1987—. Vol., cons. Hayward (Calif.) Edn. Fund, 1987; bd. dirs. Petaluma Heritage Assn., 1988. Mem. Data Processing Mgmt. Assn., Toastmasters. Republican. Home: 7123 Carillion Ct Rohnert Park CA 94928 Office: Chevron Info Tach Co 841 Standard Ave Richmond CA 94802

GARY, JAMES FREDERICK, business executive; b. Chgo., Dec. 28, 1920; s. Rex Inglis and Mary Naomi (Roller) G.; m. Helen Elizabeth Gellert, Sept. 3, 1947; children: David Frederick, John William, James Scott, Mary Anne. BS, Haverford (Pa.) Coll., 1942. With Wash. Energy Co. and predecessors, Seattle, 1947-67; v.p. Wash. Energy Co., 1956-67; pres., chief exec. officer Pacific Resources Inc., Honolulu, 1967-79, chmn., chief exec. officer, 1979-84, chmn., 1985, chmn. emeritus, 1986—; bd. dirs. Bancorp. Hawaii, Inc., Bank of Hawaii, Castle & Cooke, Inc., Wash. Energy Co., Seattle, Wash. Nat. Gas Co., Airborne Freight Corp., Seattle, Inter Island Petroleum, Inc. (chmn.), GDC, Inc., Chgo., Petroleum Industry Research Found., Inc., N.Y.; internat. bus. and energy advisor. Pres. Chief Seattle council Boy Scouts Am., 1966-67, Aloha council, 1973-74; mem. Nat. Council, 1964—, v.p. western region, 1978-85, pres., 1985—, also bd. dirs.; chmn. Aloha United Way, 1978, pres., 1979, chmn., pres., 1980; bd. regents U. Hawaii, 1981-89; trustee Linfield Coll., McMinnville, Oreg., 1983-89; bd. mgrs. Haverford Coll., 1983—; adv. bd. Kamehameha Schs., Honolulu; bd. dirs. Research Corp. of U. Hawaii, 1971-77, chmn., 1974-77; bd. dirs., officer and trustee Oahu Devel. Conf., Hawaii Employers Council, Friends of East-West Ctr., Honolulu Symphony Soc., East-West Ctr. Internat. Found.; chmn. The Hawaii Community Found., 1987—. Capt. AUS, 1942-46. Recipient Distinguished Eagle award Boy Scouts Am., 1972, Silver Beaver award, 1966, Silver Antelope award, 1976, Silver Buffalo award, 1988. Mem. Am. Gas Assn. (bd. dirs. 1970-74), Pacific Gas Assn. (pres. 1974; Pres.'s trophy 1960), Nat. LP-Gas Assn. (bd. dirs. 1967-70), Am. Petroleum Inst., Inst. Gas Tech. (trustee 1975-86), Hawaii Econ. Council, Nat. Petroleum Council, Hawaii Dist. Export Council, Japan-Hawaii Econ. Council, U.S. Nat. Com. for Pacific Econ. Cooperation, Pacific Basin Econ. Council (chmn. U.S. com. 1985-86), Japan-Am. Soc. Honolulu, Pacific Forum, Honolulu Commn. on Fgn. Relations, Hawaii C. of C. (chmn. 1979). Episcopalian. Clubs: Pacific Union (San Francisco); Oahu Country, Waialae Country, Outrigger Canoe, Pacific, Plaza (Honolulu); Seattle Tennis, Wash. Athletic (Seattle), Rainier. Office: 130 Merchant St Ste 1080 Honolulu HI 96813

GARY, KATHLEEN NOLAND, public relations executive; b. Long Beach, Calif.; d. Richard Lee and Grace Irene Noland; m. Richard N. Gary. BA, U.

Wash., 1967. Assoc. editor Kaiser News, Kaiser Aluminum & Chem. Corp., Oakland, Calif., 1968-73; dir. communications Kaiser Engrs., Oakland, 1973-74; mgr. internal communications Kaiser Industries Corp., Oakland, 1975-77; dir. pub. relations and advt. Kaiser Steel Corp., Oakland, 1977-80, v.p. pub. affairs, 1979-80; corp. v.p. pub. affairs and communications Syntex Corp., Palo Alto, Calif., 1981—. Chmn. steering com. St. Mary's Coll. Exec. Seminar.; mem. Bay Area council steering com. Nat. Investor Relations Inst.; bd. dirs. U. Washington Devel. Fund. Mem. Pub. Relations Soc. Am., World Affairs Council, Calif. Mfrs. Assn., Pharm. Mfrs. Assn. (pub. affairs sect.), Silverado Country Club, Forum West Club. Author: (with Don Fabun) Dimensions of Change, 1971, Children of Change, 1970. Office: Syntex Corp 3401 Hillview Ave Palo Alto CA 94304

GASICH, WELKO ELTON, consulting aerospace executive; b. Cupertino, Calif., Mar. 28, 1922; s. Elija J. and Catherine (Paviso) G.; m. Patricia Ann Gudgel, Dec. 28, 1973; 1 child, Mark David. A.B. cum laude in Mech. Engring. (Bacon scholar), Stanford U., 1943, M.S. in Mech. Engring., 1947, cert. in fin. and econs. (Sloan exec. fellow), 1967; Aero. Engr., Calif. Inst. Tech., 1948. Aerodynamicist Douglas Aircraft Co., 1943-44, supr. aeroelastics, 1947-51; chief aero design Rand Corp., 1951-53; chief preliminary design aircraft div. Northrop Corp., Los Angeles, 1953-56; dir. advanced systems Northrop Corp., 1956-61, v.p., asst. gen. mgr. tech., 1961-66, corp. v.p., gen. mgr. Northrop Ventura div., 1967-71, corp. v.p., gen. mgr. aircraft div., 1971-76, corp. v.p., group exec. aircraft group, 1976-79, sr. v.p. advanced projects, 1979-85, exec. v.p. programs, 1985-88, ret., 1988. Patentee in field. Chmn. adv. council Stanford Sch. Engring., 1981-83; past mem. adv. council Stanford Grad. Sch. Bus.; chmn. United Way, 1964; chmn. Scout-O-Rama, Los Angeles council Boy Scouts Am., 1964; chmn. explorer scout exec. com., 1963-64. Served to lt. USN, 1944-46. Fellow AIAA, Soc. Automotive Engrs.; mem. Nat. Acad. Engring., Navy League, Stanford Grad. Sch. Bus. Alumni Assn. (pres. 1971). Republican. Clubs: Wings, Conquistadores del Cielo, Bel Air Country. Office: 3517 Caribeth Dr Encino CA 91436

GASKILL, CAROL VALENTINE, college official; b. Zanesville, Ohio, July 16, 1946; d. Howard Franklin Valentine and Glenna Eulala (Smith) Dusenberry; m. Don Mason Gaskill. Aug. 26, 1965; children: Don Mason Jr., Carin Leigh. BS in Acctg., Weber State Coll., 1980. Journalist Ogden (Utah) Standard-Examiner, 1977-78; adminstrv. asst. Weber State Coll., Ogden, 1978-79, asst. dir. budget, 1982—; staff acct. Crane, Davis, Johnson & Christensen, Ogden, 1980-82. Bd. dirs. Weber County Vol. Svcs., Ogden, 1980-81; community bd. trainer Jr. League Ogden, 1980, devel. dir., 1986-87; organizer Women to Woman, Ogden, 1986-88. Recipient Presdl. Outstanding Profl. Staff award Weber State Coll., 1987. Mem. Consortium for Utah Women in Higher Edn. (sr. assoc., exec. dir.-elect 1988—), Faculty-Staff Assn. Weber State Coll. (pres. bd. dirs. 1987—), Leadership for a New Century (YCC Woman of Yr. 1989), Order Eastern Star, Phi Kappa Phi. Republican. Lutheran. Home: 6175 South 2400 East Ogden UT 84403-5331 Office: Weber State College 3750 Harrison Blvd Ogden UT 84408-1006

GASKILL, HERBERT LEO, accountant, engineer; b. Seattle, July 1, 1923; s. Leo Dell and Vesta Rathbone (Dahlen) G.; m. Margaret Helen Jenkins, Mar. 1, 1944 (div.); children—Margaret V., Herbert Leo. B.S. and M.S. in Chem. Engring., U. Wash., 1949, M.B.A., 1976. C.P.A., Wash. asst. prof. dental materials, exec. officer dept. dental materials Sch. Dentistry, U. Wash., 1950-56; ops. analyst The Boeing Co., Seattle, 1958-71, mktg. cons. govt. programs, 1972-74; pvt. practice acctg., Seattle, 1976-80; hazardous waste mgr. Boeing Co., Seattle, 1980-86, project mgr. western processing remediation, 1986—. Active Seattle Art Mus., Pacific Northwest Aviation Hist. Found. Served to lt. (j.g.) USNR, 1941-46. TAPPI fellow, 1956; U. Wash. Engring. Expt. Sta. fellow, 1957. Mem. Wash. Soc. C.P.A.s. Contbr. articles to profl. jours. Home: 1100 University St 15 K Seattle WA 98101

GASPARI, RUSSELL ARTHUR, electrical engineer, educator; b. Redding, Calif., Jan. 15, 1941; s. Richard Anthony and Elena Adelaide (Biancalana) G.; B.S., U. Calif., Berkeley, 1963; M.S., San Diego State Coll., 1965; Ph.D., U. Calif., Los Angeles, 1970; m. Carole Anne Sterni, Feb. 20, 1965; children—Heather Elizabeth, Catherine Annette. Electronic engr. astronautics div. Gen. Dynamics, San Diego, 1963-65; instr. engring. No. Ariz. U., Flagstaff, 1965-67; engring. specialist data systems div. Litton Systems, Van Nuys, Calif., 1968-71; sr. staff scientist microwave applications group Chatsworth, Calif., 1971-72; vis. prof. engring. Calif. State U., San Diego, 1972-73; sr. scientist Hughes Space & Communications Group, Los Angeles, 1973—. Litton fellow, 1969-70. Registered profl. engr., Calif. Mem. IEEE (sr. mem., officer, Outstanding Engr. award San Diego computer chpt. 1973, outstanding engr. award Los Angeles Harbor Sect. 1980, mgr. winter communications conf.; Region 6 achievement award 1984, Centennial medal 1984). Patentee in field. Home: 6656 W 87th Pl Los Angeles CA 90045

GAST, NANCY LOU, chemical company executive; b. Appleton, Wis., Aug. 13, 1941; d. Harvey William Gast and June Louella (Mohr) Webster. Med. technologist Palo Alto/Stanford (Calif.) Hosp., 1963-65; med. technologist St. Vincent Hosp., Portland, Oreg., 1965-70, chemistry supr., 1970-81; tech. rep. DuPont-Diagnostic Systems, Claremont, Calif., 1981-83, sales rep., 1983-85, account rep., 1985-87, acct. mgr., 1987—. Vol. med. technologist Health Help Ctr., Portland, 1984-88; bd. dirs. Assocs. of the Sisters of Holy Names of Jesus and Mary, Marylhurst, Oreg., 1984—. Mem. Am. Soc. Med. Tech., Assn. Oreg. Med. Technologists. (treas. 1976-78), Am. Soc. Clin. Pathologists (cert. med. technologist, assoc.). Republican. Roman Catholic. Office: EI DuPont Diagnostic Systems 1480 N Claremont Blvd Claremont CA 91711-9990

GATES, ALLEN BENSON, aerospace company executive; b. Westwood, Calif., Feb. 6, 1940; s. St. Clair and Dora Lavaun (Morey) G.; m. Elizabeth Ankers, July 4, 1960 (div. 1982); children: Allison, Tod, Jeffrey; m. Nancy Marie Sigman, Aug. 20, 1983. BSME, U. Nev., 1961, MS, 1963; PhD in Systems Engring., Case Western Res. U., 1971; MS in Mgmt., MIT, 1977. Control systems engr., program mgr. Naval Weapons Ctr., China Lake, Calif., 1962-78; long range planning mgr. Ford Aerospace, Newport Beach Calif., 1978-80, v.p. tech. affairs, Detroit, 1980-81, dir. advanced devel., 1981-84, asst. gen. mgr., Houston, 1984-85; v.p. E-O System, 1985-88; v.p. engring., 1988—. Capt. U.S. Army, 1963-66. Naval Weapons Ctr. fellow, 1966-68, Sloan fellow MIT, 1976-77; recipient Tech. Dir. award, 1974. Mem. Assn. U.S. Army, AIAA, Nat. Security Indsl. Assn., Am. Def. Preparedness Assn., Profl. Rodwo Cowboys Assn., Rotary. Republican. Office: Ford Aerospace & Communications Corp Ford Rd Newport Beach CA 92658-9983

GATES, CHARLES CASSIUS, rubber company executive; b. Morrison, Colo., May 27, 1921; s. Charles Cassius and Hazel LaDora (Rhoads) G.; m. June Scowcroft Swaner, Nov. 26, 1943; children: Diane, John Swaner. Student, MIT, 1939-41; BS, Stanford U., 1943; DEng (hon.), Mich. Tech. U., 1975, Colo. Sch. of Mines, 1985. With Copolymer Corp., Baton Rouge, 1943-46; with Gates Rubber Co., Denver, 1946—, v.p., 1951-58, exec. v.p., 1958-61, chmn. bd., 1961—, now also chief exec. officer; chmn. bd. The Gates Corp., Denver, 1982—, chief exec. officer, from 1982, also bd. dirs.; bd. dirs. Hamilton Bros. Petroleum Corp., Denver, Robinson Brick Co., Denver. Pres., trustee Gates Found.; trustee Denver Mus. Natural History, Calif. Inst. Tech., Pasadena. Recipient Community Leadership and Service award Nat. Jewish Hosp., 1974; Mgmt. Man of Year award Nat. Mgmt. Assn., 1965; named March of Dimes Citizen of the West, 1987. Mem. Conf. Bd. (dir.), Conquistadores del Cielo. Clubs: Denver Country, Cherry Hills Country, Denver, Outrigger Canoe, Waialae Country, Boone and Crockett, Club Ltd, Country Club of Colo, Roundup Riders of Rockies, Shikar-Safari Internat. (dir.), Augusta Nat. Golf, Castle Pines Golf. Office: Gates Corp 900 S Broadway Denver CO 80209

GATES, DARYL FRANCIS, police chief; b. Aug. 30, 1926. B.S. in Pub. Adminstrn., U. So. Calif., also postgrad. in Pub. Adminstrn. With Dept. Police City of Los Angeles, 1949—, lt., 1959-63, capt., 1963-65, comdr., 1965-68, dep. chief, 1968-69, asst. chief, 1969-78, chief, 1978—. Bd. councilors U. So. Calif. Inst. Saftey and Systems Mgmt.; bd. dirs. YMCA, Los Angeles; mem. Children's Village Adv. Bd. Served with USN, World War II. Mem. Calif. Peace Officers Assn., Internat. police Assn., Calif. Police Chief Assn., Internat. Assn. Chiefs of Police, Women's Peace Officers Assn. Calif., Los Angeles C. of C. Lodge: Rotary. Office: City of Los Angeles Police Dept 150 N Los Angeles St Los Angeles CA 90012 *

GATES, MILO SEDGWICK, construction company executive; b. Omaha, Apr. 25, 1923; s. Milo Talmage and Virginia (Offutt) G.; m. Anne Phleger, Oct. 14, 1950 (dec. Apr. 1987); children: Elena, Susan, Virginia, Mariquita Anne, Milo T.; m. Robin Templeton Quist, June 18, 1988. Student, Calif. Inst. Tech., 1943-44; B.S., Stanford U., 1944, M.B.A., 1948. With Swinerton & Walberg Co., San Francisco, 1955—, pres., 1976—, chmn., 1988—. Bd. dirs., trustee Children's Hosp. San Francisco; bd. trustees Grace Cathedral, San Francisco. Lt. (j.g.), USNR, 1944-46. Republican. Clubs: Pacific-Union, Bohemian (San Francisco). Home: 3757 Washington St San Francisco CA 94118 Office: Swinerton & Walberg Co 580 California St San Francisco CA 94104

GATES, ROBERT JOHN, service company executive; b. Edgewood, Iowa, Sept. 3, 1939; s. John W. and Sybil Garnet (Griffith) G.; m. Linda Kaye Hall; children: Kristi Lynn, John W. Instr. Amphitheater Community Schs., Tucson, 1976-77, coord., 1977-79; owner A Service Co., Lakeside, Ariz., 1980—; organizer, developer Fall Festival 2-Day Auto Show, Pinetop-Lakeside. Pres. Amphitheater Schs. Coord. Coun., Tucson, 1979-80; bd. dirs. Lakeside Fire Dept., Pinetop Lakeside, 1989. Mem. C. of C., Greater Tucson Jaycees (v.p. 1965-66), White Mountain Club. Republican. Home: Rte 2 PO Box 1581 Lakeside AZ 85929

GATES, THEODORE ALLAN, JR., data processing executive; b. Washington, May 24, 1933; s. Theodore Allan and Margaret (Camp) G.; m. Anne Bissell, Sept. 8, 1955; children: Virginia Anne, Nancy Bissell, Theodore Allan III, Margaret Kenyon. Student, U. Md., 1951-53, 56-57, 68-69. Mem. staff Arthur D. Little Systems, Burlington, Mass., 1976-77, Corp. Tech. Planning, Portsmouth, N.H., 1977-78; project mgr. Honeywell Info. Systems, Phoenix, 1978-81; tech. mgr. Honeywell Info. Systems, Seattle, 1981-83; mgr. data and software engring. ISC Systems Corp., Spokane, Wash., 1983—. Served with U.S. Army, 1953-56, Korea. Recipient Superior Performance award Census Bur., 1958. Mem. IEEE, Assn. Computing Machinery, Data Processing Mgmt. Assn., Boston Computer Soc., Internat. Platform Assn., Nat. Trust for Hist. Preservation, Berkeley Macintosh Users Group, Common Cause, Gorilla Found., Smithsonian Assocs., Nature Conservancy, Pi Kappa Alpha. Democrat. Lutheran. Club: Commodores (Boston). Lodges: Shriners, Masons. Home: S 4505 Farr Rd Spokane WA 99206 Office: ISC Systems Corp Box TAF-C8 Spokane WA 99220

GATES, THOMAS EDWARD, civil engineer, researcher; b. Tachikawa AFB, Japan, June 25, 1953; came to U.S., 1954; s. Harold Charles and Masako (Endo) G.; m. LeAnn Faye Eakins, Aug. 19, 1981 (div. 1986). BS, Kans. State U., 1979, MS, 1981. Registered profl. engr., Wash., Kans., Alaska. Advt. salesman Junction City (Kans.) Daily Union, 1972-74; co-op student Burns & McDonnell, Kansas City, Mo., 1975-76; state insp. Riley County Pub. Works, Manhattan, Kans., 1977-78, field supr., 1978, cons., 1979; grad. rsch. asst. Kans. State U., Manhattan, 1979-81; engr. Batttelle Pacific N.W. Labs., Richland, Wash., 1981-83, rsch. engr., 1983-85, sr. rsch. engr., 1985-86; mgr. Waste Package Projects BWIP, 1986-88; acting mgr. Support Projects BWIP, 1988; mgr. for def. programs Westinghouse Hanford Co., Richland, 1988—; cons. Elec. Power Rsch. Inst., Washington, Atomic Energy of Can. Ltd. Rsch. Co., Ottawa, Can.; lead jusge Wash. State Sci. Talent Search, Richland. Contbr. 4 articles to profl. jours., 12 tech. reports; session works, obtaining accelerated data on concrete degradation, 1981, concrete durability and degradation processes, 1986. Councilman City of Richland, 1988—; mem. Phys. Planning Com., Richland, 1982-87, vice chmn. 1983-84, chmn. 1984-87; precinct. chmn. Rep. Cen., Richland, 1984—, dep. registrar 1985—, state del. 1988, county del. 1986, 88; instr. christian catechism doctrine Christ The King Ch., Richland, 1981-82; chmn. Sausage Festival Vol., 1984-86; bd. dirs. Salvation Army Adv. Coun., Richland, 1987—, chmn., 1987—; vice chmn., program chmn. Benton-Franklin Community Action Com., Pasco, Wash., 1988—; mem. March of Dimes, Junction City, 1976-80, Walk-A-Thon, 1973-80, campaign chmn., 1978-79, chmn. bd., 1979-80; chmn. dept. campaign United Way, Richland, 1984, Cen. Bus. Dist. Master Plan Team, Richland C. of C., 1987. Named one of Outstanding Young Men of Am., Montgomery, Ala., 1987. Mem. Am. Concrete Inst. (tech. com. 118 computers 1983—, 227 radioactive waste mgmt. 1983—, E801 student concrete projects 1984—, Harry F. Thomson Scholarship 1980), ASCE (tech. coun. on computer practices pub. com. N.Y.C. area 1986), Kiwanis, KC. Roman Catholic. Home: 1937 Forest Ave Richland WA 99352 Office: PO Box 1970 Richland WA 99352

GATES, WILLIAM HENRY, software company executive; b. Seattle, Oct. 28, 1955; s. William H. and Mary M. (Maxwell) G. Grad. high sch., Seattle, 1973; student, Harvard U., 1975. Chmn. bd. Microsoft Corp., Redmond, Wash., 1976—, now chief exec. officer. Recipient Howard Vollum award, Reed Coll., Portland, Oreg., 1984. Office: Microsoft Corp 16011 NE 36th Way Redmond WA 98073-9717 *

GATHERS, LESLIE HOWARD, real estate developer; b. Phila., Aug. 17, 1945; s. Howard Leslie and Lois Edna (Cunningham) G. BA, California State Tchrs. Coll., Pa., 1967; postgrad., Parsons Design Sch., 1969. Buyer, supr. Lamport Textile Import, N.Y.C., 1968-70; interior designer, prin. Leslie Howard Assocs. N.Y., Ridgewood, N.J., 1970-74; v.p. pub. rels. Safeco Title Ins. Co., Panorama City, Calif., 1974-77; pres. Calif. Conversion Co. Real Estate Devel. and Svc., L.A., 1977-83; ptnr. Trumps Restaurant, L.A., 1979—, K.C. Nightclub, Phoenix, Ariz., 1986—; pres. Leslie Howard Assocs., L.A., 1983-86, Leslie Gathers Assocs., Phoenix, 1986—; cons., L.A. County Bd. Suprs., 1978-82, L.A. County Housing Task Force, 1978-82, Multi Housing News, N.Y.C., 1979; founder, dir., Bank of L.A., 1980-83. Contbr. articles to various publs.; author condominium conversion legislation, L.A. County. Bd. dirs. Mcpl. Elections Com. L.A., 1979-83; mem. ad hoc com., L.A. Bd. Suprs., 1980. Mem. Camelback Businessmen Assn., Phoenix C. of C. Republican. Methodist. Home: 2404 N 18th Dr Phoenix AZ 85007

GATTI, DANIEL JON, lawyer; b. Racine, Wis., Apr. 22, 1946; s. Daniel John and Rosemary J. (Moore) G.; m. Donna Jeane Gatti, Mar. 30, 1984; children: Danny, DiAndra, Stephanie, David. BS, Western Oreg. State U., 1968; JD, Willamette U., 1973. Bar: Oreg. 1973, U.S. Dist. Ct. Oreg. 1973, U.S. Ct. Appeals (9th cir.) 1974, U.S. Ct. Appeals (2d cir.) 1985, U.S. Supreme Ct. 1979; cert. trial specialist. Tchr. Lake Oswego (Oreg.) High Sch., 1970; specialist in edn. law Oreg. Dept. Edn., Salem, 1973-75; pres., atty., ptnr. Gatti & Gatti, P.C., Salem, 1975—. Co-author: The Teacher and The Law, 1972, Encyclopedic Dictionary of School Law, 1975, New Encyclopedic Dictionary of School Law, 1983. V.p., bd. trustees Western States Chiropractic Coll., Portland, Oreg., 1976—. Mem. Oreg. Bar Assn., Assn. Trial Lawyers Am., Am. Bd. Trial Advocacy (cert. as trial specialist 1987), Am. Adjudicature Soc., Illahe Club. Office: Gatti Gatti Maier & Assocs 1761 Liberty St Salem OR 97302

GAUDIO, JOSEPH GILBERT, accountant; b. Chgo., Apr. 24, 1965; s. Alexander Louis and Mary Grace (Dimasi) G. BS in Acctg., Ariz. State U., 1987. Staff acct. Arthur Andersen and Co., Phoenix, 1987—. Republican. Roman Catholic.

GAUGER, GREGORY SCOTT, military officer; b. Plymouth, Mich., Apr. 2, 1961; s. Jay Grant and Faith Anne (Pasma) G. BSME, Mich. Tech. U., 1984. Commd. lt. USN, 1984; asst. adminstrv. officer Attack Squadron One Four Five, Naval Air Station Whidbey Island, Wash., 1988—. Mem. U.S. Naval Inst. Home: 1130 Crosswoods Dr Oak Harbor WA 98277 Office: Hqrs EUCOM APO New York NY 01928

GAULKE, MARY FLORENCE, library administrator; b. Johnson City, Tenn., Sept. 24, 1923; d. Gustus Thomas and Mary Belle (Bennett) Erickson; m. James Wymond Crowley, Dec. 1, 1939; 1 son, Grady Gaulke (name legally changed); m. 2d, Bud Gaulke, Sept. 1, 1945 (dec. Jan. 1978); m. 3d, Richard Lewis McNaughton, Mar. 21, 1983. B.S. in Home Econs., Oreg. State U., 1963; M.S. in L.S., U. Oreg., 1968, Ph.D. in Spl. Edn., 1970. Cert. standard personnel supr., standard handicapped learner, Oreg. Head dept. home econs. Riddle Sch. Dist. (Oreg.), 1963-66; library cons. Douglas County Intermediate Edn. Dist., Roseburg, Oreg., 1966-67; head resident, head counselor Prometheus Project, So. Oreg. Coll., Ashland, summers 1966-68; supr. librarians Medford Sch. Dist. (Oreg.), 1970-73; instr. in psychology So. Oreg. Coll., Ashland, 1970-73; library supr. Roseburg Sch. Dist., 1974—; resident psychologist Black Oaks Boys Sch., Medford, 1970-75; mem. Oreg. Gov.'s Council on Libraries, 1979. Author: Vo-Ed Course for Junior High, 1965; Library Handbook, 1967; Instructions for Preparation of Cards For All Materials Cataloged for Libraries, 1971; Handbook for Training Library Aides, 1972. Coordinator Laubach Lit. Workshops for High Sch. Tutors, Medford, 1972. Mem. So. Oreg. Library Fedn. (sec. 1971-73), ALA, Oreg. Library Assn., Pacific N.W. Library Assn., Delta Kappa Gamma (pres. 1980-82), Phi Delta Kappa (historian, research rep.). Republican. Methodist. Clubs: Lodge: Order Eastern Star (worthy matron 1956-57). Home: 1625 Days Creek Rd Days Creek OR 97429 Office: Roseburg Pub Schs 1419 Valley View Dr Roseburg OR 97470

GAUSTAD, EDWIN SCOTT, historian; b. Rowley, Iowa, Nov. 14, 1923; s. Sverre and Norma (McEachron) G.; m. Helen Virginia Morgan, Dec. 19, 1946; children—Susan, Glen Scott, Peggy Lynn. B.A., Baylor U., 1947; M.A., Brown U., 1948, Ph.D., 1951. Instr. Brown U., 1951-52, Am. Council Learned Socs. scholar in residence, 1952-53; dean Shorter Coll., 1953-57; prof. humanities U. Redlands, 1957-65; asso. prof. history U. Calif., Riverside, 1965-67; prof. U. Calif., 1968-89, prof. emeritus, 1989—. Author: The Great Awakening in New England, 1957, Historical Atlas of Religion in America, 2d edit, 1976, Dissent in American Religion, 1973, Baptist Piety: The Last Will and Testimony of Obadiah Holmes, 1978, George Berkeley in America, 1979, Faith of Our Fathers, 1987; editor books, most recent being: Documentary History of Religion in America, 2 vols., 1982, 83; editor: Arno Press, 1970-79; editorial bd.: Jour. Ch. and State, 1970—; contbr. articles to profl. publs. Served to 1st lt. USAAC, 1943-45. Decorated Air medal; Am. Council Learned Socs. grantee, 1952-53, 72-73; Am. Philos. Soc. grantee, 1972-73. Mem. Am. Hist. Assn., Am. Acad. Religion, Am. Soc. Ch. History (pres.), Orgn. Am. Hist., Phi Beta Kappa. Democrat. Baptist. Office: U Calif Dept History Riverside CA 92521

GAUTHIER, VICTOR JOSEPH, mining executive, consultant; b. Berlin, N.H., Jan. 8, 1941; s. Omer Daniel and Alice (DuBois) G.; m. Sandra Frances Dusek, Aug. 15, 1964 (div. Dec. 1980; children: Kathryn K., Nina E. Student, Ryder Coll., Trenton, N.J., 1962. Mgr. State Loan & Fin. Mgmt. Corp., Trenton, N.J., 1962-66; customer engr. AT&T Bell Systems, Manchester, N.H., 1966-84; chmn., pres. Calif. Gold Producers, Inc., Seal Beach, 1984—; mineral explorer Gauthier Exploration Co., Sacramento, 1984-85; cons. Mine Systems Assoc., L.A., 1985—, L.A. County, 1985—; cons. E.C.M. Group, Inc., Cerritos, 1988—; bd. dirs. Gauthier, Hicks & Pipher Assocs., Seal Beach, Hadi Fin. Co., Compton, Calif., Little Bear Devel. Co., Santa Ana, Calif. With USAF, 1958-62. Roman Catholic. Office: Calif Gold Producers Inc PO Box 55 Seal Beach CA 90740

GAY, DON ALAN, metals industry executive; b. L.A., Aug. 17, 1946; s. Dominic and Elizabeth Mary (Parsons) G.; m. Sharon Lynn Doss, Jan. 24, 1969; children: Christie, Brett, Don. AA, St. Mary's Coll., Moraga, Calif., 1967; AS, Los Angeles Trade Tech., 1971. With Downey Steel Treating Co., Inc., Calif., 1960-70; quality control mgr. Orange Empire Heat Treating Co., Anaheim, Calif., 1970-73; gen. mgr. Continental Heat Treating Co., Norwalk, Calif., 1973-75; sales mgr., quality control mgr. Varco Internat., Inc., Orange, Calif., 1975-84; pres., chief exec. officer Diversified Metall. Svcs., Inc., Garden Grove, Calif., 1984—. Mem. Metal Heat Treating Assn. (pres. 1979-80), Am Soc. Metals. Republican. Roman Catholic. Office: Diversified Metall Svcs Inc 12101 Industry St Garden Grove CA 92641

GAY, JAMES EDWARD, manufacturing executive; b. Richmond, Calif., Oct. 7, 1949; s. Raymond L. and Jennie Lee (Gillock) G.; m. Bonnie S. Werth, Oct. 10, 1976; 1 child, Courtney Anne. BS, U. Calif., Berkeley, 1972; M in Bus., St. Mary's Coll., Moraga, Calif., 1979. Merchandise mgr. Lucky Stores, Inc., Dublin, Calif., 1972-79; assoc. A.T. Kearney Inc., Chgo., 1979-83, Slavin Assocs., San Francisco, 1982-83; mgr. Amdahl Corp., Santa Clara, Calif., 1983—. Mem. Am. Prodn. and Inventory Control Soc. (cert. mgmt. 1983, coll. liaison 1983-85), St. Mary's Coll. Grad. Sch. Alumni Assn. (bd. dirs. 1983-84). Home: 60 Wood Ranch Circle Danville CA 94526 Office: Amdahl Corp MS #190 1250 E Arques Ave Sunnyvale CA 94086

GAY, PHILIP THOMAS, oil company executive; b. Manchester, Conn., Apr. 27, 1949; s. Bert Duayne and Rosemary (Wise) G.; m. Shirley Marie Dirks, Mar. 17, 1973 (div. 1977); 1 child, Nathan W. 7SBA cum laude, U. Colo., 1976, MBA, 1980. CPA, Colo.; lic. real estate broker, Colo. Revenue agt. IRS, Denver, 1974-78; auditor Golden Dist. Atty.'s Office, Golden, Colo., 1978-82; supervisory auditor KN Energy, Inc., Lakewood, Colo., 1982-83; dir. acctg. Western Oil Corp., Lakewood, 1983-85, v.p. acctg., 1985—; ad hoc prof. Met. State Coll., Denver, 1982, Aurora (Colo.) Community Coll., 1988. Pres. Golden Pines Homeowners Assn., Golden, 1980-82; advisor bd. dirs. Jefferson County Housing Authority, Lakewood, 1981-82, others.With U.S. Army, 1969-71. Mem. AICPA, Colo. Soc. CPA's, Assn. MBA Execs., Beta Gamma Sigma. Republican. Roman Catholic. Home: 20A S Nome St Aurora CO 80012 Office: Western Oil Corp 12055 W 2d Pl PO Box 15277 Lakewood CO 80215

GAYNOR, JOSEPH, chemical engineering consultant; b. N.Y.C., Nov. 15, 1925; s. Morris and Rebecca (Schnapper) G.; m. Elaine Bauer, Aug. 19, 1951; children—Barbara Lynne, Martin Scott, Paul David, Andrew Douglas. B.Ch.E., Polytechnic Inst. Bklyn., 1950; M.S., Case-Western Res. U., 1952, Ph.D., 1955. Research asst. Case Inst., Cleve., 1952-55; with Gen. Engring. Labs. Gen. Electric Co., Schenectady, N.Y., 1955-66, sect. mgr. research and devel., 1962-66; group v.p. research Bell & Howell Co., 1966-72; mgr. comml. devel. group, mem. pres.' office Horizons Research, Inc., Cleve., 1972-73; pres. Innovative Tech. Assos., Sierra Madre, Calif., 1973—; mem. nat. materials adv. bd. com. Nat. Acad. Scis.; chmn. conf. com. 2d internat. conf. on bus. graphics 1979, program chmn. 1st internat. congress on advances in non-impact printing techs., 1981, mem. adv. com. 2d internat. congress on advances in non-impact printing techs., 1984, chmn. publs. com. 3rd internat. congress on advances in non-impact printing techs., 1986. Editor, Advances in Non-Impact Printing Technologies (Procs.), 1983; editor Advances in Non-Impact Printing Technologies (Procs.), Vol. II., 1988; patentee in field. Served with U.S. Army, 1944-46. Fellow AAAS, Am. Inst. Chem. Engrs.; mem. Am. Chem. Soc., Soc. Photographic Scientists and Engrs. (sr., gen. chmn. 2d internat. conf. on electrophotography 1973, chmn. bus. graphics tech. sect. 1976—, chmn. edn. com. Los Angeles chpt. 1978—), Am. Soc. Photobiology, Sigma Xi, Tau Beta Pi, Phi Lambda Upsilon, Alpha Chi Sigma. Home: 108 La Brea Oxnard CA 93035 Office: 3639 E Harbor Blvd #203E Ventura CA 93001

GAZUNIS, KATHERINE-TERESSA, economic development executive, consultant; b. Washington, Apr. 9, 1954; d. George Nicholas and Florence Irene (Frampton) G. BA, Mary Washington Coll., 1976; MA, U. Utah, 1982; diploma in econ. devel., U. Okla., 1988. Cert. econ. devel. fin. profl. Owner, mgr. Griffin and Phoenix Cons., Salt Lake City, 1981-83; mgr. Forward Delta County, Delta, Colo., 1984-85; econ. devel. specialist Region 10 Econ. Devel. Dist., Montrose, Colo., 1985-87; exec. dir. Eagle County Econ. Devel. Corp., Eagle, Colo., 1987—; mem. Colo. Gov.'s High Tech. Task Force, 1986, Colo. Gov.'s Econ. Devel. Tech. Task Force, 1987-88; mem. president's small bus. coun. U. Colo., Boulder, 1988-89. Mem. Tony Tafel Athletic Scholarship Com., Eagle, 1988-89, Region 12 Revolving Loan Fund, Frisco, Colo., 1988-89, Eagle County Airport Commn., 1989; mem. bus. adv. coun. Colo. Mountain Coll., 1989. Recipient President's Outstanding Pub.-Pvt. Partnership award HUD, 1984; Order of Ahepa scholar, 1972, Western Interstate Commn. on Higher Edn. scholar, 1976. Mem. Am. Econ. Devel. Coun., Econ. Developers Coun. Colo. (pres. 1988-89, Disting. Svc. award 1986), Bus. and Profl. Women Vail. Am. Orthodox. Office: Eagle County Econ Devel Co PO Box 1440 Eagle CO 81631

GDOWSKI, DIANA, tax specialist; b. Utica, N.Y., Aug. 16, 1951; d. Michael and Frances Mary (Carzo) G. BA, U. San Diego, 1972; MA, U. So. Calif., 1979, MBA, 1981, M Bus. Taxation, 1986. CPA, Calif. Instr. French lang. Bishop Montgomery High Sch., Torrance, Calif., 1973-76, U. So. Calif., L.A., 1977-79; auditor Ernst & Whinney, L.A., 1981-82, mgmt. cons., 1982-83; tax specialist Fox & Co., L.A., 1983-84; sr. tax specialist Kenneth Leventhal & Co., L.A., 1984-87; tax mgr. Deloitte, Haskins & Sells, Costa Mesa, Calif., 1987-88; mgr. tax acctg. Fluor Corp., Irvine, Calif., 1988—. Vice-pres., Village Ct. Homeowners' Assn., L.A., 1982. Mem. AICPA, Calif. Soc. CPAs. Republican. Roman Catholic. Office: Fluor Corp 3333 Michelson Dr Irvine CA 92730

GEAKE, ROBERT WILLIAM, lawyer, utility executive; b. Xenia, Ohio, Dec. 7, 1952; s. Arthur William and Pauline (Irwin) G.; m. Lynette Sherbo, June 2, 1979; 1 child, Jonathan. BS, West Liberty State Coll., 1975; JD, W.Va. U., 1978; MBA, W.Va. Coll. Grad. Studies, 1983. Bar: W.Va., Ariz. Staff atty. Pub. Svc. Commn. W.Va., Charleston, 1979-81; dep. commr. securities W.Va. State Auditor, Charleston, 1981-84; v.p., gen. counsel Ariz. Water Co., Phoenix, 1984—. Mem. Maricopa County Bar Assn., Omicron Delta Epsilon, Delta Mu Delta, Theta Xi. Home: 1029 E Taro Ln Phoenix AZ 85024 Office: Ariz Water Co 3805 N Black Canyon Hwy Phoenix AZ 85038

GEAR, MARSHA LYNN, editor, university official; b. Berwyn, Ill., Dec. 31, 1952; d. Roy Frank and Lorraine Edna (Bubenik) Kveton; m. Arthur Leon Gear, III, Dec. 9, 1972; children: Arthur Leon IV, Mary Rebecca. BA cum laude, San Diego State U., 1985. Publ. asst. San Diego State U., 1979-85, communications officer, editor alumni mag., 1985--. Sunday sch. tchr. College Ave. Bapt. Ch., San Diego, Calif. Mem. Pub. Relations Soc. Am., Golden Key. Democrat. Office: San Diego State U Office Communications San Diego CA 92182

GEARY, GREG GERARD, education educator; b. Long Beach, Calif., Oct. 20, 1959; s. Charles Francis and Gladys (Herbert) G.; m. Diane Leticia Holly. BS in Physical Edn., U. Redlands, 1982; MS in Exercise Physiology, Fullerton State U., 1986; PhD in Physiology, Loma Linda U., 1988. Tchr. San Bernardino City (Calif.) Sch., 1989—. Mem. NEA, Calif. Edn. Assn., Am. Coll. Sports Medicard. Republican.

GEBAUER, ANDREA MADELEINE, hairdesigner; b. L.A., June 19, 1950; d. Werner Ludwick and Danna (McGraw) G.; m. Michael Leach (div. 1977); children: Joshua Christopher, Adam Michael. Grad., Lapin Bros. Beauty Sch., 1975. Asst. Numero Uno Hair, Glendale, Calif., 1977-78; men's hairdesigner Ryals, Glendale, 1978-80; hairdesigner Gallery, Pasadena, Calif., 1980-85, owner, 1985--. Mem. Pasadena C. of C., Nat. Fedn. Ind. Bus., Nat. Hairdresser Assn. Democrat. Jewish. Office: Gallery 696 E Colorado Pasadena CA 91101

GEBBIE, KRISTINE MOORE, health official; b. Sioux City, Iowa, June 26, 1943; d. Thomas Carson and Gladys Irene (Stewart) Moore; children: Anna, Sharon, Eric. BSN, St. Olaf Coll., 1965; MSN, UCLA, 1968. Project dir. USPHS tng. grant, St. Louis, 1972-77; coordinator nursing St. Louis U., 1974-76, asst. dir. nursing, 1976-78, clin. prof., 1977-78; adminstr. Oreg. Health Div., Portland, 1978—; assoc. prof. Oreg. Health Scis. U. Portland, 1980—; mem. Presdl. Commn. on Human Imunodeficiency Virus Epidemic, 1987-88. Author: (with Deloughery and Neuman) Consultation and Community Orgn., 1971, (with Deloughery) Political Dynamics: Impact on Nurses, 1975; (with Scheer) Creative Teaching in Clinical Nursing, 1976. Bd. dirs. Luth. Family Svcs. Oreg. and S.W. Wash., 1979-84; bd. dirs. Oreg. Psychoanalytic Found., 1983-87. Recipient Disting. Alumna award St. Olaf Coll., 1979. Mem. Assn. State and Territorial Health Ofcls., 1988 (pres. 1984-85, exec. com. 1980-87, McCormick award 1988), Am. Pub. Health Assn., Hastings Ctr., N.Am. Nursing Diagnosis Assn. (treas. 1983-87), Oreg. Pub. Health Assn., Am. Soc. Pub. Adminstrn. (adminstrn. award II 1983), City Club of Portland. Office: Oreg State Health Div 1400 SW 5th St Portland OR 97207

GEBHARD, DAVID, museum director, educator; b. Cannon Falls, Minn., July 21, 1927; s. Walter J. and Ann (Olson) G.; m. Patricia Peeke, July 7, 1954; children: Ellen Jean, Tyra Ann. B.A., U. Minn., 1949, M.A., 1951, Ph.D., 1957. Curator, instr. art U. N.Mex., 1953-55; dir. Roswell (N.Mex.) Mus., 1955-61; prof. art, dir. art galleries U. Calif. at Santa Barbara, 1961-80; curator archtl. drawing collection Art Mus., 1980—; field research in archeology, summers 1949-57; Fulbright prof. Tech. U. Istanbul, Turkey, 1960-61; cons. hist. preservation, 1970—. Author: Prehistoric Cave Paintings of the Diablo Region of Texas, 1960, A Guide to the Architecture of Purcell and Elmslie, 1960, A Guide to Architecture in Southern California, 1964, R.M. Schindler: Architect; Architecture in California, 1868-1968, 1968, Kem Weber and the Moderene, 1969, The Richfield Building, 1928-1968, 1969, Charles F.A. Voysey, Architect, 1970, Architecture in Los Angeles, A Complete Guide, 1985, An Arcadian Landscape: The Gardens of A.E. Hanson, 1920-31, 1985, Santa Barbara: El Pueblo Viejo, 1986, Romanza: The California Architecture of Frank Lloyd Wright; co-author: Lloyd Wright, Architect, 1972, High Style Design, Whitney Museum American Art, 1985, A Guide to Architecture in San Francisco and Northern California, 1973, 2d edit., 1986, Indian Art of the Northern Plains, 1974, Los Angeles in the 30's; Bay Area Houses, 1976, A Guide to Architecture in Los Angeles and Southern California, 1977, A Guide to Architecture in Minnesota, 1977, 200 Years of American Architectural Drawing, 1977, A View of California Architecture, 1960-1976, 1977, Picturesque California Homes, 1978, The Architecture of Samuel and J.C. Newsom, 1878-1908, 1979, The Architecture of Gregory Ain, 1980, California Crazy, 1980, Tulsa Art Deco, 1980, Santa Barbara, the Creation of a New Spain in America, 1980, Legacy of Minneapolis, 1983, Romanza, The California Architecture of Frank Lloyd Wright, 1988, L.A. in the 30s, 1989; co-author: Frank Lloyd Wright in California, 1987; editor: California Architects & Architecture Series; contbr. articles to profl. jours. Pres. Citizens Planning Assn. Santa Barbara County, Inc., 1970-76; vice chmn. Historic Landmark Commn., Santa Barbara, 1973—, Citizens Planning Assn., 1980—; bd. dirs. Regional Plan Assn., So. Calif., Western Found.; chmn. Montecito Archl. Bd., 1988—. Served with AUS, 1945-47. Research grantee NSF; Research grantee NEA; Research grantee Nat. Endowment Humanities; Nat. Park Service grantee; Ford found. grantee study Turkish architecture, 1965; Guggenheim Found. fellow, 1980-81. mem. AIA (hon. (nat.) 1989, M. Riggs award), Soc. Am. Archaeology, Am. Anthrop. Assn., Coll. Art Assn., Soc. Archtl. Historians (pres. 1980-81, dir.), Archtl. Found. Santa Barbara (bd. dirs.). Home: 895 E Mountain Dr Santa Barbara CA 93103 Office: U Calif Archtl Drawing Collection Santa Barbara CA 93106

GEBHART, DOUGLAS ALAN, air force officer; b. Chillecothe, Ohio, Sept. 18, 1962; s. Robert Lee and Ann (Spetnagel) Lane. BS in Aero. and Astron., Ohio State U., 1984; MS in Systems Mgmt., U. So. Calif., 1987. Commd. 2d. lt. USAF, 1984, advanced through grades to capt., 1988; space systems staff officer Hdqrs. Air Force Space Command, Peterson AFB, 1984-87, mission controller, 1987-88; space ops. officer 3d Satellite Control Squadron, Falcon AFB, 1988--; project warrior coord. Hdqrs. Air Force Space Command, 1984-87. Mem. Peterson AFB Protestant Funds Coun., 1987--; capt. Peterson AFB Protestant Chapel Ushers, 1987--. Mem. Air Force Assn., Ohio State U. Alumni Assn. Republican. Office: 2d Space Wind/ 3SCS (MCC2) Falcon AFB CO 80914

GEDDES, BARBARA SHERYL, communications executive, consultant; b. Poughkeepsie, N.Y., May 27, 1944; d. Samuel Pierson and Dorothy Charlotte (Graham) Brush; m. James Morrow Geddes, Feb. 24, 1968 (div. Dec. 1980); 1 child, Elisabeth. BA, Skidmore Coll., 1968. Project leader Four-Phase Systems, Cupertino, Calif., 1976-77, Fairchild Co., San Jose, Calif., 1979-80; mgr. tech. publs. Mohawk Data Scis., Los Gatos, Calif., 1977-79, Sytek Inc., Mountain View, Calif., 1981-83; project mgr. Advanced Micro Computers, Santa Clara, Calif., 1980-81; v.p. communications systems Strategic Inc., Cupertino, 1983-86; pres., mng. ptnr. Computer and Telecommunicatios Profl. Services, Mountain View, Calif., 1986—; cons. H-P, Varian, Aydin Energy, Chemelex, also others, 1972—; v.p. Conf. Recorders, Santa Clara, 1975-77; advisor Tele-PC, Morgan Hill, Calif., 1983—. Editor: Mathematics/Science Library, 7 vols., 1971. Contbr. numerous articles to mags. Mem. Santa Clara County Adoptions Adv. Bd., 1971-73, Las Cumbres Archtl. Control Commn., Los Gatos, 1983; advisor Los Altos Hills Planning Commn., Calif., 1978-79. N.Y. State Regents merit scholar, 1962. Mem. Assn. for Computing Machinery (editor 1970-72), Nat. Soc. for Performance and Instrn., Bus. and Profl. Advt. Assn., Women in Communications (pres. San Jose 1983—). Democrat. Home: 1052 Colorado Pl Palo Alto CA 94303 Office: Computer Telecommunications Profl Services 2672 Bayshore Pkwy #1050 Mountain View CA 94043

GEDDES, GARY LEE, wildlife park director; b. Peoria, Ill., Aug. 23, 1950; s. Robert and Mary O. (McCartney) G.; m. Debbie L. Lush, Sept. 7, 1974; children: Jake Austin, Cody Robert, Katelyn Jane. AS, Ill. Cen. Jr. Coll., 1970; BA in Zoology, So. Ill. U., 1972. Dir. Wildlife Prairie Park, Hanna City, Ill., 1973-81, N.W. Trek Wildlife Park, Eatonville, Wash., 1981—; co-chmn. bd. dirs. Region 6 Tourism Council, Olympia, Wash., 1984-86; vice chmn. Bates Vocat. Sch. Tourism Adv. Bd.; exec. bd. mem. Regional Tourism Council, Olympia, Wash., 1983-88; chmn. tourism and travel adv. bd. Knapp Bus. Coll. Leader Cub Scouts Am. Fellow Am. Assn. Zool. Parks and Aquariums. Club: Mountaineers (Tacoma). Home: 6502 255th St Ct E Graham WA 98338 Office: Northwest Trek Wildlife Pk 11610 Trek Dr E Eatonville WA 98328

GEDDES, JOHN WILLIAM, pharmacist; b. Denver, Apr. 11, 1949; s. William A. and Audrey J. (Mattson) G.; m. Gail J. Naaden, Nov. 23, 1973; children: Christopher, Mark, Carrie, Janine, Jeffrey, Audrey. AA, northeastern Jr. Coll., Sterling, Colo., 1967-69; BS in Pharmacy, U. Colo., 1973. Lic. pharmacist, Colo. Pharmacy mgr. Geddes Drug, Inc., Evergreen, Colo., 1974-75; pharmacist K-Mart Corp., Englewood, Colo., 1975; pharmacy mgr. K-Mart Corp., Longmont, Colo., 1975-78; prin. Geddes Drug Store, Lamar, Colo., 1978—; mem. U. Colo. Sch. Pharmacy Adv. Council, Boulder, 1985—; v.p. Colo. Bd. Pharmacy, Denver, 1983-85. Active Lamar Utilities Bd., 1985—. Mem. SE Colo. Pharm. (pres. 1979-83, 88—), Am. Pharm. Assn. (William S. Apple Meml. Program in Community Pharmacy Mgmt. award, 1987), Nat. Assn. Retail Druggists, Colo. Pharm Assn. (del.). Republican. Roman Catholic. Lodges: Rotary (pres. Lamar club 1987-88), KC (treas. local chpt. 1978-80). Home: 301 S 3d St Lamar CO 81052 Office: Geddes Drug 119 S Main St Lamar CO 81052

GEE, ÉLWOOD GORDON, university president; b. Vernal, Utah, Feb. 2, 1944; s. Elwood A. and Vera (Showalter) G.; m. Elizabeth Dutson, Aug. 26, 1968; 1 dau., Rebekah. B.A., U. Utah, 1968; J.D., Columbia U., 1971, Ed.D., 1972. Asst. dean U. Utah, Salt Lake City, 1973-74; jud. fellow U.S. Supreme Ct., Washington, 1974-75; assoc. dean Brigham Young U., Provo, Utah, 1975-79; dean W.Va. U., Morgantown, 1979-81, pres., 1981-85; pres. U. Colo., 1985—. Author: Education Law and Public Schools, 1978, Law and Public Education, 1980, Violence, Values and Justice in American Education, 1982, Fair Employment Practice, 1982. W.K. Kellogg fellow, 1971-72; Mellon fellow, 1977-78. Mem. ABA, Adminstrv. Conf. U.S., Phi Delta Kappa, Phi Kappa Phi. Mormon. Home: PO Box 128 Boulder CO 80309 Office: U Colo 914 Broadway Campus Box B-35 Boulder CO 80309

GEELAN, PETER BRIAN KENNETH, publisher; b. London, May 28, 1929; arrived in U.S., 1979; s. Michael John and Elsie Doreen (Bath) G.; m. Joan Norris, Apr. 2, 1953; children: Michael Anthony, Jeremy Paul, Christopher Patrick; m. Marjorie Wells, Apr. 20, 1980; 1 child, Jane Lesley. G-rad., Kilburn Grammar, London. Advtg. mgr. Ward, Lock & Co., London, 1949-50; sales mgr. Staples Press, London, 1951-57; European mgr. Prentice-Hall Internat., N.Y.C., 1958-60, London, 1958-60; v.p. European ops. CBS Holt Publishing Group, N.Y.C., London, 1961-70; mng. dir. Eurospan Group of Publishers, London, 1970-79; pres. Peter Geelan, Inc., Las Vegas, 1980—; chmn. Eurospan Group of Publishers, London,1980—, Adamantine Press Ltd, London, 1980—. Sgt. British Army, 1947-49. Home: 7445 Valhalla Ln Las Vegas NV 89123 Office: 3 Henrietta St, Covent Garden, London WC2E8LU, England

GEFFERS, ELIZABETH DI GIACOMO, health care administrator; b. N.Y.C., Nov. 8, 1939. BA in Health Edn., Jersey City State Coll., 1961; MPH in Adminstrn., Johns Hopkins U., 1966. Grad. fellow environ. medicine Johns Hopkins U., Balt., 1966-67; adminstr. North Hudson Hosp., med. staff officer SS US Lines, Inc.; assoc. dir. nursing svcs. Cedars-Sinai Med. Ctr., L.A., 1970-81; nat. and internat. health care cons. Monterey Park, Calif., 1981-88; dir. ambulatory nursing, assoc. dir. ops. FHP Internat. Inc., Monterey Park, 1988—; exec. dir., chief operating officer Queen of Angels Clinic and Family Care Ctr., L.A., 1986-87. Bd. dirs. Good Shepherd Ctr.; AIDS task force advisor La Habra Unified Sch. Dist.; mem. adv. bd. Echo Park Com. Coordinating Coun. Mem. Royal Soc. Health, AAUW, Emergency Nurses Assn., Calif. Soc. Nursing Svc. Adminstrs., Sigma Theta Tau. Home: 20961 Morningside Dr Trabuco Canyon Area CA 92679

GEHL, BARBARA SUE, accountant, bookkeeper; b. Delta, Colo., July 20, 1959; d. William Boyd and Ida Rose (Holvoet) Cruse; m. Russell C. Gehl, May 21, 1988. BS in Acctg., Mesa Coll., 1981. Staff acct. Smith, Hawkins & Co., Hotchkiss, Colo., 1981-83; mgr. office bookkeeper H&R Precision, Paonia, Colo., 1984; tax preparer Tax Preparation, Hotskiss, Colo., 1984; acct., paraplanner Herndon Fin. Planning, Paonia, 1984-86; bookeeper Aronowitz, Helgeson & Pearson, Arvada, Colo., 1986-88; bus. asst. Pacific Mountain Network, Lakewood, Colo., 1988—. Mem. AAUW (v.p. programs 1985-86). Roman Catholic. Home: 2231 Depew St Edgewater CO 80214 Office: Pacific Mountain Network 12596 W Bayard #215 Lakewood CO 80228

GEHR, DAVID EDWARD, telecommunications executive; b. Lorain, Ohio, July 18, 1948; s. Earl Edward and Dorothy Marie (Hammel) G.; m. Dorothy Leeann Soder, Oct. 9, 1971; children: Jason Michael, Leah Suzann. Student, Internat. Correspondence Sch., Scranton, Pa., 1973-75, Lorain County Community Coll., 1976-77, U. Calif., Berkeley, 1989—. Assembler Ford Motor Co., Lorain, 1968-72; cen. office technician Lorain (Ohio) Telephone Co., 1973-79; equipment engr. No. Telecom Inc., Raleigh, N.C., 1979-80; quality auditor No. Telecom Inc., Research Triangle Park, N.C., 1980-81; quality mgr. No. Telecom Inc., Research Triangle Park, 1981-83; mgr. program mgmt. No. Telecom Inc., Seattle, 1983-86; mgr. customer service No. Telecom Inc., San Ramon, Calif., 1986-87; dir. customer service No. Telecom Inc., San Ramon, 1987—; mem. Am. Soc. for Quality Control, Raleigh, 1980-83; founding mem. No. Telecom Mgmt. Assn., Research Triangle Park, 1982—; adv. mem. First Application System Test Tech. Adv. Council, Research Triangle Park, 1988—, Nat. Emergency Svc. and Adminstn. Ctr. Com., Research Triangle Park, 1988—. Mem. Parent Tchr. Assn., San Ramon, 1988, No. Telecom Polit. Action Com., Washinton, 1986—, Unity Ch. Walnut Creek, KQED, Cousteau Soc., Smithsonian Inst., Nat. Rifle Assn., Nat. Wildlife Fed. With USN, 1968-71. Mem. Am. Mgmt. Assn. Home: 317 Almond Ct San Ramon CA 94583 Office: Northern Telecom Inc 2305 Camino Ramon PO Box 5070 San Ramon CA 94583

GEHRES, JAMES, lawyer; b. Akron, Ohio, July 19, 1932; s. Edwin Jacob and Cleora Mary (Yoakam) G.; m. Eleanor Agnew Mount, July 23, 1960. B.S. in Acctg., U. Utah, 1954; M.B.A., U. Calif.-Berkeley, 1959; J.D., U. Denver, 1970, LL.M. in Taxation, 1977. Bar: Colo. 1970, U.S. Dist. Ct. Colo. 1970, U.S. Tax Ct. 1970, U.S. Supreme Ct. 1973, U.S. Ct. Appeals (10th cir.) 1978. Atty. IRS, Denver, 1965-80, atty. chief counsel's office, 1980—. Served with USAF, 1955-58, capt. Res. ret. Mem. ABA, Colo. Bar Assn., Am. Inst. C.P.A.s, Colo. Soc. C.P.A.s, Am. Assn. Atty.-C.P.A.s, Am. Judicature Soc., Am. Acctg. Assn., Order St. Ives, Beta Gamma Sigma, Beta Alpha Psi. Democrat. Contbr. articles to profl. jours. Office: 935 Pennsylvania St Denver CO 80203

GEHRIG, ALLEN JOHN PETER, finance and marketing executive; b. N.Y.C., Nov. 4, 1944; BA, U. N.Mex., 1968; MPA, Golden Gate U., 1980, MBA, 1983. Regional v.p. Mastercard Internat., Inc., San Francisco. Pres., San Francisco Spl. Olympics, 1977-81, chmn. bd., 1981-82; state treas. Calif. Spl. Olympics, 1982-89; trustee St. Francis Hook and Ladder Soc., San Francisco, 1981-83; mem. Civil Grand Jury, City and County of San Francisco, 1982-83; active Rep. Nat. Com.; chmn. San Francisco Spl. Olympics Ann. Golf Tournament, 1986-89. Recipient cert. of commendation U.S. Senator S.I. Hayakawa, 1978, 81; KABL Citizen of Day, 1978; joint resolution of commendation Calif. State Legislature, 1979; San Francisco Mayoral Proclamation of Commendation, 1979; letter of commendation U.S. Senator Alan Cranston, 1979, 81; cert. of appreciation Joseph P. Kennedy Jr. Found., 1979; plaque of appreciation San Francisco Spl. Olympics, 1980, 82, 83, 85, 86, 87, 88; President's award for social service Wells Fargo Bank, 1981, Outstanding Vol. award Macy's of Calif., 1981; resolution San Francisco Bd. Suprs., 1979; communications award Easter Seals Soc. San Francisco, 1979; San Francisco Vol. Activist award Bay Area Vol. Bur. and Macy's Calif., 1981; recognition of valuable contbn. to community through vol. service cert. No. Calif. Council Vol. Burs., 1981; Nat Commendation for vol. service in the community Pres. Reagan; award of merit City and County of San Francisco, 1981; resolution Bd. Suprs. City and County of San Francisco, 1981; San Francisco mayor's commendation for public services, 1981; commendation resolution Calif. Spl. Olympics, 1981; resolution Calif. Senate, 1981; letter of commendation Eunice Kennedy Shriver/Spl. Olympics, Inc., Washington, 1981, numerous others. Mem. San Francisco Jaycees (pres. 1977-79, chmn. bd. 1979-80, Mem. of Yr. 1978, Officer of Yr. 1978, Disting. Service award 1979), Smithsonian Instn., Am. Mus. Nat. History. Clubs: Olympic, Commonwealth of Calif. Roman Catholic. Home: 1550 Bay St #338 San Francisco CA 94123

GEHRING, GEORGE JOSEPH, JR., dentist; b. Kenosha, Wis., May 24, 1931; s. George J. and Lucille (Martin) G.; DDS, Marquette U., 1955; m. Ann D. Carrigan, Aug. 2, 1982; children: Michael, Scott. Pvt. practice dentistry, Long Beach, Calif., 1958—. Author: The Happy Flosser. Chmn. bd. Long Beach affiliate Calif. Heart Assn.; mem. Long Beach Grand Prix com. of 300. Served with USNR, 1955-58. Fellow Internat. Coll. of Denists; mem. Harbor Dental Soc. (dir.), Pierre Fauchard Acad., Delta Sigma Delta. Club: Rotary. Home: 1230E Ocean Blvd #603 Long Beach CA 90802 Office: 532 E 29th St Long Beach CA 90806

GEHRY, FRANK OWEN, architect; b. Toronto, Ont., Can., Feb. 29, 1929; came to U.S., 1947; s. Irving and Thelma (Caplan) G.; children—Leslie, Brina; m. Berta Aguilera, Sept. 11, 1975; children—Alejandro, Samuel. B. in Architecture, U. So. Calif., 1954; postgrad., Harvard U., 1956-57. Registered profl. architect, Calif. Designer Victor Gruen Assn., Los Angeles, 1953-54, planning, design and project dir., 1958-61; project designer, planner Pereira & Luckman, Los Angeles, 1957-58; prin. Frank O. Gehry & Assocs., Venice, Calif., 1962—. Architect, California Aerospace Mus., 1984, Loyola Law Sch., 1981-84, Mus. of Contemporary Art, 1983, Frances Howard Goldwyn Regional Br. Library, 1986, Info. and Computer Sci. Engring. Research Facility-U. Calif. Irvine, 1986. Trustee Hereditary Disease Found., Santa Monica, Calif., 1970—. Recipient Arnold W. Brunner Meml. Architecture prize, 1983, Eliot Noyes Desigh Chair award Harvard U., 1984; awarded Charlotte Davenport Chair, Yale U., 1982, 85, Pritzker Architecture prize, 1989. Fellow AIA. Office: Frank O Gehry & Assocs 1520-B Cloverfield Blvd Santa Monica CA 90404

GEIDUSCHEK, E(RNEST) PETER, biophysics and molecular biology educator; b. Vienna, Austria, Apr. 11, 1928; came to U.S., 1945, naturalized, 1946; s. Sigmund and Frieda (Tauber) G.; m. Joyce Barbara Brous; 2 children. B.A., Columbia U., 1948; A.M., Harvard U., 1950, Ph.D., 1952. Instr. chemistry Yale U., New Haven, 1952-53, 55-57; asst. prof. chemistry U. Mich., Ann Arbor, 1957-59; asst. prof. biophysics U. Chgo., 1959-62, assoc. prof., 1962-64, prof., 1964-70; prof. biology U. Calif.-San Diego, 1970—, chmn. dept., 1981-83; cons. USPHS, 1963-69. Editorial bd. Biophys. Jour., 1967-69, Ann. Revs. Biophysics and Bioengring., 1971-74, Virology, 1972—, Science, 1977-84. Served with U.S. Army, 1953-55. Recipient research award Am. Postgrad. Med. Assn., 1962, USPHS, 1962; Guggenheim fellow, 1964-65. Fellow AAAS; mem. Nat. Acad. Scis., Am. Soc. Biochemistry and Molecular Biology (pub. affairs com. 1988—), Biophys. Soc. (council 1964-66), Am. Soc. Microbiology, Am. Soc. Virology (council 1985-87). Office: U Calif Dept Biology Ctr for Molecular Genetics La Jolla CA 92093

GEIGER, ALLEN RICHARD, research physicist; b. Sayre, Pa., Dec. 31, 1951; s. Richard A. and Francis M. (Aumick) G. BS in Physics, N.Mex. State U., 1975. Research aid N.Mex. State U., Las Cruces, 1975-76; research physicist Deep Space Systems, Las Cruces, 1977-79; chmn. bd. dirs. G.E.I., Las Cruces, 1979-81, PetroLaser, Inc., El Paso, Tex., 1987—; research physicist Atmospheric Sci. Lab., White Sands Missile Range, N.Mex., 1980-89; pvt. practice cons. to petroleum industry, 1981—. Patentee in field. Mem. U.S. Naval Inst. (assoc.), World Space Found. (charter), Planetary Soc. (charter). Republican. Home: PO Box 2425 Las Cruces NM 88004 Office: PO Box 4998 University Park NM 88003

GEIGER, EDWARD R., telecommunications company executive; b. Allentown, Pa., Apr. 14, 1942; s. Donald R. and Katharine J. (Ealer) G.; m. Edri C. Pappenberger, June 19, 1965; children: Suzanne C., Heather R. BS in Acctg., Lehigh U., 1964, MBA, 1965. CPA, Alaska. Acct. Berg Schultz & Green, CPAs, Allentown, 1964-65, GE, Cleve., 1965-66; mgr. acctg. Pillsbury Co., Mpls., 1970-72; controller Fairbanks (Alaska) Mcpl. Utilities, 1972-76; v.p. fin. Alascom, Inc., Anchorage, 1976-82; v.p. adminstrn. Pacific Telecom, Inc., Vancouver, Wash., 1982-89, contr., 1989—; supr. Columbia Credit Union, Vancouver, 1987—. Bd. dirs. Clark Coll. Found., Vancouver, 1987—; mem. adv. bd. Wash. State U., Vancouver, 1987—. Served to lt. USN, 1966-70. Mem. AICPA, Alaska Soc. CPAs, Fin. Execs. Inst. (treas. 1988, v.p. 1989—), Vancouver C. of C. (bd. dirs. 1987—).

GEIGER, KURT BEREN, journalist; b. Durham, N.C., June 15, 1964; s. Keith Winfield and Pamela Mary (Ehrgott) G. Student, U. Houston, 1982-84; BA in Communications, Pepperdine U., 1986. Mktg. asst. Investor's Daily Newspaper, L.A., 1986; circulation asst. Bon Appetit Mag., L.A., 1987; editorial coord. Archtl. Digest Mag., L.A., 1987—. Lutheran. Office: Archtl Digest KCC 5900 Wilshire Blvd Los Angeles CA 90036

GEIGER, RICHARD GEORGE, librarian; b. Los Angeles, Sept. 13, 1946; s. George L. and Thelma E. (Klots) G.; m. Susan L. Woods, Dec. 21, 1974; 1 child, Brendan. BA in Biology, U. Calif., Santa Barbara, 1970; BA in Art, U. Calif., 1970; M in Library and Info. Sci., UCLA, 1975. Circulation supr. art library UCLA, 1971-73, photographer/cataloger slide library, 1973-74; librarian Nat. Maritime Mus., San Francisco, 1975-76; librarian San Francisco Chronicle, 1976-80, library dir., 1984—; library mgr. San Jose Mercury News, San Jose, Calif., 1980-84. Mem. Spl. Libraries Assn. (treas. news div. 1985-87, chmn. 88-89), ALA. Clubs: Blue Water Cruising Club, Strybing Arboretum Soc. Office: San Francisco Chronicle 901 Mission St San Francisco CA 94119

GEIS, LINDA SUSAN, rancher, educator; b. Merced, Calif., July 31; d. John E. and Elsie I. (Worthy) G. BA, U. Fresno, 1971; MS, Calif. State U., Fresno, 1972; postgrad., U. Calif., Santa Cruz, 1972-73, U. Calif., Davis, 1983, 84, 87. Substitute tchr. Fresno County-City Schs., 1971—; elem. bilingual tchr. Merced County Schs., Merced, 1972—; cattle buyer 1972—; tutor Valley Med. Ctr., 1969-70, San Joaquin Valley Youth Authority, 1970-71; liaison person Head Start, Fresno, 1970-71; researcher for Am. counsel gen., 1974—; spl. edn. tutor Fresno City Schs., 1982—; pvt. tutor, Madera, 1982—. Chmn. agr. com. Calif. Republican Com., 1972-80, energy chmn., 1978; v.p. Merced Rep. Com., 1975-76; chmn. Calif. senatorial campaign, 1978-80; mem. Merced County Supervisory Bldg. Selection Com., 1978-79; vol. St. Agnes Hosp., Fresno, 1982--; mem. Community Bicultural Com., 1973-74. Mem. Calif. Women for Agr. (area rep. 1978-80), Merced County Farm Bur. (bd. dirs. 1975-79), Calif. Farm Bur. (del. 1975-79), LWV, AAUW (br. pres. 1976-77, v.p. home tour Firebaugh, Calif. 1978--), Duck Club, Square Dancing Club (sec. 1987-88).

GEISLER, DICK G., petroleum products company executive; b. 1928. With Am. Breeders, Pocatello, Idaho, 1949-51, Ea. Idaho Svcs., 1951-55; now pres. Cowboy Oil Co., Pocatello, Id. Office: Cowboy Oil Co 2806 S Fifth St Pocatello ID 83205 *

GEISSERT, KATY, mayor; b. Wash., 1926; m. Bill Geissert; children: Bill Jr., Jack, Holly, Doug, Ann. BA in Journalism, Stanford U., 1948. Mem. Torrance (Calif.) City Council, 1974-86; mayor City of Torrance, 1986—; mem. Gov.'s Infrastructure Rev. Task Force, Calif. Past chmn. Torrance Park & Recreation Commn.; past mem. fin. adv. com. Torrance Sch.; past chmn. adv. bd. Calif. State U., Dominguez Hills, Torrance Salvation Army; mem. bond steering com. Torrance Library, 1967; chmn. local park bond issue steering com., 1971, Los Angeles County Sanitation Dist. Bd.; community cons. South Bay Harbor Vol. Bur.; mem. adv. bd. Torrance YWCA; bd. dirs. Switzer Ctr., region III United Way, Torrance LWV; mem. city selection com. Los Angeles County. Recipient PTA Hon. Service award, Woman of Distinction award Soroptimists, Community Service award Riviera Homeowners Assn., spl. citation Nat. Recreation & Park Assn.; named Disting. Citizen of Yr. Torrance Area C. of C., 1973, Woman of Yr. YWCA, Woman of Achievement award Redondo Marina Bus. & Profl. Women's Club. Mem. U.S. Conf. Mayors, League Calif. Cities (del., cities transp. com.), Calif. Elected Women's Assn. (bd. dirs.). Office: City of Torrance 3031 Torrance Blvd Torrance CA 90503 *

GEIST, JERRY DOUGLAS, electric company executive; b. Raton, N.Mex., May 23, 1934; s. Jacob D. and Jessie Kathleen (Wadley) G.; m. Sharon Ludell Kaemper, June 12, 1956; children: Douglas, Bruce, Robert. Student, U. Mo., 1952-54; BEE, U. Colo., 1956. Registered profl. engr., N.Mex. With Pub. Service Co. N.Mex., Albuquerque, 1960—, v.p. engring. and ops., 1970-71, v.p. corp. affairs, 1971-73, exec. v.p., 1973-76, pres., 1976-82, chmn., pres., 1982—, also bd. dirs., mem. exec. com.; bd. dirs. Ch2M Hill, Lectrosonics Inc., Venture Advisors Investment Funds, Aegis Ins. Services, Inc.; chmn. Utech Venture Capital Corp. Ltd.; mem. Pres.'s Export Council. Bd. dirs. Nat. Symphony, S.W. Community Health Services; chmn. adminstrv. bd. 1st United Meth. Ch.; co-chmn. N. Mex. Com. Nat. Holocaust Mus., Albuquerque, 1987; chmn. growth devel. com. Albuquerque Econ. Forum; chmn. U. N.Mex. Found. Lt. USN, 1952-59. Mem. Edison Electric Inst., Albuquerque C. of C. (pres. 1972-73), Bus. Roundtable, Four Hills Country Club, Albuquerque Country Club, Alubquerque Petroleum Club, Links, Tau Beta Pi, Sigma Tau, Eta Kappa Nu, Pi Mu Epsilon. Methodist. Office: Pub Svc Co NMex Alvarado Sq Albuquerque NM 87158

GELBER, DON JEFFREY, lawyer; b. Los Angeles, Mar. 10, 1940; s. Oscar and Betty Sheila (Chernitsky) G.; m. Jessica Jeasun Song, May 15, 1967; children: Victoria, Jonathan, Rebecca, Robert. Student UCLA, 1957-58, Reed Coll., 1958-59; AB, Stanford U., 1961, JD, 1963. Bar: Calif. 1964, Hawaii 1964, U.S. Dist. Ct. (cen. and no. dists. Calif.) 1964, U.S. Dist. Ct. Hawaii 1964, U.S. Ct. Appeals (9th cir.) 1964. Assoc. Greenstein, Yamane & Cowan, Honolulu, 1964-67; reporter Penal Law Revision Project, Hawaii Jud. Council, Honolulu, 1967-69; assoc. H. William Burgess, Honolulu, 1969-72; ptnr. Burgess & Gelber, Honolulu, 1972-73; prin. Law Offices of Don Jeffrey Gelber, Honolulu, 1974-77; prin., pres. Gelber & Wagner, Honolulu, 1978-83; prin., pres. Gelber & Gelber, Honolulu, 1984—; legal counsel Hawaii State Senate Judiciary Com., 1965; adminstrv. asst. to majority floor leader Hawaii Senate, 1966, legal csl. Edn. Com., 1967, 68; majority counsel Hawaii Ho. of Reps., 1974; spl. counsel Hawaii State Senate, 1983. Contbr. articles to legal publs. Mem. State Bar Calif., ABA (sect. bus. law), Am. Bankruptcy Inst., Hawaii Bar Assn. (sect. corps. and securities). Clubs: Pacific, Plaza (Honolulu). Office: Gelber & Gelber 745 Fort St Ste 1400 Honolulu HI 96813

GELDERMANN, JOEL FREDRICK, rancher; b. Alameda, Calif., Nov. 10, 1956; s. Harlan Stolp and Audrey Ruth (Skupa) G.; m. Sheila Jean Smith, July 12, 1985; children: Nathan, Jason, Mathew. Owner El Nido Rancho, San Ramon, Calif., 1986—. Mem. Rep. Presdl. Task Force, Washington. Address: 19251 San Ramon Valley Blvd San Ramon CA 94583

GELFAND, MARSHALL M., accountant; b. Claremont, N.H., Dec. 14, 1927; s. I.N. and Annie (Senoff) G.; m. Judy Jaffe, Dec. 17, 1955; children: Todd, Elizabeth, Dean. BS, Syracuse U., 1950; JD, NYU, 1955. CPA, N.Y., Calif. Bar: N.Y. 1958. Ptnr. H.H. Lawin & Co., N.Y.C., 1958-67; mng. ptnr. Gelfand Rennert & Feldman, CPA's, Los Angeles, 1967—; dir. Palm Springs Savs. Bank, Calif. Trustee Syracuse U., N.Y., 1983—; bd. dirs. Palm Springs Friends of Los Angeles Philharm., 1981—; v.p. Bob Hope Cultural Ctr. Inc., 1988—; pres. Desert Mus., Palm Springs 1988—. Mem. Calif. CPA Soc., Sigma Alpha Mu (trustee 1979—). Democrat.

GELFOND, LAWRENCE PETER, accountant; b. Bklyn.; s. Morris B. and Florence (Siegel) G.; m. Joyce Cook (div.); children: Marcie A., Monica L.; m. Karen Lynn Milzer, Dec. 20, 1972; children: Kimberly H., Tammy Jo. BSBA, U. Denver, 1964. CPA, Colo. Ptnr. Munishor & Gelfond, Denver, 1967-69, Milzer, Gelfond, Pangburn & Co., Denver, 1969-80, Laventhol & Horwath, Denver, 1980--; cons. Colonial Nat. Bank, Denver, 1985--; appointee State Bd. Acctg., 1988--. Pres. Colo. Rep. Jewish Coalition, 1988-; chmn. Rocky Mountain States Israel Bonds, 1988--; treas. BMH Congregation, Denver, 1988--; bd. dirs. Anti-Defamation League, Denver, 1988--. Recipient Humanitarian award Colo. Lubavitch Soc., 1987. Mem. AICPA, Colo. Soc. CPAs, Green Gables County Club, Denver Athletic, B'nai B'rith. Home: 13 Cherrymoor Dr Englewood CO 80110 Office: Laventhol & Horwath 370 17th St Ste 2100 Denver CO 80202

GELLER, FLOYD STUART, optometrist; b. Portland, Oreg., Oct. 16, 1933; s. Jack J. and Gussie (Frager) G.; m. Dorothy Ruth Jermulowske, June 10, 1956; children—Carol Sue, Cynthia Sharon, Craig Steven. B.S., Pacific U., 1958, O.D., 1958. Mgr., Columbian Optical of Gateway (Oreg.), 1964-77, owner, mgr., 1977-83; optometrist Mall 205 Optical, Portland, 1981—. Commr. Multnomah County Parks; pres. Greater Gateway Boosters; mem. adv. com. Portland Community Coll. Jewish. Lodges: Elks, Masons, Shriners, Lions (pres. Parknose chpt. 1987-88, citizens adv. com. multicounty sheriff's office). Home: 13209 SE Ankeny Ct Portland OR 97233 Office: 9978 SE Washington Portland OR 97216

GELLMAN, GLORIA GAE SEEBURGER SCHICK, marketing professional; b. La Grange, Ill., Oct. 5, 1947; d. Robert Fred and Gloria Virginia (McQuiston) Seeburger; m. Peter Slate Schick, Sept. 25, 1980 (dec. 1980); 3 children by previous marriage; m. Irwin Frederick Gellman, Sept. 9, 1989. BA magna cum laude, Purdue U., 1969; student, Lee Strasberg Actors Studio; postgrad., UCLA. Mem. mktg. staff Seemac, Inc. (formerly R.F. Seeburger Co.). Profl. actress, singer; television and radio talk show hostess, Indpls., late 1960s; performer radio and television commls., 1960s—. Mem. Orange County Philharm. Soc., Orange County Master Chorale, Orange County Performing Arts Ctr., treas.; bd. dirs., v.p. membership, mem. acquisition coun., Newport Harbor (Calif.) Art Mus.; bd. dirs., mem. founders soc., Opera Pacific. Named one of Outstanding Young Womem of Am., 1972. Mem. Screen Actors Guild, AFTRA, Actors Equity, AAUW, U. Calif. Irvine Chancellor's Club, U. Calif. Irvine Humanities Assocs. (founder, pres., bd. dirs.), Mensa, Orange County Mental Health Assn., Alpha Lambda Delta, Delta Rho Kappa. Home: PO Box 1993 Newport Beach CA 92663

GELL-MANN, MURRAY, theoretical physicist; b. N.Y.C., Sept. 15, 1929; s. Arthur and Pauline (Reichstein) Gell-M.; m. J. Margaret Dow, Apr. 19, 1955 (dec. 1981); children: Elizabeth, Nicholas. BS, Yale U., 1948; PhD, Mass. Inst. Tech., 1951; ScD (hon.), Yale U., 1959, U. Chgo., 1967, U. Ill., 1968, Wesleyan U., 1968, U. Turin, Italy, 1969, U. Utah, 1970, Columbia U., 1977, Cambridge U., 1980. Mem. Inst. for Advanced Study, 1951, 55, 67-68; instr. U. Chgo., 1952-53, asst. prof., 1953-54, assoc. prof., 1954; assoc. prof. Calif. Inst. Tech., Pasadena, 1955-56; prof. Calif. Inst. Tech., 1956—, now R.A. Millikan prof. physics.; vis. prof. MIT, spring 1963, CERN, Geneva, 1971-72, 79-80; Mem. Pres.'s Sci. Adv. Com., 1969-72; mem. sci. and grants com. Leakey Found., 1977—; chmn. bd. trustees Aspen Ctr. for Physics, 1973-79. Author: (with Y. Ne'eman) Eightfold Way. Regent Smithsonian Instn., 1974-88; bd. dirs. J.D. and C.T. MacArthur Found., 1979—. NSF post doctoral fellow, vis. prof. Coll. de France and U. Paris, 1959-60; recipient Dannie Heineman prize Am. Phys. Soc., 1959; E.O. Lawrence Meml. award AEC, 1966; Overseas fellow Churchill Coll., Cambridge, Eng., 1966; Franklin medal, 1967; Carty medal Nat. Acad. Scis., 1968; Research Corp. award, 1969; Nobel prize in physics, 1969. Fellow Am. Phys. Soc.; mem. NAS, Royal Soc. (fgn.), Am. Acad. Arts and Scis. (v.p., chmn. Western ctr. 1970-76), Council on Fgn. Relations, French Phys. Soc. (hon.). Clubs: Cosmos (Washington); Century Assn., Explorers (N.Y.C.); Athenaeum (Pasadena). Office: Calif Inst Tech Dept Physics Pasadena CA 91125

GELNETT, RONALD HOWARD, geologist, consultant; b. Minot, N.D., May 16, 1933; s. Raymond Edgar Gelnett and Edith E. (Foster) Mark; m. Isabel Johnson, June 6, 1965; children: Jay Crandall, Joel Sydney. BS in Geology, Utah State U., 1957, MS in Geology, 1958; postgrad., U. Calif., Berkeley, 1964-66. Registered geologist, Calif., Ariz.; cert. engring. geologist, Calif. Chief geologist U.S. Army C.E., San Francisco, 1958-74; chief geologist, v.p., bd. dirs. Motorola Aerial Remote Sensing, Inc. (now Mars Assocs. Inc.), Phoenix, 1974-85, pres., chief exec. officer, chmn. bd., 1985—; cons., lectr. NASA Hdqrs., Govt. of Philippines, Govt. of Can., Japanese Geol. Survey, Govt. Electronics div. Motorola, Inc., Scottsdale, Ariz., Environ. Rsch. Inst. Mich., Woodward-Clyde Cons., San Francisco, Intera Technologists, Austin, Tex., Calgary, Alta., Can. Contbr. articles to profl. jours. With U.S. Army, 1954-56. Recipient Wheeler medal Soc. Am. Mil. Engrs., 1974. Mem. Am. Assn. Petroleum Geologists, Assn. Engring. Geologists (chmn. San Francisco sect. 1968, nat. bldg. codes com. 1969, nat. tech. remote sensing com. 1982-88). Republican. Office: Mars Assocs Inc 1422 N 44th St Ste 109 Phoenix AZ 85008

GEMMELL, DARRELL VANCE, real estate executive; b. Pendleton, Oreg., May 17, 1926; s. Chester Hugh and Katherine (McIntyre) G.; m. Marieta Jean Marlow; children: Tia, Douglas, David. Student, Oreg. State U., 1946-47. Real estate broker Gem Real Estate, Salem, Oreg., 1960—; pres. 11-80 Corp., Pendleton, 1973-87; mng. ptnr. Indian Hills Investment Co., 11-80 Properties, Pendleton. Served with USMCR, 1943-46. Named Builder of the Yr., Salem Homebuilders, 1962. Mem. Elks. Republican. Home and Office: 2304 Crestview Dr S Salem OR 97302

GEMPLER, GREGORY JAMES, pilot; b. Akron, Ohio, Jan. 28, 1951; s. Kenneth Ernest and Marie Esther (Kettring) G.; m. Sharon Lee Stewart, Aug. 25, 1973; 1 child, Keith Stewart. BS, USAF Acad., 1973; MBA, UCLA, 1974. Commd. 2d lt. USAF, 1973, advanced through grades to capt., 1977, resigned, 1981; field engr. Schlumberger Well Svcs., Inc., Ft. Morgan, Colo., 1981; flight instr. USAF Acad. Aero Club, Colorado Springs, Colo., 1981-83; air traffic contr. FAA, Pueblo, Colo., 1983-84; pilot Colo. Interstate Gas Co., Colorado Springs, 1984-85, Delta Airlines, Inc., Dallas, 1985—. Mem. Airline Pilots Assn. Republican. Home: 15630 Teak Pl Elbert CO 80106

GENEST, KAREN DIANE, educational administrator; b. San Francisco, Oct. 24, 1950; d. Arthur Oakley and Marjorie Louise (Thurston) Lemmon; m. Jeffrey Lee, Aug. 4, 1978; children: Twyla Chantelle and Janelle Rose (twins). BA in Speech and Hearing, U. Calif., 1976; BS in Edn., Oreg. State Coll., 1979; MS in Edn., So. Oreg. State U., 1986. Tchr. Corvallis (Oreg.) Open Sch., 1978, Greater Albany (Oreg.) Sch. Dist., 1979; Tchr. Klamath County Sch. Dist., Klamath Falls, Oreg., 1979-82, media specialist, 1986--; instr. computers So. Oreg. State Coll., Ashland, 1987, instr. media, 1988; presenter NW Computer Consortium Edn., Portland, Oreg., 1987. Mem. Klamath Falls Dem. Cen. Com., 1985. Mem. Oreg. Edn. Assn., Oreg. Ednl. Media Assn., Oreg. Assn. for Edn. Young Children (sec.), LWV (facilitator Klamath Falls 1987), AAUW (pres. Klamath Falls), Klamath Falls Jaycees. Office: Klamath County Sch Dist 3641 Crest St Klamath Falls OR 97603

GENGOR, VIRGINIA ANDERSON, financial planning executive, educator; b. Lyons, N.Y., May 2, 1927; d. Axel Jennings and Marie Margaret (Mack) Anderson; m. Peter Gengor, Mar. 2, 1952 (dec.); children: Peter Randall, Daniel Neal, Susan Leigh. AB, Wheaton Coll., 1949; MA, U. No. Colo., Greeley, 1975, 77. Chief hosp. intake service County of San Diego, 1966-77, chief Kearny Mesa Dist. Office, 1977-79, chief Dependent Children of Ct., 1979-81, chief child protection services, 1981-82; registered rep. Am. Pacific Securities, San Diego, 1982-85; assoc. Pollock & Assocs., San Diego, 1985-86; pres. Gengor Fin. Advisors, 1986—; cons. instr. Nat. Ctr. for Fin. Edn., San Diego, 1986—; instr. San Diego Community Coll., 1985—. Mem. allocations panel United Way, San Diego, 1976-79; chmn. com. Child Abuse Coordinating Council, San Diego, 1979-83; pres. Friends of Casa de la Esperanza, San Diego, 1980-85, bd. dirs., 1980—; 1st v.p. The Big Sister League, San Diego, 1985-86, pres., 1987—. Mem. Inst. Cert. Fin. Planners, Internat. Assn. Fin. Planning, Inland Soc. Tax Cons., AAUW (bd. dirs.), Nat. Assn. Securities Dealers (registered prin.), Nat. Ctr. Fin. Edn., Am. Bus. Women's Assn., Nat. Assn. Female Execs., Navy League, Freedoms Found. Valley Forge, Internat. Platform Assn. Presbyterian. Avocations: community service, travel, reading. Home: 6462 Spear St San Diego CA 92120 Office: Gengor Fin Advisors 4950 Waring Rd Ste 7 San Diego CA 92120

GENINI, RONALD WALTER, history teacher, historian; b. Oakland, Calif., Dec. 5, 1946; s. William Angelo and Irma Lea (Gays) G.; m. Roberta Mae Tucker, Dec. 20, 1969; children: Thomas, Justin, Nicholas. BA, U. San Francisco, 1968, MA, 1969. Cert. secondary edn. tchr., Calif. Tchr. Cen. Unified Sch. Dist., Fresno, Calif., 1970—; judge State History Day, Sacramento, 1986—; bd. dirs. Calif. Coun. for Social Studies, Fresno; mem. U.S. History devel. team Golden State U., San Diego, 1989—. Author: Romualdo Pacheco, 1985; contbr. articles to profl. jours. Bd. dirs. Fresno Area 6 Neighborhood Coun., 1973-74, Fresno City and County Hist. Soc., 1975-78, St. Anthony's Ch., Fresno, 1980-84. Named one of Outstanding Young Educators Am., Fresno Jaycees, 1978. Mem. Calif. Hist. Soc. Republican. Office: Cen High Sch 2045 N Dickenson Fresno CA 93722

GENNARO, ANTONIO L., biology educator; b. Raton, N.Mex., Mar. 18, 1934; s. Paul and Mary Lou (Gasperetti) G.; m. Virginia Marie Sullivan, May 15, 1955 (div. 1979); children—Theresa Ann, Carrie Marie, Janelle Elizabeth; m. Marjorie Lou Cox, Sept. 27, 1980. B.S., N.Mex. State U., 1957; M.S., U. N.Mex., 1961, Ph.D., 1965. Tchr. biology Las Cruces High Sch., N.Mex., 1957-58; asst. prof. biology St. John's U., Collegeville, Minn., 1964-65; prof. biology Eastern N.Mex. U., Portales, 1965—. Contbr. articles to sci. jours. Served to capt. U.S. Army, 1958-59; mem. Res., 1959-66. Recipient Presdl. Faculty award Eastern N.Mex. U., 1970, Pres.'s Faculty award for excellence in rsch., 1988; Outstanding Sci. award N.Mex. Acad. Sci., 1975. Mem. Southwestern Naturalists (treas. 1974-78), Am. Soc. Mammalogists, Herpetologists League, Sigma Xi, Phi Kappa Phi (pres. 1970-74). Roman Catholic.

GENOVESE, ANTHONY, JR. (BUD GENOVESE), auditor; b. Cleve., Sept. 17, 1947; s. Anthony Sr. and Bernice G.; m. Carla Jane Batchelder, Dec. 14, 1969; children: Gregory, Erin. BBA in Fin., Ohio U., 1969; MBA in Mgmt., Golden Gate U., 1978; postgrad., U. Wis., 1982. Chartered bank auditor; cert. internal auditor; cert. info. systems auditor. Engring. analyst Memorex Corp., Santa Clara, Calif., 1970-72; prodn. analyst Am. Microsystems, Santa Clara, 1972-74; EDP auditor Federal Home Loan Bank of San Francisco, 1974-78; sr. v.p., chief auditor County Bank & Trust, Santa Cruz, Calif., 1978-87; v.p., gen. auditor Pacific Western Bancshares, San Jose, Calif., 1987—. Mem. EDP Auditors Assn. (v.p. 1985, pres. 1987), Bank Auditors Roundtable (chmn. 1983-84, bd. dirs. 1985—), Inst. Internal Auditors, Bank Adminstrn. Inst., Ohio U. Alumni Assn. (pres. San Jose chpt.), Bay Area Browns Backers Assn. (pres. EVP 1988—). Democrat. Office: Pacific Western Bank PO Box 1260 Santa Cruz CA 95061

GENSMER, RICHARD PAUL, engineer; b. Horicon, Wis., May 8, 1946; s. Alvin Robert and Kathleen Mary (Caughlin) G.; m. Linda Ann Rogers, June 23, 1973; children: Kristin Ann, Steven Rogers. BS in Geology, U. Wis., 1972; MS in Geochemistry, No. Ill. U., 1977. Engr. Nobel Drilling Corp., Denver, 1978—. Contbr. articles to profl. jours. With USN, 1964-68. Mem. Internat. Assn. Drilling Contractors (com. chmn. 1987-88), Am. Petroleum Inst. (com. chmn. 1988). Republican. Home: 7219 S Zephyr Way Littleton CO 80123 Office: Noble Drilling Corp Ste 2810 1660 Lincoln St Denver CO 80254

GENTILE, CATHERINE ANN, Olympic skier; b. Los Angeles, June 28, 1962; d. Lawrence Thomas and Diane Marie (Smith) G. BS in Mktg. and Fin., U. So. Calif., 1984. Adminstrv. asst. Redgat Meml. Hosp., Long Beach, Calif., 1987; programmer computer Winter Pk. (Colo.) Cen. Reservations, 1984-87; adminstrv. asst. Office of Pres. Behavioral Health Services, Gardena, Calif., 1988; participant U.S. Disabled Ski Team, Colo., 1984—. Recipient Silver medal Ladies Disabled Giant Slalom XV Winter Olympics, Calgary, Can., 1988, 4th Paralympics for Disabled, Innsbruck, Austria, 6th Giant Slalom, 5th Downhill Skiing, in U.S. Nationals: 2nd Combined, 2nd Slalom, 4th Giant Slalom, 5th Super Giant Slalom, 1987-88, 3rd Slalom, 3rd Giant Slalom, 2nd Downhill, 1986-87, 3rd Slalom, 3rd Giant Slalom, 2nd Downhill, 1985-86, Foreran both Giant Slalom and Slalom Third World Games Disabled, Salen, Sweden, 6th Slalom, 6th Giant Slalom, 6th Downhill, 1984-85, Can. Nationals: 6th Slalom, 7th Giant Slalom, 6th Downhill, Pres.'s award Far West Ski Assn., 1988. Home: 2331 239th St Torrance CA 90501

GENTRY, CURTIS MARSENA, author; b. Lamar, Colo., June 13, 1931; s. Curtis Herman and Coral Eloise (McMillin) G.; m. Laura Wilson Spence, Oct. 30, 1954 (dec. 1975); m. Gail Stevens, June 13, 1976 (div. 1982). Student, U. Colo., 1949-50; BA, San Francisco State U., 1957. Sports writer Lamar (Colo.) Daily News, 1947-49; Boulder corr. Denver Post, 1949-50; salesman Paul Elder, Books, San Francisco, 1954-57, Tro Harper, Books, San Francisco, 1957-62; book reviewer San Francisco Chronicle, 1957-65. Author numerous books, 1962—, including The Madams of San Francisco, 1964, The Vulnerable Americans, 1966, Frame-Up: The Incredible Case of Tom Mooney and Warren Billings, 1967 (Mystery Writer's award 1968), The Last Days of the Late, Great State of California, 1968, The Killer Mountains, 1968, Official/Confidential: The Secret Files of J. Edgar Hoover; co-author: Jade: Stone of Heaven, 1962, John M. Browning: American Gunmaker, 1964, A Kind of Loving, 1970, Operation Overflight, 1970, Second in Command, 1971, Helter Skelter: The True Story of the Manson Murders, 1974 (Edgar Allen Poe award Mystery Writers Am. 1975). With USAF, 1950-54, Korea. Mem. Authors Guild Am., ACLU, E Clampus Vitus (Jackson, Calif.). Democrat. Office: care Irving S Feffer 609 N Alta Beverly Hills CA 90211

GENTRY, DARRELL WAYNE, city official; b. Ft. Smith, Ark., Dec. 30, 1942; s. Amos Franklin Gentry and Lorraine (Waldrip) Cullen. AA, Mt. San Antonio Coll., 1974; BS, Calif. Poly. State U., 1977. Asst. planner to assoc. planner City San Marcos, Calif., 1977-80, dir. planning to project mgr., 1980-88; redevel. mgr. City of Whittier, Calif., 1988—. Contbr. articles to profl. jours. Mem. environ. quality policy com. Rep. League of Calif. Cities, 1988—. Decorated D.S.M. Mem. Am. Planning Assn., Mcpl. Mgmt. Assn. So. Calif., Kiwanis. Republican. Home: 4129 1/2 E Shaw St Long Beach CA 90803

GENTRY, JAMES WILLIAM, state official; b. Danville, Ill., Aug. 14, 1926; s. Carl Lloyd and Leone (Isham) G.; A.B., Fresno State Coll., 1948; M.J., U. Calif., Berkeley, 1956; m. Dorothie Shirley Hechtlinger, Mar. 18, 1967; 1 stepdau., Susan Mushkin. Field rep. Congressman B.W. Gearhart, Fresno, Calif., 1948, Assemblyman Wm. W. Hansen, Fresno, 1950, sec., 1953-56; exec. asst. Calif. Pharm. Assn., Los Angeles, 1956-69, editor, pub. jour., 1956-69; pub. relations dir. PAID Prescriptions, 1963-64; dir. pub. info. comprehensive Health Planning Council, Los Angeles County, 1969; asst. adminstr., dir. pub. info. So. Calif. Comprehensive Health Planning Council, 1969-71, acting adminstr., 1971-72; exec. sec. Calif. State Health Planning Council, 1972-73, Calif. Adv. Health Council, 1973-85, fed. cons., 1986-88; Calif. Health Care Commn., 1973-75; acting public info. officer Calif. Office Statewide Health Planning and Devel., 1978-79; interim dir. Calif. Office Statewide Health Planning and Devel., 1983; mem. L.A. Civil Svc. Police Interview Bd., 1967-72; asst. sgt.-at-arms Calif. State Assembly, 1950; exec. sec. Calif. Assembly Interim Com. on Livestock and Dairies, 1954-56; mem. adv. bd. Am. Security Council; mem. Calif. Health Planning Law Revision Commn.; former mem. Calif. Bldg. Safety Bd. Mem. Fresno County Republican Central Com., 1950; charter mem. Rep. Presdl. Task Force. Served to col. AUS, 1949-50, 50-53; Korea. Decorated Legion of Merit, Bronze Star medal, Commendation Ribbon with metal pendant ; recipient pub. awards Western Soc. Bus. Publns. Assn., 1964-67. Mem. Am. Assn. Comprehensive Health Planning, Pub. Relations Soc. Am., Ret. Officers Assn. (life), Allied Drug Travelers So. Calif., L.A. Press Club, Mil. Police Assn., Res. Officers Assn. (life), Assn. U.S. Army, U.S. Senatorial Club, The Victory Svcs. Club of London, Pi Gamma Mu, Phi Alpha Delta. Sigma Delta Chi. Editor: Better Health, 1963-67; Orientation Conf. Comprehensive Health Planning, 1969; Commentary, 1969-71. Editorial adv. Pharm. Svcs. for Nursing Homes: A Procedural Manual, 1966. Editor: Program and Funding, 1972; Substance Abuse, 1972. Home: 902 Commons Dr Sacramento CA 95825-6647

GENTRY, MARTHA IMOGEN, teacher, writer; b. San Francisco, Dec. 23, 1926; d. Guy Vernellon and Mary Edna Whaley; m. Herbert D. Nightingale, Sept. 10, 1951 (div. 1962); children: Carolyn Marie Schleif, David Edwin. Cert., Rudolph Schaeffer Sch. of Design, San Francisco, 1945-46; BA cum laude, Whitman Coll., Walla Walla, Wash., 1950; MFA, U. Wash., 1953; postgrad., UCLA, 1959-68. Cert. elem. and secondary tchr., Calif., Oreg.; ordained to ministry Christian Ch. of Universal Philosophy, 1987. Tchr. L.A. City Schs., 1960-72; supr. tchr. tng. UCLA, 1961-72; writer L.A. City Schs., 1968; profl. tutor for exceptional children Grants Pass (Oreg.) City Schs., 1978-79; lectr. several orgns., Western U.S. and Can., 1984-85; researcher Flower Essence Soc., Nevada City, Calif., 1987; dir. edn. Ch. of Light and Love, Grants Pass, 1987—; pres., founder Universal Inst. of Philosophy and Rsch., Grants Pass, 1987-88. Group leader Camp Fire Girls, Pomona, Calif., 1942-43; patron Barnstormers Theatre, Grants Pass, 1979-80; vol. Lovejoy Hospice, Grants Pass, 1989—; practitioner The Flower Essence Soc., Nevada City, Calif., 1987; congl. mem. Astara, Inc., Upland, Calif., 1989. Mem. Oreg. Assn. for Children with Learning Disabilities, Internat. Order of St. Luke the Physician, Grants Pass Camera Club (pres. 1976-77, Women's Club (pres. Sedro Woolley, Wash. 1956-57), Odd Fellows, Oreg. State Grange, Grants Pass Grange (chaplain), Women's Assn. (pres. 1976-79). Republican. Home: 722 NW Amelia Dr Grants Pass OR 97526

GENUNG, NORMAN BERNARD, management consultant; b. Dayton, Ohio, June 6, 1951; s. Paul Kenneth and Mary Elizabeth (Rose) G.; m. Sharon Rose Lynch, June 9, 1973; 1 child, Jeffrey Patrick. BS in Psychology, Mich. State U., 1973; MS in Ops. Mgmt., U. Ark., 1977. Chief plans br. Western Space and Missile Ctr., Lompoc, Calif., 1980-84; chief engring. div. Fgn. Tech. Div., Fairborn, Ohio, 1984-87; chief ops. div. 5S Satellite Control Sq, Spokane, Wash., 1987-88; pres. Genung Assocs., Spokane, 1989—. Maj. USAF, 1973-88. Mem. Nat. Mgmt. Assn. Office: Genung Assocs W 937 33d Ave Spokane WA 99203

GEOFFRION, CHARLES ALBERT, university development director; b. Cambridge, Mass., Apr. 21, 1943; s. Louis Felix and Irene Gertrude (Mercier) G.; m. Moira Marti, July 31, 1965; children: Sabrina, Damien Marcel. AB, Boston U., 1965; PhD, Indiana U., 1971. Lectr. So. Ill. U., Edwardsville, Ill., 1972-74, St. Mary's Coll., South Bend, Ind., 1975-78, Ind. U., South Bend, 1975-78; vis. lectr. Inst. on Africa, Notre Dame, Ind., 1979-86; fin. systems mgr. St. Joseph County Govt., South Bend, 1979-82; cons. Resource Mgmt. Assocs., South Bend, 1982-83; cons. faculty research U. Notre Dame, South Bend, 1984-86; assoc. dir. devel. U. Ariz., Tucson, 1987—; cons. Festival for Performing Arts, South Bend, 1979-84, Performing Arts Tng. Ctr., East St. Louis, Ill., 1970-75; mentor Acad. Preparation for Excellence, Tucson, 1987—. Author: Study Guide to Africa, (videotape) Guide to India. Mem. long range planning com. South Bend Art Ctr., 1982-83, Council Advancement and Support of Edn.; cons. Jr. Achievement Project Bus., South Bend, 1986; bd. dirs. County Park Found. South Bend, 1984-86; mem. adv. panel WNIT-TV (PBS), Elkhart, Ind., 1983-84; vol. U.S. Peace Corps, Sierra Leone, West Africa, 1965-67; gantee numerous grants and founds. Mem. Assn. Am. Colls. (council liberal learning), Nat. Council Univ. Research Adminstrs. Roman Catholic. Home: 4460 N Territory Pl Tucson AZ 85715

GEOFFRION, SONDRA JANE, teacher; b. Williamstown, Mass., May 5, 1939; d. Donald Edwin and Edith Mae (McKane) Cary; m. David Louis Geoffrion, Dec. 30, 1960; children: Steven David, Joyce Mae. BA in English, Edn., U. Mass., 1961. Pvt. tutor Armed Forces Adults, U.S., Germany, 1962-69; tchr. various pub. schs., Mass., 1970-79; ednl. rsch., tchr., tutor Wayland, Mass., 1970-79; founder, dir. Access Success Assocs., Goleta, Santa Barbara, Calif., 1986—; cons. to GATE, Santa Barbara pub. schs., 1987--; cons. in field; lectr. in field. Author: Get Smart Fast: a Handbook for the Academic Success, 1986, five Power Study to Up Your Grades booklets, 1989. Scholarship advisor Alpha Chi Omega, Santa Barbara, 1981-88. Mem. Women's Fed. Svc. Republican. Mem. Christian Ch. Home: 6565 Camino Caseta Goleta CA 93117

GEORGALLIS, JOANN, lawyer; b. Sacramento, Aug. 6, 1956; d. Pericles and Katherine Mary (Thompson) G. AB in Rhetoric cum laude, U. Calif., Davis, 1978; JD, U. Santa Clara, 1981. Bar: Calif. 1981, U.S. Dist. Ct. (cen. dist.) Calif. 1982, U.S. Dist. Ct. (ea. dist.) Calif. 1983, U.S. Dist. Ct. (no. dist.) Calif. 1988. Assoc. Surr & Hellyer, San Bernardino, Calif., 1981-83, Porter, Scott, Weiberg & Delehant, Sacramento, 1983-86, Ramsey, Morrison, Keddy & Wallis, Sacramento, 1986-87, Metheny, Poidmore & Sears, Sacramento, 1987—. Mem. legis. relations com. U. Calif., Davis, 1985-88; bd. dirs. Jr. League, Sacramento, 1988-89. Mem. Sacramento County Bar Assn., Am. Hellenic Profl. Soc. (bd. dirs. 1986—), Hellenic Law Soc., Calif. Aggie Alumni Assn. (bd. dirs. 1988-89), Crocker Art Mus. Assn., Delta Delta Delta. Republican. Greek Orthodox. Office: Metheny Poidmore & Sears 2100 Northrop Ave Sacramento CA 95825

GEORGE, ALEXANDER LAWRENCE, political scientist, educator; b. Chgo., May 31, 1920; s. John and Mary (Sargis) G.; m. Juliette Lombard,

Apr. 20, 1948; children—Lee Lawrence, Mary Lombard. A.M., U. Chgo., 1941, Ph.D., 1958; DHL (hon.), U. San Diego, 1987. Research analyst OSS, 1944-45; dep. chief research br. Info. Control Div., Office Mil. Govt. for Germany, 1945-48; specialist study decision-making and internat. relations RAND Corp., Santa Monica, Calif., 1948-68; head dept. social sci. RAND Corp., 1961-63; prof. polit. sci. Stanford, 1968—; Lectr. U. Chgo., 1950, Am. U., 1952-56. Author: (with Juliette L. George) Woodrow Wilson and Colonel House: A Personality Study, 1956, Propaganda Analysis, 1959, The Chinese Communist Army in Action, 1967, (with others) The Limits of Coercive Diplomacy, 1971, (with Richard Smoke) Deterrence in American Foreign Policy: Theory and Practice, 1974 (Bancroft prize for Deterrence in Am. Fgn. Policy 1975), Towards A More Soundly Based Foreign Policy: Making Better Use of Information, 1976, Presidential Decisionmaking in Foreign Policy, 1980; author: Managing U.S.-Soviet Rivalry, 1983, (with Gordon Craig) Force and Statecraft, 1983; editor: (with others) U.S.-Soviet Security Cooperation: Achievements, Failures, Lessons, 1988. Ctr. for Advanced Study Behavioral Scis. fellow, 1956-57, 76-77; Founds. Fund for Research in Psychiatry grantee, 1960; NIMH spl. fellow, 1972-73; NSF research grantee, 1971-73, 75-77, MacArthur Found. fellow, 1983-88. Mem. Am. Acad. Arts and Scis., Council on Fgn. Relations, Am. Polit. Sci. Assn., Internat. Studies Assn. (pres. 1973-74), AAUP, Phi Beta Kappa. Home: 944 Lathrop Pl Stanford CA 94305

GEORGE, DICK STANLEY, marketing executive; b. Grants, N.Mex., Oct. 29, 1947; s. Stanley Henry and Violet Lanham (Maddox) G.; m. Penny Lee Jordan, Sept. 2, 1970; children: Brandy, Robin, Sarah, Katie, Joshua, Rebecca, Megan. BS, Brigham Young U., 1972. With Burroughs Corp., 1972-77; sr. acct. mgr. Burroughs Corp., San Jose, Calif., 1976-77; sr. terr. mgr. Data Gen. Corp., Salt Lake City, 1977-80; mktg. mgr. Automated Language Processing, Provo, Utah, 1980-81; dist./br. mgr. Harris Corp., Salt Lake City, 1981-88; sr. acct. mgr. Novell Corp., Salt Lake City, 1988—. Home: 280 S Alpine Dr Alpine UT 84004 Office: Novel Inc 5215 W Wiley Post Way Salt Lake City UT 84116

GEORGE, GERALD EUGENE, high school distict administrator; b. St. Paul, Kans., July 21, 1935; married; 6 children. BS in Edn., Kans. State Coll., 1959, MS in Edn., 1962; EdD in Adminstrn. and Supervision, Ariz. State U., 1970. Assoc. prin. Moon Valley High Sch., Phoenix, 1972-73; adminstr. fed., state and vocat. programs Glendale (Ariz.) Union High Sch. Dist., 1973-74, adminstr. ednl. mgmt. system, from 1974, supt. of schs., 1982—. Office: Glendale Union High Sch Dist 7650 N 43d Ave Glendale AZ 85301 *

GEORGE, MARY SHANNON, state senator; b. Seattle, May 27, 1916; d. William Day and Agnes (Lovejoy) Shannon; B.A. cum laude, U. Wash., 1937; postgrad. U. Mich., 1937, Columbia U., 1938; m. Flave Joseph George; children—Flave Joseph, Karen Van Hook, Christy, Shannon Lowrey. Prodn. asst., asst. news editor Pathe News, N.Y.C., 1938-42; mem. fgn. editions staff Readers Digest, Pleasantville, N.Y., 1942-46; columnist Caracas (Venezuela) Daily Jour., 1953-60; councilwoman City and County of Honolulu, 1969-74; senator State of Hawaii, 1974—, asst. minority leader, 1978-80, minority policy leader, 1983-84, minority floor leader, 1987, minority leader, 1987—, chmn. transp. com., 1981-82; mem. Nat. Air Quality Adv. Bd., 1974-75, Intergovtl. Policy Ady. Com. Trade, 1988—, White House Conf. Drug FreeAm., 1988—. Vice chmn. 1st Hawaii Ethics Commn., 1968; co-founder Citizens Com. on Constl. Conv., 1968; vice-chmn. platform com. Republican Nat. Conv., 1976, co-chmn., 1980; bd. dirs. Hawaii Planned Parenthood, 1970-72, 79-86, Hawaii Med. Services Assn., 1972-86; mem. adv. bd. Hawaii chpt. Mothers Against Drunk Driving, 1984—. Recipient Jewish Men's Club Brotherhood award, 1974; Outstanding Legislator of Yr. award Nat. Rep. Legislators Assn., 1985; named Woman of Yr., Honolulu Press Club, 1969, Hawaii Fedn. Bus. and Profl. Women, 1970; Citizen of Yr., Hawaii Fed. Exec. Bd., 1973, 76. Mem. LWV (pres. Honolulu 1966-68), Mensa, Phi Beta Kappa, Kappa Alpha Theta. Episcopalian. Author: A Is for Abrazo, 1961. Home: 782-G N Kalaheo Ave Kailua HI 96734 Office: Hawaii State Capitol Honolulu HI 96813

GEORGE, PETER T., orthodontist; b. Akron, Ohio; s. Tony and Paraskeva (Ogrenova) G.; BS Kent State U., 1952; DDS, Ohio State U., 1956; cert. in orthodontics Columbia U., 1962; children: Barton Herrin, Tryan Franklin. Pvt. practice orthodontics, Honolulu, 1962—; cleft palate cons. Hawaii Bur. Crippled Children, 1963—; asst. prof. Med. Sch., U. Hawaii, Honolulu, 1970—. Mem. Hawaii Gov.'s Phys. Fitness Com., 1962-68; mem. Honolulu Mayor's Health Council, 1967-72; mem. med. com. Internat. Weightlifting Fedn., 1980-84; chmn. bd. govs. Hall of Fame of Hawaii, 1984; bd. dirs. Honolulu Opera Theatre, 1986—; chmn. bd. Hawaii Internat. Sports Found., 1988—. Served to capt. Dental Corps, U.S. Army, 1956-60. Olympic Gold medallist in weightlifting, Helsinki, 1952, Silver medallist, London, 1948, Melbourne, 1956; six times world champion; recipient Disting. Service award Hawaiian AAU, 1968; Gold medal Internat. Weightlifting Fedn., 1976; named to Helms Hall of Fame, 1966. Diplomate Am. Bd. Orthodontics. Fellow Am. Coll. Dentistry, Internat. Coll. Dentistry; mem. Hawaii Amateur Athletic Union (pres. 1964-65), U.S. Olympians (pres. Hawaii chpt. 1963-67, 80—), Am. Assn. Orthodontists, Honolulu Dental Soc. (pres. 1967-68), Hawaii Dental Assn. (pres. 1978), Hawaii Soc. Orthodontists (pres. 1972). Editor Hawaii State Dental Jour., 1965-67. Inventor appliance to prevent sleep apnea. U.S. weightlifting coach USSR, 1979, asst. coach Olympic weightlifting team, 1980. Home: 1441 Kapiolani Blvd Ste 520 Honolulu HI 96814 Office: 1441 Kapiolani Blvd Rm 520 Honolulu HI 96814

GEORGE, VANCE, symphony chorus conductor. Formerly assoc. dir. Cleve. Orch. Chorus; now dir. San Francisco Symphony Chorus; formerly chmn. vocal div. Blossom Festival Sch.; dir. choral activities U. Wis., Madison, Kent State U. Office: San Francisco Symphony Chorus 201 Van Ness San Francisco CA 94102 *

GEORGE, WILFRED RAYMOND, investment advisor; b. Grinnell, Iowa, Apr. 1, 1928; s. Raymond Lawrence and Doris Love (Durey) G.; m. Ann Ingraham, Sept. 5, 1987. BS in Engring., Iowa U., 1950; MBA, Harvard U., 1955; PhD, Golden Gate U., 1979. Registered profl. engr., Va. Engr. Westinghouse Electric, Pitts., 1950-51; mech. design engr. 5th Naval Dist., Norfolk, Va., 1952-53; budget supr. sales and employment adminstr. Lockheed Missile and Space Div., Sunnyvale, Calif., 1955-59; registered rep. Shearson Hammill and Co., Menlo Park, Calif., 1963; v.p., mgr. Bache and Co., San Francisco, 1964-72; v.p. investments Prudential Bache Securities, San Francisco, 1972—. Author: Profit Box System for Forecasting Stock Prices, 1976, Tight Money Timing, 1982; patentee in field. Trustee Brit. Benevolent Soc., San Francisco, 1979—; chmn. bd. trustees St. Andres Soc. San Francisco, 1983-89. Served to lt. (j.g.) USNR, 1951-52. Mem. Tech. Securities Soc. of San Francisco (founder 1970, pres. 1974, bd. dirs. 1975—). Republican. Clubs: San Francisco Bond, Harvard Bus. Sch. (San Francisco), Fremont Hills Country (bd. dirs. 1968-70). Home: 73 Telegraph Pl San Francisco CA 94133

GEORGES, ROBERT AUGUSTUS, professor, researcher, writer; b. Sewickley, Pa., May 1, 1933; s. John Thomas and Pauline Pantzis G.; m. Mary Virginia Ruth, Aug. 11, 1956; 1 child, Jonathan Gregory. BS, Ind. U. of Pa., 1954; MA, U. Pa., 1961; PhD, Indiana U., 1964. Tchr. Bound Brook (N.J.) High Sch., 1954-56, Southern Regional High Sch., Manahawkin, N.J., 1958-60; asst. prof. U. Kans., Lawrence, 1963-66; asst. prof. UCLA, 1966-70, assoc. prof., 1970-76, prof., 1976—; vice chmn. Folklore and Mythology Program UCLA, 1966-82, chmn. 1983-86. Author: Greek-American Folk Beliefs and Narratives, 1980; co-author: People Studying People: The Human Element in Fieldwork, 1980, American and Canadian Immigrant and Ethnic Folklore: An Annotated Bibliography; editor: Studies on Mythology, 1968; translator: Two Studies on Modern Greek, Folklore by Stilpon P. Kyriakides, 1968; contbr. numerous articles in folklore periodicals. With U.S. Army, 1956-58. NDEA fellow, 1962-63, Guggenheim fellow, 1969-70. Fellow Am. Folklore Soc.; mem. Calif. Folklore Soc. Home: 906 Fiske St Pacific Palisades CA 90272 Office: Folklore and Mythology Program UCLA 405 Hilgard Ave Los Angeles CA 90024-1459

GEORGESON, ADAMONT NICHOLAS, lawyer; b. Albuquerque, Aug. 21, 1946; s. Agamemnon James and Frances (Dellas) G.; m. Tracy Denise McDonald, July 1, 1984. BA, U. Mich., 1968, JD, 1972. Bar: Calif., Mich. Atty. Monterey County Dist. Atty., Monterey, Calif., 1974-76; assoc. Hancock Rothert & Bunshoft, San Francisco, 1977-80; pvt. practice law Mill Valley, Calif., 1981—. Mem. Marin County Bar Assn. (bd. dirs. 1987-89), San Francisco Bar Assn., Olympic Club. Office: 591 Redwood Hwy Ste 2250 Mill Valley CA 94941

GERALD, DEAN, JR., judge; b. Hobbs, N.Mex., July 30, 1942; s. Gerald and Mary (Wallace) D.; m. Kathryn Stone, Sept. 3, 1962; children: Grant, Rodney, Tahmra. Student, Lubbock Christian Coll., 1960-62; JD, N.Mex. Jud. Coll., 1988. Mgr. Dean Hardware, Capitan, N.Mex., 1960-77; owner Dean Oil Co., Capitan, 1978-86; magistrate judge N.Mex. Supreme Ct., Carrizozo, N.Mex., 1987—. Mem. NRA, Rotary. Republican. Mem. Ch. of Christ.

GERALD, JEFFREY PAUL, military officer; b. Jersey City, Dec. 27, 1952; s. Alan Fredrick and Joan Nina (Dow) G.; m. Diane Susan Dillon, Jan. 26, 1985. BS in Polit. Sci., Jacksonville U., 1974; MS in Criminal Justice, Nova U., 1983. Parole officer Fla. Parole Commn., Jacksonville, Fla., 1974-76; pvt. investigator Investigative Svcs., Inc., Miami, Fla., 1976-77; intelligence officer, 35 tactical fighter squadron USAF, George AFB, Calif., 1978-80; electronic warfare officer USAF, Mather AFB, Calif., 1980-81; F-4 phantom aviator, 561st tactical fighter squadron USAF, George AFB, 1982-85; instr., flight examiner, 3rd tactical fighter wing USAF, Clark AB, Philippines, 1985-87; flight comdr., 90th tactical fighter squadron USAF, Clark AB, 1987-88; stealth fighter, unit electronic warfare officer USAF, Nellis AFB, Nev., 1988—. Author: Deployment Checklist: Korean Air Combat Guide, 1986. Chmn. ARC, Clark AB, Philippines, 1986. Mem. Assn. Old Crows, Soc. Wild Weasels. Republican. Office: USAF 4450 Tactical Group Nellis AFB NV 89191

GERARD, JEFFREY MCKEIGHAN, healthcare facility executive; b. Fresno, Calif., July 5, 1960; s. Vergil Lee and Doris Ann (Johnston) G. AB in Human Biology, Stanford U., 1982. Asst. mgr. facilities Gov's. Corner housing project Stanford (Calif.) U., 1982-83; devel. dir. Am. Emergicenter Inc., La Habra, Calif., 1983-85; mgr. med. facilities Fischer Mangold Group, Pleasanton, Calif., 1985-86; contracting officer Davies Med. Ctr., San Francisco, 1987-88, v.p. corp. affairs, 1988—, 1988—; chief operating officer Davies Med. Network, San Francisco, 1986—; guest lectr. Golden Gate U., San Francisco, 1986, 88, 89. Mem. Nat. Assn. for Ambulatory Care, The Healthcare Forum, Soc. for Ambulatory Care Profls., Bay Area Healthcare Contracting Assn., Am. Coll. Healthcare Execs. Home: 495 Frederick St 1 San Francisco CA 94117 Office: Davies Med Network Castro and Duboce Sts San Francisco CA 94114

GERARDI, RALPH, aerospace company executive; b. Huntington, N.Y., Aug. 10, 1941; s. Anthony and Mary (Clarke) G.; m. Joan I. Leeson, Feb. 14, 1965; children: Chad, Greg. BBA, Manhattan Coll., 1962. Various contract mgmt. positions Hughes Aircraft Co., Fullerton, Calif., 1968-71, 72-73, Raytheon Co., Santa Barbara, Calif., 1973-76; exec. dir. Nelson Assocs. (govt. contracts cons. co.), Anaheim, Calif., 1971-72; dir. contracts and pricing Northrop Corp., Anaheim, 1976—; mem. adv. coun. contract mgmt. career program U. Calif., Irvine, 1985—, West Coast U., L.A., 1986—. Lt. col., USAFR. Mem. Nat. Contract Mgmt. Assn., Nat. Estimating Soc., Northrop Mgmt. Club. Home: 34 Choate St Santa Ana CA 92720 Office: Northrop Corp 500 E Orangethorpe Anaheim CA 92801

GERBA, CHARLES PETER, microbiologist, educator; b. Blue Island, Ill., Sept. 10, 1945; s. Peter and Virginia (Roulo) G.; m. Peggy Louise Scheitlin, June 6, 1970; children: Peter, Phillip. BS in Microbiology, Ariz. State U., 1969; PhD in Microbiology, U. Miami, 1973. Postdoctoral fellow Baylor Coll. Medicine, Houston, 1973-74, asst. prof. microbiology, 1974-81; assoc. prof. U. Ariz., Tucson, 1981-85, prof., 1985—; cons. EPA, Tucson, 1980—; advisor CRC Press, Boca Raton, Fla., 1981—. Editor: Methods in Environmental Virology, 1982, Groundwater Pollution Microbiology, 1984, Phage Ecology, 1987; contbr. numerous articles to profl. and sci. jours. Mem. Pima County Bd. Health, 1986—; mem. sci. adv. bd. EPA, 1987—. Named Outstanding Research Scientist U. Ariz., 1984; environ. science and engring. fellow AAAS, 1984. Mem. Am. Soc. Microbiology (div. chmn. 1982-83, 87-88, pres. Ariz. br. 1984-85, councilor 1985-88), Inst. Food Technologists, Internat. Assn. Water Pollution Research (sr. del. 1985—). Home: 1980 W Paseo Monserrat Tucson AZ 85704 Office: U Ariz Dept Microbiology and Immunology Tucson AZ 85721

GERBER, BARRY ELDON, data processing executive; b. L.A., May 12, 1942; s. Harry and Elsie (Lubin) G.; m. Jane Bernette Margo, June 7, 1962; children: Margot, Karl, Georg. BA, UCLA, 1964, MA, 1966, CPil, 1972. Prof. Calif. State U., Fullerton, 1968-77; dep. dir. Community Cancer Control, L.A., 1977-82; v.p. info. systems Zenith Ins., Encino, Calif., 1983-85; rsch. assoc. Neuropsychiatric Inst. UCLA, L.A., 1982-83; adminstrv. dir. Social Sci. Computing UCLA, Encino, 1985—; cons. in field. Contbg. editor PC week Ziff Davis, 1988—; contbr. articles to profl. jours. Office: UCLA Soc Sci Computing 2121 Bunche Hall Los Angeles CA 90024

GERBER, DONALD LINDAHL, ergotect; b. N.Y.C., June 16, 1930; s. Stephen Ward and Hilma Louise (Lindahl) G.; ed. San Francisco Jr. Coll., Stanford U., Pacific Western U.; BSIE, MBA Pres. Mgmt. Rsch. Frontiers, Inc. Registered indsl. engr., profl. engr., Calif.; cert. systems profl. Mem. Am. Inst. Indsl. Engrs., Assn. Systems Mgmt., Assn. Quality and Participation, Improvement Inst. Home: 160 Caldecott Ln Apt 214 Oakland CA 94618 Office: 160 Caldecott Ln Ste 214 Oakland CA 94618

GERBER, STEVEN HIRAM, investment company executive; b. N.Y.C., Apr. 2, 1938; s. Newcom Lifton and Dorothy (Horowitz) G.; m. Susan Marr, Nov. 26, 1981 (div. Oct. 1985). ABA, Nichols Coll., 1959; BS, Syracuse U., 1961; postgrad., CUNY, 1965. Registered investment advisor. Sales mgr. Xerox Corp., N.Y.C., 1962-68; dir. mktg. Fox & Carskadon Corp., Menlo Park, Calif., 1969-73; sr. v.p. Robert A. McNeil Corp., Los Angeles, 1974-83; pres. Tandam Capital Funding Corp., Los Angeles, 1985--; mem. adv. bd. City Savs. & Loan, Westlake Village, Calif., 1983-. Bd. dirs. Thalians, Cedars-Sinai Hosp., Los Angeles. Recipient Top Fund Raiser award Cedars-Sinai Hosp., 1980. Mem. Nat. Assn. Fin. Wholesalers (found, pres. 1983-86), Internat. Assn. Fin. Planners (bd. dirs.), President's Club, Cellar Club (pres.), Vikings, Racquet Club Palm Springs (pres. 1979--). Home: 10701 Wilshire Blvd Los Angeles CA 90024 Office: Tandam Capital Funding Corp 1631 161st St Santa Monica CA 90401

GERBERDING, WILLIAM PASSAVANT, university president; b. Fargo, N.D., Sept. 9, 1929; s. William Passavant and Esther Elizabeth Ann (Habighorst) G.; m. Ruth Alice Albrecht, Mar. 25, 1952; children: David Michael, Steven Henry, Elizabeth Ann, John Martin. B.A., Macalester Coll., 1951; M.A., U. Chgo., 1956, Ph.D., 1959. Congl. fellow Am. Polit. Sci. Assn., Washington, 1958-59; instr. Colgate U., Hamilton, N.Y., 1959-60; research asst. Senator E.J. McCarthy, Washington, 1960-61; staff Rep. Frank Thompson, Jr., Washington, 1961; faculty UCLA, 1961-72, prof., chmn. dept. polit. sci., 1970-72; dean faculty, v.p. for acad. affairs Occidental Coll., Los Angeles, 1972-75; exec. vice chancellor UCLA, 1975-77; chancellor U. Ill., Urbana-Champaign, 1978-79; pres. U. Wash., Seattle, 1979—; dir. Wash. Mut. Savs. Bank, Safeco Corp., Seattle; cons. Def. Dept., 1962, Calif. Assembly, 1965; mem. Wash. State exec. com. U.S. West Communications. Author: United States Foreign Policy: Perspectives and Analysis, 1966; co-editor, contbg. author: The Radical Left: The Abuse of Discontent, 1970. Trustee Macalester Coll., 1980-83. Served with USN, 1951-55. Recipient Distinguished Teaching award U. Calif., Los Angeles, 1966; Ford Found. grantee, 1967-68. Mem. Am. Polit. Sci. Assn., Assn. Am. Univs. (mem. exec. com. 1985—), Am. Coun. on Edn. (bd. dirs. 1985-89). Office: U Wash Pres Office 301 Adminstrn Bldg AH-30 Seattle WA 98195

GERDEL, MIGUEL ANTONIO, manufacturing research engineer, researcher; b. Roblecito, Guarico, Venezuela, July 26, 1957; came to U.S., 1975; s. Miguel and Maria (Machado) G.; m. Theresa Randolph, Nov. 8, 1984; 1 child, Dalia Elena. BS in Materials Engring., U. Mich., 1979; MS in Metall. Engring., U. Nev., 1985. Materials and processing assoc. engr. Lear Fan Ltd., Reno, 1980-82, aircraft structures engr., 1983, materials and processing engr., 1983-85; mfg. rsch. engr. Rohr Industries Inc., Riverside, Calif., 1985-87; sr. mfg. rsch. engr. Rohr Industries Inc., Riverside, 1987—. Grad. fellow U. Nev. McKay Sch. Mines, 1980-83. Mem. Am. Soc. Metals, Soc. Advancement of Materials and Process Engring., The Metall. Soc. of Am. Inst. Mech. Engrs., U. Mich. Alumni Assn. Home: 3610 Banbury Dr #8D Riverside CA 92505 Office: Rohr Industries Inc 8200 Arlington Ave Riverside CA 92503

GERDES, HENRY CARSTEN, sales executive; b. Bremen, Fed. Republic Germany, June 20, 1940; came to U.S., 1948; s. Frank and Elsa Frieda (Kelch) G.; m. Dulcy Martha Alvarez, June 20, 1975; children: Lisa, Frank. BA, L.I. U., 1965; MA, U. Conn., 1966. Sales rep. Shell Oil Co., N.Y.C., 1966-69; asst. div. mgr. Gallo Wine Co., Los Angeles, 1969-73; div. mgr. Colgate Palmolive Pangburn div., Los Angeles, 1973-76; v.p. west Barton, N.Y.C., 1976-77; region mgr. Kraft Foods, C.M.D., Glenview, Ill., 1977-79, Bigelow Inc., Los Angeles, 1979—; cons. New Brand Devel., Los Angeles, San Francisco, 1986-88. Republican. Lutheran. Home: 1379 Darlington Upland CA 91786

GERDES, RICHARD CONWELL, electronics engineer; b. Waukegan, Ill., Feb. 23, 1939; s. Richard Conwell and Dorothy (sampson) G.; m. Suzanne Elizabeth Smith, 1962 (div. 1977); children: Ryckie Christina, Roberta Coe; m. Mary Kathryn Heuser, June 25, 1983; children: Michelle Lee, John Paul. BEE, U. Ariz., 1962. Pres. Optical Electronics, Inc., Tucson, 1964-79, Analog Systems, Tucson, 1979-86, Third Domain, Inc., Tucson, 1982-86; v.p. Prodn. Svcs., Inc., Tucson, 1983—. Patentee in field. Mem. IEEE, Soc. Motion Picture & TV Engrs., Audio Engring. Soc. Office: Prodn Svcs Inc 3275 W Ina Rd Ste 209 Tucson AZ 85741

GERDTS, DONALD DUANE, television station executive; b. Janesville, Minn., Oct. 18, 1932; s. Ernest William and Gertrude Louise (Bartsch) G.; B.S., Mankato (Minn.) State U., 1957; postgrad. UCLA, 1958-59; M.A., Calif. State U., Fullerton, 1970; m. Marilyn June Anderegg, June 15, 1957; children—James, Paul, Julie. Chmn. fine arts El Rancho High Sch., Pico Rivera, Calif., 1959-66; sr. producer, dir. ITV Center, Santa Ana, Calif., 1967-70; dir. prodn. Sta. KOCE-TV, Huntington Beach, Calif., 1971-75, asst. sta mgr., exec. producer, 1976-78, exec. v.p., sta. mgr., 1978—; exec. producer Bill Alexander's Magic of Oil Painting TV series; lectr. in field. Served with USMC, 1951-54. Recipient Emmy award (2) Acad. TV Arts and Scis., 1978, 1979. Mem. Acad. TV Arts and Scis. Conglist. Exec. producer 12 ednl. television series used by 800 colls. and univs., also 21 documentary films for Pub. Broadcasting Service. Office: Sta KOCE-TV Box 2476 Huntington Beach CA 92647

GERE, JAMES MONROE, civil engineering educator; b. Syracuse, N.Y., June 14, 1925; s. William S. and Carol (Hixson) G.; m. Janice M. Platt, June 1, 1946; children—Susan M., William P., David S. B.S., Rensselaer Poly. Inst., 1949, M.S., 1951; Ph.D., Stanford, 1954. Registered profl. engr., Calif., N.Y. Instr. Rensselaer Poly. Inst., 1949-51; faculty Stanford, 1954—; prof. civil engring. 1962—; assoc. dean Sch. Engring., 1960-67, exec. head dept. civil engring., 1967-72; cons. and lectr. in field, 1954—. Author 7 textbooks in field, also tech. papers. Served with USAAF, 1943-46, ETO. Fellow ASCE; mem. Am. Soc. Engring. Edn., Earthquake Engring. Research Inst., Sigma Xi, Tau Beta Pi. Home: 932 Valdez Pl Stanford CA 94305

GERETY, EDWARD JOSEPH, surgeon, computer consultant; b. Shelton, Conn., Dec. 20, 1918; s. Peter Leo and Charlotte Ursula (Daily) G.; m. Margaret Helen Schneider, Sept.4, 1945; children: Edward J. Jr., Michael T., Richard L., Meghan B., M. Colin, Moira C., Brigid M. BA, U. Bridgeport, 1953; MD, Yale U., 1954; postgrad., U.N.Mex., 1981-83. Cert. Diplomate, Am. Bd. Surgery, Nat. Bd. of Med. Examiners. Intern Naval Med. Ctr., Bethesda, Md., 1954-55; pvt. practice Fairfield, Conn., 1955-61; surgical resident U. N. Mex., Albuquerque, 1961-65; surgeon Surgical Assn., Albuquerque, N.M., 1965-83; computer ops. cons. N.M. Capital Mgmts., Albuquerque, 1986--; rep. Clark Fin. Corp., Salt Lake City. Bd. dirs. Santa Fe (N.M.) Opera (pres. 1983-86, chmn. 1986--); mem. Goals for Albuquerque Task Force, 1983-84, PTO. Capt. USMC, 1943-50. Col. USAF, 1964-78. Decorated with DFC, 4 bronze oak leaf clusters. Fellow Am. Coll. of Surgeons; mem. Yale Club of N. M. (Albuquerque) (pres. 1981-84). Demorat. Roman Catholic. Home: 2041 Los Poblanos Pl NW Albuquerque NM 87107

GERHARDT, WILLIAM THEODORE, chemical engineer; b. Porterville, Calif., Sept. 3, 1937; s. Walter Theodore and Edna J. (Coe) G.; m. Janet Nash Denhoff, Dec. 22, 1969; 1 child, Stephen John. AA, Porterville Coll., 1957; BS in Chem. Engring., U. Calif., Berkeley, 1960. Registered profl. engr., Calif. Technologist Shell Chem., Torrance, Calif., 1960-64, asst. dept. mgr., 1964-68; sr. engr. Shell Oil, Carson, Calif., 1968-80, staff engr., 1980—. Mem. Am. Inst. Chem. Engrs., Robert Sproul Assocs. U. Calif. Berkeley, Catalina 30 Fleet, So. Seas Club, Shoreline Yacht Club. Home: 535 Ultimo Ave Long Beach CA 90814 Office: Shell Oil Co 20945 S Wilmington Ave Carson CA 90745

GERHART, JAMES BASIL, physics educator; b. Pasadena, Calif., Dec. 15, 1928; s. Ray and Marion (van Deusen) G.; m. Genevra Joy Thomesen, June 21, 1958; children: James Edward, Sara Elizabeth. B.S., Calif. Inst. Tech., 1950; M.A., Princeton, 1952, Ph.D., 1954. Instr. physics Princeton, 1954-56; asst. prof. physics U. Wash., Seattle, 1956-61; asso. prof. U. Wash., 1961-65, prof., 1965—; Exec. officer Pacific Northwest Assn. for Coll. Physics, 1972—, bd. dirs., 1965—, chmn., 1970-72; governing bd. Am. Inst. Physics, 1973-76, 78-81. Recipient Disting. Teaching award U. Wash. Regents and Alumni Assn., 1983. Fellow Am. Phys. Soc, AAAS; mem. Am. Assn. Physics Tchrs. (sec. 1971-77, v.p. 1977, pres.-elect 1978, pres. 1979, Millikan medal 1985). Home: 2134 E Interlaken Blvd Seattle WA 98112

GERING, JOSEPH MICHAEL, service executive; b. Queens, N.Y., Apr. 11, 1958; s. Gustave Joseph Jr. and Helen (Weilandt) G.; m. JudyAnn Starr, Aug. 1, 1980 (div. Aug. 1985); m. Mirna Lissette Gonzalez, May 19, 1989. Diploma religion, Life Bible Coll., 1978, BA in Theology, 1980; MA in Psychology, Azusa (Calif.) Pacific U., 1988. Youth pastor N. Heights Foursquare Ch., Albuquerque, 1978-80; typographer Meredith Publs., Albuquerque, 1981; assoc. pastor Corona Bible Ch., Phoenix, 1984-85; instr. aerobics Jack La Lanne's European Spa, Glendale, Calif., 1985-87; pvt. practice typographer 1985—; intern Alpha Counseling Ctrs., Mission Viejo, Calif., 1989—. Mem. Toastmasters (pub. speaker La Crescenta, Calif. chpt. 1988—). Republican. Home: 8545 Cedros Ave #206 Panorama City CA 91402

GERKEN, WALTER BLAND, insurance company executive; b. N.Y.C., Aug. 14, 1922; s. Walter Adam and Virginia (Bl) G.; m. Darlene Stolt, Sept. 6, 1952; children: Walter C., Ellen M., Beth L., Daniel J., Andrew P., David A. BA, Wesleyan U., 1948; MPA, Maxwell Sch. Citizenship and Pub. Affairs, Syracuse, 1958. Supr. budget and adminstrv. analysis Wis., Madison, 1950-54; mgr. investments Northwestern Mut. Life Ins. Co., Milw., 1954-67; v.p. finance Pacific Mut. Life Ins. Co., L.A., 1967-69, exec. v.p., 1969-72, pres., 1972-75, chmn. bd., 1975-87; chmn. exec. com. Pacific Mut. Life Ins. Co., Los Angeles, 1987—, also dir.; bd. dirs. Whittaker Corp., Carter Hawley Hale Stores, So. Calif. Edison Co., Times Mirror Co. Bd., Mgmt. Compensation Group, DAC; mem. bd. overseers Rand/Ulla Ctr. for Study of Soviet Internat. Behavior. Bd. Dirs. Keck Found., James Irvine Found., Hoag Meml. Presbyn. Hosp.; chmn. bd. overseers U. Calif.-Irvine; trustee Occidental Coll., L.A., Wesleyan U., Middletown, Conn., United Way Am. Capt. USAAF, 1942-46. Decorated D.F.C., Air medal. Mem. Calif. Club, Dairymen's Country Club (Boulder Junction, Wis.), Met. Club (Washington), Balboa Bay Club (Newport Beach, Calif.), Automobile Club (So. Calif. chpt., bd. dir.), Calif. Roundtable, Pauma Valley Country Club, Calif. Stock Exch. Club (L.A.), Pacific Union Club (San Francisco). Office: Pacific Mut Life Ins Co 700 Newport Center Dr Newport Beach CA 92660

GERLOCK, RHEDA S., optometrist; b. Lamar, Colo., Aug. 25, 1959; d. Dave and Lydia (Weimer) G.; m. Robert D. McQuaid. Student, Adams State Coll., 1977-78, Colo. State U., 1978-80; OD, So. Calif. Coll. Optometry, 1984. Optometrist Robert Larson, Optometrist, Lamar, 1984-85, Vision Care Specialist, Aurora, Colo., 1985—. Vol. Colo. Soc. to Prevent Blindness, Denver, 1985—; mem. Jr. Symphony League, Denver, 1985—; active local political campaigns. Mem. Am. Optometric Assn., Colo. Optometric Assn. (legis. com. 1986-88). Democrat. Office: Vision Care Specialists 1550 S Potomac #155 Aurora CO 80012

GERMAN, THOMAS LOTELL, plant pathology educator; b. Aurora, Ill., Aug. 23, 1941; s. Kempton L. and Winefred (Bray) G.; m. Mary Catherine Diezel, June 19, 1983. BS, U. Wis., 1963, PhD, 1974; MS, Mich. State U., 1968. Assoc. prof. dept. plant pathology U. Hawaii, Honolulu, 1985--. Contbr. articles to profl. jours., chpts. to books. U. Hawaii grantee, 1985, USDA grantee 1986. Mem. Am. Soc. Virology, Am. Soc. Plant Pathology, AAAS.

GERMAN, WILLIAM, newspaper editor; b. N.Y.C., Jan. 4, 1919; s. Sam and Celia (Norack) G.; m. Gertrude Pasenkoff, Oct. 12, 1940; children: David, Ellen, Stephen. B.A., Bklyn. Coll., 1939; M.S., Columbia U., 1940; M.S. Nieman fellow, Harvard U., 1950. Reporter, asst. fgn. editor, news editor, mng. editor, exec. editor San Francisco Chronicle, 1940—; editor Chronicle Fgn. Service, 1960-77; mng. editor KQED, Newspaper of the Air, 1968; lectr. U. Calif., Berkeley, 1946-47, 68-70. Editor: San Francisco Chronicle Reader, 1962. Served with AUS, 1943-45. Mem. Am. Soc. Newspaper Editors, A.P. Mng. Editors Assn. Home: 150 Lovell Ave Mill Valley CA 94941 Office: San Francisco Chronicle 901 Mission St San Francisco CA 94103

GERRINGER-BUSENBARK, ELIZABETH JACQUELINE, systems analyst, consultant; b. Edmund, Wis., Jan. 7, 1934; d. Clyde Elroy and Matilda Evangeline Knapp; student Madison Bus. Coll., 1952, San Francisco State Coll., 1953-54, Vivian Rich Sch. Fashion Design, 1955, Dale Carnegie Sch., 1956, Arthur Murray Dance Studio, 1956, Biscayne Acad. Music, 1957, L.A. City Coll., 1960-62, Santa Monica (Calif.) Jr. Coll., 1963; Hastings Coll. of Law, 1973, Wharton Sch., U. Pa., 1977, London Art Coll., 1979; Ph.D., 1979; attended Goethe Inst., 1985; m. Roe (Don David) Devon Gerringer-Busenbark, Sept. 30, 1968 (dec. Dec. 1972). Actress, Actors Workshop San Francisco, 1959, 65, Theatre of Arts Beverly Hills (Calif.), 1963, also radio; cons, and systems analyst for banks and pub. accounting agys.; artist, singer, songwriter, playwright, dress designer. Pres., tchr. Environ Improvement, Originals by Elizabeth, Dometrik's, JIT-MAP, San Francisco, 1973—; steering com. explorations in worship, ordained min. 1978. Author: Explorations in Worship, 1965, The Magic of Scents, 1967, New Highways, 1967; Happening - Impact-Mald, 1971; Seven Day Rainbow, 1972; Zachary's Adversaries, 1974; Fifteen from Wisconsin, 1977; Bart's White Elephant, 1978; Skid Row Minister, 1978; Points in Time, 1979; Special Appointment, A Clown in Town, 1979; Happenings, 1980, Votes from the Closet, 1984, Wait for Me, 1984, The Stairway, 1984, The River is a Rock, 1985, Happenings Revisted, 1986, Comparative Religion in the United States, 1986, Lumber in the Skies, 1986, The Fifth Season, 1987, Summer Thoughts, 1987, Toast Thoughts, 1988. Address: PO Box 1640 7th and Mission Sta San Francisco CA 94101

GERSHON, DANIEL E., lawyer; b. Manhattan, N.Y., Sept. 10, 1959; s. N. Richard and Monique Beatrice (Erzberger) G. BA, U. Colo., 1981; JD, U. Creighton, 1984, U. Denver, 1986. Bar: N.Mex., Colo. Publicist Feyline Presents, Inc., Denver, 1981-83; ski instr. Loveland Ski Basin, Georgetown, Colo., 1985-86; assoc. Montgomery & Andrews, P.A., Santa Fe, N.Mex., 1986—; ski instr. Santa Fe Ski Basin, 1987—. Mem. ABA, N.Mex. Trial Lawyers Assn., 1st Jud. Dist. Bar Assn., Pro Ski Instrs. Am., Amnesty Internat., U. Colo. Alumni Assn. Democrat. Office: Montgomery & Andrews PA 325 Paseo de Peralta Santa Fe NM 87501

GERSHWIN, JERRY, motion picture producer; b. N.Y.C., Apr. 20, 1926; s. Max and Rose (Sachs) Grishman; m. Jackie Joslin Gershwin, June 17, 1955 (div. June 1973); 1 child, Gina Gershwin Varney. Student, UCLA. Mail room clk. MCA Agy., Beverly Hills, Calif., 1950-52, N.Y.C., 1953-56; v.p. MCA-Universal Prodn., Universal City, Calif., 1957-58; exec. asst. to chief exec. officer 1958-65; ind. motion picture producer Sweet November, The Bobo, Sol Madrid, Michael Kohlaas, Laughter in the Dark, Where Eagles Dare, Your Three Minutes Are Up, Breakheart Pass, 8 Bells Toll, A Severed Head, Harper, Nomads, Kaleidoscope, 1965—. Mem. Acad. Motion Picture Arts and Scis. Home: 6503 Point Lechuza Dr Malibu CA 90265

GERSON, GUS J., JR., leisure studies educator; b. Dec. 12, 1935; s. Gus and Theresa Alicia (Costa) G.; m. Diane E. Gerson, Mar. 21, 1958; children: Alicia, Eric, Dirk. BS, U. So. Calif., 1958; MS, Calif. State U., 1968; EdD, Brigham Young U., 1975. Recreation dir. Dept. Recreation & Parks, L.A., 1959-65; dir. recreation program Pasadena (Calif.) Unified Sch. Dist., 1965-72; asst., then assoc. prof. Calif. State U., Northridge, 1972-79; coordinator, prof. Calif. State Poly. U., Pomona, 1979-85; prof. health, phys. edn. and recreation Calif. State Poly. U., 1985--; cons. in field; adj. prof. Brigham Young U., Provo, Utah, 1976, 77; grant author, evaluator Ross Snyder Recreations Ctr., L.A., 1988; presenter, panelist profl. confs. Author: Understanding Leisure, 1988, Effective Park and Recreation Commissioners and Board Members (with others), 1987; contbr. articles to profl. publs. Mem. Community Svcs. Commn., City of Monrovia, Calif., 1974-85. Mem. World Leisure and Recreation Assn., Calif. Parks and Recreation Soc. (dist.dir. 1985-86), Nat. Parks and Recreation Soc. Home: 6107 Meadow Lark Dr LaVerne CA 91750 Office: Calif State Poly U Dept HPER 3801 W Temple Ave Pomona CA 91768-4079

GERST, PAUL RENE, electrical engineering company executive; b. Chgo., Aug. 20, 1927; s. Paul Ernest and Francine Claire (Niemard) G.; m. Shirley Louise Lucki, June 29, 1963; children: Paul Vernon, John William, Cathleen Claire. BS in Elec. Engring., Northwestern U., 1952; MBA, Washington U., 1955. Registered profl. engr., Ill., Calif.; diplomate Am. Assn. Environ. Engrs. Advt. mgr. Century Electric Co., St. Louis, 1953-56; sales mgr. indsl. wire Kaiser Aluminum and Chem., Chgo., 1957-60; mng. dir. Paul E. Gerst & Co., Chgo., 1961-63; chief exec. officer Energy Systems Corp., Chgo., 1964-72, Enercology Assocs., Ltd., Chgo., Los Angeles, 1973—; mng. dir. Western Energy Engrs., Costa Mesa, Calif., 1983-88; chmn. bd. Oceanside Refrigeration, Inc., Newport Beach, Calif., Klondike Equity Enterprises, Balboa Island, Calif. Patentee in field. Supr. Lake County Bd., Waukegan, Ill., 1976-80; mem. No. Ill. Planning Commn., Chgo., 1976-80; advisor South Coast Air Quality Mgmt. Dist, El Monte, Calif., 1984—. Served to 1st lt. USAF, 1952-53. Mem. Am. Cogeneration Assn. (pres.), Los Angeles Cogeneration Assn. (bd. dirs.), Sigma Chi. Republican. Roman Catholic. Lodge: KC. Office: Western Energy Engrs Inc 3158 Redhill #100 Costa Mesa CA 92626

GERSTELL, A. FREDERICK, cement, aggregates, asphalt and concrete manufacturing company executive; b. 1938. Vice pres. mktg., dir. Alpha Portland Cement Co., 1960-75; v.p. Calif. Portland Cement Co., L.A., 1975-81, pres., chief operating officer, 1981-84; pres., chief operating officer CalMat Co., L.A., 1984-88, pres., chief exec. officer, chief operating officer, 1988—. Office: CalMat Co 3200 San Fernando Rd Los Angeles CA 90065

GERSTENBERG, GEORGE JAMES, district director federal agency; b. N.Y.C., Feb. 17, 1933; s. Frank David and Anna Marie (Gaussmann) G.; m. Janis Ann Silverthorn, May 2, 1959; children: Susan Ann, Christopher James. BS, UCLA, 1959. Inspector U.S. Food & Drug Adminstrn., Los Angeles, 1957-58, Phila., 1958-67; chief inspector U.S. Food & Drug Adminstrn., N.Y.C., 1967-71, dist. dir., 1971-86; dist. dir. U.S. Food & Drug Adminstrn., Los Angeles, 1986—. Scoutmaster Boy Scouts Am., Centerport, N.Y., 1975-85. Recipient Award of Merit U.S. Food & Drug Adminstrn., 1985, Commr.'s Citation U.S. Food & Drug Adminstrn., 1988. Mem. Western Assn. Food & Drug Officials, Lions. Republican. Roman Catholic. Home: 435 Todd Ln Monrovia CA 91016 Office: US Food & Drug Adminstrn 1521 W Pico Blvd Los Angeles CA 91016

GERTH, DONALD ROGERS, university president; b. Chgo., Dec. 4, 1928; s. George C. and Madeleine (Canavan) G.; m. Beverly J. Hollman, Oct. 15, 1955; children: Annette, Deborah. BA, U. Chgo., 1947, AM, 1951, PhD, 1963. Field rep. S.E. Asia World Univ., 1950; asst. to pres. Shimer Coll., 1951; Admissions counselor U. Chgo., 1956-58; assoc. dean students, admissions and records, mem. dept. polit. sci. San Francisco St. U., San Francisco, 1958-63; assoc. dean instnl. relations and student affairs Calif. State Univ., 1963-64; chmn. commn. on extended edn. Calif. State Univs. and Colls., 1977-82; dean of students Calif. State U., Chico, 1964-68, prof. polit. sci., 1964-76, assoc. v.p. for acad. affairs, dir. internat. programs, 1969-70, v.p. acad. affairs, 1970-76; co-dir. Danforth Found. Research Project, 1968-69; coordinator Inst. Local Govt. and Public Service, 1968-70; pres., prof. polit. sci. and public adminstrn. Calif. State U., Dominguez Hills, 1976-84; pres. Calif. State U., Sacramento, 1984—; mem. Accrediting Commn. for Sr. Colls. and Univs. of Western Coll. Assn.; chmn. admissions coun. Calif. State U.; chmn. No. Am. coun. of Internat. Assn. Univ. Pres.; mem. edn. com. Commn. of Californias; assoc. West Coast coord. Higher Edn. Exec. Assos. of Chgo., 1967-71; bd. dirs. Ombudsman Found., L.A., 1968-71; com. continuing edn. Calif. Coordinating Coun. for Higher Edn., 1963-64; lectr. U. Philippines, 1953-54, Claremont Grad. Sch. and Univ. Ctr., 1965-69. Coauthor: The Learning Society, 1969; author, editor: An Invisible Giant, 1971; contbg. editor Education for the Public Service, 1970, Papers on the Ombudsman in Higher Education, 1979. Mem. pers. commn. Chico Unified Sch. Dist., 1969-76, chmn., 1971-74; adv. com. on justice programs Butte Coll., 1970-76; mem. Varsity Scouting Coun., 1980-84; chmn. United Way campaign Calif. State Univs., Los Angeles Co., 1981-82; bd. dirs. Sacramento Area United Way, Sacramento Symphony Assn.; mem. bd. dirs., South Bay Hospital Found., 1979-82; mem. The Cultural Commn., Los Angeles, 1981-84. Capt. USAF, 1952-56. Mem. Nat. Assn. Schs. Pub. Affairs and Adminstrn., Am. Polit. Sci. Assn., Am. Soc. Pub. Adminstrn., Soc. Coll. and Univ. Planning, Western Govtl. Rsch. Assn., World Affairs Coun. L.A., Calif. Assn. Pub. Adminstrn. Edn. (chmn. 1973-74), Western Polit. Sci. Assn., Western Assn. Schs. and Colls., Sacramento Met. C. of C. (bd. dirs.), Sacramento Club, Comstock Club. Democrat. Episcopalian. Home: 11463 Forty Niner Circle Gold River CA 95670 Office: Calif State U 6000 J St Adm 206 Sacramento CA 95819-2694

GERWICK, BEN CLIFFORD, JR., construction engineer, educator; b. Berkeley, Calif., Feb. 22, 1919; s. Ben Clifford and Bernice (Coultrap) G.; m. Martelle Louise Beverly, July 28, 1941; children: Beverly (Mrs. Robert A. Brian), Virginia (Mrs. Roy Wallace), Ben Clifford III, William. B.S., U. Calif., 1940. With Ben C. Gerwick, Inc., San Francisco, 1939-70; pres. Ben C. Gerwick, Inc., 1952-70; exec. v.p. Santa Fe-Pomeroy, Inc., 1968-71; prof. civil engring. U. Calif., Berkeley, 1971—; sponsoring mgr. Richmond-San Rafael Bridge substructure, 1953-56, San Mateo-Hayward bridge, 1964-66; lectr. constrn. engring. Stanford U., 1962-68; cons. major bridge and marine constrn. projects; cons. constrn. engr. for ocean structures and bridges, also offshore structures in North Sea, Arctic Sea, Japan, Australia, Indonesia, Arabian Gulf, Southeast Asia, South Am.; mem. U.S. Arctic Research Com. Author: Russian-English Dictionary of Prestressed Concrete and Concrete Construction, 1966, Construction of Prestressed Concrete Structures, 1971; Construction and Engineering Marketing for Major Project Services, 1981, Construction of Offshore Structures, 1986; contbr. articles to profl. jours. Served with USN, 1940-46; comdr. Res. ret. Recipient Lockheed award Marine Tech. Soc., 1977, Frank P. Brown medal Franklin Inst., 1988. Fellow ASCE (hon. mem.; Karp award 1976), Am. Concrete Inst. (dir. 1960, hon. mem., Turner award 1974, Corbetta award 1981); mem. Federation Internationale de la Precontrainte (pres. 1974-78, now hon. pres., Freyssinet medal 1982), Prestressed Concrete Inst. (pres. 1957-58, hon.), Deutscher Beton Verein (hon., Emil Mörsch medal 1979), Concrete Soc. U.K. (hon.), Association Francaise pour Constrn. (hon.), Verein Deutscher Ingenieure (hon.), Norwegian Acad. of Tech. Sci., Royal Acad. Tech. Sci. (Sweden), Nat. Acad. Engring., Moles, Soc. Naval Architects and Marine Engrs. (Blakely Smith award 1981), Beavers (Engring. award 1975), Phi Beta Kappa, Tau Beta Pi, Sigma Xi, Chi Epsilon, Kappa Sigma. Congregationalist. Clubs: Bohemian (San Francisco); Claremont Country (Oakland). Home: 5727 Country Club Dr Oakland CA 94618 Office: U Calif 217 McLaughlin Hall Berkeley CA 94720 also: 500 Sansome St San Francisco CA 94111

GERWICK-BRODEUR, MADELINE CAROL, marketing and sales professional; b. Kearney, Neb., Aug. 29, 1951; d. Vern Frank and Marian Leila (Bliss) Gerwick; m. David Louis Brodeur; 1 child, Maria Louise. Student, U. Wis., 1970-72, U. Louisville, 1974-75; BA in Econs. magna cum laude, U. N.H., 1979; postgrad., Internat. Trade Inst., Seattle. Indsl. sales rep. United Radio Supply Inc., Seattle, 1980-81; mfrs. rep. Ray Over Sales Inc., Seattle, 1981-82; sales engr. Tektronix, Inc., Kent, Wash., 1982-83; mktg. mgr. Zepher Industries, Inc., Burien, Wash., 1983-85, Microscan Systems Inc., Tukwila, Wash., 1986—; market devel. URS Electronics, Inc., Portland, 1986-88; sr. product specialist John Fluke Mfg. Co. Inc., 1989—; bd. dirs., sec. Starfish Enterprises Inc., Tacoma, 1984-87; com. chmn. Northcon, Seattle and Portland, 1984-86, 88; speaker to Wash. Women's Employment and Edn., Tacoma, 1983—. Recipient Jack E. Chase award for Outstanding Svc. and Contbn. Northern Founder's Orgn., 1988. Mem. Electronic Mfrs. Assn. (sec. 1982, sec.-treas. 1988, v.p. 1989—), Phi Kappa Phi. Office: John Fluke Mfg Co Inc PO Box C9090 MS 266D Everett WA 98206

GESHELL, RICHARD STEVEN, lawyer; b. Colorado Springs, Colo., Aug. 6, 1943; s. Peter Steven and Ann Elizabeth (Irwin) G.; m. Carol Ann Reed, Sept. 6, 1965; 1 child, Carmen Marie. BA in Chemistry, Ariz. State U., 1965; JD, U. Nebr., 1968. Bar: Nebr. 1968, U.S. Dist. Ct. Nebr. 1968, Hawaii 1983, U.S. Dist. Ct. Hawaii 1983. Mem. Robak and Geshell, Columbus, Nebr., 1968-83; ptnr. R. Steven Geshell, Honolulu, 1983—. Served to capt. USAR, 1974-83. Mem. Assn. Trial Lawyers Am., Nebr. Bar Assn., Hawaii Bar Assn., Blue Key (pres. 1964-65), Phi Sigma Kappa (past house mgr, past v.p.). Republican. Lodge: Elks (chief forum 1984, past exalted ruler, trustee). Home: 1155 Kaluanui Rd Honolulu HI 96825 Office: 1088 Bishop St Ste 1104 Honolulu HI 96813

GESSERT, AUTUMN ROBERTA, telecommunications administrator; b. Milw., Nov. 25, 1958; d. Sherman Albert and Nancy Ann (Darnold) G.; divorced; 1 child, Phillip Patrick. Student, Marquette U., 1982-83, Nat. Ctr. Degree Studies. Telex operator Aqua-Chem, Inc., Milw., 1981-82, translator French, 1982-83, project coordinator, 1983-85, coordinator telecommunications, 1985-86; mgr. telecommunications Mark Travel Corp., Milw., 1986-87; instr. computer networks and literacy U.S. Fed. Govt., Yuma, Ariz., 1987—. Served as pfc. U.S. Army, 1977-78. Mem. Wis. Telecommunications Assn., Nat. Assn. for Female Execs. Republican. Lutheran. Office: Info Systems Command Attn: ASNC-TYU-OA-T Yuma Proving Ground Yuma AZ 85365

GETCHES, DAVID HARDING, law educator, state environmental executive, lawyer; b. Abington, Pa., Aug. 17, 1942; s. George Winslow Getches and Ruth Erskine (Harding) Fossette; m. Ann Marks, June 26, 1964; children: Matthew, Catherine, Elizabeth. AB, Occidental Coll., 1964; JD, U. So. Calif., 1967. Bar: Calif. 1968, U.S. Supreme Ct. 1971, D.C. 1972, Colo. 1973. Assoc. Luce, Forward, Hamilton & Scripps, San Diego, 1967-69; directing atty. Calif. Indian Legal Services, Escondido, 1969-70; founding dir. Native Am. Rights Fund, Boulder, Colo., 1970-76; ptnr. Getches & Greene, Boulder, 1976-78; prof. U. Colo. Sch. Law, Boulder, 1978—; exec. dir. Colo. Dept. Natural Resources, Denver, 1983-87. Author: Water Law in a Nutshell, 1984; Co-author: Cases and Materials on Federal Indian Law, 1986, Water Resources Management, 1988; mem. editorial bd. Felix S. Cohen's Handbook on Federal Indian Law, 1982, Am. Law Mining, 1985; contbr. articles to profl. jours. Chmn. state govt. campaign United Way, Denver, 1984; mem. Colo. River Basin Salinity Control Forum, Salt Lake City, 1983-87, Colo. Water Conservation Bd., Denver, 1983-87, Colo. Groundwater Commn., Denver, 1983-87, Colo. Mined Land Reclamation Bd., Denver, 1985-87. Mem. Colo. Bar Assn., D.C. Bar, Calif. Bar. Democrat. Home: 627 Pine St Boulder CO 80302 Office: U Colo Sch Law Boulder CO 80309-0401

GETREU, IAN E(DWIN), electronics engineer; b. Melbourne, Australia, Sept. 14, 1943; s. Leo and Matylda Getreu; m. Beverly S. Salmenson, June 5, 1983. BE with honors, U. Melbourne, 1965, M Engring. Sci., 1967; postgrad., UCLA, 1966-67; PhD, U. Calif., Berkeley, 1972. Sr. engr. Tektronix Inc., Beaverton, Oreg., 1972-79, mgr. integrated cir. computer aided design devel., 1979-83, mgr. advanced products mktg., 1983-85, scientist advanced products, 1985-86; v.p., research and devel., modeling Analogy, Inc., Beaverton, 1986—, also bd. dirs.; lectr. U. New South Wales, Sydney, Australia, 1974-75; chmn. ComputerAided Network Design Com., 1980-82. Author: Modeling the Bipolar Transistor, 1976. Bd. dirs. Jewish Fedn. of Portland, 1986—. Mem. IEEE (sr.), Internat. Conf. Computer Aided Design (chmn. 1986). Home: PO Box 1356 Beaverton OR 97075

GETREU, SANFORD, city planner; b. Cleve., Mar. 9, 1930; s. Isadore and Tillie (Kuchinsky) G.; B.A. in Architecture, Ohio State U., 1953; M.A. in Regional Planning, Cornell U., 1955; m. Gara Eileen Smith, Dec. 8, 1952 (div. Feb. 1983); children—David Bruce, Gary Benjamin, Allen Dana; m. Kelly Heim, Aug. 8, 1988. Resident planner Mackesey & Reps., consultants, Rome, N.Y., 1955-56; planning dir., Rome, 1956-57; dir. gen. planning, Syracuse, N.Y., 1957-59, dep. commr. planning, 1959-62, commr. planning, 1962-65; planning dir. San Jose, Calif., 1965-74; urban planning cons., 1974—; pres. Sanford Getreu, AICP, Inc., vis. lectr., critic Cornell U., 1960-65, Syracuse U., 1962-65, Stanford, 1965—, San Jose State Coll., 1965—, Santa Clara U., Calif. State Poly. Coll., DeAnza Coll., San Jose City Coll., U. Calif. at Berkeley; pres. planning dept. League of Calif. Cities, 1973-74; advisor State of Calif. Office of Planning and Research. Past bd. dirs. Theater Guild, San Jose, Triton Mus., San Jose. Mem. Am. Soc. Cons. Planners, Am. Planning Assn., Am. Inst. Cert. Planners, Bay Area Planning Dirs. Assn. (v.p. 1965-74, mem. exec. com. 1973-74), Assn. Bay Area Govts. (regional planning com. 1967-74). Club: Rotary. Home: 105 Coronado Ave Los Altos CA 94022 Office: 399 Main St Los Altos CA 94022

GETTY, DONALD ROSS, provincial premier; b. Westmount, Que., Can., Aug. 30, 1933; s. Charles Ross and Beatrice (Hampton) G.; m. Margaret Inez Mitchell, Aug. 18, 1955; children: Dale, David, Darin, Derek. BBA, U. Western Ont., 1955. With Imperial Oil Ltd., 1955-61; with Midwestern Indsl. Gas Ltd., 1961-63; pres., mng. dir. Baldonnel Oil & Gas Ltd., 1964-67; ptnr. Doherty Roadhouse & McCuaig Ltd., 1967; minister fed. and intergovtl. affairs Province of Alta., 1971-75, minister energy and natural resources, 1975-79, premier, 1985—; past pres. D. Getty Investments Ltd.; chmn. bd. dirs. Ipsco, 1981-85; former chmn. Nortek Energy Corp. Former mem. Alta. Legislature, mem., 1985—; active Alta. No. Lights Wheelchair Basketball Team. Recipient Outstanding Can., Western Canada Football League award. Conservative. Clubs: Edmonton Petroleum (former bd. govs.), Derrick Golf and Winter (former bd. dirs.). Home: 52 Westbrook Dr, Edmonton, AB Canada T6J 2C9 Office: Office of the Premier, 307 Legislature Bldg, Edmonton, AB Canada T5K 2B6 *

GETZ, BERT ATWATER, investment company executive; b. Chgo., May 7, 1937; s. George Fulmer Jr. and Olive Cox (Atwater) G.; m. Sandra Maclean, July 17, 1958; children: Lynn Getz Polite, George F., Bert A. Jr. BSBA, U. Mich., 1959. V.p. Globe Corp., Scottsdale, Ariz., 1960-74, pres., 1974—, also bd. dirs., 1974--; bd. dirs. CalMat Co., L.A., Security Pacific Corp., Security Pacific Nat. Bank, L.A., Iliff, Thorn & Co., Phoenix, Ellsworth Fin. Corp., Phoenix, Security Pacific Bancorp. S.W., Security Pacific Bank Ariz. Trustee Lawrenceville (N.J.) Sch., 1972—, pres. bd., 1984—; chmn. bd. Phoenix Community Found. Mem. Phoenix Thunderbirds, Paradise Valley Country Club, John Gardiners Tennis Ranch, Sigma Chi, Theta Theta. Republican. Episcopalian. Home: 4529 E Clearwater Pkwy Scottsdale AZ 85253 Office: Globe Corp 3634 Civic Center Pla Scottsdale AZ 85251

GETZ, GEORGE FULMER, JR., holding company executive; b. Chgo., Jan. 4, 1908; s. George Fulmer and Susan Daniel (Rankin) G.; m. Olive Cox Atwater, Jan. 17, 1933 (dec. Sept. 22, 1980); children: George Fulmer, III (dec.), Bert Atwater. Pres. Eureka Coal & Dock Co., 1935-45; chmn. bd., chief exec. officer Globe Corp.; chmn. bd. Getz Coal Co., 1939-48, pres., 1948-53; dir. Chgo. Nat. League Ball Club, 1940-72; mem. exec. com., dir. A.T. & S.F. Ry., 1955-80, Sante Fe Industries, Inc., 1968-80; dir. Upper Ave. Nat. Bank, Chgo., 1936-74, Chgo. Transit Authority, 1945-47. Mem. United Republican Fund Ill.; mem. citizens bd. U. Chgo., 1956-71; bd. dirs. Jr. Achievement Chgo., 1939—, v.p., 1947-49; v.p. Met. Jr. Achievement, 1942-44; mem. Pres.'s Commn. White House Fellowships, 1982, 83; bd. dirs. Getz Found., Ind. U. Found.; pres., dir. Arthur R. Metz Found.; hon. trustee Chgo. Zool. Soc.; past v.p. finance, treas. Nat. Safety Council; pres. Geneva Lake Water Safety Com., Inc., 1949-54, bd. dirs., 1949-69, hon. dir., 1969—; mem. Ill. Com. Crusade for Freedom, Inc., 1957, 58; pres., dir. Nat. Hist. Fire Found., Globe Found.; bd. dirs. Ariz. Zool. Soc., 1966-81, 84-88, emeritus, 1988; trustee Am. Grad. Sch. Internat. Mgmt., vice chmn. bd., 1976-78; mem. organizing com., mem. Chgo. Rotary Found., 1936-45; mem. Nat. Rep. Fin. Com., 1976—; trustee Grand Cen. Art Galleries, N.Y.C., 1982—(mem. emeritus) ; bd. dirs. Scottsdale Meml. Health Found., 1984—. Mem. Chgo. Assn. Commerce and Industry (com. mem. govtl. affairs council); emeritus mem. Phoenix 40. Episcopalian. Clubs: Chgo., Tavern, Chgo. Yacht, Economic (Chgo.); Los Rancheros Visitadores (Santa Barbara, Calif.); Paradise Valley Country (Ariz.); Circumnavigators; Phoenix Symphony Assn. 400; Valley Field Riding and Polo (Ariz.); Balboa (Mazatlan, Mexico). Home: 80 Mountain Shadows W Scottsdale AZ 85253 Office: Globe Corp 3634 Civic Center Blvd Scottsdale AZ 85251 also: 16555 W Hwy 120 Libertyville IL 60048

GEVING, STEVE WILLIAM, executive chef; b. Harvey, N.D., May 10, 1952. Cert. exec. chef. Exec. chef L.A. Biltmore Hotel, 1975-76, City Centre Club, 1976-78, Maldonado's Restaurant, Pasadena, Calif., 1978-80; corp. exec. chef 1st Interstate Bancorp, L.A., 1980—; cons. chef 1984 Summer Olympica, L.A. Team adv. Les Togues Blanches, Carnation U.S.A., 1988 IKA-HOGA, Frankfurt, Profl. Culinary Team, Internat. Culinary Olympics. Recipient gold medal Am. Culinary Fedn., 1984, Culinary Olympics, 1988. Mem. Chefs Cuisine Assn. Calif. (pres. 1980-82, Chef of Yr. award 1983), Toques Blanches Internat. (pres. 1985-86, Chef of Yr. award 1985), Chaines de Rotisseurs, Acad. Chefs, Epicurean Club L.A., Sommelier Assn. Calif. (bd. dirs.), Amis de Escoffier. Office: 1st Interstate Tower 707 Wilshire Blvd 60th Fl Los Angeles CA 90017

GEYMAN, JOHN PAYNE, physician, educator; b. Santa Barbara, Calif., Feb. 9, 1931; s. Milton John and Betsy (Payne) G.; m. Emogene Clark Deichler, June 9, 1956; children: John Matthew, James Caleb, William Sabin. A.B. in Geology, Princeton U., 1952; M.D., U. Calif., San Francisco, 1960. Diplomate: Am. Bd. Family Practice. Intern Los Angeles County Gen. Hosp., 1960-61; resident in gen. practice Sonoma County Hosp., Santa Rosa, Calif., 1961-63; practice medicine specializing in family practice Mt. Shasta, Calif., 1963-69; dir. family practice residency program Community Hosp. Sonoma County, Santa Rosa, 1969-71; asso. prof. family practice, chmn. div. family practice U. Utah, 1971-72; prof., vice chmn. dept. family practice U. Calif., Davis, 1972-77; prof., chmn. dept. family medicine U. Wash., 1977—. Author: The Modern Family Doctor and Changing Medical Practice, 1971, Family Practice: Foundation of Changing Health Care, 1980, 2d edit., 1985; editor: Content of Family Practice, 1976, Family Practice in the Medical School, 1977, Research in Family Practice, 1978, Preventive Medicine in Family Practice, 1979, Profile of the Residency Trained Family Physician in the U.S, 1970-79, Funding of Patient Care, Education and Research in Family Practice, 1981, The Content of Family Practice: Current Status and Future Trends, 1982, Archives of Family Practice, 1980, 81, 82; founding editor: Jour. Family Practice, 1973—; co-editor: Behavioral Science in Family Practice, 1980; editor: Family Practice: An International Perspective in Developed Countries, 1983. Served to lt. (j.g.) USN, 1952-55, PTO. Recipient Gold-headed Cane award U. Calif. Sch. Medicine, 1960. Mem. Am. Acad. Family Physicians, AMA, Soc. Tchrs. Family Medicine, Inst. Medicine of Nat. Acad. Scis. Republican. Unitarian. Home: 2325 92d Ave NE Bellevue WA 98004 Office: U Wash Dept Family Medicine Sch Medicine RF 30 Seattle WA 98195

GHANDOUR, ZIAD, transportation executive; b. Beirut, Aug. 2, 1961; came to U.S., 1977; s. Sakeena Yashruti. BS, Syracuse, 1982. Sales account exec. Alia Airlines, Los Angeles, 1982-84; asst. to pres. Metito Industries, Riyadh, Saudi Arabia, 1984-86; account exec. DHL Airways, Van Nuys, Calif., 1986-87; pres. GMDC Aviation, Los Angeles, 1987—. Home: 616 Veteran Ave #217 Los Angeles CA 90024

GHANTIWALA, PRAVIN RATILAL, electrical engineer; b. Surat, India, Feb. 7, 1951; came to U.S., 1979; s. Ratilal Lallubha and Taraben Ratilal (Reshamwala) G. m. Chandrika Pravin Ghantiwala, May 14, 1977; children: Pinki, Swati. BSEE, S.V.R. Coll. Engring., Surat, India, 1974. Engr. in Tng., Calif. Field engr. The Surat (India) Electricity Co., 1977-78; elec. engr. jr. Gujarat Electricity Bd., Bardoli, India, 1978-79; elect. engring. asst. City of Glendale, Calif., 1980-86; elect. engring. assoc. City of Glendale, 1986—; alternate dir. So. Calif. Joint Pole com., Pasadena, 1985—. Hindu. Home: 361 S Greendale Dr La Puente CA 91746 Office: City of Glendale 119 N Glendale Ave Glendale CA 91206

GHERARDI, GINGER, transportation executive; b. Bronx, N.Y., Apr. 11, 1943; d. John Peter and Eleanor Virginia (Boll) Apuzzo; m. Charles Anthony Gherardi, June 27, 1965 (div. Mar. 1979); children: Andrew, John. BS, Pratt

Inst., 1964, MS, 1965. Tchr. various locations, 1964-74, Moorpark (Calif.) High Sch., 1974-80; program mgr. So. Calif. Assn. Govts., L.A., 1980-84; transp. cons. N.Y.C., 1984-85; fund devel. mgr. N.Y.C. Transit Authority, Bklyn., 1985; mgr. L.A. County Transp. Commn., 1985—; pres. Women's Transp. Seminar, L.A., 1987-88, dir.-at-large Washington, 1988. Illustrator Arts & Crafts Activities Desk Book, 1970. Councilwoman, mayor City of Simi Valley, Ventura County, Calif., 1972-79, mem. planning commn.; mem. Ventura County Assn. Govts., 1972-79. Named Outstanding Young Woman in Calif., 1978, Tchr. of Yr. Moorpack High Sch., 1976, One of Ten Outstanding Young Women in Am., 1978. Mem. Inst. Transp. Engrs., Assn. For Commuter Transp., Women's Transp. Seminar (pres. 1984-88), Transp. Rsch. Bd. (com. mem. 1988), Am. Assn. Univ. Women. Democrat. Unitarian.

GHIL, MICHAEL, environmental engineer, educator; b. Budapest, Hungary, June 10, 1944; s. Louis and Ilona V. (Dobo) Cernat; m. Michèle J. Denizot, July 8, 1982; children: Emmanuel A., Mirella J. BSc cum laude, Technion-Israel Inst. Tech., Haifa, Israel, 1966, MSc in Mech. Engring., 1971; MS, NYU, 1973, PhD in Math., 1975. Registered profl. engr., Israel. Rsch. asst. to instr. Technion-Israel Inst. Tech., Haifa, 1966-71; rsch. assoc. NASA Goddard Inst. Space Studies, N.Y.C., 1975-76; rsch. asst. prof. math. Courant Inst. Math. Scis., N.Y.C., 1976-79, rsch. assoc. prof. atmos. sci., 1979-82; rsch. prof. Courant Inst. Math. and Scis., N.Y.C., 1982-86; prof. atmos. sci. and geophysics UCLA, 1985—; chmn. dept. atmospheric scis., UCLA, 1988—; dir. Climate Dynamics Ctr., UCLA, 1986—; disting. vis. sci. Jet Propulsion Lab, Calif. Tech./NASA, Pasadena, Calif., 1988—. Author: Topics in GFD: Atmospheric Dynamics, Dynamo Theory and Climate Dynamics, 1987; editor: Turbulence and Predictability in Geophysical Fluid Dynamics and Climate Dynamics, 1985, Dynamic Meteorology: Data Assimilation Methods, 1981. Adv. bd. Calif. Space Inst., San Diego, 1986—; coord. com. profl. Climate Systems Modeling Program, Boulder, Colo., 1988—. Mem. Am. Meteorological Soc. (profl. com. 1989—), Am. Geophysical Union, Nat. Acad. Sics. (climate res. com. 1989—), Soc. for Indsl. and Applied Math., Sigma Xi. Democrat. Jewish. Office: UCLA Dept Atmospheric Scis 405 Hilgard Ave Los Angeles CA 90024-1565

GHORMLEY, JOHN HARNED, building contractor; b. Greenfield, Iowa, Aug. 11, 1936; s. Clarence E. and Dorothy (Harned) G.; student Purdue U., 1954; B.S., U. Wis., 1959; m. Anne Doran, May 25, 1960; children—Dorothy Lynne, Rebecca Anne. Assoc. engr. Douglas Aircraft Co., El Segundo, Calif., 1959; civil engring. assoc. City of Torrance, Calif., 1959-62; dir. pub. works-city engr. City of Gardena, Calif., 1962-66, adminstrv. officer, 1966-70; cons. civil engring. practice, Gardena, 1962-66; ptnr. Benner and Ghormley, Santa Paula, Calif., 1970-75; v.p. Ervin, Ghormley, Johnson & Assocs., Los Angeles, 1975-77; pres. Bonita Homes, Inc., 1977—, Bonita Am., 1986—, Computer Terminal, 1986—. Adviser, Boy Scout Splty. Explorer Post, 1968-70; bd. mgrs. Gardena Valley YMCA; pres. South County Econ. Devel. Assn., 1984-85. Recipient award for outstanding service Gardena Valley C. of C., 1968. Registered profl. engr., Calif., Fla., Ind. Mem. Sigma Phi. Republican. Presbyterian. Clubs: Masons, Ojai Optimist (pres. 1976), Kiwanis. Home: 980 Branch Mill Rd PO Box 356 Arroyo Grande CA 93420 Office: 550 Camino Mercado PO Drawer FF Arroyo Grande CA 93420

GIALANELLA, PHILIP THOMAS, newspaper publisher; b. Binghamton, N.Y., June 6, 1930; s. Felix and Frances (Demuro) G.; 1 son, Thomas Davis. B.A., Harpur Coll., 1952; M.A., State U. N.Y., 1955. Promotion dir. Evening Press and Sta. WINR-TV, Binghamton, 1957-62; v.p., gen. mgr. Daily Advance, Dover, N.J., 1962-66; v.p. Hartford (Conn.) Times, 1966-70; pres., pub. Newburgh (N.Y.) News, 1970-71; exec. v.p. Hawaii Newspaper Agy., Honolulu, 1971-73, pres., 1974-86; pub. Honolulu Star-Bull., 1975-86; pres. USA Today, 1982-83, pub., 1983; exec. v.p., pub. Honolulu Advertiser, 1986—; exec. v.p., chief operating officer Persis Corp., Honolulu, 1986—, pres. Persis Media div., 1986—; v.p., chief operating officer Northwest Media, Inc., Bellevue, Wash., 1986—, Knoxville (Tenn.) Jour., 1988—; bd. dirs. Capital Investment Co., Hawaii Newspaper Agy. Found., Inc., Hawaii Newspaper Agy., Inc., Waterhouse Properties, Persis Corp., Honolulu Advertiser Inc., Northwest Media, Inc.; v.p., bd. dirs. ASA Properties, Inc., Bay-Area Steuart, Inc., Shiny Rock Mining Corp. Past chmn., exec. com. mem. Nat. Alliance Businessmen for Hawaii and Micronesia; v.p. Hawaii Newspaper Agy. Found.; mem. Japan Hawaii Econ. Coun.; bd. govs. Pacific Asian Affairs Coun.; bd. dirs. Hawaii Theatre Ctr., Honolulu Boy Choir, Honolulu Symphony, Aloha United Way, Aloha Coun. Boy Scouts of Am.; mem. adv. group Western Command U.S. Army. With U.S. Army, 1952-54. Mem. Am. Newspaper Pubs. Assn., Hawaii Pubs. Assn., AP Assn. Calif., AP Assn. Ariz., AP Assn. Hawaii, AP Assn. Nev., Sigma Delta Chi. Roman Catholic. Office: The Honolulu Advertiser Honolulu HI 96802

GIANARIS, NICHOLAS JAMES, mining engineer; b. Pitts., Mar. 12, 1963; s. Demetrios Nicholas and Maria (Meragias) G. BS in Metallurgical Engring. and Materials Sci., Carnegie Mellon U., 1985. Registered engr.-in-tng., Pa. Project engr. Echoram Tecn., Inc., North Huntington, Pa., 1985-88; project engr. II aircraft div. Northrop Corp., El Segundo, Calif., 1988—; com. mem. task group com. on eddy current testing ASME, Pitts., 1988. Vol. Pitts. Vintage Grand Prix, 1984-88; mem. World Affairs Coun. Pitts., 1980-88. Mem. Am. Soc. for Nondestructive Testing, Am. Soc. for Metals, Minerals, and Metals Soc.-Am. Inst. Mining, Metallurgical and Petroleum Engrs., Alpha Phi Omega. Republican. Greek Orthodox. Home: 26014 Pennsylvania Dr Lomita CA 90717 Office: Northrop Corp Aircraft Div 1 Northrop Ave 3881194 Hawthorne CA 90250

GIARDE, JEFFREY LYLE, municipal court judge; b. Seattle, Oct. 7, 1941; s. Lyle Herschel and Mertie Mae (Okerman) G.; m. Leigh R. Dahl, Apr. 7, 1978; 1 child, Sandra. AB, San Diego State U., 1964; JD, Calif. Western Law Sch., San Diego, 1967. Bar: Calif. 1968, U.S. Dist. Ct. (so. dist.) Calif. 1969. Pvt. practice law La Jolla, Calif., 1968-69; staff atty. San Diego Legal Aid Soc., 1969-71, Calif. Ct. Appeal, 4th Appellate Dist., Div. 2, San Bernardino, Calif., 1971-73; prin. atty. Calif. Ct. Appeal, 4th Appellate Dist., Div. 2, San Bernardino, 1973-87; judge San Bernardino Mcpl. Ct. Dist., Redlands, Calif., 1987—; instr. law Western States U., San Diego, 1970-71; contracts instr. Citrus Belt Law Sch., Riverside, Calif., 1973-78; supervising judge east div. San Bernardino Mcpl. Ct. Dist., Redlands, 1988. Author: Glass Milk Bottles: Their Makers and Marks, 1980. Mem. Calif. Bar Assn., Calif. Judges Assn. Republican. Office: San Bernardino County Mcpl Court 216 Brookside Ave Redlands CA 92373

GIARDINA, RICHARD CONO, university official; b. N.Y.C., Aug. 28, 1944; s. Cono and Nancy (Biondi) G. Cert., Inst. Polit. Studies, Paris, 1964; AB, Fordham U., 1965; PhD, Princeton U., 1969. Acting chmn. polit. sci. dept. Bowling Green (Ohio) State U., 1970-71, dir. Little Coll., 1971-72, dir. modular achievement program, 1972-74, dir. Univ. div. gen. studies, 1974-76; assoc. v.p. acad. affairs San Francisco State U., 1976—; Edwin S. Corwin teaching fellow Princeton U., 1968; mem. Chancellor's Master Planning Commn., San Francisco Community Coll. Dist., 1982-83; mem. tech. adv. com. on accreditation and pub. policy Calif. Post-Secondary Edn. Commn., Sacramento, 1983-84; mem. vocat. adv. com. San Francisco Unified Sch. Dist., 1985—. Author: The Dynamics of Baccalaureate Reform, 1973; contbr. articles to profl. jours. Bd. dirs. Actors Ark Theatre, San Francisco, 1982-84; trustee Saybrook Inst. and Grad. Sch., San Francisco, 1986—. Recipient Outstanding Mentor award San Francisco State U., 1986. Mem. Internat. Studies Assn., Am. Assn. for Higher Edn., Assn. for Gen. and Liberal Studies (nat. exec. bd. 1981-84), World Affairs Coun. No. Calif., Phi Beta Kappa. Democrat. Roman Catholic. Home: 403 Arkansas St San Francisco CA 94107 Office: San Francisco State U 1600 Holloway Ave San Francisco CA 94132

GIBB, DOUGLAS GLENN, police chief; b. Makaweli, Hawaii, June 5, 1940; s. Douglas Stormont and Gwendolyn Elizabeth (Bedell) G.; m. Melanie Ululani Hardy, Nov. 16, 1963; children—Diane Nalani, Glenn Kale. BS in Bus. Adminstrn., U. Denver, 1966; cert., Nat. Execs. Inst., FBI, 1984. Patrolman Honolulu Police Dept., 1967-71, sgt., 1971-76, lt., 1976-80, capt., 1980-83, chief police, 1983—; cons. on sting projects Office Justice Assistance, Dept. Justice, 1983—; mem. Hawaii Gov.'s Planning Commn. on Crime, 1983—, Juvenile Justice Interagy. Bd., 1983—. Bd. dirs. ARC, Honolulu, 1983—; mem. exec. bd. Boy Scouts Am., Honolulu, 1983—; mem. sr. adv. council CAP, Honolulu, 1983—. Recipient cert. of merit Law Enforcement Assistance Adminstrn., Washington, 1979; named Police Officer of Yr., 200 Club, Honolulu, 1982. Mem. Hawaii Law Enforcement Officer Assn. (pres. 1983-85), Internat. Assn. Chiefs of Police (membership com. 1985), Major City Chiefs, Honolulu C. of C. (crime com. 1983—). Episcopalian. Home: PO Box 510 Kaawa HI 96730 Office: Honolulu Police Dept 1455 S Beretania Honolulu HI 96814 *

GIBB, RICHARD DEAN, university president; b. Smithshire, Ill., Dec. 6, 1928; s. Edward Dale and Anna Marie (Anderson) G.; m. Betty G. Epperson, Dec. 22, 1951; children: Richie William, Connie Marie. Student, Western Ill. U., 1947-50; B.S., U. Ill., 1951, M.E., 1955; Ph.D., Mich. State U., 1958. Faculty agrl. econs. Western Ill. U., Macomb, 1958-68; prof. Western Ill. U., 1965-68, adminstrv. asst. to pres., 1964-67, dean adminstrn., 1967-68, acting coordinator internat. programs, 1964-65; S.D. commr. for higher edn. Pierre, 1968-74; Ind. commr. for higher edn. Indpls., 1974-77; pres. U. Idaho, 1977-89. Served with AUS, 1952-53. Mem. Am. Assn. Higher Edn., Statewide Higher Edn. Assn., Am. Agrl. Econs. Assn., Delta Sigma Phi. Home: 1026 Nez Perce Dr Moscow ID 83843 Office: U Idaho Office of Pres Moscow ID 83843

GIBBLE, WALTER PAUL, oil and gas industry consultant; b. Atglen, Pa., July 26, 1916; s. Walter Paul and Mabel Teresa (Wise); m. Jeanne A. van Dyck, Dec. 31, 1960. BS, U. Pa., 1941; MS, U. Ariz., 1951, PhD, 1956. Dir. research Vegetable Oil Products, Wilmington, Calif., 1955-57, VA Hosp., Tucson, 1957-62; sr. chemist Hunt-Wesson Foods, Fullerton, Calif., 1962-76; tech. cons. Govt. of India, New Delhi, 1979-80; indsl. cons. Edible Oil Cos., 1980—; cons. Hunt-Wesson Foods, Fullerton, Wilsey Food Inc., City of Industry, Calif., Surya Agroils Ltd., New Delhi, Modipon Ltd., Modingar, India. Contbr. articles to sci. jours.; patentee in field. Served to commdr. USN, 1942-49. Recipient Highest Merit award Hunt-Wesson Foods, Fullerton, 1971. Mem. Service Corps Retired Execs. (chmn. local satellite chpt. 1983—), Am. Chem. Soc., Am. Oil Chemists Soc., Sigma Xi. Lutheran. Home and Office: 2931 Viking Way Carson City NV 89701

GIBBONS, DON CARY, sociology educator, writer; b. Newport, Wash., June 6, 1926; s. George and Mildred (Snow) G.; m. Carmen L. Baker, Sept. 1, 1951; children: Michael, Diane. BA, U. Wash., 1950, MA, 1953, PhD, 1956. Mem. faculty U. B.C., Can., 1956-57, San Francisco State Coll., 1957-69; prof. sociology and urban studies Portland (Oreg.) State U., 1969—. Author: Changing the Lawbreaker, 1965, Soc., Crime and Criminal Careers, 1968, Deliquent Behavior, 1970, Becoming Delinquent, 1970, The Study of Deviance, 1975, Criminal Justice Planning, 1977, The Criminological Enterprise, 1979; editor: Crime and Delinquency. With USNR, 1944-46. Mem. Am. Sociol. Assn., Pacific Sociol. Soc. (pres. 1982-83), Soc. Study Social Problems. Home: 1100 SW Hillcroft Dr Portland OR 97225

GIBBONS, GARY EUGENE, investment counseling executive; b. Tucson, May 5, 1949; s. Lawrence Lee and Naomi (Price) G.; m. Amy Smith, Sept. 1, 1979; children: Lawrence Smith, Ryan Smith. BS, U. Ariz., 1973; MS, Calif. State U., Carson, 1982. chmn. Uni-Net, Inc., 1986-89; chief fin. officer Hanseatic Corp., Albuquerque; dir. , chief fin. officer Richmark Corp., L.A.; v.p. CPB, Inc., L.A.; lectr. fin. Calif. State U.-Fullerton, 1983—, U. So. Calif., L.A., 1984—. Editor: Strokes and Strategies, 1973; contbr. numerous articles on econs., investments to publs. Fellow Fin. Analysts Fedn.; mem. Fin. Mgmt. Assn., U.S. Profl. Tennis Assn., Coll. Fin. Planning (adj. faculty), Calif. State U. Alumni Assn. & Bus. Alumni Coun. Republican. Episcopalian. Clubs: Santa Monica Yacht, Old Ranch Country. Office: 4425 Jamboree #125 Newport Beach CA 92660-2042

GIBBONS, MARIBETH VIVIAN, environmental consulting company executive; b. Teaneck, N.J., Apr. 19, 1952; d. Stephen John and Veronica Marie (Henke) Hanussak; m. Harry Lawrence Gibbons, Aug. 4, 1973; children: Ryan, Michael. BA in Math., Wash. State U., 1977, MS in Environ. Sci., 1980, MS in Environ. Engring., 1984. Cert. engr.-in-tng., Wash. Lab. technician Wash. State U., Pullman, 1977-84, research asst. civil and environ. engring., 1979-82; pres. Water Environ. Services, Inc., Bainbridge Island, Wash., 1984—, Enviroscan, Inc., Kent, Wash., 1987—. Contbr. articles to profl. jours. Mem. N.Am. Lake Mgmt. Soc., Aquatic Plant Mgmt. Soc., Sigma Xi, Phi Kappa Phi, Tau Beta Pi. Roman Catholic. Home: 9515 Windsong Loop NE Bainbridge Island WA 98110

GIBBONS, PAUL PHILIP, consultant; b. Worcester, Mass., Feb. 27, 1929; s. Albert Paul and Phyllis (Berling) G.; m. Ellen Marilyn Pike, Apr. 8, 1974; children: Michael Dale, Steven Carl. Student, Worcester Jr. Coll., 1958-59, Spokane Community Coll., 1979-80; AS, Community Coll. Air Force, Maxwell AFB, Ala., 1981. Enlisted USAF, 1961; advanced through grades to sgt. USAF, Fairchild AFB, Wash., 1961-80; ret. 1980; sr. project mgr. Itron, Spokane, 1981-87; cons. A-Five, Otis Orchards, Wash., 1988—. Mem. VFW (life). Democrat. Roman Catholic. Home: E 19711 Fairview Ct Otis Orchards WA 99027 Office: Itron, 4 Rue de Tuvenne, 59200 Tourcoing Nord France

GIBBS, BARBARA KENNEDY, art museum director; b. Newton, Mass., Feb. 15, 1950; d. Frederic Alexander and Jane Jarvis (Ensinger) K. A.B. magna cum laude, Brown U., 1972; M.B.A., UCLA, 1979. Dep. dir. Portland Art Assn., Oreg., 1979-83; dir. Crocker Art Mus., Sacramento, 1983—. Guggenheim intern fellow Solomon R. Guggenheim Mus., 1978. Mem. Assn. Art Mus. Dirs., Am. Assn. Mus. Home: 1036 56th St Sacramento CA 95819 Office: Crocker Art Mus 216 O St Sacramento CA 95814

GIBBS, ELINOR THAL, rehabilitation center administrator; b. Bismarck, N.D., Sept. 27, 1930; d. Alfred Alexander and Bertha (Rigler) Thal; m. Seymour B. Gibbs, July 14, 1951 (dec. 1978); children: Curtis, Guru Prem Singh, Douglas, Patrice. BS in Edn., Northwestern U., 1953; MS in Kinesiology, UCLA, 1973. Dir. Neuro-Kinesthetics, Inc., Burbank, Calif., 1976-81, The Gibbs Inst., L.A., 1982-85; exec. dir. Clinic for Neuromuscular Disorders, Inc., L.A., 1986—; cons., Los Angeles County Probation Dept., 1974-75. Troop leader, Boy Scouts Am., Blue Birds/Camp Fire Girls, L.A. area, 1960-76; vol. local Democratic campaigns, 1956-72. Mem. So. Calif. Rehab. Assn. (recipient Outstanding Achievement award 1988), Nat. Rehab. Assn., Rehab. Nurses Soc., UCLA Alumni Assn. Jewish. Home: Apt B 310 3716 Barham Blvd Los Angeles CA 90068 Office: Clinic for Neuromuscular Disorders Ste 118 6430 Sunset Blvd Los Angeles CA 90028

GIBBS, JANNE ROBERTA, nurse, educator; b. San Francisco, June 2, 1949; d. Henri Robert Larmuseau and D. Lee (Fitzpatrick) Garrison; m. David Nicholas Gibbs, Dec. 19, 1970; children: Evan David, Alysia Marie. Diploma, St. Luke's Sch. Nursing, San Francisco, 1970; BS in Nursing, Humboldt State U., 1979; MS in Nursing, Calif. State U., Dominguez Hills, 1987. RN, Calif.; cert. pub. health nurse; cert. community coll. instr. Staff nurse, ICU-CCU nurse St. Luke's Hosp., San Francisco, 1970, Mad River Hosp., Arcata, Calif., 1972-74, St. Joseph's Hosp., Eureka, Calif., 1977-83; nurse, co-dir. cardiac rehab. Calif. State U.-Humboldt, Arcata, 1973-83; instr. nursing Coll. Redwoods, Eureka, 1979—; part-time instr. nursing Calif. State U.-Humboldt, 1979-85. Past pres., v.p., instr. CPR and Basic Cardiac Life Support Systems Eureka chpt. Am. Heart Assn., 1975—; troop leader Eureka area Girl Scouts U.S., 1987-88. 1st lt. Nurse Corps, U.S. Army, 1969-72. Kellogg Found. grantee, 1986-87, Nightengale Soc. fellow, 1988. Mem. Am. Nurses Assn. (cert. med.-surg. nurse), Nat. League Nursing, Humboldt Fire Dist. Ladies Aux., Cal Cts. Health Club. Office: Coll Redwoods Tompkins Hill Rd Eureka CA 95501

GIBLER, AMY CAROL, college bookstore director; b. Basin, Wyo., May 10, 1959; d. John S. and Dorothy C. (Michaels) G.; m. William T. Brown, Apr. 25, 1987. AA in Bus., N.W. Community Coll., Powell, Wyo., 1979; BA in Bus. Adminstrn., Ea. Montana Coll., 1982. Text book mgr. Ea. Mont. Coll. Bookstore, Billings, 1979-85, dir. bookstore, 1985—. Elected Mont. Coll. Found. Bd. dirs., 1989—. Named Outstanding Young Women Am., 1986. Mem. Nat. Assn. Coll. Bookstores, Nat. Assn. Exec. Females, Mont. Assn. Coll. Bookstores (chairperson annual mtgs., 1985, 87), Jr. League Billings, Ea. Mont. Coll. Bd. Dirs. (v.p. and sec. 1981—), Ea. Mont. Coll. Fed. Credit Union. Democrat. Office: Ea Mont Coll Bookstore 1500 N 30th St Billings MT 59101

GIBLETT, ELOISE ROSALIE, hematology educator; b. Tacoma, Wash., Jan. 17, 1921; d. William Richard and Rose (Godfrey) G. B.S., U. Wash., 1942, M.S., 1947, M.D. with honors, 1951. Mem. faculty U. Wash. Sch. Medicine, 1957—, research prof., 1967-87, emeritus research prof., 1987—; asso. dir., head immunogenetics Puget Sound Blood Center, 1955-79, exec. dir., 1979-87, emeritus exec. dir., 1987—; former mem. several research coms. NIH. Author: Genetic Markers in Human Blood, 1969; Editorial bd. numerous jours. including Blood, Am. Jour. Human Genetics, Transfusion, Vox Sanguinis; Contbr. over 190 articles to profl. jours. Recipient fellowships, grants, Emily Cooley, Karl Landsteiner, Philip Levine and Alexander Wiener immunohematology awards, distinguished alumna award U. Wash. Sch. Med., 1987. Fellow AAAS; Mem. Nat. Acad. Scis., Am. Soc. Human Genetics (pres. 1973), Am. Soc. Hematology, Am. Assn. Immunologists, Brit. Soc. Immunology, Internat. Soc. Hematologists, Am. Fedn. Clin. Research, Western Assn. Physicians, Assn. Am. Physicians, Sigma Xi, Alpha Omega Alpha. Home: 6533 53rd St NE Seattle WA 98115 Office: Puget Sound Blood Ctr Terry and Madison Sts Seattle WA 98104

GIBLETT, PHYLIS LEE WALZ, teacher; b. Denver, July 17, 1945; d. Henry and Leah (Pabst) Walz; B.S.B.A. (Estelle Hunter scholar 1963, Denver Classroom Tchr.'s scholar 1963, Outstanding Bus. Edn. Student scholar 1967), U. Denver, 1967, M.B.A., 1969; m. Thomas Giblett, May 31, 1975; children—Leann Ruth, Douglas Henry, John Peter. Tchr. bus. Aurora (Colo.) South Middle Sch., Aurora Pub. Schs., 1967-80, 82-86, 88—, on leave, 1980-82, 86-88, chmn. bus. dept., 1972-79; evening tchr. S.E. Met. Bd. Coop Services, 1967-68, post secondary/adult classes Aurora Pub. Schs., 1972-75, Community Coll. Denver, North Campus, 1973, Aurora Pub. Schs. Adult Edn., 1983-84; mem. Dist. Tchr. Adv. Com., 1975-79; adviser chpt. Future Bus. Leaders Am., 1976-78; mem. Colo. Curriculum Specialist Com., 1976-77. Treas. Aurora Coun. PTA, 1987-89, Century Elem. Sch. PTA, 1988-89. Named Miss Future Bus. Tchr., Phi Beta Lambda of Colo., 1965. Mem. Nat., Mountain-Plains (participant leadership conf. 1977), Colo. (pres. 1976-77) bus. edn. assns., Colo. Educators for/About Bus., Am., Colo. vocat. assns., NEA, Colo., Aurora edn. assns., Delta Pi Epsilon (pres.-elect Eta chpt. 1978, pres. 1980-81). Republican. Lutheran.

GIBNEY, FRANK BRAY, publisher, editor, writer, foundation executive; b. Scranton, Pa., Sept. 21, 1924; s. Joseph James and Edna May (Wetter) G.; m. Harriet Harvey, Dec. 10, 1948 (div. 1957); children: Alex, Margot; m. Harriet C. Suydam, Dec. 14, 1957 (div. 1971); children: Frank, James, Thomas; m. Hiroko Doi, Oct. 5, 1972; children: Elise, Josephine. BA, Yale U., 1945; DLitt (hon.), Kyung Hee U., Seoul, Korea, 1974. Corr., assoc. editor Time mag., N.Y.C., Tokyo and London, 1947-54; sr. editor Newsweek, N.Y.C., 1954-57; staff writer, editorial writer Life mag., N.Y.C., 1957-61; pub., pres. SHOW mag., N.Y.C., 1961-64; pres. Ency. Brit. (Japan), Tokyo, 1965-69; pres. TBS-Brit., Tokyo, 1969-75, vice chmn., 1976—; v.p. Ency. Brit., Inc., Chgo., 1975-79; vice chmn., bd. editors Ency. Brit., Chgo., 1978—; pres. Pacific Basin Inst., Santa Barbara, Calif., 1979; adj. prof. Far Eastern studies U. Calif., Santa Barbara, 1986—; bd. dirs. Hudson Reports Internat., Paris, 1981—; cons. Com. on Space and Aero Ho. of Reps., Washington, 1957-59; vice chmn. Japan-U.S. Friendship Commn., 1984—, U.S.-Japan Com. on Edn. and Cultural Interchange, 1984—. Author: Five Gentlemen of Japan, 1953, The Frozen Revolution, 1959, (with Peter Deriabin) The Secret World, 1960, The Operators, 1961, The Khrushchev Pattern, 1961, The Reluctant Space Farers, 1965, Japan: The Fragile Super-Power, 1975, Miracle by Design, 1983; editor: The Penkovskiy Papers, 1965; Presdl. speech writer, 1964. Served to lt. USNR, 1942-46. Decorated Order of the Rising Sun 3d Class Japan, Order of Sacred Treasure 2d Class Japan. Mem. Council on Fgn. Relations, Tokyo Fgn. Corr. Club, Am. C.of C. (Tokyo), Japan-Am. Soc., Japan Soc. Roman Catholic. Clubs: Century Assn., Yale (N.Y.C.); Tokyo; Tavern, The Arts (Chgo.). Home: 1901 E Las Tunas Rd Santa Barbara CA 93103

GIBSON, ARTHUR CHARLES, biologist, educator; b. Bronx, N.Y., Oct. 16, 1947; s. Richard Goodwin and Rosalie (Reinhardt) G.; m. Linda Lee Corey, Aug. 15, 1970; children—Heather Elizabeth, Erin Kathryn. B.A. in Botany, Miami U., 1969; Ph.D. in Botany, Claremont (Calif.) Grad. Sch., 1973. Asst. prof. U. Ariz., Tucson, 1973-79, assoc. prof., 1979-80; assoc. prof. UCLA, 1980-82, prof., 1982—, also dir. Mildred E. Mathias Bot. Garden. Mem. Bot. Soc. Am. Author: (with J.H. Brown) Biogeography, 1983; (with P.S. Nobel) The Cactus Primer, 1986; contbr. articles to profl. jours. Office: UCLA Mildred E Mathias Bot Garden/Botany Bldg Rm 124 Los Angeles CA 90024

GIBSON, CAROL SUE ANDERSON, teacher; b. Moline, Ill., Sept. 15, 1950; d. Edwin Carl and Mary Helen (Abbott) Anderson; m. James Patrick Gibson, Sept. 15, 1982; 1 child, James P. Jr. BA in Liberal Arts, Ariz. State U., 1972, postgrad., 1973-82. Cert. tchr., Ariz. Tchr. Paradise Valley High Sch., Phoenix, 1973-74, Shadow Mountain High Sch., Phoenix, 1974—; contbg. cons. Gen. Ednl. Devel. Testing Service, Washington, 1986—. Contbr. articles to profl. jours. Named High Sch. Tchr. of Yr. Ariz. English Tchrs. Assn., 1988. Mem. NEA, Nat. Council Tchrs. of English, Ariz. English Tchrs. Assn., Ariz. Edn. Assn., Shadow Mountain Edn. Assn. Office: Shadow Mountain High Sch 2902 E Shea Blvd Phoenix AZ 85028

GIBSON, CATHERINE ANTIONETTE, realtor; b. Los Angeles, Aug. 7, 1954; d. Joseph Anthony and Hortense Julia A. (Gallardo) Moran; m. Henry R. Bowman, Dec. 19, 1971 (div.); children: Jessica Lynn, Eric R.; m. Thomas R. Gibson, Apr. 30, 1983 (div. Sept. 1986); 1 child, Julie Ann. Auditor Progressive Savs. and Loan, Alhambra, Calif., 1985; realtor Red Carpet Eastwood Realty Inc., West Covina, Calif., 1985—, Re/Max Estate Services, Upland, Calif., 1988—. Mem. Covina San Gabriel Valley Bd. Realtors, Inland Empire West Bd. Realtors. Home: 1464 Lawford Glendora CA 91740 Office: ReMax Estate Svcs 974 W Foothill Blvd Upland CA 91786

GIBSON, DENNIS JAMES, systems engineer; b. Los Angeles, July 22, 1952; s. James Carl and Jacqueline Diane (Nenzell) G.; m. Marian Lynette Young, Jan. 29, 1978; children: Amy, Diane. BS in Applied Mechanics, U. So. Calif., 1974. Group leader engr. Bechtel Power Corp., Los Angeles, 1980-85; lead systems engr. div. autonetics marine systems Rockwell Internat., Anaheim, Calif., 1985—. Served to lt. USN, 1974-80. Republican. Methodist. Home: 213 S Mountain View Pl Fullerton CA 92631 Office: Rockwell Internat-AMSD 3370 Miraloma Ave Anaheim CA 92803

GIBSON, EDWARD FERGUS, physicist, educator; b. Colorado Springs, Colo., Apr. 2, 1937; s. George Merrick and Elsie Ida (Schnurr) G.; m. Harriette Graham DuShane, June 1, 1963; children: Sascha, Graham, Clark, Eileen. B.A., U. Colo., 1959, M.A., 1964, Ph.D., 1966. Physicist Nat. Bur. Standards, Boulder, Colo., 1958-64; research asst., research assoc. U. Colo., Boulder, 1964-66; postdoctoral research assoc. U. Oreg., Eugene, 1966-68; scientist-in-residence Naval Radiol. Def. Lab., San Francisco, 1968-69; prof. physics Calif. State U., Sacramento, 1969—, chmn. dept., 1979-88; cons. on alternative energy sources Calif. Energy Commn., 1977-78; cons. computer-assisted instrn. Control Data Corp., 1981-87. Assoc. Western Univs. fellow, 1971- 72, 73. Mem. Am. Phys. Soc., Phi Beta Kappa, Sigma Xi, Sigma Pi Sigma. Home: 527 Blackwood St Sacramento CA 95815 Office: Calif State U Dept Physics 600 J St Sacramento CA 95819

GIBSON, ELISABETH JANE, principal; b. Salina, Kans., Apr. 28, 1937; d. Cloyce Wesley and Margaret Mae (Yost) Kasson; m. William Douglas Miles, Jr., Aug. 20, 1959 (div.); m. Harry Benton Gibson, Jr., July 1, 1970. AB, Colo. State Coll., 1954-57; MA (fellow), San Francisco State Coll., 1967-68; EdD, U. No. Colo., 1978; postgrad. U. Denver, 1982. Cert. tchr., prin., Colo. Tchr. elem. schs., Santa Paula, Calif., 1957-58, Salina, Kans., 1958-63, Goose Bay, Labrador, 1963-64, Jefferson County, Colo., 1965-66, Topeka, 1966-67; diagnostic tchr. Cen. Kans. Diagnostic Remedial Edn. Ctr., Salina, 1968-70; instr. Loretto Heights Coll., Denver, 1970-72; co-owner Ednl. Cons. Enterprises, Inc., Greeley, Colo., 1974-77; resource coordinator Region VIII Resource Access Project Head Start Mile High Consortium, Denver, 1976-77; exec. dir. Colo. Fedn. Council Exceptional Children, Denver, 1976-77; asst. prof. Met. State Coll., Denver, 1979; dir. spl. edn. Northeast Colo. Bd. Coop. Edn. Services, Haxtun, Colo., 1979-82; prin. elem. jr. high sch., Elizabeth, Colo., 1982-84; prin., spl. projects coordinator Summit County Schs., Frisco, Colo., 1985—; prin. Frisco Elem. Sch., 1985—; cons. Colo. Dept. Edn., 1984-85; cons. Colo. Dept. Edn., 1984-85, Montana Dept. Edn., 1978-79, Love Pub. Co., 1976-78, Colo. Dept. Inst.,

1974-75; pres. Found. Exceptional Children, 1980-81; pres. bd. dirs. Northeast Colo. Services Handicapped, 1981-82; bd. dirs. Dept. Ednl. Specialists, Colo. Assn. Sch. Execs., 1982-84; mem. Colo. Title IV Adv. Council, 1980-82; mem. Mellon Found. grant steering com. Colo. Dept. Edn., 1984-85. Mem. Colo. Dept. Edn. Data Acquisition Reporting and Utilization Com., 1983, Denver City County Commn. for Disabled, 1978-81; chmn. regional edn. com. 1970 White House Conf. Children and Youth; bd. dirs. Advocates for Victims of Assault, 1986—; mem. adv. bd. Alpine Counseling Ctr., 1986—; mem. placement alternatives commn. Dept. Social Services, 1986—; mem. adv. com. Colo. North Cen. Assn., 1988—. Recipient Ann. Service award Colo. Fedn. Council Exceptional Children, 1981. Mem. Colo. Assn. Retarded Citizens, Assn. Supervision Curriculum Devel., Nat. Assn. Elem. Sch. Prins., Kappa Delta Pi, Pi Lambda Theta, Phi Delta Kappa. Republican. Methodist. Club: Order Eastern Star. Author: (with H. Padzensky) Goal Guide: A minicourse in writing goals and behavioral objectives for special education, 1975; (with H. Padzensky and S. Sporn) Assaying Student Behavior: A minicourse in student assessment techniques, 1974. Contbr. articles to profl. jours. Home: 2443 S Colorado Blvd Denver CO 80222 Office: Frisco Elem Sch PO Box 7 Frisco CO 80443

GIBSON, FRANCES, nurse; b. Junction, Tex., Sept. 28, 1936; d. August and Juanita (Corpus-Garcia) Rehwoldt; m. Richard Gibson, July 4, 1954 (dec. July 25, 1962); childreN; Kenneth, René, Allison. AA, East Los Angeles Coll. Lic. vocat. nurse, 1969; registered nurse 1976, operating room technician, 1971; cert. adult edn. tchr., paralegal. Instr., profl. expert East Los Angeles Coll., Monterey Park, Calif., 1971-74; hostess talk show (in Spanish) Sta. KMEX-TV, Los Angeles, 1970-76; tchr. adult edn. Garvey Sch. Bd., Rosemead, Calif., 1976-77; clin. nurse L.A. County/U. So. Calif. Med. Ctr., 1981-89; vol. nurse Lung Assn., Los Angeles, 1970-76, ARC, Los Angeles, 1969—; instr. health classes, ARC, also instr. Spanish to ARC personnel, mgr. info. booths at health fairs and conventions, provide first aid at various gatherings, immunization clinics, etc., chmn. adv. bd., 1971-72, bd. dirs., 1972-75, 80-82; med. review/legal asst. Ivie & McNeill, Los Angeles, 1986—. Author: Spanish for English-Speaking Personnel, 1972. Recipient Spotlight award ARC, 1972, Clara Barton award, 1976, Associate Womens Students award, 1969; named one of Ten Prettiest Chicanas in East Los Angeles, 1970. Mem. Nursing Edn. Associates, Chicana Nurses Assn., AFL CIO, ACLU, Alpha Gamma Sigma. Democrat. Roman Catholic. Home: 2241 Charlotte Ave Rosemead CA 91770

GIBSON, GORDON DAVIS, anthropologist; b. Vancouver, B.C., Can., June 22, 1915; came to U.S., 1922; s. Ross Clark and Rebecca (Davis) G.; m. Bethune Millen, 1938 (div. 1973); children: Linda Caroline, Roger Eliot; m. Mary Horgan, Mar. 31, 1978. Student, Calif. Inst. Tech., 1933-35; BA, U. Chgo., 1937, MA, 1950, PhD, 1952. Asst. prof. anthropology U. Utah, Salt Lake City, 1955-58; curator Smithsonian Instn., Washington, 1958-82, emeritus curator, 1982—. Film review editor: American Anthropologist, 1965-69; author, editor: The Kavango Peoples, 1981; translator: The Ethnography of Southwestern Angola, 1976-81; creator numerous mus. displays on the cultures of Africa, 1961-80; producer numerous documentaries, 1969-82; contbr. articles and reviews to profl. jours. Social Sci. Res. Council grantee, 1952, NSF grantee, 1961, NIH grantee, 1972, Smithsonian Instn. grantee, 1960, 71. Fellow Am. Anthrop. Assn. Home: 2640 Loma Vista Dr Escondido CA 92025

GIBSON, GRANT SINGLETON, communications executive; b. Moses Lake, Wash., Sept. 27, 1956; s. Samuel Wallen Gibson and Patricia (Singleton) Romanov; m. Suzanne Marie McDonnell, May 14, 1988. BA, U. Oreg., 1978. Advt., promotion mgr. Wheelsport Distbg., Portland, Oreg., 1978-84; advt. mgr. Floating Point Systems, Beaverton, Oreg., 1984-86; mktg. communications mgr. Floating Point Systems, Beaverton, 1986-88; dir. mktg. communications Protocol Systems, Beaverton, 1988—. Mem. Pub. Rels. Soc. Am., Portland Advt. Fedn. Republican. Methodist. Home: 11085 SW Cottonwood Ln Tigard OR 97223 Office: Protocol Systems 14924 NW Greenbrier Pkwy Beaverton OR 97006

GIBSON, JAMES ISAAC, chemical manufacturing company executive; b. Golden, Colo., Mar. 22, 1925; s. Fred Daniel and May Emma (Borsberry) G.; m. Audrey June Brinley, June 23, 1947; children: James Brinley, David Scott, Robin Lee, Terry Lynn, Cynthia Rae, Holly Jo. BS, U.S. Naval Acad., 1947; BCE, MCE, Rensselaer Poly. Inst., 1950; LLD (hon.), U. Nev., Las Vegas, 1988. Registered profl. engr., Nev., Ariz. Ensign C.E., USN, 1947, advanced through grades to lt., 1953, resigned, 1953; asst. chief engr. Western Electro-Chem. Co., Henderson, Nev., 1953-56; chief engr. Am. Potash and Chem. Corp., Henderson, 1956-61; chief engr. Pacific Engring. and Prodn. Co. Nev., Henderson, 1961-66, exec. v.p., 1966-85, pres., 1985—, also bd. dirs.; pres. Henderson Ventures, Inc., 1968—. Mem. assembly Nev. Legis., Carbon City, 1958-66, mem. senate, 1966—; majority leader Nev. Senate, 1976—; chmn. council state govts., Lexington, Ky., 1985, vice chmn., 1984, governing bd., 1968—. Recipient Silver Beaver award Boulder Dam Area council Boy Scouts Am., 1970; named Disting. Nevadan, U. Nev., 1973. Mem. NSPE, Nev. Soc. Profl. Engrs., Sigma Xi. Democrat. Mormon. Home: 806 Park Ln Henderson NV 89015 Office: Pacific Engring Prodn Co Nev PO Box 797 Henderson NV 89015

GIBSON, JEFFREY NEAL, mechanical engineer; b. Bakersfield, Calif., Jan. 28, 1959; s. Lester Howard and Elizabeth Ann (Jones) G.; m. Lynn Ann Halverson, Mar. 15, 1986. BSME, Calif. Poly. Inst., San Luis Obispo, 1982. Mfg. engr. Spectra Physics, Mountain View, Calif., 1982-85; sr. mfg. engr. Coherent Med., Palo Alto, Calif., 1985-86; engring. mgr. Coherent Laser Products, Palo Alto, Calif., 1986-89; mfg. devel. engr. Hewlett-Packard Co., Palo Alto, 1989—. Contbr. articles to profl. publs. Mem. Inst. Indsl. Engrs., ASME, Internat. Optical Engring. Soc., Peninsula Boardsailing Assn. Republican. Mem. Christian Ch. (Disciples of Christ). Home: 7569 Kirwin Ave Cupertino CA 95014

GIBSON, JOHN WILLIAM, aircraft maintenance engineer, technician, consultant; b. Christchurch, Canterbury, New Zealand, July 13, 1950; came to U.S., 1976; s. Marcus Hampton and Monica Alice (Cawood) G.; m. Deborah Renae (New), Dec. 12, 1971; 1 child, Sarah Renae. Cert. aircraft maintenance engr., New Zealand; lic. aircraft and power plant mechanic, U.S. Aircraft engr. Air New Zealand, Christchurch, 1973-76; aircraft mechanic Flightcraft, Inc., Portland, Oreg., 1976-77, aircraft maintenance foreman, 1977-78; aircraft maintenance foreman Flightcraft, Inc., Seattle, 1978-82; asst. mgr. Burlington No., Inc., Seattle, 1982-84, aircraft maintenance mgr., 1984—; cons. Fed. Express Corp., Seattle, 1984—, La. Land Devel. Co., New Orleans, 1987; aviation adv. com. South Seattle Community Coll., 1986—. Fairwood Crest Homeowner's Assn. (comm. mem.), Renton, Wash., 1982. Mem. Profl. Aviation Maintenance Assn. (technician of yr. award, 1983). Mem. Ch. of Eng. Home: 16528 133d Pl SE Renton WA 98058 Office: Burlington No Inc 7777 Perimeter Rd S Seattle WA 98108

GIBSON, KIRK HAROLD, professional baseball player; b. Pontiac, Mich., May 28, 1957; s. Robert and Barbara Gibson; m. JoAnn Sklarski. Student, Mich. State U., 1975-78. Player Lakeland (Fla.) Tigers, 1978, Evansville (Ind.) Triplets, 1979, Detroit Tigers, 1979-88, World Series, 1984, 1988, Los Angeles Dodgers, 1988—. Named Nat. League Most Valuable Player, 1988. Office: Los Angeles Dodgers Dodger Stadium 1000 Elysian Park Ave Los Angeles CA 90012 *

GIBSON, LOUISE, lawyer; b. Flushing, N.Y., Apr. 15, 1947; d. Rubin H. and Beatrice T. (Chorna) G. BA, U. Mich., 1969; JD, Northeastern U., 1974. Bar: Ariz. 1975, U.S. Dist. Ct. Ariz. 1975, N.Mex. 1978, U.S. Dist. Ct. N.Mex., U.S. Ct. Appeals (10th cir.) 1979, U.S. Supreme Ct. 1985. Atty. DNA-People Legal Svcs., Tuba City, Ariz., 1975-77; law clk. State of N.Mex., Santa Fe, 1977-78; assoc. Butt, Thorton & Baehr, Albuquerque, 1978-82, ptnr., dir., 1982—. Bd. mem. YWCA, Albuquerque, 1983—. Mem. ABA, Ariz. Bar Assn., N.Mex. Bar Assn., N.Mex. Def. Lawyers Assn., Albuquerque Bar Assn. Democrat. Jewish. Office: Butt Thorton & Baehr PC PO Box 3170 Albuquerque NM 87190

GIBSON, MELVIN ROY, pharmacognosy educator; b. St. Paul, Nebr., June 11, 1920; s. John and Jennie Irene (Harvey) G. B.S., U. Nebr., 1942, M.S., 1947, D.Sc. (hon.), 1985; Ph.D., U. Ill., 1949. Asst. prof. pharmacognosy Wash. State U., Pullman, 1949-52; assoc. prof. Wash. State U., 1952-55, prof., 1955-85, prof. emeritus, 1985—. Editor: Am. Jour. Pharm. Edn, 1956-61; editorial bd., co-author: Remington's Pharm. Sci, 1970, 75, 80, 85; editor, co-author: Studies of a Pharm. Curriculum, 1967; author over 100 articles. Served as arty. officer AUS, 1942-46. Decorated Bronze star, Purple Heart; sr. vis. fellow Orgn. for Econ. Cooperation and Devel., Royal Pharm. Inst., Stockholm, Sweden and U. Leiden (Holland), 1962; recipient Rufus A. Lyman award, 1972, Wash. State U. Faculty Library award, 1984; named Wash. State U. Faculty Mem. of Yr., 1985. Founder, charter mem. Am. Diplomates in Pharmacy.; fellow AAAS; assoc. fellow Am. Coll. Apothecaries; mem. N.Y. Acad. Sci., Am. Pharm. Assn., Am. Soc. Pharmacognosy (pres. 1964-65), Am. Assn. Coll. Pharmacy (exec. com. 1961-63, bd. dirs. 1977-79, chmn. council of faculties 1975-76, pres. 1979-80, Disting. Educator award 1984), U.S. Pharmacopeia (revision com. 1970-75), Am. Found. Pharm. Edn. (hon. life, bd. dirs. 1980-85, exec. com. 1981-85, vice chmn. 1982-85), AAUP, Acad. Pharm. Sci., Am. Public Health Assn., Fedn. Internat. Pharm., Am. Inst. History of Pharmacy, Am. Acad. Polit. and Social Sci., Sigma Xi, Kappa Psi (Nat. Service citation 1961), Rho Chi, Phi Kappa Phi, Omicron Delta Kappa. Democrat. Presbyterian. Club: Spokane. Home: W 707 6th Ave Apt 41 Spokane WA 99204

GIBSON, PAUL RAYMOND, international trade and investment development executive; b. Cathay, Calif., Apr. 10, 1924; s. Otto and Louella (Vestal) G.; m. Janice Elizabeth Carter, Dec. 19, 1952; children—Scott C., Paula S. B.S. in Internat. Commerce, Sch. Fgn. Service Georgetown U., 1956. Export mgr. Asia Philip Morris Co., San Francisco, 1952-54; founder, v.p., gen. mgr. McGregor and Werner Internat. Corp., Washington, 1954-62, v.p., dir. McGregor and Werner Corp., 1955-62; v.p. fin. Parsons & Whittemore, Inc., N.Y.C., 1962-65; founder, pres. Paul R. Gibson and Assocs., Washington, 1965-70; mng. dir. Black Clawson Pacific Co., Sydney, Australia, 1970-72; pres. Envirotech Asia Pacific, Sydney, 1972-74, pres. Envirotech Internat., Menlo Park, Calif., 1975-80; founder, pres. INTERACT, Burlingame, Calif., 1980—; pres. The Manchester Group, Ltd., Washington, 1987—. dir. Eimco K.C.P., Ltd., India. Mem. Pacific Basin Econ. Council v.p. program and vice chmn. govt. liaison U.S. Sect., 1976—; trustee World Affairs Council No. Calif., 1978—; mem. San Francisco Com. Foreign Relations, 1980—. Served to sgt. USMC, 1941-45. Mem. U.S. C. of C. (chmn. Asia-Pacific council Am. C. of C. 1974, mem. adv. com. 1975—). Clubs: Internat. (Washington); Am. Nat. (Sydney, Australia); Sharon Heights Golf and Country (Menlo Park, Calif.). Home: #9 Brent Ct Menlo Park CA 94025 Office: INTERACT 1350 Old Bayshore Hwy Ste 750 Burlingame CA 94010

GIBSON, ROY BERRETT, communications educator; b. North Ogden, Utah, Feb. 17, 1924; s. John William and Hazel (Berrett) G.; m. Bena Le Bowring, Mar. 22, 1948; children: Robert Barrett, Kathy Danielle, Cory Denise, Wendy Jo, Laurie Lee, Susan Kaye. Comml. announcer sta. KTVT-TV, Salt Lake City, 1952-57; newscaster KDYL Radio, Salt Lake City, 1957; news dir. KTVT-TV, 1958-62, KCPX-TV, Salt Lake City, 1962-72; guest lectr. U. Utah Sch. Journalism, 1968-72, vis. prof., 1972-73, assoc. prof. communication, 1973-89; prof. communication, 1989—. Served with AUS, 1943-46. Mem. Radio-TV News Dirs. Assn., Assn. Edn. in Journalism, Nat. Broadcast Editorial Assn., Sigma Delta Chi (chpt. pres. 1965, regional dir. 1970-72). Club: Exchange (pres. Salt Lake City 1968-69). Author: Radio and Television Reporting, 1989. Home: 561 Northmont Way Salt Lake City UT 84103

GIBSON, SALLY BARRETT, physical therapist; b. Boulder, Colo., Nov. 4, 1947; d. Holger William and Coranelle Cambell (Barrett) Munson; m. James Bradley Gibson, Sept. 21, 1970 (div. Aug. 1987); 1 child, Lindsey Barrett. BS, U. Colo., 1969. Reg. phys. therapist, Colo. Reg. phys. therapist various hosps. and nursing homes, Colorado Spring, Colo., 1971-87, Gates Med. Ctr., Denver, 1987-88; pvt. practice Dr. Robert Powers, Denver, 1987—. Fundraiser Colo. Opera Festival, Colorado Springs, 1980-84; ch. officer Colorado Springs, 1980-86; vol. Colorado springs Schs., 1980-86; bd. dirs. Jr. League, Colorado Springs, 1972-80. Served to lt. (j.g.) USN, 1969-71. Mem. Am. Phys. Therapy Assn. (Colo chpt., orthopaedic sect.). Republican. Home: 5789 E Powers Ave Englewood CO 80111 Office: Dr Robert Powers 601 E Hampden Ave #220 Englewood CO 80110

GIBSON-DAVIS, JAN GAIL, recruiting executive; b. Los Angeles, Apr. 20, 1944; d. Phillip Howard Gibson and Marion Enid (Child) Sesma; m. Andrew Joseph DoBan, May 22, 1971 (div. July 1973); m. Lee Allan Davis, Apr. 1, 1981. AA, Calif. State U., Long Beach, 1966. Bookkeeper Gen. Fin. Corp., Long Beach, 1964-66, Webber Showcase & Fixture, Los Angeles, 1966, Nationwide Investment Co., Beverly Hills, Calif., 1967, Booktrails, Ltd., Beverly Hills, 1968-69; exec. asst. to pres. Regis Corp., Beverly Hills, 1969-76; profl. recruiter Bus. & Profl., Inc., Los Angeles, 1976-79; exec. recruiter, founder, exec. v.p. DBG The Search Corp., Malibu, Calif., 1979—. Mem. Los Angeles County Mus. Art. Mem. Nat. Assn. for Female Execs., Armed Forces Communications and Electronics Assn., Malibu Woman's Club (1st v.p. 1984-85), Assn. Old Crows. Democrat. Lutheran. Office: DBG The Search Corp 22761 Pacific Coast Hwy Malibu CA 90265

GIBU, GARY KAZUO, chemical company executive; b. Honolulu, July 17, 1954; s. Charles Yoshio and Joyce (Fukushima) G.; m Kay Shizue, Mar. 18, 1978; children: Christopher Kameo, Kimberly Yoshie. BBA, U. Hawaii, 1980. Sales trainee Dubois Chem. Co., Honolulu, 1980-82, jr. dist. mgr., 1982-83, 1982-83, dist. mgr., 1983-85, div. mgr., 1985-87, asst. v.p., gen. mgr., 1987—. Mem. U. Hawaii Found., U.O.A. Club. Republican. Office: Dubois Chem Co 120 Mokauea St Honolulu HI 96819

GIDEON-HAWKE, PAMELA LAWRENCE, fine arts, small business owner; b. N.Y.C., Aug. 23, 1945; d. Lawrence Ian Verry and Lily S. (Stein) Gordon; m. Jarrett Redstone, June 27, 1964; 1 child, Justin Craig Hawke. Student, U.S. Mil. Acad., 1973—. Owner Gideon Gallery Ltd., L.A., 1975—. Sec. Design Alliance to Combat Aids, L.A., 1986—. Named Friend of Design Industry Designers West Mag., 1987. Mem. Am. Soc. Interior Designers (publicist), Internat. Soc. Interior Designers (trade liaison 1986-88), Nwtwork Exec. Women in Hosp., Internat. Furnishings and Design Assn. (programs chmn.). Office: Gideon Gallery Ltd 8748 Melrose Ave Los Angeles CA 90069

GIDUMAL, SHYAM HIRA, management consultant; b. N.Y.C., May 21, 1959; s. Hira and Lila (Hathiramani) G. BA magna cum laude, Columbia U., 1979; MBA, Harvard U., 1983. Assoc. Bluth Eastman Dillon & Co., Internat., Athens, Greece, 1979-80, Blyth Eastman Dillon & Co., Internat., London, 1980-81; cons. Boston Cons. Group, Boston, 1982; cons. Boston Cons. Group, L.A., 1983-86, mgr., 1986—. Mem. Phi Beta Kappa. Office: Boston Cons Group 333 S Grand Ave Ste 4262 Los Angeles CA 90071

GIELISSEN, A. JAMES, construction executive; b. Dubuque, Iowa, Sept. 11, 1928; s. Fred Hubert and Theresse Mary (Sonnemans) G.; m. Dolores Parachini, 1952 (div. 1955); m. Betsy Jane Chambers, June 20 1958; children: Stephen Jeffrey, Bradley Randolph, Dana Lee. BS in Archtl. Engring., U. Colo., 1957. Carpenter Conlon Constrn. Co., Dubuque, 1946-50; account exec. Ludwig & Patterson, Denver, 1957-62; pres., chief exec. officer Charles Hughes & Co., Denver, 1962—; mem. adv. bd. Pitts. State U., 1985—; chmn. exec. com. Colo. State Carpenters Apprentice Tng., Denver, 1982—. Pres. Listen Found., Englewood, Colo., 1976—. With USAF, 1950-54. Mem. Nat. Assn. Store Fixtures Mfrs. (pres., dir. 1981—), Assn. Gen. Contrs. (exec. com. 1987—), Lakewood Country Club, Mt. Vernon Country Club. Office: Hughes & Co 500 E 76th Ave Denver CO 80229

GIEM, ROSS NYE, JR., surgeon; b. Corvallis, Oreg., May 23, 1923; s. Ross Nye and Goldie Marie (Falk) G.; student U. Redlands, Walla Walla Coll.; BA, MD, Loma Linda U.; children: John, David, Paul, James, Ross Nye, Matthew, Julie. Intern, Sacramento Gen. Hosp., 1952-53; resident in ob-gyn, Kern County Gen. Hosp., Bakersfield, Calif., 1956-57, in gen. surgery, 1957-61; practice medicine specializing in gen. surgery, Sullivan, Mo., 1961-70; staff emergency dept. Hollywood Presbyn. Med. Center, 1971-73, Meml. Hosp., Belleville, Ill., 1973—, St. Elizabeth Hosp., Belleville, Ill., 1973—; St. Luke Hosp., Pasadena, Calif., 1973—; instr. nurses, physicians, paramedics, emergency med. technicians, 1973—. Served with AUS, 1943-46. Diplomate Am. Bd. Surgery. Fellow ACS, Am. Coll. Emergency Physicians; mem. AMA, Ill. Med. Assn., Pan Am. Med. Assn., Pan Pacific Surg. Assn., Royal Coll. Physicians (Eng.)

GIERSON, EUGENE DOBSON, physician; b. L.A., Oct. 7, 1940; s. Hyman William and Sylvia Gierson. BA, Occidental Coll., 1962; MD, U. So. Calif., 1966. Diplomate Am. Bd. Surgery. Instr. in surgery NYU, 1967-71; resident in surgery NYU Hosp., 1967-71, Bellevue Hosp., N.Y.C., 1967-71; asst. prof. surgery UCLA, 1971-74; asst. clin. prof. surgery UCLA-Harbor, Torrance, Calif., 1974-80, U. Calif., Irvine, 1981-83; mem. surg. staff Valley Hosp., Van Nuys, 1984—; oncologic surgeon The Breast Ctr., Van Nuys, 1984—. Fellow ACS. Office: The Breast Ctr 14624 Sherman Way #600 Van Nuys CA 91405

GIESE, HERBERT ADOLPH, JR., pediatrician; b. Alexandria, Va., Dec. 22, 1937; s. Herbert Adolph and Vohnda Avonelle (Pilgrim) G.; m. Carol Jean Dauenhauer, Aug. 10, 1959; children: Paul Thomas (dec.), Vohnda Maria, Rosanne Celeste, Scott Damian, Mark Michael, Brent Edward. BS, Loyola U. of South, New Orleans, 1960; MD, La. State U., 1963; MPH, Tulane U., 1970. Diplomate, Am. Bd. Pediatrics. Intern Keesler USAF Hosp., Biloxi, Miss., 1963-64; resident in pediatrics Wilford Hall USAF Hosp., San Antonio, 1964-66; pediatrician 3535th USAF Hosp., Mather AFB, Calif., 1966-68, Holzer Med. Clinic, Gallipolis, Ohio, 1970-72; dir. pediatric edn. St. Jude Children's Hosp., Memphis, 1972-73; pediatrician Beaver Med. Clinic, Redlands, Calif., 1973-75; assoc. dir. pediatrics San Bernardino (Calif.) County Med. Ctr., 1975-79; pediatrician Washington Pediatric Med. Assn., Colton, Calif., 1979—; med. dir., Children in Crisis Ctr., San Bernardino, 1988—; bd. dirs., Coalition for Prevention of Abuse toWomen and Children, San Bernardino, 1977-84; cons. in infectious diseases. Mem. Child Abuse and Neglect Prevention and Intervention Commn., San Bernardino, 1984-86; mem. Juvenile Justice and Delinquency Prevention Commn., San Bernardino, 1988—; bd. dirs., Bethlehem House Battered Women's Shelter, San Bernardino, 1988—. Maj. USAF, 1963-68. USPHS trainee in pediatric infectious diseases, Tulane U., 1968-70. Fellow Am. acad. Pediatrics; mem. Am. Soc. Microbiology, Internat. Soc. Prevention of Child Abuse and Neglect, Calif. Profl. Soc. Against Child Abuse, Hinterlands Pediatric Soc. Office: Washington Pediatric Assn 1880 Washington St Colton CA 92324

GIESELMAN, LESLIE ALLEN, pharmacist; b. Bloomfield, Nebr., Nov. 8, 1951; d. Winfred Paul and Laura Alice (Peitzmeier) G.; m. Janet Ann Nelson, Feb. 14, 1976; children: Adam Paul, Anna Kathryn. BS, U. Nebr., 1974. Resident U. Nebr. Med. Ctr., Omaha, 1975, instr. coll. of pharmacy, 1975-77, staff pharmacist, 1975-77; staff pharmacist St. Luke's Regional Med. Ctr., Boise, Idaho, 1977-84, clin. pharmacist, 1984—; mem. regional adv. com. regional med. library Nat. Library of Medicine, Seattle, 1986—; mem. pharmacy, therapeutics, libr. coms. St. Luke's Regional Med. Ctr., Boise, 1984—. V.p. Immanuel Luth. Ch., Boise, 1987-88, chmn. stewardship com., 1987-88, mem. choir, 1986—. Mem. Am. Soc. of Hosp. Pharmacists, Idaho Soc. Hosp. Pharmacists (permanent workshop imputology 1988—). Lutheran. Home: 216 Twin Willow Boise ID 83706 Office: St Lukes Regional Med Ctr 190 E Bannock St Boise ID 83712

GIESLER, GREGG CARL, nuclear chemist, computer systems consultant; b. Chgo., Sept. 11, 1944; s. Carl and Vivian Marie (Gregersen) G.; m. Maryjane Anne Vlk, June 22, 1968; children: Susananne, Janaanne, Jeffrey, Jonathan. BS in Chemistry, U. Ill., 1966; PhD in Chem. Physics, Mich. State U., 1971. Staff mem. Los Alamos Nat. Lab., 1972-86; computer systems engr. Jomar Systems, Los Alamos, 1986-88; cons. Salem Tech. Svcs., Albuquerque, 1988—. Com. mem. pack 229, Cub Scouts Am., Los Alamos, 1982-85; com. chmn. troop 329, Boy Scouts Am., Los Alamos, 1986--. Mem. Am. Chem. Soc. (local membership chmn. 1980-81), Am. Phys. Soc., Digital Equipment Computer Users Soc. (local users group chmn. 1979—, spl. interest group com. 1979--). Lutheran. Office: Salem Tech Svcs 4004 Carlisle Blvd NE Albuquerque NM 87107

GIFFIN, ROBERT LEWIS, engineer consultant; b. Somerville, Mass., Aug. 1, 1937; s. Burpee Lewis and Hilda May (Woods) G.; m. Jean Ruth Scott, Dec. 21, 1958; children: William Robert, Robin, Donna. BS, Ind. Inst. of Tech., 1959; postgrad., UCLA, 1968. Project engr. D.S. Kennedy & Co., Cohasset, Mass., 1957-64; chief engr. Electronic Specialty Co., Glendale, Calif., 1964-67; engring. mgr. Canoga Electronics, Chatsworth, Calif., 1967-69; dir. engring. Radtec Inc., Sun Valley, Calif., 1969-75; v.p. engring. Tecom Industries Inc., Chatsworth, 1975-84; cons. engr. Giffin Assoc., Canoga Park, 1984—. Recipient scholarship Am. Soc. of Tool Engrs., Boston, 1956. Mem. ASME, Assn. of Old Crows. Democrat. Roman Catholic. Home: 21820 MaryLee St Woodland Hils CA 91367 Office: Giffin Assocs 7246 Remmet Ave Canoga Park CA 91303

GIFFORD, ARTHUR ROY, aircraft executive; b. Buffalo, Jan. 27, 1937; s. William Howard and Dorothy Ellen (Logan) G.; m. Anna Marie Boone, July 9, 1960 (div. Feb. 1974); 1 child, Douglas Alan; m. Carolyn Elaine Crowe, Dec. 20, 1974; children: Christine Michelle, Stephen Michael. BA, Butler U., 1964; postgrad., Pacific Luth. U., Tacoma, 1970; MA, U. Wash., 1975. Provisional, standard and secondary tchr. certs., Wash. Passenger svc. agt. United Airlines, Seattle, 1966-67; indsl. engr. The Boeing Co., Seattle, 1967-70, com. dir., 1987—; tchr. Fed. Way (Wash.) Sch. Dist., 1971-87. Bd. dirs. Lyric Theatre and Conservatory, Midway, Wash., 1980-82; treas. Wash. Edn. Theatre Assn., 1973-77, 85-89; treas. ArtsTime '89 Wash. State Centennial All-Arts Conf., 1987-89, long-range planning com., Kent (Wash.) View Christian Sch., 1987—; mem. precinct com. Dem. Orgn. King County, Wash., 1973-75. Democrat, Methodist. Home: 13904 SE 241st St Kent WA 98042 Office: The Boeing Co PO Box 3707 M/S 6X-34 Seattle WA 98124-2207

GIFFORD, BECKY JENSEN, infosystems specialist; b. Akron, Ohio, Apr. 30, 1947; d. Henry Hartwig and Dorothy Myrtle (Surber) Jensen; m. James Roy Gifford, Jan. 18, 1986. BA, U. Nebr., 1970; MLS, UCLA, 1977. Cert. info. scientist. Librarian Instructional Materials Ctr. for Spl. Edn., U. So. Calif., Los Angeles, 1970-73; cons. Los Angeles, 1972-77; mgr. info. services NASA Indsl. Application Ctr., Los Angeles, 1977-81; dir. info. systems Savage Info. Services, Rolling Hills, Calif., 1981-85, v.p., 1985—. Mem. So. Calif. Online User Group (founding), Spl. Libraries Assn., Assn. Records Mgrs. and Adminstrs. Office: Savage Info Svcs 2510 W 237th St Ste 200 Torrance CA 90505

GIFFORD, GERALD FREDERIC, environmental program director; b. Chanute, Kans., Oct. 24, 1939; s. Gerald Leo and Marion Lou (Browne) G.; m. Cinda Jean Lowman, June 26, 1982. Student, Kans. U., 1957-60; BS in Range Mgmt., Utah State U., 1962, MS in Watershed Mgmt., 1964, PhD in Watershed Sci., 1968. Asst. prof. watershed sci. Utah State U., Logan, 1967-72, assoc. prof., 1972-80, prof., 1980-84, chmn. watershed sci. unit, 1967-84, dir. Inst. Land Reclamation, 1982-84; head range, wildlife and forestry U. Nev., Reno, 1984—; exchange scientist NSF, Canberra, Australia, 1974; cons. Smithsonian Inst., Nat. Park Service, Office of Tech. Assessment, Tex. Tech U., U. Minn., Bur. Land Mgmt. AMAX Coal Co., Nat. Commn. Water Quality, 1967—. Author: Rangeland Hydrology, 1981; assoc. editor Arid Soil Research and Rehab., 1985—; contbr. papers to profl. publs. Mem. Am. Water Resources Assn., Soc. Range Mgmt. (assoc. editor 1982-86), Soil Conservation Soc. Am. Home: 3880 Squaw Valley Circle Reno NV 89509 Office: U Nev Range Wildlife and Forestry 1000 Valley Rd Reno NV 89512

GIFFORD, JAMES ROY, manufacturing executive; b. Muskegon, Mich., May 23, 1945; s. Theron Fairweather and Margaret (Grierson) G.; m. Ellen D. Richardson, Dec. 14, 1973 (div. Dec. 1982); m. Rebecca Joanne Jensen, Jan. 18, 1986. BA, Dartmouth Coll., 1967; MS, U. Southern Calif., 1976. Commd. ensign USN, 1967, advanced through grades to lt., 1970, resigned, 1975; cons. Advanced Logistics Mgmt., San Diego, 1975-76; analyst Cubic Corp., San Diego, 1976-77; logistics analyst aircraft div. Northrop Corp., Hawthorne, Calif., 1977-80; dep. mgr. logistics Northrop Corp., Pico Rivera, Calif., 1980-88; ATF logistics mgr. Northrop Corp., Hawthorne, 1988—. Mem. U.S. Naval Inst., Soc. Logistics Engrs., Tailhook Assn., Smithsonian Inst., Northrop Mgmt. Club. Republican. Home: 4048 Miraleste Dr Rancho Palos Verdes CA 90274 Office: Northrop Corp 1 Northrop Ave Hawthorne CA 90250

GIFFORD, JONATHAN BERRY, architect; b. Aurora, Ill., Dec. 10, 1942; s. William Carleton and Jewel Gordon (Berry) G.; m. Helen Grube, Sept. 10, 1966; children: Jonathan Knell, Peter Berry. AB, Stanford U., 1964.

Draftsman CSS Assocs. Architects, Palo Alto, Calif., 1966-71, assoc., 1971-78, v.p., 1978-79, pres., 1979—; dir. Palo Alto-Stanford Heritage, Palo Alto, 1988. Pres. Palo Alto YMCA, 1980, sr. dir., 1988--; chmn. City of Palo Alto Historic Resources Bd., 1988. Mem. AIA, Rotary. Office: CSS Assocs Architects 940 E Meadow Ave Palo Alto CA 94303

GILBERD, KATHLEEN MICHELE, legal worker; b. Oakland, Calif., July 30, 1949; d. Philip Murray and Elizabeth (Whitson) G.; m. Terrence Christian, July 29, 1972. BA, U. Calif., Berkeley, 1971; law study program, U. Calif., San Diego, 1985. Legal worker Law Offices of Charles Bumer, San Diego, 1984—. Editor (legal manual) Fighting Back, 1985, (jour.) On Watch, 1979—; contbg. editor (jour.) The Objector, 1985—. Bd. dirs. ACLU, San Diego, 1987—; mem. Com. Opposed to Militarism and Draft, San Diego, 1981—; mem. adv. bd. Com. Against Registration and Draft, 1986—, N.L.G. AIDS Project, 1986—; chmn. N.L.G. Mil. Law Task Force, 1980—. Recipient Community Svc. award Greater San Diego Bus. Assn., 1986. Mem. Nat. Lawyers Guild (regional v.p. 1980-81), Phi Beta Kappa. Office: 1168 Union Ste 201 San Diego CA 92101

GILBERG, ARNOLD L., psychiatrist; b. Chgo., Sept. 11, 1936; s. Jack and Anne (Schwartz) Gilberg; children: Suzanne, Jonathan. MD, U. Ill., 1961; PhD, So. Calif. Psychoanalytic Inst., 1973. Practice medicine specializing in adult psychiatry, psychoanalysis Berverly Hills, Calif., 1965—; assoc. clin. prof. psychiatry UCLA Sch. Medicine, 1978—; tng., supervising psychoanalyst, pres. So. Calif. Psychoanalytic Inst., Beverly Hills, 1988—; vis. prof. human relations Hebrew Union Coll., L.A., 1965—; bd. govs. U. Judiasm; examiner Am. Bd. Psychiatry and Neurology, 1978—. Contbr. articles to profl. jours. Appointed Bd. Med. Quality Assurance Calif. Med. Quality Review Com. Fellow APA, Am. Coll. Psychoanalysts; mem. Am. Psychoanalytic Assn., Internat. Psychoanalytic Assn. Jewish. Office: 9915 Santa Monica Blvd Beverly Hills CA 90212

GILBERT, CLIFFORD WARD, lawyer; b. Detroit, Sept. 30, 1954; s. Gilbert J. and Helen Susan (Myers) G.; m. Patricia Gottridge; 1 child, Christopher Ward. AB summa cum laude, UCLA, 1976; JD, U. Calif., Berkeley, 1979. Assoc. Rosenfeld, Meyer and Susman, Beverly Hills, Calif., 1979-83, Gilbert and Hoeland, Sherman Oaks, Calif., 1983-84; counsel Walt Disney Co., Burbank, Calif., 1984-86; assoc. Ziffren Brittenham and Brunca, L.A., 1986-88, ptnr., 1988—. Contbr. Calif. Law Rev. Mem. Order of the Coif, Phi Beta Kappa. Office: Ziffren Brittenham & Branca 2121 Ave of the Stars Ste 3200 Los Angeles CA 90067

GILBERT, DAVE (DONALD WILLIAM GILBERT), actor; b. Cin., Jan. 22, 1930; s. Courtney and Jewel (Maxwell) G. BA, Ohio State U., 1955. Actor B'way, off-B'way, N.Y., 1956-62; creative dir. Kaleidoscope Films, Ltd., L. A., 1971-82; self employed actor L.A., 1981--. Author: The Candid Cannibal, 1987; actor (film) "D.B. Cooper," "Listen To Me". Pub. relations exec. Am. Cancer Soc., N.Y. Epilepsy Found. Mem. Nat. Press Club, Writers Guild of Am., Screen Actors Guild, AFTRA. Democrat. Office: Internat Creative Mgmt 8899 Beverly Blvd Los Angeles CA 90048

GILBERT, HEATHER CAMPBELL, manufacturing company executive; b. Mt. Vernon, N.Y., Nov. 20, 1944; d. Ronald Ogston and Mary Lodivia (Campbell) G.; BS in Math. (Nat. Merit scholar), Stanford U., 1967; MS in Computer Sci. (NSF fellow), U. Wis., 1969. With Burroughs Corp., 1969-82, sr. mgmt. systems analyst, Detroit, 1975-77, mgr. mgmt. systems activity, Pasadena, Calif., 1977-82; mgr. software product mgmt. Logical Data Mgmt. Inc., Covina, Calif., 1982-83, dir. mktg., 1983, v.p. bus. devel., 1983-84; v.p. profl. services, 1984-85; mgr. software devel. Unisys Corp., Irvine, Calif., 1985—. Mem. Assn. Computing Machinery, Am. Prodn. and Inventory Control Soc., Stanford U. Alumni Assn. (life), Stanford Profl. Women Los Angeles County (pres. 1982-83), Nat. Assn. Female Execs., Town Hall. Republican. Home: 21113 Calle de Paseo El Toro CA 92630 Office: Unisys Corp 19 Morgan Irvine CA 92718

GILBERT, JAMES FREEMAN, geophysics educator; b. Vincennes, Ind., Aug. 9, 1931; s. James Freeman and Gladys (Paugh) G.; m. Sally Bonney, June 19, 1959; children: Cynthia, Sarah, James. BS, MIT, 1953, PhD, 1956. Research assoc. MIT, Cambridge, 1956-57; asst. research geophysicist Inst. Geophysics and Planetary Physics at UCLA, 1957, asst. prof. geophysics, 1958-59; sr. research geophysicist Tex. Instruments, Dallas, 1960-61; prof. Inst. Geophysics and Planetary Physics at U. Calif. San Diego, La Jolla, 1961—, assoc. dir., 1976-88; chmn. grad. dept. Scripps Inst. Oceanography, La Jolla, 1988—; chmn. steering com. San Diego Supercomputer, 1984-86, Nat. Research Council Com. on Seismology, 1976-78, Nat. Acad. Scis. Panel on U.S.-USSR Exchange Program of the Bd. of Internat. Sci. Exchange, 1978-81; mem. NSF adv. com. Advanced Sci. Computing, 1983-85, NSF network subcom., 1985. Contbr. numerous articles to profl. jours. Recipient Arthur L. Day medal Geol. Soc. Am., 1985; Fairchild scholar Calif. Inst. Tech., Pasadena, 1987; fellow NSF, 1956, Guggenheim, 1964-65, 72-73, Overseas fellow Churchhill Coll. U. Cambridge, Eng., 1972-73. Fellow AAAS, Am. Geophys. Union; Nat. Acad. Scis., European Union Geoscis. (hon.); mem. Seismology Soc. Am., Soc. Exploration Geophysicists, Am. Math. Soc., Royal Astron. Soc. (recipient Gold medal 1981), Nat. Research Council (mem. ad hoc com. of Govt./Univ. Round Table, 1986), Sigma Xi. Home: 780 Kalamath Dr Del Mar CA 92014 Office: U Calif Inst Geophysics and Planetary Physics A-025 La Jolla CA 92093

GILBERT, PHILLIP NOLAND, architect; b. Richmond, Ky., May 19, 1949; s. Henry C. and Katherine May (Mullins) Green. BArch, U. Ky., 1972. Registered architect, Ky.,Calif. With Lexington-Fayette Planning Commn., Lexington, Ky., 1972-74; prin. Gilbert Designs, Lexington, 1974-75; draftsman, designer New & Assocs., Berea, Ky., 1975-77; prin. Gilbert Design and Build, Lexington, 1977-79, Form Guild, Inc., Irvine, Calif., 1987--; project mgr. Hamill/McKinney A and E, Lexington, 1979-82; dir. Hamill/McKinney A and E, Santa Monica, Calif., 1982-84; dir. architecture and engring. Pepsico, Irvine, 1984-87; pub. Open Ground, 1976. Recipient Best of Industry award Point Purchase Advt. Inst., 1986. Mem.AIA, Constrn. Specifications Inst., Nat. Coun. Archtl. Registration Bds., Nat.ist. Soc. Home: 34092 Mazo Ave Dana Point CA 92629 Office: Form Guild Inc 34094 Mazo Ave Dana Point CA 92629

GILBERT, ROBERT WOLFE, lawyer; b. N.Y.C., Nov. 12, 1920; s. L. Wolfe and Katherine L. (Oestreicher) Wolfe; m. Beatrice R. Frutman, Dec. 25, 1946; children: Frank Richard, Jack Alfred. BA, UCLA 1941; JD, U. Calif., Berkeley, 1943. Bar: Calif. 1944, U.S. Ct. Apls. (9th cir.) 1944, U.S. Ct. Apls. (D.C. cir.) 1976, U.S. Sup. Ct. 1959. Pres. Gilbert & Sackman, P.C. and predecessors, L.A., 1944—; judge pro tem Los Angeles Mcpl. Ct., Commr. City of L.A. Housing Authority 1953-63; bd. dirs. Calif. Housing Coun. 1955-63. Mem. Internat. Bar Assn., Interam. Bar Assn. (co-chmn. labor law and social security com.), ABA (co-chmn. internat. labor law com.), Fed. Bar Assn., L.A. Bar Assn. (past chmn. labor law sect.), Am. Judicature Soc., Order of Coif, Pi Sigma Alpha. Club: Nat. Lawyers. Contbr. articles to profl. jours. Home: 7981 Hollywood Blvd Hollywood CA 90046 Office: 6100 Wilshire Blvd Ste 700 Los Angeles CA 90048-5107

GILBERT, THOMAS ANGUS, military officer; b. Pensacola, Fla., Aug. 5, 1948; s. Randall DeWayne and Catherine (Allan) G.; m. Teresita Lee, July 1, 1970 (div. Aug. 1981); 1 child, Kenneth Thomas; m. Lilia Rey; 1 child, Rowelina. BABA, Columbia Coll., 1979, BA in Adminstrn. of Justice. Enlisted U.S. Navy, 1966, commd., 1985; leading petty officer USS Waccamaw AO-109, FPO, N.Y.C., 1974-75; supr. sales commissary store NCS, Harold E. Holt, Exmouth, Western Australia, 1975-77; supr. recruit clothing Naval Adminstrv. Command, Orlando, Fla., 1977-79; leading storekeeper USS Voge FF-1047, FPO, Miami, Fla., 1979-82, USS Platte AO-186, FPO, N.Y.C., 1982-84; asst. internal rev. officer Fleet Combat Direction System Support Activity, Virginia Beach, Va., 1984-85; cargo officer USS Nimitz CVN-68, FPO, Seattle, 1985-88. Republican rep. exec. com., Lake County, Fla., 1973; asst. cubmaster Exmouth Cub Scouts, 1975-77. Named one of Outstanding Young Men of Am., Jaycees, 1980. Methodist. Home: 2081 Crosscreek Rd Chula Vista CA 92013 Office: CACI Inc Fed 8755 Aero Dr Ste 200 San Diego CA 92123

GILBERT, WILLIAM ALLAN, agronomist, consultant; b. Batavia, N.Y., Sept. 6, 1954; s. Reed Davies and Frances (Owens) G.; m. Lucinda Russell, June 2, 1973; children: Seth, Jesse, Caleb. BS, Cornell U., 1976; MS, Colo. State U., 1978. Cert. profl. agronomist. Research asst. agronomic research Colo. State U., 1976-78; asst. scientist, room control supr. Castle & Cooke Inc., East Windsor, Conn., 1978-80; cons. agronomist Inter-Am. Labs., Ft. Collins, Colo., 1980-82; owner Applied Agronomics, Ft. Collins, 1982-88; cons. agronomist Mid-Am. Cons. Inc, Ft. Collins, 1988—. Med. Colo. Dry Bean Adv. Bd. 1986-87. Gt. Western Sugar Co. grantee Colo. State U., 1976-78. Mem. Am. Soc. Agronomy, Crop Sci. Soc. Am., Soil Sci. Soc. Am., Nat. Alliance Ind. Crop Cons. (sec./treas. 1986-87). Democrat. Contbr. articles to profl. jours.

GILBERTSON, OSWALD IRVING, marketing executive; b. Bklyn., Mar. 23, 1927; s. Olaf and Ingeborg (Aase) Gabrielsen; m. Magnhild Hompland, Sept. 11, 1954; children: Jan Ivar, Eric Olaf. Electrotechnician, Sorlandets Tekniske Skole, Norway, 1947; BSEE, Stockholms Tekniska Institut, Stockholm, Sweden, 1956. Planning engr. test equipment design and devel. Western Electric Co., Inc., Kearny, N.J., 1957-61, planning engr. new prodn., 1963-67, engring. supr. test equipment, 1963-67, engring. supr. submarine repeaters and equalizers, 1967-69; engring. mgr. communication cables ITT Corp., Oslo, Norway, 1969-71, mktg. mgr. for ITT's Norwegian co., Standard Telefon og Kabelfabrik A/S (STK), 1971-87, STK Factory rep., 1987—; div. mgr. Eswa Heating Systems, Inc., 1980-87, pres., 1987—. Hon. Norwegian consul, 1981—. Served with AUS, 1948-52. Registered profl. engr., Vt. Mem. IEEE, Norwegian Soc. Profl. Engrs., Soc. Norwegian Am. Engrs., Sons of Norway. Patentee in field. Home: 6240 Brynwood Ct San Diego CA 92120 Office: Eswa Heating Systems Inc STK Cables Royal Norwegian Consulate 4380 Viewridge Ave Ste D San Diego CA 92123-1620

GILBODY, WENDOLYN MARIE, insurance executive; b. Santa Ana, Calif., Jan. 20, 1945; d. Wendell Cecil and Phyllis Elizabeth (Farquhar) Westlake; m. Richard Arthur Presnell, Nov. 17, 1963 (div. 1970); children: Deborah, David; m. Karl John Gilbody, May 14, 1971; 1 child, John. Grad. high sch., Garden Grove, Calif. Cert. gen. underwriter. Asst. office mgr. Garden Grove Elks Lodge, 1962-63; nurses aide Royale Oaks Convalescent Hosp., Glendale, Calif., 1964-67; med. billing clk. Pacific Med. Mgmt., Glendale, 1967-68; exec. sec. Century Convalescent Ctrs., Marina del Rey, Calif., 1968-70; office mgr. Willow Glen Convalescent Hosp., San Jose, Calif., 1970-74; comml. account underwriter State Farm Ins., Costa Mesa, 1975—. Recipient Betty Crocker Jr. Bake Off award, 1961. Office: State Farm Ins 3333 Hyland Ave Costa Mesa CA 92626

GILBREATH, PATRICIA LOU, accountant; b. Fargo, N.D., Nov. 20, 1941; d. Samuel Preston Colwell and Berdelle Marcella (Jacobson) Smith; m. Rex Lynn Pedersen, Aug. 25, 1959 (div. 1969); children: Clark, Jessie, Eric; m. John R. Gilbreath, June 6, 1970; 1 child Samantha. BS, Calif. Poly. U., 1975; M in Taxation, U. So. Calif, 1980. CPA, Calif. Staff acct. Ross Landis & Pauw, Riverside, Calif., 1975-77; tax ptnr. Eadie and Payne, Redlands, Calif., 1977—; bd. dirs. Allied Constrn. Industries, San Bernardino, Calif. Mem. Calif. Gov.'s Council on Devel. Disabilities, 1984-87; active in United Way (campaign chmn. Redlands Area, 1987, pres. 1988). Recipient Outstanding Svc. award, Calif. Council on Devel. Disabilities, 1988. Mem. Am. Inst. CPA's, Calif. Soc. CPA's (bd. dirs. 1983-86), Estate Planning Council San Bernardino (treas. 1988—), Nat. Assn. Women in Constrn. (pres. San Bernardino 1984-85), Nat. Soc. Accts. for Coops. (chmn. tax program 1988). Republican. Office: Eadie and Payne 300 E State St Ste 212 Redlands CA 92373

GILBRIDE, JOHN THOMAS, JR., aircraft company executive; b. Bklyn., Mar. 9, 1945; s. John Thomas and Rosemary (Shelare) G.; m. Victoria N. Caragol, Aug. 26, 1967; children—John Thomas III, Michael J., Elizabeth Shelare, Matthew T. BS in Indsl. Engring. cum laude, Lehigh U., 1968, BSBA cum laude, 1968. Registered profl. engr., Wash. Ship supt. Todd Pacific Shipyards, Seattle, 1969-70, asst. gen. supt., 1970-71, gen. supt., 1972-75, asst. gen. mgr. prodn., 1975-79, v.p., gen. mgr., 1979-86, pres., chief ops. officer, Jersey City, 1986-89; dir. ops. support Boeing Helicopters, Phila., 1989—. Mem. Western Shipbuilders Assn. (pres., bd. dirs. 1983-85), Soc. Naval Architects and Marine Engrs., Am. Soc. Naval Engrs., Greater Seattle C. of C. (trustee 1985), Nat. Propeller Club U.S., Wash. Athletic Club (dir. 1984). Roman Catholic. Home: 3 E Spring Oak Circle Media PA Office: Boeing Helicopters PO Box 16858 MS P30-46 Philadelphia PA 19142-0858 also: Todd Shipyards Corp 11025 W Massachusetts Seattle WA 98134

GILCREST, LINDA RAE, construction company executive; b. Spokane, Wash., Oct. 4, 1946; d. Martin J. and Patricia J. (Sullivan) McFee; m. James D. Gilcrest, Nov. 30, 1970; children: Krystal Marie, Brenda Jean. Dir. personnel, asst. EEO officer Carl N. Swenson, Inc., San Jose, Calif., 1967-81; v.p. constrn. IDEVCO, Inc., Scotts Valley, Calif., 1981-86; dir. U.S. facilities Seagate Tech., Inc., Scotts Valley, 1986—. Mem. Exec. Women Internat. (pres. San Jose), LWV (speaker's bur. San Jose). Lutheran. Office: Seagate Tech Inc 920 Disc Dr Scotts Valley CA 95066

GILES, GERALD LYNN, mathematics, psychology, computer educator; b. Manti, Utah, Jan. 2, 1943; s. Bert Thorne and Sarah Jenett (Carlen) G.; m. Sharon Ruth Bleak, June 12, 1967; children: Kim, David, Kristie, Becky, Michael, Andrew, Brent. BA, U. Utah, 1968, MA, 1971. Tchr. Granite Sch. Dist., Salt Lake City, 1968-72; prof. Utah Tech. Coll. (now Salt Lake Community Coll.), Salt Lake City, 1972—; adj. prof. U. Utah, 1985—; cons. QUE Enterprises, Salt Lake City, 1976—; mem. faculty U. Phoenix, Salt Lake City, 1986—. Author: The Vicious Circle of Life, 1986, The Computer Productivity Planner, 1988. Chmn. Rep. voting dist., Salt Lake City, 1984-86; bishop Mormon Ch. Recipient Teaching Excellence award, 1986; named Outstanding Tchr. of Yr., 1986. Mem. Assn. Coll. Unions Internat., NADE. Home: 4342 Beechwood Rd Salt Lake City UT 84123 Office: Utah Tech Coll PO Box 30808 Salt Lake City UT 84130-0808

GILES, JAMES PAUL, JR., management educator; b. Texarkana, Tex., Nov. 24, 1919; s. James Paul and Mabel (Legg) G.; m. Joan Epperson, June 24, 1946; children: Christopher, William Epperson, Allison Conrey. BS, Tex. A&M U., 1941; MBA, Harvard U., 1948; postgrad., UCLA, 1974. Various mgmt. postions Hercules div. Am. Cement Corp., Phila., 1951-58, pres. Hercules div., 1958-60; pres., chief exec. officer Am. Cement Corp., Los Angeles, 1961-69; assoc. prof. mgmt. Claremont (Calif.) Grad. Sch., 1974-80, prof. fin., 1980—; mgmt. cons. Skye Investment Advisors, Cupertino, Calif., 1985—; bd. dirs. Union Bank, Los Angeles, Kasler Corp., San Bernardino, Calif. Served to lt. col. U.S.Army, 1941-45. Decorated Legion of Merit; Mil. Valor Cross (Italy). Republican. Home: 1695 Lafayette Claremont CA 91711 Office: Claremont Grad Sch Claremont CA 91711

GILGER, PAUL DOUGLASS, architect; b. Shelby, Ohio, Oct. 13, 1954; s. Richard Douglass and Marilyn Joan (Hawkins) G. BArch, U. Cin., 1978. Registered architect, Ohio. Architect Soulen & Assocs., Mansfield, Ohio, 1976-81, PGS Architecture/Planning, Los Gatos, Calif., 1981-82, Bottomline Systems, Inc., San Francisco, 1983-85; set designer Nomad Prodns. Scenic Studios, San Francisco, 1985—; pvt. practice in set designer San Francisco, 1985—; booking mgr. 1177 Club, San Francisco, 1985-86, City Cabaret, San Francisco, 1986-87; bd. dirs. San Francisco Coun. Entertainment. Author: "Tune the Grand Up". Recipient Ohio Community Theatre Assn. award, 1980, Theatrewest Acting award, 1983, Bay Area Critics Cir. award, 1984, 85, Cabaret Gold awards San Francisco Coun. Entertainment, 1985,86, Hollywood Dramalogue award, 1985, San Francisco Focus award, 1985. Home and office: 4155 26th St San Francisco CA 94131

GILKERSON, TOM MOFFET, economist, company executive, education consultant; b. Stratford, Calif., May 2, 1910; s. Thomas John and Winifred Nora (Hall) G.; m. Ethel White, Sept. 1, 1931 (div. 1942); children: Tom Moffet Jr., Sandra Lee Gilkerson Sullivan; m. Laura Marion Oberlander, Apr. 29, 1945; children: Obie Grant, Jerry Bruce, David Vance, Andrew Jules. BA in Phys. Edn., U. Ill., 1935; MS in Agrl. Econs., Mont. State U., 1944. Social studies tchr., asst. coach Fergus County High Sch., Lewistown, Mont., 1935-39; researcher, instr. Mont. State U., Bozeman, 1939-44; program dir. Berkeley (Calif.) YMCA, 1944-46; sales mgr. W.T. Rawleigh Co. No. Calif., Oakland, Calif., 1946-50; econ. analyst 6th U.S. Army, San Francisco, 1950-53; sales and dist. mgr. Internat. Corr. Schs., Scranton, Pa., 1953-79; adminstr., editor Bay Area Community Services, Inc., Oakland, 1979-88; pres., author newsletter Alchemics, Berkeley, 1953--; cons. Golden Gate Sch. Lock Tech., Oakland, 1957--; incorporator Emeritus Enterprises, Alameda County, Calif., 1976--; coordinator, interviewer Bay Area Media Ctr. Cable TV, Berkeley, 1980-84. Contbr. to profl. publs . Co-initiator Lewistown Town Meeting, 1935-39; past organizer searchlight vigil Unitarian Ch., Berkeley, past chmn. peace com.; mem. pub. rels. com. Bay Area Community Services, Inc., Alameda, Calif., 1980--, editor newsletter, 1983-86; bd. dirs. Sr. Companions, Oakland, 1980-86; past mem. adv. bd. Alameda County Area on Aging. Recipient citation Oakland Bd. Suprs., 1985, 86, 87. Mem. Am. Soc. Tng. Dirs., Scroll and Quill, Delta Theta Epsilan, Phi Epsilon Kappa, Theta Xi, Toastmasters (Berkeley) (pres. 1975-77, Able Toastmaster award 1979). Home: 917 Tulare Ave Berkeley CA 94707

GILL, DAVID WALTER, theology educator; b. Omaha, Feb. 2, 1946; s. Walter Leonard and Vivian Erna (Wurz) G.; m. Lucia Lynn Paulson, Sept. 9, 1967; children: Jodie Lynn, Jonathan Christopher. BA in History, U. Calif., Berkeley, 1968; MA in History, San Francisco State U., 1971; PhD in Religion and Social Ethics, U. So. Calif., 1979. Co-editor Radix Mag., Berkeley, 1971-73; founder, project dir. New. Coll. Berkeley, 1977-79, dean and asst. prof. Christian Ethics, 1979-82, dean and assoc. prof., 1982-86, pres., prof., 1986—. Author: The Word of God in the Ethics of Jacques Ellul, 1984, Peter the Rock, 1986, The Opening of the Christian Mind, 1989. Mem. Am. Acad. Religion, Pacific Coast Theol. Soc., Soc. Christian Ethics, Evang. Theol. Soc., Conf. on Faith and History. Mem. Evang. Covenant Ch. Office: New Coll Berkeley 2606 Dwight Way Berkeley CA 94704

GILL, GEORGE WILHELM, anthropologist; b. Sterling, Kans., June 28, 1941; s. George Laurance and Florence Louise (Jones) G.; B.A. in Zoology with honors (NSF grantee), U. Kans., 1963, M.Phil. Anthropology (NDEA fellow, NSF dissertation research grantee), 1970, Ph.D. in Anthropology, 1971; m. Pamela Jo Mills, July 26, 1975; children—George Scott, John Ashton, Jennifer Florence, Bryce Thomas. Mem. faculty U. Wyo., Laramie, 1971—, prof. anthropology, 1985—; forensic anthropologist law enforcement agencies, 1972—; sci. leader Easter Island Anthrop. Expdn., 1981. Served to capt. U.S. Army, 1963-67. Recipient J.P. Ellbogen meritorious classroom teaching award, 1983; research grantee U. Wyo., 1972, 78, 82, Nat. Geog. Soc., 1980, Center for Field Research, 1980, Kon-Tiki Mus., Oslo, 1987. Diplomate Am. Bd. Forensic Anthropology (bd. dirs. 1985—). Fellow Am. Acad. Forensic Scis. (sec. phys. anthropology sect. 1985-87, chmn. 1987-88); mem. Am. Assn. Phys. Anthropologists, Current Anthropology (assoc.), Plains Anthrop. Soc., Wyo. Archael. Soc. Republican. Presbyterian. Author articles, chpts. in books. Home: 649 Howe Rd Laramie WY 82070 Office: U Wyo Dept Anthropology Laramie WY 82071

GILL, KEITH HUBERT, lawyer; b. Pocatello, Idaho, May 31, 1929; s. Hubert Samuel and Myrtle Frances (Olsen) G.; m. Glenna Jean Lowery, June 16, 1956; children—Suzanne Marie, Gina Michelle. B.A., Idaho State U., 1952; M.B.A., UCLA, 1962; J.D., U. So. Calif., 1968. Bar: Calif. 1969, U.S. Dist. Ct. (cen. dist.) Calif. 1969, U.S. Ct. Appeals (9th cir.) 1972, U.S. Supreme Ct. 1973, U.S. Tax Ct. 1974. Assoc. Kadison, Pfaelzer, Woodard, Quinn & Rossi, Los Angeles, 1968-73, ptnr., 1973-80; of counsel Mitchell, Silberberg & Knupp, Los Angeles, 1980-81; prin. Rodi, Pollock, Pettker, Galbraith & Phillips, Los Angeles, 1981-85; sole practice, Woodland Hills, Calif., 1985-87, 89—; ptnr. Pelletier, Supancic & Gill, 1987-89; lectr. UCLA Law Sch. Clin. Program; dir. Sunland Ford, Inc. Judge pro tem Los Angeles Mcpl. Ct., 1977—; chmn. ballot measures Town Hall Calif., Los Angeles; mem. World Affairs Council Los Angeles County Art Mus. Bd. dirs. Las Virgenes Ednl. Fund, Calabasas Park Homeowners Assn. Mem. Calif. Bar Assn., Los Angeles County Assn., ABA, Calif. Conf. Dels., Phi Alpha Delta. Republican. Mormon. Office: 21550 Oxnard St Ste 300 Woodland Hills CA 91367

GILL, REBECCA LALOSH, aerospace engineer; b. Brownsboro, Tex., Sept. 17, 1944; d. Milton and Dona Mildred (Magee) La Losh; m. Peter Mohammed Sharma, Sept. 1, 1965 (div.); m. James Fredrick Gill, Mar. 9, 1985; children: Erin, Melissa, Ben. BS in Physics, U. Mich., 1965; MBA, Calif. State U., Northridge, 1980. Tchr., Derby, Kans., 1966; weight analyst Beech Aircraft, Wichita, Kans., 1966; weight engr. Ewing Tech. Design, assigned Boeing-Vertol, Phila., 1966-67, Bell Aerosystems, Buffalo, 1967; design specialist Lockheed-Calif. Co., Burbank, 1968-79; sr. staff engr. Hughes Aircraft Missile Systems, Canoga Park, Calif., 1979-82, project mgr. AMRAAM spl. test and tng. equipment, 1982-85, project mgr. GBU-15 guidance sect., Navy IR Maverick Missile, Tucson, 1985—; sec. Nat. Cinema Corp. Com. chmn. Orgn. for Rehab. through Tng., 1971-75; speaker ednl. and civic groups. Pres. Briarcliffe East Homeowners Assn. Recipient Lockheed award of achievement, 1977. Mem. Soc. Allied Weight Engrs. (dir., sr. v.p., chmn. pub. rels. com.), Aerospace Elec. Soc. (dir.), Nat. Assn. Female Execs, Hughes Mgmt. Club (bd. dirs., chmn. spl. events, chmn. programs, 1st v.p.). Republican. Club: Tucson Racquet. Office: Hughes Aircraft Missile Systems Bldg 805 MS L5A Tucson AZ 85734

GILLAND, BRUCE, guidance counselor, education officer; b. Marion, Ky., Mar. 8, 1933; s. Roy T. and Francis A. (Horning) G.; m. Anita D. Hendrickson, Jan. 31, 1959; children—Cynthia Ann, Brent Stuart, Kristi Faye. B in Gen. Studies, Rollins Coll., 1973. B.S., 1976; BA, SUNY-N.Y.C., 1977; MA, Calif. State U. Consortium-Sacramento, 1979, postgrad. U. Calif., Davis, 1987. Enlisted U.S. Air Force, 1950; ret., 1974; guidance counselor U.S. Army, Korea, 1977-78, 85-87, U.S. Air Force, Malstrom AFB, Mont., 1979, edn. officer, Sunnyvale AFS, Calif., 1980-81, guidance counselor, Travis AFB, Calif., 1982-84. Mem. Am. Personnel and Guidance Assn., Nat. Vocat. Guidance Assn., Am. Vocat. Assn., Am. Mgmt. Assn. Republican. Baptist. Club: DAV. Office: 60th ABG/DPE Travis AFB CA 94535

GILLARD, FREDERICK BUTLER, dentist; b. Winslow, Ariz., Jan. 14, 1910; s. Alfred Ernest and Anno Elizabeth (Killorin) G.; m. Elizabeth Metcalfe, Aug. 6, 1930; children: Carol Anne, Thomas F., James M., William F. BS, Marquette U., 1934, DDS, 1935. Pvt. practice dentistry Milw., 1935-36, Ajo, Ariz., 1936-41, Inglewood, Calif., 1942-55, Phoenix, 1957—. Served to col. U.S. Army, 1955-57. Mem. ADA, Ariz. Dental Assn. (life), Lions, Elks, Dons of Ariz., Ariz. Club, Ariz. Historical (Pioneer). Republican. Home: 7357 E Tuckey Ln Scottsdale AZ 85253 Office: 5051 E Thomas St Phoenix AZ 85018

GILLASPIE, RICHARD C., banker. Pres., chmn. First Nat. Bank Colorado Springs, Colo.; regional v.p. Affiliated Bankshares Colo. Inc., Denver. Office: First Nat Bank PO Box 1699 Colorado Springs CO 80942 *

GILLCRIST, PAUL THOMAS, manufacturing executive, retired naval officer; b. Chgo., Mar. 22, 1929; s. James Joseph and Florence Genevieve (Casey) G.; m. Nancy May Murtagh, Dec. 31, 1955; children—James, Mary, Thomas, Peter. B.S., U.S. Naval Acad., 1952; M.A., Am. U., 1964. Commd. ensign U.S. Navy, 1952, advanced through grades to rear adm., 1979; test pilot 1958-61; comdg. officer Fighter Squadron 53, 1967-68; comdr. Carrier Air Wing 3, 1970-71; comdg. officer Naval Air Sta., Cecil Field, Fla., 1975-76; exec. asst. to asst. sec. research and devel. Dept. Navy, Washington, 1973-74, exec. asst. to undersec., 1974-75; asst. chief of staff U.S. Atlantic Fleet, Norfolk, Va., 1976-78; comdr. Fighter Airborne Early Warning Wing, U.S. Pacific Fleet, San Diego, 1979-81; comdr. naval base USN, San Diego and San Francisco, 1981-82, dir. aviation plans and programs, 1982-83; asst. dep. chief naval ops. (air warfare) USN, Washington, 1983-85; ret. USN, 1985; dir. corp. test and evaluation Northrop Corp., L.A., 1986—. Decorated D.F.C., Bronze Star with oak leaf cluster, Air medal with 12 oak leaf clusters, Legion of Merit with oak leaf cluster, Vietnam Air Gallantry Cross. Mem. Soc. Exptl. Test Pilots (assoc., guest editor Jour. Def. Research 1975). Republican. Roman Catholic. Home: 300 S Lucerne Blvd Los Angeles CA 90020 Office: Northrop Corp 1840 Century Park E Los Angeles CA 90067

GILLE, JOHN CHARLES, scientific researcher; b. Akron, Ohio, Oct. 12, 1934; s. Merrill Charles and Marjorie Ruth (Tragler) G.; m. Ellen Cole Fetter, Aug. 24, 1963; children: Sarah T., Edward P. BS, Yale U., 1956; BA, Cambridge U., 1958, MA, 1966; PhD, MIT, 1964. Postdoctoral researcher Harvard U., Cambridge, Mass., 1964; from asst. to assoc. prof. Fla. State U., Tallahassee, 1964-72; sr. scientist, sect. head Nat. Ctr. Atmospheric Research, Boulder, Colo., 1972—; mem. coms. Nat. Acad. Scis., Washington, 1970—; mem. adv. groups NASA, Washington, 1969—; mem. Com. on Space Research, 1974—; sabbatical U. Kyoto, Japan, 1988. Contbr.

articles to profl. jours. Recipient Tech. Achievement award Nat. Ctr. Atmospheric Research, 1978, Exceptional Sci. Achievement award NASA, 1982. Fellow AAAS (electorate nominating com. 1986-89), Am. Meteorol. Soc. (assoc. editor Jour. Atmospheric Sci., 1974-79); mem. Am. Geophys. Union (assoc. editor Jour. Geophys. Research 1980-83), Internat. Union Geology and Geophysics (internat. com. meteorol. upper atmosphere 1975-83, internat. radiation commn. 1979-87), Phi Beta Kappa, Sigma Xi. Office: Nat Ctr Atmospheric Rsch PO Box 3000 Boulder CO 80307

GILLELAND, RICHARD A., health care company executive. Chmn., chief exec. officer Am. Med. Internat. Inc., Beverly Hills, Calif., 1989—. Office: Am Med Internat Inc 414 N Camden Dr Beverly Hills CA 90210 *

GILLEN, KATHERINE ELIZABETH, librarian; b. Washington, D.C., May 16, 1951; d. Hugh Chisholm and Norma Marie (Provost) G. BS, U. Md., 1973, MLS, 1976; MA, U. Phoenix, 1989. Librarian Maricopa County Community Coll., Phoenix, 1982-84; librarian reference and serials Mesa (Ariz.) Pub. Library, 1981—. Author short stories to mags. Mem. AAAS (reviewer 1982—), Ariz. State Library Assn., Serials Specialists of Maricopa County, Mensa (book reviewer Phoenix chpt. 1987—). Home: 1010 N 26th St Mesa AZ 85213

GILLEN, ROBERT LEONARD, communications executive; b. St. Paul, Aug. 19, 1946; s. Arthur F. and Lois (Powers) G.; m. Mary Margaret Lenertz, June 1, 1968 (div. 1979), 1 child Aric C.; m. Jean M. King, Nov. 8, 1980; children: Patrick, Timothy. BA in Journalism, Coll. St. Thomas, 1968; MSJ, Northwestern U., 1969. Editor Tennis Trade/Tennis Times, Mpls., 1972-74; editorial dir. Chilton Publishing Co., Radnor, Pa., 1974-79; exec. editor SKI Magazine, Times Mirror, N.Y.C., 1979-81; rsch. dir. Best Pub. Co., N.Y.C., 1981-82; editor SKI BUSINESS Mag., Dairen, Conn., 1982-84, NON-FOODS MERCHANDISING, N.Y.C., 1984-85; communications dir. Crested Butte (Colo.) Mt. Resort, 1985—; pub. rels. dir. USAF/NATO Joint Exercise, Germany & France, 1972; press dir. U.S. Pro Indoor Tennis Cham., Phila., 1977-79, Subaru U.S. Alpine Championships, Crested Butte, 1986—; mktg. dir. Ski Industry Newsletter, Colo. & N.Y., 1988—. Author, editor: Winning Tennis, 1978; editor: The Tennis Book, 1982, The Ski Book, 1984. V.p. Sta. KBUT Pub. Radio, 1988—. Capt. USAF, 1969-72. Mem. Am. Soc. Travel Editors, U.S. Ski Writers, Ea. Ski Writers (bd. dirs., 1984-85), U.S. Tennis Writers Assn (1st v.p., 1979), Crested Butte C. of C. (bd. dirs., 1987—), Crested Butte Nordic Coun. (sec. 1989). Roman Catholic. Office: Crested Butte Mt Resort PO Box A Crested Butte CO 81225

GILLETTE, DEAN, educator, consultant; b. Chgo., Aug. 11, 1925; s. Frank Kenneth and Ruth (Whitmore) G.; m. Helen Klamt, Dec. 19, 1949; 1 child, Troy. B.S. in Chemistry, Oreg. State U., 1948; M.A. in Math., U. Calif.-Berkeley, 1950, Ph.D. in Math., 1953. Mem. tech. staff Bell Labs., Holmdel, N.J., 1953-84; exec. dir. labs. Bell Labs., 1966-84; prof. Harvey Mudd Coll., Claremont, Calif., 1984-88; Henry R. Luce prof. info. technology and soc. Harvey Mudd Coll.; prof. Claremont McKenna Coll., Calif., 1984-88; prof. info. sci. Claremont Grad. Sch., 1988—; mem. coms. Dept. Def.; mem. coms. Office Tech. Assessment; mem. coms. Nat. Rsch. Coun.. Author papers on math., systems engring., mgmt.; editorial com. Networks, Telecom. Policy. Served with USN, 1944-46; PTO. Mem. IEEE , Am. Math. Soc., Soc. Indsl. and Applied Math. Repubican. Office: Claremont Grad Sch Dept Info Sci Claremont CA 91711

GILLETTE, ERIC ALLISON, computer scientist, consultant; b. Rochester, N.Y., May 4, 1935; s. George A. and Mildred (Lockwood) G. BA, Alfred U., 1958; MBA, Syracuse U., 1960. Computer systems analyst Ford Motor Co., Dearborn, Mich., 1960-67; project mgr. Bell & Howell, Lincolnwood, Ill., 1967-69; comml. systems mgr. G.D. Searle, Skokie, Ill., 1969-74; internal cons. Fed. Res. Bank of Chgo., 1974-78; sr. systems info. specialist Computer Scis. Corp., El Segundo, Calif., 1978-84; sr. systems specialist Beneficial Standard, L.A., 1985-88, Exec. Life, L.A., 1988—; assoc. prof. Calif. State U., Dominguez Hills. Mem. Assn. Systems Mgmt., Am. Prodn. Inventory Control Soc.

GILLETTE, W. MICHAEL, judge; b. Seattle, Dec. 29, 1941; s. Elton George and Hazel Irene (Hand) G.; m. Susan Dandy Marmaduke, 1989; children: Kevin, Saima. AB in German, Polit. Sci., Whitman Coll., 1963; LLB, Harvard U., 1966. Bar: Oreg. 1966, U.S. Dist. Ct. Oreg. 1966, U.S. Ct. Appeals (9th cir.) 1966, Samoa 1969, U.S. Supreme Ct. 1970, U.S. Dist. Ct. Vt. 1973. Assoc. Rives & Rogers, Portland, Oreg., 1966-67; dep. dist. atty. Multnomah County, Portland, 1967-69; asst. atty. gen. Govt. of Am. Samoa, 1969-71, State of Oreg., Salem, 1971-77; judge Oreg. Ct. Appeals, Salem, 1977-86; assoc. justice Oreg. Supreme Ct., Salem, 1986—. Office: Oreg Supreme Ct Supreme Ct Bldg Salem OR 97310

GILLIAM, CHARLES STANLEY, columnist; b. Sacramento, Apr. 29, 1924; s. Charles Bilby and Flora Helen (Rippon) G.; m. Joan Cecelia Jonen, July 29, 1950; children: John Anthony, Ann Dolora Banks, Stuart Charles. BA, St. Mary's Coll., Moraga, Calif., 1945; MA, Calif. State U., Sacramento, 1957. Cert. tchr., Calif. Instr. Grant Tech. Coll. and Grant Union High Sch., Sacramento, 1948-65; copy editor, dealer Sacramento Bee, 1965-78, columnist, 1978—; regent Christian Bros. Sch., 1978-81; judge Calif Newspaper Pubs. Assn., 1965—. Mem. Calif. Retired Tchrs. Assn., The Newspaper Guild, St. Mary's Coll. Alumni Assn. (Sacramento chpt.), Sigma Delta Chi. Democrat. Roman Catholic. Lodge: Elks. Office: Sacramento Bee PO Box 15779 Sacramento CA 95852

GILLIAM, DENNIS EUGENE, public administrator; b. Cheyenne, Wyo., Jan. 4, 1945; s. Andrew Eugene and Kathryn (Innes) G. AB, U. Calif.-Berkeley, 1967; MPA, U. Southern Calif., 1976. Tchr. Modesto (Calif.) City Schs., 1969-73; forms systems analyst Calif. Dept. of Social Svcs., Sacramento, 1974-79, contracts officer, 1980—; project adminstr. Immigration, Reform, Health and Welfare Agy., Sacramento, 1988—. Recipient Cost Savs. prize Am. Pub. Welfare Assn., 1979. Mem. U. Calif. Alumni Club Sacramento (bd. dirs. 1988-89), Sacramento Old City Assn. (sec. 1982). Democrat. Home: 8409 Sunblaze Way Sacramento CA 95823 Office: Calif Dept Social Svcs 744 P St Sacramento CA 95814

GILLIN, KATHRYN LORRAINE, realtor; b. Vallejo, Calif., Oct. 23, 1945; d. Dana and Betty Lucille (Jones) Roberts; m. James R. Gillin Dec. 13, 1963 (div. June 1980); 1 child, Christina Lynn. BA, Sacramento State Coll., 1967. Sales assoc. Century 21 Real Estate, Vallejo, 1980-82, sales mgr., 1980—; bd. dirs. Solano Bd. of Realtors, (pres. 1988, v.p. 1987) Vallejo; bd. dirs. Calif. Assn. Realtors, Sacramento, 1986-89. Author: My Life in South Africa, 1986. Bd. dirs. Vallejo Women's Bowling Assn., 1984-86. Mem. Nat. Assn. Realtors (bd. dirs.), Calif. Assn. Realtors, Vallejo C. of C. Republican. Club: Blue Rock Golf (Vallejo). Home: PO Box 4385 Vallejo CA 94590 Office: Century 21 Egidio Realty Inc 95 Flemingtowne Ctr Vallejo CA 94589

GILLIN, PHILIP HOWARD, lawyer; b. Council Bluffs, Iowa, Apr. 11, 1937; s. Nathan E. and Louise (Herzoff) G.; student U. Ariz., 1955-57, U. Calif., San Francisco, 1957-59; J.D., U Santa Clara, 1960; m. Joycelyn Hall, July 4, 1977; children—Jamie Lynn, Julia Ann. Andrea Leigh. Admitted to Calif. bar, 1961; mem. firm Gillin & Scott, Hollywood, Calif., 1959-60; sole practice law, Hollywood, 1970-75; mem. firm Gillin, Gottesman & Menes, Los Angeles, 1975-81; sole practice, 1981—; tchr. real estate law Calif. Continuing Edn. for the Bar; pres. Church Lane Music Inc., Berkeley Square Music Inc., Kings Road Music; pres. Scott Gillin Ltd. Chmn. March of Dimes, Sherman Oaks, 1964-69. Mem. Am. (nat. sec. student assn. 1958-59), Hollywood (dir. 1963-66, sec. 1967-68, pres. 1971) bar assns., Century City Bar Assn., Los Angeles Bar Assn., Calif. Copywright Conf. Office: 1901 Ave of the Stars #1600 Los Angeles CA 90067

GILLIO, CAROLYN IRENE, psychotherapist; b. Wells, Minn., Jan. 1, 1931; d. William Frederick and Antonia Willemina (Augst) Moll; m. Cesar Padilla, June 28, 1953 (div. 1967); children: Paula, Mark, Julie; m. Frank Gillio, May 24, 1969. BA, Gustavus-Adolphus Coll., 1952; postgrad., U. Chgo., 1952-53; MSW, U. Calif., Berkeley, 1955. Psychotherapist Agnews St. Hosp., San Jose, Calif., 1955-56; supr. San Jose Family Services, 1956-68; Psychotherapist Mid-Peninsula Psychotherapy Clinic, Sunnyvale, Calif., 1968-76; pvt. practice psychotherapy Sunnyvale, 1976—; adj. instr. U. Calif.-Santa Cruz Extension, Sunnyvale, 1979-80; cons. Santa Clara County (Calif.) Mental Health, 1975-78, other orgns. in field. Mem. Cen. Core Comprehensive Mental Health Planning Commn., Santa Clara, Calif., 1965-67; chmn. Sunnyvale Coordinating Council, 1968; bd. dirs. No. County Social Planning Council, Santa Clara, 1968-69. Recipient Disting. Service award Santa Clara County Family Service, 1968; named Disting. Woman on Mid-Peninsula, Girls Club of the Mid-Peninsula, 1973. Fellow Nat. Assn. Social Workers (bd. dirs. 1970-71), Soc. Clin. Social Workers (legis. com. 1975-77), Soc. Clin. Social Work (bd. dirs. 1977-81); mem. AAUW (mem. com. 1986-87, book reviewer 1988), Alphas. Home: 435 Logan St Santa Cruz CA 95062 Office: 869 Cumberland Dr Sunnyvale CA 94087

GILLIS, JOHN WILLIAM, computer software/hardware company executive; b. Lexington, Ky., Mar. 9, 1937; s. John Louis and Mamie (Hawkins) G.; m. Patsy J. Gillis; children: John Jr., Felicia Mayott. AA, E. L.A. Coll., 1968; BA, Calif. State U., 1970; MS, U. So. Calif., L.A., 1973. Mail carrier U.S. Postal Svc., N.Y.C., 1959-60; police officer Port Authority N.Y., N.Y.C., 1960-62; police officer, lt. Police Dept., L.A., 1962-88; chief exec. officer Gillis Enterprises, Alhambra, Calif., 1988—; lectr. Community Coll. Dist., L.A., 1976-78. Developer office automation L.A. Police Dept., 1974. Bd. dirs. Gov.'s Roundtable on Crime Prevention, Sacramento, 1988, Justice for Homicide Victims, Beverly Hills, Calif., 1986; bd. dirs., co-founder Coalition on Victim Equal Rights, L.A., 1988; pres. HUD Adv. Bd., Alhambra, 1985—. With U.S. Army, 1955-58. Recipient Disting. Svc. award Bd. Suprs. L.A. County, 1988, Svc. to Law Enforcement award Calif. Senate, 1988, Dedicated Svc. L.A. City Coun., 1988, Community Svc. Alhambra City Coun., 1988. Mem. Assn. Black Law Enforcement Execs., Calif. Peace Officers Assn., Nat. Orgn. Victim Assistance, Western Govtl. Reseach Assn., Alhambra C. of C. (computer cons. 1988—), Optimist Club, Rotary (sec. Alhambra chpt. 1989—). Office: Gillis Enterprises PO Box 1001 Alhambra CA 91802

GILLIS, PAUL LEONARD, accountant; b. Montevideo, Minn., Nov. 20, 1953; s. Joseph Hans and Verna Ruth (Sjolie) G.; m. Deborah Ann Roller, Sept. 9, 1978. BA, Western State Coll., 1975; MS, Colo. State U., 1976. CPA, Colo. Tax cons. Price Waterhouse, Denver, 1976-78; tax mgr. Price Waterhouse, Singapore, 1978-82; internat. tax mgr. Price Waterhouse, San Francisco, 1982-84; sr. mgr. Price Waterhouse, Denver, 1984-88, mng. tax ptnr., 1988—; dir. Colo.-Taiwan Investment Council; lectr. World Trade Inst., San Francisco, 1982-84. Author: Accounting for Income Tax, 1988. Recipient 50 for Colo. award, Colo. Assn. Commerce and Industry. Fellow Colo. Soc. CPAs; mem. AICPAs, Am. Club (Singapore) (treas. 1981-82), Pinehurst Country Club, Denver Club. Democrat. Lutheran. Home: 5320 W Princeton Denver CO 80235 Office: Price Waterhouse 950 17th St Denver CO 80202

GILLISS, CATHERINE LYNCH, nurse, educator; b. New Britain, Conn., Apr. 18, 1949; d. James A. and Lorraine (Balocki) Lynch; m. Thomas P. Gilliss, June 6, 1970. BS in Nursing, Duke U., 1971; MS in Nursing, Cath. U. Am., Washington, 1974; D of Nursing Sci., U. Calif., 1983. Cert. adult nurse practitioner, 1979. Staff and charge nurse Duke U. Med. Ctr., Durham, 1971, VA Hosp., Washington, 1971-72; asst. prof. U. Md., Balt., 1974-76, The Cath. U. Am., 1976-79; assoc. prof. U. Portland, Oreg., 1979-83; lectr. in nursing Sonoma State U., Rohnert Park, Calif., 1983-84; asst. prof. U. Calif., San Francisco, 1984—; bd. dirs. Nat. Council Family Relations, St. Paul. Co-author Toward a Science of Family Nursing, 1989; contbr. articles to profl. jours. Recipient NRSA award NIH, 1981-83, Pres. fellow U. Calif. Regents, 1983, Disting. Practitioner Nat. Acad. Practice, 1985; NIH rsch. grantee, 1986-89. Mem. Am. Nurses' Assn., Am. Heart Assn. Office: U Calif San Francisco Sch Nursing San Francisco CA 94143-0606

GILLMAR, STANLEY FRANK, lawyer; b. Honolulu, Aug. 17, 1935; s. Stanley Eric and Ruth (Scudder) G.; m. Constance Joan Sedgwick; children: Sara Tamsin, Amy Katherine. AB cum laude with high honors, Brown U., 1957; LLB, Harvard U., 1963. Bar: Calif. 1963. Ptnr. Graham & James, San Francisco, 1970—. Co-author: How To Be An Importer and Pay For Your World Travels, 1979; co-pub.: Travelers Guide to Importing, 1980. Sec. Calif. Council Internat. Trade, 1973—; mem. Mayor San Francisco Adv. Council Econ. Devel., 1976-82; mem. Title IX Loan Bd., 1982—, sec. 1986—. Served with USNR, 1957-60. Mem. ABA, Calif. State Bar, Bar Assn. San Francisco. Clubs: Bankers (San Francisco); Villa Taverna, Inverness Yacht. Office: Graham & James 1 Maritime Pla Alcoa Bldg Ste 300 San Francisco CA 94111

GILLMER, VIRGINIA, marketing account manager; b. Coral Gables, Fla., Aug. 4, 1949; d. Richard Earle and Margaret (Vittur) G. BA in Sociology, U. South Fla., 1971; MSW, Fla. State U., 1977. Social worker Fla. Dept. Health/Rehab. Svcs., Miami, 1973-75; child abuse supr. N.Mex. Social Svcs. div. Human Svcs., Albuquerque, 1977-78; bur. chief children's med. svcs. N.Mex. Health & Environ. Dept., Santa Fe, 1978-83; div. dir. Human Svcs. Dept., N.Mex. Social Svcs., Santa Fe, 1983-85; mgmt. cons. Santa Fe, 1985-86; account mgr. Digital Equipment Corp., Albuquerque, 1986—; adv. bd. Nat. Resources Ctr. on Family Based Svcs., Iowa City, 1983-86, Am. Indian Law Ctr., Albuquerque, 1984-85;. Mem. League of Women Voters, Albuquerque, 1986—, Sierra Club, Albuquerque, 1986—, Hist. Preservation Soc., Albuquerque, 1985—, NOW, Albuquerque, 1975—. Recipient Svc. award Pediatric Pulmonary Ctr., U. N.Mex. Med. Sch., Albuquerque, 1983. Mem. Acad. Cert. Social Workers, Nat. Assn. Social Workers (pres. N.Mex. chpt. 1983-1984, bd. dirs. 1979-82), Devel. Disabilities Planning Council N.Mex., Am. Pub. Welfare Assn., Am. Pub. Health Assn. Democrat. Episcopalian. Home: 1328 Camino Ecuestre NW Albuquerque NM 87107 Office: Digital Equipment Corp Box 499 Albuquerque NM 87103

GILLOW, GEORGE BRACEY, electrical engineer; b. Potrerillos, Chile, Oct. 27, 1945; s. Joseph Robert and Annie Rachel (Taylor) G.; came to U.S., 1957; B.S. in Elec. Engring., San Diego State U., 1970, M.S. in Elec. Engring., 1973; m. Pamela Jean Kennedy, Sept. 24, 1982. Project leader, design central processing units for computer, advanced devel. dept. Data Processing div. NCR Corp., San Diego, 1970-78; group mgr., design of large central processing units for computer Nat. Semi-condr. Corp., San Diego, 1978-80; with JRS Industries, San Diego, 1980-82; mgr. engring. DDG Corp., San Diego, 1982—; v.p. Digidyne Corp., San Diego, 1983—; dir. engring. Questron Corp., 1984-86; instr. Southwestern Coll., evenings, 1974, 75. Chmn. Environ. Control Commn. Chula Vista, 1975-78, chmn. Hist. Sites Bd., 1975-78; mem. Chula Vista City Council, 1978-82, vice mayor, 1979-80. Mem. Tau Beta Pi. Democrat. Home: 250 Camino Del Cerro Grande Bonita CA 92002 Office: 3910 Sorrento Valley Blvd San Diego CA 92121

GILMAN, JOHN JOSEPH, national laboratory senior research scientist; b. St. Paul, Dec. 22, 1925; s. Alexander Falk and Florence Grace (Colby) G.; m. Pauline Marie Harms, June 17, 1950 (div. Dec. 1968); children: Pamela Ann, Gregory George, Cheryl Elizabeth; m. Gretchen Marie Sutter, June 12, 1976; 1 son, Brian Alexander. B.S., Ill. Inst. Tech., 1946, M.S., 1948; Ph.D., Columbia, 1952. Research metallurgist Gen. Electric Co., Schenectady, 1952-60; prof. engring. Brown U., Providence, 1960-63; prof. physics and metallurgy U. Ill., Urbana, 1963-68; dir. Materials Research Center Allied Chem. Corp., Morristown, N.J., 1968-78; dir. Corp. Devel. Center, 1978-80; mgr. corp. research Standard Oil Co. (Ind.), Naperville, Ill., 1980-85; assoc. dir. Lawrence Berkeley Lab., Calif., 1985-87; mem. solid state physics com. Nat. Acad. Scis., 1979-82. Author: Micromechanics of Flow in Solids, 1969; Editor: The Art and Science of Growing Crystals, 1963, (with D.C. Drucker) Fracture of Solids, 1963, Atomic and Electronic Structures of Metals, 1967; editorial bd.: Jour. Applied Physics, 1969-72; Contbr. papers, articles to tech. jours. Served as ensign USNR, 1943-46. Recipient Mathewson gold medal Am. Inst. Metal Engrs., 1959, Disting. Service award Alumni Assn. Ill. Inst. Tech., 1962, Application to Practice award, 1985. Fellow Am. Phys. Soc., Am. Soc. for Metals (Campbell lectr. 1966); mem. Nat. Acad. Engring., Phi Kappa Phi, Tau Beta Pi. Home: 780 Spruce St Berkeley CA 94707 Office: U Calif Lawrence Berkeley Lab Berkeley CA 94720

GILMAN, PETER A., national laboratory administrator, scientist. BA in Physics, Harvard U., 1962; MS in Meteorology, MIT, 1964, PhD, 1966. Asst. prof. U. Colo., Boulder, 1966-69, lectr., 1970-77; various positions Nat. Ctr. for Atmospheric Research, Boulder, 1969—, sr. scientist, 1973—, dir. high altitude obs., 1987—; adj. prof. U. Colo., 1977—; chmn. program com. div. advanced sci. computing NSF, 1986-88. NASA trainee, 1964-66; Ford Found. fellow, 1962-64, NSF fellow, 1962; recipient Detur prize, 1960. Mem. Am. Meteorol. Soc., AAAS, Am. Astron. Soc., Am. Geophys. Union, Ineternat. Astron. Union. Office: Nat Ctr Atmospheric Rsch High Altitude Obs 1850 Table Mesa Dr Boulder CO 80307

GILMAN, RICHARD CARLETON, college president; b. Cambridge, Mass., July 28, 1923; s. George Phillips Brooks and Karen Elise (Theller) G.; m. Lucille Young, Aug. 28, 1948 (dec. 1978); children: Marsha, Bradley Morris, Brian Potter, Blair Tucker; m. Sarah Gale, Dec. 28, 1984 (dec. 1986). B.A., Dartmouth, 1944; student, New Coll., U. London, Eng., 1947-48; Ph.D. (Borden Parker Bowne fellow philosophy), Boston U., 1952, L.H.D., 1969; LL.D., Pomona Coll., 1966, U. So. Calif., 1968, Coll. Idaho, 1968; L.H.D., Chapman Coll., 1984, Occidental Coll., 1988. Teaching fellow religion Dartmouth, 1948; mem. faculty Colby Coll., 1950-56, assoc. prof. philosophy, 1955-56; exec. dir. Nat. Council Religion Higher Edn., New Haven, 1956-60; dean coll., prof. philosophy Carleton Coll., 1960-65; pres. Occidental Coll., Los Angeles, 1965-88, pres. emeritus, 1988—; Past bd. dirs. Am. Coun. on Edn., Assn. Am. Colls., Assn. Ind. Calif. Colls. and Univs., Coun. for Fin. Aid to Edn., Coun. on Postsecondary Accreditation, Nat. Coun. Ind. Colls. and Univs., Ind. Coll. Funds Am.; mem. Intergovtl. Adv. Coun. on Edn., 1980-84; Pres.'s Commn. NCAA, 1983-87; exec. asst. and couselor to sec. of edn., 1979-80. Past bd. dirs. Calif. Mus. Found., L.A. World Affairs Coun., Westridge Sch.; bd. dirs. Cape of Good Hope Found., Exec. Svc. Corps of So. Calif., S.W. Mus., Pacific Am. Income Shares. With USNR, 1944-46. Fellow Soc. Values in Higher Edn.; mem. Newcomen Soc., Calif. C. of C. (past bd. dirs.), Calif. Club Los Angeles, Phi Beta Kappa. Home: 131 Annandale Rd Pasadena CA 91105

GILMARTIN, KEVIN JARVUS, social scientist; b. Morristown, N.J., Dec. 16, 1947; s. Thomas Maran and Cornelia Kahle (Peck) G.; m. Barbara Lynn Bessey, Jan. 18, 1975. BA, Lawrence U., 1970; MS, Carnegie-Mellon U., 1971, PhD, 1974. Postdoctoral fellow Carnegie-Mellon U., Pitts., 1974-75; assoc. rsch. scientist Am. Insts. for Rsch., Palo Alto, Calif., 1975-77, rsch. scientist, 1977-79, sr. rsch. scientist, 1979-83, prin. rsch. scientist, 1983-88, sr. rsch. fellow, 1988—; dir. Social Indicators Rsch. Program, Palo Alto, Litigation Support Program, Palo Alto; dir. Applied Behavioral Sci. Group, Palo Alto, 1988—. Author: Social Indicators: An Annotated Bibliography of Current Literature, 1979, Handbook of Social Indicators, 1980, Monitoring Educational Outcomes and Public Attitudes, 1982, Agencies Working Together: A Guide To Coordination and Planning, 1982. Vol. ranger Henry W. Coe State Park, Morgan Hill, Calif., 1989—. NSF fellow, 1970-74. Mem. Law and Soc. Assn., AAAS, Am. Ednl. Rsch. Assn., Pine Ridge Assn., Calif. Acad. Sci., Phi Beta Kappa, Sigma Xi, Phi Kappa Tau (pres. 1969-70). Democrat. Home: 127 Glenwood Ave Woodside CA 94062 Office: Am Insts for Rsch PO Box 1113 Palo Alto CA 94302

GILMORE, CHRISTOPHER JOHN, marketing professional; b. Denver, Dec. 25, 1961; s. William Francis and Mary Adell (Larsen) G. AS, Mesa Coll., 1983. With Vivid Color, 1985—, v.p. mktg., 1988—. Fellow Soc. Photo Finishing Engrs., Photo Mktg. Assn. Republican. Roman Catholic. HOme: 3000 S High St Denver CO 80210 Office: Vivid Color 816 Federal Blvd Denver CO 80204

GILMORE, JOHN THOMAS, college dean; b. Alamosa, Colo., July 24, 1945; s. William Cammon and Lenora Martha (Steffens) G.; m. Patrice Diane Lester, Sept. 29, 1970; children: Jeffrey, Mark, Erin. BA, Adams State Coll., 1967, MA, 1968; PhD, Colo. State U., 1976. Asst. v.p. 1st Nat. Bank, Alamosa, 1970-73; econ. devel. specialist So. Colo. Econ. Devel. Dist., Alamosa, 1973-76; asst. prof. Sch. Bus. Adams State Coll., Alamosa, 1976-78, dean, 1978—; bd. dirs. San Luis Valley Fed. Savs. & Loan, Alamosa. Contbr. articles to profl. jours. Chmn. bd. dirs. San Luis Valley Ctr. for Handicapped, 1971-77; mem. Alamosa Devel. Corp., 1973-76, Six County Area Regional Devel. Commn., 1982-84; chmn. fin. com. Ch. of Sacred Heart, Alamosa, 19756. Mem. Midwest Finance Assn., Alamosa C. of C. (bd. dirs. 1981-84), Small Bus. Devel. Ctr. Network. Democrat. Home: 3666 S 105th St Alamosa CO 81101 Office: Adams State Coll Sch Bus Alamosa CO 81102

GILMORE, JOHN VAUGHN, JR., psychologist; b. Boston, Aug. 6, 1948; s. John Vaughn and Eunice Chandler (Crocker) G. MDiv, Gordon-Conwell Sem., 1976; MTh, Princeton Theol. Sem., 1977; PhD, Mich. State U., 1984. Lic. psychologist, Calif. Clin. chaplain intern Princeton (N.J.) U. Med. Ctr., 1976-77; counseling intern Personality Dynamics, Southfield, Mich., 1978-79; psychologist Profl. Psychol. Cons., East Lansing, Mich., 1980-81, Los Angeles County Dept. Mental Health, L.A., 1984-85; clin. psychology intern Psychol. Ctr., Pasadena, Calif., 1981-82; adminstrv. dir. I-Can Program, Pasadena, 1982-84; supervising psychologist Pacific Clinics, Pasadena, 1985-87; pres. John V. Gilmore Psychology Corp., Covina, Calif., 1987—. Ednl. Testing Svc. rsch. grantee, 1976. Mem. Am. Psychol. Assn., Calif. Psychol. Assn., Am. Soc. for Psychology and Law. Office: 260 S Glendora Ave Ste 103 West Covina CA 91790

GILMORE, MIKAL GEORGE, critic, journalist, author; b. Portland, Oreg., Feb. 9, 1951; s. Frank Harry and Bessie (Brown) G.; m. Erin Cowley, Aug. 21, 1982 (div. 1985). Student, Portland State U., 1969-72. Freelance writer Rolling Stone Mag., San Francisco, 1976-77; assoc. editor Rolling Stone Mag., Los Angeles, 1977-80, contbg. editor, 1980—; music editor L.A. Weekly, Los Angeles, 1980-82; music critic Los Angeles Herald Examiner, 1982-87; freelance journalist, author Los Angeles and N.Y.C., 1987—. Author non-fiction history rock group Grateful Dead, 1988. Recipient Deems Taylor award ASCAP, N.Y., 1983, 84. Democrat. Mormon. Home: 834 N Sweetzer Los Angeles CA 90069

GILMORE, SUSAN ASTRID LYTLE, speech and language pathologist; b. Phila., July 12, 1942; d. Ford Bertrand and Astrid Elizabeth (Hammerstrom) Lytle; m. Stuart Irby Gilmore, June 6, 1970 (div. Dec. 1981); 1 child, Ford Lytle. BA, U. Pacific, 1964, MA, 1965; PhD, Ohio U., 1968. Cert. pub. sch. adminstr., elem. tchr., speech-lang. pathologist, Calif. Asst. prof. spl. edn., speech-lang. pathology La. State U., Baton Rouge, 1968-76, assoc. prof., 1976-79; supr. spl. edn. Sacramento City Unified Sch. Dist., 1979—, acting adminstrv. specialist Spl. Edn. Dept., 1988—; cons. State Dept Health, Baton Rouge, 1970-75, State Dept. Hosps., Baton Rouge, 1973-75; instr. U. Pacific, Stockton, Calif., 1979, ind. examiner Sacramento City Unified Sch. Dist., 1979; acting adminstrv. specialist Spl. Edn. Dept. Sacremento City Unified Sch. Dist., 1988—. Editor: (asst.) Lang., Speech and Hearing Services in Schs., 1983—; contbr. articles to profl. jours. Vestry mem. Trinity Episcopal Cathedral Ch., Sacramento, 1983-85, altar guild mem. 1980—; bd. dirs. Friends of People With Chronic Mental Illness, Sacramento, 1983-85. Mem. Assn. Calif. Sch. Adminstrs., Am. Speech-Lang.-Hearing Assn., Calif. Speech-Lang.-Hearing Assn. (cert. of appreciations 1985—), Council for Exceptional Children (sec.), Am. Assn. Mental Deficiency, Kappa Alpha Theta (pres. 1961-62), Phi Delta Kappa. Republican. Home: 6333 Driftwood St Sacramento CA 95831 Office: Sacramento City Unified Sch Dist 4701 Joaquin Way Sacramento CA 95822

GILMORE, TIMOTHY JONATHAN, executive recruiter; b. Orange, Calif., June 24, 1949; s. James and Margaret (Swanson) G.; m. Blanche Jean Panter, Sept. 3, 1984; children: Erin, Sean and Brian (twins). BA, St. Mary's Coll., Moraga, Calif., 1971. Adminstrv. asst. Gov. Ronald Reagan, Sacramento, Calif., 1971-73; salesman Penn Mutual, Anaheim, Calif., 1973-76; asst. devel. dir. St. Mary's Coll., Moraga, 1976-81; devel. dir. St. Alphonsus Hosp., Boise, Idaho, 1981-83; adminstr. Blaine County Hosp., Hailey, Idaho, 1983-86; exec. dir. Poudre Hosp. Found., Ft. Collins, Colo., 1986-87; nat. recruiting dir. Power Securities Corp., Denver, 1987-89; pres. Gilmore and Assocs., Ft. Collins, 1989—. Republican. Roman Catholic. Lodge: Kiwanis (pres. Moraga club 1980-81, sec. Boise club 1982-83). Home: 2914 Bassick St Fort Collins CO 80526

GILPIN, CHARLES HARRY, tax accountant; b. Saxton, Mo., May 21, 1927; s. Bernard Vincent and Mary (Baldwin) G; m. Shirley Ann Wilson, Nov. 23, 1956; 1 child, Cynthia Gilpin Miller. BS, U. Calif., Berkeley, 1959; postgrad., Golden Gate U., San Francisco, 1974, U. Mo., 1947-50. Systems rep. Burroughs Corp., San Francisco, 1959-67; treas. Mail Delivery Svc., Inc., San Francisco, Calif., 1967-72; sales rep. The Research Inst. Am., San Leandro, 1972-78; cons. Charles H. Gilpin, San Leandro, 1977-78; v.p. Clyde

B. Mitchell & Assocs., Hayward, Calif., 1978-84; owner Charles H. Gilpin, San Leandro, 1984—. Sgt.-maj. U.S. Army, 1946-47. Mem. Calif. Soc. Enrolled Agts., Nat. Assn. Enrolled Agts., Nat. Assn. Accts. (bd. dirs. 1970-71), Cal 23 Club (v.p. 1953-54). Republican. Home: 855 Lee Ave San Leandro CA 94577 Office: 897 MacArthur Blvd #105 San Leandro CA 94577

GILSON, JAMES RUSSELL, lawyer; b. Cleve., Dec. 27, 1951; s. Richard Allen and Barbara (Rose) G.; m. Nancy E. Holland, Sept. 24, 1983. BA, Wesleyan U., Middletown, Conn., 1974; MA in Urban Studies, Occidental Coll., Los Angeles, 1975; JD, Washington U., St. Louis, Mo., 1978. Bar: D.C. 1978, Calif. 1983. Spl. asst. to gen. counsel U.S. Dept. Transp., Washington, 1978-80; lawyer U.S. CAB, Washington, 1980-81; sr. dep. to chmn. bd. suprs. Los Angeles county, Los Angeles, 1981-87; lawyer Tuttle & Taylor, Los Angeles, 1987—. Bd. dirs. Coro Found. (fellow 1974-75), Marina Found., 1983-84, Beverly-Roxbury Assn., 1987—. Mem. Los Angeles Bar Assn., ABA, Wesleyan U. Alumni Assn., Order of the Coif. Office: Tuttle & Taylor 355 S Grand Ave 40th Floor Los Angeles CA 90071

GILTZOW, RAYMOND ALAN, architect; b. Salt Lake City, Dec. 19, 1944; s. Frederick Harold and Margaret (Hansen) G.; m. Sheila Giltzow, Sept. 21, 1968 (div. Oct. 1974); m. Benita Elaine Shaw, Nov. 27, 1976; children: Camden Shaw, Jeanne Shaw. BArch, U. Idaho, 1970. Registered architect, Idaho. Draftsman Pritchard and Blanton, Moscow, Idaho, 1968-69, Cline, Smull, Hamill, Shaw, Boise, Idaho, 1969-71; jr. partner Thurber, Marler, Boise, Idaho, 1971-73; ptnr. Zabala, Giltzow, Boise, Idaho, 1973-76; pres. Zabala, Giltzow, Albanese, Boise, Idaho, 1976--. Mem. Boise City Historic Preservation Commn., 1985--; v.p. Idaho Historic Preservation Council, 1985--. Recipient numerous awards for drawings and watercolors; Dropping scholar, 1967. Mem. AIA (corp.); (chmn. ethics com. Idaho, 1976-79, design awards 1988; mem. nat. historic resources com. 1979-84), Nat. Trust for Historic Preservation, Theta Chi, Rotary (roster chmn. Boise 1988--). Home: 919 W Hays St Boise ID 83702 Office: Zabala Giltzow Albanese 815 Park Blvd Ste 350 Boise ID 83712

GINGELL, PATRICIA JO, art museum administrator; b. Bethesda, Md., Mar. 20, 1946; d. Thomas Henry and Priscilla Alden (Tibbals) Gingell; m. Willard Edwards Jr., May 14, 1966 (div. March 1984); children: Arthur, Thomas, Adam, Leanna. AA in Liberal Studies, Allan Hancock Jr. Coll., 1967; BA in English, U. Calif., Santa Barbara, 1985; postgrad., Sonoma State U., 1986-89. Adminstrv. asst. Edn. Abroad Program U. Calif., Santa Barbara, 1984-85, art dir. Summer Art Program, 1985; office asst. Sonoma State U. Art Gallery, Rohnert Park, Calif., 1987—; adminstr. Calif. Mus. Art, Santa Rosa, Calif., 1988—; co-editor newsletter Highlighter: Ednl. Opportunity Program, Sonoma State U., Rohnert Park, 1987—. Playwrite: If It Hadn't Happened That Way, 1988 (Outstanding Script award 1988). Executed mural The Journey, 1987-88. Recipient Service award Ch. Jesus Christ Latter-day Saints, 1988, Vol. Service award County of Sonoma, 1988. Mem. Art Union (Sonoma State U. chpt.). Mormon. Home: 1378 Southwest Blvd Rohnert Park CA 94928 Office: Calif Mus Art Luther Burbank Ctr 50 Mark W Springs Rd Santa Rosa CA 95403

GINN, SAM L., telephone company executive; b. St. Clair, Ala., Apr. 3, 1937; s. James Harold and Myra Ruby (Smith) G.; m. Meriann Lanford Vance, Feb. 2, 1963; children: Matthew, Michael, Samantha. B.S., Auburn U., 1959; postgrad., Stanford U. Grad. Sch. Bus., 1968. Various positions AT&T, 1960-78; with Pacific Telephone & Telegraph Co., 1978—; exec. v.p. network Pacific Telephone & Telegraph Co., San Francisco, 1979-81, exec. v.p. services, 1981-82, exec. v.p. network services, 1982, exec. v.p., strategic planning and adminstrn., 1983, vice chmn. bd., strategic planning and adminstrn., 1983-84; vice chmn. bd., group v.p. PacTel Cos. Pacific Telesis Group, San Francisco, 1984-86, vice chmn. bd., pres., chief exec. officer PacTel Corp., 1986, pres., chief operating officer, 1987-88, chmn., chief exec. officer, 1988—; mem. adv. bd. Sloan program Stanford U. Grad. Sch. Bus., 1978-85; bd. dir. 1st Interstate Bank. Trustee Mills Coll., 1982—. Served to capt. U.S. Army, 1959-60. Sloan fellow, 1968. Republican. Clubs: Blackhawk Country (Danville, Calif.); World Trade, Pacific-Union; Rams Hill Country (Borrego Springs, Calif.), Bankers. Office: Pacific Telesis Group 130 Kearny St San Francisco CA 94108

GINNIS, CLEO AQUILA, textile corporate director of training; b. Chewelah, Wash., May 19, 1938; d. John Henry and Aquila Talitha (Wilson) Lyda; m. Joseph Edward Clauson, June 24, 1957 (div. 1966); 1 child, Joseph Edward II; m. Jack Thomas Ginnis, Aug. 8, 1971. BS, Oreg. State U., 1960. Home service rep. So. Calif. Gas Co., L.A., 1960-61; asst. hostess kitchen program Sta. KOIN-TV, Portland, Oreg., 1967-89; sr. mfg. engr. Jantzen Inc., Portland, 1969—. Mem. Inst. Indsl. Engrs., Beaverton Jr. Woman's, Tualatin Twirlers (past pres.) (Beaverton, Oreg.). Democrat. Office: Jantzen Inc PO Box 3001 Portland OR 97232

GINSBURG, FLORENCE EHRLICH, small business owner; b. Columbus, Ohio, Mar. 21, 1943; d. Harry Mark and Hilda (Ehrlich) Grayson; m. Sheldon W. Ginsburg, 1971 (div. 1980); 1 child, Bret Gordon. BA, UCLA, 1965. With Wells Fargo Alarm Services, Los Angeles, 1980-84; security cons. Honeywell Protection Services, Los Angeles, 1985-86; owner Quality Constrn. by K & F, Los Angeles, 1986—, Florence Ginsburg & Assocs., Los Angeles, 1986—. Mem. The Network Group (pres. 1985-86), AAUW (chmn. pub. info. 1984-85). Home: 1342 10th St Apt 308 Santa Monica CA 90401 Office: Florence Ginsburg & Assocs 1342 10th St Ste 308 Santa Monica CA 90401

GINZTON, EDWARD LEONARD, engineering corporation executive; b. Dnepropetrovsk, Ukraine, Dec. 27, 1915; came to U.S., 1929; s. Leonard Louis and Natalie P. (Philipova) G.; m. Artemas A. McCann; children: Anne, Leonard, Nancy, David. BS, U. Calif., 1936, MS, 1937; EE, Stanford U., 1938, PhD, 1940. Research engr. Sperry Gyroscope Co., N.Y.C., 1940-46; asst. prof. applied physics and elec. engring. Stanford U., 1946-47, assoc. prof., 1947-50, prof., 1951-68; dir. Microwave Lab., 1949-59; with Varian Assocs., Palo Alto, Calif., 1948—, chmn. bd. dirs., 1959-84, chief exec. officer, 1959-72, pres., 1964-68, chmn. exec. com., 1984—, also bd. dirs.; dir. project M Stanford Linear Accelerator Ctr., 1957-60; mem. commn. 1 U.S. nat. com. Internat. Sci. Radio Union, 1958-68; mem. Lawrence Berkeley Lab. Sci. and Adv. Com., 1972-79; chmn. adv. bd. Sch. Engring., Stanford, 1968-70; bd. dirs., mem. exec. com. co-chmn. Stanford Mid-Peninsula Urban Coalition, 1968-72; bd. dirs. Nat. Bur. Econ. Research, 1981-87; mem. sci. policy bd. Stanford Synchrotron Radiation Lab., 1985—. Author: Microwave Measurements, 1957; contbr. articles to tech. jours.; patentee in field. Bd. dirs. Mid-Peninsula Housing Devel. Corp., 1970—, Stanford Hosp., 1975-80; trustee Stanford U., 1977-86. Recipient Morris Liebmann Meml. prize I.R.E., 1958, Calif. Manufacturer of Yr. award, 1974. Fellow IEEE (bd. dirs. 1971-72, chmn. awards bd. 1971-72, medal of Honor 1969); mem. Nat. Acad. Scis. (chmn. com. on motor vehicle emissions 1971-74, co-chmn. com. nuclear energy study 1975-80, com. on sci. and nat. security 1982-84, com. on use of lab. animals in biomed. and behavioral research 1985-88), Am. Acad. Arts and Scis. (mem. exec. com. Western Ctr. 1985—), Nat. Acad. Engring. (mem. council 1974-80), Sigma Xi, Eta Kappa Nu, Tau Beta Pi. Home: 28014 Natoma Rd Los Altos Hills CA 94022 Office: Varian Assocs 611 Hansen Way Palo Alto CA 94303

GIOVINCO, JOSEPH, non-profit administrator, writer; b. San Francisco, Oct. 12, 1942; s. Joseph Bivona Giovinco and Jean Andrews; m. Sally Garey, Aug. 31, 1970 (div. Mar. 1982); 1 child, Gina Lorraine. BA, U. Oreg., 1964; MA in History, San Francisco State U., 1968; PhD in History, U. Calif., Berkeley, 1973. Asst. prof. history SUNY, Albany, 1974-76; instr. multicultural studies Sonoma State U., Cotati, Calif., 1976-79; exec. dir. Hist. Mus. Found., Sonoma County, Santa Rosa, Calif., 1977-80; exec. dir. no. Calif. affiliate Am. Diabetes Assn., San Francisco, 1980-81; exec. dir. San Francisco Sch. Vols., 1981-85, Calif. Hist. Soc., San Francisco, 1985-87. Contbr. articles to profl. publs. Fellow, NEH and Harvard U., 1973; recipient scholarship U. Minn. Ctr. for Immigration History, Mpls., 1975; Rockefeller Found. grantee, 1977; recipient Covello prize Italian Am. Hist. Assn., 1976; named Alumnus of Yr., San Francisco State U., 1987. Roman Catholic. also: Calif Hist Soc 2090 Jackson St San Francisco CA 94109

GIRARD, MAUREEN ROBERTA, English educator; b. Hollywood, Calif., May 22, 1940; d. Robert Le Roy and Mary Irene (Van Brunt) Hooker; m. Gary Lee Girard, Aug. 29, 1959; children: Amanda Lynn, Gabrielle Anne, Michele Lisa. BA in Humanities, San Jose State U., 1979, MA in English Lit., 1985. Prof. English San Jose (Calif.) State U., 1983-86, Monterey (Calif.) Peninsula Coll., 1986--. Author: Practicing the Process (instr. manual), 1988, Writing Wisely and Well, 1989; contbr. articles to profl. jours. Pres., bd. dirs. Parent-Faculty Clubs, Carmel (Calif.) Unified Schs., 1975-81; organizer, pres. Parents Who Care drug awareness program, Carmel, 1980-83; founding mem. Friends of Carmel Unified Schs. Mem. NEA, Nat. Council Tchrs. English, Calif. Reading Assn. Democrat. Home: 26030 Atherton Dr Carmel CA 93923 Office: Monterey Peninsula Coll 980 Fremont St Monterey CA 93940

GIRAULT, LAWRENCE JOSEPH, aircraft engineer; b. Washington, Aug. 27, 1915; s. Alexandre Arsene and Elizabeth Jeanette (Pilcher) G.; m. Lenora Josephine Keahey, Jan. 19, 1946 (dec. 1981); m. Lois Ione Rasmussen, Aug. 5, 1984. Ground engr. Q.A.N.T.A.S., Brisbane, Queensland, Australia, 1932-41; engring. test operator Commonwealth Aircraft, Port Melbourne, Australia, 1941-42; aircraft insp. Douglas Aircraft Corp., Park Ridge, Ill., 1944; design engr. Belmont Radio Corp., Chgo., 1944-45; engr.-in-charge liaison engring. dept. Aeronca Aircraft Corp., Middletown, Ohio, 1945-46; designer Waco Aircraft Corp., Troy, Ohio, 1946; self-employed airplane and power plant mechanic, Williams, Calif., 1946-47; asst. mech. engr. Phelps Dodge Corp., Ajo, Ariz., 1947-48; designer Fairchild Aircraft Corp., Hagerstown, Md., 1948-50; lead designer Chance Vought Aircraft Corp., Dallas, 1950-60; lead designer The Boeing Co., Renton, Wash., 1960-63, sr. engr., 1967-71; mem. staff N.Mex. State U., Las Cruces, 1963-67, 84-86, YOH, Inc., 1986-87; self-employed gen. aviation aircraft mechanic insp., Las Cruces, 1971—; broker O'Donnell Realty, Las Cruces, 1971-83; owner, founder Shoestring Ranch Airport Realty, 1983-87; inspection authorization gen. aviation aircraft, 1987—. With USAAF, 1942-44. Lic. ground engr., Australia; lic. pilot; real estate broker, N.Mex.; lic. aircraft mechanic. Mem. U.S. Naval Inst., Aircraft Owners and Pilots Assn. Adventist. Inventor main landing gear uplock, outer panel-wing and wing fold prototype, other inventions in field of aircraft mechanics. Home: Courtney Rd PO Box 666 Bingen WA 98605

GIROD, FRANK PAUL, surgeon; b. Orenco, Oreg., Aug. 13, 1908; s. Leon and Anna (Gerig)úG.; m. Nadine Mae Cooper, Aug. 26, 1939; children: Judith Anne, Janet Carol, Franklin Paul, John Cooper. AB, Willamette U., Salem, Oreg., 1929; MD, U. Colo., 1938. Diplomate Am. Bd. Family Practice. Tchr. physics and chemistry, athletic coach Cortez High Sch., Colo., 1929-34; intern U. Colo., Denver, 1938-39; resident surgeon U.S. Marine Hosp., Balt., 1939-41; pvt. practice specializing in family practice and surgery Lebanon, Oreg., 1946—. trustee, sec. Blue Shield Ops., Oreg. Maj. U.S. Army, 1942-46. Decorated Bronze Star. Mem. Oreg. Med. Assn., AMA, Am. Acad. Family Practice, Kiwanis (pres. 1947-48). Republican. Methodist. Home: 625 E Rose St Lebanon OR 97355 Office: 325 Park St Lebanon OR 97355

GIRVIGIAN, RAYMOND, architect; b. Detroit, Nov. 27, 1926; s. Manoug and Margaret G.; m. Beverly Rae Bennett, Sept. 23, 1967; 1 son, Michael Raymond. AA, UCLA, 1947; BA with honors, U. Calif., Berkeley, 1950; M.A. in Architecture, U. Calif.-Berkeley, 1951. With Hutchason Architects, Los Angeles, 1952-57; owner, prin. Raymond Girvigian, Los Angeles, 1957-68, South Pasadena, Calif., 1968—; co-founder, advisor Los Angeles Cultural Heritage Bd., 1961—; vice chmn. Historic Am. Bldgs. Survey, Nat. Park Service, Washington, 1966-70; mem. Calif. Hist. Resources Commn., 1970-78; chmn. adv. bd. Calif. Hist. Bldgs. Code, 1976—; bd. dirs. Calif. Heritage Council, 1979—. Co-editor, producer: film Architecture of Southern California for Los Angeles City Schs, 1965; historical monographs of HABS Landmarks, Los Angeles, 1958-80; historical monographs of Califs. State Capitol, 1974, Pan Pacific Auditorium, 1980; designed: city halls for Pico Rivera, 1963, LaPuente, 1966, Rosemead, 1968, Lawndale, 1970 (all Calif.); architect for restoration of Calif. State Capitol, 1975-82; Workman/Temple Hist. Complex, City of Industry, Calif., 1974-81. Mem. St. James Episc. Ch., South Pasadena, Calif. Served with AUS, 1945-46. Recipient Archtl. Design medal U. Calif., Berkeley, 1947, Outstanding Achievement in Architecture award City of Pico Rivera, Calif., 1968, Neasham award Calif. Hist. Soc., 1982. Fellow AIA (Calif. state preservation chmn. 1970-75, state preservation coordinator 1975—, co-recipient nat. honor award for restoration Calif. State Capitol 1983); mem. Soc. Archtl. Historians, Assn. for Preservation Tech., Nat. Trust for Historic Preservation, Archtl. Guild, U. So. Calif., S.W. Mus., Los Angeles. Independent Democrat. Office: PO Box 220 South Pasadena CA 91031-0220 *

GITTINS, DEANNA CHRISTINE, technical publications company executive; b. Carrizozo, N.Mex., July 11, 1957; d. Roland Clinton and Edna Elaine (Shults) Erwin; m. William Thomas Lewis, May 6, 1979 (div. 1987); m. Jeffery Michael Gittins, June 6, 1988; children: Julietta Ann, Adam Thomas. BS in Comml. Arts, Eastern N.Mex. U., 1978. Adminstrv. asst. Fairchild Data Corp., Scottsdale, Ariz.; tech. illustrator, sr. tech. illustrator, graphics supr. Fairchild Data Corp., Scottsdale, 1980—. Mem. Nat. Computer Graphics Assn. Republican. Office: Fairchild Data Corp 350 N Hayden Rd Scottsdale AZ 85257

GIULIANO, FRANK DAVID, mortgage banker; b. Walsenburg, Colo., Oct. 25, 1948; s. Lawrence G. and Kathryne (Giardino) G.; m. Jan Rosser Wedge, Aug. 16, 1987; 1 child, Amy A. BS, U. So. Colo., 1971. Auditor Am. Fed., Pueble, Colo., 1971-74; asst. v.p. Otero Savs., Colorado Springs, Colo., 1974-80; regional v.p. Empire Savs., Denver, 1980-83; br. mgr. Cityfed Mortgage, Colorado Springs, 1983-86; state mgr. Cityfed Mortgage, Denver, 1986-89; sr. loan officer ICA Mortgage, Las Vegas, Nev., 1989—. Democrat. Roman Catholic. Office: ICA Mortgage 2300 Paseo Del Prado Ste C107 Las Vegas NV 89102

GIULIANO, NEIL GERARD, constituent relations; b. Bloomfield, N.J., Oct. 26, 1956; s. Jacqueline Ann (Enright) G. BA, Ariz. State U., 1979, MEd, 1983. Pres. Circle K. Internat., Chgo., 1977-78; conv. cons. Circle K. Internat., 1983-87; counselor disabled students Ariz. State U., Tempe, 1980-81; pres. associated students Ariz. State U., 1982-83, coordinator leadership devel., 1983-87, constituent dir., 1988—; pres. Valley Achievement, Tempe, 1987—; speaker, trainer in field. Bd. dirs. Tempe Community Council, 1987—, Tempe Leadership, Inc., 1987—, Valley Big Bros.-Big Sisters, Tempe, 1987—. Recipient Selected Participant award Ctr. for the Study of the Presidency Symposium, Washington, 1983. Mem. Am. Assn. of Polit. Con., Tempe C. of C., Kiwanis (pres. 1986-87), Sigma Nu (conv. cons. 1988), Key Club Internat. (conv. cons. 1983-87). Republican. Roman Catholic. Home: PO Box 921 Tempe AZ 85281

GIVANT, PHILIP JOACHIM, mathematics educator, real estate investment executive; b. Mannheim, Fed. Republic of Germany, Dec. 5, 1935; s. Paul and Irmy (Dinse) G.; m. Kathleen Joan Porter, Sept. 3, 1960; children: Philip Paul, Julie Kathleen, Laura Grace. BA in Math., San Francisco State U., 1957, MA in Math., 1960. Prof. math. San Francisco State U., 1958-60, Am. River Coll., Sacramento, 1960—; pres. Grove Enterprises, Sacramento, 1961—; pres. Am. River Coll. Acad. Senate, Sacramento, 1966-69; v.p. Acad. Senate for Calif. Community Colls., 1974-77; mem. State Chancellor's Acad. Calendar Com., Sacramento, 1977-79. Founder, producer Annual Sacramento Blues Music Festival, 1976—; producer Sta. KVMR weekly Blues music program, 1978—, music festivals Folsom Prison, 1979-81, Vacaville Prison, 1985. Pres. Sacramento Blues Festival, Inc., 1985—; mem. Lake Tahoe Keys Homeowners Assn., 1983—, Sea Ranch Homeowners Assn., 1977—. Recipient Spl. Service Commendation, Acad. Senate Calif. Community Colls., 1977, Spl. Human Rights award Human Rights-Fair Housing Commn., Sacramento, 1985, W.C. Handy award for Blues Promoter of Yr. Nat. Blues Found., Memphis, 1987. Mem. Faculty Assn. Calif. Community Colls., Am. Soc. Psychical Research, Nat. Blues Found. (adv. com., W.C. Handy Blues Promoter of Yr. 1987). Home and Office: 3809 Garfield Ave Carmichael CA 95608

GIVEN, RICHARD LEWIS, marketing professional; b. El Paso, Tex., Aug. 10, 1936; s. Edmund Lionel and Doretta (Boretz) G.; m. Cynthia Levitan, Sept. 3, 1956 (div. 1974); children: Michael, Deborah, Kimberly; m. Darlene Anne Johnson, Dec. 31, 1975; children: Richard, Nancy, Patti, Gail, Scott, Gregory, Mary, Michael, Jean. BSEE, MIT, 1958; postgrad., U. N.M., 1958-60. Engr. Telecomputing Corp., Alamogordo, N.M., 1957-59; engring. sect. head Consol. Systems Corp., Monrovia, Calif., 1959-64; mgr., systems engr. Packard Bell Computer Corp., Santa Ana, Calif., 1964-65; dir. product mktg. Control Data Corp., Mpls., 1965-69; v.p. Tally Corp., Seattle, 1969-74; nat. sales mgr. Lockheed Electronics Corp., City of Commerce, Calif., 1974-75; v.p. Randal Data Systems, Torrence, Calif., 1975-80, BDT Products, Irvine, Calif., 1980—. Inventor Linear Transmission Gate. Mem. Am. Mktg. Assn., Chi Phi. Lodge: Kiwanis (pres. 1964-65). Home: 12103 Stonegate Ln Garden Grove CA 92645 Office: BDT Products Inc 17152 Armstrong Ave Irvine CA 92714

GIVENS, JOYCE SHELMERDENE, elementary school teacher; b. La Grande, Oreg., Jan. 2, 1932; d. Fred McKinley and Jeanne Margaret Bellinger (May) Graham; m. Loren Thomas Givens, Nov. 12, 1950 (dec. 1975); children: Jeffrey Keith, Noreen Jeanne, Jolene Lynette. BS in Edn., Ea. Oreg. State Coll., 1963, MS in Edn., 1968. Cert. tchr., Oreg. Elem. sch. tchr. Crook County Schs., Powell Butte, Oreg., 1963-76, Prineville, Oreg., 1976—. Mem. NEA, Oreg. Edn. Assn., Crook County Edn. Assn., Am. Legion Aux. (treas. 1961-62), Eagles (treas. 1950-62), Delta Kappa Gamma (sec. Sigma chpt. 1984-86, treas. 1986--). Democrat. Home: 4216 NW Pershall Way Redmond OR 97756

GLAD, DAIN STURGIS, aerospace engineer; b. Santa Monica, Calif., Sept. 17, 1932; s. Alma Emanuel and Maude La Verne (Morby) G.; BS in Engring., UCLA, 1954; MS in Elec. Engring., U. So. Calif., 1963. Registered profl. engr., Calif. m. Betty Alexandra Shainoff, Sept. 12, 1954 (dec. 1973); 1 child, Dana Elizabeth; m. Carolyn Elizabeth Giffen, June 8, 1979. Electronic engr. Clary Corp., San Gabriel, Calif., 1957-58; with Aerojet Electro Systems Co., Azusa, Calif., 1958-72; with missile systems div. Rockwell Internat., Anaheim, Calif., 1973-75; with Aerojet Electrosystems, Azusa, 1975-84; with support systems div. Hughes Aircraft Co., 1984—. Contbr. articles to profl. jours. Ensign, U.S. Navy, 1954-56; lt. j.g. Res., 1956-57. Mem. IEEE, Calif. Soc. Profl. Engrs., Soc. Info. Display. Home: 1701 Marengo Ave South Pasadena CA 91030 Office: Hughes Aircraft Co 1100 W Hollyvale St Azusa CA 91702

GLANCY, MARK HAROLD, quality assurance engineer; b. Phoenix, June 28, 1962; s. Harold Wade and Marlene Amelia (Holmes) G. BSE in Indsl. Engring., Ariz. State U., 1985. Quality assurance engr. Goodyear Aerospace Corp., Litchfield Park, Ariz., 1985-87, Loral Def. Systems, Litchfield Park, 1987-89; cen. tech. ops. Honeywell, Inc., Phoenix, 1989—. Vol. Spl. Olympics, Tempe, Ariz., Easter Seals, Phoenix. Mem. Inst. Indsl. Engrs. (sec.), Am. Soc. for Quality Control, Am. Mgmt. Assn., Tau Beta Pi, Alpha Pi Mu (pres.), Ariz. State U. Alumni Assn. Republican. Home: 5935 W Indianola Phoenix AZ 85033

GLASER, DONALD A(RTHUR), physicist; b. Cleve., Sept. 21, 1926; s. William Joseph Glaser. B.S., Case Inst. Tech., 1946, Sc.D., 1959; Ph.D., Cal. Inst. Tech., 1949. Prof. physics U. Mich., 1949-59; prof. physics U. Calif. at Berkeley, 1959—, prof. physics and molecular biology, 1964—. Recipient Henry Russel award U. Mich., 1955; Charles V. Boys prize Phys. Soc., London, 1958; Nobel prize in physics, 1960; NSF fellow, 1961; Guggenheim fellow, 1961-62. Fellow Am. Physics Soc. (prize 1959); mem. Nat. Acad. Scis., Sigma Xi, Tau Kappa Alpha, Theta Tau. Office: U Calif Dept Molecular Physics Berkeley CA 94720 *

GLASER, EDWARD LEWIS, electrical engineer; b. Evanston, Ill., 1929; s. James and Margaret (Barnes) G.; m. Anne Sims MacIntyre, Nov., 1950; children: Eliot, Cheryl Anne. AB in Physics, Dartmouth Coll., 1951; DSc (hon.), Heriot-Watt U., 1980. Mem. planning group on large size computers IBM, 1951-55; extension instr. computer architecture UCLA, 1958-59; cons. to dir. engring. ElectroData Corp. div. Burroughs Corp., 1958-60; mgr. systems research dept. Burroughs Corp., 1960-63; assoc. prof. elec. engring. MIT, Cambridge, 1963-67; dir. Andrew R. Jennings Computer Ctr., Case Western Res. U., Cleve., 1967-75; mgr. dept. product engring. and devel. System Devel. Corp., Santa Monica, Calif., 1975-78, chief tech. officer, v.p. products group, 1978-79; dir. advanced computer systems tech. Memory Products div. Ampex Corp., El Segundo, Calif., 1979-82; chmn. bd. IRI, Inc., 1982-84; chmn. bd., chief tech. officer Nucleus Internat. Corp. (formerly Marcus Info. Systems), Santa Monica, 1984-85, co-chmn., chief tech. officer, 1985—; vis. prof. UCLA, 1982-85, adj. prof., 1985—. Contbr. articles to profl. jours. Trustee Seeing Eye, Morristown, N.J., 1964. Named Computer Man of Yr., Data Processing Assn., 1976. Fellow IEEE; mem. Nat. Acad. Engring. Christian Scientist. Office: Nucleus Internat Corp 1639 11th St Santa Monica CA 90404

GLASER, EDWIN V., rare book dealer; b. N.Y.C., June 7, 1929; s. Simon and Dorothy (Goldwater) G.; m. Janice Briggs, May 1, 1959 (div. 1975); children: Peter, Daniel. BA, U. N.Mex., 1950; MS, Columbia U., 1951. Reporter Providence Jour.-Bulletin, 1951-55; sales mgr. R.E.C. Corp., New Rochelle, N.Y., 1955-69; owner Edwin V. Glaser Rare Books, Sausalito, Calif., 1969—; faculty mem., antiquarian book seminar, U. Denver, 1979—. Contbr. numerous articles profl. jours. Mem. Antiquarian Booksellers Assn. Am. (pres. 1986-87, gov.). Office: Glaser Rare Books PO Box 1765 Sausalito CA 94966

GLASER, NANCY ELLEN, venture capitalist; b. Hawthorne, N.J., Apr. 24, 1945; d. John Joseph and Marie (Schilde) G. BS, Marshall U., 1967; MBA, Stanford U., 1985. Tchr. spl. edn. Quincy (Mass.) Sch. System, 1967-68; mgr. sales Macy's Dept. Store, Atlanta, 1968-71; group mgr. Daly City, Calif., 1971-73; buyer merchandising The Gap, Inc., San Bruno, Calif., 1973-75, dir. mdse. control, 1976-78; mng. dir. Lord & Taylor, Stamford, Conn., 1978-81; dir. retail and franchise Barton's Candy Corp., Bklyn., 1981-83; gen. ptnr. U.S. Venture Ptnrs., Menlo Park, Calif., 1985—; sec. Home Express, Inc., Hayward, Calif., 1986—; cons. Harvard U. Bus. Sch. Alumni Community Helpers, San Francisco, 1987—; bd. dirs. Gymboree Corp, Burlingame, Calif. mem. New Enterprise Forum Stanford (Calif.) U. Bus. Sch., 1986—, exec. mem. bd. alumni cons. team, 1987—; mem. student selection com. Am. Field Service, Palo Alto, Calif., 1987; bd. dirs. Exploratorium Mus., San Francisco, 1988. Mem. Western Assn. Venture Capitalists. Republican. Home: 54 Cape Hatteras Ct Redwood Shores CA 94065 Office: US Venture Ptnrs 2180 Sand Hill Rd Ste 300 Menlo Park CA 94025

GLASER, ROBERT JOY, physician, foundation executive; b. St. Louis, Sept. 11, 1918; s. Joseph and Regina G.; m. Helen Louise Hofsommer, Apr. 1, 1949; children: Sally Louise, Joseph II, Robert Joy. SB, Harvard U., 1940, MD magna cum laude, 1943; DS (hon.), U. Health Scis.-Chgo. Med. Sch., 1972, Temple U., 1973, U. N.H., 1979, U. Colo., 1979; LHD, Rush Med. Coll., 1973; DS, Mt. Sinai Med. Sch., 1984; DS (hon.), Washington U., 1988. Med. intern Barnes Hosp., St. Louis, 1944, asst. resident physician, 1945-46, resident physician, 1946-47, asst. physician, 1949-57; asst. resident physician Peter Bent Brigham Hosp., Boston, 1944-45; NRC fellow med. scis. Wash. U. Med. Sch., 1947-49, instr. medicine, 1949-50, asst. prof., 1950-56, asst. dean., 1947, 53-55, assoc. prof., 1956-57, assoc. dean, 1955-57; dean, prof. medicine Med. Sch. U. Colo., 1957-63, v.p. for med. affairs, 1959-63; vis. physician Washington U. Med. Service, St. Louis City Hosp., 1950, chief service, 1950-53, cons., 1953-57; attending physician Colo. Gen. Hosp., Denver, 1957-63; prof. social medicine Harvard U., Boston, 1963-65; pres. Affiliated Hosps. Ctr., Inc., 1963-65; v.p. med. affairs, dean Sch. Medicine, prof. medicine Stanford U., 1965-70, acting pres., 1968, cons. prof., 1972—; bd. dirs. Henry J. Kaiser Family Found., 1970-83, pres., chief exec. officer, 1972-83; attending physician Columbia-Presbyn. Med. Ctr., N.Y.C., 1971-72, clin. prof. medicine, 1971-72; dir. for med. sci. Lucille P. Markey Charitable Trust, 1984—; bd. dirs. Hewlett-Packard Co., Alza Corp., Calif. Water Service Co.; cons. medicine VA Hosp., Denver, 1957-63, Fitzsimons Army Hosp., Aurora, Colo., 1957-63, Lowry AFB, Denver, 1957-63; mem. nat. adv. council NIMH, 1970-72, Harvard Fund Council, 1953-56, Harvard Med. Alumni Council, 1956-59; assoc. mem. streptococcal commn. Armed Forces Epidemiologic Bd., 1958-61; chmn. com. study nat. needs biomed. and behavioral research personnel Nat. Acad. Scis.-NRC, 1974-77; mem. vis. com. Med. Sch. Harvard U., 1968-74, Sch. Pub. Health, 1971-77; bd. visitors Charles Drew Postgrad. Med. Sch., 1972-79; mem. com. on med. affairs Yale U., 1969-82, adv. bd. Sch. Orgn. and Mgmt., 1976-84; vis. com. Tufts Med. Sch., 1974-84. Editor: Pharos, 1962—; contbr. articles to sci. jours. and chpts. to books. Bd. regents Georgetown U., 1976-78; bd. dirs. Kaiser Found. Hosps., Kaiser Found. Health Plan, 1967-79, Council on Founds., 1974-79, Packard Humanities Inst., 1987—; trustee Commonwealth Fund,

1969-88, v.p., 1970-72; trustee David and Lucille Packard Found., 1984—, Pacific Sch. Religion, 1972-77, Washington U., St. Louis, 1979-87, 88—; mem. Sloan Commn. on Govt. in Higher Edn., 1977-79. Fellow AAAS, Am. Acad. Arts and Scis. (exec. bd., v.p. 1972-76); mem. Am. Clin. and Climatological Assn. (pres. 1982-83), Am. Fedn. Clin. Research (chmn. midwestern sect. 1954-55), Central Soc. Clin. Research (councillor 1955-58), Am. Soc. Clin. Investigation, Assn. Am. Med. Colls. (asst. sec. 1956-60, chmn. com. edn. and research 1958-63, mem. exec. council 1959-63, 76-79, v.p. 1963-64, chmn. exec. council and assembly 1968-69), Assn. Am. Physicians, Western Assn. Physicians (councillor 1960-63), Am. Soc. Exptl. Pathology, Nat. Inst. Allergy and Infectious Disease (tng. grant com. 1957-60), Inst. Medicine, Nat. Acad. Sci. (mem. exec. com. 1971-73, chmn. membership com. 1970-72, acting pres. 1970-71), Harvard Club, Century Club, Sigma Xi, Alpha Omega Alpha (bd. dirs. 1963-77). Office: 525 Middlefield Rd Ste 130 Menlo Park CA 94025

GLASS, GARY BERTRAM, geologist, state official; b. Pitts., Mar. 6, 1940; s. George Addison and Beverly Martha (Gauding) G.; m. Judith Cobb; children: Susan Lynne, Gary Bertram, William Charles. BS in Geology, Bucknell U., 1962; MS in Geology, Lehigh U., 1964. Cert. profl. geologist. Part time assoc. geologist Pa. Geol. Survey, Harrisburg, 1964; coal geologist, 1967-71; staff coal geologist Wyo. Geol. Survey, Laramie, 1971-78, dep. dir./coal specialist, 1978-81, state geologist, exec. dir., Laramie, 1981—; commr. Wyo. Oil and Gas Conservation Commn., Casper. Served with C.E., U.S. Army, 1964-67. Decorated Bronze Star, Air medal. Mem. Assn. Am. State Geologists, Am. Inst. Profl. Geologists (editor 1985-86, v.p. 1988), Geol. Soc. Am. (sec. coal geology div. 1980-82), Wyo. Geol. Assn., Am. Assn. Petroleum Geologists (energy minerals div.), Sigma Xi. Mem. editorial bd. Elsevier's Internat. Jour. Coal Geology. Office: Geol Survey of Wyo Univ Sta Box 3008 Laramie WY 82071

GLASS, STEPHEN JOSEPH, realtor; b. Commodor, Pa., Apr. 27, 1917; s. Matthew and Veronica (Eastman) G.; m. Catherine Rebecca Lentz, Mar. 27, 1943; children: Louis, Richard, Daniel, Christopher. BS, Indiana (Pa.) U., 1939; MA, Case Western Reserve U., Cleve., 1955. Enlisted USMC, 1942, advanced through the ranks to maj., 1952, ret., 1952; vocat. advisor VA, Cleve., 1946-56; tng. dir. USAF, San Benadino, Calif., 1956-67; dir. mgmt. devel. Def. Contracts Adminstrn., Los Angeles, 1967-72; dir. orgn. devel. County of Riverside, Calif., 1972-84; realtor Red Hill Realty, Tustin, Calif., 1980—; instr. Santa Ana (Calif.) Community Coll., 1958-68. Mem. ASPA (accredited personnel diplomate), Nat. Assn. Realtors, Calif. Realtors Assn., East Orange County Bd. Realtors, Real Estate Investment Assn. Orange County, Am. Soc. Tng. and Devel. (founder Orange County chpt., pres. 1972). Republican. Club: Phoenix (Anaheim, Calif.). Home: 13582 Diamond Head Dr Tustin CA 92680

GLASSMEYER, JAMES MILTON, aerospace and electronics engineer; b. Cin., Mar. 31, 1928; s. Howard Jerome and Ethel Marie (Nieman) G.; m. Anita Mary Tschida, Apr. 21, 1979. Student U. Cin., 1947-49; BSEE with spl. honors, U. Colo., Boulder, 1958, MS in Aeronautics and Astronautics, MIT, 1960. Commd. 2d lt. U.S. Air Force, 1950, advanced through grades to lt. col., 1971; astron. engr. Air Force Space Systems Div. Hdqrs., Los Angeles, 1960-64, astronautical engr. and astronautics tech. intelligence analyst Air Force Rocket Propulsion Lab., Edwards AFB, Calif., 1967-73; ret., 1973; pvt. practice aerospace and electronics research and analysis, 1973—. Contbr. articles to jours. in field. Recipient Air Force Inst. Tech. scholarship, U. Colo., 1956-58, MIT, 1958-60, USAF Master Missileman badge, Air Force Rocket Propulsion Lab., 1970. Mem. AIAA, Air Force Assn., Planetary Soc., Ret. Officers Assn., Tau Beta Pi (1st grand prize Greater Interest in Govt. Nat. Essay Contest 1957), Eta Kappa Nu, Sigma Tau, Sigma Gamma Tau, Sigma Xi. Roman Catholic. Home: 5801 E N Wilshire Dr Tucson AZ 85711 Office: 5610-B E Glenn St Tucson AZ 85712

GLATZER, ROBERT ANTHONY, marketing and sales executive; b. N.Y.C., May 19, 1932; s. Harold and Glenna (Beaber) G.; m. Paula Rosenfeld, Dec. 20, 1964; m. Mary Ann Murphy, Dec. 31, 1977; children: Gabriela, Jessica, Nicholas. BA, Haverford Coll., 1954. Br. store dept. mgr. Bloomingdale's, N.Y.C., 1954-56; media buyer Ben Sackheim Advt., N.Y.C., 1956-59; producer TV commls. Ogilvy, Benson & Mather Advt., N.Y.C., 1959-62; dir. broadcast prodn. Carl Ally Advt., N.Y.C., 1962-63; owner Chronicle Prodns., N.Y.C., 1963-73; dir. Folklife Festival, Smithsonian Inst., Washington, 1973, Expo 74 Corp., Spokane, Wash., 1973-74; pres. Robert Glatzer Assocs., Spokane, 1974—; ptnr. Delany/Glatzer Advt., Spokane, 1979-84; dir. sales/mktg. Pinnacle Prodns., Spokane; adj. faculty Ea. Wash. U., 1987—. Bd. dirs. Riverfront Arts Festival, 1977-78; bd. dirs. Comprehensive Health Planning Council, 1975-78, Spokane Quality of Life Council, 1976-82, Allied Arts of Spokane, 1976-80, Art Alliance Wash. State, 1977-81, Spokane chpt. ACLU, 1979-83, Wash. State Folklife Council, 1983—; commr. Spokane Arts, 1987—; mem. Spokane Community Devel. Bd., 1988—; mem. Shorelines Update Commn., 1988—. Recipient CINE Golden Eagle award (2). Mem. Dirs. Guild Am. Democrat. Jewish. Author: The New Advertising, 1970; co-scenarist Scorpio and other TV prodns. Office: W 905 Riverside Ave Spokane WA 99201

GLAZER, REA HELENE See KIRK, REA HELENE

GLEASON, A. M., electric utility and telecommunications company executive; b. 1930; married. Student, U. Oreg. With Pacific Power & Light Co. Inc., Portland, Oreg., from 1949, asst. to v.p., 1952-65, mgr. pub. accounts, 1965-68, v.p., 1968-73; pres. Pacific Telecom, Inc. (formerly Telephone Utilities, Inc.), Vancouver, Wash., 1973-82, chmn., 1982—, chief exec. officer, 1973-82, also bd. dirs.; pres. parent co. Pacificorp, Portland. Office: Pacificorp 851 SW 6th Ave Portland OR 97204 *

GLEASON, DEANN MAY, realtor; b. Geneva, Ohio, July 21, 1937; d. Nathan Bishop and Eva (Koblek) Williams; m. Carl David Gleason, July 17, 1955; children: Carl Nathan, Lee William, Jeannie Marie Devon, D'Aun Lynn Devon, Patrick Don. Student, U. Alaska; grad., Realtors Inst. Lic. realtor, Alaska; accredited land counselor. Realtor Witt Realty, Inc., Madison, Ohio, 1966-70; real estate broker Tanner and Magowan Realtors, Talkeetna, Alaska, 1975-76, Krenik Realtors, Wasilla, Alaska, 1976-77; real estate assoc. broker Barry and Assocs., Wasilla, 1977-79; prin. County Realty (later merged with Heritage Homes), Wasilla, 1979—. Chairwoman Vocat. Edn., Mat Su Borough, Alaska, 1985-86; active Wasilla City Planning Commn., 1985-87, Mat Su Borough Bd. Equalization, 1986-88, Vocat. Edn. Adv. Bd., 1985-88. Mem. Alaska Bd. Realtors (sec. 1981, v.p. 1983), Valley Bd. Realtors. (pres. 1979), Anchorage Bd. Realtors, (Alaska Chpt. Realtors Land Inst. (pres. 1988), DAR. Republican. Lutheran. Home: 807 Barrow St Anchorage AK 99501 Office: Heritage Real Estate 3230 C St Ste 102 Anchorage AK 99503

GLEASON, DOUGLAS RENWICK, marketing professional; b. Worcestor, Mass., Oct. 27, 1956; s. Sherman M. and Dolores E. (Murad) G. BA, Stanford U., 1978; MBA, UCLA, 1982. Asst. product mgr. Pepsi USA, Purchase, N.Y., 1982-83, assoc. product mgr., 1983-85; product mgr. Carnation Co., Los Angeles, 1985-87; dir. promotion Walt Disney Home Video, Burbank, Calif., 1987—. Mem. Beta Gamma Sigma. Office: Walt Disney Home Video 500 S Buena Vista St Burbank CA 91521

GLEESON, WILLIAM MARK, marketing executive; b. Merced, Calif., Apr. 23, 1952. BA, Calif. State U., Chico, 1974. Vice pres. mktg. Valley Health Care Corp., Sacramento, Calif., 1986—. Author travel books: Small Hotels of California, 1984, Backroad Wineries of California, 1985, 89, The Great Family Getaway Guide, 1988; contbr. articles to newspapers. Mem. Internat. Assn. Bus. Communicators (award of merit 1985, 88). Home: PO Box 186 Carmichael CA 95608

GLEICHER, BEN, electronics executive; b. Bklyn., May 3, 1953; s. Morton William and Thelma (Schechter) G.; m. Mei-Lin Chan, May 28, 1974; children: Shaina, Sonya. BS, Washington U., St. Louis, 1973; MA, U. So. Calif., 1975. Sr. programmer Hughes Aircraft Co., Fullerton, Calif., 1977-80, mem. tech. staff, 1981-88; sr. sci. programmer Lockheed Aircraft Svcs. Co., Ontario, Calif., 1980-81; engr. specialist electronics div. Northrop, Hawthorne, Calif., 1988—. Jewish. Home: 12858 Clear Springs Ln Chino Hills CA 91709

GLEIN, RICHARD JERIEL, lawyer; b. L.A., Aug. 20, 1929; s. Henry Carl Glein and Elsie B. (Brummond) Schurman; divorced; children: Valerie, Kimberley, Richard Jr., Stacy. Student, U. Wash., 1953-58. Bar: Wash. 1963, U.S. Dist. Ct. (ea. and we. dists.) Wash. 1963, U.S. Ct. Appeals (9th cir.) 1963. Dep. pros. atty. King County, Wash., 1963-65; from assoc. to ptnr. Clinton, Fleck & Glein, Seattle, 1965—. Sgt. USAF, 1946-49, U.S. Army, 50-51. Mem. ABA, Wash. State Bar Assn., Fed. Bar Assn., Seattle-King County Bar Assn., Internat. Footprint Assn. (pres. Seattle chpt. 1969-70, grand pres. 1982-83), Wash. State Def. Attys., Assn. Trial Lawyers Am., Wash. State Trial Lawyers Assn., Footprinter Club (San Francisco, grand pres. 1983-84), Masons (master 1973), Elks. Republican. Home: 12300 28th NE #104 Seattle WA 98125 Office: Clinton Fleck & Glein 2112 3d Ave Ste 500 Seattle WA 98121

GLENN, GUY CHARLES, pathologist; b. Parma, Ohio, May 13, 1930; s. Joseph Frank and Helen (Rupple) G.; B.S., Denison U., 1953; M.D., U. Cin., 1957; m. Lucia Ann Howarth, June 13, 1953; children—Kathryn Holly, Carolyn Helen, Cynthia Marie. Intern, Walter Reed Army Med. Center, Washington, 1957-58; resident in pathology Fitzsimons Army Med. Center, Denver, 1959-63; commd. 2d lt. U.S. Army, 1956, advanced through grades to col., 1977; demonstrator pathology Royal Army Med. Coll., London, 1970-72; chief dept. pathology Fitzsimons Army Med. Center, Denver, 1972-77; pres. med. staff St. Vincent Hosp.; past mem. governing bd. Mont. Health Systems Agy. Diplomate Am. Bd. Pathology, Am. Bd. Nuclear Medicine. Fellow Coll. Am. Pathologists (chmn. chemistry resources com., chmn. commn. sci. resources, mem. budget program and review com., council on quality assurance), Am. Soc. Clin. Pathology, Soc. Med. Cons. to Armed Forces, Colo. Assn. Continuing Lab. Edn., Midland Empire Health Assn. (past pres.), Rotary (bd. dirs. local chpt.). Contbr. to profl. jours. Home: 3225 Jack Burke Ln Billings MT 59102 Office: St Vincent Hosp Billings MT 59102

GLENN, JAMES D., JR., lawyer; b. Oakley, Idaho, July 1, 1934; s. Vernal D. and Vilate H. Glenn; student U. Utah, 1952-57, JD, 1960. Bar: Utah 1960, Calif. 1961, Idaho 1978. m. Alice Rexine, Dec. 14, 1956; children: Sheilagh Ann Glenn Thornock, Michelle Glenn Larson, James D. III, Deirdre, David R., Alison. Assoc. counsel Fed. Trade Commn., San Francisco, 1960-61; ptnr. Ferguson & Vohland, 1961-63, Ferguson & Glenn, 1963-65; pvt. practice, Oakland, Hayward and Fremont, Calif., 1965-77, Twin Falls, Idaho, 1987—; ptnr. Webb, Burton, Carlson, Pedersen & Paine, Twin Falls, Idaho, 1977-83; sr. ptnr. Glenn & Henrie, Twin Falls, 1983-87; ; sec. Virga Land Corp., Calif.; counsel Norton Enterprises, Inc., A & B Bean & Grain, Inc., Haney Seed Co., Klein Bros., Ltd., Beta Western, Inc., Loughmiller Farm, Inc. Bd. dirs. So. Alameda County (Calif.) Legal Svcs. Corp., 1969-73. Mem. Idaho Trial Lawyers Assn., Phi Kappa Phi. Republican. Mormon. Office: 715 Shoshone St PO Box 1538 Twin Falls ID 83303-1538

GLENN, RICHARD WRIGHT, dentist; b. Berkeley, Calif., July 26, 1952; s. Harold James and June Ball (Wright) G.; m. Verna Lynne Ogden, Dec. 27, 1975; children: Lindsay, Kristen, Shelli, David, Bradley. BS, Brigham Young U., 1976; DDS, U. Pacific, 1979. Gen. practice dentistry Middleton, Idaho, 1979-84, Prescott, Ariz., 1984—. Office: 1055 Ruth St Prescott AZ 86301

GLENNON, MICHAEL JOHN, educator; b. Chgo., Dec. 19, 1947; s. William John and Catherine (Feil) G. BA summa cum laude, St. Thomas Coll., 1970; JD, U. Minn., 1973. Asst. counsel Office Legis. Coun., Washington, 1973-77; legal counsel Senate Fgn. Rels. Com., Washington, 1977-80; atty. Busby Rehm & Leonard, Washington, 1980-81; assoc. prof. law U. Cinn., 1981-83; prof. law U. Cinn. Coll. Law, 1983-86, U. Calif., Davis, 1987—. Co-author: U.S. Foreign Relations and National Security Law, 1987; mem. bd. editors Am. Jour. Internat. Law, 1986—. Recipient Cert. merit Am. Soc. Internat. Law, 1981. Mem. Am. Law Inst., D.C. Bar Assn., Minn. Bar. Assn. Democrat. Home: 2406 Overhill Ln Davis CA 95616 Office: U Calif Davis CA 95616

GLESSNER, PAUL THOMAS, aerospace engineer; b. Chester, Pa., Mar. 15, 1961; s. Thomas John and Mildred (Weidel) G. BS, Pa. State U., 1984; MS in Aerospace Engring., Poly. U., Bklyn., 1988. Coop. engr. Boeing Vertol Co., Ridley Park, Pa., 1981, 83; aerodynamic engr. Grumman Aerospace Corp., Bethpage, N.Y., 1984-87, Lockheed Aero. Systems Co., Burbank, Calif., 1987—. Mem. Condominium Assn., Lakeview Terrace, Calif., 1988. Mem. AIAA, Am. Helicopter Soc., Soc. Automotive Engrs., Soc. Am. Mil. Engrs., Aircraft Owners and Pilots Assn. Republican. Roman Catholic. Office: Lockheed Aero Systems Co 2550 N Hollywood Way Burbank CA 91520

GLICK, ANDREW JUSTUS, composer, computer systems consulting executive; b. Culver City, Calif., Oct. 25, 1948; s. George Gordon and Josephine (Griner) G. BA in Music Composition, Calif. State U., Long Beach, 1969; BSEE, U. So. Calif., Los Angeles, 1977. Quality engr. supr. Thomas Organ Co., Sepulveda, Calif., 1974-75; sr. systems analyst Tektronix, Inc., Woodland Hills, Calif., 1978-80; supr. computer graphics Lockheed Calif. Aircraft, Burbank, 1980-82; regional tech. support mgr. Digital Research, Inc., Los Angeles, 1982-84; pres. Justus Engring., La Canada, Calif., 1984—; prof. computer sci. Northrop U., Inglewood, Calif., 1984-86; cons. Glenray Prodns., Pasadena, Calif., 1985—, Teledyne Camera, Arcadia, Calif., 1985, Hughes Aircraft, Conoga Park, Calif., 1980. Composer: Cosmogony Oratorio, 1979, Solstitium, 1986 (MASCA commn. 1986); inventor, video encoder; contbr. articles to profl. jours. V.p. Mus. Arts Soc. Los Angeles, 1986, bd. dirs., 1984—; librarian Cambridge Singers, Los Angeles, 1984-86, commd. composer, 1986; dir. services and music Throop Meml. Unitarian Ch., Pasadena, 1982-84. Served with U.S. Army, 1969-71. Recipient Outstanding Scholar. in Materials Sci. award Am. Soc. for Testing Materials, 1976; performance grantee Meet the Composer, 1986. Mem. AAAS, Assn. for Computing Machinery, Audubon Soc., Minn. Composers Forum. Democrat. Unitarian. Club: Nature Conservancy. Office: Justus Engring PO Box 1451 La Canada-Flintridge CA 91011-5451

GLICK, M. LAURIE, investment banker; b. New Rochelle, N.Y., Nov. 24, 1960; d. Frederick and Dolores Phyllis (Messinger) G. BS in Econs., U. Pa., 1982; MBA, Stanford U., 1986. Analyst, pub. fin. Smith Barney Harris Upham & Co., N.Y.C. and San Francisco, 1982-84; assoc., corp. fin. Drexel Burnham Lambert Inc., Beverly Hills, Calif., 1986—. Mem. Jr. League, L.A., 1987—. Office: Drexel Burnham Lambert Inc 131 S Rodeo Dr Ste 300 Beverly Hills CA 90212

GLICKMAN, HARRY, professional athletics executive; b. Portland, Oreg., May 13, 1924; s. Sam and Bessie (Karp) G.; m. Joanne Carol Matin, Sept. 28, 1958; children: Lynn Carol, Marshall Jordan, Jennifer Ann. B.A., U. Oreg., 1948. Press agt. 1948-52; pres. Oreg. Sports Attractions, 1952—; mgr. Multnomah (Oreg.) Civic Stadium, 1958-59; pres. Portland Hockey Club, 1960-73; exec. v.p. basketball team Portland Trail Blazers, from 1970, now pres. Trustee B'nai B'rith Jr. Camp, 1965; bd. dirs. U. Oreg. Devel. Fund. Served with AUS, 1943-46. Named to Oreg. Sports Hall of Fame, 1986. Mem. Portland C. of C. (bd. dirs. 1968-72), Sigma Delta Chi, Sigma Alpha Mu. Jewish. Office: Portland Trail Blazers 700 NE Multnomah St Lloyd Bldg Ste 950 Portland OR 97232 *

GLICKMAN, JAMES MICHAEL, insurance executive; b. Chgo., May 1, 1953; s. Daniel Elliott and Arlyne (Iranow) G.; m. Marlene Gonik, Aug. 15, 1976; children: Steven, Marc, Robert. BA, U. Mich., 1975. CLU. Mgr. Maccabees Mut. Life, Southfield, Mich., 1975-80; asst. v.p. Pacific Standard Life, Davis, Calif., 1980-82; v.p. Pa. Life, Santa Monica, Calif., 1982-87; pres. Glickman Fin. Group, Calabasas, Calif., 1987—; pres. 21st Century Life and Health, Woodland Hills, Calif., 1988—, also bd. dirs.; bd. dirs. Life Care Assurance Co., Phoenix. Fellow Soc. Actuaries, Life Mgmt. Inst. Loma; mem. Am. Acad. Actuaries, Chartered Life Underwriters. Republican. Jewish. Home: 5030 Orrville Ave Woodland Hills CA 91367

GLICKMAN, JEFFREY BRUCE, computer engineer, college official, photographer; b. Cleve., Mar. 20, 1948; s. Irving Julius Glickman and Rhoda (Hecht) Unger. BS in Math., Ohio State U., 1972; MS in Compute Engring., Case Western Res. U., 1976. Computer operator Predicasts, Inc., Cleve., 1975; solar constrn. worker Ben Larsen, Santa Fe, 1976, Charles Van Maanen, Santa Fe, 1978; mgr. photography sch. and labs. Ctr. of Eye Photography Collaborative, Santa Fe, 1977-78; instr. Computer Sch., Santa Fe, 1979-80; 3-D milling machine computer programmer United Centrifugal Pumps, Santa Fe, 1980-81; mgr. computer system Coll. Santa Fe, 1981—; owner Photographer's View, Santa Fe; instr. computer operating systems and computer architecture Coll. Santa Fe. Home: Rte 1 Box 189-B Santa Fe NM 87501 Office: Coll Santa Fe St Michaels Dr Santa Fe NM 87501

GLIHA, JOHN LEE, management information consultant, researcher; b. Sidney, N.Y., Feb. 18, 1953; s. Edward Richard and Agnes (Bennett) G. BA, SUNY, Oswego, 1976; postgrad., Ariz. State U., 1977—. Grad. asst. Boulton Collection Mus. Instruments, Ariz. State U., 1977-78; supr. research info. ctr. music library Ariz. State U., 1979-83, cataloger music library, 1979-83, project coordinator collection devel. univ. library, 1983-84, dir. devel. research devel. office, 1984—; cons. AT&T, Phoenix, 1985. Contbr. book reviews to library jour. Mem. Grievance com. Ariz. State U., 1983-84, ombudsman, chmn. staff personnel com., 1980-84, adv. bd. aux. services, 1981-82, also platform speaker univ. inauguration commn., 1981-82. Mem. Am. Mgmt. Assn., Assoc. Records Mgrs. and Adminstrs., Am. Prospect Research Assn. (pres. 1989), Ariz. State U. Library Assocs., Ariz. State U. Friends Music, Friends KAET, Ariz. State U. Club. Republican. Home: PO Box 1009 Tempe AZ 85280-1009 Office: Ariz State U Devel Office Tempe AZ 85287

GLIWA, KEVIN ANDREW, lawyer; b. Oceanside, N.Y., Aug. 30, 1956; s. Thaddeus Lawrence and Ursula Valerie Lynn (Walsh) G.; m. Denise Lynn. Student, U. Leicester, 1976-77; AB, Colby Coll., 1978; JD, Boston U., 1982. Assoc. Breed, Abbott & Morgan, N.Y.C., 1982-86; assoc. Otten, Johnson, Robinson, Neff & Ragonetti, P.C., Denver, 1986-88, ptnr., dir., 1989—. Atty. Hist. Paramount Found., Denver, 1987—; vol. for Outdoor Colo. Mem. ABA, Colo. Bar Assn., Denver Bar Assn., Phi Beta Kappa. Office: 950 17th St Ste 1600 Denver CO 80202

GLOUDEMAN, JOSEPH FLOYD, mechanical engineer; b. West Allis, Wis., Oct. 19, 1935; s. Martin Peter and Anna Marie (Kieweg) G.; m. Jeanette Therese Markert, June 14, 1958; children: Mike, Mark, John. BSME, Marquette U., 1958; MSME, U. So. Calif., 1962; Dr.-Ing., U. Stuttgart, Republic of Germany, 1970. Engring. trainee Kearney & Trecker, Milw., 1955-58; engr. Northrop Corp., Los Angeles, 1958-61; sect. mgr. The Aerospace Corp., Los Angeles, 1961-67; dir. data mgmt. Rockwell Internat., Los Angeles, 1967-78; v.p. mktg. MacNeal-Schwendler, Los Angeles, 1978-83, pres., chief exec. officer, 1983—, also bd. dirs. Contbr. articles to profl. jours. Mem. pres.'s coun. Loyola Marymount U., Los Angeles, 1985; pres. adv. coun. U. La Verne, 1985; dean's adv. coun. Marquette U.; active Town Hall of Calif., 1985. Recipient Spl. Achievement award USAF Space Systems Div., The Aerospace Corp., 1966, Apollo Achievement award NASA, 1969, Significant Achievements to Space Div. Program, N.Am. Rockwell, 1973. Fellow: AIAA (assoc.); mem. Structural Mechanics in Reactor Tech. (dept. orgn. chmn. 1977—), Computer Aided Engring. Reactor Structures (seminar co-organizer 1977—). Republican. Roman Catholic. Home: 731 Hillcrest La Canada Flintridge CA 91011 Office: MacNeal-Schwendler Corp 815 Colorado Blvd Los Angeles CA 90041

GLOVER, JEFF CURTISS, computer engineer; b. Milw., Dec. 26, 1962; s. Clifford E. and Helen J. (Lewis) G. BS in Computer Sci., U. Cen. Fla., Orlando, 1984. Software engr. Interactive Scis., Inc., Orlando, Fla., 1981-84; software engr. II Tektronix/CBI, Beaverton, Oreg., 1984-87; software engr. III Tektronix/IDG, Wilsonville, Oreg., 1987—. Mem. IEEE. Home: 10700 SW N Dakota Tigard OR 97223 Office: Tektronix 26600 SW Pkwy Wilsonville OR 97070

GLOWIK-JOHNSON, LINDA ANN, actress, educator, dancer, choreographer; b. Cleve., Mar. 30, 1951; d. Joseph and Frances (Trovato) Glowik. BA in Theatre Arts and Communications with honors, Cleve. State U., 1974; MA in Theatre Arts with honors, NYU, 1985; pvt. studies, Herbert Berghof/Uta Hagen Studio, N.Y.C. Dir., actress, choreographer, dancer N.Y.C., 1971-81; drama chmn., tchr., dir. Bronxville (N.Y.) High Sch., 1981-84; artistic dir. in residence TASIS Internat., Eng., 1984-85; chmn. performing arts dept. The Rhodes Sch., N.Y.C., 1985-86; artistic dir., founder The Youth Actors Guild, N.Y.C., 1982-86; artist/tchr. theatre New Orleans Ctr. for Creative Arts, 1986-88, Mid-Pacific Inst., Honolulu, 1988—. Appeared in lead roles in (off-Broadway) Homecoming, Little Difference, Carousel, Kiss Me Kate, (summer stock) Gertrude Stein & A Companion, Children of a Lesser God, Noises Off, Fallen Angels, Stage Door, Godspell; was prin. dancer Cleve. Ballet Co., lead dancer Jerry Ames Tap/Jazz Co.; dir., choreographer Little Difference, Toby Tyler, A Midsummer Night's Dream, Noises Off, On the Verge, Cabaret, Where the Girls Were, The Importance of Being Earnest, Pippin. Home: 1600 Ala Moana #4004 Honolulu HI 96815

GLUCK, HENRY, resort complex executive; b. Aurich, Germany, May 11, 1928; married. BS, U. Pa., 1950. Former pres., chief operating officer Monogram Industries, Inc.; chmn., pres., chief exec. officer Magnasync-Moviola, Inc.; chmn. Standun, Inc., from 1978; chief exec. officer Caesars World, Inc., 1982—, now also chmn., bd. dirs., 1982—; chmn. Caesars N.J. Inc., Atlantic City, 1983—, now also chief exec. officer. Served with U.S. Army, 1950-53. Office: Caesars World Inc 1801 Century Pk E Los Angeles CA 90067 *

GLUCKSMAN, STEPHAN ALAN, insurance executive; b. Los Angeles, June 25, 1958; s. Herbert Charles and Carol (Lupkin) G.; m. Serena Brooks, Nov. 8, 1981 (div. Mar. 1985). BBA, U. Tex., 1980. Dept. mgr., asst. buyer J.W. Robinson's Dept. Store, Los Angeles, 1980-81; account exec. Pacific Mut., Phoenix, 1981-88, Ins. West, Phoenix, 1988—. Mem. Sunkist Fiesta Bowl, Phoenix, 1984—, Scottsdale (Ariz.) Active 20/30. Mem. Ariz. Group Assn., Greater Phoenix Health Underwriters Assn. (bd. dirs. 1988, v.p. 1988), Life Underwriters Assn. Republican. Jewish. Home: 6249 N 78th St #15 Scottsdale AZ 85253 Office: Ins West 2730 E Camelback Rd Phoenix AZ 85016

GLUSHIEN, ARTHUR SAMUEL, cardiologist, educator; b. Bklyn., July 15, 1911; s. Isaac and Minnie (Hoffman) G.; m. Edith Risk, Dec. 25, 1938 (dec. July 1978); 1 son, Thomas Michael. B.S. cum laude, N.Y. U., 1930, M.D., 1936. Intern, Kings County Hosp., Bklyn., 1936-37, Ellis Hosp., Schenectady, 1937-38; physician VA Hosp., Pitts., 1939-44, cardiologist, 1944-55, chief med. service, 1955-59; pvt. practice medicine, Pitts., 1959-64; chief cardiology sect. VA Hosp., East Orange, N.J., 1964-74; pvt. practice medicine specializing in cardiology, San Diego, 1974-78; council Inst. Continued Learning U. Calif.-San Diego, 1978—; assoc. clin. prof. medicine U. Pitts. Sch. Medicine, 1952-64; asso. prof. medicine N.J. Coll. Medicine, 1965-74; chief staff Russellton Med. Group, 1959-64. Pres. Western Pa. Heart Assn., 1961-62. Served to maj. U.S. Army, 1944-46. Recipient Distinguished Service award Western Pa. Heart Assn., 1962; Superior Performance award East Orange VA Hosp., 1969. Diplomate Am. Bd. Internal Medicine. Fellow A.C.P., Am. Coll. Cardiology; mem. Am. Heart Assn., Phi Beta Kappa, Alpha Omega Alpha. Independent. Jewish. Contbr. articles to med. jours. Home: 6761 Caminito del Greco San Diego CA 92120

GMBER, MARK STEPHEN, manufacturing company executive, land developer; b. N.Y.C., Sept. 29, 1951; s. Simon and Claire Rebecca (Israel) G.; m. Nancy Melee Robertshaw, June 21, 1981; 1 child, Stephen Spencer. BS, U. Bridgeport, 1973. Dept. supr. Del Monte Corp., Hartsdale, N.Y., 1974-75; office mgr. Del Monte Corp., Balt., 1976-77; staff auditor Del Monte Corp., San Francisco, 1977-78, sr. auditor, 1979-80, supervising sr. auditor, 1980-81; asst. contr. A-1 Carbide Corp., Placentia, Calif., 1981-82; contr. A-1 Carbide Corp., Placentia, 1982-85, treas., chief fin. officer, 1985—; also bd. dirs. A-1 Carbide Corp., Placentia, Calif. Coach Am. Youth Soccer, Long Beach, Calif., 1988; mgr. Little League, 1989. Office: A-1 Carbide Corp 1649 Miraloma Ave Placentia CA 92670

GNAM, ADRIAN, orchestra director and conductor; b. N.Y.C., Sept. 4, 1940; s. Hugo and Annette (Nussbaum) G.; m. Catharine Dee Morningstar, Aug. 16, 1984; children: Evan Julian, Geneva Nicole. MusB, U. Cin., 1961, BS and MusM, 1962. Asst. condr. N.E. Chamber Orch., Maine, 1966-67;

asst. music dir. Nat. Endowment for the Arts, Washington, 1976-82, music dir., 1982-84; prin. guest condr. Concerto Soloists of Phila., 1980—; music dir., condr. Midland (Mich.) Symphony, 1982-86, Macon (Ga.) Symphony Orch., 1983—, Eugene (Oreg.) Symphony Orch., 1985—; music dir. Shreveport (La.) Summer Music Festival, 1987—; prin. oboe Am. Symphony, N.Y.C., 1964-65, Cleve. Orch., 1965-67. Rec. artist for Decca, Opus One, Piper and Epic labels. Recipient Presdl. citation Nat. Fedn. Music Clubs; Corbett scholar Univ. Cin., 1960-62. Mem. Am. Symphony Orch. League, Condrs. Guild, Chamber Music Am. Lodge: Rotary. Home and Office: 85440 Appletree Ct Eugene OR 97405

GNEHM, MAX WILLI, financial consultant; b. Switzerland, July 15, 1943; s. Max Hans and Frieda Gnehm; m. Henrietta D. Schwarz, July 1, 1984; children: Alexandra Barbara, William Anthony. MBA, Swiss Sch. Bus., 1963; postgrad. Swiss Inst. Mktg. and Fgn. Trade Research. Asst. mgr. Maxwell Sci. Internat. Book Co., 1964-66; mgr. book and periodical div. Internat. Univ. Booksellers, N.Y.C., 1966-69; dir. Internat. div. Richard Abel Co., 1969-74; v.p. mktg. Blackwell of N.Am., Inc., Beaverton, Oreg., 1974-76, pres., 1976-79, also bd. dirs.; pres., chmn. bd. Swiss-Am. Investment Group Inc.; bd. dirs. Swiss Am. Data Net, Swiss Am. Data Exchange, Atlin Investment Group, Inc.; pres., bd. dirs. Transpacific Holding Group Ltd., Malcolm Smith, Inc, Concorde Pacific Exploration, Inc., Interpacific Printing, Inc., Hong Kong Fin. Group Ltd., Pacific Mining, Inc., 1987—; bd. dirs. Macedon Resources Ltd., Lore Corp. Author: New Reference Tools for Librarians, 1965. Mem. ALA, Pres.'s Assn. Home: Rte 2 Box 376 Forest Grove OR 97116 Office: TransPacific Holding Group Inc 10 Thomas Rd Irvine CA 92718

GNIFFKE, TERRY LEE, marketing professional; b. Clarkfield, Minn., Mar. 22, 1952; s. Glenn Duane and Eunice Josephine (Halvorson) G.; m. Peggy Lynn Haugen, Aug. 25, 1973; children: Chad, Jennifer, Christopher. Student, S.W. State U., Marshall, Minn., 1974-76. Lic. real estate broker, Calif. Asst. sales mgr. Rogers Gardens, Newport Beach, Calif., 1976-77; gen. mgr. Wilderness Pines, Idyllwild, Calif., 1978-79; regional mgr. Thousand Trails, Seattle, 1979-82; sales rep. Robert Shank Co. Heating & Air Conditioning, Orange, Calif., 1982-83; sales mgr. Air Mgmt., Anaheim, Calif., 1983-85, Pro Heating & Air Conditioning, Anaheim, 1985-86; sales and mktg. mgr. IrvineWest Heating & Air Conditioning, Inc., Anaheim, 1986—. Mem. men's com. Christian Bus. Sgt. USMC, 1970-74, Vietnam. Mem. Execs. Assn. of Orange (bd. dirs. 1988—). Republican. Home: 12661 Shelly Ln Santa Ana CA 92705 Office: IrvineWest Heating & Air Conditioning Inc 638 Southern Ave Orange CA 92665

GOBAR, ALFRED JULIAN, economic consultant, educator; b. Lucerne Valley, Calif., July 12, 1932; s. Julian Smith and Hilda (Millbank) G.; B.A. in Econs., Whittier Coll., 1953, M.A. in History, 1955; postgrad. Claremont Grad. Sch., 1953-54; Ph.D. in Econs., U. So. Calif., 1963; m. Sally Ann Randall, June 17, 1957; children—Wendy Lee, Curtis Julian, Joseph Julian. Asst. pres. Microdot Inc., Pasadena, 1953-57; regional sales mgr. Sutorbilt Corp., Los Angeles, 1957-59; market research assoc. Beckman Instrument Inc., Fullerton, 1959-64; sr. marketing cons. Western Mgmt. Consultants Inc., Phoenix, Los Angeles, 1964-66; ptnr., prin., chmn. bd. Darley/Gobar Assocs., Inc., 1966-73; pres., chmn. bd. Alfred Gobar Assocs., Inc., Brea, Calif., 1973—; asst. prof. finance U. So. Calif., Los Angeles, 1963-64; assoc. prof. bus. Calif. State U.-Los Angeles, 1963-68, 70-79, assoc. prof. Calif. State U.-Fullerton, 1968-69; mktg., fin. adviser 1957—; pub. speaker seminars and convs. Contbr. articles to profl. publs. Home: 1100 W Valencia Mesa Dr Fullerton CA 92633 Office: 201 S Brea Blvd Brea CA 92621

GOBAR, SALLY RANDALL, school principal; b. Santa Maria, Calif., Nov. 27, 1933; d. Vernon Blythe Randall and Leona Margaret (Jackson) Batchman; m. Alfred Julian Gobar, June 17, 1957; children—Wendy Lee, Curtis Julian, Joseph Julian. B.A., Whittier Coll., 1955; M.A., Claremont Grad. Sch., 1967, Ph.D., 1979. Tchr., So. San Francisco High Sch., 1956-57, Santa Ana High Sch., Calif., 1957-61; counselor Sunny Hills High Sch., Fullerton, Calif., 1961-66; head counselor Troy High Sch., Fullerton, 1967-83; asst. prin. Buena Park High Sch., Calif., 1983-84; prin. Fullerton High Sch., 1984—; cons. Coll. Bd., N.Y., 1972-77. Mem. Pres.'s Assocs., Calif. State U.-Fullerton. Recipient Golden Book award Exchange Club, 1978, Outstanding Service award Calif. Personnel and Guidance Assn., 1980. Mem. Assn. Calif. Sch. Adminstrs., Whittier Coll. Alumni Assn., Claremont Grad. Sch. Alumni, Fullerton C. of C. Republican. Avocations: travel; classical music; piano. Home: 1100 Valencia Mesa Dr Fullerton CA 92633 Office: Fullerton Union High Sch 201 E Chapman Fullerton CA 92634

GOBLE, JOHN LEWIS, pediatric ophthalmologist; b. Delaware, Ohio, July 18, 1926; s. John Lester and Esther Pauline (Freese) G.; m. Elise Joan Hollenberg, Oct. 4, 1956; children: John Robert, Michael William. AB, Ohio Wesleyan U., 1948; MD, U. Rochester, 1952. Diplomate Am. Bd. Ophthalmology. Intern U. Va. Hosp., Charlottesville, 1952-53; resident in Ophthalmology Columbia Presbyn. Hosp., N.Y.C., 1956-58; practice medicine San Mateo, Calif., 1959—; instr. ophthalmology, Stanford U., 1960-68, Am. Acad. Ophthalmology, 1970-74; pres. Peninsula Eye Soc., Calif., 1973-74; chief ophthalmology, Mills Hosp., San Mateo, 1974-75. Author: Visual Disorders in the Handicapped Child, 1984. Served to lt. U.S. Army, 1953-55. Fellow Am. Coll. of Surgeons, Am. Acad. for Cerebral Palsy, Am. Acad. of Ophthalmology; affiliate fellow Am. Acad. of Pediatrics; charter mem. Am. Assn. for Pediatric Ophthalmology, Peninsula Club. Republican. Unitarian. Home: 2007 New Brunswick Dr San Mateo CA 94402 Office: Goble & Goble Inc 100 S Ellsworth Ste 507 San Mateo CA 94401

GOBLE, THOMAS LEE, clergyman; b. Anderson, Ind., July 5, 1935; s. Carl Wilbur and Agnes Irene (McVey) G.; m. Esther Charlene Callaway, June 12, 1956; children: Jeffreay Mark, Jeanette Marcelle Goble Pittman. BA, Pasadena Coll., 1956; BD, Nazarene Theol. Sem., 1959; DMin, Calif. Grad. Sch. Theology, 1972. Ordained to ministry Ch. of Nazarene as deacon, 1960. Pastor various congregations Ch. of Nazarene, 1959-87; supt. Anaheim dist. Ch. of Nazarene, Orange, Calif., 1987—; prof., Point Loma Nazarene Coll., Nazarene Bible Coll.; chmn. bd. dirs., Asian Nazarene Bible Coll., Long Beach, Calif., 1987—. Trustee, Idyllwild (Calif.) Christian Camp, 1987—, Point Loma Nazarene Coll., San Diego, 1987—. Mem. Point Loma Coll. Alumni Assn., Rotary. Office: Anaheim Dist Ch Nazarene 524 E Chapman Ave Orange CA 92666

GODAGER, JANE ANN, social worker; b. Blue River, Wis., Nov. 29, 1943; d. Roy and Elmyra Marie (Hood) G. BA, U. Wis., 1965; MSW, Fla. State U., 1969. Lic. clin. social worker. Social worker III State of Wis. Dept Corrections, Wales, 1965-71; supervising psychiat. social worker I State of Calif., San Bernardino, 1972-75, La Mesa, 1975-77; psychiat. social worker State of Calif., San Bernardino, 1978-85; supr. mental health services Riverside (Calif.) County Dept. Mental Health, 1985-86; mental health counselor Superior Ct. San Bernardino County, 1986—. Mem. Nat. Assn. Social Workers, Acad. Cert. Social Workers (diplomate), Kappa Kappa Gamma Alumnae Assn. Office: Office Mental Health Counselor 700 E Gilbert St Bldg 1 San Bernardino CA 92415

GODBEY, ROBERT CARSON, lawyer; b. Houston, June 7, 1953; s. Charles Perry and Bobbye Lee (Wendland) G.; m. Ellen Carson, June 2, 1979. BS, BSEE, So. Meth. U., 1975; JD, Harvard U., 1980. Bar: D.C. 1980, U.S. Patent Office 1983, Hawaii 1988. Telecommunications engr. Southwestern Bell, Dallas, 1975-76, Tex. Instruments, Dallas, 1976-77; assoc. Peabody, Lambert & Meyers, Washington, 1980-84; asst. U.S. atty. U.S. Dept. of Justice, Washington, 1984-87, Honolulu, 1987—. Mem. IEEE. Office: US Attys Office US Courthouse Honolulu HI 96850

GODBOLD, MONIQUE TOI, chemical engineer; b. Detroit, Apr. 20, 1960; d. Donald Horace and Delores Roxanna (Cofer) G.; m. Randolph Villaranda Simmons, Mar. 27, 1981 (div.); 1 child, Christian Thomas. BSChemE, U. Tex., Austin, 1984. Chem. engr. Sacramento Air Logistics Ctr., McClellan AFB, Calif., 1985—. Author: Images, 1988. Mem. Western Council Scientists and Engrs. (treas. 1988—), McClellan Mgmt. Soc., Tex.-Ex Alumni Club. Democrat. Home: 5325 Stoney End Ct North Highlands CA 95660 Office: Sacramento Air Logistics Ctr MAQCE Bldg 368 McClellan AFB CA 95652

GODDARD, TERRY, mayor. Mayor City of Phoenix. Office: Office of Mayor 251 W Washington St Phoenix AZ 85003 *

GODDARD, THOMAS GLEN, lawyer, public affairs consultant; b. Wichita Falls, Tex., Aug. 8, 1955; s. Glen and Florence Ellen (Cowgill) G.; m. Alice Ann Milton, May 31, 1981 (div. 1986); m. Barra Kahn, June 14, 1987. BA in Polit. Sci., U. Ariz., 1976, JD, 1979. Bar: Ariz. 1979, U.S. Dist. Ct. Ariz. 1979, U.S. Ct. Appeals (9th cir.) 1979. Assoc., Law Offices of Walter B. Nash, III, P.C., Tucson, 1979-81; pvt. practice, Tucson, 1981; spl. asst. to Ariz. Gov. Bruce Babbitt, Tucson, 1981-83; state legis. counsel Assn. of Trial Lawyers of Am., Washington, 1983-85; dir. Alliance for Consumer Rights, N.Y.C., 1985-86; pres. Goddard Pub. Affairs Corp., Tucson, 1986—; exec. dir. Tucson Adminstrs., Inc., 1989. Contbr. articles and columns to legal publs. Charter mem. Crime Resistors, Tucson, 1982-83; mem. exec. com. Pima County Democratic Party, Tucson, 1982-83, Dems. of Greater Tucson, 1982-83, bd. govs., 1989, legis. Dist. 12 Dem. Club., Tucson, 1982-83. Recipient William Spaid Meml. award U. Ariz. Coll. Law. Mem. So. Ariz. Criminal Def. Lawyers Assn., Assn. Trial Lawyers Am., Blue Key, Phi Kappa Phi. Office: Goddard Pub Affairs Corp 118 S La Creciente Tucson AZ 85711

GODDARD, WILLIAM ANDREW, III, chemist, applied physicist, educator; b. El Centro, Calif., Mar. 29, 1937; s. William Andrew and Barbara Worth (Bright) G.; m. Yvonne Amelia Correy, Oct. 27, 1957; children: William Andrew, Susan Yvonne, Cecelia Moniqué, Lisa Sharéll. B.S. in Engring. with highest honors, UCLA, 1960; Ph.D. in Engring. Sci, Calif. Inst. Tech., 1964. Mem. faculty Calif. Inst. Tech., Pasadena, 1964—; asso. prof. theoretical chemistry Calif. Inst. Tech., 1971-75, prof. theoretical chemistry, 1975-78, prof. chemistry and applied physics, 1978-84, Charles and Mary Ferkel prof. chemistry and applied physics, 1984—, dir. Caltech-NSF materials research group, 1985—; vis. staff mem. Los Alamos Sci. Lab., 1973—; cons. Gen. Motors Research Labs., 1978—, Argonne Nat. Lab., 1978-82, Sandia Labs., 1979-84, Bell Labs., 1979-83, Gen. Electric Research and Devel. Labs., 1982—, Shell Devel., 1982-88, Triton Bioscis. Inc., 1984-87, Allied Signal Engineered Materials Research Ctr., 1984-85—, Biodesign, 1985—, also Exxon, Sohio; mem. adv. com. for chemistry NSF, 1984-86, chmn., 1985-86; mem. council Gordon Research Confs., 1985-87, trustee, 1987-89. Mem. adv. editorial bd. Chem. Physics, 1972—, Jour. Phys. Chemistry, 1976-80, Langmuir, 1984-87, Jour. Am. Chem. Soc., 1985-87. Recipient Buck-Whitney medal for major contbns. in chemistry, 1978; NSF fellow, 1960-61, 62-64; Shell Found. fellow, 1961-62; Alfred P. Sloan Found. fellow, 1967-69. Fellow Am. Phys. Soc.; mem. Nat. Acad. Scis., Materials Research Soc., Am. Chem. Soc. (award for computers in chemistry 1988), Am. Vacuum Soc., Calif. Catalysis Soc., Sigma Xi, Tau Beta Pi. Home: 955 Avondale Dr San Marino CA 91108 Office: Calif Inst Tech Mail Code 127-72 Pasadena CA 91125

GODDEN, MARTHA THERESE, real estate agent; b. Honolulu, May 6, 1942; d. Manuel Paul and Martina (Fernandez) Ruiz; m. Kenneth Allan Ornellas Sr., Apr. 22, 1961 (div. 1969); m. Kevin Godden, Nov. 26, 1985. BA in Religious Studies, U. Santa Clara, Calif., 1982. Lic. real estate agt. Account corrdinator and trainer Revlon, Inc. Borghese div., New York, 1983-84; Cypress Gardens housing mgr. Housing Authority Santa Clara County, San Jose, Calif., 1983-87; realtor Gibson Properties / Better Homes and Gardens, San Jose, Calif., 1987—. Edward Alverez grant U. Santa Clara, 1978-82; scholar State of Calif. , 1978-82. Mem. San Jose Real Estate Bd., Women's Club, Santa Clara Club. Republican. Roman Catholic. Home: PO Box 514 Santa Clara CA 95052 Office: Gibson Properties/Better Homes and Gardens 5570 Sanchez Dr San Jose CA 95123

GODEKE, RAYMOND DWIGHT, poultry company executive; b. San Diego, Nov. 26, 1947; s. Robert Carroll and Julia Mae (Caeser) G.; m. Norma Dean Rhodes, Oct. 31, 1966(div. 1970); 1 child, Melyssa Dawn; m. Vicki Lorraine Coleman, Feb. 19, 1972; 1 child, Kristin Francine. AA, Fullerton Coll., 1976; BA, Calif. State U.-Fullerton, 1978; MBA, Pepperdine U., 1980. Cert. internal auditor, cert. mgmt. accountant. Acct. Robert Johnston & Assocs., Lynwood, Calif., 1974-75; mem. acctg. staff Denny's, Inc., La Mirada, Calif., 1975-82, div. controller, 1982-87; div. controller Foster Farms, Livingston, Calif., 1987—, controller sales and mktg., 1988--. Chmn. Arrowhead dist. Boy Scouts Am., 1986. Mem. Nat. Assn. Accts. (bd. dirs. 1982-83), Inst. Internal Auditors (cert. internal auditor), Inst. Cert. Mgmt. Accts., Masons, Scottish Rite. Republican. Presbyterian. Office: Foster Farms 1000 Davis St Livingston CA 95334

GODFREY, BRUCE LEE, III, marine corps officer; b. Enid, Okla., June 27, 1951; s. Bruce Lee Jr. and Margaret Roberta (Ryan) G.; m. France Ingrid Karotsch, June 30, 1977; children: Bruce Lee IV, Stephanie Marie, Charles Brian, Paul Ryan. BS, SUNY, Albany, 1989. Commd. 2d lt. USMC, 1975, advanced through grades to maj., 1988; adjutant Marine Wing Support Group 37, El Toro, Calif., 1982-83; ops. officer detachment A, Marine Tactical Reconaissance Squadron 3, USS Midway (CV-41), 1983-84; ops. officer detachment C Marine Tactical Reconaissance Squadron 3, USS Midway (CV-4l), Iwakuni, Japan, 1986-87; exec. officer Marine Air Base Squadron ll, El Toro, 1984-86, Marine Air Base Squadron 11, El Toro, 1984-86; ops. officer 7th Marine Expeditionary Brigade, Twenty Nine Palms, Calif., 1988—. Mem. Marine Corps Assn., Nat. Geog. Soc., Aircraft Owners and Pilots Assn., Mensa. Home: 7930 Grand Ave Yucca Valley CA 92284 Office: 7th MEB (G-3) MCAGCC Twentynine Palms CA 92278

GODFREY, RICHARD GEORGE, real estate appraiser; b. Sharon, Pa., Dec. 18, 1927; s. Fay Morris and Elisabeth Maguerite (Stefanak) G.; m. Golda Fay Goss, Oct. 28, 1951; children: Deborah Jayne, Gayle Rogers, Bryan Edward. BA, Ripon Coll., 1949. V.p. 1st Thrift & Loan Assn., Albuquerque, 1959-61; pres. Richard G. Godfrey & Assocs., Inc., Albuquerque, 1961—. Mem. Am. Inst. Real Estate Appraisers (v.p. 1981-82), Valuation Network, Inc., Am. Right of Way Assn., Am. Soc. Real Estate Counselors (cert.). Baptist. Home: 1700 Columbia Dr SE Albuquerque NM 87106 Office: 523 Louisiana Blvd SE Albuquerque NM 87108

GODFREY, WILLARD H., JR., marketing company executive; b. Salt Lake City, Jan. 10, 1938; children: Ben, Shawn, Kim, Mike, Michelle. Student, Colo. State U., 1956-58; BS, Brigham Young U., 1963; MS, U. Ariz., 1965; PhD, Montana State U., Bozeman, 1969. Mktg. specialist U. Ariz., Tucson, 1963-65, Montana State U., Bozeman, Mont., 1965-69; asst. prof. bus. Central Wash. State, Ellensburg, Wash., 1968-70; prof. mktg. Boise State U., Boise, Idaho, 1971-78; v.p. mktg. Murdock Internat., Provo, Utah, 1978-83; owner, exec. Bus. Venture Systems, Irvine, Calif., 1983--; owner, mgr. Fly Fishing Ctr. Internat., Island Park, Idaho, 1967-86; v.p. mktg. Fedn. of Fly Fishers, West Yellowstone, Mont., 1970-83; bd. Am. Museum of Fly Fishers, Vt., 1973-78. Author numerous articles in field. Chmn. Pacific Marine Fisheries Commn., Idaho, 1976-78, Idaho Fish and Game Commn., State of Idaho, Boise, 1975-79. Recipient Educator of Yr. award, Boise State U., Boise, Idaho, 1977, NEA, 1971, 1973, Man of Yr. award, Fedn. of Fly Fishers, West Yellowstone, Mont., 1971, President's Pin, 1971. Mem. Am. League of Anglers (bd. mem. 1972-76), Toastmasters. Mormon. Office: Bus Venture Systems 6262 Sierra Siena Irvine CA 92715

GODLEWSKI, KRYSTOF JAN, physician; b. Krakow, Poland, Apr. 6, 1957; s. Julian and Barbara Jadwiga (Preisner) G.; m. M. Catherine Gornet, Apr. 23, 1988. BA, Copernicus Med. Sch., Krakow, 1975-80; MD, Bowman Gray Sch. of Medicine, Winston-Salem, N.C, 1983. Resident in internal medicine U. Conn. Med. Ctr., Farmington, 1983-84, Cleve. Clinic Found., 1984-86; practicing internist Cleve., Libby, Mont., Ketchikan, Ala., 1986-87; fellow in cardiology U. Calif., Irvine, 1987—. Democrat. Office: U Calif Irvine Med Ctr The City Dr Orange CA 92668

GODWIN, JOYCE, health and business services executive; b. Washington, July 25, 1943; m. Earl R. Godwin. BA in Govt., Fla. State U., 1965; MA in Polit. Sci. and Pub. Adminstrn., George Washington U., 1967. Dir. inquiry service Nat. League Cities, Washington, 1965-68; mem. polit. sci. faculty Calif. State Coll., San Jose, 1968-71; mgr. govtl. and pub. affairs San Jose (Calif.) C. of C., 1968-69, gen. mgr., 1969-70, acting exec. v.p., 1970-71; dir. staff devel. Meml. Med. Ctr., Corpus Christi, Tex., 1971-73; dir. edn. Southwest Community Health Services, Albuquerque, 1973-74, dir. personnel, 1974-79, v.p. mgmt. services, 1979-85, v.p. diversification, 1985-86, sec. corp., bd. dirs., 1982—; pres. Southwest Bus. Ventures Inc., 1986—, Vanguard Properties Inc., 1986—; v.p. Southwest Health Found., 1981—; pres., chmn. bd. dirs. MedWest, Inc., 1984—, Total Bus. Systems, Inc., 1981—. Contbr. articles to profl. publs. Chmn. orchestra relations com. N.Mex. Symphony Orch., 1985—, exec. com., 1985-86, bd. dirs., 1983—; assoc. gen. chmn. United Way, 1987. Mem. Greater Albuquerque C. of C. (chmn. roadrunners, bd. dirs., exec. com. 1984, chmn. statewide econ. devel. task force 1985, officer 1985-86, v.p. econ. affairs div. 1985, v.p. ednl. affairs div. 1986, v.p. membership 1987). Office: Southwest Bus Ventures Inc PO Box 26027 Albuquerque NM 87125-6027

GOEBEL, RICHARD MCNEIL, real estate broker; b. Grand Junction, Colo., Feb. 27, 1955; s. Douglas McNeil and Sally Ann (St. John) G.; m. Virginia Lee Biddle, June 13, 1981; children: Jennifer Lorraine, Stephen Richard. BA in History, Colo. Coll., 1977; graduate, Jones Sch. Real Estate, 1984; postgrad., Comm. Investment Real Estate Council. Lic. real estate broker Colo. Community developer Voice Calvary Ministries, Jackson, Miss., 1977-81; with real estate sales Leech Real Estate and Parker Real Estate, Jackson, 1981-83; broker real estate Moore and Co., Denver, 1984—; instr. Moore Sch. Real Estate, Denver, 1987—. Author, marketer: (marketing newsletter) Homestead Market Report, 1984—. Vol. chaplain Swedish Med. Str., Denver, 1988—; Stephen's minister St. Andrew United Meth. Ch., Littleton, Colo., 1988—, also head of ch. and soc. work area, 1987. Mem. Jackson Assn. Realtors, Miss. Assn. Realtors, Nat. Assn. Realtors, S. Suburban Bd. Realtors, Colo. Bd. Realtors, Nat. Assocs. Realtors, Rocky Mt. Urantia Soc. Republican. Home: 7131 S Forest Ct Littleton CO 80122 Office: Moore & Co 7300 E Arapahoe Rd Englewood CO 80112

GOECKS, JAMES RALPH, electronics engineer; b. Portland, Oreg., May 10, 1953; s. Roy C. and Barbara (Aspinwall) G.; m. Jean Shute, Aug. 18, 1973; children: Kristine, Heather, Jeremy, Gabriel. BS in Physics, Harvey Mudd Coll., 1975; MSEE, U. Portland, 1983. Electronics engr. Challenger Electronics, Portland, 1979-80, Hewlett-Packard, Vancouver, Wash., 1980-85; sr. electronics engr., project mgr. Saba Techs., Beaverton, Oreg., 1985—; cons. North Pacific Communications, Portland, 1980-85. Bd. dirs. Servant Mgmt. Group, Camas, Wash.; chmn. stewardship com. Camas Friends Ch., 1987—. Served to 1st lt. U.S. Army, 1975-79. Mem. Lions, Masons (sec. Clarke club 1988—), Order Ea. Star (assoc. patron 1988—). Home: 21021 SE 41st St Camas WA 98607 Office: Saba Techs 9300 SW Gemini Dr Beaverton OR 97005

GOERING, LEONARD LOWELL, clergyman, psychotherapist, philosophy educator; b. McPherson, Kans., June 22, 1938; s. Ellis Elbert and Esther Elva (Wedel) G.; m. Imogene Helen Ediger, June 10, 1957 (div. 1969); children: Preston, Angela; m. Jane Ellen Kurtz, Dec. 15, 1979; children: David, Jonathan, Rebecca. PhB, Northwestern U., 1964; postgrad., Northeastern Ill. U., 1969-71; MDiv, McCormick Theol. Sem., 1973; postgrad., Vanderbilt U., 1975-77. Ordained to ministry Presbyn. Ch., 1977. Campus minister United Ministries in Higher Edn., Emporia, 1973-75; instr. philosophy, coll. chaplain Coll. Emporia, Kans., 1973-74, Univ. Christian Ministries, Carbondale, Ill., 1977-80; pastor United Presbyn. Ch., Trinidad, Colo., 1981—; instr. philosophy Trinidad State Jr. Coll., 1983—; pres. Family Guidance Services, Trinidad, 1985-87; exec. dir. Family Guidance Services, Trinidad, 1987—. Editorial adv. bd. Collegiate Press. Coord. congl. dist. Bread for the World, Illinois, 1979-81; chmn. local bd. Emergency Food & Shelter Program Fed. Emergency Mgmt. Agy., Las Animas County, Colo., 1983-86; behavioral specialist human rights com. So. Colo. Devel. Disabilities Svcs. Mem. Acad. Parish Clergy, Assn. Mental Health Clergy, Am. Assn. Profl. Hypnotherapists, Trinidad Ministerial Assn., Internat. Platform Assn. Lodge: Kiwanis. Home: 721 Pine St Trinidad CO 81082 Office: United Presbyn Ch 224 N Commercial Trinidad CO 81082

GOETZINGER, JAMES HERMAN, educational administrator; b. Cascade, Iowa, May 27, 1941; s. Gerald F. and Margaret (Soll) G.; m. Patricia Rose O'Farrell, Apr. 30, 1966; chldren: Janet Lee, Cheryl Lynn. BA, Loras Coll., 1963; MA, Vanderbilt U., 1969; PhD, 1972. Cert. tchr., adminstr., N.Mex. Writer Commerce Clearinghouse, Chgo., 1964-65; tchr., coach Winston Park Sch., Palatine, Ill., 1964-68, St. Viator High Sch., Arlington Heights, Ill., 1966-68; tchr. Los Alamos (N.Mex.) High Sch., 1971-87, athletic dir., 1987-88, asst. prin., 1988—; instr. U. N.Mex., Los Alamos, 1972-87; asst. prof. N.Mex. State U., Las Cruces, 1989—; cons. N.Mex. Dept. Edn., Santa Fe, 1974-82. Mem. state com., N.Mex. Dem. party, 1982-86; subcom. chair, Project 2000, Los Alamos Schs., 1988—. Mem. Nat. Assn. Athletic Dirs., N.Mex. Assn. Sch. Adminstrs., N.Mex. Coun. Social Studies (pres. 1976-77), Phi Delta Kappa. Roman Catholic. Home: Rte 11 Box 325 F Santa Fe NM 87501 Office: Los Alamos High Sch 1300 Diamond Dr Los Alamos NM 87544

GOETZKE, GLORIA LOUISE, medical social worker; b. Monticello, Minn.; d. Wesley and Marvel (Kreidler) G. BA, U. Minn., 1964; MSW, U. Denver, 1966; MBA, Coll. St. Thomas, 1977. Med. social worker VA Med. Ctr., Los Angeles, 1980—; income tax preparer and instr. H&R Block, Santa Monica, Calif., 1980—; preceptor for grad. social work students at UCLA and U. So. Calif. Mem. Nat. Assn. Social Workers (cert.; dip.), Nat. Assn. of Enrolled Agts. Lutheran.

GOFF, FRANK WARD, banker; b. Mullen, Idaho, Aug. 26, 1936; s. Floyd Edward and Evelene (Ochs) G.; m. Arvilla Anne Michael, Mar. 24, 1956; children: Carol Anne, David Franklin, Diane Michele, Shari Lynn. BBA, U. Puget Sound, 1958; MBA, Pacific Luth. U., 1972. Systems mgr. Nat. Bank Wash., Tacoma, 1963-67; programmer/analyst Seattle 1st Nat. Bank, 1967-72, corr. bank svcs. mgr., 1972-76, systems mgr., 1976-78, spl. projects mgr., 1978-83, mgr. fin. acctg. projects, 1983-86; fin. planning officer Puget Sound Nat. Bank, Tacoma, 1986-88, mgr. fin. acctg. projects, 1988—. Mem. Data Processing Mgmt. Assn. (pres. Puget Sound chpt. 1965-66), Bank Adminstrn. Inst. (pres. Puget Sound chpt. 1984-85). Mem. Christian Ch.

GOFF, HARRY RUSSELL, manufacturing company executive; b. San Francisco, May 24, 1915; s. Harry Roy and Ethel S. (Ludwigsen) G.; B.A., Stanford U., 1937; M.B.A., Harvard U., 1939; m. Kathleen K. Kloster, Feb. 10, 1940; children: Kathleen, Karen, Betsi. With Nat. Lead Co., San Francisco, 1939-41; prtnr. James D. Dole & Assocs., San Francisco, 1946-60; pres. James Dole Corp., San Francisco, 1955-79; chmn. bd., Pacific Sci. Co., Anaheim, Calif., 1979—; vice chmn. Stanford U. Library Assn., 1979—; mem. Nat. Pub. Adv. Com. on Regional Econs. Devel., 1974-76. Served with USNR, 1941-46. Mem. Inst. Food Technologists. Republican. Clubs: Bohemian, University (San Francisco); Los Altos Golf and Country; California (Los Angeles). Home: 868 Southampton Dr PO Box 50095 Palo Alto CA 94303 Office: Pacific Sci Co 3603 Haven Ave Menlo Park CA 94025

GOFF, STEVEN LEE, real estate executive; b. Rupert, Idaho, Oct. 10, 1958; s. James Roland and Lanell (Doane) G.; m. Melanie Lee Pierce; children: Brandon James, Whitney Lee. BS in Bus. Fin., Brigham Young U., 1984. Property mgr. Tomlinson and Assocs., Boise, Idaho, 1985-88, First Columbia Mgmt., Seattle, 1988-89, Puget Sound Bank, Tacoma, 1989—. Varsity scout coach Boy Scouts Am., Meridian, Idaho, 1986-88. Mem. Inst. Real Estate Mgmt., Bldg. Owners and Mgrs. Assn., Nat. Apt. Assn. (nat. pres. coun. 1988), Idaho Multi-Housing Assn. (pres. 1987-88), Boise C. of C. (grad. Leadership 1986-88), Ducks Unltd. (banquet com. 1987). Mormon. Home: 4346 S 347th St Auburn WA 98001 Office: Puget Sound Bank PO Box 11500 Tacoma WA 98411

GOGGIN, JOHN R., systems engineer; b. Lynwood, Calif., June 26, 1951; s. John R. and Pauline Ruth (Robinson). BA in Math. and Computer Sci., U. Tex., 1974. Programmer, analyst Potomac Electric Power Co., Washington, 1974-75; assoc. Analytics, Inc., McLean, Va., 1975-79; sr. analyst Pattern Analysis & Recognition, Colorado Springs, 1979-80; research assoc. Colo. State U., Ft. Collins, 1980-81; software engr. Ford Aerospace, Colorado Springs, 1982-84; software design engr. Hewlett Packard Co., Colorado Springs, 1985-88; sr. software engr. Kentek Info. Systems, Boulder, Colo., 1988—. Various positions Am. Lung Assn., Colorado Springs, 1980—. Mem. Mensa, Colo. Mountain Club.

GOGOLIN, MARILYN TOMPKINS, educational administrator, language pathologist; b. Pomona, Calif., Feb. 25, 1946; d. Roy Merle and Dorothy (Davidson) Tompkins; m. Robert Elton Gogolin, Mar. 29, 1969. BA, U. LaVerne, Calif., 1967; MA, U. Redlands, Calif., 1968; postgrad., U. Washington, 1968-69; MS, Calif. State U., Fullerton, 1976. Cert. clin. speech pathologist; cert. teaching and sch. adminstrn. Speech/lang. pathologist Rehab. Hosp., Pomona, 1969-71; diagnostic tchr. Los Angeles County Office of Edn., Downey, Calif., 1971-72, program specialist, 1972-75, cons. lang., 1975-76, cons. orgns. and mgmt., 1976-79, asst. to supt., 1979—; cons. lang. sch. dists., Calif., 1975-79; cons. orgn. and mgmt. and profl. assns., Calif., 1976—; exec. dir. Los Angeles County Sch. Trustees Assn., 1979—. Founding patron Desert chpt. Kidney Found., Palm Desert, Calif., 1985. Doctoral fellow U. Washington, 1968; named One of Outstanding Young Women Am., 1977. Mem. Am. Mgmt. Assn., Am. Speech/Hearing Assn., Calif. Speech/Hearing Assn., Am. Edn. Research Assn. Baptist. Home: 15 Sweetwater Irvine CA 92715 Office: Los Angeles County Office Edn 9300 E Imperial Hwy Downey CA 90242

GOGTE, SUDHEER TRIMBAK, cardiologist; b. Amravati, India, Oct. 16, 1947; came to U.S., 1971; s. Trimbak Mahadev and Eashadaya (Lele) G.; m. Manju Sudheer Gupta, June 21, 1971; children: Sushrut, Ravi. BS, Vidarbha Maha Vidyalva, Amravati, 1965; MBBS, All-India Inst. Med. Sci., New Delhi, 1969. Diplomate Am. Bd. Internal Medicine, Am. Bd. Cardiology. Tutor All-India Inst. Med. Sci., Delhi, 1971-73; asst. research officer ICMR, Delhi, 1971; pvt. practice Sierra Vista, Ariz., 1981—; vice chief of staff Sierra Vista Community Hosp., 1983-85, chief of staff, 1988-89. Research fellow All-India Inst. Med. Sci. Fellow Am. Coll. Cardiology, Am. Coll. Chest Physicians, Clin. Council on Cardiology. Office: 2585 E Wilcox Dr Ste A Sierra Vista AZ 85635

GOGUE, GEORGE PAUL, electrical engineer; b. Basrah, Iraq, Oct. 3, 1949; came to U.S., 1981.; S. Paul Essa and Mary (Francis) G.; m. Kathryn Sayles, Apr. 25, 1981. BSEE, U. Basrah, 1969; MSEE, U. Aston, Birmingham, Eng., 1976, PhD, 1980. Lectr. U. Basrah, 1969-75; design engr. Walter Jones Co., London, 1980; rsch. engr. Electro-Craft, Hopkins, Minn., 1981-83; mgr. materials devel. Synektron Corp., Portland, Oreg., 1983-87; founder, owner G2 Cons., Beaverton, Oreg., 1987—. Patentee in field. Mem. IEEE. Home and Office: 9775 SW Rodeo Pl Beaverton OR 97005

GOHIL, PUNIT, physicist; b. Bhullarai, India, Apr. 8, 1957; came to U.S., 1983; s. Chaman Lal and Mohinder (Kuar) G. BSc in Physics, Imperial Coll., London, 1978, PhD and DIC in Physics, 1982. Rsch. fellow Sci. Rsch. Coun., Swindon, Eng., 1982-84; staff scientist II Lawrence Berkeley (Calif.) Lab., 1984-85; sr. scientist Gen. Atomics, San Diego, 1985—. Mem. AAAS, Am. Phys. Soc. Home: 3913 Carmel Brooks Way San Diego CA 92130 Office: Gen Atomics MS13-413 PO Box 85608 San Diego CA 92138

GOHL, ROGER E., interior designer; b. Sturgis, Mich., July 19, 1943; s. John Ernest and Nola Mae (Edwards) G.; m. Marlene Carole Wiley, Feb. 15, 1964; 1 child, Lance Eric. BFA, Art Ctr. Coll. Design, Pasadena, Calif., 1969. Fashion illustrator L.S. Ayres, Fort Wayne, Ind., 1963-66; interior designer Morganelli-Heuman Assocs., L.A., 1969-72; project designer Welton Becket Assocs., L.A., 1972-77, John Carl Warnecke Assocs., L.A., 1977-80, Gensler & Assocs., L.A., 1980-82, Integrated Design Assocs., L.A., 1982-88; owner, designer Intrasphere, Santa Monica, Calif., 1988—; design instr. UCLA, 1978-82. Designer: Indpls. city flag, 1962. Mem. Art Ctr. Alumni Assn. Home: 2643 Stoner Ave Los Angeles CA 90064 Office: Intrasphere 1750 B 14th St Santa Monica CA 90404

GOLABI, KAMAL, management scientist, consultant; b. Tehran, Iran, July 6, 1942; came to U.S., 1970; s. Haji Agha and Rafat (Mansuri) G.; children: Leila, Kavé. BS, Abadan (Iran) Inst. Tech., 1967; MS, U. Calif., Berkeley, 1971; PhD, UCLA, 1976. Process engr. Iranian Oil Refining Co., Abadan, 1967-70; asst. prof. Calif. State U., Northridge, 1974-75; asst. rsch. prof. UCLA, 1976-77; sr. scientist Woodward-Clyde Cons., San Francisco, 1977-81; assoc. prof. U. Pitts., 1981-84; pres. Optima, Inc., San Francisco, 1984—; consulting prof. Stanford U., Palo Alto, Calif., 1984-88; cons. to several fed., internat. and pub. policy agys.; pioneer in infrastructure and pub. policy decision systems. Contbr. articles to profl. jours. Regents fellow U. Calif., 1971; winner Franz Edelman award, 1982. Mem. Inst. Mgmt. Scis., Ops. Rsch. Soc. Am., Transp. Rsch. Bd., Internat. Soc. Inventory Rsch. (founding mem.). Home: 57 Richardson Rd Kensington CA 94707 Office: Optima Inc 517 Washington St Ste 205 San Francisco CA 94111

GOLD, ERIC JOSEPH, real estate developer; b. Chgo., June 3, 1962; s. Robert Elmer and Marsha Diane (Miller) G. BSBA, U. Denver, 1984. Mktg. asst. Bill L. Walters Co., Denver, 1983; exec. property mgr. Falcon Ventures, Denver, 1984-85; sales assoc. Comml. Property Leasing, Denver, 1985; broker assoc. Anderson Investments, Denver, 1985-86; pres., owner Sheldon Gold Realty, Inc., Denver, 1986—. Mem. Aurora C. of C. Office: Sheldon Gold Realty Inc 7979 E Tufts Ave #602 Denver CO 80237

GOLD, MICHAEL NATHAN, biomedical engineer; b. Chgo., May 3, 1952; s. Julius and Sarah (Blitzblau) G.; m. Cynthia Bilicki, June 19, 1976; children: Aaron Michael, Nathan Matthew. BA, Kalamazoo Coll., 1976; cert. in exec. mgmt. UCLA, 1989. Research fellow Sinai Hosp., Detroit, 1976; research assoc. Molecular Biological Inst., UCLA, Los Angeles, 1976-77; lab mgr., adminstr. Biomed. Engring. Ctr., U. So. Calif., Los Angeles, 1977-80; asst. dir. Crump Inst., UCLA, 1980-84, assoc. dir., exec. officer Crump Inst. for Med. Engring., UCLA, Los Angeles, 1984-89; chmn., pres. Therapeutic Environments Inc., 1989—. Mem. IEEE, Assn. for Advancement of Med. Instrumentation, Clin. Ligand Assay Soc., Am. Assn. for Med. Systems and Informatics, Sea Edn. Assn., Biomed. Engring. Soc., Internat. Soc. for Optical Engring. Office: Therapeutic Environments Inc 6222 Mammoth Ave Van Nuys CA 91401

GOLD, RICHARD HORACE, radiologist; b. N.Y.C., Nov. 20, 1935; s. Samuel Joseph and Edith (Vogel) G.; m. Gittelle Schneider, June 27, 1965; children: Lara, David. BA, NYU, 1956; MD, U. Louisville, 1960. Diplomate Am. Bd. Radiology. Intern Pa. Hosp., Phila., 1960-61; resident in radiology Yale-New Haven (Conn.) Hosp., 1963-66; fellow in skeletal radiology U. Calif., San Francisco, 1967-68, asst. prof. radiology, 1968-72; asst. prof. radiology UCLA, 1972-74, assoc. prof. radiology, 1974-78, prof. radiology, 1978—, chief div. gen. diagnostics radiology, 1986—; cons. Wadsworth Vets. Hosp., Sepulveda V.A. Hosp., 1979—. Author: Roentgen Appearance of Hand in Diffuse Disease, 1975, Clinical Arthrography, 2d edition, 1986, Breast Ultrasound, 1986, Breast Cancer Detection, 2 edit., 1987, MRI Atlas of the Musculoskeletal system, 1989; bd. adv. editors Clin. Orthopaedics and Related Research, 1987—; bd. editors Investigative Radiology, 1987—; contbr. articles to profl. jours. Active Breast Task Force Am. Joint Com. on Cancer, 1979—; chmn. breast cancer task force Calif. div. Am. Cancer Soc., 1984-87, nat. task force breast cancer control, 1977-82. Capt. USAF, 1961-63. Recipient Commr.'s Spl. Citation USPHS, 1981. Fellow Am. Coll. Radiology; mem. Assn. Univ. Radiologists, Radiol. Soc. N.Am., Am. Roentgen Ray Soc., Internat. Skeletal Soc., Alpha Omega Alpha. Office: UCLA Sch Medicine Dept Radiol Scis Los Angeles CA 90024

GOLD, ROBERT J., inventor; b. N.Y.C., Mar. 10, 1953; s. E. Frank and Etta (Hirsch) G. Student, Queens Coll., 1971-73. Pres. Gold Research and Devel., N.Y.C., 1973-81; dir. research Neoteric Inc., N.Y.C., 1981-83; pres. Neoteric Inc. (name changed to Power Staf Inc.), Phoenix, 1983-87; also bd. dirs. Neoteric Inc., Phoenix; pres. GoldMind Assocs., Glendale, Ariz., 1987—; v.p. First Am. Counter-Terrorist Systems, Inc. (FACTS Inc.), 1988—; cons. Law Enforcement Tech. Mag., N.Y.C., 1985-88; speaker Nat. Orgn. Wardens, San Antonio, 1984, Am. Def. Preparedness Assn., Virginia Beach, Va., 1986, others. Contbg. editor L.E.T. mag.; contbr. articles to profl. jours.; patentee non-lethal equipment. Mem. Internat. Non-Lethal Weapons Assn., Tactical Response Assn., Am. Soc. Law Enforcement Trainers. Office: GoldMind Assocs Box 88 Cedar Creek TX 78612

GOLDAPER, GABRIELE GAY, clothing executive, consultant; b. Amsterdam, The Netherlands, May 4, 1937; came to U.S., 1949; d. Richard and Gertrud (Sinzheimer) Mainzer; married, 1957; children: Carolyn, Julie, Nancy. BA in Econs., Barnard Coll., 1959; BS in Edn., U. Cin., 1960; postgrad., Xavier U., 1962. V.p. planning, systems and material control High Tide Swimwear div. Warnaco, Los Angeles, 1974-79; v.p., customer support cons. Silton AMS, Los Angeles, 1979-80; exec. v.p., ptnr. Prisma Corp., Los Angeles, 1980-84; exec. v.p. Mindstar Prods., Los Angeles, 1984-85; gen. mgr. Cherry Lane, Los Angeles, 1985-86; dir. inventory mgmt. Barco Uniforms, Los Angeles, 1986; mgmt. cons. to clothing industry Santa Monica, Calif., 1986—; instr. Calif. State U., 1978-79, UCLA Grad. Bus. Mgmt. Sch., 1979-86, Fashion Inst. Design and Merchandising. 1985—; chmn. data processing com. Calif. Fashion Creators, 1980; mediator Los Angeles County Bar Assn.; cons. Exec. Service Corps; lectr. various colls. Author: A Results Oriented Approach to Manufacturing Planning, 1978, Small Company View of the Computer, 1979; also articles. Elected mem. Commn. on Status Women, 1985—. Mem. Apparel Mfrs. Assn. (mgmt. systems com. 1978-80), Calif. Apparel Industries Assn. (exec. com., bd. dirs. 1980), Am. Arbitration Assn. Home: 37 Village Pkwy Santa Monica CA 90405

GOLDBERG, DAVID BEN, record company executive; b. Eutin, Fed. Republic Germany, Oct. 6, 1956; came to U.S., 1957; s. Herbert H. and Leah (Gerlach) G.; m. Karin Ezra, Dec. 28, 1987. AB, Columbia U., 1978; AM, U. So. Calif., 1981; postgrad., Harvard U., 1983-84. Pres., chief exec. officer Merkava Prodns., Tarzana, Calif., 1981—. Producer, vocalist (record albums) Israel's Gold, 1986, Hallel, 1989; organizer world tour band MERKAVA, 1988-89. Recipient Disting. Performance award Royal Musical Conservatory, Manchester, Eng., 1986. Office: Merkava Prodns PO Box 81 Tarzana CA 91357-0081

GOLDBERG, EDWARD DAVIDOW, geochemist, educator; b. Sacramento, Aug. 2, 1921; s. Edward Davidow and Lillian (Rothholz) G.; m. Kathe Bertine, Dec. 26, 1973; children—David Wilkes, Wendy Jean, Kathi Kiri, Beck Bertine. B.S., U. Calif.-Berkeley, 1942; Ph.D., U. Chgo., 1949. Mem. faculty Scripps Instn. Oceanography, La Jolla, Calif., 1949—; prof. chemistry Scripps Instn. Oceanography, 1960—; provost Revelle Coll., U. Calif. at San Diego, 1965-66; condr. research and author publs. on subjects including marine pollution, chem. composition of sea water, sediments, marine organisms, environmental management; vis. prof. chemistry U. Otago Dunedin, New Zealand, 1988. Author: (with J. Geiss) Earth Sciences and Meteorites, 1964, Guide to Marine Pollution, 1972, North Sea Science, 1973, The Sea: Marine Chemistry, Vol. V, 1974, The Health of the Oceans, 1976; Black Carbon in the Environment, 1985. Contbr. numerous articles to profl. jours. Guggenheim fellow, 1961; NATO fellow, 1970; U.S. Nat. Acad. Scis. exchange scholar, 1987. Fellow Am. Geophys. Union, AAAS; mem. Geochem. Soc., U.S. Acad. Scis., Sigma Xi. Home: 750 Val Sereno Dr Encinitas CA 92024

GOLDBERG, FRED SELLMANN, advertising executive; b. Chgo., Jan. 22, 1941; s. Sydney Norman and Birdie (Cohen) G.; m. Jerrilyn Toby Tager, Apr. 12, 1964; children—Robin Lynn, Susanne Joy. B.S., U. Vt., 1962; M.B.A., NYU, 1964. Mktg. research mgr. P. Ballantine & Sons, Newark, 1964-67; sr. v.p., mgmt. supr. Young & Rubicam, N.Y.C., 1967-78; sr. v.p., gen. mgr. Young & Rubicam, Los Angeles, 1978-82; exec. v.p., gen. mgr. Chiat-Day, Inc., San Francisco, 1982-85, exec. v.p., chief operational officer, 1985-87, pres., chief exec. officer, 1987—; vice chmn. Chiat/Day Advt., Los Angeles, 1987—. Republican. Jewish. Office: Chiat-Day Advt 77 Maiden Ln San Francisco CA 94108

GOLDBERG, GLENN ALAN, advocacy organization administrator; b. New Haven, Conn., Dec. 1, 1947; s. Herbert B. and Lillian Grace (Chauser) G.; m. Kari Zeh; 1 child, Jesse Zeh. BA with honors, U. Conn., 1969; JD, Columbia Law Sch., 1972. Bar: Conn. 1979, D.C. 1979. Trial atty. Bur. of Consumer Protection, FTC, Washington, 1972-74; instr. in law George Washington U., Washington, 1974-75; gen. counsel Action on Smoking & Health, Washington, 1974-75; adj. prof. Antioch Sch. of Law, Washington, 1975; exec. dir. Nat. Ctr. for Law & the Deaf, Gallaudet U., Washington, 1975-77, Deaf Counseling, Advocacy & Referral Agy., Oakland, Calif., 1978-80; non profit cons. Goldberg & Assocs., Pacific Grove, Calif., 1980-86; exec. dir. NorCal Ctr. on Deafness, Sacramento, Calif., 1986—; bd. dirs. Sacramento Community Cable Found. (chmn. fundraising com.), 1987—. Contbr. articles to profl. jours. Coord. Students for Ribicoff, Storrs, Conn., 1974; Senate Intern Senator Abraham Ribicoff, Washington, 1968; congressional intern Rep. Joseph Monahan, Washington, 1968. Mem. Nat. Assn. of the Deaf, Calif. Assn. of the Deaf, Self Help for Hard of Hearing People, Phi Beta Kappa. Democrat. Jewish. Office: NorCal Ctr on Deafness 2045 Hallmark Dr Sacramento CA 95825

GOLDBERG, HARVEY, financial executive; b. Bklyn., Jan. 30, 1940; s. Joseph and Regina (Goldkrantz) G.; m. Joyce Baron, Nov. 22, 1962; children—Keith, Jodi. BS in Acctg., Bklyn. Coll., 1962; postgrad. CCNY, 1963. CPA, N.Y. Sr. acct. Schwartz, Zelin & Weiss CPA's, N.Y.C., 1962-66; mgr. fin. analysis Columbia Records div. CBS, Inc., N.Y.C., 1966-70; asst. controller Revlon, Inc., N.Y.C., 1970-71; treas. Central Textile, Inc., Jersey City, 1971-74; controller Marcade Group, Inc., Jersey City, 1974-81, v.p., controller, 1981-86; v.p., chief fin. officer Paul Marshall Products, Inc., subs. Marcade Group, Long Beach, Calif., 1982-86, sr. v.p. chief fin. officer, 1988—; v.p., chief fin. officer, Players Internat., Inc., Calabasas, Calif., 1986-88, sr. v.p., chief fin. officer, 1988—. County committeeman Monmouth County Dem. Com., N.J., 1979-80; chmn. adv. bd. High Point Ctr., Marlboro, N.J., 1978-82; mem. Marlboro Twp. Bd. Edn., 1980-82, v.p., 1981-82; bd. dirs. Family Consultation Ctr., Freehold, N.J. , 1982-83. Mem. AICPA, N.Y. State Soc. CPA's, Met. Retail Fin. Execs. Assn. Home: 19798 Greenbriar Dr Tarzana CA 91356 Office: Players Internat Inc 23901 Calabasas Rd Calabasas CA 91302

GOLDBERG, KENNETH JAY, psychologist; b. N.Y.C., Apr. 18, 1953; a. Ira and Rosalind Edith (Spector) G.; m. Margaret Rose Krueser, July 13, 1980; children: Geoffrey William, Matthew Alan. BA summa cum laude, Boston U., 1975, MEd, 1977, EdD, 1982. Cert. psychologist, Ariz. Data base mgr. New Bedford (Mass.) Ctr. for Human Svcs., 1975-77; dir. Stoughton (Mass.) Youth Commn., 1977-79; assoc. dir. Counseling & Family Svcs., Inc., Brockton, Mass., 1979-81; chief psychol. cons. Ariz. Dept. Corrections, Phoenix, 1981-82; pres. Counseling & Family Resources Ltd., Tempe, Ariz., 1981—. Contbg. author: Handbook on Violent Juvenile Offenders, 1984. Recipient Kenneth B. Pickard innovative program award Mass. Mcpl. Assn., 1978. Fellow Am. Orthopsychiat. Assn.; mem. Am. Psychol. Assn., Ariz. Psychol. Assn., Acad. Family Psychologists, Pi Lambda Theta. Jewish. Office: Counseling & Family Resources Ltd 6101 S Rural Rd Ste 128 Tempe AZ 85283

GOLDBERG, LEE WINICKI, furniture company executive; b. Laredo, Tex., Nov. 20, 1932; d. Frank and Goldie (Ostrowiak) Winicki; student San Diego State U., 1951-52; m. Frank M. Goldberg, Aug. 17, 1952; children—Susan Arlene, Edward Lewis, Anne Carri. With United Furniture Co., Inc., San Diego, 1953-83, corp. sec., dir., 1963-83, dir. environ. interiors, 1970-83; founder Drexel-Heritage store Edwards Interiors, subs. United Furniture, 1975; founding ptnr., v.p. FLJB Corp., 1976—, founding ptnr., sec. treas., Sea Fin., Inc., 1980, founding ptnr., First Nat. Bank San Diego, 1982. Den mother Boy Scouts Am., San Diego, 1965; vol. Am. Cancer Soc., San Diego, 1964-69; chmn. jr. matrons United Jewish Fedn., San Diego, 1958; del. So. Pacific Coast region Hadassah Conv., 1960, pres. Galilee group San Diego chpt., 1960-61; supporter Marc Chagall Nat. Mus., Nice, France, Smithsonian Instn., Los Angeles County Mus., La Jolla (Calif.) Mus. Contemporary Art, San Diego Mus. Art. Recipient Hadassah Service award San Diego chpt., 1958-59. Democrat. Jewish.

GOLDBERG, MAX LOUIS, marketing executive; b. Bellefonte, Pa., Jan. 7, 1952; s. Earl Joseph Goldberg and Phyllis Leah (Rothner) Kirson; m. Lisa Beth Howard, Oct. 19, 1986. BA, George Washington U., 1973. Regional mktg. dir. Ringling Bros. Circus, Washington, 1973-75; mktg. dir. Am. Freedom Train, Washington, 1975; media dir. Advt. Agy. Assn., Boston, 1975-77; western mgr. Arbitron Ratings Co., L.A., 1977-80; sr. v.p. marketing Ice Capades, L.A., 1986-88; pres., chief exec. officer Max Goldberg and Assocs., L.A., 1981—. Mem. Common Cause, Handgun Control, People for the Am. Way. Mem. Acad. Magical Arts and Scis. Office: Max Goldberg & Assocs Inc 4289 Bakman Ave Studio City CA 91602

GOLDBERG, MAXINE SHEILA, advertising executive; b. Bronx, Aug. 2, 1941; d. Arnold and Beatrice (Fischel) Kesten; m. Arthur Stewart Goldberg, Apr. 11, 1964; children: Randy Michael, Kelly Sue. BA cum laude, Hunter Coll., 1962; postgrad., San Diego State U., 1966; MBA, Ariz. State U., 1980. Tchr. pub. schs. various locations, 1961-67, office mgr. various cos., 1968-77; with Capricchio, 1977-80; assoc. faculty Ariz. State U., Tempe, 1981-85; buyer/sr. buyer The Dial Corp., Phoenix, 1980; purchasing mgr. The Dial Corp., dir. purchasing, dir. spl. projects, v.p., dir. purchasing/advt. Mem. Nat. Assn. Purchasing Mgrs., Nat. Assn. MBA Execs., Purchasing Mgmt. Assn. Ariz., Packaging Inst., Internat. Food Technologists, Phi Beta Kappa, Kappa Delta Phi, Pi Lambda Theta, Beta Gamma Sigma, Sigma Iota Epsilon. Republican. jewish. Office: The Dial Corporation 111 W Clarendon Phoenix AZ 85077

GOLDBERG, MORRIS, internist; b. N.Y.C., Jan. 23, 1928; s. Saul and Lena (Schanberg) G.; B.S. in Chemistry cum laude, Poly. Inst. Bklyn., 1951; M.D., SUNY, Bklyn., 1956; m. Elaine Shaw, June 24, 1956; children—Alan Neil, Seth David, Nancy Beth. Intern, Jewish Hosp. Bklyn., 1956-57, resident, 1957-58, 61-62, renal fellow, 1958-59; practice medicine, specializing in internal medicine, N.Y.C., 1962-71, Phoenix, 1971—; instr. to asst. clin. prof. internal medicine State U. N.Y. Coll. Medicine, Bklyn., 1962-71; clin. investigator, metabolic research unit Jewish Hosp. Bklyn., 1962-71; cons. in field; mem. staff Phoenix Bapt., Maryvale Samaritan, Good Samaritan, St. Joseph's hosps. Served to capt. M.C., U.S. Army, 1959-61. Diplomate Am. Bd. Internal Medicine. Fellow ACP; mem. Am. Soc. Internal Medicine, AMA, Am. Coll. Nuclear Physicians, Internat. Soc. Internal Medicine, Am. Soc. Nephrology, Am. Soc. Hypertension, Ariz. Med. Assn., 38th Parallel Med. Soc. S. Korea, Ariz., Maricopa County med. assns., N.Y. Acad. Sci., Sigma Xi, Phi Lambda Upsilon, Alpha Omega Alpha. Jewish. Contbr. articles to med. jours. Home: 24 E Wagonwheel Dr Phoenix AZ 85020 Office: 11209 N Tatum Blvd Ste 150 Phoenix AZ 85028

GOLDBLATT, HAL MICHAEL, photographer, accountant; b. Long Beach, Calif., Feb. 6, 1952; s. Arnold Phillip and Molly (Stearns) G.; m. Shawn Naomi Doherty, Aug. 27, 1974; children: Eliyahu Yonah, Tova Devorah, Raizel, Shoshana, Reuven Lev, Eliezer Noach, Esther Bayla, Rochel Leah. BA in Math., Calif. State U., Long Beach, 1975. Owner Star Publs., Long Beach, 1975-80; treas. Goldblatt, Inc., Long Beach, 1980—. Photographer: (photo essays) Mikveh Yisroel, 1978, Chassidic Fabrengen, 1979; producer, engr.: (audio cassettes) From the Heart of My Dreams, 1980, Middle Class Dreams, 1981, Uforatzta Trio, 1982. Founder, pres. Jews for Judaism, Long Beach, 1975-82; fundraising chmn. Friends of Lubavitch, Long Beach, 1977; bd. dirs. Congregation Lubavitch, Long Beach, 1987. Recipient Gold Press Card award Forty Niner Newspaper, 1973, 74.

GOLDEN, JULIUS, advertising and public relations executive, lobbyist, investor; b. N.Y.C., Feb. 25, 1929; s. Nathan and Leah (Michlin) G.; m. Constance Lee Carpenter, Dec. 31, 1954 (div. Mar. 1965); children—Andrew Mitchell, Juliet Deborah; m. Diana Zana George, Apr. 30, 1973; 1 child, Jeremy Philip. B.A., U. N.Mex., 1952. Asst. dir. info. U. N.Mex., Albuquerque, 1952-53; writer AP, Albuquerque, part-time 1952-53, staff writer, 1953-55, fgn. corr., S.Am., 1956-59; pres. Group West Advt./Pub. Relations Albuquerque, 1959—; dir. Telemarks, Inc., Albuquerque, Diagnostek, Inc., Albuquerque, Galaxy Broadcasting Co., Albuquerque. Author: A Time to Die, 1975. Active Bernalillo County Lung Assn., 1961-64; mem. Met. Crime Commn., Albuquerque, 1967-71; chmn., 1970-71; mem. Albuquerque Police Commn. Task Force, 1988—. Served with AUS, 1945-48, PTO, Korea. Recipient Nat. Feature Writing award Sigma Delta Chi, 1952, E.H. Shaffer award N.Mex. Press Assn., 1953. Mem. Pub. Relations Soc. (pres. N.Mex. chpt. 1972), Profl. Journalism Soc. (pres. 1969-70), Pub. Relations Soc. N.Mex. pres. 1972), Am. Advt. Fedn., Sigma Delta Chi. Democrat. Jewish. Clubs: Overseas Press of Am., Albuquerque Press, Petroleum, 4 Hills Country. Home: 1408 Stagecoach Ln SE Albuquerque NM 87123 Office: Group West 7005 Prospect Pl NE Albuquerque NM 87110

GOLDEN, MORTON JAY, museum director; b. Bklyn., Apr. 11, 1929; s. Sam Carl and Anna (Denmark) G.; m. Evelyn Lois Gould, Oct. 6, 1956; children: Caron, Linda, Jay. BS, U. So. Calif., 1952. Dep. dir. Los Angeles County Mus. Art, 1972-82; dir. Palm Springs (Calif.) Desert Mus., 1982—; cons. M.A.P., 1984—. Treas., mem. exec. com. Greater Palm Springs Conv. and Visitors Bur., 1985—. Honor of Republic, nation of Egypt, 1978. Mem. Am. Assn. Mus. (cons. 1985-86, mem. accreditation rev. com. 1986), Calif. Assn. Mus. (chmn. bd. 1979-83, bd. dirs. 1985—), Mus. Mgmt. Inst. (sr. assoc.), Assn. Sci. Mus. Dirs. Democrat. Jewish. Office: Palm Springs Desert Mus Inc 101 Museum Dr PO Box 2288 Palm Springs CA 92263

GOLDEN, RALPH WILARD, electrical engineer; b. Superior, Wis., Sept. 24, 1937; s. Floyd W. and Ruth M. (Harper) G.; m. Mary Jane Sethre, Aug. 13, 1961 (dec. Jan. 1985); children: Gloria G., Jeffery T.; m. Coy M. Peterson, Apr. 4, 1987; children: Linda M. Peterson Carpender, Kathleen D. Peterson Miller, Steven O., Eric G. AAS in electronic tech., Milw. Tech. Coll., 1968; BSEE, U. Idaho, 1975; MEE, U. Idaho, Idaho Falls, 1981. Registered profl. engr., Idaho. Grain inspector Wis. State Grain Commn., Superior, 1959; material handler Am. Motor Corp., Milw., 1959-61, painter, 1962-67; receiving inspector AC Electronics of Gen. Motor Corp., Oak Creek, Wis., 1967-68; sr. engring. specialist EG&G Idaho, Inc., Idaho Falls, 1968; instrument technician Idaho Nat. Engring. Lab., 1968-70, assoc. engr. Idaho Nuclear Corp./ Aerojet Nuclear Corp., 1970-74, engr. Aerojet Nuclear Corp., 1975, sr. engr. Aerojet Nuclear Corp./EG&G Idaho, Inc., 1975-88, engring. specialist, 1988—. Contbr. articles to profl. jours. Asst. scoutmaster Boy Scouts Am., Idaho Falls, 1982—; camp pres. Gideons Internat., Idaho Falls, 1980—, bistate sec. Idaho-Utah Gideons, Idaho and Utah, 1987—. Served with USNG, 1955-62. Mrm. Inst. Soc. Am. (sr., sec.-pres. 1981-82). Mem. Alliance Covenant Ch. Club: Idaho Alpine (Idaho Falls). Home: 8051 S Ammon Rd Idaho Falls ID 83406 Office: EG&G Idaho Inc PO Box 1625 Idaho Falls ID 83415

GOLDEN, RENATA MICHELE, photographer, journalist; b. Chgo., Nov. 3, 1952; d. Michael Frances and Eileen Rose (Foley) G. Student, U. N.Mex., 1974-76; BS, Ariz. State U., 1978. Photojournalist The Mesa (Ariz.) Tribune, 1978-80; research asst. Mus. for Contemporary Art, Chgo., 1981; darkroom printer for Olympics AP, Los Angeles, 1984; instr. photography City of Phoenix, 1983-87; owner photographer Renata Golden Photography, Phoenix, 1980—. One-woman photography exhibitions Phoenix Pub. Library, 1984, Austin Gallery, Scottsdale, Ariz., 1987, Tempe Fine Arts Ctr., 1988; author, photographer articles and pictures for numerous publs. including Scottsdale Progress, USA Today, U.S. News and World Report, Christian Science Monitor, N.Y. Photo Dist. News. Office: 1222 E Edgemont Phoenix AZ 85006

GOLDEN, ROBERT LEON, astrophysicist; b. Alameda, Calif., July 28, 1940; s. Herbert Leon and Helen Maria (Haarala) G.; children: Lisa, John. BA, U. Calif., Berkeley, 1963, PhD, 1966. Researcher Johnson Space Ctr., NASA, Houston, 1968-75; chief space physics br. Johnson Space Ctr., NASA, 1975-77; assoc. prof., then prof. elec. engring. N. Mex. State U., Las Cruces, 1978—; dir. particle astrophysics lab. N. Mex. State U., 1986—; pres., Golden Aero, Inc., Las Cruces, 1977—. Contbr. to numerous profl. publs. Mem. IEEE, AIAA, Am. Phys. Soc., Am. Astron. Soc. Office: Particle Astrophysics Lab NMex State U Dept 3-PAL Las Cruces NM 88003

GOLDEN-MOORE, CINDI LOU, furniture retailer; b. Ann Arbor, Mich., Sept. 23, 1956; d. William R. Golden and Vedra (Hunt) Britton; m. David Wayne Moore, June 22, 1980; 1 child, Benjamin Jason. BA magna cum laude, Calif. State U., Northridge, 1985. Dental asst. Gene Harrington DDS, Hot Springs, Ark., 1976-79; prodn. mgr. Hi-Torque Publs., Encino, Calif., 1979-83; typographer Marchese Graphics, Los Angeles, 1983; supr. Bernard Hodes Advt., Encino, 1983-86; owner, operator GML Office Furniture, San Marcos, Calif., 1987—. Mem. Advt. Prodn. Assn., San Marcos C. of C. Republican. Home: 2344-C Caringa Way Carlsbad CA 92009 Office: GML Office Furniture 133-A Newport Dr San Marcos CA 92069

GOLDFARB, ROBERT STEVEN, broadcast executive; b. Hartford, Conn., Oct. 27, 1951; s. Samuel and Sophie (Maron) G. AB, Harvard Coll., 1973; MBA, Harvard U., 1978. Music dir. WCRB Radio, Boston, 1972-76; spl. asst. to exec. v.p. Nat. Pub. Radio, Washington, 1978-79; gen. mgr. WFCR

Radio, Amherst, Mass., 1979-82; exec. dir. Eastern Pub. Radio, Boston, 1982-84; chief oper. officer KUSC Radio, L.A., 1984-85; v.p. radio Western N.Y. Pub. Broadcasting, Buffalo, 1986; v.p. programming and ops. KFAC Radio, L.A., 1986—; broadcast cons., 1985—. Mem. Concert Music Broadcasters Assn. (treas. 1988—). Democrat. Jewish. Home: 1215 S La Cienega Blvd #C Los Angeles CA 90035 Office: Sta KFAC Radio 6735 Yucca St Los Angeles CA 90028

GOLDIE, RAY ROBERT, lawyer; b. Dayton, Ohio, Apr. 1, 1920; s. Albert S. and Lillian (Hayman) G.; student U. So. Calif., 1943-44, J.D., 1957; student San Bernardino Valley Coll., 1950-51; JD U. So. Calif., 1957; m. Dorothy Roberta Zafman, Dec. 2, 1941; children—Marilyn, Deanne, Dayle, Ron R. Elec. appliance dealer, 1944-54; teaching asst. U. So. Calif. Law Sch., 1956-57; admitted to Calif. bar, 1957; dep. atty. gen. State of Calif., 1957-58; sole practice, San Bernardino, 1958-87. Pres., Trinity Acceptance Corp., 1948-53. Mem. World Peace Through Law Center, 1962—; regional dir. Legion Lex, U. So. Calif. Sch. Law, 1959-75; chmn. San Bernardino United Jewish Appeal, 1963; v.p. United Jewish Welfare Fund San Bernardino, 1964-66, Santa Anita Hosp., Lake Arrowhead, 1966-69. Bd. dirs. San Bernardino Med. Arts Corp. Served with AUS, 1942-43. Fellow Internat. Acad. Law and Sci.; mem. ABA, San Bernardino County Bar Assn., Riverside County Bar Assn., State Bar Calif., Am. Judicature Soc., Am. Soc. Hosp. Attys., Calif. Trial Lawyers Assn. (v.p. chpt. 1965-67, pres. 1967-68), Am. Arbitration Assn. (nat. panel arbitrators), Coachella Valley Desert Bar Assn., Order of Coif, Nu Beta Epsilon (pres. 1956-57). Club: Lake Arrowhead Country (pres. 1972-73, 80-81), Lake Arrowhead Yacht, Club at Morningside. Home and Office: 1 Hampton Ct Rancho Mirage CA 92270

GOLDING, GEORGE EARL, journalist; b. Oakdale, Calif., Aug. 26, 1925; s. Herbert Victor and Elva M. (Leydecker) G.; m. Joyce Mary Buttner, July 15, 1948; children: Earlene Golding Bigot, Brad Leslie, Dennis Lee, Frank Edwin, Charlton Kenneth, Daniel Duane. AA, Modesto Jr. Coll., 1950; BA San Francisco State Coll., 1959. Advt. salesman Riverbank News, 1949; galley bank boy, cub reporter San Bernardino Sun, 1951; editor Gustine Standard, 1952; photographer-reporter Humboldt Times, 1952-56; reporter, asst. city editor San Mateo (Calif.) Times, 1956-63; staff writer, corr. UPI; contbg. writer, photographer Nat. Motorist mag.; aviation writer, columnist Flight Log. Pub. relations adviser Powder Puff Derby start. 1972. Served with U.S. Maritime Service, 1943, USAAF, 1944-46, AUS, 1950. Recipient John Swett award Calif. Tchrs. Assn., 1964; nominee McQuaid award Cath. Newsmen, 1965, 68; A.P. and Ency. Brit. photography awards, 1954-55, A.P. newswriting award, 1964. Mem. Am. Newspaper Guild, San Francisco-Oakland News Guild, Aviation/Space Writers Assn. (various awards 1983-84), Peninsula Press Club (founding dir., pres. 1976, co-chmn. awards and installation 1986-87), San Mateo County Arts Council (charter). Home: 1625 Ark St San Mateo CA 94403 Office: 1080 S Amphlett Blvd San Mateo CA 94402

GOLDING, LOIS HAMBLETT, professional pianist; b. Calgary, Sept. 24, 1921; d. Reginald William and Florence Jessica (Hayes) Hamblett; m. William Roy Goodwin, Mar. 21, 1941 (dec. 1944); m. Thomas Alexander Stewart Golding, Sept. 11, 1947; children: Ross Hamblett, Bruce Stewart, Mark Alexander, Lyn Alison. A in Music, McGill U., Montreal, 1939, LMus, 1940; ATCL, Trinity Coll., London, 1938, LTCL, 1965, FTCL, 1966. Concert pianist TV, radio concertos with orchs. and solo performances, 1936—; instr. McGill U., 1941-42, 46-47; pvt. tchr., coach piano, lectr. in field; prof. piano, U. South Fla., Tampa, 1962-84. Editor: No Gods, No Angels, No Glory, 1975; contbr. articles to profl. jours.; concerts with Orchs. McGill U. Orch., 1940, Calgary Symphony Orch., 1952, Fla. Philharm. Orch., Clearwater and St. Petersburg, 1958; community concert series regular CBC appearances on Distinguished Artist series, 1952-56, internat. shortwave broadcasts, 1945-46; recitals Isabella Stewart Gardiner Mus., Boston, 1948, VAncouver Art Gallery series, Friday Morning Musicale series; numerous other recitals. Lt. CRC Corps, 1942-46. Fellow Trinity Coll.; recipient Gold medals Nat. Music Soc., Durban, Republic of South Africa, 1936, Victoria City Medallion, 1939, Highest Nat. Achievement medal Lt. Gov. Can., 1940. Mem. Olympic Peninsula Music Tchrs, Music Tchrs. Nat. Assn., Am. Matthay Assn., European Piano Tchrs. Assn. (charter), AAUW, Mu Phi Epsilon. Address: 108 Southwestern Pl Sequim WA 98382

GOLDING, SUSAN, county official; b. Muskogee, Okla., Aug. 18, 1945; d. Brage and Hinda Fay (Wolf) G.; m. Richard T. Silberman, July 22, 1984; children: Samuel, Vanessa. Cert. Pratique de Langue Francaise, U. Paris, 1965; BA in Govt. and Internat. Relations, Carleton Coll., 1966; MA in Romance Philology, Columbia U., 1974. Asssoc. editor Columbia U. Jour. of Internat. Affairs, N.Y.C., 1968-69; teaching fellow Emory U., Atlanta, 1973-74; instr. San Diego Community Coll. Dist., 1978; assoc. pub., gen. mgr. The News Press Group, San Diego, 1978-80; city council mem. City of San Diego, 1981-83; dep. sec. bus., transp., housing State of Calif., Sacramento, 1983-84; county supr. dist. 3 County of San Diego, 1984—; founder Internat. Trade Commn., San Diego, 1985; chmn. San Diego Drug Strike Force, 1987-88, Alcohol and Drug Abuse Prevention Task Force, 1988, San Diego Earthquake Preparedness Com., 1986—, San Diego Unified Disaster Council, 1989—, San Diego Regional Justice Facility Financing Agy., 1989—, Calif. Environ. Quality Act Task Force, San Diego County Bd. Suprs., 1989—; dir. Svc. Auth. for Freeway Emergencies, San Diego, 1987; mem. Gov.'s Pub. Infrastructure Task Force, Mortgage Capital Task Force, Calif. Housing Fin. Agy., Calif. Coastal Commn.; mem. San Diego County Commn. on the Status of Women. Bd. dirs. Child Abuse Prevention Found., San Diego Conv. and Vis. Bur., Crime Victims Fund, United Cerebral Palsy; adv. bd. Girl Scouts U.S.; trustee So. Calif. Water Comm.; mem. Rep. State Cen. Com. Named one of Ten Outstanding Rep. County Ofcls. in U.S.A., Rep. Nat. Com., 1987, San Diego Woman of Achievement Soroptimists Internat., 1988, One of San Diego's Ten Outstanding Young Citizens, 1981; recipient Calif. Women in Govt. Achievement award, 1988, Alice Paul award Nat. Women's Polit. Caucus, 1987, Willie Velasquez Polit. award Mex. Am. Bus. and Profl. Assn., 1988. Mem. Nat. Assn. of Counties (chair Op. Fair Share, mem. taxation and fin. com.), Nat. Women's Forum, Kiwanis, Sigma Delta Chi. Jewish. Office: San Diego County Bd Suprs 1600 Pacific Highway Rm 335 San Diego CA 92101

GOLDISH, ELIHU, chemical educator; b. Marietta, Ohio, Oct. 18, 1928; s. Louis and Sona (Lebow) G.; m. Dorothy May Bowman, Dec. 20, 1958; children: Judith, Matthew David. BS, Marietta Coll., 1949; PhD, Calif. Inst. Tech., 1956. Postdoctoral fellow Ohio State U., Columbus, 1956-57, U. So. Calif., Los Angeles, 1958-60; research chemist Union Oil Co. of Calif., Brea, 1960-86; postdoctoral fellow UCLA, Los Angeles, 1966, Calif. Inst. Tech., Pasadena, 1974; adj. prof. Calif. State U., Long Beach, 1986—. Contbr. articles to profl. jours. Mem. Mineral. Soc. Am., Clay Minerals Soc., Royal Soc. Chemistry, Am. Crystallographic Assn. Office: Calif State U Dept Geol Scis Long Beach CA 90840

GOLDMAN, LEON, dermatologist, laser surgeon; b. Cin., Dec. 7, 1905; s. Abraham and Fannie (Friedman) G.; m. Belle Hurwitz, Aug. 23, 1936; children—John, Steve, Carol. M.D., U. Cin., 1929. Intern, U. Cin. Hosp., 1929-30, resident, 1930-36, chief resident, 1933-36; asst. prof. dermatology U. Cin., 1949-50, assoc. prof., 1950-51, prof., 1951-76, prof. emeritus, 1976—, dir. dermatology U. Cin. Med. Center, 1951-76, dir. laser lab., 1971-76; dir. Laser Treatment Ctr., Jewish Hosp. Cin., 1980—; laser cons. dept. dermatology Naval Hosp., San Diego, 1988—. Served with M.C., USAR, 1943. Recipient award for devel. laser medicine Internat. Soc. Laser Surgery, Tokyo, 1981, Finnerud award Dermatology Found., 1984, Xanar Gold medal, 1985, Leon Goldman medal Am. Soc. Dermatol. Surgery, 1985, Daniel Drake medal Coll. Medicine U. Cin., 1988; named Father of Laser Medicine, Opto-Elektronic Conf., Munich, 1979; named honored citizen Cin. Bicentennial, 1988. Fellow Laser Inst. Am.; mem. Am. Dermatol. Assn., Am. Soc. Laser Medicine and Surgery (pres. 1979-80, editor newsletter 1980—) W. D. Mark medal 1982), Soc. Investigative Dermatology, Am. Soc. Dermatol. Surgery, Internat. Confedn. Council Laser Medicine (pres. 1982-86), Laser Inst. Am. (formerly Laser Industry Assn., award for valuable service 1977, Schawlow medal 1985), Sigma Xi, Alpha Omega Alpha. Jewish. Club: Losantiville. Author books, including: The Biomedical Laser; Applications of the Laser; Laser Medicine and Surgery in Dermatology; Laser Medicine; contbr. numerous articles on dermatology and laser tech. to profl. jours., articles on history and art to sci. jours. Avocations: sculpture, photography, laser art. Office: US Naval Hosp Dept Dermatology Code 43 San Diego CA 92134

GOLDOJARB, DAVID MICHAEL, vocational rehabilitation counselor; b. Los Angeles, May 28, 1952; s. L. William and Muriel F. (Margolis) G.; m. Sherry Gray, July 21, 1985; children: Bari Marnina, Tali Shoshana. BS, U. Redlands, 1974; MS, Calif. State U., Los Angeles, 1980. Cert. rehab. counselor, ins. rehab. specialist. Supr. tech. Spastic Children's Found., Chatsworth, Calif., 1974-76; rehab. counselor INTEP Inc., Los Angeles, 1976-78, V.R.S., Inc., Woodland Hills, Calif., 1978-80; counselor II No. Los Angeles County Regional Ctr., Panorama City, Calif., 1980-82; rehab. counselor Vector, Inc., Huntington Beach, Calif., 1982-83, RTW, Inc., Los Angeles, 1983-84; owner Goldojarb and Assocs., Van Nuys, Calif., 1984—. Mem. Nat. Assn. Rehab. Profl. in Private Sector, Nat. Rehab. Assn., Orgn. of Bilingual Rehab. Assocs. Home: 20608 Leadwell St Canoga Park CA 91306 Office: Goldojarb and Associates 5400 Van Nuys Blvd Ste 415 Van Nuys CA 91401

GOLDSCHMIDT, NEIL EDWARD, governor of Oregon; b. Eugene, Oreg., June 16, 1940; s. Lester H. and Annette (Levin) G.; m. Margaret Wood; children: Joshua, Rebecca. A.B. in Polit. Sci., U. Oreg., 1963; LL.B., U. Calif., 1967. Atty. Legal Aid Oreg., 1967-70; commr. City of Portland, 1971-72, mayor, 1973-79; sec. transp. Washington, 1979-81; v.p. internat. mktg. NIKE/BRS, Inc., Beaverton, Oreg., from 1981; gov. State of Oreg., 1987—; dir. Nat. Semi-Condr. Corp., Gelco Corp. Civil rights worker, Miss., 1964; former chmn. transp. com. U.S. Conf. Mayors, also chmn. housing and community devel. com.; former co-chmn. energy task force Nat. League Cities; bd. dirs. Kaiser Permanente Found. Health Plan, 1981—. Named Outstanding Young Man Am., 1972. Home: 3900 SW Murray Blvd Beaverton OR 97005 Office: Office of Gov 254 State Capitol Bldg Salem OR 97310 *

GOLDSMITH, BRAM, banker; b. Chgo., Feb. 22, 1923; s. Max L. and Bertha (Gittelsohn) G.; m. Elaine Maltz; children: Bruce, Russell. Student, Herzl Jr. Coll., 1940, U. Ill., 1941-42. Asst. v.p. Pioneer-Atlas Liquor Co., Chgo., 1945-47; pres. Winston Lumber and Supply Co., East Chicago, Ind., 1947-50; v.p. Medal Distilled Products, Inc., Beverly Hills, Calif., 1950-75; pres. Buckeye Realty and Mgmt. Corp., Beverly Hills, 1952-75; exec. v.p. Buckeye Constrn. Co., Inc., Beverly Hills, 1952-75; chmn. bd., chief exec. officer City Nat. Corp., Beverly Hills, 1975—; dir. City Nat. Bank, Beverly Hills, 1964—, chmn. bd., chief exec. officer, 1975—; bd. dirs. Cedars/Sinai Med. Ctr.; past dir. Los Angeles br. San Francisco Fed. Res. Bank. Pres. Jewish Fedn. Council of Greater Los Angeles, 1969-70; nat. chmn. United Jewish Appeal, 1970-74; regional chmn. United Crusade, 1976; co-chmn. bd. dirs. NCCJ; chmn. Am. com. for Weizman Inst. Sci. Served with Signal Corps U.S. Army, 1942-45. Mem. Los Angeles Philharmonic Assn. (v.p., bd. dirs.). Jewish. Clubs: Hillcrest Country, Masons (Los Angeles), Balboa Bay. Office: City Nat Corp 400 N Roxbury Dr Beverly Hills CA 90210

GOLDSMITH, MELISSA, nurse; b. Ann Arbor, Mich., Apr. 8, 1954; d. Neal A. and Gertrude F. (Julow) G. BEd, Oreg. Coll. Edn., Monmouth, 1976; Assoc. Nursing, Central Oreg. Coll., 1982. RN, Oreg. Tchr. Glendale High Sch., Oreg., 1976-77; nurse Central Oreg. Dist. Hosp., Redmond, 1978-83, Rogue Valley Med. Ctr., Medford, 1983—. Author books poetry. Mem. Nat. Orgn. Women, Am. Nurses Assn., Oreg. Nurses Assn. Home: 2525 Siskiyou Blvd Medford OR 97501

GOLDSTEIN, AVRAM, pharmacology educator; b. N.Y.C., July 3, 1919; s. Israel and Bertha (Markowitz) G.; m. Dora Benedict, Aug. 29, 1947; children—Margaret, Daniel, Joshua, Michael. A.B., Harvard, 1940, M.D., 1943. Intern Mt. Sinai Hosp., N.Y.C., 1944; successively instr., assoc., asst. prof. pharmacology Harvard U., 1947-55; prof. dept. pharmacology Stanford U., Palo Alto, Calif., 1955-89, exec. head dept., 1955-70, prof. emeritus, 1989—; dir. Addiction Research Found., Palo Alto, Calif., 1973-87. Author: Principles of Drug Action. Served from 1st lt. to capt., M.C. AUS, 1944-46. Mem. Nat. Acad. Scis., Am. Soc. Pharmacolology and Exptl. Therapeutics, AAAS, Am. Soc. Biol. Chemists. Home: 735 Dolores St Stanford CA 94305

GOLDSTEIN, BARRY BRUCE, biologist, researcher; b. N.Y.C., Aug. 2, 1947; s. George and Pauline (Kolodner) G.; m. Jacqueline Barbara Aboulafia, Dec. 21, 1968; children: Joshua, Jessica. BA, Queens Coll., 1968; MA, CCNY, N.Y.C., 1974; PhD, CUNY, N.Y.C., 1980. Microbiologist CPC Internat., Yonkers, N.Y., 1968-71; rsch. scientist U. Tex., Austin, 1977-80; v.p. Systems Culture Inc., Honolulu, 1980-83; bioenergy/aquaculture program mgr. N.Mex. Solar Energy Inst., Las Cruces, 1983-89; pres. Ancient Seas Aquaculture Inc., Roswell, N.Mex., 1989—. Contbr. articles to profl. jours. Recipient Nat. Energy Innovation award Dept. Energy, Washington, 1985; Grad. fellow CUNY, 1971, Jesse Smith Noyes fellow, 1975, Regents scholar, N.Y. State U., 1964. Mem. World Aquaculture Soc., Am. Soc. Microbiology, AAAS. Office: Ancient Seas Aquaculture Inc Roswell Test Facility PO Box 2707 Roswell NM 88202

GOLDSTEIN, MICHAEL, caterer, consultant, teacher; b. Bronx, N.Y., Mar. 20, 1945; s. Jack and Juanita (Klieman) G.; m. Carol Fretz (div.). BA in History, Mich. State U., 1973. Owner, operator 464 Magnolia Restaurant, Larkspur, Calif., 1973-85; chef, cons. Moscone Ctr., San Francisco, 1985-86; exec. chef, food/beverage dir. Olema Inn, Calif., 1987; caterer, cons. Innverness Inn Restaurant, Calif., 1987-88—; ptnr. Tandem Catering, San Rafael, Calif., 1988—; cons. Tomales Bay Oyster Co., Marshall, Calif., 1987-88, MT Shasta Pure Spring Water Co., 1988—; winetaster Calif. Living mag., San Francisco Examiner/Chronicle, 1983-86. Democrat. Home: Box 45 Point Reyes Station CA 94956 Office: Tandem Catering 130 Bay View Dr San Rafael CA

GOLDSTEIN, MICHAEL STUART, systems executive; b. N.Y.C., Apr. 22, 1945; s. David and Anne (Klotz) G.; BA, UCLA, 1966; m. Penelope Donaldson, May 4, 1968; children: David John, Darren Stuart. Cert. data processor, computer programmer, computer profl. Promotions mgr. Transamerica Fin., Los Angeles, 1966-70; Western regional mgr. Trans Union Systems, Corp., L.A., Chgo., 1970-78; pres. Mutogo Data Corp., Santa Ana, Calif., 1978—; condr. seminars in field; cons. in field. Mem. Am. Mgmt. Assn., Data Processing Mgmt. Assn., Data Entry Mgmt. Assn. Office: 1801 Newport Circle Santa Ana CA 92705

GOLDSTEIN, NORMAN, dermatologist; b. Bklyn. July 14, 1934; s. Joseph H. and Bertha (Docteroff) G.; B.A., Columbia Coll., 1955; M.D., SUNY, 1959; m. Ramsay, Feb. 14, 1980; children—Richard, Heidi. Intern, Maimonides Hosp., N.Y.C., 1959-60; resident Skin and Cancer Hosp., 1960-61, Bellevue Hosp., 1961-62, NYU. Postgrad. Center, 1962-63 (all N.Y.C.); partner Honolulu Med. Group, 1967-72; practice medicine specializing in dermatology, Honolulu, 1972—; asso. clin. prof. dermatology U. Hawaii Sch. Medicine, 1973—; bd. dirs. Pacific Laser. Bd. dirs. Skin Cancer Found., 1979—; trustee Dermatol. Found., 1979-82; pres. Hawaii Theater Ctr., Hawaii Med. Library, 1987—; mem. Oahu Heritage Council, 1986—. Recipient Henry Silver award Dermatol. Soc. Greater N.Y., 1963; Husik award NYU, 1963; Spl. award Acad. Dermatologia Hawaiiana, 1971. Served with U.S. Army, 1960-67. Fellow Am. Acad. Dermatology (Silver award 1972), ACP, Royal Soc. Medicine; mem. Internat. Soc. Tropical Dermatologists (Hist. and Culture award), Soc. Investigative Dermatologists, Assn. Mil. Dermatologists, AAAS, Am. Soc. Photobiology, Environ. Health and Light Research Inst., Internat. Soc. Cryosurgery, Am. Soc. Micropigmentation Surgery, Nat. Fedn. Ind. Bus., Small Bus. Council Am. (bus. adv. council), Pacific and Asian Affairs Council, Navy League, Assn. Hawaii Artists, Nat. Stereoscopic Soc., Am. Assn. Clin. Oncology, Biol. Photog. Assn., Internat. Solar Energy Soc., Photog. Soc. Am., Societe Internationale de la Photographie, Friends of Photography, Health Sci. Communication Assn., Internat. Pigment Cell Soc., Am. Med. Writers Assn., Physicians Exchange of Hawaii, N.Y. Acad. Sci., Am. Coll. Cryosurgery, Internat. Soc. Dermatol. Surgery, Am. Soc. Preventive Oncology, Soc. for Computer Medicine, Am. Assn. for Med. Systems and Info., computer Security Inst., Pacific Telecom Council, Hawaii State Med. Assn. (mem. public affairs com.), Hawaii Dermatol. Soc. (sec.-pres.), Hawaii Public Health Assn., Pacific Dermatol. Assn., Pacific Health Research Inst., Honolulu County Med. Soc. (gov.), Nat. Wildlife Fedn., Am. Forestry Assn., C. of C., Preservation Action, Pan Pacific Surg. Assn., Am. Coll. Sports Medicine. Jewish. Clubs: Outrigger Canoe, Rotary, Plaza, Honolulu, Chancellor's, Japan-Am., Oahu Country. Contbr. articles to profl. jours. Office: Hist Stangenwald Bldg 119 Merchant St Honolulu HI 96813

GOLDSTEIN, STEVEN EDWARD, psychologist; b. Bronx, N.Y., Nov. 25, 1948; s. Maurice and Matilda (Weiss) G.; B.S. in Psychology, CCNY, 1970, M.S. in Sch. Psychology, 1971; Ed.D. in Sch. Psychology, U. No. Colo., 1977. Tchr., N.Y.C. Public Schs., 1970-71, 72-73, tchr., counselor, 1974; extern in sch. psychology N. Shore Child Guidance, 1972; sch. psychologist Denver Public Schs., 1975; asst. prof. psychology Northeastern Okla. State U., Tahlequah, 1976-78; coordinator inpatient, emergency services Winnemucca (Nev.) Mental Health Center, 1978-80; dir. Desert Devel. Ctr., Las Vegas, Nev., 1980-82; sr. psychologist Las Vegas Mental Health Ctr., 1982—; pvt. practice psychology, Las Vegas, 1983—; participant NSF seminar on biofeedback, 1977. Sec. grad. council CUNY, 1971; pres. grad. council in edn. CCNY, 1971. Lic. psychologist, Nev.; cert. sch. psychologist, N.Y., Calif. Mem. Am. Psychol. Assn. (Nev. coordinator office of profl. practice 1987-88), Nat. Assn. Sch. Psychologists, Biofeedback Soc. Nev. (membership dir. 1982—), Nev. Soc. Tng. and Devel. (dir. 1982-83), Biofeedback Soc. Am., Biofeedback Soc. Nev. (membership dir. 1982-84), So. Nev. Soc. Cert. Psychologists (pres. 1984-86). Presenter papers to profl. confs. Office: 6161 W Charleston Blvd Las Vegas NV 89158 also: 2225 E Flamingo Ste 200 Las Vegas NV 89119

GOLDSTEIN, WARREN DALE, radiologist; b. Montgomery, Ala., Dec. 8, 1951; s. Howard Jerome and Florence (Felt) G.; m. Bobbie Joyce Meshad, Nov. 18, 1979; children: Rebecca, Nathan. BS, U. Ala., 1974, MD, 1978. Intern St. Vincent Hosp., Birmingham, Ala., 1978-79; chief resident U. Ala. Hosps., Birmingham, 1979-82; dir. radiology dept. Meml. Hosp., Colorado Springs, 1982—; chmn. radiology dept. Doctors Hosp., Colorado Springs, 1987—; bd. dirs. Med. Network PPO, Colorado Springs, Health Network HMO, Colorado Springs. Bd. dirs. Temple Shalom. Mem. Colorado Springs Radiol. Soc. (founder, dir.), El Paso County Med. Soc., Colo. Radiol. Soc., Radiol. Soc. N.Am., Am. Coll. Radiologists, Plaza Club (bd. dirs.), Phi Beta Kappa, Phi Eta Sigma, Gamma Sigma Epsilon. Jewish. Home: 4115 Three Graces Dr Colorado Springs CO 80904

GOLDSTONE, PHILIP DAVID, physicist; b. Bklyn., Mar. 5, 1950; s. Herman and Carolyn Martha (VanGelderen) G.; m. Joyce Ann Roberts, Aug. 26, 1972 (div. Jan. 1989). BS in Physics, Polytechnic Inst. of Bklyn, 1971, MS in Physics, 1972; PhD, SUNY, Stony Brook, N.Y., 1975. Nuclear physics group postdoctoral appointee Los Alamos (N.Mex.) Nat. Lab., 1976-77, laser ops. group staff mem., 1977-78, high energy density physics group staff mem., 1978-81, laser matter interaction and fusion physics group leader, 1981—, inertial fusion expts. program mgr., 1986-89, staff mem. weapons tech. program, 1989—. Contbr. articles to profl. jours. Chief adminstrv. officer La Cueva (N.Mex.) Vol. Fire Dept., 1984-87. Fellow Woodrow Wilson, Woodrow Wilson Found., 1971. Mem. Am. Physical Soc. Div Of Plasma Physics (exec. com. 1984-85)., Optical Soc. of Am., Am. Assn. For Advancement of Sci., Sigma XI (assoc. mem.). Office: P-4/WT MS-F629 Los Alamos National Lab Los Alamos NM 87545

GOLDSTRAND, DENNIS JOSEPH, financial planning executive; b. Oakland, Calif., July 12, 1952; s. Joseph Nelson and Frances Marie (Royce) G. BSBA, Calif. State U., 1975; CLU, Am. Coll., 1986, CFC, 1988. Asst. mgr. Household Fin. Corp., San Leandro, Calif., 1975-76; registered rep. Equitable Fin. Svcs., San Francisco, 1976-79; dist. mgr. Equitable Fin. Services, San Francisco, 1979-85; ptnr. Goldstrand & Small Ins. and Fin. Services, Stockton, Calif., 1986-89; owner Goldstrand Fin. & Ins. Svcs., Stockton, 1989—. Speaker Stockton Assn. Life Underwriters, 1986; contbr. articles to Life Ins. Selling mag., 1986, 88. Mem. Rep. Nat. Com., Des Plaines, Ill., 1987—, Political Action Com., Des Plaines, Million Dollar Round Table Found., 1986—, Univ. Pacific Athletic Found., Stockton, 1986—. Mem. Nat. Assn. Life Underwriters (1st v.p. Stockton chpt. 1989—), Am. Soc. Chartered Life Underwriters (pres. Stockton chpt. 1989—), Greater Stockton C. of C. Home: 2828 Appling Circle Stockton CA 95209 Office: Goldstrand Fin Svcs & Ins Svcs Ste 212 W Stockton CA 95207

GOLDWARE, DAVID, insurance company executive; b. Omaha, Aug. 22, 1916; s. Joseph and Fannie Goldware; m. June Goldware; 2 children. BS in Acctg., U. Nebr., 1937. Pvt. practice acctg. Omaha, 1937-39; with Govt. Printing Office, Washington, 1939-42; store mgr. 1946-56; pvt. practice ins. agt. Riverside, Calif., 1956-64; ins. agt., founder David Goldware Ins. Services, Riverside, 1964—; bd. dirs. Inland Empire Nat. Bank. Bd. dirs. Temple Beth El Congregation, Riverside, past pres., past chmn. fin. com., past chmn. fund raising com., past mem. archtl. com.; mem. Parkview Community Found., past sec. bd. dirs., chmn. long-range planning com., endowment com.; mem. founders club Riverside Community Hosp. Found., 1979—; mem. citizens adv. com. Loma Linda (Calif.) U. Hosp., bd. dirs. So. Calif. div. St. Jude's Children's Research Hosp. Found., 1977—, past. v.p.; mem. City of Hope, 1957-59, past. v.p. Riverside chpt.; founding bd. dirs., v.p. exec. com. Janet Goeske Ctr. Srs. and Handicapped Persons; past bd. dirs. YMCA; mem. chancellor's assocs. U. Calif. Riverside, town and gown com., boosters club; v.p. World Affairs Council Inland So. Calif.; active United Way, 1956—, Monday Morning Group; past. pres., past. chmn. mil .affairs com. Greater Riverside C. of C.; pres. Riverside Civic Ctr. Authority, past mem.; vol. Mayor's Council on Human Relations; mem. Mayor's com. Housing, 1976—, Mayor's Com. Establish Performing Arts Ctr., 1976—, Mayor's Com. UN Mgmt. Com., 1964; past mem. mgmt. com., devel. com., Mission Inn Found.; bd. dirs., past fin. com. mem. Riverside Citizens Goals Com. Named So. Calif. Man of Yr., St. Jude Children's Research Hosp. Found., 1976, Man of Yr., Inland Empire Mag., 1980, Man of Yr. So. Calif. Inland Area Boy Scouts Am., 1982. Mem. Air Force Assn. (chmn. bd. dirs. Riverside chpt.). Lodges: Kiwanis (past pres. Univ. Area), B'nai Brith (past pres.), Masons (active various coms.). Home: 3815 Westwood Dr Riverside CA 92504

GOLDWATER, BARRY MORRIS, former U.S. senator; b. Phoenix, Jan. 1, 1909; s. Baron and Josephine (Williams) G.; m. Margaret Johnson, Sept. 22, 1934 (dec. 1985); children: Joanne, Barry, Michael, Margaret (Mrs. Bob Clay). Student, Staunton Mil. Acad., U. Ariz., 1928. With Goldwater's, Inc. (name now Robinson's), from 1929, pres., 1937-53; U.S. senator from Ariz., 1953-65, 69-87; chmn. Armed Services Com.; mem. Commerce Com.; former chmn. Select Com. on Intelligence; mem. Select Com. Indian Affairs; Councilman, Phoenix, 1949-52; mem. adv. com. Indian affairs Dept. Interior, 1948-50. Author: Arizona Portraits (2 vols.), 1940, Journey Down the River of Canyons, 1940, Speeches of Henry Ashurst, The Conscience of a Conservative, 1960, Why Not Victory?, 1962, Where I Stand, 1964, The Face of Arizona, 1964, People and Places, 1967, The Conscience of the Majority, 1970, Delightful Journey, 1971, The Coming Breakpoint, 1976, Barry Goldwater and the Southwest, 1976, With No Apologies, 1979, autobiography (with Jack Casserly) Goldwater, 1988. Rep. candidate for President of the U.S., 1964; bd. dirs. Heard Mus., Mus. No. Ariz., St. Joseph's Hosp. Served as pilot USAAF, 1941-45; col., chief staff Ariz. NG, 1945-52; maj. gen. Res. Recipient award U.S. Jr. C. of C., 1937, Presdl. Medal of Freedom, 1986; named Man of year Phoenix, 1949. Mem. Royal Photog. Soc., Am. Assn. Indian Affairs (dir.), Am. Legion, V.F.W., Municipal League (v.p.), Am. Inst. Fgn. Trade (dir.), Eta Mu Pi, Sigma Chi. Lodges: Masons, Shriner, Elks. *

GOLDWYN, RALPH NORMAN, financial company executive; b. Chgo., Jan. 24, 1925; s. Herman and Rissie F. Goldwyn; B.S., UCLA, 1948; m. Joan J. Snyder, Dec. 25, 1954; children—Bob, Greg, Lisa. Partner, Arc Loan Co., Los Angeles, 1948-52; v.p. Arc Discount Co., Los Angeles, 1952-73; pres. Arc Investment Co., Los Angeles, 1952-73; partner First Factors, Los Angeles, 1960-78; pres. First Comml. Fin., Los Angeles, 1978—; dir. Roy J. Maier, Inc.; trustee UCLA Found. Served to lt. (j.g.) USN, 1943-46. Mem. World Affairs Council, UCLA Chancellor Assos., Anti-Defamation League. Jewish. Clubs: Town Hall of Calif. (life), Brentwood Country, Los Angeles. Office: First Comml Fin 4221 Wilshire Blvd Suite 470 Los Angeles CA 90210

GOLDY, DANIEL LOUIS, economist, consultant; b. Butler, N.J., Aug. 7, 1915; s. Morris A. and Gussie (Silverman) G.; m. Genevieve Beatrice Rustvold, Aug. 14, 1944; 1 child, Daniel Rustvold. BA in Econs. summa cum laude with honors, U. Wis., 1936. Spl. asst. to dir. U.S. Employment

Service, Washington, 1946-47; dep. asst. sec. U.S. Dept. Interior, Washington, 1947-48; regional adminstr. Bur. of Land Mgmt., Washington, 1949-51; adminstr. econ. coop. Office of the Spl. rep. of Pres. for Europe, Paris, 1951-52; regional dir. bur. of employment security U.S. Dept. of Labor, Seattle and N.Y.C., 1952-58; v.p. Pacific No. Lumber Co., Wrangell (Alaska) and Portland, Oreg., 1959-61; dep. adminstr. area redevel. adminstrn. U.S. Dept. of Commerce, Washington, 1961-62, adminstr. bus. and def. services, adminstr. and dep. asst. sec. of commerce, 1962-64; nat. export expansion coordinator, exec. dir. cabinet com. on export expansion The White House, Washington, 1964-65, v.p. for econs. and planning, 1965-69, mem. Pres.'s adv. coun. for trade negotiations, 1975-80; pres., dir. Internat. Systems and Controls Corp., Houston, 1969-76; dir. dept. of econ. devel. State of Oreg., Portland, 1976-78; pres. Daniel L. Goldy, Inc. Cons. Economists, Portland, Oreg., 1979—; ptnr. Mountain Fir Lumber Co., Independence, Oreg., 1955-69; bd. overseers World Affairs Council, Portland, 1987—. Adv. council Internat. Trade Inst. Portland State U., Portland City Club; bd. dirs. Marquam Nature Park, Portland, 1986—. Served to lt. USN, 1943-46. Recipient John Lendrum Mitchell Meml. award U. Wis., 1936. Mem. Nat. Assn. Bus. Economists, U.S. C. of C. (chmn., past. bd. dirs.). Democrat. Home: 2225 SW Scenic Dr Portland OR 97225 Office: Daniel L Goldy Inc 519 SW Park Ste 410 Portland OR 97205

GOLGERT, BARBARA JANE, educator; b. Oakland, Calif., Mar. 27, 1939; d. Robert Harold and Mary Emmaline (McCall) Inman; m. Donald Edwin Golgert, Sept. 29, 1962; children: Donald Edwin Jr., Lisa Helen. BS in Music Edn., U. Oreg., 1959, MEd, 1963, postgrad., 1966-67; postgrad., Portland State U., 1965-66. Cert. tchr., Oreg., Wash. Tchr. Vancouver (Wash.) Sch. Dist., 1961-62, Tacoma (Wash.) Sch. Dist., 1962-63, Lakwood (Wash.) Sch. Dist., 1963-64; tchr. Evergreen Sch. Dist., Vancouver, Wash., 1964-65, 68—, volleyball coach, 1983—; tchr. Springfield (Oreg.) Sch. Dist., 1965-68. Leader Camp Fire Girls, 1965-68; vol. Am. Cancer Soc., Multiple Sclerosis Found., Muscular Dystrophy Found.; mem. Brahm's Singers, Vancouver, 1969-81; co-chmn. mother's March of Dimes, Springfield, 1966, pub. rels. Hospice S.W., Vancouver, 1987—; mem. pub. rels. com. YWCA, Vancouver, 1988—, Racial Justice Task Force, 1988—; chmn. ch. and soc. com. Pacific N.W. Ann. Conf., United Meth. Ch., Vancouver, 1988; founder F.I.S.H., Vancouver, 1968. Mem. NEA, Wash. Edn. Assn., Evergreen Edn. Assn. (rep.), Wash. Orgn. for Reading Devel., Delta Kappa Gamma, Delta Zeta, Sauvie Island Yacht Club (membership chmn. Portland, Oreg. chpt. 1984-87). Republican. Home: 13417 NE 19th St Vancouver WA 98684 Office: Image Elem Sch 4400 NE 122d Ave Vancouver WA 98682

GOLITZ, LOREN EUGENE, dermatologist, pathologist, clinical administrator, educator; b. Pleasant Hill, Mo., Apr. 7, 1941; s. Ross Winston and Helen Francis (Schupp) G.; MD, U. Mo., Columbia, 1966; m. Deborah Burd Frazier, June 18, 1966; children: Carrie Campbell, Matthew Ross. Intern, USPHS Hosp., San Francisco, 1966-67, med. resident, 1967-69; resident in dermatology USPHS Hosp., Staten Island, N.Y., 1969-71; dep. chief dermatology, 1972-73; vis. fellow dermatology Columbia-Presbyn. Med. Ctr., N.Y.C., 1971-72; asst. in dermatology Coll. Physicians Surgeons, Columbia, N.Y.C., 1972-73; vice-chmn. Residency Rev. Com. for Dermatoloby, 1983—. Earl D. Osborne fellow dermal. pathology Armed Forces Inst. Pathology, Washington, 1973-74; assoc. prof. dermatology, pathology Med. Sch. U. Colo., Denver, 1974-88; prof., 88—; chief dermatology Denver Gen. Hosp., 1974—; attending physician dermatology Denver VA Hosp., 1974—; Diplomate Am. Bd. Dermatology. Nat. Bd. Med. Examiners. Mem. Am. Soc. Dermatopathology (sec., treas. 1985-89, pres.-elect 1989), Am. Acad. Dermatology (chmn. coun. on clin. and lab. svcs., coun. sci. assembly 1987—, bd. dirs. 1987—), Soc. Pediatric Dermatology (pres. 1981), Soc. Investigative Dermatology, Pacific Dermatol. Assn. (exec. com. 1979—, sec.-treas. 1984-87, pres. 1988), Noah Worcester Dermatol. Soc. (publs. com. 1980), Colo. Dermatol. Soc. (pres. 1978), Am. Bd. Dermatology Inc. (bd. dirs. 1987—), Colo. Med. Soc., Denver Med. Soc., AMA (residency rev. com. for dermatology 1982—, dermatopathology test com. 1979-85), Denver Soc. Dermatopathology, Am. Dermatol. Assn. Editorial bd. Jour. Pediatric Dermatology, editorial bd. Jour. Am. Acad. Dermatology, Current Issues in Dermatology. Contbr. articles to med. jours. Home: 11466 E Arkansas Ave Aurora CO 80012

GOLL, J. PAUL, manufacturing executive; b. Havre, Mont., Aug. 31, 1956; s. Jim and Shirley (Winkel) G.; m. Kathi Lynn, May 22, 1982. BS in Indsl. Engring., U. Wash., Seattle, 1979. Production team mgr. Proctor & Gamble, Ventura, Calif., 1979-82; indusl. engr. Am. Can Co., Halsey, Oreg., 1982, Lamb-Weston, Portland, Oreg., 1982-85; facilities mgr. CD-Med., Portland, 1985-86, mfg. mgr., 1986-87, materials mgr., 1987-88, ops. mgr., 1989—; pres. The Bus Bench Advt., Inc., Portland, Oreg., 1983-85; co-owner Household Svcs., Inc., Portland, 1985-87. Coach Recreational Volleyball Assn., Portland, Oreg., 1983-88. Mem. Am. Production & Inventory Control Soc., Purchasing Mgmt. Assn. Oreg. Republican. Home: 20351 S Henrici Oregon City OR 97045 Office: CD-Med 13520 SE Pheasant Ct Portland OR 97222

GOLNICK, LON FREDERICK, corporate communications leader; b. Albert Lea, Minn., Sept. 7, 1940; s. Fritz Louis and Betty Jo (Nelson) G.; m. Sandra Kay Taylor, Jan. 26, 1964; children: Kirsten Kay, Heidi Lynn. BS in Engring., U. Redlands, 1962. Engr. to sr. engr. Lockheed Propulsion Co., Redlands, Calif., 1963-68; rep. Lockheed Aircraft Corp., Washington, 1968-71; mktg. project mgr. Lockheed Missiles and Space Co., Sunnyvale, Calif., 1971-74; dept. mgr. Werner Erhard & Assocs., San Francisco, 1975-78, trainer, 1978-84, forum leader, 1985—. Republican. Lutheran. Office: Werner Erhard & Assocs 62 First St San Francisco CA 94105

GOLONDZINIER, LILY DELIA, management executive; b. South Gate, Calif., Nov. 15, 1943; d. Willard Kenneth and Minnie (Ophaug) Anderson; m. Theodore M. Golondzinier, June 25, 1966; children: Lori, Traci. BA, Calif. State U., L.A., 1966. Regional rep. ManPak Tailoring Products, Inc., Dayton, Ohio, 1972-75; office mgr. Cornerstone, Panama City, Fla., 1980-82; site mgr. SRS Techs., Colorado Springs, Colo., 1987-89; mgr. office adminstrn. SRS Techs., 1989—. Founder vol. parents program, Ramstein AFB, Fed. Republic Germany, 1975-78; fin. dir., mem. presenting team Worldwide Marriage Encounter, Fed. Republic Germany, 1976-78. Mem. NAFE. Republican. Roman Catholic.

GOLTERMANN, CARL WILLIAM, real estate developer; b. Decatur, Ill., June 23, 1952; s. Carl Herbert and Virginia Hutt (Johnson) G.; m. Joann Bailey, Nov. 21, 1981; children: Carl, Jessica. BArch, U. Ill., 1974; MBA, U. So. Calif., 1979. Asst. project mgr. CM Assocs., Dhahran, Saudi Arabia, 1975-77; spl. project mgr. The Irvine Co., Newport Beach, Calif., 1979-81; regional project mgr. World Savs. & Loan Co., Santa Ana, Calif., 1982-84; project devel. mgr. McDonnell Douglas Realty, Irvine, Calif., 1984—; speaker in field. Chmn. archtl. com., Woodbridge Village Assn., Irvine, 1985—. Mem. Nat. Assn. Indsl. and Office Parks, Urban Land Inst., Bldg. Owners mgmt. Assn. Republican. Presbyterian.

GOLUBA, RAYMOND WILLIAM, engineer; b. Streator, Ill., Oct. 5, 1939; s. William Nickolas and Lois Bryant (Jones) G.; m. Diane Elizabeth Fries, June 18, 1961; children: Todd, Alaine, Ross. BS, U. Ill., 1961, MS, 1962; PhD, U. Wis., 1968. Engr. Arnold Engring. Devel. Ctr., Tullahoma, Tenn., 1962-63; instr. dept. mechan. engring. U. Wis., Madison, 1963-64; engr. Lawrence Livermore Nat. Lab., Livermore, Calif., 1968-70, group leader, 1970-77, assoc. div. leader, 1977-81, dep. div. leader, 1981-86, asst. dep. assoc. dir. for mechan. engring., 1986—; adv. bd. UCLA, 1986—. Active sch. bd. Pleasanton (Calif.) Joint Elem. Sch. Dist., 1977-83, trustee. Mem. ASME (program chmn. 1970-71, vice chmn. 1971-72, chmn. Mt. Diablo chpt. 1972-73, bd. dirs. 1981-82), Pi Tau Sigma, Sigma Tau, Tau Beta Pi, Sigma Xi. Republican. Methodist. Home: 2527 Corte Bella Pleasanton CA 94566 Office: Lawrence Livermore Nat Lab PO Box 808 Livermore CA 94550

GOLUBIC, THEODORE ROY, sculptor, designer, inventor; b. Lorain, Ohio, Dec. 9, 1928; s. Ivan and Illonka (Safar) G.; m. Rose Andrina Ieraci-Golubic, Nov. 27, 1958; children: Vincivan, Theodore E., Victor, Georjia. Student Ohio State U., Columbus, 1947-48; BFA in Painting, Miami U., Oxford, Ohio, 1951; student Syracuse U., 1955; MFA in Sculpture, U. Notre Dame, 1957. Asst. to Ivan Mestrovic, 1954-60; guest tchr. U. Notre Dame, 1959; urban planner redevel. dept., South Bend, Ind., 1960-65; sculpture cons., Rock of Ages Corp., 1965-67; instr. Cen. Mo. State U., 1969; instr. San Diego Sculptors' Guild, 1970-71; artist-in-residence Roswell (N.Mex.) Mus. and Art Ctr., 1971-72; sculptor, designer, inventor, 1958—; works include: Limestone relief sculpture Cathedral of the Nativity, Dubuque, Iowa, 4 dimensional sun environ. design, South Bend, Ind., 4 pt. positive gap surface pick-up, 3 dimensional interconnected integrated cir., Phoenix, mahogany bas relief, U. San Diego. With U.S. Army, 1951-53. Mem. Artists Equity Assn., Coll. Art Assn. Am., Internat. Sculpture Ctr. Contbr. articles to profl. jours.

GOMBRICH, PETER P., manufacturing executive, educator; b. N.Y.C., Oct. 26, 1935; s. Walter H. and Herta (Schauder) G.; m. Jacqueline Block, May 31, 1964; children: Christine, Eric, Matthew. BSEE, U. Denver, 1959, MBA, 1961. Project engr. Victoreen Instruments, Cleve., 1959-60; sales engr. Production Machinery, Cleve., 1961-63; mktg. mgr. Beckmann Instruments, Fullerton, Calif., 1963-68; dir. sales and mktg. Medtronics, Inc., Mpls., 1968-72; v.p. Pacesetter Systems, Sylmar, Calif., 1972-76; exec. v.p. and div. pres. St. Jude Med., St. Paul, Minn., 1976-80; pres. and co. exec. officer Integrated Microcircuits, Hopkins, Minn., 1980-83; sr. v.p. ADC Magnetic Controls, Mpls., 1983-85; chmn. and co. exec. officer Clinicom, Inc., Boulder, Colo., 1985—; prof. Sch. of Bus. U. Colo., Boulder; prof. and curriculum advisor St. Thomas Coll., Chaska, Minn., 1982-84. Inventor heart rate monitor, telephone pacemaker evaluation system, automatic meter reading system, portable handheld terminals and patient ID system. Dir. Minn. Wellspring, Mpls., 1981-84, Minn. High Tech. Council., Mpls., 1981-84, Make A Wish of Minn., Mpls., 1979-81. Office: Clinicom Inc 4720 Walnut St Ste 106 Boulder CO 80301

GOMES, MICHAEL JAMES, construction industry executive; b. Tullare, Calif., Jan. 12, 1954; s. John Francis and Aurora Rose (DeCoit) G. BA in History, U. Calif., Irvine, 1976. Supr. Indsl. Electric, Palm Springs, Calif., 1976-78; project mgr. Indsl. Electric, Palm Springs, 1978-80, treas., 1980-82; v.p. System Electric, Inc., Cathedral City, Calif., 1982-85; exec. v.p. System Electric, Inc., Palm Springs, Calif., 1985—. Office: System Electric Inc 1278 Montalvo Way Palm Springs CA 92262

GOMEZ, DAVID FREDERICK, lawyer; b. Los Angeles, Nov. 19, 1940; s. Fred and Jennie (Fujier) G.; m. Kathleen Holt, Oct. 18, 1977. BA in Philosophy, St. Paul's Coll., Washington, 1965, MA in Theology, 1968; JD, U. So. Calif., 1974. Bar: Calif. 1975, U.S. Dist. Ct. (cen. dist.) Calif. 1975, U.S. Dist. Ct. (ea. dist.) Calif. 1977, Ariz. 1981, US. Dist. Ct. Ariz. 1981, U.S. Ct. Claims 1981, U.S. Ct. Appeals (9th cir.) 1981, U.S. Supreme Ct. 1981; ordained priest Roman Cath. Ch., 1969. Staff atty. Nat. Labor Relations Bd., Los Angeles, 1974-75; ptnr. Gomez, Paz, Rodriguez & Sanora, Los Angeles, 1975-77, Garrett, Bourdette & Williams, San Francisco, 1977-80, Van O'Steen & Ptnrs., Phoenix, 1981-85; pres. David F. Gomez, PC, Phoenix, 1985—; mem. faculty Practicing Law Inst. Author: Somos Chicanos: Strangers in Our Own Land, 1973; mem. faculty, co-author Advanced Strategies in Employment Law, 1988. Mem. ABA, Maricopa County Bar Assn., Los Abogados Hispanic Bar Assn., Plaintiff Employment Lawyer's Assn. Democrat. Office: 2425 E Camelback R Ste 620 Phoenix AZ 85016

GOMEZ, LOUIS SALAZAR, educational administrator; b. Santa Ana, Calif., Dec. 7, 1939; s. Louis Reza and Mary (Salazar) G.; m. Patricia Ann Aboytes, June 30, 1962; children: Louis Aboytes, Diana Maria, Ramon Reza. Student, Calif. State Poly. U., 1959-65; BA, Calif. State U., San Bernardino, 1971; MA, Calif. State U., 1975; EdD, U. So. Calif., L.A., 1987. Cert. tchr., counselor, adminstr., Calif. Tchr., counselor San Bernardino City Schs., 1971-76; human rels. coord. San Bernardino Valley Coll., 1976-78, counselor, 1978-82, coord. of counseling, 1982-87; asst. dean student svcs. Crafton Hills Coll., Yucaipa, Calif., 1987—; lectr., Calif. State U., San Bernardino, 1976-81, mem. adv. bd., 1987-91. Mem. San Bernardino Valley Coll. Faculty Assn. (treas. 1980-82), Faculty Assn. Calif. Community Colls., San Bernardino Community Coll. Dist. Mgmt. Assn., Kiwanis (pres. San Bernardino chpt. 1982). Democrat. Roman Catholic. Home: 5534 N Mayfield Ave San Bernardino CA 92407 Office: Crafton Hills Coll 11711 Sand Canyon Rd Yucaipa CA 92399

GONG, MAMIE POGGIO, educator; b. San Francisco, June 26, 1951; d. Louis and Mary Lee (Lum) G.; m. Andy Anthony Poggio. BA, U. Calif., Berkeley, 1973, postgrad., 1981-83, MEd, 1982. Tchr. Oakland (Calif.) Unified Sch. Dist., 1974-84, Palo Alto (Calif.) Unified Sch. Dist., 1984—; cons., author Nat. Clearinghouse for Bilingual Edn., Washington, 1984; cons. ARC Assocs., Oakland, 1983; rsch. asst. dept. edn. Stanford U., 1987—. Co-author: Promising Practices: A Teacher Resource, 1984. Recipient Kearney Found. award, 1969, others. Mem. TESOL, Pi Lambda Theta. Democrat. Office: Palo Alto Unified Sch Dist 25 Churchill Ave Palo Alto CA 94306

GONICK, HARVEY CRAIG, nephrologist; b. Winnipeg, Man., Can., Apr. 10, 1930; s. Joseph Wolfe and Rose (Chernick) G.; m. Gloria Granz, Dec. 16, 1967; children: Stephan, Teri. BS in Chemistry, UCLA, 1951; MD, U. Calif., San Francisco, 1955. Diplomate Am. Bd. Internal Medicine, Am. Bd. Nephrology. Intern Peter Bent Brigham Hosp., 1955-56; fellow in nephrology Mass. Meml. Hosp., 1956-57; fellow in nephrology, resident in internal medicine Wadsworth VA Hosp., Los Angeles, 1959-61, clin. investigator, 1961-64, chief metabolic balance unit, 1964-67; instr. medicine Sch. Medicine, UCLA, 1961-64, asst. prof., 1964-69, assoc. prof., 1969-72, adj. assoc. prof., 1972-76, adj. prof., 1976—, assoc. chief div. nephrology, 1965-72, co-dir. Bone and Stone Clinic,, 1972-76, coordinator postgrad. nephrology edn., 1975-78; mem. staff Santa Monica (Calif.) Hosp., St. John's Hosp., Santa Monica; mem. staff Century City Hosp., Los Angeles, med. dir. dialysis unit, 1972-79, chief medicine, 1978-79; mem. staff Cedars-Sinai Med. Ctr., Los Angeles, dir. trace element lab., 1979—, clin. chief nephrology, 1983-85; practice medicine specializing in nephrology Los Angeles, 1972—; co-founder, med. dir. Berkeley East Dialysis Unit, Santa Monica, 1971-75; co-founder, cons. Kidney Dialysis Care Units Inc., Lynwood, Calif., 1971-78; co-dir. Osteoporosis Prevention and Treatment Ctr., Santa Monica; mem. numerous adv. coms. to state and fed. agys., 1969-83. Contbr. articles to profl. jours.; editor: Current Nephrology, 1977—. Served to capt. M.C., USAF, 1957-59. Fellow Charles Nelson Fund, Kaiser Found., NIH; recipient Oliver P. Douglas Meml. award Los Angeles County Heart Assn., 1959, Vis. Scientist award Deutscher Academischer Austauschendienst, 1978. Fellow ACP; mem. Internat. Soc. Nephrology (organizing com. internat. cong. 1984), Am. Soc. Nephrology, European Dialysis and Transplant Assn., Los Angeles Transplant Soc., Soc. Exptl. Biology and Medicine, AAAS, AMA, Pan-Am. Med. Assn., Calif. Med. Assn., Los Angeles County Med. Assn. (legis. com.), Nat. Kidney Found. (active ann. conf. 1963-65, sec. nat. med. adv. council 1969-70, regional rep. and legis com. nat. med. adv. council 1970-73, grantee 1963), So. Calif. Kidney Found. (chmn. sci. adv. council 1968-70, co-chmn. legis. com. 1970-73, bd. dirs. 1974-83, honoree 1979), Am. Soc. Bone and Mineral Research, Am. Coll. Toxicology, Soc. Toxicology, Am. Heart Assn. (renal sect. of council on circulation), Am. Fedn. Clin. Research, Western Soc. Clin. Research, Western Assn. Physicians, Los Angeles Soc. Internal Medicine, Phi Beta Kappa, Sigma Xi, Alpha Omega Alpha, Phi Eta Sigma, Alpha Mu Gamma, Phi Lambda Upsilon. Office: 2080 Century Pk E #707 Los Angeles CA 90067

GONOT, LINDA I., management analyst; b. Bangor, County Down, No. Ireland, Aug. 28, 1953; d. Thomas Orr Stitt and Isobel (Miller) Neill; m. Gregory Lin Gonot, Sept. 18, 1982; children: Stephanie, Jeffrey. BS, Calif. State U., Sacramento, 1975, MBA, 1981. Tchr. Sawyer's Bus. Coll., Sacramento, 1975-77; buyer Sacramento Mcpl. Utility Dist., 1977-82, mgmt. analyst, 1982—. Pres. East Ranch Homeowners Orgn., Sacramento, 1981-82; sec./v.p. Encorps Symphony Group, Sacramento, 1981-84, pres., 1988—. Republican. Episcopalian.

GONSALVES, MARY ANN BERNADETTE, educational administrator; b. St. Petersburg, Fla., May 13, 1945; d. Thomas Bernard and Helen Patricia (Crowe) Scanlon; m. David Alan Gonsalves, Aug. 27, 1966; children: Kimberly, Erin Elizabeth. BA, Calif. State U., Hayward, 1970, MS, 1977. Elem. tchr. St. John's Sch., San Lorenzo, Calif., 1970-76; learning disability tchr. New Haven Sch. Dist., Union City, Calif., 1976-80, resource specialist, 1980--; cons. neuro-linguistic programming, Cupertino, Calif., 1986--; workshop presenter Chapman Coll., Fremont, Calif. Recipient Resource Specialist Program award State of Calif., 1986, Profl. Advancement award New Haven Sch. Dist., 1988. Fellow Calif. Tchrs. Assn.; mem. AAUW, Tanglewood Tennis. Democrat. Roman Catholic. Home: 2482 Lancaster Ct Hayward CA 49542 Office: New Haven Sch Dist Alvarado Niles Rd Union City CA 94587

GONTARZ, STANLEY, former protective services official, consultant; b. Union, N.J., May 7, 1917; s. Frank I. and Katherine (Florko); children: Greer McKenna, Mary M. Iadevaia, Christopher. MA, Salve Regina U., 1976; DPA, Nova U., 1980. With N.Y.C.P.D., 1952-67; coord. Police Acad., N.Y.C., 1960-67; police chief Barrington (Rhode Island) Police, 1967-82; cons. Tucson, 1982—; adj. prof. Barrington Coll., Salve Regina Coll., 1967-82; bd. dirs. We the People, Tucson, 1986—. Author: Workbooks for Police, 1960, instruction manuals. Chmn. Police Athletic League, Barrington, 1967-82, organizer and dir. Capt. field arty. U.S. Army, 1942-46. Roman Catholic. Home: 2602 W Prato Way Tucson AZ 85741

GONZALES, MARIE GUADALUPE, public relations coordinator; b. Brawley, Calif., Oct. 20, 1963; d. Steve Baiz and Clara R. Gonzales. BA in Communications, Calif. State U., Dominguez Hills Carson, 1985. Account coord. pub. rels. and mktg. Saatchi & Saatchi, DFS Inc., Torrance, Calif., 1987-89; asst. account exec, account mgmt. Saatchi & Saatchi DFS/Pacific, Torrance, 1989—. Mem. Hispanic Pub. Relations Assn., Publicity Club Los Angeles. Office: Saatchi & Saatchi DFS Inc 3501 Sepulveda Blvd Torrance CA 90505

GONZALES, RAFAEL CHIPECO, art director, lawyer; b. Manila, Oct. 24, 1933; came to U.S., 1984; AA, U. of Philippines, 1953, BA, 1959, LLB, 1959. Bar: Philippines 1960. Prin. R.C. Gonzales and Assocs., Manila, 1960-84; owner, mgr. Heritage Art Ctr., San Diego, 1985—; pres. Uplex, Inc., Manila, 1960-67, First Philippines Adjustment Corp., Manila, 1961-78, Banner Taxicab Corp., Manila, 1964-81, Pvt. Resources, Inc., Manila, 1979-82. Pres. San Juan Jaycees Club, S.J. Rizal, Philippines, 1968; nat. chmn. Walk for a Cause Fund, Philippines, 1980, 1983; dir. Philippines Inst. Loss Adjusters, Manila, 1967-70, Philippines Historical Assn., 1980-83; v.p. Manila Taxi Assn., 1959-60, Philippines Mobil Dealer Assn., Manila, 1980-83. Mem. Integrated Bar of Philippines, Internat. Cons. Exchange . Roman Catholic. Lodge: Rotary (Paul Harris fellow 1972). Home: 1740-B Plaza Blvd National City CA 92050 Office: Heritage Art Ctr 448 W Market St San Diego CA 92101

GONZALES, RICHARD JOSEPH, lawyer; b. Tucson, Mar. 5, 1950; s. Diego D. and Helen O. (Olivas) G.; divorced; children: Adrianne Dee, Laura Renee. BA, U. Ariz., 1972, JD, 1975. Bar: Ariz. 1976, U.S. Dist. Ct. Ariz. 1976, U.S. Ct. Appeals 1976. Asst. pub. defender Pima County Pub. Defenders Office, Tucson, 1976-77; dep. atty. criminal div. Pima County Atty.'s Office, Tucson, 1977-80; ptnr. Gonzales & Villarreal, P.C., Tucson, 1980—; assoc. instr. bus. law Pima Community Coll.,Tucson, 1977, criminal law, 1978-80; judge pro tem Pima County Superior Ct., 1983—; magistrate City of South Tucson, 1982-85; spl. magistrate City of Tucson, 1982-85. Mem. Tucson Tomorrow, 1984—, citizen's adv. council sunnyside Sch. Dist. #12, 1986-88; chmn. com. Udall for Congress Ariz. 2d Congl. Dist., United Way Hispanic Leadership Devel. Program, 1984-86, Hispanic Profl. Action Com., 1984-85, vice-chairperson, 1983-84, chairperson, 1984-85; bd. dirs. Girls Club of Tucson, Inc., 1980-81, Teatro Carmen, Inc., 1981-88, Alcoholism Council of Tucson, 1982-83, Crime Resisters, 1984-85, La Frontera Ctr., Inc., 1985—, Crime Prevention League, 1985-75; gen. counsel U. Ariz. Hispanic Alumni, 1984—, Accion 80's, 1983-86. Named one of Outstanding Young Men of Am. U.S. Jaycee's, 1980; recipient Vol. of Yr. award United Way Greater Tucson, 1985. Fellow Ariz. Bar Found.; mem. ABA, Ariz. Bar Assn., Pima County Bar Assn., Assn. Trial Lawyers Am., Ariz. Trial Lawyers Assn., Nat. Orgn. on Legal Problems of Edn., Supreme Ct. Hist. Soc., Univ. Ariz. Alumni assn., Phi Delta Phi. Democrat. Roman Catholic. Lodge: Optimists (Optimist of Yr. 1981). Home: 7330 N Sonya Way Tucson AZ 85704 Office: Gonzales & Villarreal PC 261 N Court Ave Tucson AZ 85701

GONZALES, RICHARD ROBERT, academic administrator; b. Palo Alto, Calif., Jan. 12, 1945; s. Pedro and Virginia (Ramos) G.; AA, Foothill Coll., 1966; BA, San Jose (Calif.) State U., 1969; MA, Calif. Poly. State U., San Luis Obispo, 1971; grad. Def. Info. Sch., Def. Equal Opportunity Mgmt. Inst. Counselor student activities Calif. Poly. State U., San Luis Obispo, 1969-71, instr. ethnic studies, 1970-71; counselor Ohlone Coll., Fremont, Calif., 1971-72, coord. coll. readiness, 1971; counselor De Anza Coll., Cupertino, Calif., 1972-78, mem. community speakers bur., 1975-78; counselor Foothill Coll., Los Altos Hills, Calif., 1978—, mem. community speakers bur., 1978—; instr. Def. Equal Opportunity Mgmt. Inst., 1984—. Mem. master plan com. Los Altos (Calif.) Sch. Dist., 1975-76; vol. worker, Chicano communities, Calif.; fellow Masters and Johnson Inst. With Calif. Army N.G., now maj. Adj. Gen. Corps, USAR. Recipient Counselor of Yr. award Ohlone Coll., 1971-72; lic. marriage family child counselor, Calif. Mem. Am. Calif. Personnel and Guidance Assns., Am. Coll. Personnel Assn., Calif. Assn. Marriage and Family Therapists, Calif. Community Coll. Counselor Assn., Calif. Assn. Counseling and Devel.- Hispanic Caucus, Res. Officers Assn., La Raza Faculty Assn. Calif. Community Colls., Nat. Career Devel. Assn., Phi Delta Kappa, Chi Sigma Iota. Republican. Office: Foothill Coll Los Altos Hills CA 94022

GONZALEZ, ANTONIO, aeronautical engineer; b. Guadalajara, Spain, July 20, 1960; came to U.S., 1988; s. Carlos and Carmen (Molina) G. Escuela Tecnica Superior de Ingenieros Aeronauticos, Ingenieros Aeronauticos, Madrid, 1987. Registered profl. engr. Flight controls engr. Boeing Aircraft Co., Renton, Wash., 1988—. Home: 15448 NE 13th Pl Apt 1512 Bellevue WA 98007 Office: Boeing Comml Airplane Co 2 Renton Pl 700 Renton Village Pl Renton WA 98055

GONZALEZ, BRENDA KAYE, medical transcriptionist; b. Monroe, Wash., Nov. 5, 1958; d. Richard Darr and Lois Ann (Krotke) Bloomquist; m. Antonio Gonzalez, Jr.; children: Andres Navarro, Alicia Kaye, Adel Marrta. Records clk. Seattle Radiologist, Inc., 1979; med. transcriptionist Valley Gen. Hosp., Monroe, 1979-84, Providence Hosp., Everett, Wash., 1984—, Stevens Meml. Hosp., Edmonds, Wash., 1985. Sunday sch. tchr. presch. St. Timothy Luth. Ch., Edmonds, Wash., 1987—, bookkeeper/treas., 1988-89. Mem. Nat. Assn. for Med. Transcriptionists (cert.,; treas. Evergreen chpt. 1989—, newsletter editor 1983-84, del. to state orgn. 1988—), Wash. State Assn. for Med. Transcriptionists. Home: 16130 2d Pl W Lynnwood WA 98037

GONZALEZ, KIMBERLY REGINA, controller; b. Walnut Creek, Calif., Nov. 5, 1964; d. Earl Glenn and Marilynn Mae (Roberts) K.; m. George Gonzalez, May 30, 1987; children: Joshua Alan, Nathaniel James. BS in Internat. Bus. summa cum laude, Woodbury U., 1986. Controller Charisma Missions Inc., Los Angeles, 1985—, dir., treas., 1986—. Mem. Am. Soc. Profl. and Exec. Women, Nat. Assn. Female Exec., Am. Mgmt. Assn. Republican. Roman Catholic. Home: 629 Ave A Redondo Beach CA 90277 Office: Charisma in Missions Inc 1059 S Gage Ave Los Angeles CA 90023

GONZALEZ, LOUIS STEVEN, sporting equipment manufacturing company executive; b. Chicago Heights, Ill., Nov. 22, 1953; s. Joeseph Louis Gonzelez and Zita (Rodriguez) Lezeau. Student, U. Ill., Chgo., 1971-74. Mill and timber man Mountain Lumber Mill, Bailey, Colo., 1978-81; stone mason Copeland Masonry Co., Bailey, 1981-83; dir. ski patrol Geneva Basin Ski Area, Grant, Colo., 1985; pres., chief exec. officer BOA Constrn. & Design Co., Bailey, 1979—, Know Fun Club Inc., Bailey, 1987—; mem. ski patrol Winter Park (Colo.) Resort, 1985-86. Author: Official Bicycle Polo, 1988; editor Chukkar Times newsletter, 1987—; patentee bicycle polo mallet. Mem. World Bicycle Polo Fedn. (co-chmn. 1987—). Office: Know Fun Club Inc Box 1039 Bailey CO 80421

GONZALEZ, PAMELA LOUISE, mathematics teacher, consultant; b. Hartford, Conn., July 20, 1946; d. Raymond William and Anna (Bracken) Kinsley; m. Armando David Gonzalez, Nov. 1, 1975; children: Anita, Laura. BS, Boston U., 1968; postgrad., U. Calif.-Santa Barbara, 1968-88. Cert. tchr., Calif. Tchr. Huntington Park (Calif.) Pub. Schs., 1968-70, Santa Barbara Pub. Schs., 1970—; math. cons. Santa Barbara County Schs., 1988.

Mem. AAUW, Santa Barbara Tchrs. Assn. (pres. 1988--), Phi Delta Kappa. Home: 70 Surrey Pl Goleta CA 93117 Office: Santa Barbara Tchrs Assn 100 N Hope Ave Santa Barbara CA 93105

GOO, ABRAHAM MEU SEN, aircraft company executive; b. Honolulu, May 21, 1925; s. Tai Chong and Lily En Wui (Dai) G.; m. Shin Quon Wong, June 12, 1950; children: Marilynn, Steven, Beverly Cardinal. BEE U. Ill., 1951; postgrad. MIT, 1975. With The Boeing Co., Seattle, 1951-73; B-1 avionics program mgr. Boeing Aerospace Co., Seattle, 1974-75, v.p., gen. mgr. aircraft armament div., 1975-77; v.p. mil. systems Boeing Mil. Airplane Co., Wichita, Kans., 1977-79, exec. v.p., 1979-84, pres., 1984-87; pres. Boeing Advanced Systems, Seattle, 1987—. With USAAF, 1946-47. Recipient Chinese-Am. Engrs. and Scientists of So. Calif. Achievement award Sci. and Engring., 1989. Mem. Nat. Aero. Assn., Army Aviation Assn. Am., Army Sci. Bd., Air Force Assn., Am. Def. Preparedness Assn., Armed Forces Communication and Electronics Assn., Army Sci. Bd. Home: 18909 SE 282d Ct Kent WA 98042 Office: Boeing Advanced Systems PO Box 3707 Seattle WA 98124-2207

GOO, DONALD WAH YUNG, architect; b. Honolulu, Jan. 16, 1934; s. Kam Lum and Grace (Ching) G.; m. Laura Ray Luke, July 9, 1960; 1 child, Wayne. B.Arch., U. Ill., 1957. Registered architect, Hawaii, Guam, Calif., Tex., Fla. Staff mem., Skidmore Owings & Merrill, Chgo., 1957; v.p. Wimberly, Whisenand, Allison & Tong, Honolulu, 1969-71, Wimberly, Whisenand, Allison, Tong, and Goo Architects Ltd., Honolulu, 1971-80, pres., 1980—, corp. sec., 1980-85, chief exec. officer, 1985—. Pres. Arts Council Hawaii, Honolulu, 1978-84; vice chmn. Honolulu City Commn. Culture and Arts, 1985-86, chmn., 1986—. Contbr. articles to profl. jours. Served to 1st lt. USAF, 1957-59. Mem. AIA (pres. Hawaii Soc. 1977, treas. 1973-74, dir. 1984-86, fellow 1988), Constrn. Specifications Inst. (pres. Honolulu chpt. 1975-76), Hawaii Econ. Assn., Urban Land Inst. (recreational devel. coun. 1987—), Hawaii C. of C. (bd. dirs. 1988—), Honolulu C. of C., Pacific. Avocations: tennis, travel. Office: Wimberly Allison Tong & Goo Inc Architects 2222 Kalakaua Ave PH Honolulu HI 96815

GOOD, ALICE THOMPSON MCMORRIS, university official; b. L.A., Jan. 17, 1940; d. Charles R. and Kathleen (Bell) Thompson; m. Martin H. Good (div. June 1983); 1 child, Michael E. BS in Bus., UCLA, 1961; cert. with honors, Tobe-Coburn Sch., N.Y.C., 1961; MA in Journalism, U. Nev., 1978. Paralegal asst., asst. advt. dir., asst. buyer, dept. mgr. various retial stores South Lake Tahoe, L.A., N.Y.C., Calif., 1962-74; newspaper reporter, columnist, TV reporter Reno, 1975-78; legis. reporter Stas. KOLO-TV-AM, KORK-TV-AM, Reno, 1979; news dir., anchorwoman Sta. KCBY-TV, Coos Bay, Oreg., 1979-81; news announcer, reporter Sta. KQIQ, Hanford, Calif., 1981; mktg. dir. Shoppers Sq. Ctr., Reno, 1981-82; instr. journalism U. Nev., Reno, 1983, asst. dir. pub. rels. sch. medicine, 1983-84, communications coord. coll. agr., 1984—. Coord. publicity Wayne Newton Fundraiser, Reno, 1983; mktg. dir. 1st Ch. Religious Sci., Reno, 1988—. Mem. Internat. Assn. Bus. Communicators (award of excellence 1986, 87, 88, pres. Silver State chpt.), AAUW, Chi Omega. Democrat. Home: 1335 Crown Dr Reno NV 89503 Office: U Nev Coll Agr Agr Info Office Reno NV 89557

GOOD, JANET LOIS, occupational health nurse; b. Coudersport, Pa., Mar. 18, 1938; d. Warren Worth and Jeannette (Britton) Ohlman; m. Robert Jack Good, Feb. 14, 1960; children: Diana Ivy, Robert Warren. Diploma in nursing, Pa. Hosp., 1958; cert. in alcohol studies, U. N.D., 1970; cert. in nurse practition, U. Colo., 1973; BS in Health Care Adminstrn., St. Joseph Coll., 1987. Cert. instr. CPR, cert. audiometry, spirometry. Staff and recovery room nurse Children's Hosp., Phila., 1958-60; supr. male div. Pennhurst State Sch. for Mentally Retarded, Spring City, Pa., 1961-65; office nurse Pediatric Clinic, Denver, 1966-69; nurse practitioner mgr. Mountain Bell, Denver, 1969-82; adminstrv. nurse Atlantic Richfield Co., Denver, 1982—; presenter health care topics 1978—. Rep. com. woman Adams County, Northglenn, Colo., 1980; del. Rep. State Conv., Denver, 1980; counselor merit badges Boy Scouts Am., Northglenn, 1984-85. Mem. Am. Nurses Assn. (cert.), Am. Nurses Assn. Primary Council Nurse Practitioners, Am. Assn. Occupational Health Nurses (bd. dirs. 1983-87, sec. 1987—), Colo. Assn. Occupational Health Nurses (corr. sec. 1975-76, pres. elect 1977-78, pres. 1978-79, named Occupational Health Nurse of Yr. 1979, Schering Occupational Health Nurse 1985), Denver Assn. Occupational Health Nurses. Lodge: Order Eastern Star. Office: Atlantic Richfield Co 555 17th St Rm 2202 Denver CO 80202

GOOD, JOHN HENRY, advertising executive; b. Orange, Calif., Jan. 20, 1965; s. John Henry Sr. and Dorothy Helen (Fricke) G. Student, Orange Coast Coll., 1983-85. Mktg. dir. Ameritech Communications, Huntington Beach, Calif., 1988—; pub. OC AdNEWS, Irvine, Calif., 1989—. Mem. Orange County Advt. Fedn., Advt. Fedn., Los Angeles Advt. Communications Network, Desert Bus. Assn., Pub. Relations Soc. Am. Democrat. Roman Catholic. Office: 5632 Bolsa Ave Huntington Beach CA 92649

GOOD, NATHAN LAWRENCE, interior design, architect; b. Marion, Ind., Sept. 25, 1954; s. Wallace E. and Catherine (Wright) G.; m. April Diana Hunt, Aug. 16, 1980; children: Aaron Nathanial, Forrest Scott. Student, U. Copenhagen, 1976; BA in Architecture, Calif. Polytechnic U., 1978, MA in Architecture, 1989; postgrad., U. Colo., 1982. Mktg. dir. Blurock Partnership, Newport Beach, Calif., 1978-79; ptnr. Hunt-Good Interiors, Denver, 1979-84; archtl. designer Worthington, Everett, Zeigel & Tumpes Architects, Boulder, Colo., 1985; interior designer W.C. Muchow & Ptnrs., Denver, 1986; dir. interior architecture Architects Orange, Orange, Calif., 1987—; coord. lecture series Architecture Found. Orange County, Calif., 1988; instr. Interior Design Inst., Corona Del Mar, Calif., 1989; steering com. mem. Boulder Cen. Park Redevelopment Com., 1987; architect 1989 Denver Symphony Show Home; instr. Comml. Interior Design, Interior Design Inst, Corona Del Mar, Calif., 1989. Contbr. article to Crit Mag., 1983. Vis. critic U. Colo., 1985-86; panel chmn. World Affairs Conf., Boulder, 1985; steering com. mem. Internat. Pedestrian Conf. Boulder, 1986. Named to Nat. Honor Soc., 1972. Mem. Am. Soc. Interior Designers, Am. Inst. of Architects (assoc.), Artists Club (Sausalito, Calif.). Office: Architects Orange 144 N Orange St Orange CA 92666

GOODALL, JACKSON WALLACE, JR., restaurant company executive; b. San Diego, Oct. 29, 1938; s. Jackson Wallace and Evelyn Violet (Koski) G.; m. Mary Esther Buckley, June 22, 1958; children: Kathleen, Jeffery, Suzanne, Minette. BS, San Diego State U., 1960. With Foodmaker, Inc., San Diego, 1965-70, pres., 1970—, chief exec. officer, 1979—, chmn. bd., 1985—; founder, bd. dir. Grossmont Bank, La Mesa, Calif.; bd. dirs. Budget Rent A Car Corp. Bd. dirs. Faith Chapel, Greater San Diego Sports Assn., Mercy Hosp. Found.; trustee U. San Diego. Recipient Disting. Alumni of Yr. award San Diego State U., 1974, Golden Chain award, 1982, Silver Plate award Internat. Foodsvc. Mfg. Assn., 1985, Golden Chain Operator of Yr. award Multi Unit Food Svc. Operators, 1988. Mem. Am. Restaurant Assn., San Diego State U. Alumni Assn. (bd. dirs.). Republican. Club: Fairbanks Ranch Country (founder). Office: Foodmaker Inc 9330 Balboa San Diego CA 92123

GOODALL, LEONARD EDWIN, public administration educator; b. Warrensburg, Mo., Mar. 16, 1937; s. Leonard Burton and Eula (Johnson) G.; m. Lois Marie Stubblefield, Aug. 16, 1959; children: Karla, Karen, Greg. B.A., Central Mo. State U., 1958; M.A., U. Mo., 1960; Ph.D. (Kendrick C. Babcock fellow), U. Ill., 1962; A.A. (hon), Schoolcraft Coll., 1977. Asst. prof. polit. sci., asst. dir. Bur. Govt. Research, Ariz. State U., Tempe, 1962-65; dir. Bur. Bur. Govt. Research, Ariz. State U., 1965-67; assoc. prof. polit. sci., assoc. dean faculties U. Ill. at Chgo. Circle, 1968-69, vice chancellor, 1969-71; chancellor U. Mich., Dearborn, 1971-79; pres. U. Nev., Las Vegas, 1979-85; prof. mgmt. and pub. administrn. U. Nev., 1985—; cons. Ariz. Acad., Phoenix, 1964-67; dir. Peace Corps tng. program for Chile, 1965. Author: The American Metropolis: Its Governments and Politics, 1968, rev. edit., 1975, Gearing Arizona's Communities to Orderly Growth, 1965, State Politics and Higher Education, 1976, When Colleges Lobby States, 1987; editor: Urban Politics in the Southwest, 1967. Mem. univ. exec. coun. United Fund, 1966-67; v.p. Met. Fund, Inc.; mem. Mich. Gov.'s Commn. Long Range Planning, 1973-75, Tempe Planning and Zoning Commn., 1965-67, New Detroit Com., 1972-79; mem. Wayne County (Mich.) Planning Commn., 1973-79, vice chmn., 1976-79; mem. exec. bd. Clark County chpt. NCCJ, 1979-86; bd. dirs. Nev. Devel. Authority, 1980-86; Boulder Dam council Boy Scouts Am., 1980—, Nev. Power Co. Consumer Adv. Council, 1984—. Served with AUS, 1959. Mem. Am. Polit. Sci. Assn., Am. Soc. Pub. Adminstrn., Western Govtl. Research Assn. (exec. council 1966-68), Dearborn C. of C. (dir. 1974-79), Phi Sigma Epsilon, Phi Kappa Phi. Lodge: Rotary. Home: 6530 W Darby Ave Las Vegas NV 89102 Office: U Nev Las Vegas NV 89154

GOODBODY, TERRY GEORGE, data processing executive; b. San Diego, Aug. 18, 1944; s. Francis Patrick Goodbody and Jeanne Louise (Lane) Eidsmoe; m. Nancy Carder, July 21, 1968 (div. Jan. 1979); m. Anita Marie Miknuk, May 15, 1982; children: Sean M., Terri M. Programmer IBM Corp., Poughkeepsie, N.Y., 1968-72; mgr. fin. systems Nat. Steel and Shipbldg. Co., San Diego, 1972-76; cons. CACI U.S. Navy, Harrisburg, Pa., 1976-79, NALCOMIS, Washington, 1980-81; mgr. databases Carter, Hawley, Hale Stores, Anaheim, Calif., 1980-83; sr. v.p. administrn. Calif. Fed. Savs. & Loan, Rosemead, Calif., 1983-85; pres., chief exec. officer I-See Corp, Orange, Calif., 1983—; dir. info. svcs. Orange County Register, Santa Ana, Calif., 1986—; guest lectr. various computer mgmt. orgns., Japan, Europe, U.S., 1982—; speaker in field. Author: Managing the Four Resources of Data Processing, 1985; creator, developer common non-industry specific data architecture. With USMC, 1961-68, Vietnam. Mem. Data Adminstrn. Mgmt. Assn., Data Processing Mgmt. Assn., Systems Mgmt. Assn. Republican. Roman Catholic. Home: 5308 Shoshone Ave Orange CA 92667 Office: Orange County Register 625 N Grand Ave Santa Ana CA 92701

GOODELL, CAROL GUYTON, educational administrator, consultant; b. River Forest, Ill., Feb. 18, 1936; d. Robert Harmar and Margaret (Thomas) Guyton; m. William Dudley Goodell, Dec. 20, 1958; children—Douglas Sewall, Elizabeth Ormond. B.S., B.A., Ohio State U., 1958; M.A. in Ednl. Adminstrn., Stanford U., 1969, M.A. in Anthropology, 1974, Ph.D., 1979. Tchr., pub. schs., DeCoto, San Mateo, Hillsborough, Calif., 1958-67; pres. Real World Learning, Inc., San Carlos, Calif., 1968-72; co-ordinator Early Childhood Project, Mass. State Dept. Edn., Boston, 1977-79; co-founder Coll. Campus Tours, Inc., 1979-84; pres. Carol Goodell & Assocs. Coll. Advising Svc., 1979—; bd. dirs. Nueva Learning Ctr., Hillsborough, Calif. Quaker. Editor: The Changing Classroom, 1973, 75, 79.

GOODEN, REGINALD HEBER, bishop; b. Long Beach, Calif., Mar. 22, 1910; s. Robert Burton and Alice Leonard (Moore) G.; m. Victoria Elena F. de Mendia y Miranda (dec. 1982); children: Reginald Heber, Hiram Richard; m. Sandra Marie Wojcik Roberts, July 23, 1988. A.B., Stanford U., 1931; S.T.B., Berkeley Div. Sch., New Haven, 1934, S.T.D., 1946; student, U. Madrid, 1934-35, Centro de Estudios Historicos, Madrid (Spain), 1934-35; D.D., Trinity Coll., Hartford, 1963. Ordained to ministry Episcopal Ch., 1934; hon. asst. chaplain Brit. Embassy Ch., Madrid, 1934-35; priest in charge St. Paul's Ch. and Sch., Camaguey, Cuba, 1935-39; dean Holy Trinity Cathedral, Havana, Cuba, 1939-45; bishop of missionary dist. Episc. Ch., Panama C.Z., 1945-72; also bishop in charge Episc. Ch., Ecuador, 1956-64; bishop in charge Central Central-Am., 1956-57; asst. bishop Diocese La., Shreveport, 1972-75, acting bishop, 1975-76, ret., 1976; bishop-in-residence Ch. of Holy Cross, Shreveport, 1976—. Decorated Gran Cruz Order Vasco Nunez de Balboa, Panama; recipient Distinguished Community Service award Govt. C.Z., 1972; John Henry Watson fellow Berkeley Div. Sch. Club: The Breakers (Stanford U.). Lodge: Masons. Home: The Episcopal Home 1428 S Marengo Ave Alhambra CA 91803 also: Friars 9999 Smitherman Dr #700 Shreveport LA 71115

GOODEY, ILA MARIE, psychologist; b. Logan, Utah, Feb. 1, 1948; d. Vernal P. and Leona Marie (Williams) Goodey. BA with honors in English and Sociology, U. Utah, 1976; Grad. Cert. Criminology, U. Utah, 1976, MS in Counseling Psychology, 1984, PhD in Psychology, 1985. Speech writer for dean of students U. Utah, Salt Lake City, 1980—, psychologist Univ. Counseling Ctr., 1984—; cons. Dept. Social Services, State of Utah, Salt Lake City, 1983—; pvt. practice psychology Consult West, Salt Lake City, 1985-86; pub. relations coordinator Univ. Counseling Ctr., 1985—; cons. Aids Project, U. Utah, 1985—; pvt. practice psychology, Inscapes Inst., Salt Lake City, 1987—; writer civic news Salt Lake City Corp., 1980—. Author book: Love for All Seasons, 1971; play: Validation, 1979; musical drama: One Step, 1984. Contbr. articles to profl. jours. Chmn. policy bd. Dept. State Social Service, Salt Lake City, 1986—; campaign writer Utah Dem. Party, 1985. Recipient Creative Achievement award Utah Poetry Soc., 1974, English SAC, U. Utah, 1978. Mem. Am. Psychol. Assn., Utah Psychol. Assn., AAUW, Internat. Platform Assn., Mortar Board, Am. Soc. Clin. Hypnosis, Utah Soc. Clin. Hypnosis, Soc. Psychol. Study Social Issues, League of Women Voters, Phi Beta Kappa, Phi Kappa Phi, Alpha Lambda Delta. Mormon. Clubs: Mormon Theol. Symposium, Utah Poetry Assn. Avocations: theatrical activities, creative writing, travel, political activities. Office: U Utah $S1Counseling Ctr $S2450 SSB Salt Lake City UT 84112 also: Inscapes Inst 34 S 600 E Salt Lake City UT 84102

GOODIN, WILLIAM CHARLES, oil company consultant; b. Louisville, Sept. 18, 1917; s. Edward C. and Bertha (Vorhies) G.; m. Emily Ellen Percefull, Sept. 8, 1946; children: Sue Ellen Goodin Baird, Charles W. B.A. in Econs., U. Colo., 1941. Owner, operator Petroleum Info. Corp., Denver, 1946-68; ptnr., v.p. Petroleum Info. Corp., subs. A.C. Nielsen Co., Denver, 1968-75, pres., 1975-79; chmn. bd., chief exec. officer Petroleum Info. Corp., subs. A.C. Nielsen Co., Littleton, Colo., 1979-83, chmn. bd., 1983-86; cons. 1986—; mem. Colo. Oil and Gas Commn., 1972-76, Interstate Oil Compact Commn. Bd. dirs. Swedish Med. Ctr. Found., Englewood, Colo., 1979-86, U. Colo. Found., Inc., Boulder, 1983—. Served to 1st lt. CIC, AUS, 1942-46, Philippines, Korea. Recipient Betty McWhorter award Denver chpt. Desk & Derrick, 1979. Mem. Rocky Mountain Oil and Gas Assn. (dir. 1982—), Denver Landmen's Assn., Soc. Petroleum Engrs., Am. Assn. Petroleum Geologists, Rocky Mountain Petroleum Pioneers, Assn. Petroleum Writers, Ind. Petroleum Assn. Mountain States (Wildcatter of Yr. award 1987); hon. life mem. Rocky Mountain Assn. Petroleum Geologists. Republican. Presbyterian. Clubs: Denver Petroleum (bd. dirs. 1958-62, v.p. 1961, pres. 1962), Cherry Hills Country (Englewood, Colo.); Garden of God's (Colorado Springs, Colo.); 25 Yr. Club of Petroleum Industry (Solvang, Calif.). Home: 11 Parkway Dr Englewood CO 80110 Office: Petroleum Info Corp 600 Denver Club Bldg Denver CO 80202

GOODLAD, JOHN ERLE, commercial real estate company executive; b. L.A., Oct. 7, 1929; s. Clarence Erle and Adda Louise (Baughman) G.; m. Nancy Lou Lanzit, July 7, 1956; children: Lisa, Lynn, John Jr. BA, UCLA, 1953; MBA, Pepperdine U., 1978. Asst. art dir. Whitman Pub. Co., Beverly Hills, Calif., 1953-55; sales supr. Shell Oil Co., San Diego, 1955-57; sec., treas. Lanzit Printing Co., L.A., 1957-63; asst. to pres. Holga Metal Products, Van Nuys, Calif., 1963-80; comml. sales rep. Sterpa Real Estate Co., Glendale, Calif., 1980-85, Prudential-Stevenson Real Estate Svcs., Glendale, 1985—. Author: Plant Site Selection, 1978. Mem. adv. coun. Glendale YWCA; trustee Glenpac, Glendale, 1984—; bd. dirs. Rep. Buck and Ballot Brigade, Glendale, 1985-87; bd. dirs., v.p. Assn. for Retarded, Glendale, 1985--; mem. Design Rev. Bd., Glendale, 1986--. Sgt. USAF, 1951-52. Mem. Am. Indsl. Real Estate Assn., Glendale Bd. Realtors (bd. dirs. 1984, 86, R.A.P. award 1986), Calif. Assn. Realtors, Nat. Assn. Realtors, Glendale C. of C. (bd. dirs. 1984-85), Oakmont Country Club, Verdugo Club, Rotary (bd. dirs. Glendale chpt. 1985-87), Masons. Mem. Ch. of Christ. Office: Prudential-Stevenson Real Estate Svc 1025 N Brand Blvd Glendale CA 91202

GOODLEY, PAUL C., engineer; b. Henderson, Ky., Feb. 23, 1941; s. Charles S. and Barbara (Griggs) G. BS, Murray State U., 1972. Scientist research and devel. Abbott Labs., North Chicago, Ill., 1972-80; lab. dir. Murray (Ky.) State U., 1978-80; research and devel. engr. Hewlett-Packard Co., Palo Alto, Calif., 1980—; chmn. North Chicago Sci. Seminar series, 1974-78. Author: Analytical Chemistry, 1971; patentee in field. Mem. AAAS, Am. Chem. Soc., Am. Soc. Mass Spectrometry (exec. bd. 1987-88), Bay Area Mass Spectrometry (chmn. 1988—), Joint Com. Atomic Molecular Physics (exec. bd. 1987—), Brenda Ct. Homeowners Assn. (pres. 1981—), Sigma Xi. Office: Hewlett-Packard Co 1601 California Ave Palo Alto CA 94304

GOODLEY, PAUL HARVEY, physician; b. Bklyn., Feb. 6, 1932; s. Israel Harry and Ruth (Reiter) G.; m. Dolores Henrietta Ledfors, Apr. 2, 1955; children—Mark David, Pamela Susan, Diane Deborah, Caryn Lynn, Lisa Louise. B.A. cum laude, U. So. Calif., 1955; M.D., UCLA, 1959. Diplomate Am. Bd. Phys. Medicine and Rehab., Am. Bd. Family Practice. Intern, Harbor Gen. Hosp., Torrance, Calif., 1959-60; gen. practice indsl. medicine, Torrance, 1960, Wilmington, Calif., 1961-72; resident phys. medicine and rehab. U. So. Calif.-Los Angeles County Med. Ctr., 1972-73, U. Calif.-Davis, 1974; practice medicine specializing in phys. medicine and rehab., Los Angeles, 1975—; med. dir. rehab. ctr. Glendale Adventist Med. Ctr., Calif., 1975-76; med. cons. orthopedic medicine U.S. VA, 1981-84; founder Pain Diagnostics and Rehab. Inst., Los Angeles, 1977, dir., 1977-84; adj. prof. orthopedic medicine Coll. Osteo. Medicine of Pacific; exam. physician Los Angeles County Sheriff's Dept., 1962-79; exec. dir. Am. Coll. Orthopaedic Medicine, 1987—. Inventor Goodley Polyaxial Cervical Traction System; (with others) Goodley/Shemet Lumbar Lift. Mem. Founders Club of Music Ctr. Performing Arts; Recipient Award of Valor, Los Angeles County Sheriff's Dept., 1968. Mem. Am. Assn. Orthopedic Medicine (founding, 1st pres., pres. emeritus), Am. Acad. Phys. Medicine and Rehab. (chmn. task force and spl. interest group musculoskeletal medicine), Internat. Rehab. Medicine Assn. (chmn. com. musculoskeletal medicine), AMA, Los Angeles County Med. Assn., Am. Assn. Electromyography and Electrodiagnosis, Am. Congress Rehab. Medicine, Soc. Orthopedic Medicine, Internat. Assn. Study of Pain, Am. Pain Soc., Am. Thermographic Soc., Nat. Rifle Assn. (life master, Gold medal Calif. championships 1968), Phi Delta Epsilon. Office: Bear Valley Orthopedic Medicine 41609 Big Bear Blvd Box 2909 Big Bear Lake CA 92315

GOODMAN, ARLENE See SCOTT, LAURIE

GOODMAN, BEATRICE MAY, realtor; b. Rehoboth, Mass., Nov. 12, 1933; s. Manuel Silva and Mercy Elizabeth (Mayers) Bettencourt; m. Sam R. Goodman, Sept. 15, 1957; children: Mark, Stephen, Christopher. Pres. Bettencourt Draperies, Rehoboth, Mass., 1955-56; asst. mgr. Leo H. Spivack Furniture, L.I., N.Y., 1956-57; asst. designer Lillian Decorators, L.I., N.Y., 1957-58; asst. buyer Macy's N.Y., N.Y.C., 1958-59; pres. Beatrice & Beverly, Mt. View, Calif., 1980-82; realtor Coldwell Banker, Menlo Park, Calif., 1984—; pres. The Added Touch, Atherton, Calif., 1982—. Den mother Boy Scouts Am., N.Y.C., 1970-76; active Peninsula Vols., Palo Alto, 1974—. Mem. Nat. Bd. Realtors, Orgn. for Rehab. Tng. Home: 60 Shearer Dr Atherton CA 94025 Office: Coldwell Banker 1295 El Camino Real Menlo Park CA 94025

GOODMAN, GWENDOLYN ANN, nursing educator; b. Davenport, Iowa, Aug. 7, 1955; d. Merle Erwin and Loraine Etta (Mahannah) Langfeldt; m. Mark Nathan Goodman, Oct. 24, 1982; 1 child, Zachary Aaron. BS in Nursing, Ariz. State U., 1977. RN, Ariz. Staff nurse surgical floor and intensive care unit St. Luke's Hosp. and Med. Ctr., Phoenix, 1977-81; staff nurse intensive care unit Yauapai Regional Med. Ctr., Prescott, Ariz., 1981-82; instr. nursing Yauapai Coll., Prescott, 1982-88, cons., 1986; part time staff nurse Ariz. Poison Control Ctr., Phoenix, 1980-81. Mem. Ariz. Nurses Assn. Democrat. Home: PO Box 450 Prescott AZ 86302

GOODMAN, JAMIE LYNN, advertising executive; b. N.Y.C., Sept. 13, 1963; d. Harris and Naomi (Zeidenberg) G. BS, U. Calif., Berkeley, 1985. Sr. acct. exec. Thomas/Rahm Mktg. Communications, Oakland, Calif., 1988—. Mem. NAFE, Prytanean Soc., Big Brothers/Big Sisters. Home: 1056 Fulton # 2 San Francisco CA 94117 Office: Thomas/Rahm Mktg Communications 499 14th St Oakland CA 94612

GOODMAN, JOEL HARRY, JR., university administrator; b. Seattle, Apr. 18, 1944; s. Joel H. and Edith (Kullmann) G.; m. Barbara Guzofsky, May 8, 1976; children: Elliott James, Julia Rose. BA with distinction, Stanford U., 1966; MAT, Harvard U., 1967; MA, Stanford U., 1973 and 76; postgrad., U. Chgo., 1975-76. Asst. dir. admissions Stanford U., Palo Alto, Calif., 1972-74; mktg. services mgr. Bell & Howell Edn. Group, Chgo., 1974-80; dir. planning and devel. Western State U., Fullerton, Calif., 1980-83, dean of admissions, 1983—; v.p. adminstrn. Western State U., 1984—. Bd. dirs. Orange County chpt. Am. Diabetes Assn. Mem. Stanford Club of Orange County. Office: 1111 N State College Blvd Fullerton CA 92631

GOODMAN, JOSEPH WILFRED, electrical engineering educator; b. Boston, Feb. 8, 1936; s. Joseph and Doris (Ryan) G.; m. Hon Mai Lam, Dec. 5, 1962; 1 dau., Michele Ann. B.A., Harvard U., 1958; M.S. in E.E., Stanford U., 1960, Ph.D., 1963. Postdoctoral fellow Norwegian Def. Research Establishment, Oslo, 1962-63; research assoc. Stanford U., 1963-67, asst. prof., 1967-69, assoc. prof., 1969-72, prof. elec. engring., 1972—; vis. prof. Univ. Paris XI, Orsay, France, 1973-74; dir. Info. Systems lab., dept. elec. engring., Stanford U., 1981-83, chmn., 1988—; William E. Ayer prof. elec. engring. Stanford U., 1988—; cons. to govt. and industry, 1965—; v.p. Internat. Comm. for Optics, 1985-87, pres., 1988—; mem. internat. adv. com. on phys. scis. and engring. Sci. Council Singapore. Author: Introduction to Fourier Optics, 1968, Statistical Optics, 1985; contbr. articles to profl. jours. Recipient F.E. Terman award Am. Soc. Engring. Edn., 1971. Fellow Optical Soc. Am. (dir. 1977-83, editor jour. 1978-83, Max Born award 1983), IEEE (edn. medal 1987), Soc. Photo-optical Instrumentation Engrs. (bd. govs. 1979-82, 88—, Dennis Gabor award, 1987); mem. Nat. Acad. Engring. Home: 570 University Terr Los Altos CA 94022 Office: Stanford U Dept Elec Engring Durand 127 Stanford CA 94305

GOODMAN, JULIUS, nuclear engineer, consultant, researcher; b. Odessa, USSR, July 19, 1935; came to U.S., 1979, naturalized, 1986; s. Isaac and Eugenia (Lusher) Guttmann; m. Rachel Bezpalko, July 4, 1959; 1 dau., Marina. M.S. in Theoretical Physics, State U., Odessa, 1958, Ph.D., Inst. Nuclear Physics, Tashkent, USSR, 1962, Inst. Tech. Odessa, 1965. Sr. researcher Inst. Nuclear Physics, Tashkent, Acad. Sci., USSR, 1958-63; prof. Inst. Tech., Odessa, 1963-70, Poly U., 1970-76; sr. engr. Bechtel Power Corp., Norwalk, Calif., 1980-86; prof. Calif. State U. Long Beach, 1986—. Author: Professional Education, 1975, (with P.U. Arifov) Positron Diagnostic, 1978; contbr. numerous articles to profl. jours. Pres. Hatchiya (Revival), Orange County, Calif., 1982—. Mem. Am. Nuclear Soc., Internat. Soc. Reliability Engrs., Internat. Platform Assn., Com. on Internat. Freedom of Scientists, AAAS, N.Y. Acad. Scis., Los Angeles Council Engrs. and Scientists (publicity chmn. 1983-84). Club: Toastmasters (Fullerton, Calif.). Lodge: B'nai B'rith. Research on probabilistic risk assessment, reliability, statistics, artificial intelligence, simulation; gen. relativity, atomic and nuclear physics, physics of space nuclear reactors. Patentee nuclear reactor with UF-6.

GOODMAN, MARK N., lawyer; b. Phoenix, Jan. 16, 1952; s. Daniel H. and Joanne G.; m. Gwendolyn A. Langfeldt, Oct. 24, 1982; 1 child, Zachary A. BA, Prescott Coll., 1973; JD summa cum laude, Calif. Western Sch. Law, 1977; LL.M., U. Calif.-Berkeley, 1978. Bar: Ariz. 1977, Calif. 1977 U.S. Dist. Ct. (no. dist.) Calif. 1977, U.S. Dist. Ct. Ariz. 1978, U.S. Ct. Appeals (9th cir.) 1978, U.S. Dist. Ct. (so. dist.) Calif. 1981, U.S. Supreme Ct. 1981, U.S. Dist. Ct. (ce. dist.) Calif., 1982, Nebr. 1983, U.S. Dist. Ct. Nebr. 1983. Practice Law Offices Mark N. Goodman, Prescott, Ariz., 1978-79, 81-83, Mark N. Goodman, Ltd., Prescott, 1983-86; ptnr. Alward and Goodman, Ltd., Prescott, 1979-81; ptnr. Perry, Goodman, Drutz & Musgrove, Prescott, 1986-87, Goodman, Drutz & Musgrove, 1987-88; ptnr. Sears & Goodman, P.C., Prescott, 1988—. Author: The Ninth Amendment, 1981. Contbr. articles to profl. jours. Bd. dirs. Yavapai Symphony Assn., Prescott, 1981-84. Notes and comments editor Calif. Western Law Review, 1976. Mem. ABA, Assn. Trial Lawyers Am., Yavapai County Bar Assn. (v.p. 1981-82). Office: Sears & Goodman P C PO Box 2489 Prescott AZ 86302-2489

GOODMAN, NONG SUWANNAKORN, controller; b. Bangkok, Aug. 29, 1956; came to U.S., 1981; d. Samak and Khanitsri (Puntudit) Suwannakorn; m. William Alan Goodman, May 24, 1987. BA in Econs. and Bus. Adminstrn., Simon Fraser U., 1981; MBA, Calif. State U., Northridge, 1985. Medicare provider auditor Blue Cross Calif., Woodland Hills, 1982-87; fin. mgmt. analyst Cedar-Sinai Med. Ctr., L.A., 1987-88; asst. contr. Greater El Monte (Calif.) Community Hosp., 1988—; cons. Goodman and Goodman Ltd., Valencia, Calif., 1987—. Mem. Healthcare Fin. Mgmt. Assn. Republican. Roman Catholic. Office: Nong Goodman 26510 Strambino Ct Valencia CA 91355

GOODMAN, RONALD BURTON, engineering consultant; b. Bklyn., July 2, 1932; s. Herbert Samuel and Rose (Shiller) G.; m. Hannah Indig, Nov. 19, 1960; children: Doreen Goodman Townley, Karen Goodman Ingamells. B-SChemE, Bucknell U., 1954; postgrad. in engring., Columbia U., 1954-55; postgrad. in bus., NYU, 1957-60. Mgr. proposals and estimating Foster Wheeler Corp., Livingston, N.J., 1957-77; prin., combustion engr. C.F. Braun, Inc., Alhambra, Calif., 1977-87; pvt. practice cons. heat transfer equipment Northridge, Calif., 1987—. Patentee in field. Pres. Troy Hills Civic Assn. Parsippany, N.J., 1965; treas. Chpt. F City of Hope, Northridge, 1983-85. 1st lt. U.S. Army, 1955-57. Mem. Am. Petroleum Inst. (mem. subcom. on fired heaters 1981—), Valley Socialites, Masons, Shriners. Democrat. Home and Office: 19500 Turtle Ridge Ln Northridge CA 91326

GOODMAN, SEYMOUR EVAN, computer science and international studies educator, researcher, consultant; b. Chgo., June 19, 1943; s. Paul S. and Shirley (Young) G.; m. Diane Margot Samuel, Dec. 18, 1966; children—Richard Michael, Steven Neal. B.S., Columbia U., 1965, M.S., 1966; Ph.D., Calif. Inst. Tech., 1970. Asst. prof. applied math. U. Va., Charlottesville, 1970-75, assoc. prof. applied math. and computer sci., 1975-81; vis. prof. pub. and internat. affairs, Princeton (N.J.) U., 1977-79, research fellow, 1978-79; vis. scholar U. Chgo., 1979; prof. mgmt. info. systems U. Ariz., Tucson, 1981—; mem. adv. com. Internat. Trade Adminstrn., Dept. Commerce, 1979—; mem. adv. com. Def. Sci. Bd., Dept. Def., 1981-84, Def. Intelligence Agy., 1983-87, NRC coms., 1985—, Dept. State, 1987—; chmn. NRC com. Intrenat. Devel. in Computer Sci. and Tech., 1987-88; cons. govtl. agys. Danforth Assoc., 1977-82; Sesquicentennial Assoc. State of Va., 1977; NSF grantee, 1978-79, 83; numerous grant and research contracts Office Tech. Assessment, U.S. Congress, 1979-81, Los Alamos Nat. Lab., U.S. Air Force, Battelle Meml. Labs., IBM, Nat. Council for Soviet and East European Research; U.S. participant U.S.-USSR IREX program, 1988—. Mem. Assn. for Computing Machinery (nat. lectr. 1981-82, com. computing and pub. policy 1981-83), Am. Assn. for Advancement Slavic Studies, Computer Soc. of IEEE (com. on pub. policy 1987—). Contbr. numerous articles to profl. jours. Office: U Ariz MIS BPA Tucson AZ 85721

GOODMAN, WILLIAM LEE, commercial pilot; b. Butte, Mont., May 15, 1946; s. William Lonzo and Phyllis Hilma (White) G.; m. Susan Margaret Thompson, Nov. 29, 1969; children: Kathryn, Margaret, William. BS in Computer Sci., Oreg. State U., 1968; MBA, City U., Seattle, 1982; postgrad., Seattle U.; postgrad. in def. econs., U.S. Naval War Coll., 1986. Cert. airline transport pilot, flight engr., control tower operator, flight instr., FAA. Systems analyst Mohawk Data Scis. Corp., Portland, Oreg., 1974-76; air traffic controller FAA, Pendleton, Oreg., 1976-78; pilot Trans Internat. Airlines, Oakland, Calif., 1978; aerospace engr. Boeing Comml. Airplane Co., Seattle, 1978-86; pilot USAIR, Washington, 1986—. Editor Boeing Tng. Ctr. newsletter Intercom, 1980-82; contbg. editor Boeing Customer Service mag. Advisor, 1982-86. V.p. Homeowners Assn., Auburn, 1982-85. Served to comdr. USNR, 1968-89, Vietnam. Mem. Airline Pilots Assn., Naval Res. Officers Assn., Soaring Soc. Am. Republican. Home: 33720 135th Ave SE Auburn WA 98002

GOODMAN, WILLIAM ROBERT, electronics company executive; b. Las Vegas, Nev., Nov. 1, 1952; s. George Harrison and Edna Muriel (Bentley) G.; m. Norinne Williams, June 18, 1974; children: Marissa, Patrick, Mark. BS in Fin., Lewis and Clark Coll., 1974. Tax acct. Hyster Corp., Portland, Oreg., 1974-75; corp. acct. Hyster Corp., Portland, 1975-78; dealer analyst Freightline Corp., Portland, 1977-78, fin. analyst, 1978-80, corp. planning mgr., 1980-83, dir. fin. and costing, 1983-85; controller, chief fin. officer Lab Oscilloscope div. Tektronix Corp., Beaverton, Oreg., 1985—; bd. dirs. Consol. Freightways Credit Union, Portland, 1983-84. Bd. dirs. Celebrations Unltd., child abuse prevention program, Portland, 1988—. Mem. Planning Execs. Inst. (v.p. membership 1984-85), Planning Forum, Econ. Roundtable, Delta Mu Delta, City Club (Portland), West Hills Tennis Club (Beaverton). Home: 1704 SW Elizabeth Portland OR 97201 Office: Tektronic Corp Lab Oscilloscope Div PO Box 500 MS39-811 Beaverton OR 97077

GOODPASTURE, JESSIE CARROL, biochemist; b. Oak Park, Ill., Nov. 27, 1952; d. James Slocum and Elizabeth Virginia (Goddard) G. BA, So. Ill. U., 1973, MS, 1975; PhD, U. Ill., Chgo., 1979. Research asst. U. Ill. Med. Ctr., Chgo., 1976-80; asst. prof. Sch. Medicine U. Essen, Fed. Republic Germany, 1980-81; staff researcher I Syntex Research, Palo Alto, Calif., 1981-83, staff researcher II, 1983—; cons. HDC Corp., Mountain View, Calif., 1986—; mem. fellowships award panel AAUW, Washington, 1988—; mem. sci and math adv. bd. Mills Coll., Oakland, Calif., 1985—; mem. speakers bur. Assn. Women in Sci., Palo Alto, 1988—. Author: (with others) Reversal of Sterilization, 1978, IUD Technology, 1982, Long Acting Contraceptive Delivery Systems, 1984, Male Contraception: Advances and Future Prospects, 1986; contbr. articles to profl. jours. Scholar So. Ill. U., 1971-73, U. Ill., 1975-79. Mem. Internat. Soc. Andrology, Am. Soc. Andrology, Am. Fertility Soc., Soc. for the Study Reprodn., Scis. Ctr. Animal Welfare. Home: 12 Antique Forest Ln Belmont CA 94002 Office: Syntex Rsch 3401 Hillview Ave Palo Alto CA 94304

GOODRICH, JOY BENTON, service executive, educator; b. Yellville, Ark., Mar. 4, 1937; d. Floyd Dewey and Myrtle Ruth (Baughman) Benton; m. Paul Thomas Peckman, June 17, 1956; children: Thomas Michael, Martin Roy, Douglas Benton, Virginia Ruth; m. Quentin Allan Goodrich, Nov. 23, 1978; stepchildren: Lynn Elizabeth, Dean Vernon. Student, Ark. Poly. Coll., 1954-55, Yakima Valley Jr. Coll., 1955; AA, Green River Community Coll., 1976; BA, Evergreen State Coll., 1978. Stenographer FBI, Little Rock, 1955; sec., bookkeeper Firemans Fund Ins., Seattle, 1958-60; sec. Boeing Co., Renton, Washington, 1961-63; supr. Avis Rent-a-Car, SeaTac Airport, Seattle, 1970-75; adminstrv. asst. Luth. Community Svcs., Tacoma, 1975-77; owner Speedy Office Svcs., Port Townsend, Wash., 1978—; instr. typing Peninsula Community Coll., Port Townsend, 1986—. Bd. dirs. North Olympic Health Planning Coun., Clallam and Jefferson Counties, Wash.; Pub. chmn. Jefferson County United Good Neighbors, 1982-86, sec. exec. com. 1985—; mem. vocat. adv. com. Port Townsend High Sch., 1984—, citizen's adv. com. Townsend Br. Peninsula Coll., 1986—; pres. bd. trustees Community United Meth. Ch., Hadlock, Wash., 1986-88, sec. adminstrv. coun., 1984-85sec. personnel and nominations, 1989—; chmn. communications com. Jefferson County United Good Neighbors, 1987. alt. del. state Dem. conv., 1984, 88. Mem. AAUW (pres. Port Townsend br.), Nat. Assn. Quick Printers, Nat. Fedn. Ind. Bus., Port Townsend C. of C. (chair edn. com. 1984-89, trustee 1987), Port Ludlow Yacht Club. Home: 70 Keefe Ln Port Ludlow WA 98365 Office: Speedy Office Svcs 712 Washington Port Townsend WA 98368

GOODRICH, NORMA LORRE (MRS. JOHN H. HOWARD), French and comparative literature educator; b. Huntington, Vt., May 10, 1917; d. Charles Edmund and Edyth (Riggs) Falby; m. J.M.A. Lorre, Dec. 10, 1943 (div. June 1946); 1 son, Jean-Joseph; m. John Hereford Howard, Jan. 20, 1964. BS cum laude, U. Vt., 1938; postgrad. (U. Vt. fellow), U. Grenoble, France, 1938-39; PhD (Ellis fellow), Columbia U., 1965. Tchr. high schs., Vt., 1939-43, Bentley Sch., N.Y.C., 1943-47; owner dir. Am. Villa in Normandy, Trouville, France, 1947-53; tchr. Fieldston Sch., N.Y.C., 1954-63; asst. prof. French U. So. Calif., 1964-66, assoc. prof., 1966-71; dean faculty Scripps Coll., Claremont, Calif., 1971-72; prof. French and comparative lit. Claremont Colls., 1972, prof. emeritus, 1982—; vis. scholar Calif. Luth. Coll., 1965, Isle of Man, U.K., 1986, Claremont McKenna Coll., 1986; vis. prof. John Carroll U., Cleve., 1987, Calif. State U., Long Beach, 1986, 87, 88. Author: Ancient Myths, 1959, rev. edit., 1977, Medieval Myths, 1960, rev. edit., 1977, Doctor and Maria Theresa, 1961, Myths of the Hero, 1961, Ways of Love, 1963, Charles of Orleans: A Study of Themes in His French and English Poetry, 1967, Giono: Master of Fictional Modes, 1973, Afterword for The Man Who Planted Trees (Jean Giono), 1985 (New Eng. Book award), London edit., 1989, King Arthur, 1986, 2d edit. 1989 Merlin, 1987, 2d edit., 1989, Il Mito della Tavola Rotonda (transl. of King Arthur), 1989, Castle Eppstein (transl. of Alexander Dumas), 1989; contbr. articles to internat. profl. jours.; guest appearances various TV and radio shows, Eng., 1986. Mem. pub. rels. staff Worthington Corp., N.Y.C., 1953-54; bd. dirs., patron West End Opera Assn., 1973-74, program dir., 1975-76. Mem. Assn. Study of Dada and Surrealism (sec. 1970-72), Philol. Assn. Pacific Coast (nominating com. 1971-72), MLA (mem. del. assembly's election com. 1975), The Prehistoric Soc., Am. Assn. Tchrs. French, Medieval Assn. Pacific, Medieval Acad. Am., Columbia U. Alumni Assn., Dante Soc., Clan Mac Arthur, Clan Mac Kay (hon.), Tordarrach Trust (Scotland and U.S.), Met. Opera Guild, Phi Kappa Phi. Home: 620 Diablo Dr Claremont CA 91711

GOODSELL, THEODORE CLAIR, aerospace company official; b. Geneva, N.Y., Feb. 3, 1947; s. Clair Everett and Mildred (Hoppins) G.; m. Judith Lynn Callaghan, July 24, 1971; children: Michael Clair, Michelle Marie. Student, Alfred State Coll., 1964-65. Enlisted with USN, 1966-86; assignments in USN, U.S., Spain, Vietnam, 1966-86; retired USN, 1986; quality assurance field rep. Rohr Industries Inc., Chula Vista, Calif., 1986--. treas. Mesa View Home Owners Assn., Mira Mesa, Calif., 1985--. Mem. Nat. Mgmt. Assn., K.C. (charter San Diego, trustee 1987-88). Republican. Home: 8921 Libra Dr San Diego CA 92126 Office: Rohr Industries Inc PO Box 878 Chula Vista CA 92012-0878

GOODSITT, ROBERT DONALD, real estate developer; b. Milw., Feb. 18, 1933; s. William Bradley and Caroline (Werba) G.; m. Barbara A. Wolfe, Dec. 19, 1954 (div. 1968); m. Dorothy June Jensen, Dec. 7, 1969; children: Sherri Jo, Jeffrey Bruce. BS, U. Wis., 1954. Pres. various cos., 1954-73; v.p. Arthur Rubloff Co., Chgo., 1973-84; sr. v.p. Robert A. McNeil Co., San Mateo, Calif., 1984-86; western v.p. Integrated Resources, L.A., 1986-87; pres. Fed. Securities Mortgage Corp., L.A., 1987—. 1st Lt. U.S. Army, 1954-56. Mem. Inst. Real Estate Mgmt. (cert. property mgr.). Home: 660 Harbor St Marina Del Rey CA 90291 Office: Fed Securities Mortgage Corp 1888 Century Park E Los Angeles CA 90067

GOODSON, MARK, television producer; b. Sacramento, Jan. 24, 1915; s. Abraham Ellis and Fannie (Gross) G.; children by previous marriages: Jill, Jonathan, Marjorie. BA, U. Calif., 1937. Announcer, newscaster, dir. Sta. KFRC, San Francisco, 1938-41; radio announcer, dir. N.Y.C., 1941-43; radio dir. U.S. Treasury War Bond Drive, 1944-45; 1st v.p. Mid-Atlantic Newspapers, Inc.; chmn. bd. Cen. States Pub. Co.; 1st v.p. Capitol City Pub. Co.; v.p. New Eng. Newspapers, Inc. Formed Goodson-Todman Prodns., 1946; originated radio shows Winner Take All, 1946, Stop the Music, 1947, Hit the Jackpot, 1947-49; creator of TV game programs What's My Line, It's News to Me, The Name's the Same, I've Got a Secret, Two for the Money, The Price is Right, Password, Match Game, To Tell the Truth, Family Feud, Child's Play, others; producer TV film series The Web, The Rebel, Richard Boone Theater, Branded. Trustee Mus. Broadcasting, 1985—; bd. dirs. Am. Film Inst., 1975—. Recipient Nat. TV award Gt. Britain, 1951, Emmy award Acad. TV Arts and Scis., 1951, 52, Sylvania award. Mem. Acad. TV Arts and Sci. (pres. N.Y.C. 1957-58), Phi Beta Kappa. Office: 375 Park Ave New York NY 10152 also: 5750 Wilshire Blvd Los Angeles CA 90036

GOODSON, RAY ANDREW, business owner; b. Tracy, Calif., Oct. 27, 1957; s. Raymond Herbert and Colleen Joan (Dougherty) G.; m. Pamela Jane Murphy, Sept. 19, 1981; children: Christopher Chase, Michael William. BSBA, U. N.D., 1989. With sales dept. Georga A. Hormel & Co., Denver, 1980-81, Active Bus. Forms, San Ramon, Calif., 1981-83, Chase Manhattan Bank, Atlanta, 1984-86, Barclays Bank, Atlanta, 1986-87; owner Landmark Bus. Forms, San Ramon, 1987—. Mem. Nat. Bus. Forms Assn. Episcopalian. Office: Landmark Bus Forms PO Box 5008A-80 San Ramon CA 94583

GOODWILL, MARGARET JANE, artist; b. L.A., Sept. 27, 1950; d. David and Erna Pauline (Kremser) G.; m. James Vincent Erickson, Sept. 6, 1980. Student, U. Calif., Santa Barbara, 1968-70; BFA cum laude, Calif. Coll. Arts and Crafts, 1972. Graphic artist Proarts, Oakland, Calif., 1970-71; creative art dir. Am. Analysis Corp., San Francisco, 1974-76; dir. Lone Wolf Gallery, San Francisco, 1982-84. One-woman show Lone Wolf Gallery, 1985, Wrubel Gallery, Berkeley, Calif., 1988; two-woman show St. Mary's Coll., Moraga, Calif., 1973; exhibited in group shows San Francisco Art Festival, 1971, 72, A Gallery, Palm Desert, Calif., 1986, Banaker Gallery, Walnut Creek, Calif., 1988; mural for Prevention Cruelty to Animals Hdqrs., San Francisco, 1980. Recipient 1st prize Ossining (N.Y.) Women's Club, 1968, Poughkeepsie (N.Y.) Art Ctr., 1968, merit award Delta Art Show, Antioch, Calif., 1971; N.Y. State Regent's scholar, 1968, Walnut Creek Civic Arts scholar, 1970. Mem. Calif. Coll. Arts and Crafts Alumni Assn., Oakland Mus., Mus. Modern Art San Francisco, Nat. Geog. Soc., Smithsonian Assocs.

GOODWIN, ALFRED THEODORE, judge; b. Bellingham, Wash., June 29, 1923; s. Alonzo Theodore and Miriam Hazel (Williams) G.; m. Marjorie Elizabeth Major, Dec. 23, 1943 (div. 1948); 1 son, Michael Theodore; m. Mary Ellin Handelin, Dec. 23, 1949; children—Karl Alfred, Margaret Ellen, Sara Jane, James Paul. B.A., U. Oreg., 1947; J.D., 1951. Bar: Oreg. 1951. Newspaper reporter Eugene (Oreg.) Register-Guard, 1947-50; practiced in Eugene until 1955; circuit judge Oreg. 2d. Jud. Dist., 1955-60; assoc. justice Oreg. Supreme Ct., 1960-69; judge U.S. Dist. Ct. Oreg., 1969-71; judge U.S. Ct. Appeals (9th cir.), 1971-88, chief judge, 1988—. Contbr.: articles to Oreg. Law Rev, 1949-51; student editor, 1950-51. Bd. dirs. Central Lane YMCA, Eugene, 1956-60, Salem (Oreg.) Art Assn., 1960-69; adv. bd. Eugene Salvation Army, 1956-60, chmn., 1959. Served to capt., inf. AUS, 1942-46, ETO. Mem. Am. Judicature Soc., Am. Law Inst., ABA (ho. of dels. 1986-87), Order of Coif, Phi Delta Phi, Sigma Delta Chi, Alpha Tau Omega. Republican. Presbyn. Club: Multnomah Athletic (Portland, (Oreg.). Home: 311 E Glenarm St #6 Pasadena CA 91106 Office: US Ct Appeals 125 S Grand Ave PO Box 91510 Pasadena CA 91109-1510

GOODWIN, GREGORY LANG, educator; b. Galesburg, Ill., Oct. 29, 1939; s. William Lang and Eileen Elizabeth (Foley) G.; m. Peggy Joan Calvin, June 15, 1963; children: Katherine, Paul. BS, Northwestern U., 1961; MA in History, Stanford U., 1962; PhD in Edn., U. of Ill., 1972. Tchr. of history Bakersfield (Calif.) High Sch., 1962-64; prof. Bakersfield (Calif.) Coll., 1964—; chmn. Social Sci. Dept., Bakersfield Coll., 1973-79; pres. Acad. Senate, Bakersfield Coll., 1985-87. Contbr. articles to profl. jours.; editor: Two Decades of Innovation, 1988. Bd. dirs. Lori Brock Jr. Mus., Bakersfield, 1976-78; community advisor Jr. League, Bakersfield, 1987—; polit. analyst KGET-TV, Bakersfield, 1980—. Recipient Woodrow Wilson fellowship, Ford Found., Stanford U., 1961, NEH research grant, 1973, del. NEH Summer Inst., U.Cal., Santa Barbara, 1978. Mem. Community Coll. Social Scis. Assn. Home: 1808 Club View Dr Bakersfield CA 93309 Office: Bakersfield Coll 1801 Panorama Dr Bakersfield CA 93305

GOODWIN, JAMES TIPTON, college official; b. Plainview, Tex., Jan. 9, 1936; s. Herbert Marshall and Wynelle (Tipton) G.; m. Elizabeth Sushiela Mancha, June 27, 1970. Student, San Diego State Coll., 1955. Actor, writer, musician 1955-66; v.p. sales Calif. State Automobile Leasing Co., L.A., 1966-68; environ. designer Phoenix Design Assocs., N. Hollywood, Calif., 1968-70, Laurel Plaza May Co., N. Hollywood, 1970-77; dir. mktg. and design Swedlow Group, L.A., 1977-80; v.p., dir. mktg. and communications Pacific Design Ctr., L.A., 1980-88; sr. v.p. instnl. affairs Art Ctr. Coll. Design, Pasadena, Calif., 1988—; bd. dirs. West Hollywood (Calif.) Mktg. Corp. Curator design confs.; creator Westweek mag. Pres. Design Alliance to Combat AIDS, 1987—. Mem. Design Am. (founders coun. 1988). Home: 2062 N Vine St Hollywood CA 90068 Office: Art Ctr Coll Design 1700 Lida St Pasadena CA 91108

GOODWIN, JOHN ROBERT, lawyer, educator; b. Morgantown, W.Va., Nov. 3, 1929; s. John Emory and Ruby Iona G.; m. Betty Lou Wilson, June 2, 1952; children—John R., Elizabeth Ann Paugh, Mark Edward, Luke Jackson, Matthew Emory. B.S., W.Va. U., 1952, J.D., 1964. Bar: W.Va., U.S. Supreme Ct. Formerly city atty., county commr., spl. pros. atty., then mayor City of Morgantown; prof. bus. law W.Va. U.; prof. hotel and casino law U. Nev., Las Vegas; Author: Legal Primer for Artists, Craftspersons, 1987, Hotel Law, Principles and Cases, 1987. Served with U.S. Army; Korea. Recipient Bancroft-Whitney award in Constl. Law. Democrat. Author: Twenty Feet From Glory; Business Law, 3d edit.; High Points of Legal History; Travel and Lodging Law; Desert Adventure; Gaming Control Law; editor Hotel and Casino Letter; past editor Bus. Law Rev., Bus. Law Letter. Home: 5250 E Lake Mead Blvd Casa Linda 48 Las Vegas NV 89115 Office: 5250 E Lake Mead Blvd Las Vegas NV 89115

GOODWIN, SANDRA JOAN, management trainer, consultant; b. St. Louis, Sept. 30, 1937; d. Robert Earl and Irma Josephine (Modray) Balencia; m. Earl Victor Goodwin II, July 22, 1980; children: Kathleen Anne, Kristine Annette. Student, Wash. U.; MS in exec. mgmt., U. Calif., Riverside, 1986. Adminstrv. aide Washington U., St. Louis, 1955-65; mgmt. cons. Hughes Heiss & Assocs., San Mateo, Calif., 1975-79; budget analyst San Bernardino (Calif.) County, 1979-80, mgmt. cons., 1980-82, data processing projects mgr., 1982-83, chief edn. and info. services, 1983-87, exec. post dep. county admnstr. officer, 1987-88; owner Mgmt. Assocs. Tng. and Cons. Services, San Bernardino, 1982—. State chairperson Calif. Regional Criminal Justice Planning Bd., San Mateo, 1974-78, regional vice chairperson; San Mateo Bd. Suprs., 1978. Coro Found. scholar, 1976. Mem. Am. Soc. Pub. Adminstrn., Nat. Acad. Polit. Scientists, Am. Soc. Tng. Devel., LWV (chairperson fin., tng. bur. 1973-78), Bus. and Profl. Women, League of Women Voters. Democrat. Lutheran. Home: 648 Palo Alto Redlands CA 92373 Office: Mgmt Assocs PO Box 8505 San Bernardino CA 92412

GOOKIN, GEORGE EDWIN, JR., livestock marketing specialist, rancher; b. Oakdale, Calif., Feb. 27, 1961; s. Geroge Edwin Sr. and Barbara Ann (Stadler) G.; m. DeeAnn Marie Dias, May 6, 1984. Student, Modesto (Calif.) Jr. Coll., 1979-81. Fieldman Oakdale Livestock Aution, 1981—; co-owner Gookin Bros Livestock Co., Farmington, Calif., 1984—. Booster Oakdale 4-h & FFA Boosters, 1979-88. Mem. Nat. Cattleman's Assn., Calif. Cattleman's Assn., Stanislaus County Farm Bur., Valley Home (Calif.) 4-H Club (pres. 1973-75). Republican. Roman Catholic. Home: 658 David dr Oakdale CA 95361 Office: Oakdale Livestock Auction 6001 Albers Rd Oakdale CA 95361

GOOKIN, THOMAS ALLEN JAUDON, civil engineer; b. Tulsa, Aug. 5, 1951; s. William Scudder and Mildred (Hartman) G.; m. Leigh Anne Johnson, June 13, 1975 (div. Dec. 1977); m. Sandra Jean Andrews, July 23, 1983. BS with distinction, Ariz. State U., 1975. Registered profl. engr., Calif., Ariz., Nev. Civil engr., treas. W.S. Gookin & Assocs., Scottsdale, Ariz., 1968—. Chmn. Ariz. State Bd. Tech. Registration Engring. adv. com., 1984—. Mem. NSPE, Ariz. Soc. Profl. Engrs. (sec. Papago chpt. 1979-81, v.p. 1981-84, pres. 1984-85, named Young Engr. of Yr. 1979, Outstanding Engring. Project award 1988), Order Engr., Ariz. Congress on Surveying and Mapping, Am. Soc. Civil Engrs., Ariz. Water Works Assn., Tau Beta Pi, Delta Chi (Tempe chpt. treas. 1970-71, sec. 1970, v.p. 1971), Phi Kappa Delta (pres. 1971-73). Republican. Episcopalian. Home: 10760 E Becker Ln Scottsdale AZ 85259 Office: W S Gookin & Assocs 4203 N Brown Ave Scottsdale AZ 85251

GOOKIN, WILLIAM SCUDDER, hydrologist, consultant; b. Atlanta, Sept. 8, 1914; s. William Cleveland and Susie (Jaudon) G.; m. Mildred Hartman, Sept. 4, 1937; children: William Scudder Jr., Thomas Allen Jaudon. BSCE, Pa. State U., 1937. Registered profl. engr. and hydrologist. Engr. U.S. Geol. Survey, Tucson, 1937-38; inspector City of Tucson, 1938-39; steel designer Allison Steel Mfg. Co., Phoenix, 1939-40; engr. Bur. Reclamation, various locations, 1940-53; chief engr. San Carlos Irrigation and Drainage Dist., Coolidge, Ariz., 1953-58; chief engr. Ariz. Interstate Stream Commn., Phoenix, 1956-62, state water engr., 1961-68; adminstr. Ariz. Power Authority, Phoenix, 1958-60; cons. engr. Scottsdale, Ariz., 1968—; bd. dirs. Cen. Ariz. Project Assn., Phoenix, 1985—. Contbr. articles to profl. jours. Dem. committeeman State of Ariz., 1979-84. Served to 2d lt. C.E., U.S. Army, 1938-42. Fellow Am. Soc. Civil Engrs.; mem. NSPE (bd. dirs.), Nat. Water Resources Assn. (small projects com.), Colo. River Water Users' Assn., State Bar Ariz. (assoc., environ. natural resources sect.), Culver Legion, Order of the Engr., Chi Epsilon. Home: 9 Casa Blanca Estates Paradise Valley AZ 85253

GOPALAKRISHNAN, CHENNAT, professor; b. Ernakulam, India, Oct. 9, 1936; came to U.S., 1963; d. Palliyil Narayana Menon and Chennat (Sarada) Amma; m. Malini Varma Gopalakrishnan, Sept. 15, 1962; 1 child, Shalini. BA, Kerala U., 1955, MA, 1957; PhD, Mont. State U., 1967. Asst. prof. of nat. resource econ. Mont. State U., Bozeman, 1967-69; assoc. prof. U. Hawaii, Honolulu, 1969-74; visiting prof. U. So. Calif., Los Angeles, 1976-77, U. Wyo., Laramie, 1982-83; prof. U. Hawaii, 1974—; reviewer NSF, Washington, 1981; cons. Argonne (Ill.) Nat. Lab., 1986—, Gas Reasearch Inst., Chgo., 1983-84. Author: Natural Resource and Energy: Theory and Policy, 1980; editor: The Emerging Marine Economy of the Pacific, 1984; contbr. over 50 articles to profl. jours. Named Outstanding Researcher Gamma Sigma Delta, 1980; recipient Outstanding Service award Marine Tech. Soc., 1981; Law Inst. for Economists national fellow, 1986, Summer Inst. for Univ. Faculty national fellow, 1988. Mem. Internat. Assn. Energy Economists, Am. Agrl. Econs. Assn., Am. Water Resources Assn., Western Regional Sci. Assn., Internat. Agrl. Econs. Assn. Home: 2333 Kapiolani Blvd #1101 Honolulu HI 96826 Office: U Hawaii Dept Agrl and Resource Econ 3050 Maile Way Gilmore 112 Honolulu HI 96822

GORANS, GERALD ELMER, accountant; b. Benson, Minn., Sept. 17, 1922; s. George W. and Gladys (Schneider) G.; m. Mildred Louise Stallard, July 19, 1944; 1 child, Gretchen. BA, U. Wash., Seattle, 1947. CPA, Wash. With Touche, Ross & Co., CPAs and predecessor, Seattle, 1947-88; ptnr. Touche, Ross & Co., 1957-88, in charge Seattle office, 1962-82, mem. policy group, adminstrv. com., 1964-69, dir., 1974-83, sr. partner, 1979-88, chmn. mgmt. group, 1982-88, ret., 1988. V.p. budget and fin. Seattle Worlds Fair, 1962; chmn. budget and fin. com. Century 21 Ctr., Inc., 1963-64; mem. citizens adv. com. Seattle Lic. and Consumer Protection Com., 1965; head profl. div. United Way King County, Seattle, 1963-64, head advanced gifts div., 1965, exec. v.p., 1966, pres., 1967; trustee United Way Endowment Fund, 1984—; adv. bd. Seattle Salvation Army, 1965-80, treas., 1974-80; fin. com. Bellevue Christian Sch., 1970-77; citizens adv. bd. pub. affairs Sta. KIRO-TV, 1970-71; treas., bd. dirs., exec. com. Scandinavia Today in Seattle, 1981-83; treas., bd. dirs. Seattle Citizens Coun. Against Crime, 1972-80, pres., 1976, 77; bd. dirs. U. Wash Alumni Fund, 1967-71, chmn., 1971; trustee U. Wash. Pres.'s Club, 1980-83; bd. dirs., chmn. devel. com. N.W. Hosp. Found., 1977-83, trustee hosp., 1989—, treas. bd., 1981-84, vice-chmn. bd. hosp., 1984-89, chmn. bd. trustees, 1989—, chmn fin. com., 1987-89; chmn. fin. com. Com. for Balanced Regional Transp., 1981—; co-chmn. United Cerebal Palsy Seattle Telethon, 1986; chmn. fin. com. fund raising Mus. Flight, 1983-87; mem. assoc. bd. Pacific Scis. Ctr., Seattle, 1986—; active Japanese/Am. Conf. Mayors. Lt. (j.g.) USNR, 1943-45. Mem. Assoc. Am. Inst. CPA's (chmn. nat. def. com. 1969-75, mem. spl. investigation com. 1984-87), Nat. Office Mgmt. Assn. (past pres.), Wash. Soc. CPA's (Outstanding Pub. Svc. award 1988), Seattle C. of C. (chmn. taxation com. 1970-71, bd. dirs. 1971-74, 76-79, 80-81, 85—, mem. exec. com. 1980-83, v.p. 1981-84, 1st vice-chmn. 1983-84, chmn. 1984-85, vice-chmn. facilities fund drive, 1982-84), Nat. Def. Exec. Res., Nat. Club Assn. (bd. dirs. 1984—), Assn. Wash. Bus. (bd. dirs. 1983-86). Clubs: Seattle Golf, Wash. Athletic (pres. 1975-76), Rainier (treas. 1976-77), Lake. Home: 9013 NE 37th Pl Bellevue WA 98004 Office: Touche Ross & Co 1111 3rd Ave Seattle WA 98101

GORDAN, JUDITH ALLISON, entertainment industry executive; b. Cleve., Feb. 21, 1956; d. Andrew Leb and Clina Ann (De La Mater) G. BA in Communications, Ursuline Coll., 1979. Acctg. adminstr. Tandem Prodns., Inc., L.A., 1980-82; supr. residuals and payroll Embassy Communications, L.A., 1982-84, dir. contract acctg., 1984-86; dir. prodn. acctg. Columbia Pictures TV, L.A., 1986—; alt. mgmt. trustee, mem. audit and deliquency com., mem. communications com. Writers' Guild Am. Health Fund; alt. mgmt. dir., mem. audit and deliquency com., mem. communications com. Producers' Writers' Guild Am. Pension Funds. Mem. Am. Film Inst., Acad. TV Arts and Scis., Toastmasters Internat. (local sec. 1986, local treas. 1987). Democrat. Roman Catholic. Home: 6013 Babbitt Ave Encino CA 91316 Office: Columbia Pictures TV 1438 N Gower St Los Angeles CA 90028

GORDIS, DAVID MOSES, religious organization executive; b. N.Y.C., June 4, 1940; s. Robert and Fannie (Jacobson) G.; m. Felice Witztum, Sept. 3, 1962; children: Lisa, Elana. BA, Columbia U., 1960, MA, 1966; MHL, Jewish Theol. Sem., 1962, PhD, 1980. Ordained rabbi, 1964. Dean of students Tchrs. Inst., Jewish Theol. Sem., N.Y.C., 1966-72; exec. dir. Found. for Conservative Judaism, 1981-84; assoc. prof., v.p. U. of Judaism, L.A., 1972-84; v.p. Jewish Theol. Sem., N.Y.C., 1981-84; exec. v.p. Am. Jewish Com., N.Y.C., 1984-87; v.p. U. Judaism, L.A., 1988—, dir. Wilstein Inst. of Jewish Policy Studies, 1988—. Bd. dirs. Interns for Peace, N.Y., Project Mazon, N.Y., Jewish TV Network, Los Angeles, Bet Tzedek Legal Project,

Los Angeles; chmn. exec. com. Am. Found. for Polish-Jewish Studies, 1988—. Mem. Rabbinical Assembly Am., Assn. Jewish Studies.

GORDON, ANNE P., social work adminstrator, counseling psychotherapist; b. Massillon, Ohio, Jan. 8, 1943; d. William jerome and Ethelyn Anna (Horst) Paul; m. Michael Peter Gordon, May 28, 1966 (div. Sept. 1988); children: James Alan, Suzanne Marie. BA, Antioch U., 1965; MA, San Francisco State Coll., 1969; MSW, U. Wash., 1975; BA in Computer Sci., Grifin Coll., 1982. Lic. counselor, Wash. Reading cons. Jefferson Elem. Sch. Dist., Daly City, Calif., 1966-72; therapist Learning Devel. Ctr., Seattle, 1972-75; dir. Solo Ctr. for Single Adults, Seattle, 1975-81; coord. Family Life Edn. Network, Seattle, 1981-86; dir. World for Women, Lynnwood, Wash., 1986—; founder Discovery Singles Group, Des Moines, Wash., 1980—, Unitarian Counseling Affiliates, Seattle, 1982—; affiliate field instr. intern Sch. Social Work, U. Wash., Seattle and Lynnwood, 1982-88; cons., presenter workshops. State rep. Nat. Displaced Homemaker Network, Seattle, 1983, Region X nat. bd., 1988; mem. Snohomish County Children's Commn., 1987-88, Snohomish County Homeless Task Force, 1987-88. Mem. Am. Orthopsychiat. Assn., Nat. Assn. Social Workers, Exec. Dirs. Assn. United Way, AAUW, Snohomish County Women's Bus. Assn., Zonta. Office: World for Women PO Box 5627 Lynnwood WA 98046

GORDON, CLAUDE EUGENE, musician; b. Helena, Mont., Apr. 5, 1916; s. James Austin and Nellie G. (Elge) G.; m. Genevieve Alice Pentecost, Apr. 19, 1936; children: Gary Anthony, Steven Robert. Trumpeter NBC, CBS, Motion Pictures, Los Angeles, 1937-69; 1st trumpet big bands, stage shows, hotels, Los Angeles, 1937-44, CBS, Hollywood, 1944-56; orchestra leader Los Angeles and nationwide, 1950-69; conductor TV mus., stage shows for stars, Los Angeles and Las Vegas, Reno, Nev., 1960-69; lectr., instr. in clinics Mich. U., No. Ill. U., Fla. State U., N. Tex. State U., others, 1970-87; instr. Claude Gordon Internat. Brass Camp, Idyllwild (Calif.) Sch.; recorded for all major labels. Author: Brass Playing Is No Harder Than Deep Breathing, The Physical Approach to Elementary Brass Playing, Systematic Approach to Daily Practice, Daily Trumpet Routines, Tongue Level Exercises, 30 Velocity Studies; annotator: Arban Complete Method, 1982; instrument designer: CG Benge trumpet, 1960, Claude Gordon Selmer trumpet, 1977. Office: CG Music Enterprises 19522 Leadwell St Reseda CA 91335

GORDON, CLYDE HOWARD, management consultant; b. Longview, Tex., Nov. 26, 1933; s. Thomas Foyil and Edna (Hester) G.; m. Norma Huff, Dec. 28, 1953; children: Clyde Howard Jr., Penelope Gordon Chumbley, Kerry, Marcus, Anastasia Gordon Clark. BS in Archtl. Engring., U. Tex., 1956; MBA, U. New Orleans, 1968. With various constrn. cos., New Orleans, 1956-62, Mason & Hanger, Lexington, Ky., 1962-73; pres. Total Facility Svcs., Inc., Dallas, 1973-75; regional v.p. ARA Bldg. Svcs., Dallas, 1975-77; sr. cons. Svc. Engring. Assocs., Atlanta, 1977-78; prin. Groover Engring. Co., Atlanta, 1978-81; spl. cons. Calif. State U., Long Beach, 1981-84; prin., owner Gordon & Assocs., Concord, Calif., 1984—; assoc. prof. extended edn. Calif. State U., Hayward, fall 1986. Contbr. articles to profl. publs., chpts. to books. Elder El Monte Ch., Concord, 1986—. Republican. Office: Gordon & Assocs PO Box 6003 Concord CA 94524

GORDON, CONSTANCE MARY BRAND, media consultant, video producer; b. Chgo., Oct. 26, 1956; d. Thomas Anthony and Kathleen (Dunn) Brand; m. Jeffrey Lawrence Gordon, Sept. 14, 1986. Student, Reed Coll., 1974-78; BA, Portland State U., 1980. Freelance video producer Portland, Oreg., 1979-83; ptnr., mktg. dir. Interact Communications, Portland, 1983-88; mcpl.-ednl. access coord. Bd. Suprs. City and County San Francisco, 1985—; owner, mgr. Constance Brand Media & Communications, Oakland, Calif. Active Ind. Precinct Orgn., Chgo., 1969-74; coun. mem. Temple Sinai Sisterhood, Oakland, 1988—, pres., 1989—; vol. Oakland Dem. Com., 1986. N.W. Area Found. grantee, 1981-83. Mem. Nat. Fedn. Local Cable Programmers (N.W. regional coord. 1980-83, chmn. nat. advocacy com. 1983-84, Far West regional bd. dirs. 1987—, nat. bd. dirs. 1983-84), Bay Area Video Coalition, Media Alliance, Film Arts Found. Home and Office: 6151 Buena Vista Ave Oakland CA 94618

GORDON, DENNIS DOUGLAS, historian, author; b. Spokane, Wash., July 2, 1944; s. Matthew Henry and Lucille Caroline (Davis) G.; m. Pauline Ann Miller, July 3, 1964; children: Scott Douglas, Brett Charles, Kert, Cybelle Lenore, Damon Anthony. BA in English, U. Mont., 1969, MFA, 1970. Pres. G.O.S. Inc. Book Publs., Missoula, Mont., 1977—, Missoula Gun & Antique Shows, 1980—; advisor Mil. Aviation Heritage Ctr., USAF Acad., Colo., 1986—; appraiser Missoula Antique Assn., 1972—. Editor: Doughboy Quar. Publ., 1978—; author: Quartered in Hell, 1982, World War I Collector's Handbook I and II, 1977, 79, 88, Experimental Helmets/Body Armor, 1978; contbr. World War I aviation biographies to profl. jours. Founder, pres. Doughboy Hist. Soc., Missoula, 1978—. Mem. League World War I Aviation Historians (charter), Co. Mil. Historians, Elks. Republican. Roman Catholic. Home: 1246 North Ave Missoula MT 59801 Office: GOS Inc PO Box 3912 Missoula MT 59806

GORDON, DONALD HOWARD, podiatrist; b. Ft. Smith, Ark., Nov. 16, 1954; s. Halton Howard and M. Janelle (Carter) G.; m. Carol Ann Miller, Aug. 15, 1975; children: Stephanie, Andrew. BS in Chemistry, Okla. Christian Coll., 1977, BSE in Science, 1977; BS in Basic Medicine, Calif. Coll. Podiatric Medicine, 1981, D in Podiatric Medicine, 1983. Tchr. chemistry, football coach Midwest City (Okla.) High Sch., 1977-79; resident in surgery Calif. Podiatry Hosp., San Francisco, 1983-84, sr. resident in surgery, 1984-85; podiatrist Ambulatory Family Podiatry Group, Daly City, Calif., 1985-87; pvt. practice podiatry Pacifica, Calif., 1987-88; asst. prof. Calif. Coll. Podiatric Medicine, San Francisco, 1987—. Named one of Outstanding Young Men of Am., 1985. Mem. Am. Podiatric Med. Assn., Calif. Podiatric Med. Assn., San Francisco/San Mateo County Podiatry Assn., Am. Coll. Foot Surgeons (assoc.), Pacifica (Calif.) C. of C. (dir. membership com., edn. com. 1985-86, chmn. edn. com. 1986-87), Calif. C. of C. (v.p. 1988). Mem. Ch. of Christ. Office: 1210 Scott St San Francisco CA 94105

GORDON, DONNA GRACE, retired nurse, civic worker; b. Thomson Station, N.S., Can., Aug. 30, 1934; came to U.S., 1967; d. Hugh Ross and Doris Geneve (Smith) Patterson; m. John Edward Bourne, Apr. 30, 1956 (div. Aug. 1966); m. Steve Sol Gordon, June 6, 1967 (dec. Aug. 1973); children: Kathy Penelope (dec.) Kristopher David (dec.), Jery Lynn (dec.). Grad., Halifax Children's Hosp. Nursing Sch., 1955. RN, N.S., Calif. Staff nurse Halifax (N.S.) Children's Hosp., 1955-56, house supr., 1957-66; in-svc. dir., staff nurse Granada Hills (Calif.) Community Hosp., 1967-69; staff nurse infection control Encino (Calif.) Hosp., 1971-77; staff nurse Valley Presbyn. Hosp., Van Nuys, Calif., 1978; nat. dir. Nu-Med Systems, Inc., Van Nuys, 1980-83; fin. cons. Northridge, Calif., 1982-84, ret., 1984. Bd. dirs. San Fernando Teen Ctr., Van Nuys, 1977-83, acting exec. dir., 1983-84; bd. dirs. ARC, Redwood Empire, Calif., 1986—, chmn. vols., 1988—, chmn. disaster action team, 1986—, emergency mgmt. vol., 1986—; ruling elder St. Andrew Presbyn. Ch., also chmn. fellowship; coord. disaster vols. No. Calif. Floods, 1986; staffing officer L.A./Whittier Earthquake, 1987. Named Vol. of Yr. ARC, 1987-88; recipient Clara Barton award for outstanding svc. ARC, 1988.

GORDON, FRANK X., JR., judge; b. Chgo., Jan. 9, 1929; s. Frank X. and Lucille (Gburek) G.; m. Joan C. Gipe, Sept. 17, 1950; children: Frank X., Candace Gordon Lander. BA, Stanford U., 1951; LLB, U. Ariz., 1954. Bar: Ariz. 1954. Assoc. Gordon and Gordon, Kingman, Ariz., 1954-62; atty. City of Kingman, 1955-57; judge Superior Ct. Mohave County (Ariz.), Kingman, 1962-75; justice Ariz. Supreme Ct., Phoenix, 1975—, now chief justice; mem. various coms. Ariz. State Bar; Ariz. rep. to Council for State Ct. Reps., Nat. Ctr. State Cts. Bd. visitors U. Ariz. Law Sch., 1972-75; trustee Chester H. Smith Meml. Scholarship Fund; past bd. dirs., pres. Mohave County Mental Health Clinic, Inc.; past mem. Gov.'s Commn. Mental Health; state bd. dirs. Ariz. Heart Assn.; active Boulder Dam Area council Boy Scouts Am. Mem. ABA, Ariz. Bar Assn. Maricopa County Bar Assn., Am. Judicature Soc., Mohave County C. of C. (past pres.). Democrat. Methodist. Lodges: Rotary, Elks. Office: Ariz Supreme Ct State Capitol 201 W Wing Phoenix AZ 85007 *

GORDON, JACK FRANCIS, trade association administrator; b. Portland, Oreg., June 30, 1921; s. James Samuel and Mabel Ann (Ratchford) G.; grad. Seattle U., 1950, U. Wash., 1955; m. Roberta M. Gordon, May 1, 1948; children—John, Mary, Ann, Joseph. City editor Catholic NW Progress, Seattle, 1947-48; dir. pub. relations Seattle U., 1948-50, Greater Seattle, Inc., 1950-64; commr. employment security State of Wash., 1964-65; dir. spl. events Seattle Ctr., 1965; exec. v.p. Restaurant Assn. Wash., Seattle, 1966—; spl. asst. to gov. Wash., 1973-74, spl. agt., 1980; v.p., bd. dirs. Wash. Trade Fair, 1950-78; mem. Seattle Human Rights Commn., 1966-79, Wash. Am. Bicentennial Commn., 1975-76; bd. dirs. Seattle-King County Conv. and Visitors Bur., 1976—, Seafair FEstival, 1988, Bob Hope Heart Ctr., 1986-89; mem. Wash. State Personnel Appeals Bd., 1981-82. Pres., Providence Med. Found., 1980-81; bd. dirs. Seattle Youth Symphony Orch.; pres. Pacific Internat. Hospitality Indsl. Expn., 1982—. Served with USNR, World War II; maj. NG. Named Alumnus of Year, Seattle U., 1969, Newsmaker of Tomorrow, Time Mag., 1953. Mem. Am. Soc. Assn. Execs., AGVA, Seattle C. of C., Internat. Platform Assn., Am. Security Council, U.S. Security and Intelligence Fund, Musicians Assn., Am. Legion (past post comdr.), Rainier Club, Wash. Athletic Club, Rotary, KC. (Seattle). Roman Catholic. Home: 6814 44th Pl NE Seattle WA 98115 Office: 722 Securities Bldg Seattle WA 98101

GORDON, LARRY JEAN, public health administrator and educator; b. Tipton, Okla., Oct. 16, 1926; s. Andrew J. and Deweylee (Stewart) G.; m. Nedra Callender, Aug. 26. 1950; children: Debra Gordon Dunlap, Kent, Gary. Student, U. Okla., 1943-44; BS, U. N.Mex., 1949, MS, 1951; MPH, U. Mich., 1954. High sch. sci. tchr. N.Mex., 1949-50; various positions N.Mex. Dept. Health, 1950-55; commd. officer, cons. USPHS, 1957—, advanced through grades to Dir. Grade (Navy capt.), dir. Albuquerque Environ. Health Dept., 1955-68, 82-86; dir. Environ. Improvement Agy., Santa Fe, 1968-71; adminstr. for health and environ. programs N.Mex. HHS Dept., Santa Fe, 1976-78; dir. N.Mex. Sci. Lab. System, Albuquerque, 1973-76; dep. sec. N.Mex. Health and Environ. Dept., Santa Fe, 1978-82, sec., 1987-88; vis. prof. pub. health adminstrn. U. N.Mex., Albuquerque, 1988—; cons. Sandia Corp., Albuquerque, 1960-68, Profl. Exam. Svc., N.Y., 1964-80, Assn. State Territorial Health Officers, 1973-75, Nat. Sanitation Found., Mich., 1966-73, 81-86, Los Alamos (N.Mex.) Sci. Labs., 1969-74, adv. group Health Services Adminstrn. U. N.Mex., 1984—; cons. USPHS Bur. Community Environ. Mgmt., 1971, Health Programs Ctr., 1968-71, Comprehensive Health Planning, Dallas, 1967-75, spl. cons. Washington, 1962-65; bd. dirs. Coun. Edn. for Pub. Health, 1973-75, 82-85; guest lectr. Ctr. for Disease Control, 1958-66, U. N.Mex. Peace Corps Tng. Ctr., 1964-67; dir. 1st Govs.' Conf. on Environ. Health Planning, 1966; clin. assoc. Sch. Medicine U. N.Mex., 1968—; mem. environ. health rev. com. Bur. Health Professions, Edn. and Manpower Tng., 1970, pub. health rev. com. NIH, 1970, Gov.'s Energy Task Force, 1972-73; chmn. N.Mex. Coal Surface Mining Commn., 1971-73, N.Mex. Water Quality Commn., 1971-73; mem. Albuquerque Area Comprehensive Health Planning Coun., 1966-73; adv. panel on water related techs. for sustaining agriculture in arid and semi-arid lands Congl. Office Tech. Assessment, 1981-83; subcom. on pub. health NRC, 1985—; adj. instr. Pub. Adminstrn. div. U. N.Mex., 1983. Asst. editor Jour. Environ. Health, 1975-78; cons. editor Environ. News Digest, 1970-82; editorial cons. Jour. Pub. Health Policy, 1980—; author over 100 articles, reports, newsletters. Recipient Samuel J. Crumbine award for Outstanding Devel. of Comprehensive Program for Environ. Sanitation, 1959 and 65, Sanitarians Disting. Service award Internat. Assn. Milk, Food, and Environ. Sanitarians, 1962, Outstanding Contrbn. award N.Mex. Assn. Pub. Health Sanitarians, 1967, Boss of Yr. award Santa Fe chpt. Nat. Secs. Assn., 1970, Walter F. Snyder award For Achievement in Environ. Quality, 1978, Commendation for Leadership in Health Care N.Mex. Hosp. Assn., 1981, N.Mex. Outstanding Pub. Svc. award, 1988. Mem. Nat. Assn. Pub. Health Policy (pres. 1981-83), Am. Pub. Health Assn. (exec. bd. 1975-82, pres. 1980-81, John J. Sippy Meml. award 1962, co-chmn. Action Bd. 1970-72, other coms., Sedgwick award 1987), Am. Acad. Sanitarians (founder, Davis Calvin Wagner Excellence award 1984), N.Mex. Pub. Health Assn. (past pres., Disting. Svc. award 1970, Spl. award 1978, D.A. Larrazola award 1989), N.Mex. Environ. Health Assn. (past-pres.), Rocky Mountain Assn. Milk and Food Sanitarians (past-pres.), Nat. Environ. Health Assn. (chmn. sect. 1970-71, Walter S. Mangold award 1961), Am. Assn. Comprehensive Health Planning (environ. health com. 1972-74), Am. Lung Assn. N.Mex. (bd. dirs. 1982—, Clinton R. Anderson award for Outstanding Contbn. to Lung Health 1987), Nat. Accreditation Coun. Environ. Health Curricula, Nat. Audubon Soc. (pres. coun. 1982-86), U. Mich. Sch. Pub. Health Alumni Assn. (bd. govs. 1985-88), Royal Soc. Promotion of Health, London (hon.), Delta Omega, Phi Kappa Phi, Phi Sigma. Democrat. Home: 7100 Carriveau NE Albuquerque NM 87110 Office: U NMex Pub Adminstrn Div Albuquerque NM 87131

GORDON, LEONARD, sociology educator; b. Detroit, Dec. 6, 1935; s. Abraham and Sarah (Rosen) G.; m. Rena Joyce Feigelman, Dec. 25, 1955; children: Susan Melinda, Matthew Seth, Melissa Gail. B.A., Wayne State U., 1957; M.A., U. Mich., 1958; Ph.D., Wayne State U., 1966. Instr. Wayne State U., Detroit, 1960-62; research dir. Jewish Community Council, Detroit, 1962-64; dir. Mich. area Am. Jewish Com., N.Y.C., 1964-67; asst. prof. Ariz. State U., Tempe, 1967-70, assoc. prof., 1970-77, prof., 1977—, chmn. dept. sociology, 1981—; cons. OEO, Maricopa County, Ariz., 1968. Author: A City in Racial Crisis, 1971, Sociology and American Social Issues, 1978; co-author: (with A. Mayer) Urban Life and the Struggle to Be Human, 1979, (with others) Confronting Social Problems, 1984. Sec. Conf. on Religion and Race, Detroit, 1962-67; mem. exec. bd. dirs. Am. Jewish Com., Phoenix chpt., 1969-70. Grantee NSF, 1962, Rockefeller found., 1970, 84. Fellow Am. Sociol. Assn.; mem. Pacific Sociol. Assn. (v.p. 1978-79, pres. 1980-81), AAUP, Soc. Study Social Problems (chair C. Wright Mills award com. 1988, treas. 1989—), Ariz. State U. Alumni Assn. (faculty dir. 1981-82). Democrat. Jewish. Home: 5262 N Woodmere Fairway Scottsdale AZ 85253 Office: Ariz State U Dept Sociology Tempe AZ 85287

GORDON, RONALD, insurance executive; b. Los Angeles, Apr. 18, 1927; s. Aleck and Sadie (Philips) G.; m. Mary Charmaine Wells, June 18, 1973; 1 child, Allison Claire. BS, U. So. Calif., 1971. Broker Mutual Life N.Y., Los Angeles, John Hancock, Los Angeles, Mutual Omaha, Los Angeles; pres. Imperial Agts. Inc., Los Angeles, 1956-64, Gordon & Harrow, Los Angeles, 1964-69, Gordon Co., Los Angeles, 1969-84; chmn. Sentinel Group Cos., Los Angeles, 1984—. Bd. dirs. Save Heart, 1986—; bd. govs. Cedars Sinai Med. Ctr., 1986—; mem. Vista Del Mar Child Service. Served to sgt. U.S. Air Force, 1945-46. Mem. Friends Israel Def. (chmn. bd. dirs. Western region), Thalians Pres. (bd. dirs.), Cedars Sinai Medalions (bd. dirs. 1986—), Presidents Club. Clubs: Regency Friars, Mt. Gate. Office: Sentinel Group 1925 Century Pk E #1000 Los Angeles CA 90067

GORDON, RUTH I., librarian; b. Chgo., May 13, 1933; d. Samuel M. and Charlotte (Blank) G. AB, Tufts U., 1954; MA, Brown U., 1961; MLS, U. Calif., Berkeley, 1967, PhD, 1977. Cert. tchr., Calif. Tchr. Portola Valley (Calif.) Sch. Dist., 1956-62, Aviano (Italy) Dependents' Sch., 1962-66; lectr., dir. practicum U. San Francisco, 1968-74; dir. sch. librs. Lassen County Office Edn., Susanville, Calif., 1976-84; dir. librs. Cloverdale (Calif.) Unified Sch. Dist., 1984-85; libr. Petaluma (Calif.) Sch. Dist., 1985-89; lectr. U. Md., Aviano, 1965-66; cons. Gorco Library Cons., Cloverdale, 1984--. Author: Paul Elder: Editor, Bookseller, 1978; editor: Under All Silences, 1987; contbr. articles to profl. jours. NDEA scholar, 1968-70. Mem. Assn. Library Svcs. to Children (chmn. notable children's book com., Newbery com.), Assn. for Children's Librarians No. Calif., Sierra Club, Beta Phi Mu. Jewish.

GORDON, STEVEN ERIC, animator and designer; b. Hollywood, Calif., Mar. 23, 1960; s. Wilfred Isadore and Tamara (Bernstein) G.; m. Judith Katherine Ball, June 27, 1981; children: Scott Conrad, Eric Alexander. G-rad. high sch., Granada Hills, Calif. Asst. animator Bakshi Prodns., Hollywood, 1977-79, animator, 1979-80; animator, dir. Bakshi Prodns., Sun Valley, Calif., 1981-82; layout artist Filmation Studios, Hollywood, 1980-81; animator Disney Pictures, Burbank, Calif., 1982-87; prodn. designer Rich Entertainment, Encino, Calif., 1987—; story board artist, Disney TV, Burbank, 1984—, DIC Enterprises, Burbank, 1986-88; comml. animator, Playhouse Pictures , Hollywood, 1986-88, Baer Animation Co., Inc., Hollywood, 1989. Democrat. Home: 32449 Scandia Dr Running Springs CA 92382 Office: PO Box 2829 Running Springs CA 92382

GORDON, WILLIAM S., III, air force officer; b. Cin., Oct. 26, 1939; s. William and Lillian Ann (Giraitis) G.; m. Linda Lisa Taylor Dec. 28, 1972 (div. 1981); 1 child, William Taylor. BA in Econs., Tufts U., Medford, Mass., 1961; MBA, Auburn U., 1973. Commd. USAF, 1961, advanced to lt. col., to date; fighter pilot USAF, various locations, 1963-68; F4 fighter weapons sch. instr. 414th FWS, Nellis AFB, Nev., 1968-70; F4 operational test and evaluation pilot 422th Fighter Weapons Squadron, Nellis AFB, 1970-72; fighter requirements staff officer R&D Hq. USAF, Pentagon, 1973-77; F4 squadron ops. officer 36 TFS, Osan, Korea, 1977-78; ops. officer, asst. dep. comdr. ops. and F4E wing dep. base comdr. 347 TFW, Moody AFB, Ga., 1978-82; sr. Air Force advisor Colo. ANG 140TFW (A-7), Buckley ANGB Denver, 1983—. Decorated Silver Star, D.F.C. (3), Purple Heart, Air medals (16). Home: 2800 S Oakland Pl Aurora CO 80014

GORINGE, RUTH ELLEN, educator; b. Milw., June 13, 1931; d. William and Lillian Mable (Hibbard) Organ; m. Barry Thomas Goringe, Aug. 5, 1960 (div. 1977); children: Tracey Ruth Skoog, Thomas Ricks. BS, Pacific U., 1970; MEd, Portland State U., 1977, postgrad., 1979. Cert. elem. tchr. Oreg. Advertising sales Bell Systems, Portland, Oreg., 1953-60; remedial reading tchr. Yamhill (Oreg.) Grade Sch. Dist, 1970, tchr., 1971-74; learning disabilities specialist Forest Grove (Oreg.) Sch. Dist., 1974-84, tchr., 1984—; negotiations chairperson Yamhill Edn. Assn., 1972-73, Forest Grove Edn. Assn., 1984-87; child svc. demonstration program title VI Oreg. State Dept. Edn., 1976. Donator NEA polit. action com., 1984-88, OSPIRG, Greenpeace, thousand friends of Oreg. Mem. NEA, Oreg. Edn. Assn., Forest Grove Edn. Assn. Republican. Roman Catholic. Home: 2640 SW 175th Aloha OR 97006 Office: Forest Grove Sch Dist Forest Grove OR 97116

GORLICK, LAURENCE KARL, internist, educator; b. N.Y.C., Feb. 4, 1951; s. Eugene and Rose (Kantrowitz) G.; m. Laura Jean Dunaway, Dec. 11, 1983; children: Sara, Zachary. AA, Kingsborough Community Coll., 1971; BA in Psychology, Bklyn. Coll., 1973; MD, Autonoma U. Guadalajara, 1977. Diplomate Am. Bd. Internal Medicine, Am. Bd. Geriatric Medicine. Intern L.I. Coll. Hosp., N.Y., 1978-79; resident Norwalk Hosp., 1979-81; pvt. practice Los Alamitos, Calif.; clin. instr. internal medicine UCLA, 1987—. Bd. dirs. Am. Heart Assn., Long Beach, Calif., 1985-87. Mem. L.A. County Med. Assn. Republican. Jewish. Avocations: golf, martial arts, scuba diving, softball. Home: 216 Roycroft Ave Long Beach CA 90803 Office: Assocs in Internal Medicine 3801 Katella Ave Los Alamitos CA 90720

GORMAN, GERALD OTIS, coffee and vending company owner; b. Pine Bluff, Ark., Feb. 1, 1937; s. Alvin and Inez (Carr) G.; m. Elizabeth Jean Rider, Dec. 3, 1958; children: Crystal D., Jill R., Geralynn J. Student, Santa Ana Coll., 1960-63. Sales rep. Arrowhead Water Co., L.A., 1966-75; nat. sales mgr. Servatron, Long Beach, Calif., 1975-76; founder, owner Gorman & Daus., Inc. (Coffee Cupboard of Ariz.), Phoenix, 1976—; cons. City of Yorba Linda, Calif., 1968-76. Bd. dirs. Equestrian Trail, Inc., L.A., 1971-74. Mem. Nat. Coffee Assn. (design cons.), Kiwanis (New River). Democrat. Baptist. Home: 1626 E McDowell Rd Phoenix AZ 85006 Office: Gorman & Daus Inc 1626 E McDowell Rd Phoenix AZ 85006

GORMAN, MICHAEL STEPHEN, construction executive; b. Tulsa, Aug. 3, 1951; s. Lawrence Matthew and Mary Alice (Veith) G.; m. Sheryl Lane McGee, Feb. 19, 1972; children: Kelley Lane, Michael Ryan. Student, Colo. State U., 1971. With McGee Constrn. Co., Denver, 1972-74, with sales and estimating dept., 1974-78, gen. mgr., 1978-80, pres., owner, 1980—. Mem. Nat. Assn. Remodeling Industry (bd. dirs. Met. Denver chpt. 1982—, chmn. membership svcs. com. 1987—, regional v.p. 1987—, Man of Yr. 1982, Regional Contractor of Yr. 1988). Roman Catholic.

GORMÉZANO, KEITH STEPHEN, publisher; b. Madison, Wis., Nov. 22, 1955; s. Isadore and Miriam (Fox) G.; m. Emma Lee Rogers, Aug. 17, 1986. BGS U. Iowa, 1977; postgrad. in law U. Puget Sound, 1984-86. Pub. Le Beacon Presse, Seattle, 1980—; real estate agt. Jim Stacy Realty, 1988—; arbitrator Better Bus. Bur. Greater Seattle, 1987—, Puget Sound Multi Listing Assn., 1988-89, Nat. Assn. Securities Dealers, 1989—, PSMLA, 1988-89, NASD, 1989—. Op. Improvement Found., 1980-81; pub. info. officer chmn. Iowa City Young Ams. for Freedom, 1979-81; vol. VISTA, 1982-83; dir. ACJS, Inc., 1981-82. Vice chmn. Resource Conservation Commn., Iowa City, 1979-80; bd. dirs. Seattle Mental Health Inst., 1981-83, Youth Advocates, Seattle, 1984, Atlantic St. Ctr., 1984; mem. City of Seattle Animal Control Commn., 1984-86, vice chmn., 1985-86, chmn. 1986; mem. Selective Svc. System, 1982—, vice chmn. civilan rev. bd. 742, 1985—. Named Citizen of the Day Sta. KIXI Radio, 1982. Mem. League United Latin Am. Citizens Amigos (chair 1984-86), U. Iowa Alumni Assn. (life). Republican. Jewish. Editor, M'godolim, 1980-81. Home: 7520 37th Ave NE #3 Seattle WA 98115-8023 Office: PO Box 15945 Seattle WA 98115-0945

GORMLEY, BRIAN F., advertising executive; b. Norwalk, Conn., Feb. 21, 1945; s. Daniel J. and Helen (Saltes) G.; m. Marlitt Dellabough, Aug. 31, 1986; 1 child, Elona Kassia. BA, Boston Coll., 1967; MA, Fairfield U., 1970; Cert., Sch. Visual Arts, 1978. Dean of students Sch. Visual Arts, N.Y.C., 1973-77; pres. Lake Placid (N.Y.) Sch. of Art, 1977-79; co-dir. arts program XIII Olympic Winter Games, Lake Placid, 1979-81; dir. pub. affairs Calif. Inst. of the Arts, Valencia, 1981-84; pres. Gormley/Takei Inc., Los Angeles, 1984—, Valencia Airport Shuttles, Los Angeles, 1987—; bd. dirs. Cons. Consortium, Los Angeles. Author: (poems) Popsicle in My Pocket, 1970. Founder Explorations Art Festival, Los Angeles, 1983; co-founder Los Angeles High Sch. for the Arts, 1985, Chamber Music Los Angeles Festival, 1986, pres. 1987—, Dance Resource Ctr. Los Angeles, 1987, bd. dirs. 1986-87. Served with USAF, 1968-70. Democrat. Roman Catholic.

GORMLEY, DANIEL EUGENE, dermatologist; b. Oakland, Calif., Nov. 30, 1935; s. David Eugene and Dorothy Elizabeth (McGuire) G.; children: Brendan Daniel, Christopher Patrick. BS, St. Mary's Coll., 1958, U. Calif., Berkeley, 1959; MD, U. Calif., San Francisco, 1963. Diplomate, Am. Bd. Dermatology. Rotating intern SUNY, Syracuse, 1963-64, resident in radiology, 1964-65; asst. resident in medicine U. Utah Hosp., Salt Lake City, 1965-67; resident in dermatology Washington U. Med. Ctr., St. Louis, 1967-70; pvt. practice Glendora, Calif., 1970—; asst. clin. prof. Ctr. Health Scis., UCLA, 1984-88; mem. staff, Foothill Presbyn. Hosp., San Dimas Community Hosp., Glendora Community Hosp., UCLA Ctr. Health Scis. Patentee biol. surface contour measurement device; contbr. articles to med. publs. Fellow Am. Acad. Dermatology, Pacific Dermatologic Assn., Met. Dermatol. Soc., Am. Soc. Dermatologic Surgery (bd. dirs. 1973-76, v.p. 1980), Soc. Investigative Dermatology; mem. Calif. Med. Assn., Internat. Soc. Bioengring. and Skin, Pacific Dermatologic Soc., L.A. Met. Dermatologic Soc. Republican. Office: 412 W Carroll St Ste 207 Glendora CA 91740

GORMLEY, FRANCIS XAVIER, JR., social worker; b. Boston; s. Francis Xavier and Catherine Caroline (Ireland) G. Student, Massasoit Community Coll., 1973; BA in Psychology, U. Mass., Boston, 1981; MSW, U. Wash., 1984. Coordinator Gerontology Career Program Elder Fest, Chico, Calif., 1981; mgr. Arnold's Restaurant, Cardiff, Wales, 1981-82; med. social worker Harborview Med. Ctr., Seattle, 1983-84; psychotherapist Seattle Counseling Service, 1982—; clin. social worker Pain Ctr. Swedish Hosp., Seattle, 1984-88, Valley Med. Ctr., Renton, Wash., 1987-88; clin. social worker AIDS program, virology clinic Univ. Hosp., Seattle, 1988—; speaker U. Wash. Sch. Social Work Graduation Class, 1984, Social Sensitivity in Health Care U. Wash, 1985—; coordinator Coping with AIDS Swedish Hosp. Tumor Inst., 1985; guest speaker Sta. KIRO-TV, Seattle, 1985, Sta. KPLZ, Seattle, 1985; cons. Assn. Workers Resources, Seattle, 1985—. Editor abstract form Comprehensive Multi-Disciplinary Documentation, Western U.S.A. Pain Soc., 1986. Mem. Seattle Aids Network, 1985—. Mem. Acad. Cert. Social Workers, Nat. Assn. Social Workers, Occupational Social Work Orgn. of Nat. Assn. Social Workers, U. Wash. Alumni Assn., U. Mass. Alumni Assn., Green Key Soc. Democrat.

GORMLEY, MYRA DEVEE, newspaper columnist; b. Muskogee, Okla., Feb. 7, 1940; d. John Oscar and Doris Jean (Fricks) Vanderpool; m. John Carl Goerges, Nov. 9, 1958 (div. Oct. 1966); m. Leo Claude Gormley, Mar. 1, 1975; stepchildren: Kirk, Rick, Kyle. Student, Muskogee Jr. Coll., 1957-58, Okla. U., 1960-61, U. Md. extension, Darmstadt, Fed. Republic Germany, 1962. Cert. Genealogist. Copy editor, proofreader, typesetter Stars & Stripes, Darmstadt, 1961-64; proofreader, typesetter San Antonio Light, 1964-65, Seattle Times, 1965-66, News Tribune, Tacoma, 1966—; syndicated columnist L.A. Times, 1985—. Author: Family Diseases: Are You At Risk? 1989. Loaned exec. United Way, Tacoma, 1984. Mem. Nat. Geneal. Soc., Assn. Profl. Genealogists, Oral History Assn., Fedn. Geneal.

Socs., Am. Name Soc., Wash. State Hist. Soc., Tacoma/Pierce County Geneal. Soc. (v.p. 1979-80, 87-89, editor 1989—), DAR, Coun. Genealogy Columnists (pres. 1987—). Democrat. Home: 8402 57th St W Tacoma WA 98467 Office: LA Times Syndicate Times Mirror Sq Los Angeles CA 90053

GORMLY, WILLIAM MOWRY, financial consultant; b. Pitts., Mar. 15, 1941; s. Thomas Wilson and Lourene (Blaine) G.; m. Barbara Diesner, Aug. 21, 1965; children: Kirsten Eve, Kellie Blaine. BA in Econs., Dickinson Coll., Carlisle, Pa., 1963; postgrad. Northwestern U., 1967, DePaul U., 1968; grad. banking degree, Rutgers U., 1978. Regional mgr. Harris Bank, Chgo., 1967-69; corp. banking officer Wells Fargo Bank N.A., San Francisco, 1969-73; v.p. 4th Nat. Bank of Wichita, 1973-74, Union Nat. Bank of Pitts., 1974-79; v.p., sr. nat. accts. officer Ariz. Bank, Phoenix, 1979-82; pres. Cons. in Pub. Fin., Ltd., Scottsdale, Ariz., 1982—. Mem. Dickinson Coll. Alumni Council, 1975-80; bd. dirs. Ariz. Theatre Co., Phoenix, 1980-83; trustee Northland Pub. Library, Pitts., 1975-79. 1st lt. U.S. Army, 1963-65. Mem. Am. Hosp. Assn., Econ. Club Phoenix, Phi Delta Theta. Republican. Methodist. Office: Cons Pub Fin Ltd 23150 N Pima Rd Suite 1 Scottsdale AZ 85255

GORRELL, JOHN ELLISON, physician, writer; b. Chgo., July 14, 1903; s. Talbot John Howe and Katherin (Parmenter) G.; m. L. Larguerite Cook, Sept. 1930; children: Elizabeth Gorrell Kot, Joan, John David. BS in Physiology and Anatomy, U. Chgo., 1928; MB, Northwestern U., Chgo., 1929, MD, 1930. Lic. physician, Calif. Prof. Loma Linda (Calif.) U.; professorial lectr. Tchrs. Coll. Columbia U., N.Y.C.; prof. Coll. of Physicians and Surgeons Columbia U., N.Y.C.; professorial lectr. Tchr's. Coll. St. John's U., Bklyn.; lectr. U. Calif., Riverside and Santa Barbara; now lectr. and writer for the gen. pub. about health and medicine. Author: Manual on Insurance; author confidential report for the bus. div. U.S. Census Bureau; pub. 11 vols. on community surveys on Health and Hosps. for Nausa County, Onondoga County, and others; contbg. editor New Physican Jour.; contbr. 10 articles to profl. jours. Bd. dirs. Sci. Engring. Council, Santa Barbara, Calif. Republican. Home and Office: 900 Calle De Los Amigos Santa Barbara CA 93105

GORSKY, BENJAMIN HOWARD, anesthesiologist; b. Hartford, Conn., July 28, 1944; s. Samuel and Bae (Botuck) G.; m. Susan R. Gorsky, Dec. 20, 1965. BS, Trinity Coll., Hartford, 1965; MS, Case Western Res. U., 1968, MD, 1970. Diplomate Am. Bd. Anesthesiology. Intern Univ. Hosps. Cleve., 1970-71, resident, dept. anesthesiology, 1971-73; mem. faculty dept. anesthesiology Case Western Res. U., Cleve., 1973-80; anesthesiologist Carlisle (Pa.) Hosp., 1980-83; chief anesthesiologist Shriners Hosp. for Crippled Children, Honolulu, 1983—; med. cons. pain mgmt. program Rehab. Hosp. of Pacific, Honolulu, 1987—. Author: Pain Origin and Treatment, 1982, Introduction to Medical Hypnosis (with Susan R. Gorsky), 1983. Home: 1629 Wilder Ave Apt 1003 Honolulu HI 96822 Office: Shriners Hosp Crippled Children 1310 Punahou St Honolulu HI 96826

GORSLINE, SAMUEL GILBERT, JR., school administrator; b. San Jose, Calif., Oct. 20, 1921; s. Samuel Gilbert Sr. and Gladys Zeiters (Wolf) G.; m. Barbara Jeanne Clifton, Mar. 22, 1946 (div. 1969); children: Samuel Gilbert III, John Clifton, James Scott; m. Ann Moyes Todd, Sept. 3, 1969; children: Carroll Ann, Robert Todd. BS, U.S. Naval Acad., 1944. Commd. ensign USN, 1944, advanced through grades to capt., 1965; naval aviator USN, Korea, 1949-74; commanded fleet oiler USN, Vietnam, 1968-69, commanded attack carrier USS Coral Sea, 1969-70; ops. officer U.S. Atlantic fleet USN, 1971-72; commdr. naval tng. ctr. USN, Great Lakes, Ill., 1972-73; ret. USN, 1974; owner, operator Panmure Arms Hotel, Edzell, Scotland, 1974-81; adminstr.v.p. Army and Navy Acad., Carlsbad, Calif., 1986—. Troop com. chmn. Boy Scouts Am., Fallbrook, Calif., 1987-88; steering com. Fallbrook Incorp. Coalition, 1986-88; elder Fallbrook Presbyn. Ch., 1989—. Decorated 3 Legions of Merit, distg. Flying Cross; honored during Sam Gorsline Day proclaimed by mayor, Battle Creek, Mich., 1972. Mem. Mil. Order World Wars, Naval Acad. Alumni Assn. Republican. Loges: Rotary, Masons (sr. warden 1979-81). Home: 225 Deddie Terr Fallbrook CA 92028 Office: Army and Navy Acad 2605 Carlsbad Blvd Carlsbad CA 93008

GORSUCH, NORMAN CLIFFORD, law educator; b. Pitts., Oct. 3, 1942; s. Clifford Lee and Helen (Berzac) G.; children by a previous marriage: Elizabeth, Kieth, Jennifer, Deborah, David; m. Lenore W. Boston, Oct. 18, 1985. B.A. with honors, U. N.C., 1964; J.D., Columbia U., 1967. Bar: Alaska 1968, U.S. Dist. Ct. Alaska 1968, U.S. Ct. Internat. Trade 1968, U.S. Ct. Appeals (9th cir.) 1969, U.S. Supreme Ct. 1973. Assoc. Ely, Guess & Rudd, Anchorage, 1967-70, ptnr., 1970-71; ptnr. Ely, Guess & Rudd, Juneau, Alaska, 1974-82; dep. atty. gen. State of Alaska, Juneau, 1971-73, atty. gen., 1973-74, 82-85; assoc. prof. law and pub. adminstn. U. Alaska, Juneau, 1985—; owner Capitol Assocs., Juneau, 1986—. Editor-in-chief Alaska Pub. Affairs Jour., 1987—; contbr. articles to profl. jours. Trustee Alaska Permanent Fund, Juneau, 1982—, 85; mem. Alaska Democratic Central Com., 1982; commr. Alaska Fed.-State Land Use Planning Commn., 1977-79. Mem. Alaska Bar Assn., Alaska C. of C. (bd. dirs. 1980-81, Juneau C. of C. (bd. dirs. 1979-82), Westends CSG (mem. monitoring bd.), Rotary, Phi Beta Kappa. Democrat. Methodist.

GORTON, H. CLAY, engineering manager; b. Soda Springs, Idaho, Mar. 7, 1923; s. Rees Dubois and Sarah Dorleska (Sterrett) G.; m. Hilda Edna Frances Foot, April 7, 1949; children: David, Deborah, Stephen, Rebecca, Elizabeth. BA, Brigham Young U., 1952, MA, 1953. Research physicist Battelle Meml. Inst., Columbus, Ohio, 1953-63, asst. div. chief, 1963-69; mission pres. Ch. of Jesus Christ of Latter-Day Saints, Cordoba, Argentina, 1969-72; mgr. component reliability Victor Comptometer Corp., Des Plaines, Ill., 1972-75; engr. TRW Elecs. & Def., Redondo Beach, Calif., 1975-78, section head, 1978-86; chief scientist, tech. cons. TRW Components Internat., Inc., Torrance, Calif., 1986—. Editor: Reliability Physics Notebook, 1965; contbr. articles to profl. jours.; patentee in field. Served to sgt. USAF, 1942-46. Home: 19501 Donora Ave Torrance CA 90503 Office: TRW Components Internat Inc 19951 Mariner Ave Torrance CA 90503

GORTON, SLADE, U.S. senator; b. Chgo., Jan. 8, 1928; s. Thomas Slade and Ruth (Israel) G.; m. Sally Jean Clark, June 28, 1958; children: Tod, Sarah Jane, Rebecca Lynn. AB, Dartmouth Coll., 1950; LLB with honors, Columbia U., 1953. Bar: Wash. 1953. Assoc. law firm, Seattle, 1953-65; ptnr. law firm 1965-69; atty. gen. State of Wash., Olympia, 1969-81; U.S. Senator from Wash. 1981-87, 89—; ptnr. Davis, Wright & Jones, Seattle, 1987-89; Mem. Wash. Ho. of Reps., 1959-69, majority leader, 1967-69. Trustee Pacific Sci. Center, Seattle, found. mem., 1977-78; mem. Pres.'s Consumer Adv. Council, 1975-77; mem. Wash. State Law and Justice Commn., 1969-80, chmn., 1969-76; mem. State Criminal Justice Tng. Commn., 1969-80, chmn., 1969-76. Served with AUS, 1945-46; to 1st lt. USAF, 1953-56; col. Res. Mem. ABA, Wash. Bar Assn., Nat. Assn. Attys. Gen. (pres. 1976-77, Wyman award 1980), Phi Delta Phi, Phi Beta Kappa. Clubs: Seattle Tennis, Wash. Athletic (Seattle). Office: US Senate Office Senate Mems Washington DC 20510

GOSE, JOAN CATHERINE, retired educator; b. Milw., Nov. 20, 1933; d. John Sylvester and Eleanor Helen (Toschik) Wolf; m. Joe Lewis, Sept. 6, 1952; children: David Anthony, Robert John, Paul Martin, Carol Ann, Thomas Edward. BA in Edn., Ariz. State U., 1971, MA in Edn., 1976; EdS in Adminstrn. and Supervision, NOVA U., 1979. Cert. elem. prin., supr., spl. edn. supr., tchr., Ariz. Tchr. Mesa (Ariz.) Pub. Schs., 1971-76, learning disabilities program specialist, 1976-78, in-svc. presenter, 1976-89, regional dir., 1978-89. Active local community projects. Mem. Council Exceptional Children (sec. chpt. 86), Spl. Edn. Adminstrn. of Ariz. (pres. 1986, treas. 1984, sec. 1981-83), Phi Delta Kappa, Phi Kappa Phi. Democrat. Mem. Christian Ch. Office: Mesa Pub Schs 549 N Stapley Mesa AZ 85203

GOSE, RICHARD VERNIE, lawyer; b. Hot Springs, S.D., Aug. 3, 1927. BS, U. Wyo., 1950; MS in Engring., Northwestern U., 1955; LLB, George Washington U., 1967; JD, George Washington U., 1968; children—Beverly Marie, Donald Paul, Celeste Marlene. Bar: N.Mex. 1967, U.S. Supreme Ct. 1976, Wyo. 1979. Exec. asst. to U.S. Senator Hickey, Washington, 1960-62; mgr. E.G. & G., Inc., Washington, 1964-66; asst. atty. gen. State of N.Mex., Santa Fe, 1967-70; sole practice law, Santa Fe, 1967—; assoc. prof. engring. U. Wyo., 1957-60; owner, mgr. Gose & Assocs., Santa Fe, 1967-78; pvt. practice law, Casper, Wyo., 1978-83; co-chmn. Henry Jackson for Pres., M.Mex., 1976, Wyo. Johnson for Pres., 1960. With U.S. Army, 1950-52. Registered profl. engr., N.Mex., Wyo. Mem. 1st Jud. Dist. Bar Assn. (past pres.), N.Mex. Bar Assn., Wyo. Bar Assn., Phi Delta Theta, Pi Tau Sigma, Sigma Tau. Methodist. Lodge: Masons. Home and Office: PO Box 8301 Santa Fe NM 87504

GOSHI, KEIICHI, physician; b. Taikyu, Korea, Jan. 17, 1927; came to U.S., 1955, permanent resident, 1962.; s. Yoshihiro and Haruko G.; m. Eloise Yachie Nekomoto, Nov. 16, 1957; 1 child, Allen Keiichi. MD, Kobe Med. Coll., Japan, 1949, PhD, 1961. Intern Kobe Med. Coll., Japan, 1949-50; research asst. in biochemistry Kobe Med. Coll., 1950-55; intern St. Francis Hosp., Honolulu, 1955-56, resident in med., 1957-58; resident in allergy Med. Coll. of Va., Richmond, 1956-57, asst. prof., 1962-65; resident in med. Sinai Hosp., Balt., 1958-59; fellow in med., infectious disease and allergy Johns Hopkins Med. Sch., Balt., 1959-62; pvt. practice internal med. and allergy Honolulu, 1965—; cons., vocational rehabilitation, State of Hawaii, Honolulu, 1966-72; asst. clin. prof., U. Hawaii Sch. of Med., Honolulu, 1967-73. Author: (med. rsch.): Nutritional Requirements in Exercise, 1950-55, Pathogenesis of Staphylococcal Infection, 1959-65, History of Medicine in Hawaii and Japan, 1982—; contbr. articles to profl. jours. and studies. Nippon Ikueikai scholar, Tokyo, 1946-50. Mem. Am. Acad. of Allergy, Internat. Congree of Allergology, AMA, Am. Soc. Internal Med. Home: 46-511 Haiku Plantation Dr Kaneohe HI 96744 Office: 1010 S King St 215 Honolulu HI 96814

GOSLINE, WILLIAM JAMES, JR., educator; b. Santa Monica, Calif., Aug. 8, 1953; s. William James and Celesta (Thayer) G.; m. Bonnie McKeever Ostrander, May 7, 1988. BA in English, U. Calif., Santa Barbara, 1975; M in Profl. Writing, U. So. Calif., 1987. Head waiter Chart House Restaurants, Inc., various, Calif., 1977-81; mgr. Station House Inn Restaurant, South Lake Tahoe, Calif., 1981-83, U. Calif. Food Svc., Santa Barbara, 1983-85; lectr. U. So. Calif., L.A., 1985; cons. U. So. Calif. dept. bus. communications, L.A., 1985—, Communication Training and Consulting, Anaheim Hills, Calif., 1988—. Author: (short story) The Hobart, 1986, (play) House Pets, 1986. Home: 16176 - B Sunset Blvd Pacific Palisades CA 90272 Office: Univ So Calif Sch Bus Adminstrn Los Angeles CA 90089-1421

GOSPE, SIDNEY MALOCH, JR., child neurologist; b. San Francisco, Oct. 7, 1952; s. Sidney Maloch and Ruth Marie (Winger) G.; m. Mary Elizabeth Williams, Apr. 12, 1980; children: Sidney III, Jessica. BS, Stanford U., 1974, MS, 1975; PhD, Duke U., 1980, MD, 1981. Diplomate Am. Bd. Pediatrics, Am. Bd. Psychiatry and Neurology. Pediatric resident Baylor Coll. of Med., Houston, 1981-83, child neurology resident, 1983-86; asst. prof. Albany (N.Y.) Med. Coll., 1986-87, U. Calif., Davis, 1987—. Fellow Am. Acad. Pediatrics; mem. Am. Acad. Neurology, Child Neurology Soc. Democrat. Jewish. Office: Dept of Neurology Univ Calif Med Ctr 2315 Stockton Blvd Sacramento CA 95817

GOSS, CHARLES ALBERT, chemistry educator; b. N.Y.C., Dec. 24, 1962; s. Albert Edward and Mary E. W. Goss; m. Karen Lessall Weiner, June 18, 1988. BA, Cornell U., 1985. Rsch. asst. Cornell U., Ithaca, N.Y., 1984-85; grad. teaching asst. in chemistry U. Calif., Berkeley, 1985—. Mem. Am. Chem. Soc., AAAS. Home: 1121 Chaucer St Berkeley CA 94702

GOSS, DOUGLAS ALAN, electrical engineer; b. Des Moines, May 21, 1963; s. David Alan Sr. and Patricia Ann (Middleworth) G. BSEE, U. Okla., 1985. Engr. digital design Delco Systems Ops., Goleta, Calif., 1985—. Mem. IEEE. Home: 5455 8th St #68 Carpinteria CA 93013 Office: Delco Systems Ops 6767 Hollister E503 Goleta CA 93117

GOSS, JEROME ELDON, cardiologist; b. Dodge City, Kans., Nov. 30, 1935; s. Horton Maurice and Mary Alice (Mountain) G.; m. Lorraine Ann Sanchez, Apr. 20, 1986. BA, U. Kans., 1957; MD, Northwestern U., 1961. Diplomate Am. Bd. Internal Medicine, Am. Bd. Cardiology (fellow, bd. govs. 1981-84). Intern Met. Gen. Hosp., Cleve., 1961-62; resident Northwestern U. Med. Ctr., Chgo., 1962-64; fellow in cardiology U. Colo., Denver, 1964-66; asst. prof. medicine U. N.Mex., Albuquerque, 1968-70; practice medicine specializing in cardiology N.Mex. Heart Clinic, 1970—; mem. bd. alumni counsellors Northwestern U. Med. Sch., 1977—; chief dept. medicine Presbyn. Hosp., Albuquerque, 1978-80, mem. exec. com. 1980-82, bd. dirs. cardiac diagnostic services; cons., cardio-pace med. lectr., Marion Labs., Kansas City (Mo.) and Mpls.; lectr. Winthrope Labs., N.Y.C. Contbr. articles to profl. jours. Bd. dirs. Presbyn. Heart Inst., Ballet West N.Mex., N.Mex. Symphony Orch. Served to lt. comdr. USN, 1966-68. Nat. Heart Inst. research fellow, 1965-66; named one of Outstanding Young Men Am., Jaycees, 1970; recipient Alumni Service award Northwestern U. Med. Sch., 1986. Fellow ACP, Council Clin. Cardiology of Am. Heart Assn., Soc. Cardiac Angiography; mem. Albuquerque-Bernalillo County Med. Soc. (sec. 1972, treas. 1975, v.p. 1980), Alpha Omega Alpha. Republican. Methodist. Lodge: Rotary. Office: NMex Heart Clinic 1001 Coal SE Albuquerque NM 87106

GOSSELIN, KENNETH STUART, minister; b. Altus, Okla., Aug. 9, 1932; s. George Clairo and Florence May (Stebbins) G.; m. P. Rodene Tayar, Sept. 8, 1962; children: Mark Alan, Kimberly Sue, Anna Jouree, Sabrina Kay. BA, Oklahoma City U., 1954; STM, Perkins Sch. Theology, 1958; MA, Claremont (Calif.) Grad. Sch., 1967. Cert. tchr., Calif. Campus minister Wesley Found., Tex. Christian U., Ft. Worth, 1958-64; minister to youth 1st Meth. Ch., Riverside, Calif., 1964-66; assoc. minister Community Meth. Ch., Sepulveda, Calif., 1967-69; minister St. Matthew's Meth. Ch., Newbury Park, Calif., 1969-71; assoc. minister Christ Ch. United Meth., Tucson, 1971-73; minister Nestor United Meth. Ch., San Diego, 1973-83, Pacific Beach (Calif.) United Meth. Ch., 1983-85; sr. minister Christ United Meth. Ch., San Diego, 1985—; radio announcer, editor San Diego County Ecumenical Conf., 1979—; mem. ordained ministry com. United Meth. Dist., San Diego, 1982—; mem. communications com. Calif.-Pacific Conf. U. Meth. Ch., Pasadena and L.A., 1988—. Entertainer, clown Muscular Dystrophy Assn. Telethon, San Diego, 1973—, Spl. Olympics, Am. Cancer Soc., Am. Heart Assn., Children's Hosp., KPBS, San Diego Symphony, etc. Danforth Found. grantee, 1956-57. Mem. Am. Acad. Religion, Calif.-Pacific Ann. Conf. U. Meth. Ch., Clowns Am., World Clown Assn. Democrat. Home: 3283 Meade Ave San Diego CA 92116 Office: Christ United Meth Ch 3295 Meade Ave San Diego CA 92116

GOSSELIN, PETER PAUL, electronics company executive, consultant; b. Boston, Feb. 10, 1941; s. Robert Louis and Margaret Regina (Tahmezian) G.; m. June D. Anderson, Jan. 14, 1960 (div. Sept. 1985); children: Julie, Sharon, Lynda, Valerie. BS in Mgmt., Northeastern U., 1973. Product mgr. ITT Semicondrs., Lawrence, Mass., 1963-72; plant mgr. Semicon, Inc., Lawrence, Mass., 1972-75; pres., chief exec. officer Park Electronic Products, Salem, N.H., 1975-85, Parkwest Microcomponents, Inc., Pacentia, Calif., 1985--; cons. Caluctta, India, 1979-81, Iskra, Zagreb, Yugoslavia, 1983-86. Mem. Am. Electronics Assn., K.C., The Exec. Com. Roman Catholic. Home: 28956 Live Oak Cir Trabuco Canyon CA 92679 Office: Parkwest Microcomponents Inc 1921 Petra Ln Placentia CA 92670

GOSSWEILER, ROBERT MARTIN, oil company executive; b. La Paz, Bolivia, July 13, 1949; s. Robert Fritz and Hildegard (Zewrkowsky) G.; m. Dawn Ann Phillips, Sept. 21, 1974; children: Brant, Robert. BA in Lit., San Andres U., La Paz, 1967; BS in Econs., U. Pa., 1972, MBA, 1974. Purchasing agt. Samincorp Inc., N.Y.C., 1974-75; v.p. mktg. J. Mueller Corp., Zurich, 1976-78; v.p. Closomat USA Inc., Franklin Lakes, N.J., 1979-83; pres. Aquamatics Co., Tallman, N.Y., 1984-85, Sodiesa Petroleum, N.Y.C., 1986—; pres. Sodiesa Petroleum. Contbr. articles to profl. jours. Coord. ednl. programs for Mexican/Americans NMSU-DONA ANA chpt., Las Cruces, N.Mex., 1988. Recipient Spl. Mention, Phila. chpt. SBA, 1974. Mem. Wharton Alumni Club. Home: PO Box 8234 Las Cruces NM 88006 Office: Cosmana Ent Ltd PO Box 8234 Las Cruces NM 88006 also: Sodiesa Petroleum PO Box 8275 Naples FL 33941

GOTHAM, PAMELA HELEN, insurance company executive; b. Tacoma, July 15, 1953; d. Alfred Wilson and Margaret Jena Rix; m. D. Terry Gotham, Sept. 29, 1979. Grad. high sch., Tacoma, 1971. Statistician Weyerheauser Corp., Federal Way, Wash., 1972-73; mgr. Pacific Fin. Corp., Burien, Wash., 1973-75; dep. sheriff Pierce County Sheriff's Dept., Tacoma, 1975-77; internal auditor Fred Meyer, Inc., Seattle, 1975-77; account exec. Bus. Mens Clearing House, Seattle, 1977-79; sr. assoc. Alaska Exec. Search, Anchorage, 1979-83; regional dir. Wash., Alaska Colonial Life nd Accident Co., Tacoma, 1983—. Chmn. Salaries and Emoluments Commn., anchorage, 1983—; pres. LWV, Anchorage, 1983. Mem. LWV (v.p. Anchorage 1979-87), Assn. Health Underwriters, Nat. Assn. of Life Underwriters, Pierce County C. of C.,. Republican. Office: Colonial Life & Accident Co World Trade Ctr 209 3600 Port of Tacoma Rd Tacoma WA 98424

GOTO, KENJI, former hospital administrator and consultant, cultural society executive; b. Puako, Hawaii, Oct. 10, 1904; s. Unokichi and Yana (Inaba) G.; B.A. in Bus. and Econs., U. Hawaii, 1927, postgrad., 1930-31; m. Hagino Mikami, Feb. 23, 1935; children—Irving Ken, Alan Jiro. Salesman, Theodore H. Davies & Co., Honolulu, 1927-29; mgr. U. Goto Store, Kona, Hawaii, 1929-30; tchr. Konawaena High Sch., 1931-42; prin. Hookena Elementary Sch., 1942-43; supr. On-Job Tng. Program for Vets., Honolulu, 1947-48; adminstr. Kuakini Hosp. and Home, 1948-69, cons., 1970-73. Pres., Oahu Health Council, 1959-61; mem. Mayor's Adv. Com. on Community Renewal Program, 1964-65; vice chmn. Hawaii Adv. Council Hosp. and Med. Facilities, 1965-76; mem. Honolulu Com. on Aging, 1970-78, chmn., 1976-78; chmn. adv. com. Honolulu Heart Research Programs, 1964-77, state and Oahu chmn. Com. for Centennial Celebration of Japanese Immigration to Hawaii, 1967-68; chmn. Centennial Celebration Arrival of Govt.-contract (Kanyaku)Japanese Immigrants to Hawaii, 1983-86; leader U.S. Army Pacific Friendship Mission to Japan, 1968; chmn. adv. com. Japan-Hawaii Cancer Study, 1971-77; mem. Crown Prince Akihito Scholarship Fund, 1972—, chmn., 1980—; treas., chmn. membership com. Japanese Immigrant Heritage Preservation Ctr., 1975-86, sec., 1980-85, v.p., 1985-88, pres. 1988—; bd. dirs. Kuakini Med. Center, 1973-79; chmn. bd. Hawaii Sr. Services, Inc., 1977-79. Served with AUS, 1943-45. Decorated Order of Rising Sun Fourth Class, Japanese Govt., 1983; named Hawaii Man of Year, 1970; recipient Outstanding Older Am. award for County of Honolulu, 1979; honored with resolution State of Hawaii Ho. of Reps., 1988; elected to McKinley High Sch's. Hall of Honor, 1988. Mem. United Japanese Soc. Hawaii (pres. 1967-68, adviser 1969—), Am. Coll. Hosp. Adminstrs. (life), Hosp. Assn. Hawaii (pres. 1957, 67), Japan-Am. Soc. Honolulu (trustee 1976-84, sr. advisor 1984—), Teiko Kai (pres. chpt. 1978—). Home: 99-869 Lalawai Dr Aiea HI 96701

GOTSHALL, CORDIA ANN, publishing company executive; b. Greenwood, Ark., Jan. 21, 1931; d. Harrison Wages and Mabel Magdalene (Boswell) Wages Moreland; m. Daniel W. Gottshall, Apr. 12, 1952. AA with honors, Foothill Jr. Coll., Los Altos Hills, Calif., 1966; BA magna cum laude, Humboldt State U., Arcata, Calif., 1969; student, Humboldt State U., 1969-71. Clk., typist Indentification Bur. Stanislaus County Sheriff's Office, Modesto, Calif., 1950-55; credit dept. mgr. Brizard's Dept. Store, Arcata, 1955-56; sec.-coord. City of Eureka (Calif.) Recreation Dept., 1956-60; seasonal aide State of Calif. Dept. Fish and Game, Palo Alto, 1961; owner, v.p. Sea Challengers Pub. Co., Monterey, Calif., 1976-83, pres., 1983—; co-editor (with Daniel W. Gotshall) Fishwater's Guide, 1977; U.S. rep. Moscow Internat. Book Fair, 1985. Palo Alto area Dem. vol. Mem. Chi Sigma Epsilon. Home and Office: 4 Somerset Rise Monterey CA 93940

GOTTFRIED, EUGENE LESLIE, physician, educator; b. Passaic, N.J., Feb. 26, 1929; s. David Robert and Rose (Chill) G.; m. Phyllis Doris Swain, Aug. 16, 1957. AB, Columbia U., 1950, MD, 1954. Cert. Nat. Bd. Med. Examiners, Am. Bd. Internal Medicine. Intern Presbyn. Hosp., N.Y.C., 1954-55, asst. resident in medicine, 1957-58; resident Bronx (N.Y.) Mcpl. Hosp. Ctr., 1958-59, fellow in medicine, 1959-60; asst. instr. medicine Albert Einstein Coll. Medicine Yeshiva U., N.Y.C., 1959-60, instr., 1960-61, assoc., 1961-65, asst. prof., 1965-69; assoc. prof. medicine Cornell U. Med. Coll., N.Y.C., 1969-81, assoc. prof. pathology, 1975-81; clin. prof. dept. lab. medicine U. Calif., San Francisco, 1981—, vice chmn. dept. lab. medicine, 1981—; hosp. appointments include asst. vis. physician Bronx Mcpl. Hosp. Ctr., 1960-66, assoc. attending physician, 1966-69; assoc. attending physician N.Y. Hosp., N.Y.C., 1969-81, assoc. attending pathologist, 1975-81, dir. lab. clin. hematology, 1969-81; chief lab. medicine San Francisco Gen. Hosp. Med. Ctr., 1981—, dir. clin. labs., 1981—. Assoc. editor Jour. Lipid Research, 1971-72, 75-77; mem. editorial bd. Jour. Lipid Research, 1972-77. Served to lt. comdr. USNR, 1955-57. Recipient Career Scientist award Health Research Council City of N.Y., 1964-72. Fellow Am. Soc. Hematology, Internat. Soc. Hematology, ACP, Acad. Clin. Lab. Physicians and Scientists; mem. AAAS, Phi Beta Kappa, Alpha Omega Alpha. Office: San Fráncisco Gen Hosp Clin Labs 1001 Potrero Ave San Francisco CA 94110

GOTTFRIED, IRA SIDNEY, management consulting executive; b. Bronx, N.Y., Jan. 4, 1932; s. Louis and Augusta (Champagne) G.; m. Judith Claire Rosenberg, Sept. 19, 1954; children: Richard Alan, Glenn Steven, David Aaron. B.B.A., CCNY, 1953, M.B.A., U.S.C., 1959. Sales mgr. Kleerpak Plastics, North Hollywood, Calif., 1956-57; head systems and procedures Hughes Aircraft Co., Culver City, Calif., 1957-60; mgr. corp. bus. systems The Aerospace Corp., El Segundo, Calif., 1960-61; dir. adminstrn. Eldon Industries, Inc., Hawthorne, Calif., 1962; mgr. info. systems Litton Industries Inc., Woodland Hills, Calif., 1963-64; exec. v.p. Norris & Gottfried, Inc., Los Angeles, 1964-69; pres. Gottfried Cons., Inc., 1970-85; exec. ptnr. Coopers & Lybrand, CPA's, 1985-88; v.p. Cresap/Towers Perrin, 1988—; chmn., dir. Mgmt. Adv. Services, Inc., 1968—; vice chmn. ACME Inc., 1984-85; dir., mem. exec. com. Blue Cross of Calif., 1968-77. Contbr. articles in field to prof. jours. Bd. dirs. ARC, 1980—, Univ. Synagogue, 1986—. Served with USNR, 1953-56. Recipient Pres.'s award United Hosp. Assn. Mem. Inst. Mgmt. Cons. (cert.), Am. Arbitration Assn., Data Processing Mgmt. Assn. (life), Alpha Phi Omega (life). Jewish. Clubs: Brentwood Country, Palm Valley Country. Lodge: Rotary. Home: 12118 La Casa Ln Los Angeles CA 90049

GOTTI, MARGARET LYNN, library administrator; b. Detroit, July 31, 1944; d. Frank Matthias and Betty Louise (Lee) Sieger; m. Cyriac Thannikary, Nov. 13, 1965 (div. Feb. 1973); 1 child, Luke Anthony; m. Marcos T. Perez, Mar. 1973 (dec. Oct. 1973); m. Lui Gotti, Dec. 23, 1984. AB, U. Detroit, 1968; MLS, Pratt Inst., 1969; postgrad., NYU, 1976-77. Cert. librarian, N.Y. Sr. librarian Queens Pub. Library, Jamaica, N.Y., 1969-77; library dir. El Centro Pub. Library, El Centro, Calif., 1977—; vice chmn., chmn. Serra Coop. Library System, San Diego, 1980-82. Pres. His. Site Found., El Centro; fin. sec. St. Elizabeth Luth. Ch., El Centro; active numerous civic coms., fund raising events. Title IIB fellow Pratt Inst., 1968-69. Mem. ALA, Calif. Library Assn., AAUW (v.p. El Centro 1988), El Centro Toastmasters (v.p. 1987-88), Soroptomists (treas. El Centro 1978), Women of Moose (sr. regent El Centro 1988--). Democrat. Lutheran. Home: 1531 Heil Ave El Centro CA 92243 Office: El Centro Pub Libr 539 State St El Centro CA 92243

GOTTLIEB, ALAN MERRIL, association executive; b. Los Angeles, May 2, 1947; s. Seymour and Sherry (Schutz) G.; m. Julie Hoy Versnel, July 27, 1979; children: Amy Jean, Sarah Merril, Alexis Hope. BS in Nuclear Engring., U. Tenn., 1971; postgrad. Georgetown U. Nat. dir. Young Ams. for Freedom, Washington, 1971-72; nat. treas. Am. Conservative Union, Washington, 1971—; chmn. Citizens Com. for Right to Keep and Bear Arms, Bellevue, Wash., 1974—; pres. Ctr. Def. of Free Enterprise, Bellevue 1976—; pres. Second Amendment Found., Bellevue, 1974—; pub. Gun Week, 1985—; bd. dirs. Nat. Park User Assn., 1988—, Am. Polit. Action Com., 1988—. With U.S. Army, 1968-74. Recipient Good Citizenship award Citizens Home Protective Assn., 1978, Cicero award Nat. Assn. Federally Licensed Firearms Dealers, 1982; Second Amendment award Scope, 1983, Roy Rogers award 1987. Mem. NRA. Republican. Author: The Gun Owners Political Action Manual, 1976, The Rights of Gun Owners, 1981, The Gun Grabbers, 1986, Gun Rights Fact Book, 1988; co-author: Guns For Women, 1988, The Wise Use Agenda, 1989.

GOTTLIEB, MARILYNN PAYNE, medical photographer; b. Santa Rosa, Calif., Feb. 17, 1956; d. Jack Weston and Patricia (Bruce) P.; m. Daniel Seth, July 21, 1985;. BA, U. Calif., 1978; AA with honors, Bellevue Community Coll., 1980. Med. photographer Virginia Mason Med. Ctr., Seattle, Wash., 1987. Home: 4428 Greenwood Ave N Seattle WA 98103

GOTTSCHALK, LOUIS AUGUST, psychiatrist, psychoanalyst; b. St. Louis, Aug. 26, 1916; s. Max W. and Kelmie (Mutrux) G.; m. Helen Reller, July 24, 1944; children—Guy H., Claire A., Louise H., Susan E. A.B., Washington U., St. Louis, 1940, M.D., 1943; Ph.D., So. Calif. Psychiat. Inst., 1977. Asst. in neuropsychiatry Washington U. Sch. Medicine, 1944-46; commd. asst. surgeon USPHS, 1946, advanced through grades to med. dir., 1979; instr. psychiatry S.W. Med. Coll., Dallas, 1947-48; research psychiatrist NIMH, Bethesda, Md., 1950-53; coordinator research, research prof. psychiatry U. Cin. Coll. Medicine, 1953-67; attending psychiatrist Cin. Gen. Hosp., 1953-67; faculty Inst. Psychoanalysis, Chgo., 1957-67, So. Calif. Psychiat. Inst., Los Angeles, 1970—; chmn. research com. Hamilton County (Ohio) Diagnostic Center, 1958-67; prof. psychiatry, social sci. and social ecology, dept. psychiatry and human behavior U. Calif. - Irvine Coll. Medicine, 1967—, chmn. dept., 1967-78; also program dir. psychiat. residency tng.; dir. psychiat. services U. Calif. - Irvine Med. Center, 1967-78, dir. cons. and liaison program, 1978-87; sci. co-dir. U. Calif. - Irvine Med. Center (Nat. Alcoholism Research Center), 1978-84; Mem. clin. psychopharmacology study sect. NIMH, 1968-71; mem. research rev. com. Nat. Inst. Drug Abuse, 1973-77, Mental Health Study Center, 1978-84. Author: (with G. C. Gleser) The Measurement of Psychological States through the Content Analysis of Verbal Behavior, 1969, How to Understand and Analyze Your Own Dreams, 1975, Greek edit., 1978, Spanish edit., 1981, 3d rev. edit., 1985; editor: Comparative Psycholinguistic Analysis of Two Psychotherapeutic Interviews, 1961, (with A. H. Auerbach) Methods of Research in Psychotherapy, 1966, (with S. Merlis) Pharmacokinetics of Psychoactive Drugs: Blood Levels and Clinical Responses, 1976, Pharmacokinetics of Psychoactive Drugs: Further Studies, 1979, The Content Analysis of Verbal Behavior: Further Studies, 1979, (with F.L. McGuire and others) Drug Abuse Deaths in Nine Cities: A Survey Report, 1980; (with R. Cravey) Toxicological and Pathological Studies on Psychoactive Drug-Involved Deaths, 1980; (with Winget, Gleser and Lolas) Analisis de la Conducta Verbal, 1984; The Tree of Knowledge, 1985, (with F. Lolas and L.L. Viney) The Content Analysis of Verbal Behavior: Significance in Clinical Medicine and Psychiatry, 1986, (with Lolas) Estudios Sobre Analisis del Comportamiento Verbal, 1987, How to do Self-Analysis and Other Self-Psychotherapies, 1989; editorial bd. Psychosomatic Medicine, 1960-70, Psychiatry, 1967—, Am. Jour. Psychotherapy, 1975—; others; contbr. numerous articles to tech. lit. Recipient Hofheimer Research award, 1955, Franz Alexander Essay prize So. Calif. Psychoanalytic Inst., Los Angeles, 1973; Disting. Research award U. Calif. Irvine Alumni Assn., 1974; named Disting. Practitioner, Nat. Acad. Med. Practice, 1984; Rockefeller fellow Bellagio Study Ctr., Italy, 1985; NIMH Research Career award, 1960-67. Fellow AAAS, Am. Psychiat. Assn. (Found. Fund prize research 1978), Am. Coll. Neuropsychopharmacology, Am. Coll. Psychiatrists; mem. Assn. for Research Nervous and Mental Diseases, Am. Psychosomatic Soc., Cin. Soc. Neurology and Psychiatry (past pres.), Am. Psychoanalytic Assn., AMA, Orange County Med. Assn., So. Calif. Psychiat. Soc., Am. Assn. Child Psychoanalysts, So. Calif. Psychoanalytic Soc., Phi Beta Kappa, Sigma Xi, Alpha Omega Alpha., Omicron Delta Kappa. Clubs: Cosmos, Balboa Bay. Home: 4607 Perham Rd Corona Del Mar CA 92625 Office: U Calif Coll Medicine Dept Psychiatry & Human Behavior Irvine CA 92717

GOTTSCHALK, MAX JULES, new development specialist, industrial designer; b. St. Louis, Dec. 14, 1909; s. Max William and Kelmie (Mutrux) G.; m. Josephine Pipkin, 1933 (div. 1940); children: Sandra, Jules; m. Cecil Cornsweet, June 8, 1979. BA in Design, Washington U., St. Louis, 1933, postgrad. in psychology and history of art, 1936-38, Sch. Engring., 1942-44. With Knapp Monarch Elec. Co., St. Louis, 1934-36; chief tech. advisor govt. Nfld., Can., 1938-42; chief devel. engr. Hussman Co., St. Louis, 1942-44; sr. engr. devel. Walter Dorwin Teague, N.Y.C., 1942-44; chief engr. Gerald C. Johnson Assocs., N.Y.C., 1946-48; sr. engr. in charge field handling equipment Hughes Aircraft, Tucson, 1952-60; sr. research product design engr. Bell Aerosystems Co., Buffalo, 1962-64; pres. Max's Enterprises, 1986; instr. in design, drafting, perception, electronics, coordinator design and drafting dept., cons. sound recording systems Pima Coll., Tucson, 1967-77; prof., chmn., applied design dept. Pima Jr. Coll., Tucson, 1969-89; cons. Mark A. Simpson Mfg. Co., L.I., N.Y., 1944-52, Plymold Corp., Lawrence, Mass., Wheeldex Corp., White Plains, N.Y., Simpla Research and Mfg. Co., N.Y.C., 1944-52; cons. engr. Burr-Brown Research Corp., Lee Supply, 1964-67; lectr. Coop. Summer Coll., St. John's and Corner Brook, Nfld., 1937-39; cons. art and design Sullivan, Stauffer, Colwell and Bayless, Foote, Cone, and Belding, Gardner Advt., Darcy Advt., 1948-52; indsl. designs and devels. include: new modular chassis systems, electronic test equipment, paper towel holder, rotary card file, 1st open case frozen food refrigeration, 1st self service electronic checkout, use of cellophane for wrapping cheeses and meats, lunar escape vehicle, air cushion vehicle, curtain wall air cooling, intensive care cooling systems, electronics packaging systems; pres. Imagineering, Tucson, 1960—; chief engr. Godesca and Gottschalk Engring., 1970—; owner Max's Enterprises (M.E.), 1980—; work exhibited St. Louis Artist Guild, 1935, St. Louis Art Mus., 1936, St. John's, Can., 1940-42, Mus. Modern Art, N.Y.C., 1948-50, Internat. Canvas Exhibit, Tokyo, 1975, Pima Coll., Rosequist Wohlheim Gallery, Tucson, 1970—, Udinotti Gallery, Scottsdale, Ariz., San Francisco and L.A., Kaibob Art Gallery. Mem. Radio Engring. Soc., Plastic Engring. Soc., Audio Engring Soc. (life). Home: 5620 N Campbell Ave Tucson AZ 85718

GOTTSTEIN, BARNARD JACOB, retail and wholesale food company executive, real estate executive; b. Des Moines, Dec. 30, 1925; s. Jacob B. and Anna (Jacobs) G.; children—Sandra, James, Ruth Anne, David, Robert; m. Rachel Landau, July, 1986. B.A. in Econs. and Bus., U. Wash., 1949. Pres. J.B. Gottstein & Co., Anchorage, 1953—; chmn. bd. Carr-Gottstein Inc., Anchorage, 1974—; dir. United Bank Alaska, Anchorage, 1975-86. Commr. Alaska State Human Rights Commn, 1963-68; del. Dem. Nat. Conv., 1964, 68, 76, 88; committeeman Dem. Nat. Com., 1976-80; v.p. State Bd. Edn., Alaska, 1983-87, pres., 1987—. Served with USAF, 1944-45. Jewish. Office: J B Gottstein & Co 6411 A St Anchorage AK 99518

GOUBRAN, EMILE ZOLA, anatomy educator; b. Cairo, Nov. 26, 1942; came to U.S., 1979; s. Emile Goubran and Isis Zaki (Ibrahim) Khoury; m. Isabelle George Haddad, Oct. 23, 1969; children: Edmond, George. MD, Alexandria U., 1965, MS, 1970, PhD, 1973. Med. officer Egyptian Ministry Health, Cairo, 1966-67; demonstrator Alexandria (Egypt) U. Med. Sch., 1967-70, asst. lectr., 1970-73, lectr., 1973-75; lectr. Tripoli (Libya) Med. Sch., 1975-78; sr. lectr. Ahmadu Bello U. Med. Sch., Nigeria, 1978-79; assoc. prof. anatomy L.A. Coll. Chiropractic, Whittier, Calif., 1979-8l, prof., 198l—, chmn. basic scis., 198l—. Author: Introduction to Human Histology, 198l, Histology Laboratory Manual, 1982, Histology Study Guide, 1988, Anatomy II Study Guide, 1988. Mem. Egyptian Syndicate Physicians, AAAS, Inst. Noetic Scis., N.Y. Acad. Scis. Republican. Christian Orthodox. Office: LA Coll Chiropractic l6200 E Amber Valley Dr Whittier CA 90604

GOUGH, BRYAN RAY, graphic designer; b. San Rafael, Calif., Feb. 4, 1954; s. Robert Ray and Effie Scott (Kuehn) G.; m. Molly Diane Davis, July 18, 1987; 1 child, John Robert. BFA, U. Colo., 1976. Pvt. practice illustration & design Boulder, Colo., 1976-80; production artist Horizon Graphics & type Co., Boulder, 1980-84; designer, illustrator Communication Arts, Inc., Boulder, 1984-86, assoc., 1986—. Recipient merit award Art Dirs. Club Houston, 1985-86, award of excellence Art Dirs. Club Denver, 1986, 88, 88, cert. design excellence Print Mag., 1986, 88, award of excellence Dallas Soc. Visual Communications, 1986, cert. of distinction Art Direction Mag., 1986-87, Am. Corp. Identity/3 award 1987, cert. of merit Art Dirs. Club L.A., 1987, cert. of merit. Communication Arts Design Annual, 1988. Mem. Soc. Environ. Graphic Designers. Office: Communication Arts Inc 1112 Pearl St Boulder CO 80302

GOUGH, HARRISON GOULD, psychologist, educator; b. Buffalo, Minn., Feb. 25, 1921; s. Harry B. and Aelfreda (Gould) G.; m. Kathryn H. Whittier, Jan. 23, 1943; 1 child, Jane Kathryn Gough Rhodes. AB summa cum laude, U. Minn., 1942, AM (Social Sci. Research Council fellow 1946-47), 1947, PhD, 1949. Asst. prof. psychology U. Minn., 1948-49; asst. prof. U. Calif.-Berkeley, 1949-54, assoc. prof., 1954-60, prof., 1960-86, prof. emeritus, 1986—, assoc. dir. Inst. Personality Assessment and Research, 1964-67, dir., 1973-83, chmn. dept. psychology, 1967-72; cons. VA, 1951—; dir. cons. Psychologists Press, Inc., 1956—; mem. research adv. com. Calif. Dept. Corrections, 1958-64, Calif. Dept. Mental Hygiene, 1964-69, Gov.'s Calif. Adv. Com. Mental Health, 1968-74, citizens adv. council Calif. Dept. Mental Hygiene, 1968-71; clin. projects research review com. NIMH, 1968-72. Served to 1st lt. AUS, 1942-46. Recipient U. Calif. the Berkeley citation, 1986, Bruno Klopfer Disting. Contbn. award Soc. Personality Assessment, 1987; Fulbright research scholar, Italy, 1958-59, 65-66; Guggenheim fellow, 1965-66. Mem. Am., Western psychol. assns., Soc. Personality Assessment, Internat. Assn. Cross-Cultural Psychology, Académie National de Psychologie, Soc. Mayflower Desc., Phi Beta Kappa. Clubs: Commonwealth (San Francisco), Capital Hill (Washington). Author: Adjective Check List, California Psychological Inventory, other psychol. tests; chmn. bd. editors U. Calif. Publs. in Psychology, 1956-58; cons. editor Jour. Cons. and Clin. Psychology, 1956-74, 77-84, Jour. Abnormal Psychology, 1964-74, Jour. Personality and Social Psychology, 1981-84, Med. Tchr., 1978-84, Cahiers d'Anthropologie, 1978-84, Population and Environment: Behavioral and Social Issues, 1977-80; Current Psychol. Research and Revs., 1985-89, Pakistan Jour. Psychol. Research, 1985—, Jour. Personality Assessment, 1986—; assoc. editor Jour. Cross-Cultural Psychology, 1969-81. Home: PO Box 909 Pebble Beach CA 93953 Office: U Calif Dept Psychology Berkeley CA 94720

GOULD, CLIO LAVERNE, electric utility and irrigation dist. exec.; b. Madison, S.D., Feb. 20, 1919; s. Howard Bennett and Moneta Kay (Herrick) G.; student Walla Walla Coll., 1948, U. Wash. Extension, 1954, U. Calif. at San Diego Extension, 1962, Capital Radio Engring. Inst. Corr., 1958-62; diploma elec. engring. Internat. Corr. Schs., 1958; m. Mildred May Newell, Apr. 13, 1942; children—George Marcus, Deanna May (Mrs. Terry L. Paxton). With astronautics div. Gen. Dynamics Corp., San Diego, 1957-66, sr. design engr. research and devel. Atlas and Centaur space vehicles, 1958-66; supt. power and pumping depts. Wellton Mohawk Irrigation & Drainage Dist., Wellton, Ariz., 1966-76, gen. mgr., 1976—. treas. Liga Internat., Inc., San Diego, 1964-65; mem. Colorado River Task Force, 1987. Served with AUS, 1941-45; PTO. Recipient Performance award Gen. Dynamics Corp., 1963. Registered profl. engr., Ariz. Mem. IEEE (sr.), AIAA, Nat., Ariz. (pres. chpt. 1977-78) socs. profl. engrs., Photog. Soc. Am., Nat. Water Resources Assn., Ariz. State Reclamation Assn., Colorado River Water Users Assn. (bd. dirs. 1982—, exec. com. 1984—), Ariz. Agri-Bus. Council (exec. bd. 1980—, v.p. 1981). Republican. Seventh-day Adventist (elder 1956—, chmn. bldg. com. 1970-73). Home: Rte 1 Box 4 Wellton AZ 85356 Office: Rte 1 Box 19 Wellton AZ 85356

GOULD, GARY HOWARD, state official; b. Dayton, Oreg., Apr. 1, 1938; s. Calvin J. and Alice Viola G.; student North Idaho Coll., 1957-59; B.A. in Govt., Idaho State U., 1965, M.A. in Edn., 1971; m. Marcella Jean Gould, July 24, 1963; children—Susan Marie, Jon Calvin. Dir. fin. aids and scholarships Idaho State U., 1969-78, spl. asst. to v.p. for adminstrn., 1978-79; ins. agent, realtor Paul Smith Agy., Pocatello, Idaho, 1979—; mem. Idaho Ho. of Reps., 1977-80, Idaho Senate, 1980-84; dir. Idaho Dept. Labor and Indsl. Services, 1984—. Precinct committeeman, Bannock County, Idaho, 1972-74; chmn. Democratic Central Com., 1974-77. Served with U.S. Army, 1959-61. Mem. Idaho Realtors Assn., Ind. Ins. Agts. Assn., Western Council State Legislators, Phi Delta Kappa. 116 Clubs: Masons (Scottish Rite 32 deg.), Elks. Office: Idaho Dept Labor Statehouse Mail 2401 Ellis Ave Boise ID 83720

GOULD, JAMES WARREN, international relations educator; b. Boulder, Colo., May 14, 1924; s. Douglas W. and Elsa (Dohne) G.; m. Anne Garrison, Jan. 5, 1951; children: Robert D., Steven C., Christopher W., C. Linn, Elizabeth A. Cert. des etudes, U. Paris, 1946; AB, U. Pa., 1946; MA, Fletcher Sch. Law and Diplomacy, 1947, PhD, 1955. Fgn. service officer U.S. Fgn. Service, Sumatra, Hong Kong and Java, 1947-52; internat. oil legislator Mobil Oil Co., N.Y.C., 1955; asst. prof. internat. relations Claremont (Calif.) Men's Coll., 1955-60; assoc. prof. Scripps Coll., Claremont, 1960-64, prof., 1967—; Fulbright prof. U. Munich, 1960-61. Author: The U.S. and Malaysia, 1969, Americans in Sumatra, 1960, America Interests in Sumatra, 1955, Altruistic Statecraft, 1986. Chmn. Coalition for Peace with Justice, Pomona Valley, Calif., 1985, 86; coordinator Interfaith Peace Ctr., Pomona Valley, 1986; sec. Interfaith Legis. Action, Pomona Valley, 1985-86, pres., 1988; bd. dirs. Peace Corps, Malaysia, 1964-66, Council of Chs., Pomona Valley, 1979—. Served as sgt. inf. U.S. Army, 1941-45, ETO. Fellow Asia Found., 1953; Fulbright Found., 1959, Danforth Found., 1963. Mem. Consortium on Peace Research and Edn., Conf. Peace Research in History, Internat. Peace Research Assn., UN Assn. (v.p. 1965—). Mem. Soc. of Friends. Office: Scripps Coll Dept Internat Rels Claremont CA 91711

GOULD, JOHN BRANT, lawyer, accountant; b. Pitts., Nov. 21, 1955; s. Albert William and Jane (Oellig) G.; m. Jana King, Mar. 21, 1981. BS in Bus. Adminstrn., Portland State U., 1980; JD cum laude, Lewis and Clark Coll., 1987. Bar: Oreg.1987; CPA, Oreg. Auditor, tax researcher Arthur Young and Co., Portland, Oreg., Moss Adams, Portland; ind. CPA Portland, 1981—; bd. dirs. Go Ye Air Service, Inc.; disting. guest lectr. Portland Community Coll., 1984. Eagle scout Boy Scouts Am.; bd. dirs. Christian Conciliation Service, Portland, 1985—. Served with USN. Mem. Chamber Music Soc. Oreg. (bd. dirs. 1987—), Delta Tau Delta. Club: U.S.A. Oreg. Athletic. Home: 3800 SW Kilkenny Dr Lake Oswego OR 97034

GOULD, MARTHA B., librarian; b. Claremont, N.H., Oct. 8, 1931. BA in Edn., U. Mich., 1953; MS in Library Sci., Simmons Coll., 1956; cert., U. Denver Library Sch. Community Analysis Research Inst., 1978. Childrens librarian N.Y. Pub. Library, 1956-58; adminstr. library services act demonstration regional library project Pawhuska, Okla., 1958-59; cons. N.Mex. State Library, 1959-60; childrens librarian then sr. childrens librarian Los Angeles Pub. Library, 1960-72; acctg. dir. pub. srvices, reference librarian Nev. State Library, 1972-74; pub. services librarian Washoe County (Nev.) Library, 1974-79, asst. county librarian, 1979-84, county librarian, 1984—. Contbr. articles to jours. Treas. United Jewish Appeal, 1981; bd. dirs. Temple Sinai, RSVP; trustee N. Nevadans for ERA. Recipient Nev. State Library Letter of Commendation, 1973, Washoe County Bd. Commrs. Resolution of Appreciation, 1978. Mem. ALA (bd. dirs. intellectual freedom round table 1977-79, intellectual freedom com. 1979-83, council 1983-86), Nev. Library Assn. (chmn. pub. info. com. 1972-73, intellectual freedom com. 1975-78, govt. relations com. 1978-79, v.p., pres.-elect 1980, pres. 1981, Spl. Citation 1978, 87), ACLU (bd. dirs., Civil Libertarian of Yr. Nev. chpt.), NCCJ (chair No. div. govs. conf. for women 1989). Office: Washoe Country Libr 301 S Center St PO Box 2151 Reno NV 89505

GOULD, MAXINE LUBOW, lawyer, marketing professional, consultant; b. Bridgeton, N.J., Feb. 28, 1942; d. Louis A. and Bernice L. (Goldberg) Lubow; B.S., Temple U., 1962, J.D., 1968; m. Sam C. Gould, June 17, 1962 (div. Dec. 1984); children—Jack, Herman, David. Head resident dept. student personnel Temple U., 1962-66; dir., treas. Hilltop Interest Program, Inc., Los Angeles, 1973-74; law clk. law firms, Los Angeles, 1975-77; with Buffalo Resources Corp., Los Angeles, 1978-82, corp. sec., 1979-82; corp. sec., securities prin. Buffalo Securities Corp., Los Angeles, 1979-82; corp. sec. LaMaur Devel. Corp., Los Angeles, 1979-82; contracts analyst, land dept. Texaco Inc., Los Angeles, 1982-83; exec. dir. Sinai Temple, West Los Angeles, 1983-85; pres. Cutting Edge, Los Angeles, 1986; adminstr. law firm Robinson, Wolas & Diamant, Century City, 1986, acctg. firm Roth, Bookstein & Zaslow, Los Angeles, 1986-87; project coordinator Cipher, 1987; mktg. dir. Am. Bus. Capital, Beverly Hills, Calif., 1988—. Mem. Roscomare Valley Assn. Edn. Com., Bel Air, Calif., 1975-76; subcom. chmn. Roscomare Rd. Sch. Citizens Adv. Council, Bel Air; active various community drives. Recipient Joseph B. Wagner Oratory award B'nai B'rith, 1959, Voice of Democracy award, 1958-59, award Commentator Club, 1959. Mem. ABA (law office econs. sect.), Los Angeles Bar Assn. (assoc., law office econs. sect.), Nat. Assn. Legal Adminstrs. (Beverly Hills chpt.), Nat. Assn. Female Execs. (network dir.), Nat. Assn. Law Firm Mktg. Adminstrs., Calif. Women Lawyers, Women in Bus. (co-chmn. membership com.), Calif. CPA Soc. (adminstr. com.), Nat. Assn. Synagogue Adminstrs., Am. Assn. Petroleum Landmen, Los Angeles Assn. Petroleum Landmen, Textile Profl. Soc., Comml. Fin. Assn., Phi Alpha Theta, Alpha Lambda Delta. Jewish. Home: 2501 Roscomare Los Angeles CA 90077 Office: Am Bus Capital 400 S Beverly Dr #208 Beverly Hills CA 90212

GOULD, ROBERT JAY, video production executive, lawyer; b. N.Y.C., May 8, 1946; s. Harry E. and Lucille (Quartucy) G.; m. Charlotte Edith Horton, June 9, 1979; children: Brandon Jay, Loren Blake. BA, Harvard U., 1967; JD, Columbia U., 1970. Bar: N.Y. 1971. Assoc. Guggenheimer & Untermeyer, N.Y.C., 1971; v.p., gen. counsel Gould Paper Corp., N.Y.C., 1975-77; pres. Visions Ltd. & MultiVisions Inc., Anchorage, 1977-85; owner The Bralor Group, Anchorage, 1985—; pres. The Videoplex, Anchorage, 1986—, Connections, Ltd., Anchorage, 1988—. Bd. dirs. Performing Arts Ctr., Anchorage, 1987—. Served to lt. JAGC, USN, 1971-75.

GOULDING, MERRILL KEITH, engineer, consultant; b. Erie, Pa., Jan. 21, 1933; s. Forest Clute and Felicita Clara (Johnson) G.; BS, UCLA, 1968, PhD, 1979; children: Merrill, Robert, Nida, Gina. Asst. to v.p. Internat. Controls Corp., 1963-69; chmn. bd. Village Verde Corp., 1963-64; pres. Merrill K. Goulding & Assocs., Inc., Los Angeles, 1974—; chief exec. officer Coin Cop Electronics Co., 1975-88; bd. dirs. Mid City Travel Industry; cons. FAA, DOT, DNA. Bd. dirs. Rio Hondo Area Action Com., 1970; guiding counselor Inst. Cultural Affairs; past pres. Request Computer Users Group. Served with USMC, 1953. Registered profl. engr., N.Y., Calif. Mem. ASME, IEEE, AIAA, NSPE, Calif. Soc. Profl. Engrs., Am. Soc. Metals, Constrn. Specifications Inst., Soc. Material and Process Engrs., Vols. in Tech. Assistance, Mensa, Am. Legion, Blue and Gold Circle Alumni Assn. UCLA. Republican. Clubs: Calif. Yacht. Lodges: Shriners, Los Angeles Consistory. Address: PO Box 577 Glendale CA 91209

GOULDTHORPE, KENNETH ALFRED PERCIVAL, publisher; b. London, Jan. 7, 1928; s. Alfred Edward and Frances Elizabeth Finch (Callow) G.; came to U.S., 1951, naturalized, 1956; m. Judith Marion Cutts, Aug. 9, 1975; children: Amanda Frances, Timothy Graham Cutts. Student U. London, 1948-49, Bloomsbury Tech. Inst., 1949-50; diploma City and Guilds of London, 1949; student, Washington U., 1951-53. Staff photographer St. Louis Post-Dispatch, 1951-55, picture editor, 1955-57; nat. and fgn. corr. Life mag., Time, Inc., N.Y.C., 1957-65, regional editor Australia-New Zealand, 1966-68, editorial dir. Latin Am., 1969-70; editor Signature mag., N.Y.C., 1970-73; mng. editor Penthouse mag., N.Y.C., 1973-76, pub. cons., 1976-79; editor, exec. pub. Adventure Travel mag., Seattle, 1979-80; sr. ptnr. Pacific Pub. Assocs., Seattle, 1981-83; editor, pub. Washington mag., 1984-89; vice chmn. Evergreen Pub. Co., 1984-89; tchr. design, editorial techniques Parsons Sch. Design, N.Y.C.; lectr. Served with Royal Navy, 1946-48. Decorated Naval Medal and bar; recipient awards of excellence Nat. Press Photographers Assn., AP and UP, 1951-57; certs. excellence, Am. Inst. Graphic Arts, 1971, 72, 73, Communication Arts, 1980, 81, 84; spl. award, N.Y. Soc. Publs. Designers, 1980. Mem. Regional Pubs. Assn. (v.p., pres., Best Typography award 1985), Western Publs. Assn. (Best Consumer Mag. award, Best Travel Mag. awards, 1980, Best Regional and State Mag. award 1985, 86, 88, Best New Publ. award 1985, Best Column award 1985, Best Signed Essay 1986, 87, Best Four-Color Layout 1985, Best Four Color Feature Design), City and Regional Mag. Assn. (William Allen White Bronze awards), Time/Life Alumni Soc., Sigma Delta Chi. Episcopalian. Nominated for Pulitzer Prize for coverage of Andrea Doria disaster, 1956; contbr. articles, photographs to nat. mags., books by Life mag. Home: 3049 NW Esplanade Seattle WA 98117

GOULET, WILLIAM DAWSON, marketing professional; b. Hartford, Conn., Sept. 24, 1941; s. Henry J.K. and Elizabeth Bryne (Dawson) G. BA in English, Marietta Coll., 1963. Field service rep. Conn. Gen. Life Ins. Co., Hartford, 1963-65; sales promotion assoc. Phoenix Mut. Life Ins. Co., Hartford, 1965-69; dir. sales promotion Pacific Nat. Life Ins. Co., San Francisco, 1969-70; v.p. sales and mktg. E.F. Hutton Life Ins. Co., San Francisco, 1970-79; sr. v.p., fin. planning Prudential-Bache, San Francisco, 1979; v.p. GUMP's, San Francisco, 1980—, mem. exec. com., 1981—; pres. Campton Advt. Agy., 1980—; dean ins. faculty Life Ins. Industry Sch., Williamsburg, Va., 1974; mktg. cons. U. of the Pacific, Stockton, Calif., 1972-80. bd. dirs. Mus. Soc. San Francisco; v.p. bd. Friends of Recreation and Parks, 1986—; mem. adv. bd. The McLean Home, Simsbury, Conn., 1985—; mem. hon. bd. govs. The World Corp. Games, San Francisco, 1988. Served to sgt. USAR, 1963-69. Recipient Lawrence award Life Advertisers Assn., Vancouver, B.C., Can., 1979, Disting. Alumni Lectr. award Marietta Coll., 1985. Mem. San Francisco Grand Prix Assn. (adv. bd. 1986—), Western Retail Mktg. Assn. (bd. dirs. 1989—). Democrat. Roman Catholic. Home: PO Box 155 Ross CA 94957 Office: GUMP's 250 Post St San Francisco CA 94108

GOUNDER, RAJ N., aerospace engineer; b. Erode, Tamilnadu, India, Jan. 15, 1944; m. Nicole Andre Pantanelli, Oct. 7, 1972; Children: Celine, Sabine, Stephanie. BSc, U. Madras, India, 1964; BE, Indian Inst. of Sci, Bangalore, India, 1967; MASc, U. Toronto, Toronto, Can., 1968; PhD, Northwestern U., 1972. Rsch. Assoc. Lord Corp., Erie, Pa., 1972-77; sr. tech. staff Sikorsky Helicopters, Stratford, Conn., 1977-79; adv. composites mgr. RCA Astro-Elect., Princeton, N.J., 1979-81; structures & Materials mgr. RCA Astro-Elect., Princeton, 1981-84, spl. programs mgr., 1984-85; mech. subsystem mgr. Boeing Aerospace, Seattle, 1985-87, structures & thermal mgr., 1987—; lectr. spacecraft design RCA Astrop-Elect. Princeton, 1983-85; chmn. AIAA Panel, space & missile investment strategy, 1988—. Author: 40 tech. papers; patentee: 6 U.S. patents; authors and inventors award 1982, 1984. Mem. U.S. Jaycees, Erie, 1973-76. Mem. AIAA, SAMPE. United Methodist. Office: Boeing Aerospace PO Box 3999 Seattle WA 98042

GOURLEY, RONALD ROBERT, architect, educator; b. St. Paul, Oct. 5, 1919; s. Robert Thomas and Eva Irene (Cardle) G.; m. Phyllis Mary McDonald, Apr. 10, 1950; children: Robert McDonald, Karen Ellen, Geoffrey James. BArch, U. Minn., 1943; MArch, Harvard U., 1948. Instr. architecture MIT, Cambridge, 1948-53; vis. prof. Royal Acad., Copenhagen, Denmark, 1952; prof. architecture Harvard U., 1953-70; ptnr., co-founder Sert, Jackson & Gourley, Cambridge, 1958-64, Integrated Design Svcs. Group, Cambridge, 1966-72; ptnr. Gourley/Richmond, 1972-76, Gourley, Richmond & Mitchell, 1976-82; tech. coord. Boston Archtl. Ctr., 1976-77; prof. architecture U. Ariz., Tucson, 1977—, dean Coll. Architecture, 1977-87, pres. Architecture Lab., 1986-89; pvt. practice Cambridge, 1954-58, 64-66. Prin. works include U. N.H. Meml. Union Bldg., Harvard U. Married Student Housing (Nat. Honor award AIA 1965), Cunningham Found. Bldg., Radcliffe Coll. Faculty Housing (Nat. Honor award AIA 1973), Brookline (Mass.) Pub. Libr., Kingston Housing for Elderly, Wheaton Coll. Libr., Mass. Hosp Sch. Recreation Bldg. With AUS, 1944-46. Fellow AIA; mem. Boston Archtl. Ctr. (hon.). Home: 2522 E 3d St Tucson AZ 85716 also: Middle Rd Martha's Vineyard Chilmark MA 02535 Office: U Ariz Coll Architecture Tucson AZ 85721

GOURLIE, REBECCA ELIZABETH, writer, editor; b. Tampa, Fla., Oct. 19, 1948; d. Phillip James O'Reagan and Rosalind Theresa (Gallo) Field; m. Dale Ray Gourlie, Oct. 19, 1965; children: Jordan Dale, Heather Noelle, Meagan Nicole, Brian David. M in Journalism, UCLA, 1974. Dist. asst. Am. Internat. Pictures, Hollywood, Calif., 1965-68; property asst. Paramount Pictures, Beverly Hills, Calif., 1968-71; writer, prodn. asst. Mark VII Prodns., Universal City, Calif., 1971-76; editor Tile & Decorative Surfaces Mag., Hollywood, 1976-82; writer Aries Prodns., Pacific Palisade, Calif., 1982—. Mem. Burbank (Calif.) Kennel Club (v.p. 1975-78). Republican. Roman Catholic. Office: Aries Prodns 919 Rivas Canyon Pacific Palisades CA 90222

GOURSAUD, ANNE RENEE MAURICETTE DOMINIQUE, film editor; b. Tours, France; came to U.S., 1979.; d. Leon and Madeleine (Boutin) G.; divorced. Licence D'Histoire De L'Art, U. Sorbonne, Paris, 1968, MA in Fine Arts, 1970; MA in Fine Arts, Columbia U., 1973. Editor: (Film) The Night the Lights Went Out in Georgia, 1980, One From the Heart, 1981, Outsiders, 1982-83, Am. Dreamer, 1983-84, Just Between Friends, 1985-86, Crimes of the Heart, 1986 (3 acad. award nominations), Ironweed, 1987 (2 acad. award nominations), Her Alibi, 1988. Mem. Acad. Motion Picture Arts and Scis., Am. Cinema Editors.

GOWERS, MONT A., home improvement company executive; b. Eureka, Utah, Oct. 27, 1915; s. Alfred Joseph and Laura (Hinckley) G.; m. Rachel Smith, June 1936 (div. Dec. 1945); 1 child, Jane Gowers Bogdanoff; m. Mary Jane Roeder, Dec. 21, 1946 (dec. June 1987); children: Richard M., Robyn Gowers White. Student mktg., George Washington U., 1946-47; BS in Bus., U. Utah, 1948. Salesman Ketchum Builders Supply, Salt Lake City, 1936-37; br. sales mgr. Union Lime & Material Co., Ogden, Utah, 1938-39; mgr. Morrison Merrill & Co., Salt Lake City, 1940-44; naval recruiter Naval Supply Depot, Clearfield, Utah, 1944-45; hardware rep. Vimcar Sales Co.,

L.A., 1948-54; sales mgr. Utah Lumber Co., Salt Lake City, 1954-69; owner, mgr. A.A. Home Improvement Co., Inc., Salt Lake City, 1969—, Vulcan Distbg. Co., Salt Lake City, 1972—. With U.S. Army, 1945-46. Mem. Utah Home Improvement Coun. (pres. 1979-8l), Nat. Fedn. Ind. Bus. (guardian), South Salt Lake C. of C. (pres. 1958), Hoo Hoo Lumbermans Club (pres. l960), Footprinters Club, Elks (chmn. charities Salt Lake City 1958-59, exalted ruler l959-60, pres. Utah chpt. 1967-68, dist. dep. 1968-69), Beta Theta Pi. Republican. Mormon. Home: l8l0 E 27th South St Salt Lake City UT 84106 Office: AA Home Improvement Co Inc 465l Riverside Dr Unit l0 Murray UT 84107

GOYER, ROBERT STANTON, communication educator; b. Kokomo, Ind., Oct. 7, 1923; s. Clarence V. and Genevieve M. (Sober) G.; m. Patricia Ann Stutz, Aug. 12, 1950; children: Karen, Susan, Linda, Amy. BA, DePauw U., 1948; MA, Miami U., Oxford, Ohio, 1950; PhD, Ohio State U., 1955. Instr. Miami U., Oxford, 1949-51; instr., then asst. prof. Ohio State U., Columbus, 1955-58, rsch. assoc., cons. rsch. found., 1956-63; from asst. to assoc. to prof. Purdue U., Lafayette, Ind., 1958-66; prof. Ohio U., Athens, 1966-81, dir. ctr. communication studies, 1966-74, 79-81, assoc. dean grad. coll., 1978, dean grad. coll., acting dir. rsch., 1979, acting assoc. provost grad. and rsch. programs, 1979; chmn. dept. communication Ariz. State U., Tempe, 1981-89, prof., 1981—; cons. in field. Author books; contbr. articles to profl. jours. 1st lt. U.S. Army, 1943-46, 52-53. Decorated Bronze Star. Fellow Internat. Communication Assn. (past pres.), AAAS; mem. Am. Psychol. Assn., Acad. Mgmt., Speech Communication Assn. Presbyterian. Home: 517 W Summit Pl Chandler AZ 85224 Office: Ariz State U Dept Communication Tempe AZ 85287

GRABARZ, DONALD FRANCIS, pharmacist; b. Jersey City, Sept. 18, 1841; s. Joseph and Frances (Zotynia) G.; m. Joan Isoldi, Aug. 13, 1966; children: Christine, Robert, Danielle. BPharm, St. Johns U., N.Y.C., 1964. Lic. pharmacist, N.Y., Vt. Dir. qualtiy control and assurance Johnson and Johnson Co., New Brunswick, N.J., 1965-72; dir. quality assurance and regulatory affairs Bard Parker div. Becton Dickinson, Franklin Lakes, N.J., 1972-80; asst. corp. dir. regulatory affairs Becton Dickinson, 1972-80; corp. dir. regulatory affairs C.R. Bard Inc., Murray Hill, N.J., 1980-85; v.p. regulatory affairs, qualtiy assurance Symbion Inc., Salt Lake City, 1985-86; cons. DFG & Assocs., Salt Lake City, 1986—; lectr. Inst. for Applied Tech. Author, editor Inspection and Recall Film. Bd. dirs. v.p., asst. treas. Am. Lung Assn., N.J., 1972-75; chmn. Drug Edn., DuPage County, Ill., 1968. Mem. Health Industry Mfg. Assn. (chmn. Legal and Regulatory commn. 1983), Regulatory Affairs Profl. Soc., Am. Soc. Quality Control, Am. Mfr. Med. Instrumentation Assn., Am. Pharm. Assn. Office: DFG & Assocs PO Box 17801 Salt Lake City UT 84117-0801

GRACE, CORINNE BISSETTE, oil and gas owner; b. Middlesex, N.C., Nov. 9, 1929; d. Oscar and Mary (Massey) Bissette; m. Michael Paul Grace II, April 26, 1954 (div. 1987); children: Michael Paul III, Corinne Yvonne, Winston R., Janette Patrice, John Zacharias. BA, U. N.C., 1952. Ptnr. Grace Oil, Dallas and Carlsbad, N.Mex., 1961-83; owner Grace Oil, Carlsbad, 1983—. Sponsor various civic orgns.; mem. Centennial Planning Bd. and Spl. Events Com., U. N.C., Greensboro, 1988—. Mem. Carlsbad C. of C., N.Mex. Oil and Gas Engring. Com., Ind. Petroleum Assn. N.Mex., N.Mex. Geol. Soc., Riverside Country Club. Office: Grace Oil 3722 National Parks Hwy Carlsbad NM 88220

GRACE, JOHN WILLIAM, electrical company executive; b. Swissville, Pa., May 29, 1921; s. Joseph and Ruth Margaret (Bailey) G.; student Am. TV Inst. Tech., 1950; BEE, Drexel U., 1960; m. Ruth Delores Schroeder, Nov. 25, 1950; children: Martha, Joan, Nancy, John William. Technician missiles and surface radar div. RCA, Moorestown, N.J., 1950-56, design engr., 1956-60, project engr., 1960-66; mgr. engring. and sci. exec. EG & G, Inc., Las Vegas, Nev., 1966-73, mgr. bus. devel. operational test and evaluation, Albuquerque, 1973-77; engring. mgr. Instrumentation div., Idaho Falls, Idaho, 1977-79, mgr. systems project office, 1979, mgr. instrumentation program office, 1979-82, mgr. engring. spl. products div., 1982-84, mgr. tech. resources, 1984—. Active Boy Scouts Am., 1969-71. Served with USNR, 1941-45. Mem. IEEE, Instrument Soc. Am. (dir. sci. instrumentation and research div.), Assn. Old Crows, Am. Legion (post adj. vice comdr. 1950). Episcopalian (pres. couples retreat 1969-70). Patentee contradirectional waveguide coupler. Home: 2900 S Valley View 154 Las Vegas NV 89102 Office: EG&G Spl Projects Div 2755E Desert Inn Las Vegas NV 89121

GRACE, ROBIN M., venture capitalist; b. N.Y.C., May 26, 1951; d. Robert Morgan and Jane Ewing (Rovensky)úG.; m. Thomas G. B. Wheelock, DEc. 20, 1974 (div. Nov. 1978). BA, Prescott Coll., 1972; MBA, UCLA, 1983. Assoc. Warburg, Paribas & Becker, Century City, Calif., 1982-84; ptnr. The Phoenix Ptnrs., Seattle, 1983-84; v.p. Vanaar, Inc., Santa Monica, Calif., 1984-85; v.p. mktg. and sales Bitstream, Inc., Cambridge, Mass., 1985-87; gen. ptnr. The Rainbow Investment Fund, Santa Monica, 1983—; chmn. bd. dirs. Magic Years Child Care & Learning Ctrs., Inc., Plains, Pa., 1987—. Office: The Rainbow Investment Fund 528 San Vincente Blvd Santa Monica CA 90402

GRACIAS, MAURICE, economist; b. Nairobi, Kenya, July 16, 1923; came to U.S., 1969, naturalized, 1975; s. John Ludgero and Olga Rosalina (Themudo) G.; m. Angela Coutinho, Aug. 22, 1954; children: Loretta, Belinda, Marina. BA, U. Internat. Studies, Geneva, 1962; postgrad., Inst. Transport, London, 1956. Asst. to controller East African Rys. and Harbours, Nairobi, 1948-63; contr. East African Rd. Svcs., Nairobi, 1963-65; chief auditor U.S. State Dept., Africa, 1965-69, Econ. Devel. Orgn., San Francisco, 1970-71; sr. acct. Coopers & Lybrand CPAs, Oakland, Calif., 1969; corp. audit mgr. Blue Cross, Oakland, 1971-80; owner, pres. Gracias & Assocs., Oakland, 1976—; bd. dirs. Land Title Ins. Co., Oakland, 1986-88; pres. Internat. Investment Assocs., Oakland, 1976—; cons. Asian Devel. Bank, U.N., 1978—, coord. econ. devel. funding projects with U.N., World Bank, European Econ. Commn., White House Conf. on Small Bus., 1979, 86. Author: Life-Search for Its Glory, 1989; contbr. articles to newspaper publs. Active local Roman Cath. Ch., community affairs; pres. Goan Inst., Inc., San Francisco, 1975-78. Named Outstanding Immigrant to U.S., Calif. State Legislature, 1978; Royal Econ. Soc. fellow, Eng., 1964-68. Republican.

GRACIDA, JOAQUIN CHAUSSEE, marine corps officer, information systems specialist; b. Mexico City, June 14, 1940; came to U.S., 1958, naturalized, 1962; s. Joaquin O. and Esperanza (Chaussee) G.; m. Ann Marie Smith, May 11, 1963; children: Joaquin Gerard, Leon Edward. BS in Math., U. Idaho, 1966; MA in Counseling, Pepperdine U., 1976; MS in Computer Sci., Naval Postgrad. Sch., 1978. Enlisted USMC, 1958, advanced through grades to col., 1987; programming analyst, hdqrs. USMC, Washington, 1978-81; sr. analyst, fin. ctr. USMC, Kansas City, Mo., 1981-83; dep. dir. Regional Automated Services Ctr. USMC, Camp Pendleton, Calif., 1983-86, dir., 1986-88; asst. chief staff MWR Services, MCB Camp Butler, Okinawa, Japan, 1988—; instr. data processing Johnson County (Kans.) Community Coll., 1981-83, Miracosta Coll., Oceanside, Calif., 1983-84. Mem. Cardiff (Calif.) Town Council, 1986-87. Mem. Data Processing Mgmt. Assn. Republican. Roman Catholic. Lodge: Elks. Address: HQSVS BN MCB Camp Butler FPO Seattle WA 98773

GRACY, MICHAEL LEE, sales executive; b. Burbank, Calif., Oct. 20, 1962; s. Russell Lee Gracy and Janet Lucille (Pohren) Myers. Asst. mgr. Mt. Waterman Ski Lifts, La Canada, Calif., 1980-82; fire fighter U.S. Forest Svc., La Canada, 1982-83; mgr. West Coast Electric Sales, Inc., Burbank, 1983—; owner On-Line Guns & Munitions, Burbank, 1985-87. Mem. Nat. Assn. Federally Lic. Firearms Dealers. Republican. Office: West Coast Electric Sales 2802 N Naomi St Burbank CA 91504

GRAD, LAURIE BURROWS, food editor; b. L.A., June 17, 1944; d. Abe and Ruth (Levinson) Burrows; m. Peter N. Grad, Feb. 11, 1968; 1 child, Nicholas Newfield. BA, U. Pa., 1966. Fashion model N.Y.C., 1965-67, food writer, 1973—; food editor L.A. Mag., 1977—; TV chef Hour Mag., L.A., 1980-87. Author: Dining in Los Angeles, 1979, Make it Easy in the Kitchen, 1982, Make it Easy Entertaining, 1984 (Tastemaker award 1985), Make it Easy, Make it Light, 1987. Mem. Mem. Am. Inst. Wine and Food, Internat. Assn. Cooking Profls., Alzheimer's Disease and Related Disorders Assn. (hon. bd. dirs.). Home: 1250 Beverly Green Dr Los Angeles CA 90035

GRADIN, JOSEPH LLOYD, microbiologist; b. Portland, Oreg., Nov. 22, 1941; s. Melvin Daniel and Amy Lillian (Noreen) G.; m. Claudia N. James, June 24, 1967. BS, Oreg. State U., 1973, MS, 1976. Rsch. asst. Coll. Vet. Medicine, Oreg. State U., Corvallis, 1974-84, sr. rsch. asst., 1984—. Contbr. articles to profl. publs. Bd. dirs. 1st Bapt. Ch., Philomath, Oreg., 1977—, moderator, 1978—; capt. Mounted Posse, Corvallis, 1981, sec.-treas., 1983-85. Mem. Am. Soc. Microbiology, Arabian Horse Breeders Oreg. (bd. dirs. 1978-81). Republican. Home: 23869 Neuman Rd Corvallis OR 97333 Office: Oreg State U Coll Vet Medicine Corvallis OR 97331-4802

GRAF, ERVIN DONALD, municipal administrator; b. Crow Rock, Mont., Mar. 9, 1930; s. Emanuel and Lydia (Bitz) G.; m. Carolyn Sue Robinson, Mar. 15, 1956 (div. 1958); m. Eleanor Mahlein, Apr. 13, 1959; children: Debra, Belinda, Corrina, Melanie, Ervin Jr. Enlisted U.S. Army, 1948; served two tours of duty in Vietna; ret. U.S. Army, 1972; with office and maintenance staff Greenfields Irrigation Dist., Fairfield, Mont., 1972-77, sec. to Bd. Commrs., 1977—. Decorated Bronze star with oak leaf cluster. Mem. Am. Legion (all offices Post #80 and Dist. 8 incl. dist. comdr.). Democrat. Lutheran. Home: 211 6th St N Fairfield MT 59436 Office: Greenfields Irrigation Dist Central Ave W Fairfield MT 59436

GRAF, OTTO WALTER, JR., retired entomologist, biologist, educator; b. San Francisco, May 26, 1925; s. Otto Walter and Mildred Ilyne (Morrison) G.; m. Anne Marie Minaker, Mar. 7, 1953; children: Catherine, David, Paul, Lloyd, John, Walter, Matthew, Robert. AB, San Francisco State Coll., 1952; MA, U. San Francisco, 1979; postgrad. Stanford U., Duke U., U. Calif., Berkeley, Calif. State U., Hayward. Secondary teaching credential, Calif. Profl. asst. San Francisco State Coll., 1950-51; film librarian, supr. student sect. Calif. Acad. Scis., 1954-62; instr. U. Calif., Berkeley, 1956-61, Washington High Sch., Fremont, Calif. 1955-84. Active Boy Scouts Am., Rep. Party. With USN, 1943-46; to 1st lt., U.S. Army, 1951-54. Decorated Pacific Theatre ribbon, Am. Theatre ribbon, Korean ribbon, 2 Presidential Unit citations, Presidential citation, Korean Merit citation; recipient Silver Beaver award, Boy Scouts Am., 1971; Outstanding Secondary Tchr. award, 1974; NSF grantee; Biol. Scis. Curriculum Studies grantee. Mem. Pan Pacific Entomol. Soc., Nat. Sci. Tchrs. Assn., Korean War Vets. Assn., Nat. Assn. Biology Tchrs., E. Africa Wild Life Soc., Internat. Wildlife Fedn., Nat. Wildlife Fedn., VFW, Am. Legion. Roman Catholic. Author: Key to the Mosquitos of Korea, 1951, Flies of Medical and Veternary Importance of Japan & Korea, 1952; Nature Games for the Secondary School, 1979; designed trap for live mice in Korea. Home: 5151 Tenaya Ave Newark CA 94560-2653

GRAFF, MARC DAVID, psychiatrist, educator; b. Chgo., Nov. 2, 1948; s. Norman and Phyllis Lenore (Firestone) G.; m. Laura Lee Kunstler, Sept. 24, 1972; children: Rebecca Sara, Benjamin Louis. Student, Coll. of San Mateo, 1965-67; BA in Zoology with honors, U. Calif., Berkeley, 1970; postgrad., U. Wis., 1971; MD, U. Chgo., 1974. Diplomate Am. Bd. Psychiatry and Neurology. Intern U. Rochester (N.Y.), 1974-75, resident in psychiatry, 1975-78; asst. prof. psychiatry Western Psy. Inst. and Clinic, U. Pitts., 1978-80; grad. fellow Rand Grad. Inst., Santa Monica, Calif., 1980; cons. Rand Corp., Santa Monica, 1981; pvt. practice Inglewood, Calif., 1981-83, Van Nuys, Calif., 1983-; asst. clin. prof. Neuropsychiat. Inst., UCLA, 1983--. Mem. profl. adv. bd. peer counseling orgn. Thishpachah Sh'lemah,Temple Ahavat Shalom, Northridge, Calif., 1987—. Mem. Am. Psychiat. Assn., So. Calif. Psychiat. Soc. (co-chmn. pub. info. com. 1986-88), Assn. for Pub. Policy Analysis, AAAS, Calif. Turble and Tortoise Club (v.p. San Fernando Valley chpt. 1982-83, pres. Canoga Park 1983--). Democrat. Home: 17259 Ballinger St Northridge CA 91325 Office: So Calif Permanente Med Grp 13746 Victory Blvd Van Nuys CA 91401

GRAF VON AHNENBERG, FRANCIS, computer information scientist; b. Vienna, Va., Dec. 13, 1948; s. Phillip and Gertrude E. (Von Dvorak) Graf Von A. MA in History, MA in Sociology/Psychology, U. Paris, 1971, MA in Philosophy, 1973; PhD in Scis., U. Holistic Studies, Vienna, 1982; PhD in Metaphysics, U. La Verne, 1986. Pres. United Founds., St. Helier Jersey, 1977—; cons. Supercomputer Rsch. Group, London, 1981; pres, chief exec. officer Inst. for Gen. Epistemology, St. Helier Jersey, 1977—; pres. Inst. for Holistic Studies, Laguna Beach, Calif., 1986—; exec. v.p. Aleor Industries Internat., Laguna Beach, 1987—; dir. Parallel Systems Internat. Ltd., London, 1988—. Bd. dirs. Tchrs. without Borders, Vienna, 1974, Found. for Humanity, Vienna, 1968—; trustee Alliance for Unity, Manila, 1985. Unitarian. Office: United Founds PO Box 4162 Laguna Beach CA 92652-4162

GRAGG, ROB BILLY, corporate professional; b. Albuquerque, Dec. 2, 1953; s. Billy Max and Jeanette (Ostermann) G.; m. Jane H. Hendrix, Dec. 23, 1976; 1 child, Heather. B Univ. Studies, U. N.Mex., 1976. Cert. property mgr. Sales assoc. Roger Cox, Albuquerque, 1976-78; sales mgr. Ellis & Jones, Albuquerque, 1978-79; sec., treas. EEG, Inc., Albuquerque, 1978-81; pres. Prestige Builders, Inc., Albuquerque, 1979-81; v.p. Cauwels & Davis, Albuquerque, 1981-85, Inman Homes, Albuquerque, 1985-87; pres. GateWest Property Svcs., Inc., Albuquerque, 1987—; pres. N.Mex. Chpt. Inst. of Real Estate Mgmt., Albuquerque, 1986-87. Lobbyist, N.Mex. Multi Housing Assn., Santa Fe, 1985; legis. chmn. Inst. of Real Estate Mgmt., Albuquerque, 1984—, pres. 1986-87; consumer coun. Pub. Svc. Co. of N.Mex., Albuquerque, 1985-88. Named Outstanding Young New Mexican, N.Mex. Jaycees, 1987, Rookie of Yr., Roger Cox & Assocs., N.Mex., 1976. Mem. N.Mex. Multi Housing Assn. (pres. 1984-85, instr. 1984—). Republican. Baptist. Office: GateWest Property Svcs Inc 4401 Montgomery Blvd NE 5A Albuquerque NM 87109

GRAHAM, BEARDSLEY, management consultant; b. Berkeley, Calif., Apr. 24, 1914; s. Reuben Jacob and Kate Ellen (Beardsley) G.; m. Frances Rose McSherry, June 17, 1951 (div. Mar. 1967); children: McSherry, Heather; m. Lorraine Juliana Shaw, Oct. 22, 1973. BS in Chemistry, Physics and Math., U. Calif., Berkeley, 1935; postgrad. in Electronics, U. Calif., 1938-40, Columbia U., 1941-42; postgrad. in Chemistry, Tufts U., 1942-43. Registered profl. engr., Ariz., Calif., Ky.; lic. real estate broker, Calif. Instr. Edison Elec. Sch., Berkeley; frameman Pacific Tel. & Tel. co., San Francisco, 1937-39; chief engr. Golden Gate Internat. Expn. RCA Mfg. Co., 1939-40; devel. engr. NBC, Hollywood, Calif., N.Y.C., 1940-42; staff mem. radiation lab MIT, Cambridge, 1942-44; chief engr., head dept. spl. products devel. labs. Eclipse-Pioneer div. Bendix Avaiation Corp., Teterboro, N.J., and Pacific div., Detroit, 1946-51, chief engr. rsch. labs., tech. cons. to v.p. rsch.; asst. chmn. engring. dept. Stanford Rsch. Inst., Menlo Park, Calif., 1951-56; pres. Spindletop Rsch., 1961-67; exec. v.p. Sequoia Process Corp., Redwood City, Calif., 1956-57; spl. asst. comml. satellites Lockheed Aircraft Corp., Palo Alto and Sunnyvale, Calif., 1957-61, mgr. satellite systems planning Air Force Satellite Systems Program, mgr. specialty sales dept.; pres. Spindletop Rsch. Inc., Lexington, Ky., 1961-67; cons. Lockheed Aircraft Corp., Palo Alto and Sunnyvale, Calif., 1967—; pvt. practice mgmt. cons. Bend, Oreg., 1967—; pioneer in fields of new techs. and svcs. including econ. devel., air pollution and environ. qualities, nuclear weapons and power, satellite systems; bd. dirs., incorporator (selected by Pres. Kennedy) Communication Satellite Corp., 1962-64; founding chmn. bd. Videorecord Corp. Am.; mem. adv. com. on isotope and radiation devel. AEC, Ky., Atomic Energy and Space Authority, Ky. adv. com. on nuclear energy; rsch. prof. elec. engring. U. Ky., 1965; active in Microwave Communications Inc. (now MCI), Aetna Life Inc., numerous other. Papers on file at Bancroft Libr., U. Calif. at Berkeley. V.p. Bend Urban Area Planning Commn., 1983-87; vice chmn. engring. tech. adv. com. Cen. Oreg. Community Colls., 1983—, Citizens Com. for Cityhood, Yucca Valley, Calif., 1977; mem. energy adv. com. League Oreg. Cities, 1983-87; active various other civic orgns.; treas., bd. govs. ocn. for art Stanford U., 1956; mem. Bend Traffic-Saftey Com., 1987, Cent. Oreg. Coun. on Higher Edn., 1983—. Named to Hon. Order Ky. Cols. Fellow IEEE (life), AIAA (assoc.); mem. Internat. Solar Energy Soc. (founding sec., bd. dirs. 1953-66), Solar Energy Assn. Oreg. (parliamentarian 1986, exec. bd.), International Club (Washington), Arizona Club, University Club (L.A.). Democrat. Home: PO Box 5153 Bend OR 97708 Office: 63255 Deschutes Market Rd Bend OR 97701

GRAHAM, BILL, producer; b. Berlin, Germany, Jan. 8, 1931; came to U.S., 1941, naturalized, 1953; s. Jacob and Frieda (Zess) Grajonca; m. Bonnie McLean, June 1967 (div. 1969); 1 son, David. Statistician Pace Motor Trucking Co., from 1955; paymaster Guy F. Atkinson Constructors; office mgr. Allis-Chalmers Mfg. Co., to 1965. Concert promoter producer, mgr. maj. rock music artists, Santana, Ronnie Montrose, Eddie Money, Van Morrison; creator Fillmore Auditoriums East, N.Y.C., 1968-71, and West, San Francisco, 1965-71, pres. FM Prodns., San Francisco, from 1966, Bill Graham Presents, San Francisco, 1976—, Bill Graham Mgmt., 1976—, Wolfgang Records, San Francisco, from 1976, Brownwood Prodns., Nashville; producer outdoor musical events including Watkins Glen, N.Y., 1974, country-wide tours, Bob Dylan, Crosby, Stills, Nash and Young and George Harrison, Rolling Stones World Tour, 1981-82, 50 maj. outdoor concerts at Oakland (Calif.) Stadium, 1974-79; actor, producer concert for film A Star Is Born, 1976, Last Waltz, 1976; actor Apocalypse Now, Cotton Club, Gardens of Stone; concert prodn. cons.; organizer, producer maj. benefit concerts for causes including Center for Self-Determination, 1975, Save Our Cities, 1976, San Francisco Sch. Dist., 1976, Live Aid, 1985, Amnesty Internat., 1986, Crack-Down, 1986, Soviet-American Peace Concert, Moscow, 1987; recipient commendation of excellence Broadcast Music Inc. 1975, St. Francis of Assisi award City of San Francisco 1975, Billboard Conv. award as promoter of the Year 1975, 76, 77, others. Served with U.S. Army, 1951-53. Decorated Bronze Star medal, Purple Heart.; Recipient B'nai B'rith Lodge award, 1973, MTV Lifetime Achievement award, City of Hope Spirit of Life award; lauded in U.S. Congl. Records 1968, 85. Office: Bill Graham Presents Box 1994 San Francisco CA 94101 *

GRAHAM, CHRIS STERLING, rehabilitation facility administrator; b. Corpus Christi, Tex., July 18, 1946; s. Harry Canfield and Ethel Elizabeth (Estes) G.; children: Doug Alan, Ross Martin. BA, Ea. N.Mex. U., 1969, MA, 1973; PhD, So. Ill. U., 1983. Employment counselor Employment Security Commn., Roswell, N.Mex., 1969-72; rehab. counselor N.Mex. Div. Vocat. Rehab., Roswell, 1972-75; vocat. evaluator North Tex. State U., Denton, 1975-76, asst. dir., 1976-79; residential house mgr. Comprehensive Rehab. Svcs., Carbondale, Ill., 1980-81; ind. cons. Albuquerque, 1982-83; exec. dir. The Resource Ctr., Grants, N.Mex., 1983-85, Tresco, Inc., Las Cruces, N.Mex., 1985—; cons., Commn. on Accreditation of Rehab. Facilities, Tucson, 1977—; instr., N.Mex. State U., Las Cruces,1984—. Author: Selected Aspects of Financial Management in Rehabilitation Facilities, 1981; contbr. articles to profl. publs. Mem. Nat. Rehab. Assn., Am. Assn. on Mental Retardation, Coun. M.Mex. Svcs. to Handicapped, U.S. Assn. for Retarded Citizens, Rotary, Civitan. Democrat. Roman Catholic. Home: 440 W Ethel St Las Cruces NM 88005 Office: Tresco Inc 2325 E Nevada St Las Cruces NM 88001

GRAHAM, DENIS DAVID, curriculum specialist, marriage and family counselor; b. Santa Rosa, Calif., Oct. 21, 1941; s. Elbert Eldon and Mildred Bethana (Dyson) G.; m. Margaret Katherine Coughlan, Aug. 31, 1968; children—Kathleen Ann, Todd Cameron. B.S. in Edn., U. Nev., 1964, M.Ed., 1973, M.A., 1982. Cert. for ednl. personnel; lic. marriage and family therapist, Nev.; nat. cert. counselor Nat. Bd. for Cert. Counselors. Tchr. vocat. bus. edn. Earl Wooster High Sch., Reno, 1964-66, chmn. dept. bus. edn., 1966-67; state supr. bus. and office edn. Nev. Dept. Edn., Carson City, 1967-70, adminstr. vocat. edn. field services, 1970-74, asst. dir., 1974-78, vocat. edn. cons., 1978-85; edn. curriculum specialist Washoe County Sch. Dist., Reno, 1985—; marriage and family counselor Severance & Assocs., Carson City, 1983-85, Mountain Psychiat. Assocs., 1985-87; mem. tng. and youth employment council S.W. Regional Lab. for Ednl. Research and Devel., Los Alamitos, Calif., 1982, mem. career edn. council, 1980-81. Editor Council of Chief State Sch. Officers' Report: Staffing the Nation's Schools: A National Emergency, 1984. Contbr. articles to profl. jours. bd. dirs. U. Nev.-Reno Campus Christian Assn., 1988—; adv. com. Truckee Meadows Community Coll., Reno, 1988—; mem. Gov.'s Crime Prevention Com., Carson City, 1979-83, Atty. Gen.'s Anti-Shoplifting Com., Carson City, 1974-78, Gov.'s Devel. Disabilities Planning Council, Carson City, 1977-79. Recipient award for service Bus. Edn. Assn. of No. Nev., 1973; Service award YMCA, 1962, 63. Mem. Am. Vocat. Assn., Nat. Farmer Assn. Vocat. Edn. Spl. Needs Personnel (Outstanding Service award region V 1982), Am. Assn. Marriage and Family Therapy, Am. Assn. for Counseling and Devel., Am. Mental Health Counselors Assn., U. Nev. Reno Alumni Assn. (exec. com. 1971-75), Phi Delta Kappa, Phi Kappa Phi. Democrat. Methodist. Office: 425 E 9th St Reno NV 89520

GRAHAM, DOUGLAS JOHN, museum administrator, poet, banker, venture capitalist; b. Dunfermline, Scotland, July 6, 1934; came to U.S., 1959, naturalized, 1965; s. Hugh Merton and Ellen Charlotte Baroness (Podmaniczky) G.; children: Robert, Christopher, Anabel, Isis. BA, N.Y. Inst. Fin., 1961. Ptnr. Mitchell, Hutchins & Co., N.Y.C., William D. Witter Inc., N.Y.C., 1959-72; founder, chmn. bd. trustees The Turner Mus., Denver, 1973—; pres. Internat. Bank Holdings Ltd., Denver, 1979-84; ptnr., chmn. G.I.F.T. Venture Capital Mgmt. Co., Denver, 1988—; bd. dirs. Turner Soc., London; patrow H.R.H. The Prince of Wales, 1978—. Life mem. St. Andrew's Soc. Colo. Served with M.I., Brit. Army, 1952-59. Mem. Unity Ch. Office: The Turner Mus 773 Downing Denver CO 80218

GRAHAM, JOHN WALLACE, pathologist. MD, McGill U., Montreal, Que., Can., 1960. Diplomate Am. Bd. Pathology. Intern L.A. County-U. So. Calif. Med. Ctr., 1960-61; resident in pathology U. Oreg. Health Sci. Ctr., Portland, 1961-63, V.A. Med. Ctr. West Los Angeles, 1963-65; fellow in forensic pathology Office Med. Examiner, Balt., 1965-66; dep. med. examiner Office Med. Examiner, L.A., 1966-67, chief div. forensic medicine, 1968, 1983-84; asst. med. examiner Office Med. Examiner, Dallas, 1975-78; dep. chief med. examiner Office Med. Examiner, Calgary, Alt., Can., 1984-86; dir. Calif. Toxicology Service Inc., L.A., 1969-75; chief med. examiner State of Utah, Salt Lake City, 1978-83; asst. clin. prof. pathology, U. So. Calif., 1970-75, U. Tex. Southwestern Med. Sch., 1975-78; assoc. clin. prof. U. Utah, 1979-84, U. Calgary, 1986—. Fellow Am. Acad. Forensic Scis., Nat. Assn. Med. Examiners, Am. Soc. Clin. Pathologists, Coll. Am. Pathologists. Home: 1571 E Tomahawk Dr Salt Lake City UT 84103 Office: LDS Hosp Dept Pathology 18th Ave & C St Salt Lake City UT 84113

GRAHAM, JON FREDRICK, neurosurgeon, hospital administrator; b. Wahiawa, Hawaii, Nov. 15, 1952; s. Neff William and Jane Ellen (Wilder) G. BS, Mich. State U., 1974; MD, Wayne State U., 1978. Diplomate Nat. Bd. Med. Examiners, Am. Bd. Neurol. Surgery; lic. physician, Md., Hawaii. Commd. 2d lt. U.S. Army, 1975, advanced through grades to maj., 1984; intern Walter Reed Army Med. Ctr. U.S. Army, Washington, 1978-79, resident physician Walter Reed Army Med. Ctr., 1979-84; asst. chief neurosurgery Tripler Army Med. Ctr. U.S. Army, Honolulu, 1984-86, chief dept. neurosurgery Tripler Army Med. Ctr., 1986-87; chief neurosurgery svc. Hawaii Permanent Med. Group, Honolulu, 1987—; clin. asst. prof. surgery U. Hawaii, Honolulu, 1985—, F. Edward Hebert Sch. Medicine, Bethesda, Md., 1986—. Mem. AAAS, AMA, Am. Assn. Neurol. Surgeons, Congress Neurol. Surgeons, Am. Assn. Neurol. Surgeons, Alpha Omega Alpha. Republican. Presbyterian. Club: Mililani (Hawaii) Orchid. Office: Hawaii Permanente Med Group Chief Neurosurgery Svc 3288 Moanalua Rd Honolulu HI 96819

GRAHAM, LOIS LAVERNE, academic administrator, educator; b. Muscogee, Okla., Jan. 19, 1933; d. Louis G. and Bonnie (Hill) Reed; children: Harold Gibson, Kathryn Ann Jayson. BA in English, Calif. State U., Sacramento, 1974, M in Pub. Adminstrn., 1978. Cert. community coll., standard elem. tchr., Calif.; lic. nurse. Nurse various hosps., San Diego, 1953-63; adminstrv. asst. Joseph Bonnheim Sch., Sacramento, 1963-74; tchr., adminstr. Creative Careers, Sacramento, 1974-78; tchr. Mark Hopkins Elem. Sch., Sacramento, 1978-84; secondary tchr. Fern Bacon Jr. High, Sacramento, 1984—; instr. Los Rios Community Coll., Sacramento, 1978-85, tchr. trainor, cons., Quality Edn. Project, Calif.; bd. dirs. Ynobe Internat., Sacramento, 1984—; participant in state tchr. roundtable, Sacramento, 1983—; appointed by Gov. Calif. to Fair Employment and Housing Commn., 1984—. Contbr. articles to profl. jours. Named Tchr. of Yr. Sacramento Sch. Dist. 1984-85, Outstanding Educator Mexican Am., 1984-85; Calif. Tchr. grantee State/Sch. Dist., 1985-86, Outstanding Woman award YWCA, 1985. Mem. Black Educators (pres. 1984—, named Outstanding Educator), River City Rep. Assembly, sec., v.p., bd. dirs. 1985-86, Outstanding Work), AAUW (v.p., bd. dirs. 1983-84, 86—, pres. Capitol br. 1986—, multi-cultural award), Sacramento City Tchrs. Assn. (chmn., pub. adminstrn., bd. dirs. 1980-84, Mentor tchr. 1985-86, Spl. Media award Outstanding Work), Delta Sigma Theta. Unitarian. Home: 7408 Toulon Ln Sacramento CA 95828

GRAHAM, LOLA AMANDA (MRS. JOHN JACKSON GRAHAM), photographer, author; b. nr. Bremen, Ga., Nov. 12, 1896; d. John Gainer and Nancy Caroline Idella (Reid) Beall; student Florence Normal Sch., 1914; m. John Jackson Graham, Aug. 3, 1917 (dec.); children—Billy Duane, John Thomas, Helen (Mrs. D. Hall), Donald, Beverly (Mrs. Bob Forson). Tchr. elem. public sch., Centerdale, Ala., 1914, Eva, Ala., 1915; free lance photographer and writer, 1950—; editor poetry column Mobile Home News, 1968-69; designer jacket cover for Reader's Digest book Our Amazing World of Nature. Recipient numerous nat. prizes, 1950—; Crossroads of Tex. grand nat. in poetry for For Every Monkey Child, 1980; executed prize-winning Sioux Indian and heirloom photog. quilts. Mem. Nat. Poetry Soc. Ina Coolbrith Poetry Soc., Chapparal Poets. Author: (booklet) How to Recycle Ancestors and Grandcestors, (poetry) Recycling Center, 1988. Contbr. photographs to Ency. Brit., also numerous mags. and books. Address: 225-93 Mount Hermon Rd Scotts Valley CA 95066

GRAHAM, MARTIN LAREN, radiologist; b. Hutchinson, Kans., Mar. 5, 1942; s. George F. (Bill) and Hazel Pauline (Pittman) G.; m. Karen Mae Holben, Aug. 19, 1967; children: Sarah Jane, John Martin, Michael George. BA, UCLA, 1965; MD, U. Calif., San Francisco, 1969. Diplomate Am. Bd. Radiology. Intern U. So. Calif., L.A. County Med. Ctr., 1969-70; resident in radiology U. Mich. Med. Ctr., Ann Arbor, 1972-75; radiologist Dignostic Imaging N.W., Tacoma, 1975—. Lt. U.S. Navy, 1970-72. Mem. Am. Coll. Radiology, Wash. State Radiol. Soc., Pacific NW Radiologic Soc., Pierce County and Wash. State Med. Socs., Radiol. Soc. N.Am. Presbyterian. Office: 7424 Bridgeport Way W Tacoma WA 98467

GRAHAM, PATRICIA MULLEN, convention services company executive; b. Shanghai, People's Republic China, Oct. 24, 1936; (parents Am. citizens); d. Timothy and Imogene (Norman) Mullen; m. Garrett Graham (div. 1975); children: Garrett Jr., Molly. BA cum laude, San Jose State U., 1958. Tchr. Norwalk (Calif.) Unifed Sch. Dist., 1958-59, Tustin (Calif.) Pub. Schs., 1959-60, Richmond (Calif.) Pub. Schs., 1960-63, Tamalpais High Sch. Dist., 1964-78; instr. Marin County Coll. Dist., Kentfield, Calif., 1970-79; registration clk. San Francisco Conv. and Visitors Bur., 1976-78; co-owner, mgr. Cappa and Graham, Inc., San Francisco, 1979—. Mem. Nat. Assn. Exhibit Mgrs., San Francisco Conv. and Visitors Bur., San Francisco C. of C. (Women Owned Bus. of Yr. award 1986), The Network. Office: 401 China Basin St Ste 212 San Francisco CA 94107

GRAHAM, STEPHEN MICHAEL, lawyer; b. Houston, May 1, 1951; s. Frederick Mitchell and Lillian Louise (Miller) G.; m. Joanne Marie Sealock, Aug. 24, 1974; children: Aimee Elizabeth, Joseph Sealock, Jessica Anne. BS, Iowa State U., 1973; JD, Yale U., 1976. Bar: Wash. 1977. Assoc. Perkins Coie, Seattle, 1976-83, ptnr., 1983—. Bd. dirs. Wash. Spl. Olympics, Seattle, 1979-83, pres., 1983; mem. Seattle Bd. Ethics, 1982-88, chmn., 1983-88, Seattle Fair Campaign Practices Commn., 1982-88; trustee Cornish Coll. of the Arts, 1986—, exec. com., 1988—; trustee Epiphany Sch., 1987—; mem. exec. com. Sch. Law Yale U., 1988—; bd. dirs. Perkins Coie Community Service Fund. Mem. ABA, Wash. State Bar Assn., Seattle-King County Bar Assn. Episcopalian. Clubs: Wash. Athletic, Columbia Tower. Office: Perkins Coie 1201 3d Ave 40th Fl Seattle WA 98101-3099

GRAHAM, SUE ANN, medical technologist; b. Waterloo, Iowa, Sept. 9, 1953; d. Floyd Leon and Alberta Jean (Wiedman) T.; m. John Gary Graham, Aug. 8, 1980; children: Jeffrey John, Joseph Turner. AA, Colo. Mountain Coll., 1974; BS summa cum laude, Adams State Coll., 1976. Diplomate Am. Soc. Clin. Pathologists. Staff technologist Penrose Hosps., Colorado Springs, Colo., 1977-82, sr. technologist, 1982--. Iowa State scholar, 1971. Mem. Manitou Women's Club, Adaman. Home: 9 Dudley Rd Manitou Springs CO 80829

GRAHAM, TONI, writer; b. San Francisco, June 24, 1945; d. Joseph Foster and Maxine E. (Johnson) Avila; m. J. Richard Graham, Nov. 23, 1972 (div. 1987); 1 child, Salvatore Z. BA, New Coll. Calif., 1988; student, San Francisco State U., 1989—. Author short fictions in mags. including Playgirl, Short Story Review, Am. Fiction 88, Five Fingers Review. Harrold scholar, 1986. Mem. Golden Key Honor Soc. Home: 345 Prospect Ave San Francisco CA 94110 Office: C/O Dijkstra Literary Agy 1237 Camino Del Mar Del Mar CA 92014

GRAHAM, VERNON LEE, corporate executive; b. Oquaka, Ill., Dec. 2, 1930; s. Grover Cleveland and Pearl (Fisher) G.; m. July 27, 1952; children: Steven, Dione, Rhonda. BA, San Jose U., 1954; MS, San Diego State U., 1962. CLU, Chartered Fin. Cons. Commd. USAF, 1954, advanced through ranks to capt., 1954, resigned, 1965; exec. v.p. Kennedy Sinclaire Inc., N. Haledon, N.J., 1967-81, pres., 1981-84; sr. v.p. Am. Fin. Svcs. Inc., Honolulu, 1984-87; pres. Fund Am. Svcs. Inc., Wilton, Calif., 1988—. Author newspaper column, Dowtown Planet, Honolulu, 1986088; contbr. articles to mags. Fund raising cons. ARC, Am. Heart Assn., Am. Cancer Soc., Honolulu, 1984-87. Sgt. U.S. Army 1946-47. Recipient Upson Meml. award U.S. Jaycees, Tulsa, 1962, Dunagan Meml award, 1964, Anela award Am. Cancer Soc., Honolulu, 1986-87. Mem. Nat. Soc. Fund Raising Execs. (cert., charter pres. Hawaii 1985-86), Elks. Republican. Home: 9440 Rancheria Dr Wilton CA 95693-0316 Office: Fund Am Svcs Inc 10093 Davis Rd Wilton CA 95693

GRAINGER, SCOTT, fire protection engineer, consultant; b. Missoula, Mont., Nov. 2, 1947; s. Paul James and Lula Elizabeth (Calvert) G.; m. Barbara Elizabeth Bittner, Sept. 7, 1968; children: Seth Ryan, Heidi Elizabeth. BS in Civil Engring., Colo. State U., 1971. Registered civil engr., Ariz., Colo., N.Mex., N.Y. Engring mgr. Ferguson Wilcox Engrs., Inc., Sierra Vista, Ariz., 1973-74; owner, pvt. practice Sierra Vista, 1974-75; civil engr. U.S. Army Corps of Engrs., Sierra Vista, 1975-77; resident engr. U.S. Army Corps of Engrs., Tucson, 1977-83; project mgr. W.F. Conelly Constrn. Co., Tucson, 1983-85; owner Grainger Consulting, Fire Protection Engrs., Tucson, 1985—; mem. Ariz. state fire code rev. com., Phoenix, 1987—. Co-founder, bd. dirs. Sunnyside Found., Tucson, 1975-88, Unity Sch. of Creative Living, Tucson, 1978-83; scoutmaster Boy Scouts Am., 1978-84; mem. Rep. Senate/Inner Circle, Washington D.C., 1987-88. Mem. Am. Arbitration Assn. (arbitrator Phoenix 1986-88), Nat. Fire Protection Assn., Soc. Fire Protection Engrs., ASCE, NSPE (chpt. sec. 1973-75, pres. 1976), Am. Cons. Engrs. Assn., Order of the Engr. Lodge: Rotary (Sierra Vista) (sec. 1977, sgt.-at-arms 1975-76, bicentennial chmn. 1976). Home and Office: 9401 E Deer Trail Pl Tucson AZ 85710

GRAMATIKAS, THOMAS NICHOLAS, health club executive; b. Manchester, NH, July 16, 1942; s. Nicholas and Evangeline (Tassias) G. BA in Sociology, U. N.H., 1965; MA in Bus. Mgmt., Cen. Mich. Coll., 1978. Dir. Southeast Asia ops. Southeast Asia Computer Assocs., Honolulu, 1971-74; dir. indsl. relations Pacific Architects & Engrs., Rlyadh, Saudi Arabia, 1978-80; pres. Mark V Advt. Cons., Sierra Vista, Ariz., 1980-82; pres., gen. mgr. Cochise Racquet Club, Inc., Sierra Vista, 1981-86; pres. GVR Devel. Corp., Sierra Vista, 1983—; pres., gen. mgr. Bayshore, Inc., Sierra Vista, 1986—; fitness cons. BodyTek, Sierra Vista, 1987—; bd. dirs., mem. adv. bd. United Bank of Ariz., Sierra Vista, 1986—; v.p. Globe Trotter Travel, Inc., 1988—. Dir. adminstrn. Mission Warden Office U.S. Dept. of State, Saigon, Republic of Vietnam. Capt. U.S. Army, 1965-70, Vietnam. Decorated Bronze Star. Home and Office: 4225 Avenida Cochise Sierra Vista AZ 85635

GRAMS, THEODORE CARL WILLIAM, librarian, educator; b. Portland, Oreg., Sept. 29, 1918; s. Theodore Albert and Emma Elise (Boehne) G. B.A., U. Wash., 1947; postgrad. Harvard Law Sch., 1947-48; M.S. in L.S., U. So. Calif., 1951. Land title asst. U.S. Bonneville Power Adminstrn., Portland, 1939-45, accountant, 1948-50, librarian, 1951-52; head cataloger, lectr. Portland State U. Library, 1952-59, dir. processing services, 1960-83, prof., 1969-87, prof. emeritus, 1988—. Panelist on community action N.W. Luth. Welfare Assn. Conf., 1969; mem. adv. council Area Agy. on Aging, 1974-75; commr. City-County Commn. Aging, Portland-Multnomah County, 1975-80. Bd. dirs. Hub-Community Action Program, Portland, 1967-70, Project ABLE, 1972-74. HEW Inst. fellow, 1968-69. Mem. Am., Oreg., Pacific N.W. library assns., AAUP, Am. Soc. for Info. Sci. (panelist on impact new technologies on info. sci. 1974, Library of Congress services 1976), Portland Area Spl. Librarians (pres. 1954-55), Spl. Libraries Assn., Beta Phi Mu. Lutheran. Clubs: Multnomah Athletic, University, Portland. Author: Allocation of Joint Costs of Multiple-Purpose Projects, 1952; Textbook Classification, 1968. Editor: Procs. 4th Am. Soc. Info. Sci. Midyear Meeting, 1975; Special Collections in Libraries of the Pacific Northwest, 1979; Disaster Preparedness and Recovery 1983; Technical Services: The Decade Ahead, in Beyond 1984: The Future of Technical Services, 1983. Home: 1000 SW Vista Ave Portland OR 97205

GRANCHELLI, RALPH S., company executive; b. Framingham, Mass., Jan. 2, 1955; s. Ralph S. and Avon L. (Chadwick) G. ASEE, Wentworth Inst. Tech., Boston, 1975; postgrad., U. Mass., 1975-78. Nat. sales mgr. Teledyne Semiconductor Co., Mountain View, Calif., 1981-85; v.p. Elantel, Inc., Milpitas, Calif., 1985—. Office: Elantec Inc 1996 Tarob Ct Milpitas CA 95055

GRANDJEAN, CYRILLE MAURICE, packaged goods company executive; b. Casablanca, Morocco, Nov. 5, 1959; came to U.S. 1984; s. Bernard and Monique G.; m. Patricia DeBaux, Oct. 1, 1988; 1 child, Albane. BA, U. Paris, 1981, LLM, 1982; MBA, Calif. State U., Hayward, 1988. Mktg. rsch. analyst Mother's Cake & Cookie Co., Oakland, Calif., 1986-88; asst. product mgr. Mother's Cake & Cookie Co., Oakland, 1988—. Lt. French Armed Forces, 1982-83. Office: Mothers Cake & Cookie Co 810 81st Ave Oakland CA 94621

GRANDY, NITA MARY, antique dealer, cosmetologist; b. Rexburg, Idaho, Aug. 28, 1915; d. David and Anna (Heinz) Heffel; m. Alex Kretekos, Jan. 25, 1931 (div. Apr. 1935); m. James Scott Grandy, Dec. 21, 1940. Grad. high sch., L.A. Pvt. practice cosmetology L.A., 1931-67; salesperson Richard Hudnut, San Francisco, 1941-42; technician Gibbs & Co. Beauty Supply, L.A., 1943-46; pvt. practice investments L.A., 1940—, pvt. practice antique appraising, 1978—, pvt. practice agt., 1978-80, pvt. practice antique dealer, 1978-86. Mem. Rep. Presdl. Task Force, Washington, 1983—. Home and Office: 6720 Spring Pk Ave Los Angeles CA 90056

GRANGE, LARRY WILLIAM, electro-mechanical engineer electronics executive; b. Topeka, Kans., Nov. 19, 1937; s. William Frank and Edna Laverne (Sales) G. AACE, Los Angeles Harbor Coll.; BA in Math., U. Calif., Long Beach; MBA, Pepperdine U. Sr. draftsman Douglas Aircraft Co., El Segundo, Calif., 1958-59; designer Ramo-Woolridge, Canoga Park, Calif., 1959-60; engr. Nortronics, Northrop Corp., Hawthorne, Calif., 1960-64; sr. design engr. Northrop Aircraft Co., Hawthorne, 1966; sr. engring. designer Hughes Aircraft Co., Culver City, Calif., 1964-66; product engr. TRW Systems, Redondo Beach, Calif., 1966-70; asst. mgr., sr. engr. Ampex Computer Products Div., El Segundo, 1970-75; mgr. Xerox Corp., El Segundo, 1975—; bd. dirs. Crane Electronics; pres. Gramor Property Investments. Mem. Electric Connector Study Group (chmn. membership). Office: Xerox Corp 701 S Aviation Blvd El Segundo CA 90245

GRANGER, DAVID WILLIAM, personnel agency executive, educator; b. Reading, Pa., Feb. 22, 1951; s. David Stanley and Gertrude Norma (Zeswitz) G. Student, Bapt. Coll., Springfield, Mo., 1969-70. Ins. agt. Nat. Life and Accident Co., Savannah, Ga., 1972-75; line mgr. Kerr S.S. Co., Savannah, 1975-78; gen. line mgr. Kerr S.S. Co., Houston, 1978-81; dir. pub. affairs Port of Long Beach (Calif.), 1981-85; pres., chief exec. officer Temp. Svcs. Internat., Long Beach, 1985—; guest lectr. Travel and Trade Career Inst., Long Beach, 1985—; mem. adv. bd. Harbor Occupational Ctr., San Pedro, Calif., 1988—. Contbr. editor various mags., 1983. Mem. Sales and Mktg. Execs., Internat. Bus. Assn. (com. 1986—), Long Beach Area C. of C., Greater L.A. World Trade Ctr. (com. 1988—), Internat. Trade Club L.A. (program dir. 1982-84), Harbor Transp. Club. Republican. Baptist. Office: Temp Svs Internat 4201 Long Beach Blvd 326 Long Beach CA 90807

GRANT, BRADLEY C., physician; b. Olean, N.Y., Sept. 10, 1954; s. Murray and Trudy (Shein) G.; m. Kristine Grant, May 7, 1988. Student, La. State U., 1972-73, U. Md., 1973-75, Colo. Coll., 1974, Towson State U., Balt., 1975; BA in Biology, Western Md. Coll., Westminster, 1976; DO, Coll. Osteo. Medicine & Surgery, Des Moines, 1979; JD, MBA, Western State Coll. U., Fullerton, Calif.; MSEd, U. So. Calif., 1987. Diplomate Am. Bd. Family Practice. Intern U.S. Pub. Health Services Hosp., Staten Island, N.Y., 1979-80, Rocky Mountain Hosp., Denver, 1980; mem. staff Community Health Ctr., Garden Grove, Calif., Circle City Hosp., Corona, Calif.; practice medicine specializing in osteo. medicine Lake Elsinore, Calif., 1981—; team physician Elsinore High Sch., 1981—; U.S. Olympic physician, asst. med. dir. U. So. Calif., 1984; sports med. dir. Grant Med. Group, Corona, 1987. Contbr. numerous articles to profl. jours. Mem. Am. Osteo. Assn., Osteo. Physicians & Surgeons Calif., Calif. Med. Assn., Riverside County Med. Soc., Am. Coll. Gen. Practitioners Osteo. Medicine Surgery Calif (pres. 1984-86), Osteo. Alumni Assn., Orange County Osteo. Med. Soc., San Bernardino Osteo. Med. Soc., San Diego Osteo. Med. Soc., Denver Med. Soc., Colo. Osteo. Med. Soc. (editor newsletter 1985-87, pur. relations dir. 1985), Am. Med. Joffee Assn., Am. Soc. Preventative Medicine Health, Am. Med. Assn. Substance Abuse and Chem. Dependency, Sigma Sigma Phi. Home: 17037 Lakeshore Dr Lake Elsinore CA 92330

GRANT, BRIAN LOWELL, psychiatrist; b. Detroit, Dec. 24, 1952; s. Max and Charlotte (Greenberg) G.; m. Donna Kost, March 13, 1977 (div. 1982); 1 child, Shira; m. Lyn Ann Wiley, Dec. 21, 1986; children: Gabriel, Oliver. BA cum laude, U. Mich., 1974; MD, Mich. State U., 1978. Lic. Wash.; diplomate Am. Bd. Psychiatry and Neurology. Intern U. Wash., Seattle, 1978-79, resident in psychiatry, 1979-82; staff mem. Providence Hosp., Swedish Hosp., and Cabrini Hosp., Seattle, 1982—; pvt. practice Seattle, 1982—; clinical instr. dept. psychiatry U. Wash., Seattle, 1985—; pres., med. dir. Med. Cons. Northwest Inc., Seattle, 1985—; cons. Ctr. for Addiction Svcs., Seattle, 1980-81, Cherry Heights Intermediate Care Facility, 1982-87, Jewish Family Svcs., 1982-87; bd. dirs. Crisis Clinic of King County, Seattle, 1983-86; lectr. in field. Contbr. articles to profl. jours. Mem. Grad. Edn. Steering com. dept. psychiatry, U. Wash., 1978-80; mem. residency admissions com., U. Wash., 1980-81; vol. physician Country Dr. Clinic, Seattle, 1978-79. Rsch. fellow Nat. Found. March of Dimes, 1971. Mem. Physicians for Social Responsibility (speakers bur. 1980-82), Am. Psychiatric Assn., Wash. State Psychiatric Assn. (Wash. dist. br. newsletter editor 1985—), Am. Acad. of Psychiatry and the Law, Internat. Assn. for the Study of Pain. Office: 4105 E Madison St Ste 246 Seattle WA 98112

GRANT, CATHERINE BAIRD, lawyer; b. L.A., Mar. 1, 1948; d. Stoddard and Jane Catherine (Spencer) Baird; m. John M. Grant, Mar. 26, 1977; children: Amanda Jane, Sybil Grace. BA, SUNY, New Paltz, 1974; JD, UCLA, 1977. Bar: Calif. 1982. Exec. sec. U.S.-China People's Friendship Assn., L.A., 1978-81; risk mgr. City of Fullerton (Calif.), 1981-84; atty. Legal Aid Soc. of Orange County Calif., Compton, 1984-86; supervising atty. Community Legal Svcs., Norwalk, Calif., 1986—. Mem. Governing Bd. ABC Unified Sch. Dist., Cerritos, Calif., 1985, pres. 1987-88. Recipient hon. service award Niemes Elem. Sch. PTA, 1987. Mem. Southeast Dist. Bar Assn., Los Angeles County Bar Assn., Am. Assn. of Univ. Women, LWV (treas. Downey, Calif., 1984-85). Democrat. Home: 13603 Ranchill Dr Cerritos CA 90701

GRANT, CHERYL, producer, television syndicator; b. Phoenix, Mar. 1, 1944; d. William Edward and Mary Louise (Weldon) Grant; m. Louis Tancredi, Nov. 27, 1976; children—John Francis, Jennifer Grant. Student U. Fribourg, Switzerland, 1963-64; B.A., Coll. of Notre Dame of Md., 1965; M.S., Syracuse U., 1966. Assoc. producer Girl Talk ABC Films, N.Y.C., 1968-70, New Jersey Speaker for Itself, WNDT-TV, N.Y.C., 1966-68, Communications and Education, WNDT-TV, N.Y.C., 1967, The Virginia Graham Show, RKO, Los Angeles, 1970-71, Manhattan Townhouse, Source Internat., N.Y.C., 1971-72, Collision Course, Wolper Prodns., Los Angeles, 1972, Living Easy with Dr. Joyce Brothers, Capricorn Prodns., N.Y.C., 1972-73, Mike Douglas Show, Westinghouse, Phila., 1974, Beverly & Vidal Sassoon, Sta. KCOP, Los Angeles, 1975, Dinah, 20th Century Fox, Los Angeles, 1975; hostess A.M. Miami, Sta. WPLG-TV, Miami, Fla., 1972; exec. producer/pres. Carter-Grant Prodns., Inc., Los Angeles, 1976—, Sherry Grant Enterprises, Inc., Los Angeles, 1982—. Programs have been honored by the Freedom Found. award, Internat. Film and TV Festival of N.Y. Gold Award and Calif. Motion Picture Assn. Golden Halo award. Mem. Acad. T.V. Arts and Sci., Women in Bus., Women in Film, Am. Women in Radio and TV, AFTRA, Women in Cable. Roman Catholic. Home: 18120 Sweet Elm Dr Encino CA 91316 Office: Sherry Grant Enterprises 17915 Ventura Blvd Suite 208 Encino CA 91316 *

GRANT, CRISLYN JEAN, telecommunications executive; b. Downey, Calif., Dec. 19, 1951; d. William Beryl and Lillian Bernice (Costley) Evans; m. Barry Gerard Grant, Dec. 14, 1985; children: Evan Patrick and Andrew Ryan (twins). AA, Am. River Coll., Sacramento, 1972; BS, Calif. State U., Sacramento, 1978; M in Adminstrn., U. Calif., Davis, 1986. Residential lender Wells Fargo Bank, N.A., San Francisco, 1978-84; comml. lender SBA, Sacramento, 1986-87; comml. supr. telecommunications Citizen's Utilities Co. Calif., Elk Grove, 1987—. Rep. precinct walker, Sacramento; vol. Elk Grove Citizen's Strauss Festival; chair Elk Grove Holiday Craft Fair. Mem. Assn. MBA's, NAFE, Nat. Park and Recreation Assn., Calif. Park and Recreation Assn., Soroptomists. Roman Catholic. Office: Citizen's Utilities Co PO Box 340 Elk Grove CA 95624

GRANT, DAVID BROWNE, manufacturing executive; b. Sharonville, Ohio, Apr. 21, 1915; s. David John and Catherine Emma (Browne) G.; m. Elizabeth Ann Connolly, May 17, 1942; children: Ann Catherine, Elizabeth Bonnie, David C., Susan B., Mary Margaret, James B., Patricia Jude. AB cum laude, Colgate U., 1936; LLB, Yale U., 1939. Bar: Mich. 1939. Assoc. Edward Bryant Firm, Detroit, 1939-40, Vandeveer and Haggerty Firm, Detroit, 1940-41; sales mgr., asst. to pres. Empire Tool Co., Detroit, 1941-42; sales rep., dist. mgr. Stone Tool Corp., Los Angeles, 1946-47; owner, mgr. Tool Electrolizing Co., Los Angeles, 1947-49, Electrolizing Co. and Electrolizing Sales and Tool Co., Los Angeles, 1949-52; pres., chief exec. officer Electrolizing, Inc., Los Angeles, 1952—. Mem. Los Angeles C. of C. (Indsl. com. 1952-60). Served to lt. USNR, 1942-46. Mem. Am. Soc. Metals, Metal Finishing Assn. So. Calif., Inst. Aeronautics and Astronautics, Soc. Automotive Engrs., Phi Beta Kappa, Phi Gamma Delta. Republican. Roman Catholic. Clubs: Jonathan (Los Angeles); Braemar (Tarzana, Calif.), Spring Valley Country, Newport Beach Country. Home: 3 Northampton Ct Newport Beach CA 92660 Office: Electrolizing Inc 1947 Hooper Ave Los Angeles CA 90017

GRANT, DAVID MORRIS, chemistry educator; b. Salt Lake City, Mar. 24, 1931; s. David Lewis and Mary Lucille (Greenwood) G.; m. Reva Luella Carlow, Sept. 11, 1953; children: David James, Linda Grant Halling, Heidi Grant Cox, Karen Grant Lindstrom, John Carlow Grant. BS in Chemistry, U. Utah, 1954, PhD in Chemistry, 1957. Du Pont instr. chemistry U. Ill., Champaign-Urbana, 1957-58; asst. prof. U. Utah, Salt Lake City, 1958-62, assoc. prof., 1962-65, prof., 1965-85, disting. prof., 1985—, chmn. dept. chemistry, 1962-73, dean coll. sci., 1976-85; adj. prof. fuels engring., U. Utah, 1985-89, assoc. v.p. acad. and rsch. computing, co-investigator study to improve mgmt. of costly instrumentation trs., 1974-75; lectr. numerous univs., sci. and tech. assns. and confs., 1963—. Mem. editorial bd. Jour Am. Chem. Soc., 1975-76, Jour. Magnetic Resonance, 1969-84; mem. editorial adv. bd. Spectrochimica Acta, 1976-84. Named Sherman Fairchild Disting. Vis. Scholar Calif. Inst. Tech., 1973-74; recipient U. Utah Disting. Research award, 1971-72, Willard Gardner prize Utah Acad. Scis., Arts and Letters, 1971. Mem. AAAS, Am. Chem. Soc. (assoc. editor jour. 1975-76, accreditation rev. com. 1985, Gold Medal award Calif. sect. 1969, Utah sect. award 1973), Utah Acad. Scis., Arts and Letters (Univ. Disting. Svc. award for Biol. and Phys. Scis. 1989) Am. Phys. Soc., Sigma Xi (Ann. award Utah chpt. 1957), Phi Beta Kappa, Phi Kappa Phi. Mormon. Office: U Utah Dept Chemistry Salt Lake City UT 84112

GRANT, HOWARD W., symphony orchestra executive. Exec. dir. Honolulu Symphony Orch. Office: Honolulu Symphony Orch 1441 Kapiolani Blvd Ste 1515 Honolulu HI 96814 *

GRANT, JOHN CARRINGTON, advertising executive; b. St. Louis, Feb. 2, 1937; s. George Nelson Whitfield and Mary Frances (Tissier) G.; m. Judith Ann Thompson, Oct. 20, 1962; children: Christopher, Susan. Student Westminister Coll., 1960; BS, Washington U., St. Louis, 1969. Account mgr. Darcy, McManus & Masius, St. Louis, N.Y.C. and San Francisco, 1960-68; with Gardner Advt., St. Louis, 1963-66, McCann-Erickson, Seattle, 1974-75; stockbroker Dean Witter, San Francisco, 1968-74; with Tracy-Locke/BBDO, 1975-80; pres. Grant Pollack Advt., Denver, 1980-85; v.p. Brock & Assocs., Denver, 1985-86; dir. Univ. relations U. Denver, 1987-89; pres. Grant & Assocs., 1989—; mem. faculty Met. State Coll., Denver, 1981-82. Mem. Denver Advt. Fedn. Clubs: Denver Athletic, Oxford.

GRANT, MARK ANTONIO, organization administrator; b. Newark, June 16, 1954; s. Louis Wallace and Mary Louise (Bantum) G. Student, Glassboro State Coll., 1972-75; BA, William Paterson Coll., 1977; postgrad., UCLA, 1984. Film editor ABC, Hollywood, Calif., 1978-81, video engr., 1981-84; pub. info. specialist United Way of Los Angeles, 1984-85; blood cons. ARC, Santa Monica, Calif., 1985-86, dir., 1986—; mem. Emergency Ops. Ctr., Santa Monica, 1986—. Bd. dirs. UN Assn., West Los Angeles, 1987—; mem. adv. bd. vol. ctr. West Los Angeles, 1988. Named Outstanding Young Man Am., 1982, 84, 88. Democrat. Episcopalian. Lodge: Kiwanis. Home: 12713 Caswell St #1 Mar Vista CA 90066 Office: ARC 1450 11th St Santa Monica CA 90406

GRANT, MERWIN DARWIN, lawyer; b. Safford, Ariz., May 7, 1944; s. Darwin Dewey and Erma (Whiting) G.; m. Charlotte Richey, June 27, 1969; children: Brandon, Taggart, Christian. BA in Econs., Brigham Young U., 1968; JD, Duke U., 1971. Bar: Ariz. 1971, U.S. Dist. Ct. Ariz., U.S. Dist. Ct. (we. dist.) Tex., U.S. Ct. Appeals (5th, 7th, 8th, 9th and 10th cirs.), U.S. Tax Ct., U.S. Supreme Ct. Pres. Merwin D. Grant, P.C., Phoenix, 1977—; ptnr. Beus, Gilbert, Wake & Morrill, Phoenix, 1984—. Bd. dirs. Grand Canyon coun. Boy Scouts Am., Phoenix, 1974-76; pres., bd. dirs. Golden Gate Settlement, Phoenix, 1975-80, 84-88; charter mem. Rep. Presl. Task Force, Washington, 1984—. Mem. ABA (litigation sect.), Assn. Trial Lawyers Am., Kiwanis (bd. dirs. Phoenix chpt. 1972-79). Office: Beus Gilbert Wake & Morrill 3200 N Central Ave Ste 1000 Phoenix AZ 85012

GRANT, RICHARD EARL, nursing administrator; b. Spokane, Wash., Aug. 27, 1935; s. Conrad Morrison and Sylva Celeste (Sims) G.; m. Susan Kimberly Hawkins, Mar. 17, 1979; children: Aaron Sahmie Q., Camber Do'otsie O. BSc cum laude, U. Wash., 1961; MEd, Whitworth Coll., 1974; PhD, Wash. State U., 1980. Supr. nursing Providence Hosp., Seattle, 1970-72; asst. prof. nursing Wash. State U., Spokane, 1972-78; dir. nursing Winslow (Ariz.) Meml. Hosp., 1978-79; adminstr. psychiat. nursing Ariz. State Hosp., Phoenix, 1979-80; asst. prof. Ariz. State U., Tempe, 1980-83; assoc. prof. Linfield Coll., Portland, Oreg., 1983-86; assoc. prof. Intercollegiate Ctr. for Nursing Edn., Spokane, 1986-88, coord. med. care, 1988—; cons. Ariz. State Hosp., 1980-82, Pres.'s Commn., Washington, 1981-83, U. No. Colo., Greely, 1985-86. Author: The God-Man-God Book, 1976, Publications of the Membership (Conaa), 1983, 3d rev. edit., 1985, 4th rev. edit., 1988, Predetermined Careplan Handbook-Nursing, 1988; contbr. articles to profl. jours. Judge Student Space Shuttle Project, Portland, 1983—, Northwest Sci. Expo, Portland, 1983—. Served with U.S. Army, 1953-56. Grantee NIMH, U. Wash., 1961; named one of top Hopi Scholars, Hopi Tribe, Second Mesa, Ariz., 1981. Mem. AAAS, N.Y. Acad. Scis., Nat. League for Nursing, Council on Nursing and Anthropology (editor 1982—), Soc. for Intercultural Edn., Tng. and Research, Sigma Theta Tau.

GRANT, ROBERT LEE, business economist; b. Hempstead, N.Y., Dec. 28, 1938; s. William M. and Lillian A. (Cofield) G.; m. Liesbeth Matthieu, Nov. 17, 1985; 1 child, Jacqueline. BA, Queens Coll., 1961; Master of Social Sci., U. Stockholm, Sweden, 1964, PhD in Bus. Econs., 1968. Postal clk. U.S. Post Office, N.Y.C., 1958-61; pub. relations dir. UNICEF, Stockholm and Paris, 1963-64; Scandinavian rep. Bemis Corp. of Boston, Stockholm, 1965-66; special asst. to asst. sec. of model cities HUD, Washington, 1969-71; bus. cons. San Francisco, 1971-74; asst. prof. U. Calif., Berkeley, 1973-79; pres. Golden Gate Designs, Inc., Marin County, Calif., 1978-. Trustee Marin Community Coll. Dist., Kentfield, Calif., 1975-83. Mem. Swedish Am. C. of C., San Francisco C. of C., San Francisco Black C. of C., Rotary (local pres. 1987-88). Democrat. Office: Golden Gate Designs Inc 2547 8th St Berkeley CA 94710

GRANT, SARAH DICKINSON, judge; b. El Dorado, Kans., Nov. 10, 1942; d. Edward and Mary Louise (Motz) D.; children: Trevi, Ashley. BA,

UCLA, 1966; JD, Ariz. State U., 1970. Bar: Ariz. 1971. Assoc. Debus & Busby, Phoenix, 1970-72; staff atty. Ariz. Supreme Ct., Phoenix, 1972-79; chief staff atty. Ariz. Supreme Ct., 1974-79; judge Maricopa County Superior Ct., Phoenix, 1979-82, Ariz. Ct. Appeals, Phoenix, 1982--; chief judge Ariz. Ct. Appeals, 1988--. Membership chair Charter 100, Phoenix; bd. dirs. Ariz. Womens Forum, Phoenix. Mem. ABA, Am. Law Inst., State Bar Ariz., Nat. Assn. Women Judges. Democrat. Office: Ariz Ct Appeals State Capitol SW Wing 125 1700 W Washington St Phoenix AZ 85007

GRANTHAM, DONALD JAMES, engineering educator, author; b. Grantham, N.C., Aug. 1, 1916; s. James Clarence and Nannie (Rose) G.; children—David S., Philip L. B.A. in Chemistry, U. N.C., 1939. Radio announcer, 1940-42, 46; radio programmer, sta. gen. mgr., 1947-50; founder, pres. Grantham Coll. of Engring., Los Alamitos, 1951—. With U.S. Army, 1942-46. Mem. IEEE, ASEE. Office: 10570 Humbolt St Los Alamitos CA 90720

GRANUCI, PATRICIA, program director; b. Manchester, England, Dec. 24, 1942; came to U.S., 1971; d. Daniel and Mary (Newton) Diamond; m. Francis Clowes, Jan. 9, 1964 (dec. 1972); m. H. Thomas Granuci, Sept. 6, 1989. Assoc. in Nursing, College of the Desert, Palm Desert, Calif., 1973; BS, Redlands U., 1979, MS in Human Resource Mgmt., 1984. Staff nurse The Royal Infirmaty, Manchester, England, 1960-63; office supr. Imperial Chem. Industries, Manchester, 1963-69; program dir. Eisenhower Med. Ctr., Rancho Mirage, Calif., 1972—. Contbr. articles to profl. jours. Mem. Am. Diabetes Assn., NAFE, Am. Assn. Diabetes Educators (cert. diabetes educator), Diabetes Teaching Nurses So. Calif. (treas. 1978). Republican. Roman Catholic. Office: Eisenhower Med Ctr 39000 Bob Hope Probst 100 Rancho Mirage CA 92270

GRAPER, EDWARD BOWEN, research mechanical engineer; b. Los Angeles, June 1, 1941; s. Robert Edward and Clare (Bowen) G.; m. Barbara Lea Heyl, June 22, 1968. BS in Mech. Engring., U. Calif., Berkeley, 1965, postgrad., 1967—. Engr. Unified Science, Pasadena, Calif., 1965-67; project engr. Sloan Tech., Santa Barbara, Calif., 1967-73; pres. Lebow Corp., Golena, Calif., 1973—; expert on thin films for U.N. Indsl. Devel. Orgn., Vienna, Austria, 1986—. Contbr. articles to profl. jours. Mem. Am. Vaccum Soc., Am. Optical Soc. Home: RR 1 Box 2304 Goleta CA 93117 Office: Lebow Co 5960 Mandarin Ave Goleta CA 93117

GRASDALEN, GARY LARS, educator, astronomer; b. Albert Lea, Minn., Oct. 7, 1945; s. Lars G. and Lillie S. (Olson) G. AB, Harvard U., 1967; MS, U. Calif., Berkeley, 1969, PhD, 1972. Assoc. astronomer Kitt Peak Nat. Obs., Tucson, 1972-77; prof. U. Wyo., Laramie, 1977—. Contbr. articles to profl. jours. Republican. Office: U Wyo Dept Physics and Astronomy Laramie WY 82071

GRASKEMPER, JOSEPH PETER, dentist; b. Cleve., Oct. 18, 1951; s. Joseph George and Ruth Helen (Hasek) G.; m. Tara Hammond, Mar. 17, 1984; children: Joseph William, Gena Claire. BS, Xavier U., Cin., 1973; postgrad., Case Western Res. U., 1973-74; DDS, Ohio State U., 1977; JD, Western State U., San Diego, 1987. Assoc. Univ. Towne Dental Group, San Diego, 1979-80; v.p., ptnr. Sorrento Valley Ceramic Arts, San Diego, 1980-82; v.p., ptnr. Univ. Towne Dental Group, San Diego, 1980-84, pres., sole owner, 1984--. Bd. dirs. Franklin County Crippled Children's Dental Program; v.p. Encinitas Town Council, 1981. Lt. USN, 1977-79. Fellow Am. Endodontic Soc., Acad. Gen. Dentistry; mem. ADA, Calif. Dental Assn. Republican. Roman Catholic. Office: Univ Towne Dental Group 4525 LaJolla Village Dr San Diego CA 92122

GRASSO, CHRISTOPHER ANTHONY, non-academic administrator, fundraiser; b. Los Angeles, Oct. 28, 1950; s. Frank Anthony and Beatrice Louise (Archer) G. AB, St. Anselm Coll., 1974; MBA, N.H. Coll., 1978. Asst. to v.p. for devel. St. Anselm Coll., Manchester, N.H., 1974-77; assoc. dir. corp. and found. relations Drexel U., Phila., 1977-82; regional pres. Tau Kappa Epsilon, Indpls., 1982-83; assoc. dir. devel. Calif. State Poly. U., Pomona, 1983-84; dir. devel. phys. scis. UCLA, 1984-87; dir. devel. Univ. Heart Ctr., Ariz. Health Scis. Ctr./U. Ariz., Tucson, 1987—; cons. in field. Bd. dirs. TEKE Ednl. Found., Indpls., 1987—. Mem. Nat. Soc. Fund Raising Execs., Council for Advancement and Support of Edn., Tau Kappa Epsilon (pres. Western states 1985—). Republican. Roman Catholic. Lodge: KC. Home: 6251 N Saffron Rd Tucson AZ 85741 Office: Ariz Health Scis Ctr Coll Medicine 1501 N Campbell Ave Tucson AZ 85724

GRASSO, PAULINE VIRGINIA, civic volunteer; b. Salem, Mass., May 13, 1930; d. John M. and Mary Elizabeth (Cologey) Devitt; m. Frank Anthony Grasso, Oct. 26, 1968; 1 stepson, Christopher Anthony. BSN, Boston Coll., 1952; student, Boston U., 1954-55, Boston State Tchrs. Coll., 1953-54. RN. Staff nurse J.P. Kennedy Jr. Meml. Hosp., Brighton, Mass., 1952-53; head nurse, day supr. J.P. Kennedy Jr. Meml. Hosp., Brighton, 1953-54, day supr., 1955, clin. instr., 1955-58, adminstrv. asst., 1968, dir. nursing edn., 1958-68; vis. instr. Boston coll., Mass. State Coll., Meml. Hosp. Sch. Nursing, Newton (Mass.) Hosp. Sch. Nursing, 1955-68. Pres. Project H.O.P.E., Manhattan Beach, Calif., 1982—; cons. Manhattan beach Housing Found., 1986—, Manhattan Beach Case Mgr., 1987—; mem. adv. coun. South Bay Sr. Svcs., Torrance, Calif., 1986—; sr. advocate City of Manhattan Beach, 1982—; bd. dirs. Retired Sr. Vol. Program, Torrance, 1986-88; neighborhood chair Girl Scouts U.S.; mem. Beach City Coun. on Aging, 1983-89. Recipient Cert. of Appreciation, County of L.A., 1988, Vol. Appreciation award City of Manhattan Beach, 1988, award of honor County of L.A., 1989, State of Calif. Senate Rules Com. Resolution Commendation, 1988; named Outstanding Vol. Cath. Daus. of Am., 1986, Rose and Scroll award Manhattan Beach C. of C., 1989, Art Michel Meml. Community Svc. award Manhattan Beach Rotary Club, 1989, Cert. of Appreciation KC's Queen of Martyers Coun., 1989, Redondo Beach Lila Bell award Salvation Army, 1989, others. Mem. Am. Martyrs Altar Soc. (pres. 1983), Manhattan Beach Sr. Citizens Club Inc. (pres. 1985-86, 88-89). Democrat. Roman Catholic. Home: 329 Third St Manhattan Beach CA 90266

GRASSO, ROBERT P(HILIP), musician; b. Newark, June 9, 1938; s. Orazio Ralph and Charlotte (Zywicki) G.; m. Yvonne Roberts, Apr. 10, 1959 (div. 1970); 1 child, Gina Lynn. Grad. high sch., Hillside, N.J., 1956. Drummer Copa Cabana, N.Y.C., 1968-69; road mgr. Jimmie Rodgers, Los Angeles, 1969-74, drummer, 1969—, mus. dir., 1974—; v.p. Jimmik Prodns., Santa Monica, Calif., 1974-76. Appeared in film Show of the World, 1970, World Tour, 1973-75, 84, The World Through the Eyes of Children, 1974, U.S. Tour of Big Band Galaxy of Stars, 1988; drummer numerous TV shows and recs. Served with USNR, 1956-64. mem. Am. Fedn. Musicians, 1958-1984. Democrat. Baptist. Home: 9667 Kewen St Arleta CA 91331

GRAU, RAUL RIVERIA, real estate developer; b. Cayey, P.R., Apr. 20, 1947; s. Juan Leon and Carmen (Collazo) G.; m. Wilma Torres, Feb. 10, 1966 (div. 1976); children: Wendy Ericka, Rachel Kim, Stephanie Laurie; m. Rossana Bianchi; children: Daniel, Vanessa, Sheila. Student, U. P.R., 1967; lic. vocat. nurse, cert. med. technologist, Johns Hopkins U., 1972. Lic. vocat. nurse, Calif. Med. technologist Johns Hopkins Hosp., Balt., 1971-76; med. salesman Devco Industries, Burlingame, Calif., 1977-78; dialysis technician Ind. Contractors, Santa Cruz, Calif., 1978-79; chief dialysis technologist Santa Cruz Community Dialysis, 1979-86; bus. mgr. Sunset Realty, Santa Cruz, 1986—; cons. in field. Vol. Home and Sch. Club, Santa Cruz, 1987—. Served with U.S. Army, 1967-71, Vietnam. Mem. Bd. Nephrology Examiners. Democrat. Roman Catholic. Home: 3495 Mission Dr Santa Cruz CA 95065

GRAUNSTADT, KENNETH PAULL, JR., auctioneer; b. Oakland, Calif., Nov. 1, 1939; s. Kenneth Paull and Margaret (Kenney) G.; m. La Verne Perry, Apr. 21, 1963 (div. 1985); children: Tracy Lynn, Anthony Joseph, Nathan Frances, Michelle Marie; m. Linda Wamsley, Oct. 11, 1986. Prin. Graunstadt Enterprises, Oakley, Calif., 1969-88; auctioneer Paul Lewis Co., San Rafael, Calif., 1985—; prin. Delta Scrap & Salvage, Oakley, 1988—. Co-founder Oakley (Calif.) Wine and Jazz Festival, 1985; bd. dirs. Mount Diablo YMCA. Mem. Oakley C. of C. (founder), Inst. Scrap Iron and Recycling Industries (bd. dirs., pres. chpt.), Nat. Auctioneers Assn., Am. Conservatory Theater. Republican. Club: Commonwealth. Office: Graunstadt Enterprises Rt 1 Box 73 Oakley CA 94561

GRAVELY, HARIOETT R., company executive; b. Omaha, Dec. 27, 1946; d. Myron D. and Jeannette Elizabeth (Bucher) Hilty; m. William Hamilton Gravely, Feb. 7, 1970. With Durbins Apparel, Edmonds, Wash., 1975-85; salesperson The Mediterrean, Seattle, 1985; full-figure model Eileen Seals Internat., Seattle, 1984—; sr. dir. Noevir, Inc., Irvine, Calif., 1986—, mem. Noevir N.W. Exec. Bd., Bellevue, Wash., 1986-88. Composer piano selections: Collection of songs: "Gifts of Love.". Organizer, dir. Edmonds Charity Festival of Fashion, Wash., 1984, Edmonds 2nd Charity Festival of Fashion, 1985. Recipient Community Svc. Award, City of Edmonds, 1985. Mem. Woodinville Bus. and Profl. Women (chmn. 1987—, pres. protem 1987, pres. 1987-88), Bus. & Profl. Women of Wash. (dir. 1987-88). Office: Grande Image 13110 NE Ste 172 Woodinville WA 98072

GRAVES, CHARLES EDWARD, lawyer; b. S.I., N.Y., Mar. 22, 1931; s. Charles Edward and Helen Joyce (Rundlett) G.; m. Halene Landen, June 16, 1985; children: Elizabeth Lee McCurdy, Janet Kimberly, Ann Kristen. BS, Duke U., 1953; LLB, U. Colo., 1959. Bar: Wyo. Assoc. Roncalio, Pattno & Graves, Cheyenne, Wyo., 1959-60, Roncalio, Graves, & Smyth, Cheyenne, 1960-71, Graves & Hacker, Cheyenne, 1971-77; states atty. State of Wyo., 1977-81; Atty. Graves, Hacker & Phelan, Cheyenne, 1981-84; pvt. practice Cheyenne, 1984-88; ptnr. Graves, Santini & Villemez, P.C., Cheyenne, 1988—; bd. dirs. Frontier Bank Laramie County, Cheyenne, Cadiz Corp., Clearmont, Wyo. Trustee, Laramie County Community Coll., Cheyenne, 1982—; state chmn., The Assn. of Com. Coll. Trustees, 1985—; committeeman, Dem. State Com., 1982-86, state chmn., 1989; dir., Laramie County Comm. Coll. Found., Cheyenne, 1982—; Wyo. atty., Jimmy Carter Election Campaign., Cheyenne, 1976. Mem. ABA, Colo. Bar Assn., Wyo. Bar Assn., Wyo. Trial Lawyers Assn.,' Plaintiff Employee Attys. Assn., Lions, Elks. Unitarian. Home: 816 Skyline Dr Cheyenne WY 82009 Office: Graves Santini & Villemez 408 W 23d St Cheyenne WY 82001

GRAVES, DAN BARTHOLOMEW, insurance company executive; b. Coral Gables, Fla., Jan. 8, 1951; s. James Mortimore and Mary Jane (Pickle) G.; m. Donna Marie Pierceall, Dec. 27, 1971; children: Corey, Chad, Leah. AA, Napa Community Coll., 1973. Salesman D.D. Assocs., Palo Alto, Calif., 1973-77; field underwriter N.Y. Life Ins. Co., Palo Alto, 1977-78; v.p. Orchard Printing, Inc., San Jose, Calif., 1978--. Republican. Home: 6418 Menlo Dr San Jose CA 95120 Office: NY Life Ins Co 333 W Santa Clara St Ste 900 San Jose CA 95113

GRAVES, DENNIS JAY, lawyer, arbitrator; b. McCook, Nebr., Sept. 4, 1947; s. Claude L. and Edith L. (Merrill) G.; m. Heidi G. Howard, Nov. 24, 1979; 1 child, Christopher John. BA summa cum laude, Willamette U., 1970, JD, 1973. Bar: Oreg. 1973. Assoc. Bruce Williams, P.C., Salem, Oreg., 1973-75; ptnr. Williams, Spooner & Graves, Salem, 1975-80, Graves & Hilgemann, Salem, 1983—; pvt. practice Salem, 1980-83. Chmn. Oreg. Mental Health Adv. Bd. Mem. ABA, Oreg. State Bar Assn. (disciplinary rev. bd. 1985—, jud. adminstrn. com. 1985—), Marion County Bar Assn. (treas. 1982-83, bd. dirs. 1983-87), Oreg. Assn. Def. Counsel, Def. Rsch. Inst., Am. Arbitration Assn., Oreg. Pilot's Assn., Capitol Flying Club (pres. 1979—), Illahe Hills Country Club, Salem City Club. Office: Graves & Hilgemann 530 Center St NE Ste 409 Salem OR 97302

GRAVES, JERRY KENDALL, sales executive, consultant; b. Seminole, Okla., Apr. 23, 1932; s. Audie and Clara (Brisco) G.; m. Larene Mae Carlson, Apr. 19, 1952; children: Jeri Lynn, Cathy Rae, Michael, Susan Rae. Student, Northwest Coll., Seattle, 1957-59; degree in indsl. engring. and sales mgmt., Manhatten (N.Y.) Coll., 1964. Indsl. engr. Boeing Co., Seattle, 1960-64; regional sales mgr. Electronic Mgmt. Corp., Tampa, Fla., 1964-70, Kenite Corp., Scarsdale, N.Y., 1970-74, Multa-Metal Wire Cloth, Tappan, N.Y., 1974-78; nat. sales mgr. F.P. Research, Inc., Bellevue, Wash., 1978-82; nat. acctg. mgr. Am. Cons., Seattle, 1982-84; pres. Tower Media Corp., Bellevue, 1984—, also cons., 1982-84. Served to cpl. U.S. Army, 1950-52, Korea. Republican. Home: 20912 82d Ave W Edmonds WA 98020

GRAVES, KATHRYN MARIE, security services company executive; b. St. Louis, Apr. 5, 1954; d. Russell Byron Graves and Kathryn Julia (Coyne) MacDonald. AA, Meramec Community Coll., St. Louis, 1974; BS in Adminstrn. Justice, U. Mo., St. Louis, 1975. Cert. protection profl. Adminstr. asst. Bekins Distbn. Svcs., Phoenix, 1977-78; adminstr. asst. Pedus Svcs., Scottsdale, Ariz., from 1978, successively exec. advisor, 1979-80, v.p., 1981-83, now pres., 1984—. Mem. Am. Soc. for Indsl. Security (utility com. 1982-), Bldg. Owners and Mgrs. Assn., Am. Mgmt. Assn., Am. Nuclear Soc., NAFE. Office: Pedus Svcs 8399 E Indian School Rd Scottsdale AZ 85251

GRAVES, RONALD NORMAN, lawyer; b. Caldwell, Idaho, Nov. 11, 1942; s. Vernon E. and Mildred Elizabeth (Norman) G.; m. Diane Jo Plastino, Dec. 29, 1985. BA, Coll. Idaho, 1965; JD, U. Idaho, 1968. Bar: Idaho 1968. Staff lawyer J.R. Simplot Co., Boise, Idaho, 1968-72, corp. counsel, 1972, corp. sec., 1975—, gen. counsel, 1986—; Mem. com. Idaho Corp. Counsel Workshop, Boise, 1987—; corp. sec., v.p. Simplot Livestock Co., Simplot Finl. Corp., Simplot Can. Ltd. Bd. dirs. Idaho Ronald McDonald House, Boise, 1987—; mem. Coll. Idaho Alumni Bd., Caldwell, 1987—. Mem. ABA, Idaho Bar Assn., Am. Corp. Counsel Assn., Mountain States Legal Found. (dir. 1989—). Republican. Presbyterian. Office: JR Simplot Co 999 Main St Suite 1300 Boise ID 83702

GRAVES, ROY DANNER, public relations executive; b. Indpls., Mar. 2, 1943; s. Robert Harrison and Ardis Louise (Danner) G.; m. Rebecca Jane Cole, Oct. 30, 1971; children: Gavin Matthew, Aaron Todd. BA, Butler U., 1964; MA, U. Wash., 1972. Pub. rels. specialist Cummins Engine Co., Columbus, Ind., 1969-71; account exec. Communication N.W., Seattle, 1972, 1975-77, pres., 1978—; pub. rels. rep. naval systems div. Boeing Aerospace, Seattle, 1972-75. Pres. bd. dirs. Intiman Theatre, Seattle, 1989—; chmn. Magnolia Youth Assn., Seattle, 1984-85. Lt. USNR, 1964-69, capt. 1985—. Mem. Seattle C. of C. (v.p. pres. club, 1985-87, chmn. mil. affairs com. 1986—); Puget Sound Pub. Rels. Soc. Am. (v.p. 1976-77), Pub. Rels. Soc. Am. (bd. dirs. counselors acad. 1982-85), Coll. Club. Office: Communication Northwest 111 W Harrison St Seattle WA 98119

GRAY, DENNIS LEE, deputy sheriff; b. San Francisco, May 3, 1953; s. Lewis Leroy and Beverly Lorain (Kneckt) G.; m. Diane Christine Lesh; children: Daniel Lewis, Christine Denise, Jonathon David. AS, Mt. San Jacinto Coll., 1973; BA, Calif. State U., San Bernardino, 1982. Res. police officer Perris (Calif.) Police Dept., 1974-76; sgt. Banning (Calif.) Police Dept., 1979-82; investigator Inyo Sheriff's Office, Independence, Calif., 1982-85, sr. investigator, 1985--. Author tng. manuals. Mem. Owens Valley Sch. Bd., Independence, 1983--, pres. 1986-87. Sgt. Mil. Police Investigations, U.S. Army, 1976-79. Mem. Peace Officers Rsch. Assn., Inyo Dep. Sheriff's Assn., Calif. Sch. Bd. Assn., Lions. Republican. Methodist. Office: Inyo Sheriff's Office 101 E Market St Independence CA 93526

GRAY, EDMUND WESLEY, physician; b. Colville, Wash., Nov. 9, 1928; s. Wesley Harold and Helen (Corridan) G.; m. Jane Bloomfield, June 20, 1953; children: Timothy Paul, Sarah Jane, Terrence Wesley. Student, Gonzaga U., 1946-49; MD, U. Wash., 1953. Diplomate Am. Bd. Family Practice. Intern Indpls. Gen. Hosp., 1953-54; pvt. practice Colville, 1956—; health officer N.E. Tri-County Health Dept., Colville, 1973—; med. dir. N.W. Alloys, ALCOA, Addy, Wash., 1975—; bd. dirs. Wash. State Physicians Ins. Assn., Seattle. Mem. joint select com. on basic health Wash. Ho. of Reps., Olympia, 1986-87; mem. Wash. Bd. Health, 1986-88, Wash. Basic Health Commn., 1988-89. Capt. M.C., USAF, 1954-56. Recipient Disting. Alumni award Gonzaga U., 1988, Achievement in Pub. Health award Wash. Pub. Health Ofcls., 1988. Mem. AMA (del. 1980-87), Am. Occupational Med. Assn., N.W. Occupational Med. Assn. (trustee, sec. 1984-85), Am. Acad. Family Practice, Wash. Acad. Family Practice, Wash. Pub. Health Assn., Wash. Med. Assn. (past sec., v.p., pres. 1985-86), Stevens County Med. Assn. (You Made a Difference award 1987), Spokane County Med. Assn. (hon. life), Colville C. of C. (pres. 1966), Spokane Country Club, Spokane City Club, Elks (exalted ruler Colville 1964, dist. dep. 1968). Democrat. Roman Catholic. Home: 860 E 1st St Colville WA 99114 Office: NE Wash Med Group 1200 E Columbia Colville WA 99114

GRAY, GERALD, retail executive; b. L.A., Sept. 25, 1946; s. Homer William and Eva Beatrice (Price) G.; m. Cynthia Madsen, Dec. 21, 1980; children: Lizbeth Marie, Robert William. Grad. high sch., Norwalk, Calif. Lead man N.Am. Rockwell, Seal Beach, Calif., 1965-69; mgr. Am Parts, Norwalk, 1969-76; gen. mgr. Westwind Divers, Orange, Calif., 1976-78; chief exec. officer, chmn. bd. Calif. Novelties, Riverside, 1978--; cons. sales Gerald Gray Sales, Big Bear, Calif., 1986-88. Mem. NRA, Aircraft Owners and Pilots, Cessna Owners Assn., Cessna Pilot's Assn., Calif. Rifle and Pistol Assn. (life), Riverside C. of C., Big Bear C. of C. Republican. Home: 18093 Granite Perris CA 92730 Office: Calif Novelties 9960 Indiana #10 Riverside CA 92503

GRAY, JAMES EDWARD, real estate executive; b. Chgo., Jan. 17, 1949; s. Winton S. and Anita (McCahey) G.; m. Constance Anne Kemmerer, June 10, 1972 (div. Oct. 1983); children: James Edward Jr., Carolyn Kemmerer; m. Frances Lyon Hoppen, Nov. 16, 1985. BA, U. Denver, 1973, MA, 1978. Headmaster St. Anne's Episcopal Sch., Denver, 1973-78; exec. dir. Sun Valley (Idaho)/Ketchum C. of C., 1978-80; ptnr. Sun Valley (Idaho) Assocs., 1980—. Commr. Sun Valley Planning and Zoning Bd., 1980-84; pres. Pioneer Montessori Sch., Ketchum, 1980-87, chmn.; bd. dirs. EAR Internat. Found., Los Angeles, 1980—, past. chmn.; packmaster Boy Scouts Am., Ketchem, 1980-87. Mem. Nat. Assn. Realtors, Idaho Assn. Realtors, Sawtooth Bd. Realtors. Republican. Roman Catholic. Club: Sun Valley Ski (pres.). Home: PO Box 2700 Sun Valley ID 83353 Office: Sun Valley Assocs PO Box 326 Sun Valley ID 83353

GRAY, JAN CHARLES, lawyer; b. Des Moines, June 15, 1947. s. Charles Donald and Mary C. Gray; m. Anita Marie Ringwald, June 6, 1987. B.A. in Econs., U. Calif.-Berkeley, 1969; M.B.A., Pepperdine U., 1986, J.D., Harvard U., 1972. Bar: Calif. 1972, D.C. 1974. Law clk. Kindel & Anderson, Los Angeles, 1971-72; assoc. Halstead, Baker & Sterling, Los Angeles, 1972-75; sr. v.p., gen. counsel, sec. Ralphs Grocery Co., Los Angeles, 1975—; judge pro tem Los Angeles Mcpl. Ct., 1977—; instr. bus. UCLA, 1976—, Pepperdine MBA Program, 1985—; arbitrator Am. Arbitration Assn., 1977—; media spokesman So. Calif. Grocers Assn., Calif. Grocers Assn.; real estate broker, Los Angeles, 1973—. Trustee, South Bay U. Coll. Law, 1978-79; mem. bd. visitors Southwestern U. Sch. Law, 1983—; mem. Los Angeles County Pvt. Industry Council, 1982—, exec. com. 1984-88, chmn. econ. devel. task force, 1986—; mem. Los Angeles County Martin Luther King, Jr. Gen. Hosp. Authority, 1984—; mem. Los Angeles County Aviation Commn, 1986—; Los Angeles Police Crime Prevention Adv. Council, 1986—; Angelus Plaza Adv. Bd., 1983—; bd. dirs. RecyCAL of So. Calif., 1983—; bd. trustees Santa Monica Hosp. Found., 1986—; mem. Los Angeles County Democratic Central Com., 1980-82 ; del. Dem. Nat. Conv., 1980. Recipient So. Calif. Grocers Assn. award for outstanding contbns. to food industry, 1982; Calif./Nev. Soft Drink Assn. appreciation award for No on 11 Campaign, 1983. Mem. ABA, Calif. Bar Assn., Los Angeles County Bar Assn. (exec. com. corp. law depts. sect. 1974-76, 79—, vice-chmn. 1988—, exec. com. barristers sect. 1974-75, 79-81), San Fernando Valley Bar Assn. (chmn. real property sect. 1975-77, Los Angeles Pub. Affairs Officers Assn., Los Angeles World Affairs Council, Calif. Retailers Assn. (supermarket com.), Food Mktg. Inst. (govt. relations com., govt. affairs council), So. Calif. Businessmen's Assn. (bd. dirs. 1981—, mem. exec. com. 1982—, sec. 1986—), Town Hall Los Angeles, U. Calif. Alumni Assn., Ephebian Soc. Los Angeles, Phi Beta Kappa. Club: Harvard of So. Calif. Contbg. author: Life or Death, Who Controls?, 1976; contbr. articles to legal jours. Home: PO Box 407 Beverly Hills CA 90213 Office: PO Box 54143 Los Angeles CA 90054

GRAY, JEANNE (MRS. JOHN B. MC DONALD), television producer; b. Seattle, Sept. 10, 1917; d. George Patrick and Mary Edna (Gray) Murphy; m. John B. Mc Donald, June 30, 1951; children: Gregory Roland Stoner, Margaret Jeanne Eve. Student, Columbia U., 1940, Art Students League, 1940-43, Nat. Acad. Dramatic Art, 1945. Radio producer, commentator The Woman's Voice Sta. KMPC, Los Angeles, 1947-50; TV producer, commentator, writer The Woman's Voice Sta. KTTV-CBS, Los Angeles, 1950-51; TV producer, commentator The Jeanne Gray Show Sta. KNXT-TV CBS, Los Angeles, 1951-53; West Coast editor Home Show NBC network, Los Angeles, 1955-56; TV film producer documentaries and travelogues Virgonian Prodns., Los Angeles, 1953—. Author: The Power of Belonging, 1978. Women's chmn. Los Angeles Beautiful, 1971; mem. Women's Aux. St. John's Hosp.; trustee Freedoms Found. at Valley Forge, 1966—, founder, pres. women's chpt., Los Angeles County chpt., 1965-66, Western dir. women's chpt., 1967-68, nat. chmn. 1968-71, nat. chmn. women vols., 1973-75, hon life mem. Recipient Francis Holmes Outstanding Achievement award, 1949, Silver Mike award, 1948, Emmy award Acad. TV Arts and Scis., 1951, Lulu award Los Angeles Advt. Women, 1952, Genii award Radio and TV Women, 1956, George Washington Honor award Freedoms Found. Valley Forge, 1967, honor cert., 1972, Morale award Christians and Jews for Law and Morality, 1968, Exceptional Service award Freedoms Found., 1975, Liberty Belle award Rep. Women's Club, 1975, Leadership award Los Angeles City Schs., 1976, Theodore Roosevelt award USN League, 1986. Mem. Am. Women in Radio and TV, Radio and TV Women So. Calif. (hon. life, founder, 1st pres. 1952), Footlighters (v.p. 1958-59), Los Angeles C. of C. (dir. women's div. 1948-54, mem. exec. bd., women's div. 1954-66, pres. women's div. 1963-64, hon. past pres. women's div. 1979), Los Angeles Orphanage Guild, DAR, The Muses, Les Dames de Champagne, Bel Air Garden Club, Yacht Club. Home: 910 Stradella Rd Bel Air Los Angeles CA 90077

GRAY, JOHN DELTON, retired manufacturing company executive; b. Ontario, Oreg., July 29, 1919; s. Elmer R. and Mabel (Ridgley) G.; m. Elizabeth Neuner, Jan. 4, 1946; children—Anne, Joan, Janet, John Richard, Laurie. B.Secretarial Sci., Oreg. State Coll., 1940; M.B.A., Harvard U., 1947; LL.D., Lewis and Clark Coll., 1967. Asst. to pres. Pointer-Willamette Co., Portland, 1947; asst. gen. mgr. Oreg. Saw Chain Corp. (now Omark Industries, Inc.), Portland, 1948-50; gen. mgr. Oreg. Saw Chain Corp. (now Omark Industries, Inc.), 1950-53, pres., gen. mgr., 1953-67, chmn. bd., 1961-83, vice chmn. bd., 1983-85; chmn. Textronix, Inc., 1985-87, ret., 1987; chmn. Grayco Resources, Inc.; dir. Precision Castparts Corp., First Interstate Bank Oreg., N.A., Standard Ins. Co. Past pres. Portland area council Boy Scouts Am., 1959-61; past mem. exec. bd., also past pres. Columbia-Pacific council; trustee Com. Econ. Devel., 1967-81; mem. Chief Execs. Orgn., 1969—; trustee Reed Coll., Portland, 1961—, chmn., 1968-82, chmn. Steering Com. Capital Campaign, 1983-88; trustee Oreg. Grad. Center. Served from 2d lt. to lt. col. AUS, 1941-46. Decorated Bronze Star medal; recipient Silver Beaver award Portland Area council Boy Scouts Am. Republican. Episcopalian. Lodge: Rotary. Office: Grayco Resources Inc 5331 SW Macadam Ave Ste 200 Portland OR 97201

GRAY, MARY JANE, education administrator; b. Richmond, Va., July 13, 1934; d. John Loyd and Annie Louise (Birdsong) Prentice; m. Jimmy C. Gray, Sept. 9, 1956 (dec. 1982); children: Tommy Carroll, Jack Allison. BBS, Webber Coll., 1956. Cons. various orgns., Tucson, 1973-79; dir. coop. edn. No. Ariz. U. Coll. of Engring., Flagstaff, 1986—; mem. Solar Energy Council, Dept. of Commerce, Ariz., 1987—; minority program, Coll. of Engring. and Tech., No. Ariz. U., 1986—. Built photovoltaic power generating facility, registered 1985— FERC, with line tie to Ariz. Power Service. Recipient appreciation award Navajo Tribe div. Youth Devel. 1986, appreciation award Am. Indian Sci. & Engring. Soc., 1986, 87, 88. Home: One Lohali Trail Flagstaff AZ 86001 Office: No Ariz U Coll Engring Box 15600 Flagstaff AZ 86011

GRAY, NORMAN EUGENE, fire chief; b. Helena, Mont., Nov. 3, 1937; s. Eugene F. and Gladys I. (Lippert) G.; student public schs., Helena, Mont.; m. Sharon A. Weed, Nov. 21, 1959; children—Debra A., Norman Dean. Clk., IRS, Helena, Mont., 1959; firefighter, Helena, 1960—, fire chief, 1979—, tng. officer, 1973-79. Served with USN, 1955-58. Mem. Internat. Assn. Fire Chiefs, Western Fire Chiefs Assn., Mont. State Fire Chiefs Assn. Republican. Club: Elks. Office: Office of Fire Chief City of Helena Helena MT 59623 *

GRAY, PHILIP HOWARD, psychologist, educator; b. Cape Rosier, Maine, July 4, 1926; s. Asa and Bernice (Lawrence) G.; m. Iris McKinney, Dec. 31, 1954; children: Cindelyn Gray Eberts, Howard. M.A., U. Chgo., 1958; Ph.D., U. Wash., 1960. Asst. prof. dept. psychology Mont. State U.,

Bozeman, 1960-65; assoc. prof. Mont. State U., 1965-75, prof., 1975—; vis. prof. U. Man., Winnipeg, Can., 1968-70; pres. Mont. Psychol. Assn., 1968-70; chmn. Mont. Bd. Psychologist Examiners, 1972-74; speaker sci. and geneal. meetings on ancestry of U.S. presidents. Organized exhbns. folk art in Mont. and Maine, 1972-79; author The Comparative Analysis of Behavior, 1966, (with F.L. Ruch and N. Warren) Working with Psychology, 1963, A Directory of Eskimo Artists in Sculpture and Prints, 1974, The Science that Lost its Mind, 1985; contbr. numerous articles on behavior to psychol. jours., poetry to lit. jours. Served with U.S. Army, 1944-46. Recipient Am. and Can. research grants. Fellow Am. Psychol. Assn., AAAS, Internat. Soc. Research on Aggression; mem. History of Sci. Soc., Nat. Geneal. Soc., New Eng. Hist. Geneal. Soc., Gallatin County Geneal. Soc. (charter), Deer Isle-Stonington Hist. Soc., Psychonomic Soc., Internat. Soc. for Human Ethology, Descs. of Illegitimate Sons and Daus. of Kings of Britain, Piscataqua Pioneers, Animal Behavior Soc., Flagon and Trencher, Friends of Freud Museum, Am. Legion, SAR (trustee Mont.), Sigma Xi. Home: 1207 S Black Ave Bozeman MT 59715 Office: Mont State U Dept Psychology Bozeman MT 59717

GRAY, RICHARD ARDEN, retired protective services official; b. Ft. Bragg, Calif., Oct. 29, 1935; s. Arden Howard and Marion Florence (Coolidge) G.; m. Roberta Jeanne Montna, Feb. 5, 1955; children: Mark Alan, Laura Ann, Deborah Marie, Lisa Lynn. AA, Yuba Coll., 1955; BA, Calif. State U., 1957. Cert. spl. designated subjects tchr., Calif. Deputy sheriff Yuba County Sheriffs Dept., Marysville, Calif., 1957; traffic officer Calif. Hwy. Patrol, Ventura, 1958-60, Yuba City, 1961-68; sgt. field ops. officer Calif. Hwy. Patrol, Gardena, 1969-71; lt. exec. officer Calif. Hwy. Patrol, Van Nuys, 1972-76; lt. area comdr. Calif. Hwy. Patrol, Chico, 1977-88; wholesale, retail distbr. Dick Gray Enterprises, Chico, 1989—; instr. Yuba Coll., Marysville, 1965-67, Calif. fish and game hunter safety program, Chico, 1982-86. chmn. citizen review com. United Way of Butte County, Chico, 1984, (outstanding achievement 1984-86), fundraising campaign chmn., 1986, pres., bd. dirs., 1985; v.p., bd. dirs. No. Calif. Counties Exch. Club Child Abuse Prevention Ctr., Chico, 1987—. With USNR, 1953-61. Mem. Calif. Hwy. Patrolmen Assn., RV Club, Elks (honors 1988, pres. 1988-89), Exch. Club (pres. 1980-81). Republican. Office: Dick Gray Enterprises 236A W E Ave Ste 344 Chico CA 95926

GRAY, SONIA LEE, data processing executive; b. Torrance, Calif., Jan. 28, 1957; d. Gene Charles and Shirley (Levon) Young; m. Danny Lee Gray, July 31, 1982. Cert. profl. acct., Merritt Davis Coll. Bus., Medford, Oreg., 1983; student, Calif. Coast U. Restaurant mgr. F & H Enterprises, Medford, Oreg., 1980-82; staff acct. Tepa Jalisco, Inc., Medford, Oreg., 1984-85; ops. mgr. Kasam, Inc. (doing business as Computerland), Medford, Oreg., 1985-88, mgr. support svcs., 1988—. Office: Computerland 707 Medford Ctr Medford OR 97504

GRAY, THOMAS STEPHEN, newspaper editor; b. Burbank, Calif., Aug. 22, 1950; s. Thomas Edgar and Lily Irene (Ax) G.; m. Barbara Ellen Bronson, Aug. 27, 1977; children: Jonathan Thomas, Katherine Marie. BA, Stanford U., 1972; MA in English, UCLA, 1976. Teaching assoc. UCLA, 1976-77; reporter L.A. Daily News, 1977-79, editorial writer, 1979-84, editorial page editor, 1984—. Recipient 1st Place award Editorial Writing Greater L.A. Press Club, 1988. Mem. Nat. Conf. Editorial Writers, Phi Beta Kappa. Office: Daily News Editorial Pages PO Box 4200 Woodland Hills CA 91365

GRAY, WILLIAM ERNEST, fine jewelry designer, goldsmith; b. Denver, July 10, 1949; s. Ernest Marian and Jean Elizabeth (Nygren) G.; m. Katherine M., Aug. 22, 1981 (div. Oct. 1984); 1 child, Corinda Faun. BA in Biology, We. State Coll., 1971, course in drama, 1973. Counselor of personal values INSIGHT/MAI Seminars, Dallas, 1973-76; tchr., counselor PACE Alternative High Sch., Denver, 1976-78; jewelry designer, goldsmith Anjevine Ltd., Denver, 1978—; founder, dir. INnerTOUCH Seminars, Denver, 1983-85; co-founder Healing Horse, Idaho Springs, Colo., 1988—. Office: Anjevine Ltd 600 Downing Ste B Denver CO 80218

GRAY, WILLIAM PERCIVAL, judge; b. Los Angeles, Mar. 26, 1912; s. Jacob L. and Catherine (Percival) G.; m. Elizabeth Polin, Nov. 8, 1941; children—Robin Marie, James Polin. A.B., U. Calif. at Los Angeles, 1934; LL.B. cum laude, Harvard, 1939. Bar: Calif. bar 1941. Legal sec. to judge U.S. Ct. Appeals, Washington, 1939-40; with firm O'Melveny & Myers (lawyers), Los Angeles, 1940-41; pvt. practice Los Angeles, 1945-49; partner Gray, Pfaelzer & Robertson, Los Angeles, 1950-66; U.S. dist. judge Central Dist. Calif., 1966—; spl. asst. to atty. gen. U.S., 1958-64; chmn. Calif. Conf. State Bar Dels., 1952. Trustee Ch. of Lighted Window, La Canada. Served from 1st lt. to lt. col. AUS, 1941-45. Fellow Am. Bar Found.; mem. Am. Law Inst., Am. Bar Assn., Los Angeles County Bar Assn. (pres. 1956), State Bar Calif. (bd. govs. 1960-63, pres. 1962-63). Office: US Dist Ct 312 N Spring St Los Angeles CA 90012

GRAYBILL, DAVID WESLEY, chamber of commerce executive; b. Council Bluffs, Iowa, Apr. 8, 1949; s. John Donald and Dorothy Lorraine (King) G.; m. Kortney Loraine Steinbeck, Aug. 17, 1974; 1 child, Darcy Lorraine. BA in Journalism, U. Iowa, 1971. Cert. indsl. econ. developer, Chamber exec. Adminstrv. asst. Iowa City C. of C., 1972-74; exec. v.p. Brighton (Colo.) C. of C., 1974-77; pres. Fremont (Nebr.) C. of C., 1977-83; pres., chief exec. officer Tacoma-Pierce County C. of C., 1983—; pres. Nebr. C. of C. Execs., 1981-82; treas. NE Nebr. Econ. Devel. Dist., 1980-83. Mem. Gov.'s Small Bus. Improvement Com., Wash., 1984-88. Mem. Am. C. of C., Am. Econ. Devel. Council (bd. dirs. 1985-87), Wash. C. of C. Execs. (bd. dirs. 1988-89), Econ. Devel. Execs. Wash., Pacific NW Indsl. Devel. Council. Mem. Reorganized Ch. Jesus Christ Latter-day Saints. Lodge: Rotary. (bd. dirs. Tacoma club 1985-87). Office: Tacoma-Pierce County C of C PO Box 1933 Tacoma WA 98401

GRAYSON, DONALD KENNETH, archaeologist, educator; b. N.Y.C., Apr. 10, 1945; S. S.A. and Marion Grayson; m. Barbara E. Proller, Mar. 24, 1968. BA, SUNY, Buffalo, 1966; MA, U. Oreg., 1969, PhD, 1973. Asst. prof. anthropology Kirkland Coll., Clinton, N.Y., 1971-74; archaeologist Bur. Land Mgmt., Portland, Oreg., 1974-75; asst. prof. U. Wash., Seattle, 1975-78, assoc. prof., 1978-83, prof., 1983—; adj. asst. prof. Quaternary Research Ctr., U. Wash., 1975-78, adj. assoc. prof., 1978-82; adj. prof., 1983—; vis. assoc. prof. NYU, 1981; adj. asst. curator environ. archaeology Thomas Burke Meml. Mus., U. Wash., 1977-78, adj. assoc. curator 1978-83, adj. curator 1983—; research assoc. dept. anthropology, Am. Mus. Nat. History, 1979—; cons. U. Oreg. archaeol. crew, 1973; dir. Kirkland Coll. archaeol. crew, 1973, Bur. Land Mgmt. archaeol. crews, 1975, U. Wash. archaeol. field sch., 1978, 79, 80; dir. various small mammal censuses throughout Oreg., Nev., Calif., 1975-87. Author: The Establishment of Human Antiquity, 1983 (Book of Yr. in anthropology, Am. Library Assn., 1983), Quantitative Zooarchaeology, 1984, Danger Cave, Last Supper Cave, Hanging Rock Shelter: The Faunas, 1988; editor Volcanic Activity and Human Ecology, 1979, Studies in Archaeological Science, 1983-85; assoc. editor Quaternary Research, 1983—; mem. editorial bd. Advances in Archaeolog. Method and Theory, 1983—; contbr. articles to profl. jours. Grantee NSF 1977-80, 80-82, 81-83, 83-84, 85-87, 88-90, U. Oreg. 1969, Wenner-Gren Found. 1971, Mellon Found. 1973, Am. Philosophical Soc. Penrose Fund 1976, Am. Mus. Nat. History 1977-78, Mr. Bingham's Trust for Charity 1982-83, U.S. Forest Service 1983-84. NDEA Title IV fellow, 1966-69. Mem. NSF (archaeology panel 1985-87), Soc. Am. Archaeology (exec. officer 1979-81, Fryxell award for Interdisciplinary Research 1986), Am. Soc. Conservation Archaeology (v.p. 1977-78, pres. 1978-79), Am. Soc. Mammalogists, Council for Mus. Anthropology, Soc. Systematic Zoology, History of Sci. Soc., Internat. Council Archaeozoology, Sigma Xi. Office: U Wash Dept Anthropology Seattle WA 98195

GRAYSON, ELLISON CAPERS, JR., human resources executive; b. St. Paul, Sept. 7, 1928; s. Ellison Capers and Inez (Santos) G.; m. Jean Mason, Dec. 26, 1952; children: Darby, William. BA, U. Minn., 1950; PhD (hon.), Nat. U., San Diego, 1984. CLU. Gen. agt. Home Life Ins. Co. N.Y., San Francisco, 1955-81; prin. dep., asst. sec. USN, Washington, 1981-84; cons. Washington, 1985-86; sr. v.p. Boyden Internat., San Francisco, 1987—. Commr. City and County of San Francisco, 1978-81; pres. bd. dirs. St. Mary's Hosp. and Med. Ctr., San Francisco, 1972-75; co-chmn. nat. finance com. Bush for Pres; bd. regents St. Ignatius Coll. Preparatory, San Francisco. Capt. USN, 1952-55. Named Eagle Scout Boy Scouts Am., 1944; recipient Nat. Brotherhood award Nat. Assn. Christians and Jews, San Diego, 1984. Mem. Sovereign Mil. (knight 1978), Order of St. John of Jerusalem, Knights of Malta, Bohemian Club, Met. Club (Washington), St. Francis Yacht Club, Army Navy Club. Republican. Roman Catholic. Home: 95 Sea Cliff Ave San Francisco CA 94121 Office: Boyden Internat 1 Maritime Pla San Francisco CA 94111

GRAYSON, JOHN WESLEY, business consultant, computer science educator; b. N.Y.C., Sept. 7, 1941; s. Roger Henry and Dorothy Mae (Kenny) G.; children—John Wesley Jr., Carleton Avery. M.A., SUNY-Stony Brook, 1974; postgrad. U. West Los Angeles Sch. Law, 1979. Programmer, Data Stats., Inc., N.Y.C., 1961-62; sr. programmer Computech, Inc., N.Y.C., 1962-65; systems analyst Nat. Shoes, Inc., Bronx, N.Y., 1965-68; sr. systems analyst Acad. Press, Inc., N.Y.C., 1968-69; sr. systems cons. Grumman Aerospace Corp., 1969-71; sr. mgmt. cons. FRB, N.Y.C., 1971-72; coll. lectr., mgr. mgmt. info. systems SUNY-Stony Brook, 1972-76; communications cons. Gen. Telephone Calif., Los Angeles, 1976-79; owner, pres. Bus. Cons. Firm, Glendale, Calif., 1980; lectr. Compton (Calif.) Community Coll., Long Beach City Coll., El Camino Coll., SUNY-Stony Brook; instr. Long Beach City Coll. Treas., Sunset Baseball Little League, Redondo Beach, Calif.; pres. 147th Bd. Election Dist. Insps., N.Y.; trustee Middle Island (N.Y.) Pub. Library; SBA pres. U. West Los Angeles Sch. Law, 1979; com. examiner Glendale (Calif.) Unified Sch. Dist.; mem. usher bd. St. Francis Episcopal Ch., also mem. choir; scoutmaster Cub Scouts Am., St. James, N.Y.; mem. West High Sch. Band Assn., Torrance, Calif., West High Sch. PTA. Mem. Data Processing Mgmt. Assn., Assn. Systems Mgmt., ACM (treas.). Republican. Clubs: Suffolk County Republican (Brook Haven, N.Y.); Pioneer Track (N.Y.); Los Verdes Men's Golf; Masons, Shriners. Home and Office: 1533 S Pearl Ave Compton CA 90221

GREANEY, MARGARET JEAN, science educator; b. Newburyport, Mass., Jan. 15, 1941; d. Dennis Christopher and Edna Jean (Hall) Finnegan; m. William F. Greaney, May 18, 1968; 1 child, Kara-Ann. BA, U. N.H., 1962. Cert. tchr., Mass., Colo. Research asst. Tufts-New Eng. Med. Ctr., Boston, 1962-63, Harvard Med./Thordike Lab., Boston, 1964-66; tchr. sci. Newburyport High Sch., 1966-68, Killingworth (Conn.) Elem. Sch., 1968-69; substitute tchr. Amherst (N.Y.) Cen. Sr. High Sch., 1969-70; gen. chmn. St. Mary's Acad., Denver, 1984-85; tchr. sci. Marycrest High Sch., Denver, 1986—; tech. asst. New Eng. Jour. Medicine, 1966. Mem. swim parents com. Bear Creek Swim and Tennis Club, Lakewood, Colo., tennis capt. 1985, 86, 87, bd. dirs. 1970-72, Denver Ballet Guild; fundraiser St. Mary's Acad., 1981-84; bd. dirs. Les Cygnetts, 1984-87. Mem. AAUW, U.S. Tennis Assn. Roman Catholic. Home: 8753 E Cornell Ave #4 Lakewood CO 80227

GREAT, DON CHARLES, music company executive, composer; b. Medford, Oreg., Mar. 11, 1951; s. Donald Charles Sr. and Anna Marie (Huff) G.; m. Andrea Louise Gerber, Oct. 31, 1970. Student, UCLA, 1975-76, 83-86, Dick Grove Sch. Music, 1983-87. Freelance songwriter Metro-Goldwyn-Mayer Records, 20th Century Records, Bell Records, Los Angeles, 1968—; pres. Don Great Music, Inc., Los Angeles, 1972—. Composer music for TV shows including Who's the Boss? (ABC), 227 (NBC), The Jeffersons (CBS), Diff'rent Strokes (NBC), Real People (NBC), Gimme a Break (NBC), 1978—, Facts of Life (NBC), Married with Children (Fox Network), Small Wonder, Amen's (NBC), Saved by the Bell (NBC), Freddie's Nightmare (Warner Bros.); theatrical features include: Alls Fair Movie Store, Fright Nite (part 2-TriStar) Kareem, Reflestions from Within (CBS/Fox), Nightmare on Elm StreetPart 2 (Lorimar). Mem. Broadcast Music, Inc. (Best Music Score of Yr. award 1986, named TV Composer of Yr. 1986). Home: 3867 Rhodes Ave Studio City CA 91604 Office: 1800 N Argyle Ste 202 Hollywood CA 90028

GREAVES, PETER DAVID, architect; b. Flint, Mich., Mar. 5, 1953; s. Roland Edwin and Patricia June (Albugh) G. AA in Architecture, Ohio U., 1972; BArch, Syracuse U., 1977. Registered architect, Wash. Drafter, checker Roland E. Greaves, Inc., Rochester, N.Y., 1968-72; exec. asst. L.M. Lawrence Corp., Rochester, 1972-74; drafter Connell & Light, Rochester, 1974; architect Schuchart & Assocs., Inc., cons. engrs., Seattle, 1977-83, Ibsen Nelsen & Assocs., P.S., architects and planners, Seattle, 1983-86; ptnr. Workshop 3D, Seattle, 1986-89; mng. dir. Architects on Line, Seattle, 1986-89; pres. Workshop 3D Software Inc., Seattle, 1987—; ptnr. Olsen, Compton, Greaves, Seattle, 1989—. Prin. works include Inn at the Market improvements, Seattle, 1986—, Oysterville House, Seattle, 1986, Inn at the Market Penthouse, Seattle 1987, Zebraclub, Seattle, 1987, MPCurtis Studio, Seattle, 1987, Texaco Puget Sound Plant, 1987--, numerous others. Recipient Home of Month award Seattle chpt. AIA-Seattle Times, 1986. Mem. AIA, Soc. for Mktg. Profl. Services. Democrat. Episcopalian. Home: 3832 39th Ave S Seattle WA 98118-1110 Office: Olsen Compton Greaves 215 Second Ave Ste 307 Seattle WA 98104

GRECO, ANNA MARIA, electrical engineer, program manager; b. East Chicago, Ind., Dec. 25, 1958; d. Dominick Antonio and Concetta Giovanna (Libri) G. BSEE magna cum laude, San Diego State U., 1981. Assoc. engr. Electron Inc., San Diego, 1979-81; engr. Burroughs Corp., San Diego, 1981-85; staff engr. Tacan Corp., Carlsbad, Calif., 1985-88; program mgr. Tacan Corp., Carlsbad, 1988—, also corp. sec., 1986—. Recipient scholarship, R. H. Fleet Found., San Diego, 1979, Nat. Elec. Contractor's Assn., San Diego, 1980. Mem. IEEE, Tau Beta Pi, Eta Kappa Nu. Democrat.

GREELY, MICHAEL TRUMAN, lawyer, former state attorney general; b. Great Falls, Mont., Feb. 28, 1940; s. Myril Jay and Laura Harriet (Haugh) G.; m. Marilyn Jean Myhre, Dec. 1, 1972; children: Winston Truman, Morgen, Anna Lee. B.A., Yale U., 1962; J.D., U. Mont., 1967. Bar: Mont. 1967. Tchr. pub. schs. Oklahoma City, 1962-63; asst. atty. gen. Mont., 1968-70, atty. gen., 1977-88; chmn. Mont. Justice Project, 1975; dep. county atty. Cascade County, Mont., 1970-74. Mem. Mont. Ho. of Reps., 1971-74; mem. Mont. Senate, 1975-77; Pres. 8th Dist. Youth Guidance Home, Great Falls, 1971-72. Mem. Nat. Assn. Attys. Gen. (pres. 1983-84), Mont., Cascade County bar assns. Democrat. Address: PO Box 162 Helena MT 59624

GREEN, BARRY, lawyer; b. Bklyn., Oct. 24, 1957; s. Joseph Allen and Anne (Polsky) G. BA in Am. Studies, Brandeis U., 1978; JD, Tulane U., 1982. Bar: N.Mex. 1982, U.S. Dist. Ct. N.Mex. 1986. Asst. dist. atty. Dist. Atty.'s Office, Santa Fe, 1983; pvt. practice Santa Fe, 1983—. Active Greenpeace, 1986, Amnesty Internat., 1987, Wilderness Soc., 1986, Jacques Cousteau Soc. Recipient Pro Bono award Lawyer Referral Project for Elderly, N.Mex., 1987. Mem. Assn. Trial Lawyers Am., N.Mex. Trial Lawyers Assn., N.Mex. Bar Assn., Greenpeace. Democrat. Jewish.

GREEN, CECIL DENNIS, management, marketing and investment counselor, educator; b. Balt., Dec. 12, 1936; s. Cecil Zachary and Catherine L. (Follin) G.; A.A., Pasadena City Coll., 1958; B.A. with honors, U. Calif.-Santa Barbara, 1960; M.A., Calif. State U.-Los Angeles, 1963; Ph.D., U.S. Internat. U., 1974; m. Janet Mary Yoest, July 21, 1977; children—Tony, Donald, Denise. Dean occupational edn. Riverside (Calif.) Community Coll., 1966-76; prof. master degree program U. Calif.-Long Beach, 1974-76; pres. Real Estate Edn. Corp., Mgmt. and Investment Counseling Co.; gen. partner Research and Devel. Jojoba Tax Shelter Project; now mgmt. and investment cons. Bd. dirs. San Bernardino-Riverside Counties Industry Edn. Council. Served with USMC, 1959-62. NSF scholar, 1959-60. Mem. Phi Delta Kappa. Republican. Clubs: Rialto, Riverside, Canyon Crest Country; Lions, Rotary, Elks., Masons. Cons.: Human Behavior in Organizations, 1981. Home: 17334 Ranchero Rd Riverside CA 92504 Office: 4800 Magnolia Ave Riverside CA 92506

GREEN, CORENA CRASE, management consultant; b. Grass Valley, Calif., Apr. 7, 1917; d. James Carter and Drucilla Grace (Hicks) Crase; m. Harold Francis Green, Dec. 6, 1950; children: Elizabeth, James, Richard. BA, Stanford U., 1938. Cert. tchr. Calif. Tchr. Oakland (Calif.) Pub. Schs., 1939-43; sec. Am. Trust Co., San Francisco, 1945-48; reporter Independent Journal, San Rafael, Calif., 1958-63; editor Palos Verdes Peninsula (Calif.) News, 1964-74; officer pub. info. Unified Sch. Dist., Palos Verdes Peninsula, 1974-77; sec./treas. LOSALCO Inc., Palo Alto, Calif., 1984—. Pres. Marin County (Calif.) Council Girl Scouts U.S., 1962; v.p. Marin County ARC, 1963. Served as lt. U.S. Navy, 1943-45. Recipient Thanks Badge Marin County Girl Scouts U.S., San Rafael, Calif., 1962, numerous writing and editing awards Calif. Newspaper Publishers, Nat. Presswomen, Calif. Presswomen; named hon. life mem. Palo Verdes (Calif.) PTA Council, 1974. Mem. Calif. Pubs. Assn. (editor's com. 1972-75), AAUW (Status Women award 1975). Club: Women's Nine Hole Golf Assn. (No. Calif., pres. 1988). Home: 10410 Albertsworth Ln Los Altos Hills CA 94022

GREEN, CYRIL KENNETH, retail company executive; b. Portland, Oreg., June 11, 1931; s. Lionel and Nora Evelyn (Walker) G.; m. Beverly Ann Hutchinson, July 24, 1950; children: Kenneth James, Teri Ann, Tamara Jo Green Easton, Kelly Denise Green Van Horn. Student pub. schs., Portland. Salesperson Fred Meyer Inc., Portland, Oreg., 1947-53, mgr. food dept., 1953-57, supr. food div., 1957-60, buyer food div., 1960-64, head buyer food div., 1964-67; gen. mgr. Roundup Co. subs. Fred Meyer Inc., Spokane, Wash., 1967-70; dir. ops. Fred Meyer Inc., Portland, Wash., 1970-72, pres., 1972—, chief operating officer, from 1972; vice chmn., bd. dirs. Oreg. Trail chpt. ARC, Portland, 1984—; bd. dirs. Marylhurst Coll., Portland, 1987—. Office: Fred Meyer Inc 3800 SE 22d Ave PO Box 42121 Portland OR 97242

GREEN, DEBORAH LYNN, real estate banker; b. Portland, Oreg., Oct. 7, 1951; d. John Claude and Margaret Pauline (Polley) Cannon; 1 child, Nathaniel J. Student, Oreg. State U., 1969, Centralia (Wash.) Community Coll., 1974-77; BBA, U. Alaska, 1987. Office asst. Fed. Land Bank, Chehalis, Wash., 1974-77; loan closer People's Bank & Trust, Anchorage, 1977-78, Alaska Bank of Commerce, Anchorage, 1978-79; asst. v.p. First Nat. Bank Anchorage, 1979-84; v.p. Alaska State Bank, Anchorage, 1987-88, Nat. Bank Alaska, Anchorage, 1988—. Chairperson career awareness com. for Explorer Scouts, Boy Scouts Am. Mem. Alaska Mortgage Bankers Assn. (edn. com.), Rotary (vocat. dir. 1987-88, sec. 1988—). Home: 4365 Constellation Ave 27 Anchorage AK 99517 Office: Nat Bank Alaska 301 W Northern Lights Blvd Anchorage AK 99503

GREEN, EDWARD WISNER, insurance adjuster; b. N.Y.C., Aug. 20, 1962; s. Emmett Wisner and Clare (Godsell) G. BS in Fin., Ariz. State U., 1985. Chief exec. officer Raven Group, Scottsdale, 1984—. Precinct committeeman Ariz. Rep. Party, 1987—. Republican. Presbyterian. Home: 7900 E Princess Dr #1012 Scottsdale AZ 85255

GREEN, FRANCES MARION, lawyer; b. Milledgeville, Ga., Oct. 14, 1945; d. Frank M. and Alice (Kelley) G. BA in Econs., Wellesley Coll., 1966; postgrad. in econs., George Washington U., 1967-68, JD with honors, 1972. Bar: D.C. 1973, Colo. 1983. Mgmt. intern U.S. Dept. Labor, Washington, 1968-69; clk. to judge U.S. Dist. Ct., Montgomery, Ala., 1972-73; assoc. Wilmer, Cutler & Pickering, Washington, 1973-77; dep. assoc. atty. gen. U.S. Dept. Justice, Washington, 1977-79; spl. asst. U.S. Atty. U.S. Dept. Justice, Alexandria, Va., 1979-80; dep. gen. counsel U.S. Dept. Commerce, Washington, 1980-81; counsel natural resource clinic Nat. Wildlife Fedn., Boulder, Colo., 1982-84; pvt. practice Boulder, Colo., 1985—. assoc. editor George Washington Law Rev., 1970-71, notes editor, 1971-72; editor natural resource law notes Colo. Lawyer, 1986—. Mem. energy adv. bd. City of Boulder, 1987; bd. dirs. So. Poverty Law Ctr. Trustee scholar, 1970-72. Mem. ABA (vice chmn. environ. values com. 1988—), Colo. Bar Assn. Democrat. Home: 3755 Silver Plume Ln Boulder CO 80303 Office: 1405 Arapahoe Ste 200 Boulder CO 80302

GREEN, FRANCIS WILLIAM, investment consultant; b. Locust Grove, Okla., Mar. 17, 1920; s. Noel Francis and Mary (Lincoln) G.; B.S., Phoenix U., 1955; M.S. in Elec. Engring., Minerva U., Milan, Italy, 1959; M.S. in Engring., West Coast U., Los Angeles, 1965; m. Alma J. Ellison, Aug. 26, 1950 (dec. Sept. 1970); children—Sharmon, Rhonda; m. Susan G. Mathis, July 14, 1973 (div. July 1979). With USN Guided Missile Program, 1945-49; design and electronic project engr. Falcon missile program Hughes Aircraft Co., Culver City, Calif., 1949-55; sr. electronic engr. Atlas missile program Convair Astronautics, San Diego, 1955-59; sr. engr. Polaris missile program Nortronics div. Northrop, Anaheim, Calif., 1959-60; chief, supr. electronic engr. data systems br. Tech. Support div. Rocket Propulsion Lab., USAF, Edwards AFB, Calif., 1960-67, dep. chief tech. support div., 1967-69; tech. adviser Air Force Missile Devel. Ctr., Holloman AFB, N.Mex., 1969-70, 6585 Test Group, Air Force Spl. Weapons Ctr., Holloman AFB, from 1970; pvt. investment cons., 1978—. Bd. examiners U.S. CSC; mem. Pres.'s Missile Site Labor Relations Com.; cons. advanced computer and data processing tech. and systems engring.; mem. USAF Civilian Policy Bd. and Range Comdrs. Council. Served as pilot USAAF, 1941-45. Fellow Am. Inst. Aeros. and Astronautics; mem. IEEE, Nat. Assn. Flight Instrs. Contbr. articles to profl. jours. Home and Office: 2345 Apache Ln Alamogordo NM 88310

GREEN, GEORGE, radio executive; b. N.Y.C., May 23; m. Mim, Aug. 23, 1958; children—Jeff, Randy, Jamie. B., UCLA, 1955. Acct. exec. Sta. KPAL, Palm Springs, Calif., 1956-57, KDAY-KRHM, Los Angeles, 1957-59; salesman Sta. KABC-TV, Los Angeles, 1959-60, acct. exec. Sta. KABC, Los Angeles, 1960-65, gen. sales mgr., 1965-79, gen. mgr., 1979—, v.p., 1979-86, pres., 1986—. Mem. exec. com. United Cerebral Palsy/Spastic Children's Found., Los Angeles, 1980—. Recipient Lifesaver award Advt. Industry Emergency Fund, Los Angeles, 1983. Mem. So. Calif. Broadcaster's Assn. (chmn. 1983—), Ad Club (bd. dirs. 1980—). *

GREEN, HOWARD I., television executive; b. Detroit, Mar. 9, 1936; s. Albert and Fanya (Newman) G. BA, U. Mich., 1957, MA, 1958, JD, 1961. Artistic dir. Counterpoint Theater Co., N.Y.C., 1974-81; v.p. sales, contract & systems adminstrn. Paramount Pictures Corp., L.A., 1982—.

GREEN, JACQUELINE ANNE, public relations executive; b. London, May 14, 1940; came to U.S., 1962; d. Francis John and Joan Margaret (Bott) G. Diploma, S.W. Essex Tech. Coll. and Sch. of Art, London, 1958. Pub. relations sec. Sands Hotel, Las Vegas, Nev., 1962-65; pub. relations asst. Riviera Hotel, Las Vegas, 1965-70; asst. to pres. Price, Stern, Sloan Pub. Co., Los Angeles, 1970-74; prodn. exec. Atkins Gilbert, Beverly Hills, Calif., 1974-77; pub. relations exec. Hanson & Schwam, Beverly Hills, 1977-79; pres. Jacqueline Green Pub. Relations Inc., Beverly Hills, 1979—. Mem. Acad. TV Arts and Scis., Publicists Guild, Women in Film, Hollywood Women's Press Club. Office: Jacqueline Green Pub Rels Inc 9320 Olympic Blvd Ste 202 Beverly Hills CA 90212

GREEN, JAMES CRAIG, data systems company executive; b. Gladstone, Mich., Apr. 19, 1933; s. Albert Keene and Margaret Josephine (Craig) G.; student Coll. of Gt. Falls, 1951-53, UCLA, 1962; m. Catherine Maxwell, Nov. 1, 1957; children—Cindi, Shelley, Nancy, James W., Robert. Clk., carrier U.S. Post Office, Gt. Falls, Mont., 1951-57; clk. office and sales Mont. Liquor Control Bd., Gt. Falls, 1957-59; payroll clk. Herald Examiner, Hearst Publs., Los Angeles, 1959-67, data processing mgr., 1967-75, data processing ops. mgr. corp. hdqrs. Hearst Publs., N.Y.C., 1975-78; gen. mgr., v.p. Computer/Data Inc., Billings, Mont., 1978-83; mgr. customer service Big Sky Data Systems, Billings, Mont., 1983-84; pres. FACTS, Inc., 1985—; tax cons., Los Angeles, 1962-75. Cub Scout leader, com. chmn., Los Angeles council Boy Scouts Am., 1973-75; pres. Bus. Office Employees Assn. Los Angeles, 1963-66. Area commr. Black Otter Council Boy Scouts Am., 1982-84, com. chmn., 1982-84. Served with USNR, 1951-59. Recipient degree of Chevalier, Order De Molay, 1951, Legion of Honor degree.; cert. data processing mgr. Mem. Data Processing Mgrs. Assn., Los Angeles Masonic Press Club. Clubs: Masons, Blue Lodge, York Rite, Scottish Rite, Shrine (Grotto charter mem. Gt. Falls), DeMolay (chpt. advisor 1983—, state advisor 1982—). Writer, negotiator contract Bus. Office Employees Assn., Los Angeles, 1965. Office: 2110 Wiligate Ln Billings MT 59102

GREEN, JOHN MORRISH, marketing professional; b. Butte, Mont., May 10, 1948; s. Morrish and Verna Maxine (Yeager) G.; m. Sandra Wynn McGuin, Dec. 28, 1968; children: Shawna Renee, Marnee Joell. BS in Bus. Mgmt., Mont. State U., Bozeman, 1970. Sr. buyer Dayton-Hudson Corp., Mpls., 1970-73; div. mgr. F.A. Buttrey Co., Great Falls, Mont., 1973-75; sales mgr. Lawrence Jewelry Co., Denver, 1975-78; pres. Direction 25, Aurora, Colo., 1978-84, Johnson Enterprises, Aurora, 1979—. Pres. Mont. Young Reps., 1969; precinct leader Colo. Reps., 1988; deacon Presbyn. Ch., Aurora, 1976-79, elder, 1979-82. Named Outstanding Young Man in Am., 1975. Mem. World-Wide Deacon and Elders, Mont. State U. Alumni Assn.,

Elks, Phi Beta Lambda, Sigma Chi Alumni Assn. Colo. Home: 15407 E Jarvis Pl Aurora CO 80013

GREEN, KENNETH HARLON, forest products industry executive; b. Fargo, N.D., Sept. 7, 1948; s. Wilfred Harlon and Harriet Jean (McKenzie) G.; m. Jeanine Madeleine Gauthier, Jan. 30, 1971; children: Brian Harlon, Juline Michelle. BS, U. Mont., 1970. With nat. park svc. Glacier Nat. Park, 1968; forest intern Weyerhauser Co., Longview, Wash., 1969; cruiser U.S. Forest Svc., Great Falls, Mont., 1970; forester Burlington No., Inc., Missoula, Mont., 1971-78; supr. engring. and access Burlington No. Timberlands, Inc., Missoula, 1979-85; supt. prodn. Plum Creek Timer Co., Missoula, 1985-88; indsl. analyst Plum Creek Timer Co., Inc., Missoula, 1988—. Hill leader Nat. Ski Patro, Missoula, 1985-88; vice chmn. bd. trustees Dist. 4, Missoula, 1985-88; bd. dirs. Mont. Sch. Bds. Assn., Helena, Mont., 1986-88. Mem. Soc. Am. Foresters, Mont. Forestry Alumni Assn. (pres. 1986-88). Roman Catholic. Home: 2305 Houston Circle Whitefish MT 59937 Office: Plum Creek Timber Co PO Box 160 Columbia Falls MT 59912

GREEN, LESLIE CLAUDE, political science and international law educator; b. London, Nov. 6, 1920; arrived in Can., 1965; s. Israel Willie and Raie (Goldberg) G.; m. Lilian Denise Meyer, Sept. 1, 1945; 1 child, Anne Roslyn. LLB with honors, U. Coll. London, 1941; LLD, U. London, 1971. Lectr. U. Coll. London, 1946-60; prof. internat. law U. Singapore, 1960-65; prof. polit. sci. U. Alta., Edmonton, Can., 1965-69; univ. prof. U. Alta., Edmonton, 1969—; legal advisor Can. Delegation Conf. on Humanitarian Law, Geneva, 1975-77; acad. in residence to Legal Dept., dept. external affairs, 1974-75, JAG, Nat. Def. Hdqrs., Ottawa, Can., 1979-80; vis. prof. Kyung Hee U., Seoul, Republic of Korea, 1985; hon. prof. of law U. Alta., 1982—. Author: International Law Through the Cases, 4th rev. edit., 1978, Law and Society, 1975, Superior Orders in National and International Law, 1976, International Law-A Canadian Perspective, 2d rev. edit., 1988, Essays on the Modern Law of War, 1985; (with O.P. Dickason) The Law of Nations and the New World, 1989. Served to maj. Brit. Army, 1941-46. Recipient Cecil Peace prize U. Bur. Brit. Empire, 1941, Grotius Found. medal, 1954, U. Alta. Research Prize, 1982; fellow Royal Soc. Can., 1980. Jewish. Club: Athenaeum (London). Home: 7911 119 St, Edmonton Can T6G 1W6 Office: U Alta, Dept Polit Sci, Edmonton, AB Canada TGG 2H4

GREEN, MARJORIE BILLER, educational administrator; b. Boston, Nov. 5, 1939; d. David Wolfe and Martha S. (Rosenthal) Biller; m. Jason I. Green, Mar. 17, 1963; children: Nancy Elke, David Charles, Matthew Adam. AB cum laude, Boston U., 1961, MA, 1964; postgrad., U. Calif., Berkeley, 1961-62, UCLA, 1973-78. Ednl. cons. Rand Corp., Los Angeles, 1977-78; coordinator Wilshire Community Edn. Complex, Los Angeles, 1979-80; cons. Los Angeles Unified Sch. Dist., 1980-83; exec. dir. Calif. Coalition Pub. Edn., Los Angeles, 1985-87; dir. western states edn. Anti-Defamation League of B'nai B'rith, Los Angeles, 1987—. Mem. Mayor Bradley's Edn. Adv. Com., Los Angeles, 1979—; del. Dem. Nat. Conv., San Francisco, 1984; chairperson 24th Congl. Dist. Women-to-Women campaign, Los Angeles, 1984; mem. Los Angeles Commn. Sex Equity, 1984—; bd. dirs. Community Relations Conf. So. Calif., 1984, bd. dirs., 1985—; bd. dirs. Para los Niños, Los Angeles, 1984—; bd. dirs. community relations com. Jewish Fedn. Council So. Calif., 1986, chmn. edn. commn., 1986—. Recipient Outstanding Service award Los Angeles Unified Sch. Dist., 1981-82, Outstanding Contbn. award Los Angeles Commn. Sex Equity, 1983, citation Calif. Assembly, 1986, Euclan award U. Calif., 1986. Mem. LWV, Phi Beta Kappa, Phi Delta Kappa. Home: 218 S Lorraine Blvd Los Angeles CA 90004 Office: Anti-Defamation League Dir Western States Edn 6505 Wilshire Blvd #814 Los Angeles CA 90048

GREEN, MICHAEL JAY, foundation administrator; b. Cleve., Aug. 7, 1947; s. Philip Erman and Leah (Gertzlin) G. BA, U. Ariz., 1976, JD, 1983. Chief exec. officer Tucson (Ariz.) Landscape Constrn., 1976-81; plant broker, chief exec. officer Kickass Cactus Inc., Tucson, 1976-81; pvt. practice Tucson, 1983-85; pub. defender Territory of Am. Samoa, Pago Pago, 1985-86; exec. dir. Jewish Community Found., Tucson, 1986—; counsel Pago Pago Yacht Club, 1985-86, So. Ariz. Woodworkers Assn., Tucson, 1987—; dir. M. Revak & Co., Tucson. Editor art catalogue Jerusalem Print Workshop, 1988. Chmn. Amnesty Now, Tucson, 1975-78; mem. Nuclear Free State, Tucson, 1976-78; chmn. Jewish Com. on Scouting, Tucson; mem. Catalina coun. Boy Scouts Am., Tucson; race chmn. Pago Pago Yacht Club, 1985-86. With USN, 1967-73, Vietnam. Mem. ABA, Ariz. Bar Assn., So. Ariz. Estate Planners, Phi Beta Kappa, Phi Kappa Phi. Jewish. Office: Jewish Community Found 635 N Craycroft Rd Tucson AZ 85711

GREEN, NEIL LYLE, anesthesiologist; b. Winnipeg, Man., Canada, June 1, 1952; s. Harry Nathan and Rebecca (Claman) G.; m. Mary Jean Walker, Feb. 10, 1982 (div. 1985); m. Lauri Anne Durdahl, July 31, 1986; 1 child, Jennifer Lynn. BS, UCLA, 1974; MD, U. N.Mex., 1979. Intern, categorical anesthesiology U. Utah Sch. Med., 1979-80, anesthesiology resident, 1980-82; practicing medicine specializing in anesthesiology Bremerton, Wash., 1982-84, Albuquerque, 1985-87, Colorado Springs, Colo., 1987--; staff anesthesiolgist U. N.Mex., Albuquerque, 1984-85. Mem. Am. Soc. Anesthesiologists, Am. Soaring Soc., Alpha Omega Alpha. Home: 3942 Broadmoor Valley Rd Colorado Springs CO 80906 Office: Saint Frances Hosp 825 E Pikes Peak Colorado Springs CO 80903

GREEN, PAUL CECIL, management consultant; b. Oconto, Nebr., Sept. 8, 1919; s. Paul Simpson Green and Ruth Adelaide (Kennedy) Elder; m. Carole Jean Pass, Dec. 21, 1964. BSBA, U. Nebr., 1941; MBA, Harvard U., 1948. CLU. Dir. sales Continental Assurance Co., Chgo., 1948-62, v.p. mktg., 1962-73; v.p. mktg. USLIFE Corp., N.Y.C., 1973-75; sr. v.p. Helmich, Miller and Pasek, Inc., Chgo., 1975-81; pres. Paul C. Green and Assocs., Ltd., Green Valley, Ariz., 1981—; chmn. bd. CLU Jour., Bryn Mar, Pa. Contbr. articles to profl. jours. Precinct capt. Young Repubs., Chgo.; bd. dirs. Green Valley Recreation, Inc.; exec. bd. Green Valley Coordinating Council; pres. Foothills IV Homeowners Assn., Green Valley. Lt. col. USAF, 1942-46. Recipient Achievement award City of Hope, 1977, 78. Mem. Am. Soc. Chartered Life Underwriters, Internat. Assn. Fin. Planners, Life Ins. Mktg. and Research Assn. (chmn. various coms.), Harvard Bus. Sch. Club (Phoenix chpt.), Country Club of Green Valley. Presbyterian. Home: 551 Paseo del Cobre Green Valley AZ 85614 Office: PO Box 1448 Green Valley AZ 85622

GREEN, RICHARD, psychiatrist, lawyer, educator; b. Bklyn., June 6, 1936; s. Leo Harry and Rose (Ingber) G.; 1 child, Adam Hines. AB, Syracuse U., 1957; MD, Johns Hopkins U., 1961; JD, Yale U., 1987. Diplomate, Am. Bd. Psychiatry and Neurology. Intern Kings County Hosp., Bklyn., 1962-64; resident in psychiatryand neurology Nat. Inst. Mental Health, Bethesda, Md., 1965-66; asst. prof., assoc. prof., then prof. dept. psychiatry UCLA, 1968-74; prof. psychiatry and psychology SUNY, Stony Brook, 1974-85; prof. psychiatry UCLA, 1986—, prof. law, 1988—. Author: Sexual Identity Conflict in Children and Adults, 1974, Impotence, 1981, Sissy Boy Syndrome and the Development of Homosexuality, 1987; co-author, co-editor: Transsexualism and Sex Reassignment, 1969, Human Sexuality: A Health Practitioner's Text, 1975, 2d edit. 1979; editor Jour. Archives of Sexual Behavior, 1981—. Vol. atty., ACLU, LA. Vis. scholar, U. Cambridge, Eng., 1980-81; fellow, Ctr. Advanced Study in Behavioral Scis., Stanford, Calif., 1982-83. Fellow Am. Psychiat. Assn., Soc. Sci. Study Sex (past pres.), Am. Coll. Legal Medicine; mem. Internat. Acad. Sex Rsch. (founding pres. 1973), Calif. Bar Assn. Office: UCLA Neuropsychiatric 760 Westwood Pla Los Angeles CA 90024

GREEN, SIMON POM, talent agency executive; b. N.Y.C., Sept. 29, 1965; s. Daniel and Jane (Oliphant) G. BA, Vassar Coll., 1987. Sales rep. Giorgio Armani, N.Y.C., 1987; v.p. St. James, N.Y.C., 1987-88; agt.-in-tng. Triad Artists, L.A., 1988—.

GREEN, TEREK VON, electrical engineer; b. Balt., Dec. 25, 1964; s. Clyde Von and Eleanor Marie (Offer) G. BEE, Morgan State U., 1985; cert., Motorola Engring. tng. program, 1986. Registered profl. engr., Ariz. Elect. engr. NASA Goddard Space Flight Ctr., Greenbelt, Md., 1985-86; large scale integration design engr. Motorola Strategic Electronic div., Chandler, Ariz., 1986—; cons. Phoenix Bus. Exchange, 1987—. Ariz. rep. Nat. Black Caucus, Washington, 1987. Mem. IEEE, Ariz. Council of Black Engrs. (co-chmn. 1986-87, youth motivation award, 1986), Soc. of Black Engrs. (Motorola Corp. rep.), Soc. of Profl. Engrs., Phi Sigma Phi (v.p. 1984-85), Eta Kappa Nu, Alpha Phi Alpha, Tau Beta Pi. Democrat. Roman Catholic. Home: 4422 E St Anne Ave Phoenix AZ 85040

GREEN, WILLIAM PORTER, lawyer; b. Jacksonville, Ill., Mar. 19, 1920; s. Hugh Parker and Clara Belle (Hopper) G.; m. Rose Marie Hall, Oct. 1, 1944; children: Hugh Michael, Robert Alan, Richard William. B.A., Ill. Coll., 1941; J.D., Northwestern U., 1947. Bar: Ill. 1947, Calif. 1948, U.S. Dist. Ct. (so. dist.) Tex. 1986, Ct. Customs and Patent Appeals 1948, U.S. Patent and Trademark Office 1948, U.S. Ct. Appeals (fed. cir.) 1982, U.S. Ct. Appeals (5th and 9th cirs.), U.S. Supreme Ct. 1948, U.S. Dist. Ct. (cen. dist.) Calif., U.S. Dist. Ct. (so. dist.) Tex., 1986. Practice patent, trademark and copyright law Los Angeles, 1947—; mem. firm Wills, Green & Mueth, 1974-83; of counsel Nilsson, Robbins, Dalgarn, Berliner, Carson & Wurst, Los Angeles, 1984—; del. Calif. State Bar Conv., 1982-88, delegation chair 1986. Bd. editors Ill. Law Rev, 1946. Mem. Los Angeles World Affairs Council, 1975—; del., chmn. Calif. State Bar Conv., 1986. Lt. USNR, 1942-46. Mem. ABA, Calif State Bar, Am. Intellectual Property Law Assn., Los Angeles Patent Law Assn. (past sec.-treas., bd. govs.), Lawyers Club Los Angeles (past treas., past sec., bd. govs., pres.-elect 1983-84, pres. 1985-86), Los Angeles County Bar Assn (trustee 1986-87), Am. Legion (past post comdr.), Phi Beta Kappa, Phi Delta Phi, Phi Alpha. Republican. Presbyn. (deacon 1961-63). Clubs: Big Ten of So. Calif, Northwestern U. Alumni of So. Calif, Phi Beta Kappa Alumni of So. Calif, Town Hall of Calif. Home: 3570 E Lombardy Rd Pasadena CA 91107 Office: Nilsson Robbins Dalgarn Berliner Carson & Wurst 201 N Figueroa St 5th Fl Los Angeles CA 90012

GREENAWALT, DAVID FRANKLIN, food products executive; b. 1933; married;. BS in Econs., U. Pa., 1955. Dist. operating mgr. Sealtest Foods div. Dart-Kraft Co., 1959-67; v.p. ops. Farmbest Inc., 1967-73; exec. v.p. Dairylea Coop. Inc., 1973-77; v.p. product engring. William Underwood Co., 1977-79; sr. v.p. mfg. Knudsen Foods Inc., Los Angeles, 1979-80, exec. v.p. ops., 1980-82, pres., chief operating officer, 1982; pres., chief operating officer Santee Dairies, Los Angeles. Served with USMC, 1956-59. Mem. Merchants and Mfrs. Assn. (bd. dirs.), Internat. Ice Cream Assn. (bd. dirs.), Milk Industry Found. (bd. dirs.). Office: Santee Dairies Inc PO Box 60310 Terminal Annex Los Angeles CA 90060

GREENBERG, DAVID ETHAN, communications consultant; b. N.Y.C., Oct. 8, 1949; s. Abraham M. and Norda B. (Jacovitz) G.; m. Kerri Shwayder, Apr. 24, 1983; children: Alison Leigh, Zachary Scott. BA cum laude, Columbia U., 1971; JD, Harvard U., 1975. Bar: Colo. 1975. Speechwriter Gov. Richard D. Lamm, Denver, 1977-78, legal counsel, 1978-79; dir. mktg. Colo. Ski Country U.S.A., Denver, 1979-82; sr. ptnr. Greenberg, Baron and Simon, Denver, 1982—; assoc. prof. U. of Colo., Denver, 1984—. Columnist, The Denver Post, 1985-88. Spl. asst. to adminstr. for communications EPA, Washington, 1989; pres. Childrens' Mus. Denver, 1988; bd. dirs. Am. Ctr. for Internat. Leadership, Columbus, Ind., 1987—. Named Nat. Merit Scholar, N.Y.C., 1967. Mem. Denver C. of C. (leadership Denver com.). Office: Greenberg Baron Simon 535 16th St Denver CO 80202

GREENBERG, EDWARD SEYMOUR, political science educator; b. Phila., July 1, 1942; s. Samuel and Yetta (Kaplan) G.; m. Martha Ann Baker, Dec. 24, 1964; children: Joshua, Nathaniel. BA, Miami (Ohio) U., 1964, MA, 1965; PhD, U. Wis., 1969. Asst. prof. polit. sci. Stanford (Calif.) U., 1968-72; assoc. prof. Ind. U., Bloomington, 1972-73; prof. U. Colo., Boulder, 1973—, dir. research program polit. and econ. change Inst. Behavioral Sci., 1980—, chair dept. polit. sci., 1985-88. Author: Serving the Few, 1974, Understanding Modern Government, 1979, Capitalism and the American Political Ideal, 1985, The American Political System, 1989, Workplace Democracy, 1986 (Dean's Writing award Social Scis. 1987); contbr. aticles to profl. jours. Recipient fellowship In Recognition of Disting. Teaching, 1968; Russell Sage Found. grantee, 1968, U. Wis. grantee, 1968; grantee NSF, 1976, 82, 85. Mem. Internat. Polit. Sci. Assn., Am. Polit. Sci. Assn., Western Polit. Sci. Assn. (mem. exec. bd. 1986—). Home: 755 11th St Boulder CO 80302 Office: U of Colo Dept of Polit Sci Box 333 Boulder CO 80309

GREENBERG, ELINOR MILLER, college administrator; b. Bklyn., Nov. 13, 1932; d. Ray and Susan (Weiss) Miller; m. Manuel Greenberg, Dec. 26, 1955; children: Andrea, Julie, Michael. BA, Mt. Holyoke Coll., 1953; MA, U. Wis.-Madison, 1954; EdD, U. No. Colo., 1981; LittD (hon.), St. Mary-of-the-Woods, Ind., 1983; LHD (hon.), Profl. Sch. Psychology, Calif., 1987. Exec. dir. Arapahao Inst. for Community Devel., Littleton, Colo., 1969-71; founding dir. Univ. without Walls, Loretto Heights Coll., Denver, 1971-79, asst. acad. dean, 1982-84, asst. to pres., 1984-85; regional exec. officer, mgr. Council for Adult and Experiential Learning, Columbia, Md., 1979—; program adminstr. U.S. West Communication CWA, Pathways to the Future, 1986—, Communications Workers Am.; cons. in field. Co-editor, contbr.: Educating Learners of All Ages, 1980; co-author: Designing Undergraduate Education, 1981, Widening Ripples, 1986, Leading Effectively, 1987; editor, contbr.: New Partnerships: Higher Education and the Nonprofit Sector, 1982; contbr. articles to profl. jours. Bd. dirs., exec. com. Anti Defamation League of B'nai B'rith, Denver, 1981—; vice chair Colo. State Bd. for Community Colls. and Occupational Edn., 1981-86; bd. dirs. Internat. Women's Forum, Griffith Ctr., Golden, Colo., 1982-86, Colo. Bd. Continuing Legal and Jud. Edn., 1984—; pres. Women's Forum of Colo., 1986; v.p. Women's Forum Colo. Found., 1987; mem. adv. bd. Anchor Ctr. Blind Child, Colo. Coalition Prevention Nuclear War; mem. Nat. Conf. on Edn. for Women's Devel., Community Adv. Bd. Colo. Woman News, Gov.'s Women's Econ. Devel. Taskforce; co-chair Women's Econ. Devel. Council, 1988—. Named Citizen of Yr. Omega Psi Phi, Denver, 1966; Woman of Decade Littleton Ind. Newspapers, 1970; grantee W. K. Kellogg Found., 1982, Weyerhauser Found., 1986, Fund for Improvement of Post Secondary Edn., 1977, 80; recipient Sesquicentennial award Mt. Holyoke Coll. Alumni Assn., 1987. Mem. Am. Assn. for Higher Edn., Assn. for Experiential Edn. (editorial bd. 1978-80), ACLU, Am. Council in Edn., Kappa Delta Pi. Democrat. Jewish. Home: 6725 S Adams Way Littleton CO 80122

GREENBERG, IRA ARTHUR, psychologist; b. Bklyn., June 26, 1924; s. Philip and Minnie (S.) G.; BA in Journalism, U. Okla., 1949; MA in English, U. So. Calif., 1962; MS in Counseling, Calif. State U. L.A., 1963; PhD in Psychology, Claremont (Calif.) Grad Sch., 1967. Editor, Ft. Riley (Kans.) Guidon, 1950-51; reporter, copy editor Columbus (Ga.) Enquirer, 1951-55; reporter Louisville Courier-Jour., 1955-56, L.A. Times, 1956-62; free-lance writer, L.A., Montclair, Camarillo, Calif., 1960-69, 76—; counselor Claremont Coll. Psychol. Clinic and Counseling Ctr., 1964-65; lectr. psychology Chapman Coll., Orange, Calif., 1965-66; psychologist Camarillo State Hosp., 1967-69, supervising psychologist, 1969-73, part-time clin. psychologist, 1973—; part-time asst. prof. edn. San Fernando Valley State Coll., Northridge, Calif., 1967-69, lectr. psychodrama, social welfare U. Calif. Extension Div., Santa Barbara, 1968-69; vol. psychologist Free Clinic, L.A., 1968-70; staff dir. Calif. Inst. Psychodrama, 1969-71; tng. cons. Topanga Ctr. for Human Devel., 1970-75, bd. dirs., 1971-74, faculty Calif. Sch. Profl. Psychology, 1970—; founder, exec. dir. Behavioral Studies Inst., mgmt. cons., L.A., 1970—; pvt. practice cons. in psychology, psychodrama, hypnosis, 1970—; founder, exec. dir. Psychodrama Ctr. for L.A., Inc., 1971—, Group Hypnosis Ctr., L.A., 1976—; producer, host TV talk show Crime and Pub. Safety, Century Cable, Channel 3, 1983—. Vol. humane officer State of Calif., 1979—; res. officer L.A. Police Dept., 1980-86; bd. dirs. Human Ecutors Coun., 1982-86; capt. Calif. State Mil. Res., 1986—. With AUS, 1943-46; ETO; USAR, 1950-51. Fellow Am. Soc. Clin. Hypnosis; mem. Am. Soc. Group Psychotherapy and Psychodrama, Assn. Rsch. and Enlightenment, L.A. Soc. Clin. Psychologists (dir. 1975), Am. Psychol. Assn., Western Psychol. Assn., Calif. Psychol. Assn., Los Angeles Psychol. Assns., Am. Soc. for Psychol. Rsch., Group Psychotherapy Assn. So. Calif. (dir. 1974-76, 82-87, pres. 1987-87), Am. Mgmt. Assn., Am. Soc. Bus. and Mgmt. Cons. (nat. adv. coun. 1977—), So. Calif. Soc. Clin. Hypnosis (dir., exec. v.p. 1973-76, pres. 1977-78), So. Calif. Psychotherapy Affiliation (dir. 1976-85), Assn. for Humanistic Psychology, Mensa, Am. Zionist Fedn., Nat. Rifle Assn., Calif. Rifle and Pistol Assn., SW Pistol League, Animal Protection Inst. Am., Airport Psychol. Assocs., Sigma Delta Chi. Clubs: Sierra, Greater L.A. Press; B'nai B'rith; Beverly Hills Gun. Author: Psychodrama and Audience Attitude Change, 1968. Editor, author: Psychodrama: Theory and Therapy, 1974; Group Hypnotherapy and Hypnodrama, 1977. Address: Camarillo State Hosp Box A Camarillo CA 93011 also: BSI & Group Hypnosis Ctr 11692 Chenault St Ste 206 Los Angeles CA 90049

GREENBERG, MARVIN, music educator; b. N.Y.C., June 24, 1936; s. Samuel and Rae (Sherry) G.; B.S. cum laude, N.Y. U., 1957; M.A., Columbia U., 1958, Ed.D., 1962. Tchr. elem. schs., N.Y.C., 1957-63; prof. music edn. U. Hawaii, Honolulu, 1963—, research cons. Center for Early Childhood Research, 1969-71; edn. adminstr. Model Cities project for disadvantaged children Family Services Center, Honolulu, 1971-72. Cons. western region Volt Tech. Services, Head Start program, 1969-71; Head Start worker, 1972-75; Child Devel. Assoc. Consortium rep., 1975—. Recipient several fed. and state grants for ednl. research and curriculum projects. Mem. Hawaii Music Educators Assn., Music Educators Nat. Conf., Soc. for Research in Music Edn., Council for Research in Music Edn., Nat. Assn. for Edn. Young Children. Author: Teaching Music in the Elementary School: Guide for ETV Programs, 1966; Preschool Music Curriculum, 1970; Music Handbook for the Elementary School, 1972; Staff Training in Child Care in Hawaii, 1975; Your Child Needs Music, 1979; also articles. Home: 2575 Kuhio Ave 19-2 Honolulu HI 96815 Office: 2411 Dole St MB203 Honolulu HI 96822

GREENBERG, MILTON, corporation executive; b. Carteret, N.J., Apr. 21, 1918; s. David and Eva (Salzer) G.; m. Maxine Carol Baer, June 30, 1948; children: Eve Diane, David Max, Alan Baer. Student, CCNY, 1934-40; B.A., NYU, 1943; M.P.A., Harvard U., 1954; Sc.D. (hon.), Canaan Coll., 1961, Merrimack Coll., North Andover, Mass., 1981; D.H.L. (hon.), U. Lowell, 1985. Research and devel. planner Air Force Cambridge Research Center, 1947-49, dep. dir. operations and planning Geophysics Research div., 1947-54, dir. Geophysics Research Directorate, 1954-58; pres. GCA Corp., 1958-84, chmn., chief exec. officer, 1958-86; First chmn. tech. mgmt. council Air Research and Devel. Command, 1957-58; U.S. del. to XIth Gen. Assembly, Internat. Union Geodesy & Geophysics, 1957; mem. Upper-Air Rocket & Satellite Research Panel; mem. central radio propagation lab. adv. panel of Nat. Acad. Scis., 1963-1968; mem. exec. com. Mass. Tech. Park Corp., 1982-86, currently dir. Editor-in-chief Planetary and Space Science, 1957-62; mem. editorial adv. bd. 1962-75. Bd. dirs. Mass. High Tech. Council, 1978-86, mem. exec. com., 1981-86; Selectman Town of Andover, Mass., 1971-77; Trustee Canaan (N.H.) Coll., 1960-72, Merrimack Coll., 1983—. Served from cadet to maj. USAAF, 1943-47; geophysicist. Recipient Exceptional Civilian Service medal USAF, 1957. Asso. fellow AIAA; fellow AAAS; mem. Sigma Xi, Mu Chi Sigma, Beta Lambda Sigma.

GREENBERG, MYRON SILVER, lawyer; b. Los Angeles, Oct. 17, 1945; s. Earl W. and Geri (Silver) G.; m. Shlomit Gross; children: David, Amy. BSBA, UCLA, 1967, JD, 1970. Bar: Calif. 1971, U.S. Dist. Ct. (cen. dist.) Calif. 1971, U.S. Tax Ct. 1977; CPA, Calif. Staff acct. Touche Ross & Co., Los Angeles, 1970-71; assoc. Kaplan, Livingston, Goodwin, Berkowitz, & Selvin, Beverly Hills, 1971-74; ptnr. Dinkelspiel, Steefel & Levitt, San Francisco, 1975-80; ptnr. Steefel, Levitt & Weiss, San Francisco, 1981-82; pres. Myron S. Greenberg, a Profl. Corp., Larkspur, Calif., 1982—; professorial lectr. tax. Golden Gate U.; instr. U. Calif., Berkeley, 1989—. Author: California Attorney's Guide to Professional Corporations, 1977, 79; bd. editors UCLA Law Rev., 1969-70. Mem. San Anselmo Planning Commn., 1976-77; bd. dirs. Bay Area Lawyers for Arts, 1979-80, Marin County chpt. Am. Heart Assn. (bd. dirs., pres. 1984—). Mem. ABA, Marin County (Calif.) Bar Assn., Bus. Execs. Assn. of Marin, Am. Inst. CPA's, Calif. Soc. CPA's, Real Estate Tax Inst. of Calif. Continuing Edn. Bar (planning com.), Larkspur C. of C. (bd. dirs. 1985-87). Democrat. Jewish. Office: 80 E Sir Frances Drake Blvd Larkspur CA 94939

GREENE, ALVIN, service company executive, management consultant; b. Pitts., Aug. 26, 1932; s. Samuel David and Yetta (Kroff) G.; B.A., Stanford U., 1954, M.B.A., 1959; m. M. Louise Sokol, Nov. 11, 1977; children—Sharon, Ami, Ann, Daniel. Asst. to pres. Narmco Industries, Inc., San Diego, 1959-62; adminstrv. mgr., mgr. mktg. Whittaker Corp., L.A., 1962-67; sr. v.p. Cordura Corp., L.A., 1967-75; chmn. bd. Sharon-Sage, Inc., L.A., 1975-79; exec. v.p., chief operating officer Republic Distbrs., Inc., Carson, Calif., 1979-81, also dir.; chief operating officer Memel, Jacobs & Ellsworth, 1981-87, 87—; pres. SCI Cons., Inc.; dir. Sharon-Sage, Inc., True Data Corp.; vis. prof. Am. Grad. Sch. Bus., Phoenix, 1977-81. Chmn. bd. commrs. Housing Authority City of L.A., 1983-88 . Served to 1st lt., U.S. Army, 1955-57. Mem. Direct Mail Assn., Safety Helmet Mfrs. Assn., Bradley Group. Office: 10960 Wilshire Blvd Ste 1226 Los Angeles CA 90024

GREENE, BILL, state senator; b. Kansas City, Mo., Nov. 15, 1931; m. Yvonne LaFargue; children—Alisa Rochelle, Jan Andrea. Ed. Lincoln Jr. Coll., U. Mich. Mem. Calif. State Assembly, 1967-75, chmn. indsl. relations com., mem. govt. orgn. and fin. coms., elections and reapportionment, chmn. fin. subcom. on health and welfare; now mem. Calif. State Senate; del. Democratic Nat. Conv., 1980. Clk. Calif. State Assembly; labor cons., legis. adv., legis. asst. to Assemblyman Mervyn Dymally; field rep. Los Angeles County Dem. Central Com.; former regional dir. Calif. Fedn. Young Dems.; mem. YMCA, NAACP, CORE, Urban League. Served with U.S. Air Force. Home: 8514 Broadway Los Angeles CA 90003 Office: Office of State Senate State Capitol Sacramento CA 95814

GREENE, D. EDWARD, marketing executive; b. Benton Harbor, Mich., Oct. 17, 1940; s. Kenneth Elsworth and Ruth Alice (Peterson) G.; m. Rea Sue Green (div. June 1, 1965; 1 child, Steven Dale; m. Betty Jean Domeny, June 22, 1968; children: David Edward, Michael Alan. BS, Southern Ill. U., 1963. Sales rep. Mt. Vernon (Ill.) Electric Supply Co., 1955-62; sales/mktg. trainee Olivetti Corp., San Diego, 1968-72; regional mgr. Worthington Biochem. Co., San Diego, 1973-83; cons. Abacus Data Systems, Del Mar, Calif., 1984-86; dir. sales Sensatron, Inc., San Diego, 1986--. Lt. USN 1963-68. Mem. Sales and Mktg Execs. (bd. dirs.), Armed Forces Aero Club, San Diego Yacht Club, Quail Unlimited (chmn. 1988—), Optimist (bd. dirs.). Republican. Methodist. Home: 3538 Elsinore Pl Unit L-21 San Diego CA 92117

GREENE, FRANK S., JR., information systems business executive; b. Washington, Oct. 19, 1938; s. Frank S. Sr. and Irma O. Greene; m. Phyllis Davison, Jan. 1958 (dec. 1984); children: Angela, Frank; m. Nilene D. Fitzpatrick, Sept. 1985; children: Christopher, David. BS, Washington U., St. Louis, 1961; MS, Purdue U., 1962; PhD, U. Santa Clara (Calif.), 1970. Part-time lectr. Washington U., Howard U., Am. U., 1959-65; dir., chmn. Tech. Devel. Corp., Arlington, Tex., 1985—; pres. Zero One Systems, Inc. (formerly Tech. Devel. of Calif.) Santa Clara, Calif., 1971-87, Zero One Systems Group subs. Sterling Software Inc., 1987—; asst. chmn., lectr. Stanford U., 1972-74; dir. Networked Picture Systems Inc. Author two indsl. textbooks; also articles; patentee in field. Bd. dirs. NCCJ, Santa Clara, 1980—, NAACP, San Jose chpt., 1986-88; bd. regents U. Santa Clara, 1983—; mem. adv. bd. Urban League, Santa Clara County, 1986—. Capt. USAF, 1961-65. Mem. Assn. Black Mfrs. (dir., 1974-80), Am. Electric Assn. (indsl. adv. bd., 1975-76), Fairchild Research and Devel. (tech. staff, 1965-71), IEEE, IEEE Computer Soc. (governing bd., 1973-75), Bay Area Purchasing Council (dir. 1978-84), Security Affairs Support Assn. (dir. 1980-83), Sigma Xi, Eta Kappa Nu. Office: ZeroOne Systems Group Sterling Software Inc 4401 Great American Pkwy Santa Clara CA 95054

GREENE, HOWARD BERKLEY, engineering test pilot; b. Mt. Sterling, Ky., Jan. 13, 1940; s. Harold Crail and Catherine (Howell) G.; m. Margaret Ratcliff, June 7, 1964; children: Mary Ann, Kathleen. BSEE, Purdue U., 1963; grad., USAF Pilot Tng. Sch., 1964; postgrad., Ohio U., 1968; grad., USAF Test Pilot Sch., Edwards AFB, Calif., 1970. Test pilot FAA, Seattle, 1970—. Served to capt. USAF, 1963-68. Decorated Air medal. Mem. IEEE, Soc. Automotive Engrs., Soc. Exptl. Test Pilots. Office: FAA ANM-1605 17900 Pacific Hwy S Seattle WA 98168

GREENE, JAMES FIEDLER, real estate executive; b. Rochester, Minn., Feb. 15, 1958; s. Laurence Francis and Rosalyn Estelle (Ravits) G. BA, Colo. Coll., 1980; MBA, U. Denver, 1987. Lic. real estate broker, Colo. Exec. broker Coldwell Banker Comml. Group, Denver, 1982—. Mem. Alumni awards com. Colo. Coll., Denver, 1986—. Club: Colo. Coll. Gold, Denver Athletic Colo. Office: Coldwell Banker Comml Group 1775 Sherman Ste 2700 Denver CO 80203

GREENE, JOHN CLIFFORD, dentist, university dean; b. Ashland, Ky., July 19, 1926; s. G. Norman and Ella R. G.; m. Gwen Rustin, Nov. 17, 1957; children: Alan, Lisa, Laura. A.A., Ashland Jr. Coll., 1947; student, Marshall Coll., 1948; D.M.D., U. Louisville, 1952, Sc.D. (hon.), 1980; M.P.H., U. Calif., Berkeley, 1961; Sc.D. (hon.), U. Ky., 1972, Boston U., 1975. Diplomate: Am. Bd. Dental Public Health (pres.). Intern USPHS Hosp., Chgo., 1952-53; staff USPHS Hosp., San Francisco, 1953-54; asst. regional dental cons. Region IX, San Francisco, 1954-56; asst. to chief dental officer Region IX, Washington, 1958-60; chief epidemiology program Dental Health Center, 1961-66; dep. dir. Div. Dental Health, 1966-70, acting dir., 1970, dir., 1970-73; acting dir. Bur. Health Resources Devel., 1973-74, dir., 1974-75; chief dental officer USPHS, 1974-81, dep. surgeon gen., 1978-81; with Epidemic Intelligence Service, Communicable Disease Center, Altanta and Kansas City, Mo., 1956-57; epidemiology and biometry br. Nat. Inst. Dental Research, NIH, Bethesda, Md., 1957-58; dean. Sch. Dentistry, U. Calif., San Francisco, 1981—; spl. cons. WHO, India, 1957; faculty Calif., U. Mich., U. Pa.; cons. Am. Dental Assn. Council, Nat. Health Professions Placement Network. Contbr. writings to profl. publs. Served with USN, 1945-46. Recipient citation Sch. Grad. Dentistry Boston U., 1971, citation U. of the Pacific, 1977, Meritorious and Disting. Service awards HEW, 1972, 75, Outstanding Alumnus award U. Louisville, 1980, award of merit FDI, 1978; Alumnus of Yr. award U. Calif. Sch. Pub. Health, Berkeley, 1984. Fellow Am. Coll. Dentists; mem. ADA, Calif. Dental Assn., San Francisco Dental Soc., Internat. Assn. Dental Research, Am. Assn. Dental Research (pres.), Am. Assn. Public Health Dentists, Am. Acad. Periodontology, Am. Assn. Dental Schs. (v.p.), Inst. of Medicine of Nat. Acad. Sci., Federation Dentaire Internationale (chmn. commn. on public dental health, mem. WHO panel of experts on dental health), Omicron Kappa Upsilon, Delta Omega. Home: 103 Peacock Dr San Rafael CA 94901 Office: U Calif Sch Dentistry 513 Parnassus Ave Rm S-630 San Francisco CA 94143-0430

GREENE, JOHN THOMAS, JR., judge; b. Salt Lake City, Nov. 28, 1929; s. John Thomas and Mary Agnes (Hindley) G.; m. Kay Buchanan, Mar. 31, 1955; children: Thomas B., John B., Mary Kay. B.A., U. Utah, 1952, J.D., 1955. Bar: Utah 1955. Law clk. Supreme Ct. Utah, Salt Lake City, 1954-55; asst. U.S. atty. Dist. Utah, Salt Lake City, 1957-59; partner firm Marr, Wilkins & Cannon, Salt Lake City, 1959-69, Cannon, Greene & Nebeker, Salt Lake City, 1969-74, Greene, Callister & Nebeker, Salt Lake City, 1974-85; judge U.S. Dist. Ct. Utah, 1985—; spl. asst. atty. gen. State of Utah, 1965-69; spl. grand jury counsel Salt Lake County, 1970; pres. Utah Bar Found., 1971-74, trustee, 1971-88. Author: sect. on mining rights American Law of Mining, 1965; contbr. articles to profl. jours. Pres. Community Svcs. Coun., Salt Lake City area, 1971-73; chmn. Utah Bldg. Authority, 1980-85; mem. Utah State Bd. Regents, 1983-86. Mem. Utah Bar Assn. (pres. 1970-71, chmn. judiciary com. 1971-76, chmn. com. post. law sch. tng. 1985-89), ABA (Utah del. to ho. of dels. 1975-81, 82-88, mem. bd. govs., 1988—, mem. spl. com. delivery legal service 1975-81, council gen. practice sect. 1974-82, chmn. spl. com. on environ. law 1971-75, mem. adv. com. Nat. Legal Service Corp. 1975-81, chmn. standing com. on jud. selection, tenure and compensation 1985-88), Am. Inn Ct. II (pres. 1983-84, bd. govs. 1988—), U. Utah Alumni Assn. (dir. 1968-69), Utah State Bd. Regents, Order of Coif, Phi Beta Kappa, Phi Kappa Phi. Mormon. Clubs: Ft. Douglas Country, Salt Lake Tennis. Office: US Dist Ct 220 US Courthouse 350 S Main St Salt Lake City UT 84101

GREENE, MICHAEL THRONTON, lawyer; b. N.Y.C., Feb. 8, 1941; s. Irving B. and Mildred (Stern) G.; m. Lori S. Morris, May 6, 1984; children: Sage Margot, Winston Zachary. BA, Antioch Coll., Ohio, 1963; LLB, Harvard U., 1966. Bar: Calif. 1966. Dep. dist. atty. County of L.A., 1966-67; asst. U.S. atty. City of L.A., 1967-68; founding ptnr. Greene & Pancer, L.A., 1969-75; mng. ptnr. Greene Properties, Pagosa Springs, Colo., 1975-78; ptnr. DeCastro & Greene, L.A., 1978-81; mng. ptnr. Western Investment Assocs., Farmington, N.Mex., 1981—. Mem. Calif. State Bar Assn., Real Estate Broker N.Mex., Sierra Club, Trout Unlimited Club, Fedn. Fly Fisherman Club. Home: 3211 Mountainview Dr Farmington NM 87401

GREENE, ROBERT HARGRAVE, JR., savings and loan executive; b. Newark, July 7, 1929; s. Robert Hargrave Greene Sr. and Lillie Mae (Snead) Greene-Bureau; m. June M. Brennan, Sept. 27, 1952; children: Susan Ann Greene Rump, Robert Hargrave III, Pamela Mae Greene Waggoner. BS, U. San Francisco, 1982; MA, Calif. State U., Carson, 1988. Asst. auditor Howard Savs. Bank, Newark, 1950-68; v.p., auditor Bank of Commonwealth, Detroit, 1968-73; v.p., gen. auditor Security Nat. Bank, Walnut Creek, Calif., 1974-81, Republic Bank, Torrance, Calif., 1981-83; v.p., dir. auditing Foothill Group, L.A., 1983-85; sr. v.p., gen. auditor 1st Security Savs. Bank, Pleasant Hill, Calif., 1986--. Treas. Pleasant Hill Homeowners Assn. (treas. 1987-88). Mem. Inst. Internal Auditors (cert.). Home: 161 Southwind Dr Pleasant Hill CA 94523 Office: 1st Security Savs Bank 622 Contra Costa Blvd Pleasant Hill CA 94523

GREENFELD, SUSAN THERESA, management educator; b. Pitts., July 21, 1946; d. Robert Duane and Theresa Lillian (Duquette) Robertson; div. 1976; 1 child, Darcy Lee. BA in Psychology, Whittier Coll., 1968; MBA, Calif. State U., 1973; D Bus. Adminstrn., U. So. Calif., 1978. Asst. prof. Tex. A&M U., 1977-80; asst. prof. U. Balt., 1980-81, dir. women's program mgmt., 1983, acting chair dept. mgmt., 1983-84, assoc. prof., 1981-86; prof. Sch. Bus. Salisbury State U., 1986-87; prof. Calif. State U., San Bernardino, 1987—; dividend analyst, customer svc. rep. Mitchum, Jones & Templeton, 1969-71; job developer, West L.A. Coll., 1977; adj. faculty U. So. Calif., 1983, Johns Hopkins U., 1987; speaker, presenter in field. Contbr. articles to numerous publs. Mem. Acad. Mgmt. (bd. dirs. Women in Mgmt. div.), AAUW (legis. chair Redlands br. 1988—),Beta Gamma Sigma, Sigma Iota Epsilon, Phi Delta Gamma. Office: Calif State Univ 5500 University Pkwy San Bernardino CA 92407

GREENFIELD, GERALD RICHARD, computer systems analyst; b. Miami Beach, Fla., July 8, 1939; s. Arthur and Martha Silvia (Marcus) G.; m. Corinne Sue Elzer, Dec. 22, 1963; 1 child, Katrina Louise. BA, Dartmouth Coll., 1961, B of Indsl. Adminstrn., 1962, MBA, 1965; JD, U. W. Los Angeles, Culver City, 1977. Bar: Calif. 1977. Sr. engr. Rockwell Internat., Downey Calif., 1962-66; asst. project mgr. Teledyne Corp., Santa Monica, Calif., 1966-67; planning officer Security Pacific Nat. Bank, Los Angeles, 1967-68; mgmt. cons. Mgmt. Computer Tech., Santa Monica, 1968-72; sr. data processor, bus. research analyst TRW Inc., Redondo Beach, Calif., 1972-78; sr. systems analyst Westinghouse Hanford Co., Richland, Wash., 1978—; adj. instr. Santa Monica Coll., 1970-78, Cen. Wash. U., Ellensburg, 1979-87, U. Wash., Seattle, 1984-85. Bd. dirs. Richland Community Concerts Assn., 1985-88, Richland Sunfest Assn., 1988; chmn. Richland Sausage Fest, 1985; bd. dirs. Mid-Columbia Symphony Soc., Richland, 1984—, pres. 1987, treas. 1988. Mem. Assn. for Systems Mgmt. Jewish. Home: 2112 Davison Richland WA 99352

GREENFIELD, PATRICIA ANN MARKS, psychology educator; b. Newark, July 18, 1940; d. David and Doris Jeannette (Pollard) Marks; m. Sheldon Greenfield, Mar. 13, 1965 (div.); children; Lauren, Matthew Michael. AB summa cum laude, Radcliffe Coll., 1962; PhD in Social Psychology, Harvard U., 1966. Research fellow in psychology Ctr. for Cognitive Studies Harvard U., Cambridge, Mass., 1968-72; vis. asst. prof. psychology Stanford (Calif.) U., 1972-73; asst. prof. U. Calif., Santa Cruz, 1973-74; assoc. prof. UCLA, 1974-78, prof., 1978—; bd. dirs. Westside Women's Clinic; external examiner U. Lagos, 1977-79; collaborating scientist Yerkes Regional Primate Ctr., Emory U., 1979—. Contbr. articles to profl. jours. Recipient 1st award Am. Insts. Research, 1967, award div. 2 Am. Psychol. Assn., 1986; named Sci. scholar Bunting Inst. Radcliffe Coll., 1986-87. Fellow AAAS, Am. Psychol. Assn.; mem. Soc. Research in Child Devel. Home: 42 Park Ave Venice CA 90291

GREENHILL, J. RAYMOND, retail executive, consultant; b. Cross plains, Tex., Mar. 20, 1913; s. Jesse Monroe and Alice (Steen) G.; m. Mary Foster, Sept. 15, 1935; children: Robert F., Raymond M. Buyer Golden Rule Dept. Store, St. Paul, 1935-36; buyer Powers Dry Goods Dept. Store, Mpls., 1937-47, v.p., merchandise mgr., 1947-50; v.p., dir. Stewart & Co., Balt., 1950-57, pres., 1958-66; v.p. J.W. Robinson Co., L.A., 1966-80; owner Greenhill Design Cons., Palos Verdes, Calif., 1980—; v.p. Assoc. Dry Goods Corp., N.Y.C., 1958; pres. Delivery of Balt.; bd. dirs. Cavendish Trading Corp., N.Y.C., Gibson Island Corp. Bd. dirs. Greater Balt. Com., com. for Downtown, Better Bus. Bur. Greater L.A., Mayor's Coordinating Coun., Howard St. Assn.; chmn. United Fund Appeal, Eye Bank of Md. Commr., Balt. Econ. Devel. Commn.; bd. govs. Palos Verdes Community Arts Assn.; adv. commn. El Pueglo de L.A. State Hist. Monument Commn. Mem. Retail Mchts. Balt. (pres., bd. dirs.), Nat. Retail Mchts. Assn., Maryland Club, Univ. Club Balt., Gibson Island Club (bd. govs.), Riviera Tennis Club., L.A. Athletic Club, Lambda Phi Alpha. Home: 1825 Via Visalia Palos Verdes CA 90274

GREENLAND, DAVID EDWARD, geography educator; b. Bournemouth, Eng., Aug. 19, 1940; came to U.S., 1965; s. Edward Henry and Grace Ada (Haggar) G.; m. Risa I. Palm, June 28, 1976; 1 child, John. BS, U. Birmingham, Eng., 1963, MS, 1965; PhD, U. Canterbury, Christchurch, New Zealand, 1971. Sr. lectr. U. Canterbury, 1966-75; prof. geography, chmn. Geography dept. U. Colo., Boulder, 1976—. Author: Guidelines for Modern Resource Management, 1983; co-author: The Earth inProfile, 1977. Rsch. grantee USDA Forest Svc., 1978, NSF, 1980—. Mem. Assn. Am. Geographers, Am. Meteorol. Soc., Am. Geophys. Union, Royal Meteorol. Soc., Internat. Mountain Soc. Episcopalian. Office: U Colo Dept Geography Campus Box 260 Boulder CO 80302-0260

GREENLAND, THOMAS ROY, real estate executive; b. Tucson, Dec. 4, 1954; s. Roy and Henrietta (Holtrop) G.; m. Eunice Carol Brouwer, Aug. 17, 1977; children: Jason, Kevin. BSBA, U. Ariz., 1977; MBA, Golden Gate U., 1984. Mktg. rep. Mobil Oil Co., Las Vegas, Nev., 1978-83; real estate rep. Southland Corp., Las Vegas, 1983-86; mgr. real estate div. Southland Corp., Pleasanton, Calif., 1986—; instr. Golden Gate U., Las Vega, 1985-86. Mem. Nat. Assn. Real Estate Execs., Internat. Council Shopping Ctrs. Republican. Home: 2560 Toltec Circle San Ramon CA 94583 Office: Southland Corp 5820 Stoneridge Mall Rd Ste 310 Pleasanton CA 94566

GREENLAW, ROGER LEE, interior designer; b. New London, Conn., Oct. 12, 1936; s. Kenneth Nelson and Lyndell Lee (Stinson) G.; children—Carol Jennifer, Roger Lee. B.F.A., Syracuse U., 1958. Interior designer Cannell & Chaffin, 1958-59, William C. Wagner, Architect, Los Angeles, 1959-60, Gen. Fireproofing Co., Los Angeles, 1960-62, K-S Wilshire, Inc., Los Angeles, 1963-64; dir. interior design Calif. Desk Co., Los Angeles, 1964-67; sr. interior designer Bechtel Corp., Los Angeles, 1967-70; sr. interior designer, project mgr. Daniel, Mann, Johnson, & Mendehall, Los Angeles, 1970-72, Morganelli-Heumann & Assos., Los Angeles, 1972-73; owner, prin. Greenlaw Design Assos., Glendale, Calif., 1973—; lectr. UCLA; mem. adv. curriculum com. Mt. San Antonio Coll., Walnut, Calif., Fashion Inst. Design, Los Angeles; bd. dirs. Calif. Legis. Conf. Interior Design. Past scoutmaster Verdugo council Boy Scouts Am.; pres. bd. dirs. Unity Ch., La Crescenta, Calif., 1989. Mem. Am. Soc. Interior Designers (treas. Pasadena chpt. 1983-84, pres. 1986-87, 1st v.p. 1985, chmn. So. Calif. regional conf. 1985, nat. dir. 1987—, nat. com. legis., nat. com. jury for catalog award, speaker ho. dels., nat. bd. dirs., medallist award, v.p. Calif. legislative conf. interior design, chmn. standards task force,), Glendale C. of C. (bd. dirs.), Adm. Farragut Acad. Alumni Assn., Delta Upsilon. Republican. Lodge: Kiwanis. Home: 2100f Valderas Dr Glendale CA 91208 Office: 3901 Ocean View Blvd Montrose CA 91020

GREENLEAF, VICKI DARLENE, public relations executive, writer; b. Lancaster, Pa., June 8, 1959; d. E.F. and E. Yvonne (Cramer) G.; m. Julien Bohbot, Dec. 26, 1984. BA in Journalism, Shippensburg U., 1981. Reporter Lancaster (Pa.) newspaper, 1979-82; staff publicist Kragen & Co., L.A., 1982; freelance publicist and writer 1983; dir. publicity Media Home Entertainment, L.A., 1984-85, 20th Century Fox, 1985-86; v.p. publicity, staff publicist Internat. Video Entertainment, 1987—; simultaneously v.p. corp. communications Live Entertainment Inc., 1988—. Contbr. articles to profl. jours. and mags. Home: 4119 Beverly Glen Los Angeles CA 91423 Office: 15300 Sherman Way Ste 500 Van Nuys CA 91400

GREENSLADE, DAVID LESLIE, mechanical engineer; b. Long Beach, Calif., June 30, 1957; s. Ronald Stuart and Jeanette Florence (Timm) G.; m. Dannette Marie Chapin, Dec. 13, 1986; 1 child, Amadee Marie. BS with highest honors, U. Calif.-Santa Barbara, 1979. Assoc. engr. applied systems devel. Westinghouse Hanford Co., Richland, Wash., 1979-81; engr. Westinghouse Hanford Co., 1981-84, advanced engr., 1984-87, sr. engr., 1987-88, prin. engr., 1988--. Office: Westinghouse Hanford Co PO Box 1970/300 Area 306 E Bldg L6-37 Richland WA 99352

GREENSPAN, STEPHEN BARRY, computer technology executive; b. N.Y.C., July 19, 1941; s. Saul Abraham and Gertrude (Smith) G.; m. Ann Soskil, July 1, 1967; children: Alison, Melissa. BSEE, N.J. Inst. Tech., 1967; MSEE, Syracuse U., 1970. With IBM, 1967-86; engr. circuits East Fishkill, N.Y., 1967-70; circuit tech. mgr. Manassas, Va., 1970-78; circuit tech. mgr. Boca Raton, Fla., 1978-83, mgr., CMC, 1983-86; v.p. ops. Tandon Corp., Chatsworth, Calif., 1986-87; v.p. process devel. Seagate Tech., Inc., Scotts Valley, Calif., 1987—. Served with USAF, 1960-63. Recipient invention achievement awards IBM, 1978, 80. Mem. IEEE, Courtside Tennis Club, Eta Kappa Nu, Tau Beta Pi. Republican. Jewish. Home: 13935 Damon Ln Saratoga CA 95070 Office: Seagate Tech Inc 920 Disc Dr Scotts Valley CA 95066

GREENTREE, LEANNE MARIE, health care administrator; b. Calgary, Alta., Can., Oct. 30, 1960; came to U.S., 1979; d. William Wayne Chris and Patricia Ann (Hugo) G. BS, U. Tulsa, 1983; MBA, Golden Gate U., 1987. Dir. arts and crafts Easter Seal Soc., New Durham, N.H., 1979-82; tchr. spl. edn. Sand Springs Pub. Schs., Tulsa, 1983-84; dir. horseback riding program Hissom Meml. Ctr., Tulsa, 1983-84; dir. activities Highland Manor Nursing Ctr., Phoenix, 1984-86; dir. program Royal Oaks Healthcare Ctr., Sun City, Ariz., 1986; cons. Bayview Hunters Point Sr. Ctr., San Francisco, 1988; mgr. mktg. Nat. Emergency Services, Tiburon, Calif., 1987-89; mktg. dir. San Francisco Magnetic Resonance Ctr., 1989—. Artist: works exhibited at U. Tulsa, 1979-82; contbr. articles to profl. jours. Mem. com. Ariz. Spl. Olympics, Phoenix, 1985. Mem. N. Am. Riding Handicapped (conf. speaker 1986), Am. Mktg. Assn., N. Calif. Health Care Mktg. Assn. Home: 353 29th Ave #B San Francisco CA 94121

GREENWALD, SUSAN, former aircraft company executive; b. Long Beach, Calif., Aug. 7, 1945; d. Marinus and Anna (Mair) van Leeuwen; m. Kenton Lee Greenwald, Dec. 9, 1967 (div. June 21, 1977); 1 child, Julie Anna. Student Mt. St. Mary's Coll., 1963-64. Systems service rep. NCR Corp., Los Angeles, 1966-69; self-employed systems cons., Long Beach, Calif., 1969-72; controller Berney-Karp & Assocs., Los Angeles, 1972-78; v.p. mgmt. info. systems Century 21 Real Estate Corp., Irvine, Calif., 1978-82; dir. tech. mktg. support Microdata, Corp., Irvine, 1982-85; dir. tech. services McDonnell Douglas Field Service Co., Irvine, 1985-88. Treas. Friends Irvine Pub. Library, Calif., 1982-88, Parents for the Advancement of Latin Studies U. High Sch., Irvine, 1986-87; dir. Orange County Camp Fire Council, Tustin, Calif., 1980. Mem. Data Processing Mgmt. Assn. (chpt. pres. 1980), MICRU Internat. (pres. 1980-82). Republican. Roman Catholic. Clubs: The 99's Incorporated (chpt. treas. 1974-75; chpt. chmn. 1976-77) (Long Beach, Calif.). Avocation: flying. Home: 12 Oak Tree Ln Irvine CA 92715

GREENWELL, ROGER ALLEN, scientist; b. Santa Maria, Calif., Dec. 4, 1941; s. George C. and Bessie Florence (Sutton) G.; m. Jeannine Pendleton, July 25, 1969; 1 child, George Eli. AA, Hancock Jr. Coll., 1961; BS, Calif. Poly. Coll., 1968; MS, U.S. Internat. U., 1974, DBA, 1981. Mathematician Naval Weapons Ctr., China Lake, Calif., 1968, ops. research analyst, Corona, Calif., 1969-70; ops. research analyst Comdr. Naval Forces, Vietnam, 1968-69; mathematician Naval Electronics Lab. Ctr., San Diego, 1970-77; scientist Naval Ocean Systems Ctr., San Diego, 1977-84; sr. scientist Sci. and Engring. Assoc., Inc., 1984—; cons. fiber optics and econ. analysis; mem. NATO Research Study Group, 1983—. Served with U.S. Army, 1964-67. Decorated Bronze Star. Mem. Ops. Research Soc. Am., Inst. Mgmt. Sci., AIAA, Soc. Allied Weight Engrs., Soc. Photo Optical and Instrumentation Engrs., Optical Soc. Am. Home: 3778 Eagle St San Diego CA 92103 Office: 3838 Camino del Rio North Suite 120 San Diego CA 92108

GREER, DONALD MERRILL, plastic surgeon; b. Chgo., Nov. 14, 1936; s. Donald M. and Mary Elizabeth (Adams) G.; m. Anne Lindsay, June 11, 1966 (div. 1979); children: Donald, William; m. Jane Deely Carr, July 17, 1981; 1 child, Steven. BSc, U. Chgo., 1958; MD, U. Cin., 1962. Diplomate Am. Bd. Plastic Surgery. Resident in surgery U. Chgo., 1962-66, 68-70; resident in plastic surgery U. Mich., Ann Arbor, 1970-72; asst. prof. U. Fla., Gainesville, 1972-75; assoc. prof. U. Tex., San Antonio, 1975-87; pvt. practice Casper, Wyo., 1987—. Lt. comdr., USNR, 1966-68. Fellow ACS; mem. Am. Burn Assn., Am. Soc. Plastic and Reconstructive Surgeons, Am. Cleft Palate Assn. Office: 1300 E A St Casper WY 82601

GREER, ELSIE MARJORIE, small business owner; b. Toepka, July 16, 1915; d. James Henry and Dora Mabel (Nichols) McCoy; m. Harry Adrian Greer, Feb. 7, 1934; children: Etha Kathleen, Edith Karen. Grad. high sch., Tieton, Wash. Self-employed laundry Umatillo, Oreg., 1947-57; self employed cafe Plymouth, Wash., 1957-62; bookkeeper Umatillo Hosp., 1955-56; owner Greer Rentals, Plymouth, 1960—; with Plymouth Post Office, 1975-85, postmaster, 1978-85. Mem. Women's Club of Plymouth, Emblem Club (Hermiston, Oreg.) (pres. 1957-58), Order Eastern Star, Lions Aux. (state v.p. 1956-57). Republican. Home: Christy Rd Plymouth WA 99346

GREER, LINDA JEAN, nurse; b. Seattle, Sept. 6, 1950; d. Norman Joseph and Eileen Louise (Mullen) Foerstel; m. Stephen William Greer, Aug. 25, 1984; children: Amanda Lynne, Michael William James. BS in Nursing, U. Wash., 1972. Asst. head nurse U. Wash. Hosp., Seattle, 1975-79; RN staff Children's Hosp. Seattle, 1981-83; RN clinic Mollie Scott Clinic, Sun Valley, Idaho, 1984—; RN staff Moritz Community Hosp., Sun Valley, 1984—; sec., treas. Flair Inc., Sun Valley, 1987—; mem. audit com. U. Hosp., Seattle, 1976-79. Mem. Sun Valley C. of C., Alpha Xi Delta. Republican. Home: PO Box 602 Sun Valley ID 83353

GREER, MONTE ARNOLD, physician, educator; b. Portland, Oreg., Oct. 26, 1922; s. William Wallace and Rose (Rasmussen) G.; m. Margaret Johnson, Dec. 31, 1943; children: Susan Elizabeth, Richard Arnold. Student, Oreg. State U., 1940-43; A.B., Stanford U., 1944, M.D., 1947. Intern San Francisco Gen. Hosp., 1946-47; research fellow endocrinology New Eng. Med. Center, Boston, 1947-49; resident internal medicine Mass. Meml. Hosp., Boston, 1949-50; research assoc. in endocrinology New Eng. Med. Center Hosp., 1950-51; sr. investigator, sr. asst. surgeon USPHS, Nat. Cancer Inst., NIH, Bethesda, Md., 1951-55; chief radioisotope unit VA Hosp., Long Beach, Calif.; clin. asst. prof. medicine UCLA, 1955-56; faculty, head div. endocrinology U. Oreg. Med. Sch., Portland, 1956-80; prof. medicine U. Oreg. Med. Sch., 1962—; head div. endocrinology, metabolism and clin. nutrition Oreg. Health Scis. U., 1980-84, head sect. endocrinology, 1984—. Author: (with H. Studer) The Regulation of Thyroid Function in Iodine Deficiency, 1968, (with P. Langer) Antithyroid Drugs and Naturally Occurring Goitrogens, 1977; Editor: (with D.H. Solomon) The Thyroid, 1974; Mem. editorial bd.: Endocrinology, 1960-72, Neuroendocrinology, 1965-76; Contbr. articles to profl. jours. Recipient Oppenheimer award Endocrine Soc., 1958, Research Career award NIH, 1962-81, Discovery award Med. Research Found. Oreg., 1985, DeMolay Legion of Honor award, 1988. Mem. Am. Fedn. for Clin. Research (chmn. Western sect. 1958-59), Western Soc. for Clin. Research (v.p. 1963-64, pres. 1967-68), Endocrine Soc. (mem. council 1965-68, v.p. 1976-77), Am. Thyroid Assn. (past v.p., dir. 1974-77, pres. 1980, Disting. Service award 1985), Am. Soc. Clin. Investigation, Soc. Exptl. Biology and Medicine, Western Assn. Physicians (sec.-treas. 1974-77), Assn. Am. Physicians, Internat. Brain Research Orgn., Internat. Soc. Neuroendocrinology, AAAS, European Thyroid Assn., Japan Endocrine Soc. (hon.), Czechoslovak Endocrine Soc. (hon.), Rotary, Sigma Chi. Home: 2706 Glen Eagles Rd Lake Oswego OR 97034 Office: Oreg Health Scis U Portland OR 97201

GREER, WESLEY DWAINE, art educator; b. Weyburn, Canada, Nov. 25, 1937; came to U.S., 1970; s. Wesley Burton and Gloria Cecelia (Lemke) Staples G.; m. Beverley Jean Snowdon, Apr. 13, 1963; children: Todd Alexander, Kevin Anthony. BEdn, U. British Columbia, 1964, MEdn, 1967; PhD, Stanford U., 1974. Life cert. art specialist, British Columbia. Tchr., dept chmn. art Vancouver Sch. Bd., Vancouver, British Columbia, 1956-70; instr. Stanford, Palo Alto, Calif., 1970-72; sr. mem. profl. staff SWRL Ednl. Research & Devel., Los Alamitos, Calif., 1972-82; prof. art U. Ariz., Tucson, Ariz., 1982—; dir. Improving Instruction in the Visual Arts Project, Los Angeles, 1988—. Co-author: Discipline Based Art Education, 1987. Named Pacific Region Higher Edn. Art Educator of the Year Nat. Art Edn. Assn., 1987; recipient Award of Merit Calif. Art Edn. Assn., 1981. Mem. Council for Policy Studies in Art Edn., Nat. Art Edn. Assn., Am. Soc. For Aesthetics. Democrat. Presbyterian. Home: 1240 W San Lucas Dr Tucson AZ 85704 Office: Univ Arizona #104 Art Dept Tucson AZ 85721

GREERAN, JUDITH RAE, blueprint company executive; b. Santa Barbara, Calif., Oct. 22, 1939; d. Fred Homer and Iona Minnie (Wallace) Miller; m. Elio R. Giusti, Dec. 21, 1957 (div. June 1962); m. Thomas P. Greeran, June 1, 1980. Student, U. Calif.-Berkeley, 1961-65. Adminstrv. asst. U. Calif., Berkeley, 1961-69; asst. booking agt. Sal Carson Orch., 1969-70; constrn./archtl. analyst Michael Goodman Architect, Berkeley, 1970-74; budget analyst U. Calif., San Francisco, 1974-76; sec.-treas. Berkeley Blue Print, 1976—, also bd. dirs. Bd. mem. Marina Gardens Assn., San Leandro, Calif., 1988—; active Earth Island Inst., San Francisco, 1988, U.S. Humane Soc., Washington, 1985—. Mem. East Bay 49er Booster Club. Democrat. Office: Berkeley Blue Print Co 1798 University Ave Berkeley CA 94703

GREGG, DEAN OAKLEY, consulting company executive, hydrogeologist; b. Indpls., Apr. 6, 1937; s. James H. and Edna (M.) G.; m. Kathleen Gail Noble, Aug. 30, 1958; children: Karin, John, Andrew, Paula. BS, Colo. Sch. Mines, 1959. Registered profl. engr., Ga., Calif., Ariz.; registered geologist, Calif. Asst. engr. Climax Colo. Molybdenum, 1959-60; hydrologist U.S. Geol. Survey, Denver, 1960-63, Brunswick, Ga., 1963-70, Tacoma, 1970-74; sr. hydrogeologist Dames & Moore, Park Ridge, Ill., 1974-79; assoc. Earth Tech. Corp., Long Beach, Calif., 1979-83; v.p. Hunter Environmental Services, Inc., Fountain Valley, Calif., 1988—; pres. Gregg & Assocs., Inc., Fountain Valley, 1983—; cons. in field, 1974—. Contbr. articles on hydrogeology studies to profl. mags. Pres. Altama PTA, Brunswick, 1969. Mem. Nat. Water Well Assn. Club: Toastmasters (Brunswick) (pres. 1969). Lodge: Rotary. Home: 19732 Rumford Ln Huntington Beach CA 92646 Office: Gregg & Assocs Inc 18350 Mt Langley St Ste 100 Fountain Valley CA 92708

GREGG, MARC BOYCE, computer programmer/analyst; b. Woonsocket, R.I., Feb. 8, 1955; s. Boyce and Jeanne Marie (Plasse) G. BS in Biology, Lowell Tech. Inst., 1977; BA in Computer Sci., U. Calif., San Diego, 1981; MS in Computer Sci., West Coast U., 1984. Programmer Sci. Applications, San Diego, 1979-81; programmer/analyst NCR Corp., San Diego, 1982—. Mem. NRA (life), Nat. Assn. Fed. Licensed Firearms Dealers, Escondido Fish and Game Assn., Sigma Xi (assoc.). Republican. Roman Catholic. Home: 721 Fresca St Solana Beach CA 92075 Office: NCR Corp 16550 W Bernardo Dr San Diego CA 92127

GREGGS, ELIZABETH MAY BUSHNELL (MRS. RAYMOND JOHN GREGGS), librarian; b. Delta, Colo., Nov. 7, 1925; d. Joseph Perkins and Ruby May (Stanford) Bushnell; m. Raymond John Greggs, Aug. 16, 1952; children: David M., Geoffrey B., Timothy C., Daniel R. BA, U. Denver, 1948. Children's librarian Grand Junction (Colo.) Pub. Library, 1944-46, Chelan County Library, 1948, Wenatchee (Wash.) Pub. Library, 1948-52, Seattle Pub. Library, 1952-53; children's librarian Renton (Wash.) Pub. Library, 1957-61, dir., 1962, br. supr. and children's services supr., 1963-67; area children's supr. King County Library, Seattle, 1968-78, asst. coordinator children's services, 1978-86; head librarian Valley View Library of King County Library System, Seattle, 1986—; cons., organizer Tutor Ctr. Library, Seattle South Community Coll., 1969-72; mem. Puget Sound (Wash.) Council for Reviewing Children's Media, 1974—, chmn., 1974-76; cons. to children's TV programs. Editor: Cayas Newsletter, 1971-74; cons. to Children's Catalog, Children's Index to Poetry. Chmn. dist. advancement com. Kloshee dist. Boy Scouts Am., 1975-78; mem. Bond Issue Citizens Group to build new Renton Library, 1958, 59. Recipient Hon. Service to Youth award Cedar River dist. Boy Scouts Am., 1971, Award of Merit Kloshee dist., 1977. Mem. ALA (Newbery-Caldecott medal com. 1978-79, com. chmn. 1983-84; membership com. 1978-80, Boy Scouts com. children's services div. 1973-78, chmn. 1976-78, exec. bd. dirs. Assn. for Library Service to Children 1979-81, mem. council 1985—, chmn. nominating com. Assn. Library Service to Children 1986-87, councillor 1989—, exec. bd. 1989—, exec. com.

1989—), Wash. Library Assn. (exec. bd. children's and young adult services div. 1970-78, chmn. membership com. 1983—, publs. com. 1988—), King County Right to Read Council (co-chmn. 1973-77), Pierce-King County Reading Council, Wash. State Literacy Council (exec. bd. 1971-77), Wash. Library Media Assn. (jr. high levels com. 1980-84), Pacific Northwest Library Assn. (young readers' choice com. 1981-83, chmn. div. 1983-85, exec. bd. 1983-85). Methodist. Home: 800 Lynnwood Ave NE Renton WA 98056 Office: Valley View Libr 17850 Military Rd S Seattle WA 98188

GREGORY, CALVIN, insurance service executive; b. Bronx, N.Y., Jan. 11, 1942; s. Jacob and Ruth (Cherchian) G.; m. Rachel Anna Carver, Feb. 14, 1970 (div. Apr. 1977); children—Debby Lynn, Trixy Sue; m. 2d, Carla Deane Deaver, June 30, 1979. A.A., Los Angeles City Coll., 1962; B.A., Calif. State U.-Los Angeles, 1964; M.Div., Fuller Theol. Sem., 1968; M.R.E., Southwestern Sem., Ft. Worth, 1969; Ph.D. in Religion, Universal Life Ch., Modesto, Calif., 1982; D.Div. (hon.), Otay Mesa Coll., 1982. Notary pub., real estate lic., casualty lic., Calif.; ordained to ministry Am. Baptist Conv., 1970. Youth minister First Bapt. Ch., Delano, Calif., 1964-65, 69-70; youth dir. St. Luke's United Meth. Ch., Highland Park, Calif., 1969-70; tchr. polit. sci. Maranatha High Sch., Rosemead, Calif., 1969-70; aux. chaplain U.S. Air Force 750th Radar Squadron, Edwards AFB, Calif., 1970-72; pastor First Bapt. Ch., Boron, Calif., 1971-72; ins. agt. Prudential Ins. Co., Ventura, Calif., 1972-73, sales mgr., 1973-74; casualty ins. agt. Allstate Ins. Co., Thousand Oaks, Calif., 1974-75; pres. Ins. Agy. Placement Service, Thousand Oaks, 1975—; head youth minister Emanuel Presbyn. Ch., Los Angeles, 1973-74; owner, investor real estate, U.S., Wales, Eng., Can., Australia. Counselor YMCA, Hollywood, Calif., 1964, Soul Clinic-Universal Life Ch., Inc., Modesto, Calif., 1982. Mem. Apt. Assn. Los Angeles, Life Underwriter Tng. Council. Republican. Clubs: Forensic (Los Angeles); X32 (Ventura). Lodge: Kiwanis (club speaker 1971). Home: 3307 Big Cloud Circle Thousand Oaks CA 91360 Office: Ins Agy Placement Svc PO Box 4407 Thousand Oaks CA 91359

GREGORY, CANDACE LYNN, firefighter; b. Gridley, Calif., Sept. 10, 1957; d. Wallace Edward and Cynthia Rosemary (Wicker) G. BS, Humboldt State U., 1980. Firefighter U.S. Forest Service, Waldport, Oreg., 1976, Calif. Dept. Forestry, Oroville, Calif., 1977-78; forestry aid Calif. Dept. Forestry, Redding, Calif., 1979, fire apparatus trainer, 1980-81; graduate trainee Calif. Dept. Forestry, Fresno, Calif., 1982, fire capt., 1983; fire capt. Calif. Dept. Forestry, Oroville, 1984-86; battalion chief Dept. Forestry and Fire Protection, Crestline, Calif., 1987—. Mem. Calif. Dept. Forestry Employees Assn., Calif. State Employees Assn., So. Calif. Forestry & Fire Wardens. Democrat. Presbyterian. Office: Calif Dept Forestry and Fire Protection 3800 Sierra Way San Bernardino CA 92405

GREGORY, NELSON BRUCE, motel owner, retired naval officer; b. Syracuse, N.Y., Aug. 4, 1933; s. Nelson Bruce and Josephine (Sully) G.; m. Bonnie K. Bannowsky, May 2, 1961 (div. 1970); children: Elizabeth Jo, Jennifer Kay; m. Patricia Ann Greenhalgh, Oct. 15, 1977; children: Peter Ward, Annette Frances, Michael John, Geoffrey Charles. BS, N.Y. Maritime Coll., 1955; student naval aviator, USN Pilot Tng., Pensacola, Fla., 1955-57; diploma, USN Counter Insurgency, Little Creek, Va., 1968, USAF Space Ops., Montgomery, Ala., 1969. Commd. ensign USN, 1955, advanced through grades to lt. comdr., 1964; operational pilot airborne Early Warning Squadron 2 USN, Patuxent River, Md., 1957-60; flight instr. Airborne Early Warning Tng. Unit USN, Patuxent River, 1960-63; command pilot Air Devel. Squadron 6 USN, McMurdo Sound, Antarctica, 1963-64; airspace control officer NATO USN, Naples, Italy, 1964-68; chief pilot Naval Support Activity USN, Danang, Vietnam, 1968-69; space intelligence analyst NORAD USN, Colorado Springs, Colo., 1969-71; operational pilot Electronic Warfare Squadron 33 USN, Norfolk, Va., 1971-74; ops. officer Nat. Parachute Test Range USN, El Centro, Calif., 1974-75; ret. USN, 1975; owner, gen. mgr. Bonneville Motel, Idaho Falls, Idaho, 1975—. Patron Idaho Falls Symphony/Opera Theater, 1980—; mem. Better Bus. Bur., 1989. Decorated Air medals (3) USN; recipient Vietnamese Gallantry Cross Republic of Vietnam, 1969; Gregory Ridge in Antarctica named for him, 1964. Mem. Retired Officers Assn. (life), Idaho Falls C. of C., Elks. Republican. Presbyterian. Home: 2000 S Yellowstone Hwy Idaho Falls ID 83402

GREGORY, RICHARD WALLACE, infosystems specialist; b. Chgo., Sept. 28, 1936; s. Oscar Wallace and Muriel (Sale) G.; m. Beverly Verne Smith, Aug. 3, 1957; children: Julie Lynne, James Richard. BS, Colo. State U., 1958, PhD, 1969; MS, U. Wash., 1962. Field tech. N.Mex. Dept. Fish and Game, Raton, N.Mex., 1953-59; fishery biologist Fisheries Research Inst., U. Wash., Seattle, 1960-63; wildlife researcher Colo. Div. Wildlife, Ft. Collins, Colo., 1963-69; asst. unit leader Maine Cooperative Fishery Research Unit, Orono, Maine, 1969-74; unit leader Mont. Cooperative Fishery Research Unit, Bozeman, Mont., 1974-79, Fla. Cooperative Fish and Wildlife Research Unit, Gainesville, Fla., 1979-84; leader Information Transfer Section, Ft. Collins, Colo., 1984-87; dep. chief Office of Information Transfer, Ft. Collins, 1987-88, chief, 1987-88; chmn. St. Croix salmon restoration com., Orono, 1974; mem. Environ. Edn. Curriculum com., Bangor, 1973-74, adv. com., MSU Water Research Ctr., Bozeman, 1976, grad. programs com., U. Fla., Gainesville, 1981-84. Referee (editing) J. Fish. Research Bd. Canada, 1972-73; assoc. editor: Progressive Fish-Culturist, 1983-87; contbr. articles to profl. jours. Chmn. Citizens Adv. Com., Bangor, 1972, Pilot Recycling Com., Bangor, 1972; mem. City Charter Rev. Com., Bangor, 1972-74. With USN, 1958-60. Recipient contracts: rock mining impacts, Fish and Wildlife Svc., So. Fla., 1980, manatee population index, Fish and Wildlife Svc., Marine Mammal Com., Fla. Ea. Coast, 1981, IPN virus, Fish and Wildlife Svc., Leetown, W.Va., 1983, sea turtles, USAF, Fla. Ea. Coast, 1983. Mem. Am. Fisheries Soc. (2nd v.p. 1988-89). Democrat. Home: 1600 Quail Hollow Dr Fort Collins CO 80525 Office: Office Information Transfer 1025 Pennock Pl Ste 212 Fort Collins CO 80524

GREGORY, RICK DEAN, lawyer; b. Edmond, Okla., Feb. 22, 1954; s. Jerry D. and Elaine (Hall) G. B.A. in History, Central State U., 1977; J.D., Oklahoma City U., 1981. Bar: Okla. 1982, U.S. Dist. Ct. (ea. and we. dist.) Okla. 1982, U.S. Ct. Appeals (10th cir.) 1982. Juvenile parole officer dept. human services State of Okla., Oklahoma City, 1977-81; law clk. Jess Horn, Inc., Oklahoma City, 1981-82; atty. in sole practice, Oklahoma City, 1982—. Editor: Policy Options on Political Reform, 1974; author: A Historical, Legal and Moral Analysis of Unauthorized Audio Duplication in the United States, 1975. Mem. ABA, Am. Trial Lawyers Assn., Am. Judicature Soc., Okla. Bar Assn., Okla. Trial Lawyers Assn., Okla. County Bar Assn., Can. County Bar Assn., Okla. Criminal Defense Lawyers Assn. Democrat. Methodist. Avocations: skiing, tennis, swimming.

GREGORY, THOMAS L., restaurant chain executive; b. Detroit, 1935. Grad., Mich. State U., 1957. Pres. Sizzler Restaurants Internat., L.A.; v.p. Collins Foods Internat. Inc. Office: Sizzler Restaurants Internat Inc 5400 Alla Rd Los Angeles CA 90066 *

GREGORY, WILLIAM GEORGE, air force officer; b. Lockport, N.Y., May 14, 1957; s. William and Kathleen Joan (Kracht) G.; m. Mary Beth Harney, Feb. 6, 1982; 1 child, William Philip. BS in Engring., U.S. Air Force Acad., 1979; MS in Engring., Columbia U., 1980; MS in Mgmt., Troy State U., 1984. Commd. 2d lt. USAF, 1975, advanced through grades to capt., 1983; fighter pilot U.S. Air Force, RAF Lakenheath, Eng., 1982-85, Cannon AFB, N.Mex., 1985-86; test pilot U.S. Air Force, Edwards AFB, Calif., 1987--. Guggenheim fellow, 1979. Democrat. Home: 6879 Lindbergh Dr Edwards CA 93523 Office: 6515 Test Sq Edwards AFB CA 93523-5000

GREIG, WILLIAM HAROLD, lawyer; b. Fayetteville, Ark., Nov. 15, 1951; s. James Kibler Greig and Betty Sue (Hamm) G.; m. M. Francine Stuckey, May 16, 1976; children: Elizabeth Anne, William David. BS, Kans. State U., 1973; JD, Washburn U., 1976; MBA, Eastern N.Mex. U., 1982. Bar: N.Mex. 1976, Kans. 1977, U.S. Dist. Ct. Kans. 1977, U.S. Dist. Ct. N.Mex. 1977. Ptnr. Van Soelen, Greig & Gutierrez Law Firm, Clovis, N.Mex., 1976—. Contbr. numerous articles to profl. and sci. jours. Mem. ABA, Assn. Trial Lawyers Am., N.Mex. Trial Lawyers Assn. (state bar and supreme ct. coms.), Curry County Bar Assn. (v.p. 1976-77, pres. 1980-81). Democrat. Methodist. Home: PO Box 423 Clovis NM 88101 Office: Van Soelen Greig & Gutierrez PO Box 1080 Clovis NM 88101

GREMBAN, JOE LAWRENCE, utilities company executive; b. Goodman, Wis., June 3, 1920; s. Joseph and Anna (Kryzyak) G.; m. V. June Smith, June 8, 1945; children: Ronald D., Keith D., Brian D. BBA, U. Wis., 1948; postgrad., U. Mich., 1973, U. Mich., 1974. Spl. acct. in budgeting, income tax reports, analysis Cen. Ill. Electric & Gas Co., Rockford, 1948-62; asst. treas. Sierra Pacific Power Co., Reno, 1962-63, corp. sec., 1963-69, v.p., 1969-71, v.p., sec., treas., 1971-72, fin. v.p., treas., 1972-73, exec. v.p., 1973-75, pres., 1975-76, pres., chief exec. officer, 1976-80, chmn., pres., chief exec. officer, 1980-86, chmn., chief exec. officer, 1986-87, chmn. bd., 1987-89; mem. faculty industry adv. com. Pub. Utilities Edn., U. Mich., 1974; bd. dirs. WEST Assocs., Western Regional Coun., Econ. Devel. Authority of Western Nev., pres. 1988; mem. adv. bd., past pres. Coll. Bus. Adminstrn. U. Nev., Reno. Past pres., past commr., mem. exec. bd. Nev. Area coun. Boy Scouts Am.; past dir. Reno Better Bus. Bur.; dir., past pres. United Way of No. Nev.; bd. dir. Internat. Winter Spl. Olympic Games, 1989; chmn. Salvation Army capital campaign com. With USAAF, 1942-45. Mem. Nat. Assn. Accts. (past pres. Reno chpt.), Reno Execs. Club (past pres.), Edison Electric Inst., Pacific Coast Gas Assn. (past dir.), Greater Reno-Sparks C. of C. Lodge: Rotary. Home: 2865 Juliann Way Reno NV 89509 Office: Sierra Pacific Resources 6100 Neil Rd PO Box 30150 Reno NV 89520-3150

GREMBOWSKI, EUGENE, insurance company executive; b. Bay City, Mich., July 21, 1938; s. Barney Thomas and Mary (Senkowski) G.; m. Teresa Ann Frasik, June 27, 1959; children: Bruce Allen, Debora Ann. AA, Allan Hancock U., 1963; BA, Mich. State U., 1967; MBA, George Washington U., 1972. Enlisted USAF, 1955, commd. 2d lt., 1968, advanced through grades to capt., 1971; personnel officer USAF, Goldsboro, N.C., 1968-70; chief of procurement USAF, Cheyenne, Wyo., 1971-73; contract analyst USAF, Omaha, 1973-76; chief of contracting USAF, Atwater, Calif., 1976-79; ret. USAF, 1979; office supr. Farmers Ins. Group of Cos., Merced, Calif., 1980-85, office mgr., 1985-86; fleet mgr. Los Angeles, 1986—. Author: Governmental Purchasing: Its Progression Toward Professional Status, 1972. Cubmaster Boy Scouts Am., Goldsboro, 1968; com. chmn. Am. Heart Assn., Merced-Mariposa, Calif., 1985, sec.-treas., 1986. Recipient Meritorious Service medals Office of the Pres., 1973, 76. Mem. Nat. Contract Mgmt. Assn., Nat. Assn. Fleet Administrs. Home: 14633 Mountain Spring St Hacienda Heights CA 91745 Office: Farmers Ins Group 4750 Wilshire Blvd Los Angeles CA 90010

GREMEL, VICKI CAROL, interior designer; b. Seward, Nebr., Sept. 6, 1962; d. Ted R. and Virginia Carol (Heidemann) Hughes; m. Douglas Dean Gremel, May 28, 1984. BS in Interior Design, Colo. State U., 1984. Cert. interior designer. Space planner John Ruth Corp., San Jose, Calif., 1984-85; v.p. for design, sec. Productive Environments Inc., San Jose, 1985-87; facilities designer Fujitsu Am. Inc., San Jose, 1987-88; pvt. practice interior design Seward, 1988—. Mem. Inst. Bus. Designers, Alpha Chi Omega. Republican. Lutheran.

GRENLEY, PHILIP, urologist; b. N.Y.C., Dec. 21, 1912; s. Robert and Sara (Schrader) G.; BS, N.Y.U., 1932, MD, 1936; m. Dorothy Sarney, Dec. 11, 1938; children: Laurie (Mrs. John Hallen), Neal, Jane (Mrs. Eldridge C. Hanes), Robert. Intern, Kings County Hosp., Bklyn., 1936-38, resident, 1939; resident in urology L.I. Coll. Hosp., Bklyn., 1939-41; practice medicine specializing in urology, Tacoma, Wash., 1946—; urologist Tacoma Gen. Hosp., St. Joseph Hosp., Tacoma, Good Samaritan Hosp., Puyallup, Wash.; pres. med. staff St. Joseph Hosp., Tacoma, 1968-69, mem. exec. bd., 1950-54, 67-68; cons. urologist to Surgeon Gen., Madigan Army Med. Center, Tacoma, 1954-87, USPHS McNeil Island Penitentiary, 1955-82, Good Samaritan Rehab. Center, Puyallup, 1960—; lectr. in sociology U. Puget Sound, Tacoma, 1960—. Trustee Wash. Children's Home Soc., 1951-60, Charles Wright Acad., 1961-69, Wash. State Masonic Home, 1984—; trustee Pierce County Med. Bur., 1949-51, 59-61, 71-73, pres., 1973-74, mem. exec. bd., 1975-77. Served with AUS, 1941-46. Diplomate Am. Bd. Urology. Fellow ACS; mem. Am. Urol. Assn., AMA, Wash., Pan Am. med. assns., Pierce County Med. Soc., Masons, Shrine (med. dir. 1965-78, imperial council 1982-85, potentate 1983), Royal Order Jesters (dir. 1986, 87), Lions, Elks, Red Cross of Constantine (knight). Home: 40 Loch Ln SW Tacoma WA 98499 Office: Allenmore Med Ctr S 19th and Union Ste A206 Tacoma WA 98405

GRENNAN, CYNTHIA, school superintendent; b. Sterling, Ill., Jan. 4, 1938; d. Francis John and Elza (Pippert) G. B.S., Ill. State U., 1959; M.A., Ariz. State U., 1964. Tchr. Palatine Sch. Dist., Ill., 1959-61, Chandler Sch. Dist., Ariz., 1961-64, Anaheim Union High Sch. Dist., Calif., 1964-67, counselor, 1972-76, psychologist, 1972-76, asst. prin. to asst. supt., 1976-79, supt., 1979—; state supt. com. Assn. Calif. Sch. Adminstrs., Burlingame, Calif., 1984—. Episcopalian. Office: PO Box 3520 Anaheim CA 92803

GRESKA, THOMAS FRANCIS, astronautical engineer; b. Providence, Mar. 26, 1940; s. Stanly S. and Pearl (Geatar) G.; m. Pam Greska (div. 1987); children: Stephanie Ann, Brian Thomas; m. Caroline Mayer, June 1, 1988. M in Engring., Calif. State U., Hayward, 1964; postgrad, El Camino Coll., 1982-84. Registered profl. engr., Calif. Design engr. Fleetwood Enterprise, Riverside, Calif., 1969-72, Fores Mfg.-Yacht, Tustin, Calif., 1973-80, Mattel Toys, Hawthorne, Calif., 1980-85; design dept. mgr. Astronautics Corp. Am., Torrance, Calif., 1986-87; project designer Condor Pacific Ind., Canoga Park, Calif., 1987—; owner, ptnr. Skywords, L.A., 1986—; instr. astronomy El Camno Coll., 1985-87; cons. in field. With U.S. Army, 1960-64. Mem. Polaris Obs. Assn. (chmn. 1983-84), Aircraft Owners & Pilots Assn., Exptl. Aircraft Assn. Home and Office: 6347 W 82d St Westchester CA 90045

GRETHER, DAVID MACLAY, economics educator; b. Phila., Oct. 21, 1938; s. Ewald T. and Carrie Virginia (Maclay) G.; m. Susan Edith Clayton, Mar. 24, 1961; children: Megan Elizabeth, John Clayton. B.S., U. Calif., Berkeley, 1960; Ph.D., Stanford U., 1969. Research staff economist Cowles Found., Yale U., 1966-70; lectr. econs. Yale U., 1966-68, asst. prof., 1968-70; assoc. prof. econs. Calif. Inst. Tech., Pasadena, 1970-75; prof. econs. Calif. Inst. Tech., 1975—, exec. officer for social scis., 1978-82, chmn. Humanities and Social Scis. div., 1982—. Author: (with M. Nerlove and J.L. Carvalho) Analysis of Economic Time Series: A Synthesis, 1979; contbr. articles to profl. jours. Mem. Econometric Soc., Am. Statis. Assn., Am. Econ. Assn. Home: 2116 N Craig Ave Altadena CA 91001 Office: Calif Inst Tech Humanities & Social Scis Div Pasadena CA 91125

GRETZKY, WAYNE, professional hockey player; b. Brantford, Ont., Can., Jan. 26, 1961; s. Walter and Phyllis G.; m. Janet Jones, July 16, 1988; 1 child, Paulina. Center Peterborough Petes, Jr. Ont. Hockey Assn., 1977-78, Sault Ste. Marie Greyhounds, 1977-78, Indpls. Racers, World Hockey Assn., 1978-79, Edmonton Oilers (Alta., Can.), NHL, 1979-88, Los Angeles Kings, NHL, 1988—. Player NHL All-Star Game, 1980-87; named Rookie of Yr. World Hockey Assn., 1979, Hart Trophy for Most Valuable Player NHL, 1980-87, 89, Sportsman of Yr. Sports Illus., 1982; recipient Lady Byng Meml. trophy NHL, 1980, Art Ross Meml. trophy NHL, 1981-87, Conn Smythe trophy, 1985, 88. Office: care Los Angeles Kings 3900 West Manchester Blvd The Forum Inglewood CA 90306 *

GREVE, EINAR, utilities executive; b. Bergen, Norway, 1928. Grad., Tech. Inst. Norway, 1951, MIT, 1953. Formerly pres., chief exec. officer Tucson Electric Power Co., now chmn., pres., chief exec. officer, also bd. dirs.; chmn., chief exec. officer Escavada Leasing Co., Ariz., Valencia Energy Co., Ariz. Office: Tucson Electric Power Co PO Box 711 Tucson AZ 85702 *

GREY, RONALD BRIAN, small business owner; b. Garden Grove, Calif., May 1, 1962; s. Judson Clifford and Helen Anne (Petersen) G. BS, U. So. Calif, 1985. Pres. Energrey Enterprises, Inc., Stanton, Calif., 1985—; bd. dirs. Modern Alloys, Inc., Stanton. Named #2 in state Entrepreneur of Yr. World Trade Ctr. Orange County, SBA, 1987. Mem. Assn. Collegiate Entrepreneurs (Top 100 in nation 1987, 88), Young Entrepreneurs Orgn. (Top 100 in nation 1987,88). Republican. Home: 1926 W Oceanfront Newport Beach CA 92663 Office: Energrey Enterprises Inc 11140 Western Ave Stanton CA 90680

GRIBBLE, CAROLE L., wholesale distributing executive; b. Toppenish, Wash., May 19, 1940; d. Harold Max and Gertrude Louisa (Spicer) Smith; m. Duane E. Clark, Aug. 1959 (div. 1963); 1 child, David Allen; m. Vance William Gribble, May 19, 1966. Student, Seattle Pacific Coll. With B.F. Shearer, Seattle, 1959-60, Standard Oil, Seattle, 1960-62, Seattle Platen Co., 1962-70; ptnr. West Coast Platen, Los Angeles, 1970-87, Waldorf Towers Apts., Seattle, 1970—, Cascade Golf Course, North Bend, Wash., 1970-88, Pacific Wholesale Office Equipment, Seattle and Los Angeles, 1972-87; owner Pacific Wholesale Office Equip.dba Bob Bianco Sales, Seattle and Los Angeles, 1988—, Pac Electronic Service Ctr., Commerce and San Pablo, Calif., 1988—. Republican. Methodist. Office: Pacific Wholesale Equipment 1512 7th Ave Seattle WA 98101

GRIBBLE, T. JOHN, pediatrician, educator; b. Cardiff, Wales, Apr. 6, 1937; s. James W. and Doris (Riseley) G.; m. Geraldine Godek, Nov. 26, 1966; children: Joseph James, Julie Marie, Brian John. BS in Chemistry, U. of the South, 1959; MD, Stanford U., 1964. Cert. Am. Bd. Pediatrics, Am. Bd. Pediatric Hematology/Oncology. Intern in pediatrics Bellevue Hosp. Ctr., N.Y.C., 1964-65; resident Stanford U. Med. Ctr., 1965-66, research fellow in pediatric hematology, 1968, instr., 1968-69, chief resident in pediatrics, 1969, asst. prof. pediatrics, 1969-74, clin. assoc. prof., 1974-76; assoc. prof. U. N.Mex., Albuquerque, 1976—; dir. pediatric hematology/oncology U. N.Mex., 1976-87; dir. Ted R. Montoya Hemophilia Program, U. N.Mex., 1980—. Bd. dirs. Ronald McDonald House, Albuquerque, 1980-86; mem. State of N.Mex. AIDS Task Force, 1983-85; advisor to bd. dirs. Carrie Tingley Hosp., Albuquerque, 1982-86. Served with USPHS, 1966-68. Mem. Am. Acad. Pediatrics, Am. Soc. Hematology, N.Mex. Pediatric Soc., Western Soc. Pediatric Research, Alpha Omega Alpha, Sigma Pi Sigma, Phi Beta Kappa. Republican. Episcopalian. Office: U New Mexico Dept Pediatrics Albuquerque NM 87131

GRIEVE, HAROLD WALTER, retired interior designer; b. Los Angeles, Feb. 1, 1901; s. Alexander and Maria (Chapman) G.; m. Jetta Goudal, Oct. 11, 1930. Student Los Angeles art schs., 1920-21, Chouinard Sch. Art, 1920-21, Camillo Innocentie, Rome, 1923-24. Art dir. M.P. Studios, 1920-28; art dir. for motion pictures including: Dorothy Vernon of Haden Hall, Lady Windemer's Fan, So This is Paris; interior designer, Los Angeles, now ret.; decorated Colleen Moore Doll House interiors, 1935; interior design work includes homes of George Burns, Jack Benny, Bing Crosby, Erving Thalberg, Norma Schearer, others. Fellow Am. Inst. Interior Designers (life mem., past nat. pres., past local pres.), Acad. of Motion Pictures (founder mem., life mem.), Hist. Soc. So. Calif. Republican. Clubs: Los Angeles Athletic; Beach (Santa Monica, Calif.).

GRIFFIN, JOHN HENRY, medical researcher; b. Seattle, June 26, 1943; s. John Henry and Lillian Louise (O'Connell) G.; m. Antonia Lastreto, 1965 (div. 1984); children—John, Deanna, Paul. B.S., U. Santa Clara, 1965; Ph.D., U. Calif.-Davis, 1969. Teaching asst. U. Calif., 1967-69; research fellow Harvard U. Med. Sch., 1969-71; guest worker NIH, 1971-73; on staff Service de Biochimie Centre d'Etudes Nucleaires, Saclay, France, 1973-74; asst. dept immunopathology Scripps Clinic and Research Found., La Jolla, Calif., 1974-75, assoc. depts. immunopathology and molecular immunology, 1975-80, assoc. mem. dept. immunology, 1980—; peer rev. com. NIH, 1979—. Contbr. articles to profl. jours. Treas. San Diego Assn. Gifted Children, 1978-81; active Pub. Sch. Cluster Com., University City, S.D., 1984-85; mem. adv. com. High Sch. Community, University City, 1979-82, 86-88 . Recipient Research Career Devel. award NIH, 1976-81. RCA physics scholar 1961-64; fellow NIH, 1966-69, 72-73, Helen Hay Whitney Found. 1969-72. Mem. Am. Chem. Soc., Am. Soc. Biol. Chemists, Am. Assn. Pathologists, Am. Assn. Immunologists, Internat. Soc. Thrombosis and Hemostasis, Am. Heart Assn., Sigma Xi, Alpha Sigma Nu, Phi Kappa Phi. Current work: Basic and clinical research on regulation of hemostasis and thrombosis. Subspecialties: Biochemistry (medicine); Hematology.

GRIFFIN, VERNICE DOLORES, nurse; b. Cin., Apr. 22, 1951; d. Vernon W. and Clarice E. (Schultheis) G.; m. Darold E. Hills, Dec. 20, 1970 (div. 1984); children: Tara, Caine. AS in Nursing, Community Coll. Denver, 1974-77. R.N., Colo. Psychiatric nurse Mt. Airy Hosp., Denver, 1980-82; staff nurse U. Colo. Health Scis. Ctr. Addiction Rsch. Treatment Svcs., Denver, 1982-84, Highlands Horizon Hosp., Denver, 1984-86, VA Hosp., Denver, 1986-87; psychiatric nurse Nursing Svcs., Inc., Denver, 1987—; adviser, Nurses of Colo. Corp., Denver, 1982-84; cons., Denver Police and Fire Dept. support program, 1985-86. Contbr. articles to various jours. Home and Office: 17652 E Bethany Pl Aurora CO 80013

GRIFFIS, KEITH NEWLON, aerospace engineer; b. Joplin, Mo., Aug. 13, 1937; s. Newlon Ira and Viola Oscar (Hosey) G.; m. Jacquelyn Dean McCann, July 3, 1957; children: Dean Newlon, Melissa Lynn. Student, Joplin Jr. Coll., 1955-57, U. Kansas City, Mo., 1958-59; certificate, U. Okla., 1968. Reporter Constitution-Press, Lawton, Okla., 1966-70; reporter oil and bus. Tulsa Tribune, 1970-74; field editor Engring. News, Little Rock, 1974-75; publisher, editor Clymer Pub. Co., El Dorado, Kans., 1975-76; engr. Boeing Military Aircraft Co., Wichita, Kans., 1976-81; sr. engr. Martin-Marietta, Vandenberg AFB, Calif., 1981-84; sr. engr., scientist Tracor Inc., Austin, Tex., 1984-85; engr., scientist Verac Inc., Edwards AFB, Calif., 1985-87; sr. engr. Northrop Aircraft Div., Hawthorne, Calif., 1987—. Scoutmaster Boy Scouts Am., Joplin, Mo. and Tulsa. Recipient AP award for State News Feature, Mo., 1964. Mem. Assn. Old Crows, Am. Defense Preparedness Assn. Republican. Baptist. Lodge: Masons. Home: 3221 W 132d Hawthorne CA 90250 Office: Northrop Corp Hawthorne CA 90250

GRIFFITH, CARL DAVID, civil engineer; b. Hill City, Kans., Mar. 1, 1937; s. Wilfred Eugene and Veda May (Jackson) G.; m. Mariana Segall, Mar. 26, 1988; stepchildren: Laurie Ann Segall, Allen Segall. BSCE summa cum laude, West Coast U., 1978; MSCE in Water Resources, U. So. Calif., 1980, MS in Engring. Mgmt., 1983. Profl. engr., Calif. Chief draftsman Bear Creek Mining Co., Spokane, Wash., 1959-64; right-of-way technician So. Calif. Edison Co., Los Angeles, 1964-65; engr. treatment plant design of spl. projects br. Metropolitan Water Dist. So. Calif., Los Angeles, 1965—, com. chmn. employees assn.; assoc. prof. Sch. Engring., West Coast U. Sustaining mem. Calif. Republican party. Served with USAF, 1957-58. Mem. ASME, ASCE, NSPE, Am. Water Works Assn., Nat. Mgmt. Assn., Metropolitan Water Dist. Mgmt. Club. Lodge: Masons. Home: PO Box 923122 Sylmar CA 91392 Office: PO Box 54153 Los Angeles CA 90054

GRIFFITH, DON MONTAGUE, institutional investor; b. Los Angeles, 1943; married. BA, Stanford U., 1965; MA, U. Calif., 1966; MBA, Harvard U., 1971. Mgr. Citibank NA, 1971-74; v.p. Bank of America, 1974-79; with First Interstate Bancorp, Los Angeles, 1979—, v.p. fin. planning, then sr. v.p. corp. planningand devel., exec. v.p. and chief fin. officer; fin. instn. investor Kohlberg Kravis Roberts & Co., N.Y.C., 1988—; bd. dirs. First Interstate Bank of Denver. *

GRIFFITH, DONALD ARTHUR, orthodontist; b. Mena, Ark., Nov. 15, 1943; s. Freeman Arthur and LaVern Loretta (Presley) G.; m. Elaine Vivian Johnson, Mar. 16, 1968; children: Brian, Kirsten, Todd. BS, U. Oreg., 1964, MD, 1968. Resident in orthodontics U. Oreg. Health Sci. Ctr., Portland, 1971-73; pvt. practice Portland, 1973—. Coach Happy Valley Soccer Club, 1980—. Lt. comdr. USPHS, 1968-71. Mem. ADa, Am. Assn. Orthodontists, Oreg. Dental Assn., Oreg. Dental Soc., Multnomah Dental Soc. (membership chmn. 1975-80), Rotary (Paul Harris fellow 1988). Republican. Presbyterian. Office: 13908 SE Stark #B Portland OR 97233

GRIFFITH, GRATIA HANNAN, consultant; b. Pierre, S.D., Nov. 9, 1924; d. William Seaton and Dorliska Cecilia (Crandall) Hannan; m. William Alexander Griffith, Jan. 27, 1949; children: Georgeanne Reid, James William, Wade Andrew. BA, De Pauw U., 1945; MA, Whitworth Coll., 1985. Cert. Spanish and social studies tchr., Idaho. Tchr. Silver Hills Jr. High Sch., Osburn, Idaho, 1970-74; instr. Spanish, needlepoint North Idaho Coll., Osburn, 1974-76; cons. Idaho Dept. Health & Welfare, Coeur d'Alene, 1987—, mem. adv. bd.; mem. Regional State Mental Health Adv. Bd., Coeur d'Alene. Bd. dirs. Cancer Community Charities, Coeur d'Alene, 1987—, Woman's Aux. to Am. Inst. Mining and Metallurgical Engrs., N.Y.C., 1979-87, v.p., editor newsletter. Mem. Am. Assn. Counseling and Devel. Republican. Clubs: PEO, WAAIME.

GRIFFITH, JOHN CHADWICK, JR., lawyer; b. Bern, Switzerland; s. John Chadwick and Jane Ann (Berg) G. BA, Boston U., 1980; JD, U. Va., 1985, MA, 1989. Bar: Ariz. 1986, Calif. 1988. Assoc. Winston & Strawn, Phoenix, 1985-88, Graham & James, L.A., 1988—. Editor Va. Jour. Internat. Law, 1984-85. Mem. ABA, Ariz. State Bar Assn., Calif. State Bar Assn., Pi Sigma Alpha, Psi Chi. Office: Graham & James 725 S Figueroa Ste 3400 Los Angeles CA 90017

GRIFFITH, MICHAEL VERNON, controller; b. Richland, Wash., June 16, 1955; s. Rowland James and Sharon Ann (Snorf) G.; m. Christine Diane King, June 11, 1983; children: Nicole, Richard. BA bus. adminstrn., acctg, U. Wash., 1977. CPA, Wash. Auditor Sears-West Coast Reg., L.A., 1977-79; controller TVI, Inc., Bellevue, Wash., 1979--. Mem. Am. Inst. CPAs, Wash. State Soc. CPAs, Bellevue Athletic Club. Republican. Presbyterian. Home: 229 W Lk Sammamish Pkwy SE Bellevue WA 98008 Office: TVI Inc 11400 SE 6th St 220 Bellevue WA 98004

GRIFFITH, OSBIE HAYES, chemistry educator; b. Torrance, Calif., Sept. 14, 1938; s. Osbie and Mary Belle (Neathery) G.; m. Karen Hedberg; 2 sons; B.A., U. Calif.-Riverside, 1960; Ph.D., Calif. Inst. Tech., 1964. NAS-NRC postdoctoral Stanford U., 1965; asst. prof. chemistry U. Oreg., Eugene, 1966-69, assoc. prof., 1969-72, prof. Inst. Molecular Biology, 1972—. Co-editor: Lipid-Protein Interactions, 1982; mem. editorial bd. Biophysical Jour., 1974-78, Chemistry & Physics of Lipids, 1974—. Contbr. articles to profl. jours. Recipient scholarship Camille and Henry Dreyfus Found., 1970; Career Devel. award Nat. Cancer Inst., 1972-76; fellow Sloan Found., 1967-69, Guggenheim Found., 1972-76; Faculty Achievement award for Teaching Excellence, Burlington No. Found., 1987. Mem. Am. Chem. Soc., Biophys. Soc., Electron Microscopy Soc. Am., Am. Soc. Cell Biology. Home: 2550 Charnelton Eugene OR 97405 Office: U Oreg Inst Molecular Biology Eugene OR 97403

GRIFFITH, RICHARD L., service executive; b. 1931; married. BA, U. Colo.; JD, Georgetown U., 1959. With Cades Schutte Fleming and Wright, 1960-85, Amfac Inc., San Francisco, 1985—; formerly exec. v.p. Amfac Inc., now pres., chief exec. officer, dir.; chmn., chief exec. officer Amfac Hi Inc.; bd. dirs. HAL Inc., Honolulu, Calif. and Hawaiian Sugar Co., Concord, Calif. Office: Amfac Inc 44 Montgomery St San Francisco CA 94104 also: Amfac Inc 700 Bishop PO Box 3230 Honolulu HI 96801 *

GRIFFITH, WILLIAM ALEXANDER, mining company executive; b. Sioux Falls, S.D., Mar. 28, 1922; s. James William and Adeline Mae (Reid) G.; m. Gratia Frances Hannan, Jan. 27, 1949; children—Georgeanne Reid, James William, Wade Andrew. B.S. in Metall. Engring., S.D. Sch. Mines and Tech., 1947; M.S. in Metallurgy, M.I.T., 1950; Mineral Dressing Engr. (hon.), Mont. Coll. Mineral Sci. and Tech., 1971; D in Bus. Adminstrn. (hon.), S.D. Sch. Mines & Tech., 1986. With N.J. Zinc Co., 1949-57, chief milling and maintenance, 1956-57; metallurgist Rare Metals Corp. Am., Tuba City, Ariz., 1957-58; dir. rsch. and devel. Phelps Dodge Corp., Morenci, Ariz., 1958-68; with Hecla Mining Co., Wallace, Idaho, 1968-87; exec. v.p. Hecla Mining Co., Wallace, 1978, pres., chief exec. officer, 1979-86, chmn., 1985-87; chmn., chief exec. officer Hecla Mining Co., 1986-87, also bd. dirs.; pres. Granduc Mines Ltd., 1987-88, bd. dirs. ; bd. dirs. The Coeur d'Alenes Co., Consol. Silver Corp. Bd. dirs. Kootonai Med. Ctr. Found. With USNR, 1943-46. Mem. AIME (Gaudin award 1977, Richards award 1981, Disting. mem. 1977, Hon. 1987), Am. Mining Congress (past dir.), Idaho Mining Assn. (past pres.), Idaho Assn. Commerce and Industry (past bd. dirs.), Western Regional Coun. (chmn. 1986-87), Nat. Strategic Materials and Minerals Adv. Com. to Sec. Interior, Silver Inst. (past pres., past chmn.), Sigma Tau, Theta Tau. Republican. Lodge: Rotary. Home: 630 S 14th St Coeur d'Alene ID 83814 Office: 6500 Mineral Dr Box C-8000 Coeur d'Alene ID 83814-1931

GRIFFITHS, FRANK A., professional sports team executive. Chmn. bd. Vancouver Canucks, Nat. Hockey League, B.C., Can. Office: care Vancouver Canucks, 100 N Renfrew St, Vancouver, BC Canada V5K 3N7 *

GRIGGS, WALTER ALAN, marketing professional; b. Rupert, Idaho, Jan. 17, 1952; s. Walter Harrison and Lois (Krupp) G.; m. Kathy Lynne Hankins, Apr. 22, 1979. Grad. High Sch., Grand Junction, Colo. Pres. Custom Sweeping, Tucson, 1976-87, Freeland (Wash.) Enterprises, 1987—; ptnr. Dura-Shed mini storage bldgs., Freeland, 1989—. Republican. Home: 3686 S Oceanside Dr Greenbank WA 98253 Office: Freeland Enterprises PO Box 545 Freeland WA 98249

GRIGGS, WELDON MICHAEL, state agency administrator; b. Monahans, Tex., Aug. 25, 1939; s. Edward Jackson and Evelyn Miller (Haubelt) G.; m. Sara Allen Mayers, Dec. 16, 1961; children: Lewis Edward, Shannon Carol, Kristen Sara. BS, Oreg. State U., 1961. Inventory forester Wash. Dept. Natural Resources, Ellensburg, 1961-62; forest practices forester Wash. Dept. Natural Resources, Vancouver, 1964-65, recreation survey forester, 1965; forest mgmt. forester Wash. Dept. Natural Resources, Sedro Woolley, 1965-68; forest mgmt. asst. Wash. Dept. Natural Resources, Sultan, 1968-72; dist. mgr. Wash. Dept. Natural Resources, Monroe, 1973-77; asst. area mgr. Wash. Dept. Natural Resources, Enumclaw, 1977-83, region mgr., 1983—. Served as lt. col. USAR, 1961—. Mem. No. Puget Sound Soc. Am. Foresters (chmn. 1970), Soc. Am. Foresters, NRA (life, team capt. U.S. shooting team 1987), Reserve Officers Assn. (life), Assn. U.S. Army. Republican. Home: 623 B Watson St N Enumclaw WA 98022 Office: Wash Dept Natural Resources Hwy 410 Enumclaw WA 98022

GRIGORIAN, VREJ, surgeon; b. Tehran, Iran, Apr. 15, 1938; came to U.S., 1957; s. Hairapet and Varsening (Sayranian) G.; m. Setta Daghestanian, June 29, 1963; children: Vera, Sonia, Vivian, Armen. AA, El Camino Coll., 1959; BA, U. Calif., L.A., 1961; D in Medicine, Wayne State U., 1965. Diplomate Am. Bd. Surgery. Intern Hosp. Good Samaritans, L.A., 1965-66; resident in gen. surgery Zion Hosp., San Francisco, 1966-70; pvt. practice Lombard Med. Group, Thousand Oaks, Calif., 1970—, chmn. bd., 1980-85; attending surgeon Los Robles Hosp. and Regional Med. Ctr., Thousand Oaks, 1970—; chmn. bd. dirs. Lombard Med. Group, Inc., 1980-85. Fellow ACS; mem. Soc. Clin. Vascular Surgery. Republican. Office: Lombard Med Group Inc 2230 Lynn Rd Thousand Oaks CA 91360

GRILL, LEWIS JOSEPH, trucking industry executive; b. Scranton, Pa., Aug. 26, 1949; s. Joseph John and Florence Marie (Gobinski) G.; children: Nathan Joseph, Adam Matthew. Cert., Northeastern Tech. Inst., Fleetville, Pa., 1974; cert. archl. drafting, Tom. P. Haney Vo-Tech. Trade Sch., Panama City, Fla., 1976. Interstate trucker Gen. Equipment Co., Old Forge, Pa., 1969-76, Pepsi Cola, Panama City, Fla., 1976-77; owner, operator Midwestern Distribution, Fort Scott, Kans., 1977-79; contractor, driver Internat. Transport, Rochester, Minn., 1979-82; dir. tng. U.S. Truck Driving Sch., Denver, 1982-84; dir. edn. Jay Truck Driving Sch., Kansas City, Mo., 1984-85; dir. ops. U.S. Truck Driving Sch., Denver, 1985-88; v.p. Driver Resource Ctr., Billings, Mont., 1988-89; dir. Rocky Mountain Coll., Billings, 1989—; tng. cons. Panama Canal Commn., Balboa, Panama, 1988, Perrot Truck Co., Valparaiso, Chile, S.Am., Togs-R-US, Paramus, N.J. Author: Essential techniques for the Professional Driver, 1987, Owner-Operator: Successful Operation of 1 to 50 Trucks, 1988, New Truck Operators Log, 1987, Motor Carrier Adminstration and Management, 1989, Owner-Operator Instructors Manual, 1989, Owner-Operator Student Manual, 1989, Training the Professional Driver, 1987; photographer: Comstock, 1976—; nat. corres. Am. Trucker Magazine, Brea, Calif., 1982—. Active Boy Scouts Am., Moosic, Pa., 1962-68. Mem. Am. Trucking Assn., Interstate Carriers Conf., Nat. Saftey Coun., Nat. Assn. Truck Driving Schs. (exec. dir. 1986), Profl. Truck Driving Inst. Am. (bd. dirs. 1987—). Republican. Roman Catholic. Home: 5533 Walter Hagen Dr Billings MT 59106 Office: Driver Resource Ctr 5220 Midland Rd Billings MT 59104

GRILLMEYER, OLIVER, computer science educator; b. San Rafael, Calif., July 30, 1961; s. Hans Reinhold and Maria (Spachmann) G. BS, U. Calif.-Berkeley, 1984. Software engr. Teradyne Inc., Agoura Hills, Calif., 1984-87; instr. in computer sci. Univ. Calif.-Berkeley, 1988--. Author papers in field. Home: 135 Atherton Oaks Dr Novato CA 94945 Office: Univ Calif Computer Science Dept Berkeley CA 94720

GRILLO, LEO FRANCIS, Actor; b. Lawrence, Mass., Feb. 6, 1949; s. Leo F. Sr. and Carmela M. (DeLucia) G.; m. Patricia Ellen Jeans; 1 child, Craig. BS in speech, Emerson Coll., Boston, 1970. Actor Glendale, Calif., 1965—; pres. and founder Dedication and Everlasting Love to Animals Inc., Glendale, 1979—. Author: Delta, 1988; author and editor: (with others) Landscam, 1988; contbr. articles to mags. Mem. Screen Actors' Guild, AFTRA, Actors Equity Assn. Home: PO Box 11523 Glendale CA 91226 Office: DELTA PO Box 9 Glendale CA 91209

GRILLO, PHYLLIS PRETZEL, nurse, educator; b. Chgo.; m. Victor J. Grillo; children: Jodie Klimek, Dann. Diploma, Grant Hosp. Sch. Nursing, Chgo., 1947; BS in Nursing, U. Ill., Chgo., 1975; MS in Nursing, U. Tex., San Antonio, 1982. Staff nurse operating room Belmont Hosp., Chgo., 1962-63, John F. Kennedy Med. Ctr., Chgo., 1968-71, U. Ill. Hosp., Chgo., 1973-75, Martha Washington Hosp., Chgo., 1971-73, 75-76, Loyola U. Hosp., Maywood, Ill., 1980-81; supr. surgery Meml. Med. Ctr., Long Beach, Calif., 1983-87; perioperative educator Saddleback Hosp. & Med. Ctr., Laguna Hills, Calif., 1987—; part-time clin. specialist, cons. U. Chgo. Hosp. Clinics, 1977-78; part time instr. Harper Coll., Palatine, Ill., 1976-78, 81; guest lectr., mem. adv. curriculum com. Saddleback Coll., Laguna Hills, 1988. Mem. Long Beach, Orange County Consortium, 1987—, chmn. legis. com. 1988—. Mem. Calif. Nurses Assn. (pres. region I, 1988—, comnr. govt. relations 1986—)), Assn. Operating Room Nurses (pres. Long Beach chpt. 1986-87, bd. dirs. 1988—, scholarships 1974, 75, 79, 82), Nat. League Nursing, So. Calif. Nursing Diagnosis Assn. (charter), Sigma Theta Tau. Home: 8581 Vogel Ave Westminster CA 92683 Office: Saddleback Hosp & Health Ctr 24451 Health Center Dr Laguna Hills CA 92653

GRIMES, GARY JOE, communications executive; b. Aug. 19, 1947; s. Joseph E. Jr. and Norma M. (Good) G.; m. Sharon J. Hanson; children: David, Jennifer. BS in Physics, Colo. Coll., 1969; MS in Physics, U. Wis., 1970; PhD in Elec. Engring., U. Colo., 1973. Project mgr., sr. engr. Kappa Systems Inc., Colorado Springs, Colo., 1974-78; disting. mem. tech. staff AT&T, Denver, 1978—. Contbr. articles to profl. jours. and chpts. to books. Patentee in field. Mem. IEEE, Soc. Photo-optical Instrumentation Engrs., Phi Beta Kappa. Office: AT&T 11900 N Pecos St Westminster CO 80234

GRIMES, JOSEPH EDWARD, computer science educator; b. Bloomington, Ill., Sept. 28, 1941; s. Edward A. and Mary C. (Kleemann) G.; m. Mary Rae Tures, Aug. 8, 1964; children: Joe, Therese, Christine, Michael, Matthew, Mark. BA, St. Ambrose U., Davenport, Iowa, 1963; MS, Ill. State U., 1968; PhD, Iowa State U., 1973. Tchr., coach Cen. Cath. High Sch., Bloomington, 1963-66; civil engr. McLean County Hwy. Dept., Bloomington, 1966-68; instr. Iowa State U., Ames, 1968-73; prof. computer sci. Calif. Poly. State U., San Luis Obispo, 1973-85, 87—, mgr. computer svcs., 1986-87; cons. NASA, Moffett Field, Calif., 1974—; mem. Naval Ship Weapons Systems Engring. Sta., Port Hueneme, Calif., 1987; expert witness Nat. Cash Register Corp., San Luis Obispo, 1983-85. Contbr. articles to profl. jours. Dir. referees San Luis Obispo Youth Soccer, 1982—; chmn. Fin. coun., mem. pastoral coun. Old Mission, San Luis Obispo, 1985—. Mem. Am. Statis. Assn., Assn. for Computing Machinery, Mu Sigma Rho. Roman Catholic. Home: 650 Evans Rd San Luis Obispo CA 93401 Office: Calif Poly State U Dept Computer Sci San Luis Obispo CA 93407

GRIMES, RUTH ELAINE, city planner; b. Palo Alto, Calif., Mar. 4, 1949; d. Herbert George and Irene (Williams) Baker; m. Charles A. Grimes, July 19, 1969 (div. 1981); 1 child, Michael; m. Roger L. Sharpe, Mar. 20, 1984; 1 child, Teresa. AB summa cum laude, U. Calif.-Berkeley, 1970, M in City Planning, 1972. Research and evaluation coordinator Ctr. Ind. Living, Berkeley, 1972-74; planner City of Berkeley, 1974-76, sr. planner, 1983—, analyst, 1976-83; pres. Vets. Assistance Ctr., Berkeley, 1978—, also bd. dirs.; treas. Berkeley Design Advs., 1987—, also bd. dirs.; bd. dirs. Ctr. Ind. Living. Author: Berkeley Downtown Plan, 1988; contbr. numerous articles to profl. jours. and other publs. Edwin Frank Kraft scholar, 1966. Mem. Am. Planning Assn., Am. Soc. Pub. Adminstrn., Mensa, Phi Beta Kappa. Club: Lake Merritt Joggers and Striders (sec. 1986—). Home: 1330 Bonita Ave Berkeley CA 94709 Office: City of Berkeley 2180 Milvia St Berkeley CA 94704

GRIMM, DAN K., state treasurer; b. Aberdeen, Wash., Apr. 5, 1949; s. Rupert T. and Lillian Mae (Brownlee) G.; m. Kathy Raines; 1 child, Whitney K. Student, U. Wash., 1967-69, Uppsala U., Sweden, 1971; BA in English Lit., Columbia U., 1972. State rep. Ho. Reps., Olympia, Wash., 1977-89; state treas. 1989—. Chmn. Ho. Ways & Means Com., Olympia, Wash., 1983-87, State Econ. & Revenue Forecast Coun., 1983-87, Ho. Dem. Caucus, 1981-83, Ho. Dem. Campaign Com., 1981-83, Ho. Higher Edn. Com., 1978-81. Mem. Nat. Assn. State Treasurers. Democrat. Methodist. Office: Treasury Dept Legislature Bldg PO Box 1009 Olympia WA 98504

GRIMM, LARRY LEON, psychologist; b. Goshen, Ind., Aug. 16, 1950; s. Warren Arden and Elizabeth Ann (Rassi) G.; m. Ann Mae Nelson, July 16, 1977; 1 dau., Kirsten Ann. B.S. in Elem. Edn., No. Ariz. U., 1975, M.A., 1977, Ed.D. in Ednl. Psychology, 1983. Cert. psychologist, sch. psychologist, cert. elem. tchr. Ariz. Tchr. elem. sch. Page (Ariz.) Unified Dist., 1975-76; grad. asst. Coll. Edn., No. Ariz. U., Flagstaff, 1976; tchr. elem. sch. Litchfield Sch. Dist., Litchfield Park, Ariz., 1976-80; grad. assoc. dept. ednl. psychology No. Ariz. U., Flagstaff, 1980-81; sch. psychologist intern Peoria (Ariz.) Unified Dist., 1981-82; adj. faculty Grand Canyon Coll., Phoenix, 1982; sch. psychologist Child Study Services, Prescott (Ariz.) Unified Sch. Dist., 1982-87; adj. faculty No. Ariz. U., Flagstaff, 1984—, asst. prof. , 1987-88; post doctoral fellow in pediatric psychology Child Devel. Ctr. Georgetown U. Med. Ctr., Washington, 1988-89; pediatric psychologist Prescott Neurol. Inst., 1989—; cons. in field; presenter at convs. Mem. Am. Psychol. Assn. (publs. com. div. 16), Ariz. Assn. Sch. Psychologists (bd. dirs. No. Ariz., pres. 1986-87, newsletter editor, 1983, Pres.'s award 1985, 88), Nat. Assn. Sch. Psychologists (Ariz. del. fiscal adv. com. 1987-88, Capitol Network 1988-89, pres. award 1988), Christian Assn. Psychol. Studies. Republican. Contbr. articles to profl. jours. Home: 660 Dragonfly Dr Prescott AZ 86301 Office: Prescott Neurol Inst 1000 Ainsworth Dr Ste 100 Prescott AZ 86301

GRIMM, ROYDEN ARCHIE, newspaper editor; b. Roseburg, Oreg., Aug. 5, 1925; s. Royden Alexandria and Sylvia Ada (Myers) G.; m. Joanne Rossmann, Apr. 11, 1954; children—Margaret Sylvia Rose, Scott Thomas, Joseph Conrad. Student, U. Calif.-Berkeley, 1950. Reporter, city editor Daily Rev., Hayward, Calif., 1953-56; from reporter to mng. editor The Tribune, Oakland, Calif., 1956-88, sr. editor, 1989—; instr. Laney Coll., Oakland, 1969-70. With U.S. Army, 1951-53. Mem. Am. Soc. Newspaper Editors, Associated Press Mng. Editors, Soc. Profl. Journalists, Calif. Soc. Newspaper Editors. Democrat. Office: The Tribune PO Box 24304 Oakland CA 94623

GRIMSBO, RAYMOND ALLEN, forensic scientist; b. Portland, Oreg., Apr. 25, 1948; s. LeRoy Allen and Irene Bernice (Surgen) G.; m. Barbara Suzanne Favreau, Apr. 26, 1969 (div. 1979); children: John Allen, Kimberly Suzanne; m. Charlotte Alice Miller, July 25, 1981; children: Sarah Marie, Benjamin Allen. BS, Portland State U., 1972; D of Philosophy, Union for Experimenting Colls. & Univs., Cin., 1987. Med. technician United Med. Labs., Inc., Portland, 1969-74; criminalist Oreg. State Police Crime Lab., Portland, 1975-85; pvt. practice forensic science Portland, 1985-87; pres. Intermountain Forensic Labs., Inc., Portland, 1987—; adj. instr. Oreg. Health Scis. U., Portland, 1985—; adj. instr. Portland State U., 1986-88, adj. asst. prof., 1988—; clin. dir. Intermountain Forensic Labs., Inc., 1988—. Contbr. articles to profl. jours. Fellow Royal Microscopical Soc.; mem. Am. Acad. Forensic Scientists, Soc. Forensic Haemogenetics, N.W. Assn. Forensic Scientists, Pacific N.W. Forensic Sci. Soc., Internat. Assn. Bloodstain Pattern Analysts, Electrophoresis, New Horizons Investment Club. Republican. Roman Catholic. Clubs: Pacific N.W. Forensic Study (Portland), New Horizons Invitational (Portland). Home: 16936 NE Davis St Portland OR 97230 Office: Intermountain Forensic Labs Inc 11715 NE Glisan St Portland OR 97220

GRIMSHAW, DONALD HARVEY, logistics engineer; b. Turtlecreek Twp., Ohio, June 22, 1923; s. Percy and Louella Rose (Harvey) G.; m. Jean Dolores Mrazek, Nov. 18, 1950; children—Randall, Kimberley, Stuart, Paul, Heather, Matthew. A.B. in Govt., Calif. State U.-Los Angeles, 1959; post-grad. in pub. adminstrn. U. So. Calif., 1960-62. Research asst. Hughes Aircraft, Culver City, Calif., 1951-54, Douglas Aircraft, Santa Monica, Calif., 1954-57; research engr. Northrop Corp., Hawthorne, Calif., 1957-62; research writer Calif. Dept. Water Resources, Los Angeles, 1962-65; mgr. logistics TRW Def. Systems Group, Redondo Beach, Calif., 1965—. Mem. exec. com. Calif., Los Angeles County and 53d Assembly dist. Republican Party, 1978—; Rep. nominee for U.S. Rep. from Calif.'s 31st Dist., 1978, 80. Served with USN, World War II; Korea. Mem. Soc. Logistics Engrs. (mng. editor SPECTRUM 1966-68), AIAA, Soc. Tech. Communications, U.S. Naval Inst., VFW.

GRINDEL, JOHN ANTHONY, priest, educator; b. Kansas City, Mo., Sept. 14, 1937; s. Edward Anthony and Inez Elizabeth (Weber) G. STL, Cath. U. Am., 1965, MA, 1966; SSL, Pontifical Bibl. Inst., Rome, 1967. Ordained priest Roman Cath. Ch., 1964. Prof. Scripture. St. John's Sem., Camarillo, Calif., 1968-78, pres., 1973-78; provincial superior Vincentian Fathers and Bros., L.A., 1978-87; vis. scholar Jesuit Sch. Theology, Berkeley, Calif., 1987-89; dir. Inst. for Leadership of Religious Orgns. DePaul U., Chgo., 1989—; lectr. Mt. St. Mary's Coll., L.A., 1973—; cons. Inter-Community Cons., St. Louis, 1982—; rsch. assoc. Am. Sch. Oriental Rsch., Jerusalem, 1967. Author: I and II Chronicles, 1973, Joshua Judges, 1985; contbr. articles to religious jours. Trustee DePaul U., Chgo., 1988—. Mem. Cath. Bibl. Assn. (exec. bd. 1987—), Soc. Bibl. Lit. Office: 243 S Wabash Ste 803 Chicago IL 60604

GRINDHEIM, DIANE LEE, computer analyst; b. Hempstead, N.Y., June 10, 1955; d. Ingolf and Irma Lee (Henry) G. Student, Diablo Valley Coll., 1973-74, Butte Coll., Oroville, Calif., 1974-76, Calif. State U., Chico, 1976-78. Computer specialist, systems analyst Sverdrup Corp., San Francisco, 1978—. Mem. Assn. of Small Systems Users, Common. Republican. Office: Sverdrup Corp 417 Montgomery St San Francisco CA 94104

GRISEZ, MARIANNE, nurse; b. Canton, Ohio, Oct. 10, 1948; d. Marion Vincent and Helen Genevieve (Stalder) G. BA, St. Joseph Coll., 1970; cert., Frontier Nursing Sch., Hyden, Ky., 1978; MPH, Loma Linda U., 1989. Mem. nursing staff Childrens Hosp., Washington, 1970, Bethesda (Md.) Naval Hosp., 1970-72; charge nurse St. John Hosp., Santa Monica, Calif., 1972-73; charge nurse, mem. staff Gambo (Ethiopia) Leprosy Control Ctr., 1973-76; intern nurse practitioner Mary Breckenridge Hosp., Hyden, Ky., 1978; family nurse practitioner FHP, Laguna Hills, Calif., 1978—; rsch. nurse Healthworks, Laguna Beach, Calif., 1981. Mem. Am. Nurses Assn., Nat. Coun. Internat. Health, Calif. Coalition Nurse Practitioners, Calif. Nurses Assn. (ballot com. 1981-83, nurse practitioner interest group chmn. 1982), Cath. Alumnae (sec. 1984-85, conv. del. 1985). Roman Catholic. Office: FHP 22932 Alcalde Dr Laguna Hills CA 92653

GRISHAM, MARC STEPHEN, engineering company executive; b. Long Beach, Calif., Aug. 18, 1950; s. Donald Steven and Lois Darlene (German) G.; m. Dana Lue Enscoe, Apr. 7, 1974; children: Gavin Marc, Darah Lesley. BA in History, Calif. State U., Long Beach, 1973, MPA, 1981. Account exec. Long Beach Econ. Devel. Corp., 1973-75; econ. devel. specialist City of Long Beach, 1975-78, adminstrv. officer, 1978-79; prin. ACS, Inc., Irvine, Calif., 1979-83; dir. devel. planning Community Devel. Com., L.A. County, 1983-84; dir. econ. community devel. County of Riverside (Calif.), 1984-88; v.p. devel. service J.F. Davidson Assocs., Inc., Riverside, 1988—. Bd. dirs., scout master Calif. Inland Empire council Boy Scouts Am., 1988; mem. UCR adv. com., Rancho Calif., 1988. Mem. Calif. Assn. Local Econ. Devel., Nat. Assn. Indsl. and Office Parks, Nat. Council Local Econ. Devel., Rancho Calif. C. of C., Rotary. Democrat. Office: JF Davidson Assocs Inc 3880 Lemon St Ste 300 PO Box 493 Riverside CA 92502

GRISSOM, LEE ALAN, association executive; b. Pensacola, Fla., Sept. 7, 1942; s. Levi Aaron and Virginia Sue (Olinger) G.; m. Sharon Kay Hasty, May 14, 1966; children: David, Jonathan, Matthew, Andrew. BA in Pub. Adminstrn., San Diego State U., 1965, M in City Planning, 1971. Sr. research assoc. Western Behavioral Scis. Inst., La Jolla, Calif., 1965-73; mgr. planning div. Greater San Diego C. of C., 1973-74, gen. mgr., 1974-75, pres., chief operating officer, 1975—; mem. NFL Super Bowl Task Force; mem. bd. and exec. com. San Diego Holiday Bowl. Host (TV program) The City Game, 1972-75. Trustee Calif. State U., mem. campus planning, bldgs. and grounds com., fin. com.; chmn. collective bargaining com. Calif. State U. Found., mem. gifts and pub. affairs com., chmn. com. on coms., trustee liaison Commn. on Pacific Rim; bd. dirs. Armed Forces YMCA, Econ. Devel. Corp.; chmn. San Diego Housing Commn., 1983-86, Pres.'s adv. bd., San Diego State U., 1983—; mem. Calif. Econ. Devel. Task Force, 1983—; adv. com. Fed. Home Loan Mortgage Corp.; mem. exec. com. Am.'s Cup Task Force. Named Outstanding Young Citizen San Diego Jaycees, 1976; named Outstanding Young Citizen Calif. Jaycees, 1977, one of 10 Outstanding Young Men in Am. U.S. Jaycees, 1978, Outstanding Alumnus San Diego State U., 1987. Mem. Am. Bd. C. of C. Execs. (bd. dirs.), Calif. Assn. C. of C. Execs. Republican. Lodge: Rotary. Office: San Diego C of C 110 W C St Ste 1600 San Diego CA 92101

GRISWOLD, GEORGE BULLARD, geologist, educator; b. Ponca City, Okla., Dec. 9, 1928. B.S. in Mining Engring., N.Mex. Inst. Mining and Tech., 1955; M.S. in Mining Engring., U. Ariz., 1957, Ph.D. in Geol. Enging. 1967. Vice pres., mgr. Getty Mines, Ltd., Vancouver, B.C., 1970-73; sr. staff mem. Sandia Labs., Albuquerque, 1974-77; pres. Tecolote Corp., N.Mex., 1978-83; mining and geol. engring. dept. chmn. N.Mex. Inst. Mining and Tech., Socorro, 1983-88; dir. Potash Mining div., 1989— Office: NMex Inst Mining and Tech Socorro NM 87801

GRISWOLD, MARTHA KERFOOT, social worker; b. Oklahoma City, Mar. 22, 1930; d. John Samuel III and Frances (Mann) Kerfoot; m. George Littlefield Griswold, Jan. 28, 1967. AB, Occidental Coll., 1951; MRE, U. So. Calif., 1956, postgrad., 1962. Cert. social worker. Teen dir. Toberman Settlement, San Pedro, Calif., 1954-56; social worker County of Los Angeles, 1956-62, 1969-72; dir. program to integrate disabled children Internat. Inst., Los Angeles, 1979-80; cons. community orgn. Los Angeles, 1980-84; dir. L.I.V. Disability Resources Ctr., Altadena, Calif., 1984—; instr. Calif. State U., Los Angeles, 1966-68, 1983-84; chair Childrens' Adv. Com. Los Angeles County Dept. Mental Health, 1985-86; coordinator So. Calif. Conf. on Living Long Term with Disability, 1985-87. Co-host, producer radio program on disability Challenge, Sta. KPFK, 1987—. Mem. Pasadena (Calif.) City Disability Issues Com., 1984-86, Pasadena Strategic Planning Task Force, 1985-86; mem. task force on aging, long term care United Way Region 2, Los Angeles. Recipient 1986 award So. Calif. Rehab. Assn. Mem. Nat. Assn. Soc. Workers, Nat. Assn. for Edn. Young Children, Calif. Assn. Physically Handicapped, Acad. Cert. Social Workers, Health and Social Service Workers with Disabilities. Congregationalist. Office: LIV Ctr 943 E Altadena Dr Altadena CA 91001

GROAT, ROBIN ROBBINS, travel agency executive; b. Bronxville, N.Y., Oct. 7, 1930; d. George V. and Elizabeth L. (Chase) Robbins; m. William B. Groat III, June 28, 1952 (div. 1974); 1 child, Janet L. Student, Queens Coll., 1953-54. Cons. FNCB Travel Svcs., N.Y.C., 1967; owner Esq. Travel Service, N.Y.C., 1969-73; mgr. Don Travel Service, N.Y.C., 1973-83, Walco, Palm Springs, Calif., 1983, Anderson Travel Service, LaQuinta, Calif., 1983—. Mem., usher McCullam Theatre, Palm Desert, Calif., 1988—; sec. Casa Sonora Homeowners Assn., Palm Springs, Calif., 1985—; active La Quinta Arts Found., La Quinta, Calif., 1983—; dir. La Quinta Classic Jazz Festival, 1987—. Mem. La Quinta C. of C. (dir. 1985-86, 2nd v.p. 1986-87, sec. 1987-88, 1st v.p. 1988—, vol. 1988), Palm Springs Country Club, O'Donnell Country Club. Republican. Episcopalian. Home: 1713 Capri Circle Palm Springs CA 92264

GROBE, WILLIAM HOWARD, retired state government official; b. Winnett, Mont., Feb. 19, 1916; s. Wesley H. and Leota H. (Smith) G.; m. Jane Singleton, May 7, 1967 (dec. Nov. 1987); stepchildren: John C. Singleton (dec.), Linda G. Moore; children from previous marriage: William H., Robert. Student, Simpson Coll., Indianaola, Iowa, 1934-37, Mo. State U., 1937-39, Mont. State Tchrs. Coll., 1940-41; BS, Mont. State U., 1948; BS in Health and Phys. Edn., Miss. Coll., 1951; postgrad., U. Nev., summers 1958-62. Clk. N.P. Ry., Livingston, Mont., 1946-47; student and line coach Mont. State U., Bozeman, 1947-48; coach, phys. edn. tchr. Edgar (Mont.) High Sch., 1948-51; athletic dir., coach, phys. edn. tchr., guidance counselor

Bridger (Mont.) High Sch., 1951-57, Lassen Union High Sch. Dist., Herlong, Calif., 1957-62; supt. recreaton and phys. edn. Calif. Conservation Ctr., State Dept. Corrections, Susanville, 1962-75, ret., 1975. Served with USAAF, 1941-45. Mem. Calif. Employees Assn., Nat. Recreation Assn., Calif. Correctional Assn. Lodge: Masons. Home: 3485 Lakeside Dr Apt 300 Reno NV 89509

GROBIN, ROBERT ALES, chemical executive; b. Ljubljana, Yugoslavia, Nov. 7, 1963; came to U.S., 1987; s. Tomaz and Anica (Gabrijel) G. Gimnasium Degree, Gimnasium Ivan Cankar, 1982; Associated Degree, Sch. of Econs., 1985. Asst. tchr. in Econs. of Enterprise Sch. of Econs., Ljubljana, Yugoslavia, 1984-85; internat. mktg. and chemical buyer ICN Biomedicals Inc., Costa Mesa, Calif., 1987—. Mem. Orgn. Economists of Ljubljana, AAAS, Am. Purchasing Soc. Home: 3045 Carob St Newport Beach CA 92660 Office: ICN Biomedicals Inc 3300 Hyland Ave Costa Mesa CA 92626

GROFER, EDWARD JOSEPH (TED GROFER), publisher; b. Cin., Sept. 20, 1934; s. Edward Joseph and Margaret Mary (McGinley) G.; m. Mary Janet Procissi, Aug. 18, 1962; children—Catherine Mary, Laura Marie, Daniel McGinley. B.A., U. Cin., 1957; M.A., U. Iowa, 1959. Asst. dir. pub. relations Champion Paper, Hamilton, Ohio, 1959-61; mktg. dir. The Jam Handy Orgn., Detroit, 1961-69; dir. promotion and research Detroit News, 1969-74; v.p., pub. Desert Sun, Palm Springs, Calif., 1974-80; pres. Ted Grofer Assocs., Inc., Palm Springs, 1980-88; pub. Desert Community Newspapers, Inc., Palm Desert, Calif., 1981-85; pres. Desert Mailing Svcs., Inc., Cathedral City, Calif., 1982-88; gen. ptnr. The Graphic Arts Ctr., Cathedral City, 1985—; pres. Communications Mktg. Inc., Palm Springs, 1988—; cons. several major newspapers; compiler of Newspaper Market Analysis Report, 1980—. Bd. dirs., pres. Palm Springs chpt. Am. Cancer Soc., 1985-87. Mem. Calif. Newspaper Pubs. Assn. (bd. dirs. 1978-80), Internat. Newspaper Promotion Assn. (bd. dirs. 1972-74), Palm Springs C. of C. (pres. 1979-80), Pi Kappa Alpha (nat. v.p. 1982-86). Republican. Roman Catholic. Clubs: The Springs (Rancho Mirage, Calif.); Palm Springs. Lodge: Rotary. Home: 584 Fern Canyon Dr Palm Springs CA 92264 Office: The Graphic Arts Ctr 68-816 Summit Dr Cathedral City CA 92234

GROGAN, STANLEY JOSEPH, JR., educator; b. N.Y.C., Jan. 14, 1925; s. Stanley Joseph and Marie (Di Giorgio) G.; AA, Am. U., 1949, BS, 1950, MA, 1955; degree, Air War Coll., 1972; MS, Calif. State Coll., Hayward, 1973; EdD, Nat. Christian U., 1974; m. Mary Margaret Skroch, Sept. 20, 1954; 1 child, Mary Maureen. Personnel asst., recruitment asst. CIA, Washington, 1954-56; asst. prof. air sci. U. Calif., Berkeley, 1963-64, Oakland Tech. Adult Sch., Chabot Coll., 1964-70, Oakland Unified Sch. Dist., 1964—, Hayward Unified Sch. Dist., 1965-68; prof. Nat. Christian U., 1975—, Nat. U. Grad. Studies, Belize, 1975—; pres. SJG Enterprises, Inc., cons., 1967—. Asst. dir. Nat. Ednl. Film Festival, 1971. Pub. rels. cons., 1963—. Bd. dirs. We T.I.P., Inc., 1974, Calif. Vets. Coalition, 1978. With AUS, 1945; also to lt. col. USAFR, 1948-76; col. Calif. State Mil. Res. Decorated Air medal with oak leaf cluster; recipient citation Korea, 1963. Named to Hon. Order Ky. Cols. Commonwealth of Ky., 1970. Mem. Aviation Space Writers Assn., NRA (life), Am. Def. Preparedness Assn. (life), Night Fighter Assn. (nat. publicity chmn. 1967), DAV (life), Air Force Assn., Res. Officers Assn., Phi Delta Kappa, VFW (life), Am. Soc. Indsl. Security, Disabled Am. Vets (life), Nat. Def. Exec. Res., Marines Meml., Presidio Officers, Assn. Nat. Def. Exec. Res., Nat. Def. Exec. Res., Toastmasters. Contbr. articles to profl. jours. and newspapers. Home: 2585 Moraga Dr Pinole CA 94564

GROH, JOHN EDWARD, real estate broker, minister; b. Freistatt, Mo., Apr. 11, 1939; s. Irwin Benjamin and Margaret Barbara (Weidman) G.; m. Nancy Irene Asher, Aug. 22, 1964; children: Brett Timothy, Marguerite Elizabeth. BA, Concordia Sr. Coll., Fort Wayne, Ind., 1961; MDiv, Concordia Sem., St. Louis, 1965, MST, 1966; MA, U. Chgo., 1968, PhD, 1972. Ordained to ministry Evang. Luth. Ch., 1966. Pastor Savior Divine Luth. Ch., Palos Hills, Ill., 1966-70; asst. prof. theology Concordia Tchrs. Coll., River Forest, Ill., 1970-74; assoc. prof. hist. theology Concordia Sem. in Exile, St. Louis, 1974-78; broker Realty Execs., Scottsdale, Ariz., 1978—; lectr. La Casa de Cristo Luth. Ch., Scottsdale, 1978—. Author: The Lutheran Church in North American Life, 1979, Nineteenth Century German Protestantism, 1982, Air Force Chaplains Volume IV: Air Force Chaplains 1971-80, 1986; contbr. articles, book reviews to profl. jours., encys. Col. chaplain USAFR, 1966—. Named Divinity Sch. fellow, U. Chgo., 1966-70, Younger Humanist fellow Nat. Endowment Humanities, 1973-74; Disting Grad. Res. Component Nat. Security Course. Avocations: walking, traveling. Home: 10104 E Sahuaro Dr Scottsdale AZ 85260 Office: Realty Execs 7800 E McCormick Pkwy Scottsdale AZ 85258

GROHMAN, ROBERT T., business executive; b. 1924; married. Student S.D. State Coll., U. Nebr., U. Calif., Davis. Gen. mgr. weaving ops. Duplan, 1946-57; v.p. gen. mgr. ops. Internat. Playtex Corp., 1957-69; pres. BVD Co., 1969-74; v.p. parent co., pres. internat group Levi Strauss & Co., 1974—, exec. v.p., chief operating officer, from 1976, pres., chief exec. officer, 1976-1984; dir. Clorox Co., Bank of Calif. Tri-State Corp.; cons. Henkel of Am. and others. Address: 1100 Larkspur Landing Circle Ste 275 Larkspur CA 94939 also: 142 Island Dr Ste B Hilton Head Island SC 29926

GRONINGER, WILLIAM GENE, management consultant, retired military officer; b. Port Royal, Pa., Apr. 13, 1941; s. Benjamin Edward and Marian (Van Ormer) G.; m. Eleanor Rhinesmith, June 24, 1962 (div. 1968); 1 child, Christina Hatch; m. Barbara Phillips, Apr. 20, 1968 (div. 1980); 1 child, Gene; m. Carolyn Bryce, June 3, 1984. BS in Edn., Shippensburg U., 1963; MS in Psychology, Troy State U., 1975. Commd. 2nd lt. USAF, 1963, advanced through grades to lt. col., 1980, pilot, navigator, missile launch officer, 1980-83, ret., 1983; v.p. ops. and tng. Foxfield Products, Inc., Rancho Cordova, Calif., 1984; dir. human resources Mgmt. Service Co., Tustin, Calif., 1985; pres. Team Systems Unltd., Orange, Calif., 1986—; prof. Golden Gate U., Sacramento, 1981-85. Author: Mach 3 Motivation, 1984; creator audio tape series: Trust Me, 1985. Bd. dirs. Spl. Olympics, Sacramento, 1984, Sacramento Mgmt. Conf., 1982-85. Decorated DFC, 10 Air Medals. Republican. Mem. Ch. of Religious Sci. Lodge: Kiwanis. Home and Office: 190-16 N Singingwood St Orange CA 92669

GROOM, DAVID MICHAEL, insurance agency executive; b. Leeds, Eng., June 6, 1949; came to U.S., 1977; s. James Kenneth and Dorothy (Gray) G.; m. Judith Ann Trafford, Mar. 23, 1974; children: Amy Laura, Christopher David. Grad. high sch., Leeds, Eng. Account clk. Sun Alliance & London Ins. Co., Leeds, 1967-72; area sales rep. Provident Mut. Life Ins. Co., Leeds, 1972-77; mgr. West Coast Furniture Co., Santa Barbara, Calif., 1977-80; owner, mgr. David Groom Ins. Agy., Santa Barbara, 1980—. Bd. dirs. Santa Barbara coun. Campfire, 1985. Fellow Life Underwriters Tng. Coun.; mem. Santa Barbara Assn. Life Underwriters (sec. 1986-87, 88-89, Multi-Line Agt. of Yr. award 1988), Rotary (bd. dirs. Santa Barbara 1987-88, sec., pres.-elect 1988-89). Home: 460 Gwyne Ave Santa Barbara CA 93111 Office: 5370 Hollister Ave Ste 5 Santa Barbara CA 93111

GROOMS, IRA GLENN, manufacturing company executive; b. Ambler, Pa., Oct. 15, 1927; s. Ira Wesley and Emma Lou (Miller) G.; m. Lois Marie Brumbaugh, Aug. 30, 1952; children: Lucinda, Rebecca, Jennifer, Jeffrey. BA, Pa. State U., 1953; JD, U. San Fernando Valley, 1970. Spl. apprentice Am. Brake Shoe Co., N.Y.C., 1953-54; office mgr. Sintermet div. Am. Brake Shoe Co., Cleve., 1954-56; asst. to corp. controller Am. Brake Shoe Co., N.Y.C., 1956-59; comptroller Raymond Atchley, Inc., L.A., 1959-62; dir. systems and procedures aerospace div. Abex Corp., Oxnard, Calif., 1962-69, asst. v.p. mktg., 1969-74, v.p. mktg., 1974-79; sr. v.p. adminstrn. Abex Corp., N.Y.C., 1979-83; mgmt. cons. Ira G. Grooms, Somis, Calif., 1983—; mgmt. cons. Sigma Assocs., San Diego, 1983-86. Scoutmaster Boy Scouts Am., Camarillo, Calif., 1964-67; precinct auditor Rep. Com., Ventura County, Calif., 1988; treas. Blackberry Ln. Property Owners Assn., Somis, 1986—. With USN, 1946-49, PTO. Mem. Nat. Assn. Accts. (nat. dir. 1967-68, Most Valuable Mem. 1963), Las Posas Country Club (Camarillo, Calif.). Methodist. Home and Office: 4208 Blackberry Ln Somis CA 93066

GROSS, AMY LORETAN, electrical engineer; b. Northampton, Mass., Aug. 3, 1965; d. Hubert Auxilious and Margaret Lucille (Ruditis) Loretan; m. Harry Neil Gross, July 5, 1987. BSEE cum laude, Tufts U., 1987. Electronic engr. Lear Engring., Dayton, Ohio, 1986-87; engring. cons. Dayton, 1987; test engr. U.S. Air Force, Robins AFB, Ga., 1987—. With USNR, 1987. Democrat. Jewish.

GROSS, CATHERINE MARY (KATE GROSS), writer, educator; b. Seattle, Jan. 21, 1931; d. Daniel Bergin Hutchings and Eleanor Paris (Miller) Bold. Student, Northwestern U., Evanston, Ill., 1958; BA, U. Wash., 1962, postgrad, 1984. Cert. vocat. tchr. Copywriter Pacific Nat. Advt., Seattle, 1963; prodn. coordinator Sta KRON-TV, San Francisco, 1963-65, acting program mgr., 1965; chief copywriter, TV and radio producer Teawell-Shoemaker Advt., San Diego, 1966-68; asst. pub. relations dir. San Diego Zoo, 1968-70; pub. relations dir. Univ. Village, Seattle, 1975-77, Seattle/King County Bd. Realtors, 1978; cons. advt. various orgns. including Internat. Assn. Osteopaths, Seattle, 1980-85; adj. instr. bus. Seattle Pacific U., 1980—. Author: Advertising for a Small Business, 1984, Fund Raising Magic, 1984; editor: Hiking and Bushwalking in Papua, New Guinea, 1987; contbr. short stories to Compass and Sea, 1982. Vol. sponsor Big Sisters of Puget Sound, Seattle, 1978-87; vol. coordinator World Affairs Council, Seattle, 1986; bd. dirs. Seattle Aquarium, 1985-87. Recipient Non-Fiction Book award Pacific Northwest Writers' Conf., 1979, Juvenile Story award Pacific Northwest Writers' Conf. 1984. Mem. AAUW (internat. rep. 1988), Japan Am. Soc., Seattle Freelance Writers' Assn., Wash. Press. Assn., Mountaineers. Republican.

GROSS, HERBERT GERALD, space physicist; b. Chgo., Dec. 9, 1916; s. William Theodore and Lucille Eleanor (Powalski) G.; m. Regina Marie Dwyer, Sept. 22, 1951 (div. Dec. 1962); children: Regina Marie, Gerald, Paul, Robert; m. Alice Marie Molway, June 13, 1964; stepchildren: Susan, Margaret, Judith, Joseph. BA in Philosophy, Cath. U. Am., 1940, MS in Physics, 1950; postgrad., Mass. Inst. Tech., 1952-53, Northeastern U., 1954-55, UCLA, 1968, Colo. State U., 1968. Registered profl. engr., Mass. Physicist, project engr. Raytheon Co., Newton, Mass., 1951-58, Edgerton, Germeshausen & Greir Co., Boston, 1958-59; staff scientist Geophysics Am., Bedford, Mass., 1959-64; prin. scientist McDonnell Douglas Astronautics Co., Huntington Beach, Calif., 1964-75; dir. advanced devel.H Koch & Sons div. Wickes Mfg. Co., Anaheim, Calif., 1977—; cons. Harvard Coll. Obs., Cambridge, Mass., 1962-63, Sci. & Applications, Inc., La Jolla, Calif., 1975-76, Planning Rsch., Inc., L.A., 1976, Planning Systems & Sci., Inc., Newport Beach, Calif., 1977-78. Inventor in field; contbr. articles to profl. jours. Pres. Cedarwood Assn., Waltham, Mass., 1951-54, Waltham Mus. Club., 1954-55; founder Waltham Community Symphony, 1955; dist. dir. Waltham Hosp. Fund Drive, Mass., 1956, Citizens Edn. Adv. Group, Tustin, Calif., 1967; treas. South Coast Homeowner's Assn., Santa Ana, Calif., 1974-76, pres., 1976-78; mem. SAE A-20 Aircraft Lighting Com., Laguna Beach Arts Festival. Mem. The Planetary Soc., Survival & Flight Equipment Assn., Illuminating Engring. Soc., Elks (Palm Springs, Calif.). Roman Catholic. Home: 2011 Summerwind Santa Ana CA 92704 Office: Wickes Mfg Co H Koch & Sons Div 5410 E La Palma Ave Anaheim CA 92807

GROSS, MARC JONATHON, periodontist; b. L.I., Oct. 18, 1961; s. Kenneth Robert and Susan Jane (Roslow) G.; m. Sharon Marie Carroll, Sept. 4, 1987. BA, U. Calif., San Diego, 1983; DDS, Emory U., 1987. Resident in periodontology U. Calif. Sch. of Dentistry, San Francisco, 1987--. Named Neal Kopp clin. scholar Emory U., Atlanta, 1987. Mem. ADA, Am. Acad. Periodontology, Ephebian Soc., Alpha Omega, Omicron Kappa Upsilon. Office: UCSF Sch Dentistry D-3013 707 Parnassus St San Francisco CA 94143-0762

GROSS, PAUL, transportation company executive; b. N.Y.C., July 2, 1953; s. Morris and Fannie (Morra) G.; m. Catheirne Aiss, July 12, 1976; children: Derek, Allison. BBA in Mktg. Mgmt., CUNY, 1977, MBA in Mktg. Rsch., 1986. Sales rep. Olivetti Corp. Am., N.Y.C., 1977-78; mktg. analyst Sea-Land Svc., Edison, N.J., 1978-84; mktg. mgr. Sea-Land Agys., Edison, N.J., 1984-87; v.p. mktg. systems Australia-New Zealand Direct Line, San Francisco, 1987—; lectr. NYU, 1984. Mem. Am. Mktg. Assn. Home: 275 Linda Ln Pleasant Hill CA 94523 Office: Australia-NZ Direct Line 456 Montgomery Plaza San Francisco CA 94104

GROSS, RANDY, mayoral assistant; b. Waltham, Mass., May 28, 1955; s. Isadore and Norberta (Salk) G.; m. Beth Deborah Karnell, Sept. 25, 1988. BA, Brandeis U., 1977; MBA, Cornell U., 1979. Performance auditor Ariz. Auditor Gen., Phoenix, 1979-82; mgmt. asst. I City of Tempe, Ariz., 1982-83; mgmt. asst. II City of Tempe, 1983-84, asst. to mayor and coun., 1984-88, asst. to mayor, 1988—. Pres. Family Villas Foster Care Agy., Phoenix, 1983; bd. dirs. Tempe Ctr. for the Handicapped; vice-chair United Way Appropriation Com., Tempe, 1988. Mem. Am. Soc. Pub. Adminstrn. (pres. Ariz. chpt. 1985-86). Jewish. Home: 629 E Watson Dr Tempe AZ 85283 Office: City of Tempe 31 E 5th St Tempe AZ 85281

GROSS, WILLIAM H., financial analyst, insurance company executive; b. Middletown, Ohio, Apr. 13, 1944; children: Jeff, Jennifer. BA in Psychology, Duke U., 1966; MBA in Fin., UCLA, 1971. Chartered Fin. Analyst. Investment analyst Pacific Mut. Life Ins. Co., Newport Beach, Calif., 1971-73, sr. analyst, 1973-76, asst. v.p., Fixed Income Securities, 1976-78, 2d v.p., Fixed Income Securities, 1978-80, v.p. Fixed Income Securities, 1980-82; mng. dir. Pacific Investment Mgmt. Co. subs. Pacific Mut. Life Ins. Co., Newport Beach, Calif., 1982—; regular panelist Wall Street Week with Louis Rukeyser TV program. Mem. L.A. Soc. Fin. Analysts. Office: Pacific Investment Mgmt Co 840 Newport Ctr Dr PO Box 9000 Newport Beach CA 92660

GROSS, WINTHROP ALFRED, electrical engineer; b. Exeter, N.H., Apr. 29, 1947; s. Thomas Alfred Otto and Judith Cogswell (Fiske) G.; m. Martha Gilroy, June 23, 1973; children: Elizabeth Anne, Thomas Winthrop. BA, Harvard U., 1969; MS in Engring., MIT, 1973. Design engr. Tektronix Inc., Beaverton, Oreg., 1969-82, engring. mgr., 1982—. Patentee in field; contbr. articles to profl. jours. Office: Tektronix Inc 59-316 PO Box 500 Beaverton OR 97077

GROSSBART, JACK ELLIOT, television producer; b. Newark, Apr. 18, 1948; s. Edward and Marilyn Frances (Urbach) G. BA, Rutgers U., 1970. Mailroom asst. Internat. Famous Agy., N.Y.C., 1972-73, theater agt., 1973-75; tv and motion picture agt. Hesseltine, Baker Agy., N.Y.C., 1975-76; tv agt. William Morris Agy., L.A., 1976-80; personal mgr. Litke-Grossbart Mgmt., L.A., 1980-87; TV Producer Jack Grossbart Prodns., L.A., 1987-88, Grossbart/Barnett Prodns., L.A., 1989—. Producer: Mail Order Bride, 1983; Seduction of Gina, 1984; Shattered Vows, 1984; Rockaybe, 1985; Killer in the Mirror, Something in Common, 1986, Echoes In The Darkness, 1987, Dangerous Affection, 1987, I Was Marked for Murder, 1988, Sorry, Wrong Number, 1989, The Preppy Murder, 1989. Mem. Acad. of TV Arts & Science, Caucus of Writers, Producers & Dirs.

GROSSETETE, GINGER LEE, gerontology administrator, consultant; b. Riverside, Calif., Feb. 9, 1936; d. Lee Roy Taylor and Bonita (Beryl) Williams; m. Alec Paul Grossetete, June 8, 1954; children: Elizabeth Gay Blech, Teri Lee Zeni. BA in Recreation cum laude, U. N.Mex., 1974, M in Pub. Adminstrn., 1978. Sr. ctr. supr., Office of Sr. Affairs, City of Albuquerque, 1974-77, asst. dir. Office of Sr. Affairs, 1977—; conf. coordinator Nat. Consumers Assn., Albuquerque, 1978-79; region 6 del. Nat. Council on Aging, Washington, 1977-84; conf. chmn. Western Gerontol. Soc., Albuquerque, 1983; mem. Council on Phys. Fitness and Health. Contbr. articles to mags. Pres. Albuquerque Symphony Women's Assn., 1972; exec. com. mem. Jr. League Albuquerque, 1976; campaign dir. March of Dimes N.Mex., 1966-67. Recipient N.Mex. Disting. Pub. Service award N.Mex. Gov.'s Office, 1983, Disting. Woman on the Move award YWCA, 1986. Fellow Nat. Recreation and Park Assn. (bd. dirs. Southwest Regional Council, pres. N.Mex. chpt. 1983-84, Outstanding Profl. 1982); mem. U. N.Mex. Alumni Assn. (bd. dirs. 1978-80, Disting. Alumni award 1985), Southwest Soc. on Aging (pres. 1984-85, bd. dirs.), Am. Soc. Pub. Adminstrn. (pres. N.Mex. Council 1987—), Las Amapolas Garden Club (pres. 1964), Pi Alpha Alpha, Chi Omega (pres. alumni 1959-60). Home: 517 La Veta NE Albuquerque NM 87108 Office: Office of Sr Affairs 714 7th St SW Albuquerque NM 87102

GROSSMAN, HAL J., electrical engineer; b. Huntington, Ind., Mar. 21, 1948; s. Harold and Amantta (Pinkerton) G.; children from previous marriage: Beth, Kate. Student, Tri-State U., 1966-68; BSEE, Purdue U., 1971; postgrad., Carnegie Mellow U., 1971-72, U. Pitts., 1971-72, Purdue U., 1982-83. Tech. spl. products mgr.. Endress & Hanser, Greenwood, Ind., 1973-81; engr. Applied Metals, Santa Clara, Calif., 1983-84, Controls Mfg., Belmont, Calif., 1984-85; R&D engr. Ramco Mfg., San Jose, Calif., 1985-86; sr. elec. engr. Southwall, Palo Alto, Calif., 1986-87; engr. Western Polymer, Newark, Calif., 1987-88; sr. controls engr. Raychem Corp., Menlo Park, Calif., 1988—; cons. computer programming, Los Altos, Calif., 1986-88. Mem. IEEE, Instrument Soc. Am. Internat. Republican. Methodist. Home: 100 First St PO Box 208 Los Altos CA 94022 Office: Raychem Corp 300 Constitution Dr Menlo Park CA 94025

GROSSMANN, JOHN RICHARD, corporate planner; b. Morristown, N.J., Apr. 15, 1951; s. John and Viola Louise (Glassmann) G.; m. Kathleen E. O'Neil, Apr. 24, 1980; children: Jessica, Megan. BArch., Pa. State U., 1974; M in City and Regional Planning, Harvard U., 1977. Project mgr. Energy and Environ. Analysis Inc., Arlington, Va., 1977-85; v.p. Blackstone Assocs. Inc., Arlington, 1985-86; mgr. bus. devel. Colo. Interstate Gas, Colorado Springs, Colo., 1986—. EPA fellow, 1976-77. Mem. Internat. Assn. Energy Economists, Capital PC Users Group, Greater Denver C. of C. Home: 535 Royal Oak Dr Colorado Springs CO 80906 Office: Colo Interstate Gas 2 N Nevada St Colorado Springs CO 80903

GROSSMANN, ROBERT HORST, service executive; b. Rennerschule, Hannelore, Austria, Sept. 11, 1960; came to U.S., 1980; s. Peter and Hannelore (Egger) Grossmann. Grad. high sch., Rennerschule. Chef de rang Ratskeller, Saarbrücken, Fed. Republic Germany, 1978-79; capt. Black Forest Inn, Los Angeles, 1980-83; mgr. restaurant Hilton Internat., Los Angeles, 1983-84, dir. restaurants, 1984-85; ptnr., gen. mgr. Sculpture Garden Restaurant & Gallery, Venice, Calif., 1986—; ptnr., bd. dirs. Kid-z-ersize-Gym for Children, Beverly Hills, Calif., Rainwater Records & Prodn., Santa Monica, Calif.; Groo Enterprises, West Los Angeles; v.p. Royal Import & Export, Los Angeles, 1985—. Served with Austrian Special Force, 1977. Recipient award cert. Biathalon World Assn., 1977, Olympic Com., 1984. Mem. Dining Profls. Am. Roman Catholic. Home: 10751 Rose Ave #124 Los Angeles CA 90034

GROTH, BARBARA MARGARET, marketing professional; b. San Jose, Calif., Sept. 24, 1954; d. Henry and Lorene Field (Davis) G.; m. Keith Claus, Jan. 18, 1974 (div. 1979). AA, Deanza Coll., 1974; BS in Bus., San Jose State U., 1981; MBA, Santa Clara U., 1985. Tech. support specialist Four Phase, Cupertino, Calif., 1974-78; product specialist Four Phase, Cupertino, 1978-79; mkgt. mgr. Motorola Co., Cupertino, 1979-83, Gavilan Co., Campbell, Calif., 1983-84, Sun Microsystems, Inc., Mountain View, Calif., 1984-88; strategic mktg. mgr. Apple Computer, Cupertino, Calif., 1989—. Mem. Am. Mgmt. Assn., Am. Mktg. Assn. Office: Apple Computer 20575 Mariani Ave Cupertino CA 95014

GROTH, ROBERT JOHN, geologist; b. Hartford, Wis., Sept. 24, 1944; s. Roland Adolfus and Lillian (Terlinden) G.; m. Jeanne Elizabeth Harris, Dec. 15, 1987; 1 child, David Roland Harris Groth. BS, U. Wis., 1967; postgrad., U. N.Mex., 1970-72. Cert. petroleum geologist. Geologist, mine pit Utah Internat., Shirley Basin, Wyo., 1972-73; field geologist Chen & Assocs., Denver, 1974-75; wellsite geologist Tooke Engring., Casper, Wyo., 1975-79; geologist Berge Exploration, Denver, 1979-81; area geologist ANR Prodn. Co., Denver, 1981-85; chief geologist, v.p. ops. G & H Prodn. Co., Denver, 1986—. With U.S. Army, 1968-70, West Germany. Recipient Disting. Svc. award, Assn. for Women Geoscientists, Denver, 1985. Mem. Wyo. Geolog. Assn., Rocky Mountain Assn. Geologists (treas. 1988-89), Am. Assn. Geologists, Soc. Econ. Paleontologists and Mineralogists (Rocky Mountain section, field trip coordinator 1988—), Assn. for Women Geoscientists. Home: 12803 Milwaukee Ct Thornton CO 80241

GROTJAHN, MARTIN, medical writer, retired psychiatrist and analyst; b. Berlin, July 8, 1904; s. Alfred and Charlotte (Hartz) G.; M.D., Kaiser Friedrich U., Berlin, 1929; came to U.S., 1936, naturalized, 1942; m. Etelka Gross, Aug. 18, 1927; 1 son, Michael. Intern, Hosp. Reinikendaf, Berlin; resident Charité Hosp., Berlin, 1933-36, Menninger Clinic, Topeka, 1936-38, Chgo. Psychoanalytic Inst.; head physician Berlin U. dept. psychiatry and neurology, 1933-36; mem. staff Chgo. Inst. Psychoanalysis, 1938-46; mem. faculty U. So. Calif., 1946-86, now prof. emeritus, tng. analyst emeritus; practice psychiatry, Topeka, Chgo., now Los Angeles, Calif. Served with M.C., AUS, 1942-46. Recipient Sigmund Freud award Psychoanalytic Physicians, 1976. Mem. Am. Psychoanalytic Assn. (life), Am. Psychiat. Assn. (life), So. Calif. Psychiat. Assn. (life), So. Calif. Psychoanalytic Soc. (life). Author: Beyond Laughter, 1957; Psychoanalysis and the Family Neurosis, 1960; A Celebration of Laughter, 1970; The Voice of the Symbol, 1972; The Art and the Technique of Analytic Group Therapy, 1977; My Favorite Patient: The Memoirs of an Analyst, 1987; author, co-editor Psychoanalytic Pioneers, 1966. Contbr. 400 articles to profl. jours. Home: 2169 Century Hill Los Angeles CA 90067

GROUT, STEPHEN C., lawyer; b. Phoenix, Sept. 18, 1955; s. George C. and Geraldine L. (Barker) G. BA, U. Calif., San Diego, 1977; JD, U. Ariz., 1982. Bar: Ariz. 1982. Research assoc. biology dept. Stanford (Calif.) U., 1977-78; real estate salesman Bud Grout Inc., Phoenix, 1978-79; assoc. atty. O'Connor, Cavanagh, Phoenix, 1981-84; v.p. Grout Properties, Inc., Phoenix, 1984—; bd. dirs. Grout Properties, Inc., v.p. 1984—. Mem. Ariz. Dem. Council, 1987-88. Mem. Ariz. State Bar, Order of Coif, Phi Alpha Delta. Clubs: Phoenix Chess (treas. 1986—), University (Phoenix). Office: Grout Properties Inc 3225 N Central #900 Phoenix AZ 85012

GROVE, ANDREW S., electronics company executive; b. Budapest, Hungary, 1936; married; 2 children. B.S., CCNY, 1960; Ph.D., U. Calif.-Berkeley, 1963. With Fairchild Camera and Instrument Co., 1963-67; pres., chief operating officer Intel Corp., Santa Clara, Calif., 1967-87, pres., chief exec. officer, 1987—, also dir. Recipient Medal award, Am. Inst. Chemists, 1960; cert. of merit, Franklin Inst.,1975; Townsend Harris medal, CCNY, 1980. Mem. Nat. Acad. Engring.; fellow IEEE (achievement award 1969, J. J. Ebers award 1974). Office: Intel Corp 3065 Bowers Ave Santa Clara CA 95051 *

GROVE, JACK STEIN, naturalist, marine biologist; b. York, Pa., Oct. 29, 1951; s. Samuel Hersner and Myrtle Elenor (Stein) G. AS, Fla. Keys Coll., 1972; BS, U. West Fla., 1976; postgrad., Pacific Western U. Chief naturalist Galapagos Tourist Corp., Guayaquil, Ecuador, 1977-84; expedition leader Soc. Expeditions Cruises, Seattle, 1985—; marine biologist, underwater photographer Eye on the World, Inc., L.A., 1986—; rsch. assoc. L.A. County Mus. Natural History, 1982—, Sea World Rsch. Inst., San Diego, 1981—; assoc. investigator Nat. Fisheries Inst., Guayaquil, 1982-85; park naturalist Galapagos Nat. Park, Ecuador, 1977-85. Editor: Voyage to Adventure/Antarctica, 1985; photographer film documentaries. NSF grantee, 1986. Mem. Acad. Underwater Scis., Profl. Assn. Diving Instrs. (divemaster), U.S. Nat. Recreation and Parks Assn. Office: Mus Natural History-Fishes 9000 Exposition Blvd Los Angeles CA 90007

GROVES, FORREST DAVID WOLFE, dental surgeon; b. Durango, Colo., June 16, 1954; s. William David and Nila Mae (Wolfe) G.; m. Sheron Ann Deeg Groves, May 22, 1987. AA, Mesa Community Coll., 1974; BA, U. Colo., 1976, DDS, 1982. Capt., dir. U.S. Pub. Health Service (Park Hill Clin.), Denver, 1982-86; gen. practice dentistry Boulder, Colo., 1987--; faculty U. Colo. Sch. of Dentistry, Denver, 1987--. Mem. ADA, Colo. Dental Assn. Avocations: skiing, sailing, carpentry. Office: 1136 Alpine St Ste 310 Boulder CO 80302

GROW, DAVID PARNELL, electrical engineer; b. Portland, Oreg., Nov. 28, 1951; s. Gene P. and Mildred V. (Goff) G.; m. Tracey M. Riley, Mar. 31, 1972; children: James D., Christopher M. BSEE, Calif. Poly. State U., San Luis Obispo, 1974; postgrad., Santa Clara U., 1983-88. Elec. engr. Naval Reactors Facility, Westinghouse Co., Idaho Falls, Idaho, 1981-82; threat analyst Dalmo Victor Co., Belmont, Calif., 1982-83, dep. program mgr., 1983-85; program mgr. Teledyne CME, Santa Clara, Calif., 1985-88, Altus Corp., San Jose, Calif., 1988; sales and mktg. bus. mgr. Power-One, Inc., Camarillo, Calif., 1988-89; electronics engr. Pacific Missile Test Ctr., Point Mugu, Calif., 1989—; cons. D.P. Grow & Assocs., Modesto, Calif., 1985-88, Camarillo,

1988—. 1st lt. USMC, 1975-81. Mem. IEEE, Assn. Old Crows. Republican. Mem. Ch. of Christ. Office: Pacific Missile Test Ctr PO Box 4034 Point Mugu CA 93042-5000

GRUA, O. E., surgeon; b. Salt Lake City, Aug. 11, 1917; s. Oscar Ernest and Suzanna Mae (Clark) G.; m. Jeanette C. Cross, Feb. 10, 1945; children: Roger, William, James. BS, U. Utah, 1939; MD, Temple U., 1943. Diplomate Am. Bd. Surgery. Pvt. practice Ogden, Utah; chief surgery St. Benedict's Hosp. Ctr., Ogden, 1975-80; chief surgery McKay Dee Hosp. Ctr., Ogden, 1981-85, chief staff, 1985—. Capt. USMC, 1943-47. Fellow ACS, S.W. Surg. Congress (past pres.); mem. AMA, Utah Med. Assn., Rotary. Republican. Mormon. Office: 3905 Harrison Blvd Ogden UT 84403

GRUBB, L(EWIS) CRAIG, financial company executive, consultant; b. Canton, Ohio, June 1, 1954; s. Lewis G. and Janet M. (Hornback) G.; m. Carol Elizabeth Norvell, Dec. 19, 1981; children: Carie Lynne, Chelsea Michelle. Student, W.Va. Wesleyan Coll., 1972-74. Regional rep. IDS/Am. Express Corp., Tucson, 1982-84; v.p. Mut. Benefit Fin. Group, Tucson, 1984-86, Am. Fin. Cos. (formerly Estate Fin. Services Ltd.), Tucson, 1986—; also bd. dirs. Estate Fin. Services Ltd., Tucson. Bd. dirs. Desert Survivors Inc., Tucson, 1984-86. Mem. Internat. Assn. Fin. Planners, Gen. Agts. and Mgrs. Assn. Republican. Lodge: Masons. Home: 6573 Calle Herculo Tucson AZ 85710 Office: Estate Fin Svcs Ltd 950 N Finance Center Dr Ste 180 Tucson AZ 85710

GRUBB, THOMAS JAMES, office automation executive, consultant; b. Richmond Heights, Mo., Nov. 5, 1959; s. James Lee and Dixie (Westbrook) G.; m. Nicola Bridges, Oct. 5, 1985. BS in Bus., Eastern Ill. U., 1982. Microcomputer analyst Bechtel Petroleum, San Francisco, 1982-83, Computerland Internat., Oakland, Calif., 1983-85; mgr. of end user computing RREEF Funds, San Francisco, 1985—. Mem. Microcomputer Mgmt. Assn. (program dir. 1987—). Home: 4479 17th St #2 San Francisco CA 94114 Office: The RREEF Funds 650 California St San Francisco CA 94108

GRUBEN, FRED JAY, real estate investment executive; b. Clinton, Ark., Nov. 20, 1953; s. John Henry and Sylvia Jean (Heinry) G.; m. Carol Anne Gay, Dec. 3, 1985. Grad. high sch., Walla Walla, Wash. Owner, operator Blue Mountain Iron Works, Bainbridge Island, Wash., 1976-81; with title unit dept. Chgo. Title Ins. Co., Seattle, 1981-84; examiner Commonwealth Land Title Co., Seattle, 1984--. Republican. Methodist. Home: 7027 179th St NW Edmonds WA 98020

GRUBER, HELEN ELIZABETH, medical researcher; b. Wallace, Idaho, Nov. 6, 1946; d. Hugo J. and Margaret A. (Dorsey) G. BS, U. Idaho, 1969; MS, Oreg. State U., 1974, PhD, 1976. Research asst. Oreg. State U., Corvallis, 1974-76; NIH postdoctoral fellow U. Iowa, Iowa City, 1976-78; research instr. U. Wash., Seattle, Tacoma, 1978-81; assoc. researcher, research medicine U. So. Calif., Los Angeles, 1981-86; dir. skeletal dysplasia morphology lab., assoc. researcher Cedars-Sinai Med. Ctr., UCLA, Los Angeles, 1986—; vol. tchr. Los Angeles Schs., Griffin Ave., 1986; mem. Cedars-Sinai Med. Ctr. Research Com., 1987—; mem. Cedars-Sinai Biosci. Library Task Force, 1988—. Contbr. articles to profl. jours. Recipient Appreciation award Griffin Ave. Sch., Los Angeles, 1986. Mem. Soc. Exptl. Biology and Medicine (editorial bd. 1986—), AAAS, Am. Fedn. Clin. Research, Am. Soc. Bone and Mineral Research, Am. Soc. Cell Biology, Women in Cell Biology, So. Calif. Bone and Mineral Club. Roman Catholic. Office: Cedars Sinai Med Ctr Med Genetics Birth Defects Ctr ASB 3d Fl Los Angeles CA 90048

GRUCHALLA, MICHAEL EMERIC, electronics engineer; b. Houston, Feb. 2, 1946; s. Emeric Edwin and Myrtle (Priebe) G.; m. Elizabeth Tyson, June 14, 1969; children: Kenny, Katie. BSEE, U. Houston, 1968; MSEE, U. N.Mex., 1980. Registered profl. engr., Tex. Project engr. Tex. Instruments Corp., Houston, 1967-68; group leader EG&G Washington Analytical Services Ctr., Albuquerque, 1974-88; engring. specialist EG&G Energy Measurements Inc., Albuquerque, 1988—; cons. engring., Albuquerque; lectr. in field, 1978—. Contbr. articles to tech. jours; patentee in field (3). Judge local sci. fairs, Albuquerque, 1983—. Served to capt. USAF, 1968-74. Mem. IEEE, Instrumentation Soc. Am., Planetary Soc., N.Mex. Tex. Instruments Computer Group (pres. 1984-85), Sigma Xi, Tau Beta Pi, Eta Kappa Nu. Office: EG&G Energy Measurements Inc Kirtland Ops PO Box 4339 Sta A Albuquerque NM 87196

GRUE, DOUGLAS HARRISON, publishing executive, consultant; b. L.A., May 25, 1959; s. Robert I. and Barbara (Friedman) G. BA, Trinity U., 1981. Rsch. assoc. Baylor Med. Coll., Houston, 1981; account exec. E.F. Hutton, L.A., 1982-84; pres. Innovative Amenities, Santa Monica, Calif., 1984—; cons. Hot Data Software, Santa Monica, 1988—. Editor: All About Me--Children, 1986, Full Life Senior Health Journal, 1988. Mem. Soc. Healthcare Planning and Mktg. of Am. Hosp. Assn., Soc. Pub. Rels. of Am. Hosp. Assn., Am. Mktg. Assn., Med. Mktg. Assn. Republican. Office: Innovative Amenities II Inc PO Box 1280 Santa Monica CA 90406

GRUENWALD, GEORGE HENRY, new products management consultant; b. Chgo., Apr. 23, 1922; s. Arthur Frank and Helen (Duke) G.; m. Corrine Rae Linn, Aug. 16, 1947; children: Helen Marie Gruenwald Orlando, Paul Arthur. B.S. in Journalism, Northwestern U., 1947; student, Evanston Acad. Fine Arts, 1937-38, Chgo. Acad. Fine Arts, 1938-39, Grinnell Coll., 1940-41. Asst. to pres. Uarco, Inc., Chgo., 1947-49; creative dir., mgr. mdse. Willy-Overland Motors Inc., Toledo, 1949-51; new products, brand and advt. mgr. Toni Co., Chgo., 1951-53; v.p., creative dir., account supr. E.H. Weiss Agy., Chgo., 1953-55; exec. v.p., supr. mgmt. North Advt., Chgo., 1955-71; pres., treas., dir. Pilot Products, Chgo., 1963-71; pres., dir. Advance Brands, Inc., Chgo., 1963-71; exec. v.p., dir. Campbell Mithun Inc., Mpls. and Chgo., 1971-72; pres., dir. Campbell Mithun Inc., 1972-79, chmn., dir., 1979-81, chief exec. officer, dir., 1981-83, chief creative officer, dir., 1983-84; vice-chmn., dir. Ted Bates Worldwide, N.Y.C., 1979-80; mgmt. cons. new products 1984—. Author: New Product Development-What Really Works, 1985, Guide to New Product Success - Comprehensive Checklist, 1990; (videos) New Products Seven Steps to Success, 1988, New Product Development, 1989; editor-in-chief Oldsmobile Rocket Circle mag., 1956-64, Hudson Family mag., 1955; expert columnist Mktg. News, 1988—; contbr. articles to profl. jours.; creator numerous packaged consumer products. Trustee Chgo. Pub. TV Assn., 1969-73, Mpls. Soc. Fine Arts, 1975-83, Linus Pauling Inst. Sci. and Medicine, Palo Alto, 1984—; chmn., v.p., chmn. class reps. Northwestern U. Alumni Fund Council, Chgo., 1965-68; trustee, chmn., pres., chief exec. officer, chmn. exec. com. Twin Cities Pub. TV Corp., 1971-84; trustee Minn. Pub. Radio Inc., 1973-77, vice chmn., 1974-75; bd. dirs., exec. com. Pub. Broadcasting Service, Washington, 1978-86, bd. dirs., 1988—; bd. dirs. St. Paul Chamber Orch., 1982-84,, San Diego Chamber Orch., 1986-88; mem. adv. bd. San Diego State U. Pub. Broadcasting Community, 1986—. Served with USAAF, 1943-45, MTO. Recipient Hermes award Chgo. Federated Advt. Clubs, 1963; Ednl. TV awards, 1969, 71, 86. Mem. Am. Assn. Advt. Agys. (mgmt. com. 1976-84), NSPE (project mem.), Nat. Soc. Profl. Journalists, Internat. Assn. Cooking Profls., Am. Inst. Wine and Food (bd. dirs. 1985—). Office: PO Box 1696 Rancho Santa Fe CA 92067

GRUETTER, RICHARD ALLEN, chemical company executive; b. Atlanta, Oct. 11, 1946; s. Walter and Betty Marie (Joseph) G.; m. Mary Louise Sanchez, Apr. 6, 1979. AA in Bus., Delta Jr. Coll., Stockton, Calif., 1966. Inventory control clk. Baker Commodities, L.A., 1970-71; buyer Hehr Internat., L.A., 1971-75; sr. buyer Paul-Monroe Hydraulics, Whittier, Calif., 1975-78; sr. project buyer Ralph M. Parsons, Pasadena, Calif., 1978-80; sr. buyer Occidental Engring., Irvine, Calif., 1980-82, Phone Mate, Inc., Torrance, Calif., 1983; purchasing supr. Centon Electronics, Irvine, 1983-84; sr. buyer Santa Fe/Braun Engrs., Alhambra, Calif., 1984-87; contract adminstr. U.S. Borax & Chemical Corp., L.A., 1987—. With U.S. Army, 1966-67, Vietnam. Mem. Mensa. Democrat. Home: 776 E San Bernardino Rd Covina CA 91723

GRUMBLES, LYNNELLE DAHLGREN, food service executive, dietitian; b. Kingsburg, Calif., Aug. 1, 1959; d. Reuben Emmanuel and Marian Cecilia (Almquist) Dahlgren; m. Randal Wayne Grumbles, May 22, 1982; 1 child, Amanda Michelle. BS, Calif. Poly. State U., San Luis Obispo, 1981. Registered dietitian, Calif. Food svcs. supr. Beverly Enterprises, Fresno, Calif., 1981-84; asst. dir. food svcs. Kaweah Delta Dist. Hosp., Visalia, Calif., 1984-87; food svc. dir. Cutler-Orosi (Calif.) Unified Sch. Dist., 1987—. Mem. Am. Dietetic Assn., Calif. Dietetic Assn., Calif. Sch. Foodsvc. Assn. (sec. 1987-88, treas. 1989-91), Tulare-Kings Nutrition Coun. (pres. 1987-88). Republican. Mem. Covenant Ch. Office: Cutler-Orosi Unified Schs 41855 Rd 128 Orosi CA 93647

GRUND, WALTER JAMES, JR., gynecologist; b. Denver, Colo., Apr. 27, 1927; s. Walter James and Anita Margretha (Strong) G.; m. Mary Frances Sethman, Feb. 18, 1949 (div. 1980); children: John Walter, Steven Michael, Cheryl Lee; m. Gloria Ann Johansen, Mar. 29, 1987. BA, U. Colo., 1951; MD, U. Colo., Denver, 1955. Diplomate Am. Bd. Ob-Gyn. Intern St. Lukes Hosp., Denver, 1955-56; resident U. Nebr., Omaha, 1956-59; trainee Nat. Cancer Inst., 1957-58; pvt. practice ob-gyn. Denver, Littleton, Colo., 1959-76; pvt. .practice gynecology Littleton, 1976—; assoc. clin. prof. Univ. Colo. Health Scis. Ctr., Denver, 1983—; chmn. dept. ob-gyn. Swedish Med. Ctr., Englewood, Colo., 1972-76, Porter Meml. Hosp., Denver, 1972-76. Contbr. articles to profl. pubs. Ensign USNR, 1945-52, PTO. Fellow Am. Coll. Ob-Gyn. (vice chmn. Colo. sect. 1988—) ; mem. AMA, Colo. Med. Soc., Cen. Assn. Ob-Gyn., Am. Soc. for Colposcopy and Colpomicroscopy, Am. Med. Tennis Assn., Colo. Gynecol. and Obstet. Soc. (pres. 1981, treas. 1981—), Arapahoe Med. Soc. (pres. 1984-86), Denver Athletic Club, Denver Tennis Club, Phi Beta Kappa, Alpha Omega Alpha. Republican. Episcopalian. Office: 191 E Orchard Rd Littleton CO 80121

GRUNDER, ROBERT DOUGLAS, real estate executive; b. Valley Forge, Pa., Aug. 17, 1953; s. Richard Rudolph and Alice Gertrude (Jablow) G.; m. Becky Ann Nelson, May 29, 1982; children: Katherine Victoria, Christopher Nelson. Student, U. Alaska, 1986-87. Lic. real estate broker, Hawaii; Grad. Realtor's Inst., 1980. Ptnr. Grunder Investment Co., Fairbanks, Alaska, 1975-; realtor Luke & Luke Realty, Inc., Honolulu, 1979-83; pres. Grunder Devel., Inc., Fairbanks and Honolulu, 1983--. Bd. dirs. Ilikai Marina Owners Assn., Honolulu, 1988--. Mem. Nat. Assn. Realtors, Hawaii Assn. Realtors, Honolulu Bd. Realtors. Congregationalist. Home: 1480 Ihiloa Loop Honolulu HI 96821 Office: 2222 Kalakaua Ave Ste 715 Honolulu HI 96815

GRUSSENDORF, BENJAMIN FRANKLIN, JR., state house speaker; b. Grand Rapids, Minn., Feb. 23, 1942; s. Benjamin F. Sr. and Fern (Ross) G.; m. Karen Solem; children: Timothy, Karla. AA, BA, U. Minn., 1964, MA, 1966; postgrad., Wash. State U., 1970. Tchr. Sitka (Alaska) High Sch., 1967-80, Sitka Community Coll.; state legislator Alaska Ho. Reps., Juneau, 1981—, speaker House, 1985—; pres. Alaska Conf. Mayors, Sitka; mem. Alaska Mcpl. League Legis. Com. Assemblyman City and Borough Sitka, 1971, dep. mayor, 1971-75, mayor, 1975-79; chmn. Sitka Charter Commn. Mem. Alaska Jaycees (state chmn. govtl. affairs). Democrat. Club: Alaska Native Brotherhood (Sitka). Lodges: Moose, Elks. Office: Alaska Ho of Reps State Capitol PO Box V Juneau AK 99811

GRUWELL, CHARLES PETER, interior designer; b. Pacific Grove, Calif., Nov. 24, 1953; s. Clinton JAmes and Lucy Elizabeth (Ventimiglia) G. AA in Psychology, Monterey Peninsula Coll., 1972; BA in Psychology, Calif. State U., Fresno, 1975; tchr. cert. in art, Chapman Coll., 1978. Art tchr. Notre Dame High Sch., Salinas, Calif., 1976-79; interior designer, dir. mktg. Falls, Grant & Lucas, Los Altos, Calif., 1979-82; owner, designer Gruwell Design Assocs., Pacific Grove, Calif., 1982-87; co-prin., dir. design and mktg. Gruwell-Pheasant Design, Pacific Grove, 1988—; hon. set designer Monterey Film Festival, 1986—; Gourmet Gala exhibitor Monterey March of Dimes, 1986—; judge Gold Key awards Am. Hotel and Motel Assn., 1988; judge Designer Circle awards Lodging Hospitality Mag., 1988. Recipient numerous design awards Am. Hotel and Motel Assn., Lodging Hospitality Mag., Modern Salon Mag., Bldg. Industry of Am. Mem. Am. Soc. Interior Designers, Hospitality Industry ASsn. (assoc.), Sigma Alpha Epsilon (Cal-Iota chot. Alumni). Democrat. Office: Gruwell-Pheasant Design 311 Forest Ave Pacific Grove CA 93950

GU, ZU HAN, research scientist; b. Shanghai, China, July 29, 1941; came to U.S., 1980; s. Hong Shou Gu and Jian Ming Zhang; m. Ying Lin, Dec. 16, 1969; children: Jenny, Belinda. BEE, Jiaotong U., Shanghai, 1964; MS, U. Calif., San Diego, 1983, PhD in Elec. Engring., 1986. Lectr., asst. prof. laser lab. dept. applied physics Jiaotong U., 1964-80; sr. rsch. staff scientist Surface Optics Corp., San Diego, 1986—; cons. 14 articles to profl. jours. Author: (with others) Laser Optics of Condensed Matter, 1988; contbr. articles to profl. jours. Recipient Capt. Nelson Tsui Found. award, 1983. Mem. Optical Soc. Am., Internat. Soc. for Optical Engring. Office: Surface Optics Corp 9929 Hibert St San Diego CA 92131

GUAY, GORDON HAY, postal service executive, educator, consultant; b. Hong Kong, Aug. 1, 1948; came to U.S., 1956; s. Daniel Bock and Ping Gin (Ong) G. AA, Sacramento City Coll., 1974; BS, Calif. State U., Sacramento, 1976, MBA, 1977; PhD, U. So. Calif., 1981. Mgmt. assoc. U.S. Postal Service, Sacramento, 1980-82, br. mgr., 1982-83, fin. mgr., 1983-84, mgr. quality control, 1984-86, mgr. tech. sales and services div., 1986—; assoc. prof. bus. adminstrn., mktg. and mgmt. Calif. State U., Sacramento, 1981-85; prof. mktg. Nat. U., San Diego, 1984—; sr. cons. Gordon Guay & Assocs., Sacramento, 1979—; cons. Mgmt. Cons. Assocs., Sacramento, 1977-79. Author: Marketing: Issues and Perspectives, 1983; also articles to profl. jours. Served with U.S. Army, 1968-70. Recipient Christopher Columbus award U.S. Postal Service, Potomac, Md., 1982, Cert. Accomplishments, U.S. Postal Service, Los Angeles, 1983, Outstanding Merits award U.S. Postal Service, Sacramento, 1985, Cert. of Appreciation, U.S. Postal Service, Sacramento, 1986, Patriotic Service award U.S. Treasury Dept., San Francisco, 1985. Fellow Acad. Mktg. Sci.; mem. NEA, AAUP, Soc. Advancement Mgmt. (Outstanding Mem., 1976), Am. Mgmt. Assn., Am. Mktg. Assn., Assn. MBA Execs., Am. Soc. Pub. Adminstrn. Democrat. Office: US Postal Service 555 Capitol Mall Ste 550 Sacramento CA 95814-4560

GUDDE, ROBERT LOUIS, engineering project executive; b. Holden, Mo., Apr. 5, 1934; s. Jerome Louis and Verna (Goff) G.; m. Margaret Elissa Pucci, Aug. 6, 1955; children: Robert Michael, Anthony Louis, Angela Marie, David Allen, Ronald Eugene. AA, San Diego City Coll., 1955; BSME, San Diego State U., 1963. Design engr. Gen. Dynamics Convair, San Diego, 1955-63; design engr. to project mgr. Rohr Industries, Chula Vista, Calif., 1963—; designated engr. rep. FAA, 1986—. Patentee two locking systems. Players agt. Santee (Calif.) Pioneer Little League, 1968-69; chmn. rd. com. Santee Citizens Planning com., 1970-71. Mem. NRA (life), Nat. Mgmt. Assn. (charter). Democrat. Roman Catholic. Home: 9555 Maureen Ct Santee CA 92071 Office: Rohr Industries Inc Foot H St Chula Vista CA 92010

GUDER, DARRELL LIKENS, educational administrator, clergyman; b. Ventura, Calif., Nov. 12, 1939; s. Russell Otto and Eileen (Likens) G.; m. Linda Evans, Dec. 20, 1963 (div. 1978); children: Terrence Evan, Megan Claer; m. Judith Johnson, Nov. 10, 1979. PhD, U. Hamburg, Fed. Republic Germany, 1965; DD (hon.), Jamestown (N.D.) Coll., 1988. Ordained to ministry, Presbyn. Ch. (U.S.A.), 1965. Student pastor Ch. of Schleswig-Holstein, Hamburg, 1964-67; minister Christian edn. First Presbyn. Ch., Hollywood, Calif., 1967-71; prof. theology and edn. Karlshohe Coll., Ludwigsburg, Fed. Republic Germany, 1971-75; dir. inst. youth ministries Young Life & Fuller Sem., Colorado Springs, Colo., 1976-85; v.p. acad. affairs, dean of faculty Whitworth Coll., Spokane, Wash., 1985—; mem. com. theol. edn., Presbyn. Ch. (U.S.A.), Louisville, 1987—; mem. ch. relations com. Young Life, Colorado Springs, 1985—. Author: Be My Witnesses, 1985; translator: Foundations of Dogmatics (Weber, 2 vols.), 1980-84, God as the Mystery of the World (Jungel), 1984. Mem. Presbytery of Inland Empire. Democrat. Home: W 215 Hawthorne Rd Spokane WA 99218 Office: Whitworth Coll Spokane WA 99251

GUENTHER, NANCY STEPHENSON, education educator, real estate agent; b. Omaha, Apr. 26, 1936; d. Robert Kirk and Lucile Helen (Dailey) Stephenson; m. Alfred Walter Guenther, Dec. 13, 1958. BS, U. Wis., 1958; MS, U. So. Calif., 1963, EdD, 1979. Cert. tchr., Calif.; lic. real estate agent, Calif. Tchr. coordinator Van Deene Ave. Elem. Sch., Los Angeles, 1960-68; chmn. art dept. White Jr. High Sch., Los Angeles, 1968-80; asst. prin. Bellflower (Calif.) Unified Sch. Dist., 1980-83; prin. Hawthorne (Calif.) High Sch., 1983-86; dir. instructional svcs. Centinela Valley Union High Sch. Dist., Lawndale, Calif., 1985-88; univ. lectr., student tchr. supr. Loyola-Marymount U., L.A., 1988—; with Marler & Assoc. Estates Realty, Inc., Palos Verdes, 1988—; cons. in field. Author: Guess Who's Not Hiding Behind the Classroom Door, 1981; co-editor Take Five: A Methodology for the Humane School, 1979. Pres. Palos Verdes (Calif.) Jr. Womans Club; mem. com. for incorp. of Rancho Palos Verdes; founder LaCresta Homeowners Assn.; bd. dirs. Palos Verdes Community Arts Assn.; sec. South Bay Young Reps., Palos Verdes Rep. Club; cen. com. mem. Calif. State Reps.; trustee Little Co. of Mary Hosp. Recipient Outstanding Personal Contbns. award Palos Verdes Community Arts Assn., 1981-83, Outstanding Jr. award Palos Verdes Jr. Womans Club. Mem. Dist. Art Textbook Evaluation Com., Assn. Calif. Sch. Adminstrs. (chmn. area IX curriculum leaders com., mem. state curriculum leaders com.), Assn. Supervision and Curriculum Devel., Nat. Assn., Secondary Sch. Prins., Hon. Assn. Women Educators, Educare, Trojan League of South Bay, Palos Verdes Woman's Club , Delta Epsilon, Delta Kappa Gamma, Phi Delta Kappa. Office: Marler & Assoc Estates Realty Inc 24 Mabga Cove Pla Palos Verdes CA 90274

GUENTHER, ROBERT STANLEY, II, investment manager; b. Orange, Calif., Sept. 29, 1950; s. Robert Stanley and Fanny Newnan (Shaw) G. BA in Psychology, U. Calif., Santa Barbara, 1975; BA in Sociology, U. Calif., 1975. Pvt. practice Grover City, Calif., 1975—. Republican. Home and Office: 762 Trouville Grover City CA 93433

GUERIN, CHARLES ALLAN, artist, museum director; b. San Francisco, Feb. 27, 1949; s. John Warren and Charlene (Roovaart) G.; m. Katherine Riccio. BFA, No. Ill. U., 1971, MA, 1973, MFA, 1974. Co-dir. Guerin Design Group, Colorado Springs, Colo., 1972-77; dir. exhbns. Colorado Springs Fine Arts Ctr., 1977-80, curator fine arts, 1980-86; dir. U. Wyo. Art Mus., Laramie, 1986—. Author catalogues including various Colorado Springs Fine Arts Ctr. catalogues; contbg. author The Encyclopedia of Crafts, 1974; exhbns. include Purdue U. West Lafayette, Ind., 1974, 76, DePauw U., Greencastle, Ind., 1976, Colorado Springs Fine Arts Ctr., 1977, Mus. of Fine Arts, Santa Fe, N.Mex., 1978, Wis. State U., Platteville, 1972, Suburban Fine Arts Ctr., Highland Park, Ill., 1974, Colo. Woodworking Invitational, Silver Plume, 1977, Colo. Craft Invitational, Arvada, 1981, Leslie Levy Gallery, Scottsdale, Ariz., 1983, Robischon Gallery, Denver, 1983, Adams State Coll., Alamosa, Colo., 1984, U. Wyo. Art Mus., 1986—; represented in permanent collections Lloyds of London, Dallas, Art Inst. Chgo., Marriott Hotel, Albany, N.Y., Ill. State Mus., Springfield, U.S. West Corp., Denver, Thresholds, Chgo., others. Grantee Nat. Endowment for the Arts, Ill. Arts Council, 1973. Mem. Coll. Art Assn. Am., Am. Assn. Mus., Western Mus. Conf. Home and Studio: 612 S 11th Laramie WY 82070 Office: U Wyo Art Mus Univ Sta Box 3897 Laramie WY 82071

GUERIN, JOHN P., air transportation company executive. Chmn., dir. PS Group Inc., San Diego; also dir. Pacific Southwest Airlines, San Diego. Office: PS Group Inc 4370 La Jolla Village Dr Ste 1050 La Jolla CA 92122 •

GUERNSEY, LLOYD BRUCE, lawyer; b. Henryville, Ind., Oct. 19, 1919; s. Thomas Brucilla and Cloe Ann (Turner) G.; Mickey McKee, Aug. 22, 1947 (dec. 1964); 1 child, Larry Bruce; m. Doris Mildred Shain, June 18, 1976. BS in Physics, Ind. State U., 1942, MS in Physics, 1947; LLB, LaSalle U., Chgo., 1958; MSEE, Purdue U., 1962. Sci tchr. St. Bernice High Sch., Ind., 1942-43, Thornton Sch., Terre Haute, Ind., 1943-44; instr. Purdue U., West Lafayette, Ind., 1944-45, 57-62; test engr. Allison Aircraft Co., Indpls., 1945; instr. Valparaiso (Ind.) Tech. Inst., 1947-57; patent atty. Gen. Elec. Co., Phoenix, 1962-70; sr. patent agt. Honeywell Corp., Phoenix, 1970-74; group patent counsel FMC Corp., San Jose, Santa Clara, Calif., 1974--. Patentee in field. Mem. Peninsula Patent Law Assn., Bapt. Men's Club (sec. 1986--). Republican. Baptist. Home: 881 Kingfisher Dr San Jose CA 95125 Office: FMC Corp 900 Lafayette St Ste 608 Santa Clara CA 95050

GUERRERO, JUAN TENORIO, territorial senator; b. Saipan, Northern Mariana Islands, Dec. 10, 1949; s. Herman Reyes and Maria Camacho (Tenorio) DeLeon Guerrrero; m. Roberta Kay Janssen, Dec. 28, 1972; children: Vincent, Tracy, Jolene, John, Michael. Student, Nebr. Bus. Coll., 1969-70, 71-72. Pres., gen. mgr. Herman's Modern Bakery, Inc., Saipan, 1972-84; mem. 4th Northern Marianas Ho. of Reps., Saipan, 1984-86; senator Northern Marianas Legislature, Saipan, 1986—; pres. Marianas Internat. Travel, Saipan, 1982—, Saipan Stevedore Co., Inc., 1982-84, also bd. dirs.; bd. dirs. Tinian (Northern Mariana Islands) Marine Stevedore, Inc., Saipan Hotel Corp. Chmn. No. Mariana Islands chpt. ARC, Saipan, 1985—; coord. Boy Scouts Am. Troop 903, Saipan, 1985-86; treas. Dems. of Northern Mariana Islands, 1986-88, chmn., 1989—. Mem. Am. Soc. Travel Agts., Am. Soc. Bakery Engrs., Pacific Asia Travel Assn., Rotary Club. Roman Catholic. Home: PO Box 1218 Airport Rd San Vicente MP 96950 Office: Northern Mariana Islands Legislature Capitol Bldg Saipan MP 96950

GUERRIERI, TERESA ELLEN, transportation company executive; b. Espanola, N.Mex., Nov. 22, 1934; d. George M. and Irma P. (Muth) Witzke; m. Gasper J. Guerrieri, May 13, 1950; children: Gasper L., Jimmy George, Robin B. Grad. high sch. Pres., treas. G&G Truck Leasing Inc., Thornton, Colo., 1967—. Recipient Golden Poet award World of Poetry, 1985-88. Republican. Office: G&G Truck Leasing Inc 5974 Marion Dr Denver CO 80216

GUESS, PAUL RICHARD, hydro equipment manufacturing executive; b. Terre Haute, Ind., Oct. 6, 1945; s. Paul and Laura Lucille (Turner) G.; m. Terri Anne Alexander, Aug. 31, 1968. AA, San Diego Mesa Coll., 1967; BS in Bus., San Diego State U., 1969. Lic. real estate broker, Wyo. Mgmt. trainee Sears & Roebuck, Chula Vista, Calif., 1968-71; store mgr. Sears & Roebuck, Poway, Calif., 1977; oper. mgr. Sears & Roebuck, Barstow, Calif., 1978-79, San Mateo, Calif., 1979-81, Cheyenne, Wyo., 1981-83; real estate broker Coldwell Banker, Cheyenne, Wyo., 1983-86; pres. Rice Hydro Equipment Mfg. Co., El Cajon and Yorba Linda, Calif., 1986—. With U.S. Army, 1969-71, Korea. Mem. Nat. Utility Contractors Assn., Am. Water Works Assn., Internat. Assn. Fire Chiefs, Assoc. Equipment Distbrs., Am. Rental Assn. Home: 3324 Longridge Dr Orange CA 92667 Office: Rice Hydro Equipment Mfg Co 22720 Savi Ranch Pkwy Ste B Yorba Linda CA 92686

GUEST, DIANA L. ROTH, sales manager, interior design consultant; b. Fremont, Nebr., Nov. 17, 1950; d. Arlan L. and Betty L. (Prieb) Roth; m. William K. Guest, Nov. 23, 1971 (div. July 1981). BS, U. Nebr., 1968-72. Interior design cons. Colo., Nebr., Tex., 1972-85; regional mgr. Boris Kroll Fabrics, Colo., Mont., Wyo., N.Mex., Utah., 1981-83; territory mgr. Mohasco Carpet Corp., Colo., Tex., Calif., 1983-87; western regional mgr. U.S. Axminster, Greenville, Miss., 1987—; asst. instr. U. Nebr., 1974-75; profl. advisor Student Chpt. Am. Soc. Interior Designers; basic interior design instr., Houston, 1976. Mem. Jr. League (Denver chpt. 1981-85, Austin, Tex. chpt. 1985-86, Long Beach, Calif. chpt. 1986-87). Recipient Marquis award Mohawk Carpet, 1984. Mem. Am. Soc. Interior Designers, Network Exec. Women in Hospitality (fin. chmn. 1986—), Delta Gama Alumni (Houston chpt. fin. advisor Advisory Bd., chmn. Archtl. Planning Com.; Lincoln, Nebr. chpt. chmn. newsletter). Office: US Axminster E Union Extended PO Box 877 Greenville MS 38702

GUEVARA, ANNE MARIE, librarian; b. Lynwood, Calif., Dec. 7, 1949; d. Conrad and Philomene (Timko) Goracke; m. Rey Guevara, Jan. 11, 1975; children: Gregory Rey, Angela Marie. BA, Calif. State U., Long Beach, 1971; MLS, U. So. Calif., 1974. Reference libr. L.A. County Pub. Libr., Norwalk, 1974-76, periodicals libr., 1976-77; info. specialist City of Long BeachPub. Libr., 1977-79; libr. Sacred Heart Sch., Medford, Oreg., 1981—; reference libr. Jackson County Pub. Libr., Medford, 1985-88, children's libr., 1988—. Chmn. arts & crafts Children's Festival, Jacksonville, Oreg., 1981-84. Mem. ALA, Oreg. Libr. Assn., Oreg. Ednl. Media Assn., Medford Storytelling Guild (bd. dirs. 1981-85). Democrat. Roman Catholic. Home: 4460 Dark Hollow Rd Medford OR 97501 Office: Sacred Heart Sch 431 S Ivy St Medford OR 97501

GUGAS, CHRIS, criminologist; b. Omaha, Aug. 12, 1921; s. Nicholas and Vera (Henas) G.; student U. So. Calif., 1946-49, U. Calif. at Northridge, 1955-56; BA, MA in Pub. Adminstrn., U. Beverly Hills, 1977; DDiv, Ch. Living Sci., 1968; PhD, U. Beverly Hills, 1983; m. Anne Claudia Setaro, June

27, 1942; children: Chris, Steven Edward, Carol Ann Gugas Hawker. Asst. dir. security Los Angeles Bd. Edn., 1948-49; spl. agt. CIA, Washington, 1950-54; criminol. cons., Los Angeles, 1955-61; pub. safety dir., Omaha, 1962-65; dir. polygraph services Profl. Security Cons., Los Angeles, 1966—; exec. dir. Calif. Acad. Polygraph Scis., Los Angeles, 1974-76, The Truthseekers, 1975—; instr. Los Angeles Inst. Polygraph, 1979—, Gormac Polygraph Sch., Los Angeles, 1972-73; chief instr. Las Vegas Acad. Polygraph Sci., 1982-83; chmn. Polygraph Legal Def. Fund, 1988—; columnist Los Angeles Daily Jour., Security World mag., The Truthseekers. Mem. advisory bd., sec. Calif. Dept. Consumer Affairs, 1971-76; tech. advicor to Pres. MIA/POW Commn., 1986. With USMCR, 1940-45, 47-49. Mem. Marine Corps League (comdr. 1946), Marine Corps Combat Corr.'s Assn. (pres. Los Angeles chpt. 1975-77), Nat. Bd. Polygraph Examiners (pres. 1958), Security Officers Assn. (pres. 1968), Am. Polygraph Assn. (pres. 1971, exec. dir. 1972-73), Nat. Polygraph Assn. (pres. 1989—), Am. Soc. Indsl. Security, LA Press. Author: The Silent Witness; co-author: The National Corruptors; Pre-Employment Polygraph; The Polygraphist in Court; Our National Rebellion, 1982; contbr. numerous articles to various jours. Home: 4018 Dixie Canyon Sherman Oaks CA 91403 Office: 6253 Hollywood Blvd Ste 311 Hollywood CA 90028

GUGGENHEIM, ALAN ANDRE ALBERT PAUL EDOUARD, company executive; b. Paris, France; Arrived in U.S., 1981.; s. Jacques and Micheline (Raffalovich) G.; m. Suzanne Marton, Mar. 20, 1974. BS, U. Paris, France, 1971; MS in Civil Engring., Sch. Pub. Works Constrn. & Industry, Paris, France, 1974, MBA in Finance, 1975; Diploma D'Etat Major, Army Command and Gen. Staff Coll., Paris, France, 1981. Asst. prof. maths. Nat. Sch. of Arts & Architecture, Paris, 1972-75; civil engr. Societe Routiere Colas, Paris, 1976-77, French Antilles, 1977-78; chief exec. officer, exec. dir. C.R.P.G., Pointe A Pitre, Guadeloupe, 1979-81; chief exec. officer, chmn. D BCS, Inc., Stockton, Calif., 1982-88, San Joaquin Software Systems, Inc., Stockton, Calif., 1982-86, Calcar Investment Services, Inc., Lodi, Calif., 1983—; Bd. mem. SUCMANU, Paris, 1976-82, Pacific State Bank, Stockton, Calif... Exec. Editor; newslette, L'Action Universitaire, 1970-76. mem. French Def. Commn. Paris, 1969-77, French Ministry of Def. Recipient: Gold Medal, OTH, Paris, 1975. Fellow: Engr. & Scientist, France, Yosemite Club, Lodi Lions Club. Home: 1995 W Larson Rd Lodi CA 95242

GUGGENHIME, RICHARD JOHNSON, lawyer; b. San Francisco, Mar. 6, 1940; s Richard E. and Charlotte Guggenhime; m. Emlen Hall, June 5, 1965 (div.); children: Andrew, Lisa, Molly. AB in Polit. Sci. with distinction, Stanford U., 1961; LLB, Harvard U., 1964. Bar: Calif. 1965, U.S. Dist. Ct. (no. dist.) Calif. 1965, U.S. Ct. Appeals (9th cir.) 1965. Assoc. Heller, Ehrman, White & McAuliffe, 1965-71, ptnr., 1972—; spl. asst. to U.S. Senator Hugh Scott, 1964; bd. dirs. Comml. Bank of San Francisco, 1980-81, Global Savings Bank, San Francisco, 1984-86. Mem. San Francisco Bd. Permit Appeals, 1978-86; bd. dirs. Marine World Africa USA, 1980-86; mem. San Francisco Fire Commn., 1986-88, Recreation and Parks Commn., 1988—; chmn. bd. trustees San Francisco Univ. High Sch.; trustee St. Ignatius Prep. Sch., San Francisco, 1987—. Mem. Am. Coll. Probate Counsel, San Francisco Opera Assn. (dir.). Clubs: Bohemian, University, Wine and Food Soc., Olympic, Chevaliers du Tastevin (San Francisco); Silverado Country (Napa, Calif.); Vintage (Palm Springs). Home: 3957 Washington St San Francisco CA 94118 Office: Heller Ehrman White & McAuliffe 333 Bush St San Francisco CA 94104

GUICHARD, ALAIN ALFONSE, chef, restaurateur, consultant, educator; b. Paris, July 2, 1945; came to U.S., 1978; s. Raymond Guichard; m. Barbara Lorene Robinson, May 29, 1978; 1 child, Mikael Raymond. Apprentice pastry cook La Petit Monge, Paris, 1959-62; with Ermitage de Robinson Paris, 1962-63; asst. chef Restaurant Noel-Peters, Paris, 1963û67; with Nationale Usines Renault Billancourt, France, 1967; chef Compagnie Internationale Informatique, Louvieinnes, France, 1967-74, Auberge de Carpe d'Or, Paris, 1974-75; sauce chef L'Archiduc, Paris, 1976-77; exec. chef Plaza Four Restaurant, Los Angeles, 1977-79, Albion's Restaurant, Sherman Oaks, Calif., 1979-81; chef, owner, mgr. L'Horizon Restaurant, San Jose, Calif., 1986--; ;instr. intermediate cuisine Mission Coll., San Jose, 1986--. Advisor Ctr. Employment Tng., San Jose, 1988--. Mem. Food and Wine Soc. Santa Clara (Purple Foot award 1987), Rotary. Office: L'Horizon Restaurant 1250 Aviation Ave San Jose CA 95110

GUIDO-CLARK, LAURA ANNE, textile executive; b. Dearborn, Mich., Mar. 2, 1958; d. Emilio and Elena (Tosto) G.; m. Daniel James Clark, Sept. 9, 1983. BFA, Wayne State U., 1981. Rep. textile Ferguson Hildreth, San Francisco, 1983-86; v.p. design Deepa Textiles, San Francisco, 1986—. Recipient IBD Silver award Inst. Bus. Design, 1987. Office: Deepa Textiles 280 Utah St San Francisco CA 94103

GUILBERT, IRENE WEST, educational administrator; b. Camp Verde, Ariz., Oct. 11, 1930; d. Irving Coleman and Amy Elaine (Stock) West; m. Lionel Ward Guilbert, Apr. 12, 1952 (div. May 1985); children: Marion Elizabeth, Lynelle Marie, Marjorie Ann. BA in Secondary Edn., U. Ariz., 1952; MEd in Elem. Edn., Ariz. State U., 1982. Cert. elem. and secondary tchr., prin., Ariz. Tchr. pub. schs. Ariz., 1954-78, 81-83; developer, demonstrator nat. diffusion network U.S. Office Edn., Mesa, Ariz., 1978-85, asst. state facilitator, 1983-85; instrnl. specialist Ariz. Dept. Edn., Phoenix, 1985-88; pres. Ednl. Directions, Inc., Glendale, Ariz., 1985-88, prin., 1988—; adj. prof. No. Ariz. U., Flagstaff, 1985-88; cons. math., lang. arts, mgmt. and motivation. Author: Big Tee Math Books, 1986, Math Pages, 1987. Pres. local PTA, 1957; community chmn. Girl Scouts U.S.A., 1958-71. Mem. Assn. for Supervision and Curriculum Devel., Assn. for Vocat. Educatos, Computer Users in Edn., Federated Woman's Club (local pres. 1956), Mensa, Phi Delta Kappa, Pi Lambda Theta, Alpha Delta Kappa (pres. Alpha Gamma chpt. 1974; southwestern regional scholar 1980). Republican. Unitarian.

GUILFORD, WILLIAM JOSEPH, chemical researcher; b. Oakland, Calif., July 8, 1954; s. Adrian Peter and Frances Mary (Salel) G. BS, U. Calif., Berkeley, 1976; PhD, U. Ill., 1982. Research fellow Swiss Fed. Inst. Tech., Zurich, 1981-83, Harvard U., Cambridge, Mass., 1984-85; sr. research chemist Sogetal, Inc., Hayward, Calif., 1985—. Contbr. articles to profl. jours. Fellow NIH, 1982-83, Merck, 1979-80, Eastman Kodak, 1978-79, 3M, 1977-78. Mem. AAAS, Am. Chem. Soc., Calif. Acad. Sci. Office: Sogetal Inc 3872 Bay Ctr Pl Hayward CA 94545

GUILLAUME, DOROTHY NOFZIGER, teacher, artist; b. Burbank, Calif., Aug. 23, 1939; d. Roland Joseph and Alice Polly (Slate) Bolgiano; m. Gary Lee Nofziger, Aug. 28, 1959 (div. 1982); children: Phillip Gary, Karen Annette, Eric David; m. Donald Frank Guillaume, Jan. 1, 1985. BA, Calif. State U., Los Angeles, 1964. Cert. tchr., Calif. Tchr. Ocean View Sch. Dist., Huntington Beach, Calif., 1972-80, Los Angeles Unified Sch. Dist., 1983-86, Long Beach (Calif.) Unified Sch. Dist., 1986—; free-lance artist, 1965—. Works include series prints of Calif. Missions, 1984. Mem. Friends Bolsa Chica, Huntington Beach, 1986—. Artist prints Calif. Missions, 1984; freelance artist 1965—. Mem. AAUW, Tchrs. Assn. Long Beach, Audubon Soc. (membership chmn.), Friends of Bolsa Chica. Democrat. Home: 19243 Meadowood Circle Huntington Beach CA 92648

GUILLEMIN, ROGER, physiologist; b. Dijon, France, Jan. 11, 1924; came to U.S., 1953, naturalized, 1963; s. Raymond and Blanche (Rigollot) G.; m. Lucienne Jeanne Billard, Mar. 22, 1951; children—Chantal, Francois, Claire, Helene, Elizabeth, Cecile. B.A., U. Dijon, 1941, B.Sc., 1942; M.D., Faculty of Medicine, Lyons, France, 1949; Ph.D., U. Montreal, 1953; Ph.D. (hon.), U. Rochester, 1976, U. Chgo., 1977, Baylor Coll. Medicine, 1978, U. Ulm, Germany, 1978, U. Dijon, France, 1978, Free U. Brussels, 1979, U. Montreal, 1979, U. Man., Can, 1984, U. Turin, Italy, 1985. Intern, resident univs. hosps. Dijon, 1949-51; asso. dir., asst. prof. Inst. Exptl. Medicine and Surgery, U. Montreal, 1951-53; asso. dir. dept. exptl. endocrinology Coll. de France, Paris, 1960-63; asst. prof. physiology Baylor Coll. Medicine, 1953-57, assoc. prof., 1957-63, prof., dir. labs. neuroendocrinology, 1963-70, adj. prof., 1970—; adj. prof. medicine U. Calif. at San Diego, 1970—; rsch. fellow, chmn. labs. neuroendocrinology Salk Inst., 1970—. Decorated chevalier Legion of Honor (France), 1974, officier, 1984; recipient Gairdner Internat. award, 1974; U.S. Nat. Medal of Sci., 1977; co-recipient Nobel prize for medicine, 1977; recipient Lasker Found. award, 1975; Dickson prize in medicine, 1976; Passano award med. sci., 1976; Schmitt medal neurosci., 1977; Barren gold medal, 1979; Dale medal Soc. for Endocrinology U.K., 1980. Fellow AAAS; Mem. Am. Physiol. Soc., Endocrine Soc. (pres.) 1986), Soc. Exptl. Biology and Medicine, Internat. Brain Research Orgn., Internat. Soc. Research Biology Reprodn., Soc. Neuro-scis., Nat. Acad. Scis., Am. Acad. Arts and Scis., Académie Nationale de Médecine (fgn. assoc.), Swedish Soc. Med. Scis. (hon.), Académie des Scis. (fgn. assoc.), Académie Royale de Médecine de Belgique (corr. fgn.), Club of Rome. Office: Salk Inst Box 85800 San Diego CA 92138 *

GUINN, KENNY C., utility company executive; b. 1934; married. BA, Fresno U., MA; PhD., Utah State U. Supt. Clark County Sch. Dist.; v.p. adminstrn. Nev. Savs. and Loan Assn., 1978-80, pres., chief operating officer, 1980-85, chief exec. officer, 1985—; pres. Southwest Gas Corp., 1987-88, chmn., chief exec. officer, 1988—. Office: Nev Savs & Loan Assn 201 Las Vegas Blvd S PO Box 2191 Las Vegas NV 89125-2191 other: Southwest Gas Corp 5241 Spring Mountain Rd Las Vegas NV 89102 *

GUINN, SUZANNE KAY, speech language pathologist; b. Kalamazoo, Mar. 4, 1944; d. Kenneth Jeremiah and Ruth Minnie (Baker) Yeomans; m. Howard Christopher Guinn, Apr. 26, 1968; 1 child, Ian Christopher. BS, Western Mich. U., 1966; MS, U. Wis., 1967. Presch. supr. Kalamazoo Valley Intermediate Sch. Dist., 1967-68; speech-lang. pathologist State operated schs., Eielson AFB, Alaska, 1968-74; coordinator speech-lang. and presch. services Fairbanks (Alaska) North Star Borough Sch. Dist., 1974-88; dir., owner Communicaid, 1988—. Recipient DiCarlo award Am. Speech and Hearing Found., 1983. Mem. NEA, Alaska Speech Lang. Hearing Assn. (pres. 1974-75, 80-81), Am. Speech and Hearing Assn. (Frank Kleffner award 1987), Delta Kappa Gamma (pres. Fairbanks chpt. 1978-80). Home: 1438 Dupont Ln Fairbanks AK 99709 Office: Communicaid 600 University Ave Fairbanks AK 99709

GUINOUARD, DONALD EDGAR, psychologist; b. Bozeman, Mont., Mar. 31, 1929; s. Edgar Arthur and Venabell (Ford) G.; m. Irene M. Egeler, Mar. 30, 1951; children: Grant M., Philip A., Donna I. BS, Mont. State U., Bozeman, 1954; MS, Mont. State U., 1955; EdD, Wash. State U., Pullman, 1960; postdoctoral, Stanford U., 1965; grad., Indsl. Coll. of the Armed Forces, 1964, Air War Coll., 1976. Lic. psychologist, Ariz., counselor, Wash., Mont.; cert. secondary tchr. and sch. adminstr., Wash., Mont. Advanced through grades to col. USAFR, 1946-84, ret., 1984; dir. counseling Consol. Sch. Dist., Pullman, Wash., 1955-60; assoc. prof. Mont. State U., Bozeman, 1960-66; field selection officer Peace Corps, U.S., S.Am., 1962-68; prof. counseling, counseling psychologist Ariz. State U., Tempe, 1966—; coowner Forensic Cons. Assocs., Tempe, 1970—; admissions liaison officer USAF Acad., Colo. Springs, 1967-84; assessment officer Fundamental Edn. Ctr. for the Devel. of the Latin American Community, Patzcuaro, Mex., 1963-64; expert witness on vocat. and psychol. disability for fed. and state cts. Contbr. articles to profl. jours. Mem. Ariz. Psychol. Assn., Am. Assn. Counseling & Devel., Reserve Officers Assn. Democrat. Methodist. Home: 112 E Cairo Dr Tempe AZ 85282

GULBRANDSON, L. C., justice Montana Supreme Court; b. Vida, Mont., Oct. 28, 1922; s. E.O. and May (Farnham) G.; m. Wilma Loomans, Apr. 20, 1976; 1 son by previous marriage, Stephen. B.S.L., U. Minn., 1950, LL.B., 1952. Bar: Mont. 1953. Judge Dist. Ct. 7th Dist. Mont., 1959-83; justice Mont. Supreme Ct., Helena, 1983—. Served to capt. USAAF, 1942-48, PTO. Home: 2034 Gold Rush Ave Helena MT 59601 Office: Mont Supreme Ct 215 N Sanders St Justice Bldg Rm 323 Helena MT 59601

GULBRANSON, JAMES BERNHARD, retail executive; b. Glendale, Calif., June 28, 1942; s. Bernard Theodore and Frances (Slang) G.; m. Kathleen Berg, May 6, 1967; children: Kirsten, Erik, Ingrid. AA, Antelope Valley Jr. Coll., Lancaster, Calif., 1962; BA, Calif. Luth. U., 1964. Pres. San Fernando Valley Glass Co., Panorama City, Calif., 1967—, Van Nuys Glass Co. Inc., Panorama City, 1979—. Mem. nominating com. Mission District, Boy Scouts Am., 1972—; mem. San Fernando Valley Hist Soc., v.p. 1969, 83, pres. 1970, bd. dirs. 1983-85; bd. dirs. Heritage Mus. Fine Arts; commr. City of San Fernando hist. bldgs. and sites; active many historical groups and societies; mem. Los Angeles County Rep. Com. Served to 1st lt. U.S. Army, 1964-67, Vietnam. Decorated Silver Star, Air medal; recipient Disting. Service award San Fernando Jaycees, 1973. Mem. So. Calif. Glass Assn. (bd. dirs. 1987—), San Fernando Valley Internat. Soc. Interior Designers (bd. dirs. 1987—), San Fernando Valley Bus. and Profl. Assn., Calif. Luth. Coll. Alumni Assn. Lutheran. Lodge: Rotary (San Fernando) (treas. 1971-72, Paul Harris fellow, 1976). Office: Van Nuys Glass Co 9051 Van Nuys Blvd Panorama City CA 91402

GULBRANSON, REX ALAN, arts administrator; b. Flandreau, S.D., Sept. 22, 1951; s. George J. Gulbranson and Shirley U. (White) De Zotell; m. Beverly Ann Parry, June 12, 1976; 1 child, Lea Ann. BA, S.D. State U., 1973. Asst. dir. S.D. Meml. Art Ctr., Brookings, 1974-79; dir. visual arts Ariz. Commn. on Arts, Phoenix, 1979-84, dir. spl. projects, 1984-88, dir. design and orgn. devel., 1988—. Bd. dirs. Aid to Adoption Spl. Kids, Phoenix, 1986—. NEA fellow, 1976. Mem. Phoenix City Club. Office: Ariz Commn on Arts 417 W Roosevelt St Phoenix AZ 85003

GULL, PAULA MAE, nurse; b. Los Angeles, Mar. 7, 1955; d. Gerald Henry and Artemis (Cubillas) Balzer; m. Randell Jay Gull, July 10, 1976. AA, Cypress (Calif.) Coll., 1976; AS with high honors, Rancho Santiago Coll., Santa Ana, Calif., 1985. Staff RN U. Calif. Irvine Med. Ctr., Orange, Calif., 1986-87, asst. nurse mgr., 1987-88, nurse mgr., 1988. Mormon. Home: 24974 Enchanted Way Moreno Valley CA 92387

GULLARD, J(AMES) MICHAEL, venture capital company executive; b. Townsend, Mont., Feb. 11, 1945; s. James H. and Helen G. (Barker) G.; m. Pamela Kathleen Knudson, Dec. 9, 1972; children: Erik James, Benjamin Knute. B.A., Stanford U., 1967, M.B.A., 1970. Fin. controller Intel Corp., Santa Clara, Calif., 1972-79; v.p. fin. and adminstrn. Telecommunications Tech., Inc., Sunnyvale, Calif., 1979-81, gen. mgr., 1981-83, pres., chief exec. officer, 1983-84; chmn., ptnr. Cornerstone Ventures, Menlo Park, Calif., 1984—. Mem. bd. advisors Santa Clara (Calif.) Univ. Levy Sch. Bus.; chmn. bd. dirs. SiScan Systems, Inc., Campbell, Calif; bd. dirs. IntelliMed Corp, Ft. Lee, N.J., DIS, Bellingham, Wash., Custom Solutions, Inc. Mountain View, Calif, Gen. Info., Inc., Kirkland Wash., Cunningham Communication, Inc., Santa Clara, Calif. VLSI Packaging Materials Inc., San Jose, Calif.; mem. adv. bd. Levy Sch. Bus. at Santa Clara U., 1985—. Vol. VISTA, Oakland, 1968-70. Mem. Am. Electronics Assn., Western Assn. Venture Capitalists. Club: Foothills Tennis and Swim (Palo Alto, Calif.). Avocations: classical guitar, skiing, tennis, golfing. Office: Cornerstone Ventures 2420 Sand Hill Rd Ste 202 Menlo Park CA 94025

GULLERS, KARL WERNER, book publisher; b. Stockholm, Sept. 5, 1916; came to U.S., 1973; s. W. Emil and Anna Charlotta (Agren) G.; m. Ingvor Margareta Gullers, Feb. 3, 1937 (div. 1972); children: Birgitta, Peter, Kristina, Ingela, Lena Pia; m. Barbara Karen Howard, Apr. 29, 1973. Student pub. sch.s, Stockholm. Owner, mgr. Gullers Studio, Gullers Pictorial, Stockholm, 1938—; owner, mgr., producer Gullers Pictorial, Phoenix, 1973—. Exhibited photographs in London, N.Y.C., Chgo., San Francisco, Rome, Rio de Janeiro, Stockholm, Gothenburg, Oslo; pub. 92 books. Named to Hall of Fame of Photography. Mem. Am. Soc. Photographers, Profl. Photographers Am., Rotary. Home and Office: Gullers Pictorial 4963 E Palomino Rd Phoenix AZ 85018

GULLIFORD, ANDREW JELLIS, museum director; b. St. Paul, Nov. 2, 1953; s. David Oliver and Mildred Christine (Jellis) G.; m. Stephanie Bruce Moran, Aug. 13, 1977; children: Tristan David, Duncan Jewett. BA, Colo. Coll., 1975, MA in Teaching, 1976; PhD, Bowling Green State U., 1986. Tchr. 4th grade Silt (Colo.) Elem. Sch., 1976-83; historian, folklorist Am. House, Inc., Lima, Ohio, 1986-87; mus. dir. Western N.Mex. U., Silver City, 1987—; instr. Colo. Mountain Coll., Rifle, 1977-83; grant writer Colo. Endowment Humanities, Boulder, 1977-78; project dir. Country Sch. Legacy, 1980-83, As Far As the Eye Can See, 1975-76, The Years Ahead, 1977-79; writer, photographer El Paso County (Colo.) Hist. sites, 1975-76. Author: America's Country Schools, 1984, Boomtown Blues: Colorado Oil Shale 1885-1985, 1989. Grantee Can. Embassy, Victoria, B.C., 1987, NEH, 1982, Colo. Endowment for the Humanities, 1975, 77; fellow Smithsonian Instn., 1986. Mem. Am. Culture Assn. (bd. govs.), Western History Assn., Am. Studies Assn., Colo. Hist. Soc., Mt. Plains Mus. Assn. Democrat. Home: 621 Cain Dr Silver City NM 88062 Office: Western NMex U Mus Coll Arts and Letters Fleming Hall Silver City NM 88062

GUMUCIO, FERNANDO RAUL, foods and beverage company executive; b. Bolivia, Sept. 9, 1934; s. Julio F. G.; children: Linda, Julie, Cynthia, Beverly. B.S., U. San Francisco, 1957; M.B.A., St. Mary's Coll., 1977. Dir. mktg. Latin Am. Del Monte, Mexico, 1963-68; group product dir. Del Monte Corp., San Francisco, 1971-73, dir. sales and product mgmt., 1973-74, v.p. mktg., 1973-80, pres. dry grocery and beverage products group, 1980-85, group v.p., 1985-87, pres. Del Monte U.S.A. operating group, 1985-87; dir. Basic Am. Foods, San Francisco; mem., exec. bd. Nat. Food Producers Assn., Washington. Active Boy Scouts Am.; bd. regents St. Mary's Coll. Republican. Roman Catholic. Clubs: St. Francis Yacht; World Trade (San Francisco). Office: Del Monte Corp 1 Market Pla PO Box 3575 San Francisco CA 94119 *

GUND, GEORGE, III, financier; b. Cleve., May 7, 1937; s. George and Jessica (Roesler) G.; m. Mary Theo Feld, Aug. 13, 1966; children: George, Gregory. Student, Western Res. U., Menlo (Calif.) Sch. Bus. Engaged in personal investments San Francisco, 1967—; cattle ranching Lee, Nev., 1967—; partner Calif. Seals, San Francisco, 1976-77; pres. Ohio Barons, Inc., Richfield, 1977-78; chmn. bd. Northstar Fin. Corp., Bloomington, Minn., from 1978, Minn. North Stars, Bloomington; dir. Ameritrust Cleve.; vice-chmn. Gund Investment Corp., Princeton, N.J.; chmn. North Stars Met Center Mgmt. Corp., Bloomington; v.p. hockey Sun Valley Ice Skating, Inc., Idaho. Chmn. San Francisco Internat. Film Festival, 1973—; mem. sponsors council Project for Population Action; adv. council Sierra Club Found.; mem. internat. council Mus. Modern Art, N.Y.C.; collectors com. Nat. Gallery Art; bd. dirs. Calif. Theatre Found., Bay Area Ednl. TV Assn., San Francisco Mus. Art, Cleve. Health Museum, George Gund Found., Cleve. Internat. Film Festival, Sun Valley Center Arts and Humanities, U. Nev. Reno Found., Sundance Inst. Served with USMCR, 1955-58. Clubs: Calif. Tennis (San Francisco), University (San Francisco), Olympic (San Francisco); Union (Cleve.), Cleve. Athletic (Cleve.), Kirkland Country (Cleve.), Rowfant (Cleve.); Ranier (Seattle). Office: 1821 Union St San Francisco CA 94123 also: Minn North Stars 7901 Cedar Ave S Bloomington MN 55420 *

GUNDERSON, CLEON HENRY, management consultant corporation executive; b. Great Falls, Mont., June 5, 1932; s. Leon H. and Mona (Emmett) G.; m. Virginia Ellen Hudson, Aug. 26, 1972; children: Craig H., Robert S., Laura E. BS, Inst. Tech., Dayton, Ohio, 1971, Mont. State U., 1957; MAPA, U. Okla., 1975. Communications engr. Mountain States Tel & Tel, Helena, Mont., 1953-54; aerospace engr. Boeing Co., Seattle, 1957-58; commd. 2nd lt. USAF, 1958, advanced to col., 1974, ret., 1976; pres. Precision Prodn. & Engring., Walla Walla, Wash., 1976-79, Western Skies Energy Systems, Spokane, Wash., 1979-88, Computer Central, Olympia, Wash., 1988—; Mem. Am. Inst. Elec. Engrs., Seattle, 1957-60, Am. Inst. Indsl. Engrs., Spokane, 1982-85. Inventor heatexchange solar panels, comml. solar panels. Decorated Silver Stars, Disting. Flying Crosses, Purple Heart, Air medals. Mem. Soc. Mfg. Engrs. (sr. mem.), Soc. Mil. Engrs., Nat. Assn. Small Businesses, Toastmasters Internat., Walla Walla C. of C., Canto Blanco Gun Club (Madrid, v.p. 1973-75, Scott Air Force Base Gun Club (v.p. 1975-76), Spokane Gun Club. Republican. Home: 13001 Littlerock Rd Box 246 Littlerock WA 98556 Office: Computer Central 3700 Pacific Ave SE Ste A Olympia WA 98501

GUNDERSON, ELMER MILLARD, state justice, law educator; b. Mpls., Aug. 9, 1929; s. Elmer Peter and Carmaleta (Oliver) G.; m. Lupe Gomez, Dec. 29, 1967; 1 son, John Randolph. Student, U. Minn., U. Omaha, 1948-53; LL.B., Creighton U., 1956; LL.M., U. Va., 1982; LL.D., Calif. Western Sch. Law; student appellate judges seminar, N.Y. U., 1971; LL.D., U. Pacific. Bar: Nebr. 1956, Nev. 1958. Atty.-adviser FTC, 1956-57; pvt. practice Las Vegas, 1958-71; justice Nev. Supreme Ct., 1971-89, now sr. justice; instr. bus. law So. regional div. U. Nev.; lectr., author bulls. felony crimes for Clark County Sheriff's Dept.; counsel Sheriff's Protective Assn.; mem. legal staff Clark Council Civil Def. Agy.; legal counsel Nev. Jaycees. Compiler, annotator: Omaha Home Rule Charter; project coordinator: Jud. Orientation Manual, 1974. Chmn. Clark County Child Welfare Bd., Nev. central chpt. Nat. Multiple Sclerosis Soc.; hon. dir. Spring Mountain Youth Camp. Served with U.S. Army. Recipient A.J.S. Herbert Harley award. Mem. Am., Nebr., Nev. bar assns.; Mem. Inst. Jud. Adminstrn., Am. Law Inst., Am. Trial Lawyers Assn., Am. Judicature Soc., Phi Alpha Delta, Alpha Sigma Nu. Office: Nev Supreme Ct 100 N Carson St Carson City NV 89710

GUNDERSON, LESLIE CHARLES, engineering company executive, electrical engineer; b. Rahway, N.J., Aug. 1, 1935; s. Ainslie Carl and Anna Helena (Jacobsen) G.; m. Edith Van Muiswinker, Oct. 8, 1957; children: Lynn Suzanne, Diane Joy, David Charles. B in Engring., Stevens Inst., 1957, MS, 1960; MSEE, Columbia U., N.Y.C., 1964; PhD in Elec. Engring., N.C. State U., 1971. Sr. engr. ITT Labs., Nutley, N.J., 1957-62; with Corning (N.Y.) Glass Works, 1964-88, dir. product devel. div., 1975-82, dir. bus. devel. div., 1982-88; pres., chief exec. officer MetriCor, Inc., Woodinville, Wash., 1987—. Inventee in field. Mem. IEEE (sr.), Am. Phys. Soc., Optical Soc. Am. Office: MetriCor Inc 18800 142d Ave NE Woodinville WA 98072

GUNDERSON, MAURICE EDWARD PHILLIPS, mechanical engineer; b. Kodiak, Alaska, Dec. 10, 1951; s. Maurice Darst and Marjorie (Lieber) G.; m. Rebecca Phillips, Aug. 31, 1985. BA, Oreg. State U., 1974, MS in Mech. Engring., 1975; MBA, Stanford U., 1985. Registered engr., Calif., Oreg. Project engr. CH2M Hill, Corvallis, Oreg., 1974-77; project mgr. Garrett AiResearch, Torrance, Calif., 1977-80; dir. Airco Cryogenics, Irvine, Calif., 1980-83; pres. Edison Systems Corp., South San Francisco, Calif., 1985—. Patentee in field; contbr. articles to profl. jours. Mem. ASME, AIAA, Soc. Automotive Engrs. Republican. Home: 1036 Grebe St Foster City CA 94404 Office: Edison Systems Corp 379 Oyster Point Blvd South San Francisco CA 94080

GUNDERSON, STAMY SAM, transportation executive; b. Denver, Mar. 13, 1963; d. Theodore and Jane (Ganas) Andrew: m. Theodore Dale Gunderson, Feb. 14, 1982 (divorced); 1 child, Marie. Student, Metro State Coll., 1981-82, Aurora (Colo.) Community Coll., 1987. Sales mgr. Foxmoor Casuals, Englewood, Colo., 1981-82, 24 Hr. Nautilus, Denver, 1982-85; adminstr., control tower agt. Continental Airlines, Denver, 1985—; treas. Denver Airport Ticket Office Distress Fund Com., 1986-88. Aide Legal Aid Soc., Denver, 1988—. Republican. Greek Orthodox. Home: 17874 E Crestline Pl Aurora CO 80015 Office: Stapleton Internat Airport Denver CO 80207

GUNDERSON, TED LEE, security consultant; b. Colorado Springs, Colo., Nov. 7, 1928. BBA, U. Nebr. Sales rep. George A. Hormel Co., Austin, Minn., 1950-51; spl. agt. in charge U.S. Dept. Justice FBI, Los Angeles, Dallas, Memphis, Phila., 1951-79; internat. security cons. Ted L. Gunderson & Assocs., Santa Monica, Calif., 1979—; pres. Scandanavian-Am. Mgmt. Corp.; bd. dirs. St. Peters Life and Casualty Co.; cons. Calif. Narcotic Authority. Author: How to Locate Anyone Anywhere, 1989; appeared on numerous nat. and local TV, radio talk shows. Mem. Bel Air U.S. Navy League (pres.), Internat. Assn. Chiefs of Police, Am. Soc. Indsl. Security, Internat. Footprinters Assn., Nat. Football Found. and Hall of Fame, Philanthropic Soc. (Los Angeles chpt.), Sigma Alpha Epsilon.

GUNDVALDSON, LISA KAY, accountant; b. Corona, Calif., Aug. 10, 1955; d. Joseph William and Mary (McMartin) Copeland; m. Lynn F. Gundvalson, May 10, 1977. AA, Ariz. Western Coll., 1975; BA, U. Ariz., 1982. CPA, Ariz. Bookkeeper Hinkle & Perius, P.C., Yuma, Ariz., 1972-78; acct. Safari Club Internat., Tucson, 1978-79; staff acct. Zele Stokes & Harbour, P.C., Tucson, 1979-87; owner, mgr. Lisa Gundvaldson, CPA, Tucson, 1987—. Mem. AICPA, Ariz. Soc. CPA's, Am. Soc. Women Accts., Greater Ariz. Bicycling Assn. (treas. 1985-86). Republican. Office: 6133 E Grant Rd Tucson AZ 85712

GUNJA, DONALD EDWARD, military officer, consultant; b. Kansas City, Kans., Feb. 8, 1949; s. Edward John and Rosemary (Miller) G.; m. Gracia D. Arias, Apr. 10 1971. AA, SUNY, 1983; BS in Aviation Mgmt., So. Ill. U., 1985. Lic. radar approach contr. Air traffic contr. Naval Air Sta., Key West, Fla., 1970-74; air traffic mgr./supr. Naval Sta., Rota, Spain, 1974-78; air traffic asst. Air Route Traffic Control Ctr., Indpls., 1979-81; air traffic contr.tactical air control squadron 11 USN, Coronado, Calif., 1982-85; mem. fleet project team for ATC tng. devices USN, Memphis, 1983-85; air traffic tng. supr. fleet area control and surveillance facility USN, San Diego, 1985-88, naval tactical data systems QA, combat systems analyst, 1988—; cons. Naval Ocean Systems Command on ATC short-term memory sci-study, San Diego, 1987-88. Recipient Navy Commendation Medal, U.S. Navy, 1985. Mem. Am. Assn. of Airport Exec., Air Traffic Control Assn., Aircraft Owners and Pilots Assn., Non Commd. Officers Assn., Rota Flying Club (Spain), Fleet Res. Assn. (Indpls.). Roman Catholic. Office: FCDSSA 200 Catalina Blvd San Diego CA 92147

GUNN, DENNIS MICHAEL, manufacturing executive, consultant; b. Covington, Ky., May 22, 1949; s. Richard Anthony and Dorothy May (McCudden) G.; m. Judy Carol Cotlow, Feb. 23, 1975 (div. Jan., 1983); m. Melanie Irene Tissot, Jan. 1, 1986. AA, Santa Monica Community Coll., Calif., 1978; BS, U. Redlands, 1979; postgrad., Pepperdine U., 1983; PhD, Am. Coll., Birmingham, 1988. Assoc. analyst First Interstat So. Calif. Edison, L.A., 1975-76; systems analyst Pencorp Fin., Santa Monica, Calif., 1976-78; dir. devel. Positive Systems, L.A., 1978-80; mgr. planning, devel. Armstrong Data Svcs., Pacoima, Calif., 1980-82; pres., cons. Consultant Elite Ltd., Manhattan Beach, Calif., 1982-83; head fin. systems Hughes Aircraft, El Segundo, Calif., 1983—; pres. Consultant Elite, Ltd, Manhattan Beach, 1978—. Mem. Calif. Realtors Assn., Manhattan Beach C. of C., Alpha Phi Omega. Republican. Roman Catholic. Home: One Arbolado Ct Manhattan Beach CA 90266 Office: Hughes Aircraft 999 Sepulveda El Segundo CA 90245

GUNN, GILES BUCKINGHAM, English educator, religion educator; b. Evanston, Ill., Jan. 9, 1938; s. Buckingham Willcox and Janet (Fargo) G.; m. Janet Mears Varner, Dec. 29, 1969 (div. July 1983); 1 child, Adam Buckingham; m. Deborah Rose Sills, July 9, 1983; 1 child, Abigail Rose. BA, Amherst Coll., 1959; student, Episc. Theol. Sch., Cambridge, Mass., 1959-60; MA, U. Chgo., 1963, PhD, 1967. Prof. religion and lit. U. Chgo., 1966-74; prof. religion and Am. studies U. N.C., Chapel Hill, 1974-85; prof. English and Religion U. Fla., 1984-85; prof. English U. Calif., Santa Barbara, 1985—; vis. asst. prof. religion Stanford U., Palo Alto, Calif., 1973; Benedict Disting. vis. prof. Religion Carleton Coll., Northfield, Minn., 1977; William R. Kenan Disting. vis. prof. Humanities Coll. William and Mary, Williamsburg, Va., 1983-84; Humanities Disting. vis. prof. U. Colo., 1989; dir. NEH summer sems. for coll. and univ. tchrs., 1979, 81, 85, for sch. tchrs., 1987, 88, 89. Author: F.O. Matthiessen: The Critical Achievement, 1975, The Interpretation of Otherness: Literature, Religion and the American Imagination, 1979, The Culture of Criticism and the Criticism of Culture, 1987; editor: Literature and Religion, 1971, Henry James, Senior: A Selection of His Writings, 1974, New World Metaphysics: Readings on the Religious Meaning of the American Experience, 1981, The Bible and American Arts and Letters, 1983, Church, State, and American Culture, 1984; contbr. numerous articles to profl. jours. Edward John Noble Leadership grantee, 1959-63; Amherst-Doshisha fellow, Kyoto, Japan, 1960-61, Kent fellow, Danforth Found., 1963-65, Guggenheim fellow, 1978-79, Nat. Endowment for Humanities fellow, 1990, U. Calif. Pres.'s Rsch. fellow, 1990. Mem. MLA, Am. Acad. Religion (dir. research and pubs. 1974-77), Am. Studies Assn., Soc. Religion, Arts and Contemporary Culture, Soc. Am. Phil. Democrat. Home: Walking M Ranch 2851 Tapadero Rd Los Olivos CA 93441 Office: U Calif Dept English Santa Barbara CA 93106

GUNN, PATRICIA ALICE, transportation executive, small business owner; b. San Diego, Dec. 15, 1948; d. Leonard James and Wilba Alice (Toomey) Bailey; m. Daniel Joseph Gunn, Nov. 22, 1970; children: Andrea Marie, Michelle Leigh. Student, Southwestern Jr. Coll., Chula Vista, Calif., 1968-70; grad. in med. asst., Pacific Coll. Medicine, 1969; Cert. lic. vocat. nurse, Long Beach City Coll., 1987. Med. asst., X-ray technician Dr. J. Ravenna, La Mirada, Calif., 1976-86, X-ray technician, LVN, 1986—; sec., treas. Sun Van Moving and Storage, Long Beach, Calif., 1980-88; claims adjuster Gunn Van Lines, Inc., Wilmington, Calif., 1980-88; v.p. Gunn Worldwide Forwarding, Wilmington, 1987—; owner Nationwide Claim Adjustors, Wilmington, 1986—; cons. Gunn Van Lines, 1984—; bd. dirs. Gunn Worldwide Forwarding, 1987—. Democrat. Roman Catholic. Office: Gunn Van Lines 1020 McFarland Ave Wilmington CA 90744

GUNNING, DIANE DOROTHY, real estate company executive; b. Tonasket, Wash., May 31, 1941; d. Benjamin Fred Helm and Lydia Erma Matilda (Fedderson) Wallace; m. Robert R. Sack, April 27, 1965 (div. May 15, 1975); children: Benjamin Wayne, Raymond Robert; m. Theodore G. Gunning, July 10, 1976; stepchildren: Gary L., Diane C. Harwood. AA, San Jose State U., 1961; BS, Concordia Tchrs. Coll., 1964. Tchr. St. Matthew Luth. Elem. Sch., Lodi, Calif., 1961-63, Edmund, Wash., 1964-65; instr. off-campus U. Ariz., Tucson, 1965-66; tchr. Ft. Huachuca (Ark.) Pub. Sch., 1966-68; owner Spokandles Whs., Spokane, 1972-75; sec., treas. Northwood Properties, Spokane, 1977—; owner., mgr. Quality Inn Valley Stes., Spokane, 1989—. Sec., treas. Redemmer Luth. Ch., Spokane, 1978, contbr. to newsletter, 1978, chmn. fellowship, 1986—; bd. dirs. Spokane Lilac Assn., 1984, Spokane Valley Gen. Hosp., 1985, dir., 1986—; dir. Lilac Festival, 1985—; mem. Spokane Convention and Bus. Bur., 1987—; executor Holly Caudill Trust Fund, 1981—. Mem. Exec. Women's Club, Valley Garden Club, Moose, United Women's Club (pres., sec.), Spokane C. of C. Office: Northwood Properties Quality Inn Valley Stes E 9616 Montgomery Spokane WA 99206

GUNSTREAM, ROBBY DEAN, music society executive; b. Pasadena, Calif., Sept. 23, 1951; s. Robby Nelman and Dorothy Jean (Poole) G.; m. Mareth Sinclair, June 6, 1981; children: Corbin Sinclair, Caroline E. Stuart. MusB, U. So. Calif., 1974; MusM, Yale U., 1976. Staff assoc. Nat. Assn. Schs. of Music, Reston, Va., 1976-79; asst. dean Conservatory of Music Wheaton (Ill.) Coll., 1979-83; exec. dir. Coll. Music Soc., Boulder, Colo., 1983—. Recipient cert. Ctr. for Black Music Research, Chgo., 1987. Episcopalian. Office: Coll Music Soc 1444 15th St Boulder CO 80302

GUNTHER, HERBERT CHAO, advertising agency executive; b. Taipei, Republic of China, Dec. 10, 1951; came to U.S., 1966; s. Walter and Emerald Jade (Chao) G. AB in Philosophy, U. Calif., Berkeley, 1973. Organizer Target: Banking in Am., San Francisco, 1971-73; adminstr. Alternative Banking Project, San Francisco, 1973-75; copywriter Pub. Media Ctr., San Francisco, 1975-78, exec. dir., 1978—, also dir.; chmn. bd. dirs. Urban Designs Inc., San Francisco, 1983—; bd. dirs. Ctr. for Investigative Reporting, San Francisco, 1984—, Media Alliance, Fairness and Accuracy in Reporting; instr. Dept. Journalism City Coll. San Francisco; past mem. consumer adv. panel Pacific Bell; media cons. various orgns.; lectr. various orgns.; dir. various workshops; expert witness. Exec. editor: Index of Progressive Funders, 1984, Talking Back: Citizen's Guide to the Fairness Doctrine, 1985; exec. producer short films for govt. agys., various media campaigns; contbr. articles to profl. jours. Bd. dirs. Chinese for Affirmative Action, San Francisco, 1984—, Ctr. for 3d World Organizing, Oakland, Calif., 1983—, Cath. Social Services, San Francisco, Asian Neighborhood Design, San Francisco Study Ctr., Telegraph Hill Family Assn.; past bd. dirs. Friends of Earth, Support Ctr., Campaign Against Nuclear War; assoc. dir. Sunflower Found., N.Y.C. Office: Pub Media Ctr 466 Green St San Francisco CA 94133

GUNTY, CHRISTOPHER JAMES, newspaper editor; b. Hometown, Ill., Oct. 13, 1959; s. Harold Paul and Therese Agnes (Kohs) G.; m. Nancy Louise Blanton, July 10, 1982; children: William, Amy. BA, Loyola U., Chgo., 1981. Circulation mgr. The Chgo. Catholic, 1981-83, assoc. mnging. editor, 1983, mng. editor, 1983-85; editor, mng. editor The Catholic Sun, Phoenix, 1985—. Author: He Came to Touch Us, 1987; co-author videotape script The Pope in Arizona, 1987. Contbr. articles to spl. Catholic news svcs. as well as papers when employed. Mem. Fiesta Bowl Com., Phoenix, 1987—. Named Honoree Summer U. Internat. Cath. Union of the Press, Switzerland, 1988. Mem. Cath. Press Assn. (bd. dirs. 1988—), Assoc. Ch. Press, Ariz. Newspapers Assn., Ariz. Press Club, Soc. of Profl. Journalists. Roman Catholic. Office: The Catholic Sun 400 E Monroe St Phoenix AZ 85004

GUPTA, ANIL, electrical engineer; b. Ferozepur, India, Mar. 21, 1948; came to U.S., 1969; s. Uttam Chand and Prakash (Agarwal) G.; m. Anita Guptal, Dec. 25, 1977; children: Samir, Sasha. BS, Indian Inst. Tech., Kaaragpur, 1969; MS, Clemson U., 1971; PhD, Syracuse U., 1975. Research asst. Tex. A&M U., College Station, 1971-72, Syracuse (N.Y.) U., 1972-74; mem. tech. staff Rockwell Internat., Anaheim, Calif., 1974-79; sr. mem. tech. staff Hughes Aircraft Co., Carlsbad, Calif., 1979—. Contbr. articles to profl. jours. Recipient Merit scholarship Indian Inst. Tech, 1964. Mem. IEEE (1st prize paper award 1975, sr., gen. chmn. SOS/SOI workshop 1987). Hindu. Office: Hughes Aircraft Co 6155 El Camino Real Carlsbad CA 92008

GUPTA, BIMLESHWAR PRASAD, mechanical engineer, researcher; b. Jaipur, Raj, India, May 17, 1946; s. Hari Prasad and Sarla D. (Agarwal) G.; m. Rajni Garg, Dec. 10, 1974; children: Anjli, Neeraj. BSME, U. Jodhpur, India, 1968; MSME, U. Minn., 1971, MBA, 1974. Registered profl. engr., Colo. Engr. Honeywell Inc., Mpls., 1971-76, sect. mgr., 1976-78; program mgr. Solar Energy Rsch. Inst., Golden, Colo., 1978—; lectr. in field; chairperson nat. and internat. confs. on solar thermal rsch. Guest editor spl. edit. The Energy Jour., 1987; contbr. articles to profl. jours. Mem. ASME (assoc. editor jour. 1983-85, guest editor spl. issue 1984,), Internat. Solar Energy Soc., India Assn. Colo. (exec. com. 1983-84), Minn. Alumni Assn., Toastmasters Club (Lakewood, Colo., pres. 1985, area gov. F-2 1988-89). Club: Toastmasters (Lakewood, Colo.) (pres. 1985, area gov. 1988-89). Home: 14373 W Bayaud Pl Golden CO 80401 Office: Solar Energy Rsch Inst 1617 Cole Blvd Golden CO 80401

GUPTA, DILIP K., financial consultant. came to U.S., 1977; s. Bishwanath and Suraj G.; m. Prema Gupta. BS in Metallurgical Engring., IIT, Kanpur, India, 1977; MS in Metall. Engring., Ohio State U., 1979; MBA, U. So. Maine, 1988. Cert. fin. planner. Chief engr. Philips Elmet Corp., Lewiston, Maine, 1980-86; sales engr. Philips-N.Am., Hollywood, Calif., 1987; staff engr. Hughes Aircraft Co., El Segundo, Calif., 1987-88; fin. cons. Merrill Lynch, Hemet, Calif., 1988—; rsch. asst. Dept. Elec. and Computer Engring. U. Calif., Santa Barbara, 1986-87. Mem. Am. Soc. Metals (treas. Maine chpt. 1984-85), Hughes Investment Club, Alpha Sigma Mu, Phi Kappa Phi. Home: 41459 Shadow Palm Way Hemet CA 92344 Office: Merrill Lynch 1565 W Florida Ave Hemet CA 92343

GUREVITCH, ARNOLD WILLIAM, dermatology educator; b. Los Angeles, Apr. 3, 1936; s. Leon and Freda Stella (Goldman) G.; m. Camille Abbott, June 12, 1960; children: Douglas Neal, Lara Judith. AB, Harvard U., 1958; MD, UCLA, 1962. Diplomate Am. Bd. Dermatology. Intern Los Angeles County Gen. Hosp., 1962-63; resident specializing in dermatology Los Angeles County Harbor Gen. Hosp., Torrance, Calif., 1963-66; practice medicine specializing in dermatology Los Angeles, 1966-67; staff physician Harbor-UCLA Med. Ctr., Torrance, 1969-73, acting chief dermatology, 1973-77, chief dermatology, 1977—; asst. prof. dermatology UCLA Sch. Medicine, Los Angeles, 1969-76, assoc. prof. to prof. dermatology, 1976—; head task force on teaching Nat. Program for Dermatology, 1971-75; cons. USAF Clinic, Los Angeles, 1969—, U. So. Calif. div. med. research in edn., Los Angeles, 1975-76, GMENAC, Dept. Health Edn. and Welfare, 1979. Contbr. articles to profl. jours. Chmn. Community Sch., Los Angeles, 1975-76; pres. adv. council Bancroft Jr. High Sch., 1978-80, Fairfax High Sch., 1981-84. Fellow Am. Acad. Dermatology; mem. Soc. Investigative Dermatology, Pacific Dermatol. Assn., Los Angeles Dermatol. Assn. (pres. 1978-79), Assn. Profs. of Dermatology. Office: Harbor-UCLA Med Ctr 1000 W Carson St Torrance CA 90509

GUREVITCH, RUSS, veterinary surgeon; b. Berkeley, Calif., Nov. 28, 1945; s. Leo and Evelyn (Schneider) G.; m. Terry Baker Van Horn, Sept. 25, 1988. BA, U. Calif., Berkeley, 1967; DVM, U. Calif., Davis, 1974. Intern Sch. of Vet. Medicine Purdue U., West Lafayette, Ind., 1974-75; resident in surgery Coll. of Vet. Medicine Ohio State U., Columbus, 1975-78; staff surgeon Northtown Animal Hosp., Santa Rosa, Calif., 1978-82; owner, staff surgeon Vet. Referral Surg. Svc., Petaluma, Calif., 1982—; surg. cons. various San Francisco Bay Hosps., 1982—. Recipient Vol. award Guide Dogs for the Blind, San Rafael, Calif., 1982-88, Canine Companions for Independence, Santa Rosa, 1988. Mem. Assn. for Vet. Orthopedic Rsch. and Edn. (sec. 1987—, trustee 1987-89), Vet. Orthopedic Soc., Am. Animal Hosp. Assn., Am. Vet. Med. Assn., Redwood Empire Vet. Med. Assn. (v.p. 1981-82), Breakfast Club (pres. 1985-86). Home: 71 Bay Rd Fairfax CA 94900 Office: Vet Referral Surg Svc 343 S McDowell Blvd Petaluma CA 94952

GURNEY, DANIEL SEXTON, race car manufacturing company executive, racing team executive; b. L.I., Apr. 13, 1931; s. John R. and Roma (Sexton) G.; m. Evi B., July 7, 1970; children: Justin B., Alexander R.; children by previous marriage: John, Lyndee, Danny, Jimmy. Grad., Menlo Jr. Coll., 1951. Profl. race car driver 1955-70; pres., owner Dan Gurney's All Am. Racers, Inc. (doing bus. as); Dan Gurney Eagle Racing Cars, U.S.A., Santa Ana, Calif., 1964—; mgr. Eagle Racing Team (Indpls. 500 winners 1968, 73, 75, U.S. Auto Club Nat. Championship winners 1968, 74), Formula A Championship winners 1968, 69); sports commentator CBS Sports; mem. Automobile Competition Com. for U.S.A. Served with U.S. Army, 1952-54, Korea. Recipient numerous racing awards including GTO Driving championship Internat. Motor Sports Assn., 1987 (driver Chris Cord), GTO Mfrs.' championship Internat. Motor Sports Assn., 1987 (mfr. Toyota), Norelco Cup championship, 1987 (driver Willy T. Ribbs). Mem. Screen Actors Guild, AFTRA, U.S. Auto Club, Sports Car Club Am., U.S. C. of C., Championship Auto Racing Teams, Inc., Soc. Automotive Engrs., Fedn. Internationale de L'Automobile, Internat. Motor Sports Assn. Clubs: Balboa Bay, Eagle.

GUSTAFSON, CONRAD LEE, insurance executive; b. Portland, Oreg., Dec. 12, 1944; s. Richard Franklin and Lula Elizabeth (Herold) G.; m. Melody Rae Diegel, Sept. 28, 1968. BS, Oreg. State U., 1968. Premium auditor Argonaut Ins. Co., Portland, 1971-73, premium audit, credit/collection mgr., 1973-77, spl. rep., 1977-78, asst. div. mgr., San Francisco, 1978-79, br. mgr., San Jose, Calif., 1979-85, div. mgr., San Jose, 1985-86; v.p. Ins. Equities Corp., Palo Alto, Calif., 1986-88; v.p. mktg. MMI/Multi-Systems Ady., San Rafael, 1988—. Served with U.S. Army, 1968-71. Mem. Soc. CPCU's. Republican. Lutheran. Office: Multi-Systems Agy 175 N Redwood Dr Ste 280 San Rafael CA 94903

GUSTAFSON, EVELYN MARIE, teacher; b. L.A., June 16, 1943; d. Ernest Albert and Ella Dorothy (Johnson) Anderson; m. William Ivor Gustafson, July 10, 1965; children: William Jr., Mark. BA, UCLA, 1966; MA, U. LaVerne, Calif., 1989. Cert. gen. elem. tchr., adminstrv. master tchr., Calif. Tchr. L.A. Unified Schs., 1966, tchr. gifted program, 1976-79; tchr. Inglewood (Calif.) Unified Schs., 1966-71; tchr. Saugus (Calif.) Union Schs., 1981—, master tchr., 1982, 85-86, learning specialist, 1986-88, head tchr., 1988—; master tchr. The Master's Coll., Newhall, Calif. 1982, 85-86. Pres. Calif. State U. Faculty Wives, Northridge, 1978-79; active L.A. Bapt. High Sch. Parent Grp., Sepulveda, 1986-87, Parent Adv. Grp. Granada Hills (Calif.) Presbyn. Weekday Sch., 1977-84; edn. chairperson and coord. St. Stephen's Luth. Ch., Granada Hills, 1984-88. Recipient Meritorious Svc. Teaching award Masons, 1987. Mem. Assn. for Supervision and Curriculum Devel. Republican. Office: Skyblue Mesa Elem Sch 28040 Hardesty Ave Canyon Country CA 91351

GUSTAFSON, LEWIS BRIGHAM, geologist; b. Timmins, Ont., Can., Sept. 4, 1933; s. John Kyle and Elizabeth (Brigham) G.; m. Ursula Lenkert, Jan. 21, 1961; children: Katrin, Kirsten, Irene. BSE, Princeton U., 1955; MS, Calif. Inst. Tech., 1958; PhD, Harvard U., 1962. Geologist to chief geologist Andes Copper Mining Co., El Salvador, Chile, 1962-69; sr. project geologist to chief geologist rsch./tech. The Anaconda Co., Tucson, 1969-74; prof. econ. geology Australian Nat. U., Canberra, 1975-81; rsch. group ldr. Conoco Inc., Exploration Rsch. div., Ponca City, Okla., 1981-82; sr. staff geologist to chief rsch. geologist Freeport Exploration Co., Reno, Nev., 1982-86; ptnr. Annapurna Exploration, Reno, 1987—; v.p. REX Resources, Inc., Reno, 1988—; councillor Australian Mineral Found., 1977-79. Contbr. articles to profl. jours. With U.S. Army, 1955-57. Fellow Geol. Soc. Am., Soc. Econ. Geologists (Lindgren award 1962); mem. Soc. Mining Engrs., Geol. Soc. Nev. Home: 3520 San Mateo Ave Reno NV 89509 Office: Annapurna Exploration 2995 Skyline Blvd #202 Reno NV 89509

GUSTAFSON, RANDALL LEE, city manager; b. Sidney, Nebr., Nov. 11, 1947; s. Robert John and Hilda Lydia (Sims) G.; m. Cynthia Ann Taylor, Oct. 18, 1974. Student, U. Kans., 1965-68, Rockhurst Coll., 1968-70. City mgr. City of Bonner Springs, Kans., 1970-77; bus. owner The Lambquarters, Dix, Nebr., 1977-83; city mgr. City of Aurora, Mo., 1983-85, City of Sterling, Colo., 1985—; chmn. bd. dirs. Bus. Incubator Ctr., Sterling, Logan Area Devel. Co., Sterling, 1986—. Bd. dirs. Fire and Police Pension Assn. of Colo., Denver, 1987—, 13th Juducial Dist. Community Corrections, Brush, Colo., 1988—; mem. Colo. Mcpl. League Policy Com., Denver, 1987—. Recipient Disting. Svc. award Jaycees, 1976. Mem. Internat. Assn. City Mgmt. (full mem.), Colo. Assn. City Mgmt., Am. Soc. for Pub. Adminstrn., Rotary, Elks. Republican. Lutheran. Office: City of Sterling Centennial Sq Sterling CO 80751

GUSTAFSON, RICHARD PAUL, utilites administrator; b. St. Paul, July 20, 1957; s. Clarence John and Grace Esther (Benson) G.; m. Joan Kay Barnett, Apr. 23, 1977; children: Kari, Jennifer. BBA, Westen Internat. U., Phoenix, 1982, MBA, 1988. Teller Valley Nat. Bank, Phoenix, 1976-77; with Ariz. Pub. Svc., Phoenix, 1978—, credit analyst, 1984-85, office mgr., 1985-86, adminstr. credit and collections, 1986-89, bus. office supr., 1989—; bd. dirs. Consumer Credit Counseling Svcs., Phoenix. Active Bus. and Mktg. Adv. Coun. Glendale (Ariz.) Union High Sch. Dist., 1987-88. Mem. Nat. Assn. Credit Mgmt. Republican. Home: 3910 E Thrush Ln Flagstaff AZ 86004

GUSTAFSON, STUART REID, real estate developer; b. San Diego, July 15, 1936; s. Carl Earl and Florence Vance (Ambrose) G.; m. Marilyn Ann Breedlove, Dec. 14, 1975 (div.); children: Damon, Fletcher; m. Sandra C. Abernethy, June 28, 1960. BS, U. Calif., Davis, 1962. Mgr. Palomar Mortage, San Diego, 1962-64, Colonial Mortgage, San Diego, 1964-66; sr. v.p. Nat. Community Builders, San Diego, 1966-74; v.p. Broadmoor Homes, Irvine, Calif., 1974-79; cons. Orange County, Calif., 1979-81; pres. Shea Homes, San Jose, Calif., 1981—. Chmn. YMCA, San Jose, 1988-89, bd. mgrs., 1985—; bd. dirs. San Jose Symphony, 1988—, LEED, San Jose, 1987—; bd. govs. O'Connor Hosp., San Jose, 1988—. Served with U.S. Army, 1957-60. Mem. Bldg. Industry Assn. (pres. South div. 1984, bd. dirs. Calif. chpt. 1986—, chmn. No. Calif. chpt. 1987, Builder of Yr. 1987, Pres.'s award 1985), Nat. Assn. Home Builders (bd. dirs. 1986—). Republican. Office: Shea Homes 2502 Stevens Creek Blvd San Jose CA 95128

GUSTAVSON, DEAN LEONARD, architect; b. Salt Lake City, June 27, 1924; s. Ernest L. and Leona (Hansen) G.; m. Barbara Knight, Apr. 28, 1944; children—Mark Steven, Lisa Ann, Clint Knight. Student, U. Utah, 1946-47; B.Arch., U. Calif-Berkeley, 1951. Pvt. practice architecture Salt Lake City, 1953—; also architectural practice in Utah, Ariz., Calif.; pres. Gustavson Assocs., Inc. (formerly Dean L. Gustavson Assos. architects and planners), Salt Lake City, 1957-86, Gustavson, Nelson and Panushka, Inc. (architects), Salt Lake City, 1976-82, Gustavson Group Inc. (design and constrn. mgrs.), 1978-82; mng. architect U. Utah Med. Center Additions Project, 1975-82; pres. Nat. Council Archtl. Registration Bds., 1969-70; project mgr. U. Calif.-Berkeley Bioscis. Additions Complex, 1982—; co-chmn. Internat. Com. Archtl. Registration, 1970; chmn. World Conf. on Edn. and Reciprocity of Architects, Amsterdam, Holland, 1971; Chmn. planning Salt Lake City's Second Century Plan, 1960-62; mem. Utah Air Travel Commn., 1987—. Served with USAAF, 1942-46. Dean L. Gustavson award established in his honor, NCARB, 1974. Fellow A.I.A. (pres. Utah chpt. 1959-60, chmn. chpt. task force on objectives and means 1974); mem. Salt Lake C. of C. (chmn. econ. devel. steering com. 1980-85, com. of 100), U.S. C. of C. Clubs: Ft. Douglas (Salt Lake City); Bloomington (Utah) Country. Home: 5775 Highland Dr Salt Lake City UT 84121 also: 3638 Sugar Leo Rd Bloomington UT 84770 Office: 630 E South Temple Salt Lake City UT 84102

GUSTAVSON, PHILLIP RONALD, toy manufacturing executive, accountant; b. Glendale, Calif., May 31, 1944; s. Paul Rozzelle and Marjorie Maureen (Smith) G.; m. Sara Jane Van Ornum, Sept. 10, 1966; children: Jan Erik, Nicholas-Tait, Rosemary Iola. BS in Acctg., U. So. Calif., 1967; grad. advanced mgmt. Claremont Grad. Sch., 1984. CPA, Calif. Mgr., Price Waterhouse, Newport Beach, Calif., 1973-82; v.p. fin. Tungsten Carbide Mfg. div. Smith Internat., Inc., Newport Beach, Calif., 1982-87, asst. corp. contr. Mattel Inc., Hawthorne, Calif. 1988— ; lectr. seminars in field. Contbr. articles to profl. jours. Mem. Orange County Philharm. Soc. (Calif.), 1980—; vol. scoutmaster, fundraiser, dist. chmn. Orange County council Boy Scouts Am., 1981—; mem. World Affairs Council Orange County, 1982—. Served as capt. USAF, 1967-73. Mem. Am. Inst. CPAs, Calif. Soc. CPAs (tech. com. 1979-82), Acctg. Circle U. So. Calif. Home: 1132 St Vincent Pl Santa Ana CA 92705 Office: Mattel Inc 5150 Rosecrans Ave MS 01-197-R05 Hawthorne CA 90250-6692

GUTHRIE, JAMES BRYAN, architect; b. Chgo., Jan. 26, 1957; s. Thomas Allan and Marilyn L. (Murphy) G. BS, U. Ill., 1979, MArch, 1982. Designer Martinez, Wong & Assocs., San Diego, 1983-84; architect Kromenhoek, McKeown Architects, San Diego, 1984-85, M.W. Steele, Inc., San Diego, 1985-87, Sillman Wyman Architects, San Diego, 1987-88; assoc. Gast, Urban Design & Architecture, San Diego, 1988-89; prin. San Diego, 1989—; instr. New Sch. of Architecture, 1987—. Contbr. articles to profl. jours.; Bd. dirs. Norman Heights Community Devel. Corp, 1988—, Save Our Heritage Orgn. Mem. San Diego Archt. Club (pres. 84-86), AIA, Nat. Trust Hist. Preservation, San Diego Sailing Club.

GUTHRIE, JERRY RALPH, electronic engineer; b. Percell, Okla., Jan. 26, 1949; s. Ray Aron and Stella Opal (Schoonover) G.; m. Doreen Vivian Peters, June 8, 1973 (div. Sept. 1977); m. Margo Lynn Timbrook, Sept. 8, 1978; 1 child, Raymond Benjamin. BEE, Oreg. Inst. Tech., Klamath Falls, 1969. Lic. pilot. Technician Western Electric Co., Vancouver, Wash., 1971-74; engr. Cardiac Resuscitator Corp., Portland, Oreg., 1974-77, Smallcomb Electric Co., L.A., 1977-78; owner, mgr. Guthrie Elec. Svc., Bloomington, Calif., 1978—. Sgt. USMCR 1970-71. Mem. Riverside C. of C., Riverside Art Alliance, Canyon Crest Golf Club. Office: Guthrie Electronic Svc PO Box 389 Bloomington CA 92316

GUTIERREZ, FRANCISCO XAVIER, lawyer; b. El Paso, Tex., Jan. 18, 1957; s. Candelario and Guadalupe (Saenz) G.; m. Eugenia Garcia, Dec. 10, 1977; children: Trina Marie, Manuel Javier, Vanessa Monique. BS, Ariz. State U., 1980, JD, 1983. Bar: Ariz. 1984, U.S. Dist. Ct. Ariz. 1984. Assoc. Daniel Ortega, P.C., Phoenix, 1982-84; ptnr. Gutierrez, Contreras & Salaiz, P.C., Phoenix, 1984—; bd. dirs. State of Ariz. Bd. Psychologist Examiners; hearing officer S. Phoenix Justice Ct., 1986-87. Chmn. adv. bd. S. Mountain Community Coll., 1988—. Mem. Assn. Trial Lawyers Am., Ariz. Trial Lawyers Assn., Maricopa County (Ariz.) Bar Assn., Los Abogados Hispanic Bar Assn. Ariz., South Mountain C. of C., Kiwanis. Democrat. Roman Catholic.

GUTIERREZ, RAMON ARTHUR, history educator; b. Albuquerque, Apr. 19, 1951; s. Arthur and Nellie (Alderete) G. BA, U. N. Mex., 1973; MA, U. Wis., 1976, PhD, 1980. Lectr. in history U. Wis., Madison, 1980; asst. prof. history Pomona Coll., Claremont, Calif., 1980-82; from asst. to assoc. prof. U. Calif. San Diego, La Jolla, 1982--. Author: When Jesus Came the Corn Mothers Went Away, 1988; contbr. articles to profl. jours. Fellow Fulbright Found., 1973, Danforth Found., 1974-80, MacArthur Found., 1983-88. Mem. Am. Hist. Assn., Latin Am. Studies Assn., We. History Assn., Chicano Studies Assn. Office: U Calif San Diego Dept History C 004 La Jolla CA 92093

GUTIERREZ, RENAE DOLORES, health and patient educator; b. Oakland, Calif., July 23, 1954; d. Raymond Clifford and Veronica (Sabo) Christianson. BS, U. Oreg., 1975, MS, 1976; PhD, U. Utah, 1983. Instr. U. Wis., LaCrosse, 1977-80; teaching fellow, lectr. U. Utah, Salt Lake City, 1980-83; asst. prof. Ariz. State U., Tempe, 1983-85; assoc. dir. Ariz. Emergency Med. Systems, Phoenix, 1985-87; dir. patient edn. Mayo Clinic Scottsdale, Ariz., 1987—; vis. lectr. U. Oreg., Eugene, 1976-77, Lane Community Coll., Eugene, 1976-77; vis. instr. Lewis & Clark Coll., Portland, 1977; adj. prof.

Ariz. State U., Tempe, 1986-88; cons. in field. Contbr. articles to profl. jours. Bd. dirs. Am. Cancer Soc., Tempe, 1983—; mem. com. Planned Parenthood, Phoenix, 1984—; chmn. com. Ariz. Coalition for Seatbelt Use, Phoenix, 1985-86; mem. com. Ariz. Emergency Med. Svcs., 1985-87. Named Vol. of Yr., Am. Cancer Soc., 1985. Mem. AAHPERD (chmn. S.W. dist. 1984-85), Assn. for Advancement of Health Edn., Ariz. Alliance AAHPERD (v.p. 1985-86). Office: Mayo Clinic Scottsdale 13400 E Shea Blvd Scottsdale AZ 85250

GUTIERREZ, RITA, early childhood education specialist; b. L.A., Feb. 3, 1962; d. Armando and Mary Bertolli G. BA, U. Calif., Irvine, 1986. Bilingual operator Gen. Tel. Co., Westminster, Calif., 1984-85; adminstr. asst. Tomas Rivera Ctr., Claremont, Calif., 1985-86; early childhood edn. specialist Irvine Unified Sch. Dist., Irvine, Calif., 1987—. Designer: Greeting Cards. Translator, missionary outreach Calvary Chapel of San Clemente, Mexico (La Mision B.C.), 1988-89. Mem. Internat. Montessori Inst. (cert. Primary Edn. Program). Democrat. Home: 2355 Calle Lobina San Clemente CA 92672 Office: Early Childhood Edn Irvine Unified Sch Dist #3 Lemongrass Irvine CA 92714

GUTIN, RAYMOND S., ., physician; b. Cin., Oct. 25, 1935; s. Frank Joseph and Betty (Bederman) G.; m. Linda Lee Gold, June 22, 1963; children: Alissa, Gregory. BS, Ohio State U., 1958; MD, U. Cin., 1962. Diplomate Am. Bd. Internal Medicine. Intern San Francisco County Hosp., 1962-63; resident in internal medicine U. Colo. Med. Ctr., Denver, 1963-66; fellow in endocrinology 1966-67, pvt. practice, 1967--; chief internal medicine Mercy Med. Ctr., 1984-88; asst. clin. prof. medicine U. Colo. Health Scis. Ctr., Denver, 1975--. Mem. ACP, Am. Diabetes Assn., Am. Soc. Internal Medicine. Jewish. Office: 3005 E 16th St Denver CO 80206

GUTTENPLAN, JACK DAVID, chemical engineer; b. Baton Rouge, Oct. 10, 1925; s. Murray Louis and Harriet (Hirsch) G.; m. Shirley Lenore Rosenthal, Jan. 23, 1949; children: Stuart, Karen, Mark. BS, Case Inst. of Tech., 1945, postgrad., 1947-49, MS, 1948. Registered profl. engr., Calif. Assoc. engr. C.F. Prutton & Assocs., Cleve., 1948-49; group leader Chrysler Corp., Highland Park, Mich., 1949-61; mgr. devel. Magna Corp. (TRW), Anaheim, Calif., 1961-62; mem. tech. staff. Rockwell Internat., Anaheim, 1962—; Westec chmn. ASM Internat., L.A., 1985; chmn. corp. corrosion panel, Rockwell Internat., L.A., 1985—; career training instr., Rockwell Internat., Anaheim, 1978-86. Contbr. electronics corrosion articles to profl. jours.; patentee in field. Comdr. State of Calif., Jewish War Vets., L.A., 1972-73, 1981-82; nat. exec. committeeman, Jewish War Vets., Washington, 1973-76, 82-83 (state comdr. of yr. award, 1973, 82). Comdr. USN. Fellow ASM Internat. (chpt. chmn. 1978-79), Nat. Assn. of Corrosion Engrs. (chmn. com. T-9E 1981-83), Sigma Xi, Tau Beta Pi. Home: 2210 W Avalon Ave Santa Ana CA 92706 Office: Rockwell Internat Auto Elect Sys MS 031-GA25 3370 Miraloma Ave Anaheim CA 92803

GUYAN, CHERYL ANN, nurse; b. Worcester, Mass., June 4, 1964; d. Ronald John and Linda Ellen (Stone) Denault; m. William James Guyan, July 19, 1986. BS in Nursing, Salve Regina Coll., Newport, R.I., 1986. RN. RN St. Joseph's Hosp., Tucson, 1986-87; nurse Univ. Med. Ctr., Tucson, 1987—; mem. quality assurance com., Univ. Med. Ctr., Tucson, 1987—, nursing rep. infection control bd. Mem. Am. Assn. Critical Care Nurses, Tuscon Humane Soc., Sigma Phi Sigma. Republican. Home: 5188 W Wood Owl Dr Tucson AZ 85741 Office: Univ Med Ctr 1501 N Campbell Ave Tucson AZ 85719

GUYETTE, WAYNE CHARLES, consulting company executive; b. Providence, Aug. 31, 1942; s. Irvin and Laura (Farley) G.; m. June M. Silver, Mar. 10, 1970. BSc, U. Nev., 1973; MSc, Fla. Internat. U., 1977; PhD, Fla. State U., 1979. Dir. hospitality mgr. Clark County Community Coll., Las Vegas, 1972-75; state dir. Sch. Food Service Tng., Tallahassee, 1977-78; chmn., bd. dirs. Guyette and Assocs., Inc., Metairie, La., 1979-86; dean, prof. Widener U., Wilmington, Del., 1986; pres. GEO, Inc., Cannon Beach, Oreg., 1986--; prof. hotel adminstrn. U. New Orleans, 1979-86; exec. dir. Corp. Food and Beverage Dirs., Las Vegas, 1981-85; trustee Am. Culinary Fedn. Ednl. Inst., Fla., 1981-83; chmn. bd. trustees Culinary Apprenticeship Program La., New Orleans, 1983-85. Author: Management for Culinarians, 1982, Property-Level Food and Beverage Reduction, 1983, Cost Reduction for Culinarians, 1983; contbr. articles to profl. jours. Mem. Cannon Beach Budget Com., 1987--. With U.S. Army, 1966-69, Vietnam. Statler Found. fellow, 1965, Nat. Inst. for Foodservice Industry, 1977; Club Mgmt. Assn. Am. grantee, 1978. Mem. Am. Hotel and Motel Assn. (cert. hotel adminstr., grantee 1978, sr. advisor exec. bd. food and beverage com. 1980-85), Council on Hotel, Restaurant and Instnl. Edn. Office: GEO Inc PO Box 1000 Cannon Beach CA 97110

GUYN, LEW JAMES, project engineer, consultant; b. Ann Arbor, Mich., June 10, 1953; s. Wade and Margaret (Mead) G.; m. Beverly Anne Jones, Aug. 4, 1972; children: Kimberly, Kevin. BS, Chapman Coll., 1986. Designer Del Mar Avionics, Irvine, Calif., 1975-77, Data Tech., Santa Ana, Calif., 1977-80; mgr. Orange Coast Electronics, Huntington Beach, Calif., 1980-81; project engr. Bard, Inc., Santa Ana, 1981-84, EECO Inc., Santa Ana, 1984—; pres. Lew Guyn and Assoc., Anaheim, Calif., 1988—. Asst. Scoutmaster BoyScouts Am. Troop 1149, Anaheim, 1986—. Served with USAF, 1971-75. Mem. Soc. Mfg. Engrs. (map/top users group). Home: 2007 W Binnacle Way Anaheim CA 92801 Office: EECO Inc 1601 E Chestnut Santa Ana CA 92701

GUZMAN, DAVID ANDREW, career officer; b. L.A., Mar. 15, 1940; s. Arturo Carlos and Angela Dolores (Santos) G.; m. Sumiko Tamura, Jan. 26, 1960 (div. 1978); m. Niamh Marie Prossor, June 26, 1978 (div. Aug. 1982); m. Cathy Ann Taggart, June 27, 1983. BA in Mgmt., U. Phoenix, Albuquerque, 1988. Personnel sgt. major Sembach AFB, German Dem. Republic, 1978-82; noncommissioned officer-in-charge Hickam AFB, Honolulu, 1983-85, sr. enlisted advisor, 1985-86; office mgr. N.M. State U., Albuquerque, 1987-88. Recipient Legion of Merit award USAF, 1987. Mem. Air Force Assn., Air Force Sgts. Assn., VFW. Lodges: Elks. Home: 421 N Hayes St Moscow ID 83843-3236

GUZY, MARGUERITA LINNES, teacher; b. Santa Monica, Calif., Nov. 19, 1938; d. Paul William Robert and Margarete (Rodowski) Linnes; m. Stephen Paul Guzy, Aug. 25, 1962 (div. 1968); 1 child, David Paul. AA, Santa Monica Coll., 1959; student, U. Mex., 1959-60; BA, UCLA, 1966, MA, 1973; postgrad. in psychology, Pepperdine U., 1988—. Cert. secondary tchr., Calif. Tchr. Inglewood (Calif.) Unified Sch. Dist., 1967—, chmn. dept., 1972-82, mentor, tchr., 1985—; clin. instr. series Clin. Supervision Levels I, II, Ingelwood, 1986-87; clin. intern Chem. Dependency Ctr., St. John's Hosp., Santa Monica, 1988—; tchr. Santa Monica Coll., 1975-76; cons. bilingual edn. Inglewood Unified Sch. Dist., 1975—; mem. ednl. teaching com. Monroe Jr. High Sch., 1985-86, staff devel. com., 1985—, chmn. drug and alcohol awareness com., 1986—. Author: Elementary Education: "Pygmalian in the Classroom", 1975, English Mechanics Workbook, 1986. Recipient Teaching Excellence cert. State of Calif., 1986; named Tchr. of Yr., 1973, 88. Mem. NEA, Calif. Tchrs. Assn., Inglewood Tchrs. Assn. (local rep. 1971-72, tchr edn. and profl. services com. 1972-78), UCLA Alumnae Assn. (life), Prytanean Alumnae Assn. Republican. Club: Westside Alano (Los Angeles)(bd. dirs., treas. 1982-83). Lodge: Masons. Office: Monroe Jr High Sch 10711 10th Ave Inglewood CA 90303

GWIN, LARRY BOYD, optometrist; b. Denver, June 4, 1940; s. E.M. and E.A (Ball) G.; m. Sandra Solberg, June 11, 1968 (div. Nov. 1973); m. Donna M. Davis, Sept. 18, 1980. AB, Doane Coll., 1962; BS, Columbia U., 1963, MS, 1964; PhD, Stanford U., 1973; OD, New Eng. Coll. Optometry, 1979. Assoc. structural engr. astronautics div. Gen. Dynamics Corp., San Diego, 1964-65; sr. engr. structural dynamics rsch. Martin Marietta Co., Denver, 1965-67, structural engr. for Skylab loads analysis, 1969; engring. cons. on vibration analysis Sperry Rand Co., Salt Lake City, 1958-59; rsch. fellow NASA Ames Rsch. Ctr., Sunnyvale, Calif., 1973-74; vis. prof. civil engring. U. B.C. (Can.), Vancouver, 1974-75; asst. prof. aero engring. and engring. mechanics U. Tex., Austin, 1975-76; pvt. practice Boulder, Colo., 1979—; clin. investigator Bausch & Lomb, Sola Syntex, Barnes Hind, Multi-Optics, 1981; clin. investigator Wesley-Jesson, Chgo., 1981—, cons., 1985; trustee, bd. dirs. Omni Eye Svcs., Denver; rsch. asst. Stanford (Calif.) U., 1968-72. Contbr. articles to engring. and optometric jours. Chmn. UNICEF, Boulder County, 1980-84; regional chmn. Am. Cancer Soc. of Boulder County, 1981-82. S.W. Mudd scholar, 1961-68; NSF fellow, 1973. Mem. Aerospace Med. Assn., Am. Optometric Assn. (recognition award for continuing edn. 1988), Colo. Optometric Assn. (trustee 1988-89). Democrat. Home: 2421 Briarwood Dr Boulder CO 80303 Office: Table Mesa Med Ctr 4150 Darley Ave Boulder CO 80303

GWINN, PAULA, musician; b. Portsmouth, Ohio, Mar. 7, 1923; d. Everett Richard and Erma (Nickell) Smith; m. Lawrence Morris Gwinn, Dec. 29, 1951; 1 child, Nancy Ellen. MusB, Coll. Wooster, 1939-43; postgrad., Cleve. Inst. Music, 1943-45, U. Mich., 1945-46, Berkshire Music Ctr., summer 1946. First violinist Denver Symphony, 1946-61; organist, choir dir. Wheatridge (Colo.) Lutheran Ch., 1955; concertmaster South Bay Civic Symphony, Torrance, Calif., 1963-76; pvt. instr. violin Los Angeles, 1963-84; freelance violinist various operas, ballets, symphonies, Calif., 1963—; founder, condr. South Bay Jr. Chamber Orch., Calif., 1964-75; first violinist Long Beach (Calif.) Symphony, 1966-84; contest judge various local music contests, Calif., 1966-80. Composer numerous string orch. works and violin solos, 1964-80. Tchrs. aide Lomita (Calif.) Elem. Sch., 1967; leader 4-H Club, 1967-72. Recipient Superior awards state and nat. violin contests, 1930-39, Outstanding Achievement award Nat. Congress Parents and Tchrs., Calif., 1968, Cert. Appreciation Lomita City Council, 1971, Community Recognitioin plaque Lions, Lomita, 1974. Mem. Sigma Alpha Iota. Democrat. Lodge: Order Ea. Star (organist).

GWYNN, ANTHONY KEITH (TONY GWYNN), professional baseball player; b. Los Angeles, May 9, 1960; m. Alicia; children: Anthony, Anisha Nicole. Student, San Diego State U. Player San Diego Padres, Nat. League 1982—, World Series, 1984, All-Star Game, 1984-88. Holder Nat. League batting title, 1984, recipient Gold Glove, 1986-87. Office: San Diego Padres PO Box 2000 San Diego CA 92120 *

GYLSETH, DORIS (LILLIAN) HANSON, librarian; b. Helena, Mont., May 26, 1934; d. Richard E. and Lillie (Paula) Hanson; m. Arlie Albeck, Dec. 26, 1955 (div. Apr. 1964); m. Hermann M. Gylseth, Apr. 29, 1983 (dec. Aug. 1985). BS in Edn., Western Mont. Coll. Edn., 1958; MLS, U. Wash., 1961. Tchr. Helena Sch. Dist., 1955-56, Dillon (Mont.) Elem. Sch., 1957-59, Eltopia (Wash.) Unified Sch. Dist., 1959-60; sch. libr. Shoreline Sch. Dist., Seattle, 1960-64, Dept. of Def., Chateauroux, France, Hanau, Fed. Republic Germany, Tachikawa, Japan, 1964-68, Long Beach (Calif.) Unified Sch. Dist., 1968-70; br. libr. Long Beach Pub. Libr., 1970-74, coord. children's svcs., 1974-85; libr. Long Beach (Calif.) Unified Sch. Dist., 1986—. Bd. dirs. Children's Svcs. Div. Calif. Libr. Assn., 1985; co-chmn. Long Beach Authors Festival, 1978-86; mem. planning com. Third Pacific Rim Conf. on Children's Lit., UCLA, 1986. Mem. So. Calif. Coun. on Lit. for Children and Young People (bd. dirs. 1974-88, pres. 1982-84), Helen Fuller Cultural Carrousel (bd. dirs. 1985—), Zonta (pres. 1978-80), Sons of Norway. Home: 5131 Kingscross Dr Westminster CA 92683

HA, CHONG WAN, insurance company executive; b. Chin-ju, Kyung-Nam, South Korea, Oct. 26, 1938; came to U.S., 1963; s. Kyung-sik and Kyung-Nam (Park) H.; m. Karen Hye-Ja Han, Aug. 19, 1968; children: Jean Frances, Julie Ann. BA in Econs., UCLA, 1970; cert. in exec. mgmt., The Peter F. Drucker Mgmt. Ctr., 1984; MA in Mgmt., Claremont (Calif.) Grad. Sch., 1985. Sr. systems analyst Atlantic Richfield Co., Los Angeles, 1972-78; asst. v.p. 1st Interstate Services Co., Los Angeles, 1978-85; v.p. Ticor Title Ins. Co., Los Angeles, 1985—. Res. police officer Monterey Park (Calif.) Police Dept., 1981-82; bd. dirs. Asian Pacific Alumni Assn. UCLA, Los Angeles, 1988, Asian Pacific Am. Legal Found., Los Angeles, 1988—. Mem. Soc. of Info. Mgmt., Leadership Edn. for Asian Pacifics, UCLA Chancellers Circle. Democrat. Home: 7801 Via Foggia Burbank CA 91504

HAACK, DAVID WILFORD, biomedical consultant; b. Denver, Nov. 22, 1945; s. Robert Daniel and Jane Evangeline H.; m. Sharon Dee Sollars, June 19, 1987; children: Shelly, Stacey, Alexis. BS, Colo. State U., 1968, MS, 1971, PhD, 1974. Postdoctorate U. Mich., Ann Arbor, 1974-75, asst. prof. dept. anatomy, med. sch., 1975-80; research assoc. dept. physiology, med. ctr. U. Ariz., Tucson, 1980-83; new product devel., product specialist W.L. Gore & Assocs., Inc., Flagstaff, Ariz., 1983-86, coord. worldwide clin. trials, med. products div., 1986-88; founder, pres. Life Tech. Internat., Inc., Flagstaff, 1988—; coordinator worldwide clin. trials W.L. Gore & Assoc. med. product div., Flagstaff, 1986—. Contbr. numerous articles to profl. jours.; speaker in field; patentee in field, 1986. Nat. Research Service award Nat. Inst. Health, 1974, 1980-83.

HAAG, ARTHUR W., business owner; b. Chgo., Sept. 1, 1931; s. Anne (Sohr) Haag; 1 child, Jennifer. BS in Econs., Lake Forest Coll., 1956. Registered real estate broker, Colo. Pres. Western Communities, Inc., Denver, 1959—, Western Housing, Inc., Denver, 1985-86; pres., owner Western Real Estate and Mgmt. Co., Denver, 1986—. Tennis coach Special Olympics, Denver, 1988; mem. tennis tournament com. March of Dimes, Denver, 1982—. Served with U.S. Army, 1952-55. Mem. Colo. Manufactured Housing Assn. (bd. dirs. 1982—, sec. 1988). Republican. Home: 12311 E Bates Circle Aurora CO 80014

HAAG, JACQUELINE VERA, educator, publisher; b. Washington, May 9, 1951; d. Leonard Nicholas and Patricia Levia (Pymm) Block; Gerald Robert Haag, Sept. 1, 1971; children: Laura Jean, Krista Michelle, Julie Ann, Ashley Elizabeth. BA in Lang. Arts, S.D. State U., 1973. Pvt. practice The Colony, Tex., 1979-83; pre-natal instr. Childbirth Edn. Assn. Cen. Mass., Worcester, 1984-85; childbirth instr. Worcester Ob-Gyn Assocs., Worcester, 1985-86; pre-natal instr. Penrose Community Hosp., Colorado Springs, Colo., 1988—; guest speaker Barre (Mass.) Emergency and Rescue Squad, 1985, pub. and pvt. schs., Mass., Tex. and Colo.; pub. Mother House Pub., Colorado Springs. Author graphic Comfort Suggestions for Labor, 1986, calendar My Pregnancy Year, 1986. Mem. Am. Soc. Psychoprophylaxis in Obstetrics, Childbirth Edn. Assn. of Cen. Mass. (bd. dirs. 1984). Democrat. Roman Catholic.

HAAK, HAROLD HOWARD, university president; b. Madison, Wis., June 1, 1935; s. Harold J. and Laura (Kittleson) H.; m. Betty L. Steiner, June 25, 1955; children—Alison Marie, Janet Christine. B.A., U. Wis., 1957, M.A., 1958; Ph.D., Princeton U., 1963. From asst. prof. to assoc. prof. polit. sci., pub. adminstrn. and urban studies San Diego State Coll., 1962-69, dean coll. profl. studies, prof. pub. adminstrn. and urban studies, 1969-71; acad. v.p. Calif. State U., Fresno, 1971-73, pres., 1980—; v.p. U. Colo., Denver, 1973, chancellor, 1974-80; mem. joint council on food and agrl. scis. U.S. Dept. Agr., 1985—. Trustee William Saroyan Found., 1981—; chmn. AASCU Com. on Agr. Renewable Resources and Rural Devel., 1985—; mem. NCAA Pres.' Commn., 1987—; bd. dirs. Fresno Econ. Devel. Corp., 1981—, Found. for the 21st Century, 1987—. Recipient U. Colo. medal, 1980. Mem. Phi Beta Kappa, Phi Kappa Phi. Office: Calif State U Office of Pres Fresno CA 93740 *

HAAPANEN, LAWRENCE WILLIAM, communication educator; b. Seattle, Apr. 24, 1945; s. Morris William and Helen Marie (Stearns) H.; m. Beverly Ann Biggi, Aug. 19, 1972; children: Laurell, Holly. BA in History, U. Wash., 1967; MA in Speech, Wash. State U., 1972, PhD in Speech, 1974. Tchr. Neah-Kah-Nie High Sch., Rockaway, Oreg., 1974-76; asst. prof. Utah State U., Logan, 1976-81; assoc. prof., chmn. dept. communication Baker U., Baldwin City, Kans., 1981-87, chmn. div. fine & performing arts Lewis Clark State Coll., Lewiston, Idaho, 1987—. Contbr. chpt. to textbook. Del. State Democratic Conv., Salt Lake City, 1978. Served to capt. USAF, 1967-71. Decorated Air Force Commendation medal; summer fellow NEH, 1980. Mem. Speech Communication Assn. (chmn. commn. on govt. communication 1984-85). Democrat. Lutheran. Avocation: genealogy. Home: 1826 Powers Ave Lewiston ID 83501 Office: Lewis Clark State Coll Div Fine & Performing Arts 8th Ave and 6th St Lewiston ID 83501

HAARSAGER, DENNIS LEE, broadcasting executive; b. Wadena, Minn., Apr. 18, 1947; s. Ralph Oliver and Doris Blanche (Johnson) H.; m. Julie Carol Wince, July 16, 1966 (div. 1976); 1 child, Jennie Ella; m. Sandra Lynn Smith Watkinson, Jan. 1, 1977; children: Anna Lynn, Andrew Lee. BS, U. S.D., 1972, MA, 1975. Dir. adminstrn. S.D. Pub. TV Network, Vermillion, 1972-75; state coordinator pub. broadcasting Idaho State Bd. Edn., Boise, 1975-78; gen mgr. radio-TV, Wash. State U., Pullman, 1978—; pres. H2A Communications, Moscow, Idaho, 1982—; pres. Wash. Ednl. Network, 1980-82, 83-84; bd. dirs. Sta. Resource Group, 1986—; bd. dirs. and sec. West Coast Public Radio, 1986—; bd. dirs. Pacific Mountain Network; telecommunications cons. to numerous orgns., 1977—. Author: (software) H2A Microwave Transmission Planner, 1983. Mem. City Cable Refranchise Com., 1983; dir. Washington-Idaho Symphony, 1984-87. Served with USAF, 1966-69. Avocations: computer programming, amateur radio. Home: 1171 Border Ln Moscow ID 83843 Office: Wash State U Sta KWSU/Radio-TV Svcs Pullman WA 99164-2530

HAAS, DAVID WILLIAM, court clerk; b. Beaverdam, Wis., Mar. 22, 1950; s. William Ralph and Mary Jane (Miller) H.; m. Mary Ellen Arvold, May 31, 1981; children: Elizabeth Arvold Haas, Jacob Arvold Haas. BA in polit. sci., U. Wis., 1972. Adminstr. asst. Wis. Assembly Com., Madison, 1974-76; assoc. dir. of legal affairs Wis. State Assembly, Madison, 1977-78; state fed. coordinator Gov.'s Office, Juneau, Alaska, 1980-82; ombudsman asst. Office of the Ombudsman, Juneau, 1983-86; clk. of Ct. System Juneau, 1986—. Rescue dog handler trainer, Seadogs, Juneau, 1980—. Office: Juneau Trial Cts 4th and Main St Juneau AK 99801

HAAS, DEBORAH LYNN, banker; b. Chgo., June 11, 1952; d. William Hermann and Elizabeth Dorothy (Badali) H. BA, U. Dayton, 1973; MA, U. Ariz., 1976; MIM, Am. Grad. Sch. Internat. Mgmt., 1979. Advt. mgr. Flyer News, U. Dayton (Ohio), 1970-73; instr. U. Ariz., Tucson, 1974-79; consumer lending officer Valley Nat. Bank, Phoenix, 1980-82, comml. lending officer, 1982-83, asst. mgr., med. banking specialist, 1984-88; comml. banking officer Sun State Savs. & Loan, 1988—; tchr. ESL, 1975-79; tchr. German, U. Ariz., 1974-76. Mem. Ariz. Sonora Desert Mus., 1984—, Nat. Wildlife Fedn.; sec. Friends of Refugees, 1982; instr. Vols. for Refugee Self-Sufficiency, 1982-83. Mem. Am. Assn. Tchrs. German, Phoenix Thunderbird Alumni Assn. (sec. steering com. 1983-85, balloon race com. 1986—, pres.-elect 1986-87, pres. 1987-88, giving adv. bd. 1989—, chmn. bd. 1988-89, trustee 1989—), Friends of Thunderbird (coord. fgn. student luncheons, 1986, mem. planned giving bd. 1989—), Delta Phi Alpha, Phi Beta Alpha. Lodge: Civitan (bd. dirs. local chpt. 1984—, pres.-elect 1985—, pres. 1985-86, chmn. bd. 1987-88). Offices: Sun State Savs & Loan 15015 N 7th Pl Phoenix AZ 85022

HAAS, PETER E., manufacturing company executive; b. San Francisco, Dec. 20, 1918; s. Walter A. and Elise (Stern) H.; m. Josephine Baum, Feb. 1, 1945; m. Mimi Lurie, Aug., 1981; children: Peter E., Michael Stern, Margaret Elizabeth. Student, Deerfield Acad., 1935-36; A.B., U. Calif., 1940; MBA cum laude, Harvard, 1943. With Levi Strauss & Co., San Francisco, 1945—; exec. v.p. Levi Strauss & Co., 1958-70, pres., 1970-81, chief exec. officer, 1976-81, chmn. bd., 1981—; dir. emeritus AT&T. Former mem. Golden Gate Nat. Recreation Area Adv. Com.; Former pres. Jewish Welfare Fedn.; former trustee Stanford U.; former v.p., trustee San Francisco Bay Area Council, United Way of San Francisco Bay Area; pres. Aid to Retarded Citizens; currently bd. govs. United Way of Am; mem. distrbn. com. San Francisco Found. Recipient Alexis De Tocqueville Soc. award, United Way Am., 1985; named Chief Exec. Officer of Yr., Fin. World mag., 1981; Baker scholar, 1940. Office: Levi Strauss & Co PO Box 7215 San Francisco CA 94120

HAAS, ROBERT DOUGLAS, apparel manufacturing company executive; b. San Francisco, Apr. 3, 1942; s. Walter A. Jr. and Evelyn (Danzig) H.; m. Colleen Gershon, Jan. 27, 1975; 1 child, Elise Kimberly. BA, U. Calif., Berkeley, 1964; MBA, Harvard U., 1968. With Peace Corps, Ivory Coast, 1964-66; with Levi Strauss & Co., San Francisco, 1973—, sr. v.p. corp. planning and policy, 1978-80, pres. new bus. group, 1980, pres. operating groups, 1980-81, exec. v.p., chief operating officer, 1981-84, pres., chief exec. officer, 1984-89, chief exec. officer, 1989—, chmn. bd.; bd. dirs. Levi Strauss Found. Hon. dir. San Francisco AIDS Found; mem. U.S. adv. coun., Bay are com. '89 Internat. Indsl. Conf. White House fellow, 1968-69. Mem. Am. Apparel Mfrs. Assn. (bd. dirs.), Brookings Inst. (trustee), Bay Area Com., Conf. Bd., Council Fgn. Affairs, Trilateral Commn., Meyer Friedman Inst. (bd. dirs.), Phi Beta Kappa. Office: Levi Strauss & Co PO Box 7215 San Francisco CA 94120

HAAS, ROBERTA KARLIN, real estate broker; b. Bklyn., Sept. 10, 1941; d. Jack David Karlin and Sophie (Eisenstadt) Weinstein; m. Gordon Lee Haas, Mar. 21, 1963; 1 child, Courtney Lee. Student, U. Miami, 1960-61, Hofstra Coll., 1961-62. Co-owner, v.p. Creative Counseling Pers. Agy., San Francisco, 1965-72; v.p., producer children's books Haas Enterprises, Inc., Tokyo, 1973-74; co-owner, founder, pres., prin. broker Hanalei (Hawaii) North Shore Properties, Ltd., 1981—. Editor: Courtney Flower Books, 1975. Mem. Am. Rose Soc., Am. Horticulture Soc., Pacific Tropical Botanical Soc. Home: PO Box 237 Hanalei HI 96714 Office: Hanalei North Shore Properties Ltd Princeville Ctr Hanalei HI 96714

HAAS, WALTER A., JR., retired apparel company executive, professional baseball executive; b. San Francisco, Jan. 24, 1916; s. Walter Abraham and Elise (Stern) H.; m. Evelyn Danzig, 1940; children: Robert D., Elizabeth Haas Eisenhardt, Walter J. BA, U. Calif., Berkeley, 1937; MBA, Harvard U., 1939; hon. degree, Wheaton Coll., 1983. Chief exec. officer Levi Strauss & Co., San Francisco, 1958-76, now hon. chmn. exec. com. bd. dirs.; owner, mng. gen. ptnr. Oakland (Calif.) Athletics Baseball Co.; dir. Bank of Am., Bank Am. Corp., UAL, Inc., Mauna Kea Properties, Pacific Telephone Co. Active Trilateral Commn.; mem. exec. com., regional chmn. Nat. Alliance Businessman; mem. Presdl. Adv. Council for Minority Enterprise, Presdl. Task Force in Internat. Devel., 1970, Nat. Ctr. for Voluntary Action, Citizens Commn. on Pvt. Philanthropy and Pub. Needs; mem. vis. com. Harvard Bus. Sch.; mem. intercollegiate athletics adv. bd. U. Calif.; dir. Hunters Point Boys' Club, San Francisco Boys' Club, Bay Area Urban League, Mt. Zion Hosp.; campaign chmn. United Bay Area Crusade, 1965, also bd. dirs.; chmn. Radio Free Europe, No. Calif.; commr. San Francisco Parking Authority, 1953; trustee Ford Found., Com. for Econ. Devel.; co-chmn. bus. steering com. Nat. Cambodia Crisis Com. Named a Leader of Tomorrow Time mag., 1953, Chief Exec. Officer of Yr. Fin. World mag., 1976, Alumnus of Yr., U. Calif. at Berkeley, 1984; recipient Jefferson award Am. Inst. Pub. Service, 1977, Alumni Achievement award Harvard Grad. Sch. Bus., 1979, Chancellor's award U. Calif. at Berkeley Found., 1982, The Alexis De Tocqueville Society award United Way Am., 1985. Mem. San Francisco C. of C. (bd. dirs.), Mfrs. and Wholesalers Assn. San Francisco, (pres. 1951), Nat. Urban League (dir.), Phi Beta Kappa, Alpha Delta Phi. Office: Levi Strauss & Co PO Box 7215 San Francisco CA 94120

HAAS, WALTER J., professional sports team executive. S. Walter A. Jr. and Evelyn (Danzig) H.; m.; 3 children. Former pres. Goldmine Records; exec. v.p. Oakland (Calif.) A's, Am. League, 1980-88, chief oper. officer, 1988—. Office: care Oakland A's Oakland-Alameda County Coliseum Oakland CA 94621 *

HAASE, DONALD WYMAN, real estate broker; b. Rawllings, Wyo., Mar. 9, 1948; s. Fredrick Darwin and Anne Adeline (Bolton) H.; m. Sept. 23, 1972 (div. 1979); children: Danial William, Douglas Nels. Student, Cen. Tex. Coll., Killeon, 1969, Lane Community Coll., Eugene, Oreg., 1982. Grad. Realtors Inst. Pres. Eugene Cascade Inc., 1972-82, Statelyn Homes, Inc., Eugene, 1972-86, STATE Realty, Inc., Eugene, 1982—; area mgmt. broker U.S. HUD, Portland, 1982—; sec. Twin Butte Mtg.. Inc., Eugene, 1984—; bd. dirs. Diamond Butte Constrn., Eugene, Eugene Springfield Multiple Listing, Nimbus, Inc. Coach Eugene Sports Prog., 1987-88. With U.S. Army, 1966-69. Named Boss of the Yr., Am. Bus. Women Assn., 1980, 87. Mem. Eugene Springfield Multiple Listing Svcs., Eugene C. of C., Singles Connection, Odd Fellows. Democrat. Foursquare Ch. Office: State Realty Inc 143 Madison Eugene OR 97402

HAASE, EDWARD FRANCIS, mining company ecologist; b. Milw., Apr. 29, 1937; s. William Meinrad and Eleanore Ann (Treml) H.; m. Joann Marie Meister, Aug. 21, 1965; children: Mark, Timothy, Julie. BS in Botany, Marquette U., 1959; MS in Botany, U. Wis., Milw., 1965; PhD in Biology, U. Ariz., 1969. Ecologist SW Watershed Res. Ctr., USDA, Tucson, 1969-70; research assoc., asst. prof. U. Ariz., Tucson, 1970-76; head dept. smoke investigation Phelps Dodge Corp., Douglas, Ariz., 1976-79; coord. land use and reclamation Phelps Dodge Corp., Phoenix, 1979-85, sr. environ. analyst,

1985—; cons. Oak Ridge Nat. Lab., Tenn., 1973-74; chmn. APCA Ecol. Effects Tech. Com., Pitts., 1984-86. Contbr. articles to profl. jours. Recipient Fellowship, NSF, 1968, grantee NASA, Corp of Engrs., HEW, 1971-76. Mem. Air Pollution Control Assn., Ecol. Soc. Am., Sigma Xi, Beta Beta Beta, Phi Sigma. Roman Catholic. Office: Phelps Dodge Corp 2600 N Central Ave Phoenix AZ 85004

HAASE, MARILEE ELLEN, real estate broker; b. Madison, Wis., Mar. 2, 1947; d. Joseph Aloysius and Janis Eleanor (Adams) H. BS, U. Colo., 1970; MSW, U. Denver, 1978. Mem. treatment team, coord. div. youth svcs. State of Colo., Denver, 1973-84; pres., owner First Home Realty, Denver, 1984—. Mem. Nat. Assn. Realtors, Colo. Assn. Realtors, Denver Bd. Realtors (co-chmn. inner city mktg. session 1987—). Office: First Home Realty 1732 Pearl St Denver CO 80203

HABECK, FREDERIC HARVEY, sales executive; b. Milw., Mar. 20, 1933; s. Edgar Allen and Edna (Koehn) H.; m. Sharon Lee Fuchs, Aug. 6, 1966 (div. 1978); 1 child, Deborah Ann. BA, Knox Coll., Galesburg, Ill., 1956. Sales rep. Parke Davis Pharm., Detroit, 1958-68; sales mgr., mktg. mgr. Marine Collins, Inc., Detroit, 1968-78; regional mgr. Fidco, Inc., White Plains, N.Y., 1978—; mem. sales mktg. D.A. Ent., Huntington Beach, Calif., 1978—. Mem. Inst. Food Tech., Food & Drug Law Inst., Shoreline Yacht Club. Home: 21342 Greenspray Ln Huntington Beach CA 92646

HABERMANN, NORMAN, restaurant group executive; b. Hillside, N.J., 1933. Grad., Rutgers U., 1955; postgrad., Golden Gate U. Sch. Bus. Adminstrn., 1968. Pres. Restaurant Enterprises Group Inc., Irvine, Calif.; chief oper. officer Carrows Restaurants, Santa Barbara, Calif.; bd. dirs. Elephant Bar Restaurants Inc., Taco Villa Inc., Jeremiah's Restaurants Inc., Grace Food Co., Bruner Corp. Inc., Rayne Aquatechs. Inc. Office: Restaurant Enterprises Group Inc 2701 Alton Irvine CA 92714 *

HABLUTZEL, ROSALEE ANN, nurse, personal care company official; b. Livingston, Mont., May 11, 1941; d. Walter William and Celine Marie (Parenteau) Hart; m. Bruce John Hablutzel, Aug. 29, 1964; children: Michael Todd, JoAnn Marie, Brian John, Patrick William (dec.). BS in Nursing, Mary Coll., Bismarck, N.D., 1964; postgrad. in health bus. adminstrn., City U., Bellevue, Wash. RN, N.D. Staff nurse, charge nurse St. Alexius Hosp., Bismarck, 1966-70; staff nurse Heartview Alcohol & Drug Addiction Ctr., Mandan, N.D., 1970-72, St. Joseph's Hosp., Dickinson, N.D., 1978-80; instr. nursing U. N.D., Dickinson, 1973-75; state rev. coord. N.D. Peer Rev., Inc., Minot, 1975-77; coord. to expand home health program S.W. Health Nurse Office, Dickinson, 1981-83; co-owner, mgr. Nurse Corps, Dickinson, 1983-84; owner, mgr. Nurse Tech, Dickinson, 1984-86; nurse ter. mgr. extended care div. Johnson & Johnson Products, Inc., Mukilteo, Wash., 1985—; owner Spry Spat Nurse Clinic, 1986—; mem. U.S. Congl. Adv. Bd., 1987-89. Pres., bd. dirs. Dickinson Nutrition Svc., 1973-78; bd. dirs., chmn. artists series Dickinson Fine Arts Coun., 1974-76; sec. Coun. Aging Svcs. Planning Com. Bd., Dickinson, 1980; founder Dickinson League for Nursing, 1973; bd. dirs. N.D. League for Nursing Bd., 1973-78. Mem. Nat. League for Nursing (chairwoman 1974), Wash. State Nurses Assn., Wyo. Nurses Assn., NAFE (charter), Toastmasters (recorder Dickinson 1984-85). Roman Catholic. Office: 9502 49th Ave W Apt 19K Mukilteo WA 98275

HABSBURG-LOTHRINGEN, CHRISTOPHER, cabinet making and home building company executive; b. Boston, Jan. 26, 1957; s. Stefan and Jerrine (Soper) H.-L.; m. Elizabeth Ann Blanchett, May 1, 1987; 1 child, Saygan. Owner, mgr. Habsburg Constrn. and Woodworking Co., Sausalito, Calif., 1982—. Office: 2350 Marinship Way Sausalito CA 94965

HACHTEN, RICHARD ARTHUR, II, hospital administrator; b. Los Angeles, Mar. 24, 1945; s. Richard A. and Dorothy Margaret (Shipley) H.; m. Jeanine Hachten, Dec. 12, 1970; children: Kristianne, Karin. BS in Econs., U. Calif.-Santa Barbara, 1967; MBA, UCLA, 1969. Mgmt. intern TRW Systems Group, Redondo Beach, Calif., 1969-72; adminstrv. asst. Methodist Hosp., Arcadia, Calif., 1972-73, asst. adminstr., 1973-74, assoc. adminstr., 1974-76, v.p. adminstrn., 1976-80, exec. v.p., adminstr., 1980-81, pres., adminstr., 1981-84; chief exec. officer Tri-City Hosp. Dist., Oceanside, Calif., 1984—; instr. health care mgmt. Pasadena City Coll. Bd. dirs., pres. Hospice of Pasadena, Inc. Bd. dirs. ARC, Arcadia. Mem. Am. Coll. Healthcare Execs., Hosp. Council San Diego and Imperial Counties (chmn., bd. dirs.), Calif. Assn. Hosps. and Health Systems (bd. dirs.), Beta Gamma Sigma. Republican. Methodist. Club: Rotary. Home: 1130 Sugarbush Dr Vista CA 92084 Office: Tri-City Med Ctr 4002 Vista Way Oceanside CA 92056

HACKETT, CAROL ANN HEDDEN, physician; b. Valdese, N.C., Dec. 18, 1939; d. Thomas Barnett and Zada Loray (Pope) Hedden; B.A., Duke, 1961; M.D., U. N.C., 1966; m. John Peter Hackett, July 27, 1968; children—John Hedden, Elizabeth Bentley, Susanne Rochet. Intern. Georgetown U. Hosp., Washington, 1966-67, resident, 1967-69; clinic physician DePaul Hosp., Norfolk, Va., 1969-71; chief spl. health services Arlington County Dept. Human Resources, Arlington, Va., 1971-72; gen. med. officer USPHS Hosp., Balt., 1974-75; pvt. practice family medicine, Seattle, 1975—; mem. staff, chmn. dept. family practice Overlake Hosp. Med. Ctr., 1985-86; clin. instr. U. Wash. Bd. dirs. Mercer Island (Wash.) Preschool Assn., 1977-78; coordinator 13th and 20th Ann. Inter-profl. Women's Dinner, 1978, 86; trustee Northwest Chamber Orch., 1984-85 . Mem. Wash. Med. Soc., King County Med. Soc. (chmn. com. TV violence), DAR, Bellevue C. of C., NW Women Physicians (v.p. 1978), Seattle Symphony League, Eastside Women Physicians (founder, pres.), Sigma Kappa. Episcopalian. Clubs: Wash Athletic, Lakes. Home: 4304 E Mercer Way Mercer Island WA 98040 Office: 1128 112th Ave NE Bellevue WA 98004

HACKETT, JOHN PETER, dermatologist; b. N.Y.C., Feb. 10, 1942; s. John Thomas and Helen (Donohue) H.; m. Carol A. Hedden, July 27, 1968; children: John, Elizabeth, Susanne. AB, Holy Cross Coll., 1963; MD, Georgetown U., 1967. Diplomate Am. Bd. Internal Medicine, Am. Bd. Dermatology. Intern Georgetown U. Hosp., 1967-68, resident, 1968-69; fellow Johns Hopkins Hosp., 1972-75, chief resident, 1975; practice medicine specializing in dermatology Seattle, 1975—; chmn. bd. dirs. NW Dental Ins. Co.; asst. prof. dermatology U. Wash., 1975; active staff Swedish Hosp.; active staff Providence Hosp.; pres. Psoriasis Treatment Ctr., Inc., 1978-80; cons. physician Children's Orthopedic Hosp. Contbr. articles to profl. jours. Bd. dirs. Mercer Island Boys and Girls Club, 1976-81, Seattle Ctr. for Blind, 1979-80. Served to lt. condr. USNR, 1969-71. Mem. Am. Acad. Dermatology, Seattle Dermatol. Soc. (pres. 1981-82), Soc. Investigative Dermatology, Wash. State Med. Soc., King County Med. Soc. (chmn. media relations com. 1977-80), Wash. Physicians Ins. Assn. (chmn. actuarial subcom. 1983-85, chair subscribers adv. com. 1986-89). Club: Wash. Athletic, Seattle Yacht. Lodge: Rotary. Office: 1500 Cabrini Tower 901 Boren Ave Seattle WA 98104

HACKL, SYLVIA LEE, lawyer; b. Indpls., Aug. 6, 1955; d. Charles Leslie and Nancy (Hill) Miller; m. Thomas Joseph Hackl, May 24, 1980. BA summa cum laude, Lewis & Clark Coll., Portland, Oreg., 1977; JD, U. Wyo., 1980, MPA, 1988; student, Mt. Holyoke Coll., South Hadley, Mass., 1973-75. Bar: Wyo. 1980, U.S. Dist. Ct. Wyo., 1980, U.S. Ct. Appeals (10th cir.) 1985, U.S. Supreme Ct. 1986. Asst. pub. def. Wyo. State Pub. Def., Cheyenne, 1980-81; appellate counsel Wyo. State Pub. Def., 1981-84; asst. atty. gen. Wyo. Atty. Gen., Cheyenne, 1984-85; sr. asst. atty. gen. Wyo. Atty. Gen., 1985-87, adminstrv. asst. to atty. gen., 1987—; pres. Legal Svcs. for S.E. Wyo., Inc., Cheyenne, 1985-87; adj. prof. U. Wyo. Coll. Law, 1987-88. Co-author book: Wyoming Appellat Practice Manual, 1985, Wyoming Public Defender Criminal Manual, 1979; contbr. articles to profl. jours. Treas., bd. dirs. Cheyenne Capital Chorale, 1985—; mem. Cheyenne City Bd. Adjustment, 1985-86, Cheyenne City Neighborhood Conservation com., 1984-85;/ pres., incorporator Valley-View Homeowners Assn., 1984. Mem. Laramie County Bar Assn., Am. Judicature Soc., Phi Kappa Phi. Republican. Presbyterian. Office: Office of Attorney General 123 Capitol Bldg Cheyenne WY 82002

HACKNEY, CLINT RUDOLPH, III, consulting company and marketing company executive; b. El Paso, Tex., Mar. 10, 1953; s. Clint R. Jr. and Ginny T. H.; m. Robin Clifford, Dec. 21, 1973 (div. June 1977); m. Sunne Dee Griffith, Feb. 14, 1980. Student, So. Meth. U., 1971-75, San Jacinto Jr. Coll., Houston, 1976, Coll. of the Mainland, Texas City, Tex., 1977, Tex. A&M, Bryan, 1978, North Seattle Community Coll., 1987. V.p. H & H Music Co., Inc., Houston, 1975-77; police officer City of Friendswood, Tex., 1977-79, City of Lake Jackson, Tex., 1979-80; store mgr. Gonters Music City, Tacoma, 1980-81; gen. mgr. sales Murray Pub. Co., Seattle, 1981-83; pres. Tourism Mktg. Unltd., Inc., Tacoma, 1983—, Hackney, Halbert & Assocs., Tacoma, 1987—; chmn. travel and tourism adv. bd. Knapp Sch. Bus., Tacoma, 1985-88, chmn. bus. adv. bd. 1988—; chmn. mktg. com. Tacoma-Pierce County VCB, 1984-85; adv. bd. Ohop Indian Village/Dove, Eatonville, Wash., 1987—. Pub. Tacoma Visitors Guide, 1984, Tacoma All-Am. City Poster, 1984. Mem. NW Internat. Trade Assn. (v.p.), Pacific NW Speakers Assn., Tacoma-Pierce County C. of C. Methodist. Home: 54 Loch Ln SW Tacoma WA 98499 Office: Hackney Halbert & Assocs PO Box 600 Tacoma WA 98401

HACKNEY, ROBERT WARD, plant pathologist, nematologist, parasitologist, commercial arbitrator; b. Louisville, Dec. 11, 1942; s. Paul Arnold and Ovine (Whalen) H.; m. Cheryl Lynn Hill, June 28, 1969; 1 child, Candice Colleen. B.A., Northwestern U., 1965; M.S., Murray State U., 1969; Ph.D., Kans. State U., 1973.; Postgrad. research nematologist U. Calif., Riverside, 1973-75; plant nematologist Calif. Dept. Food and Agr., Sacramento, 1975-85, sr. plant nematologist, 1985—, comml. arbitrator Am. Arbitration Assn., 1980—; chmn. Calif. Nematode Diagnosis Adv. Commn., Sacramento, 1981—. Contbr. articles to profl. jours. Hon. dep. Sheriff, Sacramento, 1982-83. Served with USMC, 1966. NSF grantee, 1974. Mem. Soc. Nematologists, Internat. Council Study of Viruses and Virus Diseases of the Grape, Delta Tau Delta. Democrat. Methodist. Home: 2024 Flowers St Sacramento CA 95825-0422 Office: Calif Dept Food and Agr 1220 N St Rm 340 Sacramento CA 95814

HACKWOOD, SUSAN, electrical and computer engineering educator; b. Liverpool, Eng., May 23, 1955; came to U.S., 1980; d. Alan and Margaret Hackwood. BS with honors, Leicester Poly., Eng., 1976, PhD in Solid State Ionics, 1979. Research fellow Leicester Poly., Eng., 1976-79; postdoctoral research fellow AT&T Bell Labs., Homdel, N.J., 1980-81, mem. tech. staff, 1981-83, supr. robotics tech., 1983-84, dept. head robotics tech., 1984-85; prof. elec. and computer engring. U. Calif., Santa Barbara, 1985—, dir. Ctr. Robotic Systems in Microelectronics, 1985—. Editor: Jour. of Robotic Systems, 1983, Recent Advances in Robotics, 1985; contbr. 64 articles to tech. jours.; 7 patents in field. Mem. IEEE, Electrochem. Soc. (treas. 1985-87). Office: U Calif Ctr Robotic Systems 6740 Cortona Santa Barbara CA 93106

HACKWORTH, THEODORE JAMES, JR., city official; b. Denver, Nov. 7, 1926; s. Theodore James and Thelma B. (Hill) H.; m. Doris Evelyn Larson, Dec. 31, 1947; children—James Robert, Joan Evelyn Grady, Linda Jean Hoffman. B.A., U. Denver, 1955. Sales mgr. Continental Baking Co., Denver, 1950-64; mktg. exec. Sigman Meat Co., Denver, 1964-76; v.p. sales Pierce Packing Co., Billings, Mont., 1976-79; city councilman City of Denver, 1979—, pres., 1983-84; cons. EPA. Mem. Denver pub. schs. bd. edn., 1971-77; dir. Urban Drainage and Flood Control Dist., 1981-84; dir. Met. Sewer dist., 1982—, sec., 1984-85, chmn. elect 1988-89; mem. Denver Regional Council Govts., 1979—, vice chmn., 1981-83, chmn., 1984-86; neighborhood commr. Boy Scouts Am., 1968-69, Western Dist. commr., 1970-71; pres. Harvey Park Improvement Assn., 1969; chmn. Denver Met. Library Task Force, 1982. Served with USAF, 1945-47. Mem. Nat. Assn. Regional Council (bd. dirs. m., chmn. surface trans. task force, pres. 1987-89). Republican. Club: Mt. Vernon Country. Contbr. articles to EPA jours. Home: 3955 W Linvale Pl Denver CO 80236 Office: 1800 S Sheridan Blvd Ste #107 Denver CO 80226

HADDAD, ANEACE, data processing executive; b. Austin, Tex., Jan. 19, 1960; s. Hadi Majid and Judith (Hobgood) H.; m. Zameena Ally, Aug. 5, 1979 (div. Jan. 1986); children: Iman, Nadia. Student, u. Colo., 1979-81. Cons. Boulder, Colo., 1981-84; v.p. Integrated Mgmt. Systems, Denver, 1984-86; v.p. James P. Magee Assocs., Golden, Colo., 1986-88, with, 1988—. Home: 4801 S Wadsworth 4-309 Littleton CO 80123

HADDAD, EDMONDE ALEX, public affairs executive; b. Los Angeles, July 25, 1931; s. Alexander Saleeba and Madeline Angela (Zail) H.; m. Harriet Ann. AA, Los Angeles City Coll., 1956; BA, U. Southern Calif., 1958; MA, Columbia U., 1961. co-author, How Peace Came to the World, 1985. Staff writer WCBS Radio News, New York, 1959-61; news commentator, editor KPOL AM/FM Radio, Los Angeles, 1961-67, dir., pub. affairs, 1967-73; exec. dir. Los Angeles World Affairs Council, 1973-84; pres. Los Angeles World Affairs Coucil, 1984-88; deputy asst. sec. of State for Pub. Diplomacy Dept. State, U.S. Govt., Wash., 1987-88; Steering com. mem., moderator, Conf. Environment., Los Angeles, 1989. Recipient Am. Polit. Sci. Assn. award for Disting. Reporting of Pub. Affairs, 1967. Mem. Wilton Pk. Alumni of So. Calif. (exec. com.). Democrat. Home: 12730 Halkirk St Studio City CA 91604 Office: Saint Francis Med Ctr Found 3630 E Imperial Hwy Lynwood CA 90262

HADDAD, LILLIAN LAILA, retired company executive; b. Bentleyville, Pa., Aug. 10, 1922; d. Nesseme George and Mahussen Haddad; m. George Ofiesh, Feb. 25, 1942 (div. 1945); 1 child, Sheri; m. Sami Haddad, 1947 (div. 1969); children: Marwan, Alissar, Ragidia, Aida. Owner, mgr. vaious grocery stores, restaurants and clubs, 1940—. Mem. pub. rels. com. Rep. Nat. Orgn.; counselor for handicapped, Las Cruces, N.Mex., 1989—. Syrian Orthodox. Home: 1570 San Acacio St Las Cruces NM 88001

HADDAD, LOUIS NICHOLAS, newspaper executive; b. Beggs, Okla., Sept. 3, 1923; s. Abraham and Tammam (Lelo) H.; m. Jacqueline Marie Pratali, Sept. 22, 1945 (div. 1952); children: Carole, Shirley, Charles; m. Martha Maria Laengst, Dec. 31, 1954; children: Sheila, Stephanie. Co-owner Haddad Bros. Wholesalers, Lancaster, Calif., 1955-57; regional v.p. Nulite Corp., No. Calif., 1957-60; owner, mgr. Shamrock Motors, Seaside, Calif., 1960-68, Gateway Liquors, Seaside, 1968-70, Wagontown Auto Sales, Seaside, 1971-73, Camptown West Motor Homes, Seaside, 1973-79; co-owner, mgr. Monterey (Calif.) Bay Tribune, 1983—. Councilman City of Seaside, 1964-66, 78-80, mayor, 1966-72; charter bd. dirs. Monterey Peninsula Boys Club; bd. dirs. Alliance on Aging, Assn. Monterey Bay Area Govts.; chmn. Laguna Grande Agy., Seaside County Sanitation Dist., Monterey Overall Econ. Devel. Com.; chmn. adv. com. Project Aquarius; mem. Seaside Planning Comn.; vice chmn. So. Monterey Bay Water Pollution Control Agy.; chmn. tri-county bd. Calif. Coun. on Criminal Justice; former vice chmn. Monterey County Local Agys. Formation. Commn. Capt. U.S. Army, 1940-46, 50-55. Mem. VFW, NCO Assn. Am. (hon.), Am. Legion, VFW, Seaside C. of C. (bd. dirs.), Commonwealth Calif., Elks, K.C., Lions (past pres. Seaside chpt.), Rotary (past pres. Seaside chpt.). Republican. Roman Catholic. Home: 5 Deer Stalker Path Monterey CA 93940 Office: Monterey Bay Tribune 551 Foam St Monterey CA 93940

HADDIX, CHARLES E., legislative and regulatory consultant; b. Astoria, Oreg., Nov. 23, 1915; s. Charles H. and Mattie Lee (Wilson) H.; grad. U.S. Maritime Officers Sch., 1943; grad. in traffic mgmt. Golden Gate U., 1951; m. Betty Lee Wylie, Aug. 22, 1948; children—Bruce W., Anne C., C. Brian. Nat. sales mgr. Radio Sta. KLX, Oakland, Calif., 1953-55; West Coast mgr. Forjoe & Co., 1955-60; v.p. Calif. Spot Sales, 1958-60, Radio Calif., KLIP, Fowler, Calif., 1961-63; med. sales rep. Ives Labs., Inc., Sanger, Calif., 1964-73; state govt. relations cons. Marion Labs., Inc., 1973—; Calif. legis. advocate, 1968-85; Ariz., Nev., N.Mex., Oreg., Wash., Idaho, Utah and Mont. legis. advocate, 1975-85. Mem. Central Calif. Forum on Refugee Affairs, 1983—, chmn. 1987-88, state forum chmn., 1988; mem. Calif. State Adv. Council on Refugee Assistance and Svcs., 1988—; field cons. U.S. Sen. Alan Cranston, 1987—. Served with Marina Mercante Nat., Republic of Panama, 1945, U.S. Mcht. Marine, 1939-41, USCG, 1942-45. Mem. U.S. Naval Inst., Internat. Oceanographic Found., Am. Mus. Natural History, Oreg. Hist. Soc., Manuscript Soc., Columbia River Maritime Mus., U.S. Sen. Staff Club, Commonwealth Club of Calif. (San Francisco). Address: 3218 N McCall Sanger CA 93657

HADDOCK, PATRICIA ANN, writer; b. San Francisco, Nov. 3, 1946; d. Albert Newton and Audrey Agnes (O'Callaghan) H. BA, Lone Mountain Coll., 1968. Mgr. The Travelers, San Francisco, 1968-71, Lumber Industry HWP Funds, San Francisco, 1971-75; asst. v.p. Bank of Am., San Francisco, 1976-85; writer 1986—. Author: Standing Up for America, 1986, San Francisco, 1988;co-author: Leadership Skills for Women, 1989; contbr. to Lincoln Homework Ency., 1988; contbr. articles to Sylvia Porter's Personal Finance, Woman's Day, Consumers Research. Bd. dirs. Directions, San Francisco, 1985; vol. Calif. Acad. Scis., 1987—. Mem. Am. Soc. Journalists and Authors, Authors Guild, Soc. Children's Book Writers. Democrat. Home: 3193 16th St San Francisco CA 94103

HADELER, JOHN EXELBY, financial executive; b. Dayton, Ohio, May 29, 1952; s. William Edward and Cecelia (McCrate) H. BA, Brown U., 1974; MBA, Ohio State U., 1978. Systems analyst Burroughs Corp. Detroit, 1978-82, mgr. systems analysis, Irvine, Calif., 1982-85, mgr. fin. svcs. br., San Francisco 1985—. Mem. Data Processing Mgmt. Assn. Republican. Unitarian. Home: 956 Sacramento St #504 San Francisco CA 94108 Office: Unisys Corp 1000 Marina Blvd Brisbane CA 94005

HADGES, THOMAS RICHARD, media consultant; b. Brockton, Mass., Mar. 13, 1948; s. Samuel Charles and Ethel Toli (Prifti) H. BA in Biology magna cum laude, Tufts U., 1969; student, Harvard Sch. Dental Med., 1969-71. Announcer Sta. WOKW, Brockton, 1965-67, Sta. WTBS-FM, MIT, Cambridge, 1966-68; announcer, program dir. Sta. WTUR, Medford, Mass., 1967-69; announcer Concert Network, Sta. WBCN-FM, Boston, 1968-78, program dir., 1977-78; program dir. Sta. WCOZ-FM, Blair Broadcasting, Boston, 1978-80, Sta. KLOS-FM, ABC, Los Angeles, 1980-85; sr. programming advisor Pollack Media Group, Pacific Palisades, Calif., 1985-89; pres. Pollack/Hadges Enterprises, Pacific Palisades, 1985-89, Pollack Media Group, 1989—. Named Program Dir. of Yr., Los Angeles Times, 1981. Mem. Phi Beta Kappa. Office: Pollack Media Group 984 Monument St #105 Pacific Palisades CA 90272

HADLEY, HENRY LEE, urologist; b. Washington, Aug. 21, 1922; s. Henry Gilbert and Anna Virginia (Hafemayr) H.; m. Bonnie Rae Barnes, Mar. 8, 1945; children: Dean, Jeralyn, Roger, Merrilee. BS, Columbia Union Coll., Takoma Park, Md., 1942; MD, Loma Linda U., 1946. Resident urology Urology Clinic White Meml. Ctr., L.A., 1948-51; chief urology White Meml. Ctr., 1951-70; practice medicine, specialising in urology Loma Linda, Calif., 1951—; sr. attending physician L.A. Gen. Hosp., 1960-70; chmn., prof. dept. urology Loma Linda Sch. Medicine, 1970—; chief urology VA Hosp., Loma Linda, 1978-85, San Bernardino County Hosp., 1980—, Riverside County Hosp., 1988—. Author: Textbook of Urology, 1960; contbr. articles to profl. jours. Capt. U.S. Army, 1946-48. Mem. Soc. U.Urologists, Am. Urol. Assn., ACS, Internat. Soc. Urology, Loma Linda U. Alumni Assn. (pres. 1980). Home: 1329 Arroyo Crest Redlands CA 92373 Office: Loma Linda Univ Urology Grp 11370 Anderson St #1100 Loma Linda CA 92354

HADLEY, SUSAN MARIE, librarian; b. Buffalo, Nov. 25, 1952; d. Frank Joseph and Antionette (Gerace) Coniglio; m. Steven R. Hadley, Sept. 1, 1984. BA, SUNY, Buffalo, 1975; MLS, U. Mich., 1976; cert., U. Calif., Berkeley, 1986. Reference libr. Mont. Coll. Mineral Sci. and Tech., Butte, 1977-78; research libr. Sandia Nat. Labs., Livemore, Calif., 1978-85; cons. Townsend & Townsend, San Francisco, 1987—, Howe-Lewis Internat., Palo Alto, Calif., 1988—. Mem. Spl. Libraries Assn. Home: 2385 Kilkare Rd Sunol CA 94586 Office: Townsend & Townsend 1 Market Pla 20th Fl San Francisco CA 94105

HADLEY, WILLIAM KEITH, microbiologist, educator; b. Eugene, Oreg., Nov. 12, 1928; s. Olin Clair and Elma Ruby (Paulsen) H.; m. Marilyn JoAnn Norville, Nov. 15, 1952; Joan Elizabeth, Ruth Sarah. AB, U. Calif., Berkeley, 1950, PhD, 1967; MD, Yale U., 1959. Diplomate Am. Bd. Pathology. From asst. prof. to prof. lab. medicine U. Calif., San Francisco, 1967-77, prof., 1977; chief microbiology div. San Francisco Gen. Hosp., 1967—. Contbr. articles to profl. jours. Fellow Am. Soc. Clin. Pathology, Acad. Clin. Lab. Physicians Scientists; mem. Am. Soc. Microbiology (nat. counselor 1980). Home: 18 Reed Ranch Rd Tiburon CA 94920 Office: San Francisco Gen Hosp Microbiology Div 1001 Potrero Ave San Francisco CA 94110

HAEUSER, JOHN H., bank executive; b. Phoenix, Oct. 30, 1957; s. John H. and Eleanore M. (Pascale) H. AA in Bus., Glendale Community Coll., 1977; BS in Fin., Ariz. State U., 1979; cert. comml. lending, Am. Inst. Banking, 1984. Consumer loan officer Valley Nat. Bank Ariz., Phoenix, 1980-82, comml. loan officer, 1983-84, corp., nat. loan officer, 1984-87; corp. loan officer First Interstate Bank Ariz., Phoenix, 1987-88; v.p. First Interstate Bank Ariz., Scottsdale, 1988—; assoc., Robert Morris Assocs., Phoenix, 1984—. Mem. Am. Electronics Assn. Republican. Lutheran. Home: 19630 N 19th Pl Phoenix AZ 85024 Office: First Interstate Bank Ariz 6060 N Scottsdale Rd Scottsdale AZ 85261

HAFEY, EDWARD EARL JOSEPH, precision tool company executive; b. Hartford, Conn., June 7, 1917; s. Joseph Michael and Josephine (Pyne) H.; B.S. in Mech. Engring., Worcester Poly. Inst., 1940; postgrad. Johns Hopkins U., 1943, 44; m. Loyette Lindsey, Oct. 21, 1971; children—Joseph M., Barbara Hafey Beard, Edward F. Instr. dept. mech. enging. Worcester Tech. Inst., 1940-41; mgr. Comfort Air Inc., San Francisco, 1946-47; owner, mgr. Hafey Air Conditioning Co., San Pablo, Calif., 1947—, pres. Hafey Precision Tool, Inc., Laguna Beach, Calif., 1982—; cons. air conditioning U.S. Navy, C.E., Japan, Korea, Okinawa. Served to comdr. USNR, 1941-46. Registered profl. engr., Calif.; named Man of Year, San Pablo, 1962. Mem. Assn. Energy Engrs., Calif. Air Conditioning Service Engring. Soc., World Trade Center Orange County, Am. Legion, Ret. Officers Assn., Sigma Alpha Epsilon. Republican. Roman Catholic. Clubs: Exchange of Laguna Beach, Marine's Meml. Office: PO Box 417 Laguna Beach CA 92652

HAFEY, JOSEPH M., health association executive; b. Annapolis, Md., June 25, 1943; s. Edward Earl Joseph and Verna (Hedlund) H.; m. Mary Kay Miller, Dec. 30, 1978; children: Erin Catherine, Ryan Michael. BA, Whittier Coll., 1965; MPA, UCLA, 1967. Sr. asst. health officer HHS, Washington, 1967-69; dir. govt. relations Alliance for Regional Community Health, St. Louis, 1969-71; exec. dir. Contra Costa Comprehensive Health Coun., Richmond, Calif., 1971-74, Bay Area Comprehensive Health Planning Coun., San Francisco, 1974-76, Western Ctr. for Health Planning, San Francisco, 1976-86, Calif. Pub. Health Found., Berkeley, 1986-88, Western Consortium for Pub. Health, Berkeley, 1980—; chmn. Contra Costa Pub. Health Adv. Body, Martinez, Calif., 1987—; mem. Calif. Coalition for Future of Pub. Health, Sacramento, 1988—; prin. investigator Calif. Healthy Cities Program, Berkeley. Chmn. United Way Com. for the Uninsured, San Francisco, 1987-88; bd. dirs. Eugene O'Neill Found. With USPHS 1967-69. Recipient fellowship WHO, Geneva, 1987. Mem. Am. Pub. Health Assn. (governing coun. 1984-87), Am. Health Planning Assn. bd. dirs., chmn. annual meeting 1982). Home: 1749 Toyon Rd Lafayette CA 94549 Office: West Consortium Pub Health 2001 Addison # 200 Berkeley CA 94103

HAFF, STEPHEN LYMAN, research engineer; b. Northport, N.Y., Mar. 23, 1941; s. Clifton Stephen Leander and Ruth Allen (Chapell) H.; m. Lillian Louise Beaufrere, June 17, 1967 (div. 1981). BS in Aero. Engring., Tri-State U., 1962; MS in Systems Mgmt., U. So. Calif., 1980. Registered profl. engr. Flight test engr. Gyrodyne Co. Am., Inc., St. James, N.Y., 1962-71; systems test engr. Naval Air Test Ctr., Patuxent River, Md., 1971-78, Ames Rsch. Ctr., Moffett Field, Calif., 1978-85; tech. asst. Aerospace Systems, Moffett Field, 1985-86; rsch. engr. McDonnell Douglas Helicopter Co., Mesa, Ariz., 1986—. Contbr. articles to profl. jours. Pres. So. Md. Water Ski Club, Hollywood, 1972; sec. Cub Scouts Am., San Jose, Calif., 1983; pres. Villa Coronado Homeowner's Assn., Scottsdale, Ariz., 1987—. Named Outstanding Young Man in Am., U.S. Jaycees, 1975. Mem. AIAA (sr., facilities chair Phoenix chpt. 1987-88, treas. 1988-89), Am. Helicopter Soc. (prse. San Francisco chpt. 1984-85). Home: 7632 E Edgemont Ave Scottsdale AZ 85257 Office: McDonnell Douglas Helicopter Co 5000 E McDowell Mesa AZ 85205

HAFSTAD, GUNNAR ANDREAS, aeronautical engineer; b. Egersund, Norway, Feb. 27, 1922; came to U.S., 1956; s. Gunnar ad Anna (Haave) H.; m. Liv Gusta Marie Andersen, July 29, 1949; children: Berit, Gunnar Eilif, Grethe. BSME, Schous Inst. TEch., Oslo, Norway, 1947; BS in Aeros., MIT, 1949; MS in Aero-Astro Engring., Stanford U., 1961; MS in Engring.

Mgmt., U. So. Calif., 1975. Aero. engr. Saab Aircraft Corp., Linkoping, Sweden, 1949-56, Lockheed Aircraft Corp., Burbank, Calif., 1956-58; with Lockheed Missile & Space Co., Sunnyvale, Calif., 1958—, staff engr., 1975; rsch. dir. Santa Clara Solar Energy Rsch. Inst., Saratoga, Calif., 1978-85. Mem. AIAA, Photovoltaic Info. & Edn. Assn. Home: 15401 Via Caballero Monte Sereno CA 95030 Office: Lockheed Missile & Space Co 1111 Lockheed Way Bldg 598 Sunnyvale CA 94089

HAGA, ENOCH JOHN, computer educator, author; b. L.A., Apr. 25, 1931; s. Enoch and Esther Bouncer (Higginson) H.; student Sacramento Jr. Coll., 1948-49; AA, Grant Tech. Coll., 1950; student U. Colo., Denver, 1950, U. Calif., Berkeley, 1954, Midwestern U., 1950-54; AB, Sacramento State Coll., 1955, MA, 1958; PhD, Calif. Inst. Integral Studies, 1972, diploma tchr. Asian Culture, 1972; m. Elna Jo Wright, Aug. 22, 1957. Tchr. bus. Calif. Med. Facility, Vacaville, 1956-60; asst. prof. bus. Stanislaus State Coll., Turlock, Calif., 1960-61; engring. writer, publs. engr. Hughes Aircraft Co., Fullerton, Calif., 1961-62, Lockheed Missiles & Space Co., Sunnyvale, Calif., 1962, Gen. Precision, Inc., Glendale, Calif., 1962-63; sr. adminstrv. analyst Holmes & Narver, Inc., L.A., 1963-64; tchr., chmn. dept. bus. and math. Pleasanton Unified Dist., Pleasanton, Calif., 1964—, coordinator computer svcs., adminstrn. and instrn., 1984-85; vis. asst. prof. bus. Sacramento State Coll., 1967-69; instr. bus. and computer sci. Chabot Coll., Hayward, Calif., 1970-89; instr. bus. and philosophy Ohlone Coll., Fremont, Calif., 1972; prof., v.p., mem. bd. govs. Calif. Inst. Asian Studies, 1972-75; pres., prof. Pacific Inst. East-West Studies, San Francisco, 1975-76, also mem. bd. govs.; dir. Certification Councils, Livermore, Calif., 1975-80; mem., chmn. negotiating team Amador Valley Secondary Educators Assn., Pleasanton, Calif., 1976-77, pres., 1984-85. With USAF, 1949-52, with USNR, 1947-49, 53-57. Mem. Assn. Computer Educators (exec. dir. 1970-74). Coordinating editor: Total Systems, 1962; editor: Automation Educator, 1965-67; Automated Educational Systems, 1967; Data Processing for Education, 1970-71; Computer Techniques in Biomedicine and Medicine, 1973; contbg. editor Jour. Bus. Edn., 1961-69, Data Processing mag., 1967-70. Author and compiler: Understanding Automation, 1965. Author: Simplified Computer Arithmetic, Simplified Computer Logic, Simplified Computer Input, Simplified Computer Flowcharting, 1971-72. Editor: Data Processor, 1960-62, Automedica, 1970-76, FBE Bull., 1967-68. Home: 983 Venus Way Livermore CA 94550 Office: 4375 Foothill Rd Pleasanton CA 94566

HAGAN, ALFRED CHRIS, federal judge; b. Moscow, Idaho, Jan. 27, 1932; s. Alfred Elias and Irene Lydia (Wells) H.; m. Doreen M. Auve, July 10, 1953; children: Chris E., Martha Ann, Peter M. BA, U. Idaho, 1953, JD, 1958. Bar: Idaho 1958, U.S. Dist. Ct. Idaho 1958. Asst. atty. gen. State of Idaho, Boise, 1958, dist. judge, 1967-77; dep. pros. atty. Ada County, Boise, 1959; pvt. practice Boise, 1960-67, 77-84; U.S. magistrate for bankruptcy Dist. of Idaho, Boise, 1984-85, U.S. bankruptcy judge, 1985—. 1st lt. USAF, 1953-62. Mem. Nat. Conf. Bankruptcy Judges. Office: Federal Bldg 550 W Fort St Boise ID 83724

HAGAN, PATRICIA KITTREDGE, health facility administrator; b. Milo, Maine, May 12, 1935; d. Milton Donald and Beatrice Alma (Ingalls) Kittredge; B.S., U. Maine, 1961; M.P.A., Calif. State U., 1982. Food service mgr. U. Maine, Orono, 1961-62, Ind. U., 1962-64, U. Tex., Austin, 1965; adminstr. dietary services Cabrillo Med. Center, San Diego, 1965-69, adminstr. gen. services, 1969-70, adminstr. for ops., 1970-73, assoc. adminstr., 1973-76, adminstr., 1976-82; health services con. Cons. Health Services Adminstrn., San Diego, 1982—; chief exec. officer Specialty Med. Clinic, La Jolla, Calif., 1986-87. Served with USAF, 1954-58. Mem. Am. Coll. Hosp. Adminstrs., Am. Acad. Med. Adminstrs., Am. Hosp. Assn., Med. Group Mgmt. Assn., Am. Dietetic Assn., Asso. Western Hosps. Episcopalian. Club: Altrusa Internat. Home: 1275 Alexandria Dr San Diego CA 92107 Office: 2726 Shelter Island Dr #288 San Diego CA 92106

HAGAN, THOMAS PATRICK, advertising executive; b. Covington, Ky., Apr. 4, 1931; s. Michael Henry and Ruby V. Louise (Kailer) H.; m. Mary E. Maloney, June 1, 1957 (div. Mar. 1987); children: Kathleen Rundles, Kelly Hagan, Susan Hagan. BA in Journalism, Wayne U., 1956. Cert. bus. communicator. With pub. rels. Burroughs Corp., Detroit, 1956-57, copywriter, 1959-62; pers. adminstr. Chrysler Corp., Highland Park, Mich., 1957-58; ins. agt. State Farm Ins. Co., Detroit, 1958-59; copywriter Kenyon & Eckhardt, Detroit, 1962-64; assoc. creative dir. Campbell-Ewald, Detroit, 1964-73; creative dir. Frye-Sills, Denver, 1973-77; co-chmn. Karsh & Hagan Advt., Denver, 1977—. V.p. Ronald McDonald House, Denver, 1983—. With U.S. Army, 1952-54. Recipient many creative awards from advt. orgns. Mem. Bus./Profl. Advt. Assn., Denver Advt. Fedn. Roman Catholic. Office: Karsh & Hagan Inc 5500 Greenwood Plaza Blvd Ste 200 Englewood CO 80111-2106

HAGE, STEPHEN JOHN, radiology administrator, consultant; b. Chgo., July 22, 1943; s. Steve and Irene (Lewandowski) H.; m. Constance Louise Simonis, June 10, 1967. AAS, YMCA Community Coll., Chgo., 1970. Registered radiol. tech. Staff tech. Highland Park (Ill.) Hosp., 1966-68; chief radiotherapy tech. VA Hines (Ill.) Hosp., 1968-70; chief radiology tech. Gottlieb Meml. Hosp., Melrose Park, Ill., 1970-71; radiology adminstr. S. Chgo. County Hosp., 1971-79; adminstrv. dir. radiology Cedars-Sinai Med. Ctr., Los Angeles, 1979—; cons. Computer Sci. Corp., El Segundo, Calif., 1983—. Contbr. articles to profl. jours. Served with USMC, 1961-64. Recipient 1st pl. Essay award Ill. State Soc. Radiol. Technicians, 1966. Mem. Am. Hosp. Radiology Adminstrs. (charter), Am. Soc. Radiol. Technologists, AAAS, Phi Theta Kappa. Home: 22115 Halsted St Chatsworth CA 91311 Office: Cedars Sinai Med Ctr 8700 Beverly Blvd Los Angeles CA 90048

HAGEMAN, FRED SHAW, rancher; b. Douglas, Wyo., July 22, 1928; s. Fred August and Ruth Elizabeth (Shaw) H.; m. Veora Ileen Pilcher, July 20, 1952; children: Deborah L., Barbara G., Laura L. Grad., Converse County High Sch., Douglas, Wyo., 1947. Owner ranch Douglas, Wyo.; pres. Farmers Mut. Fire Ins. Co. of Albin, Wyo., 1963—. Mem. Converse County Sch. Bd., 1963-77, Predatory Animal Bd., Douglas, 1965-75; chmn. State Fair Improvement Com., Douglas, 1978-80; rep. We. Fairs Assn., Billings, 1978; v.p. Niobrara Rural Elec. Assn., Lusk, Wyo., 1975-87; state exec. bd. Wyo. Rural Elec. Assn., 1984-87; mem. Wyo. Bd. Agr., 1976-80, others. Recipient Achievement award, Niobrara Elec. Assn., 1986; Outstanding Svc. award, Gov. Wyo., 1980. Mem. Country Club of Douglas, Am. Legion, Cottonwood Country Club, Moose. Republican. Congregationalist.

HAGEN, ELEANOR HERTA, software engineer; b. N.Y.C., Dec. 28, 1933; d. Carl Ottomar and Herta Helene (Goetze) Badura; m. Armin A. Hagen, Mar. 11, 1956 (div. 1982); children: Eleanor, Eileen. BA in Anthropology, BS in Computer Sci., SUNY, Stony Brook, 1974. Software engr. Grumman Aerospace Corp., Calverton, N.Y., 1974-81, Grumman Aircraft Systems, Point Mugu, Calif., 1981—. Mem. Soc. Women Engrs. (sr. mem.). Club: Old Crows. Office: Grumman Aircraft Systems PO Box 42232 Point Mugu CA 93042

HAGEN, JOHN ROBERT, electronics executive; b. Denver, Feb. 27, 1948; s. Robert Harry and Ethel Irene (Martin) H.; m. Dawn Carolyn Bush (div. 1979); m. L. Ann Saltvick, Apr. 1980. Technician Stenocord Corp., Seattle, 1966-67; prodn. illustrator Boeing Co., Everett, Wash., 1967-68; mgr. Radio Shack, Everett, 1968-69; proprietor Bothel-Tronics, Everett, 1969-71; technician Westyway TV, Edmonds, Wash., 1971-72, John Fluke, Everett, 1972-75; proprietor Hagen Electronics, Kirkland, Wash., 1975-78; engring. v.p. Gen. Security Controls Corp., Bellevue, Wash., 1978-79; proprietor Hagen Electronics, Lynnwood, Wash., 1978--. Mem. 44th Dist. Dem. Com., Bothell, Wash., 1984—. Methodist. Home and Office: Hagen Electronics 2505 196th Ave SW #14 Lynnwood WA 98036

HAGEN, LARRY WILLIAM, manufacturing and retail executive; b. Pyote, Tex., May 5, 1945; s. Lawrence Herbert and Marjorie Fern (MacFarland) H.; m. Lynda Barbara Hagen; 1 child, Bret William. AA, Highline Coll., 1965; BS cum laude, Seattle U., 1969; MBA, Pacific Luth. U., 1987. Dir. ops. group III The Bon Marche, Seattle, 1967-75; dir. distbn. Brittania Sportswear, Seattle, 1975-77; exec. v.p., chief fin. officer, ptnr. Schoenfeld Neckwear Corp., Seattle, 1977—; also bd. dirs. Schoenfeld Neckwear, Seattle, 1984—; bd. dirs. Mallory & Church Ltd., London, 1985—; cons. Jeans Warehouse, Seattle, 1979-81. Loaned exec. United Way, Seattle, 1966-69; collector YMCA Disadvantaged Youth, Seattle, 1983-86. Served with USNG, 1964-74. Mem. Am. Prodn. Inventory Control Soc., Pacific NW Personnel Mgmt. Assn., Am. Soc. Personnel Adminstrn. (v.p. Seattle chpt. 1970-71, pres. Columbian Basin 1981-82). Democrat. Lutheran. Home: 5731 111th Ave SE Bellevue WA 98006 Office: Schoenfeld Neckwear Corp 676 S Industrial Way Seattle WA 98108

HAGEN, NICHOLAS STEWART, clinical educator, consultant; b. Plentywood, Mont., Aug. 6, 1942; s. William Joseph and June Janette (Reuter) H.; m. Mary Louise Edvalson, July 26, 1969; children: Brian Geoffrey, Lisa Louise, Eric Christopher, Aaron Daniel, David Michael. BS in Chemistry, Ariz. State U., 1964; MBA in Internat. Bus., George Washington U., 1969; MD, U. Ariz., 1974. Lic. physician Ariz., Utah, Idaho.; diplomate Nat. Bd. Med. Examiners. Resident Good Samaritan Hosp., Phoenix, 1974-75; pvt. practice Roy, Utah, 1975-77; dir. clin. rsch. Abbott Labs., North Chicago, Ill., 1977-84; v.p. med. affairs Rorer Group, Inc., Ft. Washington, Pa., 1984-88; clin. prof. Ariz. State U., Tempe, 1988—; pres. Southwestern Clin. Rsch., Tempe, 1987—. Author: Valproic Acid: A Review of Pharmacologic Properties and Clinical Use in Pharmacologic and Biochemical Properties of Drug Substances, 1979; contbr. articles to med. jours.; patentee in field. Bishop Ch. Jesus Christ of Latter-day Saints, Gurnee, Ill., 1981-84; various positions with local couns. Boy Scouts Am., 1988—; active Rep. campaigns, Mesa, Ariz., 1988—. Lt. comdr. USCG, 1965-69. Joan Mueller-Etter scholar Ariz. State U., 1960, Phelps-Dodge scholar Ariz. State U., 1961; NASA fellow Brigham Young U., 1964. Mem. Am. Coll. Sports Medicine, Eagle Forum, Nat. Right-to-Life Assn., Free Congress Found., Am. Conservative Union, Utah Hist. Soc., Nat. Geneal. Soc., Bucks County Geneal. Soc., Sons Norway, Soc. Descendants Emigrants from Numedal Norway, Beta Beta Beta, Alpha Epsilon Delta, Phi Eta Sigma, Kappa Sigma, Blue Key, Sophos. Republican. Mormon. Office: PO Box 26224 Tempe AZ 85285

HAGEN, PAULA LYNN, advertising executive, consultant; b. Seattle, Sept. 4, 1962; d. Donald Herman and Anna Lillian (Kopp) H. BA in History, U. Conn., 1985. Jr. copywriter and media asst. Donahue, Inc., Hartford, Conn., 1985; copywriter and broadcast librarian Cronin and Co., Inc., Glastonbury, Conn., 1985-86; copywriter and pres. FirstWords, Englewood, Colo., 1986—. Active Jr. League Denver, 1988—. Recipient Gold award Art Dirs.' Club Hartford, 1987, Merit award Art Dirs.' Club Hartford, 1987. Mem. Bus. Profl. Advt. Assn., Art Dirs.' Club Denver (Merit award 1988), Rocky Mountain Figure Skating Club, Am. Morgan Horse Assn. Republican.

HAGENBUCH, JOHN JACOB, investment banker; b. Park Forest, Ill., May 31, 1951; s. David Brown and Jean Iline (Reeves) H.; m. Elisabeth Root Luce, May 23, 1981; children: Henry, Hunter, Hilary. AB magna cum laude, Princeton U., 1974; MBA, Stanford U., 1978. Assoc., Salomon Bros., N.Y.C., 1978-80, v.p., San Francisco, 1980-85; gen. ptnr. Hellman & Friedman, 1985—; bd. dirs. Am. Pres. Cos. Bd. govs. San Francisco Symphony. Mem. Burlingame Country Club, Pacific-Union Club. Home: 3476 Jackson St San Francisco CA 94118 Office: Hellman & Friedman 1 Maritime Pla San Francisco CA 94111

HAGENS, WILLIAM JOSEPH, state official, public health educator; b. Bay City, Mich., June 3, 1942; s. Francis Bernard and Lillian May (O'Neill) H.; m. Noel Scantlebury, Apr. 15, 1967; children: Clara O'Neill, Nicholas Barlow. BA, Saginaw Valley Coll., 1969; MA, Wayne State U., 1971. Mem. adj. faculty Wayne State U., Detroit, 1971; VISTA vol. Pierce County Legal Assistance, Tacoma, 1971-73; sr. policy analyst Wash. Ho. of Reps., Olympia, 1974—; instr. Pacific Luth. U., Tacoma, 1979-81; clin. prof. Sch. Pub. Health, U. Wash., Seattle, 1984—; reviewer Policy Studies Rev., Chgo., 1983—; mem. health policy project George Washington U., Washington, 1985—; bd. dirs. Area Health Edn. Ctr., Seattle, 1988—. Contbg. author: Analyzing Poverty Policy, 1975. Recipient President's award Wash. State Pub. Health Assn., 1986; NIMH fellow, 1979. Mem. Am. Pub. Health Assn., Am. Polit. Sci. Assn., Policy Studies Orgn., English Speaking Union, World Affairs Coun., Pi Sigma Alpha. Home: 3214 N 27th St Tacoma WA 98407 Office: Wash Ho of Reps MS AS-33 Olympia WA 98504

HAGENSTEIN, WILLIAM DAVID, consulting forester; b. Seattle, Mar. 8, 1915; s. Charles William and Janet (Finigan) H.; m. Ruth Helen Johnson, Sept. 2, 1940 (dec. 1979); m. Jean Kraemer Edson, June 16, 1980. BS in Forestry, U. Wash., 1938; MForestry, Duke, 1941. Registered profl. engr., Wash., Oreg. registered forester, Calif. Field aid in entomology U.S. Dept. Agr., Hat Creek, Calif., 1938; logging supt. and engr. Eagle Logging Co., Sedro-Woolley, Wash., 1939; tech. foreman U.S. Forest Svc., North Bend, Wash., 1940; forester West Coast Lumbermen's Assn., Seattle and Portland, Oreg., 1941-43, 45-49; sr. forester FEA, South and Central Pacific Theaters of War and Costa Rica, 1943-45; mgr. Indsl. Forestry Assn., Portland, 1949-80; exec. v.p. Indsl. Forestry Assn., 1956-80, hon. dir., 1980-87; pres. W. D. Hagenstein & Assocs., Inc., Portland, 1980—; H.R. MacMillan lectr. forestry U. B.C., 1952, 77; Benson Meml. lectr. U. Mo., 1966; S.J. Hall lectr. indsl. forestry U. Calif. at Berkeley, 1973; cons. forest engr. USN, Philippines, 1952, Coop. Housing Found., Belize, 1986; mem. U.S. Forest Products Trade Mission, Japan, 1968; del. VII World Forestry Congress, Argentina, 1972, VIII Congress, Indonesia, 1978; mem. U.S. Forestry Study Team, West Germany, 1974; mem. sec. Interior's Oreg.-and Calif. Multiple Use Adv. Bd., 1975-76; trustee Wash. State Forestry Conf., 1948—, Keep Oreg. Green Assn., 1957—, v.p., 1970-71, pres., 1972-73; adv. trustee Keep Wash. Green Assn., 1957—; dir. World Forestry Ctr., 1965—, v.p., 1965-79. Author: (with Wackerman and Michell) Harvesting Timber Crops, 1966; Assoc. editor: Jour. Forestry, 1946-53; columnist Wood Rev., 1978-82; contbr. numerous articles to profl. jours. Trustee Oreg. Mus. Sci. and Industry, 1968-73. Served with USNR, 1933-37. Recipient Forest Mgmt. award Nat. Forest Products Assn., 1968, Western Forestry award Western Forestry and Conservation Assn., 1972, 79, Gifford Pinchot medal for 50 yrs. Outstanding Svc. Soc. Am. Foresters, 1987, Charles W. Ralston award Duke Sch. Forestry, 1988. Fellow Soc. Am. Foresters (mem. coun. 1958-63, pres. 1966-69); mem. Am. Forestry Assn. (life, hon. v.p. 1966-69, 74—), Commonwealth Forestry Assn. (life), Internat. Soc. Tropical Foresters, Portland C. of C. (mem. forestry com. 1949-79, chmn. 1960-62), Nat. Forest Products Assn. (mem. forestry adv. com. 1949-80, chmn. 1972-74, 78-80), West Coast Lumbermen's Assn. (v.p. 1969-79), Lang Syne Soc., Hoo Hoo Club, Xi Sigma Pi (named outstanding alumnus Alpha chpt. 1973). Republican. Home: 3062 SW Fairmount Blvd Portland OR 97201 Office: 225 SW Broadway Rm 412 Portland OR 97205

HAGER, JOHN PATRICK, engineering educator; b. Miles City, Mont., Oct. 2, 1936; s. John Herman and Agnes C. (Hart) H.; m. Mary Anna McCloskey, Aug. 26, 1961; children: Patrick, Michael, Charles, Justine, Brendan, Thomas, John Jr. BS, Mont. Sch. Mines, 1958; MS, Mo. Sch. Mines, 1960; ScD, MIT, 1969. Asst. scientist AVCO Corp., Wilmington, Mass., 1961; instr. MIT, Cambridge, 1961-64, research asst., 1964-66; asst. prof. Colo. Sch. Mines, Golden, 1966-69, assoc. prof., 1969-71, dept. head, prof., 1971-74, prof. metallurgy, 1974-87, Hazen research prof. extractive metallurgy, 1988—. Named Prof. Extractive Metallurgy St. Joe Minerals Corp., 1974—. Mem. AIME. Republican. Roman Catholic. Home: 2054 Crestvue Circle Golden CO 80401 Office: Colo Sch Mines Dept Metallurgy Golden CO 80401

HAGERTY, BRIAN PATRICK, comsumer products company executive; b. Aurora, Ill., Dec. 14, 1958; s. Thomas Arthur and Joyce Ann H. BBA, U. Iowa, 1981; postgrad. bus. adminstrn., Purdue U., 1982-83, Keller Grad. Sch., Chgo., 1983-84. Supr. key accounts Dial Corp., Chgo., 1981-84; mgr. key and nat. accounts Gillette Co., Chgo., 1984-86; mktg. organizer Innovators Mktg. Group, Scottsdale, Ariz., 1986-87; v.p. mktg. JAD Mfg. Corp., Scottsdale, 1987—, also bd. dirs.; cons. Idle Eyes Sunglasses, Scottsdale, 1988—. Co-inventor Shave 'n Cream complete shaving system. Vol. Phoenix Rep. Com., Ariz. Archaeol. Soc. Home: 9468 E Camino del Santo Scottsdale AZ 85260 Office: JAD Mfg Corp Box 4818 NRS2 Phoenix AZ 85029

HAGGARD, CLAUDE COLLINS, electrical engineering consultant; b. Ranfurly, Alta., Can., Feb. 6, 1908; s. Joshiah Collins and Adella Elizabeth (Prescott) H.; m. Yvonne May Pickell, Oct. 11, 1933; children: Gloria, Merrill. Student Oreg. schs. With Mountain States Power Co., Tillamook, Oreg., 1926-29; elec. plant operator Calif. Oreg. Power Co., North Bend, Oreg., 1929-39; dir. safety Calif.-Oreg. Power Co., 1939-63; safety specialist Pacific Power and Light Co., 1963-73; elec. cons. and internat. lectr. on safe use of electricity Haggard's Seminars, Medford, Oreg., 1973—; instr. War Manpower Commn. Recipient Oreg. Accident Commn. award, 1965; Oreg. Workmen's Compensation award, 1967; named to Hall of Fame, Internat. Assn. Elec. Insps., 1974. Mem. Edison Electric Inst. (cardiopulmonary resuscitation com.), IEEE (sr. mem.; Contbn. award 1972), Am. Soc. Safety Engrs., NW Electric Light and Power Assn., Nat. Fire Protection Assn., Vets. of Safety. Republican. Mem. Christian Ch. Producer TV programs; developer safety devices. Home and Office: 2607 Eastover Terr Medford OR 97501

HAGGIS, PAUL EDWARD, writer, director, producer; b. London, Ont., Can., Mar. 10, 1953; came to U.S., 1979; s. Edward H. and Mary Yvonne (Metcalf) H.; m. Diane Christine Gettas, Apr. 9, 1977; children: Alissa Sullivan, Lauren Kilvington, Katy Elizabeth. Story editor TV show One Day at a Time/CBS, L.A., 1982-84; exec. story editor, producer TV show The Facts of Life/NBC, L.A., 1984-86; supervising producer TV shows Sweet Surrender/NBC, 1986-87, Nothing is Easy/CBS, 1987, thirtysomething/ABC, 1987-88, Los Angeles; screenwriter feature films Personal Column/New Horizon Pictures, 1988. creator, exec. producer Desperate Women, CBS, 1989. Trustee Found. for Religious Freedom; mem. adv. bd. Mus. Broadcasting. Recipient Emmy award for outstanding writing in a dramatic series Nat. Acad. TV Srts and Scis., 1988, Emmy award for producer outstanding drama series, 1988, Humanitas prize, 1988, People's Choice award for best new dramatic program, producer, 1988.

HAGINO, GERALD TAKAO, state senator; b. Puunene, Maui, Hawaii, July 31, 1949; s. Masao and Lynette (Higashida) H.; m. Cynthia H. Haraguchi, June 30, 1973; children: Steven, Danielle, Sharyse. BS in Biology, U. Hawaii, 1971. Operator Hawaiian Ind. Refinery, 1972-88; researcher Oceanic Inst., 1988—. mem. Hawaii Senate, 1982—, senate majority leader, chmn. legis. mgmt. Bd. dirs. Wahiawa Gen. Hosp., West Oahu (Hawaii) YMCA; active Wahiawa Community and Businessmen's Assn. Mem. Lions. Democrat. Office: Office of State Senate State Capitol Honolulu HI 96813

HAGLER, ABIGAIL, physician; b. Cleve., Sept. 26, 1943; d. John Alexander Gibbons and Maria (le Duc) O'Neill; m. Benjamin Lucien Hagler (div. 1976). BA in Art, Manhattanville Coll., 1964; MD, Emory U., 1981. Diplomate Am. Bd. Internal Medicine. Advt. copywriter Ga. Power Co., Atlanta, 1967-71; freelance med. illustrator 1977-81; intern in medicine Grady Hosp., Atlanta, 1981-82, resident in medicine, 1982-84; pvt. practice internal medicine Yuma, Ariz., 1986—; chief of staff Yuma Regional Med. Ctr., 1988—. Med. dir. Alzheimers Unit Hillhaven Nursing Home, Yuma; mem. Yuma County Bd. Health. Mem. Yuma County Med. Soc., AMA, Ariz. Med. Soc., Am. Soc. for Internal Medicine. Office: 2451 S Ave A Yuma AZ 85364

HAGNER, DONALD ALFRED, New Testament educator; b. Chgo., July 8, 1936; s. Carl Sture and Marie (Gondek) H.; m. Beverly Jean Smith, Sept. 2, 1962. BA, Northwestern U., Evanston, Ill., 1958; BD, Fuller Theol. Sem., Pasadena, 1966; ThM, Fuller Theol. Sem., 1967; PhD, U. Manchester, Eng., 1969. Instr. to assoc. prof. Wheaton (Ill.) Coll., 1969-76; assoc. prof. to prof. New Testament Fuller Theol. Sem., Pasadena, 1976—; dean summer inst. Young Life, Colorado Springs, Colo., 1977—. Author: Use of O.T. and N.T. in Clement of Rome, 1973, Jewish Reclamation of Jesus, 1984, Hebrews (Commentary), 1983; co-editor: Pauline Studies, 1980. With USN, 1958-62. Mem. Soc. N.T. Studies, Soc. Bibl. Lit., Tyndale Fellowship (U.K.), Inst. Bibl. Research (fellow), Swedish Exegetical Soc. Democrat. Presbyterian.

HAGOPIAN, DAVE MALCOLM, military officer; b. June 16, 1960; s. Bearge M. and Eugenie B. Hagopian. AS in Engring., Fresno City Coll., 1980; BSME, Calif. State U., Fresno, 1983; postgrad., Advanced Communications Officer's Course, 1989—. Long haul trucker Market Express, Inc., Fresno, 1980-83; commd. 2nd lt. USMC, 1983, advanced through grades to capt., 1988; basic officer Marine Corps Devel. and Edn. Command, Quantico, Va., 1983-84; communications officer Fleet Marine Force, Okinawa, Japan, 1984-85; ops. officer U.S. Marine Recruiting Sta., Seattle, 1985-87; exec. officer U.S. Marine Recruiting Sta., 1985-88. Counselor Christian Berets Camp, Sonora, Calif., 1973-75.

HAGUE, JOHN BRIAN, energy company executive; b. Lethbridge, Alta., Can., Aug. 15, 1944; s. John Rayson and Rose (Knowlden) H. BA in Honors Econs., U. B.C., 1965; postgrad., U. Minn., 1965-66. Bus. analyst Pacific Region Office Imperial Oil Ltd., 1966-69; asst. dir. price rev. div. Prices & Income Commn., Ottawa, Ont., Can., 1969-72; fin. analyst Can. Devel. Corp., Toronto, Ont., 1972-75, mgr. fin. analysis, 1976, v.p., 1976-79, exec. v.p., 1979-86; dir. gen. prices and profits br. Anti-Inflation Bd., Ottawa, 1975-76; pres., chief operating officer Canterra Energy Ltd., Calgary, Alta., Can., 1986—; also bd. dirs. Canterra Energy Ltd., Calgary, Alta., Can.; bd. dirs. Cansulex Ltd., Vancouver, B.C., Can. *

HAGUE, MICHAEL R., illustrator; b. Los Angeles, Sept. 8, 1948; s. Riley Herbert and Daisy Marie (King) H.; m. S. Kathleen Burdick, Dec. 5, 1970; children: Meghan Micaela, Brittany Michael, Devon Heath. BFA, Art Ctr. Coll. of Design, Los Angeles, 1972. Illustrator Hallmark Cards, Kansas City, Mo., 1973-75, Current, Inc., Colorado Springs, Colo., 1975-77; freelance illustrator Colorado Springs, 1977—. Illustrator of numerous children's books including The Cabbage Moth and the Shamrock, 1978, A Necklace of Fallen Stars, 1979, Beauty and the Beast, 1980, The Wind in the Willows, 1980, The Wizard of Oz, 1982, The Lion, the Witch and the Wardrobe, 1983, Mother Goose: A Collection of Classic Nursery Rhymes, 1984, The Legend of the Veery Bird, 1985, Out of the Nursery, Into the Night, 1986, Peter Pan, 1987, Rootabaga Stories, 1988. Recipient Book of the Yr. award A Child's Study Assn., 1983, Children's Choices award, 1983, Children's Books Mean Bus. Group Show, 1984.

HAHN, ANITA LOUISE, radiologic technologist; b. Eugene, Oreg., Feb. 15, 1947; d. William Harry Manley and Louise Helen (Weimer) Shultz; m. Patrick Dale, Feb. 11, 1967; children: Brian, Derek. Student, U. Oreg., 1965-66; AS, Kapiolani Community Coll., 1974; postgrad., U. Hawaii, 1978-85. Cert. radiologic technologist, Hawaii. Chief mammography technologist Breast Cancer Detection and Demonstration Project Pacific Health Rsch. Inst., Honolulu, 1974-79; computerized tomography technician Kapiolani Med. Ctr., Honolulu, 1979-85, mammography technologist, 1985-87; mammography specialist Kaiser Permanente, Honolulu, 1987—. Recipient award of Excellence Mallinckodt, 1975. Mem. Hawaii Soc. Radiologic Technologist (pres. 1980-81), Hawaii Humane Soc., Friends of the Library. Democrat. Methodist. Home: 7523 Laielua Pl Honolulu HI 96825 Office: Kaiser Permanente Radiology 1010 Pensacola St Honolulu HI 96814

HAHN, ELLIOTT JULIUS, lawyer; b. San Francisco, Dec. 9, 1949; s. Leo Wolf and Sherry Marion (Portnoy) H; m. Toby Rose Mallen; 1 child, Brittany Atira Mallen. BA cum laude, U. Pa., 1971, JD, 1974; LLM, Columbia U., 1980. Bar: N.J. 1974, Calif. 1976, D.C. 1978, U.S. Dist. Ct. N.J. 1974, U.S. Dist. Ct. (cen. dist.) Calif. 1976, U.S. Supreme Ct. 1980. Assoc. von Maltitz, Derenberg, Kunin & Janssen, N.Y.C., 1974-75; law clk. Los Angeles County Superior Ct., Los Angeles, 1975-76; atty. Atlantic Richfield Co., Los Angeles, 1976-79; prof. Summer in Tokyo program Santa Clara Law Sch., 1981-83; assoc. prof. law Calif. Western Sch. Law, San Diego, 1980-85; atty. Morgan, Lewis & Bockius, Los Angeles, 1985-87; assoc. Whitman & Ransom, Los Angeles, 1987-88, ptnr., 1989—; adj. prof. law Southwestern U. Sch. Law, 1986—, Pepperdine U., 1986—. Author: Japanese Business Law and the Legal System, 1984; contbr. chpt. on Japan to The World Legal Ency.; contbr. articles to Law Rev. Vice-chmn. San Diego Internat. Affairs Bd., 1981-85; bd. dirs. San Diego-Yokohama Sister City Soc., 1982-85, Los Angeles-Nagoya Sister City Soc., 1986—; mem. master planning com. City of Rancho Palos Verdes, Calif., 1989—. Vis. scholar Nihon U., Tokyo, 1982; vis. lectr. Internat. Christian U., Tokyo, 1982. Mem. L.A. County Bar Assn. (bd. dirs. internat. sect.), Assn. Asian Studies, ABA, U. Pa. Alumni Club (pres. San Diego chpt. 1982, pres. council Phila., 1983), Anti-Defamation League, State Bar Calif., Japanese-Am. Soc. Legal Studies (book rev. editor Seattle, 1983—). Jewish. Office: Whitman & Ransom 444 S Flower St Los Angeles CA 90071

HAHN, ERWIN LOUIS, physicist, educator; b. Sharon, Pa., June 9, 1921; s. Israel and Mary (Weiss) H.; m. Marian Ethel Failing, Apr. 8, 1944 (dec. Sept. 1978); children: David L., Deborah A., Katherine L.; m. Natalie Woodford Hodgson, Apr. 12, 1980. B.S., Juniata Coll., 1943, D.Sc., 1966; M.S., U. Ill., 1947, Ph.D., 1949; D.Sc., Purdue U., 1975. Asst. Purdue U., 1943-44; research assoc. U. Ill., 1950; NRC fellow Stanford, 1950-51, instr., 1951-52; research physicist Watson IBM Lab., N.Y.C., 1952-55; assoc. Columbia U., 1952-55; faculty U. Calif. at Berkeley, 1955—, prof. physics, 1961—, assoc. prof., then prof. Miller Inst. for Basic Research, 1958-59, 66-67, 85-86; vis. fellow Brasenose Coll., Oxford (Eng.) U., 1981-82; Eastman vis. prof. Oxford U., 1988-89; cons. Office Naval Research, Stanford, 1950-52, AEC, 1955—; spl. cons. USN, 1959; adv. panel mem. Nat. Bur. Standards, Radio Standards div., 1961-64; mem. NAS/NRC com. on basic research; adv. to U.S. Army Research Office, 1967-69. Author: (with T.P. Das) Nuclear Quadrupole Resonance Spectroscopy, 1958. Served with USNR, 1944-46. Recipient Oliver E. Buckley prize Am. Phys. Soc., 1971; prize Internat. Soc. Magnetic Resonance, 1971; award Humboldt Found., Germany, 1976-77; co-winner Wolf Found. prize in physics, 1983-84; named to Calif. Inventor Hall of Fame, 1984; Guggenheim fellow, 1961-62, 69-70; NSF fellow, 1961-62; vis. fellow Brasenose Coll., Oxford, 1969-70; lifetime hon. fellow Brasenose Coll., Oxford, 1984, Alumni Achievement award, Juniata Coll., 1986. Fellow Am. Phys. Soc. (past mem. exec. com. div. solid state physics); mem. Am. Acad. Arts and Scis., Nat. Acad. Scis., Slovenian Acad. Scis. and Arts (fgn.). Home: 69 Stevenson Ave Berkeley CA 94708 Office: U Calif Dept Physics Berkeley CA 94720

HAHN, HAROLD THOMAS, physical chemist, chemical engineer; b. N.Y.C., May 31, 1924; s. Gustave Hahn and Lillie Martha (Thomas) H.; m. Bennie Joyce Turney, Sept. 5, 1948; children: Anita Karen, Beverly Sharon, Carol Linda, Harold Thomas Jr. Student, Hofstra U., 1941-43; BSChemE, Columbia U., 1943-44; PhD in Chemistry, U. Tex., 1950-53. Chem. engr. Manhattan Dist. U.S. Army, Los Alamos, N.Mex., 1945-47; chem. engr. U. Calif., Los Alamos, 1947-50; sr. scientist Gen. Electric Co., Hanford, Wash., 1953-58; sect. chief, chem. research dept. Phillips Petroleum Co., Idaho Falls, Idaho, 1958-64; sr. staff scientist Lockheed Missiles & Space Co., Palo Alto, Calif., 1964—. Contbr. articles to profl. jours.; patentee in field. Pres. Edgemont Gardens PTA, Idaho Falls, 1963-64; commr. cub scout div. Stanford area council Boy Scouts Am., Palo Alto, 1973-76, also cubmaster pack 36, 1973-80, chmn. troops 36 and 37, 1975-77; mem. adminstrv. bd. Los Altos Meth. Ch. Served to col. U.S. Army, 1944-46, with res., 1946-84, col. res. ret. Humble Oil Co. fellow, 1952, Naval Bur. Ordnance fellow, 1953. Fellow Am. Inst. Chemists; mem. Calif. Acad. Scis., Internat. Platform Assn., Am. Chem. Soc., AIAA, Sigma Xi, Phi Lambda Upsilon, Kappa Rho. Republican. Home: 661 Teresi Ln Los Altos CA 94022 Office: Lockheed Rsch Lab Dept 93-50 Bldg 204 3251 Hanover St Palo Alto CA 94304

HAHN, JOAN CHRISTENSEN, drama educator, travel agent; b. Kemmerer, Wyo., May 9, 1933; d. Roy and Bernice (Pringle) Wainwright; m. Milton Angus Christensen, Dec. 29, 1952 (div. Oct. 1, 1971); children—Randall M., Carla J. Christensen Teasdale; m. Charles Henry Hahn, Nov. 15, 1972. B.S., Brigham Young U., 1965. Profl. ballroom dancer, 1951-59; travel dir. E.T. World Travel, Salt Lake City, 1969—; tchr. drama Payson High Sch., Utah, 1965-71, Cottonwood High Sch., Salt Lake City, 1971—; dir. Performing European Tours, Salt Lake City, 1969-76; dir. Broadway theater tours, 1976—. Dir. Salem City Salem Days, Utah, 1965-75; regional dir. dance Latter-day Saints Ch., 1954-72. Named Best Dir. High Sch. Musicals, Green Sheet Newspapers, 1977, 82, 84; recipient 1st place award Utah State Drama Tournament, 1974, 77, 78, 89; Limelight award, 1982; Exemplary Performance in teaching theater arts Granite Sch. Dist., Salt Lake City, 1982. Mem. Internat. Thespian Soc. (sponsor 1968—, internat. dir. 1982-84, trustee 1978-84), Utah Speech Arts Assn. (pres. 1976-78, 88—), NEA, Utah Edn. Assn., Granite Edn. Assn., Profl. Travel Agts. Assn., Utah High Sch. Activities Assn. (drama rep. 1972-76), AAUW (pres. 1972-74). Republican. Mormon. Avocations: reading; travel; dancing. Home: 685 S 1st E Box 36 Salem UT 84653 Office: Cottonwood High Sch 5715 S 1300 E Salt Lake City UT 84121

HAHN, ROGER, historian, educator; b. Paris, Jan. 5, 1932; came to U.S., 1941, naturalized, 1953; s. John P. and Thérèse E.L. (Lévy) H.; m. Ellen Isabel Leibovici, Sept. 11, 1955; children: Elisabeth L., Sophie A. B.A. magna cum laude, Harvard U., 1953, M.A. in Teaching, 1954; certificate, Ecole Pratique des Hautes Etudes, Paris, 1955; Ph.D., Cornell U., 1962. Instr. history U. Del., 1960-61; mem. history faculty U. Calif. at Berkeley, 1961—, prof., 1974—; spl. asst. to dir. sci. affairs Bancroft Library, Berkeley, 1972—; chief U.S. del. XVth Internat. Congress History of Sci., Edinburgh, 1977, co-chmn. XVIIth Internat. Congress, Berkeley, 1985; bd. dirs. Centre de Synthèse, Paris, 1976—; vis. prof. Collège de France, 1984. Author: L'Hydrodynamique au XVIIIè Siècle, 1965, Laplace as a Newtonian Scientist, 1967, The Anatomy of a Scientific Institution: The Paris Academy of Sciences 1666-1803, 1971, paperback edit., 1986; A Bibliography of Quantitative Studies on Science and Its History, 1980, Calendar of the Correspondence of Laplace, 1982; (with R. Taton) Ecoles Techniques et Militaires au XVIIIè Siècle, 1986; adv. editor: Isis, 1971-75, 18th-Century Studies, 1976-80; cons. editor: History of Sci, 1972—; editorial advisor: Social Studies of Science, 1974—. Served with AUS, 1955-57. Fulbright scholar, 1954-55, 83-84; NSF fellow, 1959-60, 64-65; Am. Council Learned Socs. fellow, 1973-74; decorated chevalier Ordre des Palmes Académiques, 1977; recipient book prize Pacific Coast br. Am. Hist. Assn., 1972. Fellow AAAS (council 1967-73); mem. History Sci. Soc. (council 1967-70, 77-80), Am. Soc. 18th Century Studies (pres. 1982-83), Western Soc. 18th Century Studies (pres. 1977-78), West Coast History of Sci. Soc. (pres. 1982-84), Acad. Internat. d'Histoire des Scis. Office: U Calif Dept History 3229 Dwinelle Berkeley CA 94720

HAHN, THOMAS MARTIN, sales supervisor; b. Pensacola, Fla., July 20, 1945; s. Walter Lewis and Grace E. Evelyn (Freese) H.; m. Lori Margrot Ross, Aug. 9, 1970; children: Scott Christopher, Kyle Gerrard. AA, Deanza Jr. Coll., Cupertino Coll., 1970; BA in History, Hayward Coll., 1972. Salesman Emporium, Mountain View, Calif., 1970-72, selling supr., 1972-73, dept. sales mgr., 1973-74; selling supr. Emporium-Capwell, Mountain View, Calif., 1974-88; asst. mgr. Wohl Shoe Co., Mountain View, 1988—. Served with USNR, 1965-69, Vietnam. Republican. Episcopalian. Home: 2831 El Vista Way San Jose CA 95148 Office: Wohl Shoe Co 701 E El Camino Rd Mountain View CA 95148

HAIG, DAVID MACKINNON, estate trustee, investment management specialist; b. New Rochelle, N.Y., May 20, 1951; s. Alexander Salusbury and Joan (Damon) H.; m. Myrna B. Murdoch, Oct. 1, 1982. Student, Marlboro Colll., 1974. bd. dirs. First Hawaiian Bank, Honolulu. Trustee Estate of S.M. Damon, Honolulu, 1982&; Trustee Hawaii Pacific Coll., Honolulu, 1988; bd. dirs. YMCA Met. Honolulu, 1985—, Hawaii Foodbank Inc., Honolulu, 1987, Molokai Mus. and Cultural Ctr., Hawaii, 1988, Oahu Country Club, Waialae Country Club, Rotary. Home and Office: Estate SM Damon 165 S King St Ste 1215 Honolulu HI 96813

HAIGHT, JAMES THERON, corporation executive, lawyer; b. Racine, Wis., Dec. 10, 1924; s. Walter Lyman and Geraldine (Foley) H.; m. Patricia Aloe, Apr. 26, 1952; children: Alberta, Barbara, Catherine, Dorothy, Elaine. Student, U. Nebr., 1943-44, U. Bordeaux, France, 1947; diplome d'Etudes, U. Paris, 1948; B.A., U. Wis., 1950, LL.B., 1951. Bar: D.C. 1952, U.S. Supreme Ct. 1955, Calif. 1968. Atty. Covington & Burling, Washington, 1951-56, Goodyear Tire & Rubber Co., Goodyear Internat. Corp., Akron, Ohio, 1956-61; gen. counsel, sec. George J. Meyer Mfg. Co., Milw., 1961-66; sr. v.p., sec., chief corp. counsel Thrifty Corp., Los Angeles, 1966—; Mem. adv. bd. Internat. and Comparative Law Center, Southwestern Legal Found. Contbr. articles to legal books and profl. jours.; Editor: Current Legal Aspects of Doing Business with Sino-Soviet Nations, 1973; mem. bd. editors: Internat. Lawyer, 1967-76. Served with C.E. AUS, 1943-46. Fellow Am. Bar Found. (life); mem. ABA (vice chmn. 1965-67, chmn. 1974-75, internat. law sect.), Calif. Bar Assn., Los Angeles County Bar Assn., Pasadena Bar Assn., Los Angeles Town Hall, Los Angeles World Affairs Council, Internat. Law Assn., Am. Soc. Corp. Secs., Order of Coif. Home: 1390 Ridge Way Pasadena CA 91106 Office: 3424 Wilshire Blvd Los Angeles CA 90010

HAIKEN, MARVIN BURTON, lawyer; b. N.Y.C., Feb. 3, 1932. s. Michael and Anne (Starobin) H.; m. Jean McEwen, Dec. 17, 1960 (div. 1980); children: Melanie, Elizabeth, Sally Anne, Claire; m. Sallie Harrison Weissinger, Jan. 16, 1982. AB, Columbia U., 1953, JD, 1955. Bar: N.Y. 1955, D.C. 1960, Calif. 1964. Trial atty. U.S. Dept. Justice, Washington, 1962-63; asst. U.S. atty. No. Dist. Calif., San Francisco, 1963-65; mem. firm Zang, Friedman, Haiken & Damir, McKenna & Fitting, San Francisco, 1965-74; atty.-editor Calif. Continuing Edn. of Bar, 1974-78; sole practice, Berkeley, Calif., 1974—; asst. dir. Calif. Ctr. Jud. Edn. and Rsch., Berkeley, 1978—; coord. New Trial Judges Orientation Programs, 1978—, Calif. Jud. Coll., 1982—; counsel On Lok Sr. Health Svcs., San Francisco, 1975-82, 1st Unitarian Ch., San Francisco, 1970-73; lectr. Sch. Law and Grad. Sch. Acctg., Golden Gate U., 1976-78. Editor: Basic Techniques of Public Contracts Practice, 1977; co-editor: Operating Problems of California Corporations, 1978; supervising editor: California Judges Benchguides-Municipal and Justice Courts, Vol. 1, II, 1980. Bd. dirs. San Francisco Neighborhood Legal Assistance Found., 1975-77. 1st lt. JAGC, U.S. Army, 1956-59. Mem. State Bar Calif., Berkeley-Albany Bar Assn. Democrat. Unitarian. Office: Calif Ctr Jud Edn & Rsch 2000 Powell St Ste 850 Emeryville CA 94608

HAILE, LAWRENCE BARCLAY, lawyer; b. Atlanta, Feb. 19, 1938; m. Ann Springer McCauley, March 28, 1984; children: Gretchen Vanderhoof, Eric McKenzie, Scott McAllister. B.A. in Econs, U. Tex., 1958, LL.B., 1961. Bar: Tex. 1961, Calif. 1962. Law clk. to U.S. Judge Joseph M. Ingraham, Houston, 1961-62; pvt. practice law San Francisco, 1962-67, L.A., 1967—; mem. firm Simon, Buckner & Haile, Marina Del Rey, Calif., 1984—; instr. U. Calif. at Los Angeles Civil Trial Clinics, 1974, 76; lectr. law Calif. Continuing Edn. of Bar, 1973-74, 80-88; mem. nat. panel arbitrators Am. Arbitration Assn., 1965—. Asso. editor: Tex. Law Rev, 1960-61; Contbr. articles profl. publs. Mem. State Bar Calif., Tex., U.S. Supreme Ct. Bar Assn., Internat. Assn. Property Ins. Counsel (founding mem., pres. 1980), Phi Delta Phi, Delta Sigma Rho. Club: Vintage Auto Racing Assn. (bd. dirs.). Office: 4551 Glencoe Ave #300 Marina Del Rey CA 90292

HAILE, MARCUS ALFRED, chemistry educator; b. Haviland, Kans., Oct. 14, 1930; s. William Oral and Myrna May (Stotts) H.; m. Lynne Helene Hunsucker, Mar. 20, 1964; children: Marta Helene, Cavan William. BS, Pepperdine U., 1955; Master, U. No. Iowa, 1968. Cert. secondary tchr., Calif. Tchr. chemistry Hamilton High Sch., Los Angeles, 1957-67; prof. chemistry Los Angeles City Coll., 1969—, also pres. acad. senate, 1972-73. Author: Experimental General Chemistry, 1973, 76, Gen. Analytical Chemistry, 1987; contbr. articles to profl. jours. Chmn. Amateur Athletic Union So. Calif. Swimming U.S. Swim, Los Angeles, Ventura and Santa Barbara Counties, Calif., 1980-81. Served with U.S. Army, 1950-52. NSF grantee, 1967-68. Mem. Am. Chem. Soc., Am. Fedn. Tchrs., Calif. Thoroughbred Breeders Assn. Democrat. Home: 22404 Kearny St Woodland Hills CA 91364 Office: Los Angeles City Coll 855 N Vermont Ave Los Angeles CA 90026

HAIMOVITZ, JULES, broadcasting company executive; b. Tel Aviv, Dec. 25, 1950; came to U.S., 1955; s. Louis and Josephine (Ratz) H.; m. Susan Lovett, July 3, 1974 (div. Jan. 1978); m. Elizabeth Webster, Apr. 9, 1982. BA in Math., Bklyn. Coll., 1971, MA in Math., 1974. Research analyst ABC TV Network, N.Y.C., 1971-75, mgr. statis. ops., 1975-76; dir. pay TV programming Viacom Internat., Inc., N.Y.C., 1976-77; sr. v.p. Showtime Entertainment, N.Y.C., 1976-81; v.p. Viacom Internat., Inc., N.Y.C., 1981-82; exec. v.p. Viacom Entertainment Group, N.Y.C., 1982-84, pres., 1984-86; pres. Viacom Networks Group, N.Y.C., 1986-87; pres., chief oper. officer Spelling Entertainment, Inc., L.A., 1988—. Office: Spelling Entertainment Inc 1041 N Formosa Ave West Hollywood CA 90046

HAINES, BEVERLEY BENEZET, activities and program director; b. Phila., Nov. 23, 1940; d. William Spence and Myrtle (Hewes) H. BA in Edn., Western Oreg. State Coll., 1972, MA in Counseling, 1976. Tchr. Sleighton Farm Sch., Darling, Pa., 1964-65; dir. phys. fitness Portland (Oreg.) Dept. Parks and Recreation, 1965-66; dir. recreation dept. Hillcrest Sch. Oreg., Salem, 1966-72; tchr., team dir. MacLaren Sch. Oreg., Woodburn, 1972-79; coop. work experience coord. Chemeketa Community Coll., Salem, 1979—. Pace setter United Way, Salem, 1986, campus coord., 1985, loaned exec., 1984, mem. allocations com., 1983. Mem. Work Experience Coords. Oreg. (pres. 1987-88, pres. elect 1986-87, sec. 1984-85, Outstanding Svc. award 1984), AAUW (chmn., bd. dirs. 1988--). Republican. Presbyterian. Home: 292 Hylo Rd SE Salem OR 97306 Office: Chemeketa Community Coll 4000 Lancaster Dr Salem OR 97309

HAIR, KITTIE ELLEN, secondary educator; b. Denver, June 12, 1948; d. William Edward and Jacqueline Jean (Holt) H. BA, Brigham Young U., 1971; MA in Social History, U. Nev., Las Vegas, 1987. cert. tchr., Nev. Health educator Peace Corps, Totota, Liberia, 1971-72; tchr. Clark County Sch. Dist., Las Vegas, Nev., 1972-77, 1979—; missionary Ch. Jesus Christ Latter-Day Saints, Alta., Can., 1977-79. Mem. NEA, Nat. Council for Social Scis., Clark County Tchr.'s Assn., ACLU, Phi Kappa Phi, Phi Alpha Theta. Democrat. Office: Eldorado High Sch 1139 Linn Ln Las Vegas NV 89110

HAISLEY, FAY BEVERLEY, academic dean; b. Sydney, Australia, Feb. 20, 1933; came to U.S., 1971; d. Reginald Charles and Edna Irene (Kidd) Sambrook; m. Ian George Haisley, May 11, 1963 (div. 1973). BA, U. Papua New Guinea, Port Moresby, 1970; MEd with honors, U. Oreg., 1971, PhD, 1973. Cert. elem. tchr., spl. edn., Oreg., New South Wales, Australia. Tchr., prin. Dept. Edn., Australia, 1952-70; prin., lectr. Dept. Edn., Port Moresby, Papua New Guinea, 1969-70; lectr. early childhood U. Calif., Santa Barbara, 1973-75; from asst. prof. to assoc. prof. learning disabilities and elem. edn. U. Oreg., Eugene, 1975-80, assoc. dean tchr. edn., 1981-84; dean Sch. of Edn. U. Pacific, Stockton, Calif., 1984—, dir. dean's grant, 1977-83; commr. Calif. Commn. on Tchr. Credentialling, 1985-87; dir. spl. project Am. Nepalese Edn. Found., Eugene, 1982-84; dir. doctoral dept. edn. program U. Guam, 1983-84; bd. dirs. Far West Ednl. Labs, 1986—. Contbr. articles to profl. jours. Trustee Stockton Civic Theatre, 1986-88. Grantee U.S. Office Edn., 1979-82, Nat. Inst. Edn., 1981, Oreg. State Dept. Edn., 1978. Mem. Am. Ednl. Research Assn., Assn. Tchr. Educators, Am. Assn. Colls. Tchr. Edn., Calif. Assn. Tchr. Educators (pres. 1988-89), Phi Delta Kappa, Phi Kappa Phi. Anglican. Office: U Pacific Sch Edn Pacific Ave Stockton CA 95211

HAKIN, DAVID LAWRENCE, mortgage company executive; b. Morgantown, W.Va., Aug. 1, 1929; s. John and Anna Mabel (Martin) H.; m. Mary Ann Megginson, Aug. 9, 1949; children: Dennis Kent, Evelyn Kay. Grad. high sch., Morgantown, W.Va. Enlisted USN, 1947, advanced through grades to lt. comdr., 1972, ret., 1975; owner, prin. Ramona (Calif.) Bldrs., 1975-77; mgr. Realty World-Shamrock, Poway, Calif., 1978-80; owner Hakin Ins. Agy., Eugene, Oreg., 1980-82; v.p. Gemini II, Albuquerque, 1982-83; broker PCA Mortgage Co., Albuquerque, 1982-87; pres., chief exec. officer Interstate Mortgage Co., Albuquerque, 1988—. Mem. U.S. Submarine Vets. Republican. Office: Interstate Mortgage Funding 5801 Osuna Rd Ste #209 Albuquerque NM 87109

HAKKILA, EERO ARNOLD, nuclear safeguards technology chemist; b. Canterbury, Conn., Aug. 4, 1931; s. Jack and Ida Maria (Lillquist) H.; m. Margaret W. Hakkila; children: Jon Eric, Mark Douglas, Gregg Arnold. BS in Chemistry, Cen. Conn. State U., 1953; PhD in Analytical Chemistry, Ohio State U., 1957. Staff mem. Los Alamos (N.Mex.) Nat. Lab., 1957-78, assoc. group leader safeguard systems, 1978-80, dep. group leader, 1980-82, group leader, 1982-83, project mgr. internat. safeguards, 1983-87, project coordinator, 1987—. Editor: Nuclear Safeguards Analysis, 1978; contbr. numerous articles to profl. jours. Fellow Am. Inst. Chemists; mem. N.Mex. Inst. Chemists (pres. 1971-73), Am. Chem. Soc., Am. Nuclear Soc. (exec. com. fuel cycle and waste mgmt. div. 1984-86), Inst. Nuclear Materials Mgmt. Office: Los Alamos Nat Lab PO Box 1663 Los Alamos NM 87545

HAKODA, HARVEY NOBUO, lawyer, real estate broker; b. Kona, Hawaii, Nov. 8, 1943; s. Konao and Doris Harumi (Mori) H. BA, U. Hawaii, 1965; MS, U. So. Calif., 1973; JD, U. San Francisco, 1980. Bar: Hawaii 1980, U.S. Dist. Ct. Hawaii, 1980, U.S. Ct. Appeals (9th cir.) 1982. Pres. Spaces, Ltd., Honolulu, 1972-76, house counsel, 1983—; sole practice Honolulu, 1980-81; lawyer Office of Pub. Defender, Kona, 1981-82; bd. dirs. Spaces Ltd., Honolulu, 2Y Hawaii, Inc., Honolulu, Space Travel, Inc., Honolulu. Capt. USAF, 1966-72. Mem. ABA, Phi Delta Phi. Buddhist. Office: 1522 Makaloa St Ste 206 Honolulu HI 96814

HAKOMORI, SEN-ITIROH, immunochemist, biochemist, researcher, educator; b. Sendai, Japan, Feb. 13, 1929; came to U.S., 1963, naturalized, 1978; s. Shinichiro and Kiku (Amae) H.; m. Mitsuko Ito, June 16, 1956; children—Yoichiro, Kenjiro, Naoko. M.D., Tohoku U., Sendai, 1952, D. Med. Sci., Inst. Biochemistry, 1957. Intern, Sendai City Hosp., Japan, 1952-53, asst. prof. Tohoku U., 1957-59, prof. Coll. Pharmacy, 1959-63; research assoc. Med. Sch., Harvard U., Boston, 1963-66; vis. prof. Brandeis U., Waltham, Mass., 1966-68; assoc. prof., then prof. U. Wash., Seattle, 1968-75; program head, prof. pathobiology and microbiology F. Hutchinson Cancer Ctr. and U. Wash., Seattle, 1975-86; scientific dir. The Biomembrane Inst., Seattle, 1986—; mem. study sect. NIH, Bethesda, Md., 1975-78, mem. adv. com., 1984. Author: Sphingolipid Biochemistry, 1983; contbr. numerous articles to profl. publs. Recipient Philip Levin award Am. Soc. Clin. Pathology, 1984, Outstanding Investigator Nat. Cancer Inst., 1986. Mem. Am. Soc. Biol. Chemists, Am. Assn. Cancer Research, Am. Soc. Immunology.r Research, Am. Soc. Immunology. Office: The Biomembrane Inst 201 Elliott Ave W Seattle WA 98119

HALBE, SHERRILL BALDWIN, interior designer; b. Hot Springs, S.D., Aug. 25, 1941; d. Clarence James and Margaret Marie (Arbuckle) Baldwin; m. Raymond Gordon Rector, Nov. 20, 1958 (div. 1976); children: Kelli Rae, Michelle Rector Davis, Garric Paul; m. Stephen Augustus Halbe, Apr. 22, 1978; stepdau., Denise Marie. BS, Mont. State U., 1967; MA, San Francisco State U., 1987. Tchr. spl. edn. Napa County (Calif.) Supt. Schs., 1968-70; tchr. mid. sch. St. Helena (Calif.) Unified Sch. Dist., 1970-78; restaurateur Girdle Mountain Summer House Restaurant, Belt, Mont., 1975-88; pvt. practice as studio oil painter Novato, Calif., 1979-82; student asst. San Francisco State U., 1987; prin., interior designer Sherrill Baldwin Halbe Interior Design, San Francisco, 1983—. Active Sunset-Parkside Edn. Action Com., San Francisco, 1987-89; San Francisco Mus. Modern Art, 1986-89. Recipient Best of Show award Terra Linda Art Assn., 1982. Mem. Am. Soc. Interior Designers, Inst. Bus. Designers (student), San Francisco Substitute Tchr. Orgn., Commonwealth Club Calif., Phi Delta Kappa, Pi Lamda Theta. Democrat. Home and Office: 1202 23 Ave San Francisco CA 94122

HALBERT, SHERRILL, retired federal judge; b. Terra Bella, Calif., Oct. 17, 1901; s. Edward Duffield and Ellen (Rhodes) H.; m. Verna Irene Dyer, June 7, 1927; children—Shirley Ellen (Mrs. Stanley J. Eager), Douglas James. A.B., U. Calif. at Berkeley, 1924, J.D., 1927; LL.D., McGeorge Coll. Law, 1962. Bar: Calif. bar 1927. Practiced in Porterville, 1927-41, San Francisco, 1942-44; pvt. practice Modesto, 1944-49; dist. atty. Stanislaus County, 1949; judge Superior Ct. of Calif., 1949-54; judge U.S. Dist. Ct. (ea. dist.) Calif., Sacramento, 1954-89, ret. sr. judge; Chmn. bd. advisers McGeorge Sch. Law, Sacramento. Contbg. author: Lincoln for the Ages, 1960, Lincoln: A Contemporary Portrait, 1962. Mem. Am. Camellia Soc. (pres. emeritus), Native Sons of Golden West, Nat. Pony Express Centennial Assn. (pres.), Selden Soc., Calif. Hist. Soc., Alpha Chi Rho, Phi Delta Phi. Clubs: Lion (Sacramento) (hon.), Ambassador's (Sacramento); Book of Calif. (San Francisco), Commonwealth (San Francisco). Office: US Dist Ct US Courthouse 650 Capitol Mall Sacramento CA 95814

HALE, CARL DENNIS, electronics company executive; b. Oakland, Calif., July 12, 1949; s. William Francis and Irene Helegard (Knoth) H.; children: Telissa, Desiree, Michael. BS, San Jose State U., 1974; mfg. studies program, Gen. Electric Co., San Jose, 1976. Prodn. planner Gen. Electric, San Jose, Calif., 1974-77; mfg. engr. Gen. Electric, Paterson, N.J., 1977-78; advisor, prodn. mgr. Gen. Electric Co., San Jose, 1978-79; materials mgr. Spectra Physics, Mountain View, Calif., 1979-81; factory parts mgr. Hewlett-Packard, Mountain View, 1981-82; materials mgr. Hewlett-Packard, Santa Clara, 1982-88; mgr. prodn. sect. Hewlett-Packard, San Jose, 1986—, materials mgr. rsch. and devel., 1988—; part time instr. San Jose State U., 1985—. Author: (manuals) Material Requirements Planning, 1981, Conceptual Manufacturing, 1983, How to Professionally Qualify Suppliers, Apics International Conference, 1987. Mem. Am. Prodn. and Inventory Control Soc. (cert. prodn. and inventory mgmt.). Republican. Roman Catholic. Club: Schobers. Office: Hewlett-Packard 370 W Trimble Rd San Jose CA 95131

HALE, DAVID CLARENCE, electronics manufacturing executive; b. Danville, Vt., Aug. 28, 1940; s. Clarence H. and Louise (Houston) H.; m. Darla C. Jones, Mar. 9, 1962; children: Ramona, Morgan. BA, U. Tex., 1968. Indsl. engr. Merck, Sharp & Dohme, West Point, Pa., 1970-74; cons. Sci. Mgmt. Corp., Moorestown, N.J., 1974-78, Delta Mgmt. Systems, Metairie, La., 1978-79; mfg. cons. Coopers & Lybrand, Atlanta, 1979-83; sr. dir. materials and distbn. Racal-Milgo, Ft. Lauderdale, Fla., 1983-88; v.p. ops. Republica Telecom Systems Corp., Boulder, Colo., 1988—; speaker in field, U.S. and Europe. With USN, 1959-62. Mem. Am. Prodn. and Inventory Control Soc. Republican. Home: 1224 Twin Peaks Circle Longmont CO 80501 Office: Republic Telecom Systems 6150 Lookout Rd Boulder CO 80301

HALE, DAVID FREDRICK, health care company executive; b. Gadsden, Ala., Jan. 8, 1949; s. Millard and Mildred Earline (McElroy) H.; BA, Jacksonville State U.; m. Linda Carol Sadorski, Mar. 14, 1975; children: Shane Michael, Tara Renee, Erin Nicole, David Garrett. Dir. product mgmt. Ortho Pharm. Corp. div. Johnson & Johnson, Raritan, N.J., 1978-80; v.p. mktg. BBL Microbiology Systems div. Becton Dickinson & Co., Cockeysville, Md., 1980-81, v.p., gen. mgr., 1981-82; sr. v.p. mktg. and bus. devel. Hybritech, Inc., San Diego, 1982, pres., 1983-86, chief executive officer, 1986-87; pres., chief exec. officer Gensia Pharmaceuticals, Inc., San Diego, 1987—; bd. dirs. Gen-Probe, Inc., Immunetech Pharmaceuticals, Viagene, Inc., Access Medical Systems, Inc. Bd. dirs. San Diego Econ. Devel. Corp., So/Cal/Ten; founding sponsor CONNECT. Mem. Biomed. Mktg. Assn., Young Pres.'s Orgn. Republican. Episcopalian. Home: 18778 Olmeda Pl San Diego CA 92128 Office: Gensia Pharms Inc 11075 Roselle St San Diego CA 92121

HALE, DEAN EDWARD, social services administrator; b. Balt., Aug. 4, 1950; s. James Russell and Marjorie Elinor (Hoerman) H.; BASW, U. Pa., 1975; postgrad. U. Oreg., 1976, U. London, 1974, U. Mont., 1968-71; m. Lucinda Hoyt Muniz, 1979. Dir. recreation Hoffman Homes for Children, Gettysburg, Pa., 1970; social worker Holt Adoption Program, Inc., Eugene, Oreg., 1975-78; supr. social svcs. Holt Internat. Children's Svcs., Eugene, 1978-84, Asia rep., 1984—; guest lectr. U. Oreg.; cons. internat. child welfare, 1982—; co-founder Family Opportunities Unltd. Inc., 1981—. Author: Adoption, A Family Affair, 1981, When Your Child Comes Home, 1986. Pres. Woodtique Heights Homeowners Assn., 1980-82, Our Saviour's Luth. Ch., 1981-85; bd. dirs. Greenpeace of Oreg., 1979-84; cons., campaign worker Defazio for Congress 1988, 1987-88. Named Outstanding New Jaycee, Gettysburg Jaycees, 1971. Mem. Nat. Assn. Social Workers (bd. dirs. 1978-80, sec. 1979-80), Nat. Assn. Christian Social Workers. Home: 931 Taylor St Eugene OR 97402 Office: PO Box 2880 1195 City View St Eugene OR 97402

HALE, IRVING, investment executive, writer; b. Denver, Mar. 22, 1932; s. Irving Jr. and Lucile (Beggs) H.; B.A. with distinction, U. Colo., 1964; m. Joan E. Domenico, Dec. 29, 1954; children—Pamela Joan, Beth Ellen. Security analyst Colo. Nat. Bank, Denver, 1955-58; asst. sec. Centennial Fund, Inc., Second Centennial Fund, Inc., Gryphon Fund, Inc., Meridian Fund, Inc., 1959-68; portfolio mgr. Twenty Five Fund, Inc. (formerly Trend Fund, Inc.), Denver, 1969-72; v.p. Alpine Corp., Denver, 1971-72; dir. research Hanifen, Imhoff & Samford, Inc., Denver, 1973-77; v.p. research First Fin. Securities, Inc., 1977-82; arbitrator Nat. Assn. Securities Dealers; contbg. editor Nat. OTC Stock Jour., 1982-83; exec. v.p. research/corp. Fin. R. B. Marich, Inc., 1983—. lectr., Denver Public Schs. Community Talent, 1975—; bd. dirs. Community Resources, Inc., 1981-88, v.p. 1988—. Fellow Fin. Analysts Fedn.; mem. Denver Soc. Security Analysts, Radio Hist. Assn. Colo. (pres. 1977-78), Nat. Assn. of Securities Dealers (abitrator), Mensa, Baker St. Irregulars, Beta Sigma Tau. Republican. Episcopalian. Club: Denver Press (assoc. mem.). Columnist, Denver Post; contbr. articles to profl. jours. Home: 1642 Ivanhoe St Denver CO 80220 Office: RB Marich Inc 1512 Larimer St Ste 800 Denver CO 80202

HALE, VERNON STEVEN, avionics and computer systems engineer; b. Selma, Ala., Dec. 18, 1961; s. Vernon Levon and Dorothy Ann (Johnson)

H. BS in Elec. Engring., U. Tex., El Paso, 1985. Computer data enterer Interfirst Bank El Paso, 1981, with computer ops. and mgmt. dept., 1983-84; with mktg. sales support dept. IBM, El Paso, 1982; computer systems and programmer researcher Analysis Maintenance Co., El Paso, 1985; avionics computer engr., mfg. design engr. Lockheed Aero. Systems Co., Burbank, Calif., 1985--. Stevens scholar, 1980-84. Mem. IEEE, Lockheed Mgmt. Assn., Tau Beta Pi, Eta Kappa Nu. Office: Lockheed Aero Systems Dept 7082 Plant A1 Bldg 652 PO Box 551 Burbank CA 91520

HALE, WILLIAM BRYAN, JR., newspaper editor; b. Stephenville, Tex., Apr. 26, 1933; s. William Bryan and Gladys (Tittle) H.; divorced; children: Shandra Hale Reiss, Tamara Hale Cameron, Nicholas, Sabrina. Grad. high sch., Stephenville. Police beat/courts reporter Santa Monica (Calif.) Outlook, 1953-58; gen. reporter Ontario (Calif.) Daily Report, 1958-59; criminal court writer L.A. City News Service, 1959-60; gen. reporter L.A. Times, 1960-61; reporter Houston Chronicle, 1961-62; news editor Somerset (Pa.) American, 1962-63; night city editor Elmira (N.Y.) Star-Gazette, 1963-64; copy editor, investigative reporter Milw. Jour., 1964-70; Tucson corr. Time mag., 1970-71; night city editor Tucson Citizen, 1970-71; sr. lectr. U. So. Calif., 1974-88; nat. desk copy editor Los Angeles Times, 1971—; pres. Nat. Copy Editors Sch., Thousand Oaks, Calif., 1984—. Cpl. USMC, 1951-53. Home: 2219 Thousand Oaks Blvd Ste 371 Thousand Oaks CA 91362 Office: LA Times Nat Desk Times-Mirror Sq Los Angeles CA 90053

HALEY, FREDERICK THOMAS, confectionery manufacturing company executive; b. Tacoma, June 29, 1912; s. Jonathan Clifford and Margaret Mae (Hamilton) H.; m. Dorothy Jean Geyer, June 28, 1946; children: Susan Marie Haley Headley, Mark Tyler, Evan Woodruff, Marian Mae. BA, Dartmouth Coll., 1935; postgrad., U. Wash.; PhD (hon.), U. Puget Sound, 1970, Prometheus Coll., 1977. Sales mgr. Brown & Haley, Tacoma, 1946-52, gen. mgr., 1952-54, pres., gen. mgr., 1954-84, chmn. bd., chief exec. officer, 1984—; pres. Pacific States Radio Corp., 1954-57. Trustee Saul Haas Found., Pacific Sci. Ctr., Seattle; mem. adv. bd. Citizens Edn. Ctr. N.W., N.W. Sch., Seattle; bd. dirs. Apogee Inst.; mem. vis. com. dept. history U. Wash.; mem. nat. task on higher edn and pub interest Coun. for Advancement and Support Edn.; former founding chmn. bd. Prometheus Coll.; past trustee Linfield Coll., Seattle Symphony, N.W. Grand Opera Assn.; past mem. met. bd. Tacoma-Pierce County YMCA; formerly active numerous other orgns. Lt. USNR, 1941-46, PTO. Recipient William O. Douglas award Wash. chpt. ACLU, 1985; John Hay fellow, 1963. Mem. Tacoma Yacht Club, Harbor Club (Seattle), Rainier Club (Seattle). Unitarian. Office: Brown & Haley PO Box 1596 Tacoma WA 98401

HALEY, JOHN DAVID, petroleum consulting executive; b. Denver, Mar. 16, 1924; s. Peter Daniel and Margaret Dorothy (O'Haire) H.; m. Annie Loretta Breeden, June 20, 1951; children—Laura, Patricia, Brian, Sharon, Norine, Kathleen. Profl. engr. Colo. Sch. Mines, 1948. Registered profl. engr., Colo., Okla. Petroleum engr. Creole Petroleum, Venezuela, 1948-50, Texaco Corp., 1950-52; staff engr. Carter Oil (Exxon), Tulsa, 1954-56; petroleum cons. Earlougher Engring., Tulsa, 1956-61, resident mgr., Denver, 1961-62; v.p. prodn. Anschutz Corp., Denver, 1962-86; v.p. Circle A Drilling, Denver, 1967-78; dir. Circle A Mud, Denver, 1983-86; pres. Greylock Pipeline, Denver, 1983-86, Anschutz Pipeline, Denver, 1984-86; pres. Haley Engring. Inc., 1987—; bd. dirs. Future Devel., 1985—, Polar Bear, 1986—; mem. adv. bd. Paratine Tech., 1988; mem. pres.'s council Colo. Sch. Mines, 1985—. Rep. committeeman, Littleton. Lt. comdr. USNR, 1943-46, 52-54. Mem. Soc. Petroleum Engrs. (dir. Denver chpt.), Soc. Petroleum Evaluation Engrs., Ind. Petroleum Assn. Am., Ind. Petroleum Assn. Mountain States, Am. Petroleum Inst. (citation for service), Internat. Assn. Drilling Contractors, Soc. Profl. Well Log Analysts. Petroleum Club (Denver chpt.). Roman Catholic. Home: 561 E Caley Dr Littleton CO 80121

HALEY, LINDA FAY, resort manager, accountant; b. Spokane, Wash., Feb. 11, 1951; d. Delwyn Glenn and Sara Betty (Garske) Biddle; m. Joseph Brennan Haley, Sept. 5, 1974; children: Jolin Erin, Joseph Glenn. BA in Speech Pathology, Wash. State U., Pullman, 1973; MBA in Acctg., Ea. Wash. U., 1976. Speech therapist Sch. Dist. 181, Deer Park, Wash., 1973-75; teaching fellow Ea. Wash. State U., Cheney, 1975-76; acct. Kaiser Aluminum & Chem. Corp., Spokane, 1977-82; mgr. Granite Point Park Corp., Loon Lake, Wash., 1982—, v.p., 1984—; tax acct. Loon Lake Sewer Dist., 1982—. Chmn. Dist. #183 Sch. Bd., 1989—. Office: Granite Point Park Corp Granite Point Park Rd Loon Lake WA 99148

HALEY, ROSEMARY ELIZABETH, corporate executive; b. N.Y.C., June 25, 1926; d. James Alfred and Rosalie (Graham) Hayes; children: Michael, Mark, Meg, Myles. BS in Nursing and Edn., Manhattanville Coll., 1948. RN. Newscaster Sta. WABC-TV, N.Y.C., 1960-62; host. Sta. WCAU-TV, Phila., 1962-66; producer, host Sta. KMVT-TV, Twin Falls, Idaho, 1968-76; owner, mgr. Haley Livestock, Rupert, Idaho, 1970-85; pres., mgr. Acequia Inc., Rupert, 1983—. Editorial columnist: Times News, 1966-70, Inter-Mountain Observer. Founder Grasshopper Task Force, Rupert, 1985; mem. com. Idaho Bruise Com., 1968-70; lectr. Nat. Air Pollution Control Assn., Washington, 1963; hon. Christmas Seal chmn. Am. Lung Assn., Boise, 1970; bd. dirs. N.Y. State Air Pollution Bd., Albany, 1962, Moritz Community Hosp., Sun Valley, Idaho, 1982-85. Mem. Am. Women in Radio-TV, Am. Sugar Assn. (spokesperson), Am. Assn. Agri-Women, Am. Farm Bur., Idaho Wheat Growers Assn., Ethanol Fuel Assn. (bd. dirs.). Home: PO Drawer 226 Sun Valley ID 83353 Office: Acequia Inc PO Drawer C Rupert ID 83350

HALEY, TENISON, college administrator. Student, Calif. Poly. State U., San Luis Obispo, 1948-50, U. Colo., 1951-52; BS, Washington U., St. Louis, 1954; MEd, U. Oreg., 1958, DEd in Higher Edn. and Counseling Psychology, 1963. Lic. psychologist, Oreg.; cert. marriage and family therapist, Oreg. Tchr., counselor, dir. guidance services The Dalles (Oreg.) Pub. Schs., 1955-61; counseling psychologist, asst. prof. Oreg. State U., Corvallis, 1963-64; assoc. prof., dir. counseling and testing Cen. Oreg. Community Coll., Bend, 1964-67; assoc. prof., dean of student services Southwestern Oreg. Community Coll., Coos Bay, 1967-71; mem. faculty dept. psychology Rogue Community Coll., Grants Pass, Oreg., 1971-75, dean of student services, 1971-88, dean of students and community svcs., 1988—; coll. evaluator Northwest Assn. Schs. and Colls. Regional Accreditation Assn., 1978—; chmn. student personnel services adv. com., Oreg. Dept. Edn., 1976-78; mem. Community Coll. Commn. for at Risk Youth Oreg. Dept. Edn., Oreg. Am. Coll. Testing Council, 1982-83, ann. conf. Oreg. Community Coll. Student Personnel Services, 1973; mem. regional adv. bd. So. Oreg. State Coll., 1976—; practicum dir. CAUSE II tng. program paraprofl. counselors, Oreg. State U., 1965; sec., treas. N.W. Assn. Community and Tech. Colls., 1987—; cons. Am. Assn. Community and Jr. Colls., 1969-73, State Oreg. Vocat. Rehab. div., 1970-71, Nat. Alliance Businessmen, Josephine County, Oreg., 1972-73; ednl. tour organizer to People's Republic China, 1984, 86; mem. ednl. tours Japan, 1984, 86, Mex., Cuba, 1960; bd. dirs. Am. Coll. Testing Program, 1984—; mem. Oreg. dept. edn. Community Coll. Commn. for at Risk Youth, 1987—. Contbr. articles to profl. bulls., jours., revs. Exec. dir. Rogue Community jColl. Found., 1986—; bd. dirs. Rogue Valley Council Govts. Area Agy. on Aging. Adv. Council, 1982-88, chmn., 1984-86; bd. dirs. Josephine County Council on Alcoholism, 1977-85, pres., 1980-82; bd. dirs. Josephine County Council on Drug Abuse, 1973-75; mem. gov.'s adv. com. on Vocat. Rehab., Oreg., 1967-68; mem. State Oreg. Selective Service System Appeals Bd., 1972-74; vol. dir. staff tng. and devel. Southwestern Oreg. Community Action Com., Coos Bay, 1967-70; chmn. bd. dirs. Northwest Social Systems, Inc., Seattle, 1970-71; mem. mental health adv. bds. various programs, Josephine, Coos and Deschutes counties, 1965-75; active in Boy Scouts Am., 1955-82; bd. dirs. Josephine Coun. on Alcohol and Drug Abuse, 1985—; mem. Josephine County Adv. Coun., Retired Sr. Vol. Program, 1988—. Served as sgt. USAF, 1951-54. Recipient Bold Journey award, 1959. Mem. NEA (life), Nat. Assn. Student Personnel Adminstrs., Nat. Vocat. Guidance Assn. (cert. profl.), Am. Coll. Personnel Assn. (life), Am. Assn. Counseling and Devel. of Am. Personnel and Guidance Assn. (life, sen. 1973-76, chmn. western region br. assembly 1970-71), Am. Psychol. Assn. (Counseling Psychology div.), Am. Assn. Marriage and Family Therapy (clin.), Am. Coll. Personnel Assn. (commr. student devel. in 2-yr. colls. 1967-70, commr. counseling 1971-74), Northwest Coll. Personnel Assn., Oreg. Personnel and Guidance Assn. (life, cert. sch. counselor, pres. 1970-71), Oreg. Psychol. Assn., Oreg. Assn. Marriage and Family Therapy, Oreg. Council Student Services Adminstrs. (chmn. 1986-87), Phi Delta Kappa (life, pres. So. Oreg. region chpt. 1974-75), Oreg. Community Coll. Deans of Students Consortium (chmn. The Displaced Worker 1982-83), N.W. Assn. Community and Tech. Colls. (sec./treas. 1987—), Alpha Phi Omega. Office: Rogue Community Coll 3345 Redwood Hwy Grants Pass OR 97527

HALFANT, GARY D., small business owner; b. Washington, Aug. 1, 1953; s. Manny and Jean Frances (Eddinger) H.; m. Gwyn Reneé Jones, Dec. 24, 1987; 1 child, Garic David. Grad. high sch., Sacramento. Pres. G's Herbs, Sacramento, 1974-78, G's Herbs Internat., Ltd., Portland, Oreg., 1978—. Office: G's Herbs Internat Ltd 2344 NW 21st Pl Portland OR 97210

HALFPENNY, JAMES C., scientist, educator; b. Shreveport, La., Jan. 23, 1947; s. Donald Frazier and Dorothy (Carson) H. BS, U. Wyo., 1969, MS, 1970; PhD, U. Colo., 1980. Various positions govt. conservation agys., parks and univ. conservation programs, 1966-80; coord. long-term ecol. rsch. program U. Colo., Boulder, 1980—; rsch. assoc. Inst. Arctic and Alpine Rsch., U. Colo., 1980-87, fellow, 1987—; instr. Teton Sci. Sch., Kelly, Wyo., 1980—, Aspen (Colo.) Ctr. for Environ. Studies, 1984-88, Yellowstone (Wyo.) Inst., 1984—, Rocky Mountain Nature Assn., 1987; pres. A Naturalist's World, Boulder, 1985—; staff trainer Colo. Div. Wildlife, Sterling, 1979, 83, sci. advisor 1982-85; staff trainer Yellowstone Nat. Park, 1985-86, 88; grant proposal rev. bd. NSF, 1984—, Nat. Geog. Sci., 1984—; trustee Thorne Ecol. Inst., Boulder, 1982-84; mem. Indian Peaks Wilderness Area Adv. Panel, Boulder, 1982-86, others; speaker mammal tracking, Alpine and winter ecology, Republic of China's endangered wildlife. Author: A Field Guide to Mammal Tracking, 1986; editor (booklets) Mountain Research Sta.; its environment and research, 1982, Long Term Ecol. Research in the U.S.: a network of research sites, 1982, 83, 84; contbr. articles to profl. jours. Mem. Sci. Adv. Panel to EOP Program U. Colo., 1982-84, Sci. Coun. Greater Yellowstone Coalition; bd. advisors Teton Sci. Sch., Moran, 1985—; bd. dirs. Nat. Outdoor Leadership Sch., Lander, Wyo., 1975-80, chmn. 1978-79. With USNR, 1969-71, Vietnam. Decorated Navy Achievement medal with combat "v", Vietnamese Gallantry Cross with palm (Republic Vietnam); recipient Roosevelt Meml. grant Am. Mus. Natural History, 1979, Walker Van Riper grant U.Colo., 1979, Kathy Lichty Fund grant U. Colo., 1979. Mem. Am. Inst. Biol. Scis., AAAS, Am. Soc. Mammalogists, Internat. Soc. Cryptozoology, Southwestern Assn. Naturalists, N.W. Sci. Assn., Colo.-Wyo. Acad. Sci., Orgn. Biol. Field Stas., Sci. Council Greater Yellowstone Coalition, Sigma Xi. Office: U Colo Inst Arctic/Alpine Rsch PO Box 450 Boulder CO 80309

HALKER, WILLIAM HENRY, JR., lawyer, educator; b. Hollywood, Calif., Mar. 13, 1940; s. William Henry and Dorothy Irene (Melcher) H.; m. Veryla Lee Hewitt Henry, Dec. 21, 1963 (div. 1974); 1 child, William Henry IV; m. Muriel Helen Zetter, Mar. 21, 1975; 1 child, Liberty L. Zetter-Halker. BGS, U. Nebr., 1971; JD, U. Pacific, 1983. Bar: Md. 1984, Calif. 1986, U.S. Dist. Ct. (ea. dist.) Calif. 1986. Enlisted man U.S. Army, 1960, advanced through grades to lt. col., 1980; assigned to U.S., Japan, Vietnam, 1960-80; ret. 1980; owner, founder Will Pass Bar Rev. Program, Sacramento, 1985--, Halker Law Offices, Sacramento, 1987--; prof. law, dean U. No. Calif., Sacramento, 1986-87. Decorated Meritorious Svc. medal with two oak leaf clusters; Vietnam Cross of Gallantry with palm. Mem. Calif. Bar, Md. Bar Assn., Sacramento County Bar Assn. (exec. com. small practice sect. 1987--). Presbyterian. Office: 3311-A Julliard Dr Sacramento CA 95826

HALL, ADRIENNE ANN, advertising agency executive; b. Los Angeles; d. Arthur E. and Adelina P. Kosches; m. Maurice Hall; children: Adam, Todd, Stefanie, Victoria. B.A., UCLA. Founding ptnr. Hall & Levine Advt., L.A., 1960-80; vice chmn. bd. Eisaman, Johns & Laws Advt. Inc., L.A., Houston, Chgo., N.Y.C., 1980—; dir. Calif. Mfrs. Assn. Svc. Corp., Inc.; chmn. Eric Bovy Inc., 1986—. Trustee UCLA; bd. regents Loyola-Marymount U., Los Angeles; mem. Blue Ribbon of Music Ctr., Pres. Circle, Los Angeles County Mus. Art, Calif. Gov.'s Commn. on Econ. Devel.; bd. dirs. Wonder Women Found., N.Y.C.; mem. adv. council Girl's Clubs Am., Girl Scouts U.S.; mem. adv. bd. Asian Pacific Women's Network, fashion group Downtown Women's Ctr. and Residence, Leadership Am., Washington; mem. exec. bd. Greater Los Angeles Partnership for Homeless, Los Angeles Shelter Partnership Bd.; mem. Nat. Network for Hispanic Women. Recipient Nat. Headliner award Women in Communications, 1982; recipient Profl. Achievement award UCLA Alumni, 1979; named Woman of Yr. Am Advt. Fedn., 1973, Ad Person of the West award Mktg. and Media Decisions, 1982; Bus. Woman of Yr. award Boy Scouts Am., 1983; Women Helping Women award Soroptimist Internat., 1984; Bullock's 1st ann. portfolio award for exec. women, 1985; Communicator of yr. award Ad Women, 1986; Leader award YWCA, 1986; named One of 20 Top Corp. Women, Savvy mag., 1983. Mem. Internat. Women's Forum (bd. dirs., Woman Who Made a Difference award 1987), Am. Assn. Advt. Agys. (bd. dirs., chmn. bd. govs. western region), Western States Advt. Agys. Assn. (pres.), Hollywood Radio and TV Soc. (dir.), Nat. Advt. Rev. Bd., Overseas Edn. Fund, Com. 200 (western chmn.), Women in Communications, Orgn. Women Execs., Calif. Women's Forum (founder, chmn. The Trusteeship), L.A. Area C. of C. (bd. dirs. 1987—), Rotary (L.A. chpt.), Internat. Bus. Fellows (mem. adv. bd.), Women's Econ. Alliance. Clubs: Calif. Yacht; Stock Exchange, Los Angeles Advt. (pres.) (Los Angeles). Lodge: Rotary. Office: Eisaman Johns & Laws Advt 6255 Sunset Blvd Los Angeles CA 90210

HALL, BLAINE HILL, librarian; b. Wellsville, Utah, Dec. 12, 1932; s. James Owen and Agnes Effie (Hill) H.; married, 1959; children: Suzanne, Cheryl, Derek. BS, Brigham Young U., 1960, MA, 1965, MLS, 1971. Instr. English, Brigham Young U., Provo, Utah, 1963-72, humanities librarian, 1972—; book reviewer Library and Info. Sci. Ann., 1984—. Author: Collection Assessment Manual, 1985, Saul Bellow Bibliography, 1987; editor Utah Libraries, 1972-77 (periodical award ALA 1977); contbr. articles to profl. jours. Bd. dirs. Orem (Utah) Pub. Library, 1977-84; mem. Orem Media Rev. Commn., 1984-86; chmn. Utah Adv. Commn. on Libraries. With U.S. Army, Korea. Mem. ALA (coun. 1988—), Utah Library Assn. (pres. 1980-81, Disting. Svc. award 1989), Mountain Plains Library Assn. (bd. dirs. 1978-83, editor newsletter 1978-83, grantee 1979, 80), Phi Kappa Phi. Mormon. Home: 230 East 1910 South Orem UT 84058 Office: Brigham Young U Provo UT 84602

HALL, BOBBY GENE, insurance executive; b. Corinth, Miss., May 17, 1933; s. Harvey and Lillie Belle (Laster) H.; m. Farrel Jean Suiter, Feb. 9, 1959; children: Gregory, Keith, Robin. B Gen. Scis., Chaminade Coll., 1973; MBA, Golden Gate U., 1980. Enlisted USAF, 1954, advanced through grades to sr. master sgt., 1974, ret., 1976; agt. State Farm Ins. Co., Sacramento, 1976-80; agy. mgr. State Farm Ins. Co., Dublin, Calif., 1980—. Republican. Baptist. Home: 5074 Blackhawk Dr Danville CA 94526

HALL, CYNTHIA HOLCOMB, judge; b. Los Angeles, Feb. 19, 1929; d. Harold Romeyn and Mildred Gould (Kuck) Holcomb; m. John Harris Hall, June 6, 1970 (dec. Oct. 1980); 1 child, Harris Holcomb; 1 child by previous marriage, Desma Letitia. A.B., Stanford U., 1951, J.D., 1954; LL.M., NYU, 1960. Bar: Ariz. 1954, Calif. 1956. Law clk. to judge U.S. Ct. Appeals 9th Circuit, 1954-55; trial atty. tax div. Dept. Justice, 1960-64; atty.-adviser Office Tax Legis. Counsel, Treasury Dept., 1964-66; mem. firm Brawerman & Holcomb, Beverly Hills, Calif., 1966-72; judge U.S. Tax Ct., Washington, 1972-81, U.S. Dist. Ct. for central dist. Calif., Los Angeles, 1981-84; U.S. circuit judge 9th Circuit, Pasadena, Calif., 1984—. Served to lt. (j.g.) USNR, 1951-53. Office: US Ct of Appeals 125 S Grand PO Box 91510 Pasadena CA 91109-1510

HALL, CYRUS BACH, systems analyst; b. Chadron, Nebr., Dec. 30, 1944; s. Cyrus Boothby and Edith (Bach) H.; m. Mary Ann Hodgson, Aug. 21, 1980; children: Jamie Kathryn, Cyrus Bach II. BA, U. Nebr., 1963; MS, Johns Hopkins U., 1972. Commd. 2nd lt. U.S. Army, 1967, advance through grades to maj., 1984, assigned to Vietnam and Balt., 1967-71; assigned U.S. Mil. Acad., West Point, N.Y., 1973-84; systems analyst U. Nebr., Lincoln, 1971-73, Foodland Ltd., Honolulu, 1986-87, HSMA, Honolulu, 1987—; lectr. math. U. Md., Republic Korea, 1985-87; lectr. computer sci. Roosevelt U., Honolulu, 1986-87. Vol. Honolulu Marathon Assn., 1987-88. Decorated Bronze Star, Meritorious Svc. medal with oak leaf cluster; U. Nebr. Regents scholar 1963, Ford Found. career scholar, 1964. Office: HMSA 818 Keeaumoku Honolulu HI 96808

HALL, DAVID CARROLL, statistics educator; b. Amarillo, Tex., Nov. 1, 1933; s. Everett S. and Oma Lee (Reed) H.; m. Barbara Sue Fleming, Sept. 1, 1957; children: Lisa, Marcy, Jill. BS in Math, West Tex. State U., 1957; MS in Ednl. Research, N. Mex. State U., 1966, PhD in Research and Statistics, 1969. Physicist in physical sci. lab N. Mex. State U., Las Cruces, 1957-66, assoc. dir. in ERIC Retrieval Ctr., 1966-80, prof. statistics, 1980—. Served with USN, 1952-54. Mem. Am. Statistical Assn. Democrat. Methodist. Home: 16 Lebanon Arc Las Cruces NM 88005

HALL, FREDERICK COLUMBUS, plant ecologist; b. Milw., Apr. 19, 1927; s. Nelson Clarence and Carol (Conlee) H.; m. Katherine Fodor, July 1950 (div. 1965); children: Wayne Fodor, Conlee Adair Hall Steenberg; m. Virginia May Munday, June 2, 1984. BS, Purdue U., 1951; MS, Oreg. State Coll., 1956, PhD, 1966. Range conservationist USDA Forest Service, Prineville, Oreg., 1956-59; area ecologist USDA Forest Service, Portland, Oreg., 1961-72, regional ecologist, 1972—; asst. prof. U. Idaho, Moscow, 1959-61. Author: Plant Communities, 1973, Growth Basal Area Handbook, 1987; contbg. author Wildlife Habitat in Forests (cert. merit 1978), 1979. Served to maj. USMC, 1951-54. Recipient Superior Service award U.S. Dept. Agr., 1976. Mem. Soc. Am. Foresters, Soc. Range Mgmt., Ecol. Soc. Am., Wildlife Soc. Baha'i. Club: Sauvie Island Yacht (Portland). Home: 550 Tomahawk Island Moorage Portland OR 97217 Office: USDA Forest Svc Ecology Sect PO Box 3623 Portland OR 97208

HALL, GEORGE PEYTON, JR., architect; b. Richmond, Va., June 20, 1951; s. George Peyton and Alice Christine (Roberts) H. BArch, U. Va., 1974; Master of Environ. Design, Yale U., 1980. Lic. architect, Calif. Intern Giuliani Assocs., Washington, 1974-77; coordinator architecture div. G.K. Design Internat., Inc., Santa Monica, Calif., 1980-84; dir. architecture and planning David Hyun Assocs., Inc., L.A., 1984-87, John Ash AIA Assocs., L.A., 1987—. Mem. L.A. Conservancy, Soc. Archtl. Historians.

HALL, GORDON R., state supreme court chief justice; b. Vernal, Utah, Dec. 14, 1926; s. Roscoe Jefferson and Clara Maud (Freestone) H.; m. Doris Gillespie, Sept. 6, 1947; children: Rick Jefferson, Craig Edwin. B.S., U. Utah, 1949, LL.B., 1951. Bar: Utah 1952. Sole practice Tooele, Utah, 1952-69; city atty. City of Grantsville, Utah, 1954-69; town atty. Town of Wendover, Utah, 1955-69, Town of Stockton, Utah, 1955-69; legal adviser Tooele Army Depot, 1953-58; county atty. Tooele County, 1958-69; judge 3d Jud. Dist. Utah, 1969-77; assoc. justice Supreme Ct. Utah, 1977-81, chief justice, 1981—; pres. Conf. Chief Justices, 1988—; chmn. Nat. Ctr. State Cts., 1988—; pres. Utah Assn. Counties, 1965; mem. Pres.'s Adv. Com. OEO, 1965-66; trustee Am. Inns of Ct. Found., 1988—; mem. exec. com. Coun. of State Govts., 1988—. Served with U.S. Maritime Service, 1944-46. Mem. ABA, Utah Bar Assn. Office: Utah Supreme Ct 332 State Capitol Salt Lake City UT 84114

HALL, GWENDOLYN LOUISE, communication specialist; b. Washington, July 14, 1948; d. Baxter Austin and Virginia Dare (Dunston) Yarborough; m. Ronald E. Hall, June 5, 1976 (dec. July 1979). Student, U. D.C., 1973-79, Alameda Coll., 1982, Laney Coll., 1983; cert. tchr., Calif. State Poly. U., Pomona, 1985. Stenographer FCC., Washington, 1966-73; adminstrv. asst. Bd. Trustees U. D.C., Washington, 1973-77; spl. asst. to pres. U. D.C., Washington, 1978-80; prin. Gwendolyn Hall & Assocs., Alameda, Calif., 1980—; bd. dirs. DaMontel Engrs., Oakland; administrv. asst. Dani Perkins & Assocs., Oakland, Calif., 1984—; workshop facilitator on career devel. crown Zellerbach Paper Co. MVO Personnel Svcs., San Francisco, 1986; computer instuction adminstr. MAC Bus. Inst., Fairfield, Calif., 1987; guest speaker BET (Black Entertainment TV); mem. Tuckegee Airmen, Inc. Ronald McNair Chpt., Travis AFB. Contbg. poet Widow-Hearts of Fire, 1980, 85; announcer Pub. Affairs Program Sta. KJAZ-FM, Alameda, 1981; choreographer Lord's Prayer, 1983. Bd. dirs. Everybody's Creative Art Ctr., Oakland, 1982; mem. YMCA. Recipient Appreciation award Flag of U.S. at request of Congressman Fortney H. Stark, 1985, Vet. award U. D.C., 1979, Outstanding Svc. award U. D.C. Bd. Trustees, 1978; recipient Recognition award Anacostia High Sch., 1986, Appreciation award Holy Land Reunion Allen Temple Baptist Ch., 1987, Black Educator award Solano County, Recognition award RL Prodns. and Mrs. Solano Pageant; named one of Outstanding Young Women of Am., 1984. Mem. Widows Network, Bay Area Black Journalist Assn., Black Filmmakers Hall of Fame, Women in Telecommunications (charter), Soc. Humanistic Mgmt., Nat. Bus. Edn., Nat. Assn. Trade and Tech. Schs., Am. Fedn. State, County and Mcpl. Employees. Baptist. Office: PO Box 1738 Travis AFB CA 94535

HALL, HAL, writer, economic, political, social and religious critic; b. Colby, Kans., June 7, 1911; s. Robert Ellsworth and Sarah (Myers) H.; m. Liane Hanft, May 23, 1947; children: Robert Eric, Alan Rae, Ronald Frederick. Student Lewis Inst., 1933-34; BA in Econs. U. Ill., 1939. Journeyman welder various shipyards, Oakland, Calif., 1941-43; with Mil. Govt., 16th Armored Div., 1943-46; journeyman carpenter, San Jose, Calif., 1946-49; house designer and builder, Calif., Colo., 1949-53; co-owner, co-operator Red Mountain Lodge, Ouray, Colo., 1953-80. Author: The Great Conflict, 1943, Even to the Last Man, 1960, The Wealth of Persons, 1968, Collectivism and Freedom, 1976, The Sleeping Dragon, 1981, rev. edit., 1986, The Road to Freedom, 1989. Contender for equalitarian and econ. democracy. Address: Box 129 Ouray CO 81427

HALL, HAROLD ROBERT, computer engineer; b. Bakersfield, Calif., Feb. 7, 1935; s. Edward Earl and Ethel Mae (Butner) H.; m. Tenniebee May Hall, Feb. 20, 1965. BS, U. Calif., Berkeley, 1956, MS, 1957, PhD, 1966. Chief engr. wave-filter div. Transonic, Inc., Bakersfield, 1957-60; chief design engr. Circuit Dyne Corp., Pasadena and Laguna Beach, Calif., 1960-61; sr. devel. engr. Robertshaw Controls Co., Anaheim, Calif., 1961-63; research engr. Naval Ocean Systems Ctr. Navy Research Lab., San Diego, 1966—; bd. dirs. Circuit Dyne Corp., Pacific Coil Co. Recipient Thomas Clair McFarland award U. Calif., Berkeley, 1956, NSF fellow, 1957. Mem. IEEE, Acoustical Soc. Am., Phi Beta Kappa. Home: 5284 Dawes St San Diego CA 92109 Office: Naval Ocean Systems Ctr San Diego CA 92152

HALL, IVAN SCOTT, physician; b. Moscow, Idaho, Feb. 8, 1947; s. John Ivan and Phyllis Mary (Cluer) H.; m. Catherine Ann, Sept. 13, 1980; children: Abby Kathryn, Samuel Cluer. BS with honors, U. Redlands, 1969; MD, UCLA, 1973. Diplomate Am. Bd. of Internal Medicine. Intern Harbor Gen. Hosp., Torrance, Calif., 1973-74; resident U. Wash. Hosp., Seattle, 1976-79; pvt. practice Seattle, 1979—; clin. instr. in medicine U. Wash., Seattle, 1979—; chief of medicine Swedish Hosp. Med. Ctr., Seattle, 1987-89, asst. chief of staff, 1989—. With USPHS, 1974-76. Mem. Am. Coll. Physicians, Am. Soc. Internal Medicine, Wash. State Med. Assn., King County Med. Assn., North Pacific Soc. Internal Medicine, Seattle Acad. Internal Medicine. Home: 6230 79th SE Mercer Island WA 98040 Office: 1221 Madison #92D Seattle WA 98104

HALL, JACK HENRY, retired television executive, foundation administrator; b. South Gate, Calif., Sept. 29, 1926; s. Lamont Dupere and Mildred Elizabeth (Hooker) H.; B.A., Calif. State U., Fresno, 1949; m. Peggy Jean Walterscheid, Dec. 27, 1974; children—Julie Anne, Jeffrey Adams; stepchildren—Robert, Jeffrey, April, Steven. Radio singer Sta. KECA, Los Angeles, summer 1938; announcer Sta. KARM, Fresno, 1943-44; asst. theatre mgr. Fox West Coast Ltd., 1944, 46-48; announcer Sta. KSGN, Sanger, Calif., 1949-50, Sta. KMJ, Fresno, 1950-53; dir., announcer Sta. KMJ-TV, Fresno, 1953-81, sta. KSEE, 1981-88, community affairs mgr., 1979-88; exec. dir. VMC Found., 1989—; performer, stage dir. Fresno Community Theater, 1960-85, pres., 1963-64, 73-74; mem. Fresno Community Chorus, 1955-60, pres., 1959-60. Mem. Easter Seal Soc. Central Calif., 1980—, pres., 1982-84, 1988—, sec. Easter Seal Soc. Calif., 1984-86, pres. 1986-88. Served with AUS, 1944-45. Recipient Best Actor award Fresno Community Theater, 1965, Pres.'s award, 1971, 72, 77, J.U. Berry award, 1987. Mem. Am. Community Theatre Assn. Producer TV documentary Opus 20, 1974; producer, narrator film documentary Lost, 1976. Home: 1435 Park St Sanger CA 93657

HALL, LARRY BRUCE, clergyman; b. Georgetown, Ky., Dec. 11, 1942; s. Bruce Browning and Juanita Ann (Patrick) H.; m. Sara Kay Yarbrough, Mar. 26, 1966; children: Larissa Kathleen, Lary Bruce Jr. BA, Georgetown Coll., 1964; grad., Lexington Theol. Sem., 1974; MDiv, Emory U., 1977; postgrad., Emory U., Grad. Theol. Found., Notre Dame, Ind., 1978.

Ordained deacon United Meth. Ch., 1974, elder, 1979. Pastor Centerville United Meth. Ch., Paris, Ky., 1972-74; assoc. pastor Sandy Springs United Meth. Ch., Atlanta, 1974-77, First United Meth. Ch., Pampa, Tex., 1977-80; pastor Agape United Meth. Ch., Lubbock, Tex., 1980-82; sr. pastor First United Meth. Ch., Dumas, Tex., 1982-84, Artesia, N.Mex., 1986—; dir. Wesley Found., W. Tex. State U., Canyon, 1978-80; chmn. evangelism Lubbock dist. United Meth. Ch., Tex., 1980-82; chmn. ethnic minority chs. N.W. Tex. Conf., 1982-86; dir. spiritual life Clovis (N.Mex.) Dist. United Meth. Ch., 1987. Editor: Services in Texas Panhandle, 1984; author, editor Theol. Thoughts, 1978—, Acad. of Faith, 1980—. Bd. dirs. Commn. on Mental Health, Dumas, Tex., 1983-86; found. dir. Com. on Volunteerism, Dumas, 1985; bd. dirs. YMCA, Dumas, 1985-86, Good Samaritan Ctrs., Artesia, N.Mex., 1987—. Capt. U.S. Army, 1965-69. Recipient Youth Leadership award United Meth. Ch., Tex., 1979-80, Evangelism Growth award, 1981, 82, 84, Leadership award Tex. Meth. Coll., 1984. Fellow Grad. Theol. Found.; mem. Am. Assn. Christian Counselors, Order St. Luke, Disciplined Order of Christ, Rotary. Democrat. Office: First United Meth Ch 500 W Grand PO Box 499 Artesia NM 88211-0499

HALL, LARRY D., energy company executive; b. Hastings, Nebr., Nov. 8, 1942; s. Willis E. and Stella W. (Eckoff) H.; m. Jeffe D. Bryant, July 5, 1985; children: Scott, Jeff, Mike, Bryan. BA in Bus., Kearney (Nebr.) State Coll.; JD, U. Nebr. Bar: Nebr., Colo. Ptnr. Wright, Simmons, Hancock & Hall, Scottsbluff, Nebr., 1967-71; atty., asst. treas. KN Energy Inc., Hastings, Nebr., 1971-73; dir. regulatory affairs KN Energy Inc., Hastings, 1973-76; v.p. law div. KN Energy Inc., Lakewood, Colo., 1976-82, sr. v.p., 1982-85, exec. v.p., 1985-88, pres., chief ops. officer, 1988—, also bd. dirs.; bd. dirs. Midwest Gas Assn., Mpls., INGAA. Mem. ABA, Fed. Energy Bar Assn., Nebr. Bar Assn., Colo. Bar Assn., Pres. Assn., Midwest Bar Assn. (bd. dirs. 1986-88), Columbine Country Club, Elks, Masons. Democrat. Presbyterian. Home: 1892 Sugar Bush Dr Evergreen CO 80439 Office: KN Energy Inc PO Box 15265 Lakewood CO 80215

HALL, LESLIE CHARLES, police officer, educator; b. Tahlequah, Okla., Oct. 12, 1945; s. Leslie Charles Sr. and Hazel June (Ballew) H.; m. Sandra Kay Coale, Apr. 14, 1967; children: Wendy Christine, Bobby Lynn. AA in Police Sci., Riverside (Calif.) Community Coll., 1973; BS in Pub. Adminstrn., U. La Verne (Calif.), 1981; Cert. in Mgmt., Peace Officers Standards and Tng. Command Coll. at Calif. Poly. U., Pomona, 1987, Advanced Cert., 1987. Successively police officer, detective, sgt., lt. City of Riverside, 1967-85, police capt., 1985—. Recipient Award of Merit Am. Legion, Riverside, 1989. Mem. Calif. Narcotics Officers Assn., Command Coll. Alumni Assn. (v.p.), Kiwanis. Republican. Office: City of Riverside Police Dept 4102 Orange St Riverside CA 92501

HALL, LOIS RIGGS, symphony orchestra administrator, state senator; b. Beeville, Tex., May 22, 1930; d. Ira Franklin and Pearl Ophelia (McCoy) Riggs; student Tex. Women's U., 1947-49, U. Tex., Austin, 1949-50; m. Walter William Hall, Dec. 28, 1950 (dec.); children—Robert Macfarlane, Elaine Denise, Judith Lea. Exec. sec. N.Mex. Symphony Orch., Albuquerque, 1975—; mem. N.Mex. Senate, 1980-85. Active Boy Scouts Am., Girl Scouts U.S.A., Officers Wives Clubs; 2d v.p. Albuquerque Symphony Women's Assn.; bd. dirs. Friends of Music, 1986-88; treas., publicity dir. N.Mex. Aviation Assn. Republican. Home: 620 Ortiz NE Albuquerque NM 87108 Office: PO Box 769 Albuquerque NM 87103

HALL, MARIAN ELLA See ROBERTSON, MARIAN ELLA

HALL, MARLENE MALOUF, physician assistant; b. L.A., Feb. 2, 1933; d. Bert B. and Marion (Nassour) Malouf; m. Gerald Lowell Hall, Jan. 20, 1956; children: John, Jeanne, Jacqueline. BS, UCLA, 1955; cert. in nursing assisting, L.A. Valley Coll., 1971; cert. in physician, Drew Med. Sch., 1976. RN, Calif.; cert. physician asst. Physician asst. Kaiser Permanete, Woodland Hills, Calif., 1976-78; physician asst., nursing mgr. Dr. Patrick S. Zaccalini, L.A., 1978—. Pres. aux. ARC, 1967-69, benefit chmn., 1984, 88; pres. St. Michael's Sch. PTA, 1970-72; benefit chmn. L.A. Orphanage Guild, 1963. Mem. Delta Delta Delta (reference chmn. 1987-88). Republican. Presbyterian. Home: 10101 Galaxy Way 5-104 Century City CA 90067 Office: 11645 Wilshire Blvd #1050 Los Angeles CA 90025

HALL, PHILIP LYLE, lawyer; b. Silver Creek, N.Y., Sept. 25, 1955; s. A. Ray and Margaret Elizabeth (Boecraft) H.; m. Joyce Ann Mandell, July 22, 1979; children: Stacy Elizabeth, Jennifer Lynn, Raymond Christopher. BS in Pub. Adminstrn., U. Ariz., 1977; JD, Cornell U., 1981. Bar: Ariz. 1981. Dep. county atty. Yuma County, Yuma, Ariz., 1981-86, chief dep. county atty., 1986—. Bd. dirs. Casa de Yuma County, 1986—; deacon Sierra Vista Presbyn. Ch., Yuma, 1988—. Mem. State Bar Ariz., Yuma County Bar Assn. Republican. Home: 1489 42d Ave Yuma AZ 85364 Office: Yuma County Atty 168 S 2d Ave Yuma AZ 85364

HALL, RALPH CORBIN, forest entomologist, consultant; b. Ellenville, N.Y., May 7, 1899; s. James Harvey and Anna (Newkirk) H.; m. Dorothy Dane Colby, Sept. 7, 1930 (dec. Aug. 1981); children: James Dane, Judith Gilmore Thomson, John Colby, Joanne Newkirk Parrish (dec.). BS, Syracuse U., 1925; MF, Harvard U., 1927; PhD, U. Mich., 1931. Registered profl. entomologist, U.S.; registered profl. forester, Calif. Research forest entomologist Bur. Entomology and Plant Quarantine, Columbus, Ohio, 1931-38, Berkeley, Calif., 1938-53; with U.S. Forest Service, 1953-64; entomologist San Francisco, 1961-64; v.p., dir. Natural Resources Mgmt. Corp., Orinda, Calif., 1970-74; cons. forest entomology Orinda, 1974—; cons. research grants NSF, 1951—. Mem. nat. council Boy Scouts Am., 1955-66, mem. exec. council Mt. Diablo Council, 1947-71; bd. dirs. Wildernees Found., Calif. Forestry Found., Forest Landowners Calif. Named Man of Yr. by City of Orinda, 1949; recipient Silver Beaver award Boy Scouts Am., 1957; award of Merit SUNY, award of Merit Calif. Acad. Scis., award of Merit N.Y. Acad. Scis. Fellow Soc. Am. Foresters (Golden Membership award 1978), AAAS, Internat. Platform Assn., Fedn. Am. Scientists, Explorers Club; mem. Assn. Cons. Foresters, Wildlife Soc., Wilderness Soc., Am. Forestry Assn., Entomol. Soc. Am., Sierra Club, Sigma Xi, Gamma Sigma Delta, Phi Sigma. Address: 72 Davis Rd Orinda CA 94563

HALL, RICHARD DENNIS, journalist; b. Troy, N.Y., Apr. 12, 1935; s. Dennis John and Clara Eleanor (Hanson) H.; m. Joyce Ann Huntington, June 7, 1957; children: Brian Huntington, Roger Hanson. BS, Boston U., 1957. Gen. assignment reporter Worchester (Mass.) Telegraph and The Evening Gazette, Mass., 1957-60; city hall reporter, columnist Springfield (Mass.) Union, 1960-65; reporter Fresno (Calif.) Bee, 1965-77, agr. water reporter, 1977-79; Washington corr. McClatchy Newspapers, 1979-83; agribus. writer Fresno (Calif.) Bee, 1983—; mem. Ninth Annual Conf. European and Am. Journalists, Maastricht, The Netherlands, 1985. Author: Fresno County in the 20th Century, 1987; contbg. editor California Farmer mag., 1986—. Docent show ofcl. local history tours, Hanford, Calif., 1987. Recipient Agribus. Invitation award, Taiwan, 1983. Mem. Garden of the Sun Corral Western History Club. Home: 1978 Mulberry Dr Hanford CA 93230 Office: Fresno Bee 1626 E St Fresno CA 93786

HALL, ROBERT EMMETT, JR., investment banker, realtor; b. Sioux City, Iowa, Apr. 28, 1936; s. Robert Emmett and Alvina (Faden) H.; m. Marna Thiel, 1969. BA, U. S.D., 1958, MA, 1959; MBA, U. Santa Clara, 1976; grad. Am. Inst. Banking, Realtors Inst. Grad. asst. U. S.D., Vermillion, 1958-59; mgr. ins. dept., asst. mgr. installment loan dept. Northwestern Nat. Bank of Sioux Falls, S.D., 1959-61, asst. cashier, 1961-65; asst. mgr. Crocker Nat. Bank, San Francisco, 1965-67, loan officer, 1967-69, asst. v.p., asst. mgr. San Mateo br., 1969-72; v.p., Western regional mgr. Internat. Investments & Realty, Inc., Washington, 1972—; owner Hall Investment Co., 1976—; pres. Almaden Oaks Realtors, Inc., 1976—; instr. West Valley Coll., Saratoga, Calif., 1972-82, Grad. Sch. Bus., U. Santa Clara (Calif.), 1981—. Treas., Minnehaha Leukemia Soc., 1963, Lake County Heart Fund Assn., 1962, Minnehaha Young Republican Club, 1963. Mem. Am. Inst. Banking, San Mateo C. of C., Calif. Assn. Realtors (vice chmn.), Beta Theta Pi. Republican. Roman Catholic. Clubs: Elks, Rotary (past pres.), K.C., Almaden Country, Mercedes Benz Calif. Home: 6951 Castlerock Dr San Jose CA 95120 Office: Almaden Oaks Realtors Inc 6501 Crown Blvd 100 San Jose CA 95120 Home (summer): 8864 Rubicon Bay Lake Tahoe CA 95733

HALL, ROBERT PIERCE, camera manufacturing company sales executive; b. La Jolla, Calif., Jan. 16, 1963; s. Robert Rankin and Elisse Marie (Vogel) H.; m. Laura Joanne Johnson, Aug. 23, 1986. BBA, U. San Diego, 1985. Sales rep. for consumer electronics Eastman Kodak Co., Sacramento, 1985-86, Tampa, Fla., 1986; sales account exec. Eastman Kodak Co., Hollywood, Calif., 1986—. Mem. U. San Diego Alumni Assn. (career counselor 1986—). Republican. Roman Catholic. Home: 24001 Cape May Ct Valencia CA 91355 Office: Eastman Kodak Co 12100 Rivera Rd Whittier CA 90606

HALL, STEVEN ALAN, real estate appraisal executive, consultant; b. Butte, Mont., Aug. 11, 1952; s. Gregory McLaren and Rita Irene (Schnieder) h.; m. Sheila Kay Stephens, Aug. 6, 1976; children: Matthew Steven, Abigail Leigh, Jared Patrick, Caitlin Mary. BSBA, U. MOnt., 1975. Staff appraiser Wilcox and Assocs., Missoula, Mont., 1975-76, Wells Fargo Bank, San Leandro, Calif., 1977, R.D. Kembel and Assocs., Missoula, 1977-80; owner, mgr. Hall Agy., Missoula, 1981-82, Hall-Widdoss & Co., Missoula, 1986—. Chmn. fin. com. Christ the King Ch., Missoula, 1986—. With U.S. Army, 1971-73. Mem. Am. Inst. Real Estate Appraisers (chmn. admissions Rocky Mountain chpt. 1983-85, pres. 1987-89, N.W. regional com. 1987—), Urban Land Inst. (assoc.), Nat. Assn. Realtors, Missoula C. of C., Kiwanis (bd. dirs. Sentinel club 1987-88). Republican. Roman Catholic. Office: Hall-Widdoss & Co 929 SW Higgins Ave Ste C Missoula MT 59803

HALL, STEVEN ANTHONY, university official; b. Ceiba, P.R., June 15, 1964; s. Charles Marvin Jr. and Sylvia Racquel (Morales) H. AAS with honors, Oxnard Coll., 1985; BA in History, Calif. State Poly U., 1988. Office supr. recreational sports Calif. State Poly U., San Luis Obispo, 1965-67, pub. rels. rep. for ann. giving, 1987--. Scottish Rite scholar, 1985. Mem. Pi Gamma Mu, Phi Delta Theta (pres., charter mem.). Presbyterian. Home: 4401 Boston Way Oxnard CA 93033

HALL, STUART CAMPEN, lawyer, public affairs and travel consultant; b. San Jose, Calif., June 18, 1935; s. Marshall Spencer and Helen Bernice (Campen) H. B.A., U. Calif. at Berkeley, 1957; M.A., Stanford U., 1961; J.D., Harvard U., 1964. Bar: Alaska 1984, U.S. Dist. Ct. Alaska 1984, U.S. Ct. Appeals (9th cir.) 1986. Legis. asst. Calif. Legislature Assembly, 1958-59, asst. clk. 1960, 1st asst. clk., 1961; adminstrv. analyst Office of Pres., U. Calif. at Berkeley, 1960, grad. research analyst, 1960; investigator Office of Dist. Atty., County of Santa Clara, San Jose, 1962-63; cons. Calif. Constn. Revision Commn., Calif. Legislature, San Francisco, 1964-65; lectr. polit. sci., dept. polit. sci. San Jose State Coll., 1965-69; cons. com. on elections and constl. amendments Calif. Assembly, 1969-70; adminstrv. asst. to Calif. State Senator John A. Nejedly, 1970-71; legis. counsel, legis. affairs, agy. Alaska Legislature, 1971-75, sr. legis. counsel, 1975-76; mem. Alaska Pub. Utilities Commn., 1976-83; adj. lectr. pub. adminstrn. U. Alaska, Juneau, 1973-76; adj. lectr. polit. sci. Anchorage Community Coll., U. Alaska, Anchorage, 1984-85. Mem. Rep. Cen. Com. Santa Clara County, 1967-70. Trustee Jr. Statesmen Found., 1970-80; bd. dirs. S. Cen. Alaska chpt. ARC, 1986-88. Served with USAFR, 1959—, now lt. col. Woodrow Wilson fellow, 1957-58. Mem. ABA, Alaska Bar Assn., Calif. Hist. Soc., Nat. Civic League, Am. Soc. for Pub. Adminstrn., Western Govtl. Research Assn., Am. Philatelic Soc., Harvard Law Sch. Assn., Stanford U. Alumni Assn., U. Calif. Alumni Assn., Ripon Soc. (nat. governing bd. 1979-81), Sigma Delta Chi. Episcopalian. Clubs: Masons, Rotary, Lions, Commonwealth (San Francisco). Home: 815 Colwell St PO Box 300 Anchorage AK 99510 Office: 310 G St Ste 310 Anchorage AK 99501

HALL, SUSAN JEAN, teacher; b. Long Beach, Calif., Jan. 12, 1951; d. Owen Parson and Goldie Marie (Lutz) H. BA in Music, U. of the Pacific, 1973, MA in Polit. sci., 1981; postgrad., U. So. Calif., 1981-83. Tchr. Lincoln Unified Sch. Dist., Stockton, Calif., 1973-80; writer Teledyne Inet, Torrance, Calif., 1981-82; data mgmt. coordinator Northrop Corp., Hawthorne, Calif., 1982-83; proposal adminstr. Rockwell Internat. Corp., El Segundo, Calif., 1983; tchr. Lodi (Calif.) Unified Sch. Dist., 1983—, fine arts dir., 1984—; chairperson Lodi PTA, 1985—. Author: National Socialism the German Tragedy, 1981; composer: Sonata in C, 1975. Dem. campaigner, Lodi, 1976-80; donator, drive chmn. Lodi Life Mission, 1986; 1st violinist Stockton Symphony. Mem. Nat. Tchrs. Assn., Calif. Tchrs. Assn., Music Educators Assn. Home: 1753 Cape Cod Lodi CA 95242 Office: Nichols School 1301 S Crescent Lodi CA

HALL, TERESA MARIE, dentist; b. Reno, July 19, 1957; d. Maurice George and Ruby Merle (Bowman) H. BS, Calif. State U., Long Beach, 1980; DDS, Loyola U., Maywood, Ill., 1986. Resident in dentistry Rancho Los Amigos Med. Ctr., Downey, Calif., 1986-87; gen. practice dentistry Sacramento, 1988—. Mem. ADA, Calif. Dental Assn., Am. Assn. Hosp. Dentists, So. Calif. Acad. Oral Pathology, Physicians for Social Responsibility (Sacramento chpt.), Delta Sigma Delta. Democrat. Roman Catholic. Home: 1300 Rodeo Way Sacramento CA 95819 Office: 2525 K St Ste 305 Sacramento CA 95816

HALL, THOMAS HENRY, political consultant; b. Alameda, Calif., Aug. 1, 1958; s. Gordon Edwin and Rita Marie (Kelly) H.; m. Karin Macalka, Sept. 12, 1987. BA in Polit. Sci., Calif. State U., Hayward, 1981; cert. fund raising, U. So. Calif., 1985. Sr. analyst Pacific Coast Cons., San Francisco, 1981-82; dep. campaign dir. Freeman for Gov., Anchorage, 1982-83; exec. dir. Sportsmen's Club for the City of Hope, L.A., 1983-85; dir. devel. New Sch. for Child Devel., Sherman Oaks, Calif., 1985-86; field dir., fund raiser Woodward & McDowell Campaigns, L.A., 1986-87; state field dir., fund raiser Calif. Movement for Ednl. Reform, L.A., 1987; state field dir. Fong for U.S. Senate, L.A., 1987; polit.-pub. affairs dir. First Tuesday, Inc., Santa Monica, Calif., 1987-88; dir. campaign unit Cerrell Assocs., Inc., L.A., 1988—. City commr. Human Resources Commn., City of Hayward, 1981. Mem. Am. Assn. Polit. Cons., Nat. Soc. Fund Raising Execs. Democrat. Roman Catholic. Home: 933 Ocean Ave Santa Monica CA 90403-2412

HALL, WILLIAM SPENCER, electrical engineer; b. Ancon, Panama, Oct. 9, 1935; s. William Evens and Helena Spencer (Callaway) H.; m. Mary Helena Steketee, July 27, 1963 (div. 1984); children: Christopher Andrew, Mark Evens; m. Ewa Hanna Tarczynska, Dec. 19, 1987. BEE, U. Va., 1958; BA Honours, Cambridge U., Eng., 1965; PhD, Brown U., 1968; MS in Engring., U. Mich., 1985. Assoc. prof. math. U. Pitts., 1968-82; assoc. editor Math. Revs., Ann Arbor, Mich., 1982-85; mem. tech. staff AT&T Info. Systems, Lincroft, N.J., 1985-87; sr. engr. Olivetti Advanced Tech. Ctr., Cupertino, Calif., 1987-89, CONNECT Inc., Cupertino, 1989—. Contbr. articles to profl. jours. Election judge City of Pitts., 1973-82. 1st lt. USAF, 1958-63. Internat. Rsch. and Exchs. Bd. fellow 1975, 78, NAS fellow, 1978. Mem. Sigma Xi, Phi Eta Sigma, Tau Beta Pi. Democrat. Home: 3665 Benton St #66 Santa Clara CA 95051 Office: CONNECT Inc 10101 Bubb Rd Cupertino CA 95014

HALL, WILTON EARL, JR., engineering company executive; b. San Antonio, Mar. 20, 1941; s. Wilton Earl Sr. and Ada Allen (Goodman) H.; m. Donna Lee Thatcher, May 15, 1981 (div.); m. Laura Elizabeth Baker, Oct. 17, 1982; children: Alicia, Kimberly. BS, MIT, 1962; MS, So. Meth. U., 1965; PhD, Stanford U., 1971. Registered profl. engr., Calif. Research engr. Bell Helicopter Co., Ft. Worth, 1962-66; research assoc. Stanford U., Stanford, Calif., 1971-72; v.p. Systems Control, Palo Alto, Calif., 1972-81, Scicon, Palo Alto, 1981-88; lectr. Hewlett-Packard, Palo Alto, 1984. Coauthor: Advances in Control Systems, 1980-81; contbr. articles to profl. jours. Recipient Kelly award Am. Helicopter Soc., Ft. Worth, 1965. Mem. Am. Inst. Aero. and Astronautical Engrs. (assoc.), IEEE, Am. Mgmt. Assn. Episcopalian.

HALL, YONG OK, social worker; b. Korea, Apr. 20, 1950; d. Gabe M. and Seung Sun (Shim) H. BA in Sociology, U. Wash., 1973, MSW, 1974-76. Bilingual counselor City of Seattle, 1973; geriatric social worker Good Samaritan Hosp., Puyallup, Wash., 1974-75; med. social worker Seatoma Convalescent Ctr., Kent, Wash., 1974-76; geritatric mental health cons. Lutheran Community Services, Bremerton, Wash., 1976-78; ombudsman Dept. Social & Health Services, Olympia, Wash., 1978—; instr. Highline Community Coll., Kent, Wash., 1976, S. Puget Sound Community Coll., Tumwater, 1977; faculty mem. U. Wash., Seattle, 1978, St. Martin's Abbey Coll, Lacey, 1986-87; founder, advisor Wash. State Nursing Home Family Council, 1982—; bd. dirs. Nat. Tardive Dyskinesia Assn. Vol. USO, Tacoma, 1984—. Nat. Mental Health grantee, 1974-76. Mem. Nat. Acad. Social Work, Am. Geriatric Soc., Nat. Assn. State Omubdsman (bd. dirs. 1984-86), Am. Assn. For Univ. Women (bd. dirs. 1981-82). Office: Wash Dept Social and Health Svcs Mail Stop OB31-C Olympia WA 98504

HALLACY, EDWIN RICHARD, sales executive; b. Yonkers, N.Y., Nov. 19, 1951; s. Edwin Richard and Rosalie Theresa H.; m. Minerva Argentina Tenorio,. Student, Archbishop Stepinac high sch., White plains, N.Y., 1965-69; BSc., U. Mass. at Amherst, 1973-77. Life Mem. Vietnam Vet. Am., Wash., Disabled Am. Vett. Cin., Am. Legion. Mem. KC. (deputy grand knight). Republican. Roman Catholic. Home: 1642 Judah St San Francisco CA 94122 Office: 2215-R Market St San Francisco CA 94114

HALLAUER, ALAN DOUGLAS, data processing executive; b. Rochester, N.Y., Feb. 7, 1953; s. John William and Irma Rose (Musclow) H. BS, Colo. State U., 1976, MEd, 1978. Hall dir. U. Wis.-Stout, Menomonie, 1978-80; programmer, analyst McDonnell-Douglas Corp., Denver, 1980-85, KRM Software Devel. Co., Englewood, Colo., 1985-88; mgr. tech. support Telesis Cons., Inc., Denver, 1988-89; sr. systems analyst Dept. of State State of Colo., Denver, 1989—; ind. cons., Denver, 1987—. Mem. Nat. Prime Users Group. Office: PO Box 22502 Denver CO 80222

HALLBERG, DALE MERTON, sculptor; b. Spokane, Wash., Aug. 30, 1927; s. Gustaf Philip and Thelma (Bauman) H.; student U. Idaho, 1947-49, Wash. State U., 1949-50, U. Oreg., 1952-54; B.S. in Landscape Architecture, U. Calif., Berkeley, 1955; B.A. in Art, B.Ed., Eastern Wash. State Coll., 1956; postgrad. Claremont Grad. Sch., 1960-62, 62-67; M.A., Calif. State Coll. at Long Beach, 1967; m. Mildred May Lemmon, May 1, 1955. Tchr. art LaHabra (Calif.) High Sch., 1956-62; instr. landscape architecture Calif. State Poly. Coll., 1962-64; art instr. Troy High Sch., Fullerton, Calif., 1964-84; sculptor, 1967—; pvt. practice landscape architecture, Orange, Calif., 1955-78, Fullerton, 1978—; orchidist, 1978—; exhibited sculpture Muckenthaler Cultural Center, Fullerton, 1966, Calif. State Coll. at Long Beach, 1967, Galleria Numero, Venice, 1971, Galleria Fiamma Vigo, Rome, 1971, Art Alliance Safari for Calif. State U. at Fullerton, 1975, Common Ground Artists' Coop., Fullerton, 1978, 79, 80, others; prin. works include sculpture commn. Art in Pub. Places, Brea, Calif., 1985, Pvt. Commn. Bronze Gate, 1987-88. Served with USMC, 1945-47, 50-52. Mem. Am. Soc. Landscape Architects, Art. Alliance of Fullerton State U., Laguna Beach Art Assn., Orange County Orchid Soc. (bd. dirs.), Specie Orchid Soc. (bd. dirs.). Republican. Presbyterian. Address: 1630 Skyline Dr Fullerton CA 92631

HALLBOM, HAROLD RAYMOND, JR., printing company executive; b. Evanston, Ill., Nov. 8, 1951; s. Harold Raymond and Helen (Hoffman) H.; m. Denise C. Carlson, Oct. 31, 1952; children: Heather Jean, James Erick. BA, Loyola U., Chgo., 1974. Profl. engring. recruiter Profl. div. Businessmaus, Chgo., 1974-76; nat. sales mgr. Control Process Co., Elk Grove Village, Ill., 1975-78; exec. dir. U.V. Process, Inc., Chgo., 1978-82; v.p. Svecia USA, Inc., San Marcos, Calif., 1982—; cons. Argonne Nat. Labs., Batavia, Ill., 1984; advisor Screen Printing Tech. Found., Fairfax, Va., 1986—. Contbr. articles to profl. jours. Recipient Commendation Binday Inst. Am., 1985. Mem. Screen Printing Assn. Internat. (moderator, Commendation 1984), Soc. Mfg. Engrs. (sr., Cert. of Appreciation 1987), Screen Print Tech. Found. (advisor 1986—), Assn. for Finishing Processes, Alpha Delta Gamma (c. mgr. 1971-73). Democrat. Home: N 626 Lancaster Dr Winfield IL 60190 Office: Svecia USA Inc 220 Distribution St San Marcos CA 92069

HALLENBECK, LANE WILLIAM, aerospace company executive; b. Ft. Belvoir, Va., Apr. 19, 1955; s. Ralph J. and Corabelle (Harback) H. BA, U. Colo., 1977. Process engr. NCR Microelectronics, Colorado Springs, Colo., 1977-79; quality engr. Harris Semiconductor, Palm Bay, Fla., 1979-81, product engr., 1981-84; program mgr. TRW-Electronic Products, Colorado Springs, 1985-88, TRW-Space and Def., Redondo Beach, Calif., 1988—. Republican. Methodist. Home: 23135 Madison St Torrance CA 90505 Office: TRW Space and Def Sector 1 Space Park Redondo Beach CA 90278

HALLIDAY, JOHN MEECH, investment company executive; b. St. Louis, Oct. 16, 1936; s. William Norman and Vivian Viola (Meech) H.; m. Martha Layne Griggs, June 30, 1962; children: Richard M., Elizabeth. BS, U.S. Naval Acad., 1958; MBA, Harvard U., 1964. Dir. budgeting and planning Automatic Tape Control, Bloomington, Ill., 1964-66; dir. planning Ralston-Purina, St. Louis, 1966-67, v.p. subsidiary, 1967-68, dir. internat. banking, 1967-68; v.p. Servicetime Corp., St. Louis, 1968-70; assoc. R.W. Halliday Assocs., Boise, Idaho, 1970-87; v.p. Sawtooth Communications Corp., Boise, 1970-73, Commdr. Corp., 1979-81; pres., chief exec. officer, bd. dirs. Sonoma Internat., San Francisco, 1971-77, ML Ltd., San Francisco, 1974—, Halliday Labs., Inc., Reno, 1980—, Alta Packaging Corp., San Francisco, 1986-89, H.W.L. Inc., San Francisco, 1985—; exec. v.p., bd. dirs. Franchise Fin. Corp. Am., Phoenix, 1980-85; bd. dirs., v.p. Harvard Bus. Sch. Assn. of No. Calif., 1980-87; bd. dirs. 1st Fidelity Fin. Corp., San Diego. Bldg. com. YMCA, 1965; pres. Big Bros. of San Francisco, 1978-81; trustee U. Calif. Santa Cruz Found., 1988—. Served to lt. comdr. USNR, 1958-66. Mem. Nat. Restaurant Assn., Soc. Advancement Food Research, Heart Ill. Restaurant Assn. (v.p. 1969-70). Republican. Episcopalian. Clubs: Family, Olympic (San Francisco), Scott Valley Tennis (Mill Valley, Calif.). Home: 351 Corte Madera Ave Mill Valley CA 94941 Office: 625 Market St Ste 602 San Francisco CA 94105

HALLIDAY, KEITH, finance company executive; b. Albuquerque, Oct. 4, 1938; s. Henry F. and Cleo (Pead) H.; m. LLana Charlene Moorhouse Armitage Halliday, (div. 1965); m. Nancy Thelma Wolfe Halliday, May 10, 1969; 1 child, Laurie P. Student, Am. River Coll., 1958-60. Cert. consumer credit exec. Credit mgr. Sears Roebuck & Co., 1960-65, Montgomery Ward & Co., 1965-70; exec. v.p. Carte Blanche Corp., Los Angeles, 1970-74; gen. credit mgr. Liberty House Dept. Stores, Oakland, Calif., 1974-78; sr. v.p. Am. Express Co., Phoenix, 1978—. Mem. council 100 Ariz. State U., Temple, 1984—; mem. Phoenix 40 Ariz. State U., 1986—; council of bus advisors U. Ariz., 1987; bd. dirs. United Way, Phoenix, 1984—. Mem. Phoenix C. of C. Republican. Club: Biltmore Country (Phoenix). Lodge: Elks. Office: Am Express Co 2423 E Lincoln Dr Phoenix AZ 85016

HALLIDAY, WILLIAM ROSS, retired physician, speleologist; b. Atlanta, Ga., May 9, 1926; s. William Ross and Jane (Wakefield) H.; m. Eleanore Hartvedt, July 2, 1951 (dec. 1983); children: Marcia Lynn, Patricia Anne, William Ross III; m. Louise Baird Kinnard, May 7, 1988. BA, Swarthmore Coll., 1946; MD, George Washington U., 1948. Diplomate Am. Bd. Vocat. Experts. Intern Huntington Meml. Hosp., Pasadena, Calif., 1948-49; resident King County Hosp., Seattle, Denver Childrens Hosp., L.D.S. Hosp., Salt Lake City, 1950-57; practice medicine Seattle, 1957-65, 83-84; with Wash. Dept. Labor and Industries, 1965-76; med. dir. Wash. Div. Vocat. Rehab., 1976-82, Comprehensive Med. Rehab. Ctr., Brentwood, Tenn., 1984-87; dep. coroner, King County, Wash., 1964-66. Author: Adventure Is Underground, 1959, Depths of The Earth, 1966, 76, American Caves and Caving, 1974, 82; Editor: Jour. Spelean History, 1968-73; contbr. articles to profl. jours. Mem. Gov.'s North Cascades Study Com., 1967-76; mem. North Cascades Conservation Council, v.p., 1962-63; Dir. Western Speleological Survey, Seattle, 1955-81, pres., 1981-87; Internat. Speleological Found. asst. dir. Internat. Glaciospeleological Survey, 1972-76. Served to lt. comdr. USNR, 1949-50, 55-57. Fellow Am. Coll. Chest Physicians, Am. Acad. Compensation Medicine, Nat. Speleological Soc., Explorers Club; mem. Soc. Thoracic Surgeons, AMA, Am. Congress Rehab. Medicine, Am. Coll. Legal Medicine, Wash. State Med. Assn., Tenn. State Med. Assn., King County Med. Soc., Am. Fedn. Clin. Research, Am. Spelean History Assn. (pres. 1968), Brit. Cave Research Assn., Nat. Trust (Scotland), Am. Pain Soc., Internat. Soc. for the Study of Pain, Am. Acad. Algology. Clubs: Mountaineers (past trustee), Seattle Tennis. Home: 308 Aaron Ct Sterling VA 22170

HALLIGAN, JAMES EDMUND, university administrator, chemical engineer; b. Moorland, Iowa, June 23, 1936; s. Raymond Anthony and Margaret Ann (Crawford) H.; m. Ann Elizabeth Sorenson, June 29, 1957; children: Michael, Patrick, Christopher. M.S. in Chem. Engring, Iowa State U., 1962, M.S., 1965, Ph.D., 1968. Process engr. Humble Oil Co., 1962-64; mem. faculty Tex. Tech U., 1968-77; dean engring. U. Mo., Rolla, 1977-79; dean engring. U. Ark., Fayetteville, 1979-82, vice chancellor for acad. affairs, 1982-83, interim chancellor, 1983-84; pres. N.Mex. State U., Las Cruces,

1984—; v.p. engring. Kandahar Cons. Ltd.; mem. Gov. Tex. Energy Adv. Council, 1972-74. Served with USAF, 1954-58. Recipient Disting. Teaching award Tex. Tech U., 1972, Disting. Research award, 1975, 76; Disting. Teaching award U. Mo., Rolla, 1978. Mem. Am. Inst. Chem. Engrs., Am. Soc. Engring. Edn., Tau Beta Pi, Phi Kappa Phi, Pi Mu Epsilon. Roman Catholic. Club: Rotary. Home: Drawer 3CG Las Cruces NM 88003 Office: NMex State U 208 Hadley Hall Box 3Z Las Cruces NM 88003

HALLIGAN, THOMAS WALSH, construction company executive; b. Davenport, Iowa, Oct. 20, 1922; s. Eugene Joseph and Gertrude (Walsh) H.; m. Mary E. McClelland, Apr. 17, 1947; children: Carol, Mary Beth, Susan, Nancy, Timothy, Kathleen. A.B., Georgetown U., 1943. With Walsh Constrn. Co., Trumbull, Conn., 1946-80, pres., 1975-80; pres. Guy F. Atkinson Co., South San Francisco, until 1987, chief exec. officer, chmn. bd., until 1989, dir. Pres.-elect The Beavers, 1989—. Office: Guy F Atkinson Co of Calif 10 W Orange Ave South San Francisco CA 94080 *

HALLORAN, JAMES VINCENT, III, business analyst; b. Greenwich, Conn., May 12, 1942; s. James Vincent and Rita Lucy (Keator) H.; m. Barbara Sharon Case, Sept. 7, 1974. BME, Cath. U. Am., 1964; MBA, U. Chgo., 1973. Mktg. rep. Rockwell Internat., El Segundo, Calif., 1973-76, bus. area mgr., 1976-80, bus. analysis mgr., 1980-84; asst. dir. market analysis H. Silver & Assocs. Inc., Torrance, Calif., 1984-87, dir. mktg., 1987—. Commr. Redondo Beach Housing Adv. and Appeals Bd., 1985—; mem. citizens adv. bd. South Bay Union High Sch. Dist., Redondo Beach, 1983. Served to capt. USAF, 1964-68. Mem. Am. Def. Preparedness Assn., Internat. Windsurfer Class Assn. Libertarian. Home: 612 S Gertruda Ave Redondo Beach CA 90277 Office: H Silver & Assocs Inc 2044 Century Park E Los Angeles CA 90067

HALLUMS, BURGESS NATHANIEL, securities brokerage principal; b. Boston, Apr. 24, 1958; s. Nathaniel Burgess and Joyce Pauline (Woodson) H. BS in Fin., San Diego State U., 1981, BSME, 1981. V.p. fin. San Diego State U., 1979-81; account mktg. rep. IBM, San Diego, 1981-86, fin. adv. and money mgr., 1984-87, brokerage firm prin. and money mgr., 1987—; bd. dirs. ICR Tracking Scis., San Diego, 1986—, San Diego State U. Alumni, 1986—. Bd. dirs. Neighborhood Use Assn., San Diego, 1987—, v.p. fin., treas. exec. bd. comprehensive human assistance programs and svcs. project, 1989—; chmn. fund raising United Negro Coll. Fund, San Diego, 1987. Mem. Am. Mktg. Assn., Am. Mgmt. Assn. Home: 12610 Torrey Bluff Dr 374 San Diego CA 92130-4234

HALOPOFF, WILLIAM EVON, industrial designer, consultant; b. Los Angeles, May 31, 1934; s. William John Halopoff and Dorothy E. (Foote) Lawrence; m. Nancy J. Ragsdale, July 12, 1960; children: Guy William and Carolee Nichole. BS, Art Ctr. Coll. Design, 1968. Internat. indsl. design cons. FMC Corp. Cen. Engring. Lab., Santa Clara, Calif., 1969-81; mgr. indsl. design Tandem Computers, Cupertino, Calif., 1981-84; design cons. Halopoff Assocs., San Jose, Calif., 1984—. Patentee in field. Served with U.S. Army, 1957-59. Mem. Indsl. Designers Soc. Am., Soc. Automotive Engrs. (chmn. subcom. 29 1979-85). Home: 17544 Holiday Dr Morgan Hill CA 95037

HALPERIN, ROBERT MILTON, electrical machinery company executive; b. Chgo., June 1, 1928; s. Herman and Edna Pearl (Rosenberg) H.; m. Ruth Levison, June 19, 1955; children: Mark, Margaret, Philip. Ph.B., U. Chgo., 1949; B.Mech. Engring., Cornell U., 1949; M.B.A., Harvard U., 1952. Engr. Electro-Motive div. Gen. Motors Corp., La Grange, Ill., 1949-50; trust rep. Bank of Am., San Francisco, 1954-56; adminstr. Dumont Corp., San Rafael, Calif., 1956-57; pres. Raychem Corp., Menlo Park, Calif., 1957—; also bd. dirs. Raychem Corp., Menlo Park, 1961—; bd. dirs. Molecular Design Ltd. Trustee U. Chgo.; bd. dirs. Harvard Bus. Sch. Assocs., Stanford U. Hosp. Served to lt. USAF, 1952-53. Club: Harvard of New York City. Home: 80 Reservoir Rd Atherton CA 94025 Office: Raychem Corp 300 Constitution Dr Menlo Park CA 94025

HALPERIN, WARREN LESLIE, management consultant; b. Bklyn., Apr. 12, 1938; s. Abraham and Bertha Gertrude (Aronowitz) H.; m. Sherry Lee Weshner, Mar. 31, 1968; children: Jonathan David, Justin Edward. PhB, Adelphi U., 1959. Dir. mktg. Faust-Day Inc., Los Angeles, 1969-71; product mgr. Hunt-Wesson Foods, Fullerton, Calif., 1972-74; sr. v.p. Searchmasters Inc., Newport Beach, Calif., 1975-79; ptnr. MCS Assocs., Newport Beach, 1979-83; pres. The Halperin Co. Inc., Newport Beach, 1983-88; exec. v.p. Mercury Savs. and Loan, Huntington Beach, Calif., 1988—; bd. dirs. Capital Savings & Loan Assn., West Helena, Ark. Contbr. articles to profl. jours. Mem. nat. bd. trustees Leukemia Soc. Am., N.Y.C., 1980-85; trustee Amigos De Las Americas, Irvine, Calif., 1975-78; pres. Leukemia Soc. Am. Tri-County chpt., Garden Grove, Calif., 1979, Jewish Nat. Fund, Orange City, Calif., 1988. Recipient Exec. of Yr. Exec. Mag., 1986. Mem. U.S. League of Savings Insts., Mortgage Bankers Assn. Am., Bank Adminstrn. Inst. Office: Mercury Savs & Loan Assn 7812 Edinger Ave Huntington Beach CA 92647

HALPIN, CHARLES AIME, archbishop; b. St. Eustache, Man., Can., Aug. 30, 1930; s. John S. and Marie Anne (Gervais) H. BA, U. Man., 1950; BTh, U. Montreal, 1956; Licentiate Canon Law, Gregorian U., Rome, 1960. Ordained priest Roman Catholic Ch., 1956; named monsignor Roman Cath. Ch., 1969, consecrated bishop, 1973; asst. St. Mary's Cathedral, Winnipeg, Man., 1956-58; vice chancellor, sec. to archbishop Archdiocese Winnipeg, 1960; officialis Archdiocesan Matrimonial Tribunal, 1962; vice-officialis Regional Matrimonial Tribunal, Regina, Sask.; archbishop of Regina, 1973—. Mem. Western Cath. Conf. Bishops (past pres.), Can. Conf. Cath. Bishops (dir., pastoral team, chairperson ministries commn.).

HALPIN, DARCY MICHELLE, financial analyst; b. Trona, Calif., Feb. 26, 1961; d. Jerome Leon and Alice Henrietta (Jacobs) H. Student, U. Calif., Santa Barbara, 1979-80; BS in Ornamental Hort., Calif. State Poly U., San Luis Obispo, 1985. Greenhouse maintenance worker Calif. State Poly U., San Luis Obispo, 1980-81; nursery mgr. Karleskint-Crum Color Garden, San Luis Obispo, 1984-85; with sales dept., inventory clk. Bonita Nursery, Nipomo, Calif., 1984-85; prodn. facilities clk. Naval Weapons Ctr., China Lake, Calif., 1985-87; budget analyst Nanval Aviation Depot, San Diego, 1987—; landscape designer, Ridgecrest, Calif., 1985-87. Vol. local children's hosp.; vol. tutor reading Laubach Soc. Mem. Am. Soc. Mil. Comptrollers, Am. Hort. Soc., Pi Alpha Xi, Phi Kappa Phi. Democrat. Lutheran. Home: 10045 Rio San Diego Dr #248 San Diego CA 92108

HALPRIN, LAWRENCE, landscape architect, planner; b. N.Y.C., July 1, 1916; s. Samuel W. and Rose (Luria) H.; m. Ann Schuman, Sept. 19, 1940; children: Daria, Rana. B.S. in Plant Scis, Cornell U., 1939; M.S. in Plant Scis, U. Wis., 1941; B.Landscape Architecture, Harvard U., 1942. Sr. assoc. Thomas D. Church & Assocs., San Francisco, 1946-49; prin. Lawrence Halprin & Assos., San Francisco, 1949-76; co-founder Round House, San Francisco, 1976-78; founder Lawrence Halprin Studios, 1978—; lectr. U. Calif.-Berkeley, 1960-65, Regents prof., 1982-83. Dir., Halprin Summer Workshop, 1966, 1968; prin. works include Ghirardelli Sq., San Francisco, Sea Ranch, Calif., Nicolett Mall, Mpls., Old Orchard Shopping Center, Skokie, Ill., Lovejoy Fountain, Pettigrove Park, Forecourt Fountain, Portland, Oreg., Market St. reconstrn, San Francisco, Seattle Freeway Park, Rochester Manhattan Park, Franklin Delano Roosevelt Meml, Washington, Levi Park and Plaza, San Francisco, Haas Promenade, Jerusalem, Bunker Hill Stairs, Central Library, Hope St. and Olympic Park, Los Angeles; author: Cities, 1963; rev. edit., 1972, Freeways, 1966, New York, New York, 1968, The RSVP Cycles, 1970, Lawrence Halprin Notebooks, 1959-71, 1972; co-author: The Freeway in the City, 1968, Taking Part: A Workshop Approach to Collective Creativity, 1974, The Sketch Books of Lawrence Halprin, 1981; filmmaker: Le Pink Grapefruit, Franklin Delano Roosevelt Memorial, How Sweet It Is!, Designing Environments for Everyone. Panelist White House Conf. Natural Beauty, 1965; mem. bd. urban cons. Bur. Pub. Roads, 1966-67; design cons. Calif. Div. Hwys., 1963-65; landscape architect, urban cons. San Francisco Bay Area Rapid Transit Dist., 1963-66; mem. Gov.'s Conf. Calif. Beauty, 1966, Nat. Council Arts, 1966—, Adv. Council, Historic Preservation, 1967—; bd. dirs., San Francisco Dancers Workshop Co., 1959—. Served to lt. (j.g.) USN, 1943-46. Named One of Leaders of Tomorrow, Time mag. 1953, recipient awards including Allied Professions Gold medal AIA 1964, Thomas Jefferson award in architecture 1979; Richard J. Neutra award for Excellence, 1986; honored Changing Places Exhbn., San Francisco Mus. Modern Art, 1986. Fellow Am. Soc. Landscape Architects; mem. Am. Acad. Arts and Scis., Sierra Club. Democrat. Jewish. Address: 444 Brannan San Francisco CA 94107

HALSEY, ROBERT HARRY, controller, communications executive; b. St. Louis, Apr. 6, 1950; s. Robert and Dorothy (Stephens) H.; m. Anita C. Crafts, Oct. 19, 1985. BBA, Lincoln U., Jefferson City, Mo., 1972. Sr. acct. Ole's Home Ctrs., Pasadena, Calif., 1978-82; asst. controller Corona (Calif.)-Foothill Co., 1982-84; ptnr. Bookkeeping Plus, San Dimas, Calif., 1984; contr. Pasadena Media, Inc., 1984-89; with Ramco Music Distbr's., Pasadena, 1989—; pres. Macro Media, Inc., Pasadena, 1986—, also bd. dirs. Republican. Office: Ramco Music Distbr's 35 N Arroyo Pkwy Pasadena CA 91103

HALSTEAD, DAVID STEWART, educational administrator; b. Hillsboro, Oreg., Jan. 28, 1949; s. Herbert Charles Lockwood and Vernona Sina (Stewart) H.; m. Linda Louise Barker, June 5, 1971; children: Jeffrey Stewart, Michael David. BA in Edn., Pacific Luth. U., 1971, MA in Edn., 1975; EdD, Portland State U., 1988. Standard teaching prin., supt. credentials, Wash. Tchr., coach Yelm (Wash.) Jr.-Sr. High Sch., 1971-74; asst. prin. Yelm Sr. High Sch., 1974-77; prin. Nooksack (Wash.) Valley Jr.-Sr. High Sch., 1977-82, Hudson's Bay High Sch., Vancouver, Wash., 1982—. Author: Principal's Survival Kit, 1979. Named Clark County Rising Star, Columbian newspaper, Vancouver, 1989. Mem. Nat. Assn. Secondary Sch. Prins. (nat. conv. speaker, presenter 1980-83), Wash. Assn. Secondary Sch. Prins. (pres. 1982-83, chmn. coll. rels. com. 1987-89, exec. bd. Wash. coun. on high sch. coll. rels. 1986-89), Assn. Wash. Sch. Prins. (exec. bd. 1980-84), Phi Delta Kappa (editor St. Helen's chpt. 1984-85, dir. rsch. 1988-89). Lutheran. Office: Hudson's Bay High Sch 1206 E Reserve St Vancouver WA 98661

HALSTEAD, JOHN HENRY, non-profit foundation administrator; b. Fruita, Colo., July 13, 1944; s. Marshall H. and Susie E. (Ball) H.; m. Rebecca L. Halstead, Jan. 7, 1967 (div. June 1988); children: Michael, Leah. BS in Edn., So. Oreg. Coll., 1966, MS in Polit. Sci., 1974; postgrad., Portland State U., U. Oreg. Grand asst. So. Pacific R.R., Portland, Oreg., 1962-71; with sales dept. J.C. Penney & Co., Grants Pass, Oreg., 1962-71; tchr. Redmond (Oreg.) Sch. Dist. 2J, 1966-71; project coord. Cen. Oreg. Consortium-NABS, Redmond, 1971-72; vocat. dir. Opportunity Found. of Cen. Oreg., Redmond, 1972-73, exec. dir., 1973—; exec. dir. Housing Opportunities, Inc., Redmond, 1984—, Residential Housing, Inc., Redmond, 1987—; bd. dirs. COCAAN-Community Action, Bend, Oreg.; mem. coun. Oreg. Pvt. Industry Coun., Albany, 1988—, Supported Employment Coun. Cen. Oreg., 1986—. Mem. com. St. Charles Med. Ctr., Bend, 1987—; mem. planning commn. City of Redmond, 1986—; bd. dirs. County STF Coms., 1986—; mem. ARC, 1972—. Named one of Outstanding Adminstrs. Deschutes County, 1980, 81. Mem. Oreg. Assn. Rehab. Facilities (pres. 1987-88), Oreg. Providers Assn. (treas. 1983—), Kiwanis, Elks. Democrat. Office: Opportunity Found Cen Oreg PO Box 430 Redmond OR 97756

HALVER, JOHN EMIL, nutritionist; b. Woodinville, Wash., Apr. 21, 1922; s. John Emil and Helen Henrietta (Hansen) H.; m. Jane Loren, July 21, 1944; children: John Emil, Nancylee Halver Hadley, Janet Ann Halver Fix, Peter Loren, Deborah Kay. B.S., Wash. State U., 1944, M.S. in Organic Chemistry, 1948; Ph.D. in Med. Biochemistry, U. Wash., 1953. Plant chemist Asso. Frozen Foods, Kent, Wash., 1946-47; asst. chemist Purdue U., 1948-49; instr. U. Wash., Seattle, 1949-50; affiliate prof. U. Wash., 1960-75, prof. Sch. Fisheries, 1975—; condr. research on vitamin and amino acid requirements for fish; identified aflatoxin B1 as specific carcinogen for rainbow trout hematoma, identified vitamin C2 for fish; dir. Western Fish Nutrition Lab., U.S. Fish and Wildlife Service, Dept. Interior, Cook, Wash., 1950-75, sr. scientist, nutrition, Seattle, 1975-78; cons. FAO, UNDP, Internat. Union Nutrition Scientists, Nat. Fish Research Inst., Hungary, World Bank, Euroconsult, UNDP, IDRC; affiliate prof. U. Oreg. Med. Sch., 1965-69; vis. prof. Marine Sci. Inst., U. Tex., Port Arkansas; pres. Fisheries Devel. Technology, Inc., 1980—, Halver Corp., 1978—. Served from pvt. to capt. U.S. Army, World War II; col. USAR. Decorated Purple Heart, Bronze Star with oak leaf cluster, Meritorious Service Conduct medal. Fellow Am. Inst. Fishery Research Biologists; mem. Soc. Exptl. Biol. Medicine, Nat. Acad. Sci., Am. Sci. Affiliation, Am. Chem. Soc., Am. Fishery Soc., Am. Inst. Nutrition, Phi Lambda Upsilon, Pi Mu Epsilon, Alpha Chi Sigma. Methodist (lay leader). Club: Rotary. Home: 16502 41 Ave NE Seattle WA 98155 Office: U Wash Sch Fisheries WH-10 Seattle WA 98195

HALVERSON, LAWRENCE HOLTON, II, sales executive; b. N.Y.C., May 2, 1958; s. Lawrence Holton and Diane (Kraut) H. BBA in Econs., N. Tex. State U., Denton, 1981. With Indsl. Bolt & Nut Co., Newark, 1982; salesman Moore Bus. Forms, Denver, 1982-85; sr. salesman Honeywell, Inc., Denver, 1985—; trainer, group leader Dale Carnegie Sales Orgn., Denver, 1988. Sun. sch. tchr. Mission Hills Bapt. Ch., Littleton, Colo., 1988. Mem. Mission Hills Singles, Cherry Creek Coloradans Soccer Team (capt. 1984—). Republican. Christian Ch. Office: Honeywell Inc 7108 S Alton Way Bldg B Englewood CO 80112

HALVERSON, LOWELL KLARK, lawyer, writer; b. Tacoma, May 4, 1942; s. Sidney Lawrence and Jeannette (Thompson) H.; m. Diane Edna Vosburgh, June 13, 1964; children: Liana Kay, Ward Vosburgh. AB, Harvard U., 1964; JD, U. Wash., 1968. Bar: Wash. 1968, N.Y. 1981, U.S. Supreme Ct. 1979, Alaska 1989. Sr. ptnr. Halverson & Strong, Seattle, 1970—; bd. dirs. Wash. Legal Found., 1984—. Author, editor: Washington Lawyer Practice Manual, 3 vols., 1972-78; author: (with others) Divorce in Washington-A Humane Approach, 1985; (with others) Divorce in New York, 1987. Fellow Am. Acad. Matrimonial Lawyers; mem. ABA, Wash. State Bar Assn. (gov. 7th congl. dist. 1977-80, merit award 1988, editor-in-chief Family Law Deskbook), Alaska State Bar Assn., N.Y. State Bar Assn., Seattle-King County Bar Assn. (trustee 1975-77, chmn. young lawyers sect. 1974-75, Disting. Service award 1986). Clubs: Harvard of Wash. (pres. 1974), Rainier. Home: 3014 90th Pl SE Mercer Island WA 98040 Office: Halverson & Strong 900 Hoge Bldg 705 2d Ave Seattle WA 98104

HAMACHEK, TOD RUSSELL, manufacturing executive; b. Jan. 3, 1946; m. Barbara Callister, 1969; children: Mark, Elizabeth. BA, Williams Coll., 1968; MBA, Harvard U., 1970. Nat. sales mgr. Harris Corp., Westerly, R.I., 1970-74; asst. to pres. Gt. Western Malting Co., Vancouver, Wash., 1974-76; v.p. sales Gt. Western Malting Co., Vancouver, Oreg., 1976-79, pres., chief exec. officer, 1979-84; pres., chief ops. officer Penwest, Ltd., Bellevue, Wash., 1984-85, pres., chief exec. officer, 1985—; sr. v.p. Univar Corp., Seattle, 1982-84; bd. dirs. N.W. Natural Gas Co., First Interstate Bank of Wash. Trustee Lewis and Clark Coll., Portland, Oreg., Lakeside Sch., Seattle, Seattle Found., Va. Mason Ctr., Washington Pub. Paper Found.; past trustee Portland Opera Assn., Pacific Crest Outward Bound Sch., Outward Bound, Inc.; bd. dirs. Va. Mason Hosp. Mem. Young Pres.' Orgn., Wash. Roundtable, Wash. Pulp & Paper Found. Office: Penwest Ltd 777 108th Ave NE Ste 2390 Bellevue WA 98004

HAMADANI, SIAVOSH MOSHFEGH, electronics company executive; b. Teheran, Iran, May 24, 1949; came to U.S., 1971; s. Raby Moshfegh Hamadani and Farrokh (Faezi) Ekbatani; m. Vida Amid, Sept. 16, 1978; children: Kambiz, Kiarash. BS, U. Rome, 1971; PhD, MIT, 1976. Research asst. European Space Research Inst., Rome, 1970-71, MIT, Boston, 1972-76; group leader Atomic Energy Orgn. Iran, Teheran, 1976-84; research assoc. U. Rome, 1984; assoc. prof. Western Ky. U., Bowling Green, 1984-85; pres., chmn., chief exec. officer Laseronics Inc., Torrance, Calif., 1985—; cons. Oak Ridge (Tenn.) Nat. Lab., 1985, sci. corr. Keyhan Internat., Teheran, 1978-79; researcher in field; lectr. Nat. U. Iran, Teheran, 1980. Editor Iranian Jour. Physics, 1983-84; translator: The Ascent of Man, 1979. Grantee Iran Def. Industries, 1983-84, NSF, 1985. Mem. Laser Inst. Am. Jewish. Office: Laseronics Inc 2808 Oregon Ct Ste L-12 Torrance CA 90503

HAMBIDGE, DOUGLAS WALTER, archbishop; b. London, Mar. 6, 1927; emigrated to Can., 1956; s. Douglas and Florence (Driscoll) H.; m. Denise Colvill Lown, June 9, 1956; children—Caryl Denise, Stephen Douglas, Graham Andrew. A.L.C.D., London U., 1953, B.D., 1958, D.D., 1969. Ordained deacon Church of England, 1953, priest, 1954, consecrated bishop, 1969; asst. curate St. Mark's Ch., Dalston, London, 1953-55; priest-in-charge St. Mark's Ch., 1955-56; incumbent All Saints Ch., Cassiar, B.C., Can., 1956-58; rector St. James Parish, Smithers, B.C., 1958-64, North Peace Parish, Ft. St. John, B.C., 1964-69; canon St. Andrew's Cathedral, 1965; lord bishop of Caledonia, 1969-80, New Westminster, B.C., 1980-81; lord archbishop of New Westminster and metropolitan of B.C., 1981—. Office: 302-814 Richards St, Vancouver, BC Canada V6B 3AY

HAMBLIN, JAMES R., radio producer; b. Bell, Calif., Oct. 31, 1936; s. John H. and Fredericka L. (Zwally) H.; (div. 1979); 1 child, Lee. Student, San Bernardino Valley Coll., 1955, Long Beach State Coll., 1969; AA, Coll. of San Mateo, 1970; BA, San Francisco State U., 1975. Disc jockey Sta. KRNO, San Bernardino, 1954; newsman Stas. KNRO, KMEN, KFXM, San Bernardino, 1955-63, Sta. KRLA Radio, L.A., 1963-68; news editor Sta. KCBS, San Francisco, 1968, newsman, 1969-80; press sec. Tom Lantos Congress Campaign, Burlingame, Calif., 1980; TV news writer Sta. KPIX-TV, San Francisco, 1981-82; newsman Sta. KFBK Radio, Sacramento, 1982-86; producer State Lottery Radio Network, Sacramento, 1986—; capitol corr. Sta. KCBS Radio, San Francisco, 1987—. Mem. Bench-Bar-Media Com., Sacramento, 1982—. Recipient Best Interpretive Reporting award, San Francisco Press Club, 1972. Mem. Soc. Profl. Journalists, Radio TV News Dirs. Assn., Capitol Corrs. Assn., Sons of the Desert (Sacramento). Republican. Office: State Lottery Radio Network 925 L St Ste A Sacramento CA 95814

HAMBLIN, KEVIN LAVAR, dentist; b. Burley, Idaho, Oct. 20, 1954; s. Ernest A. and Elizabeth Hellen (Siddoway) Hale; m. Marlene Bingham, Mar. 4, 1957; children: K. Scott, Shane M., Chelsea, Shantae, Brittany, Krista. BS in Zoology, Biology, Idaho State U., 1982; DDS, U. Tenn., Memphis, 1987. Cubmaster Boy Scouts Am., Burley, 1987-88. Named one of Outstanding Young Men in Am., 1982, 83. Mem. ADA, South Idaho Dental Assn., Idaho S. Cen. Dental Assn. (v.p.). Republican. Home: 749 Mae Dr Twin Falls ID 83301 Office: Sawtooth Dental Group 1218 Filer Ave E Twin Falls ID 83301

HAMBROOK, ERNEST CECIL, oil company executive; b. Calgary, Alta., Can., Mar. 29, 1937; came to U.S., 1982; s. Ernest Cecil and Lilian Evelyn (Dundas) H.; m. Carole Anne Mitchell, Aug. 27, 1960 (div. 1985); children: Keith Gordon, Carolyn Fay; m. Constance Marie Chernosek, May 2, 1987. BCommerce, U. Alta., 1960. From acct. to v.p. adminstrn. Home Oil Co. Ltd., Calgary, Alta., Can., 1961-82; sr. v.p. fin. adminstrn. Home Oil Co. Ltd., Denver, 1982-83, sr. v.p., chief ops. officer, 1983-87, pres., chief exec. officer, 1987—; bd. dirs. Home Petroleum Corp., HPC, Inc., Denver. Active United Way of Calgary, 1980-82. Mem. Calgary Personnel Assn. (pres. 1969-70). Office: Home Petroleum Corp 1225 17th St Denver CO 80202

HAMBY, M. CHARLES, school administrator; b. Ludlow, Okla., Aug. 10, 1933; s. Edward Wilder Hamby and Dovie Mae (Mowdy) Rone; m. Ellen Rose Hamby, May 27, 1955 (div. Aug. 1982); children: Stephen Vaughn, Kevin Charles, Valerie Lynn; m. Janet Rae, June 5, 1987. BS, Southeastern U., 1956; MA in Bus., Ea. Wash. U., 1966; MA in Adminstrn., U. Oreg., 1975. Tchr., coach Delta (Colo.) County Schs., 1958-61, Tekoa (Wash.) Schs., 1961-66; dept. chmn. Eugene (Oreg.) Pub. Schs., 1966-69, bus. adminstr., 1969—; prof. acctg. Lane Community Coll., Eugene, 1967-82; tax acct. Eugene, 1966—; collective bargaining cons., Eugene, 1974—. Contbr. articles to profl. jours. Served with AUS, 1956-58. Mem. Nat. Assn. Sch. Bus. Ofcls., Confederation Sch. Adminstrs., Oreg. Assn. Sch. Bus. Ofcls., Oreg. Assn. Sch. Adminstrs. Republican. Baptist. Home: 85813 Territorial Rd Eugene OR 97402 Office: Eugene Schs 200 N Monroe Eugene OR 97402

HAMERLY, MICHAEL T., librarian; b. Seattle, Sept. 23, 1940; s. James Charles Riley and Harriet Elinor (Jackson) H.; m. Carmen Victoria Flores Rosero, Jan. 19, 1963; 1 child, Michael Charles. BA, U. Wash., 1963, MA, 1965, M in Librarianship, 1979; PhD, U. Fla., 1970. From instr. to asst. prof. U. No. Colo., Greeley, 1970-74; dir. Archivo Arzobispal, Ecuador, 1975-78; researcher Departamento de Historia Maritima, Armada del Ecuador, 1975-77; vis. sr. lectr. dept. Spanish and Latin Am. studies Hebrew U., Jerusalem, 1981; cataloguer Pre-Columbian studies Dumbarton Oaks Rsch. Library and Collections, 1983-84; bibliographer, cataloguer Latin Am. Bibliographic Found., Redlands, Calif., 1985-88; catalog librarian, assoc. prof. Pacific collections Micronesian Area Rsch. Ctr., U. Guam, Mangilao, 1988--. Contbr. articles to profl. jours.; Andean area editor The Americas; a quar. rev. of Inter-Am. Cultural history, 1974-88; assoc. editor Revista del Archivo Historico del Guayas, 1975—; contbg. editor handbook of Latin Am. Studies, 1971—. NDEA, Title VI, Doherty and Fulbright-Hays grantee, fellow; Am. Coun. Learned Socs. and Social Sci. Rsch. Coun. grantee. Mem. Latin-Am. Studies Assn., Conf. on Latin-Am. History, Centro de Investigaciones Historicas de Guayaquil, Beta Phi Mu. Home: 9416 1st Ave Unit 113 Seattle WA 98115

HAMILTON, BRADLEY JAMES, restaurant corporation executive; b. San Francisco, Feb. 3, 1967; s. Donald E. and Susan D. (Schafer) B. Student, Fresno State U., 1985—. Dir. ops., unit gen. mgr. Dining Concepts, Inc., Fresno, Calif., 1985—; owner Dining Concepts, Inc., Merced, Calif., 1988—, Arroyo Grande, Calif., 1988—. Mem. Racquettime. Republican. Methodist. Home: 475 W Sierra St Apt 272 Fresno CA 93711 Office: Dining Concepts Inc 5665 N Blackstone St Fresno CA 93710

HAMILTON, BRUCE EDWARD, sociologist; b. Logan, Ohio, Mar. 2, 1950; s. Edward Kenley and Alice Alberta (Van Atta) H.; m. Carolyn Manuel, Dec. 24, 1976 (div. Apr. 1981); m. Christine Addie Nolte, May 16, 1987. BS, Ariz. State U., 1972; MA, Western Mich. U., 1974; PhD, Am. U., 1976. Instr. N.J. Med. Sch., Coll. Medicine and Dentistry, Newark, 1976-78; mem. research staff East Orange (N.J.) VA Hosp., 1976-78; adj. prof. Seton Hall U., Orange, N.J., 1978; sr. human factors engr. Sikorsky Aircraft div. United Techs., Stratford, Conn., 1983-87; human factors scientist Lockheed Aero Systems Co., Burbank, Calif., 1987—; mem. aeromed del. to People's Republic China, 1987. Contbr. articles to profl. jours.; patentee helmet mounted display symbols and techniques. Capt. U.S. Army, 1978-83. Mem. Am. Helicopter Soc., Human Factors Soc. Republican. Baptist. Home: 28088 Wildwind Rd Canyon Country CA 91351

HAMILTON, CHARLES HOWARD, metallurgist; b. Pueblo, Colo., Mar. 17, 1935; s. George Edwin and Eva Eleanor (Watson) H.; m. Joy Edith Richmond, Sept. 7, 1968; children: Krista Kathleen, Brady Glenn. BS, Colo. Sch. Mines, 1959; MS, U. So. Calif., 1965; PhD, Case Western Res. U., 1968. Research engr. Space div. Rockwell Internat., Downey, Calif., 1959-65; mem. tech. staff Los Angeles div. Rockwell Internat., 1968-75; tech. staff, phys. metallurgy Sci. Ctr., Thousand Oaks, Calif., 1975-77, group mgr. metals processing, 1977-79, prin. scientist, 1979-81, dir. materials synthesis and processing dept., 1982-84; assoc. prof. Washington State U., Pullman, 1984-87, prof., 1987—; chmn. Rockwell Corp. tech. panel, materials research and engring; co-organizer 1st Internat. Symposium Superplastic Forming, 1982, Internat. Conf. on Superplasticity and Superplastic Forming, 1988. Sr. editor Jour. Materials Shaping Tech.; dep. editor Scripta Metallurgica, 1989—; contbr. tech. articles to profl. publs.; patentee advanced metalworking and tech. Named Rockwell Engr. of Yr., 1979; recipient IR 100 award Indsl. Research mag., 1976, 80. Fellow Am. Soc. Metals; mem. AIME (shaping and forming com.), Sigma Xi. Home: 410 SE Crestview Pullman WA 99163

HAMILTON, DARDEN COLE, flight test engineer; b. Pitts., Nov. 28, 1956; s. Isaac Herman Hamilton and Grace Osborne (Fish) Thorp; m. Linda Susanne Moser, Aug. 8, 1976; children: Christopher Moser Hamilton, Elijah Cole Hamilton. BS in Aeronautics, St. Louis U., Cahokia, Ill., 1977; postgrad. in aeronautical tech., Ariz. State U. Licensed pilot; licensed airframe and power mechanic. Engr. McDonnell Douglas Aircraft Co., St. Louis, Mo., 1977-80; group leader, engring. Cessna Aircraft Co., Wichita, Kans., 1980-83, sr. flight test engr., 1983-85; sr. flight test engr. Garrett Turbine Engine Co., Phoenix, 1986—. Mem. Covenant of Grace Christian Fellowship; sr. comdr. Royal Rangers Boys Ministry. Mem. Soc. Flight Test Engrs. Republican. Lodge: Masons. Home: 4501 W Paradise Ln Glendale AZ 85306 Office: Garrett Turbine Engine Co 111 S 34th St Phoenix AZ 85010

HAMILTON, DAVID MIKE, publishing company executive; b. Little Rock, Feb. 25, 1951; s. Ralph Franklin and Mickey Garnet (Chappell) H.; m. Carol Nancy McKenna, Oct. 25, 1975; children: Elisabeth Michelle, Caroline Ellen. BA, Pitzer Coll., 1973; MLS, UCLA, 1976. Cert. tchr. library sci., Calif. Editor Sullivan Assocs., Palo Alto, Calif., 1973-75; curator Henry E. Huntington Library, San Marino, Calif., 1976-80; mgr. prodn., mktg. William Kaufmann Pubs., Los Altos, Calif., 1980-84; pres. The Live Oak Press, Palo Alto, 1984—; pub. cons. Am. Assn. Artificial Intelligence, Menlo Park, Calif., 1984—; cons. editor, gen. ptnr. Sensitive Expressions Pub. Co., Palo Alto, 1985—. Author: To the Yukon with Jack London, 1980, The Tools of My Trade, 1986; contbg. author (jour.) Small Press, 1986; (books) Book Club of California Quarterly, 1985, Research Guide to Biography and Criticism, 1986. Sec. Vestry of Trinity Parish, Menlo Park, 1986, bd. dirs., 1985-87; trustee Jack London Ednl. Found., San Francisco; bd. dirs. ISYS Forum, Palo Alto, Calif., 1987—. Mem. ALA, AAAI, Bookbuilder's West (book show com. 1983), Author's Guild, Soc. Tech. Communication (judge 1984), Assn. Computing Machinery (chmn. pub. com. 1984), COSMEP, 1986, Book Club of Calif., Sierra Club. Democrat. Episcopalian. Home: 2620 Emerson St Palo Alto CA 94306 Office: The Live Oak Press PO Box 60036 Palo Alto CA 94306

HAMILTON, GAIL HILDEGARD, photographer; b. Chgo., Mar. 19, 1943; d. Goerdt Herbert and Elsie Johanna (Hartig) Carstanjen; m. Gary Gordon Hamilton, Aug. 10, 1962 (div. 1975); 1 child, Mark Curtis; m. Daniel Edward Jones, Aug. 27, 1983. Grad. high sch., Ava, Mo. Photographer Del Carlo Studios, San Jose, Calif., 1964-75; sales and mktg. asst. Shapell Industries, Sunnyvale, Calif., 1975-76; freelance photographer San Jose, Calif., 1976-. Served with USAF, 1961-62. Mem. Profl. Photographers Greater Bay Area, Wedding Photographers Internat. Republican. Office: Gail Hamilton Photography PO Box 23807 San Jose CA 95153

HAMILTON, JACKSON DOUGLAS, lawyer; b. Cleve., Feb. 5, 1949; m. Margaret Lawrence Williams, Dec. 19, 1971; children: Jackson Douglas Jr., William Schuyler Lawrence. BA, Colgate U., 1971; JD, U. Pa., 1974. Bar: Calif. 1974, U.S. Dist. Ct. (cen. dist.) Calif. 1974, U.S. Tax Ct. 1978. Ptnr. Kadison, Pfaelzer, Woodard, Quinn & Rossi, L.A., 1986-87, Spensley, Horn, Jubas & Lubitz, L.A., 1987—; adj. prof. law U. San Diego, 1981, Golden Gate U., San Francisco, 1981-85; cons. Calif. Continuing Edn. Bar, 1983-84, select com. on sports Calif. Senate, 1983-85. Editor Entertainment Law Reporter, 1979—; contbr. articles to profl. jours. Mem. ABA (tax sect., internat. law sect.), Los Angeles County Bar Assn. (tax sect., internat. law sect.). Republican. Presbyterian.

HAMILTON, JAMES CHARLES, healthcare facilities administrator; b. Aberdeen, Wash., Apr. 1, 1952; s. David William Hamilton and Marion Lavonne (Brown) Price; m. Doris June Deering, Sept. 8, 1972; children: Jaymi Danielle, Keri Lynne. AS, Grays Harbor Community Coll., Aberdeen, Wash., 1973; AA, Highline Community Coll., Midway, Wash., 1980; BS, Cen. Wash. U., 1982; postgrad. in bus., Seattle Pacific U., 1988—. Cert. biomed. equipment technician, electronic technician. Communications technician Rad-Com Electronics, Aberdeen, 1973-74, Pacific Communications, Port Angeles, Wash., 1974-76; biomed. technician Swedish Hosp. Med. Ctr., Seattle, 1976; mgr. biomed. svcs. Group Health Coop., Seattle, 1976-81, asst. mgr. plant ops., 1982; dir. bldg. svcs. Overlake Hosp. Med. Ctr., Bellevue, Wash., 1982—; mem. adv. bd. Carnachan Assocs., Seattle, 1987—. Pres. Alderwood Acres Homeowners Assn., Woodinville, Wash., 1986—. With USN, 1970-71. Mem. ASHRAE, Am. Soc. for Hosp. Engring. (bd. dirs. region 9, 1989—), Assn. Energy Engrs., Wash. State Soc. Hosp. Engrs. (pres. 1988/89). Home: 22811 NE 202d St Woodinville WA 98072 Office: Overlake Hosp Med Ctr 1035 116th Ave NE Bellevue WA 98004

HAMILTON, MARGARET LAWRENCE, psychologist; b. Pottstown, Pa., Oct. 12, 1948; d. Mansfield Wiggin and Margaret Lawrence (VanVechten) Williams; m. Jackson Douglas Hamilton, Dec. 19, 1971; children: Jake, Will. BA, Skidmore Coll., 1970; MA, Bryn Mawr Coll., 1974; PhD, Internat. Coll., 1983. Cert. marriage, family counselor, Calif.; lic. psychologist, Calif. Research assoc. Fels Inst., Phila., 1971-72, Bryn Mawr (Pa.) Child Study, 1972-74; psychotherapist Santa Monica, Calif., 1976—. Supr. Bel Air Presbyn. Ch. Counseling Ctr., Bel Air, Calif., 1980—; leader Santa Monica (Calif.) counsel Boy Scouts Am., 1984—; pres. PTA, Santa Monica, 1988—; moderator Bel Air Presbyn. Deacon Bd., 1987; elder Bel Air Presbyn. Ch., 1989—. Mem. Am. Psychol. Assn., Internat. Transaction Analysis Assn., Christian Psychol. Assn., Calif. Psychol. Assn., AAUW (study chmn. 1978-82). Home: 1760 Sunset Ave Santa Monica CA 90405 Office: 1452 26th St 105 Santa Monica CA 90404

HAMILTON, MARIAN JOAN ETTER, arts consultant, designer; b. Dorris, Calif., June 21, 1938; d. Benjamin Walter and Eva Louise (Larson) Etter; m. William John Hamilton III, Nov. 23, 1956; children: John Douglas, Susan Marie. BA, Dominican Coll., San Rafael, 1954; teaching cert., Notre Dame Coll., San Bruno, Calif., 1956; student in Fine Arts, U. Calif., Davis. Exec. dir. Davis Art Ctr., 1972-80; African travel specialist U. Pacific, Stockton, Calif., 1981-83; owner Hamilton Design, Winters, Calif., 1983—. Mem. Civic Arts Commn., Davis, 1976-82; chmn. Yolo County Arts Council, Woodland, Calif., 1982-83; bd. dirs. Yolo County chpt. ACLU, 1988—. Democrat. Home and Office: Blue Oak Ranch Winters CA 95694

HAMILTON, NANCY JEANNE, structural engineer; b. Rochester, Minn., Jan. 1, 1959; d. Michael Joseph and Joanne Marguerite (Brunger) H.; m. Robert Scott Edwards; 1 child, Sarah Marie Hamilton Edwards. BS in Archtl. Engring., Calif. Poly. State U., San Luis Obispo, 1981; MSCE, MIT, 1984. Registered civil and structural engr., Calif. Project engr. KPFF Cons. Engrs., Los Angeles, 1984-85, project mgr., 1986-88; project mgr. Ove Arup and Ptnrs. Internat., Los Angeles, 1988-89, assoc., 1989—; vis. critic architecture Calif. Poly. State U., 1986. Recipient scholarships Rotary Club Redding, Calif. chpt., 1977, Women's Archtl. League So. Calif., 1980. Mem. Earthquake Engring. Research Inst., Am. Concrete Inst., ASCE, Sigma Xi, Tau Beta Pi. Republican. Roman Catholic. Home: 9523 Lucerne Ave Culver City CA 90230 Office: Ove Arup & Ptnrs Calif 10780 Santa Monica Blvd #300 Los Angeles CA 90025

HAMILTON, RICHARD LEE, surgeon; b. Hamilton, Ohio, June 20, 1939; s. Irvin Chester and Helen Grace (Yochum) H.; divorced; children: Kimberly Lynn, Kari Lee. Student, Ohio State U., 1958, DDS, 1963, MS, 1968. Instr. dental hygiene Clark County Community Coll., Las Vegas, Nev., 1978-80; pres. Nev. State Soc. Oral and Maxillofacial Surgeons, Las Vegas, 1982-83; asst. clin. prof. surgery sch. of medicine U. Nev., Las Vegas, 1985—; asst. dir. Pain Inst. Nev. U. Nev., Las Vegas, 1987-88. Mem. pub. edn. com. Am. Cancer Soc., Las Vegas, 1985-88; bd. dirs., Las Vegas, 1985-88, dir. pub. oral cancer screening program, 1987-88. Lt. comdr. USNR, 1963-65. Fellow Am. Assn. Oral and Maxillofacial Surgeons, Am. Dental Soc. Anesthesiology, Ohio State U. Alumni Assn. (pres. Las Vegas chpt. 1985-88). Republican. Office: 2330 Rancho Re Ste 106 Las Vegas NV 89102

HAMILTON, ROBERT EDWARD, oral and maxillofacial surgeon; b. St. Petersburg, Fla., June 24, 1946; s. Orman and Alice Katherine (Edmiston) H.; m. Martha Laine Wood, Sept. 13, 1975; children: Katherine Elizabeth, Melissa Ann. BA, Centre Coll., 1968; DDS, Case Western Res. U., 1978. Commd. comdr. USN, 1978—, dental officer, 1978—; head oral surgery sect. naval hosp. USN, Camp Pendleton, Calif., 1989—; cons. in field. Sr. warden of Vestry St. John's Episcopal Ch., Fallbrook, Calif., 1988—. Capt. USMC, 1968-74. Decorated D.F.C. with Gold Star, Air medal, 50 awards. Mem. Assn. Oral and Maxillofacial Surgeons, Am. Dental Soc. Anesthesia, Boys and Girls Club. Republican. Episcopalian. Office: Naval Hosp Dental Dept Camp Pendleton CA 92055

HAMILTON, RONALD RAY, minister; b. Evansville, Ind., May 6, 1932; s. Floyd Ray Hamilton and Ruby Dixon (Chism) Hahn; m. Norma Jean Robertson, Mar. 25, 1956; children: Ronnetta Jean, Andrea, Robert Rae. BA, U. Evansville, 1955; BD, Garrett Theol. Sem., 1958, MDiv, 1972. Ordained elder United Meth. Ch. Minister Scobey (Mont.) Meth. Ch., 1958-61, St. Andrew Meth. Ch., Littleton, Colo., 1961-67; sr. minister First Meth. Ch., Grand Junction, Colo., 1967-75, Christ United Meth. Ch., Salt Lake City, 1975-80, Littleton United Meth., 1980-86, U. Park United Meth., Denver, 1986—. Author: The Way to Success, 1972, The Greatest Prayer, 1983, A Chosen People, 1986; editor jour., 1978. Recipient Spl. award Mental Health Assn., Mesa County, Colo., 1974, Goodwill Rehab. Inc., 1975. Mem. Lions Club, Rotary Club, Civitan (chaplain 1964-67). Republican. Home: 7558 S Cove Circle Littleton CO 80122 Office: U Park Meth Ch 2180 S University Blvd Littleton CO 80210

HAMILTON, WILLIAM LARDNER, perfumer; b. Chgo., Jan. 17, 1952; s. Robert Alexander Hamilton and Joan Marie (Lardner) Beachley; m. Rita Megerdichian, July 1, 1971; children: Courtney Chris, Dane William. BA in Organic Chemistry, CUNY, 1975. Apprentice perfumer perfumer Bush Boake Allen, Montvale, N.J., 1976-80; perfumer Dial Corp., Scottsdale, Ariz., 1980-82, sr. perfumer, 1982-84, chief perfumer, 1984--. Recipient bronze award Internat. Perfumery Congress, 1984. Mem. Am. Soc. Perfumers, Mensa. Home: 16020 N 52nd Pl Scottsdale AZ 85254 Office: Dial Tech Ctr 15101 N Scottsdale Rd Scottsdale AZ 85254

HAMISTER, DONALD BRUCE, electronics company executive; b. Cleve., Nov. 29, 1920; s. Victor Carl and Bess Irene (Sutherl) H.; m. Margaret Irene Singiser, Dec. 22, 1946; children: Don Bruce, Tracy. A.B. cum laude, Kenyon Coll., 1947, LLD (hon.), 1989; postgrad., Stanford U., 1948-49, U. Chgo., 1957. Application engr. S.E. Joslyn Co., Cin., 1947-48; regional sales mgr. Joslyn Mfg. and Supply Co., St. Louis, 1950-52; mktg. mgr. Joslyn Mfg. and Supply Co., Chgo., 1953-55, asst. to pres., 1956-57, mgr. aircraft arrester dept., 1958-62, gen. mgr. electronic systems div., 1962-71; v.p., gen. mgr., dir. Joslyn Mfg. and Supply Co., Goleta, Calif., 1973-78, group v.p. indsl. products, 1974-78, pres., chief exec. officer, 1978-85, chmn., 1979—; chmn. Joslyn Mfg. and Supply Co. named changed to Joslyn Corp., 1986; pres. Joslyn Stainless; pres., dir. Joslyn Stamping Co.; pres., chmn., dir. Joslyn Def. Systems, Inc., 1981—; dir. Brewer Tichener Corp. Served to lt. USNR, 1942-46. Mem. IEEE, Airline Avionics Inst. (pres., chmn. 1972-74). Club: Univ. (Chgo.). Office: PO Box 817 Goleta CA 93017

HAMLIN, EDMUND MARTIN, JR., engineering manager; b. Utica, N.Y., June 9, 1949; s. Edmund Martin and Catherine Mary (Humphreys) H.; m. Nancy Ann Christensen, June 26, 1971; 1 child, Benjamin John. BSEE, Clarkson U., 1971; postgrad., U. So. Calif., 1972-73, RPI Hartford Grad. Ctr., 1980-82, UCLA, 1987-8. Engr. NASA Flight Rsch. Ctr., Edwards, Calif., 1971-75, Edwards, 1976-79; project engr. Sundstrand Energy Systems Div., Belvidere, Ill., 1975-76; sr. engr. Teleco Oilfield Svcs., Meriden, Conn., 1979-80; mgr. electronic systems Teleco Oilfield Svcs., Meriden, 1980-83, the sr. staff engr., 1984; sr. engr. NASA Ames-Dryden, Edwards, Calif., 1984-85; asst. chief flight systems NASA Ames-Dryden, Edwards, 1985—; prin. Technology Unlimited, Tehacapi, Calif., 1984—. Inventor: position measurement system, 1976, method for determining and correcting magnetic interference in boreholes, 1984, method for computing borehole azimuth while rotating, 1985. Com. mem. Tehachapi (Calif.) Unified Sch. Dist., 1987-88. Capt. U.S. Army, 1971-75. Mem. Instrument Soc. of Am., Am. Assn. Aeros. and Astronautics, Aircraft Owners and Pilots Assn. Republican. Home: 22220 Valley Vista Dr Tehachapi CA 93561 Office: NASA Ames-Dryden Flight Rsch Facility PO Box 273 Edwards CA 93523-5000

HAMM, CHARLES R., military academy administrator; b. Little Rock, Dec. 23, 1933; m. Sandra D. Hughes; children: Charles Jr., Rebecca; 1 stepchild, Russell D. Beer. Grad., U.S. Mil. Acad., West Point, N.Y., 1956; MS in Polit. Sci., Auburn U., 1969. Commd. USAF, 1956, advanced through grades to lt. gen., 1987; with 50th Tactical Fighter Wing USAF, Toul-Rosieres Air Base, France, 1958-60, Hahn Air Base, Fed. Republic Germany, 1960-61; with 474th Tactical Fighter Wing USAF, Cannon AFB, N.Mex., 1961-62; forward air controller 101st Airborne Div. USAF, Ft. Campbell, Ky., 1962-64; mem. Air Demonstration Squadron USAF, Nellis AFB, Nev., 1964-66; aide 7th Air Force Comdr. USAF, Republic of Vietnam, 1966; flight comrd. 416th Tactical Fighter Squadron USAF, Vien Hoa Air Base, Republic of Vietnam, 1966; instr., flight comdr. air-to-air flight Fighter Weapons Sch. USAF, Nellis AFB, 1966-68; staff officer for asst. chief of staff for studies and analysis USAF, Washington, 1969-70; dep. comdr. ops. 4th Tactical Fighter Wing USAF, Seymour Johnson AFB, N.C., 1972-73; dir. ops. 5th Air Force Hdqrs. USAF, Fuchu Air Sta., Japan, 1973-74; comdr. 8th Tactical Fighter Wing USAF, Kunsan Air Base, Republic of Korea, 1975-76; dep. dir. readiness devel. Office of the Dep. Chief of Staff Plans and Ops. USAF, 1976-78; dir. fighter and reconnaissance ops. hdqrs. tactical air command USAF, Langley AFB, Va., 1978-79; comdr. 33d Tactical Fighter Wing USAF, Eglin AFB, Fla., 1979-80; def. attache USSR USAF, 1981-83, dep. dir. pland Office of Dep. Chief of Staff, 1983-84, dir. ops., 1984-85; vice-comdr. Air Tng. Command USAF, Randolph AFB, Tex., 1985-87; supt. USAF Acad. USAF, Colorado Springs, 1987—. Decorated DSM, DFC, Def. Superior Svc. medal, Legion of Merit, Bronze Star medal, 5 air medals. Office: USAF Acad Office of Supt Colorado Springs CO 80840-5651

HAMM, GEORGE ARDEIL, teacher, hypnotherapist, consultant; b. San Diego, Aug. 13, 1934; s. Charles Ardeil and Vada Lillian (Sharrah) H.; m. Marilyn Kay Nichols, July 1, 1972; children—Robert Barry, Charles Ardeil II, Patricia Ann. B.S. in Music, No. Ariz. U., 1958, M.A. in Music Edn., 1961; M.A. in Ednl. Adminstrn., Calif. Lutheran Coll., 1978, M.S. in Guidance and Counseling, 1981. Cert. secondary sch. tchr., adminstr. pupil personnel services, Calif. Tchr. music Needles (Calif.) High Sch., 1958-61; tchr. career guidance and psychology, counselor Hueneme High Sch., Oxnard, Calif., 1961—; founder Nat. Judo Inst., Colorado Springs, Colo.; cons. applied sport psychology. Served with USMC, 1953-55; Korea. Mem. Am. Personnel and Guidance Assn., N.Am. Soc. Psychology of Sport and Phys. Activity, Am. Fedn. Tchrs., Assn. for Humanistic Edn. and Devel., Am. Council Hypnotist Examiners, U.S. Judo Assn. Inc. (6th Degree Black Belt; named sr. level coach of Judo, 1980), Phi Delta Kappa, Kappa Delta Pi. Republican. Mormon. Contbr. numerous articles to nat. and internat. Judo jours. Pioneer ednl. hypnosis. Home: 1864 S Bearden Ct Oxnard CA 93035 Office: Hueneme High Sch 500 Bard Rd Oxnard CA 93033

HAMM, WIL D., electronic engineer; b. Hamburg, Ger., Apr. 10, 1932; came to U.S. 1934; s. B. Frankline and Lyta (Rosler) H.; m. Sheryl R. DeWitt; children: Lyta L., Linda E., Laura E. BS in Physics, U. Wash., 1954. Pres., chief engr. Medistar Instrument Co., Inc., Seattle, 1957-75, W. H. Autopilots Inc., Seattle, 1976—. Mem. Queen City Yacht Club. Home: 4243 NE 92nd St Seattle WA 98115 Office: W-H Autopilots Inc 655 NE Northlake Pl Seattle WA 98105

HAMMACK, FELIX M., paper products company executive; b. Bolton, Miss., 1928. Grad., La. Tech. U., 1953. Exec. v.p. Williamette Industries, Portland, until 1987, vice chmn., 1987—. Office: Willamette Industries Inc 1300 SW 5th Ave Portland OR 97201

HAMMAN, STEVEN ROGER, vocational rehabilitation specialist; b. Santa Monica, Calif., Nov. 2, 1946; s. Roy Ernest H. and Joan Barbara (Werner) Scott; m. Christine Frances Solomon, May 29, 1976; children: Zachary Charles, Tamara Edith, Bryan Joseph. AA, Northeastern Colo. U., 1967; BA, Colo. State Coll., 1970; MA, U. No. Colo., 1972; MS, Drake U., 1981. Social worker Poudre-Thompson Transp. Corps, Ft. Collins, Colo., 1974-78; placement specialist Missoula (Mont.) Rehab. Ctr., 1978-80; rehab. counselor Adolph Coors Co., Golden, Colo., 1981; rehab. counselor, br. mgr. Nat. Rehab. Cons., Duluth, Minn., 1981-82; Mont. case svcs. dir. Nat. Rehab. Cons., Missoula, 1982-83; case svcs. dir. Northwest U.S. Nat. Rehab. Cons., Spokane, Wash., 1983-86; rehab. cons., pres., chief exec. officer Vocability, Inc., Post Falls, Idaho, 1986—; counselor, trainer Community Corrections Program, Ft. Collins, 1976. Community organizer VISTA, Clay, W.Va., 1973-74; pres., bd. dirs. Mountain Van Spl. Transp., Missoula, 1980. Mem. Nat. Rehab. Assn., Nat. Rehab. Counseling Assn. Office: Vocability Inc PO Box 772 Post Falls ID 83854

HAMMELL, GRANDIN GAUNT, financial services company executive, financial consultant; b. Rumson, N.J., Aug. 10, 1945; s. Grandin Kenneth and Catherine Elizabeth (Conklin) H.; m. Darlene Faye Settje, Nov. 21, 1972; children: Grandin Jeffrey, Heidi Grechen. B of Bus. Sci., Calif. State U., Los Angeles, 1979. V.p. Security Pacific Bank, N.A., Los Angeles, 1973-87; exec. v.p. The Wellington Group, Rolling Hills Estate, Calif., 1987—; speaker seminars on estate planning, So. Calif., 1983—. Exec. producer radio program The World of Money. Mem. planned giving com. of So. Calif. chpt. Arthritis Found., 1987—; v.p. Burbank Ednl. Found., 1984—; vol. Polit. Service. Glendale, 1988—. Mem. Glendale Estate Planning Commn. Lodges: Kiwanis, Elks. Office: The Wellington Group 4010 Palos Verdes Dr N Rolling Hills Estates CA 90274

HAMMER, ALVIN NEIL, metallurgist; b. Des Moines, Sept. 1, 1933; s. Lester G. and Norah G. (Mortishead) H.; m. Rita D. Malinauskas, Sept. 4, 1954 (div. May 13, 1977); children: Theodore W.E., Diana M., Christopher, Mathew F.; m. Virginia J. Buchanan, Dec. 1, 1979. Student, Iowa State U., 1951-52, Case Inst. Tech., 1952-54, U. Minn., 1954-56, St. Paul Coll. Law, 1955-56. Metallurgist mech. div. Gen. Mills, Mpls., 1955-56; mfg. engr. Convair div. Gen. Dyamics, San Diego, 1956-63; sr. research engr. Solar Turbines, Inc., San Diego, 1963—; product liability cons. to various pvt. law practices, San Diego, 1970—. Vol. Ilan Lael, San Diego, 1984—, Point Loma Assn., 1983—. Mem. Am. Soc. Metals Internat. (chmn. 1969-70, vice chmn. 1988—), Am. Soc. Non-destructive Testing (editorial reviewer, 1962-68). Democratic. Roman Catholic. Home: 3455 Valemont St San Diego CA 92106 Office: Solar Turbines Inc 2200 Pacific Hwy San Diego CA 92138

HAMMER, ARMAND, petroleum company executive, art patron; b. N.Y.C., May 21, 1898; s. Julius and Rose (Robinson) H.; m. Olga von Root, Mar. 14, 1927; m. Angela Zevely, Dec. 19, 1943; m. Frances Barrett, Jan. 26, 1956; 1 child. BS, Columbia U., 1919, MD, 1921, LLD, 1978; LLD, Pepperdine U., 1978, Southeastern U., Washington, 1978, U. Aix-en-Provence, 1981; D in Pub. Service, Salem (W.Va.) Coll., 1979; HHD, U. Colo., Boulder, 1979; DSc (hon.), U. S.C., 1983; PhD (hon.), Tel Aviv U., 1986. Pres. Allied Am. Corp., N.Y.C., 1923-25, A. Hammer Pencil Co., N.Y.C., London and Moscow, 1925-30, Hammer Galleries, Inc., N.Y.C., 1930—, J. W. Dant Distilling Co., N.Y.C. and Dant, Ky., 1943-54; pres., chmn. bd. Mut. Broadcasting System, N.Y.C., 1957-58; chmn. bd., chief exec. officer Occidental Petroleum Corp., Los Angeles, 1957—; chmn. M. Knoedler & Co., Inc., N.Y.C., 1972—, Knoedler-Modarco S.A., N.Y.C., 1977—; dir. Nat. State Bank, Perth Amboy, N.J., 1949-56, City Nat. Bank, Beverly Hills, Calif., 1962-71, Can. Occidental Petroleum Ltd., Calgary, Alta.; dir. Raffinerie Belge de Petroles, Antwerp, Belgium, 1968-79, Cities Service Co., Tulsa; hon. dir. Fla. Nat. Bank of Jacksonville, 1966-72; mem. Nat. Petroleum Council, 1968—, Com. on Arctic Oil and Gas Resources, 1980—. Author: The Quest of the Romanoff Treasure, 1936, autobiography (with Neil Lyndon) Hammer, 1987, (with Neil Lyndon) Hammer: Witness to History, 1987; subject of biography: The Remarkable Life of Dr. Armand Hammer (Robert Considine), 1975; Brit. edit. Larger than Life, 1976; The World of Armand Hammer (John Bryson), 1985. Pres. N.J. Aberdeen Angus Assn., 1948-49; Bd. govs. Monmouth County Orgn. Social Service, Red Bank, N.J., 1949-61, Monmouth Meml. Hosp., Long Branch, N.J., 1946-58, Eleanor Roosevelt Cancer Found., N.Y.C., 1960—, Ford's Theatre Soc., 1970—, UN Assn. U.S.A., 1976—; bd. dirs., exec. com. Internat. Council United World Colls., 1983—; mem. Royal Acad. Trust, Eng., 1980—; mem., fellow Met. Mus. Art, 1985; trustee U. North Africa Assn., 1968-71, Los Angeles County Mus. Art, 1968—, UCLA Found., 1973-76, Nat. Symphony, 1977—, United for Calif., 1977—, Capitol Children's Mus., 1978—; chmn. wine and spirits div. Vis. Nurse Service Greater N.Y., 1946, Am. Aid to France, 1947; mem. Citizens Food Com., 1946-47, Cardinal Spellman's Com. of Laity for Catholic Charities, 1946-48, Public Adv. Com. on U.S. Trade Policy, 1968-69, Am. Com. for Nat. Archives, 1974-76, Los Angeles County-U. So. Calif. Cancer Assos., 1975—, George C. Marshall Assos., James Smithson Soc. of Smithsonian Nat. Assos., 1977—, U. Okla. Assos., 1981—, Bus. Adv. Commn. for 1984 Olympics, 1981—, Los Angeles Olympic Citizens Adv. Commn., 1981—; hon. trustee Denver Art Mus., 1980—; mem. adv. bd. Inst. of Peace, 1950-54, Los Angeles Beautiful, Inc., 1969-75, Com. for a Greater Calif., 1969—, Fogg Art Mus. and Fine Arts Library, Cambridge, Mass., 1977—, The Friendship Force, 1977—, Am. Longevity Assn., Inc., 1980—, Center Strategic and Internat. Studies, Georgetown U., 1981—; mem. fine arts com. U.S. Dept. State, 1981—; chmn. Pres.'s Cancer Panel, 1981—; mem. exec. com. Econ. Devel. Bd. City of Los Angeles, 1968-73; trustee, chmn. exec. com. Salk Inst. Biol. Studies, San Diego, 1969—; bd. dirs. Los Angeles World Affairs Council, 1969—, Planned Parenthood World Population/Los Angeles, 1970—, U.S.-USSR Trade and Econ. Council, 1973—, Assos. Harvard Bus. Sch., 1975—, Calif. Roundtable, 1976—, Century City Cultural Commn., 1977—, Corcoran Gallery Art, Washington, 1978—, Keep Am. Beautiful, Inc., 1979—, Bus. Com. for Arts, N.Y.C., 1980—; bd. visitors Grad. Sch. Mgmt., UCLA, 1957—, UCLA Sch. Medicine Center for Health Scis., 1980—; exec. mem. Energy Research and Edn. Found., 1978—; charter mem. Nat. Visiting Council of Health Scis. Faculties, Columbia U., 1978—; mem. univ. bd. Pepperdine U., 1979—; mem. fellows for life New Orleans Mus. Art, 1980—; bd. dirs. Nat. Coordinating Ctr. forat. support council U.S. Com. for UNICEF, 1980—; founder mem. Pepperdine Assos., 1976—; pres. Found. of Internat. Inst. Human Rights, Geneva, 1977—; mem. exec. bd. dirs. UN Assn. Los Angeles; mem. Bd. Mcpl. Arts Commrs. Los Angeles, 1969-73; mem. budget and fin. com. of bd. trustees Los Angeles County Mus. Art, 1972-74; sponsor Internat. Inst. Human Rights Peace Conf., Oslo, 1978, Campobello Peace Park, 1979, Warsaw, 1980, Aix-en-Provence, France, 1981. Served with M.C. U.S. Army, 1918-19. Endowed Armand Hammer Center for Cancer Biology, Salk Inst., 1969; Armand Hammer prof. bus. and public policy UCLA, 1968; Frances and Armand Hammer wing Los Angeles County Mus. Art, 1969; Armand Hammer Animal Facility Salk Inst., 1976; Calif. Inst. Cancer Research UCLA, 1976; Ann. Armand Hammer Cancer Conf. and Fund Salk Inst., 1976; Harvard/Columbia Russian Study Fund, 1977; Julius and Armand Hammer Health Scis. Center Columbia U., 1977; Five-Yr. Funding Program UN Assn., 1978; Five-Yr. Funding Program Corcoran Gallery Art, 1979; Five-Yr. Funding Program Jacquemart-André Mus., Paris, 1979; Ann. Armand Hammer Award Luncheon Los Angeles, 1980; Los Angeles City Dept. Parks and Recreation, 1981, Armand Hammer Cancer Prize, 1982; Hammer-Rostropovich Cello Scholarship award U. So. Calif., 1982; Theatre du Gymnase, Marseille, France, 1983, Armand Hammer chair Leonardo Ctr., UCLA, 1985; Armand Hammer Ctr. for Advanced Studies in Nucelar Energy and Health, Los Angeles, 1986; recipient Humanitarian award Eleanor Roosevelt Cancer Found., 1962; city commendation Mayor of Los Angeles, 1968; decorated comdr. Order of Crown Belgium, 1962; comdr. Order of Andres Bellos Venezuela, 1975; Order of Aztec Eagle Mex., 1977; officer Legion of Honor France, 1978; Order of Friendship Among Peoples USSR, 1978; Royal Order of Polar Star Sweden, 1979; officer Grand Order of Merit Italy, 1981; Knight Comdr.'s Cross Austria, 1982; comdr. Nat. Order French Legion Honor, 1983; named Hon. Citizen and Seal Bearer of City of Vinci, Italy, 1982; Disting. Honoree of Yr. Nat. Art Assn., 1978; Golden Plate award Am. Acad. Achievement, 1978; Aztec award Mexican-Am. Opportunity Fond., 1978; Appeal of Conscience award N.Y.C., 1978; Spirit of Life award Oil Industry Council of City of Hope, 1979; award Antique Monthly, 1980; Entrepreneur of Yr. award U. So. Calif., 1980; Maimonides award Los Angeles Jewish Community, 1980; Golden Achievement award Andrus Gerontology Center, U. So. Calif., 1981; Ambassador of Arts award State of Fla., 1981; recipient John Jay award Columbia Coll., 1981, Disting. Citizen award Greater N.Y. Councils Boy Scouts Am., 1982, James Ewing Soc. Layman's award, Soc. Surgical Oncology, 1983, Medaille d'Or Mayor of Marseille and French Minister of Interior, 1983, Golda Meir award Israeli Prime Minister, 1984, Hilal-i-Quaid-i-Azam award Pres. Pakistan, 1985, Jubilee Medal Ambassador Zhulev of Bulgaria, 1985, Golden Archigymnaseum Decoration Mayor Renzo Imbeni of Bologna, 1985, Humanitarian award LWV, 1986, Human Achievement award Op. Calif., 1986, Nat. Recognition award Pres. United States Mexico, 1987, 1987 Humanitarian award Internat. Physicians for Prevention of Nuclear War, Inc., 1987, Emma Lazarus Statue Liberty award Nat. Jewish Hist. Soc., 1987, Nat. Arts Medal, 1987, Eleanor Roosevelt Humanitarian award United Nations Assn. San Francisco, 1987, Norman Vincent Peale award Insts. for Religion and Health, 1987, Spl. award Gen. Hosp. Mexico City, Ministry Health, 1987, Franklin and Eleanor Roosevelt Freedom from Fear award, 1988. Mem. Los Angeles Petroleum Club, Royal Acad. Arts (London), hon. corr., Am. Petroleum Inst. (dir. 1975—), Navy League U.S. (Los Angeles council 1980—), Fifty-Yr. Club Am. Medicine, Royal Scottish Acad. (hon.), AMA (life), N.Y. County Med. Assn., Internat. Inst. Human Rights, Alpha Omega Alpha, Mu Sigma, Phi Sigma Delta. Office: Occidental Petroleum Corp 10889 Wilshire Blvd Suite 1500 Los Angeles CA 90024 *

HAMMER, SAMUEL K., certified public accountant; b. Miami, Nov. 17, 1960; s. Oscar and Barbara (Weiser) H.; m. Deborah Reiser, May 24, 1987; 1 child, Daniel Jon. BBA in Acctg. & Fin., Emory U., 1982. CPA, Fla., Calif. Staff acct. Price Waterhouse, Miami, 1982-84; v.p., dir. Stern Hammer Acct. Corp., Los Angeles, 1984—; sec.-treas. Prime Cut Music, Inc., Los

Angeles, 1987—; chief fin. officer Integrated Fin. Mgmt., Inc., Los Angeles, 1988—. Mem. Am. Inst. CPA's, Nat. Soc. Pub. Accts., Fla. Inst. CPA's, Calif. Soc. CPA's, Sherman Oaks (Calif.) C. of C. Office: Stern Hammer Acctg Corp 14144 Ventura Blvd #255 Sherman Oaks CA 91423

HAMMER, WILLIAM AUSTIN, accountant; b. Des Moines, Jan. 9, 1953; s. Dale Austin and Ida Clara (Powers) H. BS in Acctg. with honors, Northwest Mo. State U., 1975. CPA, Ill. Mem. staff State Auditor of Iowa, Des Moines, 1975; asst. inventory controller Younker Bros., Inc., Des Moines, 1975-77; revenue dept. mgr. Cen. Tractor, Des Moines, 1977-78; mgr. acctg. svcs. Hawkeye Nat. Life Ins. Co., Des Moines, 1978-81; treas. Preferred Bus. Svcs., Des Moines, 1981; mgr. acctg. Capitol Life Ins. Co., Denver, 1981-82; chief acct., auditor, analyst The Navigators, Colorado Springs, 1982—; chmn. supervisory com. Mountain Bell Fed. Credit Union, Colo. Springs, 1988—, supervisory com., 1986—, exec. com., 1988—, treas., bd. dirs., 1988—. Mem. Colo. Soc. CPAs, Pikes Peak Obedience Club, Bernese Mountain Dog Club Am., Bernese Mountain Dog Club of Rockies, Pikes Peak Road Runners. Home: 2819 Straus Ln Colorado Springs CO 80907 Office: The Navigators 3820 N 30th St Colorado Springs CO 80904

HAMMERBACK, JOHN CLARK, communications educator; b. San Francisco, Oct. 6, 1938; s. William Joseph and Susan (Ridzik) H.; m. Jean Melton, Aug. 29, 1965; children: Kristen, Karen. BA, San Francisco State Coll., 1962; MA, U. Okla., 1965; PhD, Ind. U., 1970. Teaching asst. dept. speech communication U. Okla., Norman, 1963-65, Ind. U., Bloomington, 1965-68; prof. speech communication Calif. State U., Hayward, 1968-71, 79—, chmn. dept. speech and drama, 1972-79, affirmative action liason officer, 1986-88; lectr. U. N.Mex., Albuquerque, 1977, Oreg. State Coll., 1989, to local Rotary, Kiwanis and Lions clubs; speech writer for local polit. candidates, Fremont, Calif., 1978—; dir. conf. in rhetorical criticism U. N.Mex., 1987-88. Author: A War of Words: Chicano Rhetoric of the 1960s and 1970s, 1985, In Search of Justice: Studies in Speech Communication in the Indiana Tradition, 1987; contbr. articles, papers, and book reviews to profl. publs. Faculty Research grantee Calif. State U., Hayward, 1975; Meritorious Service award, 1985. Mem. Western Speech Communication Assn. (2d v.p. 1979-80, chmn. legis. assembly 1980, 1st v.p. 1981-82, chief conv. planner 1982-83, pres. 1983-84, assoc. jour.editor 1979-81, 84-87, disting. service award com. 1985, nominating com. 1984, chmn. membership com. 1980, mem. legis. assembly 1974-77, editor search com. 1989), Rhetoric Soc., Speech Communication Assn. (nominating com. 1984, com. on coms. 1984, mem. com. 1989), Calif. Speech Assn. (com. on intercultural communication 1976, bd. dirs. community counseling and edn. ctr., Fremont), Greater Kimber Area Homeowners' Assn. (v.p. 1984). Home: 203 Fisalia Ct Fremont CA 94539 Office: Calif State U Hayward CA 94539

HAMMERS, OLIVER BERTRAND, retired mechanical contracting company executive; b. St. Joseph, Mo., Nov. 23, 1924; s. Earl E. and Lola M. (Hetherington) H.; BS in Elec. Engring., U. Kans., 1950; m. Patricia Ruth Dillman, Nov. 27, 1954; children: Patrick James, David Earl. With Natkin & Co., 1950-84, v.p. spl. assignments, Omaha, 1966-68, exec. v.p., mgr. S. Central div., Dallas, 1968-80, res., chief exec. officer, Denver, 1980-84, chmn. bd., 1980-84, also pres.; bd. dirs. Natkin Service Co., Johansen Co., Fuel Economy Contracting Co.; Colo. pres., chief exec. officer Natkin Group, Inc., 1984-89; officer, dir. Charter Page, Inc. Served with AUS, 1942-46. Mem. Mech. Contractors Assn. (Man of Year award Tex. chpt. 1979), Denver C. of C. Club: Columbine Country. Office: Natkin Group Inc 2700 S Zuni St Englewood CO 80150

HAMMETT, BENJAMIN COWLES, psychologist; b. Los Angeles, Nov. 18, 1931; s. Buell Hammett and Harriet (Cowles) Graham; m. Ruth Finstrom, June 18, 1957; children: Susan, Sarah, Carol, John. BS, Stanford U., 1957; PhD, U. N.C., 1969. Lic. psychologist, Calif. Staff psychologist Children's Psychiat. Ctr., Butner, N.C., 1965-67; sr. psychologist VA Treatment Ctr. for Children, Richmond, Va., 1968-71; asst. prof. child psychiatry Va. Commonwealth U., Richmond, 1968-71; instr. psychology Western Grad. Sch. Psychology, 1980—; pvt. practice psychology Palo Alto, Calif., 1972—; affiliate staff mem. O'Connor Hosp., San Jose, Calif., 1980—; v.p. bd. dirs. Mental Research Inst., Palo Alto, 1982-83, pres. bd. dirs., 1983-85, vol. svcs. coord., 1984—, chmn. fin. com., 1986—. Co-author chpts. to two books. Vol. Boy Scouts Am., 1952-54, Peninsula Conservation Ctr., Palo Alto, 1983—, Calif. Acad. Scis., San Francisco, 1987—; treas. Cary Sch. PTA, Richmond, 1969-70. Named Eagle Scout, 1947; grantee NIMH, 1970. Mem. Am. Psychol. Assn., Am. Group Psychotherapy Assn. (cert. clin. mem.), Internat. Transactional Analysis Assn., Biofeedback Soc. Am. (BCIA cert.), Biofeedback Soc. Calif., Calif. State Psychol. Assn. Republican. Unitarian. Club: El Tigre (Stanford) (sec. 1954). Home: 301 Lowell Ave Palo Alto CA 94301 Office: 555 Middlefield Rd Palo Alto CA 94301

HAMMING, RICHARD WESLEY, computer scientist; b. Chgo., Feb. 11, 1915; s. Richard J. and Mabel G. (Redfield) H.; m. Wanda Little, Sept. 5, 1942. B.S., U. Chgo., 1937; M.A., U. Nebr., 1939, Ph.D. in Math, 1942. With Manhattan Project, 1945-46; with Bell Telephone Labs., 1946-76; mem. faculty Naval Postgrad. Sch., Monterey, Calif., 1976—; adj. prof. computer sci. Naval Postgrad. Sch., 1976—. Author books, papers in field. Fellow IEEE (Piore award 1979, $10,000 prize medal named in his honor 1986, 1st recipient of same 1988); mem. Assn. Computing Machinery (Turing prize 1968), Nat. Acad. Engring., Am. Math. Assn., AAAS. Office: Naval Postgrad Sch Code 52 Hg Monterey CA 93943

HAMMOCK, JANICE DEE, librarian; b. Seattle, Sept. 1, 1943; d. James Davis and Noel Mary (Carmichael) H. BS in math., U. Wash., 1965; MLS, 1968. Standard teaching cert. 1967. Math tchr. Bellingham (Wash.) Sch. Dist. 501, 1965-67; research asst. to chief of tech. svcs. Wash. State Libr., Olympia, Wash., 1968-69; cataloger 1969-72, systems libr., 1972-76, mgr. cataloging, 1976—. Recipient: Alcoa Scholarship, U. Wash., 1961-62. Mem. Wash. Libr. Assn. (vice-chmn. Tech Svcs. Interest Group, 1980-81, chmn. 1981-82, Interest Group Rep. 1981-83, treas., 1983—), Northwest Libr. Assn., Am. Libr. Assn., Am. Rhododendron Soc. (Olympia, Wash. chpt. sec., 1986—), Nib'n Inks, Beta Phi Mu. Office: Wash State Library AJ-11 Olympia WA 98504-0111

HAMMON, PATRICIA JANE, art consultant, appraiser; b. Cleve., Oct. 21, 1946; d. Arthur James and Jane Mary (Price) McClaskey; m. William M. Hammon, Jan. 7, 1971. Cert., Yale-New Haven Sch. Nursing, 1967; BFA, U. Hawaii, 1981. Staff nurse VA Hosp., Washington, 1969-71; edn. program coord. Honolulu Emergency Med. Svcs., 1976-78; edn. coord. CPR program Hawaii Heart Assn., Honolulu, 1978-79; cons. Honolulu Acad. of Arts, 1979-81; owner, cons., appraiser The Art Loft, Honolulu, 1981—; v.p. Arts Coun. Hawaii, Honolulu, 1984—. Air evacuation nurse vol., Honolulu chpt. ARC, 1972-75; docent, Honolulu Acad. of Arts, 1975-81; bd. dirs. Spl. Olympics, Honolulu, 1981-84; chmn. bd. dirs. Hawaii Heart Assn., Honolulu, 1986-88. 1st lt. nurses corps, U.S. Army, 1966-69, Vietnam. Mem. Internat. Soc. Appraisers, Hawaii Mus. Assn., Am. Soc. Interior Design (chmn. industry found. 1987—), Plaza Club, Maunalua Bay Club, Beaver Creek Club, Co. Office: The Art Loft Bldg 4 1020 Auahi St Honolulu HI 96814

HAMMOND, CHARLES EDGAR, data processing executive; b. Kellogg, Idaho, Dec. 24, 1943; s. Charles William and Irene Elizabeth (Hoffman) H.; m. Jennifer Lee Giard, Aug. 12, 1967; children: Christa Lee, Robert Charles. BBA, Washington State U., 1967; MBA, Golden Gate U., 1973. Programmer, analyst Boeing Airplane Co., Seattle, 1967-68, Chevron Corp., San Francisco, 1969-70; div. mgr. Chevron Info. Tech. Co., San Ramon, Calif., 1980—. Mem. adv. com. Re-entry Program for Women and Minorities, Computer Sci. U. Calif., Berkeley, 1983—. Recipient Award of Merit Calif. Dept. Rehab., Sacramento, 1981. Mem. Beta Theta Pi. Club: Crow Canyon Country (San Ramon). Home: 2749 Tumwater Dr Walnut Creek CA 94598

HAMMOND, DAVID GREENE, engineering company executive, consultant; b. Paterson, N.J., Sept. 8, 1913; s. Nelson Davis and Frances Edna (Greene) H.; m. Joan Constance Morse, Jan. 7, 1947; children—David, Peter, Victoria. B.S. in Civil Engring., Pa. State U., 1934; M. of Civil Engring., Cornell U., 1939; postgrad., Army-Navy Staff Coll., 1945, Army War Coll., 1957. Registered profl. engr., Md., Calif. Instr. civil engring. Pa. State U., University Park, 1934-37; commd. 2d lt. C.E. U.S. Army, 1937, advanced through grades to col., 1952, ret., 1964; dist. engr. Omaha Dist. C.E., 1957-60; chief installations Continental Army Command, Fortress Monroe, Va., 1963-64; asst. gen. mgr. ops. and engring. San Francisco Bay Area Rapid Transit Dist., 1964-73; v.p. Daniel, Mann, Johnson & Mendenhall (DMJM), Balt., 1973—, Los Angeles; chmn. U.S. Nat. Com. on Tunneling Tech. Contbr. articles to profl. jours. Recipient Award of Merit, San Francisco Bay Area Rapid Transit Dist.; named Man of Yr., Kiwanis Internat. and Am. Pub. Works Assn., 1969. Fellow ASCE (co-chmn. specialty conf. on risks and liability), Nat. Soc. Profl. Engrs., Soc. Am. Mil. Engrs.; mem. Am. Pub. Transit Assn. (elected Transit Hall of Fame 1986), Am. Pub. Works Assn., Nat. Acad. Engring. Republican. Clubs: Center (Balt.); The Moles, Athletic (Los Angeles). Home: 364 Noren St La Canada CA 91011 Office: DMJM 3250 Wilshire Blvd Los Angeles CA 90010

HAMMOND, JUDY MCLAIN, business services executive; b. Downey, Calif., June 24, 1956; d. Ernest Richard and Bernice Elaine (Thompson) McLain; m. Dennis Francis Hammond, Aug. 15, 1981. BS in Mgmt., Pepperdine U., 1982; MBA, U. So. Calif., 1986. Br. mgr. Kelly Svcs., Encino, Calif., 1978-81; mktg. mgr. Payco Am. Corp., Encino, 1981-83, GC Svcs. Corp., Santa Ana, Calif., 1983-86; pres. Resource Mgmt. Svcs., Norwalk, Calif., 1986—; qualified mgr. Bur. Collection & Investigative Systems. Mem. adv. com. Cerritos Coll. Mem. Am. Soc. Tng. Devel., Women in Mgmt., Toastmaster, Club.

HAMMONS, STACY ANN, social worker; b. Poplar Bluff, Mo., Oct. 26, 1961; d. Glenn Alton and Emogene (Boyer) B. BSW summa cum laude, U. Mo., 1984; MSW, U. Denver, 1985. Counselor The Shelter, Columbia, Mo., 1983-84; victim advocate intern Denver City Atty.'s Office, 1985; caseworker Gateway Battered Women's Shelter, Aurora, Colo., 1985—. Mem. Nat. Assn. Social Workers, Colo. Orgn. for Victim's Assistance, N.Am. Assn. Christians in Social Work. Democrat. Mem. Ch. of Nazarene. Office: Gateway Battered Women's Shelter PO Box 914 Aurora CO 80040

HAMPDEN-SMITH, MARK JONATHAN, chemistry educator; b. London, July 1, 1960; came to U.S., 1986; s. Francis Willington and Joan (Briscombe) H-S.; m. Tessa Catherine Ward, Aug. 30, 1986. BSc, U. London, 1981, PhD, 1984. Post-doctoral fellow U. Guelph Dept. Chemistry, Ont., Can., 1984-86, Ind. U. Dept. Chemistry, Bloomington, 1986-88; asst. prof. chemistry U. N.Mex., Albuquerque, 1988—. Contbr. articles to profl. jours. Mem. Am. Chem. Soc., Materials Rsch. Soc. Office: U New Mexico Dept of Chemistry & Ctr Micro-Engineered Ceramics Albuquerque NM 87131

HAMPL, PETER FRANCIS, oral surgeon; b. Saint Paul, May 13, 1942; s. Stanley R. and Mary T. (Marmum) H.; m. Jeanne T. Hampl, Aug. 24, 1968; children: TIm, Theresa. BS, U. Minn., 1967; DDS, NYU, 1969. Diplomate Am. Bd. Oral and Maxillofacial Surgery, Am. Bd. Forensic Odontology. Pvt. practice in oral and maxillofacial surgery, odontology Tacoma, Wash., 1970—. Fellow Am. Assn. Oral and Maxillofacial Surgeons, Am. Acad. Forensic Scis.; mem. ADA, Wash. State Dental Assn. (del. 1986), Pierce County Dental Soc. (trustee 1975-78, 83-86), Wash. State Soc. Oral and Maxillofacial Surgeons (pres. 1978-79). Office: 1901 S Cedar #106 Tacoma WA 98405

HAMPLE, STEPHEN R., investment firm manager, educator; b. Jamestown, N.D., Sept. 7, 1947; s. Ross M. and Helen (Johnson) H.; m. Carol Jean Dismore, 1978. Student, Chapman Coll., Orange, Calif., 1967; BA, Jamestown Coll., 1965-69; MA, U. N.D., 1969-70; EdD, Mont. State U., 1971-76. Instr. U. N.D., Grand Forks, 1970-71, Mont. State U., Bozeman, 1971-73; sr. staff specialist for higher edn. research Md. State Bd. Higher Edn., Annapolis, 1974-78; dir. of instl. research, adj. assoc. prof. Mont. State U., Bozeman, 1978-86; cons. finance and planning Bozeman, 1986-87; br. mgr. Fin. Network Investment Corp., Bozeman, 1987—; vice chmn. Bozeman Med. Arts Ctr, 1984—. Author: (with others) A Study Guide to Algebra and Trigonometry. Bd. dirs. Sourdough Vol. Fire Co., Bozeman, 1979-83; program coordinator Build A Better Bozeman, 1987—; mem. Gallatin Devel. Corp. Grantee Kellogg Found., 1979, N.W. Area Found., 1981, Nat. Ctr. for Higher Edn. Mgmt. Systems, 1983. Mem. Bozeman Area C. of C., Mont. State U. Alumni Assn., Assn. for Instl. Research (bd. dirs. 1984-86), Internat. Assn. Fin. Planning, Inst. Cert. Fin. Planners. Lodge: Rotary. Home: 2 Hodgman Canyon Bozeman MT 59715 Office: Fin Network Investment Corp 300 N Willson Ste 3003 Bozeman MT 59715

HAMPSHIRE, HOWARD MICHAEL, corporate security director; b. Atlanta, Aug. 23, 1947; s. Oliver Milton and Katie Lou (Hall) H.; m. Lynda Louise Lester, Aug. 9, 1968; children: Amy Carroll, Katie Allison, Michael Bradley. Student, Gordon Military Coll., 1966-67, Bob Jones U., 1967-69, Zonn Inst. Polygraph, 1978. Lic. polygraph examiner. Sgt. forensic div. Greenville County (S.C.) Sheriff's Dept., 1969-73; owner H.M. Hampshire & Assoc., Greenville, S.C., 1973-79; dir. security Ellmon's Inc., Atlanta, 1979-83; security cons. Security Concepts, Atlanta, 1983-86; dir. corp. security Western Stone & Metal Corp., Denver, 1986—; lectr. in field. Contbr. articles to mags. Precinct delegate Colo. Rep. Com., 1988. Named Outstanding Young Men of Am., U.S. Jaycees, 1973. Mem. Am. Soc. Indsl. Security, Ga. Polygraph Assn. (bd. dirs. 1980-81), Jewelry Security Alliance, Nat. Assn. of Chiefs of Police, Wade-Hampton Taylors Jaycees (v.p. 1972, Outstanding Chmn. of Yr. award 1982, Key Man of Yr. 1972, Pres. Award of Honor 1972), Masons. Republican. Baptist. Office: Western Stone & Metal Corp 7400 E Orchard Rd Ste 360 Englewood CO 80111

HAMPTON, CALVIN J., surveyor; b. Longview, Wash., Nov. 2, 1950; s. Rollen G. Hampton and Larene (Quigley) Wegdahl; m. Donna Jean Marcus, June 17, 1973; children: Christy Jean, Cally Jo, Jenny Lee. AA in Engring. Surveying Tech., Oreg. Inst. Tech., 1974. Land surveyor Crown Zellerbach Corp., Cathlamet, Wash., 1974-80; resident engr. Brusco Corp., Kelso, Wash., 1980-83; pres. Hampstur Corp., Longview, 1983—. Mem. Wahkiakum County Sch. Bd., 1977-80; dir. Kelso Girls Softball Assn., 1979—. Mem. Land Surveyors' Assn. of Wash. (pres. Lower Columbia chpt. 1988-89, sec. 1986-87), Nat. Soc. Profl. Surveyors, Am. Congress Surveying/Mapping. Office: Hampstur Corp 1010 Douglas A-3 Longview WA 98632

HAMPTON, HARLA DEE, school system administrator; b. Huntington Park, Calif., Sept. 15, 1943; d. Hubert Horace and Lulu Marjorie (Carey) H.; m. Glen William Funkhouser, July 3, 1960 (div. Sept. 14, 1972); children: Michael William, Lisa Marie Brannan, Michele Marjorie; m. John Bruce Morelli, Dec. 15, 1974. Grad. high sch., Santa Barbara, Calif. Adminstrv. asst. Laguna Blanca Sch., Santa Barbara, 1983-86, Bishop Garcia Diego High Sch., Santa Barbara, 1986—. Pres. Santa Barbara Birth Resource Ctr., 1987-88. Mem. South Coast Bus. Network (v.p. 1981-83, pres. 1983-84). Democrat. Home: 230 Los Alamos Santa Barbara CA 93109

HAMPTON, WILLIAM CHRISTOPHER, aerospace engineer; b. Walnut Creek, Calif., Oct. 25, 1954; s. William Edmund and L. June (Schneider) H.; m. Marcella Louise Moody, Nov. 2, 1986. BS, UCLA, 1979; postgrad., U. So. Calif., 1984-85. Commd. ensign USN, 1979, advanced through grades to lt., 1983; naval flight officer USN, San Diego, 1979-83; space test program mgr. USN, El Segundo, Calif., 1983-87, resigned, 1987; spacecraft integration mgr. McDonnell Douglas Space Systems Co., Huntington Beach, Calif., 1987—. Lt. comdr. aviation USNR, 1987—. Mem. AIAA., Planetary Soc. Office: McDonnell Douglas Space Systems Co 5301 Bolsa Ave Huntington Beach CA 92647

HAMREN, NANCY VAN BRASCH, bookkeeper; b. L.A., Feb. 2, 1947; d. Milton Carl and Winifred (Taylor) Van Brasch; m. Jerome Arthur Hamren, Feb. 14, 1981; children: Emily Allison, Meredith Ann. Student, Pasadena City Coll., 1964-65, San Francisco State Coll., 1966-67, U. Oreg., 1975-79. Bookkeeper Springfield Creamery, Eugene, Oreg., 1969—, also bd. dirs.; originator Nancy's Yogurt, Nancy's Cultured Dairy Products. Active mem. Oreg. Shakespearean Festival, Ashland, 1986. Mem. LWV, Audubon Soc., N.Am. Truffling Soc. Democrat. Unitarian. Home: 50 Lynnbrook Dr Eugene OR 97404 Office: Springfield Creamery 29440 Airport Rd Eugene OR 97402

HAMRICK, JOSEPH EUGENE, dentist; b. Shelby, N.C., Dec. 30, 1931; s. Drewry Joseph and Louise (Allen) H.; m. Emily Cole, Aug. 30, 1952 (div. 1972); children: Joseph Jr., Christie Leigh, Mark Stephen, Karla Anne; m. Ruth Brooks, July 16, 1972. BS, U. N.C., 1953, DDS, 1957; MS, Ohio State U., 1961. Instr. U. N.C. Dental Sch., Chapel Hill, 1955-57, Ohio State Dental Sch., Columbus, 1959-61; commd. 2d lt. USAF, 1957, advanced through grades to col., 1974, surgeon gen., 1965-80, retired, 1980; cons. to gen. dentists Am. Dental Assn., Colo., 1980—; researcher in field. Mcpl. judge Town of Monument (Colo.), 1981-88. Fellow Am. Bd. Prosthodontists; mem. Am. Dental Assn. (life), Am. Prosthodontic Assn., Am. Coll. Prosthodontists, Sertoma. Republican. Home and Office: 19130 Shadowood Dr Monument CO 80132

HAMRICK, JOSEPH EUGENE, JR., information services specialist; b. Chapel Hill, N.C., Feb. 4, 1954; s. Joseph Eugene Sr. and Emily Southerland (Cole) H.; m. Elaine Kay Metcalf, Oct. 2, 1982; children: Aubrie Nicole, Allison Laurel. Student, Met. State Coll., Denver, 1983—. Programmer, analyst Aviation Mgmt. Systems, Denver, 1980-83; mgr., AVsoft devel. PHH Aviation Systems, Golden, Colo., 1983-86; programmer, analyst Columbine Systems, Inc., Golden, 1986-88; dir., info. svcs. Cairn Mgmt. Co., Denver, 1988—; cons., pres. Bridgeware, Denver, 1985—. Cons. Terry Considine U.S. Senate Campaign, Denver, 1985-86. Sgt. USAF, 1975-79. Presbyterian. Home: 2299 S Yosemite Cir Denver CO 80231 Office: Cairn Mgmt Co 1873 S Bellaire St Denver CO 80222

HAN, ITTAH, political economist, high technology, computer engineering and financial strategist; b. Java, Indonesia, Jan. 29, 1939; came to U.S., 1956, naturalized, 1972; s. Hongtjioe and Tsuiying (Chow) H. BS in Mech. Engring. and Elec. Engring., Walla Walla Coll., 1960; MA in Math., U. Calif., Berkeley, 1962; BA in French, U. Colo., 1965, MS in Elec. Engring., 1961; MSE in Computer Engring., U. Mich., 1970; MS in Computer Sci., U. Wis., 1971; MBA in Mgmt., U. Miami, Fla., 1973; BA in Econs., U. Nev., 1977; MBA in Tax, Golden Gate U., 1979, MBA in Real Estate, 1979, MBA in Fin., 1980, MBA in Banking, 1980, MPA in Adminstrv. Orgn. and Mgmt., 1984. Cert. fin. planner. Salesman, Watkins Products, Walla Walla, Wash., 1956-60; instr. Sch. Engring. U. Colo., Denver, 1964-66; systems engr. IBM Corp., Oakland, Calif., 1967-69, Scidata Inc., Miami, Fla., 1971-72; chief of data processing Golden Gate Bridge, Hwy. and Transp. Dist., San Francisco, 1973-74; mgr. info. systems tech. and advanced systems devel. Summa Corp., Las Vegas, Nev., 1975-78; mgr. systems devel. Fred Harvey Inc., Brisbane, Calif., 1978-80; chmn. corp. systems steering com., mgr. systems planning Amfac Hotel & Resorts, Inc., 1978-80; tax strategy planner, innovative turnaround fin. strategy planner, chief exec. Ittahhan Corp., 1980—; exec. v.p. Developers Unltd. Group, Las Vegas, 1982-84; v.p. Fidelity Fin. Co., Las Vegas, 1984-85; exec. v.p. John H. Midby and Assocs., Las Vegas, 1982-84; sec., treas., dir. River Resorts Inc., Las Vegas, 1983-84; sec., treas. Goldriver Ltd., Las Vegas, 1983-84; pres. Weststar Gen. Ptnr. Co., 1984-85, Developers Group Service Co., 1984-86; chief exec. officer, pres. Very High Tech. Polit. Economy Turnaround Management Strategist, Inc., 1986—; chief exec. officer, pres. Artificial Intelligence Computer Engring. and Expert Systems Engring., Inc., 1986—; pres. Orion Land Devel. Co., Las Vegas, 1987—, Very High Tech. Computer Engring., Inc., Las Vegas, 1988—; instr. U. Nev. Sch. Elec. Engring., Reno, 1981; systems designer, cons. in field. Mem. IEEE, Assn. Computing Machinery, Am. Assn. Artificial Intelligence, Am. Math. Assn., Inst. Cert. Fin. Planners, Am. Contract Bridge League. Republican. Home and Office: PO Box 27025 Garside Sta Las Vegas NV 89126

HANAUER, JOE FRANKLIN, real estate executive; b. Stuttgart, Fed. Republic Germany, July 8, 1937; came to U.S., 1938; s. Otto and Betty (Zurndorfer) H.; m. Jane Boyle, Oct. 20, 1972; children: Jill, Wendy, Jason, Elizabeth. BS, Roosevelt U., 1963; postgrad., U. Chgo. Gen. sales mgr. Thorsen Realty, Oak Brook, Ill., 1966-74, pres., 1974-80; sr. v.p. Coldwell Banker, Newport Beach, Calif., 1980-83, pres., 1984, chmn. bd., chief exec. officer, 1984-88; chmn. bd., chief exec. officer Coldwell Banker Residential Group, Newport Beach, Calif., 1985-89; with Combined Investments LP, Laguna Beach, Calif., 1989—; bd. dirs. Homart Devel. Co., Chgo.; mem. policy adv. bd. Joint Ctr. for Housing Studies Harvard U. Bd. dirs. Chgo. Chamber Orch., 1976-82; trustee North Cen. Coll., Naperville, Ill. Mem. Nat. Assn. Realtors, Realtors Nat. Mktg. Inst. (v.p. fin. 1977). Home: 105 S La Senda Dr South Laguna CA 92677 Office: Combined Investments LP 570 Glenneyre St Ste 101 Laguna Beach CA 92651

HANCE, ANTHONY JAMES, pharmacologist, educator; b. Bournemouth, Eng., Aug. 19, 1932; came to U.S., 1958; s. Walter Edwin and Jessie Irene (Finch) H.; m. Ruth Anne Martin, July 17, 1954; children—David, Peter, John. B.Sc., Birmingham U., 1953, Ph.D., 1956. Research fellow in electrophysiology Birmingham U., Eng., 1957-58; research pharmacologist UCLA, 1959-62; research assoc. pharmacology Stanford U., Palo Alto, Calif., 1962-65, asst. prof., 1965-68; assoc. prof. U. Calif., Davis, 1968—. Contbr. articles to profl. jours. Mem. AAAS, Am. Soc. for Pharmacology and Exptl. Therapeutics, Biomed. Engring. Soc., Assn. for Computing Machinery. Home: 1103 Radcliffe Dr Davis CA 95616 Office: U Calif Med Sch Dept Pharmacology Davis CA 95616

HANCOCK, DON RAY, researcher; b. Muncie, Ind., Apr. 9, 1948; s. Charles David and June Lamoine (Krey) H. B.A., DePauw U., 1970. Community worker Fla. Meth. Spanish Ministry, Miami, 1970-73; seminar designer United Meth. Seminars, Washington, 1973-75; info. coordinator SW Research and Info. Ctr., Albuquerque, 1975—; cons. State Planning Council on Radioactive Waste Mgmt., Washington, 1980-81; task force mem. Gov.'s Socioecon. Com., Santa Fe, 1983; pub. adv. bd. WIPP Socioecon. Study, Albuquerque, 1979-81. Author mag. articles. Bd. chmn. Roadrunner Food Bank, Albuquerque, 1981—, N.Mex. Coalition Against Hunger, 1978-85; bd. dirs. Univ. Heights Assn., Albuquerque, 1977-82, 85, 88-89, United Meth. Bd. of Ch. and Society, Washington, 1976-80. Democrat. Office: SW Rsch and Info Ctr PO Box 4524 Albuquerque NM 87106

HANCOCK, JOY ELIZABETH, real estate associate, writer; b. Pomona, Calif., Dec. 24, 1957; d. William Kenneth and Margaret Ann (Brooks) Turner; m. David George Hancock, Sept. 15, 1979 (div. Nov. 1986); 1 child, David Alan. AA, Citrus Community Coll., 1977. Salesperson Ken Turner Real Estate, Glendora, Calif., 1977-79; bank clk., customer svc. rep. Bank Am. 241, 1979-81; acctg. asst. Santa Fe Internat. Corp., Alhambra, Calif., 1981-82; air traffic controller trainee Air Traffic Control Ctr., Palmdale, Calif., 1982; freelance writer Glendora, 1988—. Author: The Loudest Little Lion, 1988. Mem. Soc. Children's Book Writers, Azusa Glendora Bd. Realtors. Office: Ken Turner Real Estate 137 N Glendora Ave Glendora CA 91740

HANCOCK, LONI, city mayor; b. N.Y.C., 1940; children: Leita, Mara. BA, Ithaca Coll.; MA, Wright Inst. Mem. Berkeley City Council, 1971-79, co-sponsor Fair Representation Ordinance, introduced affirmative action program, mem. subcom. for creation of Ohlone Park; mem. Berkeley's Waterfront Adv. Commn., 1984-86; mayor City of Berkeley, 1986—. Mem. Berkeley Parent Nursery Schs., 1964-68, Berkeley Citizens Action Com., 1975—; mem., past pres. New Dem. Forum, 1982—; mem. adv. bd. Working Assets, 1984—; bd. dirs., v.p. Berkeley Office of Econ. Opportunity, 1969-71, Local Gov. Commn., Literacy Vols. of Am., Youth Project; past regional dir. of ACTION; exec. dir. Shalan Found., San Francisco, 1981—; mem., cofounder LeConte Neighborhood Assn., 1969-71. Mem. Sierra Club, Nat. Women's Polit. Caucus. Office: City of Berkeley 2180 Milvia St Berkeley CA 94704

HANCOCK, MICHAEL ANTHONY, real estate developer; b. Inglewood, Calif., Sept. 20, 1953; s. George Lincoln and Mary Eileen (Frost) H.; m. Janele Ann Geer, Oct. 20, 1972; children: Kevin Michael, Brent Anthony. Sales assoc. MacPhersons, Inc., Everett, Wash., 1974-75; title officer Transam. Title Ins. Co., Everett, 1975-77, Bellevue, Wash., 1977-79; title officer Chgo. Title Agy. Snohomish County, Everett, 1979-81; v.p., mgr. Chgo. Title Agy. Kitsap County, Silverdale, Wash., 1981-86; pres. Am. Redicorp, Inc., Silverdale, 1986—; chmn. Am. Asset Mgmt., 1989—, Am. Classic Homes Inc., 1989—; bd. dirs. Cen. Kitsap Pub. Facilities, Kitsap Futures. Mem. Bldg. Industry Assn. Am. (dir. 1989), Bldg. Industry Assn. Washington (dir. 1989), Bldg. Industry Assn. Kitsap County (dir. 1985-86, 89—), Peninsula Regional Escrow Assn. (pres. 1986, Escrow Achiever of Yr.

1985), Escrow Assn. Wash. (dir. 1985-86), Homebuilder Assn. Kitsap, Kitsan Golf and Country Club, Ducks Unltd., Rotary (dir. 1986-89, sec. 1989-90). Office: Am Redicorp Inc PO Box 1428 Silverdale WA 98383

HANCOCK, N(EWELL) LES(LIE), accountant; b. Pitts., Apr. 13, 1943; s. Newell Francis and Mildred Helen (Bouveroux) H.; m. Margaret Ann Kendrick, Nov. 30, 1968; children: Michelle Lynn, Jennifer Ann, Marie Noelle. BSBA, U. Denver, 1966; postgrad., various schs., 1969—. CPA, Colo., Nev. Supr. Pannell, Kerr, Forster, Denver and Atlanta, 1969-78; mgr. Wolf & Co. of Colo., Inc., Denver, 1978-79, 83-84; supr. Kafoury, Armstrong & Co., Reno, 1979-82; pvt. practice acctg. Arvada, Colo. and Reno, 1982—; mgr. Ashby, Armstrong & Co., Denver, 1984-87; asst. contr. 1st Resorts Inc., Great Am. Mgmt. Group Inc., Lakewood, Colo., 1987—. Served to 1st lt. U.S. Army, 1966-69. Mem. Am. Inst. CPA's, Colo. Soc. CPA's (mem. report rev. com. 1984—), Nev. Soc. CPA's (bd. dirs. Reno chpt. 1982-83, mem. auditing standards com. 1981-82, vice chmn. acctg. prins. com. 1981-83), Hospitality Accts. Assn. (sec. 1976-77). Republican. Baptist. Office: PO Box 968 Arvada CO 80001-0968

HAND, EARL PARSONS, electrical engineer; b. New Eagleboro, Pa., Apr. 9, 1943; s. Frederick Carlton and Genevieve (Parsons) H.; m. Phyllis Marilyn Kaupa, Aug. 15, 1964; children: Tracy Hand Blue, Christopher E., Jodie Hand Ludwig, Stephen N. BSEE, So. Colo. State, 1972. Commd. sgt. USAF, 1962, advanced through grades to capt., 1973; autopilot tech. USAF, McClellan AFB, Calif., 1962-70; autopilot shop USAF, Peterson Field Col., 1970-74; maintenance officer USAF, Minot AFB, N.D., 1974-76; chief of maintenance USAF, King Salmon AFB, Alaska, 1976-77; maintenance and logistics officer USAF, Tinker AFB, Okla., 1977-79; engring. officer USAF/Boeing, Seattle, 1979-83; engr. Boeing Aerospace, Seattle, 1983—; quality circle leader, Seattle, 1986; avionics team leader, AWACS Maintenance Facility Survey Team, Saudi Arabia, 1985-87. Del. Republican Party, Black Diamond, Wash., 1988; bd. dirs. Black Diamond Community Ctr., 1988-89; elder Black Diamond Presbyn. Ch., 1985-86. Mem. Seattle Profl. Engring. Employees Assn., Air Force Assn. Republican. Assembly of God. Home: 33019 Pacific Pl PO Box 271 Black Diamond WA 98010-9722 Office: Boeing Aerospace PO Box 3999 M5-23-39 Seattle WA 98124-2499

HANDEL, WILLIAM KEATING, sales executive; b. N.Y.C., Mar. 23, 1935; s. Irving Nathaniel and Marguerite Mary (Keating) H.; m. Margaret Inez Sitton; children: William Keating II, David Roger. BA in Journalism, U. S.C., 1959, postgrad., 1959-60. With Packaging div. The Mead Corp., Atlanta, 1960-64, Ketchum, MacLeod & Grove, Pitts., 1964-67, Rexall Drug & Chem. Corp., L.A., 1967-68; owner Creative Enterprises/Mktg. Communications, L.A., 1968-71; creative dir., sales promotion mgr. Beneficial Standard Life Ins., L.A., 1971-72; mgr. advt. and pub. rels. ITT Gen. Controls, Glendale, Calif., 1972-80; mgr. corp. recruitment advt. Hughes Aircraft Co., L.A., 1980-81; mgr. corp. communications Fairchild Camera and Instrument Corp., 1981-83; dist. mgr. Cahners Pub. Co., 1984—; pub. rels. counsel Calif. Pvt. Edn. Schs., 1978-87; chmn. exhibits Mini/Micro Computer Conf., 1977-78. Bd. dirs. West Valley Athletic League; bd. dir. L.A. chpt. USMC Scholarship Found.; pub. rels. cons. Ensenada, Mexico Tourist Commn., 1978; chmn., master of ceremonies U.S. Marine Corps Birthday Ball, L.A., 1979-82. With USMC, 1950-53. Decorated Silver Star, Bronze Star, Purple Heart (4), Navy Commendation medal with combat V; recipient Pub. Svc. award L.A. Heart Assn., 1971-73. Mem. Bus. and Profl. Advt. Assn. (cert. bus. communicator, past pres.), 1st Marine Div. Assn., Navy League (dir.), Sigma Chi (chpt. adv.). Republican. Roman Catholic. Clubs: AdLinx Golf of So. Calif., Torrey Pines Golf, Griffith Pk. Golf, Nueva España Boat, Baiamar Country, Ensenada Country, Ensenada Fish and Game (Baja, Mexico), Torrey Pines Golf. Home: 2428 Badajoz Pl Rancho La Costa CA 92009

HANDFORD, JACK, fashion educator; b. Piedmont, Mo., Aug. 4, 1917; s. Jack and Ethel Collins (Bunyard) H.; m. Virginia Lee Snigg, Sept. 19, 1942 (dec. 1983). BFA, Chouinard Art Inst., L.A., 1946; MFA, Kensington U., Glendale, Calif., 1977; EdD, Kensington U., 1978. Apparel designer Chic Lingerie, L.A., 1946-50; instr. Chouinard Art Inst., L.A., 1946-61; apparel designer Calif. Girl, L.A., 1952-56; designer/owner Handford Ent., Inc., L.A., 1956-72; dir./owner Calif. Fashion Inst., L.A., 1961-72; instr. UCLA Ext., 1972-83; assoc. chmn. fashion dept. Otis/Parsons, L.A., 1981—; guest lectr. Calif. Dept. Edn., Sacramento, 1964-69, Calif. State U., L.A., 1969-79; part-time instr. Fullerton Coll., 1975-83; conductor/planner in field; mem. various fashion adv. bd.s; adv. bds. Author: Professional Patternmaking, 1974, 2nd edit. 1984, Professional Pattern Grading, 1980; contbr. articles to profl. jours. With USNR, 1942-45. Mem. Calif. Fashion Designers (pres. 1950-52), Costume Soc. Am. (nat. bd. dirs. 1977-86, reg. pres. 1977-79), Costume Council (bd. dirs. 1978-80). Episcopalian. Home: 447 S Saint Andrews Pl Los Angeles CA 90020 Office: Otis Parsons Sch of Design 2401 Wilshire Blvd Los Angeles CA 90057

HANDLEY, JOHN R., commercial real estate broker; b. Denver, May 29, 1940; s. Robert W. and Jeanne (Rudolph) H.; m. Merilyn L. Rademacher, Sept. 1, 1961; children: Tori L., Derek S. Student, Colo. State U., Ft. Collins, 1959-62. Sec.-treas. Intermountain Specialty Equip. Co., Inc., Englewood, Colo., 1967-87; pres. Colo. Golf & Turf, Englewood, 1987-88; broker assoc. Dawson & Co., Comml. div., Littleton, Colo., 1988—. Mem. Assn. Gen. Contrs., Am. Subcontrs. Assn., Nat. Assn. Credit Mgrs., Nat. Assn. Ind. Bus., S. Suburban Bd. Realtors, Colo. Assn. Realtors, Nat. Assn. Realtors, Englewood Jaycees, Masons, Rotary. Republican. Methodist. Home: 6101 Rosewood Dr Littleton CO 80121 Office: Dawson & Co 609 W Littleton Blvd Littleton CO 81120

HANDSCHUMACHER, ALBERT GUSTAVE, corporate executive; b. Phila., Oct. 20, 1918; s. Gustave H. and Emma (Streck) H.; children: Albert, David W., Megan, Karin, Melissa. B.S., Drexel Inst. Tech., 1940; diploma, U. Pitts., 1941, Alexander Hamilton Inst., 1948. Prodn. mgr. Jr. Motors Corp., Phila., 1938-40; sales engr. Westinghouse Electric Co., Pitts., 1941; with Lear, Inc., Grand Rapids, Mich., 1945-57; beginning as sales mgr. central dist., successively asst. to pres., asst. gen. mgr., v.p. and gen. mgr., sr. v.p., dir. sales, pres., dir. Lear, Inc., 1959-62; v.p., gen. mgr. Rheem Mfg. Co., 1957-59; pres., dir. Lear Siegler, Inc., 1962-65; chmn. bd. Aeronca, Inc.; dir. First Exec. Corp., Lear Siegler, Inc., Exec. Life Ins. Co., Flight Dynamics Inc.; underwriting mem. Lloyd's of London; chmn. exec. com. First Fin. Group, Inc. Trustee Drexel U.; trustee City of Hope; nat. adv. chmn. Am. Heart Assn.; mem. bus. adv. council UCLA Internat. Student Ctr., Los Angeles World Affairs Council; trustee Nat. Asthma Assn. Served to maj. USAAF, 1942-45. Recipient 60th Anniversary Alumni award for outstanding achievements and services field of indsl. mgmt. Drexel U., 1951, Outstanding Alumni award, 1971; Man of Year award City of Hope, 1970; Man of Year award Nat. Asthma Assn., 1978. Mem. Am. Mgmt. Assn., ASHRE. Clubs: Jonathan, Calif. Yacht, Bel Air (Calif.) Country; Wings (N.Y.C.), Metropolitan (N.Y.C.); Confrerie de la Chaine des Rotisseurs, Beverly Hills; Le Mirador Country (Switzerland); Astro (Phila.). Home: 1100 Stone Canyon Rd Los Angeles CA 90077 Office: 844 Moraga Dr Los Angeles CA 90049

HANDY, VERA SHARP, music educator, civic worker; b. Mayfield, Ky., Oct. 21, 1912; d. Delmus Prince and Zoda (English) McGee; m. 2d Jamison Handy Jr., June 2, 1983; 1 child by previous marriage, John Sharp. Grad., Mayfield Bus. Coll., 1930; studied voice culture with various tchrs. including, Paschal Monk, Julia Monroe; studied piano and organ; vocal studies, Prof. Pascal Monk. Piano tchr., sole creator audio-visual music course Little Princess Symphony Adventures, Pacific Palisides, Calif. Performed in operas: The Marriage of Figaro, Don Giovanni, The Magic Flute; entertainer various service clubs; soloist Esperanto Club, Sacramento. Actice Sacremento Suymphony League; led citizens com. to form Sacramento Civic Opera Co.; active various fundraising events, Sacramento; organizer Jr. Music Sponsors (sponsor childrens' concerts); chmn. citizen's com. Sacremento Civic Opera Co.; mem. Sacremento League of Women. Recipient award The Pres. Commn. on the Arts and Humanities, 1986, Maestro Mehli Mehta Am. Youth Symphony, 1984, Symphony Mag., 1985. Mem. Calif. Fedn. Music Clubs, Nat. Fedn. Music Clubs, Music Tchrs. Assn. Calif. (W. Los Angles br., various offices), Women's Club of Pacific Palisides, Viennese Culture Club of Los Angeles, Opera Reading Club of Hollywood, Inc. Republican. Mem. Christian Science Church. Home: 17350 Sunset Blvd 204C Pacific Palisades CA 90272

HANEY, ROBERT LOCKE, insurance company executive; b. Morgantown, W.Va., June 14, 1928; s. John Ward and Katherine Eugenia (Locke) H. BA, U. Calif., Berkeley, 1949. Sr. engr. Pacific Telephone Co., San Francisco, 1952-58; mgmt. analyst Lockheed Missiles & Space Co., Sunnyvale, Calif., 1958-64; sr. cons. John Diebold, N.Y.C., 1964-65; sr. indsl. economist Mgmt. & Econs. Research, Inc., Palo Alto, Calif., 1965-67; prin. economist Midwest Research Inst., Kansas City, Mo., 1967-69; dir. mktg. coordination Transam. Corp., San Francisco, 1969-73; staff exec. Transam. Ins. Corp., L.A., 1974-82; div. mgr. Transam. Life Cos., L.A., 1982—; cons. in field. Co-author: Creating the Human Environment, 1970. Lt. (j.g.) USN, 1949-52. Mem. Scabbard & Blade. Republican. Episcopalian. Home: 2743 Tiburon Ave Carlsbad CA 92008 Office: Transamerica Life Cos 1150 S Olive St Los Angeles CA 90015

HANF, JAMES ALPHONSO, poet, government official; b. Chehalis, Wash., Feb. 3, 1923; s. William G. and Willa DeForest (Davis) H.; grad. Centralia Jr. Coll., 1943, DLitt (hon.) World U. Ariz.; m. Ruth G. Eyler, Aug. 16, 1947; 1 child, Maureen Ruth. Naval architect technician P.F. Spaulding, naval architects, Seattle, 1955-56, Puget Sound Bridge & Dredge Co. (Wash.), 1953-55, Puget Sound Naval Shipyard, 1951-53, 56—; cons. Anderson & Assocs., ship bldg.; cons. The Research Bd. Advs., Am. Biographical Inst., Inc.; guest lectr. on poetry and geneal. research methods to various lit. socs., 1969—; contbr. hundreds of poems to lit. jours., anthologies and popular mags.; poetry editor Coffee Break, 1977-82. Recipient Poet Laureate award, 1978, Poet Laureate Wash. State award Internat. Poetry Soc. India and World, 1981, grand prize World Poetry Soc. Conv., 1985, 86, Golden Poet award World of Poetry in Calif., 1985-88, numerous other awards. Judge poetry contest, Australia and India, 1985. Mem Internat. Poetry Soc., World of Poetry Soc. (Golden Poet award 1985, 86, 87, 88), Kitsap County Writers Club (pres. 1977-78), Internat. Fedn. Tech. Engrs., Nat. Hist. Locomotive Soc., Kitsap County Hist. Soc., Puget Sound Geneal. Soc., Western World Haiku Soc., Olympic Geneal. Soc. (pres. 1974-75), N.Y. Poetry Forum, World Poets Resource Center, Literarische Union, Internat. Platform Assn., Calif. Fedn. Chaparral Poets, Internat. Biog. Assn., Am. Biog. Inst. (Silver and Gold medals of honor). Baptist. Home: PO Box 374 Bremerton WA 98310

HANFF, PETER EDWARD, librarian, bibliographer; b. Jacksonville, Fla., Jan. 23, 1944; s. George E. and Mildred Todd (Stringer) H.; m. Judith A. Baker, Jan. 22, 1974 (div. 1979). BA, U. Calif., Santa Barbara, 1966; MLS, UCLA, 1967. Librarian Library of Congress, Washington, 1967-69; librarian, fellow Lilly Library, Ind. U., Bloomington, 1969-70; librarian Bancroft Library, U. Calif., Berkeley, 1970—; lectr. on book collecting U. Calif. Extension, 5 campuses, 1978, 79. Author: Bibliographia Oziana, 1976; mem. editorial bd. Rare Books and Manuscripts Librarianship, 1986—; contbr. articles to various publs. Mem. ALA, Assn. Coll. and Rsch. Libraries (appointments and nominating com. 1989—), Internat. Wizard of Oz Club (bibliography editor 1976—, pres. 1978-86, Grolier Club (N.Y.C., recipient L. Frank Baum Meml. award, 1978), Colophon Club (San Francisco), Roxburghe Club (San Francisco). Democrat. Home: 1083 Euclid Ave Berkeley CA 94708 Office: U Calif Bancroft Library Berkeley CA 94720

HANIFEN, RICHARD CHARLES, bishop; b. Denver, June 15, 1931; s. Edward Anselm and Dorothy Elizabeth (Ranous) H. B.S., Regis Coll., 1953; S.T.B., Cath. U., 1959, M.A., 1966; J.C.L., Pontifical Lateran U., Italy, 1968. Ordained priest Roman Catholic Ch., 1959; asst. pastor Cathedral Parish, Denver, 1959-66; sec. to archbishop Archdiocese Denver, 1968-69, chancellor, 1969-76; aux. bishop of Denver, 1974-83; 1st bishop of Colorado Springs, Colo., 1984—. Office: 29 W Kiowa St Colorado Springs CO 80903 *

HANKIN, JERRY DEAN, city official; b. Cheyenne, Wyo., Oct. 9, 1956; s. Howard W. Hankin and Ruthanne (McIver) Wold; children: Lark M. Rambo, Jeremy P. Rambo. Constrn. foreman Reiman Constrn. Co., Cheyenne, 1978-80; bldg. ins. City of Laramie (Wyo.), 1980-83, bldg. ofcl., chief bldg. insp. and zoning adminstr., 1983—; cons. constrn. mgmt., Boulder, Colo., 1985-88. Mem. Internat. Conf. Bldg. Ofcls., Wyo. Conf. Bldg. Ofcls. (Colo. chpt. ICBO), Wyo. Outdoor Coun. Democrat. Home: 2354 Riverside Dr Laramie WY 82070

HANKINS, MARY KATHERINE, association executive, consultant; b. San Diego, June 3, 1940; d. Henry Francis and Katherine (Walton) LaRose; m. George Leo Kinder, Feb. 22, 1958 (div. 1965); m. Leslie Dale Hankins, May 6, 1978; children: Richard Dennis, Rebecca Anne, Leslie Michael Francis. Office mgr. Calif. Pools, San Diego, 1977-78; exec. sec. Geremia Pools, Sacramento, 1980-81; adminstrv. tech. Calif. State Employees Assn., Sacramento, 1981—; mktg. cons. Leslie Ent., Sacramento, 1988—. Calif. State Employees Assn. chmn. United Way, Sacramento. Mem. Royal Scottish Country Dance Soc. (Scotland), DAR, Order Eastern Star (Worthy matron 1989). Republican. Office: Calif State Employees Assn 1108 O St Sacramento CA 95833

HANKOFF, JEFFREY FRANK, physician; b. Charlotte, N.C., Sept. 15, 1948; s. Robert Raymond and Blanche (Osheroff) H.; m. Jane Louise Caplan, Aug. 29, 1977; children: Robert Aaron, Essie Sarah. BS, MIT, 1970; MD, U. Calif., Davis, 1976. Diplomate Am. Bd. Family Practice. Resident Ea. Ma. Med. Ctr., Bangor, 1976-79; Family physician Orono Family Practice, Orono, Maine, 1979-81; family physician Sansum Med. Clinic, Inc., Santa Barbara, Calif., 1981—; chief family practice svc. Santa Barbara Cottage Hosp., 1987—. Fellow Am. Acad. Family Practice; mem. AMA, Calif. Med. Assn. Office: Sansum Med Clinic Inc 317 W Pueblo St Santa Barbara CA 93105

HANKS, EUGENE RALPH, land developer, cattle rancher, retired naval officer; b. Corning, Calif., Dec. 11, 1918; s. Eugene and Lorena B. Hanks; m. Frances Elliot Herrick, Mar. 4, 1945; children: Herrick, Russell, Stephen, Nina. Student, Calif. Poly. Coll., 1939-41, U. So. Calif., 1949-50, Am. U., 1958-59; grad., Command and Staff Coll., Norfolk, Va., 1960. Served as enlisted man USN, 1941-42, commd. ensign, 1942, advanced through grades to capt., 1963; carrier fighter pilot, test pilot Naval Air Test Ctr., 1946-48; mem. Navy Flight Exhbn. Team Blue Angels, 1950; comdg. officer fighter squadrons, San Diego, 1957-61; ops. officer U.S.S. Constellation, 1961-62; dir. ops. Naval Missile Ctr., 1963-66; test dir. Joint Task Force Two, Albuquerque, 1966-69; ret. 1969; owner, developer Christmas Tree Canyon, Cebolla Springs and Mountain River subdivs., Mora, N.Mex., 1969—. Decorated Navy Cross, D.F.C. with star (2), Air medal (7), Legion of Merit; named Citizen of Yr. Citizen's Com. for the Right to Keep and Bear Arms, 1987. Mem. Ret. Officers Assn., Am. Fighter Aces Assn., Combat Pilots Assn., Assn. Naval Aviation, Am. Forestry Assn., NRA, Blue Angels Assn. Democrat. Home and Office: Christmas Tree Canyon Box 239 Mora NM 87732

HANKS, LARRY BERKLEY, life insurance company executive; b. Idaho Falls, Idaho, Sept. 25, 1940; s. Victor Franklin and Marjorie (Burke) H.; AB, Brigham Young U., 1964; Master in Fin. Sci., Am. Coll., 1982; CLU; chartered fin. cons.; m. Georgia Lee Gammett, Dec. 29, 1965; children—Tiffany, Berkley, Colli, Andrea, Rachel, Jared, Cyrus. Owner, mgr. Larry B. Hanks, CLU, ins. and employee benefits, Salt Lake City, 1969—; pres. Am. Pension Adminstrs. Inc., Salt Lake City 1978—, Integrated Fin. Designs, Inc., 1982—; gen. agt. Mass. Mut. Life Ins. Co., Salt Lake City, 1980—; instr. CLU classes Am. Coll., Bryn Mawr, Pa., 1975—. With U.S. Army, 1968-69. Mem. Am. Soc. CLU (dir. Magic Valley chpt.), Nat. Assn. Life Underwriters, Am. Soc. Pension Actuaries, N.E. Idaho Assn. Life Underwriters (dir., officer), Million Dollar Roundtable, Estate Planning Coun. Boise, Gen. Agts. and Mgrs. Assn. Republican. Mormon. Home: 7628 Riverwood Dr Sandy UT 84092 Office: Integrated Fin Designs Inc 4 Triad Ctr Ste 600 Salt Lake City UT 84180

HANLIN, RUSSELL L., citrus products company executive; b. Sioux Falls, S.D., 1932; married. Student, U. Wash., Los Angeles City Coll. With Sunkist Growers, Inc., Van Nuys, Calif., 1951—, asst. mgr., 1964-72, v.p. mfg., mkt. research and devel., products group, 1972-78, former chief exec. and chief operating officer, pres., 1978—, also dir. Served with U.S. Army, 1953-55. Office: Sunkist Growers Inc 14130 Riverside Dr Box 7888 Van Nuys CA 91409 *

HANLON, CHARLES JOSEPH, former state senator; b. Pa., Sept. 15, 1918; s. Charles Hugh and Anna (Darby) H.; m. Neila Margaret Gaines, Mar. 11, 1943; children: Kathy, Jeffrey. grad. high sch., Greensburg, Pa. With rock, sand and gravel industry, 1946-58; rancher, Cornelius, Oreg., 1958—; mem. Oreg. Senate, 1975-86. Served with Aviation Engrs., AUS, 1941-46; PTO. Author: (short fiction collections) Love, Time and Again, 1987, The Sapphire People, 1988. Democrat. Polit. writer for state newspapers.

HANN, DON ROBERT, electrical engineer; b. Ancon, Republic of Panama, Apr. 28, 1946; s. Lyle Ray and Olive Louise (McNicholl) H.; m. Bettye Darlene Wilcox, June 15, 1968; children: Valerie Michelle, Robert Douglass. AS, Barstow (Calif.) Jr. Coll., 1970; BS in Elec. Engring., Calif. Poly. State U., Pomona, 1973; MS in Elec. Engring., San Diego State U., 1977. Registered elec. engr., Calif. Engr. San Diego Gas & Electric, 1973-77, meters and test supr., 1977-82, distbn. engring. supr., 1982-85, project engr., 1985—. Served with N.G., 1964-70. Mem. IEEE, Tau Beta Pi, Eta Kappa Nu, Kappa Mu Epsilon. Republican. Mem. Assembly of God ch. Home: 3155 Mount Acmar Ct San Diego CA 92111 Office: San Diego Gas and Electric Co PO Box 1831 San Diego CA 92112

HANNA, EDWARD ALOYSIUS, computer executive; b. Pitts., Mar. 12, 1958; s. Edward Aloysius and Nelda Louise (Shore) H.; m. Janice Lynne Gay, Sept. 1, 1977; children: Paul, Scott, Corinne. Grad. high sch., Santa Ana, Calif. Computer operator Sisters of St. Joseph, Orange, Calif., 1977-79; tech. support Pacific Mut., Newport Beach, Calif., 1979-82; systems mgr. Nat. Capacitor, Garden Grove, Calif., 1982-84, Paul-Munroe Hydraulics, Whittier, Calif., 1984-85; EDP mgr. Harte-Hanks/NCA, Santa Clara, Calif., 1985—; programmer, contractor Federated Group, Commerce, Calif., 1984-85; sub-contractor Pilgrim Computer, West Covina, Calif., 1984-85; cons., contractor Nat. Capacitor, 1984-85. Cubmaster Boy Scouts Am., San Jose, 1987-88; parent rep. Gate Adv. Council, San Jose, 1987-88, Brooktree Sch. Site Council, San Jose, 1988; mem. PTA, San Jose, 1987-88. Mem. Interex. Roman Catholic. Office: Harte-Hanks/NCA 1350 Duane Ave Santa Clara CA 95054

HANNA, JOHN ROBERT, lawyer; b. San Diego, May 17, 1951; s. Wallace John and Gloria L. (Schotz) H. BA, Calif. State U., Fullerton, 1974; JD, Loyola U., Los Angeles, 1979. Bar: Calif. 1980. Congl. aide Rep. Jerry Patterson, Santa Ana, Calif., 1976-80; pub. info. officer Ho. of Reps., Washington, 1979-80; with Horton, Barbaro & Reilly, Santa Ana, 1980—. V.p. St. Joseph Ballet Co., Santa Ana, 1984—; pres. Dem. Assocs., Orange County, 1985; mem. Calif. Dem. Cen. Com., 1975—; mem. Orange County Dem. Cen. Com., 1976—, chmn. 1986-88. Mem. ABA, Calif. State Bar Assn., Orange County Bar Assn. Roman Catholic. Office: Horton Barbaro & Reilly 200 N Main 2d Fl Santa Ana CA 92701

HANNA, ROBERT CECIL, lawyer, construction company executive; b. Albuquerque, July 28, 1937; s. Samuel Gray and Orvetta (Cecil) H.; B.A., U. N.Mex., 1959, J.D., 1962. Bar: N.M1962, Hawaii 1974, U.S. Supreme Ct. 1970; practiced in Albuquerque, 1962-70, 72—; organizer, dep. dir. Micronesian Legal Services Corp., Trust Ter. Pacific Islands, 1970-71; practiced in Hilo; Hawaii, 1974; partner Cotter, Atkinson, Kelsey & Hanna, Ortega, Snead, Dixon & Hanna, Albuquerque, 1975-77; owner, pres., prin. Robert C. Hanna & Assocs., Albuquerque, 1978-80, 88—; pres. Sedco International. USA, Inc., Albuquerque, 1977-79, Suncastle Builders, Inc., Albuquerque, 1978—; pres. Am. Legal Consortium, A Chartered Law Firm, 1984—; N.Mex. Real Estate Consortium Ltd., 1986—; mem. Bd. Bar Commrs., Trust Ter. Pacific Islands, 1971-72. Recipient award Rocky Mountain Mineral Law Found., 1962; Public Service award Micronesian Legal Services Corp. Bd. Dirs., 1972. Mem. Hawaii Bar Assn., N.Mex. Bar Assn., Albuquerque Bar Assn. Home and Office: 310 Rio Grande Blvd SW Albuquerque NM 87104

HANNA, STANLEY SWEET, physicist, educator; b. Sagaing, Burma, May 17, 1920; s. Alexander Carson and Hazel (Ames) H.; m. Jane Reeves Martin, Dec. 27, 1942; children: David Stanley, Peter Alexander, Susan Lee. A.B., Denison U., 1941, D.Sc., 1970; Ph.D., Johns Hopkins U., 1947. Mem. faculty Johns Hopkins U., 1943-55, asst. prof. physics, 1948-55; asso. physicist Argonne Nat. Lab., 1955-60, sr. physicist, 1960-63, cons., 1963-68; prof. physics Stanford U., 1963—; researcher on nuclear structure, giant resonances, polarizations of nuclear radiations, positron polarization, lifetimes of nuclear states, resonance absorption, analogue states, electron scattering, nuclear moments, intermediate energy physics, weak and hyperfine interactions; cons. Los Alamos Sci. Lab., 1967-74. Chmn. nuclear physics panel, com. on physics Nat. Acad. Scis., 1964-65. Served with AUS, 1945-46. Guggenheim fellow, 1958-59; Humboldt awardee, 1977; fellow Inst. for Advanced Study, Ind. U., 1983. Fellow Am. Phys. Soc. (organizing com. nuclear physics div. 1966-67, exec. com. 1967-68, 75-82, vice chmn. 1975-76, chmn. 1976-77, nuclear physics councillor 1978-82, publ. com. 1980-83, chmn. com. 1981-83, mem. exec. com. 1979-82); mem. Phi Beta Kappa, Sigma Xi, Omicron Delta Kappa. Home: 784 Mayfield Ave Stanford CA 94305

HANNAN, CECIL JAMES, school system administrator, small business owner; b. Sydney, Mont., Oct. 3, 1925; s. Cecil George and Isabelle Mary (Finch) H.; m. Molly M. Roberts, Dec. 16, 1974; children: Matthew G., Kelley J., Marguerite M. BA, Western Wash. State U., 1947, MS, 1948; DEd, Wash. State U., 1961. Exec. sec. Wash. State Edn. Assn., Seattle, 1959-67; assoc. exec. sec. NEA, Washington, 1967-71; pres. NTL Learning Resources Co., Washington, 1971-75; exec. sec. Colo. Edn. Assn., Denver, 1975-77; vice chancellor San Diego Community Coll. Dist., 1977-85; chmn., chief exec. officer Edn. Systems Tech. Co., San Diego, 1985—; ptnr. Tech. Specialists Inc., Phila., 1988—; pres. Tchrs. Services Corp., Washington, 1968-71. Author: Teach Spelling By All Means, 1952, Merit Pay for Teachers, 1953, Cross Value Dialog, 1963, Twenty Exercises for Classroom, 1966. Chmn. Educators Humphrey for Pres., Washington 1964, Educators Jackson for Pres., Washington, 1968. Served to lt. USAF, 1943-46. Recipient Disting. Service award Wash. State Legis., 1967. Mem. NEA (exec. com. 1964-68, bd. dirs. 1960-64), Nat. Tng. Labs. (exec. com. 1964-72), Fla. Edn. Assn. (life), Mass. Tchrs. Assn. (life), Nat. Congress PTA (life). Democrat. Methodist. Home: 2433 7th St Olivenhain CA 92024 Office: Edn Systems Tech Corp 5230 Carroll Canyon Rd San Diego CA 92121

HANNAY, N(ORMAN) BRUCE, chemist, industrial research and business consultant; b. Mt. Vernon, Wash., Feb. 9, 1921; s. Norman Bond and Winnie (Evans) H.; m. Joan Anderson, May 27, 1943; children: Robin, Brooke. BA, Swarthmore Coll., 1942, DSc (hon.), 1979; MS, Princeton U., 1943, PhD, 1944; PhD (hon.), Tel Aviv U., 1978; DSc (hon.), Poly. Inst. N.Y., 1981. With Bell Telephone Labs., Murray Hill, N.J., 1944-82; exec. dir. materials research div. Bell Telephone Labs., 1967-73, v.p. research and patents, 1973-82, ret., 1982; researcher on dipole moments and molecular structure, thermionic emission, mass spectroscopy, analysis of solids, solid state chemistry, semiconductors, superconductors; mem. sci. adv. com. SRI Internat., tech. adv. council Chrysler Corp.; rsch. adv. com. United Techs., Regents' prof. UCLA, 1976, U. Calif., San Diego, 1979; cons. Alexander von Humboldt Found.; bd. dirs. Plenum Pub. Co., Gen. Signal Corp., Rohm and Haas Co., Alex Brown Cash Res. Fund, Tax-Free Investments Trust, and Flag Investors Telephone Income Trust, Internat. Trust, Corp. Cash Trust and Emerging Growth Fund. Author: Solid State Chemistry, 1967, also articles.; Mem. numerous editorial bds.; editor: Semiconductors, 1959, Treatise on Solid State Chemistry, 1974. Recipient Acheson medal, 1976; Perkin medal, 1983; Gold medal Am. Inst. Chemists, 1986. mem. Nat. Acad. Engring. (past fgn. sec.), Nat. Acad. Scis., Am. Acad. Arts and Scis., Mexican Nat. Acad. Engring., Electrochem. Soc. (past pres.), Indsl. Research Inst. (past pres., medal 1982), Dirs. of Indsl. Research (past chmn.).

HANNEN, JOHN EDWARD, bishop; b. Winnipeg, Man., Can., Nov. 19, 1937; s. Charles Scott and Mary Bowman (Lynds) H.; m. Alana Susan Long, June 24, 1977; children—Rebecca Meghann, Meredith Alana. B.A., McGill U., 1959; G.O.E., Coll. of Resurrection, Mirfield, Eng., 1961. Ordained deacon Anglican Ch., 1961, ordained priest, 1962. Asst. curate Diocese of Birmingham, Eng., 1961-64; rector Hart Hwy. Diocese of Caledonia, Chetwynd, B.C., Can., 1965-67; assoc. priest Diocese of Caledonia, Greenville, B.C., 1967-68; rector Diocese of Caledonia, Port Edward, B.C., 1968-

71, Kincolith, B.C., 1971-81; bishop Diocese of Caledonia, Prince Rupert, B.C., 1981—; senator Vancouver Sch. Theology, B.C., 1981-85; mem. inter ch.-interfaith relations com. Gen. Synod, Anglican Ch. of Can., 1983—. Chmn. bd. trustees Nisgha Sch. Dist., Naas River, B.C., 1977-78; mem. exec. com. Nishga Tribal Council, Naas River, 1974—. Office: Synod Office, PO Box 278, Prince Rupert, BC Canada V8J 3P6 *

HANNIBAL, JOSEPH HARRY, educator, artist; b. Bklyn., May 4, 1945; s. Mayme (Glover) H. AA, Hiwassee Coll., 1965; BS, Austin Peay State U., 1968; MFA, U. Tenn., 1972. Prof. U. Wis., Menomonie, 1972-81; prof., chmn. Calif. St. Polytech. U., Polmona, 1981—; guest artist, prof. Cen. Sch. Art & Design, London, 1976-77; juror Mid-Valley Arts League, Glendora, Calif., 1988. Works include: (photos) Southwest Series, 1988, European Series, 1988, (paintings) Distg. Artist Forum, 1985, McDonnell-Douglas Exhibition, 1987. Recipient 1st prize Laps Juried Competion Multicultural Inst., 1982, Gold medal Academia Italia Delle Arti del Lavoro, Parma, 1980. Mem. L.A. Printmaking Assn., Coll. Art Assn. Office: Calif St Polytech U Dept Art 4801 W Temple Pomona CA 92648

HANNIGAN, JOSEPH C., military officer; b. Marshall, Tex., Sept. 12, 1945; s. Joseph C. and Carrie Lou (McBride) H.; m. Sally I. Holmquist, Feb. 14, 1969; children: Michael C., Marissa E. BS in Journalism, Calif. Poly. State U., San Luis Obispo, 1968; MA in Procurement Mgmt., Webster U., St. Louis, 1978. Commd. USAF, 1968, advanced through grades to lt. col.; space surveillance officer Aerospace Def. Command, Clear, Alaska, 1974-75; contract adminstr. Space Command, Colorado Springs, Colo., 1976-78; chief contract ops. Alaskan Air Command, Anchorage, 1978-81; chief subcontract mgr. AFPRO, Martin Marietta, Littleton, Colo., 1981-83; chmn. joint acquisition coordinating bd. Europe/Africa U.S. European Command, Stuttgart, Fed. Republic of Germany, 1983-86; dir. contracting Alaskan Air Command, Anchorage, 1988—; vol. examiner FCC, Anchorage, 1987-89. Active Iditarod Trail Sled Dog Race, Anchorage, 1988-89. Mem. Nat. Contract Mgmt. Assn., Amateur Radio Relay League, Anchorage Amateur Radio Club, Sigma Delta Chi, Delta Sigma Phi. Home and Office: 9636 Etolin Cir Eagle River AK 99577

HANOWELL, ERNEST GODDIN, physician; b. Newport News, Va., Jan. 31, 1920; a. George Frederick and Ruby Augustine (Goddin) H.; m. Para Jean Hall, June 10, 1945; children: Ernest D., Daborah J. Hanowell Orick, Leland H., Dee P. Hanowell Martinmaas, Robert G. Diplomate Am. Bd. Internal Medicine. Intern USPHS Hosp., Norfolk, Va., 1948-49; resident in internal medicine USPHS Hosp., Seattle, 1952-55; chief medicine USPHS Hosp., Ft. Worth, 1955-57; dept. chief medicine USPHS Hosp., Boston, 1957-59; chief medicine USPHS Hosp., Memphis, 1964-65, Monterey County Gen. Hosp., 1969-70; mem. IM and Cardiology staff Kaiser Permanente Med. Group, Sacramento, 1971-87; clin. asst. Tufts Med. Sch., 1960-61; cons. chest disease Phila. Gen. Hosp., 1960-61; asst. prof. U. Md. Med. Sch., 1961-64; instr. U. Tenn. Med. Sch., 1964-65; asst. clin. prof. Sch. Medicine, U. Calif., Davis, 1973-81; mem. attending staff Cardiac Clinic Stanford U. Med. Sch. 1967-69. Mem. sch. bd. Salinas, Calif., 1968-69; bd. dirs. Am. Heart Assn., Tb and Health Assn. Served with AUS, 1943-46. Fellow ACP, Am. Coll. Chest Diseases; mem. AWA, Crocker Art Mus. Assn., Phi Chi. Clubs: Commonwealth (San Francisco), Comstock (Sacramento). Home: 1158 Racquet Club Dr Auburn CA 95603

HANSCOME, THOMAS CHANDLER, mortgage company executive; b. Washington, July 2, 1943; s. Thomas Dixon and JoAnn Elizabeth (Chandler) H.; m. Margaret Lee McDonald, Aug. 25, 1973; children: Heather Chandler, Jennifer Chandler, Kimberly McDonald, Lindsey Anne. BA in Mgmt. and Mktg., Parsons Coll., 1968. Lic. real estate broker, Calif.; registered rep. SEC, Nat. Assn. Securities Dealers. Mgr. project devel. Disneyland, Anaheim, Calif., 1961-72, Disneyworld, Orlando, Fla., 1969-72; owner, cons. Thomas Hanscome Enterprises, Santa Ana, Calif., 1972-76; owner, broker Sheltered Investments, Santa Ana, 1976-82; founder, pres. T.H.E. Investments Specialists Internat., Irvine, Calif., 1982—; cons. Taft Broadcasting-Kings Prodn., Cin., 1972-74. Mem. Nat. Assn. Realtors, Internat. Assn. Amusement Parks and Attractions, Nat. Assn. Fin. Wholesalers, Internat. Assn. for Fin. Planning. Republican. Episcopalian.

HANSEL, PAMELA KAY, marriage, family and child therapist; b. Denver, Dec. 23, 1942; d. Delmar Dean and Frances Evelyn (Low) Givens; m. Timothy Jon Hansel, Apr. 28, 1970; children: Zachary McClean, Joshua Givens. BS, Calif. Bapt. Coll., 1984; MS, Calif. Family Study Ctr., 1987. Rsch. asst. sec. Stanford U., Palo Alto, Calif., 1964-70; tchr.'s aide Menlo Atherton High Sch., Menlo Park, Calif., 1970-71; saleswoman Bath Store, Menlo Park, 1971; adminstrv. asst. Summit Expdn., La Jolla, Calif., 1971-73, A.L. Williams Co., Pasadena, Calif., 1983-84; field rep. Children's Village, Glendora, Calif., 1980-83; devel. officer Azusa (Calif.) Pacific U., 1984-85; intern Georgiana Rodiger Ctr., Pasadena, 1985-89, Creative Counseling Ctr., Claremont, Calif., 1989—; chmn. Young Life, La Verne, Calif., 1980-82, co-chmn., 1988—. Mem. Am. Assn. Marriage and Family Therapy, So. Calif. Assn. Marriage and Family Therapy. Democrat. Home: 1307 Aldersgate Dr La Verne CA 91750 Office: Creative Counseling Ctr 250 W 1st St Ste 214 Claremont CA 91711

HANSEN, ANNA MARIE, insurance company executive; b. Fresno, Calif., Oct. 16, 1958; d. Herman Christian and Tena Tilda (Brumm) H. AA in Bus. Adminstrn., Fresno City Coll., 1979; BS in Mktg., Calif. State U., Fresno, 1981. Underwriter Comml. Union Ins., Fresno, 1981-84; mktg. rep. Atlantic Cos., Irvine, Calif., 1984-86; mgr. mktg. Kemper Group, City of Industry, Calif., 1986—. Mem. Ins. Women of Fresno (bd. dirs 1982-86, chmn. community service 1983, sec. 1984, Rookie of Yr. 1984). Republican. Office: Kemper Group 17800 Castleton St City of Industry CA 91748

HANSEN, CLIFFORD PETER, rancher; b. Zenith, Wyo., Oct. 16, 1912; s. Peter Christofferson and Sylvia Irene (Wood) H.; m. Martha Elizabeth Close, Sept. 24, 1934; children: Mary Elizabeth, Peter Arthur. BS, U. Wyo., 1934, LLD (Hon.), 1965. Chmn. Teton County Bd. of Commissioners, Jackson, Wyo., 1943-51; pres. U. Wyo. Bd. of Trustees, Laramie, Wyo., 1955-63; commissioner Snake River, Idaho, Wyo., Columbia Interstate, 1943-50; pres. Wyo. Stock Growers Assn., Cheyenne, Wyo., 1953-55; chmn. Sec. of Agg. Adv. com., Washington, 1956-62; v.p. Jackson State Bank, Jackson, 1953-69; gov. State of Wyo., Cheyenne, 1963-66; U.S. Senator State of Wyo., Washington, 1967-78; rancher; mem. (Pres. appt.) Com. on Federalism Washington 1981, Bd. of Dirs. Pacific Power & Light Portland, 1979-83, Bd. Dir. 1st Wyo. Bank Corp. Cheyenne 1979-83. Recipient Medallion Svc. Award U. Wyo. Laramie 1965, Stockman of the Century Wyo. Stock Growers Assn. Cheyenne 1972. Republican. Episcopalean. Home: 1000 Spring Gulch Rd Jackson WY 83001 Office: Peter A. Hansen Bldg. 280 E Broadway Jackson WY 83001

HANSEN, DANIEL LEE, naval officer; b. Wichita, Kans., July 9, 1955; s. Robert Lee and Verde Joanne (Ritter) H.; m. Cheryl Ann Carlough, Dec. 5, 1981; children: Jason Thomas, William Eugene, Matthew Robert. BS in Ocean Engring., U.S. Naval Acad., 1977; MEE, Naval Postgrad. Sch., 1988. Commd. ensign USN, 1973, advanced through ranks to lt. comdr., 1987; vertical replenishment helicopter pilot Helicopter Combat Support Squadron, USN, Norfolk, Va., 1979-82; helicopter instr. pilot USN, Milton, Fla., 1982-84; aircraft handling officer U.S.S. Inchon, USN, Norfolk, 1984-86; student space engring. U.S. Naval Postgrad. Sch., Monterey, Calif., 1986—; asst. design engr. space dept., 1987—. Unit commr. Boy Scouts Am., Pensacola, Fla., 1982-84. Mem. IEEE, Am. Soc. Naval Engrs., Planetary Soc., Eagle Scouts Am., Naval Helicopter Assn. Republican. Methodist. Home: 579-C Wilkes Ln Monterey CA 93940 Office: US Naval Postgrad Sch C3Dept Monterey CA 93943

HANSEN, DARREL CHANCY, teacher; b. Lewisville, Idaho, July 13, 1933; s. Chancy Hans and Edith Viola (Forsgren) H.; BS, Brigham Young U., 1955, MS, 1971; m. Margaret Doxey, Dec. 20, 1954 (div. 1983); children: Julie, Steven, Eric, Wayne; m. Lisa Young McCarrey, Mar. 23, 1984. Commd. 2d lt. USAF, 1955, advanced through grades to lt. col.; pilot Robins AFB, Ga., 1957-60; chief maintenance, Spain, 1961-64; maintenance control officer, France, 1964-65; chief pilot Hill AFB, Utah, 1965-66; resigned, 1966; civilian chief publs. mgmt. sect. Hill AFB, 1966-70; tchr. earth sci. and geography Shelley (Idaho) Jr. High Sch., 1973—. Chmn. troop com. Boy Scouts Am., 1970-71; bd. dirs. S.E. Idaho UNISERV. Decorated Air Force Commendation medal, Meritorious Service medal. Mem. Assn. Am. Geographers, Idaho Edn. Assn. (dir.), Shelley Edn. Assn. (pres. 1976-77), S.E. Idaho Res. Officers Assn. (pres.), Idaho State Res. Officers Assn. (pres. 1980), Sigma Gamma Upsilon, Gamma Theta Upsilon. Mormon. Contbr. articles to profl. jours. Home: 874 W Goldie St Idaho Falls ID 83402 Office: 350 E Pine St Shelley ID 83274

HANSEN, DONNA, educator organizational behavior; b. Washington, Jan. 12, 1950; d. Robert Hartvig and Rose Mary (Cashioli) H.; m. Harold Young McCulloch, Jr., Sept. 14, 1974 (div. Mar. 1981); m. Richard David Gritta, May 7, 1988. BA, Cornell U., 1972; MA, U. Mich., 1974, PhD, 1978. Asst. prof. Wayne State U., Detroit, 1979-83; asst. prof. U. Portland (Oreg.), 1983-86, assoc. prof., 1986—. Contbr. articles to profl. jours. Recipient Best Paper award Western Acad. Mgmt., 1988. Mem. Acad. Mgmt., Am. Psychological Assn., Decision Scis. Inst. Republican. Roman Catholic. Home: 13915 SW Secretariat Ct Beaverton OR 97005 Office: Univ Portland 5000 N Willamette Blvd Portland OR 97203

HANSEN, EDWARD ALLEN, music educator, organist; b. Tacoma, Feb. 21, 1929; s. Peter Ingolf and Olaug Elsie (Axness) H.; m. Jeanne Martinelli, June 21, 1953; children: Kathryn Elise Hansen Del Beccaro, Roberta Claire Hansen Downey, Paul Edward. BA in Music, U. Wash., 1950, 1951, MA in Music, 1952, PhD, 1965. Tchr. Seattle Pub. Schs., 1952-55; organist First Meth. Ch., Seattle, 1952-57, Seattle Symphony Orch., 1959-69; musician King Broadcasting Co., Seattle, 1965-70; organist, choirmaster Plymouth Congl. Ch., Seattle, 1957—; prof. music U. Puget Sound, Tacoma, 1970—; performer organ recitals, US and Europe, 1957—. Mem. Am. Guild Organists (pres. 1981-86), Am. Fedn. Musicians, Nat. Music Council (bd. dirs. 1984-86), Phi Mu Alpha. Office: U Puget Sound 1500 N Warner St Tacoma WA 98416

HANSEN, ERIC GUSTAV, communications executive; b. Phila., Feb. 19, 1937; s. Hans Peter and Isabella Marie (Nilsson) H.; m. Margaret Noreen Dana, Mar. 22, 1959; children: Christopher, Jeffrey, Karen. BA, San Jose State U., 1961. Engring. assoc. Western Electric, Sunnyvale, Calif., 1963-66; engr. Pacific Telesis, Alhambra, Calif., 1966-69; plant supr. Pacific Telesis, San Gabriel Valley, Calif., 1969-73; budget analyst Pacific Telesis, Pasadena, Calif., 1973-76; traffic engr. Pacific Telesis, Pasadena, 1976-77; with acctg. dept. Nev. Bell, Reno, 1977-79, fin. mgr., 1979-85, dir. finance, 1985—; bd. dirs. Great Basin Fed. Credit Union, Reno, 1981-84. Bd. dirs., treas. Reno Philharmonic Assn., 1988—. Cpl. USMC, 1954-57. Mem. Reno Tennis Club, Bally's Tennis Club, Alpha Gamma Sigma. Republican. Episcopalian. Home: 390 Chevy Chase Reno NV 89509 Office: Nev Bell 645 E Plumb Ln Reno NV 89502

HANSEN, EVELYN MARGARET, food products executive; b. Aberdeen, Wash., June 6, 1948; d. Robert Louis and Margaret Issable (Roberson) Hatfield; m. Randall George Hansen, Sept. 19, 1970; 1 child, Margaret Evelyn. Student, Grays Harbor Jr. Coll., 1967, Seattle Pacific U., 1968-69. Instr. in spl. edn. Seattle Pub. Schs., 1970-77; cons. Nat. Seafood Educators, Richmond Beach, Wash.; cons. seafood Quality Food Ctrs., Bellevue, Wash., 1986-87; coord. project Am. Heart Assn., Seattle, 1984-85; educator seafood Safeway, Haggens, various food stores around the N.W. Author: Seafood Treasurers, 1977, Selling Seafood, 1986; co-author: Seafood-A Collection of Heart Healthy Recipes, 1986, Light Hearted Seafood, 1989. Mem. Women's Fisheries Network (v.p. 1986), Coalition Fishermens Wives (v.p. 1982), Puget Sound Gillnetters Wives (pres. 1977-79). Office: Nat Seafood Educators PO Box 60006 Richmond Beach WA 98160

HANSEN, FLORENCE MARIE CONGIOLOSI (MRS. JAMES S. HANSEN), social worker; b. Middletown, N.Y., Jan. 7, 1934; d. Joseph James and Florence (Harrigan) Congiolosi; B.A., Coll. New Rochelle, 1955; M.S.W., Fla. State U., 1960; m. James S. Hansen, June 16, 1959; 1 dau., Florence M. Caseworker, Orange County Dept. Pub. Welfare, N.Y., 1955-57, Cath. Welfare Bur., Miami, Fla., 1957-58; supr. Cath. Family Service, Spokane, Wash., 1960, Cuban Children's Program, Spokane, 1962-66; founder, dir. social service dept. Sacred Heart Med. Ctr., 1968-85, dir. Kidney Ctr., 1967—. Asst. in program devel. St. Margaret's Hall, Spokane, 1961-62; trustee Family Counseling Service Spokane County, 1981—, also bd. dirs.; mem. budget allocation panel United Way, 1964-76, mem. planning com., 1968-77, mem. admissions com., 1969-70, chmn. projects com. 1972-73, active work with Cuban refugees; mem. kidney disease adv. com. Wash.-Alaska Regional Med. Program, 1970-73. Mem. Spokane Quality of Life Commn., 1974-75. Mem. Nat. Assn. Social Workers (chpt. pres. 1972-74), Acad. Cert. Social Workers (charter). Roman Catholic. Home: 5609 Northwest Blvd Spokane WA 99205 Office: Sacred Heart Med Ctr W 101 8th St Spokane WA 99204

HANSEN, FREDERIC J., state environmental agency director; b. Portland, Oreg., Mar. 22, 1946; s. Vernon Edward and Ella Freda (Schacher) H. BA in Math. and History, U. Oreg., 1968; MA in History, McMaster U., 1969; postgrad., Johns Hopkins U., 1970. Asst. historian U.S. Nat. Park Service, Washington, 1970; office mgr. U.S. Senate, Washington, 1970-71; exec. asst. U.S. Ho. of Reps., Washington, 1971-75; spl. asst. to pres. Clemency Bd. for Vietnam Era Veterans, Washington, 1975; exec. officer Peace Corps., Washington, 1975-77; dep. dir. office of the pres. Fed. Cash Mgmt. Project, Washington, 1977-78; chief dep. state treas. State of Oreg., Salem, 1978-84; dir. Oreg. Dept. of Environ. Quality, Portland, 1984—. Woodrow Wilson Nat. Found. vis. fellow, 1987—. Mem. Phi Eta Sigma, Phi Beta Kappa. Office: Oreg Environ Quality Dept 811 SW 6th Ave Portland OR 97204

HANSEN, HOBERTA LOUISE, information specialist; b. Seattle, May 22, 1939; d. Hobart McKinley Wiseman and Emma Angela (Fladebo) Rishor; m. Neil Peter Heimdahl Hansen, Nov. 10, 1958; children: Neil, Craig, John, Amber. BA magna cum laude, Eastern Wash. U., 1986. Motivational trainer, info. and referral specialist Mesa (Ariz.) Community Coun., 1987—; supr., coord. vols., Spokane County Courthouse Info. Booth, Wash., 1984-86. Campaign worker, Booth Gardner for Gov., Wash., 1984; mem. Gov.'s Com. on Employment of Handicapped, 1985, 86; staff support Mayor's Com. on Handicap Awareness, Mesa, 1987, 88; mem. demonstration project Mesa United Way Women off Welfare, 1988-89. Home: 730 N 96th Pl Mesa AZ 85207

HANSEN, JAMES V., congressman; b. Salt Lake City, Aug. 14, 1932; s. J. Vear and Sena C. H.; m. Ann Burgoyne H., 1958; children—Susan, Joseph James, David Burgoyne, Paul William, Jennifer. B.S., U. Utah, 1960. Mem. Utah Ho. of Reps., 1973-80, speaker of house, 1979-80; mem. 97th-101st Congresses from 1st Utah dist., Washington, 1981—; pres. James V. Hansen Ins. Agy., Woodland Springs Devel. Co. Office: 2421 Rayburn House Office Bldg Washington DC 20515

HANSEN, JEFFREY R., clinical pharmacist; b. Albany, Oreg., Apr. 10, 1953; s. Melvin Jesse Hansen and Delores Virginia (Reierson) LaGrange; m. Kelley MarieKroger, Sept. 11, 1977 (div. Feb. 1979). BS, Oreg. State U., 1978. Registered pharmacist, Oreg., Calif. Pharmacist Gilroy (Calif.) Med. Ctr. Pharmacy, 1979-80, Good Samaritan Hosp., San Jose, Calif., 1980-81; clin. pharmacist VA Hosp., Palo Alto, Calif., 1981—. Recipient Superior Performance award VA, 1985-87. Mem. Calif. Soc. of Hosp. Pharmacists. Democrat. Office: VA Hosp 119 3801 Miranda Ave Palo Alto CA 94301

HANSEN, JOANN BROWN, financial officer; b. Gallup, New Mex., July 7, 1929; d. William Brown and Stefi Marie (Schuster) Shillingburg; m. Gordon Eddy Hansen, March 2, 1951; 1 child, Erling Wilhelm Hansen II. BS in Microbiology, U. Ariz., 1950, MS in Microbiology, 1954, PhD in Microbiology and Virology, 1966. Lab. technician Hartman Labs., Tucson, 1950-54; rsch. asst. U. Ariz., Tucson, 1953, teaching fellow, 1954, instr., 1954-55, program dir. Cancer Ctr., 1977-82, rsch. assoc. Coll. Med., 1975-76; pres. Hansen's Auto & Tool Supply, Tucson, 1958—; dir. budget and fin. La Frontera Ctr., Inc., Tucson, 1982-89; mem. adv. bd. Ariz. Head injury Found., Tucson, 1983—; bd. dirs. Catalina Bank of Commerce, Tucson; cons.Nat. Cancer Inst., 1982—; cons., grant reviewer NSF, 1982—, and others; participant numerous confs. in field; lectr. in field. Producer (videotapes): Cancer's Impact on You, 1978, 79, 81; contbr. articles to profl. jours. Vol. allocations div. United Way, 1979-82; mem. Good Govt. League, Tucson, 1976-80; dir. Pima County Unit, Am. Cancer Soc., Tucson, 1978-86, Profl. Edn. com., 1978-81, Pub. Edn. Com., 1978-82, Crusade com., 1982-86; pres. com. on Aflatoxin, U. Ariz.; mem. adv. bd. St. Joseph Community Hosp., Com. of 100, Women's Commn. Health Task Force. Grantee Instl. Biomed.. Rsch. Support, 1980, 81, U.S. Dept. Labor, 1978, 79, 80, 81, U. Ariz. Found., 1977, NSF, 1976, Am. Cancer Soc., 1964, USPHS, 1962. Mem. AAUW (founder's fellow 1975), Am. Soc. Profl. and Exec. Women, Profl. and Bus. Women's Orgn. (elected to Key Group 1982), Nat. Assn. Corp. Dirs., 99's Club, Am. Soc. Microbiology, Assn. Women Sci., Women in Sci. and Engring. (chmn. adv. bd., Southwestern Inst. Rsch. on Women), Mensa, Sigma Delta Epsilon, Chi Omega (pres. 1949-50, 68-69), Iota Sigma Pi (cons. Washington chpt. 1982—, elected nat. del. 1981). Republican. Episcopalian. Home: 4926 E Bermuda Tucson AZ 85712 Office: Hansen's Auto & Tool Supply 5193 E 22nd St Tucson AZ 85711

HANSEN, KIM LOREN, agency administrator; b. Mpls., Jan. 23, 1953; s. Cecil Harold Hansen and Marilyn Ruth (Latham) Rippon. BS, Creighton U., 1975; MPH, U. Pitts., 1976. Adminstrv. asst. Planned Parenthood Omaha, 1977-78; exec. dir. Planned Parenthood So. Nev., Las Vegas, 1978-87; adminstr. So. Nev. Health Svcs., North Las Vegas, 1987—; mem. Primary Care Adv. Coun., Reno, 1987—. Mem. gov.'s adv. b. on White House Conf. on Families, Las Vegas, 1980; mem. Clark County Dem. Cen. Com., Las Vegas, 1982-86. Mem. Am. Pub. Health Assn., Nev. Pub. Health Assn., Nat. Assn. Community Health Ctrs., Nat. Eagle Scout Assn. Office: So Nev Health Svcs Inc 2414 E Cheyenne Ave North Las Vegas NV 89030

HANSEN, LEONARD JOSEPH, writer, editor, educator, marketing consultant; b. San Francisco, Aug. 4, 1932; s. Einar L. and Margie A. (Wilder) H.; A.B. in Radio-TV Prodn. and Mgmt., San Francisco State Coll., 1956, postgrad. 1956-57; cert. IBM Mgmt. Sch., 1967; m. Marcia Ann Rasmussen, Mar. 18, 1966; children: Barron Richard, Trevor Wilder. Jr. writer (part-time) Sta. KCBS, San Francisco, 1952-54; assoc. producer and dir. Ford Found. TV Research Project, San Francisco State Coll., 1955-57; air promotion dir. and writer Sta. KPIX-TV, San Francisco, 1959-60, crew chief on live and remote broadcasts, 1957-59; pub. relations mgr. Sta. KNTV-TV, San Jose, Calif., 1961; radio and TV promotion mgr. Seattle World's Fair, 1962; pub. relations and promotion mgr. Century 21 Ctr., Inc., Seattle, 1963-64; pub. relations dir. Dan Evans for Gov. Com., Seattle, 1964; propr., mgr. Leonard J. Hansen Pub. Relations, Seattle, 1965-67; campaign mgr. Walter J. Hickel for Gov. Com., Anchorage, 1966; exec. cons. to Gov. of Alaska, Juneau, 1967; gen. mgr. No. TV, Inc., Anchorage, 1967-69; v.p. mktg. Sea World, Inc., San Diego, 1969-71; editor and publisher Sr. World Publs., Inc., San Diego, 1973-84; chmn. Sr. Publishers Group, 1977-84; speaker and mktg. cons. to sr. citizens, 1984—; panelist, pub. affairs radio programs, 1971—; lectr. journalism San Diego State U., 1975-76. Writer weekly syndicated column Mainly for Seniors, 1984—, syndicated column Travel for Mature Adults, 1984—; contbg. editor Mature Life Features, news/feature syndicate, 1987—; chmn. Mature Mkt. Seminars, 1987—; author Life Begins at 50-The Handbook for Creative Retirement Planning, 1989. Founding mem. Housing for Elderly and Low Income Persons, San Diego, 1977-78; mem. Mayor's Ad Hoc Adv. Com. on Aging, San Diego, 1976-79; vice chmn. Housing Task Force, San Diego, 1977-78; bd. dirs. Crime Control Commn., San Diego, 1980, San Diego Coalition, 1980-83; del. White House Conf. on Aging, 1981. Served with U.S. Army, 1953-55. Recipient numerous service and citizenship awards from clubs and community orgns. Mem. Public Relations Soc. Am. (accredited), Soc. Profl. Journalists (Best Investigative Reporting award 1979), Internat. Platform Assn., San Diego Press Club (Best Newswriting award 1976-77, Headliner of Yr. award 1980), Am. Assn. Travel Editors (profl. mem.). Home: 959 Braemar Ln San Diego CA 92109 Office: 1326 Garnet Ave San Diego CA 92109

HANSEN, MARILYN JEANNE, securities brokerage executive; b. L.A., Oct. 24, 1941; d. Fred Visser and Ernestine (Neal) Kline; m. Steven A. Hansen (div.); children: Kristin, Jason. Student, Biola U., 1959-62. Mgr. securities dept. Fin. Mgmt. Svcs., Inc., Encino, Calif., 1984-87; asst. v.p. Quincy Cass Assocs., Inc., L.A., 1987—; supt. Newport Dog Shows, Pasadena, Calif., 1979—. Mem. Nat. Notary Assn., NAFE. Democrat. Office: Quincy Cass Assocs Inc 11111 Santa Monica Blvd Los Angeles CA 90025

HANSEN, MARK DOUGLAS, human factors engineer; b. Port Arthur, Tex., Oct. 3, 1956; s. Henry Arnold and Evelyn Inez (Young) H. BS in Psychology, Tex. A&M U., 1980, MS in Indsl. Engring., 1982. Registered profl. engr., Tex. Engr. human factors Ford Aerospace Corp., Houston, 1982-84; lead, human factors and systems safety engr. Ford Aerospace Corp., Colorado Springs, Colo., 1984—; sr. human engr. Harris Corp., Melbourne, Fla., 1984; cons. Computer Software Assocs., Inc., Houston, 1982-84. Contbr. rsch. articles to tech. jours. Aide Reps., Houston, 1982-84, Colorado Springs, 1984—. Selected for Citizen Ambassador Program People to People Internat., Europe, 1985, Peoples Republic of China, 1988. Mem. Human Factors Soc. (cert.), System Safety Soc., NSPE, Tex. Soc. Profl. Engrs., Am. Soc. Safety Engrs. (sec. Pikes Peak chpt. 1987, v.p. 1987-88, pres. 1988-89, Safety Profl. of Yr. Pikes Peak chpt. 1988), Inst. Indsl. Engrs. (chmn. awards com. Pikes Peak chpt. 1987-88, sec. local chpt. 1988—, pres. 1989—), Am. Psychol. Assn., Assn. Aviation Psychologists, Sons. of Norway. Lutheran. Home: 2451 Astron Dr Colorado Springs CO 80906 Office: Ford Aerospace Corp 10440 State Hwy 83 Colorado Springs CO 80908

HANSEN, R. ERIC, wine educator; b. Winchester, Mass., Aug. 5, 1946; s. Ralph Ernest and Jane (Carroll) H.; m. Jane Cowan, Sept. 19, 1970; 1 child, Sarah Lane. BFA, Phila. Coll. Art, 1970. Dir. of wine Kapalua (Hawaii) Bay Hotel, 1978-86; specialist in nat. hotel accounts Robert Mondavi Winery, Oakville, Calif., 1986—; wine judge Los Angeles County Fair, 1983-88, Los Angeles Times, 1987, Nat. Restaurant Assn., Chgo., 1984-85; chmn. wine symposium Kapalua Bay Hotel, 1981—. Mem. Maui (Hawaii) County Planning Bd., 1985-86. Mem. Brotherhood Knights of the Vine (master knight 1983—), Soc. Wine Educators (instr. 1982—), Comfrerie de la Chaine des Rotisseurs (mem. Ordrie Mondail des Gourmet, chevalier 1987—). Home: 15 Oakcliff Dr Laguna Niguel CA 92677 Office: Robert Mondavi Winery PO Box 106 Oakville CA 94562

HANSEN, RALPH WALDEMAR, librarian; b. N.Y.C., May 14, 1927; s. Waldemar and Minna Klara (Zimmermann) H.; m. Lillian Strong, Sept. 16, 1949; children: Diane, Lynn. BA, Brigham Young U., 1951, MA, 1954; MLS, U. Calif., Berkeley, 1970. Tchr. social sci. Orem (Utah) High Sch., 1952-53; reference librarian Brigham Young U., Provo, Utah, 1953-56, Univ. archivist, 1956-62; Univ. archivist Stanford (Calif.) U., 1962-79, acquisitions librarian, 1967-79; assoc. librarian Boise (Idaho) State U., 1979—; mem. Idaho State Hist. Records Adv. Bd., Boise, 1980—; project supr. Frank Church Papers Processing Project, Boise, 1985-88; mem. Calif. Heritage Preservation Commn., Sacramento, 1963-77; city historian Palo Alto (Calif.) Hist. Assn., 1963-67; rsch. assoc. Oreg. Collection, U. Oreg., Eugene, 1959-60, Baker Library, Harvard U. Grad. Sch. Bus., Cambridge, Mass., 1962. Contbr. articles to profl. jours. Bd. dirs., sec. Boise Chamber Music Soc., 1984—. Sgt. AUS, 1945-47, MTO. Mem. ALA, Soc. Am. Archivists, Idaho Library Assn. Home: 251 Arrowrock Ln Boise ID 83706 Office: Boise State U Library 1910 University Dr Boise ID 83725

HANSEN, REED ELLIOTT, economist, consultant; b. Omaha, Apr. 17, 1944; s. Ernest William and Alice May (Nielson) H.; m. Brigitte Bachmann, Sept. 6, 1974; children: Jens, Todd. BA, Wash. State U., 1968; MA, George Washington U., 1972. Assoc. research Urban Inst., Washington, 1970-83; prin. R.E. Hansen Research Assocs. Inc., Bainbridge Island, Wash., 1983—. Author numerous research reports. Peer and mem. rev. panel State of Nev. Technical Rev. Com. for proposed High Level Nuclear Waste Repository, 1986—. Office: RE Hansen Rsch Assocs 755 Winslow Way E Ste 206 Bainbridge Island WA 98110

HANSEN, RICHARD OLAF, geophysics professor; b. Ottawa, Ont., Can., Oct. 4, 1946; came to U.S., 1968; s. Hyllard Olaf and Muriel Lenora (Helson) H.; m. Kathleen Jean Thoms, June 15, 1968. BSc with honors, Carleton U., 1968; MS, U. Chgo., 1969, PhD, 1973. Research assoc. U. Pitts., 1973-75; postdoctoral research asst. U. Oxford, Oxford, Great Britian, 1975-76; lectr. U. Calif., Berkeley, Calif., 1976-78; staff scientist EG&G Geometrics, Sunnyvale, Calif., 1979-85; prof. Colo. Sch. of Mines, Golden, Colo., 1985—; Assoc. editor Geophysics, 1987-89. Mem. Soc. Exploration

Geophysicists, Am. Geophys. Union, Am. Physical Soc., Am. Math. Soc., Soc. for Indsl. and Applied Math. Office: Colo Sch of Mines Dept of Geophysics Golden CO 80401

HANSEN, ROBERT DENNIS, educational administrator; b. San Francisco, July 17, 1945; s. Eiler Cunnard and Muriel Lenore (Morrison) H.; BA, U. San Francisco, 1967, MA in Counseling and Guidance, 1971, MA in Supervision and Adminstrn., 1973; EdD, U. La Verne, 1988; m. Diane Armstrong Messinger, Aug. 14, 1971; children—April Michelle, Alison Nicole. Tchr., dept. chmn., counselor, dir. student affairs, attendance officer South San Francisco Unified Sch. Dist., 1968-74, coordinator, asst. prin. Jurupa Unified Sch. Dist., Riverside, Calif., 1974-78; prin., asst. supt. San Gabriel (Calif.) Sch. Dist., 1978—; adj. prof. U. La Verne, Calif., 1988—. Exec. bd. South San Francisco PTA, 1968-74. Named hon. chpt. farmer Future Farmers Am.; recipient Hon. Service award Calif. State PTA. Mem. U. San Francisco Edn. Alumni Soc. (pres. 1972-73), U. San Francisco Alumni Assn., Am. Assn. Sch. Adminstrs., Assn. Calif. Sch. Adminstrs., Assn. for Supervision and Curriculum Devel., Phi Delta Kappa. Republican. Episcopalian. Mason (32 deg.). Home: 2012 Cobblefield Way Glendora CA 91740 Office: 102 E Broadway San Gabriel CA 91776

HANSEN, ROBERT GUNNARD, philatelist; b. Chgo., Aug. 16, 1939; s. Earl F. and Mildred E. (Hargrave) H.; A.A., Lincoln Coll., 1960; B.A., Culver Stockton Coll., 1962; M.B.A., U. So. Calif., 1966; postgrad. UCLA Extension, 1962-67; m. Bertha Golds, Aug. 10, 1960; children—Karin Lee, Lisa Marie. With Litton Industries, 1962-63, Sterer Engring., 1963-69; mktg. and contracts ofcl. Santa Barbara Research Ctr., 1969-73; pres., chief exec. officer, R.G. Hansen & Assocs., Santa Barbara, 1974— ; pres., owner The Silver Penny and Santa Barbara Stamp & Coin, 1969—; guest lectr. Santa Barbara City Coll. Mem. Am. Vacuum Soc., Am. Philatelic Soc. (life), Am. Numismatic Assn., Hawaii Numismatic Assn., Token and Medal Soc., Masons, York Rite. Scottish Rite, Shriners, Royal Order of Scotland, Channel City, Royal Arch Masons, Rotary Internat. Research and publs. on cryogenics, electro-optics, infrared radiation; patentee in field. Republican. Presbyterian. Office: 631 Chapala St Santa Barbara CA 93101

HANSEN, RONALD GREGORY, civil engineer; b. Waipahu, Hawaii, Aug. 22, 1929; s. Erling M. and Geraldine J. (Nettleton) H.; m. Theresa J. Cunningham, Feb. 5, 1955; children: Eric L., Karen A., Maureen A., Timothy E. BCE, U. Santa Clara, 1952; MSCE, U. So. Calif., 1958, postgrad., 1958-66; M in Pub. Adminstrn., U. Alaska, 1981. Registered civil engr., Alaska, Wash., Oreg., Calif. Engr. Calif. Dept. Water Resources, Los Angeles, 1957-67; sr. engr. Water Quality Control Bd., Los Angeles, 1967-71; chief water pollution control State of Alaska, Juneau, 1971-79; sr. engr. KCM Inc. and EMPS Engring, Juneau, 1980-85; pres. Hansen Engring., Juneau, 1985—. Former scoutmaster, mem. bldg. com. S.E. Alaska, Boy Scouts Am.; chmn. Juneau Parks and Recreation Adv. Com., 1983—. Served to lt. col., C.E., U.S. Army. Mem. Am. Water Works Assn., ASCE, Water Pollution Control Fedn., Am. Acad. Environ. Engrs., Am. Water Resources Assn., Internat. Water Resources Assn., NSPE. Republican. Roman Catholic. Home and Office: Hansen Engring 4117 Birch Ln Juneau AK 99801

HANSEN, SIGVARD THEODORE, JR., orthopaedic surgeon, educator; b. Spokane, Wash., Nov. 30, 1935; s. Sigvard Theodore and Beverly Esther (Means) H.; m. Mary Jane Weinmann, Aug. 20, 1960; children: Christopher Michael, Eric Theodore; m. Dalia Maria Nalis, Sept. 19, 1987. BA cum laude, Whitman Coll., 1957; MD, U. Wash., 1961. Diplomate Am. Bd. Orthopaedic Surgery. Intern, King County Hosp., Seattle, 1961-62; resident in surgery U. Wash., Seattle, 1965-69, asst. prof. orthopaedic surgery 1971-75, assoc. prof., 1975-79, prof., 1979—, chmn. dept., 1981-85; cons. Madigan Army Hosp., 1975—; bd. overseers Whitman Coll., 1985—. Served with USN, 1962-65. NIH summer research fellow, 1957, 58. Mem. Am. Acad. Orthopaedic Surgery, Am. Orthopaedic Assn., Assn. Bone and Joint Surgeons, Western Orthopaedic Assn., Am. Orthopaedic Foot and Ankle Soc., AO-N. Am. Found. (pres. 1986—), Assn. for Study Internal Fixation (bd. dirs. 1984—), M.E. Mueller Found. (bd. dirs. 1986—), Phi Beta Kappa. Contbr. articles to med. jours., chpts. to books. Home: 1 W Highland Dr Seattle WA 98119 Office: 325 9th Ave Ste 6S Seattle WA 98104

HANSEN, W(ARREN) EUGENE, lawyer; b. Tremonton, Utah, Aug. 23, 1928; s. Warren Eugene and Ruth (Steed) H.; m. Jeanine Showell, Sept. 8, 1950; children: Christian, Jeff, Matthew, Susan, Steven, Stanton. BS, Utah State U., Logan, 1950; JD, U. Utah, 1958. Assoc. Nielsen & Conder, Salt Lake City, 1958-61, ptnr., 1961-75; ptnr. Hansen & Orton, Salt Lake City, 1975-78, Hansen & Thompson, Salt Lake City, 1978-80, Hansen, Thompson & Dewsnup, Salt Lake City, 1980-84, Hansen & Dewsnup, Salt Lake City, 1984—; bd. dirs. First Continental Life & Accident Ins. Co., Salt Lake City and Houston, 1977-87. Co-author The Utah Insurance Commissioner, 1957. Chmn. Utah State Bd. Regents, Salt Lake City, 1987-89; pres. Utah State Bar, Salt Lake City, 1979-80; mem. Utah State U. Inst. Council, Logan, Utah, 1981-85. Fellow Am. Coll. Trial Lawyers, Am. Bar Found.; mem. Am. Bd. Trial Advocates, Order of Coif, Bonneville Knife and Fork (pres. 1976-77). Republican. Office: Hansen & Dewnup 2020 Beneficial Life Tower Salt Lake City UT 84111

HANSEY, RENEE JEANNE, corporate executive; b. Tacoma, Wash., Apr. 24, 1927; d. Francis J. and Genevieve (Hewitt) Payette; m. James Burpee, Mar. 13, 1947 (dec. 1950); children: James, Victoria; m. Orville D. Hansey (div. 1987); children; Dan, Terri, John, Bill. Student in Layout and Design, Art Inst. Chgo., 1943; BS in Psychology, St. John's U., 1988; postgrad. in Graphics, U. Alaska, 1985. Copy writer Sta. KIT, Yakima, Wash., 1942-44; program mgr. Sta. KING, Seattle, 1945-47; advt. mgr. Sequim (Wash.) Press, 1967-70, editor, 1970-76; tv producer Municipality of Anchorage, 1976-86; publisher Voice, Port Angeles, Wash., 1986—; also dir. Retired Sr. Vol. Program, Port Angeles, Wash.; founder Widowed Persons Svc., Anchorage, 1983-85; owner Frontier Pub., Anchorage, 1983-85; dir. Far North Network, Anchorage, 1982-86. Author: Go to the Source, 1977, One Way to the Funny Farm, 1978; producer (tv show) Opportunities for Seniors, 1981-86 (TV Prodn. award, 1982-85). Sec. Dem. Cen. Com. Clallam County, Wash., 1965-76; founder Olympic Women's Resource Ctr., Port Angeles, 1966-75; councilwoman City Sequim, 1973-76; active Affirmative Action Clallam County, Wash., 1974, Sr. Companions, Elder Abuse Task Force; bd. dirs. Port Angeles Sr. Ctr. With WAC, 1944. Mem. Alaska Press Women (pres. 1981-82, 85-86), Nat. Fedn. Press Women, Alaska Press Club. Roman Catholic. Home: 235 N Sunnyside Sequim WA 98382 Office: RSVP 215 1/2 S Lincoln Port Angeles WA 98362

HANSON, DAVID JON, computer consultant; b. Ames, Iowa, May 22, 1955; s. Harley Odean and Lavina Helena (Geiszler) H.; m. Gabrielle Marie Droulers, Mar. 24, 1984; 1 child, Alexandra Patricia. BA in Math. and Computer, Luther Coll., 1976. Cert. data processor. Cons. Consumer Systems, Chgo., 1977-80; sr. systems analyst Arabian Am. Oil Co., Dhahran, Saudi Arabia, 1980-82; ind. cons. IBM, Stuttgart, Fed. Republic Germany, 1982-83; cons. Knauer Cons., San Francisco, 1983-85; pres., owner Structured Solutions, Inc., San Francisco, 1985—. Author (ednl. software) Caravan: The Travels of Marco Polo, 1986. Mem. Data Processing Mgmt. Assn. (treas. 1988, sec. 1987). Home and Office: 4090 26th St San Francisco CA 94131

HANSON, EUGENE WILLIAM, JR., sales administrator; b. St. Louis, June 11, 1950; s. Eugene William Sr. and Mary Jayne (Drummond) H.; m. Linda Kelley, Apr. 17, 1982; children: Eugene W. III, Jennifer, Marc. BSBA in Acctg., Calif. State Coll., Bakersfield, 1977. Br. systems coordinator Coca-Cola Bottling Co., Los Angeles, 1976-81, mgr. br. controls, 1981-83, mgr. sales adminstrn., 1983-88; br. mgr. Coca-Cola Bottling Co., Bakersfield, 1988—. Democrat. Roman Catholic. Office: Coca-Cola Bottling Co 414 19th St Bakersfield CA 93301

HANSON, FRANK ERWIN, JR., mining company executive; b. Tulsa, Aug. 20, 1943; s. Frank Erwin and Marie Regina (Segmiller) H.; m. Virginia Lee Feeser, July 15, 1967; children: Frank III, Gretchen, Tiffany. Student, Coll. of Great Falls, 1972-75, Montant Tech. Inst., 1971; BSBA, U. Phoenix, 1982. Weighmaster The Anaconda Co., Great Falls, Mont., 1969-70, traffic clk., 1970-75; traffic coordinator Inspiration Consol. Copper Co., Claypool, Ariz., 1975-77, traffic mgr., 1977-78, dir. transp. and customer svcs., 1978-88; mgr. transp. svcs. Cyprus Copper Co., Claypool, 1988—; bd. dirs., cons. San Carlos (Ariz.) Lake Devel. Corp., 1988. Rifle coach Jr. Olympics; youth leader Holy Angels Cath. Ch., Globe, Ariz., 1987-88; merit badge counselor Boy Scouts Am., Globe, 1988—. Served with USMC, 1964-68. Named Jaycee of Yr., Shelby (Mont.) Jaycees, 1968. Mem. Nat. Indsl. Traffic League, Wire Assn. Internat., Nat. Rifle Assn. (rifle instr.), Ariz. Rifle and Pistol Assn., VFW. Republican. Club: Globe-Miami Gun (pres. 1985—). Lodge: Elks. Office: Cyprus Copper Co Hwy 60 at Inspiration Rd Box 4444 Claypool AZ 85532

HANSON, GEORGE PETER, retired research botanist, real estate investor; b. Conde, S.D., July 20, 1933; s. George Henry and Rosa Wilhelmina (Peterson) H.; m. Barbara Jean Graves, Aug. 20, 1958; children: David, Carole, Heather, Peter; m. Gloria Ann Gauntt, June 1, 1969. BS in Agronomy, S.D. State U., 1956, MS in Plant Breeding, 1958; PhD in Genetics, Ind. U., 1965. Asst. prof. biology Thiel Coll. Greenville, Pa., 1962-65; asst. prof. botany Butler U., Indpls., 1965-67; sr. biologist L.A. State and County Arboretum, Arcadia, Calif., 1968-82; real estate investor, 1971—. Mem. Apt. Assn. of Greater L.A. Methodist. Contbr. numerous articles in field to profl. jours. Home: 1345 W Haven Rd San Marino CA 91108

HANSON, GERALD WARNER, county official; b. Alexandria, Minn., Dec. 25, 1938; s. Lewis Lincoln and Dorothy Hazel (Warner) H.; m. Sandra June Wheeler, July 9, 1960. AA, San Bernardino Valley (Calif.) Coll., 1959; BA, U. Redlands (Calif.), 1979; MA, U. Redlands, 1981. Cert. advanced metrication specialist. Dep. sealer San Bernardino (Calif.) County, 1964-80, div. chief, 1980-85, dir. weights and measures, 1985—. Mem. Redlands Rent Rev. Bd., 1985—; bd. dirs. House Neighborly Svc., Redlands, 1972-73, Boys Club, Redlands, 1985-86. With USN. Fellow U.S. Metric Assn. (treas. 1986-88); mem. Nat. Conf. on Weights and Measures (asst. treas. 1986—), Western Weights and Measures Assn. (pres. 1987—), Calif. Assn. Weights and Measures Ofcls. (1st v.p. 1987—), Masons, Shriners, Kiwanis (treas. Redlands club). Home: 225 E Palm Ave Redlands CA 92373 Office: San Bernardino County Dept Weights and Measures 777 E Rialto Ave San Bernardino CA 92415-0790

HANSON, JANET CURTIS, lawyer; b. Chgo., Jan. 9, 1948; d. Bruce B. and Marie Katherine (Marsh) Curtis. BA magna cum laude, Denison U., 1969; MA, U. Minn., 1970; AA, Edmonds Community Coll., 1978; JD, Stanford U., 1981. Bar: Oreg. 1981, D.C. 1987, Calif. 1987. Instr., So. Conn. State Coll., New Haven, 1973-74; parent edn. instr. N. Seattle Community Coll., 1974-76; paralegal George Wm. Cody, Lynwood, Wash., 1978, Davis, Wright, Todd, Riese & Jones, Seattle, 1977-78; assoc. Miller, Nash, Wiener, Hager & Carlsen, Portland, Oreg., 1981-84; assoc. gen. counsel N.W. Power Planning Council, Portland, 1984-86; atty. Fed. Home Loan Bank San Francisco, 1987—. Contbr. articles to profl. jours. Bd. dirs., crime watch chmn., historic preservation chmn. Irvington Community Assn., Portland, 1982-86. Mem. ABA, Oreg. State Bar Assn., D.C. Bar Assn., Calif. State Bar Assn., Lawyers' Club San Francisco, San Francisco Bar Assn., Multnomah County Bar Assn., Nat. Trust Hist. Preservation, Phi Beta Kappa, Sigma Xi, Psi Chi, Kappa Delta Pi. Presbyterian. Home: 3840 Market St #3 San Francisco CA 94131 Office: Fed Home Loan Bank One Montgomery St Ste 400 PO Box 7948 San Francisco CA 94120

HANSON, JOHN RANDALL, bank executive; b. Taos, N.Mex., Aug. 15, 1952; s. John Edward and Carol Jean (Anderson) H.; m. Katherine Hinsch, Sept. 17, 1971; children: Julie Ann, Kristin Jean. BS in Bus. Mgmt., Hawthorne U., 1986. Mgr. Beneficial Mgmt. Corp., Ogden, Utah, 1972-74; regional credit mgr. GE Credit, Salt Lake City, 1974-79; sr. v.p. Valley Bank and Trust Co., Salt Lake City, 1979—; lectr. Small Bus. Devel. Council, Salt Lake City, 1985—, Small Bus. Adminstrn., Salt Lake City, 1984—, Inst. of Banking, Kuwait, 1988, U. Utah Grad. Sch. Bus., Salt Lake City, 1984—, cons. Mem. bd. regents Hawthorne Acad., 1987—. Recipient 1st Divisional prize Am. Inst. Banking, Salt Lake City, 1985, Pub. Relations award Utah Consumer Fin. Assn., Salt Lake City, 1972-75, 78. Mem. Robert Morris Assn. Republican. Presbyterian. Home: 3224 South 4840 West Salt Lake City UT 84120 Office: Valley Bank and Trust Co 3620 S State St Salt Lake City UT 84115

HANSON, KEITH DUNSDEN, dentist; b. Boulder, Colo., Oct. 24, 1956; s. Russell Harland and Lois Helene (Olsen) H. BA in Biology, Union Coll., Lincoln, Nebr., 1979; DDS, Loma Linda U., 1983. Lic. dentist, Calif., Colo. Dentist Internat. Clerkship Program, Nairobi, Kenya, 1982; pvt. practice Denver, 1984--; dentist Aspen Dental Assocs., Estes Park, Colo., 1984-86, Westminister Dental Assocs., Colo., 1984--. Recipient Cert. of Appreciation, Calif. Dental Assn., 1982, Humanitarian Service award Nat. Found. of Dentistry for Handicapped, State Colo., 1986. Mem. ADA (meritorious service award 1982-83), Colo. Dental Assn., Nat. Denver Dental Assn., Englewood C. of C. Seventh Day Adventist. Office: 3470 S Sherman St Ste 4 Englewood CO 80110

HANSON, LAURIE WOOD BAILEY, consultant healthcare, banking and transactional law; b. Washington, Jan. 20, 1946; d. William Russell and Adelaide (Wood) Bailey; m. Martin F. Hanson, Dec. 28, 1974 (div. Sept. 1984); 1 child, Nancy. BS in Biology and Chemistry, Purdue U., 1970; postgrad., Harvard U., 1970-71, Boston U., 1971-72. Rsch. biochemist Scripps Clinic, La Jolla, Calif., 1972-74, U. So. Calif. Med. Sch., L.A., 1974, Vet.'s Hosp., L.A., 1975-77, UCLA, 1978-80, Cedars Sinai Hosp., L.A., 1980-82; investment analyst L.A., 1981-84; corp. recruiter Search West, Century City, Calif., 1984-85; pvt. practice corp. recruitment L.A. area, 1985—; cons. Paracelsus Healthcare Corp., Pasadena, Calif., 1985—, Am. Med. Internat., Santa Monica, Calif., 1985—, Nat. Med. Enterprises, Santa Monica, 1985—, Blue Cross, Woodland Hills, Calif., 1987—, Jupiter Healthcare Corp., 1987—, Summit Healthcare Corp., 1988—, Long Beach Meml. Hosp., 1988—, Luth. Hosp. Soc., 1987—. Rsch. grantee Nat. Cancer Inst., UCLA, 1978, NIH, Cedars Sinai Hosp., 1980, U. So. Calif. Med. Sch., 1977. Republican. Congregationalist. Office: PO Box 3885 Torrance CA 90510

HANSON, LLOYD ELDRED, insurance executive; b. Fordville, N.D., Apr. 4, 1945; s. Irvin Marcus and Annie Joanne (Ness) H.; m. Carrol Lynn Proffitt, June 20, 1970; children: Erik, Kristopher, Sarah, Emily. BBA, U. N.D., 1966, postgrad., 1966-67; postgrad., U. Va., 1972-73; MBA, Pacific Western U., 1982. Acct. Dean Van Lines, L.A., 1967-68; gen. mgr. Delta Van & Storage (subs. of Dean Van Lines), Alexandria, Va., 1970-73; acctg. mgr. Gulf Oil Real Estate, Reston, Va., 1973-77; controller Carl M. Freeman Assoc., Silver Spring, Md., 1977-78; dir. cost acctg. Geico Ins. Group, Washington, 1978-81; controller Celina (Ohio) Ins. Group, 1981-86; v.p., controller TransAmerica Ins. Group, L.A., 1986—. Patrol dad Boy Scouts Am., Calif., 1987—; tchr., usher Community Ch., Va., Calif. and Ohio, 1977-88. Served with U.S. Army 1968-70. Mem. Ins. Acctg. and Systems Assn. (bd. dirs. 1988—), Nat. Assn. Accts. (controllers council 1983—), Mensa, Toastmasters (pres. 1985-86). Republican. Office: TransAm Ins Group 6300 Canoga Ave Box 6300 Woodland Hills CA 91367

HANSON, MARCY, actress, model; b. Galveston, Tex., Dec. 22, 1952; d. James Carrol and Gladys Henrietta (Hensel) Jones; m. Ron Albrect Aug. 1, 1969 (div. 1973); m. Chuck Hanson, Aug. 2, 1974 (div. 1975); m. Shep Gordon, Mar. 2, 1979 (div. 1981). Student, La Marque (Tex.) Coll., U. Tex. TV actress, model Ben Shaws Modeling Agy., Houston, 1972-75, Joan Mangun Agy., Beverly Hills, Calif., 1975—; cover girl, playmate Playboy Enterprises, Los Angeles, 1976—; star of TV series NBC, Los Angeles, 1978, First Choice of Can., Toronto, 1984; counselor Models For Christ, Los Angeles, 1988. Adminstr. Hope Luth. Social Services, Hollywood, 1988. Mem. Screen Actors Guild, AFTRA. Republican. Office: Hope Lutheran Church 6720 Melrose Ave Hollywood CA 90038

HANSON, NOEL RODGER, management consultant; b. Los Angeles, Jan. 19, 1942; s. Albert and Madelyne Gladys (Pobanz) H.; B.S. in Indsl. Mgmt., U. So. Calif., 1963, M.B.A. in Fin., 1966; m. Carol Lynn Travis, June 17, 1967; 1 son, Eric Rodger. Asst. dir. alumni fund, then dir. ann. funds U. So. Calif., 1964-66; asst. to Walt Disney for Cal-Arts, Retlaw Enterprises, Glendale, Calif., 1966-68; asst. dir. joint devel. Claremont U. Center, 1968-69; v.p. adminstrn. Robert Johnston Co., Los Angeles, 1969-70; partner Hale, Hanson & Co., Pasadena, Calif., 1970-82, Hanson, Olson & Co., 1982—; pres. Pasadena Services, Inc., 1977—; dir. Pasadena Fin. Cons., Inc., Wilihire Funding, Inc., 1988—. Trustee Oakhurst Sch., Pasadena, 1973-75; bd. advisers Girls Club Pasadena, 1977—; mem. U. So. Calif. Assos., 1979—, U. So. Calif. Commerce Assos., 1965—. Republican. Presbyterian. Club: Jonathan (Los Angeles). Address: 1051 LaLoma Rd Pasadena CA 91105

HANSON, PETER GRIFFITH, lawyer; b. Sacramento, July 25, 1947; s. Samuel Griffith and Emmy Lou (Hotchkiss) H. AB, San Francisco State U., 1969; JD, U. Calif., Hastings, 1973. Bar: Calif. 1973, U.S. Dist. Ct. (ea. dist.) Calif. 1973. Analyst Coun. of State Administrs. of Vocat. Rehab., Washington, 1974-75; pros. atty. Office of San Francisco Dist. Atty., 1976-81; pntr. Disler & Hanson, San Francisco, 1982-86; sole practice San Francisco, 1986—. Author mag. column San Francisco Bus.; speechwriter for civic leaders. Bd. dirs. Legal Svcs. for Children, San Francisco, 1983-84; pres. City Dem. Club, 1982-84, Big Bros. of San Francisco, 1980-82, Small Bus. Network, 1986-87; v.p. San Francisco Planning & Urban Rsch. Assn., 1989; mem. adv. com. on capital expenditures San Francisco Unified Sch. Dist., 1988-89. Mem. San Francisco C. of C. (bd. dirs. 1988—). Office: 1388 Sutter St #900 San Francisco CA 94109

HANSON, ROBERT DAREN, real estate developer; b. Santa Maria, Calif., Oct. 7, 1965; s. Palmer Bennie and Janette Elinor (Tronnes) H. BS in Fin., Ariz. State U., 1987. Teller The Stockmen's Bank, Kingman, Ariz., 1980-83; computer programmer Citizens Utilities Co., Kingman, 1983-84; bookkeeper Casino Properties Ltd. Ptnrships, Bullhead City, Ariz., 1988—; real estate agt. Western Tierra Properties, Inc., Bullhead City, 1987—; gen. mgr. Mohave Cars, Inc., Bullhead City, 1986-89; developer Nev. Ninety-Five, Laughlin, 1988—. Mem. Nat. Assn. of Realtors, Ariz. Assn. of Realtors, Alpha Lambda Delta. Republican. Methodist. Office: PO Box 2509 Bullhead City AZ 86430

HANSON, RONDELL BLAIR, lawyer, real estate executive; b. Rexburg, Idaho, Sept. 1, 1937; s. Edward Blair and Alice (Barnett) H.; m. Joyce Pugmire, June 25, 1960; children: Jennifer, Elizabeth, Matthew, Andrew. AB, Stanford U., 1959; JD, U. Calif.-Berkeley, 1962. Bar: Calif. 1962. Assoc. Kindel & Anderson, Santa Ana., Calif., 1962-67, ptnr., 1968-70; gen. counsel, exec. v.p. Diversified Communities, Newport Beach, Calif., 1970-75; ptnr. Layman, Hanson & Jones, Newport Beach, 1975-78; pvt. gen. real estate corp. mgmt., Newport Beach, 1978—; founder, dir. Westlands Bank, Santa Ana, 1970-75; dir. Orange County Performing Arts Ctr.; Contbr. articles to profl. jours. Pres., mgr. Little League Baseball, 1978-83; bishop Ch. of Jesus Christ of Latter-day Saints, 1975-80, 85-86; pres. Emerald Bay Community Assn., 1986-87. Mem. Stanford U. Alumni Assn. Republican. Clubs: Stanford Assocs., Center. Home: 529 Emerald Bay Laguna Beach CA 92651 Office: PO Box 1960 Newport Beach CA 92660

HANSON, RUSSELL GLEN, organizational development consultant; b. Havre, Mont., Mar. 31, 1952; s. James Russell and Mavis Maxine (Bishop) H.; m. Margaret Anne Shields, Dec. 28, 1974; children: Erik Russell, Emily Elizabeth. BS in Indls. Engring., Mont. State U., 1974; MS in Indsl. Engring., Ariz. State U., 1977. Mfg. engr. Honeywell Info. Systems, Phoenix, 1974-77, mgr. ops., 1977-79, orgn. devel. cons., 1979-85, dir. orgn. devel., 1985, sr. cons. mfg. systems, 1986; owner, pres. TransTech, Glendale, Ariz., 1986—. Contbr. articles to profl. jours. Lector, usher St. Helens Roman Cath. Ch., Glendale, 1980—; umpire, coach Thunderbird Little League, Phoenix, 1987-88. Mem. Assn. Quality and Productivity, Tau Beta Pi, Alpha Pi Mu. Democrat. Lutheran. Office: TransTech 5311 W Aire Libre Glendale AZ 85306

HANSON, SCOTT R., restaurant general manager; b. Boise, Idaho, Oct. 27, 1956; s. Merle Lee and Barbara Ann (Hegoestad) H.; m. Robin Lee Eschenbaugh, Feb. 4, 1984; children: Kathleen, Michael. AA in Sci., Math., Ariz. State U., 1977; AA in Acctg., Mesa Community Coll., 1979; AA in Restaurant Mgmt., Northwestern U., 1980; BS, U. Phoenix, 1987. Beverage mgr. The Other Place/Fiesta Inn, Tempe, Ariz., 1974-75; asst. mgr. Rodehouse Restaurant, Inc., Phoenix, 1975-77; kitchen, gen. mgr. Hunter Inn, Phoenix, 1976-80; cons. Hunter Inn, 1980-82; food, beverage dir. P.V. Baptist Retirement Ctr., Paradise Valley, Ariz., 1980-82; gen. mgr. Tequila Dan's Inc., Tempe, 1982—; tournament dir. Tequila Dan's Inc., 1987—; Cons. Lincoln Properties, Phoenix, 1981-83. Author: Rodehouse Restaurant Guide, 1979. Democrat. Lutheran. Office: Tequila Dan's Inc 825 S 48th St Tempe AZ 85281

HANSON, SIMON PETER, chemical engineering educator; b. Torquay, Eng., June 13, 1953; came to U.S., 1969; s. Jack Aubrey and Eliza Ellen (Hall) H.; m. Nancy Ann Dean, Dec. 7, 1980. SB, MIT, 1974, ScD, 1982. Asst. prof. chem. engring. U. Ariz., Tucson, 1982—; bd. dirs. rsch. Researchers Am., Tucson; pres. Deltek, Tucson, 1988—. Halcon Internat. fellow, 1976. Mem. AIAA, Am. Inst. Chemists, Am. Inst. Chem. Engrs., Combustion Inst., Sigma Xi. Home: PO Box 41041 Tucson AZ 85717-1041 Office: U Ariz Dept Chem Engring M/S Geo 108B Tucson AZ 85721

HANSON, STEPHEN RAYMOND, biomedical engineer, educator; b. Missoula, Mont., Aug. 22, 1949; s. Raymond Oscar and Eileen (Crego) H.; m. Bonnie Diane Sawin, Aug. 7, 1976; children: Angela Rae, Neal Anthony. BS, U. Pa., 1971; MS, Stanford U., 1972; PhD, U. Wash., 1977. Rsch. asst. prof. medicine U. Wash., Seattle, 1979-82, affiliate assoc. prof. bioengring., 1985—; staff scientist Rsch. Inst. of Scripps Clinic, LaJolla, Calif., 1982—; cons. in field. Contbr. articles to profl. jours., chpts. to books. Recipient numerous med. rsch. grants, 1977—. Mem. Am. Inst. Chem. Engrs., Am. Heart Assn., AAAS, Internat. Soc. for Thrombosis and Hemostasis, Soc. for Biomaterials. Republican.

HANSON, THOMAS JEFFREY, data processing executive; b. Madison, Wis., June 11, 1950; s. Francis T. and Frances G. (Joerg) H. BS, U. Wis., 1972, MS, 1974. Cert. Data Processor, 1986. Programmer, analyst Nat. Forest Products Assn., Washington, 1976-79; mgr. data processing IFA Nurseries, Inc., Portland, Oreg., 1979—. Designed, developed and wrote the Quanta Payroll System; also, first full network database system used by a reforestation nursery in U.S. Mem. Am. Univacs Users Assn., CUBE, Inc. Inst. Certification Computer Profls. Office: IFA Nurseries Inc 10700 SW Beaverton Hillsdale Hwy Beaverton OR 97005

HANTZ, ROBERT HOWARD (PETER HANTZ), hairdesign manufacturing company executive; b. Scott City, Kans., Dec. 27, 1930; s. Howard Marshall and Sarah Audrey (Sheils) H.; m. Sallie Ponce, Dec. 1, 1958; children: Jennifer Diane, Robyn Kelly, Dane Ashley. Grad. high sch., Liberal, Kans. Cert. hairdresser and cosmetologist; cosmetology instructor. Designer, stylist Kay-Michaels Hair Design, Long Beach, Calif., 1957-58; model San Mateo, Calif., 1958-79; instr. Ponce Interfashion, San Mateo, 1958-79; product cons., educator Peter Hantz Co., Tempe, Ariz., 1980—; cons., artist Revlon, N.Y.C., 1970-80; chmn. Calif. Hairfashion Commn., 1960-62; manufacturer, stylist Intercoifure Am./Can. Author haircutting technique books. Recipient Rose d'Or Du Festival award French Internat. Assn., 1967; named Stylist of Yr. CHFC, 1962. Mem. Nat. Cosmetologist Assn., Audobon Soc., Hist. Soc. Ariz. Republican. Roman Catholic. Office: Peter Hantz Co 1930 W 3d St Tempe AZ 85281

HANTZ, SALLIE PONCE, hairdesign manufacturing company executive; b. Gobe, Ariz., Mar. 24, 1930; d. Francisco and Elena (Leon) Ponce; m. Robert Howard Hantz, Dec. 1, 1958; children: Jennifer, Robyn Kelly, Dane Ashley. Student, Coll. San Mateo, Calif. Cert. hairdresser & cosmetologist; cosmetology instr. Cosmetologist Al Tate Acad., Pasadena, Calif., 1953-56; platform artist instr. Ponce Interfashion, San Mateo, 1953-56; model major manufacturers, U.S., 1959-80; pres. Peter Hantz Co., Tempe, Ariz., 1985—. Author (manual) View and Do, 1967, Prentis Hall Cosmetology Theory Book, 1974. Mem. Nat. Cosmetologist Assn. (USA team mem., trainer 1964-76). Republican. Seventh-day Adventist. Office: Peter Hantz Co 1930 W 3d St Tempe AZ 85281

HAQUE, MASOOD ATHAR, aerospace engineer; b. Kuwait, Jan. 12, 1960; came to U.S., 1971; s. Zia Ul and Farrakh (Hamid) H.; m. Denyce Dianne Reno, Mar. 27, 1987; 1 child, Alyxandra Yasmin. BS in Aerospace Engring., SUNY, Buffalo, 1982. Engr. 4950th test wing/aircraft modification structures div. USAF, 1982-85; engr. McDonnell Douglas Aircraft Co., Long Beach, Calif., 1985-87; sr. design engr. Lockheed Aero. Systems Co., Ontario, Calif., 1987—. Republican. Muslim. Home: 1831 Pali Dr Norco

CA 91760 Office: Lockheed Aero System Co Bldg 15 Dept 1355 PO Box 33 Ontario CA 91762-8022

HARA, GEORGE, venture capital executive, industrialist; b. Osaka, Japan, Oct. 10, 1952; s. Nobutaro and Mitsuko (Kuroda) H.; m. Junko Hara, Oct. 8, 1988. LLB, Keio U., Tokyo, 1975; MS, MBA, Stanford U., 1981. Fin. officer UN Capital Devel. Fund, N.Y.C., 1980-81; founder, pres. Gekee Fiberoptics Inc., Palo Alto, Calif., 1981-83; pres. Data Control Ltd., Osaka, 1984-85; v.p. Pacific Catalyst Group, L.A., 1984—; gen. ptnr. Japan Incubation Capital, Tokyo, 1985-88; pres., chief exec. officer Data Control Ltd., Osaka, Tokyo and Palo Alto, 1985—; mng. ptnr. DEFTA, Palo Alto and San Francisco, 1986—; founder, advisor Control Tech. Ltd., Osaka, 1986—; bd. dirs. Wollongong Group Inc., Palo Alto, IDA Bldg. (USA) Corp., San Francisco, Plantec Inc., Tokyo, NIIC, Redwood City, Calif. Advisor coll. bus. U. San Francisco, 1987—; advisor to pres., 1988—; advisor to gov. Prefecture of Osaka, 1986—; active task force for econ. devel. Osaka Kankai Keizaidoyukai, 1981. Mem. Japan-Cen. Am. Soc. (pres. 1976-78), Shotosha Found. (chmn. 1977—), Japan Software Rsch. Found. (bd. dirs. 1988—), Networking Japan (pres. 1985), Alliance Japan (pres. 1986), Smithsonian Inst., Calif. Acad. Sci., Shangri-La Train Mus. (bd. dirs. 1987—), Am. Inst. Archaeology, Stanford Assn. of Japan, U.S.-Japan High-tech. Trade and Strategic Alliance Com. (pres. 1989—), Cen. Am. Mita Assn., Kansai Stanford Assn., Nat. Venture Capital Assn. Home: 3737 Fillmore St San Francisco CA 94123 Office: Wollongong Group PO Box 51238 Palo Alto CA 94303 also: One Embarcadero Ctr San Francisco CA 94111

HARADA, YASUE, trade organization executive; b. Kobe City, Japan, Dec. 9, 1939; came to U.S., 1970; d. Ryoichi and Sumie (Nagatani) Yamashita; m. Nobuyuki Harada, Oct. 12, 1963; 1 child, Mariko. BA, Osaku (Japan) U., 1962; postgrad., Santa Monica City Coll., 1973-74. Cert. tchr. of English as a second lang., Calif. Tchr. Japanese and English bus. info. dept. Japan External Trade Orgn., Los Angeles, 1985-88; bus. cons., pres. Nihongo Plus, Santa Monica, Calif., 1988--. Translator: Access Tokyo, 1984.

HARASETH, RONNIE ANDREW, communications executive; b. Helena, Mont., May 25, 1950; s. Edwin H. and Irena (Gentry) H.; m. Judy Beatty, June 26, 1971; 1 child, Benjamin A. Grad. high sch., Helena. Communications engr. Mont. Dept. Adminstrn., Helena, 1976-81; radio technician Mont. Dept. Hwys., Helena, 1972-76, asst. chief communications, 1981-82, supr. communications, 1982—. Scout master coun., Boy Scouts Am., East Helena, Mont., 1988. Mem. Associated Pub. Safety Communications Officers Am. (frequency coord., Mont., 1984—). Lutheran. Home: 3876 Flaxstem East Helena MT 59635 Office: Mont Dept Hwys 2701 Prospect Ave Helena MT 59620

HARASZTI, JOSEPH SANDOR, psychiatrist; b. Ocsa, Hungary, Apr. 23, 1944; came to U.S., 1956; s. Alexander Sandor and Rosalie (Baan) H.; m. Linda J. Franklin, Mar. 8, 1969 (div. Oct. 1976); children: Christopher Joseph, Samantha Jane; m. Thelma Jane Cebula, Apr. 26, 1985. BS, Emory U., 1966; MD, Johns Hopkins U., 1971. Diplomate Am. Bd. Psychiatry and Neurology. Intern in medicine Cornell Med. Ctr., N.Y.C., 1971-72; resident in psychiatry U. Chgo., 1972-75; fellow in psychopharmacology Ill. State Psychiat. Inst., Chgo., 1975-76; asst. prof. dept. psychiatry U. Chgo., 1975-78; pvt. practice Chgo., 1976-82, Rosemead, Calif., 1982—; med. dir. Ingleside Hosp., Rosemead, 1982-87. Mem. AMA, Calif. Med. Assn., L.A. County Med. Soc., Am. Psychiat. Assn., So. Calif. Psychiat. Soc. (councillor 1985), Quadrangle Club. Office: 3907 N Rosemead Blvd Rosemead CA 91770

HARBAUGH, DANIEL PAUL, lawyer; b. Wendell, Idaho, May 18, 1948; s. Myron and Manuelita (Garcia) H. BA, Gonzaga U., 1970, JD, 1974. Bar: Washington 1974. Asst. atty. gen. State of Wash., Spokane, 1974-77; ptnr. Richter, Wimberley & Ericson, Spokane, 1977-83, Harbaugh & Bloom, P.S., Spokane, 1983—; bd. dirs. Spokane Legal Svcs., 1982-86; bd. govs. LAWPAC, Seattle, 1982—. Bd. dirs. Spokane Ballet, 1983-88; chpt. dir. Les Amis du Vin, Spokane, 1985—. Mem. ABA, Wash. State Bar Assn., Spokane County Bar Assn., Wash. State Trial Lawyers Assn. (v.p. 1988—), Am. Trial Lawyers Assn., Nat. Orgn. Social Security Claimants Reps., Internat. Wine & Food Soc. (pres. local chpt. 1989—), Alpha Sigma Nu, Phi Alpha Delta. Democrat. Roman Catholic. Clubs: Spokane, Spokane Country. Office: Harbaugh & Bloom PS N 9 Post Ste 210 Spokane WA 99201

HARBORD, ANNE MARIE, consulting dietetics company executive; b. Detroit, Nov. 9, 1954; d. Lionel Joseph and Mary Ellen (Beaushaw) H.; m. Scott H. Reed, May 27, 1978 (div. Apr. 1980); m. Charles Bloom, June 18, 1988. BS in Dietetics, Mich. State U., 1976; MS Nutrition, Food Mgmt., Calif. Poly. U., 1985. Registered dietition, Calif. Clin. dietitian Saga Foods Co., Kalamazoo, 1976-78; cardiac dietition Anaheim (Calif.) Meml. Hosp., 1978; dir. dietary svcs. Care Enterprises, Orange, Calif., 1978-88; owner, mgr. Geriatric Nutrition Mgmt., Encinitas, Calif., 1988—; speaker in field; quality assurance cons. Health Care div. ARA Living Ctrs. and Retirement Homes, Verduga Hills, Calif., 1979. Editor: Dietary Policy and Procedure Manual for Long-Term Care, 1984, Recipes Standardized for Long-Term Care, 1986. Calif. Dietetic Assn. grad. scholar, 1984. Mem. Am. Dietetic Assn., Calif. Assn. Health Facilities (chmn. cons. dietitian practice group 1981-85), Am. Soc. Enteral and Parenteral Nutritrion, San Diego Diatetic Assn. (edn. chmn. 1988—). Roman Catholic. Home and Office: Geriatric Nutrition Mgmt 2095 Wandering Rd Encinitas CA 92024

HARCOURT, ROBERT NEFF, educational administrator, author; b. East Orange, N.J., Oct. 19, 1932; s. Stanton Hinde and Mary Elizabeth (Neff) H. BA, Gettysburg Coll., 1958; MA, Columbia U., 1961. Cert. guidance, secondary edn., career and vocat. guidance, N.Mex. Social case worker N.J. State Bd. Child Welfare, Newark and Morristown, 1958-61; asst. registrar Hofstra U. and asst. to evening dean of students CCNY, 1961-62; housing staff U. Denver, 1962-64; fin. aid and placement dir. Inst. Am. Indian Arts, Santa Fe, 1965—; appointed by corp. pres. to adv. bd. Genre Ltd. Art Pubs., L.A., 1986—; nat. color ad participant The Bradford Exchange, Chgo., 1986—. Donor Am. Indian Library collection Gettysburg (Pa.) Coll. With U.S. Army, 1954-56; Ger. Named hon. Okie, Gov. Okla., 1970; decorated Nat. Def. medal; postmasters fellow U. Denver, 1962-64; col. a.d.c. to N.Mex. Gov. David F. Cargo, 1970. Mem. Am. Contract Bridge League (exec. bd. Santa Fe unit; advance sr. master), SAR, Santa Fe Council Internat. Relations, Am. Assn. Counseling and Devel., Assn. Specialists in Group Work (charter), Adult Student Personnel Assn. (charter), Southwestern Assn. Indian Affairs, Phi Delta Kappa (holding exec. bd. membership), Alpha Tau Omega, Alpha Phi Omega, Safari Internat. Home: 2980 Viaje Pavo Real Santa Fe NM 87505 Office: Inst Am Indian Arts CSF Campus Santa Fe NM 87501

HARCROW, HARRY WILLIAM, astronautical engineer, consultant; b. Little Rock, Mar. 29, 1930; s. Harry Eugene and Addie Mae (French) H.; m. Maxine Marie Ford, Aug. 17, 1952; children: Kelly Eugene, David William Daniel Craig, Harry Scott. BS in Math. and Physics, U. Wichita, 1959; postgrad. in mechanics, U. Ala., 1962-63; postgrad. engring. design, U. Colo., 1974-76; postgrad., U. Denver, 1982-85. Aide, assoc. engr. Boeing Airplane Co., Wichita, Kans., 1954-59; engr. Avco Corp., Cin., 1959-60; structures project engr. Wright-Patterson Aeronautical Systems Div., Dayton, Ohio, 1960-61; mem. tech. staff NASA Marshall Space Flight Ctr., Huntsville, Ala., 1961-66; mem. sr. rsch. staff Martin Marietta Astronautics, Denver, 1966—; cons. engr. U. Colo., Boulder, 1979—, MIT, Cambridge, 1979-80, USAF Office of Sci. Rsch., Bolling AFB, 1981-82, Intelsat, Munich, 1985-86. Contbr. articles to profl. publs. Fellow Inst. Aero. Scis. (assoc.), AIAA (assoc. fellow, chmn. tech. com. 1987-89, dep. dir. materials and structures 1987—, Outstanding Survey Paper award 1985), Pinehurst Country Club, Masons. Democrat. Methodist. Office: Martin Marietta Astronautic PO Box 179 Denver CO 80201

HARDARDT, JUDITH L., pharmaceutical research consultant, nurse; b. Teaneck, N.J., Mar. 23, 1938; d. Olof W. and Elizabeth M. (Dayspring) Hogrelius; m. William L. Hardardt, Sept. 26, 1959; children: Lisa Hardardt Pillmore, Laura Hardardt Fisher, Andrew J. Diploma, Englewood Hosp., 1959; AB in History with honors, Douglass Coll., 1973; EdM in Psychology, Rutgers U., 1979; postgrad., Cambridge U., summer 1975. RN, N.J.; cert. secondary tchr., N.J. Former tchr. social studies, hosp. staff nurs; clin. rsch. assoc. Ortho Pharm. Corp., Raritan, N.J., 1979-81; sr. clin. rsch. assoc., clin. projects mgr. Berlex Labs. Inc., Cedar Knolls, N.J., 1981-83; mgr. med. studies Janssen Pharmaceutica, Inc. div. Johnson & Johnson Inc., Piscataway, N.J., 1983-84, dir. med. devel., 1984-86, dir. rsch. planning and adminstrn., 1986; cons. to pharm. industry Philo, Calif., 1986—; pres. Rsch. Mgmt. Assocs., Inc., Irvine, Calif., 1988—; cons. Johnson & Johnson Corp., 1986—, Biophysica Found., La Jolla, Calif., 1986-87, McNeil Consumer Products Co., Ft. Washington, Pa., 1987—, Phila. Assn. for Clin. Trials, 1988—; speaker on clin. pharmacology, 1980—. N.J. Hist. Commn. grantee, 1972. Mem. Assocs. Clin. Pharmacology (trustee 1983-85, chmn. continuing edn. com., President's award 1988), Phi Beta Kappa. Episcopalian. Home and Office: 8550 Hwy 128 PO Box 166 Philo CA 95466-6000 also: 3400 Treetops Circle Apt 303 San Bruno CA 94066

HARDCASTLE, ALAN JOHN, career counselor; b. Ketchikan, Alaska, Mar. 5, 1958; s. Richard Minkler and Vera (Finzel) H.; m. Karen D'Huyvetter, May 17, 1987. BA in Psychology, Western Wash. U., 1981; MS, Calif. State U., Long Beach, 1984. Computer lab. cons. Calif. State U., Long Beach, 1983-84; counselor Career Devel. Ctr., Calif. State U., Long Beach, 1983—. Mem. Calif. Coll. Personnel Assn. (treas. 1988--), Calif. Assn. for Counseling and Devel., Western Coll. Placement Assn. Democrat. Home: 4161 Los Coyotes Diagonal Lakewood CA 90713 Office: Calif State U Career Devel Ctr 1250 Bellflower Blvd Long Beach CA 90840

HARDEN, KATHLEEN MARIE, data processing executive; b. Corvallis, Oreg., Jan. 31, 1964; d. Roland Wayne and Jeris Janeen (Daily) Carpenter; m. George Henry Harden, June 12, 1982; children: Paul Michael, Amanda Christine. Dipl. Computer Ops., Computer Learning Ctr., L.A., 1982. Lead operator Rockwell Internat., Seal Beach, Calif., 1982-84; data ctr. mgr. CH2M Hill, Corvallis, Oreg., 1984--; cons. HBS So., Clearwater, Fla., 1984-- . Mem. Data Processing Mgrs. Assn., Digital Equip. Corp. Users Symposium. Office: CH2M Hill 2300 NW Walnut St Corvallis OR 97330

HARDEN, MARVIN, artist, educator; b. Austin, Tex.; s. Theodore R. and Ethel (Sneed) H. B.A. in Fine Arts, UCLA, also M.A. in Creative Painting. Tchr. art Calif. State U., Northridge, 1968—, Santa Monica (Calif.) City Coll., 1968; mem. art faculty UCLA Extension, 1964-68; mem. visual arts fellowship/painting panel Nat. Endowment Arts, 1985. One-man shows include Ceeje Galleries, Los Angeles, 1964, 66, 67, Occidental Coll., Los Angeles, 1969, Whitney Mus. Am. Art, N.Y.C., 1971, Eugenia Butler Gallery, Los Angeles, 1971, Irving Blum Gallery, Los Angeles, 1972, Los Angeles Harbor Coll., 1972, David Stuart Galleries, Los Angeles, 1975, Coll. Creative Studies, U. Calif., Santa Barbara, 1976, James Corcoran Gallery, Los Angeles, 1978, Newport Harbor Art Mus., 1979, Los Angeles Mcpl. Art Gallery, 1982, Conejo Valley Art Mus., 1983, Simard Gallery, Los Angeles, 1985; group shows include U.S. State Dept. Touring Exhbn., USSR, 1966, Oakland (Calif.) Mus. Art, 1966, UCLA, 1966, Mpls. Inst. Art, 1968, San Francisco Mus. Art, 1969, Phila. Civic Ctr. Mus., 1969, Mus. Art, R.I. Sch. Design, 1969, N.S. State Mus., 1969, Everson Mus. Art, Syracuse, 1969, La Jolla (Calif.) Mus., 1969, 70, High Mus. Art, Atlanta, 1969, Flint (Mich.) Inst. Arts, 1969, Ft. Worth Art Center Mus., 1969, Contemporary Arts Assn., Houston, 1970, U. N.Mex., 1974, U. So. Calif., 1975, Bklyn. Mus., 1976, Los Angeles County Mus. Art, 1977, Newport Harbor Art Mus., 1977, Frederick S. Wight Gallery, UCLA, 1978, Cirrus Editions, Ltd., Los Angeles, 1979, Franklin Furnace, N.Y.C., 1980, Art Ctr. Coll. Design, Los Angeles, 1981, Alternative Mus., N.Y.C., 1981, Laguna Beach Mus. (Calif.), 1982, Los Angeles Inst. Contemporary Art, 1982, Mus. Contemporary Art, Chgo., 1983, Mint Mus., Charlotte, N.C., 1983, DeCordova and Dana Mus. and Park, Lincoln, Mass., 1983, Equitable Gallery, N.Y.C., 1984, Los Angeles Municipal Art Gallery, 1984, 1985, Cirrus, Los Angeles, 1986; represented in permanent collections include Whitney Mus. Am. Art, N.Y.C., Mus. Modern Art, N.Y.C., Los Angeles County Mus. Art, Atlantic Richfield Co. Corp. Art Coll., Grunwald Ctr. Graphic Arts UCLA, City of Los Angeles, Metromedia, Inc., Los Angeles, San Diego Jewish Community Center, Berkeley (Calif.) U. Mus., Home Savs. & Loan Assn., Los Angeles, also pvt. collections. Bd. dirs. Images & Issues, 1980-86; mem. artists adv. bd. Los Angeles Mcpl. Art Gallery Assn., 1983-86. Recipient UCLA Art Council award, 1963, Disting. Prof. award Calif. State U. Northridge, 1984, Exceptional Merit Service award Calif. State U. Northridge, 1984; Nat. Endowment Arts fellow, 1972; awards in Visual Arts, 1983; Guggenheim fellow, 1983. Mem. Los Angeles Inst. Comtemporary Art (co-founder 1972). Home: PO Box 1793 Cambria CA 93428 Office: Calif State U Northridge 18111 Nordhoff St Northridge CA 91330

HARDEN, PATRICK ALAN, journalist, news executive; b. Twickenham, Eng., Aug. 13, 1936; s. Ernest William and Annie Ceridwen (Jones) H.; m. Connie Marie Graham, Nov. 2, 1963; children: Marc Graham, Ceri Marie. Cert. in journalism, Ealing (Eng.) Tech. Coll., 1957. With UPI, 1960-78; regional exec. UPI, London, 1968-69; European picture mgr. UPI, London and Brussels, 1969-72; regional exec. UPI, Detroit, 1973-75; gen. mgr. UPI Can. Ltd., Montreal, 1976-78, UP Can., Toronto, 1979-82; dir., sec. UP Can., 1979-82; treas. UP Can. Ltd.; gen. mgr. Edmonton (Alta.) Sun, 1982-84, pub., 1984—, corp. v.p., 1989; v.p. Toronto Sun Pub. Corp., 1989—. With RAF, 1957-59. Clubs: Edmonton Centre; Edmonton (bd. govs.); Wig and Pen (London). Office: The Edmonton Sun, 9405 50th St, Edmonton, AB Canada T6B 2Y2

HARDEN, THOMAS ALLEN, lawyer; b. Clovis, N.Mex., Jan. 15, 1946; s. Thomas Adrain and Sybil Lorene (Rutherford) H.; m. Charlotte Janette Edwards, Feb. 27, 1971; children: Tyler Adrain, Tiffany Lorene, J Wesley. BBA, Baylor U., 1968, JD, 1970. Bar: Tex. 1970, N.Mex. 1974. Clk. N.Mex. Atty. Gen. Office, Santa Fe, 1973; asst. dist. atty. Bernalillo County, Albuquerque, 1974-75; pvt. practice Clovis, N.Mex., 1975—; commr. City of Clovis, 1980-84. Mem. ABA, N.Mex. Bar Assn., Tex. Bar Assn., Curry County Bar Assn. (pres. 1976-77). Republican. Baptist. Home: 1208 Concord St Clovis NM 88101 Office: 1100 Mitchell St Clovis NM 88101

HARDER, MICHAEL UPHAM, airline executive, pilot; b. Mt. Kisco, N.Y., Jan. 21, 1953; s. John Worthington and Joan Lewis (Hopkinson) H.; m. Nora Mary Kochanik, Sept. 20, 1981. Student, U. Wash., 1971-75, Seattle Community Coll., 1976-77. Pilot All Alaskan Seafoods, Inc., Kodiak, 1979, Yute Air Alaska, Inc., Dillingham, 1980-81, S.W. Airways, Inc., Dillingham, 1981-83, Armstrong Air Svc., Inc., Dillingham, 1983-84, Hermens Air, Inc., St. Marys and Bethel, Alaska, 1985; pilot, chief pilot Manokotak Airways, Inc., Dillingham, 1985-87; pres., chief pilot, dir. ops. Starflite, Inc., Dillingham, 1987--. Mem. Dillingham City Planning Commn., 1985-87. Recipient Flight Safety award FAA, Dept. Transp., 1983. Mem. Alaska Air Carriers Assn. (safety award 1987), Alaska Aviation Safety Found. Democrat. Episcopalian. Home: PO Box 824 Dillingham AK 99516 Office: Starflite Inc PO Box 824 Dillingham AK 99576

HARDIE, GEORGE GRAHAM, gaming club executive, mayor; b. Cleve., Aug. 19, 1933; children: George Graham Jr., Jennifer. With sales dept. Hardie Bros., Pitts.; later various mgmt. positions, operator sales agys, owner, driver, trainer, racer standardbred horses, 1963--; owner, mgr. advt. and pub. relations co. (merged into Profile, Inc. 1978), Bell Gardens, Calif., 1973--; mng. ptnr., gen. mgr. Bell Gardens Bicycle Club, 1981--; mayor City of Cathedral City (Calif.), 1988--. Active community and civic affairs. Recipient Congl. award, 1987; commendation L.A. County Suprs., 1987, Los Angeles County Office Dist. Atty., 1987; resolution Calif. Senate, 1987, cert. of recognition City of Bell Gardens, 1987. Mem. Calif Harness Drivers Guild (past pres.), Western Standardbred Assn. (past bd. dirs.), Golden State Greyhound Assn. (organizer, pres. 1973), Bell Gardens C. of C. (pres. 1986). Office: Bell Gardens Bicycle Club 7301 Eastern Ave Bell Gardens CA 90201

HARDIN, GARRETT, biology educator; b. Dallas, Apr. 21, 1915; s. Hugh and Agnes (Garrett) H.; m. Jane Swanson, Sept. 7, 1941; children: Hyla, Peter, Sharon, David. ScB, U. Chgo., 1936; PhD, Stanford U., 1941. Staff mem. Carnegie Instn., Washington and Palo Alto, Calif., 1942-46; prof. biology U. Calif., Santa Barbara, 1946-78, emeritus, 1978—. Author: Biology: Its Principles and Implications, 1949, 2d edit., 1966, Biology: Its Human Implications, 1949, Nature and Man's Fate, 1959, Population, Evolution and Birth Control, 1964, Birth control, 1970, Exploring New Ethics for Survival, 1972, Stalking the Wild Taboo, 1973, Mandatory Motherhood, 1974, Managing the Commons, 1977, The Limits of Altruism, 1977, Promethean Ethics, 1980, Naked Emperors, 1982, Filters against Folly, 1985; (classic essay) The Tragedy of the Commons, 1968. Office: U Calif Dept Biol Sci Santa Barbara CA 93106

HARDIN, TAMMY JO, small business owner; b. Baton Rouge, Dec. 10, 1963; d. Emile Gene and Carol Jean Hardin; children: Nicole Jean, Sean Michael. Grad. high sch., Mattoon, Ill. Customer service rep. Domino's Pizza, Hammond, La., 1982; mgr. in tng. Domino's Pizza, Hammond, 1982-83, mgr., 1983; mgr. Domino's Pizza, Baton Rouge, 1984; franchisee-7919 Domino's Pizza, Pacifica, Calif., 1984—; franchisee-8222 Domino's Pizza, Pacifica, 1986—. Sponsor Calif. Parks, Beaches and Recreation, Pacifica, 1985—, Pros for Kids, Pacifica, 1988-89, Pacifica Resource Ctr., 1988-89; troop leader, Girl Scouts Am., Pacifica, 1989—. Mem. Pacifica C. of C. Republican. Roman Catholic. Home and Office: 1368 Castro Ct Pacifica CA 94044

HARDING, JAMES GEORGE, financial executive; b. Iowa City, Iowa, Oct. 3, 1949; s. Joe Petsel and Florence Lorena (Yarwood) H.; children from previous marriage: Paige Annette, Pamela Suzanne; m. Cynthia Gail Balzer, Feb. 14, 1987; children: Kelly Kristin Cannon, Matthew Patrick Perry Cannon. BBA in Fin., U. Iowa, 1972, BBA in Ins., 1972; postgrad. in acctg., Colo. State U., 1974-76. Asst. nat. bank examiner U.S. Dept. Treasury, Albuquerque, 1972-74; dir. fin. City of Ft. Collins, Colo., 1974-76; fin. dir., city treas., city clk. City of Canon City, Colo., 1977-79; bus. dir. West Central Mental Health Ctr., Canon City, 1979-81; dir., exec. v.p., chief fin. officer Peak Health Care, Inc., Colorado Springs, Colo., 1981-87; v.p., dir. Talis Corp., Colorado Springs, 1986—; dir. Sunset Met. Dist., Colorado Springs, 1988—; v.p., chief fin. officer Excell, Inc., Colorado Springs, 1988—; cons. in field. Co-treas. Rep. Party of Fremont County, Canon City, 1978; officer United Way, Canon City, 1978. Mem. Winter Night Club, Lions (officer Canon City chpt. 1977-80). Mem. Christian Ch. (Disciples of Christ). Home: 3270 Northern Outlook Dr Black Forest CO 80921

HARDING, WAYNE EDWARD, III, accountant; b. Topeka, Sept. 29, 1954; s. Wayne Edward and Nancy M. (Gean) H.; BS with honors in Bus. Adminstrn., U. Denver, 1976, MBA, 1983; m. Janet Mary O'Shaughnessy, Sept. 5, 1979 (div. Mar. 1985); m. Karen Ruttan, Oct. 17, 1987. Partner, HKG Assocs., Denver, 1976-77; staff auditor Peat, Marwick, Mitchell & Co., Denver, 1976-78; auditor Marshall Hornstein, P.C., Wheat Ridge, Colo., 1978-79; sr. auditor Touche Ross & Co., Denver, 1979-80; controller Mortgage Plus Inc., 1980-81; sec.-treas. Sunlight Systems Energy Corp., 1980-81; ptnr. Harding, Newman, Sobule & Thrush, Ltd., Denver, 1981-82; pvt. practice specializing in microcomputer applications and litigation support, 1982—; dir. Harding Transp., Harding Tech. Leasing, Crown Parking Products; lectr. in field. Class agt., mem. alumni council Phillips Exeter Acad., Exeter, N.H., 1973-83; bd. dirs., treas. Legal Center for Handicapped Citizens, Denver, 1979-80; vol. Denver Bridge, 1984-85. Mem. AICPAs, Colo. Soc. CPAs (chmn. CPE com. 1987-89), Beta Alpha Psi, Pi Gamma Mu, Beta Gamma Sigma. Republican. Contbr. articles in field of microcomputers to profl. jours. including Jour. Acctg. on Micro Computers. Home: 6029 S Kenton Way Englewood CO 80111 Office: 6000 E Evans Penthouse Ste 1-425 Denver CO 80222

HARDMAN, PHYLLIS ANNE, real estate executive; b. Columbus, Ohio, Mar. 8, 1945; d. James Stanley and Elizabeth B. (Chaffe) McKee; m. Roy Stephen Hardman, Aug. 2, 1975; 1 child, James Stanley. BA, U. Ariz., Tucson, 1973. Adminstrv. asst. Adsco Properties, Inc., Tucson, 1970-74; propery mgr. Richard Huff Realty, Inc., Tucson, 1974-76, The Jim Matison Co., Tucson, 1976-77, GT Realty Assoc., Tucson, 1978-82; property mgr., owner Hardman Real Estate Service, Tucson, 1982-84; property mgr., owner, sec. SHS Mgmt., Inc., Tucson, 1984-88; property mgr., v.p. LJ Hooker Internat. Real Estate Mgmt., Tucson, 1988—. Mem. appropriations com. United Way, Tucson, 1984-86. Mem. Inst. Real Estate Mgmt. (pres. local chpt. 1984), Bldg. Owners and Mgrs. Assn. (pres. local chpt. 1983). Republican, Episcopalian. Office: LJ Hooker Internat Real Estate Mgmt D-440 1200 N El Dorado Pl Tucson AZ 85715

HARDT, ATHIA L., writer; b. Globe, Ariz., July 29, 1948; d. August V. and Athia (Vallery) H.; m. Charles G. Case II, Nov. 19, 1977; children: Nancy Vallery, Jessica Hardt. BA in Journalism, Ariz. State U., 1970; MA in Communications, U. Ill., Champaign, 1971. Reporter Ariz. Rep., Phoenix, 1971-77; press sec. Gov. Bruce Babbit, Phoenix, 1978-80; freelance writer Phoenix, 1980-88, 88—; transition press sec. Gov. Rose Mofford, Phoenix, 1988; asst. to Mayor Terry Goddard Phoenix, 1989—; stringer N.Y. Times, Phoenix, 1976-78, 80-88. Editor Ariz. Waterline, 1980—; contbr. articles in field to profl. jours. and mags. Bd. dirs. Ariz. Bus. Coun., Phoenix, 1988—, Phoenix Library Adv. Bd., 1982-86; bd. mem., pres. Friends of the Phoenix Pub. Library, 1982—; mem. bd. Encanto Carousel Fund, Inc., Phoenix, 1986—; vice-chmn. Mayor's Task Force on Drug Abuse, Phoenix, 1988; mem. City Arts Dist. Coordinating Com., Phoenix, 1988—; mem. Madison Sch. Dist. Bond Com., Phoenix, 1988. Recipient 1st Pl. News award Ariz. Edn. Assn., 1975-77, Margaret Sanger award Planned Parenthood, Phoenix, 1975, Gov.'s award Women Who Communicate, 1986. Mem. Ariz. Press Club (prs. 1973-74, 1st pl. feature award 1973), Charter 100 Club, Sigma Delta Chi. Democrat.

HARDWICK, WILLIAM ROBERT, mining engineer; b. Phoenix, Mar. 30, 1907; s. William and Exilda May (Hocken) H.; m. Adda Jane Giroux, Dec. 23, 1939. Student, U. Ariz., 1928-35. Asst. mining engr., chemist, mine engr. Phelps Dodge Corp., 1935-42, 47; devel. engr. Kennecott Copper Corp., Ray, Ariz., 1948-50, cons. engr., 1950-51; field engr. Sterns-Roger Mfg. Co., Silver Bell, Ariz., 1951-52; mineral exam. and devel. engr. U.S. Bur. Mines, Tucson, 1953-57, mining methods research engr., 1957-60, project leader div. mineral resources, 1961-62, project leader application of nuclear explosives to mining, 1963-72. Contbr. numerous articles on mining methods, costs. Capt. ordnance U.S. Army, 1942-46. Mem. Ariz. Geol. Soc., N.Mex. Geol. Soc., Ariz. Pioneer Hist. Soc., Am. Legion, Theta Tau, Elks. Democrat. Episcopalian. Home: 1802 E Spring St Tucson AZ 85719 Office: 1722 E Copper St Tucson AZ 85719

HARDY, BEN (BENSON B. HARDY), orchid nursery executive; b. Oakland, Calif., Nov. 22, 1920; s. Lester William and Irene Isabell (Bliss) H.; student pub. schs., Oakland, Calif., Concord, Calif.; grad. photo Intelligence Sch., Denver, 1949. Served as enlisted man U.S. Navy, 1942-48; joined USAF, 1948, advanced through grades to capt., 1957; with 67th Reconnaisance Squadron, Korea, 1951-52, Hdqrs. Squadron, Thule AFB, 1956, resigned, 1957; material requirements analyst-coordinator Teledyne Ryan Aero. Co., San Diego, 1958-73, 83—; dispatcher-coordinator Cubic Western Data Co., San Diego, 1977-80; owner-partner orchid nursery. Pres. San Diego County Orchid Soc., 1972-73, 75-76, Exotic Plant Soc., 1976-78, 81-84, San Diego Gesneriad Soc., 1978; dir. 23d Western Orchid Congress, 1979. Decorated Bronze Star; recipient Letter of Commendation NASA, also others. Mem. Am. Orchid Soc., N.Z. Orchid Soc., Orchid Soc. SE Asia, Pacific Orchid Soc. Hawaii, Hoya Soc. Internat. (pres. 1981-83), Mexicana de Orquideologia, Sociedad Colombiana de Orquideologia, Cymbidium Soc. Am., Orchid Digest Corp. Contbr. articles to orchid jours.; pub. Western Gesneriad Gazette, 1978-79. Home: 9443 E Heaney Circle Santee CA 92071

HARDY, DUANE HORACE, federal agency administrator, educator; b. Ogden, Utah, June 8, 1931; s. Willis and Julia Mary (Garder) H.; m. Janet Myrnel Slater, Aug. 3, 1951; children: Rochelle Anne Leishman, Leslie Kaye Woolston, Kathy Korinne Davis. AA, Weber State Coll., 1951. Cert. EEO investigator/counselor. Ordained Mormon bishop, 1987. Enlisted U.S. Army, 1951, advanced through grades to lt. col., 1967, ret., 1971; EEO investigator U.S. Postal Service, San Bruno, Calif., 1978—, EEO instr., 1982—. Mem. EEO civic council, Salt Lake City, 1978—. Republican. Mormon. Lodge: Kiwanis. Home: 120 W 5200 S Ogden UT 84405 Office: US Postal Svc 3680 Pacific Ave Ogden UT 84401

HARDY, GORDON ALFRED, music educator, music school president; b. Hudson, Ind., Aug. 18, 1918; s. Carl Alfred and Gayle (Pike) H.; m. Lillian Studebaker, May 19, 1945; children—John Studebaker, Christopher Bartlett, Susan, Jeffrey Pike. B.A., B.Mus., U. Mich., 1941, M.Mus., 1946; B.S., Juilliard Sch. Music, 1952. Teaching fellow Juilliard Sch. Music, 1952-53, teaching asst., 1953-54, mem. faculty lit. and materials of music dept., 1954—, asso. dean, 1963-69, dean students, 1970-76; dean Aspen (Colo.) Music Sch., 1963-66, exec. v.p., 1966-75, pres., 1976—. Author: (with

Arnold Fish) Music Literature-A Workbook for Analysis, vol. I, Homophony, 1963, vol. II, Polyphony, 1966. Bd. dirs. Juilliard Repertory Project, 1968, Juilliard Inst. Spl. Studies, 1969. Served to lt. USNR, 1942-45. Mem. Theta Chi. Home: 149 E 73 St New York NY 10021 Office: Aspen Music Festival PO Box AA Aspen CO 81612

HARDY, LOIS LYNN, educational seminar training company executive; b. Seattle, Aug. 20, 1928; d. Stanley Milton and Helen Bernice (Conner) Croonquist; m. John Weston Hardy, July 29, 1951 (div. 1974); children: Sarah Lynn, Laura Lynn; m. Joseph Freeman Smith, Jr., Apr. 18, 1981; stepchildren: Nancy Smith Willis, Martha Smith Dahlquist. BA, Stanford U., 1950, MA, 1952; postgrad., U. Calif., Berkeley, 1957-78, U. San Francisco, 1978-81. Cert. life secondary tchr., life counselor, adminstr., Calif.; lic. career and ednl. counselor, Calif. Tchr., counselor Eastside Union High Sch. Dist., San Jose, Calif., 1951-55; dir. Lois Lynn Hardy Music Studio, Danville, Calif., 1955-69; high sch. tchr. San Ramon Unified Sch. Dist., Danville, 1969-71, counselor, 1971-83; dir. Growth Dynamics Inst., Alamo, Calif., 1976—; instr. Fresno (Calif.) Pacific Coll., 1976-79, Dominican Coll., San Rafael, Calif., 1979—; cons., trainer Personal Dynamics Inst., Mpls., 1976—, Performax Internat., Mpls., 1979—, San Jose Unified Sch. Dist., 1986-86, Novato (Calif.) Unified Sch. Dist., 1985-86, IBM, San Francisco, 1984, corp. and ednl. cons., 1951—. Author: How To Study in High School, 1952, 3d edit., 1973, (with B. Santa) How To Use the Library, 1954; author: How To Learn Faster and Succeed, 1982, 85; contbr. numerous articles to profl. jours. Choir dir., organist Community Presbyn. Ch., Danville, 1966-68, elder, 1974-75; speaker to numerous orgns., 1955—. Named Musician of Yr., Contra Costa County, 1978, Counselor of Yr., No. Calif. Personnel and Guidance Assn., 1980; Olive S. Lathrop scholar, 1948, AAUW scholar, 1950; recipient Colonial Dames prize in Am. history, 1950. Mem. Am. Assn. Counseling and Devel., Calif. Assn. Counseling and Devel., Calif. Tchrs. Assn., Calif. Career Guidance Assn., Nat. Speakers Assn., Am. Guild Organists, Stanford U. Alumni Assn., Delta Zeta. Democrat. Presbyterian. Office: Growth Dynamics Inst PO Box 1053 Alamo CA 94507

HARDY, VERNON ERNEST, engineering executive, consultant; b. Okla. City, Apr. 5, 1937; s. Ernest Alexander and Sadie Mildred (Patterson) H.; m. Fleta Kate Garrison, July 30, 1966; children: Stephani Layne, Laura Michelle. BSEE, U. Okla., 1960, MSEE, 1962. Staff engr. Tex. Instruments, Dallas, 1962-69, Electronic Memories & Magnetics, El Segundo, Calif., 1969-71; engr. mgr. Standard Memories, Santa Ana, Calif., 1971-75; dir. engring. Trendata/Standard Memories, Santa Ana, 1975-83, M.S.I. Data, Costa Mesa, Calif., 1983-85; cons. M.S.I., Costa Mesa, 1985-87; engring. mgr. Rockwell SPD, Newport Beach, Calif., 1987—; cons. Electrocom Automation, 1987. Lt. USAR, 1960-75. Mem. IEEE, Tau Beta Pi, Sigma Tau. Republican. Baptist. Home: 18912 Santa Mariana Fountain Valley CA 92708 Office: Rockwell SPD 4311 Jamporee Blvd Newport Beach CA 92660

HARE, SUSAN YVONNE, trade association administrator; b. Casper, Wyo., Apr. 8, 1953; d. Edward J. and Jeanne Marie (Miller) Cajthaml; divorced; 1 child, Kacie Jeanne. Cert., Cen. Bus. Coll., Denver, 1972. Sec. CU Med. Ctr., Denver, 1972-73; trade show coordinator Denver Mdse. Mart, 1973-80; exec. dir. Mountain States Mens, Boys and Western Apparel Club, Denver, 1985—. Mem. Nat. Assn. Expns. Mgrs., Colo. Soc. Assn. Execs. Republican. Office: Mountain States Apparel Club 451 E 58th Ave #4595 Denver CO 80216

HARELSON, HUGH, magazine publisher; b. Phoenix, Oct. 25, 1930; s. C. L. and Frances (Gilbert) H.; m. Dorothy Jan Dedman, Aug. 24, 1957; children—Matthew, Scott. B.A., U. Ariz., 1952. News editor Bisbee Daily Rev., Ariz., 1955-56; writer, editor Ariz. Republic, Phoenix, 1956-70; news editor Scottsdale Daily Progress, Ariz., 1961-62; news. dir. Sta. KTAR-TV subs. NBC, Phoenix, 1970-73; dir. info. services U. Ariz., 1973-81, exec. dir. univ. relations, 1981-82; pub. Ariz. Hwys. Mag., Ariz. Dept. Transp., Phoenix, 1982—; v.p., bd. dirs. Ariz. Nature Conservancy; bd. dirs. Walter Cronkite Ctr. for Telecommunications and Journalism. Past pres. Vol. Bur. Maricopa County. Served to 1st lt. U.S. Army, 1952-54. Mem. Ariz. Newspapers Assn., Ariz. Acad., U. Ariz. Alumni Assn. (past pres.), Soc. Profl. Journalists. Republican. Methodist. Home: 943 W Coronado Phoenix AZ 85007 Office: Ariz Hwys Mag 2039 W Lewis Ave Phoenix AZ 85009

HARGETT, LOUIE THOMAS, agricultural chemistry corporation executive, entomologist; b. Wilmington, N.C., Oct. 19, 1932; s. Louie Fulton and Catherine Cordelia (Thomas) H.; m. Anna Catherine Hazel, June 26, 1954; children—Cheryl Ann, Robert Thomas, Catherine Lynn. B.A., Bridgewater (Va.) Coll., 1953; M.S., Va. Poly. Inst., 1958; Ph.D., Oreg. State U., 1962; A.M.P., Harvard Bus. Sch., 1976. Cert. profl. entomologist. Mem. faculty dept. entomology Va. Poly. Inst., Blacksburg, 1955-58, Oreg. State U., Corvallis, 1958-60; dir. field devel., asst. to v.p. mktg. Geigy, Inc., N.Y.C., 1961-70; dir. devel., gen. mgr. Rhodia, Inc., Monmouth Junction, N.J., 1970-77; asst. to pres. Environ. Research and Tech., Concord, Mass., 1977-78; dir. research, devel. crop protection Sandoz, Inc., San Diego, 1979-84; dir. product devel. Zoecon Corp. div. Sandoz Co., Palo Alto, 1984-86, dir. product devel. Sandoz Crop Protection, 1986—. Served with AUS, 1953-55. NIH fellow, 1960-61. Mem. Am. Inst. Biologists, Entomology Soc. Am., Weed Sci. Soc. Am., Sigma Xi. Republican. Protestant.

HARGISS, JAMES LEONARD, ophthalmologist; b. Manhattan, Kans., June 15, 1921; s. Meade Thomas and Julia Baldwin (Wayland) H.; m. Helen Natalie Berglund, July 19, 1947; children: Phillip M., Craig T., D. Reid. BS, U. Wash., 1942; MD, St. Louis U., 1945; MSc in Medicine, U. Pa., 1952. Diplomate Nat. Bd. Med. Examiners, Am. Bd. Opthalmology. Intern U.S. Naval Hosp., PSNS Bremerton, Washington, 1945-46; resident physician G.E. Geisinger Meml. Hosp. and Foss Clinic, Danville, Pa., 1949-51; practice medicine specializing in ophthalmic surgery Seattle, 1951-58; ophthalmic surgeon Eye Clinic of Seattle, 1958—, pres., 1962—, chief exec. officer, 1985—; cons. U. Wash. Sch. Medicine, 1958—. Contbr. chapter to book, 1987, articles to Ophthalmology, 1964-80. Dist. chmn. King County Rep. Cen. Com., 1962-70. Served as physician/surgeon with USNR, 1945-48. Recipient Citation of Merit Washington State Med. Ctr., 1959, Cert. of Award Am. Acad. Ophthalmology and Otolaryngology, 1975; Wendell F. Hughes fellow, 1960. Fellow AMA (Cert. of award 1960), Am. Coll. Surgeons, Am. Acad. Ophthalmology (honor award), Am. Soc. Ophthalmic Plastic and Reconstructive Surgery (charter) (Lester T. Jones award 1979), Lions (lake City pres. 1960-61), Alpha Omega Alpha. Office: Eye Clinic of Seattle 1601 16th Ave Seattle WA 98122-4098

HARGRAVES, SHERILYN, public television executive; b. Corsicana, Tex., Dec. 4, 1943; d. John F. and Jean (Scott) H.; divorced; children: Lissa Ball, John Ball. BFA, Ohio U., 1974; MFA, Syracuse U., 1978. Media dir. Analy High Sch. Dist., Sebastopol, Calif., 1978-81; video cons. Sonoma Office of Edn., Santa Rosa, Calif., 1981-84; pub. access exec. producer Rancho Santiago J.C., Santa Ana, Calif., 1984-86; community access coord. Foothills Cablevision, Redlands, Calif., 1986-87; cable TV adminstr. City of Riverside, Calif., 1987—; bd. dirs. Sta. KUCR Radio U. Calif. Riverside; mem. adv. bd. Greater Riverside Edn. Cable TV Access, 1987—. Producer (film) Ford Grant, 1977, 1984 Dem. Conv. coverage by students of Analy High Sch., Sebastopol; executed sculpture at Mellon Pitsberg Mus. (Best Show award), 1976. Bd. dirs. Juvenile Diabetes Assn., Riverside, 1988—; adv. Coalition on Pub. Access, Riverside, 1989—. Mem. Nat. Assn. Telecommunication Officers and Advisors (producer 4 video programs, recipient awards, 1988), Calif. Assn. Pub. Info. Officers (mem. cable TV com., 1988—, bd. dirs.). Home: 19951 Via De Las Montanas Yorba Linda CA 92686

HARGREAVES, GEORGE JULIAN, landscape architect; b. Atlanta, Nov. 12, 1952; s. George Julian and Carolyn Lucille (Snyder) H.; children: Joseph, Rebecca, Kate. B of Landscape Architecture, U. Ga., 1977; M of Landscape Architecture, Harvard U., 1979. Prin. Hargreaves Assocs., San Francisco, 1980—; vis. prof. Calif. Polytech. Inst., 1981, U. Ill., 1984, U. Va., 1985, Harvard U., 1986-88; lectr. in field. One man shows include Harvard U., 1987, Ohio State U., 1988, U. Minn., 1988, Iowa State U., 1988, U. Toronto, 1988, N.C. State U., 1988, Pa. State U., 1988; works published in European, Am. and Japanese jours.; contbr. articles to profl. jours. Recipient Henry Herring Meml. medal Nat. Sculpture Soc., 1988, Design award Am. Inst. Architects, 1985, Pacific Coast Builders Gold Nugget award, 1984; Hubert B. Owens fellow, 1977. Mem. Am. Soc. Landscape Architects (chmn. jury, Excellence award 1986, 87), Am. Acad. Rome (Landscape Architecture award 1988). Office: Hargreaves Assn 855 Folsom St San Francisco CA 94107

HARGROVE, JOHN JAMES, federal judge; b. Bay Shore, N.Y., May 4, 1942; s. John A. and Cecelia L. Hargrove; m. Jane A Nagle, Oct. 21, 1967; children: David, Kristin, Kelly, Kathryn. BAin Polit. Sci., U. Notre Dame, 1964, JD, 1967. Bar: N.Y. 1968, Calif. 1971. Atty. Grant & Asaro, San Diego, 1972-76; ptnr. Weeks, Willis, Hoffman & Hargrove, San Diego, 1976-79, Strauss, Kissane, Davis & Hargrove, San Diego, 1979-83, Britton & Hargrove, San Diego, 1983-84; prin. John J. Hargrove & Assocs., San Diego, 1984-85; judge Bankruptcy Ct., City of San Diego., 1985—; adj. prof. Calif. Western Sch. Law, 1986. Coach University City Bobby Sox Softball Team; lector Our Mother of Confidence Roman Cath. Ch.; trustee U. Notre Dame, 1987-89. Lt. col. USMCR, 1968-72. Mem. U. Notre Dame Alumni Assn. (bd. dirs. 1985-89, pres. 1988-89). Republican. Home: 5537 Stresemann St San Diego CA 92122 Office: US Bankruptcy Ct 940 Front St Rm 5-N-22 San Diego CA 92189

HARGROVE, WILLIAM GREGORY, operations management executive; b. Vancouver, Wash., Mar. 6, 1947; s. William Earl Hargrove and Marsha Ruth (Crabill) Bullard; m. Gretchen Heider, Sept. 6, 1975 (div. Oct. 1988). BSBA, U. Phoenix, 1986; LLB, Peninsula U., 1084. Cert. in prodn. and inventory control. Systems integration supr. Gen Rad Corp., Santa Clara, Calif., 1976-78; prodn. mgr. Solfan Systems, Inc., Mountain View, Calif., 1978-82, Dictaphone Corp., Mountain View, 1982-84; dir. mfg. Advanced Imaging Devices, Mountain View, 1984-86; sr. tech. cons. Ask Computers, Inc., Los Altos, Calif., 1986-89; v.p. ops. Westcor Corp., Los Altos, 1989—. Bd. dirs. Mountain View Revitalization Com., 1984; bd. trustees Los Altos Ch. Religious Sci., 1985—. Named Sales Course Champion, Dale Carnegie Assn., 1988. Mem. Am. Prodn. and Inventory Control Soc. (v.p. Santa Clara chpt. 1987-88, bd. dirs.), Sierra Club. Home: 255 S Rengstorff Mountain View CA 94040 Office: Westcor Corp 485 100 Alberto Way Los Gatos CA 95030

HARKEMA, JACK ROBERT, veterinarian, pathologist; b. Kalamazoo, Jan. 17, 1953; s. James and Beatrice (Stehouwer) H.; m. Laurie Joy Hofman, Aug. 27, 1976; children: Leslie Joy, Lindsay Renee. MS, Mich. State U, 1977, DVM cum laude, 1980; PhD, U. Calif., Davis, 1985. Diplomate Am. Coll. Vet. Pathologists. Resident in vet. pathology U. Calif., Davis, 1982-85; staff pathologist Lovelance Inhalation Toxicology Research Inst., Albuquerque, 1985--. Contbr. articles to sci. jours. Recipient New Investigator award in inhalation toxicology Soc. Toxicology, 1987. Fellow Morris Animal Found.; mem. AVMA, Am. Thoracic Soc., AAAS, Microbeam Analysis Soc. Mem. Christian Reformed Ch. Home: 1328 Michael Hughes Dr NE Albuquerque NM 87112 Office: Lovelace Inhalation PO Box 5890 Albuquerque NM 87185

HARKINS, MICHAEL EUGENE, construction professional; b. Trenton, Mo., Jan. 3, 1955; s. Otto Reid and Rohama (Adams) H.; m. Sonna Loyce Brown; children: Justin, Jacob. Student, U. Mo., 1975. Lic. contractor, Ariz. Owner, contractor Harkins Constrn., Trenton, 1975—, Mesa, Ariz., 1983—. Republican. Mem. Assembly of God Ch. Home and Office: Harkins Constrn 2223 E Flossmore St Mesa AZ 85602

HARLAN, DAVID, reporter; b. Portland, Oreg., July 24, 1955; s. Dale Morgan and Joyce (Niedemeyer) H. BJ, U. Oreg., 1983, B in History, 1983. News editor The Clackamas County Review, Milwaukie, Oreg., 1984-85; reporter, community editor The Enterprise Courier, Oregon City, Oreg., 1985-86; corr. The Oregonian, Oregon City, Oreg., 1985-86; bus. reporter The Daily Astorian, Astoria, Oreg., 1986—. Recipient 1st and 2d pl. Bus. and Econ. Reporting awards Oreg. Newspaper Pubs. Assn., 1986, 1st pl. Consumer and Environ. Affairs Reporting award Pacific N.W. Soc. of Profl. Journalists "Excellence in Journalism Competition", 1988. Democrat. Presbyterian. Office: The Daily Astorian 949 Exchange St Astoria OR 97103

HARLAN, DONALD MICHAEL, JR., management consultant; b. Monterey, Calif., Aug. 21, 1956; m. Sarah Harrow, Feb. 16, 1986. BS in Aeronautics, MIT, 1978; MBA, Stanford U., 1984. Mgmt. cons. McKinsey & Co., Inc., Los Angeles, 1984—. Lcdr. USNR, 1978—. Mem. AIAA. Home: 245 Churchill Glen Sierra Madre CA 91024 Office: McKinsey & Co Inc 400 S Hope St Los Angeles CA 90071-2890

HARLAN, ESTLE MAE, business consultant, legal assistant; b. Portland, Oreg., Aug. 7, 1939; d. Vaughn Estle and Mae Marie (VanHorn) A.; m. Robert T. Butler, June 21, 1957 (div. 1972); children: Randy, Cindy; m. Dale Morgan Harlan, June 13, 1975; stepchildren: Janice Harlan Raisl, David, James, Nancy Harlan Henderson. AS, Clackamas Community Coll., Oreg., 1977; BS, Marylhurst Coll., 1984; MPA, Lewis and Clark Coll., 1988. Bar: Oreg 1978; cert. legal asst. Legal asst. Dale M. Harlan, P.C., Milwaukie, Oreg., 1958--; owner, mgr. Harlan Bus. Cons. Inc., Milwaukie, Oreg., 1982—. Contbr. articles to trade publs.; columnist: In My Opinion, Oregonian, 1988. Mem. Milwaukie (Oreg.) Parks and Recreation Commn., 1982; precinct committeewoman Clackamas County Dem. Com., 1982--; campaign chmn. for county commr., 1982, 86--; mem. Solid Waste Adv. Com. Met. Service Dist., Portland, 1986--, Recycling Adv. Com. Portland Dept. Environ. Quality, 1986--, Gresham (Oreg.) Solid Waste Citizens Adv. Com.,1988--, Portland Solid Waste Oversight Com.; organist, various Milwaukie (Oreg.) chs., 1980-. Mem. Oreg. San. Service Inst. (cons. 1982—), Clackamas County Legal Secs. Assn.(pres. 1977-79, legal sec. of year, 1979), North Clackamas C. of C. (adminstv. affairs com. 1982—), Am. Hist. Soc. Germans from Russia, Portland Soild. Waste Oversight Com., Rotary (Milwaukie) (Paul Harris fellow, 1988, organist). Democrat. Mem. Evangelical Ch. Office: Harlan Bus Cons Inc 2202 SE Lake Rd Milwaukie OR 97222

HARLAN, KATHLEEN T. (KAY HARLAN), business consultant, professional speaker and seminar leader; b. Bremerton, Wash., June 9, 1934; d. Floyd K. and Rosemary (Parkhurst) Troy; m. John L. Harlan, Feb. 16, 1952 (div. 1975); children: Pamela Kay, Kenneth Lynwood, Lianna Sue. Owner, operator Safeguard N.W. Systems, Tacoma, 1969-79; devel., mgr. Poulsbo (Wash.) Profl. Bldg., 1969-75; pres. Greenapple Graphics, Inc., Tacoma, 1976-79; owner, mgr. Iskrem Hus Restaurant, Poulsbo, 1972-75; pres. Bus. Seminars, Tacoma, 1977-82; owner, mgr. Safeguard Computer Ctr., Tacoma, 1982-86; owner Total Systems Ctr., Tacoma, 1983—; mem. Orgnl. Renewal, Inc., Tacoma, 1978-81; assoc. mem. Effectiveness Resource Group, Inc., Tacoma, 1979-80; pres. New Image Confs., Tacoma, 1979-82; speaker on mgmt. and survival in small bus. Contbg. author: Here is Genius!, 1980; author small bus. manuals. Mem. Wash. State Bd. Boundary Rev. for Kitsap County, 1970-76, Selective Service Bd. #19, 1971-76; co-chair Wash. State Small Bus. Improvement Council, 1986 apptd. sec. by gov., 1987; del. to White House Conf. on Small Bus., 1986; chair Wash. State Conf. on Small Bus., 1987. Recipient Nellie Cashman award; named Woman Entrepreneur of Yr. for Wash. State, 1986, 87. Mem. Nat. Speakers Assn., Better Bus. Bur. (exec. bd.), Tacoma-Pierce County C. of C. (exec. bd. 1985—, chair spl. task force on small bus. for Pierce County, 1986-87, treas. 1987-88, chair-elect 1988-89), Pacific Northwest Speakers' Assn. Office: Old City Hall Ste 310 625 Commerce St Tacoma WA 98402

HARLAN, NEIL EUGENE, consumer products company executive; b. Cherry Valley, Ark., June 2, 1921; s. William and Mary Nina (Ellis) H.; m. Martha Almlov, Sept. 27, 1952; children: Lindsey Beth, Neil Eugene, Sarah Ellis. Student, U. Edinburgh, Scotland, 1946; B.S., U. Ark., 1947, LL.D., 1969; M.B.A., Harvard U., 1950, D.B.A., 1956. Mem. faculty Harvard U. Grad. Sch. Bus. Adminstrn., 1951-62, asst. prof., 1954-58, assoc. prof., 1958-61, prof., 1962; asst. sec. Air Force Washington, 1962-64; v.p., chief fin. officer, dir. Anderson, Clayton & Co., 1964-66, exec. v.p., 1966-67; dir. McKinsey & Co., Inc., 1967-74; with McKesson Corp., San Francisco, 1974-88, chmn., 1979-88, also dir.; chief exec. officer 1984-86. Author: Management Control in Air Frame Subcontracting, 1956, (with R.H. Hassler) Cases in Controllership, 1958, (with R.F. Vancil) Cases in Accounting Policy, 1961, (with Christenson and Vancil) Managerial Economics, 1962. Trustee San Francisco Ballet, World Affairs Council; bd. dirs. Bay Area Council, Nat. Park Found.; bd. govs. San Francisco Symphony; mem. Calif. Com. on Campaign Fin., Calif. Roundtable, San Francisco Bay Area Council; mem. nat. adv. com. YMCA. Sch. Served with AUS, 1943-46. Mem. Conf. Bd., San Francisco C. of C. (bd. dirs., trustee). Clubs: Congressional Country (Bethesda, Md.); Webhannet Golf, Edgecomb Tennis (Kennebunk Beach, Maine); Bankers, Bohemian, Pacific Union (San Francisco); Menlo Country (Woodside, Calif.); Links (N.Y.C.); Johns Island Golf (Vero Beach, Fla.). Home: 1170 Sacramento St #13D San Francisco CA 94108 also: 400 Ocean Rd Unit 170 Johns Island Vero Beach FL 32973 *

HARLANDER, LESLIE ALBERT, architectural consultant; b. Crockett, Calif., Jan. 26, 1923; s. Albert Charles and Hilma Louise (Hedstrom) H.; m. June Hildegarde Rodgers, Oct. 3, 1943 (div. Mar. 1983); children: George, Penny, Leslie. BSME, U. Calif., Berkeley, 1951; MS in Naval Architecture and Marine Engring., MIT, 1955; postgrad., Sch. Nuclear Sci. and Engring., 1956. Design draftsman Moore Drydock Co., Oakland, Calif., 1951-54; engr. Matson Navigation Co., San Francisco, 1955-56, mgr. engring. devel., 1957-63, v.p. engring. and maintenance, 1964-67, v.p. engring. and marine ops., 1968-70; v.p. ops. Am. Pres. Lines, San Francisco, 1971-77; cons., prin. L.A. Harlander & Assocs., Richmond, Calif., 1977—; owner Cal-Coast Marine, Inc., Richmond, 1977—. Contbr. numerous articles to profl. jours.; patentee in field. Recipient Gibbs medal NAS, 1988. Mem. Soc. Naval Architects and Marine Engrs. (MIT scholarship 1954, Jerry Land medal 1987), St. Francis Yacht Club, Richmond Yacht Club, Sigma Xi. Republican. Home and Office: LA Harlander & Assocs 310 W Cutting Blvd Richmond CA 94804

HARLESS, KEITH WESTON, physician; b. Seattle, Apr. 12, 1946; s. Hubert R. and Eda Irene (Tasker) H.; m. Susan Jean Ettinger, Aug. 29, 1970; children: Wendy Eileen, Brian Richard. BS, Lewis and Clark Coll., 1968; MD, U. Oreg. Health Scis. Ctr., 1972. Diplomate Am. Bd. Internal Medicine, Pulmonary Disease, Critical Care Medicine. Intern Dartmouth-Mary Hitchcock Med. Ctr., Hanover, N.H., 1972-73; resident U. Oreg. Health Scis. Ctr., Portland, 1973-75; pulmonary fellowship U. Oreg. Health Scis. Ctr. and Utah Med. Ctr., Salt Lake City, 1975-77; physician ptnr. Bend (Oreg.) Meml. Clinic, 1977—; clin. asst. prof. medicine U. Oreg. Health Scis. Ctr., Portland, 1983—; bd. dirs. Cardiopulmonary Svcs. St. Charles Med. Ctr., Critical Care Units. Contbr. articles to profl jours. Recipient Clean Air award Am. Lung Assn. of Oreg., 1985. Fellow ACP, Am. Coll. Chest Physicians; mem. AMA, Am. Soc. Internal Medicine, Am. Thoracic Soc. Office: Bend Meml Clinic 1501 NE Med Ctr Dr Bend OR 97701

HARLESS, SUSAN ETTINGER, museum curator; b. Chgo., Nov. 26, 1947; d. Richard Howard and Marjorie Jean (Larsen) Ettinger; m. Keith Weston Harless, Aug. 29, 1970; children: Wendy Eileen, Brian Richard. BA in Biology, Lewis and Clark Coll., Portland, Oreg., 1969; MEd, Oreg. State U., 1988. Research asst. U. Oreg. Med. Sch., Portland, 1970-72, Dartmouth-Mary Hitchcock Meml. Hosp., Hanover, N.H., 1972-73; vol., co-chmn. Oreg. High Desert Mus., Bend, Oreg., 1979-84; collections intern The High Desert Mus., Bend, Oreg., 1986-87, collections coordinator, 1987-88, asst. curator, 1988—. Mem. Am. Inst. Conservation, Can. Conservation Inst., Internat. Inst. for Conservation, Oreg. Hist. Soc., Am. Assn. Mus. (AAM registrar's com. western region). Republican. Club: P.E.O (Bend) (chpt. AI). Home: 20140 Mathers Dr Bend OR 97701 Office: The High Desert Mus 59800 S Hwy 97 Bend OR 97702

HARLEY, ROBISON DOOLING, JR., lawyer, educator; b. Ancon, Panama, July 6, 1946; s. Robison Dooling and Loyde Hazel (Goehenauer) H.; m. Suzanne Purviance Bendel, Aug. 9, 1975; children—Arianne Erin, Lauren Loyde. B.A., Brown U., 1968; J.D., Temple U., 1971; LL.M., U. San Diego, 1985. Bar: Pa. 1972, U.S. Ct. Mil. Appeals 1972, Calif. 1976, U.S. Dist. Ct. (cen. and so. dists) Calif. 1976, N.J. 1977, U.S. Dist. Ct. N.J. 1977, U.S. Supreme Ct. 1980, D.C. 1981, U.S. Ct. Appeals (9th cir.) 1982, U.S. Dist. Ct. (ea. dist.) Pa. 1987, U.S. Ct. Appeals (3rd cir.) 1986. Cert. criminal law specialist Calif. Bd. Legal Specialization; cert. criminal trial adv. Nat. Bd. Trial Advocacy. Asst. agy. dir. Safeco Title Ins. Co., Los Angeles, 1975-77; ptnr. Cohen, Stokke & Davis, Santa Ana, Calif., 1977-85; ptnr. Harley and McDermott, Santa Ana, Calif., 1985—; instr. Orange County Coll. Trial Advocacy, paralegal program U. Calif.; judge pro-tem Orange County Cts. Author: Orange County Trial Lawyers Drunk Driving Syllabus; contbr. articles to profl. jours. Bd. dirs. Orange County Legal Aid Soc. Served to lt. col. JAGC, USMCR, 1975—; trial counsel, def. counsel, mil. judge, asst. staff judge adv. USMC, 1971-75, regional def. counsel Western Region, 1986—. Mem. ABA, Orange County Bar Assn. (judiciary com., criminal law sect., adminstrn. of justice com.), Orange County Trial Lawyers Assn., Calif. Trial Lawyers Assn., Assn. Trial Lawyers Am., Calif. Attys. for Criminal Justice, Calif. Pub. Defenders Assn., Nat. Assn. for Criminal Def. Attys., Assn. Specialized Criminal Def. Advs., Orange County Criminal Lawyers Assn. (found. com.), Res. Officers Assn., Marine Corps Reserve Officers Assn. Republican. Avocations: sports, physical fitness, reading. Home: 12 Bayberry Way Irvine CA 92715 Office: Harley & McDermott 825 N Ross St Santa Ana CA 92701

HARLOW, STEVEN MARK, insurance company executive; b. Mexico, Maine, June 11, 1954; s. Walter Benjamin and Christine (Chicoine) H. BS summa cum laude, U. So. Maine, 1976. Music educator Portland (Maine) Pub. Schs., 1976-77; claim svc. rep. United Chambers Ins. Svcs., Inc., Redwood City, Calif., 1978-79; group benefits, lead benefits examiner Lincoln Nat., San Francisco, 1979-81, trainee, 1981-82; auditing specialist Lincoln Nat., San Mateo, Calif., 1982-83, claim mgr. trainee, 1982-83; regional mgr. Lincoln Nat., Dallas, 1983-85, Orange, Calif., 1985-86, San Mateo, Calif., 1987—. Vol. project Open Hand, San Francisco, 1988—. Mem. San Francisco Claims Assn. Democrat. Home: 3718 20th St San Francisco CA 94110

HARMON, BARBARA, nurse; b. Merced, Calif., Oct. 12, 1945; d. Basil L. and Phyllis G. (Wilsey) Sullens.; m. Robert A. Harmon, Oct. 7, 1967; children: David A., Mark A. Student, Highland Sch. Nursing, 1966; BS in Nursing, SUNY, 1986. RN, Calif. Staff nurse Merced Community Med. Ctr., 1966-70; nurse ICU Community Hosp. Monterrey Penn, Carmel, Calif., 1970, Holy Family Hosp., Spokane, Wash., 1970-71; indsl. nurse Kaiser Aluminum, Spokane, 1971-72; instr. Merced Coll., 1980-83; vis. nurse Hospice Merced-Mariposa County, 1986—. Den leader Boy Scouts Am., 1978-80, chair com., 1986—; vol. ARC.; mem. PTA. Merced County Bd. Suprs. scholar, 1963. Mem. Presby. Women's Club. Republican. Presbyterian. Home: 831 University Dr Merced CA 95348 Office: Hospice 2011 Canal St #1 PO Box 763 Merced CA 95341

HARMON, JACK D., emergency services executive, computer consultant; b. Hawthorne, Calif., Feb. 5, 1953; s. Robert I. and Margeret (Sheiff) H.; m. Linda Lee Sims, Mar. 14, 1973; children: Cassandra Kay, Jessica Diane. AA, U. Alaska, Anchorage, 1978; BA, Western Oreg. State Coll., 1985. Firefighter Anchorage Fire Dept., 1974-84, capt., 1984—; cameo instr. NOAA, Seattle, 1986—; computer cons. Fire Svcs., Inc., Anchorage, 1988—; instr. Nat. Fire Acad., Emmitsburg, Wash., 1986—. Vol. Muscular Dystrophy Assn., Anchorage, 1976—; bd. dirs. Campbell Elem. Sch. PTA, Anchorage, 1980-84. Mem Internat. Assn. Fire Chiefs, Internat. Assn. Fire Svc. Instrs., Internat. Assn. Firefighters, Internat. Fire Svc. Tng. Assn., Anchorage Macintosh Users Group (sec. 1985-87). Office: Anchorage Fire Dept 1301 E 80th Ave Anchorage AK 99518

HARMON, KEITH JAMES, artist; b. Michigan City, Ind., Sept. 7, 1950; s. Frederick Dean and Christine Marie (Arcuri) H. BA, Purdue U., 1972; MA, UCLA, 1977. Executed murals, decorative motifs and borders, exhibited paintings nationally and internationally, 1978—. With U.S. Army, 1972-74. Roman Catholic. Home: 1033 1/2 N Croft Ave West Hollywood CA 90069

HARMON, SCOTT MCKNEELY, health science facility administrator; b. Dothan, Ala., May 20, 1951. BA, Huntingdon Coll., Montgomery, Ala., 1973; MHA, U. Ala., 1978. Cert. hosp. adminstr. With systems devel. lab Jackson Hosp. & Clinic, Montgomery, 1974-76; resident in hosp. adminstr. VA Wadsworth Med. Ctr., L.A., 1977-78; regional adminstr., ops. VA Med. Dist., Lexington, Ky., 1979-81; regional health care planner, rsch devel. VA Med. Dist., L.A., 1981-85; hosp. adminstr. Sign of the Dove, Inc., Chatsworth, Calif., 1985-86, Fountain View Mgmt., L.A., 1986-88, Health Care Group, San Diego, 1988—; prin. McKneely Harmon Assocs., West Hollywood, Calif., 1986—. Editor & contbr.: Healthcare Strategic Plan, MEDIPP83; editor & author: MEDIPP84; contbr. articles to profl. jours. U. Ala. fellow, 1977-78. Mem. Am. Hosp. Assn., Calif. Assn. Health Facilities (assoc.), So. Calif. Soc. for Hosp. Planning & Mktg. (charter), Sigma Sigma Sigma, Chi Delta Phi. Presbyterian. Home: 727 Westbourne Dr West Hollywood CA 90069

HARMON, TERRY, retail groceries executive; b. 1940. With Harmon City Inc., West Valley City, Utah, 1952—, pres., 1971—, also bd. dirs. Office: Harmon City Inc 3540 S 4000 W Ste 500 West Valley City UT 84120 *

HARMON, WARREN WAYNE, educator; b. Colton, Calif., Feb. 13, 1936; s. Renick Elkin and Henrietta Frances (Stûwich) H.; m Margaret Ann Schonberger, Nov. 21, 1959; children: Andrea Jane, Fritz Warren. AA, San Bernardino Valley Coll., 1958; BA, San Diego State Coll., 1961, MA, 1964. Lic. secondary tchr., Calif. Chmn. social sci. Roosevelt Jr. High Sch., San Diego, 1962-66; geography instr. Mesa Coll., San Diego, 1966; geography instr. Grossmont Coll., El Cajon, Calif., 1967-84, div. coord., 1984, prof. geography, dept. chmn. of earth scis., 1984—; geog. cons. UCLA, 1986-88. Author: Geography of California, 1976; co-author Geographic Perspectives on American Westward Expansion, 1986; contbr. articles to profl. jours. Co-founder So. Calif. Tourette Syndrome Assn., Mission Viejo, Calif, 1974; chief Indian Guides, La Jolla, Calif., 1978. Named Outstanding Educator of Am., Fuller and Dees, 1974, Disting. Chair of Sci. Grossmont Coll., 1988-89. Mem. San Diego County Social Sci Adv. Coun., Nat. Coun. for Geog. Edn., Calif Geography Soc. (exec. bd. mem. 1978), Calif. Geog. Alliance (charter mem.), Fulbright Alumni Assn. (Fulbright scholar 1970-71), La Jolla Play Readers Club, Gamma Theta Upsilon. Democrat. Methodist. Office: Grossmont Coll 8800 Grossmont Coll Dr El Cajon CA 92020

HARMOUSH, RALPH JOSEPH, realtor; b. Beirut, Lebanon, May 6, 1953; came to U.S., 1971; s. Joseph R. and Vicky (Hajal) H. BA, Loretto Heights Coll., 1977. Lic. real estate broker. Dir. ops. Colo. region Internat. Investment Promotions Corp., Denver, 1980-84; real estate broker Jones Real Estate, Denver, 1983-84; founder, pres. R.H. Assocs. Ltd. Partnership, Investments, Denver, 1984-88; owner, operator Remax Cen., Inc., Denver, 1984—. Mem. Nat. Assn. Realtors, Colo. Bd. Realtors, Denver Bd. Realtors, Million Dollar Roundtable Club. Home: 6063 Glencoe Way Little County CO 80121 Office: Remax Cen Inc 3801 E Florida Ave #200 Denver CO 80210

HARMS, DENNIS WALTER, computer executive; b. Waverly, Iowa, Dec. 16, 1946; s. Walter Gerhard and Dora (Thompson) H.; m. Carol Jean Mardorf, July 19, 1969; children: Deborah, Catherine. BA, Wartburg Coll., 1969; MD, Iowa State U., 1971, PhD, 1974. Instr. Iowa State U., Ames, 1969-73; numerical analyst Hewlett-Packard, Cupertino, Calif., 1973-77; project mgr. Hewlett-Packard, Corvallis, Oreg., 1977-81; v.p. Intelledex, Corvallis, 1981-85, Pacific Crest Software, Corvallis, 1985-88; project leader Hewlett-Packard, Corvallis, 1988—; sec. bd. Pacific Crest Software, Corvallis, 1981—. Inventor, patentee four-function calculator. Mem. Soc. Mech. Engrs., Am. Contract Bridge League (life). Democrat. Lutheran. Office: Hewlett Packard 1000 NE Circle Blvd Corvallis OR 97330

HARNEY, DAVID MORAN, lawyer; b. Marysville, Calif., June 30, 1924; s. George Richard and Eileen M. (Daly) H.; m. Evelyn Brint Turner, Mar. 17, 1945; children: Brian Patrick, David Turner. Student Loyola U., Los Angeles, 1942-43, Ariz. State U., 1943-44, Southwestern La. U., 1944; J.D., U. So. Calif., 1948. Bar: Calif. 1949. Ptnr. Harney Law Offices, Los Angeles, 1950—. Served to 1st lt. USMC, 1942-45. Mem. Internat. Acad. Trial Lawyers (pres.-1983-84). Democrat. Roman Catholic. Club: Jonathan (Los Angeles). Home: 880 W 1st St 705 Los Angeles CA 90012 Office: 201 N Figueroa St #1300 Los Angeles CA 90012

HARNLY, CAROLINE DAY, librarian; b. Palo Alto, Calif., June 22, 1951; d. John Curtis and Eleanor Allin (Smith) H. BA in Math., McPherson Coll., 1973; MSL, Western Mich. U., 1974. Sci. indexer The Upjohn Co., Kalamazoo, Mich., 1974-75; asst. librarian McPherson (Kans.) Coll., 1975-78; sci. librarian Miami U., Oxford, Ohio, 1978-82; reference librarian San Francisco State U., 1982—, reference program coordinator, 1986—. Co-author: Mount St. Helens: An Annotated Bibliography, 1984; author: Space Weapons (Oryx Science Bibliographies vol. 2), 1985, Agent Orange and Vienam: An Annotated Bibliography, 1988. Mem. AAUW, Am. Library Assn., Assn. Coll. and Research Libraries (sci. and tech. sect.), Sci. and Engring. Acad. Librarians (pres. No. Calif. CARL Interest Group 1986), Calif. Acad. and Research Librarians (interest groups rep. 1987), Beta Phi Mu. Democrat. Methodist. Office: San Francisco State U J Paul Leonard Libr 1630 Holloway Ave San Francisco CA 94132

HARNSBERGER, THERESE COSCARELLI, librarian; b. Muskegon, Mich.; d. Charles and Julia (Borrell) Coscarelli; B.A. cum laude, Marymount Coll., 1952; M.L.S., U. So. Calif., 1953; postgrad. Rosary Coll., River Forest, Ill., 1955-56, U. Calif., Los Angeles Extension, 1960-61; m. Frederick Owen Harnsberger, Dec. 24, 1962; 1 son, Lindsey Carleton. Free-lance writer, 1950—; librarian San Marino (Calif.) High Sch., 1953-56; cataloger, cons. San Marino Hall, South Pasadena, Calif., 1956-61; librarian Los Angeles State Coll., 1956-59; librarian dist. library Covina-Valley Unified Sch. Dist., Covina, Calif., 1959-67; librarian Los Angeles Trade Tech. Coll., 1972—; med. librarian, tumor registrar Alhambra (Calif.) Community Hosp., 1975-79; tumor registrar Huntington Meml. Hosp., 1979—; pres., dir. Research Unltd., 1980—; free lance reporter Los Angeles' Best Bargains, 1981—; med. library cons., 1979—. Chmn. spiritual values com. Covina Coordinating Council, 1964-66. Mem. ALA, Calif. Assn. Sch. Librarians (chmn. legis. com.), Covina Tchrs. Assn., AAUW (historian 1972-73), U. So. Calif. Grad. Sch. Library Sci. (life), Am. Nutrition Soc. (chpt. Newsletter chmn.), Nat. Tumor Registrars Assn., So. Calif. Tumor Registrars Assn., Med. Library Assn., So. Calif. Librarians Assn., So. Calif. Assn. Law Libraries, Book Publicists So. Calif., Am. Fedn. Tchrs. Coll. Guild, Faculty Assn. Calif. Community Colls., Inc., Loyola, Marymount Alumnae Assn. (coordinator), Pi Lambda Theta. Author: (poetry) The Journal, 1982, To Julia: in Memoriam; contbr. articles to profl. jours. Office: 2809 W Hellman Ave Alhambra CA 91803

HARO, ROBERTO PEDRO, university official, education educator; b. Sacramento, Sept. 9, 1936; s. Tereso Nunez and Catalina (Herreros) H.; m. Pauline J. Kessemeier, June 10, 1961 (div. Aug. 1972); children: Richard, Robert. BA, U. Calif., Berkeley, 1958, MA, 1959, MLIS, 1962; EdD, U. San Francisco, 1979. Librarian Calif. State U., Hayward, 1962-63; adminstrv. intern Columbia U., N.Y.C., 1963-65; head librarian InterGovtl. Affairs Library, U. Calif., Davis, 1965-69; dir. rsch. President's Cabinet Com. on Spanish-Speaking, Washington, 1969-71; assoc. dir. libraries U. So. Calif., L.A., 1972-75; assoc. dir. profl. devel. program U. Calif., Berkeley, 1976-79, mgmt. fellow Chancellor's Office, 1980-81, asst. vice chancellor, 1982-87, asst. chancellor, 1988—, also sr. lectr., 1982; rsch. cons. Border States Consortium, San Diego, 1978-79, Calif. Spanish Lang. Data, Hayward, 1981-84; prin. investigator Hispanic Info. Exchange, Oakland, Calif., 1984-86; vice chmn. adv. com. Coll. Bd., N.Y.C., 1986-89. Author: Latin Americana Resources, 1971, Developing Library and Information Services, 1981; contbr. articles to profl. jours. Chmn. New Oakland Community Ednl. Task Force, 1984-89. Sgt. U.S. Army, 1959-61. Am. Coun. on Edn. fellow, 1987, Inst. for Ednl. Mgmt. fellow, 1988. Mem. Am. Assn. Higher Edn., Nat. Assn. Student Personnel Adminstrs. Roman Catholic. Home: 771 Grizzly Peak Blvd Berkeley CA 94708-1336 Office: U Calif Chancellor's Office 200 California Hall Berkeley CA 94720

HAROLD, JOHN GORDON, internist, cardiologist; b. Petaluma, Calif., Aug. 17, 1955; s. John and Anne (Callaghan) H.; m. Ellen Teresa Cox, Dec. 28, 1977. BS, CCNY, 1977; MD, SUNY, Stony Brook, 1979. Diplomate Nat. Bd. Med. Examinrs, Am. Bd. Internal Medicine, Am. Bd. Cardiology, Am. Bd. Critical Care Medicine, Am. Bd. Geriatric Medicine. Intern medicine Mt. Sinai Hosp., N.Y.C., 1979-80, resident medicine, 1980-82; cardiology fellow div. cardiology, dept. medicine Cedars-Sinai Med. Ctr., L.A., 1982-85, assoc. cardiologist, 1985—; asst. clin. prof. medicine Sch. Medicine UCLA, 1987—; attending physician UCLA Med. Ctr., Cedars-Sinai Med. Ctr., Century City Hosp., Beverly Hills Med. Ctr., Midway Hosp. Med. Ctr., L.A., 1986—. Editor: Two-Dimensional Echocardiography and Cardiac Doppler, 1989; contbr. articles to profl. jours. Mem. Rep. Nat. Com., Washington, 1982-89; active Nat. Eagle Scout Assn. Recipient Nat. Rsch. Svc. award NIH, 1984-85. Fellow ACP, Am. Coll. Cardiology, Am. Coll. Chest Physicians, Am. Heart Assn. (coun. on clin. cardiology); mem. L.A. County Med. Assn., Nat. Geographic Soc. Republican. Roman Catholic. Office: Cedars Sinai Med Office 8635 W 3d Jupiter Dr Ste 750-2 Los Angeles CA 90048-6178

HARP, ROBERT GEORGE, JR., hospitality corporation executive; b. Balt., May 28, 1959; s. Robert George and Delores (Creutzer) H.; m. Jill Stephenson, June 4, 1983; 1 child, Preston Robert. BA in Econs., Wheaton Coll., 1980, MA in Communications with high honors, 1981; ThM, Dallas Theol. Sem., 1985. Lic. real estate broker. Real estate broker The Swearingen Co., Dallas, 1986-87; dir. of devel., v.p. of real estate Global Hospitality Corp., San Diego, 1987—. Contbr. book reviews to jours. in field. Precinct capt. San Diego Count Rep. Com. Named one of Outstanding Young Men of Am., 1985. Mem. Nat. Assn. Realtors, Realtors Nat. Mktg. Inst., Calif. Assn. Realtors, San Diego Bd. of Realtors (edn. com., govt. and polit. affairs com.), Cert. Comml. Investment Mem. (San Diego chpt.). Republican. Baptist.

HARP, RUFUS WILLIAM, set decorator; b. Bastrop, La., Nov. 28, 1923; s. Robert Edward and Anna Lee (Kirkpatrick) H. BA, La. State U., 1947, MA, 1951. Asst. prof. U. Ga., Atlanta, 1952-54; set decorator Ford Found. Radio & TV, N.Y.C., 1954-55, CBS-TV, N.Y.C., 1955-69, Carol Burnett Show, Hollywood, Calif., 1969-78; pvt. practice set decorator Hollywood, 1978-85; set decorator ABC Circle Film "Moonlighting", Hollywood, 1985—, Joe Hamilton Prodn. "Mama's Family", Hollywood, 1985—; pres., chief exec. officer Prop Services West, Los Angeles, 1978—; pres. Billy Wolf Inc., Los Angeles, 1980—; dir. Marbil Prodn., Los Angeles, 1986—. Served to 1st. lt., USAF, 1943-46, ETO. Mem. Nat. Acad. TV Arts and Scis. (Emmy award 1965, 77, 79, with 22 nominations 1964-88). Democrat. Baptist. Office: Prop Svcs West 915 N Citrus Ave Hollywood CA 90038

HARPER, CHARLES LA-SHEAR, small business owner; b. Pensacola, Fla., Dec. 31, 1962; s. Charles William and Helen Earlene (Stallworth) H.; m. Amanda Marie G.; children: Charles Andre Devon III, Christopher Andrew Damone. Student, Monterey (Calif.) Acad., 1981, Monterey Peninsula Coll., 1982. Mgr. Royal Beauty Salon, Seaside, Calif., 1980-82; owner, operator, tchr. Chardon Salon/Supply, Seaside, 1983—; tchr. Leisure Curl, Chgo., 1986—; Le-Do Products, Seaside, 1986—. Pres. NAACP, Seaside, 1987. Mem. Kiwanis. Republican. Roman Catholic. Home: 1188 Broadway Seaside CA 93955 Office: PO Box 1981 Seaside CA 93955

HARPER, DONALD JACQUES, holding company executive; b. Knoxville, Tenn., June 30, 1928; s. Raymond James and Pauline Jean (Huffstuttler) H.; m. Jayne C. Combs; children—Nancy Lynn (Mrs. Norman Mehl), Danial Ray, Larry F., Lenny G., Lindsay J. Student Wichita (Kans.) State U., 1946-47, Kansas City Coll. Engring., 1948; Indsl. Engr., U. Okla., 1950. Indsl. engr. Coleman Co., Inc., Wichita, 1953-56; agt. Penn Mut. Life Ins. Co., Wichita, 1956-60; gen. agt. Crown Life Ins. Co., Wichita, 1960-62; pres. Fin. Unification Corp., Mark V group of cos., holding co.'s, Scottsdale, Ariz., 1963—. Bd. dirs. Scottsdale Symphony. Served with USNR, 1942-45. Mem. Ariz. Law Soc., Am. Mgmt. Soc., Profl. Consultants, Nat. Soc. Bus. Consultants, Scottsdale C. of C. Home: 5320 E Camelback Rd Phoenix AZ 85018 Office: 6060 E Thomas Scottsdale AZ 85251

HARPER, HAL DISHON, chemist; b. Princeton, Ind., Feb. 24, 1950; s. Hallie Herbert and Anna Bell (Dishon) H.; m. Sally Morton Farmer, Nov. 29, 1968 (div. 1971); 1 child, Ginger Elaine Duncan; m. Pamela Elaine Scott, May 27, 1979. Student, U. Evansville, 1967-68; BS, Oakland City Coll., 1977. Lab. technician Gen. Tire Co., Evansville, Ind., 1978-81, Consol. Coal Co., Pinckneyville, Ind., 1980-81; chemist Veco, Inc., Anchorage, 1983-86, Northwest Tech. Services, Anchorage, 1986, Arco Alaska, Inc., Anchorage, 1986--. Vol. emergency med. technician Oakland City (Ind.) Emergency Med. Services, 1976; vol. firefighter Prudhoe Bay (Alaska) Fire Dept., 1986-87. Mem. Am. Chem. Soc., Alaska Flyfishers, Nordic Ski Club (Anchorage). Office: Arco Alaska Inc 701 G St Anchorage AK 99501

HARPER, HOWARD LAYNE, psychotherapist, social worker; b. Waco, Tex., May 13, 1938; s. William Earnest and Opal Zuela (Howard) H.; m. Betty Faye Jordan, June 6, 1958; children: Kelly, Vicki Harper Barry. AA, Orange Coast Coll., 1974; BS in Human Svcs. with honors, BA in Psychology with honors, U. Calif., Fullerton, 1980, MS in Counseling, 1982; PhD, Columbia Pacific U., 1985. Lic. marriage and family therapist. Program cons. Beverly Enterprises, Riverside, Calif., 1980-81; pvt. practice Fullerton, 1983—; cons. Merrill Community Svc., Fontana, Calif., 1984-85; mem. Calif. Behavioral Bd. Sci. Examiners, 1985; asst. dir. Charter Grove Hosp., Corona, Calif., 1988, Charter Counseling, Anaheim Hills, Calif., 1988. Contbr. articles and poetry to various publs. Mem. Riverside Interagy. Sexual Abuse Coun., 1980—; chmn. pub. awareness Child Abuse Coun., Riverside, 1983-85; group therapist Parent's United, Orange County, Calif., 1985—. Mem. Am. Assn. for Counseling and Devel., Calif. Assn. for Counseling and Devel. (editor Psyche 1986—), Calif. Assn. Marriage and Family Therapists, Yorba Linda C. of C., Psi Chi. Office: Family Therapy Ctr 17621 Irvine Blvd Ste 202 Tustin CA 92680

HARPER, KENNETH CHARLES, minister; b. Detroit, Aug. 31, 1946; s. Charles Burdett and Marion Anna (Pankau) H.; m. Sharon Kay Royse, June 14, 1969; children: Charles William, David Peter, Andrew Scott. BSE, Ill. State U., 1969; MDiv, Trinity Evang. Div. Sch., Deerfield, Ill., 1973; ThM, Princeton Theol. Sem., 1976; DMin., San Francisco Theol. Sem., 1986. Ordained to ministry Presbyn. Ch., 1974. Asst. pastor First Presbyn. Ch., Mt. Holly, N.J., 1974-77; pastor First Presbyn. Ch., Herrin, Ill., 1977-82; sr. pastor First Presbyn. Ch., Westminster, Calif., 1982—. Contbr. to book HIS Guide to Evangelism, 1977; contbr. articles to profl. jours. Mem. Presbyns. for Renewal, Evang. Theol. Soc., Conf. on Faith and History, Assn. Psychol. Type. Democrat. Office: First Presbyn Ch 7702 Westminster Blvd Westminster CA 92683

HARPER, KENNETH EDWARD, former university chancellor, renewal center executive; b. Pocahantas, Ill., Aug. 21, 1921; s. Thomas Edward and Myra (Martin) H.; m. Mary Jane Kimbell, May 26, 1946; children: Susan, Sandra, Steven, Sara. BA, Asbury Coll., 1943, BD, 1946; MA, U. Ky., 1947, PhD, 1959. Ordained to ministry United Meth. Ch., 1947. Dean U. Ky., Lexington, 1959-65; dir. tng. VISTA, Washington, 1966-69; pres. Pima Coll., Tucson, 1969-72; pres., prof. Riverside (Calif.) Coll., 1972-83; chancellor Golden State U., Los Angeles, 1983-87; pres. Natural Renewal Ctr., Oceanside, Calif., 1987—. Author: Son Get A Hold of the Self, 1987. Civil rights organizer, Lexington, 1962; organizer human rights, Reston, Va., 1969. Mem. Omicron Delta Kappa, Kappa Delta Pi, Phi Delta Kappa. Home: 1200 Harbor Dr N Apt 13-A Oceanside CA 92054

HARPER, RICHARD HENRY, film producer, director; b. San Jose, Calif., Sept. 15, 1950; s. Walter Henry and Priscilla Alden (Browne) H.; m. Ann Marie Morgan, June 19, 1976; children: Christine Ann, Paul Richard, James Richard. Student, Cal. Inst. Arts, 1970-71. Show designer Walt Disney Imagineering, Glendale, Calif., 1971-76; motion picture producer, dir. Harper Films, Inc., La Canada, Calif., 1976—. Producer, dir. films (in 360 degree Circle-Vision) Magic Carpet 'Round the World, Disneyland, Tokyo, 1983, American Journeys, Disneyland, Calif., 1985; (in 200 degree Wrap-Around) Impressions de France, Disney World, Fla., 1982; Collecting America, Nat. Gallery Art, Washington, Side By Side, Osmond Entertainment Complex, Utah, World of Speed, Disneyland, Calif. Recipient more than 130 awards world-wide for outstanding motion picture prodn. including Silver trophy Cannes, France Internat. Film Festival, Cert. of Excellence Edinburgh, Scotland Internat. Film Festival, two Best of Category awards San Francisco Internat. Film Festival.

HARPER, ROBERT CHARLES, design drafting executive; b. Darby, Pa., June 23, 1943; s. James Ingram and Mary (Winsmore) H.; m. Martha Lynn Sadler, Dec. 30, 1966; 1 child, Tamara Lynn. AA, U. Mich., 1968, LaSalle Coll., Chgo., 1970, La Pierce Coll., Woodland Hills, Calif., 1972. Drafter Lockheed Calif. Co., Burbank, 1968-71; buyer Sinclair Paints, Los Angeles, 1971-78; pres. Ye Old Wood Mill, Ltd., Westlake Village, Calif., 1978-83; design drafting mgr. Am. Semiconductor Equipment Technologies, Woodland Hills, Calif., 1983—. Sec., tres. Ventura County Sheriff Underwater Search and Rescue, 1988—. Served as sgt. USMC, 1963-67, Socialist Republic Vietnam. Avocations: sailing, scuba. Office: ASET 6110 Variel Ave Woodland Hills CA 91367

HARPER, ROBERT LEVELL, pharmaceutical company executive; b. Wichita, Kans., Nov. 11, 1942; s. Cleo Levell and Mary Florence (Weaver) H.; m. Margaret Lucille Madden, Jan. 20, 1961 (div. 1980); children: Douglas Warren, Susan Denise; m. Maria Elain Davis, June 20, 1981; stepchildren: Laura Elaine Emery, Melissa MacAlpin Emery. Cert. med. rep., Sterling Mgmt. Inst. Sales rep. Dorsey Labs. div. Sandoz Pharms., Tulsa, 1967-70; mgr. key accounts Sandoz Pharms., Houston, 1970-72; div. mgr. Dorsey Pharms. div. Sandoz Pharms., Kansas City, Mo., 1972-85; mgr. govt. affairs Sandoz Pharms., Sacramento, 1985—; rotating mgr. Sandoz Pharms., East Hanover, N.J., 1985. Donor Kansas City Coll. Osteo. Medicine, 1973; co-founder first aid program state CAP, Oklahoma City, 1973; leader youth program YMCA, Johnson County, Mo., 1977-79; leader youth baseball Johnson County, 1976-79; del. Nat. Baseball Congress, Houston, 1971, 72, 73; mem. med. edn. for srs. SRx Regional Program, 1985—. With USAFR, 1960-64. Recipient appreciation award Calif. State Firemen's Assn., Sacramento, 1987. Mem. Nat. Assn. Legis. Svcs., Calif. Medication Edn. Coalition, Calif. Mfrs. Assn., Pharm. Mfrs. Assn., Calif. Derby. Home: 11370 Tunnel Hill Way Rancho Cordova CA 95670

HARPER, W. TROY, environmental consultant. BS (2d hons.), U. Mo., Rolla, 1953. Mem. staff Los Alamos Sci. Lab., N.M., 1953-56; engr. Lockheed Aircraft Corp., Marietta, Ga., 1956-58; dep. project mgr. Lockheed Missiles and Space Co., Sunnyvale, Calif., 1958-71; mgr. regulatory affairs Bechtel Power Corp., San Francisco, 1977-88; prin. Regulatory Interface Assocs., San Leandro, Calif., 1988—; cons. San Leandrans for Reasonable Growth, San Leandro, 1984-85. Inventor graphite prodn., 1969. Advisor San Leandro City Coun., 1985-88. Mem. Nat. Assn. Environ. Profls., Calif. Environ. Affairs Agy. (registered environ. assessor). Office: Regulatory Interface Assocs 13517 Aurora Dr Ste 105 San Leandro CA ▲ 94577

HARR, KELVIN SINCLAIR, engineering company executive; b. Denver, Feb. 16, 1935; s. Ulysses Grant and Nettie Ester (Wages) H.; m. Sharon Linda Worster, June 2, 1961 (div. Dec. 1970); children: Eric Allen, Shawn Michel, Shelly Marie; m. Edna Hege Parker, Sept. 26, 1971; children: Mireille Margarita, Sebastian Grann-Kieth. BS in Tech. Mgmt., Regis Coll., 1983; MS in Systems Mgmt., U. Southern Calif., 1987. Surveyor U.S. Geol. Survey, Grand Junction, Colo., 1953-56; tech. specialist Ball Aerospace Corp., Boulder, Colo., 1959-72; owner Skyline Lodge, Platoro, Colo., 1972-75; supr.-instr. Macco div. Ortloff Corp., Fruita, Colo., 1975-77; rsch. engr. Louisiana-Padivic-Pabco div., Fruita, Colo., 1977-80; sr. rsch. engr. Solar Energy Rsch. Inst., Golden, Colo., 1980-84; staff test engr. Martin Marietta Astronautics, Denver, 1984—. Contbr. articles to profl. jours. With U.S. Army, 1956-59. Mem. Instrument soc. Am., Am. Vacuum Soc. (organizing com. 1964-65). Democrat. Unitarian Universalist. Home: 2140 Ellis St Golden CO 80401 Office: Martin Marietta PO Box 179 M/S H0361 Denver CO 80201

HARRELL, JERRY WAYNE, hotel company executive; b. Lake Charles, La., Dec. 31, 1953; s. Wayne Allen and Maxine Mary (Barnes) H. Gen. mgr. various Sheraton hotels GGCMC, Inc., La., Tex., 1981-85; resident mgr. Sheraton Mockingbird LPT, Inc., Dallas, 1985-86; gen. mgr. Holiday Inn Tucson (Ariz.) North Ritter Investments, 1986-87; gen. mgr. Holiday Innde Las Cruces Ritter Investments, N.Mex., 1987; v.p., dir. ops. Ritter Investments, Las Cruces, 1987—. Vice-chmn. bd. dirs., Las Cruces Conv. and Visitors Bur., 1988. Mem. N.Mex. Restaurant Assn., Las Cruces Hotel/Motel Assn. (v.p. 1988—), N.Mex. Hotel/Motel Assn. (bd. dirs. 1988—), Skal Club. Democrat. Southern Baptist. Office: Ritter Investments PO Box HI Las Cruces NM 88004

HARRIGAN, JOHN FREDERICK, banker; b. Eau Claire, Wis., June 22, 1925; s. Frederick H. and Marion F. (Farr) H.; m. Barbara Heald, July 1, 1950; children—Sarah H. Gruber, Peter Christopher. Student, U. Wis., 1946-49; grad., Rutgers U. Stonier Grad. Sch. Banking, 1965. With First Nat. Bank Oreg., Portland, 1949-71, exec. v.p., 1971; chmn. bd., chief exec. officer Pacific Nat. Bank Wash., Seattle, 1971-74, dir., 1971-80; vice chmn. bd. dirs. United Calif. Bank, Los Angeles, 1974-75; pres., dir. Western Bancorp., Los Angeles, 1975-80; dir. Union Bank, Los Angeles, 1980—; dir. Nordstrom, Inc. Bd. dirs. Los Angeles Civic Light Opera Assn., So. Calif. chpt. Nat. Multiple Sclerosis Soc.; bd. visitors Grad. Sch. Mgmt., U. Calif., Los Angeles; mem. Peregrine Fund. Served with USMCR, 1943-45. Mem. Assn. Res. City Bankers. Episcopalian. Clubs: Calif, Los Angeles Country, Eldorado Country. Office: Union Bank 1900 Ave of Stars Ste 210 Los Angeles CA 90067

HARRILL, JOHN WILLIAM, controller; b. Lincolnton, N.C., Feb. 8, 1932; s. Robert Lee and Vera Catherine (Michael) H.; m. Helene Harbart, Mar. 15, 1961; children: Holly Ann, Jason Charles. BS, U. Md., 1958; postgrad., U. Mich., Dearborn, 1961-62. Regional controller Sealtest Foods, Cleve., 1958-64; sr. auditor White Motor Corp., Cleve., 1964-65; dir. audits, asst. treas. Carling Brewing Corp., Waltham, Mass., 1965-73; treas., bd. dirs. Hutch Founds., Montpelier, Vt., 1973-76; asst. to v.p. fin. Cedar Point, Sandusky, Ohio, 1976-78; v.p., controller CMPI, Littleton, Colo., 1978; corp. controller Goldco Industries Inc., Loveland, Colo., 1979—, sec., treas., bd. dirs., 1981—; bus. cons., 1971—. bd. dirs. Kessen Enterprises Inc., Englewood, Colo.; pres. Solar Vista Condominiums Assn., Lakewood, Colo., 1985—. Served with USN, 1950-54, Korea. Mem. Nat. Assn. Accts. (pres. Denver chpt. 1986-87, (Rocky Mountain Council 1988-89, nat. del. 1989—). Republican. Lutheran. Home: 8721 S Westwind Ln Highlands Ranch CO 80126 Office: Goldco Industries Inc 5605 Goldco Dr Loveland CO 80537

HARRIMAN, CHARLES JARVIS, JR., cultural organization administrator; b. Newport, R.I., Sept. 3, 1922; s. Charles Jarvis and Kathryn (Cocroft) H.; m. Nancy Anne Dole, Dec. 10, 1966. BA, Trinity Coll., 1943. Gen. prodn. mgr. Moral Re-Armament, N.Y.C., 1946-56, staff mem., 1956-68; staff mem. Up With People, Tucson, 1968; exec. dir. Tucson Festival Soc., 1970-86; exec. v.p. Westerners Internat., Tucson, 1973-86. mem. Tucson Mus. Art, Ariz-Sonora Desert Mus.; bd. dirs. St. Lukes in the Desert, Tucson, 1980-84, Friends of Western Art, 1980—, Tucson Trade Bur., 1980—, Ariz.-Mex. Commn., Phoenix, 1983-86. Served to sgt. Med. Dept., U.S. Army, 1943-46. Mem. Internat. Festivals Assn. (pres. 1984-85, bd. dirs. 1981-86), Southwestern Mission Research Ctr. Republican. Episcopalian. Home: 6941 E Third St Tucson AZ 85710

HARRIMAN, WILLIAM CASWELL, educational administrator; b. Cornish, Maine, Nov. 10, 1930; s. Lester Boardman and Marguerite (Pendexter) H.; m. Pamela Joan Cook, Feb. 25, 1954; children: Anthony W., Debra A., David W. BS, U. Maine, 1952; MSBA, Boston U., 1975. Commd. 2d lt. U.S. Army, 1952, advanced through grades to lt. col., 1967; chief svcs. dir. U.S. Army, Ft. Sam Houston, Tex., 1974-77; ret. U.S. Army, 1977; extension agt. mktg. Colo. State U., Delta, 1977-88; acting area extension dir. Colo. State U., Grand Junction, 1988-89; chmn. dist. conf. Colo. State U., Glenwood Springs, 1970-88. Facilitator, Gov.'s Agrl. Rural Econ. Devel. Com., Grand Junction, 1987. Decorated Legion of Merit with oak leaf cluster, Bronze Star, Air medal. Mem. Retired Officers Assn., Assn. County Agrl. Agts., Am. Legion, Western Colo. Horticultural Soc., Rotary, Masons. Democrat. Episcopalian. Home: 678 1900 Rd Delta CO 81416 Office: Colo State U Courthouse Annex 6th and Dodge Sts Delta CO 81416

HARRINGTON, HELEN CAROLYN, librarian; b. Basin, Wyo., Jan. 29, 1927; d. Charles Lamb and Helen Orr (Dyer) Brome; m. Jack William Harrington, Aug. 26, 1948; children: John Charles, Thomas Warren, Susan Kay. BS, U. Wyo., 1969; MLS, U. Denver, 1973. Librarian Big Horn County Library, Basin, 1947-48; tchr. Washakie County (Wyo.) Sch. Dist., Worland, 1969-71, librarian, 1971—. Author: (annotated bibliography) Middle Sch. Reading, 1986. Trustee Washakie County Library, 1954-63; den mother Worland council Cub Scouts Am., 1957-64; dir. Girl Scout Day Camp, Worland, 1965-66. Mem. NEA, ALA, Wyo. Library Assn. (sch. library chmn. 1975-76, Librarian of Yr. 1987), Internat. Reading Assn., Washakie County Reading Council (chmn. various coms.). Republican. Methodist. Club: PEO Sisterhood (pres. Worland chpt. 1960, 65, 73). Office: Worland Middle Sch 1200 Culbertson Worland WY 82401

HARRINGTON, J. B., preacher, counselor; b. Weatherford, Tex., Aug. 30, 1930; s. Joe Boyd and Ida Mae (Galbreaith) H.; m. Ruth Lenora Ferguson, Dec. 21, 1954; children: Lisa, Boyd, Alan, Dale, Elyn. BA, Abilene Christian Coll., 1950. Preacher Ch. of Christ, Texhoma, Okla., 1951-53, Elkhart, Kans., 1953-55, Loveland, Colo., 1955-63, Farmington, N. Mex., 1963-71, Big Spring, Tex., 1971-74, Albany, Tex., 1974-75, Los Alamos, N. Mex., 1975—. Mem. Kiwanis (Los Alamos pres. 1986-87), Toastmasters (Los Alamos pres. 1984). Republican. Home & Office: PO Box 918 Los Alamos NM 87544

HARRINGTON, JOHN LEONARD, JR., hospital administrator; b. Pitts., Feb. 1, 1955; s. John Leonard and Marilyn (Rice) H.; m. Krisann Jacobs, May 31, 1980 (div. July 1987); m. Coleen Christine Attanucci, Dec. 31, 1988; children: Jennifer Lynne, Zachary Scott Dyer. BS magna cum laude, U. Pitts., 1977, MPH, 1980. Adminstrv. resident Phoenix Gen. Hosp., 1979-80, asst. v.p., 1980-83; asst. adminstr. Good Samaritan Med. Ctr., 1983-85, assoc. adminstr., 1985-89; assoc. adminstr. Thunderbird Samaritan Med. Ctr., Glendale, Ariz., 1989—. Mem. Ariz. Sr. Olympics Steering Com., Phoenix, 1983—, chmn., 1988-89, bd. dirs. 1989—; mem. planning com. of bd. YMCA, Phoenix, 1988-89. Mem. Health Adminstrs. Forum Ariz. (sec.-treas. 1983, pres. 1984), Am. Coll. Healthcare Execs. (regents adv. com. 1984—, Fache fellow, 1989), Ariz. Hosp. Assn. Republican. Roman Catholic. Home: 433 E Tierra Buena Dr Phoenix AZ 85022 Office: Thunderbird Samaritan Med Ctr 5555 W Thunderbird Rd Glendale AZ 85306

HARRINGTON, LAMAR, curator, visual arts administrator; b. Guthrie Center, Iowa, Nov. 2, 1917; d. Arthur Sylvester and Anna Mary (Landkamer) Hannes; m. Stanley John Harrington, 1938 (div. 1972); 1 dau., Linda Harrington Chace. Student music, Cornish Sch. Fine Arts, Seattle, 1945-50; B.A. in History of Art, U. Wash., 1979. Mem. staff Henry Art Gallery, U. Wash., Seattle, 1957-75; assoc. dir. Henry Art Gallery, U. Wash., 1969-75; curator, research assoc. Archives Northwest Art, U. Wash. Libraries, 1975-77; dir., chief curator Bellevue Art Mus., Wash., 1985—; cons. in arts 1977—; mem. panel visual arts div. Nat. Endowment Arts, 1976-78; pres. Western Assn. Art Museums, 1973-75; trustee Pacific Northwest Arts Center, 1971-74; exec. com. Pacific Northwest Arts Council of Seattle Art Mus., 1976, mem. steering com. photography council, 1977-78; v.p. Pottery Northwest, 1977-78; participant 1st Symposium on Scholarship and Lang., Nat. Endowments for Humanities and Arts, 1981; mem. adv. com. N.W. Oral History Project, Archives Am. Art, 1981; trustee, chmn. archives Pilchuck Glass Sch., 1981-87, Internat. Council, 1987—; Santa Fe Chamber Music Festival, 1981-87, Puget Sound Chamber Music Soc., 1987-88; lectr. in field, organizer exhbns., leader seminars, mem. art juries, appearances on TV, 1963—. Author: Ceramics in the Pacific Northwest: A History, 1979, Washington Craft Forms: an Historical Perspective, 1981; founder: Archives of Northwest Art, U. Wash., 1969, Index of Art in Pacific Northwest, U. Wash. Press, 1970; curator Third Wyoming Biennial Exhbn., 1988-89, James W. Washington Jr.: The Spirit in the Stone Bellevue Art Mus., 1989; resident curator, mgr. Frank Lloyd Wright: In the Realm of Ideas Bellevue Art Mus., 1989. Recipient Gov. Wash. Art award, 1989, Gov. Writer's award, 1980, Friends of Crafts award Seattle, 1972, Woman of Achievement award Women in Communications, 1974, Arts Service award King County Arts Commn., 1987. Hon. fellow Am. Crafts Council; mem. Am. Assn. Museums, Pacific Northwest Arts and Crafts Assn. (pres. 1957-59), Allied Arts Seattle (trustee 1962-81), Japan-Am. Soc. Wash. (trustee 1986-88). Office: 511 Galer St Seattle WA 98109

HARRINGTON, RODNEY ELBERT, biochemist, educator; b. Mayville, N.D., Jan. 9, 1932; s. Elbert W. and Marjorie (Mayberry) H.; m. June 6, 1953 (div.); children: Tiffany Anne, Jennifer Ellen; m. Ilga Butefis, Jan. 26, 1979. BA, U. S.D., 1953; PhD, U. Wash., Seattle, 1960. Rsch. assoc. chemist U. Calif.-San Diego, La Jolla, 1960-62; asst. prof. chemistry U. Ariz., Tucson, 1962-64; asst. prof. chemistry U. Calif., Davis, 1964-68, assoc. prof. chemistry, 1968-72, prof. chemistry, 1972; prof., chmn. chemistry dept. U. Nev., Reno, 1972-82, prof. biochemistry, 1982—. Bd. dirs. Reno Opera Co., 1973-77. NIH and NSF grantee, 1962—. Mem. Am. Chem. Soc., Am. Med. Soc., Biophys. Soc., Am. Soc. for Biochemistry and Molecular Biology, Phi Beta Kappa. Lutheran. Office: U Nev Dept Biochemistry Reno NV 98557

HARRINGTON, THOMAS LLOYD, psychologist, educator; b. Kalispell, Mont., Dec. 30, 1933; s. Charles John and Leona Lois (Tidrick) H.; m. Marcia Sheila Keilson, Nov. 4, 1959; 1 child, Leslie Sheryl. BA, U. Mont., 1959; MA, U. Oreg., 1965, PhD, 1967; postgrad., Johns Hopkins U., 1968. Postdoctoral fellow Johns Hopkins U., Balt., 1967-69; scientist Tokyo Met. Inst. for Neuroscis., 1979; sr. scientist dept. physiology Melbourne (Australia) U. Med. Sch., 1979; Scass fellow Swedish Collegium Advanced Study, Uppsala, 1987; sr. rsch. scientist Hong Kong U., 1987; rsch. fellow psychology Victoria U., Wellington, New Zealand, 1988; prof. psychology U. Nev., Reno, 1969—; cons. in field. Contbr. articles to profl. jours. Served with U.S. Army, 1954-56. Naval Rsch. grantee, 1980, NASA grantee, 1985—. Mem. AAAS, NSEA, Human Factors Soc., Sigma Xi. Home: 4715 Mayberry Dr Reno NV 89509

HARRINGTON, WALTER HOWARD, JR., municipal judge; b. San Francisco, Aug. 14, 1926; s. Walter Howard and Doris Ellen (Daniels) H.; B.S., Stanford, 1947; J.D., Hastings Coll., U. Calif., 1952; m. Barbara Bryant, June 1952 (div. 1973); children—Stacey Doreen, Sara Duval; m. 2d, Hertha Bahrs, Sept. 1974. Admitted to Calif. bar, 1953; dep. legislative counsel State of Calif., Sacramento, 1953-54, 55; mem. firm Walner & Harrington, Sacramento, 1954; dep. dist. atty. San Mateo County, Redwood City, Calif., 1955-62; asso. firm Wagstaffe, Daba & Hulse, Redwood City, 1962-67; practiced in Redwood City, 1967-84; judge San Mateo County Mcpl. Ct., 1984—. Chmn., San Mateo County Criminal Justice Council, 1971-76, San Mateo County Adult Correctional Facilities Com., 1969-71; pro tem referee San Mateo County Juvenile Ct., 1967-72. Served as ensign USNR, 1944-46. Mem. San Mateo County Bar Assn. (pres. 1969, editor publs. 1964-74), State Bar Calif. (editorial bd. 1968-81, vice chmn. 1969, 74-75, chmn., editor 1975-76), San Mateo County Legal Aid Soc. (pres. 1971-72), Order of Coif, Delta Theta Phi. Republican. Episcopalian. Office: Courthouse 750 Middlefield Rd PO Box 1064 Redwood City CA 94064

HARRINGTON-LLOYD, JEANNE LEIGH, interior designer; b. L.A., Sept. 24, 1946; d. Peter Valentine and Avis Lorraine (Brown) Harrington; m. James Wilkinson, Dec. 17, 1966 (div. Mar. 1976); m. David Lloyd, Nov. 27, 1985. BS in Psychology, U. Utah, 1984; cert., Salt Lake Sch. Interior Design, 1985. With Mary Webb-Davis Agy., L.A., 1970; model, actress McCarty Agy., Salt Lake City, 1983-85; contract designer Innerspace Design, Salt Lake City, 1985—. Democrat. Home: 1082 S 500 East Salt Lake City UT 84105

HARRIS, ANDREW VAN VLEET, JR., nuclear submarine officer; b. Seattle, Oct. 14, 1953; s. Andrew Van Vleet and Kathleen Elizabeth (Billings) H.; m. Mary Elizabeth Tucker, June 21, 1975; children: Michael, Kathleen. BS in Physics, U. Wash., 1975; student, Naval Nuclear Power Sch., Mare Island, Calif., 1975-76. Cert. nuclear submarine commander. Commd. ensign USN, 1975, advanced through grades to lt. comdr., 1984; div. officer USS Kamehameha, Groton, Conn., 1976-79; navigator USS Haddo, San Diego, 1982-86; staff instr. Naval Submarine Sch., Groton, 1979-82, Trident Tng. Facility, Bangor, Bremerton, Wash., 1986-88; exec. officer USS Mich., Bangor, Wash., 1988—. Mem. U.S. Naval Inst. Republican. Episcopalian. Office: USS Mich (SSBN727) (Blue) FPO Seattle Bangor WA 98799-2097

HARRIS, BARBARA HULL (MRS. F. CHANDLER HARRIS), social agency administrator; b. Los Angeles, Nov. 1, 1921; d. Hamilton and Marion (Eimers) Baird; student UCLA, 1939-41, 45-47; m. F. Chandler Harris, Aug. 10, 1946; children—Victoria, Randolph Boyd. Pres., Victoria Originals, 1955-62; partner J.B. Assos., cons., 1971-73; statewide dir. vols. Children's Home Soc. Calif., 1971-75. Los Angeles County Heart Sunday chmn. Los Angeles County Heart Assn. (recipient Outstanding Service award 1965), 1965, bd. dirs., 1966-69; mem. exec. com. Hollywood Bowl Vols., 1966-84, chmn. vols., 1971, 75; chmn. Coll. Alumni of Assistance League, 1962; mem. exec. com. Assistance League So. Calif., 1964-71, 72-80, 83—, pres., 1976-80; bd. dirs. Nat. Charity League, Los Angeles, 1965-69, 75, sec., 1967, 3d v.p., 1968; ways and means chmn., dir. Los Angeles Am. Horse Show, 1969; dir. Coronet Debutante Ball, 1968, ball bd. chmn., 1969-70, 75, 84, mem. ball bd., 1969—; pres. Hollywood Bowl Patroness com., 1976; v.p. Irving Walker aux. Travelers Aid, 1976, 79, pres., 1988-89; pres. So. Calif. alumni council Alpha Phi, 1961, fin. adviser to chpts. U. So. Calif., 1961-72, UCLA, 1965-72; benefit chmn. Gold Shield, 1969, 1st v.p., 1970-72; chmn. Golden Thimble III Needlework Exhbn., Hosp. of Good Samaritan, 1975; bd. dirs. UCLA Affiliates, 1976-78, KCET Women's Council, 1979-83, Region V United Way, 1980-83; pres. Jr. Philharmonic Com., 1981-82; bd. dirs. Los Angeles Founder chpt. Achievement Rewards for Coll. Scientists, 1980—, pres., 1984-85. Recipient Ivy award as outstanding Alpha Phi alumna So. Calif., 1969; outstanding alumni award for community service UCLA, 1978; Mannequin's Eve award, 1980. Mem. Hollywood C. of C. (dir. 1980-81). Home: 7774 Skyhill Dr Hollywood CA 90068

HARRIS, BRUCE ALLYN, data processing executive; b. Bklyn., Mar. 3, 1955; s. Martin J. and Marge (Vegh) H. Student, U. Bergen, Norway; BA in Social Ecology, U. Calif., Irvine, 1976, MS in Adminstrn., 1978. Dir. installation Profl. Health Services, Los Angeles, 1978-80; rep. client service McDonnell Douglas, Palo Alto, Calif., 1980, sr. client service rep., 1980-84; hosp. fin. specialist McDonnell Douglas, Santa Clara, Calif., 1984-85, account mgr., 1985-86; dir. data processing Good Samaritan Hosp., San Jose, Calif., 1986—; bd. dirs., v.p. McDonnell Douglas HFC User Group, Hayward, Calif., 1986-87. Mem. Hosp. Fin. Mgmt. Assn., Alvarado Village Homeowners Assn. (bd. dirs., v.p. 1986—). Republican.

HARRIS, DALE RAY, lawyer; b. Crab Orchard, Ill., May 11, 1937; s. Ray B. and Aurelia M. (Davis) H.; m. Toni K. Shapkoff, June 26, 1960; children—Kristen Dee, Julie Diane. BA in Math., U. Colo., 1959; LLB, Harvard U., 1962. Bar: Colo. 1962, U.S. Dist. Ct. Colo. 1962, U.S. Ct. Appeals (10th cir.) 1962, U.S. Supreme Ct. 1981. Assoc. Davis, Graham & Stubbs, Denver, 1962-67, ptnr., 1967—, chmn. mgmt. com., 1982-85; speaker, instr. various antitrust seminars. Mem. cabinet Mile High United Way campaign, 1986-87, chmn., atty. adv. com., 1988, sec., legal counsel, bd. trustees Mile High United Way, 1989—; mem. devel. council U. Colo. Arts and Scis. dept., 1985—; trustee The Spaceship Earth Fund, 1986-89; area chmn. law sch. fund Harvard U., 1978-81. With USAR, 1962-68. Fellow Am. Bar Found.; mem. Colo. Bar Assn. (chmn. antitrust com. 1980-84; coun. corp. banking and bus. law sect. 1978-83), Denver Bar Assn., Colo. Assn. Corp. Counsel (pres. 1973-74), Denver Law Club (pres. 1976-77), Phi Beta Kappa, Univ. Club, Union League Club (Chgo.), Rotary (Denver). Home: 2032 Bellaire St Denver CO 80207 Office: Davis Graham & Stubbs 370 17th St PO Box 185 Denver CO 80201

HARRIS, DEBRA CORAL, physical education teacher; b. Portland, Oreg., Feb. 4, 1953; d. Raymond Dale and Kathleen Caroline (Himpel) H. AA, Cen. Oreg. Community Coll., 1974; BS in Health and Phys. Edn., So. Oreg. State Coll., 1976, MST in Health Edn., 1982. Tchr. phys. edn., coach Franklin High Sch., Portland, 1976-79; instr. health, phys. edn., tennis coach Mt. Hood Community Coll., Gresham, Oreg., 1979-80; health and phys. edn. specialist, coach Inza R. Wood Middle Sch., Wilsonville, Oreg., 1980-86; tchr. health and phys. edn. West Linn (Oreg.)High Sch., 1986—; mem. planning com. SeasideHealth Conf., Oreg. Dept. Edn., 1985-87; writer AIDS curriculum, 1987-88; cons. health edn. textbooks Holt, Reinhart & Winston, N.Y.C., 1987-88. Mem. AIDS subcom. ARC, Portland, 1988—, safety svcs. com. 1988—, sex edn. coalition com. Planned Parenthood, Portland, 1988—, com. women's sport leadership network U. Oreg., Eugene, 1988—. Recipient Vol. of Month award ARC, 1984, Profl. Leadership award Oreg. Gov's. Coun. for Health Phys. Edn. Fitness & Sport, 1986, Outstanding Health/Phy. Edn. award Portland State U., 1988. Mem. Am. Alliance Health, Phys. Edn., Recreation & Dance (nat. pub. affairs & legis. com. 1987—), Oreg. Alliance Health, Phys. Edn., Recreation & Dance (pres. 1984-85), Oreg. Assn. Advanced Health Edn. (pres. 1987-89), AAUW, Oreg. Edn. Assn. (uniserv treas. 1985-86), Kappa Delta Pi. Home: 8315 SE Mill St Portland OR 97216 Office: West Linn High Sch 5464 West A St West Linn OR 97068

HARRIS, EDWARD A., producer, writer, director; b. Elizabeth, N.J., Dec. 14, 1946; s. Howard E. and Bernice W. Harris; m. Chris Garrison, May 16, 1987. Student music composition and theory, U. Okla., 1964-67, Los Angeles Community Coll., 1977, UCLA, 1978. Singer, songwriter, 1962—; pres., exec. producer Myriad Prodns., Los Angeles, 1965—; creative dir. Myriad Graphics, Los Angeles, 1976—; producer, assoc. dir. Columbia Music Hall, Hartford, Conn., 1972-75; film and TV producer, 1971—; multi-media entertainment cons., Los Angeles, 1977—; field producer Good Morning Am., also Good Night Am., ABC-TV, 1975-77; exec. producer, dir. The Act Factory, Los Angeles, 1977-83; sr. ptnr. Myriad-Fritz Prodns., Los Angeles, 1977-83; v.p. Sports Prodns., Am. Videogram, Inc., Los Angeles, 1986-87; ptnr. Myriad/Knox Prodns., Los Angeles, 1987—, H-two-O Prodns., L.A., 1987—; exec. producer Gateway Group, San Francisco, 1974-75; dir. Performance Evaluation Workshop, Los Angeles Songwriter's Expo, 1978-83; co-dir. SPVA Performing Arts Workshop, Los Angeles, 1980. Composer over 30 songs; producer: (TV sports mag.) The Clubhouse, 1982—, (TV show) Boating World, ESPN, 1987—. Pres. Wintonbury Mall Mchts. Assn., Bloomfield, Conn., 1971-72. Mem. Am. Fedn. Musicians, AGVA, Soc. for Preservation of Variety Arts, Alpha Epsilon Pi, Kappa Kappa Psi.

HARRIS, EILEEN LEEPER, interior designer, consultant; b. Akron, Ohio, Aug. 4, 1941; d. Morton Samuel and C. Leeper; children: Deborah Anne, Tamara Lynn. Student, Ohio State U., 1959-61; BFA cum laude, Ariz. State U., 1977. Freelance designer Scottsdale, Ariz., 1973-78; interior designer Roche Bobois, Scottsdale, 1978-79; prin. Eileen Harris Art & Design Cons., Scottsdale, 1979—; tchr. art in high schs., jr. colls.; motion picture and TV film prodn. and set design John White Prodns., 1978; set decorator TV commls. E.A.T.S., Inc. for Madison, Coleman Muyskins, N.Y.C., 1978; prodn. coordinator, set designer TV commls. Madison, Muyskins, Jones, N.Y.C., 1980. Exhibited art at Scottsdale Ctr. for Arts, 1974-77, Ariz. State U., 1974-77; author monthly column Phoenix Living Mag. Chmn. Phoenix Council for Soviet Jews, 1972; task force photo chmn. City of Phoenix Motion Picture Promotion Office, 1979—. Recipient 2d Place award in Drawing Ariz. State U. Juried Art Exhbn., 1976. Mem. Am. Soc. Interior Designers (assoc. mem. local bd. 1975), Scottsdale Assn. Merchants (bd. dirs. 1980-81). Republican. Office: 4305 N Brown Ave Scottsdale AZ 85251

HARRIS, EMMA EARL, nursing home executive; b. Viper, Ky., Nov. 6, 1936; d. Andrew Jackson and Zola (Hall) S.; m. Ret Haney Marten Henis Harris, June 5, 1981; children: Debra, Joseph, Wynona, Robert Walsh. Grad. St. Joseph Sch. Practical Nursing. Staff nurse St. Joseph Hosp., Bangor, Maine, 1973-75; office nurse Dr. Eugene Brown, Bangor, 1975-77; dir. nurses Fairborn Nursing Home, Ohio, 1977-78; staff nurse Hillhaven Hospice, Tucson, 1979-80; asst. head nurse, 1980; co-owner Nu-Life Elderly Guest Home, Tucson, 1980—. Vol. Heart Assn., Bangor, 1965-70, Cancer Assn., Bangor, 1965-70. Mem. NAFE, Assn. Sr. Resources (cons. 1983—). Democrat. Avocations: theatre; opera. Home: 1082 E Seneca Tucson AZ 85719

HARRIS, ERIC ALBERT, hardware engineer; b. Budapest, Hungary, Apr. 3, 1920; s. Victor Michael V. and Rela (Ettinger) Loewe H.; m. Nelly Chender, June 28, 1946 (div. 1961); 1 child, David Alan; m. Beatrix Sybil Berger, Sept. 29, 1967. BEE, UCLA, 1948; PhD in Nuclear Physics, U. Innsbruck, 1949. Engr. KMTR Corp., Hollywood, Calif., 1948-50; engr. TV CBS, Inc., N.Y.C., 1950-61; recording cons. CBS-TV, Munich, 1960-61; video mktg. mgr. AMPEX Corp., Fribourg, Switzerland, 1961-72; sr. engr. AMPEX Corp., Redwood City, Calif., 1980-83; cons. Mayo Clinic, Rochester, Minn., 1972-80; sr. software writer Gould Inc., Santa Clara, Calif., 1983-84; sr. systems engr. CAE/Tektronix, Santa Clara, Calif., 1984-87; cons. Eribea Assocs., Half Moon Bay, Calif., 1984—. Capt. OSS, 1943-46. Mem. IEEE, Computer Soc., Soc. Motion Picture and TV Engrs. Democrat. Jewish. Home and Office: 132 Ocean View Ave Half Moon Bay CA 94019

HARRIS, ERIC NATHAN, banker, marketing executive; b. Phoenix, Mar. 9, 1959; s. Edward Nathan and Barbara Lee (Kohler) H.; m. Janet Marie Houle, Apr. 26, 1986; 1 child, Elliot Nathan. BA cum laude in Econs., Whitman Coll., Walla Walla, Wash., 1981. Rsch. asst. John D. Herbert & Assocs., Phoenix, 1980, rsch. assoc., 1981-82; product devel. officer, corp. officer Valley Nat. Bank, Phoenix, 1982-84, product mgr., asst. v.p., 1984-87, sr. market mgr., asst. v.p., 1987—. Mem. Am. Inst. Banking (chmn. mktg. com. Ariz. 1987—), Phi Beta Kappa, Wiharu Toastmasters (pres. 1988—), Valley Tennis Assn. (rules com. 1987-88), Valley Bowling League, Phoenix Direct Mktg. Club. Republican. Episcopalian. Office: Valley Nat Bank 241 N Central Phoenix AZ 85004

HARRIS, ERNEST ALEXANDER, real estate developer; b. Hot Springs, Ark., July 29, 1939; s. Ernest Alexander and Hazel Jean (Sherman) H.; m. Shelly Kay Stadheim, June 6, 1961 (div. Aug. 1982); children: Mary Beth, John; m. Paula Mills Withrow, Jan. 19, 1986. BSCE, Oreg. State U., 1961. Registered profl. engr., Hawaii; lic. gen. contractor. Commd. USMC, 1961, advanced through grades to capt., 1966; with USMC, Vietnam, 1964, 66, 68; resigned USMC, 1969; supr. Hawaiian Dredging, Honolulu, 1969-74; v.p. Pacific Constrn. Co., Honolulu, 1974-78, The Lusk Co., Honolulu, 1978-87; pres. The Harris Co., Honolulu, 1987—. Decorated Bronze star, Purple Heart; recipient Presdl. Unit citation, Navy Commendation medal. Fellow ASCE; mem. Nat. Soc. Profl. Engrs., Oahu Country Club (chmn. structures), Vietnam Vets. Leadership Orgn. (bd. dirs. 1980-83). Republican. Office: The Harris Co 1605 Quincy Pl Honolulu HI 96816

HARRIS, F. CHANDLER, emeritus university administrator; b. Neligh, Nebr., Nov. 5, 1914; s. James Carlton and Helen Ayres (Boyd) H.; m. Barbara Ann Hull, Aug. 10, 1946; children: Victoria, Randolph Boyd. AB, UCLA, 1936. Assoc. editor Telegraph Delivery Spirit, Los Angeles, 1937-39; writer, pub. service network radio programs University Explorer, Sci. Editor, U. Calif., 1939-61; pub. information mgr. UCLA, 1961-75, dir., 1975-82, dir. emeritus, 1982—. Mem. pub. relations com., western region United Way, 1972-75; bd. dirs. Am. Youth Symphony, Los Angeles, 1978—, v.p., 1983—; bd. dirs. Hathaway Home for Children, 1982-88. Recipient 1st prize NBC Radio Inst., 1944; Harvey Hebert medal Delta Sigma Phi, 1947, Mr. Delta Sig award, 1972; Adam award Assistance League Mannequins, 1980, Univ. Service award UCLA Alumni Assn., 1986. Mem. Western Los Angeles Regional C. of C. (dir. 1976-80), U. Calif. Retirees Assn. Los Angeles (pres. 1985-87), Sigma Delta Chi, Delta Sigma Phi (nat. pres. 1959-63). Club: UCLA Faculty (sec. bd. govs. 1968-72). Editor Interfraternity Research Adv. Council Bull., 1949-50, Carnation, 1969-80, Royce Hall, 1985. Home: 7774 Skyhill Dr Hollywood CA 90068

HARRIS, GEORGE CLINTON, bishop; b. Dec. 19, 1925; s. Clinton George and Meta Grace (Werner) H.; m. Mary Jane Shotwell, June 27, 1953; 6 children. BSCE, Rutgers U., 1950, STB, Gen. Theol. Sem., N.Y.C., 1953, STM, 1970. Ordained to ministry Episcopal Ch. as deacon, 1953, as priest. Curate Heavenly Rest Ch., N.Y.C., 1953-55; chaplain Easter Sch.; asst. Epiphany Ch., Baguio City, The Philippines, 1956-57; priest-in-charge Mary Virgin Ch., Sagada, The Philippines, 1957-62; prin. St. Francis High Sch., Uti Cotabato, The Philippines, 1963-69; rector Lower Luzerne Parish, Hazelton, Pa., 1970-74; dir. Dakota Leadership Program, 1974-81; bishop Diocese of Alaska, Fairbanks, 1981—. Office: Box 441 Fairbanks AK 99707 *

HARRIS, GODFREY, public policy consultant; b. London, June 11, 1937; s. Alfred and Victoria H.; came to U.S., 1939, naturalized, 1945; BA with gt. distinction, Stanford U., 1958; MA (disting. mil. grad.), UCLA, 1960; m. Linda Berkowitz, Dec. 21, 1958 (div. 1982); m. Barbara DeKovner-Mayer, Nov. 5, 1984; children—Gregrey, Kennith, Mark. Fgn. svc. officer U.S. State Dept., Washington, Bonn, Fed. Republic of Germany and London, 1962-65; mgmt. analyst Office Mgmt. and Budget, Washington, 1965-67; spl. asst. to pres. IOS Devel. Co., Geneva, 1967-68; pres. Harris/Ragan Mgmt. Corp., L.A., 1968—; lectr. Rutgers U., 1960-61. Mem. adv. com. on gifted Santa Monica Unified Sch. Dist. (chmn. 1978-79); mem. L.A. World Affairs Coun., Town Hall L.A.; former W. Coast rep. Panamanian Export Promotion and Investment Devel. Ctr. 1st lt. U.S. Army, 1958-60. Decorated Commendation medal. Fellow Am. Acad. Cons.'s; mem. Assn. Mgmt. Cons.'s, Stanford U. Alumni Assn. (membership sec. N.Am. chpt.), London C. of C. and Industry. Democrat. Jewish. Author: History of Sandy Hook, N.J., 1961; (with F. Fielder) The Quest for Foreign Affairs Officers, 1966; Panama's Position, 1973; (with C. Sonabend) Commercial Translations, 1985; (with B. DeKovner-Mayer) From Trash to Treasure, 1985; (with K. Katz) Promoting International Tourism, 1986, The Panamanian Perspective, 1987, The Ultimate Black Book, 1988; founder, editor Almanac of World Leaders, 1957-62, Consultants Directory, 1975-76. Office: 9200 Sunset Blvd Los Angeles CA 90069

HARRIS, HARRIET LOUISE, teacher, real estate broker; b. Los Angeles, Sept. 19, 1950; d. Willie M. Jackson and Inez L. (Stephens) Reed; 1 child, Mieesha Latreessce. BA, Calif. State U., 1973, MA, 1980. Lic. real estate agt. Tchr., counselor Los Angeles Unified Sch. Dist., 1978—; real estate broker Jolly Escrow Realty, Inglewood, Calif., 1984—. Author booklets and teaching aids. Mem. Bus. Profl. Women, Calif. Assn. Adult Educators Membership, Women Educators, Los Angeles C. of C. Office: Israel Jolly Realty 2509 W Manchester Blvd Inglewood CA 90305

HARRIS, HELEN JOSEPHINE, foundation administrator; b. Phila.; d. John and Grace Melley; m. Robert Irvin Harris; children: Robert, Jim, Rich. Grad. high sch., Phila. Pres., founder Retinitis Pigmentosa Internat., Woodland Hills, Calif., 1973—; advisor Calif. Dept. Rehab., 1980-88; dir. Michael Maning Ministries, Inc., Calif., 1983—. Recipient Humanitarian award, Pierce Coll., Woodland Hills, 1984, Leadership award, YWCA, L.A., 1986. Mem. L.A. C. of C., Woodland Hills C. of C. Democrat. Roman Catholic. Office: RP Internat 5950 Canoga Ave #230 Woodland Hills CA 91367

HARRIS, HOWARD JEFFREY, marketing and printing company executive; b. Denver, June 9, 1949; s. Gerald Victor and Leona Lee (Tepper) H.; m. Michele Whealen, Feb. 6, 1975; children: Kimberly, Valerie. BFA with honors, Kansas City Art Inst., 1973; M. of Indsl. Design with honors, Pratt Inst., 1975; postgrad. Graphic Arts Research Center, Rochester Inst. Tech., 1977; cert. mktg. exec., U. Utah, 1987. Indsl. designer Kivett & Myers, Architects, 1970-71; indsl. designer United Research Corp., Denver, 1971-72; indsl. designer, asst. to v.p., pres. JFN Assos., N.Y.C., 1972-73; dir. facility planning Abt & Assos., Cambridge, Mass., 1973-74; v.p. design, prodn., and research Eagle Lithographics, Denver, 1974—; pres. HSR Corp., Denver. Bd. dirs. Friends of C. Henry Kemp Ctr., Denver. Mem. Indsl. Designers Soc. Am., Graphic Arts Tech. Found., Design Methods Group, The Color Group, Nat. Assn. Counsel for Children, Am. Advt. Fedn. Democrat. Jewish. Office: 5105 E 41st Ave Denver CO 80216

HARRIS, JAMES HOWARD, small business owner; b. St. Paul, Oct. 31, 1952; s. Robert Charles and Dorothy Harriet (Greenagle) H.; m. Debra Lee Berke, Dec. 2, 1972; children: Andrea, Evan, Nathan. Parts runner, daily rental mgr. United Truck Leasing, Mpls., 1972-75; with sales dept. Gelco Truck Leasing, St. Paul, 1975-79; asst. dist. mgr. Gelco Truck Leasing, St. Louis, 1979-81; dist. mgr. Gelco Truck Leasing, Denver, 1981-86; owner, operator Colo. Nationalease, Denver, 1987—. Active Citizens Budget COm. Arapahoe County, Littleton, Colo., 1986—. Office: Colo Nationalease 17751 E Colfax Aurora CO 80011

HARRIS, JAMES STEWART, JR., engineering educator, researcher; b. Portland, Oreg., Aug. 22, 1942; s. James Stewart and Jane Ann (Gordon) H.; m. Joyce Emelyn Christensen, June 12, 1965; children: Geoffrey Stuart, Gregory Alan. BS, Stanford U., 1964, MS, 1965, PhD, 1969. Mem. tech. staff Rockwell Internat., Thousand Oaks, Calif., 1969-73, mgr. infrared devices, 1973-79, prin. scientist, 1979-81, dir. optoelectronics, 1981-82; prof. elec. engring. Stanford (Calif.) U., 1982—, dir. solid state lab., 1984—; cons. Varian Assocs., Palo Alto, Calif., 1982—, NRC, Washington, 1980, 85, Citicorp., N.Y.C., 1988—. Author: International Conference on GaAs, 1976, 78, 80, 82; contbr. articles to profl. jours.; patentee in field. Scoutmaster Boy Scouts Am., Palo Alto, 1982-88; coach Am. Youth Soccer Orgn., Palo Alto, 1980—. Recipient Terman Engring. award Stanford U., 1964; Tektronix fellow Stanford U., 1965-66. Fellow IEEE (mem. exec. com. 1980—); mem. Electrochem. Soc. (editor jour. 1978-86), Am. Phys. Soc., Am. Vacuum Soc., Materials Rsch. Soc., Union Concerned Scientists, Fedn. Am. Scientists, Physicians for Social Responsibility. Mem. United Ch. Christ. Home: 763 Esplanada Way Stanford CA 94305 Office: Solid State Electronics Lab McCullough 224 Stanford CA 94305

HARRIS, JOE NEWTON, naval officer; b. Konawa, Okla., June 7, 1946; s. George William and Oberia Mae (Sanders) H.; m. Tacy Lynn Cook, Nov. 2l, 1983; 1 child, Cassandra Simone. BA, Duke U., 1968; MBA, Nat. U., 1975; MS, Naval Postgrad. Sch., Monterey, Calif., 1979. Commd. ensign USN, 1968, advanced through grades to comdr., 1983; avionics officer E-2 Aircraft Squadron, San Diego, 1970-73, head ops. dept., 1980-82; contract monitoring officer Fleet Combat Direction Systems, San Diego, 1973-76; tactical data systems officer USS Enterprise, Alameda, Calif., 1976-78; mem. staff Naval Postgrad. Sch., 1978-80, 82-84, mem. faculty, 1982-84; program mgr. Security Assistance Acctg., Denver, 1984-88; fin. compt. Naval Air Sta. Miramar, San Diego, 1988—. Treas. Navy Relief Aux., 1988—. Decorated Air medal with six oak leaf clusters. Mem. Am. Soc. Mil. Compts. (pres. San Diego chpt. 1989—), Delta Sigma Phi. Home: 933 Tarento Dr San Diego CA 92106 Office: Naval Air Sta Miramar Code 100 San Diego CA 92145

HARRIS, JOHN FRANKLIN, architect; b. Pomona, Calif., Apr. 10, 1941; s. H. L. and Frances I. (Cooper) H.; m. Donna Sue Hayes; children: Michael Leroy, Vicki Lynn. Lic. architect; lic. gen. contractor. Project mgr. William P. Ficker, AIA, Newport Beach, Calif., 1970; project mgr., coordinator Griffin & Banks Architects, AIA, Buena Park, Calif., 1971-72, Willdan Engring. Assocs., Anaheim, Calif., 1972-74; project architect Rolly Pulaski Architect, AIA, Newport Beach, Calif., 1974-76; prin. John F. Harris Architect, AIA, Placentia, Irvine, Calif., 1976-79, Irvine, 1976—; project mgr., chief architect The Austin Co., Irvine, Calif., 1979-83; project mgr., estimator Carpenter & Smallwood, West Los Angeles, Calif., 1983-84, AHL Constrn. Co., Inc., Pismo Beach, Calif., 1984-88, Marathon Enterprises, South Gate, Calif., 1988—. Architect, Redevel. Agy., City of Anaheim, 1978; archtl. chmn. Winnwood Homeowners Assn., Santa Ana, Calif., 1976-80, pres., 1976-80. Mem. AIA (coms.). Office: 4521 Campus Dr Ste 519 Irvine CA 92715

HARRIS, JOHN WALTER, administration manager, training specialist; b. Petersburg, Va., Jan. 16, 1925; s. William Hodges Harris Sr. and Mable Elizabeth (Thompson) H.; m. India Martin (div. July 15, 1954); 1 child, Orban Dale; m. Cynthia Joy Carruthers, June 4, 1960; children: Ronald C. and Cyndy J. BS, NYU, 1049, MA, 1957; MS, U. So. Calif., Los Angeles, 1971. Cert. tchr., Calif. Acct. Patrow Transmission Co., N.Y.C., 1947-51; tchr., adminstr. Clark Coll., Atlanta, 1951-60; asst. bus. mgr. Los Angeles Trade Tech. Coll., 1960—; tng. specialist Hughes Aircraft Co., El Segundo, Calif., 1962-68, head tng., 1969-71, prodn. line mgr., 1971-78, mgr. support materials processing dept., 1979—. Served to cpl. USMC, 1943-45, PTO. Mem. Alpha Phi Alpha, Am. Soc. for Tng. and Devel. Democrat. Club: Hughes Mgmt. (bd. dirs. 1974-75). Home: 4236 Terraza Dr Los Angeles CA 90008 Office: Radar Systems Group PO Box 92426 Bldg RC R50 MS 1607B Los Angeles CA 90009

HARRIS, JONATHAN, actor; b. N.Y.C., Nov. 6, 1919; s. Sam and Jennie (Parker) H.; m. Gertrude Bregman, June 19, 1938; 1 child, Richard. PhG, Fordham U., 1937. Appeared in Broadway plays The Heart of a City, 1942, Madwoman of Challot, Teahouse of the August Moon, many others; appeared in live TV programs Studio One, Pulitzer Prize Playhouse, Omnibus, U.S. Steel Hour, many others, TV series The Third Man, The Dana Show, Battlestar Galactica, Lost in Space, Space Acad., many others; films include Botany Bay, 1957, The Big Fisherman, Catch Me If You Can; appeared in many TV films, commls., cartoon and animated series. Recipient Outstanding TV Performance award Acad. Sci. Fiction, Fantasy and Horror Films, 1977. Democrat.

HARRIS, JUDY GILLIS, financial analyst; b. Miami, Sept. 5, 1945; d. Avery Eugene and Mary Ellen Latonia (Watson) Gillis; m. Douglas Iven Harris, June 9, 1963; children: Steven Douglas, Nora Diane. Grad. high sch., Homestead, Fla. Clk. Pacific Bell Telephone, Sacramento, 1964-67; service sta. attendant Harris Shell, Roseville, Calif., 1968-74; tax profl. J. Harris Tax Service and Fin. Mgmt. Systems, Inc., Roseville, 1974—; singer various rock groups, Sacramento, 1968-71; musician Leni and Judy, Roseville, 1974-85. Mem. Nat. Fed. of Ind. Bus., Nat. Assn. Enrolled Agts., Calif. Soc. Enrolled Agts., Roseville C. of C., Citrus Heights C. of C., MENSA. Republican. Baptist. Home: 8385 Cook Riolo Rd Roseville CA 95678 Office: J Harris Tax Svc Inc 735 Sunrise Ave #115 Roseville CA 95661

HARRIS, MALCOLM STEPHEN, lawyer, publisher; b. Long Beach, Calif., June 10, 1943; s. Norman Clifton and Dorothy Pauline (Dodgen) H.; m. Karen Kristine Nordquist, Nov. 26, 1977; children: Spencer Phillip, Stephanie Marie. BA, Yale U., 1965; JD, U. Mich., 1972. Bar: Wash. 1972, U.S. Dist. Ct. Appeals (9th cir.) 1975, U.S. Supreme Ct. 1988. Assoc. Preston, Thorgrimson, Ellis & Holman, Seattle, 1972-76; ptnr. Harris, Orr & Wakayama, Seattle, 1980—; owner Parkside Publs. Dir. Separation and Loss Inst., Seattle, 1983—. Lt. USNR, 1965-69. Mem. ABA, Wash. State Bar Assn., Wash. Athletic Club, Columbia Tower Club. Office: Harris Orr & Wakayama 999 3d Ave #3210 Seattle WA 98104

HARRIS, MICHAEL GENE, optometrist, educator, lawyer; b. San Francisco, Sept. 20, 1942; s. Morry and Gertrude Alice (Epstein) H.; B.S., U. Calif., 1964, M. Optometry, 1965, D. Optometry, 1966, M.S., 1968; J.D., John F. Kennedy U., 1985; m. Andrea Elaine Berman, Nov. 29, 1969; children—Matthew Benjamin, Daniel Evan. Bar: Calif., U.S. Dist. Ct. (no. dist.) Calif. Assoc. practice optometry, Oakland, Calif., 1965-66, San Francisco, 1966-68; instr., coordinator contact lens clinic Ohio State U., 1968-69; asst. clin. prof. optometry U. Calif., Berkeley, 1969-73, dir. contact lens extended care clinic, 1969-83, chief contact lens clinic, 1983—, assoc. clin. prof., 1973-76, asst. chief contact lens service, 1970-76, assoc. chief contact lens service, 1976—, lectr., 1978-80, sr. lectr., 1980—, vice chmn. faculty Sch. Optometry, 1983-85, prof. clin. optometry, 1984-86; clin. prof. optometry, 1986—; John de Carle vis. prof. City U., London, 1984; pvt. practice optometry, Oakland, Calif., 1973-76; lectr., cons. in field; mem. regulation rev. com. Calif. State Bd. Optometry; cons. hypnosis Calif. Optometric Assn., Am. Optometric Assn.; cons. Nat. Bd. Examiners in Optometry, Soflens div. Bausch & Lomb, 1973—, Barnes-Hind Hydrocurve Soft Lenses, Inc., 1974-87, Sola-Barnes Hind, 1987—, Contact Lens Research Lab., 1976—, Wesley-Jessen Contact Lens Co., 1977—, Palo Alto VA, 1980—, Primarius Corp., Cooper Vision Optics Alcon, 1980—; co-founder Morton D. Sarver Research Lab., 1986; Planning commr. Town of Moraga, Calif., 1986, vice-chmn., 1987-88, chmn. 1988—; founding mem. Young Adults div. Jewish Welfare Fedn., 1965—, chmn. 1967-68; commr. Sunday Football League, Contra Costa County, Calif., 1974-78. Charter Mem. Jewish Community Ctr. Contra Costa County; founding mem. Jewish Community Mus. San Francisco, 1984; Para-Rabbinic, Temple Isaiah, Lafayette, Calif., 1987; life mem. Bay Area Council for Soviet Jews, 1976; bd. dirs. Jewish Community Relations Council of Greater East Bay, 1979—, Campolindo Homeowners Assn., 1981—; pres. student council John F. Kennedy U. Sch. Law, 1984-85. Fellow U. Calif., 1971; Calif. Optometric Assn. Scholar 1965, George Schneider Meml. scholar, 1964. Fellow Am. Acad. Optometry (diplomate cornea and contact lens sect.; chmn. contact lens papers; mem. contact lens com. 1974—, vice chmn. contact lens sect. 1980-82, chmn. 1982-84, immediate past chmn. 84-86, chmn. jud. com. 1989—, chmn. by-laws com. 1989—), Assn. Schs. and Colls. Optometry (council on acad. affairs), AAAS; mem. Assn. for Research in Vision and Ophthalmology, Am. Optometric Assn. (proctor 1969—, cons. on hypnosis, mem. contact lens sect.), Calif. Optometric Assn., Assn. Optometric Contact Lens Educators, Am. Optometric Found., Mexican Soc. Contactology (hon.), Nat. Council on Contact Lens Compliance, Internat. Soc. Contact Lens Research, Calif. State Bd. Optometry (regulation rev. com.), Calif. Acad. Scis., U. Calif. Optometry Alumni Assn. (life), ABA, Assn. Trial Lawyers Am., Calif. Trial Lawyers Assn., Calif. Young Lawyers Assn., Contra Costa Bar Assn., Mus. Soc., JFK U. Sch. Law Alumni Assn., Benjamin Ide Wheeler Soc. U. Calif., Mensa. Democrat. Lodge: B'nai B'rith. Editor current comments sect. Am. Jour. Optometry, 1974-77; editor Eye Contact, 1984-86, assoc. editor The Video Jour. Clin. Optometry, 1988—, consulting editor Contact Lens Spectrum, 1988—; contbr. chpts. to books; author various syllabuses; contbr. articles to profl. pubs. Home: 43 Corte Royal Moraga CA 94556 Office: U Calif Sch Optometry Berkeley CA 94720

HARRIS, NICK STEVEN, technical director; b. Chgo., June 2, 1942; s. Jack Morton and Miriam Janet (Heyman) H.; m. Aline Susan Kite, Aug. 15, 1965; children: Steven Jeffry, Craig Stuart. BS, U. Wis., 1964; MS, U. Ill., 1967, PhD, 1969; post doctoral, U. Minn., 1971. Diplomate Am. Bd. Med. Lab. Immunology. Asst. prof. surgery and human biol. chemistry and genetics U. Tex. Med., Galveston, Tex., 1971-76, assoc. prof. surgery and human biol. chemistry and genetics, 1976-78; chief, immunology and electron microscopy sects. Health Cen. Inst., Mpls., 1978-79; dir. dept. of immunology Bio-Sci. Labs., Van Nuys, Calif., 1979-83; dir. lab. svcs. Allergenetics Ref. Lab., Mountain View, Calif., 1983-84; tech. dir. Allergenetics div. Axonics, Inc. (now 3M, Inc.), Mountain View, Calif., 1983; tech. dir. 3M Diagnostic Systems, Inc., Mountain View, Calif., 1984—, dir. clin. studies program, 1985—, dir. lab. svcs., 1986—; cons. Kalestad, Mpls., 1969-71, Associated Biomedical, Buffalo, N.Y., 1972-73, El Paso (Tex.) Inst. for Med. Research, 1986—. Contbr. articles to profl. jours. and publs. Membership chmn. Bnai mina, Galveston, 1971-72; v.p. Jewish Welfare League, Galveston, 1972-73. U.S. Public Health Svc. Predoctoral fellowship U. Ill., 1964-65, 66-69, U. Minn., 1969-71; named Am. Men of Sci., 1969. Fellow Am. Coll. Allergists; mem. AAAS, AAUP, Am. Soc. Microbiologists, Am. BurnAssn., Reticuloendothelial Soc., Internat. Soc. for Experimental Hematology, Internat. Burn Assn., Am. Assn. of Immunology, Am. Assn. of Tissue Banks, Am. Assn. Clin. Immunology and Allergy, Am. Acad. of Allergy and Immunology, Am. Acad. of Otolaryngic Allergy, Clin. Immunology Soc., Transplantation Soc., Am. Assn. of Clin. Chemistry, Masons, Shriners, Sigma Xi. Republican. Jewish. Home: 12546 Miller Ave Saratoga CA 95070 Office: 3M Diagnostic Systems 3380 Central Expressway Santa Clara CA 95051

HARRIS, ROBERT G., economist, educator; b. Bryan, Ohio, Mar. 30, 1943; s. Gerald E. and Mary (Merillat) H.; m. Linda Kathleen Baxter, Mar. 29, 1969; children: Kirsten, Brandon. BA in Social Sci., Mich. State U., 1965, MA in Social Sci., 1973; MA in Econs., U. Calif., Berkeley, 1975, PhD in Econs., 1977. Rep. pub. rels. Gen. Motors Corp., Detroit, 1965-66; cons. pub. rels. Washington and N.Y.C., 1967-69; pres. Young Am. Corp., St. Louis, 1969-71; prof. bus. adminstrn. U. Calif., Berkeley, 1977—, chmn. bus. and pub. policy group Sch. Bus. Adminstrn., 1986—; dep. dir. Interstate Commerce Commn., Washington, 1980-81; pres. Econom Inc., Berkeley, 1981—. Contbr. numerous articles to profl. jours.; assoc. editor Calif. Mgmt. Rev., 1983—. Del. Mich. Dem. Conv., Lansing, 1972; mem. campaign staff Humphrey Presdl. Com., Washington, 1968, Rockefeller Presdl. Com., N.Y.C., 1968, Hatfield Senatorial Com., Salem, Oreg., 1966. Mem. Internat. Telecommunications Soc., Am. Econ. Assn., Strategic Mgmt. Soc. (chmn. internat. conf. 1988-89), Acad. Mgmt. Claremont Tennis Club, Squaw Ridge Homeowners Assn. Home: 2841 Forest Ave Berkeley CA 94705 Office: U Calif Sch Bus Adminstrn Berkeley CA 94720

HARRIS, ROBERT MYER, engineer; b. Dryden, Ont., Can., Dec. 15, 1935; came to U.S., 1955; s. Reginald Derwood and Martha Evelyn (Adair) H.; m. Louise Clare Peterson, Oct. 15, 1960; children: Alison Marie, Tracey Jo, Robert William, Lisa Joan. BS in Geolog. Engring., U. N.D., 1960. Reg. Control System Engr., Calif. Sales mgr. Fischer & Porter (Can.) Ltd., Toronto, 1960-68; regional mgr. Electronic Automation Systems, Inc., Beaverton, Oreg., 1968-71; v.p. sales Electronic Automation Systems, Inc., Grand Island, N.Y., 1971-72; v.p. mktg. Electronic & Electronic Assocs. (Can.), Toronto, 1972-73, asst. to pres., 1973-74; v.p. Harris Group, Inc. (formerly Schuchart & Assocs., Inc.), Seattle, 1975-80, pres., 1980-87, chmn. and chief exec. officer, 1987—. Exec. contact, United Way of King County, Seattle, 1988; bd. dirs. Evergreen Safety Council, Seattle, 1986-89. Mem. Tech. Assn. of Pulp and Paper Industry, Canadian Pulp and Paper Assn., Rainier Club, Wash. Athletic Club. Home: 16319 70th Pl W Edmonds WA 98020

HARRIS, SANDY ELLEN, retail executive; b. Hays, Kans., Jan. 28, 1956; d. Kenneth and Mabel (Owen) H.; m. Larry Ohmie (div. Aug. 1987); children: Brandon, Austin. Student, Career DEvel. Ctr., 1974, Colo. U., 1975; BS in Bus., Colo. U., 1979, BS in Mktg., 1979. Mgr. Zales Corp., Dallas, 1974-78; wholesale, import rep. Fine Lines, Denver, 1978-80; pres., chief exec. officer ACL, Inc., Denver, 1980-86, FFI, Inc., Boulder, Colo., 1986—; cons. sales Tindalls, Inc., Madeira Beach, Fla., 1988—. Authors: Manufacturing Processes, 1973, Marketing and Consumer Purchasing, 1974. Republican. Home: 1705 14th St #292 Boulder CO 80302

HARRIS, SIGMUND PAUL, physicist; b. Buffalo, Oct. 12, 1921; s. Nathan N. and Ida (Lebovitz) H.; m. Florence Katcoff, Sept. 19, 1948; 1 child, Roslyn (Mrs. Arnold Hurwitz). BA cum laude, SUNY, Buffalo, 1941, MA, 1943; postgrad., Yale U., 1943; PhD, Ill. Inst. Tech., 1954. Physicist Metall. Lab. U. Chgo., 1943-44; jr. scientist Los Alamos (N.Mex.) Nat. Lab., 1944-46; assoc. physicist Argonne Nat. Lab., Chgo., 1946-53; sr. physicist Tracer Lab., Inc., Boston, 1954-56; sr. research engr. Atomics Internat., Canoga Park, Calif., 1956-64; head physics sect. research div. Maremont Corp., Pasadena, Calif., 1964-66; from asst. prof. to full prof. L.A. Pierce Coll., Woodland Hills, Calif., 1966-86, prof. physics emeritus, 1986—; cons. Space Scis. Inc., Monrovia, Calif., 1968—. Author: Introduction to Air Pollution, 1973. Patentee method for measuring power level of nuclear reactor, apparatus for producing neutrons. Mem. Am. Nuclear Soc., Am. Assn. Physics Tchrs., Am. Phys. Soc., Phi Beta Kappa, Sigma Xi. Home: 5831 Saloma Ave Van Nuys CA 91411 Office: 6201 Winnetka Ave Woodland Hills CA 91371

HARRIS, WARREN EDWARD, restaurant company executive; b. Prescott, Ariz., Nov. 26, 1961; s. Edward Dean and Patricia Ann (Lambson) H.; m. Rowane Gail Parkes, Oct. 20, 1984. BS in Bus. Adminstrn., U. Ariz., 1986, postgrad. Karl Eller Ctr., 1986. Owner Prescott (Ariz.) Concessions, 1977-80; missionary Ch. of Jesus Christ of Latter-day Saints, 1981-83; dir. ops. Village Inn Pizza Parlors, Prescott, 1986—. Mem. Golden Key (life). Republican. Office: Village Inn Pizza Parlors 730 Miller Valley Rd PO Box 4371 Prescott AZ 86302

HARRIS, WILLIAM DAVID, aerospace engineer; b. Phila., July 26, 1933; s. Benjamin and Edith (Garfield) H.; (div. 1961); children: Jonathan M., Hilliary, Hugh R., Steven E. Student, Drexel U., 1951-52, 52-54, U.S. Naval Acad., 1952; BCE, U. Pa., 1956, MCE, 1959. Instr. U. Pa., Phila., 1956-59; supr. Vertol Div. Boeing Co., Ridley Park, Pa., 1959-62; supr. North Am. Aviation, Downey, Calif., 1962-64; chief of stress Vertol Div. Boeing Co., Ridley Park, 1964-71; staff engr. Fairchild Industries, Germantown, MD, 1971-72; group engr. Lockheed Calif. Co., Van Nuys, Calif., 1972; cons. Calspan Corp., El Segundo, Calif., 1972-73; lead engr. Rockwell Internat., Downey, 1973-74; dept. mgr. McDonnell Douglas Helicopter Co., Mesa, Ariz., 1974—; stress analyst various civil engring. cons. firms, Phila., 1954-59. Contbr. articles to profl. jours. Mem. Am. Helicopter Soc., Soc. of Allied Weight Engrs. Home: 9448 N 105th Pl Scottsdale AZ 85258 Office: McDonnell Douglas Helicopter Co 5000 E McDowell Rd Mesa AZ 85205

HARRIS, WILLIAM T., hydrologist, soil scientist; b. San Jose, Calif., Oct. 13, 1948; s. Harry William and Virginia Ann (Cirone) H.; m. Karen Jones, Sept. 27, 1975 (div. Sept. 1981); 1 child, Sara Ann. Student, U. Calif., Davis, 1973. With Ray's TV Lab., San Jose, 1966-68; tutor W. Valley Coll., San Jose, 1970-71; lab technician U. Calif., Davis, 1973; soil scientist SCS, 1973-77; hydrologist, soil scientist BLM, Shoshone, Idaho, 1977-88; pvt. practice San Jose, 1988—. Community developer Citizens of Shoshone, 1982-88. Home: 2735 Ori Ave San Jose CA 95128

HARRISON, CAROLE ALBERTA, museum curator, restaurateur, civic worker; b. Dayton, Ohio, Jan. 16, 1942; d. Chester Arthur and Mildred Irene (Focke) Shaw; student U. Dayton, 1959-60, U. Colo., 1960-61; m. Darrell Harrison, Apr. 24, 1962; children: Amelia Holmes, Ann Elizabeth, Abigail Shaw. With Council for Pub. TV, Channel 6, Inc., Denver, 1972-78, Hist. Denver, Inc., 1973-88; owner Old Number One Fire House Restaurant, The Christmas Catalog, Two Forks Restaurant, The Third Oasis; dir. devel. Sewall Rehab. Center, Denver, 1979-80; exec. v.p. Marilyn Van Derbur Motivational Inst., Inc., 1980-82. Bd. dirs. Center for Public Issues, Denver, 1979-82, Passages, 1982-88, Hall of Life, 1981-83, Historic Denver, 1982-84, Denver Firefighters Mus., 1979—; bd. dirs. KRMA-TV Vols., 1970—, pres., 1973-74; founder Com. for Support of Arts, Denver, 1978-79; chmn. Graland Country Day Sch. Auction, 1979, 80, Channel 6 Auction, 1971, 72, Colo. Acad. Auction, 1980, The Hundred Most Interesting Women in Denver, 1988; mem. Denver Mayor's Task Force on Infrastructure Fin., 1988—; bd. dirs. Met. Denver and Colo. Conv. and Visitors Bur. Mem. Leadership Denver Alumni Assn. (dir. 1980-82), Denver C. of C. (govt. relations com. 1983-87, state local affairs council 1987-88). Club: Pinehurst Country. Home: 5303 W Oberlin Dr Denver CO 80235 Office: 1326 Tremont Pl Denver CO 80204

HARRISON, CHARLES WAGNER, JR., applied physicist; b. Farmville, Va., Sept. 15, 1913; s. Charles Wagner and Etta Earl (Smith) H.; m. Fern F. Perry, Dec. 28, 1940; children—Martha R., Charlotte J. Student, U.S. Coast Guard Acad., 1934-36; B.S. in Engring., U. Va., 1939, E.E., 1940; S.M., Harvard U., 1942, M.E., 1952, Ph.D. in Applied Physics, 1954. Registered profl. engr., N.Mex., Va., Mass. Engr. Sta. WCHV, Charlottesville, Va., 1937-40; commd. ensign U.S. Navy, 1939, advanced through grades to comdr., 1948; research staff Bur. Ships, 1939-41, asst. dir. electronics design and devel. div., 1948-50; research staff U.S. Naval Research Lab., 1944-45, dir.'s staff, 1950-51; liaison officer Evans Signal Lab., 1945-46; electronics officer Phila. Naval Shipyard, 1946-48; mem. USN Operational Devel. Force Staff, 1953-55; staff Comdg. Gen. Armed Forces Spl. Weapons project, 1955-57; ret. U.S. Navy, 1957; cons. electromagnetics Sandia Nat. Labs., Albuquerque, 1957-73; instr. U. Va., 1939-40; lectr. Harvard U., 1942-43, Princeton U., 1943-44; vis. prof. Christian Heritage Coll., El Cajon, Calif., 1976. Author: (with R.W.P. King) Antennas and Waves: A Modern Approach, 1969; contbr. numerous articles to profl. jours. Founder Fellowship Bible Ch., chmn. steering com., 1976-77, deacon, 1978-81, 83-86; mem. Famous Families Va. Fellow IEEE (Electronics Achievement award 1966, best paper award electromagnetic compatibility group 1972); mem. Soc. Harvard Engrs. and Scientists, Internat. Union Radio Sci. (commn. B. and H), Sigma Xi. Home: 2808 Alcazar St NE Albuquerque NM 87110

HARRISON, CRAIG DONALD, water rights broker, real estate and land use planner; b. Balt., May 9, 1956; s. Charles R. and Iris (Gable) H.; m. Christina Seidel, Sept. 11, 1979; children: Craig Russell, Charles Marshall. Grad. high sch., Balt. Lic. real estate broker, Colo. V.p. Russell William Ltd., Balt., 1974-80; sole proprietor Harrison Land Co., Ft. Collins, Colo., 1980-82; pres. Harrison Resource Corp., Ft. Collins, 1982—; speaker in water market field. Mem. Colo. Water Congress. Republican. Methodist. Home: 5329 S County Rd 3F Fort Collins CO 80525 Office: Harrison Resource Corp 760 Whalers Way Ste A200 Fort Collins CO 80525

HARRISON, DEE, jewelry designer, sales professional; b. Miami, Fla., June 23, 1963; d. Henry and Shirley B. (Seifman) H. BS, U. Ariz., 1983. Salesperson Levys Fine Jewelry, Tucson, 1979-80; v.p. Gem I Jewelry, Tucson, 1980—; founder mail order div. Gem I Jewelry, 1986; designer Wholesale Antique Jewelry, Las Vegas, Nev., 1987—. Mem. Park Mall Mdse. Assn. (bd. dirs. 1981), Meadows Mall Mdse. Assn. Jewish. Office: Gem I 5870 E Broadway Tucson AZ 85711

HARRISON, EARLE, former county official; b. Rainsville, Ala., May 20, 1905; s. Robert Lee and Sarepta Ophelia (Hansard) H.; m. Joan Mary Jackson, Jan. 24, 1942. AB, Northwestern U., 1929, postgrad. in bus. adminstrn., 1942; LLB, Chgo.-Kent Coll. Law, 1935. With Marshall Field & Co., Chgo., 1929-68; div. operating mgr. Marshall Field & Co., 1958-60, v.p. operations, 1960-64, v.p., treas., 1964-68; bd. dirs. Credit Bur. Cook County, 1949-69, pres., 1958-69; mem. bd. suprs., chmn. planning and zoning com. Lake County, Ill., 1970—; cons. finance and adminstrn. to hosps. and health care instns. Commr. Northeastern Ill. Planning Commn., 1970—; pres. Northeastern Ill. Plan Commn., 1973, now mem. exec. com.; ret. pres., bd. dirs. Family Fin. Counseling Service Greater Chgo.; bd. dirs. Condell Meml. Hosp., Libertyville, Ill., 1971—, adminstr., 1973—, pres., 1975-78, bus. cons., 1978—. Mem. Phi Delta Phi. Episcopalian. Home: 2801 N Kentucky Apt 121 Roswell NM 88201

HARRISON, ERNEST ROBERT, police officer; b. Huntington Park, Calif., Jan. 11, 1953; s. Terry and Wilma Ruby (Raymond) H.; m. Janet Marie Cheeks, Mar. 2, 1985; children: Danial Ryan, James Michael. AA in Adminstrn. Justice, Cerritos Coll., Norwalk, Calif., 1978; BA in Mgmt., U. Redlands, 1981. Police officer City of Hawthorne (Calif.), 1974-76; police sgt. City of Newport Beach (Calif.), 1976-88; police lt. City of Coronado (Calif.), 1988—. Author tng. videotapes. Chmn. 1986 Calif. Police Olympics. San Diego Police Mgmt. Grad. scholar, 1989. Mem. Calif. Peace Officers Assn., Peace Officers Rsch. Assn. Calif. Republican. Office: Coronado Police Dept 578 Orange Ave Coronado CA 92118

HARRISON, JOHN CONWAY, state justice; b. Grand Rapids, Minn., Apr. 28, 1913; s. Francis Randall and Ethlyn (Conway) H.; m. Ethel M. Strict; children—Nina Lyn, Robert Charles, Molly M., Frank R., Virginia Lee. LLD, George Washington U., 1940. Bar: Mont. 1947, U.S. Dist. Ct. 1947. County atty. Lewis and Clark County, Helena, Mont., 1934-60; justice Mont. Supreme Ct., Helena, 1961—. Pres. Mont. TB Assn., Helena, 1951-54; Am. Lung Assn., N.Y.C., 1972-73, local coun. Boy Scouts Am., Great Falls, Mont., 1976-78. Col. U.S. Army. Mem. ABA, Mont. Bar Assn., Kiwanis (pres. 1953), Sigma Chi Fraternity. Home: 215 S Cooke Helena MT 59601 Office: Mont Supreme Ct 215 N Sanders St Justice Bldg Rm 323 Helena MT 59620

HARRISON, KEN L., holding company and electric utility executive; b. Bakersfield, Calif., Oct. 14, 1942. BS, Oreg. State U., 1964, MA, 1966. Cert. fin. analyst. V.p. 1st Interstate Bank, Portland, Oreg., 1966-75; asst. to pres. Portland Gen. Electric Co., 1975-78, v.p., 1978, chief fin. officer, 1978-80, sr. v.p., 1980-87, pres., 1987-88, also bd. dirs., chmn. bd., pres., chief exec. officer; chmn. bd., chief exec. officer Portland Gen. Corp., also bd. dirs. Office: Portland Gen Corp 121 SW Salmon St Portland OR 97204

HARRISON, LOU SILVER, composer, educator; b. Portland, Oreg., May 14, 1917. Student, San Francisco State U., 1934-35, Henry Cowell and Arnold Schoenberg; PhD (hon.), Mills Coll., 1988. Prof. music Black Mountain Coll., 1947-48, San Jose State U., Calif., 1967-80, Mills Coll., Oakland, Calif., 1980—; Am. rep. League of Asian Composers Conf., 1975. Composer Third Symphony, 1981-82; puppet opera Young Caesar, 1970-71; Four Strict Songs (commn. from Louisville Orch.), 1955, Suite for Piano, Violin and Small Orch., 1951. Grantee Guggenheim, 1952, 54, Rockefeller, Korea, 1962-63; Fulbright sr. scholar N.Z., 1983. Mem. Nat. Inst. Arts and Letters (music mem.).

HARRISON, LOUIS D., insurance executive; b. Logansport, Ind., June 18, 1970; s. Earl H.; m. Kas J. Harrison, June 18, 1970. BSBA, Ball State U., 1965. CPCU-CLU. Claims rep. State Farm Ins. Co., Jackson, Mich., 1965-67, Indpls., 1967-75; ins. agt. Lou Harrison CPCU-CLU, Peru, Ind., 1975-81, Western Ins. Agy., Tucson, 1981-83, Custard Ins. Adjusters, Tucson, 1983-86; owner So. Ariz. Claims Service, Tucson, 1986—; pres. CPCU Claim Mgr. Council, Tucson, 1986. Mem. Chartered Property Casualty Underwriters, Calif. Ind. Adjusters Assn., CLU's Soc., Ariz. Ins. Claims Assn., Ind. Ins. Agts. Ariz., Profl. Ins. Agts. Ariz. Clubs: Extra Point, Rebounders. Home and Office: So Ariz Claims Svc PO Box 26783 Tucson AZ 85726-0783

HARRISON, NORMAN DON, therapist; b. Tulsa, May 19, 1945; s. Alexander Norman and Wanda (Hanmor) H.; m. Janice Ellen Riddle, June 8, 1968; children; Robert Norman, Liz (dec.). BA, N. Tex. State U., 1967-71. Pvt. practice Las Cruces, N.Mex., 1982—; owner Back Therapy Ctr., 1989—; bd. dirs. Cornerstone Bank; lectr. in field Las Cruces, 1984—; staff M.G.H. Hosp., past pres. Author: Back Care, 1978. V.p. Full Gospel Businessmen's Fellowship Internat.; tchr. sunday sch. United Meth. Ch.; tchr. healing Hunter Healing. Home and Office: 1001 E Boutz Las Cruces NM 88001

HARRISON, PHILIP LEWIS, writer, researcher; b. Lynn, Mass., Nov. 30, 1945; s. Michael and Florence (Moline) H.; m. Margaret Anne Taylor, Aug. 19, 1977; children: Michael, Jennifer. BSc, Bklyn. Coll., 1969. Assoc. editor ASHRAE, N.Y.C., 1967-69, Ry. Age, N.Y.C., 1969-71, Reader's Digest, N.Y.C., 1971-72; asst. dir. Worcester (Mass.) Sci. Ctr. Planetarium, 1972-74; assoc. engr. Goodyear Aerospace, Litchfield, Ariz., 1974-76; free-lance writer 1976—. Author: Official Evan Mecham Joke Book, 1987; also hundreds of articles for local, regional, nat. and internat. jours.; ghost-writer books in sci. and tech., bus. and econs. Served with U.S. Army, 1965-67, Vietnam. Recipient Gold Pen award Phoenix Gazette, 1986, Copper Quill award Internat. Assn. Bus. Communicators, Phoenix, 1986, 88. Home and Office: 3370 W Grandview Rd Phoenix AZ 85023

HARRISON, WARREN, computer scientist; b. San Diego, Nov. 26, 1956; s. Frank and Elizabeth Harrison; m. Teresa Harrison; 1 child, Samuel. BS, U. Nev., 1978; MS, U. Mo., Rolla, 1981; PhD, Oreg. State U., 1986. Computer programmer Nev. Coop. Ext. Service, Reno, 1976-78; mgr. data processing Electrodyne Surveys Co., Reno, 1978-79; computer scientist Lawrence Livermore (Calif.) Nat. Lab., 1981, 83; mem. tech. staff Bell Labs., Lincroft, N.J., 1982; v.p. research SET Labs. Inc., Portland, Oreg., 1987—; asst. prof. bus. adminstrn. U. Portland, 1984-88; asst. prof. computer sci. Portland State U., 1988—. Co-author computer program PC-METRIC, 1987. Mem. IEEE, Assn. for Computing Machinery. Office: SET Labs Inc PO Box 83627 Portland OR 97283

HARROD, LAWRENCE WAYNE, government contractor; b. Gillette, Wyo., July 14, 1950; s. Lawrence Lester and Bonnie LaVell (Lamb) H.; div., Dec. 1977; children: Darrell, Shannon. BA in Psychology, Columbia Coll., Denver, 1980; doctoral study, U. Colo., 1982-83; MA in Psychology, U. No. Colo., 1986; postgrad., U. Denver, 1983—. Sales rep. Micrographics div. 3M Co., Denver, 1971-73; mgmt. analyst U.S. Dept Defense, Washington, 1973-76; with mental health and behavioral sciences VA Med. Ctr., Denver, 1976-80; pvt. cons. in mental health Denver, 1980-82; health care program specialist OCHAMPUS, Aurora, Colo., 1982-84; interim chief operating officer, cons. Respond Industries Corp./Respond Franchise Co., Denver, 1987-88; law clk. to judge Colo. Dist. Ct., Brighton, 1988; bd. dirs. Respond Industries Corp., Respond Franchise Corp., Denver.; faculty Nat. Inst. Trial Advocacy, Denver, 1984; coord. legal efforts litigations against Computer Sci. Corp., Colo. Dept. Social Svcs., Denver, 1987. Dist. capt. dist. 8 Republican Party, Denver, 1989; vol. Spl. Olympics, Denver, Washington, 1976—; legal researcher U.S. Senate Republican Policy Com., Washington, 1985; mem. steering com. "Let's Vote No Inc." Denver Airport election, 1989. With USMC, 1968-71, Vietnam. Decorated Bronze Star, Purple Hearts; named Outstanding Young Man Am., U.S. Jaycees, 1980. Mem. ABA, Colo. Bar Assn., Colo. Trial Lawyers Assn., Disabled Am. Vets. (life mem.), 3rd Marine Div. Assn. (life mem.). Republican. Episcopalian. Home: 2431 California St Denver CO 80205 Office: 999 18th St Ste 501 N Denver CO 80202

HARROD, SCOTT BRYANT, air force officer; b. Shelbyville, Ky., Feb. 18, 1955; s. Clarence B. and Nancy Lee (Byrnside) H.; m. Sherry Anita Thompson, Apr. 27, 1985; 1 child, Kimberly Renee. BS in History, USAF Acad., 1977; M.Pub.Adminstrn., U. Colo., 1988; postgrad., Air U., 1983, 85. Commd. 2d lt. USAF, 1977, advanced through grades to maj., 1988; instr. pilot Columbus AFB, Miss., 1978-81, Randolph AFB, San Antonio, 1981; air ops. staff officer Randolph AFB, 1982-84; exec. officer Lackland AFB, San Antonio, 1984; comdr. hdqrs. sq. Lackland AFB, 1985; air ops. staff officer USAF Acad., Colorado Springs, Colo., 1985-88; comdr. cadet squadron USAF Acad., 1988—. Democrat. Baptist. Home: 4409 A USAF Acad Colorado Springs CO 80840 Office: USAF Acad CWDS-35 Colorado Springs CO 80840

HARROP, CLAYTON KEITH, minister, educator; b. Berryton, Kans., Feb. 18, 1924; s. Joseph and Rose Belle (Fetrow) H.; m. Shirley Ann Jacobs, Dec. 24, 1944; children: Judith Ann, Joyce Elaine, Janice Louise. AB, William Jewell Coll., Liberty, Mo., 1949; BD, So. Bapt. Theol. Sem., 1952, PhD, 1956; postgrad., U. Chgo., 1964, Cambridge U, 1965, U. Gottingen, Fed. Republic Germany, 1973-74. Ordained to ministry, Baptist Ch. Pastor Birmingham (Mo.) Bapt. Ch., 1947-49, New Hope Bapt. Ch., Newtonville, Ind., 1951-55; instr. Golden Gate Bapt. Theol. Sem., Berkeley, Calif., 1955-56; asst. prof. Golden Gate Bapt. Theol. Sem., Mill Valley, Calif., 1956-61, assoc. prof., 1961-68, prof., 1968—, dir. PhD studies, 1984—; vis. prof. So. Bapt. Theol. Sem., Louisville, 1986. Author: The Letter of James, 1969, History of the New Testament in Plain Language, 1984; contbr. articles to Holman Bible Dictionary and Mercer Dictionary of the Bible. Capt. U.S. Army, 1942-46, Philippines. Recipient award of Excellence, Calif. Bapt. Found., 1986. Mem. Soc. Biblical Literature, Nat. Assn. Bapt. Profs. of Religion. Republican. Office: Golden Gate Bapt Theol Sem Seminary Dr Mill Valley CA 94941-3197

HARROP, JANICE CHERI, educator, counselor; b. Rigby, Idaho, June 18, 1940; d. Wilburn Gerald and Edith Lettie (Cleveland) Jenkins; m. Larry Neal Harrop, Apr. 8, 1960; children: Laurie Cheri, Penny Lea, Peggy Lyn, Shannon Kae. BA, Utah State U., 1969; MS, Idaho State U., 1979. Cert. paramedic, Ga. Physical edn. faculty Ricks Coll., Rexburg, Idaho, 1960-75; health sci. faculty Ricks Coll., Rexburg, 1970—, emergency med. service coord., 1972—, paramedic program coord., 1985—, search and rescue dir. instr., 1976—; profl. counselor Rexburg, 1979—. Author: EMT-Ambulance Manual, 1980, EMT-Intermediate Manual, 1980, EMT-Paramedic Manual, 1985, Learned Helplessness, 1979. Program cons. ARC, 1958—, water safety instr. and trainer, 1960—, first aid and CPR instr. trainer, 1965—, chmn. disaster, Jefferson County, 1985—. Recipient Service award, ARC, 1980. Mem. Assn. for Mormon Counselors and Psychologists, Am. Assn. Health, Physical Edn., and Recreation. Mormon. Office: Ricks Coll Rexburg ID 83440

HARRY, DORIS JANE, music school director; b. St. Clairsville, Ohio, Nov. 14, 1938; d. Ralph Johnson and Arvanna (Fulton) Roman; m. Paul A. Harry, June 11, 1961; children: Jill Elaine Denny, Julie Lyn, Steven Jay. BS in Mus. Edn., U. Cin., 1960, M in Music, 1976. Tchr. music Ohio Pub. Schs., 1960-70; cons. early childhood Baldwin Piano and Organ Co., Cin., 1970-76; instr. San Francisco State U., Cin., 1977-78; dir. The Music Sch. at Sunnyvale (Calif.) Presbyn., 1978—; pres. Active Learning in the Arts, Cupertino, Calif., 1981—; founding ptnr. Candle Power Press, Cupertino, 1985—; cons. music edn., arts for the handicapped. Author: The Young Musician, 1983, (music curriculum) Pathways, 1971; author, performer ednl. TV series Pathways, 1974, We Can Do It, 1980; performer rec. Music Play, 1979; contbr. articles to profl. jours. Commr. Fine Arts Commn. City of Cupertino, 1987—; pres. Monta Vista High Sch. Music Boosters, Cupertino, 1982, 83-85. Mem. AAUW (cultural chair 1985-86, Citizen of Achievement 1985), Music Tchrs. Nat. Assn. (state group chair 1978-80), Sigma Alpha Iota (v.p. 1984). Democrat. Presbyterian. Home: 8147 Hyannisport Dr Cupertino CA 95014 Office: The Music Sch 728 W Fremont Ave Sunnyvale CA 94087

HARSEY, STEVEN ANDREW, small business owner; b. Los Angeles, Feb. 2, 1948; s. Verne Andrew Harsey and Betty June (Mechura) McRuer; m. Rosemary Hawkins, June 6, 1970; children: Joanna, Monica, Tricia. AA, El Camino Coll., Gardena, Calif., 1968; BS, Brigham Young U., 1970. Sales mgr. Van Waters and Rogers, Carritos, Calif., 1970-79; prin. Harsey and Assocs., Inc., Steven Harsey/Orient Express Silk Collection, Placentia, Calif., 1979—, Mary Rose Interior Products, Inc., Harsey and Harsey, Laguna Niguel, Calif., 1982—. Mormon. Office: Harsey & Assocs Inc 570 S Melrose St Placentia CA 92670

HARSHA, PHILIP THOMAS, aerospace engineer; b. N.Y.C., Feb. 22, 1942; s. Palmer and Catherine (Redinger) H.; m. Jean Ann Quinn, Oct. 23, 1965; children: Peter Charles, Evan Michael. BS in Engring. Sci., SUNY, Stony Brook, 1962, MS in Engring. Sci., 1964; PhD in Aerospace Engring., U. Tenn., 1970. Combustion rsch. engr. Gen. Electric Co., Cin., 1964-67; lead rsch. engr. Aro, Inc., Arnold Engring. Devel. Ctr., Tenn., 1969-74; rsch. specialist R&D Assoc., Marina Del Rey, Calif., 1974-76; div. mgr. Sci. Applications Internat. Corp., Chatsworth, Calif., 1976-85; chief aero. scientist Lockheed Aero. Systems Group, Burbank, Calif., 1985-88; chief project engr. Rocketdyne div. Rockwell Internat., Canoga Park, Calif., 1988—. Contbr. articles to profl. jours. Recipient Disting. Alumnus award U. Tenn. Space Inst., 1984. Mem. AIAA, ASME, N.Y. Acad. Sci., Sigma Xi. Republican. Methodist. Home: 7235 Cirrus Way West Hills CA 91307 Office: Rockwell Internat Rocketdyne Div 6633 Canoga Ave Canoga Park CA 91304

HARSHMAN, ARTHUR LINCOLN, JR., art historian, educator; b. Muncie, Ind., Aug. 12, 1940; s. Arthur Lincoln and Geraldine Olive (Buckles) H.; m. Lorraine Ann Markulis, Aug. 31, 1975 (div. Oct. 1982). BA, Antioch U., Yellow Springs, Ohio, 1964; MA, Mich. State U., 1964, U. Chgo., 1968; PhD, U. Chgo., 1977. Asst. prof. Calif. State U.-Dominguez Hills, Carson, 1971-81, assoc. prof., 1981-86, chairperson art dept., 1984-86, prof. art history, coordinator humanities gen. studies, MA programs, 1986-89, coord. humanities,GE/MA external degree programs, 1989—; gallery dir. Calif. State U.-Dominguez Hills, Carson, 1972-74. Lilly Fedn. grantee Stanford U., 1977, Program for Faculty Renewal grantee Stanford U., 1982, NEH grant, Zurich, Switzerland, 1978. Mem. Nat. Assn. Schs. of Art and Design, Assn. of Art Historians, Am. Soc. for Aesthetics, Nat. Council of Art Adminstrs., Coll. Art Assn. Home: 26116 Narbonne Ave Unit D Lomita CA 90717 Office: Calif State U-Dominguez Hills 1000 E Victoria St Carson CA 90747

HART, ARTHUR ALVIN, museum director; b. Tacoma, Feb. 13, 1921; s. Albert Arthur and Erma Lola (Maltby) H.; m. Novella D. Cochran, Feb. 26, 1944; children—Susanna, Robin, Catherine, Allison. B.A., U. Wash., Seattle, 1948, M.F.A., 1948; postgrad., Biarritz Am. U., Hans Hofmann Sch. Fine Arts, U. Calif., Berkeley; H.H.D. honoris causa, Coll. Idaho, 1985. Head art dept., chmn. div. fine arts Coll. Idaho, 1948-53; instr. art Colby Jr. Coll. Women, New London, N.H., 1953-54; head art dept., dir. adult edn. Bay Path Jr. Coll., Longmeadow, Mass., 1955-69; dir. Idaho Hist. Mus., Boise, 1969-75, Idaho Hist. Soc., 1975-86; lectr. Am. architecture Boise State U., 1970-86 ; mem. Boise Allied Arts Council, 1970-78, Idaho Historic Preservation Council, 1971-87, Boise Bicentennial Commn., 1975-76, Idaho Centennial Commn., 1985—, Idaho Humanities Council, 1985-86; mem. adv. bd. Snake River Regional Studies Center, 1969—, Boise Redevel. Agy., 1986-87, Basque Mus. and Cultural Ctr., 1985—. Author: Steam Trains in Idaho, 1971, Space, Style and Structure: Building in Northwest American, 1974, Fighting Fire on the Frontier, 1976, Historic Boise, 1979, The Boiseans: At Home, 1984, Idaho, Gem of the Mountains, 1985, Basin of Gold, 1986, Life in Old Boise, 1989; also numerous articles. Served with USAAF, 1942-44; Served with AUS, 1944-46. Recipient Idaho Statesman Disting. Citizen award, 1973; Allied Arts Council award for hist. writing, 1972; Phoenix award for leadership in conservation Soc. Am. Travel Writers, 1982. Mem. AIA (hon.), AAUP, Coll. Art Assn., Soc. Archtl. Historians (pres. No. Pacific Coast chpt. 1974-76), Am. Assn. Museums (mem. council 1980-82, pres. Western regional conf. 1979-81).

HART, DANIEL MARTIN, aerospace engineer; b. N.Y.C., Mar. 1, 1961; s. Allen M. and Mildred (Dickstein) H.; m. Deborah Susan Babich. BS in Physics, SUNY, Albany, 1983. Res. asst. Inst. for Study of Defects in Solids, Albany, 1982-83; spacelab elec. systems engr. McDonnell Douglas Astronautics Co., Kennedy Space Ctr., Fla., 1983-88; engr. specialist McDonnell Douglas Space Systems Co., Huntington Beach, Calif., 1988—; integration and test engr. Dornier Systems, Immenstaadt, West Germany, 1983-84; Delta rocket elec. engr. launch support McDonnell Douglas Astronautics Co., Cape Canaveral Air Force Sta., Fla., 1986-87. Mem. Soc. Physics Students (pres. 1982-83). Democrat. Jewish. Home: 928 Badger Pass Ln Orange CA 92665 Office: McDonnell Douglas SSC 5301 Bolsa Ave Huntington Beach CA 92647

HART, DONALD PURPLE, bishop; b. N.Y.C., Apr. 22, 1937; s. Donald Buell Hart and Ann Wentworth (Ayres) Herrick; m. Elizabeth Ann Howard, Sept. 8, 1962; children: Sarah, Thomas. BA, Williams Coll., 1959; B of Divinity, Episc. Div. Sch., Cambridge, Mass., 1962. Curate Ch. of the Redeemer, Chestnut Hill, Mass., 1962-64; priest-in-charge Good Shepherd Mission, Huslia, Alaska, 1964-69; diocesan staff Native Ministry, Anchorage, Alaska, 1969-73; rector St. Matthew's Ch., Fairbanks, Alaska, 1973-83, St. James Ch., Keene, N.H., 1983-86; bishop Diocese of Hawaii, Honolulu, 1986—. Chmn. St. Andrew's Priory Sch., Honolulu, 1986—, Seabury Hall Sch., Makawao, Hawaii, 1986—, St. John's Sch., Tumon Bay, Guam, 1986—; bd. govs. Iolani Sch., Honolulu, 1986—. Home: 3337 Niolopua Dr Honolulu HI 96817 Office: Episcopal Ch in Hawaii 229 Queen Emma Sq Honolulu HI 96813

HART, EDWARD B., retail drug store company executive; b. 1924; married. BS, Oreg. State U., 1948. With Pay Less Drug Stores NW, Inc., 1948—, pharmacist, then asst. store mgr., Lewiston, Idaho, then mgr. trainee, Portland, Oreg., 1951-53, store mgr., Coos Bay, Oreg., 1953-63, corp. v.p., 1963-67, pres., 1967-86, chief exec. officer, 1969—, chmn., 1980—, also bd. dirs. Served to lt. (j.g.) USN, 1943-46, USNR, 1946-56. Office: Pay Less Drug Stores NW Inc 9275 SW Peyton Ln Wilsonville OR 97070 *

HART, GARY W., former senator, lawyer; b. Ottawa, Kans., Nov. 28, 1936; m. Lee Ludwig, 1958; children: Andrea, John. Grad., Bethany Nazarene Coll., Okla.; LLB, Yale U., 1964. Bar: Colo. 1964. Began career as atty. U.S. Dept. Justice, Washington; then spl. asst. to sec. U.S. Dept. Interior; practiced in Denver 1967-70, 72-74; nat. campaign dir. Senator George McGovern Democratic Presdl. Campaign, 1970-72; U.S. senator from Colo. 1976-84; of counsel Davis, Graham & Stubbs, Denver, 1985—; founder, 1st chmn. Environ. Study Conf., 1975; congl. adviser Salt II Talks, 1977; adviser UN Spl. Session on Disarmament, 1978; chmn. Nat. Commn. on Air Quality, 1978-81; founder Congl. Mil. Reform Caucus, 1981. Author: Right From the Start, 1973, A New Democracy, 1983, America Can Win, 1986, The Strategies of Zeus, 1987; co-author: The Double Man, 1985. Student vol. John F. Kennedy Presdl. Campaign, 1960; vol. organizer Robert F. Kennedy Presdl. Campaign, 1968; bd. visitors U.S. Air Force Acad., 1975—, chmn., 1978-80; nat. co-chmn. Share Our Strength, 1985; candidate for Democratic presdl. nomination, 1983-84, 87-88. Office: Davis Graham & Stubbs 370 17th St Ste 4700 Denver CO 80201-0185

HART, HOWARD ARTHUR, personnel executive; b. Newark, Oct. 20, 1934; s. Irving J. and Helen (Franklin) H. BS, U. Pa., 1956; MBA, Fla. Atlantic U., 1973; postgrad., Golden Gate U., 1983. Mgr. mktg., cons. edn. and sales tng. IBM Corp., N.Y.C. and N.J., 1956-65; tng. chief N.J. Community Action Tng. Inst., Trenton, 1965-66; mgr. copr. manpower devel. ESB Ray-O-Vac Mgmt. Corp., Phila., 1966-82; mgr. corp. tng. and devel. Atari Inc., Sunnyvale, Calif., 1982-83; v.p., sr. cons. Drake Beam Morin Inc., San Francisco, 1983—; lectr., cons. in field; guest prof. Temple U., Phila., 1975-76. 1st lt. Q.M.C., U.S. Army. Recipient Leadership Conf. Achievement award Am. Mgmt. Assn. Mem. Indsl. Relations Assn. (past v.p. Phila. chpt.), Am. Soc. Tng. and Devel., Am. Soc. Personnel Adminstrs., No. Calif. Human Resources Council, San Francisco C. of C. (arts and culture council). Office: Drake Beam Morin Inc 4 Embarcadero Ctr Ste 450 San Francisco CA 94111-4111

HART, JACK ROBERT, editor; b. Tacoma, Sept. 7, 1946; s. John Sebald and Alice Agnes (Hurlbut) H.; m. Cherie Denise Boston, Dec. 27, 1970 (div. 1978); children: Joshua John, Aaron Lee, Jesse Robert. BA in journalism, U. Wash., 1968; PhD in Mass Communications, U. Wis., 1975. Instr. Calif. State U., Northridge, 1971-74; from asst. prof. to assoc. prof. journalism U. Oreg., Eugene, 1974-82, acting dean Sch. Journalism, 1982; reporter Register-Guard, Eugene, 1980; arts and leisure editor The Oregonian, Portland, 1981-82, editor N.W. Mag., 1982-89, staff devel. dir., 1989—; cons. and speaker in field; vis. faculty The Poynter Inst., St. Petersburg, Fla., 1984—, Oreg. State U., Corvallis, 1985—, Lewis and Clark Coll, Portland Oreg., 1986—. Author: The Information Empire, 1979; contbr. articles to profl. jours. and mags. Served to 2d lt. USAR, 1968-70. Recipient Ruhl Fellowship Disting. Vis. Prof. U. Oreg. Sch. Journalism, 1988, Nat. Teaching award Am. Soc. Newspaper Editors, 1981, Excellence in Newspaper Writing award Am. Assn. Schs. and Depts. Journalism. Home: 2376 SW Cedar Portland OR 97205 Office: The Oregonian 1320 SW Broadway Portland OR 97205

HART, JAMES DAVID, library director, educator; b. San Francisco, Apr. 18, 1911; s. Julien and Helen Louise (Neustadter) H.; m. Ruth Arnstein, June 14, 1938 (dec. 1977); children: Carol Helen (Mrs. John L. Field), Peter David; m. Constance Crowley Bowles, Feb. 9, 1985. A.B., Stanford U., 1932; M.A., Harvard U., 1933, Ph.D., 1936; L.H.D., Mills Coll., 1978. Mem. faculty U. Calif.-Berkeley, 1936—, chmn. dept., 1955-57, 65-69, vice chancellor, 1957-60; acting dir. Bancroft Library, 1961-62, dir., 1969—; vis. prof. Harvard U., 1964; Phi Beta Kappa vis. scholar, 1980-81; chmn. Marshall Scholarship Com. Western U.S., 1959-63, 79-86, adv. council Brit. Ambassador, 1986—. Author: The Oxford Companion Am. Literature, 1941, rev. edits, The Popular Book, 1950, 61, America's Literature, (with C. Gohdes), 1955, American Images of Spanish California, 1960, The Private Press Ventures of Samuel Lloyd Osbourne and R.L.S, 1966, A Companion to California, 1978, rev. edit., 1987; New Englanders in Nova Albion, 1976, Fine Printing: The San Francisco Tradition, 1985; editor: My First Publication, 1961, The Oregon Trail (Francis Parkman), 1963, From Scotland to Silverado (Robert Louis Stevenson), 1966, A Novelist in the Making (Frank Norris), 1970; contbr. articles to mags., revs. Trustee Mills Coll., 1970-78, 79-86, pres. bd., 1973-76; trustee Fine Arts Mus. San Francisco, 1983—. Decorated comdr. Order Brit. Empire. Fellow Am. Antiquarian Soc., Am. Acad. Arts and Scis., Calif. Hist. Soc.; mem. Modern Lang. Assn., Philol. Assn. Pacific Coast, Book Club of Calif. (pres. 1956-60). Clubs: Bohemian (San Francisco); Grolier (N.Y.C.); Century Assn., Faculty (Berkeley). Home: 740 San Luis Rd Berkeley CA 94707

HART, JEAN MACAULAY, clinical social worker; b. Bellingham, Wash.; d. Murry Donald and Pearl N. (McLeod) Macaulay; m. Richard D. Hart, Feb. 3, 1940 (dec. Mar. 1973); children: Margaret Morrison, Pamela Horton, Patricia L. Hart; m. Lawrence Duling, Jan. 20, 1979; children: Lenora Daniel, Larry, Jayne. BA, Wash. State U., 1938; MSW, U. So. Calif., 1961. Lic. clin. social worker, Calif. Social worker Los Angeles County, 1957-58; children's service worker Dept. Children's Services, Los Angeles, 1958-59; program developer homemakers services project Calif. Dept. Children's Services, Los Angeles, 1962-64, developer homemaker cons. position, 1964-66; supr. protective services Dept. Children's Services, Los Angeles, 1966-67; dep. regional service adminstrn. Dept. Los Angeles County Children's Services, 1967-76. Mem. Portals Com., Los Angeles, 1974, Travelers Aid Bd., Long Beach, Calif. 1969. Recipient Nat. award work in community, spl. award for work with emotionally disturbed Com. for Los Angeles, 1974. Mem. AAUW, Nat. Assn. Social Workers (former delegate), Acad. Cert. Social Workers. Republican. Congregationalist. Club: Wing Point Golf and Country (Bainbridge Island, Wash.). also: 7300 Quill Dr Downey CA 90242

HART, JOHN, artistic director; b. London, 1924. Student, Sch. Sadler's Wells Ballet. Dancer Sadler's Wells Royal Ballet, London, 1938-42, from 1946; created roles in ballets of Ninette de Valois, appeared in premieres of works by Frederick Ashton, including The Wanderer, 1941, Sylvia, 1952 Sadler's Wells Royal Ballet, later asst. dir., then adminstr., from 1975; artistic dir. Ballet West, Salt Lake City, 1985—; formerly artistic dir. PACT Ballet Co., S. Africa; formerly chmn. dance div. U.S. Internat. U., San Diego; formerly dance dir. San Diego Opera. Author: Ballet and Camera, The Royal Ballet. Recipient 1st Adeline Genee Gold Medal Royal Acad. Dancing, Queen Elizabeth award outstanding achievement in ballet, 1970; decorated comdr. Order Brit. Empire, 1971. Office: Ballet West 50 W 200 S Salt Lake City UT 84101 *

HART, JOSEPH H., bishop; b. Kansas City, Mo., Sept. 26, 1931. Ed., St. John Sem., Kansas City, St. Meinrad Sem., Indpls. Ordained priest Roman Catholic Ch., 1956; consecrated titular bishop of Thimida Regia and aux. bishop Cheyenne Wyo., 1976; apptd. bishop of Cheyenne 1978. Office: Bishops Residence Box 468 Cheyenne WY 82003 *

HART, MARGIE RUTH, publisher, writer; b. Chesterfield, S.C., Oct. 28, 1943; d. Lonnie Carson and Carrie Jane (Hancock) Sellers; m. Ben Tucker, Mar. 9, 1963 (div. 1980); children: Chipman D., Sandra L.; m. Len Hart, Dec. 21, 1980; children: Richard W., Leonard P., Carl S., Karen J. H. Student, Greenville Tech. Sch., 1964-65, Pickens Vocat. Sch. Barstow Jr. Coll. Br. mgr. Caroline Emmons Jewelry Co., western S.C., 1978-79; microwave sales specialist western N.C. and S.C., Whirlpool Corp., 1978-79; sales rep. Cleaves Office Products, 1979; asst. mgr. D & L Assocs., 1977-78; substitute tchr. Picken Jr. High Sch., Pickens, S.C., 1975-79; asst. mgr., co-pub. The Am. Patriot Mag., Barstow, Calif., 1982-84. Chmn. 1st supervisorial dist., mem. cen. com. Am. Independent Party, San Bernardino County, Calif., also mem. state exec. bd. congl. dist. coordinator Freedom Counsel, San Bernardino County; chmn. first supervisoral dist. San Bernardino County Am. Ind. Party, 1983-87; mem. nat com. woman Am. Ind. Party, 1986-87; candidate for Calif. Assembly, 1984, 1986; chmn. SARB Barstow Schs., 1987; parlimentarian PTA Exec. Bd., Barstow Area, mem. area council PTA; advisor to 61st dist. assemblyman Bill Leonard, 1985-87. Recipient Good Establishment cert., Pickens, S.C., 1977; certs. of appreciation Picken PTA, 1978, Second Amendment Found., 1982. Mem. Concerned Women for Am., Nat. Congl. Women, A.I.P., Moral Majority. Baptist. Home: PO Box 370 Barstow CA 92312 Office: PO Box 370 Barstow CA 92311

HART, N. BERNE, banker; b. Denver, Jan. 6, 1930; s. Horace H. and Eva (Saville) H.; m. Wilma Jean Shadley, Sept. 17, 1952; children: Linda Lea Hart Frederick, Patricia Sue Hart Sweeney, David Bruce. B.A., Colo. Coll., 1951; postgrad., Colo. Sch. Banking, 1958-60. Sales trainee U.S. Rubber Co., 1953; exec. trainee United Bank of Denver N.A., 1954-56, asst. operations mgr., 1956-58, asst. cashier, 1958-61, asst. v.p., 1961, cashier, 1961-65, v.p. ops., 1965-69, sr. v.p. personal banking div., 1969, sr. v.p., trust officer, 1969-73; v.p. United Banks Colo. Inc., 1974, exec. v.p., 1975-77, pres., 1977-78, chmn., 1979—; mem. fed. adv. council Fed. Res. Bd., 1983-85. Past chmn. bd. dirs. St. Joseph Hosp., Denver; past chmn. bd. trustees Colo. Sch. Banking. Served to capt. USMCR, 1951-53. Named Denver Met. Exec. of Year Denver chpt. Nat. Secs. Assn., 1968; recipient Torch of Liberty award Anti-Defamation League, 1986, Colo. Bus. Leader of 1988 award, 1988. Mem. Colo. Bankers Assn. (past pres.), Adminstrv. Mgmt. Soc. (past pres. Denver chpt.), Colo. Assn. Commerce and Industry (chmn. 1985-86), Bank Adminstrn. Inst. (chmn. 1980-81), Beta Theta Pi. Republican. Clubs: Rotary (Denver) (pres. 1982-83), University (Denver); Denver Country. Home: 2552 E Alameda Ave #99 Denver CO 80209 Office: United Banks Colo Inc 1 United Bank Ctr 1700 Lincoln Ste 3200 Denver CO 80274-0010

HART, NICOLLE SAULS, chef, artist's agent; b. Courthezon, Vaucluse, France, Aug. 19, 1941; came to U.S., 198l; d. Henri Jean and Kamille (Sier) Pouzol; m. Jacques Mansillon, Aug. 4, 1960 (div. Oct. 198l); l child, Gilles; m. Ralph Hart, Dec. 2l, 1985. BEC, Coll. Tech. Jeanne d'Arc, Marseille, France, 1960. Acct., auditor pvt. office, Paris, 196l-80; mgr., exec. chef Le Koala, Paris, 1970-78, Le Restaurant du Nardie, Asmeres, France, 1970-78; agt. rep. of Frederick Sauls 1982—; cons. animator bus. seminars, Paris, 1970-78; tchr. French, L.A., 1983-84; exec. mgr. Gille Mansillon Fine Art Gallery, Santa Monica, Calif., 1983-85; dir. Saul's Gallery, Santa Fe, 1989—; exec. chef Tree and Pool Restaurant, Hollywood, Calif., 1985-88, Oliver's Whole Earth Café, Santa Fe, 1989—. Buddhist. Office: Box 16572 Santa Fe NM 87506

HART, R. DEAN, chief financial officer; b. Belleville, Ill., Dec. 17, 1932; s. Orville C. and Mildred (Allen) H.; m. Sinone Yen, Feb. 21, 1979. AA, C.I.M. of L.A., 1957; BS, Calif. State U., 1959. CPA. Acct. State Bd. Accountancy, Calif., 1967; with Earth Tech. Corp., Long Beach, Calif., 1967—; bd. dirs. Clinic Control Corp., Stanton, Calif., 1972-73, Internat. Ocean Industries. Contbr. articles to profl. jours. Cpl. USMC, 1953-56. Mem. Calif. Soc. CPA's, Nat. Assn. Accts., Toastmasters, Lions Club (treas. 1966-68). Republican. Home: 2220 E Chapman Ave #55 Fullerton CA 92631 Office: Earth Tech Corp 3777 Long Beach Blvd Long Beach CA 90807

HART, RAY LEE, religious studies educator; b. Hereford, Tex., Mar. 22, 1929; s. Albert Mann and Ruby Douglas (Bracken) H.; m. Juanita Fern Morgan, Sept. 8, 1951; children: Douglas Morgan, Stuart Bracken. B.A., U. Tex., 1949; B.D., So. Methodist U., 1953; Ph.D., Yale U., 1959. Instr., then asst. prof. Drew U. Theol. Sch., 1956-63; asso. prof. philos. and systematic theology Vanderbilt U. Div. Sch., 1963-69; prof., chmn. dept. religious studies U. Mont., 1969—; Cons. on religious studies SUNY, 1972—. Author: Unfinished Man and the Imagination, 1968; trans. into Chinese, editor: Selections from Thomas Aquinas, 1966, The Critique of Modernity, 1986, Trajectories in the Study of Religion, 1987. Mayor, Polebridge, Mont., 1969-70. Mem. Am. Acad. Religion (editor jour. 1970-80, pres. 1983-84, del. to Am. Council Learned Socs. 1980—, mem. exec. com., bd. dirs.), Metaphys. Soc. Am., Soc. Sci. Study Religion, Soc. Values in Higher Edn., Ctr. of Study of World Religions (bd. dirs. 1986—). Home: 16 Carriage Way Missoula MT 59801

HART, RICHARD LAVERNE, college dean; b. Cozad, Nebr., Dec. 10, 1929; s. David Lane and Carrie Belle (Queale) H.; m. Ramona Jean Fecht, July 28, 1956; children: Jay Huston, David Lane. BA, Nebr. Wesleyan U., 1950; EdM, U. Nebr, 1955, EdD, 1960. Tchr. Wakefield (Nebr.) High Sch., 1950-51, Cozad (Nebr.) High Sch., 1954-57; supr. social studies U. High Sch. U. Nebr., Lincoln, 1957-60; asst. prof. edn. U. Maine, Orono, 1960-62; from asst. prof. to assoc. prof., chmn. dept. curriculum and instrn. U. Wis., Milw., 1962-69; prof., chmn. dept. sec. edn. Kent (Ohio) State U., 1969-73, assoc.

dean Coll. Edn., 1973-78; dean Coll. Edn. Boise (Idaho) State U., 1978—; bd. dirs. N.W. Regional Ednl. Lab., Portland, Oreg., 1984—; mem. profl. standards commn. State of Idaho, Boise, 1981-84, 87—. Co-editor: Student Unrest: Threat or Promise, 1970. Bd. dirs. Boise Sch. Vols., 1979—, Ada County United Way, Boise, 1983-87. Cpl. U.S. Army, 1951-53, Korea. Named Ednl. Adminstr. of Yr., Assn. Ednl. Office Personnel, 1986. Mem. Tchr. Edn. Council State Colls. and Univs. (pres. 1988—), Idaho Assn. Supervision and Curriculum Devel. (pres. 1978-80), Idaho Assn. Colls. of Tchr. Edn. (pres. 1982-84), Rotary (chmn. Boise chpt. scholarship com. 1987—). Democrat. Lutheran. Home: 1517 Oriole Way Boise ID 83709 Office: Boise State U Coll Edn 704 Edn Bldg Boise ID 83725

HART, ROBERT RAY, finance executive; b. Wichita Falls, Tex., Jan. 31, 1936; s. John F. and Mattye O. (O'Kelly) H.; m. Faye I. Wohlers, Jan. 26, 1955; children: Candace A., Denise L., Lawrence A. BS, Calif. State U., Fullerton, 1980. Corp. mgr. Thorpe Insulation Co., L.A., 1965-75; owner Viking Bus. Systems, Fullerton, Calif., 1970—; ops. mgr. Authorized Supply Corp., Los Angeles, 1975-85; v.p. Freight Masters, Inc., La Habra, Calif., 1985—; cons. in field. Mem. The Indsl. Coun., City of Commerce, Calif., 1980. Sgt. U.S. Army Airborne, 1954-57. Fellow Soc. Profl. Credit Mgrs.; mem. Soc. Profl. Personnel Mgrs., Nat. Credit Mgrs. Assn. Am., Nat. Accts. Assn. Am., Fullerton C. of C. Republican. Episcopalian. Office: Viking Bus Systems PO Box 712 Brea CA 92622

HART, RUSS ALLEN, telecommunications educator; b. Seguin, Tex., June 30, 1946; s. Bevelly D. and Hattie V. (Reeh) H.; m. Judith Harwood, 1984 (div. 1986); m. Patricia Barrios, Mar. 22, 1987. BA, Tex. Tech. U., 1968; MA, U. Ariz., 1976; PhD, U. Wyo., 1984. Chief cinematographer, producer-dir. dept. med-TV-film, health sci. ctr. Univ. Ariz., Tuscon, 1973-77; instr., coordinator ednl. TV and cinematography Univ. Wyo., Laramie, 1977-81; assoc. prof., dir. biomed. communication Mercer Univ., Macon, Ga., 1981-84; prof., dir. instructional telecommunications Calif. State Univ., Fresno, 1984—; condr. of numerous ednl. confs., 1978—. Contbr. articles to profl. jours. Served to capt. USAF, 1968-73. Recipient Cert. Merit, Chgo. Internat. Film Festival, 1975, 1st place INDY Indsl. Photography award, 1976, 2d place INDY Indsl. Photography award, 1975, Silver plaque Chgo. Internat. Film Festival, 1978. Mem. Assn. for Ednl. Communications and Tech. (research session chmn. 1983), Am. Assn. Adult and Continuing Educators (mem. Eval. Task Force 1986), Broadcast Edn. Assn., Health Sci. Communication Assn. (mem. continuing edn. subcom. 1983), Biol. Photog. Assn. (film judge 1975), Phi Delta Kappa, Phi Kappa Phi. Office: Calif State U Dept Instructional Telecom Fresno CA 93740-0050

HART, TIMOTHY RAY, college official, lawyer; b. Portland, Jan. 5, 1942; s. Eldon V. and Wanda J. (Hillyer) H.; m. Mary F. Barlow, Aug. 31, 1964 (div. Dec. 1975); children: Mark, Matthew, Marisa, Martin; m. Annette Bryant, Aug. 8, 1981. AA, San Jose City Coll., 1968; BA, San Jose State U., 1970; MA, Wash. State U., 1973; JD, San Joaquin Coll. Law, Fresno, Calif., 1983. Bar: Calif. 1983, U.S. Dist. Ct. (ea. dist.) Calif. 1983. Police officer City of Santa Clara, Calif., 1965-71; chief of police U. Idaho, Moscow, 1971-73; crime prevention officer City of Albany, Oreg., 1973-75; instr. criminal justice Coll. of Sequoias, Visalia, Calif., 1975-81, dir. paralegal dept., 1981-83, chmn., dir. adminstrn. justice div., 1983-88; assoc. dean instruction, 1988—; sole practice, Visalia, 1983—. Bd. dirs. Sprout Ranch for Deaf Children, Tulare County Humane Soc. With USAF, 1960-63. Mem. ABA, Calif. Bar Assn., Assn. Trial Lawyers Am., Assn. Criminal Justice Educators, Am. Criminal Justice Assn., Delta Phi. Mennonite. Home: 3527 McCormick Ave Visalia CA 93277 Office: Coll of Sequoias 915 S Mooney Blvd Visalia CA 93277

HARTFORD, MARGARET ELIZABETH, social work educator, gerontologist; b. Cleve., Dec. 12, 1917; d. William A. and Inez (Logan) H. BA, Ohio U., 1940; MS, U. Pitts., 1944; PhD, U. Chgo., 1962. Dir. youth service YWCA, Canton, Ohio, 1940-42; program cons. Intercultural Relations Am. Service Inst., Pitts., 1943-48, exec. dir., 1948-50; prof. social work Case Western Res. U., Cleve., 1950-75; founding dir. Sch. Gerontology U. So. Calif., Los Angeles, 1975-77, prof. gerontology, social work, 1977-83, prof. emeritus, 1983—; instr. Claremont (Calif.) Adult Sch. Dist., 1983—; instr. retirement Pasadena (Calif.) City Coll., 1983-84, Mt. San Antonio Coll., 1988—; cons. pre-retirement, retirement planning to corps. and ednl. systems, various cities, 1980—; cons., lectr. 1970—. Author: Groups in Social Work, 1973, (workbook) Making the Best of the Rest of Your Life, 1982, Leaders Guide to Making the Best of the Rest of Your Life, 1986; also numerous articles. Commr. Human Services, City of Claremont, 1986—; trustee Mt. San Antonio Gardens Retirement Com., 1985, sec. 1988—; trustee Corp. Pilgrim Pl. Ret. Community, chmn. health and svcs. com., 1987—; bd. dirs. Vol. Assn. Rancho Santa Ana Botanic Gardens. Named Outstanding Contbn. to Social Work, Alumni Assn. Schs. Social Work U. So. Calif., 1984, Outstanding Contbr. Social Group Work, Com. Advancement of Group Work, Toronto, Ont., Can., 1985, Woman of Yr., Trojan Women U. So. Calif., 1976; recipient Dart award for Inovative Teaching, U. So. Calif., 1974, 1st pl. award at juried show Am. Assn. Chinese Brush Painting, 1987. Fellow Gerontol. Soc. Am.; mem. Nat. Assn. Social Workers (cert., nat. chmn. 1962-64, group work sect., chmn. Cleve. chpt. 1969-72), Am. Soc. Aging (chmn. program com. 1983-85, City of Claremont com. on aging), AAUW, Delta Kappa Gamma, Alpha Xi Delta. Episcopalian. Home: 413 Willamette Ln Claremont CA 91711 Office: U So Calif Gerontology Ctr Los Angeles CA 90007

HARTGEN, STEPHEN ANTHONY, newspaper editor; b. Balt., Sept. 30, 1944; s. Vincent Andrew and Frances Caroline (Lubanda) H.; m. Janice Elaine Herbert, Oct. 4, 1980;children: Tiffany Rose, Rachel Frances. BA in Am. Studies cum laude, Amherst Coll., 1966; MA in Am. History, Brandeis U., 1968; PhD in Am. Studies, U. Minn., 1976. Staff writer Mpls. Star, 1967-73; lectr. sch. journalism U. Minn., Mpls., 1973-75; asst. prof. sch. journalism Ohio State U., Columbus, 1975-77; asst. prof., grad. chmn. dept. journalism U. Wyo., 1978; mng. editor Star-Tribune, Casper, Wyo., 1978-79, Star, Anniston, Ala., 1980-82, Times-News, Twin Falls, Idaho, 1982—; dir. editorial staff devel. Howard Pub., Inc., Twin Falls, 1984—; pres. Twin Cities Journalism Review, Mpls., 1972-75. Author: A Guide to Minnesota Records, 1975; co-author: New Strategies for Public Affairs Reporting, 1976; editor: Idaho Media Law Handbook, 1986; contbr. The Reporters Hand Book, 1983. Chmn. Wyo. Freedom Info. com., 1978, Idaho Sci. Rsch. Adv. Com., 1986, Idaho Atty. Gen's. Victim Rights Task Force, 1988; mem. excellence com. Twin Falls Schs., 1986—, agr. adv. com. So. Idaho Coll., 1987. Recipient First Amendment award People for Am. Way, 1985. Mem. AP Mng. Editors Assn., Idaho Allied Dailies Assn. (edn com. 1987—, freedom info. 1988—), Am. Soc. Newspaper Editors, Investigative Reports & Editors, Idaho-Utah AP Dailies Assn. (pres. 1988, Editorial Writing award 1986), Idaho Press Club (pres. 1985, EditorialWriting award 1986), Rotary. Home: 2147 E Addison Ave Twin Falls ID 83301 Office: Times-News 132 W 3d St PO Box 548 Twin Falls ID 83303

HARTLEY, FRED LLOYD, oil company executive; b. Vancouver, B.C., Can., Jan. 16, 1917; came to U.S., 1939, naturalized, 1950; s. John William and Hannah (Mitchell) H.; m. Margaret Alice Murphy, Nov. 2; children: Margaret Ann, Fred Lloyd. BS in Applied Sci., U. B.C., 1939. Engring. supr. Union Oil Co. Calif., 1939-53, mgr. comml. devel., 1953-55, gen. mgr. rsch. dept., 1955-56, v.p. in charge rsch., 1956-60, sr. v.p., 1960-63, exec. v.p., 1963-64, pres., chief exec. officer, 1964-73, chmn. bd. dirs., pres., 1974-85, chief exec. officer, 1985-88, chmn. bd. dirs., 1985-89, chmn. emeritus, 1989—. Bd. dirs. L.A. Philharm. Assn.; sr. trustee Calif. Inst. Tech., Com. Econ. Devel.; ambassador and commr. gen. U.S. exhibition EXPO 86. Mem. Am. Petroleum Inst. (bd. dirs., former chmn. bd. dirs., hon. dir.), Coun. Fgn. Rels., Calif. C. of C. (bd. dirs.). Office: Unocal Corp PO Box 7600 Los Angeles CA 90051

HARTLEY, GRACE VAN TINE, foundation administrator; b. San Francisco, Aug. 24, 1916; d. Ellis Charles and Nadine (Allen) Van Tine; m. Frank Brooke Hartley (div. 1974); children: Shirley Hartley Hill, Linda Hartley Sims, Brooke Hartley Hudson, Jessie Hartley Brady, Frank. Student, De Anza Coll., 1975-77, Coll. of Marin, 1985-86. V.p. Barron & Hartley Builders, Alameda, Calif., 1946-72; pres. Aurley Apt. Houses, Sunnyvale, Calif., 1974-86; exec. dir. George Demont Otis Found., San Francisco, 1974—; pres. Western Arts Acad. Found., San Rafael, Calif., 1982—, Grace Group of Calif., Inc., Corte Madera, Calif. and San Rafael, 1983—. Author, producer: (audio visual) American Artists National Parks, 1976 (Bicentennial award 1976); exhibited in group shows at Golden Gate Collection, 1974 (Soc. Western Artists award 1974), Otis Centennial, 1980 (Calif. History Ctr. award 1980). Pres. Rep. Women's Club, Alameda, 1960-62; active Rep. State Cen. Com., Alameda, 1964, Ronald Reagan Presdl. Task Force, Corte Madera, 1978-80. Recipient cert. Achievement Internat. Platform Assn., Washington, 1982, Presdl. Achievement award Rep. Party, Corte Madera, 1987. Presbyterian.

HARTLEY, JAMES HARRISON, data processing executive; b. Denver, Sept. 28, 1946; s. John Robert and Ossie Lee (Petty) H.; m. Dianne Louise Spearman, June 10, 1967 (div. 1985); children: Shana Renee, Krista Rae; m. Merry Elizabeth Briggs, Dec. 21, 1985; stepchildren: Terrence Lee Tuytschaevers, Tamara Lynn Tuytschaevers. Dipl., Nettleton Bus. Sch., Omaha, 1968; student, Omaha Bapt. Bible Coll., 1964-67. Computer prog. specialist U.S. Army Sec. Agy., Frankfurt, W. Ger., 1968-72; computer programmer Karman Western Apparel, Denver, 1972-74; data processing mgr. Karman Western Apparel, 1974-80; MIS dir. Carefree of Colo. div. Scott Fetzer, Broomfield, 1980-84; data processing mgr. Arapahoe County Sheriff's Dept., Littleton, Colo., 1985—; cons. JH Ent., Littleton, 1985—, Depco Oil, Denver, 1985. With U.S. Army, 1968-72. Recipient award Arapahoe County Sheriff's Dept., 1984. Baptist. Home: 1556 Mount Evans Blvd Pine CO 80470

HARTLEY, JERRY LESTER, insurance executive; b. Sedro Woodley, Wash., Aug. 1, 1937; s. Robert Earl and Lydia (Goode) H.; m. Kathryn Isabelle Hartley, Aug. 11, 1956; children: Karol Lynn, Kenneth Dean, Kristine Louise. Student, N.W. Nazarene Coll., Nat. Coll. Life Underwriters. Agt. Prudential Ins. Co., Salem, Oreg., 1963-72; pvt. practice ins. agt. Salem, 1972-73; office mgr. Mathis Bros., Inc., Salem, 1973-75; owner Capitol Roofing, Inc., Salem, 1975-77; v.p. sales div. J.B. Internat. (Instant Lawn), Salem, 1977-83; agy. mgr. Regional Health Svc., Salem, 1983-88, co-owner, mng. gen. agt., 1988—. Chmn. Pack 12 Cub Scouts, Salem, 1965-69, N. Salem Am. Cities Planning Commn., 1968; co-chmn. com. to re-elect Mark Hatfield, Salem, 1972; fundraising chmn. Marion County Rep. Cen. Com., Salem, 1972. Mem. Salem Assn. Life Underwriters (sec., v.p., pres. health com. 1988—). Republican. Baptist. Office: Regional Health Svc Agy 1725 Capitol St NE Salem OR 97303

HARTLEY-LINSE, BONNIE JEAN, nurse; b. Chgo., July 26, 1923; d. Frank and Anna Kathleen (Koutecky) Kadlec; m. Robert William Hartley, June 23, 1949 (div. Feb. 1961); children: Robert Greig, Franklin James; m. Howard Albert Linse, June 10, 1978 (dec. Nov. 1985); stepchildren: Michael Howard, Janet Stokes. BS in Nursing, St. Xavier Coll., Chgo., 1945; cert. edn. Portland State Coll., 1965; MS in Nursing Edn., U. Oreg., 1972; cert. coll. health nurse practitioner program Brigham Young U., 1976. R.N., Oreg. Mem. faculty nursing St. Xavier Coll., 1945-47; head nurse U. Chgo. Clinics, 1947-48; nurse research newborn neurology U. Oreg. Med. Sch., Portland, summer 1961; coordinator dental assistant program, instr. biology Portland Pub. Schs., Oreg., 1965-67; health service clinician, adminstr. Clackamas Community Coll., Oregon City, Oreg., 1970-84; cons. Health Services Community Colls. of Oreg., 1972-84; pres. Coll. Health Nurses, State of Oreg., 1976-78. Vol. Task Force for Medically Needy of Clackamas County, Oreg.; mem. svc. vol. environ. learning ctr., Clackamas Community Coll. Mem. N.W. Oreg. Health Systems, Clackamas County Sub-Area Council, Oregon City, 1980-86. Recipient Recognition for Outstanding Service award Clackamas Community Coll., 1984; USPHS grantee, 1968. Mem. Am. Nurses Assn., Oreg. Nurses Assn. (Clackamas County unit 26), Pacific Coast Coll. Health Assn. (ann. conf. program coordinator 1980), Oreg. Coll. Health Dirs. Assn., Oreg. Health Decisions. Avocations: travel, piano, choral singing, swimming. Home: 18633 Roundtree Dr Oregon City OR 97045

HARTLOFF, STEPHEN ALEXANDER, insurance company executive; b. Wamego, Kans., June 16, 1947; s. William Henry and Lila Jane (Craig) H.; m. Judith Harrington, Oct. 20, 1973; children: Jacquelyn Colleen, Kathleen Alexandra. BA in Fin., Calif. State U, 1971. Lab. techician Aeronetronics, Newport Beach, Calif., 1967-69; surety underwriter U.S. Fidelity & Security, Fullerton, Calif., 1973-78, Albuquerque, 1974-84; home office underwriter Fireman's Fund, San Francisco, 1978, br. office mgr., 1978-85; br. office mgr. Ins. Co. of the West, Sacramento, 1985—. Mem. Planning Adv. Council, Carmichael, Calif., 1987. Mem. Bldg. Industry Assn. Republican. Lutheran.

HARTMAN, BRENDA ALANE, newspaper executive, human resource specialist; b. Spokane, Wash., Oct. 27, 1952; d. Wilbert James and Letitia May (Taft) H.; m. Richard Allen Frishman, Sept. 24, 1983. Cert., U. Wash., 1987. Customer service rep. The Herald, Everett, Wash., 1972-76, dist. mgr., 1976-78, newsdealer supr., 1978-80, personnel mgr., 1981-85, dir. human resources, 1985—; bd. dirs. Ctr. Career Alternatives, Everett, 1986—. vocat. adv. bd. Everett Community Coll., 1985-86. Mem. vocat. adv. bd. Everett Community Coll., 1985-86, Mukilteo (Wash.) Sch. Dist., 1988—. Mem. Am. Soc. Personnel Adminstrn., Am. Soc. Tng. and Devel., Newspaper Personnel Relations Assn., Pacific NW Personnel Mgmt. Assn. (sec. 1983, v.p. mem. 1984), Cascade (Everett). Club: Cascade. Office: The Herald Grand and California Everett WA 98201

HARTMAN, CHERRY, clinical social worker; b. Portland, Oreg., Sept. 26, 1947; d. Dale Chester and Dorothy Ella (Buterbaugh) H. BA, Lewis & Clark Coll., 1968; MSW, Portland State U., 1975. Caseworker State of Oreg., Grants Pass, 1968-71; dir. counseling Luth. Family Svcs., Portland, 1971-80, Phoenix Rising Found., 1980-89; pvt. practice Phoenix, 1989—. Author: Be-Good-To-Yourself Therapy, 1987; contbr. articles to profl. jours. Named Woman of Yr., Cascade Voice Newspaper, 1985. Mem. Registered Clin. Social Workers Assn. Democrat. Home: 2318 NE 20th Ave Portland OR 97212 Office: 333 SW 5th Ave Ste 401D Portland OR 97204

HARTMAN, DUANE LEVI, service company executive; b. Pt. Arthur, Tex., Feb. 13, 1957; s. Levy and Geneva (Vincent) H.; m. Debby Darlene Massey; children: Shanae Lee, Hunter Levi. Lic. real estate, Colo. Project mgr. H&H Welding & Fab Inc., Bridge City, Tex., 1972-75, Hartman Marine & Construction Inc., Bridge City, 1975-81; owner DLH Engerprises, Aurora, Colo., 1981-84; property mgr. Johnstown Properties Colo., Englewood, Colo., 1984-86; v.p. ops. Grounds Mgmt. Inc., Englewood, 1986—. Mem. Apartment Assn. Metro. Denver, Assoc. Builders and Contractors, Assoc. Landscape Contractors Colo., Profl. Grounds Mgmt. Soc., Profl. Lawn Care Assn. Am., Englewood C. of C., NRA, Internat. Athletic Club. Republican. Methodist. Home: 1670 Witter Gulch Rd Evergreen CO 80439

HARTMAN, GEORGE JOHN, former financial consultant; b. Rankin, Pa., Apr. 15, 1918; s. William Edward and Caroline Christine (Zapf) H.; m. Evelyn Maude Kearney, Nov. 26, 1941; children: Robert, John (dec.), Edward. BS, U. Pitts., 1940; MS, San Fernando State U., 1967. Lic. real estate assoc.; cert. tchr., Calif., Ariz. Mgr. cost dept. Doehler-Jarvis Co., Grand Rapids, Mich., 1945-48; pres. Hartman-Ricker Co., Grand Rapids, 1948-51; budget dir., asst. treas. Lear, Inc., Santa Monica, Calif., 1951-58; sec., treas., bd. dirs. Canoga Electronics, Van Nuys, Calif., 1956-61, Coast Pro Seal & Mfg. Co., L.A., 1961-66; pres., bd. dirs. Ideal Financing, Encino, Calif., 1966-84; owner, mgr. Hartman Assocs., L.A., 1967-77; bd. dirs. Blue Cross-Blue Shield, Phoenix; instr. Valley Jr. Coll., Vna Nuys, 1969-73. Author: Budgeting for Small Business, 1967. Bd. dirs. Sun City (Ariz.) Homeowners Assn., 1980-83; candidate for Ariz. Senate, 1962; mem. Maricopa County Bd. Adjustment, 1983-85. Recipient numerous awards. Mem. Am. Inst. Mgmt. (assoc.), Lions (pres. Sun City chpt. 1985, bd. found., 1986). Republican. Roman Catholic. Home: 9639 Country Club Dr Sun City AZ 85373

HARTMAN, GUY LESLIE, pediatrician; b. Big Flats, N.Y., Sept. 11, 1922; s. Fred Charles and Ruth Agnes (Andrews) H.; m. Shirley Fenn Baldwin, Dec. 23, 1943; children: Eric Vreeland, Fenn Elizabeth, Christina Louise, Peter Bain, Juliana Middaugh. BA in Zoology, Alfred U., 1943; MD, U. Buffalo, 1946. Diplomate Am. Bd. Pediatrics. Served to maj. USAF, 1943-52; intern Med. Ctr., Jersey City, 1946-47; pediatrics resident Children's Hosp., Los Angeles, 1957-59; pediatrician So. Calif. Permanente Med. Group, Fontana, 1952-87; chmn. Cen. Valley Child Abuse Team, Fontana, 1975-87, San Bernardino County Child Abuse Council, 1986-87; bd. dirs., v.p. Calif. Consortium Child Abuse, 1981-86; pres. Southwestern Pediatric Soc. Los Angeles, 1984-85. Contbr. articles to profl. jours. and mags. Speaker civic orgns. nationally. Recipient Citation Domestic Violence Task Force San Bernardino, 1984, Martha Lou Berkey award Inland Empire Child Abuse Task Force, 1985. Fellow Am. Acad. Pediatrics; mem. Southwestern Pediatric Soc. (chmn. 1984-85), Los Angeles Pediatric Soc., Hinterland Pediatric Soc., Internat. Soc. Prevention of Child Abuse and Neglect, Def. of Children. Republican. Mormon. Home: 1425 Ashland Ave Claremont CA 91711

HARTMAN, HEDY ANN, museum chief executive officer; b. Sept. 24, 1954; d. Alan Stuart Hartman and Joan Marcia (Lederman) Hartman Goldsmith; m. Jon Abbott Mersereau, Nov. 27, 1976 (div. June 1981); m. William Bainbridge Everett, June 2, 1984. B.A. with distinction, U. Pa., 1975; M.A., U. Wash., 1982, Ph.C., 1983. Researcher Am. Mus. Natural History, N.Y.C., 1974; curatorial asst. Univ. Mus., U. Pa., Phila., 1974-75; instr. Children's Mus., Indpls., 1976; curatorial asst. Indpls. Mus. Art, 1975-76; program adminstr. statewide services S.C. State Mus., Columbia, 1977-80; pres. Hartman Planning & Devel. Group Ltd., Bellevue, Wash., 1980—; S.C. state rep. Southeastern Mus. Conf., 1979-80. Author: Funding Sources and Technical Assistance for Museums and Historical Organizations, 1979; Fund Raising for Museums, 1985. Editor: Official Museum Guide to Products and Services, 1980. Mem. Am. Assn. Museums, Am. Assn. State and Local History (bd. dirs. 1983—), Western Museums Conf. (bd. dirs. 1980-83), Wash. Mus. Assn. (bd. dirs. 1985—; sec. 1986—). Office: Hartman Planning & Devel Corp PO Box 3401 Redmond WA 98073-3401

HARTMAN, MATTHEW ALOYSIUS, real estate administrator; b. N.Y.C., July 18, 1922; s. Matthew Aloysius and Mary Agnes (Linskey) H.; m. Lillian Marie Broderick, Apr. 17, 1948 (div. 1958); children: Nancy Marie, Susan Marie; m. Margaret Gail Obert, Nov. 8, 1974; stepchildren: Kenneth Mark Wooden, Lorelei Jean Kaczmarski. LLB, St. John's U., Bklyn., 1945. Bar: N.Y. 1946. Law clk., atty. Burlington, Veeder, Clark & Hupper, N.Y.C., 1945-46; mng. atty. Michelsen & Elliot, N.Y.C., 1946-48; pvt. practice Huntington, N.Y., 1948-57; examiner Lane Title & Trust Co., Phoenix, 1958-60; sr. title examiner Ariz. State Hwy. Dept., Phoenix, 1961-71; real estate adminstr. Maricopa Co. Hwy. Dept., Phoenix, 1972—. Mem. Rep. Nat. Com., 1978—. Mem. Internat. Right Way Assn., Maricopa Assn. Govts., Scottsdale Yacht Club (commodore 1977). Roman Catholic. Home: 6120 E Monterey Way Scottsdale AZ 85251 Office: Maricopa County Hwy Dept 3325 W Durango St Phoenix AZ 85009

HARTMAN, PAULA A., teacher; b. Panama City, Fla., June 7, 1953; d. Paul F. and Mary A. Lane; m. Daniel S. Hartman. BS, U Ind., 1975; MS, Ind. U., 1977; postgrad., Portland State U., 1985—. Cert. tchr. Spl. Edn., Elem. Edn. Supr. Ind. U.; supr. Ind. U., Bloomington, 1976, area coordinator, 1977; elem. tchr. LaFayette (Ind.) Sch. Corp., 1975-76; vocat./ spl. edn. tchr. Owen Valley Schs., Spencer, Ind., 1977-78, multicategorical resource tchr., 1978-81; resource tchr. Portland (Oreg.) Pub. Schs., 1984-86; resource/consulting tchr. Portland (Oreg.) Pub. Schs., Oreg., 1986-87, diagnostic specialist, 1987—. Mem. NEA, Portland Assn. Tchrs.

HARTMAN, ROBERT LEROY, artist, educator; b. Sharon, Pa., Dec. 17, 1926; s. George Otto and Grace Arvada (Radabaugh) H.; m. Charlotte Ann Johnson, Dec. 30, 1951; children: Mark Allen, James Robert. B.F.A., U. Ariz., 1951, M.A., 1952; postgrad., Colo. Springs Fine Arts Center, 1947, 51, Bklyn. Mus. Art Sch., 1953-54. Instr. architecture, allied arts Tex. Tech. Coll., 1955-58; asst. prof. art U. Nev., Reno, 1958-61; mem. faculty dept. art U. Calif., Berkeley, 1961—; prof. U. Calif., 1972—, chmn. dept., 1974-76; mem. Inst. for Creative Arts, U. Calif., 1967-68. One man exhbns. include, Bertha Schafer Gallery, N.Y.C., 1966, 69, 74, Santa Barbara Mus. Art, 1973, Cin. Art Acad., 1975, Hank Baum Gallery, San Francisco, 1973, 75, 78, San Jose Mus. Art, 1983, Bluxome Gallery, San Francisco, 1984, Bluxome Gallery, San Francisco, 1984, 86, U. Art Mus., Berkeley, 1986, Instituto D'Arte Dosso Dossi, Ferrara, Italy, 1989; group exhbns. include Richmond Mus., 1966, Whitney Mus. Biennial, 1973, Oakland Mus., 1976, San Francisco Arts Commn. Gallery, 1985 (award); represented in permanent collections, Nat. Collections Fine Arts, Colorado Springs Fine Arts Center, Corcoran Gallery, San Francisco Art Inst., Roswell Mus. U. Calif. humanities research fellow, 1980. Office: U Calif Dept Art Berkeley CA 94720

HARTSOUGH, GAYLA A. KRAETSCH, management consultant; b. Lakewood, Ohio, Sept. 16, 1949; d. Vernon W. and Mildred E. (Austin) Kraetsch; m. James N. Heller, Aug. 20, 1972 (div. 1977); m. Jeffrey W. Hartsough, Mar. 12, 1983. BS, Northwestern U., 1970; EdM, Tufts U., 1973; MEd, U. Va., 1978, PhD, 1978. Vol. VISTA, Greeneville, Tenn., 1970-71; asst. tchr. Perkins Sch. for the Blind, Watertown, Mass., 1971-72; team ldr., resource tchr. Fairfax County (Va.) Pub. Schs., 1972-76; asst. dir. Am. Psychological Assn. clinic U. Va., Charlottesville, 1976-78; sr. program officer Acad. for Edn. Devel., Washington, 1978-80; mgmt. cons. Cresap div. TPF&C Co., Washington and L.A., 1980-86; pres. KH Cons. Group, L.A., 1986—; cons. Los Angeles Community Coll. Dist., 1988—, Am. Motors Corp., Bramalea, Can., 1987, others; joint ventures cons. Arthur D. Little, U.S., Pak-Poy & Kneebone, Australia, Bernard Krief, France. Contbr. over 24 articles to profl. jours. Vol. assoc. chair United Way, Los Angeles County, 1984—; co-founder Los Angeles Higher Edn. Roundtable, Los Angeles, 1988—. Woodrow Wilson fellow, 1978-80. Mem. Orgn. Women Execs. Home: 15624 Royal Ridge Rd Sherman Oaks CA 91403 Office: KH Cons Group 1901 Ave of the Stars #1774 Los Angeles CA 90067

HARTWELL, ROBERT SIMPSON, piano educator; b. Memphis, Jan. 12, 1952; s. Lindley Stearns and Alice Cary (Simpson) H.; m. Eileen M. Beaudry, July 16, 1988. BA, Sonoma State U., 1980; MA, San Francisco State U., 1987. Pvt. tchr. Menlo Park, Calif., 1975—; guest lectr., musicologist, performing pianist various schs., Calif., 1980—. Composer songs and instrumental works, 1984—. Mem. Music Tchrs. Assn. Unitarian. Home: 1036 Berkeley Ave Menlo Park CA 94025

HARTWICK, THOMAS STANLEY, aerospace company executive; b. Vandalia, Ill., Mar. 19, 1934; s. William Arthur and Bernice Elizabeth (Daniels) H.; m. Alberta Elaine Lind, June 10, 1961; children: Glynis Anne, Jeffrey Andrew, Thomas Arthur. BS, U. Ill., 1956; MS, UCLA, 1958; PhD, U. So. Calif., 1969. Mgr. quantum electronics dept. Aerospace Corp., El Segundo, Calif., 1973-75, asst. dir. electronics research lab., 1975-79; mgr. electro-optical devel. lab. Hughes Aircraft Co. subs. Gen. Motors Corp., El Segundo, 1979-82, chief sci. advanced tactical programs, 1982-83; mgr. electro-optics research ctr. TRW Corp., Redondo Beach, Calif., 1983-86, mgr. microelectrics ctr., 1986—; bd. dirs. Laser Tech. Inc., Hollywood, Calif.; cons. mem. U.S. Dept. Def. Adv. Group on Electronic Devices, Washington, 1977—, group chmn., 1988—; mem. Japan/U.S. Tech. Assessment team, Washington, 1984. Contbr. articles to profl. jours.; inventor FAR Infrared Laser, 1975. Mem. adv. com. Calif. State U., Long Beach, 1983-85, U. So. Calif. Photonics Inst., 1985-88, U. Colo. Opto-Electronics Inst., Boulder, 1986-87. Mem. Am. Phys. Soc., Optical Soc. Am., (com. mem. 1976-79), Am. Def. Preparedness Assn. (dep. chmn. West Coast chpt. 1987-88). Office: TRW Inc Microelectronics Ctr One Space Park Redondo Beach CA 90278

HARTZELL, DOUGLAS KEITH, interior designer; b. Harrisburg, Pa., May 31, 1946. AS, Mohegan Community Coll., Norwich, Conn., 1981; BA with hons., Calif. State U., Sacramento, 1988. Enlisted USN, 1966; shift supr. USN, Hawaii, 1966-69; adminstrn. supr., equal opportunity and human resources mgmt. specialist USN, Calif., Hawaii, 1971-83; quality control mgr. Gen. Battery Corp., Reading, Pa., 1970-71; mgr. corp. adminstrn. services Dysan Corp., Santa Clara, Calif., 1983-85; assoc. designer Rae Designs, Citrus Heights, Calif., 1987—. sr. chief petty officer USNR, 1983—. Mem. Am. Soc. of Interior Designers. Republican. Lutheran. Home: PO Box 2068 Fair Oaks CA 95628

HARVEY, CLIFFORD SHERRILL, protective services official; b. Boston, Apr. 2, 1943; s. Clifford Akers and Helen Elizabeth (Sherrill) H.; m. Mary Jack, May 18, 1964; children: Ronald James, Helen Elizabeth. Student, Mont. Sch. Mines, 1961-62; AA in fire sci. tech., Red Rocks Community Coll., Denver, 1972, AA, 1973. Firefighter Boulder (Colo.) Fire Dept., 1968-73, rescue squad tech., 1973-74, asst. fire marshal, 1974-79, chief fire marshal, 1979—; pres. FireMeasure, Inc., Boulder, 1981-85, Fire Mark Ltd., Boulder, 1988—. Contbr. numerous articles to profl. jours. Staff sgt.

USAF, 1962-66. Mem. Soc. Fire Protection Engrs. (vice chmn. computer users com., sec. Rocky Mt. chpt.), Nat. Fire Protection Assn. (health care sect., fire service sect., mem.'s adv. council), Met. Arson Investigators Assn., Fire Service Tng. Bd., Fire Marshals' Assn. Colo., Fire Marshals' Assn. North Am., Internat. Conf. Bldg. Officials, Nat. Assn. Fire Investigators, Masons. Republican. Methodist. Home: 1090 Edinboro Dr Boulder CO 80303 Office: Boulder Fire Dept PO Box 791 Boulder CO 80306

HARVEY, ELAINE LOUISE, artist, educator; b. Riverside, Calif., Mar. 1, 1936; d. Edgar Arthur and Emma Louise (Shull) Siervogel; m. Stuart Herbert Harvey, June 16, 1957; children: Kathleen Robin, Laurel Lynn, Mark Stuart. BA with highest honors, with distinction, San Diego State U., 1957. Cert. gen. elem. tchr., Calif. Tchr. Cajon Valley Schs., El Cajon, Calif., 1957, 58; free-lance artist El Cajon, 1975—; juror various art exhbns., Calif., 1983—; lectr., 1984—; tchr. painting seminars, 1987—. Editor: Palette to Palate, 1986; contbr. The Artists Mag., 1987. Trustee San Diego Mus. Art, 1985, 86; leader El Cajon council Girl Scouts of U.S., 1968; vol. art tchr., San Diego area pub. schs., 1973-76. Recipient Merit award La. Watercolor Soc., 1984, Arches Canson Rives award Midwest Watercolor Soc./Tweed Mus., Greenbay, Wis., 1984, Winsor Newton award Midwest Watercolor Soc./Neville Mus., Duluth, Minn., 1985; McKinnon award Am. Watercolor Soc. 1985, Creative Connection award Rocky Mountain Nat. Exhibition 1986, 1st Juror's award San Diego Internat. Watercolor Exhibition 1986, Dassler Mochs award Adirondacks Exhibition of Am. Art. Mem. Nat. Watercolor Soc. (bd. dirs. 1987, 88), Watercolor West (bd. dirs. 1986, 87, 88), West Coast Watercolor Soc., San Diego Watercolor Soc. (pres., 1979, 80, chmn. 1980, 81, Silver Recognition award 1986), San Diego Mus. Art Artist's Guild (pres. 1985, 86, bd. dirs. 1986-87), Western Fedn. Watercolor Socs. (del. 1983—), Rocky Mountain Nat. Watermedia Soc., Allied Artists of Am. Club: Grossmont Garden (La Mesa, Calif.) (Elson Trophy 1977, 79). Home and Studio: 1602 Sunburst Dr El Cajon CA 92021

HARVEY, GREGORY ALAN, microcomputer technology educator, consultant; b. Harvey, Ill., Feb. 15, 1949; s. Kenneth Herman and Mildred Faye (Pounds) H. BA, U. Ill., 1970; teaching credential, San Francisco State U., 1982. Mem. drafting and design staff Bechtel Engring., San Francisco, 1973-81; computer cons., prin. Harvey & Assocs., San Francisco, 1981—; instr., Golden Gate U., San Francisco, 1987—; computer cons., PCTeach, Inverness, Calif., 1988—. Author Sybex computer books: Communication in Writing, 1984, Mastering SuperCalc3, 1985, Mastering Q&A, 1986, Lotus 1-2-3 Desktop Companion, 1987, WordPerfect Desktop Companion, 1987, Mastering WordStar, 1987, Lotus 1-2-3- Instant Reference, 1988, WordPerfect Instant Reference, 1988, DOS Instant Reference, 1988, Understanding HyperCard, 1988, HyperTalk Instant Reference, 1988, The Complete Lotus 1-2-3 Release 2 Handbook, 1989. Mem. Macs of Marin, Berkeley Macintosh Users Group. Democrat. Zen Buddhist. Home: 60 Kyleswood Pl Inverness CA 94937 Office: Harvey & Assocs PO Box 1175 Point Reyes Station CA 94956

HARVEY, JAMES GERALD, educational consultant, counselor, researcher; b. California, Mo., July 15, 1934; s. William Walter and Exie Marie (Lindley) H. BA Amherst Coll., 1956; MAT (fellow), Harvard U., 1958, MEd, 1962. Asst. to dean grad. sch. edn. Harvard U., Cambridge, Mass., 1962-66, dir. admissions, fin. aid, 1966-69; dir. counseling service U. Calif., Irvine, 1970-72; ednl. cons., Los Angeles, 1972—. 1st lt. USAF, 1958-61. Amherst Mayo-Smith grantee, 1956-57; UCLA Adminstrv. fellow, 1969-70. Mem. Am. Ednl. Research Assn., Nat. Council Measurement in Edn., Am. Assn. for Counseling and Devel. Address: 1845 Glendon Ave Los Angeles CA 90025

HARVEY, JAMES ROSS, financial company executive; b. Los Angeles, Aug. 20, 1934; s. James Ernest and Loretta Berniece (Ross) H.; m. Charlene Coakley, July 22, 1971; children: Kjersten Ann, Kristina Ross. B.S. in Engring., Princeton U., 1956; M.B.A., U. Calif.-Berkeley, 1963. Engr. Chevron Corp., San Francisco, 1956-61; acct. Touche, Ross, San Francisco, 1963-64; chmn. bd., chief exec. officer, dir. Transamerica Corp., San Francisco, 1965—; bd. dirs. Sedgwick Group, Pacific Telesis Group, McKesson Corp., SRI Internat., Charles Schwab. Bd. trustees St. Mary's Coll.; bd. dirs. U. Calif. Bus. Sch., Calif. State Parks Found., Bay Area Council, Mt. Land Reliance, Nat. Park Found. Served with AUS, 1958-59. Mem. San Francisco C. of C. (dir., pres.), Bohemian Club, Pacific-Union Club, Union League Club. Office: Transam Corp 600 Montgomery St San Francisco CA 94111

HARVEY, MONA REATHIA, community liaison worker; b. Carthage, Miss., Jan. 16, 1955; d. Lacy McDonald and Shirley B. (Earnest) Fuller; m. Torie Lee Harvey, June 15, 1974; 1 child, Torrie Lavone. Grad. high sch., Colorado Springs, Colo. Nurses' aide Four Seasons Nursing Ctr., Colorado Springs, 1973; campus supr. Wm. J. Palmer High Sch., Colorado Springs, 1973-84, community liaison, 1984—; team mem. Mil. Liaison, 1980—, Intervention Team, 1985—; instr. Get Set Team, 1987—. Recipient Outstanding Support award, U.S. Army, 1986, 87, Support award Navy, 1988, Honorary Navy Recruiter Cert., USAF, 1987. Office: Palmer High Sch 301 N Nevada Ave Colorado Springs CO 80903-1299

HARVEY, PAMLA, engineer; b. St. Petersburg, Fla., Apr. 6, 1963; d. Samuel Stedman and Susan Ann (Shollenberger) H. AA, Eastern Ariz. Coll., Thatcher, 1983; BS in Engineering, Northern Ariz. U., 1987. Test engr. Rockwell Internat., Rocketoyne, Canoga Park, Calif., 1987—. Vol. Habitat for Humanity, Atlanta, 1988. Mem. Soc. Women Engrs. (pres. student chpt. 1986-87), IEEE, Rockwell Orgn. for Women. Democrat. Baptist. Home: 1508 2nd St Simi Valley CA 93065 Office: Rockwell Rocketdyne Div 6633 Canoga Ave Canoga Park CA 91303

HARVEY, PATRICIA JEAN, educational association administrator; b. Newman, Calif., Oct. 27, 1931; d. Willard Monroe and Marjorie (Greenlee) Clougher; m. Richard Blake Harvey, Aug. 29, 1965; children: G. Scott Floden, Timothy P. Harvey. BA, Whittier Coll., 1966, MA, 1971. Resource specialist Monte Vista High Sch. and Whittier High Sch., Whittier, Calif., 1977—; dept. chairperson spl. edn. Whittier High Sch., Whittier, Calif., 1982—. Author: (tchrs. manual) The Dynamics of Calif. Govt. and Politics, 1970; co-author: Meeting The Needs of Special High School Students in Regular Education Classrooms, 1988. Active Whittier Fair Housing Com., 1972; pres. Women's Aux. Whittier Coll., 1972-73, sec., 1971-72; historian Docian Soc. Whittier Coll., 1963-64, pres. 1965-66. Democrat. Episcopalian. Home: 424 Avocado Crest Rd La Habra Heights CA 90631 Office: Whittier Union High Sch 12417 E Philadelphia St Whittier CA 90601

HARVEY, RICHARD DUDLEY, marketing consultant; b. Atlanta, Sept. 24, 1923; s. Robert Emmett and June (Dudley) H.; BA, U. Denver, 1947; postgrad. various bus. seminars Harvard U., Stanford U.; m. Donna Helen Smith, Oct. 12, 1944; 1 child, Louise Dudley. Various positions in sales, sales promotion and mktg. The Coca-Cola Co., St. Louis, Denver and Atlanta, 1948-60, v.p., brand mgr., mktg. mgr., mktg. dir., Atlanta, 1965-70, v.p. orgn. and mktg. devel., 1970-75; sr. v.p. mktg. Olympia Brewing Co., Olympia, Wash., 1975-78; with Sound Mktg. Services Inc., Seattle; dir. Lone Star Brewing Co., San Antonio. Mem. mayor's housing resources com., Atlanta, 1968-70; program chmn. United Way, Atlanta, 1969; trustee Episcopal Radio-TV Found., Atlanta, 1961-88, vice chmn. 1975-84, emeritus trustee, 1988—; bd. dirs. Oreg. Shakespearean Festival Assn., 1982-86; chmn. mktg. com., trustee Seattle Symphony, 1983-88; mem. assistance com. Albers Sch. Bus. Seattle U., 1988—; gov.'s adv. com. bus. devel. and job retention, State of Wash., 1988—. Served with USAAF, 1942-45. Mem. Am. Mktg. Assn. (pres. 1983-84), Mktg. Communications Execs. Internat. (pres. 1984-85), Inst. Mgmt. Cons., Phi Beta Kappa, Omicron Delta Kappa. Democrat. Episcopalian. Clubs: The Rainier, Seattle Tennis (Seattle). Home: 3837 E Crockett St Seattle WA 98112-2422 Office: Sound Mktg Svcs Inc PO Box 22443 Seattle WA 98122

HARVEY, ROBERT J., medical supplies company executive. Chmn., chief exec. officer Thoratec Labs. Corp., Berkeley, Calif. Address: Thoratec Labs Corp 2023 8th St Berkeley CA 94710 *

HARVEY, VALERIE DIONNE, educator, home economist; b. Grants, N.Mex., Jan. 7, 1958; d. Wesley C. and Vivian (Porter) Andrews; m. William C. Harvey, Jan. 7, 1978. BS in Home Econs. Edn., U. N.Mex., 1985, postgrad., 1985—. Cert. social studies and vocat. home econs. tchr., N.Mex. Fashion model Flair Acad. & Agy., Albuquerque, 1974—; med. sec. James D. Harvey, Albuquerque, 1976-85; interior decorator Wallpaper Plus, Albuquerque, 1985-86; shopping cons., fashion coord., dir. teenboard Broadway S.W., Albuquerque, 1986-87; tchr. spl. edn. Albuquerque Pub. Sch. System, Albuquerque, 1987—; lectr. N.Mex. Restaurant Assn., 1987. Vol. probation officer Juvenile Ct., Albuquerque, 1987-88. Helen Easterly Meml. scholar, Home Econs. Meml. scholar, Ives scholar U. Nex., 1985, spl. edn. crisis grantee, 1988. Mem. Am. Home Econs. Assn. (cert. in health edn., home econs. and spl. edn.), N.Mex. Home Econs. Assn. (treas. ednl. sect. 1987-88), Albuquerque Home Economists (chmn. scholarship 1989-90), Kappa Omicron Phi. Republican. Baptist. Home: 3553 San Pedro Dr NE Albuquerque NM 87110 Office: Wash Mid Sch 1101 Park SW Albuquerque NM 87102

HARWICK, MAURICE, lawyer; b. Los Angeles, Feb. 6, 1933; m. Saowapa Butranon, July 4, 1970; children: Manasnati, Manasnapa. AA, Los Angeles City Coll., 1954; JD, Southwestern U., 1957. Bar: Calif., 1958; U.S. Supreme Ct. bar, 1962. Dep. dist. atty. County of Los Angeles, 1958-60; individual practice law, Santa Monica, Calif., 1960—; judge pro tem Municipal Ct., 1966-67, 80, 81, 85, 86, 87. Chmn. bd. rev. Los Angeles Community Colls. and City Schs.; mem. Project Safer Calif. gov.'s com., 1974-75. Mem. ABA, Calif. Bar Assn., Los Angeles County Bar Assn., Criminal Cts. Bar Assn. (pres. 1972, bd. govs.), Assn. Trial Lawyers Am., Los Angeles County Dist. Attys. Assn., Vikings. Office: 2001 Wilshire Blvd Ste 600 Santa Monica CA 90403

HARWOOD, ALLAN DALE, video systems manager, consultant; b. Portland, Oreg., Nov. 28, 1939; s. Franklin Barton and Ruth (Fickel) H.; m. Lois Evelyn Rowley, Sept. 4, 1958; children: Leroy Allan, Craig Steven, Kenneth Dale. Student, U. Wash., 1966, Seattle Community Coll., 1967, 85. N.W. region svc. mgr. Dictaphone Corp., Seattle, 1961-64; sales mgr. Aero Marc Co., Seattle, 1964-70, mgr. video systems, 1971-73; v.p. engring. Gowar Corp., Seattle, 1970-71; sales engr. Wash. Sch. Supply, Seattle, 1973-74; pres., chief exec. office Custom Video Systems, Inc., Seattle, 1974-88; video systems mgr. Photo & Sound Co., Seattle, 1988—. With USN, 1958-61, PTO. Mem. Soc. Broadcast Engrs. (bd. dirs. Seattle chpt. 1987—), Internat. TV Assn., Internat. Communications Industry Assn. (exec. video com. Washington chpt. 1984—). Methodist. Home: 11400 Bella Coola Rd Edmonds WA 98020 Office: Photo & Sound Co 19221 66th Ave S Seattle WA 98138

HARWOOD, IVAN RICHMOND, pediatric cardiologist; b. Huntington, W.Va., July 3, 1939. BA, Dartmouth Coll., 1961; MD, U. W.Va., 1965. Diplomate Nat. Bd. Med. Examiners; lic. physician, Calif., Can.; cert. Am. Bd. Pediatrics. Intern in pediatrics U. W.Va. Hosp., Morgantown, 1965-66; resident in pediatrics Yale-New Haven (Conn.) Hosp., 1966-68, sr. resident outpatient dept., 1968-69; chief pediatrics USAF Hosp. 3646, Del Rio, Tex., 1968-70; asst. prof. pediatrics U. Calif. Med. Ctr., San Diego, 1971-78, chief pediatric pulmonary div., 1972—, dir. pediatric intensive care unit, 1972-78, assoc. adj. prof. pediatrics, 1978-86, prof., 1987—; mem. library com., staff bylaw com. and numerous others U. Calif. Med. Ctr., 1976—; co-dir. Cystic Fibrosis Ctr., San Diego, 1972-73, dir., 1973—; mem. Cystic Fibrosis Young Adult Com., Atlanta, 1974-80, chmn., 1976-80; mem. San Diego County Tuburculosis Control Bd., 1974-78; presenter, lectr. in field. Producer: (videos) Issues in Cystic Fibrosis Series; cons., The Cardiopulmonary Jour., 1981; mem. rev. bd., CF Film, 1980; contbr. chpts. to books, and numerous articles to profl. jours. Mem. Air Quality Adv. Com., State of Calif., 1974-80; mem. Genetically Handicapped Persons Program Adv. Com., Calif., 1977-87; mem. adv. bd. Grossmont Coll. Inhalation Therapy Sch., San Diego, 1975-76; mem. inpatient adolscent adv. com., Mercy Hosp., 1982-85. U. Calif. fellow in pediatric cardiology, 1970-71; recipient 1st Prize Internat. Rehab. Film Library Competition, 1980. Mem. Calif. Med. Assn. (patient care audit com. 1975-78), Nat. Cystic Fibrosis Found. (consumer focus com. 1976-80, med. adv. com. 1976-80. planning ad hoc com. 1976-77, ctr. com. 1986—, patient registry sub-com. 1986—), San Diego Found. for Med. Care (major med. rev. com. 1978-84), San Diego Lung Assn. (pediatric com. 1976-80, chmn. Project Breath-Easy 1976-78), Am. Thoracic Soc. Home: PO Box 431 Jamul CA 92035 Office: 4130 Front St San Diego CA 92130

HARZ, G. MICHAEL, real estate developer; b. N.Y.C., Apr. 18, 1951; s. Victor and Arlene (Nadohl) H. BSCE, Cornell U., 1973. Pres. Zibeq Enterprises, N.Y.C., 1975—. Regent scholar N.Y. State Edn. Dept., 1969-73; recipient Nat. Collegiate Legal Studies award U.S. Achievement Acad., 1988, Home: 1156 Aspen Dr Evergreen CO 80439

HASEMEIER, DONNA RAE, counselor; b. Covington, Ky., Feb. 14, 1942; d. Estill D. Mitts and Edythe Louise (Kuchenmeister) Edwards; m. John Robert Hasemeier, Nov. 3, 1962; children: Martin John, Scott Alan, Jo Ellen, Robert Jay. Grad., Christ Hosp. Sch. Nursing, Cin., 1962; Assoc Social Work, Glendale Coll., 1979; BA, Ottawa U., Phoenix, 1986, MA, 1989. RN, Ariz., Ohio; cert. addiction counselor, Ariz. Underwriting asst. Union Cen. Life Ins. Co., Cin., 1959; nursing supr. Children's Convalescent Hosp., Cin., 1962-63; staff nurse Dunham County Hosp., Cin., 1963-64, Christ Hosp. Med. Ctr., Cin., 1964-65; med.-surg. charge nurse Phoenix Bapt. Med. Ctr., 1968-69; coord. chem. dependency Camelback Psychiat. Hosp., Phoenix, 1976-80; pvt. nurse Dr. J.F. Szymanski, M.D., Ltd., Phoenix, 1980-81; evening nursing supr. Women's Ctr. for Addiction Treatment, Phoenix, 1980-81; dir. counseling svcs. Sun City Area Interfaith Svcs., Inc., Sun City West, Ariz., 1985—; rehab. cons. Injury Mgmt. and Rehab. Corp., Phoenix, 1980-83. Editor: Human Services Professionals, 1987—. Webelo scout leader Boy Scouts Am., 1973-75, mem. Cactus-Pine coun., 1973-74; mem. parent adv. coun. Washington Sch. Dist., 1976-78; former ch. sch. tchr., coord. vacation ch. sch., mem. bd. and sec. Women's Fellowship, Ch. of Beatitudes. Mem. Human Svcs. Profls. (news editor 1987—), Ariz. Group Psychotherapy Soc., Ariz. Poetry Soc. (treas. Phoenix br. 1985-86), Phi Theta Kappa. Republican. Congregationalist. Home: 3019 W Wescott Dr Phoenix AZ 85027 Office: Sun City Area Interfaith Svcs Inc 17635 El Mirage Rd Surprise AZ 85374

HASHIMOTO, LLOYD KEN, communications executive; b. Cheyenne, Wyo., Sept. 21, 1944; s. Harry H. and Bettie M. (Kadota) H. Prin. Teltron Electronics, Laramie, Wyo., 1972—; audio visual technician U. Wyo., Laramie, 1972—; instr. workshops and seminars High Tech to a Lay Person, 1978; instr. workshop radio direction finding, 1988—. Contbr. articles to profl. jours. Program chmn., unit and dist. commr. Snowy Range Dist. Boy Scouts Am., Laramie, 1985—, eagle scout, 1961, active, Wood Badge, N.C., 1987. With U.S. Army, 1965-69. Mem. IEEE, Assn. Ednl. Communications Tech., Assn. for Field Svc. Mgrs. Internat., Am. Legion. Home: 504 S 26th St Laramie WY 82070 Office: Teltron Electronics PO Box 1049 Laramie WY 82070

HASKELL, PETER ABRAHAM, actor; b. Boston, Oct. 15, 1934; s. Norman Abraham and Rose Veronica (Golden) H.; m. Ann Compton, Feb. 27, 1960 (div. 1974); m. Dianne Tolmich, Oct. 26, 1974; children: Audra Rosemary, Jason Abraham. BA, Harvard U., 1962; student, N.Y. Law Sch., 1982-83. Actor (films) Finnegans Wake, 1965, Legend of Earl Durand, 1972, Christina, 1974, Forty Days of Musa Dagh, 1982, Riding the Edge, 1987, (TV series) Bracken's World, NBC, 1968-70, Rich Man Poor Man, Book II, ABC, 1976-77, Ryan's Hope, ABC, 1982-83, Search for Tomorrow, NBC, 1983-85, Rituals, Metromedia, 1985, The Law and Harry McGraw, CBS, 1987-88. Served with U.S. Army, 1954-56. Mem. Screen Actors Guild, Actors Equity, AFTRA, Am. Film Inst., Acad. TV Arts and Scis. Democrat. Office: care Belson-Klass Assocs 211 S Beverly Dr Ste 106 Beverly Hills CA 90212

HASKINS, THOMAS ALEXANDER, creativity company executive; b. Plainfield, N.J., Dec. 14, 1950; s. Lewis Byron and June Alice (Cuthbertson) H. BArch, Carnegie-Mellon U., 1972; MBA, UCLA, 1978. Apprentice architect Carl W. Fischer, Architect, Denver, 1972-74; project leader Rocky Mountain Prestress Co., Denver, 1974-76; teaching asst. Grad. Sch. Mgmt., UCLA, 1977-78; program dir. Performance Systems Improvement, Tustin, Calif., 1978-81; pres. Haskins Orgn., Denver, 1981—; cons. constrn. industry, motivational speaker. Author: Marketing Professional Services, 1982, How To Raise Your Fees, 1986; contbr. articles to profl. publs.; puppet video producer; screenwriter videos, 1982—. Office: 7280 S Jay St Littleton CO 80123-4659

HASLAM, GERALD PETER, marketing executive; b. Rotherham, England, Feb. 5, 1945; came to Can., 1952; s. Hubert Sterland and Muriel Croft (Baker) H.; m. Patricia Ann Wheatley, June 22, 1968. B.A., McGill U., Montreal, 1967. Vice pres. corp. communications MacMillan Bloedel, Vancouver, B.C., Can., 1977-79; dir. videotex services Southam Inc., Toronto, Ont., Can., 1979-82; publisher The Province, Vancouver, B.C., Can., 1982-85; v.p., publisher Pacific Press Ltd., Vancouver, B.C., Can., 1985-88, v.p. mktg., 1988—; bd. dirs. Canadian Press, Toronto, Ont., Vancouver Community Coll. Ednl. Found., vice-chmn., 1988—. Patron Vancouver Aquarium. Named Mktg. Exec. of Yr. Vancouver Sales & Mktg. Execs., 1987. Mem. Commonwealth Press Union, Internat. Press Inst., Can. Daily Newspaper Publishers Assn., Am. Press Inst. (chmn. Western adv. bd. 1985—). Anglican. Clubs: Royal Vancouver Yacht, Can. of Vancouver (bd. dirs. 1985—); Royal Can. Yacht (Toronto); Shaughnessy Golf and Country. Office: Pacific Press Ltd, 2250 Granville St, Vancouver, BC Canada V6H 3G2

HASSAN, LYNDA BAHEERAH, pre-school owner, educator; b. Jackson, Miss., Oct. 24, 1949; d. James and Lena Mae (Hayes) Smith; m. Aubrey Kenneth Hassan, Jan. 28, 1969; 1 child, Omar Sharieff. Student, Jackson State U., 1966-68, Armstrong Bus. Coll., Berkeley, Calif., 1966-68; BS in Health Services Adminstrn., St. Mary's Coll., Morgaga, Calif., 1984. Charge receptionist Johnson and Mosley Pub. Relations Co., Jackson, Miss., 1966-70; charge sec. Dickerson and Dickerson Pub. Relations Co., Jackson, 1970-71; asst. supr. Richmond (Va.) Pub. Sch. Dist., 1971-73; acting office mgr., supr. Children's Hosp., Oakland, Calif., 1973-80; telecommunications officer Samuel Merritt Hosp., Oakland, 1980-81; radiology clerical supr. Kaiser Permanente Hosp., Oakland, 1981-83; telecommunications analyst Kaiser Permanente Health Plan, Oakland, 1983-85; owner, prin. A.M.I.P. Daycare Nursery Services, Oakland, 1986—; chairperson Well-Being Com. Am. Muslim Community, Oakland, 1985—, mem. leadership council, 1985—; bd. dirs Masjidul Waritheen, Childcare Employee Project, Oakland; coord. mem. Oakland Bus. Devel. Corp. Bd. dirs. Chinatown Oakland Community Devel. Council, 1987—, Oakland Bus. Devel. Corp., 1988—, Masjidul Waritheen; chairperson Well-Being Com. Am. Muslim Community. Mem. Oakland Lic. Daycare Assn. (bd. dirs. 1985, pres.), Piedmont Women's Fitness Club. Democrat. African Am. Muslim. Home and Office: 3344 Harrison St Oakland CA 94611

HASSETT, ROBERT JAMES, real estate executive; b. Madison, Wis., Dec. 6, 1955; s. Edward Cecil and Doris Ann (Nisen) H.; m. Cheryl A., June 15, 1985; 1 child, Michael Edward. BA in Bus., Madison Bus. Coll. Sales mgr. Newell Cos., Atlanta, 1980-84, Ray-o-Vac Corp., Houston, 1984-86; sales Russ Lyon Realty, Scottsdale, Ariz., 1986—. Col. U.S. Army, 1974-80. Republican. Roman Catholic.

HASSOUNA, FRED, architect, educator; b. Cairo, Mar. 26, 1918; s. Amin Sami and Dawlat (Mansour) H.; came to U.S., 1948, naturalized, 1953; diploma in architecture with honors Higher Sch. Fine Arts, Cairo, 1940; diploma in Egyptology with 1st class honors U. Cairo, 1944; diploma in civic design U. Liverpool (Eng.), 1946; M.Arch., M.S. in Pub. Adminstrn., U. So. Calif., 1950; m. Verna Arlene Dotter, Mar. 9, 1950. Architect, curator Cairo Mus., Egypt, 1940-44; lectr. archaeology and architecture Alexandria U., Egypt, 1944-45, 47-48; dir. planning Huyton-with-Roby Urban Dist. Council, Huyton, Eng., 1946-47; lectr. city planning U. So. Calif., 1950-55; architect Kistner, Wright and Wright, architects and engrs., Los Angeles, 1952-53; project architect Welton Becket and Assocs., architects and engrs., Los Angeles, 1954-56, Albert C. Martin and Assocs., architects and engrs., 1956-58; faculty architecture East Los Angeles Coll., 1958-75, prof. architecture, head dept. architecture; prof., head dept. architecture Saddleback Coll., 1975-83; pvt. planning cons., architect, Los Angeles, 1950-75, Laguna Niguel, 1975—. Mem. indsl. tech. adv. bd. Calif. State U. at Long Beach, 1963-83; mem. adv. bd. on environ. and interior design U. Calif., Irvine, 1976-83; pres. Calif. Council Archtl. Edn., 1977; mem. liaison com. architecture, landscape architecture, urban and regional planning in Calif. higher edn., 1976-83. Registered architect, Calif.; recipient hon. cultural doctorate World U. Roundtable, Tucson, 1983. Fellow Internat. Inst. Arts and Letters (life); mem. emeritus AIA, Am. Planning Assn. Home and Office: 31242 Flying Cloud Dr Laguna Niguel CA 92677

HASSRICK, PETER HEYL, museum director; b. Phila., Apr. 27, 1941; s. Royal Brown and E. Barbara (Morgan) H.; m. Elizabeth Drake, June 14, 1963; children: Philip Heyl, Charles Royal. Student, Harvard U., 1962; BA, U. Colo., 1963; MA, U. Denver, 1969. Tchr. Whiteman Sch., Steamboat Springs, Colo., 1963-67; also bd. dirs. Whiteman Sch., Steamboat Springs; curator of collections Amon Carter Mus., Ft. Worth, 1969-75; dir. Buffalo Bill Hist. Ctr., Cody, Wyo., 1976—. Author: Frederic Remington, 1973, The Way West, 1977, (with others) The Rocky Mountains, 1983, Treasures of the Old West, 1984, (with others) Frederic Remington, The Masterworks, 1988, (with others) Frontier America, 1988, Charles M. Russell, 1989. Mem. Yellowstone Assn., Cody C. of C., Am. Fedn. Arts. Office: Buffalo Bill Hist Ctr Box 1000 Cody WY 82414

HASTINGS, JAMES HOWARD, broadcasting executive; b. Winnipeg, Man., Can., Dec. 9, 1947; came to U.S., 1978; s. Donald James and Isobel M. (Carver) H.; m. Sharmain C. Mitchell; 1 child, Coutney. BA, U. Man., 1970; cert. french lang., U. Montreal, 1972. V.p. mktg. CZI Programming, Dallas, 1979-83; freelance cons. 1983-87; gen. mgr. KLFF/KONC, Phoenix, 1987—. Office: KLFF-KONC 7401 W Camelback Ave Phoenix AZ 85033

HASTINGS, MERRILL GEORGE, JR., publisher, marketing consultant; b. Dedham, Mass., May 12, 1922; s. Merrill G. and Emita E. (Zeil) H.; m. Priscilla G. Brayton, July 31, 1948; children: William, Deborah. BA, Bowdoin Coll., 1946. Pres. Skiing Pub. Co., Denver, 1950-64, Colorado Mag., Inc., Denver, 1964-77, Mountain Bus. Pubs., Denver, 1972-77, Hastings, Johnson & White, Vail, Colo., 1977-79, Energy Pub. Co., Denver, 1980-82, Pulse Pubs., Denver, 1985-87. Founder Nat. Cancer Survivors Day, 1988. Served with Brit. Army, 1944-45. Recipient Austrian IXth Winter Olympic medal, Innsbruck, 1964. Mem. Colo. Press Assn., Denver Club. Home: Sunnyvail Ranch McCoy CO 80463 Office: 11280 W 20th Ave Ste 27 Denver CO 80215

HASTRICH, JEROME JOSEPH, bishop; b. Milw., Nov. 13, 1914; s. George Philip and Clara (Dettlaff) H. Student, Marquette U., 1933-35; BA, St. Francis Sem., Milw., 1940, MA, 1941; postgrad., Cath. U. Am., 1947. Ordained priest Roman Cath. Ch., 1941; assigned to Milw. Chancery, 1941; curate St. Ann's Ch., Milw., St. Bernard's Ch., Madison, Wis.; asst. chaplain St. Paul U. Chapel, then U. Wis.; sec. to bishop of Diocese U. Wis., Madison, 1946-52; chancellor Diocese Madison, Wis., 1952-53; apptd. vicar gen. Diocese Madison, 1953, domestic prelate, 1954, protonotary apos., 1960; aux. bishop 1963-67, titular bishop of Gurza and aux. of Madison, 1963; pastor St. Raphael Cathedral, Madison, 1967-69; bishop Gallup, N.Mex., 1969—; diocesan dir. Confraternity Christian Doctorine, 1946—, St. Martin Guild, 1946-69; aux. chaplain U.S. Air Force, 1947-67; pres. Latin Am. Mission Program; sec. Am. Bd. Cath. Missions; vice chmn. Bishop's Com. for Spanish Speaking; mem. subcom. on allocations U.S. Bishops Com. for Latin Am.; founder, episcopal moderator Queen of Americas Guild, 1979—; pres. Nat. Blue Army of Our Lady of Fatima, 1980—. Mem. Gov. Wis. Commn. Migratory Labor, 1964—. Club: K.C. (hon. life mem.). Address: PO Box 1338 Gallup NM 87301

HATAI, THOMAS HENRY, marketing professional; b. Tokyo, Dec. 27, 1937; came to U.S., 1951; s. Isamu Herbert and Kiyoko (Kume) H.; m. Geraldine Hatai (div. 1978); 1 child, Dickson Y. BS, Woodbury Coll., 1965. Supr. internat. dept. Union Bank, L.A., 1964-66; sales rep. United Airlines, L.A., 1966-69; v.p. far east Travel Systems Internat., Oakbrook, Ill., 1969-75; pres. Hatai Internat., L.A., 1975-78; pres., chief exec. officer Pace Mktg., Inc., La Habra, Calif., 1978—; chmn. Pace Products, Inc., La Habra, 1983—; bd. dirs. Taiyo Estate Devel., Inc., Del.; pres. D.B.H. Global, Ltd., La Habra, 1983—. Illustrators: The Marty Story, 1954, The St. Meinrad Story, 1954. Mem. United Internat. Club (bd. dirs. 1969 Japan), U.S. C. of C. Republican. Home: 8544 Buena Tierra Pl Buena Park CA 90621 Office: Pace Mktg Inc 1251-C S Beach Blvd La Habra CA 90631

HATCH, DAVID PAUL, financial planner; b. Sacramento, Calif., June 12, 1937; s. Dean F. and Ida (Berreth) H.; m. Charlotte A. Wittsche, Jan. 21, 1959 (div. Oct. 1975); children: Cynthia K., Jeannette L. Brazil, Christina M. Currier, Scott D.; m. Sherry Wagner, Sept. 17, 1976 (div. June 1978); 1 child, Echo L. AA, Stockton Coll., 1958; student, Golden Gate U., 1984-87. Asst. v.p. Wells FArgo Bank, Sacramento, 1959-86; cert. fin. planner Titan Capital Corp., Sacramento, 1987—. Bd. dirs. Am. Cancer Soc., Sacramento, 1988. Named Outstanding Jaycee Stockton Jaycees, 1965. Mem. Internat. Assn. Fin. Planning, Inst. Cert. Fin. Planners(cert.). Republican. Presbyterian. Clubs: 50/50 (pres. 1988), Natomas Toastmasters (Sacramento) (pres. 1980). Office: Titan Capital Corp 3000 Arden Way Ste 2 Sacramento CA 95825

HATCH, DAVID PORTER, artist, educator; b. N.Y.C., Dec. 5, 1926; s. Gladstone Fielding and Esther Quinby (Huston) H.; m. Kia Dorothy Kennelly, Aug. 7, 1965; children: Laura Anne, Eloise Quinby. Student, U. Calif., Berkeley, 1946-48; BA, UCLA, 1951, MA, 1953. Instr. Los Angeles State Coll., 1951; asst. prof. U. Oreg., Eugene, 1952-58; assoc. prof. Antioch Coll., Yellow Springs, Ohio, 1958-60; prof. San Jose (Calif.) State U., 1960—; instr. Iran-Am. Inst., Mandalay State Coll., Burma, Iran, 1956-57, Oreg. Tech. Inst., Klamath Falls, 1958; adj. lectr. Calif. Coll. Arts and Crafts, Oakland. Exhibited in shows at Smithsonian Instn., Toledo (Ohio) Art Mus., Oakland Art Mus., Portland Art Mus., San Francisco Mus. Art, Am. House, N.Y.C., Crocker Art Gallery, Sacramento, St. Paul Gallery, Dayton (Ohio) Art. Inst., Los Angeles County Mus., Cin. Art Mus., Seattle World's Fair, Calif. State Fair, Oreg. State Fair, Mus. Fine Arts, St. Petersberg, Fla., Los Angeles City Coll., UCLA, U. Del., U. Oreg., San Jose City Coll., Oreg. State U., East Tenn. State U., U. Wash., Works Gallery, San Jose, 1978, 82, 83, San Jose Inst. Contemporary Art, 1984, travelling exhbn. San Jose League Art Gallery, 1988-89, numerous others; film exhibitins include Marin Film Festival, 1974, San Jose U., 1989, represented in permanent collections nationally in comml. and community ctrs. Bd. dirs. San Ramon, Contra County and Calif. State Fair Arts Councils. Served with USN, 1944-46, PTO. Recipient Fulbright award, 1956, Tiffany award, 1960, Archey Bray Found. award, Pacific Internat. award, Am. House award, N.Y.C., others. Mem. Works Gallery, Mus. Modern Art. Office: San Jose State U 1 Washington Sq San Jose CA 95192

HATCH, EASTMAN NIBLEY, physics educator; b. Salt Lake City, June 14, 1927; s. Joseph Eastman and Florence (Nibley) H.; m. Anne Clawson, June 21, 1952; children: Joseph Eastman II, Richard Clawson, Anne Florence. Student, U. Utah, 1946-48, 51-52; B.S., Stanford, 1950; Ph.D., Calif. Inst. Tech., 1956. Postdoctoral fellow in physics Calif. Inst. Tech., 1956-57; research asso. physics Brookhaven Nat. Lab., Upton, N.Y., 1957-58; sci. liaison with USN in Frankfurt/Main, Germany, 1958-60; guest physicist Heidelberg U., Germany, 1960-61; assoc. prof. physics Iowa State U., 1961-66, prof. physics, 1966-69; asst. dean Grad. Coll., 1967-69; physicist Ames Lab., 1961-66, sr. physicist, 1966-69; prof. physics Utah State U., Logan, 1969—; head dept. physics Utah State U., 1972-74, dean sch. grad. studies, 1974-79; vis. prof. physics Freiburg U., W. Ger., 1979-80; vis. research assoc. Los Alamos Sci. Lab., 1971-83; vis. prof. U. Cologne, Fed. Republic Germany, 1987. Served with USNR, 1945-46. Fellow Am. Phys. Soc., Phi Beta Kappa, Sigma Xi. Home: 1795 Country Club Dr Logan UT 84321

HATCH, GEORGE CLINTON, television executive; b. Erie, Pa., Dec. 16, 1919; s. Charles Milton and Blanche (Beecher) H.; m. Wilda Gene Glasmann, Dec. 24, 1940; children: Michael Gene Zbar Arnow, Diane Glasmann Orr, Jeffrey Beecher, Randall Clinton, Deepika Hatch Windstone. AB, Occidental Coll., 1940; MA in Econs., Claremont Coll., 1941; HHD, So. Utah State Coll., 1988. Chmn. Intermountain Network, Inc., Salt Lake City, 1941—; pres. Communications Investment Corp., Salt Lake City, 1945—; chmn. Sta. KUTV, Inc., Salt Lake City, 1956—; dir. Republic Pictures Corp., Los Angeles, 1971-88; pres. Sta. KVEL, Inc., 1978, KUPI, Inc., Idaho Falls, 1985—; treas. Standard Corp., Ogden, 1984—; mem. Salt Lake adv. bd. First Security Bank Utah; past chmn. Rocky Mountain Pub. Broadcasting Corp.; past chmn. bd. govs. Am. Info. Radio Network; past bd. govs. NBC-TV Affiliates. Past pres. Salt Lake Com. on Fgn. Relations; mem., past chmn. Utah State Bd. Regents, 1964-85; past mem. Utah Symphony Bd., Salt Lake City; mem. Utah Tech. Coll. Found., Salt Lake City (Disting. Service award 1984). Recipient Service to Journalism award U. Utah, 1966, Silver Medal award Salt Lake Advt. Club, 1969, Disting. award Utah Tech. Coll., 1984. Mem. Nat. Assn. Broadcasters (past pres., radio bd. dirs., Ambassador to Inter-Am. Meetings in Latin Am. 1962), Utah Broadcasters Assn. (past pres.; Mgmt. award 1964, Hall of Fame award 1981), Phi Beta Kappa, Phi Rho Pi (life). Democrat. Club: Salt Lake City Advt. (Silver medal award 1969). Lodge: Rotary. Office: Sta KUTV Inc 2185 S 3600 W Salt Lake City UT 84119

HATCH, JENNIFER SEYLER, display designer, artist; b. Lake Geneva, Wis., Aug. 21, 1947; d. David Warren and Rosemary (Dickman) S.; m. Jerry Hatch, 1968 (div. 1973). Student, U. Nebr., 1966-67, San Francisco Art Inst., 1978, John O'Connell Tech. Inst., San Francisco, 1979, De Young Mus. Sch., San Francisco, 1980. Designer display dept. Hovlands, Lincoln, Nebr., 1968-74; art dir. Sta. KOLN-TV, CBS, Lincoln, 1974; freelance designer and visual merchandiser San Francisco Trade Ctr., 1978—; display designer Wilkes Bashford Clothing, San Francisco, 1984-86; display dir. Bullock & Jones Clothing, San Francisco, 1986—; lectr. Skyline Coll., San Bruno, Calif., 1976-77; stylist Humbert-Clark, San Francisco, 1986—. One-woman show Walker Art Ctr., Mpls., 1966, Mushroom Gallery, Missoula, Mont., 1973-76; exhibited in group shows Miller and Paine Gallery, Lincoln, 1955, 65, Brandeis Co., Lincoln, 1966, Mushroom Gallery, 1973; represented in pvt. collections. Archivist San Francisco dance Archives, 1978; vol. San Francisco Pub. Library. Mem. San Francisco Mechanics Inst., Smithsonian Inst., Nat. Trust for Hist. Preservation. Office: Bullock & Jones 340 Post St San Francisco CA 94108

HATCH, KENNETH L., television executive; b. Vernal, Utah, Aug. 4, 1935; s. Lois and Alva Le Roy Hatch; m. Marsha Kay Rich, Dec. 7, 1974; children: Sean, Ryan, James, Michael, Elizabeth-Ann. BS in Banking and Fin., U. Utah, 1957; postgrad. Stanford U., Harvard Grad. Sch. Bus. Gen. sales mgr. KSL, Salt Lake City, 1963-64; gen. sales mgr. KIRO-TV, Seattle, 1964-66, asst. gen. mgr., 1965-67, gen. mgr., 1967-71, sr. v.p., 1971-80, pres., chief exec. officer, 1980-87; chmn. bd., mem. exec. com., KIRO, Inc.; sr. v.p. Bonneville Internat. Corp.; bd. dirs. Bear Creek, Inc., Wash., Olympic Bank. Bd. dirs. United Way King County, 1984-86, chmn. mktg. com., 1987, co-chmn. communications com., 1988; assoc. chmn. Boy Scouts Annual Fundraising Event, 1985; bd. dirs. Seattle Opportunities Industrialization Ctr., Seattle Conv. & Bus. Bur.; mem. adv. bd. Providence Hosp. Found.; amb. Children's Found. Assocs., 1986. Mem. Nat. Assn. Broadcasters Television & Radio Polit. Action Com., Torbet Radio Reps., Inc. (bd. dirs. N.Y.C. chpt. 1982-84), Sales & Mktg. Execs. Internat. (pres. 1969), Seattle C. of C. (bd. trustees 1986-88). Recipient Spl. Svc. award United Way, 1986, Bus. Man of Yr. award BYU, 1986, Keynote Speaker award Eastside Ins. Women's Pub. Rels. Banquet, 1986. Mem. Ch. of Christ. Clubs: Seattle Advt. Club (bd. dirs. 1967), Rainier of Seattle, Bellevue Athletic, Wash. Athletic, Overlake Golf and Country.

HATCH, ORRIN GRANT, senator; b. Homestead Park, Pa., Mar. 22, 1934; s. Jesse and Helen (Kamm) H.; m. Elaine Hansen, Aug. 28, 1957; children: Brent, Marcia, Scott, Kimberly, Alysa, Jesse. B.S., Brigham Young U., 1959; J.D., U. Pitts., 1962; LLD (hon.), U. Md., 1981; MS (hon.), Def. Intelligence Coll., 1982. Bar: Pa. 1962, Utah 1962. Ptnr. firm Thomson, Rhodes & Grigsby, Pitts., 1962-69, Hatch & Plumb, Salt Lake City, 1976; mem. U.S. Senate from Utah, 1977—; past chmn. labor and human resources com.; ranking minority mem. Senate Labor and Human Resources Com, mem. Senate Judiciary Com., Select Com. on Intelligence, Spl. Senate Com. Investigating Iran Arms Deal. Author ERA Myths and Realities, 1983; contbr. articles to newspapers and profl. jours. Recipient Outstanding Legislator award Nat. Assn. Rehab. Facilities, Legislator of teh Yr. award Am. Assn. Univ. Affiliated Programs, Legis. Leadership award Health Profl. Assn., many others. Mem. Am., Nat., Utah, Pa. bar assns., Am. Judicature Soc. Republican. Mormon. Office: US Senate 135 Russell Senate Bldg Washington DC 20510

HATCH, RANDALL CLINTON, journalist; b. Salt Lake City, Oct. 15, 1951; s. George Clinton and Wilda Gene (Glasmann) H.; m. Ann Darger, Apr. 11, 1975; children—Sarah, George, William, Spencer, Robert. BA, U. Utah, 1975; MBA, Columbia U., 1977, MS in Journalism, 1976. Reporter, Salt Lake Tribune, 1977-78; ad salesman Newspaper Agy., Salt Lake City, 1978-79; promotion dir. Ogden Standard, Utah, 1979-80, mng. editor, 1980—. Dir., Communications Investment Corp., Salt Lake City, Nat. Video Clearinghouse, Syosset, N.Y., 1978—, bd. dirs. Standard Corp. 1988—. Bd. dirs. Union Sta. Devel. Corp., 1981-83, Ogden Arts Commn., 1981-83, McKay Dee Hosp. Found., Ogden, 1981-83. Served with AUS, 1970-78. Mem. Soc. Profl. Journalists (1st v.p. 1984, bd. dirs. Utah chpt. 1984-85, pres. 1985-86). Mormon. Lodge: Rotary. Office: Ogden Standard Examiner 455 23d St Ogden UT 84401

HATCH, RICHARD, obstetrician/gynecologist; b. Stockton, Calif., Jan. 28, 1948; s. Elmer Webb and Tressa (Farr) H.; m. Jennifer Stevens Adams, Mar. 13, 1981; children: Richard Elmer, Dorothy Allison, John Adams, Elizabeth Amanda, Abigail Sariah. BS cum laude, Brigham Young U., 1970; MD, U. Utah, 1974. Diplomate Am. Bd. Ob-gyn, subspecialty Reproductive Endocrinology. Resident in ob-gyn U. Chgo., 1974-78, fellow in reproductive endocrinology, 1978-81, asst. prof. ob-gyn, 1981-85; practice medicine specializing in ob-gyn and reproductive endocrinology Vernal, Utah, 1985-87, Provo, Utah, 1988—. Contbr. articles to profl. jours. Fellow Am. Coll. Obsetricians and Gynecologists; mem. Rotary, Phi Kappa Phi. Mormon. Office: 930 N 500 W Provo UT 84604

HATCH, RICHARD ALLEN, business communications educator; b. Anderson, Ind., Aug. 18, 1940; s. Clarence Wilbur and Mildred Marie (Sutton) H.; m. Ann Marie Menchinger, Aug. 27, 1960; children: Karen Marie, Kevin Ryan. BS, Boston U., 1961; PhD, U. Ill., 1969. Instr. U. Ill., Urbana, 1967-69; assoc. prof. Western Mich. U., Kalamazoo, 1969-75; prof. bus. San Diego State U., 1975—. Author: Business Communication: Theory and Technique, 1988, Using Basic on the IBM PC, 1985, Business Writing, 1983, Using Basic on Cyber, 1982, Communicating in Business, 1977, Basics for Communication in the Church, 1971. Mem. Assn. for Bus. Communication (v.p. 1975, 77). Mem. United Ch. of Christ. Office: San Diego State U San Diego CA 92182

HATCH, STEVEN GRAHAM, publishing company executive; b. Idaho Falls, Idaho, Mar. 27, 1951; s. Charles Steven and Margery Jane (Doxey) H.; BA, Brigham Young U., 1976; postgrad. mgmt. devel. program U. Utah, 1981; m. Rhonda Kay Frasier, Feb. 13, 1982; children: Steven Graham, Kristen Leone. Founder, pres. Graham Maughan Enterprises, Provo, Utah, 1975—, Internat. Mktg. Co., 1980—; dir. Goldbrickers Internat., Inc. Sec., treas. Zions Estates, Inc., Salt Lake City, Kansas City, Mo. Eagle Scout Boy Scouts Am., 1970; trustee Villages of Quail Valley, 1984-88. Recipient Duty to God award, 1970. Mem. Provo Jaycees, Internat. Entrepreneurs Assn., Mormon Booksellers Assn., Samuel Hall Soc. (exec. v.p. 1979), U.S. C. of C., Provo C. of C. (chmn. legis. action com. 1981-82). Republican. Mormon (missionary France Mission, Paris 1970-72, pub. rels. dir. 1972). Club: Rotary. Office: Graham Maughan Pub Co 50 E 500 S Provo UT 84606

HATCHER, HERBERT JOHN, biochemist, microbiologist; b. Mpls., Dec. 18, 1926; s. Herbert Edmond and Florence Elizabeth (Larson) H.; m. Beverly J. Johnson, Mar. 28, 1953 (dec. July 1985); children: Dennis Michael, Steven Craig, Roger Dean, Mark Alan, Susan Diane, Laura Jean; m. Louise Fritsche Nelson, May 24, 1986; children: Carlos Howard Nelson, Kent Robert Nelson, Carolyn Louise Tyler. BA, U. Minn., 1953, MS, 1964, PhD, 1965. Bacteriologist VA Hosp., Wilmington, Del., 1956-57; microbiologist Smith, Kline, French, Phila., 1957-60, Clinton (Iowa) Corn Processing, 1966-67; microbiologist, biochemist Econs. Lab. Inc., St. Paul, 1967-84; biochemist EG&G Idaho Inc., Idaho Falls, 1984—; affiliate prof. U. Idaho; cons. Henkel Corp. N.J., 1986. Chmn. bd. edn. Cross of Christ Luth. Ch., Coon Rapids, Minn., 1974-76; pres. chpt. Aid Assn. Luths., Idaho Falls, 1986; pres.-elect St. Johns Luth. Ch., 1988. Served with USNR, 1945-46. Mem. Am. Soc. Microbiologists, N.Y. Acad. Scis., Idaho Acad. Scis., Am. Chem. Soc. (fuel div., microbial tech. and biochem. div.). Office: EG&G Idaho Inc Box 1625 Idaho Falls ID 83415

HATCHER, JOHN CHRISTOPHER, psychologist; b. Atlanta, Sept. 18, 1946; s. John William and Kay (Carney) H.; BA, U. Ga., 1968, MS, 1970, PhD, 1972. Psychologist, Clayton Mental Health Ctr., Atlanta, 1971-72; dir. intern tng. psychology svc. Beaumont Med. Center, El Paso, Tex., 1972-74; dir. family therapy program Langley Porter Inst., U. Calif., San Francisco, 1974—; adj. prof. dept. psychology U. Tex., 1972-74, dept. ednl. psychology and guidance, 1972-74; asst. clin. prof. psychology U. Calif., San Francisco, 1974-80, assoc. clin. prof., 1980-86, clin. prof., 1986—; cons. city and state govts. in U.S., Europe, Mexico, Asia, Far East; internat. cons. in hostage negotiation and terrorism chmn., Mayors Commn. on Family Violence, San Francisco; advisor arson task force San Francisco Fire Dept.; adv. bd. Nat. Firehawk Found., Kevin Collins Found. for Missing Children; advisor CBS-TV; spl. asst. to Mayor of San Francisco in charge of People's Temple Jonestown Case; mem. Calif. State Legis. Task Force on Missing Children; prin. investigator U.S. Dept. Justice Families of Missing Children Project, Reunification of Missing Children Project. Mem. Am. Psychol. Assn. (chmn. com. hostage families), Calif. State Psychol. Assn. (chmn. task force on terrorism), Soc. Police and Criminal Psychology, Assn. Advancement Psychology, Am. Family Therapy Assn., Internat. Council Psychologists, Phi Kappa Phi. Author: (with Himelstein) Handbook of Gestalt Therapy, 1976; (with Brooks) Innovations in Counseling Psychology, 1977, (with Gaynor) Psychology of Child Firesetting, 1987; assoc. editor Am. Jour. Family Therapy; sr. editor Family Therapy Jour., mem. editorial bd. Family Psychology Jour. Office: U Calif Dept Psychiatry 401 Parnassus San Francisco CA 94143

HATELEY, DONALD PATRICK, investment banker, restaurant industry consultant; b. Long Beach, Calif., Sept. 28, 1957; s. James Charles Jr. and Enid Ellen (Shephard) H.; m. Wendy Joy Seretan, May 25, 1985. BS, U. So. Calif., 1979. CPA, Calif. Asst. acct. Peat, Marwick, Mitchell & Co.,, Los Angeles, 1979-81, staff acct., 1981-82; assoc. ENI Corp., Los Angeles, 1982-83; pres. Cambridge Resources, Inc., Los Angeles, 1983—, Cambridge Group, Inc., Los Angeles, 1984—; pres., bd. dirs. Coll. Ctrs. So. Calif., Los Angeles, 1984—, Calif. Hoagies, Inc., Los Angeles, 1987—; bd. dirs. City Resources, Inc., Newport Beach, Calif., Coll. Counseling Ctrs. Am., Los Angeles. Mem. AICPA, Calif. Soc. CPAs (securities com. 1982-83, entertainment and sports com. 1987—). Republican. Office: Cambridge Group Inc 11150 W Olympic Blvd Los Angeles CA 90064

HATFIELD, ELAINE CATHERINE, psychology educator; b. Detroit, Oct. 22, 1937; d. Charles E. and Eileen (Kalahar) H.; m. Richard L. Rapson, June 15, 1982. B.A., U. Mich., 1959; Ph.D., Stanford U., 1963. Asst. prof. U. Minn., Mpls., 1963-64, assoc. prof., 1964-66; asso. prof. U. Rochester, 1966-68, U. Wis., Madison, 1968-69; prof. U. Wis., 1969-81; now prof. U. Hawaii at Manoa; chmn. dept. U. Hawaii of Manoa, 1981-83. Author: Interpersonal Attraction, 1969, 2d edit., 1978, Equity: Theory and Research, 1978, A New Look at Love, 1978, Human Sexual Behavior, 1985, Mirror, Mirror: The Importance of Looks in Everyday Life, 1986, The Psychology of Emotions, 1990. Contbr. articles to profl. jours. Fellow Am. Psychol. Assn. Home: 3334 Ano'ai Pl Honolulu HI 96822 Office: U Hawaii 2430 Campus Rd Honolulu HI 96822

HATFIELD, JOHN ALAN, civil engineer, consultant; b. Denver, Dec. 23, 1944; s. Alan Edwin and Evelyn Louise (Nunn) H.; m. Jean Elaine McKinney, Jan. 24, 1981; children: Joel Nathan, Julianne Kathleen. AS in Civil Engring., Mesa Coll., 1969; BS in Civil Engring., U. Colo., 1971. Registered profl. engr., Colo. Wyo. Chief exec. officer Materials Testing Lab., Denver, 1971-80, Bldg. Dept. Inc., Denver, 1976-85; chief bldg. ofcl. City of Glendale, Colo., 1976-81, City of Edgewater, Colo., 1981-83, City of Sheridan, Colo., 1983-85; staff engr. and code engr. Bldg. Code Cons., Inc., Conifer, Colo., 1985—; instr. fire sci. tech. Community Coll. Denver, Red Rocks, Colo., 1979-80, constrn. mgmt. div. U. Denver, 1981-83, Colo. Chpt. Assoc. Bldg. Contractors, 1981-85. Author: contbr. articles to trade jours. Mem. Internat. Conf. Bldg. Ofcls. (cert. bldg. insp., plans examiner, plumbing insp., spl. ins. reinforced concrete and prestressed concrete; code changes com. Colo. Chpt. 1977-85, pres. 1982; mem. nat. code com. 1979-82, chmn. fire and life safety com. 1980-82), Council Am. Bldg. Ofcls. (cvert. solar specialist), Nat. Fire Protection Assn., Internat. Assn. Plumbing and Mech. Ofcls., Home Bulders Assn. Denver (edu. com. 1982-85), Masons. Shriners. Office: Bldg Code Cons Inc PO Box 400 Conifer CO 80438

HATFIELD, MARK, senator; b. Dallas, Oreg., July 12, 1922; s. Charles Dolen and Dovie (Odom) H.; m. Antoinette Kuzmanich, July 8, 1958; children: Mark, Elizabeth, Theresa, Charles. A.B., Willamette U., 1943; A.M., Stanford U., 1948. Instr. Willamette U., 1949, dean students, asso. prof. polit. sci., 1950-56; mem. Oreg. Ho. of Reps., 1951-55, Oreg. Senate, 1955-57; sec. State of Oreg., 1957-59, gov., 1959-67; U.S. senator from Oreg. 1967—, ranking minority mem. appropriations com.; mem. energy and natural resources com., rules and adminstrn. com. Author: Not Quite So Simple, 1967, Conflict and Conscience, 1971, Between A Rock and A Hard Place, 1976; co-author: Amnesty: The Unsettled Question of Vietnam, 1973, Freeze! How You Can Help Prevent Nuclear War, 1982, The Causes of World Hunger, 1982. Served to lt. j.g. USN, 1943-45. Recipient numerous hon. degrees. Republican. Baptist. Office: US Senate 711 Hart Senate Bldg Washington DC 20510

HATFIELD, PAUL GERHART, judge, lawyer; b. Great Falls, Mont., Apr. 29, 1928; s. Trueman LeRoy and Grace Lenore (Gerhart) H.; m. Dorothy Ann Allen, Feb. 1, 1958; children—Kathleen Helen, Susan Ann, Paul Allen. Student, Coll. of Great Falls, 1947-50; LL.B., U. Mont., 1955. Bar: Mont. bar 1955. Asso. firm Hoffman & Cure, Gt. Falls, Mont., 1955-56, Jardine, Stephenson, Blewett & Weaver, Gt. Falls, 1956-58, Hatfield & Hatfield, Gt. Falls, 1959-60; chief dep. county atty. Cascade County, Mont., 1959-60; dist. ct. judge 8th Jud. Dist., Mont., 1961-76; chief justice Supreme Ct. Mont., Helena, 1977-78; U.S. Senator from Mont., 1978-79; U.S. dist. judge for Dist. of Mont., Gt. Falls, 1979—; Vice chmn. Pres.'s Council Coll. of Great Falls. Author: standards for criminal justice, Mont. cts. Served with U.S. Army, 1951-53. Korea. Mem. Am., Mont. bar assns., Am. Judicature Soc. Roman Catholic. Office: US Dist Ct PO Box 1529 Great Falls MT 59403

HATHAWAY, JAMES DAVID, judge, lawyer; b. Santa Cruz County, Ariz., Feb. 17, 1927; s. William H. and Mary L. (McIntyre) H.; m. Carolyn H. Gum, Mar. 30, 1956; children: Roseanne, David, Thomas, Joseph, Jennifer. JD, U. Ariz., 1954; LLM in Judiciary, U. Va., 1984. Bar: Ariz. 1954. Asst. atty. gen. State of Ariz., Phoenix, Ariz., 1954; pvt. practice Nogales, Ariz., 1955-64; judge div. II, Ariz. Ct. Appeals, Tucson, 1965—; county atty. Santa Cruz County, Nogales, 1956-64; mem. Jud. Ethics Adv. Commn., Tucson, 1988—; charter mem. Commn. on Jud. Qualifications, Tucson, 1970-88. Active 4-H Club, Nogales, 1965-67; leader Boy Scouts Am., Nogales, 1982-86; v.p. bd. dirs. Ariz. Head Injury Found., Tucson, 1982—. Mem. ABA, Am. Judicature Soc. (bd. dirs. 1960—), Rotary, Elks. Democrat. Office: Ariz Ct Appeals Div II 416 W Congress Tucson AZ 85701

HATHAWAY, LOLINE, zoo and botanic park curator; b. Whitter, Calif., June 27, 1937; d. Richard Franklin and F. Nadine (Applegate) H.; m. A. Roger Kundtz, Nov. 25, 1976; 1 child, Patrick Paul. BA, Reed Coll., Portland, Oreg., 1959; PhD, Washington U., St. Louis, 1969. Instr. St. Louis U., 1966-68; curator of edn. Chgo. Zool. Soc., Brookfield, Ill., 1968-71; cons. on terrestrial biology Ryckman, Edgerly, Tomlinson & Assocs., St. Louis, 1972-75; marina mgr. Lake Piru (Calif.) Recreation Area, 1976-77; curator, dir. Navajo Nation Zool. and Botanical Park, Window Rock, Ariz., 1983—. v. chmn., chmn. City of Santa Fe Springs (Calif.) Traffic Commn., 1979-83; mem. Navajo Estates Vol. fire Dept., Yah-ta-hey, N.Mex., 1984-85; treas. McKinley Co. Assn. Gifted and Talented Students, 1986—; bd. dirs. Hathaway Ranch Mus., Santa Fe Springs, 1986—. Mem. AAAS (vice chmn. Southwest-Rocky Mountain div. sci. edn. sect. 1983-84, chmn. 1984-85), Am. Assn. Zool. Parks and Aquariums, Am. Assn. Bot. Gardens and Arboretums, Assn. Living Hist. Farms and Agr. Mus., Am. Inst. Biol. Scis., Sierra Club (Ozarks chpt. founder, bd. dirs., sec. Great Lakes chpt. 1963-72). Democrat. Lodge: Kiwanis. Home: 127 LaChee PO Box 4172 Yah-ta-hey NM 87375 Office: Navajo Nat Zool and Bot Park PO Box 308 Window Rock AZ 86515

HATTER, TERRY JULIUS, JR., judge; b. Chgo., Mar. 11, 1933. A.B., Wesleyan U., 1954; J.D., U. Chgo., 1960. Bar: Ill. 1960, Calif. 1965, U.S. Dist. Ct. 1960, U.S. Ct. Appeals 1960. Adjudicator Chgo., 1960-61; assoc. Harold M. Calhoun, Chgo., 1961-62; asst. pub. defender Cook County Chgo., 1961-62; asst. U.S. atty. No. Dist. Calif., San Francisco, 1962-66; chief counsel San Francisco Neighborhood Legal Assistance Found., 1966-67; regional legal svcs. dir. Exec. Office Pres. OEO, San Francisco, 1967-70; exec. dir. Western Ctr. Law and Poverty, L.A., 1970-73; exec. asst. to mayor, dir. criminal justice planning L.A., 1974-75; spl. asst. to mayor, dir. urban devel. 1975-77; judge Superior Ct. Calif., L.A., 1977-80, U.S. Dist. Ct. (cen. dist.) Calif., L.A., 1980—; assoc. clin. prof. law U. So. Calif. Law Ctr., L.A., 1970-74; prof. law Loyola U. Sch. Law, L.A., 1973-75; mem. faculty Nat. Coll. State Judiciary, Reno, 1974; lectr. Police Acad., San Francisco Police Dept., 1963-66, U. Calif., San Diego, 1970-71, Colo. Jud. Conf., 1973; mem. bd. councilors U. So. Calif. Law Ctr. V.p. Northbay Halfway House, 1964-65; vice chmn. Los Angeles Regional Criminal Justice Planning Bd., 1975-76; mem. Los Angeles Mayor's Cabinet Com. Econ. Devel., 1976-77, Mayor's Policy Com., 1973-77, chmn. housing econ. and community devel. com., City Los Angeles, 1975-77, chmn. housing and community devel. tech. com., 1975-77; vice chmn. Young Dems. Cook County, 1961-62; chmn. bd. Real Estate Coop; bd. dirs. Bay Area Social Planning Coun., Contra Costa, Black Law Center L.A., Nat. Fedn. Settlements & Neighborhood Ctrs., Edn. Fin. & Governance Reform Project, Mexican Am. Legal Def. & Ednl. Fund, Nat. Health Law Program, Nat. Sr. Citizens Law Ctr., Calif. Law Ctr., L.A. Regional Criminal Justice Planning Bd.; mem. exec. com. bd. dirs. Constl. Rights Found; trustee Wesleyan Univ. Meth. Ch.; mem. bd. visitors U. Chgo. Law Sch. Mem. NAACP (exec. com., bd. dirs. Richmond chpt.), Nat. Legal Aid & Defender Assn. (dir., vice chmn.), L.A. County Bar Assn. (exec. com.), Am. Judicature Soc., Charles Houston Law Club, Phi Delta Phi, Order Coif. Office: US Dist Ct 312 N Spring St Los Angeles CA 90012

HATTON, GERALD NORMAN, sales executive; b. Norwalk, Conn., Sept. 9, 1936; s. William Norman and Paula (Gunderson) H.; m. Laurie H. Hatton, Feb. 7, 1959; children: Christopher, Jennifer, Stephanie. BSCE, U. Colo., 1959. Sales mgr. IBM Corp., Denver, 1962-78, Leeds and Northrop, Denver, 1978-86, Hatton & Co., Lakewood, Colo., 1986--; speaker Success Motivation, Inc., 1986--. Bd. dirs. Opera Colo., Denver, 1980-81. 1st lt. U.S. Army, 1959-61. Mem. Am. Assn. Retired Persons (asst. state dir. pub. rels. media Colo. chpt. 1989—). Republican. Episcopalian. Office: 2675 Van Gordon Dr Lakewood CO 80215-7001

HAUBERG, JOHN HENRY, forestry management company executive; b. Rock Island, Ill., June 24, 1916; s. John Henry and Suzanne Christina (Denkmann) H.; m. Ann Homer Brinkley, Dec. 1, 1979; children—Fay Page, Sue B. Student Princeton U., 1939; B.S. in Forestry, U. Wash., 1949. Founder Pacific Denkmann Co., Seattle, 1948, pres., 1952—; mem. vis. com. U. Wash. Coll. Forest Resources, 1960—. Vice chmn. Republican Nat. Fin. Com., 1956-64; trustee Seattle Art Mus., 1956—, pres., 1973-78, chmn. bd. trustees, 1978-81; mem. adv. com. for Child Devel. and Mental Retardation Ctr., U. Wash.; trustee, founder, pres. Pilchuck Glass Sch., Stanwood, Wash.; trustee Bush Sch., Seattle, 1950-62, pres. 1954-57, Reed Coll., 1962-74; trustee Am. Fedn. Arts, 1984—, Am. Craft Council, 1979-87 ; mem. vestry Epiphany Parish Episcopalian Ch., Seattle. Served to 2d lt. F.A. and inf. U.S. Army, 1943-46. Mem. Soc. Am. Foresters, Northwest Hardwoods Assn. (founder, trustee), Phi Beta Kappa, Phi Sigma, Xi Sigma Pi. Clubs: Seattle Tennis, Seattle Golf, Univ., Rainier. Pub. Pilchuck Tree Farm Notes, 1981—. Office: 216 1st Ave Ste 230 Seattle WA 98104

HAUCK, DENNIS WILLIAM, data processing engineer; b. Hammond, Ind., Apr. 8, 1945; s. Floyd William and Wilma (Frey) H. BS, Ind. U., 1969; postgrad., U. Innsbruck, Austria, 1970; PhD in Math., U. Vienna, Austria, 1973. Systems analyst Tran Am. Corp., East Chicago, Ind., 1973-75; rsch. supt. U.S. Gypsum Co., East Chicago, Ind., 1975-79; elec. engr. Howmet Turbine, Reno, 1979-80; engring. mgr. EPCO, Reno, 1980-81; project engr. Campbell Soup Co., Sacramento, Calif., 1981-83; process mgr. Odenberg, Inc., Sacramento, Calif., 1983—; cons. math. GSW, Inc., Phoenix, 1977—; speaker Internat. Conf. on OFO's, Acapulco, Mex., 1978. editor: Jour. Ufology, 1975-77, MufonJour., 1976—, four mags., 1976-78; appeared in documentary Gold of the Gods, 1978. Mem. Greenpeace, San Francisco, 1987—. Mem. AAAS, Instrument Engrs. Soc., Inst. Transpersonal

Psychology. Home: 5550 Franklin Blvd Apt. #101 Sacramento CA 95820 Office: Odenberg Inc 6890 Luther Dr Sacramento CA 95823

HAUENSTEIN, DONALD HERBERT, JR., aerospace manufacturing executive; b. Canton, Ohio, Dec. 29, 1942; s. Donald Herbert and Mary Alice (Andrichs) H.; m. Maria Del Socorro Moreno, June 5, 1965 (div. Apr. 1979); children: Carlos Ian, Marissa Renee; m. Carol King, May 28, 1988. B in Indsl. Engring., Ohio State U., 1970, MS in Indsl. Engring., 1970; MBA, U. Houston, 1977; exec. mgmt. program, UCLA, L.A., 1986. Indsl. engr. Schlumberger Well Svcs., Houston, 1970-72, supr. of methods, 1972-75; mgr. engring. svcs. Dresser Atlas, Houston, 1975-80; mgr. mfg. engring. VETCO Offshore, Ventura, Calif., 1980-83; dir. mfg. engring. HR Textron, Valencia, Calif., 1983-88; dir. spl. projects HR Textron, Valencia, 1988—. Pres. St. Christopher's Sch. Bd., Houston, 1976-79, bd. dirs. Orchard Ln. Condominium Assn., Oxnard, Calif., 1986, Arbor Park Condominium Assn., 1987. With USAF, 1961-65. Mem. Inst. Indsl. Engrs. (sr.), Soc. Mfg. Engrs. (cert.) (sr. mem.), Nat. Mgmt. Assn., Tau Beta Pi, Alpha Pi Mu. Republican. Roman Catholic. Home: 28025 Tupelo Ridge Dr Valencia CA 91355 Office: HR Textron 25200 W Rye Canyon Rd Valencia CA 91355

HAUER, ANDREAS, employee benefit consultant; b. Oslo, June 25, 1946; came to U.S., 1948, naturalized, 1958; s. Karl Andreas and Ellen Bertha (Neilsen) H.; B.S., Linfield Coll., 1967; M.B.A., Golden Gate U., 1974. Asst. brokerage mgr. Pacific Mut. Ins. Co., San Francisco, 1970-72; employee benefit cons. Johnson & Higgins, San Francisco, 1972-80; v.p. employee benefits Bayly, Martin & Fay, Oakland, Calif., 1980-81, Fireman's Fund Ins. Co., San Rafael, Calif., 1981—; sr. benefits cons. Coopers & Lybrand, 1984— . Chmn., World Championship Domino Tournament, San Francisco; bd. dirs. Stonestown YMCA. Served with USNR, 1968-69; Vietnam. Mem. C.L.U. Soc. (dir. San Francisco chpt. 1975-76), Olympic Club. Republican. Lutheran. Home: 2032 Baker St San Francisco CA 94115 Office: Coopers & Lybrand 333 Market St San Francisco CA 94109

HAUK, A. ANDREW, U.S. district judge; b. Denver, Dec. 29, 1912; s. A.A. and Pearl (Woods) H.; m. Jean Nicolay, Aug. 30, 1941; 1 dau., Susan. A.B. magna cum laude, Regis Coll., 1935; LL.B., Catholic U. Am., 1938; J.S.D. (Sterling fellow), Yale U., 1942. Bar: Calif. 1942, Colo. 1939, D.C. 1938, U.S. Supreme Ct. 1953. Spl. asst. to atty. gen., counsel for govt. antitrust div. U.S. Dept Justice, Los Angeles, Pacific Coast, Denver, 1939-41; asst. U.S. atty., Los Angeles, 1941-42; with firm Adams, Duque & Hazeltine, Los Angeles, 1946-52; individual practice law Los Angeles, 1952-64; asst. counsel Union Oil Co., Los Angeles, 1952-64; judge Superior Ct., Los Angeles County, 1964-66; U.S. dist. judge Central Dist. Calif., 1966—, chief judge, 1980-82, now sr. judge, chief judge emeritus; instr. Southwestern U. Law Sch., 1939-41; lectr. U. So. Calif. Law Sch., 1947-56; Vice chmn. Calif. Olympic Com., 1954-61; ofcl. VIII Olympic Winter Games, Squaw Valley, 1960; Gov. Calif.'s del. IX Olympic Games, Innsbruck, Austria, 1964. Bd. dirs. So. Calif. Com. for Olympic Games. Served from lt. to lt. comdr., Naval Intelligence USNR, 1942-46. Recipient scroll Los Angeles County Bd. Suprs., 1965, 66, 75; Alumnus of Yr. Regis Coll., 1967; named to Nat. Ski Hall of Fame, 1975. Mem. Los Angeles Town Hall, World Affairs Council, Los Angeles County Bar Assn. (chmn. pleading and practice com. 1963-64, chmn. Law Day com. 1965-66), State Bar Calif. (corps. com., war work com. past vice-chmn.), ABA (com. criminal law sect.), Fed. Bar Assn., Lawyers Club Los Angeles, Am. Judicature Soc., Am. Legion, Navy League, U.S. Lawn Tennis Assn., So. Calif. Tennis Assn. (dir., bd. govs. 1972—), So. Calif. Tennis Patrons Assn. (bd. govs.), Far West Ski Assn. (Nat. Sr. Giant Slalom champion 1954), Yale Law Sch. Assn. So. Calif. (dir., past pres.), Town Hall. Clubs: Yale of So. Calif. (dir. 1964-67), Newman; Valley Hunt (Pasadena); Jonathan (Los Angeles). Office: US Dist Ct 312 N Spring St Los Angeles CA 90012

HAULENBEEK, ROBERT BOGLE, JR., government official; b. Cleve., Feb. 24, 1941; s. Robert Bogle and Priscilla Valerie (Burch) H.; BS, Okla. State U., 1970; m. Rebecca Marie Talley, Mar. 1, 1965; children—Kimberly Kaye, Robert Bogle, III. Micro paleon. photographer Pan Am. Rsch. Co., Tulsa, 1966-67; flight instr. Okla. State U., 1970; air traffic control specialist FAA, Albuquerque, 1970-73, Farmington, N.Mex., 1973-78, flight svc. specialist, Dalhart, Tex., 1978-80, Albuquerque, 1980—; staff officer CAP, Albuquerque, 1970-73, Farmington, 1974-78, advanced through grades to col., 1988, dir. ops. for hdqrs., 1981-86, N.Mex. Wing dep. commdr., 1986-88, N.Mex. Wing comdr., 1988—; mem. faculty Nat. Staff Coll., Gunter Air Force Sta., Montgomery, Ala., 1981-82; dir. South West Region Staff Coll., Albuquerque, 1986. With U.S. Army, 1964-65. Recipient Meritorious Svc. award CAP, 1978, 81, 82, Lifesaving award, 1982. Mem. Exptl. Aircraft Assn., Nat. Assn. Air Traffic Specialists (facility rep. 1978-86), Aircraft Owners and Pilots Assn. Republican. Presbyterian. Home: 5229 Carlsbad Ct NW Albuquerque NM 87120

HAUN, JOHN DANIEL, petroleum geologist, educator; b. Old Hickory, Tenn., Mar. 7, 1921; s. Charles C. and Lydia (Rhodes) H.; m. Lois Culbertson, June 30, 1942. AB, Berea Coll., 1948; MA, U. Wyo., 1949, Ph.D., 1953. Registered profl. engr., Colo. Geologist Stanolind, Amoco, Vernal, Utah, 1951-52; v.p. Petroleum Research Corp., Denver, 1952-57; mem. faculty dept. geology Colo. Sch. Mines, Golden, 1955-80; prof. Colo. Sch. Mines, 1963-80, part time, 1980-85, emeritus prof., 1983—; chmn. bd. Barlow & Haun, Inc., Evergreen, Colo., 1957—; cons. Potential Gas Agy., 1966-78; mem. exec. adv. com. Nat. Petroleum Council, 1968-70; mem. adv. com. Colo. Water Pollution Control Commn., 1969-70; mem. adv. council Kans. Geol. Survey, 1971-76; del. Internat. Geol. Congress, Sydney, Australia, 1976; U.S. rep. Internat. Com. on Petroleum Res. Classification UN, N.Y.C., 1976-77; mem. oil shale adv. com. Office of Tech. Assessment, Washington, 1976-79, mem. U.S. natural gas availability adv. panel, 1983; mem. Colo. Oil and Gas Conservation Commn., 1977-87, vice-chmn., 1983-85, chmn. 1985-87; mem. energy resources com. Interstate Oil Compact Commn., 1978—; mem. Nat. Petroleum Council, 1979—, mem. com. on unconventional gas sources, 1978-80; com. on Arctic oil and gas resources, 1980-81; mem. U.S. Nat. Com. on Geology Dept. Interior and NAS, 1982-89, chmn., 1985-87; del. Internat. Geol. Congress, Paris, 1980, Moscow, 1984. Editor: The Mountain Geologist, 1963-65, Future Energy Outlook, 1969, Methods of Estimating the Volume of Undiscovered Oil and Gas Resources, 1975; asst. editor: Geologic Atlas of the Rocky Mountain Region, 1972; co-editor: Subsurface Geology in Petroleum Exploration, 1958, Symposium on Cretaceous Rocks of Colorado and Adjacent Areas, 1959, Guide to the Geology of Colorado, 1960; contbr. articles to profl. jours. Served with USCG, 1942-46. Recipient Disting. Service award Am. Assn. Petroleum Geologists, 1973, Alumnus award U. Wyo., 1986, Disting. Alumnus award Berea Coll., 1989, Outstanding Prof. award Colo. Sch. Mines, 1973, Halliburton award Colo. Sch. Mines, 1985. Fellow Geol. Soc. Am., AAAS; mem. Am. Assn. Petroleum Geologists (editor 1967-71, pres. 1979-80, hon. mem. 1984), Am. Inst. Profl. Geologists (v.p. 1974, pres. 1976, exec. com. 1981-82, Ben H. Parker Meml. award 1983), Am. Geol. Inst. (governing bd. 1976, 79-82, sec.-treas. 1977-78, v.p. 1980-81, pres. 1981-82, Ian Campbell medal, 1988), Rocky Mountain Assn. Geologists (sec. 1961, 1st v.p. 1964, pres. 1968, hon. mem. 1974), Soc. Econ. Paleontologists and Mineralogists, Am. Petroleum Inst. (com. exploration 1971-73, 78-88), Geochem. Soc., Nat. Assn. Geology Tchrs., Wyo. Geol. Assn. (hon. life), Colo. Sci. Soc. (hon. life), Sigma Xi, Sigma Gamma Epsilon, Phi Kappa Phi. Home: 1238 County Rd 23 Evergreen CO 80439 Office: Colo Sch of Mines Golden CO 80401

HAUPTSCHEIN, MARTIN, internist; b. N.Y.C., Mar. 30, 1953; s. Arthur and Rosalyn (Chapnick) H.; m. Rachel Shemash, Dec. 26, 1987. AB, Rutgers Coll., 1975; MD, Georgetown U., 1979. Diplomate Am. Bd. Internal Medicine. Intern, then resident in internal medicine Westchester County Med. Ctr., Valhalla, N.Y., 1979-82; internist So. Calif. Permanente Med. Group, Panorama City, Calif., 1982-85; pvt. practice L.A., 1985—; consultative specialist Olive View Med. Ctr., Sylmar, Calif., 1986—; physician urgent care sect. Burbank (Calif.) Med. Clinic, 1987-88; med. staff Cedars Sinai Med. Ctr., 1988—. Vol. physician Venice (Calif.) Family Clinic, 1983—, Summer Olympics, L.A., 1984, Camp Ramah, L.A., 1984—, L.A. Jewish Festival, 1985—, Am. Heart Assn., L.A., 1987—. Recipient Physician's Recognition award Am. Bd. Internal Medicine, 1982. Mem. ACP, AMA, Phi Delta Epsilon. Jewish. Home: 1831 Barry Ave #14 Los Angeles CA 90025 Office: 8631 W 3d St #840E Los Angeles CA 90048

HAUSAM, NEAL ALLEN, civil engineer, real estate developer; b. Peoria, Ill., Oct. 17, 1939; s. George Melville and Elizabeth (Miklas) H.; m. Beverly Jo Beyer, Apr. 1962, (div. 1967); children: Kelly Kathleen, Neal Curtis. BSCE, Bradley U., 1962. Registered profl. civil engr., Alaska, Wash., Calif.; registered surveyor, Alaska, Oreg.; registered contractor, Calif. Owner Constrn. Testing Lab., Anchorage, 1973-81, Alaska Engring. Svcs., Anchorage, 1973-81, Neal Hausam Realty, Anchorage, 1978-82; developer Hamack, Vista View, Bay View, Holiday Park, Alaska, 1974-80; owner Crystal Water Lodge, Iliamna Lake, Alaska, 1976-79; assoc. broker Century 21 Heritage Homes and Investments, Inc., Anchorage, 1979-81; mgr. Oil Field Contractors of Alaska, Anchorage, 1979-81; owner Residential Housing Devel. Co., Salem, Oreg., 1981-85; constrn. and projects mgr. Fleming Foods, Inc., Pleasanton, Calif., 1982-86; mgr. Contractor's Quality Control, Taywood, Berg and Riedel, Alaska, 1988; mem. Municipality of Anchorage Constrn. Adv. Com., 1979-81; surveying trainer, Alaska Laborers Union, Anchorage, 1979-81. Inventor inflation device, 1963. Mem. Joe Hayes Mayorial Campaign, Anchorage, 1982. Mem. Porsche Club of Am. Republican. Home: 3605 Williams St Anchorage AK 99508 Office: Oreg Investments 2054 Mousebird Ave NW Salem OR 97304

HAUSDORFER, GARY LEE, mortgage banker; b. Indpls., Mar. 26, 1946; s. Walter Edward and Virginia Lee (Bender) H.; A.A., Glendale Coll., 1966; B.S., Calif. State U.-Los Angeles, 1968; m. Debora Ann French, Dec. 17, 1966; children—Lisa Ann, Janet Lee. Research officer Security Pacific Bank, Los Angeles, 1968-73; v.p., mgr. W. Ross Campbell Co., Irvine, Calif., 1973-81; sr. v.p. Weyerhaeuser Mortgage Co., Irvine, 1982-87; exec. v.p., ptnr. L.J. Melody & Co. of Calif., 1987—. Councilman, City of San Juan Capistrano, 1978—, mayor, 1980-81, 84-85, 88—; chmn. Capistrano Valley Water Dist., 1980-81, San Juan Capistrano Redevel. Agy., 1983-84, 85—, South Orange County Leadership Conf.; bd. dirs. Orange County Trans. Corridor Agy. Recipient cert. of commendation Orange County Bd. Suprs., 1981, congl. commendation, 1985. Mem. Mortgage Bankers Assn. Am., Calif. Mortgage Bankers Assn., Orange County Mortgage Bankers Assn. (dir. 1979-80), Calif. League of Cities. Republican.

HAUSEL, WILLIAM DAN, economic geologist; b. Salt Lake City, July 24, 1949; s. Maynard Romain and Dorthy (Clark) H.; m. Patricia Kemp, Aug. 14, 1970; children: Jessica Siddhartha, Eric Jason. BS in Geology, U. Utah, 1972, MS in Geology, 1974. Teaching asst. U. N.Mex., Albuquerque, 1974-75; astronomy lectr., Hansen Planetarium, Salt Lake City, 1968-72; project geologist Warnock Cons., Albuquerque, 1975; geologist U.S. Geol. Survey, Casper, Wyo., 1976-77; staff geologist Geol. Survey of Wyo., Laramie, 1977-81, dep. dir., 1981—; cons. geologist Western Gold Exploration and Mining, Anchorage, 1988, 89; assoc. curator mineralogy Wyo. State Mus., Cheyenne, 1983—. Author: Partial Pressures of Some Lunar Lavas, 1972, Petrogenesis of Some Representative Lavas, Southwestern Utah, 1975, Exploration for Diamondiferous Kimberlite, 1979, Gold Districts of Wyoming, 1980, Ore Deposits of Wyoming, 1982, Geology of Southeastern Wyoming, 1984, Minerals and Rocks of Wyoming, 1986, The Geology of Wyoming's Precious Metal Lode and Placer Deposits, 1989; numerous articles to profl. jours. With U.S. Army, 1971-73. Grantee NASA, 1981, Office of Surface Mining, 1979, U. Wyo., 1981—, U.S. Geol. Survey COGEOMAP, 1985-88. Mem. N.Mex. Geol. Soc., Wyo. Geol. Assn., Utah Geol. Assn., Am. Inst. Mining Engrs., U. Utah Geology (pres. 1969-71), U. Utah Karate, Laramie Bushido Dojo Karate (pres. 1985-88), Campus Club, Shotokan Karate Club (instr. 1988—). Home: 4238 Grays Gables Rd Laramie WY 82070 Office: Geol Survey of Wyo Box 3008 Laramie WY 82071

HAUSER, DIANA LOUISE, aerospace engineer; b. Latrobe, Pa., Apr. 29, 1964; d. Ronald Kent and Diana Hera (Kalokerinos) H. BSCE, Cornell U., 1986; MSME, Calif. State U., Long Beach, 1988; postgrad., Calif. State U., 1988—. Engr. scientist McDonnell Douglas, Corp., Cypress, Calif., 1986—. Contbr. articles to profl. jours. Mem. Assn. Computing Machinery, Nat. Physique Com., Tau Beta Pi. Republican. Home: 9802 Bloomfield Ave #66 Cypress CA 90630 also: 482 Gaviota St Long Beach CA 90802 Office: McDonnell Douglas Corp 10855 Bus Park Dr Cypress CA 90630 also: Cornell U 130 Upson Hall Ithaca NY 14853

HAUSER, ROBERT FRANCIS, chemical engineer; b. Oak Park, Ill., June 29, 1943; s. Francis Stanley and Veronica Rose (Lucarz) H.; m. Marie Antoinette Racut, July 23, 1966; children: Michael, Mary, John, Jeanmarie, Michelle. BSChemE, Case Western Res. U., 1965. Devel. engr. Eveready Battery div. Union Carbide, Cleve., 1965-74; chem. engr. Harshaw Chem., Cleve., 1974-79; materials engr. PCC Sherwood Refractories, Cleve., 1979-83; pilot plant engr. Oseonics Biomaterials, Livermore, Calif., 1983-89; supr. Beckman Instruments, San Ramon, Calif., 1989—. Patentee in field. Mem. Am. Inst. Chem. Engrs. Democrat. Roman Catholic. Home: 4323 Arleda Ln Concord CA 94521 Office: Beckman Instruments 2350 Camino Ramon San Ramon CA 94583

HAUSER, VICTORIA KAY, infosystems executive; b. Rhinelander, Wis., Feb. 6, 1958; d. Maurice Henry and Luella Francis (Papineau) H. BS in Acctg., U. Wis., Eau Claire, 1981. Corp. cost acct. Schreiber Foods, Green Bay, Wis., 1981-82, systems acct., 1982-83; mgr. cons. svcs. Seidmarr and Seidmarr, Milw., 1983-84; dir. mgmt. info. systems Kaibab Industries, Phoenix, 1984—; chmn. Sotas Hewlett Packard User Group Host Com., Las Vegas, Nev., 1987—. Mem. Data Processing Mgmt. Assn. Office: Kaibab Industries 4602 E Thomas Rd Phoenix AZ 85018

HAUSLE, VIVIAN ZADA, ceramics store executive; b. Levenworth, Wash., Mar. 11, 1919; d. Earenst A. and Zada (Irwin) Wells; m. Dean D. Hausle, June 14, 1940; children: Susan, Carol, Nancy. Grad. high sch., Seattle. Owner, mgr. World of Porcelain, Inc., Seattle, 1951--; staff writer Ceramics Arts and Crafts, Lavonia, Mich., 1964--; porcelain tchr. Author: World of Porcelain, 1980, Unlimited Technique, 1982, Vivian's Patterns, 1984, Porcelain Porcelain Porcelain, 1985, Love of Porcelain, 1986; producer video tapes on porcelain. Recipient numerous awards for porcelain, Alaska, P.R., N.Z., Australia, Eng., Hawaii, Owl award Pen Women Am. Mem. Internat. Ceramic Assn. (chmn. tchr.'s div., judge). Home: 12003 Palatine Ave Seattle WA 98133

HAUSMAN, ARTHUR HERBERT, electronics company executive; b. Chgo., Nov. 24, 1923; s. Samuel Louis and Sarah (Elin) H.; m. Helen Mandelowitz, May 19, 1946; children: Susan Lois, Kenneth Louis, Catherine Ellen. B.S. in Elec. Engring, U. Tex., 1944; S.M., Harvard U., 1948. Electronics engr. Engring. Research Assos., St. Paul, 1946-47; supervisory electronics scientist U.S. Dept. Def., Washington, 1948-60; now advisor, v.p., dir. research Ampex Corp., Redwood City, Calif., 1960-63, v.p. ops., 1963-65, group v.p., 1965-67, exec. v.p., 1967-71, exec. v.p., pres., chief exec. officer, 1971-83, chmn. bd., 1981-87, chmn. bd. emeritus, 1987—; chmn. tech. adv. com. computer peripherals Dept. Commerce, 1973-75; mem. Pres.'s Export Council; chmn. Subcom. on Export Adminstrn.; bd. dirs. Drexler Tech. Inc., T.C.I. Inc., Synthetic Vision Systems Inc., Calif.-Amplifier, Inc. Trustee United Bay Area Crusade.; mem. vis. com. dept. math. MIT; Bd. dirs. Bay Area Council. Served with USNR, 1944-54. Recipient Meritorious Civilian Service award Dept. Def. Mem. IEEE, Army Ordnance Assn. (dir. chpt. 1969-71), Am. Electronics Assn. (dir.). Clubs: Commonwealth of Calif.; Cosmos. Office: Ampex Corp 401 Broadway Redwood City CA 94063

HAUSMAN, MICHAEL ZAHN, sales executive, preservationist; b. L.A., June 27, 1947; s. Allan Harry and Mary Ann Margaret (Zahn) H. Student, U. Calif., Santa Barbara, 1965-66. Sales rep. Gen. Tire & Chem. Plastic, Orange, Calif., 1970-72; gen. mgr. Pacific Urethane, Gardena, Calif., 1972-74; owner Ram Enterprises, Tustina, Calif., 1975-78; v.p. PPS Packaging Co., Fresno, Calif., 1978—. Mem. Internat. Erosion Control Assn. Home: 8635 W Sahara #453 Las Vegas NV 89117

HAUSMAN, WILLIAM, psychiatry educator, consultant; b. N.Y.C., July 25, 1925; s. Jacob Henry and Tillie (Hoffman) H.; m. Lillian Margaret Fuerst, June 12, 1947; children: Steven David, Peter Douglas, Linda Louise Hausman Johnson, Clifford Alan. MD, Washington U., St. Louis, 1947. Diplomate Am. Bd. Psychiatry and Neurology. Commd. capt. U.S. Army, 1949, advanced through grades to col., 1964, ret., 1966; intern Coney Island Hosp., Bklyn., 1947-48; resident Worcester (Mass.) State Hosp., 1948-49, Inst. Pa. Hosp., Phila., 1949-50, 51-52; assoc. prof. Johns Hopkins U., Balt., 1966-69; prof. psychiatry, head dept. U. Minn., Mpls., 1969-80, prof. psychiatry, 1980-88, prof. emeritus, 1988—; cons. Levinson Inst., Belmont, Mass., 1975—. Contbr. articles to profl. jours. Fellow Am. Coll. Psychiatrists, Am. Psychiat. Assn., Am. Assn. Social Psychiatry; mem. Minn. Psychiat. Soc. Home and Office: 3785 Ranch Crest Dr Reno NV 89509

HAVELOCK, JOHN ERIC, lawyer; b. Toronto, Ont., Can., July 30, 1932; s. Eric Alfred and Ellen (Parkinson) H.; m. Patricia Minotti, 1959 (div. 1968); children: Eric, Brian, Scott, Bruce, Jennifer; m. Judith Luginbuhl, 1969 (div. 1984); m. Robyn Johnson, 1985. AB, Harvard U., 1956, JD, 1959. Bar: Alaska 1961, U.S. Dist. Ct. Alaska 1961, U.S. Ct. Appeals (9th cir.) 1963, U.S. Supreme Ct. 1972. Dep. atty. gen. State of Alaska, Juneau, 1959-63, atty. gen., 1970-73; ptnr. Ely, Guess, Rudd & Havelock, Anchorage, 1963-70; dir. legal studies, prof. U. Alaska, Anchorage, 1974-84; pvt. practice Anchorage, 1984—; dir. Alaska Ind. Pub. TV Corp., Anchorage, 1986—; cons. on criminal justice planning State of Alaska, 1974—. Author: Legal Education for a Frontier Society, 1975; co-author: Alaska Native Land Claims, 1974; weekly columnist: Policy Profiles, 1975-80, Alaska Bar newspaper, 1982-85. Pres., bd. dirs. Alaska World Affairs Coun., Anchorage, 1968-88; vice chmn., Alaska Commn. on Post-Secondary Edn., Juneau, 1985-88; bd. vis., U. Puget Sound Law Sch., Tacoma, 1979-88; chmn., Alaska Commn. to Celebrate U.S. Constitution, 1986-88, Alaska Mcpl. League, Anchorage Fedn. Community Couns., 1986-88; dem. nominee to U.S. Senate, Alaska, 1984; spl. counsel, Anchorage Equal Rights Commn., 1983—; mem. Bartlett Dem. Club, dir. 1986—; pres. SANE-Alaska, 1989—. Named White House fellow Dept. Agrl., 1967-68. Mem. ABA (mem. ho. of dels. 1968-69), Alaska Bar Assn. (fonder), White House Fellows Assn., Am. Judicature Soc., Am. Soc. for Pub. Adminstrn. Presbyterian (elder 1989—).

HAVENS, CANDACE JEAN, city official; b. Rochester, Minn., Sept. 13, 1952; d. Fred Z. and Barbara Jean (Stephenson) H.; m. Bruce Curtis Mercier, Feb. 22, 1975 (div. Apr. 1982); 1 child, Rachel; m. James Arthur Renning, Oct. 26, 1986; 1 child, Kelsey. Student, U. Calif., San Diego, Darmouth Coll., Am. U., Beirut, 1973-74; BA in Sociology, U. Calif., Riverside, 1977. Project coord. social svc. orgn. Grass Roots II, San Luis Obispo, Calif., 1976-77; planning enforcement technician City San Luis Obispo, 1977-81, asst. planner, 1981-83, assoc. planner, 1983-86, coord. parking program, 1986-88; project mgr. City-County Libr. Bldg. Commn., San Luis Obispo, 1985-89, 1989—. Past pres. Nat. Charity League, Riverside; mem. San Luis Obispo Med. Aux., 1986—, San Luis Obispo Arts Coun., 1986—; spl. asst. to City Adminstr. Mem. Calif. Pub. Parking Assn., Instn. & Mcpl. Parking Congress, AAUW, Cen. Coast Women's League Club, Toastmaster (sec. 1986-87, v.p. 1987-88, pres. 1989—). Office: City of San Luis Obispo 990 Palm St San Luis Obispo CA 93401

HAWE, DAVID LEE, consultant; b. Columbus, Ohio, Feb. 19, 1938; s. William Doyle and Carolyn Mary (Hassig) H.; m. Margret J. Hoover, Apr. 15, 1962; children: Darrin Lee, Kelly Lynn. Project mgr. ground antenna systems W.D.L. Labs., Philco Corp., 1960-65; credit mgr. for Western U.S., Am. Hosp. Supply Corp., Burbank, Calif., 1965-74; owner, mgr. Hoover Profl. Equipment Co., contract health equipment co., Guasti, Calif., 1974-75; pres. Baslor Care Services, owners convalescent homes, Santa Ana, Calif., 1975-80; pres. Application Assocs., 1980—; bd. dirs., chmn. of bd. Xiron, Inc., 1984—; dir. Medisco Co., Casa Pacifica, Broadway Assocs. Bd. dirs. Santa Ana Community Convalescent Hosp., 1974-79, pres., 1975-79. With USN, 1954-56. Lic. real estate broker, Calif. Mem. Am. Vacuum Soc. Republican. Roman Catholic. Home: 18082 Hallsworth Cir Villa Park CA 92667

HAWES, GRACE MAXCY, archival specialist, writer; b. Cumberland, Wis., Feb. 4, 1926; d. Clarence David and Mabel Hannah (Erickson) Maxcy; student U. Wis., 1944-46; BA, San Jose State U., 1963, MA, 1971: m. John G. Hawes, Aug. 28, 1948 (dec.); children: Elizabeth, John D., Mark, Amy. Library asst. NASA, Langley, Va., 1948-49; archival specialist Hoover Archives, Stanford U., 1976-80, adminstrv. asst., 1980-89; rsch. asst. Hoover Inst., 1989—. Mem. Soc. Am. Archivists, Western Assn. Women Historians, Women in Hist. Research, Calif. Archivists Assn., Inst. Hist. Study. Author: The Marshall Plan for China: Economic Cooperation Administration, 1948-1949, 1977. Home: 410 Sheridan Apt 220 Palo Alto CA 94306 Office: Stanford U Hoover Instn Archives Stanford CA 94304

HAWKE, ROBERT FRANCIS, dentist; b. Pasadena, Calif., Oct. 26, 1946; s. George Herbert and Milded Estelle (Wood) H.; m. Emily Sue Wilkins, Aug. 17, 1973; 1 child, Kristen. BA, U. Ariz., 1969; DDS, Baylor U., Dallas, 1973. Assoc. B.J. Barber, Tucson, 1976-78; ptnr. Barber-Hawke, P.C., Tucson, 1978-87; pvt. practice Tucson, 1987--; bd. dirs., pres. Delta Dental Ariz., Phoenix, 1985-87. Mem. Tuscon Bus. Alliance, 1981—, pres., 1983, Community Auto Immune Deficiency Syndrome Adv. Coun., Tucson, 1987—, Auto Immune Deficiency Syndrome Edn. Project, Tucson, 1988—. Maj. U.S. Army. Mem. ADA (alt. del. 1988), Ariz. State Dental Assn. (bd. of trustees 1988), So. Ariz. Dental Soc. (bd. dirs. 1983-89, pres. 1987-88), Rotary. Republican. Evangelical. Home: 6745 E Tivani Pl Tucson AZ 85715 Office: 5255 E Knight Dr Tucson AZ 85712

HAWKES, GLENN ROGERS, psychology educator; b. Preston, Idaho, Apr. 29, 1919; s. William and Rae (Rogers) H.; m. Yvonne Merrill, Dec. 18, 1941; children—Kristen, William Ray, Gregory Merrill, Laura. B.S. in Psychology, Utah State U., 1946, M.S. in Psychology, 1947; Ph.D. in Psychology, Cornell U., 1950. Asst. prof. to prof. child devel. and psychology Iowa State U., Ames, 1950-66, chmn. dept. child devel., 1954-66; prof. human devel., research psychologist U. Calif.-Davis, 1966—, assoc. dean applied econs. and behavioral scis., 1966-83, chmn. dept. applied behavioral scis., 1982-86, chmn. teaching div., 1970-72; prof. behavioral scis. dept. family practice Sch. Medicine U. Calif.-Davis; vis. scholar U. Hawaii, 1972-73, U. London, 1970, 80, 86; bd. dirs. Creative Playthings Inc., 1962-66. Author: (with Pease) Behavior and Development from 5 to 12, 1962; (with Frost) The Disadvantaged Child: Issues and Innovations, 1966, 2d edit., 1970; (with Schultz and Baird) Lifestyles and Consumer Behavior of Older Americans, 1979; (with Nicola and Fish) Young Marrieds: The Dual Career Approach, 1984. Contbr. numerous articles to profl. and sci. jours. Served with AUS, 1941-45. Recipient numerous research grants from pvt. founds. and govtl. bodies; recipient Iowa State U. faculty citation, 1965, Outstanding Service citation Iowa Soc. Crippled Children and adults, 1965, citation Dept. Child Devel., 1980, Coll. Agrl. and Environ. Scis., 1983; named hon. lt. gov. Okla., 1966. Home: 1114 Purdue Dr Davis CA 95616 Office: U Calif Dept Applied Behavioral Scis Davis CA 95616

HAWKINS, AUGUSTUS FREEMAN, congressman; b. Shreveport, La., Aug. 31, 1907; s. Nyanza and Hattie H. (Freeman) H.; m. Pegga A. Smith, Aug. 28, 1945 (dec. Aug. 1966); m. Elsie Taylor, June 30, 1977. A.B. in Econs., UCLA, 1931. Engaged in real estate and retail bus. Los Angeles, from 1945—; mem. Calif. Assembly from, Los Angeles County, 1935-62; chmn. rules com. Calif. Assembly from, 1961-62; mem. 88th to 93d congresses from 21st dist. Calif., 94th—; chmn. House Edn. and Labor Com.; chmn. Subcom. on Elem., Secondary and Vocational Edn. Democrat. Methodist. Club: Masons. Office: 2371 Rayburn House Office Bldg Washington DC 20515

HAWKINS, JAMES LOWELL, JR., bank executive; b. Kansas City, Mo., Apr. 25, 1950; s. James Lowell and Jean Marion (Schweitzer) H.; m. Linda Faye Cottrill, July 27, 1974; children: Paul Madison, Brian Lowell. BBA, N.Mex.State U., 1973; postgrad., Grad. Sch. Banking, 1982. Fin. intern U. S. Treasury Dept., Denver, 1970-73, asst. nat. bank examiner, 1973-74; asst. cashier Republic Bank & Trust, Tulsa, 1974-76; v.p., cashier Bank Cushing (Okla.) & Trust Co., 1977-83; v.p. Union Bank & Trust, Bartlesville, Okla., 1983-86; sr. v.p. First Nat. Bank Alamogordo, N.Mex., 1987—; bd. dirs., com. on payment systems Fed. Reserve Bank Dallas, 1987—. Dir. Retired Sr. Vol. Program, Alamogordo, 1987; mem. budget com. United Way, Bartlesville and Cushing, 1980-86. Mem. ABA, State U. Alumni Assn. (pres. Otero County 1987), Lions Club (Alamogordo), Rotary (Cushing), Masons. Republican. Prebyterian. Home: 404 Sunglow Ave Alamogordo NM 88310 Office: First Nat Bank Alamogordo 414 10th St Alamogordo NM 88310

HAWKINS, JOSEPH GAILYARD, electrical engineer, educator; b. Kansas City, Mo., Feb. 2, 1956; s. Joseph Gailyard and Dorothy Sue (Frantz) H.; m. Donna Lee Weihs, Sept. 8, 1984. BS, U. Alaska, Fairbanks, 1982; MS,

Stanford U., 1984, PhD, 1988. Asst. prof. elec. engring. U. Alaska, Fairbanks, 1987—. Mem. Am. Geophys. Union, IEEE, AIAA. Office: Univ of Alaska Fairbanks Elec Engring Dept Fairbanks AK 99775

HAWKINS, KAREN L., videotape production company executive. With Security Pacific Nat. Bank, L.A., 1969-86; ops. mgr., loan mgr. Security Pacific Nat. Bank, Downey, Calif., 1978-79; asst. v.p. ednl. design and devel. Security Pacific Nat. Bank, L.A., 1979-86; co-owner, mgr. ednl. media prodn. co. AbHawk Prodns., Inc., Lakewood, Calif., 1986—; instr. regional occupational programs, L.A. Unified Sch. Dist. Mem. parent adv. coun. Long Beach Unified Sch. Dist. Mem. NAFE, Am. Soc. for Tng. and Devel. Office: AbHawk Prodns Inc PO Box 8654 Long Beach CA 90808-0654

HAWKINS, ROBERT LEE, social work administrator; b. Denver, Feb. 18, 1938; s. Isom and Bessie M. (Hugley) H.; A.A., Pueblo Jr. Coll., 1958; B.S., So. Colo. State Coll., 1965; M.S.W., U. Denver, 1967; m. Ann Sharon Hoy, Apr. 28, 1973; children—Robert, Jeanne, Julia, Rose. Psychiat. technician Colo. State Hosp., Pueblo, 1956-58, 1962-63, occupational therapist asst., 1964-65, clin. adminstr. psychiat. team, 1969-75, dir. community services, 1975—, supr. vol. services, 1975—, mem. budget com., 1975—; counselor (part-time) Family Service Agy., Pueblo, 1968-69, exec. dir., 1969-70; mem. faculty U. So. Colo., 1968-75; partner Human Resource Devel., Inc., 1970-75. Mem. Pueblo Positive Action Com., 1970; chmn. adv. bd. Pueblo Sangre de Cristo Day Care Center, 1969-72; chmn. Gov.'s So. Area Adv. Council of Employment Service, 1975-76, chmn. Pueblo's City CSC, 1976-77, Pueblo Community Corrections, 1985-87, Pueblo Civil Service Commn., 1988—; commr. Pueblo Housing Authority, 1986—, Colo. Commn. Higher Edn., 1987—; mem. gov's. adv. com. Mental Health Standards, 1981—; mem. Colo. Juvenile Parole Bd., 1977; bd. dirs. Pueblo United Fund, 1969-74, pres., 1973; bd. dirs. Pueblo Community Orgn., 1974-76, Spanish Peaks Mental Health Center, 1976—, Neighborhood Health Center, 1977-79, Pueblo Community Corrections, 1983—, Pueblo Legal Services, 1983—. Served with U.S. Army 1958-62. Mem. Nat. Assn. Social Workers (nominating com. 1973-76), ACLU (dir. Pueblo chpt. 1980—), NAACP, Broadway Theatre Guild. Democrat. Methodist. Club: Kiwanis. Home: 520 Gaylord St Pueblo CO 81004 Office: Colo State Hosp 1600 W 24 St Pueblo CO 81003

HAWKSLEY, BARBARA JEAN, entrepreneur, educator; b. Riverside, Calif., Feb. 3, 1956; d. Robert Leonard and Virginia (Peterson) H. BA, Calif. State U., San Bernardino, 1987. Pres. B.J. Hawksley Profl. Secretarial Service, Palm Springs, Calif., 1982—; asst. dir. edn. Profl. Career Coll., Palm Desert, Calif., 1988—. Home: 28795 Avenida Condesa Cathedral City CA 92234-3702 Office: Hawksley Profl Secretarial Svc PO Box 8182 Palm Springs CA 92263

HAWLEY, BERNARD RUSSELL, clergyman; b. Ludlow, Mass., Nov. 22, 1926; s. Charles Arthur and Barbara Dickinson (Kimball) H.; m. Lois Jeanne Dick, Nov. 19, 1950; children: Steven Alan, Diane Kathleen, John Fredrick, James Russell. AB, Ottawa U., 1949; BD, McCormick Theol. Sem., 1958; DD, Sterling Coll., 1970. Ordained to ministry, Presbyn. Ch., 1954. Asst. pastor, then sr. pastor Woods Meml. Presbyn. Ch., Severna Park, Md., 1958-64; head of staff First Presbyn. Ch., Salina, Kans., 1965-87; interim pastor San Marino (Calif.) Community Ch., 1987—; bd. dirs., McCormick Theol. Sem., Chgo., 1969-77; trustee, Presbyn. Manors Mid Am., Newton, Kans., 1978-86, chmn. bd. trustees, 1978-79. Contbr. articles, sermons to religious publs. Republican. Office: San Marino Community Ch 1750 Virginia Rd San Marino CA 91108

HAWLEY, PHILIP METSCHAN, retail executive; b. Portland, Oreg., July 29, 1925; s. Willard P. and Dorothy (Metschan) H.; m. Mary Catherine Follen, May 31, 1947; children: Diane (Mrs. Robert Bruce Johnson), Willard, Philip M. Jr., John, Victor, Edward, Erin, George. B.S., U. Calif., Berkeley, 1946; grad., Advanced Mgmt. Program, Harvard U., 1967. With Carter Hawley Hale Stores, Inc., Los Angeles, 1958—, pres., 1972-83, chief exec. officer, 1977—, chmn., 1983—, also dir.; bd. dirs. Atlantic Richfield Co., BankAm. Corp., AT&T, The Economist; dir. Johnson & Johnson. Trustee Calif. Inst. Tech., U. Notre Dame, Huntington Library and Art Gallery; bd. dirs. Assocs. Harvard U Grad Sch. Bus. Adminstrn.; adv. council Grad. Sch. Bus. Stanford U.; vis. com. UCLA Grad. Sch. Mgmt., Bus. Council, Bus. Roundtable, Conf. Bd.; chmn. Los Angeles Energy Conservation Com. 1973-74. Decorated hon. comdr. Order Brit. Empire, knight comdr. Star Solidarity Republic Italy; recipient award of merit Los Angeles Jr. C. of C., 1974, Coro Pub. Affairs award, 1978, Medallion award Coll. William and Mary, 1983; named Calif. Industrialist of Year Calif. Mus. Sci. and Industry, 1975. Mem. Phi Beta Kappa, Beta Alpha Psi, Beta Gamma Sigma. Clubs: California, Los Angeles Country; Bohemian Pacific-Union (San Francisco); Newport Harbor Yacht (Newport Beach, Calif.); Multnomah (Portland); Links (N.Y.C.). Office: Carter Hawley Hale Stores Inc 550 S Flower St Los Angeles CA 90071

HAWLEY, ROBERT CROSS, lawyer; b. Douglas, Wyo., Aug. 7, 1920; s. Robert Daniel and Elsie Corienne (Cross) H.; m. Mary Elizabeth Hawley McClellan, Mar. 3, 1944; children—Robert Cross, Mary Virginia, Laurie McClellan. B.A. with honors, U. Colo., 1943; LL.B., Harvard U., 1949. Bar: Wyo. 1950, Colo. 1950, U.S. Dist. Ct. Colo. 1950, U.S. Dist. Ct. Wyo. 1954, U.S. Ct. Appeals (10th cir.) 1955, Tex. 1960, U.S. Ct. Appeals (5th cir.) 1960, U.S. Supreme Ct. 1960, U.S. Dist. Ct. (so. dist.) Tex. 1961, U.S. Ct. Appeals (D.C. cir.) 1961, U.S. Ct. Appeals (8th cir.) 1979, U.S. Ct. Appeals (11th cir.) 1981, U.S. Dist. Ct. (we. dist.) Tex. 1987. Assoc. Barrister Weller & Friedrich, Denver, 1949-50; sr. atty. Continental Oil Co., Denver, 1952-58, counsel, Houston, 1959-62; ptnr., v.p. Ireland, Stapleton & Pryor, Denver, 1962-81; ptnr. Dechert Price & Rhoads, Denver, 1981-83, Hawley & VanderWerf, Denver, 1983—; pres. Highland Minerals, Denver; dir. Yorker Mfg., Denver, Bank of Denver; speaker oil and gas insts. Contbr. articles to Oil & Gas Bd. dirs. Am. Cancer Soc., Denver, 1967-87, treas., 1981-82; chmn. U. Colo. Devel. Found., 1960-61, Rocky Mountain Arthritis Found., 1987—. Served to lt. col. U.S. Army, World War II. Recipient Alumni Recognition award U. Colo., Boulder, 1958, Meritorious Service award Monticello Coll., Godfrey, Ill., 1967; Sigma Alpha Epsilon scholar, 1941-43. Mem. Denver Assn. Oil and Gas Title Lawyers (pres. 1983-84), Denver Petroleum Club (pres. 1978-79), Harvard Law Sch. Assn. Colo. (pres. 1980-81), Associated Alumni U. Colo. (pres. and bd. dirs. 1956-57), Law Club, Denver (pres. 1958-59), ABA, Colo. Bar Assn., Denver (pres. 1958-59), Bar Assn., Tex. Bar Assn., Wyo. Bar Assn., Fed. Energy Bar Assn. (legal and lands com.), Interstate Oil Compact Comn., Mile High Alumni Assn., Rocky Mountain Oil and Gas Assn., Chevaliers du Tastevin. Republican. Episcopalian. Clubs: Denver Country, Petroleum, Gyro, Univ. (Denver); Colo. Arlberg (Winter Park). Author, co-author: Landman's Handbook, Law of Federal Oil and Gas Leases, Problems of Surface Damages, Federal Oil and Gas Leases--The Sole Party in Interest Debacle. Office: Hawley & VanderWerf 730 17th St Suite 730 Denver CO 80202 Home: 4401 E 3d Ave Denver CO 80220 *

HAWLEY, SHARON LOUISE, small business owner; b. San Diego, May 1, 1950; d. William Dwight Jr. and Mildred Louise (Andreson) H. BA in English, U. Kans., 1972. Permits editor Peabody Coal Co., Denver, 1976-79; projects mgr. Ertec Rocky Mountain, Inc., Denver, 1979-81; property mgr., pub. lands coordinator Anaconda Minerals Co., Denver, 1981-82; interior designer Homestead House, Denver, 1982-85; regional mktg. mgr. Right Assocs., Denver, 1985-86; owner, mgr. Sunshine Prodns., Denver, 1986—. Tour vol., Historic Denver, 1985.

HAWLEY, STEPHEN LA THAIR, plumbing contractor; b. Ely, Nev., Oct. 5, 1936; s. Rollo Earl and Margaret Ella (Lawrence) H.; m. Sidney Ann Delgado, July 11, 1964; children: Kelli Ann, Aaron La Thair. Grad. High Sch., Las Vegas, Nev. Plumbing foreman Local 525 Plumber & Pipefitter, Las Vegas, Nev., 1964-79; pres., chief exec. officer Classic Plumbing Inc., Las Vegas, 1979-84, Rakeman Plumbing, Las Vegas, 1984—; bd. dirs. Las Vegas Master Plumbers, 1982, Las Vegas Plumbing Code Com., 1984, Clark County Plumbing Bd., 1988. Served in U.S. Army, 1959-60. Named Plumbing Rep., People to People, Republic of China, USSR, 1983. Mem. Plumbing Heating Cooling Contractors of Nev. (pres. 1982-84), Las Vegas Exec. Assn., Plumbing Mech. Contractors of Nev. Democrat. Episcopalian. Home: 2208 Verdinal Dr Las Vegas NV 89102 Office: Classic Plumbing Inc 3823 Losee Rd Las Vegas NV 89030

HAWORTH, ROBERT HAINES, data processing executive; b. Portland, Oreg., Apr. 12, 1947; s. Berton James and Beckie (J.) H.; m. Katherine A. Kingsbury, Dec. 17, 1967; children: Susan, Scott, Sally. BS in Chemistry, Portland State U., 1969. Ptnr. Haworth & Harris Investments, Portland, 1972-80; field svc. mgr. Kockums Industries, Tualatin, 1980-81; prodn. and dept. mgr. Automatic Data Processing, Portland, 1981-85; dir. prodn. Automatic Data Processing, 1985-86, dir. customer engring. support, 1986-88; dir. product assurance McDonnell Douglas Computer Systems, Santa Ana, Calif., 1988—. Mem. Am. Soc. Quality Control, Willamette Valley DX Club. Democrat. Adventist. Office: McDonnell Douglas 1801 E St Andrew Pl PO Box 35020 Santa Ana CA 92705

HAWTHORNE, DONALD BRUCE, healthcare executive; b. L.A., Dec. 31, 1955; s. Donald Claire and Elene Ruth (Roussey) H. BS, Harvey Mudd Coll., 1977; MBA, Stanford U., 1981. Fin. planner Westinghouse Electric Corp., Sunnyvale, Calif., 1978-79; fin. analyst, sr. fin. analyst treasury dept. Arco, L.A., 1981-83; sr. fin. analyst corp. planning Syntex Corp., Palo Alto, Calif., 1983-84; fin. planning mgr. ophthalmics div. Syntex Corp., Phoenix, 1984-85, div. controller, 1985; mgr. fin. and adminstrn. Genelabs Inc., Redwood City, Calif., 1985-87; dir. fin. Genelabs Inc., Redwood City, 1987-89, chief fin. officer, 1989—. Sen. dist. dir. Calif. Rep. Assembly, San Mateo County, 1988, treas. Peninsula chpt., 1988, bd. dirs., 1987-88; trustee Harvey Mudd Coll., Claremont, Calif., 1986-89, pres. student body, 1976-77. Mem. Am. Soc. Engring. Edn., Stanford Bus. Sch. Alumni Assn., Harvey Mudd Coll. Alumni Assn. (bd. govs. 1981-87, pres. 1984-86, v.p. 1983-84, treas. 1982-83), Pi Sigma Alpha. Republican. Home: PO Box 1056 Belmont CA 94002-1056 Office: Genelabs Inc 505 Penobscot Dr Redwood City CA 94063

HAWTHORNE, DOUGLAS BRUCE, journalist, author; b. Mineola, N.Y., Aug. 12, 1948; s. Frank Douglas and Jean Rae (Spencer) H.; m. Marjorie Jo Rheinscheld, Dec. 21, 1979. AA in Journalism, Pima Community Coll., 1981; BA in Broadcast Communications, U. Ariz., 1983, MA in Journalism, 1985. City editor, reporter The Tombstone (Ariz.) Epitaph, 1985; copy editor, reporter Territorial Pubs., Inc., Tucson, 1986—; freelance writer Tucson, 1987—. Author: Men and Women of Space, 1989. With USNR, 1965-69. Fellow Brit. Interplanetary Soc.; mem. Nat. Space Coun., Golden Key Nat. Honor Soc., Phi Theta Kappa, Phi Kappa Phi. Republican. Home and Office: 4532 E La Estancia Tucson AZ 85718

HAWTHORNE, MARION FREDERICK, chemistry educator; b. Ft. Scott, Kans., Aug. 24, 1928; s. Fred Elmer and Colleen (Webb) H.; m. Beverly Dawn Rempe, Oct. 30, 1951 (div. 1976); children: Cynthia Lee, Candace Lee; m. Diana Baker Razzaia, Aug. 14, 1977. B.A., Pomona Coll., 1949; Ph.D. (AEC fellow), U. Calif. at Los Angeles, 1953; D.Sc. (hon.), Pomona Coll., 1974. Research asso. Iowa State Coll., 1953-54; research chemist Rohm & Haas Co., Huntsville, Ala., 1954-56; group leader Rohm & Haas Co., 1956-60; lab. head Rohm & Haas Co., Phila., 1961; vis. lectr. Harvard, 1960, Queen Mary Coll., U. London, 1963; vis. prof. Harvard U., 1968; prof. chemistry U. Calif. at Riverside, 1962-68, U. Calif. at Los Angeles, 1968—; vis. prof. U. Tex., Austin, 1974; Mem. sci. adv. bd., USAF, 1980-86, NRC Bd. Army Sci. and Tech., 1986—. Editor: Inorganic Chemistry, 1969—; Editorial bd.: Progress in Solid State Chemistry, 1971—, Inorganic Syntheses, 1966—, Organometallics in Chemical Synthesis, 1969—, Synthesis in Inorganic and Metalorganic Chemistry, 1970—. Recipient Chancelors Research award, 1968, Herbert Newby McCoy award, 1972, Am. Chem. Soc. award in Inorganic Chemistry, 1973, Tolman Medal award, 1986, Nebr. sect.Am. Chem. Soc. award, 1979, Disting. Service in the Advancement of Inorganic Chemistry award Am. Chem. Soc., 1988, Disting. Achievements in Boron Sci. award, 1988; Sloan Found. fellow, 1963-65, Japan Soc. Promotion Sci. fellow, 1986; named Col. Confederate Air Force, 1984. Fellow AAAS; mem. U.S. Nat. Acad. Scis., Am. Acad. Arts and Scis., Aircraft Owners and Pilots Assn., Sigma Xi, Alpha Chi Sigma, Sigma Nu. Club: Cosmos. Home: 3415 Green Vista Dr Encino CA 91436

HAXTON, RONALD SCOTT, pediatrician; b. L.A., Mar. 15, 1942; s. Alexander Scott and Jacqueline Alice (Adams) H.; m. Betty Jane Glenn, . BA, Whittier Coll., 1963; MD, U. Calif., 1967. Intern Los Angeles County-U. So. Calif. Med. Ctr., 1967-68; resident in pediatrics U. Calif. Med. Ctr., Irvine, 1970-72; pvt. practice Mission Viejo, Calif., 1972—. With U.S. Navy, 1968-70. Fellow: Am. Academy of Pediatrics; mem. Orange County Medical Assn.. Republican. Office: 27800 Medical Center Rd Mission Viejo CA 92691

HAY, ANDREW MACKENZIE, merchant banking and commodities company executive; b. London, Apr. 9, 1928; came to U.S., 1954, naturalized, 1959; s. Ewen Mackenzie and Bertine (Buxton) H.; MA in Econs., St. John's Coll., Cambridge U., 1950; m. Catherine Newman, July 30, 1977. Commodities trader, London and Ceylon, 1950-53; v.p. Calvert Vavasseur & Co. Inc., N.Y.C., 1954-61, pres., 1962-78, pres. Calvert-Peat Inc., N.Y.C., 1978—, Andrew M. Hay, Inc.; chmn. Barretto Peat Inc., N.Y.C., 1974-88; Pacific NW cons. Am. Assn. Exporters and Importers, 1982—; radio and TV appearances. Mem. adv. com. on tech. innovation Nat. Acad. Scis., 1978; bd. dirs. Winston Churchill Found.; treas., trustee World Affairs Coun. Oreg., 1986—; apptd. Her Majesty's hon. Brit. consul., 1987. Capt. Brit. Army. Decorated comdr. Order Brit. Empire. Mem. Am. Importer Assn. (pres. 1977-79), Pacific N.W. Internat. Trade Assn. (exec. dir. 1986—), Brit. Am. C. of C. (pres. 1966-68), Philippine Am. C. of C. (pres. 1977-79), St. George's Soc. (bd. dir.), St. Andrew's Soc. (bd. dir.), Recess Club, Downtown Assn. (N.Y.C.), U. Club, Arlington Club. Episcopalian. Author: A Century of Coconuts, 1972. Home and Office: 3515 SW Council Crest Dr Portland OR 97201

HAY, JOHN LEONARD, lawyer; b. Lawrence, Mass., Oct. 6, 1940; s. Charles Cable and Henrietta Dudley (Wise) H.; m. Millicent Victoria, Dec. 16, 1967; 1 child, Ian. AB with distinction, Stanford U., 1961; JD, U. Colo., 1964. Bar: Colo. 1964, Ariz. 1965, D.C. 1971. Assoc. Lewis and Roca, Phoenix, 1964-69, ptnr., 1969-82; ptnr. Fannin, Terry & Hay, Phoenix, 1982-87, Allen, Kimerer & LaVelle, Phoenix, 1987—; bd. dirs. Ariz. Life and Disability Ins. Guaranty Fund. Mem. Dem. Precinct Com., 1966-78, Ariz. State Dem. Com., 1968-78; chmn. Dem. Legis. Dist., 1971-74; mem. Maricopa County Dem. Cen. Com., 1971-74; bd. dirs. ACLU, 1973-78; bd. dirs. Community Legal Svcs., 1983—, pres. 1987-88. Mem. ABA, Maricopa County Bar Assn. (bd. dirs. 1972-85), State Bar of Ariz., Ariz. Licensors and Franchisors Assn. (bd. dirs. 1985—, pres. 1988-89), Ariz. Civil Liberties Union (bd. dirs. 1967-84, pres. 1973-77, Disting. Citizen award 1979). Home: 201 E Hayward Ave Phoenix AZ 85020 Office: Allen Kimerer LaVelle 2715 N 3d St Phoenix AZ 85004

HAY, JOHN WOODS, JR., banker; b. Rock Springs, Wyo., Apr. 23, 1905; s. John Woods and Mary Ann (Blair) H.; A.B., U. Mich., 1927; m. Frances B. Smith, Dec. 28, 1948; children—Helen Mary, John Woods III, Keith Norbert, Joseph Garrett. Pres., dir. Rock Springs Nat. Bank, 1947—, Rock Springs Grazing Assn., 1939—, Blair & Hay Land & Livestock Co., Rock Springs, 1949—. Trustee, v.p. William H. and Carrie Gottsche Found. Mem. Sigma Alpha Epsilon. Republican. Episcopalian. Clubs: Masons, Shriners, Jesters, Rotary. Home: 502 B St Rock Springs WY 82901 Office: 333 Broadway Rock Springs WY 82901

HAY, LOUISE, lecturer, author, therapist; b. L.A., Oct. 8, 1926; d. Henry Lunney and Vera (Chawala) Hay; m. Andrew Mackenzie Hay, 1953 (div. 1968). Student, Maharishis' Internat. U., Fairfield, Iowa, 1977. Model Bill Blass Fashions, N.Y.C., 1944-53; pvt. practice counselor, tchr. N.Y.C., 1970-80; founder, lectr., author, pub. Hay House, L.A., 1980—; bd. dirs. Inside Edge, Pacific Palisades, Calif., 1980—; pres. Hay Found., Santa Monica, Calif., 1984—. Author: Heal Your Body, 1976, You Can Heal Your Life, 1984, I Love My Body, The AIDS Book: Creating a Positive Approach, Colors and Numbers, 1989; creator self-healing audio and video tapes: Conversations on Living; participant video: Doors Opening: A Positive Approach to AIDS; subject of articles in People mag., L.A. Times, N.Y. Daily News, others. Bd. dirs. L.A. Ctr. for Living, 1987—; facilitator Hayride AIDS Support Group, West Hollywood, Calif., 1984—; participant crafts and health expo, Circle of Light Found., L.A., 1987. Recipient Honoraria Brandeis U., 1988, From the Heart, 1988. Office: Hay House 501 Santa Monica Blvd Apt 602 Santa Monica CA 90401

HAY, RICHARD LAURENCE, theater scenic designer; b. Wichita, Kans., May 28, 1929; s. Laurence Charles and Ruth Mary (Rhoades) H. BA, Stanford U., 1952, MA, 1955. Tech. dir., designer Oreg. Shakespeare Festival, Ashland, 1953-55, prin. scenic designer, 1970—; instr. drama Stanford U., Palo Alto, Calif., 1957-62, assoc. prof., 1965-69; assoc. artistic dir. for design Denver Ctr. Theater Co., 1984—; freelance scenic designer Guthrie Theater, Mpls., Am. Conservatory Theater, San Francisco, Mo. Repertory Theater, Kansas City, Mark Taper Forum, Los Angeles, Old Globe Theater, San Diego, Berkekey (Calif.) Repertory Theater, others. Author: (with others) A Space for Magic: Stage Settings by Richard L. Hay, 1979; exhibitor Prague Quadriennial, 1987, U.S. Inst. Theatre Tech. Biennial Scenography Expn., 1984, 88. Recipient Critics award Hollywood (Calif.) Drama-Logue, 1982, 85, 86, Gov's. award for the Arts State of Oreg., 1989; Fulbright grantee, 1955. Mem. United Scenic Artists, U.S. Inst. Theatre Tech., League Hist. Am. Theaters. Democrat. Congregationalist. Home: 9 Hillcrest Ashland OR 97520 Office: Oreg Shakespeare Festival PO Box 158 Ashland OR 97520

HAY, WILLIAM WINN, natural history and geology educator; b. Dallas, Oct. 12, 1934; s. Stephen J. and Avella (Winn) H. B.S., So. Meth. U., 1955; postgrad. U. Zurich, Switzerland, 1955-56; M.S., U. Ill., 1958; Ph.D., Stanford U., 1960. Mem. faculty Rosenstiel Sch. Marine and Atmospheric Sci., U. Miami., Fla., 1968-82, chmn. div. marine geology, 1974-76, interim dean, 1976-77, dean, 1977-80; pres. Joint Oceanographic Instn., Inc., Washington, 1979-82; dir. U. Colo. Mus., Boulder, 1982-87; mem. faculty dept. geology U. Ill., Urbana, 1960-73; mem. adv. panel sediment and ocean history Joint Oceanographic Instns. for Deep Earth Sampling, Washington, 1984-88; mem. sci. adv. com. Ocean Drilling Program, 1979-83; mem. exec. com. div. ocean sci. NSF, 1982-85. Editor: Studies in Paleo-Oceanography, 1974. Univ. Coll. London fellow, 1972—; recipient Francis P. Shepard medal Soc. Econ. Paleontologists and Mineralogists, 1981, Best Paper award Gulf Coast sect., 1970. Fellow AAAS, Geol. Soc. Am., Geol. Soc. (London), Coop. Inst. Rsch. in Environ. Scis.; mem. Am. Assn. Petroleum Geologists, Internat. Nannoplankton Assn., Cosmos Club. Office: Univ of Colo Mus Campus Box 218 Boulder CO 80309

HAYASHI, KENNETH SHIGENORI, real estate corporation officer; b. Tokyo, Feb. 1, 1946; came to U.S., 1966; s. Norio and Kimi (Mori) H.; m. Marie Angele Lewis, Jan. 25, 1969; children: Kenneth S. II, Hilary A. Student, Chuo U., Tokyo, 1964-66; BS in Fin. and Mgmt., Woodbury Coll., Los Angeles, 1972. Auditor Peat, Marwick, Mitchell & Co., Los Angeles, 1972-74; pres. Service Master Bldg. Maintenance Co., Los Angeles, 1975-77; real estate broker H. Bruce Hanes, Inc., Los Angeles, 1977-78; pres., chmn. bd. Kenneth S. Hayashi Corp., Los Angeles, 1978—. Author: Apartment House Investment, Management and Taxation, 1978. Office: Kenneth S Hayashi Corp 1900 Sepulveda 2d Fl Los Angeles CA 90025

HAYDEN, GOULD DWIGHT, ophthalmologist; b. Asbury, Mo., Oct. 23, 1933; s. Claud Wray and Mollie Edna (Bateman) H.; m. Sherry Lynn Trogdon, Dec. 20, 1958; children: Laurie Ann, Bret Wray, Dana Marie. BS, Kans. State Coll., 1955; MD, Ind. U., Indpls., 1958. Diplomate Am. Bd. Opthalmology. Intern Orange County Gen. Hosp., Orange, Calif., 1958-59; resident in ophthalmology Parkland Meml. Hosp., Dallas, 1962-64; instr. Sch. of Aerospace Medicine, San Antonio, 1966-67; chief of staff Sierra Vista Hosp., San Luis Obispo, Calif., 1981; ophthalmologist Cen. Coast Eye Associates, San Luis Obispo, 1968—. Maj. USAF, 1959-68, Vietnam, Europe, U.S. Fellow Am. Acad. Ophthalmology; mem. AMA, Calif. Med. Assn., Calif. Assn. Ophthalmology, Cal-Nev.-Ha Kiwanis (lt. gov. div. 29, 1988-89). Republican. Office: Cen Coast Eye Assocs 628 Calif Blvd San Luis Obispo CA 93401

HAYDEN, TOM, state legislator, author; b. Royal Oak, Mich., Dec. 11, 1939; m. Jane Fonda; children: Troy, Vanessa. Grad., U. Mich. Co-founder Students for a Democratic Soc., 1961, pres., 1962, 63; staff Student Nonviolent Coordinating Com., 1963; co-founder Econ. Research and Action Project, 1964; leader Newark Community Union Project, 1964-67; founder Indochina Peace Campaign; candidate for U.S. Senate in Calif. Democratic Primary, 1976; founder, chmn. Calif. Campaign for Econ. Democracy, 1977—; chmn. SolarCal Council, State of Calif., 1978-82; mem. Calif. State Assembly, 1982—, chmn. labor & employment com., chmn. subcom. on higher edn. Author: Port Huron Statement, 1962, Rebellion in Newark, 1967, Rebellion and Repression, 1969, Trial, 1970, The Love of Possession is a Disease with Them, 1972, The American Future, 1980, Reunion: A Memoir, 1988; co-author: The Other Side, 1967; contbr.: articles to periodicals including Washington Post, Los Angeles Times, N.Y. Times. Office: State Capitol Rm 2196 Sacramento CA 95814 *

HAYEK, CAROLYN JEAN, judge; b. Portland, Oreg., Aug. 17, 1948; d. Robert A. and Marion L. (DeKoning) H.; m. Steven M. Rosen, July 21, 1974; children: Jonathan David, Laura Elizabeth. BA in Psychology, Carleton Coll., 1970; JD, U. Chgo., 1973. Bar: Wash. 1973. Assoc. firm Jones, Grey & Bayley, Seattle, 1973-77; sole practice law, Federal Way, Wash., 1977-82; judge Federal Way Dist. Ct., 1982—. Task force mem. Alternatives for Wash., 1973-75; mem. Wash. State Ecol. Commn., 1975-77; bd. dirs. 1st Unitarian Ch. Seattle, 1986-89, vice chair 1987-88, pres., 1988-89; den leader Cub Scouts Mt. Ranier coun. Boy Scouts Am., 1987-88, scouting coord., 1988-89; bd. dirs. Twin Lakes Elem. Sch. PTA. Mem. ABA, Wash. Women Lawyers, Wash. State Bar Assn., AAUW (br. pres. 1978-80, chmn. state level conf. com. 1986-87), King County Dist. Ct. Judges Assn. (treas., exec. com., com. chmn.), Elected Wash. Women (dir. 1983-87), Nat. Assn. Women Judges (nat. bd. dirs., dist. bd. dirs. 1984-86, chmn. rules com. 1988—), Women's Profl. and Managerial Network, Fed. Way Women's Network (bd. dirs. 1984-87, 88—, pres. 1985, program co-chair 1989—), Greater Fed. Way C. of C. (dir. 1978-82, sec. 1980-81, v.p. 1981-82). Republican. Office: Federal Way Dist Ct 33506 10th Pl S Federal Way WA 98003

HAYES, BYRON JACKSON, JR., lawyer; b. L.A., July 9, 1934; s. Byron Jackson and Caroline Violet (Scott) H.; m. DeAnne Saliba, June 30, 1962; children: Kenneth Byron, Patricia DeAnne. Student, Pomona Coll., 1952-56; B.A. magna cum laude, Harvard U., LL.B. cum laude, 1959. Bar: Calif. 1960, U.S. Supreme Ct. 1963. Assoc., McCutchen, Black, Verleger & Shea, L.A., 1960-68, ptnr., 1968—. Trustee L.A. Ch. Extension Soc. United Meth. Ch., 1967-77, pres., 1974-77; Dir., pres. Pacific and S.W. United Meth. Found., 1978-83, chancellor annual conf., 1979-86. Served to capt. U.S. Army, 1959-65. Named layperson of yr. Pacific and S.W. Annual Conf., United Meth. Ch., 1981. Mem. Am. Coll. Mortgage Attys. (regent 1984—), Calif. Bar. Assn., ABA, Assn. Real Estate Attys., L.A. County Bar Assn. (chmn. real property sect. 1982-83), Pomona Coll. Alumni Assn. (pres. 1984-85), Lakeside Golf Club (Toluca Lake, Calif.), Univ. Club (L.A.). Office: 600 Wilshire Blvd 9th Fl Los Angeles CA 90017

HAYES, CLAUDE QUINTEN CHRISTOPHER, research scientist; b. N.Y.C., Nov. 15, 1945; s. Claude and Celestine (Stanley) H. BA in Chemistry and Geol. Sci., Columbia U., 1971, postgrad., 1972-73; postgrad., N.Y. Law Sch., 1973-75; JD, Western State Law Sch., 1978. Cert. community coll. tchr. earth scis., phys. sci., law, Calif. Tech. writer Burroughs Corp., San Diego, 1978-79; instr. phys. scis. Nat. U., San Diego, 1980-81; instr. bus. law, earth scis. Miramar Coll., 1978-82; sr. systems analyst Gen. Dynamics Convair, 1979-80, advanced mfg. technologist, sr. engr., 1980-81; pvt. practice sci. and tech. cons. Calif., 1979—; instr. phys. sci., geography, bus. law San Diego Community Coll. Dist., 1976-82, 85-89; U.S. Dept. Def. contractor Def. Nuclear Agy., Strategic Def. Initiative Agy., USAF, Def. Advance Projects Agy., 1986—; adj. prof. phys. chemistry San Diego State U., 1986-87; adj. prof. internat. bus. and computer sci. U. Redlands (Calif.) Grad. Sch., 1986-88; def. research contractor to Maxwell Labs., Naval Oceans Systems Ctr. Contbr. articles to profl. jours.; patentee in field. Mem. Am. Chem. Soc., N.Y. Acad. Sci., Am. Inst. Aero. and Astronautics. Home: 7980 Linda Vista Rd #49 San Diego CA 92111

HAYES, ERNEST M., podiatrist; b. New Orleans, Jan. 21, 1946; s. Ernest M. and Emma Hayes; B.A., Calif. State U., Sacramento, 1969; B.S., Calif. Coll. Podiatric Medicine, San Francisco, 1971, D.P.M., 1973; m. Bonnie Ruth Beigle, Oct. 16, 1970. Resident in surg. podiatry Beach Community Hosp., Buena Park, Calif., 1973-74, dir. residency program, 1974-75; practice podiatry, Anaheim, Calif., 1974-80, Yreka, Calif., 1980—; sr. clin. instr. So. Calif. Podiatric Med. Center, Los Angeles, 1975-78; vice chmn. podiatry dept. Good Samaritain Hosp., Anaheim, Calif., 1978-79; mem. med. staff Mercey Med. Ctr., Mt. Shasta, Calif. Bd. dirs. Little Bogus Ranches Home Owners Assn., 1981-83, pres., 1983—. Fellow Nat. Coll. Foot Surgeons; mem. Am. Assn. Podiatric Physicians and Surgeons (cert.). Baptist. Club: Kiwanis. Home: PO Box 958 Yreka CA 96097 Office: 1009 S Main St Yreka CA 96097 also: The Plaza 108 Siskiyou Ave Stes A&B Mount Shasta CA 96067

HAYES, GORDON GLENN, civil engineer; b. Galveston, Tex., Jan. 2, 1936; s. Jack Lewis and Eunice Karen (Victery) H. BS in Physics, Tex. A & M U., 1969. Registered profl. engr., Alaska. Rsch. technician Shell Devel. Co., Houston, 1962-68; rsch. assoc. Tex. Trans. Inst., College Station, 1969-71, asst. rsch. physicist, 1971-74, assoc. rsch. physicist, 1974-80; traffic safety specialist Alaska Dept. Transp. & Pub. Facilities, Juneau, 1981-83, state traffic engr., 1983-85, traffic, safety standards engr., 1985—. Authors of numerous pubs. in the hwy. safety field; producer of numerous documentary films in the hwy. safety field. Petty officer USN, 1953-57. Mem. Am. Assn. State Hwy. & Transp. Officials (state rep., traffic engring. com.), Inst. Transp. Engrs., Juneau Sea Kayak Club, Territorial Sportsmen Club. Home: PO Box 211363 Auke Bay AK 99821

HAYES, HUGH (JOSEPH), actor, singer, hair salon executive; b. Chgo., Sept. 28, 1937; s. James T. and Ella (Williams) H.; divorced; 1 child, Michael Francis. BA, Mt. Carmel Coll., Niagara Falls, Ont., Can., 1955; postgrad., Am. Conservatory, Chgo., 1957, Chgo. Conservatory, 1958. Resident actor Mus. Theatre Ariz., Temple, 1987—; pres. Salon Shears Internat., Phoenix, 1986—; prin. All That Glitters, Scottsdale, Ariz. Appeared in over 70 theatrical prodns., mus. comedy and dramatic roles, N.Y.C., Chgo., Dublin, Ireland, nat. tours U.S.; starred as Tevye in Fiddler on the Roof tour. Recipient Premier Performer of Yr. award Am. Platform Assn., 1976, Jeff award Jefferson Com., 1973, Award of Honor Variety Clubs Am. Mem. AFTRA, AGVA, Actor's Equity. Roman Catholic. Home and Office: 14818 N 47th St Paradise Valley Phoenix AZ 85032 also: All That Glitters 7125 E 5th Ave Scottsdale AZ 85251

HAYES, JACK WARREN, company executive; b. Mpls., Jan. 8, 1928; s. Jabez Claire and Mildred Lucille (Robinson) H.; m. Charlotte Joanne King, Aug. 29, 1948; children: Gregory King, Beverly Joanne, Jeffry Warren. Dir. human resources The Bekins Co., L.A., 1958-61; ea. reg. mgr. The Bekins Co., N.Y.C., 1961-63; pres. Source Devel. Corp., San Diego, 1963-73, The Summit Group, San Francisco, 1973-80, Vector Systems Inc., LaJolla, Calif., 1980—; bd. dirs. IDT Corp., Base 8 Corp., Omed Corp., San Diego. With USN, 1945-46. Mem. Nat. Assn. Corp. Dirs. (pres. San Diego chpt. 1986-88, chmn. 1988—). Presbyterian. Home: 8685 Robin Hood Ln La Jolla CA 92037 Office: Vector Systems Inc Corporate Ctr Box 1029 La Jolla CA 92038

HAYES, JOAN EAMES, state official; b. Cin., Feb. 29, 1916; d. Alastair Chatham and Emma (Faber) Eames, m. Nathan Harris David, July 3, 1937 (div. 1952); children: Deborah David Dewar, Steven Matthew, Anthony Peter; m. John Newton Hayes, Sept. 14, 1964 (dec. 1979); m. Robert Burch Hewett, Nov. 12, 1983. AB, Harvard U., 1936. Mng. editor Am. Fgn. Svc. Jour., Washington, 1948-52; registered lobbyist Nat. Counsel Assocs., Washington, 1952-60; stockbroker Bache & Co., Washington, 1960-67; founder, pres. Citizens Against Noise, Honolulu, 1970-86; state rep. Hawaii State Legis., Honolulu, 1982—. Author: (booklet) Inside the State Department, 1952; contbr. articles to mags, 1952-57. Legis. chairwoman AAUW, State of Hawaii, 1968-70; bd. dirs. Outdoor Circle. Recipient Thomas Jefferson award Nat. Vol. Activitist Germaine Monteill, 1977. Mem. Japan-Am. Soc., English Speaking Union, Harvard Club (Honolulu). Democrat. Home: 1860 Ala Moana Blvd #2001 Honolulu HI 96815 Office: Hawaii Legis State Capitol Rm 324 Honolulu HI 96813

HAYES, JOHN EDWARD, III, lawyer; b. St. Louis, Feb. 22, 1949; s. John Edward and Norma Virginia (Blackwell) H.; m. Carolee Burns, June 21, 1969; children: David Scott, Heather Erin. BA cum laude with honors, Knox Coll., 1971; JD, U. Denver, 1973. Bar: Colo. 1974, U.S. Dist. Ct. Colo. 1974, U.S. Ct. Appeals (10th cir.) 1984. Assoc. Nelson, Haring, Marchetti, Leonard & Tate, Denver, 1974, McMartin & Burke, Englewood, Colo., 1975-76; assoc. McMartin, Burke, Loser & Fitzgerald, Englewood, 1977-79, ptnr., 1980-85; pres. Hayes & Phillips, P.C., Denver, 1985—, also bd. dirs.; atty. City of Wheat Ridge, Colo., 1980, City of Sheridan, Colo., 1982; gen. counsel Parker Water and Sanitation Dist., Colo., 1982. Contbr. articles to profl. jours. Trustee Knox Coll., Galesburg, Ill., 1983-87. Recipient Leadership award Metro City Atty.'s Assn., 1986. Mem. ABA, Denver Bar Assn., Colo. Bar Assn. Democrat. Methodist. Office: Hayes & Phillips PC 1350 17th St Ste 450 Denver CO 80202-1517

HAYES, JOHN PATRICK, JR., broadcasting executive; b. Cleve., Aug. 14, 1949; s. John Patrick and Margaret Barisard (Butler) H. BA, U. Detroit, 1971. Account exec. Sta. WEBR, Buffalo, 1972; account exec., sales mgr. Sta. WGRQ, Buffalo, 1973-77; gen. mgr. Sta. KZOK-AM & FM, Seattle, 1977-78; v.p., gen. mgr. Sta. KYUU, San Francisco, 1979-84, Sta. WNBC, N.Y.C., 1984-87, pres., dir. Fairmont Communications Corp., San Francisco, 1987—; dir. Puget Sound Radio Broadcasters Assn., 1978; dir. No. Calif. Broadcasters Assn., 1979-80, treas., 1981, v.p., 1982, chmn., 1983, dir., 1984. Roman Catholic.

HAYES, MITCH, entrepreneur; b. Atlanta, May 14, 1961; s. Edward Alvin and Michiko (Ishibashi) Gonder H.; 1 child, Chezray Yujiro. Student, Hawaii Pacific Coll., 1986. Photographer Kahala Kai Photo, Honolulu, 1979-84; ptnr., photography dir. Charisma Hawaii Prodns., Honolulu, 1983-85; owner Profl. Glass Tint, Honolulu, 1984-85; owner, producer M&M Prodns., Honolulu, 1985—; pub. rels. ptnr. C.E. M. Auto Body & Paint, Honolulu, 1986-88; onwer, producer MC's Unltd., Honolulu, 1986-87; flight crew Hawaiian Airlines, Honolulu, 1987—; owner, chef Resturant "Jalapenos", Honolulu, 1988—. Inventor cellular phone covers, 1988. Home: 1253 Ala Aolani St Honolulu HI 96819 Office: Resturant Jalapenos 99-115 Aiea Heights Dr #227 Aiea HI 96701

HAYES, SAUNDRA MADDEN, insurance company executive; b. Little Rock, Dec. 31, 1935; d. Winfred Harris and Ermina Mayr (Madden) Owen; m. Thomas Ramer Clark, July 5, 1958 (div. 1967); 1 child, Tom; m. Robert James Hayes, Aug. 19, 1967; children: Harris, Guy. AA, U. Ark., 1954. Exec. sec., model Sta. KATV-TV, Little Rock, 1954-60; asst. mgr. Sta. KMMK-FM, Little Rock, 1960-67, Sterling Floors, Va., 1974-77; tech. editor, writer Space Inst., U. Tenn., Tullahoma, 1978-82; officer, personnel mgr., asst. sec. Alaska Nat. Ins. Co., Anchorage, 1982—. Mem. Soroptimist. Democrat. Roman Catholic. Home: 10618 Tradition Ave Eagle River AK 99577 Office: 7001 Jewel Lake Rd Anchorage AK 99502

HAYES, STEVEN CHARLES, psychologist, educator; b. Phila., Aug. 12, 1948; s. Charles Aloysius and Ruth Ester (Dryer) H.; m. Angela Fe Butcher (div.); 1 dau., Camille Rose; m. Linda Jean Parrott; 1 child, Charles Frederick. B.A. cum laude in Psychology, Loyola U., Los Angeles, 1970; postgrad. Calif. State U., San Diego, 1971-72; M.A. in Clin. Psychology, W.Va. U., 1974, Ph.D., 1977. Lic. psychologist, N.C., Nev. Intern psychology Brown U. Sch. Medicine, Providence, 1975-76; asst. prof. U. N.C.-Greensboro, 1976-82, assoc. prof., 1982-86; prof. U. Nev., Reno, 1986—, dir. clin. tng., 1986—. W.Va. U. Found. Inc. grantee, 1975; NIMH grantee, 1976-77; U. N.C. grantee, 1976-77, 77-78, 81-82, 82-83. Mem. AAAS, Am. Psychol. Assn. (sec.-treas. 1988—, div. 25 student affairs coordinator, 1977, 78, continuing ed. chmn. 1980-82, program co-chmn. 1980-82, chmn. long-term planning com. 1982, mem.-at-large 1982-85, pres. 1987, council of reps., 1988—, fellow divs. 12, 24, and 25), Assn. Behavior Analysis, Assembly of Sci. and Applied Psychology (sec.-treas. 1987-88), Assn. Advancement Behavior Therapy (student affairs coordinator 1978, assoc. program chmn. 1979, program chmn. 1980, chmn. task force student involvement 1980-81), Soc. Exptl. Analysis Behavior (sec. 1985), Southeastern Assn. for Behavior Analysis (sec. 1985-86), Sigma Xi. Democrat. Author: The Effects of Monthly Feedback, Rebate Billing and Consumer Directed Feedback on the Residential Consumption of Electricity, 1977; Research Opportunities in Clinical Psychology Internships, 1979; Abnormal Psychology, 1979; (with J.D. Cone) Environmental Problems/Behavioral Solutions, 1980; (with D.H. Barlow and R.O. Nelson) The Scientist Practitioner: Research and Accountability in Clinical and Educational Settings, 1984, (with R.O. Nelson) Conceptual Foundations of Behavioral Assessment, 1986, Rule-Governed Behavior, 1989; contbr. chpts. to books, articles to profl. jours.; editor APS Observer, 1988—; assoc. editor Jour. Applied Behavior Analysis, 1982-85; editorial bd. Behavioral Assessment, Behavior Modification, Jour. Cons. and Clin. Psychology, The Behavior Analyst, Behaviorism. Home: Box 6501 Incline Village NV 89450-6501 Office: U Nev Dept Psychology Reno NV 98557-0062

HAYES, THOMAS WILLIAM, state treasurer. m. Mary Hawkins, 1969; children: Christy, Shannon. Student, Oreg. State U., 1964-66; BS in Mgmt., Calif. State U., San Jose, 1968, MBA in Fin. (first in class), 1972. Analyst supervisory mgmt. U.S. Gen. Acctg. Office, 1972-76; program evaluation mgr. and analyst offices of legis. analyst and auditor gen. Calif. State Legislature, Sacramento, 1976-77; asst. auditor gen. State of Calif., Sacramento, 1977-79, auditor gen., 1979-89, treas., 1989—; chairperson, mem. several state bds. and commns.; advisor, cons. The Republic of Philippines, Kingdom of Thailand, Governmental Acctg. Standards Bd., Controller-Gen. of U.S., Rutgers U. Eagleton Inst.; instr. part-time Calif. State U., San Jose, 1973-82. 1st lt. USMC, 1968-71. Mem. Nat. Assn. State Auditors, Comptrollers and Treas. (past pres.), Nat. State Auditors' Assn. (past pres.), San Jose State U. Alumni Assn. (Disting. Alumnus award 1985). Office: Treasury Dept PO Box 191 Sacramento CA 94812-0191

HAYHURST, JOHN BLAKE, aircraft company executive; b. Parkersburg, W.Va., Jan. 4, 1948; s. Blake and Jane Katherine (Collinson) H.; m. Linda Lee Spaeth, Sept. 11, 1970; children: Anne Christina, Thomas Christopher. BS in Aero. Engring., Purdue U., 1969; MBA, U. Wash., 1971. With Boeing Comml. Airplanes, Seattle, 1969—; mgr. mktg. Boeing Comml. Airplanes, 1977-82, regional sales dir., 1983-86, dir. customer tng., 1987, v.p. mktg., 1987—. Office: Boeing Comml Airplanes PO Box 3707 Seattle WA 98124-2207

HAYNER, JEANNETTE C., state legislator; b. Jan. 22, 1919; m. Herman H. Hayner, 1942; children—Stephen A., James K., Judith A. B.A., U. Oreg., 1940, J.D., 1942. Atty., Bonneville Power Co., Portland, Oreg., 1943-47; mem. Wash. Ho. of Reps., 1972-76, Wash. Senate from Dist. 16, 1977—. Mem. Walla Walla Dist. 140 Sch. Bd., 1956-63, chmn. bd. 2 yrs.; mem. adv. bd. Walla Walla Youth and Family Services Assn., 1968-72; active YWCA, 1968-72; majority leader Wash. State Senate, 1981-82, 87—, minority leader 1979-80, 83-86; dist. chmn. White House Conf. on Children and Youth, 1970; chmn. Walla Walla County Mental Health Bd., 1970-72; former mem. Wash. Council on Crime and Delinquency, Nuclear Energy Council, Bonneville Power Regional Adv. Council, State Wash. Organized Crime Intelligence Adv. Bd.; mem. Coun. State Govts. Governing Bd.; former asst. whip Republican Caucus. Mem. Wash. State Centennial Commn. Recipient Merit award Walla Walla C. of C., Pioneer award U. Oreg., 1988; named Legislator of Yr. Nat. Rep. Legislators' Assn., 1986, Wash. Young Rep. Citizen of Yr., 1987. Mem. Oreg. Bar Assn., Delta Kappa Gamma (hon.), Kappa Kappa Gamma. Lutheran. Office: State Senate State Capitol Olympia WA 98504 also: PO Box 454 Walla Walla WA 99362

HAYNES, CALEB VANCE, JR., geology and archaeology educator; b. Spokane, Wash., Feb. 29, 1928; m. Elizabeth Hamilton, Jan. 11, 1954; 1 child, Elizabeth Anne.. Student, Johns Hopkins U., 1947-49; degree in geol. engring., Colo. Sch. Mines, 1956; PhD, U. Ariz., 1965. Mining geology cons. 1958-60; sr. project engr. Am. Inst. Research, Golden, Colo., 1956-60; sr. engr. Martin Co., Denver, 1960-62; geologist Nev. State Mus. Tule Springs Expedition, 1962-63; research asst. U. Ariz., Tucson, 1963-64, asst. prof. geology, 1965-68, prof. geoscis., anthropology, 1974—; assoc. prof. So. Meth. U., Dallas, 1968-73, prof., 1973-74. Served with USAF, 1951-54. Guggenheim fellow 1980-81, Smithsonian sr. post doctoral fellow, 1987 ; grantee NSF, Nat. Geographic Soc., others. Fellow Geol. Soc. Am. (Archeol., Geology award 1984); mem. AAAS, Am. Quaternary Assn. (pres. 1976-78), Soc. Am. Archaeology (Fryxell award 1978), Sigma Xi. Office: U Ariz Dept Anthropology Tucson AZ 85721

HAYNES, GARY ANTHONY, archaeologist; b. Long Beach, Calif., Sept. 30, 1948; s. Ellsworth Wallace and Martha Louise (Ryan) H. BA, U. Md., 1970; MA, Cath. U. Am., 1978, PhD, 1981. Vis. asst. prof. anthropology Cath. U. Am., Washington, 1981; assoc. prof. lectr. George Washington U., Washington, 1982; research assoc. anthropology dept. Smithsonian Inst., Washington, 1981-85; asst. prof. anthropology U. Nev., Reno, 1985-88, assoc. prof. anthropology, 1988—; dir. Zimbabwe (Africa) Nat. Parks Research Trust, 1987—. Editor: Nev. Archaeologist, 1987—; contbr. articles to profl. jours. Active Scientist Exchange Acad. Scis. U.S. Nat. Research Council, 1987. Fellow Smithsonian Inst., 1980; Nat. Geog. Soc. grantee, 1981-88; Fulbright scholar African Regional Rsch. Program, 1989—. Mem. Soc. Am. Archeology (Fryxell com. chmn. 1986-89), Am. Quaternary Assn., Soc. Vertebrate Paleontology, Zimbabwe Sci. Assn., Nev. Archaeol. Assn. (exec. com. 1987—). Office: U Nev Dept Anthropology Bus Bldg Rm 502 Reno NV 89557

HAYNES, GARY RONALD, engineer; b. Quincy, Ill., Aug. 16, 1944; s. Orrin Robie and Marjorie Helen (Lyons) H.; m. Lenetta Kay Keller, Mar. 28, 1970; children: Gregory, Aaron. BSCE, BSBA, U. Colo., 1967. Profl. engr., Colo. Design engr. Sun Oil Co., DX Div., Tulsa, Okla., 1967-70; civil engr. II City Engring. Div., Colorado Springs, Colo., 1970-74; civil engr. III City Engring. Div., Colorado Springs, 1974-79, asst. city engr., 1979-83, city engr., 1983—. Bd. dirs. Partnership For Community Design, Colorado Springs, 1987,88. Mem. ASCE (branch pres. 1974-75, svc. award 1978, contact mem. for USAF Acad. Cadet Civil Engring. Chpt., 1974—), Am. Pub. Works Assn. (chpt. dir., recipient svc. award 1987), Computer Club (Colorado Springs).

HAYNES, HAROLD WALTER, aircraft manufacturer; b. Snoqualmie, Wash., Jan. 23, 1923; s. Ralph and Bertha (Sewell) H.; m. Barbara J. Tatham, Oct. 11, 1943; children—Christine, Steven, Kevin. B.A., U. Wash., 1948. C.P.A., Wash. With Touche, Ross, Bailey & Smart (C.P.A.'s), Seattle, 1948-54; with Boeing Co., Seattle, 1954—, v.p. finance, 1960-70, sr. v.p. finance, 1970-75, exec. v.p., chief finance officer, 1975—, also dir.; dir. First Interstate Bank of Wash., Safeco, Itel Corp. Served as pilot USMCR, 1942-45. Mem. Financial Execs. Inst. Home: Highlands Seattle WA 98177 Office: The Boeing Co 7755 E Marginal Way S Seattle WA 98108

HAYNES, JAMES EARL, JR., association executive; b. Bakersfield, Calif., Oct. 11, 1943; s. James E. and Ruth M. (Campbell) H.; m. Norma Beth Jordan, Feb. 10, 1978; 1 child, Andrew Jordan. B.A. in Journalism, Los Angeles State Coll., 1967. Asst. mgr. West Covina C. of C., Calif., 1966-68; mgr. Monterey Park C. of C., Calif., 1968-72; gen. mgr. ops. San Francisco C. of C., 1972-76; pres. Phoenix C. of C., 1976—; mem. bd. regents Insts. for Orgn. Mgmt. U.S. C. of C.; vice chmn. Western Internat. U. Bd. dirs. Western Internat. U. Mem. Am. C. of C. Execs. (bd. dirs., past chmn.), Ariz. C. of C. Mgrs. Assn. Office: Phoenix C of C 34 W Monroe St Phoenix AZ 85003

HAYNES, KENT TAYLOR, dentist; b. San Diego, Feb. 3, 1954; s. Buster Eugene and Iness Lorraine (Curtis) H.; m. Judith Ann Gates, Jan. 31, 1987; 1 child, Brittany Morgan. BS in Agronomy, U. Nebr., 1976, DDS, 1981. Lic. dentist, Colo. Pvt. practice Durango, Colo., 1981—. Mem. Am. Dental Assn., Colo. Dental Assn. (com. mem.), San Juan Basin Dental Soc., Acad. Gen. Dentistry. Office: 143 CR 250 Durango CO 81301

HAYNES, LINDA JEAN, communications executive; b. Berkeley, Calif., Apr. 6, 1954; d. John William Haynes and Hope (Webster) Sinclair. Student, Lewis & Clark Coll., 1972-73; BS in Psychology, Oreg. State U., 1977. Support worker, counselor Housing for Handicapped, Corvallis, Oreg., 1977-80; asst. dept. mgr. Joseph Magnin Co., Palo Alto, Calif., 1980-81; sales rep. Creative Systems, Inc., San Carlos, Calif., 1981-82, Introlink, San Francisco, 1982-86; sales mgr. Bay Area Teleport, Alameda, Calif., 1986—. Home: 5372 Laurel Dr Concord CA 94521 Office: Bay Area Teleport 1141 Harbor Bay Pkwy Alameda CA 94501

HAYNES, RICHARD GLEN, JR., real estate broker, teacher; b. Albany, Oreg., July 19, 1948; s. Richard Glen and Marjorie Bell (Prowell) H.; m. Barbara Lee Johnson, Sept. 14, 1974 (div. 1982); 1 child, Stephanie Lynne. Student, Oreg. State U., 1966-70; BS, Ea. Oreg. State Coll., 1976. Salesman Farmterials, Inc., Baker, Oreg., 1971-74; tchr. Adrian (Oreg.) Sch. Dist., 1976-77; owner, operator Rich Haynes Contracting, Baker, 1977-83; sales assoc. Michael Nelson Real Estate, Baker, 1983-86; pres., broker Northwest Properties, Inc., Baker, 1986—; bd. dirs. Small Bus. Advisory Council, Baker. Fundraiser Baker YMCA, 1983-88. Mem. Baker County Bd. Realtors (pres. 1986, state dir. 1988). Democrat. Episcopalian. Lodges: Rotary, Elks. Home: 2950 Grandview Baker OR 97814 Office: NW Properties Inc 1937 Washington PO Box 430 Baker OR 97814

HAYNES, RONALD EUGENE, medical devices manufacturing company executive; b. Des Moines, Nov. 20, 1927; s. Robert Eugene and Frances (Wright) H.; m. Laura May Herbert (div. 1975); children: Deborah, Laura, Stephen, Paul; m. Dorothy Lillian Gerhard Norager, Dec. 3, 1978. Student, San Jose State U., 1946-48, 52-53. Sr. designer Westinghouse Co., Sunnyvale, Calif., 1953-55; designer Varian Assocs., Palo Alto, Calif., 1955-60, sr. designer, 1960-65, design engr., 1965-70, mgr. engring., 1970-79; pres., founder Haynes Radiation Ltd., Inc., Alameda, Calif., 1982—; cons. radiation therapy to pvt. facilities, 1982—. Contbr. articles on radiation therapy to med. jours. Cubmaster Boy Scouts Am., Palo Alto, 1960, scout commr., 1965-70; founder Young People's Mountaineering, Palo Alto, 1969-75. With USN, 1948-52. Recipient Indsl. Design award Wescon Electronics, 1968. Mem. Single Handed Sailing Soc. (commodore 1983-84). Republican. Home: PO Box 953 Groveland CA 95321 Office: Haynes Radiation Ltd Inc 2033 Clement Ave Bldg 31 Alameda CA 94501

HAYS, FRANKLIN ERNEST, minister, chaplain; b. Invokern, Calif., Aug. 8, 1947; s. Franklin Burley and Eileen Pauline (Munsterman) H.; m. Peggy Kay, Nov. 4, 1968 (div. Jan. 1972); m. Marsha Ann, Aug. 23, 1983; children: Noel, Robert, Shelley, Jane. BS, San Jose (Calif.) State U., 1971; MS in Divinity, Golden Gate Theology Seminary, 1977; MS of Theology, U. Chgo., 1983. Ordained to ministry Evangelical Luth. Ch., 1978. Pastor Chapel Hills, Mill Valley, Calif., 1977-78; enlisted U.S. Navy, 1978; chaplain Fleet Religious Support Actvity U.S. Navy, Norfolk, Va., 1978-80, Credo Great Lakes, Chgo., 1980-82, 3rd Marine Div., Okinawa, Japan, 1982-83, U. Chgo., 1983-84, Naval Air Sta., Alameda, Calif., 1984-86, Naval Mec Det, San Francisco, 1986-88, CNRA-8, Oakland, Calif., 1988—. Named One of Outstanding Young Man Am. U.S. Jaycess, 1979. Lodges: Lions, Elks, Kiwanis. Home: 116 Pearl Harbor Rd Alameda CA 94501 Office: CNRA-8 7677 Oakport St Ste 650 Oakland CA 94621-1929

HAYS, GEORGE WILLIAM, air force officer; b. Enterprise, Oreg., July 23, 1952; s. Marion E. and Ethel M. (Wise) H.; divorced; children: Juli Ann, Jared William; m. Mary Lynn Wise; 1 child, Nicole Michelle. AAS, Community Coll. Air Force, 1981; AA in Bus., U. Md.-Europe, 1981, BS in Bus., 1982. Enlisted U.S. Air Force, 1971, commd. 2d lt., 1982, advanced through grades to capt., 1986; telecommunications specialist, Korea, Thailand, Colo., Wash., 1971-79; non-commd. officer in charge switchboard ops., Alconbury, Eng., 1979-82; program mgr. tactical air control system, Sacramento, 1983; officer in charge info.-systems maintenance br., Spokane, Wash., 1983-86, airborne parachutist, joint communications unit field ops. officer, Ft. Bragg, N.C., 1986—. Named Disting. Grad., USAF Officer Tng. Sch., 1982; Squadron NCO of Yr, 1977, 81, Officer of Yr., 1985; decorated Meritorious Svc. medal (3), Air Force Achievement medal, others; Vietnam Svc. medal. Mem. Arm Forces Assn., Armed Forces Communications and Electronics Assn., Phi Kappa Phi. Republican. Baptist.

HAYS, PATRICK GREGORY, healthcare executive; b. Kansas City, Kans., Sept. 9, 1942; s. Vance Samuel and Mary Ellen (Crabbe) H.; m. Penelope Ann Hall, July 3, 1976; children—Julia L., Jennifer M. Meyer, Emily J. Meyer, Drew D. Meyer. B.S. in Bus. Adminstrn, U. Tulsa, 1964; M.H.A., U. Minn., 1971; postgrad., U. Mich. Grad. Sch. Bus. Adminstrn., 1977. Mfg. analyst N.Am. Rockwell Corp., Tulsa, 1964-66; asst. adminstr., adminstr. for ops. Henry Ford Hosp., Detroit, 1971-75; exec. v.p. Meth. Med. Ctr. of Ill., Peoria, 1975-77; adminstr. Kaiser Found. Hosp., Los Angeles, 1977-80; pres. Sutter Community Hosps. and Sutter Health, Sacramento, 1980—; trustee Central Area Teaching Hosps., Inc., Los Angeles, 1977-79; clin. preceptor U. Minn., Med. Coll. Va., Ariz. State U.; adj. prof. grad. program in health services adminstrn. U. So. Calif.; bd. dirs. New Center Area Council, Detroit, 1973-75, Arthritis Found. Central Ill., 1976-77; chmn. bd. Calif. Hosps. Polit. Action Com., 1983-87; mem. exec. com. St. Jude Children's Research Hosp. Midwest Affilate, Peoria, 1975-77; chmn. adv. bd. grad. program in health services adminstrn. U. So. Calif.-Sacramento; bd. dirs. Hosp. Council No. Calif., 1986, The Healthcare Forum; chmn. bd. Option Care, Inc. Contbr. articles on health services to publs. Mem. Pvt. Industry Council, Sacramento Employment and Tng. Agy., 1984-85; bd. dirs. Consumer Credit Counselors Sacramento, 1984-87, United Way Sacramento Area, Comstock Club; pres. Sacramento Camellia Festival Assn., 1987-88; chmn. Whitney M. Young, Jr. Award, 1987. Served with U.S. Army, 1966-69. Decorated Army Commendation medal, cert. of appreciation Dept. Army; USPHS fellow, 1969-71; recipient Commendation resolution Calif. Senate, 1979; Recipient Whitney M. Young award Sacramento Urban League, 1983. Fellow Am. Coll. Healthcare Execs. (Calif. regents); mem. Sacramento-Sierra Hosp. Assn. (exec. com., bd. dirs., pres. 1984), Royal Soc. Health (U.K.), Am. Mgmt. Assn. (pres.' club), Hollywood C. of C. (Hollywood revitalization com. 1979), Calif. Assn. of Hosps. & Health Systems (bd. dirs., treas.), Sacramento C. of C. (bd. dirs. 1982-85, 87-88), Vol. Hosps. Am. (bd. dirs.), Vol. Hosps. No. Calif. (bd. dirs.), Kappa Sigma. Presbyterian. Lodge: Rotary (bd. dirs. Sacramento chpt. 1987-89). Office: Sutter Community Hosp Office of Pres 1111 Howe Ave Ste 600 Sacramento CA 95825

HAYS, RICK F., public relations executive; b. St. Joseph, Mo., Oct. 27, 1952; s. William Andy and Alma LaVonne (Temple) H.; m. Jane Reid, Aug. 16, 1975; children: Matthew Patrick, Benjamin Reid, Lara Elizabeth. BS in Journalism, U. No. Colo., 1973. Editor Town & Country News, Greeley, Colo., 1973-74; pub. relations rep. Mountain Bell, Greeley, 1974-77; pub. relations supr. Mountain Bell, Tucson, 1977-79; pub. relations mgr. Mountain Bell, Denver, 1979-83; pub. relations dir. U S WEST Communications, Boise, Idaho, 1983—; bd. dirs. Boise Neighborhood Housing, Idaho Bus. Week. Mem. fund dist. com. Ada County United Way, Boise, 1988—, mktg. com. Boise Area Econ. Devel. Coun., 1987—, Capital Youth Soccer, Boise, 1987—; asst. scoutmaster Boy Scouts Am., 1989—. Mem. Pub. Relations Soc. Am. (bd. dirs. 1988—), Pub. Relations Roundtable, Jaycees (bd. dirs. Greeley, Colo. 1976-77). Roman Catholic. Office: US WEST Communications 999 Main 11th Fl Boise ID 83702

HAYS, WAYNE EDGAR, audit manager; b. Dayton, Wash., Sept. 1, 1950; s. Clarence Joseph and Margaret Mary (Jorgensen) H. BA, Wash. State U., 1972, BS in Acctg., 1981; MBA, U. Wash., 1974. CPA, Wash. Commd. 2d lt. U.S. Army, 1972, advanced through grades to capt., 1976; artillery officer U.S. Army, Baumolder, Fed. Republic Ger., 1974-75; fin. officer 7th Corps, Fed. Republic Ger., 1975-77; budget officer Def. Lang. Inst., Monterey, Calif., 1978-80; ret.; auditor Arthur Anderson & Co., Seattle, 1981-83, audit sr., 1983-87, audit mgr., 1987—. With USAR, 1980—. Named Disting. Alumnus, Beta Alpha Psi, Pullman, Wash., 1988. Mem. Assn. Mil. Controllers, Nat. Assn. Accts. (dir. Seattle chpt. 1986-88, v.p. edn. 1988-89), Inst. Internal Auditors, Electronic Data Processing Auditor Assn., Phi Kappa Phi, Saber and Blade (sec. 1970-71). Office: Arthur Anderson & Co 801 2d Ave Norton Bldg Seattle WA 98104

HAYUM, GEORGE THEODORE, lawyer; b. N.Y.C., Feb. 21, 1945; s. Gustave Isidore and Pauline Celine L. (Patoir) H. AB with honors, Princeton U., 1967; postgrad., U. Bordeaux, France, 1968; JD, Yale U., 1972. Bar: N.Y. 1972, D.C. 1975, Calif. 1979. Assoc. Donovan, Leisure, Newton & Irvine, N.Y.C., 1972-75; assoc. Ginsburg, Feldman & Bress, Washington, 1975-77; studio counsel Columbia Pictures Corp., Burbank, Calif., 1977-79; assoc. Schiff, Hirsch & Schreiber, Beverly Hills, Calif., 1979-80; ptnr. Armstrong, Hirsch & Levine, L.A., 1980—. McConnell fellow, Niamey, Niger, 1966; Fulbright scholar U. Bordeaux, 1968. Mem. Calif. State Bar Assn., N.Y. State Bar Assn., D.C. Bar Assn., L.A. Bar Assn., Franco-Am. Com. on 1789 French Revolution. Office: Armstrong Hirsch & Levine 1888 Century Park E 18th Floor Los Angeles CA 90067

HAYWARD, GEORGE ERNEST, real estate corporation officer; b. Idaho Falls, Idaho, June 18, 1923; s. George Louis and May Eliza (Abercromie)

Stevenson; m. Esther Louise Martin, Dec. 11, 1947; children: Linda Elisa, Stephen George. Student, Utah State Coll., 1946-47; Diploma in Sci. Crime Detection, Inst. Applied Sci., Chgo., 1951; LLB, Blackstone Coll., 1953. Owner, operator Hayward's Food Markets, Idaho Falls, 1947-49; inspector, security div. Atomic Energy Commn., Idaho Falls, 1949-51; dir. security Am. Cyanamid Co., N.Y.C. and Idaho, 1951-54; pres., gen. mgr. MoneySaver Stores, Idaho Falls, 1955-64; dir. gen. services div. Supreme Foods, Inc., Santa Monica, Calif., 1964-67; pres. Cl-Ida Packing Co., Santa Monica, 1967-68; pvt. practice cons. internal controls retail L.A., 1968-74; pres. G.E. Enterprises, L.A., 1974-86. Active Rep. Nat. Com. 1980-86; sponsor Little League Baseball, Westchester Calif., 1987—. With U.S. Navy, 1943-46, ETO, Natousa. Named Hon. Chief N.J. State Police Chiefs Assn., 1953, Hon. N.Y. Sheriff N.Y. State Sheriff's Assn., 1953. Mem. Am. Assn. Retired Persons, Nat. Com. to Preserve Social Security and Medicare, Elks Lodge. Presbyterian. Lodge: Elks (Westchester, Calif.). Home and Office: GE Enterprises 7906 Nardian Way Westchester CA 90045

HAYWARD, PEGGY FREER, student personnel administrator; b. Neptune, N.J.; m. Stanley D. Hayward; children: Cary G., Brooks A. BS, Rutgers U., 1961; MS, Ind. U., 1967; postgrad., U. So. Calif., 1983—. Dir. edn. Planned Parenthood of Cen. Calif., Fresno, 1974-76; cons. vocat. equity State of Calif., Sacramento, 1979-81; instr., career counselor Kings River Community Coll., Reedley, Calif., 1976-81, project dir., 1980-81; coordinator orientation Calif. State U., Fresno, 1981—. Mem. Am. Field Service, Fresno, 1985-87; bd. dirs. Univ. Religious Ctr., Fresno, 1982-84, Planned Parenthood Cen. Calif., Fresno, 1973-74, 1976-79. Bynam and Reed scholar U. So. Calif., 1985, 86, Norman Russell scholar, 1983. Mem. AAUW, Nat. Assn. Student Personnel Adminstrs., Nat. Assn. Orientation Dirs. Office: Calif State U Shaw and Maple Sts Fresno CA 93740-0006

HAZEL, CHARLES RICHARD, natural resourses engineer; b. Indpls., May 19, 1929; s. Samuel Joshua and Lucile Frances (Daniels) H.; m. Doris Dianne Pierre, Sept. 15, 1951; children: Charlotte C. Newbill, Roberta R. Hicks, Suzanne M. Ryans. AA, Santa Rosa Jr. Coll., Santa Rosa, Calif., 1958; BS, Humboldt State U., 1961, MS, 1963; PhD, Oreg. State U., 1969. Rsch. assoc. Humboldt State U., Arcata, Calif., 1961-63; assoc. biologist Calif. Dept. Fish & Game, Stockton, 1963-64; ast. in fisheries Oreg. State U., Corvallis, 1964-67; sr. biologist Calif. Dept. Fish & Game, Sacramento, 1967-70; prin. Jones & Stokes Assocs., Inc., Sacramento, 1970-76, v.p., 1976-82, pres., 1982—; bd. dirs. Jones & Stokes Assocs., Inc., Sacramento, 1976—. Mem. Sacramento County Phoenix Field Safety Com., Fair Oaks, Calif. 1980-84; deacon Christ Community Ch., Carmichael, Calif., 1986-88. Sgt. USAF, 1947-56. Recipient Luther Burbank award Mrs. L. Burbank and Santa Rosa Jr. Coll., 1958; named Disting. Alumnus, Humboldt State U., 1986. Mem. TEC (exec. com.), Assn. Environ. Profls., Am. Fisheries Soc. (chpt. sec. 1974), Pacific Fishery Biologists (pres. 1982), Ecol. Soc. Am., Calif. C. of C. (natural resources com. 1982—). Republican. Mem. Reformed Ch. of Am. Office: Jones & Stokes Assocs Inc 1725 23rd St Ste 100 Sacramento CA 95816

HAZELRIGG, CHARLES RICHARD, banker; b. Cadiz, Ohio, 1933; married. B.S., Miami U., Ohio, 1955. Security analyst United Bank of Denver, 1958-61, portfolio mgr., 1961-65, mgr. bus. devel., 1965-68, v.p., 1968-70, group v.p., 1970-74, sr. v.p., 1974-77, exec. v.p., 1977-81, sr. exec. v.p., 1981-82, pres., 1982-87; with United Banks of Colo., Inc., 1986—, pres., 1986-87, pres., chief operating officer, 1987—, also dir. Served to capt. USAF, 1956-58. Office: United Banks Colo Inc 1700 Lincoln St Ste 3200 Denver CO 80274

HAZEN, PAUL MANDEVILLE, banker; b. 1941; married. BA U. Ariz., 1963, MBA U. Calif., Berkeley, 1964. Asst. mgr. Security Pacific Bank, 1964-66; v.p. Union Bank, 1966-70; chmn. Wells Fargo Realty Advisors, 1970-76; with Wells Fargo Bank, San Francisco, 1979—, exec. v.p., mgr. Real Estate Industries Group, 1979-80, mem. exec. office, 1980, vice-chmn., 1980-84, pres., chief operating offficer, 198—, also dir.; pres., treas. Wells Fargo Mortgage & Equity Trust, 1977-84; with Wells Fargo & Co. (parent), San Francisco, 1978—, exec. v.p., then vice-chmn., now pres., chief operating officer, dir.; trustee Wells Fargo Mortgage & Equity Trust. Office: Wells Fargo & Co 420 Montgomery St San Francisco CA 94163 *

HAZEWINKEL, VAN, manufacturing executive; b. Los Angeles, Oct. 2, 1943; s. Ben J. and Betty J. (Bishop) H.; m. Linda Bennett, Sept. 11, 1965; children: Van, Karey. BS, Calif. State U., Long Beach, 1967. With Daily Indsl. Tools Inc., Costa Mesa, Calif., 1959—, v.p., 1966-78, pres., 1978—. Founding mem. bd. dirs. Greater Irvine (Calif.) Indsl. League, 1970-73. Mem. Soc. Mfg. Engrs. Office: 3197-D Airport Loop Dr Costa Mesa CA 92626

HEAD, JACK SINGLETON, computer software company executive; b. Winnipeg, Manitoba, Can., Sept. 2, 1934; s. William Leslie and Mary Adelaide (Pumpelly) H.; m. Sharon C. Schwenger (div. July 1982); children: Kelley Elizabeth, Kimberly Anne, John Singleton; m. Elizabeth Ann Benton, May 27, 1988. Diploma in bus. adminstrn., Ryerson Inst., Toronto, Can., 1957; BS in Math. and Computers, York U., Toronto, 1969. Sales rep. Can. Petrofina Co., Toronto, 1957-60; supr. sales Cities Service Oil Co., Toronto, 1960-62; computer programmer Lever Bros., Toronto, 1962-65; sr. systems analyst Toronto-Dominion Bank, 1965-69; supr. mgmt. info. systems Municipality of Met. Toronto, 1969-77; gen. mgr. HIS, Inc., Denver, 1977-80; founder, pres. Headline Bus. Computer Systems, Inc., Denver, 1980—. Chief of staff, mission pilot Denver squadron CAP, 1985—. Recipient Comdr.'s commendation CAP, 1988. Mem. Data Processing Mgmt. Assn. (cert., chpt. pres. 1971-72), Internat. Standards Orgn. (chmn. task group 1986), Can. Standards Assn. (chmn. standards com. 1974-77). Republican. Episcopalian. Lodges: Masons, Shriners. Office: Headline Inc 9145 E Kenyon Ave Ste 202 Denver CO 80237

HEAD, LAURA DEAN, educator; b. Los Angeles, Nov. 3, 1948; d. Marvin Laurence and Helaine Dean (Springer) H.; B.A., San Francisco State Coll., 1971; M.A., U. Mich., 1974, Ph.D., 1978. Teaching asst., asst. project dir. U. Mich., Ann Arbor, 1970-73; instr. U. Calif.-Riverside, 1973-76; project dir., research scientist Urban Inst. Human Services, San Francisco, 1978-80; sr. research scientist, project dir. Far West Lab. Ednl. Research and Devel., San Francisco, 1980-81; assoc. prof.Black Studies, San Francisco State U., 1982-85, prof. black studies, 1985—; mem. Com. on Sch. Crime and Violence, Calif. State Dept. Edn., 1981-82. Mem. com. on sch. crime and violence Dept. Edn. Calif. State, 1982-83. Chmn. Bay Area Black Child Devel. Inst., 1978-81; chmn. bd. dirs. mem. Marin City Multi-Service Ctr. Calif. 1982—; bd. dirs. Oakland Men's Project. State scholar, 1966, Nat. Cath. scholar for Negroes, 1966. Mem. NAACP, Am. Psychol. Assn. (minority fellow), Assn. Black Psychologists, Children's Def. League, Nat. Black Child Devel. Inst., Soc. Research in Child Devel., Black Women's Forum, Alpha Kappa Alpha. Home: 3614 Randolph Ave Oakland CA 94602 Office: San Francisco State U Dept Black Studies 1600 Holloway Ave San Francisco CA 94132

HEADDING, LILLIAN SUSAN, writer; b. Milw., Jan. 1, 1944; d. David Morton and Mary Davis (Berry) Coleman; m. James K. Hill (div. 1976); children: Amy Denise; m. John Murray Headding (div. 1987). BA, U. Nev., 1975; MA, U. Pacific, 1976. With Gimbels, Milw., 1963-65; retail mgr. Frandisco Corp., N.Y.C., 1965-66; store mgr. Anita Shops, Los Angeles, 1966-68, Clothes Closet, Sunnyvale, Calif., 1969-70; owner Lillian Headding Interiors & Comml. Design, Pittsburg, Calif., 1976-88; instr. 1st degree black belt, 1972—. Author (as Sara Davis): When Gods Fall; short stories. Bd. dirs. Community Action Against Rape, Las Vegas, Nev., 1972-75; self-def. expert Las Vegas Met. Police Dept., 1972-75, North Las Vegas (Nev.) Police Dept.; co. supr. Family & Children's Services, Contra Costa County, Calif., 1985-86. Mem. Walnut Creek Writers Group (pres.), Philippine Hawaiian Black Belters Assn. Republican. Jewish.

HEADINGTON, BONNIE JAY, psychologist; b. Alameda, Calif., Sept. 22, 1940; d. Jerome Willard and Beth Arlene (Dye) Headington; children: Christopher James, Tai Sirima. BA, San Francisco State, 1961; MEd, Ohio U., 1967, PhD, 1969. Lic. psychologist, Calif. Prof. psychology Humboldt State U., Arcata, Calif., 1972-86; psychologist, dir. North Coast Mental Health Clinic, McKinleyville, Calif., 1975-84; psychologist Counseling Services, Arcata, Calif., 1984-87, Nev. Dept. of Prisons Indian Springs, Las Vegas, 1987—; cons. West Coast Cancer Found., Calif., 1978-80, U.S. Forest Service, 1982-83, Humboldt County Welfare Dept., 1982-84. Author: (book) Communication in Counseling Relationship, 1979, (monograph) Cancer consulting for health care professionals, 1980; contbr. articles to profl. jours. Mem. Am. Psychological Assn., Am. Assn. Counseling Devel. (editor newsletter 1979-83), Phi Kappa Phi. Democrat. Roman Catholic. Office: Dept of Prisons PO Box 208 Indian Springs NV 89018

HEADLEE, ROLLAND DOCKERAY, association executive; b. Los Angeles, Aug. 27, 1916; s. Jesse W. and Cleora (Dockeray) H.; m. Alzora D. Burgett, May 13, 1939; 1 dau., Linda Ann (Mrs. Walter Pohl). Student, UCLA, 1939. Asst. mgr. Par Assocs., Los Angeles, 1935-43, Finance Assocs., 1946-58; financial cons., lectr. 1958-63; account exec. Walter E. Heller & Co., Los Angeles, 1963-66; exec. dir. emeritus Town Hall Calif., Los Angeles, 1966—; dir. Am. Internat. Bank, Mfrs. Assocs., R.H. Investment Corp. Mem. adv. bd., bd. dirs., Los Angeles council Boy Scouts Am. Served to 1st lt. AUS, 1943-46. Mem. Mensa, Los Angeles World Affairs Council, Newcomen Soc. Methodist. Clubs: Commonwealth of Calif, Economic of Detroit, Los Angeles Stock Exchange. Home: 8064 El Manor Ave Los Angeles CA 90045

HEAFEY, THOMAS ROBERT, nursing administrator; b. Montague, Mass., Mar. 24, 1948; s. Robert Thomas and Anna Christine (Draper) H.; m. Kazimiera Monica Bigaj, July7, 1984; children: Scott E., Gary Thomas. AA, Spokane Falls Community Coll., Wash., 1976; AS in Nursing, Greenfield Community Coll., Mass., 1973; BS in Pub. Health, U. Mass., 1976; postgrad., Columbia Pacific U., 1987—. Psychiatric aide Northampton (Mass.) State Hosp., 1965-67, staff nurse, 1973-74, head nurse, 1974-76; nursing supr. Deaconess Med. Ctr., Spokane, Wash., 1976-86; asst. dir. nursing Deaconess Med. Ctr., Spokane, 1986-87; asst. adminstr. Forks (Wash.) Community Hosp., 1987-89; investigator State of Wash., Spokane, 1989—; eye bank tech. Lion's Eye Bank, Spokane, 1983-84; instr. Spokane Community Coll., 1978-84. Dep. coroner Spokane County, 1987; chair pub. health adv. bd. Clallam County, Wash., 1988-89. With USAF, 1967-71. Mem. Health Svcs. Consortium, N.W. Hosp. Council, Nat. Rural Health Assn., Sigma Theta Tau, Lions, K.C. (sec. 1987). Roman Catholic. Home: PO Box 14956 Spokane WA 99214 Office: Dept of Licensing E 11530 Sprague Spokane WA 99206

HEALD, SUSAN BAUTER, biomedical company official; b. Ogden, Utah, Jan. 12, 1948; d. Robert Whitney and Jane (Wright) Bauter; m. Robert Millard Heald, June 12, 1971 (div. June 1983); children: Michael Whitney, Allison. BS in Biology, U. Utah, 1970; MT, McKay-Dee Hosp., 1971. Med. technologist McKay-Dee Hosp., Ogden, 1971-76; med. technologist St. Benedict's Hosp., Ogden, 1978-80, donor recruiter, 1980-83; sales rep. Curtin Matheson Sci., Inc., Salt Lake City, 1983—. Chmn. capital fund Camp Tuttle, Brighton, Utah, 1986-87. Named Am. Field Svc. student, Finland, 1965, Miss Rodeo Ogden, Miss Rodeo Utah 1966; recipient First Yr. Leadership award, Curtin Matheson-Midwestern Area, 1984, Vendor award, Hynson, Wescott & Dunning, 1985, CMS Presidents Team, 1985. Mem. Utah Soc. Med. Technologists (exhibit chmn. 1987, social chmn. 1988). Home: 1371 Browning Ave Salt Lake City UT 84105 Office: Curtin Matheson Sci Inc 20100 E 35th Dr Aurora CO 80011

HEALY, BARBARA ANNE, insurance company executive, financial planner; b. Chgo., May 21, 1951; d. William James Healy and Eileen Mary (Dooley) Dashiell; m. Gerald Lally Angst, June 9, 1973 (div. Sept. 1977). BA, No. Ill. U., 1973; MBA, DePaul U., 1976. Cert. fin. planner. Dept. head, instr. St. Benedict High Sch., Chgo., 1973-76; account rep. Xerox Corp., Chgo., 1976-78, mktg. specialist, 1978-79, high volume sr. sales exec., 1979-81; western dist. mgr. McGraw Hill, N.Y.C., 1981-82; fin. planner United Resources Ins. Service, Torrance, Calif., 1982-83, sales mgr., 1983-85, exec. v.p., 1985-86, regional v.p., 1986—; instr. Trenton Coll., Riverside, Ill., City Coll. Chgo., Northeastern Ill. U., Chgo., Prairie State Coll., Chicago Heights, 1976-81. Author: Financial Planning for Educators, 1987; contbr. articles to prof. jours.; speaker in field. Mem. Internat. Assn. Fin. Planners, Inst. Cert. Fin. Planners, Registry Fin. Planning Practitioners, Nat. Council Fin. Edn. Republican. Roman Catholic. Home: 815 Sea Spray Ln #215 Foster City CA 94404 Office: United Resources Ins Svcs 950 Tower Ln Ste 1120 Foster City CA 94404

HEALY, DANIEL FRANCIS, chemical engineer; b. Milw., June 26, 1954; s. Daniel Francis and Ruth (Bjornstad) H.; m. Susan Winkelman, Apr. 13, 1985. B in Chemistry and Math., U. Wis., Milw., 1977, M in Chemistry, 1986. Registered profl. chem. engr. Instr. chemistry U. Wis., Milw., 1979-82, rsch. asst., 1982-84; supr. quality assurance Intel Corp., Santa Clara, Calif., 1984-87; environ. chemist Lockheel Missiles and Space Corp., Sunnyvale, Calif., 1988—. Grantee U. Wis.-Milw., 1982, 83; recipient Div. award Intel Corp., 1986. Grantee U. Wis., Milw., 1982, 83. Mem. Am. Vacuum Soc.

HEALY, ELIZABETH CAMORIN, radio station account executive, consultant; b. Berkeley, Calif., May 5, 1954; d. Donald Clayton and Connie Jean (Dunford) Bentley; m. Richard Thomas Healy, Jan. 30, 1988. BA, U. Calif., Berkeley, 1977; teaching credential, Calif. State U., Chico, 1980. Mktg. coord. Bentley Engring., San Francisco, 1980-82; media planner Goedert Advt., Redding, Calif., 1983; account exec. Summit Info. Systems, San Francisco, 1983-84, Sta. KEWB, Redding, 1984-87, Sta. KNCQ, Redding, 1987—; mktg. cons. Exec. and Adminstrv. Support Enhancement, San Francisco. Bd. dirs. Shasta County Arts Coun., Redding, 1983-84. Mem. Shasta Profl. Assn., AAUW (bd. dirs. Redding chpt. 1986-87). Office: Sta KNCQ 1588 Charles Dr Redding CA 96003

HEALY, JAMES BRUCE, cooking school administrator, writer; b. Paterson, N.J., Apr. 15, 1947; s. James Burn and Margaret Mercy (Patterson) H.; m. Alice Fenvessy, May 9, 1970; 1 child, Charlotte Alexandra. BA, Williams Coll., 1968; PhD, The Rockefeller U., 1973. Mem. faculty Inst. Advanced Study, Princeton, N.J., 1973-75; J.W. Gibbs instr. physics Yale U., New Haven, Conn., 1975-77, research affiliate, 1977-80; dir. Healy-Lucullus Sch. French Cooking, New Haven, 1978-80, Boulder, Colo., 1980—; cons. Claudine's, Denver, 1985-86; vis. instr. Salem (Mass.) State Coll., 1984, and various culinary schs. Author: Mastering the Art of French Pastry, 1984; contbr. articles and revs. on restaurants and cooking to mags. and profl. jours. Mem. Internat. Assn. Cooking Profls. (cert.), Confederation Nationale des Patissiers, Glaciers, et Confiseurs de France. Presbyterian. Home and Office: Healy-Lucullus Sch French Cooking 840 Cypress Dr Boulder CO 80303

HEALY, KIERAN JOHN PATRICK, lighting designer, consultant; b. London, June 6, 1957; came to U.S., 1980; s. Denis Finbarr and Dawn Josephine (O'Hannigan) H. Student, Isleworth Polytechnic, Middlesex, Eng., 1975-76. V.p. Showlites, L.A., 1980-81; freelance in TV, lighting designer 1982-89; dir. photography Klages Group Inc, Hollywood, Calif., 1989—; lighting designer Mus., The Who, London, 1976-80, The Rolling Stones, U.S.A., 1981-82. lighting designer for TV includes Live Aid, Liberty Weekend Opening Ceremonies, Top of the Pops & MTV Awards. Mem. Nat. Acad. Cable Programming (ACE Nomination 1988), Acad. TV, Arts & Scis. (Emmy Nominations 1984, 87), Assn. Cinemotograph Techs. & Allied Trades. Roman Catholic. Office: The Klages Group Inc 1438 N Gower St Hollywood CA 90028

HEALY, WINSTON, JR., educational administrator; b. Evanston, Ill., Oct. 20, 1937; s. Winston and Margaret (Lee) H.; m. Judith Becker, June 24, 1976; children—Nathaniel, Sarah, Jason, Elisabeth. B.A., Williams Coll., 1960; M.A., U. Hawaii, 1968; Ed.D., U. Mass., 1982. Tchr. English, Punahou Sch., Honolulu, 1960-67, chmn. dept. English, 1966-67, dean adminstrn., 1967-69, secondary sch. prin., 1969—. Chmn. bd. Early Sch.; v.p., Hawaii Pub. Radio, 1978-88; mem. Joint Econ. Council; mem. exec. bd. Honolulu Community Scholarship Program. Served with Hawaii Air N.G., 1960-71. Coe fellow; Nat. Assn. Ind. Schs. fellow, 1972-73. Mem. Nat. Assn. Secondary Sch. Prins., Assn. Supervision and Curriculum Devel., Nat. Council Tchrs. English (nat. adv. bd. achievement awards), Hawaii Council Tchrs. English (past pres.). Congregationalist. Home: 45 Piper's Pali Honolulu HI 96822 Office: 1601 Punahou St Honolulu HI 96822

HEALY EIGE, SHARON JANET, software engineer, consultant; b. Naylor, Mo., Nov. 16, 1946; d. Leonard Nelson and Lena (Walker) Healy; m. Howard Allen Eige, May 13, 1987. BA in Psychology, Columbia U., 1968; postgrad., U. Calif., Davis, 1979. Electronics engr. Signetics, Sunnyvale, Calif., 1979-81; software developer AT&T, Pleasanton, Calif., 1982--. Mem. IEEE. Home: 720 Keeler Ave Berkeley CA 94708

HEANEY, DOROTHY PHELPS, nurse, nursing administrator; b. Elmer, N.J., Apr. 8, 1963; d. Joseph Francis and Dorothy Ruth (Andrews) Phelps; m. Bradley George Heaney, June 8, 1985. AS in Nursing, Gloucester County Coll., Sewell, N.J., 1984. Nursing asst. Pine Crest Nursing Home, Sewell, 1982-84, staff nurse, 1984, charge nurse, 1984-85; charge nurse Le Havre Convalescent Hosp., Menlo Park, Calif., 1985-86, dir. staff devel., 1986-87, asst. dir. nursing, 1986, dir. nursing, 1986-87; dir. nursing Hillhaven Convalescent Hosp., Menlo Park, 1987—. Mem. Calif. Assn. Health Facilities, Council Longterm Care Nursing Calif. Home: 433-116 Sylvan Ave Mountain View CA 94041 Office: Hillhaven Convalescent Hosp 16 Coleman Pl Menlo Park CA 94025

HEARD, RONALD ROY, motion picture producer; b. Denver, Oct. 3, 1947; s. John Arthur and Louise Marie (Smith) H.; m. Kim Widing Aug. 12, 1967 (div. 1969). BS, Colo. State U., 1969; postgrad., U. Colo., 1969-72, U. Paris/Sorbonne, 1964-65. Prodn. design/stage mgr. The Rolling Stones, London, 1969-86; property/set dresser Universal Studios, Universal City, Calif., 1978-79, Warner Bros. Studios, Burbank, Calif., 1979-80; producer stage plays Hollywood, 1980-85; music video cons. L.A., 1984—; corres. CBS Network News, Chgo., 1971-72; writer/photographer UPI/Nat. Geographic/Denver Post, 1969-73; ptnr. Silver Screen Ptnrs. II and III, L.A., 1986—; owner Yankee Pride Ent., North Hollywood, Calif., 1986—. Exec. com. Dem. Party, Larimer County, Colo., 1972-79. Named honorary citizen of S.D. by Gov. Richard Kneip, 1972. Mem. Am. Film Inst., Smithsonian Instn., Statue of Liberty/Ellis Island Cen. Commn. Democrat.

HEARN, CHARLES VIRGIL, minister; b. Westport, Ind., Sept. 4, 1930; s. Forrest V. and Emma Florence (Marsh) H.; Ph.D., Thomas A. Edison U., 1972; D.D., Trinity Hall Coll. and Sem., 1977; diploma Palm Beach Psychotherapy Tng. Center, 1976; m. Linda Elmendorf; children by previous marriage—Debra Lynn, Charles Gregory, Martin Curtis. Ordained to ministry Methodist Ch., 1958; pastor various Meth. chs., Ind., Tex., Wyo., Calif., 1958-70; interpersonal minister St. Alban's Ch. of the Way, San Francisco, 1974—; clergyman and counselor Green Oak Ranch Boys Camp, Calif., 1969-70; dir. rehab. Mary-Lind Found., Los Angeles, 1970-71; med. asst. Fireside Hosp., Santa Monica, Calif., 1971-72; dir. alcoholism program Patrician Hosp., Santa Monica, 1972-74; propr., exec. dir. Consultation & Referral, Santa Monica, 1974—. Vice chmn. Western Los Angeles Alcoholism Coalition, 1974-78; pres. bd. dirs. Trinity Hall Coll. and Sem. Served with U.S. Army, 1951-53; Korea. Decorated Bronze Star; diplomate Am. Bd. Examiners in Psychotherapy, Bd. Examiners in Pastoral Counseling. Fellow Am. Acad. Behavioral Sci., Internat. Council Sex Edn. and Parenthood of Am. U.; mem. Am. Ministerial Assn. (pres. 1981—), Nat. Assn. Alcoholism Counselors, Calif. Assn. Alcoholism Counselors, Cons. on Alcoholism for Communities, Nat. Council Family Relations, Am. Coll. Clinic Adminstrs., Assn. Labor-Mgmt. Adminstrs. Democrat. Contbr. numerous articles on psychotherapy to profl. publs. Address: 1244 11th St Ste D Santa Monica CA 90401

HEARN, ROBERT VINCENT, financial executive; b. Portland, Oreg., June 21, 1930; s. Berthold Edgar and Linda (Anderson) H.; m. Maryann Talbot, Jan. 18, 1963; children: Bruce, Mark, Susan. BA, Willamette U., 1952. Project acct. Pine Flat Contractors, Sanger, Calif., 1952-53; corp. acct. Guy F. Atkinson Co., South San Francisco, Calif., 1953-57; project acctg. mgr. Guy F. Atkinson Co., Cougar, Wash., 1957-58, Pasco, Wash., 1953-62; acct. Guy F. Atkinson Co., South San Francisco, Calif., 1962-76, mgr. central acctg., 1976-86, cash mgr., 1986--. Contbr. articles to profl. publs. Cert. cash mgr., treas. Highlands Community Assn., San Mateo, Calif., 1967-68. Named Grand Marshall, Highlands Community Assn., 1968. Mem. Nat. Corp. Cash Mgmt. Assn., Phi Delta Theta. Republican. Home: 2216 Cobblehill Pl San Mateo CA 94402 Office: Guy F Atkinson Co 10 W Orange Ave South San Francisco CA 94080

HEARST, JAMES ELDON, compensation consultant; b. Toronto, Ont., Can., June 2, 1930; s. John Eldon and Beatrice Margaret (Way) H.; m. Mary Carol Dressel, Aug. 7, 1953 (div. 1969); children: John Eric, Caryl Lee; m. Betty Ann Robinson Arbaugh, May 27, 1972; 1 stepchild, Randolph Bradford Arbaugh. BA, Albion Coll., 1953. Salary analyst Chrysler Corp., Detroit, 1957-60; compensation analyst, then labor rels. rep. Brunswick Corp., Chgo., 1960-65; mgr. indsl. rels. Owens Yacht Co., Balt., 1966-69; personnel mgr. Rixon Electronics, Silver Spring, Md., 1969-71, Arundel Corp., Balt., 1972-74; compensation cons. Comml. Credit Corp., Balt., 1974-75; mgr. compensation, benefits Blue Cross/Blue Shield, Balt., 1975-78, Dillingham Corp., Honolulu, 1979-84, Hawaiian Electric, Honolulu, 1984-86; asst. v.p., mgr. compensation and benefits Bank of Hawaii, Honolulu, 1986-89; speaker in field. Chmn. personnel mgmt., Hawaii chpt. Am.Heart Assn., 1986—, Vol. Info. and Referral Svcs., Honolulu, 1986—. Mem. Am. Compensation Assn., Elks. Home and Office: 735 Nunu St Kailua HI 96734

HEARST, RANDOLPH APPERSON, publishing executive; b. N.Y.C., Dec. 2, 1915; s. William Randolph and Millicent (Willson) H.; m. Catherine Campbell, Jan. 12, 1938 (div. Apr. 1982); children: Catherine, Virginia, Patricia, Anne, Victoria; m. Maria C. Scruggs, May 2, 1982 (div. Oct. 1986); m. Veronica de Uribe, July, 1987. Student, Harvard U., 1933-34. Asst. to editor Atlanta Georgian, 1934-38; asst. to pub. San Francisco Call-Bull., 1940-44, exec. editor, 1947-49, pub., 1950-53; asso. pub. Oakland Post-Enquirer, 1946-47; pres., dir., chief exec. officer Hearst Consol. Publs., Inc. and Hearst Pub. Co., Inc., 1961-64; pres. San Francisco Examiner, 1972—; dir. The Hearst Corp., 1965—, chmn. exec. com., 1965-73, chmn., 1973—; Dir. Hearst Found., 1945—, pres., 1972—; dir. Wm. Randolph Hearst Found., 1950—. Served as capt., Air Transport Command USAAF, 1942-45. Roman Catholic. Clubs: Piedmont Driving (Atlanta); Burlingame Country, Pacific Union. Office: The Hearst Corp 110 5th St San Francisco CA 94103 also: The Hearst Corp 959 8th Ave New York NY 10019 *

HEARST, ROSALIE, philanthropist, foundation executive; b. Oklahoma City, Mar. 7; d. Mathis O. and Audell Bertha (Clary) Wynn; m. George Randolph Hearst, Sr., July 16, 1958. Student, Oklahoma City Coll., UCLA. Hearst rep. U.S. Senate Youth Program; pres. George Randolph Hearst Meml. Found. for Diabetic Edn.; pres. Rosalie Hearst Ednl. Found.; bd. dirs. Elvirita Lewis Found; life mem. Eisenhower Med. Ctr., Pathfinders, Tiempo de Los Ninos, Desert Hosp. Aux., Desert Press Club, Coll. of the Desert Aux., Internat. Orphans; bd. dirs. Pathfinder's Ranch Boys' Club; past bd. dirs. numerous charitable orgns.; trustee emeritus The Bob Hope Cultural Ctr.; coord. Officers' Wives Vol. Svcs. Dibble Gen. Hosp., Palo Alto; coord. Am. Women's Vol. Svcs. Sawtelle Hosp. L.A.; created Rosalie and George Hearst Fellowship in Ophthalmology U. Calif Berkeley. Named Woman of Yr. City of Hope, 1971, Disting. Woman Northwood Inst. Midland, Mich., 1988; recipient award for Lifetime Achievement in Community Service Palm Springs Women's Press Club. Home: 550 Camino del Sur Palm Springs CA 92262

HEARST, WILLIAM RANDOLPH, III, newspaper publisher; b. Washington, June 18, 1949; s. William Randolph and Austine (McDonnell) H.; m. Nan Peletz, Aug. 2, 1975; children—William, Adelaide. A.B., Harvard U., 1972. Reporter, asst. city editor San Francisco Examiner, 1972-76, publisher, 1984—; editor Outside Mag., 1976-78; asst. mng. editor Los Angeles Herald Examiner, 1978-80; mgr. devel. Hearst Corp., 1980-82; v.p. Hearst Cable Communications Div., 1982-84. Office: San Francisco Examiner 110 5th St San Francisco CA 94103

HEARTH, BEVERLY KAY, software engineer; b. Klamath Falls, Oreg., Sept. 14, 1960; d. Kenneth Dwight and Genevieve Ann (Williams) H. BS in Computer Sci., Oreg. State U., 1982, BA in Computer Sci., 1982. Software engr. Intel Corp., Hillsboro, Oreg., 1982-84, Metheus Computervision, Beaverton, Oreg., 1984-87; software engr., cons. Advance Computer Engrg., Inc., Portland, Oreg., 1987—; cons. Washington County Fed. Credit Union, Hillsboro, 1982-86. Mem. Oreg. State Polit. Interest Rsch. Group, Portland, 1981-89; mem. Friends of Washington Park Zoo, Portland, 1988-

89. Mem. League Conservation Voters. Democrat. Office: Advance Computer Engring PO Box 10736 Portland OR 97210

HEASLEY, MICHELE ANNE, navy petty officer; b. Fall River, Mass., Feb. 9, 1961; d. Aime Denery and Claire Annette (Higgins) Cantin; m. Timothy Joseph Heasley, Oct. 16, 1984. Airman recruit USN, Orlando, Fla., 1980-81; airman apprentice USN, Orlando, 1981, Aviation Maintenance Adminstrn., USN, Meridian, Miss., 1981; airman apprentice Tng. Squadron 9, USN, Meridian, 1981, airman, 1981, 3rd class petty officer, 1981-83, 2nd class petty officer, 1983; 1st class petty officer Aircraft Intermediate Maintenance Dept., Naval Air Sta., Agana, Guam, 1988—; 1st class petty officer Anti-Submarine Light Squadron 43 NAS, San Diego, 1988—. Democrat. Roman Catholic. Home: 641 11th St Apt C Imperial Beach CA 92032 Office: HSL 43 NAS North Island San Diego CA 92135

HEATER, KURT DUANE, real estate broker; b. Grants Pass, Oreg., Feb. 26, 1957; s. Sherman Ross and Geraldine Francis (Newell) H.; m. Martina Helena Burton, July 10, 1976; children: Rebecca, Amy, Timothy. BBA, So. Oreg. State U., 1979. Assoc. broker Sherm Heater Inc., Realtors, Grants Pass, 1979—. Real estate solicator United Way, Grants Pass, 1981-82; sec. Grants Pass High Sch. Scholarship Found., 1982—. Republican. Club: Active (Grants Pass) (sec. 1987). Office: Sherm Heater Inc Realtors 705 NE 7th St Grants Pass OR 97526

HEATH, CLYDE DWAYNE, manufacturing supervisor; b. Hawthorne, Calif., Mar. 7, 1961; s. Kenneth Heath and Rose (Peterson) Holmes; m. Tammie Kaye Marbut, July 4, 1980; children: Darci Michele, Tiffany Rose, Caitlin Alyse. Student, Nat. U., Anaheim, Calif. Electronic assembler Rockwell Internat., Anaheim, Calif., 1981-82, adv. elec. processor and assembler, 1982-83; electric motor mechanic Hemet Electric Motor, Hemet, Calif., 1983-84; electronic assembler Rockwell Internat., Anaheim, Calif., 1984, methods analyst, 1984-85, electronic assemby sr. leader, 1985-88, inertial measurement unit mfg. supr., 1988—. Republican. Home: 16282 Main St #24B Tustin CA 92680 Office: Rockwell Internat 3370 Miraloma Anaheim CA 92803

HEATH, DONALD MALONE, computer industry executive; b. Willmar, Minn., Nov. 11, 1940; s. Drew Malone and Miranda Henrietta (Denbrook) H.; m. Judith Ann Augustson, June 7, 1958; children: Jeffrey Malone, Christopher David. B in Math., U. Minn., 1963; postgrad., U. Houston, 1979. Mgr. energy br. Sperry Corp., Houston, 1962-79; v.p. ops. Tymnet, Inc., Cupertino, Calif., 1979-82; v.p. devel. and ops. Integrated Software Systems Corp., San Diego, 1982-85; pres. XtraSoft, Inc., Santa Clara, Calif., 1985—, bd. dirs.; bd. dirs. Diversified Software Systems, Inc., San Jose, Calif., XtraSoft, Inc. Rep. precinct capt., Silver Spring, Md., 1972 pres. Wilchester West Homeowners Assn., Houston, 1979-81; bd. dirs. San Diego Master Chorale, 1984-85, also chmn. fund-raising, 1984-85. Mem. Nat. Assn. Corp. Dirs., U. Minn. Alumni Assn. (life). Presbyterian. Office: XtraSoft Inc 4701 Patrick Henry Dr Bldg 21 Santa Clara CA 95054

HEATLEY, THOMAS WILLIAM, therapist; b. Boston, July 31, 1954; s. Thomas Henri and Elizabeth (Webster) H. BA, Boston U., 1977; MS, Emerson Coll., 1982. Cert. speech therapist, hypnotherapist and neurolinguistic programmer. Cons. Judith Wisnia Assocs., Burlington, Mass., 1983-84; cons. Valley Hosp. Med. Ctr., Van Nuys, Calif., 1984-85, dir. communication disorders, 1985; process cons. HealthWest Found., Chatsworth, Calif., 1985-86; cons. Cedars Sinai Med. Ctr., Beverly Hills, Calif., 1986—; co-dir. Los Angeles Neurolinguistic Programming Inst., 1985—, PROSPEAK, Studio City, Calif., 1986—. Mem. Am. Speech, Lang. and Hearing Assn., Soc. Neurolinguistic Programmers. Democrat. Home: 807 N Vista St Los Angeles CA 90046 Office: Cedars Sinai Med Ctr 8700 Beverly Blvd Beverly Hills CA 90048

HEATON, FRITZ CHARLES, publishing executive; b. Pasadena, Calif., Aug. 24, 1954; s. Charles E. and Rose J. (Hinzo) H. BA in Journalism, San Diego State U., 1977. Editor compilations Internat. Pulp and Paper Directory; prodn. editor Buyers' Guide, promotion asst., asst. print buyer coord., mgr. market rsch. Miller Freeman Publs., San Francisco, 1980-84; mgr. circulation and promotions The Western Journal, San Francisco, 1984-89, mgr. advt. and promotions, 1989—; location and prodn. asst. LM Prodn. Svcs., San Francisco, 1986—. Feature writer, assoc. editor: Am. Zine mag.; appearances as extra in films A View to a Kill, Hard to Hold, Presidio, Burglar, Leonard VI, also TV commls.; contbr. articles to profl. jours. including Am. Zine mag. Office: Western Jour Medicine PO Box 7602 San Francisco CA 94120-7602

HEATON, SHARON MARIE, naval education administrator; b. Dallas, Feb. 14, 1956. MusB, North Tex. State U., 1976; M Music Edn., U. North Tex., 1979. Cert. tchr., Tex. Music tchr. Desoto (Tex.) Ind. Sch. Dist., 1979-80, Houston Ind. Sch. Dist., 1980-81; geophys. data technician Western Geophys. Co. U.S.A., Houston, 1981-86; dep. clk. of ct. U.S. Dept. Justice Immigration sect., San Diego, 1987; edn. specialist U.S. Dept. Navy, San Diego, 1987; spl. projects adminstr. Navy Campus, San Diego, 1987—. Mem. Enable Users' Group Microcomputer Users' Group, Navy Microcomputer Users' Group (co-chmn.), Mu Phi Epsilon (pledge pres. 1977). Republican. Clubs: Chula Vista Women's , Houston Gem and Mineral, Mariner's (San Diego). Home: 713 Austrian Rd Grand Prairie TX 75050-2330 Office: Navy Campus 921 W Broadway Blvd #110 San Diego CA 92132-5105

HEAVNER, ROBERT OWEN, finance company executive; b. Akron, Ohio, Nov. 20, 1941; s. Clarence Owen and Lena (Coburn) H.; m. Elaine Louise Conrad, July 3, 1964; children: Jocelyn, Kristin, Amanda. BS, USAF Acad., 1963; MA in Econs., Georgetown, 1964; PhD in Bus., Econs., Stanford U., 1976. Commd. 2d lt. USAF, 1959, advanced through ranks to col., 1980; asst. to dir. OMB, Office of the Pres., USAF, Washington, 1977-79; speech writer Chief of Staff, USAF, Washington, 1979-80; asst. dep. ops. 81st TFW, USAF, Bentwaters, Eng., 1980-81, resource mgr., 1981-82; dir. plans Europe USAF, Ramstein, Fed. Republic Germany, 1982-83; ret. USAF, 1983; prof. Westmont Coll., Santa Barbara, Calif., 1983-88; pres. Heavner & Assoc., Santa Barbara, 1984-88; sr. v.p. Calif. Thrift and Loan, Santa Barbara, 1988—; chmn. bd. KSB, Inc., Bakersfield, Calif., 1985—, Presentek, Inc., Santa Barbara, 1987—. Decorated Silver Star, Legion of Merit, Disting. Flying Cross with oak leaf cluster. Home: 840 Woodland Dr Santa Barbara CA 93108 also: PO Drawer B Santa Barbara CA 93102

HEBERT, ARCHILLE WILLIAM, retired electronics engineer; b. Pineville, La., July 24, 1909; s. Archille and Clara Lucy (Tillman) H.; m. Marjorie Lorraine Ball, Oct. 1, 1934 (dec. 1987); children: Archille W. III, Josef E., Norman A., Cecilia L., Angelita L. BEE, Pacific State U., 1953; MDS, DD, Metaphysical Bible Inst., L.A., 1981. Letter carrier U.S. Postal Svc., L.A., 1934-41; fire protection engr. L.A. Fire Dept., 1941-61; spacecraft reliability analyst Rockwell Internat., Downey, Calif., 1961-74; film projectionist Edward Circuit Theatres, Newport Beach, Calif., 1929—; pres. McGregor's Constrn., Inc., Inglewood, Calif., 1988. Active U.S. Congl. Adv. Bd., Boston, 1980—, U.S. Def. Com., 1980—, Am. Security Coun., 1980—, Boy Scouts Am. Recipient Apollo Eleven Spacecraft Medallion NASA, 1974. Mem. Soc. Motion Picture and T.V. Engrs. (assoc.), Am. Planetary Soc., Am. Astronomical Soc., Am. Astronautical Soc., IEEE, Am. Air Force Assn. (patron), Masons, Knights of Pythagoras, Kappa Alpha Psi. Democrat. Home: 1751 Buckingham Rd Los Angeles CA 90019 Office: MK McGregor's Constrn Inc 718 E Manchester Blvd Inglewood CA 90301

HEBERT, BUDD HANSEL, business executive, state senator; b. Detroit, Aug. 19, 1941; s. L. Hansel and Trudy Hebert; B.Sc. with distinction, Ariz. State U., 1963, M.A., 1964; Ph.D., Ohio State U., 1972; m. Doris Ann Brackeen, Oct. 5, 1963; children—Shirley, Julia. Asst. prof. U. Cin., 1968-71; asst. prof. urban econs. Va. Commonwealth U., 1971-74; economist, project mgr. Dames & Moore, Cin., 1974-77, assoc., Artesia, 1988—; landman Yates Petroleum Corp., Artesia, N.Mex., 1977-80; land mgr. Marbob Energy Corp., Artesia, 1980-81; v.p. Security Nat. Bank, Roswell, N.Mex., 1981-83; ind. oil and gas operator, 1983-88; state senator Dist. 33, N.Mex., 1980-88; caucus chmn. state sen. Reps., N.Mex.; mem. senate fin. com.; mem. senate conservation com.; mem. interim com. on Sci. and Tech. Oversight. Active Conquistador council Boy Scouts Am., Artesia, 1977-83. NSF grantee, 1968-69. Mem. Am. Assn. Petroleum Landmen. Republican. Mem. Ch. of Christ. Club: Kiwanis.

HEBERT, HENRY RAYMOND, army officer; b. Providence, Jan. 5, 1951; s. Henry Raymond and Kathleen Mae (Williamson) H.; m. Gail Rogers, Aug. 3, 1975; 1 child, Laura. BA in Anthropology, U. R.I., 1976. Commd. 2d lt. U.S. Army, 1976, advanced through grades to maj., 1987; command and staff positions U.S. Army, Fed. Republic Germany, 1977-80; co. comdr. Boston Army Recruiting Bn., Providence, 1983-84; ops. officer L.I. Recruiting Bn., Bklyn., 1984-85; dep. pub. affairs officer 2d Inf. Div., Camp Casey, Republic of Korea, 1985-86; asst. pub. affairs officer 7th Light Inf. Div., Ft. Ord, Calif., 1986-88; pub. affairs officer Def. Lang. Inst., Monterey, Calif., 1988—. Contbr. numerous articles and photographs to mil. publs. Mem. Monterey Parks and Recreation Com., 1988—. With U.S. Army, 1969-73. Fellow Mil. Order World Wars, Monterey Peninsula C. of C. (mil. affairs com. 1987—), Naval Postgrad. Sch. Sailing Assn. Office: Def Lang Inst Presidio of Monterey Monterey CA 93944

HEBNER, PAUL CHESTER, oil company executive; b. Warren, Pa., Dec. 29, 1919; s. Henry G. and Mabel (Gross) H.; m. Dorothy Farrell, Feb. 16, 1943; children—Richard P., Kathleen D., Susan M., Christine L., Elizabeth A., Jeannie M. Acct., adminstrv. asst. Altman-Coady Co., Columbus, Ohio, 1940-41; mgr. acctg., exec. adminstr. T&T Oil Co. (and assoc. cos.), L.A., 1954-57; with Occidental Petroleum Corp., L.A., 1957—, sec.-treas., 1958-68, v.p., sec., 1968-80, exec. v.p., sec., 1980-88, exec. v.p., 1988—, dir., 1960-88, dir. emeritus, 1988—; bd. dir. subs. cos.; sec.-treas., bd. dir. The Armand Hammer United World Coll. of Am. West. Mem. L.A. Beautiful; trustee Calif. Mus. Found. Maj. USAAF, 1942-45. L.S.B. Leakey Found. fellow. Mem. Am. Soc. Corp. Secs., C. of C. (bd. dir. L.A. Bus. Coun.). Home: 12 Amber Sky Dr Rancho Palos Verdes CA 90274 Office: Occidental Petroleum Corp 10889 Wilshire Blvd Los Angeles CA 90024

HEBNER, ROBERT JOHN, lawyer; b. L.I., N.Y., Nov. 21, 1948; s. Robert Gross and Sarah Bridget (Roscoe) H.; m. Susan Ann Wendt, Oct. 9, 1970; children: Heather, Racheal, Robert Jr. BA in English, Calif. State U., Fullerton, 1974; JD, Western State U., Fullerton, 1980. Bar: Calif. 1980, U.S. Dist. Ct. (cen. dist.) Calif. 1980, U.S. Ct. Appeals (9th cir.) 1980. Claims examiner Underwriters Adjusting Co., Santa Ana, Calif., 1974-76; claims supr. Eldorado Ins., Anaheim, Calif., 1976-78, Fremont Indemnity, Orange, Calif., 1978-80; assoc. Zonni, Ginocchio & Taylor, Glendale, Calif., 1980-82; prin. Kriner & Hebner, Inc., Santa Ana, 1982—; tchr. Ins. Ednl. Assn., Newport Beach, Calif., 1988. Mem. ABA, Orange County Bar Assn. Democrat. Roman Catholic. Home: 25202 Calle Busca El Toro CA 92630 Office: Kriner & Hebner 2006 N Broadway #212 Santa Ana CA 92706

HECHT, CHIC, ambassador, former U.S. senator; b. Cape Giradeau, Mo., Nov. 30, 1928; m. Gail Hecht; children: Lori, Leslie. B.S., Washington U., St. Louis, 1949; postgrad., Mil. Intelligence Sch., Ft. Holibird, Mo., 1951. Mem. Nev. State Senate, 1966-74, Rep. minority leader, 1968-72; mem. U.S. Senate from Nev., 1982-89, mem. Banking, Housing and Urban Affairs Com., chmn. housing and urban affairs subcom., mem. Energy and Natural Resources Com., mem. Senate Select Com. on Intelligence; ambassador to The Bahamas 1989—. Served with U.S. Army, 1951-53. Mem. Nat. Counter Intelligence Corps. (past pres.), Nat. Mil. Intelligence Assn. Address: Ambassador to The Bahamas Dept of State Washington DC 20520-5110 *

HECHT, LEONARD NORMAN, investment banker; b. N.Y.C., Dec. 28, 1936; s. Abraham and Sylvia (Moskowitz) H.; m. Linda Sharon Lodge, Nov. 19, 1966; children: Marni Susan, Andrew Michael, Brian Mitchell. BBA, Baruch Sch. of Bus., 1957. Mktg. mgr. IBM Corp., L.A., 1960-69; v.p. Cantor Fitzgerald & Co. Inc., L.A., 1969-71; pres. Gen. Analytics Corp., L.A., 1971-72; spl. asst. to pres. Republic Corp., L.A., 1972-73; sr. v.p., chief operating officer Scott Pub. Co., N.Y.C., 1973-76; founding prin. Xerox Devel. Corp., L.A., 1976-80; chmn. The Donalen Group, L.A., 1980-83; vice chmn., chief exec. officer Quantech Electronics Corp., N.Y.C., 1983-87; sr. v.p. Houlihan, Lokey, Howard & Zukin Capital, L.A., 1987—; bd. dirs. Instant Cir. Corp., San Diego, World Trade & Data Inc., San Francisco, Meret Optical Communications Inc., Santa Monica, Physicians Office Computer Inc., L.A. With USCG, 1959-60. Office: Houlihan Lokey Howard & Zukin Capital 1930 Century Park W Los Angeles CA 90067

HECHT, MYRON JAY, engineer, consultant; b. Oceanside, N.Y., May 11, 1954; s, Herbert and Esther (Indman) H.; m. Sara Hochhauser, Dec. 29, 1985; children: Ariel, Vivian. BS in Chemistry, UCLA, 1975, MS in Nuclear Engring., 1976, MBA, 1982. Assoc. engr. Westinghouse Co., Richland, Wash., 1977-78; staff engr. Sci. Applications Internat., La Jolla, Calif., 1978-80, SoHaR, Inc., L.A., 1980-85; v.p. SoHaR, Inc., 1985—; instr. Santa Monica (Calif.) Coll., 1984-85; cons. FAA, Washington, 1985--, U.S. Army Strategic Def. Command, Huntsville, Ala., 1985. Author: Data Base Managers for IBM PC, 1985, Fault Tolerant Computing, 1986; contbr. articles to profl. publs. Recipient Small Bus. Innovative Research award, NASA, 1987, Dept. of Energy, 1988. Mem. IEEE. Democrat. Jewish. Office: SoHaR Inc 8500 Wilshire Blvd Ste 1027 Beverly Hills CA 90211

HECHTER, MICHAEL NORMAN, sociologist; b. Los Angeles, Nov. 15, 1943; s. Oscar Milton and Gertrude (Horowitz) H.; children: Joshua, Rachel, Eliana. AB, Columbia U., 1966, PhD, 1972. From asst. prof. to prof. U. Wash., Seattle, 1970-84; prof. sociology, dir. research group for instnl. analysis U. Ariz., Tucson, 1984—; vis. prof. U. Bergen, Norway, 1984; vis. scholar Russell Sage Found., 1988—. Author: Internal Colonialism, 1975, Principles of Group Solidarity, 1987; editor: The Microfoundations of Macrosociology, 1983, Social Institutions, 1989. Mem. Am. Sociol. Assn., Internat. Sociol. Assn., Am. Economic Assn., Pub. Choice Soc. Office: U Ariz Dept Sociology Tucson AZ 85721

HECKER, ANNE, professional society administrator; b. Dallas, Oreg., July 6, 1924; d. Elwyn Gordon and Dorothy Ida (Dick) Craven; m. Robert F. Hecker, Sept. 28, 1946; children: Sandra, Barbara, Nancy. BA, U. Oreg., 1945. Staff correspondent UPI, Portland, Oreg., Madison, Wis., 1945-46; publ. editor Nat. Aeronautics Assn., Washington, 1947; dept. editor Pacific Builder & Engr., Seattle, 1951-53; mng. editor NW Medicine, Seattle, 1953-54; contbg. editor Argus, Seattle, 1961-65; dir. pub. relations Wash. State Dental Assn., Seattle, 1965-77, asst. exec. dir., 1977-85, cons. pub. relations, 1985-87, exec. dir., 1987—. Bd. dirs. Camp Fire Inc., Kansas City, 1980-81, Seattle, 1980-84, 86—. Mem. Am. Soc. Assn. Execs., Women in Communications (pres. 1977-78, Disting. Service award 1986). Democrat. Home: 13065 15th Ave NE Seattle WA 98125 Office: Wash State Dental Assn 2033 Sixth Ave #333 UAL Bldg Seattle WA 98121

HECKER, BERNICE RUTH, anesthesiologist; b. Yakima, Wash., July 31, 1949; d. Leonard and Rose Marie (Kuntz) H.; m. Robert Leonard Thompson, May 24, 1975; children: Nicholas Robert, Elayna Marie. BA in Ind. Studies, U. Wash., 1971, MD, 1975. Intern Univ. Va. Med. Ctr., Charlottesville, 1975-76; gen. med. officer USN, Naples, Italy, 1976-79; staff physician Cen. Va. Community Health Ctr., New Canton, 1979-80; resident Univ. Va. Med. Ctr., Charlottesville, 1980-82, fellow in pain mgmt. & cardiovascular anesthesia, 1982-83; attending anesthesiologist Virginia Mason Med. Ctr., Seattle, 1983—; clin. asst. prof. various univs.; post-anesthesia unit med. dir. Va. Mason Hosp., Seattle, 1985-88. Contbr. articles to profl. jours. Assoc. examiner Am. Bd. Anesthesiology; mem. NOW, 1970—; bd. sponsors Physicians for Social Responsibility, 1986; officer comp. Knights St. Lazarus, 1987. Fellow Am. Coll. Cardiology; mem. Internat. Anesthesia Research Soc., Am. Soc. Anesthesiologists, Am. Soc. Regional Anesthesia, Soc. Cardiovascular Anesthesia, Wash. State Soc. Anesthesiologists, King County Med. Assn., Wash. State Med. Assn., Internat. Assn. for the Study of Pain. Democrat. Roman Catholic. Office: Virginia Mason Med Ctr Dept Anesthesiology 1100 9th Ave Seattle WA 98111

HECKER, SIEGFRIED STEPHEN, metallurgist; b. Tomasow, Poland, Oct. 2, 1943; came to U.S., 1956; s. Robert and Maria (Schaller) Mayerhofer; m. Janina Kabacinski, June 19, 1965; children—Lisa, Linda, Lori, Leslie. B.S., Case Inst. Tech., 1965, M.S., 1967; Ph.D., Case Western Res. U., 1968. Postdoctoral assoc. Los Alamos Sci. Lab., 1968-70, mem. staff, 1973-80, assoc. div. leader, 1980-81, dep. div. leader, 1981-83, div. leader, 1983-85, chmn. Ctr. for Materials Sci., 1985-86, dir., 1986—; sr. research metallurgist Gen. Motors Research Labs., Warren, Mich., 1970-73; bd. dirs. Carrie Tingley Hosp.; Coun. Superconductivity for Am. Competitiveness; bd. regents U. N.Mex., 1987—. Author, editor: Formability, 1977. Bd. regents U. N.Mex.; bd. dirs. Carrie Tingley Hosp.; bd. dirs. Coun. on Superconductivity for Am. Competitiveness. Recipient E. O. Lawrence award Dept. Energy, 1984; named One of 100 Top Innovators, Sci. Digest, 1985. Fellow Am. Soc. Metals (mem. nat. commn. superconductivity 1989—); mem. Metall. Soc. (bd. dirs. 1983-84), Nat. Acad. Engring. Republican. Roman Catholic. Clubs: Los Alamos Ski (pres. 1980-81). Home: 117 Rim Rd Los Alamos NM 87544 Office: Los Alamos Nat Lab Mail Stop A100 Los Alamos NM 87545

HECKMAN, RICHARD AINSWORTH, chemical engineer; b. Phoenix, July 15, 1929; s. Hiram and Anne (Sells) H.; BS, U. Calif. at Berkeley, 1950, cert. hazardous mgmt. U. Calif., Davis, 1985; m. Olive Ann Biddle, Dec. 17, 1950; children—Mark, Bruce. With radiation lab. U. Calif. at Berkeley, 1950-51; chem. engr. Calif. Research & Devel. Co., Livermore, 1951-53; assoc. div. leader Lawrence Livermore Nat. Lab., Livermore, 1953-77, project leader, 1977-78, program leader, 1978-79, energy policy analyst, 1979-83, toxic waste group staff engr., 1984-86, waste minimization project leader, 1986—; mem. Calif. Radioactive Materials Forum. Bd. dirs. Calif. Industries for Blind, 1977-80, Here and Now Disabled Services for Tri-Valley, Inc., 1980. Registered profl. engr., Calif. Fellow Am. Inst. Chemists, Acad. Hazardous Materials Mgmt.; mem. AAAS, Am. Acad. Environ. Engrs. (diplomate), Am. Chemistry Soc., Am. Inst. Chem. Engrs., Soc. Profl. Engrs., Water Pollution Control Assn., Air Pollution Control Assn., Internat. Union Pure and Applied Chemistry (assoc.), Nat. Hist. Soc., N.Y. Acad. Scis., Am. Nuclear Soc., Better World Soc., Internat. Oceanographic Soc. Clubs: Commonwealth (San Francisco); Island Yacht (Alameda, Calif.) (commodore 1971), Midget Ocean Racing Club (sta. 3 commodore 1982-83), U.S. Yacht Racing Union, Midget Ocean Racing Assn. No. Calif. (commodore 1972). Co-author: Nuclear Waste Management Abstracts, 1983; patentee in field. Home: 5683 Greenridge Rd Castro Valley CA 94552 Office: Livermore Nat Lab PO Box 808 Livermore CA 94550

HECKMAN, WILLIAM JOSEPH, oil and chemical company executive; b. N.Y.C., Aug. 29, 1909; s. John Herman and Margaret Lauretta (Ferguson) H.; m. Mildred Berta Rogers, Sept. 3, 1938; children: William Rogers, Laura Graham Nokes. Student, CCNY, 1927-29. Office mgr. Scandia Mfg., N.Y.C., 1927-29; asst. sec. Gerry Estates, Inc., N.Y.C., 1929-38; asst. gen. purchasing agt. Texaco, N.Y.C., 1938-45; prodn. mgr., various other positions Warner-Hudnut, N.Y.C., 1945-50; v.p. purchasing and transp. Aramco Overseas Corp., The Hague, Holland, 1950-53; dir. purchasing Olin Mathieson Chems., Balt. and N.Y.C., 1953-60; v.p. spl. projects Olin Corp., N.Y.C. and Stamford, Conn., 1960-74; dir. Ormet Corp. and subs., 1961-74; bus. cons. Sun City, Ariz., 1974—; dir. purchasing and transp. Arabian-Am. Oil Co., N.Y.C., 1950-53. Dir., v.p. Sun City Recreation Ctrs., Inc., 1984-86; trustee Ohio Valley Improvement Assn. Mem. Lake Club, N.Y. Athletic Club. Republican. Roman Catholic. Home and Office: 16014 Nicklaus Ln Sun City AZ 85351

HECKSCHER, ERIC, personnel executive, writer; b. Brussels, Apr. 23, 1923; came to U.S., 1948; s. Ray and Germaine (Scaron) H; m. K. Donovan, 1959 (dec. 1960); children: Daniela, Gail, Shary Lynn, Ingrid. Cert. naval scis., U. Southampton, Eng., 1942; PhD in Psychology, Inst. Des Etudes Superieures En Sciences Humaines, Montreal, Can., 1974; cert., Learning Systems Inst., Paris. Cert. in clin. child psychology. Asst. dir. Marshen Found. for Gifted Youth, Santa Barbara, Calif., 1952-55; mgr. video sonics Hughes Aircraft Co., Culver City, Calif., 1955-58; exec. producer Auca Films Inc, Hollywood, Calif., 1958-63; producer Plan Alto Producoes, São Paulo, Brazil, 1963-65; dir. devel. Playboy Enterprises, Chgo., 1965-67; dir. manpower Booz Allen Hamilton, London and Paris, 1967-71; chief mgmt. communication UN, Geneva, 1971—; pres. Media and Talent Orgn. Inc., Beverly Hills, Calif., 1980—; dir. edn. Valley Coll., Los Angeles, 1986—; prof. psychology Cath. U., Sao Pãulo, 1960-63; exec. producer Eric Heckscher Prodn. Internat., Beverly Hills, 1958—. Author: Sleep with the Angels, My Love..., 1963; scriptwriter (TV film) 'Twas the Night After Christmas, 1985; producer, dir., writer numerous films; contbr. articles to profl. jours. Served to capt. U.S. Army, 1941-46, ETO, PTO. Fellow Am. Orthopsychiat. Assn., Internat. Council Psychologists; mem. Internat. Communications Inst., Soc. of Motion Picture and TV Engrs., Am. Mgmt. Assn., Soc. Internat. Applied Psychology. Republican. Home and Office: Media & Talent Orgn Inc PO Box 2310 Beverly Hills CA 90213-2310

HEDBERG, ALLAN GEORGE, clinical psychologist. AA, Wright Jr. Coll., 1957; BS in Edn., Northern Ill. U., 1960, MA in Psychology, 1963; PhD in Clin. Psychology, Queen's U., Kingston, Ont., Can., 1969. Instr. dept. psychology Wheaton Coll., Wheaton, Ill., 1963-65; lectr. dept. psychology Queens U., 1966-69; clin. psychologist Sioux Trails Mental Health Ctr., New Ulm, Minn., 1969-72; asst. prof. dept. psychology Mankato State Coll., Mankato, Minn., 1969-72, Baylor U., Waco, Tex., 1972-73; pvt. practice clin. and consulting psychology Waco, Tex., 1972-73; program dir. Schick Alcohol Program St. Vincent's Hosp., Waco, 1973-75; instr. Calif. Profl. Sch. Psychology, Fresno, Calif., 1975-79; mgr. psychological svcs. Leon S. Peters Rehab. Ctr., Fresno, Calif., 1976-81; pvt. practice clin. and consulting psychology Fresno, 1975—. Contbr. numerous articles in profl. jours. Mem. Calif. State Psychological Assn. (cert. recognition, 1983, Silver Psi award, meritorious contribution to psychology, 1988), Am. Psychological Assn., Assn. for the Advancement of Behavior Therapy, Behavior Therapy and Research Soc., Western Psychological Assn., San Joaquin Psychological Assn., Calif. Head Injury Found. Republican. Home: 281 W Ellery Fresno CA 93704 Office: 5100 N 6th St Ste 130 Fresno CA 93710

HEDBERG, KENNETH WAYNE, chemistry educator; b. Portland, Oreg., Feb. 2, 1920; s. Gustave N. and Ruth (Haagsma) H.; m. Jean Read, Dec. 24, 1943 (div. 1952); m. Lise Smedvik, Aug. 11, 1954; children: Erik, Katrina. BS, Oreg. State Coll., 1943; PhD, Calif. Inst. Tech., 1948. Chemist Shell Devel. Co., Emeryville, Calif., 1943-46; research fellow Calif. Inst. Tech., 1948-52, sr. research fellow, 1954-56; asst. prof. Oreg. State U., Corvallis, 1956-58, assoc. prof., 1958-63, prof., 1964-87, prof. emeritus, 1987—. Fellow J.S. Guggenheim Found., Norway, 1952-53; recipient Fulbright Research Scholarship, U.S. Edn. Found., Norway, 1952-53. Fellow AAAS, Am. Phys. Soc.; mem. Norwegian Acad. Arts and Scis., Am. Chem. Soc., Sigma Xi. Home: 1715 NW 27th St Corvallis OR 97330 Office: Oreg State U Dept Chemistry Corvallis OR 97331-4003

HEDGES, CARL DEVON, inventor, manufacturing executive; b. Rochester, Ind., Sept. 2, 1924; s. Samuel Pope and Cora Myrtle (Wood) H.; grad. King Coll., 1963; m. Margery Eileen Corliss, Aug. 15, 1953; children: Karl Eugene, Karen Eileen. Insp., trainee U.S. Border Patrol, Rochester, N.Y., 1950-53; woodworker, designer Klok Inst., Grand Rapids, Mich., 1954-57; research dir. KARLEEN Enterprises, 1964-67; research and devel. plastic mktg. mgmt., 1967-70; new product developer, corp. and patent and invention cons., 1970-74; pres., gen. mgr. World-Wide Meml., Inc., Pueblo, Colo., 1974—, maj. stockholder, new product devel. mgr. successor firm World Wide Industries, Inc., 1980—. Inventor and holder 30 patents in field. First aid instr. ARC, 1941-73, recipient 10,000 Hr. Vol. Service award, 1965; merit badge counselor Boy Scouts Am. Served with AUS, 1943-46; PTO. Recipient Internat. Gold Medal award for inventions Internat. Patent and Lic. Expn., 1967, 73. Mem. Ind. Inventors Am., Internat. Ind. Inventors, Am. Plastics and Fiberglass Research and Tech. Assn., DAV (past comdr., life mem., past Ind. state treas.), VFW (life, past comdr.). Republican. Methodist. Selected as 1st Boy Mayor in U.S., 1941. Home: 1806 E 3d St Pueblo CO 81001 Office: PO Box 322 Pueblo CO 81002

HEDGPETH, HARDING BRENT, air force officer; b. Corvallis, Oreg., Nov. 15, 1947; s. Lewis Floyd and Charlotte Edna (Knapp) H.; m. Jacalyn Sue Jordan, Aug. 29, 1970; children: Gregory, Pamela, Jeffrey, Katherine, Daniel. BS in Math. and Physics, U. Oreg., 1973; MA in Math., U. Wash., 1984. Chief warrant officer U.S. Army, U.S., Vietnam, Korea, 1966-69; commd. officer U.S. Air Force, 1973, advanced through grades to lt. col., 1988; C-9 instr. pilot 375th Aeromed. Evacuation Wing, Scott AFB, Ill., 1975-77; test pilot 6512th Test Squadron, Edwards AFB, Calif., 1978-81; govt. flight rep. detachment 9 Air Force Contract Mgmt. Div., Seattle, 1981-84; B-

1B prodn. test pilot detachment 15 Air Force Contract Mgmt. Div., Palmdale, Calif., 1985-87; chief Palmdale ops., govt. flight rep. Northrup B-2 Div., Palmdale, Calif., 1987-89; comdr., dir. spl. ops. combined test force 6518th Test Squadron, Edwards Air Force Base, Calif., 1989—; assigned to Air Command and Staff Coll., Montgomery, Ala., 1984-85; adj. instr. Antelope Valley Coll., Lancaster, Calif., 1986-. Trumpet player Antelope Valley Coll. Jazz Band, 1986-88; bd. dirs., mem. strategic planning com. Am. Cancer Soc., Lancaster, 1987-. Mem. Soc. Exptl. Test Pilots, Toastmasters. Republican. Roman Catholic. Home: 43721 Fenner Ave Lancaster CA 93536 Office: 6518th Test Squadron Edwards AFB CA 93523

HEDRICK, GARY LEE, employee relations company executive, consultant; b. Seattle, May 7, 1946; m. Betty J. Ruud, June 23, 1984. BA, Seattle U., 1977; MBA, Cornell U., 1980. Vol., staff mem. Peace Corps, Korea, 1967-73; owner, mgr. Aged East, Seattle, 1974-78; internal auditor 2550 Eastern, Tokyo, 1980-81; pres. N.W. Employee Rels., Inc., Mercer Island, Wash., 1981—. Bd. dirs. Boys and Girls Club, Mercer Island, 1981-83; pres. bd. dirs Youth Advocates, Seattle, 1983-86. Anglican. Home and Office: 7525 SE 24th St Ste 401 Mercer Island WA 98040

HEDRICK, JOSEPH WATSON, JR., judge; b. Fresno, Calif., Nov. 29, 1924; s. Joseph Watson and Kathryn (Watson) H.; m. Coleena Alice Wade, June 17, 1949; children—Joseph Wade, Robert S. B.S., U. Calif.-Berkeley, 1950; LL.B., U. Calif.-San Francisco, 1952. Bar: Calif. 1953. Assoc. Rowell Lamberson & Thomas, Fresno, 1953; mcht., Fresno, 1954; atty. Fresno County Legal Services, Inc., 1967; ptnr. Lerrigo, Thuesen & Thompson, Fresno, 1971, Lerrigo, Thuesen, Walters, Nibler & Hedrick, Fresno, from 1972; judge Modesto div. Ea. Dist. Calif., U.S. Bankruptcy Ct., 1980—. Served with AUS, 1943-46. Office: US Dist Ct PO Box 5276 Modesto CA 95352

HEDRICK, WALLACE EDWARD, director state lottery; b. Malad, Idaho, Nov. 11, 1947; s. Clarence Franklin and Beth S. Hedrick; B.S., U. Nev., Reno, 1970; M.A., U. No. Colo., Greeley, 1974; m. Jerrie S. Deffenbaugh, Nov. 20, 1980; children: Ann Elizabeth, Ryan Wallace, Hallie Sue. Regional dir. No. Idaho, Idaho Planning and Community Affairs Agy., Moscow, 1970-73, assoc. chief, Boise, 1973-75; project dir. Pacific N.W. Regional Commn., Boise, 1975-76; pres. Resources N.W., Inc., Boise, 1976-88; dir. Idaho State Lottery, 1988—. Sec.-treas. Idaho Citizens for Responsible Govt., 1978-80; trustee, chmn. Joint Sch. Dist. 2, 1985—; trustee Meridian Sch. Bd.; bd. dirs. Nat. Vandal Boosters, Inc. Served with USAR, 1971. Mem. Am. Planning Assn. Democrat. Home: 9413 Knottingham St Boise ID 83704 Office: Idaho State Lottery 1199 Shoreline Ln Ste 100 Boise ID 83702

HEDSTROM, KENNETH GERALD, insurance company executive; b. Spokane, Wash., Oct. 27, 1939; s. Elof Gerald Hedstrom and Audrey Ellen (Cox) Crawford; m. Sandra Elaine Vandersluys, Oct. 17, 1964; children: Kelli Anne, Kristina Suzanne. Grad. high sch., Spokane, 1957. Collection mgr. Pacific Fin., Spokane, 1960-63; credit mgr. Sears, Medford, Oreg., 1963-76; field underwriter Mony Fin. Services, Medford, Oreg., 1976—. Bd. dirs. Consumer Credit Counseling Service, Medford, 1984, 1st Ch. of the Nazarene, Medford, 1986, Blossom Hill Child Devel. Ctr., Medford, 1986. Served with USCG, 1958-60. Recipient Mony Top Club award Mony Fin. Services, 1986. Mem. Rogue Valley Life Underwriters (pres. 1984-86), Jackson County C. of C., Oreg. Life Underwriters (bd. dirs. 1980-86), Nat. Assn. Life Underwriters (Nat. Sales Achievement award 1978, 87, Nat. Quality award 1978, 87), Million Dollar Round Table (1984-88). Republican. Home: 1445 N Keeneway Dr Medford OR 97504 Office: Mony Fin Svcs 1175 E Main Ste 2F Medford OR 97504

HEDVA, BETH, psychotherapist; b. Detroit, Aug. 27, 1955; d. Harold Chaim and Tova Sylvia (Snyder) Milinsky; m. Matthew John Prest, Nov. 14, 1949. BS in Psychology magna cum laude, Mich. State U., 1977; MA in Clin. Psychology, John F. Kennedy U., 1981, MA in Transpersonal Psychology, 1981. Ward clerk Alta Bates Hosp., Berkeley, Calif., 1978-80; field placement asst. John F. Kennedy U., Orinda, Calif., 1978-80, dir. of field placement, 1980-81; counselor Contra Costa Alternative Sch., Orinda, Calif., 1980-83; dir. of internships Antioch U., San Francisco, 1984-89, faculty dept. of psychology, 1984—; dir. Psychic Hot Line, Oakland, Calif., 1982-88; psychotherapist Oakland, 1983—; clin. cons. Psychic Hot Line, Oakland, 1988—, founder, dir., 1982-88; adv. bd. clin. internship Antioch U., San Francisco, 1986; bd. dirs. Contra Costa Alternative Sch., Orinda, 1984. Foster parents, 1988; religious vol. Pleasanton Prison, 1986-89. Mem. Montclair Bus. Assn., Calif. Assn. of Marriage Family Therapists, Assn. Transpersonal Psychology, Parapsychology Found., Inst. of Noetic Scis., Aquarian Minyan Club, Ancient and Mystical Order Rosea Crucis, Acad. of Religion and Psychial Rsch., White Eagle Lodge (group leader 1983-84), Phi Beta Kapa, Phi Kapa Phi.

HEE, THOMAS WAH SUNG, accountant; b. Honolulu, Feb. 9, 1955; s. Clifford S.C. and Blanche K.Q. (Ching) H. BBA, U. Hawaii, 1978; grad. with high honors, Sch. of Bank Adminstrn., 1988. CPA Hawaii. Programmer First Hawaiian Bank, Honolulu, 1979-80, sr. fin. analyst, 1980-83, officer acctg., 1983-88, asst. v.p., 1988—. Chair fin. com. Hemophilia Found. Hawaii, 1981-85, also bd. trustees 1985—. Mem. Nat. Assn. Accts., Honolulu Marathon Assn. (chair data processing 1980), Ala Moana Jaycees (pres. 1985). Home: 3173 Olu St Honolulu HI 96816 Office: First Hawaiian Bank 165 S King St Honolulu HI 96813

HEEKIN, VALERIE ANNE, communications company technician; b. Santa Monica, Calif., Nov. 7, 1953; d. Edward Raphael and Jane Eileen (Potter) H. AA, L.A. Valley Coll., 1980; BS magna cum laude, Calif. Baptist Coll., 1987. Communications technician Pacific Bell Co., Canoga Park, Calif., 1971—; pres. Odyssey Adventures, Inc., Sylmar, Calif., 1987-89. Pres. Parkwood Sylmar Homeowners Assn., 1981—; activist Civil Rights. Republican. Roman Catholic. Office: Pacific Bell Co 7222 Remmet Ave Canoga Park CA 91303

HEENAN, DAVID A., diversified products company executive; b. 1940. AB, Coll. William and Mary, 1961; MBA, Columbia U., 1966; PhD, Wharton Sch. Bus., U. Pa., 1972. Sales rep., then sales mgr., mktg. mgr. Caltex Petroleum Corp., 1966-69; with Citicorp, 1972-75; v.p. acad. affairs U. Hawaii, 1975-82; with Theodore H. Davies and Co., Ltd., Honolulu, 1982—; now chmn. bd., pres., chief exec. officer, also bd. dirs. Theodore H. Davies and Co., Ltd. Capt. USMC, 1961-65. Office: Theodore H Davies & Co Ltd 841 Bishop St Honolulu HI 96802 *

HEERE, KAREN R., astrophysicist; b. Teaneck, N.J., Apr. 9, 1944; d. Peter N. and Alice E. (Hall) Heere; m. Gary L. Villere, Aug. 28, 1967 (div. Feb. 1988). BA, U. Pa., 1965; MA, U. Calif., Berkeley, 1968; PhD, U. Calif., Santa Cruz, 1976. Research assoc. Nat. Research Council NASA Ames Research Ctr., Moffett Field, Calif., 1977-79; research astronomer U. Calif., Santa Cruz and Moffett, Field, 1979-86; assoc. prof. San Francisco State U., 1986-87; scientist Science Applications Internat. Corp., Los Altos, Calif., 1774-76, 1987—; visiting prof. TATA Inst. for Fundamental Research, Bombay, India, 1984; adj. prof., San Francisco State U., 1987-. Author numerous articles in field. Mem. Am. Astron. Soc. Home: 226 Flynn Ave Mountain View CA 94043 Office: Sci Applications Internat Corp Ste B-31 5150 El Camino Real Los Altos CA 94022

HEERMANN, DALE FRANK, agricultural engineer; b. Scribner, Nebr., Mar. 2, 1937; s. Frank H. and Esther M. (Bock) H.; m. Betty Marie Tuchenhagen, July 21, 1957; children: Sara Heermann Buchleiter, Philip, Laura. BS in Agrl. Engring., U. Nebr., 1959; MS in Agrl. Engring., Colo. State U., 1964, PhD, 1968. Instr. Colo. State U., 1965-68; engr. Agrl. Research Service, USDA, Ft. Collins, Colo., 1968-80; research leader Agrl. Research Service, USDA, Ft. Collins, 1980—; cons. Rainbird, Glendora, Calif., 1973-75, Valmont Industries, Valley, Nebr., 1984-85. Author numerous sci. jours., 1967-85 (Outstanding Paper awards 1968-85). Chmn. accountability com. Pourde Ri, Ft. Collins, 1981-85. Mem. Am. Soc. Agrl. Engrs. (bd. dirs. 1974-76), Irrigation Assn. (chmn. program com., Man of Yr. award 1985), Am. Soc. Agronomy, U.S. Com. for Irrigation and Drainage. Lutheran. Home: 4780 Hogan Dr Fort Collins CO 80525 Office: USDA-ARS AERC-Colo State U Fort Collins CO 85023

HEERWAGEN, DEAN REESE, university educator, consultant; b. Summit, N.J., Dec. 27, 1942; s. Arthur Robert and Jane Roberts (Thoman) H.; m. Judith Ann Hannula, Aug. 21, 1971; 1 child, Margaret Jane Reese. B in Metall. Engring., Cornell U., 1965; MS, MIT, 1967, MArch, 1971. Asst. prof. arch. Cornell U., Ithaca, N.Y., 1971-73; pvt. practice in engring. 1973-75; acting assoc. prof. to assoc. prof. arch. U. Wash., Seattle, 1975—; cons. Seattle, 1980—; cons. in field. Mem. Soc. Bldg. Sci. Educators, Am. and Internat. Solar Energy Socs., ASHRAE, U.S. Working Group on Daylight Measurement, Acoustical Soc. Am., Internat. Soc. Biometerology. Home: 2716 NE 91st St Seattle WA 98115 Office: U Wash 208 Gould Hall JO-20 Seattle WA 98115

HEET, KATHLEEN MARIE, air traffic controller; b. Phoenix, Oct. 20, 1960; d. George Adrian and Thelma Mary (Vidovrek) H. high sch., Coolidge, Ariz. Sgt. USAF, 1978-82. Mem. Nat. Air Traffic Controllers Assn. (treas. 1988-89). Democrat. Roman catholic. Home: 1252 Garnet Ave Palmdale CA 93550

HEFFERN, CLARA BERNARD, interviewer; b. Wahpeton, N.D., Aug.18, 1910; d. Arnold and Gertrude (Schiller) Bernard; m. Marion Cadwell Heffern, June 25, 1935; children: Barbara J., Gertrude A., Nancy C., Mary M., Kathryn S. Student, N.D. State Sch. of SCi., 1926-28; BS, U.N.D., 1930; postgrad., Vassar Coll., 1955, Coll. of Great Falls, 1955-56. Tchr. Fairmount (N.D.) High Sch., 1930-32, Wahpeton (N.D.) High Sch., 1932-35, Ursuline Acad., Great Falls, Mont., 1954-64; dir., curator Cascade County Hist. Mus., Great Falls, 1976-80; interviewer N.W. Ursuline History Found., Great Falls, 1987—; con. Paris Gibson Sq., Great Falls, 1976-88; bd. dirs. Cascade County Hist. Soc., Coll. of Great Falls Guild. Active Citizen's Involvement Com. Preservation of Hist. Bldg., Great Falls, 1975-76; cons. Great Falls Genealogy Soc., 1976-88. Mem. AAUW, Coll. Great Falls Pres.' Council (fund raising com. 1975-88), Alpha Chi Omega, Ursuline Assn., 20th Century Book Club (pres. 1967-68). Roman Catholic. Home: 2115 3d Ave S Great Falls MT 59405

HEFFERNAN, RUTH MARIE, aerospace engineer; b. Worcester, Mass., Mar. 20, 1963; d. John Timothy and Marie Ann (Considine) H. BSME, MIT, 1985; MS in Aeronautics, Stanford U., 1989. Aerospace engr. NASA Ames Rsch. Ctr., Moffett Field, Calif., 1985—. Contbr. articles to profl. publs. Scholar, Texaco Philanthropic Found., 1984-85, Soroka Meml. Found., 1983-84. Mem. Am. Helicopter Soc., AIAA, ASME, Pi Tau Sigma, Delta Psi. Democrat. Office: NASA Ames Rsch Ctr Moffett Field CA 94035

HEFFLINGER, LEROY ARTHUR, agricultural manager; b. Omaha, Feb. 14, 1935; s. Leroy William and Myrtle Irene (Lampe) H.; m. Carole June Wickman, Dec. 23, 1956; children: Dean Alan, Andrew Karl, Roger Glenn, Dale Gorden. BS in Fin., U. Colo., 1957. Mgr. Hefflinger Ranches, Inc., Toppenish, Wash., 1963-73; pres. Hefflinger Ranches, Inc., 1973—; bd. dirs., Hop Adminstrv. Com., Portland, Oreg., 1980-86; truste, Agr. and Forestry Edn. Found., Spokane, Wash., 1988—. Vestryman, bd. dirs. St. Michael's Ch., Yakima, Wash., 1964-74. Capt. USAF, 1958-63. Mem. Hop Growers Am. (bd. dirs., past pres.), Hop Growers Wash. (bd. dirs., past treas.), Beta Theta Pi. Republican. Episcopalian. Office: Hefflinger Ranches Inc PO Box 47 Toppenish WA 98948

HEFFNER, ROSLYN, rehabilitation counselor; b. Bklyn.; m. Claude H. Heffner, Mar. 12, 1966; children: Steven, Deborah. Diploma in nursing, Buffalo (N.Y.) Gen. Hosp., 1963; BA, San Francisco State U., 1977, MS, 1979. Nurse Pacific Med., San Francisco, 1973-79; nurse, dept. head Mercy Hosp., Roseburg, Oreg., 1979-80; nurse Douglas Community Hosp., Roseburg, 1980-85; rehab. counselor Vocational Planning, Roseburg, 1980-81; dep. dir. services Siskiyou Rehab., Roseburg, 1982-85; rehab. counselor Cooley/Assocs., Roseburg, 1985-86, Richter & Assoc., Portland, Oreg., 1986, Crawford Rehab., Portland, 1987; pvt. practice rehab. counselor R. Heffner Vocational Counseling Service, Tualatin, Oreg., 1987—; cons. Adult and Family Services, Roseburg, 1984; instr. Gerontology Class, Roseburg, 1982. Mem. Douglas County Mental Health, Roseburg, 1981-85, Health Systems Agy., Roseburg, 1982-84. Mem. AAUW, Nat. Rehab. Assn., Nat. Rehab. Counseling Assn. Lodge: Lioness. Office: R Heffner Vocat Counseling PO Box 1391 Tualatin OR 97062

HEFFRON, MICHAEL EDWARD, software company executive; b. Battle Creek, Mich., Dec. 18, 1949; s. Michael Richard and Maxine Beverly (Piper) H.; m. Louella Mae Thompson, Apr. 12, 1969; children: Karen, Jennifer. BS in Engring., Computer Sci., Ariz. State U., 1986. Engring. aide Motorola, Inc., Scottsdale, Ariz., 1977-81; calibration lab. supr. ADR Ultrasound, Tempe, Ariz., 1981-82; engr. MEH Cybernetics, Scottsdale, 1982-86; v.p. CyberSoft, Inc., Scottsdale, 1986—. Served with USAF, 1970-77. Mem. Assn. Computing Machinery. Office: CyberSoftInc 1820 W Drake Dr Building 6 Ste 108 Tempe AZ 85283-4312

HEFLEY, JOEL M., congressman; b. Ardmore, Okla.; s. J. Maurice and Etta A. (Anderson) H.; m. Lynn Christian, Aug. 25, 1962; children: Janna, Lori, Juli. B.A., Okla. Baptist U., 1957; M.S., Okla. State U., 1963. Exec. dir. Community Planning and Research, Colorado Springs, Colo., 1966-86; mem. Colo. Ho. of Reps., 1977-78, Colo. Senate, 1979-87, 100th, 101st Congresses from 5th Colo. dist., 1987—. Republican. Presbyterian. Clubs: Rotary, Colorado Springs Country. Office: 508 Cannon Bldg Washington DC 20515

HEFNER, CASSANDRA JEWELL, mortgage banker, marketing executive; b. Dubuque, Iowa, Aug. 7, 1956; d. Milton Dudley and Aderine Lorraine (Lang) Ebner; m. Jack Eugene Hefner, Aug. 29, 1975; 1 child, Andrew Jackson. Student, Glendale Community Coll., 1975, 83-85, Ariz. State U., 1984. Loan officer Sutter Trust Co., Phoenix, 1977-78; asst. v.p. Saguaro Savs. & Loan, Phoenix, 1978-81; account exec. Verex Assurance Co., Phoenix, 1981-84; v.p. Citibank (Ariz.), Phoenix, 1984—. Mem. Ariz. Mortgage Bankers Assn. (bd. dirs. 1986-), Assn. Profl. Mortgage Women (pres. 1983). Methodist. Office: Citibank (Arizona) 3300 N Central Ave Ste 590 Phoenix AZ 85016

HEFNER, ROBERT ALAN, judge; b. Los Angeles, May 24, 1929; s. Earl C. and Igerna Nellie (Ferguson) H.; m. Elizabeth Sykes, Dec. 17, 1955; children—Coral E., Robert Alan. B.A., U. Calif., Los Angeles, 1955, LL.D., 1958. Bar: U.S. Dist. Ct. bar, So. Dist. Calif 1959, Calif. bar 1959, U.S. Supreme Ct. bar 1964. Practiced law Escondido, Calif., 1959-68, 71-74; asst. atty. gen. Saipan (Mariana Islands) Trust Terr., Pacific Islands, 1968-69; dep. atty. gen. Saipan (Mariana Islands) Trust Terr., 1969-70, atty. gen., 1970-71; assoc. justice High Ct. Trust Terr., Pacific Islands, Palau, Western Caroline Islands, Saipan, Mariana Isla, 1974-79; chief judge Commonwealth Ct., Saipan, 1979—; temp. judge Dist. Ct., Mariana Islands, High Ct., Trust Terr., Supreme Ct., Republic of Palau; instr. in real estate law and gen. law Palomar Jr. Coll., 1965-66. Pres. Escondido Republican Club, 1962-63; campaign mgr. Republican Congl. Candidate, N. San Diego County, 1972; chmn. Escondido Planning Commn., 1963-68. Served with USN, 1950-54, Korea. Recipient Man of Yr. award Jr. C. of C. of Escondido, 1963. Mem. Calif. Bar Assn., No. San Diego County Bar Assn. (pres. 1962-63), San Diego County Bar Assn. (v.p. 1963-64), Am. Judicature Soc., Trust Terr. Bar Assn., Escondido C. of C. (pres. 1963-64). Office: Courthouse Saipan MP 96950

HEGRENES, JACK RICHARD, educator; b. Fargo, N.D., Feb. 27, 1929; s. John and Ivy Anna (Jacobson) H.; B.S., U. Oreg., 1952, M.S., 1955; M.A., U. Chgo., 1960, Ph.D., 1970. Caseworker, Clackamas County Public Welfare Commn., Oregon City, Oreg., 1956-59, casework supr., 1960-62; instr. dept. psychiatry U. Oreg. Med. Sch., Portland, 1962-64, instr. Crippled Children's div., 1966-68, asst. prof., 1969-73, asso. prof. dept. public health and preventive medicine, and Crippled Children's div. Oreg. Health Scis. U., 1973—; adj. asso. prof. social work Sch. Social Work, Portland State U., 1973—. La Verne Noyes scholar, U. Chgo., 1958-60; NIMH fellow, U. Chgo., 1964-66. Fellow Am. Orthopsychiat. Assn.; mem. Nat. Assn. Social Workers, Am. Public Health Assn., Soc. for Gen. Systems Research, Am. Assn. for Advancement of Behavior Therapy, Am. Assn. Marriage and Family Therapists. Lutheran. Contbr. articles to profl. jours. Home: 3101 McNary Pkwy 12 Lake Oswego OR 97035 Office: Oreg Health Scis U PO Box 574 Portland OR 97207

HEIBERG, CHRISTOPHER JAN, mechanical engineer; b. Huntington, N.Y., Aug. 28, 1961; s. Milton Jean and Brenda Diane (Fink) H.; m. Jennifer Ann Harvey, June 27, 1987. BS in Mech. Engring., U. Ariz., 1984. Mech. engr. tech. staff Hughes Aircraft Co., Tucson, 1985-87; mech. engr. satellite systems div. Honeywell, Glendale, Ariz., 1987—. Mem. ASME (sec. Ariz. sect. 1986-87, adminstrv. conf. chmn. Ariz. sect. 1987-88, coll. rels. chmn. Ariz. sect. 1988—). Republican. Club: Ariz. Nature Conservancy. Home: 4576 W Maryland Glendale AZ 85301-4129

HEIDER, TONY KARL, lawyer; b. San Francisco, May 14, 1948; s. Charles Ivery and Elizabeth (Filice) H.; m. Kathleen Louise Kavern, Aug. 15, 1981; 1 child, Eric. BA in Polit. Sci. magna cum laude, San Francisco State Coll., 1970; JD, U. San Francisco, 1973. Bar: Calif. 1973. Prin. atty. Kern County Pub. Defender, Bakersfield, Calif., 1974-86, 88—; assoc. Law Office of Fred S. McAtee, Bakersfield, 1986-87, Goldberg, Fisher & Quirk, Bakersfield, 1987-88. Treas. Bakersfield Dem. Club, 1985-86. Mem. Kern County Bar Assn., Kern County Pub. Defenders Assn. (pres. 1980-86), La Raza Lawyers Assn. (sec. 1986-87). Democrat. Roman Catholic. Office: Office of the Pub Defender 1215 Truxtun Ave 3rd Fl Bakersfield CA 93301

HEIDT, RAYMOND JOSEPH, insurance company executive; b. Bismarck, N.D., Feb. 28, 1933; s. Stephen Ralph and Elizabeth Ann (Hirschkorn) H.; BA, Calif. State U., San Jose, 1963, MA, 1968; PhD, U. Utah, 1977; m. Joyce Ann Aston, Jan. 14, 1956; children: Ruth Marie, Elizabeth Ann, Stephen Christian, Joseph Aston. Claims supr. Allstate Ins. Co., San Jose, Calif., 1963-65; claims mgr. Gen. Accident Group, San Francisco, 1965-69; owner, mgr. Ray Heidt & Assos., Logan, Utah, 1969-76; v.p. claims Utah Home Fire Ins. Co., Salt Lake City, 1976—; with Utah State U., 1970-76; dir. Inst. for Study of Pacifism and Militarism; vice-chmn. Benton County Parks and Recreation Bd., 1987—. Active, Republican Party; mem. Kennewick Historic Preservation Commn., 1989—. With U.S. Army, 1952-57. Decorated Bronze Star. Mem. Southeastern Wash. Adjusters' Assn. (pres. 1988—), Utah Claims Assn. (pres. 1977-78), Lions, Am. Legion. Mormon. Home: 4103 S Sharon Kennewick WA 99337

HEIECK, PAUL JAY, wholesale distributing company executive; b. San Francisco, Aug. 6, 1937; s. Erwin N. and Ann C. (Retchless) H.; student Golden Gate Coll., 1958; m. Kathleen Pawela, Oct. 14, 1967; children: Valerie, Yvonne, Elizabeth, Krista, Justin. Sales rep. Heieck & Moran, San Francisco, 1958-63, sec.-treas., 1963-69, Heieck Supply, San Francisco, 1969-76, pres. 1976—; 1st v.p., dir. San Francisco Bd. Trade, 1978-82. Dir., San Francisco Boys Club, 1972—. With U.S. Army, 1955-57. Mem. Nat. Assn. Wholesalers, Am. Supply Assn. (dir. 1984—, v.p. 1987—), Western Supplier's Assn. (pres. 81-83, dir. 1981-85). Republican. Episcopalian. Clubs: Rotary, San Mateo County Mounted Posse, Sharon Heights Country, Olympic. Office: Heieck Supply 1111 Connecticut St San Francisco CA 94107

HEILEMAN, JOHN PHILLIP, endocrinologist; b. Phoenix, Feb. 2, 1930; s. Leonidas McAffee and Rose Madelaine (Murphy) H.; m. Ann Frances O'Hara, Nov. 4, 1961; children: Jeanne Marie, James Andrew, Denise Ann, Matthew John. BS, Ariz. State U., 1951; MD, Loyola U., Chgo., 1955; postgrad., USN Sch. Aviation Medicine, Pensacola, Fla., 1956. Diplomate Am. Bd. Internal Medicine. Intern U.S. Naval Hosp., Gt. Lakes, Ill., 1955-56; resident in internal medicine Cook County Hosp., Gt. Lakes, 1958-60, Vet. Rsch. Hosp., Gt. Lakes, 1960-61; fellow in endocrinology 1961-62; practice madicine specializing in internal medicine and endocrinology Phoenix, 1962—; pres. Endocrinology Assocs. P.A., Phoenix, 1971—. Pres. Ariz. chpt. Am. Diabetes Assn., 1975-77. Lt. comdr., flight surgeon USNR, 1955-58. Fellow ACP; mem. Ariz. Med. Assn. (sec. 1967-69), Maricopa County Med. Soc., Ariz. Soc. Internal Medicine, Ariz. Country Club. Republican. Roman Catholic. Office: Endocrinology Assocs 3522 N 3d Ave Phoenix AZ 85013

HEILIG, HARRY LUTHER, lawyer; b. Harrisburg, Pa., Apr. 3, 1930; s. Harry Luther and Katharine Kinter (Famous) H.; m. Doris Evelyn Fulcher, May 30, 1948 (div. Mar. 1950); m. Nancy Scott Keech Selden, Nov. 4, 1963 (dec. June 1987). AB, U. N.C., 1953; LLB, Wake Forest U., 1956. Bar: N.C. 1956. Sole practice Durham, N.C., 1956-71; counsel mid-Atlantic states TICOR Title Ins. Co., Wilmington, Del., 1971-73; assoc. gen. counsel Chelsea Title & Guarantee Co., Atlantic City, 1973-75; gen counsel, v.p. Ariz. Legal Posting, Phoenix, 1983—, also bd. dirs.; gen. counsel, bd. dirs. Country Care Found., Phoenix, Fair Automotive, Inc., Ariz. Life, Inc., Bukhari Importing and Exporting, Phoenix, others. Served with USNR. Mem. N.C. Bar Assn., N.C. State Bar Assn., Delta Phi Alpha. Republican. Baptist. Home: 2211 W Campbell Ave #1026 Phoenix AZ 85015 Office: PO Box 34801 Phoenix AZ 85067

HEILMAN, EDWARD GEORGE, forestry consultant; b. Butte, Mont., Mar. 25, 1929; s. Edward James and Miriam Andree (McDonald) H.; m. Donna Marie Dever, Nov. 5, 1951; children: Anne Patricia, Edward Mark. BS in Forestry, U. Mont., 1950. Registered profl. forester, Calif. With U.S. Forest Svc., various locations, 1945-84; fire control officer U.S. Forest Svc., Redding, Calif., 1961-67; fire tng. officer U.S. Forest Svc., Marana, Ariz., 1967-70; asst. regional forester U.S. Forest Svc., Milw., 1970-74; staff dir. U.S. Forest Svc., Missoula, Mont., 1974-84; ret. U.S. Forest Svc., 1984; sr. cons. FMA Internat., Inc., Gardnerville, Nev., 1984—. Prin. author tng. manuals on forest fire control, 1967-70. Pres., Missoula County Park Bd., 1984—, Friends of Hist. Mus., Missoula, 1984—; mem. disaster svcs. com. Missoula unit ARC, 1985—. Capt. USAF, 1950-53, Korea. Mem. Soc. Am. Foresters, Kiwanis (bd. dirs. Missoula chpt. 1983—), Elks. Roman Catholic. Home: 112 Michelle Ct Missoula MT 59803

HEILPERN, STEPHEN, real estate developer, television producer; b. N.Y.C., June 1, 1935; s. Carl Kalman and Ruth (Fine) H.; m. Maria Ortiz, May 236, 1968 (div. 1978); 1 child, Jaime Ortiz; m. Barbara J. Van Orden, May 5, 1984. BA in Speech, U. Mich., 1957. With bus. affairs dept. MCA, Inc., Universal City, Calif., 1957-68; producer MCA, Inc., 1968-75; ptnr. FBN Ltd., Studio City, Calif., 1976-85; pres. S & M Builders Co., Inc., Upland, Calif., 1985-88, Dovercrest Corp., Inc., L.A., 1988-. Steering com. D'Agostino for Dist. Atty., L.A., 1988. Mem. Acad. TV Arts and Scis., Producers Guild Am., Friars Club, St. James' Club. Democrat. Jewish.

HEIM, GEORGE EDWARD, engineering geologist; b. Buffalo, N.Y., Mar. 25, 1934; s. G. Edward and Marion Ruth (Stauffiger) H.; m. Linda Lou Hiler; children: Stephen E., Rebecca S. Heim Whyte, Katherine M. Heim Carbonaro. BS, U. Mich., 1956, MS, 1957; PhD, U. Ill., 1963. Cert. engring. geologist, Calif. Geologist Harza Engring. Co., Chgo., 1967-70, Dames & Moore, Chgo., 1970-72; mgr. geotech. div. Sargent & Lundy, Chgo., 1972-77; mgr., Chgo. div. Harding-Lawson Assocs., Chgo., 1978-82; tech. assurance coun. Battelle Meml. Inst., Columbus, Ohio, 1982-86; geologist ERM, West Chester, Pa., 1986-87; v.p. Leighton & Assocs., Inc., Irvine, Calif., 1987—; cons. Internat. Atomic Energy Agy., Vienna, Austria, 1984—. Author and contbr. tech. articles and guidance manuals. Fellow Geol. Soc. Am.; mem. ASCE, Am. Nuclear Soc., Assn. Engring. Geologists. Republican. Methodist. Home: 22561 La Brusca Mission Viejo CA 92692

HEIM, PATRICIA JANE, management consultant; b. LaJolla, Calif., Jan. 14, 1950; d. Charles Jr. and Mary Jane (Richard) H.; m. Sergius Lashutka, Jan. 8, 1983. BA in English Lit., San Diego State U., 1972; MA in Communication, 1974; PhD in Communication, U. Colo., 1977. Asst. prof. Loyola Marymount U., Los Angeles, 1977-79; advisor Rockwell Internat., Downey, Calif., 1979-81; asst. v.p. Am. Med. Internat., Beverly Hills, Calif., 1981-85; pres. Heim & Assoc., Pacific Palisades, Calif., 1985—. Mem. Organizational Devel. Network, Speech Communication Assn. Home and office: Heim & Assoc 1024 Kagawa St Pacific Palisades CA 90272

HEIM, WERNER G(EORGE), biology educator; b. Muhlheim Ruhr, Germany, Apr. 7, 1929; came to U.S., 1940, naturalized, 1946; s. Fred and Recha (Hirsch) H.; m. Julie I. Blumenthal, June 25, 1961; children: Susan L., David L.; m. 2d, Suzanne M. Levine, June 24, 1973; children: Elise B. Ginsburg, Lynn A. Ginsburg. BA in Zoology, UCLA, 1950, MA in

Zoology, 1952, PhD in Zoology, 1954. Instr. Brown U., Providence, 1956-57; asst. prof. biology Wayne State U., Detroit, 1957-63, assoc. prof. biology, 1963-67, vice chmn. biology dept., 1961-62, planning coordinator biology bldg. program, 1964-67; mem. faculty Colo. Coll., Colorado Springs, 1967—, prof. biology, 1967—, chmn. biology dept., 1971-76, 87—; vis. prof. biophysics and genetics dept. U. Colo. Sch. Medicine, 1978, 86; cons., geneticist regional genetic counseling program U. Colo. Health Scis. Ctr., Denver, 1978—, Del., Republican State Conv., Denver, 1982, 84, 86. USPHS-Nat. Cancer Inst. fellow, 1952-54; NIH grantee, 1958-67, NSF grantee, 1963-70, Am. Cancer Soc. grantee, 1963-65, Colo. Coll. grantee, 1979-83. Fellow AAAS; mem. Am. Soc. Zoologists, Soc. Devel. Biology, Internat. Soc. Devel. Biologists, Colo.-Wyo. Acad. Sci. (v.p. 1968-69), Nat. Soc. Genetic Counselors (assoc. mem.), Am. Soc. Human Genetics, Sigma Xi. Contbr. book revs., sci. articles to profl. publs. Office: Colo Coll Dept Biology Colorado Springs CO 80903

HEIN, MARK WILLIAM, newspaper editor; b. San Francisco, Nov. 23, 1944; s. William John Hein and Eileen Barbara (Fink) Woodington; m. Dawn Caroline Hudson, Apr. 5, 1968 (div. Nov. 1988); children: Michael Joseph, Genevieve Kathleen, Victoria Christine, William Whitehorse;. BA in Am. Studies, San Francisco State U., 1964; MA in History, Claremont Grad Sch., Claremont, Calif., 1966; PhD in Lit., Claremont Grad Sch., 1980. Cert. community coll. teaching, Calif. Instr., Am. studies program dir. Cañada Community Coll., Redwood City, Calif., 1969-72; editor, Surface Miner trade jour. Bucyrus-Erie Co., Milw., 1972-74; asst. editor The Living Church Episcopal Ch., U.S.A., Milw., 1974-76; copy editor, asst. editor features Milw. Sentinel, 1976-78; asst. dean faculty Alverno Coll., Milw., 1978-83; chair dept. English King Faisal U., Dammam, Saudi Arabia, 1983-84; copy editor, asst. editor features Ariz. Republic, Phoenix, 1984—; cons. non-profit fund-raising, Phoenix, 1984-88. Author: James Gould Cozzens, 1980; author, editor: Liberal Learning at Alverno, 1976-83; contbr. poems to several jours. Bd. dirs. Milw. Ballet Co., 1972-75; exec. bd. mem. Episcopal Diocese Milw., 1975-80; mem. Phoenix City Club, 1986—; bd dirs. Ariz. Spl. Events Network, Phoenix, 1985-88, City Arts/Phoenix, 1988-89; jury mem. Ariz. Arts Commn., Phoenix, 1987—; mgr. several polit. campaigns, 1968-75. Mem. SDX/Soc. Profl. Journalists (bd. dirs. Valley of Sun chpt. 1988—), Nat. Assn. Hispanic Journalists. Democrat.

HEIN, NICKOLAS EDWARD, aeronautical engineer; b. Monroe, Wis., July 27, 1957; s. Willaim Edward and Audrey Claire (Nix) H.; m. Susan Patricia Brennan, Aug. 6, 1983; 1 child, Peter William. BS in Aerospace Engrng. and Mechanics, U. Minn., 1980. Aerodynamicist Boeing Corp., Seattle, 1980-84, Douglas Aircraft Co., Long Beach, Calif., 1984-87, Aerolift Inc., Tillamook, Oreg., 1987—. Mem. AIAA, Jaycees, Internat. Human Power Vehicle Assn., U.S. Hang Gliding Assn., Phi Gamma Delta. Roman Catholic. Clubs: Cloudbase Country (Seattle). Office: Aerolift Inc 4105 Blimp Rd Tillamook OR 97141

HEIN, ROBERT ELDOR, electrical engineer; b. Portland, Oreg., Oct. 31, 1943; s. Eldor William and Beulah Gertrude (Billeter) H.; m. Bernice Alfreda Naessens, June 19, 1965; 1 child, Trent Robert. BSEE, U. Colo., 1966. Registered profl. engr., photographer. Design engr. Woodward Gov., Ft. Collins, Colo., 1970-71; dir. design engring. Coors Container Co. div. Coors Corp., Golden, Colo., 1971-81; mgr. advanced tech. Martin Marietta Corp., Denver, 1981-85; dir. research support Solar Energy Research Inst., Golden, 1985-88; mgr. computer automation Martin Marietta Astronautics Group, Denver, 1988—. Vestry coun. St. John Chrysostum Episcopal Ch.; mem. adv. bd. Red Rock Community Coll., Denver, 1976-80; bd. mgrs. N.W. YMCA, Arvada, Colo., 1978-81. Served to Capt. USAF, 1966-70, Vietnam. Mem. IEEE (sr., pres. IAS-GLASS com. 1982), Profl. Photographers Am., Denver Apple Users Group (pres. 1984-85), Am. Mgmt. Assn. Lodge: Elks. Home: 11735 W 72d Pl Arvada CO 80005-3204 Office: Martin Marietta Astronautics Group Space Launch Systems PO Box 179 Denver CO 80201-0179

HEIN, THOMAS JOE, dentist; b. Ft. Riley, Kans., Mar. 7, 1954; s. Marvin August and Jean Eileen (Barta) H.; m. Cherrie Kay Burchett, May 30, 1976; children: Nicholas Ryan, Candice Christine. BA, U. Colo., Boulder, 1976; DDS, U. Colo., Denver, 1980. DDS. Owner Thomas Hein, DDS, Englewood, Colo., 1980-85, Thomas Hein, DDS, PC, Englewood, 1985—; mem. restorative clin. staff Sch. Dentistry U. Colo., 1980—; chmn. Dental Sch. Colo. U., MDDS Liason, 1987-89. Mem. Am. Dental Assn., Colo. Dental Assn., Metro. Denver Dental Soc., Colo. Prost. Soc., Rocky Mt. Dental Study Club, M.D.D.S. Dental Study Club (chmn. 1987-88), Sertoma. Republican. Office: 8200 E Belleview Ave Ste 334 Englewood CO 80111

HEINBERG, PAUL JULIUS, communications educator; b. Birmingham, Ala., Aug. 25, 1924; s. Benjamin Fries and Juliette (Isaacs) H.; m. Joyce Suwal, July 8, 1945; 1 child, Juliet Caye. BS, Columbia U., 1949, MA, 1950; PhD, U. Iowa, 1956. Instr. speech Tex. Women's U., Denton, 1950-52; asst. prof. speech Okla. State U., Stillwater, 1952-57; asst. prof. speech and drama U. Iowa, Iowa City, 1957-65; asst. prof. speech and communications U. Hawaii, Honolulu, 1965-69, prof. communications, 1969—; merchandising analyst Amos Parrish, Inc., N.Y.C., 1948-50; v.p. Internat. Learning Systems, Honolulu, 1968-72; pres. Human Devel., Ltd., Honolulu, 1976-80, Heinberg Assocs., Ltd., Honolulu, 1984—. Author: play Man UNMANNED, 1964 (1st prize 1964); patentee audiovisual playback device, random access playback device, language teaching method and apparatus. 1st lt. USAF, 1941-47, ETO. AT&T grantee, 1963-69, Hawaii State Dept. Edn. grantee, 1971-72, State of Hawaii grantee, 1975-76, FAA grantee, 1980-81. Mem. Am. Psychol. Assn., Soc. for Gen. Systems Rsch. (referee 1975—), Internat. Communication Assn., Optimist (pres. Iowa City chpt. 1964-65), Hawaii chpt. Am. Ex-POW's (comdr. Honolulu chpt. 1988—). Democrat. Jewish. Home: 1530 Ahuawa Loop Honolulu HI 96816-5604 Office: U Hawaii Dept Communication 2560 Campus Rd Rm 307 Honolulu HI 96822

HEINDL, CLIFFORD JOSEPH, physicist; b. Chgo., Feb. 4, 1926; s. Anton Thomas and Louise (Fiala) H. B.S., Northwestern U., 1947, M.S., 1948; A.M., Columbia U., 1950, Ph.D., 1959. Sr. physicist Bendix Aviation Corp., Detroit, 1953-54; orsort student Oak Ridge Nat. Lab., 1954-55; asst. sect. chief Babcock & Wilcox Co., Lynchburg, Va., 1956-58; research group supr. Jet Propulsion Lab., Pasadena, Calif., 1959-65, mgr. research and space sci., 1965—. Served with AUS, 1944-46. Mem. AIAA, Am. Nuclear Soc., Health Physics Soc., Planetary Soc., Am. Phys. Soc. Home: 179 Mockingbird Ln South Pasadena CA 91030 Office: 4800 Oak Grove Dr Pasadena CA 91109

HEINE, GUNTER KARL, computer company executive; b. Ellenserdamm, Nieder., West Germany, Feb. 9, 1941; came to U.S., 1984; s. Max Oscar and Frieda (Kohlrenken) H.; m. Edelgard Hannelore Woop, July 7, 1965; children: Gero, Thorsten. Diploma engenieur, Univ. Hamburg, West Germany, 1965. Devel. engrng. AEG-Telefunken, Oldenburg, West Germany, 1965-66; mgr. research and devel. AEG-Telefunken, Oldenburg, 1967-68; dir. engring. Berger-Lahr, Lahr, West Germany, 1968-74; v.p. engring. Berger-Lahr, Lahr, 1975-83; dir. engring. Seagate Tech., Scotts Valley, Calif., 1984-86; v.p. Seagate Tech., Scotts Valley, 1986—; cons. Oriental Motors, Tokyo, 1978-82, EPFL (Univ.), Lausanne, Switzerland, 1980-84, Berger-N.H., Jeffrey, N.H., 1976-83. Co-author: Step-Motors & Control Systems, 1979, Electrical Kleinmotoren, 1979; contbr. articles to profl. jours. Home: 143 Driftwood Ct Aptos CA 95003 Office: Seagate Tech 920 Disc Dr Scotts Valley CA 95066

HEINER, ROBERT T., banker; b. 1925. Student, Weber State Coll. With First Security Bank of Utah NA, Salt Lake City, 1946—, chmn. bd., chief exec. officer, dir.; pres., chief adminstrv. officer 1st Security Corp., Salt Lake City, 1986—. Office: 1st Security Corp 79 S Main St PO Box 30006 Salt Lake City UT 84130 *

HEINEY, OTTO KELCHNER, aerospace engineer, researcher; b. Allentown, Pa., Nov. 11, 1940; s. Edmund C. and Emma (Kelchner) H.; m. Judith L. Kampmann, Sept. 12, 1964; children: Kristine, Edmund. BS in Engring. Physics, Lehigh U., 1962; MS in Aerospace Engring., U. So. Calif., L.A., 1966; diploma, Indsl. Coll. of Armed Forces, 1980. Registered profl. engr., Fla. Sr. propellant engr. Jet Propulsion Lab., Pasadena, Calif., 1966-70; interior ballistic br. chief USAF, Elgin AFB, Fla., 1970-84; sr. staff scientist Rockwell Corp., L.A., 1984—. Author: Interior Ballistics of Aircraft Cannon, 1982. With USAF, 1962-65, col. USAFR, 1962—. Named Air Force Armament Lab. Scientist of Yr., 1978. Mem. Am. Def. Preparedness Assn. Republican. Lutheran. Home: 20040 Community St #66 Canoga Park CA 91306 Office: Rocketdyne div Rockwell 6633 Canoga Ave Canoga Park CA 91304

HEINLEIN, OSCAR ALLEN, former air force officer; b. Butler, Mo., Nov. 17, 1911; s. Oscar A. and Katherine (Canterbury) H.; B.S., U.S. Naval Acad., 1932; M.S., Calif. Inst. Tech., 1942; M.S. in Mech. Engring., Stanford, 1949; certificate in mining U. Alaska, 1953; grad. Air War Coll., 1953; student spl. studies U. Ariz., 1956-57, Eastern Wash. U., Clark County Community Coll., Las Vegas, Nev., 1988, U. Nice, France; D.D., Universal Sem., 1970; AA Clark County Community Cm. Catharine Anna Bangert, May 1, 1933 (div. Apr. 1937); 1 dau., Catharine Anna; m. 2d, Mary Josephine Fisher, Aug. 25, 1939 (dec. Dec. 1977); 1 son, Oscar Allen III; m. 3d, Suzanne Birke, Feb. 23, 1980; 1 son, Michael Andre Bertin. Marine engr. Atlantic Refining Co., Phila., 1934; civil engr. Annapolis Mineral Devel. Co., Calif., 1935-37; enlisted as pvt. U.S. Army, 1937, advanced through grades to col., 1944; comdr. Ladd AFB, Alaska, 1953-54, 11th Air Div., Fairbanks, Alaska, 1954, Air Force Logistics Command Support Group, Vandenberg AFB, Calif., 1960-65, prof. air sci. U. Ariz., Tucson, 1955-58; insp. Gen. Mobile Air Materiel Area, Ala., 1958-60; ret. 1965; now cons.; pres. O.A. Heinlein Merc. Co., Butler, Mo., 1934—; vis. prof. U. Nev., Reno; dep. dir. civil def. Boulder City, Nev., 1967; dir., sec. Boulder Dam Fed. Credit Union, 1973-79; mem. Boulder City Police Adv. Com., 1976; ordained minister Bapt. Ch., 1976. Active Boy Scouts Am. Mem. Clark County (Nev.) Republican Central Com., 1966, Exec. com., 1970; mem. Rep. Central Com., 1966; Rep. candidate Nev. Assembly, 1972; mem. Boulder City Charter Commn. Mem. community coll. adv. bd. U. Nev., 1970. Served with USN, 1928-32; to 2d lt. USMC, 1932-34. Decorated Legion of Merit, Air medal, Army, Navy and Air Force commendation medals. Mem. Inst. Aero. Scis., Am. Meteorol. Soc., Nat. Research Assn., Am. Radio Relay League, SAR, Am. Polar Soc., VFW, Daedalians, Mensa, So. Nev. Amateur Radio Club, Inst. Amateur Radio, Quarter Century Wireless Assn., Ret. Officers Assn., Air Force Assn., Nat. Rifle Assn. (life), Armed Forces Communications and Electronics Assn., USS Nevada Assn., CAP, Am. Legion, Am. Assn. Ret. Persons, West Coast Amateur Radio Service, Soc. Wireless Pioneers. Mason, Nev. Rifle and Pistol Assn. (bd. dirs.), Vet. Wireless Operator's Assn. Clubs: MM (San Diego); Intertel (Ft. Wayne, Indiana); Missile Amateur Radio (pres. 1961-65 Vandenberg AFB); Explorers (N.Y.C.); Arctic Circle Prospectors', High Jumpers (Fairbanks, Alaska); Boulder City Gem and Mineral; Stearman Alumnus; Marines Memorial (San Francisco). Author: Big Bend County, 1953. Inventor. Home: 107 Wyoming St Boulder City NV 89005

HEINOLD, S. LYNN, realtor, educator, home economist; b. Shelton, Wash., Oct. 27, 1951; d. Robert Lloyd and Cora Irene (Cole) Deffinbaugh. BA, Seattle Pacific U., 1974; postgrad., U. Wash. Cert. elem., high sch. tchr., Wash. Supr., tchr. Highline Vocat. Skills Ctr., Seattle, 1976-77; tchr. Kent Jr. High Sch., Seattle, 1977-78; substitute tchr. various schs., Seattle, 1978-79; tchr. Shelton (Wash.) High Sch., 1979-85, Mt. View Grade Sch., Shelton, 1985-86; realtor Classic Realty, Olympia, Wash., 1987—. Mem. Olympia C. of C. (bus. edn. devel., mil. affairs coms.), Thurston County Bd. Realtors (edn. com.), AAUW, Women's Network, Beta Sigma Phi, Thurston County Multiple Sales Club (sec. 1988). Club: Thurston County Multiple Sales (sec. 1988). Office: Classic Realty 3905 Martin Way E Olympia WA 98506

HEINRICH, JOHN WILLIAM, JR., management consultant; b. Oakland, Calif., Oct. 19, 1943; s. John William Sr. and Ernestine Lillian (Loehwing) H.; children: John William III, David. BA, Antioch Coll., 1966; MBA in Fin., U. Pa., 1968. Supr. Ford Motor Credit Co., Dearborn, Mich., 1972-78; v.p. sales John Heinrich Co., Sparks, Nev., 1978-83, pres., 1983-86; pres. J.H. Assoc., Phoenix, 1987—; sales v.p. Tahoe Products, Sparks, Nev., 1986, Computer Data Networks, Tempe, Ariz., 1987; mktg. dir. VSLA Architects, Phoenix, 1987—, Data Images, Inc., 1988—, Lawforms, Phoenix, 1988—, Primatemp, Inc., 1989—. Author: Navy Special Purpose Communications, 1972; patentee in field. Mem. Phoenix Soc. for the Arts, 1986—, Downtown YMCA Bd. dirs., 1988—. Comdr. USNR, 1968-72. Fellow U.S. Naval Inst.; mem. Enterprise Network, Ariz. Innovation Network. Republican. Home and Office: 6523 N 14th St #101 Phoenix AZ 85014

HEINRICHER, JACK EDWARD, government audit executive; b. Centralia, Wash., June 25, 1935; s. Raymund August Heinricher and Irma Pauline (Sparber) Brown; m. Larieta Yvonne Saeger, Apr. 15, 1955 (div. Sept. 1974); children: Gregory, Deborah, Jackie, Jami. BA, Cen. Wash. U., 1958. Cert. info. systems auditor, internal auditor. Acct., auditor, systems analyst Shell Oil Co., Seattle, N.Y.C. and Palo Alto, Calif., 1958-67; auditor Office of the State Auditor, Olympia, Wash., 1967—. Author: Control Objectives, 1984. Campaign dir. Com. to Re-elect Bob Graham, Olympia, 1988. Served to cpl. U.S. Army, 1954-56. Mem. EDP Auditors' Assn. (pres. 1979, nat. v.p. 1981, audit standards com. 1986-88), Nat. State Auditors' Assn. (single audit com. 1988), Assn. Govt. Accts. (nat. exec. com. 1987—). Democrat. Roman Catholic. Lodge: Rotary. Home: 301 W Lee #30 Tumwater WA 98501 Office: Office of State Auditor Legis Bldg AS21 Olympia WA 98504

HEINS, MARILYN, college dean, pediatrics educator, author; b. Boston, Sept. 7, 1930; d. Harold and Esther (Berow) H.; m. Milton P. Lipson, 1958; children: Rachel, Jonathan. A.B., Radcliffe Coll., 1951; M.D., Columbia U., 1955. Diplomate Am. Bd. Pediatrics. Intern, N.Y. Hosp., N.Y.C., 1955-56; resident in pediatrics Babies Hosp., N.Y.C., 1956-58; asst. pediatrician Children's Hosp. Mich., Detroit, 1959-78; dir. pediatrics Detroit Receiving Hosp., 1965-71; asst., assoc. dean student affairs Wayne State U. Med. Sch., Detroit, 1971-79; assoc. dean acad. affairs U. Ariz. Med. Coll., Tucson, 1979-83, vice dean, 1983—, prof. pediatrics, 1985— . Author: (with Anne M. Seiden) Child Care/Parent Care, 1987; mem. editorial bd. Jour. AMA, 1981—; contbr. articles to profl. jours. Bd. dirs. Planned Parenthood So. Ariz., 1983—, pres., 1988—; mem. adv. com. Tucson Assn. Child Care, Inc., 1984—, Nat. Bd. Med. Examiners, 1983—; mem. adv. bd. Ariz. State Hosp., 1985-88. Recipient Alumni Faculty Service award Wayne State U., 1972, Recognition award, 1977, Women on the Move Achievement award YWCA Tucson, 1983. Fellow Am. Orthopsychiat. Assn., Am. Acad. Pediatrics; mem. Assn. Am. Med. Colls. (chair group on student affairs 1976-79), Am. Hosp. Assn. (chmn. com. med. edn. 1985), Soc. Health and Human Values, Women in Sci. and Engring. U. Ariz. (bd. dirs. 1979—), Exec. Women's Council Tucson, Ariz. Med. Assn. (com. on med. service 1985—), Pima County Med. Soc., Pima County Pediatric Soc., Ambulatory Pediatric Assn., AAAS, Am. Pub. Health Assn., Assn. Am. Med. Colls., Med. Soc. U.S. and Mex., Western Soc. Pediatric Research. Club: Second Tuesday (co-founder). Home: 6530 N Longfellow Dr Tucson AZ 85718 Office: U Ariz Med Coll 1501 N Campbell Ave Tucson AZ 85724

HEINZ, DON J., agronomist; b. Rexburg, Idaho, Oct. 29, 1931; s. William and Berniece (Steiner) H.; m. Marsha B. Hegsted, Apr. 19, 1956; children: Jacqueline, Grant, Stephanie, Karen, Ramona, Amy. BS, Utah State U., 1958, MS, 1959; PhD, Mich State U., 1961; grad., Stanford U. Exec. Program, 1982. Assoc. plant breeder Experiment Sta. Hawaiian Sugar Planters' Assn., Aiea, 1961-66, head dept. genetics and pathology, 1966-78, asst. dir., 1977-78, v.p. and dir., 1979-85, pres., dir. experiment sta., 1986—; cons. Phillippines, Egypt, Colombia, Reunion; mem. adv. com. plants Hawaii Dept. Agr., 1970—, Pres. Nat. Commn. Agriculture and Rural Devel. Policy, 1988. Contbr. articles to sci. jours. on sugarcane breeding, cytogenetics, cell and tissue culture techniques. Served with USAF, 1951-54. Mem. Internat. Soc. Sugar Cane Technologists (chmn. com. germplasm and breeding 1975-86), Am. Soc. Agrl. Cons., Crop Sci. Soc. Am., AAAS, Sigma Xi. Mormon. Home: 224 Ilihau Kailua HI 96734 Office: Hawaiian Sugar Planters Assn 99-193 Aiea Heights Dr Aiea HI 96701

HEINZE, HAROLD C., petroleum industry transportation company executive; b. 1942. BS, Colo. Sch. Mines, 1964. Jr. engr. South L.A. dist. ARCO Oil & Gas Co., 1965-67, jr. engr. North Permian dist., 1967-69, reservoir engr. Alaska dist., 1969-72, staff engr., 1972-73, mgr. reservoir engring., engring. mgr. Alaska dist., 1973-81, planning mgr., 1981-82; pres. ARCO Alaska, from 1983; now pres. ARCO Transportation Co.; sr. v.p. Atlanta Richfield Co. 1st Lt., U.S. Army, 1965-67. Office: ARCO Transp Co 300 Oceangate Long Beach CA 90802 *

HEIPLE, CLINTON RIE, metallurgist; b. Tacoma, Wash., Nov. 12, 1939; s. Uriah M. and Mildred J. (Allgood) H.; m. Joanne Watkins, Feb. 1966 (div. 1979); children: Robin, Penny. BS, Stanford U., 1961; MS in Metallurgy, Sheffield (Eng.) U., 1962; PhD, U. Ill., 1967. Postdoctoral fellow N.Am. Rockwell Sci. Ctr., Thousand Oaks, Calif., 1966-68; research metallurgist Dow Chem. Co., Rocky Flats, Colo., 1968-76; sr. research specialist Rockwell Internat., Rocky Flats, Colo., 1976-79, assoc. scientist, 1979—. Contbr. articles to profl. jours., chpts. to books. Mem. Am. Soc. Metals, Am. Welding Soc. (William Spraragen award 1983, McKay-Helm award 1987), Internat. Inst. Welding, Acoustic Emission Working Group, Colo. Mycological Soc., Sierra Club. Republican. Home: 1785 Deer Valley Rd Boulder CO 80303 Office: Rockwell Internat Corp Bldg 779 PO Box 464 Golden CO 80402

HEISERMAN, FREDERICK VON, physician; b. Princeton, Ind., Jan. 10, 1927; s. Fred E. and Maud M. (Miller) H.; m. Margaret Jeanne Flanders, Feb. 5, 1950; children: John, Jane. AB in Zoology, Ind. U., 1951, BS in Pub. Health, 1952; D in Osteopathic Medicine, Kirksville (Mo.) Coll., 1966. Diplomate Am. Bd. Med. Examiners, Am. Bd. Gen. Practice. Pres. Romero Rd. Med. Clinic, P.C., Tucson, 1967—; aviation med. examiner FAA, 1968; med. dir. Border Bapt. Free Clinic, Nogales, Ariz., 1976—, Ariz. Coll. Med. and Dental Careers, Tucson, 1988—, Buenos Samaritinos, Nogales, 1989—; mem. exec. com. Tucson Gen. Hosp., 1986—. Mem. Internat. Disaster Med. Relief Assn., Richmond, Va., 1978—; med. examiner Spl. Olympics, Tucson, 1979—. Mem. Am. Acad. Family Physicians, Am. Coll. Osteopathy, Am. Osteo. Med. Assn., Ariz. Osteo. Med. Assn., Am. Coll. Sclerotherapy, Aerospace Med. Assn., Pima County Med. Soc., World Med. Assn., Greater Ariz. Bicycling Assn. Republican. Southern Baptist. Office: Romero Rd Med Clinic PC 4006 N Romero Rd Tucson AZ 85705

HEISTAND, JOSEPH THOMAS, bishop; b. Danville, Pa., Mar. 3, 1924; s. John Thomas and Alta (Hertzler) H.; B.A. in Econs., Trinity Coll., Hartford, Conn., 1948, D.D. (hon.), 1978; M.Div., Va. Theol. Sem., 1952, D.D. (hon.), 1977; m. Roberta Crieger Lush, June 1, 1951; children—Hillary Heistand Long, Andrea Deferrier, Virginia Redmon. With Internat. Harvester Co., 1948-49; ordained to ministry Episcopal Ch., 1952; rector Trinity Ch., Tyrone, Pa., 1952-55; chaplain Grier Sch., Birmingham, Pa., 1952-55; asso. rector St. Paul's Ch., Richmond, Va., 1955, rector, 1955-69; rector St. Philip's in the Hill Ch., Tucson, 1969-76; bishop coadjutor Episcopal Diocese Ariz., Phoenix, 1976-79; bishop of Ariz., 1979—. Served with AUS, 1943-45. Decorated Bronze Star with oak leaf cluster, Purple Heart; Croix de Guerre (France). Office: Box 13647 Phoenix AZ 85002

HEITMAN, GREGORY ERWIN, state official; b. Lewiston, Idaho, June 7, 1947; s. Elmer William and Carmelita Rose Ann (Kinzer) H.; m. Phyllis Ann Pryor, Sept. 25, 1982. BS in Math., U. Idaho, 1969, MBA, 1971; student, Wash. State U., 1965-67. Student communications dir. Assoc. Students U. Idaho, Moscow, 1970-72, advisor, apt. mgr. dept. housing, 1971-72; traffic fatality analyst Idaho Dept. Transp., Boise, 1973-74; ops. mgr. Region IV Health & Welfare State of Idaho, Boise, 1974-78, supr. computer svcs., div. environ. in health and welfare, 1978-85; supr. field svcs., program dir. Idaho Vital Statistics, Boise, 1985—; acting dir. Idaho Ctr. for Health Statistics, Boise, 1988; mem. med. records adv. com. Boise State U., 1987—, cons., lectr. 1987—. Active various charitable orgns.; precinct committeeman Dem. of Latah County, 1972; election day coord. Ada County, 1986. Mem. Idaho Pub. health Assn., Assn. Vital Records and Health Statistics, Idaho Pub. Employees Assn., Assn. Govt. Employees. Roman Catholic. Home: 5103 Shalecrest Ct Boise ID 83703 Office: Idaho Vital Statis 450 W State St Boise ID 83702

HEITMAN, HUBERT, JR., animal science educator; b. Berkeley, Calif., June 2, 1917; s. Hubert and Blanche (Peart) H.; m. Helen Margaret McCaughna, Aug. 7, 1941; children: James Hubert (dec.), William Robert. B.S., U. Calif.-Davis, 1939; A.M., U. Mo., 1940, Ph.D., 1943. Asst. instr. animal husbandry U. Mo., 1939-43; mem. faculty U. Calif. at Davis, 1946—, prof. animal sci., 1961-87, prof. emeritus, 1987—, chmn. dept., 1963-68, 81-82, acad. asst. to vice chancellor acad. affairs, 1971-78; livestock supt. Calif. State Fair, 1948-59; v.p. at large Nat. Collegiate Athletic Assn., 1975-77; pres. Far Western Intercollegiate Athletic Conf., 1971-72, 77-78, Golden State Conf., 1979-80. Pres. Yolo County Soc. Crippled Children, 1954-56; Bd. dirs. Calif. Soc. Crippled Children and Adults, 1954-56. Served to capt., San. Corps AUS, 1943-46. Mem. AAAS, Am. Soc. Animal Sci. (pres. Western sect. 1953), Animal Behavior Soc., Internat. Soc. Biometeorologists, Calif., N.Y. acads. scis., Nutrition Soc. (Gt. Britain), Brit. Soc. Animal Prodn., Sigma Xi, Alpha Zeta, Gamma Sigma Delta, Gamma Alpha, Sigma Chi. Home: 518 Miller Dr Davis CA 95616

HEITNER, DONALD H., manufacturing company executive, controller; b. Yonkers, N.Y., Feb. 26, 1959; s. Joel Heitner and Alice (Greenberg) Drake. BS, U. Tenn., 1981. CPA, Ariz. Tax auditor II, Tenn. Dept. Revenue, Nashville, 1981; staff acct. Luton, Knolton, Keeney & Assocs., Memphis, 1982-83; gen. acct. Syncorp, Inc., Memphis, 1983-84; acctg. mgr. Cooper Office Equipment Co., Memphis, 1984-85, Jordan Cos., Memphis, 1985-86; contr. Jordan Cos., Phoenix, 1986—. Bd. dirs. Black Tie Optional, Phoenix, 1988—. Mem. AICPA, Ariz. Soc. CPA's. Office: Jordan Cos 4235 E Winslow Ave Phoenix AZ 85040

HELFERT, ERICH ANTON, management consultant, author, educator; b. Aussig/Elbe, Sudetenland, May 29, 1931; came to U.S., 1950; s. Julius and Anna Maria (Wilde) H.; m. Anne Langley, Jan. 1, 1983; children: Claire L., Amanda L. BS, U. Nev., 1954; MBA with high distinction, Harvard U., 1956, DBA, 1958. Newspaper reporter, corr., Neuburg, Fed. Republic of Germany, 1948-52; rsch. asst. Harvard U., 1956-57; asst. prof. bus. policy San Francisco State U., 1958-59; asst. prof. fin. and control Grad. Sch. Bus. Adminstrn., Harvard U., 1959-65; internal cons., then asst. to pres., dir. corp. planning Crown Zellerbach Corp., San Francisco, 1965-78, asst. to chmn., dir. corp. planning, 1978-82, v.p. corp. planning, 1982-85; cons. mgmt., San Francisco, 1985—; founding dir. Modern Soft, Inc.; mem. adv. bd. Quadrant Tech., Inc., Antares Telecom, Inc.; mem. Dean's adv. coun. San Francisco State Bus. Sch., sch. fin. Golden Gate U. Author: Techniques of Financial Analysis, 1963 , 6th edit., 1987, Valuation, 1966, (with others) Case Book, 1963, Controllership, 1965; contbr. articles to profl. jours. Exch. student fellow U.S. Inst. Internat. Edn., 1950; Ford Found. doctoral fellow, 1956. Mem. Assn. Corp. Growth (past pres., bd. dirs. San Francisco chpt.), Inst. Mgmt. Cons., World Bus. Acad. (bd. dirs.), Phi Kappa Phi. Roman Catholic. Clubs: Commonwealth, Harvard U. Bus. Sch. of No. Calif. (chmn. bd. dirs., past pres.). Home: 111 W 3rd Ave #401 San Mateo CA 94402 Office: 1777 Borel Pl 508 San Mateo CA 94402

HELFORD, PAUL QUINN, financial advisor, insurance planner; b. Chgo., June 27, 1947; s. Norman and Eleanor (Kwin) H.; m. Leslie Gale Weinstein, July 11, 1971; children: Ross Michael, Benjamin Keith. BA, U. Ill., 1969; MA, Northeastern Ill. U., 1977. Cert. tchr., Ill., Oreg. Tchr. John Hersey High Sch., Arlington Heights, Ill., 1969-73; freelance writer Mill Valley, Calif., 1973-75; mgr., program dir. Sta. KOZY-TV, Eugene, Oreg., 1976-88, mktg., sales, and program dir. Group W Cable, 1984-88; fin. advisor, ins. planner, agt. N.Y. Life, 1988—. Writer, producer Paul Helford's Hollywood Oldies, 1976-81, In Review, 1981, Live from the Fair, 1981-85, Group W Cable Minutes, 1984-85, Bad Horror and Sci. Fiction, 1985 (Award for Cable Excellence 1986), KOZY movie promotional spots 1976-88 (Award for Cable Excellence 1984, 88, Clio award nomination 1988, 1989); contbr. articles to profl. jours. Recipient CLIO award 1984, 86, Cable Mktg. Grand award, 1981, 85. Mem. Nat. Assn. Cable Programmers. Home: 940 Madison Eugene OR 97402 Office: NY Life 1600 Executive Pkwy Ste 400 Eugene OR 97401

HELGASON, DEAN EUGENE, technical writer; b. Chgo., May 21, 1940; s. Kristvin S. Helgason and Alice (Joscelyne) Shultz; m. Carole Anne Schwocher, Feb. 10, 1970; children: Carlie, Kerstin, Branden. Student, U. N.Mex., 1969-72; BSBA, U. Phoenix, 1987. Tech. writer Sun Electric Corp., Chgo., 1965-68; instr. Albuquerque Tech.-Vocat. Inst., Albuquerque, 1970-71; dept. head Ariz. Automotive Inst., Glendale, Ariz., 1972-75; mgr. Hamilton Test Systems, Tucson, 1976—; instr. Pima Community Coll., Tucson, 1987—; cons. Automotive Tech. Data, Phoenix, 1976-80; automotive adv. com. Pima Coll., 1981—. Contbr. articles to profl. jours. Cpl. USMC, 1961-64. Mem. Soc. Automotive Engrs. Home: 751 N Banff Ave Tucson

AZ 85748 Office: Hamilton Test Systems 2202 N Forbes Blvd Tucson AZ 85745

HELGESON, DUANE MARCELLUS, librarian; b. Rothsay, Minn., July 2, 1930; s. Oscar Herbert and Selma Olivia (Sateren) H.; B.S., U. Minn., 1952. Librarian, Chance-Vought Co., Dallas, 1956-59, System Devel. Corp., Santa Monica, Calif., 1959-62, Lockheed Aircraft, Burbank, Calif., 1962-63, C.F. Braun Co., Alhambra, Calif., 1963-74; chief librarian Ralph M. Parsons Co., Pasadena, Calif., 1974-79; pres. Mark-Allen/Brokers-in-Info., Los Angeles, 1976-80; phys. scis. librarian Calif. Inst. Tech., Pasadena, 1980-84; corp. librarian James M. Montgomery Cons. Engrs., Pasadena, 1985—; mem. adv. bd. Los Angeles Trade Tech. Coll., 1974-79, U. So. Calif. Library Sch., 1974-79. Served with USAF, 1952-54. Mem. Spl. Libraries Assn. (chmn. nominating com. 1974). Co-editor: (with Joe Ann Clifton) Computers in Library and Information Centers, 1973. Home: 2706 Ivan Hill Terr Los Angeles CA 90039 Office: James M Montgomery Cons Engrs 250 N Madison Pasadena CA 91101

HELIN, JAMES DENNIS, advertising agency executive; b. Carmel, Calif., Aug. 30, 1942; s. Richard James and Helen Margaret (Noonan) H.; m. Sally Katharine Pope, July 2, 1966; children: Laurie Ann, Jennifer Katharine, Holly Margaret, Christopher James, Kathleen Patricia. BS, San Jose State U., 1964. Mktg. asst. Diamond Internat. Co., San Francisco, 1965; product mgr. Purex Corp., Lakewood, Calif., 1966-69; sr. v.p., mgmt. supr. Doyle Dane Bernbach Co., Los Angeles, 1969-81; exec. v.p., account group dir. 1981-85; Dailey & Assocs., Los Angeles, 1981-85; mng. dir., D'Arcy Masius Benton & Bowles, Los Angeles, 1985— ; instr. 4A's Inst. Advanced Advt. Studies U. So. Calif. Served with USAR, 1964-70. Recipient Alumni of Yr. award, bus. div. San Jose State U., 1979. Mem. Am. Assn. Advt. Agys. (gov., pres.), Western States Advt. Agys. Assn. (bd. dirs.), Beta Gamma Sigma. Republican. Roman Catholic. Office: D'Arcy Masius Benton & Bowles Inc 6500 Wilshire Blvd Ste 1000 Los Angeles CA 90048

HELINSKI, DONALD RAYMOND, biologist; b. Balt., July 7, 1933; s. George L. and Marie M. (Naparstek) H.; m. Patricia G. Doherty, Mar. 4, 1962; children—Matthew T., Maureen G. B.S., U. Md., 1954; Ph.D. in Biochemistry, Western Res. U., 1960; postdoctoral fellow, Stanford U., 1960-62. Asst. prof. Princeton (N.J.) U., 1962-65; mem. faculty U. Calif., San Diego, 1965—; prof. biology U. Calif., 1970—, chmn. dept., 1979-81, dir. Ctr. for Molecular Genetics, 1984—; mem. com. guidelines for recombinant DNA research NIH, 1975-78. Author papers in field. Mem. Am. Soc. Biol. Chemists, Am. Soc. Microbiology, AAAS, Am. Acad. of Arts and Scis., Nat. Acad. Scis., Genetics Soc. Office: U Calif Ctr for Molecular Genetics M-034 Dept Biology San Diego CA 92093

HELLENTHAL, S. RONALD, finance company executive; b. Santa Cruz, Calif., Oct. 26, 1949. BA in Bus., Baylor U., 1969, MBA, 1975; BA in Bus., U. Air Force, Colorado Springs, Colo., 1973; postgrad., Portland State U., 1980—. Investigator, dept. def. fed. govt. 1970-73; with law enforcement county govt., 1973-75; transp. cons. 1975-78; owner Rohn Mgmt. Co., Portland, 1978-80; pres. Rohn Mgmt. Corp., Portland, 1980—, Northwest Tours, inc., Portland, Seattle, 1984—; pres., treas. Monty D. Moore & Co., Portland, 1984—; pres. Rohn Marine Svcs., Seattle, 1986—; chmn. bd. dirs. Rohn Mgmt. Corp., Portland, Northwest Tours, Inc., Seattle. Staff sgt., U.S. Army, 1966-70, Vietnam, USAFR ret. Mem. Nat. Tour Assn., Portland/Oreg. Visitors Assn., Seattle/King County Visitors Assn., Griffith Park Club. Democrat. Roman Catholic. Office: Rohn Mgmt Corp PO Box 8637 Portland OR 97207

HELLER, JEFFREY ALAN, government official; b. Peoria, Ill., May 8, 1958; s. Michael William and Joyce (Mendeloff) H.; m. Frances Trevino, June 21, 1984. BA, Northwestern U., 1980; postgrad., Spertus Coll. Judaica, 1980-81; MA, Brandeis U., 1984; postgrad., U. Calif., Berkeley, 1985. Tax examiner IRS, Fresno, Calif., 1984-86; revenue officer IRS, Oakland, Calif., 1986—. Vol. tax educator IRS, Oakland, 1987-88. Recipient 1st Prize Best Running Story, Sportscape Mag., Boston, 1984. Mem. Beta Theta Pi. Jewish. Office: IRS 1330 Broadway Ste 600 Oakland CA 94612

HELLER, STANLEY, hardware manufacturer's representative; b. N.Y.C., Oct. 3, 1929; s. David N. Heller and Mildred (Steinman) Poland; m. Estelle David, Jan. 30, 1955; children: David N., Felice A. BA, Pa. State U., 1951. V.p. research and devel. Madway Main Line Homes, Inc., Wayne, Pa., 1954-63; divisional sales mgr. Lifetime Doors, Inc., Livonia, Mich., 1964-71; dist. rep. Kwikset Corp., Anaheim, Calif., 1971—. Mem. N.J. Crime Prevention Officers Assn., Howell, 1977-87 (named Crime Prevention Practioner of the Year 1980); pres. Pine Brook (N.J.) Jewish Ctr., 1967. Served with U.S. Army, 1951-53. Mem. Sigma Alpha Mu (nat. treas. 1962-64). Home: 62 Douglas Dr Towaco NJ 07082 Office: Kwikset Corp 516 E Santa Ana St Anaheim CA 92803

HELLICKSON, KAZUKO SATO, contract administrator; b. Tokyo, Apr. 9, 1947; d. Jun and Misao (Kobayashi) Sato; m. Howard Adrian Hellickson, Apr. 4, 1970 (dec. Oct. 1974). BA in English Lit., Macalester Coll., 1969; BS in Consumer Sci., U. Wis., 1978. Sr. engr. in contract tech. requirements, sr. contract specialist Martin Marietta Corp., Denver, 1979-82, sr. contract specialist, 1984-86, contract adminstr., 1986—; configuration engr. Gen. Telephone and Elec., Westborough, Mass., 1982-84. Bd. dirs. Congress Park Neighbors, Denver, 1979. Mem. Nat. Def. Preparedness Assn., Nat. Contract Mgmt. Assn. (sec. 1986-87, historian pub. rels. 1987-88), Omicron Nu. Office: Martin Marietta Corp PO Box 179 Denver CO 80201

HELLON, MICHAEL THOMAS, tax consultant; b. Camden, N.J., June 24, 1942; s. James Bernard and Dena Louise (Blackburn) H.; BS, Ariz. State U., 1972; m. Toni L. Carson; 3 children. Ins. investigator Equifax, Phoenix, 1968-69; exec. v.p. Phoenix Met. C. of C., 1969-76; ins. co. exec. London Ins. Group, 1976-78; pres. Hellon and Assocs., Inc., 1978—; nat. def. exec. res. U.S. Dept. of Commerce, 1986—; bd. dirs. Equity Benefit Life Ins. Co., Modern Income Life Ins. Co. of Mo., First Equity Security Life Ins. Co. Mem. Ariz. Occupational Safety and Health Adv. Council, 1972-76, mem. Speaker's Select Com. Auto Emissions, 1976; Phoenix Urban League, 1972-73, Area Manpower Planning Council, 1971-72, Phoenix Civic Plaza Dedication Com., 1972, Phoenix Air Quality Maintenance Task Force, 1976. Pres. Vis. Nurse Service, 1978-79; Rep. precinct capt., 1973—; state campaign dir. Arizonans for Reagan Com., 1980; alt. del. Rep. Nat. Conv., 1980, 84, 88; mem. staff Reagan-Bush Nat. Conv., 1984. campaign mgr. for various candidates, 1972-82; mem. Rep. state exec. com., 1989—. Bd. dirs. ATMA Tng. Found., 1981-84. Served with USAF, 1964-68. Decorated Bronze Star medal, Purple Heart. Recipient George Washington Honor medal Freedom's Found., 1964; commendation Fed. Bar Assn., 1973. Mem. U.S. C. of C. (pub. affairs com. western div. 1974-76), Inst. of Property Taxation, Internat. Assn. Assessing Officers, U.S. Dept. Commerce Exec. Res., Ariz. C. of C. Mgrs. Assn. (bd. mem. 1974-76), Tucson C. of C. Club: Trunk 'N Tusk; Catalina Soccer (bd. dirs. 1984-88). Home: 5775 Camino Real Tucson AZ 85718 Office: PO Box 37123 Tucson AZ 85740

HELLSTROM, PAMELA DONWORTH, human resource development executive; b. Bangor, Maine, Apr. 4, 1948; d. Clarence Arlowe and Margaret Mary (Donworth) Small; m. Michael Willard Hellstrom, Oct. 12, 1978; 1 child, Kirsten Elyse. BA in English Edn., Merrimack Coll., 1970. Lic. vocat. educator, Wash. Asst. dir. pub. relations, employment counselor Meals-On-Wheels, Seattle, 1970-72; social services asst. Madigan Army Med. Ctr., Tacoma, 1972-73, social work asst., 1974-81; chief counselor drug and alcohol treatment ctr. Am. Lake VA Health Ctr., Tacoma, 1973-74; trainer, cons. alt. chief examiner Gen. Equivalency Diploma program L.H. Bates Vocat. Tech. Inst., Tacoma, 1983-84; founder, pres. Growth Techs., Inc., Tacoma, 1984—, dir. trainer edn. program and ednl. rsch. project. Mem. Am. Mgmt. Assn., Am. Soc. Tng. and Devel., Tacoma-Pierce County C. of C. Democrat. Roman Catholic.

HELLYER, CONSTANCE ANNE, writer, publication manager; b. Puyallup, Wash., Apr. 22, 1937; d. David Tirrell and Constance (Hopkins) H.; m. Peter Andrew Corning, Dec. 30, 1963 (div. 1977); children: Anne Arundel, Stephanie Deak; m. Don W. Conway, Oct. 12, 1980. BA with honors, Mills Coll., 1959. Grader, researcher Harvard U., Cambridge, Mass., 1959-60; reporter, researcher Newsweek mag., N.Y.C., 1960-63; author's asst. Theodore H. White and others, N.Y.C., 1964-69; freelance writer, editor Colo., Calif., 1969-75; writer, editor Stanford (Calif.) U. Med. Ctr., 1975-79; communications dir. No. Calif. Cancer Program, Palo Alto, 1979-82; pubs. dir. Stanford Law Sch., Palo Alto, 1982—. Founding editor (newsletter) Insight, 1978-80, Synergy, 1980-82; editor (mag.) Stanford Lawyer, 1982—; contbr. articles to profl. jours. and mags. Recipient Silver Medal award Council Advancement and Support of Edn., 1985, 89. Mem. No. Calif. Sci. Writers Assn. (co-founder, bd. dirs. 1979—), Nat. Sci. Writers Assn. (assoc.), Phi Beta Kappa. Democrat. Home: 2080 Louis Rd Palo Alto CA 94303 Office: Stanford Law Sch Stanford CA 94305-8610

HELM, JANE COLE, real estate associate; b. Woodbury, Conn., Dec. 13, 1954; d. Ralph Edwin and Julia Constance (Skripkunis) C.; m. Richard Hamilton Helm, (div. Dec. 1982). Student, St. Anselm's Coll., 1972-74, Hesser Bus. Coll., 1974, Truckee Meadows Community Coll., 1986. Assoc. Fuetsch-Argeres and Assoc. Realty, Reno, Nev., 1987—. Democrat. Roman Catholic. Home: 12751/2 S Arlington Ave Reno NV 89509 Office: Fuetsch Argeres & Assocs 222 California Ave Reno NV 89509

HELMLINGER, WILLIAM KEITH, company executive; b. Bremen, Ind., July 9, 1949; s. William Edward and Helein Louise (Dobelstein) H.; m. Lois Elaine Eggers, Nov. 29, 1969 (div. Aug. 1987); m. Suzanne Jo Ribstein, Feb. 29, 1988; children: William Kai, Arick Wade. BA in German, Cen. Mo. State U., 1971; MS in Bus. Mgmt., U. LaVerne, 1988. Mgr. new bus. Household Fin. Corp., Chgo., 1971-77; employment mgr., asst. v.p. Lloyds Bank, Los Angeles, 1977-83; asst. v.p., recruitment mgr. Union Bank, Los Angeles, 1983-85; employment supr. R&B Enterprises, Los Angeles, 1985--. Area rep. Youth for Understanding Exchange Program, Los Angeles, 1985--. Mem. Employment Mgmt. Assn. Republican. Lutheran. Home: 3168 Barry Ave Los Angeles CA 90066

HELSELL, ROBERT M., construction executive; b. Seattle, Mar. 29, 1937; s. Frank P. and Ellen (Bringloe) H.; m. Linda M. Clark, Dec. 19, 1961; children—Kristina, Ingrid, Spencer, Alexa. B.A., Dartmouth Coll., 1959, M.B.E., 1960. C.P.A., Wash. With Haskins & Sells, 1961-64; treas. Cascade Natural Gas Co., 1964-68; successively sec.-treas., exec. v.p., pres. and chief exec. officer Howard S. Wright Constrn. Co., Seattle, 1974-84; pres., chief exec. officer Wright Schuchart, Inc., 1980-84; chmn., chief exec. officer Sprague Resources Corp., 1984—; vice chmn. bd. Schuchart & Assocs., 1980-87; vice chmn., chief exec. officer Wright Schuchart Inc., 1984—, Howard S. Wright Constrn. Co., 1984—; dir. Rainier Nat. Bank, Rainier Bancorp. Bd. dirs. Virginia Mason Hosp., 1984-87, Virginia Mason Med. Found., 1984—, Va. Mason Med. Ctr., 1987—, Lakeside Sch., 1969-73; bd. dirs. Seattle Children's Home, 1968-77, pres., 1972-75; bd. dirs. Corp. Council for Arts, 1981—, pres., 1984, chmn., 1985; trustee Seattle Art Mus., 1973—; mem. men's adv. com. Children's Orthopedic Hosp., 1980—. Served to lt. comdr. USCG, 1961-68. Mem. Assoc. Gen. Contractors. Republican. Episcopalian. Clubs: Univ., Rainier, Seattle Tennis, Seattle Yacht, Columbia Tower, Wash. Athletic (Seattle). Office: Wright Schuchart Inc PO Box 3764 Seattle WA 98124 *

HELTON, MAX EDWARD, minister, consultant; b. Conasauga, Tenn., Nov. 24, 1940; s. Herman Marshall and Nellie Gladys (Haddock) H.; m. Jean Bateman, June 8, 1962; children: Elaine, Melanie, Crista, Becky. BA, Tenn. Temple U., 1963; DD (hon.), Hyles-Anderson Coll., 1973. Ordained minister Bapt. Ch., 1963. Sr. pastor Koolau Bapt. Ch., Kaneohe, Hawaii, 1964-71; exec. v.p. Hyles-Anderson Coll., Crown Point, Ind., 1971-77; sr. pastor Grace Bible Ch., White Plains, N.Y., 1977-83; pastor outreach program Grace Bapt. Ch., Glendora, Calif., 1986—; sr. pastor West Park Bapt. Ch., Bakersfield, Calif., 1983-86; bd. dirs. Final Frontiers, Bartow, Ga.; pres. Motor Racing Outreach, Charlotte, N.C., 1988—. Author: Thirty Qualities of Leadership, 1975; contbr. articles to profl. jours.; keynote speaker Commonwealth Youth Day, Cayman Brac, B.W.I., 1964. Mem. adv. bd. legislation N.Y., Albany, 1980-82, sch. bd. Bakersfield Christian Sch. Dist., 1985-86; dep. sheriff Lake County (Ind.) Sheriff Dept., Crown Point, 1974-77. Mem. Internat. Sports Coalition, Conservative Bapt. Assn. (cons. 1983—, chmn. fellowship com. 1985-87), Nat. Assn. for Stock Car Auto Racing. Republican. Office: Motor Racing Outreach Smith Tower Ste 400 Hwy 29 N Harrisburg NC 28075

HELZER, JAMES DENNIS, hospital executive; b. Fresno, Calif., Apr. 27, 1938; s. Alexander and Katherine (Scheidt) H.; m. Joan Elaine Alinder, Feb. 25, 1967; children: Amy, Rebecca. B.S., Fresno State Coll., 1960; M.Hosp. Adminstrn., U. Iowa, 1965. Adminstrv. asst. Twilight Haven, Fresno, Calif., 1960-61; asst. adminstr. U. Calif. Hosps. and Clinics, San Francisco, 1965-68; asst. adminstr. Fresno Community Hosp., 1968-71, exec. adminstr., 1971-82, pres., chief exec. officer, 1982—; pres., chief exec. officer Community Hosps. Cen. Calif., 1983—. Served with U.S. Army, 1961-63. Mem. Am., Calif. hosp. assns., Am. Coll. Hosp. Adminstrs. Presbyterian. Club: Rotary. Home: 5909 E Hamilton Fresno CA 93727 Office: Fresno Community Hosp & Med Ctr PO Box 1232 Fresno CA 93715

HEMANN, RAYMOND GLENN, aerospace company executive; b. Cleve., Jan 24, 1933; s. Walter Harold Marsha Mae (Colbert) H.; B.S., Fla. State U., 1957; postgrad. U.S. Naval Postgrad. Sch., 1963-64, U. Calif. at Los Angeles, 1960-62; M.S. in Systems Engring., Calif. State U., Fullerton, 1970, M.A. in Econs., 1972; m. Lucile Tinnin Turnage, Feb. 1, 1958; children—James Edward, Carolyn Frances; m. Pamela Lehr, Dec. 18, 1987.Aero. engring. aide U.S. Navy, David Taylor Model Basin, Carderock, Md., 1956; analyst Fairchild Aerial Surveys, Tallahassee, 1957; research analyst Fla. Rd. Dept., Tallahassee, 1957-59; chief Autonetics div. N.Am. Rockwell Corp., Anaheim, Calif., 1959-69; v.p., dir. R. E. Manns Co., Wilmington, Calif., 1969-70; mgr. avionics design and analysis dept. Lockheed-Calif. Co., Burbank, 1970-72, mgr. advanced concepts div., 1976-82; gen. mgr. Western div. Arinc Research Corp., Santa Ana, 1972-76; dir. future requirements Rockwell Internat., 1982-85; dir. Threat Analysis, Corp. Offices, Rockwell Internat., 1985-89; pres. Advanced Systems Rsch. Corp., 1989—; cons. various U.S. govt. agys.; mem. naval studies bd. Nat. Acad. Scis., 1985—; asst. prof. ops. analysis dept. U.S. Naval Postgrad. Sch., Monterey, Calif., 1963-64, Monterey Peninsula Coll., 1963; instr. ops. analysis Calif. State U., Fullerton, 1963, instr. quantitative methods, 1969-72; adj. fellow Ctr. Strategic and Internat. Studies, Washington, 1987—; pres. Asso. Aviation, Inc., Fullerton, 1965-74; lectr. Brazilian Navy, 1980, U. Calif., Santa Barbara, 1980, Yale U., 1985, Princeton U., 1986, U.S. Naval Postgrad. Sch., 1986; cons. to various corps. and govt. agys. Served with AUS, 1950-53. Syde P. Deeb scholar, 1956; Honor awards Nat. Assn. Remotely Piloted Vehicles, 1975, 76. Comml., glider and pvt. pilot. Fellow AAAS; mem. Ops. Research Soc. Am., IEEE, AIAA, Air Force Assn., N.Y. Acad. Scis., Nat. Acad. Scis. (Naval Studies Bd. 1985—), Assn. Old Crows, Phi Kappa Tau (past pres.). Episcopalian. Contbr. articles to profl. jours. and news media. Home: 1215 Hartwood Point Dr Pasadena CA 91107

HEMION, DWIGHT ARLINGTON, television producer, director; b. New Haven, Mar. 14, 1926; s. Dwight Arlington and Bernice Ruby (Berquist) H.; m. Katherine Bridget Morrissy, Sept. 1, 1973; children—Katherine, Dwight Gustav. Student pub. schs., Verona, N.J. Asso. dir. ABC-TV, N.Y.C., 1946-49; TV dir. Tonight Show, NBC-TV, N.Y.C., 1950-60; dir. Perry Como TV show, N.Y.C., 1960-67; producer/dir. Yorkshire Prodns., N.Y.C., 1967-70; producer/dir. TV spls. in assn. with ATV, London; producer/dir. Smith-Hemion Prodns., Los Angeles, 1975—. Dir.: Frank Sinatra: A Man and His Music, 1965 (Emmy award TV Acad. Arts and Scis.); The Sound of Burt Bacharach, 1969, Singer Presents Burt Bacharach, 1970, Barbra Streisand and Other Musical Instruments, 1973, Steve and Eydie-Our Love is Here to Stay, 1975, America Salutes Richard Rodgers: The Sound of His Music, 1976, Bette Midler-Ol' Red Hair is Back, 1977, Ben Vereen ... His Roots, 1977, Steve and Eydie Celebrate Irving Berlin, 1978, IBM Presents Baryshinikov on Broadway, 1979 (Emmy award), Goldie and Kids ... Listen to Us!, 1982 (Emmy award), Sheena Easton...Act I, 1983 (Emmy award), Anne Murray's Winter Cranival...From Quebec, 1984, many others. Served in AC U.S. Army, 1944-46. Named Dir. of Year in TV Dirs. Guild Am., 1965. Club: Bel-Air Country. Office: Smith-Hemion Prodns 1438 N Gower Box 15 Los Angeles CA 90028 *

HEMMERDINGER, WILLIAM JOHN, artist; b. Burbank, Calif., July 7, 1951; s. William John Jr. and Eileen Patricia (Fitzmaurice) H.; m. Catherine Lee Cooper, Aug. 8, 1981. Student Art Ctr. Coll. Design, 1967-69, Nat. Palace Mus., Taiwan, 1973; A.A., Coll. of Desert, 1971; B.A., U. Calif.-Riverside, 1973; M.F.A., Claremont Grad. Sch., 1975, Ph.D., 1979; post-grad. Harvard U., 1977. Curator Calif. Mus. Photography, 1973-74; instr. Coll. of Desert, 1974-79, 80-84, Calif. State U., Long Beach, 1979-80, Otis Art Inst. Parsons Sch. Design, 1979-80, U. Calif., Riverside, 1981-82, co-owner William & Catherine Hemmerdinger Gallery, Palm Desert, Calif. One-man shows include: Cirrus Editions, Ltd., 1982, 84; group shows include: NAD, N.Y.C., Whitney Mus. Am. Art, N.Y.C., UNESCO Mus., Paris, Am. Watercolor Soc., N.Y.C., L.A. County Mus. Art, Boyusan Citizens Hall, Internat. Contemporary Art Fair; works in permanent collections Tate Gallery, London, UCLA, Smithsonian Instn., Washington, Mobil Oil Co., N.Y.C., Fed. Reserve Bank, San Francisco. Recipient Calif. Nat. Watercolor Soc. award, 1974, 1979; Ford Found. grantee, 1979; NEA grantee, 1979, NEH grantee, 1980. Mem. Nat. Watercolor Soc. (v.p. 1981-82, 83). Contbr. articles to profl. jours. Studio: 42-240 Green Way Ste D Palm Desert CA 92260 Office: Cirrus Editions Ltd 540 S Alameda St Los Angeles CA 90013

HEMMERT, MAX L., auditor; b. Soda Springs, Idaho, June 29, 1945; s. George Eugene and Lucille (Nelson) H.; m. Nancy R. Smith, June 28, 1967 (div. 1982); m. Debra R. Rasmussen, Feb. 9, 1985; 1 child, Gauin Max; stepchildren: Braydn, Megan, Trevor, Brooke. A in Acctg., Steven Henager Bus. Coll., Salt Lake City, 1973. Acct., office mgr. Walker Bank & Trust Co., Salt Lake City, 1969-74, Mark III, Inc., Constrn., Soda Springs, 1974-84; v.p. ops., auditor Security State Bank, Soda Springs, 1984—. Coach, Soda Springs Little League Baseball Assn., 1976—, All Star, 1977, 88. With USAF, 1965-69. Mem. Masons, Shriners, Scottish Rite, Soda Springs Golf Club (sec.-treas. 1981—). Republican. Mormon. Home: 141 Soda Creek Dr Soda Springs ID 83276 Office: Security State Bank 101 N 1st W Soda Springs ID 83276

HEMMINGS, PETER WILLIAM, orchestra and opera administrator; b. London, Apr. 10, 1934; s. William and Rosalind (Jones) H.; m. Jane Frances Kearnes, May 19, 1962; children—William, Lucy, Emma, Rupert, Sophie. Grad. Gonville and Caius Coll., Cambridge, 1957; LL.D. (hon.), Strathclyde U., Glasgow, 1978. Clk., Harold Holt Ltd., London, 1958-59; planning mgr. Sadlers Wells Opera, London, 1959-65; gen. adminstr. Scottish Opera, Glasgow, 1962-77; gen. mgr. Australian Opera, Sydney, 1977-79; mng. dir. London Symphony Orch., 1980-84; gen. dir. Los Angeles Music Ctr. Opera Assn., 1984—; gen. mgr. New Opera Co., London, 1956-65, dir. Royal Acad. Music. Served to lt. Brit. Signal Corps, 1952-54; Fed. Republic Germany. Mem. Internat. Assn. Opera Dirs., 1977-79, Opera Am. (bd. dirs.). Anglican. Club: Garrick (London). Home: 775 S Madison Ave Pasadena CA 91106 Office: Los Angeles Music Ctr Opera 135 N Grand Ave Los Angeles CA 90012

HEMPHILL, ALAN POLK, management consultant; b. Montgomery, Ala., Aug. 22, 1933; s. Alan Polk and Elizabeth Evans (Orr) H.; m. Jean Tilden Baker, June 8, 1957; children—Elizabeth, Alan, Laurie. BSEE, U.S. Naval Acad., 1957; MA in Mgmt., Nat. U., 1987. Commd. ensign U.S. Navy, 1957, advanced through grades to lt. comdr., 1977; various assignments, San Diego, 1957-77; mgr. Prestige Properties, Poway Calif., 1977-80; founder Orion Bus. Systems, San Diego, 1980-82; pres., chief exec. officer Sta. KBSC-TV, Glendale, Calif. (sta. received 12 Emmy awards), 1982-83; chmn., bd. dirs. Oak Broadcasting Systems, Glendale, 1983-84; pres. Community Bus. Cons., San Diego, 1984-85; prof. computer sci. Nat. U., Vista, Calif., 1984—; trustee Sta. KBSC-TV Stock of Oak Industries, San Diego, 1982-84; panelist TV series On Edge, 1986—; cons. Oak Industries, San Diego, 1984; bd. dirs. Community Bus. Cons., San Diego, 1984. Contbr. articles and columns to profl. jours., chpts. to books. Gen. mgr. Remember the Pueblo, San Diego, 1968; pres., chmn. bd. Green Valley Civic Assn., Poway, 1974-75; pres., bd. dirs. North County Bd. of Jr. Achievement, 1979. Lodge: Kiwanis (pres. Rancho Bernardo chpt. 1980-81).

HEMPHILL, THOMAS WILSON, financial company executive, consultant; b. Portland, Oreg., Dec. 3, 1930; s. Oliver and Elsie Mae (Baguley) H.; m. Shirley Mae Miller, Nov. 11, 1960; children: Mae, Thomas, Paul. BBA, U. Oreg., 1958. Vice pres. sales Pacific Assocs., Palm Springs, Calif., 1958-62, Continental Mortgage Ins. Co., Madison, Wis., 1962-66; pres. Excel Investment Co., Bettendorf, Iowa, 1966-74; sr. mgmt. advisor Security Pacific Corp., L.A., 1974-75; pres. Thomas W. Hemphill Bus. Cons., Eugene, Oreg., 1976-83, Alpha Health Care, Eugene, 1983-84, Capital One Corp., Eugene, 1985—; cons. W.W. Capital Corp., Dodge City, Kans., 1986—, World Power Co., 1987—; bd. dirs. Pacific Energy Resources Ltd., Eugene, Glen Eden Corp., Eugene. Author: The Ultimate, 1987. Sgt. USAF, 1950-53. Republican. Presbyterian. Office: Capital One Corp 695 Country Club Rd Eugene OR 97401

HEMPHILL, WILLIAM ALFRED, III, marketing executive; b. Pitts., Mar. 3, 1949; s. William Alfred II and Virgie Mae (Fisher) H.; m. Sandra Lynn von Lohen, Feb. 17, 1973; 1 child, Michelle Ellise. BS, USAF Acad., 1972; MBA, Air Force Command and Staff Coll., 1985. Commd. 2d lt. USAF, 1972, advanced through grades to capt., 1976; B-52 radar navigator SAC USAF, Blytheville AFB, Ark., 1974-77; bomb radar navigator SAC USAF, Rapid City, S.D., 1977-79; resigned USAF, 1979; maj. USAFR, 1988; mktg. rep. Sperry Def. Systems, Phoenix, 1979-82, Sperry Space Div., Phoenix, 1982-83; product devel. mgr. Motorola Govt. Electronics Group, Tempe, Ariz., 1983-84; mktg. dir. Conrac SCD Div., Duarte, Calif., 1984-88; cons. Upland, Calif., 1988; nat. sales mgr. TEAC Am., Inc., Montebello, Calif., 1989—. Author: (with other); A Programmable Display Generator System, 1982. Position paper writer Rep. Nat. Com., 1980; mem. West End Rep. Club, Ontario, Calif.; chairperson St. Mark's Episc. Ch., Upland, Calif., 1988—. Mem. Am. Mgmt. Assn., Tech. Mktg. Soc. Am., Air Force Assn., USAF Acad. Grad. Assn. Episcopalian. Lodge: Elks.

HENAGER, CHARLES HENRY, civil engineer; b. Spokane, Wash., July 11, 1927; s. William Franklin and Mary Agnes (Henry) H.; m. Dorothy Ruth Parker, May 6, 1950; children: Charles Henry, Jr., Donald E., Roberta R. BS in Civil Engring., Wash. State U., 1950. Registered profl. engr., Wash. Instrumentman Wash. State Dept. Hwys., Yakima, 1950-52; engr. Gen. Electric Co., Richland, Wash., 1952-62, shift supr., reactor, 1962-63; sr. engr. Gen. Electric Co., Richland, 1963-65; sr. devel. engr. Battelle, Pacific N.W. Labs., Richland, 1965-68, sr. rsch. engr., 1968—. Contbr. articles to profl. jours.; patentee in field. With USN, 1945-46. Mem. Am. Concrete Inst. (tech. activities com. 1987-89, Del Bloem award 1986), ASTM (subcom. 1980-89), ASCE (pres. Columbia sect. 1961-62), Kennewick Swim Club (pres. 1962-63), Sigma Tau, Tau Beta Pi, Phi Kappa Phi. Republican. Methodist. Home: 1306 N Arthur Pl Kennewick WA 99336 Office: Battelle Pacific NW Labs Battelle Blvd Richland WA 99352

HENCH, PHILIP KAHLER, physician; b. Rochester, Minn., Sept. 19, 1930; s. Philip Showalter and Mary Genevieve (Kahler) H.; m. Barbara Joan Kent, July 10, 1954; children: Philip Gordon, John Kahler, Amanda Kent. BA, Lafayette Coll., 1952; MD, U. Pitts., 1958; MS in Medicine, Mayo Grad. Sch. of Medicine, Rochester, 1965. Intern U. Colorado Med. Ctr., 1958-59; resident, fellow in internal medicine and rheumatology Mayo Graduate Sch. Medicine, Rochester, Minn., 1959-63; asst. mem. Rheumatology div. Scripps Clinic and Research Found., La Jolla, Calif., 1965-66, assoc., 1966-74, head, 1974-82, sr. cons., 1982—; asst. clin. prof. San Diego Sch. Medicine U. Calif., 1973—; adj. asst. mem. Dept. of Basic and Clin. Research, La Jolla, 1987—, mem. dept. acad. affairs; cons. Pharms. Cos., Oradell, N.J., 1987—, Rheumatology Revs., 1974-84, Arthritis and Rheumatology, 1982; participating mem. People to People Mission to China on Study of Aging, 1982; guest investigator Nat. Inst. for Arthritis and Metabolic Diseases NIH, Bethesda, Md., 1963-64; asst. mem. div. rheumatology Scripps Clinic & Research Found., 1965-66, assoc. mem. 1966-74. Bd. editors Patient CARE mag., 1987—; editorial com. Rheumatism Revs., 1974-84; editorial reviewer arthritis and rheumatism Jour. Rheumatology, 1985—; contbr. 73 articles on rheumatic diseases, pain and sleep disorders to profl. jours. Mem. Arthritis Found., San Diego Hist. Soc., 1970, San Diego Mus. of Fine Arts, 1970, San Diego Opera Assn., 1970. P.S. Hench scholar Mayo Grad. Sch. of Medicine, 1965; recipient Arthritis Found. award (6), San Diego, 1971-80. Fellow ACP, Am. Rheumatic Assn. (non-articular rheumatic study group com. 1975-82, council on prevention and rehab. medicine 1984-85, com. on rheumatic practice 1975-77); mem. AMA, Am. Pain Soc., San Diego County Med. Soc., Calif. Med. Assn., Nat. Soc. Clin. Rheumatologists. Republican. Home: 7856 La Jolla Vista Dr La Jolla CA

92037 Office: Scripps Clinic & Rsrch Found 10666 N Torrey Pines Rd La Jolla CA 92037

HENDERSON, ARDEN GORDON, electric utility executive; b. Gainesville, Tex., June 22, 1928; s. William Gordon and Bertha Belle (West) H.; m. Melba June Chehak, Nov. 28, 1951 (div. Apr. 1984); children—Garth, Dorothy, Karen; m. Alma K. Cooper, Apr. 23, 1986. B.S. in Elec. Engring., U. Okla., 1951; postgrad. Pepperdine U., 1977, Harvard Advanced Mgmt. Program, 1969. Registered profl. engr., Hawaii. Elec. engr. Bonneville Power Adminstrn., Portland, Oreg., 1951-53, 57-59; distbn./customer engr. Hawaiian Elec. Co., Honolulu, 1960-77; exec. v.p. Maui Electric Co., Kahului, Hawaii, 1977-78, pres., 1978—, also dir. Bd. dirs. Maui Econ. Devel. Bd., Kahului, 1982—; bd. dirs., campaign chmn. Maui United Way, Wailuku, 1983-84, pres., bd. dirs.; mem. exec. bd. Maui council Boy Scouts Am., 1979. Named PSI Exec. of Yr., 1985. Mem. Nat. Soc. Profl. Engrs. (Maui Engr. of Yr. 1984), IEEE of Hawaii, Maui C. of C. (dir. 1982-85), Rotary (pres. Wailuku 1988-89). Republican. Presbyterian. Office: Maui Electric Co Ltd 210 Kamehameha Ave PO Box 398 Kahului HI 96732

HENDERSON, CECELIA ELIZABETH, small business owner, bookseller; b. Los Angeles, Sept. 20, 1956; d. Charles E. Jr. and Marjorie C. (Hewitt) H.; m. James L. Wiedel, Jan. 16, 1982; children: Jacqueline G.H. Wiedel, Christopher J.H. Wiedel, Kathleen A.H. Wiedel. BS in Computer Sci., U. So. Calif., 1977; MEE, Computer Sci., MIT, 1982. Systems programmer U. So. Calif., Los Angeles, 1975-77, supr. programming group, 1979-80, mem. research group, 1981-82, supr. research group, 1982-83; mem. tech. staff Bell Telephone Labs., Naperville, Ill., 1977-79; co-owner, v.p. Carlson Publ. Co., Los Alamitos, Calif., 1983—; owner, operator Blind Moth Books and Drinks, Cypress, Calif., 1987—, also bd. dirs. Editor (newsletter): Sunlite, 1987-88; contbr. articles to profl. jours. Mem. Bus. and Profl. Women U.S.A. (pres. local chpt. 1988-89, editor newsletter 1985-88, Young Careerist award 1986, Best Local Newsletter award 1988), Am. Booksellers Assn., Soc. Women Engrs., Assn. for Computing Machinery, Phi Beta Kappa. Office: Blind Moth Books & Drinks PO Box 1531 Cypress CA 90630-1531

HENDERSON, DONALD WAYNE, cosmetologist; b. Havre, Mont., May 24, 1951; s. Robert Charles and Octa Beverly (Francois) H. Cert., Dahls Beauty Coll., Great Falls, Mont., 1975. Owner, mgr. Penthouse Hair Designers, Great Falls, 1979—; presenter workshops, seminars, tng. sessions. Sgt. U.S. Army, 1968-72, Vietnam. Decorated Silver Star medal. Mem. Paris Gibson Sq. (bd. dirs. 1988—), Great Falls C. of C., Mont. Cosmetologists Assn., Great Falls City Ctr. Assn., Great Falls Leadership Program, Great Falls Ad Club. Office: Penthouse Hair Designers 313 Central Ave Great Falls MT 59401

HENDERSON, HARVEY EARL, JR., lawyer; b. Taylor, Tex., June 10, 1943; s. Harvey Earl and Jean (Bouchier) H.; m. Candace A. Mitchell, June 17, 1967 (div. Feb. 1984); children: Shannon L., Heather E. AA, Menlo Coll., 1963; BA, U. Calif., Berkeley, 1965; JD, U. Calif., San Francisco, 1968. Bar: Calif. 1969, Hawaii 1970, U.S. Dist. Ct. Hawaii 1970, U.S. Ct. Appeals (9th cir.) 1978, U.S. Supreme Ct. 1987. Assoc. Cades, Schutte, Fleming & Wright, Honolulu, 1968-76; pvt. practice Honolulu, 1976-77; ptnr. Lee, Henderson & Wong, Honolulu, 1977—. With USAR, 1968-74. Mem. Hawaii State Bar Assn., State Bar Calif., Def. Research Inst., Nat. Inst. for Trial Advocacy. Democrat. Office: Lee Henderson & Wong 345 Queen St Ste 700 Honolulu HI 96813

HENDERSON, HERBERT BERNARD, physician; b. Charlotte, N.C., June 11, 1911; s. Gad Herbert and Rosa (Thompson) H.; m. Vivian Brown, Apr. 15, 1955 (div. 1962); m. Claire Marguerite Goode, Dec. 31, 1965; children: Edward, Randall, Pamela, Herbert Lewis. AB, Johnson C. Smith U., 1931; MD, Howard U., 1935. Intern Freedman's Hosp., Washington, 1935-36; resident Harlem Hosp., N.Y.C., 1936-37; physician N.Y.C. Dept. Social Hygiene, 1938-41; pvt. practice N.Y.C., 1941, San Francisco, 1947-79; chief dept. medicine Vets. Hosp., Roanoake, Va., 1946-47; physician State of N.Y. Dept. Alcoholism, N.Y.C., 1979-82, Dept. Immigration, Long Beach, Calif., 1987—; physician Long Beach Plasma Ctr., 1983-87. Founder, asst. to dir. Sammy Davis Jr. Nat. Liver Inst. at N.J. Med. Sch. Served to capt. U.S. Army Med. Corps, 1941-46, ETO. Decorated 4 battle stars. Mem. N.J. U. Med. (asst. to med. dir., 1984—, dir.), Alpha Phi Alpha, Mason. Republican. Episcopalian. Home: 600 E Ocean Blvd Long Beach CA 90802 Office: Pacific Med Assocs 434 E Broadway Long Beach CA 90802

HENDERSON, JAMES FRANCIS, SR., fraternal organization administrator; b. LaJunta, Colo., Nov. 15, 1944; s. William F. and Francis (Hill) H.; m. Wanda G. Sizemore, July 7, 1964 (div. July 1971); m. Linda C. Cronk, Aug. 19, 1973; children: James C., Mark A., Terri L., Sandie M., Stephanie, James Jr. Student, Wayne State U., 1961-62. Ops. mgr. I.D.A. Pub. Warehouse, Hamtramck, Mich., 1963-72; collateral mgr. S.L.T. Warehousing, Detroit, 1972-74; gen. supt. Nat. Archtl., Phoenix, 1974-76; regional mgr. Rusco Industries, Sun City, Ariz., 1976-83; adminstr. Lodge #2243 Loyal Order Moose, Glendale, Ariz., 1976-86; adminstr. Lodge #708 Loyal Order Moose, Phoenix, 1986—; apptd. mem. of Mooseheart; mem. Moosehaven Endowment Fund, Chgo. Bd. dirs. Phoenix Better Health, 1983-84. Mem. Ariz./N. Mex. Moose Assn. (Moose of Yr. 1979, pres. 1985-86), Eagles. Presbyterian. Office: Phoenix Moose Lodge #708 4501 E McDowell Rd Phoenix AZ 85008

HENDERSON, JUDY HILL, financial company executive, consultant; b. Yakima, Wash., Mar. 1, 1947; d. Noble Grey and Lois (Van Meter) Hill; m. Stephen John Henderson, Feb. 14, 1970; children: Stephanie Anne, Drew Thomas. BA magna cum laude, U. Wash., 1969, MA cum laude, 1982. Cert. home economist, Wash. Staff clk. U.S. Congress, Washington, 1967; media specialist McCann-Erickson Advt., San Francisco, 1969-70; dir. consumer affairs State of Wash. Dept. Agr., Olympia, 1970-76; media cons. Consumer Product Safey Commn., Olympia, 1976-78; mktg. dir. Capital N.W. Mgmt. Co., Olympia, 1978-82; owner, pres. Capital Fin. Group, Olympia, 1982—. Pres., bd. dirs. Wash. State Food and Nutrition Coun., 1970-76, POSSCA Charity Auction, 1980-88; treas., bd. dirs. Wash. Ctr. for Performing Arts, Olympia, 1982-88, State Capital Mus. Found., 1986—; mem. disciplinary bd. Wash. Collection Agy., 1984-88; bd. dirs. donations com. Puget Sound Nat. Bank, 1988—; mem. bd. trustees St. Peter Hosp. Found., 1988—. Recipient State Young Career Woman award Wash. Bus. and Profl. Women, 1974, Nat. award Consumer Product Safety Commn., 1976, Disting. Citizen award Thurston Kiwanis, 1986; Raitt Meml. scholar U. Wash., 1965-69. Mem. Internat. Assn. Fin. Planning (treas. 1980-83, bd. dirs. 1981-85), Am. Home Econs. Assn. (pres. Wash. chpt. 1976-77), Wash. State Home Econs. Assn. (pres., bd. dirs. 1970-78). Republican. Office: Capital Fin Group 1401 E 4th St Olympia WA 98501

HENDERSON, PATRICIA MCGOVERN, state human rights agency executive; b. Mobile, Ala., Aug. 6, 1940; d. Thomas Joseph and Babe Hope (Lowery) McGovern; children—Thomas Bain III, Patrick Sean. Student, Loretto Coll., Nerinx, Ky., 1958-61; B.A. in Psychology, Hawaii Pacific Coll., 1976; M.A., in Psychology, Antioch U., Honolulu, 1981. Cert. mgmt. Queen's Med. Ctr., 1977; cert. U. Ala. Sch. Medicine, 1979; cert. Neuropsychiat. Inst., UCLA, 1980. Dir., exec. sec. Mission and Youth Office for Catholic Diocese and Charities, Mobile, 1961-64; spl. edn. tchr. Ala. State Dept. Pub. Edn., Mobile, 1966-69; spl. edn. tchr., adminstr., social worker St. Peter Claver Sch. and Ctr., Tampa, Fla., 1970-72; chief adminstr., dir., prin., ednl. dir., social worker Salvation Army Kauluwela Corps, Kula Kokua Therapeutic Sch., Malama Makua Rehab. Ctr., 1973-77; exec. dir., chief exec. officer Protection and Advocacy Agy. of Hawaii and State Client Assistance Agy. of Hawaii, Honolulu, 1977—, pres., 1988—; cons. in field. Author, editor: A Self Advocate-You Have the Right to Speak for Yourself, 1978. Co-author, co-editor The Answer Book for Parents on the Right to Education for the Handicapped Child, 1983. Bd. dirs. State Dept. Health Adv. Com., Honolulu, 1979—, Gov.'s State Planning Council on Developmental Disabilities, 1986—; chmn. human rights com. State Dept. Health, 1982—; co-chmn. Mayor's City and County Transp. for Handicapped/ Elderly Task Force, 1984—. Recipient Disting. Service award Salvation Army, 1977; Keen, Dedicated, Outstanding Profl., Highest Calibre award Salvation Army, 1977; Spl. Contbns. Internat. Yr. of Disabled Persons award State Hawaii and Internat. Yr. Disabled Persons Council, 1981; Promotion and Advancement of Women award Hawaiian Telephone Co., 1984; Disting. American award Am. Biog. Inst., 1985; Quality Advocacy Service award Nat. Assn. Protection and Advocacy Systems, 1987. Mem. Nat. Tourette Syndrome Assn. (exec. dir. 1984—, NW regional dir. 1984—), Nat. Assn. Protection and Advocacy Systems (exec. bd. dirs., officer 1987—), Nat. Client Assistance Orgn. (exec. bd. dirs., officer 1987—). Avocations: travel; theater; music; art collecting; photography. Office: Protection & Advocacy Agy Hawaii 1580 Makaloa St Ste 1060 Honolulu HI 96814

HENDERSON, PAUL, III, journalist, private investigator; b. Washington, Jan. 13, 1939; s. Paul and Doris Olive (Gale) H.; m. JoAnn Burnham, Sept. 10, 1964; children: Leslee, Jill, Polly Ann; m. 2d Janet Marie Horne, Jan. 22, 1982; children: Peter Paul, Brady Thomas. Student Wentworth Mil. Acad. Jr. Coll., Lexington, Mo., 1957-59, Creighton U., 1963, U. Nebr.-Omaha, 1964-67. Reporter Council Bluffs (Iowa) Nonpareil, 1962-66, Omaha World-Herald, 1966-67; investigative reporter Seattle Times, 1967-85; pvt. practice investigator, Seattle, 1985. Co-founder Seattle Forgotten Children's Fund, 1976. Featured investigator in Home Box Office Crime Documentary, 1986. Served with U.S. Army, 1959-62. Recipient 1st Place C.B. Blethen award, 1977, 82, Pulitzer prize for spl. local reporting, 1982, 1st Place Roy W. Howard Pub. Service award Scripps-Howard Found., 1982; named one of 50 Outstanding Achievers Am., Am. Acad. Achievement, 1982. Methodist. Office: PO Box 70 Seattle WA 98111

HENDERSON, PHILLIPS BROOKS, JR., company sales executive; b. Seymour, Ind., June 8, 1944; s. Phillips Brooks and Barbara Florence (Putnam) H.; m. Jane Mary Mulligan, Aug. 5, 1967; children: Jeffrey Phillips, Joshua Peter. Student, U. Vermont, 1964, U. Bristol (Eng.), 1965; BS, Castleton State Coll., 1967. Tchr. Gorham (N.H.) Sch. Dist., 1966-68, Franklin (Mass.) Sch. Dist., 1970-79; asst. prin. Vergennes (Vt.) Sch. Dist., 1968-70; salesman Tech. Aid Corp., Nashua, N.H., 1979-80; mgr. Tech. Aid Corp., Marwick, R.I., 1980-82; br. mgr. EDP Contract Svcs., Sherman Oaks, Calif., 1982-87; nat. sales mgr. Mediscript, Chatsworth, Calif., 1987--. Recipient Distinctive Svc. award Franklin Jaycees, 1975. Mem. Nat. Assn. Tech. Svcs. (com. mem. L.A. 1985-87), Med. Group Mgmt. Assn. (pres. 1988). Republican. Baptist. Home: 79 Larkhill St Thousand Oaks CA 91360

HENDERSON, THELTON EUGENE, federal judge; b. Shreveport, La., Nov. 28, 1933; s. Eugene M. and Wanzie (Roberts) H.; 1 son, Geoffrey A. B.A., U. Calif.-, Berkeley, 1956, J.D., 1962. Bar: Calif. 1962. Atty. U.S. Dept. Justice, 1962-63; assoc. firm FitzSimmons & Petris, 1964, assoc., 1964-66; directing atty. San Mateo County (Calif.) Legal Aid Soc., 1966-69; asst. dean Stanford (Calif.) U. Law Sch., 1968-76; ptnr. firm Rosen, Remcho & Henderson, San Francisco, 1977-80; judge U.S. Dist. Ct. (no. dist.) Calif., San Francisco, 1980—; asso. prof. Sch. Law, Golden Gate U., San Francisco, 1978-80. Served with U.S. Army, 1956-58. Mem. ABA, Nat. Bar Assn., Charles Houston Law Assn. Office: US Dist Ct 450 Golden Gate Ave PO Box 36060 San Francisco CA 94102

HENDERSON, THOMAS JAMES, construction company executive; b. 1931. BS, MS, MIT, 1954. From project mgr. to exec. asst. J.L. Simmons Co., Decatur, Ill., 1958-61; with Guy F. Atkinson Co., South San Francisco, Calif., 1961—, various mgmt. positions, 1961-75, v.p., gen. mgr. Lake Ctr. Industries, 1975-83, sr. v.p., 1983-85, group v.p., 1985-86, exec. v.p., 1986-87, pres., chief oper. officer, 1987-88, pres., chief exec. officer, 1988-89, chmn., pres., chief exec. officer, 1989—, also bd. dirs. Served to Lt. USN, 1955-58. Office: Guy F Atkinson Co Calif 10 W Orange Ave South San Francisco CA 94080

HENDLER, ROSEMARY NIELSEN, business owner; b. Sydney, Australia, Oct. 18, 1946; came to U.S., 1954, naturalized, 1970; d. Robert Stanley McFarlane and Joyce Elizabeth (Annetts) Nielsen; m. Joel Arnold Hendler, June 1, 1977; 1 child, Stewart Maxwell. BA, U. Calif., Berkeley, 1968; postgrad., Acad. Art San Francisco, 1974-76, UCLA, 1985-87. Buyer linens Breuners Home Furnishings, Oakland, Calif., 1969-72, Palo Alto, Calif., 1973-77; buyer textiles Liberty House, San Francisco, 1971-73; graphic artist Montclarion Pubs., Oakland, 1974-76; pres., owner Cordeaux River Trading Co., L.A., 1986—. Bd. dirs. docent coun. L.A. County Mus. Art, 1981—; VIP hostess Olympic Games, L.A., 1984; bd. dirs. Young Audiences, L.A., 1985-87. Recipient Design award Levi Strauss, 1975. Mem. Jr. League L.A., NAFE, Costume Coun., L.A. County Mus. Art. Republican. Presbyterian. Office: Cordeaux River Trading Co 13763 Raywood Ave Los Angeles CA 90049

HENDREN, ROBERT LEE, JR., college president, furniture company executive; b. Reno, Oct. 10, 1925; s. Robert Lee and Aleen (Hill) H.; student U. Idaho, 1943-44, 46-47; BA magna cum laude Coll. Idaho; m. Merlyn Churchill, June 14, 1947; children: Robert Lee IV, Anne Aleen. Pres., Hendren's Furniture Co., Boise, Idaho, 1947-87, Hendren's Inc., 1988—; pres. Coll. Idaho, Caldwell, 1988—; dir. Shore Club Lodge, Inc., 1st Interstate Bank Idaho., Blue Cross of Idaho. Trustee Boise Ind. Sch. Dist.; charter dir. Boise Valley Indsl. Found.; chmn. bd. trustees Coll. of Idaho; dir. Idaho Blue Cross; mem. Boise Redevel. Agy., Ada County Marriage Counseling, Ada County Planning and Zoning, Boise Area Econ. Devel. Council, Mountain View Council Boy Scouts Am., Southwest Idaho Multiple Sclerosis Assn. Mem. Boise Retail Mchts. (chmn.), Boise C. of C. (pres., dir.), Am. Inst. Interior Designers, Idaho Sch. Trustees Assn., Arid Club, Hillcrest Country Club, Masons, K.T., Shriner, Rotary. Home: 3504 Hillcrest Dr Boise ID 83705 Office: The Coll of Idaho Caldwell ID 83605-9990

HENDRICKS, CHARLES DURRELL, JR., nuclear engineering educator; b. Lewiston, Utah, Dec. 5, 1926; s. Charles Durrell and Louise (McAlister) H.; m. Leah Funk, Mar. 4, 1948; children—Katherine, Martha Jane. B.S., Utah State U., 1949; M.S., U. Wis., 1951; Ph.D., U. Utah, 1955. Research asst. U. Utah, 1953-55; staff mem. Lincoln Lab., Mass. Inst. Tech., 1955-56; faculty U. Ill. at Urbana, 1956—, prof. dept. elec. engring., 1961-79, prof. nuclear engring., 1965-79, prof. emeritus, 1979—, also dir. charged particle research lab., 1964-79; asso. program leader for fusion target fabrication U. Calif. Lawrence Livermore Nat. Lab., 1974-82, sr. scientist, 1982—; vis. prof. Mass. Inst. Tech., 1967-68; sr. research fellow U. Southampton, Eng., 1971-72; editor Blaisdell Pub. Co.; cons. indsl. firms.; vis. research fellow U. Tokyo, 1985. Fellow AAAS, Am. Phys. Soc., Am. Inst. Aeros. and Astronautics (asso.), IEEE; mem. Am. Assn. Physics Tchrs., Electrostatics Soc. Am. (exec. council 1970—), Phi Beta Kappa, Sigma Xi, Tau Beta Pi, Phi Kappa Phi, Eta Kappa Nu. Mormon. Home: 2817 Pardee Pl Livermore CA 94550

HENDRICKS, DAVID WARREN, civil engineering educator; b. Springfield, Mo., Sept. 10, 1931; s. E. Warren and Helen D. (Hardison) H.; m. Betty Ann Omo, June 24, 1959; children: Bridgette, Philip, Sara,. BS in Civil Engring., U. Calif., Berkeley, 1954; MS in Irrigation Engring., Utah State U., 1960; PhD in San. Engring., U. Iowa, 1965. Registered profl. engr., Colo.; diplomate Am. Acad. Environ. Engrs. Jr. civil engr. Calif. Dept. Water Resources, Sacramento, 1954; rsch. asst. Utah State U., Logan, 1956-57, assoc. prof. civil engring., 1966-70; asst. prof. civil engring. U. Idaho, Moscow, 1958-61; research asst. U. Iowa, Iowa City, 1961-65; prof. civil engring. Colo. State U., Ft. Collins, 1970—; cons. on water supply and pollution control to pvt. cons. firms and govtl. orgns., U.S., Brazil, Venezuela, Mex., Can., Italy, Saudi Arabia, 1967--; Fulbright-Hays sr. lectr. Istanbul Tech. U. 1986-87. Co-author: Technology Assessment for Water Supplies, 1977, Operation of Complex Water Systems, 1983; editor: Environment Design for Public Projects, 1974; contbr. numerous articles to profl. jours. With U.S. Army, 1955-56. Grantee NSF, USPHS, EPA, C.E., 1966--; NATO sr. scientist fellow, Italy, 1978. Fellow ASCE; mem. Am. Water Works Assn. (best paper resources div. award 1983), Rocky Mountain Water Pollution Control Assn., Am. Inst. Chem. Engrs., Assn. Environ. Engring. Profs., Internat. Assn. Water Pollution Research and Control (U.S.nat. com. 1982--). Presbyterian. Office: Colo State U Dept Civil Engring Fort Collins CO 80525

HENDRICKS, FANNY See FANNY-DELL

HENDRICKS, KATHERINE, lawyer; b. Logan, Utah, Apr. 12, 1949; d. Charles Durrell and Leah Grace (Funk) H.; m. O. Yale Lewis, Jr., Sept. 7, 1985. BS, MS, MIT, 1972; JD, Boston U., 1975. Bar: Mass. 1976, Colo. 1982, Wash. 1984, U.S. Dist. Ct. Mass. 1979, U.S. Dist. Ct. (no. dist.) N.Y., U.S. Dist. Ct. Colo., U.S. Dist. Ct. Wash., U.S. Ct. Appeals (1st cir.), 1978, U.S. Ct. Appeals (9th cir.), 1984. Assoc. Palmer & Dodge, Boston, 1975-81, Garfield & Hecht, Aspen, Colo., 1981-84, Wickwire, Lewis, Goldmark & Schorr, Seattle, 1984-86; ptnr. Hendricks & Lewis, Seattle, 1986—; mem. panel arbitrators Mandatory Arbitration Program of King County. Fellow Delta Gamma Found.; mem. ABA, Wash. Bar Assn. (interprofl. com.), Wash. Vol. Lawyers Arts (dir. 1988—), MIT Enterprise Forum of N.W. (dir. 1988—), Seattle-King County Bar Assn. Office: Hendricks & Lewis 2675 First Interstate Ctr Seattle WA 98104

HENDRICKS, MARILYN LOUISE, small business owner; b. Juneau, Alaska, Feb. 24, 1952; d. Tarleton Friend and Doris Jean (Gregg) Smith; m. John Leland Hendricks, Mar. 28, 1970; 1 child, Debbie Pruett. Student, Griffin Bus. Coll., Seattle, 1969-70, Midway Adult Sch., San Diego, 1970-71, Bellingham (Wash.) Vocat. Tech. Inst., 1977. Circulation mgr. La Jolla (Calif.) Light Newspaper, 1972-74; sec., receptionist The Petersburg (Alaska) City Manager, 1976; owner Northwest Off-Road Specialties, Inc., Bellingham, 1978—; coordinator Toyota Jamboree, British Columbia. Republican. Office: NW Off-Rd Specialties 1999 Iowa St Bellingham WA 98226

HENDRICKS-ANDRUS, DIANE MARIE, data communications executive; b. Long Beach, Calif., Mar. 20, 1953; d. Norman Lee and Joyce (Best) Hendricks; m. Charles Hartley Marsden, Mar. 2, 1981 (div. 1982); m. Ursel Paul Andrus, Dec. 28, 1985; 1 child, Kevin Maurice. A Computer Sci., Long Beach City Coll., 1981. Supr. western div. computer ops. Healthcare Svcs., Torrance, Calif., 1981-83; data communications, computer operator Drexel Burnham Lambert, Beverly Hills, Calif., 1983--. Mem. So. Calif. Users Micom (sec. 1986--). Republican. Roman Catholic. Home: 15710 Ada St Santa Clarita CA 91351-1890

HENDRICKSON, CHARLES MICHAEL, mechanical engineer; b. Longview, Wash., June 7, 1945; s. Toivo Ilmer and Viola Irja (Linder) H.; m. Carol Ann Mench, Nov. 1969 (div. May, 1984). AA, Clark Coll., 1966. Clk. Boehm's Grocery, Amboy, Wash., 1960-65; attendent Al's Service Station, Vancouver, Wash, 1963-66; chief engr. P&G Mfg., Lake Oswego, Oreg., 1966-68; product mgr. Columbia Steel Casting Co., Portland, Oreg., 1968—. Patentee in field. Mem. Slo-Poks Club. Republican. Home: 2607 NE Whitman Ave Vancouver WA 98662 Office: Columbia Steel Casting Co. 10425 N Bloss Ave Portland OR 97203

HENDRICKSON, ELIZABETH ANN, teacher; b. Bismarck, S.D., Oct. 21, 1936; d. William Earl and Hilda E. (Sauter) Hinkel; m. Roger G. Hendrickson, Apr. 18, 1960; 1 child, Wade William. BA, Jamestown Coll., 1958; postgrad., U. Calif., Davis, 1962, Calif. State U., Sacramento, 1964, U. San Diego, 1985-88, Ottawa U., 1986-88. Cert. tchr., Calif. Tchr. Napoleon (N.D.) High Sch., 1958-59, Kulm (N.D.) High Sch., 1959-61, Del Paso Jr. High Sch., Sacramento, 1961, Mills Jr. High Sch., Rancho Cordova, Calif., 1961—. Mem. NEA, AAUW, Calif. Assn. for Gifted, Calif. Edn. Assn., Sacramento Area Gifted Assn., Soroptimists (news editor Rancho Cordova club 1985, sec. 1986). Democrat. Lutheran. Home: 2032 Kellogg Way Rancho Cordova CA 95670

HENDRICKSON, JEROME ORLAND, trade association executive, lawyer; b. Eau Claire, Wis., July 25, 1918; s. Harold and Clara (Halverson) H.; student Wis. State Coll., 1936-39; J.D., U. Wis., 1942; m. Helen Phoebe Harty, Dec. 27, 1948 (dec. Oct. 1988); children—Jaime Ann, Jerome Orland. Bar: Wis., 1942, U.S. Supreme Ct., 1955; sole practice, Eau Claire, 1946; sales and advt. mgr. Eau Claire Coca-Cola Bottling Co., Inc., 1947-48; exec. sec. Eau Claire Community Chest, 1948-49; in charge dist. office Am. Petroleum Inst., Kansas City, Mo., 1950-53, Chgo., 1953-55; exec. dir. Nat. Assn. Plumbing-Heating-Cooling Contractors, 1955-64; sec. Joint Apprentice Text, Inc., 1955-64; exec. v.p. Cast Iron Soil Pipe Inst., Washington, 1964-74; pres. Valve Mfrs. Assn., McLean, Va., 1975-80; exec. v.p. Plumbing and Piping Industry Council, Inc., 1981—. Treas., Wis. Community Chest, 1948-49. Treas., All-Industry Plumbing & Heating Modernization Com., 1956-57; co-sec. Joint Industry Program Com., 1958-64. Served to lt. USNR, 1943-46. Mem. ABA, Wis. Bar Assn.,, Am. Soc. Assn. Execs., Washington Soc. Assn. Execs., Wis. State Soc. Washington (pres. 1966-68), Nat. Conf. Plumbing-Heating-Cooling Industry (chmn. 1967-69), NAM, U. Wis. Alumni Assn., U. Wis. Law Sch. Alumni Assn. Washington (pres. 1970-74), C. of C. of U.S., Gamma Eta Gamma (pres. Upsilon chpt. 1941-42). Episcopalian. Mason (32 deg., Shriner). Clubs: Washington Golf and Country, Internat. (Washington). Home: 4621 N 33d St Arlington VA 22207 Office: Plumbing and Piping Industry Coun 501 Shatto Pl Ste 405 Los Angeles CA 90020

HENDRICKSON, JOHN FREDERICK, real estate associate, business owner; b. Plainview, Minn., Aug. 3, 1925; s. Clarence A. and Hilda C. (Heaser) H.; m. Patricia Ann Almeter, Aug. 11, 1949; children: JoAnn, David, Jill, Mary, Susan. BS, Winona (Minn.) State Coll., 1949. Crown ambassador Amway Corp., Orange, Calif., 1965—. Served U.S. Army AC, 1944-45. Mem. SE Bd. Realtors (pres. 1960), Winona C. of C. (bd. dirs.). Republican. Roman Catholic. Club: Exchange. Home: 10041 Sycamore Villa Park CA 92667

HENDRIX, JAMES LEE, physicist, consultant; b. Lompoc, Calif., May 10, 1961; s. James Herman and Ruby Jo (Seals) H.; m. Terri Anne Marie May, Apr. 26, 1983; 1 child, James Thomas V. BS in Physics, U. So. Calif., Los Angeles, 1983. Devel. engr., staff physicist, tech. supr. Apollo Lasers Inc. Allied, Chattsworth, Calif., 1982-84; tech. supr. Hughes Aircraft Co., El Segundo, Calif., 1984—; cons. Santa Barbara (Calif.) Research Ctr., 1984—, Hughes Missile Systems Group, Canoga Park, Calif., 1984—, Hughes Indsl. Products Div., Carlsbad, Calif., 1984—, Computer Solutions, Northridge, Calif., 1988—. Author and editor: LFU Laser Transmitter Module Design, 1988; contbr. articles to profl. jours.; patentee in field. Mem. Am. Phys. Soc., IEEE, Soc. Photo-Optical Instrumentation Engrs., Calif. Scholarship Fedn. Home: 18432 Lemarsh St 56 Northridge CA 91325 Office: Hughes Aircraft Co PO Box 902 El Segundo CA 90245

HENDRIX, LOUISE BUTTS, teacher, author; b. Portland, Tenn., June 16, 1911; d. Luther Edward and Johnny Henrietta (McNeill) B.; m. Edwin Alonzo Hendrix, Sr., Aug. 1, 1934; children: Lynette Louise, Edwin Alonzo. AB, Chico (Calif.) State Coll., 1932; postgrad., Sacramento State U., 1934-62, Coll. Pacific, 1934-62; Diploma of merit, U Delle Arti, Parma, Italy, 1982. Tchr. jr. high sch. Rio Vista, Calif., 1932-34; newspaper worker Chico Enterprise, 1930-32; tchr. jr. high sch. Alpaugh, Calif., 1944-45; newspaper corr. Sacramento Bee, Marysville Appeal Dem., Live Oak, Calif., 1945-52, Oroville Mercury Register Marysville Appeal Dem., Biggs, Calif., 1935-40; tchr. jr. high sch. Live Oak, 1952-69. Author: Better Reading and Writing of Journalism, 1974; Sutter Buttes--Land of Histum Yani, 1980, revised edit., 1987, Petals and Blossoms, 1983, Squaw Man, 1987; contbr. poetry to profl. jours. Mem. Sutter County Parks and Recreation Commn., Yuba City, 1977-80; founder Save Sutter Buttes Assn., Inc., Yuba City, 1978, sec., treas., 1978—,. Recipient Poet of Yr. award World Congress Poets, Orlando, Fla., 1986, Gold Poet award World of Poetry Conv., Anaheim, Calif., 1988. Fellow Internat. Poetry Soc.; mem. AAUW, Calif. Retired Tchrs. Assn., Sierra Club (Conservationist of Yr. 1974), Woman's Club (pres. Yuba City chpt. 1978-79). Democrat. Roman Catholic. Home: 1354 Geneva Ave Yuba City CA 95991

HENEGHAN, JOHN JAMES, geotechnical engineer; b. Warrington, Eng., Oct. 11, 1940; came to U.S., 1951; s. Thomas and Jessie (Duckworth) H.; m. Marie Theresa Feltes, June 27, 1964; children: Sean, Kevin, Brian. BCE, Ill. Inst. Tech., 1963. Registered profl. engr., Calif., Hawaii, Oreg., Wash., Minn., Idaho. Civil engr. Glendale (Calif.) Rocketdyne, 1963-66; assoc. engr. Calif. Div. Safety of Dams, L.A., 1966-70; mgr., project engr. Geolabs, Inc., L.A., 1970-74; sr. project engr. R.M. Hardy & Assocs., Bernaby, B.C., Can., 1974-76; v.p. Wahler Assocs., Palo Alto, 1976--, sec., treas., 1983--; sec., treas. Unitech Soils, Inc., Palo Alto, 1985--. Fellow ASCE; mem. Calif. Geotech. Engrs. Assn. (past pres.), Can. Geotech. Soc., Internat. Soc. Soil Mechanics and Found. Engring., U.S. Commn. Large Dams, Soil and Found. Engrs. Assn. Calif. (pres. 1982-830), Irish Social, Rotary. Home: 1789 Los Gatos Almaden Rd San Jose CA 95124

HENKE, ANA MARI, education educator; b. Albuquerque, Apr. 21, 1954; d. David Ernest and Mary Anne (Gallegos) Sanchez; m. Michael John

Henke, Aug. 14, 1976; children: Kristin Mari, Michelle Lee. BA in Spl. Edn., U. N.Mex., 1976, MA in Spl. Edn., 1983. Cert. elem. and secondary spl. edn. tchr., N.Mex.; cert. elem. and secondary phys. edn. tchr., N.Mex.; cert. elem. and secondary behavior disorder tchr., N.Mex. Tchr., supr. Perceptual Motor Learning Sch. U. N.Mex., Albuquerque, 1976, 82, tchr. phys. edn., 1980-82; tchr. phys. edn. Nat. Youth Sports Program, Albuquerque and San Diego, 1976-82; tchr. multihandicapped Chula Vista (Calif.) Pub. Schs., 1976-77; tchr. adaptive phys. edn. San Diego City Schs., 1977-78; lab asst. Presbyn. Hosp., Albuquerque, 1979-80; tchr. Hermosa Jr. High Sch., Farmington, N.Mex., 1983-85, Heights Jr. High Sch., Farmington, 1985—; in-service exercise therapist Four Corners Regional Ednl. Conf., Farmington, 1985-86; supr. parents workshop Intervention/awareness for Subtance Abuse, Heights Jr. High Sch., 1985-86; instr. workshop Farmington Schs., 1986; active nat. youth sports program Leaders Are in Demand, NCAA-U. N.Mex., 1989; active programs Bldg. Self Esteem by Taking Risks-AWAREL, 1989, Leadership/Self-Esteem Multicultural Settings. Mem. new educator support program, 1988. Named Young Career Woman of San Juan County Nat. Fedn. Bus. & Profl. Women, 1988-89. Mem. Phi Delta Kappa (sec. 1987—, v.p. 1988—). Republican. Roman Catholic. Home: 4406 N Dustin Ave Farmington NM 87401

HENLEY, ERNEST MARK, physics educator, former university dean; b. Frankfurt, Germany, June 10, 1924; came to U.S., 1939, naturalized, 1944; s. Fred S. and Josy (Dreyfuss) H.; m. Elaine Dimitman, Aug. 21, 1948; children: M. Bradford, Karen M. B.E.E., CCNY, 1944; Ph.D., U. Calif. at Berkeley, 1952. Physicist Lawrence Radiation Lab., 1950-51; research assoc. physics dept. Stanford U., 1951-52; lectr. physics Columbia U., 1952-54; mem. faculty U. Wash., Seattle, 1954—; prof. physics U. Wash., 1961—, chmn. dept., 1973-76, dean Coll. Arts and Scis., 1979-87; researcher and author numerous publs. on symmetries, nuclear reactions, weak interactions and high energy particle interactions; bd. dirs. Associated Univs. , Inc.; chmn. Nuclear Sci. Adv. Com., 1986-89. Author: (with W. Thirring) Elementary Quantum Field Theory, 1962, (with H. Frauenfelder) Subatomic Physics, 1974, Nuclear and Particle Physics, 1975. Bd. dirs. Pacific Sci. Ctr., 1984-87, Wash. Tech. Ctr., 1983-87. Recipient sr. Alexander von Humboldt award, 1984, T.W. Bonner prize Am. Physics Soc., 1989; F.B. Jewett fellow, 1952-53; NSF sr. fellow, 1958-59; Guggenheim fellow, 1967-68; NATO sr. fellow, 1976-77. Fellow Am. Phys. Soc. (chmn. div. nuclear physics 1979-80), AAAS (chmn. physics sect. 1989); mem. Nat. Acad. Scis., Sigma Xi. Office: U Wash Physics Dept FM 15 Seattle WA 98195

HENLEY, PRESTON VANFLEET, former banker, financial consultant; b. Fort Madison, Iowa, July 7, 1913; s. Jesse vanFleet and Ruth (Roberts) H.; m. Elizabeth Artis Watts, Mar. 31, 1940 (div. June 1956); children: Preston Edward VanFleet, Stephen Watts, John vanFleet; m. 2d, Helena Margaret Greenslade, Nov. 29, 1964; 1 adopted son, Lawrence D. Student Tulane U., 1931-34, Loyola U., New Orleans, 1935-36; A.B., Calif. State Coll. at Santa Barbara, 1939; postgrad. U. Wash., 1939-40, N.Y. U., 1943, 46. Teaching fellow U. Wash., 1939-40; sr. credit analyst, head credit dept. Chase Nat. Bank, 45th St. br. N.Y.C., 1942-49; Western sales rep. Devoe & Raynolds, Inc., N.Y.C., 1949-51; v.p., comml. loan officer, mgr. credit dept. U.S. Nat. Bank, Portland, Oreg., 1951-72; loan adminstr. Voyageur Bank Group, Eau Claire, Wis.; v.p. Kanabec State Bank, Mora, Minn., Montgomery State Bank (Minn.), Park Falls State Bank (Wis.), Montello State Bank (Wis.), 1972; v.p., mgr. main office, sr. credit officer So. Nev. region Nev. Nat. Bank, Las Vegas, 1973-75; bus. and fin. cons., 1975—; loan cons. Continental Nat. Bank, Las Vegas, 1983—; instr. Am. Inst. Banking, Portland, 1952-65, Multomah Coll., Portland, 1956-62, Portland State U., 1961-72, Mt. Hood Community Coll., 1971-72, Clark County Community Coll., 1979-83; adv. dir. Vita Plus, Inc., 1979-83; exec. dir. Nev. Minority Purchasing Council, 1979-80; dir., treas. Consumer Credit Counselling Service of Oreg. 1965-72. Treas., Ore. chpt. Leukemia Soc., 1965-66; mem. Menninger Found. 1965-67; trustee, exec. com. St. Rose delima Hosp. Found., 1982-87;dir. So. Nev. chtp. Assn. Part-Time Profls., 1985-87. Served with USNR, 1943-45. Mem. Oreg. Bankers Assn., Robert Morris Assos. (pres. Oreg. chpt. 1959-60, nat. dir. 1961-64), Nat., Oreg. assns. credit mgmt., Credit Research Found., Inst. Internal Auditors, S.A.R., Am. Legion, Navy League, Beta Mu, Leaf and Scarab, Alpha Phi Omega, Portland C. of C., Oreg. Retail Council. Republican. Episcopalian. Mason (32 deg., Shriner), Elk. Club: International. Contbr. articles to profl. jours. Home and Office: 4235 Gibraltar St Las Vegas NV 89121

HENLEY, WILLIAM BALLENTINE, lawyer, rancher; b. Cin., Sept. 19, 1905; s. William Herbert and May G. (Richards) Ballentine (later assumed name of stepfather, Charles E. Henley); m. Helen McTaggart, 1942. A.B., U. So. Calif., 1928; postgrad., Sch. Religion, 1928-29, Yale, 1929-30; M.A., U. So. Calif., 1930, J.D., 1933, M.S. in P.A, 1935; LL.D., Willamette U., 1937; Sc.D., Kansas City Coll. Osteopathy and Surgery, 1949; R.Sc.D., Inst. Religious Sci. and Philosophy, 1949; L.H.D. Los Angeles Coll. Optometry, 1958; Sc.D., Pepperdine Coll., 1966. Lectr. pub. adminstrn., asst. to coordination officer U. So. Calif., 1928-29; dir. religious edn. First Meth. Ch., New Haven, 1929-30; lectr. in pub. adminstrn. U. So. Calif., 1930-33; exec. sec. U. So. Calif. (Women's Civic Conf.), 1930-40; acting dean U. So. Calif. (Sch. of Govt.), 1937-38; dir. U. So. Calif. (8th and 9th Inst. Govt.), 1937-38; asst. to dean U. So. Calif. (Sch. Govt., in charge in-service tng., Civic Center), 1934-36, asst. prof. pub. adminstrn., 1935-39, asso. prof., 1939-40, dir. co-ordination, 1938-40; pub. speaking instr. and debate coach Am. Inst. Banking, 1928-40; pres. Calif. Coll. Medicine, Los Angeles, 1940-66, Coll. Osteopathic Surgeons, 1940-66; provost U. Calif. at Irvine-Calif. Coll. Medicine, 1966-69; pres., chmn. bd. trustees United Ch. Religious Sci., 1969—; prof. United Ch. Religious Sci. (Sch. Ministry), 1972—; exec., speakers' panel Gen. Motors Corp., 1956-75. Author: The History of the University of Southern California, 1940, Man's Great Awakening, or Beautiful Mud, 1974, also mag. articles. Bd. dirs. Glendale Community Hosp., Glendale Adventist Med. Center, 1978-85; mem. Bd. Water and Power Commrs., Los Angeles, 1944-62, pres., 1946, v.p., 57-58; mem. Employees' Pension and Retirement Bd. Mgmt, 1946; mem. adv. bd. Los Angeles County Gen. Hosp., 1940-65; v.p. Los Angeles County Safety Council, 1971—; mem. Los Angeles Def. Council, 1941-44, War Council, 1944-45, Calif. Civil Def. Com.; guest observer UN Conf., San Francisco, 1945, A.T. Still Meml. lectr., Washington, 1958. Mem. Am., Calif., Los Angeles bar assns., NEA, Am. Pub. Health Assn., AAAS, Am. Saddle Horse Breeding Futurity Assn. (dir.), Am. Aberdeen Angus Breeders Assn., Sigma Alpha Epsilon, Phi Delta Phi, Phi Kappa Phi, Phi Sigma Gamma, Sigma Sigma Phi, Delta Sigma Rho, Phi Delta Kappa, Pi Sigma Alpha, Alpha Delta Sigma, Phi Eta Sigma, Sigma Sigma, Skull and Dagger. Republican. Clubs: Mason (32 deg.), Los Angeles Rotary (pres. 1955-56, chmn. conf. dist. 160-A, gov. dist. 528 1959-60, mem. internat. community service consultative group, chmn. host club exec. com. for 1962 internat. conv., mem. world community service com.). Home and Office: Creston Circle Ranch Paso Robles CA 93446

HENNEMAN, STEPHEN CHARLES, air force officer; b. Chgo., June 17, 1949; s. Charles Philip and Charlotte Smiley (Hitchcock) H.; m. Patrica Ann York, Feb. 14, 1975 (div. Sept. 1980); 1 child Charles Philip III; m. Marion Jean McDermand, Oct. 4, 1980; stepchildren: Ervin F. Schrock Jr., Lisa Ann Schrock, Thomas M. Schrock. BA in Journalism, Colo. State U., 1971; MA in Counseling, U. N.D., 1987. Commd. 2d lt. USAF, 1971, advanced through grades to maj., 1984; missile launch officer 570th Strategic Missile Squadron, Davis Monthan AFB, Ariz., 1972-76; info. officer 321st Strategic Missile Wing, Grand Forks AFB, N.D., 1976-79; missile combat crew flight comdr. 446th Strategic Missile Squadron, Grand Forks AFB, 1980-82; missile combat crew comdr. evaluator 321st Strategic Missile Wing, Grand Forks AFB, 1982, wing nuclear surety officer, 1982-83, chief weapon safety branch, 1983-85; asst. ops. officer 320th Strategic Missile Squadron, F E Warren AFB, Wyo., 1985-86; dep. wing inspector 90th Strategic Missile Wing, F E Warren AFB, 1986-88; ops. officer 319th Strategic Missile Squadron, F E Warren AFB, 1988—. Advocate, counselor Safehouse/Sexual Assault Svcs., Inc., Cheyenne, 1985-89. Mem. Newcomen Soc. Am., Air Force Assn., Nat. Coalition Against Domestic Violence, Nat. Coalition Against Sexual Assault, USAF Officers Club. Office: 319th Strategic Missile Squadron F E Warren AFB WY 82005

HENNES, JOHN PETER, aerospace scientist; b. Seattle, Apr. 27, 1933; s. Albert Frank and Elma (Hawkins) H.; m. Judith Mosler, June 22, 1958 (div. July 1977); children: Scott Norman, Lisa Beth; m. Margaret Lahde, Apr. 15, 1989. BS in Physics, U. Wash, 1955, MS in Physics, 1957; postgrad., U. Md., 1956-59. Materials scientist Nat. Bur. Standards, Washington, 1956-57; research asst. physics dept. U. Md., College Park, 1957-59; aerospace scientist Goddard Space Flight Ctr., NASA, Greenbelt, Md., 1959-65; space scientist Boeing Aerospace Co., Seattle, 1965—. Contbr. articles to profl. sci. jours. Bd. mem. Cen. Area Sch. Council, Seattle, 1968-71; precinct com. mem. King County Dems., Seattle, 1968-72; bd. dirs. Seattle Marathon Assn., 1981-85. Mem. AAAS, Optical Soc. Am., Planetary Soc., Seattle Profl. Engring. Employees Assn. Democrat. Home: 1412 N 52d St Seattle WA 98103 Office: Boeing Aerospace Co M/S 8A-24 PO Box 3999 Seattle WA 98124

HENNIGAN, MICKEY LEE, restaurateur; b. Hayward, Calif., Apr. 28, 1943; s. Charles Leslie Hennigan and Aloha Etta (Cox) Smith; m. Shannon Herring, Mar. 10, 1962 (div. 1970); m. Karen Sui Lan Lau, July 19, 1980; 1 child, Sean Michael. Grad. high sch., Sutter Creek, Calif. Waiter, capt. Nick's Fishmarket, Honolulu, 1969-72; waiter Mama's Fish House, Kuau, Hawaii, 1972-73, mgr., 1978-80; mgr. dining rm. Silver Sword Inn, Kula, Hawaii, 1973-74; mgr. restaurant Anchor Cove, Kihei, Hawaii, 1974-76; asst. mgr. Kihei (Hawaii) Village Fish House, 1976-78; ptnr., mgr. Island Fish House, Kihei, 1981-88; owner, mgr. Mickey's Restaurant, Kahului, Hawaii, 1988—. With U.S. Army, 1960-61. Mem. Valley Isle Vintage Car Club (founder). Home: 420 Mopua St Haiku HI 96708 Office: Mickey's Restaurant 33 Lono Ave Kahului HI 96732

HENNING, DAN, professional football coach; b. Bronx, June 21, 1942; m. Sandy Henning; children: Mary, Patty, Terry, Donny, Mike. Student, Coll. William and Mary. Player San Diego Chargers, 1964-67, head coach, 1989—; asst. coach Homer L. Ferguson High Sch., Newport News, Va., 1967, Fla. State U., Tallahassee, 1968-70, 74, Va. Tech. U., 1971, 73, Houston Oilers, NFL, 1972, N.Y. Jets, 1976-78, Miami (Fla.) Dolphins, 1979-80, Washington Redskins, 1981-82, 87; head coach Atlanta Falcons, 1983-86. Office: San Diego Chargers Jack Murphy Stadium PO Box 20666 San Diego CA 92120 *

HENNINGS, HELEN AGNES, choreographer, educator; b. Jersey City, July 17, 1925; d. King George and Gertrude C. (McNaney) MacIlwraith; m. Roy Hennings, May 18, 1946; children: Donna J. Hennings Lee, Claire H. Hennings Dayton. Grad. high sch., Jersey City. Med. sec. Pathologists Community Hosp., Boulder, Colo., 1974--; dance instr. Armary Park Sr. Ctr., Tucson, 1985--, Green Valley (Ariz.)Recreation Dept., 1987--. Bd. dirs. Tucson Met. Ballet Co., 1979-84; bd. dirs. Tucson Met. Dance Co., 1987--, sec., 1984-85; bd. dirs. Tucson Zool. Soc., 1987--, sec., 1988--; trainer, leader Saguaro council Girl Scouts U.S., 1978--; tchr. handicapped, Gump Sch., Tucson, 1986. Recipient Civics award, City of Tucson, Vol. Hosp. award Vassar Bros. Hosp., Poughkeepsie, N.J., Community Hosp., Boulder. Mem. Cert. Dance Masters Am., Newcomers Club Tucson. Democrat. Roman Catholic. Home: 7149 E River Canyon Circle Tucson AZ 85715

HENNINGSEN, WALTER FREDERICK, medical company executive; b. Portland, Oreg., Aug. 14, 1933; s. Walter Frederick and Amy (Gard) H.; m. Sally Jan Hoy, Apr. 12, 1958; children: Sandra Anne, Linda Marie. BS, U. Oreg.; Hosp. Adminstrn. Degree, Gunter USAF, Montgomery, Ala., 1957. Asst. hosp. adminstr. U.S. Air Force, Fairchild, Wash., 1957-60; sales rep. Parke Davis, Portland, 1960-62, Schemerhoen Bros., Portland, 1962-64; sales rep., brand mgr. Continental Cordage, San Francisco, 1964-65; sales rep., dist. mgr. Convertors, Portland, 1965-88; chief exec. officer Henningsen & Assocs., Tigard, Oreg., 1972—, Tri-Med Corp., Tigard, 1979—. Author: Surgical Draping with Non-Wovens, 1968; contbr. articles to profl. jours. Capt. USAF, 1956-60. Knighted Illustrious Order of the Medusa, Province, France, 1987; named in book dedication The Am. Legal Environment, 1986. Mem. Health Ind. Mfrs. Reps. (pres., bd. dirs. 1979-87), Lions (charter pres. 1963), Royal Rosarian. Republican. Roman Catholic. Office: Tri-Med Corp 9382 SW Tigard Ave Tigard OR 97223

HENNRICH, CARL P., insurance executive; b. Rochester, N.Y., Sept. 23, 1947; s. Warren Carl and Nancy Elizabeth (Potter) H.; m. Secret B. Nelson, May 30, 1970 (div. 1979); children: Stacy N., Nicole J.; m. Alice Nei Wen Kuo, Oct. 27, 1984; 1 child, Emily Jade. BA, Claremont McKenna Coll., Calif., 1969. CPCU. Wide receiver Buffalo Bills, 1974; pres. Carl H. Hennrich, Inc., Rochester, 1970-79; v.p. Frank B. Hall & Co., Inc., Honolulu, 197-83, Rollins Burdick Hunter, Inc., Honolulu, 1983-88; v.p., sr. account exec. John H. Connors, Inc., Honolulu, 1988—. With U.S. Army, 1970-72. Mem. Assn. CPCU's (pres. 1989—), Clark Hatch Fitness Ctrs., Honolulu Club, Genesee Valley Club, Rotary. Republican. Episcopalian. Home: 4815 Aukai Ave Honolulu HI 96816

HENOCH, MIRIAM ALICE, audiologist, researcher; b. Santa Barbara, Calif., May 9, 1939; d. Herbert Joseph and Lorraine Antoinette (Howard) H. BA, North Tex. State U., 1971, MA, 1972; PhD, Wayne State U., Detroit, 1976. Asst. prof. Ball State U., Muncie, Ind., 1975-76; assoc. dir. Detroit Hearing and Speech Ctr., Detroit, 1976-77; assoc. prof. coordinbator audiology North Tex. State U., Denton, 1977-87; assoc. prof. San Jose (Calif.) State U., 1987-88; research audiologist VA Med. Ctr., Palo Alto, Calif., 1988—, cons., 1987—; cons. Scott Inst. Corp., Denton, 1984—. Author: Aural Rehabilitation for the Elderly, 1978. Served with USAF, 1957-59. Mem. Am. Speech-Langs.-Hearing Assn., Acad. Rehab., Tex. Speech and Langs., Assn., Calif. Speech and Lang. Assn. Democrat. Home: 201 S 4th St #707 San Jose CA 95112 Office: VA Med Ctr 795 Willow Rd Menlo Park CA 94025

HENRICH, STEPHEN BROWN, aircraft systems engineer; b. Cin., Mar. 20, 1950; s. Kenneth Fred and Sarah Eloise (Brown) H.; m. Rose Marie Bingham, May 5, 1979. AS in Aerospace Sci., Spartan Aero. Sch., Tulsa, 1981; BSBA, U. La Verne, 1988. Fin. mgr. Citicorp, Tulsa, 1975-79; systems engr. N.Am. Aircraft div. Rockwell Internat., Edwards AFB, Calif., 1982—. Republican. Methodist. Home: 1255 Herzel Ave Lancaster CA 93535 Office: Rockwell Internat NAm Aircraft div Edwards AFB CA 93523

HENRIE, KIM BARTON, direct marketing professional; b. Ely, Nev., Aug. 17, 1951; s. Keith Larsen and Faye (Barton) H.; m. Linda Maree Casper, Aug. 2, 1974; children: Justin, Seth, Asher. BS, Brigham Young U., 1975, MBA, 1977. Mgr. Y-Tex Corp., Cody, Wyo., 1977-80; mktg. mgr. Reliance Co., Walnut Creek, Calif., 1980-81; pres., owner K.B. Henrie & Assocs., Inc., San Ramon, Calif., 1981—; chmn., owner Brit. Am., San Ramon, 1983—. Author: The Insiders Guide to Greater Wealth and Bargains, 1985, Small Business Savvy, 1988. Club: Blackhawk (Calif.). Office: 7 Crow Canyon Ct Ste 250 San Ramon CA 94583

HENRY, BRENDA GAY, social worker; b. Eagle Pass, Tex., May 14, 1962; d. Tom Ray and Wanda Fay (Schlup) Zumbro; m. Frank W. Henry, July 20, 1985. BSW, N.Mex. State U., 1984. Sec. Shriners Club, Las Cruces, N.Mex., 1984; behavior edn. counselor Nutri Sytems Weight Loss Ctr., Las Cruces, 1984-85; with new accounts dept. Sun West Bank, Las Cruces, 1985; social worker N.Mex. Dept. Human Svcs., Las Cruces, 1985-87; clin. social worker Denton (Tex.) State Sch., 1988—. Mem. Nat. Assn. Social Workers. Republican. Baptist. Office: Denton State Sch PO Box 368 Denton TX 76202-0368

HENRY, CHARLES EDISON, horticulturist, consultant; b. Colefax, Wash., Apr. 7, 1929; s. Harold Harris and Alta (Cress) H.; m. Melva Elizabeth Freligh, July 15, 1955 (dec. Nov. 1982); children: Preston Charles, Heidi Elizabeth, Lucinda Ann, Randolph Harold; m. Bernice E. Gregory, July 2, 1983; children: Gregory Dayton, Karen Nelson. BS, Oreg. State U., 1950, postgrad., 1953-54. With field dept. Producers Corp., Salem, Oreg., 1953-55; prodn. supt. Pinnacle Packing Co., Medford, Oreg., 1956-62; dist. mgr. Stauffer Chem. Co., Portland, Oreg., 1962-87; pres. Agrl. Safety Cons., Inc., Scio, Oreg., 1987—. Lay del. United Meth. Ch. Ann. Conf., Salem and Boise, Idaho, 1964-88; bd. dirs. Am. Field Svc., Stayton, Oreg., 1977-78. Capt. USAR, 1950-70, Korea. Decorated Bronze Star; recipient N. Star award Western Agrl. Chems. Assn., 1986; named Family of Yr., Meth. Ch., 1961, Hon. Farmer, Future Farmers Am., 1975. Mem. Oreg. Horticultural Soc. (pres. 1986-87), Oreg. Agrl. Chem. Assn. (pres. Salem chpt. 1971, legis. chmn. 1974-80), Oreg. Soc. Weed Sci., Western Agrl. Chem. Assn. (pres. Salem chpt. 1974, 84), Mid Willamette Fieldmans Assn., Stayton C. of C., Rotary (bd. dirs. 1984-87), Lions (bd. dirs. 1974-83). Home and Office: 40385 Queener Dr Scio OR 97374

HENRY, IRENE VALERIA, insurance company executive; b. Chicago Heights, Ill., July 8, 1958; d. Roger Herbert and Mary Guadalupe (Rocha) H. BA in Criminal Law, Governor's State Coll., Park Forest, Ill., 1981; JD, Santa Barbara Coll. Law, 1986. Dept. mgr. Ace Hardware, Chicago Heights, Ill., 1973-79; office mgr. State Farm Ins., Matteson, Ill., 1979-81; legal process specialist Santa Barbara County, Calif., 1982-87; agt. State Farm Ins., Santa Barbara, 1987—. Commr. Park Forest City Council, 1979-81; pujb. relations com. Santa Barbara Dem. Women, 1988—; active Nuclear Age Peace Found., 1987—. Mem. Beta Sigma Phi, Delta Theta. Democrat. Roman Catholic. Office: State Farm Ins 1810 Cliff Dr Ste B Santa Barbara CA 93109

HENRY, KAREN HAWLEY, lawyer; b. Whittier, Calif., Nov. 5, 1943; d. Ralph Hawley and Dorothy Ellen (Carr) Hawley; m. John Dunlap, 1968; m. Charles Gibbons Henry, Mar. 15, 1975; children—Scott, Alexander, Joshua. B.S. in Social Scis., So. Oreg. Coll., 1965; M.S. in Labor Econs., Iowa State U., 1967; J.D., Hastings Coll. of Law, 1976. Instr., Medford (Oreg.) Sch. Dist., 1965-66; research asst. dept. econs. Iowa State U., Ames, 1966-67; dir. research program Calif. Nurses Assn., San Francisco, 1967-72; labor relations coordinator Affiliated Hosps. of San Francisco, 1972-79; ptnr. Littler, Mendelson, Fastiff & Tichy, San Francisco, 1979-86; mng. ptnr. labor and employment law Weissburg and Aronson, Inc., San Francisco, 1986—, also bd. dirs. Mem. Calif. Soc. Healthcare Attys. (bd. dirs. 1986-87, pres. 1987-88), Am. Hosp. Assn. (ad hoc labor atty. com.), State Bar of Calif., San Francisco Bar Assn., Contra Costa Bar Assn., Thurston Soc., Order of Coif. Author: Health Care Supervisor's Legal Guide, 1984, Nursing Administration Law Manual, 1986.. Office: Weissburg & Aronson Inc 555 California St Ste 2400 San Francisco CA 94108

HENRY, PHILIP LAWRENCE, marketing professional; b. Los Angeles, Dec. 1, 1940; s. Lawrence Langworthy and Ella Hanna (Martens) H.; m. Claudia Antonia Huff, Aug. 9, 1965 (div. 1980); children: Carolyn Marie, Susan Michelle; m. Carrie Katherine Hoover, Aug. 23, 1985. BS in Marine Engring., Calif. Maritime Acad., 1961. Design engr. Pacific Telephone Co., San Diego, 1963-73; service engr. Worthington Service Corp., San Diego, 1973-78; pres. Realmart Corp., San Diego, 1978-81; dir. mktg. Orbit Inn Hotel and Casino, Las Vegas, 1981-84; pres. Comml. Consultants, Las Vegas, 1984—, Gray Electronics Co., Las Vegas, 1986—. Inventor electronic detection device, 1986. Served to lt. (j.g.) USNR, 1961-67. Republican. Mem. Christian Sci. Ch. Home: 1843 Somersby Way Green Valley NV 89014

HENRY, SHIRLEY ANN, press executive; b. Los Angeles, Apr. 23, 1937; d. Austin Perry Shaver and Ann (Pitrucka) Wilhelm; m. Walter Sigman Henry, July 1, 1955 (dec. Oct. 1985); children—Debbie Henry Johnson, Shelly Henry Dozier, Derek Sigman; m. Charles J. Vitale, Feb. 11, 1989. AA with honors, Contra Costa Coll., San Pablo, Calif., 1969. Lic. R.N., Calif. Nurse, VA Hosp., Martinez, Calif., 1970-73; chief exec. officer Lamorinda Press, Lafayette, Calif., 1976—. Baptist. Avocations: skiing, scuba diving. Office: Lamorinda Press 3409 C Mt Diablo Blvd Lafayette CA 94549

HENRY, WALTER L., cardiologist, educator; b. Cumberland, Md., Feb. 20, 1941; s. Walter and Virginia Mae (Keller) H.; BSEE cum laude, U. Pitts., 1963; MD, Stanford U., 1969. Intern, Bronx Mcpl. Hosp., N.Y.C. and Albert Einstein Coll. Medicine, 1969-70, resident in internal medicine, 1970-71; clin. asso. Nat. Heart, Lung and Blood Inst., Bethesda, Md., 1971-73, sr. investigator, 1973-78; prof. medicine, chief div. cardiology U. Calif., Irvine, 1978—, vice chancellor health scis., dean Coll. Medicine. With USPHS, 1971-78. Diplomate Am. Bd. Internal Medicine. Recipient Disting. Alumnus award U. Pitts. Engring. Alumni Assn, 1985, Profl. Achievement award U. Calif., Irvine, 1986. Bd. dirs. Opera Pacific. Mem. Am. Soc. Echocardiography (pres. 1981-83), N. Am. Soc. Cardiac Radiology, Am. Heart Assn., Am. Coll. Cardiography (area gov. So. Calif. 1985-88), Am. Fedn. Clin. Rsch., Pres.'s Circle of NAS (co-founder), Eta Kappa Nu, Alpha Omega Alpha, Omicron Delta Kappa. Editorial bd. Am. Heart Jour. Contbr. articles to profl. jours. Office: U Calif Irvine Med Ctr Cardiology Div 101 City Dr S Orange CA 92717

HENRY-JOHN, EMMANUEL SYLVESTER, preacher, counselor; b. Ootacamund, Madras, India, Dec. 15, 1949; came to U.S., 1980; s. Isaac and Sama Thanam (Asirvatham) Henry-J.; m. Laura Elia Garza, Feb. 4, 1984; children: Sarai Samathanam, Isaac Max, Shalani Esther. AS, Schs. for Officers Tng.; ACP, Assoc. Coll. of Preceptors; BA, U. Madras. Sales rep. Baba's Ice Cream Factory, Bangalore, India, 1972; tchr. Woizero Comprehensive Higher Dessie Secondary Sch., Ethiopia, 1973-77, Mopa Secondary Sch., Illorin, Kwara, Nigeria, 1977-80; fin. planner John Hancock, Cerritos, Calif., 1982; respiratory therapy technician Burbank (Calif.) Community Hosp., 1983-84; counselor The Salvation Army Rehab. Ctr., Canoga Park, Calif., 1985-86; pastor The Savlation Army, Bakersfield, Calif., 1988-89; comdg. officer The Savlation Army, Gilroy, Calif., 1989—; spiritual counselor Adult Rehab. Ctr., The Salvation Army, Canoga Park, 1980, youth minister ch. for homeless, Bakersfield, 1983, mem. adv. bd., 1988. Vol. food for homeless The Salvation Army, Bakersfield, 1988, spiritual and social work to the needy. Named Best Tchr., Wollo Province, 1974. Mem. Coun. of Chs. Greater Bakersfield, Jay Strack Evangelistic Com., Soc. Internat. Missionaries, Lions, Masons, Kiwanis. Republican. Home: 781 Lawrence Dr Gilroy CA 95020

HENSEL, STEVEN MARK, artist, interior, textile, furniture and graphic designer; b. Seattle, Aug. 8, 1955; s. Frank John and Lois Eleanor (Hayden) H. Owner, designer Xenox Designs, Seattle, 1978-79, Studio Steel by Steven Hensel, Seattle, 1987--; pres., head designer Artex Designs Ltd., Seattle, 1981-- . Group exhbn. Foster/White Functional Art Show, 1983, Foster/White Studio Steel Show, 1989. Artist, designer Mayor Royer Reelection Campaign, Seattle, 1985; designer N.W. Harvest, Seattle, 1988. Recipient Internat. ROSCOE award Resource Coun. Inc., 1987, 2 Neocon Spec Nat. awards. Mem. Am. Soc. Interior Designers (industry, internat. product design award 1987), Allied Arts. Home and Office: Artex Designs Ltd 2202 N Pacific St Seattle WA 98103

HENSING, JOHN ANDREW, physician; b. Ames, Iowa, Sept. 8, 1947; s. Andrew Magnus and Kathryn Teresa (Judge) H.; m. Barbara Sue Brown, Aug. 9, 1969; children: Natalie, Garett, Gavin, Angela. BS in Zoolology, Iowa State U., 1969; MD, U. Iowa, 1972. Diplomate Am. Bd. Internal Medicine. Resident Maricopa County Hosp., Phoenix, 1975-77; gen. practice medicine Tempe, Ariz., 1977—; chief med. staff Desert Samaritan Hosp., Mesa, Ariz., 1988—. Capt. USAF, 1973-75. Mem. ACP, Am. Soc. Internal Medicine. Republican. Office: 2600 E Southern Ave Tempe AZ 85282

HENSLEY, DALE EUGENE, sales representative; b. Nebraska City, Nebr., Aug. 27, 1960; s. Leroy Elliot and Mildred (Lauman) H. AA with honors, Iowa Western U., 1980; BS, Wayne (Nebr.) State Coll., 1983. With Hormel Corp., 1983—; deli sales mgr. Hormel Corp., San Francisco, 1986-88; retail account mgr. Hormel Corp., Salt Lake City, 1988—. Republican. Methodist. Home: 6862 S Country Woods Circle Midvale UT 84047

HENSLEY, WILLIAM L., state senator, corporate executive; b. Kotzebue, Alaska, June 17, 1941; s. John and Priscilla Hensley; m. Abigale Ryan; children: Priscilla, Mary Lynn, James, Elizabeth. Student, U. Alaska, 1960-62; BA, George Washington U., 1966; postgrad., U. Alaska, spring 1966, LLD (hon.), 1980; postgrad., UCLA, fall 1968. Mem. Akaska Ho. of Reps., 1966-70; senator State of Alaska, 1970-74, 86—; chmn. United Bank Alaska, Anchorage, 1976-86; pres. N.W. Alaska Native Assn. Devel. Corp., Kotzebue, 1976—, N.W. Alaska Native Assn. Regional Corp., Kotzebue, 1986—; pres. Alaska Village Electric Coop., 1967-71; chmn., chmn., bd. dirs. Tundra Times, 1979—. Chmn. Alaska Dem. Party, 1968, 84-86, Rural Affairs Commn., 1968-74, Capital Site Selection Com., 1975-76, Reapportionment Commn., 1985; bd. regents U. Alaska, 1985-87; bd. dirs. Nat. Coun. on Indian Opportunity, 1968-70, N.W. Regional Ednl. Lab., 1969-71, Alascom, 1977—, Alaska Fedn. Natives, 1966-80; mem. Providence Hosp. Adv. Bd., 1979-87. Recipient Rockefeller Pub. Service award, 1980; named

Citizen of Yr. Alaska Fedn. Natives, 1981. Home: PO Box 710 Kotzebue AK 99752 Office: NANA Regional Corp PO Box 49 Kotzebue AK 99752

HENSLEY-JONES, CONSTANCE IRENE, biotechnology company executive; b. Hillsboro, Oreg., Sept. 24, 1950; d. Wayne D. and Irene M. (Ott) Hensley; m. Dennis D. Jones, Feb. 24, 1979; children: Andrew, Allison. BS, U. Oreg., Eugene, 1972. Media specialist Batten, Barton, Durstine and Osborn, San Francisco, 1972-73; advt. exec. Foote, Cone and Belding/Honig, San Francisco, 1974-75; media sales exec. Meredith Corp., San Francisco, 1976; owner The Cloth Mcht., Inc., Corvallis, Oreg., 1977-81; bus. mgr. Antivirals, Inc., Corvallis, 1986—; bd. dirs. Anti-Gene Devel. Group, Corvallis. Chairperson edn. com. Grace Luth. Ch., Corvallis, 1986—. Mem. Sigma Kappa. Democrat. Lutheran. Lodge: Zonta (treas. Corvallis chpt. 1968—). Club: Timberhill Athletic (Corvallis). Home: 774 SW Lookout Dr Corvallis OR 97333 Office: Antivirals Inc 249 SW Avery Ave Corvallis OR 97333

HENSON, MARY BLUNT, educator; b. Washington, June 23, 1925; d. Wilfrid Mason and Elizabeth Pollard (Fleming) Blunt; m. Jack Elliott Henson, June 26, 1947; children: Laurel, Mark, Katherine, Robin, Polly, Joel, Abigail, John. AB, Colo. Coll., 1947; student, Stanford u., 1947-48; MA in Edn., Calif. State U., Sacramento, 1974. Cert. elementary tchr., Calif. Lab technician Santa Fe Hosp., L.A., 1948-49, L.A. County Hosp., 1949-50; tchr. San Juan Unified Sch. Dist., Sacramento, 1970—. With USN, 1945-46. Mem. Rep. Women's Club, DAR, Del Norte Swim and Tennis. Democrat. Roman Catholic.

HENZE, RAYMOND F., III, food products company executive. Exec. v.p. Flexi Van, N.Y.C., 1983-84, pres., chief operating officer, from 1984, also bd. dirs.; from v.p. to exec. v.p. Pacific Holding Corp., Los Angeles, 1984-86; exec. v.p. Castle & Cooke Inc., San Francisco, 1985—, also bd. dirs. Office: Pacific Holding Corp 10900 Wilshire Blvd Los Angeles CA 90024 *

HENZEL, NANCY L., educator; b. Reedsburg, Wis.; d. Paul and Verona (Schuette) Richert; m. George R. Henzel; 1 child, Aaron Daniel. Grad. high sch. Cert. travel counselor. With Am. Airlines, Chgo., Phoenix, 1959-76; travel counselor Travel Studio, Phoenix, 1978—; travel isntr. SST Travel Sch. of Ariz., Scottsdale, 1985—. Mem. Inst. Cert. Travel Agts., Internat. Fed. Women's Travel Orgns., Ariz. Women in Travel. Lutheran. Office: SST Travel Sch of Ariz 7975 N Hayden Rd Scottsdale AZ 85258

HEPLER, KENNETH RUSSEL, manufacturing executive; b. Canton, Ohio, Mar. 31, 1926; s. Clifton R. and Mary A. (Sample) H.; m. Beverly Best, June 9, 1945; 1 child, Bradford R. Student, Cleve. Art Inst., 1946-47, Case Western Res. U., 1948-50. V.p., adminstr. A. Carlisle and Co., San Francisco, 1954-67; pres. K.R. Hepler and Co., Menlo Park, Calif., 1968-73, Paramount Press., Jacksonville, Fla., 1974-75; pvt. practice printing broker 1976-80; chmn. Hickey and Hepler Graphics Inc., San Francisco, 1981—; instr. printing prodn., San Francisco City Coll. With USAAC, 1943-45. Mem. San Francisco Litho Club (pres. 1972), Phila. Litho Club (sec. 1975-76), Newtown Exchange Club (pres. 1976), Elks. Republican. Presbyterian. Office: Hickey & Hepler Graphics Inc 1485 Bayshore Blvd San Francisco CA 94124

HEPLER, MERLIN JUDSON, JR., real estate broker; b. Hot Springs, Va., May 13, 1929; s. Merlin Judson and Margaret Belle (Vines) H.; m. Lanova Helen Roberts, July 25, 1952; children: Nancy Andora, Douglas Stanley. BS in Bus., U. Idaho, 1977; grad., Realtors Inst., 1979. Cert. residential specialist. Enlisted USAF, 1947, advanced through grades to sgt., 1960, ret., 1967; service mgr. Lanier Bus. Products, Gulfport, Miss., 1967-74; sales assoc. Century 21 Singler and Assn., Troy, Idaho, 1977-79; broker B&M Realty, Troy, 1979—. Mem. Nat. Assn. Realtors, Am. Legion, U. Idaho Alumni Assn., Air Force Sgts. Assn. Republican. Lodge: Lions. Home: Rte 1 Box 119 Troy ID 83871 Office: B&M Realty PO Box 187 102 A St Troy ID 83871

HEPPE, RALPH RICHARD, aeronautical engineer; b. Kansas City, Mo., Mar. 4, 1923. BS, Stanford U., 1944, MS, 1945; MS, Calif. Inst. Tech., 1947. V.p. Lockheed Corp., from 1974, v.p., gen. mgr. govt. projects, 1974-79, v.p. ops., 1979-81, v.p., asst. gen. mgr. advanced devel. projects, 1981-84; pres. Lockheed-Calif. Co. (now Lockheed Aero. Systems Co.), Burbank, Calif., from 1984. Fellow AIAA, mem. NAE, Sigma Xi. Office: Lockheed Aero Systems Co PO Box 551 Burbank CA 91520 *

HEPWORTH, LORNE, Canadian provincial politician; b. Assiniboia, Sask., Can., Dec. 20, 1947; s. Henry Bramall and Eileen (Malesh) H.; m. Fern Dianne Margeurite Presber, Dec. 23, 1969; children: Graeme, Alana. Student, U. Regina, Sask., 1965-67; DVM, U. Sask., 1971. Veterinarian Hepworth, Pulfer, Weyburn, Sask., 1982; minister of agr. Provincial Govt. of Sask., Regina, 1983-85; minister of energy and mines Provincial Govt. of Sask., 1985-86, minister of edn., 1986—; Mem. Province of Sask. Legis. Assembly; also minister of agr. Mem. Sask. Vet. Medicine Assn. (ex-officio), Can. Vet. Medicine Assn. Progressive Conservative. Home: 4349 Castle Rd, Regina, SK Canada S4S 4W2 Office: Province of Sask, Legislative Bldg Rm 361, Regina, SK Canada S4S 0B3

HERB, EDMUND MICHAEL, optometrist, educator; b. Zanesville, Ohio, Oct. 9, 1942; s. Edmund G. and Barbara R. (Michael) H.; divorced; children—Sara, Andrew; m. Jeri Herb. O.D., Ohio State U., 1966. Pvt. practice optometry, Buena Vista, Colo., 1966—; prof. Timberline campus Colo. Mountain Coll., 1988—. Mem. Am. Optometric Assn., Colo. Optometric Assn. Home: Lost Creek Ranch Buena Vista CO 81211 Office: 115 N Tabor St Buena Vista CO 81211 also: Leadville Colorado Med Ctr Leadville CO 80461

HERBER, STEVEN CARLTON, physician; b. L.A., Aug. 25, 1960; s. Raymond and Marilyn Joyce (Dart) H.; m. Katherine Carol Jones, Apr. 23, 1989. BS, Pacific Union Coll., 1982; Dr.med., Loma Linda U., 1986. Diplomate Nat. Bd. Med. Examiners, 1987. Resident surgeon Med. Ctr. Loma Linda (Calif.) U., 1986—; researcher Dept. of Surgery, Loma Linda, Calif., 1987—; bd. dirs. MacPherson Rsch. Soc., 1988—. Contbr. articles to profl. jours. NIH grantee, 1988. Mem. Am. Med. Student Assn. (resident), San Bernardino County Med. Soc., Calif. Med. Assn. Republican. Adventist. Home: 2506 Mound St Loma Linda CA 92354 Office: Univ Med Ctr 11234 Anderson St Loma Linda CA 92354

HERBERGER, KENNETH STEPHEN, marketing specialist; b. Bklyn., Aug. 27, 1936; s. Fredrick Jacob and Marguerite Virginia (Skippon) H.; m. Christine Godsey, Sept. 9, 1961 (div. 1967); children: Maryann, William F.; m. Sherry LaVelle Kelley, Sept. 1, 1973; children: David, Robert. BS in Engring., U.S. Mil. Acad., 1958; MS in Systems Mgmt., U. So. Calif., 1975. Commd. 2nd lt. U.S. Army, 1958, advanced through grades to lt. col., 1979, various program mgmt. and communications assignments, 1958-79, ret., 1979; electronic warfare program mgr. Raytheon Co., Wayne, N.J., 1979-83; ground systems group Hughes Aircraft, Fullerton, Calif., 1983-87; mktg. mgr. support systems div. Hughes Aircraft, Long Beach, Calif., 1987—. Contbr. articles to profl. jours. Active Cub Scouts Am., Mission Viejo, Calif., 1984—, Boy Scouts Am., Mission Viejo, 1985—, Puddingstone Puddle Chorale, Kinnelon, N.J., 1982-83, Smoke Rise (N.J.) Players, 1982. Decorated Bronze star with oak leaf cluster, Legion of Merit. Mem. Security Affairs Support Assn., Armed Forces Communication Electronics Assn., West Point Soc., Orange County (bd. dirs. 1984-87), Army/Navy Country Club, Assn. Old Crows. Republican. Roman Catholic. Home: 26965 Recordo Ln Mission Viejo CA 92691

HERBERT, GAVIN SHEARER, JR., health care products company executive; b. Los Angeles, Mar. 26, 1932; s. Gavin and Josephine (D'Vitha) H.; children by previous marriage Cynthia, Lauri, Gavin, Pam; 2d. m. Ninetta Flanagan, Sept. 6, 1986. B.S., U. So. Calif., 1954. With Allergan Pharms., Inc., Irvine, Calif., 1950—; v.p. Allergan Pharms., Inc., 1956-61, exec. v.p., pres., 1961-77, chmn. bd., chief exec. officer, 1977—, pres., from 1977, pres. eye and skin care products group, from 1981; exec. v.p. Smith Kline Beckman Corp., 1986—, also bd. dirs. Trustee U. So. Calif.; bd. dirs. Richard Nixon Presdl. Found., Estelle Doheny Eye Found., Beckman Laser Inst. and Med. Clinic. Served with USN, 1954-56. Mem. Beta Theta Pi. Republican. Clubs: Big Canyon Country, Balboa Bay, Newport Harbor Yacht, Pacific. Office: Allergan Inc 2525 DuPont Dr Irvine CA 92715

HERBERT, SAMUEL ALFRED, psychologist; b. Modesto, Calif., Apr. 7, 1943; s. Ira and Kathryn Elizabeth (Worthley) H.; m. Muriel Tomaszewski, Dec. 6, 1964 (div. 1979); children: Annette Marie, David Samuel, Andrew James. BA with distinction, San Diego State U., 1973; MA, Calif. Sch. Profl. Psychology, 1979, PhD, 1981. Lic. psychologist, Calif. Patrolman Calif. Hwy. Patrol, San Diego, 1968-73; spl. investigator Calif. Dept. Human Affairs, San Diego, 1973-74; sales rep. G.S. Parsons & Co., San Diego, 1974-76; psychologist Mathis & Assocs., Napa, Calif., 1981-85; pres. Synergetics, Ventura, Calif., 1981—; lectr. in field. Contbr. articles to profl. jours. Mem. Disaster Response Team, Ventura, 1988. Served with U.S. Army, 1963-66. Mem. Am. Psychol. Assn., Calif. State Psychol. Assn., Ventura County Psychol. Assn., Calif. Peace Officers Assn., Am. Mgmt. Assn., Ventura C. of C. Office: Synergetics 2021 Sperry Ave #5 Ventura CA 93003

HERBIG, RONALD F., conference facility administrator; b. Tooele, Utah, Sept. 11, 1947; s. Merle L. and Ruth N. (Pummel) H.; m. Christie L. Alber, Feb. 14, 1975; children: Kate, Marie, Paul. AA, Everett (Wash.) Community Coll., 1971; BA, Cen. Wash. U., 1973. Investigator Boeing Aircraft Co., Seattle, 1967-69; asst. mgr. Household Internat., Seattle, 1973-75; br. mgr. Household Internat., Spokane, Washington, 1975-84; conf. adminstr. Cannon Beach (Oreg.) Conf. Ctr., 1984—; corp. treas. Cannon Beach Conf. Ctr., 1986—. Bd. dirs. Spokane Neighborhood Accountability Bd., 1976; chmn. bd. deacons Seaside Community Bapt. Ch., 1987—, Cannon Beach; pres. Portland, Oreg. chpt. Christian Ministries Mgmt. Assn., 1986—; bd. dirs. Riverview Bible Camp, 1983-84. Staff sgt. USAR Army, 1967-73. Mem. Cannon Beach C. of C. (bd. dirs. 1987—), Kiwanis Club (North Spokane, Wash., bd. dirs. 1976-84, pres. 1981). Republican. Home: PO Box 908 Cannon Beach OR 97110 Office: Cannon Beach Conf Ctr PO Box 398 Cannon Beach OR 97110

HERBRANSON, KAI WOLD, hotel executive; b. Bagley, Minn., Apr. 27, 1935; s. Joseph H. and Kari (Wold) H.; m. Donna Lou Stamos, Sept. 2, 1961; children: Shawn, Adam, Jill. B.A., St. Olaf Coll., Northfield, Minn., 1957, Mich. State U., 1960; M.A., Mich. State U., 1961. With Sheraton Hotel Corp., 1961—; v.p., gen. mgr. Lord Baltimore Hotel, Balt., 1969-71, Royal Hawaiian Hotel, Honolulu, 1971-73; sr. v.p. Sheraton Hotels Ltd.; sr. v.p., area mgr. North and East Am. div., mng. dir. Sheraton Centre, Toronto, Ont., Can., 1973-87; sr. v.p. North Am. div. for Ramada Internat., 1987—; v.p., dir. Met. Toronto Conv. Bur., 1976—; dir., mem. exec. com. ITT Industries Can. Ltd. Past pres. Met. Toronto Boy Scouts. Served with AUS, 1958. Recipient Medal of Merit Boy Scouts Can.; Hotelier of Yr. award, 1984; Silver Goblet award. Mem. Am. Hotel and Motel Assn. (trustee ednl. inst., vice chmn. natural resources com., chmn. chpt. adv. council Ednl. Inst.), Hotel Assn. Can. (dir.), Ont. Hotel and Motel Assn. (v.p. 1977-78),. Address: 3838 E Vanburen St Phoenix AZ 85008

HERBST, LAWRENCE ROBERT, entrepreneur; b. Haverhill, Mass., Aug. 8, 1946; s. Morton and Ruth I. (Cooper) H. Attended UCLA, Alexander Hamilton Bus. Inst.; DVM, N.Am. Sch. Animal Scis.; DD, Missionaries of New Truth, Chgo. Owner, pres. Best-way Records, Data Time Info., Lawrence Herbst Records, Total Sound Records, Beverly Hills Records, Beverly Hills Music Pub. Co., Plus K-Larrco Rec. Studios, Future World Stores, Larry's Family Restaurant, Heavenly Waterbed Showrooms, K-Larrco Satellite Radio and TV Stas.; pres., adminstr. LH Investment Trust Fund of Tex., Inc., Larrco Industries of Tex.; pres., founder House of Robots, Larr Robots, Larry's Merchandising Data Base; founder, pres., dir. chief adminstr. Holy Bible Gospel Ministry of the Body of Christ, 1989—. Author: (book and movie) Legend of Tobby Kingdom, 1975; The Good, The Bad, The True Story of Lawrence Herbst; news columnist World of Investments, 1976. Designer 1st musical electronic amplifier with plug in I.C.'s; inventor Larrco AM/FM satellite car radio, one-man air car, 2-foot satellite dish and system, flat satellite dish and system. Mem. Broadcast Music, Inc.; pres. Lawrence Herbst Farms; producer Spacee the Lion Cartoon. Pres., adminstr. Lawrence Herbst Found. Mem. Nat. Acad. TV Arts and Scis., Los Angeles Press Club, Internat. Platform Assn., Nat. Assn. Broadcasters, Epsilon Delta Chi. Office: PO Box 3842 Houston TX 77253-3842

HERD, JAMES LESLIE, manufacturing executive; b. Lennox Town, Scotland, Mar. 29, 1952; came to U.S., 1979; BSMIE, Luton Tech. Coll., London, 1973, BSIE, 1975; MBA, Gen. Motors Inst., 1977. Engr. apprentice Vauxhall Motors, Luton, Eng., 1968-73, indsl. engr., 1973-75; sr. indsl. engr. Vauxhall Motors, Luton, 1977-79; indsl. engr. Gen. Motors, Flint, Mich. and Detroit, 1975-77; mgr. indsl. engring. Diablo Systems, Hayward, Calif., 1979-81; mgr. indsl. engring. facilities Diablo Systems, Fremont, Calif., 1981-84; mgr. mfg. ops. Xerox Corp., Fremont, 1985-86, mgr. strategic planning, 1986—; cons. various mfrs. Silicon Valley, Calif., 1984—. Contbr. chpt. to book. Mem. Am. Inst. Indsl. Engrs. (sr.), Tau Beta Pi. Office: Xerox Corp 901 Page Ave Fremont CA 94537

HERDEG, HOWARD BRIAN, physician; b. Buffalo, Oct. 14, 1929; s. Howard Bryan and Martha Jean (Williams) H.; student Paul Smith's Coll., 1947-48, U. Buffalo, 1948-50, Canisius Coll., 1949; DO, Phila. Coll. Osteopathic Medicine, 1954; MD, U. Calif.-Irvine Coll. Medicine, 1962; m. Beryl Ann Fredricks, July 21, 1955; children: Howard Brian III, Erin Ann Kociela. Intern, Burbank (Calif.) Hosp., 1954-55; practice medicine specializing in family practice, Woodland Hills, Calif., 1956—; chief med. staff West Park Hosp., Canoga Park, Calif., 1971-72, trustee, 1971-73; chief family practice dept. Humana Hosp. West Hills, Canoga Park, 1982-83, 84-85, 88-89, mem. exec. com., 1984-85, 88-89. Mem. Hidden Hills (Calif.) Pub. Safety Commn., 1978-82, chmn. family practice dept., 1988—, chmn., 1982, exec. com. 1982—; bd. dirs. Hidden Hills Community Assn., 1971-73, pres., 1972; bd. dirs. Hidden Hills Homeowners Assn., 1973-75, pres., 1976-77; bd. dirs. Woodland Hills Freedom Season, 1961-67, pres., 1962; mem. Hidden Hills City Council, 1984—, mayor pro tem, 1987—. Recipient disting. service award Woodland Hills Jr C. of C., 1966. Mem. Woodland Hills C. of C. (dir. 1959-68, pres. 1967), Theta Chi, Gamma Pi. Republican. Home: 24530 Deep Well Rd Hidden Hills CA 91302 Office: 22600 Ventura Blvd Woodland Hills CA 91364

HEREDY, LASZLO A., fuel scientist, consultant; b. Gödöllő, Hungary, Nov. 20, 1921; s. Kalman and Lenke (Fekete) H.; m. Ethel S. Szügyi, May 26, 1947 (dec. Jan. 1984); 1 child, Laszlo G.; m. Klara Toth, Oct. 3, 1985. MS in Chemical Engring., Tech. U., Budapest, Hungary, 1944; PhD in Phys. Chemistry, Carnegie-Mellon U., 1962. Dept. dir. Coal and Inorganic Research Inst., Veszprem, Hungary, 1950-56; sr. scientist Cons. Coal Co. Research Div., Pitts., 1957-63; mgr. phys. chemistry Rocketdyne div. Rockwell Internat., Canoga Park, Calif., 1963-84; cons. fuel sci. Irvine, Calif., 1984—; mem. Coal Mine Safety Adv. Com., Washington, 1972-75. Contbr. articles to profl. jours; patentee in field. Mem. Atomics Internat. (pres. 1971-72), Sigma Xi. Republican. Roman Catholic. Home and Office: 41 Mirador Irvine CA 92715

HERGER, WALLY W., JR., congressman; b. Yuba City, Calif., May 20, 1945. Formerly mem. Calif. State Assembly; mem. 100-101st Congresses from 2d Calif. dist., mem. agr., mcht. marine and fisheries coms.; owner Herger Gas, Inc. Office: US Ho of Reps Office of House Mems Washington DC 20510 *

HERGET, CHARLES JOHN, engineer, research; b. L.A., Dec. 2, 1937; s. Anton and Blanche (Morton) H.; m. Marlene Jean Sternberg, Aug. 29, 1964 (div. 1984); children: Laura Jane, Edward Charles; m. Patricia Gail Bowling, Nov. 8, 1986. BS, UCLA, 1959, MS, 1965, PhD, 1967. Registered control systems engr., Calif. Mem. of tech. staff, group leader Hughes Aircraft Co., Culver City, Calif., 1959-69; asst. prof. to assoc. prof. Dept. of Elect. Engring. Iowa State U., Ames, Iowa, 1969-78; engr., group leader, project engr. Lawrence Livermore Nat. Lab., Livermore, Calif., 1978—. Mem. IEEE (bd. govs. 1986—), Sigma Xi, Tau Beta Pi. Office: Lawrence Livermore Nat Lab PO Box 808 Livermore CA 94550

HERING, WILLIAM MARSHALL, human resource development executive; b. Indpls., Dec. 26, 1940; s. William Marshall and Mary Agnes (Clark) H.; m. Suzanne Wolfe, Aug. 10, 1963. BS, Ind. U., 1961, MS, 1962; PhD, U. Ill., Urbana, 1973. Tchr. Indpls. pub. schs., 1962-66; asst. dir. sociol. resources project Am. Sociol. Assn., 1966-70; dir. social sci. curriculum Biomed. Interdisciplinary Project, Berkeley, Calif., 1973-76; staff assoc. Tchrs. Ctrs. Exchange, San Francisco, 1976-82; dir. research Far West Lab. Ednl. Research and Devel., San Francisco, 1979-82, sr. research assoc., 1982-85; mgr. human resource devel. Bank Am., San Francisco, 1985—; mem. Nat. Adv. Bd. Educ. Resource Info. Ctr.; cons. U.S. Dept. Edn.; pres. Social Sci. Educ. Consortium, 1981-82, bd. dirs., 1979-81; bd. dirs. Sinfonia, San Francisco, 1986—. Nat. Inst. Educ. grantee, 1979-82, 82—. Mem. Am. Soc. Tng. and Devel. (v.p. 1986), Golden Gate Soc., Nat. Audubon Soc., Phi Delta Kappa. Republican. Episcopalian. Contbr. over 100 articles on social studies edn., staff devel., ednl. research and evaluation to profl. jours. Home: 731 Duboce Ave San Francisco CA 94117 Office: PO Box 37000 Dept 3850 San Francisco CA 94137

HERLIHY, JAMES PATRICK, banker; b. N.Y.C., Oct. 27, 1948; s. Patrick John and Elizabeth (Murphy) H.; m. Catherine Pottier, Oct. 11, 1975; 1 child, Jennifer Rachel Sabine. LLB with honors, London Sch. Econs., 1972; postgrad., St. Mary's Coll., Great Crosby, Eng., 1965-69. V.p. Bank of Am., San Francisco, 1973-86, Citibank, San Francisco, 1986—; Mem. Urban Land Inst., Washington, 1987—, World Affairs Coun., San Francisco. Contbr. articles to profl. jours. Mem. State Dem. Cen. Com., Calif., 1986—; chmn. Econ. Plank Platform Com., Calif., 1986-88, Bus. and Profl. Caucus, Calif., 1989—; bd. mem. St. Mary's Hosp. Found., San Francisco, 1988. Office: Citicorp N Am 1 Sansome St San Francisco CA 94104

HERMAN, ANNALEE WOLFF, employee benefits executive; b. Compton, Calif., Mar. 24, 1950; d. Kurt and Anita Elois (Oberlander) Wolff; m. Allen Floyd Herman, Dec. 25, 1983. BS in Mgmt., Pepperdine U., 1984. Employee benefits adminstr. Petrolane Inc., Long Beach, Calif., 1973-86; benefits supr. 1st Interstate Bnk, L.A., 1986-88; benefits mgr. Meml. Med. Ctr., Long Beach, Calif., 1988—. Republican. Jewish. Office: Meml Med Ctr 2801 Atlantic Ave Long Beach CA 90801

HERMAN, DAVID JAY, dentist; b. Rome, N.Y., Oct. 4, 1954; s. Maurice Joseph and Bettina S. (Stiener) H.; m. Mary Beth Appleberry, Apr. 11, 1976; children: Jeremiah D., Kellin A. BA in Biology, San Jose State U., 1976; DDS, Emory U., 1981. Commd. lt. USPHS, 1981, advanced to lt. commdr., 1985; advanced gen. practice resident Gallup (N. Mex.) Indian Med. Ctr., 1983-84; clin. service specialist Ames Co., Santa Clara, Calif., 1976-77; service unit dental chief Keams Canyon (Ariz.) Service Unit USPHS Indian Health Service, 1981-82; staff dental officer Crownpoint (N. Mex.) Service Unit, 1982-83; service unit dental program chief Winslow (Ariz.) Service Unit, 1984-85; Navajo area dental br. chief Window Rock, Ariz., 1986—; mem. health adv. bd. Navajo Reservation Headstart, 1984—; health promotion/disease prevention cons. USPHS-Indian Health Service Navajo Area, Window Rock, 1986-89; cons. Ariz. Healthy Mothers/Healthy Babies Coalition, 1987-88. Asst. wrestling coach Gallup High Sch., 1983-84, 87-89, Winslow High Sch., 1985-86; bd. dirs. Telluride Lodge Homeowners Assn., 1986—, pres., 1988. Named Nat. Health Service Corp. scholar, Emory U., 1977-81; recipient Outstanding Community Health award HHS, 1987-88, USPHS Achievement medal, 1985, Headstart Achievement award, 1986. Mem. Am. Assn. Pub. Health Dentists, Commd. Officers Assn., ADA, Navajo Area Dental Soc. (pres. 1985). Democrat. Jewish.

HERMAN, ELVIN EUGENE, consulting radar engineer; b. Sigourney, Iowa, Mar. 17, 1921; s. John Lawrence and Martha Elizabeth (Conner) H.; m. Grace Winifred Eklund, Sept. 29, 1945; 1 child, Jane Ann. BSEE, U. Iowa, 1942. Staff engr. Naval Research Lab., Washington, 1942-51; sect. head Corona (Calif.) Labs., Nat. Bur. Standards, 1951-53; sr. scientist Hughes Aircraft Co., El Segundo, Calif., 1953-56, dept. mgr., 1956-58, lab. mgr., 1958-70, tech. dir. radar div., 1970-73; tech. dirs. radar systems group Hughes Aircraft Co., Pacific Palisades, Calif., 1973-83; cons. in field, Pacific Palisades, 1983—. Patentee in field. Fellow IEEE; mem. Research Soc. Am., Eta Kappa Nu. Address: 1200 Lachman Ln Pacific Palisades CA 90272

HERMAN, JAMES RICHARD, union executive; b. Newark, Aug. 21, 1924; s. Milton Matthew and Larraine Catherine (Kelly) H. Student public schs., N.J. Pres. Internat. Longshoremen's and Warehousemen's Union, San Francisco, 1977—. Bd. dirs. Delancey St. Found., St. Anthony's Dining Rm., Columbia Pk. Boys Club; mem. Dem. State Central Com., Calif. Named Labor Man of Yr. Alameda County Central Labor Council, 1973. Mem. Maritime Inst. for Research and Indusl. Devel. (dir.). Democrat. Roman Catholic. Club: Concordia. Office: Internat Longshoremen's and Warehousemen's Union 1188 Franklin St San Francisco CA 94109 *

HERMAN, WILLIAM JOSEPH, technology consulting company executive, aerospace engineer; b. Pitts., Dec. 24, 1941; s. Milton and Jane B. (Broudy) H.; m. Katherine D. White, Sept. 1, 1963; children: Michael, Stephanie, Mark. BS in Aerospace Engring., Pa. State U., 1963; MS in Aerospace Engring., Air Force Inst. Tech., 1968; MBA, U. N.Mex., 1977. Commd. 2d. lt. USAF, 1963, advanced through grades to capt., 1970; aeronautical engr., capt. USAF, Kirtland AFB, N.M., 1963-66, 68-73; resigned USAF, 1973; mem. tech. staff Sci. Applications Inc., Albuquerque, 1973-74; gen. engr. USAF Weapons Lab., Kirtland AFB, 1974-79; sr. assoc. Booz, Allen & Hamilton, Albuquerque, 1979-85, prin., 1985—. Treas. Com. to Elect Herb Hughes, 1975, Duke City Soccer League, 1979-81; founder and coach Sierra Vista Soccer Club, 1979-82; coach Sandia Peak Jr. Nordic Team, 1985-86; team coach Albuquerque Jr. Nordic, 1986—. Mem. IEEE, AIAA, Internat. Test and Evaluation Assn., Am. Def. Preparedness Assn. Democrat. Presbyterian. Club: Norski Racing. Office: Booz Allen & Hamilton Inc 2201 Buena Vista Dr SE Albuquerque NM 87106

HERMANSEN, DAVID N., management; b. Murray, Utah, May 14, 1956; s. Donald N. and Helen Augusta (Reich) H.; m. Cheryl Berrett. BS in Acctg., Utah State U., 1983. Staff acct. Price Waterhouse, Salt Lake City, 1983-87, tax cons., 1987-89; corp. controller Varsity Contractors, Inc., Pocatello, Idaho, 1987—. Mem. AICPA, Utah Assn. CPA's. Home: 1945 Ardella Pocatello ID 83201 Office: Varsity Contractors Inc 253 W Halliday Pocatello ID 83204

HERMANSON, JOHN CARL, physicist, educator; b. Stevens Point, Wis., June 2, 1940; s. Robert Bardeen and Oleeta (Johansen) H.; m. Patricia Carol Wiersig, July 4, 1965; children: Jenny, Heidi, John. BS, MIT, 1962; MS, U. Chgo., 1964, PhD, 1966. Research assoc. dept. physics U. Ill., Urbana, 1966-68; Miller fellow U. Calif., Berkeley, 1968-70; asst. prof. physics Montana State U., Bozeman, 1970-73, assoc. prof., 1973-80, prof., 1980—; vis. prof. U. Munich, 1978-79; cons. Michelson Lab., China Lake, Calif., 1973-82. Mem. Am. Phys. Soc. Office: Mont State U Dept Physics Bozeman MT 59717

HERMS, THOMAS CHRISTIAN, electrical engineer; b. Chula Vista, Calif., June 21, 1946; s. Charles Christian and Marjorie Mae (Laughlin) H.; m. Marcia Lyn Morehead, Sept. 24, 1971; children: Jamie Kristin, Victoria Anne. AS in Electronics, Merced Coll., 1967; BS in Elec. Engring., San Diego State U., 1983. Elec. engr. Western Tech. Assocs., San Diego, 1974-77; elec. engr. Control Data Corp., San Diego, 1977-82, Roseville, Minn., 1982-84; sr. test engr. Honeywell, Colorado Springs, Colo., 1984-88; sr. programmer/analyst Cray Research Inc., Colorado Springs, 1988—. Dep. comdr. CAP, Colorado Springs, 1985. Served with USN, 1967-74. Republican. Home: 8465 Stratus Dr Colorado Springs CO 80920 Office: Cray Rsch Colo Ops PO Box 17500 Colorado Springs CO 80935

HERNANDEZ, H. PAUL, mechanical engineer; b. San Jose, Jan. 28, 1918; s. Herman Paul and Anna Loretta (Williams) H.; m. Barbara Jane Ross, July 26, 1942; children: Richard Paul, Maryann, John Ross. BSME, U. Calif., Berkeley, 1943. Registered profl. engr., Calif. Project mech. engr. RF transmission lines Nat. Testing Accelerator div. Lawrence Livermore (Calif.) Nat. Lab., 1950-52, project mech. engr. 90-inch cyclotron, 1952-55; project mech. engr. bubble chamber Lawrence Berkeley (Calif.) Lab., 1955-64. project mgr. time projection chamber, 1977-82, head. mech. engring dept., 1972-86; staff sr. scientist emeritus, cons. —, 1986—. Contr. articles to profl. jours.; patentee and inventor in field. Capt. U.S. Army, 1943-45.

Fellow ASME; mem. U. Calif. Alumni Assn., Commonwealth Club of Calif. Republican. Roman Catholic.

HERNANDEZ, JAIME MANUEL, management executive; b. Mexico City, July 29, 1944; came to U.S., 1956; s. Luis Alonso and Dolores Maria (Perez Castro) H.; m. Lois Grace Hart, Dec. 3, 1966; children: Delores Grace, Debra Ann, Jaime Manuel Jr. BSME, U.S. Mcht. Marine Acad., 1966. Mgr. Dresser Industries Inc., Mexico City, 1974-80, regional mgr., 1980-85; plant mgr. Dresser-Rand Co., Seattle, 1986-88; assoc. broker comml. and residential real estate sales dept. The Landmark Group., Seattle, 1988—. Lt. USNR, 1966—. Roman Catholic. Home: 1913 161st Ave Bellevue WA 98008 Office: The Landmark Group 1031 Madison St Seattle WA 98112

HERNANDEZ, MARIELA GLORIA, advertising executive; b. Argentina, Mar. 24, 1951; parents Am. citizens; d. Oscar and Juana (Reynoso) Hernandez. BA, U. Calif., Santa Barbara, 1983. Staff career developer seminars on adult edn. City Coll. Santa Barbara, 1983; dir. Olympic Neighbor Com., Santa Barbara, 1984; cons. job devel. Santa Barbara, 1985; real estate assoc. Sunset Realty, Santa Barbara, 1985; promotions cons. Procter & Gamble account Noble & Assocs., Newport Beach, Calif., 1986; advt. cons. Smith & Myers Advt., Santa Ana, Calif., 1987; pres. Hernandez & Assoc. Hispanic Promotions, Torrance, 1987—. Contbr. articles to profl. jours. Asst. Santa Barbara City Hall, 1983-84. Mem. Young Execs. Am. Republican. Mem. Christian Ch. Office: Hernandez & Assoc 23825 Anza Ave Torrance CA 90505

HERNANDEZ, RUDY, JR., accountant; b. Aug. 7, 1950; s. Rudy F. and Chonita (Salazar) H.; m. Vivian N. Najera, Apr. 24, 1976; 1 child, Jayme Marie. AA, Glendale Community Coll., 1970; BS in Acctg., Ariz. State U., 1973. CPA, Ariz. Ptnr. GBS Acctg. and Tax Svc., Glendale, Ariz., 1973-78; acct. Salt River Project, Phoenix, 1973-78, audit supr., 1978—; mem. sub-com. State Bd. Accountancy, Phoenix, 1986—. Mem. AICPA, Nat. Assn. Accts. (bd. dirs. socio-econ. program 1794-75), Inst. Internal Auditors (cert.). Democrat. Roman Catholic. Home: 2712 W Plata Ave Mesa AZ 85202 Office: Salt River Project PO 52025 Phoenix AZ 85072-2025

HERON, GEOFFREY B., psychiatrist; b. Pitts., June 3, 1944; s. Ronald and Lillian (Tanner) H.; m. Susan A. Menne, May 23, 1981; 1 child, Theodore Menne. BA, U. Chgo., 1966, MD, 1971; postgrad., Denver Inst. Psychoanalysis, 1987. Diplomate Am. Bd Psychiatry and Neurology. Resident in psychiatry U. Colo. Health Scis. Ctr., Denver, 1972-76, clin. asst. prof. psychiatry, 1981—; pvt. practice Denver and Boulder, 1976—; psychiatrist Denver VA Hosp., 1976-82; pres. med. staff Mt. Airy Psychiat. Ctr., Denver, 1982; psychiat. cons. United Airlines, Denver, 1977, 86, 89; assoc. Denver Inst. for Psychoanalysis, 1988—. Mem. Am. Psychiat. Assn., Am. Psychoanalytic Assn., Am. Assn. Psychiatry and Law, Colo. Psychiat. Soc., Denver Psychoanalytic Soc., Denver Inst. for Psychoanalysis (inst. assoc.). Office: 4495 Hale Pkwy Ste 310 Denver CO 80220

HERR, LORRAINE ANGELA, financial manager, consultant; b. Weisbaden, Germany, Dec. 5, 1953; came to U.S., 1955; d. William Frederick and Lydia (Pirazzini) Kuster; m. David Frank Herr, Nov. 22, 1981. BA in English Lit., Concordia Coll., 1976; postgrad., Utah State U., 1987—. Ops. asst. United Americas Bank, N.Y.C., 1976-7; office mgr. Transcommerce Inc., N.Y.C., 1977-78; asst. dir. legal dept. Quality Care Inc., Rockville Centre, N.Y., 1978-81; fin. mgr. Porphyrin Products Inc., Logan, Utah, 1982—; ins. cons., Logan, 1985—. Mem. Nat. Assn. Female Exec., Am. Assn. Bus. and Profl. Women, LWV (v.p. 1985). Lutheran. Home: 903 SE Sweetbriar Troutdale OR 97060 Office: Porphyrin Products Inc PO Box 31 Logan UT 84321

HERRERA, GUILLERMO OSVALDO, messenger company executive, clinical psychologist; b. Buenos Aires, Feb. 13, 1952; came to U.S., 1963; s. Marcos and Edith Mary (Arango) H.; m. Adriana Elisa Kenney, Dec. 15, 1986. BA in Psychology and Biology, Elmhurst (Ill.) Coll., 1972; PhD in Clin. Psychology, Profl. Sch. Psychol. Studies, L.A., 1986. Dispatcher, mgr. asst. Archer Air Courier, L.A., 1976-78; sales mgr. Metro Messenger Inc., Studio City, Calif., 1978-80; psychologist's asst., cons. Dr. Michael S. Cohn, Beverly Hills, Calif., 1982—; pres. Alert Messenger Inc., L.A., 1980—; psychologist cons. Dr. Noemi Contreras, Glendale, Calif., 1986—. Author: Child Neglect, Abuse and I.Q., 1986. Mem. Assn. Messenger and Courier Svcs. (chmn. bd. 1988). Republican. Roman Catholic. Office: Alert Messenger Inc 373 N Western Ave #4 Los Angeles CA 90004

HERRERA, MICHAEL DENNIS, optometrist; b. So, N.Mex., Apr. 8, 1950; s. Teodulo Segundo and Mary Lou (Marquez) H.; m. Helen Gonzales Ortiz, Dec. 26, 1970 (div. June 1971); 1 child, Michelle Renee; m. Jeneane Marie Cole, May 15, 1975; children: Ruth, Nathan, Jesse, Hannah. BS, Pacific U., OD. Diplomate Nat. Bd. Optometry, N.Mex. State Bd. Optometry. Pvt. practice Santa Fe, N.Mex., 1978—; researcher CIBA Vision, Atlanta, Santa Fe, 1986—; mem. discussion panel CIBA/Syntex, Bermuda, 1985. Elder Berean Bapt. Ch., Santa Fe, 1980-88; tchr. Calvary Chapelde Santa Fe, 1989—. Capt. USAF, 1975-78. Mem. N.Mex. Optometric Assn. Republican. Office: Michael D Herrera & Assocs 4250 Cerrillos Rd Ste 1004 Santa Fe NM 87505

HERRERA, ROBERT BENNETT, retired educator; b. L.A., July 24, 1913; s. Royal Robert and Rachel (Mix) H.; AA, L.A. City Coll., 1934; AB, UCLA, 1937, MA, 1939; m. Agnes Mary MacDougall, May 18, 1941; children: Leonard B., Mary Margaret, William R. Tchr. high sch., Long Beach, Calif., 1939-41; statistician U.S. Forest Survey, Berkeley, Calif., 1941-45; faculty L.A. City Coll., 1946-79, prof. math., 1966-79, chmn. math. dept., 1975-79, ret., 1979; lectr. math. UCLA, 1952-75; cons. Ednl. Testing Svc., Princeton, 1965-68, Addison Wesley Pub. Co., 1966-68, Goodyear Pub. Co., 1970-76. Mem. Math. Assn. Am. (past sec. So. Calif. sect., past gov.), Am. Math. Soc., AAAS, Internat. Oceanic Soc., Phi Beta Kappa, Pi Mu Epsilon. Democrat. Author: (with C. Bell, C. Hammond) Fundamentals of Arithmetic for Teachers, 1962. Home: 1206 Anita Ave Ojai CA 93023 Office: 855 N Vermont Ave Los Angeles CA 90029

HERRICK, TRACY GRANT, fiduciary; b. Cleve., Dec. 30, 1933; s. Stanford Avery and Elizabeth Grant (Smith) H.; B.A., Columbia U., 1956, M.A., 1958; postgrad. Yale U., 1956-57; M.A., Oxford U. (Eng.), 1960; m. Maie Kaarsoo, Oct. 12, 1963; children—Sylvi Anne, Alan Kalev. Economist, Fed. Res. Bank, Cleve., 1960-70; sr. economist Stanford Research Inst., Menlo Park, Calif., 1970-73; v.p., sr. analyst Shuman, Agnew & Co., Inc., San Francisco, 1973-75; v.p. Bank of Am., San Francisco, 1975-81; pres. Tracy G. Herrick, Inc., 1981—; lectr. Stonier Grad. Sch. Banking, Am. Bankers Assn., 1967-76; commencement speaker Memphis Banking Sch., 1974; bd. dirs. Jefferies Group, Inc., Jefferies & Co., Inc., Bank Valuation, Inc., B & H Communications Inc., Desk Top Broker, Inc., Anderson Capital Mgmt., Inc., Money Analyst Inc. Fellow Fin. Analysts Fedn.; mem. Columbia Coll. Alumni Assn., Nat. Assn. Bus. Economists, San Francisco Bus. Economists Assn., San Francisco Soc. Security Analysts. Republican. Congregationalist. Author: Bank Analyst's Handbook, 1978; Timing, 1981; Power and Wealth, 1988; contbr. articles to profl. jours. Home: 1150 University Ave Palo Alto CA 94301

HERRIN, LEXIE ELBERT, engineering firm executive; b. Donna, Tex., May 17, 1925; s. Lexie E. and Mary Frances (Scates) H.; BSME, U. Mich., 1951, postgrad. 1951; MBA, U. So. Calif., 1964; m. Charlotte Frances Campbell, Mar. 9, 1946; children: Christopher Patrick, Timothy Michael, Bradley Terrence. Commd. 1st lt. USAF, 1951, advanced through grades to lt. col., 1967, ret., 1969; pres. KOHM Mining and Devel., 1966-69; exec. v.p. Oil Producers & Refiners, Glendale, Calif., 1969-70; gen. mgr. Broadmore Homes of Tex., Waco, 1970-72; pres. Exec. Mobile Home Service, Lighthouse Point, Fla., 1972-74; pres. L.E. Herrin Engr. Cons., Redlands, Calif., 1974-76; v.p., gen. mgr., dir. von Haenel-Herrin & Assocs., Glendale, Calif., 1977-83; pres. Herrin-Stanton & Assocs. 1983—; dir. Seagull Industries, 1966-75; chmn. sub-com. on traffic accident reporting Nat. Hwy. Safety Adv. Com.; lectr. U. Calif., Northridge; arbitrator Am. Arbitration Assn., 1978—; del. com. on transp. Calif. Commn. on the Califs. Active, Boy Scouts Am., 1951-64; co-chmn. Reagan for Pres., San Bernardino County, 1976, asst. to chmn., 1980; del. Calif. Rep. Conv., 1981—; presdl. appointee Dept. Transp. 1981-85. Decorated Air Force Commendation medal with oak leaf clusters. Mem. ASME, AIAA, Internat. Soc. Air Safety Investigators, Am. Inst. Indsl. Engrs., Soc. Automotive Engrs., Am. Assn. Automotive Medicine, Triangle, Sphinx, Michigama, Phi Sigma Kappa. Republican. Clubs: Officers, March AFB Flying, Wheeler Flying, Masons. Editor-in-chief U. Mich. Technic, 1949-51. Office: Herrin-Stanton & Assocs 302 Alabama Ste 10 Redlands CA 92373

HERRING, CHARLES DAVID, lawyer, educator; b. Muncie, Ind., Mar. 18, 1943; s. Morris and Margaret Helen (Scherbaum) H.; children—David, Margaret, Christopher. B.A., Ind. U., 1965, J.D. cum laude, 1968. Bar: Ind. 1968, U.S. Dist. Ct. (so. dist.) Ind. 1971, Calif., 1971, U.S. Dist. Ct. (so. dist.) Calif. 1971. Research assoc. Ind. U., 1965-68; intern Office of Pros. Atty., Monroe County, Inc., 1967-68; ptnr. Herring, Stubel & Lehr, and predecessor Herring and Stubel, San Diego, 1972-88; pvt. practice, San Diego, 1988—; prof. law Western State U., 1972—. Vice chmn. Valle de Oro Planning Com., Spring Valley, Calif., 1972-75; chmn. Valle de Oro Citizens Exec. Com. for Community Planning, Spring Valley, 1975-78. Served with JAGC, U.S. Army, 1968-72. Mem. ABA (nat. best brief award 1968), Ind. Bar Assn., Calif. Bar Assn., San Diego County Bar Assn., Conf. Spl. Ct. Judges, Calif. Trial Lawyers Assn., Order of Coif. Author: (with Jim Wade) California Cases on Professional Responsibility, 1976. Republican. Avocations: computers, gardening, swimming, golf. Home: 1968 Treseder Circle El Cajon CA 92021 Office: Law Offices C David Herring 101 W Broadway Ste 1770 San Diego CA 92101

HERRING, LÁWRENCE SHEPARD, sales manager; b. Phila., Aug. 14, 1946; s. Nathan and Ruth (Shepard) H. BS, Rider Coll., 1968; MBA, Seton Hall U., 1973. Fraternal ins. counselor. Mgr. fin. analysis Dobbs-Life Savers Inc., N.Y.C., 1974-80; dir. fin. planning Macmillan Pub. Co., N.Y.C., 1980-84; acct. exec. Prudential-Bache Securities, N.Y.C., 1985-86; sales mgr. Ind. Order of Foresters, Phoenix, 1986—. Mem. Nat. Assn. Fraternal Ins. Counselors. Home: 1533 E Royal Palm Rd Phoenix AZ 85020 Office: Ind Order Foresters 4120 N 20th St Phoenix AZ 85016

HERRING, WILLIAM CONYERS, physicist, emeritus educator; b. Scotia, N.Y., Nov. 15, 1914; s. William Conyers and Mary (Joy) H.; m. Louise C. Preusch, Nov. 30, 1946; children—Lois Mary, Alan John, Brian Charles, Gordon Robert. A.B., U. Kans., 1933; Ph.D., Princeton, 1937. NRC fellow Mass. Inst. Tech., 1937-39; instr. Princeton, 1939-40, U. Mo., 1940-41; mem. sci. staff Div. War Research, Columbia, 1941-45; prof. applied math. U. Tex., 1946; research physicist Bell Telephone Labs., Murray Hill, N.J., 1946-78; prof. applied physics Stanford (Calif.) U., 1978-81, prof. emeritus, 1981—; mem. Inst. Advanced Study, 1952-53. Recipient Army-Navy Cert. of Appreciation, 1947; Distinguished Service citation U. Kans., 1973; J. Murray Luck award for excellence in sci. reviewing Nat. Acad. Scis., 1980; von Hippel award Materials Research Soc., 1980, Wolf prize in Physics, 1985. Fellow Am. Phys. Soc. (Oliver E. Buckley solid state physics prize 1959), Am. Acad. Arts and Scis.; mem. AAAS, Nat. Acad. Scis. Home: 3945 Nelson Dr Palo Alto CA 94306 Office: Stanford U Dept Applied Physics Stanford CA 94305

HERRINGER, FRANK CASPER, diversified financial services company executive; b. N.Y.C., Nov. 12, 1942; s. Casper Frank and Alice Virginia (McMullen) H.; m. Maryellen B. Cattani, Feb. 11, 1989; children: William Laurence, Sarah Cattani. A.B. magna cum laude, Dartmouth, 1964, M.B.A. with highest distinction, 1965. Prin. Cresap, McCormick & Paget, Inc. (mgmt. cons.), N.Y.C., 1965-71; staff asst. to Pres., Washington, 1971-73; adminstr. U.S. Urban Mass Transp. Adminstrn., Washington, 1973-75; gen. mgr., chief exec. officer San Francisco Bay Area Rapid Transit Dist., 1975-78; exec. v.p., dir. Transamerica Corp., San Francisco, 1979-86, pres., 1986—; dir. Sedgwick Group plc (London), Unocal Corp., Occidental Life Ins. Co., Transam. Ins. Corp., Transam. Fin. Group, Transam. Leasing. Trustee Pacific Presbyn. Med. Ctr., Amos Tuck Sch. Bus. Adminstrn. Dartmouth Coll., Mills Coll. Mem. Phi Beta Kappa. Republican. Clubs: San Francisco Golf, Olympic, Bankers. Home: 224 Hillside Ave Piedmont CA 94611 Office: Transam Corp 600 Montgomery St San Francisco CA 94111

HERRMANN, GEORGE, mechanical engineering educator; b. USSR, Apr. 19, 1921. Dipl. C.E., Swiss Fed. Inst. Tech., 1945, Ph.D. in Mechanics, 1949. Asst., then asso. prof. civil engring. Columbia, 1950-62; prof. civil engring. Northwestern U., 1962-69; prof. applied mechanics Stanford, 1969—; cons. SRI Internat., 1970-80. Contbr. 200 articles to profl. jours; editorial bd. numerous jours. Fellow ASME (Centennial medal 1980); mem. ASCE (Th. v. Karman medal 1981), Nat. Acad. Engring., AIAA. Office: Stanford U Div Applied Mechanics Durand Bldg Stanford CA 94305-4040

HERRMANN, WALTER, laboratory administrator; b. Johannesburg, Republic of South Africa, May 2, 1930; came to U.S., 1953; s. Gottlob Friedraich and Gertrud Louise (Retzlaff) H.; m. Betty Allard (div.); children: Peter Friedrich, Inga Louise. BSc in Engring. cum laude, U. Witwatersrand, Republic South Africa, 1950; PhD in Mech. Engring., U. Witwatersrand, 1955. Rsch. engr. MIT, Boston, 1953-55, sr. rsch. engr., 1957-64; lectr. U. Cape Town, Rep. South Africa, 1955-57; div. supr. Sandia Nat. Labs., Albuquerque, 1964-67, dept. mgr., 1967-82, dir. engring. svcs., 1982—; W.W. Clyde prof. U. Utah, Salt Lake City, 1971-72. Contbr. articles to profl. jours. Mem. ASME, Am. Phys. Soc., Soc. Natural Philosophy, Am. Acad, Mechanics. Office: Sandia Nat Labs Albuquerque NM 87185

HERRON, DREW JONATHAN, advertising development company executive; b. Perth, Australia, Dec. 8, 1956; came to U.S., 1979; s. Douglas Alexander and Mem Kathlyn (McRohan) H.; m. Sharon Anne Blewitt, May 8, 1984. Student, U. We. Australia, Perth, 1975-79. Chief exec. officer, chmn. Custom Characters Inc., L.A., 1985—. Mem. East Side Conservative Club (N.Y.C.). Republican. Ch. of England.

HERRON, ELLEN PATRICIA, retired judge; b. Auburn, N.Y., July 30, 1927; d. David Martin and Grace Josephine (Berner) Herron; A.B. Trinity Coll., 1949; M.A., Cath. U. Am., 1954; J.D., U. Calif.-Berkeley, 1964. Asst. dean Cath. U. Am., 1952-54; instr. East High Sch., Auburn, 1955-57; asst. dean Wells Coll., Aurora, N.Y., 1957-58; instr. psychology and history Contra Costa Coll., 1958-60; dir. row Stanford, 1960-61; assoc. Knox & Kretzmer, Richmond, Calif., 1964-65; admitted to Calif. bar, 1965; ptnr. Knox & Herron, 1965-74, Knox, Herron and Masterson, 1974-77 (both Richmond, Calif.); judge Superior Ct. State of Calif., 1977-87; gen. ptnr. Real Estate Syndicates, Calif., 1967-77; owner, mgr. The Barricia Vineyards, 1978—. Active numerous civic orgns.; bd. dirs. Rhonoh Sch., Richmond, YWCA, Econ. Devel. Council Richmond; alumnae bd. dirs. Boalt Hall, U. Calif.-Berkeley, 1980-84. Mem. ABA, Contra Costa Bar Assn. (exec. com. 1969-74), State Bar Calif., Calif. Trial Lawyers, Nat. Assn. Women Lawyers, Nat. Assn. Women Judges, Calif. Women Lawyers, Applicants Attys. Assn., Calif. Judges Assn. (ethics com. 1977-79, criminal law procedure com. 1979-80), Queen's Bench, Juvenile Ct. Judges Assn. Democrat. Home: 51 Western Dr Point Richmond CA 94801

HERRON, MARGARET CATHERINE, nurse; b. Aberdeen Proving Grounds, Md., Mar. 27, 1954; d. Thomas James and Virginia (Owen) Herron. BS in Nursing, San Diego State U., 1977. RN, Calif. Nurse Tri-City Hosp. Mental Health Unit, Oceanside, Calif., 1983-86; pub. health nurse Vis. Nurse Assn., Vista, Calif., 1986—. Capt. USAF, 1978-83. Mem. Am. Nurses Assn. (cert. mental health nurse). Democrat. Office: Vis Nurse Assn 401 S Sante Fe Ave Ste 201 Vista CA 92083

HERSCHENSOHN, BRUCE, film director, writer; b. Milw., Sept. 10, 1932. Ed., Los Angeles. With art dept. RKO Pictures, 1953-55; dir., editor Gen. Dynamics Corp., 1955-56; dir., writer, editor Karma for Internat. Communications Found.; editor, co-dir. Friendship Seven for NASA; dir., editor Tall Man Five-Five for Gen. Dynamics Corp. and SAC; dir. motion picture and TV Service USIA, 1968-72, spl. cons. to dir., 1972—; staff asst. to Pres. U.S., 1972; dep. spl. asst. to Pres., 1973-74, mem. transition team, 1981; tchr. U. Md., 1972; spl. cons. to Rep. Nat. Conv., 1972; polit. analyst KABC-TV. Directed and wrote films for USIA, including Bridges of the Barrios, The Five Cities of June, The President, John F. Kennedy: Years of Lightning, Day of Drums, Eulogy to 5:02; recipient Acad. award for Czechoslovakia 1968 as best documentary short 1969; author: The Gods of Antenna, 1976; contbg. editor: Conservative Digest. Bd. govs. Charles Edison Meml. Youth Fund. Served with USAF, 1951-52. Recipient Arthur S. Flemming award as 1 of 10 outstanding young men in fed. govt., 1969; Distinguished Service medal USIA, 1972; Ann. award Council Against Communist Aggression, 1972. Office: Sta KABC-TV 4151 Prospect Ave Los Angeles CA 90027

HERSH, BRUCE R., corporate professional; b. Dragerton, Utah, Aug. 7, 1947; s. Leroy M. and Ruth May (Lewis) H.; m. Halley Kay Hersh; children: Kacie Lin, Brooke, Amidey. Student, Coll. Ea. Utah, Price, 1965-67, U. Utah, 1967-69. Mgr. Grand Cen. Stores, Salt Lake City, 1967; buyer Keith Warshaw Co., Salt Lake City, 1974-76; store designer Gen. Mills, Lee Wards, Chgo., 1976-80; store mgr. Pamida, Rexburg, Idaho, 1980; sales mgr. Artio, H.B. Hewitt, Rexburg, Idaho, 1981; gen. mgr., pres. Hortense B. Hewitt, Rexburg, Idaho, 1988—. Mem. Idaho Dist. Export Coun., 1986-87. Office: Hortense B Hewitt 1 Stationery Pl Rexburg ID 83441 Home: 250 Apache Rexburg ID 83440

HERSHISER, OREL LEONARD, IV, professional baseball player; b. Buffalo, Sept. 16, 1958; s. Orel Leonard H. III and Millie H.; m. Jaimie (Byars) Hershiser, Feb. 7, 1981; 2 sons, Orel Leonard V, Jordan Douglass. Student, Bowling Green State U. Pitcher minor league teams Clinton, Ia., 1979, San Antonio, 1980-81, Albuquerque, 1982-8; with Los Angeles Dodgers, 1983—; mem. Nat. League All-Star Team, 1987, 88. Named Nat. League Cy Young award winner, 1988, Most Valuable Player 1988 World Series. Office: Los Angeles Dodgers Dodger Stadium 1000 Elysian Park Ave Los Angeles CA 90012 *

HERSKOVITZ, MARSHALL SCHREIBER, screenwriter, director, producer; b. Phila., Feb. 23, 1952; s. Alexander and Frieda (Schreiber) H.; m. Susan Amanda Shilliday, Feb. 15, 1981; children: Elizabeth Gray, May Myles. B.A., Brandeis U., 1973; M.F.A., Am. Film Inst., 1975. Freelance writer, dir., producer various TV shows. Writer Family, ABC-TV, 1978, also dir.; writer White Shadow, CBS-TV, 1980, 81; writer-producer Special Bulletin NBC-TV, 1983 (2 Emmys for best writing, best dramatic spl. Acad. TV Arts and Scis), exec. prod., co-writer, dir. thirtysomething, 1987— (2 Emmy awards for best writing, best dramatic series Acad. TV Arts and Scis. 1988, Humanitas award Human Family Inst. 1988, Dirs. Guild Am. award 1988). Recipient Humanitas award Human Family Inst. 1983. Mem. Writers Guild of Am. (Writers Guild of Am. award), Dirs. Guild Am. Democrat. Jewish.

HERTLEIN, FRED, III, industrial hygiene laboratory executive; b. San Francisco, Oct. 17, 1933; s. Fred and Herta (Komning) H.; m. Clara Kam Fung Tse, Apr. 1958 (div. Apr. 1982); children: Fritz, Hans Wernher, Lisa Marie, Gretel Marga. BS in Chemistry, U. Nev., 1956; postgrad., U. Hawaii, 1956-58. Cert. profl. chemist, indsl. hygienist, safety profl., hazard control mgr. Grad. teaching ast. in chemistry U. Hawaii, Honolulu, 1956-58; air pollution sampling sta. operator Truesdail Labs., Honolulu, 1957; chemist oceanographical research vessels Dept. Interior, 1957-59; with Bechtel-Hawaiian Dredging, 1959; co-owner marine survey co. Honolulu, 1959-60; radiochemist Pearl Harbor (Hawaii) Naval Shipyard, 1959-62, indsl. hygienist med. dept., 1962-69, head indsl.hygiene br., 1969-72; indsl. hygiene program mgr. Naval Regional Med. Clinic, Pearl Harbor Naval Sta., 1972-78; pres., dir. lab. and indsl. hygiene, co-owner Indsl. Analytical Lab., Inc., Honolulu, 1978–; pres. F. Hertlein & Assocs., 1970-78. Contbr. articles to profl. jours. Named Outstanding Male Fed. Employee, Honolulu Fed. Exec. Council, 1967, Citizen of Day citation Sta. KGU76, Honolulu, 1972, cert. of achievement Toastmasters Internat., 1974, expression of appreciation U. Hawaii Sch. Pub. Health, 1985. Fellow Am. Inst. Chemists; mem. Am. Acad. Indsl. Hygiene, Am. Chem. Soc., AAAS, Am. Indsl. Hygiene Assn. Fedn. Am. Scientists, Gesellschaft fur Aerosolforschung, Gesellschaft Deutscher Chemiker, Profl. Assn. Diving Instrs. Home: 1493 Kaweloka St Pearl City HI 96782 Office: Indsl Analytical Lab Inc 3615 Harding Ave Ste 304 Honolulu HI 96816

HERTWECK, E. ROMAYNE, psychology educator; b. Springfield, Mo., July 24, 1928; s. Garnett Perry and Nova Gladys (Chowning) H.; m. Alma Louise Street, Dec. 16, 1955; 1 child, William Scott. BA, Augustana Coll., 1962; MA, Pepperdine U., 1963; EdD, Ariz. State U., 1966; PhD, U.S. Internat. U., 1978. Cert. sch. psychologist, Calif. Night editor Rock Island (Ill.) Argus Newspaper, 1961; grad. asst. psychology dept. Pepperdine Coll., Los Angeles, 1962; counselor VA, Ariz. State U., Tempe, 1963; assoc. dir. Conciliation Ct., Phoenix, 1964; instr. Phoenix Coll., Phoenix, 1965; prof. Mira Costa Coll., Oceanside, Calif., 1966—, mem. senate council, 1968-70, 85-87, 89—, chmn. psychology-counseling dept., 1973-75, chmn. dept. behavioral sci., 1976-82, 87-88; part-time lectr. dept. bus. adminstrn. San Diego State U., 1980-84, Sch. Human Behavior U.S. Internat. U., 1984—; prof. psychology Chapman Coll. World Campus Afloat, 1970; pres. El Camino Preschs., Inc., Oceanside, Calif., 1985—. Bd. dirs. Lifeline, 1969, Christian Counseling Center, Oceanside, 1970-82. Mem. Am., Western, North San Diego County (v.p. 1974-75) psychol. assns., Am. Personnel and Guidance Assn., Nat. Educators Fellowship (v.p. El Camino chpt. 1976-77), Am. Coll. Personnel Assn., Phi Delta Kappa, Kappa Delta Pi, Psi Chi, Kiwanis (charter mem. Carlsbad club, dir. 1975-77). Home: 2024 Oceanview Rd Oceanside CA 92056 Office: Mira Costa Coll 1 Barnard Dr Oceanside CA 92056 Office: El Camino Preschs Inc 2002 California St Oceanside CA 92054

HERTZ, BRADLEY ALLEN, consultant; b. Mar. 5, 1948; s. Raymond Allen and Sylvia (Nadler) H.; m. Dana Jean Schulack, June 21, 1981. BS, San Jose State U., 1970. Sales rep. J.M. Smucker Co., Orville, Ohio, 1970-76; regional sales mgr. Alex Foods, Anaheim, Calif., 1976-78, Allied Mills, Chgo., 1978-79; nat. sales mgr. Calif. Gift/Orlando Foods, Fresno, Calif., 1979-80; cons. Hertz Mktg., Walnut Creek, Calif., 1980—; cons. Pine Mountain Corp., Oakland, Calif., 1980—, Valley Travel, Kerman, Calif., 1980—, Ram Group, Oakland, 1982—. Home and Office: 190D Park Lake Cir Walnut Creek CA 94598

HERZ, MICHAEL JOSEPH, marine environmental scientist; b. Saint Paul, Aug. 12, 1936; s. Malvin E. and Josephine (Daneman) H.; m. Joan Klein Levy, Feb. 3, 1962 (div. 1982); children: David M., Daniel J., Ann K.; m. Naomi Brodie Schalit, Aug. 21, 1984; children: Nathaniel B., Hallie R. BA, Reed Coll., 1958; MA, San Francisco State U., 1962; PhD, U. So. Calif., 1966. Program coordinator postdoctoral tng. program U. Calif., San Francisco, 1969-73, asst. prof., 1969-73, assoc. prof. in residence, 1973-74; exec. dir., dir. water quality tng. program San Francisco Bay. chpt. Oceanic Soc., 1974-77; exec. v.p., co-dir. research and policy (Nat.) Oceanic Soc., San Francisco, 1977-84; sr. research scientist Tiburon Ctr. for Environ. Studies San Francisco State U., San Francisco, 1984—; bd. trustees Oceanic Soc., Washington, 1984-88; chmn. bd. govs. Tiburon Ctr. Environ. Studies, San Francisco State U., 1985-86; Nat. Research Council com. mem. Effectiveness of Oil Spills Dispersants, Washington, 1985—; Calif. Dept. Health Services com. Ocean Disposal of Radwaste, Sacramento, 1985—; bd. dirs. Aquatic Habitat Inst., 1986—; pres., bd. dirs. San Francisco Bay-Delta Preservation Assn., Sausalito, Calif., 1986-89, exec. dir., 1989—; bd. dirs. Citizens for a Better Environment, San Francisco. Author, co-editor: Memory Consolidation, 1972, Habituation I & II, 1973, Analysis of the Puerto Rican Oil Spill, 1985, Analysis of Influence of Freshwater Flow on the Delta-San Francsico Bay & Their Fisheries Production, 1987; contbr. articles to profl. jours. Chmn. community adv. bd. Sta. KQED (Pub. Broadcast System affiliate), 1979-85, San Francisco, citizens adv. com. San Francisco Bay Conservation and Devel. Commn., 1979—, chmn. 1984; mem. tech. adv. com. San Francisco Bay Regional Water Quality Control Bd., Oakland, Calif., 1979-82, Assn. Bay Area Govts., Oakland, 1983—; mem. bay area adv. com. Sea Grant Marine Adv. Program, San Francisco, 1983—; mem. com. Bur. Land Mgmt., Pacific States Regional Tech. Working Group, 1979-83. Served with U.S. Army, 1958-59. Predoctoral fellow NIMH, U. So. Calif., 1963-64; postdoctoral fellow NIMH, UCLA Brain Research Inst, 1966-68. Mem. AAAS, Calif. Acad. Scis., San Francisco Bay and Estuarine Assn., Sigma Xi.

HERZBERG, DOROTHY CREWS, financial services administrator; b. N.Y.C., July 8, 1935; d. Floyd Houston and Julia (Lesser) Crews; m. Hershel Zelig Herzberg, May 22, 1962 (div. Apr. 1988); children: Samuel Floyd, Laura Jill, Daniel Crews. AB, Brown U., 1957; MA, Stanford U., 1964; JD, San Francisco Law Sch., 1976. Legal sec. various law firms, San Francisco, 1976-78; tchr. Mission Adult Sch., San Francisco, 1965-66; tchr. secondary and univ. levels Peace Corps, Nigeria, 1961-63; investigator Office of Dist. Atty., San Francisco, 1978-80; sr. adminstr. Dean Witter Reynolds Co., San Francisco, 1980-83; registered rep. Waddell and Reed, Oakland, Calif., 1983-84; fin. services rep. United Resources, Hayward, Calif., 1984-85, Ind. Planning Corp., San Francisco, 1985-86; tax preparer H&R Block, 1987; revenue officer IRS, 1987—. Editor: (newsletters) Coop. Nursery Sch. Council, 1969-71, Miraloma Life, 1976-82, Dem. Women's Forum, 1980-81, Stanford Luncheon Club, 1984-85. Bd. dirs. LWV, San Francisco, 1967-69, mem. speakers bur., 1967-80; pres. Council Coop. Nursery Schs., San Francisco, 1969-71; bd. dirs. Miraloma (Calif.) Improvement Club, 1977-88, pres., 1980-81; alt. for supr. San Francisco Mayor's Commn. on Criminal Justice, 1978. Mem. San Francisco C. of C. Democrat. Unitarian. Club: West Portal Toastmistress. Home: 2237 Haste St #4 Berkeley CA 94704 Office: 1255 Post St Ste 700 San Francisco CA 94109

HERZBERG, KEVIN LEROY, electrical engineer; b. Kansas City, Mo., May 13, 1963; s. Alfred Henry and Carol Ann (Bertha) H. BS in Elec. Engring., UCLA, 1986. Lic. life and disability ins. agent, Calif. Life ins. agent Ultra Ins. Svc., Gardena, Calif., 1983-86; project engr. Behavioral Rsch. Assoc., Inc., Canoga Park, Calif., 1986—; elec. engr. Hughes Aircraft Co., Canoga Park, 1986—. Active Life Underwriters Polit. Action Com., head coach Woodland Hills (Calif.) Little League. Mem. IEEE, Order of the Engr., Nat. Assn. Life Underwriters, Phi Gamma Delta (chief justice 1985-86). Republican. Home: 10745 Kling St #103 Toluca Lake CA 91602-1471 Office: Hughes Aircraft Co 8433 Fallbrook Ave Bldg #265/P60 Canoga Park CA 91304-0445

HESS, DARLENE RUTH, health care administrator; b. Mt. Vernon, Ohio, Oct. 6, 1947; d. Dean M. Hess and Florence A. (Rohring) Beach; children: Darren, Damon. BS in Nursing, Troy State U., 1974; MS in Nursing, U. Ala., Birmingham, 1978. Cert. nurse practitioner. In service dir. Downtown Nursing Home, Montgomery, Ala., 1974, Elmore County Hosp., Wetumpka, Ala., 1974-76; nursing instr. Troy State U., Montgomery, Ala., 1976-77; family nurse practitioner USPHS, Tuskegee Inst. and Mobile, Ala., 1978-82; nursing dir. Lynwood Nursing Home, Mobile, 1982-83; patient care coordinator Mid South Home Health, Mobile, 1983-85; adminstr., dir. clin. services VNS Health Svcs., Inc., Santa Fe, 1986—; bd. dirs. Mid South Home Health; adj. nursing faculty U. So. Ala., Mobile; cons. U.S. Sports Acad.; lectr. Health Edn. for Community Based Nurses. Health team dir. Great Peace March, Los Angeles, 1986. Recipient USPHS Commd. Officer award, 1981. Mem. N.Mex. State Nurses Assn., Am. Pub. Health Assn., N.Mex. Home Care Assn., Ala. State Nurses Assn. (Outstanding Nurse Practitioner 1985), Phi Kappa Phi, Sigma Theta Tau. Home: 2491 Sawmill Rd #1308 Santa Fe NM 87505 Office: VNS Health Svcs Inc 811 St Michaels Dr Santa Fe NM 87501

HESS, DENNIS WILLIAM, chemical engineering educator; b. Reading, Pa., Mar. 1, 1947; s. John William and Dorothy E. (Miller) H.; m. Patricia Ruth Weidner, June 1, 1968; children: Amy R., Sarah E. BS in Chemistry, Albright Coll., 1968; MS in Phys. Chemistry, Lehigh U., 1970, PhD in Phys. Chemistry, 1973. Staff researcher Fairchild Semiconductor, Palo Alto, Calif., 1973-77; from asst. prof. to prof. chem. engring. U. Calif., Berkeley, 1977—; prin. investigator Materials and Molecular Research div. Lawrence Berkeley Lab., 1978-84, Ctr. for Adv. Materials, Lawrence Berkeley Lab., 1983-85. Contbr. articles to profl. jours. Office: U Calif Dept Chem Engring Berkeley CA 94720

HESS, EILEEN SWEETEN, computer consultant, software developer; b. Malad, Idaho, Jan. 1, 1949; d. Colen Hagel Jr. and Ruth (Gerber) Sweeten; m. Don Lee Hess, Sept. 13, 1968 (div. Nov. 1972); 1 child, Sonya. Student, Brigham Young U., 1967-70. Cert. in data processing Inst. for Cert. Computer Profls. Tchr. Burley Sch. Dist., Oakley, Idaho, 1970-71; keypunch operator DHI Computing Service, Provo, Utah, 1972-76; computer operator Trammel Crow, Inc., Clearfield, Utah, 1976-77; programmer, analyst Davis Computer Services, Provo, 1977-78; owner The Data Doctor, Orem, Utah, 1978-83; programmer, analyst Data Fin. Systems, Scottsdale, Ariz., 1983-84; info. systems dir. Harbor Fin. Group, Phoenix, 1984-85; owner Software Magic, Phoenix, 1985—. Music booster, chaperone Phoenix Country Day Sch., 1985-86. Mem. Data Processing Mgmt. Assn. (newsletter columnist 1986), Ind. Computer Cons. Assn., Micro-Adapt Users Internat. (pres. 1986—), Nat. Assn. Female Execs. Republican. Mormon. Home: 4201 E Camelback Rd Phoenix AZ 85108 Office: Software Magic PO Box 44378 Phoenix AZ 85064

HESS, HENRY LEROY, JR., bankruptcy judge; b. LaGrande, Oreg., Mar. 29, 1924; s. Henry Leroy and Estrid (Johanson) H.; m. Betty Lou Stone, Oct. 15, 1949; children: David Leroy, Steven Lee. BS, U. Oreg., 1947, JD, 1949. Ptnr. Conklin & Hess, Pendleton, Oreg., 1949-52; sole practice Pendleton, 1952-73; bankruptcy judge U.S. Dist. Ct. Oreg., Pendleton, 1958-73, Portland, 1973—. Chmn. Pendleton United Fund, 1956, Umatilla County Dec. Cen. Com., Pendleton, 1952-54. Ensign USN, 1943-46, PTO. Mem. Oreg. State Bar Assn., Comml. Law League, Nat. Conf. of Bankruptcy Judges, Tualitin Country Club, Elks. Home: 7790 SW Miner Way Portland OR 97225 Office: US Dist Ct Oreg 900 Orbanco Bldg 1001 SW 5th Ave Portland OR 97204

HESS, TED HAROLD, chief executive officer; b. Harrisburg, Pa., Feb. 7, 1932; s. Harold Leroy and Ferol Avalon (Stickel) H.; m. Joy Garber, May 21, 1955; children: Dianne Marie, Lorilee Evelyn, Ted Douglas. BA in Fine Arts, Pa. State U., State Coll., Pa., 1953; MBA, Ohio State U., 1967. Logistics mgr. Canadian Air Defense Command, North Bay, Ontario, Canada, 1967-70; mgmt. cons. Air Force Inspector Gen., Norton AFB, Calif., 1970-72; logistics dir. Mil. Equipment Delvery Group, Phnon Penh, Cambodia, 1972-73; asst. dir. Tactical Air Command, Langely AFB, Va., 1973-76; material mgmt. dir. Davis-Monthan AFB, Tucson, 1976-80; mgr. IBM Prodn. Control, Tucson, 1980-84, IBM Product Transfers, Tucson, 1984-86; coordinator IBM Strategic Planning, Tucson, 1986-87; pres. Ted Hess Consulting, Tucson, 1987—; instr. in field; assoc. faculty U. Phoenix, Tucson, 1985-89. Author: Meeting the Leadership Challenge, 1988, Strategic Planning, 1988, Managing Your Most Precious Resource-Time, 1988. Recipient Men of Achievement award Internat. Biog. Centre, 1987. Leadership award Am. Biog. Inst., 1987. Mem. Am. Soc. for Tng./Devel., Nat. Speakers Assn., Am. Soc. Prodn. and Inventory Control, Toastmasters (pres. 1985-86). Republican. Methodist. Home and Office: Ted Hess Consulting 4300 Camino Yermo Tucson AZ 85715

HESSE, CHRISTIAN AUGUST, mining company executive; b. Chemnitz, Germany, June 20, 1925; s. William Albert and Anna Gunhilda (Baumann) H.; B. Applied Sci. with honors, U. Toronto (Ont., Can.), 1948; m. Brenda Nora Rigby, Nov. 4, 1964; children: Robin Christian, Bruce William. In various mining and constrn. positions, Can., 1944-61; jr. shift boss N.J. Zinc Co., Gilman, Colo., 1949; asst. layout engr. Internat. Nickel Co., Sudbury, Ont., 1949-52; shaft engr. Perini-Walsh Joint Venture, Niagara Falls, Ont., 1952-54; project engr. B. Perini & Sons (Can.) Ltd., Toronto, Ottawa, and New Brunswick, 1954-55; field engr. Aries Copper Mines Ltd., No. Ont., 1955-56; instr. in mining engring. U. Toronto, 1956-57; planning engr. Stanleigh Uranium Mining Corp. Ltd., Elliot Lake, Ont., 1957-58, chief engr., 1959-60; field engr. Johnson-Perini-Kiewit Joint Venture, Toronto, 1960-61; del. Commonwealth Mining Congress, Africa, 1961; with U.S. Borax & Chem. Corp., 1961—, gen. mgr. Allan Potash Mines Ltd., Allan, Sask., Can., 1974, chief engr. U.S. Borax & Chem. Corp., Los Angeles, 1974-77, v.p. engring., 1977-81, 87—, v.p. and project mgr. Quartz Hill project, 1981—; v.p. Pacific Coast Molybdenum Co., 1981—, v.p. mining devel., 1984—. Sault Daily Star scholar, Sault Sainte Marie, Ont., Can., 1944. Mem. AIME, Can. Inst. Mining and Metallurgy (life), Assn. Profl. Engrs. Ont., The L.A. Club, L.A. Tennis Club. Lutheran. Office: US Borax & Chem Corp 3075 Wilshire Blvd Los Angeles CA 90010

HESSE, MARGARET MARY, real estate sales management, financial planner; b. Mineola, N.Y., Aug. 19, 1938; d. Donald Purdy Gager and Margaret Helen (Schroeder) Gager; m. John Lamborn Hesse, Jan. 19, 1957 (dec. Jan. 1982); children: John Donald, Judith Anne Young, Shana Marie. BA, San Jose State U., 1969; MA, N.Mex. State U., 1971. Cert. fin. planner, cert. residential broker. Instr. N.Mex. State U., Las Cruces, 1970-72; sales assoc. Drue Self Real Estate, Las Cruces, 1976-77, sales mgr., 1984—; br. mgr. N. Cen. Mortgage Co., Las Cruces, 1977-78; sr. planner Hesse & Assocs. Fin. Planners, Inc., Las Cruces, 1984-88. Bd. dirs. ARC, Dona Ana Chpt., Las Cruces, N.Mex., 1987-88, SMF counselor, Pasadena Chpt., Calif., 1982-83. Mem. Las Cruces C. of C., Nat. Assn. Realtors, Realtors Nat. Mktg. Inst., Realtors Assn. N.Mex. (southwestern chpt.), Internat. Assn. Fin. Planning (pres. 1986-88, v.p. programs 1985-86, v.p. edn. 1984-85) Western Assn. Fin. Planners, Inst. Cert. Fin. Planners, Phi Kappa Phi, Phi Beta Kappa. Republican. Protestant. Home: 3990 Nemesh Las Cruces NM 88005 Office: Drue Self Real Estate Inc 795 S Soland Las Cruces NM 88001

HESSE, MICHAEL GEORGE SAMUEL, real estate investor; b. Buffalo, Wyo., Aug. 21, 1939; s. George Sutherland and Grace (Garvey) H.; m. Betty Chamberlain Richards, Mar. 23, 1964; children: Michael, Jennifer. BA, U. Ariz., 1962. Cert. comml. investment mem. Owner Hesse & Assocs., Concord, Calif., 1968-71; co-owner Monroe Realtors, Walnut Creek, Calif., 1971-77; v.p., mgr. Security Pacific Real Estate, Walnut Creek, 1977-85; co-owner Briner & Hesse, Walnut Creek, 1985—; pres. Hesse Corp., Walnut Creek, 1980—. Bd. dirs. Unity Ctr., Walnut Creek, 1986. Mem. Rental Housing Assn. (bd. dirs.), Contra Costa Bd. Realtors, Nat. Assn. Realtors, Realtors Nat. Mktg. Assn., Internat. Assn. Shopping Ctrs. Office: Hesse Corp 1850 Mt Diablo Blvd Ste 230 Walnut Creek CA 94596

HESSEE, STEPHEN LAWRENCE, utility executive; b. Lincoln, Nebr., Nov. 23, 1942; s. Robert Thomas and Agnes Mathilda (Thompson) H.; m. Nanette L. Binger, July 8, 1966 (div. July 1984); children: Mark S., Blaine T., Megan L. BA in Psychology, U. Nebr., 1965. Adjudicator VA Regional Offices, Lincoln, 1969-70; personnel asst. Cen. Telephone and Utilities Corp., Lincoln, 1970-76; personnel staff mgr. Cen. Telephone and Utilities Corp., Chgo., 1976-78; personnel and pub. relations mgr. Cen. Telephone of Ohio, Lorain, 1978-82; gen. personnel, adminstrv. staff mgr. Centel Electric of Colo., Pueblo, 1982—; officer Ohio Telephone Assn., Columbus, 1980-82. V.p. Firelands Council Boy Scouts Am., Vermilion, Ohio, 1981; pres. Jr. Achievement Pueblo County, 1988; company rep. Savings Bond Drive, United Way Pueblo, 1983, 84. Served to capt. USAF, 1965-69. Mem. Am. Soc. for Personnel Adminstrn., Rocky Mountain Elec. League (com. chmn. 1988—), Pueblo C. of C., Kappa Sigma (Dist. Grand Master 1987—). Republican. Presbyterian. Office: Centel Electric Colo PO Box 75 Pueblo CO 81002

HESSELINK, LAMBERTUS, aeronautics, astronautics and electrical engineering educator; b. Enschede, The Netherlands, Dec. 4, 1948; came to U.S., 1971; s. Lambertus and Wilhelmina (ten Tye) H.; m. Marieke van Heerde, Aug. 18, 1971. BSME, Twente Inst. Tech., Enschede, 1970, BS in Applied Physics, 1971, postgrad., 1974; MSME, Calif. Inst. Tech., 1972, PhD in Applied Mechs., Physics, 1977. Research fellow Calif. Inst. Tech., Pasadena, 1977-78, instr. applied physics, 1978-80, sr. research fellow fluid mechs., 1979-80; asst. prof. aeros. and astronautics Stanford (Calif.) U., 1980-85, asst. prof., 1985—, assoc. prof. elec. engring., 1980-85, asst. prof., 1985—; cons. Hughes Aircraft Corp., Culver City, Calif., 1978-79, MCC Corp., 1986—; cons. to industry and govt. Patentee in field. Recipient Stheeman prize Twente Inst. Tech., 1970; Fulbright fellow 1971-74; fellow Josephine de Karman fellow, 1974-75. Mem. AIAA (Engr. of Yr. 1982), Optical Soc. Am., Soc. Photo-Optical Instrumentation Engrs. Optical Soc. Am., Am. Phys. Soc., Sigma Xi. Office: Stanford U Dept Aeros and Astronautics Durand 359 B Stanford CA 94305

HETHERINGTON, CHERYL KEIKO, lawyer; b. Honolulu, July 24, 1952; d. Sidney Ichiro and Shizuko (Murakami) Hashimoto; m. J. George Hetherington, Nov. 25, 1978. Student Whitman Coll., 1970-72; B.A. U. Wash.-Seattle, 1974; J.D., Hastings Coll. Law, San Francisco. Bar: Hawaii 1979, U.S. Dist. Ct. Hawaii 1979. Counselor Planned Parenthood of Seattle-King County, 1974-76; atty. Law Offices Sidney I Hashimoto, Honolulu, 1979-82; sole practice, Honolulu, 1982—. Mem. Hawaii State Bar Assn., Hawaii Women Lawyers, ABA (Family Law div.), Nat. Assn. Women Lawyers, Hastings Alumni Assn., U. Wash. Alumni Assn., Mortar Board, Alpha Chi Omega Found., Alpha Kappa Delta. Democrat. Club: Kailua Racquet. Contbg. author articles in field. Office: 1001 Bishop St 480 Pauahi Tower Honolulu HI 96813

HETLAND, JOHN ROBERT, lawyer, educator; b. Mpls., Mar. 12, 1930; s. James L. and Evelyn (Lundgren) H.; m. Mildred Woodruff, Dec. 1951 (div.); children: Lynda Lee, Robert John, Debra Ann.; m. Anne Kneeland, Dec. 1972; children: Robin T. Kneeland, Elizabeth J. Kneeland. B.S.L., U. Minn., 1952, J.D., 1956. Bar: Minn. bar 1956, Calif. bar 1962. Practice law Mpls., 1956-59; assoc. prof. law U. Calif., Berkeley, 1959-60, prof. law, 1960—; ptnr. Hetland & Hensen, PC, Berkeley, 1959—; vis. prof. law Stanford U., 1971, 80, U. Singapore, 1972, U. Cologne, Fed. Republic Germany, 1988. Author: California Real Property Secured Transactions, 1970, Commercial Real Estate Transactions, 1972, Secured Real Estate Transactions, 1974, 1977; co-author: (with Maxwell, Riesenfeld, and Warren) California Cases on Security Transactions in Land, 2d edit., 1975, 3d edit., 1984; contbr. articles to legal, real estate and fin. jours. Served to lt. comdr. USNR, 1953-55. Mem. state bars Calif. and Minn., Am. Bar Assn., Order of Coif, Phi Delta Phi. Republican. Home: 20 Redcoach Ln Orinda CA 94563 Office: 2600 Warring St Berkeley CA 94704

HETT, JOAN MARGARET, civic administrator; b. Trail, B.C., Can., Sept. 8, 1936; s. Gordon Stanley and Violet Thora (Thors) Hett; B.Sc., U. Victoria (B.C., Can.), 1964; M.S., U. Wis., Madison, 1967, Ph.D., 1969. Ecologist, Eastern Deciduous Forest Biome, Oak Ridge Nat. Lab., 1969-72; coor. sites dir. Coniferous Forest Biome, Oreg. State U., Corvallis and U. Wash., Seattle, 1972-77; ecol. cons., Seattle, 1978-84; plant ecologist Seattle City Light, 1984-86; supr. Rights-of-Way, Seattle City Light, 1986—. Mem. Ecol. Soc. Am., Brit. Ecol. Soc., Am. Inst. Biol. Scis., Am. Forestry Assn., Sigma Xi. Contbr. articles to profl. jours.; research in plant population dynamics, land use planning, forest sucession.

HETT, ROSLIN MARTYN, finance company executive; b. Kamloops, B.C., Can., Nov. 22, 1931; s. Roslin Martyn and Phyllis Maude (Slater) H.; came to U.S., 1966; ed. Brentwood Coll., Victoria, B.C., 1950; m. Sophia Penelope Jane Harvey, July 10, 1953; children—Jane, Caroline, John, Jennifer, Mary. Field rep. Niagara Finance Corp., Victoria, 1953; with collections dept. Gen. Motors Acceptance Corp., Vancouver, 1953-55, from field rep. to dist. rep., 1956-60; sales mgr. Morrison Motors, Ltd., Duncan, B.C., 1955-56; with Avco Fin. Services, Inc., and predecessors, Newport Beach, Calif., 1960-79, pres., 1975-79, also dir.; pres., dir. Avco Corp., 1979-81; prin. Hett Fin. Cons., Laguna Niguel, Calif., 1981—. Episcopalian. Clubs: Balboa Bay, Masons. Home: 30882 Cypress Pl Laguna Niguel CA 92677 Office: Hett Fin Cons 30101 Town Center Dr Ste 103 Laguna Niguel CA 92677

HETTICH, RANDALL ROY, social worker; b. Seattle, June 15, 1959; s. Roy Allen Hettich and Mildred Margaret (Schroeder) Lane. BA, U. Puget Sound, 1981; MS, Oreg. State U., 1984. Nat. cert. counselor. Evening supr. Community Outreach, Inc., Corvallis, Oreg., 1982-83; counselor Redmond (Wash.) Counseling Svc., 1984-85; vocat. rehab. counselor Action Rehab. Cons., San Diego, 1985-86; counselor Southwood Residential Treatment, Chula Vista, Calif., 1986; social worker San Diego County Child Protective Svcs., 1986—; counselor, vol. Daughters and Sons United, El Cajon, Calif., 1986-87; community speaker San Diego County D.S.S. Speaker's Bur., San Diego, 1986-88. Blood drive recruiter San Diego Blood Bank, San Diego County, 1987-88; M.D.A. bachelor auction fund Raiser, San Diego, 1988-89. Democrat. Home: 5445 Baltimore Dr 33 La Mesa CA 92042 Office: San Diego County Child Protective Svcs 6950 Levant St San Diego CA 92111

HETZEL, RICHARD LEE, special government agent; b. Jefferson City, Mo., Sept. 14, 1952; s. Gordon Hetzel and Claire Louis (Howery) Sullens; m. Kathleen Ann Kliethermes, Feb. 20, 1971; children: Richard Lee II, Kristina Robin. AA cum laude, Johnson County Community Coll., 1975; BA, Columbia Coll., 1976; MA, Webster U., 1980; grad., FBI Nat. Acad., 1988. Spl. agt. U.S. Army Criminal Investigation Div., Ft. Leavenworth, Kans., 1976-79, Ft. Bragg, N.C., 1979-81; spl. agt. in charge U.S. Army Criminal Investigation Div., Garmisch, Fed. Republic Germany, 1981-85, Fulda, Fed. Republic Germany, 1985-87; investigative supr. U.S. Army Criminal Investigation Div., Ft. Carson, Colo., 1987—; cons. Family Advocacy Program, Ft. Carson, 1987—. Pres. Parent Tchr. Student Assn. Garmisch Elem. Schs., 1982-83; scoutmaster Boy Scouts Am., Fulda and Colorado Springs, Colo., 1985—. Chief warrant officer III U.S. Army, 1970—, Vietnam. Decorated Vietnamese Cross Gallantry Govt. South Vietnam, 1972. Mem. Internat. Assn. Chiefs Police, Criminal Investigative Div. Agts. Assn., Am. Acad. Forensic Scis., Rocky Mountain Assn. Bloodstain Pattern Analysts, Masons. Baptist. Office: US Army USACIDC Criminal Investigation Div 6th Region Fort Carson CO 80913-5000

HEUER, RICHARDS JOHN, III, management consultant; b. Washington, Dec. 30, 1957; s. Richards John Jr. and Mystia Nafeesie (Farnsworth) H.; m. Michelle Marta Carey; 1 child, Sasha Carey. BA, U. Calif., Berkeley, 1979; MBA, Monterey Inst. Internat. Studies, 1982. Adminstrv. supr. Trans-Arabia Co. Ltd., Jeddah, Saudi Arabia, 1979-80; owner Computer Mgmt. Cons., Carmel, Calif., 1982—; outside contractor Cambridge Plan Internat., Monterey, Calif., 1983-84; owner Data Concepts, Carmel, 1983—; chief fin. officer Computer Deisgn Ctrs. Inc., Carmel, 1984; spl. projects dir. Joseph Imports, Beverly Hills, Calif., 1986-88; gen. mgr. MicroAge Computer Stores, Salinas, Calif., 1987-88; v.p. Gilbert Enterprises, Inc., Monterey, 1988—. Mem. Archtl. Rev. Commn., Monterey, 1985-87, Planning Commn., Monterey, 1987—; United Way spokesman Ft. Ord (Calif.) Youth Ctr., 1986. Mem. Monterey Soccer League (v.p. 1982-83), Pi Kappa Phi. Republican. Office: Computer Mgmt Cons 201 Van Buren Monterey CA 93940

HEUMAN, DONNA RENA, entrepreneur; b. Seattle, May 27, 1949; d. Russell George and Edna Inez (Armstrong) H. BA in Psychology, UCLA, 1972; JD, U. Calif., San Francisco, 1985. Owner, Heuman & Assocs., San Francisco, 1978-86. Mem. Hastings Internat. and Comparative Law Rev., 1984-85; bd. dirs. Saddleback, 1987-89. Jessup Internat. Moot Ct. Competition, 1985. Mem. Nat. Shorthand Reporters Assn., Women Entrepreneurs, Calif. Shorthand Reporters Assn., Calif. State Bar Assn., Nat. Mus. of Women in the Arts, Calif. Lawyers for the Arts, ABA, San Francisco Bar Assn., Assn. Trial Lawyers Am., NAFE, Commonwealth Club, World Affairs Council, Zonta (bd. dirs.). Home: 611 Cedar Ct Daly City CA 94014 Office: 3 Embarcadero Ctr Ste 470 San Francisco CA 94111

HEUSCHELE, WERNER PAUL, veterinary researcher; b. Ludwigsburg, Federal Republic of Germany, Aug. 28, 1929; came to U.S., 1932, naturalized, 1951; s. Karl August and Margarete Anna (Wagner) H.; m. Carolyn René Bredeson, Jan. 1, 1983; children: Erick W.K., Mark R., Jennifer M. Student, San Diego State Coll., 1947-50; BA in Zoology, U. Calif., Davis, 1952, DVM, 1956; student, NIH, Bethesda, Md., 1966; PhD in Med. Microbiology, Virology, Immunology, U. Wis., 1969. Diplomate Am. Coll. Vet. Microbiologists. Mgr. veterinary hosp. Zool. Soc. San Diego, 1956-61, head, microbiology/virology, 1981-86, dir. research, 1986—; research veterinarian Plum Island Animal Disease Lab., Orient Point, N.Y., 1961-71; tng. resident in vet. pathology Armed Forces Inst. Pathology, Washington, 1965-66; assoc. prof. infectious disease Kansas State U., Manhattan, 1970-71; head, virology, research and devel. Jensen-Salsbery Labs., Kansas City, Kans., 1971-76; prof. vet. preventive medicine Ohio State U., Columbus, 1976-81; cons. Syntro Corp., San Diego, 1985—; SIBIA, San Diego, 1983—; UN-FAO-UNDP, Maracay, Venezuela, 1979, 80; grant rev. panelist USDA, Washington. Contbr. articles to profl. jours. Fellow Am. Assn. Zool. Parks and Aquariums; mem. USDA (VS adv. blue-ribbon panel 1987—), Am. Assn. Zoo Veterinarians (pres. 1958-59, sec., treas. 1959-61, American Vet. Med. Assn., Wildlife Disease Assn. (vice-pres. 1985-87), Vet. Specialist Group (species survival com.), Columbus Zoo Assn. (bd. dirs), Am. Coll. Vet. Microbiologists (bd. govs. 1984-87), U.S. Animal Health Assn., Sigma Xi, Phi Zeta. Home: 4690 59th St San Diego CA 92115 Office: Zool Soc San Diego PO Box 551 San Diego CA 92112

HEUSMANN, RICHARD W., counselor; b. Amityville, N.Y., Aug. 23, 1948; s. Richard Warren and Peggy Ann (Cox) H.; m. Janet Rose Lopipero; children: Darlene, Stephanie, Joseph. AAS, Community Coll. Air Force, San Antonio, 1978; postgrad., U. Ariz., 1976-80; MA, U. No. Colo., 1982; postgrad., Saybook Inst., San Francisco, 1983—. Habilitation tech. Ariz. Tng. Program, Tucson, 1979-80; patient rep. Dialysis Found. So. Ariz., Tucson, 1980-83; counselor Life Enrichment Counseling, Tucson, 1982—; exec. dir. Reachout, Tucson, 1988—; cons. Diocese of Tucson Schs., 1987—, St. Elizabeth of Hungary, Tucson, 1986—; bd. dirs. Rainbows for All Children, Tucson, 1987—. Author, facilitator: Positive Self-Esteem, 1984, Adolescent Sexuality, 1985, Controlling Depression, 1988, Attention Deficit Guideline, 1988. Active Mayor's Youth Task Force, Tucson, 1988—, Bishop's Council for Divorced and Separated, Tucson, 1987—; youth minister Our Mother of Sorrows Ch., Tucson, 1983-85; counselor Our Mother of Sorrows Sch., Tucson, 1983—. With USAF, 1972-78. Mem. Am. Psychol. Assn., So. Ariz. Psychol. Assn. Republican. Roman Catholic. Office: Life Enrichment Counseling 8800 E 22d St #201 Tucson AZ 85710

HEWITT, LINDA JEAN, accountant; b. Broken Bow, Nebr., Sept. 10, 1940; d. Leland James and Gladys E. (Eichelberger) H. BS in Acctg., Colo. State U., Ft. Collins, 1962; MBA, UCLA, 1964. CPA, Ariz. Staff auditor Segal, Wasserman & Co. CPAs, Beverly Hills, Calif., 1964-67; mgr. Mgmt. Info. Systems and Mgmt. Acctg. Systems dept. Singer, Lewak & Co CPAs, Beverly Hills, 1967-72; controller Engineered Systems, Inc., Omaha, 1973-75; v.p. controller Homecraft Corp., Houston, 1975-78; chief fin. officer Universal Metals and Machinery, Inc., Houston, 1978-83; pvt. practice cons. Houston and Phoenix, 1983—. Mem. Big Sisters of Houston. Mem. AICPAs, 100 Club of Houston, Houston Bus. Womens Assn., NAFE. Office: Hewitt Cons 4416 N Scottsdale Rd Ste 443 Phoenix AZ 85251

HEWLETT, T.J., transportation executive; b. Oak Grove, La., Mar. 21, 1941; s. R. E. and Ruby Thelma (Hutson) H.; m. Leonor Rita Yanes, Nov. 18, 1967 (div. Oct. 1986); children: Rudy, John. Degree in Warehousing and Distrbn., Cornell U., 1971. Fleet maintenance mgr. Ralph's Grocery Co., L.A., 1967-82; dist. mgr. Hertz Penski Truck Leasing, City of Industry, Calif., 1982-84; corp. fleet mgr. Mission Industries, Santa Barbara, Calif., 1984-85; owner, chief exec. officer Hamco United, Inc., City of Industry, 1985—; instr. L.A. Police Acad., 1981-82; chmn. Nat. Safety Coun. Pres. West Covina (Calif.) Homeowners' Assn., 1986-87. With U.S. ARmy, 1959-67. Mem. Western Coun. Pvt. Fleet Operators (pres. 1981-82, chmn. 1982-87, hall of fame 1984, man of yr. 1985), Pvt. Truck Coun. Am. (bd. dirs.). Baptist. Home: PO Box 250 Walnut CA 91788-0250 Office: Hamco United Inc 18021 Cortney Ct City of Industry CA 91748

HEWLETT, WILLIAM (REDINGTON), manufacturing company executive, electrical engineer; b. Ann Arbor, Mich., May 20, 1913; s. Albion Walter and Louise (Redington) H.; m. Flora Lamson, Aug. 10, 1939 (dec. 1977); children: Eleanor Hewlett Gimon, Walter B., James S., William A., Mary Hewlett Jaffe; m. Rosemary Bradford, May 24, 1978. BA, Stanford U., 1934, EE, 1939; MS, MIT, 1936; LLD, U. Calif., Berkeley, 1966, Yale U., 1976, Mills Coll., 1983; DSc (hon.), Kenyon Coll., 1978, Poly Inst. N.Y., 1978; LHD, Johns Hopkins U., 1985; EngD, U. Notre Dame, 1980, Utah State U., 1980, Dartmouth Coll., 1983; PhD, Rand Grad. Inst. Electromed. researcher 1936-39; co-founder Hewlett-Packard Co., Palo Alto, Calif., 1939, ptnr., 1939-46, exec. v.p., dir., 1947-64, pres., 1964-77, chief exec. officer, 1969-78, chmn. exec. com., 1977-83, vice chmn. bd. dirs., 1983-87, emeritus dir., 1987—; mem. internat. adv. council Wells Fargo Bank, 1986—; trustee Rand Corp., 1962-72, Carnegie Inst., Washington, 1971—, chmn. bd. trustees, 1980-86; dir. Overseas Devel. Council, 1969-77; bd. dirs. Inst. Radio Engrs. (now IEEE), 1950-57, pres. 1954. Contbr. articles to profl. jours.; patentee in field. Trustee Stanford U., 1963-74, Mills Coll., Oakland, Calif., 1958-68; mem. Pres.'s Gen. Adv. Com. on Fgn. Assistance Programs, Washington, 1965-68, Pres.'s Sci. Adv. Com., 1966-69; mem. San Francisco regional panel Commn. on White House Fellows, 1969-70, chmn., 1970; pres. bd. dirs. Palo Alto Stanford Hosp. Ctr., 1956-58, bd. dirs., 1958-62; dir. Drug Abuse Council, Washington, 1972-74, Kaiser Found. Hosp. & Health Plan Bd., 1972-78; chmn. The William and Flora Hewlett Found., 1966—; bd. dirs. San Francisco Bay Area Council, 1969-81, Inst. Medicine, Washington, 1971-72, The Nat. Acads. Corp., 1986—, Monterey Bay Aquarium Rsch. Inst., 1987—, Univ. Corp. for Atmospheric Rsch. Found., 1986—. Lt. col. AUS, 1942-45. Recipient Calif. Mfr. of Yr. Calif. Mfrs. Assn., 1969, Bus. Statesman of Yr. Harvard Bus. Sch. No. Calif., 1970, Medal of Achievement Western Electronic Mfrs. Assn., 1971, Industrialist of Yr. (with David Packard) Calif. Mus. Sci. and Industry and Calif. Mus. Found., 1973, Award with David Packard presented by Scientific Apparatus Makers Assn., 1975, Corp. Leadership award MIT, 1976, Medal of Honor City of

Boeblingen, Germany, 1977, Herbert Hoover medal for disting. service Stanford U. Alumni Assn., 1977, Henry Heald award Ill. Inst. Tech., 1984, Nat. Medal of Sci. U.S. Nat. Sci. Com., 1985. Fellow IEEE (pres. 1954, Founders medal with David Packard 1973), Franklin Inst. (life, Vermilye medal with David Packard 1976), Am. Acad. Arts and Scis.; mem. Nat. Acad. Scis. (panel on advanced tech. competition 1982-83), Nat. Acad. Engring., Instrument Soc. Am. (hon. life), Am. Philos. Soc., Calif. Acad. Sci. (trustee 1963-68), Assn. Quadrato della Radio, Century Assn. N.Y.C. Clubs: Bohemian, Pacific-Union (San Francisco); Menlo Country (Woodside, Calif.). Office: Hewlett-Packard Co 1501 Page Mill Rd Palo Alto CA 94304

HEXTER, ALFRED CHARLES, epidemiologist; b. Portland, Oreg., Dec. 24, 1925; s. Edgar Carl and Bessie (Rogoway) H.; m. Stella Stender, Oct. 1, 1953; children: Barbara, Theodore. BS, U. Calif.-San Francisco, 1948; MA, U. Calif.-Berkeley, 1958, PhD, 1977. Researcher Calif. Dept. Health, Berkeley, 1961-73, U. Calif., Berkeley, 1973-79; epidemiologist Birth Defects Monitoring Program Calif. Dept. Health Svcs., Berkeley, 1980--. Mem. Am. Pharm. Assn., Am. Statis. Assn., Royal Statis. Soc., Inst. Math. Stats., Biometric Soc. Home: 58 Arlington Ave Kensington CA 94707 Office: Calif Birth Defects Monitor 5900 Hollis St Ste A Emeryville CA 94608

HEYCK, THEODORE DALY, lawyer; b. Houston, Apr. 17, 1941; s. Theodore Richard and Gertrude Paine (Daly) H. B.A., Brown U., 1963; J.D., N.Y. Law Sch., 1979. Bar: N.Y. 1980, Calif. 1984, U.S. Ct. Appeals (2nd cir.) 1984, U.S. Supreme Ct. 1984, U.S. Dist. Ct. (so. and ea. dists.) N.Y. 1980, U.S. Dist. Ct. (we. and no. dists.) N.Y. 1984, U.S. Dist. Ct. (cen. and so. dists.) Calif. 1984, U.S. Ct. Appeals (9th cir.) 1986. Paralegal dist. atty. Bklyn., 1975-79; asst. dist. atty. Bklyn. dist., Kings County, N.Y., 1979-85; dep. city atty., Los Angeles, 1985—; bd. dirs. Screen Actors Guild, N.Y.C., 1977-78. Mem. ABA, AFTRA, Bklyn. Bar Assn., Assn. Trial Lawyers Am., N.Y. Trial Lawyers Assn., N.Y. State Bar Assn., Calif. Bar Assn., Fed. Bar Council, Los Angeles County Bar Assn., Screen Actors Guild, Actors Equity Assn., Nat. Acad. TV Arts and Scis., Screen Actors Guild, Home: 2106 Live Oak Dr E Los Angeles CA 90068 Office: Office of City Atty City Hall East 200 N Main St Los Angeles CA 90012

HEYER, CAROL ANN, illustrator; b. Cuero, Tex., Feb. 2, 1950; d. William Jerome and Merlyn Mary (Hutson) H. BA, Calif. Lutheran U., 1974. Freelance artist various cos., Thousand Oaks, Calif., 1974-79; computer artist Image Resource, Westlake Village, Calif., 1979-81; staff writer, artist Lynn-Davis Prodns., Westlake Village, Calif., 1981-87; art dir. Northwind Studios Internat., Camarillo, Calif., 1988-89; illustrator Touchmark, Thousand Oaks, 1989—; cons. art dir., writer Lynn-Wenger Prodns., 1987-89. Illustrator (children's books) A Star in the Pasture, 1988, The Dream Stealer, 1989, The Golden Easter Egg, 1989, Prancer, 1989, also cover art for Dragon mag., Dungeon mag., Aboriginal Science Fiction mag.; writer (screenplay) Thunder Run, 1986; illustrator, writer (children's book) Beauty and the Beast, 1989, The Easter Story, 1989. Mem. Soc. Children's Book Writers (Magazine Merit award 1988), Assn. Sci. Fiction and Fantasy Artists, Soc. of Illustrators, Westlake Village Art Guild (mem. family liturgy com.). Home and Office: Touchmark 925 Ave Arboles Thousand Oaks CA 91360

HEYL, ALLEN VAN, JR., geologist; b. Allentown, Pa., Apr. 10, 1918; s. Allen Van and Emma (Kleppinger) H.; student Muhlenberg Coll., 1936-37; BS in Geology, Pa. State U., 1941; PhD in Geology, Princeton U., 1950; m. Maxine LaVon Hawke, July 12, 1945; children: Nancy Caroline, Allen David Van. Field asst., govt. geologist Nfld. Geol. Survey, summers 1937-40, 42; jr. geologist U.S. Geol. Survey, Wis., 1943-45, asst. geologist, 1945-47, assoc. geologist, 1947-50, geologist, Washington and Beltsville, Md., 1950-67; staff geologist, Denver, 1968—; disting. lectr. grad. coll. Beijing, China and Nat. Acad. Sci., 1988; chmn. Internat. Commn. Tectonics of Ore Deposits. Fellow Instn. Mining and Metallurgy (Gt. Brit.), Geol. Soc. Am., Am. Mineral. Soc.; mem. Inst. Genesis of Ore Deposits, Soc. Econ. Geologists, Geol. Soc. Wash., Colo. Sci. Soc., Rocky Mountain Geol. Soc., Friends of Mineralogy (hon. life), Evergreen Naturalist Audubon Soc., Sigma Xi, Alpha Chi Sigma. Lutheran. Contbr. numerous articles to profl. jours., chpts. to books. Home: PO Box 1052 Evergreen CO 80439 Office: US Geol Survey Cen Mineral Resources Br MS 905 Denver Fed Br Denver CO 80225

HEYMAN, IRA MICHAEL, university chancellor; b. N.Y.C., May 30, 1930; s. Harold Albert and Judith (Sobel) H.; m. Therese Helene Thau, Dec. 17, 1950; children—Stephen Thomas, James Nathaniel. AB in Govt., Dartmouth Coll., 1951; JD, Yale U., 1956; LLD (hon.), U. Pacific, 1981; LHD (hon.), Hebrew Union Coll., 1984; LLD (hon.), U. Md., 1986. Bar: N.Y. 1956, Calif. 1961. Legis. asst. to U.S. Senator Ives, 1950-51; assoc. Carter, Ledyard & Milburn, N.Y.C., 1956-57; law clk. to presiding justice U.S. Ct. Appeals (2d cir.), New Haven, 1957-58; chief law clk. to Supreme Ct. Justice Earl Warren, 1958-59; acting assoc. prof. law U. Calif. at Berkeley, 1959-61, prof. law, 1961—, prof. city and regional planning, 1966—, vice chancellor, 1974-80, chancellor, 1980—; vis. prof. Yale Law Sch., 1963-64, Stanford Law Sch., 1971-72; bd. dirs. Pacific Gas & Electric Co., 1985—. Editor Yale Law Jour.; contbr. articles to profl. jours. Sec. Calif. adv. com. U.S. Commn. Civil Rights, 1962-67; trustee Dartmouth Coll., 1982—, Lawyers' Commn. for Civil Rights Under Law, 1977—; chmn. exec. com. Nat. Assn. State Univs. and Land Grant Colls., 1986; chmn. Div. I subcom. Nat. Collegiate Athletic Assn. Pres.'s Commn., 1986-88; chmn. Human Rights and Welfare Commn. City of Berkeley, 1966-68. 1st lt. USMC, 1951-53, capt. USMCR, 1953-58. Named Chevalier de la Legion D'Honneur Govt. France, 1985. Mem. Am. Law Inst. (asst. reporter). Democrat. Office: U Calif Office of Chancellor Berkeley CA 94720

HEYMAN, KAREN STACIE, business consultant; b. Inglewood, Calif., Feb. 28, 1955; m. Mark Edward Heyman, Feb. 20, 1982. BA, UCLA, 1975; MS, U. So. Calif., 1979. Asst. dir. HSS Calif. State U., Fullerton, 1980-81; freelance cons. Westminster, Calif., 1981-82; air traffic controller FAA, San Diego, 1982-83; pres., chief exec. officer Marvelous Muffins, Inc., Carlsbad, Calif., 1983—, cons., 1988—; freelance writer, bus. cons. Los Osos, Calif., 1988—. Office: Heyman & Co 200 Butte Dr Los Osos CA 93402

HEYMAN, MATTHEW DAVID, real estate executive, economist; b. Orange, Calif., Nov. 1, 1961; s. Harris B. and Esther (Podvin) H. BS in Econs. cum laude, NYU, 1983; postgrad. in social scis., U. Wis., 1984. Lic. real estate broker, Calif., N.Y., Mass. Teaching asst. econs. dept. NYU, N.Y.C., spring 1983; econ. analyst fin. markets div. Chase Manhattan Bank, N.A., N.Y.C., 1984; loan officer Govt. Funding Corp., L.A., 1985; real estate analyst devel. planning div. Community Devel. Commn., Commerce, Calif., 1985-86; dir. real estate real estate div. Cineplex Odeon Corp., L.A. and N.Y.C., 1986-88; chief exec. officer The Heyman Group, L.A. and N.Y.C., 1988—. Helbein scholar, 1983. Mem. Internat. Coun. Shopping Ctrs., Urban Land Inst. (assoc.), Nat. Assn. Realtors, Calif. Assn. Realtors, Venice-Marina Del Rey Assn. Realtors, Beta Gamma Sigma, Omicron Delta Epsilon. Home: 50 Ave A #4D New York NY 10009 Office: The Heyman Group 311 Bora Bora Way Ste 215 Marina Del Rey CA 90292

HEYMAN, MELVIN BERNARD, pediatric gastroenterologist; b. San Francisco, Mar. 24, 1950; s. Vernon Otto and Eve Elsie Heyman; m. Jody Ellen Switky, May 8, 1988. BA in Econs., U. Calif., Berkeley, 1972; MD in Medicine, UCLA, 1976, MPH in Nutrition, 1981. Diplomate Am. Bd. Pediatrics. Intern, resident Los Angeles County-U. So. Calif. Med. Ctr., 1976-79; fellow UCLA, 1979-81; asst. prof. U. Calif., San Francisco, 1981-88, assoc. prof., 1988—; assoc. dir. Pediatric Gastroenterology/Nutrition, San Francisco, 1986-89; mem. cons. staff San Francisco Gen. Hosp., Oakland (Calif.) Children's Hosp., Sonoma County Med. Ctr., Santa Rosa, Calif., Natividad Med. Ctr., Salinas, Calif. Contbr. articles to profl. jours. Chmn. scientific adv. com. San Francisco chpt. Nat. Found. Ileitis and Colitis, 1987—, bd. dirs., 1986—. Research grantee Children's Liver Found., 1984-85, John Tung grantee Am. Cancer Society, 1985-89. Office: U Calif Dept Pediatrics M 680 Box 0136 San Francisco CA 94143-0136

HEYNEMAN, DONALD, parasitology educator; b. San Francisco, Feb. 18, 1925; s. Paul and Amy Josephine (KLauber) H.; m. Louise Davidson Ross, June 18, 1971; children: Amy J., Lucy A., Andrew P., Jennifer K., Claudia G. AB magna cum laude, Harvard U., 1950; MA, Rice U., 1952, PhD, 1954. Instr. zoology UCLA, 1954-56, asst. prof., 1956-60; head dept. parasitology U.S. Navy Med. Research unit, Cairo; also co-dir. U.S. Navy Med. Research unit, Malakal, Sudan, 1960-62; assoc. research parasitologist Hooper Found. U. Calif., San Francisco, 1962-64, assoc. prof., 1966-68, prof., 1968—, asst. dir. Hooper found., 1970-74, acting chmn. dept. internat. health, 1976-78; assoc. dean Sch. Pub. Health U. Calif., Berkeley and San Francisco, 1987—; chmn. joint med. program, 1987—; research coordinator U. Calif. Internat. Ctr. Med. Research and Tng., Kuala Lumpur, Malaysia, 1964-66; cons. physiol. processes sect. NSF, 1966—; environ. biology div. NIH, 1968—; mem. tropical medicine and parasitology study sect. NIAID-NIH, 1973-76; mem. adv. sci. bd. Gorgas Meml. Inst., 1967—; cons. WHO, 1967, mem. sci. tech. rev. com. on Leishmaniases, 1984; cons. UN Devel. Program, 1978—, US-AID, others; panel reviewer Internat. Nomenclature of Diseases, 1984—; Am. cons. and U.S. prin. investigator U. Linkage Project, Egypt-U.S., 1984—; mem. Calif. Health Adv. Com., 1983—. Author: (with R. Boolootian) An Illustrated Laboratory Text in Zoology, 1962, An Illustrated Laboratory Text in Zoology, A Brief Version, 1977, International Dictionary Medicine and Biology, (with R. Goldsmith) Textbook of Tropical Medicine and Parasitology, 1989;co-author, contbg. editor Phytolacca dodecandra: Edod, 1984, Endod II, 1987; contbr. articles to jours., chpts. to books.; editorial cons. Am. Jour. Tropical Medicine and Hygiene, Jour. Parasitology, Jour. Exptl. Parasitology, Sci. Jour., 1968—. Served with AUS, 1943-46. NIH grantee, 1966-85. Mem. Am. Soc. Parasitologists (council 1970-74, pres. 1982-83), Am. Micros. Soc. (exec. com. 1971-75), Am. Soc. Tropical Medicine and Hygiene (councilor 1981-84), So. Calif. Parasitol. Soc. (pres. 1957-58), No. Calif. Parasitologists (sec., treas. 1969-72, pres. 1977-78), Phi Beta Kappa. Home: 1400 Lake St San Francisco CA 94118 Office: U Calif Health and Med Scis Program Bldg T-7 Rm 106 Berkeley CA 95720

HIARING, PHILIP, editor, wine industry consultant; b. Madison, S.D., Aug. 27, 1915; s. Philip Martin and Olene (Bergheim) H.; m. Claire Muriel Riebe, Aug. 28, 1941; children—Philip Edmund, Anne Claire Hiaring Hall. B.A., U. Idaho, 1937; diploma Air War Coll., Indsl. Coll. Armed Forces. Reporter, editor Salt Lake Tribune, Utah, 1937-39; editor, writer AP, Salt Lake City, Boise, Idaho, San Francisco, 1939-55; pub. relations staff Bank of Am., San Francisco, 1955-58; publicity chief Wine Inst., San Francisco, 1958-66; pub. relations mgr. Calif. Canners and Growers, San Francisco, 1966-69; pub., chmn. Wines & Vines Mag., San Rafael, Calif., 1969—; chmn., founder Wine Industry Tech. Symposium, San Francisco, 1973—. Past bd. dirs. Marin United Crusade, San Rafael, Marin council Boy Scouts Am. Served to col. USAF, 1942-46, 47-75. Mem. San Francisco Pub. Relations Round Table (past pres.). Sigma Nu, Sigma Delta Chi (founder/pres. U. Idaho chpt.). Clubs: San Francisco Commonwealth, San Francisco Marines Meml., Order of Mil. Wine Tasters (founder/exec. sec. 1959-65), Presidio Army Golf. Home: 95 Suffield Ave San Anselmo CA 94960 Office: Wines & Vines 1800 Lincoln Ave San Rafael CA 94901

HIATT, DOUGLAS PIERCE, interior designer. s. Oliver and Beatrice Hiatt. BA, Foothill Coll., 1964; BFA, Art Ctr. Coll. of Design, 1969. Pres., chief exec. officer Hiatt Enterprises Internat., Inc., Paris, France, Beverly Hills and Palm Springs (Calif.). Bd. dirs. H.E.Y Found., John Bosco Found. Mem. Am. Soc. Interior Designers (bd. dirs.), Nat. Home Fashions League (1st male mem., bd. dirs.), Internat. Soc. Interior Designers (internat. ambassador, pres. 1983, 85), Internat. Furnishings Design Assn., Brit. Inst. Interior Designers.

HIATT, PETER, library educator; b. N.Y.C., Oct. 19, 1930; s. Amos and Elizabeth Hope (Derry) H.; m. Linda Rae Smith, Aug. 16, 1968; 1 child, Holly Virginia. B.A., Colgate U., 1952; M.L.S., Rutgers U., 1957, Ph.D., 1963. Head Elmora Br. Library, Elizabeth, N.J., 1957-59; instr. Grad. Sch. Library Service Sci. Rutgers U., 1960-62; library cons. Ind. State Library, Indpls., 1963-70; asst. prof. Grad. Library Sch., Ind. U., 1963-66, assoc. prof., 1966-70; dir. Ind. Library Studies, Bloomington, 1967-70; dir. continuing edn. program for library personnel Western Interstate Commn. for Higher Edn., Boulder, Colo., 1970-74; dir. Grad. Sch. Library and Info. Sci., U. Wash., Seattle, 1974-81, prof., 1974—; prin. investigator Career Devel. and Assessment Center for Librarians, 1979-83; dir. library insts. at various colls. and univs.; adv. project U.S. Office Edn.-ALA, 1977-80; bd. dirs. King County Libr. System, 1989—. Author: (with Donald Thompson) Monroe County Public Library: Planning for the Future, 1966, The Public Library Needs of Delaware County, 1967, (with Henry Drennan) Public Library Services for the Functionally Illiterate, 1967, (with Robert E. Lee and Lawrence A. Allen) A Plan for Developing a Regional Program of Continuing Education for Library Personnel, 1969, Public Library Branch Services for Adults of Low Education, 1964; dir., gen. editor: The Indiana Library Studies, 1970; mem. editorial bd.: Coll. and Research Libraries, 1969-73; co-editor: Leads: A Continuing Newsletter for Library Trustees, 1973-75, Octavio Noda; author chpts., articles on library continuing edn. and staff devel. Mem. ALA (officer), Pacific N.W. Library Assn., Spl. Libraries Assn., Assn. Library and Info. Sci. Educators (officer, Outstanding Service award 1979), Am. Soc. Info. Sci., Adult Edn. Assn., ACLU.

HIBBARD, BURNETT JAMES, teacher; b. Hornell, N.Y., May 6, 1956; s. Merton Will and Doris Elizabeth (Waight) H.; m. Julie Anne Olson, June 6, 1980; children: Jonathan James, Janelle Anne. BA in Math., Kings Coll., Briarcliff Manor, N.Y., 1978; M. in Math., No. Ariz. U., 1985. Cert. prin., elem. tchr., Ariz. Tchr. New Life Home-Snell Farms, Bath, N.Y., 1978; tchr. Shore Shore Christian Sch., N. Bellmore, N.Y., 1978-79; tchr., coach Bagdad Unified Sch. Dist., Bagdad, Ariz., 1979—; instr. Yavapai Coll., Prescott, Ariz., 1980—; dir. Class B-C No. Region Tennis Tourney, Phoenix. Mem. Math. Assn. Am., U.S.T.A., Am. Volleyball Coaches Assn., Ariz. Volleyball Coaches Assn., Yauapai Tennis Assn., Bagdad Men's Golf Club. Republican. Mem. Ch. of the Nazarene. Home: Box 535 Bagdad AZ 86321

HIBBARD, FLORENCE LOUISE, teacher; b. Madelia, Minn., Dec. 16, 1944; d. Theodore J. and Mary Louise (Housfelt) Forstner; m. Elden Richard hibbard, July 31, 1965; children: Patricia, Pamela, Robert. AA in Gen. Studies, No. Nev. Community Coll., 1984; BS, So. Utah State Coll., 1985; MS, Nova U., 1988. Lic. practical nurse Ea. Med. Group, Ely, Nev., 1970-84; spl. edn. specialist Clark County Sch. Dist., Boulder City, Nev., 1985—. Active PTA Boulder City, Nev., 1986—; del. Dem. Party, White Pine County, 1968. Mem. AAUW, Young Ladies Inst. (pres. 1980-82). Democrat. Roman Catholic. Office: Andrew Mitchell Elem Sch 900 Ave B Boulder City NV 89001

HIBBARD, RICHARD PAUL, industrial ventilation consultant, lecturer; b. Defiance, Ohio, Nov. 1, 1923; s. Richard T. and Doris E. (Walkup) H.; BS in Mech. Indsl. Engring., U. Toledo, 1949; m. Phyllis Ann Kirchoffer, Sept. 7, 1948; children: Barbara Rae, Marcia Kae, Rebecca Ann, Patricia Jan, John Ross. Mech. engr. Oldsmobile div. Gen. Motors Corp., Lansing, Mich., 1950-56; design and sales engr. McConnell Sheet Metal, Inc., Lansing, 1956-60; chief heat and ventilation engr. Fansteel Metall. Corp., North Chicago, Ill., 1960-62; sr. facilities and ventilation engr. The Boeing Co., Seattle, 1962-63; ventilation engr. environ. health div. dept. preventive medicine U. Wash., 1964-70, lectr. dept. environ. health, 1970-82, lectr. emeritus, 1983—; prin. Indsl. Ventilation Cons. Svcs., 1983—; chmn. Western Indsl. Ventilation Conf., 1962; mem. com. indsl. ventilation Am. Conf. Govtl. Indsl. Hygienists, 1966—; mem. staff Indsl. Ventilation Conf., Mich. State U., 1955—. With USAAF, 1943-45, USAR, 1946-72. Recipient Disting. Svc. award Indsl. Ventilation Conf., Mich. State U., 1975. Mem. Am. Soc. Safety Engrs. (R.M. Gillmore Meml. award Puget Sound chpt.), ASHRAE, Am. Inst. Plant Engrs., Am. Indsl. Hygiene Assn. (J.M. Dallevalle award 1977), Am. Foundryman's Soc. Lodges: Elks, Masons. Contbr. articles on indsl. hygiene and ventilation to profl. jours. Home: 41 165th Ave SE Bellevue WA 98008

HIBBS, JOHN DAVID, software executive, engineer, business owner; b. Del Norte, Colo., Jan. 26, 1948; s. Alva Bernard and Frances Ava (Cathcart) H.; m. Ruthanne Johnson, Feb. 28, 1976. BSEE, Denver U., 1970. Elec. engr. Merrick and Co., Denver, 1972-73; lighting engr. Holophane div. Johns Manville, Denver, 1973-79; lighting products mgr. Computer Sharing Svcs., Inc., Denver, 1979-83; pres., owner Computer Aided Lighting Analysis, Boulder, Colo., 1983-86, Hibbs Sci. Software, Boulder, 1986—. Author CALA and PreCALA lighting programs. With USNR, 1970-72. Recipient 1st prize San Luise Valley Sci. Fair, 1963. Mem. Illuminating Engring. Soc. N.Am. (chmn. computer com. 1988—), IEEE, Computer Soc. of IEEE. Methodist.

HIBER, JHAN WILLIAM, broadcast consultant, writer; b. Joliet, Ill., Dec. 29, 1946; s. William M. and Marcia Jane (Slappey) H. Student U. Md., 1964-68; B.A. cum laude, Central Fla. U., 1973; M.A., Am. U., 1977. Cert. radio mktg. cons. Newsman various TV stas., 1969-73; account exec., gen. mgr. radio and TV properties, 1973-76; mgr. radio ratings div. Arbitron Ratings, 1977-78; editor/weekly columnist Radio & Records, Los Angeles, 1979-86; pres. Jhan Hiber & Assocs. Ltd., Pebble Beach, Calif., 1979—, Calif. Lit. Enterprises, Inc., 1982—. Author: Hibernetics: A Guide to Media Research, 1984. Recipient 3 Addy awards, 1972-73; Abraham Lincoln award, 1975. Mem. Internat. Radio and TV Soc., Am. Mktg. Assn., Nat. Assn. Broadcasters, Nat. Radio Broadcasters Assn., Alpha Epsilon Rho. Republican. Presbyterian. Clubs: Sports Car Am., Brit. Sch. Motor Racing. Office: 8029 Kirkton Ct Sacramento CA 95828

HICK, JOHN HARWOOD, theologian, educator; b. Scarborough, Yorkshire, Eng., Jan. 20, 1922; arrived in U.S., 1979; s. Mark D. and Mary Aileen (Hirst) H.; m. Joan Hazel Bowers, Aug. 30, 1953; children: Eleanor, Mark, Peter, Michael. MA, Edinburgh (Scotland) U., 1948; DPhil, Oxford (Eng.) U., 1950; postgrad., Westminster Theol. Coll., 1950-53; PhD, Cambridge U., 1964; DLitt, Edinburgh (Scotland) U., 1975; Theol. Dr. hon., Uppsala U., Sweden, 1977. Ordained to ministry Presbyterian Ch., 1953. Minister Belford Presbyn. Ch., Northumberland, Eng., 1953-56; asst. prof. philosophy Cornell U., Ithaca, N.Y., 1956-59; Stuart prof. Christian philosophy Princeton Theol. Sem., 1959-64; lectr. divinity Cambridge (Eng.) U., 1964-67; H.G. Wood prof. theology Birmingham (Eng.) U., 1967-82; Danforth prof. religion Claremont (Calif.) Grad. Sch., 1979—; James W. Richard lectr. U. Va., 1969; Arthur Stanley Eddington Meml. lectr. Cambridge U., 1972, Stanton lectr., 1974-77; Ingersoll lectr. Harvard U., 1977; Teape lectr., New Delhi, 1975; Montefiore lectr. U. London, 1980; Brooks lectr. U. So. Calif., 1982; Niebuhr lectr. Elmhurst Coll., 1986; Gifford lectr. U. Edinburgh, 1986-87; vis. prof. Benares Hindu U., Visva-Bharati U., Punjabi U., India, U. Sri Lanka; Fritz Sarti lectr. U. So. Ill., 1989. Author: Faith and Knowledge, 1957, 66, Philosophy of Religion, 1963, 73, 83, 89, Evil and the God of Love, 1966, 77, The Center of Christianity, 1968, 83, Arguments for the Existence of God, 1971, God and the Universe of Faiths, 1973, Death and Eternal Life, 1976, God Has Many Names, 1980, (with Michael Goulder) Why Believe in God ?, 1983, Problems of Religious Pluralism, 1985, An Interpretation of Religion, 1989; editor: The Existence of God, 1963, Faith and the Philosophers, 1963, The Myth of God Incarnate, 1977, Truth and Dialogue, 1974, (with H. Askari) The Experience of Religious Diversity, 1983, (with Paul Knitter) The Myth of Christian Uniqueness, 1987. Chmn., pres. All Faiths for One Race, Birmingham, Eng., 1972-73, 80-85. Fellow Guggenheim Found., 1963-64, 85-86; vis. fellow Brit. Acad. Overseas, 1974; Leverhulme Research fellow, 1974; Select preacher Oxford U., 1970; Hulsean preacher Cambridge U., 1969. Mem. Soc. for Study of Theology England (pres. 1975-76), Am. Acad. Religion, Soc. for Psychical Research, Am. Soc. for Study of Religion, West Coast Theol. Soc. Office: Claremont Grad Sch Claremont CA 91711

HICK, KENNETH WILLIAM, business executive; b. New Westminster, B.C., Can., Oct. 17, 1946; s. Les Walter and Mary Isabelle (Warner) H. BA in Bus., Eastern Wash. State Coll., 1971; MBA (fellow), U. Wash., 1973, PhD, 1975. Regional sales mgr. Hilti, Inc., San Leandro, Calif., 1976-79; gen. sales mgr. Moore Internat., Inc., Portland, 1979-80; v.p. sales and mktg. Phillips Corp., Anaheim, Calif., 1980-81; owner, pres., chief exec. officer K.C. Metals, San Jose, Calif., 1981-87; owner, pres., chief exec. officer Losli Internat. Inc., Portland, Oreg., 1987—; communications cons. Assn. Public Safety Communication Officers, Inc., State of Oreg., 1975-77; numerous cons. assignments, also seminars, 1976-81. Contbr. to numerous publs., 1976—. Mem. Oreg. Gov.'s Tax Bd., 1975-76; pres. Portland chpt. Oreg. Jaycees, 1976; bd. fellows U. Santa Clara, 1983—. Served with USAF, 1966-69. Decorated Commendation medal. Mem. Am. Mgmt. Assn., Am. Mktg. Assn., Assn. M.B.A. Execs., Assn. Gen. Contractors, Soc. Advancement Mgmt. Roman Catholic. Home: 17627 SW Kelok Lake Oswego OR 97034 Office: Losli Internat 4BSW Monroe Pkwy Ste 228 Box 200 Lake Oswego OR 97034

HICKEL, WALTER JOSEPH, investment firm executive, former governor Alaska; b. nr. Claflin, Kans., Aug. 18, 1919; s. Robert A. and Emma (Zecha) H.; m. Janice Cannon, Sept. 22, 1941 (dec. Aug. 1943); 1 son, Theodore; m. Ermalee Strutz, Nov. 22, 1945; children: Robert, Walter, Jack, Joseph, Karl. Student pub. schs., Claflin; D.Eng. (hon.), Stevens Inst. Tech., 1970, Mich. Tech. U., 1973; LL.D. (hon.), St. Mary of Plains Coll., St. Martin's Coll., U. Md., Adelphi U., U. San Diego, Rensselaer Poly. Inst., 1973, U. Alaska, 1976; D.Pub. Adminstrn. (hon.), Willamette U. Builder, owner Traveler's Inn, Anchorage, 1953-82, Fairbanks, Alaska, 1955-82, Hickel Investment Co., Anchorage, 1947—, Hotel Captain Cook, Anchorage, No. Lights Shopping Ctr., Univ. Shopping Ctr., Anchorage, Valley River Shopping Ctr.; chmn. bd. Hickel Investment Co., Yukon Pacific Corp.; gov. State of Alaska, 1966-69; sec. U.S. Dept. Interior, 1969-70; bd. dirs. Rowan Cos., Inc.; mem. world adv. council Internat. Design Sci. Inst.; mem. com. on sci. freedom and responsibility AAAS. Mem. Republican Nat. Com., 1954-64; bd. regents Gonzaga U.; bd. dirs. Salk Inst. Named Alaskan of Year, 1969; recipient DeSmet medal Gonzaga U., 1969, Horatio Alger award, 1972; named Man of Year, Ripon Soc., 1970. Mem. Pioneers of Alaska, Alaska C. of C. (chmn. econ. devel. com.), Equestrian Order Holy Sepulchre, Knights Malta. Clubs: KC, Capitol Hill, Washington Athletic (Washington).

HICKEY, WINIFRED E(SPY), state senator, social worker; b. Rawlins, Wyo.; d. David P. and Eugenia (Blake) Espy; children—John David, Paul Joseph. B.A., Loretto Heights Coll., 1933; postgrad. U. Utah, 1934, Sch. Social Service, U. Chgo., 1936. Dir. Carbon County Welfare Dept., 1935-36; field rep. Wyo. Dept. Welfare, 1937-38; dir. Red Cross Club, Europe, 1942-45; commr. Laramie County, Wyo., 1973-80; mem. Wyo. Senate, 1980—; dir. United Savs. & Loan, Cheyenne. Pres., bd. dirs. U. Wyo. Found., 1986-87; pres. Meml. Hosp. of Laramie County, 1986-88; chmn. adv. council div. community programs Wyo. Dept. Health and Social Services; pres. county and state mental health assn., 1959-63; trustee, U. Wyo., 1967-71; active Nat. Council Cath. Women. Named Outstanding Alumna, Loretto Heights Coll., 1959, Woman of Yr. Commn. for Women, 1988, Legislator of Yr. Wyo. Psychologists Assn., 1988. Democrat. Club: Altrusa (Cheyenne). Pub. Where the Deer and the Antelope Play, 1967.

HICKLIN, RONALD LEE, music production company executive; b. Burlington, Wash., Dec. 4, 1937; s. Wendell C. and Theodora (Van Voorhis) H.; m. Marlene Paige Folk, July 10, 1959; children: Jennifer Lynn, Mark Allan. Student, U. Wash., 1956-57. Pres. S.A.T.B. Inc., L.A., 1979—, HLC/Killer Music, Hollywood, Calif., 1982—. Lead tenor The Eligibles, 1958-62; vocal dir., singer Piece of Cake Inc., 1968-81; arranger, producer Calif. Raisin Adv. Bd., 1982 (recipient 2 Clios 1983); producer/co-writer Wheaties, 1983 (Clio award); producer/composer Gatorade, 1983; producer/performer Levi's 501 Blues, 1984. With USAF, 1959-65. Mem. NARAS (MVP award 1973, 75), AFTRA (nat. bd. dirs. 1970-85, local bd. dirs. 1968-85), Screen Actors Guild (nat. bd. dirs. 1975), Am. Fedn. Musicians, Hollywood C. of C.

HICKMAN, KENNETH JOHN, nurse, hypnotherapist; b. Reading, Mass., May 3, 1934; s. Ernest Stewert and Mildred Elizabeth (Legro) H.; m. Joyce Lorraine Colson, Nov. 10, 1952 (div. Feb., 1972); children: Roger Kenneth, Lois Ann; m. Judith Ann Berninger, May 5, 1972. Student, Atlantic Union Coll., 1955-59; diploma, New England Meml. Hosp., Melrose, Mass., 1961, Carney Sch. of Anesthesia, Dorchester, Mass., 1964; certificate, Greater New England Sch. of Hypnosis, Mass., 1984 '85 '86. Cert. registered nurse anesthetist. Oper. room supr. New Meml. Hosp., Stoneham, Mass., 1961-62; anesthesia mgr. Melrose-Wakefield (Mass.) Hosp., 1964-66, '68-73, Winthrop (Mass.) Community Hosp., 1974-77; contract anesthetist Kino Community Hosp., Tucson, 1977-78; anesthesia mgr. Meml. Gen. Hosp., Las Cruces, N.M., 1978-82, Las Cruces Anesthetist Assn., 1982-84; staff anesthetist Kaiser Permanente, Bess Kaiser Hosp., Portland, Oreg., 1984—. Disaster dir. ARC, Dona Anna County, N.M., 1978-82; co-dir., coord. Dept. Civil Preparedness, Dona Anna County, 1978-82; workshop chmn. N.M. Assn. Nurse Anesthetists, Las Cruces, 1981; bd. dirs., pub. relations dir., 1981-83;

pres. Vista View Home Owners Assn., Portland, 1986—. Capt. U.S. Army, 1966-68, Vietnam. Decorated Vietnam Combat Medal, 1966, U.S. Army, Cu Chi, Vietnam, Bronze Star Medal, U.S. Army, Letterman Gen. Hosp., San Francisco, 1967. Mem. Am. Assn. Nurse Anesthetists (cert. anesthetist), Oreg. Assn. Nurse Anesthetists (bd. dirs., pub. relations dir. 1984-85). Democrat. Home: 10907 SE Azar Dr Portland OR 97266

HICKMAN, SHARON ROSE, design consultant; b. Kansas City, Kans., May 24, 1951; d. Wilmont and Rose Marie (Cyhel) Lohoefener; m. Billy Ray Lee, July 14, 1969; m. Dan Patrick Hickman, Aug. 7, 1976; children: Jonathon Bryan, Nicole Kristen. Student pub. schs. Overland Park, Kans. Gen. mgr. Bull & Boar Restaurant, Lawrence, Kans., 1971-75, Internat. Restaurant, Lawrence, 1975-76, Sirloin Stockade, Lawrence, 1976-78, Chandler, Ariz., 1978-80; mgr. T.G.I.Friday's, Phoenix, 1980-81; pres., founder Nature's Elves, Inc., Gilbert, Ariz., 1981—; design cons. interior plantscape. Mem. NOW, Assn. Landscape Contractors Am., Gilbert C. of C. Democrat. Roman Catholic. Home: 2631 N Carriage Ln Chandler AZ 85224 Office: 13722 E Williams Field Rd Gilbert AZ 85234

HICKS, BETHANY GRIBBEN, lawyer; b. N.Y., Sept. 8, 1951; d. Robert and DeSales Gribben; m. William A. Hicks III, May 21, 1982; children: Alexandra Elizabeth, Samantha Katherine. AB, Vassar Coll., 1973; MEd, Boston U., 1975; JD, Ariz. State U., 1984. Bar: Ariz. 1984. Sole practice Scottsdale and Paradise Valley, Ariz., 1984—. Mem. Jr. League of Phoenix, 1984—; bd. dirs. Phoenix Children's Theatre, 1988—; parliamentarian Girls Club of Scottsdale, Ariz., 1985-87, bd. dirs. 1988—. Mem. ABA (family law sect.), State Bar Ariz. (family law sect.), Maricopa County Bar Assn. Democrat. Episcopalian. Club: Paradise Valley Country. Office: 4824 E Sparkling Ln Paradise Valley AZ 85253

HICKS, DAVID E., author, inventor; b. Indpls., Jan. 1, 1931; s. John Arthur and Marguerite (Barnes) H.; m. Shirlene Lavan Barlow, Jan. 22, 1958 (div. June 1973); children: Sharon Lynn, Brenda Kay; m. Margaret Leigh Payne, Feb. 17, 1977; children: David Bradley, Leslie Ann, Brian Patrick. Grad., Nat. Radio Inst., 1953; student, Purdue U., 1959-60, Miami-Dade Community Coll., 1971-72. Cert. advanced paramedic. Tech. writer, editor Howard W. Sams, Inc., Indpls., 1958-64; tech. writer Systems Engring. Labs, Inc., Ft. Lauderdale, Fla., 1964-67; publs. mgr. Novatronics, Inc., Pompano Beach, Fla., 1967-69; pres. Datatek, Inc., Ft. Lauderdale, 1969-71; tech. writer Systems Devel. Corp., Colorado Springs, Colo., 1973-74, Ford Aerospace Corp., Colorado Springs, Colo., 1974-75; pres. Nutronics Corp., Colorado Springs, Colo., 1982-87; tech. writer Digital Equipment Corp., Colorado Springs, Colo., 1978-88; pres. Inovation USA Mag., Colorado Springs, Colo., 1989—; pvt. practice tech. con., inventor Colorado Springs, 1964-65, 75-78, 87—; tech. cons. Japan Electronics, Tokyo, 1962-63, Nutronics Corp., Longmont, Colo., 1987. Author of eight tech. books (two on best seller list) including: Citizens Band Radio Handbook, 1961, Amateur Radio-VHF and Above, 1965, CB Radio Operating Procedures, 1976; contbr. articles to electronics jours.; inventor of new electric charging system, 1978, awarded U.S. patent, 1981; lectr. numerous sci. and invention seminars, 1978—. Communications officer CD, Indpls., 1962-63; judge sci. fair Pub. Sch. System, Colorado Springs, 1986-87. Served with USN, 1948. Recipient Red Cross Hall of Fame, Indpls., 1963; grantee U.S. Dept. of Energy, 1984, Nat. Energy Resources Tech. Innovation award, 1989. Mem. Soc. of Am. Inventors (bd. dirs.), Am. Radio Relay League. Republican. Home and Office: 5244 Cracker Barrel Circle Colorado Springs CO 80917

HICKS, GREGORY TYLER, architect; b. N.Y.C., Jan. 3, 1948; s. Tyler Gregory and Saretta Maude (Gratke) H.; m. Doreen Frankel, May 25, 1969 (div. 1971); m. Jacqueline Marie Wright, Aug. 9, 1978; children: Tyler Griffin, Elijah Gregory. BA, SUNY, Albany, 1970; MArch, U. N.Mex., 1977. Registered architect, N.Mex., Colo., Ariz. Constrn. worker Sun Mountain Design, Breckenridge, Colo., 1974; draftsman William McConnell Architect, Albuquerque, 1975, Morrow & Worley Landscape Architecture, Albuquerque, 1975-77, Holmes & Gianini, Albuquerque, 1977-78; staff architect Archi-Tekton, Albuquerque, 1978-80; ptnr. Garner/Hicks Architects, Albuquerque, 1980-84; prin. Gregory T. Hicks & Assocs., Albuquerque, 1984-85, pres., 1985—; v.p. Albuquerque Conservation Assn., 1981-82, pers., 1982-83. Contbr. Standard Handbook Engring. Calculations, 1985. Pres. Mirasol Pre-Sch., Inc., Albuquerque, 1987. Democrat. Home: 5824 Isleta SW Albuquerque NM 87105 Office: Gregory T Hicks & Assocs 112 2d St SW Albuquerque NM 87102

HICKS, ROGER DALE, mechanical engineer; b. Moorland, Iowa, July 31, 1935; s. Glen Everette and Elsie Caroline (Walrod) H.; m. Judith Helen Coerber, Mar. 9, 1963; children: Cynthia June, Kenneth Dale. BSME, Iowa State U., 1957; postgrad., U. So. Calif., 1957-59. Project engr. X-15, B-58, T-38 propulsion systems, power plant br. Air Force Flight Test Ctr., Edwards AFB, Calif., 1961-63; subsystem mgr. descent propulsion system NASA Johnson Space Ctr., Houston, 1963-65, vehicle mgr. flight and ground test Apollo project, 1965-71, earth resources tech. mgr., 1972-75; mfg. project engr. NASA Space Shuttle Orbiter Resident Office, Palmdale, Calif., 1975-86, mgr. Palmdale ops., 1983-86, 87—; acting mgr., resident office NASA Nat. Space Transp. System, Vandenberg AFB, Calif., 1986-87. Coach Am. Youth Soccer Orgn., Lancaster, Calif., 1975-81. 1st lt. USAF, 1957-60. Mem. Tau Beta Pi. Presbyterian. Home: 1764 Virginia St Wrightwood CA 92397 Office: NASA Resident Office PO Box 1240 Palmdale CA 93550

HIDDLESTON, RONAL EUGENE, drilling and pump company executive; b. Bristow, Okla., Mar. 21, 1939; s. C.L. and Iona D. (Martin) H.; m. Marvelene L. Hammond, Apr. 26, 1959; children: Michael Scott, Mark Shawn, Matthew Shane. Student, Idaho State U., 1957-58. With Roper's Clothing and Bishop Redi-Mix, Rupert, Idaho, 1960-61; pres., chmn. bd., gen. mgr. Hiddleston Drilling, Rupert, 1961-66, Mountain Home, Idaho, 1966—. Mem. Mountain Home Airport Adv. Bd., 1968—; hon. mem. Idaho Search and Rescue. Mem. Nat. Water Well Assn. (treas.), Idaho Water Well Assn. (dir., past pres.), Pacific N.W. Water Well Assn. (dir.), N.W. Mining Assn., Nat. Fedn. Ind. Businessmen, Nat. Water Well Assn. (treas.), Aircraft Owners and Pilots Assn., Ducks Unltd. Club: Nat 210 Owners. Lodges: Optimists, Masons, Shriners. Home: 645 E 17th St N Mountain Home ID 83647 Office: Rte 1 Box 610D Mountain Home ID 83647

HIDY, GEORGE MARTEL, chemical engineer, executive; b. Kingman, Ariz., Jan. 5, 1935; s. John William and Margaret (Coqueron) H.; m. Dana Sexton Thomas, Oct. 15, 1958; children—Anne, Adrienne, John. A.B., Columbia U., N.Y.C., 1956, B.S., 1957; M.S.E., Princeton U., N.J., 1958; D.Eng., Johns Hopkins U., Balt., 1962. Asst. dir. chemistry and microphysics Nat. Ctr. Atmospheric Research, Boulder, Colo., 1967-69; group leader chem. physics Rockwell Internat. Sci. Ctr., Thousand Oaks, Calif., 1969-73, assoc. dir., 1973-74; gen. mgr. Environ. Research & Tech., West Lake, Calif., 1974-76, v.p., 1976-84; pres. Desert Research Inst., Reno, Nev., 1984-87; v.p. Electric Power Research Inst., Palo Alto, Calif., 1987—. Commr., Calif. Youth Soccer Assn., Los Angeles, 1982-84. Mem. Am. Meteorol. Soc., Am. Chem. Soc., Am. Geophys. Union, AAAS, Air Pollution Control Assn. Club: Cosmos (Washington). Home: 419 Burning Tree Ct Half Moon Bay CA 94019 Office: Electric Power Rsch Inst 3412 Hillview Ave Palo Alto CA 94303

HIGDON, BERNICE COWAN, retired teacher; b. Sylva, N.C., Feb. 26, 1918; d. Royston Duffield and Margaret Cordelia (Hall) Cowan; m. Roscoe John Higdon, Aug. 12, 1945; children: Ronald Keith, Rod Knox, Krista Dean. BS, Western Carolina U., 1941; Cert. Tchr., So. Oreg. Coll., 1967; Cert. Life Tchr., Chapman Coll., 1971. Prin., tchr. Dorsey Sch., Bryson City, N.C., 1941-42; expeditor Glenn L. Martin Aircraft Co., Balt., 1942-45; tchr. elem. sch. Seneca, S.C., 1945-46, Piedmont, S.C., 1946-47; tchr. elem. sch. Columbia, S.C., 1950-51, Manteca, Calif., 1967-68; kindergarten tchr. 1st Bapt. Ch., Medford, Oreg., 1965-67; tchr. elem. sch. Marysville (Calif.) Unified Sch. Dist., 1968-83; tchr. Headstart, Manteca, 1968. Former counselor Youth Svc. Bur., Yuba City, Calif.; troop leader Girl Scouts U.S.A., Medford, 1962-63; past Sunday sch. tchr. 1st Bapt. Ch., Medford; bd. dirs. Christian Assistance Network, Yuba City, 1984-85; aux. vol. Fremont Med. Ctr., Yuba City, 1984-88. Recipient cert. of appreciation Marysville Unified Sch. Dist., 1983, Christian Assistance Network, 1985; cert. of recognition Ella Elem. Sch., Marysville, 1983. Mem. Calif. Ret. Tchrs. Assn., Nat. Ret. Tchrs. Assn., Sutter Hist. Soc., AAUW, Am. Assn. Ret. Persons. Home: 1264 Charlotte Ave Yuba City CA 95991

HIGDON, POLLY SUSANNE, judge; b. Goodland, Kans., May 1, 1942; d. William and Pauline Higdon; m. John P. Wilhardt (div. May 1988); 1 child, Liesl. BA, Vassar Coll., 1964; postgrad., Cornell U., 1967; JD, Washburn U., 1975; LLM, NYU, 1980. Bar: Kans. 1975, Oreg. 1980. Assoc. Corley & Assocs., Garden City, Kans., 1975-79, Kendrick M. Mercer Law Offices, Eugene, Oreg., 1980-82; pvt. practice law Eugene, 1983; judge U.S. Bankruptcy Ct., Eugene, 1983—. Active U.S. Peace Corps, Tanzania, East Africa, 1965-66. Mem. Am. Bankruptcy Inst., Nat. Assn. Bankruptcy Judges, Nat. Assn. Women Judges. Office: US Bankruptcy Ct 211 E 7th Rm 404 PO Box 1335 Eugene OR 97440

HIGGINBOTHAM, LLOYD WILLIAM, mechanical engineer; b. Haydentown, Pa., Nov. 24, 1934; s. Clarence John and Nannie Mae (Piper) H.; m. Genevieve Law, Oct. 17, 1953 (div.); 1 child, Mark William; m. Mary Bannaian, July 23, 1966; 1 child, Samuel Lloyd. BSME, Case Western Res. U.; MBA, West Coast U., L.A. With rsch. and devel. TRW Inc., Cleve., 1953-57; pres. Higginbotham Rsch., Cleve., 1957-64; pres., chief exec. officer Lloyd Higginbotham Assocs., Woodland Hills, Calif., 1964—; cons. grad. engring. programs UCLA, Calif. State U., L.A., U. So. Calif.; pres. adv. com. Pierce Coll., L.A.; adv. com. So. Calif. Productivity Ctr.; cons. various Calif. legislators. Mem. Town Hall Calif. Recipient Community Service award City of Downey (Calif.), 1974, Archimedes award NSPE, Outstanding Contribution Recognition, 1986, Outstanding Leadership Recognition, 1987. Fellow Inst.' Advancement of Engring. (exec. dir. 1984—); mem. Soc. Carbide and Tool Engrs. (chmn. 1974-76), Soc. Mfg. Engrs. (chmn. San Fernando Valley chpt. 1977-79, numerous awards), San Fernando Valley Joint Coun. Engrs. (advisor, pres. 1981-82), Profl. Salesmen's Assn., Am. Soc. Assn. Execs., L.A. Coun. Engrs. and Scientists (exec. mgr. 1984—), L.A. Area C. of C., Toastmasters, Masons. Republican. Office: Lloyd Higginbotham Assocs PO Box 1305 Woodland Hills CA 91365

HIGGINS, BARBRA IRENE, lawyer, accountant, sports company executive; b. Panama City, Panama, July 22, 1957; came to U.S., 1976; d. Victor and Dora (Arana) H. Student, C.Z. Jr. Coll., 1975-76; BBA, Fla. Internat. U., 1979; JD, U. Miami, 1983. Tax mgr. Price Waterhouse, 1983-87; pres. Athlon Sports Mgmt. Group, San Francisco, 1987—. Com. mem. Bay Area Sports Hall of Fame/San Francisco C. of C., 1987—; bd. dirs., treas. No. Calif. Olympians, 1988—; olympian, L.A., 1984. Mem. Nat. Assn. Female Execs., Phi Alpha Delta. Office: Athlon Sports Mgmt Group 650 5th St Ste 514 San Francisco CA 94107

HIGGINS, DENNIS ROY, academic administrator; b. Spokane, Wash., Jan. 21, 1937; s. Clarence James and Vivian Grace (Rogers) H.; m. Carol Louise Land Smith, 1959 (div. 1972); m. Sandra Lee Jones Sloan, May 14, 1983. BA in Acctg., Eastern Wash. U., 1962; postgrad. in mgmt. program, U. Wash., 1980-81; grad., Stanford (Calif.) Bus. Mgmt. Inst., 1988. Asst. chief acct. U. Wash., Seattle, 1964-73, dir. acctg., 1973-87, assoc. controller, 1988—; chair State of Wash. Higher Edn. Budget, Acctg. and Reporting Com., 1987-88, Office Fin. Mgmt. Accounts Payable Com., 1987-88. Served to 1st lt. U.S. Army, 1962-64. Mem. Govt. Fin. Officers Assn., Assn. Govt. Accts., Western Assn. Coll. and Univ. Bus. Officers (host com. 1988—). Republican. Methodist. Home: 7741 22d NE Seattle WA 98115 Office: U Wash 3917 University Way NE Seattle WA 98105

HIGGINS, ERROL MICHAEL, photographer; b. Johannesburg, Transvaal, Republic of South Africa, Apr. 19, 1942; came to U.S., 1984; s. Peter Godfrey and Miriam (Katz) H.; m. Suzanne Beryl Higgins (div. 1986); children: Lee Peter, Samantha Jay. Grad. high sch., Johannesburg. Owner, operator Errol Higgins Pty. Ltd., Johannesburg, 1963-84, Photo Corp. of Calif., Inc., Irvine, 1984—. Photographer: Art & Artists of South Africa, 1984, The Right to Look Human, 1975, Sun on the Grid, 1970, The Finishing Touch, 1982 (Silver award 1982). Mem. Am. Soc. Mag. Photographers, Profl. Photographers Am. Office: Photo Corp of Calif Inc 12 Hughes D104 Irvine CA 92718

HIGGINS, GREGORY T., graphic arts company executive; b. Santa Monica, Calif., July 28, 1954; s. Glen T. and Beverly Jean (Carr) H.; m. Susan Jean Sutton, Sept. 4, 1988. AS in Mktg., Moorpark Coll., 1974. Rep. Head Shampoo, Carson, Calif., 1974-78; mgr. Maho Sales, Carson, 1978-81; owner, mgr. Gregory Higgins & Assocs., Tarzana, Calif., 1981-87; pres. G. Cee Graphics Inc., Tarzana, 1987—. Republican. Baptist.

HIGGINS, KAREN LYNN, software development executive, electrical engineer; b. Scottsbluff, Neb., Aug. 10, 1948; d. Eldon Jack and Freda (Schreiner) Rogers; m. Heinz-Juergen Roeser, Oct. 18, 1969 (div. 1977); m. Timothy R. Higgins, Mar. 4, 1978; stepchildren: Joanne, Donna. AS in Math., Casper Jr. Coll., 1968; BS in Math., U. Idaho, 1972, MSEE, 1973. Software engr. Naval Weapons Ctr., China Lake, Calif., 1973-82, systems engr., 1982-84, head communications br., 1984-85, head software br., 1985-87, head. software div., 1987—. Named Fed. Woman of Yr., Naval Weapons Ctr., 1977, 80, recipient Tech. Dirs. award, 1986. Mem. Ridgecrest chpt. IEEE (presenter 1987-88), AAUW, Bus. and Profl. Women., Assn. Old Crows (v.p. 1988—), Sigma Xi, Phi Beta Kappa. Lutheran. Home: 1000 Randall Ridgecrest CA 93555 Office: Naval Weapons Ctr Code 356 China Lake CA 93555

HIGGINS, KENNETH MILTON, foundation administrator; b. Kosse, Tex., Dec. 31, 1936; s. Leland A. and Florine Higgins; m. Jarrene S. Pearce, Feb. 1, 1958; children: Kathrine E., Kenneth Milton Jr., Janneth G. BA, Baylor U., 1959; BD, Golden Gate Sem., 1962, Dr.Ministry, 1973. Ordained to ministry Bapt. Ch. as pastor, 1959. Misic dir. East Waco (Tex.) Bapt. Chapel, 1955-57; music and youth dir. Bosqueville Bapt. Ch., 1957-59, Gilroy (Calif.) Bapt. Ch., 1959-60; pastor Bapt. Ch., Calif., 1960-79, Richland (Wash.) Bapt. Ch., 1979-84; exec. v.p. Calif. Bapt. Found., Fresno, 1984—; also bd. dirs. Calif. Bapt. Found.; bd. dirs. Calif. Plan of Ch. Fin., Fresno, 1984—. Sunday sch. dir. San Francisco Peninsula Bapt. Assn., 1971-75, ch. tng. dir., 1975-76; mem. various coms. Southern Bapt. Gen. Convention Calif., 1960-78; mem. com. Northwest Satellite Ctr., 1980-82; pres. Frontier Elem. Sch. PTA, 1965-67. Mem. Assn. Bapt. Found. (exec. 1984—), Sacramento So. Bapt. assn. (clerk 1964-68, vice moderator 1968-69), Monterey Bapt. Assn. (vice moderator 1977-78), Golden Gate Bapt. Theol. Sem. Alumni Assn. (pres. 1969-70). Office: Calif Bapt Found 680 E Shaw Ave Fresno CA 93710

HIGHAM, JOHN SCOTT, mechanical engineer; b. Bakersfield, Calif., Aug. 2, 1960; s. Leonard Byron and Marilyn Joyce (Blackburn) H. BSME, Utah State U., 1988. Rsch. engr. Ctr. for Space Engring., Logan, Utah, 1986—. Editor, co-author: Manned Assembly Service and Repair Module, 1988. Mem. AIAA, ASME (v.p. local chpt. 1987-88). Republican. Mormon. Home: 1495 Highland Dr Logan UT 84321 Office: Ctr Space Engring UMC 4130 Logan UT 84322-4130

HIGHLAND, DAVID C., software developer, entrepreneur; b. Cleve., Sept. 24, 1954; s. Claude and Beverly Cassirer. Faculty Berklee Coll. of Music, Boston, 1973-75; with Support Station Software, Aspen, Colo., 1975—. Inventor: FileBank to FileBank electronic file cabinets, 1987; designer software for personal computers. Democrat. Jewish. Office: Support Station Software PO Box 8282 Aspen CO 81612

HIGHLANDER, RICHARD WILLIAM, communications executive; b. Beckley, W.Va., Feb. 17, 1940; s. Ronald William and Lucille Bernice (Bland) H.; m. Ida Mae Canterbury, June 26, 1965; one child, Alison Renee. BA, Rutgers U., 1963; MA, U. Ga., 1972. Commd. 2d lt. U.S. Army, 1963, advanced through grades to lt. col., 1979, ret., 1984; dir. communications, def. systems group FMC Corp., Santa Clara, Calif., 1984—; bd. govs. Hispanic Devel. Corp. Contbr. articles to profl. jours., Freedom Found. award 1966, 81. Trustee San Jose Repertory Co., 1985; bd. govs. Hispanic Devel. Corp. Decorated Legion of Merit with bronze oak leaf cluster, Bronze Star with two bronze oak leaf clusters, Purple Heart. Mem. Assn. of U.S. Army, Pub. Relations Soc. Am. (accredited), Internat. Assn. Bus. Communicators, Calif. Mfrs. Assn. (bd. dirs. 1985), Aerospace Industries Assn. (communications council), Internat. Platform Assn., Rotary. Republican. Methodist. Home: 1486 Oak Canyon Dr San Jose CA 95120

HIGHT, HAROLD PHILIP, security company executive; b. Crescent City, Calif., Apr. 17, 1924; s. Vernon Austin and Mary Jane (Gontau) H.; m. Margaret Rose Edelman, Nov. 19, 1945 (div. 1949); children: Linda Marie, Beverly Sue; m. Doris Louise Dunn, June 20, 1982. Student police sci., Coll. of Redwoods, 1969. With Pan Am. World Airways, South San Francisco, Calif., 1945-51, 52; officer Richmond (Calif.) Police Dept., 1952-54; aircraft electrician Internat. Atlas Svc., Oakland, Calif., 1954-56; security officer radiation lab. AEC, Livermore, Calif., 1956-58; chief police Port Orford (Oreg.) Police Dept., 1958-61; dep. sheriff, sgt., evidence technician Del Notre County Sheriff's Dept., Crescent City, 1961-85; security officer, sgt. Del Notre Security Svc., Crescent City, 1985—. With USN, 1941-45, 51-52. Mem. Internat. Footprint Assn. (sec., treas. bd. dirs. Crescent City 1985—), Navy League U.S. (2d v.p. Crescent City 1984—), Tin Can Sailors, Masons, Elks, Grange. Republican. Roman Catholic. Home: 110 Lafayette Way Crescent City CA 95531-8351

HIGHTOWER, JAMES KAY, computer executive; b. Kalamazoo, Mar. 22, 1937; s. Raymond L. and Jeanne Doris (Matthews) H.; AB, Kalamazoo Coll., 1958; MA, Claremont Grad. Sch., 1967, PhD, 1970; m. Sharon Joan Wiley, Sept. 7, 1957; children: Matthew Wiley, Elizabeth Joan. Tchr. math. Pomona (Calif.) Unified Sch. Dist., 1959-61; asst. prof. math. and econs. U. Richmond (Va.), 1964-67; asst. prof. Calif. Poly State U., Pomona, 1967-68; assoc. prof. Calif. State U., Fullerton, 1969-76, assoc. dean sch. bus., 1970-73, assoc. dir. div. info. systems, 1976-86, assoc. dir. system-wide computing svcs. and communications resources, 1986—, adj. prof. computer sci., 1986—; adj. prof. Calif. State U.-Dominguez Hills, 1984-87, Claremont Grad. Sch., 1968— . NDEA fellow, 1960-63. Mem. AAAS, IEEE, Assn. Computing Machinery, Am. Assn. Artificial Intelligence, Ops. Research Assn. Am., N.Y. Acad. Sci. Home: 798 Via Santo Tomas Claremont CA 91711 Office: PO Box 3842 Seal Beach CA 90740-7842

HIGUCHI, PETER KWAN, investment company executive; b. Honolulu, May 3, 1936; d. Hiro and Hisako (Watanabe) H. B of Engring., Yale U., 1959; MS, U. So. Calif., 1964. Design engr. Douglas Aircraft Co., Santa Monica, Calif., 1959-64; sr. assoc. Planning Research Corp., Los Angeles, 1964-68; sr. ops. research analyst Control Data Corp., Honolulu, 1968-70; cons. Hawaii Dept. Budget and Fin., Honolulu, 1970-74; sr. legis. analyst State of Hawaii, Honolulu, 1974-75; acct. exec. Bache Halsey Stuart Inc., Honolulu, 1975-77; sr. v.p. Shearson Lehman Hutton, Inc., Honolulu, 1977—. Patentee in field. Mem. Hawaii Big Brothers/Big Sisters, 1982-86. Named one of Best Stockbrokers, Money mag., 1987. Mem. Internat. Assn. Financial Planners. Democrat. Mem. United Ch. of Christ. Club: Honolulu. Office: Shearson Lehman Hutton Inc 1585 Kapiolani Blvd Ste 1812 Honolulu HI 96814

HILBRECHT, NORMAN TY, lawyer, state legislator; b. San Diego, Feb. 11, 1933; s. Norman Titus and Elizabeth (Lair) H.; m. Mercedes L. Sharratt, Oct. 24, 1980. B.A., Northwestern U., 1956; J.D., Yale U., 1959. Bar: Nev. 1959, U.S. Supreme Ct. 1963. Assoc. counsel Union Pacific R.R., Las Vegas, 1962; partner firm Hilbrecht & Jones, Las Vegas, 1962-69; pres. Hilbrecht, Jones, Schreck & Bernhard, 1969-83, Hilbrecht & Assocs, 1983—, Mobil Transport Corp., 1970-72; gen. counsel Bell United Ins. Co., 1986—; assemblyman Nev. Legislature, 1966-72, minority leader, 1971-72; mem. Nev. Senate, 1974-78; asst. lectr. bus. law U. Nev., Las Vegas. Mem. labor mgmt. com. NCCJ, 1963; mem. Clark County (Nev.) Democratic Central Com., 1959-80, 1st vice chmn., 1965-66; del. Western Regional Assembly on Ombudsman; chmn. Clark County Dem. Conv., 1966, Nev. Dem. Conv., 1966; pres. Clark County Legal Aid Soc., 1964, Nev. Legal Aid and Defender Assn., 1965-83. Served to capt. AUS, 1952-67. Named Outstanding State Legislator Eagleton Inst. Politics, Rutgers U., 1969. Mem. Am. Judicature Soc., Am. Bar Assn., Clark County Bar Assn., Am. Acad. Polit. and Social Sci., Am. Trial Lawyers Assn., State Bar Nev., Nev. Trial Lawyers (state v.p. 1966), Nat. Assn. Real Estate Appraisers (cert.), Fraternal Order Police Assos. (v.p.), Phi Beta Kappa, Delta Phi Epsilon, Theta Chi, Phi Delta Phi. Lutheran. Lodge: Elks. Office: 723 S Casino Center Blvd Las Vegas NV 89101

HILBURN, LARRY DARRELL, teacher; b. Durant, Okla., Sept. 28, 1947; s. Charles Darryl Hilburn and Mary Dee (Edwards) Purser. m. Barbara Jean. BS, U. Calif., L.A., 1969, MS, 1975; M in Physics, Calif. State U., Northridge, 1975. Communication Colg. Life Credential. System engr. Lockheed, Burbank, Calif., 1966-72; grad. asst. Calif. State U., Northridge, 1971-73; rsch. asst. physics U. Calif., L.A., 1973-75; tchr. Oxnard (Calif.) Union H.S. Dist., 1976—; Cons. in Field. 1982-89. pres. Oxnard Secondary Teachers Assn., bd. mem. Temple Beth Torah, Ventura, Calif., 1986-89. NSF Research Sci. Grant Nat. Sci. Found. 1974. mem. Am. Geophysical Union, Am. Assn. Physics Teachers, Calif. Council. Democratic. Jewish. Office: Oxnard High Sch 937 W 5th St Oxnard CA 93030

HILBURN, (CHARLES) ROBERT, music critic; b. Natchitoches, La., Sept. 25, 1939; s. Charles M. and Alice Marie (Taylor) Nelms; m. Ruthann Marie Schlegel, Nov. 19, 1958 (div. Oct. 1983); children: Kathleen Marie, Charles Robert, II; m. Mary Kathleen Barr, Oct., 1988. BA in Journalism, Calif. State U., Northridge, 1961. Reporter Valley Times Today, North Hollywood, Calif., 1961-64; pub. info. officer L.A. Bd. Edn., 1964-70; pop music critic L.A. Times, 1970—; music critic Playboy's TV Mag., 1982-84; mem. adv. panel jazz, folk, popular and rock music U.S. Internat. Communication Agy., Dept. State, 1976-79; corr. Rock and Roll Evening News TV program; mem. nominating com. Rock and Roll Hall of Fame. Author: Rolling Stone Anthology, Springsteen. Recipient award L.A. Press Club, 1972, 85. Address: LA Times Times-Mirror Sq Los Angeles CA 90053

HILBY, BRUCE TITUS, real estate investment executive; b. Chgo., June 27, 1944; s. F. Martin and Laura Elizabeth (Titus) H.; m. Paula Ann Bullock, Oct. 28, 1975; children: Anne Titus, Edwin Joseph Martin. BS in Bus., Northwestern U., 1966; student, U. Miss. Law Sch., 1966-67; JD, Northwestern U., 1973. Bar: Ariz. 1974, Ill. 1973, Wash. 1973. Analyst Boyle Investment Co., Memphis, 1966-67; registered rep. 1st Columbia Corp., Seattle, Wash., 1973-74; owner, prin. Hilby & Co., Inc., Phoenix, 1974-76; pres., dir. Tierra Assocs., Ltd., Phoenix, 1977—; mgr., gen. ptnr. Pacific Southwest Property Co., San Diego, 1985—. Author: Pay Dirt, 1988, Successful Land Investing, 1989. 1st chmn. Ariz. State Lottery Commn., Phoenix, 1980-82; mem. exec. com. Phoenix Econ. Growth Corp., 1984-86. Recipient Outstanding Area Rsch. award Indsl. Devel. Rsch. Coun., 1981. Mem. Ariz. Bar Assn., Wash. Bar Assn., Ill. Bar Assn., Ariz. Assn. for Indsl. devel. (Developer of the Year award 1982), Western Gateway Team (chmn. 1979-84), Rancho Sante Fe Golf and Tennis Club, Phoenix Country Club. Republican. Episcopalian. Home: PO Box 389 6165 Mimulus Rancho Sante Fe CA 92067 Office: Pacific SW Property Co 4370 La Jolla Village Dr Ste 400 San Diego CA 92122

HILDEBRAND, DON CECIL, helicopter company executive; b. Camp Cooke, Calif., Dec. 1, 1943; s. Cecil and Gladys Helen (Buschmeier) H.; m. Rita Ann Wojdyla, July 25, 1964; children: Jeffrey James, Denise Lynn. BA, U. Ariz., 1978. Chief pilot Tucson Police Dept., 1970-80; pres. S.W. Helicopters, Inc., Tucson, 1981—; Dir. Airborne Law Enforcement Assn., Los Angeles, 1976-78; pilot examiner FAA, Phoenix, 1979—; counselor accident prevention FAA, Phoenix, 1988. Pres. Vietnam Helicopter Pilot Assn., Phoenix, 1982. With U.S. Army, 1966-69, Vietnam. Mem. Am. Helicopter Soc., Vietnam Veterans Assn., Veterans of Fgn. Wars, Aircraft Owners & Pilots Assn., The Planetary Soc. Republican. Catholic. Home: 1911 N Old Pueblo Tucson AZ 85745 Office: Southwest Helicopters Inc 6666 S Plumer Tucson AZ 85706

HILDEBRAND, JAMES LOWELL, computer company executive; b. Tallapoosa, Ga., July 21, 1942; s. James W. Jr. and Eunice (Long) H.; m. Susan Grosz, June 26, 1981; children: Deana Cheryl, James L., Stacy Lynn. Student, Jacksonville State Coll., 1960-63. Tech. cons. Gen. Electric Co.-FSO, Washington, 1967-70; br. mgr. mktg. support Gen. Electric Co.-Honeywell, Dallas, 1970-76; dir. field mktg. support Honeywell Co., Phoenix, 1976-79; br. mgr. energy br. Honeywell Co., Houston, 1979-81; dir. engring. Honeywell Datanetwork, Mpls., 1981-83; dir. sales tng. Honeywell LCPD, Phoenix, 1983-85, dir. applications mktg., 1985-86; dir. SIVI Honeywell Bull Inc., Phoenix, 1986-87, dir. systems integration, 1987—; advisor Datapro Research, N.Y.C., 1986—; cons. Midwest Group, Phoenix, 1986—, DLM Group, Phoenix, 1987—. Deacon So. Bapt. chs., Lewisville,

Tex., Scottsdale, Ariz., 1974; pres. Ctr. for New Directions, Phoenix, 1985— Mem. Am. Soc. for Quality Control. Republican. Home: 9950 E Sundance Tr Scottsdale AZ 85262 Office: Bull HN Info Systems Inc Canyon Hwy MS-B48 Phoenix AZ 85003

HILDERBRAND, KURT ELLIOTT, sales executive; b. Oakland, Calif., Dec. 8, 1944; s. Ralph E. and Jean (Moore) H.; divorced, 1971; m. Cathleen Jo Baucom, Nov. 13, 1983; 1 child, Mark Eldon. Dispatcher Pacific Telephone, Oakland, 1963-68; salesman N.Y. Life Ins. Co., Fremont, Calif., 1968-74, Global Van Lines, Portland, Oreg., 1974-75, Honeywell, Portland, 1975-80; v.p. sales TRI-M, Inc., Portland and Seattle, 1980--. Home: 4001 239th Pl SE Issaquah WA 98027 Office: TRI M Inc 17903 Bothell Way SE Ste 104 Bothell WA 98012

HILDING, RONALD FREDERICK, psychiatrist; b. Toledo, Aug. 7, 1938; s. John Frederick and Viola Bessie (Pugh) H. B.S., U. Utah, 1961, M.D., 1965. Intern, Maricopa Gen. Hosp., Phoenix, 1965-66; resident in psychiatry Met. State Hosp., U. Calif.-Irvine, Norwalk, Calif., 1968-71, staff psychiatrist 1971-72; chief psychiat. inpatient service Maricopa Gen. Hosp., Phoenix, 1972-75; practice medicine specializing in psychiatry, Phoenix, 1975—; group mem., sec.-treas. Inst. Human Services, Inc.; mem. staff St. Luke's Behavioral Health Ctr., 1975—, pres. med. staff, 1982-83. Served with M.C., U.S. Army, 1966-68. Decorated Bronze Star. Mem. AMA, Am. Psychiat. Assn., Am. Soc. Adolescent Psychiatry, Maricopa County Med. Soc., Phoenix Psychiat. Council, Ariz. Soc. Adolescent Psychiatry. Office: 3501 N Scottsdale Rd Ste 320 Scottsdale AZ 85251

HILDNER, THOMAS G., physician; b. Saginaw, Mich., June 17, 1946; s. Harold G. and Anita (Bickel) H.; m. Nancy J. Luznak, May 21, 1977. BA, Western Mich. U., 1970; MD, Wayne State U., 1974. Rotating intern St. Luke's Hosp., Denver, 1974-75; pvt. practice Denver, 1975-77, Family Practice Assocs., Bozeman, Mont., 1977—; adj. prof. Mont. State U., Bozeman, 1978—. Mem. City County Planning Bd., Bozeman, 1987-88. Lutheran. Office: Family Practice Assocs 300 N Wilson Ste 1004 Bozeman MT 59715

HILDRETH, DONALD EDWIN, manager; b. Brattleboro, Vt., Mar. 26, 1933; s. Robert G. and Helen G. (Curley) H.; m. Mary Jane Mulvey, Aug. 5, 1956; children: John, Jim G., Kathryn, Sheila, Vicki. BA, U. N.H., 1957. Office mgr. N.Y. Life Ins. Co., Pasadena, Calif., 1958-62; mgr. Aerojet Electrosystems, Azusa, Calif., 1962—; group leader, NSIA Mgmt. Systems subcom., Washington, 1982—. Author tech. papers for nat. seminars. Leader, Boy Scouts Am., Claremont, Calif., 1967-70. Cpl., U.S. Army, 1953-55. Mem. Performance Mgmt. Assn. (v.p., chief fin. officer, 1987-88), L.A. Orange County Chpt. Performance Mgmt. Assn. (pres. 1988—). Republican. Roman Catholic. Home: 9372 Mokihana Dr Huntington Beach CA 92646 Office: Aerojet Electrosystems Co 1100 W Hollyvale St PO Box 296 Azusa CA 91702

HILGER, FREDERICK LEE, JR., real estate executive, banker, lawyer; b. Dallas, Feb. 17, 1946; s. Frederick Lee Sr. and Maryann Taylor (Ayers) H.; m. Terri Lynn Wilson, May 13, 1984; children: Matthew Charles, Kristen Leigh. BA, U. Pacific, Stockton, Calif., 1967; JD, U. Calif., Berkeley, 1970. Bar: Calif. 1971. Sr. tax acct. Touche Ross and Co., San Francisco, 1971-73; atty. F. L. Hilger Prof. Corp., Eureka, Calif., 1973-75; mng. ptnr. Moses Lake (Wash.) Farms, 1975-78; sr. cons. Sites and Co. Inc., Seattle, 1978-79; v.p. ops. mgmt. U.S. Cruises, Inc., Seattle, 1980-83; pres., chief fin. officer First Nat. Bank, Chico, Calif., 1984-86; pres., chief exec. officer FreeHill Corp., San Marcos, Calif., 1986—. Recipient Outstanding Banker award Am. Bankers Assn. First Nat. Bank, 1984, 85. Mem. ABA, Calif. Bar Assn., Sacramento Bar Assn. Republican. Presbyterian. Clubs: Olympic (San Francisco), Shadowridge Golf. Office: FreeHill Corp Box 1808 San Marcos CA 92069

HILL, ANNA MARIE, manufacturing executive; b. Great Falls, Mont., Nov. 6, 1938; d. Paul Joseph and Alexina Rose (Doyon) Ghekiere. AA, Oakland Jr. Coll., 1959; student, U. Calif., Berkeley, 1960-62. Mgr. ops. OSM, Soquel, Calif., 1963-81; purchasing agt. Arrow Huss, Scotts Valley, Calif., 1981-82; sr. buyer Fairchild Test Systems, San Jose, Calif., 1982-83; materials mgr. Basic Test Systems, San Jose, 1983-86; purchasing mgr. Beta Tech., Santa Cruz, Calif., 1986-87; mgr. purchasing ICON Rev., Carmel, Calif., 1987-88; materials mgr. Integrated Components Test System, Sunnyvale, Calif., 1988-89; mfg. mgr. Forte Communications, Sunnyvale, 1989—; cons., No. Calif., 1976—. Counselor Teens Against Drugs, San Jose, 1970, 1/2 Orgn., Santa Cruz, 1975-76. Mem. Am. Prodn. Invention Control, Nat. Assn. Female Execs., Nat. Assn. Purchasing Mgmt., Porsche Club Am., Am. Radio Relay League. Democrat. Club: Young Ladies Radio League. Home: 2922 Park Ave Soquel CA 95073 Office: Forte Communications 680 W Maude Ave Sunnyvale CA 94086

HILL, CHARLES EDWARD, municipal government official; b. Ft. Scott, Kans., June 9, 1934; s. Charles Hardin and Katherine Lucile (Allen) H.; m. Carol K. McShane, Feb. 14, 1954 (div. 1969); 1 child, Kathy; m. JoAnn Amelia Larson, June 7, 1969; children: Jennifer, Allison, Stephen. BS in Public Admin., U. Mo., 1956, MS in Public Admin., 1962. Product cost acct. Ford Motor Co., Kansas City, Mo., 1958-60; mgmt. intern City of Phoenix, 1961-63; asst. city mgr. City of Roseville (Calif.), 1963-68; fin. dir. City of Santa Cruz (Calif.), 1968-70; mgmt., budget dir. City of Phoenix, 1970—. Served to 1st lt. U.S. Army, 1956-58. Recipient Excellence in Budgeting award, Municipal Fin. Officers Assn., Toronto, Can., 1983. Mem. Internat. City Mgrs. Assn., Govt. Fin. Officers Assn. Democrat. Lutheran. Office: City of Phoenix 251 W Washington St Phoenix AZ 85003

HILL, DALE RICHARD, military officer; b. Charleston, W.Va., Dec. 20, 1939; s. Cecil Thomas Jr. and Frances Eileen (Gillespie) H.; m. Linda Lee Ergeson, Apr. 20, 1962 (dec. 1971); m. Debbie Kay Hildebrant, Feb. 19, 1972; children: Mark, Bret, Lara, Dale, Adam. BS, W.Va. State Coll., 1967; MA, Cen. Mich. U., 1977; grad., USA Command and Gen. Staff Coll., 1982. Commd. 2d lt. U.S. Army, Ft. Benning, Ga., 1968; advanced through grades to lt. col. U.S. Army, 1984; aide-de-camp USA Operational Test and Evaluation Agy., Falls Church, Va., 1976-80; ops. officer Hdqrs. 3 Bde, 2 Infantry div., Camp Howze, Republic of Korea, 1980-81; emergency action officer Hdqr. Readiness Command, MacDill AFB, Fla., 1981-82; plans tng. officer Hdqrs. Multinat. Force & Observers Sinai, El Gorah, 1982-83; chief current ops. Hdqr. I Corps., Ft. Lewis, Wash., 1983-86; commdr. Yakima (Wash.) Firing Ctr., 1986—. Democrat. Home: 941 Market St Prosser WA 99350 Office: Hdqr Yakima Firing Ctr Yakima WA 99350

HILL, DAVID KAY, sales executive; b. Kansas City, Mo., May 9, 1936; s. Kenneth M. and Ruth Inez (Wills) H.; m. Mary Theresea Wittek, Aug. 8, 1959; children: Lynne Denise, Christopher David. BS in Speech, Kans. State U., 1959. Sports dir. Sta. KNDE-AM-FM, Aztec, N.Mex., 1959-62, Sta. KHAS-TV, Hastings, Nebr., 1962-70, Sta. KTSB-TV, Topeka, 1970-74; pub. rels. dir. Amateur Softball Assn. Am., Oklahoma City, 1974-80; sales adminstr. Bunte Candies, Inc., Oklahoma City, 1980-86; sales mgr. Larson Pub., Sedona, Ariz., 1986--. Pres. PTA, Topeka, 1972; bd. dirs. Big Bros. Assn., Hastings, 1964-67. Recipient Bd. of Govs. award AAU, 1971. Republican. Roman Catholic. Home: 1705 Contention Ln Cottonwood AZ 86326 Office: Red Rock News The Jour Sedona AZ 86336

HILL, DAVID RALEIGH, police officer; b. Long Beach, Calif., June 23, 1963; s. Raleigh P. and Glorianne Lee (Soice) H. Student, U. La Verne. With City of Orange (Calif.) Police Dept., 1981—, patrol officer, 1983-86, motor officer, 1986-88, community svcs. officer, 1988—; speaker in field. Mem. Calif. Crime Prevention Officers Assn., Orange County Cities Emergency Mgmt. Orgn., City of Orange Police Assn. (sec. 1989—). Republican. Mem. Evangelical Free Ch. Office: City of Orange Police Dept 300 E Chapman Ave Orange CA 92666

HILL, DEAN ALLEN, retail executive, real estate developer; b. McGill, Nev., Feb. 3, 1934; s. Allen Glen and Eula Mae (Fister) H. AA, San Bernadino Valley Coll., 1954; BA in Psychology, U. Calif., Berkeley, 1957. Buyer Bullocks Stores, Inc., Los Angeles, 1960-67; buyer, div. mgr. Goldwaters Stores, Inc., Phoenix, 1967-70, Webbs Dept. Stores, Glendale, Calif., 1970-78; owner, mgr. various apt. bldgs. Glendale, Van Nuys, Calif. and Los Angeles, 1975-79, Casa Colina Restaurant, San Clemente, Calif., 1979-82; ops. mgr. Builders Emporium subs. Wickes, Inc., 1982—; comml., residentia interior designer various offices, stores and residences. Served to lt. (j.g.) USN, 1957-60. Recipient Cert. of Merit City of San Clemente, 1981.

HILL, DIANE SELDON, psychologist; b. Mpls., Sept. 17, 1943; d. Earl William and Geraldine (Le Veille) Seldon; m. David Reuben Hill, May 14, 1986 (div. Feb. 1988); children: Anna Marion, Jason David. BA, Mt. Holyoke Coll., 1965; MA in Psychology, U. Minn., 1968, PhD in Psychology, 1974. Lic. psychologist, Colo; diplomate in clin. psychology Am. Bd. Profl. Psychologists. Instr., counselor Student Counseling Bur. U. Minn., Mpls., 1968-70, advisor women's programs, Student Activities Bur., 1970-71; instr. psychology Augsburg Coll., Mpls., 1970-71; counselor, tchr. humanities Emma Willard Sch., Troy, N.Y., 1972-75; dir. counseling and re-engagement Colo. Women's Coll., Denver, 1976-77; clin. field supr., Sch. Profl. Psychology U. Denver, 1977—; pvt. practice Denver, 1979-89; mgmt. and organizational cons. Somerville and Co., Inc., Denver, 1989—; asst. clin. prof. psychology U. Colo. Health Scis. Ctr., Denver, 1979--; staff affiliate Ctr. for Creative Leadership, Colorado Springs, Colo., 1986--; bd. dirs. Colo. Bd. Psychologists Examiners, 1981--, vice-chmn., 1982-83, chmn., 1983-85; del. Am. Assn. State Psychology Bds., 1982-83; presenter at profl. meetings; expert witness on psychology ethics in civil litigation case in Colo., 1988; presented testimony before Colo. legis. hearing coms. and Colo. Insurance Commn. Named NDEA IV fellow U. Minn., 1967-68. Mem. Am. Psychol. Assn. (subcom. on sexual exploitation of clients by therapists div. psychology of women 1985--), Colo. Psychol. Assn. (bd. dirs. 1979-82, dir. polit. action com.), Rocky Mountain Psychol. Assn., Am. Assn. State Psychology Bds. (mem. -at-large exec. com. 1983--, pres. 1988--), Women's Forum Colo. (ret reat com. 1979--), Vail Racquet Club. Episcopalian. Home: 2052 Bellaire St Denver CO 80207 Office: Somerville & Co Inc 1625 Broadway Denver CO 80202

HILL, DONALD TRAVIS, construction company executive; b. Ord, Nebr., Aug. 18, 1930; s. Alfred Leslie and Hazel Eunice (Travis) H.; m. Ann Sanderson Hoyt, July 22, 1959 (div. 1975); m. Marian Lou Jessup, Sept. 7, 1979. BA, Nebr. State U., 1952. Sales rep. Lloyd Gordon Mfg. Co., Richmond, Calif., 1956-59, Bestwall Gypsum Co., San Jose, Calif., 1959-67, Republic Gypsum CVo., San Jose, 1967-76, Gypsum Co., San Jose, 1976-77; dir. tech. svcs. Pabco Gypsum div. of Pacific Coast Bldg. Products, Newark, Calif., 1977—. Lt. USNR, 1952-56, Korea. Mem. Gypsum Assn. (chmn. bldg. code sect. 1982-84), Am. Soc. Testing Materials, Internat. Conf. Bldg. Ofcls., Elks. Republican. Presbyterian. Home: 708 Duncanville Ct Campbell CA 95008

HILL, DOUGLAS MELVIN, emergency physician; b. Glendale, Calif., Nov. 22, 1947; s. Melvin Smith and Virginia Jeanne (Moncrieff) H.; m. Lynn Rebecca Bailey; children: Douglas, Robert, James. BA, Union Coll., 1969; DO, Kans. City Coll. Osteo. Medicine, 1973. Diplomate Am. Bd. Emergency Medicine. Staff physician Valley View Hosp., Thornton, Colo., 1974-77, assoc. dir., emergency dept., 1977-85; co-dir., emergency dept. Humana Hosp., Mountain View, Thornton, Colo., 1985-88; staff Physician St. Anthony Hosp. Systems, Denver, 1978-88; instr. Okla. State U. Coll. Osteo. Medicine & Surgery, Tulsa, 1979-88, Advanced Cardiac Life Support, 1978-88, Pediatric Advanced Life Support, Colo., 1982-88; chief of Staff, Valley View Hosp., Thornton, Colo., 1982, Humana Hosp. Mountain View, Thornton, 1985. Mem. Am. Coll. of Emergency Physicians, Colo. Soc. of Osteo. Medicine, Am. Osteo. Assn., Colo. Med. Soc., Am. Coll. of Osteo. Emergency Physicians, Am. Coll. of Emergency Medicine (Colo. chpt. sec. treas. 1986, pres. elect 1987, pres. 1988, councillor 1987—). Club: Colo. Drs. Ski Patrol. Home: 6770 Ridgeview Dr Morrison CO 80465 Office: Humana Hosp Mountain View 9191 Grant St Thornton CO 80229

HILL, EARL MCCOLL, lawyer; b. Bisbee, Ariz., June 12, 1926; s. Earl George and Jeanette (McColl) H.; m. Bea Dolan, Nov. 22, 1968; children: Arthur Charles, John Earl, Darlene Blain, Tamara Gentry. BA, U. Wash., 1960, JD, 1961. Bar: Nev. 1962, U.S. Ct. Clms. 1978, U.S. Ct. Apls. (9th cir.) 1971, U.S. Sup. Ct. 1978. Law clk. Nev. sup. ct., Carson City, 1962; assoc. Gray, Horton & Hill, Reno, 1962-65, ptnr. 1965-73; ptnr. Hill Cassas de Lipkau and Erwin, Reno, 1974—, Sherman & Howard, Denver, 1982—; judge pro tem Reno mcpl. ct., 1964-70; lectr. continuing legal edn.; Mem. Nev. Commn. on Jud. Selection 1977-84; trustee Rocky Mountain Mineral Law Found. 1976—, sec. 1987-88. Mem. ABA, State Bar Nev. (chmn. Com. on Jud. Adminstrn. 1971-77), Washoe County Bar Assn., Am. Judicature Soc., Soc. Mining Law Antiquarians. Club: Prospectors. Contbr. articles to profl. publs. Office: Holcomb Profl Ctr Ste 300 PO Box 2790 333 Holcomb Ave Reno NV 89505

HILL, ERNEST ELWOOD, nuclear engineer; b. Oakland, Calif., May 15, 1922; s. George Leslie and Ollie Isis (Moreland) H.; m. Bettejean Schaegelen, Mar. 27, 1942; children: Eric Evan, Steven Richard, Lawrence Martin. BSME, U. Calif., Berkeley, 1943, MS in Nuclear Engring., 1959. Registered profl. engr., Calif. Prodn. supr. Fed. Pacific Electric, San Francisco, 1947-55; reactor supr. Lawrence Livermore Nat. Lab., Livermore, Calif., 1955-64; br. chief AEC, Berkeley, 1964-67; engring. div. leader Lawrence Livermore Nat. Lab., Livermore, 1967-82; pres. Hill Assocs., Danville, Calif., 1982—; bd. dirs. Hill Assocs., Danville; admistrv. judge U.S. Nuclear Regulatory Commn., Washington, 1972—. Contbr. articles to profl. jours. Capt. USAAF, 1943-46, PTO. Mem. Am. Nuclear Soc. (2nd chair 1967). Office: Hill Assocs 210 Montego Dr Danville CA 94526

HILL, EUGENE DUBOSE, health care executive; b. Louisville, Nov. 5, 1951; s. Eugene DuBose Jr. and Margaret (Preston) H.; m. Joan Luise, Oct. 12, 1980; children: Eugene David, Alyssa Anne. BA, Middlebury (Vt.) Coll., 1973; MBA, Boston U., 1980. Asst. dir. Boston Dept. Health and Hosp., 1978-83; adminstr. Nu-Med Med., Encino, Calif., 1983-84; pres., dir. Sierra Health Svcs., Las Vegas, 1984-85; pres., chmn. Sierra Health and Life, Las Vegas, 1985-87; pres., chief exec. officer U.S. Behavioral Health, Emeryville, Calif., 1988—. Mem. Am. Coll. Healthcare Adminstrs., Am. Pub. Health Assn., Nev. Pub. Health Assn. Office: US Behavioral Health 2000 Powell St Ste 1180 Emeryville CA 94608

HILL, FREDRIC WILLIAM, nutritionist, poultry scientist; b. Erie, Pa., Sept. 2, 1918; s. Vaino Alexander and Mary Elvira (Holmstrom) H.; m. Charlotte Henrietta Gummoe, Apr. 1, 1944; children: Linda Charlotte, James Fredric, Dana Edwin. B.S., Pa. State U., 1939, M.S., 1940; Ph.D., Cornell U., 1944. Rsch. asst. Pa. State U., 1939-40, Cornell U., 1940-44; head nutrition div. rsch. labs. Western Condensing Co., Appleton, Wis., 1944-48; assoc. prof., then prof. animal nutrition and poultry husbandry Cornell U., 1948-59; prof. poultry husbandry, chmn. dept. U. Calif. at Davis, 1959-65, prof. nutrition, 1965—, chmn. dept. nutrition, 1965-73, assoc. dean Coll. Agr., 1965-66, assoc. dean research and internat. programs, 1976-80, coordinator internat. programs, 1976-80, prof. nutrition emeritus, 1989—; Mem. subcom. hormonal relationships and applications com. on Animal Nutrition, NRC, 1953, subcom. poultry nutrition, 1953-74; mem. Food and Nutrition Bd., 1975-78; commr. Calif. Poultry Improvement Commn., 1959-65; participant 8th Easter Sch. Agrl. Scis., U. Nottingham, Eng., 1961, World Conf. Animal Prodn., Rome, Italy, 1963, U.S. AID-Nat. Acad. Sci. Seminar on Protein Foods, Bangkok, 1970, USIA Asia Seminars on Food, Population and Energy, 1974-75; Japan Soc. Promotion Sci. vis. prof. Nagoya U., 1974-75; vis. scientist FDA, 1975, 88, Nutrition Inst., USDA, 1975; cons. Institut National de Recherche Agronomique, France, 1982; plenary speaker 3d Asian-Australian Animal Sci. Congress, Seoul, Republic of Korea, 1985. Contbr. articles profl. jours.; Editorial bd.: Poultry Sci. Jour, 1960-64; editorial bd.: Jour. of Nutrition, 1964-68; editor, 1969-79. Fellow Danforth Found., 1938; recipient Nutrition Research award Am. Feed Mfrs. Assn., 1958, Newman Internat. Research award British Poultry Assn., 1959; Guggenheim Found. fellow, 1966-67; Alumni fellow Pa. State U., 1983. Fellow AAAS, Poultry Sci. Assn. (Research prize 1957, Borden award 1961), Am. Inst. Nutrition (councillor 1982-85); mem. Soc. Exptl. Biology and Medicine, Nutrition Soc. (Gt. Britain), Council Biology Editors, World's Poultry Sci. Assn., Am. Inst. Biol. Scis., Am. Soc. Animal Sci., Am. Chem. Soc., Sigma Xi, Phi Eta Sigma, Gamma Sigma Delta, Phi Kappa Phi, Delta Theta Sigma, Gamma Alpha. Clubs: Cosmos (Washington); El Macero (Calif.). Home: 643 Miller Dr Davis CA 95616 Office: U Calif Dept Nutrition Davis CA 95616

HILL, GEORGE RICHARD, chemistry educator; b. Ogden, Utah, Nov. 24, 1921; s. George Richard and Elizabeth (McKay) H.; m. Melba Parker, Aug. 25, 1941; children: George Richard IV, Margaret Hill Nielson, Robert Parker, Carolyn Hill Allen, Susan Hill Mann, Nancy Hill Bauman, David Parker. AB in Chemistry, Brigham Young U., 1942, DSc (hon.), 1980; PhD in Phys. and Inorganic Chemistry, Cornell U., 1946. Chemist Am. Smelting & Refining Co., 1937-42; asst. part-time instr. Cornell U., Ithaca, N.Y., 1942-46; mem. faculty U. Utah, Salt Lake City, 1946-72, prof. chemistry, 1950-72, chmn. fuels engring., 1951-65, dean Coll. Mines and Mineral Industries, 1966-72, Envirotech. endowed prof., 1977-82, Eimco endowed prof., 1982—; project dir. Air Force Combustion Rs.h, 1952-57; dir. Office Coal Rsch., Dept. Interior, Washington, 1972-73; dept. dir. fossil fuels Electric Power Research Inst., Palo Alto, Calif., 1973-77; dir. fossil fuel power plants dept. Electric Power Rsch. Inst., Palo Alto, Calif., 1976-77; project dir. Air Force Office Sci. Rsch., 1956-61, Equity Oil Shale Rsch.h, 1961; mem. NRC com. Mineral and Energy Resources, 1976-81; mem. fossil energy adv. com. Dept. Energy, 1977—; vice chmn. Utah Coun. Energy Conservation and Devel., 1978-83; chmn. Utah Task Force on Power Plant Siting, 1978; chmn. editorial com. NRC, 1977-81; com. chmn. Chemistry of Coal Utilization, 1981; mem. Nat. Coal Coun., 1985—. Contbr. papers on kinetics of coal conversion, oil shale, corrosion, catalysis. Mem. exec. bd. region XII Boy Scouts Am., 1961; chmn. Explorer activities sect. 6, 1959-61; mem. Explorer com., nat. exec. bd., 1965-72; mem. quorum of the 70 area presidency Mormon Ch., 1987—; bd. dirs. Deseret Gymnasium, 1967. Recipient Silver Beaver, Silver Antelope awards Boy Scouts Am.; Disting. Svc. award Utah Petroleum Coun., 1968; Outstanding Profl. Engr. award Utah Engring. Coun., 1970. Fellow Am. Inst. Chemists; mem. AAAS, AIME, Am. Chem. Soc. (Utah award Salt Lake sect. 1969, Henry H. Storch award 1971), Am. Inst. Chem. Engrs., Nat. Coal Council, Nat. Acad. Eng., Sigma Xi, Phi Kappa Phi, Sigma Pi Sigma, Alpha Phi Omega. Home: 1430 Yale Ave Salt Lake City UT 84105 Office: U Utah Dept Chem Engring 3062 Merrill Engring Bldg Salt Lake City UT 84112

HILL, HARRY DAVID, human resources executive; b. Whittier, Calif., Oct. 29, 1944; s. Harry Boreman and Winifred Nell (Purvis) Hill; m. Linda Mae Price, Nov. 8, 1969; 1 child, Jon Ryan. AA, Los Angeles Harbor Coll., Wilmington, Calif., 1964; BA in Polit. Sci., UCLA, 1966; M of Pub. Adminstrn. in Human Resources, U. So. Calif., 1972. Personnel aide City of Anaheim, Calif., 1966-67, personnel analyst, 1967-71, sr. personnel analyst, 1971-75, personnel services mgr., 1975-83, asst. human resources dir., 1983-88, asst. labor rels. dir., 1988—; Surpervisory com. chmn. Anaheim Area Credit Union, 1981. Mem. So. Calif. Pub. Labor Council (treas. 1986-87, pres. 1988), Internat. Personnel Mgmt. Assn. (western region pres. 1983-84), So. Calif. Personnel Mgmt. Assn. (pres. 1978-79), Coop. Personnel Services (bd. dirs. 1987). Democrat. Office: City of Anaheim 100 S Anaheim Blvd 320 Anaheim CA 92805

HILL, HENRY ALLEN, physicist, educator; b. Port Arthur, Tex., Nov. 25, 1933; s. Douglas and Florence (Kilgore) H.; m. Ethel Louise Eplin, Aug. 23, 1954; children—Henry Allen, Pamela Lynne, Kimberly Renee. B.S., U. Houston, 1953; M.S., U. Minn., 1956, Ph.D., 1957; M.A. (hon.), Wesleyan U., 1966. Research asst. U. Houston, 1952-53; teaching asst. U. Minn., 1953-54, research asst., 1954-57; research assoc. Princeton U., 1957-58, instr., then asst. prof., 1958-64; assoc. prof. Wesleyan U., Middletown, Conn., 1964-66; prof. physics Wesleyan U., 1966-74, chmn. dept., 1969-71; prof. physics U. Ariz., 1966—; researcher on nuclear physics, relativity and astrophysics. Contbr. articles to profl. jours. Sloan fellow, 1966-68. Fellow Am. Phys. Soc.; mem. AAAS, Am. Astron. Soc., Royal Astron. Soc., Optical Soc. Am., Am. Assn. Advancement Sci. Office: U Ariz Dept Physics Tucson AZ 85721

HILL, JAMES LEDYARD, executive chef; b. Atlanta, Dec. 14, 1946; s. Walter Hakes and Alice (Guillard) H.; m. Esther Demetra Andriopolus (div. Dec. 1987); children: Heather, Christopher. AB in Polit. Sci., Wabash Coll., 1969. Chef, owner Piktor's Metamorphosis, San Diego, 1975-79; chef Blue Man Restaurant, Lemon Grove, Calif., 1980; sous chef Piret's commissary, San Diego, 1980-82; exec. chef Piret's, San Diego, Costa Mesa, Calif., 1982-84, Pax Bar and Grill, La Jolla, Calif., 1984-86, Vic's restaurant, La Jolla, 1986, John Culbertson Winery, Fallbrook, Calif., 1987, Rainwaters on Kettner, San Diego, 1987-89, Vic's & Fisherman's Grill, La Jolla, Calif., 1989—, Fargo Restaurants, Inc., La Jolla, Calif., 1989—. Contbr. articles to San Diego Mag., 1981-87. Recipient grand prize Ensanada (Mex.) Seafood Fair, 1980; named on of San Diego's three top chef's San Diego Home Garden Mag., 1984. Mem. Am. Inst. Wine and Food. Office: Fargo Restaurants Inc 7825 Fay Ave La Jolla CA 92037

HILL, JAYNE LILLES, teacher; b. Portland, Oreg., July 23, 1948; d. Thomas Peter and Mary Jean (Manos) Lilles; m. James John Hill, May 9, 1971; children: Andrew James, Megan Elizabeth. Student, Willamette U., 1966-68, Chapman Coll., 1968; BS, Western Oreg. State Coll., 1971. Mgr. Clark Jr. Clothing, Salem, Oreg., 1971-173, Meier and Frank, Salem, 1973-74; tchr. elem. grades Salem-Keizer Schs., 1974-82; tchr. English and social studies Judson Middle Sch., 1984—, social studies and English team leader grade 7, 1988—; property mgr. Hill Haus, Inc., Salem and Portland, 1982—; sec., bd. dirs. Lancaster Mall, Salem, 1971-72. Mem. Salem Wellness Com., 1984-86, Salem Hosp. Aux.; pres. Parent Club, Candalaria Sch., 1986-87. Mem. Salem Edn. Assn. (grievance com. 1985-87), Assn. Am. Bus. Women, Illahe Hills Country Club (women's bd. 1985-88). Republican. Episcopalian. Home: 985 Holiday Ct Salem OR 97302 Office: Judson Middle Sch Salem OR 97302

HILL, JOHN EARL, mechanical engineer; b. Ely, Nev., July 18, 1953; s. Earl M. and Florence (Lagos) H.; m. Terry Lynn Biederman, Oct. 3, 1981; 1 stepchild, Felicia Biederman. BA in Social Psychology, U. Nev., 1974, BSME, 1981. Cert. engr. in tng. Machinist B&J Machine and Tool, Sparks, Nev., 1977-78; designer, machinist Screen Printing Systems, Sparks, Nev., 1978, Machine Svcs., Sparks, 1978-81; computer programmer U. Nev., Reno, 1980-81; design engr. Ford Aerospace and Communications Corp., Palo Alto, Calif., 1981-82; contract design engr. Westinghouse Electric Corp., Sunnyvale, Calif., 1982-83; contract project engr. Adcotech Corp., Milpitas, Calif., 1983-84; sr. engr. Domain Tech., Milpitas, 1984-85; project engr. Exclusive Design Co., San Mateo, Calif., 1985-86; automation mgr. Akashic Memories Corp., Santa Clara, Calif., 1988—. Mem. Robotics Internat. of Soc. Mech. Engrs. of Soc. Mfg. Engrs., Tau Beta Pi, Pi Mu Epsilon, Phi Kappa Phi. Home: 147 Wildwood Ave San Carlos CA 94070 Office: Akashic Memories Corp 3570 Ryder St Santa Clara CA 95051

HILL, JOHN EDWIN, JR., cardiologist, air force officer; b. Chattanooga, Jan. 12, 1933; s. John Edwin and Frances Altman (Hall) H.; m. Brenda Brandt Goerdel, Feb. 8, 1959; children: John Edwin III, Karl Goerdel, Kevin Michael O'Malley, Robert Douglas. MD, U. Tenn., 1958. Diplomate, Am. Bd. Internal Medicine. Commd. 2d lt. USAF, 1958, advanced through grades to col.; chief cardiology U.S. Army Gen. Hosp., Landstuhl, Fed. Republic Germany, 1964-67; asst. chief med. cons., then chief med. cons. Office of Surgeon Gen., Washington, 1967-70; chief div. of medicine U.S. Army Med. Rsch. Inst. Infectious Disease, 1972-73; chief med. svc. Amarillo (Tex.) VA Med. Ctr., 1983-85; chief cardiology svc. USAF Regional Hosp., Carswell AFB, Tex., 1985-88; chief of staff USAF Hosp./USAF Acad., Colorado Springs, Colo., 1988—; cardiologist, Internal Medicine Group El Paso, Tex., 1973-83; adj. prof. medicine, Tex. Tech. U., 1983-85; bd. dirs. Sierra Med. Ctr., El Paso, Internal Medicine Group El Paso. Bd. dirs. El Dorados, U. Tex.-El Paso, 1979-83. Fellow ACP; mem. Rotary. Republican. Episcopalian. Office: USAF Hosp USAF Acad Colorado Springs CO 80840

HILL, JONEL C., gas company executive; b. Mankato, Minn., 1925. Attended, Mankato State Coll.; LLB, St. Paul Coll. of Law, 1950. Formerly editor West Publishing Co.; past public utilities commr. State of Oreg.; former atty. Am. Telephone & Telegraph Co.; exec. asst. So. Calif. Gas Co., 1968-70, asst. v.p., 1970-74, v.p. regulatory affairs, 1974-80, sr. v.p., 1980-83, exec. v.p., 1983-85; pres. So. Calif. Gas Co., Los Angeles, 1985—, also dir. Office: So Calif Gas Co 810 S Flower St Los Angeles CA 90017 *

HILL, JUDITH DEEGAN, lawyer; b. Chgo., Dec. 13, 1940; d. William James and Ida May (Scott) Deegan; m. Dennis M. Havens, June 28, 1986; children by previous marriage: Colette M., Cristina M. BA, Western Mich.

U., 1960; cert. U. Paris, Sorbonne, 1962; JD, Marquette U., 1971. Bar: Wis. 1971, Ill. 1973, Nev. 1976, D.C. 1979. Tchr., Kalamazoo (Mich.) Bd. Edn., 1960-62, Maple Heights (Ohio), 1963-64, Shorewood (Wis.) Bd. Edn., 1964-68; corp. atty. Fort Howard Paper Co., Green Bay, Wis., 1971-72; sr. trust adminstr. Continental Ill. Nat. Bank & Trust, Chgo., 1972-76; atty. Morse, Foley & Wadsworth Law Firm, Las Vegas, 1976-77; dep. dist. atty., criminal prosecutor Clark County Atty., Las Vegas, 1977-83; atty. civil and criminal law Edward S. Coleman Profl. Law Corp., Las Vegas, 1983-84; pvt. practice law, 1984-85; atty. criminal div. Office of City Atty., City of Las Vegas, 1985-89, pvt. practice law, 1989—. Bd. dirs. Nev. Legal Services, Carson City, 1980-87, state chmn., 1984-87; bd. dirs. Clark County Legal Services, Las Vegas, 1980-87; mem. Star Aux. for Handicapped Children, Las Vegas, 1986—; Greater Las Vegas Women's League; jud. candidate Las Vegas Mcpl. Ct, 1987. Scholar Auto Specialties, St. Joseph, Mich., 1957-60; St. Thomas More Scholarship, Marquette U. Law Sch., Milw., 1968-69; juvenile law internship grantee Marquette U. Law Sch., 1970. Mem. ABA, Nev. Bar Assn., Woman's Bar Assn. of Ill., So. Nev. Assn. Women Attys., Ill. Bar Assn., Washington Bar Assn. Democrat. Club: Children's Village (pres. 1980) (Las Vegas, Nev.). Home: 1110 S 5th Pl Las Vegas NV 89104

HILL, MONICA MARY, marketing executive; b. Wilmington, Del., Nov. 25, 1958; d. Charles Arthur and Gladys Ruth (Bernard). BS in Graphic, Advt., U. Del., 1980. Designer Gregory Assoc., Phila., 1980-81; designer, account exec. Gregory Assoc., Wilmington, Del., 1980-81; art dir. sales Community Press Newspapers, Denver, 1981-83, A.I.M. Resources, Denver, 1983-85; graphic cons. ACCU-Type, 1986-87; mktg. profl. Q.J., Inc., 1987, Inter Cap Investment Group, Inc., Aurora, Colo., 1988—; freelance designer Aurora, 1989—. Designer Couch Potato Pillow. Vol. numerous civic assns. Mem. Civitan Internat. Republican. Presbyterian.

HILL, RALPH HAROLD, wholesale grocery company executive; b. Miller, Mo., Dec. 22, 1914; s. Richard Henry and Geneva Gertrude (Woodard) H.; m. Velma Lee Friar, Sept. 20, 1937; children: James Ralph, Richard Lee, Janice Louise. Student pubs. schs. With San Diego div. Alfred M. Lewis, Inc., Riverside, Calif., from 1935, mgr. dept. frozen food, 1953-56; mgr. Ariz. div. Alfred M. Lewis, Inc., Phoenix, 1956-63; pres., chief exec. officer Alfred M. Lewis, Inc., Riverside, 1963-82, 83-86, chmn. bd., from 1980; v.p., bd. dirs. Orange Empire Fin. Inc., Riverside; pres. Alfred M. Lewis Properties, Inc., Riverside; pres., chief executive officer Lewis Retail Foods, Inc., Riverside, 1988—; dir. M&M, L.A., Riverside. Served with USNR, 1943-45. Mem. So. Calif. Grocers Assn., Pres. Assn., Am. Mgmt. Assn., Riverside C. of C. (bd. dirs. 1970-76, pres. 1974-75). Lodge: Rotary (pres. 1972-73). Home: 1891 Fairview Riverside CA 92506 Office: Alfred M Lewis Inc 3021 Franklin Ave Riverside CA 92507

HILL, ROBERT GILBERT, aeronautical engineer; b. N.Y.C., Oct. 30, 1934; s. Walter Henry and Catherine (Ebbrell) H.; m. Elizabeth York Grimes, Oct. 5, 1957; children: Connie, Deborah, Jennifer. BS in Aero. Engring., Rensselaer Poly. Inst., 1957. Aerodynamicist Republic Aviation, N.Y., 1957; with Lockheed Missile and Space, Sunnyvale, Calif., 1960—, mgr., 1984—. Vol. Big Bros./Big Sisters, San Jose, Calif., 1986—. Lt. USAF, 1958-60. Mem. Nat. Mgmt. Assn., Santa Cruz Yacht Club, Sigma Alpha Epsilon. Republican. Baptist. Home: 1014 Teal Dr Santa Clara CA 95051

HILL, ROBERT JAMES, sales executive; b. Winnipeg, Man., Can., Nov. 9, 1951; came to U.S., 1977; s. Edward James and Alice Clara (Schatoske) H.; m. Patricia Helen Hartwick, Apr. 28, 1973; children: Susanna Christine, Dianna Lynn. BA in Econs., Brandon U., 1973. Sales rep. Bekins Moving Storage, Winnipeg, 1973; agt. N.Y. Life, Winnipeg, 1974; dist. mgr. Allis-Chalmers, Regina, Sask. and Winnipeg, Can., 1974-76, product mgr., 1977-79; sales mgr. Allis-Chalmers Corp., Atlanta, 1979-80, 1979-80, Des Moines, 1980-82; regional sales mgr. Allis-Chalmers Corp., Haywood, Calif., 1982-83; gen. mgr. Can. Allis-Chalmers Corp., Regina, Sask., 1984; west gen. mgr. Allis-Chalmers Corp., Independence, Mo., 1985; region sales mgr. Deutz-Allis Corp., Independence, Mo., 1986; agricultural equipment sales mgr. Kubota Tractor Corp., Compton, Calif., 1987-88, dir. mktg., 1989—. Mem. Nat. Agr. Mktg. Assn. Republican. Lutheran. Lodge: Masons. Home: 24902 Calle Vecindad El Toro CA 92630

HILL, ROBERT MARTIN, police detective, consultant. lecturer; b. Hammond, Ind., Dec. 10, 1949; s. Donald Edwin and Norma Jeanne (Beal) H.; m. Connie Carolina Nordquist, Dec. 19, 1970. BA, U. Minn., 1974; postgrad., U. Phoenix; cert. in fin. fraud, IRS, Glynco, Ga., 1984; cert. in questioned documents, U.S. Secret Service, Glynco, Ga., 1986. Cert. police officer, Ill., Minn., Ariz. Police officer Rolling Meadows (Ill.) Police Dept., 1970-72, St. Paul Police Dept., 1972-79; police officer Scottsdale (Ariz.) Police Dept., 1980-81, police fraud detective, 1981—; com. mem. Fraud Ariz. Banker's Assn., 1985-86; lectr. various colls. and orgns. Recipient Dirs. Commendation U.S. Secret Service, Washington, 1986. Mem. Internat. Assn. Credit Card Investigators (v.p. 1985-86, pres., bd. dirs. 1986-88, Nat. Law Enforcement Officer of Yr. 1986, Police Office of Yr. Ariz. chpt. 1984, 86), Econ. Crime Investigators Assn. Republican. Baptist. Office: Scottsdale Police Dept 9065 E Valinda Scottsdale AZ 85258

HILL, ROBERT PHILIP, milling company executive; b. Idaho Falls, Idaho, Nov. 4, 1952; s. Francis Robert and Phyllis (Hopkins) H.; m. Barbara Irene Ball, June 15, 1974; children: Megan Irene, Paige Diana. B. in Animal Sci., U. Idaho, 1975. Vice-pres., plant mgr. Hill Milling Co., Terreton, Idaho, 1975—. Grad. fellow U. N.J., 1975. Mem. Nat. Fedn. Independent Bus., Idaho Feed & Grains Dealers, Idaho Wool Growers Assn. (assoc.), Idaho Cattlemen's Assn., Nat. Cattlemen's Assn., Nat. Wool Growers Assn. Episcopalian. Home: PO Box 70 Terreton ID 83450 Office: Hill Milling Co PO Box 70 Terreton ID 83450

HILL, STEVEN ALLEN, chemical engineer; b. Corvallis, Oreg., Feb. 6, 1956; s. Donald Charles and Helen Arlene (Sallee) H.; m. Diane Vivian Smith, Mar. 26, 1977 (div. Dec. 1980); m. Carolyn Lee Cox, June 5, 1983. BS in Engring., UCLA, 1976; MS in Chem. Engring., U. Calif., Berkeley, 1978. Registered profl. chem. engr., Calif. Research engr. Chevron Research Co., Richmond, Calif., 1977-79; air quality engr. Bay Area Air Quality Mgmt., San Francisco, 1980-83; sr. air quality engr. Bay Area Air Quality Mgmt., 1983-86, mgr. air toxics evaluation, 1986—. Be. dirs. Actors Ensemble, Berkeley, 1985-86, 88-89. Office: Bay Area Quality Mgmt Dist 939 Ellis St San Francisco CA 94109

HILLER, J. B., computer analyst; b. N.Y.C., May 11, 1947; s. Nathan Max and Ruth (Kaiser) H.; m. Mimi F. Hiller, Dec. 27, 1969; children: Adam, Jennifer, April. BA, SUNY, Fredonia, 1969; cert. Data Processing, Cantnsville (Md.) Community Coll., 1981. Tchr. Balt. City Pub. Schs., 1969-81; sr. programmer/analyst Johns Hopkins Med. Ctr., Balt., 1981-84; computer application systems analyst Cedars-Sinai Med. Ctr., Los Angeles, 1984—. Scout master Boy Scouts Am. Troop #648, Newhall, Calif., 1987; v.p. Santa Clarita (Calif.) Chamber Singers, 1987-88. Mem. Electronic Computer Health Oriented. Democrat. Jewish. Home: 27527 Cherry Creek Dr Valencia CA 91354 Office: Cedars-Sinai Med Ctr ASB3-Beverly Blvd Los Angeles CA 90048

HILLER, STANLEY, JR., financial company executive; b. San Francisco, Nov. 15, 1924; s. Stanley and Opal (Perkins) H.; student Atuzed Prep. Sch., U. Calif., 1943; m. Carolyn Balsdon, May 25, 1946; children: Jeffrey, Stephen. Dir. Helicopter div. Kaiser Cargo, Inc., Berkeley, Calif., 1944-45; organized Hiller Aircraft Corp. (formerly United Helicopters, Inc.), Palo Alto, Calif., 1945, became pres. and gen. mgr., pres., 1950-64 (co. bought by Fairchild Stratos 1964), mem. exec. com. Fairchild Hiller Corp., 1965; chmn. bd., chief exec. officer Reed Tool Co., Houston, Nekins, 1980, York Internat., 1985; chmn. bd. Baker Internat. Corp., 1975, Levolor Lorentzen, Inc.; ptnr. Hiller Investment Co.; dir. Boeing Co. Recipient Fawcett award, 1944; Distinguished Svc. award Nat. Def. Transp. Soc., 1958; named 1 of 10 Outstanding Young Men U.S., 1952. Hon. fellow Am. Helicopter Soc.; mem. Am. Inst. Aeros. and Astronautics, Am. Soc. of Pioneers, Phi Kappa Sigma. Office: Hiller Investment Co 3000 Sand Hill Rd Bldg 2 Ste 260 Menlo Park CA 94025

HILLINGS, PATRICK JEROME, lawyer; b. Hobart Mills, Calif., Feb. 19, 1923; s. Edward John and Evangeline (Murphy) H.; m. Celia Hentschell, Mar 10, 1935; children: Pamela, David, Jennifer. Language cert., Kenyon Coll., Gambier, Ohio, 1944; student, U. Brisbane, Australia, 1944; BA, U. So. Calif., 1947, JD, 1949. Bar: Calif. 1949, D.C. 1969. Mem. U.S. Congress, Washington, 1951-59; dir. govt. affairs Ford Motor Co., Los Angeles, 1959-73; prin. Patrick J. Hillings, A Profl. Law Corp., Los Angeles, 1949-88, Indian Wells, Calif., 1988—; mem. adv. com. bilingual edn. HEW, Washington, 1970-73. Contbr. numerous articles and columns to various newspapers, 1952-89. Rep. chmn. Los Angeles County, 1960; campaign mgr. Ronald Reagan for Pres., Tampa, Fla., 1979-80; mem. Rep. Com. on Sr. Citizens, Washington, 1988; mem. Calif. del. to Rep. Conv., 1952-88. Sgt. Signal Intelligence, U.S. Army, 1942-45. Named Outstanding Young Rep., Calif. Young Reps., 1950. Mem. Fed. Bar Assn., Am. Immigration Lawyers Assn. (mem. key com. 1972—, mem. congl. com. 1987—), Congl. Chowder and Marching Soc., U. So. Calif. Alumni Assn., Calif. Club, Capital Hill Club, Trojan Club, Kiwanis, Delta Theta Phi. Roman Catholic. Office: 74-900 Hwy 111 Ste 215 Indian Wells CA 92210

HILLMAN, BILL (CLARENCE WILLIAM HILLMAN), labor union executive; b. Rexburg, Idaho, Dec. 10, 1922; s. Clarence Lynn and Reva (Baird) H.; m. Virginia Carney, June 1948 (div. 1950); 1 son, Robert W.; m. Martha Ruth Apollonio, Dec. 31, 1959; children: Kenneth W., Nancy A. A.A., Boise Jr. Coll., 1942; B.A., U. Calif. at Berkeley, 1949. Reporter Sta. KPIX, San Francisco, 1949—; corr. Voice of Am., San Francisco, 1956-72; 1st nat. v.p. AFTRA, 1976-79, nat. pres., 1979-84; trustee health and retirement funds AFTRA, N.Y.C., 1977—. Office: AFTRA 260 Madison Ave New York NY 10016

HILLS, LINDA LAUNEY, operations specialist; b. New Orleans, June 21, 1947; d. Edgar Sebastien and Isabel (James) Launey; m. Marvin Allen Hills Sr. Jan. 29, 1977 (div. July 1982); 8 stepchildren. Student, Navy Avionics Schs., Memphis and San Diego, 1974-78; certs. in IBM Tech. Tng., System Mgmt. Schs., Chgo. and Dallas, 1987. Sec. Calhoun and Barnes Inc. Co., New Orleans, 1965; clk. typist Social Security Adminstrn., New Orleans, 1965-67, U.S. Marshal's Office, New Orleans, 1967-69; supr. U.S. Atty.'s Office, New Orleans, 1969; with clk.'s office (ea. dist.) La. U.S. Dist. Ct., New Orleans, 1969-73; steno, sr. sec. Kelly Girl and Norrell Temp Services, New Orleans, 1974; aviation electronic technician, PO2 USN, Memphis and San Diego, 1974-78; customer engr. trainee IBM, Dallas, 1979; customer engr., systems mgmt. specialist IBM, San Diego, 1979-84; system ctr. rep. NSD Washington System Ctr. IBM, Gaithersburg, Md., 1984-87; adv. system engr. mktg. dept. IBM, San Diego, 1987—; lectr., cons. in field. Author 5 books. Vol. Touro Infirmary, Dialysis Unit, New Orleans, 1965-67, New Orleans Recreation Dept. 1964-68, PALS-Montgomery County Mental Health Orgn., Bethesda, Md., 1984-87, various polit. candidates, 1963—. Mem. NAFE, ACP, ASM, ISSA, Women Computer Profls. San Diego, San Diego Zoolog. Soc., Assn. System Mgmt., Smithsonian Instn. (resident assoc.), Disabled Am. Vets. San Diego, NAS Miramar Pilots Club. Office: IBM Corp-KB7 3d Fl PO Box 85091 San Diego CA 92138-9161

HILLYARD, LYLE WILLIAM, lawyer; b. Logan, Utah, Sept. 25, 1940; s. Alma Lowell and Lucille (Rosenbaum) H.; m. Alice Thorpe, June 24, 1964; children: Carrie, Lisa, Holly, Todd, Matthew. BS, Utah State U., 1965; JD, U. Utah, 1967. Bar: Utah 1967. Pres. Hillyard, Anderson & Olsen, Logan, 1967—; senator State of Utah, Salt Lake City, 1985—. Rep. chmn. Cache County, Logan, 1970-76; Utah State Rep., 1981-84; pres. Cache County C. of C., 1977. Named one of Outstanding Young Men of Am., Utah Jaycees, 1972; recipient Disting. Svc. award, Logan Jaycees, 1972, Merit award Cache Valley coun. Boy Scouts Am., 1981. Mem. ABA, Utah State Bar Assn., Cache County Bar Assn., Assn. Trial Lawyers Am., Am. Bd. Trial Advocates. Mormon. Club: Big Blue (Logan). Lodge: Kiwanis. Office: Hillyard Anderson & Olsen 175 E First N Logan UT 84321

HILTON, BARRON, hotel executive; b. 1927; s. Conrad Hilton. Founder, pres. San Diego Chargers, Am. Football League, until 1966; v.p. Hilton Hotels Corp., Beverly Hills, Calif., 1954; pres., chief exec. officer Hilton Hotels Corp., Beverly Hills, 1966—, chmn., 1979—, also dir.; mem. gen. adminstrv. bd. Mfrs. Hanover Trust Co., N.Y.C. Office: Hilton Hotels Corp 9336 Civic Ctr Dr Beverly Hills CA 90210 *

HILTON, HART DALE, commercial interiors company executive, consultant; b. Los Angeles, May 24, 1913; s. Lewis Dale and Nora Elizabeth (Hart) H.; m. Doris King, May 20, 1939; 1 dau., Margaret Pamela. BS in Engring., U. So. Calif., 1936; diploma Naval War Coll., 1955; diploma Nat. Def. U. (Nat. War Coll.) , 1963. Commd. officer U.S. Navy, 1937, advanced through grades to capt., 1956, exec. asst. dep. chief. naval ops., 1958-59, commdg. officer USS Mauna Kea, 1959-60, aircraft carrier USS Lexington, 1960-62, asst. to chief naval ops. for Joint Chiefs of Staff matters, 1963-65, ret., 1965; v.p. alumni affairs U. So. Calif., L.A., 1967-81; v.p., div. mgr. Cannell & Chaffin Comml. Interiors, Inc., L.A., 1981-85; pres. Hart Hilton Assocs., 1985—; guest lectr. World Geography, U. So. Calif., 1975-81. Adv. bd. L.A. Philanthropic Soc. Recipient Alumni Merit award U. So. Calif., 1966, Alumni Svc. award, 1982. Mem. Am. Arbitration Assn., Aircraft Owners and Pilots Assn., Navy League (Commodore Club), Assn. Naval Aviation, World Affairs Council, Am. Arbitration Assn. (arbitrator), Newcomen Soc., U. So. Calif. Assocs. (life). Republican. Club: Wilshire Country.Lodge: Rotary. Home: 1 S Orange Grove Blvd #6 Pasadena CA 91105

HIMENO, EDWARD TORAO, child psychiatrist; b. Honolulu, May 15, 1926; s. Bunzo and Irene Yoshiko (Kudo) H.; B.A., LaSierra Coll., 1950; M.D., Loma Linda U., 1958; m. Miyoko Kusuhara, June 5, 1952; children—Cheryl Aimee, Guy Randall. Intern, Los Angeles County U. So. Calif. Med. Center, 1958-59, resident gen. psychiatry, 1959-62, child psychiatry, 1963-65; practice medicine specializing in child psychiatry, Monterey Park, Calif., 1965—, Cerritos, Calif., 1983—; assoc. prof. psychiatry Loma Linda U. Sch. Medicine, 1967-77, assoc. clin. prof. psychiatry, 1977-80, dir. child psychiatry services, 1967-77; dir. child psychiatry unit Riverside (Calif.) Gen. Hosp., 1972-81; med./clin. dir. Children's Residential Care and Intensive Day Treatment Ctr., Riverside County, Calif., 1981-83; mem. child psychiatry staff Los Angeles County, U. So. Calif. Med. Center, 1962-63, 65-67; cons. Inland Adolescent Clinic, San Bernardino, Calif., 1973-83, Desert Community Mental Health Services, Indio, Calif., 1977-80; cons. child and adolescent unit mental health services San Bernardino County Gen. Hosp., 1973-75; cons. adolescent and young adult program Patton (Calif.) State Hosp., 1968-73, Boy's Republic, Chino, 1970-74, adolescent and adult unit Ingleside Mental Health Center, Rosemead, 1962-81; bd. dirs. Ingleside Mental Health Center, Rosemead, 1974-81, 2d v.p., 1975-81; chmn. med. adv. profl. symposiums, Riverside, Calif., 1979—. Mem. City of Monterey Park Human Relations Commn., 1970. Dist. chmn. Alhambra Monterey Park council Boy Scouts Am., 1969-70. Served with AUS, 1944-45. Recipient several hons. by various profl. and civic groups. Mem. Japanese Am. Med. Assn. (v.p. 1969, 81-82, sec. 1979-80, pres.-elect 1983-85, pres. 1985-86). Home: 1142 Ridgeside Dr Monterey Park CA 91754 Office: 823 S Atlantic Blvd Monterey Park CA 91754-4721 also: 11544 South St Ste 56 Cerritos CA 90701-6612

HIMSL, MATHIAS ALFRED, state senator; b. Bethune, Sask., Can., Sept. 17, 1912; s. Victor S. and Clara C. (Engels) H.; came to U.S., 1913; B.A., St. John's U., Collegeville, Minn., 1934; M.A., U. Mont., 1940; m. Lois Louise Wohlwend, July 18, 1940; children—Allen, Marilyn Himsl Olson, Louise Himsl Robinson, Kathleen, Judith Himsl Choury. Tchr., supt. schs., Broadus, Mont., 1934-45; sec. Himsl Wohlwend Motors, Inc., Kalispell, Mont., 1945-68; pres. Skyline Broadcasters, Inc., radio sta. KGEZ, Kalispell, 1958—; part-time instr. Flathead Valley Community Coll., 1969-72; mem. Mont. Ho. of Reps. from Flathead County, 1966-72, Mont. Senate from 3d dist., 1972—; Senate pres. pro tempore, 1989. Chmn. Flathead County Republican Com., 1952-64; del. Rep. Nat. Conv., 1964; bd. govs. ARC, 1956-59. Roman Catholic. Club: Elks.

HINCH, STEPHEN WALTER, manufacturing engineer; b. Seattle, July 13, 1951; s. Harlan Delmer and Ivy Roslyn (Thrush) h.; m. Nicolette Constance Obritsch, Sept. 11, 1976; children: Gregory P., Juliana G. BS, MS in Engring., Harvey Mudd Coll., 1974. Mfg. engr. Hewlett-Packard Co., Santa Rosa, Calif., 1974-78; mfg. engring. mgr. Hewlett-Packard Co., Rohnert Park, Calif., 1978-84; corp. SMT program mgr. Hewlett-Packard Co., Palo Alto, Calif., 1984-88, Santa Rosa, Calif., 1988—; instr. Inst. Interconnection and Packaging of Electronic Circuits, Lincolnwood, Ill., 1985—. Author: Handbook of Surface Mount Technology, 1988; contbr. chpts. to books, tech. articles to profl. jours. Mem. Surface Mount Tech. Assn. (bd. dirs.), Electronics Industry Assn. (IPC surface mount council), Internat. Soc. Hybrid Electronics. Republican. Office: Hewlett Packard Co 1400 Fountaingrove Pkwy Santa Rosa CA 95403

HINCKLE, WARREN JAMES, III, journalist; b. San Francisco, Oct. 12, 1938; s. Warren James II and Angela (Devere) H.; m. Denise Libarle, Oct. 27, 1962; children: Pia Jeanne, Hilary Devere. Writer Hughes & Hinckle, San Francisco, 1960-62; reporter San Francisco Chronicle, 1962-64; editor Ramparts, San Francisco, 1964-69, pres., 1969; v.p., bd. dirs. Scanlan's Lit. House, San Francisco; editor Scanlan's Monthly, 1969-72; v.p. Madison-Hobbs Co., from 1973; editor City of San Francisco, 1975-76; with San Francisco Chronicle and Examiner, 1977—. Author: Guerrilla Warfare in the USA, 1971 (with Eliot Asinof and William Turner) The Ten Second Jailbreak, 1973, If You Have a Lemon, Make Lemonade, 1974, (with Frederick Hobbs) The Richest Place on Earth, 1978, (with William Turner) The Fish is Red, 1980. Recipient Tom Paine award Emergency Civil Liberties Com., 1967. Office: San Francisco Examiner 110 5th St San Francisco CA 94103 *

HINCKLEY, CLARK BRYANT, bank executive; b. Salt Lake City, Oct. 30, 1947; s. Gordon Bitner and Marjorie (Pay) H.; m. Kathleen Hansen, Oct. 8, 1973; children: Holly, Ann, Spencer, Ada, Joseph, Elizabeth. BS, Brigham Young U., 1971; MBA, Harvard U., 1973; grad., Stonier Grad. Sch., 1981. Asst. cashier Citibank, N.Y.C., 1973-75; assoc. Ivory & Co., Salt Lake City, 1975-77; with Mich. Nat. Corp., Bloomfield Hills, Mich., 1977-83, v.p. fin. and planning, 1983-85; v.p. Zions First Nat. Bank, Phoenix, 1985-86; pres., chief exec. officer, bd. dirs. Zions First Nat. Bank of Ariz., Mesa, 1986—. Contbr. articles to profl. jours. Bd. dirs. Mezona Found., Mesa, 1987—, Mesa Town Ctr. Corp., 1987. Mem. Brigham Young U. Mgmt. Soc. (bd. dirs. Phoenix chpt.). Mormon. Club: Harvard Bus. Sch. of Ariz. (bd. dirs.). Office: Zions First Nat Bank 5555 E Main Mesa AZ 85205

HINCKLEY, GORDON B., church official. s. Bryant S. and Ada (Bitner) H.; m. Marjorie Pay, Apr. 29, 1937; children: Kathleen Hinckley Barnes, Richard G., Virginia Hinckley Pearce, Clark B., Jane Hinckley Dudley. Asst. to Council of Twelve Apostles, Church of Jesus Christ Latter Day Saints, 1958-61, mem. council, 1961-81, now mem. First Presidency. Office: First Presidency LDS Ch 47 E S Temple St Salt Lake City UT 84150

HINDMAN, EWELL JAMES, college dean, history educator; b. Lubbock, Tex., Jan. 9, 1943; s. Ewell Andrew and Christine (Reichling) H.; m. Ann Manning Vick, Mar. 3, 1964; children: Paige, Angie. BA in History, Tex. Tech U., 1966, MA in History, 1968, PhD in History, 1972. Instr. Lamar U., Beaumont, Tex., 1970-72; prof., adminstr. Sul Ross State U., Alpine, Tex., 1972-86; prof. history, dean Coll. Liberal Arts and Scis. Ea. N.Mex. U., Portales, 1986-88; assoc. v.p. academic affairs U. No. Colo., Greeley, 1988—; cons. Commn. for Acad. Preparation for Coll. Project, N.Mex., fall 1986. Pres. bd. dirs. Alpine Pub. Library, 1978-81; trustee Alpine Ind. Sch. Dist., 1978-81. Mem. Atlantic Council U.S. (assoc.), Council of Colls. of Arts and Scis., Orgn. Am. Historians, Soc. Historians Am. Fgn. Rels., Assn. Borderland Scholars, Rotary (pres. Alpine chpt. 1983-84). Office: U No Colo Academic Affairs Carter Hall 4007 Greeley CO 80639

HINDS, HERBERT J., computer science educator; b. Northbend, Oreg., June 21, 1946; s. Herbert J. and Elsie I. (Mathes) H. BS, Oreg. Coll. Edn., 1973; MS, So. Oreg. State Coll., 1978. Instr. Whitaker Jr. High Sch., Salem, Oreg., 1972-73, Myrtle Crest Sch., Myrtle Point, Oreg., 1973-74, Talent (Oreg.) Jr. High Sch., 1974-79, Rogue Community Coll., Phoenix, Oreg., 1981-83, Phoenix High Sch., 1979—. Mem. Oreg. Council Tchrs. Maths., Nat. Council Tchrs. Maths. Republican. Office: Phoenix High Sch 745 N Rose St Phoenix OR 97535

HINDS, ROBERT JAMES, chemical engineer; b. Minot, N.D., Sept. 29, 1931; s. Lonnie Robert and Mildred Louise (Monson) H. SB, MIT, 1953, SM, 1954. Registered profl. engr., Calif. Chem. engr. E.I. duPont de Nemours & Co., Penns Grove, N.J., Antioch, Calif., Louisville, 1956-62; research engr. Chevron Research Co., Richmond, Calif., 1962-65, group supr., 1965, sr. engring. assoc., 1967, mgr. computer and systems div., 1967-74, sr. environ. engr., 1975-85; sr. staff engr. engring. tech. dept. Chevron Corp., Richmond, Calif., 1985—. Contbr. articles to profl. jours.; patentee in field. Pres. Knollwood Townhouses, Inc., San Rafael, Calif., 1977-78. Served as 1st lt. chem. corps AUS, 1954-55. Mem. Am. Inst. Chem. Engrs., Aircraft Owners and Pilots Assn., Sigma Xi, Tau Beta Pi. Club: Commonwealth (San Francisco).

HINES, JAMES MONROE, mechanical engineer; b. Long Beach, Calif., Oct. 23, 1939; s. Charles Clifford and Helena Mae (Lilla) H.; m. Geraldine Janette Rucker, May 17, 1963; children: Dessa Ann, David James. BS, Calif. State U., Long Beach, 1971; M. in Engring., UCLA, 1977. Design engr. stamping div. Norris Industries, L.A., 1960-61; project engr. Apollo program Rockwell Internat. Co., Downey, Calif., 1962-70; partner auto repair bus., Bell, Calif., 1970-73; sr. project engr. space shuttle program Rockwell Internat., Downey, 1973-74; prin. mech. engr. nuclear fuel cycle Advanced Tech. div. Fluor Daniel Inc., Irvine, Calif., 1974—; ptnr. UIT Cons.'s, 1970-78. Webelos leader Boy Scouts Am. Mem. Internat. Material Mgmt. Soc. (dir. L.A. chpt. 1974-76), Am. Nuclear Soc., Fluor Polit. Action Com., NRA (life), Calif. Rifle and Pistol Assn. (life), Fluor Suprs. Club, Toastmasters, Masons, Scottish Rite, Shriners (pres. 1983, regional bd. dirs. 1985).Republican. Baptist. Home: 9412 Dewey Dr Garden Grove CA 92641 Office: 3333 Michelson Dr Irvine CA 92730

HINES, LINDA MARIE, executive director; b. Denver, Dec. 20, 1940; d. Laurence Gerald and Betty Marie (Fish) Arnold; m. Donald Merrill Hines, June 10, 1961; children: Warren Donald, Eric Daniel, Alan Bennett. BA, Lewis & Clark Coll., 1962; MA, Ind. U., 1967. Tchr. Eisenhower High Sch., Yakima, Wash., 1962-65; teaching assoc. Ind. U., Bloomington, 1965-67; rsch. assoc. Wash. State U., Pullman, 1973-74; editor Coll. Vet. Med., Pullman, 1974-76; dir. Info. & Rsch. Services Wash. State U., Pullman, 1977-79, Vet. Pub. Relations & Devel. Wash. State U., Pullman, 1979-83; exec. dir. The Delta Soc., Renton, Wash., 1983—; cons. Sci. & Tech. Com. Holden Village, Chelan, Wash., 1978-83; planning com. mem. NIH Workshop, Bethesda, Md., 1987. Co-author: Guidelines: Animals in Nursing Homes, 1983; co-editor: Phi Kappa Phi Jour., 1986. Co-founder Fish Vols., Pullman, 1970-72; bd. dirs. Elderhostel Planning Com., Pullman, 1977-79; dir. Wash. State U. Alumni Assn. Constituent Council, Pullman, 1979-81, N. Am. Riding for the Handicapped, Denver, 1980-81; cons. Seattle Housing Authority/Pets, 1984; co-founder People-Pet Partnership, Pullman, 1979-83. Recipient Recognition award Seattle Kennel Club, 1988; SAFECO grantee, 1982, The Charles Engelhard Found. grantee, 1983-88. Mem. Am. Soc. Assn. Execs., AAUW, Wash. Soc. Assn. Execs., The Delta Soc, ALCW Club, Issaquah Alps Trail Club. Lutheran. Office: The Delta Soc 321 Burnett Ave S Ste 303 Renton WA 98055

HINES, ROBERT STEPHAN, education educator; b. Kingston, N.Y., Sept. 30, 1926; s. Harry Jacob and Gertrude (Paine) H.; m. Germaine Lahiff, Dec. 9, 1950. BS, Juilliard Sch., 1952; MusM, U. Mich., 1956. Dir. choral activities Gen. Motors Corp., Detroit, 1952-57; asst. prof. So. Ill. U., Carbondale, 1957-61; prof. Wichita State U., 1961-71; vis. prof. U. Miami, Coral Gables, Fla., 1972; prof. U Hawaii Manoa, Honolulu, 1972-80, chmn. music dept., 1980-84, dean, coll. arts and humanities, 1984—. Author, editor: The Composers Point of View: Orchestral Music, 1970, Singer's Manual of Latin Diction and Phonetics, 1975, Ear Training and Sight-Singing: An Intergrated Approach, Vol. I, II, 1979; prin. works include over 200 choral editions and arrangements. Mem. Honolulu Chamber Music Bd., 1980-84, Hawaii Pub. TV Bd., 1981. Mem. Coll Music Soc., Am. Choral Dir. Assn., Am. Assn. Higher Edn. Democrat. Home: 555 University Ave 3500 Honolulu HI 96826 Office: U Hawaii 2500 Campus Rd Honolulu HI 96822

HINKINS, MARILYN MADSEN, public relations executive; b. Manti, Utah, Nov. 11, 1934; d. Donald W. Madsen and Lula Christa (Brady) Christensen; m. Arthur Hinkins, Dec. 11, 1951 (div. June 1966); children: Arthur Lee, Ryan Tay. AA, Coll. Eastern Utah, 1965; postgrad., U. Utah, 1965-66. Pres., owner Hinkins Pub. Rels., Salt Lake City, 1969-72, Phoenix, 1980-85; accounts mgr. Western Creative Advt., Phoenix and Palo Alto, Calif., 1975-76; exec. dir. Ariz. Sign Assn., Phoenix, 1976-82; pub. affairs dir. Am. Express, Salt Lake City, 1985-86; v.p. Joanne Ralston Pub. Rels., Phoenix, 1986-87; gen. mgr. DBG&H, Phoenix, 1987-88; pres., owner Hinkins and Assoc. Pub. Rels., Phoenix, 1988—. Mem. Ariz. steering com. Mountain States Legal Found., Phoenix, 1977-83; bd. dirs. Valley Forward Assn., Phoenix, 1983-85, Salt Lake Conv. Bur., 1986, Jr. Achievement of Salt Lake City, 1986; commr. Ariz. Women's Commn., Phoenix, 1977-81, Ariz. Toll Road Study Commn., Phoenix, 1983-85. Named One of Outstanding Young Women of Am., Gen. Federated Women's Club, Salt Lake City, 1965. Mem. Pub. Relations Soc. Am., Phoenix Press Club (bd. dirs., v.p. 1982-84), Ariz. Newspaper Assn., Ariz. Soc. Assn. Execs. (bd. dirs. 1977-81), Phoenix C. of C. (bd. dirs. 1979-85). Democrat. Congregationalist. Clubs: Soroptimists, Book Cliff. Home: 4434 N 21st Pl Phoenix AZ 85016

HINKLE, CHARLES FREDERICK, lawyer, clergyman, educator; b. Oregon City, Oreg., July 6, 1942; s. William Ralph and Ruth Barbara (Holcomb) H. BA, Stanford U., 1964; MDiv, Union Theol. Sem., N.Y.C., 1968; JD, Yale U., 1971. Bar: Oreg. 1971; ordained to ministry United Ch. of Christ, 1974. Instr. English, Morehouse Coll., Atlanta, 1966-67; assoc. Stoel, Rives, Boley, Jones & Grey, Portland, Oreg., 1971-77, ptnr., 1977—; adj. prof. Lewis and Clark Law Coll. Law Sch., Portland, 1978—. Oreg. pres. ACLU, Portland, 1976-80, nat. bd. dirs., 1979-85; bd. dirs. Portland Baroque Orch., 1988—. Recipient Elliott Human Rights award Oreg. Edn. Assn., 1984, Civil Liberties award ACLU of Oreg., 1987. Mem. ABA, Fed. Bar Assn., Multnomah County Bar Assn. Democrat. Home: 14079 SE Fair Oak Way Milwaukie OR 97267 Office: Stoel Rives Boley et al 900 SW 5th Ave Portland OR 97204

HINKLE, JAMES ROBERT, II, dentist; b. Iowa City, Iowa, Sept. 26, 1948; s. James Robert and Jean (Sankot) H.; m. Randi Carlson, Aug. 6, 1985; 1 child, James Robert III. BS, U.S. Naval Acad., 1970; DDS, Georgetown U., 1981. Commd. ensign USN, 1970, advanced through grades to lt. (j.g.), 1972, served in various locations including Vietnam, 1970-75, resigned, 1975; pvt. practice gen. dentistry Alameda, Calif., 1982—. Fellow Acad. Gen. Dentistry; mem. Craniomandibular Inst., U.S. Naval Acad. Aumni Assn., Alameda City Dental Group, Navy League, Alameda Toastmasters (pres. 1987). Republican. Presbyterian. Office: 2229 Santa Clara Ave Ste D Alameda CA 94501

HINKLEY, EVERETT DAVID, JR., scientist; b. Augusta, Maine, Nov. 19, 1936; s. Everett David and Julina Margaret (Nolan) H.; m. Christine Marie Caso, June 18, 1960; children: Anne, Mark, Kristin, David. Student, Rensselaer Poly. Inst., 1954-56; BS in Engring. Physics, Washington U., St. Louis, 1958; MS in Physics, Northwestern U., 1961, PhD in Physics, 1963. Mem. rsch. staff Gen. Telephone Labs., Northlake, Ill., 1958-59; rsch.-teaching assoc. Northwestern U., Evanston, Ill., 1960-63; mem. tech. staff MIT Lincoln Lab., Lexington, Mass., 1963-76; v.p. Laser Analytics, Inc., Lexington, 1976-77; tech. mgr. Calif. Inst. Tech. Jet Propulsion Lab., Pasadena, 1976-86; chief electronics scientist Lockheed Aero. Rsch. Lab., Valencia, Calif., 1986-87; chief scientist Hughes Aircraft Co., El Segundo, Calif., 1987-89; program mgr. TRW Space & Tech. Group, Redondo Beach, Calif., 1989—. Editor: Laser Monitoring of the Atmosphere, 1976. Mem. clear air com. Pasadena Lung Assn., 1980-86. Fellow Optical Soc. Am. (co-chmn. conf. on lasers and electro-optics 1986), IEEE (sec.-treas. Lasers and Electro-Optics Soc. 1987—, sr. mem.), Sigma Xi, Tau Beta Pi. Office: TRW Space & Tech Group MS R1/1070 One Space Pk Redondo Beach CA 90278

HINSDALE, JERRY WALTER, physical education educator, swim coach; b. Sacramento, Oct. 17, 1936; s. Elmer George and Mona Delores (Ruhe) H.; m. Jane Martha Abbott, June 20, 1965; children: John Michael, Jill Ann. BA, U. Calif., Davis, 1959. Cert. phys. edn. tchr. Head coach swimming and water polo U. Calif., Davis, 1961—; chmn. NCAA Water Polo Rules com.; conducted nat. clinic for Union Nacional de Entrenadores de Natacion, Barquisimeto, Venezuela, 1983; supr. officials representing Venezuela 1983 Pan Am. Games, Caracas; conducted various internat. and domestic clinics, mem. Organizing com. 1984 Olympic Games, 1983 FINA Cup. Editor Nat. Collegiate Athletic Assn. Water Polo Rule Book, 1983-86. Named NCAA Swimming Coach of Yr., 1974, No. Calif. Athletic Conf. Coach of Yr. in Swimming, 12 yrs., No. Calif. Athletic Conf. Coach of Yr. in Water Polo, 16 yrs.; recipient Elite Coach certification U.S. Water Polo Assn., Highest Honor award, San Cristobal, Venezuela, 1983, Outstanding Contbn. to Swimming medal, Council of Pan Am. Games, 1983. Mem. Am. Swimming Coaches Assn., Coll. Swimming Coaches Assn. Am. (pres., Outstanding Achievement award), U.S. Internat. Olympic Com., Am. Water Polo Coaches Assn. Am. (pres.), U.S. Swimming Coaches Assn. (bd. dirs.), Internat. Swimming Hall Fame (bd. dirs.), Nat. Assn. Sport and Phys. Edn. (appointed to internat. tng. staff 1985). Republican. Home: 739 Elmwood Dr Davis CA 95616 Office: U Calif Athletic Dept Davis CA 95616

HINTON, BERNARD LLOYD, management educator, consultant; b. Detroit, Mar. 26, 1937; s. Bishop E. and Florence E. (Hill) H.; m. Diane J. Gysel, Aug. 20, 1960 (div. 1969); children: Linda Susan, Sandra Lee. BS, Wayne State U., 1960, MBA, 1962; PhD, Stanford U., 1966. Prof. Ind. U. Grad. Sch. Bus., Bloomington, 1962-71, 79-82, dept. chmn., 1971-79; dept. chmn. Cal. State U. Coll. Bus., Chico, 1982—; cons. in field., 1968-88. Author: Groups and Organizations, 1971; contbr. articles to profl. jours. Stanford-Sloan fellow Stanford U., 1962-64. Mem. Acad. Mgmt., Am. Psychol. Assn., Sigma Iota Epsilon, Beta Gamma Sigma. Office: Calif State U Dept Mgmt 407 Butte Hall Chico CA 95929

HINTON, JOHN PHILIP, company executive, construction consultant; b. Mankato, Minn., Dec. 2, 1947; s. Thomas R. and Hendrina A. (Nissen) H. BA, Ariz. State U., 1974; MBA, Stanford U., 1976. Auditor, cons. Coopers & Lybrand, Palo Alto, Calif., 1976-78; founder, mgr. QSI, San Francisco, 1978-79, Hinton & Assocs., Mountain View, Calif., 1987-89; comml. mgr. Bechtel Petroleum Co., San Francisco, 1980-83, Bechtel Nat., San Francisco, 1983-85; dep. project mgr. Saudi Arabian Bechtel, Dhahran, 1983-85; chief fin. officer AISI Rsch., Inc., San Ramon, Calif., 1989—. Capt. M.I., U.S. Army, 1967-72, Vietnam. Decorated Bronze Star. Mem. Palo Alto Golf Club (bd. dirs.). Democrat. Roman Catholic. Office: 2010 Crow Canyon Pl Ste 202 San Ramon CA 94043

HINTZ, LUTHER MARON, architect, medical laboratory consultant; b. San Pedro, Calif., July 24, 1945; s. Waldemar Gustav and Louise Nisamini (Werner) H.; m. Linda Mae Jewell, Sept. 9, 1967; children: Amy Meredith, Meghan Lindsay. BArch, U. Wash., 1968. Registered architect, Wash. Draftsman, architect Richard E. Baringer, AIA, St. Croix, V.I., 1971-73; architect Robert E. Bezzo, AIA, Edmonds, Wash., 1973-74, Ralph Anderson & Ptnrs., Seattle, 1974-77, Hobbs Fukui Assocs., Seattle, 1977; prin. Luther M. Hintz, AIA, Seattle, 1977—. Work pub. in Sunset mag., 1980—, Seattle Times, Seattle Post-Intelligencer, Bellevue Jour.-Am., 1979—. Recipient Environ. award King County Bd. Realtors, 1982. Mem. AIA (com. chmn. 1986—, Home of the Month award Kirkland, Wash. chpt. 1978, Renton, Wash. 1981), Swedish. Lutheran. Home: 2008 1s Ave N Seattle WA 98109 Office: 14 1/2 Boston st Seattle WA 98109

HIPPLE, ROBERT CRAIG, education educator; b. Titusville, Pa., May 31, 1944; s. Clifford E. and Zelma M. (Reynolds) H.; m. Lois Jean Woodlaand, July 23, 1971. BA, U. Ariz., 1967, MEd., 1971. Educator, tchr. San Manuel Pub. Schs., Ariz., 1967-71, Amphitheater Pub. Schs., Tucson, 1971-89; computers, tchr. Amphiteater (Summer Sch.), Tucson, 1984-87; community schs. dir. Amphitheater Schs., Tucson 1971-74. Dir. Writer Summer Sch. Computers Class for Lou Achievement 1986, Author, Dir. Curriculum, Helen Keeling Constrn., 1987; Constrn. Curriculum Dir. Vol. St. Marys Hosp. Social Svcs. Tucson 1987—; Cons. Ariz. Gen. Mem. Amphitheater E.A. Assn. (elem. rep. 1979-80), Phi Delta Kappa (v.p.). Home: 3312 W Calle Fresa Tucson AZ 85791 Office: Amphitheater Pub Schs 201 W Wetmore Rd Tucson AZ 85705

HIPPS, MICHAEL FRANCIS, management consultant; b. Woodstock, Ill., May 8, 1950; s. Edward William and Aileen (Clarke) H.; m. Lina Jean Gauna, May 24, 1975 (div. May 1984). BA in Bus. Adminstrn., U. N. Mex., 1974; MA in Bus. Adminstrn., U. Wash., 1978. Rate analyst Pub. Svc. Co. N. Mex., Albuquerque, 1974-77; sr. assoc. Theodore Barry & Assocs., Portland, Oreg., 1979-83; ptnr., bd. dirs. Coast Cons. Group, Portland, Oreg., 1982—; bd. dirs. Four Winds Enterprises, San Diego, Calif., 1987—; rep. clients Oreg. Dept. Transp., Salem, Utah Power & Light, Salt Lake City, Tri-Met, Portland, Howard Cooper Corp., Portland. Contbr. articles to tech. publs. Mem. Delta Sigma Pi. Republican. Roman Catholic. Office: Coast Cons Group One SW Colubia Suite 1200 Portland OR 97258

HIRBE, RICHARD ANDREW, JR., pastoral care associate, counselor; b. Culver City, Calif., Jan. 11, 1952; s. Richard Andrew Sr. and Dorothy (Stadler) H. Student, U. St. Thomas, 1976-78, Allan Hancock Coll., 1984-86. Hospice chaplain Mercy Med. Ctr., Redding, Calif., 1981-83; religious brother Franciscan Friars, Arroyo Grande, Calif., 1983-86; spiritual asst. Secular Franciscan Order, Arroyo Grande, 1984-86; asst. provincial minister Secular Franciscan Order, Ventura, Calif., 1985-87; chaplain St. Francis Med. Ctr., Lynwood, Calif., 1986-87; assoc. pastor Little Co. of Mary Hosp., Torrance, Calif., 1987—; co-founder Calif. Task Force, 1983-86; founder AIDS Task Force, San Luis Obispo, Calif., 1984-86; cons. Pacific Inst. for Bioethics, Solvang, Calif., 1984—; asst. dir. St. Francis House, Inc., Long Beach, Calif., 1986—. AIDS minister Monterey Diocese Calif., Arroyo Grande, 1985; active AIDS Task Force, Bros. for Christian Community. Mem. Nat. Assn. Cath. Chaplains. Democrat. Home: 155 Monterey Blvd Hermosa Beach CA 90259

HIROSE, STANLEY K., construction executive; b. Hilo, Hawaii, May 25, 1937; s. Kazuchi and Momuye (Oka) H.; m. Sharon K. Kimura, Oc.t 22, 1966; 1 child, Alison C. BBA, U. Hawaii, 1959; MBA, Northeastern U., 1963. Adminstrv. asst. Amfac, Honolulu, 1965-68, controller, 1968-70; v.p. Data Tech., Honolulu, 1970-73; controller Fujiwaka Painting, Honolulu, 1973-75, chmn., 1975—. Bd. dirs. Humane Soc. Honolulu, 1982-88, pres. 1986-87; bd. dirs. Aikane Found., 1982—; 1st v.p., bd. dirs. United Cerebral Palsy, Honolulu, 1984—. With U.S. Army, 1963-65. Mem. Cons. Fin. Mgmt. Assn., Honolulu Country Club, Elks. Office: Thos Fujikawa Painting Co 2865 Ualena St Honolulu HI 96819

HIROZAWA, BETTY FUMIKO, industrial relations executive; b. Hilo, Hawaii, Jan. 7, 1930; d. Kanichi and Midori (Koike) Fujii; m. Shurei Hirozawa, Oct. 7, 1957; children: Gail R., Joan E., Robert K. BS in Indsl. Relations, Cornell U., 1951. With Hawaii Employers Coun., Honolulu, 1951—, v.p. adminstrn., 1974—, sec.-treas., 1983—. Bd. dirs. Aloha United Way, Honolulu, Neighborhood Justice Ctr., Honolulu; trustee St. Andrew's Priory Sch., Honolulu. Mem. Indsl. Relations Research Assn., Am. Soc. Personnel Adminstrn. Episcopalian. Office: Hawaii Employers Coun 2682 Waiwai Loop Honolulu HI 96819

HIRSCH, GREGORY LEE, physician; b. Perth Amboy, N.J., Apr. 30, 1952; s. Lawrence and Marjorie Nora (Mazur) H.; m. Kathy Helene Baron, Aug. 7, 1977; children: Adam Baron, Spencer Todd. BA magna cum laude, UCLA, 1974, MD, 1978. Diplomate Am. Bd. Internal Medicine. Intern in medicine Harbor/UCLA Med. Ctr., Torrance, 1978-79, resident in medicine, 1979-81, fellow in pulmonary medicine, 1981-83; ptnr. Escondido (Calif.) Pulmonary Med. Group, 1983—; clin. instr. U. Calif.-San Diego Sch. of Medicine, 1985—; chmn. critical care com. Palomar Med. Ctr., Escondido, 1987—. Fellow Am. Coll. Chest Physicians; mem. Am. Thoracic Soc., Phi Beta Kappa. Democrat. Jewish. Office: Escondido Pulmonary Med Ctr 215 S Hickory St #112 Escondido CA 92025

HIRSCH, HORST EBERHARD, metal company executive; b. Woelsendorf, Fed. Republic Germany, July 26, 1933; came to U.S., 1984; s. Albert and Emilie (Eberhardt) H.; m. Helga G. Gruber, May 2, 1961; children: Manon K., Fabiane M., Erin A. Diploma in chemistry, Tech. U. Karlsruhe, Fed. Republic Germany, 1959, D in Chem. Tech., 1961. Postdoctoral fellow NRC of Can., 1961-62; research and devel. engr., mgr. Cominco Ltd., Trail, B.C., Can., 1962-84; pres., chief exec. officer Cominco Electronic Materials Inc., Spokane, Wash., 1984-88; pres. Johnson Matthey Electronics N.Am., Spokane, 1989—; bd. of mgmt. B.C. Research Council, Vancouver, 1980-84; senate U. B.C., Vancouver, 1981-85. Contbr. articles on chemistry and metallurgy to profl. publs., chpts. to books. Recipient Excellence in Innovation award Fed. Govt. Can., 1985. Mem. Soc. German Mining and Metall. Engrs., Chem. Inst. Can. Lutheran. Office: Cominco Electronic Materials Inc E 15128 Euclid Ave Spokane WA 99216

HIRSCH, ILONA RUTH, orthopaedic surgeon; b. St. Louis, Apr. 5, 1954; d. Werner Zvi and Hilde Esther (Zwirn) H. BA in Biology summa cum laude, UCLA, 1975, postgrad., 1975-76; MD, Stanford U., 1979. Diplomate Am. Bd. Orthopaedic Surgery. Intern Stanford U. Hosps., Palo Alto, Calif., 1979-80, resident in orthopedic surgery, 1980-84; pvt. practice Beverly Hills, Calif., 1985—; cons. surgeon Nat. Ballet Can. European Tour, 1985, Bolshoi and Moscow Ballet Am. tours, 1987-88; dir. UCLA Dance Injury Clinic, 1985—. Mem. Am. Acad. Orthopedic Surgeons, L.A. County Med. Assn. (sports medicine com., ins. rev. com. 1986-88), L.A. County Women's Med. Assn., Stanford U. Profl. Women So. Calif., Phi Beta Kappa. Office: 9001 Wilshire Blvd Beverly Hills CA 90211

HIRSCH, WALTER, economist, researcher; b. Phila., Apr. 21, 1917; s. Arnold Harry and Ann Belle (Feldstein) H.; m. Leanore Brod, Feb. 12, 1939 (dec. 1985); stepchild, Steven M. Gold; children: Paul A. Gold, Jeffrey A., Robert A.; m. June Freedman Gold, Dec. 16, 1986. BS in Econs., U. Pa., 1938; LLD (hons.), Chapman Coll., 1968. Economist U.S. Bur. Stats., Washington and N.Y.C., 1946-50, Dept. USAF, Washington, 1950-51, Nat. Prodn. Auth., Washington, 1952-53; dir. indsl. mobilization Bur. Ordnance Dept. USN, Mechanicsburg, Pa., 1954-56; ops. rsch. analyst Bur. Supplies and Accts. Dept. USN, Arlington, Va., 1956-58; economist, ops. rsch. analyst Internat. Security Affairs Office Sec. of Def., Arlington, 1958-61; chief ops., rsch. analyst Gen. Svcs. Adminstrn., Washington, 1961-63; ops. rsch. analyst Spl. Projects Office Sec. of Def., Arlington, 1963-67; dir. ednl. rsch. U.S. Office Edn., San Francisco, 1967-72; con. on loan to Office of Dean Acad. PLanning San Jose (Calif.) State U., 1972-74; pres. Am. Indian Chess Set Co., Sun City West, Ariz., 1988—. Author (book): Unit Man-Hour Dynamics for Peace or War, 1957. Vol. San Francisco's DeYoung Mus., 1981-84, Calif. Palace of the Legion of Hon., Phila. Mus. Art, 1985-86; pres. Met. Area Reform Temples, Washington, Nat. Fedn. Temple of the Brotherhoods; supporter Phila. Orch., San Francisco Symphony, San Francisco Conservatory of Music, The Curtis Inst. With USAAC, 1942-46. Mem. Pa. Athletic Club, Commonwealth Club of Calif., World Affairs Council, Press Club of San Francisco, Phi Delta Kappa. Democrat. Jewish.

HIRSCH, WERNER ZVI, economist, educator; b. Linz, Germany, June 10, 1920; came to U.S., 1946, naturalized, 1955; s. Waldemar and Toni (Morgenstern) H.; m. Hilde E. Zwirn, Oct. 30, 1945; children—Daniel, Joel, Ilona. BS with highest honors, U. Calif., Berkeley, 1947, Ph.D., 1949. Instr. econs. U. Calif., 1949-51; econ. affairs officer UN, 1951-52; economist Brookings Instn., Washington, 1952-53; asst. research dir. St. Louis Met. Survey, 1956-57; prof. econs. Washington U., St. Louis, 1953-63; economist Resources for Future, Inc., Washington, 1958-59; dir. Inst. Govt. and Pub. Affairs U. Calif., L.A., also prof. econs. Inst. Govt. and Pub. Affairs, 1963—; scholar in residence Rockefeller Study Center, 1978; cons. Rand Corp., 1958—, U.S. Senate Com. on Pub. Works, 1972, Calif. Senate Select Com. on Structure and Adminstrn. Pub. Edn., 1973, Joint Econ. Com. of Congress, 1975-76, OECD, 1977-80, Edmund G. Brown Inst. Govt., 1981-86; mem. com. to improve productivity of govt. Com. Econ. Devel., 1975-76; chmn. L.A. City Productivity Adv. Com., 1982-85. Author: Introduction to Modern Statistics, 1957, Analysis of the Rising Costs of Education, 1959, Urban Life and Form, 1963, Elements of Regional Accounts, 1964, Regional Accounts for Public Decisions, 1966, Inventing Education for the Future, 1967, The Economics of State and Local Government, 1970, Regional Information for Government Planning, 1971, Fiscal Crisis of America's Central Cities, 1971, Program Budgeting for Primary and Secondary Public Education, 1972, Governing Urban America in the 1970s, 1973, Urban Economic Analysis, 1973, Local Government Program Budgeting: Theory and Practice, 1974, Recent Experiences with National Planning in the United Kingdom, 1977, Law and Economics: An Introductory Analysis, 1979, 2d rev. edit., 1988, Higher Education of Women: Essays in Honor of Rosemary Park, 1978, Social Experimentation and Economic Policy, 1981, The Economics of Municipal Labor Markets, 1983, Urban Economics, 1984; editorial bd. Internat. Rev. Law and Econs., Pakistani Jour. Applied Econs. Bd. dirs. Calif. Coun. Environ. and Econ. Balance, 1973—; bd. dirs. Calif. Found. on Economy, 1979—; bd. dirs. U. Calif. Retirement System, 1986—; mem. UCLA Bldg. Authority, 1984-87; pres. Am. Friends Wilton Park, 1983-85, Town Hall West of Calif., 1974-79, Friends of Graphic Arts, 1974-79. Mem. Am. Econ. Assn., Am. Farm Econ. Assn., Western Region Sci. Assn. (bd. dirs., pres. 1978-80), Town Hall (chmn. econ. sect.), L.A. World Affairs Coun., Phi Beta Kappa, Sigma Xi. Home: 11601 Bellagio Rd Los Angeles CA 90049

HIRSCHFELD, A. BARRY, printing company executive; b. Denver, Aug. 18, 1942; s. Edward and Dorothy (Zinik) H.; m. Arlene Friedman, Dec. 17, 1968; children: A. Barry Jr., Hayden F. BS, Calif. Poly. U., 1964; MBA, U. Denver, 1966. Salesman A.B. Hirschfeld Press, Denver, 1966-76, v.p., 1976-84, pres., 1984—; bd. dirs. Pub. Svc. Co., Colo. Mem. exec. com., chmn. Denver Metro Conv. and Visitors Bur.; bd. dirs., v.p., exec. com. Nat. Jewish Ctr.; bd. dirs. Rocky Mountain Multiple Sclerosis Ctr., Mountain States Employees Coun., Allied Jewish Fedn., NCCJ, Boy Scouts Am., Denver, Colo. Bus. Com. for Arts, Boettcher Found.; bd. dirs., mem. exec. com., past chmn. bd. Denver Art Mus.; mem. Colo. Sci. and Cultural Facilities Dist. Bd. Named Humanitarian of Yr., Nat. Jewish Hosp., 1988. Mem. Metro Denver Execs. (past pres., bd. dirs. Denver chpt.), Green Gables Country, 100 Mile Hi Stadium (sec.).

HIRSCHFIELD, ALAN J., entrepreneur. B.S., U. Okla.; M.B.A., Harvard U. V.p. Allen & Co., Inc., 1959-67; v.p. fin., dir. Warner Bros. Seven Arts, Inc., 1967-68; with Am. Diversified Enterprises, Inc., 1968-73; pres., chief exec. officer Columbia Pictures Industries, N.Y.C., 1973-78; vice chmn., chief operating officer 20th Century-Fox Film Corp., Los Angeles, 1979-81; chmn. bd., chief exec. officer 20th Century-Fox Film Corp., 1981-84; Bd. dirs. Motown Records, Stendig Internat., Texana Internat., CPP/Belwin Inc., Tanglewood Music Ctr.; pres. Jackson Hole Land Trust. Vice chmn. Cancer Research Inst. Mem. Am. Film Inst. (bd. dirs.). Office: Box 7443 Jackson WY 83001

HIRSCHHORN, RICHARD CLARK, urologist, investment advisor; b. Bklyn., Jan. 10, 1933; s. Alexander Mordecai and Jeannette Jay (Teicher) H.; m. Ann Morris Michelson, Feb. 5, 1961; children: Abigail, Elizabeth. BA, Harvard U., 1954, MD, 1958. Diplomate Am. Bd. Urology. Intern, then resident Univ. Hosps. Western Reserve Sch. Medicine, Cleve., 1958-60; resident in surgery V.A. Hosp., Jamaica Plains, Mass., 1960-61; resident in urology Mass. Gen. Hosp., Boston, 1961-64; practice medicine specializing in urology Holyoke, Mass., 1967-87; pres., chmn. bd. Masada Realty Trust, Holyoke, 1967-87, Union Plaza Realty Trust, Holyoke, 1967-74, Antler Securities Corp., Holyoke, 1978-88, Pumpkin, Inc., Holyoke, 1978-87, Richard Hirschhorn Corp., Tucson, 1987—. Author: Handbook of Practical Urology, 1965, (novels) A Pride of Healers, 1974, Target Mayflower, 1976. Trustee Hancock Point (Maine) Library Soc. 1975-80, Mus. Fine Arts, Tucson, 1988—. Mem. Am. Urol. Assn. (1st prize for clin. research 1964), Phi Beta Kappa, Harvard Club (N.Y.C.). Home: 7491 N Catalina Ridge Dr Tucson AZ 85718 also: Hancock Point ME 04640 Office: 2509 N Campbell Ave Ste 309 Tucson AZ 85719

HIRSCHMAN, CELIA, marketing executive; b. Martinsville, Ohio, Dec. 28, 1958; d. Jack and Ruth H. Student, U. Calif., Santa Cruz, 1976-77. Retail mgr. Odyssey Records, Santa Cruz, 1977-78, Kailua and Koneohe, Hawaii, 1978-79, Santa Rosa, Calif., 1979; bus. mgr. Vision Mgmt., L.A., 1979-84, Image Mktg. & Media, 1979-84; dir. mktg. Vis-Ability, 1984-87, pres., 1987—; cons. in pub. relations, 1983-87. Co-founder, pres. L.A. Women in Music, 1986-87. Recipient Outstanding Achievement award Black Entertainment TV, 1985. Mem. L.A. Women in Music (advisor 1987-88), Nat. Acad. Recording Arts, Amnesty Internat. Office: Vis-Ability 7958 Beverly Blvd Los Angeles CA 90048

HIRSCHMANN, FRANZ GOTTFRIED, aerospace executive; b. Kempten, Fed. Republic Germany, Oct. 4, 1945; came to U.S., 1973; s. Kurt Rudolf G. and Linda (Krieger) H.; m. Martha L. Ossa, Dec. 27, 1978 (div. May 1982). BS, FWG Coll., Cologne, Fed. Republic Germany, 1965; MA, U. Bonn, Fed. Republic Germany, 1973; MBA, Pepperdine U., 1981. Mktg. mgr. Western U.S. and S. Am. regions United Techs./Ambac, L.A., 1978-80; mktg. mgr. Western U.S. and Pacific regions Buehler Inc., L.A. and N.C., 1981-83; mgr. internat. mktg. Gen. Dynamics, Pomona, Calif., 1983-84, mgr. info. svcs., 1984-88, mgr. spl. projects, 1988—. Author: Mandaic Inscription, 1970; inventor deciphering lang. computer. Vol. Lincoln Club, L.A., 1981. Mem. Nat. Mgmt. Assn., Pepperdine Alumni Assn., Sierra Club, Retinitis Pigmentosa Found. (co-founder). Republican. Lutheran. Home: PO Box 7000-391 Palos Verdes CA 90274 Office: Gen Dynamics #44 PO Box 2507 Pomona CA 91769

HIRSH, ROBERT JOEL, lawyer; b. Shamokin, Pa., May 18, 1935; s. David and Rose (Koplansky) H.; children—Christine, Jonathan, Thomas. B.S., U. Ariz., 1960, J.D., 1964. Bar: Ariz. 1964, U.S. Dist. Ct. Ariz. 1965, U.S. Ct. Appeals (9th cir.) 1965, U.S. Supreme Ct. 1971; cert. criminal specialist. Ptnr. firm Messing Hirsh & Franklin, Tucson, 1969-72, Hirsh & Hooker, Tucson, 1972-73, Hirsh, Shiner & Walker, Tucson, 1973-77, Hirsh & Bayles, Tucson, 1977-82, Hirsh & Fines, P.C., Tucson, 1982-84, Hirsh, Sherick & Murphy, P.C., 1985—. Mem. ABA, Ariz. Attys. for Criminal Justice (founder), 9th Cir. Jud. Conf. (del. 1985-88), Ariz. Supreme Ct. Commn. on Courts (task force mem.), Pima County Bar Assn. Ariz. State Bar Assn. (cert. criminal specialist), Nat. Assn. Criminal Def. Lawyers, Calif. Attys. for Criminal Justice, Am. Bd. Criminal Lawyers, Am. Coll. Trial Lawyers. Office: 177 N Church #877 Tucson AZ 85701

HIRSHFIELD, JAMES ALBERT, JR., communications company executive; b. Washington, Jan. 22, 1939; s. James Albert and Marjorie M. (Prentis) H.; m. Mary Jean Hart, July 6, 1968; children: James H., Holly L., Casey B. BA, Rice U., 1960; MBA, Harvard U., 1966. V.p. Telecable, Inc., Seattle, 1966-68, Air Mac, Inc., Seattle, 1968; pres. Crystal Cablevision, Seattle, 1969-73; v.p., controller Seafirst Bank, Seattle, 1974-76; pres. Summit Communication, Seattle, 1973—; pres. Wash. Cable Community Assn., Olympia, 1979-80. Contbr. articles to profl jours. trustee U. Preparatory Acad., Seattle, 1982-88. Lt. USN, 1960-63. Mem. Nat. Cable TV Assn. (bd. dirs. 1981-84, com. chair).

HIRSON, ESTELLE, retired educator; b. Bayonne, N.J.; d. Morris and Bertha (Rubinstein) Hirson; student UCLA, U. So. Calif., summers 1949-59, San Francisco, summer 1955, U. Hawaii, 1955; B.E., San Francisco State U., 1965. Tchr. High St. Homes Sch., Oakland, Calif., 1949-54, Prescott Sch., 1955-60, Ralph Bunche Sch., 1960-72; owner Puzzle-Gram Co., Los Angeles, 1946-49; pres. Major Automobile Co., 1948-60. Chpt. v.p. City of Hope, San Francisco, 1962-63; bd. dirs. Sinai-Duarte Nat. Med. Center, 1946-50, also parliamentarian, life mem. Mem. NEA, Calif., Oakland, Los Angeles tchrs. assns., Sigma Delta Tau. Democrat. Mem. Order Eastern Star; Scottish Rite Women's Assn. (v.p. L.A. 1982, fin. sec. 1989). Rights to ednl. arithmetic game Find the Answer 1948, 51. Home: 8670 Burton Way Apt 328 Los Angeles CA 90048

HIRST, WILMA ELIZABETH, psychologist; b. Shenandoah, Iowa; d. James H. and Lena (Donahue) Ellis; m. Clyde Henry Hirst (dec. Nov. 1969); 1 dau., Donna Jean (Mrs. Alan Robert Goss). AB in Elementary Edn., Colo. State Coll., 1948, EdD in Ednl. Psychology, 1954; MA in Psychology, U. Wyo., 1951. Elem. tchr., Cheyenne, Wyo., 1945-49, remedial reading instr., 1949-54; assoc. prof. edn., dir. campus sch. Nebr. State Tchrs. Coll., Kearney, 1954-56; sch. psychologist, head dept. spl. edn. Cheyenne (Wyo.) pub. schs., 1956-57, sch. psychologist, guidance coordinator, 1957-66, dir. rsch. and spl. projects, 1966-76, also pupil personnel, 1973-84; pvt. cons., 1984—; vis. asst. prof. U. So. Calif., summer 1957, Omaha U., summer 1958, U. Okla., summers 1959, 60; vis. assoc. prof. U. Nebr., 1961, U. Wyo., summer 1962, 64, extension div., Kabul, Afghanistan, 1970, Catholic U., Goias, Brazil, 1974; investigator HEW, 1965-69; prin. investigator effectiveness of spl. edn., 1983—; participant seminar Russian Press Women and Am. Fedn. Press Women, Moscow and Leningrad, 1973. Sec.-treas. Laramie County Council Community Services, 1962; mem. speakers bur., mental health orgn.; active Little Theatre, 1936-60, Girl Scout Leaders Assn., 1943-50; mem. Adv. Council on Retardation to Gov.'s Commn.; mem., past sec. Wyo. Bd. Psychologist Examiners, vice chmn., 1965-74; chmn. Mayor's v.p. Model Cities Program, 1969; mem. Gov.'s Com. Jud. Reform, 1972; adv. council Div. Exceptional Children, Wyo. Dept. Edn., 1974; mem. transit adv. group City of Cheyenne, 1974; bd. dirs. Wyo. Children's Home Soc., treas., 1978-84, sec. 1984—; del. Internat. Conv. Ptnrs. of Ams., Jamaica, 1987 ; bd. dirs. Goodwill Industries Wyo., chmn., 1981-83; mem. Wyo. exec. com. Partners of Americas, 1970-86; ambassador to Honduras, summer 1979; del., vice moderator, Presbyn. Ch., 1987; bd. deacons Friendship Force ambassador to Honduras, 1988; chmn. bd. SE Wyo. Mental Health Center; elder 1st Presbyn. Ch., Cheyenne, 1978—; chmn. adv. assessment com. Wyo. State Office Handicapped Children, 1980, 81; mem. allocations com. United Way of Laramie County. Named Woman of Year, Cheyenne Bus. and Profl. Women, 1974. Diplomate Am. Bd. Profl. Psychology. Fellow Internat. Council Psychologists (chmn. Wyo. div. 1980-85); mem. AAUP, Am. Assn. State Psychology Bds. (sec.-treas. 1970-73), Am., Wyo. (pres. 1962-63) psychol. assns., Laramie County (bd. mem., corr. sec. 1963-69, pres.), Wyo. mental health assns. (bd. mem.), Internat. Platform Assn., Am. Ednl. Research Assn., Assn. Supervision and Curriculum Devel., Assn. for Gifted (Wyo. pres. 1964-65), Am. Personnel and Guidance Assn., Am. Assn. Sch. Adminstrs., NEA (life, participant seminar to China 1978), AAUW, Cheyenne Assn. Spl. Personnel and Prins. (pres. 1964-65, mem. exec. bd. 1972-76), Nat. Fedn. Press Women (dir. 1979—), DAR (vice regent Cheyenne chpt. 1975-77), AARP (state coordinator 1988—, preretirement planning specialist 1986—, leadership coun., Wyo. sec. rsch. women's prisons 1989), Psi Chi, Kappa Delta Pi, Pi Lambda Theta, Alpha Delta Kappa (pres. Wyo. Alpha 1965-66). Presbyn. Lodge Soc. Colonial Dames XVII Century, Order Eastern Star, Daus. of Nile. Clubs: Wyo. Press Women, Zonta (pres. Cheyenne 1965-66, treas. dist. 12 1974). Author: Know Your School Psychologist, 1963; Effective School Psychology for School Administrators, 1980. Home and Office: 3458 Green Valley Rd Cheyenne WY 82001

HIRT, EVELYN HELEN, electrical engineer, systems engineer; b. Detroit, Mar. 16, 1952; d. Harry Joseph and Gertrude (Dennis) H.; m. Gary Alan Bonebrake, Nov. 11, 1978; children: Jacquelyn Renee, Christopher Alan. BEE cum laude, U. Detroit, 1975; postgrad., USAF Inst. Tech., 1977, U. Dayton, 1978-79, U. N.Mex., 1983-87. Elec. engr. Fisher Body div. Gen. Motors Corp., Warren, Mich., 1973-75; elec., electronics engr. USAF Wright Aero. Labs., Wright-Patterson, Ohio, 1976-80; engr., scientist Collins div. Rockwell Internat. Corp., Cedar Rapids, Iowa, 1980-82; sr. project engr. Sperry Corp., Albuquerque, 1982-84; asst. researcher elec. and computer engring. U. N.Mex., Albuquerque, 1984-85; sr. staff mem., mgr. BDM Internat., Albuquerque, 1985—. speaker in field. Troop leader Girl Scouts Am., Cedar Rapids, 1981. Mem. IEEE (various officer positions 1978—, sr. mem.), NSPE, Nat. Assn. Female Execs., Idas in Sci. and Electronics Inc. (tech. program chmn. 1985, 88, Cert. of Appreciation 1985, 88, publicity chmn. 1989), Eta Kappa Nu. Club: Basenji of Am. Office: BDM Internat 1801 Randolph Rd SE Albuquerque NM 87106

HISE, JESSE STRAWN, teacher; b. Canton, Ohio, Feb. 24, 1932; s. Jesse Strawn and Mae Elizabeth (Wagoner) Callahan H.; m. Barbara Sue Lusby, Apr. 24, 1953; children: Leslie Ann Seibert, Lisa Marie. BA, Lynchburg Coll., 1953; MA, U. Mich., 1957. Cert. secondary tchr., community coll. tchr., Ariz. Tchr. English Northville (Mich.) High Sch., 1957-58, Phoenix Union High Sch., 1958-64, Central High Sch., Phoenix, 1964-68, 1969-83; vis. lectr. English Ariz. State U., Tempe, 1968-69; tchr. English, dept. chmn. North High Sch., Phoenix, 1983—; cons. Greater Phoenix Area Writing Project, Tempe,1978—. Author: Patterns: The How to Write a Poem Book, 1982; columnist Ariz. English Bull., 1987—; contbr. short stories, humor and ednl. articles to profl. jours. Mem. Legis. Task Force on Composition, Phoenix, 1986-87. Served with U.S. Army, 1953-55. Cuthbert-Douglas scholar English Speaking Union, Phoenix, 1981, Christa McAuliffe fellow U.S. Dept. Edn., Washington, 1987; named Tchr. of Yr., North High Sch., Phoenix, 1986. Mem. Nat. Council Tchrs. English, Ariz. English Tchrs. Assn. (pres. 1973-74), Classroom Tchrs. Assn. Democrat. Unitarian-Universalist. Home: 4502 N 18th Dr Phoenix AZ 85015 Office: North High Sch 1101 E Thomas Rd Phoenix AZ 85014

HISE, MARK ALLEN, dentist; b. Chgo., Jan. 17, 1950; s. Clyde and Rose T. (Partipilo) H. AA, Mt. San Antonio Coll., Walnut, Calif., 1972; BA, U. Calif., Riverside, 1974; MS, U. Utah, 1978; DDS, UCLA, 1983. Instr. sci. NW Acad., Houston, 1978-79; chmn. curriculum med. coll. prep program UCLA, 1980-85; instr. dentistry Coll. of Redwoods, Eureka, Calif., 1983; practice dentistry Arcata, Calif., 1983—. Editor: Preparing for the MCAT, 1983-85; contbr. articles to profl. jours.; speaker in field. Henry Carter scholar U. Calif., 1973, Calif. State scholar 1973, 74, Rgents scholar U. Calif., 1973; Calif. State fellow, 1975, NIH fellow, 1975-79. Mem. ADA, Calif. Dental Assn., Acad. Gen. Dentistry, Nat. Soc. for Med. Research, AAAS. Roman Catholic. Clubs: Manatees (Maintland, Fla.); North Coast Scuba (Eureka, Calif.). Home and Office: 1225 B St Arcata CA 95521

HISLOP, DONALD LINDSAY, secondary teacher, college administrator; b. Vancouver, B.C., Can., Nov. 19, 1944; s. David Symons and Elizabeth Margaret (Proniuk) H.; m. Kare Elizabeth Branstead, Sept. 9, 1967; children: Victoria, Laurel. AA, Merritt Coll., 1965; BA, Chico State Coll., 1967; MA, Calif. State U., 1975. Cert. tchr. secondary edn., Calif. Tchr. Red Bluff (Calif.) Union High Sch., 1968—, Shasta Coll., Redding, Calif., 1972-86; supr. Outreach Program Shasta Coll., Redding, 1986—; cons. U.S. Office Edn., 1974, Calif. State Dept. Edn., 1973-76; mentor, tchr. Red Bluff Union High Sch., 1983-84. Author: The Nome Lackee Indian Reserve, 1978. Pres. Ide Adobe Interpretative Assn., Mt. Lassen Ch. Camp Inc., 1980-85; asst. leader Girl Scouts; bd. dirs. Christie Hill Ch. Camp. Mem. Calif. Tchrs. Assn. (Innovative Devel. award 1975), Orgn. Am. Historians, Nat. Council for Social Studies, Calif. Hist. Soc. Methodist. Office: Red Bluff Union High Sch 1245 Union St Red Bluff CA 96080

HITCH, THOMAS KEMPER, economist; b. Boonville, Mo., Sept. 16, 1912; s. Arthur Martin and Bertha (Johnston) H.; m. Margaret Barnhart, June 27, 1940 (dec. Nov. 1974); children: Hilary, Leslie, Caroline, Thomas; m. Mae Okudaira. Student, Nat. U. Mexico, 1932; A.B., Stanford U., 1934; M.A., Columbia U., 1946; Ph.D., U. London, 1937. Mem. faculty Stephens Coll., Columbia, Mo., 1937-42; spl. study commodity markets Commodity Exchange Adminstrn., Dept. Agr., 1940; acting head current bus. research sect. Dept. Commerce, 1942-43; labor adviser Vets. Emergency Housing Program, 1946-47; economist labor econs. Pres.'s Council Econ. Advisers, 1947-50; dir. research Hawaii Employers Council, Honolulu, 1950-59; sr. v.p., mgr. research div. First Hawaiian Bank, 1959-82; chmn. Hawaii Gov.'s Adv. Com. on Financing, 1959-62; chmn. research com. Hawaii Vistors Bur., 1962-69; chmn. Mayor's Fin. Adv. Com., 1960-68; chmn. taxation and fin. com. Constl. Conv. Hawaii, 1968. Contbr. articles to profl. jours. Trustee Tax Found. of Hawaii, 1955-80, pres., 1968; trustee McInerny Found.; chmn. Hawaii Joint Council Econ. Edn., 1964-68. Served as lt. O.R.C., 1933-38; as lt. USNR, 1943-46. Mem. C. of C. Hawaii (chmn. bd. 1971), Nat. Assn. Bus. Economists, Am., Hawaii econs. assns., Indsl. Relations Research Assn., Am. Statis. Assn., Phi Beta Kappa, Pi Sigma Alpha, Alpha Sigma Phi. Clubs: Waialae Country (pres. 1979), Pacific. Home: 5329 Olapa St Honolulu HI 96821 Office: First Hawaiian Bank Honolulu HI 96847

HITCHCOCK, VERNON THOMAS, lawyer; b. Selma, Ind., Feb. 21, 1919; s. Lucian Elmer and Loda Alice (King) H.; m. Betty Kathryn Orr, May 24, 1949; children: Brenda, Linda, Nancy, Debra, Randolph. BA in Agr., Purdue U., 1940; JD, Stanford U., 1953. Bar: Calif. 1954, U.S. Supreme Ct. 1961. Pilot Southwest Airlines, San Francisco, 1946, TWA, Kansas City, Mo., 1947-51; pvt. practice Healdsburg, Calif., 1954-55; dep. atty. gen. State of Calif., Sacramento, 1956; dep. county counsel Sonoma County, Santa Rosa, Calif., 1957-65; exec. dir. Libyan Aviation Co., Tripoli, 1966-67; legal counsel Sonoma County Schs., 1967-82; farm mgr. Selma, Ind., 1975--. Active Am. Security Council, 1965--. Served to comdr. USNR, 1941-79. Mem. Res. Officers Assn., US Naval Inst., Navy League, Naval Order U.S., Commonwealth Club San Francisco, Quiet Birdmen, Odd Fellows. Republican. Episcopalian.

HITCHINS, WILLIAM EDEN, advertising executive; b. Port-of-Spain, Trinidad and Tobago, July 27, 1935; came to U.S., 1968; s. Courtenay Eden and Ivy Godsell (Gibson) H.; m. Barbara Jocelyn Dawson, Apr. 8, 1961 (div. 1984); children: Deborah Greer Monceaux, Michael Blaine; m. Wilma Ruth Kaplan, Nov. 27, 1984. GCE, Malvern Coll., Malvern, England, 1954. Trainee reporter Trinidad Pub. Co., Ltd., Port-of-Spain, 1954-55, reporter, various editorial positions, 1955-63; br. mgr. Trinidad Pub. Co., Ltd., San Fernando, Trinidad, 1963-65; pub. rels. mgr. Kenyon & Eckhart Caribbean Ltd., Port-of-Spain, 1965-68; pub. rels. exec. Beckman Instruments, Inc., Fullerton, Calif., 1968-71; mng. dir. Hitchins Chem. Co., Ltd., Diego Martin, Trinidad, 1971; pub. rels. mgr. Celesco Industries Inc., Costa Mesa, Calif., 1972; from account mgr. to pres. Rullman & Hunger Advt., L.A., 1973-84; pres. Hitchins Co., L.A., 1985—. Mem. Optimist Club, Navy League. Republican. Anglican.

HITE, JOSEPH PIERCE, minister, consultant; b. Wenatchee, Wash., Aug. 16, 1957; s. James Edward and Clarice Ann (Shotwell) H.; m. Robin Mae Grissom, Dec. 9, 1978; children: Chelsea Lynn, Austyn Michele. AA, Wenatchee Valley Coll., 1978. Mgr. prodn. Spokane (Wash.) Parks, 1978-80; mktg. Clarklift of Wash., Seattle, 1980-83, Keebler Corp., Seattle, 1983-84; sr. assoc. pastor Puget Sound Christian Ch., Tacoma, 1984—; bd. dirs. Messenger Northwest, Tacoma, staff cons. Messenger Internat., San Jose, Calif. Producer (video) Kingdom Session, 1986, Messenger in Action, 1986; producer, engr. (record) Spirit of Truth Singers, 1979. Named Eagle Scout Boy Scouts Am., Cashmere, Wash., 1973. Republican. Home: 3524 N 7th Tacoma WA 98406 Office: Puget Sound Christian Ctr 5446 S Birmingham Tacoma WA 98409

HITTLE, LEROY MICHAEL, journalist, state official.; b. Onawa, Iowa, June 10, 1912; s. Thomas Jefferson and Mina Abigail (Covert) H.; student Morningside Coll., Sioux City, Iowa, 1934; BA, Drake U., 1938; m. Helen L.M. Beroen, June 29, 1941 (dec. 1954); 1 son, Leroy Bradley; m. 2d, Joan Byles David, Apr. 2, 1971. With AP, Des Moines, 1934-39, San Francisco, 1939-41, Reno, 1941-43, Olympia, Wash., 1946-67; mem. Wash. Liquor Control Bd., Olympia, 1967-82, chmn., 1981-82; pres. South Sound Pub. Co., pub. Lacey (Wash.) Leader, 1967-68. Promotion chmn., bd. dirs. Southwestern Wash. Evergreen State Coll. Com., 1965-67; chmn. Regional Civic Auditorium Com., 1968-72; pres. chpt. 2 Retired Pub. Employees Coun., 1987-88 . Served with AUS, 1943-46. Recipient 25 Year Svc. award AP, 1960; Sigma Delta Chi award for outstanding coverage Wash. Legislature, 1960; Gov.'s certificate of merit for 20 years reporting activities Wash. Govt., 1966; Disting. Svc. award Thurston County Citizen of Yr. Program, 1968, 73. Mem. SAR, Nat. Alcoholic Beverage Control Assn. (pres. 1979-80), Capital City Press Club (past pres.), Masons, Scottish Rite, Shriners, Rotary, Elks; Wash. Athletic Club, Olympia Country and Golf Club, Sigma Delta Chi, Tau Kappa Epsilon. Lutheran. Home: 5912 Athens Beach Dr NW Olympia WA 98502

HIX, KENNETH CHARLES, insurance company executive; b. Colorado Springs, Colo., Dec. 29, 1957; s. Jimmie Gene and Carolyn Ann (Schlieske) H. Student, Chaffey Coll., 1976-78; AA, Concordia Coll., Seward, Nebr., 1979. Salesman U.S. Safety Engring. Corp., Torrance, Calif., 1978, Met. Life Ins. Co., Claremont, Calif., 1978-79, Mut. of Omaha, Lincoln, Nebr., 1980; area mgr. United Automobile Assn., Lincoln, 1980-82; dist. mgr. Nat. Health Ins. Co., Lincoln, 1982-85; sales mgr. Am. Republic Co., Lincoln, 1985-86; exec. v.p. Pacific Ins. Svc., Grants Pass, Oreg., 1987-88; pres. So. Oreg. Solutions, Grants Pass, 1988—; chmn. Young Persons Ins. League, Grants Pass, 1987-88. Republican. Lutheran. Home: 138 Meadow Lark Dr Grants Pass OR 97526 Office: So Oreg Solutions 777 NE 7th St Ste 103 Grants Pass OR 97526

HJELMSTAD, WILLIAM DAVID, lawyer; b. Casper, Wyo., Apr. 4, 1954; s. Alvin Gordon and A. Thecla (Walz) H.; m. Cheryl Anne Wirth, May 16, 1987; children: Jennifer Ashley, Allison Caitlin. AA in Social Sci., Casper Coll., 1974; BS in Psychology, U. Wyo., 1976, JD, 1979. Bar: Wyo. 1979, U.S. Dist. Ct. Wyo. 1979. Dept. county pros. atty. Hot Springs County, Thermopolis, Wyo., 1979-80; asst. pub. defender Natrona County, Casper, Wyo., 1980-82; sole practice, Casper, 1981—. Mem. ABA (mem. family law com. 1983-84, adoption com. 1983-84), Wyo. State Bar Assn. (mem. alcohol and substance abuse com.), Natrona County Bar Assn., Wyo. Trial Lawyers Assn., Assn. Trial Lawyers Am., Am. Judicature Soc. Lodges: Elks, Kiwanis. Home: 2242 Thorndike Casper WY 82601

HLAVA, MARJORIE MAXINE KIMMEL, information scientist. Student, U. Minn., 1967; BS in Botany and Secondary Edn., U. Wis., 1970; postgrad., U. N.Mex., 1974-76. Info. scientist Tech. Application Ctr. U. N.Mex., Albuquerque, 1975-77, mgr. info., 1977-79; pres., chief ops. officer Access Innovations, Inc., Albuquerque, 1978—; dir. info. Nat. Energy Info. Ctr. affiliate U.S. Dept. Energy, U. N.Mex., 1976-78, Albuquerque, bd. dirs. Documentation Assocs. Inc. Mem. editorial bd. Info. Services and Use, 1983, Database Update, 1984; tech. columnist ONline Re. 1978-81, Info. Today, 1984; contbr. articles to profl. jours. Mem. Spl. Libraries Assn. (chmn. spl. projects com. 1976, employment com. 1978-79, membership com. 1978-79, nominations com. 1983, v.p. local chpt. 1979-80, pres. 1980-81, chmn. info. techs. div. 1984-85, editor info. techs. div. pub., nat. nominations com. 1988), S.W. Library Assn. (chmn. online bibliographic user group 1976-79), N.Mex. Library Assn. (publicity com. 1981, chmn. nominations com. 1981, chmn. online roundtable 1979, state fair com. 1981-82), Greater Albuquerque Library Assn., Western Info. Network Energy (chmn. edn. com. 1978-81, treas. 1980-84, bd. dirs. 1978-83), N.Mex. Online User Group (chmn. 1976-79), Assn. Info. and Dissemination Ctrs. (pres. 1985-86, 86-87, chmn. 1985, mem. various coms.), N.Mex. Technet Adv. Council, Am. Soc. Info. Sci. (bd. dirs. 1986—). Office: Access Innovations PO Box 40130 Albuquerque NM 87196 *

HO, DONALD TAI LOY, entertainer, singer; b. Honolulu, Aug. 13, 1930; s. James A. Y. and Emily L. (Silva) H.; m. Melvamay Kolokea Wong, Nov. 22, 1951; children: Donald Jr., Donalei, Dayna, Dondi, Dori, Dwight. Student, Springfield Coll., 1950; BS, U. Hawaii, 1954. Entertainer Honey's, Kaneohe, Hawaii, 1959-61, Flamingo Hotel, Las Vegas, Nev., 1964-72, Duke Kahanamoku's, Honolulu, 1964-70, Polynesian Palace, Honolulu, 1970-81, Donito's, Honolulu, 1981-82, Hilton Hawaiian Village, Honolulu, 1982—; with Alli's, Midway Island, 1964, Barabosa Club, San Francisco, 1965, Coconut Grace, Ambassador Hotel, L.A., 1965-68, 1967 Tour U.S./Can., Royal Box, Americana Hotel, N.Y.C., 1968, Empire Rm., Chgo., 1968; with Variety Club, Ambassador Hotel, Honolulu, 1978-87. Rec. with Reprise Co., Los Angeles, 1963-65 (Mainland, Can. tour Sept.-Dec. 1980). Served to 1st lt. USAF, 1954-59. Office: Hilton Hawaiian Village 2005 Kalia Rd Honolulu HI 96815

HO, IWAN, research plant pathologist; b. Souzhou, Jiangsu, China, Apr. 15, 1925; came to U.S., 1956; m. Mei-Chun Chang, Nov. 29, 1975; 1 child, Tomur M. BS, Nat. Shanghai U., 1946; MS, La. State U., 1958; PhD, Oreg. State U., 1984. Microbiologist Seattle Pub. Health Dept., 1962-66; research plant physiologist Forestry Scis. Lab., Corvallis, Oreg., 1970—; courtesy asst. prof. Coll. Forestry, Oreg. State U. Mem. Mycol. Soc. Am., Am. Soc. Plant Physiologists, Internat. Soc. Plant Molecular Biology, Sigma Xi. Democrat. Episcopalian. Home: 1686 Bullevard Philomath OR 97370 Office: Forestry Sci Lab Pacific NW Rsch Sta 3200 Jefferson Corvallis OR 97333

HO, MICHAEL, artistic director, choreographer, ballet teacher; b. Singapore, July 19, 1947; came to U.S., 1976; s. Charles and Sylvia (For Chin) Ho. Diploma in A level, Royal Ballet Sch., London, 1966; diploma in teaching, Royal Acad. Dancing, 1986. Solo dancer London Festival Ballet, 1967-72, Scottish Ballet, Glasgow, 1972-73; prin. dancer New London Ballet, 1974-76, Ballet Rambert, London, 1977-84; free-lance dancer various TV commls., videos, London, 1984-85; tchr. Rambert Acad., London Studios, 1986; guest dancer Sacramento Ballet, 1986, ballet master, 1987, artistic dir., 1987—. Office: Sacramento Ballet 4052 Manzanita Ave Carmichael CA 95608

HO, WILTON WUI MIN, dentist; b. Honolulu, Apr. 14; s. Wilbert Mun Sin and Helen (Youk) H.; m. Tammy Tamae Kubota, Sept. 16, 1984. DDS, Northwestern U., 1987. Sole practice dentistry Aiea and Pearl City, Hawaii, 1987—. Office: Aiea Med Bldg 99-128 Aiea Heights Dr Ste 302 Aiea HI 96701

HOAD, MARIANNA, theatre educator; b. Berkeley, Calif., June 26, 1943; d. William Marvin and Mary Jeanette (Stewart) H.; m. Robert Harry Hicks, May 14, 1982. AB, Oberlin Coll., 1965; MA, U. Mich., 1971; postgrad., Fashion Inst., N.Y.C., 1981. Teaching fellow dept. theatre U. Mich., Ann Arbor, 1968-69; instr., costumer dept. theatre Va. Commonwealth U., Richmond, 1969-71, U. Neb., Omaha, 1971-73; freelance designer Detroit and Ann Arbor, 1974-78; asst. prof., costumer Lock Haven (Pa.) State U., 1978-84; freelance artist, investor Sandy, Utah, 1984—; resident designer Detroit Repertory Theatre, 1974-78; costumer U. Mich. Opera Theatre, Ann Arbor, 1974-75. Bd. dirs. Ann Arbor Civic Theatre, 1978. Mem. United Scenic Artists, Theatrical Wardrobe Assocs., U.S. Inst. for Theatre Tech. Home: 10479 Dimple Dell Rd Sandy UT 84092

HOAGE, WILLIAM GRANT, engineer, health science consultant; b. Butte, Mont., Apr. 12, 1923; s. William Grant and Lyra Evalena (Sanborn) H.; m. Edith Rae Maple; children: Mark Steven, Carol Frances. BA, Occidental Coll, 1949; MHA, Washington U., 1951. Safety analyst Douglas Aircraft, El Segundo, Calif., 1951-59; hosp./clinic adminstr. West Covina (Calif.) Hosp./Med. Clinic, 1959-60; quality control analyst North Am. Aviation, Downey and Anaheim, Calif., 1960-71; regional med. planner U. Calif., Irvine, 1971-73; project engr. Rockwell Internat., Downey, 1973—; cons. H.A. Price Assoc., Orange, Calif., 1970, Northrop Services, Chgo., 1971; active Rockwell Employees Donate-Once Bd., El Segundo, Calif., 1987—. V.p., chmn. HMO, emergency services and facilities rev. coms. Orange County Health Planning Council, 1971-75; pres. Hoag Meml. Hosp. Presbyn. Assn., Newport Beach, Calif., 1974-84. Served as cpl. Army Air Corps, 1942-45. Republican. Presbyterian. Lodge: Masons. Home: 1617 N Shaffer Orange CA 92667

HOAGLAND, ALBERT JOSEPH, JR., psychotherapist, hypotherapist, minister; b. Clayton, N.J., July 2, 1939. Cert. psychiat. tech., Ancora State Hosp., 1958; RN, Monmouth Med. Ctr., 1961; BS, Monmouth Coll., 1964; MSW, Rutgers U., 1966; M.Div., Fuller Theol. Sem., 1978; D in Ministry, Boston U., 1981; PhD, Am. Inst. Hypnotherapy, 1989. Ordained to ministry Disciples of Christ, 1978; lic. clin. social worker, Calif., marriage, family and child counselor, Calif.; cert. sch. counselor, anger therapist. Pvt. practice counseling 1959—; psychiat. technician, RN N.J. State Hosp., 1958-66; instr., cons. Los Angeles County Dept. Probation, 1972-75; instr. psychology Calif. Grad. Inst., 1973; instr. Chapman Coll., 1972-74; instr. psychology Calif. State U., Dominguez Hills, 1974; instr. Torrance (Calif.) Adult Sch., 1977-79, 81-85; pastor Ariz., 1984-85, Calif., 1978-79, 81-84, Mass., 1979-81; subs. tchr. Marana (Ariz.) Sch. Dist., 1985; instr. Beverly Hills Adult Sch., 1984—; exec. dir. Personal Counseling Services, San Pedro, 1986—; religious educator various retreats, programs, summer camps, etc., 1975—. Author: Anger to Intimacy, 1988; editor Jonestown Collection, 1978, Professional Papers from the Desert, 1970, What's Your Problem ?, 1989; producer (film) Gestalt Therapy, 1974. Mem. Congress of Disciples Clergy, Disciples of Christ Hist. Soc., Disciples Peace Fellowship; trainer, cons. Los Angeles Council Exploring div. Boy Scouts Am., 1971-74, 88—, explorer post advisor, 1988—; coach Palos Verdes (Calif.) Soccer Program, basketball Torrance City Sports Program; dir. YWCA Delinquency Prevention Program, San Pedro, 1986-89; chair community adv. council San Pedro High Sch.; campaigned for mayor. Recipient Adult God and Svc award, 1989. Mem. Nat. Tchrs. Assn., Nat. Assn. Social Workers, Am. Assn. Marriage and Family Therapists, Am. Osteo. Assn., Nat. Assn. Christians in Soc. Work, Harbor Area Police Clergy Council (pres.), Am. Hypotherapists, Am. Bd. Hypnotherapist, Nat. Assn. Clergy, World Fedn. Mental Helath, Clowns of Am., Phi Delta Kappa. Democrat. Lodge: San Pedro Rotary (sec.). Home: 3318 W Torrance Blvd Torrance CA 90503 Office: Personal Counseling Svcs 1044 S Gaffey St #2 San Pedro CA 90731

HOAGLAND, GORDON W., mathematics educator; b. Nampa, Idaho, Oct. 22, 1936; s. Clyde Mackay and Clara Vivian (Wood) H.; m. Byrnina Louise Burningham, Aug. 1, 1962; children: David, Daniel, Deborah. BS, Brigham Young U., 1966, MS, 1968. Mem. research faculty Oreg. State U., Corvallis, 1968-69; mem. math. faculty Ricks Coll., Rexburg, Idaho, 1969—, dept. chmn., 1979-84, with campus computer planning sect., 1985—; cons. in field. Author: (lab manual) Scientific Programming, 1984; contbr. articles to profl. jours. Served with U.S. Air N.G., 1954-55. Mem. Am. Math. Assn. for 2 Yr. Colls. (editorial bd. 1986—), Soc. Indsl. and Applied Math., Pi Mu Epsilon. Republican. Mormon. Clubs: Upper Valley Sq. Dance (St. Anthony, Idaho) (caller 1978-87), Wagonwheeler Sq. Dance (Rexburg) (caller 1969—). Home: 206 E 2d South Rexburg ID 83440 Office: Ricks Coll Dept Math Rexburg ID 83440

HOAGLAND, JACK CHARLES, aerospace executive; b. L.A., Nov. 14, 1918; s. Harry and Evaline Goodborn (Bilton) H.; m. Jeanette Louise Beinhauer, June 14, 1949; children: Lawrence Eugene, Stanley E. BS in Engring., Calif. Inst. Tech., 1942; postgrad, U. Calif., L.A., 1969, U. Calif., Irvine, 1970. Registered profl. engr. (mech. and elec.), Calif. Commd. lt. USN, 1944, advanced through grades to lt. comdr., resigned, 1954; system mgr. Lockheed Missle & Space Co., Van Nuys, Calif., 1953-57; dir. systems The Ralph M. Parsons Co., Pasadena, Calif., 1957-60; cons. in electronics Orange County, Calif., 1960-62, 70-73; mgr. identification systems McDonnell Douglas Corp., Calif., Mo., 1962-70; dir. electronics and mech. engring. Rockwell Internat., Anaheim, Calif., 1973-88; program mgr., tech. dir. advance communications systems Rockwell Internat., Seal Beach and Downey, Calif., 1988—; owner Hoagland Enterprises, Tustin, Calif., 1965—. Author: ISA Flight Test, 1954, 30 tech. papers in field; patentee in field. Recipient Meritorious Svc. award NSA, 1985, spl. recognition at USAF, NASA, NSA, 1986. Fellow IEEE (Profl. Achievement awards 1967, 68, 80, Profl. Leadership awards L.A. Coun. 1975-76, chmn., chief exec. officer L.A. Coun. 1978-80, Centennial medal 1984), Inst. for Advancement Engring.; mem. Chino Airport Assn. (bd. dirs., sec./treas. 1983—), Airport Owners and Pilots Assn., Assn. of Old Crows, AIAA, Am. Astronautics Soc., Cessna Pilots Assn. Republican. Home: 12452 Ranchview SW Orange County CA 92705 Office: Rockwell Internat Aerospace Group PO Box 3644 Seal Beach CA 90740-7644

HOAGLAND, JULIA THERESA HOSKIN, social services executive; b. Oak Park, Ill., Sept. 20, 1956; d. Hiram Hodgson and Rose Frances (Boffa) Hoskin; m. William Ray Hoagland, May 21, 1977; 1 child, Theodore Dennis. Student, Coll. of DuPage, Ill., 1973-74; BA in English, No. Ill. U., 1977. Cert. secondary edn. tchr., Mont., Ill. Adj. instr. composition No. Mont. Coll., Havre, 1979-83; legal advisor COVE, Sterling, Ill., 1984; exec. dir. Big Bros./Big Sisters N. Mont., Havre, 1984—; counselor youth Women in Community Svc., Havre, 1984—. Home: 910 1st Ave Havre MT 59501 Office: Big Bros/Big Sisters N Mont PO Box 1509 Havre MT 59501

HOANG, DUC VAN, theoretical pathologist, educator; b. Hanoi, Vietnam, Feb. 17, 1926; came to U.S. 1975, naturalized 1981; s. Duoc Van and Nguyen Thi (Tham) H.; m. Mau-Ngo Thi Vu, Dec. 1, 1952; 1 child, Duc-An Hoang-Vu. M.D., Hanoi U. Sch. Medicine, Vietnam, 1953. Dean Sch. Medicine Army of the Republic of Vietnam, Saigon, 1959-63; dean Minh-Duc U. Sch. Medicine, Saigon, 1970-71; clin. prof. theoretical pathology U. So. Calif. Sch. Medicine, Los Angeles, 1978—; adj. prof. Emperor's Coll. Traditional Oriental Medicine, Santa Monica, Calif., 1988—. Author: Towards an Integrated Humanization of Medicine, 1957; The Man Who Weights the Soul, 1959; Eastern Medicine, A New Direction?, 1970; also short stories; translator: Pestis, introduction to the work of Albert Camus, Vietnamese translation of La Peste; editor: The East (co-founder); jour. Les Cahiers de l'Asie du Sud-Est. Founder, past pres. Movement for Fedn. Countries S.E. Asia; co-founder, past v.p. Movement for Restoration Cultures and Religions of Orient; active Vo-Vi Meditation Assn. Am. Served to lt. col. M.C., Army of Republic of Vietnam, 1952-63. Mem. AAUP, Assn. Clin. Scientists, Am. Com. for Integration Eastern and Western Medicine (founder), Assn. Unitive Medicine (founder, pres.). Republican. Roman Catholic. Clubs: U. So. Calif. Staff, U. So. Calif. Faculty Members (Los Angeles). Home: 3630 S Barry Ave Los Angeles CA 90066-3202 Office: U So Calif Med Ctr Interns-Residents Dormitory #127 Los Angeles CA 90033-1084

HOANG, TRUNG QUANG, mechanical engineer; b. Hanoi, Vietnam, July 24, 1950; came to U.S., 1975; s. Bao Hoang and Tru Nguyen; m. Lori Ann Jung, Aug. 8, 1981; children: Don, Charles. Student, Emporia State U., 1977-79; BS, Kans. State U., 1983, MS, 1985. Beef processor Iowa Beef

Packing Co., Emporia, Kans., 1975-77; with Cessna Aircraft Co., Wichita, 1979-81; res. asst. Kans. State U., Manhattan, 1983-85; mechanical engr. Naval Weapons Ctr., China Lake, Calif., 1985—. Mem. Nat. Soc. Profl. Engrs., Rock Club, Planetary Soc.

HOARD, DONA, city administrator; b. Bklyn., Jan. 4, 1943; d. Simon Mazer and Marcelle (Feiner) Felser; m. David Hoard, Aug. 27, 1966 (div. Nov. 1981); children: Daniel, Eliza. AB, Vassar Coll., 1964; MPA, U. Pitts., 1965. Planner Parkins, Rogers & Assoc., Detroit, 1965-66; planning dir. Lancaster (Pa.) County Community Action Agy., 1966-68; asst. to dir. Richmond Redevel. Agy., 1969-71; treas. MKGK Inc., San Francisco, 1971-82; pvt. cons. practice, Oakland, Calif., 1982-85; dir. community devel. City of Alameda, Calif., 1985—. Recipient Disting. Achievements award Council of Engrs. and Scientists, 1984, Disting. Contbn. To Engring. award Nat. Soc. Profl. Engrs., 1982, Contbn. To Engr ing. Community award, Engrs. Council, 1982, Disting. Contbns. award Soc. Mfg. Engrs., 1981. Mem. Alameda Bus. & Profl. Women (pres.-elect 1988, Woman of Yr. 1987, pres. 1989—), Calif. State Bd. Registration Engrs. & Land Surveyors (pres. 1980-81). Democrat. Jewish. Home: 5412 Proctor Ave Oakland CA 94618

HOBAN, THOMAS PATRICK, commercial real estate company executive; b. Seattle, July 3, 1935; s. Thomas A. and Vivian Elizabeth (Shaw) H.; m. Helen Maureen Pearson, Sept. 30,1961; children: Thomas Patrick Jr., Patricia Maureen, Shawn Arthur. BA in Communications, Notre Dame U., 1961; postgrad., Realtors Inst., 1980-82. Mgr. J.C. Penney Co., Honolulu, 1961-69; sr. account mgr. Hallmark Cards, Kansas City, Mo., 1969-74; sr. account and dist. mgr. Lennox China and Glass Co., Princeton, N.J., 1974-80; pres., broker Coast Comml. Properties, Everett, Wash., 1980—. Pres. Snohomish County Nat. Football Found. With USCG, 1953-57. Mem. Everett Bd. Realtors, U. Notre Dame Alumni Assn. Western Wash. (pres. 1986-88), Providence Health Club (v.p. 1987-88), Sertoma, K.C. Office: Coast Comml Properties 1602 Hewitt St PO Box 5272 Ste 511 Everett WA 98206

HOBSON, BERNARD EDWARD, lawyer; b. Austin, Tex., July 24, 1953; s. Bernard and Vivian Claire (Moran) H.; m. Pam Standley, Oct. 1, 1983. BA, Knox Coll., 1974; MA, Rice U., 1976; JD, U. Houston, 1979. Bar: Tex. 1980, U.S. Dist. Ct. (so. dist.) Tex. 1980, U.S. Ct. Appeals (5th cir.) 1980, U.S. Ct. Appeals (11th cir.) 1981, U.S. Ct. Claims 1983, U.S. Supreme Ct. 1983, Colo. 1986, U.S. Dist. Ct. (we. dist.) Tex. 1986. Assoc. Pizzitola, Hinton & Sussman, Houston, 1979-80; 1st asst. dist. atty. Ft. Bend County Dist. Atty.'s Office, Richmond, Tex., 1980-83; asst. U.S. atty. U.S. Atty.'s Office Dept. of Justice, Houston, 1983-86, El Paso, Tex., 1986-87; asst. U.S. atty. U.S Atty's. Office Organized Crime Drug Enforcement Task Force, Denver, 1987—; instr. Lamar U., Beaumont, Tex., 1983—, Atty. Gen.'s Adv. Inst., Washington, 1985—. Recipient Appreciation Cert. Gulf Coast Crime Prevention Assn., 1983, Commr.'s award U.S. Immigration and Naturalization Svc., 1985. Mem. ABA, Fed. Bar Assn. (former bd. dirs. Houston chpt. 1985-86), Tex. Bar Assn., Assn. Trial Lawyers Am., Nat. Dist. Attys. Assn., Am. Judicature Soc. Presbyterian. Home: 300 Lolard Lyons CO 80540

HOBSON, JOHN DAVID, gastroenterologist, educator; b. Seymour, Ind., Oct. 7, 1941; s. William Edwin and Jean (Davis) H.; m. Ann Wargo, Dec. 21, 1968; children: Katherine, David. BA, U. Calif., Santa Barbara, 1963; MA, U. Calif., 1965; MD, U. Calif., San Francisco, 1970. Diplomate Am. Bd. Internal Medicine, Am. Bd. Gastroenterology, Nat. Bd. Med. Examiners. Practice medicine specializing in gastroenterology Santa Barbara, 1975--; clin. prof. med. Sch. Medicine U. So. Calif., Los Angeles, 1980--; chmn. internal medicine Santa Barbara Cottage Hosp., 1978-80, v.p., 1983--, dir. gastrointestinal lab., 1987. Contbr. articles to med. jours. Fund raiser, mem. van com. Santa Barbara Amateur Radio Emergency Service, 1983--. Recipient Excellence in Teaching award Santa Barbara Cottage Hosp., 1981, 82, 84; Named U. Calif. scholar, 1969. Fellow ACP, Am. Coll. Gastroenterology; mem. Am. Gastroent. Assn., Am. Soc. for Gastrointestinal Endoscopy, Santa Barbara Amateur Radio Club (treas. 1985-87), U. Calif.-Santa Barbara Alumni Assn. (bd. dirs. 1983--, pres. 1987), Alpha Omega Alpha. Home: 4604 Via Gennita Santa Barbara CA 93111 Office: Santa Barbara Med Clinic PO Box 1200 Santa Barbara CA 93102-1200

HOBSON, MICHAEL LEE, retail executive; b. Camden, N.J., Aug. 11, 1950; s. Norman Lee and Helen Ann (Bent) H.; m. Carol Michele Pastoruis, Apor. 9, 1958; 1 child, Jennifer Carol. BS in Mktg., Drexel U., 1974. With Gimbels, Phila., 1974-77; buyer, store mdse. mgr. Bambergers subs. R.H. Macys, Newark, 1977-85; br. mdse. mgr. Meier and Frank subs. May Co., Portland, Oreg., 1985—. Home: 2505 Jolie Point Rd West Linn OR 97068 Office: Meier & Frank 621 SW 5th Ave Portland OR 97201

HOCH, ORION LINDEL, corporate executive; b. Canonsburg, Pa., Dec. 21, 1928; s. Orion L.F. and Ann Marie (McNulty) H.; m. Jane Lee Ogan, June 12, 1952 (dec. 1978); children: Andrea, Brenda, John; m. Catherine Nan Richardson, Sept. 12, 1980; 1 child, Joe. B.S., Carnegie Mellon U., 1952; M.S., UCLA, 1954; Ph.D., Stanford U., 1957. With Hughes Aircraft Co., Culver City, Calif., 1952-54; with Stanford Electronics Labs., 1954-57; sr. engr., dept. mgr., div. v.p., div. pres. Litton Electron Devices div., San Carlos, Calif., 1957-68; group exec. Litton Components div., 1968-70; v.p. Litton Industries, Inc., Beverly Hills, Calif., 1970, sr. v.p., 1971-74, pres., 1982-88, chief exec. officer, 1986—, chmn., 1988—, also dir.; pres. Intersil, Inc., Cupertino, Calif., 1974-82; bd. dirs. Measurex Corp., Maxim Integrated Products. Trustee Carnegie-Mellon U. Served with AUS, 1946-48. Mem. IEEE, Am. Electronics Assn. (bd. dirs.), Sigma Xi, Tau Beta Pi, Phi Kappa Phi. Office: Litton Industries Inc 360 N Crescent Dr Beverly Hills CA 90210

HOCHBERG, FREDERICK GEORGE, accountant; b. L.A., July 4, 1913; s. Frederick Joseph and Lottie (LeGendre) H.; 1 child, Ann C. May. BA, UCLA, 1937. Chief acct., auditor Swinerton, McClure & Vinnell, Managua, Nicaragua, 1942-44; pvt. acctg. practice, Avalon, Calif., 1946-66; designer, operator Descanso Beach Club, Avalon, 1966; v.p. Air Catalina, 1967; treas. Catalina Airlines, 1967; pres. Aero Commuter, 1967; v.p., treas., dir. bus. affairs William L. Pereira & Assocs., Planners, Architects, Engrs., L.A., 1967-72; v.p., gen. mgr. Mo. Hickory Corp., 1972-74; prin. Fred G. Hochberg Assocs., Mgmt. Cons., 1974—; v.p. Vicalton S.A. Mexico, 1976—; v.p., gen. mgr. Solar Engring. Co., Inc., 1977-79; pres. Solar Assocs. Internat., 1979-83. Chmn. Avalon Transp. Com., 1952, Avalon Harbor Commn., 1960, Avalon Airport Com., 1964-66, Harbor Devel. Commn., 1965-66; sec. Santa Catalina Festival of Arts, 1960, Avalon City Planning Commn., 1956-58; pres. Avalon Music Bowl Assn., 1961, Catalina Mariachi Assn., 1961-66; treas. City of Avalon, 1954-62, Catalina Island Mus. Soc., 1964, councilman, 1962-66, mayor, 1964-66; bd. dirs. L.A. Child Guidance Clinic, 1975-86, advisor to bd., 1986—, treas., 1978-79, pres., 1979-81; bd. dirs. Los Aficionados de L.A., 1977—, pres., 1980-83, 87-88; pres. Nat Assn. Taurine Clubs, 1982-85. With USNR, 1944-45. Named Catalina Island Man of Yr., 1956. Mem. Avalon Catalina Island C. of C. (past pres., bd. dirs. 1948-62), Soc. Calif. Accts., Mensa, Am. Arbitration Assn. (panel), El Monte C. of C., Town Hall-West (vice-chmn.). Lodge: Rotary (Avalon pres. 1956). Home: 936 Trout St Staunton VA 24401 Office: PO Box 3173 Staunton VA 24401

HOCHBERGER, JOHN RICHARD, research engineer; b. Blue Island, Ill., Oct. 18, 1960; s. John Richard and Ruth Bessie (Stevo) H.; m. Marissa Lina Planta, Jan. 11, 1986, 1 child, Jaryd James. BS MetE, U. Wis., 1983. Rsch. engr. Gen. Dynamics Corp., Pomona, Calif., 1983-88, sr. rsch. engr., 1988—. Co-inventor chip holding device, 1984. Office: Gen Dynamics MZ 50-26 PO Box 2507 Pomona CA 91769

HOCHMAN, DAVID CHARLES, data processing executive; b. San Diego, Feb. 19, 1950; s. Harry and Cecelia (Wolk) H. BS, Calif. Poly. State U., 1972; MBA, U. Fla., 1981. Applications engr. Digital Telephone Systems, San Rafael, Calif., 1973-80; mgr. product planning Harris Corp., Novato, Calif., 1980—. Contbr. articles to profl. jours. Home: PO Box 5276 Novato CA 94948 Office: Harris Corp 300 Bel Marin Keys Novato CA 94949

HOCHSCHILD, CARROLL SHEPHERD, company administrator, educator; b. Whittier, Calif., Mar. 31, 1935; d. Vernon Vero and Effie Corinne (Hollingsworth) Shepherd; m. Richard Hochschild, July 25, 1959; children: Christopher Paul, Stephen Shepherd. BA in Internat. Rels., Pomona Coll., 1956; Teaching credential U. Calif., Berkeley, 1957; MBA, Pepperdine U., 1985; cert. in fitness instrn., U. Calif., Irvine, 1988. Cert. elem. tchr., Calif. Elem. tchr. Oakland Pub. Schs. (Calif.), 1957-58, San Lorenzo Pub. Schs. (Calif.), 1958-59, Pasadena Pub. Schs. (Calif.), 1959-60, Huntington Beach Pub. Schs. (Calif.), 1961-63, 67-68; adminstrv. asst. Microwave Instruments, Corona del Mar, Calif., 1968-74; co-owner Hoch Co., Corona del Mar, 1978—. Rep. Calif. Tchrs. Assn., Huntington Beach, 1962-63. Mem. AAUW, Internat. Dance-Exercise Found., Nat. Assn. Female Execs. Republican. Presbyterian. Clubs: Toastmistress (corr. sec. 1983), Jr. Ebell (fine arts chmn. Newport Beach 1966-67).67).

HOCHSTEIN, JAMES RAYMOND, infosystems specialist; b. McMinnville, Oreg., Sept. 18, 1946; s. Raymond Peter and Mary Margaret (Versteeg) H.; m. Lucy Elizabeth Edwards, Oct. 24, 1970; children: James R. Jr., Susannah E.R., Juliana V.S., Lucyann E. BS in Math., Oreg. State U., 1968; cert. program mgmt., Def. System Mgmt. Coll., Ft. Belvoir, Va., 1978. Computer systems analyst, programmer Weapon Systems Accuracy Trials, Keyport, Wash., 1968-75; trident impact coordinator, planning dept. Naval Torpedo Sta., Keyport, Wash., 1975; tech. liaison staff mem. Naval Undersea Warfare Engring. Sta., Washington, 1976-78; asst. program mgr. Naval Undersea Warfare Engring. Sta., Keyport, 1978-81, aquisition plannerautomated data processing equipment, 1982-84, computer systems acquisition and planning br. head., 1984—; instr. in statistics Olympic Coll., Bremerton, Wash., 1988—. Editor Star of the Sea parish directory, 1980; contbr. articles to profl. publs. Mem. sch. bd. Star of the Sea Parish Sch., Bremerton, 1979; pres. Star of the Sea Parish Coun., 1980; advisor United Way of Kitsap County, Bremerton, 1984. Mem. Fed. Mgrs. Assn., Elks. Office: Naval Undersea Warfare Engr Code 543 Keyport WA 98345

HOCHSTEIN, PAUL, biochemist; b. N.Y.C., Feb. 7, 1926; s. Samuel and Ida (Leshan) H.; m. Gianna Smith, Mar. 9, 1956; children—Miles, Evon. BS, Rutgers U., 1950; MS, U. Md., 1952, PhD, 1954, PhD (hon.) U. Stockholm, 1986. Postdoctoral fellow Nat. Cancer Inst., 1954-57; research assoc. Columbia U., 1957-63; assoc. prof. Duke U., Durham, N.C., 1963-69; prof. pharmacology. U. So. Calif., Los Angeles, 1969-80, dir. Inst. for Toxicology, 1980—, assoc. dean, 1981—. Served with AUS, 1943-46. Recipient Research Career award NIH, 1965-69. Mem. Am. Soc. Biol. Chemists, Soc. for Toxicology, Am. Soc. Pharmacology and Exptl. Therapeutics, Soc. Gen. Physiologists. Contbr. numerous articles to sci. jours. Office: 1985 Zonal Ave Los Angeles CA 90033

HOCK, DELWIN D., utilities company executive; b. 1935. BS in Bus. Adminstrn., U. Colo., 1956. Acct. Gen. Electric Co., 1956-57, Arthur Young & Co., 1957-62; with Pub. Service Co. of Colo., Denver, 1962—, various mgmt. positions, 1962-79, v.p. acctg., 1979, v.p., asst. sec., 1979-80, sr. v.p., 1980-86, pres., chief operating officer, 1986—, also bd. dirs. Office: Pub Service Co of Colo 550 15th St Denver CO 80202 *

HOCKEL, JACK LEWIS, dentist; b. Menomonee, Wis., July 18, 1933; m. Judie Miner, Jan. 23, 1960; 6 children. Student, San Jose (Calif.) State U., 1951-52, U. Calif., San Francisco, 1952-55; DDS, U. Calif., San Francisco, 1959. Assoc. dentist San Francisco, 1959-60; gen. practice dentistry Berkeley, Calif., 1960-62, Concord, Calif., 1962-76, Walnut Creek, Calif., 1976—. Editor: Orthopedic Gnathology. Fellow Acad. Gen. Dentistry, Fedn. Orthodontic Assns; mem. Internat. Acad. Gnathology, Am. Acad. Gnathological Orthopedics (pres. 1983-85, diplomate 1986), Cranial Acad., Am. Equilibration Soc., Fedn. Orthodontic Assns. (diplomate 1978). Office: 2651 Oak Rd Walnut Creek CA 94598

HOCKMAN, KARL KALEVI, transportation and management services executive; b. N.Y.C., Jan. 17, 1924; s. John Laakso and Fanny Maria (Wirtanen) H.; m. Betty Lou Heyle, June 24, 1970; children: William, James Karol, Thomas, David, Kathleen. BA, Shelton Coll., 1956; BD, Bibl. Sem., 1958; cert. in indsl. relations U. Calif.-Berkeley, 1968; cert. in personnel devel. U. Calif., Santa Barbara, 1972. V.p. Schroeder Distbg. Co. No. Calif., Oakland, 1960-66; controller Inland Cities Express, Inc., Riverside, Calif., 1967-70; data processing mgr. Moss Motors, Ltd., Goleta, Calif., 1970-73; controller LKL Industries, Fontana, Calif., 1973-82; mng. ptnr. Hockman & Hockman Assocs., Rialto, Calif., 1982—; chmn. bd. Computer Networking Specialists, Inc., 1983—; sec./treas. Moreno Valley Constrn., Inc., 1986—, also bd. dirs.; bd. dirs. Raemont & Co., Inc., MI Sueno Ranch Nursery, Inc., Quest Electronics Corp. Served with AUS, 1942-45, ETO. Mem. Assn. Computing Machinery, Data Processing Mgmt. Assn., IEEE, Nat. Def. Transp. Assn., N.Y. Acad. Scis., Bibl. Archeol. Soc. Republican. Adventist. Club: Valley Transp. Office: Hockman & Hockman Assocs 1325 N Fitzgerald Ste E Rialto CA 92376

HOCKNEY, DAVID, artist; b. Bradford, Yorkshire, Eng., July 9, 1937; s. Kenneth and Laura H. Attended, Bradford Coll. Art, 1953-57, Royal Coll. Art, 1959-62. Lectr. U. Iowa, 1964, U. Colo., 1965, U. Calif. Berkeley, 1967; lectr. UCLA, 1966, hon. chair of drawing, 1980. Exhibited in one-man shows, Kasmin Gallery, 1963, Mus. Modern Art, N.Y.C., 1964, 68, Stedelijk Mus., Amsterdam, Netherlands, 1966, Andre Emmerich Gallery, N.Y.C., 1972, 83, 84, Musee des Arts Decoratifs, Paris, 1974, Mus. Gerona, Spain, 1976, Goteborg (Sweden) Mus., 1976, Gulbenkian Found., Lisbon, Spain, 1977, Susan Gersh Gallery, Los Angeles, 1982, Flanders Mus. Contemporary Arts, Mpls., 1982, Equinox Gallery, Vancouver, Can., 1988, Met. Mus. Art, 1988, others; designer: Rake's Progress, Glyndebourne, Eng., 1975; sets for Magic Flute, Glyndebourne, 1978, Met. Opera House, 1979, Tristan und Isolde, Los Angeles Music Ctr. Opera, 1987; Author: David Hockney by David Hockney, 1976, David Hockney: Travels with Pen, Pencil and Ink, 1978, Paper Pools, 1980, David Hockney Photographs, 1982; illustrator: Six Fairy Tales of the Brothers Grimm, 1969. Recipient Guinness award and 1st prize for etching, 1961, Gold medal Royal Coll. Art, 1962, Graphic prize Paris Biennale, 1963, 1st prize 8th Internat. Exhbn. Drawings Lugano, Italy, 1964, 1st prize John Moores Exhbn. Liverpool, Eng., 1967. Office: 7506 Santa Monica Blvd Los Angeles CA 90041 also: Old Bath House, Manor Ln Shipley, West Yorkshire BD18 3EA, England *

HODDER, EDWIN CLIFTON, investment company executive; b. Denver, July 1, 1955; s. Edwin James and Ruth Lowell (Lierd) H.; m. Susan L. Benson, 1984. BA cum laude, U. Denver, 1977; MBA, U. Pa., 1979. Founder, pres., bd. dirs. Hodder Sinclair Enterprises, Inc., Casper, Wyo., 1980-88; founder, mgr. Car Wash Supply Co., Casper, 1981—, Mountain Soft, 1982—; founder, mgr., bd. dirs. Hodco, Inc., Casper, 1982—; account exec. Wyo. Fin. Securities, Inc., 1988—; asst. dir. internat. affairs, Wharton Sch. U. Pa., 1978-79. Inventor turn-key box system for self-service timed bus. Francis Ferris Meml. scholar; U. Pa. Wharton fellow. Mem. Rotary, Omicron Delta Epsilon. Republican. Christian Scientist. Home: 1652 Begonia Casper WY 82604 Office: Wyo Fin Securities PO Box 407 Casper WY 82602

HODGE, GLENN ROY, postmaster; b. Billings, Mont., May 5, 1947; s. Roy William and Helen Maxine (Sarbo) H.; m. Kay Lorraine Waller, Nov. 30, 1968; children: Theresa Kay, Alan Roy. Student, Rocky Mountain Coll., 1967-68, Ea. Mont. Coll., 1968. With U.S. Postal Svc., Billings, 1968—; postmaster U.S. Postal Svc., Cut Bank, Mont., 1978-81, Livingston, Mont., 1981—. Mem. Employer Support N.G. Res., Washington, 1982—, Park County Emergency Med. Assn., Livingston, 1983—; instr. Cardio-Pulmonary Recusitation, Livingston, 1983—; pres. Park County Rural Fire Dist., Livingston, 1986-87. Mem. Nat. League of Postmasters (pres. 1984-85, 85). Baptist. Home: 119 N 5th St Livingston MT 59047-0001 Office: US Postal Svc 105 N 2d St Livingston MT 59047-9998

HODGE, RUSTY HARVEY, computer research company executive; b. Orange, Calif., July 5, 1962; s. Winston William and Lenda Sue (Harvey) H. BS in Telecommunications, Calif. Poly. Inst., 1987. Owner, corp. dir. Hodge Computer Rsch. Corp., Orange, Calif., 1980-85, SnAPP Systems, 1985-87; v.p. Hodge Computer Rsch. Corp., Orange, 1987—. Active ACLU, Amnesty Internat. Mem. IEEE Computer Soc., Amateur Radio Relay League, BMW Car Club Am. Libertarian. Mem. Ch. of Christ. Office: Hodge Computer Rsch Corp 1588 N Batavia St Orange CA 92667

HODGE, WALTER WILLIAM, counselor; b. St. Louis, Apr. 15, 1938; s. Walter William and Willie Rebecca (Smith) H.; m. Nancy Louise Paris, Apr. 5, 1985; 1 child, William Dane. BS, U.S. Mil. Acad., 1961; MA, Ariz. State U., 1968, supt.'s cert., 1985. Cert. supt., prin., supr., counselor, math. and sci. tchr., Ariz. Founder, pres. Career Exploration Acad., Phoenix, 1977-79; supr. Bur. Indian Affairs, Kayenta, Ariz., 1979-84; counselor Bur. Indian Affairs, Kayenta, 1979-84, Shonto, Ariz., 1986—; acad. supr., Kaibeto, Ariz., 1984-85; supt. schs. Paloma Dist. No. 94, Gila Bend, Ariz., 1985-86. Served from 2nd lt. to 1st lt. U.S. Army, 1961-66, Vietnam. Decorated Air medal with oak leaf cluster. Mem. Ariz. Assn. Sch. Adminstrs., Am. Fedn. Police, Boys Town Nebr. (hon.), VFW. Home: 4357 N 106th Ave Phoenix AZ 85039

HODGES, JAY ALLEN, computer information executive; b. Dallas, Oct. 30, 1964; s. Jack Creighton and Carol Ann (Moore) H. Student, El Camino Jr. Coll., 1982-83, 89; BS in Computer Sci., Tex. A&M U., 1985; postgrad., U. So. Calif., 1986. Software engr. GE, Daytona Beach, Fla., 1985; mem. tech. staff Hughes Aircraft Co., Torrance, Calif., 1985—. Mem. IEEE, Tex. A&M Univ. Alumni Assn., Century Club. Republican. Baptist. Home: 1507-B Cota St Torrance CA 90501 Office: Hughes Aircraft Co 19300 Grammercy Pl Torrance CA 90501

HODGES, STEVEN LYNN, electrical engineer, business executive; b. Wichita Falls, Tex., Sept. 23, 1950; s. Charles Elbert and Oleta (Seaberry) H.; m. Debra Carmen Marie Hone, June 16, 1957; children: Stephanie, Charles, Allison. BSEE, BBA, U. Tex., 1978. Engr. Hewlett-Packard, Boise, Idaho, 1978-84; pres., founder Computrol, Inc., Boise, 1980-87; pres., founder SynPet, Inc., Boise, 1988--, pres., 1988--. Served with USAF, 1970-74. Mem. Boise C. of C. (Small Businessman of Quarter 1987), Tau Beta Pi, Eta Kappa Nu. Home: 3125 Homer Rd Eagle ID 83616

HODGES, THOMAS WAYNE, aviation executive; b. St. Louis, Oct. 9, 1945; s. Earl Carnot and Helen Margaret (Thomas) H.; m. Sally Burrows, May 25, 1968 (div.); children: Heather, David. BS in Bus., Okla. State U., 1968; M Commerce, U. Richmond, 1975. Commd. 2d lt. U.S. Army, 1968, advanced through grades to maj., 1981, served in various locations including Vietnam, 1968-77, resigned commn., 1977; ops. analyst Cooper Airmotive to Aviall, Dallas, from 1978; mgr. data systems, sales mgr., dir. prodn., supt. mktg. Aviall, Dallas and Van Nuys, Calif., to 1985; v.p. PacAero, Burbank, Calif., 1986—. Decorated Bronze Star medal. Mem. Aero. Repair Sta. Assn. (bd. dirs. 1987—). Republican. Presbyterian. Office: PacAero 2810-20 N Lima St Burbank CA 91504

HODGES, WILLIAM FITZGERALD, professor clinical psychology; b. Pensacola, Fla., Dec. 26, 1940; s. Paul and Lilian Banks (Fitzgerald) H.; m. Linda Joan Etherage, Aug. 1, 1962; children: Heather Lynn, Wendy Lee. BA, Vanderbilt U., 1963, PhD, 1967. Cert. Clin. Psychologist, Colo. Prof. U. Colo., Boulder, 1967—, assoc. chair Dept. Psychology, 1987—, dir. Grad. Studies, 1987—. Editor: (Jr.) The Field of Mental Health Consultation, 1983; author: Interventions for Children of Divorce, 1986. Fellow Am. Psychol. Assn.; mem. Am. Psychol. Soc., Nat. Register for Health Svc.Providers in Psychology. Democrat. Office: Dept of Psychology Univ Colo Boulder CO 80309-0345

HODGES-MCLAIN, VIVAN PAULINE, educator; b. Liberal, Kans., Sept. 20, 1929; d. Paul Wright and Dora (Wilson) Arnett; m. Albert Hodges Jr. (div. 1967); children: Albert Brent, Mark Eugene; m. Charles M. McLain, June 21, 1986 (dec.). BA summa cum laude, Panhandle State U., 1958; MA summa cum laude, U. Colo., 1973, PhD summa cum laude, 1977. Tchr. pub. schs. Forgan, Okla., 1950-66, Liberal, Kans., 1966-67; tchr. reading Douglas County High Sch., Castle Rock, Colo., 1070-76; assoc. prof. Colo. State U., Ft. Collins, 1976-85; coord. dept. lang. arts Jefferson County Schs., Golden, Colo., 1985—; developer curriculum in reading and lang. arts for small and rural schs.; cons. in field; presenter workshops, seminars; mem. accreditation team, Colo. State U.; reviewer, cons. textbook series, Scott, Foresman Co., Holt, Rinehart & Winston, Macmillian Pub. Co., Zaner-Bloser Pub. Author: Improving Reading/Study Skills, 1979, A Resource Guide for Teaching Content Areas, 1980, other resource and curriculum guides; contbr. numerous articles to ednl. publs. Organizer class in reading for handicapped, Coll. for Living; supr. tutors, Alt. High Sch., Ft. Collins. Mem. Internat. Reading Assn., Colo. Coun. Internat. Reading Assn., Nat. Coun. Tchrs. English, Colo. Lang. Arts Soc., Western Writers Am., Phi Delta Kappa. Home: 1337 Yank St Golden CO 80401

HODGIN, DAVID TIMBERLAKE, service executive; b. Buffalo, June 8, 1932; s. David Reid Hodgin and Elva (Timberlake) Twamley; m. Claire Evelyn Arnold, July 19, 1953; children: David Arnold, Kathryn Anne, Elizabeth Claire, Amanda Claudia. Student, Wesleyan U., 1950-51; BA in Econs., U. Calif., Santa Barbara, 1954; B in Fgn. Trade, Am. Grad Sch. Internat. Mgmt., Phoenix, 1961; postgrad., NYU, 1964-65. Asst. to v.p. internat. div. Paul Hardeman, Inc., Stanton, Calif., 1961; dir. adminstrn. Paul Hardeman, S.A., Buenos Aires, 1962-63; supr. office svcs. Owens Corning Fiberglas Corp., N.Y.C., 1964-65; v.p. adminstrn. Fibraglas S.A., Bogota, Colombia, 1965-67; bus. analyst Owens Corning Fiberglas Corp., Toledo, 1967-68, Daire Assocs., Walnut Creek, Calif., 1968-78; pres. Am. Powerwash Corp., Concord, Calif., 1969-78; pres. Pathfinder Cos., Scotts Valley, Calif., 1977-88, chmn., 1989—; pres. Am. Holiday Resorts, Inc., Scotts Valley, 1983—, Compustudy Inc., 1989—; v.p., gen. mgr. Sunset Recreation, Inc., Menlo Park, Calif., 1973-77; sr. cons. Leisure Mgmt. Cons., Inc., Concord, 1975-77; bd. dirs. Evergreen Holding Co., Ltd., Barbados, W.I., Conifer Reinsurance, Ltd., Barbados. Contbr. numerous articles to profl. jours. Mem. Senate and Assembly Select Coms. on Small Bus., Sacramento, 1982—, Santa Cruz County (Calif.) Rep. Cen. Com., 1988—; chmn. dist. adv. council U.S. Small Bus. Adminstrn., San Francisco, 1983-87; advisor small bus. edn. program Cabrillo Coll., Aptos, Calif., 1983—; pres. Santa Cruz County Conv. and Vis. Bur., 1984, Calif. State Conf. on Small Bus., Sacramento, 1986-88, Calif. Small Bus. United, 1988—. Mem. Nat. Campground Owners Assn. (bd. dirs. 1974-83, v.p. 1976-78, pres. 1978-80), Calif. Travel Pks. Assn. (pres. 1974-76), Calif. State C. of C. (vice chair small bus. com. 1983-84), Santa Cruz Area C. of C. (bd. dirs. 1983-84), Scotts Valley C. of C. (bd. dirs. 1979-84), Exchange Club (pres., dir. Calif. and Nev. dists 1980-82). Republican. Office: Am Holiday Resorts Inc 100 Santa's Village Rd Scotts Valley CA 95066

HODGINS, GRANT MILTON, provincial cabinet minister; b. Prince Albert, Sask., Can., July 22, 1955; s. William Arnold and Betty Mildred (Finnestad) H. Diploma, Reisch Am. Sch. Auctioneering, 1973; B in Commerce, U. Sask., 1978. Pres. Hodgins Auctioneers Inc., Melfort, Sask., 1978—; Min. Hwys. and Transp. Govt. Sask., 1985-88, Min. Indian and Native Affairs, 1988—; instr. Mason City (Iowa) Coll. Auctioneering, 1985-86. Active Progressive Conservative Party, Melfort, 1982-86. Home: PO Box 3310, Melfort, SK Canada SOE 1AO Office: Ministry of Hwys & Transp, Legislative Bldg Rm 315, Regina, SK Canada S4S 0B3

HODGSON, GREGORY BERNARD, software systems engineer; b. Chgo., July 17, 1946; s. John George and Lucille (Nass) H.; m. Kathleen Patricia, Aug. 11, 1972 (div. July 1974); m. Kathryn Marie Maytum, Feb. 14, 1976. BS in Computer Engring., U. Ill., 1972. Computer programmer specialist Lockheed Missiles and Space Co., Sunnyvale, Calif., 1972-81, software systems engr., 1981-89; software systems cons. Lockheed Missiles and Space Co., Sunnyvale, 1989—; cons. in field. Served with U.S. Army, 1966-69. State of Ill. VA scholar, 1970-72. Mem. Nat. Mgmt. Assn., Ill. VA Assn. (coord. fed. and state affairs 1970-72). Republican. Roman Catholic. Home: 469 1/2 Curie Dr San Jose CA 95123

HODGSON, KENNETH P., mining executive, real estate investor; b. Canon City, Colo., Sept. 20, 1945; s. Cecil L. and Jaunita J. (Murrie) H.; m. Rebecca K. Thompson, Feb. 15, 1967; 1 child, Amber K.; m. 2d, Rita J. Lewis, Apr. 22, 1979. Student Metro Coll., 1966-68. With Golden Mining Corp., Utah, 1973-79, Windfall Group Inc., Utah, 1976-77; pres. Houston Mining, Ariz., 1979-82; v.p. Silver Ridge Mining, Inc., Gold Ridge Mining Inc., Ariz., 1979-82; pres. Ken Hodgson & Co., Inc., Canon City, 1983—; Riken Resources Ltd., 1985—. Recipient numerous safety awards. Mem. AIME. Republican. Presbyterian. Lodges: Moose, Elks. Home: 2995 Jamaica Blvd S Lake Havasu City AZ 86403

HODSON, ROY GOODE, JR., retired logistician; b. Enon, Ala., July 22, 1927; s. Roy Goode and Ilda Fern (Jinks) H.; m. Mildred Bernice Parlier, Dec. 3, 1966; children: Joan Hodson Bash, Scott Daniel, Jane Lorraine. Student, San Diego Jr. Coll., 1947-49, San Diego Vocational, 1947-49, San Diego State Coll., 1949-50. Security officer US Naval CB Ctr. (Civil Service), Port Hueneme, Calif., 1950-52; logistician Gen. Dynamics, San Diego, 1952-64, GTE Govt. Systems, Inc., Mt. View, Calif., 1964-89. Bd. dirs. San Jose Civic Light Opera Assn., 1988—. With U.S. Army, 1945-47. Mem. Assoc. Photographers Internat., Internat. Freelance Photographers Orgn. Democrat. Baptist. Home: 1527 Mount Shasta Ave Milpitas CA 95035-6934

HOECKER, THOMAS RALPH, lawyer; b. Chicago Heights, Ill., Dec. 14, 1950; s. William H. and Norma M. (Wynekoop) H.; m. V. Sue Thornton, Aug. 28, 1971; children: Elizabeth T., Ellen T. BS, No. Ill. U., 1972; JD, U. Ill., 1975. Bar: Ill. 1975, Ariz. 1985. Assoc. Davis and Morgan, Peoria, Ill., 1975-80, ptnr., 1980-84; assoc. Snell and Wilmer, Phoenix, 1984-85, ptnr., 1986—; bd. dirs. Ariz. Tax Res. Assn., Phoenix, 1987—; steering com. Western Pension Conf., Phoenix, 1986—. Fellow Ariz. Bar Found.; mem. Ariz. Bar Assn., Ill. State Bar Assn., ABA, Maricopa County Bar Assn. (investment com. 1988—), Western Pension Conf. (steering com.). Office: Snell and Wilmer 3100 Valley Bank Ctr Phoenix AZ 85073

HOEFT, STEVEN RAY, advertising executive; b. Springfield, Mo., Apr. 15, 1952; s. Norman R. and Josephine (Doria) H.; m. Jeannine Ganus, June 8, 1974; children: Jena, Jason, Jori, Janelle. BBA in Econs., U. Tulsa, 1974. With Southwestern Bell Tel. Co., various locations, 1974-84; regional mgr. Southwestern Bell Tel. Co., Ft. Smith, Ark., 1978-80; mem. gen. hdqrs. staff Southwestern Bell Tel. Co., St. Louis, 1980-84; pres. SRH Dir. Mktg., Inc., St. Louis, 1984-87, pres. div. D'Arcy Masius Benton & Bowles/USA, 1987—. Contbr. articles to profl. jours. Bd. dirs. YMCA of Ozarks, St. Louis, 1985—; chmn. fundraising U. Tulsa, 1987; mem. Congl. Awards Coun., 2d dist. Mo., 1987—. Named Vol. of Yr. St. Louis YMCA, 1987. Mem. Assn. Dir. Mktg. Agys., Dir. Mktg. Assn. St. Louis (bd. dirs. 1985-87). Office: SRH Dir Mktg One Memorial Dr Ste 600 Saint Louis MO 63102

HOEKSTRA, PIETER, geophysicist; b. Amsterdam, Netherlands, July 31, 1936; came to U.S., 1960; s. Bartele and Josephine (Poltner) H.; m. Ricki Knibbe, Sept. 20, 1960; children: Bartele Gerard, David Pieter. MSc, McGill U., Montreal, Que., Can., 1960; PhD, Cornell U., 1963. Rsch. geophysicist U.S. Army Cold Regions Rsch. and Engring. Lab., Hanover, N.H., 1960-75; assoc. Hardy & Assocs., Calgary, Alta., Can., 1975-79; pres. Geophys. Cons. Ltd., Calgary and Denver, 1979-84; prin. Earth Technology Corp., Denver, 1984-87; pres. Blackhawk Geoscis., Inc., Denver, 1987—; Mem. com. on polar programs, Nat. Acad. Scis., Washington, 1974-76. Contbr. numerous articles to profl. jours. Mem. Soc. Exploration Geophysicists, Am. Geophys. Union, Nat. Groundwater Assn., Alta. Assn. Profl. Engrs., Geologists, Geophysicists. Democrat. Lutheran. Home: 13325 Willow Ln Golden CO 80401 Office: Blackhawk Geoscis Inc 17301 W Colfax St Golden CO 80401

HOELTER, JAMES EDWARD, international shipping industry executive; b. Milw., June 26, 1939; s. Edward H. and Suzanne E. (Grabill) H.; m. Virginia Smith, June 30, 1962; Christine, Elizabeth, James. BBA in Finance, U. Wis., 1961; MBA, Harvard U., 1965. Mktg. analyst corp. staff Ford Motor Co., Dearborn, Mich., 1965-66; zone mgr. Lincoln Mercury div. Ford Motor Co., Oakland, Calif., 1966-70; chief fin. officer Mediation, Ft. Worth, 1970-71; dir. fin. leasing containver div. Itel Corp., San Francisco, 1971-75; v.p. N. Am. Trans Ocean Ltd., San Francisco, 1976-78; pres., co-founder Intermodal Equipment Assocs., San Francisco, 1979-87; pres., chief exec. officer Textainer Equipment Mgmt. NV, Netherlands Antilles, 1987—; bd. dirs. Textainer, Inc., Panama, Holmac Holdings, Inc., San Francisco, Textainer Capital Corp., San Francisco; lectr. grad. sch. mgmt. Golden Gate U., San Francisco, 1977-78. Co-author: Optical Scanning for the Businessman, 1965. Dir. sustaining membership Piedmont (Calif.) coun. Campfire Girls, 1973-76; com. chair recruiting Piedmont coun. Boy Scouts Am., 1979-85; bd. overseers Convalescent Hosp. Ministry-Alameda County, Alameda, Calif., 1981-86. 1st. lt. U.S. Army, 1961-63. Mem. World Trade Club, Chi Psi. Republican. Episcopalian.

HOEPPEL, RONALD EDWARD, soil microbiologist; b. Altadena, Calif., Aug. 30, 1944; s. Raymond Winfield and Norma Elizabeth (Burch) H.; m. Elissa Sanfilippo, Feb. 20, 1988. BS, Calif. Poly. State U., 1967; MS, N.Mex. State U., 1970; postgrad., Pa. State U., 1970-72. Microbiologist Army Corps Engrs. Waterways Exptl. Sta., Vicksburg, Miss., 1972-85; microbiologist Naval Civil Engring. Lab., Port Hueneme, Calif., 1985—, mgr. biotech. program, 1988—. Contbr. articles, reports to profl. publs. Mem. Am. Soc. Microbiology, Soc. Environ. Toxicology and Chemistry, Soc. Environ. Geochemistry and Health, Sigma Xi, Phi Kappa Phi. Democrat. Roman Catholic. Home: 607 Ridgeline Dr Oak View CA 93022 Office: Naval Civil Engring Lab Environ Systems Div L71 Port Hueneme CA 93043

HOEPPNER, IONA RUTH, publishing executive; b. Denver, Aug. 17, 1939; d. Edgar Hamlet and Thelma Marie (Arndt) Snider; m. Richard Allen Hoeppner, Dec. 10, 1975; children: Norman, Stephanie, William Scott, David, Richard, Kimberly, Tamily, Athena, Crystal. BA, U. So. Coll., Pueblo, 1978; postgrad., Western State Coll., Gunison, Colo., 1986—. Founder, owner, mgr. J&I Trucking/Hoeppner Transport, Fleming, Colo., 1958—; owner, mgr. Jim's Roundhouse Hobby Shop, Bountiful, Utah, 1969-73; tchr. sci. Briggsdale (Colo.) Schs., 1978-81, St. Patrick's Acad., Sidney, Nebr., 1983-85; founder, pres. Highlighter, Inc., Fleming, 1986—; founder, owner BookHogs Farms, Fleming, 1986—; gen. mgr. Haxtun Herald Newspaper, Colo., 1987-88; bd. dirs. Smallbird Corp., Fleming and Peetz, Colo., Over the Road, Inc., Aurora, Colo.; cons. FARE Brochure Com., Fleming, Western Ambulance Svcs., Inc., Littleton, 1985—. Author: Complete RV Handbook, 1987, Highway to Nowhere, 1986; editor, co-author: Teacher's Guide to Rural Education, 1987; contbr. articles to profl. jours. Mem. Colo. Press Assn., Rocky Mt. Biol. Lab., Nat. Writers Club. Baptist. Home and Office: 20027 County Rd 85 Fleming CO 80728

HOFER, GARY FRANS, stockbroker; b. Walla Walla, Wash., July 1, 1954; s. Glen Dale and Virginia Ann (Nelson) H.; m. Cindy Bishop, June 26, 1976; children: Gabriel Frans, Mans Daniel, Anselm Glen. BA in Psychology, East Wash. U., Cheney, 1977, BA in English, 1977; M in Internat. Mgmt., Am. Grad. Sch. Internat. Mgmt., Glendale, Ariz., 1982. Lic. security broker. Program mgr. Pre-Vocat. Tng. Ctr., Spokane, Wash., 1977-78, prodn. mgr., 1978-79; warehouseman Teamsters Local 582, Spokane, 1979-81; grain buyer, trader Harvest States Coops., St. Paul, 1982-83, futures specialist, 1983-85; stockbroker Dean Witter Reynolds, Inc., Sun City, Ariz., 1985—; pvt. practice bus. cons. Phoenix, 1987—; dir. Skyline Ranch, Inc., Fairfax, Va. Author, editor newsletters. Mem. Network, Unltd., N.W. Valley C. of C.(speaker Beware Elder Exploitation project). Republican. Roman Catholic. Office: Dean Witter Reynolds Inc 9949 W Bell Rd Sun City AZ 85351

HOFERT, JACK, consulting company executive, lawyer; b. Phila., Apr. 6, 1930; s. David and Beatrice (Schatz) H.; m. Marilyn Tukeman, Sept. 4, 1960; children: Dina, Bruce. BS, UCLA, 1952, MBA, 1954, JD, 1957. Bar: Calif. 1957; CPA, Calif. Tax supr. Peat, Marwick Mitchell & Co., Los Angeles, 1959-62, tax mgr., 1974-77; v.p. fin. Pacific Theaters Corp., Los Angeles, 1962-68; freelance cons. Los Angeles, 1969-74; tax mgr. Lewis Homes, Upland, Calif., 1977-80; pres. Di-Bru, Inc., Los Angeles, 1981-87, Scolyn, Inc., Los Angeles, 1988—; dir. Valley Fed. Savs. and Loan Assn., 1989—. Mem. UCLA Law Rev., 1956-57; contbr. articles to tax, fin. mags. Served with USN, 1948-49. Home and Office: 2479 Roscomare Rd Los Angeles CA 90077

HOFF, ELIZABETH PARSONS, import company executive; b. Wayzata, Minn., Sept. 11, 1963; d. David Coulter and Ruth Clifford (Bennett). BS in Bus. Recreation, U. Colo., 1985. Cruise hostess World Explorer Cruises, Seattle, 1985-86; event coordinator Inn At the Market, Seattle, 1986; catering mgr. Salty's on Alki, Seattle, 1986-87; acct. exec. A.J. Fritz & Co., Seattle, 1987--. Home: 938 NW 59th St Seattle WA 98107 Office: AJ Fritz & Co 1200 S 192d St Seattle WA 98148

HOFF, PHILIP HERBERT, educator; b. Washington, Mar. 12, 1941; s. Herbert Jacob and Agatha Dorothy (Hephner) H.; m. Regina Titzck, June 24, 1967; children: Paul, Elaine, Nancy Joy. BEE, Carnegie-Mellon U., 1963, MEE, 1964; PhD, U. Calif., Berkeley, 1970. Asst. prof. Calif. State U., Chico, 1966-67; lectr. Calif. State U., San Luis Obispo, 1970; assoc. prof. Calif. State U., Chico, 1970-77, prof., 1977—; fellow U. Calif., Berkeley, 1967; cons. Jet Propulsion Labs., Pasadena, Calif., 1968-73, Nowcasting, Chico, Michael Lim Inc., Chico. Contbr. articles to profl. jours. Sunday sch. supt. Forest Ranch (Calif.) Bapt. Ch., 1987—. Mem. Gideons Internat., Eta Kappa Nu. Republican. Office: Calif State U 307G Langdon Engring Ctr Chico CA 95929

HOFF, ROBERT ARTHUR, petroleum engineer; b. Moses Lake, Wash., July 31, 1957; s. Dr. Robert Arthur and Hazel Inez (Williams) H.; m. Julie Esther Hinson, June 10, 1977 (div. Oct. 1987); children: Robert III, Alexander, Candace, Eric. BS in Petroleum Engring., Winkler Inst. Mining, Houston, 1981. Svc. specialist Otis Engring., Houma, La., 1977-80; svc. engr. Schlumberger, Saudi Arabia, 1981-88; gen. ptnr. Prodn. Testing Svcs., Anchorage, 1988—; v.p. Total Health Care Ctrs. Am., Marianna, Fla., 1984—. Mem. Nat. Fedn. Ind. Businessmen, Alaska Industry Support Alliance, Anchorage C. of C. Republican. Baptist. Home: PO Box 140246 Anchorage AK 99514 Office: Prodn Testing Svcs 3200 Seward Hwy Anchorage AK 99503

HOFFENBLUM, ALLAN ERNEST, political consultant; b. Vallejo, Calif., Aug. 10, 1940; s. Albert A. and Pearl Estelle (Clarke) H. BA, U. So. Calif., 1962. StaffRep. party L.A. County, 1967-73; chief of staff assembly Rep. caucus Calif. legislature, Sacramento, 1973-75; polit. dir. Calif. Rep. Party, L.A., 1975-79; owner Allan Hoffenblum & Assocs., L.A., 1979—. Capt. USAF, 1962-67, Vietnam. Decorated Bronze Star medal. Mem. Internat. Assn. Polit. Cons., Am. Assn. Polit. Cons. Jewish. Office: Allan Hoffenblum & Assocs 6033 W Century Ste 950 Los Angeles CA 90045

HOFFLAND, DORINDA RUTH, graphic designer; b. San Diego, Sept. 25, 1961; d. David Lauren and Marie-Claire Cecil (Blouet) H. BA, San Diego State U., 1987. Prodn. artist Crest Advt., San Diego, 1987-88; graphic designer Photomation West, San Diego, 1988—; organizer Design '85 Student Art Show, San Diego, 1985. Mem. Nat. Assn. for Female Execs., Graphic Design Group, San Diego State U. (founder, pres. 1985). Democrat. Roman Catholic. Home: 10211 Caminito Rio Branco San Diego CA 92131 Office: Photomation West Co 9212 Mira Este Ct Ste 101 San Diego CA 92126

HOFFMAN, BERT ALVIN, surgeon; b. Fresno, Calif., Aug. 11, 1924; s. George Delbert and Florence Lillian (Wentworth) H.; m. Helen Claudine Hurley, Nov. 1949 (div. 1966); children: Susan, Sharyl, Brain; m. Florence Ruth Wiebe, Sept. 1, 1967; children: Gary, Stephen. BA in Chemistry, Pacific Union Coll., 1949; MD, Loma Linda U., 1954. Diplomate Nat. Bd. Med. Examiners, Am. Acad. Family Practice. Aviation med. examiner Fed. Aeros Adminstrn., Oklahoma City, 1964--; bd. dirs. Blue Shield of Calif., San Francisco. V.p. Tulare County Found. (Med. Care), Visalia, Calif., 1976, pres. 1977. Served with U.S. Army, 1944-46 PTO. Mem. AMA, Calif. Med. Assn., Tulare County Med. Soc. (v.p. 1978 pres. 1979), Tulare County Med. Assn. (chmn. polit. com. 1986--), VFW. Republican. Adventist. Office: 271 N L St Dinuba CA 93618

HOFFMAN, C. FENNO, III, architectural designer; b. Greenwich, Conn., May 28, 1958; s. Harrison Baldwin Wright and Louise Elkins (Sinkler) H.; m. Pia Christina Ossorio, Dec. 27, 1980; 1 child, Wilhelmina C. L. BA in Environ. Design, U. Pa., 1983; MArch, U. Colo., 1986. Designer Fenno Hoffman & Assocs., Boulder, Colo., 1983—; pvt. practice designer Boulder, 1985; assoc. William Zmistowski Assoc. Architects, 1987—, Anthony Pellecchia Architects, 1989—; cons. Summit Habitats, Inc., Denver, 1984—; design cons. The Denver Ptnrship, 1985, Downtown Denver, Inc., 1985. Prin. works include Ca' Venier Mus. for Venice Bienalle, 1985, Cleveland Place Connection, Denver, 1985 (1st prize 1985), hist. renovated house, Boulder, 1986, 3 Gates 3 Squares, Denver, 1986; author: Urban Transit Facility, A Monorail for Downtown Denver, 1985. Mem. AIA (assoc.), Am. Planning Assn., Constrn. Specifications Inst. Democrat. Episcopalian. Clubs: Rallysport Racquet (Boulder). Office: 2433 5th St Boulder CO 80302

HOFFMAN, CHARLES LOUIS, physician; b. Dayton, Ohio, May 10, 1925; s. Hugh Holland and Ruth Louise (Thiele) H.; m. Nancy Adele Fahrendorf, June 14, 1947; children: Thomas C., Mary Lynne Hoffman Lamb, Lori Hoffman Brustkean, William Edward. Student, U. Dayton, 1943; AB, Oberlin Coll., 1945; MD, St. Louis U., 1949. Med. intern U.S. Marine Hosp., Balt., 1949-50; chief op. dept. U.S. Marine Hosp., Kirkwood, Mo., 1950-51; chief med. officer 2nd Coast Guard Dist., St. Louis, 1951; resident internal medicine U.S. Marine Hosp., San Francisco, 1951-53, chief resident internal medicine, 1953-54, asst. chief internal medicine, 1954-55; pvt. practice internal medicine Marin County, Calif., 1955—; cons. internal medicine and pulmonology Neumiller Hosp., Tamal, Calif., 1957-83; active staff Marin Gen. Hosp., 1955—; chief of med. staff Ross (Calif.) Gen. Hosp., 1969; exec. com. Ross Gen. Hosp., 1968-71, 82-88. Lt. comdr. USPHS, 1948-55. Named Man of the Yr. in the Healing Arts, BPOE, San Rafael, Calif., 1976. Fellow AMA, Calif. Med. Assn.; mem. Calif. Soc. Intern. Med. (bd. dirs. 1976-79) Marin Med. Soc. (pres., 1975-76, bd. dirs. 1966-69, 74-77, 88—), Calif. Acad. of Med., Serra Club of Marin (pres. 1961), Richardson Bay Yacht Club, BPOE, Gen. Soc. Mayflower Descendants, Calif. Soc. Mayflower Descendants. Republican. Roman Catholic. Home: 48 Junipero Serra San Rafael CA 94901 Office: 599 S F Drake Blvd Greenbrier CA 94901

HOFFMAN, CLAUD MILTON, engineer, land surveyor; b. El Dorado Springs, Mo., Oct. 24, 1931; s. George Lawrence and Bernice Loree (Downs) H.; m. Nola May LaGrange, May 17, 1957; children: Claudia Lynn, Anthony Paul. AS in Engring., Surveying, Healds Coll., 1958; and, Alaska U., 1960-65. Registered profl. land surveyor, Alaska, Ariz., Calif., Idaho, Md., Mo., Mont., Nev., N.Mex., Oreg., Utah, Wash. Cadastral survey asst. Bur. Land Mgmt., Denver, 1953-55; survey asst. Bur. Land Mgmt., Juneau, Alaska, 1955-57; jr. cadastral surveyor Bur. Land Mgmt., Juneau, Anchorage, Alaska, 1959-60; sr. land surveyor dept. resources State of Alaska, 1960-62, state land survey supr., 1962-65, chief cadastral engr., 1965-78, dir. div. tech. svcs., 1979-81; land survey cons. C.M. Hoffman & Assocs., Anchorage, 1981—; mem. gov map adv. bd., Alaska. Contbr. numerous tech. pubs. and presentations. Mem. Am. Congress on Surveying and Mapping (past chmn.), Alaska Soc. Profl. Land Surveyors (past pres.), Am. Assn. State Surveyors. Republican. Home: PO Box 153 Ramona CA 92065 Office: CM Hoffman & Assocs 601 E Northern Lights Box 216 Anchorage AK 99503

HOFFMAN, DONALD CLINTON, physicist, researcher; b. San Francisco, June 23, 1948; s. William Walter and Myrah Ione (Johnston) H.; m. Carole Ann Reynheer, Oct. 9, 1971 (div. Oct. 1975); m. Nancy Ann Nowicki, Sept. 21 1985. BS in Physics, U. Hawaii, 1980, MS in Physics, 1983, PhD in Physics, 1985. Enlisted man USN, 1967-78, ret., 1978; rsch. asst. U. Hawaii, Honolulu, 1980-85; scientist Lockheed Co., Sunnyvale, Calif., 1985—. Mem. Am. Phys. Soc., Mensa. Republican. Office: Lockheed Co Orn 59-51 1111 Lockheed Way Sunnyvale CA 94088-3504

HOFFMAN, FRANK LLOYD, data processing executive; b. Aberdeen, Wash., July 11, 1956; s. Joseph and Grace Naomi (Wright) H. ATA in Electronic Tech., Centralia Coll., 1977. Cert. gen. radio/telephone FCC. Technician communications Cascade Loggers Supply, Chehalis, Wash., 1978-79; engr. computer Richmar Corp., Chehalis, 1979-82; technician, engr. software Pacific Sci., Chehalis, 1979-81; asst. technician communications Pacific Power and Light, Portland, Oreg., 1982-83; engr. computer Lloyd I/O Inc., Portland, 1983—; cons. computer software Gaard Automation, Portland, 1983-84, TEC Am. Inc., Torrance, Calif., 1984-85, Edge Tech., Portland, 1987—. Author: (software user manuals) K-Basic, CRASMB, CRACKER, ED, PATCH, Search and Rescue, 1981—; contbr. articles profl. jours. Precinct person Multnomah County Cen. Republican Com., Portland, 1986—. Mem. Independant Computer Cons. Assn., Oreg. Computer Cons. Assn., Portland C. of C., Chehalis Valley Amateur Radio Soc. (co-founder 1978-82). Office: Lloyd I/O Inc PO Box 30945 Portland OR 97230

HOFFMAN, GEORGE ALAN, consulting company executive; b. Albany, N.Y., May 16, 1937; s. Irving Marshall and Margaret (Coyne) H.; m. Kim Thi Nguyen, Oct. 10, 1971; children: Caroline, Christine. AB, U. Calif., Berkeley, 1980, MBA, 1982. Mgmt. analyst Am. Can Co., N.Y.C., 1966-69; cons. Vietnamese Air Force, Bien Hoa, Vietnam, 1970-74, Puslitbang, Jakarta, Indonesia, 1974-75; pres. Titan Systems, Berkeley, 1980—. Author: Indonesian Production-sharing Oil Contracts, 1982. Mem. Mensa. Club: Commonwealth (San Francisco). Office: Titan Systems 1617 6th St Berkeley CA 94710

HOFFMAN, JAY RUSSELL, mortgage investment company executive, accountant; b. Detroit, May 9, 1954; s. Joseph Howard and Gail (Klein) H.; m. Cathy Kay Heames, June 13, 1981; 1 child, Jackie. BBA, U. Mo., Kansas City, 1976. CPA, Ariz. Audit mgr. Arthur Andersen & Co., Phoenix, 1976-87, Kenneth Leventhal & Co., Phoenix, 1987-88; v.p., treas. Emerald Mortgage Investments Corp., Phoenix, 1988—. Mem. AICPA, Ariz. Soc. CPA's, Nat. Assn. Accts., Phoenix C. of C. Republican. Home: 721 E Forest Hills Dr Phoenix AZ 85022 Office: Emerald Mortgage Investment 5333 N 7th St Phoenix AZ 85014

HOFFMAN, LOU DUANE, city official; b. Albuquerque, Dec. 7, 1946; s. Louis Otto and Virginia Hunt (Mathews) H.; m. Marcia Jean Crotty, Sept. 2, 1972; children: Leslie Erin, Natalie Marie. BSME, U. N.Mex., 1968, MBA, 1977. Registered profl. engr., N.Mex. Sales engr. Pub. Svc. Co. N.Mex., Albuquerque, 1968-72; dir. mktg. research Pub. Svc. Co. N.Mex., 1972-76, supr. mktg. and econ. rsch., 1976-77, sr. advanced planner, 1977-79; sr. policy officer Four Corners Regional Commn., Albuquerque, 1979-81; dir. regulatory ops. Nev. Pub. Svc. Commn., Carson City, 1981-82; cons. Albuquerque, 1982-83; asst. sec. N.Mex. Dept. Econ. Devel., Santa Fe, 1983; rate specialist, then ops. rsch. mgr. City of Albuquerque, 1983-87, treas., 1987—; v.p. Rio Grande Trading Co., Inc., Albuquerque, 1983—, bd. dirs.; testifier com. on sci. and tech. U.S. Ho. of Reps., 1980. Contbr. numerous articles to trade mags. Bd. dirs. Amigos Ams., Albuquerque, 1972; bd. govs. Albuquerque YMCA, 1988--. Mem. Govt. Fin. Officers Assn. Republican. Methodist. Home: 3804 Glen Canyon Rd NE Albuquerque NM 87111 Office: City of Albuquerque PO Box 1293 Albuquerque NM 87103

HOFFMAN, MILTON BERNARD, television executive; b. Mineola, N.Y., Apr. 20, 1946; s. Sol Walter and Dorothy (Sokolowsky) H.; m. Stephanie Elan Cherry, Nov. 4, 1983. BS, Columbia U., 1969. Dir. drama and lit. Sta. WBAI-FM, N.Y.C., 1970-72; producer, dir. Sta. WNET-TV, N.Y.C., 1972-76; exec. producer Sta. WVIZ-TV, Cleve., 1978-81; v.p. prodn. Pacific Mountain Network, Denver, 1981-86; pres., exec. producer Milton B. Hoffman Prodns. (formerly TVI Prodns.), Denver, 1986—; judge Columbia Univ. Film Festival, N.Y.C., 1974; prodn. cons. NPO Task Force, N.Y.C., 1976-78. Producer: (marathon radio reading) War and Peace, 1970 (selected for Mus. Broadcasting collection), (home video) Perestroika Papers, 1988, The Profl. Server, 1988, (radio series) Not Without Art: Arts and the Handicapped, 1976, (cable TV series) American Viewpoints, 1984-86 (Ace award 1987); producer, dir.: (TV spls.) Lucy and the First Family, 1981, Legends of Laughter: Dick Cavett Remembers Groucho Marx and Jack Benny, 1987, National Town Meeting: How is Our Democracy Doing?, 1989. Recipient Silver Anvil award Pub. Relations Soc. Am., 1976, Spl. Ace award Nat. Acad. Cable Programming, 1985. Mem. Nat. Acad. TV Arts and Scis. (judge Cleve. chpt. 1980, Denver chpt. 1987, Emmy award 1981), Solstice Arts Found. (founder 1975). Office: Milton B Hoffman Prodns 368 S High St Denver CO 80209

HOFFMAN, PAUL RUSSELL, data processing executive; b. Hackensack, N.J., Nov. 28, 1950; s. Albert and Joan Constance (Harris) H.; m. Karen Grace Foley, Aug. 12, 1972; children: Kristin Joan, Sean Paul, Benjamin Harris. Student, Wagner Coll., N.Y.C., 1968-71. Technician AT&T, East Rutherford, N.J., 1971-72; sta. installer, Walnut Creek, Calif. AT&T, 1972-80, PBX installer, repairman, 1980-84, software technician, Concord, Calif., 1984-87, with computer tech. support dept., San Ramon, Calif., 1987-88, svc. mgr. computer tech. support, 1988-89, tech. support orgn. regional staff, svcs. mgr., Plesanton, Calif., 1989—. Home: 309 Goshen Ct San Ramon CA 94583 Office: AT&T Ctr at Pleasanton 4450 Rosewood Dr Ste 5216 Pleasanton CA 94566

HOFFMAN, RAY LINCOLN, grain market analyst; b. Hershey, Pa., Feb. 12, 1945; s. Raymond Charles and Hazel Marie (Dingledine) H.; m. Mary Helen Burke, June 24, 1972; 1 child, Thomas Ray. BS, Coll. of Great Falls (Mont.), 1972. Mem. sales and warehouse staff Nat. Porcelain Co., Great Falls, 1972-74; sales rep. Western Ranch Supply Co., Great Falls, 1974-76; traffic mgr. NFO Co., Great Falls, 1976-84; grain market analyst Cims, Great Falls, 1984—, sec., asst. treas., 1984—. Republican. Mem. United Ch. of Christ. Home: 628 33d Ave NE Great Falls MT 59404 Office: Cims 1923 10th Ave S Great Falls MT 59405

HOFFMAN, REBECCA ANN, telephone company manager; b. Moline, Ill., May 16, 1952; d. Alvin Joseph and Geraldine May (Defrates) H. AAS, Blackhawk Jr. Coll., East Moline, Ill., 1972. Programmer Royal Neighbors of 'Am., Rock Island, Ill., 1974-79; programmer, analyst Centel, Las Vegas, Nev., 1979-82, project leader, 1982-84, programming mgr., 1984—. Mem. Data Processing Mgmt. Assn. Office: Centel 330 S Valley View Las Vegas NV 89152

HOFFMAN, RICHARD MARVIN, distributing company executive; b. Mpls., Mar. 23, 1924; s. Phillip and Bess (Shedlov) H.; married; children: Cynthia J. Coleman, Thomas J., Peter B. BSME, U. Minn., 1948. Pres. R.M. Hoffman Co., Sunnyvale, Calif.; 1959--. 1st lt. U.S. Army Air Corps, 1942-46, Germany. Democrat. Jewish. Office: RM Hoffman Co 159 San Lazaro Ave Sunnyvale CA 94086

HOFFMAN, ROGER JOHN, interior designer, space planner; b. Watsonville, Calif., June 28, 1949; s. Raymon and Helen Marie (Bradley) H.; m. Nancy Jane Lee, Oct. 28, 1972 (div. Oct. 1983); 1 child, Eric Michael; m. SuAnne Black, Mar. 16, 1984; children: Erin Francis, Leah. BA, Calif. Coll. Arts and Crafts, 1972. Cert. Nat. Coun. Interior Design Qualification. Designer Hoffman Interior Designers, Watsonville, 1972-78; prin., owner Hoffman & Assocs., Watsonville, 1979--; instr. Cabrillo Coll. Aptos, Calif., 1975-80. Mem. Am. Soc. Interior Designers (treas. 1976-78, bd. dirs. 1976-79), AIA (profl. affiliate). Home: 62 Roosevelt St Watsonville CA 95077 Office: PO Box 776 Watsonville CA 95077

HOFFMAN, ROLLAND EDWARD, social services administrator; b. South Bend, Ind., Jan. 20, 1931; s. Edward William and Elsie Martha (Schultz) H.; m. Marilyn Jo McCure, Apr. 22, 1960; children: Chriss, Pamela. BS in Speech, Northwestern U., 1954, postgrad., 1954. Prodn. worker Studebaker Corp., South Bend, Ind., 1949-50; assoc. producer Mr. Wizard Show, Sta. WNBQ, Chgo., 1952-54; announcer, writer, producer WKZO Radio and TV, Kalamazoo, Mich., 1954; dir. employee and pub. relations Ball-Band Plant, U.S. Rubber Co., Mishawaka, Ind., 1956-58; assoc. exec. dir. campaign United Fund St. Joseph County Inc., South Bend, Ind., 1958-62; assoc. exec. dir. campaign and adminstrn. United Fund and Community Services Tarrant County Inc., Ft. Worth, 1962-65, exec. dir., 1965-70; pres., chief exec. officer Mile High United Way, Denver, 1970-89; prin. Found. Group, 1989—; chmn. bd. adv. com. Mut. Am., N.Y.C., 1976—; vice chmn. nat. profl. adv. com. United Way Am. Active Nat. Com. for Adoption, Washington, 1980—; trustee pres.'s leadership class U. Colo., 1985—. Sgt. AUS, 1954-56. Lodge: Rotary. Office: 384 Inverness Dr S Ste 207 Englewood CO 80211

HOFFMAN, SHARON LYNN, research center official, consultant; b. Allentown, Pa., Dec. 20, 1955; d. Harry Lawrence and Madoline (Shaner) H. BS, Pa. State U., 1978; MS, Carnegie Mellon U., 1981. Environ. educator U.S. Fish and Wildlife Service, Audubon Soc. R.I., Matonuck, summer 1978; sr. research technologist Pa. State U., University Park, 1978-79; program analyst Solar Energy Research Inst., Golden, Colo., summer 1980; research intern East West Ctr., Honolulu, 1981-82, project fellow, 1982--; research fellow Harvard U., Cambridge, Mass., summer 1983; cons. Pacific Resources, Inc., Honolulu, 1982, Saudi Arabia Ministry Planning, 1984, Temple, Barker & Sloane, Lexington, Mass., 1985, Pacific Basin Devel. Council, Honolulu, 1986-87. Author: (monograph) World Production of Synthetic Fuels, 1983, Deregulating Australia, 1987, numerous profl. papers and reports. Vol. Hawaiian Soc. for Prevention Cruelty to Animals. Mem. Internat. Assn. Energy Economists. Unitarian. Home: 4526 Aukai Ave Honolulu HI 96816 Office: East West Ctr 1777 East West Rd Honolulu HI 96848

HOFFMAN, WALTER WILLIAM, investment company executive; b. Oxnard, Calif., Aug. 17, 1922; s. Walter Henry Jr. and Edith May (Hobson) H.; m. Sheila Louise Bergin, Oct. 25, 1945; children: Katherine Hoffman Russell, Carol Hoffman Hambleton. Student, U. So. Calif., 1941-44. Asst. mgr. Casitas Ranch Co., Ventura, Calif., 1946-55, mgr., 1955—; ptnr. Hoffman, Vance and Worthington, Ventura, 1956—; bd. dirs. Bank of A. Levy, Oxnard, Automobile Club of So. Calif., Los Angeles, Ventura County Lemon Coop., St. John's Sem. Coll., Camarillo, Calif. Trustee Livingston Meml. Found., Oxnard, 1973—; bd. dirs. Ventura County Taxpayers Assn., 1950—. Served to lt. USNR, 1941-46, PTO. Decorated Knight Comdr. Order of St. Gregory, Pope John XXIII, Rome, 1960. Mem. Am. Soc. Farm Mgrs. and Rural Appraisers, Am. Right of Way Assn. (sr. mem.), U.S. Naval Acad. (Fales com. 1976—). Republican. Roman Catholic. Clubs: Calif. (Los Angeles); Newport Harbor Yacht; Cruising Am. (N.Y.C.) (dir. 1980-84), Transpacific Yacht (dir. 1976-84); St. Francis Yacht (San Francisco); Ventura Yacht. Office: Hoffman Vance Worthington 1000 Seaward Ave Ventura CA 93001

HOFFMAN, WARREN EUGENE, II, management specialist; b. Buffalo, N.Y., Apr. 5, 1954; s. Warren Eugene and Jeanne (Torrisi) H. BS in Bus. with honors, Ind. U., 1976. Restaurant mgr. Azar's Inc., Ft. Wayne, Ind., 1971-77; indsl. relations mgr. The Wickes Cos., San Diego, Calif., 1977-81; personnel dir. Dixieline Lumber Co., San Diego, 1981—. Actor, Civic Theater Stage Prodns.; dist. com., Boy Scouts Am. Named to Outstanding Young Men in Am., Jaycees, 1983. Mem. Indsl. Rel. Rsch. Assn. of San Diego, The Personnel Mgmt. Assn. of San Diego, The Lumberman's Fraternity of San Diego/Internat. (bd. dirs., club. pres., regional officer), Nico Ins. Svcs. Adv. Bd. (adv. bd. Silvergate thrift and loan com.), Greater San Diego Sports Assn., San Diego C. of C. Spkrs. Bur., San Diego Lumbermans Assn. (labor negotiations com. 1981—), Theta Chi (nat. bd. dirs., regional officer, pres. San Diego area), Alumni Assn. Ind. U. and others. Home: 2741 Bay Canyon Ct San Diego CA 92117 Office: Dixieline Lumber Co 3250 Sports Arena Blvd San Diego CA 92110

HOFFMAN, WAYNE MELVIN, retired airline official; b. Chgo., Mar. 9, 1923; s. Carl A. and Martha (Tamillo) H.; m. Laura Majewski, Jan. 26, 1946; children—Philip, Karen, Kristin. B.A. summa cum laude, U. Ill., 1943, J.D. with high honors, 1947. Bar: Ill. bar 1947, N.Y. bar 1958. Atty. I.C. R.R., 1948-52; with N.Y.C. R.R. Co., 1952-67, exec. asst. to pres., 1958-60, v.p. freight sales, 1960-61, v.p. sales, 1961-62, exec. v.p., 1962-67; chmn. bd. N.Y. Central Trans. Co., 1960-67, Flying Tiger Line, Inc. and Tiger Internat., Inc., 1967-85; trustee Aerospace Corp., 1975-86; dir. Rohr Industries; dir. Kaufman & Broad, Inc. Served to capt. inf. AUS, World War II. Decorated Silver Star, Purple Heart with oak leaf cluster. Mem. Am. Bar Assn., Phi Beta Kappa. Clubs: Calif., Bel Air Country (Los Angeles), Bohemian (San Francisco). Home: 74-435 Palo Verde Dr Indian Wells CA 92210 Office: 970 Los Vallecitos Blvd Ste 224 San Marcos CA 92069

HOFFMAN, WILLIAM CARROLL, JR., air force officer; b. Lynch, Ky., Aug. 25, 1943; s. William Carroll and Elsie Marie (Bosch) H.; m. Erika E. Kungl, June 6, 1970; children: Michelle M., Wendy A., Michael J. BGS in Econs., U. Nebr., 1975; BS in Personnel Mgmt., U. Md., 1978; MA in Procurement Mgmt., Webster U., 1983; BS Computer Sci. (hon.), Colo. Tech Coll., 1984; MA in Space System Mgmt., Webster U., 1988. Cert. vocat. instr., Colo. E-3 and aerospace technician USAF, 1962-66, E-6 and aerospace technician, 1971-80, commd. 2d lt., 1980, advance through grades to capt., 1984; officer Hdqrs. Space Command, Colorado Springs, 1980-89; chief communications br. Systems Integration Office Hdqrs. Space Command, 1988—; dir. Space & Tech. Inst., Colorado Springs, 1988—; plant layout and mech. draftsman Gen. Tire & Rubber Co., Akron, 1967-68; mktg. tech. rep. and field rep. Honeywell Inc., Akron, 1968-70; grad. prof. Webster U., Colorado Springs, 1983—. Author: Resource Manager's Guide, 1978, Electronic Data Access System Software. Cons. El Paso County Commrs., 1983-84; mem. Inf. Mgmt. Coun. Colo., 1983, Space & Tech. Inst. State Colo., 1988—. Mem. Nat. Space Soc., Armed Forces Communications and Electronics Assn., Air Force Assn., So. Colo. Data Processing Mgmt. Assn. (pres. 1982-83), Planetary Soc., Nat. Geog. Soc. Republican. Methodist. Office: Space & Tech Inst 1670 N Newport Rd #300-H Colorado Springs CO 80916

HOFFMANN, GEORGE L., surgeon, medical administrator; b. Pitts., May 15, 1926; s. George L. and Dorothy (Hurlock) H.; m. Jewel Hunt; children—Kathryn Lee, Jon Hunt. A.B., Haverford Coll., 1949; M.D., Yale U., 1953. Diplomate Am. Bd. Surgery. Resident in surgery Phila. Gen. Hosp. and Cleve. Clinic, 1954-58; practice medicine specializing in surgery, Mesa, Ariz., 1958—; pres. Surg. Inst. of Mesa, 1958—. Served to 2d lt. U.S. Army, 1944-46. Fellow ACS (bd. regents 1975-84, exec. com. 1982-84); mem. AMA, Ariz. Med. Assn., Maricopa County Med. Assn. (pres. 1981). Episcopalian. Office: 438 W 5th Pl Mesa AZ 85201

HOFFMANN, JON ARNOLD, aeronautical engineer, educator; b. Wausau, Wis., Jan. 13, 1942; s. Arnold D. and Rita J. (Haas) H.; m. Carol R. Frye. BSME, U. Wis., 1964, MSME, 1966. Register profl. engr., Calif. Research engr. Trane Co., 1966-68; prof. aeronautical engring. Calif. Poly. State U., San Luis Obispo, 1968—; research engr. Stanford U. NSF Program, 1970; research fellow Ames Research Ctr. Ctr. NASA/ASEE, 1974-75; tech. cons. NASA/AMES Research Ctr., 1977; design engr. Cal/ Poly ERDA contract, 1976-77; prin. investigator NASA-ARC Cooperative Agreement, 1983. Contbr. articles to profl. jours. Grantee NASA, NSF. Mem. ASME. Home: 960 Buck Ridge Ln Arroyo Grande CA 93420 Office: Calif Poly State U Dept Aero Engring San Luis Obispo CA 93407

HOFFORD, MEREDITH, justice program administrator, consultant; b. Portsmouth, Va., May 28, 1952; d. John Labeé and Grace Helen (George) H.; m. Thomas R. Hood, May 10, 1978 (div.). BA, Clemson U., 1974; MA, George Washington U., 1976. Program dir. County Substance Abuse Commn., Charleston, S.C., 1976-78, Trident United Way, Charleston, 1978-80; exec. dir. Juvenile Restitution Project, Inc., Charleston, 1980-84; mgr., tech. asst. Nat. Coun. Juvenile and Family Ct. Judges, Reno, 1984-87, dir. family violence project, 1987—; cons. S.C. Dept. Youth Svcs., 1982-84, Nat. Restitution, Edn., Specialized Tng. and Tech. Assistance Project, Walnut Creek, Calif., 1985-88, Juvenile Ct., Las Vegas and Minden, Nev., 1986-87, 15th Jud. Cir. Ct., Montgomery, Ala., 1987. Co-author: Restitution: a Guidebook, 1983; contbr. articles to publs. Adv. bd. United Way of No. Nev., 1986-87. Fellow Nat. Inst. Drug Abuse, Washington, 1974-76; honoree YWCA-TWIN, Charleston, S.C., 1983; selected participant Leadership, S.C., 1983-84; grantee U.S. Dept. Justice, 1979-88. Mem. Nat. Restitution Assn. (exec. steering com. 1987-88), Am. Probation and Parole Assn., Women and Founds.-Corp. Philanthropy, Ct. Appointed Spl. Advs., Jr. League Reno (various coms. 1986-88), Trident C. of C. (com. mem. 1981-84), Sierra Club. Office: Nat Coun Juvenile and Family Ct Judges PO Box 8970 Reno NV 89507

HOFINGA, TYLER HANS, marketing professional; b. Pensacola, Fla., Dec. 14, 1957; s. Peter Hans Hofinga and Shirley Philippine (Salch) Dixon; m. Elizabeth Jane Montgomery, June 27, 1987. BA, U. Calif., Berkeley, 1981. Ops. officer Bank of Am., Laguna Beach, Calif., 1978, Berkeley, Calif., 1978-81; mktg. rep. IBM Corp., San Francisco, 1981-83; internat. account mgr. IBM Corp., 1984-85; market support adminstr. IBM Corp., White Plains, N.Y., 1985-87; market devel. mgr. IBM Corp., L.A., 1987-88, regional mktg. mgr., 1988—. Assoc. cabinet mem. Music Ctr. L.A., 1988-89; v.p. In The Wings, L.A., 1988-89; team capt. United Way, L.A., 1988; big brother Big Bros. Am., San Francisco, 1984; mem. L.A. County Mus. Art, 1988-89, L.A. Mus. Contemporary Art, 1988-89. Alumni scholar U. Calif., Berkeley, 1981. Mem. U. Calif. Alumni Club (v.p. west L.A. chpt. 1988-89). Republican. Presbyterian. Home: 1131 Alta Loma Rd 521 Los Angeles CA 90069 Office: IBM Corp 355 S Grand Ave Los Angeles CA 90071

HOFMANN, ALAN FREDERICK, biomedical educator, researcher; b. Balt., May 17, 1931; s. Joseph Enoch and Nelda Rosina (Durr) H.; m. Martha Gertrude Pettersson, Aug. 15, 1969 (div. 1976); children: Anthea Karin, Cecilia Rae. BA with honors, Johns Hopkins U., 1951, MD with honors, 1955; PhD, U. Lund, Sweden, 1965; MD honoris causis, U. Bologna, Italy, 1988. Intern, then resident dept. medicine Columbia Presbyn. Med. Ctr., N.Y.C., 1955-57; clin. assoc. clin. ctr. Nat. Heart Inst., NIH, Bethesda, Md., 1957-59; asst. physician Hosp. of the Rockefeller U., N.Y.C., 1962-64; outpatient physician N.Y. Hosp., N.Y.C., 1963-64; assoc. physician Hosp. of the Rockefeller U., N.Y.C., 1964-66; cons. in medicine, assoc. dir. gastroenterology unit Mayo Clinic, Rochester, Minn., 1966-77; attending physician U. Calif.-San Diego Med. Ctr., 1977—; cons., lectr. Naval Regional Med. Ctr., San Diego, 1980—; asst. prof. dept. medicine Rockefeller U., N.Y.C., 1964-66; assoc. prof. medicine and biochemistry U. Minn. Mayo Grad. Sch., 1966-69, assoc. prof. medicine and physiology, 1969-70, prof. medicine and physiology, 1970-73; prof. medicine and physiology Mayo Med. Sch., 1973-77; cons. physiology Mayo Clinic, Rochester, 1975-77; prof. medicine U. Calif., San Diego, 1977—, adj. prof. pharmacy, U. Calif., San Francisco, 1986—; vis. prof. pharmacy U. Mich., Ann Arbor, 1980-85. Patentee solvent for direct dissolution of cholesterol gallstones, breath test for pancreatic exocrine function; contbr. numerous articles to profl. jours., books, films. USPHS fellow, 1962-63, Fogarty Internat. Sr. fellow NIH, 1985; recipient Travel award Wellcome Trust, 1961-63, Travel award NSF, 1964, Sr. Scientist award Humboldt Found., Fed. Republic of Germany, 1976, (shared prize) Eppinger Prize, Herbert Falk Co., 1976, Disting. Achievement award Modern Medicine mag., 1978 Chancellor's Rsch. Excellence award U. Calif., 1986; Rockefeller Found. scholar, Bellagio, Italy, 1980. Fellow AAAS; mem. Am. Assn. Study of Liver Disease (numerous coms.), Swedish Soc. for Gastroenterology (hon.), Soc. Gastronintestinal Radiology (hon.), Gastroenterological Soc. Australia (hon.), Chilean Soc. Gastroenterology (hon.), Peruvian Soc. Gastroenterology (hon.), Brit. Soc. Gastroenterology (hon.), Royal Flemish Acad. for Medicine Belgium (hon., fgn. corr. mem.), Am. Soc. for Clin. Investigation, Am. Assn. Physicians, Am. Liver Found. (chmn sci. adv. bd. 1986—), Am. Physiol. Soc., Am. Gastroenterological Assn. (Disting. Achievement award 1970, Beaumont prize (shared) 1979), Phi Beta Kappa, Ominon Delta Kappa. Home: 5870 Cactus Way La Jolla CA 92037 Office: U Calif Dept Medicine T-013 La Jolla CA 92093

HOFMANN, PAUL BERNARD, healthcare executive; b. Portland, Oreg., July 6, 1941; s. Max and Consuelo Theresa (Bley) H.; m. Lois Bernstein, June 28, 1969; children: Julie, Jason. B.S., U. Calif., Berkeley, 1963, M.P.H., 1965. Research assoc. in hosp. adminstrn. Lab. of Computer Sci., Mass. Gen. Hosp., Boston, 1966-68; asst. dir. Lab. of Computer Sci., Mass. Gen. Hosp., 1968-69; asst. adminstr. San Antonio Community Hosp., Upland, Calif., 1969-70; assoc. adminstr. San Antonio Community Hosp., 1970-72; dep. dir. Stanford (Calif.) U. Hosp., 1972-74, dir., 1974-77; exec. dir. Emory U. Hosp., Atlanta, 1978-87; exec. v.p., chief ops. officer Alta Bates Corp., Emeryville, Calif., 1987—; instr. computer applications Harvard U., 1968-69; lectr. hosp. adminstrn. UCLA, 1970-72, Stanford U. Med. Sch., 1972-77; assoc. prof. Emory U. Sch. Medicine, Atlanta, 1978-87. Contbr. articles to profl. jours. Served with U.S. Army, 1959. Fellow Am. Coll. Hosp. Adminstrs. (recipient Robert S. Hudgens meml. award 1976); mem. Am. Hosp. Assn., Assn. Univ. Programs in Health Adminstrn., U. Calif. Alumni Assn.

HOFSTADTER, ROBERT, physicist, educator; b. N.Y.C., Feb. 5, 1915; s. Louis and Henrietta (Koenigsberg) H.; m. Nancy Givan, May 9, 1942; children: Douglas Richard, Laura James, Mary Hinda. B.S. magna cum laude (Kenyon prize), Coll. City N.Y., 1935; M.A. (Procter fellow), Princeton U., 1938, Ph.D., 1938; LL.D., City U. N.Y., 1961; D.Sc., Gustavus Adolphus Coll., 1963; Laureate Honoris Causa, U. Padua, 1965; D.Sc. (hon.), Carleton U., Ottawa, Can., 1967, Seoul Nat. U., 1967; Honoris Causa, U. Clermont-Ferrand, 1967; D. Rerum Naturalium honoris causa, Julius Maximilians U., Würzburg, Fed. Republic Germany, 1982, Johannes Gutenberg U. Mainz, Fed. Republic Germany, 1983; D.Sc. (hon.), Israel Inst. Tech., 1985. Coffin fellow Gen. Electric Co., 1935-36; Harrison fellow U. Pa., 1939; instr. physics Princeton U., 1940-41, CCNY, 1941-42; physicist Norden Lab. Corp., 1943-46; asst. prof. physics Princeton U., 1946-50; assoc. prof. physics Stanford U., 1950-54, prof., 1954-85, Max H. Stein prof. physics, 1971-85, prof. emeritus, 1985—, dir. high energy physics lab., 1967-74; dir. John Fluke Mfg. Co., 1979-88. Author: (with Robert Herman) High-Energy Electron Scattering Tables, 1960; editor: Investigations in Physics, 1958-65, Electron Scattering and Nucleon Structure, 1963; co-editor: Nucleon Structure, 1964; assoc. editor: Phys. Review, 1951-53; mem. editorial bd.: Review Sci. Instruments, 1953-55, Reviews of Modern Physics, 1958-61. Bd. govs. Technion, Israel Inst. Tech., Weizmann Inst. Sci. Calif. Scientist of Year, 1959; co-recipient of Nobel prize in physics, 1961; Townsend Harris medal Coll. City N.Y., 1961; Guggenheim fellow Geneva, Switzerland, 1958-59; Ford Found. fellow; recipient Röntgen medal, Wurzburg, Germany, 1985, U.S. Nat. Medal Sci., 1986, Prize of Cultural Found. of Fiuggi, Italy, 1986. Fellow Am. Phys. Soc., Phys. Soc. London; mem. Nat. Acad. Scis., Am. Acad. Arts and Scis., AAUP, Phi Beta Kappa, Sigma Xi. Home: 639 Mirada Ave Stanford CA 94305 Office: Stanford U Dept Physics Stanford CA 94305

HOGAN, CLARENCE LESTER, retired electronics executive; b. Great Falls, Mont., Feb. 8, 1920; s. Clarence Lester and Bessie (Young) H.; m. Audrey Biery Peters, Oct. 13, 1946; 1 child, Cheryl Lea. BSChemE, Mont. State U., 1942, Dr. Engring. (hon.), 1967; MS in Physics, Lehigh U., 1947, PhD in Physics, 1950, D in Engring. (hon.), 1971; AM (hon.), Harvard U., 1954; D in Sci. (hon.), Worcester Poly. U., 1969. Research chem. engr. Anaconda Copper Mining Co., 1942-43; instr. physics Lehigh U., 1946-50; mem. tech. staff Bell Labs., Murray Hill, N.J., 1950-51, sub dept. head, 1951-53; assoc. prof. Harvard U., Cambridge, Mass., 1953-57, Gordon McKay prof., 1957-58; gen. mgr. semi-conductor products div. Motorola, Inc., Phoenix, 1958-60, v.p., 1960-66, exec. v.p., dir., 1966-68; pres., chief exec. officer Fairchild Inst., Mt. View, Calif., 1968-74, vice chmn. of bd. dirs., 1974-85; bd. dirs. Timeplex, Inc., Woodcliff Lake, N.J., Varian Assocs., Palo Alto, Calif., TAB Products, Palo Alto, Calif. Microdevices; gen. chmn. Internat. Conf. on Magnetism and Magnetic Materials, 1959, 60; mem. materials adv. bd. Dept. Def., 1957-59; mem. adv. council dept. electrical engring. Princeton U.; mem. adv. bd. sch. engring. U. Calif., Berkeley, 1974—, adv. bd. Dept. Chem. Engring., Montana State U., 1988—; mem. nat. adv. bd. Desert Research Inst., 1976-80; mem. vis. com. dept. electric engring. and computer sci. MIT, 1975-85; mem. adv. council div. electrical engring. Stanford U., 1976-86; mem. scientific and ednl. adv. com. Lawrence Berkeley Lab., 1978-84; mem. Pres.'s Export Council, 1976-80; mem. adv. panel to tech. adv. bd. U.S. Congress, 1976-80. Patentee in field. Chmn. Commn. Found. Santa Clara County, Calif., 1983-85; mem. vis. com. Lehigh U., 1966-71, trustee, 1971-80; trustee Western Electronic Edn. Fund; mem. governing bd. Maricopa County Jr. Coll.; bd. regents U. Santa Clara. Served to lt. (j.g.) USNR, 1942-46. Recipient Community Service award NCCJ, 1978, Medal of Merit Am. Electronics Assn., 1978, Berkeley Citation U. Calif., 1980; named Bay Area Bus. Man of Yr. San Jose State U., 1978, One of 10 Greatest Innovators in Past 50 Yrs. Electronics Mag., 1980. Fellow IEEE (Frederick Philips Gold medal 1976, Edison Silver medal Cleve. Soc., 1978), AAAS, Inst. Electrical Engrs. (hon.); mem. Am. Phys. Soc., Nat. Acad. Engring., Sigma Xi, Tau Beta Pi, Phi Kappa Phi, Kappa Sigma. Democrat. Baptist. Club: Menlo Country (Redwood City, Calif.). Lodge: Masons. Home: 36 Barry Ln Atherton CA 94025

HOGAN, CURTIS JULE, union executive, industrial relation consultant; b. Greeley, Kans., July 25, 1926; s. Charles Leo and Anna Malene (Rousselo) H.; m. Lois Jean Ecord, Apr. 23, 1955; children—Christopher James, Michael Sean, Patrick Marshall, Kathleen Marie, Kerry Joseph. B.S. in Indsl. Relations, Rockhurst Coll., 1950; postgrad., Georgetown U., 1955, U. Tehran, 1955-57. With Gt. Lakes Pipeline Co., Kansas City, 1950-55; with Internat. Fedn. Petroleum and Chem. Workers, Denver, 1955-85; gen. sec. Internat. Fedn. Petroleum and Chem. Workers, 1973-85; pres. Internat. Labor Relations Services, Inc., 1976—; cons. in field; lectr. Rockhurst Coll., 1951-52. Contbr. in field. Served with U.S. Army, 1945-46. Mem. Internat. Indsl. Relations Assn., Indsl. Relations Research Assn., Oil Chem. and Atomic Workers Internat. Union. Office: PO Box 6565 Denver CO 80206

HOGAN, JAMES LAWRENCE, physician; b. Rochester, Pa., Oct. 11, 1942; s. James L. Jr. and Kathleen T. (Logue) H.; m. Cheryl Ann Irons, Apr. 15, 1967; children: Brian D., Stacey L. BS in Math., U. Pitts., 1964, MD, 1969. Diplomate Am. Bd. Emergency Medicine. Intern Maine Med. Ctr., Portland, 1969-70, resident, 1973-74; physician St. Anthony Hosp., Westminster, Colo. Served to major U.S. Army, 1970-73, 75-76. Home: 459 Golden Ln Longmont CO 80501 Office: St Anthony Hosp 2551 W 84th Ave Westminster CO 80030

HOGAN, SHAUN CAMPBELL, mechanical engineer; b. Carbondale, Ill., Sept. 1, 1959; s. Philip Campbell Hogan and Enid Levida (Allen) Hileman; m. Karen Marie Germain, May 22, 1982. BSME, U. Wyo., 1982. Lab. technician Composite Materials Rsch. Group, Laramie, Wyo., 1980-82; design engr. Wasatch div. Morton Thiokol Inc., Brigham City, Utah, 1982-85; structural engr. chem. systems div. United Tech. Corp., San Jose, Calif., 1986-87; chief engr. EFI Corp., San Jose, Calif., 1987-88, v.p. engring., 1988—. Author computer programs; designer pressure vessels and rocket motor cases. Mem. Soc. for Advancement Material and Process Engring., Compressed Gas Assn. Republican. Office: EFI Corp 751 Charcot Ave San Jose CA 95131

HOGARTH, BURNE, cartoonist, illustrator; b. Chgo., Dec. 25, 1911; s. Max and Pauline H.; m. Constance Holubar, June 27, 1953; children—Michael, Richard, Ross. Student Art Inst. Chgo., 1925-27, Chgo. Acad. Fine Arts, 1926-29, Crane Coll., 1928-30, U. Chgo., 1930-32, Northwestern U., 1931-32, Columbia U., 1956-57. Asst. cartoonist to Lyman Young, Tim Tyler's Luck, N.Y.C., 1934; cartoonist Pieces of Eight, McNaught Syndication, N.Y.C., 1935; free lance artist King Features, N.Y.C., 1935-36; staff artist Johnstone Agy., N.Y.C., 1936-37; cartoonist Sunday Color Page, Tarzan, United Feature Syndication, N.Y.C., 1937-50, Sunday page Drago, Post-Hall Syndication, N.Y.C., 1946, Miracle Jones, United Features, N.Y.C., 1948; founder Sch. Visual Arts, N.Y.C., 1947-70, v.p., coordinator curriculum, instr., 1947-70; author Watson-Guptill, N.Y.C., 1958-89; instr. Parsons Sch., N.Y.C., 1976-79; pres. Pendragon Press Ltd., N.Y.C., 1975-79; with Art Ctr. Coll. Design, Pasadena, Calif., 1982—, Otis Art Inst., Parsons Sch. Design, Los Angeles, 1981—; numerous exhbns. worldwide including Musee des arts decoratives, Louvre, Paris, 1968, 69; one man show Paris, 1967, Bibliotheque Municipale, 1985, Palais de Longchamps, Marseille, France, 1985; represented in permanent collections: Smithsonian Instn., Mus. Cartoon Art, U. Colo., U. Wyo., Mus. Art, Gijon, Spain, others. Author: Dynamic Anatomy, 1958, Drawing the Human Head, 1965, Dynamic Figure Drawing, 1970, Drawing Dynamic Hands, 1977; Dynamic Light and Shade, 1981; creator graphic novels Tarzan of the Apes, 1972, Jungle Tales of Tarzan, 1976, Golden Age of Tarzan, 1979; Life of King Arthur, 1984. Trustee NCS Milt Gross Fund., 1980. Named Best Illustration Cartoonist, Nat. Cartoonists Soc., 1974, 75, 76, Artist of Yr., Pavilion of Humour, 1975, Premio Emilio Freixas Silver plaque V-Muestra Internat. Conv., 1978, Pulcinella award V-Mostra Internat. del Fumetto, 1983, Caran D'Ache Silver plaque Internat. Comics Conv., 1984, Adamson Silent Sam award Comics '85 Internat. Conv., 1985, Golden Palms award Cesar Illustration Group, Paris, 1988. Mem. Nat. Cartoonists Soc. (pres. 1977-79), Mus. of Cartoon Art, Am. Soc. Aesthetics, Nat. Art Edn. Assn., WHO, Graphic Arts Soc., Internat. Assn. Authors of Comics and Cartoons. Address: 6026 W Lindenhurst Ave Los Angeles CA 90036

HOGGATT, CLELA ALLPHIN, English educator; b. Des Moines, Sept. 9, 1932; d. Addison Edgar and Frances (Buckallew) Philleo; m. Charles Allphin; children: Beverly, Valerie, Clark, Arthur, Frances; m. John Hoggatt. AA, Grand View Jr. Coll., 1952; BA summa cum laude, U. No. Iowa, 1954; MA, Tex A&I U., 1961. Cert. life tchr. Iowa, Tex.; permanent life community coll. credential, Calif. Tchr. social studies Los Fresnos (Tex.) Jr. High Sch., 1954-55; tchr. English Cummings Jr. High Sch., Brownsville, Tex., 1956-59, Fickett Jr. High Sch., Tucson, 1963-66, Portola Jr. High Sch., L.A., 1956-59; instr. speech Tex. Southmost Jr. Coll., Bronsville, 1959; tchr. history and English Ysleta High Sch., El Paso, Tex., 1963-66; prof. English L.A. Trade-Tech. Coll., 1969-75, L.A. Mission Coll., 1975—. Author: Women in the Plays of Henrik Ibsen, 1975, The Writing Cycle, 1986; contbr. to Words, Words, Words, 1981. V.p. Friends West Valley Library, Reseda, Calif., 1984—. Grand View Jr. Coll. scholar, 1951-52, U. No. Iowa scholar, 1953-54. Mem. Nat. Coun. Tchrs. English, Am. Mensa, Pi Gamma Mu. Democrat. Home: 19360 Archwood St Reseda CA 91335 Office: LA Mission Coll 1212 San Fernando Rd San Fernando CA 91340

HOHLMAYER, EARL J., service company executive; b. Springfield, Ohio, June 8, 1921; s. Carl Elton and Margaret (Waggaman) H.; m. Yvonne Hohlmayer, Aug. 15, 1971 (div. 1975); m. Nikki Vramis, Feb. 14, 1976. Student, Solano Coll., 1967. V.p. Hohlmayer's Laundry Inc., Springfield, 1953-55; pres. Hohlmayer's Chevron Cleaner, Fairborn, Ohio, 1955-62; sales mgr. German Auto Parts, Long Beach, Calif., 1962-64; sales rep. Fgn. Auto Supply, Anaheim, Calif., 1964-66; sales mgr. Vern Gardner Fgn. Auto, Oakland, Calif., 1966-67; foreman Aero Mechanics, Fairfield, Calif., 1967-72; mgr., ptnr. Commodore Valet Svc., Pittsburg, Calif., 1979-80; pres. Modern Commodore Cleaner, Antioch, Calif., 1981—. Contbr. articles to Rivertown Express, 1988, Antioch Currents, 1988, Daily Ledger, 1989; producer hist. videotapes. Active Antioch Civic Arts Commn., 1988; pres. Antioch Hist. Soc., 1982-87; bd. dirs. Antioch Rivertown Dist., 1988. Tech. sgt. USAAF, 1941-46, USAF, 1948-53. Mem. Sports Car Club Am. (regional exec. 1956), Solano Yacht Club (commodore 1974), Elks, Masons, Moose. Home: 19 W 7th St Antioch CA 94509

HOHNBAUM, ANNA MARIA, mortgage company executive; b. Salt Lake City, Jan. 3, 1956; d. Martin R. Cutler and Margit H. (Modtland) Church; m. Ralph D. Kander, Apr. 26, 1974 (div. Apr. 1978); m. William G. Hohnbaum, Jan. 23, 1982. Grad. high sch., Salt Lake City. Adminstrv. asst. Wasatch Service & Supply, Salt Lake City, 1974-76; agt. Century 21 City Real Estate, Salt Lake City, 1976-77; chief loan processor Western Savs. & Loan, Salt Lake City, 1977-78; supr., acting mgr. Advance Mortgage Corp., Salt Lake City, 1978-81; br. mgr. Trans-Am. Title, Renton, Wash., 1981-82; processor, closer Rainier Mortgage, Richland, Wash., 1983-85; secondary mktg. officer United Security Mortgage, Boise, Idaho, 1985-88; loan program coordinator West One Fin. (formerly Moore Fin.), Boise, 1988—. Mem. Mortgage Bankers Assn., Assn. Profl. Mortgage Women (Boise chpt.). Republican. Reorganized Ch. of Jesus Christ of Latter-day Saints. Home: 9616 Ramsgate Dr Boise ID 83704

HOHNER, KENNETH DWAYNE, fodder company executive; b. St. John, Kans., June 24, 1934; s. Courtney Clinton and Mildred Lucile (Forrester) H.; m. Sherry Eloi Anice Edens, Feb. 14, 1961; children: Katrina, Melissa, Steven, Michael. BS in Geol. Engring., U. Kans., 1957. Geophysicist Mobil Oil Corp., New Orleans, Anchorage, Denver, 1957-72; sr. geophysicist Amerada Hess Corp., Houston, 1972-75, ARAMCO, London, 1975-79; far east area geophysicist Hamilton Bros., Denver, 1979-83; owner Hohner Poultry Farm, Erie, Colo., 1979—; pres. Hohner Custom Feed, Inc., Erie, Colo., 1982—. Mem. Soc. Exploration Geophysicists. Home and Office: 3398 Weld County Rd 4 Erie CO 80516

HOIGAARD, JAN CHRISTIAN, electronics executive; b. Stavanger, Rogaland, Norway, May 1, 1933; came to U.S., 1959; s. Jonas and Signy Leonora (Olsen) H.; m. Iris Christiansen, June 26, 1959; children: Jane Leonora, Kim Joann, Lisa Diann. BSEE, Olso Sch Tech., Oslo, 1959. bd. dirs. Equicapital Corp., Denver. Design engr. Polytronic Rsch., Rockville, Md., 1960-61, Def. Electronics, Rockville, Md., 1961-64; sr. devel. mgr. Vitro Corp., Silver Springs, Md., 1964-67; engring. mgr. Singer Instrumentation, Los Angeles, 1967-69, Vari-L Comp. Inc., Denver, 1969-73; program mgr. TRW, Colorado Springs, Colo., 1973-84; pres., chief exec. officer SpectraScan, Inc., Colorado Springs, 1984—. Patentee in field; contbr. articles to profl. jours. Republican. Lutheran. Office: SpectraScan Inc 1110A Elkton Dr Colorado Springs CO 80907

HOLADAY, BONNIE JEAN, nurse, educator; b. St. Joseph, Mich., May 27, 1947; d. George Barfoot and Barbara (Hayne) H. BSN, Ariz. State U., 1969; M in Nursing, UCLA, 1973; D in Nursing Sci., U. Calif., San Francisco, 1979. RN, Calif. Staff and charge nurse Naval Hosp., San Diego, 1969-71; instr. nursing sch. Nursing Univ. Utah, Salt Lake City, 1973-75; assoc. prof. Sch. of Nursing, Emory U., Atlanta, 1979-80; asst. prof. Sch. of Nursing, UCLA, 1980-83; assoc. prof. U. Calif., San Francisco, 1983—; clin. specialist Emory Perinatal Ctr., Atlanta, 1979-80; cons. nursing rsch. Children's Hosp., Oakland, Calif., 1988—. Author: Nursing Care of Children, 1985 (Book of Yr. award 1985); editor: Child and Family Facing Life Threatening Illness, 1987 (Book of Yr. award 1987); contbr. articles to profl. jours. Mem. task force Calif. Dept. Health Svcs., Sacramento, 1987—; bd. dirs. Calif. affiliate Am. Diabetes Assn., San Francisco, 1988—. Bur.

Health Care and Assistance rsch. grantee, 1987—, NIH grantee, 1986—. Mem. AAAS, Am. Nurses Assn., Soc. for Rsch. in Child Devel., Assn. for Care Childrens Health (founding pres. Atlanta chpt. 1979-80), Sierra, Sigma Theta Tau (pres. Alpha Eta chpt., Rsch. award 1984). Office: U Calif Dept Family Health Care N411Y San Francisco CA 94143

HOLBROOK, ANTHONY, manufacturing company executive; b. 1940; married. With Advanced Micro Devices Inc., Sunnyvale, Calif., 1973—, former exec. v.p., chief operating officer, pres., chief operating officer, 1986—. Office: Advanced Micro Devices Inc 901 Thompson Pl Sunnyvale CA 94086

HOLCOMB, CAROL MARQUARD, medical technologist; b. Mpls., June 17, 1936; d. Carl William and Ruth Lily (Benson) Marquard; m. Ralph Edwin Holcomb, Apr. 9, 1963; children: Carolyn, Karen; stepchildren: Michael, Mark, Keith, Kevin. BS in Med. Tech., U. Minn., 1958. Med. technologist U. Minn., 1985-59, War Meml. Blood Bank, 1959-60, Bishop Randall Hosp., Lander, Wyo., 1964-70, Mercy Hosp., Denver, 1971-73, Boulder Meml. Hosp., Denver, 1973-80, Evergreen Profl. Svcs., Kirkland, Wash., 1980-82, Everett Gen. Hosp., Kirkland, 1982-86, East Side Med. Lab., Redmond, Wash., 1986-87, Providence Hosp., Everett, Wash., 1987—. Mem. Am. Soc. Clin. Pathologists. Democrat.

HOLCOMB, W. R., city government executive. Mayor, City of San Bernardino, Calif., 1989— Office: Office of Mayor 300 North D St San Bernardino CA 92418 *

HOLCOMBE, HENRY JAMESON, JR., military officer; b. Bklyn., Jan. 11, 1963; s. Henry Jameson Holcombe Sr. and Patricia Ellen (Dines) Vaughan; m. Janet Teresa Flynn, Mar. 8, 1986. BS, U.S. Mil. Acad., 1985; MBA, Chaminade U. of Honolulu, 1988. Commd. 2nd lt. U.S. Army, 1985; platoon leader, 125 Signal Battalion U.S. Army, Schofield, Hawaii, 1986-88; staff officer, 1116 Signal Battalion U.S. Army, Fort Shafter, Hawaii, 1988—; instr. computer sci. Chaminade U., Honolulu, 1989—. Helper Spl. Olympics, Honolulu, 1987; v.p. Boy Scouts Am., West Point, N.Y., 1982-85. Mem. Armed Forces Communications and Electronics Assn., Hawaii Info. Intergovernmental Pacific Coun. Republican. Roman Catholic. Home: 403-J Cocos Pl Honolulu HI 96818 Office: US Army S3-Operations 1116th Signal Battalion Fort Shafter HI 96858-5415

HOLDCROFT, LESLIE THOMAS, clergyman, educator; b. Man., Can., Sept. 28, 1922; s. Oswald Thomas and Florence (Waterfield) H.; student Western Bible Coll., 1941-44; BA, San Francisco State Coll., 1950; MA, San Jose State Coll., 1955; postgrad. Stanford, 1960, 63, U. Cal., 1965-67; DDiv., Bethany Bible Coll., 1968; m. Ruth Sorensen, July 2, 1948; children: Cynthia Ruth, Althea Lois, Sylvia Bernice. Instr. Western Bible Coll., 1944-47; instr. Bethany Bible Coll., 1947-55, dean edn., 1955-68, v.p., 1967-68; pres. Western Pentecostal Bible Coll., 1968-87; pastor Craig Chapel, 1959-68; dir. Can. Pentecostal Corr. Coll., Clayburn, B.C., 1985—. Pres., Assn. Canadian Bible Colls., 1972-76. Author: The Historical Books, 1960, The Synoptic Gospels, 1962, The Holy Spirit, 1962, The Pentateuch, 1951, Divine Healing, 1967, The Doctrine of God, 1978, The Four Gospels, 1988. Home: 34623 Ascott Ave, Abbotsford, BC Canada V2S 5A3 Office: Box 123, Clayburn, BC Canada V0X 1E0

HOLDEN, ERNEST LLOYD, automotive company owner; b. Erie, Pa., May 2, 1941; s. Edmund Hudson and Ruth Marie (Mallory) H.; m. Sharon Glee Smith, Mar. 14, 1964 (div. July 1971); children: Vanessa Rene, James George; m. Carol Lee Christensen, July 9, 1985. BS, Edinboro State Coll., 1965. Cert. tchr., Pa., Ariz. Speedway mgr. U.S. Auto Raceways, Cleve., 1977-79; dir. automotive racing programs PPG Industries, Cleve., 1980-81; owner, cons. Holden Automotive, Phoenix, 1970—; owner Holden Motor Co., Inc., Phoenix, 1986—; cons. motorsports history BBC, Birmingham, England, motorsports sales White Way Sign Co., Chgo., 1985—; bd. dirs., co-founder Nat. Auto Racing Hist. Soc., Cleve., 1979—; lectr. arthritis symposium Boswell Hsop./Sun Found., Phoenix, 1983. Author: The Arthritis Survival Book, 1983; producer, dir. (video prodn.) The Racing Cars and Craft of Myron Stevens, 1981; inventor, patentee auto tire design; contbr. articles to profl. jours. Adv. bd. Harrington Arthritis Research Ctr., Phoenix, 1984; mem. New England Hist. Genealogical Soc. Mem. Vet. Motor Car Club Am. (nat. bd. govs. 1980—), Automotive Svc. Assn., Optimistic Arthritics Club (v.p. 1984-85). Republican. Office: Holden Motor Co Inc 12639 N Cave Creek Rd Phoenix AZ 85022

HOLDEN, GEORGE FREDRIC, brewing company executive, public policy specialist, consultant; b. Lander, Wyo., Aug. 29, 1937; s. George Thiel Holden and Rita (Meyer) Zulpo; m. Dorothy Carol Capper, July 5, 1959; children: Lorilyn, Sherilyn, Tamilyn. Adminstr. BSChemE, U. Colo., 1959, MBA in Mktg., 1974. Plastics lab. EDP, indsl chems. plant, prodn. process engring., tool control supervision, aerospace (Minuteman, Polaris, Sparrow), Parlin, N.J., Salt Lake City, Cumberland, Md., 1959-70; by-product sales, new market and new product devel., resource planning and devel. and pub. relations Adolph Coors Co., Golden, Colo., 1971-76; dir. econ. affairs corp. pub. affairs dept., 1979-84, dir. pub. affairs research, 1984-86; owner Phoenix Enterprises, Arvada, 1986—; mgr. facilities engring. Coors Container Co., 1976-79; instr. brewing, by-products utilization and waste mgmt. U. Wis.; cons., speaker in field. Del. Colo. Rep. Conv., 1976—; bd. dirs. Colo. Pub. Expenditures Council, 1983-86, Nat. Speakers Assn., Colo. Speakers Assn. (bd. dirs. 1987—), Nat. Assn. Bus. Economists, Colo. Assn. Commerce and Industry Ednl. Found. Mem. U.S. Brewers Assn. (chmn. by-products com., Hon. Gavel, 1975), Am. Inst. Indsl. Engrs. (dir. 1974-78). Co-author: Secrets of Job Hunting, 1972; The Phoenix Phenomenon, 1984, TOTAL Power of ONE in America, 1989; contbr. articles to Chem. Engring. Mag., 1968-76, over 200 published articles, white papers in field; over 400 speeches. Regular guest columnist La Voz, Colo. Statesman. Spkr. Heritage Found. Guide to Pub. Policy Experts, Spkrs. Bur., Commn. on the Bicentennial, U.S. Constn. Home: 6463 Owens St Arvada CO 80004 Office: Phoenix Enterprises PO Box 1900 Arvada CO 80001

HOLDEN, WINFIELD LLOYD, JR., marketing executive, educator; b. Detroit, July 16, 1926; s. Winfield Lloyd and Margaret Alida (Yerkes) H.; m. Alyce Elaine Marshall, Aug. 16, 1947; children: Winfield Lloyd III, Jeffrey, Elizabeth. BA, Mich. State U., 1948. Copywriter Chrysler Corp., Detroit, 1949, McCann-Erickson Co., Detroit, 1950; v.p. J. Walter Thompson Co., Chgo., 1951-76; sr. v.p. Margo Wood Advt., Honolulu, 1977-82; ind. mktg. cons. Honolulu, 1983, Mesa, Ariz., 1986—; v.p. Pure Systems, Modesto, Calif., 1984-85; instr. mktg., Ariz. State U., Tempe, 1986—; bd. dirs. Eagle Devel. Group, Honolulu, Polynesian Mktg., Honolulu. Trustee USS Monitor Rsch. and Recovery Found., Beaufort, N.C., 1974-77. With USNR, 1944-46. Mem. Sales and Mktg. Execs. (pres. Honolulu chpt. 1982), Ill. Soc. Founders and Patriots (gov. 1973), Pacific Club, Rotary, Sigma Delta Chi (life), Pi Sigma Epsilon (life), Phi Delta Theta. Republican. Office: 2339 W Kiowa Circle Mesa AZ 85202

HOLDEREGGER, JOHN MICHAEL, rehabilitation association administrator; b. Fresno, Calif., Dec. 9, 1951; s. Paul and Christina Mary (Friedlan) H.; m. Julie Ellen Hildreth, Oct. 19, 1979 (div. Sept. 1983). BS, U. Wyo., 1973, MS, 1975. Life skills trainer Yellowstone Assn. for Retarded Citizens, Billings, Mont., 1976-77; life skills instr. CHANCE, Inc., Dillon, Mont., 1977-78; social worker Clausen House, Oakland, Calif., 1978-79; asst. exec. dir. Cerebral Palsy Ctr. for the Bay Area, Oakland, 1979-83; v.p. Goodwill Industries of Greater Bay Area, Oakland, 1983-85; pres. Uinta County Rehab. Ctr., Evanston, Wyo., 1985—; mem. task force Gov.'s Taskforce on Habilitation Svcs., Sacramento, 1983, Gov.'s Community Support Task Force, Cheyenne, Wyo., 1986. Mem. Evanston Cowboys Days Rodeo Com., 1986-87; bd. dirs. Alameda County D.D. Planning and Adv. Coun., Oakland, 1979-84, Evanston Child Devel. Assn., 1988. Mem. Wyo. Assn. Rehab. Facilities (treas. 1986—), Nat. Soc. Fundraising Execs., Lincoln/Uinta Child Devel. Assn. (bd. dirs. Mountain View, Wyo. chpt. 1986—), Lions (sec. Oakland chpt. 1984-85, sec. Evanston chpt. 1988—), Elks (trustee 1987-89, exalted ruler 1989—). Office: 350 City View Dr #303 Evanston WY 82930

HOLDO, NELSON ANDRES, company executive; b. Pasadena, Calif., Oct. 13, 1959; s. Andres Oliver and Rosario Beatriz Holdo; m. Kelly J. Lucas, July 22, 1989. AA, Pasadena City Coll., 1977; diploma, Centre Internat. de Formation Continue Comml. pour L'Horlogie-Bijouterie, 1982. V.p. B.D. Howes and Son, Pasadena, 1979-85, Troy & Co., Pasadena, 1985—. Mem. Pasadena Tournament of Roses, 1984—; chmn. adv. bd. Escalon Sch., Pasadena, 1985-86, bd. dirs., 1985-89; gem and mineral coun. L.A. County Mus. Natural History. CFH scholar Gemolog. Inst. Am., 1982. Mem. Am. Gem. Soc. (pres. so. Calif. guild), Pasadena Jr. C. of C., Gem. Inst. Am. (diploma), South Lake Bus. Assn. (v.p.), Pasadena C. of C., Gemolog. Assn. of Gt. Britain, Athenaeum Club, Rotary. Office: Troy & Co 527 S Lake Ave Ste 105 Pasadena CA 91101

HOLDSWORTH, JANET NOTT, nurse, educator; b. Evanston, Ill., Dec. 25, 1941; d. William Alfred and Elizabeth Inez (Kelly) Nott; children—James William, Kelly Elizabeth, John David. B.S. in Nursing with high distinction, U. Iowa, 1963; M.Nursing, U. Wash., 1966; postgrad. U. Colo., 1981, U. No. Colo., 1982. Registered nurse, Colo. Staff nurse U. Colo. Hosp., Denver, 1963-64, Presbyn. Hosp., Denver, 1964-65, Grand Canyon Hosp., Ariz., 1965; asst. prof. U. Colo. Sch. Nursing, Denver, 1966-71; counseling nurse Boulder PolyDrug Treatment Ctr., Boulder, 1971-77; pvt. duty nurse Nurses' Official Registry, Denver, 1973-82; cons. nurse, tchr. parenting and child devel. Teenage Parent Program, Boulder Valley Schs., Boulder, 1980—; bd. dirs., treas. Nott's Travel, Aurora, Colo., 1980—; instr., nursing coordinator ARC, Boulder, 1979—, instr., nursing tng. specialist, 1980-82. Mem. adv. bd. Boulder County LaMaz Inc., 1980—; mem. adv. com. Child Find and Parent-Family, Boulder, 1981—; del. Republican County State Congl. Convs., 1972-86, sec. 17th Dist. Senatorial Com., Boulder, 1982—; vol. chmn. Mesa Sch. Parent Tchr. Orgn., Boulder, 1982—, bd. dirs., 1982—, v.p., 1983—. Mem. Am. Nurses Assn., Colo. Nurses Assn. (bd. dirs. 1975-76, human rights com. 1981-83, dist. pres. 1974-76), Soc. Adolescent Medicine, Council High Risk Prenatal Nurses, Council Intracultural Nurses, Sigma Theta Tau. Republican. Presbyterian (elder). Home: 1550 Findlay Way Boulder CO 80303 Office: Teenage Parent Program 3740 Martin Dr Boulder CO 80303

HOLEN, SHIRLEY LILLIAN, teacher; b. Michigan, N.D., May 19, 1931; d. Alfred and Arlotte (Helland) H.; 1 child, Michael. Student, State Sch. Sci., Wahpeton, N.D., 1953; BS, Mayville State U., 1968; postgrad., U. N.D., 1971. Tchr. Rural Schs., N.D., 1949-52, Tuttle, N.D., 1964-65; Tchr. Drayton, N.D., 1965-67; bookkeeper, sec. Lake Supply, Devils Lake, N.D., 1954-55, Grand Forks (N.D.) Supply, 1956-57, Nebr. Bridge Supply and Lumber Co., Omaha, 1958-63; tchr. high sch. Ely, Nev., 1968-70; tchr. elem. sch. Ruth, Nev., 1970-85, White Pine County Schs., East Ely, Nev., 1985--; former tchr. bookkeeping and typing No. Nev. Community Coll., Elko. Mem. NEA, Nev. Edn. Assn., AAUW (past local and state treas.), Sons Norway, White Pine Pub. Mus. Democrat. Lutheran. Office: White Pine County Schs East Ely NV 89315

HOLLADAY, DAVID HADDON, aviation safety consultant, educator; b. Orangeburg, S.C., Mar. 13, 1925; s. David James and Mary Jane (Haddon) H.; m. Lela Elizabeth Meisenholder, 1965; children: David, Kevin, Mark, Kyle. BS in Edn., U. So. Calif., 1971; MBA, Pepperdine U., Malibu, Calif., 1976. With Hawthorne Airmotive, Orangeburg, 1941-43; flight comdr. thru engring. test pilot Calif. Ea. Airways, Inc., various locations, 1951-56; head investigation prevention staff, lectr., cons. U. So. Calif., Inst. Aerospace Safety & Mgmt., Los Angeles, 1956-70; chief investigator Aircraft Accident Prevention, Gardena, Calif., 1963-64; lectr., chief instr., cons. The Royal Inst. Tech., Dept. Aeronautics, Inst. Aviation Safety, Stockholm, Sweden, 1967-85; dir. chief instr. Internat. Ctr. Aviation Safety, Libson, Portugal, 1977-87; pres., prin. cons. AVIACTION, Inc., Del Mar, Calif., 1964—. Contbr. articles to profl. jours. Served with USAAF, 1943-59. Mem. Internat. Soc. Air Safety Investigators. Republican. Office: AVIACTION Inc PO Box 3069 Del Mar CA 92014-6069

HOLLAND, BARBARA LEE, real estate executive; b. Balt., Nov. 27, 1948; d. Samuel and Shirley (Fox) Kamanitz; m. Andrew Elliot Holland; children: Michelle, Danielle. BA, U. Mass., 1970; MA, U. Conn., 1971. Dir. property mgmt. Webster Mgmt. Co., Wethersfield, Conn., 1972-74; pres., co-owner Invest Mgmt. Group, Hartford, Conn., 1974-77; dir. property mgmt. Levy Realty, Las Vegas, Nev., 1977-84; pres., owner H&L Realty & Mgmt. Co., Las Vegas, 1984—. Author: Managing Single-Family Homes, 1987; contbr. articles to profl. jours. Mem. Inst. Real Estate Mgmt. (governing councillor 1985-88, Acad. of Authors 1978, Profl. Achievement award 1983, cert.), Nev. Assn. Realtors (bd. dirs. 1986-88), Las Vegas Bd. Realtors (bd. dirs. 1986-88), Omega Tau Rho. Office: H&L Realty & Mgmt Co 720 S 4th St Ste 201 Las Vegas NV 89101

HOLLAND, EILEEN COYNE, management consultant, real estate associate; b. N.Y.C., May 6, 1959; d. Hugh James and Gloria (Clayden) Coyne; m. Edwin R. Holland, Dec., 1984 (div. Sept. 1987). Student, NYU, 1977-78. Pres. Isis Mgmt. & Cons., N.Y.C., 1986-88, Osiris Cons. Corp., L.A., 1988—. Office: Osiris Cons Corp 614 S St Andrews Pl Los Angeles CA 90005

HOLLAND, HAROLD MERVIN, urologist; b. Easton, Pa., Jan. 30, 1922; s. Ben and Leah Holland; m. Renee Holland, Apr. 2, 1967. AB, Lafayette Coll., 1943; MD, NYU, 1946. Bd. cert. in urology, 1957. Asst clin. prof. surgery (urology) U. So. Calif., 1960--. Lt. (j.g.) USN, 1947-49. Mem. Am. Coll. Surgeons, Internat. Coll. Surgeons, Am. Urol. Assn., Am. Bd. Urology. Office: 2080 Century Park East Los Angeles CA 90067

HOLLAND, JEFFREY R., religious organization administrator; b. St. George, Utah, Dec. 3, 1940; s. Frank D. and Alice (Bentley) H.; m. Patricia Terry, June 7, 1963; children: Matthew, Mary, David. B.S., Brigham Young U., 1965, M.A., 1966; M.Phil., Yale U., 1972, Ph.D., 1973. Dean religious instrn. Brigham Young U., 1974-76, pres., 1980-89; gen. authority, mem. 1st Quorum of the 70 LDS Ch., 1989—; commr. Latter Day Saints Ch. Ednl. System, 1976-80; dir. Deseret News Pub. Co., Key Bank of Utah, Key Bancshares of Utah, Inc. Bd. dirs. Polynesian Cultural Center, Laie, Hawaii. Mem. Am. Assn. Presidents of Ind. Colls. and Univs. (pres.), Nat. Assn. Ind. Colls. and Univs. (former bd. dirs.), Am. Council Edn., Phi Kappa Phi. Office: LDS Church 47 E South Temple St Salt Lake City UT 84150

HOLLAND, JUDITH RAWIE, producer; b. Long Beach, Calif., Jan. 25, 1942; d. Wilmer Ernest and Margaret Jane (Towle) Rawie; m. John Allen Holland, July 11, 1964 (div.); children: Daryn Kirsten, Dawn Malia. BBA, Marymount Coll., 1964; BA in Visual Arts and Communication, U. Calif., San Diego, 1978. Producer/writer PBS series Achieving (Emmy award 1982, ACE nominee), asst. dir. rsch. and video/producer IABC, San Francisco, 1982; bd. dir. programming Group W Cable, Westinghouse Co., 1983-85; ptnr. RH Positive Prodns. Co., 1986—; mgr. video programming Nelson/Embassy Home Entertainment, 1986-87; ptnr. Real Magic, Studio City, Calif., 1988-89. Recipient You Make the Difference award Group W, 1983. Mem. Am. Film Inst., Women in Film, Ind. Features Assn. Democrat. Episcopalian.

HOLLAND, ROBIN JEAN, personnel director; b. Chgo., June 22, 1942; d. Robert Benjamin and Dolores (Levy) Shaeffer; 1 child, Robert Gene. BA in Pub. Rels. magna cum laude, U. So. Calif., 1977. Account exec., pub. relations firm, 1977-79, Mgmt. Recruiters, 1979; owner, operator Holland Exec. Search, Marina Del Rey, Calif., 1979—; pres. Bus. Communications, 1983—; cons. on outplacement to bus.; condr. seminars on exec. search; guest lectr. and instr. on exec. recruiting at community colls. Active Ahead with Horses. Recipient numerous local honors. Mem. Am. Coaster Enthusiasts, LK.A. Can., Mensa, Peruvian Paso Horse Owners N.Am. Office: Holland Exec Search 4736 Admiralty Way Ste 9774 Marina Del Rey CA 90295

HOLLANDER, SIDNEY, computer systems engineer; b. Boston, Mar. 23, 1949; s. Morris and Edith (Feldman) H.; m. Betty Sandra Groppel, Feb. 24, 1973. BSEE, Rensselaer Poly. Inst., 1970, MEE, 1971. Commd. 2d lt. USAF, 1971, advanced through grades to capt., 1975; project mgr. satellite control facility USAF, Sunnyvale, Calif., 1974-78; resigned USAF, 1978; project engr. The Aerospace Corp., 1978—; program system engr., Unisys Def. Systems, Sunnyvale, 1987-88. Mem. IEEE (vice-chmn. Santa Clara Valley sect. 1988-89), Photographic Guild Los Gatos. Democrat. Unitarian-Universalist. Home: 1114 Keltner Ave San Jose CA 95117 Office: Aerospace Corp PO Box 3430 Sunnyvale CA 94088-3430

HOLLANDER, TYRE CHARLES, systems analyst; b. Everett, Wash., Oct. 19, 1950; s. Barry Eugene and Alfreida (Fillinger) H.; m. Bonnie Lee Huffman, Aug. 1, 1981. BA in Bus. Adminstrn., U. Wash., 1973. Data processing mgr. Reinell Boats Inc., Marysville, Wash., 1977-78; data processing mgr. Phase Linear Corp., Lynnwood, Wash., 1980-81, material control/data processing mgr., 1981-82; data processing mgr. Allsop Inc., Bellingham, Wash., 1983-84; material control/data proceesing mgr. Imperial Mfg. Co., Bremerton, Wash., 1984-85; data processing mgr. NW Bottling, Seattle, 1985-86; sys. analyst Boeing Computer Svcs., Seattle, 1986-. Mem. Am. Prodn. and Inventory Control Soc.(cert.). Republican. Home: 7520 45th Dr NW Marysville WA 98270

HOLLE, RONALD LEE, meteorologist; b. Ft. Wayne, Ind., June 4, 1942; s. Truman William and Louella Louise (Knipstein) H.; m. Shirley May Feldmann, Dec. 28, 1974; children: Laura Christine, Eric Matthew, Paul William. BS, Fla. State U., 1964, MS, 1966; postgrad., U. Miami, Coral Gables, Fla., 1969-73. Student trainee U.S. Weather Bur., Ft. Wayne, summers 1962-64; research meteorologist U.S. Weather Bur., Silver Spring, Md., 1966-67, NOAA, Coral Gables, 1967-80; meteorologist NOAA, Boulder, Colo., 1980-88, program mgr. thunderstorm studies Environ. Research Labs., 1983-88, meteorologist, 1988—. Contbr. articles to profl. jours. Pres. Mt. Hope Luth. Ch., Boulder, 1987, v.p., 1988, elder, 1989—. Mem. Am. Meteorol. Soc. (pres. Denver and Boulder chpt. 1989—), Am. Geophys. Union, Nat. Weather Assn. Home: 2897 Loma Pl Boulder CO 80301 Office: NOAA Nat Severe Storms Lab 325 Broadway Boulder CO 80303

HOLLER, DENNIS KIETH, electrical engineer; b. Woodland, Calif., July 3, 1951; s. Robert Edward Holler and Robin Verle (Loranger) Doud; m. Deborah Jane Wilbanks, Feb. 2, 1974; 1 child, Erin Michelle. AA, City Coll., Sacramento, 1978; BSEE, U. Calif., Davis, 1980; MSEE, Santa Clara U., 1985. Mem. tech. staff Argo Systems, Sunnyvale, Calif., 1980-86; sr. rsch. engr. SRI Internat., Menlo Park, Calif., 1986—. With U.S. Army, 1971-74. Mem. IEEE, Antenna Measurement Techniques Assn., Sports Car Club Am. Office: SRI Internat 333 Ravenswood Ave Menlo Park CA 94025

HOLLEY, ROBERT WILLIAM, biologist; b. Urbana, Ill., Jan. 28, 1922; s. Charles E. and Viola (Wolfe) H.; m. Ann Dworkin, Mar. 3, 1945; 1 son, Frederick. A.B., U. Ill., 1942; Ph.D., Cornell U., 1947. Fellow Am. Chem. Soc. State Coll. Wash., 1947-48; asst. prof., then assoc. prof. organic chemistry N.Y. State Agr. Expt. Sta. Cornell U., Ithaca, 1948-57, research chemist plant, soil and nutrition lab. USDA, 1957-64, prof. biochemistry, 1964-69, chmn. dept. biochemistry, 1965-66; resident fellow Salk Inst. Biol. Studies, La Jolla, Calif., 1968—; mem. biochemistry study sect. NIH, 1962-66; vis. fellow Salk Inst. Biol. Studies; vis. prof. Scripps Clinic and Research Found., La Jolla, 1966-67. Recipient Distinguished Service award U.S. Dept. Agr., 1965, Albert Lasker award basic med. research, 1965; U.S. Steel Found. award in molecular biology Nat. Acad. Scis., 1967; Nobel prize for medicine and physiology, 1968; Guggenheim fellow Calif. Inst. Tech., 1955-56. Fellow AAAS; mem. Am. Acad. Arts and Scis., Am. Soc. Biol. Chemists, Am. Chem. Soc., Nat. Acad. Scis., Phi Beta Kappa, Sigma Xi. Home: 7381 Rue Michael La Jolla CA 92037 Office: Salk Inst Biolog Studies PO Box 85800 San Diego CA 92138

HOLLINGSWORTH, PERCY MAX, computer scientist, engineer; b. Independence, Kans., Sept. 3, 1926; s. Percy Jay and Jessie Elizabeth (Denny) H.; m. Pearl G. Steinbergh, June 5, 1965; children: Mitch Leroy, Max Terry. PhD, Mo. State U., 1952; M Computer Sci., Nat. Radio inst., Washington, 1989. Engr. RCA Svc. Co., Camdon, N.J., 1952-56; with Boeing Aircraft Co., Wichita, Kans., 1956-58; rsch. and devel. engr., cons. Startronics Electronics Inc., L.A., 1959-62; chief exec. officer, projects dir. Tech. Opportunities, Inc., Carson City, Nev., 1982—. Discoverer audio principles. With USAAC, 1943-45. Mem. Soc. Motion Pictures and TV Engrs., Audio Engring. Soc. Office: T O I PO Box 1554 West Sacramento CA 95691

HOLLINS, MICHAEL, mechanical engineer; b. Chgo., Mar. 25, 1949; s. Gerald V. and Elizabeth (Armour) H.; m. Frederica Elizabeth Johnson, Mar. 25, 1969; children: Natasha, Michelle. Student, N.Y. Inst. Photography, 1968; BS, MIT, 1987. Pres. Side Angle Prodns., Inc., Santa Fe, N.Mex., 1979—; res. tech. lab. for machine productivity MIT, Cambridge, 1984-86, res. tech. Lincoln lab., 1985-87; staff mem. Los Alamos (N.Mex.) Nat. Lab., 1987-89. Mem. Am. Vacuum Soc. Home and Office: 269 Loma Entrada Santa Fe NM 87501

HOLLIS, RICHARD WHITTINGTON, JR., oil company executive; b. Little Rock, Nov. 12, 1954; s. Richard Wittington and Louise Marie (Stephens) H.; m. Kathryn Ann Bally, May 21, 1977; children: Meghan Bally, Richard Wittington III. BS with distinction, U. Kans., 1977; JD, U. Tulsa, 1981. Recording engr. KANU Radio, Lawrence, Kans., 1975-78; asst. landman Arco Exploration Co., Bakersfield, Calif., 1981-82; field landman Arco Exploration Co., Denver, 1982-83; asst. landman Arco Oil and Gas Co., Goleta, Calif., 1982; landman Arco Oil and Gas Co., Boleta, Calif., 1983-85; landman, contracts and unitization Arco Oil and Gas Co., Dallas, 1985; area landman Arco Oil and Gas Co., Bakersfield, 1985—. Mem. Am. Assn. Petroleum Landmen, Bakersfield Assn. Petroleum Landmen, Channel Island Assn. Petroleum Landmen, Kappa Tau Alpha, Alpha Epsilon Rho. Democrat. Methodist. Office: Arco Oil and Gas Co Po Box 147 Bakersfield CA 93302

HOLLIS, ROY STONE, financial analyst; b. Pasadena, Calif., Aug. 21, 1953; s. Donald Eugene and Elizabeth Caroline (Reed) H.; m. Robin Arleen Buckholtz, Sept. 20, 1975; children: Donald David, Whitney Suzanne. AB in Math., Occidental Coll., 1976. Office and br. mgr. Beneficial Fin. Co., Burbank, Calif., 1976-79; consumer credit officer lst Interstate Bank, L.A., 1979-82, comml. lender, 1982-83, analyst supr., 1983-85; fin. cons. lst Interstate Franchise Svcs., L.A., 1985—. Founder, editor PC Worker newsletter, 1987. Sec., treas. Oaktree Homeowners Assn., L.A., 1982-87. Mem. lst Interstate PC Users Group (chmn. 1987—). Republican. Home: 10242 Jardine Ave Sunland CA 91040 Office: lst Interstate Franchise 707 Wilshire Blvd W57-38 Los Angeles CA 90017

HOLLISTER, D. CHRISTINE, realtor, accountant; b. Phoenix, Aug. 31, 1952; d. Richard Davis III and Dorothy Grace (Bean) H.; children: Thomas, Brian. AA with distinction, Riverside (Calif.) Coll., 1982; cert. real estate; student, San Jose (Calif.) U., 1984-87. With Deloitte Haskins & Sells, Costa Mesa, Calif., 1979-81, Integrated System Sales, San Mateo, Calif., 1983, Estate Equity Mgmt., San Jose, 1984-88; ops. mgr. Cornish & Carey Realtors, Hollister, 1988—; realtor, computer cons., freelance writer, Hollister, 1988—. Mem. Nat. Fedn. Rep. Women. Mem. Nat. Assn. Realtors, Calif. Assn. Realtors, San Benito County Bd. Realtors, San Benito Bd. Realtors Multiple Listing Svc., Victorian Soc. in Am., Order of Eastern Star. Home: 951 Suiter St Hollister CA 95023 Office: Cornish & Carey Realtors 200 Tres Pinos Rd Hollister CA 95023

HOLLIWAY, JOHN HAROLD, insurance agency executive; b. Sitka, Kans., Feb. 25, 1927; s. James Robert and Eva Josephine (Romine) H.; m. Ruth Ellen Craig, Aug. 13, 1951; children: Kent Craig, Karen Dee. BSBA, U. Denver, 1950. Cert. ins. counselor. Journeyman butcher Safeway Stores, Inc., Denver, 1949-51; mgmt. trainee Phillips Petroleum Co., Denver, 1951-53; pres., mgr. Jefferson County Fin. Co., Arvada, Colo., 1953-66; pres. Holliway Ins. Agy., Inc., Arvada, 1966—; mem. Jefferson County R-1 participating agt. and advisor Sch. Dist., 1966-87. Mem. Charter Conv. Com. City of Arvada, 1958, 100-Man Citizen Com., 1966-67; bd. dirs., pres. Forward Arvada Bldg. Corp., 1985; pres. Arvada Rep. Club, 1977; committeeman, dist. capt., del. to convs. Rep. party, 1965-85; cubmaster, scoutmaster Boy Scouts Am., Arvada, 1965-72. With USMC, 1946-47, PTO. Named State of Colo. Agt. of Yr. Profl. Ins. Agts. Assn., Denver, 1973. Mem. Cert. Profl. Ins. Agts. (nat. pres. 1982-83), Sec. Cert. Ins. Counselors, North Jeffco Recreation Dist. Found. (dir.), Colo. Profl. Ins. Agts. (state pres. 1973, 78, chmn. 1976), Arvada C. of C. (pres. 1981, Arvada Citizen and Man of Yr. 1973), Arvada Hist. Soc., Lions (sec. 1979-80), Alpha Kappa Psi. Methodist. Home: 7027 Dudley Dr Arvada CO 80004 Office: Holliway Ins Agy Inc 5765 Olde Wadsworth Blvd Arvada CO 80002

HOLLORAN, DENNIS MICHAEL, soil scientist; b. Dayton, Ohio, Dec. 16, 1948; s. Thomas Patrick and Shirley Ann Holloran; m. Sharon Grimes, Dec. 15, 1979. B.S. in Agronomy, Ohio State U., 1974. Cert. profl. soil scientist. Soil scientist Ohio Dept. Natural Resources, 1974-77; soil scientist, soil surveyor Douglas County (Oreg.) Planning Dept. and Soil Conservation Service, 1977-81; soil scientist South Douglas Soil and Water Conservation Dist. and Soil Conservation Service, Roseburg, Oreg., 1981-83; owner Dennis Holloran Soil Cons., Idleyld Park, Oreg., 1983—; owner Northwest Soil Cons., 1984—. mem. U.S. Orienteering Fedn.; mem. U.S. team, 1978 World Orienteering Championships, Norway. Served with U.S. Army, 1969-71; Vietnam. Decorated Silver Star, DFC (5), Air medal (45). Mem. Am. Soc. Agronomy, Nat. Soc. Cons. Soil Scientists (bd. dirs. N.W. region), Oreg. Soc. Soil Scientists (west-side dir.), Soil Sci. Soc. Am. Home: PO Box 699 Roseburg OR 97470 Office: PO Box 206 Idleyld Park OR 97447

HOLLOWAY, CINDY, mortgage company executive; b. Queens, N.Y., Aug. 8, 1960; d. Richard Stephen and Beverly Bunny (Harris) Tannenbaum; m. David Milton Holloway (div. Mar. 1986); 1 child, Benjamin Jerome. BA, Calif. State U., Fullerton, 1981. Lic. real estate broker. Waitress Bob's Big Boy, San Bernardino, Calif., 1984-85; receptionist RNG Mortgage Co., San Bernardino, 1985; loan processor Quality Mortgage Co., Colton, Calif., 1985-88, loan officer, 1988—. Mem. San Bernardino Bd. Realtors spl. events com., 1988—; mem. Nat. Trust for Historic Preservation. Home: PO Box 3187 Crestline CA 92325 Office: Quality Mortgage Co 1060 E Washington Ste 125 Colton CA 92324

HOLLOWAY, DOUGLAS PATRICK, banker; b. Las Vegas, Nev., Dec. 21, 1938; s. Walker Lee and Frances Marguerite (Webber) H.; divorced; children: Gregory Stephen, Thomas Welling. B.A., U. San Francisco, 1962. Loan examiner Bank Calif., San Francisco, 1960-67, asst. v.p., 1960-70, asst. mgr., 1967-69, mgr., 1969-70; loan examiner Wells Fargo Bank, San Francisco, 1971-73, asst. v.p., 1973-76, v.p., 1976-82, dep. chief loan examiner, 1977-79, chief loan examiner, 1979—, sr. v.p., 1982—; mem. com. corp. responsibility Wells Fargo Bank, 1981-84, chmn., 1981-84. Bd. dirs. Am. Blood Commn., Arlington, Va., 1984—, chmn. fin. and audit com., 1985—, mem. exec. com., 1985—, planning com. 1986—, transition com. 1987—; bd. dirs. Irwin Meml. Blood Ctrs. of Med. Soc. San Francisco, 1984—, treas. 1984-89, pres., 1989—, chmn. fin. and audit com., 1984-89, mem. exec. com., 1984—, chmn., 1989—, mem. pers. com., 1988—, long range planning com. 1987—, chmn. community awareness task force, 1988—; bd. dirs. Blood R & D Found., 1986—; bd. dirs. Shanti Project, 1988—, chmn., 1989—, mem. fin. com., fundraising/pub. edn. coms., 1988—, chmn. vol. and direct svcs. com., 1988—, mem. nominating and bylaws coms., 1988—. Republican. Roman Catholic. Office: Wells Fargo & Co 111 Sutter St 13th Fl San Francisco CA 94163

HOLLOWAY, ROBERT WAYNE, farm owner; b. Twin Falls, Idaho, Aug. 13, 1931; s. Earl R. and Ruby Louise (Cope) H.; m. Agnes Rae Goodwin, Nov. 9, 1953; 1 child, Cindy Louise. Grad. high sch., Twin Falls. Owner, operator Holloway Farms, Quincy, Wash., 1955-88; founder, pres. Quincy Chem. Research, Inc., 1977-83; mem. Grant County Agrl. Stab. Con. Com., Ephrata, Wash., 1966-68, Wash. State, 1968-72; chmn. Cen. Wash. Prodn. Credit Assn., Yakima, 1978-79. Bd. dirs. Grant County Farm Bur., Moses Lake, Wash., 1972-75, 1985-87; pres. Quest Community Theater Group, Quincy, 1979-80; vol. fireman Grant County, 1980-85. Recipient Dairy Flood Relief award Wash. Dairy Produce Commn. and Wash. State Dairymen Fedn., 1975. Mem. Ephrata C. of C. (recipient Good Neighbor of Yr. award, 1987), Black Sands Irrigation Dist. (bd. dirs. 1987—), Elks. Republican. Presbyterian. Home and Office: 336 Dodson Rd Rte 1 Ephrata WA 98823

HOLLOWAY, ROBERT WESTER, chemist; b. Morrilton, Ark., Jan. 3, 1945; s. Otho and Bessie Vance (Woolverton) H.; m. Mary Ella Hamel, Dec. 31, 1970; children: David, Jason. BS, Harding Coll., 1967; postgrad., U. Okla., 1968; PhD, U. Ark., 1977. Asst. prof. U. Ark., Pine Bluff, 1976-79; research chemist DuPont Corp., Aiken, S.C., 1979-81; supervisory chemist EPA, Las Vegas, 1981—. Contbr. articles to profl. jours. Served to capt. USAF, 1967-72. Mem. Am. Chem. Soc. Republican. Lodge: Optimists. Home: 311 E Desert Rose Henderson NV 89015 Office: EPA PO Box 15027 Las Vegas NV 89114

HOLLOWAY, WILLIAM HAROLD, psychiatrist; b. Webster City, Iowa, Feb. 27, 1924; s. Harold Earnest and Angie (Allinson) H.; student Purdue U., 1942, Akron U., 1943-44, Pa. State U., 1943; M.D., U. Pitts., 1949; postgrad. Postgrad. Center for Mental Health, 1966-68, Western Inst. Group and Family Therapy, 1971; m. June Dessie Gibson, Dec. 5, 1944 (div. Nov. 1970); children—Gayle Lynn, Joan Lorraine, Shelley Ann; m. 2d, Martha Jeffery, Jan. 1971; children—Jeff, Stephen, Timothy, Patricia. Intern, Riverside Hosp., Toledo, 1949-50; resident Ypsilanti (Mich.) State Hosp., 1954-57; dir. Summit County Mental Hygiene Clinic, Akron, Ohio, 1957-61; practice medicine specializing in psychiatry, Akron, 1958-73, Medina, Ohio, 1973-77, Aptos, Calif., 1977-78, Garden Grove, Calif., 1978-80, Hemet, Calif., 1980—; clin. chief Riverside County Dept. Mental Health (Calif.), 1984-85; psychiat. cons. Springhill Sch., Akron, 1958-61, Boys' Village, Smithville, Ohio, 1961-67; cons. group psychotherapy Summit County Receiving Hosp., 1966-69; emeritus sr. med. staff Akron City Hosp., Akron Gen. Hosp.; active med. staff Hemet Valley Hosp.; clin. asst. prof. Ohio State U., 1968-69; clin. asst. prof. psychiatry Case Western Res. U. Sch. Medicine, 1970-76; pres. Nat. Group Psychotherapy Seminars, 1969-70; tng. cons. Family and Children's Service Soc. Summit County; founder, dir. Midwest Inst. Human Understanding Inc., Akron; cons. Medina County Family Guidance Clinic, 1974-76, Brazilian Inst. Transactional Analysis, Sao Paulo, 1976-. Served with U.S. Army, 1943-46; to maj. USAF, 1949-54. Postgrad. Center for Mental Health fellow, 1966-68. Fellow Am. Psychiat. Assn., Am. Group Psychotherapy Assn. (dir. 1970-72, treas. 1974-76); mem. Ohio State Med. Assn. (del. 1969-71), Tri-State Group Psychotherapy Assn. (pres. 1968-70), Internat. Assn. Group Psychotherapy, AMA, Internat. Transactional Analysis Assn. (teaching mem., pres. 1976-78, trustee), Summit County Med. Soc. (sec. 1964-65, mem. council 1969-72), Ohio Psychiat. Assn. (pres. 1969-70, trustee edn. and research found. 1969-73), Phi Beta Pi, Alpha Omega Alpha. Author: (with Martha M. Holloway) Change Now, 1973, Collected Monographs of the Midwest Institute, 1975; Clinical Transactional Analysis, 1974; Transactional Analysis-An Integrative View in Transactional Analysis After Eric Berue, 1977. Address: 27491 Bancroft Way Hemet CA 92344

HOLLWEDEL, CHARLES NICHOLAS, JR., aeronautical engineer; b. N.Y.C., Sept. 18, 1923; s. Charles Nicholas and Ethel (Weinschenk) H.; m. Rita Elizabeth Davis, Aug. 16, 1944; children: Cynthia, Mark. BS in Aero. Engring., U. Tulsa, 1951. Design engr. Douglas Aircraft, Tulsa, 1951-55; sr. engr. Aerojet Gen. Corp., Sacramento, 1955-60; chief engr., sales mgr. Turbocraft Inc., Monrovia, Calif., 1960-62; gen. mgr. Turbo Machine Inc., Monrovia, 1962-66; mgr. mfg. engring. Aerojet Gen. Corp., El Monte, Calif., 1966-69; gen. mgr. Marotta Sci. Controls, Santa Ana, Calif., 1969-70; asst. to pres. Control Components Inc., Los Alamitos, Calif., 1970-71; quality assurance mgr. CTI Nuclear Inc., Denver, 1971-76; cons. ASME, Denver, 1976—. Served with U.S. Army Air Corps, 1942-46, PTO. Republican. Lutheran. Lodge: Elks. Office: Hollwedel & Assocs 12 Curtis Ct Broomfield CO 80020

HOLLY, SANDOR, physicist; b. Budapest, Hungary, May 10, 1933; came to U.S. 1956; s. Sandor and Maria (Acsay) H.; m. Judith Lassovszky, Apr. 10, 1966; 1 child, Krisztina. BS, Eötvös Loránd Tudomány Egyetem, Budapest, 1955; MS in Elect. Engr., MIT, 1960; SM in Physics, Harvard U., 1962, PhD. In Physics, 1969. Staff mem. IBM Rsch. Ctr., Yorktown Heights, N.Y., 1959-61; mem. tech. staff A.D. Little Corp., Cambridge, Mass., 1962-68; tech. dir. Gen. Laser Corp., Natick, Mass., 1968-70; physics dept. faculty mem. U. Maryland, College Park, 1970-72; prin. scientist Atlantic Rsch. Corp., Alexandria, Va., 1972-76; staff scientist Rocketdyne Div. of Rockwell Internat. Corp, Canoga Pk, Calif., 1976—. Contbr. articles to profl. jours.; patentee in field. Home: 23801 Ladrillo St Woodland Hills CA 91367 Office: Rockwell Internat Rocketdyne Div 6633 Canoga Ave Canoga Park CA 91304

HOLM, ROBERT ELLSWORTH, electronic engineer; b. Toledo, Oct. 29, 1942; s. Charles Leonard and Beverly Joan (Brown) H.; m. Barbara S. Berendsen, 1969 (div. 1974); 1 child, Brian Charles. BSE Mech.-Elec. Engring., Ariz. State U., 1965; MSEE, Santa Clara U., 1968. Design engr. IBM, San Jose, Calif., 1965-66, E S L Inc., Sunnyvale, Calif., 1966-70; mgr. R & D, Argo Systems, Sunnyvale, 1970-77; engring. mgr. telecommunications Intel, Santa Clara, Calif., 1977-82; mktg. mgr. micro contrs. Intel, Chandler, Ariz., 1982-85, program mgr. microprocessors, 1985—; co-owner Homespace Furniture Store, Tempe, Ariz., 1982—; instr. Mesa (Ariz.) Community Coll., 1986;. Contbr. articles to tech. mags. Chmn. Intel United Way, Chandler, 1987, 88. Mem. U. Santa Clara Grad. Alumni Assn. (co-founder bd. dirs. 1971-75), Ariz. Outdoor and Travel Club (co-founder, bd. dirs., v.p. 1984-88). Republican. Lutheran. Office: Intel 5000 W Chandler Blvd Chandler AZ 85226

HOLMAN, ANN MARIE, supply specialist; b. Texarkana, Tex., May 19, 1930; d. Johnny and Ollie Belle (Talley) Stewart; m. Henry Holman; children: Carole, John, Joyce, Tony. Student, Tillotson Sam Houston, 1950-51. Telephone operator U.S. Dept. of Def., Anchorage, 1962-65, Loring AFB, Maine, 1965-68; telephone operator U.S. Dept. of Def., Holloman AFB, N. Mex., 1971-77; supply specialist U.S. Dept. of Def., Holloman AFB, 1977--. Active citizen rev. bd. United Way, Sacramento, 1982, 88. Mem. Elks. Democrat. Home: 6000 Hickorywood Way Citrus Heights CA 95621 Office: SM-ALC DSFO Bldg 783A McClellan AFB CA 95652-5999

HOLMAN, DONALD REID, lawyer; b. Astoria, Oreg., Jan. 30, 1930; s. Donald Reuben and Hattie Laveda (Card) H.; m. Susan Muncy Morris, Aug. 31, 1956; children: Donald Reid, Laura Morris, Holman O'Brien, Douglas Edward. B.A., U. Wash.-Seattle, 1951, J.D., 1958; postgrad., U. Oreg.-Eugene, 1955-57. Bar: Oreg. Assoc. Miller, Nash, Wiener, Hager & Carlsen, Portland, 1958-63, ptnr., 1963-87, mng. ptnr., 1987—; bd. dirs., corp. sec. La-Pacific Corp., Portland, 1973—, Byers Photo Equipment Co., Portland, 1985—; corp. sec. Brod & McLung-Pace Co., Portland, 1981—. Served to lt. (j.g.) USN, 1951-55; capt. JAGC USNR, 1977—. Fellow Am. Bar Found.; mem. Multnomah County Bar Assn., Oreg. State Bar Assn., Am. Soc. Corp. Secs., Order of Coif, The Racquet Club (pres. 1983-84, dir. 1981-83), Multnomah Athletic Club (trustee 1983-85, v.p. 1985-86), Waverly Country Club, Phi Delta Phi. Republican. Mormon. Clubs: Racquet, Multnomah Athletic, Waverley Country (all Portland). Home: 8040 SW Broadmoor Terr Portland OR 97225 Office: Miller Nash Wiener Hager & Carlsen 111 SW 5th Ave Portland OR 97204

HOLMAN, JOHN FOSTER, investment banker; b. Chgo., Dec. 11, 1946; s. William Judson and Evelyn Mae (Foster) H.; m. Paula Susan Anderson, Aug. 1, 1970 (div. Oct. 1978). BS, Ariz. State U., 1969, MBA, 1971, JD, 1975. Bar: Ariz. 1975. Trial atty. Johnson, Tucker, Jessen & Dake, Phoenix, 1975-78, Holman & Meador, Phoenix, 1978-80; nat. mktg. dir. Franchise Fin. Corp. Am., Phoenix, 1980-87; mng. dir. Fin. Resource Group, Sausalito, Calif., 1987—. Pres. Am. Wellness Assn., 1989—; mem. camp com. YMCA, Phoenix, 1968—; Inner Circle of the U.S. Senate, Washington, 1984—. Capt. U.S. Army, 1968-76. Republican. Presbyterian. Home and Office: 3500 E Lincoln Dr Phoenix AZ 85018

HOLMAN, PAUL DAVID, plastic surgeon; b. Waynesboro, Va., Mar. 13, 1943; s. Wallace D. and Rosalie S. Holman; m. Victoria Lynn Holman, Mar. 1, 1986. B.A., U. Va., 1965; M.D., Jefferson Med. Coll., 1968. Intern, George Washington U. Hosp., 1968-69, resident in gen. surgery, 1969-70, 72-74; resident in plastic surgery Phoenix Plastic Surgery Residency, 1974-76; practice medicine specializing in plastic surgery, Phoenix, 1977—; mem. staff Good Samaritan Hosp., Phoenix, St. Joseph's Hosp., Phoenix, Phoenix Children's Hosp. Served to lt. comdr. USNR, 1970-72. Diplomate Am. Bd. Surgery, Am. Bd. Plastic Surgery. Mem. AMA, ACS, Am. Soc. Plastic and Reconstructive Surgeons, Phi Beta Kappa. Office: 1010 E McDowell Rd 303 Phoenix AZ 85006

HOLME, HOWARD KELLEY, lawyer; b. Denver, May 5, 1945; s. Peter Hagner Jr. and Lena (Phillips) H.; m. Barbara Lynn Shaw, June 16, 1968; children: Timothy Peter, Lisa. AB in History with distinction Stanford U., 1967; JD, Yale U., 1972. Bar: Colo. 1972, U.S. Dist. Ct. Colo. 1972, U.S. Ct. Appeals (10th cir.) 1972, U.S. Supreme Ct. 1984. Staff Denver U. Law Sch., 1969-71; assoc. Fairfield and Woods, Denver, 1972-77; ptnr., dir. Fairfield & Woods, P.C., Denver, 1977—; cons. Fryingpan-Ark. Project, Southeastern Colo. Water Conservation Dist., 1976—. Author: New Careers in Law, 1971; contbr. articles to profl. jours. Bd. dirs. N. Cen. region Am. Friends Svc. Com., 1979-83; nat. legal adv. com. Planned Parenthood Fedn. Am., N.Y.C., 1980-82, Denver U. Ctr. for Gifted Youth, 1985-87; active Colo. Supreme Ct. law com., Denver, 1979—; advisor to Senator Barbara Holme, Colo., 1975-85. Mem. ABA (vice chmn. population com. 1976-80), Colo. Bar Assn., Denver Bar Assn., Denver Law Club, Cactus Club. Avocations: reading, squash, politics. Democrat. Quaker. Home: 1243 Fillmore St Denver CO 80206 Office: Fairfield & Woods PC 1700 Lincoln Ste 2400 Denver CO 80203

HOLMES, DALLAS SCOTT, lawyer, educator; b. L.A., Dec. 2, 1940; s. Donald Cherry and Hazel (Scott) H.; m. Patricia McMichael, Aug. 21, 1965; children: Mark Scott, Tobin John. AB cum laude, Pomona Coll., 1962; MS, London Sch. Econs., 1964; JD, U. Calif.-Berkeley, 1967. Bar: Calif. 1968. Assoc. Best, Best & Krieger, Riverside, Calif., 1968-74, ptnr., 1974—; exec. asst. to Assembly majority floor leader, Calif. State Legislature, Sacramento, 1969-70; asst. adj. prof. Grad. Sch. Mgmt., U. Calif.-Riverside, 1977-88; lectr. UCLA Extension, 1987—; city atty. Cities of Corona and Redlands, Calif.; lectr. local govt. and univ. extension groups. Pres., Pomona Coll. Alumni Coun., 1973-74, Century Club, Riverside, 1974-76, Citizens Univ. Com., 1983-85, Downtown Riverside Assn., 1987-88; chmn. legal affairs com. Assn. Calif. Water Agys., 1985—. Named Man of Yr., Riverside Press-Enterprise, 1962, Young Man of Yr., Riverside Jr. C. of C., 1972. Mem. Riverside County Bar Assn. (pres. 1982), Calif. State Bar Assn. (exec. com. pub. law sect. 1983-86), ABA, Internat. Bar Assn. Republican. Presbyterian. Contbr. articles on mass transit, assessment of farmland in Calif., exclusionary zoning and environ. law to profl. jours.; author proposed tort reform initiative for Calif. physicians. Home: 4515 6th St Riverside CA 92501 Office: Best Best & Krieger 3750 University Ave PO Box 1028 Riverside CA 92502

HOLMES, JOHN MALLORY, III, telecommunications services company executive; b. Chgo., Feb. 25, 1938; s. John Mallory Jr. and Lucie (Cook) H.; m. Pauline Garman, Nov. 24, 1967. BS in Indsl. Mgmt., Calif. State U., Sacramento, 1967. Staff engr. Pacific Telephone Co., Sacramento, 1967-69; dist. mgr. Pacific Telephone Co., San Francisco, 1969-72, AT&T, N.Y.C., 1972-76, Nev. Bell, Reno, 1976-80; v.p., gen. mgr. Nev. Tel & Tel, Tonopah, 1980-81; dir. Pub. Svc. Comm., Carson City, Nev., 1981-83; co-owner, v.p. LMSL, Inc., Carson City, 1983--; also bd. dirs. LMSL, Inc., Kansas City, Mo.; bd. dis. Am. Consol. Fin. Corp., Wilmington, Del.; v.p. True Polypay Sheep Registry, 1986-88. Contbr. articles to profl. jours. Pres., v.p., treas. Jacks Valley Vol. Fire Dept., Carson City, 1976--; chmn. Sierra Estates Gen. Improvement Dist., Carson City, 1976-80; Nev. Rep. chmn. pub. rels., 1984-86; Douglas County Rep. vice chmn., 1985-87. Served with USAF, 1956-64. Mem. Nat. Assn. Radio and TV Engrs. (charter sr., cert. engr. 1st class; bd. dirs. 1983--, v.p. 1986-88), Douglas County Farm Bur., Blue Key, Beta Gamma Sigma, Capital Club (pres. Carson City chpt. 1987-88). Home and Office: 3618 Green Acre Dr Carson City NV 89705

HOLMES, PAUL LUTHER, political scientist, educational consultant; b. Rock Island, Ill., Mar. 7, 1919; s. Bernt Gunnar and Amanda Sophia (Swenson) H.; m. Ardis Ann Grunditz, Nov. 1, 1946; children: Mary Ann, David Stephen. B.A., U. Minn., 1940; M.A., Stanford U., 1949, Ed.D., 1968; M.A., George Washington U., 1964. Career officer U.S. Navy, 1941-64, ret. as capt.; adminstr. Laney Coll., Oakland, Calif., 1965-70; dean Contra Costa Coll., San Pablo, Calif., 1970-71; pres. Coll. of Alameda (Calif.), 1971-75, prof. polit. sci., 1975-80; dir. doctoral studies program No. Calif., Nova U., 1975-80; cons. in higher edn., Gig Harbor, Wash., 1981—; regent Calif. Luth. U., 1973-76. Decorated Navy Air, Joint Service medals. Mem. AAUP, Am. Polit. Sci. Assn., Navy League, Stanford Univ. Alumni Assn., Phi Delta Kappa. Lutheran. Club: Rotary (Gig Harbor).

HOLMES, WALTER WILLIAM, JR., insurance agent; b. Salt Lake City, Nov. 16, 1939; s. Walter William Sr.and LaRhue Ferol (Smith) H.; m. Beverly Arline Lindholm, Aug. 9, 1962; children: Sheryl Lynn, Michelle Arline, Deborah LaRhue, Jeffrey Walter, Kenneth Sherman. BS, Brigham Young U., 1963. CLU. Supr. Equitable Life Assurance Soc., Denver, 1964-67; dept. mgr. Equitable Life Assurance Soc., San Francisco, 1967-76; agy. service mgr. Equitable Life Assurance Soc., Tucson, 1976-85; pres. Walter Holmes, CLU & Assocs., Tucson, 1985—. Blood drive chmn. ARC, Tucson, 1986-87; active Fruchthendler PTA. Mem. Am. Soc. CLU, CHFC, So. Ariz. Assn. Health Underwriters (bd. dirs. 1988—, continuing edn. chmn. 1987—), Gen. Agts. & Mgrs. Assn. (scc., treas. 1988—), Greater Tucson Assn. Life Underwriters, Ariz. Interscholastic Assn. (bd. dirs. 1980—), So. Ariz. CLU (pres. 1989—, chmn. 1987—). Office: Walter Holmes CLU & Assocs 3113 E First St Tucson AZ 85716

HOLMES, WILLARD, art gallery director; b. Saskatoon, Sask., Canada. Grad. in art history, U. B.C., 1972. With Fine Arts Gallery, U. B.C; head of exhbns. Nat. Gallery of Can.; curator Vancouver Art Gallery; dir. Pender St. Gallery, from 1976; chief curator, interim dir. Vancouver Art Gallery, dir., 1987—. Office: Vancouver Art Gallery, 750 Hornby St, Vancouver, BC Canada V6Z 2H7 *

HOLMES-LUPI, MARGARET HELEN, banker; b. The Dalles, Oreg., Oct. 3, 1958; d. Charles Louis Holmes and Lorita Dee (Woodside) Dunlap; m. Peter Nicola Lupi, Dec. 27, 1986. BS in Polit. Sci., Oregon State U., 1980. Loan svc. rep. Great Western Bank, Northridge, Calif., 1981-83; loan svc. officer Great Western Bank, Northridge, 1983-84, bus. analyst, 1984-86, asst. v.p., 1986—. Campaigner Atiyeh for Gov., Corvallis, Oreg., 1978; senate flr. staff Oreg. Legis. Assembly, Salem, 1979. Recipient 4-H Scholarship Union Pacific R.R., Portland, 1976. Republican. Presbyterian. Home: 21030 Gresham #804 Canoga Park CA 91304 Office: Great Western Bank 9451 Corbin Ave Northridge CA 91324

HOLMLUND, LISA LYNNE, marketing professional; b. Aberdeen, Wash., Oct. 11, 1960; d. Carl Don H. and Sharon Lynne (Markwell) Stein. BA in Communications, Wash. State U., 1983. Intern Jay Rockey Pub. Relations, Seattle, 1982-83; account exec. Arst Pub. Relations, Bellevue, Wash., 1983-86; dir. mktg. com. Princess Tours, Seattle, 1986—; cons. Boys and Girls Clubs, Kings County, Wash., 1984-86; mem. mktg. task force Bellevue C. of C., 1985-86. Bd. dirs. Eastside Theater Co., 1985-86. Office: Princess Tours 2815 2d Ave Ste 400 Seattle WA 98121

HOLO, SELMA REUBEN, museum director, educator; b. Chgo., May 21, 1943; d. Samuel and Ghita (Hurwitz) Reuben; m. Sanford Holo, June 14, 1964 (div. 1981); children: Robert, Joshua. BA, Northwestern U., 1965; MA, Hunter Coll., 1972; PhD, U. Calif., Santa Barbara, 1980. Lectr. Art Ctr. Coll. of Design, Pasadena, Calif., 1973-77; curator of acquisitions Norton Simon Mus., Pasadena, 1977-81; dir. Fisher Gallery and mus. studies program U. So. Calif., Los Angeles, 1981—; guest curator, cons. Getty Mus., Malibu, Calif. 1975-76, 81; guest curator Isetan Mus., Tokyo, 1982; cons. Nat. Mus. for Women in Arts, Washington, 1984; reviewer grants Inst. Mus. Services, Washington, 1986, 87; panel chmn. Internat. Com. on Exhbn. Exchange, Washington, 1984; panelist NEA, Washington, 1985. Author: (catalogues) Goya: Los Disparates, 1976, (co-author) La Tauromagiria: Goya, Picasso and the Bullfight, 1986; contbr. articles to profl. jours. Kress Found. grantee, N.Y., 1979; Internationes, Fed. Republic of Germany grantee, 1985. Mem. Coll. Art Assn. (survey com. mus. studies programs 1986), Am. Assn. Mus., Art Table. Jewish. Office: U So Calif Fisher Gallery 823 Exposition Blvd Los Angeles CA 90089-0292

HOLOVKA, JOHN MICHAEL, chemist; b. Binghamton, N.Y., July 3, 1940; s. Charles Jr. and Anna (Bussa) H.; m. Teresita Martinez, 1972 (div. Aug. 1985); 1 child, Julie Ann. AS in Chemistry, Broometech Community Coll., Binghamton, N.Y., 1961; BS in Chemistry, N.Mex. Highlands U., 1965; PhD in Phys. Organic Chemistry, U. Utah, 1969. Rsch. scientist Marathon Oil Co., Littleton, Colo., 1968-70; mem. tech. staff Sandia Nat. Lab., Albuquerque, 1970-84, supr., 1984—. Contbr. articles to profl. jours; patentee in field of organic chemistry. Republican. Home: PO Box 214 Sandia Park NM 87047 Office: Sandia Lab Div 9111 PO Box 9123 Albuquerque NM 87185

HOLST, SANFORD, engineering and construction executive, writer; b. Batavia, N.Y., Nov. 4, 1946; s. William Walker and Catherine (Loggie) H.; children: Suzanne, Kristina. BS in Aero., Astronautics, MIT, 1968; MBA, UCLA, 1970. Engr. advanced design group Lockheed Aircraft Corp., Los Angeles, 1968-71; analyst UCLA, Los Angeles, 1972-73, So. Calif. Assn. Govts., Los Angeles, 1973-78; systems analyst Northwest Industries, Los Angeles, 1978-80; analyst UCLA, Los Angeles, 1972-78; v.p. computer systems dept. Parsons Corp., Pasadena, Calif., 1980—. Editor Taurus mag., 1971-72; contbr. articles to various publs. Vice chmn. Beverly Hills (Calif.) Bicentennial Com., 1976. Mem. Phi Kappa Sigma (pres. Alpha Mu chpt. 1967-68). Office: Parsons Corp 100 W Walnut St Pasadena CA 91124

HOLST, WILLIAM JAMES, data processor; b. Frederick, Md., Aug. 22, 1945; s. William Walker and Catherine M. (Loggie) H.; m. Patricia Russell, Jan. 27, 1973; children—Jennifer R., Gretchen M., William R. B.S. in Bus. Adminstrn., No. Ariz. U., 1972. Computer ops. mgr. Samaritan Health Service, Phoenix, 1972-75; material requirements mgr. Pepsi-Cola, Flagstaff, Ariz., 1975-78; dir. fiscal/info. services Flagstaff (Ariz.) Med. Center, 1978-84, mgr. data processing, 1984-87, Info. Systems, 1987—. Medic Alert local rep., 1983—; mem., solicitor high tech. equipment, donations No. Ariz. Health Care Found. Served with U.S. Army, 1965-69. Mem. Data Processing Mgmt. Assn. (cert., dir.), Assn. Systems Mgmt., Health Care Fin. Mgmt. Assn., Electronic Computing Health Oriented. Roman Catholic. Office: PO Box 1268 Flagstaff AZ 86002

HOLT, ALEX A., building supply executive; b. Ciacova, Romania, Feb. 13, 1936; came to U.S., 1949; s. Frank and Magda (Theiss) Holecsek; m.June 23, 1962; children: Mark Anthony, Brian Edward. Student, U. Ill., Chgo., 1956. Ins. agt. Met. Life Ins. Co., Chgo., 1962-64; sales rep. Philip Carey Mfg. Co., Chgo., 1964-68; dist. mgr. Kaiser Aluminum & Chem. Sales Co., Chgo., 1968-76; pres., owner Aluminum Supply Co. div. Almar Corp., Denver, 1976—; pres., Alarm Engrs., Inc., L.A., 1986—; v.p., U.S. Bldg. Products, Inc., Chgo., 1984-87; v.p., gen. mgr. Prime Fin. Svcs., Inc., Denver, 1986—. With U.S. Army, 1958-60. Republican. Roman Catholic. Office: Aluminum Supply Co PO Box 16468 Denver CO 80216

HOLT, DENNIS F., media buying company executive. Student, U. So. Calif. Salesman RKO, L.A.; founder, pres. chief exec. officer Western Internat. Media Corp., L.A. Office: Western Internat Media Corp 8544 Sunset Blvd Los Angeles CA 90069 *

HOLT, JAMES FRANKLIN, numerical analyst, scientific programmer analyst; b. Alexander, Ark., Aug. 24, 1927; s. Edward Warbritton and Etta Turner (Ludi) H.; m. Gloria Anne Gaishin, May 5, 1963; children: Gregory James, Elizabeth Diana, Debora Anne. BA in Math., UCLA, 1953. With Pacific Mutual Ins. Corp., L.A., 1953-54; assoc. engr. Lockheed Aircraft Corp., Burbank, Calif., 1954-58; mem. tech. staff Space Tech. Labs., El Sedundo, Calif., 1958-61, Aerospace Corp., El Sedundo, 1961—. Author play: To Play's the Thing, 1963 (French Grand Prix award), papers in field. Mem. Young Reps., L.A., 1960-66. Cpl. USAF, 1945-48. Mem. Aerospace Profl. Staff Assn. (1st v.p. 1985—). Home: 3534 Mandeville Canyon Rd Los Angeles CA 90049

HOLT, ROBERT MCKINDLY, microscopist; b. Lodi, Calif., Sept. 24, 1956; s. Robert McKindly Holt and Cleo Virginia (Reiling) Kite; m. Cornelia Gilbert, Aug. 8, 1987. AA, San Joaquin Delta Coll., Stockton, Calif., 1983. Microscopist Raychem Corp., Menlo Park, Calif., 1983—. Mem. Sane, Washington, 1987. MJem. Electron Microscopy Soc. Am., Westcoast Microbeam Analysis Soc., No. Calif. Soc. Electron Microscopy. Democrat. Home: 726 Oak Grove Ave Menlo Park CA 94025 Office: Raychem Corp 300 Constitution Dr Menlo Park CA 94025

HOLTEL, MICHAEL RAY, physician; b. Glendora, Calif., Sept. 4, 1958; s. Robert Leonard and Nancy (Anderson) H.; m. Julie Mary Biron. BA, U. Calif., Santa Barbara, 1980; MD, Uniformed Services U. of the Health Scis., 1984. Diplomate Nat. Bd. Med. Examiners. Emergency room technician Little Company of Mary Hosp., Torrance, Calif., 1976-77; intern in surgery Naval Hosp, Bethesda, Md., 1984-85; bn. surgeon 1st Marine Amphibious Brigade, Kaneohe, Hawaii, 1985-86; resident in otolaryngology USN Hosp.,

Oakland, Calif., 1986—. Sandpiper Club scholar, 1976. Mem. Am. Acad. Otolaryngology, Am. Acad. Facial Plastics and Reconstructive Surgery, ACS. Republican. Club: Grizzly Peak Cyclists (Berkeley, Calif.). Office: Naval Hosp Box 3802 Oakland CA 94627

HOLTON, WILLIAM CHESTER, engineer, consultant; b. Caldwell, Idaho, May 2, 1939; s. Chester Clayton and Margaret Ann (MacLaren) H.; m. Rhoberta Phaigh Romo, June 1, 1958 (div. Sept. 1976); children: William Lee, Robert Charles, Ronald Clayton. AS, Regents Coll., 1986. lic. FCC. Electronic technician Litton Industries, L.A., 1963-66; applications engr. 3M Co., Camarillo, Calif., 1966-74; program analyst USN, Port Magu, Calif., 1974-75; video supr. U. Calif., Santa Barbara, 1975-77; cons. Great Am. Tech. Services, L.A., 1977—; pres. G&B Electronics Inc., Hollywood, Calif., 1987—; project engr. Amblin Entertainment, Universal City, Calif., 1983-84, Beijing (People's Republic of China) Film Studios, 1982. Creator first digitally controlled screening theater for sound/film/video at Universal Studios, first high speed sound-on-film editing suite in People's Republic of China. Mem. Soc. Motion Picture TV Engrs. (voting). Office: G&B Electronics Inc 747 N Seward Hollywood CA 90038

HOLTZAPFEL, PATRICIA KELLY, health facility executive; b. Madison, Wis., Jan. 29, 1948; d. Raymond Michael and Laura Margaret (Stegner) Kelly; m. Robert Adrian Bunker, Oct. 4, 1975 (div. June 1979); children: Donald, Theresa, Nicole, Douglas; m. Raymond Paul Holtzapfel, Mar. 12, 1983; children: David, Richard. RN; cert. pub. health nurse. Staff nurse Madison Gen. Hosp., 1970-72; bloodmobile staff nurse ARC, Madison, 1972-73; pub. health nurse Dane County Pub. Health Dept., Madison, 1973-75; field health nurse CIGNA Health Plan, Phoenix, 1975-84; dir. nursing Olsten Health Care, Phoenix, 1984-85; mgr. bus. Holtzapfel Phys. Therapy and Pain Control Clinic, Phoenix, 1985—. Bd. dirs. Deer Valley Vocat. Arts Adv. Council, Phoenix, 1986—. Mem. The Exec. Female Assn., Ariz. Networking Council. Office: Holtzapfel Phys Therapy Pain Control 4025 W Bell Rd Ste #2 Phoenix AZ 85023

HOLZ, ROLAND RAYMOND, insurance executive; b. N.Y.C., Apr. 21, 1940; s. Henry Jean and Elly (Wolz) H.; m. Alise Angelica Pfister, June 8, 1961; children: Susan Ellen, Sandra Theresa, Sherri Jean. BS, U.S. Mil. Acad., 1961; MBA in Ins. Mgmt., Coll. of Ins., N.Y.C., 1968. CPCU. Commd. U.S. Army, 1957, advanced through grades to lt., resigned, 1964; asst. underwriting mgr. Hartford Ins. Group, N.Y.C., 1967-68; underwriting mgr. Hartford Ins. Group, Mt. Kisco, N.Y., 1968-72; mgr. cons. Hartford, Conn., 1972-74; asst. gen. mgr. Newark, 1974-75, Mt. Kisco, 1975-78; branch mgr. CNA Inc., Melville, N.Y., 1978-80; asst. v.p. CNA Inc., Chgo., 1980-82; asst. div. mgr. Hartford Ins. Group, Oakbrook, Ill., 1982-85; v.p., gen. mgr. Home Ins. Co., San Francisco, 1985—. Co-chmn. Spl. Liturgy Co. St. John Vianney, Walnut Creek, Calif., 1987—, lector and eucharistic minister, 1986—. Mem. Ins. Mgrs. Assn. (v.p.), Engrs. Club of San Francisco, Huntington Crescent Club. Republican. Roman Catholic. Home: 3460 Sutcliffe Ct Walnut Creek CA 94598 Office: Home Ins Co 1 Embarcadero Ste 1400 San Francisco CA 94111

HOLZER, KENNETH DEAN, aviation executive; b. Newton, Kans., Feb. 25, 1929; s. James Lawrence and Alma Sophia (Lauer) H.; m. Marilee L. McMullen, Mar. 4, 1951 (div. 1962); children: Gregory Lawrence, Scott Clay; m. Myrna Ball (div. June 1983); 1 child, Kelly. Student, Pasadena City Coll., 1948; BS, U. Wichita, 1957. Regional sales mgr. Cessna Aircraft Co., Wichita, Kans., 1955-59; mgr. dealer sales Beech Aircraft Corp., Wichita, 1959-61, regional sales mgr., 1961-64; sales mgr. Northern Air Svc., Grand Rapids, Mich., 1964-68, v.p., gen. mgr., 1968-73; v.p., gen. mgr. Cutter Flying Svc., Inc., Albuquerque, 1973—. Bd. dirs. Air Force Assn., Albuquerque, 1982—, Presbyn. Hosp., Albuquerque, 1988—; officer, bd. mem. Albuquerque Armed Forces Adv. Assn., 1982—. Brig. Gen. U.S. Army Nat. Guard, 1951-56, Korea. Republican. Home: 1412 Hiawatha St NE Albuquerque NM 87112 Office: Cutter Flying Svc Inc 2502 Clark-Carr Loop SE Albuquerque NM 87106

HOLZER, THOMAS LEQUEAR, geologist; b. Lafayette, Ind., June 26, 1944; s. Oswald Alois and Ruth Alice (Lequear) H.; m. Mary Elizabeth Burbach, June 13, 1968; children: Holly Christine, Elizabeth Alice. BSE, Princeton U., 1965; MS, Stanford U., 1966, PhD, 1970. Asst. prof. geology U. Conn., Starrs, 1970-75; adj. environmentalist Griswold & Fuss, Manchester, Conn., 1973-75; research geol. U.S. Geol. Survey, Menlo Park, Calif., 1975-82, rsch. geologist, 1984-88; dep. asst. dir. rsch. U.S. Geol. Survey, Reston, Va., 1982-84, chief br. engring. seismology and geology, 1989—. Contbr. numerous articles to profl. jours. Coach Am. Youth Soccer Orgn., Palo Alto, Calif., 1979-82. Recipient Superior Service award U.S. Geol. Survey, 1981. Fellow: Geol. Soc. Am. (chmn. engring. geology div. 1988—); mem. AAAS, Am. Geophys. Union, Nat. Water Well Assn. Republican. Presbyterian. Home: 151 Walter Hays Dr Palo Alto CA 94303 Office: US Geol Survey 345 Middlefield Rd Menlo Park CA 94025

HOLZMAN, D. KEITH, producer, arts consultant; b. N.Y.C., Mar. 22, 1936; s. Jacob Easton and Minnette Cathryn (Sternberger) H.; m. Jo Susan Handelman, Nov. 16, 1971; children: Susanne Carla, Lucas Jon, Rebecca Leigh. BA, Oberlin (Ohio) Coll., 1957; MFA, Boston U., 1959. Asst. to gen. mgr. and stage mgr. N.Y.C. Light Opera, 1959, 62-64; dir. prodn. Elektra Records, N.Y.C., 1964-70; v.p. prodn. and mfg. Elektra/Asylum/Nonesuch Records, Los Angeles, 1970-81; sr. v.p. prodn. and mfg. Elektra/Asylum/Nonesuch Records, 1981-84; pres. ROM Records, 1987—; producer, arts cons. Treasure Trove, Inc., 1984—; pres. Treasure Trove Inc.; dir. Nonesuch Records, 1980-84; music supr. Witches of Eastwick, Warner Bros., Los Angeles, 1986; bd. dirs. Plumstead Theatre Soc., Los Angeles, 1985—, Early Music Acad., Los Angeles, 1983-86, Assn. Classical Music, N.Y.C., 1983-86. Served with AUS, 1960-62. Mem. Audio Engring. Soc., Early Music Acad. (bd. dirs.) Nat. Acad. Rec. Arts and Scis., Assn. Classical Music (bd. dirs.), Plumstead Theatre Co. (bd. dirs.). Office: ROM Records PO Box 491212 Los Angeles CA 90049

HOM, RICHARD YEE, research aerospace engineer; b. Phoenix, July 26, 1950; s. Tommy Look and Betty (Mah) H.; B.S. in Engring. Sci. and Aero. and Aerospace Tech., Ariz. State U., 1973; m. Kathleen Chien; 1 child, Matthew Thomas. Asst. engr. Sperry Flight System, Phoenix, 1973; sr. engr., composite tool engring. Boeing Comml. Airplane Co., Seattle, 1973-84; specialist engr. 1984-88, sr. specialist engr. research and devel., metall. processing and advanced projects Boeing Aerospace Co., 1984—, also automation tech. Mem. Air Force Assn., Soc. Mfg. Engrs., AIAA. Home: 28704 15th Ave S Federal Way WA 98003 Office: Boeing Aerospace Co M/S 6K-43 PO Box 3999 Seattle WA 98124

HOMAN, RALPH WILLIAM, finance company executive; b. Wilkes-Barre, Pa., June 7, 1951; s. Norman Ryan and Adelaide Bernice (Sandy) H.; m. Donna Marie Webb, Jan. 25, 1975. BS in Acctg., Wheeling Coll., 1977; MBA in Mktg., Nat. U., 1986. Paymaster Dravo Corp., Pitts., 1974-75; tax preparer H&R Block, Wheeling, W.Va., 1977; fin. services exec. NCR Credit Corp., Sacramento, 1977-84; leasing exec. CSB Leasing, Sacramento, 1984-85; pres. Convergent Fin. Services, Sedona, Ariz., 1985—. Co-winner Name the Plane Contest Pacific Southwest Airlines, 1984. Mem. The 30/40 Something Social Club (founder, pres. Sedona chpt.), Toastmasters (treas. Oak Creek chpt. 1988—), Kiwanis (sec. 1988-89). Republican. Episcopalian. Home and Office: Convergent Fin Services 210 Canyon Diablo Rd Sedona AZ 86336

HOMBS, MARGARET MAVOURNEEN, teacher; b. Evanston, Ill., May 17, 1934; d. Pat and Eloise (Taylor) O'Brien; m. Max David Garten, June 27, 1957 (div. 1968); m. John Hayden Hombs, Dec. 7, 1969; children: Eric, Lisa Andrea, Stacy, Karin, Kurt. BA in Music, Marymount Coll., 1955; MA in Edn., Loyola U., Westchester, Calif., 1956; postgrad. in library sci., Calif. State U., Los Angeles, 1984. Tchr. Baldwin (Calif.) Park Sch. Dist., 1956-57, Garden Grove (Calif.) Union Sch. Dist., 1961-74; tchr. Morongo Union Sch. Dist., Morongo Basin, Calif., 1974—, tchr., dist. curriculum and instruction, 1979—, secondary chair, 1985-86; coordinator Writing Celebration, San Bernardino, Calif., 1979-81, 1986-88; com. mem. Garden Grove Union Sch. Dist., 1964-70; CJSF advisor Garden Grove and Morongo Sch. dists., 1960—. Contbr. numerous articles to profl. jours.; editor English textbook, 1965. Soloist, choir dir., St. Christopher's Cath. Ch., Joshua Tree, Calif., 1978—, dir., soloist Hi Desert Cultural Ctr., 1978—; actress, stage mgr., Playhous Guild, Joshua Tree, 1978—. Named Best Director H. Desert Playhouse Guild, Joshua Tree. Mem. Nat. Council Tchrs. of English, Library Media Specialists, Morongo Tchrs. Assn., Calif. Media Library Educators Assn., Calif. Tchrs. Assn., NEA, 4-H Club. Republican. Home: PO Box 158 Joshua Tree CA 92252 Office: La Contenta Jr High Sch PO Box 1779 Yucca Valley CA 92252

HOMESTEAD, SUSAN, psychotherapist; b. Bklyn., Sept. 20, 1937; d. Cy Simon and Katherine (Haas) Eichelbaum; m. George Gilbert Zanetti, Dec. 13, 1962 (div. 1972); 1 child, Bruce David; m. 2d, Ronald Eric Homestead, Jan. 16, 1973 (div. 1980). BA, U. Miami-Fla., 1960; MSW, Tulane U., 1967. Lic. clin. social worker, Va., Calif. Pvt. practice, cons., Richmond, Va., 1971—; psychotherapist, cons. Family and Children's Svcs., Richmond, 1981—, Richmond Pain Clinic, 1983-84; cons. Health Internat. Va., P.C., Lynchburg, 1984-86, Santa Clara DSS, Calif., 1986-88, Franklin St. Psychotherapy & Edn. Ctr, Santa Clara, 1988— ; co-dir. asthma program Va. Lung Assn., Richmond, 1975-79, Loma Prieta Regional Ctr.; chief clin. social worker Med. Coll. Va., Va. Commonwealth U., 1974-79. Contbr. articles to profl. jours. Active, Peninsula Children's Ctr., Morgan Ctr., Council for Community Action Planning, Community Assn. for Retarded, Comprehensive Health Planning Assn. Santa Clara, Mental Health Commn., Children and Adolescent Target Group Calif., Women's Com. Richmond Symphony, Va. Mus. Theatre, mem. fin. com. Robb for Gov.; mem. adv. com. Lung Assn.; mem. steering com. Am. Cancer Soc. Va. div. Epilepsy Found., Am. Heart Assn., Cen. Va. Guild for Infant Survival. Mem. Va. Soc. Clin. Social Work, Inc. (charter mem., sec. 1975-78), Nat. Assn. Social Workers, Soc. for Psychoanalytic Psychotherapy, Am. Acad. Psychotherapists, Internat. Soc. for the Study of Multiple Personalities and Dissociations. Jewish.

HONEA, GLENN DALE, pilot; b. Jasper, Ga., Mar. 18, 1953; s. John Daniel and Era Frances (Martin) Deep H.; m. Jannie Althea Foster, Nov. 6, 1976 (div. 1979). Student, Johnson County Community Coll., 1972-73, Wichita State U., 1972-73. Cert. airline transport pilot, learjet, citation jet; flight instr.; airplanes and instruments single and multi-engine. Sgt. USAF, 1971-74; flight instr. Brown Aviation, Perry, Ga., 1974; instr. E. Ark. Community Coll., Forest City, Ark.; pres. Mid-South Aviation, Memphis, 1976; chief flight instr. Cape Cen. Airways, Cape Girardeau, Mo., 1976-78; chief pilot Blount Corp., Fort Dodge, Iowa, 1979; chief flight instr. Terra Tng., Las Vegas, 1980-81; dir. ops. and chief pilot Air Nev., Las Vegas, 1981-83; various pilot position various orgns., Calif., 1983-89; pres. Calif. Jets, Hayward, 1989—. Mem. Aircraft Owners & Pilots Assn., Smithsonian Air & Space. Republican. Home: 23924 Second St Hayward CA 94541 Office: Calif Jets 22693 Heperian Blvd Ste 260 Hayward CA 94541

HONG, NORMAN G. Y., architect; b. Honolulu, May 5, 1947; s. Kwai Ing and Patricia Y.S. (Dye) H.; m. Lorna Sachiko Yano, Aug. 11, 1973; 1 child, Christopher. T.S.C. BArch, U. Hawaii, 1969. Registered architect, Hawaii. Designer, John Tatom Architect, Honolulu, 1969-71; assoc. Group 70 Inc., Honolulu, 1971-77, prin., 1977-80, ptnr., 1980-84, mng. ptnr., 1984-88, pres., chief operating officer, 1989—. Bd. dirs. Manpower Planning Agy. Honolulu, 1972; com. mem. Ann. Gov./Mayor's Prayer, Honolulu, 1984; mem. Mayor's Adv. Com. on Chinatown Gateway, 1987, spl. design dists., 1989; mem. Epephany Epis. Sch. Bd., 1989—; mem. Haleiwa Spl. Design Adv. Com., 1986-87, Gov's Congress on Hawaii's Future, 1988. Recipient C.W. Dickey award U. Hawaii, 1977, Cert. Exemplary Performance, Dept. Navy Pacific Div., 1984. Mem. Constrn. Specifications Inst., AIA, Hawaii Soc. AIA (v.p. Hawaii 1987, pres. 1988, sec. Hawaii 1984-86, chmn. long range plan com. 1987, chmn. state conv., 1983), Plaza Club, Honolulu Country Club, Rotary. Mem. Kaimuki Christian Church. Office: Group 70 Inc 924 Bethel St Honolulu HI 96813

HONG, STEVE, manufacturing company executive; b. Stockton, Calif., Dec. 26, 1947; s. James and Ng She Hong; m. Gladys Huey, Aug. 8, 1971; children: Roger, Russell, Aimee. BS, San Jose State U., 1970. Asst. mgr. W.T. Grant Co., San Jose, 1970-71; field underwriter N.Y. Life Ins. Co., 1971-72; asst. sales mgr. N.Y. Life Ins. Co., Palo Alto, Calif., 1972; with Paul Masson Vineyards, 1972-77, chief acct., 1975-77; asst. controller NPI Corp., 1977-79; controller Forman Industries, Hayward, Calif., 1979, controller, gen. mgr., 1979-85; sec. and treas. Alerco and Hayward Steel, Inc. (name changed to A & H Steel, Inc.), Union City, Calif., 1985-86, v.p., 1986—. Mem. USNG, 1970-76. Republican. Methodist. Office: A&H Steel Inc 1000 Whipple Blvd Union City CA 94587

HONIG, BILL, state educational administrator; b. San Francisco, Apr. 23, 1937; s. Louis and Miriam (Anixter) H.; m. Nancy Catlin, June 2, 1973; children: Michael, Carolyn, Steven, Jonathan. BA, U. Calif., Berkeley, 1958, JD, 1963; MA, San Francisco State U., 1972. Bar: Calif. 1964; cert. tchr., Calif. Clk. Calif. Supreme Ct., 1963-64; atty. Calif. Dept. Fin., 1964-67; assoc. Pettit & Martin, San Francisco, 1967-71; tchr. San Francisco Unified Sch. Dist., 1972-76; dir. Staff Devel. Project, San Francisco, 1977-79; supt. Reed Union Elem. Sch. Dist., Tiburon, Calif., 1979-82; supt. pub. instrn. State of Calif., Sacramento, 1983—; mem. Calif. State Bd. Edn., 1975-82, past officer, pres. exec. sec. 1982; regent U. Calif., 1983—; trustee Calif. State Colls. and Univs., 1983—. Author: (with others) Handbook for Planning an Effective Reading Program, 1983; Last Chance for Our Children: How You Can Help Save Our Schools, 1985; contbr. articles to profl. jours. Mem. Carnegie Forum on Edn., PTA, YMCA, Nat. Commn. on Children. Served to 2d lt. U.S. Army, 1958-59. Mem. C. of C. (state edn. com.), Order of Coif. Jewish. Office: Calif State Dept Edn 721 Capitol Mall Ste 524 San Francisco CA 95814 *

HONIGSBERG, MARC STEVEN, insurance executive; b. Newark, Jan. 20, 1951; s. Henry George and Harriet (Dubin) H.; m. Cheryl Miller, Aug. 21, 1982. BA, Monmouth Coll., 1974. Lic. Nat. Assn. Security Dealers, 1975. With sales and mgmt. John Hancock Ins. Co., Millburn, N.J., 1974-77, Denver, 1977-83; P.P.G.A. Diversified Ins. Services, Denver, 1983-88; mgr. Prudential Ins. Co., Boulder, Colo., 1988—. Mem. Boulder Assn. Life Underwriters. Home: 2035 Hudson St Denver CO 80207 Office: Prudential Ins Co 3300 Mitchell Ln Boulder CO 80301

HONOR, HERBERT IRVING, electronic engineer; b. Bklyn., June 20, 1931; s. Max and Anne (Kress) H.; m. Anita Hilda Herschberg; children: Suzanne Honor Westlake, Marc Kenneth; m. Nancy Lee Schoener, Aug. 29, 1987. BS cum laude, CCNY, 1953; BSEE, MIT, 1957, MSEE, 1958. Electronic scientist USAF, Cambridge, Mass., 1956-58; mem. tech. staff Hughes Aircraft Co., Culver City, Calif., 1958-60; mgr. advanced computer devel. Nortronics, Hawthorne, Calif., 1960-65; mgr. advanced avionic systems Teledyne Systems Co., Northridge, Calif., 1965—; assoc. prof. Calif. State U., Long Beach, 1968-69. With U.S. Army, 1953-55. N.Y. State Bd. Regent's scholar, 1951, Tremaine scholar, 1952. Mem. Soc. Automotive Engrs., Tau Beta Pi, Eta Kappa Nu. Democrat. Jewish. Home: 840 20th St Apt 15 Santa Monica CA 90403 Office: Teledyne Systems Co 19601 Nordhoff St Northridge CA 91324

HONSTEAD, LOREN LEE, engineer; b. Washington, Mar. 20, 1947; s. Harold Frederick and Virginia Mae (Durk) H.; m. Lois Ann Abo, Mar. 28, 1969; children: Karla Leana, Jodi Eileen. BS in Agrl., U. Idaho, 1969; BS in Gen. Engring., Idaho State U., 1987. Asst. mgr. Hansen Farms, Pingree, Idaho, 1974-76; automotive machinist Kirkham Auto Parts, Blackfoot, Idaho, 1976-83; clk. Maverick, Blackfoot, 1984-87; engr. Rotational Molding, Inc., Caldwell, Idaho, 1988—. Parenting chmn. Idaho State PTA, 1983; pres., Pingree/Rockford PTA, 1982. Capt. USAF, 1970-74. Mem. Idaho Bd. Profl. Engrs. and Land Surveyors (engr.-in-tng.). Methodist. Home: Rt 3 PO Box 91 Caldwell ID 83605 Office: Rotational Molding Inc 716 N 11th Ave Caldwell ID 83605

HOOD, JAMES NICOL, psychiatrist; b. St. Louis, Sept. 19, 1929; s. Louis Charles and Frances Helen (Kinsman) H.; m. Claudia Chapline, Dec. 22, 1955 (div. 1974); children: Craig, Randall; m. Elinor Blake Levinson, Sept. 8, 1979; children: Gregory, Jeffrey. AB, Washington U., 1952, PHD, 1957; MD, U. So. Calif., 1959; postgrad., UCLA, 1963-65. Intern L.A. County Gen. Hosp., 1959-60; resident in psychiatry Brentwood VA Hosp., L.A., 1960-61, Cedars Sinai Hosp., L.A., 1961-62, L.A. Child Guidance Ctr., 1962-63; dir. mental health Huboldt County, Eureka, Calif., 1965-66; regional. adminstr. State of Calif., L.A., 1966-73; pvt. practice L.A., 1973-81, Oxnard, Calif., 1984—; psychiatrist Kaiser-Permanente, L.A., 1981-82; assoc. dir. student health Calif. State U., Northridge, 1982-84; asst. prof. UCLA Med. Sch., 1965-83. Contbr. articles to profl. jours. Mem. Ventura County Med. Soc., Calif. Med. Soc., Cardinal Flying Club, Phi Beta Kappa, Sigma Xi. Office: 500 E Esplanode Dr Ste 1458 Oxnard CA 93030

HOOK, CLYDE EDWARD, lawyer; b. Oklahoma City, Sept. 18, 1948; s. Edward Robert and Deliah Jane (Sampson) H.; m. Charlsie S. Dixon, Mar. 21, 1971. BBA, U. Okla., 1976, JD, 1979. Bar: Colo. 1979, U.S. Dist. Ct. Colo. 1979. Pvt. practice Denver, 1979-80; dep. dist. atty. Adams County Dist. Atty.'s Office, Brighton, Colo., 1980-84; staff counsel State Compensation Ins. Fund, Denver, 1984-86, State Compensation Ins. Authority, Denver, 1988-89; counsel, assoc. Quigley & Bruce, Denver, 1986-88; sr. assoc. Clifton & Hemphill, Denver, 1989—. 1st lt. USAF, 1969-76. Mem. Colo. Bar Assn., Adams County Bar Assn. Home: 1716 S Pennsylvania St Denver CO 80210 Office: Clifton & Hemphill 5353 W Dartmouth Ste 400 Denver CO 80227

HOOK, WILLIAM DENNIS, engineering manager; b. Cin., Dec. 25, 1951; s. Warren Dale and Marjorie Elizabeth (Dunn) H.; m. Sally Louise Drinkwine, June 19, 1976. Student, U. Cin., 1969-73. Field engr. Nalco Environ. Sci., Northbrook, Ill., 1975-77, Murray & Trettel, Northbrook, 1977-80; field engr. Applied Materials, Inc., Mesa, Ariz., 1980-86, dist. mgr., 1986-87, regional mgr., 1988—.

HOOKER, WILLIAM JONATHAN, dentist; b. Urbana, Ohio, Oct. 4, 1947; s. Malcolm DeWitt and Grace Louise (Lambert) H.; m. Kathy Irene Eckles, June 25, 1972; children: Megan Fairfide, Sara Grace. BS, Coll. of Wooster, Ohio, 1969; DDS, Ohio State U., 1974. Lic. dentist, Ariz., Ohio, Calif. Dentist Mt. Zion Hosp., San Francisco, 1977-78; gen. practice dentistry Flagstaff, Ariz., 1978--; pres., bd. dirs. Delta Dental Plan of Ariz., Phoenix, 1987--. With USPHS, 1975-77. Mem. Acad. Gen. Dentistry, Ariz. Dental Assn. (sec. 1988--), Am. Dental Assn., No. Ariz. Dental Assn. (pres. 1986-87), Flagstaff Ski Club, Kiwanis (bd. dirs. 1978-81). Republican. Methodist. Office: 718 N Humphreys St Flagstaff AZ 86001

HOOPER, BRUCE CHARLES, university loan official; b. Deadwood, S.D., July 28, 1948; s. Richard Browning and Redell H. (East) H.; m. Diana Kay Duca, Dec. 21, 1968; 1 child, Janine Marie. BS in statistics, U. Wyo., 1966-72. Program advisor U. Wyo., Laramie, Wyo., 1968-72; asst. supr. U. Wyo., Laramie, 1972-73, supr., 1973-84, mgr., 1984—, chmn., task force, 1986—; cons. U.S. Dept. of Edn., Washington, 1974—, orgn. of Am. Sts., Washington, 1987—, Nat. Coll. Credit and Collection, Aberdeen, S.D., 1975—, Info. Assocs., Rochester, N.Y., 1987—. Author: Collected Poems, 1980. treas. Albany County United Way, Laramie, 1978-80, United Methodist Ch., Laramie, 1980-81. Served to lt. U.S. Army, 1969-72. Mem. Student Info. System Users (chair-advisory), Wyo. Student Fin. Aid Adminstrs. (treas.), Rocky Mountain Assn. of Fin. Aid Adminstrs., Nat. Assn. of Student Fin. Aid Adminstrs. Republican. Methodist. Club: Optimist (sec. treas.), Laramie, 1985—. Office: U Wyo PO Box 3923 Univ Sta Laramie WY 82071

HOOPER, DAVID CHARLES, computer engineer; b. New London, Conn., Jan. 19, 1963; s. Charles Lee and Nancy Ann (Clair) H. BS in engring. cum laude, U. Conn., 1985. Assoc. field engr. Westinghouse Electric Corp., Balt., 1985--. Mem. Eta Kappa Nu, Tau Beta Pi. Home: 44256 20th St E #2 Lancaster CA 93535

HOOPES, SIDNEY LOU, marketing-advertising consultant, environmentalist; b. Monterey, Calif., Oct. 24, 1941; d. Jack Sidney Wayne Combs and Alta Virginia (Lane) Combs-Snow; m. Dan Frederick Hoppes, Oct. 11, 1969; children: Rachel Virginia, Sarah Elizabeth. BSBA in Mktg., U. Ark., 1964. Market researcher Procter & Gamble, Cin., 1964-65; asst. press sec. U.S. Senator J. W. Fulbright, Washington, 1966-68; adminstr. regional office Tex. Chapparal Basketball Team, Lubbock, 1970-71; office adminstr., sec. Tex. Tech. U., Lubbock, 1971-72; office adminstr. Hoopes Law Office, Idaho Falls, Idaho, 1973-82; cons. mktg. and advt. Idaho Falls, 1983--. Environ. educator Sch. Dist. #91, Idaho Falls, 1982-86; treas. Bonneville County Dem. Party, 1975-76, sec., 1988--; chief fund raiser Yellowstone Nat. Park Inst., 1983-84; bd. dirs. Idaho Falls Opera Theatre, 1984-85. Named One of Outstanding Young Women Dems. in Idaho, 1975; proclaimed Sidney Hoopes Appreciation Day, Idaho Falls Opera Theatre, 1988. Mem. Greater Yellowstone Coalition (charter). Episcopalian. Home: 1950 Alan Idaho Falls ID 83401

HOOVER, MARY NELL, marketing consultant; b. Ft. Worth, Oct. 30, 1946; d. Dexter E. and Nell (Thompson) H.; m. Vaughn Smith. BS, Southwest Tex. State U., 1968; MS, Iowa State U., 1972. Tchr. Northeast Ind. Sch. Dist., San Antonio, 1968-70; consumer info. specialist J.C. Penney., N.Y.C., 1972-76; asst. v.p. mktg. Security Pacific Nat. Bank, Los Angeles, 1976-80, v.p., 1980-84; v.p. product planning Great Am. Bank, Tucson, Ariz., 1984-85; sr. v.p., dir. mktg. Great Am. Bank, Tucson, 1986-87; mgmt. cons. M. Hoover, Inc., Tucson, 1988--. Recipient Cert. of Achievement, YWCA, 1982, named Outstanding Young Woman Am., 1979. Mem. Tucson Mktg. Assn. (bd. dirs. 1987--), Nat. Assn. Bank Women, Southern Ariz. club. Office: M Hoover Inc 8952 Calle Pasto Tucson AZ 85715

HOOVER, PEARL ROLLINGS, nurse; b. LeSueuer, Minn., Aug. 24, 1924; d. William Earl and Louisa (Schickling) Rollings; m. Roy David Hoover, June 19, 1948 (dec. 1987); children: Helen Louise, William Robert (dec.). Cert. nursing, U. Minn., 1945, BS in Nursing, 1947; MS in Health Sci., Calif. State U., Northridge, 1972. Dir. affiliate nursing sch. Mooselake (Minn.) State Hosp., 1948-49; nursing instr. Anchor Hosp., County Hosp., St. Paul, 1949-51; student nurse supr. and instr. Brentwood VA Hosp., L.A., 1951-52; sch. nurse L.A. Unified City Schs., 1963—. Camp nurse, United First Meth. Ch. Mem. L.A. Coun. Sch. Nurses, Calif. Sch. Nurses Orgn. Democrat. Methodist. Home: 17851 Lull St Reseda CA 91335 Office: Northridge Jr High Sch 17960 Chase St Northridge CA 91325

HOOVER, ROBERT LINVILLE, anthropology educator; b. Oakland, Calif., Mar. 26, 1943; s. Robert Francis and Betty Louise (Brown) H.; m. Christine Louise Norman, Dec. 19, 1964; children: David Norman, Ian Beard. AB, U. Calif., Berkeley, 1965; MA, U. Calif., 1969, PhD, 1971. Instr. Merritt Coll., Oakland, 1969-70; asst. prof. anthropology Calif. Poly State U., San Luis Obispo, 1970-76, assoc. prof., 1976-81, prof., 1981—; dep. chmn. social scis. dept. Calif. Poly State U., San Luis Obispo, 1976-83; vis. asst. prof. Stanford U., Palo Alto, Calif., 1971, archaeol. cons., 1972--; bd. dirs. archaeol. field sch. Mission San Antonio de Padua, Jolon, Calif., 1976—; vis. scholar Smithsonian Inst., Washington, 1981. Author: (with others) Excavations at Shilimagstush, 1976, Arms of the Apacheria, 1983; editor: Excavations of Mission San Antonio, 1985. Mem. Calif. Hist. Resources Commn., 1984—. Served with USN, 1961-62. NEH grantee, 1984-85. Fellow Am. Anthrop. Assn. (life), Royal Anthrop. Inst. Gt. Britain; mem. Soc. for Am. Archaeology, Soc. for Hist. Archaeology, Archaeol. Inst. Am., Calif. Acad. Scis., San Luis Obispo County Archaeol. Soc. (chief 1970—), Vasa Soc. Republican. Presbyterian. Office: Calif Poly State U Dept Social Scis San Luis Obispo CA 93407

HOOVER, WILLIAM R(AY), computer service company executive; b. Bingham, Utah, Jan. 2, 1930; s. Edwin Daniel and Myrtle Tennessee (McConnell) H.; m. Sara Elaine Anderson, Oct. 4; children—Scott, Robert, Michael, James, Charles. B.S., M.S., U. Utah. Sect. chief Jet Propulsion Lab., Pasadena, Calif., 1954-64; v.p. Computer Scis. Corp., El Segundo, Calif., 1964-69, pres., 1969—, chmn. bd., 1972—, now also chief exec. officer, also bd. dirs. Office: Computer Scis Corp 2100 E Grand Ave El Segundo CA 90245 *

HOOVLER, MATTHEW REED, oil executive; b. Casper, Wyo., June 21, 1952; s. Paul Vincent H. and Genevieve (Taylor) Heaney; m. Carolyn Drake Murgatroyd, Aug. 22, 1975 (div. Feb. 1978); m. Mary Michele Millison, Oct. 27, 1979. Ba in Psychology, Geology, U. Colo., 1975. Cert. profl. geol. scientist. Wellsite technician Monaco Engring., Denver, 1972-73; geol. wellsite technician Tooke Engring., Casper, 1974; geologist Chaparral Resources, Inc., Denver, 1975-76, exploration geologist, 1978-80, v.p. exploration, 1980—, treas., chief fin. officer, 1982—, also bd. dirs.; exploration geologist Sohio Petroleum Co., Oklahoma City, 1976-78; bd. dirs. Enviro-Logic, Inc., Vancouver, Wash. Active in Colo. Engergy Polit. Action Com., 1987—,

Intermountain Polit. Action Com., 1987—, Polit. Action Com., Equine Racing, Columbus, Ohio, 1986-87. Mem. Am. Inst. Profl. Geologists, Am. Assn. Petroleum Geologists, Rocky Mountain Assn. Geologists, Wyo. Geol. Assn., Ind. Petroleum Assn. Mountain States (bd. dirs.). Republican. Clubs: Valley Racquet, ACC Wellness Ctr. Home: 805 Meadow Run Golden CO 80401 Office: Chaparral Resources Inc 621 17th St Suite 1301 Denver CO 80293

HOPE, GERRI DANETTE, telecommunications executive; b. North Highlands, Calif., Feb. 28, 1956; d. Albert Gerald and Beulah Rae (Bane) Hope. AS, Sierra Coll., Calif., 1977; postgrad. Okla. State U., 1977-79. Sr. admissions clk. Bass Meml. Hosp., Enid, Okla., 1978-79; instructional asst. San Juan Sch. Dist., Carmichael, Calif., 1979-82; telecommunications supr. Calif. Dental Service, San Francisco, 1982-85; telecommunications coordinator Farmers Savs. Bank, Davis, Calif., 1985-87; telecommunications mgr. Sacramento Savs. and Loan Assn., 1987—; cons. and lectr. in field. Mem. Women in Telecommunications, Nat. Assn. Female Execs. Republican. Avocations: writing, computers, ceramics, animal behavior, participating in Christian ministry. Home: 3025 U St North Highlands CA 95660

HOPFIELD, JOHN JOSEPH, biophysicist, educator; b. Chgo., July 15, 1933; s. John Joseph and Helen (Staff) H.; m. Cornelia Fuller, June 30, 1954; children—Alison (Mrs. Charles C. Lifland), Jessica, Natalie. A.B., Swarthmore Coll., 1954; Ph.D., Cornell U., 1958. Mem. tech. staff ATT Bell Labs., 1958-60, 73—; vis. research physicist Ecole Normale Superieure, Paris, France, 1960-61; asst. prof., then asso. prof. physics U. Calif. at Berkeley, 1961-64; prof. physics Princeton U., 1964-80, Eugene Higgins prof. physics, 1978-80; Dickinson prof. chemistry and biology Calif. Inst. Tech., Pasadena, 1980—. Trustee Battelle Meml. Inst., 1982—. Guggenheim fellow, 1969, MacArthur Prize fellow, 1983; recipient Golden Plate award Am. Acad Achievement, 1985, Michelson-Morley prize, 1988. Fellow Am. Phys. Soc. (Oliver E. Buckley prize 1968, Biol. Physics prize 1985); mem. Nat. Acad. Scis., Am. Acad. Arts and Scis., Am. Philos. Soc., Phi Beta Kappa, Sigma Xi. Home: 931 Canon Dr Pasadena CA 91106 Office: Calif Inst Tech 164-30 Pasadena CA 91125

HOPKIN, LOIS ANN, nurse; b. Dell Rapids, S.D., Dec. 17, 1947. BA in Health Sci., Stephen's Coll., 1978; BS in Nursing, U. Ariz., 1980, MS in Nursing, 1986. Staff nurse urology U. Minn. Hosps., Mpls., 1969-70; staff nurse pediatrics Met. Med. Ctr., Mpls., 1970-71; staff nurse Tucson Med. Ctr., 1971-75, coord. staff devel. rsch., 1975-80, asst. dir. nursing quality assurance, 1980-82, mgr. quality assurance, 1982-83, dir. edn. svcs., 1983—. Contbr. articles to profl. jours. Mem. Nurses Assn. of the Am. Coll. Obstetricians and Gynecologists,. Office: Tucson Med Ctr 5301 E Grant Rd Tucson AZ 85712

HOPKINS, CECILIA ANN, educator; b. Havre, Mont., Feb. 17, 1922; d. Kost L. and Mary (Manaras) Sofos; B.S., Mont. State Coll., 1944; M.A., San Francisco State Coll., 1958, M.B.A., 1967; postgrad. Stanford U.; Ph.D., Calif. Western U., 1977; m. Henry E. Hopkins, Sept. 7, 1944. Bus. tchr. Havre (Mont.) High Sch., Mateo, Calif., 1942-44; sec. George P. Gorham, Realtor, San Mateo, 1944-45; escrow sec. Fox & Cars 1945-50; escrow officer Calif. Pacific Title Ins. Co., 1950-57; bus. tchr. Westmoor High Sch., Daly City, Calif., 1958-59; bus. tchr. Coll. of San Mateo, 1959—, chmn. real estate-ins. dept., 1963-76, dir. div. bus., 1976-86, coordinator real estate dept., 1986—; cons. to commr. Calif. Div. Real Estate, 1963—, mem. periodic rev. exam. com.; chmn. Community Coll. Adv. Com., 1971-72, mem. com., 1975—; projector direction Calif. State Chancellor's Career Awareness Consortium, mem. endowment fund adv. com., community coll. real estate edn. com., state community coll. adv. com.; mem. No. Calif. adv. bd. to Glendale Fed. Savs. and Loan Assn.; mem. bd. advisors San Mateo County Bd. Suprs., 1981-82; mem. real estate edn. and research com. to Calif. Commr. Real Estate, 1983—; mem. edn., membership, and profl. exchange coms. Am. chpt. Internat. Real Estate Fedn., 1985—. Recipient Citizen of Day award KABL, Outstanding Contbns. award Redwood City-San Carlos-Belmont Bd. Realtors; named Woman of Achievement, San Mateo-Burlingame br. Soroptimist Internat., 1979. Mem. AAUW, Calif. Assn. Real Estate Tchrs. (state pres. 1964-65, hon. dir. 1962—, outstanding real estate educator of yr. 1978-79), Real Estate Cert. Inst. (Disting. Merit award 1982), Calif. Bus. Edn. Assn. (certificate of commendation 1979), San Francisco State Coll. Guidance and Counseling Alumni, Theta Alpha Delta, Pi Lambda Theta, Delta Pi Epsilon (nat. dir. interchpt. relations 1962-65, nat. historian 1966-67, nat. sec. 1968-69), Alpha Gamma Delta. Co-author: California Real Estate Principles; contbr. articles to profl. jours. Home: 504 Colgate Way San Mateo CA 94402

HOPKINS, EDWINA WEISKITTEL, graphic designer; b. Cin., June 7, 1947; d. Edwin and Moody (Bowling) Campbell; m. Michael J. Weiskittel, May 1966 (dec. May 1970); 1 son, Todd Michael; m. Franklin Hopkins, June 1973 (div. June 1977). Student, U. Cin., 1965-66. Asst. to art dir. World Library Publs., Cin., 1965-68; comml. artist Campbell & Assocs. Art Studio, Cin., 1969-73; prodn. mgr. William Wilson Advt. Agy., Palos Verdes, Calif., 1973-74; ptnr. Hopkins & Hopkins Design Studio, Redondo Beach, Calif., 1975-76; owner, graphic designer Winnissa Comml. Art Studio, Rolling Hills, Calif., 1976-81; pres. Winnissa Inc., Redondo Beach, 1981—. U. Cin. hon. scholar, 1965. Home and Office: 718 Ave D Redondo Beach CA 90277

HOPKINS, HENRY TYLER, art foundation director; b. Idaho Falls, Idaho, Aug. 14, 1928; s. Talcott Thompson and Zoe (Erbe) H.; children—Victoria Anne, John Thomas, Christopher Tyler. B.A., Sch. of Art Inst., Chgo., 1952, M.A., 1955; postgrad., UCLA, 1957-60; Ph.D. (hon.), Calif. Coll. Arts and Crafts, 1984; PhD (hon.), San Francisco Art Inst., 1987. Curator exhbns., publs. Los Angeles County Mus. of Art, 1960-68; dir. Fort Worth Art Mus., 1968-74, San Francisco Mus. of Modern Art, 1974-86, Frederick R. Weisman Collection Art Found., Los Angeles, 1986—; lectr. art history, extension U. Calif. at Los Angeles, 1958-68; instr. Tex. Christian U., Fort Worth, 1968-74; dir. U.S. representation Venice (Italy) Bienniel, 1970; dir. art presentation Festival of Two Worlds, Spoleto, Italy, 1970; co-commr. U.S. representation XVI São Paulo (Brazil) Biennale, 1981; cons. Nat. Endowment for Arts, mem. mus. panel, 1979-84, chmn., 1981; cons., mem. mus. panel Nat. Endowment for Humanities, 1976. Contbr. numerous articles to profl. jours., also numerous mus. publs. Served with AUS, 1952-54. Decorated knight Order Leopold II, Belgium). Mem. Assn. Art Mus. Dirs. (pres. 1985-86), Coll. Art Assn., Am. Assn. Museums, Western Assn. Art Museums (pres. 1977-78). Home: 939 1/2 Hilgard Ave Los Angeles CA 90024 Office: Frederick R Weisman Collection Art Found 10350 Santa Monica Blvd Los Angeles CA 90025

HOPKINS, PAUL MORTIMER, mining geologist, engineer; b. Edgerton, Mo., Mar. 6, 1918; s. Walter Ashe and Vera Virginia (Denniston) H.; grad. petroleum engr., Colo. Sch. Mines, 1939, geol. engr., 1951; post grad. U. Colo., 1951-52; m. Joyce Lorraine Mundy, Nov. 16, 1946 (div. Oct. 1947); m. Marian Francis Hawk, Jan. 1, 1954 (div. Nov. 1960); m. Mary Evelyn Shurtleff Newell, Feb. 20, 1965 (div. Feb. 1977); m. Rose Marie Ashley, Oct., 1985. Employee of Socony Vacuum Oil Co., East St. Louis, Ill., 1939-41; civil engr. U.S. Air Force, Lowry Field, Denver, 1948-49; geologist Leadville Lead Corp., Park County, Colo., 1952-53; geologist engr. Silver Bell Mines, Ophir, Colo., 1952-53; jr. engr. Kennecott Copper Co., Ruth, Nev., 1953-55; cons. engr., mining geologist and engr. Colo., Utah, Nev., Wyo., S.D., N.Mex., Ariz., Idaho, Mont., Can., Alaska, Central and South Am., Africa. Capt. AUS, 1941-47. Registered profl. engr., Colo., B.C.; registered geologist, Calif. Mem. Colo. Mining Assn. (dir.), Am. Inst. Mining, Metall. and Petroleum Engrs., Nat. Soc. Profl. Engrs., Canadian Inst. Mining and Metallurgy, Mason, Shriner. Democrat. Mem. Christian Ch. Home: 3830 W Saratoga Denver CO 80123 Office: 2222 Arapahoe St PO Box 403 Golden CO 80401

HOPKINS, PHILIP JOSEPH, journalist, editor; b. Orange, Calif., Dec. 10, 1954; s. Philip Joseph and Marie Elizabeth H. BA in Journalism, San Diego State U., 1977. Cert. tissue therapist Center for Decubitis Ulcer Research, 1981. Reporter, La Jolla Light & Journal (Calif.), 1973; editorial cons. San Diego Union, 1974; asst. producer Southwestern Cable TV, San Diego, 1974; corr. Mission Cable TV, San Diego, 1975; photojournalist United Press Internat., San Diego, 1976; editor Rx Home Care mag., Los Angeles, 1981, Hosp. Info. Mgmt. mag., 1981; editor, assoc. pub. Arcade mag., 1982; mng. editor Personal Computer Age, Los Angeles, 1983-84; Bur. chief Newsbytes syndicated column, 1985-86; v.p. Humbird Hopkins Inc., Los Angeles, 1978-88; freelance editor and researcher Ind. Rsch. and Info. Svc., 1988-89; publ. cons. U. So. Calif., 1989. Recipient 1st and 4th place awards Nikon, Inc., Photo Contest, 1974; 3rd prize Minolta Camera Co. Creative Photography awards, 1975; Best Feature Photo award Sigma Delta Chi Mark of Excellence contest, 1977; Advt. of Month award Communicator mag., 1980. Pres. Ind. Writers of So. Calif., 1988. Mem. Computer Press Assn. (life, hon.). Co-author: The Students' Survival Guide, 1977, 78; photographs have appeared in Time and Omni mags., The Mythology of Middle Earth, Beginners Guide to the SLR, NBC-TV's Saturday Night Live. Office: PO Box 49229 Los Angeles CA 90049

HOPKINS, ROBERT ARTHUR, retired industrial engineer; b. Youngstown, Ohio, Dec. 14, 1920; s. Arthur George and Margaret Viola (Brush) H.; m. Mary Madelaine Bailey, Apr. 6, 1946; 1 child, Marlaine Hopkins Kaiser. BBA, Case Western Reserve U., 1949; cert. loss control engr., U. Calif., Berkeley, 1969. Lic. indsl. safety engr. Ins. agt. Nat. Life and Accident Ins. Co., Lorain, Akron, Ohio, 1951-56, San Mateo, Calif., 1951-56; ins. agt., engr. Am. Hardware Mt. Ins. Co., San Jose, Fresno, Calif., 1956-60; loss control engr. Manhattan Guarantee-Continental Ins. Co., Calif., 1967-77. Organizer Operation Alert CD, Lorain, 1951-52; prin. speaker CD, Fresno, 1957; active Pleasant Hill (Calif.) Civic Action Com., 1981-83; civilian coord. Office Emergency Svcs., Pleasant Hill, 1983-85; advisor, coord. airshows, 1980—; chmn. bd. Western Aerospace Mus., Oakland, Calif., 1988—; ops. asst. for tower and ops. 50th Anniversary Golden Gate Bridge, San Francisco, 1987; warbird coord. Port of Oakland Airshow, 1987. With U.S. Army Air Corps, 1942. Recipient Letter of Appreciation Fresno CD, 1957, cert. of appreciation City of Pleasant Hill, 1986. Mem. No. Calif. Safety Engrs. Assn. (v.p., pres., chmn. 1974-77), Confederate Air Force (staff, wing leader Pacific wing 1980—), Nat. Aero. Assn., Aero Club No. Calif., Hamilton Field Assn. (dir. ops. 1987, coord. 1988—), Kiwanis (coord., asst. to pres. 1989—, sec. treas. Pleasant Hill chpt. 1985-86), Elks (leading knight 1963-64). Republican. Roman Catholic. Home: 48 Mazie Ln Pleasant Hill CA 94523

HOPKINS, SHEILA MARIE, pharmacist; b. Mpls., Sept. 24, 1954; m. Larry I. Hopkins, Oct. 2, 1982. BS in Pharmacy, Drake U., 1976; MBA, Ill. Benedictine Coll., 1985. Registered pharmacist, Ill. Pharmacist St. Mary's Hosp., Galesburg, Ill., 1976-78; pharmacist Good Samaritan Hosp., Downers Grove, Ill., 1978-81, pharmacy supr., 1981-85, pharmacist, 1985-89; pharmacist St. Joseph Hosp., Bellingham, Washington, 1989—. Mem. exec. bd. United Meth. Women at Community United Meth. Ch. Mem. Am. Pharm. Assn., Am. Soc. Hosp. Pharmacists, No. Ill. Council of Hosp. Pharmacists, Lambda Kappa Sigma. Avocations: sports, family, outdoor activities, cooking, crafts.

HOPKINS, STEPHEN H., health facility administrator; b. Provo, Utah, June 6, 1955; s. A. Norman and Joanne (Petersen) H.; m. Margot Lillian Akarana Shaw, Mar. 30, 1984; children: Alexandra, Stephanie. BA, Brigham Young U., 1981, MPA, 1983. Fin. analyst St. John's Hosp., Santa Monica, Calif., 1984-85; budget dir. Daniel Freeman Hosps., Inc., Inglewood, Calif., 1985-86, assoc. adminstr., 1988—; asst. adminstr. Daniel Freeman Marina Hosp., Marina Del Rey, Calif., 1986-88. Republican. Mem. Ch. of Jesus Christ of Latter Day Saints. Home: 11502 Mississipi Ave Los Angeles CA 90025-6212 Office: Daniel Freeman Hosps Inc 4650 Lincoln Blvd Marina Del Rey CA 90292

HOPKINSON, SHIRLEY LOIS, educator; b. Boone, Iowa, Aug 25, 1924; d. Arthur Perry and Zora (Smith) Hopkinson; student Coe Coll., 1942-43; A.B. cum laude (Phi Beta Kappa scholar 1944), U. Colo., 1945; B.L.S., U. Calif., 1949; M.A. (Honnold Honor scholar 1945-46), Claremont Grad. Sch., 1951; Ed.M., U. Okla., 1952, Ed.D., 1957 Tchr. pub. sch. Stigler, Okla., 1946-47, Palo Verde High Sch., Jr. Coll., Blythe, Calif., 1947-48; asst. librarian Modesto (Calif.) Jr. Coll., 1949-51; tchr., librarian Fresno, Calif., 1951-52, La Mesa, Cal., 1953-55; asst. prof. librarianship, instructional materials dir. Chaffey Coll., Ontario, Calif., 1955-59; asst. prof. librarian ship, San Jose (Calif.) State Coll., 1959-64; assoc. prof., 1964-69, prof., 1969—. Dir. NDEA Inst. Sch. Librarians, summer 1966; mem. Santa Clara County Civil Service Bd. Examiners. Mem. ALA, Calif. Library Assn., Audio-Visual Assn. Calif., NEA, AAUP, AAUW (dir. 1957-58), Bus. Profl. Women's Club, Sch. Librarians Assn. Calif. (com. mem., treas. No. sect. 1951-52), San Diego County Sch. Librarians Assn. (sec. 1945-55), Calif. Tchrs. Assn., LVW (bd. dirs. 1950-51, publs. chmn.), Phi Beta Kappa, Alpha Lambda Delta, Alpha Beta Alpha, Kappa Delta Pi, Phi Kappa Phi (disting. acad. achievement award 1981), Delta Kappa Gamma. Author: Descriptive Cataloging of Library Materials; Instructional Materials for Teaching the Use of the Library. Contbr. to profl. publs. Editor: Calif. Sch. Libraries, 1963-64; asst. editor: Sch. Library Assn. of Calif. Bull., 1961-63. Office: San Jose State U Rm LN-608 San Jose CA 95192

HOPPER, STEPHEN WADE, computer innovator; b. Gallup, N.Mex., July 23, 1963; s. Manuel Curtis Hopper and Martha Faye (Medlin) Merritt. AA, Assoc. Pre-Bus., N.Mex. State U., 1987, BBA, 1988. Owner Computer Services, Las Cruces, N.Mex., 1985-88, IDEAS, Las Cruces, 1987—. Mem. Am. Prodn. and Inventory Control Soc. Home: Box 368 Gallup NM 87301 Office: IDEAS 1335 Wofford Las Cruces NM 88001

HOPPOCK, JOHN SCARBOROUGH, JR., emergency and hyperbaric medicine physician; b. Orange, N.J., July 16, 1946; s. John S. and Katherine (Crabbe) H.; m. Sarah Brooke Dorsey, Nov. 12, 1987. AB, Princeton U., 1968; MD, Columbia U., 1976. Diplomate Am. Bd. Emergency Medicine. Resident in internal medicine Good Samaritan Hosp., Portland, Oreg., 1976-78; staff physician Providence Med. Ctr., Portland, 1979—, dir. hyperbaric dept., 1987—. Editor HBO News, 1988—. 1st lt. U.S. Army, 1968-70. Fellow Am. Coll. Emergency Physicians; mem. Undersea and Hyperbaric Medicine Soc. Office: Providence Med Ctr 4805 NE Glisan St Portland OR 97213

HORA, JUDITH ANN, accounting educator; b. Harvey, Ill., Mar. 16, 1945; d. Alfred and Sophie (Jalowiec) Twardowski; m. Stephen Curtis Hora, Sept. 9, 1967; children: Erika, Greg. BA, UCLA, 1970; MS in Acctg., Tex. Tech U., 1981. CPA, Tex. Asst. to dir. acctg. programs, lectr. acctg. Tex. Tech U., Lubbock, 1981-85; asst. prof. acctg. U. Hawaii, Hilo, 1985—. Mem. Am. Ist. CPAs, Tex. Soc. CPAs, Hawaii Soc. CPAs, Am. Acctg. Assn., Hawaii Assn. Pub. Accts., AAUW (bd. dirs. Hilo 1988—). Office: U Hawaii at Hilo 523 W Lanikaula Hilo HI 96720

HORAN, ANTHONY HARDING, surgeon; b. N.Y.C., Jan. 2, 1940; s. Francis Harding Horan and Elizabeth (Selden) Rogers; m. Martha Welch, June 21, 1970 (div. Mar. 1983); 1 child, Thomas B.; m. Marcia Morrison, Aug. 1, 1986. BA, Dartmouth Coll., 1961; MD, Columbia U., 1963. Diplomate Am. Bd. Urology. Intern St. Lukes Hosp., N.Y.C., 1964-67; resident in urology Columbia Prsbyn. Hosp., N.Y.C., 1969-73; pvt. practice urologic surgeon N.Y.C., 1973-83; assoc. prof. urology Marshall U. Sch. Medicine, Huntington, W.Va., 1983-84; pvt. practice urologic surgeon South Bend, Ind., 1985-88; urologic surgeon VA Med. Ctr., Walla Walla, Wash., 1988—; instr. urology N.T. Med. Coll., Walla Walla, 1976—; cons. VA, Washington, 1985, mem. adv. group, 1984; pres. N.Am. Urologic Inst., Walla Walla, 1988—. Asst. sec. N.Y. County Med. Soc., N.Y.C., 1980-81. Capt. USAF, 1967-69, Vietnam. Population Coun. grantee, 1966-67; Eltinger fellow, 1974. Mem. Am. Urological Assn., Soc. Study of Reproduction, Am. Coll. Cryosurgery, Endourology Soc., Century Assn., Explorer's Club, Am. Alpine Club. Office: VA Hosp 77 Wainwright Dr Walla Walla WA 99362

HORAN, CLARK JAMES, III, priest, corporate executive; b. Syracuse, N.Y., Feb. 3, 1950; s. Clark James Horan Jr. and Joan Roumage (Kelsey) Bergin. BA, U. Waterloo, Ont., Can., 1972, LLD (hon.), 1982; STB, BTh, St. Peter's Sem., London, Ont., Can., 1975; MDiv, U. Western Ont., London, 1975. Ordained priest Roman Cath. Ch., 1976. Priest Diocese of Honolulu; chief exec. officer Abercrombie & Waterhouse, Del., Can. Air Travellers; v.p. The Checkley Found., Can.; chmn. bd. dirs. Horan, Macmillan, Bache & Chapman, Ottawa, Ont., Can.; cons. Wardair Internat., Calgary, Alta., Can., 1978-82; bd. dirs. Horan-in-Trust, N.Y.C. Decorated Order of Can.; named Knight Bachelor, Queen Elizabeth II, 1978, Knight of the Holy Sepulchre, Pope John Paul II, 1982, officer Order Brit. Empire, Queen Elizabeth II, 1977; ascendency 5th Earl Dunsmere and Baron Horan Antwerp, 1988. Fellow Royal Commonwealth Soc., Can. Commonwealth Council (chancellor, editor Can. Commonwealth newsletter 1978-84), Monarchist League Can. (editor Monarchy Today mag. 1979-81). Clubs: Plaza, Honolulu; Ottawa Hunt and Golf, Albany (Toronto, Can.), Empire, Confederation. Lodges: Elks, KC. Address: PO Box 38016 Honolulu HI 96837-1016

HORAN, JOSEPH PATRICK, interior designer; b. Waterloo, Iowa, Feb. 9, 1942; s. Raymond John and Anna Louise Horan. BS in Applied Art, Iowa State U., 1964. Interior designer L.S. Ayres & Co., Indpls, 1964-70, W. & J. Sloane, Inc., San Francisco, 1970-82; prin., owner Joseph Horan Interior Design, San Francisco, 1982--. Work represented in Better Homes and Gardens, San Francisco mag., Designers West mag., Christian Sci. Monitor. Mem. organizing com., com. chmn. beaux arts ball San Francisco Mus. Modern Art, 1982--; mem. organizing com. San Francisco chpt. Design Industry Found. for AIDS, 1986-88. Mem. Am. Soc. Interior Designers (profl., bd. dirs. Calif. North chpt. 1983--, v.p. 1985, 86, 88, pres. 1989—, 1st prize Asid/Flexalum Design With Blinds 1980), Nat. Trust for Historic Preservation (design assoc.). Office: 3299 Washington St San Francisco CA 94115

HORAN, MARY ANN THERESA, nurse; b. Denver, July 4, 1936; d. John Paul and Lucille (Somma) Perito; m. Stephen F. Horan, Dec. 28, 1957; children: Seanna, Dana, Michelle, Annette, Stephen Jr., Christine, Dave. BS in Nursing, Loretto Heights Coll., 1958; postgrad, Pima Community Coll., 1982. R.N., Ala. Staff nurse Med. Ctr. Hosp., Huntsville, Ala., 1978-79, Crestwood Hosp.,, Huntsville, 1980-81, St. Joseph Hosp. Eye Surgery, Tucson, 1981--; v.p. Success Achievement Ctr., Tucson, 1987--. Republican. Roman Catholic. Home: 8311 E 3d St Tucson AZ 85710 Office: Success Achievement Ctr 8311 E 3d St Tucson AZ 85710

HORAN, STEPHEN FRANCIS, technical writer; b. Denver, June 15, 1933; s. Daniel Stephen and Rose Bridget (Shanley) H.; m. Mary Ann Theresa Perito, Dec. 28, 1957; children: Seanna, Dana, Michelle, Annette, Stephen Jr., Christine, Dave. Diploma, Interior Command Sch., Gt. Lakes, Mich., 1953, Mech. Design & Draft Sch., Denver, 1956; postgrad., U. Denver, 1957. Sr. tech. writer Missile Systems Corp., Denver, 1961-62; sr. tech. publs. engr. Martin Marietta Co., Denver, 1962-64; chief editorial br. Dugway Proving Ground U.S. Army, Utah, 1964-65, chief svcs. div. Dugway Proving Ground, 1965-68; tech. publs. editorial supr. Deseret Test Ctr. U.S. Army, 1968-73; tech. publs. writer Tropic Test Ctr. U.S. Army, Ft. Clayton, C.Z., Panama, 1973-75; tech. manuals writer Missile Command U.S. Army, Huntsville, Ala., 1978-81; tech. publs. writer, editor Communications Security Log U.S. Army, Ft. Huachuca, Ariz., 1981—; pres. Success Achievement Ctr., Tucson, 1987—. Author Tour of Historic Ft. Douglas, 1976. Coach, Dugway Youth Activities, 1968-72, 75-78; pres. Dugway Parish Council, 1975, Dugway Booster Club, 1976. With USN, 1951-54. Mem. Soc. Tech. Writers and Pubs., Author's Resource Ctr., Toastmasters, KC. Roman Catholic. Home and Office: Success Achievement Ctr 8311 E 3d St Tucson AZ 85710

HORBAN, BLAISE A., air force officer; b. Rochester, Ind., Feb. 6, 1959; s. Robert Henry and Catherine Laverne (Henriott) H.; m. Lynne Carol Pompetti, Sept. 20, 1986; children: Alessandra, Peter. BS in Engring. Mechanics, Air Force Acad., Colorado Springs, 1981; MS in Aero. Engring., Air Force Inst. Tech., Dayton, Ohio, 1985. Commd. USAF, 1981, advanced through grades to capt., to date; propulsion performance engr. Aeronautical Sys. Div. USAF, Dayton, 1981-84; air-launched missile propulsion engr. Air Force Astronautics Lab., Edwards AFB, Calif., 1986-87; sect. chief Air Force Astronautics Lab., 1987-89, br. chief, 1989—. Mem. Air Force Assn., AIAA. Home: 45304 N Thornwood St Lancaster CA 93534

HORIGAN, JAMES EUGENE, lawyer, author; b. Oklahoma City, Sept. 4, 1924; s. Joseph D. Horigan and Mary (Swirczynski) Horigan McRill; stepson Albert L. McRill; student Okla. U., 1942-44, Northwestern U., 1944; J.D., Okla. U., 1949; postgrad. So. Meth. U., 1958, Colo. U., 1966; m. Joan Murry, Mar. 8, 1945; children—Susan, Daniel James, Nancy Jean Horigan Datz. Bar: Okla. 1949, Tex. 1957, N.Y. 1959, Colo. 1961, Law Soc. Eng. (hon.), 1973. Asst. county atty. Oklahoma County, 1949-51; atty. Mobil Oil Corp., Oklahoma City, 1951-57, Beaumont, Tex., 1957, Dallas, 1958; U.S. and Can. counsel, office gen. counsel, N.Y.C., 1959-61, regional gen. atty. Denver regional office, 1961-63; gen. counsel Hamilton Bros. Oil Co. and affiliates, Denver, 1963-69; ptnr. Foliart, Shepherd, McPherson & Horigan, Oklahoma City, 1963, Horigan Thompson & Miller, Denver, 1965-69; individual practice internat. law, London, 1969-70; ptnr. Horigan & Boss, 1971; sr. resident ptnr. London office law firm Vinson, Elkins, Searls, Connally & Smith, 1971-75; of counsel Burns & Wall, 1978; ptnr. Horigan, Jumonville, Broadhurst, Brook & Miller, 1978, Holland & Hart, Denver, 1979-81; sole practice law, 1981—; bd. dirs., gen. counsel Charterhall N.Am. P.L.C., 1985-87; gen. agt. Charterhall Australia Ltd. 1983-87. Trustee Town of Bow Mar (Colo.), 1976-78; mem. U.S. Congl. Adv. Bd., 1982-87; mem. adv. bd. Internat. Comparative Law Ctr., Southwestern Legal Found., 1983—. Served to lt. USNR, 1943-46. Mem. ABA, Colo. Bar Assn., Okla. Bar Assn., Denver Bar Assn., Internat. Bar Assn., Am. Soc. Internat. Law, Rocky Mountain Mineral Law Found. (gen. chmn. spl. legal inst. 1975), Internat. Platform Assn., Internat. Trade Assn. Colo. (v.p. 1979-81. bd. dirs.), Phi Delta Phi, Phi Gamma Delta, Delta Sigma Rho. Roman Catholic. Clubs: American (London); Rotary; Denver Petroleum (bd. dirs. 1987—). Author: Chance or Design?, 1979; The Key to Reconcile Modern Science and Religious Thought, 1983; Petroleum Laws of the North Sea, 1975; contbg. author: The Law of Transnational Business Transactions, 1980; Foreign Participation in Domestic Oil and Gas Ventures, 1982; contbr. articles to legal jours.; charter mem. bd. editors Okla. Law Rev., 1947-49. Home: 5230 Lakeshore Dr Littleton CO 80123

HORN, JAN ERIC, real estate executive; b. Cleve., Aug. 9, 1945; s. William and Norma (Perkoff) H.; m. Maureen Veronica Duda, Sept. 12, 1987; 1 child, Kevin Matthew. BA, UCLA, 1987. Vice pres. BAR/BRI, Inc., L.A., 1965-76; pres. Hobbs & Dobbs, L.A., 1978-81, bd. dirs., 1982--; pres. The Horn Group, L.A., 1982--; broker Mossler, Deasy & Doe, L.A., 1984--; cons. HBJ Legal Edn. and Pub., N.Y.C., 1974-76; guest speaker seminars on legal edn. Harvard U., 1967, 69, 71-74, Stanford U., Yale U., Columbia U., 1967, 69, 71-76. Mem. UCLA Lifetime Alumni Assn., Los Angeles C. of C., Calif. Assn. Realtors, Beverly Hills Bd. Realtors, Phi Delta Phi, Pi Lambda Pi. Republican. Jewish. Office: Mossler Deasy & Doe 858 N Doheny Dr Los Angeles CA 90069

HORN, RUSSELL VANCE, manufacturing sales agency president; b. Portland, Oreg., Oct. 28, 1929; s. Russell Vance and Mildred (Keith) H.; m. Anne Lorraine Buchanan, Feb. 14, 1953 (div. Nov. 1965); m. Sally Jane Willsey, June 26, 1976. Student, Lower Columbia Community Coll., Longview, Wash., 1947-48. Stock clk. Western Accessory Dist., Seattle, 1952-55, sales mgr., 1955-62; warehouse mgr. Chanslor & Lyon Co., Seattle, 1962-64, Pacific Marine Schwabavnen, Seattle, 1964-65; mfgr. salesperson Bellando, Mittelman Co., Seattle, 1965-72; owner, operator Rogovoy & Horn, Inc., Seattle, 1972—. Sgt. USAF, 1948-52. Mem. Automative Affiliated Reps., Inc. (local pres. 1980-81, 1987-88, nat. pres. 1985), Sahalee Country Club. Republican. Home: 3316 Sahalee Dr W Redmond WA 98053 Office: Rogovoy & Horn Inc 18350 Redmond Way Redmond WA 98052

HORN, (JOHN) STEPHEN, university administrator; b. Gilroy, Calif., May 31, 1931; s. John Stephen and Isabelle (McCaffrey) H.; m. Nini Moore, Sept. 4, 1954; children: Marcia Karen Horn Yavitz, John Stephen. AB with great distinction, Stanford, 1953, postgrad., 1953-54, 55-56, PhD in Polit. Sci, 1958; M in Pub Adminstrn., Harvard, 1955. Congl. fellow 1958-59; adminstrv. asst. to sec. labor Washington, 1959-60; legislative asst. to U.S. Senator Thomas H. Kuchel, 1960-66; sr. fellow The Brookings Instn., 1966-69; dean grad. studies and research Am. U., 1969-70; pres. Calif. State U., Long Beach, 1970-88, trustee prof. polit. sci., 1988--; sr. cons., host The Govt. Story on TV, The Election Game (radio series), 1967-69. Author: The Cabinet and Congress, 1960, Unused Power: The Work of the Senate Committee on Appropriations, 1970, (with Edmund Beard) Congressional Ethics: The View from the House, 1975. Mem. urban studies fellowship adv. bd. Dept. Housing and Urban Devel., 1969-70, chmn., 1969; vice-chmn. U.S. Commn. Civil Rights, 1969-80, mem., 1980-82; mem. Pres.-elect Nixon's

Task Force on Orgn. Exec. Br., 1968; mem. law enforcement edn. program, adv. commn. law enforcement assistance adminstrn. Dept. Justice, 1969-71; v.p. FHP Found.; mem. Kutak Found.; co-founder Western U.S. Com. Arts and Scis. for Eisenhower, 1956; bd. dirs. Nat. Inst. Corrections, 1971-88, chmn., 1980-87, Am. Assn. State Colls. and Univs., 1985-86; mem. Calif. Ednl. Facilities Authority, 1984—. Fellow John F. Kennedy Inst. Politics Harvard U., 1966-67. Fellow Nat. Acad. Pub. Adminstrn.; mem. Stanford Assocs., Stanford Alumni Assn. (pres. 1976-77), Phi Beta Kappa, Pi Sigma Alpha, El Capitan Eating Club (Stanford). Republican. Office: Calif State U 1250 Bellflower Blvd Long Beach CA 90840

HORNBECK, JACK LEE, manufacturing company executive; b. Covington, Ky., Feb. 4, 1929; s. Charles Gueno and Ina Belle (Claypool) H.; m. Rita June Howland, Apr. 7, 1951; children: Alicia Gail, Jeffrey Wayne, Amy Susan. Student, U. Calif., Berkeley, 1957-59. Tooling supr. Kelsey-Hayes Wheel Co., Jackson, Mich., 1953-55, maintenance supr., 1955-56; prodn. planner Dorr-Oliver, Inc., Oakland, Calif., 1956-60; factory sales rep. S.W. Card div. Union Twist Drill, San Francisco, 1960-61; factory sales rep. Pacific Grinding Wheel Co., Inc., San Francisco, 1961-65, dist. mgr. No. Calif., Nev., 1965-69, dist. mgr. Oreg., Idaho, No. Wash., 1969-71; v.p. sales Pacific Grinding Wheel Co., Inc., Marysville, Wash., 1971-73, exec. v.p., gen. mgr., 1973-86, pres., chief exec. officer, 1986-87. Mem. PTO. Sgt. USAAF, 1946-47. Mem. Lions Club, Elks. Republican. Baptist. Home: 17828 43d Ave NE Arlington WA 98223

HORNBRUCH, FREDERICK WILLIAM, III, entrepreneur, management consultant; b. Bryn Mawr, Pa., Mar. 31, 1942; s. Frederick William Jr. and Helen (Novak) H. BS in Indsl. Adminstrn., Yale U., 1964; MBA, Stanford U., 1969. Project engr., constrn. mgr. Food Mfg. div. Procter & Gamble Co., N.Y.C., 1964-66, dept. supr. Crisco oil packaging, 1966-67; v.p., sec., treas. Creative Publs., Inc., Palo Alto, Calif., 1969-77, pres., chief exec. officer, 1977-81; owner, mgr. Sundown Properties, Palo Alto, 1979—; chmn., chief exec. officer, pres. 3T Group, Palo Alto, 1985—, Phileas Fogg's Books & Maps for Traveler, Palo Alto, 1985—; bd. dirs., mgmt. cons. Investacon Inc., Irvine, Calif., 1981—, Early Learning Inst., Palo Alto, 1983-86, Landsing Corp., Menlo Park, Calif., 1983-85, Western States Endurance Run, Sacramento, 1983-88, Hidden Villa Ranch, Los Altos Hills, Calif., 1985-86. Mem. Stanford U. Alumni Assn., Yale U. Alumni Assn., Stanford U. Bus. Sch. Alumni Assn. (pres. 1981-82, chmn. alumni council 1985-86, Disting. Service award 1985), Explorers Club, World Affairs Council No. Calif., Commonwealth Club. Office: Phileas Fogg's Books & Maps 87 Stanford Shopping Ctr Palo Alto CA 94304

HORNBY, WILLIAM HARRY, newspaper editor; b. Kalispell, Mont., July 14, 1923; s. Lloyd G. and Margaret E. (Miller) H.; children: Margaret (dec.), Megan, Melinda, John, Mary Catherine. A.B. in Humanities, Stanford U., 1944, M.A. in Journalism, 1947; postgrad., U. London, Eng., 1949-50. Reporter, copyreader San Francisco News, 1947-48; reporter A.P., San Francisco, 1949; research asst. Hoover Library, Stanford, 1949-50; info. officer ECA, Paris and The Hague, 1950-52; asst. gen. mgr. Kalispell Lumber Co., 1953-56, partner, 1955-62; reporter Great Falls (Mont.) Tribune, 1957; copy-desk chief, editorial writer Denver Post, 1957-60, mng. editor, 1960-70, exec. editor, v.p., 1970-77, editor, v.p., 1977-82, sr. editor, 1982-88; v.p. Yellowstone Newspapers, Inc., Livingston, Mont.; sr. fellow Ctr. for New West. Bd. dirs. Buffalo Bill Meml. Assn., Colo. Hist. Found., Denver Found., Clayton Trust; former chmn. Colo. Hist. Soc. Mem. Am. Soc. Newspaper Editors (past pres.), Sigma Delta Chi, Sigma Nu. Republican. Episcopalian. Clubs: Denver, Univ, Denver Country. Lodge: Elks. Office: Denver Post 650 15th St Denver CO 80201

HORN-DALTON, KATHY ELLEN, rehabilitation agency administrator; b. Latrobe, Pa., Apr. 12, 1952; d. William Irving and Stella Bertha (Denisiuk) Horn; m. Glenn Holbert Dalton, Aug. 4, 1973. BS in Social Work, W.Va. U., 1975, MSW, 1976; PhD in Adminstrn., Columbia Pacific U., 1983. Registered psychotherapist. Counselor Womens Info. Ctr., Morgantown, W.Va., 1973; psychiatric aid Torrance (Pa.) State Hosp., 1974; group home counselor Sommerset Bedford Mental Health Ctr., Rockwood, Pa., 1974; shop foreman Southwest Wyo. Rehab. Ctr., Rock Springs, 1975-76, exec. dir., 1976-81, pres., administr., 1981—; researcher emotionally disturbed/mentally retarded project Div. Vocat. Rehab., Cheyenne, Wyo., 1985; CD grants adminstr. Sweetwater County, Rock Springs, Wyo., 1982-83. Author: Develop and Design an Energy Efficient Sheltered Workshop, 1983, Job Placement Results of a Job Training Partnership Act Program in a Rural Sheltered Workshop, 1985; contbr. articles to profl. jours. Mem. Wyo. Devel. Disabilities Council, 1978, Wyo. Pvt. Indsl. Council, 1983, adv. bd. U. No. Colo., Greeley, 1978; state advisor U.S. Congl. Adv. Bd., Washington, 1984, YWCA. Mem. Wyo. Assn. Rehab. Facilities (legis. chmn. 1981-83), Nat. Assn. Social Workers (cert.), Exec. Females Assn., Bus. Profl. Women's Assn., Pilot Butte Sand Drag Assn., Intermountain Sand Drag Assn., Nat. Sand Co. Assn., Nat. Hot Rod Assn. Office: SW Wyo Rehab Ctr 2632 Foothill Blvd Suite 107 Rock Springs WY 82901

HORNE, TERRY, construction company executive; b. Denver, Nov. 26, 1948; s. Van J. and Katherine G. (Stewart) H.; m. Ruth Elizabeth Booth, Aug. 15, 1970; 1 child, Lance Booth. BS in Econs., Colo. State U., 1972. Constrn. mgr. Peter Kiewit Sons Co., Sheridan, Wyo., 1972-83; v.p. Union Rock & Materials-Kiewit Co., Phoenix, 1983—; dist. mgr. Phoenix Dist.-Kiewit Co., Phoenix, 1987—; pres. Bentson Contracting Co.-Kiewit Co., Phoenix, 1987—; bd. dirs. Ariz. Contrn. Tng. Ctr., Phoenix; v.p. Sunburst Farms East Water Co., Phoenix, 1984—. Pres. Maricopa County Sheriff Posse, Phoenix, 1988; vice chmn. Boy Scouts Am., Phoenix, 1987-89; constrn. chmn. Paradise Valley Community Ch., Phoenix, 1987-89. Republican. Home: 5111 E Andora Dr Scottsdale AZ 85254 Office: Kiewit Cos 2525 W Beryl Ste 100 Phoenix AZ 85021

HORNER, ALTHEA JANE, psychologist; b. Hartford, Conn., Jan. 13, 1926; d. Louis and Celia (Newmark) Greenwald; children: Martha Horner Hartley, Anne Horner Benck, David, Kenneth. BS in Psychology, U. Chgo., 1952; PhD in Clin. Psychology, U. So. Calif., 1965. Lic. psychologist, N.Y., Calif. Tchr. Pasadena (Calif.) City Coll., 1965-67; from asst. to assoc. prof. Los Angeles Coll. Optometry, 1967-70; supr. Psychology interns Pasadena Child Guidance Clinic, 1969-70; pvt. practice specializing in psychoanalysis and psychoanalytic psychotherapy. N.Y.C., 1970-83; supervising psychologist dept. psychiatry Beth Israel Med. Ctr., N.Y.C., 1972-83, coordinator group therapy tng., 1976-82, clinician in charge Brief Adaptation-Oriented Psychotherapy Research Group, 1982-83; assoc. clin. prof. Mt. Sinai Sch. Medicine, N.Y.C., 1977—; mem. faculty Nat. Psychol. Assn. for Psychoanalysis, N.Y.C., 1982-83; sr. mem. faculty Wright Inst. Los Angeles Postgrad. Inst., 1983-85; pvt. practice specializing in psychoanalysis and psychoanalytic psychotherapy L.A., 1983—; clin. prof. dept. Psychology UCLA, 1985—. Author: (with others) Treating the Oedipal Patient in Brief Psychotherapy, 1985, Object Relations and the Developing Ego in Therapy, 1979, rev. edit., 1984, Little Big Girl, 1982, Being and Loving, 1978, new ed. 1986, Psychology for Living (with G. Forehand), 4th edit., 1977, The Wish for Power and the Fear of Having It, 1989; mem. editorial bd. Jour. of Humanistic Psychology, 1986—, Jour. of the Am. Acad. of Psychoanalysis; contbr. articles to profl. jours. Mem. AAAS, Am. Psychol. Assn., Calif. State Psychol. Assn., Am. Women Sci., Nat. Psychol. Assn. for Psychoanalysis, Am. Acad. Psychoanalysis (sci. assoc.). Office: 1314 Westwood Blvd Los Angeles CA 90024

HORNER, DONALD GORDON, banker; b. Fayetville, N.C., Sept. 29, 1950. BA, U. N.C., 1972; MBA, U. So. Calif., 1977. Trainee mgmt. 1978-88; pres., dir. First Hawaiian Creditcorp. Inc., Honolulu, 1988—; pres. First Hawaiian Leasing Inc., Honolulu, 1988—; sr. v.p. First Hawaiian Bank, Honolulu, 1988—; v.p. First Hawaiian Inc., Honolulu, 1988—; instr. fin. U. Hawaii, 1979—. Dir. Hawaii Visitors Bur., 1988—; chmn., pres. Big Bros. Hawaii, 1985; elder First Presbyn. Ch. Honolulu, 1986; mem. adv. bd. Civilian Army, 1987. Named Hawaii's Outstanding Young Person Hawaii Jaycees, 1986. Mem. Outrigger Canoe Club. Home: 2756 Tantalus Dr Honolulu HI 96813 Office: First Hawaiian Creditcorp Inc 165 S King St 18th Fl Honolulu HI 96813

HORNING, GREGORY MASON, periodontist; b. West Bend, Wis., Nov. 13, 1950; s. Donald Mitchel and Libby (Marshalek) H.; m. Diane Lynn Gach, May 11, 1974; children: Mark Gabriel, Joel Gregory. BA, Earlham Coll., Richmond, Ind., 1972; DDS, Ind. U., 1977; MS in Oral Biology, U. Mo., 1984. Diplomate Am. Bd. Periodontology. Commd. lt. USN, 1977, advanced through grades to comdr., 1977—; resident Naval Hosp., San Diego, 1977-78; dental officer Br. Dental Clinic, Adak, Alaska, 1978-80, Regional Dental Ctr., Great Lakes, Ill., 1980-82; periodontal resident U. Mo. Sch. Dentistry, Kansas City, Mo., 1982-84; dept. head Br. Dental Clinic, San Diego, 1984-87; dept. head periodontic div. dental dept. Naval Hosp., Oakland, Calif., 1987—. Contbr. articles to profl. jours. Mem. ADA, Am. Acad. Periodontology, U.S. Naval Inst., Officer's Christian Fellowship. Mem. Christian Ch. Office: Naval Hosp Dental Dept Oakland CA 94627

HORNSHUH, DAVID LAWRENCE, pharmacist, consultant; b. Portland, Oreg., Jan. 23, 1950; s. Merwyn Edward and Jeanne Elizabeth (Moran) H. BS in Pharmacy, Oreg. State U., 1973. Lic. pharmacist, Hawaii. V.p. DIROCO, Inc., Auburn, Calif., 1975-87, Interstate Pharmacy Corp., Scotts Valley, Calif., 1987—; cons. in field. Mem. Hawaii Soc. Hosp. Pharmacy, Am. Soc. Cons. Pharmacists, Hawaii Pharm. Assn. (v.p.). Home: 583 Kamoku St Apt 2603 Honolulu HI 96826

HORNUNG, RICHARD CHARLES, accountant; b. Seattle, Feb. 25, 1954; s. Richard Oscar and Marquerite Elizabeth (Blaine) H.; m. Cynthia Ann Fox, June 19, 1982; 1 child, Anne Christine. BA in Econs., U. Wash., 1978, MBA in Acctg. and Fin., 1982. CPA, Wash. Intern Arabian Am. Oil Co., Dhahran, Saudi Arabia, 1981; audit staff acct. Laventhol & Horwath, Seattle, 1983-84; asst. contr. Security Properties, Inc., Seattle, 1984-87; contr. Lakeside-Milam Recovery Ctrs., Bothell, Wash., 1987—. Subdeacon St. Paul Orthodox Ch., Lynnwood, Wash., 1987—. Mem. AICPA, Wash. Soc. CPA's. Office: Lakeside-Milam Recovery Ctrs Inc 14500 Juanita Dr NE Bothell WA 98011

HOROWITZ, BEN, medical center executive; b. Bklyn., Mar. 19, 1914; s. Saul and Sonia (Meringoff) H.; m. Beverly Lichtman, Feb. 14, 1952; children: Zacjary, Jody. BA, Bklyn. Coll., 1940; LLB, St. Lawrence U., 1935; postgrad. New Sch. Social Research, 1942. Bar: N.Y., 1941 Dir. N.Y. Fedn. Jewish Philanthropies, 1940-45; Eastern regional dir. City of Hope, 1945-50, nat. exec. sec., City of Hope Los Angeles, 1950-53, exec. dir., 1953-85, gen. v.p. of bd. dirs. City of Hope, 1985-87, pres., bd. dirs. City of Hope Nat. Med. Ctr., 1986-87; bd. dirs. Beckman Research Inst. City of Hope, 1980—. Mem. Gov.'s Task Force on Flood Relief, 1969-74. Bd. dirs., v.p. Hope for Hearing Found., UCLA, 1972—; bd. dirs. Forte Found., 1987—, Ch.-Temple Corp. Housing, 1988—. Recipient Spirit of Life award, 1970, Gallery of Achievement award, 1974, Profl. of Yr. award So. Calif. chpt. Nat. Soc. Fundraisers, 1977; Ben Horowitz chair in research established at City of Hope, 1981. Los Angeles City street named in his honor, 1986. Jewish (dir. temple 1964-67, 1986—). Home: 221 Conway Ave Los Angeles CA 90024 Office: City of Hope 208 W 8th St Los Angeles CA 90014

HOROWITZ, MYER, university president; b. Montreal, Que., Can., Dec. 27, 1932; s. Philip and Fanny Cotler H.; m. Barbara Rosen, 1956; children: Carol Anne, Deborah Ellen. BA, Sir George Williams U., 1956; MEd, U. Alta., 1959; EdD, Stanford U., 1965; LLD (hon.), McGill U., 1979, Concordia U., 1982. Tchr. elem. and high schs., Montreal, Que. area, 1952-60; lectr. in edn. McGill U., 1960-62, asst. prof., 1963-65, assoc. prof., 1965-67, prof., 1967-69, asst. dean, 1965-69; prof., chmn. dept. elem. edn. U. Alta., 1969-72, dean of edn., 1972-75, v.p. (acad.), 1975-79, pres., 1979-89, prof. edn., 1990—. Author articles in field. Fellow Can. Coll. Teachers. Jewish. Office: Univ of Alta, Dept of Edn, Edmonton, AB Canada T6G 2J9 *

HOROWITZ, NAOMI JOY, dentist, military officer; b. L.A., May 11, 1959; d. Lawrence and Roselyn Joy (Finnerman) Weinstein; m. Anthony Horowitz, July 10, 1988. BS, Loyola Marymount U., Westchester, Calif., 1981; DDS, Loyola U., Maywood, Ill., 1985. Pvt. practice Long Beach, Calif., 1985-89; commd. capt. U.S. Army Dental Corps, 1989; dentist Hanau (Fed. Republic Germany) Dental Clinic, 1989--. Inventor dental instrument. Mem. ADA, Alpha Sigma Nu. Jewish.

HOROWITZ, STEPHEN PAUL, lawyer; b. Los Angeles, May 23, 1943; s. Julius J. and Maxine (Rubenstein) H.; m. Nancy J. Shapiro, Apr. 4, 1971; children: Lindsey Nicole, Keri Lyn, Deborah Arielle. B.S., UCLA, 1966; J.D., 1970; M. Acctg., U. So. Calif., 1967. CPA, Calif. Bookkeeper, various law and acctg. firms, 1963-70; staff acct. Touche, Ross & Co., C.P.A.s, Los Angeles, 1968, 69; admitted to Calif. bar, 1971, U.S. Dist. Ct. bar, 1971, U.S. Ct. Appeals bar, 1972; individual practice law, Los Angeles, 1971-77; partner firm Horowitz & Horowitz, Los Angeles, 1978-79, prin. firm, 1979—; judge pro tem Los Angeles Mcpl. Ct.; classroom speaker Los Angeles County Bar Assn.; arbitrator Better Bus. Bur., Los Angeles County Bar Assn., Am. Arbitration Assn.; ombudsman VA, 1970. Bd. dirs. Vols. Am. Detoxification and Rehab. Center, Los Angeles, 1975-81, treas., 1979, vice chmn., 1980-81; legal adv. chmn., parliamentarian Temple Ramat Zion, Northridge, Calif., 1983-88, v.p., 1988. Served with U.S. Army, 1961-62. Mem. Calif. State Bar, Calif. Trial Lawyers Assn., Los Angeles Trial Lawyers. Jewish. Lodge: Masons. Editorial bd. UCLA-Alaska Law Rev., 1968-70, co-editor-in-chief, 1969-70. Office: 8383 Wilshire Blvd Ste 528 Beverly Hills CA 90211

HOROWITZ, ZACHARY I., record company executive; b. N.Y.C., Apr. 27, 1953; s. Ben and Beverly (Lichtman) H. BA summa cum laude, Claremont Mens Coll., 1975; JD, Stanford U., 1978. Bar: Calif. 1978. Assoc. Kaplan, Livingston, Goodwin, Berkowitz & Selvin, Beverly Hills, Calif., 1978; sr. atty. CBS Records, Los Angeles, 1978-80, dir. bus. affairs West Coast, 1980-83; v.p. bus. and legal affairs MCA Records, Universal City, Calif., 1983-84, sr. v.p. bus. and legal affairs, 1984-88; sr. v.p. bus. and legal affairs MCA Music Entertainment Group, Universal City, 1988—. Mem. bd. editors Stanford Law Rev., 1977-78. Mem. Record Industry Assn. Am. (legal com. 1983—, Calif. Strategy com. 1985—), City of Hope Music Industry Chpt. (vice chmn. 1985-86, chmn. maj. gifts com. 1986-89). Jewish. Office: MCA Records Inc 70 Universal City Pla Universal City CA 91608

HORRES, CHARLES RUSSELL, JR., health care company executive, educator; b. Charleston, S.C., Aug. 6, 1945; s. Charles Russell and Louise (Smith) H.; m. Mary Eison, June 17, 1967; 1 child, Charles Russell III. BS in Chem. Engring., Ga. Tech. U., 1967; PhD in Physiology, Duke U., 1975. Research engr. Monsanto Co., Res. Triangle Park, N.C., 1968-69; dept. mgr. Becton Dickinson, Res. Triangle Park, 1975-83; pres. Pancretec, Inc., San Diego, 1983-86; v.p. research and devel. IVAC, Inc., San Diego, 1986—; adj. assoc. prof. Duke U., Durham, N.C., 1977. Contbr. articles to profl. jours.; patentee in field. Active U. Calif. Library Devel. Council, LaJolla, 1987—. Lt. USPHS, 1969-71. Mem. Am. Soc. Artificial Internal Organ, Soc. Gen. Physiologists, Cardiac Muscle Soc., Biophys. Soc., Am. Assn. Med. Instrumentation, San Diego Yacht Club. Home: 13071 Via Grimaldi Del Mar CA 92014

HORSELL, MARY KAY, association executive; b. Roundup, Mont., Nov. 3, 1917; d. Guy Elmer and Mary Catherine (Raridan) Smith; m. Arthur Howard Horsell, June 26, 1937; children—Barbara Horsell Koon, Mary Ann Horsell Boyette, Arthur Howard. B.S., Fresno (Calif.) State U., 1939. Owner, operator Food Merchandising Service, Dublin, Calif., 1954—; chmn. bd. Oakland Diocesan Council Cath. Women, 1962-64, program chmn., 1964-65, v.p., program chmn., 1965-66, pres., 1967-69; parliamentarian, Diocesan rep. Ch. Women United Bd., 1969-71, ways and means chmn., 1971-73; province dir. San Francisco Archdiocesan Council Cath. Women, 1973-75; mem. Pres. Ford & Pres. Carter Commn. for Women, 1975, 76, 77; pres. Nat. Council Cath. Women, Washington, 1975—; U.S. rep. from Nat. Council Cath. Women to World Union Cath. Women's Orgns., 1979—; mem. Commn. for Women in Ch., Oakland Diocese, 1978—; mem. exec. bd. Women in Community Service, Washington, 1979—; bd. dirs. World Union Cath. Women's Orgns., 1979—; Mem. central com. San Francisco Bay council Girl Scouts U.S.A., 1947-55; diocesan bd. mem., health chmn., program chmn., legis. chmn. Parent Tchrs. Groups, 1949-54; pres. East Bay Pres.'s Council, 1954-56, archdiocesan pres., 1958-60; pres. Oakland Diocese, 1962-64, St. Jarlath's Mothers Club, 1946-48, Bishop O'Dowd High Sch. Mothers Club, 1956-58; co-organizer Children's Vision Center of East Bay, 1957, pres., 1971-74; pres. East Bay Motion Picture and TV Council, 1964-66; organizer Vol. Tchr. Assistance Program for elementary schs. in Oakland Diocese, 1965; bd. dirs. Met. Horseman's Assn., 1963-75, now v.p., Past Pres.'s trophy, 1975; vol. counselor juvenile delinquents awaiting trial, 1967—; sec. Fedn. Motion Picture Councils, Inc., 1975-77, nat. pres. 1977-79. Editor: Newsreel, Fedn. Motion Picture Councils, 1973-75. Pres. Fedn. Motion Picture & TV Councils, N.Y.C., 1978-80. Speaker for Pres. Johnson's Commn. for Women. Recipient Pro Ecclesia Et Pontifice, 1964, Life membership East Bay Pres.'s Council Parent Tchrs. Groups, 1964; named Oakland Mother of Year, 1970. Mem. Zonta Internat. Home: 11590 Circle Way Dublin CA 94568 Office: 1312 Massachusetts Ave NW Washington DC 20005

HORSMAN, JAMES DEVERELL, Canadian provincial government official; b. Camrose, Alta., Can., July 29, 1935; s. George Cornwall and Kathleen (Deverell) H.; m. Elizabeth Marian Whitney, July 4, 1964; children—Catherine Anne, Diana Lynn, Susan Marian. B.Com., LL.B., U. B.C. Created queen's counsel, 1980. Mem. Alta. Legis. Assembly for Medicine Hat, 1975—, minister of advanced edn. and manpower, 1979-82, minister of fed. intergovtl. affairs, 1982—, atty. gen., 1986-88, dep. govt. house leader, 1982-87, dep. premier, govt. house leader, 1989—; mem. Alta. Del. to First Ministers Conf. on Constn., 1982; chmn. Provincial Ministers Responsible for Manpower, 1982. Mem., chmn. bd. govs. Medicine Hat Coll., 1972-74; elder St. John's Ch. Medicine Hat. Mem. Medicine Hat C. of C. (pres. 1971-72). Progressive Conservative. Presbyterian. Clubs: Kinsmen (past pres., past dist. officer), Cypress. Lodge: Shriners. Office: Alta Legislature, 320 Legislature Bldg, Edmonton, AB Canada T5K 2B6

HORTON, DAVID ALAN, backhoe operator; b. San Jose, Calif., June 11, 1953; s. Elizabeth (Aman) Speck. Grad. high sch., San Jose. Foreman Green Thumb Landscaping, San Jose, 1967-77; receiving insp. various cos., 1977-79; utility clk. Alpha Beta, Sacramento, 1979; backhoe operator Galante Bros. Gen. Engring., San Jose, 1979—. Home: 510 Rodeck Way Campbell CA 95008 Office: Galante Bros Gen Engring 7107 Raich Dr San Jose CA 95120

HORTON, JACK KING, utilities executive; b. Stanton, Nebr., June 27, 1916; s. Virgil L. and Edna L. (King) H.; m. Betty Lou Magee, July 15, 1937; children: Judy, Sally, Harold. A.B., Stanford U., 1936; LL.B., Oakland Coll. Law, 1941. Bar: Calif. 1941. Treasury dept. Shell Oil Co., 1937-42; pvt. law practice San Francisco, 1942-43; atty. Standard Oil Co., 1943-44; sec., legal counsel Coast Counties Gas & Electric Co., 1944-51, pres., 1951-54; v.p. Pacific Gas & Electric Co., San Francisco, 1954-59; pres. So. Calif. Edison Co., 1959-68, chief exec. officer, from 1965, chmn. bd., 1968-80, chmn. exec. com., from 1980; dir. First Interstate Bank of Calif., Pacific Mut. Life Ins., Lockheed Aircraft Corp., First Interstate Bancorp. Trustee U. So. Calif. Mem. State Bar Calif., Tax Found. (trustee), Bus. Council. Clubs: Pacific Union, Bohemian, California, Los Angeles Country, Cypress Point. Office: So Calif Edison Co 2244 Walnut Grove Ave Rosemead CA 91770

HORTON, LAWRENCE STANLEY, electrical engineer, apartment developer; b. Hanston, Kans., July 25, 1926; s. Gene Leigh and Retta Florence (Abbott) H.; BSEE, Oreg. State U., 1949; m. Margaret Ann Cowles, Nov. 26, 1946 (dec. 1964); children: Craig, Lawrence Stanley, Steven J.; m. Julia Ann Butler Wirrkila, Aug. 15, 1965; stepchildren: Charles Wirkkila Horton, Jerry Higginbotham Horton. Elec. engr. Mountain States Power Co., Calif. Oreg. Power Co., Pacific Power and Light Co., 1948-66; mgr. Ramic Corp., 1966-69; cons. elec. engr. Marquess and Assos., Medford, Oreg., 1969-85, sec., bd. dirs.; owner, mgr. Medford Better Housing Assn.; ptnr. Eastwood Living Group, Jackson St. Properties, T'Morrow Apts., Lake Empire Apts., Johnson Manor; bd. dirs. Valley of Rogue, developer various apt. complexes, 1969—; bd. dirs. Medford Hist. Commn. Active Medford Planning Commn., Archtl. Review Commn., Housing Authority; bd. govs. State of Oreg. Citizens Utility; pres. United Fund, 1963-64. With USN, 1945-46. Named Rogue Valley Profl. Engr. of Yr., 1969. Mem. IEEE, Nat. Soc. Profl. Engrs., Profl. Engrs. of Oreg., So. Oreg. Apt. Owners Assn. (pres.), Rogue Valley Geneol. Soc. (pres.), Medford C. of C. (dir.), Rogue Valley Country Club, Rogue Valley Yacht Club (commodore 1974-55, dir., local fleet capt., champion), San Juan 21 Fleet Assn. (western vice commodore, Top Ten San Juan Sailor West Coast, 1980), Jackson Toastmasters (founder 1957), Univ. Club, Cen. Point Rotary, Kiwanis (life). Republican. Methodist. Grad. instr. Dale Carnegie course, 1955, 56; contbr. elec. articles to profl. assns., 1956-61. Office: 1118 Spring St Medford OR 97504

HORTON, NEIL FISHER, judge, lawyer; b. Chgo., June 23, 1937; s. Caesar C. and Sally (Parker) H.; m. Bronwen Margaret Taylor, July 23, 1966; children: Emma Gillian, Sarah Bronwen, David Owen. BA, Grinnell Coll., 1958; LLB, Harvard Law Sch., 1961. Bar: Calif. 1962, U.S. Dist. Ct. (no. dist.) Calif. 1962, U.S. Tax Ct. 1964, U.S. Ct. Appeals (9th cir.) 1971, U.S. Supreme Ct. 1972,. Assoc. Avakian, Johnson & Platt, Oakland, Calif., 1964-67; ptnr. Johnston and Klein, Oakland, Calif., 1967-84, Johnston, Horton & Roberts, Oakland, Calif., 1984—; arbitrator (no. dist.) U.S. Dist. Ct., San Francisco, 1980—; judge pro temp. Alameda County Superior Ct., Oakland, 1985—; lectr. Practicing Law Inst., 1975, Calif. Continuing Edn. of Bar, 1981. Chmn. Am. Friends Svc. Com. of No. Calif., San Francisco, 1966-70; mem. commn. on jud. nominees evaluation State Bar Calif., 1988. Mem. ABA, State Bar Assn. Calif. (cert. specialist in taxation law 1975—), Bar Assn. San Francisco, Alameda County Bar Assn. (pres. 1985, bd. dirs. 1981-86, lectr. 1987), ACLU (bd. dirs. San Francisco chpt. 1967-73, 75-82). Democrat. Jewish. Home: 975 Euclid Ave Berkeley CA 94708 Office: Johnston Horton & Roberts 1980 Harrison St Ste 1500 Oakland CA 94612

HORTON, ROBERT CARLTON, mining executive, geologist; b. Tonopah, Nev., July 25, 1926; s. Frank Elijah and Eathel Margaret (Miller) H.; m. Beverly Jean Burhans, Dec. 5, 1952; children: Debra, Robin, Cindy. B.S., U. Nev., 1949, D.Sc. (hon.), 1985, Geol. Engr., 1966. Registered profl. geol. engr., Nev. Assoc. dir. Nev. Bur. Mines, Reno, 1956-66; cons. Reno, 1966-76; dir. geology div. Bendix Field Engring Corp. (Grand Junction), Colo., 1976-81; dir. U.S. Bur. Mines, Washington, 1981-87; dir. strategic materials research U. Nev., Reno, 1987—, assoc. dean MacKay Sch. Mines, 1989—; mem. Nev. Gov.'s Mining Adv. Com., 1966-72. Author: Barite Deposits of Nevada, 1962, Fluorspar Deposits of Nevada, 1963, History of Nevada Mining, 1963. Republican candidate for Congress from Nev., 1958. Served to lt. USNR, 1944-46, 53-56, PTO. Kennecott scholar, 1948; named Engr. of Yr. Reno chpt. Nat. Soc. Profl. Engrs., 1967. Mem. AIME (subsect. chmn. Reno 1962-63), Soc. Econ. Geologists, Mining and Metall. Soc. Am. Methodist.

HORTON, SHARON RENE, army officer; b. DeWitt, Ark., Oct. 4, 1958; d. Clayton Haynes and Mary Lillian (Lackey) H. BS in Math., U. Ark., Pine Bluff, 1986; postgrad. bus. adminstn., Golden Gate U., 1988—. Commd. 2nd lt. U.S. Army, 1986, advanced to 1st lt., 1987; battalion adjutant 702nd Maintenance Bn.,, Camp Casey, Republic of Korea, 1986-87; tech. supply officer 702nd Maintenance Bn., "C" Co., Camp Edwards (W), Republic of Korea, 1987; maintenance platoon leader 707th Maintenance Bn., 519th Maintenance Co., Ft. Ord, Calif., 1987—; tax assistance officer 519th Maintenance Co., Ft. Ord, 1989. Mem. Nat. Assn. Female Execs., Am. Assn. Individual Investors, Alpha Kappa Mu. Democrat. Baptist. Home: 519 Maintenance Co Box 259 Fort Ord CA 93941 Office: 519th Maintenance Co Fort Ord CA 93941

HORVAT, DANIEL JAMES, architect; b. Denver, Dec. 6, 1961; s. Emil Joseph and Dorothy Mary (Gilmour) H.; m. Dawn Schulstrom, 1989. BArch, Ariz. State U., 1985. Intern Marvin Knadler & Assocs., Denver, 1983, James White Ptnrship., Lakewood, Colo., 1984, Stowe-Mettenbrink Assocs., Phoenix, 1984-85; architect Skidmore Owings & Merrill, Denver, 1985-86, Washington, 1986-88; architect Hoover, Berg, Desmond, Denver, 1988—; Registered architect, Colo., Calif. Named Funk-Sun Angel scholar, 1982-83, AIA Found. scholar, 1984-85. Mem. AIA. Democrat. Roman Catholic. Home: 620 Hudson St Denver CO 80220 Office: Hoover Berg Desmond 1645 Grant St Denver CO 80203

HORVATH, TERRENCE MICHAEL, manufacturing company executive; b. Marinette, Wis., Jan. 5, 1961; s. Frank Alexander and Marion Lydia (Chervenka) H.; m. Deborah Lynn Otte, Nov. 2 , 1987; children: Michael Alexander and Matthew Ryan (twins). BSBA, Ariz. State U., 1983; postgrad., UCLA, 1988. Jr. buyer Caoptol Machine Co., Phoenix, 1981-84; supr. Intel Corp., Albuquerque, 1984-85; buyer Lockheed Calif. Co., Burbank, 1985-86, sr. buyer, 1986-87, subcontract adminstr., 1987-88; sr. subcontract adminstr. McDonnell Douglas Aircraft Co., Long Beach, Calif., 1988-89,

McDonnell Douglas Heilcopter Co., Mesa, Ariz., 1989—. Mem. Nat. Contract Mgmt. Assn., Nat. Assn. Purchasing Mgmt., Purchasing Mgmt. Assn. Ariz. Republican. Roman Catholic. Home: 3006 N Ricardo Mesa AZ 85205 Office: McDonnell Douglas Helicoptr 5000 E McDowell Rd Mesa AZ 85205

HORWITZ, LARRY STUCKEY, electronics executive; b. Port Arthur, Tex., July 11, 1949; s. Herman and Mary Jane (Stuckey) H.; m. Mary Elizabeth Horwitz, July 16, 1983. BS in Elec. Engr., Lamer U., 1972, BS in Physics, %; MS in Elec. Engr., U. So. Calif., 1974; MS in Optical Sci., U. Rochester, 1975. Registered elec. engr., Calif. Mem. tech. staff Hughes Aircraft, Fullerton, Calif., 1972-77; research and devel. engr. Ford Aerospace subs. Ford Motor Co., Newport Beach, Calif., 1977-82; sr. staff engr. TRW, Redondo Beach, Calif., 1982-85; chief scientist Rockwell Internat., Seal Beach, Calif., 1985-86; program mgr. Analytic Sci. Corp., Reading, Mass., 1986-88; pres. Am. Tech., Long Beach, Calif., 1988—; nat. panel mem. Strategic Def. Initiative Orgn., Washington, 1987—; sci. advisor Strategic Def. Initiative Orgn., 1986—. Inventor with 30 patents in med. and sci. field. Community pres. Costa del Sol Homeowner's Assn., Long Beach, 1986—. Nat. Sci. Found. research grantee, 1971. Fellow Inst. Elec. and Electronic Engrs; mem. Optical Soc. Am., Am. Physical Soc., Am. Watchmakers Inst., Physics Hon. Soc., Engring. Hon. Soc., Eta Kappa Nu. Republican. Jewish.

HORWITZ, RICHARD ALLEN, refrigeration company executive; b. Los Angeles, Aug. 1, 1948; s. Robert J. and Ann (Leiser) H.; m. Bonnie Jean Zaler, Dec. 24, 1970; children: Rebecca Danelle, Cameron Jeffrey. BA, U. Colo., 1972, MA, 1974, PhD, 1976. Teaching asst. U. Colo., Denver, 1972-76, instr., 1976-77; asst. sec., treas. Mid-Continent Refrigerator Co., Denver, 1977-87, pres., chief exec. officer, 1987—; bd. dirs. Mid Continent Refrigerator Co., Denver, 1987—. Democrat. Jewish. Home: 7853 S Harrison Circle Littleton CO 80122

HOSFORD, HARLOW BUSS, mathematician; b. Keokuk, Iowa, Oct. 21, 1931; s. Harlow Newton and Rebecca Louise (Buss) H.; m. Barbara Annette Silvera, Apr. 10, 1960; children Michael, Heather Luann Eastwood. B in Music Edn., Knox Coll., Galesburg, Ill., 1953; M in Music Edn., U. So. Calif., 1965. Cert. secondary tchr., Calif. Music tchr. Visalia (Calif.) Pub. Sch., 1955-61; music tchr. Fresno (Calif.) Unified Sch. Dist., 1961-77, math. tchr., 1977—. Author: Developing Techniques in Junior High Wind Instrument Players, 1965. 1st lt. U.S. Army, 1953-55. Recipient Fulbright Exch. award U.S. Dept. Edn., England, 1983. Mem. Nat. Coun. of Tchrs. Math., Calif. Math. Coun. Republican. Presbyterian. Home: 3170 E Rialto Fresno CA 93726 Office: Fresno Unified Sch Dist 3232 E Fairmont Fresno CA 93726

HOSHIZAKI, BARBARA JOE, pteridologist, educator; b. Oakland, Calif., June 14, 1928; d. Wilbert and Ruby (Tom) Joe; m. Takashi Hoshizaki, June 29, 1952; children: Carol, Jon. BS, U. Calif., Berkeley, 1951; MS, U. Calif., Los Angeles, 1955. Prof. of Botany L.A. City Coll., 1960-88; curator of Pteridology U. Calif., L.A., 1975—; v.p. Pacific Hort. Found. Berkeley 1980—, Southern Calif. Hort. Inst. Los Angeles 1983-87, pres. 1987—. Author: book, Fern Growers Manual 1975; several papers on ferns. Bd. dirs. Nature Conservacy, So. Calif. Chpt. Los Angeles, 1966-68. Named hon. mem. South Fla. Fern Soc. 1979; recipient award So. Calif. Horticultural Inst. Mem. Am. Fern Soc., Brit. Pteridological Soc., Calif. Native Plant Soc., So. Calif. Botanist (bd. dir. 1980-82), L.A. Mycological Soc., Internat. Assn. Pteridologist; pres. L.A. Internat. Fern Soc. 1974-75 (Outstanding Contbr. to Hort. 1982).

HOSIE, STANLEY WILLIAM, foundation executive, writer; b. Lismore, New South Wales, Australia, Apr. 28, 1922; came to U.S., 1945; s. Stanley James and Catherine Clare (Chisholm) H. BA, U. Queensland, Brisbane, Australia, 1945; Lic. in Theology, Cath. U., Washington, 1947, MA, 1948. Dean of studies Marist Coll., Lismore, 1949-57; pres., founder Chanel Coll., Geelong, Victoria, Australia, 1958-62; writer-in-residence Casa Generalitia Societatis Mariae, Rome, 1963-66; exec. dir. The Found. for the Peoples of the South Pacific, Inc., N.Y.C., 1966—; theologian for Conf. of Pacific Cath. Bishops, 2d Vatican Council, Rome, 1963-65; dir. Am. Council of Vol. Agys., N.Y.C., 1976—, treas. 1983-84; dir. Pvt. Agys. Collaborating Together, 1977—; mem. Presdl. Adv. Com. on Vol. Aid, 1988—. Author: The Swiss Conspiracy, 1976, The Boomerang Conspiracy, 1978, (biography) Anonymous Apostle, 1966, also numerous screenplays. Recipient Best Article Vatican II award Nat. Cath. Periodicals Assn., 1964. Mem. Writers Guild Am. East, Soc. des Oceanistes, Australian Coll. Edn. Democrat. Roman Catholic. Home: 720 Palisades Beach Rd Santa Monica CA 90402 Office: Found for Peoples South Pacific 3200 Wilshire Blvd 14th Floor Los Angeles CA 90010

HOSIE, WILLIAM CARLTON, walnut growers company executive; b. Stockton, Calif., June 25, 1936; s. Fred A. and Janet (Russell) H.; m. Sherryl Rasmussen, Jan. 12, 1963; children: Shaen Case, Erin Frick. B.S., U. Calif.-Davis, 1960. Field rep. Flotill Inc., Stockton, 1960-61; orchardist Hosie Ranch Inc., Linden, Calif., 1961-83; chmn. bd. dirs. Diamond Walnut Growers Inc., Stockton, 1981—; now slao vice chmn.; dir. Sun-Diamond Growers Calif., Pleasanton; advisor U. Calif. Extension-Stockton, 1975—, Calif. Farm Bur., Sacramento, 1976—, Farmer and Mchts. Bank, Linden, 1979; dir. Walnut Mktg. Bd., San Mateo, Calif., 1981—. Pres. Stockton East Water Dist., 1969-79. Served with AUS, 1958-59. Mem. Stockton C. of C. Republican. Club: Rotary Internat. Home: PO Box 226 Linden CA 95236 Office: Diamond Walnut Growers Inc 1050 S Diamond St Stockton CA 95205 *

HOSKINS, BARBARA BRUNO, speech pathologist, learning disabilities specialist; b. Havre de Grace, Md., Feb. 21, 1948; d. Onofrio Pasquale and Marjorie (Goertler) Bruno. BS magna cum laude, Syracuse U., 1970; MS, So. Ill. U., 1971; PhD, Northwestern U., 1979. Cert. clin. competence speech/lang. pathologist. Lectr. Southern Ill. U., Carbondale, 1971-72; speech, lang. specialist Los Angeles County Schs., 1973-76; dir. tng. and research Almansor Edn. Ctr., Alhambra, Calif., 1979-86; asst. prof. Whittier (Calif.) Coll., 1980-84; vis. prof. U. Redlands, Calif., 1984-86; cons. in field, Pasadena, Calif., 1985—; affiliate staff Ingleside Hosp., Alhambra, 1982—, Las Encinas Hosp., Pasadena, 1985—. Mem. Am. Speech, Lang., Hearing Assn., Internat. Neuropsychol. Soc. Home: 285 W California #3 Pasadena CA 91105 Office: 595 E Colorado Blvd #508 Pasadena CA 91101

HOSKINS, FREDERICK HALL, food science/nutrition educator; b. Cin., May 17, 1936; s. Harold Elvin and Niota (Hall) H.; m. Mildred Ann Ball, Sept. 8, 1957; children: Michael, Darrell. BS, U. Ariz., 1958, MS, 1959; PhD, La. State U., 1963. Instr. La. State U., Baton Rouge, 1964-65, asst. prof., 1965-71, assoc. prof., 1971-76, prof. food sci., 1976-84; chmn., prof. dept. food sci. and human nutrition Wash. State U., Pullman, 1984-86, prof. food sci. and human nutrition, 1986—; cons. Ethyl Corp., Baton Rouge, 1965-67, Dairyland, Inc., St. Paul, 1977, Pillsbury Co., Mpls., 1978. Contbr. articles to profl. jours. Recipient Award of Excellence in Teaching Gamma Sigma Delta, La. State U., Baton Rouge, 1971. Mem. Inst. Food Technologists (chmn. nutrition div. 1974), Am. Inst. Nutrition (regional assoc. editor 1969-74), N.Y. Acad. Sci., Gamma Sigma Delta. Republican. Quaker. Office: Wash State U Dept Food Sci & Human Nutrition Pullman WA 99164

HOSKINS, L. CLARON, chemistry educator; b. Logan, Utah, July 27, 1940; s. Leo Cooper and Luella (Hall) H.; m. Flora Jensen, June 18, 1960; children: Duane, Daryl, Sandra. BS, Utah State U., 1962; PhD, MIT, 1965. Asst. prof. chemistry U. Alaska, Fairbanks, 1965-68, assoc. prof., 1968-75, prof., 1975—, head dept., 1984—. Mem. Am. Phys. Soc., Sigma Xi, Phi Kappa Phi, Pi Mu Epsilon. Home: 3291 Bluebird Ave Fairbanks AK 99709

HOSLEY, DAVID HENRY, broadcasting executive; b. San Jose, Calif., Dec. 20, 1949; s. Charles Thomas and Virginia Pauline (Jones) H.; m. Gayle Kim Yamada, Oct. 11, 1981. Student, Solano Coll., 1968-69; MA, Stanford U., 1972; PhD, Columbia U., N.Y.C., 1982. Lic. 1st class radio and TV operator. Bur. chief, anchor, editor, reporter Sta. KCBS-AM, San Francisco, 1971-79; news dir. Sta. WRUF-AM-FM, Gainesville, Fla., 1981-84; news dir., program dir. Sta. WINZ-AM, Miami, Fla., 1984-86; producer, writer Sta. KPIX-TV, San Francisco, 1986-87; sta. mgr. Sta. KQED, Inc., San Francisco, 1987—; asst. prof. U. Fla., Gainesville, 1981-84; instr. Stanford (Calif.) U., 1986-87; cons. ERA, Inc., San Francisco, 1974-77. Author: As Good As Any, 1983; co-author: Hard News, 1987. Coach San Francisco Women's Rugby Team, 1986-88. Recipient 1st Place award for spont news AP and UPI, 1987, 1st Place award for agr. AP, 1986, 1st Place award for investigative reporting AP, 1985; named Person of Yr. Foster Parents, Inc., 1977. Mem. Radio/TV Dirs. Assn., Am. Women in Radio (bd. dirs. 1988—), Asian Am. Journalists Assn., Family Club. Office: KQED-FM 500 8th St San Francisco CA 94103

HOSSACK, GEORGE WILLIAM, psychologist; b. Columbia Falls, Mont., Feb. 22, 1926; s. William Finley and Clarice Ada (Coulsten) H.; m. E. Corrine Moger, Dec. 23, 1949 (div. 1978); m. Janet Merrill, Mar. 16, 1979; children: Kimberly Jane, Lance Frederick, Hillary Ann. BS, Mont. State Coll., 1950; MEd, U. Maine, Orono, 1953; EdD, U. Wyo., 1966. Lic. psychologist. Supt., tchr. Harrison (Mont.) High Sch., 1950-52, 53-55; tchr., dean of boys Missoula (Mont.) County High Sch., 1956-60; guidance dir. Billings (Mont.) Pub. Schs., 1960-64; dir. personnel services Laramie (Wyo.) Pub. Schs., 1966-67; instr. dept. counseling Mont. State U., Bozeman, 1967-78; chmn. dept. counseling edn. U. Mont., Missoula, 1978-80; instr. Lewis & Clark Coll., Portland, Oreg., 1980-82; psychologist Giant Springs Counseling Assn., Great Falls, Mont., 1982—; psychologist Mont. Dept. Instns., Corrections div., Miles City, 1982-86. Served with USN, 1944-46. Mem. Internat. Council Psychologists, Internat. Transactional Analysis Assn., Am. Psychol. Assn., Council for the Nat. Register of Health Service Providers, Nat. Edn. Assn., Phi Delta Kappa. Democrat. Presbyterian. Home: 3506 Grizzly Ct Great Falls MT 59404 Office: Giant Springs Counseling Assn 510 First Ave North Ste 106 Great Falls MT 59401

HOSSLER, DAVID JOSEPH, lawyer, educator; b. Mesa, Ariz., Oct. 18, 1940; s. Carl Joseph and Elizabeth Ruth (Bills) H.; m. Gretchen Anne, Mar. 2, 1945; 1 child, Devon Annagret. BA, U. Ariz., 1969; JD, 1972. Bar: Ariz. 1972, U.S. dist. ct. Ariz. 1972, U.S. Supreme Ct. 1977. Legal intern to chmn. FCC, summer 1971; law clk. to chief justice Ariz. Supreme Ct., 1972-73; chief dep. county atty. Yuma County (Ariz.), 1973-74; ptnr. Hunt, Stanley, Hossler and Moore, Yuma, Ariz., 1974—; instr. in law and banking, law and real estate Ariz. Western Coll.; instr. in bus. law, mktg. Webster U. Mem. precinct com., Yuma County Rep. Cen. Com., 1974—, vice chmn., 1982; chmn. region II Acad. Decathalon competition, 1989; bd. dirs. Yuma County Ednl. Found., Yuma County Assn. Behavior Health Svcs., also pres., 1981; coach Yuma High Sch. mock ct. team, 1988—. With USN. Recipient Man and Boy award Boys Clubs Am., 1979, Found. award Yuma Chpt. Freedoms, 1988; named Vol. of Yr., Yuma County, 1981-82. Mem. Assn. Trial Lawyers Am., Am. Judicature Soc., Yuma County Bar Assn. (pres. 1975-76), Navy League, VFW, Am. Legion, U. Ariz. Alumni Assn. (nat. bd. dirs., past pres.), Rotary (pres. Yuma club 1987-88). Editor-in-chief Ariz. Adv., 1971-72. Episcopalian (vestry 1978-82). Home: 2802 Fern Dr Yuma AZ 85364 Office: Hunt Stanley Hossler & Moore 330 W 24th St Yuma AZ 85364

HOSTETLER, TERRY KEITH, banker; b. Louisville, Apr. 19, 1951; s. Homer Harold and Charlotte Ann (Rose) H.; m. Judith K. Farson, May 2, 1983; children: Jeremy Ryan, Megan Rose. BA, U. Ky., 1974. Loan officer Bank of Breckenridge, Colo., 1980-84; asst. v.p. Cen. Bank Centennial, Littleton, Colo., 1984-85; v.p. First Nat. Bank of Castle Rock, Colo., 1985—. Mem. adv. coun. Arapahoe Community Coll. 1986—. Mem. Castle Rock C. of C. (pres. 1988), Littleton Rotary Club, Castle Rock Rotary Club (pres.1987-88). Republican. Home: 585 Howe St Castle Rock CO 80104 Office: First Nat Bank of Castle Rock 120 S Wilcox St Castle Rock CO 80104

HOSTETTER, GENE HUBER, electrical engineering educator; b. Spokane, Wash., Sept. 14, 1939; s. John Huber and Virginia Lane (Yancey) H.; m. Donna Rae Patterson, Nov. 30, 1967; children—Colleen Rae, Kristen Lane. B.S.E.E., U. Wash., 1962, M.S., 1963; Ph.D., U. Calif.-Irvine, 1973. Dir. engring. Sta. KOL, Seattle, 1965-67; asst. prof. elec. engring. Calif. State U.-Long Beach, 1967-70, assoc. prof., 1970-75, prof., 1975-81, chmn. dept. elec. engring., 1975-81; prof. elec. engring. U. Calif.-Irvine, 1981, chmn. dept., 1983-85, acting dean engring., 1985-86. Author: Fundamentals of Network Analysis, 1980; Design of Feedback Control Systems, 1982; Engineering Network Analysis, 1984, Digital Control System Design, 1987. Recipient Outstanding Faculty award Calif. State U., 1975, 77, Engr. Faculty of Yr. award U. Calif.-Irvine, 1982. Fellow IEEE, Internat. Acad. Scis.; mem. AAAS, Am. Soc. Engring. Edn., Internat. Fedn. Automatic Control, Sigma Xi. Episcopalian. Home: 8811 Gallant Dr Huntington Beach CA 92646 Office: U Calif Dept Elec Engring Irvine CA 92717 *

HOTCHKISS, HENRY WASHINGTON, banker; b. Meshed, Iran, Oct. 31, 1937; s. Henry and Mary Bell (Clark) H. BA, Bowdoin Coll., 1958. French tchr. Choate Sch., Wallingford, Conn., 1959-62; v.p. Chem. Bank, N.Y.C., 1962-80, v.p. Chem. Bank Internat. San Francisco, 1973-80; dir. corp. rels., mgr. Crédit Suisse, San Francisco, 1980-87; dir. Indonesia-U.S. Bus. Seminar, Los Angeles, 1979. Assoc. bd. regents L.I. Coll. Hosp., 1969-71, pres., 1971, bd. regents, 1971-73, pres., bd. dirs. Gordonstown Am. Found, 1986—. Capt. USAR, 1958-69. Mem. Explorers Club (treas. North Calif. chpt. 1984-86), Calif. Council Internat. Trade (dir. 1976-87, chmn. membership com. 1977-79, treas. 1978-79), New Eng. Soc. in City Bklyn. (v.p., dir. 1968-73). Clubs: Heights Casino (bd. govs. 1971-73) (Bklyn.); St. Francis Yacht (San Francisco), Internat. Folkboat Assn. San Francisco (cruise chmn. 1976-77, pres. 1977-79, membership chmn. 1979-84, historian 1984-86). Home: 1206 Leavenworth St San Francisco CA 94109

HOTCHKISS, JOHN FARWELL, JR., aerospace company executive; b. San Francisco, June 28, 1931; s. John Farwell and Isabel Montana (Holland) H.; m. Jerra Anne Downey, July 27, 1955; children: Jeffrey Brian, Holland Anne, John Downey. BS in Engring., U.S. Mil. Acad., West Point, N.Y., 1955; student, U. Southern Calif., 1963. Commd. officer USAF, 1955, pilot Air Def. Command, 1960, resigned, 1962; sales engr. Bendix Corp., L.A., 1960-63; mktg. rep. Sperry Rand Corp., Phoenix, 1963-68; product mgr., sales mgr. Sundstrand Corp., Seattle, 1968-73; dir. govt. sales Rockwell Collins Govt. Avionics div., Cedar Rapids, Iowa, 1973-74; dir. mktg. Rockwell Collins Govt. Avionics div., Cedar Rapids, 1974-75; dir. product devel. ITT Aerospace Optical Div., Ft. Wayne, Ind., 1976; group mktg. mgr. Bendix Aerospace Group, Arlington, Va., 1976-79; dir. domestic mktg. Bendix Aerospace Group, Arlington, 1979-83, dir. advance requirements, 1983-88; dir. mil. programs Allied-Signal Aerospace Co., Torrance, Calif., 1988—. Mem. civil air patrol, Seattle, 1970-71; scoutmaster Boy Scouts Am., Mercer Island, Wash., 1971. Mem. AIAA, Assn. U.S. Army, Navy League, Air Force Assn., Aero Club Washington. Republican. Methodist. Home: 1136 Ninth St Manhattan Beach CA 90266 Office: Allied-Signal Aerospace Co 2525 W 190th St Torrance CA 90509

HOTCHKISS, RAY EUGENE, insurance company executive; b. Waterbury, Conn., Oct. 7, 1932; s. Harold Clayton and Anna S. (Wierbonics) H.; m. Grace Mary Nowicki, Feb. 21, 1959. Student, U. Conn., 1955-57; AA, El Camino Coll., 1959. Programmer, systems designer Hughes Aircraft Co., L.A., 1957-59; sales cons. Met. Life Ins. Co., Inglewood, Calif., 1959-61; brokerage mgr. Independence Life Ins. Co., Pasadena, 1961-66; mgr. Ohio Farmers Inc. Co., L.A., 1966-70; dir. mktg. Sentry Ins. Co., Orange, Calif., 1970-75; v.p. United Life Ins. Co., Orange, 1975-78; owner, adminstr. F.W.A., Tustin, Calif., 1978-81, Computer Adminstrv. Svcs., Inc., Tustin, 1981—, N.I.A.I. Ins. Adminstrs., Inc., Tustin, 1986—; cons. CAISI, Tustin, 1981—, N.Am. Ins. Adminstrs., Knoxville, 1985-86, Beneflex, Dallas, 1985-86. Mem. Ind. Adminstrs. Assn., Soc. Profl. Adminstrs., West Hills Hunt Club (bd. dirs. 1979-80). Republican. Roman Catholic. Office: NIAI Ins Adminstrs Inc 220 El Camino Real Tustin CA 92680

HOTSKO-RAGONESE, MARY LOU, marketing executive; b. L.A., Oct. 11, 1959; d. Andrew and Norma Louise (Trapp) Hotsko; m. Anthony Samuel Ragonese, Oct. 24, 1987. BA in English, UCLA, 1981. Advt. sales asst. CBS Pubs., L.A., 1981-82; media coord. Chickering/Howell Advt., L.A., 1982; mem. mktg. and circulation staff Knapp Communications Corp., L.A., 1982-84; asst. editor cable program guide, home video coord. Playboy Enterprises, Inc., L.A., 1986-87; dir. acct. svcs. Scott Mednick & Assocs., L.A., 1987-88; freelance promotion writer, mktg. cons. L.A., 1989—. Researcher video sports program Crime in Sports: Sports and Apartheid, 1985. Youth employment rep. Archdiocese of L.A., 1985. Mem. NAFE, L.A. World Affairs Coun. Democrat. Mem. Christian Ch. Home: 376 N San Vicente Blvd Los Angeles CA 90048

HOTZ, A. BRADLEY, pharmacist; b. Chicago Heights, Ill., Apr. 19, 1953; s. Robert Stewart and Carole June (Salberg) H.; m. Carolyn Rafferty, Feb. 5, 1977. BS in Pharmacy, Drake U., 1976. Registered pharmacist, Nev., Ohio, Ill., Iowa, Ariz. Pharmacist Osco Drug Store #138, Glen Ellyn, Ill., 1977, Mainland Pacific Co., Las Vegas, Nev.; asst. store mgr., pharmacist Super-X Drugs NV-1, Las Vegas, 1978-79; pharmacy mgr. Sav-On Drugs #289, Las Vegas, 1979-83; pres., pharmacist Farmer's Market Apothecary of Nev., Las Vegas, 1983; pharmacist Sav-On Drugs #235, Las Vegas, 1984; pharmacy mgr.-coord. VONS Food & Drug #196, Las Vegas, 1984—; cons. Health Systems Assocs., North Miami Beach, Fla., 1987-89. Mem. Rep. Nat. Com., 1984. Mem. Am. Pharm. Assn., Nev. Pharmacists Assn., Phi Delta Chi, Alpha Epsilon Pi.

HOTZ, HENRY PALMER, physicist; b. Fayetteville, Ark., Oct. 17, 1925; s. Henry Gustav and Stella (Palmer) H.; m. Marie Brase, Aug. 22, 1952; children: Henry Brase, Mary Palmer, Martha Marie. B.S., U. Ark., 1948; Ph.D., Washington U., St. Louis, 1953. Asst. prof. physics Auburn U., Ala., 1953-58, Okla. State U., Stillwater, 1958-64; assoc. prof. Marietta Coll., Ohio, 1964-66; physicist, scientist-in-residence U.S. Naval Radiol. Def. Lab., San Francisco, 1966-67; assoc. prof. U. Mo., Rolla, 1967-71; physicist Qanta Metrix div. Finnigan Corp., Sunnyvale, Calif., 1971-74; sr. scientist Nuclear Equipment Corp., San Carlos, Calif., 1974-79, Envirotech Measurement Systems, Palo Alto, Calif., 1979-82, Dohrmann div. Xertex Corp., Santa Clara, Calif., 1982-86; sr. scientist Rosemount Analytical Div. Dohrmann, 1986—; cons. USAF, 1958-62; mem. lectr. selection com. for Hartman Hotz Lectrs. in law, liberal arts U. Ark. Served with USNR, 1944-46. Mem. Am. Phys. Soc., Am. Assn. Physics Tchrs., AAAS, Phi Beta Kappa, Sigma Xi, Sigma Pi Sigma, Pi Mu Epsilon, Sigma Nu. Methodist. Lodge: Masons. Home: 290 Stilt Ct Foster City CA 94404 Office: Rosemount Analytical Div Dohrmann 3240 Scott Blvd Santa Clara CA 95054

HOUCHINS, R. CORBIN, lawyer, consultant; b. Charleston, W. Va., Apr. 15, 1940; s. Robert Ray and Adele (Corbin) H.; m. Paula Kimbrell, Aug. 13, 1965 (div. 1975). BA, Harvard U., 1962; LLB, U. Va., 1966. Bar: Va. 1966, Calif. 1967, Wash., 1978. Dep. pub. defender Contra Costa County Pub. Defender, Martinez, Calif., 1968-69; pvt. practice San Francisco, 1969, 1971; chief counsel Berkeley (Calif.) Neighborhood Legal Svcs., 1970; mktg. counsel Ernest & Julio Gallo Winery, Modesto, Calif., 1971-77; assoc. gen. counsel Olympia (Wash.) Brewing Co., 1977-81; ptnr. Duryea & Houchins, Olympia, Wash., 1981-85; pres. R. Corbin Houchins, P.S., Seattle, 1985—; cons. Supreme Ct. Nicaragua, Managua, 1986—. Contbr. articles to profl. jours. Recipient Jefferson prize, 1966. Mem. Calif. Bar Assn. (Assoc.), Va. Bar Assn. (assoc.), Wash. Bar Assn. Democrat. Mem. Soc. of Friends. Office: 3000 Key Tower Seattle WA 98104-1046

HOUCK, C(ARLOS THOMPSON) (CUB HOUCK), state senator, construction contractor; b. Salem, Oreg., Apr. 17, 1930; s. Roy L. and Grace F. (Thompson) H.; m. Kathleen Moore, Dec. 26, 1951; children—Ronald, Donald, Darah Ann. B.S., Oreg. State U., 1952. Vice pres. Roy L. Houck Sons' Corp., Salem, 1954-69; corp. officer Houck-Carrow Corp., Salem, Oreg., 1983—, Houck-McCall, Salem, 1983—; mem. Oreg. Senate, 1983—; owner, operator cattle ranch, 1983—; corp. officer Beaver State Sand & Gravel & Fabricators Inc.; active mgmt. real estate co., ins. agy., loan instn., state-wide devel. co. Pres. Salem City Council, 1967-69, alderman, 1966-69; chmn., mem. sch. bd., 1975-80. Served to 1st lt. USAF; Korea. Recipient Salem Disting. Service awards, 1971, 76, Council of Govt. Service award, 1965, Oreg. Gov. Ethic Commn. State Senate award, 1983. Republican. Lutheran.

HOUCK, JOHN DUDLEY, finance company executive; b. Detroit, May 5, 1939; s. Horace Alonzo and Mae Edward (Snyder) H.; m. Carol Kay Wilson, July 16, 1958; children: Sallie Mae Williams, Cheryl Ann Richard, Jonathan Matthew, Rebecca Cyrene, James Timothy. AA, L.A. Valley Coll., 1964; BS, Pacific Western U., 1982. CLU, Chartered Fin. Cons. Mgr. Met. Life Ins. Co., Glendale, Calif., 1962-66; gen. agt. Santa Clarita Ins. Agys., Newhall, Calif., 1966-71; regional field controller Calif. Western, Sacramento, 1971-73; v.p. U.S. Life Ins. Co., Pasadena, Calif., 1973-76; chief exec. officer, pres. Western Pacific Fin. Services, Inc., Lancaster, Calif., 1976—; bd. dirs. Apollo Tech., Inc., Santa Clarita; registered prin. Anchor Fin. Svcs., Inc.; mgr. OSJ, 1988—. Contbr. articles to profl. jours. Pres. Deseret Valley Bus. Assn., San Fernando Valley, Calif., 1983. With USAF, 1958-62. Fellow Underwriters Tng. Council. Republican. Mormon.

HOUGAN, TOM MCKAY, advertising executive; b. Colfax, Wash., June 23, 1935; s. Melvin C. and Laura (McKay) H.; m. Lois Jean McBride, Jan. 4, 1958; children: Debra, Scott, Mark. BA, Wash. State U., 1957; postgrad., U. Kans., 1957, Portland State U., 1968. Sr. copywriter Gen. Electric Corp., Schenectady, 1960-65; chmn. bd. dirs. Gerber Advt., Portland, Oreg., 1965—; dir., exec. com. Assn. Oreg. Industries, Salem, 1983—; Western regional chmn. Am. Advt. Fedn., Washington, 1978-80; pres. Portland Advt. Fedn., 1975-76. Pub. relations chmn. United Way Portland, 1976; trustee Citizens for a Drug-Free Oreg. Served to 1st lt. U.S. Army, 1958-60. Recipient Advt. Pres. of Yr. Silver Medal award, Am. Advt. Fedn., 1976; named Advt. Prof. of Yr., Portland. Advt. Fedn., 1976; Mayor's Corp. Citizen award Volunteer Council, Portland, 1984. Mem. N.W. Light and Power Assn., Am. Assn. Advt. Agys. (gov. Oreg. council), Pub. Utility Communicators Assn., Ducks Unlimited, Tau Kappa Epsilon (pub. relations chmn.). Republican. Presbyterian. Home: 27212 NE Bjur Rd Ridgefield WA 98642 Office: Gerber Advt Agy 209 SW Oak Portland OR 97204

HOUGH, BRUCE ROBERT, communications executive; b. Coeur d'Alene, Idaho, Apr. 6, 1954; s. Robert V. and Colleen (P.H.) Hough; m. Marriann Heaton, Aug. 19, 1976; children: Sharee Rene, Marabeth, Katherine Anne, Derek Bruce, Julianne Alexandra. Student journalism, Ricks Coll., 1977. Announcer Sta. KVNI, Coeur d'Alene, 1971-73; news reporter, editor Sta. KADQ, Rexburg, Idaho, 1975-76, sales mgr., 1976-78; sales mgr. Sta. KIGO, Rexburg, 1976-78; dir. mktg. Bonneville Prodns., Salt Lake City, 1978-80; ptnr. Gartner-Hough Advt., Salt Lake City, 1979-81; mgr. Bonneville Satellite Corp., Salt Lake City, 1980-82, v.p., gen. mgr., 1982-87; chief operating officer Bonneville Satellite Communications, Salt Lake City, 1988—. Del. Utah Rep. Conv., 1986, Nat. Rep. Conv., 1988; chmn. South Jordan (Utah) Econ. Devel. Com., 1988; mem. City Coun. City of South Jordan. Recipient Clio award, 1980, Satellite Pioneer award Telecon VII, 1988. Mem. Soc. Satellite Profls., Nat. Assn. Broadcasters, Rotary, Elephant Club (bd. dirs.). Mormon. Home: 1080 W Rivercrest Circle South Jordan UT 84065 Office: Bonneville Satellite 19 W South Temple Ste 300 Salt Lake City UT 84101-1503

HOULE, JOSEPH ADRIEN, orthopaedic surgeon; b. Ft. Saskatchewan, Alta., Can., Nov. 3, 1928; came to U.S., 1978; s. Adelard Houle and Bertha (Durocher) Guay; divorced; children: Valerie, Diane, Lorraine, Louis, Doreen; m. Marjorie Ludmilla Houle. BSc, cert. in premed., U. Ottawa, 1955; MD, Laval U., 1960, Licentiate Med. Council of Can., 1960. Cert. specialist orthopaedic surgery, Quebec, Can. Intern Hotel Dieu Hosp., Quebec City, Can., 1959-60; resident in gen. surgery St. Vincent de Paul Hosp., Sherbrooke, Que., Can., 1960-61, St. Vincent's Hosp., Bridgeport, Conn., 1961-62; resident in orthopaedic surgery Montreal Children's Hosp., Montreal Gen. Hosp. and Queen Mary's Vet. Hosp., 1962-65; practice medicine specializing in orthopaedic surgery Montreal, Can., 1965-78; chief of orthopaedic surgery Thomas Davis Med. Ctr., Tucson, 1978—. Produced film Mechanical Knee, 1969. Mem. Bd. Med. Examiners of Ariz., 1978. Served to capt. Royal Can. Forces, 1956-67. Mem. AMA, Can. Orthopaedic Assn., Ariz. Orthopaedic Assn., Pima County Med. Soc. Roman Catholic. Home: 3241 N Calle Tortosa Tucson AZ 85715 Office: Thomas Davis Med Ctr 630 N Alvernon Way Tucson AZ 85711

HOULIHAN, PATRICK THOMAS, museum director; b. New Haven, June 22, 1942; s. John T. and Irene (Rourke) H.; m. Betsy Eliason, June 19, 1965; children: Mark T. and Michael D. (twins). BS, Georgetown U., 1964; MA, U. Minn., 1969; PhD, U. Wis., Milw., 1971. Asst. commr. N.Y. State Mus., Albany, 1980-81; dir. Heard Mus., Phoenix, 1972-80, SW Mus., Los Angeles,

1981—. Mem. Am. Assn. Mus. (council mem. 1978-81), Soc. Mus. Anthropology (bd. dirs. 1982—). Office: Millicent Rogers Mus Taos NM

HOUSDEN, JOHN ERIC, pharmaceutical company executive; b. Loughborough, Leicestershire, Eng., Sept. 20, 1940; came to U.S., 1979; s. Eric Sydney and Kathleen May (Burford) H.; m. Susan Elizabeth Grimwood, Mar. 10, 1967; children: Claire Louise, Rebecca Ann, Robert William John. B in Vet. Sci., U. Bristol, Eng., 1964. Gen. practice vet. medicine and surgery Dorset, Somerset, Eng., 1964-67; research scientist Wellcome Found., London and São Paulo, Brazil, 1967-70; mgr. vet. div. Wellcome Found., Brazil, 1970-74; gen. mgr. Wellcome Found., Teheran, Iran, 1974-78; region dir. Ams. Allergan Pharm. Inc., Irvine, Calif., 1979-84, internat. v.p., 1984-86; sr. v.p. Pilkington Vision Care, Menlo Park, Calif., 1987—. Fellow Brit. Inst. Mgmt., Royal Soc. Health; mem. Royal Coll. Vet. Surgeons (Eng.), Am. Mgmt. Assn. Clubs: Balboa Bay (Newport Beach, Calif.); Farmers (London). Home: 1831 Port Stirling Pl Newport Beach CA 92660 Office: 2420 Sand Hill Rd Menlo Park CA 94025

HOUSE, ERNEST, SR., cultural organization administrator; b. Ignacio, Colo., Sept. 27, 1945; s. Thomas Sr. and Francis (Wall) H.; m. Brenda Gomez, July 17, 1965; children: Michelle, Jaque, Ernest. Student, Ft. Lewis Coll., 1968-69. Forester U.S. Dept. Interior, Towaoc, Colo., 1970-79; with Ute Mountain Tribe, Towaoc, 1960-65, tribal councilman, 1979-83, tribal chmn., 1983—. Bd. dirs. Colo. Commn. Indian Affairs, Denver, 1981—; mem. Colo. Centennial Commn., Cortez County Centennial. Served with U.S. Army, 1965-71. Mem. Nat. Tribal Chmn.'s Assn. (treas. 1984-85). Democrat. Mem. Assembly of God Ch. Office: Ute Mountain Tribal Coun Towaoc CO 81344 *

HOUSE, ERNEST R., education educator, educational evaluator; b. Alton, Ill., Aug. 7, 1937; s. Ernest House and Helen Lucille (Schumake) McDaniel) m. Donna Brown, Feb. 1, 1964; children: Kristin, Colby. AB, Washington U., St. Louis, 1959; MS, So. Ill. U., 1964; EdD, U. Ill., 1968. Cert. high sch. tchr., Ill. Tchr. English, Roxana (Ill.) High Sch., 1960-64; coms. Ill. demonstration project for gifted youth U. Ill., Urbana, 1964-65, dir. gifted program evaulation Coop. Ednl. Rsch. Lab., 1967-69, project dir., ednl. specialist, 1969-71, project dir., asst. prof. edn., 1971-75, assoc. prof., 1975-79, prof., 1979-85; vis. prof. U. Colo., Boulder, 1982, prof. edn., 1985—, dir. Lab. for Policy Studies, 1985—; vis. scholar UCLA, 1976, Harvard U., Cambridge, Mass., 1980; mem. lab. rev. panel U.S. Dept. Edn., 1987—. Author: The Politics of Educational Innovation, 1974, (with Steve Lapan) Survival in the Classroom, 1978; Evaluating with Validity, 1980, Jesse Jackson and the Politics of Charisma, 1988; mem. editorial bd. Ednl. Evaluation and Policy Analysis, 1971-81, 86—; editor-in-chief New Directions for Program Evaluation, 1982-85; columnist Evaluation Practice, 1984-88. Mem. rsch. staff Senator Adlai Stevenson of Ill., 1970, Ill. lt. gov. Paul Simon, 1972. Mem. Am. Ednl. Rsch. Assn. (program chmn. 1976, chmn. awards com. 1983), Am. Evaluation Assn., Phi Beta Kappa. Democrat. Office: U Colo Sch Edn CB 249 Boulder CO 80309

HOUSE, SUSAN JEAN, air traffic controller, government official; b. El Paso, Tex., Sept. 21, 1951; d. Paul C. House and Jean A. (Hendrick) Hawley. AS, Anchorage Community Coll., 1985; AA, U. Alaska, 1988. Air traffic control specialist trainee FAA, Anchorage, 1980-81; air traffic controller FAA, King Salmon, Alaska, 1981, Cordova, Alaska, 1982-84, Anchorage, 1984—; adj. lectr. U. Alaska, Anchorage, 1986—. Vol. Anchorage Arts Coun., 1984—. Mem. Air Traffic Control Assn., Nat. Aerospace Educators, Profl. Women Contrs. (editor Alaska newsletter 1983, bd. dirs. 1984-88, v.p. 1986-88), Women in Transp., U. Alaska Alumni Assn. (bd. dirs. 1989—). Home: 3200 Delta Dr Anchorage AK 99502-4450 Office: FAA 2016 E 5th Ave Anchorage AK 99501

HOUSE, WALTER JOHN, consulting mechanical engineer; b. Davenport, Iowa, Jan. 14, 1918; s. George and Elsie Christine (Simon) H.; m. Betty Jane Burmeister, June 28, 1941; children: Terry Lee, Jane Ann, Stephen Richard. BSME, Iowa State Coll., 1939; postgrad. mech. engring., Naval Postgrad. Sch., Annapolis, Md., 1943. Registered profl. engr., Ill. Design engr. Deere & Co., Moline, Ill., 1945-48, U.S. C.E., Rock Island, Ill., 1953-50; jr. engr. Commonwealth Edison Co., Chgo., 1939-40; sales engr. Indsl. Engring. & Equipment Co., Davenport, Iowa, 1948-51; chief utilities U.S. Army, Rock Island, 1950-79; cons. mech. engr. Sun City West, Ariz., 1979—. Registrar, precinct committeeman Maricopa County Rep. Com., 1982. Capt. USN, 1941-45, 51-53. Mem. Nat. Assn. Fed. Employees (pres. Sun City West 1983). Lutheran. Home and Office: 12522 Skyview Dr Sun City West AZ 85375

HOUSER, JOHN JOSEPH, postal service official; b. Durango, Colo., June 7, 1952; s. Robert John and Nellie Mae (Stratton) H.; m. Colleen O'Malley, May 12, 1973 (div.); m. Elaine Victoria Curran, Aug. 3, 1981; 1 child, Jennifer Jo. BS, Loras Coll., 1981. Surgical technician Finley Hosp., Dubuque, Iowa, 1978-80; quality control mgr. Pabco Gypsum, Las Vegas, Nev., 1981-82; express mail mgr. U.S. Postal Service, Las Vegas, 1982—; computer cons., Las Vegas, 1981—. Pilot and flight scheduler, Operation Angel Plane, Las Vegas, 1984-87. With USAF, 1972-76. Mem. Aircraft Owners and Pilots Assn. Democrat. Roman Catholic. Home: 4724 Pony Express St North Las Vegas NV 89030-2139 Office: US Postal Service 1001 E Sunset Rd Las Vegas NV 89199-9604

HOUSTON, ELIZABETH REECE MANASCO, teacher, consultant; b. Birmingham, Ala., June 19, 1935; d. Reuben Cleveland and Beulah Elizabeth (Reece) Manasco; m. Joseph Brantley Houston; 1 child, Joseph Brantley Houston III. BS, U. Tex., 1956; MEd, Boston Coll., 1969. Cert. elem. tchr., Calif., cert. spl. edn. tchr., Calif., cert. community coll. instr., Calif. Tchr., elem. Ridgefield (Conn.) Schs., 1962-63; staff, spl. edn. Sudbury (Mass.) Schs., 1965-68; staff intern Wayland (Mass.) High Sch., 1972; tchr., home bound Northampton (Mass.) Schs., 1972-73; program dir. Jack Douglas Ctr., San Jose, Calif., 1974-76; tchr., specialist spl. edn., coordinator classroom services, dir. Juvenile Ct. Schs. Santa Clara County Office of Edn., San Jose, Calif., 1976—; instr. San Jose State U., 1980-87, U. Calif., Santa Cruz, 1982-85; cons. Houston Research Assocs., Saratoga, Calif., 1981—. Author: (manual) Behavior Management for School Bus Drivers, 1980, Classroom Management, 1984, Synergistic Learning, 1986. Bd. dirs. Ming Quong Children's Ctr., Los Gatos, Calif. Grantee Santa Clara County Office Edn. Tchr. Advisor Program U.S. Sec. Edn., 1983-84; Recipient President's award Soc. Photo-Optical Instrumentation Engrs., 1979, Classroom Mgmt. Program award School Bds. Assn., 1984. Mem. Assn. for Supervision and Curriculum Devel., Assn. Calif. Sch. Administrs., Council Exceptional Children. Home: 12150 Country Squire Ln Saratoga CA 95070 Office: Santa Clara County Office Edn 100 Skyport Dr San Jose CA 95115

HOUSTON, GEORGE BRANSTON, computer science management executive; b. Bristol, Eng., May 12, 1944; came to U.S., 1966.; BA in Math., Pembroke Coll., Cambridge, Eng., 1966; MA in Math., Pembroke Coll., 1970; MSc in Computer Sci., U. Wash., 1971, PhD in Computer Sci., 1979. Analyst Boeing Comml. Airplane Co., Seattle, 1966-70; sr. analyst Boeing Comml. Airplane Co., 1970-73; project mgr. advanced tech. div. Boeing Computer Svcs., Seattle, 1974-79; mgr. distributed data systems Boeing Computer Svcs., 1980-86, mgr. enabling tech., comml. svcs. group, 1986-87, mgr. tech. assessment, advanced tech. ctr., 1987—. Contbr. articles to profl. publs.; patentee in field. Mem. Assn. Computing Machinery (chmn. Puget Sound chpt. 1975-76). Office: Boeing Computer Svcs PO Box 24346 Seattle WA 98124

HOUSTON, PAMELA BETH, legal assistant; b. Los Angeles, May 17, 1947; d. Ivan James and Philippa (Jones) H.; m. Joseph Paul Chretien III, Jan. 22, 1977. BA, UCLA, 1974; postgrad., U. West Los Angeles, 1987-88. Legal asst. Gibson Dunn & Crutcher, Los Angeles, 1988—. Democrat. Roman Catholic. Home: 1168 S Tremaine Ave Los Angeles CA 90019 Office: Gibson Dunn & Crutcher 333 S Grand Ave Los Angeles CA 90071

HOUTS, MARSHALL WILSON, lawyer, author, editor; b. Chattanooga, June 28, 1919; s. Thomas Jefferson and Mary (Alexander) H.; m. Mary O. Dealy, Apr. 27, 1946; children: Virginia, Kathy, Marsha, Patty, Tom, Cindy, Tim. AA, Brevard Jr. Coll., 1937; BS in Law, U. Minn., 1941, JD, 1941. Bar: Tenn. 1940, Minn. 1946, U.S. Supreme Ct. 1967. Spl. agt. FBI, Washington, Brazil, Havana, Boston, 1941-44; ptnr. Palmer & Houts, Pipestone, Minn., 1946-51; mcpl. judge Pipestone, 1947-51; gen. counsel Erle Stanley Gardner's Ct. of Last Resort, Los Angeles, 1951-60; prof. law UCLA, 1954, Mich. State U., East Lansing, 1955-57; adj. prof. Pepperdine U. Law Sch., 1972-80; clin. prof. forensic pathology Calif. Coll. Medicine, U. Calif., Irvine, 1972—; cons. police depts. Creator, editor: TRAUMA, 1959-88; author: Houts: Lawyer's Guide to Medical Proof, 4 vols., 1967, From Gun to Gavel, 1954, From Evidence to Proof, 1956, The Rules of Evidence, 1956, From Arrest to Release, 1958, Courtroom Medicine, 1958, Courtroom Medicine: Death, 3 vols., 1964, Photographic Misrepresentation, 1965, Where Death Delights, 1967, They Asked for Death, 1970, Proving Medical Diagnosis and Prognosis, 14 vols., 1970, Cyclopedia of Sudden, Violent and Unexplained Death, 1970, King's X: Common Law and the Death of Sir Harry Oakes, 1972, Art of Advocacy: Appeals; Art of Advocacy: Cross Examination of Medical Experts, 1980; Courtroom Toxicology, 7 vols., 1981, Who Killed Sir Harry Oakes?, 1988. Served with OSS, 1944-46, CBI. Decorated Bronze Arrowhead. Address: 33631 Magellan Isle Laguna Niguel CA 92677

HOVDA, DAVID ALLEN, psychologist, neuroscientist; b. Tomah, Wis., June 6, 1953; s. Allen Adelbert and Ruth Tecla (Johnson) H.; m. Cydney Clare Stewart, July 7, 1979. BA in Psychology, U. N.Mex., 1979, MS in Psychology, 1982, PhD in Psychology, 1985. Psychiat. aide Children's Psychiat. Ctr., Albuquerque, 1979-80; research asst. dept. psychology U. N.Mex., Albuquerque, 1978-84, teaching asst. dept. psychology, anatomy and physiology, 1980-84; postdoctoral scholar, instr. neurophysiology Mental Retardation Res. Ctr., Neuropsychiat. Inst., UCLA, 1985-89; asst. prof. neurosurgery UCLA, 1989—. Contbr. articles to profl. jours. Mem. Soc. Neurosci., AAAS, Brit. Brain Research Assn., European Brain and Behavior Soc., Sigma Xi, Lambda Chi Alpha. Republican. Methodist. Office: Mental Retardation Rsch Ctr 760 Westwood Pla Los Angeles CA 90024

HOWARD, BRADFORD REUEL, travel company executive; b. Honolulu, Aug. 6, 1957; s. Joseph DeSylva and Marguerite Evangeline (Barker) H.; m. Marcia Andresen, June 23, 1985. BS in Bus., U. Calif., Berkeley, 1979. Owner, operator Howard Janitorial Svcs., Oakland, Calif., 1970-80; prodn. mgr. Oakland Symphony Orch., 1976-80; brand mgr. The Clorox Co., Oakland, 1980-85; gen. mgr., corp. sec. Howard Tours, Inc./Howard Enterprises, Oakland, 1985—; co-owner Howard Mktg. Cons., Oakland, 1985—; cons. Marcus Foster Found., Oakland, 1984-85; pres., gen. mgr. Piedmont (Calif.) Community Theater, 1976—. Mem. U. Calif. Bus. Alumni Assn. (v.p. 1986-88, pres. 1988—, Bay Area chpt. 1983-84), Rotary (sec. 1985-87, pres. 1987-88), Lake Merrit Breakfast Club. Office: Howard Tours Inc 526 Grand Ave Oakland CA 94610

HOWARD, CARL MICHAEL, lawyer; b. Chgo., July 23, 1920; m. Kathleen Agnes Costello, May 10, 1953; 1 child, Carl Michael. AB, DePauw U., 1942; JD, U. Calif., San Francisco, 1949. Bar: Calif. 1951. Supervising dep. corps. commr. State of Calif., San Francisco, 1951-69; supervisory asst., asst. house counsel Fed. Home Loan Bank of San Francisco, 1970-75; legal counsel Home Fed. Savs. and Loan Assn., San Francisco, 1976-88, also bd. dirs.; chmn. bd. Home Fed. Savs. and Loan Assn., 1985-86; assoc. Kerner, Colangelo & Imlay, 1976-86; sole practice 1987—. Served to lt. USNR, 1942-46, PTO. Mem. ABA, State Bar Calif., San Francisco Bar Assn., Am. Legion Blackstone Post #143. Republican. Roman Catholic. Home: 2450 Quintara St San Francisco CA 94166-1139 Office: 114 Sansome St Ste 505 San Francisco CA 94104-3893

HOWARD, CHERI LORRAINE, marketing executive, director; b. San Francisco, Nov. 30, 1962; d. Thomas and Muriel (Weaver) H. BA in Mktg., Calif. State U., Sacramento, 1985. Sales rep. Roche Biomed. Labs., L.A., 1985-86; tech. sales rep. Dianon Systems, L.A., 1986-88; dir. mktg. Diagnostic Pathology Med. Group, Sacramento, 1988—; bd. dirs., mem. pub. rels. and fundraising com. Hospice Care Sacramento, Inc., 1988—. Office: Diagnostic Pathology Inc 2420 J St Sacramento CA 95816

HOWARD, DAVID JOHN, corporate art consultant; b. New Rochelle, N.Y., Aug. 9, 1947; s. Lee and Eleanor Francis (Leibowitz) H. AA, Mich. State U., 1967; BA in Edn. with honors, U. Fla., 1969. Tchr. Atlanta City Sch., 1969-70; assoc. dir. Homestead Family Drug Rehab. Ctr., Atlanta, 1970-71; toymaker Oakland, Calif., 1971-75; dealer Am. Indian artifacts Boulder, Colo., 1975-77; owner artifact gift store Boulder, 1977-79; mfr. rep. Jacques Jugeat Inc., Denver, 1979-81; salesman W. Graham Arader III, Inc., King of Prussia, Pa., 1981-83, sales mgr., 1983-87; fine art dealer David Howard Fine Art, Mill Valley, Calif., 1988—; v.p. Calif. Map Soc. San Francisco, 1986-87. Contbr. articles to profl. jours. Bd. dirs. advt. Downtown Bus. Assn.; precinct worker Dem. Party, Mill Valley, 1988. Mem. Calif. Map Soc., San Francisco Press Club. Democrat. Jewish. Home: 11 Somerset Ln Mill Valley CA 94941 Office: David Howard Fine Art 11 Somerset Ln Mill Valley CA 94941

HOWARD, DAVID ROGER, university administrator; b. Olympia, Wash., July 6, 1929; s. Jared Clark and Frieda (Heisig) H.; m. Kathryn Lucille Smith, July 17, 1953; children: Ann, David Jr., Michael, Paul, Margaret, Leslie. BS in Agrl. Engring., N.Mex. A&M, 1951; BSCE, U. Ill., 1957; MSCE, U. Colo., 1961. Registered profl. engr., Tex. Commd. 2d lt. USAF, 1951, advanced through grades to col., 1971, ret., 1976; base civil engr. USAF, Thule (Greenland) Air Base, 1970-71; staff civil engr. aeronautical systems div. USAF, Wright-Patterson AFB, Ohio, 1971-73; base engr. USAF, Travis AFB, Calif., 1974-76; dir. bldgs. and grounds Oakland (Calif.) Unified Sch. Dist., 1977-81; exec. dir. facilties San Francisco State U., 1981—. Contbr. articles to profl. jours. Decorated Legion of Merit, 1973, 76. Mem. Assn. Phys. Plant Adminstrs., Nat. Assn. Coll. Univ. Bus. Officials, Air Force Assn., Am. Inst. Plant Engrs. Methodist. Club: Presidio Riding Club (Marin County, Calif.) (stable official, 1980-82). Home: 890 Chamberlain Ct Mill Valley CA 94941 Office: San Francisco State U 19th and Holloway San Francisco CA 94132

HOWARD, GAIL FRANCES, artist, educator, author; b. Spokane, Wash., Jan. 18, 1946; d. Harold Elvis Stallings and Gladys S. (Klee) Jewett; Garnett James Howard, May 31, 1967; 1 child, Jan Carin. Student, Wash. State U., 1964-66, E. Wash. State U., 1965-67, 72-73, U. Wash., 1966, U. Washington D.C., 1974-75; BA in Psychology and Human Services, Marymount Coll., 1977. Information and reference specialist Arlington County, Va., 1976-77; cons. Identity Research, Inc., 1978-80; art history tchr. Children's House, 1984; art tchr., cons. Our Saviour Luth. Schs., 1985-86; art and writing tchr. Papillion LaVista Pub. Schs., 1986—; educator, cons. Hawaii Pub. Sch. Leeward Dist., 1986, ASSETS Sch. for the Gifted, Honolulu, 1985-86; tchr. Arapahoe County Parks and Recreation Dist., 1989; artist in residence, cons., tchr. Peabody Elem. Sch., Littleton, Colo., 1989; conductor seminars, Chapman Coll. Grad. Study Contg. Edn. Exhibitions include: Omaha Children's Mus., Hawaii Ronald MacDonald House Manoa Gallery, Hawaii Children's Mus., KHET-TV, PRC, Inc., Ea. Wash. State U.; author, artist (book): Me and My Pencil: I Can Draw, 1985; (art instruction booklet) Exploring Shapes in Space, 1985; promoter, artist: Spectacular Color Works, Honolulu, 1985-86, Colo. Arts Sampler, Littleton, 1989; feature artist Hawaii pub. TV, Spectrum, 1986; represented by Kyle Belding Gallery, Denver, Quinn-Morrow, Englewood, Colo. Rep. community bd., Leeward Dist., Hawaii, 1981-83; pres., Palehua Community Assn., Honolulu, 1980-82; v.p., Palehua Vista Community Assn., 1980-82; mem. Ewa Neighborhood Bd., Honolulu, 1980-82. Recipient award Hawaii Watercolor Soc., 1986. Mem. Am. Watercolor Soc. Home and Office: Artworks Unltd 5354 E Lake Pl Littleton CO 80121

HOWARD, IRVIN, education educator, consultant; b. Jamaica, N.Y., Nov. 11, 1951; s. Sol and Genia (Rotberg) H. BS in Edn., Ill. State U., 1974, MEd, 1977, EdD, 1980. Tchr., lang. arts coordinator Churchville Jr. H.S., Elmhurst, Ill., 1974-78; grad. asst., inst. Ill. State U., Normal, 1978-80; asst. prof. edn. Ball State U., Muncie, Ind., 1980-81; assoc. prof. edn. Calif. State U., San Bernardino, 1981—; cons. Paikeday Pub., Quebec, Can., 1983-87, Midwest Pub., Pacific Grove, Calif., 1984—. Author: Biographies, 1984, A Substitute Teaching Guidebook, 1987. Vol. Prof. Adv. Coun. Crisis Hotline, San Bernadino, Calif., 1982—, Inland AIDS Project, 1987. Recipient Outstanding Young Man Of Am. award Jaycees, 1985. Mem. Calif. League of Middle Schs., Assoc. for Supervision & Curriculum Devel., Internat. Reading Assoc., Profl. Adv. Council (treas.) (recipient outstanding vol. award 1987), Nat. Soc. for Study of Edn., Phi Delta Kappa. Democrat. Jewish. Office: Calif State U Sch Edn 5500 University Pkwy San Bernardino CA 92407

HOWARD, JAMES WEBB, investment banker, lawyer, engineer; b. Evansville, Ind., Sept. 17, 1925; s. Joseph R. and Velma (Cobb) H.; m. Phyllis Jean Brandt, Dec. 27, 1948; children: Sheila Rae, Sharon Kae. B.S. in Mech. Engring, Purdue U., 1949; postgrad., Akron (Ohio) Law Sch., 1950-51, Cleve. Marshall Law Sch., 1951-52; M.B.A., Western Res. U., 1962; J.D., Western State Coll. Law, 1976. Registered profl. engr., Ind., Ohio. Jr. project engr. Firestone Tire & Rubber Co., Akron, 1949-50; gen. foreman Cadillac Motor Car div. Gen. Motors Corp., 1950-53; mgmt. cons. M.K. Sheppard & Co., Cleve., 1953-56; plant mgr. Lewis Welding & Engring. Corp., Ohio, 1956-58; underwriter The Ohio Co., Columbus, 1959; chmn. Growth Capital, Inc., Chgo., 1960—; pres. Meister Brau, Inc., Chgo., 1965-73; others. Co-chmn. Chgo. com. Ill. Sesquicentennial Com., 1968. Served with AUS, 1943-46. Decorated Bronze Star, Parachutist badge, Combat Inf. badge. Mem. ASME, ABA, Nat. Assn. Small Bus. Investment Cos. (past pres.), State Bar Calif., Grad. Bus. Alumni Assn. Western Res. U. (past gov.), Tau Kappa Epsilon, Pi Tau Sigma, Beta Gamma Sigma. Methodist. Club: Masons.

HOWARD, JANE OSBURN, educator; b. Morris, Ill., Aug. 12, 1926; d. Everett Hooker and Bernice Otilda (Olson) Osburn; B.A., U. Ariz., 1948; M.A., U. N.Mex., 1966, Ph.D., 1969; m. Rollins Stanley Howard, June 5, 1948; children—Ellen Elizabeth, Susan (Mrs. John Karl Nuttall). Instr. U. N.Mex. Sch. Medicine, Albuquerque, 1968-70, mem. staff pediatrics, deaf blind children's program, Albuquerque, 1971-72, asst. dir. N.Mex. programs for deaf blind children, 1972—, instr. psychiatry, instr. pediatrics, coordinator deaf-blind children's program, 1972-76, edn. cons., 1976—, publicity and pub. relations cons., 1983—; Cons. Mountain-Plains Regional Ctr. for Services to Deaf-Blind Children, Denver, 1971-74, Bur. Indian Affairs, 1974. Active Cystic Fibrosis, Mother's March, Heart Fund, Easter Seal-Crippled Children. Recipient fellowships U. N.M., 1965, 66, 66-67, 67-68, U. So. Calif. John Tracy Clinic, 1973. Fellow Royal Soc. Health; mem. Council Exceptional Children, Am. Assn. Mental Deficiency, Nat. Assn. Retarded Children, AAUW, Pi Lambda Theta, Zeta Phi Eta, Alpha Epsilon Rho. Republican. Methodist. Home: 615 Valencia Dr SE Albuquerque NM 87108

HOWARD, MRS. JOHN H. See GOODRICH, NORMA LORRE

HOWARD, JOSEPH LEON, retired naval officer; b. New Haven, Dec. 21, 1917; s. Benjamin Ely and Eva (Bourbon) H.; m. Irene Elizabeth Silver; children: Michael Edward, Kenneth Lee, John Wayne. AB in Econs., U. Calif., Berkeley, 1940; postgrad., Naval War Coll., 1948-49, Harvard U., 1963. Commd. ensign USN, 1941, advanced through grades to rear adm., 1966; asst. planning officer Bur. Supplies and Accounts, Washington, 1959-61; exec. Naval Supply Ctr., San Diego, 1961-64; dep. chief Office Naval Materials, Washington, 1964-68; dir. procurement Office Asst. Sec., U.S. Dept. Navy, Washington, 1965-67; comdg. officer Naval Supply Ctr., Charleston, S.C., 1970-72; ret. Naval Supply Ctr., 1972. Author: Our Modern Navy, 1961, The Diamonite Conspiracy, 1980, History of San Diego Rotary, 1982; columnist United Parkinson Fedn. Newsletter, 1981--. Bd. dirs. San Diego Hist. Soc., 1985--, San Diego Cystic Fibrosis Found., 1984-86; trustee Al Lynn Charitable Trust, San Diego, 1988--. Decorated Legion of Merit with two gold stars, Bronze Star with combat V. Mem. Pearl Harbor Survivors Assn. (life), Mil. Order World Wars (life), Ret. Officers Assn. (life), Navy League, Nat. Security Indsl. Assn. (hon.), Procurement Mgmt. Assn. (hon.), Harvard (San Diego), Harvard Bus. Sch., Masons. Home: 2620 2d Ave 11A San Diego CA 92103

HOWARD, JUDITH ANN, cable television executive, consultant; b. McLean, Tex., Sept. 14, 1942; d. John Raymond and Lura Viola (Back) Glass; m. Charles R. Howard, July 23, 1960 (dec. May 1979); children: James D., Connie R. Grad. high sch., McLean, 1961. Outside plant mgr. CATV, Inc., Hill City, Kans., 1973-78; office mgr. CATV, Inc., Ruidosa, N.Mex., 1978-79, v.p., 1979-85; v.p. Cablevision Communications, Cloudcraft, N.Mex., 1983-88; v.p. Howard Enterprises, Cloudcraft, 1985—, also bd. dirs.; cons. CATV, Inc., N.Mex., 1979-84, Overall Pacific Communication, Inc., Santa Barbara, Calif., 1984, Cablevision Communication, Inc., 1985—. Charter mem. N.Mex. First, Albuquerque, 1987. Mem. Nat. Assn. Female Execs., Pilot Club (Ruidoso, v.p.1983), Cree Meadows Country Club, Inc. (bd. dirs. 1988). Home and Office: Box 567 Ruidoso NM 88345

HOWARD, KIPLAND, architect; b. Chapel Hill, N.C., Jan. 16, 1954; s. David Caldwell and Ruth (Benson) H.; m. Janice Howard, Sept. 3, 1977 (div. Sept. 1987); m. Susan Augustine, Sept. 24, 1987. BArch, U. Tenn., 1976. Registered architect, Calif. Designer Howard Oxley & Assocs., La Jolla, Calif., 1976-80; pres., chief ops. officer Torrey Enterprises, Inc., La Jolla, 1980—, also bd. dirs. Active San Diego Conv. Ctr. Task Force, 1984-87; cons. San Diego Jr. Achievement, 1987-88, bd. dirs. 1988; bd. dirs. San Diego Taxpayers, 1988. Mem. AIA, San Diego Archtl. Found. Republican. Presbyterian. Clubs: La Jolla Athletic, La Jolla Beach and Tennis. Office: Torrey Enterprises Inc 7979 Ivnahoe #250 La Jolla CA 92037

HOWARD, LAURA LYNN, electronic safe company executive; b. Bethesda, Md., May 15, 1953; d. Albert Eugene and Mary T. (Scott) H.; m. Robert Edward Burr, June 21, 1973 (div. May 1982); children: Brandon E., Ryan S. Student, Miami Dade Community Coll., 1971-72; AS in Acctg., Ft. Lauderdale Coll., West Palm Beach, Fla., 1979. Acct. Brown & Beres Comml. Design, West Palm Beach, 1980-82; saleswoman Yukon Office Supplies, Honolulu, 1982-83, Sta. KGU, Honolulu, 1983-84; acct. Elsafe Hawaii, Honolulu, 1984-86, gen. mgr., 1986-88, exec. v.p., 1988—; prin. Etcetera Unltd., Inc. Mem. Miss Hawaii U.S.A., 1987—. Mem. Hawaii Hotel Assn., Hawaii Conv. Park Coun., Hawaii Visitors Bur., Waikiki Beach Operators Assn., Hawaii C. of C. (cons. small bus. coun. 1988—). Office: Elsafe Hawaii Inc 1314 S King St Honolulu HI 96814 also: Etcetera 1314 S King St Honolulu HI 96814

HOWARD, LAWRENCE, judge, lawyer; b. Sioux City, Iowa, Apr. 11, 1931; m. Mary Teresa De La Torre, Aug. 26, 1960; children: Carmelita Howard Atkinson, Lili L. LLB, U. Ariz., 1957. Bar: Ariz. 1957. Pvt. practice Tucson, 1957-67; judge Superior Ct. Pima County, Tucson, 1967-69; judge div 2, Ariz. Ct. Appeals, Tucson, 1969—; city magistrate City of Tucson, 1964; spl. asst. atty. gen. State of Ariz., Tucson, 1964-66. Author: Arizona Condemnation Law, 1966. Former pres. Pima County Young Reps., Tucson Awareness House; former mem. Tucson Community Coun.; former bd. dirs. St. Elizabeth of Hungary Clinic, Tucson. With U.S. Army, 1950-54, Korea, col. Res. ret. Decorated Legion of Merit. Mem. Ariz. Judges Assn. (past pres.). Republican. Roman Catholic. Home: 7251 Calle Agerrida Tucson AZ 85715

HOWARD, MARGUERITE CHARLOTTE, land management company executive; b. Detroit, Oct. 25, 1932; d. Alexander and Marguerite Ellen (Oliphant) Herd; m. Alva Donald Howard, Sept. 13, 1952 (div. 1964); children; Marguerite Eileen, Alva Donald III (dec.), Jon Leslie. Student, Mich. State U., 1950, Cen. State Coll., Edmond, Okla., 1957-59, Oklahoma City U., 1956, St. Mary's U., San Antonio, 1967. Dir. Open Door Inc., Boulder, Colo., 1968-71; county chmn. White House Conf. Children and Youth, 1971; dir. Colo. Commn. Children and Youth, 1972-73; mgr. Craft and Design Ctr., Boulder, 1974-75; office mgr. Lewiston Grain Growers, Lenore, Idaho, 1975-83; ptnr., mgr. Western Land Mgmt., Culdesac, Idaho, 1984—. Bd. dirs. Youth Svcs. Bur., Boulder, 1969-72, Denver, 1971-72, Vol. and Info. Bur., Boulder, 1969-71, Jr. Dep. Sheriff's League, Boulder, 1968-71; mem. disaster team ARC, Boulder, 1968-73. Sgt. USMC, 1950-52. Mem. NAFE, Women's Marine Assn. (chpt. v.p. 1988—). Republican. Methodist. Office: Western Land Mgmt PO Box 36 Culdesac ID 83524

HOWARD, MARGUERITE EVANGELINE BARKER (MRS. JOSEPH D. HOWARD), business executive, civic worker; b. Victoria, B.C., Can., July 30, 1921; d. Reuel Harold and Frances Penelope (Garnham) Barker; brought to U.S., 1924, naturalized, 1945; BA, U. Wash., 1943; m. Joseph D. Howard, June 16, 1952; children: Wendy Doreen Frances, Bradford Reuel. Vice pres., dir. Howard Tours, Inc., Oakland, Calif., 1953—; co-owner, gen. mgr. Howard Travel Service, Oakland, 1956—, mng. dir. Howard Hall, Berkeley,

Calif., 1964-75; co-owner, asst. mgr. Howard Investments, Oakland, 1960—; sec., treas. Energy Dynamics Inc. Bd. dirs. Piedmont council Campfire Girls, 1969-79, pres., 1974-79, mem. nat. council, 1972-76, zone chmn., 1974-76, 77-83, zone coordinator, 1976, nat. v.p., 1975, nat. bd. dirs., 1976-83, bd. dirs. Alameda Contra Costa council, 1984—; bd. dirs. Oakland Symphony Guild, 1969-87, pres., 1972-74; trustee Piedmont Campfire Camp Augusta, 1988—; mem. exec. bd. Oakland Symphony Orch. Assn., 1972-74, bd. dirs., 1972-86; 1st pres. Inner Wheel Club of East Oakland, 1983-84; bd. dirs. Piedmont Jr. High Sch. Mothers Club, 1968-69. Recipient Wohelo Order award Campfire, Inc, 1985. Mem. Oakland Mus. Assn., U. Wash. Alumni Assn., East Bay Bot. and Zool. Soc., Young Audiences, Am. Symphony Orch. League, Assn. Calif. Symphony Orchs., Chi Omega Alumni Seattle, Chi Omega East Bay Alumni Berkeley. Republican. Clubs: Womens Univ. (Seattle); Womens Athletic (Oakland) (bd. dirs. 1986—). Home: 146 Bell Ave Piedmont CA 94611 Office: Howard Tours Inc 526 Grand Ave Oakland CA 94610

HOWARD, MURRAY, manufacturing, real estate, property management executive, farmer, rancher; b. Los Angeles, July 25, 1914; s. George A. J. and Mabel (Murray) H. B.S., UCLA, 1939. C.P.A., Calif. Mgr. budget control dept. Lockheed Aircraft, 1939-45; pres., chmn. bd. Stanley Foundries, Inc., 1945-59, Howard Machine Products, Inc., 1959—, Murray Howard Realty, Inc., 1959—, Murray Howard Devel., Inc., 1969—, Howard Oceanography, Inc., 1967—, Ranch Sales, Inc., 1968—, Murray Howard Investment Corp., 1961—; owner, gen. mgr. Greenhorn Ranch Co., Greenhorn Creek Guest Ranch, Spring Garden, Calif.; pres., chmn. bd. Murray Howard Cattle Co., Prineville, Oreg.; dir. Airshippers Publ. Corp., LaBrea Realty & Devel. Co., Shur-Lok Corp. Served as mem. Gov. Calif. Minority Com. Mem. Nat. Assn. Cost Accts. (dir., v.p.), NAM (dir.). Office: 1605 W Olympic Blvd Ste 404 Los Angeles CA 90015

HOWARD, PAUL SAMUEL, investment broker; b. Evanston, Ill., July 3, 1954; s. Gordon Douglass and Eleanor (Mason) H.; m. Elizabeth Jeanette Bro, Aug. 13, 1977; children: Samuel Bro, Peter Fraser, Andrew Welch. BS in Fin. with honors, U. Wyo., 1977, MBA, 1981. Head, Securities Div. Office Sec. of State, Cheyenne, Wyo., 1977-82; investment broker Boettcher & Co., Cheyenne, 1982-83, Dain Bosworth Inc., Cheyenne, 1983—; co-chmn. small bus. com. N. Am. Securities Adminstrs., 1980-82. Newspaper columnist Capital Times, 1982-84; writer newsletter Stock Talk, 1984-86. Coach Cheyenne Little League, 1980-82, Cheyenne Soccer Assn., 1987—; chmn. bldg. com. Cheyenne Sch. Dist. 1, 1988—. Mem. Nat. Assn. Securities Dealers, Cheyenne C. of C., Cheyenne Leads, Optimist club (founding Cheyenne). Congregationalist. Home: 916 Laredo Ct Cheyenne WY 82009 Office: Dain Bosworth Inc 1803 Capitol Ave Cheyenne WY 82001

HOWARD, RANDY DEWAYNE, health care executive; b. Athens, Tex., Apr. 19, 1934; s. Jesse Hardy and Jessie Viola (Harrison) h.; m. Jan. 13, 1979; div. Jan. 1987; children: Daniel Edward, Fredrick Dale. Student, So. Meth. U., 1955; BBA, Northwood Inst., Midland, Mich., 1972; MHA, Cornell U., 1974. Dir. Saginaw Gen. Hosp., Saginaw, Mich., 1969-77; adminstr. Brotman Med. Ctr., Culver City, Calif., 1977-81, Beverly Hills Med. Ctr., L.A., 1981-82; exec. dir. Los Banos Community Hosp., Los Banos, Calif., 1982-85, George Mee Meml. Hosp., King City, Calif., 1985-87; pres. Elite Health Care Svcs., L.A., 1987—; funding cons. Kinship Internat., L.A., 1987—; researcher N. Am. Coll. Law, Irvine, Calif., 1986—. Author: $2.5 Million Plan, 1982. Dir. Mizpah AIDS Network, Palm Springs, Calif., 1989; cons. Desert AIDS Project, Palm Spring, 1988. Grantee Kellogg Found., 1976. Fellow Am. Coll. Health Care Execs., Rotary. Republican. Home: PO Box 713 Desert Hot Springs CA 92240 Office: Elite Health Care Svcs 66220 3d St Desert Hot Springs CA 92240

HOWARD, TIMOTHY LEE, physicist; b. Memphis, June 11, 1955; s. Herbert Lee and Florence Elizabeth (Hargett) H.; m. Cynthia Dianne Reeves, Aug. 13, 1977 (div. Aug. 1981); m. Susan Marie Zates, Aug. 8, 1987. BS in Physics, Memphis State U., 1977, MS in Physics, 1979. Cert. in microcomputer engring., U. Calif., 1984. Mem. tech. staff Rockwell Internat., Anaheim, Calif., 1979-88; specialist GenCorp Aerojet ElectroSystems, Azusa, Calif., 1988—; instr. Rockwell Mgmt. Devel. and Tng. Program, Anaheim, 1985-87. Inventor laser gyroscope optics. Mem. Optical Soc. Am., Soc. Photo-optical Instrumentation Engrs., Am. Physical Soc., AIAA, Sigma Pi Sigma. Republican. Home: 4805 Via Del Buey Yorba Linda CA 92686 Office: GenCorp Aerojet ElectroSystems 1100 W Hollyvale B1D8451 Azusa CA 91702

HOWARD, VICTOR, management consultant; b. Montreal, Que., Can., Aug. 12, 1923; s. Thomas and Jean (Malkinson) H.; BA, Sir George Williams U., 1947; BSc, 1948; PhD, Mich. State U., 1954; m. Dorothy Bode, Dec. 25, 1953. Mech. design engr. Canadian Vickers Ltd., Montreal, 1942-46; with Aluminum Co. Can., 1946-48, E.B. Badger Co., Boston, 1948-50; asst. prof. Mich. State U., 1952-56; social scientist Rand Corp., 1956-58; staff exec., personnel dir. System Devel. Corp., Santa Monica, Calif., 1958-66; staff cons. Rohrer, Hibler & Replogle, San Francisco, 1966-69; mng. dir. Rohrer, Hibler & Replogle Internat., London and Brussels, 1969-74, ptnr. 1974, mgr. San Francisco, 1974-88, dir., 1979-88; pres. V. Howard and Assocs., 1988—, The Inst. on Stress and Health in the Work Place, 1988—. Mem. State Psychol. Examining Com., 1987. Mem. Am. Psychol. Assn., Western Psychol.Assn., Brit. Inst. Dirs., U.S. Power Squadron (comdr. Sequoia Squadron 1981, dist. comdr. 1987), Calif. State Mil. Res. (col. 1984), Reform Club, Hurlingham (London) Club, Thames Motor Yacht Club (Molesey, Eng.), Stockton Yacht Club, Masons, Scottish Rite, Shriners, Sigma Xi. Office: 1601 Old Bayshore Hwy Burlingame CA 94010

HOWATT, HELEN CLARE, library director; b. San Francisco, Apr. 5, 1927; d. Edward Bell and Helen Margaret (Kenney) H. BA, Holy Names Coll., 1949; MS in Libr. Sci., U. So. Calif., 1972; cert. advanced studies Our Lady of Lake U., 1966. Joined Order Sisters of the Holy Names, Roman Cath. Ch., 1945. Life teaching credential, life spl. svcs. credential, prin. St. Monica Sch., Santa Monica, Calif., 1957-60, St. Mary Sch., L.A., 1960-63; tchr. jr. high sch. St. Augustine Sch., Oakland, Calif., 1964-69; tchr. jr. high math St. Monica Sch., San Francisco, 1969-71, St. Cecilia Sch., San Francisco, 1971-77; libr. dir. Holy Names Coll., Oakland, Calif., 1977—. Contbr. math. curriculum San Francisco Unified Sch. Dist., Cum Notis Variorum, publ. Music Libr., U. Calif., Berkeley. Contbr. articles to profl. jours. NSF grantee, 1966, NDEA grantee, 1966. Mem. Cath. Libr. Assn. (chmn. No. Calif. elem. schs. 1971-72), Calif. Libr. Assn., ALA, Assn. Coll. and rsch. Librs. Home and Office: 3500 Mountain Blvd Oakland CA 94619

HOWDESHELL, SUZAN CHRISTINE, company executive, manufacturing executive; b. San Jose, Calif.; d. Philip and Elizabeth (Weiss) Sunseri; m. Travis D. Medley, Jr., Aug. 1, 1975;(div.); 1 child, Travis D. III; m. James Robert Howdeshell, July 18, 1987. With J & S Machining Co., Sunnyvale, Calif., 1974-77; office mgr. Assemmco, Sunnyvale, 1977-79; owner, mgr. Assoc. Fabrications (formerly SCM Fabrications), Campbell, Calif., 1979—; co-owner Foot Fetish, Folsom, Calif., 1987—.

HOWE, BRUCE IVER, government official; b. Dryden, Ont., Can., May 19, 1936; s. Norman I. and Laura A. (Locking) H.; m. Elsie Evelyn Ann Ferguson, Aug. 25, 1962; children—Karen, Norman, Kristina. BSc in Chem. Engring., Queen's U., Kingston, Ont., 1958; LLD (hon.), Lakehead U., Thunder Bay, Ont., 1983. Profl. engr., B.C. Sr. paper-making engr. Que. North Shore Paper Co., 1960-63; With MacMillan Bloedel Ltd., Vancouver, B.C., Can., 1963-80; asst. to mgr. mfg. MacMillan Bloedel Ltd., 1963-65, mgr. Island Paper Mill div., 1966, asst. div. mgr. Powell River Div., 1967-70, v.p. pulp and paper group, 1971-79, exec. v.p., 1979, pres., chief exec. officer, 1980; chief exec. officer B.C. Resources Investment Corp., 1980-86, chmn., 1986; sec., chief sci. advisor Ministry of State for Sci. and Tech., Ottawa, Ont., Can., 1986-88; dep. minister Energy Mines & Resources Can., Ottawa, Ont., Can., 1988—; chmn. bd. Westar Mining and Westar Petroleum, B.C., 1980-86; chmn. exec. com. Westar Mining, 1980-86. Contbr. numerous articles on pulp and paper to profl. jours. Past mem. internat. trade adv. com. Can. Govt.; Can. chmn. Can./Korea Bus. Council, B.C., 1983-86; commr. gen. Can. Pavilion, Expo '86, B.C., 1985-86. Office: Energy Mines & Resources Can, 580 Booth St 21st Fl, Ottawa, ON Canada K1A 1A1

HOWE, DRAYTON FORD, JR., lawyer; b. Seattle, Nov. 17, 1931; s. Drayton Ford and Virginia (Wester) H.; m. Joyce Arnold, June 21, 1952; 1 son, James Drayton. A.B., U. Calif.-Berkeley, 1953; LL.B., Hastings Coll. Law, 1957. Bar: Calif. 1958, C.P.A. Calif. Atty. IRS, 1958-61; tax dept. supr. Ernst & Ernst, San Francisco, 1962-67; ptnr. Bishop, Barry, Howe & Reid, San Francisco, 1968—; lectr. on tax matters U. Calif. extension, 1966-76. Mem. Calif. Bar Assn., San Francisco Bar Assn. (chmn. client relations com. 1977), Calif. Soc. C.P.A.s.

HOWE, RICHARD CUDDY, state supreme court justice; b. South Cottonwood, Utah, Jan. 20, 1924; s. Edward E. and Mildred (Cuddy) H.; m. Juanita Lyon, Aug. 30, 1949; children: Christine Howe Schultz, Andrea Howe Reynolds, Bryant, Valerie Howe Winegar, Jeffrey, Craig. B.S., U. Utah, 1945, J.D., 1948. Bar: Utah. Law clk. to Justice James H. Wolfe, Utah Supreme Ct., 1949-50; judge city ct. Murray, Utah, 1951; individual practice law Murray, 1952-80; justice Utah Supreme Ct., 1980—. Mem. Utah Ho. of Reps., 1951-58, 69-72, Utah Senate, 1973-78. Named Outstanding Legislator Citizens' Conf. State Legislatures, 1972. Mem. Utah Bar Assn. Mormon. Office: Utah Supreme Ct 332 State Capitol Bldg Salt Lake City UT 84114

HOWELL, ALAN PETER, lawyer, arbitrator; b. Honolulu, Aug. 1, 1927; s. Hugh and Mavis Halcyon (Shawk) H.; m. Sara Grounds, Dec. 26, 1954; children: David Wallace, Brian Cochran. BA, Yale U., 1950; LLB, Cornell U., 1953. Bar: Hawaii 1954. Law clk. to chief justice Ter. Supreme Ct. Hawaii 1953-54; asst. pub. prosecutor City and County Honolulu, 1954-58; ptnr. Hogan & Howell, 1958-71; sole practice, 1971-86; magistrate 6th dist. Dist. Ct. Honolulu, 1964-68. Rep. precinct pres., Hawaii, 1956-58; pres. chpt. 184 Exptl. Aircraft Assn. With U.S. Army, 1946-48, 1st lt. USAFR, 1950-58. Mem. Hawaii Bar Assn., Am. Arbitration Assn. (arbitrator). Christian Scientist. Clubs: Pacific, Outrigger Canoe. Office: 733 Bishop St Suite 2515 Honolulu HI 96813-4057

HOWELL, JAMES WILLIAM, physician; b. Sheridan, Wyo., Oct. 30, 1946; s. Bernard Marvin and Vivian Midge (Hamilton) H.; m. Sheryl Alice Pattinson, June 8, 1974 (div. June 1988). BS in Biology with Honors, Calif. Inst. Tech., 1968; MSEE, U. Wyo., 1976; MD, U. Utah, 1983. Diplomate Nat. Bd. Med. Examiners. Intern LDS Hosp., Salt Lake City, 1983-84; research biologist Lawrence Livermore Lab., Livermore, Calif., 1968; flight instr. Bighorn Airways, Sheridan, 1970-74; engr. Amax Corp., Gillette, Wyo., 1976-77, Combustion Engring. Co., Foster City, Calif., 1977-78, Ultrasound div. Varian Corp., Palo Alto, Calif., 1978-81; med. dir. Wyo. State Tng. Sch., Lander, 1984—. Served with U.S. Army, 1968-70, Vietnam. Decorated Bronze Star. Mem. IEEE, Am. Assn. Artificial Intelligence, Exptl. Aircraft Assn. Home: 8204 N Hwy 789 Lander WY 82520 Office: Wyo State Tng Sch Hwy 789 Lander WY 82520

HOWKINS, JOHN BLAIR, mining company executive; b. Falkirk, Stirlingshire, Scotland, Feb. 12, 1932; immigrated to Can., 1965; s. George and Jemina Maclaren (Brown) H.; m. Heather Ferguson Nicoll, Jan. 8, 1955; children: Blair Nicoll, John Alexander, Cecilia Anne. B.S. with honors, U. Edinburgh (Scotland), 1953, Ph.D., 1961. Registered profl. engr., Ont. Sr. geologist Anglo Am. Corp., Central Africa, 1965; chief geologist Hudson Bay Mining and Smelting, Ont., Can., 1965-68, v.p. exploration, 1968-76, sr. v.p., 1978-82, 83-86; sr. v.p., group exec. Inspiration Resources Corp., N.Y.C., 1986—; dir. Farley Gold, Inc., Hudson Bay Gold, Inc., Hudson Bay Mining, Tantalum Mining Corp. of Can., Inspiration Gold, Inc.; dir., pres. Hudson Holdings Corp.; chmn. bd. dirs. Black Pine Mining Co., Phoenix, Terra Internat. Inc., Sioux City, Iowa. Mem. Canadian Inst. Mining and Metallurgy, Assn. Profl. Engrs. Ont., AIME, Geol. Assn. Can. *

HOWLAND, JAMES CHASE, retired engineer, consultant; b. Oregon City, Oreg., June 2, 1916; s. Arthur Cornell and Sade (Chase) H.; m. Ruth Louise Meisenhelder, June 14, 1941; children: Joyce, Eric, Mark, Peter. BS, Oreg. State U., 1938; MS, MIT, 1939. Registered profl. engr., Oreg., Idaho. Engr. Standard Oil Co. Calif., El Segundo, 1939-41; cons. engr. CH2M Hill, Corvallis, Oreg., 1946—. Bd. dirs. Madison Ave Task Force, Corvallis, 1974—, chmn. 1974-78; trustee Linfield Coll, McMinnville, Oreg., 1979—; active Corvallis Planning Commn., 1957-70, Oreg. Water Resources Commn., Salem, 1987—. Served with U.S. Army, 1941-46, PTO. Mem. ASCE (hon., engring. mgmt. award 1987), Profl. Engrs. Oreg., Oreg. Couns. Engrs. Council (pres., engr. yr. 1988), Tau Beta Pi. Republican. Episcopal. Home: 2575 SW Whiteside Dr Corvallis OR 97333 Office: CH2M Hill PO Box 428 Corvallis OR 97339

HOWLAND, JAY ALLEN, laser physicist; b. Lorain, Ohio, Aug. 9, 1943; s. Joseph Allen and Hilda (Gram) H.; m. Rosalind Ann Dorsett, Apr. 5, 1968; children: Jason Allen, Tristan Anthony. BS in Engring. Physics, Walla Walla Coll., 1965; MS in Physics, U. Okla., 1971. Commd. 2d lt. USAF, 1965, advanced through grades to lt. col., 1986; optical physicist USAF, Kirtland AFB, N.Mex., 1971-73; missile launch officer USAF, Whiteman AFB, Mo., 1973-75; resigned USAF, 1975; sr. devel. engr.,then laser gyro project leader Honeywell, Inc., Mpls., 1976-82; laser ops. mgr., then accelerator facility mgr. Los Alamos (N.Mex.) Nat. Lab., 1982-87; laser and accelerator cons. Jay A. Howland, Cons., Welham, Gt. Britain, 1987-88; free electron laser accelerator project mgr. Ground Based Laser Project, White Sands Missile Range, N.Mex., 1988—. Author tech. reports. Communications chmn., Spl. Olympics, Mpls., 1978-81; den leader, Los Alamos area Boy Scouts Am., 1982-86. Mem. Optical Soc. Am., Honeywell Amateur Radio Club. Republican. Home: 3227 Mercury Ln Las Cruces NM 88001 Office: Ground Based Laser Project CSSD-HH-FF White Sands Missile Range NM 88002

HOWLETT, JOHN DAVID, economic development professional; b. Akron, Colo., July 16, 1952; s. John Butler and Reavis Lavina (Smith) H. BA, U. Nebr., 1975, M in Urban and Regional Planning, 1977. Urban and regional planner Oblinger-McCaleb, Denver, 1979-80; staff project mgr. Greater Denver C. of C., 1980-83; dir. econ. devel. City of Littleton, Colo., 1983-87; dir. civic and econ. devel. The Denver Partnership, Denver, 1987—; mem. Arapahoe/Douglas Pvt. Industry Coun., Englewood, Colo., 1984-87; mem. steering com., New Bus. and Industry Coun., Denver, 1985-87; mem. exec. com., Met. Denver Network, 1987—. Mem. profl. adv. coun., Coll. Architecture, U. Nebr., Lincoln, 1980—; vice-chmn. C-470 Inter-Chamber Task Force, Denver, 1984-87; trustee, AMC Cancer Rsch. Ctr., Lakewood, Colo., 1985-87; pres. Arapahoe Community Coll. Found., Littleton, Colo., 1986-87; mem. exec. bd. Friends of Auraria Library, Denver, 1989—. Mem. Am. Planning Assn. (pres. Colo. chpt. 1985-87, Karen Smith Chpt. award 1987), City Club Denver (pres. 1984-85). Democrat. Presbyterian. Home: 3026 L W Prentice Ave Littleton CO 80123 Office: Denver Partnership Ste 200 511 16th St Denver CO 80202

HOWLETT, PATRICIA ERSKINE, communications executive; b. Moscow, Maine, June 12, 1930: d. Charles Samuel and Elvina Mary (Thompson) Erskine; A.B., Colby Coll., 1952; M.A., U. San Francisco, 1979; children: Lorin Ann, Charles Erskine. English tchr. public schs., Orleans, Beverly and Brookline, Mass., 1952-57; tchr. English, Mt. Diablo Schs., Concord, Calif., 1960-67; broadcaster Radio Sta. KWUN, Concord, Calif., 1971-74; info. officer Mt. Diablo Unified Sch. Dist., Concord, 1974-79; dir. bd. devel. Calif. Sch. Bds. Assn., 1980; public relations exec. Assn. Calif. Sch. Adminstrs., 1980-84, dir. communications, 1985—; also pub./editor Thrust Mag., EDCAL edn. weekly newspaper. Bd. dirs. Sch./Community Relations Found., 1979—. Mem. Internat. Assn. Bus. Communicators, San Francisco Pub. Relations Round Table, Nat. Sch. Public Relations Assn. (accredited, bd. dirs. 1985—, Gold medalion 1986), Pub. Relations Soc. Am. (accredited, Calif. coordinator 1981-83), Calif. Sch. Public Relations Assn.(pres. 1979-80), Am. Assn. Sch. Adminstrs., Ednl. Press Assn. Am., Issue Network Calif. (bd. dirs.), Am. Soc. Assn. Execs., Internat. Platform Assn., Sigma Delta Chi, Phi Delta Kappa. Clubs: Commonwealth, San Francisco Press, Ninety Nines. Author: How to Work with the Media, 1979; Single Woman, (poetry), 1983; Independent Woman, 1983. Office: Assn Calif Sch Adminstrs 1517 L St Sacramento CA 95814

HOWSLEY, RICHARD THORNTON, lawyer, regional government administrator; b. Medford, Oreg., Jan. 31, 1948; s. Calvin Nevil and Arvilla Constance (Romine) H.; m. Susan Erma Johnson, Oct. 23, 1971; children: James Denver, Kelly Ann. B.A., Willamette U., 1970; M.S., Va. Poly. Inst. and State U., 1974; J.D., Lewis and Clark Law Sch., 1984. Bar: Oreg. 1984, Wash. 1985, U.S. Dist. Ct. (we. dist.) Wash. Tech. editor U.S. Bur. Mines, Arlington, Va., 1971-72; program mgr., sr. planner KRS Assos., Inc., Reston, Va., 1972-74; exec. dir. Rogue Valley Council Govts., Medford, 1974-78; exec. dir. Regional Planning Council of Clark County, Vancouver, Wash., 1978-84; assoc. Landerholm, Memovich, Lansverk & Whitesides, Vancouver, 1985—; vice chmn. Oreg. Council of Govts. Dirs. Assn., 1976-77, chmn., 1977-78; mem. regional adv. com. So. Oreg. State Coll., 1975-78. Mem. Medford-Ashland Air Quality Adv. Com., 1977-78. Carpenter Found. scholar, 1966-70, Leonard B. Mayfield Meml. scholar, 1966-67, Albina Page Found. scholar, 1966-70. Mem. ABA, Oreg. State Bar Assn., Wash. State Bar Assn., Am. Planning Assn., Am. Inst. Cert. Planners, Internat. City Mgmt. Assn. (10-yr. service award), Nat. Assn. Regional Councils (10-yr. service award). Democrat. Methodist. Home: 15807 NW 27th Ct Vancouver WA 98685 Office: Landerholm Memovich Lansverk & Whitesides 915 Broadway Vancouver WA 98666

HOY, MICHAEL JOHN, publisher, bookseller; b. Pontiac, Mich., Mar. 15, 1945; s. Albert Gordon and Phyllis Louise (Lease) H. BS in Acctg., Mich. State U., 1970. Owner Loompanics Unlimited, Mason, Mich., 1973-82, Port Townsend, Wash., 1982—. Author: Exotic Weapons, 1977, 79, 82, I.D. For Sale, 1983, Mail Order I.D., 1985. Served as pvt. 2nd class U.S. Army, 1968-70, Socialist Republic Vietnam. Office: Loompanics Unltd 337 Sherman St Port Townsend WA 98368

HOYE, WALTER BRISCO, college administrator; b. Lena, Miss., May 19, 1930; s. William H. and LouBertha (Stewart) H.; m. Vida M. Pickens, Aug. 28, 1954; children—Walter B. II, JoAnn M. B.A., Wayne State U., 1953. Sports/auto editor Detroit Tribune, 1958-65; sports editor Mich. Chronicle, 1965-68; assoc. dir. pub. relations San Diego Chargers Football Co., 1968-76; media liason NFL, 1972-75; community services officer San Diego Coll. Dist., 1976-78; placement officer Ednl. Cultural Complex, San Diego, 1978-80, info. officer, 1980-82, placement officer, adminstrv. asst., 1982-83, placement/program support spr., 1983—; cons. in field. Bd. dirs. San Diego County ARC; active San Diego Conv. and Tourist Bur., Joint Ctr. Polit. Studies, Am. Cancer Soc., San Diego Urban League, Neighborhood Housing Assn., Public Access TV. Named San Diego County Citizen of Month, May, 1979; recipient United Way Award of Merit, 1974. Mem. Am. Personnel and Guidance Assn., San Diego Career Guidance Assn., Nat. Mgmt. Assn., Assn. Calif. Community Coll. Adminstrs., Calif. Community Coll. Placement Assn. Home: 6959 Ridge Manor Ave San Diego CA 92120 Office: Ednl Cultural Complex 4343 Ocean View Blvd Suite 177 San Diego CA 92113

HOYT, JACK WALLACE, engineering educator; b. Chgo., Oct. 19, 1922; s. Claire A. and Fleta M. (Wheeler) H.; B.S., Ill. Inst. Tech., 1944; M.S., UCLA, 1952, Ph.D., 1962; m. Helen Rita Erickson, Dec. 27, 1945; children—John A., Katheryn M. (Mrs. Richard Everett), Annette M. (Mrs. Walter Butler), Denise M. (Mrs. Paul Kruesi). Research engr. gas turbines Cleve. Lab., NACA, 1944-47; mem. staff Naval Ocean Systems Center, Navy Dept., DOD, San Diego, 1948-79, asso. for sci. fleet engring. dept., 1967-79, now cons.; vis. prof. mech. engring. Rutgers U., New Brunswick, N.J., 1979-81; Benjamin Meaker vis. prof. U. Bristol (Eng.), 1987; prof. mech. engring. San Diego State U., 1981—. Mem. ASME (Freeman scholar 1971), N.Y. Acad. Scis., Soc. Naval Architects and Marine Engrs. Author, patentee in field. Editorial bd. Internat. Shipbldg. Progress, 1965—. Spl. research propulsion and hydrodynamics. Home: 4694 Lisann St San Diego CA 92117

HOYT-HAMEL, TERRIE LYNN, accountant; b. L.A., July 6, 1956; d. Robert Hoyt and Bobbe D. Smyer; children: Damon, Jason. Student, Foothill Coll., Los Altos Hills, Calif., 1987. Sales specialist Mervyns Dept. Store, Mountain View, Calif., 1973-74; asst. supr. No. Calif. Savs. & Loan, Palo Alto, Calif., 1975-81, Ford Aerospace Corp., Palo Alto, 1981--; producer, dir. Forever Fashions Prodns., Mountain View., 1984--. Mem. NAFE. Home: 3388 Brittan Ave #1 San Carlos CA 94070

HRISHKO, DANIEL GEORGE, furniture company executive; b. Glendale, Calif., Aug. 7, 1947; s. Daniel and Olena (Felegy) H. AA, Valley Jr. Coll., 1967; BS, Woodbury Coll., 1970; MS, Calif. State U., Northridge, 1972. Sales mgr. L.A. Times, 1968-72; v.p. Calif. Pacific Assn., Inc., L.A., 1972-76; pres. Dantek & Assocs., Inc., L.A., 1976-83, Beds 'n Bunks, Inc., Burbank, Calif., 1983—; bd. dirs. Accent Jewelry, Inc., Burbank. Mem. Toluca Lake (Calif.) Tennis Club. Republican. Roman Catholic. Office: Bed 'n Bunks Inc 330 N Golden Mall Burbank CA 91502

HRITZ, SHARON SUE, teacher; b. Evansville, Ind., Apr. 10, 1941; d. Leonard Otto and Beatrice Alice (Gibbons) Fischer; m. Thomas Donald Hritz, Nov. 22, 1962; children: Lisa, Shari, Karin. BA, Webster U., 1962; MEd, Loyola Mary Mount U., 1981. Lic. elem. tchr., Calif., Mo. Tchr. Our Lady of Lourdes Sch., University City, Mo., 1962-64, St. Peters Sch., Kirkwood, Mo., 1964-65, St. Blaise Sch., Maryland Heights, Mo., 1970-76, St. Hedwig Sch., Los Alamitos, Calif., 1976-84, Sts. Simon and Jude Sch., Huntington Beach, Calif., 1984—. Mem. Nat. Cath. Edn. Assn., Diocese of Orange Tchrs. Assn., Webster U. Alumnae Assn. Roman Catholic. Office: Sts Simon & Jude Sch 2400 Magnolia Huntington Beach CA 92646

HSIA, FREDERICK TSU, engineering consultation executive; b. Beijing, Republic of China, Oct. 8, 1941; came to U.S., 1965; s. Cheng Yin and Han-Yin (Lin) H.; m. Min Gee Kung Hsia, Apr. 6, 1968; children: Constance Yu, Eric Long. BS, Nat. Chen Kung U., Republic of China, 1963; M of Engring., Tex. A&M U., 1967; PhD, Mich. State U., 1977. Registered civil engr., Mich., Calif.; registered geotech. engr., Calif. Research asst. Tex. Transp. Inst., College Station, 1966; civil engr. Mich. Dept. Transp., Lansing, 1967-71; bridge design engr. Mich. Dept. Transp., 1971-74, transp. research engr., 1974-77; project geotech. engr. U.S. Forest Service, Pleasant Hill, Calif., 1977-86; pres. Shass Co., Danville, Calif., 1986—. Served to 2d lt. Nationalist Chinese Army, Taiwan, 1963-64. Nat. Highway Inst. Research fellow, 1973. Office: Shass Co 1262 Vailwood Dr Danville CA 94526

HSIAO, ALICE, pharmacist; b. Taipei, Republic of China, July 10, 1964; came to U.S., 1972; d. Paul T. and Katherine Hsiao. BS, UCLA, 1984; PharmD, U. So. Calif., 1988. Head intern Clin. Care Pharmacy, South Pasadena, Calif., 1986-88; clin. pharmacy resident ambulatory care U. So. Calif., Los Angeles, 1988-89; pharmacist Kaisor Permanente Med. Ctr., 1989—. Mem. Am. Pharm. Assn., Am. Soc. Hosp. Pharmacist, Calif. Soc. Hosp. Pharmacists, UCLA Alumni Assn., Lambda Kappa Sigma.

HSIAO, FRANK S. T., economics educator; b. Kao-shiong, Taiwan, Sept. 14, 1933; s. Chi-lai and Zhao-zhi (Pan) H.; m. Mei-chu Wang, July 20, 1968; children—Edward C., Victoria C. B.A., Nat. Taiwan U., 1956, M.A., 1959; M.A., U. Rochester, 1964, Ph.D., 1967. Research asst. U. Mich., Ann Arbor, 1965-66; asst. prof., then assoc. prof. U. Colo., Boulder, 1966-75, prof. econs., 1975—; vis. scholar Hoover Instn., Stanford, Calif., summer 1983; lectr. Universidad Regiomontana, Monterrey, Mex., 1979; research assoc. East Asian Research Ctr., Harvard U., summer 1977. Author articles in field. Assn. Asian Studies grantee, 1983; Fulbright-Hays research fellow, East Asia, 1975. Mem. Am. Econs. Assn., N.Am. Taiwanese Profs. Assn. Home: 5079 Holmes Pl Boulder CO 80303 Office: U Colo Campus Box 256 Boulder CO 80309

HSIAO, JAMES CHIEN, data processing executive; b. Szechwan, People's Republic China, Apr. 18, 1938; s. Tseng and Sheng-Chih (Shu) H.; m. Josefina C. Malang, Jan. 24, 1968. BS, Nat. Taiwan U., 1961; Diploma in Mineralogy, U. Freiburg, 1967, PhD, 1971. Dir. China Land Econ. Rsch. Inst., Taipei, Republic of China, 1971; sci. researcher Tech. U. Darmstadt (Fed. Republic Germany), 1971-72, Tech. U. Munich, 1972, U. Calif., Berkeley, 1973-74; asst. dir. Pertamina, N.Y.C., 1975-76; gen. mgr. Ind. Pacific Ltd., San Francisco, 1976-78; program analyst City and County of San Francisco, 1978-85; systems and processing supr. San Francisco Community Coll. Dist., 1985—. Gen. sec. Land Econ. Scholarship Fund, San Francisco, 1979. 2d lt. U.S. Army, 1961-62. Mem. Honeywell Large System Users Assn. Home: 728 Lawton St San Francisco CA 94122 Office: San Francisco Community Coll Dist 50 Phelan Ave San Francisco CA 94112

HSU, CHIEH SU, engineering educator, researcher; b. Soochow, Kiangsu, China, May 27, 1922; came to U.S., 1947.; s. Chung yu and Yong Feng (Wu) H.; m. Helen Yung-Feng Tse, Mar. 28, 1953; children—Raymond Hwa-Chi, Katherine Hwa-Ling. BS, Nat. Inst. Tech., Chungking, China, 1945; MS,

Stanford U., 1948, Ph.D., 1950. Project engr. IBM Corp., Poughkeepsie, N.Y., 1951-55; assoc. prof. U. Toledo, 1955-58; assoc. prof. Univ Calif.-Berkeley, 1958-64, prof., 1964—, chmn. div. applied mechanics, 1969-70; mem. sci. adv. bd. Alexander von Humboldt Found. of Fed. Republic Germany, Bonn, 1985—. Author 91 tech. papers; contbg. author: Thin-Shell Structures, 1974, Advances in Applied Mechanics, vol. 17, 1977; author: Cell-to-Cell Mapping, 1987; tech. editor Jour. Applied Mechanics, N.Y.C., 1976-82; assoc. editor profl. jours. Recipient Alexander von Humboldt award Fed. Republic Germany, 1986; Guggenheim Found. fellow, 1964-65; Miller research prof., U. Calif.-Berkeley, 1973-74. Fellow ASME (Centennial award 1980), Am. Acad. Mechanics; mem. Acoustical Soc. Am., Soc. Indsl. and Applied Math., U.S. Nat. Acad. Engring., Sigma Xi. Office: U Calif Dept Mech Engring Berkeley CA 94720

HSU, ISAAC HOU-AN, ophthalmologist; b. Chengtu, Szechuan, People's Republic China, Jan. 10, 1946; s. Philip Chen-Yi and Jane Yen-Cheng (Swen) H.; m. Diane Kwan-Ping Cheng, Aug. 19, 1972; children: Israel, Immanuel, Ira, Isaiah. Student, U. Oreg., 1964-67; MD, UCLA, 1971. Diplomate Am. Bd. Ophthalmology. Pediatrics intern SUNY, Syracuse, 1971-72, ophthalmology resident, 1972-73, 1973-76; pvt. practice Eye Care Inst., Tigard, Oreg., 1976—; clin. instr. Oreg. Health Scis. U., 1979—; teaching assoc. Dever's Eye Clinic, Portland, Oreg., 1976—. Fellow Am. Acad. Ophthalmology; mem. Am. Soc. Cataract & Refractive Surgery, Oreg. Med. Assn., Multnomah Med. Soc. Republican. Office: 9735 SW Shady Ln Tigard OR 97223

HSU, PAUL L., computer software engineering specialist; b. Hopei, China, Sept. 21, 1922; came to U.S., 1952; s. Kwan Hsu and Su-Yun Chang; m. Dorothy H. Yang, May 2, 1959; children: Aileen, Mimi, Victor. MBA, U. Wash., 1953, BS in Math., 1957, MS in Stats., 1961; PhD in Computer Sci., Clayton U., 1981. Instr. U.S. Army Lang. Sch., Monterey, CA, 1953-55; engr. The Boeing Co., Seattle, 1959-62; sr. research specialist Rockwell Internat., Anaheim, Calif., 1962-68; sr. staff engr. McDonnell Douglas Co., Huntington Beach, Calif., 1968—. Co-author: Tables for Testing Significance in A 2 X 2 Contingency Table; contbr.papers to jours. of Internat. Soc. for Mini and Micro Computers. Home: 1510 El Paso Ln Fullerton CA 92633

HSU, SHU-DEAN, hematologist; b. Chiba, Japan, Feb. 21, 1943; came to U.S., 1972; s. Tetzu and Takako (Koo) Minoyama; m. San-San Hsu, Mar. 3, 1973; children: Deborah Te-Lan, Peter Jie-Te. MD, Taipei (Taiwan) Med. Coll., 1968. Diplomate Am. Bd. Internal Medicine, Am. Bd. Hematology, Am. Bd. Med. Oncology. Asst. in medicine Mt. Sinai Sch. Medicine, N.Y.C., 1975-77; asst. instr. medicine U. Tex., Galveston, 1977-78; lectr. in medicine Tex. A&M U., Temple, 1978-80; asst. prof. medicine U. Ark., Little Rock, 1980-83; practice medicine specializing in hematology-oncology Visalia (Calif.) Med. Clinic, 1983—; chief hematology and oncology VA Med. Ctr., Temple, Tex., 1978-80. Contbr. articles to profl. jours. Fellow ACP; mem. N.Y. Acad. Scis., Am. Soc. Clin. Oncology, Am. Soc. Hematology, Calif. Med. Assn., Tulare County Med. Soc. Club: Visalia Racquet. Home: 3500 W Hydeway Visalia CA 93291 Office: Visalia Med Clinic 5400 W Hillsdale Visalia CA 93291

HU, EVELYN LYNN, electrical and computer engineering educator; b. N.Y.C., May 15, 1947; d. David Hosheng and Carolyn Jui-chen (Hsu) H. BA in Physics, Barnard Coll., 1969; MA in Physics, Columbia U., 1971, PhD in Physics, 1975. Mem. tech. staff AT&T Bell Labs., Holmdel, N.J., 1975-81; supr. AT&T Bell Labs., Murray Hill, N.J., 1981-84; prof. elec. and computer engring. U. Calif., Santa Barbara, 1985—; assoc. dir. Ctr. Robotic Systems in Microelectronics, 1985—; mem. MIT vis. com. EECS, 1983—; mem. program com. Nat. Research and Resource Facility for Submicron Structures; mem. steering com. Internat. Symposium on Electron, Ion and Photon Beams; chmn. Gordon Conf. on Chemistry and Physics of Microstructures, 1986. Contbr. articles to profl. jours.; patentee in field. Mem. IEEE, Am. Phys. Soc., Am. Vacuum Soc., Phi Beta Kappa, Sigma Xi. Office: U Calif Ctr Robotic Systems 6740 Cortona Goleta CA 93117 *

HU, JOHN CHIH-AN, chemist, research engineer; b. Nanchang, Hubei, China, July 12, 1922; came to U.S., 1954, naturalized, 1965; s. Chi-Ching and Chao-Xien (Tsen) H.; B.S. in Chemistry, Nat. Central U., Nanjing, China, 1946; M.S. in Organic Chemistry, U. So. Calif., 1957, postgrad., 1957-61; PhD (hon.) Marquis Giuseppe Scicluna Internat. Univ. Foundation, 1985; m. Betty Siao-Yung Ho, Oct. 26, 1957; children—Arthur, Benjamin, Carl, David, Eileen, Franklin, George. Dir. research dept. Plant 1, Taiwan Fertilizer Mfg. Co., Chilung, 1947-54; research assoc. chemistry dept. U. So. Calif., Los Angeles, 1957-61; research chemist Chem Seal Corp. Am., Los Angeles, 1961-62; research chemist Products Research & Chem. Corp., Glendale, Calif., 1962-66; sr. research engr., materials and tech. unit, Boeing Co., Seattle, 1966-71, specialist engr. Quality Assurance Labs., 1971—; cons. UN; lectr., China, profl. confs. Fellow Am. Inst. Chemists; mem. Am. Chem. Soc. (chmn. Puget Sound sect. 1988, councilor 1989—), Royal Soc. Chemistry (London), N.Y. Acad. Sci., Phi Lambda Upsilon. Patentee Chromatopyrography; contbg. author: Analytical Approach, 1983, Advances in Chromotography, vol. 23, 1984; contbr. articles on analytical pyrolysis, gas chromatography, mass spectrometry, polymer characterization, chemistry and tech. of sealants and adhesives to profl. publs. in Chinese and English; editor Puget Sound Chemist; referee profl. jours. Analytical Chemistry, Analytica Chimica Acta, Am. Chem. Soc. short courses. Home: 16212 122 SE Renton WA 98058 Office: Boeing Co M/S 8J-55 PO Box 3999 Seattle WA 98124

HUA, TIMOTHY, electrical engineer; b. Saigon, Viet-Nam, Jan. 10, 1959; came to U.S. 1980; s. Truc Tuong and Xuan Tu (Quach) H.; m. Linh My Tang, Nov. 19, 1988. BSEE, U. Wash., 1983, MSEE, 1987. Engr. The Boeing Co., Seattle, 1984-88, Mannesmann Tally, Kent, Wash., 1988—. Home: 13331 17th Ave NE Seattle WA 98125 Office: Mannesmann Tally 8301 S 180 St Kent WA 98032

HUANG, CHIEN CHANG, electrical engineer; b. Nanking, Peoples Republic of China, Feb. 16, 1931; came to U.S., 1957; s. Ling-Kuo Huang and Yi-Ching Liu; m. Li-May Tsai, June 2, 1962; children: Frederick G., Lewis G. BSEE, Taiwan Coll. Engring., Tainan, 1954; MSEE, U. Ill., 1959; postgrad., U. Pa., 1960-62. Engr. Burrough Corp., Paoli, Pa., 1960-64; sr. staff engr. Unisys Corp., San Diego, 1974—; sr. engr. Philco Ford Corp., Blue Bell, Pa., 1965-69; staff engr. Fairchild Semiconductor, Mountain View, Calif., 1969-71; sr. staff engr. Am. Micro Systems, Santa Clara, Calif., 1971-74. Contbr. articles to profl. jours. Home: 14481 Maplewood St Poway CA 92064 Office: Unisys Corp 10850 Via Frontera San Diego CA 92127

HUANG, FRANCIS FU-TSE, engineering educator; b. Hong Kong, Aug. 27, 1922; came to U.S., 1945, naturalized, 1960; s. Kwong Set and Chen-Ho (Yee) H.; m. Fung-Yuen Fung, Apr. 10, 1954; children: Raymond, Stanley. BS, San Jose State Coll., 1951; MS, Stanford U., 1952; postgrad., Columbia U., 1964. Design engr. M.W. Kellogg Co., N.Y.C., 1952-58; faculty San Jose (Calif.) State U., 1958—, assoc. prof. mech. engring., 1962-67, prof., 1967—, chmn. dept., 1973-81; hon. prof. heat power engring. Taiyuan (People's Republic of China) U. Tech., 1981—. Author: Engineering Thermodynamics—Fundamentals and Applications, 1976, 2d edit., 1988. Capt. Chinese Army, 1943-45. NSF faculty fellow, 1962-64; Named Tau Beta Pi Outstanding Engring. Prof. of Yr., 1967, 76, Pi Tau Sigma Prof. of Yr., 1985; recipient Calif. State Coll. System Disting. Teaching award, 1968-69. Mem. ASME, AIAA, Am. Soc. Engring. Edn., AAAS, AAUP, N.Y. Acad. Scis., Sigma Xi. Home: 1259 Sierra Mar Dr San Jose CA 95118 Office: San Jose State U Dept Mech Engring San Jose CA 95192

HUBBARD, CHARLES LEON, electronic engineer; b. Atlanta, May 9, 1941; s. Charles W. and Helen Allen (Walkley) H.; m. A. Christine Chewning, Feb. 16, 1962; children: Renee, Ray, Ronald, Robert, Roger, Rynette. BEE, Ga. Inst. Tech., 1965. Draftsman Blakely-Daniels Assocs., Atlanta, 1963-65; engr. McDonnell-Douglas Corp., St. Louis, 1965-69, Bell and Howell Corp., Pasadena, 1969-74, Genisco Corp., Compton, Calif., 1974-75, Northrop Corp., Newbury Park, Calif., 1975-77; engr., mgr. Dataproducts Corp., Woodland Hills, Calif., 1977-85; gen. mgr. Axiom Edwards C.P.E. Corp., San Fernando, Calif., 1985-88; pres. Creative Data Devices Inc., Camarillo, Calif., 1988—; cons. Hubbard's Cons., Camarillo, 1985—; cons., lectr., presenter in field. Contbr. articles to profl. jours. Baptist. Home: 2963 Landen St Camarillo CA 93010 Office: Creative Data Devices Inc 4750 Calle Quetzal Camarillo CA 93010

HUBBARD, CHARLES RONALD, engineering executive; b. Weaver, Ala., Feb. 4, 1933; s. John Duncan Hubbard and Athy Pauline (Lusk) Thorpe; m. Betty Lou McKleroy, Dec. 29, 1951; 1 son, Charles Ronald Hubbard II. BSEE, U. Ala., 1960. Mktg. mgr. Sperry Corp., Huntsville, Ala., 1969-71, head engring. sect., 1971-74; sr. staff engr. Honeywell Inc., Clearwater, Fla., 1974-76, mgr., 1976-79, chief engr., West Covina, Calif., 1979-83, assoc. dir. engring., 1983-84, assoc. dir. advanced systems, 1984-87, assoc. dir. programs, 1987-88; v.p. govt. systems div. Integrated Inference Machines, Anaheim, Calif., 1988—. Served as staff sgt. USAF, 1953-57. Mem. IEEE (sect. chmn. 1972-73). Methodist. Home: 5460 Willowick Circle Anaheim CA 92807 Office: Integrated Inference Machines 1468 E Katella Ave Anaheim CA 92805

HUBBARD, DONALD, marine artist, writer; b. Bronx, N.Y., Jan. 15, 1926; s. Ernest Fortesque and Lilly Violet (Beck) H.; student Brown U., 1944-45; A.A., George Washington U., 1959, B.A., 1958; student Naval War Coll., 1965-66; m. Darlene Julia Huber, Dec. 13, 1957; children—Leslie Carol, Christopher Eric, Lauren Ivy. Commd. ensign U.S. Navy, 1944, advanced through grades to comdr., 1965; served naval aviator, ret., 1967; founder Ocean Ventures Industries, Inc., Coronado, Calif., 1969, operator, 1969-77; marine artist; founder, operator Sea Eagle Pubs., Coronado, 1988; author: Ships-in-Bottles, 2d edition, 1988, A How to Guide to a Venerable Nautical Craft, 1971; Buddleschiffe: Wie Macht Man Sie, 1972; The Complete Book of Inflatable Boats, 1979; editor: The Bottle Shipwright; contbr. articles in field to publs. SCUBA instr.; lectr. on marine art. Decorated Air Medal. Mem. Ships-in-Bottles Assn. Ipres. N.Am. div. 1982—), Nature Printing Soc., Writers Guild, San Diego Watercolor Soc. (bd. dirs. 1981-82), La Jolla Art Assn., Marine Hist. Soc., San Diego Maritime Assn., Nautical Research Guild. Home and Office: 1022 Park Pl Coronado CA 92118

HUBBARD, GREGORY SCOTT, physicist; b. Lexington, Ky., Dec. 27, 1948; s. Robert Nicholas and Nancy Clay (Brown) H.; B.A., Vanderbilt U., 1970; postgrad. U. Calif., Berkeley, 1975-77; m. Susan Artimissa Ruggeri, Aug. 1, 1982. Lab. engr. physics dept. Vanderbilt U., Nashville, 1970-73; staff scientist Lawrence Berkeley Lab. Dept. Instrument Techniques, Berkeley, Calif., 1974-80; dir. research and devel. Canberra Industries, Inc., Detector Products Div., Novato, Calif., 1980-82; v.p., gen. mgr. Canberra Semicondr., Novato, Calif., 1982-85; cons., owner Hubbard Cons. Services, 1985—; cons. SRI Internat., Menlo Park, Calif., 1979-86, sr. rsch. physicist, 1986-87; div. staff scientist Ames Rsch. Ctr. Space Exploration Projects Office, NASA, Moffett Field, Calif., 1987—; lectr. in field. Recipient Founders Scholarship, Vanderbilt U., 1966. Mem. AIAA, IEEE, Nuclear Sci. Soc., Am. Phys. Soc., Commonwealth Club Calif., Hon. Order Ky. Cols.

HUBBARD, JERRY LEROY, neurosurgeon; b. Eldorado, Kans., Feb. 21, 1952; s. Jack Leroy and Bonny Jean(Riegel) H.; m. Susan Joyce Davidson, June 6, 1975; children: Emily Jean, Timothy Cole. BA in Chemistry, U. Conn., 1974; MD, U. Tex., Galveston, 1978. Resident in internal medicine Providence Hosp., Portland, Oreg., 1978-80; resident in neurosurgery Mayo Clinic, Rochester, Minn., 1980-85, U. Wash., Seattle, 1985-86; pvt. practice Salem, Oreg., 1986--; dir. neurol. ICU Salem Meml. Hosp.; advisor Oreg. Area Trauma Bd., 1987--. Contbr. articles to med. jours. Mem.AMA, Oreg. Neurol. Soc., Western Neurol. Assn. (pres. 1986--), N.W. Soc. Neurology and Psychiatry. Republican. Lutheran.

HUBBARD, LYNN, III, lawyer; b. Kent., Wash., Oct. 8, 1940; s. Lynn. J. and Barbra Jean (Elsey) H.; m. Dale Audrey Miller, Dec. 23, 1966; children: Scott Lynn, Joshua. LLB, Western State U., 1974. Bar: Calif. 1976, U.S. Dist. Ct. (ea. dist.) Calif. 1977, U.S. Ct. Claims 1977. Assoc. Law Offices A.J. Merlo, Chico, Calif., 1976-78; pvt. practice Chico, 1978—. Bd. dirs. Am. Lung Assn. Superior Calif., Chico, 1983—. Served with USN, 1959-66. Mem. Calif. Bar Assn. (cert. criminal law specialist), Assn. Trial Lawyers Am., Calif. Trial Lawyers Assn. Republican. Methodist. Home: 5 Shannon Ct Chico CA 95928 Office: 12 Williamsburg Ln Chico CA 95928

HUBBARD, N(ETTIE) LARUE FALLIN, educator; b. Coolidge, Ga., Apr. 25, 1921; d. A.C. and Minnie Louisa (Robinson) Fallin; m. Joe D. Hubbard, Mar. 4, 1944; children: Susan, Joann. BA, Ariz. State U., 1962, MA, 1965, EdD, 1976. Instr. Glendale & Phoenix Union High Sch., 1962-66, Maricopa Community Coll. Dist., Phoenix, 1966—. Pres. InterClub Council of Ariz., Phoenix, 1985-86; active Women's Polit. Caucus, Phoenix, 1984-88. Recipient Women Helping Women award Soroptimist Internat. of Phoenix, 1986, Community Contribution to Outstanding Woman award InterClub Council of Phoenix, 1986, Pub. Svc. award for Edn. Svcs. Glendale-West Maricops Bd. of Realtors, 1980. Mem. AAUW (Phoenix br. pres. 1987-89), Delta Kappa Gamma Internat. (pres. Alpha Alpha chpt. 1972-74) Delta Pi Epsilon. Republican. Methodist. Office: Glendale Community Coll 6000 W Olive Ave Glendale AZ 85302

HUBBS, DONALD HARVEY, foundation president; b. Kingman, Ariz., Jan. 3, 1918; s. Wayne and Grace Lillian (Hoose) H.; m. Flora Hubbs, June 14, 1945; children: Donald Jr., Susan Tyner, Diane Schultz, Wayne, David, Adrienne. BA in Edn., Ariz. State U., 1940; JD, Southwestern U., 1956. Bar: Calif., 1956; CPA. Acct. Wright and Hubbs, L.A., 1945-67; pvt. practice atty. L.A., 1956-81; pres. Conrad N. Hilton Found., L.A., 1981—; bd. dirs. Trans World Airlines, 1977; regent Mt. St. Mary's Coll., 1983—. 1st lt. U.S. Army. Mem. Calif. Soc. CPA's, Am. Inst. of CPA's, State Bar of Calif., Los Angeles County Bar Assn., So. Calif. Assn. for Philanthropy. Clubs: Riviera Country, Los Angeles Country. Home: 1658 San Onofre Dr Pacific Palisades CA 90272 Office: Conrad N Hilton Found 10100 Santa Monica #720 Los Angeles CA 90067

HUBEN, KEVIN MICHAEL, firefighter; b. L.A., Mar. 18, 1956; s. Michael G. and Dorothy (Withers) H. AA, L.A. Harbor Coll.; BS, Calif. State U., Long Beach. Community coll. teaching credential, Calif. Student profl. L.A. County Fire Dept., L.A., 1980-84, firefighter, 1986--; health and safety rep. TRW Inc., Redondo Beach, Calif., 1985-86. Master Protection scholar, 1981. Mem. Nat. Fire Protection Assn., Calif. Fireman's Assn., Internat. Conf. Bldg. Ofcls., Am. Soc. Safety Engrs., Aircraft Owners and Pilots Assn.

HUBER, COLLEEN ADLENE, artist; b. Concordia, Kans., Mar. 30, 1927; d. Claude Irve and Freda (Trow) Baker; m. Wallace Charles Huber, Oct. 18, 1945; children: Wallace Charles II, Shawn Dale, Devron Kelly, Candace Lynette, Melody Ann. Student, UCLA, 1974-78; BA cum laude, Calif. Tech. U., 1985. Co-owner, artist The Rocket (community newspaper), Garden Grove, Calif., 1965-78; quick sketch artist Walt Disney Prodn. Co., Burbank, Calif., 1968-69; v.p., art dir. Gray Pub. Co., Fullerton, Calif., 1968-75; tchr. North Orange County Sch. Dist., La Palma, Calif., 1981-82; art dir. Shoppers Guide, Upland, Calif., 1981-82; pub., owner Community Woman/Huber Ad Agy., Anaheim, Calif., 1976-81; artist Bargain Bulletin Pub., Fallbrook, Calif., 1981-82; graphic artist, designer Van Zyen Pub., Fallbrook, 1982-85; cons. sales East San Diego Mag./Baker Graphics, Rancho San Diego, Calif., 1978-88; owner, artist Coco Bien Objet d'Art, Laguna Beach, Calif., 1986—. Author: Gail, 1980 (1st Antoinette Viking award); artist: Yearlings (2nd place award 1985), Penning (1st place award 1987). Recipient certs. North Orange County ROP, 1976-77. Fellow Zonta, Laguna Beach C. of C. (docent gallery night 1988); mem. Exec. Women, Calif. Press. Women Assn. (Orange county chpt. chmn. jr. journalism contest 1985-86, pres. 1986-87, 2d place annual communications contest 1981). Republican. Roman Catholic. Office: PO Box 5092 Laguna Beach CA 92652

HUBER, JOSEPH VINCENT, marketing executive; b. Bethlehem, Pa., Jan. 21, 1949; s. Joseph F. and Arlene M. (McGouldrick) H.; m. Rise Storcklein, Aug. 26, 1972 (div. 1988); children: Joseph V. Jr., Katy Kinsey. BA, Shippensburg (Pa.) State Coll., 1970; JD, Duquesne U., 1973. Bar: Pa. 1974, Ohio 1979. Atty. Joseph, Makoul & Keller, Allentown, Pa., 1973-78; asst. dist. atty. Lehigh County Dist. Atty.'s Office, Allentown, 1973-78; v.p. sales CMS East, Inc., Greensburg, Pa., 1978-82; pres. CMS East, Inc., Greensburg, 1982-87; mktg. specialist Fin. Capital of Am., Folsom, Calif., 1987—. Mem. ABA, Pa. Bar Assn., Columbus Bar Assn., Aircraft Owners and Pilots Assn., Ohio Assn. of Cemeteries (pres. Columbus, Ohio chpt. 1981-82), Kanesburg (Pa.) State Assn. Cemeteries (bd. dir. 1981-86), Prearrangement Assn. Am. (pres. 1984-85). Home: 110 Blue Ravine Dr Ste 200 Folsom CA 95630 Office: Fin Capital of Am 8201 Greenbelt Ln Fair Oaks CA 95628

HUBER, LARRY GENE, controller, consultant; b. Ephrata, Pa., Nov. 7, 1953; s. John Fry and Susan Stark (Garner) H.; m. Margaret Reuter, Aug. 11, 1979; children: Abigail Starr, Jessica Starr, Emily Albright, David Garner. BS in Acctg., Pa. State U., 1975; MBA, Claremont (Calif.) Grad. Sch., 1986. Cert. Mgmt. Acct. Mem. field staff Campus Crusade for Christ, Inc., Columbus, Ohio, 1975-77; successively staff acct., mgr. fin. reporting, chief acct. Campus Crusade for Christ, Inc., San Bernardino, Calif., 1977-85, asst. controller, 1985—. Mem. Nat. Assn. Accts., Phi Eta Sigma, Beta Gamma Sigma. Republican. Home: 26277 Mirada St Highland CA 92346 Office: Campus Crusade for Christ Arrowhead Springs San Bernardino CA 92414

HUBER, NORMAN FRED, communications executive, educator; b. N.Y.C., Sept. 14, 1935; s. Fred M. Huber and Hetty (Blum) Ryan; m. Marilyn Rose Chicky, June 30, 1962; children: Norman Fred Jr., Cherlye, Karl, Karen, Daniel, Thomas. Student, West Coast U., 1963-64, Orange Coast Coll., 1965-66, UCLA, 1977-78. Mgr. systems engring. IBM Corp., South Bend, Ind., 1955-62; asst. dir. computing Rockwell Internat., Downey, Calif., 1963-69; dir. computing Computer Credit Corp., Los Angeles, 1970-74; v.p. computer services Blue Cross of Calif., Los Angeles, 1974-79; mgr., consultant Coopers & Lybrand, Los Angeles, 1979-80; pres., founder Huber Data Systems Inc., Thousand Oaks, Calif., 1980—; cons., educator Ameritech/Bell Ind., Ill., Mich., Indpls. 1986-88, Bell Atlantic/Southwestern Bell, Silver Spring, Md., Kansas City, Mo. 1986-88, Hughes Aircraft Co., Long Beach, Calif. 1986-88, State of Calif., Sacramento 1986-88. Author: Data Communications "An Intensive Introduction", 1982, Data Communications "The Business Aspects", 1983, Data Communications "Glossary of Data Communications Terms", 1985, Migration to New Technology, 1986. With USN, 1953-55. Mem. IEEE, Data Processing Mgmt. Assn. Republican. Home and Office: 931 Emerson St Thousand Oaks CA 91362

HUCK, LARRY RALPH, manufacturers representative, sales consultant; b. Yakima, Wash., Aug. 10, 1942; s. Frank Joseph and Helen Barbara (Swalley) H.; student Wash. Tech. Inst., 1965-66, Seattle Community Coll., 1966-68, Edmonds Community Coll., 1969-70; 1 child, Larry Ralph II. Salesman, Kirby Co., Seattle, 1964-68, sales mgr., 1968-69; with Sanico Chem. Co., Seattle, 1968-69; salesman Synkoloid Co., Seattle, 1970-71; tech. sales rep. Vis Queen div. Ethyl Corp., Seattle, 1971-75; Western sales mgr. B & K Films, Inc., Belmont, Calif., 1975-77; pres. N.W. Mfrs. Assocs., Inc., Bellevue, Wash., 1977-86; pres. combined sales group, 1984 ; nat. sales mgr. Gazelle, Inc., Tomah, Wis., 1979-81; dir. sales J.M.J. Mktg. E.Z. Frame div., 1984-85; pres. Combined Sales Group, Seattle, 1984; nat. accounts mgr. Upnorth Plastics, St. Paul, 1984-87. Vice pres. Bellevue Nat. Little League; basketball coordinator Cath. Youth Orgn., Sacred Heart Ch.; dir. Bellevue Baseball Assn.; Served with USMC, 1959-64. Mem. Nat. Council Salesmen's Orgns., Mfrs. Agts. Nat. Assn., Am. Hardware Mfrs. Assn., Northwest Mfrs. Assn. (pres.). Hardware Affiliated Reps., Inc., Door and Hardware Inst., Internal Conf. Bldg. Officials. Roman Catholic. Office: 14925 NE 40th Redmond WA 98052

HUCKEBY, KAREN MARIE, graphic arts executive; b. San Diego, June 4, 1957; d. Floyd Riley and Georgette Laura (Wegimont) H. Student Coll. of Alameda, 1976; student 3-M dealer tng. program, St. Paul, 1975. Staff Huck's Press Service, Inc., Emeryville, Calif., 1968—, v.p., 1975—. Mem. Rep. Nat. Task Force, 1984—. Recipient service award ARC, 1977. Mem. East Bay Club of Printing House Craftsman (treas. 1977-78), Oakland Mus. Soc., Nat. Trust Historic Preservation, Smithsonian Inst., San Francisco Mus. Soc., Internat. Platform Assn., Am. Film Inst., Commonwealth Club. Home: 105-4 Hera Ct Hercules CA 94547 Office: Staff Huck's Press Svc Inc 691 S 31st St Richmond CA 94804

HUCKER, ROBERT JOSEPH, newspaper editor; b. St. Louis, Sept. 1, 1955; s. Arthur August and Una Marie (McGrath) H.; m. Karen Kay Wind, Feb. 28, 1986. Student, U. Mo., St. Louis, 1973-74; BJ, U. Mo., 1976, AB in Polit. Sci., 1977, AM in Journalism, 1978. Copy editor St. Louis Globe-Democrat, 1978; asst. state editor Kansas City (Mo.) Times, 1978-80, copy chief, 1980-81, night sports editor, 1981-82; asst. news editor Dallas Times Herald, 1982-83; systems editor San Jose (Calif.) Mercury News, 1983-89, systems editor, budget mgr., 1989—; instr. editor Santa Clara U., Calif. 1986. Co-Editor: Kansas City Times Style Book 1981, Mercury News Editing System Manual, 1989; contbr. articles to various newspapers. Curatoros Freshman scholar U. Mo., 1973-75. Mem. Kappa Tau Alpha. Home: 6352 Jarvis Ave Newark CA 94560 Office: San Jose Mercury News 750 Ridder Park Dr San Jose CA 95190

HUDDLE, WILLIAM ROYALL, military officer; b. Pulaski, Va., June 10, 1944; s. Charles Richard and Mary Frances (Akers) H.; m. Theresa Dean Beary, Dec. 26, 1966; children: Christopher, Matthew, Andrew. BA in Psychology, U. Va., 1966; MA in Personnel Mgmt., Cen. Mich. U., 1977. Commd. 2nd lt. USAF, 1966, advanced through grades to col.; pilot systems operator 12th Tactical Fighter Wing USAF, Cam Ranh Bay, RVN, 1968-69; fighter pilot 8th Tactical Fighter Wing USAF, Upon, Thailand, 1970-71; fighter pilot wing exec. officer 4th Tactical Fighter Wing USAF, Seymour Johnson AFB, N.C., 1971-75; air liason officer 3rd Brigade, 3rd Armored Div., Freidberg, Fed. Republic Germany, 1975-77; chief comd. briefing team Hdqrs. USAF Europe, Ramstein, Fed. Republic Germany, 1977-79; instr., squadron ops. officer 56th Tactical Fighter Wing USAF, McDill AFB, Fla., 1979-83; chief fighter assignments AFMPC USAF, Randolph AFB, Tex., 1983-85; asst. dep. commdr. for ops. 8th Tactical Fighter Wing USAF, Kunsan, Republic of Korea, 1985-86; dep. commdr. ops. 388th Tactical Air Force Wing, Hill AFB, Utah, 1986—. Contbr. numerous articles to military jours. Decorated with DFC with 5 Oak Leave Clusters, Air Medal with 24 Oak Leave Clusters, Meritorious Svc. Medal with 4 Oak Leave Clusters. Mem. Air Force Assn., Order of Daedalius, Red River Rats Assn. Home: 3097 Colony Loop Hill AFB UT 84056 Office: 388th Tactical Fighter Wing Hill AFB UT 84056

HUDDLESON, SCOTT ALDEN, military officer; b. L.A., Oct. 5, 1952; s. Homer Alden and June (Hetzel) H.; m. JoAnne Elizabeth Darrow, June 11, 1977; children: Stephanie, Joshua, Nathaniel. BS in Behavioral Sci., USAF Acad., 1974; MA in Communications, U. No. Colo., 1977; MS in Space Ops., USAF Inst. Tech., 1984. Commd. 2d lt. USAF, 1974, advanced through grades to maj., 1985; missile crew comdr. 90th Strategic Missile Wing, Cheyenne, Wyo., 1974-78; chief acad. instr. 4315th Combat Crew Tng. Squadron, Lompoo, Calif., 1979-82; systems dir. 13th Missile Warning Squadron, Clear AFB, Alaska, 1984-85; mission controller, dep. dir. mission transfer Consol. Space Ops. Ctr. Cadre Air Force Satellite Network, Sunnyvale, Calif., 1985-87; chief strategic planning U.S. Space Command/Plans, Colorado Springs, Colo., 1988—. Office: US Space Command/J5X Peterson AFB CO 80914

HUDDLESTON, FOREST WILLIS, psychological researcher; b. Kingsburg, Calif., Oct. 3, 1915; s. John Samuel and Myra Jennie (Beaver) H.; m. Allene Moore, June 3, 1944 (div. 1979); children: June M., Ralph Reed, Virginia Marie; m. Jacqueline Louise Barber, Sept. 3, 1986. Student, Redley (Calif.) City Coll., 1934-36, U. Puget Sound, 1936-38, Fresno State Coll., 1940-41, 47-48. Ordained to ministry Universal Life Ch., 1978. Mem. sales staff various furniture stores, Sacramento, 1959-70; research dir. Allied Research and Counseling, Sacramento, 1970-76, Huddleston Claibourne Counseling Ctr., Sacramento, 1983-84; ret. 1984. Asst. dir. Oak Park Youth Band, Sacramento, 1968-70; active various community service orgns., Sacramento, 1958--. Sgt. USAF, 1942-45. Home: 418 N Calaveras Fresno CA 93701 Office: Universal Life Ch 601 3d St Modesto CA 95351

HUDDLESTON, LAUREN B., futurist researcher, oil company executive, human resource developer; b. Nashville, Nov. 19, 1933; d. John and Chattie (Rich) H.; m. Gilbert Taylor, Aug. 25, 1950 (div. July 1972); children: Jeffrey, Charles, Marianne; m. Robert W. Fisher, Apr. 5, 1976. BA, Stephens Coll., 1980; MSW, U. Denver, 1984, PhD, 1988. Clinician, psychotherapy tchr. Halcyon, Inc., Lafayette, Ind., 1972-76; biofeedback specialist New Orleans Ctr. for Psychotherapy, 1976-78; cons. organizational design and human resource devel., orgnl. design The Anchoring System,

Denver, 1972—; adminstrv. dir., v.p. Bradden Exploration, Denver, 1981-86; pres., chief exec. officer Fisher Energy Group, Denver, 1986—; developer wellness and peer counseling program Srs. Resource Ctr. Jefferson County, Denver, 1982-84. Co-organizer Citizens for Responsible Devel. of Bergen Park, Evergreen, Colo., 1983; dean search com. Grad. Sch. Social Work, Denver U., 1982—. Mem. Nat. Assn. Social Workers, World Future Soc., Internat. Transactional Analysis Assn. (clin. cert.), Nat. Assn. Female Execs., Ind. Petroleum Assn. Mountain States, Am. Mgmt. Assn., Internat. Platform Assn. Office: Fisher Energy Group 1020 15th St Ste 4-I Denver CO 80202

HUDGENS, MICHAEL THOMAS, SR., editor; b. Wichita Falls, Tex., July 9, 1938; s. Grady Merwyn and Iris Ann (Hawkins) H.; m. Carolyn Anne McEntire, dec. 24, 1971 (div. Aug. 1984); children: Patric, Pamela, Michael Jr., Alexander; m. Cathleen Louise Craig, Nov. 10, 1984. BA, Loyola Marymount U., Los Angeles, 1977, MA, 1980. Dir., producer TV Houston Consol. TV Co., 1958-67; theater critic, arts editor The Houston Post, 1967-73; science writer various, 1973-80; editor G.M. Hughes Electronics Corp., Los Angeles, 1980—. Contbr. articles to profl. jours., mags. and newspapers. Home: 7760 Paseo del Rey #303 Playa del Rey CA 90293 Office: GM Hughes Electronics Corp 7200 Hughes Terr Los Angeles CA 90045-0066

HUDGINS, CHRISTOPHER CHAPMAN, educator; b. Richmond, Va., Mar. 22, 1947; s. William Jesse and Cathryn (Turner) H.; m. Marsha Lee Huffman, Aug. 22, 1970 (div. Dec. 1986); 1 child, Caitlin Crawford. AB, Davidson Coll., 1968; MA, Emory U., 1969, PhD, 1976. Univ. fellow Emory U., Atlanta, 1968-69; instr. English Old Dominion U., Norfolk, Va., 1969-71; teaching asst. Emory U., Atlanta, 1971-74, lectr., 1974-75; asst. prof. English U. Nev., Las Vegas, 1976-82; assoc. prof. English U. Nev., 1982—, chair English, 1984—; cons. in field. Contbr. articles to profl. jours.; editorial bd. The Harold Pinter Review, 1986. dir., lectr. Humanities Com. and Allied Arts Council, Las Vegas, 1980-88; bd. dirs. faculty devel. seminars NEH, 1987, 88. Mem. Am. Assn. Univ. Profs., MLA, British Film Inst., Soc. for Cinema Studies. Office: Dept English Univ Nevada Las Vegas Las Vegas NV 89154

HUDSON, ARTHUR DENNIS, management executive; b. Santa Ana, Calif., Dec. 24, 1946; s. Wilfred Graham H. and Delores Kathryn (Klingman) Ferrante; m. Claudia Joan Stenberg, Dec. 4, 1971; children: Stein, Erik, Summer Rae. BS in Math., Oreg. State U., 1968; postgrad., Portland State U., 1977-81. Sales rep. E.J. Bartells Co., Portland, 1972-76, shop mgr., 1976-80, contract mgr., 1980-83, div. mgr., 1983-86; treas. Western Asbestos Abatement Co., Portland, 1985-87; pres. C.R. Kerson Co., Vancouver, Wash., 1985-87; v.p. Allwaste Asbestos Abatement, Inc., Vancouver, 1987--, also bd. dirs.; instr. asbestos abatement Wash. Indsl. Safety & Health Dept., 1987--. Author, editor: Basic Supervision Asbestos Abatement, 1987. Active Eagle Creek (Oreg.) Boy Scouts Am., 1984-85. Served with U.S. Army, 1968-70. Mem. Nat. Asbestos Coun. (founder Oreg. and SW Wash. chpt.), Western Insulation Contractors Assn. (bd. dirs. 1985-86), Elks, Phi Kappa Phi, Pi Kappa Alpha. Republican. Roman Catholic. Home: 6316 Idaho St Vancouver WA 98661 Office: Allwaste Asbestos Abatement Inc 6906 B NE 40th Ave Vancouver WA 98661

HUDSON, DONALD J., stock exchange executive; b. Vancouver, B.C., Canada, Sept. 26, 1930; s. John Richard and Olive (McCreath) H.; m. Patricia Hockridge, Aug. 20,7 1954. B.A., U. B.C., 1952. With Shell Oil Co. of Can. Ltd., 1952-53; dir. sales devel. Can. Pacific Airlines, Vancouver, 1953-64; sr. v.p. Pacific div. T. Eaton Co., Ltd., Vancouver, 1964-81; pres. Vancouver Stock Exchange, 1982—; bd. dirs. Bird Constrn., British Pacific Properties Ltd.; bd. govs. Vancouver Stock Exchange; mem. adv. bd. Sta. KCTS, Seattle. Mem. adv. council faculty Commerce and Bus. Adminstrn. U. B.C.; bd. dirs. Can. com. Pacific Basin Econ. Council, Vancouver Bd. Trade; bd. govs. Simon Fraser U.; trustee B.C. Sports Hall of Fame & Mus.; mem. B.C. and Yukon Council of The Duke of Edinburgh's Award in Can. Mem. Niagara Inst. (adv. council). Club: Can. Club of Vancouver, Vancouver Lawn Tennis. Office: Vancouver Stock Exch, Stock Exch Tower Box 10333, Vancouver, BC Canada V7Y 1H1 *

HUDSON, DOROTHY MORGAN, civic leader, business and political consultant; b. Omaha, May 23, 1928; d. Glover Sr. and Maria Elizabeth (Agee) Morgan; student U. Colo., 1967-68, Metropolitan State Coll., 1972-73, Colo. Women's Coll., 1979-80; cert. Equal Employment Opportunity Commn. Acad., 1974-75; 1 dau., Ronnette Marie Marshall Davis. Owner, proprietor D.M.H. Enterprises; pres. City Park Sundries, 1980-83; investigator, conciliator, mediator arbratrator and judicature Colo. Equal Opportunity Commn., Denver, 1974-75, pay audit technician Air Force Finance Center, Denver, 1956-74; sales person, motivational facilitator and regional dir., workshop coord. Success Motivational Inst., Inc., Waco, Tex. Dem. committeewpman; cons. numerous polit. campaigns; Presdl. Nat. Del. State of Colo., 1984. neighborhood task force rep. Denver City Council, 1973. Recipient cert. of honor City of Denver, 1976, Colo. Centennial-Bicentennial Archivist Pin, 1983; named Colo. Outstanding Woman of Yr., 1979. Mem. NAACP, Nat. Council Negro Women, Colo. Black Women for Polit. Action, Denver LWV (bd. dirs. 1977-78, editor newsletter), Colo. State League Women Voters (dir., state editor 1983-84), Colo. United Srs., Internat. Trade Assn. Imports-Exports, Nat. Soc. Notaries, Lioness. Inducted Omaha High Sch. Hall of Fame. Coord., producer TV program PH Balance, Happenings in Community.

HUDSON, EDWARD VOYLE, linen supply company executive; b. Seymour, Mo., Apr. 3, 1915; s. Marion A. and Alma (Von Gonten) H.; student Bellingham (Wash.) Normal Coll., 1933-36, also U. Wash.; m. Margaret Carolyn Greely, Dec. 24, 1939; children—Edward G., Carolyn K. Asst. to mgr. Natural Hard Metal Co., Bellingham, 1935-37; partner Met. Laundry Co., Tacoma, 1938-39; propr., mgr. Peerless Laundry & Linen Supply Co., Tacoma, 1939—; propr. Independent Laundry & Everett Linen Supply Co., 1946-74, 99 Cleaners and Launderers Co., Tacoma, 1957-79; chmn. Tacoma Public Utilities, 1959-60; trustee United Mut. Savs. Bank; bd. dirs. Tacoma Better Bus. Bur., 1977—. Pres., Wash. Conf. on Unemployment Compensation, 1975-76; pres. Tacoma Boys' Club, 1970; v.p. Puget Sound USO, 1972—; elder Emmanuel Presbyn. Ch., 1974—; past campaign mgr., pres. Tacoma-Pierce County United Good Neighbors. Recipient Disting. Citizen's cert. U.S. Air Force Mil. Airlift Com., 1977; U.S. Dept. Def. medal for outstanding public service, 1978. Mem. Tacoma Sales and Mktg. Execs. (pres. 1957-58), Pacific NW Laundry, Dry Cleaning and Linen Supply Assn. (pres. 1959, treas. 1965—), Internat. Fabricare Inst. (dir. dist. 7 treas. 1979, pres. 1982), Am. Security Council Bd., Tacoma C. of C. (pres. 1965), Air Force Assn. (pres. Tacoma chpt. 1976-77, v.p. Wash. state 1983-84, pres. 1985-86), Navy League, Puget Sound Indsl. Devel. Council (chmn. 1967), Tacoma-Ft. Lewis-Olympia Army Assn. (past pres.) Republican. Clubs: Elks (vice chmn. bd. trustees 1984, chmn. 1985-86), Shriners (potentate 1979), Masons, Scottish Rite, Tacoma, Tacoma Country and Golf, Jesters, Rotary (pres. Tacoma chpt. 1967-68), Tacoma Knife and Fork (pres. 1964). Home: 3901 N 37th St Tacoma WA 98407 Office: Peerless Laundry & Linen Supply Co 2902 S 12th St Tacoma WA 98405

HUDSON, GARY MICHAEL, corporate executive; b. Lander, Wyo., July 28, 1946; s. Frank L. and Sarah Elizabeth (Jones) H.; m. Linda Ann Shaw, July 5, 1985; 1 child, Zachary Michael. BA, U. Wyo., 1968; MA, Western Ky. U., 1970. Tchr. Hopkinsville (Ky.) Pub. Schs., 1968-69; tchr., counselor Warren County Sch., Hadly, Ky., 1969-70; counselor, social worker Wyo. State Tng. Sch., Landes, 1970-72; counselor, adminstr. Cen. Wyo. Coll., Riverton, 1972-75; chief exec. officer Dignity Inc., Riverton, 1975—. Author: Crews in Industry, 1978; contbr. articles and reviews to profl. jours.; editorial adv. bd. Sta. KTRZ-TV, Riverton, 1989—. Bd. dirs. Riverton Bicentennial Com., 1976, Wyo. Assn. Retarded Citizens, Cheyenne, 1983-86, Nat. Assn. Devel. Disability Councils, Washington, 1980-81; adv. bd. Cen. Wyo. Coll. Trades and Industry, Riverton, 1989—, Pineridge Hosp., Landes, 1986-88. Recipient Regional Dir.'s award Region 8 HEW, 1977. Mem. Wyo. Assn. Rehab. Facilities (chmn. 1984-85, sec. 1985-87), Fremont County Assn. Retarded Citizens, Lions, Masons (master 1984-85), Hugh de Payne Commandry (comdr. 1985-86). Republican. Episcopalian. Home: 2980 Sinks Canyon Rd Landes WY 82520 Office: Dignity Inc 750 College View Dr Riverton WY 82501

HUDSON, KEVIN LEWIS, architect; b. Long Beach, Calif., Feb. 18, 1957; s. Walter Greer and Carol Jean (Bartlett) H. Grad. high sch., Bellflower, Calif., 1975; Student, Cerritos Jr. Coll, 1975-77, So. Calif. Inst. of Arch., 1979-81. Architectural license, Calif., 1986. Jr. draftsman Integrated, Inc., Paramount, Calif., 1977-81; assoc. draftsman J.P. Darling, Architect, Newport Beach, Calif., 1981-84; project mgr. James R. Newmeyer, Architect, Placerville, Calif., 1984-86; prin. Kevin L. Hudson, Architect, Placerville, Calif., 1986—. Mem. Placerville Downtown Assn., 1986—, Archtl. Review Com. Oak Knoll Estates, Placerville, 1987—. Office: 319 Main St Ste 6 Placerville CA 95667

HUDSON, LAWRENCE MICHAEL, investment company executive; b. Piqua, Ohio, Aug. 17, 1945; s. Lawrence Albert and Jetta Arlene (Kerns) H.; m. Sandra Kay Thompson, July 13, 1968; children: Michael Lane, Stephanie Renee. BBA, Ohio U., 1968. Agt. Lincoln Nat. Life Ins. Co., Greenville, Ohio, 1972-73; supr. Champion Internat., Bonner, Mont., 1973-76; salesman Cliff Trexler Realty, Victor, Mont., 1976-80; broker, owner Western Land & Homes, Stevensville, Mont., 1980-82, Sapphire Realty, Hamilton, Mont., 1982-84; investment exec. Piper, Jaffray & Hopwood, Missoula, Mont., 1984-85; in charge Hamilton br. Piper, Jaffray & Hopwood, 1985—. Bd. dirs. Expdns. Internat., Hamilton, 1988-89; chmn. fin. com. Stevensville United Meth. Ch. Lt USN, 1968-72. Named Realtor of Yr., 1978. Mem. Mont. Million Dollar Club, Piper Jaffray Pacesetter Club, Rotary (bd. dirs., pres. Hamilton). Office: Piper Jaffray & Hopwood 103 Bedford St Hamilton MT 59840

HUDSPETH, JOHN RICHARD, restaurant executive; b. Prineville, Oreg., May 4, 1943; s. John Manuel and Floreine Adrienne (Powell) H. Cook Chez Panisse Restaurant, Berkeley, Calif., 1979; owner, chef Bridge Creek Restaurant, Berkeley, 1985—. Recipient Best Breakfast in East Bay award Focus Mag., 1986, 87, One of Ten Best Restaurants in Bay Area, San Francisco Chronicle, 1985, 86, One of Best Things Eaten in 1986 award, Time mag., 1986, Best Restaurant In Bay Area for Money award Zagat Restaurant Guide, 1987, 88. Home and Office: PO Box 9098 Berkeley CA 94709

HUESO, ROBERT ALAN, microbiologist; b. San Pedro, Calif., June 29, 1953; s. Julio and Rose Marie (Boccaccio) H.; m. Pamela Korth, Dec. 31, 1988. AA in Biology, Harbor Jr. Coll., Harbor City, Calif., 1974; BS in Med. Microbiology, Long Beach State U., 1980. Cert. hazardous materials mgr. Med. microbiologist Nat. Med. Enterprises, Los Altos, Calif., 1977-79; fire dept. engr. Todd Shipyard, San Pedro, Caif., 1980-84; dir., environ. protection Northrop Corp., Hawthorn, Calif., 1985—; pres. Environ. Compliance Corp. Mem. No. Employee Polit. Action Com., Hawthorn, 1980—. Mem. Calif. Aerospace Environ. Assn., Calif. State Fireman's Assn., Calif. Mfgrs. Assn., Scripps Inst. Med. Rsch. Home: 2206 Mt Shasta Dr Rancho Palos Verdes CA 90732

HUESTIS, DAVID LEE, physicist; b. St. Paul, Dec. 20, 1946; s. William D. and Dorothy M. (Fuller) H.; m. Wray Hughes, June 2, 1968. BA in Chemistry and Math., Macalester Coll., 1968; MS in Chemistry, Calif. Inst. Tech., Pasadena, 1969; PhD, Calif. Inst. Tech., 1973. Fellow in applied physics Calif. Inst. Tech., Pasadena, 1972; fellow in physics SRI Internat., Menlo Park, Calif., 1973; physicist SRI Internat., Menlo Park, 1973-77, asst. program mgr., 1977-80, program mgr., 1980-88, assoc. dir., 1988—; vis. lectr. chemistry Stanford (Calif.) U., 1978. Editor: Electronic and Atomic Collisions, 1985; contbr. articles to profl. jours., chpts. to books; patentee noble gas-halogen transfer laser. Mem. Am. Phys. Soc., Interam. Photochem. Soc. Office: SRI Internat Molecular Physics Lab Menlo Park CA 94025

HUEY, WILLIAM EDWARD, health care executive; b. Lakewood, Ohio, Apr. 14, 1930; s. William Edward and Virginia (Higgins) H. BA, Dartmouth, 1952. Sales rep. Mobil Oil Corp., L.A., Tacoma, 1954-56; ptnr. Elmer Langguth Brokearge Co., San Francisco, 1957-75, Forrest Randolph Co., San Francisco, 1957-75; cons. Dalgety Ltd., San Francisco and London, 1976-79; internat. sales/mktg. exec. William Sherman Co., San Rafael, Calif., 1980-85; with Hay Career Cons., San Francisco, 1986-87; adminstr. Fear of Flying Clinic, San Mateo, Calif., 1988-89; Huey & Asscos., San Francisco, 1989—. Adviser Black Boys' Clubs, San Francisco, 1959—; mem. Job Therapy Calif., Spl. Com. on Parolee Employment, San Quentin; pres. bd. dirs. Booker T. Washington Community Svc. Ctr.; house organ U.S. Jr. C. of C. Contbr. articles to Future mag.; editor: (internat. newsletter) Greenline, Export Fedn., (with others) San Franciscan, 1960-61. With USNR, 1952-54, Korea, 1961-62, Vietnam. Mem. U.S. Navy League, World Affairs Coun. No. Calif., Kappa Sigma. Clubs: Dartmouth of Calif., Commonwealth of Calif. (San Francisco); W. Atwood Yacht (L.A.). Lodges: Masons, Shriners, Elks. Home: 258 Chester Ave San Francisco CA 94132-3215 Office: 258 Chester Ave San Francisco CA 94132

HUFF, BRUCE O., real estate investment and management executive; b. Newton, N.J., May 28, 1946; s. Floyd Clinton and Claire Verne (Attensia) H.; m. Judy Merle Bell, Nov. 26, 1966 (div. Nov. 1986). BS, Rutgers U., 1968. Salesman Calhoun Real Estate, Willingboro, N.J., 1968-71; sales mgr. Chesley & Alloway, Mt. Holly, N.J., 1971-73; sr. v.p. Mitsch Enterprises, Inc., Marlton, N.J., 1973-77; pres. Mohawk Group Inc., Marlton, 1977-80, Club Enterprises, Inc., Sausalito, Calif., 1980-84; exec. v.p. Paradise Properties Inc., Sausalito, 1984-88; acquisitions dir. Hendricks Devel., Mill Valley, Calif., 1988--; v.p. Burlington County Bd. Realtors, Moorestown, N.J., 1978-79. Mem. N.J. Assn. Realtors. Independent. Protestant. Home: 931 Bridgeway Sausalito CA 94965 Office: Hendricks Devel 655 Redwood Hwy Mill Valley CA 94941

HUFF, KENNETH O., oilfield executive, geologist; b. Daleville, Ind., Dec. 17, 1926; s. George Byron and Mary Ethel (Smith) H.; m. Donna Mae Zimmerschied, Mar. 25, 1957; children—John, Robert, Donald, Patricia. Student Purdue U., 1944-45, Ball State U., 1947-48; B.S. in Geology, Ind. U., 1956. Well logging engr. Core Labs., Inc., Williston, N.D. and Farmington, N.Mex., 1956-64, lab. mgr., sales engr. Farmington and Casper, Wyo., 1964-67, supr. Rocky Mountain dist., Casper, 1967-69, cons. geologist, 1969-72; pres. cons. geologist Adventures, Inc., Casper, 1972—; mem. dist. export council U.S. Dept Commerce, Wyo., 1977-83. Patentee in field. Served as sgt. U.S. Army, 1944-46, 50-51; Korea. Mem. Soc. Petroleum Engrs., Am. Assn. Petroleum Geologists, Wyo. Geol. Assn., Rocky Mountain Assn. Petroleum Geologists. Republican. Club: Petroleum (Casper). Home: 1106 Payne St Casper WY 82609 Office: Adventures Inc 535 N Lennox St Casper WY 82601

HUFF, NORMAN NELSON, computer science educator; b. San Diego, Apr. 22, 1933; s. George Kleineberg Peabody and Norma Rose (Nelson) H.; BS, San Diego State U., 1957; cert. UCLA, 1972; MBA, Golden Gate U., 1972; AA, bus. cert., Victor Valley Coll., 1972; Cultural D (hon.), World U., 1987; m. Sharon Kay Lockwood, Sept. 30, 1979. Chemist, Convair, San Diego, 1954-55, astrophysicist, 1955-56; mgmt. trainee, chem. engr. U.S. Gypsum Co., Plaster City, Calif., 1957-58; instr. data processing Victor Valley Coll., Victorville, Calif., 1967-70, chmn. data processing, 1970-81; owner High Desert Data Systems, 1972-82, chmn. Computer Sci., 1984-88; dir. Dep. Gen. Internat. Biog. Ctr., 1987, Congress Proclamation, 1987; mgmt. info. systems cons. Pfizer Inc., 1970-72, Mojave Water Agy. Calif., 1972-74. With USNR, 1950-54, to capt. USAF, 1954-67; Vietnam. Decorated Life Sav. award (Spain); recipient Life Sav. award Mil. Forces Spain, 1961, Tchr. of Yr award, 1967-68, Presdl. Achievement award, 1982, Presdl. Medal of Merit, 1983, 86. Mem. Calif. Ednl. Computing Consortium, Am. Mgmt. Assn., Calif. Bus. Edn. Assn. (treas. 1967-73), Inst. Aero. Sci. (pres. 1956-57), Soaring Soc. Am. (life). Author 5 computer sci. texts. Home and Office: 16173 Rimrock Rd Apple Valley CA 92307

HUFF, OCIE BURGESS, nurse; b. Tallahassee, Fla., Aug. 21, 1935; d. James Arthur and Ellareane (Austin) Burgess; m. Willie Yancy Huff Sr., Nov. 26, 1957; children: Willie Yancey Jr., Christa Jean Huff Relford. Diploma Nursing, Grady Hosp., Atlanta, 1958; BS in Nursing, Calif. State U., Hayward, 1974, MS in Edn., 1977. RN, Calif. Staff nurse Clarksville Meml. Hosp., Tenn., 1959-60, Presbyn. Med. Ctr., Albuquerque, 1960-62, Stanford Med. Ct., Palo Alto, Calif., 1962-64; nurse researcher NIH, Bethesday, Md., 1964-66; pediatric charge nurse Children Hosp. Med. Ctr., Oakland, Calif., 1966-74; asst. dir. edn. John Muir Meml. Hosp., Walnut Creek, Calif., 1974-86; owner, exec. dir. Health Edn. Svcs., San Ramon, Calif., 1986—. Author: (manual) Diabetes Patient Teaching Curriculum, 1977. Parliamentarian mem. Childhood Injury Prevention Coalition, 1978—; chair person health edn. com. Allen Temple Bapt. Ch., 1983—; mem. Birthing Alternative Task Force, 1982, Human Rels. Commn., Contra Costa County, 1986; bd. dirs. Am. Heart Assn., San Ramon. Recipient Cert. Commendation award Mayor Wlanut Creek, 1981. Mem. AAUW (bd. dirs.), NAACP (Oakland, Calif. br.). Democrat.Baptist. Home: 5 San Peedro PL San Ramon CA 94583 Office: Health Edn Svcs PO Box 2626 Dublin CA 94568

HUFFMAN, ESTELLE FLETCHER, educator, nurse; b. Yakima, Wash., Sept. 28, 1945; d. John Dee and Edith Marie (Iverson) Fletcher; m. William Walter Huffman, June 22, 1975. BS in Nursing, Loma Linda U., 1968, MPH with honors, 1972. Standard secondary teaching, health and devel., adminstrv. credentials, Calif.; cert. tchr. gifted and talented, Calif. Sch. nurse Rialto (Calif.) Unified Sch. Dist., 1968-69, Hemet (Calif.) Unified Sch. Dist., 1969-71; sch. nurse Sweetwater Union High Sch. Dist., San Diego, 1972-83, tchr. sci. and family life edn., 1983—; chmn. sci. dept. Montgomery Jr. High Sch., San Diego, 1983-84, 86-88; guest lectr. San Diego State U., 1974-83, master tchr. life sci., 1986, 88; coord. continuing edn. sessions sch. nurses San Diego County, 1974-80. Active in support ednl. and sch. health bills in Calif., 1968—; mem. heart edn. for young com. Am. Heart Assn., San Diego, 1980-85. Recipient cert. of appreciation Am. Heart Assn., 1982. Mem. Nat. Sci. Tchrs. Assn., NEA, Calif. Tchrs. Assn., DAV Aux., Yosemite Assn., San Diego Zool. Soc., So. Calif. Convertable Club, Delta Omega. Democrat. Office: Montgomery Jr High Sch 1051 Picador Blvd San Diego CA 92154

HUFFMAN, MARK PAUL, choreographer, educator; b. Bowling Green, Ohio, Nov. 9, 1959; s. Paul Richard and Sarah Jean (Bowers) H.; m. Joyette Speirs. BA in Dance Performance, Brigham Young U., 1983, MA in Choreography, 1986. Dancer Dancer's Co., Provo, Utah, 1979-84, tchr., movement edn., 1980-84; dance tchr. Brigham Young U., Provo, 1980-86, asst. dir., 1981-84; asst. choreographer World's Fair Expo '84, New Orleans, 1984; choreographer Internat. Spl. Olympics, Salt Lake City, 1985, Jackson (Wyo.) Hole Playhouse, 1986, 88, Bowling Green (Ohio) State U. Summer Theater, 1988, Olathe (Kans.) South High Sch., 1987-88, Rick's (Idaho) Coll. Showtime, 1988-89. Artistic dir., choreographer (performance) Young Ambassadors, 1984—; choreographer (performance) Lamanite Generation, 1984—. Mormon. Home: 112 Summit St Brooklyn NY 11231 Office: Brigham Young U 26 KMB Provo UT 84602

HUFFMAN, NONA GAY, investment retirement specialist; b. Albuquerque, June 22, 1942; d. William Abraham and Opal Irene (Leaton) Crisp; m. Donald Clyde Williams, Oct. 20, 1961; children—Debra Gaylene, James Donald. Student pub. schs. Lawndale, Calif. Lic. ins., securities dealer, N.Mex. Sec. City of Los Angeles, 1960, Los Angeles City Schs. 1960-62, Aerospace Corp., El Segundo, Calif., 1962-64, Albuquerque Pub. Schs., 1972-73, Pub. Service Co. N.Mex., Albuquerque, 1973; rep., fin. planner Waddell & Reed, Inc., Albuquerque, 1979-84; broker Rauscher Pierce Refsnes, Inc., 1984-85; rep., investment and retirement specialist Fin. Network Investment Corp., 1985—; tchr. money mgmt. seminars for sr. citizens ctr.; instr. U. N.Mex. Sr. Citizen Continuing Edn. Mem. Profl. Orgn. Women (co-chmn.), Women in Bus. (Albuquerque chpt.), Internat. Assn. Fin. Planners. Office: Fin Network Investment Corp One Exec Ctr 8500 Menaul Blvd NE Ste A-301 Albuquerque NM 87112

HUFFMAN, THOMAS ALEXANDER, internist; b. Ravenna, Ohio, Jan. 21, 1927; s. Iolas M. and Margaret E (Foster) H.; m. Elizabeth Louise Nank, Dec. 28, 1957; chidlren: Peter A., Daniel T., Anthony I., Michael F. AB cum laude, Dartmouth Coll., 1949, MS, 1950; MD, U. Rochester, 1952. Diplomate Am. Bd. Internal Medicine. Intern Ohio State U., Columbus, 1952-53, fellow cardiovascular disease, 1963-65; resident St. Luke's Hosp., Cleve., 1956-59, dir. cardiology, 1965-72; med. dir. Mt. Bell Tel. Co., Denver, 1974—; cons. U.S. Vet.'s Hosp., Cleve., 1966-70, Eastman Kodak Co., Windsor, Colo., 1981-83. Contbr. articles to profl. jours. Trustee Northeastern Ohio Heart Assn., Cleve., 1969-71; bd. dirs. Longmont United Hosp., 1987—. Lt. USNR, 1954-56. Fellow ACP, Am. Coll. Cardiology. Home: 9899 Ute Hwy Longmont CO 80501 Office: Mountain Bell 1005 17th St Rm 470 Denver CO 80202

HUFFNAGLE, NORMAN PARMLEY, physicist; b. Honolulu, Dec. 26, 1941; s. Norman Sylvester and Helen Louise (Parmley) H.; m. Cleda May Walker, June 7, 1980; children: Mitchell Walker, Norman Walker, Donley Walker Jr., Kent Norman, Craig Benjamin, Christian Thomas. BA, Drake U., 1963; MS in Sci. Edn., U. Nebr., 1969. Physicist Mine Def. Lab. USN, Panama City, Fla., 1963-66; mem. tech. staff Hughes Aircraft, Canoga Park, Calif., 1969-72; staff engr. Martin Marietta Corp., Orlando, Calif., 1972-78; mgr. Electro-Optics Systems div. Boeing Mil. Airplane Co., Huntsville, Ala., 1978-83, sr. staff engr. Honeywell Def. Systems div., 1983-87; sect. head Honeywell Precision Weapons div., 1983-87; mgr. advanced concepts Northrop Electro-Mech. Div., Anaheim, Calif., 1987—; dir. Village Green Lighting Dist. Contbr. articles to profl. publs. including IEEE Jour., Acoustical Soc. of Am., and USN Auto Testcon; holder 7 patents in sonar, electronics, lasers, fuzing, signal processing, and fiber optics control systems. Mem. Acoustical Soc. Am., Soc. Auto. Test Engring., Martin Marietta Mgmt. Club, Boeing Mil. Airplane Co. Mgmt. Club, Honeywell Mgmt. Club, Sigma Xi. Republican.

HUFNAGEL, RAYMOND JOSEPH, JR., marketing executive; b. Hanover, Pa., Dec. 22, 1941; s. Raymond Joseph and Mary Gertrude (Lawrence) H.; 1 child, Raymond Joseph III. BA in Psychology, U. Ariz., 1964; MA in Supervision Mgmt., Cen. Mich. U., 1974; postgrad., Indsl. Coll. Armed Forces, 1976, Nat. War Coll., 1981. Commd. capt. USAF, 1964, advanced through grades to col., 1981; asst. for telecommunications command and control Office Sec. Air Force, Washington, 1977-79; chief police and doctrine div. Comdr. in Chief Pacific Hdqrs., 1980-81, exec. asst. to dep. comdr. in chief, 1981-84; ret. USAF, 1984; mgr. new bus. staff Command & Control Systems div. Hughes Aircraft Co., Fullerton, Calif., 1984-85, mgr. Systems Design Lab., 1985-87, mgr. Pacific and Far East ops., mgr. Advanced Systems Lab., 1987-88, mgr. mktg. div. command and control systems div., 1988—. Contbr. articles to profl. publs. Mem. Air Force Assn., Air Force Communication Electronics Assn., Air Traffic Control Assn., Tech. Mktg. Soc. Am. Republican. Roman Catholic. Office: Hughes Aircraft Co PO Box 3310 618/H325 Fullerton CA 92634

HUG, PROCTER RALPH, JR., judge; b. Reno, Mar. 11, 1931; s. Procter Ralph and Margaret (Beverly) H.; m. Barbara Van Meter, Apr. 4, 1954; children: Cheryl Ann, Procter James, Elyse Marie. B.S., U. Nev., 1953; LL.B., J.D., Stanford U., 1958. Bar: Nev. 1958. With firm Springer, McKissick & Hug, 1958-63, Woodburn, Wedge, Blakey, Folsom & Hug, Reno, 1963-77; U.S. judge 9th Circuit Ct. Appeals, Reno, 1977—; chmn. 9th Cir. Edn. Com., 1984—; chmn. Nev. State Bar Com. on Jury Inst.; dep. atty. gen., State of Nev.; v.p., dir. Nev. Tel. & Tel. Co., 1958-77. V.p. Young Democrats Nev., 1960-61; chmn. bd. regents U. Nev.; bd. visitors Stanford Law Sch.; mem. Nev. Humanities Commn., 1988—; vol. civilian aid sect. U.S. Army, 1977. Served to lt. USNR, 1953-55. Recipient Outstanding Alumnus award U. Nev., 1967, Disting. Nevadan citation, 1982; named Alumnus of Yr. U. Nev., 1988. Mem. ABA (bd. govs. 1976-78), Am. Judicare Soc. (bd. dirs. 1975-77), Nat. Judicial Coll. (bd. dirs. 1977-78), Nat. Assn. Coll. and Univ. Attys. (past mem. exec. bd.), U. Nev. Alumni Assn. (past pres.), Stanford Law Soc. Nev. (pres.). Office: US Ct Appeals 50 W Liberty St Ste 600 Reno NV 89501

HUGGINS, TIM EDWARD, electrical engineer; b. Platte, S.D., Apr. 11, 1959; s. Glen Raymond and Viola Gertrude (Roth) H.; m. Marylou Gadiano Villamor, June 16, 1979; children: Jason, Jeannie. BSEE, S.D. State U., 1986; postgrad., West Coast U., 1988—. Farming Schindler Ranch, Reliance, S.D., 1980-82; engring., technician Pub. TV, Reliance and Brookings, 1980-84; vets. coord. S.D. State U., Brookings, 1982-86; electrical engr. Vitro Corp., Oxnard, Calif., 1987-88, Advanced Tech., Inc., Camarillo, Calif., 1988—. With USN, 1976-80. Mem. Internat. Test and Evaluation Assn. Democrat. Roman Catholic. Home: 1327 W Poplar St Oxnard CA 93033 Office: Advanced Tech Inc 751 Daily Dr Ste 220 Camarillo CA 93010

HUGHELL, JAMES EDWARD, physician; b. Boise, Idaho, Dec. 4, 1924; s. Samuel Levi and Mary (Mellors) H.; m. A. Louise Towne, Dec. 27, 1946; children: James, Barbara, David, Cecilia, Michael. Student, Wilamette U., 1942-43; BS, Oreg. State Coll., 1948; MD, U. Oreg., 1952. Intern Fresno County Hosp., Fresno, Calif., 1952-53; resident Fresno County Hosp., 1953-55; pvt. practice Atascadero med. Group, Atascadero, Calif., 1955-73; residency dir. Merced Community Med. Ctr., Merced, Calif., 1974-79; med. dir. GW Harley Med. Ctr., Ganta, Liberia, 1979-82; residency dir. Merced Community Med. Ctr., 1982—; assoc. prof. sch. medicine U. Calif., Davis, 1983—. With USCGR, 1943-46. Mem. Am. Bd. Family Practice, AMA, Am. Geriatrics Soc., Am. Acad. Family Physicians, Soc. Tchrs. Family Medicine., Rotary (pres. Merced chpt. 1987-88). Democrat. Methodist. Home: 315 Eric Ct Merced CA 95348 Office: 315 E 13th St Merced CA 95340

HUGHES, ALLAN BEBOUT, chamber of commerce executive; b. Boston, June 30, 1924; s. Edwin Holt and Gladys B. (Bebout) H.; m. Margery H. Hall, Dec. 27, 1947; children: Katherine, Lee Ann, Melinda, Sally. BA, Depauw U., 1947. Commd. USMCR, 1942, advanced through grades to col., 1970; ret. USMC, 1984; sales rep. ADT Co., Los Angeles, 1954-64; sales mgr. Ernest Paper Co., Los Angeles, 1964-68; mdse. mgr. BM&T Paper Co., Los Angeles, 1968-70; pres. Hughes Paper Co., Anaheim, Calif., 1970-82, Transpark, Inc., Anaheim, 1982-84; exec. dir. C. of C., Anaheim, from 1984. Pres. Federated C. of C. of Orange County, 1988—; chmn. bd. Anaheim Meml. Hosp. Home: 18661 Eunice Pl Tustin CA 92680 Office: care Anaheim C of C 100 S Anaheim Blvd Ste 300 Anaheim CA 92805

HUGHES, AUTHOR E., university president; b. Hoopeston, Ill., Nov. 4, 1929; s. Author Ernest and Nora (Clevel) H.; m. Marjorie Ann Herman, Aug. 21, 1956; children: James Gregory, Timothy Charles, John Andrew, Susan Marie. BS, Ea. Ill. U., 1951; MA, No. Colo. U., 1954; PhD, U. Iowa, 1960. High sch. bus. tchr. 1951-54, coll. bus. tchr., 1954-66; dean No. Ariz. U. Coll. Bus., Flagstaff, 1966-69; v.p., provost No. Ariz. U. Coll. Bus., 1969-71; pres. U. San Diego, 1971—; bd. dir. Calif. First Bank, Union Bank; cons. in systems field. Co-author: Automated Data Processing, 1969. Bd. dirs. United Way, La Jolla (Calif.) Cancer Rsch. Inst., 1985-88, Am. Cancer Soc., 1985—; mem. Pres.'s Commn. on White House Fellowships. Recipient Regional Brotherhood award NCCJ; named Outstanding Citizen Cath. Community Svcs. Mem. Nat. Assn. Ind. Colls. and Univs. (bd. dir.), Assn. Cath. Colls. and Univs. (bd. dir.) Assn. Calif. Ind. Colls. and Univs., San Diego C. of C., Beta Gamma Sigma, Phi Kappa Phi, Phi Sigma Tau, Delta Pi Epsilon, Delta Sigma Pi. Office: U San Diego Casa de Alcala San Diego CA 92110

HUGHES, BRADLEY RICHARD, marketing executive; b. Detroit, Oct. 8, 1954; s. John Arthur and Nancy Irene (Middleton) H.; AA, Oakland Coll., 1974; BS in Bus., U. Colo., 1978, BJ, 1979; MBA in Fin. and Mktg., 1981; MS in Telecommunications U. Colo., 1988; m. Linda McCants, Feb. 14, 1977; children: Bradley Richard Jr., Brian Jeffrey. Cert. Office Automation Profl. Buyer, Joslins Co., Denver, 1979; mktg. adminstr. Mountain Bell, Denver, 1980-82, tech. cons. AT&T Info. Systems, mktg. exec. AT&T, 1983-86, acct. exec., 1986-87; mktg. mgr. U.S. West, 1987—. Bd. dirs. Brandychase Assn.; state del., committeeman Republican Party Colo. Mem. Assn. MBA Execs., U.S. Chess Fedn., Internat. Platform Assn., Mensa, Intertel, Assn. Telecommunications Profls., Am. Mgmt. Assn., Am. Mktg. Assn., Info. Industry Assn., Office Automation Soc. Internat., World Future Soc., Internat. Soc. Philos. Inquiry. Republican. Methodist. Home: 5759 S Jericho Way Aurora CO 80015 Office: US West 6200 S Quebec Ste 310 Englewood CO 80111

HUGHES, CAROLYN SUE, business executive; b. Cin., Sept. 30, 1945; d. LeRoy Millard and Betty Jane (West) Hughes; student Secord's Bus. Coll., 1963-64. Lic. gen. contractor, Calif. With Shilliot's, Cin., 1964-65, R.L. Polk Co., Cin., 1965, Cin. and So. Bell Tel. Co., Cin., 1965-66; buyer Sterling Electric Motors, L.A., 1966-67; credit union clk. Beckman Instruments, Fullerton, Calif., 1967-68; with Federated Dept. Stores, Cin., 1968-69, Macpro, Inc., Loveland, Ohio, 1969-71, Orange Coast Advt., Inc., Santa Ana, Calif., 1971-73; pvt. acct., Orange County, Calif., 1973-75; office mgr./acct. L. Blain Co., Paramount, Calif., 1975-77; contr. Relkoff Constrn., Santa Ana, Calif., 1977; contr. Framing Div., Warmington Devel., Irvine, Calif., 1977, Brattain Contractors, Inc., Santa Ana, 1977-78, McQueen Electric, Inc., Riverside, Calif., 1986-87; v.p., contr. L. Blain Co., Paramount, 1978-82; owner C.T. Constrn., Inc., Paramount, 1977—, Jer-Jon Motors, Inc., Garden Grove, Ca., 1976-79, Fine Line Co., Romoland, Calif., 1986—; ptnr. Quality Excavation and Heavy Equipment Rental, Romoland, 1986—; agt. Preston Trucking Co., Paramount, 1982-84, Fine Line Co., San Antonio, 1984-88; pvt. acct., Riverside County, Calif., 1987—. Mem. Nat. Assn. Women in Constrn. (treas. 1978-79, pres. chpt. 1979-81, corr. sec. 1982-83), Nat. Notary Assn., Nat. Rifle Assn., Silver Lakes Assn., Smithsonian Assn., NAFE, Internat. Platform Assn., Household Goods Forwarders. Club: No. Am. Hunt (charter). Home and Office: PO Box 1024 Romoland CA 92380

HUGHES, CHARLES CAMPBELL, anthropology educator; b. Salmon, Idaho, Jan. 26, 1929; s. Charles Frederick and Grace (Campbell) H.; m. Jane Ellen Murphy, Feb. 6, 1951 (div. July 1962); m. Patricia Diane Devereux, Aug. 8, 1964 (div. May 1969); m. Leslie Ann Medert, Mar. 7, 1970; children: John Charles Campbell, Calisse Marie. A.B. magna cum laude, Harvard Coll., 1951; M.A., Cornell U., 1953, Ph.D., 1957. Assoc. dir., sr. research assoc. Cornell Program in Social Psychiatry Cornell U., 1957-61; asst. prof. anthropology, dept. psychiatry Cornell U. Med. Coll., 1959-61; fellow Center for Advanced Study in Behavioral Scis., Stanford, Calif., 1961-62; dir. African Studies Center, Mich. State U., 1962-70, assoc. prof., 1962-64, prof. anthropology, 1964-73, prof. anthropology and psychiatry, 1970-73; prof. anthropology, chmn. behavioral sci. div. dept. family and community Medicine U. Utah Coll. Medicine, Salt Lake City, 1973-78; dir. MSPH program dept. family and preventive Medicine U. Utah Coll. Medicine, 1979—; Mem. behavioral sci. test com. Nat. Bd. Med. Examiners, 1973-77. Author: An Eskimo Village in the Modern World, 1960, (with others) People of Cove and Woodlot, 1960, Psychiatric Disorder Among the Yoruba, 1963; editor: Eskimo Boyhood: An Autobiography in Psychosocial Perspective, 1974, Make Men of Them: Introductory Readings for Cultural Anthropology, 1972, The Culture-Bound Syndromes: Folk Illnesses of Psychiatric and Anthropological Interest, 1985; editor: Custom-Made: Introductory Readings for Cultural Anthropology, 1975; contbr. articles to profl. publs. Fellow Am. Anthrop. Assn., Soc. Applied Anthropology (pres. 1969-70), Am. Sociol. Assn., African Studies Assn., Arctic Inst. N.Am., AAAS; mem. Am. Ethnol. Soc., Assn. for Behavioral Sci. and Med. Edn. (dir. 1975-78, pres. 1979-80), Soc. for Med. Anthropology (pres. 1981-82), Assn. Grad. Programs in Preventive Medicine (pres. 1987), Soc. Study Psychiatry and Culture, Phi Beta Kappa, Sigma Xi, Phi Kappa Phi. Home: 7453 Enchanted Hills Dr Salt Lake City UT 84121

HUGHES, DICKSON, actor, composer, producer; b. Akron, Ohio, Dec. 14, 1922; s. William Richard Hucks and Bessie Mercedes (Sullivan) Laird. BA, U. Redlands, Calif., 1948. Music dir. The Sacramento (Calif.) Light Opera, 1966-72; music lectr. The Leigh Bur., Princeton, N.J., 1968-80; actor Tamara Internat., Los Angeles, 1984—; entertainer, writer 1949—; owner, producer, creator The Dickson Line, N.Y.C., 1962-83, Los Angeles, 1983—; music lectr. Writer musical score: Orinoco (winner ASCAP award, 1987); lyricist numerous songs. Served with USN, 1943-47, PTO. Mem. Am. Soc. Composers, Authors, and Publishers, Actors Equity Assn., Am. Fedn. TV and Radio Artists, Screen Actor's Guild. Home and Office: 1244 N Larabee Apt 1 Los Angeles CA 90069

HUGHES, EUGENE MORGAN, university president; b. Scottsbluff, Nebr., Apr. 3, 1934; s. Ruby Melvin and Hazel Marie (Griffith) H.; m. Caroline Mae Hartwig, Aug. 1, 1954; children: Deborah Kaye, Greg Eugene, Lisa Ann. Diploma, Neb. Western Coll., 1954; B.S. in Math. magna cum laude, Chadron State Coll., 1956; M.S. in Math, Kans. State U., 1958; Ph.D. in Math, George Peabody Coll. for Tchrs., Vanderbilt U., 1968. Grad. asst. dept. math. Kans. State U. at Manhattan, 1956-57; instr. math. Nebr. State Tchrs. Coll. at Chadron, 1957-58; asst. prof. math., head dept. Chadron State Coll., 1958-66, asso. prof., 1966-69, prof. math., 1969-70, dir. research, 1965-66, asst. to the pres., 1966-68, dean adminstrn., 1968-70; grad. asst. dept. math. George Peabody Coll. for Tchrs., Nashville, 1962-63, 64-65; asst. to undergrad. dean George Peabody Coll. for Tchrs., 1964, asst. to pres., 1964-65; instr. Peabody Demonstration Sch., 1963-64; prof. math. No. Ariz. U., Flagstaff, 1970—; dean No. Ariz. U. (Coll. Arts and Scis.), 1970-71, provost univ. arts and sci. edn., 1971-72, acad. v.p., 1972-79, pres., 1979—; cons. Nebr. Dept. Edn., 1966-70; mem. adv. bd. United Bank Ariz., 1982-87; bd. dirs. Ariz. Bank, Security Pacific Bank Ariz. Mem. staff bd. trustees Nebr. State Colls., Lincoln, 1969-70; co-dir. workshop tchr. edn. N.Central Assn., U. Minn., 1968-70; officer various fed. ednl. programs, Nebr. and Ariz., 1966—; mem. com. on grad. studies Am. Assn. State Colls. and Univs., 1979—, bd. dirs., mem. com. on accreditation, 1980—; mem. Ariz. Commn. Postsecondary Edn.; bd. fellows Am. Grad. Sch. Internat. Mgmt., 1980—; mem. Gov.'s Com. on Quality Edn.; Mem. Chadron Housing Authority, 1968-70; mem. adv. bd. United Bank of Ariz.; mem. Pres.'s Commn. NCAA; bd. dirs. Flagstaff Summer Festival, Ariz. Council on Humanities and Public Policy, Mus. No. Ariz., Grand Canyon council Boy Scouts Am. Recipient Chief Manuelito award Navajo Tribe, 1976, Disting. Service award Chadron State Coll., 1982, Flagstaff Citizen of Yr., 1988; Ariz. Acad. NSF fellow, 1963, 64. Mem. Math. Assn. Am. (vis. lectr. secondary schs. western Nebr. 1962), Nat., Ariz. edn. assns., N.Central Assn. Colls and Secondary Schs. (co-ordinator 1968-72, cons.-evaluator 1977—), Nat. Council Tchrs. of Math, Flagstaff C. of C. (dir.), Blue Key, Pi Mu Epsilon, Phi Delta Kappa, Kappa Mu Epsilon, Phi Kappa Phi. Clubs: Masons, Elks, Rotary (past pres.). Home: 1407 N Aztec Flagstaff AZ 86001 Office: No Ariz U Box 4092 Flagstaff AZ 86011

HUGHES, JAMES ARTHUR, electrical engineer; b. Wayne, Nebr., Feb. 15, 1939; s. James Wallace and Ruth Genevieve H.; m. Judy Lorraine Gaskins, July 19, 1967; children: Robert Linn, Benjamin Reed, Barnaby James. BSEE, U. Nebr., 1967. Electronic technician, space tech. labs. TRW, Redondo Beach, Calif., 1963-67; mem. tech. staff systems group TRW, 1967-80, sect. mgr. electronics and def. div., 1980-82, systems engr. space and def. div., 1982--. Designer solid state thermostat, generator. Deacon First Bapt. Ch. Lakewood, Long Beach, Calif., 1975-76, 78-80, 87--; mem. exec. bd. parent-tchr. fellowship, Grace Sch., Rossmoor, Calif., 1981-87. With USN, 1959-63. Mem. AAAS, IEEE, Nat. Soc. Profl. Engrs. Republican. Office: TRW Space and Def 1 Space Park S/1869 Redondo Beach CA 90278

HUGHES, JEFFRY SCOTT, corporate executive; b. Carmi, Ill., Aug. 4, 1954; s. Glen Leon and Lola Maxine (Stull) H. BA in radio/TV prodn., U. Ariz., 1976. Show producer Sta. KUAT-AM, KUAT-TV, Tucson, Ariz., 1975-76; dir. Sta. KVOA-TV, Tucson, 1977-78, news photographer, 1978-79; talent coordinator NBC Sports, Burbank, Calif., 1979; gen. mgr. Casablanca Flowers, Ltd., Tucson, 1980-84; pres., shareholder Product Innovators, Inc., Tucson, 1985—. Recognized for best TV news and feature story Internat. Assn. Fire Fighters, 1979; named one of Top 500 Flower Shops in World FTD, 1981, Top 100 Flower Shops in World, 1984. Mem. Casa Adobes Bus. Club, Interline Club, U. Ariz. Alumni Assn., Lions. Democrat. Mem. Christian Ch.

HUGHES, KENNETH GRAHAM, screenwriter, director; b. Liverpool, England, Jan. 19, 1922; came to U.S., 1976; s. Clement Graham and Edith Mae (Kenny) H.; divorced; 1 child, Melinda; m. Charlotte Gerda Paula Epstein, June 29, 1946. Student, London (Eng.) Polytech. Coll., 1934-1938. Sound mixer, program asst. BBC, London, 1939-42; freelance film editor England, 1942-44; dir. documentary films Film Producers Guild, England, 1944-54; freelance film dir. England, 1954—. Dir., writer: (films) Joe Macbeth, 1958, The Trials of Oscar Wilde, 1961, Of Human Bondage, 1962, The Small World of Sammy Lee, 1963, Arrivederci Baby, 1964, Chitty Chitty Bang Bang, 1969, "Cromwell", 1973, The Internecine Project, 1973, The Matarese Circle, 1985, Orient Express, 1987, The Queen's Own, 1988; also for BBC, 1973-76; author: High Wray, 1952, The Long Echo, 1953, An Enemy of the State, 1987. Recipient Brit. TV Acad. award Brit. Film and TV Assn., 1958, Brit. Critics award, 1959, Emmy award, 1959, Golden Globe award, 1960. Mem. Writers Guild Am., Assn. Cinema and TV Technicians U.K., Dramatists Guild N.Y., Screenwriters Guild Great Britain. Club: White Elephant (London) (hon. mem.). Home: 2218 N Beachwood Dr #301 Los Angeles CA 90068

HUGHES, MARK BRIAN, dentist; b. Highland, Ill., Jan. 25, 1956; s. Oliver John Jr. and Lois Marilyn (Schultze) H.; m. Kris Allison Cordts, Aug. 6, 1977; children: Brooke, Brean, Lauren, Shannon. BA, U. Kans., 1979; DDS, U. Mo., 1984. Pvt. practice dentistry Phoenix, 1984—. Mem. Phoenix Art Mus., 1988, Citizens for Better Dental Health, Phoenix, 1988. Mem. ADA, Ariz. State Dental Assn. (state chmn. children's dental health month), Cen. Ariz. Dental Soc. (com. peer rev. 1988, com. membership 1987), chmn. Phoenix chpt. 1987—, com. young dentists 1987—), N.W. Phoenix C. of C., Westside Study Club, Rotary (program chmn. 1987). Republican. Lutheran. Office: 15648 N 35th Ave Ste 107 Phoenix AZ 85023

HUGHES, MARY KATHERINE, lawyer; b. Kodiak, Alaska, July 16, 1949; d. John Chamberlain and Marjorie (Anstey) H.; m. Andrew H. Eker, July 7, 1982. BBA cum laude, U. Alaska, 1971; JD, Willamette U., 1974; postgrad. Heriot-Watt U., Edinburgh, Scotland, 1971. Bar: Alaska 1975. Ptnr., Hughes, Thorsness et al, Anchorage, 1974—; trustee Alaska Bar Found., pres., 1984—; bd. visitors Willamette U., Salem, Oreg., 1980—; bd. dirs. Alaska Repertory Theatre, 1986-88, pres., 1987-88; commr. Alaska Code Revision Commn., 1987—; mem. Coll. of Fellows U. Alaska Found., 1985—. Mem. Alaska Bar Assn. (bd. govs. 1981-84, pres. 1983-84), Anchorage Assn. Women Lawyers (pres. 1975—), AAUW, Delta Theta Phi. Republican. Roman Catholic. Club: Soroptimists (v.p. 1980—, pres. 1986-87). Home: 2240 Kissee Ct Anchorage AK 99517 Office: Hughes Thorsness Gantz Powell & Brundin 509 W 3d Ave Anchorage AK 99501

HUGHES, MICHAEL TERENCE, oil company executive; b. Bell, Calif., June 17, 1935; s. Paul Benjamin and Wilma Mildred (Dosher) H.; m. Violet Orodine Bachman, Aug. 29, 1959; children: Kimberly Arden, Aaron Shane. BS in Chem. Engring. with honors, U. Calif., Berkeley, 1958. Various engring. positions Chevron, La Habra, Calif., 1958-66; supr. div. tng. Taft, Calif., 1966-68; supr. O & CC, La Habra, 1968-69; area supt. Inglewood, Calif., 1969-71; project dir. Arabian Am. Oil Co., Dhahran, Saudi Arabia, 1971-76; prodn. coord. Chevron USA, San Francisco, 1976-85; chief design and constuction engr. San Ramon, Calif., 1985-87; operation mgr. ACT Operators group, Shekou, People's Republic China, 1987—. Mem. Marin Tennis Club (San Rafael, Calif.). Republican. Office: Chevron Overseas Petroleum Co PO Box 5046 San Ramon CA 94583

HUGHES, MICHAEL WARD, banker, accountant; b. Leavenworth, Wash., Apr. 13, 1940; s. Rowland Albert and Florence Ada (Mikkelsen) H.; m. Carol Yvonne Gagnon, Dec. 23, 1961; children: Martin, Kari. BA, U. Wash., Seattle, 1962. Acct. Security Pacific Bank of Wash., Seattle, 1962-69, asst. controller, 1969-75, v.p., 1984—; dep. controller Security Pacific Bancorp. N.W., Seattle, 1974-78, asst. treas., asst. sec., 1978—. Presbyterian. Office: Security Pacific Bancorp NW 1301 Fifth Ave PO Box 3966 Seattle WA 98124-3966

HUGHES, PATRICIA TANNER, management consultant; b. Syracuse, Dec. 3, 1940; d. Kenneth R. and Bernadine Tanner; 1 child, D. Scott. BS, SUNY-Brockport, 1962; MEd, Kent State U., 1974. Tchr. pub. schs., Ravenna and Hiram, Ohio, 1962-71; asst. dir., prof. human relations Kent State U., 1971-77; mgr. orgn. devel. and tng. Norton Co., Akron, 1977-80; orgn. devel. adv. Exxon Research & Engring. Co., Florham Park, N.J., 1980-83; mgr. orgn. devel. Lockheed, Burbank, Calif., 1985—. Bd. dirs. Community Action Council Ravenna, Ohio, 1965-70. Mem. Cert. Cons. Internat., Organizational Devel. Network, Internat. Registry Organizational Devel. Cons., Am. Soc. Tng. and Devel.

HUGHES, RICHARD SMITH, electronic engineer; b. Reno, Nev., Mar. 17, 1937; m. Janet E. Gaizutis, Jan. 24, 1959; children: Stanley R., Tamara G. BSEE, U. Nev., Reno, 1960. Electronic engr. U.S. Naval Weapons Ctr., China Lake, Calif., 1960-84, analog design cons., 1984—; instr. in linear cirs. Cerro Caso Community Coll., Ridgecrest, Calif., 1968—. Author: Semiconductor Variable Gain/Logarithm Amplifiers, 1967, Logarithmic Video Amplifiers, 1971, Logarithmic Amplifications, 1986, Analog Automatic Control Loops, 1988; contbr. articles to profl. publs.; patentee in field. Recipient Grozier prize Am. Def. Preparedness Assn., 1988, Profl. Achievement Alumnus award U. Nev., 1988. Home: 912 Jessica St Ridgecrest CA 93555 Office: US Naval Weapons Ctr Code 35205 China Lake CA 93555

HUGHES, ROBERT MERRILL, mining engineer; b. Glendale, Calif., Sept. 11, 1936; s. Fred P. and Gertrude G. (Merrill) H.; AA, Pasadena City Coll., 1957; 1 child, Tammie Lynn Cobble. Engr. Aerojet Gen. Corp., Azusa, Calif., 1957-64, 66-74; pres. Automatic Electronics Corp., Sacramento, 1964-66; specialist Perkin Elmer Corp., Pomona, Calif., 1974-75; gen. mgr. Hughes Mining Inc., Covina, Calif., 1975-76; project mgr. L&A Water Treatment, City of Industry, Calif., 1976-79; dir. Hughes Industries Inc., Alta Loma, Calif., 1979—; pres. Hughes Devel. Corp., Carson City, Nev.; chmn. bd. Hughes Mining Inc., Hughes Video Corp. Registered profl. engr., Calif; lic. gen. bld. contractor. Mem. AIME, Nat. Soc. Profl. Engrs., Instrument Soc. Am., Am. Inst. Plant Engrs. Republican. Patentee in field. Home: 10039 Bristol Dr Alta Loma CA 91701 Office: Box 723 Alta Loma CA 91701

HUGHES, THOMAS ANTHONY, electrical engineer; b. Waterbury, Conn., June 19, 1940; s. Charles Kenneth and Helen Cecilia (McGrail) H.; m. Ellen Arlene Wascher, July 4, 1964; 1 child, Audrey Lynn. BS in Engring. and Physics, U. Colo., 1970; MSEE, Colo. State U., 1979. Registered profl. engr., Colo., Alaska. Electronics engr. Dow Chem. Co., Golden, Colo., 1970-73, B.K. Sweeney Mfg. Co., Denver, 1973-74; sr. elec. engr. Rockwell Internat., Golden, 1974-79, sr. prin. engr., 1984—; engring. supr. Stearns-Roger Engring. Co., Denver, 1979-84. Author: Basics of Measurement and Controls, 1988, Fundamentals of Programmable Controllers, 1988. Served with USAF, 1961-65. Mem. Instrument Soc. Am. (sr.), Sigma Pi Sigma. Roman Catholic. Club: Indian Tree Mens Golf (Arvada, Colo.). Home: 6841 Devinney St Arvada CO 80004 Office: Rockwell Internat PO Box 464 Golden CO 80004

HUGHES, THOMAS JOSEPH, mechanical engineering educator, consultant; b. Bklyn., Aug. 3, 1943; s. Joseph Anthony and Mae (Bland) H.; m. Susan Elizabeth Weh, July 1, 1972; children: Emily Susan, Ian Thomas, Elizabeth Claire. B.M.E., Pratt Inst., Bklyn., 1965; M.M.E., Pratt Inst., 1967; M.A. in Math., U. Calif.-Berkeley, 1974, Ph.D. in Engring. Sci., 1974. Mech. design engr. Grumman Aerospace, Bethpage, N.Y., 1965-66; research and devel. engr. Gen. Dynamics, Groton, Conn., 1967-69; lectr., asst. research engr. U. Calif.-Berkeley, 1975-76; assoc. prof. structural mechanics Calif. Inst. Tech., Pasadena, 1976-80; assoc. prof. mech. engring. Stanford U., Calif., 1980-82, prof., 1983—; chmn. div. applied mechanics Stanford U., 1984-88, chmn. dept. mech. engring., 1988—; cons. in field. Author: A Short Course in Fluid Mechanics, 1976, Mathematical Foundations of Elasticity, 1983, The Finite Element Method: Linear Static and Dynamic Finite Element Analysis, 1987; editor: Nonlinear Finite Element Analysis of Plate and Shells, 1981, Computational Methods in Transient Analysis, 1983; editor Jour. of Computer Methods in Applied Mechanics and Engring., 1980—; contbr. numerous articles to profl. jours. Fellow Am. Acad. Mechanics, ASME (Melville medal 1979); mem. ASCE (Huber prize 1978), AIAA, Soc. Engring. Sci., Sigma Xi, Phi Beta Kappa. Office: Stanford U Dept Mech Engring Bldg 500 Room C Stanford CA 94305

HUGHES, VINCENT PATRICK, radiologist; b. Fremont, Ohio, Mar. 14, 1927; s. George Francis and Margaret Josephine (O'Connor) H.; m. Joan Catherine Fitz, June 21, 1952; children: Mark, Fr. Benedict, Francis, Marie, Fr. Brendan, Sheila, Theresa, Margaret, Martin, Monica. BS, Notre Dame U., 1948; MD, Ohio State U., 1952. Diplomate Am. Bd. Radiology. Gen. med. practice Port Clinton, Ohio, 1953-62; radiology resident Ohio State U. Hosps., Columbus, Ohio, 1962-65; radiologist Hoffman, Birmingham Assocs., Tiffin, Ohio, 1965-76, Modern Med. Imaging, Spokane, Wash., 1976—; clin. assoc. Med. Coll. Ohio, Toledo, 1970-76; dir. Breast Cancer Screening Ctr., Spokane, 1987—; chief cons. Breast Cancer Screening Ctr., Spokane, 1987-88; chief radiologist Deer Park Health Ctr. and Hosp., 1981-88; con. VA Hosp., Spokane, 1977-88. Contbr. articles to profl. jours. Mem. Spokane Radiol. Soc. (pres. 1987), Spokane Med. Sco., Wash. State Med. Assn., Am. Coll. Radiology, Radiol. Soc. N. Am. Republican. Roman Catholic. Home: N 9305 Gerlach Rd Spokane WA 99207 Office: Modern Med Imaging W508 Sixth Ave Ste A Spokane WA 99204

HUGHES, W. JAMES, optometrist; b. Shawnee, Okla., Oct. 15, 1944; s. Willis J. and Elizabeth Alice (Nimohoyah) H. B.A. in Anthropology, U. Okla., 1966, M.A. in Anthropology, 1972; O.D., U. Houston, 1976; M.P.H., U. Tex., 1977. Lic. Optometrist, Okla., Tex., W. Va. Physician's asst., Houston, Dallas, 1969-70; teaching asst. in clin. optics U. Houston, 1973-74, contact lens research asst., 1974; Wesley Jessen Contact Lens Rep., 1974-76; extern eye clinic Tuba City Indian Hosp., 1975; teaching fellow pub. health optometry U. Houston, 1975-76; Indian Health Service optometrist, Eagle Butte, S.D., 1976; optometrist vision care project Crockett Ind. Sch. Dist., 1977; vision care program dir. Bemidji Area Indian Health Service, 1977-78; optometrist Navajo Area Indian Health Service, Chinle Health Ctr., 1978-79; adj. prof. So. Calif. Coll. of Optometry, Los Angeles, U. Houston Coll. of Optometry, 1978—, So. Coll. Optometry, Memphis, 1980—; optometrist Shiprock USPHS Indian Hosp., 1979—, chief vision care program; Navajo area Indian Health Service rep. to optometry career devel. com. USPHS. Served with U.S. Army, 1966-69. Decorated Bronze Star, Purple Heart. Recipient House of Vision award 1974; Community Health Optometry award 1976; Better Vision scholar, 1973-76. Mem. Am. Pub. Health Assn., Am. Optometric Assn., Tex. Optometric Assn. Commd. Officers Soc., Assn. Am. Indian Physicians, Beta Sigma Kappa. Democrat. Roman Catholic. Contbr. articles to profl. jours.

HUGHS, MARY GERALDINE, accountant, social service specialist; b. Marshalltown, Iowa, Nov. 28, 1929; d. Don Harold, Sr., and Alice Dorothy (Keister) Shaw; A.A., Highline Community Coll., 1970; B.A., U. Wash., 1972; m. Charles G. Hughs, Jan. 31, 1949; children—Mark George, Deborah Kay, Juli Ann, Grant Wesley. Asst. controller Moduline Internat., Inc., Chehalis, Wash., 1972-73; controller Data Recall Corp., El Segundo, Calif., 1973-74; fin. adminstr., acct. Saturn Mfg. Corp., Torrance, Calif., 1974-77; sr. acct., adminstrv. asst. Van Camp Ins., San Pedro, Calif., 1977-78; asst. adminstr. Harbor Regional Center, Torrance, Calif., 1979-87; active bookkeeping service, 1978—; instr. math. and acctg. South Bay Bus. Coll., 1976-77. Sec. Pacific N.W. Mycol. Soc., 1966-67; treas., bd. dirs. Harbor Employees Fed. Credit Union; bd. dirs. chair svcs. for developmentally disabled of Long Beach, Inc. Recipient award Am. Mgmt. Assn., 1979. Mem. Beta Alpha. Republican. Methodist. Club: Holiday Health Spas. Author: Iowa Auto Dealers Assn. Title System, 1955; Harbor Regional Center Affirmative Action Plan, 1980; Harbor Regional Center - Financial Format, 1978—; Provider Audit System, 1979; Handling Client Funds, 1983. Home and Office: 18405 Haas Ave Torrance CA 90504

HUGHSTON, BOOTS ROLF, design engineering executive; b. Burbank, Calif., June 7, 1948; s. Roland and BeBe Hughston; m. Kathie Tringal, July 3, 1949; children: Boot, Dusty. AS in Electronics Engring. Tech., Heald Inst. Tech., 1984. Mgr. Columbus Camera, San Francisco, 1970-71; pres. North Beach Photo Fair, Inc., San Francisco, 1971--; engr. Intel Corp., San Francisco, 1985; sr. design engr. Systems XIX, Inc., San Francisco, 1985-88, pres., Mill Valley, Calif., 1986--; pres. Pasta-bilities, Mill Valley, 1987--; producer Bo-Pet Music Prodn. Co., Calif., 1987--; co-owner West Coast Records, Saulitor, Calif., 1988--; cons. Andrews Heyman, R.I., 1986. Composer: Meet Rock-a-Bye, 1986. Home and Office: 54 Mountain View Ave Mill Valley CA 94941

HUHS, ROY ELBERT, JR., lawyer, mayor; b. Oakland, Wash., June 22, 1948; s. Roy Elbert and Martha Mae (Hansen) H.; m. Maryann Sobotnik, Oct. 1, 1972; children: John David, Michael Edward. BA, U. Wash., 1970; JD, UCLA, 1973. Bar: Calif. 1973, Wash. 1975. Assoc. Shidler, McBroom, Gates & Lucas, Seattle, 1975-76; counsel mgr. law dept. Security Pacific Bank Washington, Seattle, 1976-88; assoc. Keller, Rohrback, Seattle, 1989—; instr. Bellevue (Wash.) Community Coll., 1978-85, Highline Community Coll., Seattle, 1978-85, Seattle Community Coll., 1978-85, Am. Inst. Bank, Seattle, 1978-85; lectr. on bankruptcies and troubled bus. to profl., trade and fin. assns., 1981-85; councilman, mayor pro tem City of Mercer Island (Wash), 1986--. Chmn. dist. campaign Slade Gorton Campaign for Senate, Seattle, 1986; mem. fin com. Rod Chandler Campaign for Congress, Bellevue, 1988; coach Boys and Girls' Club, Meracer Island, 1986--. Fellow and assistantship scholar UCLA, 1970, 71. Mem. Mercer Island Beach Club,

Omicron Delta, Zeta Psi (pres., v.p., alumni advisor 1975-80). Republican. Congregationalist. Home: 5625 84th Ave SE Mercer Island WA 98040 Office: Keller Rohrback 1201 3d Ave Ste 3200 Seattle WA 98101-3029

HUI, NORMAN HUNG, dentist; b. Canton, People's Republic China, Sept. 23, 1944; came to U.S., 1959; s. Kai Wood and Nancy (Ho) H.; m. Lucia Tao, Mar. 29, 1970; children: Kevin, Andrea. BS in Life Sci., U. Calif., Berkeley, 1967; postgrad., Oreg. State U., 1968-69; DDS, U. Pacific, 1973. Rsch. asst. U. Calif., Berkeley, 1965-67; pvt. practice Berkeley, 1973—; cons. dental asst. program Alameda (Calif.) Jr. Coll., 1985-86, Contra Costa Coll., San Pablo, Calif., 1985—; chmn. bd. dirs. N.E. Med. Svc., San Francisco, 1986—; chmn., bd. dirs. Gidden Bay Health Plan, San Francisco, 1988—. Treas. Orgn. Chinese Ams., Oakland, 1988—. Mem. ADA, Calif. Dental Assn., Chinese Am. Edn. Assn. (sec. Berkeley 1988—), Chinese Am. Polit. Assn. Contra Costa County, Lions (pres. San Francisco 1985-86, Best Lion of Yr. award 1987). Office: 2975 Telegraph Ave Berkeley CA 94705

HUI, STEPHEN WAI, infosystems specialist; b. Hong Kong, Hong Kong, Aug. 16, 1961; came to U.S., 1976; s. Hung and Yee-man (Poon) H. BS in Computer Sci., Northrop U., 1986, MS in Computer Sci., 1989. Asst. lab coord. Northrop U., L.A.; mktg. sales asst. Nynex Bus. Ctrs., Beverly Hills, Calif.; dir. computer & info. svcs. C. Thomas Ruppert & Assocs., Beverly Hills; mem. Orbiting Aeronautical Observatory, 1987-88. Mem. IEEE, IEEE Computer Soc., Assn. Computing Machinery. Office: C Thomas Ruppert & Assocs 122 S Robertson Blvd Los Angeles CA 90048

HUIZAR, HOPE ELAINE, mycologist, researcher; b. San Antonio, May 23, 1953; d. Alfred and Hope (Hernandez) H.; m. Joe David Hernandez; 1 child, Anita Elizabeth. BS in Biology, U. Tex, El Paso, 1975, MS in Biology, 1978; PhD in Microbiology, Ariz. State U., 1983. Electron microscope technician U. Tex., El Paso, 1976-78; teaching asst. Ariz. State U., Tempe, 1978-79, research asst., 1979-82, postdoctoral assoc., 1983-84, adj. research assoc., 1985—. Contbr. articles to sci. jours. Mem. Mycol. Soc. Am., Ariz. Soc. Electron Microscopy and Microbeam Analysis, Sigma Xi. Baptist. Home: 4614 W Commonwealth Pl Chandler AZ 85226

HUKARI, ROBERT WILLIAM, fruit grower; b. Hood River, Oreg., July 4, 1922; s. William T. and Esther (Lingren) H.; m. Helen M. Gordon, Nov. 24, 1950; children: Amanda, Martta, Althea, Lori. Student, Oreg. State Coll., 1940-42, Okla. U., 1942-43, N.C. State Coll., 1943; BS, Oreg. State U., 1947. Ptnr. Indian Creek Orchards, Hood River, 1947-49; mgr. Hukari Bros., Hood River, 1949-52; ptnr. Hukari Orchards, Hood River, 1952-58; pres. Hukari Orchards Inc., Hood River, 1959—; v.p. Nat. Council Agrl. Employers, Washington, 1976-80. Bd. dirs. NW Farm Bur. Ins. Co., Salem, 1976-84, pres. 1984—; bd. dirs. (life) Western Farm Ins. Co., Denver, 1980-87. Lt. U.S. Navy, 1942-46, PTO. Mem. Hood River Grower/Shippers (pres. 1960-64), Oreg. Farm Bur. (v.p. 1976-83, pres. 1984-88), Mt. Rescue Orgn., Am. Mt. Rescue Assn., Hood River Crag Rats (pres. 1949-50), Elks, Am. Legion. Republican. Home: 4665 Kenwood Dr Hood River OR 97031

HULBERT, BRUCE WALKER, corporate executive, banker; b. Evanston, Ill., Feb. 5, 1937; s. Bruce Walker and Mary Alice (Utley) H.; m. Linnette Ott, June 19, 1963; children: Christina, Jennifer, William. B.S. in Bus., Northwestern U., 1961. Sr. v.p. 1st Interstate Bank of Calif., Los Angeles and San Francisco, 1962-78; pres., chief exec. officer, dir. First Interstate Bank of Denver, 1978-84; exec. v.p. Western Capital Investment Corp., 1984—; chmn bd. Shelter Am. Corp., 1986—; pres. PV Mortgage Corp., 1988—. Mem. nat. bd. trustees, exec. com., former Denver regional chmn. Inst. Internat. Edn., 1979—; adv. bd. Jr. League Denver, 1980—; trustee, exec. com. Denver Art Mus., 1985—; bd. dirs. Denver Partnership, 1978—, Denver Civic Ventures, Inc., 1982-88, chmn., 1984-86; exec. bd. Denver Area council Boy Scouts Am., 1981—, Nat. Jewish Ctr. Immunology and Respiratory Medicine, 1982-88; mem. exec. bd. AMC Cancer Research Ctr., 1984—, vice chmn. bd., 1988—; trustee Mile High United Way, Denver, 1980—, chmn. bd., 1987-89; bd. dirs., exec. com. NCCJ, 1983—. Mem. Colo. Assn. Bank Holding Cos. (exec. com., dir., 1978-84), Am. Bankers Assn., Mortgage Bankers Assn., Denver Clearing House Assn. (pres. 1982-83), Denver C. of C. Republican. Clubs: Confrerie des Chevaliers du Tastevin, Cherry Hills Country, Denver Petroleum. Office: Western Capital Investment Corp 1675 Broadway #1700 Denver CO 80202

HULBERT, RICHARD WILKS, company executive; b. New Haven, Mar. 21, 1951; s. Donald Corydon and Elizabeth (Wilks) H.; m. Elizabeth Harlan Batrus, Apr. 20, 1974 (div. 1982); children: Jessica Wilks, Erin Elizabeth; m. Susan Lynn Milant, June 30, 1984. BA, Seattle U., 1977. Acct. Benson & McLaughlin, Seattle, 1977-78; acctg. mgr. Almac/Stroum Electronics, Seattle, 1978-80; contr. Tanaka Kogyo (USA) Co., Ltd., Kent, Wash., 1980-83, gen. mgr., 1983-85; v.p. fin. ops. AEI Music Network, Inc., Seattle, 1985-88; pres. OPM, Inc., Seattle, 1988—; also bd. dirs. OPM, Inc. Home: 14312 173rd Pl NE Redmond WA 98052 Office: AEI Music Network Inc 900 E Pine St Seattle WA 98122

HULEN, MARJORIE JANE, health care executive; b. Denver, Sept. 23, 1921; d. Perry E. and Garnet W. (Doty) Kellogg; student pub. schs., Redondo Beach, Calif.; m. Ray Romaine Hulen, June 10, 1950; 1 child, Lynn Robert. With A. O. Smith Corp., Los Angeles, 1948-60, exec. sec., 1956-60; exec. sec. Sterling Electric Motors, Los Angeles, 1960-61; research sec. Pasadena (Calif.) Found. for Med. Research, 1961-65; exec. sec. Profl. Staff Assn., Los Angeles County/U. So. Calif. Med. Center, Los Angeles, 1965-70, office mgr., 1970-74, bus. mgr., 1974-79, exec. dir., 1979—. Instl. rep. Los Angeles Regional Family Planning, 1977-79. Nat. Pub. Relations award Nat. Assn. Accts., 1979. Mem. Am. Soc. Assn. Execs., Nat. Secs. Assn., Soc. Research Adminstrs., Nat. Assn. Accts., Nat. Council Univ. Research Adminstrs., Assn. Ind. Research Insts., Nat. Assn. Female Execs. Democrat. Home: 2311 El Paseo St Alhambra CA 91803 Office: 1739 Griffin Ave Los Angeles CA 90031

HULETT, SHIRLEY JOY, marketing communications consultant; b. San Diego, July 30, 1943; d. George C. and Dolores M. (Haury) Haas; m. David E. Hulett, July, 1965 (div.) . BA in Journalism, San Diego State U., 1965. Editor Spectator Mag., mgr. Scoreboard Promotions City of San Diego, 1974; grant writer San Diego Unified Sch. Dist., 1975-76; media specialist United Way of San Diego County, 1976-79; acct. exec. The Gable Agy., San Diego, 1979-81; dir. mktg./communications Hillside Hosp., San Diego, 1982-83; nat. pub. relations mgr. San Diego Convention and Visitors Bur., 1985-86; 1981--; prin., Hulett Communications, San Diego, 1981--. Assoc. editor The Californias, 1988, Oriental Connection, 1988; contbr. articlesin field to mags. Recipient First Place award San Diego Press Club, 1978, 79. Mem. Internat. Assn. Bus. Communicators, Pub. Relations Club San Diego, N. San Diego County Press Club (v.p. 1979). Home: 10745 Escobar Dr San Diego CA 92124

HULICK, NORMAN ARTHUR, II, portfolio manager; b. Princeton, N.J., Apr. 10, 1941; s. Norman Arthur and Edith (Clayton) H.; m. Evelyn L. Hill, Apr. 10, 1965. BBA, U. Ariz., 1963; MBA, Calif. State U., Long Beach, 1967. Loan officer United Calif. Bank, L.A., 1963-68; dir. rsch. Valley Nat. Bank, L.A., 1968-74; pres. Investment Planning and Mgmt., Scottsdale, Ariz., 1974—; bd. dirs. Ariz. Organ Bank, Phoenix. Bd. dirs. Valley Leadership, Phoenix, 1983—, Ariz. Kidney Found., Phoenix, 1973—; mem. Paradise Valley (Ariz.) Homeowners' Assn., 1971—, Arizonans for Cultural Devel., Phoenix, 1984, Rep. Caucus, 1983. Recipient A.L. Slonaker Svc. award U. Ariz., 1978. Mem. Western Pension Conf. (bd. dir.s 1982-85), Phoenix Soc. Fin. Analysts, Fin. Analysts Fedn., Cen. Ariz. Estate Planning Council, U. Ariz. Pres.'s Club, U. Ariz. Alumni Assn. (bd. dirs. Phoenix 1971-78, nat. 1977-86), Wildcat Club (bd. dris. 1982-86). Presbyterian. Office: Investment Planning & Mgmt 4455 E Camelback Rd Ste D-238 Phoenix AZ 85018

HULL, ELEANOR HORNER, writer, editor, cons.; b. Dallas; d. Lee Meridan and Frances (Connor) Horner; student So. Meth. U.; spl. courses Columbia U.; m. Leon Gay Hull, Aug. 23, 1921 (div. July 1948); 1 child, Carol Jean (Mrs. Jack Raymond Clark). Free-lance advt. rsch., 1936-40, 41-42; promoter fashion booklets, copywriter, copyreader Sterling Agy., N.Y.C., 1942-44; supr. editor govt. tng. material War Dept. Q.M. Army Corps, 1944-45; account exec. copywriter Gussow-Kahn Advt. Agy., 1945-46; advt. mgr. Kramer Bros., 1945-46; publicity dir. Henry Glass & Co., 1946-50; pres. Shoulderite, Inc., 1946-51; instr. fashion dept., extension div. CCNY, 1951-63, supr. dept., 1959-63; lectr., instr. Traphagen Sch. Fashion, 1956-67; mem. staff Fashion Digest mag., 1957-67, assoc. editor, 1962-67. Served with motor corps ARC, 1942-45. Mem. Woman's Press Club, Alpha Omicron Pi. Designer Flag of States; patentee in field. Home: 3131 N 7th Ave Phoenix AZ 85013

HULL, JOHN KENNETH, JR., chemical engineer; b. Los Angeles, Apr. 3, 1929; s. John Kenneth and Helen Virginia (Kirk) H.; m. Carolyn Jewel Dean, Sept. 12, 1953; children: John James, Michael Ridgeway. BA in Chemistry, U. Colo., 1950; postgrad., U. So. Calif., Los Angeles, 1950-51; MS in Chem. Engring., Cornell U., 1956. Jr. engr. Mobil Oil Co., Torrance, Calif., 1957-60; sr. engr. C.F. Braun & Co., Alhambra, Calif., 1960-65; mgr. chem. engring. C.F. Braun & Co., Murray Hill, N.J., 1965-68; dist. sales engr. C.F. Braun & Co., N.Y.C., 1968-73; head petroleum processing C.F. Braun & Co., Alhambra, 1973-79; engring. mgr. C.F. Braun & Co., 1983-84, asst. chief engr., 1984-85, chief process engr., 1985-88, chief engr., 1988--; v.p. engring. PCL-Braun-Simon Ltd., Calgary, Alta., Can., 1979-83; bd. dirs. Particulate Solid Research Inst., N.Y.C., 1985--, Heat Transfer Research Inst., Pasadena, Calif., 1987--. Active, Boy Scouts Am., 1959-85, Scouts Calgary, 1981-83. Served to lt. USN, 1951-54, Korea. Engr Am. Inst. Chem. Engrs., Do-Si-Do Club (Pasadena). Republican. Home: 860 Winthrop Rd San Marino CA 91108 Office: CF Braun Inc 1000 S Fremont St Alhambra CA 91802

HULL, SUZANNE WHITE, retired cultural institution administrator, writer; b. Orange, N.J., Aug. 24, 1921; d. Gordon Stowe and Lillian (Siegling) White; m. George I. Hull, Feb. 20, 1943; children: George Gordon, James Rutledge, Anne Hull Cabello. B.A. with honors, Swarthmore Coll., 1943; M.S. in L.S., U. So. Calif., 1967. Mem. staff Huntington Library, Art Gallery and Botanical Gardens, San Marino, Calif., 1969-86, dir. adminstrn. and pub. services, 1972-85, dir. pub. adminstrn. and edn., 1985-86. Author: Chaste, Silent and Obedient, English Books for Women, 1475-1640, 1982, 88; editor: State of the Art in Women's Studies, 1986. Charter pres. Portola Jr. High Sch. PTA, Los Angeles, 1960-62; pres. Children's Service League, 1963-64, YWCA Los Angeles, 1967-69; mem. community adv. council Los Angeles Job Corps Center for Women, 1972-78; mem. alumni council Swarthmore Coll., 1959-62, 83-86, mem.-at-large, 1986—; mem. adv. bd. Hagley Mus. and Library, Wilmington, Del., 1983-86; hon. life mem. Calif. Congress Parents and Tchrs.; bd. dirs. Pasadena Planned Parenthood Assn., 1978-83, mem. adv. com., 1983—; founder-chmn. Swarthmore-Los Angeles Connection, 1984-85, bd. dirs., 1985—; founder Huntington Women's Studies Seminar, 1984, mem. steering com. 1984—; bd. dirs. Pasadena Girls Club, 1988—. Mem. Monumental Brass Soc. (U.K.), Renaissance Soc., Brit. Studies Conf., Western Assn. Women Historians, Beta Phi Mu (chpt. dir. 1981-84). Home: 1465 El Mirador Dr Pasadena CA 91103 Office: 1151 Oxford Rd San Marino CA 91108

HULLAND, STEVEN ROBERT, transportation executive; b. Syracuse, N.Y., Dec. 8, 1944; s. Robert Fedrick and Barbra A. (Seitz) H.; m. Melissa Ashcraft, Mar. 15, 1967; children: Steven R. Jr., James B. AA, Pensacola Jr. Coll., 1974; BS in Aviation Mgmt., So. Ill. U., 1980. Cert. air traffic controller; lic. private pilot, real estate agt. Pvt., infantryman USMC, 1963-65, advanced through grades to capt., 1982, U.S. Embassy security, 1965-67, air traffic controller, 1967-83, air traffic control officer, 1983-86, aviation ground support equipment officer, 1977-83, ret., 1983; store mgr. U-Haul of South Ariz., Tucson, 1984; crew chief surveyor City of Tucson, Ariz., 1984-86; field maintenance supt. Tucson Internat. Airport Tucson Airport Authority, 1986--; real estate agt. Century 21, Sheldon Realty, Green Valley, Ariz., 1983-86. Scoutmaster Boy Scouts Am., Green Valley, 1983--; bd. dirs. Camp Fire South Ariz., 1988. Mem. Lions. Home: 281 Placita Sin Fin Green Valley AZ 85614 Office: Tucson Airport Authority Tucson Internat Airport Tucson AZ 85706

HULLAR, THEODORE LEE, university chancellor; b. Mar. 19, 1935; m. Joan J. Miller, Aug. 2, 1958; children: Theodore W., Timothy E. BS with high distinction, U. Minn., 1957, PhD in Biochemistry, 1963. Asst. prof. medicinal chemistry SUNY, Buffalo, 1964-69, assoc. prof., 1969-75, assoc. dean grad. sch., 1969-71; dep. commr. programs and research N.Y. State Dept. Environ. Conservation, 1975-79; assoc. dir. Cornell U. Agrl. Experiment Sta., 1979-81, dir., 1981-84; assoc. dir. research N.Y. State Coll. Agriculture and Life Scis., Cornell U., 1979-81; adj. prof. natural resources Cornell U. Agrl. Experiment Sta., 1979-81; prof. natural resources, dir. research N.Y. State Coll. Agriculture and Life Scis., Cornell U., 1981-84; exec. vice chancellor U. Calif., Riverside, 1984-85, chancellor, prof. biochem., 1985-87; chancellor, prof. environ. toxicology U. Calif., Davis, 1987—; chmn. hazardous waste mgmt. com. So. Calif. Assn. Govts., 1986-87, chmn. air quality task force, 1985-87, mem. regional adv. council, 1985-87; chmn. com. on environment Nat. Assn. State Univs. and Land Grant Colls., 1985—, com. on biotech., 1985—, chmn. program devel. subcom., 1982—, coord. Agr. Rsch. Initiative; chmn. Gov. Deukmejian's Task Force on Toxics, Waste and Tech., 1985-86; chmn. bd. agr. Nat. Rsch. Council; interim chmn. Calif. Council on Sci. and Tech.; lectr. various orgns. Contbr. articles to profl. jours. Commr. Environ. Quality Erie County, N.Y., 1974-75; alternate to Gov. N.Y. on Delaware and Susquehanna River Basin Commns., 1975-79; mem. N.Y. State Agrl. Resources Commn., 1974-75; mem. Arlington Heights Greenbelt Study Com., 1986-87; mem. Monday Morning Group, 1985-87; active various community orgns. NSF postdoctoral fellow SUNY Buffalo, 1963-64. Mem. Am. Chem. Soc., AAAS, Chem. Soc. London, Regional Inst. So. Calif., Greater Riverside C. of C., (bd. dirs. 1985-87), Sigma Xi. Home: 16 College Park Davis CA 95616 Office: U Calif Davis Office of Chancellor Davis CA 95616

HULSE, RALPH ROBERT, management consultant; b. St. Joseph, Mo., Jan. 14, 1935; s. Ralph Raymond and Eva Laduska (Hatfield) H.; m. Gwen Lea Bartosh, May 21, 1957 (div. 1959); m. Jutta-Beaujean, Jan. 14, 1961. AB, Cen. Meth. Coll., 1957; MEd, U. Mo., 1965. Continuing edn. programmer U. Mo., Columbia, 1969-71; dir. edn. tng. North Kansas City (Mo.) Meml. Hosp., 1971-74; mgmt. cons. Lawrence-Leiter, Kansas City, 1974-77; adminstr. U.S. Congress, 6th dist., Mo., 1977-78; bus. cons. Hulse & Assocs., Kansas City, 1978-88; adminstr. Sales Tng. Inst. div. Mile Hi Bus. Coll., Denver, 1988-89; bus. con. Hulse & Assocs., Denver, 1989—; founder, bd. dirs. Opportunity Industry Inc., St. Joseph, 1965-71; pres. State Adult Edn. Assn., Mo., 1978-79. Contbr. articles to profl. jours. (Nat. Pub. award 1974, 75). Served with U.S. Army, 1959-61. Mem. Colo. Cons. Assn. (founder, pres. 1985—). Republican. Methodist. Home and Office: 8706 Independence Way Arvada CO 80005

HULSEY, RUTH LENORA, state official; b. Athens, Ga., Nov. 28, 1927; d. Joseph Alonzo and Frances Rebecca (Bell) Johnson; student Pasadena Jr. Coll., 1938-40, San Bernardino Valley Coll., 1963-65; m. William A. Hulsey III, Mar. 28, 1958; children—William A., Stephen G., Alicia A. With State of Calif. Employment Devel. Office, 1960—, supr., San Bernardino Field Dept. Office, 1969-75, So. Region Office, Riverside, 1975-78, employment program mgr., asst. mgr. Ontario Field Office, 1979-80, employment program mgr., mgr. Fontana Field Office, 1980—; dir. Calif. State Employees Credit Union, 1972-75, mem. employer adv. council, 1978—. Mem. edn. com. Urban League, 1965, mem., 1965—; mem. Arrowhead Allied Arts Council, 1966-72; mem. Social Lites, 1963—, pres., 1964-66, 80-81, bd. dirs., 1980—, rec. sec., 1981—. Mem. Internat. Assn. Personnel in Employment Security, Calif. State Employees Assn., Bloomington C. of C., Fontana C. of C., Rialto C. of C., San Bernardino C. of C. Democrat. Methodist. Home: 1246 E Shamrock Ave San Bernardino CA 92410 Office: State of Calif Employment Devel Dept Office 17590 Foothill Blvd Fontana CA 92335

HULTQUIST, STEPHEN ROBERT, packaging company executive; b. Freeport, Ill., Dec. 25, 1947; s. Charles William and Patricia Rose (Fordyce) H.; m. Cathy Ann Leggett, Oct. 27, 1973; children: Robert Stephen, Mark Andrew, Kenneth William, Justin Michael. AA in Bus. Mgmt., Cerritos Coll., 1980. Cert. transp. coord. Prodn. coord. Southwest Forest Industries, Commerce, Calif., 1969-70, 77-78; prodn. mgr. George II, Cerritos, Calif., 1978-79, Ace Nat. Paper Box Co., L.A., 1979-80; plant mgr. O.E. Clark Paper Box Co., Vernon, Calif., 1980-82, 86-87; gen. mgr. Marfred Industries, No. Hollywood, Calif., 1982-83; prodn. mgr. Mid Cities Paper Box Co., Bell Gardens, Calif., 1970-77, 83-85, Gleason Industries, Hawthorne, Calif., 1985-86; asst. plant mgr. Ivy Hill Corp., Vernon, 1987—. Com. chairperson, Boy Scouts Am., La Mirada, Calif., 1984—. With U.S. Army, 1965-68. Mem. Am. Legion. Republican. Mormon. Home: 15235 Borda Rd La Mirada CA 90638

HUMBLE, JIM VERN, mining executive; b. Loxley, Ala., Dec. 27, 1932; s. Max Melvin and Esther (Sherwood) H.; m. Theresa Jean Lane, 1954 (div. 1965); children: Paris Jean, James Max; divorced; children: Jessica Paris, Shawn Christopher. Electronic technician Hughes Aircraft, Culver City, Calif., 1953-54; supr. electronic inspection guided missile div. Nortronics, Anaheim, Calif., 1954-60; cons. electronics Calif., 1960-78; pres. Action Mining Services, Los Angeles and Las Vegas (Nev.), 1978—. Author: Non-Cyanide Leaching, 1982, Science of Integrity, 1985, Modern Amalgamation, 1987; patentee in field. Served as sgt. USMC, 1950-52. Republican. Office: Action Mining Svcs 4460 W Reno Ave D Las Vegas NV 89118

HUME, STEPHEN, writer, editor; b. Blackpool, Lancashire, Eng., Jan. 1, 1947; came to Can. 1948; s. James and Joyce (Potter) H.; m. Susan Winifred Mayse, July 29, 1970. B.A., U. Victoria, B.C., 1971. Reporter Victoria Times, B.C., Can., 1968-71; Arctic corr. Edmonton Jour., Yellowknife, NWT, Can., 1971-73; city editor Edmonton Jour., Edmonton, Alta., Can., 1975-77; weekend editor Edmonton Jour., Edmonton, Alta., 1977-78, news editor, 1978-81, editor, 1981-87, gen. mgr., 1987—. Author: (poetry, essays) Signs Against An Empty Sky, 1980, And the House Sank Like a Ship in the Long Prairie Grass, 1987, Ghost Camps: Memory and Myth on Canada's Frontier, 1989. Office: Edmonton Jour, Box 2421, Edmonton, AB Canada T5J 2S6

HUMMEL, DAVID MARTIN, JR., civil engineer, consultant; b. New Haven, Nov. 22, 1940; s. David Martin and Elizabeth (Wilkinson) H.; m. Cynthia Nash, Dec. 21, 1963; children: Eric, Karl. B of Engring, Yale U., 1962; MS, Stanford U., 1963. Registered profl. engr., Mont., Wyo. Sr. engr. Bechtel Corp., San Francisco, 1963-69; chief engr. Empire Sand and Gravel, Billings, Mont., 1969-76; v.p. COP Constrn., Billings, 1976-80; sr. engr. Chen-No., Inc. (formerly No. Engring & Tersting), Billings, 1980-87, div. mgr., 1987—. Elected mem. City Charter Commn., Billings, 1975-77; trustee Rocky Mountain Coll., Billings, 1981-86. Fellow ASCE (pres. Mont. chpt. 1976); mem. Nat. Soc. Profl. Engrs. (chmn. nat. com. 1988—, one of Outstanding Engrs. 1975), Billings C. of C. (com. chmn. 1975). Club: Hilands (Billings). Lodge: Rotary. Office: Chen-No Inc 600 S 25th St PO Box 30615 Billings MT 59107

HUMMEL, JACKSON LOWE, lawyer; b. Ranger, Tex., July 19, 1933; s. Charles Andrew and Iris (Lowe) H.; m. Carol Mary Finn, Oct. 19, 1961; children: Kimberley Anne, Charles Jackson. BS in Chem. Engr., U. Tex., 1956; LLB, South Tex. Coll. Law, 1962. Bar: Tex., 1962, Ohio, 1964, Colo., 1972, U.S. Patent Office, 1967, U.S. Customs and Patent Appeals, 1976, U.S. Ct. Appeals (10th cir.) 1972, U.S. Supreme Ct., 1972. Process engr. Lubrizol Corp., Deer Park, Tex., 1956-60; project engr. Lubrizol Corp., Deer Park, 1960-63; atty. Lubrizol Corp., Wickliffe, Ohio, 1963-65; patent atty. Monsanto Chem. Co., Decatur, Ala., 1965-67; patent counsel Marathon Oil Co., Littleton, Colo., 1967—; bd. dirs. Bow Mar South, Inc.. Patentee use of high water content oil-external micellar solutions for extinguishing fires; inhibition of saline water intrusion into fresh water aquifers, use of micellar solutions to improve perforating process. Bd. dirs. Colo. div. Am. Cancer Soc., 1972-76, Lower Bowles Water Co., Littleton, 1986—, SunSet Ridge Estates, Fraser, Colo., 1984—, Town Hall Arts Ctr., Littleton, 1987—, treas., 1987—, chmn. bldg. com.; bd. dirs. Swedish Med. Ctr. Found., vice-chmn., 1982-83, chmn. ann. support com., 1976.; chmn. Swedish Med. Ctr. Devel. Council, 1976; mem. Citizens' Pub. Relations Adv. Com. Arapahoe County Sch. Dist., 1975. Capt. AUS, 1969. Mem. Tex. Bar Assn., Ohio Bar Assn., Colo. Bar Assn., Arapahoe County Bar Assn., Am. Patent Law Assn., Licensing Execs. Soc. (mem. chmn. 1986-88, trustee 1988—), Am. Corp. Counsel Assn., Am. Intellectual Property Lawyers Assn. (chmn. econ. com. 1984-86), Kiwanis (pres. 1970-71). Republican. Office: Marathon Oil Co 7400 S Broadway Littleton CO 80160

HUMPHERYS, A. RICH, state police administrator; b. Boise, Idaho, July 14, 1933; s. Rich and Evaline (Liggett) H.; m. Shirley Ann Evans, Aug. 20, 1956; children: Robert Rich, Randy Ray. Student, U. Idaho, 1973, Idaho State U., 1973-74. Roving port Idaho State Police, Boise, 1958-61; from patrolman to sgt. Idaho State Police, Lewiston and Pocatello, 1961-78; lt. Idaho State Police, Pocatello, 1978-83; capt. Idaho State Police, Boise, 1983-86, supt., 1986—; mem. Idaho Traffic Safety Commn., 1986—, Peace Officers Standards and Tng. Council, Boise, 1986-87. V.p. PTA, Lewiston, 1964, pres., 1965. With USN, 1950-54, Korea. Cited for Disting. Service Gov. Idaho, 1976. Mem. Internat. Assn. Chiefs of Police, Idaho Chiefs' Assn., Idaho Peace Officers Assn., Elks. Democrat. Mem. LDS Ch. Office: Idaho State Police 3311 W State St PO Box 55 Boise ID 83707

HUMPHREY, JOHN JULIUS, university program director; b. Booneville, Miss., Jan. 22, 1926; s. George Duke and Josephine (Robertson) H.; m. Mary Margaret Ryan, Jan. 19, 1949; children: George Duke II, Laurie Ann. BS, Miss. State U., 1945; BA, U. Wyo., 1946, MA, 1964; postgrad., U. Ariz., 1969-71. Pres. J.J. Humphrey Co., Laramie, Wyo., 1947-68; lectr. History U. Ariz., Tucson, 1969-71, asst. dir. placement, 1969-70, dir. scholarships, awards, 1970-72, dir. office of scholarships and fin. aid, 1972-84, dir. scholarship devel., 1970—. Sec. Baird Found. ,Tucson, 1970—; bd. dirs. Bendalin Fund, Phoenix, 1976—, Cecioppo Found., Tucson, 1986—; cons. De Mund Found., St. Louis, 1970—. Home: 6901 E Potawatami Tucson AZ 85715 Office: U Ariz Office Scholarship Devel Tucson AZ 85715

HUMPHREY, JOSEPH ANTHONY CHRISTIE, mechanical engineering educator; b. London, Jan. 15, 1948; came to U.S., 1977; s. Joseph A. and Madelaine I. (Curran) H.; m. Vivienne Mooney, Aug. 24, 1970; children: Luisa, Fiona, Katie. Diploma in chem. engring., Instituto Quimico De Sarria, Barcelona, Spain, 1970; MASChemE, U. Toronto, Ont., Can., 1973; PhDME, Imperial Coll. Sci. and Tech., London, 1977. Rsch. staff dept. mech. aerospace engring. Princeton (N.J.) U., 1977-78; asst. prof. mech. engring. U. Calif., Berkeley, 1978-83, assoc. prof., 1983-88, prof., 1988-89, vice chmn., 1989—; Harrison prof. mech. engring. U. Liverpool, 1987-88. Adv. editor Internat. Jour. Heat and Fluid Flow, 1988—; contbr. numerous articles to profl. jours. Fulbright fellow, 1984. Mem. ASME, AAAS, AAUP, Am. Phys. Soc., Instituto Quimico de Sarria, Pi Tau Sigma, Sigma Chi. Home: 266 Lake Dr Kensington CA 94708 Office: U Calif Dept Mech Engring Berkeley CA 94720

HUMPHREYS, TOM (DANIEL), molecular biologist, educator, biotechnology company executive; b. Arlington, Tenn., June 23, 1936; s. Tom Daniel and Libbie (Kesl) H.; m. Susie Brunner Hunt, Sept. 7, 1958 (div. 1979); 1 child, Tom Daniel III. BS, U. Chgo., 1958, PhD, 1962. Asst. prof. MIT, Cambridge, 1965-66, U. Calif., San Diego, 1966-71; assoc. prof. molecular biology U. Hawaii, Honolulu, 1971-75, prof., 1975—, dir. Cancer Rsch. Ctr. Hawaii, 1985—; pres. Hawaii Biotech. Group, Inc., Aiea, 1982-86, dir. rsch., v.p., 1986—; dir. embryology Marine Biology Lab., Woods Hole, Mass., 1975-79; mem. molecular biology study sect. NIH, 1984. Contbr. to rsch. publs. Chmn. gay rights com. ACLU, Honolulu, 1979-82. NSF grantee, 1958—, NIH grantee, 1962—. Mem. Soc. Devel. Biology, Biophys. Soc., Am. Soc. Cell Biology, Am. Soc. Zoologists, Marine Biology Labs. Corp. Office: Cancer Rsch Ctr of Hawaii 1236 Lauhala St Honolulu HI 96813

HUMPHRIES, JAMES CRANE, systems engineer, consulting company executive; b. Hollywood, Calif., Dec. 2, 1947; s. James Crane Sr. and Dorothy (Sheldon) H.; m. Connie J. Brobeck, Dec. 25, 1968 (div. 1981); 1 child, John Michael; m. Mary Emily Hanna, Feb. 27, 1982; children: Elizabeth Irene, Harriet Ann. BA in Psychology, U. Calif., Irvine, 1972, postgrad. Research and devel. engr. Rodenstock Instruments Inc., Sunnyvale, Calif., 1978-81; sr. engr. Amdata Systems Inc., Milpitas, Calif., 1981-83; mgr. engring. Sterling Fed. Systems, Palo Alto, Calif., 1983—; pres., owner Hanna/Humphries Design & Engring. Cons., Menlo Park, Calif., 1981—; cons. engr. sch. psychology Stanford U., Palo Alto, 1984-86. Contbr. articles to profl. jours.; co-developer NASA/Ames 3D display system, 1985-88. V.p. bd. dirs. Keys Sch., Palo Alto, 1981-82; pack master Boy Scout Am., Palo Alto, 1982-83. Brython P. Davis fellow, 1976. Mem. IEEE, Soc. Motion Picture and TV Engrs., Nat. Computer Graphics Assn.

Democrat. Presbyterian. Office: Sterling Fed Systems 1121 San Antonio Rd Palo Alto CA 94303

HUMPHRIES, WILLIAM R., state land commissioner; b. Hot Springs, N.Mex., Dec. 19, 1946; s. William A. and Charlta Arletta (Coleman) H.; m. Carol A. Curry, June 14, 1969; children: Heidi K., Chery L. Student, Ft. Lewis Coll., 1964-67; BS, N.Mex. State U., 1971. Ranch owner, operator Lindrith, N.Mex., 1963—; instr. Largo Canyon Sch., Counselor, N.Mex., 1971-73; v.p., br. mgr. First State Bank, Cuba, N.Mex., 1974-78; pres. Security Bank, Ruidoso, N.Mex., 1978; gen. mgr. N.Mex. State Fair, Albuquerque, 1980-82, Santa Fe Racing, Inc., 1983; commr. State Land Office, Santa Fe, 1987—; vice-chmn. State Investment Coun., Santa Fe, 1987—; mem. Oil Conservation Commn., Santa Fe, 1987—. Mem. coun. on agrl. rsch., extension and teaching Nat. Univ. Support Group, 1986—; regent N.Mex. State U., Las Cruces, 1972-84; bd. trustees Manzano Day Sch., Albuquerque, 1981-82; chmn. HUB Resource and Devel. Coun., Albuquerque, 1975-80; supr. Cuba Soil and Water Conservation Dist., 1976-80. Recipient Excellence in Grazing award Am. Soc. Range Mgmt., 1976, Pres.'s award N.Mex. State U., 1984; named one of Outstanding Young Men. Am., 1974. Mem. N.Mex. Cattlegrower's Assn., N.Mex. Farm Bur. (Outstanding Service to Agr. award 1978). Republican. Methodist. Home: PO Box 108 Lindrith NM 87029 Office: State Land Office 310 Old Santa Fe Trail PO Box 1148 Santa Fe NM 87504

HUMPHRY, DEREK JOHN, association executive, writer; b. Bath, Somerset, Eng., Apr. 29, 1930; came to U.S., 1978; s. Royston Martin and Bettine (Duggan) H.; m. Jean Edna Crane, May 5, 1953 (dec. Mar. 1975); children: Edgar, Clive, Stephen; m. Ann Wickett Kooman, Feb. 16, 1976. Student pub. schs. Reporter, Evening News, Manchester, Eng., 1951-55, Daily Mail, London, 1955-63; editor Havering Recorder, Essex, Eng., 1963-67; sr. reporter Sunday Times, London, 1967-78; spl. writer Los Angeles Times, 1978-79; founder, exec. dir. Hemlock Soc. N.Am., Los Angeles, 1980—, pres. 1988 . Author: Because They're Black, 1971 (M.L. King award 1972), Police Power and Black People, 1972; Jean's Way, 1978, Let Me Die Before I Wake, 1982, The Right to Die, 1986. Served with Brit. Army, 1948-50. Mem. World Fedn. Right-to-Die Socs. (newsletter editor 1979-84, sec.-treas. 1983-84, pres. 1988-90). Office: Hemlock Soc PO Box 11830 Eugene OR 97440

HUNEYCUTT, BOBBY TYSON, air force officer; b. Albemarle, N.C., Dec. 16, 1947; s. Glenn Tyson and Billie Camela (Helms) H.; m. Elizabeth Karen DeBruno, July 16, 1977; children: Audra Nicole, Bart Andrew, Brett Thomas, Ashley Kathryn. BSBA, U. N.C., 1970; grad., Squadron Officer Sch., Gunther AFB, Ala., 1978; MA in Pub. Adminstrn., U. No. Colo., 1980; grad., Air Command and Staff Coll., Gunther AFB, Ala., 1983. Commd. 2d lt. USAF, 1970, advanced through grades to lt. col., 1987; F-4 pilot 336 Tactical Fighter Tng. Squadron, Seymour Johnson AFB, N.C., 1972-74; F-4 instr. pilot 36 Tactical Fighter Squadron, Osan Air Base, Republic of Korea, 1974-75; F-15 instr. pilot 555 Tactical Fighter Tng. Squadron, Luke AFB, Ariz., 1975-79; chief air-to-air tng. Fighter Weapons Sch., Nellis AFB, Nev., 1979-82; action officer research and devel. Hdqrs. USAF Pentagon, Washington, 1982-83, chief programs and resources, 1984-85; legis. liaison officer legis. liaison div. sec. of Air Force, Washington, 1983-84; ops. officer 461 Tactical Fighter Tng. Squadron, Luke AFB, Ariz., 1986-88; F-15 squadron comdr. 525 Tactical Fighter Squadron, Fed. Republic of Germany, 1988—; bd. dirs. Officers Open Mess, Bitburg AFB, Fed. Republic of Germany. Author: (tech. manual) F-15 Radar Text, 1982, AIM-7F Missile Text, 1982. Decorated Air medal. Mem. Air Force Assn. Republican. Roman Catholic. Home: PO Box 572 APO NY 09132 Office: 525 Tactical Fighter Squadron APO NY 09132

HUNGERFORD, JANET MARIE, sales executive; b. Santa Monica, Calif., Jan. 28, 1958; d. Robert Lloyd and Mary Elizabeth (O'Hara) H. BA in TV Radio and Film, Calif. State U., Northridge, 1980. Various positions Calif., 1972-80; asst. mgr. Ritz Camera, Thousand Oaks, Calif., 1980-83; radio asst. Sta. KGOE, Westlake, Calif., 1980-83; asst. mgr. 5-7-9 Shops, Thousand Oaks, 1983-86; sec. Promo Attractions, Westlake, 1986; gen. mgr. Kone Corp., Newbury Park, Calif., 1986—. Democrat. Roman Catholic. Home: 28866 Conejo View Dr Agoura CA 91301-3366

HUNLEY, W. HELEN, Canadian provincial government official; b. Acme, Alta., Can., Sept. 6, 1920. Student pub. schs., Rocky Mountain House, Alta.; LL.D., U. Alta., 1985. Telephone operator Carstairs, Acme and Calgary, Alta.; with implement and truck dealership, ins. agy. Rocky Mountain House, 1948-57, owner, 1957-68; owner, mgr. Helen Hunley Agys. Ltd., ins. agy., Rocky Mountain House, 1968-71; town councillor Rocky Mountain House, 1960-66, mayor, 1966-71; elected mem. Legis. Assembly Province of Alta., Edmonton, 1971-79, minister without portfolio, 1971-73, solicitor-gen., 1973-75, minister social services and community Health, 1975-79, lt. gov., 1985—. Formerly active numerous community affairs and vol. agys., including Can. Red Cross, Can. Boy Scouts, Recreation Bd., Alta. Girls Parliament, Provincial Mental Health Adv. Council; hon. patron numerous assns. Served to lt. Can. Women's Army Corps, 1941-45. Office: Province of Alta, Legislature Bldg, Edmonton, AB Canada T5K 2B6 *

HUNNICUTT, RICHARD PEARCE, metallurgical engineer; b. Asheville, N.C., June 15, 1926; s. James Ballard and Ida (Black) H.; B.S. in Metall. Engring., Stanford, 1951, M.S., 1952; m. Susan Haight, Apr. 9, 1954; children—Barbara, Beverly, Geoffrey, Anne. Research metallurgist Gen. Motors Research Labs., 1952-55; sr. metallurgist Aerojet-Gen. Corp., 1955-57; head materials and processes Firestone Engring. Lab., 1957-58; head phys. scis. group Dalmo Victor Co., Monterey, 1958-61, head materials lab., 1961-62; v.p. Anamet Labs., Inc., 1962—; partner Pyrco Co. Served with AUS, 1943-46. Mem. Electrochem. Soc., AIME, Am. Soc. Metals, ASTM, Am. Welding Soc., Am. Soc. Lubrication Engrs. Research on frictional behavior of materials, devel. armored fighting vehicles; author: Pershing, A History of the Medium Tank T20 Series, 1971; Sherman, A History of the American Medium Tank, 1978; Patton, A History of the American Main Battle Tank, Vol. 1, 1984, Firepower, A History of the American Heavy Tank, 1988. Home: 2805 Benson Way Belmont CA 94002 Office: 3400 Investment Blvd Hayward CA 94545

HUNNICUTT, ROBERT WILLIAM, engineer; b. Pauls Valley, Okla., Aug. 12, 1954; s. James Warren Hunnicutt. BS, N.Mex. State U., 1980. Sr. assoc. engr. IBM, Tucson, 1980—. Mem. adv. bd. Community Outreach Program for Deaf; active Big Bros. Tucson. Mem. Tucson Amateur Astronomers Assn., Ariz.-Sonora Desert Mus. Republican. Home: 8421 E Stella Rd Tucson AZ 85730 Office: IBM Corp Test and Integration Lab 72Y/031-2 Tucson AZ 85744

HUNSBERGER, CHARLES WESLEY, library director; b. Elkhart, Ind., Sept. 25, 1929; s. Charles August and Emma Edna (Zimmerman) H.; m. Hilda Carol Showalter, July 3, 1949 (div.); children—Jonathan Wesley, Jerald Wayne, Jane Wannette. BA, Bethel Coll., Mishawaka, Ind., 1952; MLS, Ind. U., 1967. Mem. Ft. Wayne (Ind.) Libr. Staff, 1960-62; dir. Columbia (Ind.) City Libr., 1962-64, Monroe County Libr., Bloomington, Ind., 1964-71, Clark County Libr. Dist., Las Vegas, Nev., 1971—; cons. sch., pub. librs., 1968-70; lectr. libr. schs. Ind. U., 1970-71, U. Ariz., 1974, U. Nev., Reno, 1976; mem. Nev. Coun. on Librs., 1973-81, chmn., 1980-81. Mem. Calif. Libr. Assn., ALA, Nev. Libr. Assn. (named Libr. of Yr. 1988), Rotary (pres. 1979-80, Las Vegas-Paradise chpt.). Democrat. Home: 1544 Hialeah Dr Las Vegas NV 89119 Office: Las Vegas Clark County Libr Dist 1401 E Flamingo Rd Las Vegas NV 89119

HUNSBERGER, ROBERT EARL, mechanical engineer, manufacturing executive; b. San Diego, Nov. 9, 1947; s. Arnold and Edith Mae (Miller) H.; m. Charlotte Louise Herr, Mar. 30, 1968; children: David Arnold, Allen Robert. BS in Mech. Engring., San Diego State Coll., 1969, MBA, 1975. Project engr. Gen. Atomic Co., San Diego, 1970-75; pvt. practice commodity mktg. specialist San Diego, 1975-77; devel. engr. Solar Turbines, Inc., San Diego, 1977-82, project engr., 1982-84, project mgr., 1984—. Contbr. articles to profl. jours. Leader local Webelos, 1981-82; com. chmn. Boy Scouts Am., Ramona, Calif., 1982-83, cub master, 1983-84, com. mem., 1982—, com. chmn., 1985-86. Recipient Spirit of Courage award San Diego Inst. for Burn Medicine, 1979, Cert. of Commendation Calif. Hwy. Patrol, 1979. Mem. ASME (assoc.), Exptl. Aircraft Assn. Republican. Club: Model A Restorers.

HUNT, ANITA M., healthcare marketing executive, consultant; b. Sayre, Okla., Oct. 14, 1943; d. William Lynn and Lydia Ethel (Boyer) Heard; m. Virgil Eugene Medley, Mar. 27, 1959 (div. 1970); children: Donald Eugene, Vicki-Lea Medley Wickham, Robert Lynn, Gary Duane. AS in Med. Tech., S.W. State U., Sayre, 1972; BS in Health Career Edn., Okla. State U., 1974; postgrad., Calif. State U., Bakersfield, 1979; MPH in Health Adminstrn., U. Okla., 1985. Mgr. clin. lab. Edmond (Okla.) Med. Clinic, 1974-77; rep. prov. rels. Okla. Blue Cross-Blue Shield, Tulsa, 1977-79; med. technologist Kern County Med. Ctr., Bakersfield, Calif., 1979; med. mgmt. cons. Med. Mgmt. Group, Oklahoma City, 1980-81; clin. lab. supr. South Community Hosp., Oklahoma City, 1982-85, hosp. svcs. rep., 1985-88; dir. sales Nat. Med. Enterprises, Santa Monica, Calif., 1988—; adj. asst. prof. U. Okla. Health Scis. Ctr., Oklahoma City, 1982-85; cons. Robert M. Brice & Assocs., Louisville, 1985—; lit. agt. P. Searle/Swansea Wales G.B., 1987—; editorial reviewer Jour. Med. Tech., 1984-86. Scouting coord. Last Frontier coun. Boy Scouts Am., 1985. Recipient Disting. Achievement award Am. Med. Techs. Assn., 1978, svc. award South Community Hosp., 1988; Sci. Products Med. Tech. grantee, 1973. Mem. Am. Coll. Healthcare Execs., Lion. Republican. Office: Nat Med Enterprises 2901 28th St Santa Monica CA 90406

HUNT, DANIEL STOCKTON, publishing company executive; b. L.A., Nov. 12, 1938; s. George S. and Mireille (de Martelly) H.; m. Carolyn Sue Schutt, June 4, 1973; 1 child, Bentley Anne. BA in Psychology, Yale U., 1961. Mktg. dir. CBS Publs., Newport Beach, Calif., 1971-74; pub. Cycle World mag., Newport Beach, Calif., 1975-77, Sea mag., Newport Beach, Calif., 1977-78; mktg. cons. Newport Beach, Calif., 1978-80; v.p. TL Enterprises Inc., Agoura, Calif., 1980--; circulation cons. Western Outdoors mag., Costa Mesa, Calif., 1985-86; pub. cons. Horse and Rider mag., Temecula, Calif., 1986-87; exec. producer Motorhome video mag., Agoura, 1988. Home: 32982 Wesley St Wildomar CA 92395 Office: TL Enterprises Inc 299011 Agoura Rd Agoura CA 91301

HUNT, PETER H., director, theatrical lighting designer; b. Pasadena, Calif., Dec. 16, 1938; s. George Smith and Gertrude (Ophuls) H.; m. Virginia Osborn, Jan. 19, 1965 (div. Jan. 1972); m. Barbette Tweed, Feb. 6, 1972; children: Max, Daisy, Amy. BA, Yale U., 1961, MFA in Drama, 1963. Free-lance lighting designer N.Y.C., 1959-69, free-lance theatre dir., 1969—; free-lance motion picture dir. Los Angeles, 1972—. Dir.: (plays) "1776," 1969 (Tony award 1970), Give 'Em Hell Harry, 1975; (TV movie) Skeezer, 1981 (Peabody award 1982); (cable TV play) Bus Stop, 1982 (ACE award 1983). Recipient Christopher award, 1972, Edgar award, 1982. Office: Creative Artists Agy 1888 Century Pk E Los Angeles CA 90067

HUNT, PETER ROGER, film director, writer, editor; b. London, Mar. 11, 1925; cam to U.S., 1975; s. Arthur George and Elizabeth H.; widowed; 1 child, Nicholas Constantine. Student, London Sch. Music. Actor English Repertory Theater, London. Camera asst., asst. editor various documentaries; asst. editor various feature films. London Film Co.; scriptor various films; editor (films): Hill in Korea, Admirable Crichton, Cry From the Streets, Greengage Summer (Am. title: Loss of Innocence), Ferry to Hong Kong, H.M.S. Defiant (Am. title: Damn the Defiant); supervising editor, 2d unit dir.: Dr. No, Call Me Bwana, From Russia with Love, Goldfinger, Ibcress File, Thunderball, You Only Live Twice; assoc. producer: Chitty Chitty Bang Bang; dir.: On Her Majesty's Secret Service, Gullivers Travels (film and animated), Gold, Shout at the Devil, Death Hunt, Wild Geese II, Assassination; (TV episodes) Marlowe, Shirley's World, Persuaders; (NBC-TV movie) Beasts in the Streets; (ABC-TV mini-series) Last Days of Pompeii. Mem. Assn. Cinematic Technicians Great Britain, Motion Picture Acad. Arts, Acad. Television. Office: 2229 Roscomare Rd Los Angeles CA 90077

HUNT, ROBERT WILLIAM, theatrical producer, data processing consultant; b. Seattle, June 8, 1947; s. William Roland and Margaret Anderson (Crowe) H.; m. Marcie Loomis, Aug. 24, 1968 (div. Dec. 1975); 1 child, Megan; m. Susan Moger, June 17, 1989. BA, U. Wash., 1969. CPA, Wash. Data processing cons Arthur Anderson & Co., Seattle, 1968-78; owner, cons. Robert W. Hunt & Assocs., Seattle, 1978—; producing dir., bd. dirs. Village Theatre, Issaquah, Wash., 1979—; cons. San Francisco Mus. Modern Art, 1981—, Mus. of Flight, Seattle, 1983—, Met. Mus. N.Y.C., 1984-85. Creator arts computer software; producer (mus.) Eleanor, 1987; creator, writer (pop group music and video) The Shrimps, 1984. Chmn. com. Seattle Arts Commn., 1975-78; treas. Arts Resource Svcs., Seattle, 1976-78, Musicomedy Northwest, Seattle, 1977-79. Grantee Seattle Arts Commn., 1978-79, Wash. State Arts Commn., 1980—, King County Arts Commn., 1980—. Mem. Wash. Soc. CPAs. Office: Village Theatre 120 Front St N Issaquah WA 98027

HUNT, WILLIAM HENRY, lumber industry executive; b. Madison, Wis., July 23, 1909; s. Walter Henry and Henrietta (Milhaupt) H.; m. Mago Dolan, July 27, 1932; 1 child, William Boynton. Student, U. Wis.-RiverFalls, 1926-29; LHD (hon.), U. Portland, 1976. Tchr., athletic coach Algoma (Wis.) High Sch.; trainee, salesman Algoma Plywood & Veneer Co., 1935-38; sales v.p., dir., exec. com. Champion Internat. (formerly U.S. Plywood Corp.), N.Y.C., 1938-57; exec. v.p., pres., vice-chmn. bd. dirs. Ga.-Pacific Corp., Portland, Oreg., 1957-72; chief exec. officer, chmn. bd. dirs. La.-Pacific Corp., Portland, 1972-74. Mem. pres.'s council Columbia-Pacific council Boy Scouts Am., 1979-; bd. regents U. Portland; adv. bd. Salvation Army; fund raiser Anti-Defamation League of B'nai B'rith, NCCJ, Loyola Retreat House, Oreg. Symphony Assn. Recipient Community and Pub. Svc. award Comml. Club Portland, 1974, disting. alumnus award U. Wis.-River Falls, 1969; named Oreg. State U. Pres.'s Club founding mem., most honored mem.; named to Athletic Hall of Fame, U. Wis.-River Falls, 1981. Mem. Plywood Pioneers Assn., Arlington Club (bd. dirs. 1987--), Astoria Golf and Country Club, Edlorado Country Club (bd. dirs. 1978-81, treas. 1979-81), Multnomah Athletic Club (chmn. house com. 1970), Srs.' North West Golf Assn. (Victoria, B.C., Can.), Waverly Country Club (bd. dirs. 1972-74, chmn. house com. 1973, chmn. fin. com. 1974). Republican. Roman Catholic. Home: 2323 SW Park Pl Apt 106 Portland OR 97205 Office: 720 SW Washington St Ste 725 Portland OR 97205

HUNTER, BRIAN, aquaculture company executive; b. Memphis, Aug. 26, 1953; s. Willard Smith and Dora Lee (Allen) H.; m. Kathleen Marie Haase, Oct. 12, 1984; 1 child, Camille Marie. BS, N. Ariz. U., 1976; MS, U. Ariz., 1979, PhD, 1982. Research asst. environ. research lab. U. Ariz., Tucson, 1976-78, reseach assoc. environ. research lab., 1979-82; asst. prof. dept. surgery Health Sci. Ctr. U. Ariz., Tucson; scientist and program coord. Oceanic Inst., Waimanalo, Hawaii, 1984-86; pres. United Fisheries, Inc., Safford, Ariz., 1986—; cons. Aquastar, Ltd., Bangkok, Sylvatex, Inc., Burke, Va., UN Food & Agri. Orgn., Rome. Contbr. articles to profl. jours. Small Bus. Innovation Research grantee NSF, 1985, Fgtn. Travel grantee NSF, 1982. Mem. Ariz. Aquaculture Assn. (bd. dirs. 1989), World Aquaculture Soc. Republican. Home: Rt 1 Box 493 G Safford AZ 85546 Office: United Fisheries Inc PO Box 189 Safford AZ 85546

HUNTER, CHARLES DAN, credit company executive; b. Everett, Wash., Sept. 19, 1923; s. Charles Dan and Gail (Conover) H.; m. Irene Winifred Wigerg, July 18, 1942; children: Linda L. McCammon, Steven J. Student, Seattle U., 1942, Tex. Tech. Coll., 1943. Cert. collecter; cert. credit bur. exec.; cert. collection agy. exec. Collecter Everett Assn. of Credit Men, 1946-50; pres. Wash. Credit Inc. (formerly Eastside Credit Bur.), Redmond, 1950—; exec. bd. Consumer Credit Counseling Svc. of Seattle, 1988—; adv. com. Lake Washington Vocat. Tech. Inst., 1988; speaker credit and collection industry. Contbr. articles to profl. jours. With USAF, 1943-45. Mem. Am. Collectors Assn. (mgmt. cons. com. 1988—, legis. council 1970-75, Internat. Fellow Cert. Collectors), Wash. Collectors Assn. (legis. chmn. 1960-69, legis. com. 1988—), Seattle/King County Credit Assn. Home: 1554 West Lake Sammamish Pkwy SE Bellevue WA 98008 Office: Washington Credit Inc 2001-152 Ave NE PO Box 9729 Redmond WA 98073-9729

HUNTER, DORIAN, interior designer, educator; b. Sacramento, May 18, 1932; d. Paul Eyerly and Ramona Estelle (Haley) H. A.A., Stephens Coll., 1952; B.F.A., U. So. Calif., 1954; M.A., Mills Coll., 1956. Instr. art Oakland, Calif., 1956-57; interior designer Anaheim, Calif., 1957-60, Santa Ana, Calif., 1960-62; founder, pres. Dorian Hunter Interiors, Inc., Fullerton, Calif., 1962—; dir. Dorian Hunter Art Gallery, Fullerton, 1963-69; lectr. environ. design Calif. State U., Fullerton, 1970-74, 79-81, assoc. prof. environ. design, 1982-87; instr. comml. interior design, program cons. Orange Coast Coll., 1976-77; mem. adv. bd. certificate program in environ. and interior design U. Calif., Irvine, 1977—; mem. search com. for dean Sch. Architecture and Fine Arts, U. So. Calif., 1974-75, bd. councilors, 1976-78; mem. adv. com. art dept. Orange Coast Coll., 1974-75; mem. council Nat. Council for Interior Design Qualification, 1981-84; chmn. Am. Soc. Interior Designers Designs of Distinction, 1988, mem. fellow com., 1986—, chmn. fellow's coun., 1989. Contbr. articles to profl. publs. Chmn. Fullerton Archtl. Review Bd., 1988—; bd. dirs. Cultural Groups Found. of No. Orange County, 1966-69; hon. chmn. Night in Fullerton Art and Cultural Annual Trust, 1989. Recipient nat. design award for dental offices Fountain Valley, Calif., 1969; Alumni Achievement award Stephens Coll., 1970. Fellow Am. Soc. Interior Designers (nat. com. fellows 1976, 78, 86, 87, 88, 89 designer of distinction com. mem. 1987), Am. Inst. Interior Designers (pres. Orange County area chpt. 1967-68, nat. v.p. 1968-69, mem. exec. bd., nat. bd. govs. 1968-72); mem. Fullerton C. of C. (Distinguished Service award 1966), Archtl. Guild (U. So. Calif.) (pres. 1973-74), Art Alliance (Calif. State U. at Fullerton) (dir. 1969-71, chmn. bus. and arts com. 1975-76), League Women Voters (fin. adviser Fullerton 1966, 67). Home: 400 E Virginia Rd Fullerton CA 92631 Office: 607 E Chapman Ave Fullerton CA 92631

HUNTER, DUNCAN LEE, congressman; b. Riverside, Calif., May 31, 1948; m. Lynne Layh, 1973; children: Robert Samuel, Duncan Duane. J.D., Western State U., 1976. Bar: Calif. 1976. Practiced in San Dieg; mem. 97th Congress from 42d Dist. Calif., 98th-101st Congresses from 45th Dist. Calif. Served with U.S. Army, 1969-71, Vietnam. Decorated Air medal, Bronze Star. Mem. Navy League. Republican. Baptist.

HUNTER, FRED, mayor, lawyer. m. Jeanne Hunter; 4 children. Student, Fullerton Community Coll.; JD, Western Sch. Law, 1974. Office Anaheim (Calif.) Police Dept., 1965-75; mem. city coun. City of Anaheim, 1986—, mayor, 1988—. With USN, 1959-62. Mem. Orange County Bar Assn., Calif. Lawyers Assn., Am. Cancer Soc. Office: Office of the Mayor PO Box 3222 Anaheim CA 92803

HUNTER, GEORGE WILLIAM, III, parasitologist, educator; b. N.Y.C., Jan. 27, 1902; s. George William and Emily Isabel (Jobbins) H.; m. Adelaide Louise White, July 11, 1941 (div.); m. Fern Emily Wood, May 15, 1972; children—Anita Anderson, Gay Culp, Mina F. Sage. Student Carleton Coll., 1919-20; B.S., Knox Coll., 1923; M.S., U. Ill., 1924, Ph.D., 1927; cert. tropical and mil. medicine, 1944. Commd. 2d lt. U.S. Army Res. 1923, advanced through grades to maj. AUS, 1943, to col. U.S. Army, 1949; asst. chief dept. parasitology Army Med. Sch., 1942-45, chief, 1946-47, staff mem. tropical and mil. medicine course, 1942-47; chief sect. med. zoology 406th Med. Gen. Lab., Tokyo, 1947-51; chief sect. parasitology-entomology 4th Army Med. Lab., 1951-55; exec. officer commn. schistosomiasis Army Epidemiol. Bd., Philippines, 1945; dep. blood adminstr. Far East Command, Korea, 1950-51; ret., 1955; interim prof. biol. sci. U. Fla., Gainesville, 1956-57, lectr. biol. scis. and tropical medicine Coll. Medicine, 1957-67, prof. microbiol. Med. Sch., 1966-67, prof. emeritus, 1967—; res. coordinator, chief sect. parasitology La. State U. Internat. Ctr. Med. Research Tng., research prof. med. parasitology, sch. medicine; mem. faculty U. Costa Rica, 1961-63; clin. prof. parasitology, div. epidemiol., dept. community and family medicine U. Calif. Sch. Medicine, San Diego, 1974—. Decorated Bronze Star with oak leaf cluster; Harvard U. research fellow, 1940; NIH immunology schistosomiasis grantee, 1956-64; WHO schistosomiasis grantee, 1978-80; recipient Knox Coll. Alumni Achievement award, 1954, Carlos J. Finlay award, Cuba, 1958; named hon. citizen with distinction Kurume, Japan. Fellow Royal Soc. Tropical Medicine and Hygiene, AAAS, Am. Pub. Health Assn.; mem. Japan Soc. Parasitologists, Am. Soc. Zoologists Am. Micros. Soc., Wash. Acad. Scis., Assn. Southeastern Biologists, Southeastern Soc. Parasitologists (co-founder), Royal Inst. Pub. Health and Hygiene, Am. Soc. Parasitologists (charter, emeritus), Am. Soc. Tropical Medicine and Hygiene, Union Am. Biol. Socs. (exec. com. 1941-44), So. Calif. Parasitologists, Helminthological Soc. Wash., Japanese Soc. Parasitology, Assn. Mil. Surgeons U.S., Phi Beta Kappa, Sigma Xi, Delta Sigma Rho, Phi Eta, Beta Theta Pi. Clubs: Mil. Order Boars, Mil. Order World Wars, Mil. Order Carabao; Lions. Author: (with W.W. Frye, J.C. Swartzwelder), A Manual of Tropical Medicine, 4th edit., 1966; (with J.C. Swartzwelder and David Clyde) Tropical Medicine, 5th edit., 1976; Hunter's Tropical Medicine (G.T. Strickland) 1984. Contbr. articles to med. jours. Home: 17760 Camino Murrillo San Diego CA 92128

HUNTER, JAMES, real estate salesman, consultant; b. Paisley, Scotland, Oct. 31, 1918; came to U.S., 1927; s. James and Catherine (Cameron) H.; m. Elsie Lenora (Kelley) Feb. 1, 1953; children: Keli C.H. Barker, Kimberly Gayle. Cert., Union Jr. Coll., 1939; student, Rutgers U., 1940-42; BA in psychology, U. Colo., 1951; cert., Jones Real Estate Coll., 1981. Lab. technician Merck Inst. for Therapeutic Research, Rahway, N.J., 1937-41; salesman Merck & Co., Rahway, N.J., 1941-43; asst. mgr. Tallahassee (Fla.) C. of C., 1954-56, Fla. Devel. Commn., Tallahassee, 1956-61; exec. asst. Fla. Hotel Restaurant Commn., Tallahassee, 1961-64; mgr. Fla. Surplus Property Agy., Tallahassee, 1964-69; dir. Fla. Dept. of Transp., Tallahassee, 1970-71; adminstrv. asst. Fla. Gov.'s Office, Tallahassee, 1963-70; planner, coordinator Denver Regional Coun. Govts., 1971-73; exec. v.p. Boulder (Colo.) Bd. Realtors, 1973-83; account mgr. Ticor Title Ins. Co., Boulder, Colo., 183-87; cons. Boulder, 1987—; salesman Fowler Real Estate, Boulder, 886. Commr. Boulder Urban Renewal Authority, 1986—; bd. dirs. Ctr. for People with Disabilities, Boulder, 1986—, Presbyn. Manor for Elderly, Boulder, 1986—, U. Colo. Parents Assn., Boulder, U. Colo. Dirs. Club, 1986—. Served to 1st lt. U.S. Army, 1942-46. 1951-53. Mem. Boulder Area Bd. Realtors. Republican. Presbyterian. Lodge: Rotary (bd. dirs.). Home: 330 Lipan Way Boulder CO 80303 Office: Fowler Real Estate 2400 28th St Boulder CO 80301

HUNTER, JEAN L., nursing school director; b. Gary, Ind., Apr. 2, 1926; d. Robert Bruce and Gertrude (Slater) H. Diploma, St. Luke's Hosp., 1950; BS in Nursing, U. Ill., 1954; MA, Columbia U., 1960; PhD, U. Wash., 1972. RN, Calif. Teaching supr. sch. of nursing Highland-Alameda County Hosp., Oakland, Calif., 1956-59; nursing instr. Foothill Coll., Los Altos, Calif., 1961-63; curriculum coord. sch. of nursing Samuel Merritt Hosp., Oakland, Calif., 1963-65; nursing instr. Merritt Coll., Oakland, Calif., 1965-68; asst. prof. of nursing Calif. State U., Hayward, 1972-74; nursing dept. chmn. Holy Names Coll., Oakland, 1975-79; nursing program dir. Oreg. Inst. Tech., Klamath Falls, 1980-82; sch. of nursing dir. Dominican Coll., San Rafael, Calif., 1982—; curriculum cons. Calif. State U., Turlock, 1980, health scis. div. Contra Costa Coll., San Pablo, Calif., 1974-75. bd. sec. North Bay br. Arthritis Found., San Rafael, 1988—; adv. bd. Ross Valley Home Care, Novato, Calif., 1985-86. Special nurse rsch. fellow U. Wash. Mem. Am. Nursing Assn., Calif. Assn. Colls. of Nursing, Assn. Ind. Calif. Colls. of Nursing, Nurses Alumni of U. Wash., Sigma Theta Tal. Democrat. Home: 2100 Lincoln Village Circle #2302 Larkspur CA 94939 Office: Dominican Coll 1520 Grand Ave San Rafael CA 94901

HUNTER, JEFFREY CHARLES, chemist, technical company manager, educator; b. San Diego, Oct. 19, 1938; s. Theodore Lee and Dorothy (Wilson) H.; m. Doreen E. Lonergan, Nov. 26, 1983. BS, San Diego State U., 1962, MS, 1964; MA in Mgmt., U. Redlands, 1979. Cert. Calif. Community Coll. Tchr. of bus. and chemistry. Sr. chemist Avery Internat., Azusa, Calif., 1966-71, lab. supr., 1971-76, product devel. specialist rsch. dept. Label div., 1976-79, project mgr., 1979-84, sr. tech. assoc. Avery Comml. Products div., 1984—; undergrad. and grad. bus. instr. U. Redlands, 1980—, bus. and sci. instr. Coll. Profl. Studies U. San Francisco, 1981—, state chmn. curriculum design com. Coll. Profl. Studies, 1982-84; undergrad. sci. instr. Nat. U., 1989—. Contbr. articles to profl. jours.; co-author curriculum handbooks; patentee in field. Co-dir. East San Gabriel-Pomona Valley Back in Control Ctr., 1985-87. Mem. Assn. MBA Execs., Am. Chem. Soc., TAPPI, Ontario Pkwy. Club, Kiwanis (sec., 1980, 81, 82, Circle K Club adv. Mt. San Antonio Coll.). Republican. Episcopalian. Avocations: numismatics, raising Shar-Pei show dogs, scuba diving. Home: 17532 Calle Del Corral Riverside CA 92504 Office: Avery Comml Products div 777 E Foothill Blvd Azusa CA 91702

HUNTER, JOHN DUNDAS, government official, park and farm manager; b. Devils Lake, N.D., Feb. 9, 1937; s. Dundas and Byrdie M. (Atkins) H.; m. Ardis Doreen Benson, June 10, 1960; children—Scott D., Bruce D., Eve M., John E. A.S. in Forestry, N.D. Sch. Forestry, 1960; B.S. in Wildlife, U. Mont., 1962. With Nat. Park Service, U.S. Dept. Interior, various locations, 1961—, chief ranger Assateague Island Nat. Seashore, Berlin, Md., 1969-71, park supt. Stones River Nat. Battlefield, Murfreesboro, Tenn., 1971-74, Bandelier Nat. Monument, Los Alamos, 1974—; owner, gen. mgr. Hunter Farms, Cando, N.D., 1965—, Blue Heron Cottages, Chincoteague, Va., 1973—; mem. Fed. Exec. Bd., Nashville and Albuquerque, 1972—. Served with U.S. Army, 1957-59. Recipient Incentive awards Nat. Park Service, 1966, 67, Spl. Achievement awards, 1975, 80; Honor award Gov. N.Mex., 1977; Meritorious Service award U.S. Dept. Interior, 1985. Lutheran. Club: Kiwanis. Lodges: Moose, Elks.

HUNTER, JOHN HARNDEN, artist; b. Westmiddlesex, Pa., Sept. 26, 1934; s. John A. and Dorothea H.; children—Gregory Andrew, Christopher John. B.A., Pomona Coll., 1956; M.F.A., Claremont Grad. Sch., 1958. prof. studio art San Jose (Calif.) State U., 1965—; adviser, critic textbooks Holt, Rinehart & Winston, N.Y.C., 1972-80; Bd. dirs. San Jose Mus. Art.; guest artist Tamarind Lithography Workshop, 1969, Lakeside Studios, Mich., 1978, 79. One-person show, Cannes Film Festival, 1966; exhibited in group shows, Basel Art Fair, Documenta VI, Kassel, Germany, Cologne Art Fair, Galerie Wolfgang Ketterer, Munich; represented in permanent collections, Nat. Gallery Art, Washington, Mus. Modern Art, N.Y.C., Norton Simon Mus. Art, Pasadena, U. Minn., Mpls., Scripps Coll., Morrison Library, U. Calif., Berkeley, Los Angeles County Mus. Art, Amon Carter Mus. Western Art, Fort Worth, Grunwald Graphic Arts Found, UCLA, others. Served with AUS, 1958-62. Fulbright fellow Florence, Italy, 1963-64, 64-65. Office: San Jose State U Dept Art San Jose CA 95192

HUNTER, KATHARINE MCPHAIL, publishing company executive; b. Welland, Ont., Can., Apr. 30, 1955; came to U.S., 1964; d. Alexander Charles McPhail and Diane Mary (Ridell) Church; m. David Horace Hunter, Feb. 15, 1981. BA, Reed Coll., 1978; postgrad., Santa Clara U., 1986--. Classified advt. mgr. Willamette Week newspaper, Portland, Oreg., 1979-83; prodn. mgr. Willamette Week newspaper, Portland, 1982-84; gen. advt. staff mem. San Jose Mercury News, Calif., 1984-85; asst. mgr. advt. svcs. San Jose Mercury News, 1985-86, prodn. asst., 1986, asst. mgr product distbn., 1987—; cons. Portland Bus. Jour., 1984, Chico (Calif.) News and Rev., 1985. NSF grantee, 1977. Democrat. Office: San Jose Mercury News 750 Ridder Pk Dr San Jose CA 95190

HUNTER, KATHRYN LYNETTE, medical transcription professional; b. Visilia, Calif., Apr. 27, 1946; d. Walter Fiske Hunter and Olive Hounsome (Maley) Hazelbaker; div.; 1 child, Dawn Kathleen Richardson. AA in Med. Assisting, Coll. Med. and Dental Assts., Alhambra, Calif., 1969. Cert. med. transcription profl. Prin. KLH Med. Transcription Svc., Cornona Del Mar, Calif., 1985—. Vol., City of Hope Med. Ctr., Duarte, Calif., 1974, 75. Mem. Am. Assn. Med. Transcription, Calif. Assn. Med. Transcription, Orange County Med. Transcription Assn. (pres.-elect 1989), Western Orthopaedic Assn. (exec. sec. Orange County sect. 1982—), Newport Harbor C. of C. (health com. 1986—). Republican. Baptist. Home and Office: KLH Med Transcription Svc 605-1-2 Larkspur Ave Corona Del Mar CA 92625

HUNTER, KEN, president of city council. Grad., Pueblo (Colo.) Jr. Coll., So. Meth. U. 1st v.p. Pueblo Bank & Trust Co., ret., 1988; oil distbr. Pueblo; mem. Pueblo City Coun., 1984—, pres., 1988—; mem. Gov.'s com. on consumer credit; bd. dirs. Pueblo Bancorp., Broadway Theatre League. Mem. Pueblo C. of C. (hon. bd. dirs.), Masons, Elks, Rotary. Home: 40 Villa Dr Pueblo CO 81001 Office: Office of the Mayor 1 City Hall Pl PO Box 1427 Pueblo CO 81002

HUNTER, MICHAEL HAMILTON, historian; b. Salt Lake City, Oct. 11, 1948; s. Milton Reed and Ferne (Gardner) H.; m. Tana Walch, Aug. 26, 1980; children: Jonathan Michael, Stephen James, Christina Marie. BA in History, Brigham Young U., 1974, MA in Pub. History, 1989. Researcher Latter-Day Saints Ch. Hist. Div., Arts and Sites Div., Salt Lake City, 1975-83; internship researcher Utah State Hist. Soc., Salt Lake City, 1986. Contbr. articles to profl. jours. Mem. Am. Hist., Utah Endowment for Humanities. Mem. Simon Wiesenthal Ctr., Boys Town, Nat. Trust for Hist. Preservation, Nat. Coun. on Pub. History, Sons of Utah Pioneers, U.S. Golf Assn. Republican. Home: 1585 S 400 E Salt Lake City UT 84115

HUNTER, R. HAZE, state legislator; b. Cedar City, Utah, Oct. 5, 1924; m. Betty B. Hunter. Student, U. Utah. Chmn. bd. North East Furniture; pres. NEFCO Fin.; owner B&H Rentals; Utah state legislator 1980—; mem. State and Local Affairs standing com., 1981-82, 85-86, 87-88; chmn. Bus. and Consumer Consumer Concerns standing com., 1983-84, mem. 1981-82, 85-86; chmn. Gen. Govt. and Capitol Facilities appropriations com., 1988-89, mem. 1983-84; mem. Bus. Labor and Agriculture appropriations com., 1981-82, 85-86, Bus. Labor and Econ. Devel. standing com., 1987-88, constl. revision com., law and justice adv. com. Bishop, high councilman Ch. of Latter Day Saints. Mem. Iron Mission Park C. of C. (past pres., mem. Southern Utah devel. com.), Lions (past pres. Cedar City chpt., past dist. gov.). Office: 295 S Ridge Rd Cedar City UT 84720

HUNTER, RAYMOND EUGENE, physicist, judge; b. Moultrie, Ga., Sept. 4, 1935; s. William Jesse and Ruby (Inez) H.; m. Joyce Lee Turner, June 10, 1957; children: Allan Derek, Janis Lynn Hunter Palmer. BS magna cum laude, U. Ga., 1957, MS, 1958; PhD, Fla. State U., 1964. Staff mem. Los Alamos Nat. Lab., 1964-66, asst. div. leader, 1980-85, assoc. div. leader, 1985-88, cons. to atomic energy div. Savannah River Lab, 1988—; head dept. physics, dean grad. sch. Valdosta State Coll. (Ga.), 1966-72; Mcpl. judge County of Los Alamos, 1975-86. Contbr. articles to sci. and jud. jours. Mem. Los Alamos Republican Central Com., 1972-86; chmn. County Personnel Bd., Los Alamos, 1973-75, Los Alamos Credit Union Supervisory Com., 1972-76; mem. troup and dist. com. Boy Scouts Am., 1973-88. Served to capt. USAF, 1958-61. Recipient Research and Devel. award USAF, 1961, Outstanding Young Educator award U.S. Jaycees, 1969, Disting. Performance award Los Alamos Nat. Lab., 1981. Mem. Nat. Judges Assn. (sec. 1981-82, pres. 1983-84, sr. dir. 1984-85), Am. Judges Assn., N.Mex. Judges Assn. (bd. dirs. 1979-83), N.Mex. Mcpl. Judges Assn., Am. Nuclear Soc., Phi Beta Kappa, Omicron Delta Kappa. Baptist. Home: 111 Shirlane Pl Los Alamos NM 87544 also: 3611 Jamaica Dr Augusta GA 30909 Office: Los Alamos Nat Lab PO Box 1663 Los Alamos NM 87545 Also: 3611 Jamaica Dr Augusta GA 30909

HUNTER, RONALD LEE, telephone company executive; b. Aberdeen, Md., Mar. 1, 1949; s. Oliver M. and Imogene Hunter; m. Dorothy Marie Finley, June 19, 1971; children: Erika Marie, Jessica Ann. BS in Bus., Econs., Regis Coll., 1982; MBA, U. Phoenix, 1984. Various mgmt. positions Mountain Bell, Denver, 1972-84; dir. U S West, Denver, 1985—; bd. dirs. IPDM Inc., Denver. Mem. Mayor's Black Adv. Com., Denver, 1988; appointed mem. Gov.'s Commn. on Privatization, Denver, 1988—; chair econ. devel. Colo. Black Round Table, Denver, 1987-88; mem. NAACP, Nat. Urban League. Mem. Mountain Bell Black Employees Assn. (pres. 1986-87), Colo. Assn. Black Profl. Engrs. & Scientists (treas. 1980-85, outstanding contribution award 1985), Am. Mgmt. Assn. Home: 11435 W 76th Dr Arvada CO 80005

HUNTER, STEVEN LAWRENCE, electrical engineer; b. Albany, Calif., Feb. 11, 1955; s. Charles Rene and Carolyn (Rudolph) H.; m. Angela Jane Hodgson, Aug. 5, 1978; children: David Allen, Daniel Edward. BS, U. Calif., Berkeley, 1977; MS, Case Western Res. U., 1981. Programmer System-Donner, Concord, Calif., 1975-76; elec. engr. Varian Aerograph, Walnut Creek, Calif., 1977-78, Engring. Design Ctr., Cleve., 1978-81, Lawrence Livermore Nat. Lab., Livermore, Calif., 1981—; cons. Orion Ent., Livermore, 1981—. Patentee in field. Mem. Oxford Rsch. Inst. (dir. 1987—), Nat. Rifle Assn. Office: Lawrence Livermore Nat Lab PO Box 808 Livermore CA 94550

HUNTER, THEODORE PAUL, lawyer, energy consultant; b. St. Clair, Mich., Dec. 14, 1951; s. James Peter and Esther (Breuehner) H.; m. Ramona Holmes, Sept 5, 1977; children: Justin, Brandon. BS with honors, Portland (Oreg.) State U., 1973; JD, U. Wash., 1978. Bar: Wash 1978, U.S. Dist. Ct. (we. dist.) Wash. 1978, U.S. Ct. Appeals (9th cir.) 1979. Ptnr. Lippek, Hunter, Caryl & Raan, Seattle, 1978-83; chief counsel Wash. State Legis. Energy Com., Olympia, 1983-88; dir. Pacific Energy Inst., Seattle, 1988—; legal counsel Western Solar Network, Wash., Oreg., 1980-82; arbitrator King County Superior Cts., Seattle, 1985; prof./instr. Evergreen Coll., Olympia, 1986—. Contbr. articles to profl. jours. Fellow Environ. Law Inst., Washington, 1979. Mem. Washington State Bar Assn., Environ. Lawyers of Wash., Wash. Trial Lawyers, Klapa Sokoli. Democrat. Lutheran. Office: 403 Pioneer Bldg Seattle WA 98104

HUNTER, THORA RODELLO, writer; b. Provo, Utah, Mar. 23, 1920; d. Thomas Rollo Hicken and Venus Deon (Harris) Tripp; m. Ross A. Hunter, Jan. 27, 1939 (div. 1964); children: Sally Hunter Wenzler, Ann, Barbara Hunter Ballingham; m. Frank James Calkins, Sept. 7, 1965 (div. Aug. 1981). Student, U. Utah, 1938-39, 1956. Editorial staff Utah Fish & Game Mag., Salt Lake City, 1957-58, editorial asst., 1958-59, assoc. editor, editor, 1959-65; lectr. various orgns. and locations, 1965-88; work shop leader Creative Writing Groups, various locations, 1981-88. Author: A.A. Knoph A House of Many Rooms, 1965, Wyoming Wife, 1969, A Daughter of Zion, 1972, The Soul of Jackson Hole, 1974; newspaper columnist, 1972-74; contbr. many poems and stories to jours. and mags. Pres. Forest Sch. PTA, Salt Lake City, 1953-55; chmn. Mother's March, Salt Lake City, 1956. Recipient seven awards for wildlife books and pamphlets, Pen Women, 1963. Democrat. Home and Office: 5016 Moor Mont Circle Salt Lake City UT 84117

HUNTHAUSEN, RAYMOND GERHARDT, archbishop; b. Anaconda, Mont., Aug. 21, ,1921; s. Anthony Gerhardt and Edna (Tuchacherer) H. A.B., Carroll Coll., 1943, St. Edward's Sem., 1946; M.S., Notre Dame U., 1953; LL.D., DePaul U., 1960; postgrad. summers, St. Louis U., Cath. U., Fordham U. Ordained priest Roman Cath. Ch., 1946. Instr. chemistry Carroll Coll., 1946-57, football, basketball coach, 1953-57, pres., 1957-62; bishop Helena Diocese, Mont., 1962-75; archbishop of Seattle 1975—. Recipient Martin Luther King Jr. award Fellowship of Reconciliation, 1987. Mem. Am. Chem. Soc. Office: Chancery Office 910 Marion St Seattle WA 98104 *

HUNTLEY, ROBERT CARSON, JR., justice Idaho Supreme Court; b. Union City, Pa., Aug. 7, 1932; s. Robert Carson and Mildred (Kaltenmark) H.; m. Elfriede Garvens, Feb. 11, 1955; children: Christopher F., Anthony R. BS, U. Idaho, 1954, JD, 1959; LLM, U. Va., 1988. Bar: Idaho 1959. Ptnr. Racine, Huntley & Olson, Pocatello, Idaho, 1959-82; justice Idaho Supreme Ct., Boise, 1982—; mem. Idaho Jud. Council, 1967-81; bd. commrs. Idaho State Bar, 1982. Mem. Idaho Ho. of Reps., 1965-67; mem. Pocatello City Council, 1962-64, Gov.'s Blue Ribbon Tax Com., 1978-79, Com. to Promote Funding for Edn., 1980, Pocatello Fin. Resources Com., 1980; chmn. Idaho Energy Resources Policy Bd., 1980-82; pres. Boise Opera, 1989. Capt. USNR, 1954-79. Mem. ABA, Idaho Bar Assn., Am. Bar Found., Idaho Trial Lawyers Assn., Assn. Trial Lawyers Am. Democrat. Unitarian. Home: 604 San Felipe Way Boise ID 83712 Office: Idaho Supreme Ct 451 W State St Boise ID 83720

HUNTLEY, SCOTT ALAN, architect, human resource specialist; b. Richland, Wash., Sept. 9, 1951; s. Robin Donald and Helen Mae (Houghan) H.; m. Rebecca Louise Schultz, Aug. 7, 1976; children: Nathaniel, Andrew, Michael. BS in Architecture, Wash. State U., 1973, BArch., 1977. Registered architect. Architect McCue & Assocs., Richland, 1973-74, 75-76; plans examiner City of Richland, 1974-75; architect Seracuse Lawler, Ptnrs., Denver, 1977-79; architect The Callison Partnership, Seattle, 1979—, dir. human resources dept., 1984—, now ptnr.; bd. advisors Land Use/Transp. Plan, city of Seattle, 1981-83; mem. Nat. Trust Hist. Preservation, 1984-85. Area chmn. United Way, Seattle, 1985; mem. Leadership Tomorrow, Seattle, 1985-86. Mem. AIA (local chpt. sec.), Profl. Services Mgmt. Assn. (bd. dirs. 1986-88), Urban League, Seatle C. of C., Sigma Phi Epsilon (asst. mgr. Pullman, Wash. chpt. 1972-73). Lutheran. Clubs: Wash. Athletic (Seattle), Harbor, City. Lodge: Rotary (Emerald City). Home: 2670 Belvidere SW Seattle WA 98126 Office: The Callison Partnership Ltd 1423 3d Ave Seattle WA 98101

HUNTLEY, STIRLING LOUIS, educator consultant; b. L.A., Dec. 22, 1925; s. C. Stirling and Catharine (Somers) H.; m. Roberta Ann Baily, Sept. 16, 1950; children: Anne, Elizabeth. Student, Occidental Coll., 1943-44; BA, UCLA, 1945, MS, 1949; PhD, Stanford U., 1956. Asst. prof. Stanford (Calif.) U., 1955-58, assoc. dir. admissions, 1959-69; dir. participant svcs. East-West Ctr., Honolulu, 1969-71; assoc. dean grad. studies Calif. Inst. Tech., Pasadena, 1971-87, dir. admissions, 1973-87; dir. S.W. Mus., L.A., 1987-89; chmn. com. on internat. edn. Coll. Bd., N.Y.C., 1972-75; chmn. policy coun. Test of English and Fgn. Lang., Princeton, N.J., 1976-78. Contbr. numerous articles on univ. admissions to profl. jours. Trustee Orme Sch., Mayer, Ariz., 1973—, Met. Assocs., Pasadena, 1975—; chmn. bd. dirs. Indo-Chinese Evaluation Ctr., Long Beach, Calif., 1981—; bd. dirs. Internat. Baccalaureate, N.Y.C., 1983—. Lt. comdr. USN, 1943-40, with res. 1950-52. Recipient cert. of appreciation U.S. Dept. State, 1988. Mem. Nat. Assn. for Fgn. Student Affairs (life, pres. 1980), SAR, Athenaeum Club, Irish Club (London). Home: 1195 Arden Rd Pasadena CA 91106

HUNTON, DONALD BOTHEN, internist; b. Wheatland, Wyo., Nov. 20, 1927; s. Donald Evans and Magda Regina (Bothen) H.; m. Jean Antoinette Peachey, June 14, 1954; children: Donald Edward, Janice Annette. BS with honors, U. Wyo., 1950; MD, U. Rochester, 1954, MS in Medicine, 1961. Diplomate Am. Bd. Internal Medicine. Intern U. Rochester, Minn., 1954-55, resident, 1957-58; fellow Mayo Clinic, Rochester, 1958-61; pvt. practice, Cheyenne, Wyo., 1961—; bd. dirs. Unicover Corp., Cheyenne; mem. Flex test com. Nat. Bd. Med. Examiners, 1978—. Capt. USAF, 1955-57. Fellow ACP (bd. govs. Wyo. chpt.1985—); mem. AMA, Wyo. Med. Soc. (pres. 1975), Am. Soc. Gastrointestinal Endoscopy, Am. Gastroent. Assn., Young Men's Lit. Club, Masons, Rotary. Republican. Episcopalian. Home: 2863 Deming Blvd Cheyenne WY 82001 Office: Internal Medicine Group PC 1200 E 20th St Cheyenne WY 82001

HUNT-PELLOW, JUDY DEE, dietician; b. San Francisco, Sept. 14, 1945; d. Paul Adam and Lucille Jean (Drake) Coontz; children: Michelle, Paul. BS, U. Calif., Davis, 1966; M in Health Systems, U. San Francisco, 1987. Registered dietitian. Dietitian Sutter Gen. Hosp., Sacramento, 1968-69, Woodland Meml. Hosp., Calif., 1969-78; cons. dietician St. John's Village, Woodland, 1973-75; cons. nutritionist Drs. Blevins et al, Woodland, 1974-78; nutrition counselor Woodland Clinic, Woodland, 1978-85; nutrition counselor and pres. Nutrition For You Inc., Woodland, 1985—; pres. Calif. Dietetic Assn., Golden Empire Dist., Sacto, Calif., 1985-87. Contbr. articles to profl. jours., 1972-86. Recipient Disting. Svc. award Am. Heart Assn., 1974. Mem. Am. Dietetic Assn. (Young Dietition of Yr. 1976), Am. Soc. Bariatric Physicians (bd. dirs. 1987—, assoc.), Consulting Nutritionists (dir. No. Calif. chpt. 1979-81). Republican. Office: Nutrition For You Inc 520 Cottonwood #4A Woodland CA 95695 also: 501 Nut Tree Ct Vacaville CA 95688 also: 6500 Coyle #1 Carmichael CA 95608

HUNT-ROBINSON, DIXIE LEE, teacher; b. Pocatello, Idaho, Apr. 26, 1941; d. Leslie George and Eunice Gladys (Turner) Hunt; m. A. Lamar Robinson, Nov. 11, 1978. Student, Idaho State U., 1959-63, 65; cert., Grimm's Coll. Bus., 1962; BA in Comunications, Boise State U., 1978, cert. in secondary edn., 1980, postgrad., 1987—. Sec. Sta. KSNN, Pocatello, 1963-64, Pocatello Pub. Libr., 1964-67, Vocat.-Tech. Boise (Idaho) State U., 1968-69; receptionist Ore-Ida Foods, Inc., Boise, 1969-72; substitute tchr. Boise Sch. Dist., 1980-82; tchr. Meridian (Idaho) Sch. Dist., 1985—, tutor spl. programs, 1986—. Recipient Culinary and Gardening awards Idaho State Fair, 1985-88. Mem. AAUW (legis. chair 1983-84, cor. sec. 1984-86, nominating com. 1986-87, v.p. membership 1987-89, pres., 1989—), Garden Club, Christian Women Fellowship Club, Daughters of Nile Lodge. Democrat. Home: PO Box 423 Eagle ID 83616

HUNTSMAN, KEVIN PATRICK, physician; b. Los Angeles, Oct. 1, 1950; d. Frank Clifford and Lucille (Carpenter) Huntsman. BA, U. So. Calif., 1972; MD, U. Chgo., 1976. Diplomate Am. Bd. Internal Medicine. Staff physician Cigna Healthplan, Glendale, Calif., 1980—; bd. dirs. Cigna Healthplan. Office: Cigna Healthplan 2629 E Chapman Ave Orange CA 92669

HUO, RAE JACQUELINE, photographer; b. Taipei, Taiwan, Mar. 12, 1960; d. Mike Mao-Hsin and Shirley (Tang) H. BFA, U. So. Calif., 1981, Art Ctr. Coll. Design, Pasadena, Calif., 1984. Visual coordinator Liberty House Hawaii, Honolulu, 1981-83; advt. photographer RJH Photography, Honolulu, 1984—. Recipient photography award of merit Honolulu Mag., 1983, Hawaii Pele award of merit Hawaii Advt. Fedn. and Graphic Designers Assn., 1986, 87, 88, Hawaii Pele award of excellence, 1988. Mem. Am. Soc. Mag. Photographers. Office: RJH Photography 928 Nuuanu Ave Ste 209 Honolulu HI 96817

HUO, SHUANG, aerodynamicist; b. Kwangtung, China, July 19, 1941; came to U.S., 1974; s. Leung and Wun-chai (Chiu) H.; m. Trudy Yu-hong Tong, Oct. 28, 1971. BSME, Nat. Taiwan U., 1962; Diploma Engring., U. Stuttgart, Fed. Republic Germany, 1967; Diploma in Turbomachinery, von Karman Inst. for Fluid Dynamics, Rhode St. Genese, Belgium, 1970; DSc, Free U. Brussels, 1973. Devel. engr. Kraftwerk Union AG, Mulheim, Fed. Republic Germany, 1967-69; asst. rsch. engr. von Karman Inst. for Fluid Dynamics, Rhode St. Genese, 1970-73; sr. rsch. engr. Westinghouse Rsch. Labs., Pitts., 1974-76; supr. Garrett Turbine Engine Co., Phoenix, 1976-82; adv. engr. Westinghouse Marine Div., Sunnyvale, Calif., 1982—. Contbr. articles to profl. jours. Mem. Nat. Rep. Senatorial Com., 1983—. Mem. AIAA, ASME (turbomachinery com. 1983—). Roman Catholic. Office: Westinghouse Marine Div Hendy Ave Sunnyvale CA 94088

HUR, STEPHEN PONYI, civil engineer and management consultant; b. Peking, Hopei, China, Jan. 27, 1947; came to U.S., 1982; s. Mingan and Wenshien (Lu) H.; m. Lian Lihua Chiang, Mar. 8, 1975; children: Harry Yenhung, Cathy Chiayi. BS, Chungyuan U., 1968; MSCE, W. Va. U., 1973; Mgmt. Devel. Program cert., Taiwan U., 1982. Civil engr. Asia Cement Corp., Hsinchu, Taiwan, 1969-71; plant engr. Oriental Chem. Fiber Corp., Hsinchu, 1973-76; assoc. prof., chmn. civil engring. dept. Minghsin Coll. Engring., Hsinchu, 1976-78; gen. mgr. Join Engring. Cons., Taipei, 1978-83; sec., treas. Postech Construction Co., Belmont, Calif., 1983-86; pres. Standard Products, Foster City, Calif., 1984—; tech. adviser, Pacific Camus Corp., Taipei, 1979-82; dir. Versatile Mgmt. Cons., Taipei, 1979—; lectr., civil engring. dept. Tankang U., Taipei, 1980—; dir. Quartz Frequency Tech., Hsinchu, 1981—. Author: Construction Management, 1977, Modern Masonry, 1980, Small R.C. Building Design, 1981, Industrialized Housing, 1981. Mem. Am. Concrete Inst., Soc. Theoretical and Applied Mechanics, Chinese Inst. Engrs. Home: 1255 Beach Park Blvd Foster City CA 94404 Office: Standard Products 999C Edgewater Blvd #171 Foster City CA 94404

HURABIELL, JOHN PHILIP, SR., lawyer, corporate professional; b. San Francisco, June 2, 1947; s. Emile John and Anna Beatrice (Blumenauer) H.; m. Judith Marie Hurabiell, June 7, 1969; children—Marie Louise, Michele, Heather, John Philip Jr. J.D., San Francisco Law Sch., 1976. Bar: Calif. 1977. Sole practice, San Francisco, 1977-86; ptnr. Huppert & Hurabiell, San Francisco, 1985—; pres. San Francisco S.A.F.E., Inc., 1983-88, pres. emeritus 1988—; treas. Republican election coms.; Served with U.S. Navy, Vietnam. Decorated Navy Commendation Medal. Mem. ABA, Calif. Bar Assn., San Francisco Bar Assn., Assn. Trial Lawyers Am., Calif. Trial Lawyers Assn., San Francisco Trial Lawyers Assn., Lawyers Club San Francisco, St. Thomas More Soc., Sports Lawyers Assn., St. Franicis Hook & Ladder Soc. (trustee). Roman Catholic. Clubs: Press of San Francisco, Ferrari Owners, Golden Gate Breakfast Club, San Francisco Tennis. Lodge: KC, Alhambra (organizing regional dir. 1983-85). Editor, primary author: C.A.L.U. Business Practices Guidelines, rev. edit., 1980. Office: Huppert & Hurabiell 1355 Market St Ste 417 San Francisco CA 94103

HURLBERT, ROGER WILLIAM, direct marketing industry executive; b. San Francisco, Feb. 18, 1941; s. William G. and Mary (Greene) H.; m. Karen C. Haslag, Nov. 6, 1982; children: Chula, Monk, Morris. BS in Community Devel., So. Ill. U., 1965. Newspaper editor and reporter various, San Francisco Bay Area, 1958-62; pvt. practice investigation Ill., 1963-65; advisor San Francisco Planning Urban Rsch. Assn., 1969-87; pres. Sage Info. Svcs., San Francisco, 1988—. Compiler Western States Land Data Base, 1972—. Pres. Haight-Ashbury Neighborhood Coun., San Francisco, 1959-61. With U.S. Army, 1966-68, Vietnam. Recipient Cert. of Merit San Francisco Coun. Dist. Merchants Assn., 1972. Mem. Info. Industry Assn., Direct Mktg. Assn., Mail Advt. Svc. Assn. Internat., League of Men Voters (v.p. 1959—). Democrat. Office: Sage Info Svcs 414 Clement St #5 San Francisco CA 94118

HURLBUT, RONALD LEON, engineering executive; b. Detroit, Apr. 28, 1941; s. Leo Rogers and Norine (Duhamel) H.; m. Karen Knieriem, Sept. 25, 1965; children: Gregory, John. BSCE with high honors, Sacramento State U., 1964; MSCE, U. Calif., Berkeley, 1965. Jr. civil engr. State of Calif., Sacramento, 1963-64; assoc. civil engr. City of Oakland (Calif.), 1965-68, sr. traffic engr., 1969-72, traffic engr., dir. parking, 1973-78, dep. dir. pub. works, 1979-83, dir. pub. works, 1983—; tchr. Alameda (Calif.) Community Coll., 1970-71; lectr. U. Calif., Berkeley, 1970-81, Northwestern U., Evanston, Ill., 1974-96; commr. Calif. Const. of Accounts Com., 1986—. Asst. scout master Boy Scouts Am., Walnut Creek, Calif., 1979-83, com. chmn., Fairfield, Calif., 1983-87; bd. dirs. Woodlands Home Owners Assn., Walnut Creek, 1977-80. Served to sgt. U.S. Army, 1970-72. NSF fellow, 1964. Mem. Am. Pub. Works Assn., No. Calif. Pub. Works Soc. (pres. 1987), Inst. of Transp., Western Dist. Inst. of Transp. (pres. 1976), League of Calif. Cities. Home: 1832 Kolob Dr Fairfield CA 94533 Office: City of Fairfield 1000 Webster St Fairfield CA 94533

HURLEY, FRANCIS T., archbishop; b. San Francisco, Jan. 12, 1927. Ed., St. Patrick Sem., Menlo Park, Calif., Catholic U. Am. Ordained priest Roman Cath. Ch., 1951; with Nat. Cath. Welfare Conf., Washington, asst. sec., 1958-68; assoc. sec. Nat. Cath. Welfare Conf., now U.S. Cath. Conf., 1968-70; consecrated bishop 1970; titular bishop Daimlaig and aux. bishop Diocese of Juneau, Alaska, 1970-71; bishop of Juneau 1971-76, archbishop of Anchorage, 1976—. Office: Chancery Office PO Box 2239 Anchorage AK 99510 *

HURLEY, KEVIN CHRISTOPHER, physicist; b. N.Y.C., Oct. 12, 1942; s. Eugene and Anitra Charlotte (Freedman) H.; m. Janet Barbara Strauss, June 22, 1969; children: Sabine, Alison. BA, U. Calif., Berkeley, 1966, PhD, 1970. Asst. rsch. physicist space scis.lab. U. Calif., 1970-72, rsch. physicist, sr. fellow, 1987—; rsch. physicist Centre D'Etude Spatiale Des Rayonnements, Toulouse, France, 1972-75; vis. assoc. prof. Universite Paul Sabatier, Toulouse, 1975-78; rsch. physicist Centre Nat. De La Recherche Scientifique, Toulouse, 1978-87; cons. Schlumberger-Enertec Corp., Paris, 1982, European Space Agy., Paris, 1986. Mem. editorial bd. Jour. Astrophysical Letters and Comments, N.Y.C., 1986—; contbr. articles to profl. jours. Recipient Bronze medal French Nat. Space Agy., 1980. Mem. Am. Astronomical Assn., Phi Beta Kappa. Democrat. Jewish. Office: U Calif Space Scis Lab Berkeley CA 94720

HURLEY, MARLENE EMOGENE, oil company executive; b. Chamois, Mo., July 23, 1938; d. Eugene Arthur Harrison and Mary Elizabeth (Turner) Meredith; m. Aaron Downs Hurley, Nov. 25, 1956; children: Mitchell Kelly, Aaron Downs Jr. Cert. oil and gas acctg., frontline mgr. Acct. McGrath Constrn. Co., Tulsa, 1964-66, G&T, Inc., G&T Constrn. and Valley Supply Co., Tulsa, 1965-67; acctg. supr. Automation Industries, Inc., Boulder, Colo., 1968-73; office mgr., chief acct. Automotive Svcs., White Rock Investments, JWD Corp., 3 Constrn. Div., Boulder, 1973; freelance acct. various cos., Boulder, 1974-76; treas., contr. Quicksilver, Inc., Colo. X-Ray, Colo. Processor Svc., Broomfield, 1974-79; contr. Hartford House, Ltd., Boulder, 1979-80; adminstrv. asst., mgr. Joint Int., Acct. Payables Freeport McMoran, Inc., McMoran Oil & Gas, Midlands and Lakewood, Colo., 1980-86; chief fin. officer Transp. Engring. Systems, Inc., Broomfield, 1987-88; asst. sec./treas. Altex Industries Inc., Denver, 1989—; cons. Spruce Realty, Boulder, 1974-76, Aaron Associated Affiliates, Lafayette, Colo., 1987-88. Mem. Rebekah lodge (past madam pres. 1966-67). Democrat. Home: Rte 7 Box 405 Golden CO 80403 Office: Altex Industries Inc 1430 Larimer St Ste 201 Denver CO 80020

HUROWITZ, GEOFFREY SCOTT, artist and operations manager, country club executive, promoter; b. Sioux City, Iowa, Feb. 13, 1950; s. Nathan and Margaret Ann (Mirkin) H.; divorced. BA in Bus. and Spl. Edn., U. Okla., 1973. Booking agt. Jim Halsey Co., Tulsa, 1980; concert promoter Sound Promotions, Norman, Okla., 1972-73; artist mgr. All Night Entertainment, Tulsa, L.A., 1980—; ops. mgr. Chuck Landis' Country Club, L.A., 1987—; mgr. Bad Finger Band Atlantic Records, L.A., 1980-81, Jef Scott Epic Records, L.A., 1981-87. Mem. Okla. U. Club of So. Calif. Jewish. Home and Office: 1461 S Sherbourne Dr Los Angeles CA 90035

HURST, ROY GLENN, prosthodontist; b. Ozark, Ala., Jan. 9, 1954. BA, Northwestern U., 1976, MS, 1977; postgrad., U. So. Calif., 1983. Pvt. practice specializing in dentistry Oxnard, Calif., 1983--. Mem. ADA, Calif. Dental Assn., Santa Barbara Ventura County Dental Soc. (bd. dirs. 1986--), Am. Coll. Prosthodontists (assoc.), Internat. Coll. Prosthodontists (assoc.), Acad. Osseointegration, Somis, Riders and Ropers, Rotary (pres. Oxnard chpt.). Republican. Office: 215 Doris Ave Oxnard CA 93035

HURST, WILLIAM BARLOW, lawyer; b. Chgo., June 1, 1948; s. William Barlow and Alice Patricia (Armstrong) H.; m. Debra Lee Green, Nov. 30, 1985. BS, No. Ariz. U., 1970; JD, U. Ariz., 1973. Bar: Ariz. 1973. Dep. county atty. Coconino County, Flagstff, Ariz., 1974-76, chief dep., 1976-78; pvt. practice Flagstff, Ariz., 1978—. Candidate, Coconino County Atty., 1980. Mem. ABA, Assn. Trial Lawyers Am., Coconino County Bar Assn., Big Brothers Club. Democratic. Home: 5000 Lake County Rd Flagstaff AZ 86001 Office: 125 E Elm Ave Ste A Flagstaff AZ 86001

HURT, CHARLIE DEUEL, III, library school director; b. Charlottesville, Va., Sept. 20, 1950; s. Charlie Deuel Jr. and Timie Oletta (Young) H.; m. Susan Edith Scudamore, May 15, 1981. BA, U. Va., 1971; MLS, U. Ky., 1975; PhD, U. Wis., 1981. Engring. librarian U. Va., Charlottesville, 1975-78, automation librarian, 1977-78; asst. prof. McGill U., Montreal, Que., Can., 1981-84, assoc. prof., 1984; assoc. prof. Simmons Coll., Boston, 1984-86; dir. lib. sch. U. Ariz., Tucson, 1986—; prin. Info. Prime, Montreal, 1984—; cons. Scudamore & Assocs. Montreal, 1984-85. Contbr. articles to profl. jours. Hollowell grantee Simmons Coll., 1984. Mem. ALA, Assn. Library and Info. Sci. Edn., History Sci. Soc., N.Y. Acad. Sci. Home: 6781 E 4th St Tucson AZ 85710-2217 Office: U Ariz Grad Libr Sch 1515 E 1st St Tucson AZ 85719

HURT, ROBERT LEE, accounting educator, tax consultant; b. St. Louis, Aug. 18, 1959; s. James Leslie Hurt and Janet Irene (Markham) Immekus. BSBA, Southeast Mo. State U., 1981; MS in Bus. Adminstrn., Calif. State Poly. U., 1985; postgrad. in mgmt., Claremont Grad. Sch., 1986--. Minister youth and music Primera Iglesia Bautista, Denver, 1981-83; grad. asst. Calif. State Poly U., Pomona, 1984-85, lectr. acctg., 1987--; chmn. dept. Eldorado Coll., West Covina, Calif., 1984-86; teaching asst. Claremont (Calif.) Grad. Sch., 1986—; lectr. acctg. Claremont Colls., 1987—; tax cons., 1985-87; cons. Foxfire Industries, City of Industry, Calif., 1987. Author: computer acctg. text supplements, 1985--, Introduction to Database Management, 1985. Bd. dirs., sec. Pomona-San Gabriel Valley Gay and Lesbian Coalition, 1986. Claremont Grad. Sch. scholar, 1986—. Mem. Met. Community Ch. Home: 230 City Blvd W #101 Orange CA 92668 Office: Claremont Grad Sch Peter F Drucker Mgmt Ctr 925 N Dartmouth Claremont CA 91711

HURTADO, ALBERT LEON, history educator; b. Sacramento, Oct. 19, 1946; s. Victor Alberto and Elsie Pearl (Dickenson) H.; m. Willa Jean Kerr, May 31, 1980. BA, Calif. State U., Sacramento, 1969, MA, 1974; PhD, U. Calif., Santa Barbara, 1981. Park interpretive specialist Calif. Parks and Recreation Dept., Sacramento, 1978; cons. historian TCR, Fair Oaks, Calif., 1978-80, Pub. History Svcs. Assocs., Sacramento, 1980-82; instr. Sierra Coll., Rocklin, Calif., 1981-82, U. Md., College Park, 1983; asst. prof. history Ind. U.-Purdue U., Indpls., 1983-86, Ariz. State U., Tempe, 1986—; chmn. Calif. Com. for Promotion History, 1981-82. Author: Indian Survival on the California Frontier, 1988; contbr. articles on Indians and the west to hist. jours. Sgt. U.S. Army, 1969-71, Korea. Mem. Nat. Coun. on Pub. History (treas. 1984-86), Orgn. Am. Historians (Billington prize 1989), Am. Hist. Assn., Western History Assn. (Bolton award 1982). Democrat. Office: Ariz State U Dept History Tempe AZ 85287

HURTT, HARVEY DUANE, school system administrator; b. Delta, Utah, Jan. 5, 1928; s. Robert Filewood and Mamie Alvhilde (Huset) H.; m. Beverly Julia Montrond, June 5, 1955 (div. 1981); children: John Henry, Conrad Marlow; m. Meei-Jin Shiao, Jan. 30, 1982; 1 child, Eileen. BA, New Sch. Social Rsch., N.Y.C., 1955; MA, San Francisco State U., 1979; EdM, Columbia U., 1982. Tchr. 1953-68, various elem. schs., Morrocco, Turkey, Spain and Taiwan; tchr. social studies high sch. Seville, Spain; tchr. English and civics high sch., Bothell, Wash. and Sao Paulo, Brazil; mgr. Office Student Activities Tchrs. Coll., Columbia U., N.Y.C.; prin. adult high sch., Berkeley, Calif.; asst. supt., prin. Monterrey (Mex.) sch.; site adminstr., prin. Little Diomede (Ark.) Sch. Dist.; dist. supt., prin. Wyola (Mont.) Sch. Dist.; supt. Plumas Elem. Sch. Dist., Marysville, Calif., 1978—. Editor, pub. Ancient Coins, 1969-78; contbr. to various textbooks and encys.; photos exhibited at Mus. Modern Art, N.Y.C., 1959; pub. Century 21 Publications, Berkeley, Calif., 1961-63. Bd. dirs. Sch. for Emotionally Handicapped, Oreg.; mem. task force on urban edn. Columbia U.; mem. exec. com. Tchrs. Coll. With USMC, 1946-49. Mem. Assn. Calif. Sch. Adminstrs., San Francisco Ancient Numismatic Soc. (past pres.), Am. Soc. Monterrey (trustee), Mont. Assn. Community Edn. (trustee). Home: 1515 Ellis Lake Dr Marysville CA 95901 Office: Plumas Elem Sch Dist 2548 Hoffman-Plumas Rd Marysville CA 95901

HURTUBISE, ROBERT JOHN, chemistry educator; b. Chgo., June 7, 1941; s. Edward John and Gretta Agnes (Ward) H.; m. Paula Francine Brokhage, Aug. 14, 1965; children: Timothy, David, Suzanne. BS in Chemistry, Xavier U., 1964, MS in Chemistry, 1966; PhD in Chemistry, Ohio U., 1969. Asst. prof. chemistry Rockhurst Coll., Kansas City, Mo., 1969-71; sect. supr. Pfizer Inc., Terre Haute, Ind., 1971-74; prof. U. Wyo., Laramie, 1974—. Author: Soild Surface Luminescence Analysis: Theory, Instrumentation, Applications, 1981; reviews; contbr. chpts. to books; articles to profl. jours. Research grantee U. Wyo., Laramie Energy Tech. Ctr., 1975-77, 1977-79, numerous Dept. Energy grants, NSF, 1975, 81, also instrumentation grantee NSF, 1981, 82, 83. Mem. AAAS, Am. Chem. Soc., Soc. Applied Spectroscopy. Office: U Wyo Dept Chemistry Laramie WY 82070

HURWITZ, CHARLES EDWIN, oil company executive; b. Kilgore, Tex., May 3, 1940; s. Hyman and Eva (Engler) H.; m. Barbara Raye Gollub, Feb. 24, 1963; children: Shawn Michael, David Alan. B.A., U. Okla., Norman, 1962. Chmn. bd., pres. Investam. Group, Inc., Houston, 1965-67, Summitt Mgmt. & Research Corp., Houston, 1967-70; chmn. bd. Summit Ins. Co. of N.Y., Houston, 1970-75; with MCO Holdings, Inc. (and predecessor), Los Angeles, from 1978, chmn. bd., chief exec. officer, from 1980, dir., from 1978; chmn. bd., chief exec. officer, dir. Maxxam Inc., Los Angeles; chmn. bd. Federated Reins. Corp.; chmn. bd., pres. Federated Devel. Co.; dir. MCO Resources, Inc. Co-chmn. Com. to Establish George Kozmetsky Centennial Chair in Grad. Sch. Bus., U. Tex., Austin, from 1980. Jewish. Office: United Fin Group Inc 5718 Westheimer Houston TX 77057 other: Maxxam Inc 10880 Wilshire Blvd Los Angeles CA 90024 *

HUSAIN, RAFE ASIM, engineering executive, electrical and civil engineer; b. Kanpur, India, Jan. 20, 1959; came to U.S., 1971; s. Asim and Rafia (Khatoon) H.; m. Kishwar Jahan, Feb. 14, 1985; 1 child, Asma. BS in Math., U. Mich., 1980, BSEE, 1981; MS in Computer Engring., Wayne State U., 1983. Engr. CDA Engring., Detroit, 1982-83; lead engr. Hughes Aircraft Co., Fullerton, Calif., 1983-87; v.p. engring. Sabtech Industries, Yorba Linda, Calif., 1987—; bd. dirs. Muslim Savs. & Investment Co., Beverly Hills, Calif. Muslim. Office: Sabtech Industries 3910-B Prospect Ave Yorba Linda CA 92688

HUSCHKE, RALPH ERNEST, meteorologist, consultant; b. Utica, N.Y., Nov. 28, 1925; s. Henry Albert and Hedwig (Borchers) H.; m. Virginia-Earle Kincaid, Aug. 28, 1948; children: Peter C., Lisa E. BS, MIT, 1946. Meteorologist U.S. Weather Bur., Boston and Hartford, Conn., 1948-50, 50-52; rsch. staff mem. MIT, Cambridge, 1954-56; glossary editor Am. Meteorol. Soc., Boston, 1955-58; chief rsch. products br. Air Force Cambridge Rsch. Ctr., Bedford, Mass., 1956-59; engring. specialist Northrop Corp., Hawthorne, Calif., 1959-61; sr. phys. scientist The Rand Corp., Santa Monica, Calif., 1962-73; cons. Coronado, Calif., 1973-82; assoc. Climatol. Cons. Corp., Asheville, N.C., 1982—; pres. Huschke Assoc., Inc., Coronado, 1982—; mem. panel on weather and climate modification Nat. Acad. Sci., Washington, 1965-66; meteorol. cons. Random House, Inc., N.Y.C., 1964—; cons. The Rand Corp., Santa Monica, 1973—, Sci. Applications, Inc., Albuquerque, 1978-84. Editor: Glossary of Meteorology, 1959, Nat. Acad. Sci. Report, Weather and Climate Modification: Problems and Prospects, 1966; asst. editor Jour. Applied Meteorology, 1974-76; contbr. articles to profl. jours. Active Town Adv. Com., Scituate, Mass., 1958-59; pres. Human Rels. Coun., Palos Verdes Peninsula, Calif., 1968-70; mem. Recycling Adv. Com., Coronado, Calif., 1989—; pres. Condominios Pilar Homeowners Assn., Guaymas, Sohora, Mex., 1989—. With USNR, 1943-67. Mem. AAAS, Am. Meteorol. Soc., Am. Geophys. Union, Nat. Coun. Indsl. Meteorologists, Nat. Weather Assn., Assn. Am. Weather Observers, Mil. Ops. Rsch. Soc., Calif. Resource Recovery Assn. Democrat. Home: 6 Admiralty Cross Coronado CA 92118 Office: Huschke Assocs Inc 1001 B Ave PO Box 456 Rm 320 Coronado CA 92118

HUSHAW, JAMES STEVEN, newspaper editor; b. Bell, Calif., July 17, 1935; s. Charles Coy and Marie Katherin (Johnson) H.; m. Glenda Rose Merrick, June 14, 1958; children: Craig, Jana, Jeff. BA, San Jose State U., 1957. Mng. editor Glendale News Press, Calif., 1959-68; asst. mng. editor Riverside Press Enterprise, Calif., 1968-72; mng. editor Nev. State Jour., Reno, 1972-73, Reno Evening Gazette, 1973-74, Stockton Record, Calif., 1975-88, dir. spl. projects, 1988—. Bd. dirs. Stockton Conv. and Visitors Bur.; mem. edn. com. Bus. Coun. San Joaquin County; mem. cabinet United Way San Joaquin County. Mem. Calif. Newspaper Editors Assn. (pres. 1979), Calif. AP Editors (pres. 1978), Am. Soc. Newspaper Editors, Sigma Delta Chi (pres. Nev. chpt. 1973). Republican. Lutheran. Lodge: Rotary (bd. dirs. Stockton chpt. 1984—). Office: Stockton Newspapers Inc 530 E Market St Stockton CA 95202

HUSS, CHARLES MAURICE, municipal building official; b. Chgo., Nov. 11, 1946; s. Charles Maurice and June Pierce (Bailey) H.; m. Winifred Louise Traughber, Dec. 24, 1973; children—Amber Elaine, Ra Ja Lorraine, Micah Alexander, Gabriel Joe, Cameron M., Jordan Charles. AA, Kendall Coll., 1984; student Oregon State U., Western Oreg. State Coll., U. Cinn., U. Alaska, Western Ill. U., City U., Nat. Fire Acad., Ohio U., Chukchi Community Coll. Traffic mgr. The Harwald Co., Evanston, Ill., 1966-67, asst. v.p., 1968-69; traffic mgr. Northwestern U. Press, Evanston, 1969-71; fire chief City of Kotzebue (Alaska), 1971-76, asst. city mgr., 1973-76; dir. maintenance USPHS Hosp., Kotzebue, 1976-79; pres., gen. mgr. Action Builders, Inc., Kotzebue, 1979-82; gen. mgr. Husky Maintenance Svcs., 1982—; chief bldg. insp. City of Kotzebue, 1985—; adj. faculty Nat. Fire Acad., Emmitsburg, Md. Chmn., Kotzebue Planning Commn., 1978-82, Kotzebue Sch. Bd., 1974-79, 83—; founding vice chmn. Kotzebue chpt. ARC; mem. Alaska Criminal Code Revision Commn., 1976-78; mem. Fire Marshal's Sprinkler Task Force; mem. Alaska Fire Fighter Tng. Commn.; mem. Arctic Fire Mitigation Code Task Force; asst. chief Kotzebue Vol. Fire Dept., 1972-76, 82—; bd. dirs, instr. Alaska Craftsman Home Program 1986—; instr. Kotzebue Regional Fire Tng. Ctr., 1982—. Pullman Found. scholar, 1964-65, Blackburn Coll. scholar, 1964-65, Ill. State scholar, 1964-66. Mem. ASHRAE, AACED, Constrn. Specifications Inst., Internat. Soc. Fire Svc. Instrs., Fire Marshalls Assn. N.Am., Bldg. Ofcls. and Code Adminstrs. Internat., Alaska Firefighters Assn., Internat. Assn. Fire and Arson Investigators, Western Fire Chiefs Assn., Internat. Conf. Bldg. Ofcls. (cert. bldg. ofcl., fire, plumbing and mech. insp.), Am. Soc. Safety Engrs., Internat. Assn. Plumbing and Mech. Ofcls., Internat. Assn. Elec. Insps., Internat. Assn. Fire Chiefs, Home Builders Assn. Alaska, Nat. Fire Protection Assn., Soc. Nat. Fire Acad. Instrs., Coalition for Home Fire Safety, Masonry Soc., Kotzebue C. of C. Guest essayist: Seven Days and Sunday (Kirkpatrick), 1973; contbr. Alaska Craftsman Home Building Manual. Home and Office: PO Box 277 Kotzebue AK 99752

HUSS, CLAUDIA SPEROFF, hospital administrator, educator; b. Hammond, Ind., Jan. 2, 1959; d. Boris James and Betty Roen (Androff) Speroff; m. Patrick Lee Huss, Aug. 29, 1986; 1 child, Samantha Leigh. BS in Pub. Adminstrn., U. Ariz., 1980; M in Health Svcs. Adminstrn., Ariz. State U., 1984. Branch sec. Mercantile Nat. Bank of Ind., Griffith, 1981; analyst Equitable Life Ins. Soc. of Am., Phoenix, 1981-82; adminstrv. resident Palo Verde Hosp., Tucson, 1983-84, asst. adminstr., 1984-87; asst. adminstr. Charter Hosp. of Glendale, Ariz., 1988-89; instr. Golden Gate U., San Francisco, 1985—. Mem. Am. Soc. Healthcare Risk Mgrs. Republican. Lutheran. Home: 322 N Loquat Ave Tucson AZ 85710

HUSS, EDWARD ADOLF, instructor, researcher; b. Auburn, N.Y., June 9, 1926; s. Adolf Clement and Virginia (Geteau) H.; divorced; children: Richard, James, Anna, Leah, Teo, Christy. Cert. neuro-linguistics, hypnosis, biofeedback, Reiki therapy, extensive research into parapsychology & metaphysics. Dance instr. Arthur Murray Studios, Tulsa, 1946-48; operator Seismographic Service Corp., western U.S., 1951-53; seismic operator Century Geophysical Corp., western U.S., 1953-54, Tower Exploration, western U.S., 1954-55; airport mgr. Kimball, Nebr., 1955-57; aircraft tech., inspector Sky Ranch Airport, Denver, 1957-58; aircraft tech., inspector, lead inspector net data throughout then forman Frontier Airlines, Denver, 1958-85; instr. Colo. Aero Tech., Broomfield, 1986—; cons. SELF, non-destructive test, Denver; educator Holistic Health, SELF, Denver. Author various plays, non-fiction writings. Musician, drum major 3d Rgt. N.Y. Guard, 1944; elections examiner NLRB, Detroit, Mich., 1955. Group commdr. Civil Air Patrol, Denver. Home: 1493 Beach Park Blvd Ste 144 Foster City CA 94404

HUSSON, WILLIAM JOSEPH, educational administrator; b. Toronto, Ont., Can., Oct. 22, 1944; came to U.S., 1953; s. William Clarence and Teresa Loretta (Clarke) H.; m. Linda Mary Laury, Aug. 2, 1974; children: Michael William, Julie Christine, Mark Joseph. BA, St. Thomas U., Denver, 1966, ThM, 1970. Asst. buyer, area mgr. Joske's of Tex., San Antonio, 1972-74; edn. dir. St. Gregory's Parish, San Antonio, 1974, St. Thomas More Ctr., Englewood, Colo., 1975-79; assoc. dir. Diocese of Saginaw (Mich.) Edn. Office, 1979-82; dir. career edn. program Regis Coll., Denver, 1982—. Mem. Religious Edn. Commn. Archdiocese of Denver, 1987—. Mem. Am. Soc. Tng. and Devel., Am. Assn. Adult and Continuing Edn., The Alliance for Higher Edn., Nat. Conf. of Diocesan Dirs. of Religious Edn. Democrat. Roman Catholic. Office: Regis Coll W 50th and Lowell Blvd Denver CO 80221

HUSTON, HARRIETTE IRENE OTWELL (REE HUSTON), municipality secretary. d. Harry C. Otwell and Fannie (Mitchell) Otwell Geffert; m. Dan E. Huston, Jan. 21, 1951; children: Terry Dane, Dale Curtis, Ronald William, Randall Philip. BS, Kans. State Coll., 1951. Cert. life ins. agt., Wash.; cert. wastewater operator in tng., Wash. Tchr. Kans., Ill., 1955-58; assoc. home economist McCall's Patterns Co., N.Y.C., 1959-62; counselor, owner Dunhill of Seattle Personnel, 1968-75; enrollment officer, trainer, adminstrv. sec. Teller Tng. Insts., Seattle, 1975-76; life and health ins. agt. Lincoln Nat. Sales, Seattle, 1976-77; office mgr., adminstrv. sec. ARA Transp. Group, Seattle, 1977-78; asst. to the pres. Pryde Corp., Bellevue, Wash., 1978-80; sr. sec. Municipality of Met. Seattle, 1980—. Coauthor: Homemaking textbook, 1956; contbr. articles to profl. jours.. Sec. exec. and gen. bd. Bellevue Christian Ch. Disciples of Christ, 1976-77, 1986-87; chmn. flowers com. Bellevue Christian Ch., 1978-83, elder, 1978, diaconate, 1987.bd. mem., sec. Surrey Downs Community Club, Bellevue, 1983-85. Recipient Clothing award check McCall's Patterns Co., N.Y.C., 1962, Certs. of Merit Metro Hdqrs., Seattle, 1981, 82, 83, 86, 89. Club: Bridge (Bellevue). Home: 2424 109th Ave SE Bellevue WA 98004 Office: Municipality of Met Seattle 821 2d Ave Seattle WA 98104

HUSTON, JOHN RICHARD, physician; b. Columbus, Ohio, May 1, 1920; s. Harvey and Harriet Elizabeth (Schubert) H.; m. Patricia Wilkinson, Oct. 17, 1940 (dec. Oct. 1970); children: ShirleyJ., Bonnie L., Valerie E., John Richard; m. Martha Rankin, Oct. 16, 1971 (div. 1979); m. Beverly E. Gerrish, Apr. 21, 1982. BA, MD, Ohio State U., 1947. Diplomate Am. Bd. Internal Medicine. Intern US Naval Hosp., Phila., 1947-48; resident in pathology US Naval Hosp., Bethesda, Md., 1948-49; resident in internal medicine Phila. Naval Hosp., 1951-52, Ohio State U., 1953-54; resident in cardiology Ohio State U. Hosp., 1954-55; clin. instr. medicine Ohio State U., Columbus, 1953-60, clin. asst. prof., 1960-64, clin. assoc. prof., 1964-74; pvt. practice medicine specializing in internal medicine and cardiology Columbus, 1955-74; med. dir. United Comml. Travelers, Columbus, 1966-74; mem. staff dept. internal medicine VA Hosp., Phoenix, 1974-83, also dir. affiliated med. rsidency program, asst. chief of medicine; clin. dir. Maricopa County Alcohol and Substance Abuse Program, Phoenix, 1986—. Contbr. articles to med. jours. Served with USNR, 1944-46, 47-53. Mem. AMA, Ohio Med. Assn., Am. Heart Assn., Internat. Platform Assn., N.Y. Acad. Scis., Acad. Medicine Columbus and Franklin County (pres. 1965), Am. Med. Soc. on Alcoholism and Other Drug Dependencies (cert. 1987). Home: 2828 E Desert Cove Phoenix AZ 85028 Office: 3101 E Watkins Rd Phoenix AZ 85034

HUSTON, WILLIAM ALVIN, engineering executive; b. Braceville, Ill., Nov. 30, 1939; s. William Alvin and Betty F. (Tyler) H.; m. Delores S. Sandeno, June 18, 1960; children: John, Jeffrey. BCE, U. Ill., 1961; MS in Mech. Engring., San Diego State U., 1967. Design engr. Gen. Dynamics/Convair, San Diego, 1961-66; engring. dir. Sandaire, San Diego, 1966-82; pres. D3 Tecnologies, San Diego, 1982—. Leader Boy Scouts Am., San Diego, 1969-75; dir. Youth Sports, 1969-85; coordinator Local Campaigns, San Diego. Mem. Soc. Automotive Engrs., Am. Inst. Aeronautic and Astronautics, Am. Def. Preparedness Assn. (pres. 1984-85), Air Force Soc., Navy League Am. Republican. Lutheran. Office: D3 Techs Inc 4838 Ronson Ct San Diego CA 92111

HUTCHCRAFT, A. STEPHENS, JR., aluminum and chemical company executive; b. Orange, N.J., June 26, 1930; s. A. Stephens and Marguerite (Davis) H.; m. Mary Seaman, May 28, 1955; children: Pamela, Martha, A. Stephens. B.S., Yale U., 1952; postgrad. mgmt. devel., Harvard U., 1964. Registered profl. engr., Calif. Extrusion plant mgr. Kaiser Aluminum & Chem. Corp., Los Angeles, 1964-68; div. mgr. Kaiser Aluminum & Chem. Corp., Oakland, Calif., 1968-70, v.p., mgr. elec. products, 1970-75, v.p. aluminum, reduction and carbon, 1975-80, v.p., gen. mgr. aluminum div., 1980-82, pres., chief operating officer, 1982—; dir. Anglesey Aluminum, London, Valco, Ghana. Chmn. western region Nat. Amigos de Ser, Dallas, 1983; bd. dirs. Met. YMCA Alameda County, Calif., A Better Chance, Boston. Mem. Aluminum Assn. (chmn. 1982—). Republican. Presbyterian. Home: 15 Hillside Dr Danville CA 94526 Office: Kaiser Aluminum & Chem Corp 300 Lakeside Dr Oakland CA 94643 *

HUTCHERSON, CHRISTOPHER ALFRED, sales executive, sales and recruiting consultant; b. Memphis, June 13, 1950; s. Wayne Alfred Hutcherson and Loretta (Morris) Kindsfather; m. Glenda Ann Champ, May 22, 1971. BS, U. Houston, 1972, M in Adminstrn., 1977, postgrad., 1977-79. Pvt. music instr. Spring Br. and Pasadena Ind. Sch. Dists., Tex., 1968-75; jr. high and high sch. band dir. Deer Park (Tex.) Ind. Schs., 1972-80; recruiter M. David Lowe Personnel, Houston, 1981; sales dir. Instl. Financing Svcs., Benicia, Calif., 1982-85; sales mgr. Instl. Financing Svcs., Benicia, 1985-87; nat. tng. dir. Champion Products and Svcs., San Diego, 1987-88, west coast and midwest sales mgr., 1988-89; pres. Camelot, Inc., Auburn, Calif., 1989—. Judge Tex. jr. high and high sch. bands, 1974-81; choir dir. St. Hyacinth Ch., Deer Park, 1979-81; vice-chmn. Ch. Coun. St. Hyacinth Ch., 1980. Mem. Kappa Kappa Psi (v.p.). Republican. Roman Catholic. Home: 2491 Frontier Rd Auburn CA 95603

HUTCHESON, JERRY DEE, manufacturing company executive; b. Hammon, Okla., Oct. 31, 1932; s. Radford Andrew and Ethel Mae (Boulware) H.; B.S. in Physics, Eastern N. Mex. U., 1959; postgrad. Temple U., 1961-62, U. N.Mex., 1964-65; m. Lynda Lou Weber, Mar. 6, 1953; children—Gerald Dan, Lisa Marie, Vicki Lynn. Research engr. RCA, 1959-62; sect. head Motorola, 1962-63; research physicist Dikewood Corp., 1963-66; sr. mem. tech. staff Signetics Corp., 1966-69; engring. mgr. Litton Systems, Sunnyvale, Calif., 1969-70; engring. mgr. Fairchild Semiconductor, Mountain View, Calif., 1971; equipment engr., group mgr. Teledyne Semiconductor, Mountain View, 1971-74; dir. engring. DCA Reliability Labs., Sunnyvale, 1974-75; founder, prin. Tech. Ventures, San Jose, Calif., 1975—; chief exec. officer VLSI Research, Inc., 1981—. Democratic precinct committeeman, Albuquerque, 1964-66. Served with USAF, 1951-55. Registered profl. engr., Calif. Mem. Nat. Soc. Profl. Engrs., Profl. Engrs. Pvt. Practice, Calif. Soc. Profl. Engrs., Semiconductor Equipment and Materials Inst., Soc. Photo-Optical Instrumentation Engrs., Am. Soc. Test Engrs., Presbyterian. Club: Masons. Contbr. articles to profl. jours. Home: 5950 Vista Loop San Jose CA 95124 Office: VSLI Rsch 1754 Technology Dr Ste 117 San Jose CA 95110

HUTCHINGS, LA VERE, artist, educator; b. Lewisville, Idaho, Sept. 18, 1918; s. Marion Price and Mellie Grace (Kinghorn) H.; m. Anne Elizabeth Kirkman, Aug. 2, 1940; children—Marianne, Jeanne, Richard, Dorothy, Robert. A.A., Idaho State U., 1940; student Brigham Young U., 1940-41, Chuinard Art Inst., 1954, 55, Art Students League, summer 1970, John Pike Watercolor Sch., spring and summer 1970. Painter, art instr. Armed Forces Inst., Manila, Philippines, 1945-46, Ricks Coll., Idaho Falls, 1968-69, Hutchings Watercolor Workshops, Idaho and Calif., 1967—; painter, owner, operator Hutchings Gallery, Jamestown, Calif., 1979—; mus. collections include: Laguna Beach Mus. Fine Art, Calif., Las Vegas Mus., Nev., Merced Coll. Mus., Calif., Brigham Young U. Mus., Provo, Utah, Caldwell Library, Idaho; shows juried include: Utah Watercolor Soc., Salt Lake City, 1980, Idaho State Art Assn., Twin Falls, 1982, Wyo. State Art Assn., Pinedale, 1984; solo shows include: Brigham Young U., 1983, Merced Coll., 1982. Author: It's Fun to Paint Old Shacks and Barns, 1977; It's Fun to Paint Roads and Rivers, 1982; Make Your Watercolor Sing, 1986. Contbr. articles to newspapers and profl. jours. Pres. O.E. Bell Jr. High Sch. PTA, Idaho Falls, 1958, Toastmasters Internat., Idaho Falls, 1961, Kiwanis of E. Idaho Falls, 1968; bd. dirs. Teton Peaks Council Boy Scouts Am., Idaho Falls, 1953-60. Recipient Purchase award Inland Exhbn. VII, Elliot Block Co., 1971; Chmn.'s award and Okla. Watercolor award Okla. Watercolor Soc., 1981; 1st prize for Landscape Whiskey Painters Am., 1982. Mem. Nat. Watercolor Soc., Watercolor West (v.p. 1978-79), Soc. Western Artists (1st prize for watercolor 1984), Midwest Watercolor Soc. Mormon. Home: PO Box 249 Jamestown CA 95327 Office: Hutchings Gallery PO Box 249 Jamestown CA 95327

HUTCHINS, DAVID LEONARD, systems analyst, food products executive; b. Cambridge, Vt., Mar. 7, 1948; s. Leonard Ronald and Barbara Ruth (Sargent); H.; m. Mohini Kalwani, Oct. 14, 1978. AAS in Gen. Bus., Glendale Community Coll., Ariz., 1981. Word processing specialist 1st Interstate Bank of Ariz., Phoenix, 1973-80, word processing supr., 1980; programmer, analyst Profl. Data Processing Svc., Phoenix, 1980-81, Sun Country Fin. Svcs., Phoenix, 1981-83; sr. systems analyst Valley Nat. Bank Ariz., Phoenix, 1983-87, lead systems analyst, 1987-88, 89—; owner Bombay Bazaar Food & Spices of India, Phoenix, 1986—. With U.S. Army, 1970-73, Vietnam. Republican. Office: Valley Nat Bank Ariz 3625 N 27th Ave Phoenix AZ 85017

HUTCHINS, DONALD BRUCE, military officer, electrical engineer; b. Newton, Mass., July 31, 1947; s. Lyman Moore Jr. and Constance Ruth (Stockbridge) H.; m. Susan O'Hara, Sept. 13, 1969; children: Kimberley Anne, Ellen Townley. BSEE, Northeastern U., 1970, MS in Power Systems Engring., 1971; MS in Systems Mgmt., U. So. Calif., 1984. Registered engr.-in-tng., Wash. Commd. officer USN, 1972, advanced through grades to comdr.; asst. planning officer Naval Constrn. Bn. Ctr., Gulfport, Miss., 1972-74; staff civil engr. Naval Air Facility, Naples, Italy, 1974-76; pub. works officer Naval Communications Sta., Londonderry, No. Ireland., 1976-77; detachment officer-in-charge Naval Mobile Constrn. Bn. No. 3, Subic Bay, Philippines, 1977-79; resident officer-in-charge constrn. Naval Sta., Adak, Alaska, 1979-81; mem. pub. work staff Naval Submarine Base, Bangor, Wash., 1981-83; dep. officer-in-charge constrn. Naval Facilities Contracts Office, Silverdale, Wash., 1983-85; facilities officer Pacific Fleet Submarine Force, Pearl Harbor, Hawaii, 1985-87; dir. contracting Navy Pub. Works Ctr., Pearl Harbor, 1987-89; commanding officer Naval Mobile Constrn. Bn. 133, Gulfport, 1989—. Dir. flood recovery ops. for Navy, Ventura County, 1978; chmn. Regional Task Force on Energy Conservation, Bremerton, Wash., 1982; moderator Puget Power Co. Consumer Coun., Bremerton, 1983. Mem. Soc. Am. Mil. Engrs. (chpt. treas. 1980), U.S.

Naval Inst., Am. Pub. Works Assn. Republican. Home: 561 Mockingbird Dr Long Beach MS 39560

HUTCHINSON, JOSEPH CANDLER, retired foreign language educator; b. Hazelhurst, Ga., Jan. 10, 1920; s. George Washington and Lillie Arizona (Rowan) H.; m. June Cruce O'Shields, Aug. 12, 1950 (div. 1980); children—Junie O'Shields, Joseph Candler. B.A., Emory U., 1940, M.A., 1941; Ph.D., U. N.C., 1950; postgrad. U. Paris, summers 1951, 53. Tchr., Tech. High Sch., Atlanta, 1941-42; instr. French, German, Italian, Emory U., Atlanta, 1946-47; instr. U. N.C., Chapel Hill, 1947-50, asst. prof., 1954, assoc. prof., to 1957; asst. prof. Sweet Briar (Va.) Coll., 1950-51, 53-54; assoc. prof. Tulane U., New Orleans, 1957-59; fgn. lang. specialist U.S. Office Edn., Washington, 1959-64; acad. adv. hdqrs. Def. Lang. Inst., Washington, 1964-74, Monterey, 1974-77, dir. tng. devel. Def. Lang. Inst. Fgn. Lang. Center, Monterey, Calif., 1977-82, asst. acad. dean, 1982-85; dean of policy, from 1985-88; vis. prof. U. Va., Charlottesville, 1966, Arlington, 1970, Georgetown U., 1968, Am. U., 1971; cons. Council of Chief State Sch. Officers, 1960, U. Del., 1966, U. Colo., 1968, U. Ill., 1968; U.S. del. Bur. Internat. Lang. Coordination, NATO, 1964-79, 81-82, 86-87. Served with U.S. Army, 1942-46, 51-53. Decorated Bronze Star. Mem. Am. Council on Edn. (task force on internat. edn. 1973), NEA (sec. dept. fgn. langs. 1961-64), Higher Edn. Assn. Monterey Peninsula, Am. Council on Teaching of Fgn. Lang., MLA, Am. Mgmt. Assn., Am. Soc. Tng. and Devel., Monterey Choral Soc., Camerata Singers. Episcopalian. Clubs: Presidio of Monterey Officers and Faculty, Washington Linguistics (v.p. 1970-72). Contbr. articles to profl. jours.; author: Using the Language Laboratory Effectively, School Executives Guide, 1964; The Language Laboratory: Equipment and Utilization in Trends in Language Teaching, 1966, others; editor Dialog on Lang. Instruction, 1986-88.

HUTCHINSON, RICHARD WILLIAM, geology educator, consultant; b. London, Ontario, Can., Nov. 17, 1928; s. William Henry and Ada Georgina (Armitage) H.; m. Beryl Marie Rafuse; children: Susan Janet, Leslie Ann Hutchinson Cox, Cynthia Joan Bennett, Carla Jean. BS in Geology, U. Western Ont., 1950; MS in Geology, U. Wis., Madison, 1951, PhD in Geology, 1954. Project geologist Am. Metal Climax, Toronto, Can., 1954-60; staff geologist Am. Metal Climax, N.Y.C., 1960-64; asst. prof. U. Western Ont., London, 1964-69, prof., 1969-83; Charles F. Fogarty prof. econs., geology Colo. Sch. of Mines, Golden, 1983—; cons. geologist Chevron Resources Co., San Francisco, 1976—, UN Revolving Fund, N.Y.C., 1978—, UN Devel. Program, N.Y.C., 1976—, BHP-Utah Internat., Inc., San Francisco, 1984—; numerous others. Fellow Geol. Assn. Can. (Duncan R. Derry Gold Medal 1983); mem. Soc. of Econ. Geologists (pres. 1983, SEG Silver Medal 1985), Geol. Soc. of Am. (councillor 1987—), Can. Inst. Mining and Metallurgy (Barlow Gold Medal 1971, 79), Societee de Geologuie Applique Aux Gites Mineraux, Prospectors and Developers Assn. of Can. Office: Colo Sch of Mines Dept of Geology and Geol Engring Golden CO 80401

HUTCHINSON, WILLIAM BURKE, surgeon, research center director; b. Seattle, Sept. 6, 1909; s. Joseph Lambert and Nona Bernice (Burke) H.; m. Charlotte Rigdon, Mar. 25, 1939; children: Charlotte J. Hutchinson Reed, William B., John L., Stuart R., Mary Hutchinson Wiese. BS, U. Wash., Seattle, 1931; MD, McGill U., 1936; HHD (hon.), U. Seattle, 1982. Diplomate: Am. Bd. Surgery. Intern Balt. City Hosp., 1936-37; resident Union Meml. Hosp., Balt., 1937-39, James Walker Meml. Hosp., Wilmington, N.C., 1939-40; surgeon Swedish Hosp. and Med. Ctr., Seattle, 1941—, Providence Hosp., Seattle, 1941—; pres., founding dir. Pacific Northwest Research Found., Seattle, 1955—; founding dir. Fred Hutchinson Cancer Research Ctr., Seattle, 1972-85; dir. Surg. Cancer Cons. Service, 1982—; clin. prof. surgery emeritus U. Wash.; pres. 13th Internat. Cancer Congress, 1978-82; mem. Yarborough com. for writing Nat. Cancer Act, 1970. Contbg. editor, 13th Internat. Cancer Congress. Recipient 1st Citizen of Seattle award, 1976, Alumnus Summa Laude Dignatus award U. Wash., 1983, Wash. State award of Merit, 1988. Fellow ACS; mem. AMA, King County Med. Soc., Seattle Surg. Assn., North Pacific Surg. Assn., Pacific Coast Surg. Assn., Western Surg. Assn., Soc. Surg. Oncologists, NRC, Alpha Sigma Phi. Clubs: Men's University (Seattle); Seattle Golf and Country. Home: 7126-55th Ave So Seattle WA 98118 Office: Pacific NW Rsch Found 720 Broadway Seattle WA 98122

HUTCHISON, LOYAL DWAYNE, pharmacist; b. Stockton, Calif., Jan. 3, 1933; s. Lester and Muriel (Van Nortwick) H.; m. Jean E. McColl, Jan. 26, 1961; children: Michael, Donald. BS in Pharmacy, U. Pacific, 1966. Pharmacist Fifth St. Pharmacy, Stockton, 1966-76, prin., 1976—; prin. Hutchison Pharmacies Inc., Stockton, 1976—, McKinley Pharmacy, Stockton, 1976—, Lathrop (Calif.) Pharmacy, 1976—. Served with U.S. Army, 1957-59. Fellow Am. Coll. Apothecary; mem. Calif. Pharmacists Assn. (Pac Silver Circle), Am. Pharmacists Assn. Home: PO Box 1737 Stockton CA 95201 Office: Hutchison Pharmacies Inc 1839 S El Dorado Stockton CA 95206

HUTCHISON, MICHAEL DWAYNE, pharmacist; b. Stockton, Calif., June 15, 1952; s. Loyal Dwayne and Jean Eleanor (McColl) H.; m. Linda Carolyn Rich, Feb. 23, 1986; 1 child, Aaron. PharmD, U. Pacific, 1985. Registered pharmacist, Calif. Clk. Western Pacific R.R., Stockton, 1971-86; occupational specialist Job Corps, San Jose, Calif., 1982-86; pharmacist Thrifty Drug, Tracy, Calif., 1986-87, Tracy Community Meml. Hosp., 1986—; pharmacist mgr. McKinley Pharmacy, Stockton, 1987—. With U.S. Army, 1972-74. Mem. Am. Pharmacists Assn., Am. Soc. Hosp. Pharmacists, Calif. Pharmacists Assn., San Joaquin Pharmacists Assn., Stockton C. of C., VFW, Brotherhood of Railway and Airline Clerks. Republican. Office: McKinley Pharmacy 1964 S El Dorado St Stockton CA 95206

HUTCHISON, RICHARD LEE, electronics engineer; b. Bakersfield, Calif., Mar. 10, 1958; s. Charles Elmer and Margery Ann (Matheny) H.; m. Timma Dawn Bonzi, May 1, 1982 (div. 1987). BSEE, U. Pacific, Stockton, Calif., 1981. Program mgr. USAF 6520 Test Group, ENMD, Edwards AFB, Calif., 1981-86; chief of systems analysis USAF 6521 Range Squadron/ENRDA, Edwards AFB, Calif., 1986; program mgr. USAF 6510 Test Wing/TEXS, Edwards AFB, Calif., 1986-88, USAF 6520 Test Group ENVO, Edwards AFB, Calif., 1988—; mem. Inter-Range Instrumentation Group, White Sands Range, N.Mex., 1985-86. Clarinetist Antelope Valley Symphony, Lancaster, Calif., 1984—; saxophonist Antelope Valley Jazz Band, 1984—; pyrotechnic asst. Pismo Beach Fireworks, Calif., 1982—; cons. Antelope Valley Theater, 1984—. Mem. Assn. Old Crows, Voron Club. Home: 45541 N 35th St E Lancaster CA 93535 Office: USAF 6520 Test Group/ENVO Edwards AFB CA 93523

HUTNER, HERBERT LOEB, financial consultant, lawyer; b. N.Y.C.; s. Nathan M. and Ethel (Helhor) H.; m. Marjorie Mayer, Oct. 1, 1962 (div.); children—Jeffrey J., Lynn M. Colwell; m. 2d., Zsa Zsa Gabor, Mar. 20, 1967 (div.); m. 3d., Juli Reding, Nov. 28, 1969; 1 stepson, Christopher D. Taylor. B.A., Columbia U., 1928, J.D., 1931. Bar: N.Y. 1932. Ptnr., Osterman & Hutner, mem. N.Y. Stock Exchange, N.Y.C., 1945-57; successively pres. N.E. Life Insurance Co., N.Y.C.; chmn. bd. Sleight & Hellmuth Inc., N.Y.C.; chmn. bd. Pressed Metals of Am., Port Huron, Mich.; chmn. bd. Struthers Wells Corp., Warren, Pa., Plateau Mining Co. Inc., Oak Ridge; investor, cons., Los Angeles, 1963—; dir. United Artists Communications, Inc., 1965-87. Chmn., Pres.'s Adv. Com. on Arts for Kennedy Ctr., 1982—; founder Los Angeles Music Ctr.; chmn. profl. sports com. United Way. Decorated title DATO, Sultan of Johore, Malaysia, Highest Order of the Crown, 1981. Mem. ASCAP. Club: Deepdale Golf (Manhasset, N.Y.). Composer: The Super Bowl Song, Go Rams Go, others.

HUTSON, DAVID NATHANIEL, air force officer; b. Columbia, S.C., Nov. 27, 1945; s. Arthur Lee and Clara Evelyn (Clamp) H.; m. Marcia Ann Wehren, Dec. 2, 1986; 1 child, Heather Catherine. BSEE, U. S.C., 1969, MS in Systems Mgmt., 1979. Commd. 2d lt. USAF, 1969, advanced through grades to maj., 1980; communications engr. So. Communications Area, Tinker AFB, Okla., 1970-72; communications system engr. Combat Grande Program Office, Hanscom AFB, Mass., 1972-75, Air Force Space Div., L.A., 1976-80; comdr. Communications Site, Hortiatis, Greece, 1975-76; spacecraft sensor program mgr. Air Force Tech. Applications Ctr., Patrick AFB, Fla., 1980-83; program mgr. shuttle payloads Eastern Space & Missile Ctr., Patrick AFB, 1983-85; dir. plans Space and Missile Test Orgn., Vandenberg AFB, Calif., 1985—. Adminstrv. officer U.S. Power Squadron, Lompoc, Calif., 1989. Mem. Air Force Assn.

HUTSON, JACK KARL, publisher; b. Vancouver, Wash., Sept. 1, 1948; s. Thurl A. and Dorothy E. (Reineke) H.; m. Mary Kathleen Tobin, Nov. 5, 1969; 1 child, Jason Karl. BSME, U. Wash., 1973. Corps of engrs. U.S. Army, Vietnam, 1968-70; sr. mech. engr. The Boeing Co., Seattle, 1973-84; pub. Tech. Analysis of Stocks & Commodities mag., Seattle, 1982—; pres. Tech. Analysis, Inc., Seattle, 1982—. Editor Profitable Trading Methods, Vol. 2, 1986 Investment Techniques, Vol. 2, 1987, Successful Speculation, Vol. 4, 1988, Intelligent Trading, Vol. 4, 1989, Trading Strategies, Vol. 5, 1989, Market Timing, Vol. 6, 1989, Wyckoff Trading Method, 1989. Office: Tech Analysis of Stock & Commodities mag 9131 California Ave SW Seattle WA 98136

HUTSON, WILLIAM GARDINER, court official; b. Hollywood, Calif., July 26, 1928; s. Walter Allen and Annabelle (Gardiner) H.; m. Rita Petrosian, July 26, 1969; children: Linda, Kathryn, Natasha, Christina. MA in Sociology, U. So. Calif., 1960. Cert. marriage, family and child counselor, Calif. Dir. Cath. Youth Orgn., L.A., 1960-68; probation officer Los Angeles County Probation Dept., L.A., 1969-73, Fed. Probation System, San Bernardino, Calif., 1973-76; probation investigator Fed. Probation System, L.A., 1976-86, probation specialist, 1986-88; probation officer Fed. Probation System, San Bernardino, 1988—. Author: (novel) Julian "My Friends Call Me C.C.," 1989. Trustee Upland (Calif.) Unified Sch. Dist., 1976-77. Mem. Fed. Probation Officers Assn., Alpha Kappa Delta. Democrat. Episcopalian. Office: US Probation System 202 E Airport Dr San Bernardino CA 92408

HUTTER, JAMES RISQUE, lawyer; b. Spokane, Wash., Mar. 20, 1924; s. James R. and Esther (Nelson) H.; m. Patricia Ruth Dunlavy, Aug. 12, 1951; children: Bruce Dunlavy, Gail Anne, Dean James, Karl Nelson. B.S., UCLA, 1947; J.D., Stanford U., 1950. Bar: Calif. 1951, U.S. Supreme Ct. 1965. Assoc. Gibson, Dunn & Crutcher, Los Angeles and Beverly Hills, Calif., 1950-58, ptnr., 1959—; dir. Fifield Manors, Los Angeles, 1955—, v.p., 1964-85, pres., 1985—. Bd. dirs., chmn. fin. com. Congl. Found. for Theol. Studies, Nat. Assn. Congl. Christian Chs., 1961-68; mem. San Marino City Planning Commn., Calif., 1968—, chmn., 1976—. Served to 1st. inf. AUS, 1943-46. Decorated Purple Heart. Mem. State Bar Calif. (com. on corps. 1973-76, exec. com. bus. law sect. 1976-78), ABA, Los Angeles County Bar Assn., Beverly Hills Bar Assn. (bd. govs. 1968-70), Am. Judicature Soc., Town Hall, City Club on Bunker Hill, Valley Hunt Club, Phi Delta Phi, Beta Gamma Sigma, Phi Kappa Psi. Home: 1400 Circle Dr San Marino CA 91108 Office: Gibson Dunn & Crutcher 333 S Grand Ave 48th Fl Los Angeles CA 90071

HUTTO, FRANCIS BAIRD, JR., research director; b. Savannah, Ga., June 25, 1926; s. Francis Baird and Mary Margaret (Gnann) H.; m. Mary Jane Hall, Sept 7, 1952; children: Frank, Madeline, Roger, Nancy, Ellen, Amy. BS, Clemson U., 1848; MS, Cornell U., 1950, PhD., 1952. Sr. research chemist Manville (N.J.) Research and Devel., 1952-61, sect. chief, 1861-64, sr. sect. chief, 1964-71, research mgr., 1971-73, sr. research assoc., 1973-76; research dir. Pabco div. Fireboard Corp., Fruita, Colo., 1976—. Author: (with others) Weissberger's Techniques of Organic Chemistry, 1957. Patentee in field. Fellow Am. Inst. Chem. Engrs. (chmn N.J. sect. 1969); mem. N.Y. Filtration Soc. (pres. 1967), N.J. Am. Chem. Soc. (chmn. chem. sect. 1970). Republican. Presbyterian. Home: 676 Peony Dr Grand Junction CO 81503 Office: Pabco Insulations 1110 16 Rd Fruita CO 81503

HUTTON, JEANNETTE KAYE, systems analyst; b. Concordia, Kans., Oct. 14, 1946; d. Paul Ezra and Esther Joy (Lewis) Buss; m. Ira Randolph Hutton, Apr. 2, 1966; children: Aileen Kaye (dec.), Randolph Paul. BA in German, Phillips U., 1973; postgrad., Denver U. Cert. data processing. Tchr. St. Mary's High Sch., Colorado Springs, Colo., 1976-77; substitute tchr. various sch. dists., Colo., 1977-79; instr. Colorado Springs Coll. Bus., 1977-79; student loan collector U.S. Dept. Edn., Denver, 1979; quality control reviewer HHS, Denver, 1979-82; mem. programming staff, systems analyst Mountain Bell-U.S. West Co., Denver, 1982—. Mem. Colo. Organ Donor Families Support Group, Denver, 1987-88. Mem. Data Processing Mgmt. Assn. (instr. 1988). Mem. Disciples of Christ Church. Home: 3622 S Ouray Circle Aurora CO 80013 Office: US West Info Techs 1999 Broadway Rm HG1240 Denver CO 80202

HUYLER, JEAN WILEY, management communications consultant; b. Seattle, Mar. 30, 1935; d. Othello Phillip and Agnes Olive (Snarr) Dickert; m. Richard Wiley, Apr. 1955 (div. 1963); children: Richard Kenneth Jr., Cynthia Jean; m. Garey Heath Huyler, Mar. 2, 1968 (div. 1972). BA, Marylhurst Coll., 1978; MA in Social Scis., Pacific Luth. U., Parkland, Wash., 1979; LittD, Fairfax U., New Orleans, 1989. Bur. mgr., reporter Lynnwood (Wash.) Enterprise, 1961-63; city editor, reporter/photographer Everett (Wash.) Daily Herald, 1963-71; spl. sects. editor Seattle Post-Intelligencer, 1971; sr. econ. editor Rainier Bancorp., Seattle, 1971-72; assoc. editor, women's editor Valley Newspapers, Kent, Wash., 1973-75; chief exec. officer Jean Wiley Huyler Communications, Kent and Tacoma, 1975—, EdCom-UpCom-One Step Beyond-TravCom, Tacoma, 1981—; environ. editor-writer Bonneville Power Adminstrn.-U.S. Dept. Interior, Portland, Oreg., 1976-77; communications service dir. Wash. State Sch. Dirs. Assn., Olympia, 1977-81. Author: Communication is a People Process, 2d edit., 1981, Crisis Communications, 2d edit., 1981, De-mystifying the Media, 2d edit., 1981 (Wash. Press Assn. award 1982); editor, designer: For the Record: Tacoma Schools, 1985 (Nat. Sch. Pub. Relations Assn. medal 1985), Lifespan Learning on Centerstage of the Future, 1988. Recipient Superior Performance award Wash. Press Assn., Seattle, 1964, Torchbearer, 1981, Communicator of Achievement, 1987, Nat. Excellence in Edn. Communications award Nat. Assn. State Edn. Dept. Info. Officers, 1979; numerous other community service and communication awards throughout Pacific Northwest. Mem. Nat. Fedn. Press Women (exec. bd. 1971—, v.p. 1973-75, state pres. 1971-73, nat. pres. 75-77, elections dir. 1986-88, Woman of Achievement award 1988), Am. Mgmt. Assn., Wash. Press Assn. (pres. 1971-73), Nat. Desktop Pub. Assn., Nat. Assn. Female Execs., Tacoma C. of C. (small bus. task force 1987). Home and Office: 922 N Pearl #A-27 Tacoma WA 98406

HUYNH, JOHN, construction company executive; b. Phnom Penh, Kampuchia, Dec. 11, 1953; s. Vincent and Quan (Lam) H.; m. Carolyn Van Lang, Aug. 8, 1982; 1 child, Alexander. BS, Calif. State U., 1976, MBA, 1981. Ptnr., v.p. fin. Saarman Constrn., San Francisco. Mem. Commonwealth Club. Home: 6025 Valley View Rd Oakland CA 94611 Office: Saarman Constrn Ltd 1691 18th Ave San Francisco CA 94122

HWANG, CLAYTON CHUNG-LI, real estate broker; b. Shanghai, People's Republic of China, Dec. 7, 1930; came to U.S., 1951; s. Jin Yu and Edith (Chow) H.; m. Marian Yu-Bing Lin, June 27, 1959; children: Lydia S., Rebecca S. BS, Calif. State U., L.A., 1962; MDiv, Fuller Theol. Sem., 1967; postgrad., Sch. Theology, Claremont, Calif., 1980-82. Lab. technician Filtrol Corp., Vernon, Calif., 1957-67; pastor Chinese Christian Fellowship, Mountian View, Calif., 1967-74; sr. pastor Chinese Congl. Ch., L.A., 1974-82; salesman Coldwell Banker, Covina, Calif., 1982-86; broker, owner Far East Nat. Realty, West Covina, Calif., 1987—. Republican.

HWANG, CORDELIA JONG, chemist; b. N.Y.C., July 14, 1942; d. Goddard and Lily (Fung) Jong; m. Warren C. Hwang, Mar. 29, 1969; 1 son, Kevin. Student Alfred U., 1960-62; B.A., Barnard Coll., 1964; M.S., SUNY-Stony Brook, 1969. Research asst. Columbia U., N.Y.C., 1964-66; analytical chemist Veritron West Inc., Chatsworth, Calif., 1969-70; asst. lab. dir., chief chemist Pomeroy, Johnston & Bailey Environ. Engrs., Pasadena, Calif., 1970-76; research chemist Met. Water Dist. So. Calif., Los Angeles, 1976—; mem. Joint Task Group on Instrumental Identification of Taste and Odor Compounds, 1983-85, instr. Citrus Coll., 1974-76. Mem. Am. Chem. Soc., Am. Water Works Assn. (cert. water quality analyst level 3, Calif.-Nev.). Office: Met Water Dist So Calif 700 N Moreno St La Verne CA 91750

HYBL, WILLIAM JOSEPH, foundation executive; b. Des Moines, July 16, 1942; BA, Colo. Coll., 1964; JD, U. Colo., 1967. Bar: Colo. 1967. Asst. dist. atty. 4th Jud. Dist., El Paso and Teller Counties, 1970-72; pres., exec. v.p., dir. Garden City Co., 1973—; dir. Broadmoor Hotel, Inc., 1973—, also vice-chmn., 1987—; found. exec., pres. and trustee, El Pomar Found, 1973—. Bd. dirs. 1st Nat. Bank Colorado Springs, Affiliated Bankshares Colo., KNEnergy Inc., Lakewood, Colo.; mem. Colo. Ho. Reps., 1972-73. Trustee, vice chmn. Colo. Coll., 1978—; pres., trustee Air Force Acad. Found.; bd. dirs. Vail Valley Found., KN Energy, 1988—; sec. U.S. Olympic Found. Am., 1984—; sec., trustee Jr. Achievement; spl. White House counsel, 1981; civilian aide to sec. of army for State of Colo., 1986—. Mem. U.S. C. of C. (bd. dirs., pub. affairs com. chmn., 1985—). Home: 2 Penrose Ln Colorado Springs CO 80906 Office: 10 Lake Circle Colorado Springs CO 80906

HYDE, WILLIAM, automotive executive; b. Twin Falls, Idaho, Jan. 19, 1946; s. Cecil Lee and Nona Ida (Daley) H.; m. Betty Sue Thompson, Apr. 26, 1963 (div. 1984); children: Becky Ann, Gerry. BSME, Gen Motors Inst., Detroit, 1968; BSEE, UCLA, 1971. Engr. NASA, Houston, 1971-74; engring mgr. Dept. of Def., Dept. Transp., Midland, Tex., 1979-82; mgr. adv. rsch. engring. div. Automotive Rsch. Corp., Idaho Falls, 1982—; cons. Contbr. articles to profl. jours.; patentee in field.; author: Hydrogen Propulsion and HIgh Energy Physics, 1981. Mem. SAE, AAPS, IEEE, Sun Valley Country Club. Republican. Office: Automotive Rsch Corp 1685 Whitney St Idaho Falls ID 83402-1768

HYLAND, MARY JOAN, psychologist; b. St. Paul, Oct. 1, 1942; d. Owen J. and Eileen (Lang) H. BS in Nursing, Calif. State U., L.A., 1969, MS in Nursing, 1974; PhD in Psychology, Sierra U., 1988. R.N. Calif.; cert. clin. specialist in adult psychiat. and mental health nursing. Pub. health nurse, pediatric nurse practitioner East Los Angeles Child and Youth Clinic, 1970-74; nursing cons. L.A. County-U. So. Calif. Med. Ctr., 1974-82; sr. mental health counselor RN L.A. County Dept. Mental Health, 1982-88; clin. psychologist Augustus F. Hawkins Community Mental Health Ctr., L.A., 1988—; cons. on community care facilities, 1975-80. Named Nurse of Yr. dept. mental health Los Angeles County Bd. Suprs.; 1988. Mem. AAUW (2d v.p. 1976-77), Am. Nurses Assn., Am. Psychol. Assn., Internat. Fedn. Bus. & Profl. Women (com. chmn 1988—, treas. 1989—). Home: 5929 N Walnut Grove Ave San Gabriel CA 91775 Office: August Hawkins Health Ctr 1720 120th St Los Angeles CA 90059

HYLEN, MARIAN JOANNE, accountant; b. Coulee Dam, Wash., Sept. 18, 1939; d. Daniel Joseph and Dorothy E. (Johnson) Duggan; m. John C. Hylen, June 23, 1961 (div. 1980); children: Maria Ann, Susan Elaine. BS, U. Oreg., 1961; BBA, Boise State U., 1981. CPA, Idaho; cert. tchr., Oreg. Tchr. Lake Oswego (Oreg.) Pub. Schs., 1961-64, 65-67, Sch. Dist. Haverford (Pa.) Twp., 1964-65; auditor Idaho Pub. Utilities Commn., Boise, 1981-84; cons. Bur. Fin. Idaho Dept. Edn., Boise, 1984-88, coord. Bur. Fin., 1988—. Bd. dirs. Vis. Nurse and Homemaker Svc., Boise, 1985-88; elder, deacon First Presbyterian Ch., Boise. Mem. Idaho Soc. CPAs, Phi Kappa Phi, Phi Lambda Theta. Republican. Office: Idaho Dept Edn Len B Jordan Bldg Boise ID 83720

HYLIN, JOHN WALTER, consultant; b. Bklyn., Jan. 28, 1929; s. Hans Jacob and Lydia (Hansen) H.; m. Valia Belkoff, Jan. 30, 1954; children: E. Carl, Douglas Eric, Kenneth Leif. AB, Marietta Coll., 1950; MS, Purdue U., 1953; PhD, Columbia U., 1957. Instr. U. Tenn., Memphis, 1957-59; asst. researcher, dept. agricultural biochemistry U. Honolulu, 1959-60, asst. researcher, 1960-69, researcher, 1969-88, chmn., 1968-84, emeritus biochemist, 1984—. Founding editor, Bull. of Environmental Contamination and Toxicology, 1966-76; contbr. articles to profl. jours. Consul Royal Norwegian Consulate, Honolulu, 1968-88. Fulbright fellow, Coun. on Edn., Denmark, 1972-73; Knight, Order of St. Olaf, King of Norway, 1976. Fellow Am. Inst. Chemists; mem. Am. Chem. Soc., Collaborative Internat. Pesticide Analytical Coun., Elks, Odd Fellows. Home: PO Box 6323 Incline Village NV 89450

HYMAN, EDWARD JAY, information scientist, consultant, psychologist, educator; b. Roslyn, N.Y., Oct. 25, 1947; s. Herbert H. and Edith (Tannenbaum) H.; m. Deborah Anne McDonald, May 1, 1986; 1 child, Cameron Scott. AB, Columbia U., 1969; postgrad., Harvard U., 1969-70; PhD, U. Calif., 1975. Lic. psychologist, Calif. Editorial asst. Huntley-Brinkley Report NBC News, N.Y.C., 1969; coord. Ctr. for Ednl. Change U. Calif., Berkeley, 1970-72, sr. fellow Ctr. for Social Rsch., 1972-74, lectr., 1975-76, asst. dean, 1976-77; intern Calif. Health Dept., Santa Cruz, 1974; chmn. bd. Assn. for Advanced Tng., L.A., 1977-79; asst. prof. U. San Francisco, 1979-81; sci. dir. Ctr. for Social Rsch., Berkeley, 1981—; cons. Edison Electric Inst., Washington, 1977-80, Standard Oil Co., San Francisco, 1976-77, Pacific Gas and Electric, 1986. Co-author: Life Stress, 1983, Herbert Marcuse, 1988. Regents scholar U. Calif., 1974-75. Mem. Am. Inst. Decision Scis., Am. Psychol. Assn., Calif. State Psychol. Assn., Internat. Soc. Polit. Psychology (conv. com. 1987), Internat. Soc. Applied Psychology, Am. Child Abuse Prevention Soc. (dir. 1975—), Commonwealth Club. Office: Ctr for Social Rsch 2029 Durant Ave Berkeley CA 94704

HYNEK, FREDERICK JAMES, architect; b. Minot, N.D., May 24, 1944; s. Frederick Frank and Esther Irene (Hermanson) H.; BArch, N.D. State U., 1967; m. Jane Rebecca Lowitz, June 9, 1966; children: Tyler James, Scott Anthony. Intern archtl. firms in Bismarck, N.D., 1967-72; architect Gerald W. Deines, Architect, Casper and Cody, Wyo., 1972-73; v.p. Gerald Deines and Assos., 1973-77; propr. Fred J. Hynek, AIA/Architect, Cody, 1977-80; pres. Design Group, P.C., Architects/Planners, Cody, 1980-86; pres. CHD Architects, Cody, 1986—; Concept Interiors Inc., Cody, 1984—; mem. cert. of need rev. bd. State of Wyo., 1984-87, selection com. for archtl. students for Western Interstate Commn. for Higher Edn. Profl. Student Exchange Program, U. Wyo., 1979—; chmn. archtl. adv. commn. City of Cody. Bd. dirs. Cody Stampede, Inc., 1977-82; chmn. Cody Econ. Devel. Council, 1982-84, state coordinator Intern-Architect Devel. Program. Served with USAR, 1967-68. Mem. AIA (dir. Wyo. chpt. 1976-83, pres. 1980, 81; conf. chmn. Western Mountain region 1977, mem. awards jury 1981, treas. 1982-86; chmn. design awards jury N.D. 1981, 2 awards for Excellence in Archtl. Design Wyo. chpt.), Cody County C. of C. (dir., pres. 1982). Republican. Presbyterian. Clubs: Cody Elks, Cody Country Ambassador. Mem. editorial adv. bd. Symposia mag., 1981-82. Home: 708 Southfork Rd Cody WY 82414 Office: 1371 Sheridan Ave Cody WY 82414

IACHETTI, ROSE MARIA ANNE, teahcer; b. Watervliet, N.Y., Sept. 22, 1931; d. Augustus and Rose Elizabeth Archer (Orciuolo) Iachetti; B.S., Coll. St. Rose, 1961; M.Ed., U. Ariz., 1969. Joined Sisters of Mercy, Albany, N.Y., 1949-66; tchr. various parochial schs. Albany (N.Y.) Diocese, 1952-66; tchr. Headstart Program, Troy, N.Y., 1966; tchr. fine arts Watervliet Jr. and Sr. High Sch., 1966-67; tchr. W.J. Meyer Sch., Tombstone, Ariz., 1968-71, Colonel Johnston Sch., Ft. Huachuca, Ariz., 1971-78; tchr. Myer Sch., Ft. Huachuca, 1978—, coordinator program for gifted and talented, 1981-85. Ann. chmn. Ariz. Children's Home Assn., Tombstone, 1973-74; trustee Tombstone Sch. Dist. #1, 1972-80; active Democratic Club; mem. Bicentennial Commn. for Ariz., 1972-76, Tombstone Centennial Commn., 1979-80, chmn. Centennial Ball, 1980; pres. Tombstone Community Health Services, 1978-80; mem. Tombstone City Council, 1982-84; governing bd. Southeast Ariz. Area Health Edn. Ctr., 1985—; bd. dirs. S.E. Health Edn. Council, 1985—. Mem. Ariz. Edn. Assn. (so. regional dir. 1971-73), Ft. Huachuca Edn. Assn., Tombstone Dist. 1 Edn. Assn. (pres. 1969-71), Ariz. Sch. Bd. Assn., NEA (del. 1971-73), Ariz. Classroom Tchrs. Assn. (del. 1969-71), Internat. Platform Assn., Tombstone Bus. and Profl. Womens Club, Am. Legion Aux., Tombstone Assn. Arts, Pi Lambda Theta, Delta Kappa Gamma, (pres. 1982-84), Phi Delta Kappa (historian 1979-82, 2d v.p. 1982-83). Home: Round Up Trailer Ranch Box 725 Tombstone AZ 85638 Office: Myer Sch Fort Huachuca AZ 85613

IACONO, GEORGE DANTE, optometrist; b. Chgo., Oct. 21, 1922; s. Carl Umberto and Emma (Decrecchio) I.; m. Rosemary Marie Maksym, Nov. 28, 1928; children—Carl Dante, Georgeann Louise. O.D., Chgo. Coll. Optometry, 1948. Practice optometry, Tucson, 1948—; dir. Tucson Reading Inst., 1953-62; cons. Fellow Nat. Eye Research Found. (grand hons.) mem. Am. Optometric Assn., Ariz. Optometric Assn., Internat. Orthokeratology Assn., Am. Interprofl. Assn. (Living Treasure award). Office: 2553 E Broadway Tucson AZ 85716

IAMELE, RICHARD THOMAS, law librarian; b. Newark, Jan. 29, 1942; s. Armando Anthony and Evelyn (Coladonato) I.; m. Marilyn Ann Berutto,

Aug. 21, 1965; children: Thomas, Ann Marie. BA, Loyola U., Los Angeles, 1963; MSLS, U. So. Calif., 1967; JD, Southwestern U., L.A., 1976. Bar: Calif. 1977. Cataloger U. So. Calif., L.A., 1967-71; asst. cataloger L.A. County Law Libr., 1971-77, asst. ref. libr., 1977-78, asst. libr., 1978-80, libr. dir., 1980—. Mem. ABA, Am. Assn. Law Libraries, Calif. Library Assn., So. Calif. Assn. Law Libraries, Coun. Calif. County Law Librs. Office: Los Angeles County Law Libr 301 W 1st St Los Angeles CA 90012

IANNETTA, KIMON, graphoanalyst; b. Kailua, Hawaii, Oct. 17, 1943; a; children: Lisa, Christina, Leslie, Beau. Cert. graphoanalyst; questioned document examiner. Handwriting expert Honlulu (Hawaii) Police Dept., 1983-88; handwriting expert, cons. self-employed, Kailua, Hawaii, 1988—. Author of news column in the Windward Oahu News, 1986—. Recipient Pres.'s Cert. Merit for Excellence of Performance Internat. Graphoanalysis Soc., 1984, Graphoanalyst of the Year, 1982, Outstanding Mem. Hawaii Chpt. Internat. Graphoanalysis Soc., 1983. Mem. Internat. Graphoanalysis Soc., World Assn. Document Examiners, Am. Soc. Indsl. Security, Am. Handwriting Analysis Found., Nat. Assn. Document Examiners. Office: Handwriting Consultants PO Box 1486 Kailua HI 96734

IBBETSON, EDWIN THORNTON, construction company executive; b. Los Angeles, Apr. 17, 1923; s. Robert Edwin and Ann (Thornton) I.; student Long Beach Jr. Coll., 1941-42, Calif. Inst. Tech., 1942-43; m. Harriett Alice Hudson, Dec. 28, 1947; children: Elizabeth Ann Ibbetson Hitchcock, Douglas Hudson, Gregory Bruce, Timothy Edwin, Julia Katherine Ibbetson Zilinskas, Erika Alice Ibbetson. With Union Devel. Co., Cerritos, Calif., 1939-42, 46—, pres., 1961—; partner Paramount Constrn., Cerritos, 1948—; v.p. Valley Properties, Inc., Imperial Valley, 1962—; chmn. bd. Dutch Village Bowling Center, Inc., Lakewood, 1965-86, partner Ibbetson-Marsh Realtors, 1975—; vice chmn. bd. Equitable Savs. and Loan Assn., 1977-85. Bd. dirs. Met. Water Dist. So. Calif., 1959—, sec., 1979-82, chmn. bd., 1983-86; chmn. Bellflower Water Devel. Com., 1965—; mem. Colo. River Bd. Calif., 1987—, L.A. County Citizens Com. Real Estate Mgmt., 1974—, now chmn.; bd. dirs. armed services YMCA, Long Beach, 1962-72. Trustee St. Mary's Hosp., Long Beach. Served with USNR, 1942-46. Named Young Man of Year, Bellflower Jaycees, 1959. Realtor of Year, Bellflower Dist. Bd. Realtors, 1962, 67, 71. Mem. Am. Soc. Real Estate Counselors (gov., pres. 1977), Calif. Assn. Realtors (treas. 1972-77, dir., hon. life pres.), Internat. Real Estate Fedn., Nat. Assn. Realtors (dir.), Nat. Inst. Real Estate Brokers (cert. comml. investment mem.), Inst. Real Estate Mgmt. (cert. property mgr.), Bellflower Dist. Bd. Realtors (pres. 1961), Central Basin Mcpl. Water Dist. (dir.), Calif. Real Estate Polit. Action Com., Internat. Council Shopping Centers, Elks, Kiwanis (pres. 1958), International Traders, So. Calif. Tuna Club, Lambda Alpha. Roman Catholic. Office: 16550 Bloomfield Cerritos CA 90701

ICARD, TIMOTHY LEE, interior designer; b. Valdese, N.C., June 3, 1958; s. Richard Lee and Amanda (Hall) I. Student in Archtl. Design, N.C. State U., 1979. Pres. Icard Interiors, Houston, 1981—, Denver, 1984—. Featured designer in Rocky Mt. News, 1985, Denver Post, 1985, Colo. Homes and Life Styles, 1987. Mem. Interior Design Soc. Home and Office: 270 S Cherry St Denver CO 80222

ICE, RICHARD EUGENE, clergyman, non-profit retirement homes company executive, clergyman; b. Ft. Lewis, Wash., Sept. 25, 1930; s. Shirley and Nellie Rebecca (Pedersen) I.; m. Pearl Lucille Daniels, July 17, 1955; children—Lorinda Susan, Diana Laurene, Julianne Adele. AA, Centralia Coll., 1950; BA, Linfield Coll., 1952, LHD (hon.), 1978; MA, Berkeley Bapt. Div. Sch., 1959; grad. advanced mgmt. program Harvard U., 1971. Ordained to ministry Am. Bapt. Ch., 1954; pastor Ridgecrest Community Bapt. Ch., Seattle, 1955-59; dir. ch. extension Wash. Bapt. Conv., 1959-61; dir. loans Am. Bapt. Extension Corp., Valley Forge, Pa., 1961-64; assoc. exec. minister Am. Bapt. Chs. of West, Oakland, Calif., 1964-67; dep. exec. sec., treas. Am. Bapt. Home Mission Socs., Valley Forge, 1967-72; pres. Am. Bapt. Homes of the West, Oakland, 1972—; dir. Minister's Life Ins. Co., Mpls., 1975-87, chmn. bd. dirs. 1986-87; bd. dir. Bapt. Life Assn., Buffalo, 1988—; pres. Am. Bapt. Homes and Hosps. Assn., 1978-81. v.p. Am. Bapt. Chs. U.S.A., 1990-91; Ministers and Missionaries Benefit Bd.; mem. Bapt. Joint Com. on Pub. Affairs; trustee, chmn. com. fin. affairs Linfield Coll., 1972—; trustee Calif./Nev. Methodist Homes, 1975—, Bacone Coll., 1968-77, Grad. Theol. Union, Berkeley, Calif., 1982—; trustee Am. Bapt. Sem. of West, Berkeley, 1975—, chmn. bd. trustees, 1987—. Recipient Disting. Baconian award Bacone Coll., 1977, Disting. Alumnus award Centralia Coll., 1981, Meritorious Service award Am. Assn. Homes for Aging, 1982, Merit citation Am. Bapt. Homes and Hosp. Assn., 1985, Award of Honor Calif. Assn. Homes for the Aging, 1988. Mem. U.S. Assn. for UN, Am. Assn. Homes for Aging, Calif. Assn. Homes for Aging, Harvard Bus. Sch. Assn. No. Calif., The Oakland 100 Pi Gamma Mu. Democrat. Clubs: Harvard of San Francisco; Lakeview, Athenian Nile (Oakland). Office: 400 Roland Way Oakland CA 94621

ICHIKAWA, CHRISTIE OZAWA, nursing educator; b. Sacramento, Apr. 4, 1928; s. Walt Wataru and Pauline Kikuye (Tamura) Ozawa; m. Robert Setsuto Ichikawa, Oct. 22, 1950; children: Robert D., Ross A., Laura A. RN, L.A. County Gen. Hosp., 1950; BS, U. So. Calif., 1950; MA, Calif. State U.-Dominguez Hills, 1973; MS in Nursing, Consortium of Calif. State U., 1987. Cert. women's health care nurse practitioner, Calif. Staff nurse Seaside Hosp. (now Long Beach Meml. Hosp.), Long Beach, Calif., 1950-52; office nurse Donald J. Crawford, M.D., Long Beach, 1952-54; operating room nurse L.A. County Harbor-UCLA Med. Ctr., Torrance, 1955-56; sch. nurse L.A. Unified Sch. Dist., 1956-68; prof. nursing L.A. Community Coll. Dist., Wilmington, 1968-79; chairperson div. nursing L.A. Harbor Coll., Wilmington, 1979—; chairperson Assoc. Degree Nursing Program Dirs. L.A. Community Coll. Dist., 1981-83. Mem. adv. bd. Fairview State Hosp. Vol. Little Tokyo Health Fair, L.A., 1979-82; bd. dirs. Torrance Sister City Assn., Calif., 1982—; vol., mem. Am. Cancer Soc., Long Beach, 1983—. Named South Bay Woman of Yr. Torrance YWCA, 1982; recipient Lomita Demolay Top Hat award, 1962. Mem. Calif. Nurses Assn., Nat. League for Nursing, Am. Fedn. Tchrs., Coll. Guild, Calif. Assn. Women Adminstrs. and Counselors, Delta Kappa Gamma (2d v.p. Eta Gamma chpt. 1976-78, pres. 1978-80, parliamentarian 1980-84, chmn. fin. and budget com. 1984—). Republican. Office: Los Angeles Harbor Coll 1111 Figueroa Pl Wilmington CA 90744

ICHIKAWA, WAYNE, oral and maxillofacial surgeon; b. Palo Alto, Calif., July 25, 1954; s. Thomas Toshiaki and June Haruko (Jofuku) I.; m. Kathryn Linda Ito, Aug. 22, 1987. AA, Foothill Coll., 1974; BA, U. Calif., Berkeley, 1976; DDS, U. Calif., Los Angeles, 1981; MS, U. Ill., Chgo., 1986. Diplomate Am. Bd. Oral and Maxillofacial Surgery. Practice medicine specializing in oral and maxillofacial surgery San Leandro, Calif., 1985-86, San Jose, Calif., 1986-88, Campbell, Calif., 1988—; intern, then resident in oral and maxillofacial surgery U. Ill. Med. Ctr./VA Hosp., Chgo., 1981-85; adj. asst. prof. dept. oral and maxillofacial surgery U. Pacific, San Francisco, 1987. Contbr. articles to profl. jours. Fellow Am. Assn. Oral and Maxillofacial Surgeons, Am. Coll. Oral and Maxillofacial Surgeons; mem. ADA, Am. Dental Soc. Anesthesiology, Calif. Assn. Oral and Maxillofacial Surgeons, Calif. Dental Assn., No. Calif. Soc. Oral and Maxillofacial Surgeons, Santa Clara County Dental Soc., Western Soc. Oral and Maxillofacial Surgeons. Buddhist. Office: 1580 S Winchester Blvd Ste 101 Campbell CA 95008

IDARIUS, ERIC WILEY, real estate executive, builder, developer; b. L.A., Sept. 17, 1946; s. Bernard Wiley and Marion (Gleason) Peterson; m. Jerri-Jo Ruggenberg, May 26, 1982 (div.); 1 child, Bodhi Guido; m. Betty Jacqueline Goldberg, July 4, 1982. Student, Ariz. State U., 1964-67, Sorbonne, 1967. Lic. realtor, Ariz. Prin. Idarius Constrn., Ukiah, Calif., 1970-74; prin. ptnr. Calif. Yurt Works, Ukiah, 1974-81, Oreg. Ctr. N.L.P., Eugene, Oreg., 1982-84; realtor assoc. Russ Lyon Realty Co., Scottsdale, Ariz., 1985—, mem. adv. coun., 1989—; cons. Idarius, Inc., Scottsdale, 1987—. Mem. United Stand Owner-Builder Lobbying Group, Ukiah, 1972-79, Ukiah Bd. Bldg. Appeals, 1976-79, Scottsdale Bicycle Task Force, 1987—, Scottsdale Transp. Commn., 1989; bd. dirs. Greater Pinnacle Peak Homeowners Assn., Scottsdale, 1985—. Mem. Real Estate Land Inst., Scottsdale Bd. Realtors, Russ Lyon Realty Co. President's Club. Republican. Office: Russ Lyon Realty Co 23350 N Pima Rd Ste D Scottsdale AZ 85255

IGDALOFF, SUSAN GAIL, pediatrician; b. Toledo, Dec. 10, 1948; d. Harold Burton and Evelyn Ruth (Tarloff) Igdaloff. BS, U. Mich., 1970; MD, U. Calif., Davis, 1975. Diplomate Am. Bd. Pediatrics. Pediatric resident Children's Hosp., L.A., 1975-78; pediatrician various locations, 1978-79, Descanso Pediatric Med. Group, La Canada, Calif., 1979-80; pvt. practice pediatrics N. Hollywood, Calif., 1980—; asst. clin. prof. pediatrics U. So. Calif., L.A., 1987—. Adv. bd. L.A. Commn. Assaults Against Women, 1982—. Fellow Am. Acad. Pediatrics, Women in Pediatrics (com. chair 1985—); mem. Am. Acad. Pediatrics (chair), L.A. County Med. Assn., L.A. Pediatric Soc., Calif. Med. Assn., Am. Med. Women's Assn., L.A. County Med. Women's Assn. Office: 10711 Riverside Dr North Hollywood CA 91602

IGLER, DAVID ROLAND, service executive; b. Saskatoon, Saskatch., Can., July 25, 1936; came to U.S., 1963; s. Peter and Emma (Barth) I.; m. Jane Margaret Murdoch, Sept. 25, 1957; 1 child, Peter. BA, Walla Walla Coll., 1958; BEd, U. Toronto, 1963; MA, Andrews U., 1964. V.p. Pacific Union Coll., Angwin, Calif., 1970-82; dir. rehabilitation and mental health Glendale (Calif.) Adventist Med. Ctr., 1982-88, v.p., 1988—. Office: Glendale Adventist Med Ctr 1509 Wilson Terr Glendale CA 91206

IGNATJEV, VLADIMIR, manufacturing company executive; b. Tallinn, Estonia, Oct. 14, 1916; came to U.S., 1955; s. Feodor and Pauline (Lange) I.; m. Hedwig Pauline Ritter, Dec. 24, 1949; 1 child, Peter Vladimir. Diploma ingenieur, Technische Hochschule, Berlin, 1942. Profl. engr. Design engr. Sperry Rand Univac, Norwalk, Conn., 1955-57; research engr. Edwards Co., Norwalk, 1958-61; mechanical engr. Perkin-Elmer Co., Norwalk, 1961-64; project engr. Pitney Bowes, Inc., Stamford, Conn., 1964-71; sr. engr. Burroughs Corp., Danbury, Conn., 1972-82; pres. IGN, Inc., Norwalk, 1979-83; v.p. Smartline Products, Maui, Hawaii, 1987—. Inventor: 17 U.S. patents, 1960-81; designer: Carbon Yarn Electrode, 1981 (recipient Excellence in Design award); contbr. articles to profl. jours.

IGRAM, RICHARD ERIC, controller; b. Culver City, Calif., Apr. 9, 1954; s. Richard G. and Helen M. (Nicholson) I.; m. Debra L. McClinton, May 25, 1974; children: Stacy A., Lisa M., Laura L. AA in Liberal Arts, Santa Ana Coll., 1977, AA in Bus. Adminstrn., 1978; BA in Acctg. and Bus., Calif. State U., Fullerton, 1980. Cost supr. Datatron, Inc., Irvine, Calif., 1977-79; cost mgr. BMF Foods, Fullerton, Calif., 1979-81; asst. controller Omnimedical, Inc., Anaheim, Calif., 1981-83; controller, dir. fin. Pacific Med. Imaging, Huntington Beach, Calif., 1983-86; controller Watson Labs, Corona, Calif., 1986-87, Quintec Laminated Products, Anaheim, 1987—. Mem. Nat. Assn. Accts., Am. Mgmt. Assn. Republican. Lutheran.

IHRIG, JUDSON LA MOURE, chemist; b. Santa Maria, Calif., Nov. 5, 1925; s. Harry Karl and Luella (LaMoure) I.; m. Gwendolyn Adele Montz, July 22, 1950; children—Kristin, Neil Marshall. B.S., Haverford Coll., 1949; M.A., Princeton U., 1951, Ph.D., 1952. Asst. prof. chemistry U. Hawaii, 1952-58, assoc. prof., 1958-72, prof., 1972—, dir. honors program, 1958-64, 87—, dir. liberal studies program, 1973-79, chmn. chemistry dept., 1981-86; cons. chemistry local firms. Author publs. in field. Served with AUS, 1945-46. Mem. Am. Chem. Soc., AAUP, Phi Beta Kappa, Sigma Xi. Home: 386 Wailupe Circle Honolulu HI 96821 Office: U Hawaii 2545 The Mall Honolulu HI 96822

II, JACK MORITO, aerospace engineer; b. Tokyo, Mar. 20, 1926; s. Iwao and Kiku Ii; came to U.S., 1954, naturalized, 1966; BS, Tohoku U., 1949; MS, U. Washington, 1956; M in Aero. Engring., Cornell U., 1959; PhD in Aero. and Astronautics, U. Wash., 1964; PhD in Engring., U. Tokyo, 1980; m. Aiko Nouno, Nov. 14, 1952; children: Keiko, Yoshiko, Mutsuya. Reporter, Asahi Newspaper Press, Tokyo, 1951-54; aircraft designer Fuji Heavy Industries Ltd. Co., Tokyo, Japan, 1956-58; mem. staff structures research Boeing Advanced Systems Co., Seattle, 1962—. Mem. AIAA, Japan Shumy and Culture Soc. (pres. 1976—), Sigma Xi. Mem. Congregational Ch. Contbr. numerous articles on aerodyns. to profl. jours. Office: The Boeing Co M/S 33-04 Seattle WA 98124

IKEDA, MOSS MARCUS MASANOBU, educational administrator, consultant; b. Los Angeles, Sept. 11, 1931; s. Masao Eugene and Masako (Yamashina) I.; BE, U. Hawaii, 1960, MEd, 1962; postgrad. Stanford U., 1961-62; M in Mil. Art and Sci., U.S. Army Command and Gen. Staff Coll., 1975; grad. U.S. Army War Coll., 1976; EdD, U. Hawaii, 1986; m. Shirley Yaeko Okimoto; children—Cynthia Cecile Ikeda Tamashiro, Mark Eugene, Matthew Albert. Tchr., Farrington High Sch., Honolulu, 1962-64; vice-prin. Kailua Intermediate Sch. 1964-65; adminstrv. intern Central Intermediate Sch., Honolulu, 1965-66; vice-prin. Kaimuki High Sch., Honolulu, 1966-67; prin. Kawananakoa Intermediate Sch., Honolulu, 1967-68, Kailua High Sch., 1969-71, Kalaheo High Sch., Kailua, 1972-77; ednl. specialist Hawaii Dept. Edn., Honolulu, 1977-79; ednl. adminstr. Hawaii Dept. Edn., Honolulu, 1979—; frequent speaker on edn.; lectr. U. Hawaii, 1987—. Mem. accrediting commn. for schs. Western Assn. Schs. and Colls. Served with AUS, 1951-57, 68-69, col. Res. ret. Decorated Legion of Merit, Army Commendation medal. Mem. Nat. Assn. Secondary Sch. Prins., Assn. U.S. Army, Res. Officers Assn., Army War Coll. Alumni Assn., Hawaii Govt. Employees Assn., Phi Delta Kappa, Phi Kappa Phi. Home: 47-494 Apoalewa Pl Kaneohe HI 96744 Office: Hawaii Dept Edn 2530 10th Ave Honolulu HI 96816

IKEDA, TSUGUO (IKE IKEDA), social services center administrator, consultant; b. Portland, Oreg., Aug. 15, 1924; s. Tom Minoru and Tomoe Ikeda; m. Sumiko Hara, Sept. 2, 1951; children: Wanda Amy, Helen Mari, Julie Ann, Patricia Kiyo. BA, Lewis & Clark Coll., 1949; MSW, U. Wash., 1951. Social group worker Neighborhood House, Seattle, 1951-53; exec. dir. Atlantic St. Ctr., Seattle, 1953-86; pres. Urban Partnerships, Seattle, 1986-88, Tsuguo "Ike" Ikeda and Assoc., Seattle, 1988—; cons. Seattle, 1988—; cons. Commn. on Religion and Race, Washington, 1973, North Northeast Mental Health Ctr., Portland, 1985; affirmative action cons. Nat. Assn. Social Workers, Washington, 1977; cons./trainer various other orgns. Tsugo "Ike" Ikeda, Pub. Svc. ann. award established in 1987. Mem. Nat. Task Force to Develop Standards and Goals for Juvenile Delinquency, 1976; mem. Gov.'s Select Panel for social and health services, Olympia, Wash., 1977; chairperson Asian Am. Task Force, Community Coll., Seattle dist., 1982; div. chmn. social agys. Seattle United Way campaign, 1985; vice-chairperson Wash. State Com. on Vocat. Edn., Olympia, 1985-86, chairperson, 1986-87. Served to pvt. Mil. Intelligence Lang. Sch., 1945-46. Recipient cert. appreciation U.S. Dept. Justice, Washington, 1975-76, Am. Dream award Community Coll. Dist., Seattle, 1984, Bishop's award, PNW Conf., U. Meth. Ch., Tacoma, Wash., 1984, community service award Seattle Rotary Club, 1985, Oustanding Citizen award Mcpl. League, Seattle and King County, 1986, numerous others. Mem. Nat. Assn. Social Workers (chpt. pres., Social Worker of Yr. 1971), Vol. Agy. Exec. Coalition (pres., outstanding community service award 1979), Ethnic Minority Mental Health Consortium (chmn., Outstanding Ldr. 1982), Minority Exec. Dirs. Coalition (organizer, membership chmn. 1980-86). Democrat. Methodist.

IKLE, DAVID NORMAN, statistician; b. Mineola, N.Y., July 11, 1943; s. Adolph Max and Ruth (Clark) I.; m. Beverly Genader, 1975, (div. 1980); m. Linda Oldham, June 19, 1982. BS in Math., U. Tex., El Paso, 1971; MS in Statistics, Colo. State U., 1975; PhD in Biometrics, U. Colo., 1980. Jr. statistician Colo. Dept. Health, Greely, 1971-73; rsch. assoc. U. Colo., U. Denver, Denver, 1980-82; statistician Rockwell Internat., Golden, Colo., 1982-84; mgr. statis. applications Rockwell Internat., Golden, 1984-86, sr. statistician, 1986-88; asst. prof. sch. med. U. Colo., Denver, 1988—; chief, biostatistics Nat. Jewish Hosp., Denver, 1988—; cons. Fitzsimons Army Med. Ctr., Aurora, Colo., 1985-88. Contbr. articles to profl. jours. Sgt. U.S. Army, 1967-70, Korea. Mem. Am. Statis. Assn., The Biometric Soc., Mu Sigma Rho, Alpha Chi, Golden Retriever Club. Home: 1671 Newport St Denver CO 80220 Office: Nat Jewish Hosp 1400 Jackson St Denver CO 80206

ILETT, FRANK, JR., trucking company executive; b. Ontario, Oreg., June 21, 1940; s. Frank Kent and Lela Alice (Siver) I.; B.A., U. Wash., 1962; M.B.A., U. Chgo., 1969; m. Donna L. Andlovec, Apr. 3, 1971; children—James Frank, Jordan Lee. Accountant, Ernst & Ernst, Boise, Idaho, Cleve., Spokane, Wash., 1962-69, mgr., Boise, 1970-72, regional mgr., San Francisco, 1972-73; treas. Interstate Mack, Inc., Boise, 1973-81, pres., chief exec. officer, 1981-82; pres. Interstate NationaLease, Inc., Boise, 1975-81; pres. Contract Carriers, Inc., Boise, 1983-88, Ilett Transp. Co., Boise, 1985—; adj. lectr. Boise State U., 1964-67; chmn. Carriers/West, Inc., Salem, Oreg., 1986-89; cons. Calif. Hosp. Commn., 1973, Idaho Hosp. Assn., 1974; chmn. Mack Truck Western Region Distbr. Council, 1979-82; mem. nat. distbr. adv. com. Mack Trucks, Inc., 1980-82; dir. standards enforcement Idaho State Bd. Accountancy, 1983-84. C.P.A., Idaho, Ill., Wash. Mem. Am. Inst. C.P.A.'s, Gen. Soc. Mayflower Decendants, SAR. Episcopalian. Clubs: Hillcrest Country (Boise), Masons, Shriners. Contbr. articles in field to profl. jours. Home: 1710 Dayton Ave Almeda CA 94501 Office: 5050 Colesiom Way Oakland CA 94601

ILSTAD, GEIR ARE, investment banker; b. Mo i Rana, Norway, Mar. 19, 1955; s. Johan Julius and Rønnaug Synnøve (Kristensen) I.; m. Prudence Burnett Herman, Dec. 1, 1984; 1 child, Bergen Burnett. Degree in Econs., U. de Fribourg, Switzerland, 1980; BS, MBA, Menlo Sch. Bus., Atherton, Calif., 1982. Fin. advisor Ilstad Group, Menlo Park, 1981; mgr. Bergen Bank A/S, Oslo, 1982-85; registered rep. First Investors Corp., San Francisco, 1984; project mgr. corp. fin. A.S. Factoring Finans, Oslo, 1985-86; pres., chmn. Prudent Mgmt., Inc., Menlo Park, 1986—. Sec. Nesodden Speed Skating Club, 1969-75, Unge Høyre, Nesodden, Norway, 1971. Served with paratroopers Norwegian Army, 1975-76. Mem. Norwegian Bus. Forum, Swedish-Am. C. of C. Home: 12620 Viscaino Ct Los Altos Hills CA 94022 Office: Prudent Mgmt Inc 683 Live Oak Ave Menlo Park CA 94025

IMANA, JORGE GARRON, artist; b. Sucre, Bolivia, Sept. 20, 1930; s. Juan S. and Lola (Garron) I.; grad. Fine Arts Acad., U. San Francisco Xavier, 1950; cert. Nat. Sch. for Tchrs., Bolivia, 1952; came to U.S., 1964, naturalized, 1974; m. Cristina Imana; children—George, Ivan. Prof. art Nat. Sch. Tchrs., Sucre, 1954-56; prof. biology Padilla Coll., Sucre, 1956-60; head dept. art Inst. Normal Simon Bolivar, La Paz, Bolivia, 1961-62; propr., mgr. The Artists Showroom, San Diego, 1973—. Numerous one-man shows of paintings in U.S., S. Am. and Europe, 1952—, latest being: Gallery Banet, La Paz, 1965, Artists Showroom, San Diego, 1964, 66, 68, 74, 76, 77, San Diego Art Inst., 1966, 68, 72, 73, Contrast Gallery, Chula Vista, Calif., 1966, Central Public Library, San Diego, 1969, Universidad de Zulia, Maracaibo, Venezuela, 1969, Spanish Village Art Center, San Diego, 1974, 75, 76, La Jolla Art Assn. Gallery, 1969, 72-88, Internat. Gallery, Washington, 1976, Galeria de Arte L'Atelier, La Paz, 1977, Museo Nacional, La Paz, 1987, Casa del Arte, La Jolla, Calif., 1987; numerous group shows including: Fine Arts Gallery, San Diego, 1964, Mus. of Modern Art, Paris, 1973, exhibits in galleries of Budapest (Hungary), 1975, Moscow (USSR), 1975, Warsaw (Poland), 1976; represented in permanent collections: Museo Nacional, La Paz, Bolivia, Museo de la Universidad de Potosi, Bolivia, Muse Nacional de Bogota, Colombia, S. Am., Ministerio de Edn., Managua, Nicaragua, Bolivian embassy, Moscow, also pvt. collections in U.S., Europe and Latin Am.; executed many murals including: Colegio Padilla, Sucre, Bolivia, 1958, Colegio Junin, Sucre, Bolivia, 1959, Sindicato de Construccion Civil, Lima, Peru, 1960. Hon. consul of Bolivia, So. Calif., 1969-73. Served to lt. Bolivian Army, 1953. Recipient Mcpl. award Sucre, Bolivia, 1958. Mem. San Diego Art Inst., San Diego Watercolor Soc., Internat. Fine Arts Guild, La Jolla Art Assn. Home: 3357 Caminito Gandara La Jolla CA 92037

IMBRECHT, CHARLES RICHARD, lawyer; b. Ventura, Calif., Feb. 4, 1949; s. Earl Richard and Hazel Victoria (Berg) I.; m. Alida Margit Bergseid, Sept. 23, 1979. AB, Occidental Coll., 1971; JD, Loyola U., Los Angeles, 1974. Bar: Calif. 1974. Atty., adviser ICC, Washington, 1974-75; ptnr. Robinson, Melikan, Imbrecht & Weems, Ventura, 1975-80; assemblyman Calif. Legis., Sacramento, 1976-82; chmn. Calif. Energy Commn., Sacramento, 1983—; gov.'s energy adviser State of Calif., Sacramento, 1983—; mem. Western Interstate Energy Bd., Denver, 1983—, vice chmn., 1984-85, chmn., 1986-88; state liaison Nuclear Regulatory Commn., Washington, 1983—; bd. dirs. Alternative Energy Fin. Authority, Sacramento, 1983—. Del. Commn. of the Califs., San Diego, 1978—; mem. Ventura County Rep. Cen. Com., 1974—, Calif. State Rep. Cen. Com., Sacramento, 1976—. Richter fellow Occidental Coll., 1970; named one of Calif.'s Five Outstanding Young Men, Jaycees, 1981; recipient Outstanding Pub. Service award NSPE, 1984. Mem. Ventura County Bar Assn., Calif. State Bar Assn., Assn. Profl. Energy Mgrs. (bd. dirs.). Lutheran. Office: Calif Energy Commn 1516 9th St Sacramento CA 95814

IMLAY, GORDON LAKE, development consultant; b. Fairmont, W.Va., Oct. 12, 1937; s. Julian Mortimer and Fredricka Jane (Harveycutter) I.; m. Margaret Julia Robina, Aug. 31, 1958; children: Jane Ellen Imlay Skeen, James Elliot. BA, Mo. Valley Coll., 1959; MS, San Jose State U., 1977; EdD, U. Pacific, 1980. Registered recreator. Dist. scout exec. Boy Scouts Am., Bloomington, Ind., 1959-63; dist. scout exec. Boy Scouts Am., Detroit, 1963-68, field dir., 1968-72; exec. dir. Am. Humanics, Marshall, Mo., 1972-74, Stockton, Calif., 1974-81; v.p. YMCA of Metro Los Angeles, 1981-84; exec. dir. East Valley Family YMCA, No. Hollywood, Calif., 1984-87; v.p. Netzel/Steinhaus & Assocs., Culver City, Calif., 1987—; cons. Idaho Commn. Arts, Boise, 1982; faculty mem. YMCA Nat. Staff Tng., Foster City, Calif., 1982-84; nat. cons. Boy Scouts Am., Dallas, 1974-81; chmn. nat. teen task force YMCA U.S.A., Chgo., 1981-85. Author: Identifying the Community Power Structure, 1977; editor: YMCA Leadership Development with Teens, 1983; contbr. articles to profl. jours. Mem. Nat. Soc. Fundraising Execs., YMCA Assn. Profl. Dirs. (acad. cert. 1986). Republican. Presbyterian. Club: Sunset Hills Country (Thousand Oaks, Calif.). Lodges: Rotary (program chmn. No. Hollywood, Calif. chpt. 1987, sec. Redford Twp., Mich. chpt. 1965), Lions (key mem. Martinsville, Ind. chpt. 1960). Home: 1705 Alderwood Pl Thousand Oaks CA 91362 Office: Netzel/Steinhaus & Assocs 9696 Culver Blvd #204 Culver City CA 90232

IMLER, JEANNE E., nursing administrator, educator, nurse; b. Mt. Carmel, Pa., Oct. 26, 1932; d. Thomas Harold and Alma Rebecca (Shuler) Wetzel; m. Harper George Imler, June 13, 1959; children: Randolph, Rebecca. Cert. nursing, Jefferson Hosp. Sch. Nursing, 1953; BS in Edn., Temple U., 1956; BSN, Calif. State U., L.A., 1973, MS in Nursing Adminstrn., 1975. RN, Calif.; cert. pub. health tchr. (life), Calif. Instr. nursing Pasadena (Calif.) City Coll., 1966-68, 79-86; nurse Huntington Meml. Hosp., Pasadena, 1976-80; supr. nursing Heath Conservation, Pasadena, 1980-84; reader Huntington Library, San Marino, Calif., 1987—. Bd. dirs. in-svc. edn. Huntington Meml. Hosp., 1960-65; bd. dirs. San Marino PTA, 1977-79; speaker, vol. ARC, Pasadena, 1970—, bd. dirs., rep. for nurses, San Marino, 1987-88. Temple U. scholar. San Marino Hist. Soc. (pres. 1987—, sec. 1986-87), Calif. State U. Alumnae Assn., Temple U. Alumnae Assn., Burdette Purdum Guild of San Marino Woman's Club (chmn. 1985-86). Home: 1616 Hilliard Dr San Marino CA 91108

IMPERIAL, ROBERT SALVADORE, publisher; b. Hollywood, Calif., Sept. 18, 1945; s. Salvadore Frank and Josephine (DiPardo) I. BS, Calif. State Coll., Sherman Oaks, 1966; MBA, Calif. State Coll., Northridge, 1970. Advt. dir. Soul Publs., Hollywood, 1970-73; pres. Imperial Mktg., Hollywood, 1973-76; sr. v.p. mktg. Hotel Publs. Ltd., Long Beach, Calif., 1976-80; chief exec. officer RSI Pub., Inc., Martinez, Calif., 1980—; pres. Foxboro Assn., Hercules, Calif., 1984-85. Chmn. Young Democrats of Contra Costa County, 1988—. Served with USN, Vietnam. Decorated Bronze Star. Mem. Martinez C. of C. (exec. dir. 1986-87, v.p. 1987-88), Martinez Hist. Soc. (bd. dirs. 1986-87). Democrat. Seventh-Day Adventist. Office: RSI Pub Inc 649 Main St Martinez CA 94553

IMPERIALE, LARRY WILLIAMS, computer company executive; b. Redwood City, Calif., July 7, 1958; s. Louis George and Helen (Williams) I. BA in Computer Sci., Calif. State U., Chico, 1980; MBA in Mgmt., San Diego State U., 1987. Product mgr. Triad Systems Corp., Sunnyvale and San Diego, Calif., 1980-86; cons. Triad Systems Corp., Sunnyvale, 1986-87; pres., chief exec. officer SalePoint Systems Corp., San Diego, 1986—, also chmn., bd. dirs. Named World Frisbee Champion, 1983-85. Republican. Office: SalePoint Systems Corp 6199 Cornerstone Ct E Ste 111 San Diego CA 92121

INACKER, CHARLES JOHN, business educator, dean; b. Phila., Dec. 3, 1936; s. Charles John and Ada Anna (Matthews) I. BS in Bus. Edn., Thiel Coll., 1958; EdM in Bus. Edn. and Ednl. Adminstrn., Temple U., 1960, EdD in Bus. Edn., 1973. Cert. tchr. bus. edn. (N.J. life); cert. secondary sch. prin.; cert. sch. adminstr./supt. Tchr. bus. edn. Pitman (N.J.) High Sch., 1958-61; tchr., dept. chmn., vice prin., acting prin.. Pennsauken (N.J.) High Sch., 1961-74; from assoc. prof. to prof. dept. bus. edn. and office adminstrn.

Sch. Bus. and Econs., Calif. State U., Los Angeles, 1974—, acting chmn. dept. acctg., 1984-85, chmn. dept. bus. edn. and office adminstrn., 1982-85, dean, 1985—; dir. Ctr. for Econ. Edn. Calif. State U., Los Angeles, 1982-85; pres., bd. dirs. Aux. Services Enterprises, Inc., Los Angeles, 1985—; vis. lectr. Rider Coll., Trenton, N.J., Rutgers U., Camden, N.J., Temple U., Phila., Am. Mgmt. Assn. Ext. Inst.; mem. adv. com. Ctr. Bus. Tchr. Edn., Calif. State U., 1982-84, bus. edn. Alhambra (Calif.) High Sch., 1982-84; adv. council grad. and undergrad. programs sch. edn., Rider College, 1972-74, bus. edn. State Dept. Edn., N.J., 1972-74. Major reviewer textbooks Gregg div. McGraw-Hill Book Co., 1985, John Wiley Pub. Co., 1983-84, others; edit. bd. Business Forum, 1981—, guest editor 1983 fall issue; mem. steering and edit. com. Bus. Edn. Curriculum Guides for the 70's . N.J., 1972; contbr. articles to profl. jours. Mem. Bus. and Econ. Devel. Council, Los Angeles, 1985—. Served to maj. USAR, 1960-80, ret. Recipient Outstanding Educator in Am. award Acad. Am. Educators, 1974. Mem. Acad. Mgmt., Nat. Bus. Edn. Assn. (chmn. profl. opportunities com. 1980, nat. task force for model bus. edn. curriculum K-14 1985, Merit award 1958), Calif. Bus. Edn. Assn. (cert. recogntion 1983), Western Bus. Edn. Assn. (cert. commendation 1978), Assn. Bus. Communications, N.J. Bus. Edn. Assn. (life, state pres. 1972), AAUP, Internat. Soc. Bus. Edn., Nat. Assn. Tchr. Educators in Bus. Edn., Western Assn. Collegiate Schs. Bus., Beta Gamma Sigma, Delta Pi Epsilon (sponsor Beta Pi chpt. 1979—, nat. v.p. 1988—, Achievement award Alpha Zeta chpt. 1972), Research Found. of Delta Pi Epsilon (pres. 1984), Phi Beta Delta. Office: Calif State U Sch Bus & Econs 5151 State University Dr Los Angeles CA 90032

INDIEK, VICTOR HENRY, finance corporation executive; b. Spearville, Kans., Nov. 15, 1937; s. Ben W. and Helen Ann (Schreck) I.; m. Marlene Gould, June 2, 1962; children: Kathy, Kevin. Student, U. Nebr., 1955-57; BS in Bus., U. Kans., 1959; postgrad., U. Nebr., 1955-57. CPA, Kans. Audit mgr. Arthur Andersen & Co., Kansas City, Mo., 1961-70; pres., chief exec. officer Fed. Home Loan Mortgage Corp., Washington, 1970-77; pres., dir. Builders Capital Corp., Los Angeles, 1977-84; chief fin. officer, exec. v.p. Fin. Corp. of Am., Irvine, Calif., 1984-88; pres., chief exec. officer FarWest Savs. and Loan Assn., Newport Beach, Calif., 1988—; v.p. and pres. regional Assn. Small Businesses Investment Cos., 1979-81, bd. govs. nat. assn., 1982. Mem. Selective Service Bd., Santa Monica, Calif., 1978; capt. United Fund, Kansas City, 1968. Served with USN, 1959-61. Republican. Roman Catholic. Office: FarWest Savs & Loan Assn 4001 MacArthur Blvd Newport Beach CA 92660

INGALLS, GEGORY KENT, oral and maxillofacial sugeon; b. Denver, Apr. 13, 1955; s. Floyd Winton and Winifred (Dick) I.; m. Barbara Renard O'Donnell, Aug. 10, 1980; children: Allison Erin, Benjamin Bryant. BS, Colo. State U., 1977; DDS, U. Colo., 1982. Gen. practice resident U. Colo., Denver, 1983; oral and maxillofacial sugery resident Med. Coll. Ga., Augusta, 1986; pvt. practice oral and maxillofacial sugery Arvada, Colo., 1986--; asst. clin. prof., U. Colo. Sch. Dentistry, Denver, 1986--; clinical consultant St. Joseph's Hosp. Gen. Practice Residency, Denver, 1986--; Chief of Dentistry and oral maxillofacial surgery Lutheran Med Ctr., 1988--, trauma com., 1987--; instr. CPR, Advanced Cardiatic Life Support, 1986. Named Clin. Prof. of Yr., St. Joseph Hosp., Denver, 1986-87. Fellow Am. Assn. Oral and Maxillofacial Surgeons; mem. ADA, Colo. Soc. Oral and Maxillofacial Surgery (gen. anesthetic com. 1987--), Colo. Soc. Dental Anesesiologists (program dir. 1987--), Delta Sigma Delta, Alpha Tau Omega, Denver Athletic, Grand Lake (Colo.) Yatch. Republican. Presbyterian. Home: 1058 S High St Denver CO 80209 Office: Arvada Oral Surgery 9950 W 80th Ave Ste 14 Arvada CO 80005

INGALLS, JEREMY, poet, educator; b. Gloucester, Mass., Apr. 2, 1911; d. Charles A. and May E. (Dodge) Ingalls. AB, Tufts Coll., 1932, AM, 1933; student, U. Chgo., 1938-39; LHD, Rockford Coll., 1960; LittD, Tufts U., 1965. Asst. prof. English Lit. Western Coll., Oxford, Ohio, 1941-43; resident poet, asst. prof. English lit. Rockford (Ill.) Coll., 1948-50, successively assoc. prof. English and Asian studies, prof., chmn. div. arts, chmn. English dept., 1950-60. Author: A Book of Legends, 1941, The Metaphysical Sword, 1941, Tahl, 1945, The Galilean Way, 1953, The Woman from the Island, 1958, These Islands Also, 1959, This Stubborn Quantum, 1983, Summer Liturgy, 1985, The Epic Tradition and Related Essays, 1989; also translator, contbr. of articles and poetry to profl. jours. Recipient numerous awards for poetry; appointed hon. epic poet laureate United Poets Laureate Internat., 1965; Guggenheim fellow, 1943, Chinese classics rsch. fellow, Republic of China, 1945, 46, Am. Acad. Arts and Letters grantee, 1944. Fellow Internat. Inst. Arts and Letters; mem. Assn. Asian Studies (life), The Authors Guild, Modern Lang. Assn. (chmn. Oriental-We. lit. relations conf.), Poetry Soc. Am., New Eng. Poetry Soc., Dante Soc. Am. (life), Phi Beta Kappa, Chi Omega. Episcopalian. Home: 6269 E Rosewood St Tucson AZ 85711

INGALLS, PATRICIA MARIE, audiologist; b. Wabasha, Minn., Feb. 14, 1947; d. George Frank and Frances Abby (O'Connell) I. BA, Wash. State U., 1969; MS, U. N.Mex., 1976. Cert. clin. competence in audiology; cert. Coun. for Accreditation in Occupational Hearing Conservation, Am. Tinnitus Assn. Audiologist, coord. Butte (Mont.) Easter Seal Ctr., 1975-85; owner, mgr. Highlands Hearing Ctr., Butte, 1985—; cons. Mont. Power Co., Butte, 1979—, Safeway, Butte, 1981-85, Mont. Resources Inc., Butte, 1986—; assoc. dir., spl. projects dir. No. Rocky Mountain Easter Seal Soc., Butte, 1983-85. Bd. dirs. Mountain View Social Devel. Ctr., Butte, 1986—. Mem. Am. Speech, Lang. and Hearing Assn. (cons. congl. action network 1984—), Mont. Speech, Lang. and Hearing Assn. (pres. 1986), No. Rocky Mountain Easter Seal Employees Assn. (pres. 1981-82), AAUW, DAR, Mont. Bd. Hearing Aid Dispensers, Acad. Dispensing Audiologists, Am. Acad. Audiology. Office: Highlands Hearing Ctr 1389 Harrison Ave Butte MT 59701

INGELS, HAROLD CLAYTON, video engineer; b. Annapolis, Md., Sept. 18, 1941; s. Albert Clayton and Elizabeth Francis (Philbrick) I.; m. Clairette Eveline Ingels, Jan. 28, 1967; children: Michelle, David. AA, San Diego City Coll., 1962; student San Diego State Coll., 1962-63. With various radio stas., San Diego, 1960-65; sr. video engr. NBC Inc., Burbank, Calif., 1965—. Chmn. emergency communications Crescenta Radio Club, 1980-88. With U.S. Army, 1962-64. Recipient Emmy award for electronic camera work, 1982. Mem. Acad. TV Arts and Scis., Nat. Assn. Broadcast Employees and Technicians. (treas. 1977-88, regional v.p. 1983-86). Office: NBC Inc 3000 W Alameda Ave Burbank CA 91523

INGERMAN, MICHAEL LEIGH, business consultant; b. N.Y.C., Nov. 30, 1937; s. Charles Stryker and Ernestine (Leigh) I.; m. Madeleine Edison Sloane; Nov. 24, 1984; children by previous marriage: Shawn Marie, Jenifer Lyn. BS, George Washington U., 1963. Health planner, Marin County, Calif., 1969-70, 70-72; regional cons. Bay Area Comprehensive Health Council, San Francisco, 1972-73; hosp. cons. Booz, Allen & Hamilton, San Francisco, 1974; health planning coordinator Peralta Hosp., Oakland, Calif., 1975-76; pres. Discern, Inc., hosp. cons., Nicasio, Calif., 1976-88; ptnr. Decision Processes Internat., 1988—; instr. Golden Gate U., 1981-88. Capt. Nicasio Vol. Fire Dept., 1976-88; coord. Nicasio Disaster Commn., 1988—; dep. coroner Marin County, 1980-83; nat. bd. dirs. Am. Friends Svc. Com., 1980-81, bd. dirs. Hospice of Marin, 1983—, pres. bd. dirs., 1988—; bd. dirs. Friends Assn. Svc. for the Elderly, 1984-89 pres. 1988-89. Mem. Marin County Civil Grand Jury, 1977-78; mem. Nicasio Design Rev. Com., 1979-83; bd. dirs. John Woolman Sch., 1980-87. Office: Decison Processes Internat 2101 Nicasio Valley Rd Nicasio CA 94946

INGERSOLL, JOHN GREGORY, physicist, energy specialist, educator; b. Athens, Greece, July 25, 1948; came to U.S., 1971; s. Gregory and Catherine (Asteris) I.; m. Sally Lynn Roberts, Apr. 7, 1984. BS, Nat. Tech. U., Athens, 1970; MS, Syracuse U., 1973; PhD, U. Calif., Berkeley, 1978. Instr. physics U. Calif., 1974-75, research asst. Lawrence Berkeley Lab., 1975-77, from asst. research prof. to assoc. research prof. Lawrence Berkeley Lab., 1978-82; sr. staff scientist Hughes Aircraft Co., Los Angeles, 1983—; staff mem., advisor USN Energy Office, Washington, 1988—; cons. Calif. Energy Commn., Sacramento, 1981-82, U.S. Dept. Energy, Washington, 1981-83, Bldg. Industry, N.Y. and Calif., 1982—; prin. investigator Energy Tech. Group UCLA, 1983—. Contbr. over 60 articles on nuclear sci., renewable energy resources, indoor air quality, efficient utilization of energy in bldgs., passive solar systems and solar elec. energy to profl. jours.; contbg. author to three books on energy mgmt. in bldgs.; patentee of heat pipe devels. Mem. Rep. Presdl. Task Force, Calif., 1981-83. Served as lt. USNR, 1982—. Fellow Democritus Nuclear Research Ctr., Athens, 1970, Syracuse U., 1972, Rockefeller Found., 1974. Mem. Am. Phys. Soc. (mem. energy study group 1988—), N.Y. Acad. Scis., AAAS, ASHRAE (govt. and community liaison Calif. chpt. 1985—). Presbyterian. Home: 21315 Lighthill Dr Topanga CA 90290 Office: Hughes Aircraft Co PO Box 902 El Segundo CA 90245

INGHAM, KENNETH LEROY, systems programmer, consultant; b. Hunter AFB, Ga., May 3, 1962; s. Kenneth LeRoy and Patricia Jane (Kirk) Ingham. BS in Computer Sci. cum laude, U. N.Mex., 1985, postgrad. Student engring. trainee space projects div. NASA Ames Research Ctr. Project Tech. Br., Moffett Field, Calif., 1981-82; student cons. U. N.Mex. Computing Ctr., Albuquerque, 1980-85; from systems programmer I to systems programmer II U. N.Mex. Computer and Info. Resources and Tech. Ctr., Albuquerque, 1985—; cons. Medical Graphics, Albuquerque; instr. Berralillo County Data Processing, Albuquerque. Mem. Assn. for Computing Machinery (1st Pl. award local programming contest U. N.Mex. Chpt. 1986). Home: 1601 Rita Dr NE Albuquerque NM 87106 Office: Computer Info Resources & Tech 2701 Campus NE Albuquerque NM 87131

INGHAM, ROBERT EDWIN, cardiologist; b. Berkeley, Calif., Dec. 30, 1944; s. Theodore Alton and Mary Lou (Bailey) I.; B.A., U. Calif.-Berkeley, 1966; M.D., Cornell U., 1970; children—William Robert, Douglas James. Intern, Cornell-N.Y. Hosp., N.Y.C., 1970-71, resident internal medicine, 1971-72; fellow in cardiology Stanford (Calif.) U., 1973-74; practice medicine specializing in cardiology Naval Regional Med. Ctr., Oakland, Calif., 1974-76; mem. staff John Muir Meml. Hosp., Walnut Creek, Calif., 1976—, sec.-treas. staff, 1981, vice-chief of staff, 1982-83, chief of staff, 1983, dir. non-invasive cardiology lab., 1979-81, dir. cardiac exercise program, 1978-85, dir. invasive cardiology lab., 1986; assoc. clin. prof. medicine U. Calif.-Davis, 1976—; bd. dirs. Omega Med. Clinic, 1985—, vice chmn., 1985—. Former bd. dirs. Danville (Calif.) Fire Protection Dist.; bd. dirs., past pres. Contra Costa County chpt. Am. Heart Assn. Served with M.C., USNR, 1974-76. Diplomate Am. Bd. Internal Medicine; Leopold Schepp Found. scholar, 1968-69. Fellow Am. Coll. Cardiology, ACP; mem. Am. Heart Assn., Soc. Med. Friends of Wine. Contbr. articles to profl. jours. Office: 1515 Ygnacio Valley Rd Walnut Creek CA 94598

INGLE, ROBERT D., newspaper editor; b. Sioux City, Iowa, Apr. 29, 1939; s. Walter J. and Thelma L (McCoy) I.; m. Martha N. Nelson, Sept. 12, 1964 (div. 1984); 1 child, Julia L.; m. Sandra R. Reed, Mar. 2, 1985. B.A. in Journalism and Polit. Sci., U. Iowa, 1962. Various positions Miami Herald, 1962-75, asst. mng. editor, 1975-77, mng. editor, 1977-81; sr. v.p., exec. editor San Jose Mercury News, Calif., 1981—. Mem. AP Mng. Editors Assn., Am. Soc. Newspaper Editors. Office: San Jose Mercury News 750 Ridder Park Dr San Jose CA 95190

INGLES, JOSEPH LEGRAND, utility consumer advocate, educator; b. June 15, 1939; s. Vernal Willard and Helen Josephine (Graziano) I.; m. Hazel Jeanette Palmer, Aug. 18, 1962; children: Sally, Christine, Joette, Robert, Michael. BS, Brigham Young U., 1964; PhD, U. Mo., 1968. Research asst. U. Mo., Columbia, 1967-68; grant policy specialist HEW, Washington, 1970-71; asst. prof. govt. and politics U. Md., College Park, 1968-75; dir. human resources Wasatch Front Regional Council, Bountiful, Utah, 1975-77; utility consumer advocate Com. on Consumer Service Utah, 1977—; cons. Ellingson Kilpack Assocs., Salt Lake City, 1972, Bonneville Research Corp., Santa Monica, Calif., 1971, U.S. Dept. Commerce, 1970; spl. faculty mem. Salt Lake Ctr. Brigham Young U., 1988—. Mem. West Bountiful City Council, 1982-88; fellow NDEA, 1964-67; U. Md. grantee, 1969. Fellow Am. Soc. Pub. Adminstrn. (fellowship 1970-71); mem. Nat. Assn. Regulatory Utility Commrs. staff subcom. on consumer affairs, 1982—; mem. gas com. Nat. Assn. State Utility Consumer Advocates, 1983—. Mormon. Lodge: Snowbird Iron Blosam (budget and fin. com. 1987). Home: 1485 N 1100 W West Bountiful UT 84087 Office: Com Consumer Svcs 408 Heber Wells Bldg PO Box 45802 Salt Lake City UT 84145

INGO, ANTHONY WAYNE JR., software engineer; b. Tacoma, Jan. 3, 1960; s. Anthony Wayne Sr. and France M. (Giannetta) I. Civil engring. tech. deg., U. Southern Colo., 1983, math degree, 1985. Software engr. Martin Marietta, Denver, 1985--.

INGRAM, HELEN MOYER, political science educator; b. Denver, July 12, 1937; d. Oliver Weldon and Hazel Margaret (Wickard) Hill; m. W. David Laird; children by previous marriage: Mrill, Maia, Seth. BA, Oberlin (Ohio) Coll., 1959; PhD, Columbia U., N.Y.C., 1967. Lectr., asst. prof. polit. sci. U. N. Mex., 1962-69; cons. Nat. Water Commn., Washington, 1969-72; assoc. prof. polit. sci. U. Ariz., Tucson, 1972-77, prof. polit. sci., 1979—; acctg. dir. Udall Ctr. for studies in pub. policy, U. Ariz., 1988—; sr. fellow Resources for the Future, Washington, 1977-79; mem. panel on climate variability and U.S. water resources AAAS, 1986—. Mem. Policy Studies Orgn., (pres. 1985), Am. Polit. Sci. Assn. (council, treas. 1985-87), Western Polit. Sci. Assn. (past pres., v.p.). Author: (with Dean Mann) Why Policies Succeed or Fail, 1980; (with Nancy Laney and John McCain) A Policy Approach to Representation: Lessons from the Four Corners States, 1980; (with Martin, Laney and Griffin) Saving Water in a Desert City, 1984, (with Brown) Water and Poverty in the Southwest, 1987; book rev. editor Am. Polit. Sci. Rev., 1987—. Home: 2811 E 3d St Tucson AZ 85719 Office: U Ariz Udall Ctr Studies Pub Policy 1031 Mountain Tucson AZ 85721

INGRAM, ROBERT BRUCE, lawyer; b. Des Moines, July 19, 1940; s. Earl J. and Frances F. (Forquer) I.; married; children: Stephanie, Ashley, Robert. Student U. Iowa, 1958-61; B.A., Drake U., 1962, postgrad., 1962-63; J.D., Coll. William and Mary, 1970. Bar: Calif. 1971, Hawaii 1982. With Law Offices of Melvin M. Belli, San Francisco, 1971-78; sole practice, San Rafael, Calif., 1978—; ptnr. Stearns & Ingram, Honolulu, 1982—; Superior Ct. jud. arbitrator, San Francisco and Marin County, 1980—; judge pro-tem Mcpl. Ct., County of Marin, 1984—; keynote speaker ann. meeting Ga. State Bar, 1979; guest speaker Iowa Acad. Trial Lawyers Seminar, 1987; lead counsel Pacifica Mud Slide Litigation Class Action, 1985—. Served as capt. USAF, 1964-68. Mem. Assn. Trial Lawyers Am., Calif. Trial Lawyers Assn., San Francisco Trial Lawyers Assn., ABA, Marin County Bar Assn. Presbyterian. Club: Rafael Racquet, Honolulu. Lodge: Elks. Contbr. articles to legal jours. Office: 4340 Redwood Hwy Ste 352 San Rafael CA 94903 Office: 733 Bishop St Ste 2300 Honolulu HI 96813

INGRAM, WILLIAM AUSTIN, federal judge; b. Jeffersonville, Ind., July 6, 1924; s. William Austin and Marion (Lane) I.; m. Barbara Brown Lender, Sept. 18, 1947; children: Mary Ingram Mac Calla, Claudia, Betsy Ingram Friebel. Student, Stanford U., 1947; LL.B., U. Louisville, 1950. Assoc., Littler, Coakley, Lauritzen & Ferdon, San Francisco, 1951-55; dep. dist. atty. Santa Clara (Calif.) County, 1955-57; mem. firm Rankin, O'Neal, Luckhardt & Center, San Jose, Calif., 1955-69; judge Mcpl. Ct., Palo Alto-Mountain View, Calif., 1969-71, Calif. Superior Ct., 1971-76; judge U.S. Dist. Ct. No. Dist. Calif., San Jose, 1976-88, chief judge, 1988—. Served with USMCR, 1943-46. Fellow Am. Coll. Trial Lawyers. Republican. Episcopalian. Home: 1211 College Ave Palo Alto CA 94306 Office: US Dist Ct 280 S 1st St San Jose CA 95113

INKELES, ALEX, sociology educator; b. Bklyn., Mar. 4, 1920; s. Meyer and Ray (Gewer) K.; m. Bernadette Mary Kane, Jan. 31, 1942; 1 child, Ann Elizabeth. B.A., Cornell U., 1941, M.A., 1946; postgrad., Washington Sch. Psychiatry, 1943-46; Ph.D., Columbia U., 1949; student, Boston Psychoanalytic Inst., 1957-59; A.M. (hon.), Harvard U., 1957; prof. honoris causa, Faculdade Candido Mendez, Rio de Janerio, 1969. Social sci. research analyst Dept. State and OSS, 1942-46; cons. program evaluation br., internat. broadcasting div. Dept. State, 1949-51; instr. social relations Harvard U., Cambridge, Mass., 1948, lectr., 1948-57, prof. sociology, 1957-71, dir. studies social relations Russian Research Ctr., dir. studies social aspects econ. devel. Ctr. Internat. Affairs, 1963-71, research assoc., 1971—; Margaret Jacks prof. edn., prof. sociology Stanford U., Calif., 1971-78, prof. sociology, 1978—; sr. fellow Hoover Inst., 1978—; mem. exec. com. behavioral sci. div. NRC, 1968-75; lectr. Nihon U., Japan, 1985. Author: Public Opinion in Soviet Russia, 1950 (Kappa Tau Alpha award 1950, Grant Squires prize Columbia 1955); (with R. Bauer, C. Kluckhohn) How the Soviet System Works, 1956; (with R. Bauer) The Soviet Citizen, 1959, Soviet Society (edited with H.K. Geiger), 1961; What Is Sociology?, 1964; Readings on Modern Sociology, 1965; Social Change in Soviet Russia, 1968; (with D.H. Smith) Becoming Modern, 1974 (Hadley Cantril award 1974); Exploring Individual Modernity, 1983. Contbr. articles to profl. jours. Editor-in-chief: Ann. Rev. Sociology, 1971-79; editorial cons. Internat. Rev. Cross Cultural Studies; editorial bd. Ethos, Jour. Soc. Psychol. Anthropology, 1978; editor Founds. Modern Sociology Series; adv. editor in sociology to Little, Brown & Co. Recipient Cooley Mead award for Disting. Contbn. in Social Psychology, 1982; fellow Ctr. Advanced Study Behavioral Sci., 1955, Founds. Fund Research Psychiatry, 1957-60, Social Scis. Research Council, 1959, Russell Sage Found., 1966, 85, Fulbright Found., 1977, Guggenheim Found., 1978, Bernard van Leer Jerusalem Found., 1979, Rockefeller Found., 1982, Eisenhower Assn., Taiwan, 1984; NAS Disting. Scholar Exchange, China, 1983; grantee Internat. Rsch. and Exchs. Bd., 1989, NSF, 1989. Fellow AAAS (co-chmn. western ctr. 1984-87, chmn. Talcott Parsons award com. 1988—), Am. Philos. Soc., Am. Psychol. Assn.; mem. Nat. Acad. Scis. (corr. human rights com. 1986-88, mem. com. on scholarly communications with People's Republic of China, chmn. panel on social sci. and humanities), Am. Sociol. Soc. (council 1961-64, v.p. 1975-76), Eastern Sociol. Soc. (pres. 1961-62), World Assn. Pub. Opinion Research, Am. Assn. Pub. Opinion Research, Inter-Am. Soc. Psychology, Sociol. Research Assn. (exec. com. 1975-79, pres. 1979), Soc. for Study Social Problems. Home: 10001 Hamilton Ave Palo Alto CA 94301 Office: Stanford U Hoover Instn Stanford CA 94305

INLOW, RUSH OSBORNE, chemist; b. Seattle, July 10, 1944; s. Edgar Burke and Marigale (Osborne) I.; B.S., U. Wash., 1966; Ph.D., Vanderbilt U., 1975; m. Gloria Elisa Duran, June 7, 1980. Chemist, sect. chief U.S. Dept. Energy, New Brunswick Lab., Argonne, Ill., 1975-78, chief nuclear safeguards br. Albuquerque ops., 1978-82, sr. program engr. Cruise missile systems, 1983-84, program mgr. Navy Strategic Systems, 1984-85, dir. weapon programs div., 1985-88, dir. prodn. ops. div., 1988—, apptd. Fed. Sr. Exec. Service, 1985. Served with USN, 1966-71. Tenn. Eastman fellow, 1974-75. Mem. Am. Chem. Soc., Sigma Xi. Republican. Episcopalian. Contbr. articles to profl. jours. Home: 2024 Monte Largo NE Albuquerque NM 87112

INMAN, CHRISTOPHER CROSBY, homebuilding company executive, real estate developer; b. Indpls., Dec. 2, 1941; s. William Herman and Frances Elizabeth (Matthews) I.; m. Margie Ruth Earnest, Feb. 1, 1980; children: Jill, Karen, Craig, Mark, Melissa. BBA, U. N.Mex., 1963, MBA, 1969. Asst. v.p. Bank N. Mex., Albuquerque, 1963-68, Bank Calif., San Francisco, 1968-70; sr. v.p. 1st Nat. Bank, Albuquerque, 1970-75; pres. Inman Homes, Albuquerque, 1975—. Author: Financing Land Acquisition, 1987. Mem. Urban Land Inst., Internat. Coun. Shopping Ctrs., Nat. Assn. Homeowners (nat. bd. dirs. 1984—), Albuquerque Bd. Realtors, Phoenix Bd. Realtors, Home Owners Warranty Coun. (bd. dirs. 1980-86), Cen. N.Mex. Homebuilders Assn. (pres. 1984-85, Builder of Yr. award 1985), Albuquerque Country Club, Tanoan Country Club. Office: Inman Homes Inc 7801 Academy St NE Albuquerque NM 87109

INMON-LOEFFLER, KATHY MARIE, insurance professional; b. Phoenix, Aug. 12, 1962; d. Keith Gerald and Jean Ann (McLaughlin) Byhaug; m. Dwight E. Loeffler, Mar. 7, 1987; 1 child by previous marriage, Brookelyn Lee. AA, Phoenix Coll. Claims customer service rep. CSE Ins. Co., Phoenix, 1978-80; office mgr. Ins. Ctr. Mesa, Ariz., 1980-81; Medicare claims specialist Farnsworth-Ricks Ins. Co., Mesa, 1981-82; personal lines sales rep. Ransom Agy., Phoenix, 1982-83; benefit rep. Dave Richards Co., Scottsdale, Ariz., 1983; mgr. employee benefit sales dept. Schaefer-Smith-Ankeney Ins.Agy., Phoenix, 1983--; cons. Ryan Group, Scottsdale, 1983. Mem. Greater Phoenix Health Underwriters (sec.-treas. 1987-88, v.p. 1988, pres.-elect 1988-89), Ariz. State Assn. Health Underwriters (sec. 1988), Bus. and Profl. Women, Ariz. Group Assocs. Republican. Roman Catholic. Office: Schaefer Smith Ankeney Ins Agy 2002 E Osborn St Phoenix AZ 85026

INNES, DAPHNE JOYCE, mathematician; b. Roodepoort, Transvaal, S. Africa, Aug. 23, 1935; came to U.S., 1955; d. John Henry and Alice Maud (Stewart) Talbot; m. Robert Innes, Feb. 1955 (div. 1961); children: Mary, Mark, Janet. BA in Physics, U. Calif., Berkeley, 1958. Programmer Lawrence Radiation Lab., Berkeley, 1959-64; optical designer Spectra Physics, Mountainview, Calif., 1964-66; rsch. engr. Whittaker Corp., L.A., 1966-68; mgr. tech. systems Computer Planning Corp., Washington, 1968-69; optical physicist NASA G.S.F.C. Md., Greenbelt, 1969-71; tchr. Mariposa Free Sch., Mendocino, Calif., 1971-72; mgr. mining Johannesburg (S. Africa) Consol. Investment, 1973-75; ind. researcher in math. Berkeley, 1975—; cons. in field;. Contbr. articles to profl. jours. Co-founder 1st Global Matriarchy, Oakland, Calif., 1973.

INNIS, EILEEN SCHEFFLER, administrative analyst; b. Eau Claire, Wis., Oct. 15, 1929; d. and Elizabeth Emma (Jaeckel) Scheffler; m. Jack Mattson Innis, Feb. 12, 1950 (div. 1967); children: Jack Scheffler, Steven Wayne, Douglas Alan. Student, Orange Coast Coll., 1959, U. Calif.-San Diego, 1979-81, Mira Costa Coll., 1983-84, 86-88. Sec. U.S. Navy, Washington, 1949-51, Kaiser Aluminum & Chem. Co., Oakland, Calif., 1952-55; office mgr. Friedkin Racing Enterprises, Escondido, Calif., 1967-68; sec. U. Calif.-La Jolla, 1968-72. adminstrv. asst., 1972-84, adminstrv. analyst, 1984—; exec. bd. mem. U. Calif.-San Diego Staff Assn., La Jolla, 1984-85. Vol. Mus. of Man, San Diego, 1979—. Mem. Archeol. Inst. Am., San Diego County Archeol. Soc., Soc. Bibl. Archaeology, Nat. History Mus., Flying Samaritans Internat. (life mem.). Republican. Episcopalian. Home: 12762 Via Donada Del Mar CA 92014 Office: U Calif San Diego Sch Medicine Dept Community Family Medicine M-037 La Jolla CA 92093

INOUYE, DANIEL KEN, senator; b. Honolulu, Sept. 7, 1924; s. Hyotaro I. and Kame Imanaga; m. Margaret Shinobu Awamura, June 12, 1949; 1 child, Daniel Ken. A.B., U. Hawaii, 1950; J.D., George Washington U., 1952. Jr. asst. pub. prosecutor Honolulu, 1953-54, pvt. practice, 1954—; majority leader Territorial Ho. of Reps., 1954-58, Senate, 1958-59; mem. 86th-87th U.S. Congresses from Hawaii, U.S. Senate from Hawaii, 1963—; sec. Senate Dem. Conf., 1978-88; mem. Dem. Steering Com., Senate Com. on Appropriations; chmn. subcom. def., mem. Commerce Com.; chmn. subcom. on communications Select Com. on Intelligence, 1976-77, ranking mem. subcom. budget authorizations, 1979-84; chmn. Select Com. Indian Affairs; mem. Select Com. on Presdl. Campaign Activities, 1973-74; chmn. Sen. select com. Secret Mil. Assistance to Iran and Nicaraguan Opposition, 1987; bd. dir. Cen. Pacific Bank. Author: Journey to Washington. Active YMCA, Boy Scouts Am. Keynoter; temporary chmn. Dem. Nat. Conv., 1968, rules com. chmn., 1980, co-chmn. conv., 1984. Pvt. to capt. AUS, 1943-47. Decorated D.S.C., Bronze Star, Purple Heart with cluster; named 1 of 10 Outstanding Young Men of Yr. U.S. Jr. C. of C., 1960; recipient Splendid Am. award Thomas A. Dooley Found., 1967 Golden Plate award Am. Acad. Achievement, 1968. Mem. DAV (past comdr. Hawaii), Honolulu C. of C., Am. Legion (Nat. Comdr.'s award 1973). Methodist. Clubs: Lion. (Hawaii), 442d Veterans (Hawaii). Home: 469 Ena Rd Honolulu HI 96814 Office: US Senate 722 Hart Senate Bldg Washington DC 20510

INOUYE, HARRY MAMORU, government official, computer consultant; b. Kau, Hawaii, Apr. 5, 1940; s. Tooru and Misao (Kakizoe) I.; m. Marilyn Miyako Sakai, Nov. 27, 1970; children: Joy, Ryan. BS, U. San Francisco, 1979. Instr. credential, Calif. Computer programmer U.S. Forest Service, San Francisco, 1971-74, system analyst, 1974-78, data base mgr., 1978-83, system mgr., 1983-87; chief Hudnet br. HUD, San Francisco, 1987--; cons. HMI PROTEC, Concord, Calif., 1978--; instr. Diablo Valley Coll., Pleasant Hill, Calif., 1982-87. Chmn. Japanese Am. Club, Concord, 1988. Served with USAF, 1963-67, Vietnam. Club: Dai-Ichi Golf (Walnut Creek, Calif.) (pres. 1983). Home: 792 Terrapin Ct Concord CA 94518 Office: HUD MID 450 Golden Gate Ave San Francisco CA 94102

INTRIERE, ANTHONY DONALD, physician; b. Greenwich, Conn., May 9, 1920; s. Rocco and Angelina (Belcastro) I.; MD, U. Mich., 1944; m. Carol A. Yarmey, Aug. 1, 1945; children: Sherry Lynn, Michael, Nancy, Lisa. Intern, New Rochelle (N.Y.) Hosp., 1944-45; pvt. practice, Greenwich, Conn., 1947-53, Olney, Ill., 1956-61, Granite City, Ill., 1961-74, San Diego, 1975—; fellow in internal medicine Cleve. Clinic, 1953-55; fellow in gastroenterology Lahey Clinic, Boston, 1955-56. Capt. M.C., AUS, 1945-47.

Fellow Am. Coll. Gastroenterology (assoc.); mem. ACP (assoc.), Am. Soc. Internal Medicine. Home: 9981 Caminto Chirimolla San Diego CA 92131

INVERSO, MARLENE JOY, optometrist; b. Los Angeles, May 10, 1942; d. Elmer Encel Wood and Sally Marie (Sample) Hirons; m. John S. Inverso, Dec. 16, 1962; 1 child, Christopher Edward. BA, Calif. State U., Northridge, 1964; MS, SUNY, Potsdam, 1975; OD, Pacific U., 1981. Cert. doctor optometry, Wash., Oreg. English tchr. Chatsworth (Calif.) High Sch., 1964-68, Nelson A. Boylen Second Sch., Toronto, Ont., Can., 1968-70, Gouverneur (N.Y.) Jr.-Sr. High Sch., 1970-74, 76-77; reading resource room tchr. Parishville (N.Y.) Hopkinton Sch., 1974-75; coordinator learning disability clinic SUNY, Potsdam, 1975-77; optometrist and vision therapist Am. Family Vision Clinics, Olympia, Wash., 1982—; mem. adv. com. Sunshine House St. Peter Hosp., Olympia, 1984-86, Pacific U. Coll. Optometry, Forest Grove, Oreg. 1986. Contbr. articles to profl. jours. Mem. Altrusa Service Club, Olympia, 1982-86; tchr. Ch. Living Water, Olympia, 1983-88; mem. bd. advisors Crisis Pregnancy Ctr., Olympia, 1987—; den mother Cub Scouts Am. Pack 202, Lacey, Wash., 1987-88; vol. World Vision Countertop ptnr., 1986—. Mem. Am. Optometric Assn. (sec. 1983-84), Assn. Children and Adults with Learning Disabilities, Optometric Extension Program, Sigma Xi, Beta Sigma Kappa. Home: 4204 Timberline Dr SE Lacey WA 98503 also: 1700 C-1 Cooper Point Rd Olympia WA 98502

INZANO, KAREN LEE, advertising agency executive; b. Cleve., July 27, 1946; d. William and Edith (Fisher) Phipps; children: Thomas, Laura, Sharon. Pres., founder AK Graphics Inc., Lakewood, Colo., 1973—; instr. advt. and small bus. Red Rocks Community Coll., Golden, Colo., 1983—, mem. mktg. adv. bd., 1986—. Chmn. Ch. Adminstrv. Bd.; active caucus Colo. Rep. Com., 1980, Green Mountain Homeowners, Lakewood, 1980-84; sr. v.p. Lakewood on Parade, 1985-86; bd. dirs. Lakewood Sister Cities Internat., 1980—, Lakewood Civic Found., 1986—. Named State Champion of Free Enterprise Salesman With A Purpose, 1985; recipient Disting. Svc. award Sister Cities Internat., 1984. Mem. Lakewood/South Jefferson County C. of C. (bd. dirs. 1979—, chmn. bd. 1988-89, Small Bus. Person of Yr., 1982), Denver Advt. Fedn., Typographers Internat. Assn., Quadex Users Group, Industries for Jefferson County, Woman Bus. Owners. Home: 778 S Alkire St Lakewood CO 80228 Office: 13185 W Green Mountain Dr Lakewood CO 80228

IONESCU, CONSTANTIN, computer scientist; b. Pitesti, Arges, Romania, June 8, 1953; came to U.S., 1983; s. Petre and Constanta (Dascalu) I. MS in Math., U. Bucharest, Romania, 1976; MS in Computer Sci., West Coast U., L.A., 1985; MS in Mgmt. Info. System, West Coast U., Los Angeles, 1986; PhD in Computer and Info. Sci., Pacific Western U., 1988. Lic. mathematician. Mathematician, programmer Nat. Dept. Chemistry, Bucharest, 1976-80; sr. programmer, analyst Nat. Dept. Metallurgy, Bucharest, 1980-82; sr. software engr. Xerox Corp., El Segundo, Calif., 1983-88; computer and info. scientist Jet Propulsion Lab. NASA, Pasadena, Calif., 1988—. Contbr. articles to profl. jours. Sec. Romanian Nat. Body Bldg. Com., Bucharest, 1980-82; pres., chmn. Bucharest Mcpl. Body Bldg. Com., 1978-82. Served to lt. Romanian Army, 1978. Mem. IEEE, No. Assn. Am., Assn. Computing Machinery. Republican. Home: 34 S Mentor Ave #300 Pasadena CA 91106-2927 Office: NASA Jet Propulsion Lab 4800 Oak Grove Dr Pasadena CA 91109-8099

IRANI, RAY R., chemical company executive; b. Beirut, Lebanon, Jan. 15, 1935; came to U.S., 1953, naturalized, 1956; s. Rida and Naz I.; m. Joan D. French; children: Glenn R., Lillian M., Martin R. BS in Chemistry, Am. U. Beirut, 1953; PhD in Phys. Chemistry, U. So. Calif., 1957. Sr. research group leader Monsanto Co., 1957-67; assoc. dir. new products, then dir. research Diamond Shamrock Corp., 1967-73; with Olin Corp., 1973-83, pres. chems. group, 1978-80; corp. pres., dir. Olin Corp., Stamford, Conn., 1980-83; exec. v.p. Occidental Petroleum Corp., Los Angeles, 1983-84, pres., chief operating officer, 1984—, also dir.; chmn., chief exec. officer Occidental Chem. Corp. subs. Occidental Petroleum Corp., Dallas, 1983—; bd. dirs. Am. Petroleum Inst. Author: Particle Size; also author papers in field; numerous patents in field. Trustee St. John's Hosp. and Health Ctr. Found., Natural History Mus. Los Angeles County. Mem. Soap and Detergent Assn., Chem. Mfrs. Assn. (bd. dirs.), Am. Inst. Chemists (hon. fellow award 1983), Am. Chem. Soc., Scientific Research Soc. Am., Indsl. Research Inst., Los Angeles C. of C. (bd. dirs.). Home: 250 Lost District Dr New Canaan CT 06840 Office: Occidental Petroleum Corp 10889 Wilshire Blvd Los Angeles CA 90024 also: Can Occidental Petroleum Ltd, 500 635 8th Ave S W, Calgary, AB Canada T2P 3Z1 *

IRBY, WILLIAM OWEN, federal career administrator; b. San Antonio, Sept. 14, 1943; s. Grover and Ruby J. (Segroves) Chatman; m. Kay C. Irby, Mar. 29, 1970 (div. Jan. 1984); children: Kelly Anne, Shelly Kay; m. Sandra C. Frasier, Mar. 21, 1986; stepchildren: Sarah, Steven. AS, Barstow Jr. Coll., 1975. Commd. USMC, Barstow, Calif., 1967, pkg. inspector, planner, 1967-71, packaging specialist, 1971-75, supr. inventory mgmt. specialist, 1975-80, quality assurance specialist, 1980-81, pres. gen. foreman, 1981-89, mgr. over packaging and maintenance sect., 1985—. Pres. Barstow Jacess, 1975; dist. gov. Calif. Jaycees, 1976. Mem. Am. Soc. Quality Control, Am. Def. Preparedness Assn. USMC Packaging Com., Fed. Mgrs. Assn. (v.p. 1984, pres. 1985-86). Democrat. Lodge: Elks. Home: 28008 Church St Barstow CA 92311 Office: USMC Logistics Base Packaging and Maintenance Sect B883 Material Div Barstow CA 92311

IRONS, EDGAR TOWAR, electronics executive; b. Detroit, Oct. 11, 1936; s. William T. and Willa (McHenry) I. BS in Engring., Princeton U., 1958; MS in Engring., Calif. Inst. Tech., 1959. Mem. tech. staff Inst. Def. Analyses, Princeton, N.J., 1959-69; prof. Yale U., New Haven, Conn., 1969-80; dir. rsch. Interactive Systems, Santa Monica, Calif., 1980-84; pres. Slater Towar Ltd., Estes Park, Colo., 1984—. Contbr. articles to profl. jours. Mem. Assn. for Computing Machinery. Home: Longs Peak Rte Estes Park CO 80517 Office: Slater Towar Ltd 586 Longs Peak Rd Estes Park CO 80517

IRONS, RICHARD R., medical director; b. Providence, R.I., Sept. 25, 1948. BS magna cum laude, Kenyon Coll., 1970; MD, Dartmouth Coll., 1973. Diplomate Am. Bd. Internal Medicine. Intern in internal medicine Va. Mason Hosp., Seattle, 1973-74, resident in internal medicine, 1974-75, 76-77; attending physician St. John's Luth. Hosp., Libby, Mont., 1977-85; pvt. practice Kootenai Clinic, Libby, 1977-85; physician Mental Health Svc., Inc., 1986-88; staff physician dept. of psychiatry St. Peter's Community Hosp., Helena, Mont., 1985-88; physician dir. Mont. Physician Assistance Program, 1986-89; med. dir. Wash. Monitored Treatment Program, Seattle, 1988—; vol. coord., cons. Bd. Med. Examiners, 1985-87; wellness cons. Broadwater Athletic Club, 1985-88; cons. Mont.-Wyo. Found. Med. Care, 1985-88; physician cons. Park County Mental Health Ctr., Livingston, Mont., 1987-88; med. dir. Support Ctr.St. Peter's Community Hosp., Helena; cons. Blue Cross and Blue Shield, Mont. 1988—; speaker in field. Mem. Am. Coll. of Physicians, Mont. Med. Assn. (emergency med. svcs. com. 1980-83, health and well-being of physicians com. 1985-88), Am. Med. Soc. of Alcoholism and Other Drug Dependencies (state chairperson 1986-88, nat. credentials com. 1989—), Am. Pub. Health Assn. Internat. Div. Home: 1866 Commodore Ln Bainbridge WA 98110 Office: 901 Boren Ave Ste 1660 Seattle WA 98104

IRSFELD, LYNN IRENE, infosystems specialist, software support engineer; b. Klamath Falls, Oreg., Dec. 13, 1960; d. Paul Lambert Jr. and Gloria Rose (Lloyd) I. BS in Computer Sci., Wash. State U., 1984; MBA, City U., 1989. Coop. assoc. programmer Chevron, San Francisco, 1982-83; response ctr. support engr. Hewlett-Packard Co., Santa Clara, Calif., 1984-88; tng. specialist Microsoft Corp., Redmond, Wash., 1988—. Big sister Big Bros./Big Sisters Santa Clara, 1984-88; mem. Bellevue (Wash.) Art Mus., 1989—. Kappa Alpha Theta scholar, 1981. Mem. NAFE, Am. Soc. Tng. and Devel. Roman Catholic. Home: 11400 NE 132d St #K 204 Kirkland WA 98034 Office: Microsoft Corp 16011 NE 36th Way Box 97017 Redmond WA 98073

IRVIN, BEN FRANK, educational consultant; b. Tulsa, Sept. 28, 1945; s. Ben Frank and Betty Jean (Wise) I.; children: Marvit Door, Stellar Bull Tail, Guy Bull Tail. BA in History, Okla. Panhandle State U., 1967; MA in History, Ft. Hays State U., 1968; postgrad., U. Mont., 1989—. Cert. elem. and secondary prin., K-12 supt., psychology, history, polit. sci. and elem. tchr., Mont., Wyo. Tchr., coach pub. sch., Crow Agency, Mont., 1968-71; supervising tchr. pub. sch., Pryor, Mont., 1971-73; tchr., adminstrv. asst. pub. sch., Seeley Lake, Mont., 1973-83; prin. pub. sch., Pryor, 1983-85; supt. pub. sch., Wyola, Mont., 1985, Ashland, Mont., 1985-86; athletic dir., prin. pub. sch., Arapaho, Wyo., 1986-88; ednl. cons. Missoula, Mont., 1988—. Author: The Cheyenne of Montana, 1975, The Cree of Montana, 1975, Absaraka: The crow Tribe, 1976, The Sioux of Montana, 1976. Spokesman Wyo. Multi-Cultural Conf., Riverton, 1987. Recipient Outstanding Coaching award Seeley Lake Sch. Student Body, 1976; Mont. Office Pub. Instrn. grantee, 1974, 80, 83. Mem. Mont. Fedn. Tchrs. (v.p. Seeley Lake 1979-83), Sch. Adminstrs. Mont. Assn., Elem. Prins. Mont. Assn., Wyo. Sch. Adminstrs. Assn., Wyo. Prins. Assn., Wyo. Indian Edn. Assn. (founder). Democrat. Unitarian. Home: 228 W Beckwith St Missoula MT 59801 Office: Big Sky Edn Cons Box 2524 Missoula MT 59806

IRVINE, ROBERT GERALD, elec. engr., educator; b. Salt Lake City, July 27, 1931; s. Francis Gerald and Bernice (Henckel) I.; m. Joan Laura Granberg, Aug. 26, 1955; children: Gerald Andrew, John Robert. BSEE, Utah State U., 1956; MSEE, Calif. State U.-Los Angeles, 1975. Elec. engr. Gen. Dynamics, Ponoma, Calif., 1956-61; asst. prof. engring. Calif. State Poly. U., Ponoma, 1959-66, assoc. prof., 1976-82, prof., 1983—; sr. engr. Ling Electronics, Anaheim, Calif., 1966-70; owner, operator Stretch & Sew Fabrics, Claremont, Calif., 1971-72; sr. research and devel. engr. Safetran Systems Corp., 1972-76; mem. faculty Citrus Jr. Coll., U. LaVerne, San Bernardino Valley Coll.; cons. in field. Mem. ch. council Good Shepherd Lutheran Ch., Claremont, Calif., 1979-81; mem. exec. bd. Old Baldy council Boy Scouts Am., 1980—; mem. Los Angeles Olympic Organizing Com. Served with U.S. Army, 1949-50. Registered profl. engr., Calif. Mem. IEEE (sr.; chmn. sect. 1966-67, award of Merit 1967), Am. Soc. Engring. Edn., Precision Measurements Assn., Measurement Sci. Conf., Nat. Soc. Profl. Engrs., Tau Alpha Pi, Eta Kappa Nu. Republican. Lodges: Optimists; Masons (Salt Lake City). Author: Operational Amplifier Characteristics and Applications, 1981; co-author: Microelectric Devices and Circuit Design, 1989. Office: Calif State Poly U Dept Elec & Computer Engring 3801 W Temple Ave Pomona CA 91768

IRVINE, VERNON BRUCE, accounting educator, administrator; b. Regina, Sask., Can., May 31, 1943; s. Joseph Vern and Anna Francis (Phillip) I.; m. Marilyn Ann Craik, Apr. 29, 1967; children—Lee-Ann, Cameron, Sandra. B. Commerce, U. Sask., 1965; M.B.A., U. Chgo., 1967; Ph.D., U. Minn., 1977. Cert. mgmt. acct. Researcher, Sask. Royal Commn. on Taxation, Regina, 1964; lectr. acctg. Coll. Commerce, U. Sask., Saskatoon, 1967-69, asst. prof., 1969-74, assoc. prof., 1974-79, prof., 1979—, head dept. acctg., 1981-84; profl. program lectr. Inst. Chartered Accts., Regina, 1982-84, Soc. Mgmt. Accts., Saskatoon, 1982-84. Co-author: A Practical Approach to the Appraisal of Capital Expenditures, 1981; Intermediate Accounting: Canadian Edition, 1982, 2d edit., 1986; contbr. articles to acctg. jours. Grantee John Wiley & Sons, Ltd., 1981, 85, 87, 88, Soc. Mgmt. Accts. Can., 1979, Pres.'s Fund, U. Sask., 1978; bd. dirs. Big Sisters of Sask., 1987—. Fellow Soc. Mgmt. Accts. Can. (bd. dirs. 1979-82, 85-87, chmn. Nat. Edn. Services com.); mem. Internat. Acctg. Standards Com. (Can. rep. 1984-87), Internat. Fedn. Accts. Council (tech. advisor 1988—), Soc. of Mgmt. Accts. of Sask. (pres. 1980-81). Clubs: Sutherland Curling (treas. 1979-83), Saskatoon Golf and Country (bd. dirs. 1988—). Home: 45 Cantlon Crescent, Saskatoon, SK Canada S7J 2T2 Office: U Sask, Coll Commerce, Saskatoon, SK Canada S7N 0W0

IRWIN, BETTY J., judge; b. Fresno, Calif., Nov. 7, 1922; d. Olen Hanks and Gladys Emeline (Wotten) Carter; m. James Elliott, May 29, 1945; children: Nancy Hanks, James Carter, William Stewart. BA, Coll. of Pacific, 1944; JD, McGeorge Sch. Law, Sacramento, 1974. Dep. dist. atty. Lakeport, Calif., 1975-81; judge Southlake Jud. Dist., Clearlake, Calif., 1982—. Chmn. Lake Co. Central Com.; vice chmn. Contra Costa Rep. Central Com. Mem. Calif. Bar Assn., Calif. Judges Assn., Lake Co. Bar Assn., Kappa Alpha Theta, St. Margarets Club. Republican. Episcopalian. Home: 45501 Otter Point Cir Mendocino CA 95460

IRWIN, DAVID EDWARD, business management professional; b. Toronto, Ont., Can., Nov. 8, 1934; s. David Christopher and Mary (Dickson) I.; m. Patricia Margaret Evans, Apr. 18, 1956; children: Rosemarie Kim Billhimer, Kristal Dawn Scott, David A., Brent Richard. BA in Adminstrv. Mgmt., Cal. State U., Fullerton, 1977. Cert. purchasing mgr. Mgr. purchasing Transit Mixed Concrete, Los Angeles, 1979-80; procurement mgr. Tektronix, Inc., Beaverton, Oreg., 1980—; bd. dirs. Material Mgmt. Nat. Assn. Purchasing Mgmt., Tempe, Ariz.; advisor Portland State U. Sch. of Bus.; instr. Portland State U. Sch. Bus. Continuing Edn. Adv. com. Tualitan Valley Econ. Devel. Com., Beaverton, 1987-88. Served to cpl. U.S. Army, 1953-57. Republican. Lodge: Elks. Home: 775 SW Viewmont Dr Portland OR 97225 Office: Tektronix Inc MS39-744 Howard Vollum Park Beaverton OR 97077

IRWIN, DEBORAH JO, teacher, professional flutist; b. Ellensburg, Wash., Aug. 3, 1952; d. Robert Major and Charlotte Ruth (Klein) Panerio; m. Brent Willard Irwin, June 15, 1974; children: Tony, Nick. BA in Music Edn., Cen. Wash. U., 1974, MA in Music, 1978. Tchr. Federal Way (Wash.) Schs., 1974-75, Auburn (Wash.) Schs., 1975—; prin. flutist Tacoma Concert Band, 1982—, Renton (Wash.) Pks. Band, 1978-82; tchr. The Flute Studio, Federal Way, 1983-84; mem., historian Fireside Concert Series, Auburn, 1983-84. Mem. mus. groups Windsong, Scirrocco. Mem. NEA, Seattle Musicians Union, Seattle Flute Soc. Home: 28012 188th Ave SE Kent WA 98042

IRWIN, PHYLLIS ANN, music educator, writer; b. Manhattan, Kans., Mar. 24, 1929; d. Fred Alexander and Thelma Phyllis (Williams) I. Student, San Diego State Coll., 1945-46, Vienna State Acad., Austria, 1947-48, Hofstra Coll., 1948-49; BS, U. Houston, 1951, MEd, 1957; postgrad., Mozarteum, Salzburg, Austria, 1960; EdD, Columbia U., N.Y.C., 1963. Instr. internat. music Houston Ind. Sch. Dist., 1951-54, choral tchr., 1954-61; prof. music Calif. State U., Fresno, 1963—, asst. v.p. acad. affairs, 1971-75, asst. dean grad. sch., 1975-76, chmn. dept. music, 1981—; cons. Houston Ind. Sch., Fresno County Schs., Mariposa (Calif.) County Schs., Tulare (Calif.) County Schs. Author: Music Fundamentals: A Performance Approach, 1981, Playing the Piano, 1988; co-author: The Teacher, The Child and Music, 1986. Mem. Calif. Music Educators Assn., Music Educators Nat. Conf., Am. Choral Dirs. Assn. Office: Calif State U Dept Music Fresno CA 93740

IRWIN, R. ROBERT, lawyer; b. Denver, July 27, 1933; s. Royal Robert and Mildred Mary (Wilson) I.; m. Sue Ann Scott, Dec. 16, 1956; children—Lori, Stacy, Kristi, Amy. Student U. Colo., 1951-54, B.S.L., U. Denver, 1955, LL.B., 1957. Bar: Colo. 1957, Wyo. 1967. Asst. atty. gen. State of Colo., 1958-66; asst. div. atty. Mobil Oil Corp., Casper, Wyo. 1966-70; prin. atty. No. Natural Gas Co., Omaha 1970-72; sr. atty. Coastal Oil & Gas Corp., Denver 1972-83, asst. sec. 1972-83; ptnr. Baker & Hostetler, 1983-87; pvt. practice 1987—. Mem. ABA, Colo. Bar Assn., State Bar Wyo., Arapahoe County Bar Assn., Rocky Mountain Oil and Gas Assn. Republican. Clubs: Los Verdes Golf, Petroleum, Denver Law (Denver). Office: 9960 E Chenango Ave Englewood CO 80111

ISAAC, ROBERT MICHAEL, lawyer, mayor; b. Colorado Springs, Colo., Jan. 27, 1928; s. Isaac Albert and Sigrid Elvira (Oksa) I.; children from previous marriage: Leslie Ann Isaac Williams, Julia Hermine Isaac Harrington, Melissa Sue, Tiffany Ann, Chance Robert. Student, U. Colo., 1945-46; BS, U.S. Mil. Acad., 1951; JD, U. So. Calif., 1962. Sales engr. Trane Co., Los Angeles, 1957-62; practice law and dep. city atty. City Colorado Springs, 1962-64; asst. dist. atty. 4th Jud. Dist. Colo., Colorado Springs, 1965-66; judge Colorado Springs Mcpl. Ct., 1966-69; ptnr. Trott, Kunstle, Isaac & Hughes, Colorado Springs, 1969-72, Isaac, Walsh & Johnson, Colorado Springs, 1972-74, Isaac, Johnson & Alpern, 1974-88; councilman City of Colorado Springs, 1975-79, mayor, 1979—; chmn. adv. bd. U.S. Conf. Mayors; trustee Harry S. Truman Found.; mem. adv. bd. Nat. League of Cities; mem. adv. commn. Intergovtl. Relations. Gen. chmn. YWCA/YMCA/USO fund dr., past pres. Pikes Peak Y/USO; past pres. El Paso County Soc. Crippled Children and Adults; past mem. Nat. USO Council; chmn. Pikes Peak Area Council Govts., 1976-78. Served as officer inf. U.S. Army, 1951-57. Mem. Am. Bar Assn., Colo. Bar Assn. Calif. Bar Assn., El Paso County Bar Assn. Episcopalian. Office: PO Box 1575 Colorado Springs CO 80901

ISAACS, ABRAHAM DAVID, real estate executive, consulting engineer; b. N.Y.C., June 2, 1925; s. Isidore and Anna (Nochlin) I.; m. Arlise Goldberg, Jan. 7, 1950; children: Ellen, Dean. BA, NYU, 1949; postgrad., Columbia U., 1955-57, U. So. Calif., 1965. Registered profl. engr., Calif. Motion picture distbr. Paramount Pictures, N.Y.C., 1950-55; mgr. customer service Sensitive Research Corp., New Rochelle, N.Y., 1955-60; mgr. phys. and elec. standards Hughes Aircraft, Fullerton, Calif., 1960-64; pres. A.D. Isaacs Assoc., Laguna Niguel, Calif., 1965-78, The Isaacs Group, Laguna Niguel, 1978—. Author: (Nat. Bur. Standards publ.) Recommended Practices for Standards Labs, 1965, Built-in-test Design Guide, 1977. 1st lt. U.S. Army AC, 1943-46. Office: 30011 Ivy Glen Dr Ste 210 Laguna Niguel CA 92677

ISAACS, JAMES LAWRENCE, financial analyst; b. Chgo., Mar. 25, 1960; s. Kenneth Sidney and Ruth Elizabeth (Johnson) I.; m. Page Mailliard, Aug. 16, 1986. BA with honors, Stanford U., 1982; MBA, U. Calif., Berkeley, 1988. V.p. Kenisa Co., Northbrook, Ill., 1982-86; fin. analyst Apple Computer, Inc., Cupertino, Calif., 1988—. Tutor Vols. for Literacy, Chgo., 1986; mem. Internat. Devel. Exchange, San Francisco, 1988. Republican.

ISAACS, ROBERT WOLFE, structural engineer; b. Clayton, N.Mex., Sept. 22, 1931; s. Robert Phillip and Eva Estella (Freeman) I.; student So. Meth. U., 1949-50, Amarillo Jr. Coll., Tex. Tech U.; BS in Civil Engring., UCLA, 1959; m. Ruth Marie Peffley, Jan. 12, 1951; children: Robert Philip, Jeannette Lucille Isaacs Darlington, Charlotte Ruth Isaacs Frye, Rebecca Grace Isaacs Brund. Structural engr. N.Am. Aviation, Rockwell Internat., L.A., 1959—. Asst. scoutmaster, com. mem., fund raiser, Order of Arrow Gt. Western council Boy Scouts Am., 1964—; patron L.A.County Mus. Art; active Rep. Party. With U.S. Army, 1955. Lic. profl. engr., Tex. Recipient Pride award N.Am Aviation Orgn., 1984; named Pacemaker of Scouting, 1966. Mem. ASCE, NRA (life), Calif. Rifle and Pistol Assn. (life), Nat. Muzzleloading Rifle Assn. (endowment life, So. Calif. rep. 1976—), Western States Muzzleloading Rifle Assn. (life, charter, sportsman award 1983), Calif. Muzzleloading Rifle Assn., Colo. State Muzzleloading Rifle Assn., Bakersfield (Calif.) Muzzleloaders, Nat. Assn. Primitive Riflemen, High Desert Muzzleloaders., Santa Fe Trail Rendezvous Assn. (Bourgeous 1988), Piute Mountain Men, Sante Fe Trail Gun, Rockwell Rod and Gun, Burbank Muzzle Loader, Masons. Condr. rsch. design and devel. press diffusion bonding of titanium, aircraft design and structure; underwing and overwing inflatable seals (structure liaison B-1B, final mate, asst. checkout B-1B). Home: 1028 H-1 Lancaster CA 93534 Office: AF Plant 42 Site 9 Palmdale CA 93550 also: NAm Aircraft Ops Palmdale Facility 2825 E Ave P Palmdale CA 93550

ISAACSON, ROBERT LOUIS, investment company executive; b. Chgo., Apr. 21, 1944; s. Abe B. and Laverne (Skolka) I. BS, Mich. State U., 1966. Mktg. mgr. Florasynth, Inc., San Francisco, 1966-69; br. mgr. Florasynth, Inc., Lincolnwood and Palo Alto, Calif., 1969-72; br. office mgr. Geldermann, Palo Alto, 1972-76; founder, pres. Commodity Investment Cons., Los Altos, Calif., 1976—, Future Funding Cons., Menlo Park, Calif., 1976—; co-founder, co-chmn. Nat. Assn. Futures Trading Advisors; bd. dirs. Futures Industry Assn. Edn. and Tng.; bd. dirs., exec. com. Nat. Futures Assn.; mem. N.F.A. Regional Bus. Conduct Com.; treas. Williams & Clarissa, Inc. Contbr. articles to mags and profl. jours. Founder Fun for Lunch Bunch. With U.S. Mil., 1966-72. Mem. San Francisco Futures Soc., Peninsula Commodities Club, Elks, Kiwanis. Home: 380 La Questa Way Woodside CA 94062 Office: Future Funding Cons 3210 A Alpine Rd Menlo Park CA 94025

ISBELL, HAROLD M(AX), writer, investor; b. Maquoketa, Iowa, Sept. 20, 1936; s. H. Max and Marcella E. I.; BA cum laude (scholar), Loras Coll., 1959; MA (fellow), U. Notre Dame, 1962; grad. U. Mich. Grad. Sch. Bank Mgmt., 1982; m. Mary Carolyn Cosgriff, June 15, 1963; children—Walter Harold, Susan Elizabeth, David Harold, Alice Kathleen. Instr., U. Notre Dame, South Bend, Ind., 1963-64; assoc. prof. St. Mary's Coll., 1969-72; asst. prof. San Francisco Coll. for Women, 1964-69; with Continental Bank & Trust Co., Salt Lake City, 1972-83, v.p., 1977-83, comml. credit officer, 1978-83, also dir. Trustee Judge Meml. Cath. High Sch., Salt Lake City, 1977-84; mem. Utah Coun. for Handicapped and Developmentally Disabled Persons, 1980-81; bd. dirs. Ballet West, 1983—; founder Cath. Found. Utah, pres. 1984-86, trustee, 1984—. Mem. MLA, Mediaeval Acad. Am., Am. Assn. for the Advancement of Sci. Democrat. Roman Catholic. Club: Alta. Editor and translator: The Last Poets of Imperial Rome, 1971; contbr. to publs. in field of classical Latin lit. and contemporary Am. Lit.

ISELIN, BARRY MARTIN, audio-visual specialist; b. Troy, N.Y., Sept. 1, 1947; s. Ralph Norris and Gertrude (Dinowitz) I.; 1 child, Amy Michelle. BA in Speech and Psychology, U. Vt., 1969; MS in TV-Film Prodn., Syracuse U., 1970. Med. cinematographer Upstate Med. Ctr. div. SUNY, Syracuse, 1970-71, Ariz. U. Hosp., Tucson, 1971-76; ind. filmmaker Daehsy Film Prodns., Phoenix, 1976-78; sales and prodn. rep. I.T.S./Concor, Tempe, Ariz., 1978-79; adminstr. audio-visual services Greyhound Corp., Phoenix, 1979-83; mgr. audio-visual prodn. services MeraBank, Phoenix, 1983-87, asst. v.p., 1987—; bd. dirs Glendale (Ariz.) Community Coll., 1983—, Indsl. TV Program, mgr. corp. events, 1987—. Cinematographer, editor: (films) Trochanteric Bolt, 1975 (2d place Indy award), Total Wrist Arthroplasty, 1976 (1st place Indy award). Mem. curriculum com. Mesa (Ariz.) Schs. Vocat. Program, 1983—. Recipient Phoenix award PRSA, 1986, 87, Merit award Internat. Assn. Bus. Communicators, 1986, Cert. of Merit Multi-Media Associated Visual Communicators, 1986, Best Internal Communication award Valley of the Sun United Way, 1988. Mem. Assn. for Multi-Image, Internat. TV Assn. Office: MeraBank 3003 N Central Phoenix AZ 85012

ISELY, HENRY PHILIP, association executive, integrative engineer; b. Montezuma, Kans., Oct. 16, 1915; s. James Walter and Jessie M. (Owen) I.; m. Margaret Ann Sheesley, June 12, 1948; children—Zephyr, LaRock, Lark, Robin, Kemper, Heather Capri. Student S. Oreg. Jr. Coll., Ashland, 1934-35, Antioch Coll., 1935-37. Organizer, Action for World Fedn., 1946-50, N.Am. Coun. for People's World Conv., 1954-58; organizer World Com. for World Constl. Conv., 1958, sec. gen., 1959-66; sec. gen. World Constn. and Parliament Assn., Lakewood, Colo., 1966—, organizer worldwide prep. confs., 1963, 66, 67, 1st session People's World Parliament and World Constl. Conv. in Switzerland, 1968, editor assn. bull. Across Frontiers, 1959—; co-organizer Emergency Coun. World Trustees, 1971, World Constituent Assembly at Innsbruck, Austria, 1977, Colombo, Sri Lanka, 1978-79, Provisional World Parliament 1st session, Brighton, Eng., 1982, 2d Session New Delhi, India, 1985, 3d Session Miami Beach, Fla., 1987, mem. parliament, 1982—; sec. Working Commn. to Draft World Constn., 1971-77; pres. World Svc. Trust, 1972-78; ptnr. Builders Found., Vitamin Cottages, 1955—; pres. Earth Rescue Corps, 1984—; sec.-treas. Grad. Sch. World Problems, 1984—; cabinet mem. Provisional World Govt., 1987—; pres. World Govt. Funding Corp., 1986—; sec. preparatory com. 1990 World Constituent Assembly, 1988—; sec., preparatory com. for the 1990 World Constituent Assembly; organizer Differential Greenhouse Action Network, 1989. Author: The People Must Write the Peace, 1950; A Call to All Peoples and All National Governments of the Earth, 1961; Outline for the Debate and Drafting of a World Constitution, 1967; Strategy for Reclaiming Earth for Humanity, 1969; Call to a World Constituent Assembly, 1974; Proposal for Immediate Action by an Emergency Council of World Trustees, 1971; Call to Provisional World Parliament, 1981; People Who Want Peace Must Take Charge of World Affairs, 1982; Plan for Emergency Earth Rescue Administration, 1985; Plan for Earth Finance Credit Corporation, 1987; Climate Crisis, 1989; handbook for provisional world govt. and provisional world parliament, 1988; co-author, editor: A Constitution for the Federation of Earth, 1974, rev. edit., 1977; also author several world legis. measures adopted at Provisional World Parliament; co-author Plan for Collaboration in World Constituent Assembly in 1990; Climat Crisis, 1989. Designer prefab modular panel system of constrn., master plan for Guacamaya project in Costa Rica. Candidate, U.S. Congress, 1958. Recipient Honor award Internat. Assn. Educators for World Peace, 1975, Gandhi medal, 1977. Mem. Soc. Internat. Devel., World Union, World Federalist Assn., World Future Soc., Earth Island Inst., Internat. Assn. for Hydrogen Energy, Global Edn. Assocs., Friends of Earth, Wilderness Soc., Denver Symphony Soc., Planetary Soc., Sierra Club, SANE, Global Futures Network, Amnesty Internat., ACLU, Am. Acad. Polit. and Social Sci., Nat. Nutritional Foods Assn., Environ. Def. Fund, Greenpeace, Internat. Studies Assn., War Resistors League, Audubon Soc., Worldwatch Inst., Nation Assocs., Debt Crisis Network, Mt. Vernon Country Club. Home: 241 Zephyr Ave Lookout Mountain Golden CO 80401 Office: 1480 Hoyt St Ste 31 Lakewood CO 80215

ISENBERG, DAVID YOUNGMAN, dentist, educator; b. Seattle, Aug. 19, 1961; s. Jack Isenberg and Janet (Youngman) Hansen; m. Lorna Beckwith, Aug. 2, 1986. BA, U. Wash., 1983, DDS, 1987. Lic. dentist, Wash. Practice dentistry Renton, Wash., 1987—; assoc. dentist Dr. Howard Johnson DDS, Everett, Wash., 1987—; clin. instr. dept. oral medicine U. Wash. Dental Sch., Seattle, 1987—. Mem. ADA, Acad. Gen. Dentistry, Alpha Omega. Jewish. Office: Park Dental Assocs 150 Park Ave N Renton WA 98055

ISENGARD, CHRIS S., rehabilitation agency executive, educator; b. Denver, Mar. 14, 1948; s. William S. and Jan (Simpson) I.; m. Leslie Hunter, June 6, 1970 (div. Oct. 1985). BA, U. N. Mex., 1970; M of Mgmt., 1981. Media specialist Carlsbad (N. Mex.) Schs., 1970-73; program mgr. Teleprompter, Liberal, Kans., 1973-74; bus. communications rep. Motorola Co., Wichita, Kans., 1974-76; counsel N. Mex. Coun. of Blind, Albuquerque, 1976-77; exec. dir. Career Svcs., Albuquerque, 1977—; cons. West Oaks Hosp., Houston, 1984, Kans. Elks Tng. Ctr., Wichita, 1985, New Medico, Benton, Ark., 1986-87; instr. U. N. Mex., Albuquerque, 1985—. Mem. task force legis. Edn. Study Com., Santa Fe, 1987; mem. adv. coms. North Tex. State U., City of Albuquerque, N. Mex. Dept. Edn., Albuquerque Tech. Vocat. Recipient award of excellence Nat. Assn. Counties, 1987. Mem. Nat. Rehab. Assn. (mem. commn. on govt. affairs 1985-86, sec.-treas. 1986-87), N. Mex. Rehab. Assn. (pres. 1984, bd. dirs. 1985-86, Employer of Yr. award 1986), Coun. for Exceptional Children, United Way Agy. Dirs. (pres. Albuquerque 1986—), Albuquerque Press Club (chmn. fin. com. 1986), Blue Key, Pi Sigma Alpha. Home: 208 16th St Albuquerque NM 87104 Office: Career Svcs 4401-A Lomas Blvd NE Albuquerque NM 87110

ISERSON, KENNETH VICTOR, emergency medicine educator; b. Washington, Apr. 8, 1949; s. Isadore I. and Edith (Swedlow) I.; m. Mary Lou Sherk, June 16, 1973. BS, U. Md., 1971, MD, 1975; MBA, U. Phoenix, 1987. Diplomate Am. Bd. Emergency Medicine, Nat. Bd. Med. Examiners. Intern surgery Mayo Clinic, Rochester, Minn., 1975; resident emergency medicine Cin. Gen. Hosp., 1976-78; chmn. emergency dept. Tex. A&M Coll. Medicine, Temple, 1980-81; asst. prof. surgery U. Ariz. Coll. Medicine, Tucson, Ariz., 1981-84; residency dir. emergency medicine U. Ariz. Coll. Medicine, Tucson, 1981—, assoc. prof. surgery, 1984—; pres. Iserson Assocs. Ltd., Tucson, 1984—. Author: Getting Into a Residency: A Guide for Medical Students, 1988; sr. editor: Ethics in Emergency Medicine, 1986; mem. editorial bd. Jour. Emergency Medicine, 1985—; contbr. sci. articles to profl. jours. Med. dir. So. Ariz. Rescue Assn., Pima County, 1983—; organizing dir. Ariz. Bioethics Network, 1988—; mem. Regional EMS Council, S.E. Ariz., 1987—. Capt. USAF, 1978-80. Fellow Am. Coll. Emergency Physicians (chmn. practice mgmt. com. 1987—); mem. AMA, Soc. Tchrs. Emergency Medicine (pres. 1984-85), Wilderness Med. Soc. (bd. dirs. 1987—). Office: U Ariz Coll Medicine 1501 N Campbell Ave Tucson AZ 87524

ISHAM, DELL, independent lobbyist; b. San Rafael, Calif., Apr. 30, 1944; s. Quentin D. and Leah (Sabo) I.; m. Paulette Oblock, Dec. 17, 1966; children: Shane Gordon, Shaun Lane, Shannon Leah. Student Boise State Coll., 1962-64; BS, Weber State Coll., 1967; MA, Colo. State U., 1969. Tchr., Siuslaw High Sch., Florence, Oreg., 1971-76; ins. agt., Isham & Sprague Ins., Lincoln City, Oreg., 1977-85; mem. Oreg. State Senate, 1977-85, majority leader, 1980-83. Mem. West Lane County Planning Commn., 1977-78; mem. Oreg. State Democratic Central Com., 1974, 76-83; del. Dem. Nat. Conv., 1980; mem. Gov.'s Small Bus. Adv. Com., 1985-87; pres. Oreg. Hwy. Users Conf.; Oreg. Tourism Alliance; mayor of Lincoln City, 1987-88. Served with U.S. Army, 1969-71. Decorated Bronze Star. Mem. C. of C., North Am. Lake Mgmt. Soc. Club: Capitol. Lodges: Rotary, Elks. Author: Rock Springs Massacre, 1885, 1969. Office: PO Box 974 Lincoln City OR 97367

ISHIMARU, AKIRA, electrical engineering educator; b. Fukuoka, Japan, Mar. 16, 1928; came to U.S., 1952; s. Shigezo and Yumi I.; m. Yuko Kaneda, Nov. 21, 1956; children: John, Jane, James, Joyce. BSEE, U. Tokyo, 1951; PhDEE, U. Wash., 1958. Registered profl. engr., Wash. Engr. Electro-Tech. Lab, Tokyo, 1951-52; tech. staff Bell Telephone Lab, Holmdel, N.J., 1956; asst. prof. U. Wash., Seattle, 1958-61, assoc. prof., 1961-65, prof. elec. engring., 1965—; vis. assoc. prof. U. Calif., Berkeley, 1963-64; cons. Jet Propulsion Lab., Pasadena, Calif., 1964—, The Boeing Co., Seattle, 1984—. Author: Wave Propagation & Scattering in Random Media, 1978; editor: Radio Science, 1982. Fellow IEEE (mem. editorial bd., Region VI Achieveemnt award 1968, Centennial Medal 1984), Optical Soc. Am. (assoc. editor jour. 1983); mem. Internat. Union Radio Sci. (commn. B chmn.). Home: 2913 165th Pl NE Bellevue WA 98008 Office: U Wash Dept Elec Engring FT-10 Seattle WA 98195

ISHMAEL, WILLIAM EARL, land use planner, civil engineer; b. Mt. Sterling, Ky., Mar. 11, 1946; s. Charles William and Alice Clay (Trimble) I. BSCE, Duke U., 1968; MA in Urban Planning, U. Mich., 1975. Registered civil engr., Calif., Ky.; registered planner Am. Inst. Cert. Planners. Petroleum engr. Humble Oil (now Exxon), New Orleans, 1968-69; dep. dir. Richmond Regional Planning Commn., Richmond, Va., 1975-78; sr. planner Nolte and Assocs., Sacramento, 1978—, assoc. of the corp., 1984—; cons. to City of Lincoln, So. Pacific RR. Mem. City Planning Commn., Sacramento, 1983—, vice chmn., 1985, chmn. 1986; bd. dirs. Sacramento Heritage, 1983-88, chmn., 1985-86; chmn. Urban Design Task Force for Downtown Sacramento, 1986; mem. task force Govtl. Consolidation, 1986; mem. water sub-com., local govt. reorgn. commn., 1988; active Big Bros., 1978-83. Served to lt. USN, 1969-72. Named Mover and Shaper Heir Apparent, Exec. Pl. Mag., 1986. Mem. Sacramento C. of C. (mem. land use com. 1983—), Am. Planning Assn. (dir. pro tem 1981-83, Disting. Service award 1983), Chi Epsilon. Office: Nolte & Assocs 1730 I St Sacramento CA 95814

ISIDORO, EDITH ANNETTE, horticulturist; b. Albuquerque, Oct. 14, 1957; d. Robert Joseph and Marion Elizabeth (Miller) I. BS in Horticulture, N.Mex. State U., 1981, MS in Horticulture, 1984. Range conservationist Soil Conservation Service, Estancia, Grants, N.Mex., 1980-82; lab. aide N.Mex. State U. Dept. Horticulture, Las Cruces, 1982, 83-84; technician N.Mex. State U. Coop. Extension Service, Las Cruces, 1983-84, county agrl. extension agt., 1985; area extension agt. U. Nev., Reno, Fallon, 1985—; hay tester Nev. Agrl. Services, Fallon, 1988—. Mem. AAUW, Am. Soc. Hort. Sci., Am. Horticulture Soc., Am. Botany Soc., Am. Horticulture Therapy Assn., Alpha Zeta, Pi Alpha Psi. Home: 4675 Sheckler Fallon NV 89406 Office: Churchill County Coop Extension 1450 McLean Rd Fallon NV 89406

ISLAS, ANGEL LUERA, molecular biologist; b. San Jose, Calif., Oct. 14, 1963; parents: Bruno Nunez and Juana (Luera) I. BS, U. Calif., Davis, 1985; postgrad. biol. scis., Stanford U., 1985—. Rsch. fellow NASA Ames Rsch. Ctr., Moffett Field, Calif., 1980-85, Stanford (Calif.) U., 1985—. Patricia Harris fellow, Dept. Edn., Washington, 1987-88; Dorothy Daniel Compton Found. fellow, 1988—. Mem. Am. Soc. Microbiology, AAAS, Commonwealth Club Calif. Republican. Home: 2212 Hicks Ave San Jose CA 95125 Office: Biol Scis Stanford U Stanford CA 94305-5020

ISLEY, ERNEST D., Canadian provincial official; b. Vermilion, Alta., Can., June 29, 1937; m. Sheila; children—Floyd, Lori, Thea, Tracy. B.Edn. with distinction, U. Alta., 1969. Operator farm, Bonnyville, Alta., Can.; agt. ins. co.; prin. Bonnyville Centralized High Sch., 1971-78, Altario Sch., 1961-71; mem. Alta. Legis. Assembly, 1979—, mem. edn. caucus, agr. caucus coms., select com. of legislature on fisheries, select com. of legislature on surface rights, curriculum policies bd., Port Churchill Devel. Bd.; minister of manpower Province of Alta., Edmonton. Pres., Lakeland Tourist Assn., 1975; chmn. Bonnyville Sr. Citizens Project Com., 1976; dir., v.p. Bonnyville Progressive Conservative Assn., 1974-78; mem. Travel Alta. Zone Assistance Rev. Bd., 1976-78, chmn. bd., 1977-78. Minister Pub. Works, Supply and Services, 1986—. Office: Govt Alta, 131 Legislature Bldg, Edmonton, AB Canada T5K 2B6

ISOKANE, SAM SETSUO, real estate company executive, consultant; b. Honolulu, Feb. 11, 1925; s. Matsujiro and Shige (Yano) I.; m. Teruko Gono, Nov. 25, 1968 (div. Jan. 1975); 1 child, Lisa Yukari. BA, U. Hawaii, 1943; cert., Nat. Installment Banking Sch., U. Colo., 1971; postgrad. Japan mgmt. program, Japan-Am. Inst. Mgmt. Sci., 1975-76. Lic. realtor, Hawaii; cert. real estate appraiser (CREA). Commodity specialist commerce and industry br. Okinawa Mil. Gov., 1949-51; field rep. Japan div. Coca-Cola Export Corp., Okinawa and Yokohama, 1951-54; v.p., mgr. Svc. Fin. Ltd., Honolulu, 1968-73; real estate broker Palisades Properties, Inc., Honolulu, 1978-84; owner, CREA, prin. broker Sam S. Isokane, Realtor, Honolulu, 1985—; treas. Hawaiian Leanders Exchange, Ltd., Honolulu, 1960; mgmt. cons. Fukuyama Piano Co., Ltd., Tokyo, 1973-74. Mem. Liliha-Kapalama Neighborhood Bd., Honolulu, 1981-83; trustee Hawaii Vets. Meml. Fund, Honolulu, 1983—; precinct chmn. Honolulu Dem. Com., 1984. With M.I., AUS, 1943-46, PTO. Mem. Nat. Assn. Realtors, Honolulu Bd. Realtors, Hawaii Consumer Fin. Assn. (pres. 1962), Hawaii Econ. Study Club (pres. 1970), MIS Vets Club (1st v.p. 1987-88). Buddhist. Home: 2039 Lee Pl Honolulu HI 96817 Office: 680 Ala Moana Blvd Ste 316 Honolulu HI 96813

ISRAEL, DAVID NEAL, sales executive; b. Phoenix, Sept. 30, 1966; s. Jack Morris and Marilyn (Mayo) I. BS in BA, U. Ariz., 1988. Account rep. NCR Corp., Phoenix, 1989—. Mem. Golden Key, Delta Sigma Pi. Democrat. Jewish. Office: NCR Corp 2401 N Central Ave Phoenix AZ 85004

ISRAEL, RICHARD STANLEY, investment banker; b. Oakland, Calif., Sept. 27, 1931; s. Sybil Noble, July 29, 1962; children: Richard Lee, Lynne, Lawrence. BA, U. Calif., Berkeley, 1953, MA, 1953. Copy editor San Francisco Chronicle, 1953-59; publicist CBS TV Network, L.A., 1959-62; sr. v.p. Rogers & Cowan, Beverly Hills, Calif., 1962-69; v.p. Cantor, Fitzgerald, Beverly Hills, 1969-73; pres. Sponsored Cons. Svcs., L.A., 1973—. Pres. North Beverly Dr. Homeowners Assn., Beverly Hills, 1986-88; v.p. Temple Emanuel, Beverly Hills, 1988—, L.A. chpt. Juvenile Diabetes Found. Internat, 1987—. With U.S. Army, 1956-58. Recipient Alumni citation U. Calif. Alumni Assn., Berkeley, 1984. Mem. L.A. Venture Assn. (pres. 1987). Democrat. Office: Sponsored Cons Svcs 924 Westwood Blvd Ste 400 Los Angeles CA 90024

ISRAEL, VIVIANNE WINTERS, publishing executive; b. Inglewood, Calif., Mar. 29, 1954; d. Robert Reynolds and Annie Laura (Ripley) Winters; m. Richard Clyde Israel, May 30, 1976 (div. 1985); 1 child, Tiffany Carissa. RN, El Camino Coll., Torrance, Calif. Fashion model Los Angeles, 1957-70; critical care nurse Northridge Med. Ctr., Reseda, Calif., 1977-80, St. Joseph Med. Ctr., Burbank, Calif., 1980-81; exotic animal handler, trainer Gentle Jungle, Corona, Calif., 1980-81; coronary care nurse Mercy Med. Ctr., Reading, Calif., 1981-85; critical care nurse Norrell/CCSI, Los Angeles, 1985-87; pres. Pacific Coast Publs., Rolling Hills Estates, Calif., 1986—. Vol., co-dir. edn. Wildlife Way Sta., Little Tajunga, Calif., 1987—. Mem. Pubs. Mktg. Assn., Book Publicists of So. Calif., Book Publicists of San Diego, Execs. of South Bay, NAFE, Womens Internat. Network, Walters Internat. Speakers Bur., Internat. Assn. of Ind. Pubs., Am. Businesswomens Assn., Internat. Platformers Assn. Baptist. Home: 1180 W Locust Ave Anaheim CA 92802 Office: Pacific Coast Pubs 710 Silver Spur Rd Ste 126 Rolling Hills Estates CA 90274

ISRAELSON, NORMAN R., transportation executive; b. Petersburg, Alaska, Mar. 11, 1937; s. Arnold Joseph Israelson and Dorothy Thelma (Noreide) Brady; m. Mary Ellen Doolittle, Oct. 2, 1965 (div. 1981); m. Barbara Diane Farmer, Nov. 15, 1985; children: Michelle Maria Wendell, Stephanie Lynn Wendell. Grad. high sch., Petersburg, Alaska. Vessel operator Bellingham Canning Co., Yakutat, Alaska, 1958-62; sta. agt. Pacific No. Airlines, Yakutat, 1963-65; sr. sta. agt. Pacific No. Airlines, Kenai, Alaska, 1965-68; asst. mgr. passenger service Western Airlines, Anchorage, 1968-70; mgr. customer service Western Airlines, Juneau, Alaska, 1970-73; mgr. customer service Western Airlines, Anchorage, 1973-76, mgr. service, 1976-81, regional dir., 1981-84; pres. AVtech Alaska, Anchorage, 1984—. Mem. Anchorage/Fairbanks Airport Affairs, 1985-88, mem. industry adv. com. Dept. Trans., Anchorage, 1986-88, Rural Airports Alaska Aviation System Plan, Anchorage, 1986-88. Served to sgt. U.S. Army, 1960-62. Awarded for noteworthy contributions Gov. of Alaska, 1980, 82. Republican. Office: AVTech-Alaska PO Box 190048 Anchorage AK 99519

ISRAELY, ILAN, computer company executive; b. Haifa, Israel, Oct. 1, 1939; came to U.S., 1962; s. Meir and Frida Israely; m. Hilla Kuttenplan (div. 1985); children: Inbal, Eran, Edo. EE, Israel Inst. Tah. Tech. Sch., Haifa, Israel, 1958; MBA, Calif. State U., Dominique Hills, 1974. Sr. engr. Litton Guidance & Control, L.A., 1968, Teledyne, L.A., 1970; engring. mgr. J & H Internat., L.A., 1970-76; pres. Gen Transistor Corp., Inglewood, Calif., 1976-86, Blaser Inds., L.A., 1986-88, GTL Technology, Inglewood, Calif., 1989—. Pantentee: 3 in computer field. Republican. Office: GTC Technology 216 W Florence Ave Inglewood CA 90301

ISSARI, M. ALI, film producer, educator, consultant; b. Esfahan, Iran, Oct. 3, 1921; s. Abbas Bek and Qamar (Soltan) I.; m. Joan Gura Aamodt, 1953; children: Scheherezade, Katayoun, Roxana. B.A., U. Tehran, Iran, 1963; M.A., U. So. Calif., 1968; Ph.D., 1979. Films officer Brit. Embassy, Brit. Council Joint Film Div., Tehran, 1944-50; asst. motion picture officer USIS, 1950-65; cons. to various Iranian Govt. ministries on film and TV devels. 1950-77; liaison officer Am. and Iranian govt. ofcls., 1950-65; prof. cinema Coll. Communication Arts and Scis. Mich. State U., East Lansing, 1969-81; also dir. instructional film and multimedia prodn. Mich. State U., 1969-78; film, public relations adviser to Iranian Oil Operating Cos. in, Iran, 1963-65; spl. cons. on edn. and instructional TV Saudi Arabian Ministry of Info., 1972; tchr. Persian lang. Iran-Am. Soc., Tehran, 1949-59; introduced audio-visual edn. in Iran, 1951; established first film festivals in Iran. Producer, dir. over 1000 ednl., instructional and documentary films, 1956-78; freelance film reporter: Telenews, UPI, Iran, 1959-61; project dir., exec. producer: Ancient Iran Film Series, 1974-78; dir. film prodn. workshops, Cranbrook Inst., Detroit, 1973-74; Author: (with Doris A. Paul) A Picture of Persia, 1977, What Is Cinema Vérité?, 1979, Cinema in Iran, 1989; contbr. articles on ednl. communication and audio-visual instruction to periodicals and profl. jours. Founder, exec. sec. Youth Orgn. of Iran, 1951-52; v.p. Rugby Football Fedn., Iran, 1952-53, pres., 1954-55. Recipient Cine Golden Eagle award, 1975, Meritorious Honor award USIA, 1965; decorated Order of Magnum Cap Ord: S.F. Danaie M. Sigillum Denmark, 1960, Order of Cavalieres Italy, 1958, Order of Oranje Nassau Queen Juliana of Holland, 1959, Orders of Kooshesh and Pas HIM Shah of Iran, 1951, 57, Order of Esteghlal King Hussein of Jordan, 1960, Order of Ordinis Sancti Silvestri Papae Pope John 23d, 1959. Mem. Anglo-Iranian Dramatic Soc. (dir. 1943-50), Mich. Film Assn. (cofounder 1972, dir. 1972-73), Middle East Studies Assn. N.Am., Soc. Motion Picture and TV Engrs., Assn. Ednl. Communication and Tech., Delta Kappa Alpha (v.p. 1967). Home: 982 Golden Crest Ave Newbury Park CA 91320

ITANO, LESLIE MICHIYA, electrical engineer; b. Sacramento, Mar. 15, 1954; d. Tsuyoshi Dean and Florence (Funabiki) I.; m. W. Jerry Chang, Feb. 22, 1986. BSEE, Stanford U., 1975; MSEE, MIT, 1980, engrs. degree, 1980. Mem. tech. staff Watkins-Johnson, Palo Alto, Calif., 1975-78; research asst. MIT, Cambridge, 1978-80; mem. tech. staff Hewlett-Packard, Palo Alto, 1980-83, R & D supr., 1983-88, process productivity mgr., 1988—. Active Lively Arts, Stanford, Calif., 1981-83. John Stewart Low scholar Stanford U., 1974-75. Mem. IEEE, Internat. Soc. Hybrid Microelectronics, Sigma Xi. Home: 3913 Bibbits Dr Palo Alto CA 94303 Office: Hewlett-Packard 1501 Page Mill Rd Palo Alto CA 94304

ITOH, SEISHICHI, bank executive; b. Amagasaki, Japan, Mar. 17, 1935. Osaka U., Japan, 1957. Asst. v.p. Bank Tokyo Calif., 1972-73, v.p., 1973; with Bank Tokyo Ltd., 1957-72, 76-83, dep. gen. mgr., 1976-83; v.p. Calif. 1st Bank (now Union Bank), San Francisco, 1983—, now pres., chief exec. officer, bd. dirs. Office: Union Bank PO Box 7104 San Francisco CA 94120-1476 *

ITTNER, DWIGHT R., librarian; b. Wichita, Kans., Nov. 14, 1942; s. Ernest L. Sr. and Opal M. (Crowder) I.; m. Barbara J. Eckles, Aug. 26, 1966; children: Dexter Dwight, Douglas Dean. BS, Fort Hays State U., 1965, MS, 1967; MLS, U. Ariz., 1971. Cert. med. librarian. Instr. Biology Sul Ross State Coll., Alpine, Tex., 1967-69; sci. librarian U. Mo., Columbia, 1971-75; bio-med. librarian U. Alaska, Fairbanks, 1975—; Rapporteur, WHO, 1984. Mem. Internat. Assn. Marine Sci. Libraries and Info. Ctrs., Med. Library Assn., Alaska Library Assn., Am. Library Assn., Am. Soc. Circumpolar Health, Internat. Assn. Agricultural Librarians and Documentalists, Nordic Ski Club. Home: 4012 Teal Ave Fairbanks AK 99709 Office: U Alaska Bio-Med Library Fairbanks AK 99775-0300

IULIANO, RONALD ANTHONY, designer; b. Elkhart, Ind., Aug. 24, 1950; s. Joseph Dominic Sr. and Angela Marie (Fiorelli) I.; m. Lisa Jan George, Jan. 1, 1972 (div. Apr. 1973); 1 child, Ryan Anthony; m. Jane Elizabeth Leary, Apr. 23, 1988. AA in Architecture, Miami-Dade Community Coll., 1977; B of Design in Architecture, U. Fla., 1980. Gen. engr. U.S. Army Presidio, San Francisco, 1986-88; project mgr. Haines-Tatarian-Ipsen Architects, San Francisco, 1988—. Inventor synchro-time. With USCG, 1969-79; capt. U.S. Army, 1980-83. Mem. AIA (assoc.), Treasure Island Yacht Club. Home: 472 McGrue Cir Vallejo CA 94589 Office: Haines-Tatarian-Ipsen & Assocs 442 Post St San Francisco CA 94102-1569

IUPPA, NICHOLAS VICTOR, computer executive; b. Rochester, N.Y., May 11, 1942; s. Nicholas Victor Sr. and Irene (Gorecki) I.; m. Virginia Blum, June 27, 1964; children: Lauren, Christin Nicholas-Anthony. AB, U. Notre Dame, Ind., 1964; MA, Stanford (Calif.) U., 1966. Writer animation div. MGM, Hollywood, Calif., 1966-67, Walt Disney Prodns., Burbank, Calif., 1967-69; instructional designer Eastman Kodak, Rochester, 1969-72; mktg. edn. mgr. Bank of Am., San Francisco, 1972-76, asst. v.p., mgr. instructional design dept., 1976-77, v.p., mgr. instructional media svcs. dept., 1977-83; v.p. media dept. ByVideo, Inc., Sunnyvale, Calif., 1983-84; dir. interactive video Hewlett-Packard Co., Palo Alto, Calif., 1984-87; mgr. consumer new tech. Apple Computer, Cupertino, Calif., 1987—; lectr. numerous univs., 1985-88; lectr. vidcom and other profl. confs., 1983-88; design cons. GTE Corp. and other maj. corps., 1983-87. Author: Management by Guilt, 1984, Practical Guide to Interactive Video Design, 1985, Advanced Interactive Video Design, 1988, Corporate Video Producer's Handbook, 1990; author poetry; writer, producer Indsl. Video Prodns., 1969-87, Interactive Video, 1983, People Skills Video, 1982; designer, producer Video Shopping System, 1983; contbr. numerous articles to profl. jours. Mem. Internat. Tape/Disc Assn. (media mgr.'s coun. 1984—), Sierra Club. Republican. Roman Catholic. Office: Apple Computer 10300 Bubb Rd Cupertino CA 95014

IVERSON, CHRIS IAN, sports company executive; b. Seattle, July 17, 1968; s. Robert J. Iverson and Nancy s. (Vincent) Winters. Student, Portland State U. Waiter Piccolo Mondo, Portland, Oreg., 1984-85; mgr. Photo Master, Portland, 1986-88; pres. Premier Jet Ski, Portland, 1988—. Author: Catch The Wave, 1988. Mem. Entrepreneurship Club (Portland State U.). Democrat. Home: 5809 SE Lincoln Portland OR 97215

IVERSON, PETER JAMES, historian, educator; b. Whittier, Calif., Apr. 4, 1944; s. William James and Adelaide Veronica (Schmitt) I.; m. Kaaren Teresa Gonsoulin, Mar. 7, 1983; children: Timothy, Scott, Erika, Jens. BA in History, Carleton Coll., 1967; MA in History, U. Wis., 1969, PhD in History, 1975. Vis. asst. prof. Ariz. State U., Tempe, 1975-76; from asst. prof to prof. U. Wyo., Laramie, 1976-86; coordinator div. social and behavioral scis. Ariz. State U., Phoenix, 1986-88; prof. history Ariz. State U., Tempe, 1988—; Panelist, reviewer Nat. Endowment Humanities, Washington, 1986—. Author: The Navajos: A Critical Bibliography, 1976, The Navajo Nation, 1981, Carlos Montezuma, 1982; editor: The Plains Indians of the 20th Century, 1985; assoc. editor Social Sci. Jour., 1988—; mem. editorial bd. Pacific Hist. Rev., 1986-88, Jour. Ariz. History, 1988—. Chmn. Wyo. Council Humanities, 1981-82; mem. Mus. No. Ariz., Flagstaff, 1984—, Heard Mus., Phoenix, 1986—, Desert Botanical Garden, Phoenix, 1986—. Recipient Chief Manuelito Appreciation award Navajo Nation, 1984; Newberry Libr. fellow, Chgo., 1973-74, Nat. Endowment Humanities fellow, 1982-83, Leadership fellow Kellogg Found., Battle Creek, Mich., 1982-85. Mem. Am. Soc. Ethnohistory (chmn. prize com. 1987), Western Social Sci. Assn. (pres. 1988-89), Orgn. Am. Historians. Office: Ariz State U Dept History Tempe AZ 85287

IVERSON, THOMAS ALLEN, orthodontist; b. San Pedro, Calif., Mar. 30, 1958; s. Richard Beaumont and Barbara Ann (Chase) I.; m. Wendy Ellen Vota, May 18, 1985. BA, U. Calif., San Diego, 1980; DDS, Baylor U., 1985; MS, Northwestern U., Evanston, Ill., 1987. Pvt. practice Yuba City, Calif., 1987-. Mem. ADA, Am. Assn. Orthodontics, Calif. Dental Assn., Pacific Coast Soc. Orthodontics. Republican. Episcopalian. Office: 415 Alturas #6 Yuba City CA 95991

IVES, JOHN MILTON, engineer; b. Bayonne, N.J., Mar. 26, 1943; s. John Milton and Mary J. (Sharkey) I.; m. Dorothy Mae Davis, Nov. 27, 1971; children: RoseMae, Michael John. BS in Engring., Ariz. State U., 1969; MS, U. So. Calif., 1980. Enlisted USAF, 1964, commd. 2nd lt., 1969; advanced through grades to capt. USAFR, 1978, advanced through grade to maj., 1983; electronics engr. weapons lab. USAF, Albuquerque, 1969-73; software engr. Rome (N.Y.) Air Devel. Ctr. USAF, 1973-78; computer systems analyst weapons lab. USAF, Albuquerque, 1978-87, gen. engr. Space Tech. Ctr., 1987—. Contbr. articles to profl. jours. Leader Boy Scouts Am., Rio Rancho, N.Mex., Cibola Little League, Rio Rancho. Mem. IEEE. Roman Catholic. Lodge: KC. Home: 1660 Borealis Ave SE Rio Rancho NM 87124 Office: Air Force Space Tech Ctr SWC Kirtland AFB NM 87117-6008

IVEY, C(LARENCE) GRESHAM, JR., educator; b. Boston, Aug. 11, 1935; s. Clarence Gresham and Kathleen (Merrick) I.; m. Barbara Hampson, Sept. 12, 1959; children: Richard G., B. Suzanne, Peter G. BSE, Princeton U., 1957; MS in Oceanography, Naval Postgrad. Sch., Monterey, Calif., 1969; teaching cert., U. Utah, 1980. Commd. ensign USNR, 1958; ret. 1979; tchr. math. Cyprus High Sch., Granite Sch. Dist., Magna, Utah, 1980—. Home: 6308 Jamestown Circle Salt Lake City UT 84121

IVEY, CLAUDE TARLTON, military officer; b. Hopewell, Va., June 18, 1933; s. Sam and Dixie Lucille (Snead) I.; m. Carol L. Greiner, Aug. 25, 1956; children: Mark, Karl, Dale, Jay. BE, U. Nebr., 1965; MS in Pub. Adminstrn., U. Pa., Shippensburg, 1977. Commd. 2d lt. U.S. Army, 1956, advanceed through grades to maj. gen.; bn. commdr. 1st Bn. 61st Infantry U.S. Army, Ft. Carson, Colo., 1973-74; bn. commdr. 1st Bn. 11th Infantry U.S. Army, Ft. Carson, 1975-77; chief of staff 1st Infantry Div. U.S. Army, Goppingen, Fed. Rep. Germany, 1978; brigade commdr. 8th Infantry Div. U.S. Army, Gonsenheim, Fed. Rep. Germany, 1978-80; asst. div. commdr. ops. 101st Airborne Div. U.S. Army, Ft. Campbell, Ky., 1980-82; dept. chief of staff Hdqtrs. U.S. Army Tng. and Doctrine Commd., Ft. Monroe, Va., 1982-83; chief Office Def. Rep. U.S. Army, Islamabad, Pakistan, 1983-85; dep. corps commdr. XVIII Airborne Corps and Ft. Bragg, N.C., 1985-88; dep. commdg. gen. U.S. Army Western Commd., Ft. Shafter, Hawaii, 1988—. Recipient Sitara-I-Imtiaz Star of Distinction Pakistan Govt., 1985. Mem. Assn. U.S. Army, Army Aviation Assn. Am., Alumni Assn. Army War Coll., Union, Masons. Presbyterian. Home: 8 Palm Circle Dr Honolulu HI 96819 Office: HQ US Army Western Commd Office Dep Commdg Gen Fort Shafter HI 96858-5100

IWAO, WAYNE HARUTO, corporate executive; b. San Francisco, Mar. 30, 1957; s. Eddie Erio and Tatsuko (Ozaki) I. BA, San Francisco State U., 1984. Asst. mgr. Schoeber's Racquetball and Health Spa, South San Francisco, 1982-84; mgr. Prime Time Athletic Club, Burlingame, Calif., 1984-86; asst. mgr. Supreme Ct. Athletic Club, San Carlos, Calif., 1986-87; pres. Excalibur Corp., Millbrae, Calif., 1984—. Author: Starforce, 1986. Mem. Internat. Racquet Sports Assn., 1985—, Amateur Softball Assn., 1977—, Calif. Amateur Racquetball Assn., 1982—; baseball coach San Francisco Police Activities League, 1978-82. Mem. Calif. Amateur Racquetball Assn. Republican. Baptist. Office: Excalibur Corp PO Box 1220 Millbrae CA 94030

IWASA, SHINICHI, property management and development company executive; b. Tokyo, Mar. 25, 1947; came to U.S. 1987; s. Yoichiro and Mine I.; m. Miki Kazuyo, Oct. 15, 1972; 1 child, Miyuki. Econs. degree, Nihon U., 1970; postgrad., Pepperdine U., 1973-75. Mem. staff real estate dept. Mitsubishi Trust Banking Co., Tokyo, 1970-72; mem. sales staff Yamada Corp., L.A., 1975-78; exec. v.p. Kokudo Ryokuka Co., Tokyo, 1979-82; exec. v.p. Iwasa Mgmt., Inc., Tokyo, 1982—, L.A., 1987—. Mem. Murasaki Country Club. Office: IWS Mgmt Inc 1888 Century Park E Ste 1909 Los Angeles CA 90067

IYER, PRADEEP SATYAMURTHY, oil company research scientist; b. Tirupattur, Tamil Nadu, India, Aug. 10, 1958; came to U.S., 1979; s. Y. and Visalakshi (Mala) Satyamurthy; m. Meenakshi (Radha), Mar. 16, 1987. BS, Inst. Sci., Bombay, 1977, MS, 1979; PhD, U. So. Calif., 1984. Research assoc. Hydrocarbon Research Inst., Los Angeles, 1984-85; research scientist UNOCAL, Brea, Calif., 1986—; cons. Global Geochem. Corp, Los Angeles, 1985—, Avery Internat., Los Angeles, 1985—. Contbr. articles to profl. jours. Mem. Am. Chem. Soc., Sigma Xi, Phi Kappa Phi, Alpha Xi Sigma. Home: 1114 Reggio Pl Pomona CA 91766 Office: UNOCAL Sci and Tech Div 376 S Valencia Ave Brea CA 92621

IZUNO, CYNTHIA ANN, retail executive; b. Milw., Apr. 20, 1961; d. Gene and Nancy Hideko (Tanaka) I. BA in Special Edn., U. San Diego, 1984. Dir. legal dept., pub. relations Roberts & Assocs. of Calif., San Diego, 1985-86; v.p., chief operating officer The Mize Cos., San Diego, 1986--; dir. pub. relations Pacific Southwest Nat. AAU, San Diego, 1981. Mem. San Diego Zoological Soc., Multiple Sclerosis Brunch Soc., KPBS-TV Pub. Broadcasting. Mem. The Smithsonian Assocs., Japan Karate Orgn. (2nd degree blackbelt, grand champion world championships, 1984). Republican. Roman Catholic. Office: The Mize Cos 1340 W Valley Pkwy #208 Escondido CA 92025

IZZO, MARY ALICE, realtor; b. Mesa, Ariz., Aug. 5, 1953; d. Edward Lee and Evangeline Lauda (Gorraiz) Meeker; m. Michael David Izzo, Dec. 26, 1971; children: Michael Wade, Clinton Jarred, Antoinette Marie. Student, Pioneer Coll., 1977, Yavapai Coll., 1984. Cert. realtor, Ariz. Real estate sales agt. Babbit Bros., Flagstaff, Ariz., 1970-76; owner Cottonwood (Ariz.) Tees, 1978-84; realtor Weston Realty, Cottonwood, 1985-86, Coldwell Banker Mabery Real Estate, Cottonwood, 1986—; office mgr., sec. Izzo & Sons Contracting, 1985—. Auhtor: Current Customer Cook Book, 1984. Bd. dirs. Cub Scouts Boy Scouts Am., 1984, 87, AYSO Soccer, Verde Valley, Ariz., 1984-87, also coach; leader youth group, Cottonwood; active DAV Aux., 1988—. Mem. Women's Council Realtors. Democrat. Roman Catholic. Home: PO Box 2002 Cottonwood AZ 86326 Office: Coldwell Banker Mabery Real Estate 1075 Hwy 279 Cottonwood AZ 86326

JAACKS, JOHN WILLIAM, retired air force officer, aerospace company executive; b. Chgo., Sept. 3, 1928; s. Oren Ernst and Mathilda (Dritlein) J.; B.S. in Indsl. Adminstrn., U. Ill., 1949, B.S. in Indsl. Engring., 1962; M.B.A., U. So. Calif., 1970, M.L.A., 1984; m. Marilyn Joyce Walker, Sept. 24, 1952; children—John W. II, Jeffrey A., Holly S. Entered USAF, 1950, commd. 2d lt., 1952, advanced through grades to lt. col., 1968; navigator Fighter Interceptor Squadron, Alaska, 1952-55, pilot, fighter squadron ops. officer, Youngstown, Ohio, 1957-60, chief avionics and aircraft maintenance, Soesterberg, Holland, 1962-65, chief program mgmt. Space Systems div., Los Angeles, 1966-67, dir. program control space launch vehicles Missile Systems Orgn., L.A., from 1967; ret., 1973; asst. F/A 18 radar ILS program mgr. Aircraft Co., El Segundo, Calif. Chmn. S.W. Exploring div. L.A. counc. Boy Scouts Am. Mem. Am. Inst. Indsl. Engring., AIAA, Air Force Assn., U. Ill. Alumni Assn., U. So. Calif. Alumni Assn., Chi Gamma Iota, Phi Kappa Psi. Lutheran. Home: 3310 Seaclaire Dr Rancho Palos Verdes CA 90274 Office: Hughes Aircraft Co El Segundo CA 90009

JABARA, MICHAEL DEAN, telecommunications company executive; b. Sioux Falls, S.D., Oct. 26, 1952; s. James M. and Jean Marie (Swiden) J.; m. Gundula Beate Dietz, Aug. 26, 1984; children: James Michael, Jenna Mariel. Student, Mich. Tech. U., 1970-72; BSBA, U. Calif., Berkeley, 1974; MBA, Pepperdine U., 1979. Mgr. Sprint project So. Pacific Communications Corp., 1976-78; network product mgr. ROLM Corp., 1978-81; cons. McGraw Hill Co., Hamburg (Fed. Republic of Germany) and London, 1982-83; founder, chief exec. officer Friend Techs. Inc. (merger VoiceCom Systems, Inc.), San Francisco, 1984-88; pres. VoiceCom Ventures, San Francisco, 1988—. Patentee in field. Mem. Pepperdine Bus. Alumni, U. Calif. Berkeley Bus. Alumni. Home: 340 St Francis Blvd San Francisco CA 94127 Office: VoiceCom Systems Inc 222 Kearny St San Francisco CA 94108

JABLON, SCOTT WILLIAM, lawyer; b. Syracuse, N.Y., Aug. 10, 1954; s. Jerome Jablon and Carol Ellen (Chase) Rudy. BA in Polit. Sci., U. So. Calif., 1977; JD, O. W. Coburn Sch. Law, Tulsa, 1982. Bar: Wash. 1983. Assoc. R. S. Wilson, Lawyers, Tacoma, 1982—; bd. dirs. Centerforce, Tacoma. Mem. Wash. State Bar Assn., Am. Contract Bridge League (bd. dirs.), Kiwanis. Republican. Jewish. Office: RS Wilson Lawyers 918 N Yakima Tacoma WA 98403

JABS, JACOB, furniture store owner; b. Lodge Grass, Mont., Nov. 23, 1930; s. Adolph and Mary J.; m. Ann Pasley, Feb. 6, 1959; children: Jackie, Terri, Kim. BA in Vocat. Agrl., Mont. State, 1952. Owner Mont. Music, Bozeman, Mont., 1954-60, Mediterranean Galleries, Denver, 1968-73, Yellowstone Furniture Mfg., Bridger, Mont., 1968, Great Am. Bazaar, Billings, Mont., 1987--, Am. Furniture, Denver, 1975--. Metro. chmn. Easter Seals, Colo., 1982, telethon chmn., 1983-85, 88; bd. mem. Shepard of the Hills, Colo., 1980--; exec. com. Muscular Dystrophy, Colo., 1979-83. Served to 1st lt. USAF, 1952-53. Vol. of Year award Multiple Sclerosis Assn. 1983, Community Service award Am. Legion 1982. Mem. Colo. Furniture Dealers Assn., Childrens Hosp. Corporate Club. Republican. Lutheran. Office: Am Furniture 5445 Bannock Denver CO 80216

JACANG, AMELIA REYES, pediatrician; b. Batac, Ilocos N., Philippines, Oct. 15, 1941; came to U.S., 1964; d. Tolentino Cariaga Reyes and Cecilia (Usuquen) Asuncion; divorced; children: David, Kevin, Jay. AA, U. of East, Manila, 1958, MD, 1963. Diplomate Am. Bd. Pediatrics. Rotating intern Kuakini Hosp., Honolulu, 1964-65; resident in pediatrics N.Y. Poly. Hosp., N.Y.C., 1965-66, St. Christopher's Hosp. for Children, Phila., 1966-67; fellow in pediatric pharmacology U. Okla. Med. Ctr., Oklahoma City, 1967-68; staff Kuakini Children's Hosp., Honolulu, 1968-70; practice med. specializing in pediatrics Honolulu, 1970—; mem. Hawaii Bd. Health, 1982-85, Honolulu Drug Selection Bd., 1986—; sec. Bay Health Svcs., Honolulu, 1984-88. Bd. dirs. Aloha Med. Mission, 1982—. Recipient Outstanding Jubilarian, Mariano Marcos Meml. State U., Ilocos Norte, 1987. Fellow Am. Acad. Pediatrics (treas. Hawaii chpt. 1978-83); mem. Hawaii Med. Assn., Honolulu Pediatric Soc., Philippine Med. Assn. Hawaii (bd. dirs. 1984—), Filipino Womens League (past pres., Outstanding Mem. award 1980), Filipino C. of C. Democrat. Roman Catholic. Home: 98-1069 Palula Way Aiea HI 96701 Office: Pediatric Med Group Inc 1712 Liliha St Ste 304 Honolulu HI 96812

JACHTHUBER, RANDALL JEROME, nurse; b. Norfolk, Va., Dec. 30, 1953; s. Jerome Herbert and Carole May (Nelson) J. BSN, U. Wis., Milw., 1976. Nurse Child-Adolescent Treatment Ctr., Milw., 1977-79; supr. Adolescent Alcoholic Care Unit, Mercy Med. Ctr., Denver, 1979-82; unit dir. Mental Health Unit, St. Francis Med. Ctr., Lynwood, Calif., 1983—, acting dir. nursing, 1988—. Bd. dirs. Long Beach (Calif.) Dem. Club, 1983. Mem. Nat. Nurse's Soc. on Addictions, Nurses for Laughter, Nursing Q.A. Profls. So. Calif. Roman Catholic. Home: 4 Esperanza Ave Long Beach CA 90802 Office: St Francis Med Ctr 3630 E Imperial Hwy Lynwood CA 90262

JACK, JUDY GAYLE, nurse; b. Pasadena, Calif., Oct. 6, 1954; d. William Evans and Lois Marie (Cameron) J. AA, Cuyahoga Community Coll., 1984; BS in Nursing cum laude, Pacific U., Azusa, Calif., 1987. Staff nurse Huntington Meml. Hosp., Pasadena, 1987-89; vocat. nursing instr. Citrus Coll., Glendora, Calif., 1989—; chairperson Advocacy com., 1988--. Served with U.S. Army, 1973-76. Mem. Am. Assn. Critical Care Nurses, Sigma Theta Tau. Home: 946 E Citrus Edge Azusa CA 91702-4735

JACKMAN, MICHELE, management consultant; b. Los Angeles, Aug. 18, 1944; d. Michael and Grace (DeLeo) Pantaleo; m. Jarrell C. Jackman, Sept. 7, 1968; 1 child, Renee Grace. BA in Polit. Sci., U. Calif., Davis, 1966; MSW in Social Policy, Cath. U., 1980; MA in Human Relations Mgmt., U. Okla., 1980. Social worker Los Angeles County, 1966-70; supr., trainer Santa Barbara (Calif.) County, 1970-74; mgr. Drug/Alcohol program U.S. Army, Western Europe, 1974-78; analyst, cons. Office Dep. Chief of Staff Personnel U.S. Army, Washington, 1978-80; trainer, cons. Profit Systems, Internat., Santa Barbara, 1980—; lectr. organizational psychology U. Calif., Santa Barbara; cons. numerous agys., orgns. Co-author: Choices/Challenges Teacher's Guide, 1985; author: (tape) Humor at the Worplace, 1988; contbr. chpts. to books. Bd. dirs. Women's Community Ctr. Recipient Commdr.'s medal for Disting. Civilian Service U.S. Army, 1977. Mem. Am. Mgmt. Assn., Nat. Assn. Social Workers (chmn. local chpt.), Am. Soc. Tng. and Devel., NAFE, Santa Barbara C. of C. (Bus. award Council of High Edn./Industry 1986), University Club, Native Daus. of Golden West. Office: Profit Systems Internat Tng & Mgmt Systems 17 E Carrillo Ste 45 Santa Barbara CA 93101

JACKS, BRUCE WILLIAM, civil engineer; b. Sacramento, Apr. 15, 1947; s. Arnold Bruce and Nelda Amelia (Schroeder) J.; m. Norah M. Nolan, Dec. 18, 197; children: Brian, Aiden, Gregory, Darren. BSCE, U. Calif.-Davis, 1969. Asst. engr. Bechtel Corp., San Francisco, 1969-72; engring. estimator Teichert Constrn. Co., Woodland, Calif., 1972-74; contract. adminstr. Wismer & Becker, Sacramento, 1975-76; project mgr. Mackay & Somps Civil Engrs., Fairfield, Calif., 1976--. With U.S. Army, 1970-76. Mem. Am. Pub. Works Assn. Republican. Home: 6 Amherst Pl Woodland CA 95695 Office: Mackay & Somps Civil Engrs 707 Beck Ave Fairfield CA 94533

JACKSON, ALBERT SMITH, electronics engineer; b. Sylvia, Kans., Feb. 2, 1927; s. Oliff Harold and Nellie Blanche (Dewhurst) J.; m. Solace Patricia Smith, June 9, 1951; (div. Aug. 1978); children: Linda Michelle, Jill Sharon, Theresa Louise, Steven Thomas, Craig Michael; m. Elaine Sonia Spontak, Sept. 1, 1978. AA, John Muir Coll., 1948; BSEE, MSEE, Calif. Inst. Tech., 1952; PhDEE, Cornell U., 1956. From instr. to asst. prof. Cornell U., Ithaca, N.Y., 1952-59; dept. mgr. TRW Computers Co., Canoga Park, Calif., 1959-61; pres. Control Tech., Inc., Long Beach, Calif., 1961-65, 71-72; chief scientist Milgo Electronic Corp., Miami, Fla., 1965-71; pres. Opto Logic Corp., Long Beach, 1972-75; engring. mgr. Motorola, Inc., Orange, Calif., 1975—; cons. Naval Research Lab., Washington, 1964-69, Gen. Electric Corp., Ithaca, 1953-59; lectr. UCLA, 1972-77, U. Calif., Irvine, 1965—. Author: Analog Computation, 1960; contbr. articles to profl. jours.; inventor in field. Active Redevel. Agy., Seal Beach, Calif., 1972-74. Served with USN, 1945-46. Named Outstanding Mem. of Extension Faculty, U. Calif.-Irvine, 1985. Mem. IEEE (chmn. profl. group on human factors in engring. 1953-64, regional ednl. coordinator 1984-86). Republican. Office: Motorola Inc 2 City Blvd E Ste 258 Orange CA 92668

JACKSON, BETTY EILEEN, music educator; b. Denver, Oct. 9, 1925; d. James Bowen and Fannie (Shelton) J. MusB, U. Colo., 1948, MusM, 1949, MusB. Edn., 1963; postgrad. Ind. U., 1952-55, Hochschule fur Musik, Munich, 1955-56. Cert. educator Colo., Calif. Tchr., accompanist, tchr. H.L. Davis Vocal Studios, Denver, 1949-52; teaching assoc. U. Colo., Boulder, 1961-63, vis. lectr., 1963-69; tchr. Fontana Unified Sch. Dist., Calif., 1963—, pvt. studio, 1966—; lectr. in music Calif. State U., San Bernardino, 1967-76; performer, accompanist, music dir. numerous musical cos. including performer, music dir. Fontana Mummers, 1980—, Riverside Community Players, Calif., 1984—; performer Rialto Community Theatre, Calif., 1983—. Performances include numerous operas, musical comedies and oratorios, Cen. City Opera, Denver Grand Opera, Univ. Colo., Ind. Univ. Opera Theater (leading mezzo); oratorio soloist in Ind., Ky., Colo., and Calif., West End Opera (lead roles), Riverside Opera (lead roles); Judge, Inland Theatre League, Riverside, 1983—; mem. San Bernardino Cultural Task Force, 1981-83. Fulbright grantee, Munich, 1955-56; named Outstanding Performer Inland Theatre League, 1982-84. Mem. AAUW (bd. dirs., cultural chair 1983-86), Nat. Assn. Tchrs. Singing (exec. bd. 1985—), NEA, Music Educators Nat. Conf., Calif. Tchrs. Assn., Fontana Tchrs. Assn., Music Tchrs. Assn., San Bernardino Valley Concert Assn. (bd. dirs. 1977-83), Order Eastern Star, Kappa Kappa Iota (v.p. 1982-83). Avocations: community theater and opera, travel, collecting Hummels and plates. Home: PO Box 885 Rialto CA 92377

JACKSON, BEVERLEY JOY JACOBSON, columnist, lecturer; b. L.A., Nov. 20, 1928; d. Phillip and Dorothy Jacobson; student U. So. Calif., UCLA; m. Robert David Jackson (div. Aug. 1964); 1 child, Tracey Dee. Daily columnist Santa Barbara (Calif.) News Press, 1968—; nat. lectr. Santa Barbara history, hist. China recreated, also China today; free lance writer, fgn. corr. Bd. dirs. Santa Barbara br. Am. Cancer Soc., 1963—; mem. art mus. coun. L.A. Mus. Art, 1959—, mem. costume coun., 1983—; docent L.A. Mus. Art, 1962-64; mem. exec. bd. Channel City Women's Forum, 1969—; mem. adv. bd. Santa Barbara Mus. Natural History, Coun. of Christmas Cheer, Women's Shelter Bldg., Direct Relief Internat., Nat. Coun. Drug and Alcohol Abuse; mem adv. bd. Hospice of Santa Barbara, 1981—, Stop AIDS Coun., Arthritis Found.; bd. dirs. So. Calif. Com. for Shakespear's Globe Theatre; chmn. Santa Barbara Com. for Visit Queen Elizabeth II, 1982—. Author: Dolls and Doll Houses of Spain, 1970; (with others) I'm Just Wild About Harry, 1979. Home: PO Box 5118 Santa Barbara CA 93108

JACKSON, CLAYTON RANDALL, lawyer; b. L.A., Feb. 19, 1943; s. Leonard Glen and Isabelle Amelia (Wayne) J. BS, U. So. Calif., 1965; JD, U. Calif., San Francisco, 1968. Bar: Calif. 1969. Assoc. Parker, Milliken et al, L.A., 1969-70; ptnr. McFarland, Kuchins & Jackson, San Francisco, 1970-75, Dunne, Phelps et al, San Francisco, 1976-83, Lillick, McHose & Charles, San Francisco and Sacramento, 1983-85, Jackson & Abrams, San Francisco, 1985-89, Sullivan, Roche & Johnson, San Francisco, 1989—; dir., lectr. San Francisco Law Sch., 1970-77; dir. Superior Nat. Ins. Group, L.A., 1985—; pres., dir. SRJ Jackson, Barish & Assocs., Sacramentoand San Francisco, 1985—. Author: (book) Laws Pertaining to the California Innkeeper, 1971. Dir. Marin Symphony, San Rafael, Calif., 1984—. Mem. Am. Bar Assn., Am. Judicature Soc., Fedn. Ins. Counsel, State Bar Calif., San Francisco Bar Assn., Hastings Coll. of the Law Found., Bankers Club, World Trade Club, St. Francis Yacht Club, Sutter Club. Lutheran. Office: Sullivan Roche & Johnson 333 Bush St 18th Fl San Francisco CA 94104

JACKSON, CLIFTON PHILIP, JR., engineering specialist; b. Greenville, S.C., Nov. 29, 1942; s. Clifton Philip and Gladys (Pratt) J.; m. Song Kim, Dec. 21, 1968; children: Susanne Kim, Clifton Philip III, David Kim. BSME, U. Mich., 1965; postgrad., U.S. Army Mgmt. Engring. Coll., 1966, 68, Central Tex. Coll., 1968-69, CSC Exec. Devel. Ctr., Oak Ridge, Tenn., 1972, 77. Notary Pub. Body design engr. Pontiac Motors div., Gen. Motors Corp., Flint, Mich., 1965; applications engr. Cummins Engine Co., Columbus, Ind., 1966; chief indsl. engring. U.S. Army Mintenance Directorate, Ft. Hood, Tex., 1966-69; chief prodn. mgmt. 8th U.S. Army Engr., Seoul, Korea, 1969-74; chief mgmt. improvement U.S. Army Forces Command, Ft. McPherson, Ga., 1974-75; exec. asst. U.S. Army C.E., North Cen., Chgo., 1975-83, U.S. Army C.E., North Pacific, Portland, Oreg., 1983—; instr. Central Tex Coll., Killeen, 1968-69; propr. Just Stuff Emporium, Bartlett, Ill., 1976-82; mem. Portland Fed. Exec. Bd. Author: Procedure Manual Regulations. Coach, asst. coach Bartlett (Ill.) Youth Athletics, 1975-83. Lieut. U.S. Army, 1966-68. Mem. Soc. Automotive Engrs., Soc. Am. Mil. Engrs., Mensa, Internat. Triple Nine Soc., Portland C. of C., Chi Psi. Home: 3240 SW Malcolm Ct Portland OR 97225 Office: US Army CE North Pacific Div 220 NW Eighth Ave Portland OR 97208

JACKSON, DONALD MCCREDIE, oil and gas executive; b. Waukegan, Ill., July 7, 1942; s. Hugh McCredie and Ethyl Lynn (Hawley) J.; m. Charlotte Lee Edney, Aug. 26, 1965; children: Michael, Kellee. BS in Indsl. Engring., Lehigh U., 1964, MS, 1968; postgrad., U. So. Calif., 1972, Outward Bound Sch., 1986-87. Refinery engr. Gulf Refinery subs. Gulf Oil Co., Phila., 1964-66; mgr. ops. research Gulf Oil Co., Houston, 1968-71; mgr. devel. Gen. Atomic subs. Gulf Oil Co., San Diego, 1971-76; dir. devel. mktg. Gulf Minerals subs. Gulf Oil Co., Denver, 1976-83; gen. mgr. United Engrs. subs. Raytheon Co., Denver, 1983-86; v.p. Incinatrol subs. Phillips Petroleum, Denver, 1987—; adj. prof. U. San Diego, 1972-76. Pres. City of Bowmar Owners, Inc., Littleton, Colo.; dir. Littleton Ctr. Performing Arts, 1984-87; active Colo. Children;s Opera, Denver, 1987—; sponsor Colo. Alliance Bus., Denver, 1982-84. Recipient Engring. Design award Exxon/Soc. Profl. Engrs., 1987. Mem. Tau Beta Pi. Republican. Presbyterian. Club: Met. (Denver). Home: 5070 Bow Mar Dr Littleton CO 80123 Office: Incinatrol 8055 E Tufts Ave Pkwy Denver CO 80237

JACKSON, FRANK CLINE, JR., management consultant; b. Seattle, Aug. 14, 1920; s. Frank C. and Bertha J. (TeRoller) J.; BS in Pre-medics, U. Wash., 1942; BS in Animal Sci., Wash. State U., 1947; postgrad. Harvard U., 1954, Columbia U., 1955, Pacific Luth. U., 1966; m. Helen Elaine Bonner, Jan. 12, 1943 (dec. 1978); children: Stanley Alan, Bruce Edward, Paul Bonner, David Brian; m. 2d, Joan Marion Hurd, Dec. 29, 1979. Vets. agrl. instr. Puyallup (Wash.) High Sch., 1947-52; vet. rep. Pfizer Labs. div. Charles Pfizer Co., Inc., 1952-53, nat. sales mgr. vet. dept., N.Y.C., 1953-57, mgr. vet. dept., 1957-61; gen. mgr. Am. Wilbert Vault Co., Inc., Puyallup, 1961-65; chmn. Pierce County Co-op Extension Service, Wash. State U., Tacoma, 1966-78; chmn. Jefferson County Coop. Extension Service div. Wash. State U., Port Townsend, 1978-79; mgmt. cons., 1979—; pres. Dolphin Reach Corp.; mng. gen. ptnr. Dolphin Reach Assocs.; founder Pacific N.W. Vet. Suppliers Assn., 1955, pres., 1955-56, dir., 1956-59; founder, dir. Wash. Meml. Soc., Seattle, 1962-64. Troop chmn. Tacoma council Boy Scouts Am., 1950-60; bd. dirs. Tacoma Rescue Mission, 1970-78; Bible tchr., lectr., 1965—. Served with U.S. Army, 1942-46; PTO. Decorated Purple Heart (4), Bronze Star; recipient Disting. Citizen award Mcpl. League Tacoma, 1978, Jefferson award Am. Inst. for Public Service, 1977. Mem. Community Devel. Soc., Nat. (Disting. Service award 1979), Wash. assns. county agrl. agts., Nat. Sales Execs. Assn. Republican. Presbyterian. Club: Elks, Tacoma Yacht. Home: 2400 E Howell #K Seattle WA 98122

JACKSON, GARY BRIAN, organizational development executive, marketing professional; b. Santa Monica, Calif., Oct. 31, 1942; s. Paul Gerald and Maxine Mackenzie (Williams) J.; m. Linda Swanson, Dec. 20, 1979. BA, Calif. State U.; MS, U. Calif., Irvine, PhD. Assoc. prof. U. Redlands, Calif., 1975-79; mgr. tng. and devel. Xeorox Learning Systems, Irvine, 1979-80; dir. administrn. Canon, Inc., Irvine, 1980-82; dir. internat. mktg. Loral Instrumentation, San Diego, 1982-85; dir. human resources Doric Sci div. Emerson Electric Co., San Diego, 1985—; sr. ptnr. Jackson-MacKenzie Mgmt. Cons., San Juan Capistrano, Calif., 1984-85. Contbr. articles on Japanese soc. and bus. practices to profl. jours; choreographer (modern dance) Blue Moods. Served with USAF, 1960-64. Nominee Woodrow Wilson Fellowship, 1986; grantee U. Calif. Sch. Social Sci., USPHS, NSF. Mem. Organizational Network, Am. Soc. Tng. and Devel., Am. Psychol. Assn., Am. Anthropol. Assn. Democrat. Office: Emerson Electric Co Doric Sci Civ 3883 Ruffin Rd San Diego CA 92123

JACKSON, GORDON STUART, journalism educator; b. Cape Town, South Africa, Sept. 28, 1949; came to U.S., 1979; s. Stanley Thompson and Myrtle Daphne (Risk) J.; m. Susan Lynne Matterson, July 26, 1980; children: Sarah, Matthew. BA, U. Cape Town, 1970; BA with honors, Rhodes U., 1971; MA, Wheaton (Ill.) Coll., 1975; PhD, Ind. U., 1983. Regional dir. South African Nat. Sunday Sch. Assn., Cape Town, 1973; researcher Nat. Inst. for Personnel Research, Johannesburg, South Africa, 1973-74; writer, editor To the Point Mag., Johannesburg, 1976-79; assoc. prof. journalism Whitworth Coll., Spokane, Wash., 1983--. Contbr. articles to mags., South Africa, Eng., U.S. Mem. Assn. for Edn. in Journalism and Mass Communications, Soc. Profl. Journalists, World Assn. for Christian Communication. Presbyterian. Home: W 615 Teal Ave Spokane WA 99218 Office: Whitworth Coll Spokane WA 99251-0002

JACKSON, HARRY ANDREW, artist; b. Chgo., Apr. 18, 1924; s. Harry and Ellen Grace J.; m. Valentina Moya Lear, Feb. 22, 1974; children: Matthew, Molly, Jesse, Luke, Chloe. ArtsD (hon.), U. Wyo., 1986. Founder, ptnr. pvt. foundry, Camiore, Italy, 1964—, Wyo. Foundry Studios, Cody, 1965—, Western Fine Arts Found., 1974—, Jackson-Mariani S.R.L. Fine Art Bronze Foundry, Camaiore, 1985—. Author: Lost Wax Bronze Casting, 1972; one man exhbns. Tibor de Nagy Gallery, N.Y.C., 1952, 53, Martha Jackson Gallery, N.Y.C., 1956, Knoedler Gallery, N.Y.C., 1960, Amon Carter Mus., Fort Worth, 1961, 68, Kennedy Gallery, N.Y., 1964, 68, 69, Smithsonian Instn., Washington, 1964, Whitney Gallery Western Art/Buffalo Bill Hist. Mus., Cody, 1964, 80-81, Mont. Hist. Soc., 1964, Tryon Gallery London, 1969, J. Poole Gallery, London, 1981, S.W. Mus., Los Angeles, 1979, Smith Gallery, 1981, 86, Palm Springs Desert Mus., 1981, Mpls. Inst. Art, 1982, Trailside Gallery, Scottsdale, Ariz., 1983; retrospective exhbn. Camaiore, 1985, U. Wyo. Art Mus., 1987; represented in permanent collections Am. Mus. of Gt. Britain, U.S. Dept State, Lyndon Baines Johnson Meml. Library, Nat. Cowboy Hall of Fame, Wyo. State Mus., Whitney Mus. Western Art, Buffalo Bill Hist. Ctr., Plains Indian Mus., Amon Carter Mus., Willaroc Mus., Mont. Hist. Soc., others; commd. works include: mural, Fort Pitts Mus., Pitts., 10-foot Sacagawea polychrome bronze monument, Cen. Wyo. Coll., 1981, 21-foot monumental equestrian bronze, The Horseman, Gt. Western Fin. Corp., Beverly Hills, Calif., 1984, 10-foot patinaed Sacagawea, Sanata Barbara, Calif., 1985, Capezzano-Pianore, Camaiore, 1985; subject of books and catalogues: (by Frank Getlein) Harry Jackson, Monograph Catalogue, 1969, (by Pointer & Goddard) Harry Jackson, 1981, (by Wyo. Foundry Studios, Inc.) Harry Jackson, Forty Years of His Work 1941-81, 1981, (by City of Camaiore) Harry Jackson, Thirty Years in Versillia. Served with USMC, 1942-45. Decorated Purple Heart with gold star; recipient gold medal Nat. Acad. Design, 1968, also Presdl. citation; Best Cover Art of 1969 award for sculpture of John Wayne Am. Inst. Graphic Arts, 1969; Presdl. citation R.I. Sch. Design; Fulbright grantee, 1954; 2 bronzes presented as official gifts of state by Pres. Ronald Reagan, 1982. Fellow Nat. Acad. Western Art; mem. Nat. Sculpture Soc. Address: PO Box 2836 Cody WY 82414

JACKSON, JANE W., interior designer; b. Asheville, N.C., Aug. 5, 1944; d. James and Willie Mae (Stoner) Harris; m. Bruce G. Jackson; children: Yvette, Scott. Student, Boston U., 1964; BA, Leslie Coll., 1967; postgrad., Artisan Sch. Interior Design, 1980-82. Tchr. Montessori, Brookline, Mass., 1969-72; interior designer Nettle Creek Shops, Honolulu, 1980-82, owner, 1982—. Active Mayor's Com. for Small Bus., Honolulu, 1984. Mem. Am. Soc. Interior Design Industry Found. Democrat. Club: Honolulu. Office: Nettle Creek Shops 1221 Kapiolani Blvd Honolulu HI 96814

JACKSON, JEWEL, state youth authority official; b. Shreveport, La., June 3, 1942; d. Willie Burghardt and Bernice Jewel (Mayberry) Norton; m. Edward James Norman, May 17, 1961 (div. Nov. 1968); children—Steven, June Kelly; m. Wilbert Jackson, Apr. 6, 1969; children—Michael, Anthony. With Calif. Youth Authority, 1965—, group supr., San Andreas and Santa Rosa, 1965-67, youth counselor, Ventura, 1967-78, sr. youth counselor, Stockton, 1978-81, treatment team supr., program mgr., Whittier and Ione, 1981—, affirmative action adv. mem., Sacramento, 1976-78, equal employment adv. mem., 1978-79; speaker U. Pacific Youth Motivational Project, Stockton, Calif., 1985-86. Mem. Women in Criminal Justice-North (co-chair 1974-76), Nat. Assn. for Female Execs., Assn. Black Correctional Workers (chpt. v.p. 1979, editor newsletter 1978-80). Avocations: reading, horseback riding, writing poetry and short stories, designing clothing. Home: PO Box 898 Ione CA 95640

JACKSON, JOHN W., helicopter manufacturing company executive; b. Joplin, Mo., June 25, 1954; s. William E. and Freda May (Brown) J.; div.; 1 child, Heather Mae. BA in Bus. Adminstrn., Wichita State U., 1976. Supr.computer aided design Cessna Aircraft Co., Wichita, Kans., 1976-78; sr. tool engr. Hughes Helicopters, Inc., Culver City, Calif., 1978-79, gen. supr. systems, 1979-82, tech. specialist, 1982-84, supr. computer-integrated mfg., 1984-85; mgr. computer-integrated mfg. Hughes Helicopters, Inc., Mesa, Ariz., 1986--; chmn. corp. mfg. steering group McDonnell Douglas Corp., St. Louis, 1989--. Mem. MDC Artificial Intelligence Group, MDC Alternative to CAM-I, Soc. Mfg. Engrs. Home: 1134 E Dublin St Chandler AZ 85224

JACKSON, MARILYN DAWN, real estate broker, contracting company executive; b. Wagner, S.D., June 17, 1932; d. Fred Lewis and Anne Marie (Kostel) Eggers; m. Thomas N. Jackson, Aug. 23, 1958 (div. June 1982); children: Anita Clare, Lawrence Scott, Stephen Thomas. BS in Home Econs., S.D. State U., 1954; MS in Secondary Edn., U. Calif., Long Beach, 1955-62. Tchr. home econs. Kimball (S.D.) High Sch., 1954-55, Poly. High Sch., Long Beach, 1955-62; saleswoman Wagner Realty, Century 21, Scottsdale, Ariz., 1973-74, Realty Execs., Scottsdale, 1974-76; owner, broker, gen. contractor Majac Realty, Scottsdale, 1976--. Mem. Nat. Assn. Realtors, Ariz. Assn. Realtors, Scottsdale Bd. Realtors, Scottsdale C. of C. Republican. Roman Catholic. Home and Office: Majac Realty 11835 N 76th Pl Scottsdale AZ 85260

JACKSON, MICHAEL TERRY, real estate broker; b. Ogden, Vt., Nov. 26, 1947; s. Dean and Margaret (Terry) J.; m. Vicki Rae Huxtable, May 29, 1971; children: Tanya, Nikkol. BS in Botany, Weber State Coll., 1970; MS, U. Nev., 1972. Planner Bur. Land Mgmt., Reno, 1972-84; assoc. broker Remcor Real Estate, Reno, 1984-88; corp. broker The Real Estate Connection, Reno, 1988—; owner Wagon Wheel Mobile Home Pk., Fallon, Nev., 1986—, Five Star Mobile Pk., Silver Springs, Nev., 1987—. Office: The Real Estate Connection 888 W 2d Ste 302 Reno NV 89503

JACKSON, NANCY KAY, small business owner; b. Ames, Iowa, May 9, 1950; d. Gerald Lawrence and Betty Marie (Haugstad) Halvorson; m. Nader Khon Alai, Oct. 4, 1971 (dec. 1976); children: Timothy, Jennifer; m. Michael Curt Jackson, Dec. 31, 1980; children: Megan, Kate, Taylor. Student, Ariz. State U., 1976-80. Substitute tchr. Casa Grande (Ariz.) Elem. Dist., 1979-80; owner, operator The Property, Casa Grande, 1981—, Be Dillon's Cactus Garden & Mus., Casa Grande, 1987—. Active Friends of Arts, Casa Grande, 1987—, Phoenix Art Mus., 1987—, Casa Grande Hist. Soc., 1988—. Mem. Nat. Restaurant Assn., C. of C. of Greater Casa Grande Valley, Ariz. C. of C. Republican. Lutheran. Office: The Property 1251 W Gila Bend Hwy Casa Grande AZ 85222

JACKSON, PETER VORIOUS, III, association executive; b. Butte, Mont., May 18, 1927; s. Peter V. and Besse Portia (McLean) J.; m. Johnneta Pierce, Apr. 29, 1949; children: Ward, Michelle (Mrs. Jerry Vanhour), Johnathan. Wheat and cattle rancher 1949—; mem. Mont. Ho. of Reps., 1971-72; chief Grass Conservation bur. Mont. Dept. Natural Resources, Helena, 1972-74; supr. Conservation Dist. Madison County, Ennis, Mont., from 1957; past exec. dir. Western Environ. Trade Assn., Helena.; exec. v.p. Soc. for Range Mgmt., Denver. Author: Montana Rangeland Resources Program, 1970. Mem. Madison County Fair Bd.; pres. Grazing Lands Forum, 1988. Recipient Renner award Soc. Range Mgmt., 1971, Conservation award Mont. Wildlife Fedn., 1966. Mem. Nat. Assn. Conservation Dists. (dir.), Mont. Assn. Conservation Dists. (exec. v.p. 1974), Soc. Range Mgmt. (nat. pres.). Lodges: Masons, Elks. Home: Box 86 Harrison MT 59735 Office: 1839 York St Denver CO 80206

JACKSON, REGINALD MARTINEZ, professional baseball player; b. Wyncote, Pa., May 18, 1946; s. Martinez Jackson; m. Juanita Jackson. Student, Ariz. State U. Outfielder Kansas City, then Oakland Athletics, 1967-75, Balt. Orioles, 1976, N.Y. Yankees, 1977-81; outfielder, designated hitter Calif. Angels, 1982-86; outfielder, designated hitter Oakland A's, 1987, advisor, 1988—; mem. Am. League All-Star Team, 1969, 71-75, 77-82, 84. Author: (with Bill Libby) Reggie, 1975, (with Joel Cohen) Inside Hitting, 1975. Named Most Valuable Player Am. League, 1973, The Sporting News Major League Player of Year, 1973; Named to The Sporting News Am. League All-Star Team, 1969, 73, 75, 76, 80. *

JACKSON, ROBERT JOHN, industrial engineer; b. L.A., Dec. 24, 1922; s. John M. and Ona Blanche (Hill) J.; m. Ethel K. Beecher, Dec. 1, 1950; children: Kathryn, Bradley, Diane, Margaret, Shirley, Kelly, Riley. AA, Pasadena Coll., 1958. Supr. assembly dept. Lockheed Aircraft Co., Burbank, Calif., 1941-51; time standards engr. Bendix Pacific Co., North Hollywood, Calif., 1951-53; indsl. engr. Walsco Electronic Co., Los Angeles, 1953-55; methods and time standards engr. Lockheed-Calif. Co., Burbank, 1955-69, dir. hours rep., 1969—. Dir. Modal Investment Co., Eagle Rock, Calif., 1955-56. Served with AUS, 1944-46; PTO. Decorated Purple Heart with oak leaf cluster, Bronze Star, Silver Star. Mem. Am. Inst. Indsl. Engrs. Lodge: Masons. Home: 415 N Plymouth Blvd Los Angeles CA 90004 Office: Lockheed-Calif Co 2555 N Hollywood Way Burbank CA 91503

JACKSON, SANDEI JEAN, management specialist; b. L.A., Calif., June 3, 1940; d. Joel Julius and Jean Beryl (Shaw) Reinhard; m. Edward James Jackson, Jan. 28, 1962 (div. 1973); children: Kraig Earl, Chad Ruben. AA, Shasta Jr. Coll., 1960; student, San Jose (Calif.) State U., 1973-77. Asst. producer Sta. KVIP-TV Shasta Co. Edn., Redding, Calif., 1956-60; pub. relations Santa Clara County Data Processing, San Jose, Calif., 1968-79; sales mgr. Sta. KAYN FM, Nogales, Ariz., 1979-82, Sheraton Rio Rico Resort, Nogales, 1982-84; ins. agt. E.F. Hutton Mutual of Omaha, Nogales, 1980-85; gen. mgr. USA Hosts, Ltd., Tuscon, Ariz., 1985—. Vol. Tucson Conv. Bur., Nogales C. of C., Nogales Film Commn. 1979-85. With USAF, 1960-64. Mem. Holtel Sales Mgmt. Assn. (sec. 1986-87; Allied Exec. of Yr. 1988), Inkeepers Assn., SITE. Republican. Protestant. Office: USA Hosts 7400 N Oracle Rd Ste #336 Tucson AZ 85704-6342

JACKSON, WILLIAM LONGSTRETH, hydrologist; b. Kalamazoo, Mich., June 2, 1948; s. William Humphrey and Louise Longstreth (Cone)ú J.; m. Jane Morris Woodhams, June 24, 1972; children: David Morris, Eric Humphrey. BSME, U. Mich., 1970, MS in Natural Resources, 1971; PhD in Forest Hydrology, Oreg. State U., 1981. Natural resource planner Md. Dept. Natural Resources, Annapolis, Md., 1971-76; hydrologist USDI Bur. Land Mgmt., Denver, 1981-88; chief br. water ops. U.S. Nat. Park Svc., Denver, 1988—; chairperson tech. com. Fed. Sediment Project, Mpls., 1985-87. Editor: (monograph) Engineering Consolidations in Small Stream Management, 1987 (USDI award 1988); contbr. articles to profl. jours. Mem. AM. Inst. Hydrology, Am. Water Resources Assn., Am. Geophysical Union. Home: 1775 S Endicott St Lakewood CO 80226 Office: Nat Park Svc 301 S Howes St Fort Collins CO 80521

JACOB, GERALD REGIS, policy analyst; b. Pitts., Oct. 16, 1952; s. Bernard T. and Patricia A. (Donovan) J.; m. Kathryn Mutz, Mar., 1975. BA, U. Chgo., 1974; MS, Utah State U., 1978; PhD, U. Colo., 1988. Resource cons. Salt Lake City, 1978-83; project analyst nuclear waste policy office State of Utah, Salt Lake City, 1984; researcher Inst. Behavioral Sci., Boulder, Colo., 1984-87; policy analyst Western Interstate Energy Bd., Denver, 1987—; guest lectr. U. Colo., U. Ariz., 1987-88; instr. U. Colo., Boulder, 1985. Contbr. articles to profl. jours. U. Colo. Found. grantee, 1985, doctoral fellow, 1985-86. Mem. Assn. Am. Geographers, Western Social Sci. Assn. Home: PO Box 819 Boulder CO 80306 Office: Western Interstate Energy Bd 3333 Quebec St Ste 6500 Denver CO 80207

JACOB, NANCY LOUISE, finance educator; b. Berkeley, Calif., Jan. 15, 1943; d. Irvin Carl and Ruby (Roberts) Feustel; m. George B. Fotheringham, Dec. 22, 1972; 1 child, Randy. BA magna cum laude, U. Wash., 1967; PhD in Econs. magna cum laude, U. Calif., Irvine, 1970. Econ. analyst, summer research staff Ctr. for Naval Analysis, Arlington, Va., 1969, chmn. dept. fin., bus. econs. and quantitative methods, 1978-81; with Weyerhaeuser Co., Tacoma, 1963-65; mem. faculty U. Wash., Seattle, 1970—, dean Sch. Bus. Adminstrn., 1981-88, prof. fin., 1981—; trustee Coll. Retirement Equities Fund., N.Y., 1980—; bd. dirs. Puget Sound Power and Light Co., Bellevue, Wash., Rainier Bancorp., Seattle. Co-author: Basic: An Intro to Computer Programming Using Basic Language, 1979, Investments, 1984, 88; contbr. articles to profl. jours. Bd. dirs. Pacific Coast Banking Sch., Seattle, 1981-88, Jr. Achievement, Seattle, 1982-84, Wash. Council on Internat. Trade, Seattle, 1981—. Recipient Wall St Jour. Achievement award U. Wash., 1967; NDEA Title IV fellow, 1968-70. Mem. Am. Econ. Assn., Am. Fin. Assn. (bd. dirs. 1975-77), Western Fin. Assn. (bd. dirs. 1976-78), Seattle Soc. Fin. Analysts, Fin. Mgmt. Assn. (program com. 1977), Phi Beta Kappa, Alpha Kappa Psi. Club: Rainier, Washington Athletic, Columbia Tower (Seattle). Office: U Wash Sch Grad Bus Adminstrn Seattle WA 98195

JACOBS, ARTHUR DIETRICH, health services executive, educator; b. Bklyn., Feb. 4, 1933; s. Lambert Dietrich and Paula Sophia (Knissel) J.; m. Viva Jane Sims, Mar. 24, 1952; children: Archie (dec.), David L., Dwayne C., Dianna K. Hatfield. BBA, Ariz. State U., 1962, MBA, 1966. Enlisted USAF, 1951, commd. 2d lt., 1962, advanced through grades to maj., 1972, ret., 1973; indsl. engr. Motorola, Phoenix, 1973-74; mgmt. cons. state of Ariz., 1974-76; mgmt. cons. Productivity Internat., Tempe, Ariz., 1976-79; faculty assoc. Coll. Bus. Adminstrn., Ariz. State U., Tempe, 1977—; productivity advisor Scottsdale (Ariz.) Meml. Health Services Co., 1979-84. Bd. dirs. United Way of Tempe, 1979-85. Mem. Am. Soc. Quality Control, Ariz. State U. Alumni Assn. (bd. dirs. 1973-79, pres. 1978-79), Inst. Indsl. Engrs. (pres. Central Ariz. chpt. 1984-85), Ops. Research Soc. Am., Sigma Iota Epsilon, Beta Gamma Sigma, Delta Sigma Pi. Club: Optimist (life) (Tempe). Contbr. articles to profl. jours.

JACOBS, EDWIN MAX, oncologist, consultant; b. San Francisco, Sept. 9, 1925; s. Edwin Manheim and Floy (Sommer) J. BA, Reed Coll., 1950; MD, Cornell U., 1954. Intern Bellevue Hosp., N.Y.C., 1954-55, resident, 1956-57; resident Meml. Sloan-Kettering Cancer Ctr., N.Y.C., 1955-56, fellow in oncology, 1957-59; instr. medicine U. Calif., San Francisco, 1960-63, head clin. cancer research, 1960-76, asst. prof., 1963-69, assoc. clin. prof., 1969-76; assoc. chief clin. investigations br. Nat. Cancer Inst., Bethesda, Md., 1976-85; assoc. exec. officer No. Calif. Oncology Group, Palo Alto, Calif., 1985—; clin. prof. medicine Cancer Research Inst. U. Calif., San Francisco, 1987—; vis. physician Royal Marsden Hosp., London, 1970; cons. Monsanto Chem. Co., St. Louis, 1985—, G.D. Searle Co., Skokie, Ill., 1985—. Contbr. articles on testicular cancer to med. jours. Bd. dirs. San Francisco Symphony Found., 1968-76. Served with U.S. Army, 1944-46, ETO, PTO. Squibb-Olin fellow Meml. Sloan-Kettering Cancer Ctr., 1965; recipient Spl. Achievment award NIH, 1983. Fellow ACP; mem. AMA (Recognition award 1985—), Am. Soc. Hematology (neoplasia com. 1978-81), Am. Assn. Cancer Research, Am. Soc. Clin. Oncology, Soc. Surg. Oncology, Am. Radium Soc. (v.p. 1978-79), San Francisco Mus.'s Soc. Home: 1860 16th Ave San Francisco CA 94122 Office: No Calif Cancer Program 1301 Shoreway Rd Ste 425 Belmont CA 94002

JACOBS, JOHN HOWARD, association executive; b. Phila., June 7, 1925; s. Howard Elias and Elizabeth Pauline (Dresel) J.; m. Shirley Elizabeth Salini, Apr. 21, 1960. BS in Econs., N.Mex. State U., 1950; LLD (hon.), Golden Gate U., 1985. Adminstrv. officer U.S. Fgn. Service (NATO), London, Paris, 1951-53; gen. mgr. Vis-a-Pack Corp., Beverly, N.J., 1953-58; exec. dir. Red. Agy., City of Stockton, Calif., 1958-66, San Francisco Planning and Urban Research, 1966-81; exec. dir. San Francisco C. of C., 1981-88, pres., 1988—; pres. Pacific Region Nat. Assn. Housing and Redevel. Ofcls., Stockton, 1965-66, nat. bd. govs., San Francisco, 1966-70. Mem. San Francisco Mayor's Fiscal Adv. Com.; trustee Pacific Med. Ctr., San Francisco; trustee emeritus Fine Arts Mus. of San Francisco; bd. dirs. SPUR, San Francisco, San Francisco Devel. Fund, Pvt. Industry Council San Francisco. Served with AUS, 1943-45. Mem. Nat. Assn. Housing and Redevel. Ofcls. Home: 2823 Octavia St San Francisco CA 94123 Office: San Francisco C of C 465 California St San Francisco CA 94104

JACOBS, JOSEPH JOHN, engineering company executive; b. June 13, 1916; s. Joseph and Afiffie (Forzley) J.; m. Violet Jabara, June 14, 1942; children: Margaret, Linda, Valerie. B.S. in Chem. Engring, Poly. Inst. N.Y., Bklyn., 1937, M.S., 1939, Ph.D., 1942. Registered profl. engr., N.Y., N.J., La., Calif. Chem. engr. Autoxygen, Inc., N.Y.C., 1939-42; sr. chem. engr. Merck & Co., Rahway, N.J., 1942-44; v.p., tech. dir. Chemurgic Corp., Richmond, Calif., 1944-47; pres. Jacobs Engring. Co., Pasadena, Calif., 1947-74; chmn. bd., chief exec. officer Jacobs Engring. Group Inc., Pasadena, 1974—. Contbr. tech. articles to profl. jours. Area bd. dirs. United Way, 1978—; bd. trustees Poly. Univ. N.Y.; trustee Harvey Mudd Coll.; mem. Assocs. Calif. Inst. Tech.; bd. dirs. Genetics Inst., Inst. Contemporary Studies, Calif. Round Table, Bank Audi, Calif. Recipient Herbert Hoover medal United Engring. Socs., 1983. Fellow Am. Inst. Chem. Engrs., Am. Inst. Chemists, Inst. for Advancement Engring.; mem. Am. Chem. Soc., AAAS, Los Angeles C. of C., Pasadena C. of C., Sigma Xi, Phi Lambda Upsilon. Clubs: Altadena Town and Country, California, Annandale Golf, Pauma Valley Country. Office: Jacobs Engring Group Inc 251 S Lake Ave Pasadena CA 91101

JACOBS, KENT FREDERICK, dermatologist; b. El Paso, Tex., Feb. 13, 1938; s. Carl Frederick and Mercedes D. (Johns) J.; m. Sallie Ritter, Apr. 13, 1971. BS, N.Mex. State U., 1960; MD, Northwestern U., 1964; postgrad., U. Colo., 1967-70. Dir. service unit USPHS, Laguna, N.Mex., 1966-67; pvt. practice specializing in dematology Las Cruces, N.Mex., 1970—; cons. U.S. Army, San Francisco, 1968-70, cons. NIH, Washington, 1983, Holloman AFB, 1972-77; research assoc. VA Hosp., Denver, 1969-70; preceptor U. Tex., Galveston, 1976-77; mem. clin. staff Tex. Tech U., Lubbock, 1977—; asst. clin. prof. U. N.Mex., Albuquerque, 1972—; bd. dirs. First Nat. Bank of Dona Ana County, Las Cruces, N.Mex., 1987—. Contbr. articles to profl. jours. and popular mags. Trustee Mus. N.Mex. Found., 1987—; bd. regents Mus. N.Mex., 1987—. Served to lt. commdr. USCG, 1965-68. Invitational scholar Oreg. Primate Ctr., 1968; Acad. Dermatology Found. fellow, 1969; named Disting. Alumnus N.Mex. State U., 1985. Fellow Am. Acad. Dermatology, Royal Soc. Medicine, Soc. Investigative Dermatology; mem. AMA, Fedn. State Med. Bds. (bd. dirs. 1984-86), N.Mex. Med. Soc., N.Mex. Bd. Med. Examiners (pres. 1983-84), N.Mex. State U. Alumni Assn. (bd. dirs. 1975—), Phi Beta Kappa, Beta Beta Beta. Republican. Presbyterian. Clubs: Mil Gracias (pres. 1972-74), Pres.'s Assocs. Lodge: Rotary. Home: 3610 Southwind Rd Las Cruces NM 88005 Office: 2930 Hillrise Ste 6 Las Cruces NM 88001

JACOBS, MARIAN, advertising agency owner; b. Stockton, Calif., Sept. 11, 1927; d. Paul (dec.) and Rose (Sallah) J. AA, Stockton Coll. With Bottarini Advt., Stockton, 1948-50; pvt. practice Stockton, 1950-64; with Olympius Advt., Stockton, 1964-78; pvt. practice Stockton, 1978—; pres. Stockton Advt. Club, 1954, Venture Club, Stockton, 1955; founder Stockton Advt. and Mktg. Club, 1981. Founder Stockton Arts Comms., 1976, Sunflower Entertainment for Institutionalized, 1976, Women Execs., Stockton, 1978; founding dir. Pixie Woods, Stockton; bd. dir. Goodwill Industries, St. Mary's Dining Room, Alan Short Gallery. Recipient Woman of Achievement award San Joaquin County Women's Coun., Stockton, 1976, Achievement award San Joaquin Delta Coll., Stockton, 1978, Friend of Edn. award Calif. Tchrs. Assn., Stockton, 1988, Stanley McCaffrey Disting. Svc. award, U. of the Pacific, Stockton, 1988; named Stocktonian of the Yr. Stockton Bd. of Realtors, 1978, Outstanding Citizen Calif. State Senate & Assembly, 1978; the Marian Jacobs Writers & Poets Symposium was established in her honor; recipent Pole Model award Tierra del Oro, Girl Scout U.S., 1989. Republican. Roman Catholic. Home and Office: 4350 Mallard Creek Circle Stockton CA 95207

JACOBS, MARY MARGARET, real estate property manager; b. Beaver Dam, Wis., Apr. 26, 1939; d. Reynold Ambrose and Olive Selma (Plankel) Deniger; m. John Robert Jacobs, Oct. 20, 1962 (div. Dec. 1984); children: Jerome, James, Kathleen Thomas, Karen. BS, U. Wis., 1961. With JMB Property Mgmt. Co., Phoenix, 1979—, mgr. shopping ctr., 1981-83, mgr. shopping ctr. and office complex, 1984, area supr., 1985-88, asst. v.p., 1988—. Mem. Xavier Parents' Assn., Brophy Coll. Preparatory Mothers' Guild; chmn. bd. dirs. Franciscan Renewal Ctr., pension and profit sharing com. Mem. Inst. Real Estate Mgmt. (cert. property mgr. 1986), Bldg. Owners Mgmt. Assn., Ariz. Multihouse Assn., SW Shopping Ctr. Profls., Phoenix Bd. Realtors. Republican. Roman Catholic. Office: JMB Property Mgmt Co 4041 N Central Ave #555 Phoenix AZ 85012

JACOBS, NED L., real estate developer; b. Atlanta, Ga., Mar. 19, 1949; s. Calvin M. and Mildred C. (Jennings) J.; divorced. BBA, Ga. State U., 1971. Founder, pres. Clearview Sch., L.A., 1972; pres. Jacobs & Assocs., Malibu, Calif., 1980—; bd. dirs. Clearing House for Info. on Learning Disabilities, L.A., 1976. Dir. local chpt. ARC, 1980-82. Mem. Nat. Assn. Corp. Real Estate Execs. (L.A. chpt.), Nat. Assn. Pvt. Spl. Edn. Schs. Wash., Calif. Assn. Pvt. Spl. Edn. Schs. L.A., Kiwanis (pres. Malibu club) 1979-80. Republican. Office: Clearview Sch 2000 Stoner Ave West Los Angeles CA 90025

JACOBS, RANDALL BRIAN, lawyer; b. N.Y.C., July 8, 1951; s. John and Evelyn (Teper) J.; m. Teri Gould, July 4, 1976; 1 child, Jillian. BA, Coll. of Idaho, 1972; JD, U. West L.A., 1978. Bar: Calif., D.C., Wis. Lawyer B. Randall Jacobs Law Corp., Santa Monica, Calif., 1978—; real estate broker Morgan Reed & Co., Santa Monica, 1979—; pvt. investigator Randy Brian Assocs., Santa Monica, 1976—. Reserve deputy sheriff, L.A. County Sheriff, L.A., 1979—. Mem. Shom Rim Soc., Nat. Rifle Assn., Masons, Shriners. Office: Law Offices B R Jacobs 2309 Ocean Park Blvd Santa Monica CA 90405

JACOBS, WILLIAM PATRICK, telecommunications company executive; b. Oakland, Calif., Nov. 17, 1935; s. William Patrick Burke and Rachael Constance (Arellanes) Scott; children from previous marriage: Debra Ann, William Patrick Jr., Michael David, Nadine Louise; m. Anita Marie Fullen, June 11, 1977. AA, Chabot Coll., 1980; BS, Calif. Coast U., 1986, MBA, 1988. Technician telecommunications Pacific Telephone, Oakland, 1956-67; mgr. Pacific Telephone, San Francisco, 1967-77; cons. telecommunications Am. Bell Internat., Tehran, Iran, 1977-79; mgr. Pacific Bell, San Ramon, Calif., 1979—. Author various poems. Served with U.S. Army, France, 1953-55. Mem. Nat. Rifle Assn., Calif. Rifle & Pistol Assn.,San Ramon Libr. Assn., Los Padrinos Club, Cursillo de Christianidad (San Francisco). Republican. Roman Catholic. Home: 1004 Overlook Dr San Ramon CA 94583-2304 Office: Pacific Bell 2600 Camino Ramon Rm 3N700 San Ramon CA 94583

JACOBSEN, IAN CHRISTIAN, management consultant; b. Palo Alto, Calif., May 14, 1938; s. Lydik Stegumfeldt and Doris Isabelle (Wetzel) J.; m. Bonnie Jean Brazil, June 22, 1969. AB in Econ., Stanford U., 1961, grad. study social sci., 1961-62. Cert. mgmt. cons. From employment rep. to mgr. staff devel. Stanford U., Calif., 1963-76; personnel mgr. Duty Free Shoppers Group, Ltd., Honolulu, 1976-79; corp. v.p. personnel Duty Free Shoppers Group, Ltd., Hong Kong and Honolulu, 1979-83; pres. The HR Link, Sunnyvale, Calif., 1983--; Bd. dirs. PC-SIG, Sunnyvale. With U.S. Army, 1962-68. Mem. Am. Soc. Tng. & Devel. (Outstanding Svc. award 1985), Am. Soc. Personnel Adminstrs, Inst. Mgmt. Cons. (bd. dirs. 1987-88), Profl. & Tech. Cons. Assn. (pres. chpt. 1988—, Exceptional Svc. award 1989), Sunnyvale C. of C. (pres. elect 1988—, pres. 1989—). Home: 568 Los Olivos Dr Santa Clara CA 95050 Office: The HR Link 333 Cobalt Way Ste 107 Sunnyvale CA 94086

JACOBSEN, KIM ANDREW, educational administrator, computer consultant; b. Fresno, Calif., May 17, 1952; s. Elmer Ernest and Violet Marie (Rassmussen) J.; m. Shirley Ann Kuhns, Dec. 18, 1976; children: Timothy Andrew, Kristi Lyn. BA in English, Calif. State U., Fresno, 1975. Cert. tchr. Calif. Payroll clk. Tenneco West, Inc., Del Rey, Calif., 1970-73, office mgr., 1973-76; tchr. Washington Jr. High Sch., Sanger, Calif., 1976-80, tchr. computers, 1980-84; coord. computer edn. Sanger Unified Sch. Dist., 1984—; computer cons., Fresno, 1985—; computer technician, Fresno, 1986—; tchr. computers adult edn. Nat. U., Fresno, 1988. Editor Instrnl. Svcs., 1986-88. Treas. Little League Baseball, Fresno, 1984—. Calif. Dept. Edn. grantee, 1981, 83. Mem. Computer Using Educator (v.p. 1981-82). Republican. Lutheran. Home: 1757 S Homsy St Fresno CA 93727 Office: Sanger Unified Sch Dist 1905 7th St Sanger CA 93657

JACOBSEN, LAREN, programmer/analyst; b. Salt Lake City, June 15, 1937; s. Joseph Smith and Marian (Thomas) J.; B.S., U. Utah, 1963; m. Audrey Bartlett, July 29, 1970 (div.); children—Andrea, Cecily, Julian. Programmer, IBM Corp., 1963-70; systems programmer Xerox Computer Services, 1970-79; sr. systems analyst Quotron Systems, Los Angeles, 1979-86; programmer/analyst Great Western Bank, 1987—; pres. Prescient Investments Co., 1975-82. Served with USAR, 1961. Mem. Am. Guild Organists (dean San Jose chpt. 1967), Mensa. Home: PO Box 91174 Los Angeles CA 90009 Office: 9401 Corbin Ave Northridge CA 91328

JACOBSEN, RICHARD T., mechanical engineering educator; b. Pocatello, Idaho, Nov. 12, 1941; s. Thorleif and Edith Emily (Gladwin) J.; m. Vicki Belle Hopkins, July 16, 1959 (div. Mar. 1973); children: Pamela Sue, Richard T., Eric Ernest; m. Bonnie Lee Stewart, Oct. 19, 1973; 1 child, Jay Michael; stepchild: Erik David Lustig. BSME, U. Idaho, 1963, MSME, 1965; PhD in Engring. Sci., Wash. State U., 1972. Registered profl. engr., Idaho. Instr. U. Idaho, 1964-66, asst. prof. mech. engring., 1966-72, assoc. prof., 1972-77, prof., 1977—, chmn. dept. mech. engring., 1980-85, assoc. dean engring., 1985—, assoc. dir. Ctr. for Applied Thermodynamic Studies, 1975-86, dir., 1986—. Author: International Union of Pure and Applied Chemistry, Nitrogen-International Thermodynamic Tables of the Fluid State-6, 1979; Oxygen-International Thermodynamic Tables of the Fluid State-9, 1987, Ethylene-International Thermodynamic Tables of the Fluid State-10, 1988, ASHRAE Thermodynamic Properties of Refrigerants (2 vols.), 1986; numerous reports on thermodynamic properties of fluids, 1971—; contbr. articles to profl. jours. NSF sci. faculty fellow, 1968-69; NSF rsch. and travel grantee, 1976-83; Nat. Bur. Standards grantee, 1974-89. Mem. ASME (faculty advisor 1972-75, 78-84, chmn. region VIII dept. heads com. 1983-85, honors and awards chmn. 1985—, K-7 tech. com. thermophys. properties 1985—, chmn. 1986-89, rsch. com. properties of steam, 1988—, gen. awards com. 1985—, chmn. 1988-90, com. on honors 1988-90), Soc. Automotive Engrs. (Ralph R. Teetor Edn. award, Detroit 1968), ASHRAE (co-recipient Best Tech. Paper award 1984), Sigma Xi, Tau Beta Pi, Phi Kappa Phi Disting. Faculty award 1989). Office: U Idaho/Coll Engring Office of Dean Janssen Engring Bldg 125 Moscow ID 83843

JACOBSEN, ROBERT ALLEN, aircraft company executive, consultant; b. Kingsburg, Calif., Jan. 27, 1943; s. Everett Lewis J. and Frances Irene (Rush) Finfrock; m. Jennifer Lynn Nielsen, Jan. 30, 1965; children: Jonathan, Aaron. BS, U. Calif., Berkeley, 1965, MS, 1967. Aerospace engr. NASA, Ames Research Ctr., Moffett Field, Calif., 1967-79; dir. tech. engring. Lear Fan, Ltd., Reno, 1979-82; chief engr. Lear Fan, Ltd., 1982-85; engring. mgr. Hexcel Corp., Pleasanton, Calif., 1985-87; v.p. and gen. mgr. Sierra Composite Design, Reno, 1987-88; v.p. ops. Nevatech Industries, Reno, 1988-89; design mgr. Bruce Industries, Dayton, Nev.; cons. Walther, Key, et al, Reno, 1988—. Nation chief NW YMCA, Cupertino, Calif., 1974-75. Mem. AIAA, Soc. for Advancement of Materials and Processes Engring., Aircraft Owners and Pilots Assn., Pi Tau Sigma. Democrat. Club: Sierra Silent Soarers (Reno).

JACOBSEN, THOMAS HAROLD, genealogist; b. Ballerup, Denmark, Aug. 12, 1918; s. Anders and Anna E. M. (Sorenson) J.; brought to U.S., 1929, naturalized by Act of Congress; student U. Utah; m. Erika Elfriede Seiter, Jan. 31, 1940; children—Carma Erika, Kathryn Irene, Connie Leah, Harold Andrew. Coordinator records div. Geneal. Soc., Salt Lake City, 1936-51, coordinator microfilm div., 1951-61, asst. treas., 1956-61; Utah State archivist, records adminstr., 1963-83. Served with AUS, 1944-48, maj. Res. ret. Recipient Silver Platter award Utah Geneal. Assn., 1983, Outstanding Svc. award Nat. Micrographics Assn., 1980. Fellow Assn. Info. and Image Mgmt.; mem. Nat. Rifle Assn., Utah Hist. Soc. Inventor microfilm accessories, archival table. Author: Ancestry of Carma Erika Jacobsen, 1943, 44; Genealogical Lesson Plans, 3 vols., 1954; Manual to Microfilming, 1959; Microfilming in the State of Utah, 1964; Guide to Official Records of Genealogical Value in the State of Utah, 1980. Contbr. articles on archives, geneology, law to publs. Home: 196 W 2900 S Bountiful UT 84010

JACOBSON, ALBERT HERMAN, JR., industrial and systems engineer; b. St. Paul, Oct. 27, 1917; s. Albert Herman and Gertrude (Anderson) J.; m. Elaine Virginia Swanson, June 10, 1960; children: Keith, Paul. BS, Yale U., 1939; SM, MIT, 1952; MS, U. Rochester, 1954; PhD, Stanford U., 1976. Registered profl. engr., Calif. Pers. asst. Yale U., New Haven, 1939-40; indsl. engr. Radio Corp. Am., Camden, N.J., 1940-43; chief engr. Naval Ordnance Office, Rochester, N.Y., 1946-57; staff engr. Eastman Kodak Co., Rochester, 1957-59; assoc. dean coll. engring. and architecture Pa. State U., University Park, 1959-61; pres. Knapic Electro-Physics Inc., Palo Alto, Calif., 1961-62; prof. sch. engring. San Jose State U., 1962—, co-founder, coord. cybernetic systems grad. program, 1968—; cons. in field, Calif., Ariz., Ill., 1962—, Lockheed, Motorola, Santa Fe R.R., 20th Century Fox, Banner Container, Sci. Mgmt. Corp., Northern Telecom etc. Author: Military and Civilian Personnel in Naval Administration, 1952, Railroad Consolidations and Transportation Policy, 1975; editor: Design and Engineering of Production Systems, 1984. Chmn. Pers. Commn. City of Mountain View, 1958-68; scoutmaster, Stanford Area Coun. Boy Scouts of Am., Palo Alto, 1970-83, coun. mem. Lt. comdr. USNR, 1943-46. Alfred P. Sloan fellow Program Exec. Devel. MIT, 1951-52; fellow NSF, Stanford, 1965-66; recipient Award of Merit Stanford Coun. Boy Scouts Am., 1976. Mem. Am. Soc. Engring. Edn., Inst. Indsl. Engrs., Am. Prodn and Inventory Control Soc. (bd. dirs. 1975—), Sigma Xi, Tau Beta Pi. Lutheran. Home: 1864 Lime Tree Ln Mountain View CA 94040 Office: San Jose State U Sch Engring 1 Washington Sq San Jose CA 95192

JACOBSON, DAVID BERNARD, English educator; b. N.Y.C., Aug. 13, 1928; s. Manes and Ida Lillian (Einson) J.; m. Patricia Elaine Holcomb, Nov. 3, 1961; children: Valerie Jacobson Anderson, Melinda, Tamara. AB, Queens Coll., 1949; MA, Stanford U., 1957; post grad., U. Calif., Berkeley, 1956-59. Cert. secondary sch. tchr., Calif. Instr. U. of Puget Sound, Tacoma, Wash., 1959-60; writer, editor Sunset Books, Menlo Park, Calif., 1961-62; instr. Contra Costa Coll., San Pablo, Calif., 1962-88; writer, editor free lance, Calif., 1955—; dir., actor free lance, Calif., London, N.Y.C, 1945—; reviewer text book publs., 1962—; cons. Individual Learning Systems, San Rafael, Calif., 1971. Author: Program for Revision, 1974; Contbr. articles to profl. jours.. Pres. AFT Local 1754, San Pablo, Calif., 1977-79. Served with U.S. Army, 1951-53. Grantee CCC Found., San Pablo, 1976, 77, 86; fellow U. of Puget Sound (Danforth), Tacoma, 1961. Mem. Nat. Council of Tchrs. of English, FACCC. Democrat. Club: PH Tennis (Pleasant Hill, Calif.).

JACOBSON, DONALD THOMAS, management consultant; b. Powers Lake, N.D., June 5, 1932; s. Martin I. and Gladys E. (Thronson) J.; BA, Whitman Coll., 1954; MBA, Stanford U., 1956; m. Andrea Marie Moore, Aug. 14, 1954; 1 child, Kathryn E. Hanson. Sales and mktg. mgmt. Guy F. Atkinson Co., Portland, Oreg., 1959-63; sales control mgr. Boise Cascade Corp., Portland, 1964-66; v.p. and dir. rsch. Lund, McCutcheon, Jacobson, Inc., Portland, 1966-74; pres. Mgmt./Mktg. Assocs., Inc., Portland, 1974—; chmn. Oreg. Bus. Workshops, 1974-76; exec. com., dir. Full-Circle, Inc., 1971-77. Lt. U.S. Army, 1956-59. Decorated commendation ribbon; recipient Oreg. Econ. Devel. award, 1973; Mem. Am. Mktg. Assn. (pres. Oreg. chpt. 1972-73), Am. Mgmt. Assn., Inst. Mgmt. Cons. (cert.; founding mem., founder and pres. Pacific N.W. chpt. 1980-81), Mktg. Rsch. Assn., Nat. Assn. Bus. Economists, Portland Metro. C. of C. (bd. dirs. 1987—, chmn.'s award Outstanding Svc., 1987), Met. Chambers Econ. Devel. Coun. Portland Area (chmn. mktg. task force 1983-85, emerging issues com., 1987—, labor policy com. 1988—, chmn. Tri-Met Task Force 1985-88, chmn. transpn. com. 1987-88), The Planning Forum (v.p. Oreg. chpt. 1986-87, bd. dirs., 1986—), U.S. Dept. Commerce (nat. def. exec. res. 1966—), (chmn. Oreg.-Idaho assn. 1969-70), Oregonians for Cost-Effective Govt. (bd. dirs. 1986—), Econ. Roundtable (coord. 1982-89), Whitman Coll. Alumni Assn. (pres. 1975-77), Stanford U. Bus. Sch. Assn. (founding pres. Portland chpt. 1971-72), Phi Beta Kappa. Republican. Lutheran. Contbr. articles on mgmt. and mktg. to profl. jours. Home: 3635 SW 87th #17 Portland OR 97225 Office: Mgmt/Mktg Assocs Inc Bank Of Calif Tower Ste 1460 Portland OR 97205

JACOBSON, EUGENE DONALD, educational administrator, medical researcher; b. Bridgeport, Conn., Feb. 19, 1930; s. Morris and Mary (Mendelsohn) J.; m. Laura Kathryn Osborn, June 9, 1973; children from previous marriage: Laura Ellen, Susan Ruth, Morris David, Daniel Frederick, Miriam Louise. B.A., Wesleyan U., 1951; M.D., U. Vt., 1955; M.S., SUNY-Syracuse, 1960. Assoc. prof. UCLA Sch. Medicine, 1965-66; prof., chmn. U. Okla. Sch. Medicine, Okla. City, 1966-71, U. Tex. Med. Sch., Houston, 1971-77; vice dean Coll. Medicine U. Cin., 1977-85; dean Sch. Medicine, U. Kans., Kansas City, 1985-88; dean Sch. Medicine, U. Colo., Denver, 1988—; cons. NIH, Bethesda, Md., 1968-72, mem. nat. digestive adv. bd., 1985-87; chmn. Nat. Commn., U.S. Congress, Washington, 1977-79; cons. Upjohn Co., Kalamazoo, 1970-87, G. D. Searle and Co., Chgo., 1984-85. Contbr. articles to profl. jours. Served to maj. U.S. Army, 1956-64. NIH research grantee, 1967-89. Mem. Am. Soc. Clin. Investigation, Am. Physiol. Soc., Am. Gastroenterol. Assn.(pres. 1988-89), Assn. Am. Med. Colls. Office: U Colo Sch Medicine Office of Dean 4200 E 9th St Denver CO 80262

JACOBSON, GARY CHARLES, political science educator; b. Orange, Calif., July 7, 1944; s. Charles William and Ruth Hope (Brown) J.; m. Martha Ellen Blake, June 2, 1979. A.B. in Polit. Sci., Stanford U., 1966; M.Phil., Yale U., 1969, Ph.D. in Polit. Sci., 1972. From instr. to assoc. prof. Trinity Coll., Hartford, Conn., 1970-79; from assoc. prof. to prof. polit. sci. U. Calif.-San Diego, 1979—. Woodrow Wilson fellow, 1969; NSF grantee, 1980-82. Mem. Am. Polit. Sci. Assn. (Gladys E. Kammerer award 1981), Western Polit. Sci. Assn., Midwest Polit. Sci. Assn., So. Polit. Sci. Assn. Author: Money in Congressional Elections, 1980; (with Samuel Kernell) Strategy and Choice in Congressional Elections, 1981; The Politics of Congressional Elections, 1983, 87. Office: U Calif San Diego Dept Polit Sci Q-060 La Jolla CA 92093

JACOBSON, RONALD KEITH, mental health center executive; b. Ashland, Wis., Jan. 25, 1932; s. Albert and Madeline (Bergren) J.; m. Lorraine Gertrude Tollefson, Aug. 3, 1957; children: Steven Carl, Todd David. BA, Augsburg Coll., 1959; MSW, U. Minn., 1961. Program dir. Luth. Social Services, Wittenberg, Wis., 1961-67; interim dir. Mental Health Services, Everett, Wash., 1973-74, 1979; area dir. Luth. Social Services, Seattle, 1974-75, 1984-85; exec. dir. Luth. Child Ctr., Everett, Wash., 1967—; pres. Assn. Child Care Agy., Wash. 1971-75; chmn. Licensing task force, Wash., 1980-81; mem. council on accreditation, N.Y.C., 1982-86; exec. dir. Coll. Hill Consociation, Everett, Wash., 1982-88; pres. Coalition of Execs. (Luth. Soc. Ministry Orgns.), 1986-89. Pres. Drug Abuse Council, Everett, 1969-70; chmn. Snohomish County (Wash.) Internat. Yr. Child, 1979; mem. Am. Luth. Ch. Council, Mpls., 1984-86, Region I Coun.; mem. bd. for women Evangelical Lutheran Ch. in Am., 1988—. Mem. Alliance for Children Youth and Families (bd. dirs. 1984-86). Lodge: Rotary (pres. 1980-81). Home: 13228 Marine Dr Marysville WA 98270 Office: Luth Child Ctr 4526 Federal Everett WA 98203

JACOBSON, STEPHEN SCOTT, claims specialist; b. Hammond, Ind., Sept. 1, 1962; s. Alvin Kenneth and Gloria (Alton) J. BA in Pub. Adminstrn., San Diego State U., 1986, postgrad., present. Life guard, instr. Am. Red Cross, Hammond, 1976-80; circulation asst. Calif. Western Sch. of Law, San Diego, 1981-83; adminstrn. asst. Jewish Community Ctr., San Diego, 1981-84, San Diego (Calif.) State U., 1984-86; account clerk San Diego (Calif.) Probation Dept., 1986-87; claims specialist San Diego (Calif.) Dist. Attys. Office, 1987—. Page Ind. House of Reps., Hammond, 1976. Named Honorary Youth Adv., B'Nai B'Rith Orgn., San Diego, 1986. Democrat. Jewish. Office: San Diego Dist Atty Office 220 W Broadway PO Box X1011 San Diego CA 92112

JACOBY, IRVING, physician; b. N.Y.C., Sept. 30, 1947; s. Philip Aaron and Sylvia (Newman) J.; m. Sara Kay Vartanian; children: James Tyler, Kathryn Aaryn. BS magna cum laude, U. Miami, Coral Gables, Fla., 1969; MD, Johns Hopkins U., 1973. Diplomate Am. Bd. Internal Medicine, Am. Bd. Infectious Diseases, Am. Bd. Emergency Medicine. Intern Boston City Hosp., 1973-74, resident in medicine, 1974-75, chief resident, 1978-79; resident in medicine Peter Bent Brigham Hosp., Boston, 1975-76, fellow in infectious diseases, 1976-78; asst. dir. emergency med. svcs. U. Mass. Med. Ctr., Worcester, 1979-84; asst. dir. emergency med. svcs. U. Calif. Med. Ctr., San Diego, 1984-88, assoc. prof. med. surgery, 1988—; bd. dirs. hyperbaric med. ctr.; vis. physician, cons. infectious diseases Soroka Med. Ctr., Ben Gurion U., Beer-Sheva, Israel, 1980; flight physician New Eng. Life Flight, Worcester, 1982-84, Life Flight Aeromed. Program U. Calif., 1984-87; mem. trauma ctr. planning com., resuscitation com., pharmacy and therapeutics com., disaster com. U. Mass. Med. Ctr., 1980-84; mem. adv. bd. state communications com. Office Emergency Med. Svcs., Commonwealth Mass., 1982-84, bd. dirs. Cen. EMS Corp., 1982-84. Fellow Am. Coll. Emergency Physicians; mem. ACP, Am. Soc. Microbiology, Infectious Diseases Soc. Am., Undersea and Hyperbaric Med. Soc., Johns Hopkins Med. and Surg. Assn., Iron Arrow Leadership Soc., Omicron Delta Kappa, Phi Kappa Phi, Alpha Epsilon Delta, Phi Eta Sigma. Office: U Calif San Diego Med Ctr 225 Dickinson St H665A San Diego CA 92103

JACOBY, PETER FREDRICKSON, utilities executive; b. Laramie, Wyo., July 27, 1947; s. Glenn J. and Dorothy (Fredrickson) J.; m. Margaret E. Judd, Mar. 5, 1973 (div. 1983). BA in Music magna cum laude, U. Wyo., 1969; Diploma, U. Vienna Acad. Music, Austria, 1973. Opera coach Zurich Opera House, Switzerland, 1975-76; gen. ptnr. E.L. Price Assoc., San Francisco and Chgo., 1976-78; exec. dir. The Prelude Co., San Francisco, 1978-80; pres., chief exec. officer Bighorn Energy Co., Ft. Collins, Colo., 1980—; exec. v.p. Newcomb Securities Co., N.Y.C., 1981-84; sr. mgr. E.L. Price Bank, Galveston, Tex., 1983-87, also bd. dirs.; pres., chief exec. officer Code A Check, Inc., Cheyenne, Wyo., 1988—. Bd. ddirs. Van Ness Arts Ctr., San Francisco, 1978-79, Ft. Collins Art Inc., 1981-82. Sgt. U.S. Army, 1969-71. Republican. Episcopalian. Home: 315 W 8th Ave Cheyenne WY 82001 Office: Code A Check Inc 6101 N Yellowstone Rd Cheyenne WY 82009

JAFFE, MARK LESTER, record company executive; b. N.Y.C., Feb. 8, 1958; s. Herbert L. and Tina Jaffe. BA in Communications, UCLA, 1980; MBA in Mktg. and Fin., U. So. Calif., 1982. Asst. acct. exec. Leo Burnett, Chgo., 1982-83; acct. exec. Della, Femina & Travisano, L.A., 1983-84; dir. children's mktg. A&M Records, L.A., 1984—. Active Music Industry for the City of Hope, L.A., 1987. Mem. Nat. Acad. Recording Arts and Scis., Assn. Booksellers for Children, Nat. Assn. Record Merchandisers, Nat. Assn. Record Merchandisers, So. Calif. Assn. for Edn. Young Children. Office: A&M Records 1416 N LaBrea Hollywood CA 90028

JAFFE, MARTIN ABRAHAM, tax executive; b. Los Angeles, Sept. 15, 1953; s. Norman and Charlene R. (Hoffenburg) J. AB, Occidental Coll., 1975; JD, Hastings Coll. Law, 1981; MBA, U. Calif., Berkeley, 1981. Bar: Calif. 1981, U.S. Dist. Ct. (9th dist.); CPA. Asst. mgr. Security Pacific Nat. Bank, L.A., 1975-77; tax mgr. Arthur Anderson & Co., San Francisco, 1981-86; tax dir. The Chronicle Pub. Co., San Francisco, 1987—.

JAGER, MERLE LEROY, aerospace engineer; b. Eugene, Oreg., Sept. 22, 1942; s. Earl Christian and Alma Marie (Jensen) J.; m. Shannon Kay Jacobsen, Mar. 18, 1967; children: Holly, Peter, Melanie, Marissa.. BS in Mech. Engring., Oreg. State U., 1965; MS in Aeronautical Engring., U. So. Calif., 1967. Aerodynamicist Lockheed-Calif. Co., Burbank, 1965-68; rsch. engr. The Boeing Co., Seattle, 1968-70; aerodynamics engr. Gates Learjet Corp., Torrance, Calif., 1970; project engr. Irvin Industries, Inc., Gardena, Calif., 1971-73; aerodynamics mgr. Northrop Corp., Hawthorne, Calif., 1973—. Patentee in field. Treas. Goldenwest Assn., Westminster, Calif., 1976-78; tribal chief YMCA Indian Princess Program, Huntington Beach, Calif., 1986-87; bishopric counselor Mormon Ch., Westminster, 1986—. Mem. AIAA, Tau Beta Pi, Pi Tau Sigma, Sigma Tau. Republican. Home: 15282 Notre Dame St Westminster CA 92683 Office: Northrop Corp Aircraft Div One Nothrop Ave Hawthorne CA 90250

JAGODZINSKI, RUTH CLARK, health company administrator; b. N.Y.C., Feb. 24, 1938; d. John Kirkland and Ruth (Fishwick) Clark; m. Thomas John Jagodzinski, 1962 (div. 1974); children: Christine Ruth, James Clark. Grad., Roosevelt Hosp. Sch. Nursing, 1959. RN Nev., N.Y.; cert. substance abuse counselor, cert. program adminstr. Nev. Dir. nursing Vegas Valley Convalescent Hosp., Las Vegas, 1970-72; adminstr. Detox Unit Sunrise Hosp., Las Vegas, 1973-75; coordinator program Care Unit, North Las Vegas, 1975-77; adminstr. program Sunrise Home Health Care, Las Vegas, 1977-83, owner, adminstr., 1983—; chair State Cert. Bd. Alcohol and Drug Abuse, Carson City, Nev., 1980-86, also mem. 1976-86. Mem. Gov.'s Adv. Bd. Alcohol/Drug Abuse, Carson City, 1977—; pres./v.p. We Care Found., Las Vegas, 1974—. Mem. Home Health Care Assn. Nev. (pres. 1980-84). Office: Sunrise Home Health CAre 3101 Maryland Pkwy #104 Las Vegas NV 89101

JAKUBEK, JAMES JOSEPH, insurance agent; b. Milw., Aug. 28, 1934; s. Frank F. and Vera H. (Shutkowski) J.; m. Delores Hill, Aug. 3, 1963; children: Jennifer, Jean, Julie, Jim. BS, Marquette U., 1957. Agent Conn. Gen., Evanston, Ill., 1958-66; gen. mgr. Am. Gen., Northfield, Ill., 1966-72; sr. sales agent Allstate Ins., Scottsdale, Ariz., 1972—. Pres. Scottsdale Bus. Alliance, 1985. Republican. Roman Catholic. Club: Serra (v.p. 1988). Office: Allstate 4110 N 70th St #101 Scottsdale AZ 85251

JAMES, BRENT CARL, healthcare executive, biomedical professor; b. Shelley, Idaho, Dec. 28, 1950; s. John Carl and Barbara Joyce (Hendrickson) J.; m. Karen Anne Stephenson, Nov. 21, 1979 (Sept. 1986); 1 child, Ian Carl. BS in Computer Sci., U. Utah, 1974, BS in Med. Biology, 1975, MD, 1978, M in Statis., 1983. Sr. systems programmer 1st Security Bank, Salt Lake City, 1972-79; asst. dir. cancer dept., dir. computing dept. ACS, Chgo., 1979-83; lectr. Harvard U. Sch. of Pub. Health, Boston, 1984-85, asst. prof., 1985-86; dir. med. rsch. Intermountain Health Care, Salt Lake City, 1986—; pres. Health Care Software, Salt Lake City, 1980—; vis. lectr. dept. biostatis. Harvard U. Sch. of Pub. Health, 1986—; adj. prof. dept. family and preventive medicine U. Utah, Salt Lake City, 1987—; bd. dirs. Logical/Eustat, Inc., Salt Lake City. Contbr. numerous articles to profl. jours. Capt. USPHS, 1979-80. Nat. Merit scholar, 1969. Mem. Assn. Computing Machinery, Computer Sci. of IEEE, Am. Statist. Assn., Am. Assn. for Med. Systems and Informatics, Phi Beta Kappa. Mormons. Office: Internat Health Care 36 S State St #2200 Salt Lake City UT 84111

JAMES, CHOON HUAY, real estate broker; b. Singapore, July 18, 1957; d. Beng Chian and Lye Beoy (Oh) Chua; m. Mark Olov James, June 30, 1978; children: Robbie, Mark, Jeremy. BA in English, Brigham Young U., Laie, Hawaii, 1979. Lic. realtor. Spl. instr. Hawaii communications and lang. arts dept. Brigham Young U., Laie, 1981-86, spl. instr. bus. div., 1986—; realtor assoc. Coop. Realty, Laie, 1983-87, real estate broker, 1987-88; real estate broker Coldwell Banker, Kaneohe, Hawaii, 1988—. Program chmn. Brigham Young U. Women's Orgn., Laie, 1985; chmn. Beautification Com. Contest, Laie, 1987; mem Laie Community Assn., 1986—, PTA, Laie, 1985—, Relief Soc., Singapore, Utah, Laie, 1971—. Mem. Honolulu Bd. Realtors, Nat. Assn. Realtors. Mormon. Home: 55-047 Naupaka St Laie Point HI 96762 Office: Coldwell Banker 46-005 Kawa St Kaneohe HI 96744

JAMES, CHRISTOPHER, lawyer; b. Portland, Oreg., Nov. 26, 1948; s. Arthur Montague and Martha Rose (Lehman) J.; m. Christine Ruth Ehrsam, Jan. 28, 1972; children: Aaron Thomas, David Christopher, Daniel Jonathan. BA, U. Oreg., 1970, JD, 1974. Bar: Oreg. 1974. Assoc. James C. Maletis, P.C. Portland, 1974-8l; ptnr. Maletis and James, 198l-83, Mitchell, Lang & Smith, 1983-86; pvt. practice 1987--. Mem. ABA, Oreg. State Bar, Multnomah Athletic Club. Home: 2943 NW Imperial Terr Portland OR 97210

JAMES, CLAYTON WALLACE, resort hotel management executive; b. St. Louis, Nov. 4, 1939; s. John Rex and Jeanne (Wallace) J.; m. Sharon A. Orlin, Sept. 2, 1966; children: Scott, Jean. BS, Ariz. State U., 1962. Mgr. Rock Resorts, various locations, 1962-76; v.p., gen. mgr. Admiralty Resorts, Port Ludlow, Wash., 1976-78; exec. v.p., chief operating officer Lakeway Resorts, Austin, Tex., 1978-82; v.p., gen. mgr. Sandpiper Bay Resort, Port St. Lucie, Fla., 1982-84, Rock Resorts, Moran, Wyo., 1984—. Chmn. Teton County Visitors Coun., Jackson, Wyo., 1986—; dir. Grand Teton Natural History Assn., Moose, Wyo., 1987—. Cpl. USMC, 1962-64. Mem. Nat. Restaurant Assn., Am. Hotel/Motel Assn. (dir. 1989—), Colo./Wyo. Hotel/Motel Assn. (dir. 1986—), Rotary (Jackson). Republican. Home and Office: Box 250 Moran WY 83013

JAMES, EDGAR JEROME, oil company executive, accountant; b. Jackson, Miss., July 5, 1955; s. Thomas E. and Maurine (Cook) J.; m. Susan Denise Massey, Dec. 15, 1979; children: Christopher Robert, Jonathan Thomas. BS cum laude, U. Ala., 1977; M Profl. Accountancy, U. Tex., 1978. CPA, Colo. Tax specialist Arthur Young & Co., Denver, 1977-8l, Hamilton Bros. Oi. Co., Denver, 1981-83; chief fin. officer Club Oil & Gas, Inc., Denver, 1983—. Mem. AICPA, Colo. Soc. CPA's, Internat. Assn. for Fin. Planning, Ind. Petroleum Assn. Am., Colo. Soc. Petroleum Accts., Beta Gamma Sigma, Beta Alpha Psi, Omicron Delta Kappa. Office: Club Oil & Gas Inc 2300 S Tower 600 17th St Denver CO 80202

JAMES, GEORGE BARKER, II, apparel industry executive; b. Haverhill, Mass., May 25, 1937; s. Paul Withington and Ruth (Burns) J.; m. Beverly A. Burch, Sept. 22, 1962; children: Alexander, Christopher, Geoffrey, Matthew. AB, Harvard U., 1959; MBA, Stanford U., 1962. Fiscal dir. E.G. & G. Inc., Bedford, Mass., 1963-67; fin. exec. Am. Brands Inc., N.Y.C., 1967-69; v.p. Pepsico, Inc., N.Y.C., 1969-72; sr. v.p., chief fin. officer Arcata Corp., Menlo Park, Calif., 1972-82; exec. v.p. Crown Zellerbach Corp., San Francisco, 1982-85; sr. v.p., chief fin. officer Levi Strauss & Co., San Francisco, 1985—; bd. dirs. Pacific States Industries, Inc., Sequoia Pacific Systems, Inc. Author: Industrial Development in the Ohio Valley, 1962. Mem. Andover (Mass.) Town Com., 1965-67; mem. Select Congl. Com. on World Hunger; adv. council Calif. State Employees Pension Fund; chmn. bd. dirs. Towle Trust Fund; trustee Nat. Corp. Fund for the Dance, Cate Sch., Levi Strauss Found., Stern Grove Festival Assn.; mem. San Francisco Com. on Fgn. Relations; trustee Zellerbach Family Fund, Mid-Peninsula High Sch.; chmn. bd. trustees San Francisco Ballet Assn.; bd. dirs. Stanford U. Hosp.; mem. adv. bd. Protection Mut. Ins. Co. Served with AUS, 1960-61. Mem. Newcomen Soc. N.Am., Fin. Execs. Inst. Clubs: Pacific Union, Commonwealth Calif., Family (San Francisco); Menlo Circus (Atherton, Calif.); Harvard (Boston and N.Y.C.); Harvard (San Francisco) (bd. dirs.). Home: 207 Walnut St San Francisco CA 94118 Office: Levi Strauss & Co Levi's Pla 1155 Battery St San Francisco CA 94111

JAMES, HERB MARK (HERBERT GEORGE JAMES), foundation and insurance executive; b. Trail, B.C., Can., Jan. 30, 1936; s. George William and Violet Ethyl (Corbin) J.; student bus. adminstrn. Simon Fraser U., 1965-69; m. Patricia Helen Boyd, Nov. 1, 1958; 1 child, Brad Mark. Founder, Internat. Sound Found., Ottawa, Can., 1967—, Blaine, Wash., 1975—; mem. bus. adv. bd. U.S. Senate, 1981—; mem. Can. Internat. Devel. Agy.; founder Better Hearing Better Life projects, Fiji, Kenya, Cayman Islands, Nepal, Costa Rica, Pakistan, Guatemala. Musician B. Pops Orch. Govt. of Can. grantee, 1973-83. Mem. Blaine C. of C., Masons, Shriners, Demolay. Office: USA Am Bldg PO Box 1587 Blaine WA 98230

JAMES, JERRY HAYMAN, dentist; b. Atlanta, Jan. 21, 1954; s. Jesse Clopton and Barbara Brown (Hayman) J.; m. Laurie Burbank, Sept. 29, 1979; children: Jesse Luke, Beau Andrew, Aubrey Brooke. BA, U. Ala., 1976; postgrad., Abilene Christian U., 1976-78; DDS, Baylor Coll. Dentistry, 1981. Pvt. practice Lovington, N.Mex., 1985--. Mem. ADA, Acad. Gen. Dentistry, Am. Orthodontic Soc., N.Mex. Dental Assn., Rotary (pres. Lovington chapt. 1987--). Republican. Mem. Ch. of Christ. Home: 1006 West Ave I Lovington NM 88260

JAMES, JOHN WARREN, educator; b. Danville, Ill., Feb. 16, 1944; s. Ralph Joseph and Edith E. (Fox) J.; m. Marcy E. Marks, June 20, 1975 (div. 1978); m. Mary Jess Walton, Dec. 20, 1980. Student, Ill. State U., 1965-66, Mount. State, 1970-74. Mktg. Humble Oil Co., Orange, Calif., 1967-70; v.p. Ultrasun Tech. Inc., Culver City, Calif., 1974-75; pres. Solar Twenty, Inc., Culver City, 1975-77; dir. tng. Life Appreciation Tng., Inc., L.A., 1977-82; pres. The Grief Recovery Inst., L.A., 1982—; mem. staff Nat. Found. Funeral Service, Evanston, Ill., 1986--;. Author: The Grief Recovery Handbook, 1987. With USMC, 1962-65. Republican. Office: The Grief Recovery Inst 8306 Wilshire Blvd Suite 21-A Beverly Hills CA 90211

JAMES, JOSEPH RUSSELL, business executive; b. Seattle, July 15, 1924; s. Isaac Russell and Ruby Valerie (Standley) J.; m. Delphine Jane Houghtaling, June 30, 1946; children: Andrew Russell, Deborah Diane. BA, U. Wash., 1945. Pres., chief executive officer Ye Olde Curiosity Shop, Inc., Seattle, 1946—; dir. Emergency Med. Svcs. Found., Seattle, 1974—, King County Med. Blue Shield, Seattle, 1985—, Am. Auto. Club of Wash., 1972—, chmn., 1984-88. Lt. (j.g.) USN, 1942-46. Mem. Rotary (pres. Seattle chpt. 1971-72), Athletic Club (pres. Wash. chpt. 1985-86), 101 Club (pres. 1974-76), Scottish Rite, Shriners, Theta Chi (v.p. 1944-45), Beta Gamma Sigma. Republican. Home: 2215-28 Ave W Seattle WA 98199 Office: Ye Olde Curiosity Shop Inc 1001 Alaskan Way Seattle WA 98104

JAMES, LOUIS EARL, II, sales and marketing professional; b. Los Angeles, July 29, 1951; s. Louis Earl and Lida Faye (Snyder) J.; m. Cynthia Jean Schoenfeld, Oct. 19, 1973; children: Louis K., Kristopher, Shaun, Bonnie Jean, Rebecca. Student, El Camino Coll., 1969-70, Tulsa U., 1973, Brigham Young U., 1973-75. V.p. The Lens Man, San Diego, 1976-80; pres. Osaka Optical USA, Salt Lake City, 1981-84, Louis James and Assocs., Salt Lake City, 1984—. Missionary Mormon Ch., Okla., 1970-72. Named Eagle Scout Boy Scouts Am., Los Angeles, 1967. Office: Louis James and Assocs. 5200 Pinemont Dr Murray UT 84123

JAMES, NORMAN JOHN, aerospace engineer; b. Jamestown, N.Y., Aug. 26, 1932; s. Basil and Constance James; m. Susan Connor, June 9, 1962 (div. Sept. 1981); m. Ginna Froelich, Oct. 1, 1981. BS in Indsl. Design, Pratt Inst., 1956. Sr. designer styling GM, Warren, Mich., 1954-63; sr. designer Def. Rsch. Labs. GM, Goleta, Calif., 1963-67; account exec. Sundberg-Ferar Inc., Southfield, Mich., Burbank, Calif., 1967-73; design chief hwy. systems Rohr Industries Inc., Chula Vista, Calif., 1974-77; engring. specialist RMI, Inc., National City, Calif., 1977-86; dir. tech. svc. Tesa Design Inc., San Diego, 1986-87; group engr. Rohr Industries Inc., Chula Vista, Calif., 1988—. Patentee show car, city bus, telescope mounting system. Mem. L.A. Astron. Soc. (bd. dirs. 1968-73, pres. 1969), San Diego Astron. Assn. Republican. Office: Rohr Industries Inc Foot of H St Chula Vista CA 92012

JAMES, SANDRA ELAINE, chamber of commerce administrator; b. Long Beach, Calif., Feb. 26, 1956; d. Charles and Ruth (Gould) Eien; m. Vince James, May 27, 1979. BSBA, Calif. State U., Long Beach, 1979. Visual presentation mgr. Broadway Dept. Store, Long Beach, 1977-79; from staff mem. to exec. dir. Ashland (Oreg.) C. of C. and Vis. Bur., 1979—; mem. So. Oreg. State Coll.Regional Adv. Bd., So. Oreg. Visitors Assn. Bd., Oreg. Assn. Conv. and Visitors Burs. Bd., Oreg. Chamber Execs. Bd. Mem. Am. Soc. Assn. Execs., Oreg. Soc. Assn. Execs., Oreg. Tourism Inst. Lodge: Soroptimists. Home: 1237 Ashland Mine Rd Ashland OR 97520

JAMES, SONDRA DIANE, ballet school director; b. Long Beach, Calif., Feb. 14, 1952; d. Emerson George and Dorothy Louise (Ebbert) J. AA with Honors, Long Beach City Coll., 1974; BFA cum laude, U.S. Internat. U., 1976; MBA, Nat. U., 1978. Dancer Lakewood (Calif.) Philharm. Dance Co., 1960-64, Ballet Gala, Los Angeles, 1965-67; tchr. ballet Audrey Share Sch. Dance, Long Beach, 1966-69; artistic dir. Greta Anderson, Los Alamitos, Calif., 1967-69; dancer The Royal Ballet Co., London, 1967-69, Internat. Ballet Co., San Diego, 1973-76; artistic dir. Ice Capades Chalet, La Jolla, Calif., 1976-79; asst. to pres. Nat. U., San Diego, 1977-79; dir., owner The Ballet Conservatory, Spring Valley, Calif., 1979—; dir., choreographer South Bay Jr. Ballet Co., San Diego, 1987—, Internat. Folk Ballet, San Diego, 1981—; guest speaker Profl. Skaters Guild Am. Conv., 1979. Creator, choreographer: (ballets) The Magic Book, 1982, Carnival, 1986, Etudes, 1987, Hansel and Gretel, 1987. Mem. Better Bus. Bur., San Diego, 1985—, Friends of East County Arts, Inc., 1988—. Named one of Outstanding Young Women in Am. U.S. Jaycees, 1977. Mem. Royal Acad. Dancing (registered), San Diego Dance Alliance, San Diego Watercolor Soc. Democrat. Presbyterian. Clubs: Cottonwood Golf (El Cajon, Calif.); Entrepreneur (San Diego). Office: The Ballet Conservatory 8300 Paradise Valley Rd Spring Valley CA 92077

JAMES, WAYNE EDWARD, electrical engineer; b. Racine, Wis., Apr. 2, 1950; s. Ronald Dean James and Arlene Joyce (Mickelsen) Dawson; m. Bertie Darlene Tague, July 18, 1972; children: Terry Scott, Kevin Arthur. BS in Electronic Engring. Tech., U. So. Colo., 1976. Electronic technician Lawrence Livermore (Calif.) Nat. Lab., 1976-80; electronic technician Inmos Corp., Colorado Springs, Colo., 1980-86, assoc. CAD engr., 1986-87; CAD engr. United Techs. Microelectronics Ctr., Colorado Springs, 1988—. Sec.-treas. Stratmoor Hills Vol. Fire Dept., Colorado Springs, 1983, 84, lt., 1985, capt., 1986. Served with USN, 1968-72. Named Fireman of Yr., Stratmoor Hills Vol. Fire Dept., 1983. Lutheran. Office: United Techs Microelectronics Ctr 1575 Garden of Gods Rd Colorado Springs CO 80907

JAMES, WILLIAM LANGFORD, aerospace engineer; b. Southampton, Va., Jan. 13, 1939; s. Leroy and Worthie (Murphy) J.; m. Elaine Cecilia Reed; children: William Jr., Terri Lynne. Student, Va. State Coll., 1956, Hampton Inst., 1958; BS, Calif. State U., Los Angeles, 1962, MS, 1964; postgrad., U. Nev., Reno, 1984-86; spl. engring. studies, UCLA, 1970-82. Rsch. engr. non-metallic materials lab. N.Am. Aviation, L.A., 1960-67; project engr. program office, rsch. analyst, materials scientist, mem. tech. staff The Aerospace Corp., El Segundo, Calif., 1967—. Contbr. numerous articles and reports to profl. publs.; patentee in field. Mem. AAAS, Soc. Advancement Material and Process Engring. (vice-chmn. 1987). Home: Box 19735 Los Angeles CA 90019 Office: Aerospace Corp M5 712 Box 92957 Los Angeles CA 90009

JAMES, WILLIAM RAE, food company executive; b. Carroll, Iowa, July 1, 1950; s. Paul Emmert and Sylvia Lavonne (Boose) J.; m. Leslie J. Huey,

June 5, 1988. BA, Drake U., 1972. Div. mgr. The Bubble Machine, San Francisco, 1975-78; v.p., gen. mgr. Rod's Food Products div. Merico Inc., Industry, Calif., 1978—. Lt. (j.g.) USN, 1972-75. Mem. Calif. Restaurant Assn., So. Calif. Grocers Assn., Calif. Dairy Inst., Sigma Phi Epsilon. Republican. Office: Rods Food Products 17380 Railroad St Industy CA 91749

JAMESON, WILLIAM JAMES, retired judge; b. Butte, Mont., Aug. 8, 1898; s. William J. and Annie J. (Roberts) J.; m. Mildred Lore, July 28, 1923; children: Mary Lucille (Mrs. Walker Honaker), William James, Jr. A.B., Mont. U., 1919, J.D., 1922, LL.D., 1952; LL.D., U. Man., Can., 1954, Rocky Mountain Coll., 1969; Dr. Laws, McGeorge Coll. Law, 1965. Bar: Mont. 1922. Assoc. Johnston, Coleman and Johnston, Billings, 1922-29; mem. Johnston, Coleman & Jameson, 1929-40, Coleman, Jameson & Lamey, 1940-57; judge U.S. Dist. Ct. for Mont., 1957-69, sr. judge, 1969-87; judge Temporary Emergency Ct. Appeals, 1976-87; Bd. dirs. Nat. Jud. Coll., 1963-64; trustee Nat. Inst. Trial Advocacy, 1971-77. Mem. Mont. Ho. of Reps., 1927-30; Sch. Bd. Trustee, Billings, 1930- 32; chmn. Yellowstone County chpt. A.R.C., 1931-45. Recipient Disting. Achievement award Law Sch., Gonzaga U., 1970. Fellow Am. Bar Found.; mem. ABA (bd. govs. 1943-46, assembly del. 1946-53, pres. 1953-54, pres. endowment 1961-63, chmn. sect. jud. adminstrn. 1963-64, chmn. spl. com. on adminstrn. criminal justice 1969-73, recipient gold medal 1973), Mont. Bar Assn. (pres. 1936-37), Am. Law Inst. (mem. council 1956—), Am. Judicature Soc. (pres. 1956-58, Herbert Lincoln Harley award 1974), Am. Legion, Phi Delta Phi. Methodist. Lodges: Masons; Lion (dist. gov. 1941-42). Home: Westpark Village 2351 Solomon Ave #100 Billings MT 59102

JAMISON, DAVID W., marine scientist; b. Portland, Oreg., Apr. 23, 1939; s. Edgar W. and Nina (Ray) J.; m. Susan Elizabeth Porter, Dec. 23, 1962 (div. 1974); children—Adam, Elizabeth; m. Nancy Louise Kasper, Apr. 7, 1979; stepchildren—Kevin, Keith, Kelly. BS, Whitman Coll., 1961; postgrad. U. Oreg., 1961-62; MS, U. Wash., 1966, PhD, 1970. Remote sensing scientist Wash. Dept. Natural Resources, Olympia, 1969-70, marine scientist, 1970-74, supr. baseline studies dept. ecology, 1974-78, dir. marine rsch. and devel., 1978-80, mgr. forestry rsch. and devel., 1980-82, chief marine scientist, 1983—; gov.'s rep. U.S. Dept. Interior outer continental shelf rsch. adv. com., 1974-78; cons. NOAA Interagy. Com. on Ocean Pollution Rsch., Devel. and Monitoring, 1981; mem. adv. com. Puget Sound Water Quality Authority, 1985-86, chmn. rsch. com. 1987—; mem. tech. adv. com. Puget Sound Estuary Program, 1985—; mem. tech. work groups Puget Sound Dredge Disposal Analysis Study, 1985—. Bd. dirs. Boston Harbor Assn., 1980-88, chmn. utilities com., 1981; mem. Thurston County Shorelines adv. com., 1973-74, 82-83. Mem. Am. Soc. Photogrammetry, Marine Tech. Soc., Pacific Estuarine Rsch. Soc., Sigma Xi. Contbr. articles to profl. jours. Office: State of Wash Dept Natural Resources Olympia WA 98504

JAMISON, WARREN ROBERT, writer; b. Mitchell, S.D., Aug. 24, 1924; s. Robert William and Della Emily (Beyer) J.; m. Kitty Sue Wilkerson, Oct. 7, 1961; children: Cynthia Sue, Brian Erik. Author: (with Danielle Kennedy) How To List and Sell Real Estate in the 90's, 1989, (with Ed McMahon) Superselling, 1989, (with Michael McLaughlin and Russell S. Dynde) Screw: The Truth about Walpole Prison by the Guard Who Lived It, 1989; editor: The Official Guide To Success (Tom Hopkins), 1983, also softcover, Brit., French, Japanese and other fgn. edits., How To Master the Art of Selling (Hopkins), 1980, also softcover and numerous fgn. edits., Art of Public Speaking (Ed McMahon), 1986, softcover edit., 1987. Mem. Authors Guild, Am. Soc. Authors and Journalists. Home: 4550 Via Marina #101 Marina Del Rey CA 90292

JANECKY, DAVID RICHARD, geochemist; b. Meeker, Colo., Apr. 24, 1953; s. Richard Myron and Lois Margaret (McKenzie) J.; m. Louise Adel Anderson, Dec. 19, 1986; 1 child, Gregg David. Student, U. Bergen, Norway, 1973-74; AB, U. Calif., 1975; postgrad., U. Calif., Santa Barbara, 1975-76, Stanford U., 1977-78; PhD, U. Minn., 1982. Teaching asst. U. Calif., Santa Barbara, 1975-76; rsch. asst. Stanford U., 1976-78; rsch. asst. U. Minn., Mpls., 1978-82, rsch. assoc., 1982-84; staff mem. Los Alamos (N.Mex.) Nat. Lab., 1985—. Contbr. articles to profl. jours. Sec. Los Alamos Mountaineers, 1987. NSF grantee, 1978-84; post-doctoral rsch. fellow Los Alamos Nat. Lab., 1984-85, grnateeee U.S. Dept. Energy/Office Basic Energy Scis., 1985—, grantee Inst. Geophysics and Planetary Physics, 1986—. Mem. Am. Geophys. Union, Geochem. Soc., Internat. Assn. Geochemistry & Cosmochemistry, Soc. Econ. Geology, Norway Geol. Soc., Oceanography Soc. Democrat. Methodist. Office: Los Alamos Nat Lab Inc Isotope Geochemistry Group 7 MS J514 Los Alamos NM 87545

JANESKI, WILLIAM LOUIS, real estate broker, developer; b. Pittsburg, Kans., Nov. 28, 1932; s. William Charles and Elnora Fern (Sanders) J.; m. June Elizabeth Cover, Feb. 19, 1955; children: David Scott, Stephen Gregrey, William Andrew, Nancy Elizabeth. Student, U. Kans., 1951-52, Strayer Coll. Accountancy, 1955-56, UCLA, 1985; PhD in Bus. Mgmt., Pacific Western U., 1986. Exec. v.p. Century 21 Real Estate Co. Va., McLean, 1972-74; founder, pres., chief exec. officer Realty World Corp., Annandale, Va., 1974-80; pres. Worldwide Organizational Systems, Los Angeles and Walnut Creek, Calif., 1980-83; v.p. Very Important Properties, Rolling Hills Estates, Calif., 1984—. Mem. Realtors Polit. Action Com., 1979—. Served with USN, 1952-54, Korea. Named to Million Dollar Club, No. Va. Bd. Realtors, 1969, 70, 71, 72, 73. Mem. Nat. Assn. Realtors. Republican. Methodist. Lodge: Optimists (local pres. 1971-72). Home: 2357 Palos Verdes Dr W Unit 3 Palos Verdes CA 90274-2706 Office: Very Important Properties 609 Deep Valley Dr Rolling Hills Estates CA 90274

JANIGIAN, BRUCE JASPER, lawyer, educator; b. San Francisco, Oct. 21, 1950; s. Michael D. Janigian and Stella (Minasian) Amerian; m. Susan Elizabeth Frye, Oct. 4, 1986; 1 child, Alan Michael. AB, U. Calif., Berkeley, 1972; JD, U. Calif., San Francisco, 1975; LLM, George Washington U., 1982. Bar: Calif. 1975, U.S. Supreme Ct. 1979, D.C. 1981. Dir. Hastings Rsch. Svcs., Inc., San Francisco, 1973-75; judge adv. in Spain 1976-78; atty. advisor AID, Washington, 1979-84; dep. dir., gen. counsel Calif. Employment Devel. Dept., Sacramento, 1984—; prof. law McGeorge Sch. Law, U. Pacific, Sacramento, 1986—, Inst. on Internat. Legal Studies, Salzburg, Austria, summer 1987; designated prof. law London Inst. on Comml. Law, summer 1989; vis. prof. law U. Salzburg, Austria. Editor: Financing International Trade and Development, 1986, 87, 89. Coordinating fund raiser March of Dimes, Sacramento, 1987. Comdr. USN, 1975-79, commr. USN-USMC Ct. Mil. Rev., 1978-79, mem. Res. Recipient meritorious svc. award U.S. Dept. State, 1981; Fulbright scholar, 1989—. Mem. Calif. Bar Assn., D.C. Bar Assn., Sacramento Bar Assn. (exec. com. taxation sect. 1988-89), Sacramento Met. C. of C., Nat. Rep. Lawyers Assn., Naval Res. Officers Assn., Knights of Vartan, Phi Beta Kappa. Home: 1631 12th Ave Sacramento CA 95818 Office: Calif Employment Devel Dept 800 Capitol Mall MIC 53 Sacramento CA 94280

JANNOTTA, MARJORIE J., adult educaor; b. Alamagoroo, N.Mex., Oct. 31, 1946; d. John Wesley and Norma Evelyn (Higginbotham) Mitchell; m. Roger Louis Jannotta, Feb. 26, 1966 (div. 1970); m. Charles Albert Hundertmark, Dec. 10, 1979; 1 stepchild, Kali Hundertmark. BS, U. N.Mex., 1971, MA, 1973, PhD, 1988. Ind. ednl. program developer and designer Albuquerque, 1974-81; dir. ednl. resources Heights Gen. Hosp., Albuquerque, 1981-83; mgr. program devel. ACCLIVUS Corp., Dallas, 1983-85; mgmt. educator, program developer S.W. Community Health Svcs., Albuquerque, 1985—; nat. cons. in field; lectr. in field; conductor seminars in field; instr., guest lectr. U. N.Mex., 1980—, U. Albuquerque, 1980—. Contbr. articles to profl. jours. MBA thesis advisor U. Phoenix, Albuquerque, 1987-88. Tandy Ednl. grantee, 1985; recipient Still Media award, 1978, 77. Mem. Am. Assn. Adult and Continuing Edn., Am. Soc. Tng. and Devel., Am. Mgmt. Assn., Assn. for Psychol. Types., Rio Grande Bird Rsch. (sec. 1983-89). Democrat. Office: SW Community Health Svcs PO Box 26666 Albuquerque NM 87125-6666

JANOWICZ, PETER FRANCIS, electrical contractor; b. L.A., Sept. 14, 1940; s. Frank Francis and Kathryn Mary (Leblance) J.; m. Karen Kaye Blankenship, June 8, 1963; children: Ellen Lee, Alene Mary. Elec. apprentice Ageles Electric, Long Beach, Calif., 1963-67; foreman Ageles Electric, Long Beach, 1969-73; elec. apprentice Keith Electric, Long Beach, 1967-68; journeymam Keith Electric, L.A., 1968-69; journayman Keith Electric, Long Beach, 1969-73; elec. contractor, owner A&E Electric, Manhattan Beach, Calif., 1973—; v.p. J&E Electric, 1988; v.p. J&E Electric, elec. contractor AMBE. Sgt. with U.S. Army, 1958-61. Club: Manhattan Country. Lodge: Kanwanis. Republican. Roman Catholic. Office: A&E Electric 15233 Grevillea Lawndale CA 90260

JANSEN, GERALD JAMES, management company executive; b. Aberdeen, S.D., Jan. 26, 1940; s. John Henry and Cressie Marie J.; m. Lloydene Jansen, Nov. 28, 1987. BS, Oreg. State U., 1962, MBA, 1969. Sales mgr. Smith div. Electronic Spec., Inglewood, Calif., 1968-69; account rep. Univac div. Sperry, 'L.A., 1969-72; div. mgr. Decision Making Info., Orange, Calif., 1972-74; pres. Rsch. System, Inc., Manhattan Beach, Calif., 1974-76; dist. mgr. Honeywell, L.A., 1976-80; reg. mgr. Northern Telecom, L.A., 1980-85; pres. Janus M.I.S. Costa Mesa, Calif., 1985-87; prin. Janus Fin., Manhattan Beach, 1987-88; pres. Janus Mgmt. Svcs. Inc., Manhattan Beach, 1988—; bd. dirs. Synergetic Solution & Systems, Torrance, Calif. Capt. U.S. Army, 1963-67, Korea. Home: 231 O St Springfield OR 97477

JANSEN, ROBERT BRUCE, consulting civil engineer; b. Spokane, Wash., Dec. 14, 1922; s. George Martin and Pearl Margaret (Kent) J.; m. Barbara Mae Courtney, Sept. 18, 1943. BSCE, U. Denver, 1949; MSCE, U. So. Calif., 1955. Registered profl. engr., Calif., Colo., Wash. Chief Calif. Div. Dam Safety, Sacramento, 1965-68; chief of ops. Calif. Dept. Water Resources, Sacramento, 1968-71, dep. dir., 1971-75, chief design and constrn., 1975-77; asst. commr. U.S. Bur. Reclamation, Denver, 1977-80; cons. civil engr. 1980—; cons. Tenn. Valley Authority, Chattanooga, 1981—, So. Calif. Edison Co., Rosemead, 1982—, Pacific Gas and Electric, San Francisco, 1982—, Hydro-Quebec, Mon., Can., 1986—, Ala. Power Co., Birmingham, 1985—. Author: Dams and Public Safety, 1983; editor: Safety of Existing Dams, 1983; co-author: Development of Dam Engineering in the United States, 1988; editor and co-author: Advanced Dam Engineering for Design, Construction, and Rehabilitation, 1988. Mem. U.S. Com. on Large Dams (chmn.1979-81), ASCE, Internat. Soc. Soil Mechanics and Found. Engrng., Assn. State Dam Safety Ofcls., Nat. Acad. Engrng. (elected). Home and Office: 509 Briar Rd Bellingham WA 98225

JANSS, WILLIAM CLUFF, resort development executive; b. Los Angeles, June 9, 1918; s. Edwin and Florence (Cluff) J.; m. Anne Searls, Dec. 10, 1940 (dec. 1972); children: Suzanne Ferguson, Mary Daenzer, William Cluff Jr.; m. Glenn Candy Cooper, June 16, 1973. BA, Stanford U., 1940. Chmn. Sun Valley (Idaho) Co., 1968-77; dir. Janss Investment Co., Thousand Oaks, Calif., 1978—; bd. dirs. Manville Corp., Denver, 1978—. Mem. U.S. Olympic Ski Team, Internat. Council Mus. Modern Art, 1980—, Nat. Com. Phillips Collection, 1981—; trustee U.S. Ski Edn. Found. Park, Utah, 1981—. With USAF, 1943-45. Named to Nat. Ski Hall of Fame, 1979. Club: Bohemian (San Francisco). Home: PO Box 107 Sun Valley ID 83353

JANSSEN, WILLIAM ALBERT, investment company executive; b. Pitts., Sept. 22, 1926; s. Albert Henry and Haddassa Elizabeth (Hamilton) J.; m. Margaret Mary Baker, Sept. 12, 1953 (div. Jan. 1981); children: Janine, William Albert Jr., Felicia, Kevin, Dennis, Mary Denise, Patricia. BS, St. Francis Coll., 1959; cert. in computer programming, Columbia Inst., 1961; postgrad., U. Ariz., 1963. Compt., instr. Franciscan Order TOR's, Loretto, Pa., 1948-61; sr. acct. Troupe, Kehoe, Whiteaker & Kent, Tucson, 1961-63; pres. Western Computing Cons., Inc., Tucson, 1963-65; sec.-treas. Tucson Data Ctr., 1965-69; pres., chief exec. officer 1st Gt. Western Investment Corp., T, 1969-76, Westates Investments, Inc., T, 1976—; chmn. Tucson chpt. SBA, 1965. Bd. dirs. Tucson Awareness House, 1965-69; dist. adminstr. Little League Baseball, Tucson, 1973-87, bd. dirs., Williamsport, Pa., 1984-87. Recipient Jefferson award Am. Inst. Pub. Svc., 1980. Mem. Nat. Assn. Accts. (pres. 1966-67), Data Processing Mgmt. Assn. (pres. 1968-69), Tucson C. of C. (chmn. bus. cons. 1964), Toastmasters, Civitan, K.C. (fin. sec. 1962-72). Republican. Roman Catholic. Home: 5644 E 6th St Tucson AZ 85711 Office: Westates Investments Inc 721 N 4th Ave Tucson AZ 85705

JANTZEN, J(OHN) MARC, educator; b. Hillsboro, Kans., July 30, 1908; s. John D. and Louise (Janzen) J.; m. Ruth Patton, June 9, 1935; children: John Marc, Myron Patton, Karen Louise. A.B., Bethel Coll., Newton, Kans., 1934; A.M., U. Kans., 1937, Ph.D., 1940. Elementary sch. tchr. Marion County, Kans., 1927-30, Hillsboro, Kan., 1930-31; high sch. tchr. 1934-36; instr. sch. edn. U. Kans., 1936-40; asst. prof. Sch. Edn., U. of Pacific, Stockton, Calif., 1940-42; assoc. prof. Sch. Edn., U. of Pacific, 1942-44, prof., 1944-78, prof. emeritus, 1978—, also dean sch. edn., 1944-74, emeritus, 1974—, dir. summer sessions, 1940-72; condr. seminars; Past chmn. commn. equal opportunities in edn. Calif. Dept. Edn.; mem., chmn. Commn. Tchr. Edn. Calif. Tchrs. Assn., 1956-62; mem. Nat. Council for Accreditation Tchr. Edn., 1969-72. Bd. dirs. Ednl. Travel Inst., 1965—. Recipient Hon. Service award Calif. Congress of Parents and Tchrs., 1982; Paul Harris fellow Rotary Found., 1980. Mem. Am., Calif. edn. research assns., Calif. Council for Edn. Tchrs., Calif. Assn. of Colls. for Tchr. Edn. (sec.-treas. 1975-85), N.E.A., Phi Delta Kappa. Methodist. Lodge: Rotary. Home: 117 W Euclid Ave Stockton CA 95204

JANURA, JAN AROL, apparel manufacturing executive; b. Chgo., May 12, 1949; s. Harold Charles and Violet Mary J.; B.S., Colo. State U., 1971; M.A., Fuller Theol. Sem., 1973. Area dir. Young Life Campaign, Seattle, 1973-76; chief exec. officer, dir. Carol Anderson, Inc., Los Angeles, 1977—; chief fin. officer Fresh Retail Chain, 1988—, Outdoor Videos Inc., 1988—; pres. Los Angeles Electric Motorcar Co., 1979-80; bd. dirs. Western Leadership Found., Starr Leadership Found., SW Leadership Found., NW Fellowship, Rivergate Fellowship, Crested Butte, Colo., Glendale (Calif.) Fellowship; mem Presl. Task Force, 1986; founder Janura Library, 1986. Mem. Rep. Nat. Com., 1986, Rep. Presdl. Task Force, 1984-86; trustee Janura Library, Glendale, Colo. Weyerhaeuser fellow, 1972-73, Glendale Fellowship Found.; recipient Salesman of Yr. award, 1983, 84. Clubs: Snowcreek Athletic, Los Angeles Athletic, Wash. Athletic, N.Y. Athletic, Admirals (life), Solomon Hill Hunt, Scootney Farms Hunting. Office: 5770 Anderson St Vernon CA 90058

JAQUITH, GEORGE OAKES, ophthalmologist; b. Caldwell, Idaho, July 29, 1916; s. Gail Belmont and Myrtle (Burch) J.; BA, Coll. Idaho, 1938; MB, Northwestern U., 1942, MD, 1943; m. Pearl Elizabeth Taylor, Nov. 30, 1939; children: Patricia Ann Jaquith Mueller, George, Michele Eugenie Jaquith Smith. Intern, Wesley Meml. Hosp., Chgo., 1942-43; resident ophthalmology U.S. Naval Hosp., San Diego, 1946-48; pvt. practice medicine, specializing in ophthalmology, Brawley, Calif., 1948—; pres. Pioneers Meml. Hosp. staff, Brawley, 1953; dir., exec. com. Calif. Med. Eye Council, 1960—; v.p. Calif. Med. Eye Found., 1976—. Sponsor Anza council Boy Scouts Am., 1966—. Gold card holder Republican Assocs., Imperial County, Calif., 1967-68. Served with USMC, USN, 1943-47; PTO. Mem. Imperial County Med. Soc. (pres. 1961), Calif. Med. Assn. (del. 1961—), Nat., So. Calif. (dir. 1966—, chmn. med. adv. com. 1968-69) Soc. Prevention Blindness, Calif. Assn. Ophthalmology (treas. 1976—), San Diego, Los Angeles Ophthal. Socs., Los Angeles Research Study Club, Nathan Smith Davis Soc., Coll. Idaho Assocs., Am. Legion, VFW, Res. Officers Assn., Basenji Assn., Nat. Geneal. Soc., Cuyamaca Club (San Diego), Elks, Phi Beta Pi, Lambda Chi Alpha. Presbyterian (elder). Office: 665 S Western PO Box 511 Brawley CA 92227

JARBOE, LARRY WILLIAM, traffic systems company executive; b. Leitchfield, Ky., Nov. 29, 1952; s. Charles Henry and Agnes M. (Williams) J.; m. Mary Theresa Burke, Feb. 2, 1974; children: Jennifer Leigh, Daniel Lee. Student, U. Louisville, 1976-78, U. Phoenix, 1986—. Mgr. inventory control Safetran Systems, Inc., Louisville, 1974-82; mgr. materials control and data processing Safetran Traffic Systems, Inc., Colorado Springs, Colo., 1982—. Mem. Am. Prodn. and Inventory Control Soc. Democrat. Roman Catholic. Office: Safetran Traffic Systems PO Box 7009 Colorado Springs CO 80933

JARESS, MICHAEL FREDERICK, financial consultant; b. Detroit, Sept. 7, 1940; s. Robert Vern and Helen Wilhemina (Freedman) J.; m. Jo Ellen Schafer (div. 1974); children: Jon Cary, Michele Lea; m. Doreen Lynn Sheer, Jan. 10, 1985; 1 child, Damien Michael. Student, Wayne State U., 1958-62, Mich. State U., 1962-63. Profl. bowler Detroit, 1958-63, Los Angeles, 1963-65; fin. advisor, gen. agt. Detroit, 1965-69, Orange County, Calif., 1969-74, San Diego, 1974—; fin. advisor, cons. 1400 cos., So. Calif., 1974—; fin. advisor Found. Fin. Edn., 1980—, Nuva Internat. Plus Inc., San Diego; seminar lectr. in field. Author: Congratulations...You Made It Again, 1980. Fundraiser Winners Circle Internat., San Diego, 1986—, Family Found., San Diego, 1987—. Mem. Am. Soc. Tng. Devel., Nat. Speakers Assn. Republican. Lodge: Optimist. Office: Foundations Fin 1288 Camino Del Rio N #240 San Diego CA 92108

JARRAT, HENRI AARON, semiconductor company executive; b. Moroco, Aug. 24, 1938; came to U.S., 1968, naturalized, 1976; s. Leon El Jarrat and Hola Bendayan; children: Catherine, David. EE, Inst. Poly., Grenoble, France, 1960-64; MPhysics, Faculty Scis., Grenoble, France, 1964. Dept. mgr. optoelectronics Tex. Instruments Inc., Dallas, 1974-76; corp. v.p., gen. mgr. bipolar group Motorola, Inc., Mesa, Ariz., 1976-83; pres., chief operating officer VLSI Tech. Inc., San Jose, Calif., 1983-87; chmn., chief exec. officer United Silicon Structures, San Jose, 1988—; bd. dirs. Zymos, Sunnyvale, Calif. Bd. govs. NCCJ, Santa Clara, Calif., 1985. Jewish. Office: United Silicon Structures 1971 Concourse Dr San Jose CA 95131

JARRETT, RONALD DOUGLAS, nurse; b. Oceanside, Calif., Oct. 31, 1952; s. William Douglas and Francia Elizabeth (Ladd) J.; m. Lois Ellen Shurmaster, Dec. 23, 1984; 1 child, Emily Rose. ASN, Cabrillo Coll., 1981; BSN, SUNY, 1988; postgrad., Lincoln Law Sch. Sacramento, 1989—. Hosp. corpsman USN, 1970-74; psychiat. technician County Mental Health Dept., Santa Cruz, Calif., 1974-81; RN, ICU, CCU Watsonville Community Hosp., Calif., 1981-84, Dominican Santa Cruz Hosp., Santa Cruz, Calif., 1983-85; RN, ICU U. Calif. Davis Med. Ctr., Sacto, 1986-87; RN, ICU./ER Calif. Healthcare Cons., Sacto, 1987—; affiliate faculty Am. Heart Assn., Salinas, Calif., 1979-84; assoc. faculty Cabrillo Coll. nursing dept., Aptos, Calif., 1983-85. Served to HM3 USN, 1970-73. Fellow AMORC; assoc. Wilson Ctr. for Scholars. Republican. Home: 9400 Marcola Ct Sacramento CA 95826-5221

JARVIS, DANIEL COOK, college official, computer consultant; b. Greeley, Colo., Jan. 27, 1965; s. David LaVerl and Barbara Joy (Cook) J.; m. Evelyn Martin, Aug. 28, 1986; children: Bretton Daniel, Jenessa LyRay. A in Computer Sci., Ricks Coll., 1988. Computer cons. Information Plus, Rexburg, Idaho, 1987—; programmer, analyst Ricks Coll., Rexburg, 1987—. Author: Challenges and Progress, 1988. Jr. asst. scoutmaster Boy Scouts Am., Meridian, Idaho, 1982-84, asst., 1989—. Mormon. Home: 543 S 5th W Apt #E4 Rexburg ID 83440 Office: Ricks Coll Rexburg ID 83460-4176

JARVIS, DONALD BERTRAM, judge; b. Newark, Dec. 14, 1928; s. Benjamin and Esther (Golden) J.; B.A., Rutgers U., 1949; J.D., Stanford U., 1952; m. Rosalind C. Chodorcove, June 13, 1954; children: Nancie, Brian, Joanne. Bar: Calif. 1953. Law clk. Justice John W. Shenk, Calif. Supreme Ct., 1953-54; assoc. Erskine, Erskine & Tulley, 1955; assoc. Aaron N. Cohen, 1955-56; law clk. Dist. Ct. Appeal, 1956; assoc. Carl Hoppe, 1956-57; adminstrv. law judge Calif. Public Utilities Commn., San Francisco, 1957—; mem. exec. com. Nat. Conf. Adminstrv. Law Judges, 1986-88, sec. 1988-89; pres. Calif. Adminstrv. Law Judges Council, 1978-84; mem. faculty Nat. Jud. Coll., U. Nev., 1977, 78, 80. Chmn. pack Boy Scouts Am., 1967-69, chmn. troop, 1972; class chmn. Stanford Law Sch. Fund, 1959, mem. nat. com., 1963-65; dir. Forest Hill Assn., 1970-71. Served to col. USAF Res., 1949-79. Decorated Legion of Merit. Mem. Am. Bar Assn., State Bar Calif., Bar Assn. San Francisco, Calif. Conf. Pub. Utility Counsel (pres. 1980-81), Nat. Panel Arbitrators, Am. Arbitration Assn., Air Force Assn., Res. Officers Assn., De Young Museum Soc. and Patrons Art and Music, San Francisco Gem and Mineral Soc., Stanford Alumni Assn., Rutgers Alumni Assn., Phi Beta Kappa (pres. No. Calif. 1973-74), Tau Kappa Alpha, Phi Alpha Theta, Phi Alpha Delta. Home: 530 Dewey Blvd San Francisco CA 94116 Office: 505 Van Ness Ave San Francisco CA 94102

JASENSKY, RONALD DEAN, biotechnologist; b. Madison, Wis., Sept. 6, 1950; s. Richard John and Arlene Elizabeth (Spielde) J.; m. Dinah Lee Herron, Sept. 18, 1982; children: Nathan, Alex. BS, U. Wis., 1973, MS, 1976, PhD, 1979. Registered pharmacist, Ariz., Wis. Pharmacy intern Madison Gen. Hosp., 1979-80, pharmacist, 1980; prodn. mgr. Promega Biotech, 1980-83, Bolton Biologicals, Portland, Oreg., 1983; lab. mgr. Vega Biotechnologies, Tucson, Ariz., 1983-88; rsch. scientist U. Ariz., Tucson, 1988—. Contbr. articles to profl. jours. Vilas fellow Oscar Rennebohm Found., 1975. Mem. Am. Chem. Soc., AAAS, Sigma Xi. Home: 7444 N La Oesta Tucson AZ 85704 Office: U Ariz Dept Biotech BSW Rm 359 Tucson AZ 85721

JASINEK, GARY DONALD, newspaper executive; b. Champaign, Ill., Sept. 17, 1950; s. William Gerald and Doris Margaret (Brethorst) J.; m. Carole Riggs, Nov. 9, 1974; 1 child, Andrea Sarah. Student, San Diego State U., 1968-74. Reporter The Daily Californian, El Cajon, 1975-76, city editor, 1976-79; editor Red Oak (Iowa) Express, 1979-81; editor Los Alamos (N.Mex.) Monitor, 1981-83, editor, gen. mgr., 1983-87; asst. city editor Tacoma (Wash.) Morning News Tribune, 1987-88, metro editor, 1988—. Mem. N.Mex. AP Mng. Editors (bd. dirs. 1984, pres. 1986, 1st Pl. Column award and 2d Pl. Editorial award 1982, 2d Pl. Editorial award 1984, 1st Pl. Editorial award 1985, 86), Calif. Newspaper Pubs. (1st Pl. award 1979), Iowa Press Assn. (3d Pl. award 1981), N.Mex. Press Assn. (1st Pl. award 1982). Home: 5223 View Point Dr NW Gig Harbor WA 98335 Office: Morning Tacoma New Tribune PO Box 11000 Tacoma WA 98405

JAY, DAVID JAKUBOWICZ, management consultant; b. Danzig, Poland, Dec. 7, 1925; s. Mendel and Gladys Gitta (Zalc) Jakubowicz; came to U.S., 1938, naturalized, 1944; BS, Wayne State U., 1948; MS, U. Mich., 1949, postgrad., 1956-57; postgrad. U. Cin., 1951-53, MIT, 1957; m. Shirley Anne Shapiro, Sept. 7, 1947; children: Melvin Maurice, Evelyn Deborah. Supr. man-made diamonds GE Corp., Detroit, 1951-56; instr. U. Detroit, 1948-51; asst. to v.p. engring. Ford Motor Co., Dearborn, Mich., 1956-63; project mgr. Apollo environ. control radiators N.Am. Rockwell, Downey, Calif., 1963-68; staff to v.p. corporate planning Aerospace Corp., El Segundo, Calif., 1968-70; founder, pres. PBM Systems Inc., 1970-83; pres. Cal-Best Hydrofarms Coop., Los Alamitos, 1972-77; cons. in field, 1983—. Pres., Community Design Corp., Los Alamitos, 1971-75; life master Am. Contract Bridge League. Served with USNR, 1944-46. Registered profl. engr., Calif., Mich., Ohio. Fellow Inst. Advancement Engring.; mem. Inst. Mgmt. Sci. (chmn. 1961-62), Western Greenhouse Vegetable Growers Assn. (sec.-treas. 1972-75), Tau Beta Pi. Jewish. Patentee in air supported ground vehicle, others. Home: 13441 Roane Circle Santa Ana CA 92705

JAY, ROY, communications company executive; b. Portland, Oreg., July 22, 1947. Announcer Sta. KGAR, Vancouver, Wash., 1970-72; gen. mgr. Sta. KQIV-FM, Portland, 1972-76; v.p. Underwood-McLean Assoc., Portland, 1976-78; nat. mgr. regional ops. Mutual Credit/SNTCOR, Portland, 1978-80; pres. Trade-Mark Bus. Network, Portland, 1980—; pres., founder Data-Chek Corp., Portland, 1982—; chief exec. officer, investigator, collector Law-One, Inc., 1985—; chief exec. officer Trade-Mark Legal Adminstrs., 1985—; owner Trade-Mark Computer Sales, 1985—; ptnr. Trade-Mark Express Printing, Trade-Mark Telecommunications, 1985—. Bd. dirs. Greater Portland Vis. and Conv. Assn., 1985—, chmn. mem. com., 1988—; bd. dirs. Girls Scouts of U.S.A., Columbia Pacific Region, 1986—, chmn. nominating com., 1988; bd. dirs. Mainstream Youth Program, 1985—; mem. Multnomah County Justice Coordinating Coun., 1987—; exec. dir. Oreg. Conv. and Vis. Svcs. Network, Portland, 1988—; coordinator Miss U.S.A. Pageants, 1988-89. Mem. Pre-paid Legal Svcs. Inst., Southwest Bus. Mchts. Assn., Oreg. Legal Assts. Assn., Black Profl. Network, Oreg. Assn. Minority Entreprenurs.

JAYARAM, SUSAN ANN, professional secretary; b. Stockton, Calif., Nov. 23, 1930; d. George Leroy and Violet Yvonne (Rushing) Potter; m. M. R. Jayaram, July 2, 1960. Student Pasadena Coll., 1951-52; Woodbury Coll., 1961; A.A., Long Beach City Coll., 1979. Cert. profl. sec. Sec. to mgr. First Western Bank, Los Angeles, 1953-56; sec. to pres. Studio City Bank (Calif.), 1957-60; sec. to exec. vice-pres. Union Bank, Los Angeles, 1962-81; sec. to vice chmn. Imperial Bank, Los Angeles, 1981-82; personal sec. to Howard B. Keck, chmn. W.M. Keck. Found., 1982—. Sec., bd. advisors Citizens for Law Enforcement Needs, 1972-74; dir. Los Angeles/Bombay Sister City Com.; mem. Jeffery Found. Mem. DAR (Susan B. Anthony chpt.), Jeffery Found., Assistance League So. Calif., Freedoms Found. at Valley Forge (Los Angeles chpt.), U.S. Navy League (Long Beach and Hollywood/L.A.

Councils) League of the Americas (pres. 1988—), Los Angeles Club (dir., sec. 1967-81). Editor: Angeles Club Panorama, 1979-80; California Clarion, 1978-80. Republican. Office: HB Keck 555 S Flower St Los Angeles CA 90071

JAYME, WILLIAM NORTH, writer; b. Pitts., Nov. 15, 1925; s. Walter A. and Catherine (Ryley) J.; student Princeton, 1943-44, 47-49. With Young & Rubicam Advt., Inc., 1949, Charles W. Gamble & Assos., 1949-50; asst. circulation promotion mgr. Fortune mag., 1950-51, Life mag., 1951-53, copy dir., sales and advt. promotion CBS Radio Network, N.Y.C., 1953-55; sr. copywriter McCann-Erickson, Inc., 1955-58; established own advt. creative service, 1958-71; pres. Jayme, Ratalahti, Inc., 1971—; lectr. direct mktg. Stanford U., Radcliffe Coll., worldwide mktg. confs. Producer U.S. Army radio program Music Motorized, 1945-46; editor, producer Time, Inc. TV programs Background for Judgment, 1951, Citizen's View of '52; script editor CBS Radio-UPA motion picture Tune in Tomorrow, 1954; creator promotions that launched Smithsonian, New York, Bon Appetit, Food & Wine, California, American Health, Air & Space, other nat. mags.; author script adaptations for Studio One and other TV programs, articles and stories in periodicals. Served as sgt., 2d Armored Div., AUS, 1944-46. Democrat. Episcopalian. Club: Century Assn.,(N.Y.C.). Author: (with Roderick Cook) Know Your Toes and Other Things to Know, 1963; (with Helen McCully, Jacques Pepin) The Other Half of the Egg, 1967; (opera libretto, with Douglas Moore) Carry Nation. Address: 1033 Bart Rd Sonoma CA 95476

JAYNE, TIMOTHY RANDAL, automotive repair company executive; b. Mason City, IA, June 17, 1965; s. Donald Dale and Linda K. (Gustafson) J. AAS, Lincoln Tech. Inst., West Des Moines, Iowa, 1986. Lic. inspector and qualified test and repair mechanic. Asst. shop mgr. Andy Granatelli's Tuneup Masters, North Hollywood, Calif., 1986-87; chief exec. officer Mr. Tuneup, Inc., Saugus, Calif., 1987--. Mem. Santa Clarita Valley C. of C. Republican. Methodist. Home: 7727 Lankershim Blvd Apt 306 North Hollywood CA 91605 Office: Mr Tuneup Inc 25845 San Fernando Rd Unit 8 Saugus CA 91350

JEANLOZ, RAYMOND, geophysicist; b. Winchester, Mass., Aug. 18, 1952. BA, Amherst Coll, 1975; PhD in Geology and Geophysics, Calif. Inst. Tech., 1979. Asst. prof. Harvard U., 1979-81; from asst. prof. to assoc. prof. U. Calif., Berkeley, 1982-85, prof., 1985—. Recipient Mineral Soc. Am. award, 1988; MacArthur grantee, 1988. Fellow Am. Geophysics Union (J.B. Macelware award 1984); mem. AAAS. Office: U of Calif Dept of Geology 2120 Oxford St Berkeley CA 94720 *

JEFFERDS, IAN WALKER, food products executive; b. Columbus, Ga., July 29, 1958; s. Peter and Helen Beryl (Walker) J.; m. Karen Lee Kostelyk, Apr. 14, 1984. BS, Western Wash. U., 1981. Research analyst Koch & Assocs. Environ. Cons., Reno, 1981-83; marine research biologist Ecomar Marine Cons., Santa Barbara, Calif., 1983-85; systems research analyst Electronic Data Systems, Dayton, Ohio, 1985-86; pres., gen mgr. Penn Cove Mussels, Inc., Coupeville, Wash., 1986—. Mem. Wash. Aquaculture Council, Pacific Coast Oyster Growers, Nat. Shellfish Assn. Republican. Office: Penn Cove Mussels Inc 1900 Penn Cove Rd PO Box 148 Coupeville WA 98239

JEFFERIES, JOHN TREVOR, astronomer, astrophysicist, observatory administrator; b. Kellerberrin, Australia, Apr. 2, 1925; came to U.S., 1956, naturalized, 1967; s. John and Vera (Healy) J.; m. Charmian Candy, Sept. 10, 1949; children: Stephen R., Helen C., Trevor R. MA, Cambridge (Eng.) U., 1949; DSc, U. Western Australia, Nedlands, 1962. Sr. research staff High Altitude Obs., Boulder, Colo., 1957-59, Sacramento Peak Obs., Sunspot, N.Mex., 1957-59; prof. adjoint U. Colo., Boulder, 1961-64; prof. physics and astronomy U. Hawaii, Honolulu, 1964-83, dir., Inst. Astronomy, 1967-83; dir. Nat. Optical Astronomy Obs., Tucson, 1983-87; cons. Nat. Bur. Standards, Boulder, 1960-62. Author: (monograph) Spectral Line Formation, 1968; contbr. articles to profl. jours. Guggenheim fellow, 1970-71. Fellow AAAS, Royal Astron. Soc.; mem. Internat. Astron. Union, Am. Astron. Soc., Australian Astron. Soc. Home: 6760 N Placita Manzanita Tucson AZ 85718 Office: Nat Optical Astronomy Obs PO Box 26732 Tucson AZ 85726

JEFFERSON, M. RANAE, small business owner; b. Cody, Wyo., Jan. 30, 1954; d. Virgil LeRoy Jennings and Patricia Mae (St. John) Hess; m. Henry Marshall Jefferson III, Nov. 9, 1981; children: Henry Marshall Jefferson IV, Kelly Elaine Jefferson, Shannon Ranae. Diploma, Utah Barber Coll., Salt Lake City, 1978. Barber stylist The Clip Joint, Jackson, Wyo., 1978-79, Reid's Teton Barber Shop, Jackson, 1979-81, Wayne's Barber Shop, Newport News, Va., 1981-83; owner The Hair Loft, Idaho Falls, Idaho, 1983—; educator Excelsis Beauty Coll., Idaho Falls, 1988; advisor, educator numerous schs., Idaho, 1983-88; hair designer fashion shows, 1984-86. Mem. Idaho Falls Ski Club (v.p. 1987, pres. 1988-89). Republican. Presbyterian. Home: 4228 W Broadway Idaho Falls ID 83402 Office: The Hair Loft 1678 1st St Idaho Falls ID 83401

JEFFERY, ALAN MICHAEL, health care executive; b. L.A., May 6, 1943; s. Allen Burton and Edith Esther (Eckhaus) J.; m. Sharon Anne Brodsky, July 4, 1968 (div. Nov. 1979); 1 child, Lauren Nicole. BA, Calif. State U., 1965. Corp. benefits mgr. Security Pacific Corp., L.A., 1968-85; v.p. mktg. Admar Corp., Orange, Calif., 1985—; bd. dirs. Nu-Med Regional Med. Ctr., Canoga Park, Calif., 1984—. Mem. Kaiser Permanente Consumer Coun., L.A., 1981-85, Calif. State Chamber Cost Containment Com., Sacramento, 1983-85, Orange County Employee Benefits Coun., 1986—; v.p. Employer's Health Care Coalition, L.A., 1982-85. With USN, 1965-71. Democrat. Jewish. Home: 12602 Henzie Pl Granada Hills CA 91344 Office: Admar Corp 850 Town & Country Rd Orange CA 92668

JEFFERY, JAMES NELS, protective services official; b. Torrance, Calif., May 16, 1944; s. Daryl Fredrick and Mildred Evelyn (Sogard) J. AA, Long Beach City Coll., 1964; student, Calif. State U., Long Beach, 1964-65, Calif. State U., Sacramento, 1979-80. Capt., firefighter L.A. Fire Dept., 1965-87; dir. Long Beach (Calif.) Search & Rescue Unit, 1968—; asst. chief fire div. Calif. Office Emergency Svcs., Riverside, 1987—; rep. Firescope Communications, Riverside, 1979—. Co-author emergency plans. Chmn. svc. com. Boy Scouts Am., Long Beach, 1979-81, tng. com., 1982—; bd. dirs. Long Beach Community Episepsy Clinic, 1971-72. Recipient Disting. Svc. award Long Beach Jaycees, 1977, Community Svc. award Long Beach Fire Dept., 1978, Silver Beaver award Boy Scouts Am., 1983, Commendation Mayor City of L.A., 1985. Mem. Calif. State Firemen's Assn., Nat. Coordinating Coun. on Emergency Mgmt., So. Calif Assn. Foresters and Fire Wardens, L.A. Fire Fighters Assn., Lions, Elks. Republican. Lutheran. Home: 3916 Cerritos Ave Long Beach CA 90807 Office: Office Emergency Fire Svcs PO Box 55157 Riverside CA 92517

JEFFREDO, JOHN VICTOR, aerospace engineer, manufacturing company executive, inventor; b. Los Angeles, Nov. 5, 1927; s. John Edward and Pauline Matilda (Whitten) J.; m. Elma Jean Nesmith, (div. 1958); children: Joyce Jean Jeffredo Ryder, Michael John; m. Doris Louise Hinz, (div. 1980); children: John Victor, Louise Victoria Jeffredo-Warden; m. Gerda Adelheid Pillich. Grad. in Aeronautical Engring. Cal-Aero Tech. Inst., 1948; AA in Machine Design, Pasadena City Coll., 1951; grad. in Electronics The Ordnance Sch. U.S. Army, 1951; AA in Am. Indian Studies, Palomar Coll., 1978; postgrad. U. So. Calif., 1955-58; MBA, La Jolla U., 1980, PhD in Human Rels., 1984. Design engr. Douglas Aircraft Co., Long Beach and Santa Monica, Calif., 1955-58; devel. engr. Honeywell Ordnance Corp., Duarte, Calif., 1958-62; cons. Honeywell devel. labs., Seattle, 1962-65; supr. mech. engr. dept. aerospace div. Control Data Corp., Pasadena, Calif., 1965-68; project engr. Cubic Corp., San Diego, 1968-70; supr. mech. engring. dept. Babcock Electronics Co., Costa Mesa, Calif., 1970-72; owner, operator Jeffredo Gunsight Co., Fallbrook, Calif., 1971-81; chief engr. Western Designs, Inc., Fallbrook, 1972-81, exec. dir., 1981-88, chief exec. officer, 1988—; owner, operator Western Designs, Fallbrook, 1981-87; exec. dir. JXJ, Inc., San Marcos, Calif., 1981-88, chief exec. officer, 1988—; mgr. Jeffredo Gunsight div., 1981—, chief engr. JXJ, Inc., 1987—; owner, mgr. Energy Assocs., San Diego, 1982-86; pres. Jeffredo Internat., 1984-88; chief exec. officer John-Victor Internat., San Marcos, Calif., Frankfurt, Fed. Republica Germany, 1988—; engring. cons. Action Instruments Co., Inc., Gen. Dynamics, Alcyon Corp., Systems Exploration, Inc. (all San Diego), Hughes Aircraft Co., El Segundo, Allied-Bendix, San Marcos; bd. dirs. Indian World Corp., JXJ., Inc. Author: Wildcatting; contbr. articles to trade jours. and mags.; guest editorial writer Town Hall, San Diego Union; patentee agrl. frost control, vehicle off-road drive system, recoil absorbing system for firearms, telescope sight mounting system for firearms, breech mech. sporting firearm, elec. switch activating system, 33 others. Mem. San Diego County Border Task Force on Undocumented Aliens, 1979-80, 81-82; chmn. Native Californian Coalition, 1982—; bd. dirs. Nat. Geog. Soc., 1968. With U.S. Army, 1951-53. Recipient Superior Svc. Commendation award U.S. Naval Ordnance Test Sta., Pasadena, 1959. Mem. Am. Soc. for Metals, Soc. Automotive Engrs., Nat. Rifle Assn. (life), San Diego Zool. Soc., Sierra Club (life), Nat. Wildlife Fedn., The Wilderness Soc., Rocky Mountain Elk Found. Avocations: sculpture, chess, music, conservation, travel. Home: 1629 Via Monserate Fallbrook CA 92028 Office: 133 N Pacific St Ste D San Marcos CA 92069

JEFFRESS, JAMES VAN BUREN, JR., newspaper editor; b. Alhambra, Calif., Nov. 8, 1934; s. James Van Buren Sr. and Mildred Mae (Paine) J.; m. Mary Jane Jackson, Mar. 24, 1962; children: Laurie Jane, Jean Louise. Student, East L.A. Jr. Coll., 1957-58, L.A. State Coll., 1959-60. Make-up editor Brawley (Calif.) News, 1961-62; mng. editor Victor Press, Victorville, Calif., 1962-67; copy chief Daily Report, Ontario, Calif., 1967-71; copy editor, People editor Mercury News, San Jose, Calif., 1972—. Served with U.S. Army, 1953-56, Korea. Office: Mercury News 750 Kidder-Park Dr San Jose CA 95190

JEFFERY, DAVID GORDON, marketing executive; b. Pawtucket, R.I., July 31, 1946; s. David Gordon and Clara Ellen (Wilson) J.; m. Pamela J. Kunatz, Jan. 25, 1980; children: Alexandra Elizabeth, James Johnstone, MacAllister George David. BA, Furman U., 1968; MBA, Wake Forest U., 1971. With mktg. staff Hanes Corp., Winston-Salem, N.C., 1969-71, Levi Strauss & Co., San Francisco, 1972-74; pres., chief exec. officer Caledonia Group Inc. and subs. British Am. Trading Co., Inc., England, Jeffrey Advt., Inc., San Francisco, 1974—; bd. dirs. San Francisco Advt. Softball League, 1978-80, commr., 1981-83. 1st lt. airborne rangers U.S. Army, 1967-69. Decorated Silver Star, Bronze Star, Purple Heart. Republican. Episcopalian. Lodge: Rotary.

JEFFREY, DENNIS JOHN, purchasing executive; b. Jersey City, May 2, 1947; s. John Kenneth and Doris Louise (Ulrich) J. BA, Whittier (Calif.) Coll., 1969; MBA, U. Nev., 1980. Cert. purchasing mgr. Dep. chief clk. Orange County Mcpl. Ct., Santa Ana, Calif., 1972-77; expediter EG&G Energy Measurements, Inc., Las Vegas, Nev., 1980-81, buyer, 1981-82, sr. buyer, 1982-84, purchasing mgr., 1987—; purchasing mgr. EG&G Energy Measurements, Inc., Santa Barbara, 1984-87. Served with U.S. Army, 1970-72. State of Calif. scholar, 1965-69. Mem. Am. Film Inst., Mensa, Phi Sigma Alpha. Republican. Roman Catholic. Home: 7141 Shadow Crest Dr Las Vegas NV 89119 Office: EG&G Inc 680 E Sunset Rd Las Vegas NV 89119

JEFFREY, FRANCIS, software developer, forecaster; b. Calif., 1950. BA in Computational Neurophysiology, U. Calif., Berkeley, 1972. Research assoc. U. Calif., San Diego, 1972-73; cons. Sci. Applications, Inc., La Jolla, Calif., 1973-75; entrepreneur Big Sur, Calif., 1973-77; cons. Alive Systems Info. Scis., San Francisco, 1978-87; founder, pres., chief exec. officer Alive Systems, Inc. and Elfnet, Inc., Malibu, Calif., 1987—; cons. Inst. for Advanced Computation, Sunnyvale, Calif., 1973-75, Human-Dolphin Found., 1980-82, 87-89, Esalen Inst., 1982-83. Author: (with others) Handbook of States of Consciousness, 1986, The Biography of Dr. John C. Lilly, 1989; co-author: In the Provence of the Mind, 1989; designer computer co-pilot software; patentee isolation module. Co-founder New Forum, Monterey, Calif., 1984, Gt. Whales Found., San Francisco, 1987, Big Sur chpt. L5 Nat. Space Soc. Mem. Computer Soc. of IEEE, Control Systems Group Am. Soc. for Cybernetics (charter). Home: PO Box 6847 Malibu CA 90264

JEFFRIES, LESTER ALBERT, aerospace engineer; b. Lake Charles, La., July 27, 1931; s. Charles William and Yancey (Dunning) J.; m. Martha Abigail Richards. BS in Physics, La. State U., 1952, MS in Physics, 1954. Staff scientist Gen. Dynamics Corp., Pomona, Calif., 1957-62; chief advanced devel. Northrop Corp., Palos Verdes, Calif., 1962-74, project mgr., 1974-77; assoc. program mgr. Hughes Aircraft Co., El Segungo, Calif., 1978-88, mgr. laser programs, 1988—. Co-inventor Electron Beam SCanner, 1968, Electron Line Scanner, 1970. With USAF, 1954-56. Mem. Inst. Electrical Electronic Engrs. Democrat. Home: 29002 Firthridge Rd Rancho Palos Verdes CA 90274 Office: Hughes Aircraft Co El Segunda Blvd El Segundo CA 90245

JEFFRIES, RUSSELL MORDEN, communications company official; b. Carmel, Calif., July 15, 1935; s. Herman M. and Louise (Morden) J.; m. Barbara Jean Borcovich, Nov. 24, 1962; 1 child, Lynne Louise. AA, Hartnell Coll., 1971. Sr. communications technician AT&T, Salinas, Calif., 1955--; mayor City of Salinas, 1987--. Pres. El Gabilan Sch. PTA, Salinas, 1971-74, Salinas Valley Council PTA, 1975-76; mem. Salinas City Sch. Bd., 1975-81; mem. Salinas City Council, 1981-87; bd. dirs. Community Hosp. Salinas Found., 1987--, Salinas-Kushikino Sister City, 1987--, John Steinbeck Ctr. Found., 1987--; hon. bd. dirs. Monterey Film Festival, 1987, Calif. Rodeo Assn., 1987. Recipient hon. service award PTA, Salinas, 1976; cert. of appreciation Calif. Dept. Edn., 1980, Salinas City Sch. Dist., 1981, Calif. Sch. Bds. Assn., 1981, Steinbeck Kiwanis, Salinas, 1987; named hon. mem. Filipino community Salinas Valley, 1988. Mem. Salinas C. of C., Native Sons Golden West, K.C., Rotary, Moose, Elks. Republican. Roman Catholic. Home: 204 E Curtis St Salinas CA 93906 Office: Office of Mayor 200 Lincoln Ave Salinas CA 93901

JEFFRIS, CATHERINE MARY, consumer affairs/public relations professional; b. Medford, Oreg., June 6, 1952; d. Mearl A. and Mary Catherine (Allen) Winkel; m. Gary Bruce Jeffris, Dec. 16, 1972 (div. Oct. 1981); 1 child, Carin Nicole. AA, Wenatchee (Wash.) Valley Coll., 1979; BA, Cen. Wash. U., 1980, MS, 1983. Consumer affairs specialist Associated Grocers, Inc., Seattle, 1984—. Named one of Outstanding Young Women in Am., 1987. Mem. Am. Home Econs. Assn., Home Economists in Bus. (state sec. 1986-87, state chair elect 1987-88, chair 1988-89, state advisor 1989—), Food Mktg. Inst. (consumer affairs coun. 1987-89). Home: 10814 NE 12th Pl Bellevue WA 98004 Office: Associated Grocers Inc PO Box 3763 Seattle WA 98124

JELSEMA, C. BEN, marketing executive; b. Denver, Oct. 1, 1938; s. Ted Charles and Margaret (Pierce) J.; m. Faith E. Matthiesen, Dec. 28, 1958; children: Cindy Lyn, Charles Martin, Ted Douglas, Tod Scott, Bruce Richard. Student, U. Fla., 1956-59, Columbia U., 1969; MBA, Fairleigh Dickinson, 1977. Sales positions Quaker Oats Co., various locations, 1961-67; product/brand mgr. Burry div. Quaker Oats Co., Chgo., 1967-70, mgr. mktg., 1970-73, mgr. sales, svc. and devel., 1973-76; mgr. nat. sales Burry div. Quaker Oats Co., Elizabeth, N.J., 1976-78; dir. sales and mktg. Anderson Pretzel div. Univ. Foods Corp., Lancaster, Pa., 1978-83; v.p. mktg. Anderson Pretzel div. Nat. Home Products, Lancaster, 1983-85, Snacktime div. Culbro, Indpls., 1985-87; v.p. sales and mktg. Smoke Craft div. Curtice Burns, Albany, Oreg., 1987—. Dist. chmn. Lancaster council Boy Scouts Am., 1978-85, wood badge course dir. 1984, exec. bd. Wabasha Coun., 1986-87, v.p. program Cascade Area Coun., 1988—. Mem. Am. Mktg. Assn., Trouts Unltd. (life, nat. bd. 1974-75; recipient disting. svc. award, 1978), Elks. Republican. Mem. Ch. Christ Scientist. Home: 25000 Pioneer Rd SE Lyons OR 97358 Office: Smoke Craft PO Box 1029 Albany OR 97321

JENKINS, BRUCE STERLING, federal judge; b. Salt Lake City, May 27, 1927; s. Joseph and Bessie Pearl (Iverson) J.; m. Margaret Watkins, Sept. 19, 1952; children—Judith Margaret, David Bruce, Michael Glen, Carol Alice. B.A. with high honors, U. Utah, 1949, LL.B., 1952, J.D., 1952. Bar: Utah 1952, U.S. Dist. Ct. 1952, U.S. Supreme Ct. 1962, U.S. Circuit Ct. Appeals 1962. Individual practice law Salt Lake City, 1952-59; asso. firm George McMillan, 1959-65; asst. atty. gen. State of Utah, 1952; dep. county atty. Salt Lake County, 1954-58; bankruptcy judge U.S. Dist. Ct., Dist. of Utah, 1965-78, U.S. dist. judge, 1978—, chief judge, 1984—. Research, publs. in field; contbr. essays to Law jours.; bd. editors: Utah Law Rev, 1951-52. Mem. Utah Senate, 1959-65, minority leader, 1963, pres. senate, 1965, vice chmn. commn. on orgn. exec. br. of Utah Govt., 1965-66; Mem. adv. com. Utah Tech. Coll., 1967-72; mem. instl. council Utah State U., 1976. Served with USN, 1945-46. Mem. Utah State Bar Assn., Salt Lake County Bar Assn., Am. Bar Assn., Fed. Bar Assn., Order of Coif, Phi Beta Kappa, Phi Kappa Phi, Phi Eta Sigma, Phi Sigma Alpha, Tau Kappa Alpha. Democrat. Mormon. Office: US Dist Ct 251 US Courthouse 350 S Main St Salt Lake City UT 84101 *

JENKINS, CAROL ANNE, educator; b. Kearny, N.J., Mar. 1, 1945; d. Lawrence Augustine and Sara (Ball) J. BA, Malone Coll., 1968; MA in Religious Edn., Chgo. Grad.Sch. Theology, 1969; MA in Sociology, Western Mich. U., 1972; PhD in Sociology, Kans. State U., 1986. Asst. prof., program dir. various orgns., Grand Rapids and Livonia, Mich., 1970-73; asst. prof. Judson Coll., Elgin, Ill., 1973-74, No. State Coll., Aberdeen, S.D., 1974-75, Henry Ford Community Coll., Dearborn, Mich., 1975-76, Wheeling (W.Va.) Coll., 1976-78, Tabor Coll., Hillsboro, Kans., 1978-82; instr. Kans. State U., Manhattan, 1982-85; assoc. prof. Biola U., La Mirada, Calif., 1985—; bd. dirs., chairwoman bd. Faculty Student Union, La Mirada, Christian Conciliation Svcs. of Orange County, Calif.; cons. in field. Author: Thanatology: Discussions On Death & Dying, 1986, Social Problems: Issues and Their Opposing Viewpoints, 1987, Toward An Understanding of Social Thought, 1987, Toward an Understanding of Sociological Theory, 1989. Vol. umpire Hillsboro Recreation Dept., 1980-82; speaker Kiwanis, Hillsboro, 1981, Marquette High Sch., 1982; vol. Cedar Hill Mobile Country Club, Fullerton, Calif., 1986—. Mem. Am. Sociol. Assn., Pacific Sociol. Assn. (program chmn. 1988), Midwest Sociol. Assn. (undergrad. edn. com. mem. 1982-85), Rural Sociol. Soc. (mem. com. 1988), Assn. Christians Teaching Sociology (nat. program chmn. 1981, 82), Religious Edn. Assn., AAUW, William Lock Singers Players, Alpha Kappa Delta. Mennonite. Home: 2851-19 Rolling Hills Dr Fullerton CA 92635

JENKINS, CLAUDE, academic principal; b. McComb, Miss., May 17, 1938; s. Claude and Edna (Dillon) J.; m. Lillie B. Morris; children: Claudia, Michael Claude. BA, Calif. State U., Hayward, 1972; MA, San Francisco State U., 1976; Dr. degree, Nova U., 1986. Cert. tchr., Calif. Tchr. Oakland (Calif.) Schs., 1972-81, prin., 1981—; owner Accurate Income Tax Services, Oakland, 1988—; bd. dirs. Taylor Meml. Tutoring Program, Oakland, Shattuck Ave Ch. Tutoring Program. Pres. ELDC Dem. Club; trainer Cal-Leadership Acad.; lay leader Taylor Meml. Ch.; mem. North Oakland Community Devel. Orgn., 1983. Served to sgt. U.S. Army, 1956-59. Mem. Toastmasters, Phi Delta Kappa, Alpha Phi Alpha. Democrat. Lodge: Masons. Home: 11065 Golf Links Rd Oakland CA 94605 Office: Oakland Pub Schs 581 61st St Oakland CA 94621

JENKINS, DONALD JOHN, art museum administrator; b. Longview, Wash., May 3, 1931; s. John Peter and Louise Hazel (Pederson) J.; m. Mary Ella Bemis, June 29, 1956; children—Jennifer, Rebecca. B.A., U. Chgo., 1951, M.A., 1970. Mus. asst. Portland (Oreg.) Art Mus., 1954-56, asst. curator, 1960-69, curator, 1974-75, dir., 1975-87, curator Asian art, 1987—; assoc. curator oriental art Art Inst. Chgo., 1969-74; mem. gallery adv. com. Asia House Gallery, N.Y.C., 1977—; application reviewer NEH, Washington, 1984-86; lectr. various museums and art orgns., 1969—. Author: (exhbn. catalogues) Ukiyo-e Prints & Paintings, 1971, The Ledoux Heritage, 1973, Masterworks/China & Japan, 1976, Images of Changing World, 1983. Mem., chmn. Pittock Mansion Adv. Com., Portland, 1975—; chmn. NW Regional China Council, Portland, 1980—; mem. art selection com. Performing Arts Ctr., Portland, 1983—. Mem. Am. Assn. Museums, Art Mus. Assn., Soc. Japanese Arts and Crafts, Assn. Asian Studies. Home: 16418 NW Rock Creek Rd Portland OR 97231 Office: Portland Art Mus 1219 SW Park Ave Portland OR 97205

JENKINS, KIRK L., dentist; b. Concord, Calif., Jan. 26, 1958; s. Jack E. and Donna (Leavitt) J.; m. Judy Ann Ahlstrom, Aug. 16, 1980; children: Natalie, Lisa, David, Bryan. Student, Brigham Young U., 1979-81; DDS, U. Wash., 1986. Assoc. dentist Nampa (Idaho) Dental Health Ctr., 1986-88; gen. practice dentistry Nampa, 1988—; participator, mem. Nat. Children's Dental Health Week, Nampa, 1988. Area dir. Help Idaho Thrive, Boise, 1988. Mem. ADA, Idaho Dental Assn., SW Idaho Dental Soc., Exchange Club. Republican. Mormon. Office: Nampa Dental Health Ctr 109 12th Ave Rd Nampa ID 83651

JENKINS, MARGARET AIKENS, educational administrator; b. Lexington, Miss., May 14, 1925; d. Joel Bryant and Marie C. (Threadgill) Melton; m. Daniel Armstrong, May 21, 1944 (div. 1950); children—Marie Cynthia, Marsha Rochelle; m. Gabe Aikens, June 29, 1954 (div. 1962); m. Herbert Jenkins, May 21, 1966. Student, Chgo. Conservatory of Music, 1959, Moody Bible Inst., Chgo., 1959, Calif. State U.-Northridge, 1984; HHD (hon.), Payne Acad., 1984; HHD (hon.) Pentecostal Bible Coll., 1988. Clk., U.S. Signal Corps, Chgo., 1943-44, Cuneo Press, Chgo., 1948-52, Ford Aircraft, Chgo., 1952-58, Corps of Engrs., Chgo., 1958-64; progress control clk. Def. Contract Adminstrn. Service Region, Los Angeles, 1966-73; founder, adminstr. Celeste Scott Christian Sch., Inglewood, Calif., 1976—; founder, pres. Mary Celeste Scott Meml. Found., Inc., Inglewood, 1973—; pub., writer, founder Magoll Records, Chgo., 1958-64, M&M Aikens Music, 1957—; mem. Inglewood Coalition Against Drugs, 1987—; radio broadcast Look and Live Sta. KTYM, Inglewood, Calif., 1986—; Mayor of Inglewood Ann. Prayer Breakfast Com., 1988. Recipient Cert. Appreciation, Mayor of Inglewood, 1984, Mayor of Los Angeles, 1980, State Senator, 1975, State Rep., 1976; named Woman of Yr., Los Angeles Sentinel, 1982, Inglewood C. of C., 1982. Mem. Broadcast Music Inc., Am. Fedn. TV and Radio Artists, Nat. Assn. Pentecostal Women and Men Inc. Avocations: religion, writing and recording music, education. Home: 11602 Cimarron Ave Los Angeles CA 90047 Office: Celeste Scott Christian Sch 930 S Osage Ave Inglewood CA 90301

JENKINS, MYRA ELLEN, historian, archivist; b. Elizabeth, Colo., Sept. 26, 1916; d. Lewis Harlan and Minnie (Ackroyd) Jenkins; B.A. cum laude, U. Colo., 1937, M.A., 1938; Ph.D., U. N.Mex., 1953. Instr. pub. schs., Climax, Colo., 1939-41, Granada, Colo., 1941-43, Pueblo, Colo., 1943-50; fellow U. N.Mex., 1950-52, asst., 1952-53; free-lance historian and hist. cons., Albuquerque, 1953-59; archivist Hist. Soc. N.Mex., Santa Fe, 1959-60; sr. archivist N.Mex. Records Center and Archives, 1960-69, dep. for archives, 1968-70; N.Mex. state historian, 1967-80; ret., 1980; instr. St. Michael's Coll., 1962-63, Coll. of Santa Fe, 1966-74, 81-82; assoc. prof. N.Mex. State U., 1983; assoc. adj. prof. U.N. Mex., summer 1982, 84, 86; rsch. cons., 1980—. Mem. Western History Assn., Hist. Soc. N.Mex., Phi Beta Kappa, Phi Kappa Phi, Phi Alpha Theta, Kappa Delta Pi. Democrat. Episcopalian. Author: (with Albert H. Schroeder) A Brief History of New Mexico, 1974; Guides and Calendars to the Spanish, Mexican and Territorial Archives of New Mexico; contbr. articles to profl. jours. and book revs. Home: 1022 Don Cubero St Santa Fe NM 87501

JENKINS, NICOLETTE LEMMON, marketing consultant; b. Phoenix, Sept. 23, 1956; d. Stanley Vaughn and Emma Lou (Nims) Lemmon; m. Gregory Bart Jenkins, June 30, 1984. BS, Ariz. State U., 1978, MBA, 1983. Account exec. CORT Furniture Rental, Phoenix, 1978-79; advt. dir. Sun Lakes Mktg., Ariz., 1979-80; mktg. dir. SunWest Fed. Credit Union, Phoenix, 1980-84; pres., owner Lemmon-Aid Mktg. Svcs., Tempe, 1984—; faculty U. Phoenix, 1986—. Contbr. articles to profl. jours. Chmn. Valley of the Sun United Way dir. mktg. com., 1988-89, chmn. mktg. and communications com., 1988-89; bd. dirs., chmn. mktg. com. Ariz. Bus. and Edn. Partnership. Mem. Phoenix Direct Mktg. Club (sec./treas. 1984-87), Am. Mktg. Assn., Credit Union Exec. Soc./Fin. Suppliers Forum. Republican. Presbyterian. Office: Lemmon-Aid Mktg Svcs 1403 W 10th Pl #B114 Tempe AZ 85281

JENKINS, SAM LEON, natural health care company executive; b. Roswell, N.Mex., Feb. 20, 1943; s. Samuel Leo and Gladys Viola (Davis) J.; m. Karen Sue Quimby, Nov. 17, 1979; children: Chet Alan, Kari Sue, Heather Alena, Kevin Eugene, Lela Christina, Sean David. AS, N.Mex. Highlands U., 1963; BS, N.Mex. State U., 1967; postgrad., UCLA, 1967, Colo. State U., U. Colo., 1969, 70. Engr. Aerojet-Gen. Corp., Azusa, Calif., 1967-69, Ball Bros. Research Corp., Boulder, Colo., 1969-71; pres., owner Spirit of Am. Mktg., Longmont, Colo., 1971-79; owner, founder, mgr. Dandy Day Corp., Broomfield, Colo., 1979--. Mem. Ch. of Christ. Home and Office: 13606 Raleigh St Broomfield CO 80020

JENKINS, SPEIGHT, opera director, writer; b. Dallas, Jan. 31, 1937; s. Speight and Sara (Baird) J.; m. Linda Ann Sands, Sept. 6, 1966; children: Linda Leonie, Speight. B.A., U. Tex.-Austin; LL.B., Columbia U. News and reports editor Opera News, N.Y.C., 1967-73; music critic N.Y. Post, N.Y.C., 1973-81; TV host Live from the Met, Met. Opera, N.Y.C., 1981-83; gen. dir. Seattle Opera, 1983—; classical music editor Record World, N.Y.C., 1973-81; contbg. editor Ovation Mag., N.Y.C., 1980—, Opera Quar., Los Angeles, 1982—. Served to capt. U.S. Army, 1961-66. Recipient Emmy award for Met. Opera telecase La Boheme TV Acad. Arts and Scis., 1982. Mem. Music Critics Assn., Phi Beta Kappa. Presbyterian. Home: 903 Harvard E Seattle WA 98102-4561 Office: Seattle Opera Assn PO Box 9248 Seattle WA 98109 *

JENKINS, WILLIAM, building materials and property development company executive; b. Mystic, Iowa, Feb. 15, 1920; s. William and Agnes (Gallager) J.; m. Barbara Jane Crafts, June 4, 1944; children—Kathryn Ann, Thomas William. B.A., Drake U., 1941. Acct. Gen. Motors Corp., Kansas City, Kans., 1941-42, Menasco Mfg. Co., Los Angeles, 1946-47; pres., chief exec. officer Conrock Co., Los Angeles, 1947-84; chmn. bd., chief exec. officer CalMat Co. (merger Conrock Co. and Calif. Portland Cement), Los Angeles, 1984-88, chmn. bd., 1988—; bd. dirs. CalMat Properties Co., L.A., CalMat of Ariz., Phoenix, CalMat of Cen. Calif., Allied Concrete and Materials Co., Calif. Portland Cement Co. Trustee United for Calif., Costa Mesa. Lt. USN, 1942-46. Mem. Calif. Mfrs. Assn. (bd. dirs., chmn. 1980-81), So. Calif. Ready Mixed Concrete Assn. (bd. dirs., past pres.), Portland Cement Assn. (dir., pres., chmn.1985-88), Nat. Sand and Gravel Assn. (dir., chmn. bd. dirs. 1982-83), Calif. Club, Jonathan Club, Hacienda Golf Club, Beavers (bd. dirs.). Republican. Home: 3274 Canal Point Rd Hacienda Heights CA 91745 Office: CalMat Co 3200 San Fernando Rd Los Angeles CA 90065

JENKINS, WILLIAM MAXWELL, banker; b. Sultan, Wash., Apr. 19, 1919; s. Warren M. and Louise (Black) J.; BA, U. Wash., 1941; MBA, Harvard, 1943; m. Elisabeth Taber, Oct. 11, 1945 (div. 1976); children: Elisabeth Cordua (Mrs. John E. Nowogroski), Ann Hathaway (Mrs. George H. Rohrbacher), William Morris, Karen Louise (Mrs. Melvin A. Olanna), Peter Taber, David Maxwell, Barbara Fessenden; m. Ann Ramsay, Jan. 31, 1987. Asst. cashier, asst. v.p. Seattle-1st Nat. Bank, 1945-53, exec. v.p., mgr. Everett div., 1962, chmn., chief exec. officer, 1962-82; v.p., exec. v.p., pres. First Nat. Bank of Everett, 1953-61; chmn. Everett Trust & Savs. Bank, 1956-61, Seafirst Corp., Seattle, 1974-82; dir. United Air Lines, UAL, Inc., Scott Paper Co., SAFECO Corp. Mem. adv. com. Grad. Sch. Bus. Adminstrn., U. Wash.; incorporator, mem. exec. com. Fifth Avenue Theatre Assn.; Served to lt. (j.g.) USN, 1943-45. Decorated Navy Cross, Croix de Guerre with palm. Mem. Assn. Res. City Bankers (pres. 1973-74). Republican. Presbyterian. Clubs: The Reading Room (Maine), Bainbridge Racquet; Seattle Tennis; Harbor, Rainier, University (Seattle), Bohemian. Office: Seattle-First Nat Bank PO Box 3977 Seattle WA 98124

JENKINS, WINDSOR JAMES EDWARD, company executive; b. Rochester, N.Y., Feb. 3, 1948; s. Ronald Vernon Jenkins and Madeline Heaton; m. DeVonia Ann Reed, Sept. BS, Cornell Univ., 1975; MBA, Univ. Idaho, 1979. Personnel rep. Allied Stores, Seattle, 1975-76; personnel and safety coord. Potlatch Corp., Lewiston, 1976-78, plant employee rels. mgr., 1978-79; div. employee rels. mgr. Potlatch Corp., San Francisco, 1979-87; dir. human resources-wood products Pope & Talbot, Inc., Portland, Oreg., 1987—; dir. Timber Ops. Coun., Tigard, Ore., 1987—. With USAF, 1966-70. mem. Am. Soc. Pers. Adminstrn. Republican. Home: 6016 Clairmont Ct Lake Oswego OR 97035 Office: Pope & Talbot Inc 1500 SW First Ave Portland OR 97201

JENKS, KARL THOMAS, computer programmer, researcher; b. Los Angeles, June 29, 1948. S. Lynn Moore and Gisela Vera (Sesse) J.; m. Barbara Jean Kennedy, May 31, 1982. BA in Maths., UCLA, 1970; postgrad., Calif. State U., Los Angeles, 1970-72; cert. in Data Processing Inst. Certification Computer Profls.; money mgmt. diplomate Coneducor Corp. Programmer/analyst City of Los Angeles Data Service Bur., 1972-85, also project leader Network Communications System; sr. systems specialist data systems div., City of Los Angeles Dept. Transp., 1985—. Vol. 1 gubernatorial, 2 presdl. campaigns Democratic Party. Recipient Commendation Data Service Bur., 1984. Mem. Engrs. and Architects Assn., Assn. Inst. Cert. Computer Profls., Am. Assn. Individual Investors, UCLA Alumni Assn., Sierra Club. Office: City of Los Angeles Dept Transp 200 N Spring St Rm 1003 Los Angeles CA 90012

JENNETT, SHIRLEY MARIE, hospice executive, nurse; b. Jennings, Kans., May 1, 1937; d. William and Mabel C. (Mowry) Shimmick; m. Nelson K. Jennett, Aug. 20, 1960 (div. 1972); children: Jon W., Cheryl L.; m. Albert J. Kikral, Apr. 16, 1977 (div. 1989). Diploma, Rsch. Hosp. Sch. Nursing, Kansas City, Mo., 1958. RN, Mo., Colo., Tex., Ill. Staff nurse, head nurse Rsch. Hosp., 1958-60; head nurse Penrose Hosp., Colorado Springs, Colo., 1960-62, Hotel Dieu Hosp., El Paso, Tex., 1962-63; staff nurse Oak Park (Ill.) Hosp., 1963-64; staff nurse, head nurse, nurse recruiter Luth. Hosp., Wheat Ridge, Colo., 1969-79; owner, mgr. Med. Placement Svcs., Lakewood, Colo., 1980-84; vol. primary care nurse, admissions counselor, team mgr. Hospice Metro Denver, 1984-88, dir. patient and family svcs., 1988, exec. dir., 1988—; mem. adv. com. Linkages Assn. for Older Adults, Denver, 1989—. Community liaison person U. Phoenix, 1988—. Mem. Am. Nurses Assn., Colo. Nurses Assn. Republican. Mem. Ch. of Religious Sci. Office: Hospice of Metro Denver 450 Lincoln St Denver CO 80203

JENNINGS, B. JOELLE, educator; b. Phila., Nov. 8, 1944; d. John Joseph and Foresta (Cianfrogna) Rodgers.; m. James T. Jennings, Sept. 25, 1971 (div. 1981). B.A., Holy Family Coll., Phila., 1966; postgrad. in edn. Immaculate Heart Coll., L.A., 1977. Cert. tchr., Calif. Intake worker Mental Health Devel. Ctr., L.A., 1966-69; adminstrv. asst. L.A. Mut. Ins. Co., 1969-70; sec. med. staff Queen of Angels Hosp., L.A., 1970-76; tchr. sci. L.A. Unified Sch. Dist, 1977-79; sci. chmn. New Jewish High Sch., L.A., 1980-83; rsch. mgr. Heidrick & Struggles, L.A., 1983-87, 89—; search support coord., Heidrick & Struggles, 1988—; cons. ednl. pvt. psychotherapist, Woodland Hills, Calif., 1979—. Hospice vol. St. Joseph Med. Ctr., Burbank, Calif. Mem. NEA, Calif. Tchrs. Assn. Office: 300 S Grand Ave Ste 2400 Los Angeles CA 90071

JENNINGS, BARBARA JEAN, interior designer, art consultant, high fashion jewelry designer; b. Redondo Beach, Calif., Nov. 30, 1944; d. Harold Willard and Leone Jeanette (Kuhn) Cole; m. George Alvin Jennings, Oct. 28, 1979; children: Ian David, Euriel Leonae. Student, Pacific Christian Coll., 1962-64. Exec. sec., designer Our Saviours's Luth. Ch., Long Beach, 1966-72; prin., owner Nat. Design Assocs., Huntington Beach, Calif., 1972—; lectr. Nat. Design Assocs., Huntington Beach, 1973—. Author: The Job Connection, 1983, Where There's a Wall-There's a Way, 1986; editor: Sentenced to Life, 1987. Named one of Top Ten Recruiting Dirs. Transdesigns, 1984, 85, Girl Athlete of Yr. Can. Acad., Kobe, Japan, 1961, 62; record holder in 2 events Track and Field, 1961, 62. Mem. NAFE. Republican. Office: Nat Design Assocs 19581 Topeka Huntington Beach CA 92646

JENNINGS, JAY BRADFORD, security company executive; b. Phoenix, Apr. 6, 1957; s. John Edward and Joan (Jackson) J.; m. Kay Frances Parcks, Nov. 20, 1982. BS in Gen. Bus., U. Ariz., 1979. Sec.-treas. Assoc. Security Co., Phoenix, 1979; dir. security Safeguard Security, Phoenix, 1982-84, v.p., 1987—; pres. East Valley Security Alliance, Phoenix, 1985-87. Pres. 20/30 Internat., Phoenix, 1987, Ariz. Family Bus. Coun., Phoenix, 1989; bd. dirs. Children in Need Found., Phoenix, 1988-89; vol. Fiesta Bowl, 1989. Recipient Zajac Outstanding Achievement award 20/30 Internat., 1988, Ben Rosner Excellence award 20/30 Internat., 1987, Outstanding Contbn. award Children's Crisis Nursery, 1987, Barry Coldwater award Outstanding 20/30, 1989. Mem. Nat. Fire Protection Assn., Security Alliance (bd. dirs. 1986-87, pub. relations award 1987), Ariz. Burglar and Fire Alarm Assn., Sigma Alpha Epsilon (sec. 1976-77). Republican. Lutheran. Office: Safeguard Security 4033 N 48th St Phoenix AZ 85018

JENNINGS, MARCELLA GRADY, rancher, investor; b. Springfield, Ill., Mar. 4, 1920; d. William Francis and Magdalene Mary (Spies) Grady; student pub. schs.; m. Leo J. Jennings, Dec. 16, 1950 (dec.). Pub. relations Econolite Corp., Los Angeles, 1958-61; v.p., asst. mgr. LJ Quarter Circle Ranch, Inc., Polson, Mont., 1961-73, pres., gen. mgr., owner, 1973—; dir. Giselle's Travel Inc., Sacramento; fin. advisor to Allentown, Inc., Charlo, Mont.; sales cons. to Amie's Jumpin' Jacks and Jills, Garland, Tex. investor. Mem. Internat. Charolais Assn., Los Angeles County Apt. Assn. Republican. Roman Catholic. Home and Office: 509 Mt Holyoke Ave Pacific Palisades CA 90272

JENNINGS, MARIANNE MOODY, lawyer, educator; b. Johnstown, Pa., Sept. 11, 1953; d. James L. and Jennie (Ure) Moody; m. Terry H. Jennings, Nov. 5, 1976; children: Sarah Anne, Claire Elizabeth. BS in Fin., Brigham Young U., 1974, JD, 1977. Bar: Ariz. 1977, U.S. Dist. Ct. Ariz. 1977. Law clk. Fed. Pub. Defender, Las Vegas, 1975; U.S. Atty., Las Vegas, 1976, Udall, Shumway, Bentley, Allen & Lyons, Mesa, Ariz., 1976; asst. prof. bus. law Ariz. State U., Tempe, Ariz., 1977-80, assoc. prof., 1980-83, prof., 1983—, assoc. dean, 1986-88. Bd. dirs. Ariz. Girls Ranch, Inc.; gubernatorial appointee Ariz. Corp. Commn., 1984-85. Bd. dirs. Ariz. Pub. Service, Inc., 1987—. Named Outstanding Undergrad. Bus. Prof., Ariz. State U., 1980, 85; recipient Provost Research Incentive Fund Ariz. State U., 1982, 83, Seidman Rsch. Fund, 1988, Burlington Northern Found. Teaching Excellence award, 1986. Mem. Ariz. Bar Assn., Am. Bus. Law Assn., Pacific Southwest Bus. Law Assn., Univ. Club (bd. dirs. 1988), Beta Gamma Sigma. Republican. Mormon. Author: (with Michael Litka) Business Law, 1983, Business Strategy for the Political Arena, 1984, Real Estate Law, 1984, 2d edit., 1989, Law for Business, 1986, Business and Its Legal Environment, 1988, Avoiding and Surviving Lawsuits: An Executive Guide to Legal Strategy, 1988. Office: Ariz State U Coll Bus Tempe AZ 85287

JENNISON, BRIAN L., environmental specialist; b. Chelsea, Mass., June 13, 1950; s. Lewis L. and Myra S. (Piper) J.; m. Susan E. Erick, June 10, 1972. BA, U. N.H., 1972; PhD, U. Calif., Berkeley, 1977. Cert. hazardous materials mgr., Calif. Teaching, rsch. asst. U. Calif., Berkeley, 1972-77; staff rsch. assoc. Dept. of Molecular Biology, Berkeley, 1978-80; sr. biologist San Francisco Bay Marine Rsch. Ctr., Emeryville, Calif., 1980-81; inspector I Bay Area Air Quality Mgmt.Dist., San Francisco, 1981-83, inspector II, 1983-88, enforcement specialist, 1988—; cons. U. S. Army Corps of Engrs., L.A., 1980, San Francisco, 1981. Contbr. articles to profl. jours. Sustaining mem. Rep. Nat. Com., Washington. Postdoctoral fellow, Harbor Br. Found., 1977-78. Mem. Air and Wast Mgmt. Assn., Navy League of U.S. (life), U.S. Naval Inst. (assoc.) Phi Beta Kappa. Republican. Home: 675 Arlington Berkeley CA 94707 Office: Bay Area Air Quality Mgmt Dist 939 Ellis St San Francisco CA 94109

JENSEN, ARTHUR ROBERT, psychology educator; b. San Diego, Aug. 24, 1923; s. Arthur Alfred and Linda (Schachtmayer) J.; m. Barbara Jane DeLarme, May 6, 1960; 1 child, Roberta Ann. B.A., U. Calif., Berkeley, 1945; Ph.D., Columbia U., 1956. Asst. med. psychology U. Md., 1955-56; research fellowInst. Psychiatry U. London, 1956-58; prof. ednl. psychology U. Calif., Berkeley, 1958—. Author: Genetics and Education, 1972, Educability and Group Differences, 1973, Educational Differences, 1973, Bias in Mental Testing, 1979, Straight Talk about Mental Tests, 1981; Contbr. to profl. jours., books. Guggenheim fellow, 1964-65, fellow Ctr. Advanced Study Behavioral Scis., 1966-67. Fellow Am. Psychol. Assn., Eugenics Soc., AAAS; mem. Am. Ednl. Research Assn. (v.p. 1968-70), Psychonomic Soc., Am. Soc. Human Genetics, Soc. for Social Biology, Behavior Genetics Assn., Psychometric Soc., Sigma Xi. Office: U Calif Sch Edn Berkeley CA 94720

JENSEN, BARBARA WOOD, interior design business owner; b. Salt Lake City, Apr. 30, 1927; d. John Howard and Loretta (Sparks) Wood; m. Lowell N. Jensen, June 26, 1947; children: Brent Lowell, Robyn Lynn, Todd Wood. Interior decorator paint and wall paper co., 1947-49; cons., interior designer 1950-60; pres., treas. Barbara Jensen Interiors, Inc., Salt Lake City, 1960-79; interior designer 1979—; owner Red Hills Wholesale Distributors, St. George, Utah, Barbara Jensen Designs, St. George and Las Vegas; dir. 1st Women's Bancorp, Utah. Chmn. Utah Legis. Rep. Ball, 1970, Utah Symphony Ball, 1979. Fellow Inst. Profl. Designers (London); mem. Assistance League, Com. Fgn. Affairs, Interior Design Soc. (assoc.), Ft. Douglas Country Club, Knife and Fork Club, Hi-Steppers Dance Club, Ladies Lit. Club, Pres.'s Club of Utah, Bloomington Country Club, Elks. Mormon.

JENSEN, BEVERLY ANN, journalist, educator; b. Worthington, Minn., July 18, 1948; d. Waldo Alfred and Georgiann Mary (Ulrich) J.; m. Abdolhosain Katirayi, Mar. 23, 1975 (div. Feb. 1989); children: Leila, Angela, Laura. BJour, U. Mo., 1970, MA, 1977; PhD, U. Wash., 1987. Gen. reporter Loveland (Colo.) Reporter-Herald 1970-71; staff writer Stephens Coll., Columbia, Mo., 1972-74; news dir. Stephens Coll., Columbia, 1974-76; teaching asst. Sch. Journalism, U. Mo., Columbia, 1976-77; predoctoral teaching assoc. dept. communication U. Wash., Seattle, 1978-81; instr. journalism Mich. State U., East Lansing, 1982-83; assoc. Communication Mgmt. Rsch., Seattle, 1987-88; founder, dir. New Thought Childcare Ctr., Seattle, 1988—. Mem. Middle East Studies Assn., World Trade Club, Earthstewards Network. Democrat. Mem. Religious Sci. Ch. Home and Office: 2403 NW 197th St Seattle WA 98177

JENSEN, CYNTHIA ANN, marketing professional; b. Phoenix, Sept. 24, 1953; d. Harold Emery and Jacqueline A. (Funk) Canterbury; m. Paul Eldredge Jensen, Jan. 25, 1975; children: Elizabeth Ann. Student, Ariz. State U., 1971-72; BS, U. Ariz., 1974. From exec. trainee to asst. buyer May Co. Dept. Stores, Los Angeles, 1975-77; dept. mgr. Bullocks Dept. Stores, Phoenix, 1977-78; real estate sales assoc. Jim Daniel & Assocs. Realtors, Phoenix, 1978-79; asst. buyer Broadway Southwest, Mesa, Ariz., 1979-82; mgr. Peat, Marwick, Mitchell & Co., Phoenix, 1982-87, Lewis and Roca Lawyers, 1987—; cons. Lannan & Cleverly Property Mgmt. Inc., Tempe, Ariz., 1985-86. Mem. long range planning com. Cactus Pine council Girl Scouts U.S., 1984, new dimensions foundations com. Phoenix Symphony Orch., 1983-84, religious edn. bd. Encanto Community Ch., 1980-82, 87-89, hospitality com., 1984-87. Mem. Internat. Assn. Bus. Communicators (profl. devel. com. 1984-85, v.p. profl. devel., bd. dirs. 1985-86, treas. 1986-87, Service award 1985), Pub. Relations Soc. Am. (awards com. 1989), Meeting Planners Internat. (program com. 1984-85, mem. membership com. 1985-86, chmn. 1986-87, bd. mem. 1987-88, sec. 1988-89, awards com. 1987-88, fundraising com. chair 1987-88, by law revision com. 1988-89), Nat. Assn. Law Firm Mktg. Aminstrs. (NALFMA) (nat. awards com. 198-88, nat. awards com. chair 1988-89, 1st place award for firm newsletter, 1988), Phoenis Met. C. of C. of communications coun. 87-88. Republican. Home: 306 W Virginia Phoenix AZ 85003 Office: care Lewis & Roca 1st Interstate Bank Pla 100 W Washington Phoenix AZ 85003

JENSEN, D. LOWELL, lawyer, government official; b. Brigham, Utah, June 3, 1928; s. Wendell and Elnora (Hatch) J.; m. Barbara Cowin, Apr. 20, 1951; children: Peter, Marcia, Thomas. A.B. in Econs, U. Calif.-Berkeley, 1949, LL.B., 1952. Bar: Calif. 1952. Dep. dist. atty. Alameda County, 1955-66; asst. dist. atty. 1966-69, dist. atty., 1969-81; asst. atty. gen. criminal div. Dept. Justice, Washington, 1981-83, assoc. atty. gen., 1983-85, dep. atty. gen., 1985-86; judge U.S. Dist. Ct. (no. dist.) Calif., San Francisco, 1986—; mem. Calif. Council on Criminal Justice, 1974-81; past pres. Calif. Dist. Atty.'s Assn. Served with U.S. Army, 1952-54. Fellow Am. Coll. Trial Lawyers; mem. Nat. Dist. Atty.'s Assn. (victim/witness commn. 1974-81), Boalt Hall Alumni Assn. (past pres.). Office: US Dist Ct 450 Golden Gate Ave PO Box 36060 San Francisco CA 94130

JENSEN, DAVID LEA, mechanical engineer; b. Vermillion, Alta., Can., May 10, 1959; came to U.S., 1972; s. Alexander George and Miriam Elizabeth (Wilson) J.; m. Mariann Jean Sandvick, Dec. 18, 1981; children: Peter David, Timothy Douglas. BME, Ariz. State U., 1987. Mech. detailer ASM Am., Phoenix, 1978-79, layout designer, 1979-81, engring. asst., 1981-82, project design engr., 1982-88; mech. engr. Motorola Spectrum CVD, Phoenix, 1988—; lectr. in field. Deacon Southside Bapt. Ch., Tempe, Ariz., 1985—. Mem. Inst. Environ. Scis. Republican. Office: Motorola Spectrum CVD 3821 E Broadway Phoenix AZ 85040

JENSEN, EDMUND PAUL, bank holding company executive; b. Oakland, Calif., Apr. 13, 1937; s. Edmund and Olive E. (Kessell) J.; m. Marilyn Norris, Nov. 14, 1959; children—Juliana L., Annika M. B.A., U. Wash., 1959; postgrad., U. Santa Clara, Stanford U., 1981. Lic. real estate broker, Oreg., Calif. Mgr. fin. plan and evaluation Technicolor, Inc., Los Angeles, 1967-69; group v.p. Nat. Industries & Subs, Louisville, 1969-72; v.p. fin. Wedgewood Homes, Portland, 1972-74; various mgmt. positions U.S. Bancorp, Portland, 1974-83; pres. U.S. Bancorp, Inc., Portland, 1983—; dir. U.S. Bancorp, U.S. Nat. Bank of Oreg., VISA, U.S. Bank Washington. Bd. dirs. United Way, Portland, 1982—, chmn. campaign, 1986; bd. dirs. Saturday Acad., Portland, 1984—, Providence Child Ctr. Found., Portland, 1984—, Marylhurst Coll., Oreg. Bus. Council, Oreg. Art Inst.; bd. dirs. Oreg. Ind. Coll. Found., 1983—, treas., 1986—, chmn. 1988—; chmn. N.W. Bus. Coalition, 1987—; mem. Oreg. Tourism Alliance, 1987—, bd. visitors law sch. U. of Oreg., 1987—. Mem. Portland C. of C. (bd. dirs. 1981—, chmn. 1987), Assn. Res. City Bankers, Assn. for Portland Progress (pres. 1988). Club: Waverly country, Multnomah Athletic. Lodge: Rotary. Office: US Nat Bank Oreg 111 SW 5th St PO Box 4412 Portland OR 97204 also: US Bancorp PO Box 8837 Portland OR 97208

JENSEN, ERIK JON, artist; b. N.Y.C., Oct. 17, 1957; s. John Theisen and Olive Marie Jensen Theisen; m. Esabel Alvarez Gutierrez, Mar. 19, 1978; children: Thor Jesus Gutierrez, Jeremiah Jon Gutierrez. BFA, Tex. Tech U., 1981. Art dir. Habitat, Inc., Tempe, Ariz., 1981-83, Multigraphic Arts, Tempe, Ariz., 1983-85; studio asst. Bill Schenk, Apache Junction, Ariz., 1985-86; instr. Phoenix Inst. Tech., 1986—; owner, mgr. The Drawing Co., Chandler, Ariz., 1983—. Recipient Prisma award Communicating Arts Group Ariz., 1983. Home: 6218 W Laredo Chandler AZ 85226 Office: Phoenix Inst Tech 2555 E University Phoenix AZ 85634

JENSEN, GARY A., electrical and electronic manufacturing and construction company executive/owner; b. Reno, July 2, 1944; s. George L. and Velma K. Jensen; m. Diane Priess, Sept. 14, 1963; children: Christian, Elizabeth. Cert. pilot. Prin. Jensen Electric Co., Reno, 1968—, also chief exec. officer. Mem. U. Nev.-Reno Boosters. Mem. ASHRAE, Nat. Elec. Contractors Assn. (pres. 1976-80, bd. dirs. No. Nev.), Instrument Soc. Am. (sr.), Construction Specifiers Inst., Nat. Fire Protection Assn. Lodge: Elks. Home and Office: 140 Jensen St Reno NV 89502

JENSEN, GERALD JOSEPH, service executive; b. Toledo, Feb. 17, 1948; s. Gerald James and Thelma (Pfaff) J.; m. Barbara Jean Botts, Dec. 7, 1968; children: Troy, Heather. Student, U. Toledo, 1966-69. Catering mgr., asst. food & beverage dir. Saw Mill Creek, Huron, Ohio, 1972-73; food & beverage dir. Sheraton Hotel, Toledo, 1973-74; dir. sales Sugarloaf Village, Cedar, Mich., 1974-75; corp. mktg. dir. Boyne U.S.A. Resorts, Boyne Falls, Mich., 1975-80; dir. mktg. Sheraton at Steamboat, Steamboat Springs, Colo., 1980-81; v.p., gen. mgr. Nautical Inn Resort, Lake Havasu, Ariz., 1981—. Pres. No. Mich. Conv. Bur., Travers, 1976-80; pres. C. of C. 1987; chmn. Lake Havasu Conv. & Visitors Bur., 1985-87, Water Safety Task Force, 1987—; scout master Boy Scouts Am., 1986—. Served wtih USMC res., 1971-78. Mem. Ariz. Hotel & Motel Assn. (bd. dirs. 1982—). Republican. Roman Catholic. Home: 2385 Souchak Dr Lake Havasu City AZ 86403 Office: Nautical Inn Resort 1000 McCulloch Blvd Lake Havasu City AZ 86403

JENSEN, HELEN, musical artists management company executive; b. Seattle, June 30, 1919; d. Frank and Sophia (Kantosky) Leponis; student public schs., Seattle; m. Ernest Jensen, Dec. 2, 1939; children—Ernest, Ronald Lee. Co-chmn., Seattle Community Concert Assn., 1957-62; sec. family concerts Seattle Symphony Orch., 1959-61; hostess radio program Timely Topics, 1959-60; gen. mgr. Western Opera Co., Seattle, 1962-64, pres. 1963-64; v.p., dir., mgr. public relations Seattle Opera Assn., 1964—, preview artists Coordinator, 1981-84; bus. mgr. Portland (Oreg.) Opera Co., 1968, cons., 1967-69; owner, mgr. Helen Jensen Artists Mgmt., Seattle, 1970—. First v.p. Music and Art Found., 1981-84, pres. 1984-85. Recipient Cert., Women in Bus in the Field of Art, 1973; award Seattle Opera Assn., 1974; Outstanding Service award Music and Art Found., 1984; award of distinction Seattle Opera Guild, 1983. Mem. Am. Guild Mus. Artists, Music and Art Found., Seattle Opera Guild (pres., award of distinction 1983), Ballard Symphony League (sec.), Seattle Civic Opera Assn. (pres. 1981-84), Portland Opera Assn., Portland Opera Guild, Seattle Civic Opera Assn. (pres. 1981-89), 200 Plus One, Aria Preview, Lyric Preview Group, Past Pres. Assembly (pres. 1977-79, parliamentarian 1987-88), Pres.'s Forum (program vice chmn. 1987-88), North Shore Performing Arts Assn. (pres. 1981). Clubs: Helen Jensen Hiking, Kenmore Community. Home: 19029 56th Ln NE Seattle WA 98155 Office: 716 Joseph Vance Bldg Seattle WA 98101

JENSEN, JACQUE HAIMES, legal assistant; b. Salem, Ohio, Nov. 15, 1939; d. Sidney Stafford and Betty (Finkelman) Haimes; m. William Jay Adler, Aug. 17, 1958 (div. Nov. 1972); children: Cynthia, Susan; m. Robert Arthur Jensen, Dec. 7, 1973; children: Anne Bromley, Sara. Student, Ariz. State U., 1957-59, 68; AA, Phoenix Coll., 1972. Hygienist dental Jack Woolsey, D.D.S., Phoenix, 1972-74, J. Richard Cohen, D.D.S., Phoenix, 1972-77, Rex Brewster, D.D.S., Phoenix, 1979-84; legal asst. Jensen & Kjos, Phoenix, 1984—. Vol. coordinator Tony Mason Fed. Congl. Campaign, Ariz., 1968. Mem. Nat. Assn. Legal Assts. (cert.), Ariz. Paralegal Assn., Legal Assts. Ariz., Legal Assts. Phoenix (coordinator continuing edn. 1988), Alpha Epsilon Phi. Republican. Jewish. Office: Jensen & Kjos 3246 N 16th St Phoenix AZ 85016

JENSEN, JAKKI RENEE, retail company executive; b. Eugene, Oreg., Mar. 1, 1959; d. Philip William Jensen and Mary Katherine (Sommers) Henderson; m. Johnny Claiborne Hawthorne, May 7, 1983. Student, Oreg. State U., 1977-78; student (hon.), Portland State U., 1978-81. With Nordstrom Co., Beaverton, Oreg., 1981—; mgr. cosmetics Nordstrom Co., Beaverton, 1984; mgr. cosmetics Nordstrom Co., Walnut Creek, Calif., 1984-86, buyer cosmetics, 1986-88; buyer cosmetics Nordstrom Co., San Francisco, 1988—. Republican. Home: 213 Elderwood Dr Pleasant Hill CA 94523 Office: 865 Market St San Francisco CA 94103

JENSEN, JAMES LESLIE, chemistry educator, university administrator; b. Tulare, Calif., Oct. 17, 1939; s. Lester Eugene and Mabel Irene (Brown) J.; m. Nancy Ruth Peterson, Aug. 13, 1960; children: Randall Mark, Linda Suzanne. BA in Chemistry, Westmont Coll., 1961; MA in Chemistry, U. Calif., Santa Barbara, 1963; PhD in Organic Chemistry, U. Wash., 1967. Instr. chemistry Westmont Coll., Santa Barbara, Calif., 1962-64, U. Wash., Seattle, 1968; from asst. prof. to prof. Calif. State U., Long Beach, 1968—, assoc. dean Sch. Natural Scis., 1983-88; vis. scientist Brandeis U.-W.P. Jencks Lab., Waltham, Mass., 1974-75; vis. prof. U. Calif. Irvine, 1981-82; chmn. Calif. State U. Long Beach com. research, found. personnel com., budget adv. com., reappointment and advancement com.; invited lectr. 40 univs. and profl. confs., U.S., U.K., France, Italy, Sweden. Reviewer NSF, Jour. Am. Chem. Soc., Jour. Organic Chemistry; contbr. over 20 articles to profl. jours. Weyerhauser fellow, U. Wash., 1966-67; scholar Westmont Coll., 1957-58, 60-61; recipient Merit award Long Beach Heart Assn., 1970, Disting. Service award Am. Heart Assn., 1971; grantee: NSF, NIH. Mem. AAAS, Am. Sci. Affiliation, Internat. Union of Pure and Applied Chemistry, Am. Chem. Soc. (organic div.), Royal Soc. Chemistry (organic chemistry div., fast reactions groups), Nat. Assn. for Sci., Tech., Soc., Sigma Xi, Phi Beta Kappa, Phi Lambda Upsilon. Republican. Office: Calif State U Dept Chemistry Long Beach CA 90840

JENSEN, JUDY DIANNE, psychotherapist; b. Portland, Oreg., Apr. 8, 1948; d. Clarence Melvin and Charlene Augusta (Young) J.; m. Frank George Cooper, Sept 4, 1983; stepchildren: Pamela Cooper, Brian Cooper. BA in Sociology and Anthropology with honors, Oberlin Coll., 1970; MSW, U. Pitts., 1972; postgrad., U. Wis., 1977. Registered clin. social worker. Social worker Day Hosp. Western Psychiat. Inst. and Clinic, Pitts., 1972-73, South Hills Child Guidance Ctr., Pitts., 1973-74; mem. drug treatment program Umatilla County Mental Health Clinic, Pendleton, Oreg., 1975-77; social worker Children's Services Div. State of Oreg., Pendleton, 1978-80, therapist intensive family services project, 1980—, dir. intensive family services project, 1986—; pvt. practice Pendleton, 1980—. NIMH grantee, 1970-72; NDEA fellow 1977; Gen. Motors scholar Oberlin Coll., 1966-70. Mem. Am. Assn. Marriage and Family Therapists (clin.), Nat. Assn. Social Workers. Home: 325 NW Bailey Pendleton OR 97801 Office: PO Box 752 Pendleton OR 97801

JENSEN, KARL ERIK, travel franchise network executive, consultant; b. Battle Creek, Mich., Apr. 27, 1938; s. Ralph Christian and Alice (Kellogg)

J.; m. Holly Cummings, June 27, 1959 (div. Dec. 1984); children: Wendy Karen, Kristopher Allan; m. Suzanne Kauss, Dec. 31, 1984. BS in Aero. Ops., San Jose State U., 1961. Engring. aide Lockheed Missiles & Space Corp., Sunnyvale, Calif., 1960-61; mgr. indsl. engring. United Air Lines, Chgo., 1962-67; sr. customer engr. Boeing Co., Seattle, 1968-69, Lockheed Aircraft Corp., Burbank, Calif., 1969-72; travel industry cons. Megamerica, Seattle, 1972-79; v.p. mtkg. Travelsavers, Inc., Gt. Neck, N.Y., 1980-84; regional pres. for Western Can. Uniglobe Travel, Vancouver, B.C., 1984-86; for Pacific N.W. Uniglobe Travel, Seattle, 1986—, also bd. dirs.; cons. Travel Industry div. Western Union Corp., Dallas, 1983-85; assoc. Partnership for Air Travel, Washington, 1988—. Contbr. numerous articles on travel industry to trade publs. Advisor site com. Wash. Rep. Conv., 1988. Mem. Am. Soc. Travel Agts., Internat. Franchise Assn., Sales and Mktg. Execs. Internat. Republican. Baptist. Office: Uniglobe Travel 2815 2d Ave Ste 200 Seattle WA 98121

JENSEN, MARK ERIC, military officer; b. Orange, N.J., Sept. 11, 1955; s. Ralph Lee and Mattie Ann (Gray) J.; m. Jodie Jensen, Dec. 17, 1977; children: Britta Lee, Eric Lars, Christy Ann. BS in Polit. Sci., Utah State U., 1977. Commd. ensign USN, 1977, advance through grades to lt. comdr., 1987; deck elec. officer USS Ranger, Coronado, Calif., 1978-81; officer in charge Navy Recruiting A Sta., Butte, Mont., 1981-85; ops. officer USS Bagley, San Diego, 1985-87; deck officer USS New Orleans, San Diego, 1988—. Decorated Navy Achievement medal with Gold Star. Mem. U.S. Naval Inst., Nat. Geographic Soc., Intercollegiate Knights (pres. 1975-77), Pi Sigma Alpha, Exch. Club (Butte), Andes DX (Quito, Ecuador). Republican. Mormon. Home: 122 Rendova Cir Coronado CA 92118 Office: Deck Dept USS New Orleans LPH 11 FPO San Francisco CA 96627-1650

JENSEN, MICHAEL JAMES, engineer; b. Preston, Idaho, Aug. 18, 1943; s. Marion James and Catharine (Winward) J.; m. Jody Hood, Mar. 25, 1967; children: Richard A., Amy Jo, Juliet, Ruth, Martin. BS in Langs., Utah State U., 1970. Cert. tchr., Utah. Tchr. various schs., Costa Rica, Utah, and Idaho, 1967-74; prodn. mgr. galium line Canyonlands 21st Century High Purity Metals, Blanding, Utah, 1974-76; lab. technician Thiokol Chem. Corp., Brigham City, Utah, 1976-81; engr. Morton Thiokol, Inc., Brigham City, 1981-88, sr. engr., 1988—; ESL tchr. Box Elder Sch. Dist. Community Edn. Programs, Brigham City and Tremonton, Utah, 1980-86. Founder four troop Boy Scouts Am., Argentina, Costa Rica, 1963-65, 68, troop leader, Tremonton, 1976—, explorer council commr., 1989; bd. dirs. Northern Box Elder County Mus., Tremonton, 1982—; chmn. Rep. Precinct, Tremonton, 1978-84.. Mem. Promontory Stamp and Coin Collecting Club (pres. 1980-82), MTI Computer Club (co-pres.). LDS. Home: 326 S Tremont St Tremonton UT 84337 Office: Morton Thiokol Inc 9160 N Hwy 83 Brigham City UT 84302

JENSEN, NAOMI EILEEN, general engineer; b. Hillsboro, Oreg., Nov. 24, 1958; d. L. Wallace and E. Pauline (Wilson) Whitmore; m. Ronald E. Jensen, July 9, 1988. BSME with high honors, Portland State U., 1988. Engring tech. Tektronix, Inc., Beaverton, Oreg., 1977-86; gen. engr. HUD, Portland, Oreg., 1987—. Musician Portland Civic Theater, 1985-87. Carl G. Fanger scholar Portland State U., 1987; named Employee of the Month HUD, 1988. Mem. ASME, ASHRAE. Democrat. Presbyterian.

JENSEN, REGINA BRUNHILD, psychotherapist; b. Bredstedt, Germany, Oct. 26, 1951; came to U.S., 1973; d. Karl Adolf and Hildegard (Weiss) Schlosser; m. Benny Hvitfelt Jensen, July 31, 1976; stepchildren: Anita, Lisa. BS in Physiotherapy, Krankengymnastik Schule, Tuebingen, 1971; MA in Counseling Psychology, Vt. Coll., 1983; PhD Human Behavior, Ryokan Coll., 1984; PhD Clin. Psychology, Sierra U., 1987. Physiotherapist Urban Krankenhaus, Berlin, 1971-73; staff physiotherapist Werner & Beck Physical Therapy, Santa Maria, Calif., 1976-83; pvt. practice health cons. Santa Ynez, 1982—; cons. Jensen Enterprises, Solvang, 1975—, Alexander & Jensen Assocs., L.A., 1983-85; adolescent crisis counselor Santa Ynez Valley High Sch., 1984-86; tutor, program coordinator Sierra U., Santa Monica, 1985—; dir. Inst. for Human Systems Integration, Santa Ynez, 1985—; founder, clin. dir., The Learning Ctr., 1987—. Author: Education for the Medical Consumer, 1983, To Liberate or to Enslave, 1985, How To Buy Back Your Soul, 1987; publisher Fully Alive Publs., 1988—; pub., founder Healing Art Expressions, 1987—; contbr. articles to profl. papers and jours. Mem. Am. Psychol. Assn. (divs. for media and health psychology), Calif. Assn. For Marriage and Family Therapists, Am. Assn. for Counseling and Devel., Orgnl. Devel. Network. Home and Office: 2880 Baseline Ave #B Santa Ynez CA 93460

JENSEN, ROBERT VICTOR, lawyer; b. Tonasket, Wash., Mar. 24, 1941; s. Howard Richard and Elizabeth Augusta (Clary) J.; m. Maria Ines Vergara, Apr. 14, 1968; children: Howard Fernando, Michael Dorian, Monica Cristina. BA, Yale U., 1963; LLB, U. Wash., 1965. Bar: Wash. 1968, U.S. Dist. Ct. (ea. dist.) Wash. 1975, U.S. Dist. Ct. (we. dist.) Wash. 1977, U.S. Ct. Appeals (9th cir.) 1980, U.S. Supreme Ct. 1981. Vol. Peace Corps, Quito, Ecuador, 1966-68; trainer Peace Corps, Bozeman, Mont., 1969; asst. atty. gen. Wash. State Atty. Gen.'s Office, Olympia, 1968-82, 83—; assoc. Bustamante & Crespo, Quito, 1982-83; bd. dirs. Capitol Land Trust, Olympia. Mem. City Coun. City of Lacey, Wash., 1977-81, 86—; pres. Better Govt. League, Olympia, 1988—; precinct commr. Rep. Precinct, Lacey, 1988—. Named Pub. Offl. 1978, Wash. Environ. Coun., Seattle. Mem. Wash. State Bar Assn. (dir., bd. dirs. environl. law sect. 1978-81, bd. dirs., dir. pub. procurement and pvt. constrn. law sect. 1989—), Nusqually Delta Assn. (bd. dirs.). Roman Catholic. Home: 2307 Larch St SE Lacey WA 98503 Office: Atty Gen Highways-Licenses Bldg Olympia WA 98504

JENSEN, TIMOTHY WARD, minister; b. Seattle, Oct. 22, 1956; s. Gerald Frederick and Betty Jo (Krause) J.; m. Margaret Florence Weddell, June 21, 1985; children: Jacob Ryan Sullivan, Stephanie Jon Sullivan. BA, U. Wash., 1978; MDiv, Harvard U., 1981; MA, We. Wash. U., 1983. Ordained to ministry, First and Second. Ch. Boston, 1981. Residence hall advisor U. Wash., Seattle, 1976-78; chaplaincy intern Va. Mason Hosp., Seattle, 1979; theol. student intern First and Second Ch. in Boston, 1978-81; residence hall dir. We. Wash. U., Bellingham, 1981-82; intern minister Univ. Unitarian Ch., Seattle, 1983-84; lectr. Midland Coll., Tex., 1986; minister Unitarian Universalist Ch., Midland, 1984-88, Unitarian Universalist Community Ch., Aloha, Oreg., 1988—; bd. dirs. S.W. Unitarian Universalist Conf., 1988, Midland Assn. Chs., 1988. Treas. Midland CROP Walk, 1988; emergency rm. chaplain Midland Mcpl. Hosp., 1985-88. Mem. Unitarian Universalist Ministers Assn., Prairie Group. Office: Unitarian Universalist Ch PO Box 5190 Aloha OR 97006

JENSEN, WILLIAM SHERMAN, business educator; b. Seattle, Sept. 10, 1931; s. William Stephen and Eloise Sherman (Gibson) J.; m. Carolyn Elizabeth Moore, Nov. 23, 1958; children: Sharon, Eloise, Cynthia. AB, U. Wash., 1957; MS, Columbia U., 1959; JD, U. Calif., San Francisco, 1966; PhD, Oreg. State U., 1975. Cert. mgmt. acct. Import mgr. Washington Import-Export Corp., San Francisco, 1956-57; asst. prof. bus. Calif. State U., Hayward, 1965-67; mgr. Portland (Oreg.) Fish Co., 1967-69; prof. Lewis and Clark Coll., Portland, 1971-80, 81-88, chmn. dept. bus., 1986-88, prof. emeritus, 1988—; exec. dir. West Coast Fisheries Found., Portland, 1980-81; chief exec. officer Resource Valvations, Inc., 1988; advisor FTC, Seattle, 1972; cons. Office of Tech. Assessment, Washington, 1976, Wash. State Dept. Fisheries, Olympia, 1977-78; cons./advisor Pacific Fisheries Mgmt. Council, Portland, 1985-86; bd. dirs. Ingeborg Short Found., Seattle. Contbr. articles to profl. jours. Served as staff sgt. USAF, 1951-54. Standard & Poors fellow, Columbia U., 1958; Harriman scholar, Columbia U., 1958; grantee Am. Acctg. Assn., 1973. Mem. Acad. Polit. Sci., Inst. Mgmt. Acctg. Democrat. Episcopalian. Home: 17618 SW Lake Haven Dr Lake Oswego OR 97034 Office: Lewis and Clark Coll 0615 SW Palatine Hill Rd Portland OR 97219

JENSEN, WILMA, superintendent of schools; b. Choteau, Mont., Dec. 12, 1918; d. Robert and Edith Olive (Watson) van Scherpenzeel; m. John L. Jensen, Jan. 17, 1942 (div. 1967); 1 child, Dorothy Marie Backland. B.S., No. Mont. Coll., 1966; M.Ed., U. Mont., 1981. Tchr., Baker Sch. Dist., Dutton, Mont., 1939-40, Agawam Sch. Dist., Mont., 1940-45, Erickson Sch. Dist., Conrad, Mont., 1945-46, Pendroy Sch., Mont., 1949-52, 55-64, Troy Sch., Mont., 1964-67, Dutton Sch., Mont., 1967-78; county supt. schs. Teton County, Choteau, 1979—; sec. Big Sky Spl. Edn. Co-op, Conrad, 1981—. Mem. Soroptimist Internat. Choteau & vicinity, 1981—; sec. Teton County Women's Republican Club, Choteau, 1979—; mem. Teton County Rep. Central Com., Choteau, 1978—. Mem. Mont. Assn. County Sch. Supts., Sch. Adminstrs. Mont., Am. Assn. Sch. Adminstrs., Assn. Supervision and Curriculum Devel., Delta Kappa Gamma. Methodist. Home: PO Box 292 15 3d Ave SW Choteau MT 59422 Office: Teton County Supt Schs Courthouse Choteau MT 59422

JENSEN EIDSON, PAMELA JO, interior designer; b. Denver, June 2, 1961; d. Harry LaRoy and Jewel Kahteryn (Camp) Jensen; m. John D. Eidson, Feb. 14, 1987. BS, U. Nebr., 1983. Interior designer Conann Homes, Austin, Tex., 1984; asst. mgr. Shelly's Tall Fashions, Littleton, Colo., 1985, Pizza Hut Am., Denver, 1986; sales and mktg. coordinator Blue Willow Antique Gallery, 1986-87; mgr. Colorel, Inc., Littleton, 1987-88, The Window Cover, Westminster, Colo., 1988—. Mem. Am. Soc. Interior Designers, Nat. Trust Historic Preservation Assn., Colo. Historic Soc., Kappa Phi. Methodist. Home: 18895 W 59th Pl Golden CO 80403

JENSON, CHARLES DAVID, computer scientist; b. Ft. Riley, Kans., Nov. 19, 1952; s. Charles D. and Geniel (Wood) J.; m. Judy Thruston, Apr. 17, 1976; children: Teri, Jacque, Zakary Daniel. BS in Computer Sci., Brigham Young U., 1978. Programmer Digital Micro Systems, Orem, Utah, 1977, Brigham Young U., Provo, Utah, 1977-78; programmer analyst Tex. Instruments, Inc., Austin, 1978-79; assoc. systems programmer Sperry Univac, Salt Lake City, 1979-81; sr. devel. engr. Novell, Inc., Orem, 1981-83; sr. project engr. Technadyne Engring. Cons., Inc., Albuquerque, 1983—; cons., Technadyne/Sandia Labs., Albuquerque, 1983—. Author computer software for pharmacy prescription control, Korean lang. terminal, others. Scoutmaster, Albuquerque area Boy Scouts Am., 1987; ward membership clk., Ch. of Jesus Christ of Latter-day Saints, Albuquerque. Mem. Sandia Muzzleloaders. Republican. Home: 7201 Winans Dr NE Albuquerque NM 87109-4848 Office: Technadyne Engring Cons Inc 300 Virginia St SE Albuquerque NM 87108

JENSON, GLEN ORVIL, family life educator; b. Logan, Utah, July 31, 1939; s. Orvil Monson and Marva (Sorenson) J.; m. Kathylene Howard, June 3, 1965; children: Jennifer, Glen Eric, Natalie. BS, Utah State U., 1965, PhD, 1974; MSW, U. Utah, 1967. Marriage and family counselor Ch. Latter-Day Saints Social Svcs., Salt Lake City, 1967-72; lectr. dept. social work Utah State U., Logan, 1969-72, asst. prof., extension specialist dept. family and human devel., 1974-78, assoc. prof., extension specialist, 1978-82, prof., 1982—, dept. head, 1982-85; nat. program leader U.S. Dept. Agriculture, 1987-88. Bishop Ch. Jesus Christ of Latter-day Saints, Logan, 1980-85; Utah rep. to White House Conf. on Families, 1980. Mem. Nat. Council on Family Rels., Utah Council on Family Rels. (pres. 1979-80). Republican. Office: Utah State U College Station Logan UT 84322-2905

JENSON, RICHARD LEON, accountant, educator; b. Logan, Utah, Dec. 19, 1952; s. Richard Milton and Colleen (Hansen) J.; m. Carol Denise Daniels, Aug. 21, 1975; children: Richard Lane, Melissa, Caitlyn. BA, Weber State Coll., 1977; PhD, U. Utah, 1988. CPA, Utah. Mgr. Wiggins and Co. CPAs, Ogden, Utah, 1977-83; fin. analyst McKay-Dee Hosp., Ogden, 1983-84; asst. prof. acctg. Utah State U., Logan, 1987—. Mem. Am. Acctg. Assn., AICPA, Utah Assn. CPAs. Mormon. Office: Sch Acctg Utah State U UMC 3540 Logan UT 84322-3540

JEONG, DAVID ELDEN, manufacturing company executive; b. Chgo., Sept. 22, 1954; s. Eddie L. and Kay C. Jeong; BS in Aero. Engring., U. Mich., 1976, MBA Northwestern U., 1982. Engr. GE, Lynn, Mass., 1976-82, bus. planner, 1982-86; bus. mgr. McDonnell Douglas Helicopter Co., Mesa, Ariz., 1987—. Mem. Am. Helicopter Soc. (mem. nat. transp. rsch. bd. helicopter subcom.). Home: 3115 E Nance St Mesa AZ 85213 Office: McDonnell Douglas Helicopter Co 500 E McDowell Rd MS A290 Mesa AZ 85205-9797

JEPPSON, ROBERT BAIRD, JR., management consultant; b. Rexburg, Idaho, Apr. 23, 1920; s. Robert Baird and Elsie (Smith) J.; B.S., U. Calif., 1942; grad. Advanced Mgmt. Program, Harvard U., 1963; m. Edith Abigail French, Jan. 9, 1947; children: Jane Elizabeth, James Robert, Virginia K. Commd. ensign U.S. Navy, 1942, advanced through grades to capt., 1962; ret., 1969; bus. mgr. Reno Radiol. Assocs., 1969-78; broker Alpine Realty Assocs., 1971—; mgmt. cons., 1978—; gen. mgr., partner BHLS Investments. Republican. Mormon. Home: 2675 Everett Dr Reno NV 89503 Office: PO Box 7011 Reno NV 89510

JEPSEN, PETER LEE, court reporter; b. Virginia, Minn., Dec. 23, 1952; s. Peter Frederick and Delores Audrey (Sorenson) J.; m. Valerie Lynn Tow, Mar. 20, 1976; children: Sarah Jo, Jennifer Lynn, Elizabeth Ann. Student, Mankato State U., 1972, St. Cloud State U., 1973, Southwestern AVTI, Jackson, Minn., 1978. Registered profl. reporter; chartered shorthand reporter. Freelance ct. reporter Carney & Assocs., Rochester, Minn., 1978-79; part owner, reporter Carney & Assocs., Rochester, 1980-83; ofcl. ct. reporter State of S.D., Sioux Falls, 1979-80; realtime captioner Can. Captioning Devel. Agy., Toronto, Ont., 1984-85, mgr. live captioning services, 1985-87; captioning trainer and cons. XScribe Corp., San Diego, 1987-88, mgr. captioning products and services, 1988-. Mem. Nat. Shorthand Reporters Assn. (cat-cart com. 1986-), Chartered Shorthand Reporters Assn. Ont. Republican. Lutheran. Office: XScribe Corp 6160 Cornerstone Ct E San Diego CA 92121

JEPSON, CHARLES WARREN, electronics executive; b. Long Beach, Calif., Apr. 17, 1946; s. Milton Alvin and Janis Mae (Harry) J.; m. Judith Ann Mathews, June 5, 1976; children: Renee, Sara, Corinne. BA, San Jose (Calif.) State U., 1969; MBA, U. Calif., Berkeley, 1971. Project adminstr. Com/Link div. Singer Co., Sunnyvale, Calif., 1969-70; div. controller Hewlett-Packard Co., Boise, Idaho, 1971-78, div. mktg. mgr., 1978-80, group mktg. mgr., 1981-83; div. gen. mgr. Hewlett-Packard Co., Cupertino, Calif., 1984-85, dir. mktg., 1986-87; v.p. gen. mgr. Convergent, San Jose, Calif., 1987—. Bd. dirs. Idaho Assn. Commerce and Industry, Boise, 1980-84. Republican. Episcopalian. Office: Convergent Inc 2700 N 1st St PO Box 6685 San Jose CA 95150

JEPSON, PAUL ALVIN, gerontologist; b. Decatur, Ga., Jan. 23, 1962; s. Alvin Sayer and Mary Elizabeth (Compton) J.; m. Kathleen Carole, May 14, 1988. MS in Gerontology, U. So. Calif., 1987; BA, Gordon Coll., 1984. Research asst. U. So. Calif., Los Angeles, 1984-87, Am. Cytogenetics, North Hollywood, Calif., 1986-87; coord. older adult svcs. San Bernardino (Calif.) County Dept. of Mental Health, 1987—; Gero-Net coordinator Fuller Theol. Sem., Pasadena, 1986-87; mem. geriatric adv. bd. Fuller Theol. Sem., Pasadena, 1987—; mem. linkages adv. bd. Sr. Care Network, Pasadena, 1986; cons. Sr. Care Network, Pasadena, 1987-88; mem. adv. bd. Inland Counties Resource Ctr., 1988—; chair So. Calif. Coord. Older Adult Svcs., 1989—; mem. older adult com. Calif. Conf. Local Mental Health Dirs., 1989—; adv. bd. Inland Counties Resource Ctr. Treas. Young Reps., Wenham, Mass., 1984. Mem. Pasadena Jaycees, Am. Soc. on Aging. Presbyterian.

JERAS, KENNETH FRANCIS, service executive; b. Chgo., Oct. 24, 1961; s. Frank Joseph and Vivian Irene (Kardash) J.; m. Denise Ann Skupa, Mar. 14, 1987. BS in Bus. Adminstrn., Ariz. State U., 1986. Reservation agent Best Western Internat., Phoenix, 1982, computer operator, 1982-83, sr. computer operator, 1983-84, programmer, 1984-86, sr. programmer, 1986—. Treas. North Tatum Homeowners Assn., Phoenix, 1987-88. Mem. Supra Relational Users Group (sec. 1987, 88), Datamap. Republican. Roman Catholic. Office: Best Western Internat 6201 N 24th Pkwy Phoenix AZ 85016

JEREZ, MYRNA ROSA, real estate associate; b. Ajo, Ariz., May 11, 1956; d. Lorenzo Jerez and Maria Rosa Bon. Student, Pima Community Coll., 1976-78, Hogan Sch. Real Estate, Tucson, 1981, Pima Coll., 1988. Lic. real estate broker, Ariz. Sec. Nat. Econ. Devel., Tucson, 1979-81; asst. to chmn. Lubec Internat., Inc., Tucson, 1981-84; v.p. mktg. RDBR Investment and Mgmt., Inc., Tucson, 1984-86; pres. RDBR Investment and Mgmt., Inc., 1986—. Active community projects, Tucson, 1987. Mem. Tucson Bd. Realtors. Republican. Roman Catholic. Office: RDBR Investment & Mgmt Inc 2675 E Broadway Ste 105 Tucson AZ 85716

JERGENSEN, DIRK ORME, pharmacist; b. Rexburg, Idaho, July 2, 1950; s. Orme M. and Lu Deen (Waldram) J.; m. Laurie Zwick, Aug. 21, 1974; children: Jessica, Jeremy, Brandon, Amanda, Joshua, Jason. BS in Psychology, U. Utah, 1975, BS in Pharmacy, 1978. Registered pharmacist, Calif., Utah. Sales rep. Eli Lilly & Co., Indpls., 1978-79; mgr. Merck Sharp & Dohme, San Diego, 1979-81; pharmacist Price Rite Pharmacy Inc., Santee, Calif., 1981—; ptnr. Price Rite Pharmacy Inc., Santee, 1981-85, pres., 1985—; v.p., treas. Rx-Six Assocs. Inc., San Diego, 1984—; pres., chief exec. officer O.P.T.I.O.N. Care Santee. Mem. Am. Pharm. Assn., Calif. Pharmacists Assn., San Diego Pharmacists Assn., Santee C. of C. (bd. dirs. 1987-88). Republican. Mormon. Home: 14390 Trailwind Rd Poway CA 92064 Office: Price Rite Pharmacy Inc 8774 Cuyamaca St Santee CA 92071

JERNIGAN, JAMES PAUL, marine officer; b. Sanford, N.C., Dec. 8, 1954; s. Walter Hayes and Lilly Lois (Suggs) Jernigan Barton; m. Donna Patterson, Dec. 18, 1976. BA, U. N.C., 1977. Commd. officer U.S. Marine Corps, 1977, advanced through grades to capt., 1983; dep. pub. affairs officer Fleet Marine Force Pacific, Camp Smith, Hawaii, 1986-88; with security dept. Naval Air Sta., Moffett Field, Calif., 1988-. Mem. U.S. Marine Corps Combat Corr. Assn., U. N.C. Alumni Assn., Kappa Sigma. Republican. Home: 830 Joranollo Dr Tracy CA 95376 Office: Naval Air Sta Security Dept Moffett Field CA 94035

JERRITTS, STEPHEN G., computer company executive; b. New Brunswick, N.J., Sept. 14, 1925; s. Steve and Anna (Kovacs) J.; m. Audrey Virginia Smith, June 1948; children: Marsha Carol, Robert Stephen, Linda Ann; m. 2d, Ewa Elizabet Rydell-Vejlens, Nov. 5, 1966; 1 son, Carl Stephen. Student, Union Coll., 1943-44; B.M.E., Rensselaer Poly. Inst., 1947, M.S. Mgmt., 1948. With IBM, various locations, 1949-58, IBM World Trade, N.Y.C., 1958-67, Bull Gen. Electric div. Gen. Electric, France, 1967-70, merged into Honeywell Bull, 1970-74; v.p., mng. dir. Honeywell Info. Systems Ltd., London, 1974-76; group v.p. Honeywell U.S. Info. Systems, Boston, 1977-80; pres., chief operating officer Honeywell Info. Systems, 1980-82, also bd. dirs.; pres., chief exec. officer Lee Data Corp., 1983-85; with Storage Tech. Corp., 1985-88, pres., chief operating officer, 1985-87, vice-chmn. bd. dirs., 1988; pres., chief exec. officer NBI Corp., 1988—, also bd. dirs.; bd. dirs. First Bank, Mpls. Bd. dirs. Guthrie Theatre, 1980-83, Charles Babbage Inst., 1980—, Minn. Orch., 1980-85; trustee Rensselaer Poly. Inst., 1980-85. Served with USNR, 1943-46. Mem. Computer Bus. Equipment Mfrs. (dir. exec. com. 1979-82), Assoc. Industries Mass. (dir. 1978-80). Clubs: Wellesley (Mass.) Country; Minneapolis. Home: 650 College Ave Boulder CO 80302 Office: NBI Inc 3450 Mitchell Ln PO Box 9001 Boulder CO 80301

JESSE, MARY, electrical engineer; b. San Jose, Calif., Nov. 22, 1964; d. Eugene Lyle and Kathlyn (Leff) J.; m. Roger Edward Talmage (div. Nov. 1986). BS in Elec. Engring., U. Utah, 1986. Systems elec. engr. Unisys/CSD, Salt Lake City, 1986-88, Stanford Telecommunications, Santa Clara Calif. and San Francisco area, 1988—; speaker Women and Math, Salt Lake City, 1987—. Recipient Honors at Entrance and Elaine K. Hunter Meml. scholarships U. Utah, 1982-86. Mem. IEEE, Soc. Women Engrs. (pres. student sect. 1983-84), Eta Kappa Nu (v.p. 1984-85), Tau Beta Pi, Phi Eta Sigma. Democrat. Home: 3450 Granada Ave #89 Santa Clara CA 95051

JESSE, ROSALIE CRUISE, clinical psychologist; b. Northview, Mo., July 25, 1938; d. Harold Washington and Ida Marie (Kegley) Cruise; m. Albert F. Jesse Jr., July 17, 1958 (div. 1988); 1 child, Albert F. III; m. Roger Purnelle, Sept. 3, 1988. AA, Grossmont Coll., 1971; BA cum laude, San Diego State U., 1973; MA, Calif. Sch. Profl. Psychology, 1975, PhD, 1977. Dir. counseling and program devel. East County ACCORD, San Diego, 1977-80; dir. Inst. for Advanced Psychol. Studies Calif. Sch. Profl. Psychology, San Diego, 1978-79; dir. Family Counseling Ctr., El Cajon, 1980-81; sr. clin. psychologist forensic services San Diego County Mental Health Dept., 1981-83; dir. Alvarado Ctr. for Psychology, San Diego, 1983—. Author: Children in Rocovery, 1988; contbr. articles to profl. jours. Mem. Am. Psychol. Assn., Calif. State Psychol. Assn., Acad. San Diego Psychologists, San Diego Psychology and Law Soc. Office: Alvarado Ctr for Psychology 7171 Alvarado Rd Ste 205 La Mesa CA 92041

JESSEE, JAMES WILSON, administrative operations analyst; b. Chico, Calif., Nov. 16, 1948; s. Earl Wilson and Frances Sylvia (Brownfield) J.; m. Nelda Faye Meline, Oct. 23, 1971; children: Earl Wilson, Emma Elizabeth. BA, Calif. State Univ., Chico, 1970, MPA, 1974; postgrad., Kirili Metrodij U., Skopje, Yugoslavia, 1974-75, Montclair State Coll., Upper Montclair, N.J., 1968-69. Teaching asst., dept. speech and drama Calif. State U., Chico, 1970-71; coord. of encounter program Community Action Vols. in Edn. (CAVE), Chico, 1970-71, dir., 1971-73; research asst. No. Calif. Higher Edn. Coun., Chico, 1973-74; ptnr., systems designer EASy Assoc., Chico, 1979-83; adminstrv. asst. to v.p. for acad. affairs Calif. State U., Chico, 1975—; part-time lectr. Calif. State U., Chico, 1978—. Creator, founder, mem., bd. dirs. Chico Housing Improvement Program (CHIP), Chico, 1971—. Mem. Am. Assn. Collegiate Registrars and Admissions Officers. Democrat. Office: Calif State Univ West 1st and Normal Sts Chico CA 95929

JESSUP, ROBERT JUDD, health organization executive; b. San Francisco, Oct. 15, 1947; s. R. Bruce and Adaline (Brown) J.; m. Jeanne Bannash, Sept. 7, 1968 (div. Dec. 1987); children: Jarrett, Jody. BA, Knox Coll., 1969; MBA, U. Denver, 1971. Dir. mktg. svcs. Blue Cross-Blue Shield Colo., Denver, 1972-78, dir. alternate delivery systems, 1978-80; pres. HMO Colo, Inc. Blue Cross-Blue Shield Colo., 1980-87; exec. dir. TakeCare Corp., Oakland, Calif., 1987—. 2d lt. U.S. Army, 1972. Mem. Colo. Assn. HMO's (treas. 1985-86), Denver C. of C. (Leadership Denver 1982). Office: TakeCare Corp 2101 Webster St Oakland CA 94612

JESTE, DILIP VISHWANATH, psychiatry educator; b. Pimpalagaon, India, Dec. 23, 1944; came to U.S., 1974; naturalized Feb., 1980; m. Sonali D. Jeste, Dec. 5, 1971; children: Shafali, Neelum. B in Medicine & Surgery, U. Poona, India, 1966; D. Psychiat. Medicine, Coll. Physicians and Surgeons, 1970; MD, U. Bombay, 1970. Cer. Am. Bd. Psychiatry and Neurology, 1979; lic. physician, D.C., Md., Calif. Hon. asst. prof. KEM Hosp., G.S. Med. Coll., Bombay, 1971-74; staff psychiatrist St. Elizabeth's Hosp., Washington, 1977-82, chief movement disorder unit, 1982-86; clin. assoc. prof. psychiatry Walter Reed Med. Ctr., Bethesda, Md., 1981-84; assoc. clin. prof. psychiatry and neurology George Washington U., Washington, 1984-86; prof. psychiatry and neuroscis. U. Calif., San Diego, 1986—, dir. neuro/geropsychiatry program and neuropath. rsch. lab., 1986—; vis. scientist dept. neuropathology Armed Forces Inst. of Pathology, Washington, 1984-86; co-dir. Med. Students' Psychiatry Clerkship Program, 1987—; ad-hoc mem. Vets. Adminstrn. Neurobiology Grant Rev. Bd., 1984—; participant numerous meeting and confs.; lectr. in field. Co-author: Understanding and Treating Tardive Dyskinesia, 1982; editor: Neuropsychiatric Movement Disorders, 1984, Neurpsychiatric Dementias, 1986, Psychosis and Depression in the Elderly, 1988; contbr. articles to numerous profl. jours, reviewer numerous profl. jours. Mem. Acad. Geriatric Resource Com., U. Calif., 1986-87, mem. com. on joint doctoral program in clin. psychology, 1986-87, mgmt. com. faculty compensation fund com., 1988—, chmn. Psychiat. Undergrad. Edn. Com., 1987. Recipient Merit award NIMH, 1988; recipient numerous grants in field. Fellow Indian Psychiatric Soc. (recipient Sandoz award 1973), Am. Psychiatric Assn. (co-chmn. Tardive Dyskinesia task force 1984—), Am. Coll. Neuropsychopharm. (co-chmn. fin. com. 1988—); mem. Soc. for Neurosci., Internat. Brain Rsch. Orgn., Soc. Biolog. Psychiatry (A.E. Bennett Neuropsychiatric Rsch. award 1981), Am. Acad. Neurology, Am. Geriatrics Soc., Calif. Psychiatric Soc., Am. Assn. Geriatric Psychiatry, West Coast Coll. Biolog. Psychiatry, San Diego Soc. Psychiatric Physicians, Assn. Scientists of Indian Origin in Am. (pres. neurosci. chpt. 1988—, named Outstanding Neuroscientist 1988). Office: Vets Adminstrn Med Ctr 3350 La Jolla Village Dr V116A San Diego CA 92161

JETT, MICHAEL JAN, banker; b. Elizabethton, Tenn., Aug. 12, 1944; s. Charles E. Jett; m. Patricia Louise Squires, Sept. 2, 1967 (div. Nov. 1984); children: Carter, Charly. BA, Wake Forest U., 1966; BS, U. N.C., 1971. CPA, Tex., N.C., Ariz. Mgr. Ernst & Whinney, Cleve., 1971-79; prin.

Arthur Young & Co., Dallas, 1979-84; chief fin. officer Encore Devel. Corp., Dallas, 1984-86; v.p. Valley Nat. Bank, Phoenix, 1987—; cons. Cleve. State U., 1977-78; v.p. Nat. Assn. Accts., Dallas, 1984-86. Author: (with others) Auditing Theory and Practice, 1981. Active Men's Arts Council, 1987-88; bd. dirs. Jane Wayland Inst., Phoenix, 1988. Served to capt. U.S. Army, 1966-69, Vietnam. Mem. Am. Inst. CPA's, Phi Beta Kappa. Republican. Presbyterian. Home: 8513 E Mustang Tr Scottsdale AZ 85253

JETT, PETER PAUL, manufacturing engineer; b. Trenton, Mich., July 1, 1961; s. Robert Wayne and Gladys Marie (Hardegger) J. BME, Mich. Technol. U., 1984. Process engr. Aerojet Strategic Propusion Co., Sacramento, 1984-87; mfg. engr. Aerojet Solid Propulsion Co., Sacramento, 1987—. Vol. Aerojet Adventures in Aerospace, Auburn, Calif., 1986—. Sigma Tau Gamma. Republican. Roman Catholic. Home: 123 Pleasant Ave #3 Auburn CA 95603 Office: Aerojet Solid Propulsion Co PO Box 15699C Dept 3360 Bldg 2025-2 Sacramento CA 95813

JETT, RICHARD JAMES, bank executive; b. South Gate, Calif., May 7, 1940; s. Artie Richard and Evelyn Clara (Tuksbre) J.; m. Deborrah C. Wiesman, July 14, 1975 (div. Sept. 1982); m. Michelle Diane Hall, Oct. 25, 1984; children: Sandi, Teri, Richi. Diploma in retail banking, U. Va. Collector Dial Fin., Alhambra, Calif., 1960-62; v.p. 1st Interstate Bank, Los Angeles, 1962-79; exec. v.p. Citrus State Bank, Covina, Calif., 1979-82; pres., chief exec. officer Empire Bank, N.A., Ontario, Calif., 1982—, also bd. dirs. Mem. Am. Bankers Assn. (advisor 1979-83,), Am. Inst. Banking (bd. dirs. 1983—), Independent Bankers Assn. So. Calif. (bd. dirs. 1984—, pres. 1989), Calif. Bankers Assn. (bd. dirs. 1985-87, 88—), Covina C. of C. (pres. 1986-87, named Dir. of Yr. 1984), Western States Consu,er Law Adv. Group (dir. 1980—). Republican. Lutheran. Lodges: Lions, Masons. Home: 646 Chaparro Rd Covina CA 91724 Office: Empire Bank NA 800 N Haven Ave Ontario CA 91764

JEW, CHESTER CHUNG, government agency executive; b. Canton, China, Sept. 22, 1934; s. Jan J. and Chew Ho Jew; m. Tamie Tung, Mar. 17, 1970; 1 child, John. BS, Calif. State U., Fresno, 1958; MPA, Golden Gate U., 1966; JD, John Marshall Law Sch., 1979. Criminal investigator Calif. Dept. Motor Vehicles, L.A., 1958-60, Calif. Dept. Alcoholic Beverage Control, San Francisco, 1960-66; pub. safety advisor Agy. Internat. Devel., Dept. State, Saigon, Vietnam, 1966-71; pub. safety advisor, tng. Internat. Police Acad. Aid, Dept. State, Washington, 1971-74; chief investigator Mont. Dept. Justice, Helena, 1975-76; legal instr. Fed. Law Enforcement Tng. Ctr., Glynco, Ga., 1976-80; chief security systems br. Fed. Protective Svc., Washington, 1980-85; chief security NASA/Ames Rsch. Ctr., Moffett Field, Calif., 1985—. Recipient Police Honor medal Vietnamese Govt., 1967, Police Combat medal Vietnam Police, 1968, Civilian Svc. award Am. Embassy, 1967. Mem. Am. Soc. Indsl. Security. Home: 766 Terra Bella Dr Milpitas CA 95035 Office: NASA Ames Rsch Ctr MS-241-2 Moffett Field CA 94035

JEWELL, DOROTHY ALTHEA, writer; b. Santa Barbara, Calif., Dec. 12, 1923; d. Carl and Grace Esther (Flint) Killam; m. William Eugene, Oct. 29, 1948; children: Kathleen Althea Schwab, Marianne Susan. Student, Long Beach City Coll. Staff writer Press-Telegram, Long Beach, Calif., 1947-52; freelance writer Better Homes and Gardens, Iowa, 1948-65; assoc. editor Modern Maturity, Lakewood, Calif., 1965-87; freelance writer Crestline, Calif., 1987—.

JEWELL, HERBERT L(ESLIE), JR., medical technologist; b. Olympia, Wash., Dec. 31, 1943; s. Herbert Leslie Sr. and Marie Gergina (Inman) J.; m. Luevenia Hall, June 19, 1974 (dec. Nov. 1975); 1 child, Alisa; m. Maros Jan Hummel, Mar. 18, 1978; stepchildren: Megaera Esmond, Emmet Esmond, Roen Brown. Student, Centralia (Wash.) Coll., 1962-64; BS in Zoology, Wash. State U., 1966; BS in Fisheries, U. Wash., 1971; MPA, Evergreen State Coll., 1987. Lab. technician Gray's Harbor Community Hosp., Aberdeen, Wash., 1970; med. technologist Madigan Army Med. Ctr., Tacoma, 1971—. With U.S. Army, 1966-69, Vietnam. Mem. Am. Med. Technologists, Wash. State Soc. of Am. Med. Technologists, Ocean Shores (Wash.) Community Club (bd.dirs. 1984—), Jaycees (Tumwater, Wash. chpt. pres. 1975-76, Jaycee of the Yr. 1973, 74). Democrat.

JEWETT, LUCILLE MCINTYRE (MRS. GEORGE FREDERICK JEWETT, JR.), civic worker; b. St. Louis, Jan. 1, 1929; d. Charles Edwin and Elizabeth (Newbery) McIntyre; student U. Puget Sound, 1950; m. George Frederick Jewett, Jr., July 11, 1953; children: Mary Elizabeth, George Frederick III. Mem. Jr. League, Tacoma; mem. World Service Council, 1967—; trustee San Francisco Ballet Assn.; bd. dirs. Internat. Hospitality Center, San Francisco; collectors com. Nat. Gallery Art, Washington; trustee U. Puget Sound, Tacoma; alt. del. Rep. Nat. Conv., 1964. Mem. Order St. John of Jerusalem, Francisco Club, Pi Beta Phi. Presbyterian. Home: 2990 Broadway San Francisco CA 94115

JHAWAR, MAKHANLAL MOHANLAL, water treatment company executive; b. Ahmednagar, India, Oct. 26, 1940; came to U.S., 1965; s. Mohanlal Harikison and Mohinibai (Binnany) J.; m. Vimla M. Daga, May 31, 1964; children: Manoj Kumar, Maya Debi. BSc in Chemistry, U. Poona, India, 1963; BSChemE, U. Mo., Rolla, 1967. Assoc. engr. Fairbanks-Morse, Beloit, Wis., 1967-69; mgr., project engr. Burns & Roe Co., Paramus, N.Y., 1969-70, 70-73; sales engr. Gulf Gen. Atomic Co., San Diego, 1973-75; sales mgr. N.Am. div. Fluid Systems div. U.O.P., San Diego, 1975-78; v.p. sales and mktg. Ultraviolet Tech., San Diego, 1978-83; pres. Ultraviolet Tech., Sacramento, 1983-86, Indsl. Water Tech., San Diego, 1986—; bd. dirs. Indsl. Water Tech., San Diego, August Techs., Inc., Solana Beach, Calif. Mem. Kohinoor (advisor 1985—). Office: Indsl Water Tech Inc PO Box 1172 Encinitas CA 92024

JIANG, JOHN JIANZHONG, materials engineer; b. Kaiping, Guangdong, People's Republic China, May 7, 1960; came to U.S., 1985; s. Dong and Laiwa (Chu) J. BS in Elec. Engring., South China Inst. Tech., 1982; MS in Ceramic Engring., Alfred U., 1987. Technician Sanbu Micro Electric Motor Works, Kaiping, 1976-78, asst. engr., asst. project planner, 1982-84, tech. svc. engr., 1984-85; with Canton (People's Republic China) Research Inst. Electronics, 1982-85; rsch. and devel. engr., prin. project engr. Am. Electronic Materials, Inc., San Diego, 1987—; speaker profl. meetings. Contbr. articles to profl. jours. Mem. Materials Rsch. Soc., Am. Phys. Soc., Am. Ceramic Soc. Office: Am Electronic Materials Inc 11055 Flintkote Ave San Diego CA 92121

JIMERSON, WILLIAM ALLEN, musician; b. Albuquerque, May 19, 1950; s. William Eugene and Sue Carol (Davis) J.; children: Zia Adrian Fiorella. Paralegal, Albuquerque Career Inst., 1987. Recording engr. Paramount Recording Studios, L.A., 1974-80; court specialist O'Melveny & Myers, L.A., 1980-82; freelance paralegal Albuquerque, 1982—, freelance musician, guitarist, 1982—. Composer, writer various original songs; author book: Pervert Boot. Address: 2936 Valencia Dr NE Albuquerque NM 87110-3216

JIMMINK, GLENDA LEE, educator; b. Lamar, Colo., Feb. 13, 1935; d. Harold Dale and Ruth Grace (Ellenberger) Fasnacht; m. Gary Jimmink, Oct. 24, 1964 (div. 1984); 1 child, Erik Gerard. BA, U. LaVerne, Calif., 1955. Tchr. Pomona (Calif.) Unified Sch. Dist., 1955-61, Palo Alto (Calif.) Unified Sch. Dist., 1961-65, San Rafael (Calif.) Sch. Dist., 1966—. Artist/pubr. calendar: Dry Creek Valley, 1987, others. Mem. Marin Arts Council, San Rafael, 1989—, PTA, San Rafael, 1966—; rep. Curriculum Council of San Rafael, 1983-87; big sis. Big Bros./Big Sis., San Rafael, 1988—; mem. Citizens for a Better Environment, 1984—. Mem. Calif. Tchrs. Assn., NEA, San Rafael Tchrs. Assn., Port Sonoma Yacht Club. Republican. Office: San Rafael School Dist 225 Woodland Ave San Rafael CA 94901

JOAQUIM, RICHARD RALPH, hotel executive; b. Cambridge, Mass., July 28, 1936; s. Manuel and Mary (Marrano) J.; m. Nancy Phyllis Reis, Oct. 22, 1960; 1 dau., Vanessa Reis. BFA, Boston U., 1955, MusB, 1959. Social dir., coordinator summer resort, Wolfeboro, N.H., 1957-59; concert soloist N.H. Symphony Orch., Vt. Choral Soc., Choral Arts Soc., Schenectady Chamber Orch., 1957-60; coordinator performance functions, mgr. theatre Boston U., 1959-60, asst. program dir., 1963-64, dir. univ. programs, 1964-70; gen. mgr. Harrison House of Glen Cove; dir. Conf. Service Corp., Glen Cove, N.Y., 1970-74, sr. v.p., dir. design and devel.; v.p. Arltec, also mng. dir. Sheraton Internat. Conf. Center, 1975-76; v.p., mng. dir. Scottsdale (Ariz.) Conf. Center and Resort Hotel, 1976—; pres. Internat. Conf. Resorts, Inc., 1977, chmn. bd., 1977—; pres. Western Conf. Resorts; concert solist U.S. Army Field Band, Washington, 1960-62. Creative arts cons., editorial cons., concert mgr. Commr. recreation Watertown, Mass., 1967—; mem. Spl. Study Com. Watertown, 1967—, Glen Cove Mayor's Urban Renewal Com., Nat. Com. for Performing Arts Ctr. at Boston U., Jacob K. Kavits Fellows Program Fellowship Bd. Bd. dirs. Nat. Entertainment Conf.; trustee Boston U., 1983—, Hotel and Food Adminstrn. Program Adv. Bd., Boston U., 1986—. Served with AUS, 1960-62. Mem. Assn. Coll. and Univ. Concert Mgrs., Am. Symphonic League, Am. Fedn. Film Socs., Assn. Am. Artists, Am. Personnel and Guidance Assn., La Chaine des Rotisseurs, Knights of the Vine, Nat. Alumni Council Boston U. Clubs: The Lotos (N.Y.); The Arizona (Phoenix). Office: Scottsdale Conf Ctr & Resort Hotel 7700 McCormick Pkwy Scottsdale AZ 85258

JOBE, ALICE, transportation executive; b. Little Rock, Nov. 24, 1935; student Long Beach City Coll., 1960-61; m. K.L. Jobe, Mar. 12, 1957; 1 dau., Cathy. With Nat. Equity Life Ins. Co., Little Rock, 1954-55, Cash Wholesale Co., Little Rock, 1956-57; with Bekins Internat., subs. Bekins Co., Wilmington, Calif., 1959-77, v.p., 1971-77; v.p. Imperial Internat., Inc., Torrance, Calif., 1977-78, exec. v.p., 1978-80, dir., 1977-81; pres. Imperial Van Lines Internat., Inc., 1980-81; industry cons., 1981-82; founder, pres. Caddo Internat., freight forwarding, Los Alamitos, Calif., 1982—. Mem. Household Goods Forwarders Assn. (exec. com. 1977-78), Nat. Def. Transp. Assn. (life), Am. Soc. Profl. Women. Republican. Office: Caddo Internat 3662 Katella Ave Ste 209 PO Box 739 Los Alamitos CA 90720

JOBE, FRANK WILSON, orthopedic surgeon; b. Greensboro, N.C., July 16, 1925. MD, Loma Linda U., 1956. Diplomate Am. Bd. Orthopedic Surgery. Intern Los Angeles County Gen. Hosp., 1956-57, resident, 1960-64; staff Centinda Hosp., Daniel Freeman Hosp., Inglewood, Calif., Los Angeles County U. So. Calif. Med. Ctr., L.A.; assoc. clin. prof. U. So. Calif. Sch. Medicine; team physician, Los Angeles Dodgers. With AUS, 1943-46. Fellow ACS; mem. Am. Acad. Orthopedic Surgeons, Western Orthopedic Assn. Office: 501 E Hardy St Ste 200 Inglewood CA 90301 *

JOBS, STEVEN PAUL, computer corporation executive; b. 1955; adopted s. Paul J. and Clara J. (Jobs). Student, Reed Coll. With Hewlett-Packard, Palo Alto, Calif.; designer video games Atari Inc., 1974; co-founder Apple Computer Inc., Cupertino, Calif., chmn. bd., 1975-85, former dir.; pres. NeXT, Inc., Palo Alto, Calif., 1985—. Co-designer: (with Stephan Wozniak) Apple I Computer, 1976. Office: NeXT Inc 3475 Deer Creek Rd Palo Alto CA 94304 *

JOCHUM, LESTER H., dentist; b. Chgo., Nov. 19, 1929; s. J. Harry and Hilma O. (Swanson) J.; m. Anne Elizabeth Cannon, Sept. 20, 1952 (div. Apr. 1983); 1 child, David S. Student U. Wyo., 1947-48; BS in Bus. Adminstrn. with honors, Oreg. State U., 1952; pre-dental student Portland State Coll., 1959-60; B.S. with honors in Sci., U. Oreg., 1963, D.M.D., 1964. Staff acct. Pacific Telephone and Telegraph Co., San Francisco, 1952-59; gen. practice dentistry, San Jose, Calif., 1965-83; dental cons. Delta Dental Plan of Calif., Sacramento, 1983—; ptnr. Trinity Imports. Contbr. articles Calif. Wine Press; also others. Asst. chief Santa Clara Reserve Police Dept., Calif., 1976-83. Active No. Calif. diocese Episc. Ch. Served with U.S. Army, 1952-54. Mem. Sacramento Dist. Dental Soc., Calif. Dental Assn., ADA, Phi Kappa Phi, Psi Omega, Alpha Phi Omega, Lambda Chi Alpha (ritual chmn. 1951, soc. chmn. 1952). Republican. Office: Delta Dental Plan of Calif 7667 Folsom Blvd Sacramento CA 95826

JOCIC, DUSAN, electrical engineer, consultant; b. Belgrade, Yugoslavia, Sept. 7, 1935; came to U.S., 1963; s. Zivojin Petar and Vukosava (Stojkovic) J.; m. Coral Shirley Walker, July 2, 1966. A.S., Pierce Coll., 1985. Design engring. mgr. quality control Belfuse Inc., Jersey City, 1968-74; dir. quality assurance Vanguard Electric Co., Inglewood, Calif., 1974-75; mgr. prodn. Ferrodyne Corp., Venice, Calif., 1975-76; research and devel. assoc. Litton Guidance/Control Systems, Woodland Hills, Calif., 1976-85; mem. tech. staff def. electronics ops. Autonetics Marine Systems div. Rockwell Internat., Anaheim, Calif., 1985—; cons. Encore, San Jose, Calif., 1983—. Patentee in field. Sustaining mem. Republican Nat. Com., Washington, 1980—; mem. Rep. Senatorial Club, 1980, Rep. Congl. Com., 1980. Mem. IEEE (sr. mem., adviser to exec. bd. 1984, sec. 1986—), IEEE Magnetic Soc. (Los Angeles chpt.), Internat. Power Conversion Soc. Serbian Orthodox. Home: 1308 Cozy Terr Anaheim CA 92806 Office: Rockwell Internat Tech Staff D/379-060 031-GE 22 3370 Miraloma Ave PO Box 4921 Anaheim CA 92803-4921

JOECK, NEIL HERMANN ARCHIBALD, arms control researcher, lecturer; b. Montreal, Quebec, Can., Feb. 16, 1950; came to U.S., 1957; s. Werner Ferdinand and Nancy (Archibald) J.; m. Melinda Erickson, Sept. 16, 1972; children: Morgan Erickson, Graeme Erickson. BA, U. Calif., Santa Cruz, 1973; MA, Carleton U., Ottawa, Ont. Can., 1975; PhD, U. Calif., Los Angeles, 1986. Adminstrv. asst. U. Calif., Berkeley, 1975-78; teaching fellowship U. Calif., Los Angeles, 1979-81; research assoc. Ctr. for Internat. and Strategic Affairs, Los Angeles, 1984-86; arms control researcher Lawrence Livermore (Calif.) Nat. Lab., 1987—; asst. to editor Policy Sciences, Los Angeles, 1981-84; program cons. Com. Fgn. Relations, Los Angeles, 1986-87; cons. WGBH, Boston, 1986-87; prof. Chinese Acad. Social Sci., Beijing, 1987. Editor: Arms Control and International Security, 1984, Strategic Consequences of Nuclear Proliferation, 1986; contbr. articles to profl. jours. Vol. Dem. Party, 1972; lectr. Roosevelt Ctr., Washington, 1986, Radio and TV, various stas., Los Angeles, 1980-86. Graham fellwo UCLA, 1984-85; predoctoral research fellow Inst. On Global Conflict and Cooperation, La Jolla, Calif., 1981-83; Gimbel fellow Bank of Am., Los Angeles, 1984. Fellow Ctr. for Internat. and Strategic Affairs; mem. AAAS, Internat. Studies Assn., Dads Club (Piedmont, Calif.), LLNL Recreation Assn. (Livermore). Avocations: chess, basketball, modern lit. Office: Lawrence Livermore Nat Lab PO Box 808 Livermore CA 94550

JOFFE, LEONARD, ophthalmologist; b. Johannesburg, South Africa, May 20, 1942; came to U.S., 1976; s. David Isaac and Sonia (Levitats) J.; m. Marcelle Kusman, Dec. 16, 1964; children: Steven, Hadine, Lindy. MB, BCh, Witwatersrand U, 1985. Diplomate Am. Bd. Ophthalmology. Intern Johannesburg Group of Hosps., 1966; pvt. practice Johannesburg, 1967-72; resident in ophthalmology Johannesburg Hosp. Group, 1972-76; fellow in retina Wills Eye Hosp., Phila., 1976-78; chief retina service La. State U. Eye Ctr., New Orleans, 1978-79; pvt. practice Tucson, Ariz., 1979—; clin. asst. prof. dept. ophthalmology U. Ariz., Tucson, 1979—. V.p. Cong. Anshei Israel, Tucson, 1983-89, pres., 1989—; bd. dirs. Jewish Fedn. Ariz, 1985-88. Fellow Am. Acad. Ophthalmology, Royal Coll. Surgeons Edinburgh, Coll. Medicine South Africa; mem. AMA, Ariz. Med. Soc., Pima County Med. Soc., Ariz. Ophthal. Soc. (pres. 1988—), Tucson Ophthal. Soc. (pres. 1982-84), Ventana Golf Club (Tucson). Republican. Office: Retina Assocs SW 6561 E Carondelet Dr Tucson AZ 85710

JOHANNES, KENNETH JOHN, marketing executive; b. Fresno, Calif., July 4, 1940; s. John Peter and Anna (Gross) J.; m. Patricia A. Redman (div. 1984); children: Gregory K., Jeffery E., Kimberley A.; m. Cynthia Ellen Hackley, July 22, 1986. Grad. high sch., Fresno. Sales rep. Calif. Automobile Assn., Fresno, 1967-76; sales mgr. Woodard Chevrolet-Oldsmobile-Cadillac, Fairfield, Calif., 1976-80, Nelson Chevrolet, Richmond, Calif., 1981-82; fin. mgr., gen. sales mgr. South Lake Tahoe (Calif.) Ford-Lincoln-Mercury, 1983-84, Stockton (Calif.) Nissan, 1984-86; gen. sales mgr. Manteca (Calif.) Nissan, 1986-87; gen. mgr. Internat. Auto Brokers, Stockton, 1987-88; sales and mktg. cons. J & J Enterprises, Stockton, 1988—. Sgt. USAF, 1959-67, Vietnam. Mem. Moose. Home and Office: 2270 Lido Circle Stockton CA 95207

JOHANOS, DONALD, orchestra conductor; b. Cedar Rapids, Iowa, Feb. 10, 1928; s. Gregory Hedges and Doris (Nelson) J.; m. Thelma Trimble, Aug. 27, 1950; children—Jennifer Claire, Thea Christine, Gregory Bruce (dec.), Andrew Mark, Eve Marie; m. Corinne Rutledge, Sept. 28, 1985. Mus.B., Eastman Sch. Music, 1950, Mus.M., 1952; D.F.A. (hon.), Coe Coll., 1962. Tchr. Pa. State U., 1953-55, So. Meth. U., 1958-62, Hockaday Sch., 1962-65. Mus. dir., Altoona (Pa.) Symphony, 1953-56, Johnstown (Pa.) Symphony, 1955-56, asso. condr., Dallas Symphony Orch., 1957-61, resident condr., 1961-62, mus. dir., 1962-70, assoc. condr., Pitts. Symphony, 1970-79, mus. dir., Honolulu Symphony Orch., 1979—, artistic dir., Hawaii Opera Theater, 1979-83, guest condr., Phila. Orch., Amsterdam Concertgebouw Orch., Pitts. Symphony, Rochester Philharmonic, New Orleans Philharmonic, Denver Symphony, Vancouver Symphony, Chgo. Symphony, San Francisco Symphony, Netherlands Radio Philharmonic, Swiss Radio Orch., Mpls. Symphony, Paris Opera, Boston Symphony, others. Advanced study grantee Am. Symphony Orch. League and Rockefeller Found., 1955-58. Mem. Am. Fedn. Musicians Internat. Congress of Strings (dir.). Office: Honolulu Symphony Orch 1441 Kapiolani Blvd Ste 1515 Honolulu HI 96814

JOHANSON, DONALD CARL, physical anthropologist; b. Chgo., June 28, 1943; s. Carl Torsten and Sally Eugenia (Johnson) J. ; m. Lenora Carey, 1988. BA, U. Ill., 1966; MA, U. Chgo., 1970, PhD, 1974; DSc (hon.), John Carroll U., 1979; D.Sc. (hon.), Coll. of Wooster, 1985. Mem. dept. phys. anthropology Cleve. Mus. Natural History, 1972-81, curator, 1974-81; dir. Inst. Human Origins, Berkeley, Calif., 1981—; prof. anthropology Stanford U., 1983—; adj. prof. Case Western Res. U., 1978-81, Kent State U., 1978-81. Co-author: (with M.A. Edey) Of Lucy: The Beginning of Humankind, 1982 (Am. Book award 1982), Blue Prints: Solving the Mystery of Evolution, 1989; film producer: The First Family, 1981, Lucy in Disguise, 1982; contbr. numerous sci. articles, papers, reviews; host, narrator Pub. Broadcasting Svc. NATURE series, 1982. Recipient Jared Potter Kirtland award for outstanding sci. achievement Cleve. Mus. Natural History, 1979, Profl. Achievement award, U. Chgo., 1980, Gold Mercury Internat. ad personem award Ethiopia, 1982, Humanist Laureate award Acad. of Humanism, 1983, Disting. Svc. award Am. Humanist Assn., 1983, San Francisco Exploratorium award, 1986, Internat. Premio Fregene award, 1987; grantee Wenner-Gren Found., NSF, Nat. Geog. Soc., L.S.B. Leakey Found., Cleve. Found., George Gund Found., Roush Found., Nat. Geog. Soc. Fellow AAAS, Calif. Acad. Scis., Rochester (N.Y.) Mus., Royal Geog. Soc.; mem. Am. Assn. Phys. Anthropologists, Internat. Assn. Dental Research, Internat. Assn. Human Biologists, Am. Assn. Africanist Archaeologists, Soc. Vertebrate Paleontology, Soc. Study of Human Biology, Explorers Club, Societe de l'Anthropologie de Paris, Centro Studi Ricerche Ligabue (Venice), Founders' Coun., Chgo. Field Mus. Natural History (hon.), Assn. Internationale pour l'etude de Paleontologie Humaine, Mus. Nat. d'Histoire Naturelle de Paris (corr.), Nat. Ctr. Sci. Edn. (supporting scientist). Office: Inst Human Origins 2453 Ridge Rd Berkeley CA 94709

JOHARI, SHYAM, computer consultant, educator; b. Jodhpur, Rajasthan, India, June 30, 1948; came to U.S., 1967.; s. Mohan L. and Gauri D. (Taparia) J.; m. Kamala Baheti, Nov. 22, 1972; children: Priti, Umesh. BS, U. Jodhpur, 1965, MS, 1967; MS, U. Ill., Chgo., 1969, PhD, 1975. Sr. systems analyst western area devel. ctr. Burroughs Corp., Irvine, Calif., 1975-77; sr. specialist internat. group Burroughs Corp., Detroit, 1977-80, mktg. specialist, 1980-82, asst. to v.p. quality, 1982-84, 1982-84, mgr. data communications fin. systems group, 1984-86; sr. cons. Joseph & Cogan Assocs. sub. Unisys Corp., Naperville, Ill., 1986-87; mgr. performance group Tandem Computers Inc., Cupertino, Calif., 1987—. Assoc. editor Sigmetrics, 1987—. Mem. Assn. Computing Machinery, IEEE (mem. computer soc.), Computer Measurement Group. Hindu. Home: 3181 Heritage Valley Dr San Jose CA 95148 Office: Tandem Computer Inc 10555 Ridgeview Ct Cupertino CA 95014

JOHLER, JOSEPH RALPH, physicist; b. Scranton, Pa., Feb. 23, 1919; s. Joseph Jacob and Lillian (Dietzel) J.; B.A., Am. U., 1941; B.S.E., George Washington U., 1950; m. Nora Stella Callahan, Sept. 16, 1953; children—Dennis Ralph, Mark Stephen, Paul Norman, Annette Diane. Ballistic mathematician Ballistic Research Lab., Aberdeen Proving Grounds, Md., 1942-45; with Nat. Bur. Standards, Washington, 1946-51, electronic engr. Boulder Labs., 1951-65, chief electromagnetic theory sect., 1961-65; program leader, electromagnetic theory program Environmental Sci. Services Adminstrn., Inst. Telecommunication Scis. and Aeronomy, U.S. Dept. Commerce, Boulder, 1965-70, physicist, project scientist Office Telecommunications 1970-72, chief nav. and D-Region Sci. sect., 1972-76; pres. Colo. Research and Prediction Lab., Boulder, 1976-86; cons. Johler Assocs., 1986—. Served with USNR, 1944-46. Research Nat. Bur. Standards Disting. Authorship award, 1963, 66. Mem. Internat. Union Radio Sci., IEEE (sr. mem., life mem.), Internat. Radio Consultative Com., Wild Goose Assn. (Gold Medal of Merit award 1982). Contbr. articles to profl. jours. Home: 16796 W 74th Pl Golden CO 80403

JOHN, RONALD DAVID, police officer; b. Wenatchee, Wash., Apr. 24, 1948; s. David Willard and Phyllis Irene (Brisbine) Hewson; m. Delia. Student, Cen. Wash. St. Coll., 1966-67, Spokane Falls Community Coll., 1967-68; grad., Nat. Sheriffs Inst., 1976, Northwest Law Enforcement Exec. Command Coll., 1987; cert., Wash. St. Criminal Justice Tng. Commn., 1989. Deputy sheriff Adams county, Ritzville, Wash., 1970-71, Lincoln County, Davenport, Wash., 1971-73; undersheriff Lincoln County, Davenport, 1973-75, sheriff, 1975-77; chief of police Sedro-Woolley (Wash.) Police Dept., 1977--; Bd. dirs. NW Regional Council Law Enforcement Radio Network,. Trustee United Way Skagit County, 1981--; bd. dirs. Wash. Assn. County. Recipient cert. merit Knights of Columbus, 1982. Mem. Wash. Law Enforcement Assn., Wash. Assn. Sheriffs and Police. Republican. Home: 613 N Township Sedro-Woolley WA 98284 Office: Sedro-Woolley Police Dept 720 Murdock Sedro Woolley WA 98284

JOHNCOCK, LYNDA MARIE, service executive; b. Phoenix, Oct. 10, 1948; d. Billy James Marks and Billie Marie (Mulkey) Weigt; m. Gordon Walter Johncock, May 25, 1976 (div. 1983); 1 child, Bobby John Gardner. Grad. high sch., Phoenix. Lic. realtor, Ariz. Owner Cosmotique Plus, Coldwater, Mich., 1975-87, Am. Antiques, Phoenix, 1975—, Past and Present Interiors, Phoenix, 1982—; co. exec. Successful Singles Internat., Phoenix, 1983—; cons. in field. Chairperson 1st Indy 500 tennis tournament, 1978. Republican. Home: 2239 W Windrose Dr Phoenix AZ 85029

JOHNSEN, LEIGH DANA, historian; b. Deer Park, Calif., Jan. 14, 1952; s. Fred Ernest and Vera Evelyn (Nethercott) J.; m. Colleen Claire Brandt, Mar. 23, 1975. BA, Pacific Union Coll., 1974; MA, Andrews U., 1975; PhD, U. Calif., Riverside, 1984. Vis. scholar U. Calif., Riverside, 1987-88; asst. editor Salmon P. Chase papers The Claremont (Calif.) Grad. Sch., 1988—; cons. hist. preservation Inst. for Tech. Devel., Jackson, Miss., 1988. Mem. Loma Linda (Calif.) Hist. Commn., 1985—. Regents fellow U. Calif.-Riverside, 1980-81, Weniger fellow Andrews U., 1974-75. Mem. Assn. Documentary Editing, Am. Hist. Assn., Nat. Trust for Hist. Preservation, Orgn. Am. Historians, Phi Alpha Theta. Democrat. Office: Claremont Grad Sch History Dept Claremont CA 91711

JOHNSON, ABIGAIL RIDLEY, tour and travel executive; b. Vancouver, B.C., Can., Jan. 28, 1945; d. Frederic Neville and Cara Lee (Smith) Ridley; m. Ralph Maxwell Johnson, Sept. 17, 1971 (div.). BA in Music, Colo. Women's Coll., 1967; postgrad. San Jose State U., summer 1967. Cert. travel counselor. Co. rep. Manhattan Festival Ballet, N.Y.C., 1967-68; asst. booking mgr. Western Opera Theatre, San Francisco, 1968-69; asst. to consul and trade commr. Can. Consulate Gen., San Francisco, 1969-71; office mgr. Whitney Properties, San Francisco, 1971-72; sales mgr. Sutter Travel Service, San Francisco, 1973-80; dir., owner Tour Arts, San Francisco, 1980—; bd. dirs. Chanticleer Inc. Active San Francisco Opera, Symphony, Ballet; mem. task force Arts and Tourism Calif. Confedn. Arts. Mem. Am. Soc. Travel Agts., Inst. Cert. Travel Agts., Jr. League San Francisco. Episcopalian. Office: Tour Arts 231 Franklin St San Francisco CA 94102

JOHNSON, AGNES JAE, artist; b. Burkhardt, Wis., Mar. 30, 1921; d. Albert Kornelius and Analena Theodora (Midtun) Jacobson; m. Clinton Holver Johnson, June 12, 1945; children: Dawn Renee, Debra Lynn. Student, River Falls State U., 1942; BA, Chico (Calif.) State U., 1958; postgrad., U. Calif., 1958-75, Shasta Coll., 1976-88. Cert. elem. tchr.; reading specialist. Tchr. Cloverleaf Rural, Woodville, Wis., 1940-41, Cazenovia (Wis.) Elem. Sch., 1941-42, West Salem (Wis.) Elem. & High Sch., 1943-45; bookkeeper Aetna Ins. Co., Mpls., 1945-48; tchr. Shasta Lake Elem. Sch. Dist., Calif., 1955-58; tchr. Redding (Calif.) Elem. Sch. Dist., 1958-76, title 1 tchr., 1972-75; artist Redding, 1978—. Vol. Women's Parole Adv. Bd., Redding, 1966-69; vol. tchr. ESL, Redding. Mem. Am. Assn. Univ. Women (cultural area rep. 1986-88), Calif. Tchrs. ASsn., Shastafjell (cultural chmn. 1976-84, scholarship rep. 1980-88). Democrat. Lutheran. Home: 1449 Norman Dr Redding CA 96002

JOHNSON, ALICE ELAINE, retired academic administrator; b. Janesville, Wis., Oct. 9, 1929; d. Floyd C. and Alma M. (Walthers) Chester; m. Richard C. Johnson, Sept. 25, 1948 (div. 1974); children: Randall S., Nile C., Linnea E. BA, U. Colo., 1968. Pres., administrator Pikes Peak Inst. Med. Tech., Colorado Springs, Colo., 1968-88; mem. adv. com. to Colo. Commn. on Higher Edn., 1979-80, State Adv. Council on Pvt. Occupational Schs., Denver, 1978-86; mem. tech. adv. com. State Health Occupations, 1986-88. Mem. Colo. Pvt. Sch. Assn. (pres. 1981-82, bd. dirs. 1976-88, Outstanding Mem. 1978, 80), Phi Beta Kappa. Democrat. Unitarian.

JOHNSON, ALLEN HALBERT, surgeon; b. Atascadero, Calif., Jan. 23, 1922; s. Halbert Theodore and Julia Hallock (Kommers) J.; m. Mary Marchant McGee, Oct. 21, 1945 (dec. July 1983); children: Kathryn, Martha, Elizabeth, Kenneth. AB, U. Calif., Berkeley, 1943; MD, U. Calif., San Francisco, 1946. Diplomate Am. Bd. Surgery. Intern U. Calif., San Francisco, 1946-47, asst. resident, 1947-48, asst. resident surgery, 1950-54, chief resident, 1954-55; pvt. practice San Jose, Calif., 1955—; clin. prof. surgery Stanford, U., 1974—; chief of staff Santa Clara (Calif.) Valley Med. Ctr., 1969-72, San Jose (Calif.) Hosp., 1980-82; clin. prof. surgery Stanford U., 1970-; instr. in field. Contbr. articles to profl. jours. Bd. dirs. Boys City Boys Club, San Jose, 1962—, YMCA, San Jose, 1964—, Vis. Nurses Assn., San Jose, 1964-70, ARC, San Jose, 1960-72. Capt. Med. Corps, U.S. Army, 1948-50. Mem. San Jose Surgical Soc. (pres. 1963-64), Univ. Calif. Med. Alumni Assn. (pres. 1981-82), Naffziger Surgical Soc. (pres. 1973-74), ACS (bd. of govs. 1974-80), Pacific Coast Surg. Assn. (sec.-treas. 1980-86), San Jose Country Club (bd. dirs. 1975-78), Gustine Gun Club. Republican. Home: 1655 Emory St San Jose CA 95126 Office: Drs Johnson Seipel & Knoernschild 58 N 13th St San Jose CA 95112

JOHNSON, ANITA MARIE, foundation executive; b. Medford, Wis., May 27, 1927; d. Frank Charles and Margaret Marie (Sauer) Pernsteiner; m. Lloyd Chester Johnson, Nov. 18, 1947; children: Martin L., Lawrence J., Shelley, Janet, Robert, Andrew. Grad. high sch., Medford. Adminstrv. asst. Cath. Charities, Phoenix, 1969-80; v.p. contract mgmt. Found. for Sr. Living, Phoenix, 1981-85; adminstr. Lions Found. Ariz., Phoenix, 1985—; v.p. L.C. Johnson Constrn. Co., Phoenix, 1986—. Recipient Outstanding Contbn. award Found. for Sr. Living, 1983. Mem. Lioness (sec. Phoenix Metro club 1986-87, pres. 1987-88). Democrat. Roman Catholic. Office: Lions Found Ariz 1016 N 32d St Phoenix AZ 85008

JOHNSON, ANTHONY RICHARDO, military officer; b. Mexia, Tex.; s. Willie Larcie and Betty Jean (Cotton) J. BS in History, USAF Acad., 1976; MBA, Columbia Pacific U., 1985; MAS in Aeronautical Sci., Embry-Riddle Aeronautical U., 1989. Commd. 2d lt. USAF, 1976, advanced through grades to maj., 1980; wing combat crew instr. USAF, Minot, N.D., 1980-81; airborne missile ops. commdr. USAF, Ellsworth AFB, S.D., 1981-83, Airborne Launch Control System upgrade instr., 1983-84, chief Airborne Launch Control System standardization/evaluation, 1984-86; system safety program mgr. USAF, Norton AFB, Calif., 1986-87, chief small ICBM flight test integration br., 1988—. Recipient CAP award, Rapid City, S.D., 1982. Mem. Assn. Grads., Tuskegee Airmen Internat. Home: 2778 Irvington Ave San Bernardino CA 92407-2141 Office: BSD/MGET USAF Norton AFB CA 92409-6468

JOHNSON, ARNOLD GORDON, clergyman; b. Albert Lea, Minn., June 30, 1936; s. Arnold Clifford and Georgia (Godtland) B.; m. Mary Lou Zemke, Mar. 26, 1960; children: Dawn Marie, Eric Blair, Tanya Leigh, Mija Leah. BA, St. Olaf U., Northfield, Minn., 1958; MDiv., Luther Sem., St. Paul, 1968. Ordained to ministry, Luth. Ch. Commd. pilot USAF, 1959, chaplain, 1968, advanced through grades to col., ret., 1984; sr. pastor Cen. Luth. Ch., Spokane, Wash., 1984—; parish evangelist The Am. Luth. Ch., Seattle, 1978—; stewardship counselor Evang. Luth. Ch., Spokane, 1984—. Author: The Chaplain's Role as a Transcendant Symbol in the Military, 1974. Fundraiser United Way, Lubbock, Tex., 1979. Mem. Red River Valley Fighter Pilots Assn., Rotary, Lions (v.p. 1985—), Daedalians (v.p. 1985-86). Home: E1209 35th Ave Spokane WA 99203 Office: Cen Lutheran Ch W309 5th Ave Spokane WA 99204

JOHNSON, ARTHUR WILLIAM, JR., planetarium executive; b. Steubenville, Ohio, Jan. 8, 1949; s. Arthur William and Carol (Gilcrest) J.; B.Mus., U. So. Calif., 1973. Lectr., Griffith Obs. and Planetarium, 1969-73; planetarium writer, lectr. Mt. San Antonio Coll. Planetarium, Walnut, Calif., 1970-73; dir. Fleischmann Planetarium, U. Nev., Reno, 1973—. Organist, choirmaster Trinity Episcopal Ch., Reno, 1980—; bd. dirs. Reno Chamber Orch. Assn., 1981-87 , 1st v.p., 1984-85. Nev. Humanities Com., Inc. grantee, 1979-83. Mem. Am. Guild Organists (dean No. Nev. chpt. 1984-85), Internat. Planetarium Soc., Cinema 360, Inc. (treas. 1985—), Pacific Planetarium Assn. (pres. 1980), Planetarium Assn. Can., Rocky Mountain Planetarium Assn., Sigma Xi. Republican. Episcopalian. Writer, producer films: (with Donald G. Potter) Beautiful Nevada, 1978; Riches: The Story of Nevada Mining, 1984. Office: U Nev Fleischmann Planetarium Reno NV 89557

JOHNSON, BARBARA DIANE, interior designer, educator; b. Fairbanks, Alaska, Oct. 4, 1954; d. Karl R. and Betty L.E. (McNelly) Carlson; m. Thomas Perry Johnson, Sept. 1, 1974; children: Amanda, Carl and Perry (twins). BA in Three Dimensional Design, Kingston Poly., London, 1979. Interior designer Maurice Meyersohn & Assocs., London, 1979-80, Tectonic Designs, Berryville, Va., 1980, Jean Jongeward Interiors, Seattle, 1981-82, FORMA affiliate Westin Hotels, Seattle, 1985-86, Bus. Space Design, Seattle, 1987—, Polly McArthur Interior Design, Seattle, 1987—; instr. interior design Bellevue (Wash.) Community Coll., 1987—. Mem. Am. Soc. Interior Designers, Inst. Bus. Designers.

JOHNSON, BOB, ice hockey association executive. Formerly coach Calgary Flames, N.H.L., Alta., Can.; exec. dir. U.S.A. Hockey/Amateur Hockey Assn. of the U.S., Colorado Springs, Colo., 1987—. Office: Amateur Hockey Assn of US Inc/USA Hockey 2997 Broadmoor Valley Rd Colorado Springs CO 80906

JOHNSON, BRIAN KEITH, career planning educator; b. Jersey City, Nov. 30, 1956; s. James and Thelma (Austin) J.; m. Carroll Jean Henry, Jan. 31, 1986; children: Jasmine Camille, Brian Keith II. BA, Ottawa U., 1979. Lic. adult basic edn. instr.; lic. gen. ednl. devel. instr. Counselor Project Ujima African Am. Inst. Northeastern U., Boston, 1976-79; elem. tchr. Jersey City Bd. Edn., 1980-82; instr. gen. ednl. devel. Phoenix Job Corps Ctr., 1982-86; feature writer, reporter Ariz. Informant Newspaper, Phoenix, 1986—; career planning and placement specialist Maricopa County Community Coll. Dist., Phoenix, 1986—; dir. pub. relations Phoenix Delta Group, 1987—. Author: Come Unity of Angels, 1982, Strong, But Not Hard, 1986. Mem. Phoenix Minority Crime Task Force, 1985, Black Ednl. Task Force, 1987. Named one of Outstanding Young Men of Am., U.S. Jaycees, 1984. Mem. Nat. Assn. Sch. Employment Administrs., NAACP, Iota Phi Theta. Democrat. Episcopalian. Office: Maricopa Community Colls 3910 E Washington St Phoenix AZ 85027

JOHNSON, BRUCE PAUL, electrical engineering educator, consultant; b. Lewiston, Maine, Aug. 8, 1938; s. Albert Samuel and Francis Katherine (Powers) J.; m. Marcia Ann Duarte, Feb. 3, 1961; children: Michael, Robyn, Samuel, Rebecca. BS in Physics, Bates Coll., 1960; MS in Physics, U. N.H., 1962; PhD in Physics, U. Mo., 1967. Instr. physics Hobart/William Smith Coll., Geneva, N.Y., 1962-64; advanced scientist Gen. Elec. Med. Systems, Milw., 1967-70; leader group Solid State Lamp Project Gen. Elec., Cleve., 1970-74; prof. elec. engring./computer sci. U. Nev., Reno, 1974—, chmn. elec. engring./computer sci., 1978-83; cons. Solid State Farms, Reno, 1986—, Xebec Corp., Reno, 1984-86, Caddo Enterprises, 1987—; Pres. appointee U.S. Metric Bd., Washington, 1978, 80. Contbr. articles to sci. jours. Fellow NsF, 1961, Air Force Office Sci. Research, 1974; grantee NSF, NASA, Los Alamos Research Lab., Air Force Office Sci. Research and pvt. industry. Mem. IEEE (pres. no. Nev. sect. 1985-86, sr.), Am. Soc. Engring. Edn., Internat. Soc. Mini and MicroComputers, Masons, Sigma Xi (pres. Nev. chpt. 1984-85), Eta Kappa Nu. Republican. Home: 3190 W 7th Reno NV 89503

JOHNSON, BYRON J., state supreme court judge; b. 1937. AB, Harvard U., LLB. Bar: Idaho, 1962. Justice Idaho Supreme Ct., Boise, 1988—. Office: Idaho Supreme Ct 451 W State St Boise ID 83720 *

JOHNSON, BYRON LINDBERG, economist, educator; b. Chgo., Oct. 12, 1917; s. Theodore and Ruth Emille (Lindberg) J.; m. Catherine Elizabeth (Kay) Teter, Oct. 22, 1938; children: Steven Howard, Christine Ruth, Eric Alan. BA, U. Wis., Madison, 1938, MA, 1940, PhD, 1947. Economist, statistician State of Wisconsin, Madison, 1938-42; econ. analyst Fed. Civil Service, Washington, 1942-47; prof. econs. U. Denver, 1947-56; adm. asst. to gov. State of Colo., Denver, 1957-58; mem. U.S. Congress, Washington, 1959-60; cons. Agy. Internat. Devel. State Dept., Washington, 1961-64; prof. econs. U. Colo., Denver, 1965—; prof. econs. emeritus U. Colo., Denver, 1985—; cons. economist Commn. R.R. Retirement, Washington, 1971-72, U. Colo Regent, 1970-82. Author: Need is Our Neighbor, 1966; (with Robert Ewegen) B.S.: The Bureaucratic Syndrome, 1982; contbr. articles to profl. jours. Vice-chmn. Denver Regional Transp. Dist., 1983, chmn. 1984, bd. dirs., 1983-84. Recipient Whitehead Meml. award Colo. A.C.L.U., 1960. Mem. AAAS, Nat. Tax Assn., Advanced Transit Assn. (chmn. bd. 1986-87), Soc. Internat. Devel. (exec. com. Rocky Mountain chpt. 1986). Democrat. Mem. United Ch. of Christ. Club: City (Denver). Home: 2451 S Dahlia Ln Denver CO 80222

JOHNSON, C. BOYD, educator; b. Jamestown, N.D., July 3, 1928; s. Carl Emil and Alice Irene (Boyd) J.; m. Dec. 27, 1951 (div. 1975); children: Beth, Blair; m. Olivia M. Castle, May 25, 1976; children: Mary Kay, Daniel, Cecelia. BSME, U. N.D., 1951; MBA, U. Santa Clara, 1963, PhD, 1968. Sales engr. Westinghouse Electric Corp., L.A., 1951-53; design engr. Rheem Mfg. Co., Downey, Calif., 1953-57; engr., mgr. mktg. Sylvania Electric Prodn., Mt. View, Calif., 1957-69; cons. Kansas City, Mo., 1969-73; corp. mgmt. Bunker Ramo Corp., Oakbrook, Ill., 1973-75; prof. bus. U. N.D., Grand Forks, N.D., 1975-78, Rockhurst Coll., Kansas City, 1978-82, Cen. Wash. U., Ellensburg, Wash., 1982—; cons. City Bus. Incubator Program, Ellensburg, 1987—, SBA, Kansas City, 1978-82. Author: Principles of Marketing, 1984. With U.S. Army, 1945-47, Pacific. Mem. Am. Mktg. Assn., We. Mktg. Educators Assn., Rotary, Singing Hills Chorus (treas.). Episcopalian. Home: 506 N Walnut Ellensburg WA 98926 Office: Cen Wash U Dept Bus Adminstrn Ellensburg WA 98926

JOHNSON, CAROLYN ELIZABETH, librarian; b. Oakland, Calif., May 29, 1921; d. Ferdinand Orin and Clara Wells (Humphrey) Hassler; m. Benjamin Alfred Johnson, Feb. 12, 1943; children—Robin Rebecca, Anne Elizabeth, Delia Mary. B.A., U. Calif.-Berkeley, 1946; cert. librarian Calif. State U., Fullerton, 1960; M.L.S., Immaculate Heart Coll., 1968. Asst. children's librarian Fullerton Pub. Library, Calif., 1951-59, coordinator children's services, 1959-81, city librarian, 1981—; instr. Rio Hondo City Coll., Whittier, Calif., part time 1970-72, Calif. State U.-Fullerton, 1972-77; ; vice chmn. 3d Pacific Rim Conf. Council, 1983-86; mem. Korczak award com. U.S. Bd. Books for Young People, 1988. Author: The Art of Walter Crane, 1988. Mem. Library Tech. Tng. Adv. Com., Fullerton Coll., 1970; founding bd. dirs. Youth Sci. Ctr., Fullerton, 1958. Named Profl. Woman of Yr., N. Orange County YWCA, 1986. Mem. ALA, Calif. Library Assn. (chmn. children's service div.), Orange County Library Assn. (v.p.), So. Calif. Coun. on Lit. for Children and Young People (pres. 1979-81, Dorothy C. McKenzie award 1987), PTA (life), AAUW, LWV, Phi Beta Kappa, Theta Sigma Phi. Methodist. Home: 644 Princeton Circle E Fullerton CA 92632

JOHNSON, CHARLES FOREMAN, architect, architectural photographer, planning, architecture and systems engineering consultant; b. Plainfield, N.J., May 28, 1929; s. Charles E. and E. Lucile (Casner) J.; student Union Jr. Coll., 1947-48; B.Arch., U. So. Calif., 1958; postgrad. UCLA, 1959-60; m. Beverly Jean Hinnendale, Feb. 19, 1961 (div. 1970); children—Kevin, David. Draftsman, Wigton-Abbott, P.C., Plainfield, 1945-52; architect, cons., graphic, interior and engring. systems designer, 1952—; designer, draftsman with H.W. Underhill, Architect, Los Angeles, 1953-55; teaching asst. U. So. Calif., Los Angeles, 1954-55; designer with Carrington H. Lewis, Architect, Palos Verdes, Calif., 1955-56; grad. architect Ramo-Wooldridge Corp., Los Angeles, 1956-58; tech. dir. Atlas weapon system Space Tech. Labs., Los Angeles, 1958-60; advanced planner and systems engr. Minuteman Weapon System, TRW, Los Angeles, 1960-64, div. staff ops. dir., 1964-68; cons. N.Mex. Regional Med. Program and N.Mex. State Dept. Hosps., 1968-70; prin. Charles F. Johnson, architect, Los Angeles, 1953-68, Sante Fe, N.Mex., 1968-88, Carefree, Ariz., 1988—; free lance archtl. photographer, Sante Fe, 1971—; tchr. archtl. apprentice program, 1974—. Major archtl. works include: residential bldgs. in Calif., 1955-66; Bashein Bldg. at Los Lunas (N.Mex.) Hosp. and Tng. Sch., 1969, various residential bldgs., Santa Fe, 1973—, Kurtz Home, Dillon, Colo., 1981, Whispering Boulders Home, Carefree, 1981, Hedrick House, Santa Fe, 1983, Kole House, Green Valley, Ariz., 1984, Casa Largo, Santa Fe (used for film The Man Who Fell to Earth), 1974, Rubel House, Santa Fe, 1986, Smith House, Carefree, Ariz., 1987, Klopfer House, Sante Fe, 1988, Janssen House, Carefree, 1988, Art Start Gallery, 1988. Pres., Santa Fe Coalition for the Arts, 1977; set designer Santa Fe Fiesta Melodrama, 1969, 71, 74, 77, 78, 81; designed Jay Miller & Friends Fiesta float 1970-88 (winner of 20 awards). Mem. Delta Sigma Phi. Club: El Gancho Tennis. Contbr. articles on facility planning and mgmt. to profl. pubs.; contbr. archtl. photographs to mags. in U.S., Eng., France, Japan and Italy, contbr. articles on facility mgmt., planning info. systems, etc. to profl. jours. Recognized for work in organic architecture and siting buildings to fit the land. Club: El Gancho Tennis. Avocations: music, photography, collecting architecture books, Frank Lloyd Wright works. Home: 1598 Quartz Valley Dr The Boulders PO Box 6070 Carefree AZ 85377

JOHNSON, CHARLES ROBERT, television news anchor, reporter; b. Olivia, Minn., Apr. 6, 1954; s. Robert George and Dorothy Jean (Warner) J.; m. Karen Marie Langager, Sept. 4, 1976; children: Robert, Elizabeth. BA, U. Minn., 1976. Air personality, promotions dir. Sta. KQIC-FM Radio, Willmar, Minn., 1976-78; air personality, program dir. Sta. WJJY-FM Radio, Brainerd, Minn., 1978-79; air personality, community affairs dir. Sta. KFOR Radio, Lincoln, Nebr., 1979-80; anchor, reporter WDIO-TV, Duluth, Minn., 1980-82, KSTW-TV, Seattle-Tacoma, 1982—. Writer, producer, host pub. affairs TV program Johnson's Jour., 1984-85. Vol. University Place Sch. Dist., Tacoma, 1988-89. Lutheran. Office: Sta KSTW-TV PO Box 11411 Tacoma WA 98411

JOHNSON, CHARLES WAYNE, mining engineer, mining executive; b. Vinita, Okla., Feb. 7, 1921; s. Charles Monroe and Willie Mae (Hudson) J.; m. Cleo Faye Wittee, 1940 (div. 1952); m. Genevieve Hobbs, 1960 (dec. Sept. 1985); m. Susan Gates Johnson, Apr. 19, 1986; 1 child, Karen Candace Limon. BE, Kensington U., 1974, ME, 1975, PhDE, 1976. Owner El Monte (Calif.) Mfg. Co., 1946-49; co-owner Anjo Pest Control, Pasadena, Calif., 1946-56, Hoover-Johnson Cons. Co., Denver, 1956-59; pres. Vanguard Chem. Co., Denver, 1957-61, Mineral Products Co., Boise, Idaho, 1957-61; owner Crown Hill Meml. Park, Dallas, 1959—, Johnson Engring., Victorville, Calif., 1961—; pres. Crown Minerals, Victorville, 1985—; owner J&D Mining Co., Victorville, 1977—. Contbr. articles to profl. pubs.; patentee in field. Active Rep. VIP Club. Served with USN, 1941-45. Recipient Outstanding Achievement award East Pasadena Bus. Assn., 1948. Mem. Ch. Ancient Christianity. Office: Johnson Engring Crown Minerals PO Box 641 Wrightwood CA 92397 also: 16797 Live Oak St Hesperia CA 92345

JOHNSON, CHERYL MARIE, dietitian; b. Spokane, Wash., Jan. 9, 1961; d. Virgil Leroy and Rosemary C. (Self) King; m. Kelly Gene Johnson, Feb. 8, 1986. BS, Wash. State U., 1983. Asst. to assoc. athletic dir. Wash. State U., Pullman, 1980-83; dietetic technician, diet clk. Sacred Heart Med. Ctr., Spokane, 1983-84, clin. dietitian, 1986-89; health educator Sacred Heart Health Mgmt. Clinic, Spokane, 1989—; dietetic technician, supr. Psychiat. Ctr., Spokane, 1984-85, clin. dietitian, 1986; dietetic intern Ind. U. Med. Ctr., Indpls., 1985; cons. dietitian Riverpark Convalescent Ctr., Spokane, Wash., 1985; dietitian, supr. Southcrest Convalescent Ctr., Spokane, 1985-86; clin. dietician Holy Family Hosp., Spokane, 1986; instr. foods and nutrition Ea. Wash. U., Cheney, 1986; clin. dietitian Holy Family Hosp., Spokane, 1986; speaker Am. Heart Assn. Am. Cancer Soc. scholar, 1980. Mem. Am. Dietetic Assn., Wash. State Dietetic Assn. (Young Dietitian of Yr. award 1988), Spokane Dietetic Assn. (coun. on practice 1987-88, treas. 1988—). Roman Catholic. Office: Sacred Heart Med Ctr W 101 8th St TAF C-9 Spokane WA 99220

JOHNSON, CLAYTON ERROLD, poultry company executive; b. DeSota, Wis., Apr. 20, 1921; s. James and Louella (Goodin) J.; student U. Wis., 1940-41, Tex. A. and M. Coll., 1946; m. Betty J. Higenbotham, May 23, 1943; children—Roderick and Ronald (twins), Richard. Pres. Flavor Fresh Brand, Inc., 1949—; Calif. gen. bldg. contractor, 1947—. With USAAF, 1942-45. Home: 1008 Pine Hurst Dr Las Vegas NV 89109 Office: 830 E Sahara #3 Las Vegas NV 89104

JOHNSON, CLIFFORD DAVID, accountant; b. Angoon, Alaska, Mar. 9, 1940; s. Peter Ernest and Sophie (Frank) J.; m. Debbie Jo Rebstock, Sept. 12, 1975; children: Levada Jo, Michael David. Student, U. Alaska, Juneau, 1977—. Mem. acctg. staff State of Alask, Juneau, 1961-75; acctg. clk. U. Alaska, Juneau, 1976-77; acct. Tlingit & Haida Cen. Coun., Juneau, 1977—; sports photographer Capital City Weekly, 1987—. ACtive Vol. Income Tax Assistance, 1980; bd. dirs., Bethel Assembly of God Youth Village, Juneau, 1977, Tlingit & Haida Credit Union, Juneau, 1981-82, Big Bros./Big Sisters, Juneau, 1988, Juneau Indian Studies, 1988—, Gastineau Human Svcs., Juneau, 1988—, Juneau Parks and Recreation, 1988—, Tongass Community Counselong Svcs., Juneau, 1988—, treas., 1989—; tchr. Sunday sch. Bethel Assemby of God, 1975; asst. coach Youth Boys Basketball and Champions for the League, 1975; coach Youth Basketball and S.E. Champion, 1988. With U.S. Army, 1964-66. Mem. Alaska Native Brotherhood, Goldbelt, Lions. Democrat. Mem. Assemblies of God Ch. Home: 9153 Jerry Dr Juneau AK 99801 Office: Tlingit & Haida Cen Coun 320 Willoughby Ave Juneau AK 99801

JOHNSON, CONNIE FRANK, criminologist; b. Seymour, Iowa, July 19, 1934; s. Carl William and Una M. (Merritt) J.; m. Burnell Yvonne Knutson, Aug. 26, 1955; children: Shari Kay, Gregory, David, JoEllen. BS in Journalism, Iowa State U., 1960; student, FBI Acad., 1986. News editor Harlan (Iowa) Newspapers, 1960-62; mng. editor Democrat Herald Pub. Co., Albany, Oreg., 1962-63; pub. Blue Mountain Eagle Pub. Co., John Day, Oreg., 1963-67; assoc. pub. Iowa Farm Bur. Spokesman Press, Grundy Ctr., Iowa, 1967-69; gen. mgr. Springfield (Oreg.) News Pub. Co., 1969-72; asst. pub. Gresham (Oreg.) Outlook Pub. Co., 1972-76; criminologist Gresham Police Dept., 1976—. Patentee Computerized fingerprint device, 1987. Chmn. Grant County Rep. Com., John Day, Oreg., 1966; dir. Boys Club of Am., 1960-62; PIO Grant County Civil Defense, John Day, 1963-67. Served to sgt. USAF, 1952-56. Recipient Grant County Jr. Citizen's award, 1968, U.S. Law Enforcement Photography award Kodak Corp., 1985. Mem. Oreg. Newspaper Pub. Assn. (chmn. 1973-75, pres.'s award 1975), Internat. Assn. for Identification (mem. Pacific NWdiv., pres. 1988-89), Gresham Hist. Soc. (pres. 1987), Oreg.-Wash. Lawman's Assn., Gresham C. of C. (bd. dirs. 1973-74), Sigma Delta Chi (ann. service award Iowa state chpt. 1960), Jaycees (bd. dirs. 1964-67). Republican. Lutheran. Lodges: Elks, Rotary, Masons. Home: 471 SW 4th Gresham OR 97080

JOHNSON, COREY BENETT, university athletic administrator; b. Redwood Falls, Minn., Apr. 10, 1948; s. John Selmer Edwin and Mary Jane (Peters) J.; m. Marilyn Jane Johnson, Sept. 30, 1987; 1 child, Jeffrey Stephen-Scott. BS, Augustana Coll., 1971; postgrad., USC, 1988—. Cert. secondary tchr., Calif., Wis. Asst. coach in football, basketball, track, biology tchr. O'Gorman High Sch., Souix Falls, S.D., 1969-73; dir. athletics, head football coach, chmn. dept. physical edn. Lancaster (Wis.) High Sch. Dist., 1973-76; asst. football coach U. Iowa, Iowa City, 1976-78, U. Calif., Berkeley, 1978-82; state dir. athletics Spl. Olympics, 1982-83; asst. dir. athletics U. Miami, 1983-87; dir. intercollegiate athletics, sports and intramurals Long Beach State (Calif.) U., 1987—; Dir. Burger King Orange Bowl Basketball Tournament, 1983-87, NCAA Regional Baseball Tounament, 1984-86, West Palm Beach Basketball Classic, 1986-87, Calif. Sports Teams at Spl. Olympics, Baton Rouge, La., 1987; site dir., campus host Orange Bowl, 1984-87; adminstr., U. Miami Nat. Football Championship, 1983, U. Miami Nat. Baseball Championships, 1985, U. Miami Nat. Women's Golf Championship, 1984; mem. Internat. Track and Field Rules com., Spl. Olympics laison to all profl. sports assns., 1981-83; lectr. in field; participant in sports clinics. Author: University of Miami Policy and Procedures Manual, 1987, Recruiting Guide, 1984, NCAA Game Management Guide, 1987, Drug Testing Pamphlet, 1988, and others; contbr. articles to profl. jours. Mem. spl. presdl. task force Long Beach State U. Proposed Event Ctr., 1987—; mem. long range planning com. Long Beach State U., 1987—, Big West Promotions com., 1987—, eligibility compliance com., 1987—; mem. drug edn. testing com. Long Beach State U., 1987—, Ptnrs. for Youth Programs, Miami, 1983-87, Big Bros./Big Sisters Program, 1983-87; campus advisor Spl. Olympics, 1987—, vol., 1970—; mem. Fellowship Christian Athletes Orgn., United Way, 1983—, YMCA, Souix Falls, 1966-71, Long Beach, 1987—; participant Cancer Drive, 1983-87. Recipient scholarship Augustana Coll., 1966-71, Spl. Achievement award State of Calif. Spl. Olympics, 1982, Outstanding Service award, Orange Bowl, 1986-87, Recognition award, South Bay Athletic Club, 1987. Mem. Nat. High Sch. Coaches Assn., Nat. Athletic Dirs. Assn., Nat. Football Hall of Fame, Nat. Coaches Assn., Nat. Basketball Coaches Assn., Long Beach 49er Athletic Found. (chief exec. officer 1987—), Long Beach Sports (recreation adv. bd. 1987—), City of Long Beach Century Club, Taxi Squad, Fast Breakers Club, Webb Foots Club, Dugout Club, Spriker Brackers Club, Rotary, Lions, Long Beach Speakers Bur., Websterian Soc., Augustana Booster Club.

JOHNSON, DALE RODNEY, real estate broker; b. Duluth, Minn., Oct. 2, 1930; s. Clarence R. and Hildur (Gustafson) J.; m. Lorraine Carol Andres, Sept. 6, 1952; chidren: Brian, Kristin. Student. U. Minn., 1948-50. Chief draftsman Zalk Josephs Co., Duluth, Minn., 1950-81; supr. Marathon Steel, Phoenix, 1981-85; real estate broker Phoenix, 1985—. Mem. Phoenix Bd. Realtors. Republican. Evangelical Covenant. Home: 12222 Paradise Village PW S Apt 108A Phoenix AZ 85032 Office: Diamond Realty 3404 W Cheryl Dr Phoenix AZ 85051

JOHNSON, DANA JOYCE, policy analyst; b. L.A., Oct. 26, 1952; d. E.H. and Carolyn Joyce (Green) J.; m. Scott Norman Pace, Jan. 10, 1987. AB in Govt., U. Redlands, 1974; AM in Internat. Studies, Am. U., 1979; PhD in Internat. Relations, U. So. Calif., 1987. Diplomatic historian State Dept., Washington, 1975-80; research analyst Science Applications, Inc., La Jolla, Calif., 1980-81; ops. research analyst Rockwell Internat., Seal Beach, Calif., 1981-85; sr. policy analyst Gen. Research Corp., Hawthorne, 1985-88; researcher Rand Corp., Santa Monica, Calif., 1988—. Contbr. to profl. publs. Youth coordinator Bob Steele Gubernatorial campaign, Stratford, Conn., 1974. Recipient Leader Achievement award YWCA, 1984. Mem. U.S. Strategic Inst., Air Force Assn., Am. Astron. Soc., Women in Aerospace, Phi Delta Gamma. Republican. Baptist. Home: 2519 Kansas Ave #10 Santa Monica CA 90404 Office: Rand Corp 1700 Main St Santa Monica CA 90406

JOHNSON, DANA KAY, state agency executive; b. Denver, Nov. 19, 1940; d. Ernest Christian and E. Ione (Florine) Bergmann; m. Richard G. Johnson, June 30, 1959 (dec. 1988); 1 child, Ronald G. A Arts and Scis., Arapahoe Community Coll., 1982. From clerical to jr. personnel officer, Dept. Institutions/ Ft. Logan Mental Health Ctr. State of Colo., Denver, 1965-76, adminstrv. officer, Dept. Highways, 1976-83, dist. coord. mgr., Dept. Highways, 1983-88, cons. liaison engr., 1989—. Sec., treas. Harris Park Estates Homeowners' Assn., Bailey, Colo. Recipient Multi-Gallon Donor award Belle Bonfils Meml. Blood Ctr., Denver, 1985; named Employee of Month Colo. Dept. Highways, Denver, 1982. Mem. Colo. Assn. Pub. Employees (various offices local chpts.). Office: Colo Dept Hyws 4201 E Arkansas Ave Denver CO 80222

JOHNSON, DARRELL KURT, financial executive; b. Waukegan, Ill., Mar. 2, 1950; s. Kurt Charles and Verna Naomi (Richards) J. BA, Greenville Coll., 1972; M in Internat. Mgmt., Am. Grad. Sch. of Internat. Mgmt., 1977; MBA, So. Meth. U., 1977; BA, Baptist Christian Coll., 1984, MA, 1986; PhD, Calif. Coast U., 1989. Mgmt. cons. Peace Corps, Colombia, 1973-75; fin. cons. Peace Corps, Nicaragua, 1977-78; mgmt. cons. Peace Corps, Guatemala, 1978-80; fin. and adminstrn. cons. Agrl. Coop. Devel. Internat.,

Bolivia, 1980-81; fin. assoc. for Asia World Vision Internat., Philippines, 1982-84; fin. exec. World Vision Internat., Monrovia, Calif., 1984-86, fin. mgr. for So. Africa, Zimbabwe, 1987—. Named one of Outstanding Young Men of Am., 1985. Mem. Soc. Internat. Devel., Evangs. for Social Action. Mem. Ch. of Nazarene. Office: World Vision Internat 919 W Huntington Dr Monrovia CA 91016

JOHNSON, DARWIN LEE, systems engineer; b. Detroit, Jan. 17, 1944; s. Lloyd Eric and Marie Anna (Kresin) J.; m. Rita M. Forster, May 13, 1967; children: Robert D., Lisa M., Christina L. BS, Western Mich. U., 1966; MPA, Golden Gate U., 1979. Commd. 2d lt. U.S. Air Force, 1966, advanced through grades to lt. col., 1982; ret. 1986; served in Strategic Missile Wing McConnell AFB, Kans., 1966-71, SAC hdqrs., Nebr., 1971-75, missile launch ops. support Vandenberg AFB, Calif., 1975-80, Martin Marietta, Denver, 1980-81; stationed at Air Force test and evaluation ctr. Kirtland AFB, N.Mex., 1981-86; ret. 1986; dir. engring. Orion Internat. Techs., Albuquerque, 1986—. Mem. Internat. Test and Evaluation Assn. (founder, sr.; treas., v.p. 1983—), Am. Legion, U.S. Space Found. Republican. Lutheran. Home: 10408 La Paz Dr NW Albuquerque NM 87114

JOHNSON, DAVID FREDERICK, principal; b. Chgo., Feb. 17, 1944; s. Gustav Frederick and Jeanette Alma (Anderson) J.; m. Carol Ann Schwyn, Apr. 1, 1977; 1 child, Eric Raymond. BA, So. Ill. U., 1968, MS, 1971; EdD, U. Colo., 1986. Cert. tchr., adminstr., Ill., Colo. Secondary tchr. Peace Corps, Sierra Leone, Africa, 1968-70; middle sch. tchr. Sunset Ridge Sch., Northfield, Ill., 1971-79; elem. prin. Silverthorne (Colo.) Elem. Sch., 1979-85; middle sch. prin. Summit Middle Sch., Frisco, Colo., 1985—; mem. state adv. com. Colo. North Central Assn. of Colls. and Schs., Boulder, Colo., 1986—; adj. prof. Adams State Coll., Alamosa, Colo., 1987—. Group leader Op. Crossroads-Africa, N.Y.C., 1976; dir. Vacation Ch. Sch., Dillon, Colo., 1985—. Recipient Fulbright-Hayes grant U.S. Edn. Found., New Dehli, India, 1975. Fellow Inst. for Devel. Edn. Activities; mem. Colo. Assn. Sch. Execs., Nat. Mid. Sch. Assn., Colo. Assn. for Supervision and Curriculum Devel. (sec.), Phi Delta Kappa, Rotary Club, Frisco (blood drive chairperson Summit County, 1987-88). Lutheran. Home: PO Box 146 Dillon CO 80435 Office: Summit Middle School PO Box 7 Frisco CO 80443

JOHNSON, DAVID KENT, electric utility company executive; b. Story City, Iowa, Sept. 30, 1942; s. Marion Pierce and Mardean Mae (Fry) J.; m. Virgetta Rose Caltvedt, Feb. 29, 1964 (div. 1977); children: Jill, Maria, Richard, Christopher; m. Cynthia Joyce Wiese, Jan. 2, 1981; stepchildren: Nicole, Lucas. BSEE, Iowa State U., 1964; MBA, U. Iowa, 1974. Registered profl. engr., Calif., Wash., Oreg., Nebr., Kans., Okla., Ark., Mo., Iowa, Ga., Ala., Fla. Engr. Stanley Cons., Inc., Muscatine, Iowa, 1964-70, dept. head, 1970-73, asst. group head, 1973-74, project mgr., 1974-82, head utility mktg., 1982-84; mgr. SE region Stanley Cons., Inc., Tampa, Fla., 1984-87; engring. mgr. Bur. of Electricity, Alameda, Calif., 1987-88, asst. gen. mgr., 1988—; bd. dirs. Underground Svc. Alert No. Calif., Concord, 1987—. Mem. IEEE (sr. mem.), Nat. Soc. Profl. Engrs., Calif. Soc. Profl. Engrs., Phi Kappa Phi, Beta Gamma Sigma, Tau Beta Pi, Eta Kappa Nu. Republican. Presbyterian. Home: 3454 Capella Ln Alameda CA 94501 Office: Bur of Electricity 2000 Grand St Alameda CA 94501

JOHNSON, DAVID SELLIE, civil engineer; b. Mpls., Apr. 10, 1935; s. Milton Edward and Helen M. (Sellie) J. BS, Mont. Coll. Mineral Sci. Tech., 1958. Registered profl. engr., Mont. Trainee Mont. Dept. Hwys., Helena, 1958-59, designer, 1959-66, asst. preconstrn. engr., 1966-68, regional engr., 1968-72, engring. specialities supr., 1972—, forensic engr., 1965—, traffic accident reconstructionist, 1978—. Contbr. articles on hwy. safety to profl. jours. Adv. bd. mem. Helena Vocat.-Tech. Edn., 1972-73. Fellow Inst. Transp. Engrs.; mem. Nat. Acad. Forensic Engrs. (diplomate), Mont. Soc. Profl. Engrs., NSPE, Transp. Rsch. Bd., Wash. Assn. Tech. Accident Investigators, Corvette Club. Mem. Algeria Shrine Temple. Club: Treasure State (Helena) (pres. 1972-78). Lodges: Elks, Shriners. Home: 1921-6 Ave Helena MT 59601 Office: Mont Dept Hwys 2701 Prospect Helena MT 59620

JOHNSON, DEANDA LYNNE, nurse; b. Spokane, Wash., Aug. 26, 1957; d. Maurice Edward and Vivian Mae (Albert) Farr; m. Phillip Cary Johnson, Mar. 17, 1978 (div. 1986); children: Brianna, Brittany. Assocs. in Nursing, Umpqua Community Coll., Roseburg, Oreg., 1978. RN, Oreg. Staff nurse Rose Haven Nursing Ctr., 1978-81, Douglas Community Hosp., Roseburg, 1981--. Fellow Oreg. Nurses Assn. (com. mem.). Republican. Baptist. Home: 395 Kirby St Roseburg OR 97470

JOHNSON, DONNA MAE, nun; b. Stockton, Calif., Sept. 11, 1931; d. Ralph Wesley and Elizabeth Louise (Pucci) Johnson. BA, Calif. State U., Fullerton, 1976; MSA, U. Notre Dame, Ind., 1982. Entered Dominican Sisters, Roman Catholic Ch. Tchr. St. Elizabeth High Sch., Oakland, Calif., 1963-65; sch. treas. St. Catherine Mil. Sch., Anaheim, Calif., 1965-75; dir. devel. Immaculate Conception Acad., San Francisco, 1975-86; treas. gen. Dominican Sisters of Mission San Jose, Fremont, Calif., 1986—; bd. dirs. St. Catherines Mil. Sch., 1986—, Dominican Sisters of Mission San Jose Found., 1986—; trustee Religious Trust, San Francisco, 1986—; treas. Queen of Holy Rosary Coll., Fremont, 1986—. Mem. Conf. Religious Treas. (sec.-treas. 1987—), Nat. Assn. Treas. of Religious Insts. Home: PO Box 3908 Fremont CA 94539 Office: Dominican Sisters of Missio 43326 Mission Blvd Fremont CA 94539

JOHNSON, DOUGLAS LLOYD, utility company administrator; b. Marysville, Calif., Apr. 1, 1939; s. Lloyd Alvin and Florence Elanor (McCrank) J.; m. Judy-Lea Johnston, May 9, 1959 (div. Dec. 1986); 1 child, Paul Douglas; m. Rayne Marie Thompson, May 24, 1987. Student, Modesto Coll., 1957-58, Ohlone Coll., 1969-71. Field clk. Pacific Gas and Electric Co., San Francisco, 1958-79, supr., 1980, asst. valuation analyst, 1981, adminstrv. asst., 1983-88, suggestion plan chmn., 1988. Active Newark Sister City Assn., 1983-87. Republican. Episcopalian. Home: 34337 Gadwall Common Fremont CA 94555

JOHNSON, DREW MARTIN, lawyer; b. Canton, S.D., Aug. 18, 1939; s. Andrew Martin and Ardes Eileen (Brown) J.; divorced; children: Heather, Paige; m. Susan Johnson, Aug. 8, 1988. BJ, U. Mo., 1961; JD, U. of Pacific, 1967. Bar: Calif. 1967, Utah 1988, U.S. Dist. Ct. (no. dist.) Calif. 1967, U.S. Dist. Ct. (ea. dist.) Calif. 1968, U.S. Dist. Ct. Utah 1988, U.S. Ct. Appeals (9th cir.) 1972. Assoc. Luther & Luther, Sacramento, 1967-69; ptnr. Luther, Luther, O'Connov & Johnson, Sacramento, 1969-71, Johnson, Nash & Vinson, Sacramento, 1971-80; sole practice Sacramento, 1980—; arbitrator Sacramento Superior Ct., 1982, Am. Arbitration Assn.; judge pro tem Placer Superior Ct., Auburn, Calif., 1986. Mem. ABA, Calif. Bar Assn. (vol. voluntary legal services program 1982—), Utah Bar Assn., Sacramento County Bar Assn., Salt Lake City Bar Assn. Republican. Presbyterian. Lodge: Rotary (past pres., Paul Harris fellow1982). Office: 50 Fullerton Ct Suite 101 Sacramento CA 95825 also: 333 E 400 South St Salt Lake City UT 84111

JOHNSON, E. ERIC, insurance executive; b. Chgo., Feb. 7, 1927; s. Edwin Eric and Xenia Alice (Waisanen) J.; m. Elizabeth Dewar Brass, Sept. 3, 1949; children: Christal L. Johnson Neal, Craig R. BA, Stanford U., 1948. Dir. group annuities Equitable Life Assurance Soc., San Francisco, 1950-54; div. mgr. Equitable Life Assurance Soc., L.A., 1955-59; v.p. Johnson & Higgins of Calif., L.A., 1960-67, dir., 1968-87, chmn., 1986-87; chmn. The Benefits Group, Inc., L.A., 1988—; exec. v.p., Johnson & Higgins, N.Y.C., 1984-87; bd. dirs. Showscan Film Corp. Vice-chmn., KCET-Pub. TV, L.A., 1977—; bd. dirs., UCLA Med. Ctr. Adv. Bd., 1983—, Calif. Inst. for Cancer Rsch., L.A., 1985—, Stanford U. Grad. Sch. Bus., 1986—; trustee, Nuclear Decommissioning Trust, San Onofre, Calif., 1988—. Ensign, USN, 1944-46. Mem. Calif. Club, L.A. Country Club, Vintage Club, Riviera Town Club, Links Club N.Y.C.. Office: Benefits Group Inc 2029 Century Park E Los Angeles CA 90067

JOHNSON, EARVIN (MAGIC JOHNSON), professional basketball player; b. Lansing, Mich., Aug. 14, 1959; s. Earvin and Christine Johnson. Student, Mich. State U., 1976-78. Profl. basketball player Los Angeles Lakers, NBA, 1979—. Author: (autobiography) Magic, 1983. Mem. NCAA Championship Team, 1979, Nat. Basketball Assn. All-Star Team, 1980, 82-89, Nat. Basketball Assn. Championship Team, 1980, 82, 85, 87, 88; named Most Valuable Player, Nat. Basketball Assn. Playoffs, 1980, 82, 87, Nat. Basketball Assn., 1987, 89; Named Player of the Year, Sporting News, 1987. Office: care Los Angeles Lakers The Forum PO Box 10 Inglewood CA 90306 *

JOHNSON, EDGAR A., mechanical engineer; b. Canton, Ohio, July 27, 1925; s. Olaf and Deborah (Blomberg) J.; m. Ruth Snelgrove, Aug. 10, 1944; children: Marilyn A., Deborah A., David E., Douglas A. AAS, Rochester Inst. Tech., 1954. Registered profl. engr., Ariz., N.Y., Colo., Mass. Mech. engr. Eastman Kodak Co., Rochester, N.Y., 1946-83; tech. advisor N.Y. State Energy Office, Rochester and Lake Havasu, 1983—; cons. in field. With USAAF, 1943-46. Home: 2151 Bryce Dr Lake Havasu City AZ 86403

JOHNSON, ELIZABETH HILL, foundation administrator; b. Ft. Wayne, Ind., Aug. 21, 1913; d. Harry W. and Lydia (Buechner) Hill; m. Samuel Spencer Johnson, Oct. 7, 1944 (dec. 1984); children: Elizabeth Katharine, Patricia Caroline. BS summa cum laude, Miami U., Oxford, Ohio, 1935; MA in English Lit., Wellesley Coll., 1937; postgrad., U. Chgo., 1936. Cert. tchr., Ohio. Pres., co-founder S.S. Johnson Found., a Calif. Corp., San Francisco, 1947—. Mem. Oreg. State Bd. Higher Edn., Salem, 1962-75, Oreg. State Edn. Coordinating Com., Salem, 1975-82, Oreg. State Tchr. Standards and Practices Commn., Salem, 1982-89; bd. dirs. Lewis and Clark Coll., Portland, Oreg., 1985, Pacific U., Forest Grove, Oreg., 1982—, Oreg. Hist. Soc., Portland, 1985—, Cen. Oreg. Dist. Hosp., Redmond, 1982—, Oreg. High Desert Mus., Bend. Served to lt. USNR, 1943-46. Named Honoree March Dimes White Rose Luncheon, 1984; recipient Aubrey Watzek award Lewis and Clark Coll., 1984, Cen. Oreg. 1st Citizen award. Mem. Am. Assn. Higher Edn., Am. Assn. Jr. Colls., Assn. Supervision and Curriculum Devel., Phi Beta Kappa, Phi Delta Kappa, Delta Gamma, Beta Sigma Phi. Republican. Lutheran. Club: Francisca (San Francisco); Town, University, Waverly (Portland). Home: 415 S Canyon Dr Redmond OR 97756 Office: SS Johnson Found 441 S Canyon Dr Redmond OR 97756

JOHNSON, ELIZABETH KATHARINE, transportation executive, civic volunteer; b. Bend, Oreg., Jan. 12, 1951; d. Samuel S. and Elizabeth Avery (Hill) J.; m. John Christopher Helm, Sept. 6, 1986. Grad., Carleton Coll., 1974, Lewis & Clark U., 1977. Sr. recognizance Multnomah County Cir. Ct., Portland, Oreg., 1974-77; chief exec. officer TransWestern Helicopters, Inc., Scappoose, Oreg., 1978—. Bd. dirs. The S.S. Johnson Found., San Francisco and Redmond, Oreg., 1972—, Oreg. Symphony Assn., 1986—, Bd. of the Oreg. Mil. Mus. Found., 1986—, Planned Parenthood of the Columbia and Williamette area, 1987—, Oreg. Pub. Broadcasting Found., 1987—, St. Helens Hosp., William Temple House; bd. dirs., exec. v.p. Doernbecher Children's Hosp. Found., 1985—; treas. Whirly-Girls, Inc., 1987—; mem. Portland Downtown Heliport Citizen Adv. Com.; com. chmn. Grantmakers Oreg. and S.W. Wash.; mem. Oreg. Tourism Alliance. Named one of 100 Most Powerful Women, Oreg. Mag., 1981. Mem. Nat. Aeronautic Assn., Am. Pilot's Lobby, Helicopter Assn. Internat., Profl. Helicopter Pilots Assn., S. Columbia County Econ. Devel. Forum, Am. Helicopter Soc., Oreg. Pilot's Assn., Oreg. Hist. Soc., NRA, Asian Arts Coun., N.W. Rotorcraft Assn., Ninety-Nieds Inc., Portland Art Assn., Firends of the Zoo., Oreg. High Desert Mus., Scappoose City Club, Multnomah Athletic Club, Wings, The Town Club, Nat. Soc. Colonial Dames. Republican. Episcopalian. Office: Transwestern Helicopters 53894 Airport Way Scappoose OR 97056

JOHNSON, ERIC GORDON, geotechnical engineer; b. Fairbanks, Alaska, May 20, 1948; s. Gustav Vernor and Virginia May (Gordon) J.; m. Susan Elizabeth Parker, June 5, 1970 (div. May 1981); m. Doreen Ransom, July 13, 1981; stepchild, Kathleen Fennessy. BSCE, U. Alaska, 1970, MS in Engring. Mgmt., 1973. Registered profl. engr., Alaska. Geotech. engr. Alaska Dept. Transp., Anchorage, 1970-88, pavement mgmt. engr., 1988—. Editor: Embankment Design and Construction in Cold Regions, 1988; author papers in field. V.p. Anchorage Community Chorus, 1981. Mem. Am. Soc. Civil Engrs. (cold regions tech. coun. control group 1986—), Alaska Soc. Profl. Engrs. (pres. 1987-88, v.p. MATHCOUNTS 1984-87, state dir.), Profl. Engrs. in Govt. (Alaska dir. 1987—), Alaska Racquetball Assn., Sons of Norway. Congregationalist. Office: PO Box 196900 Anchorage AK 99519-6900

JOHNSON, F. MICHAEL, control systems engineer; b. Sacramento, Jan. 14, 1953; s. Carroll Loren and Constance (Latterell) J.; m. Donna Louise Hamilton, June 28, 1975; children: Bryan J., Cassandra L. BSChemE, U. Calif., Davis, 1975. Registered profl. control systems engr., Calif. Field engr., instrumentation Universal Oil Products, 1975-80; project engr. and leader Atkinson System Techs. Co., 1980-85; control systems project leader, system mgr. spl. project Stearns-Roger, Denver, 1985-87; digital systems engr., mgr. spl. software applications CH2M Hill, Denver, 1987—. Recipient Top Cat award Atkinson Systems Tech. Co., 1985. Mem. Am. Chem. Soc., Instrument Soc. Am., Toastmasters. Home: 8725 E Cherokee Ct Parker CO 80134 Office: Ch2M Hill PO Box 22508 Denver CO 80222

JOHNSON, FRANKLIN WILLIAM, aerospace engineer; b. Chattanooga, July 16, 1931; s. James Walter and Elizabeth Lola (Chandler) J.; m. Nancy Ann Snipes; children: Walter W., Stephen S., Elizabeth Graye. BS in Engring., Ga. Inst. Tech., 1958; MS in Engring., UCLA, 1975. Engr. Lockheed Ga. Co., Marietta, 1953-69; tech. mgr. Lockheed Calif. Co., Burbank, 1970—; panelist in field. Contbr. articles to profl. jours. Fellow Soc. Allied Weight Engrs. (pres. local chpt. 1971-72, 87-89, mem. internat. tech. com. 1980—), Atlanta Yacht Club (bd. dirs. 1965-68), Bass Lake. Republican. Episcopalian. Home: 9909 Bothwell Rd Northridge CA 91324 Office: Lockheed Calif Co PO Box 551 76-83 Burbank CA 91520

JOHNSON, GAIL DELORIES, forensic chemist, toxicologist; b. Chgo., Sept. 30, 1957; d. Roger George and Delories B. (Reppert) J. BS in Chemistry, No. Ill. U., 1980. Quality control chemist Standard Pharmacal Corp., Elgin, Ill., 1980; forensic chemist Ill. Racing Bd. Lab., Elgin, 1980-82, Analytical Techs., Inc., Tempe, Ariz., 1982-84; analytical chemist Nichols Inst., San Juan Capistrano, Calif., 1985-87; forensic chemist, toxicologist, GC/MS group leader Reference Lab., Colton, Calif., 1987—. Mem. Am. Chem. Soc., Am. Inst. Chemists. Office: Reference Labs 952 S Mt Vernon PO Box 670 Colton CA 92324

JOHNSON, GAIL LYNNE, direct mail company official; b. Chgo., Nov. 11, 1953; d. Kenneth W. and Junellen Elizabeth (Carlson) Johnson; m. Roger Bernard Demuth, July 14, 1984. Student, Gov.'s State U., 1982. Editorial asst. Jour. Communication Therapy, Park Forest, Ill., 1980-82; gen. mgr. Hanna Andersson Corp., Portland, Oreg., 1984—. Home: 3535 NW South Rd Portland OR 97229 Office: Hanna Andersson Corp 1010 NW Flanders St Portland OR 97209

JOHNSON, GARY ALLEN, social services administrator; b. Denver, May 18, 1954; s. Donald Duane and Joan Lou (Reynolds) J.; m. Cynthia Carol Ozman, June 2, 1979; children: Erin Elizabeth, Zachary Allen. B Environ. Design, U. Colo., 1976; MDiv with honors, Denver Sem., 1988. Staff mem. Campus Crusade for Christ, Colo.,Oreg, 1977-84, Student Ministries, Inc., Aurora, Colo., 1984-88; pvt. practice psychotherapy Aurora, 1988—; chaplain Care Unit Colo., Aurora, 1988—; counselor, cons., Faith Counseling Ministries. Author marriage preparation course materials. Mem. Christian Assn. Psychol. Studies, Nat. Coun. Family Rels.. Republican. Presbyterian. Home and Office: 617 S Quentin St Aurora CO 80012

JOHNSON, GARY HAROLD, sales and marketing executive; b. Elk River, Minn., Aug. 31, 1943; s. Harold August Johnson and Bernice Elizabeth (Stevens) Johnson Lavin; m. Sara Kathryn Wildman, Feb. 27, 1982; 1 child, Charles Bryant. BA, U. Minn., 1969. Nat. sales mgr. Snow Sports Publs., Mpls., 1970-74; dist. mgr. Kawasaki Motors USA, Mpls., 1974-78; regional mgr. Kawasaki Motors USA, Arlington, Tex., 1978-82; v.p. sales Kawasaki Motors USA, Irvine, Calif., 1982—. Host Inter Study program, San Francisco, 1988; mem. presdl. task force Rep. Com., 1982-86. With USMC, 1962-66. Mem. Internat. Jet Ski Boating Assn. (sec.-treas. 1985-89), Toastmasters (past pres. 1986-87, Spirit of Merit award 1987). Office: Kawasaki Motors USA 9950 Jeronimo St Santa Ana CA 92718

JOHNSON, GARY KENT, management education company executive; b. Provo, Utah, Apr. 16, 1936; s. Clyde LeRoy and Ruth Laie (Taylor) J.; m. Mary Joyce Crowther, Aug. 26, 1955; children—Mary Ann Johnson Harvey, Gary Kent, Brent James, Jeremy Clyde. Student Brigham Young U., 1954-55, U. Utah, 1955-58, 60-61, U. Calif.-Berkeley, 1962. Sales rep. Roche Labs., Salt Lake City, 1958-61, sales trainer, Denver, 1962, sales trainer, Oakland, Calif., 1962, div. mgr., Seattle, 1962-69; sec.-treas. Western Mgmt. Inst., Seattle, 1969-71; pres. WMI Corp., Bellevue, Wash., 1971—, Provisor Corp., 1983-86; speaker, cons. various nat. orgns. Bd. dirs. Big Bros.; del. King County Republican Com. Served with U.S. N.G., 1953-61. Walgreen scholar, 1955-58; Bristol scholar, 1958. Mem. Am. Soc. Tng. and Devel., Internat. Platform Assn., Phi Sigma Epsilon. Mormon. Club: Bellevue Athletic. Author: Select the Best, 1976; Antitrust Untangled, 1977; The Utilities Management Series, 1979; Performance Appraisal, A Program for Improving Productivity, 1981. Office: WMI Corp 1309 114th Ave SE Ste 212 Bellevue WA 98004

JOHNSON, GEORGE DUANE, economics educator, university administrator; b. Pagosa Springs, Colo., Aug. 7, 1938; s. Clarance William and Dolores Estelle (Coen) J.; m. Judith Nichols, June 27, 1958; children: Gregory, Justin. BA, Ft. Lewis Coll., 1966; MA, Kans. State U., 1967, PhD, 1970. Lectr. Coll. Bus., Calif. State U., Chico, 1969-70, prof. econs., 1976—; univ. acad. planner Calif. State U., Chico, 1976, dean acad. planning, 1977, assoc. v.p. acad. affairs, 1985—; coord. grad. program in bus. Coll. Bus., Calif. State U., Chico, 1973-75, chmn. dept. acctg. and mgmt. sci., 1971-73. Contbr. articles to profl. jours. Mem. Society for Coll. & Univ. Planning, Math. Assn. Am. Office: Calif State Univ Kendall Hall 106 Chico CA 95929

JOHNSON, GLADE, industrial designer, interior designer; b. Boise, Idaho, Aug. 10, 1946; s. Ralph A. and Maureen (Hogsette) J.; m. Pennie R. Johnson, Jan. 25, 1969; children: Sage, Amber. Staff designer Ford Motor Co., Dearborn, Mich., 1969-72, Chrysler Corp., Highland Park, Mich., 1972; sr. designer Walter Dorwin Teague Assocs., Seattle, 1977-76; devel. engr. Hewlett Packard Co., Boise, 1977; v.p. design Volpar Aircraft, Inc., Bellevue, Wash., 1979-84, Design Dynamics Internat., Bellevue, 1984-87; owner, prin. Glade Johnson Design, Inc., Bellevue, 1987—. Mem. Aircraft Interior Design Assn. (bd. dirs. 1984-86). Republican. Office: Glade Johnson Design Inc 11820 Northrup Way Ste 220 Bellevue WA 98005

JOHNSON, GREGG STEPHEN, company executive; b. St. Louis, Sept. 4, 1960; s. Penhale Eddy and Zita (Mulligan) J.; m. Nancy Joy Ginkel, July 16, 1983; children: Kathryn Joy, Scott Richard. BS in Hotel Adminstrn., U. Nev., Las Vegas, 1982. Mgr., trainee Ambassador Inns, Las Vegas, 1981, mgr. on duty, 1981-82; mgr. trainee Hawaii ops. Volume Svcs., Honolulu, 1982; night mgr. Waimea Falls Park Volume Svcs., Haleiwa, 1982-83, asst. gen. mgr., 1983-84, gen. mgr., 1984-86; project mgr. Oakland (Calif.) Coliseum Volume Svcs., 1986; gen. mgr. Hawaii ops. Volume Svcs., Waimanalo, 1988--; food and beverage dir. Holiday Inn-Tempe (Ariz.), 1986-88. Asst. scoutmaster Boy Scouts Am., Oakland, 1986; coord. Jr. Achievement, Tempe, 1986-88. Mem. Hawaii Restaurant Assn. (bd. dirs. 1988--), Rotary. Roman Catholic. Office: Volume Svcs 41-202 Kalanianaole Hwy Waimanalo HI 96795

JOHNSON, GWENAVERE A., artist; b. Newark, S.D., Oct. 16, 1909; d. Arthur E. and Susie Ellen (King) Nelson; m. John Wendell Johnson, Dec. 17, 1937; 1 son, John Forres' Student Mpsl. Sch. Art, 1930; BA, U. Minn., 1937; MA, San Jose State U., 1957. Cert. gen. elem., secondary, art tchr., Calif. Art tchr., supr. Austin (Minn.) Schs., 1937-38; art tchr. Hillbrook Sch., Los Gatos, Calif., 1947-52; art tchr., supr. Santa Clara (Calif.) Pub. Schs., 1952-55; art tchr., dept. chmn. San Jose (Calif.) Unified Schs., 1955-75; owner Tree Tops studio, San Jose, 1975—. Juried shows: Los Gatos Art Assn., 1976-79, 85-88, Artist of Yr., 1988 (1st and 2d awards), 83, 84 (Best of Show awards), Treeside gallery, Los Gatos, 1980, 81 (1st awards); Livermore Art Assn., 1977 (2d award), Los Gatos Art Mus., 1981 (1st award), 82 (2d award), Rosicrucean Mus., 1983, Centre d'Art Contemporian, Paris, 1983; creator Overfelt portrait Alexian Bros. Hosp., San Jose, Calif., 1977; exhibited in group shows Triton Art Mus., 1983-89. Recipient Golden Centaur award Acad. Italia, 1982, Golden Album of prize winning Artists, 1984, Golden Flame award Academia Italia, 1986, others. Mem. San Jose Art League, Los Gatos Art Assn., Santa Clara Art Assn. (Artist of Yr. 1983), Soc. Western Artists, Artists Equity, Nat. League Am. Penwomen (corr. sec., Merit Achiever award), Academia Italia. Home and Office: 2054 Booksin Ave San Jose CA 95125

JOHNSON, HARRY WILLIAM, artist; b. Spokane, Wash., Sept. 19, 1947; s. Ira William and Noreen Louise (Edwards) J.; m. Cynthia Marie Delorme, Mar. 24, 1973; children: Steve Scott, Amber Rose, Chelan Michelle. Freelance artist Leavenworth, Wash., 1969—; sr. illustrator Walter Dorwin Teague Assoc., Renton, Wash., 1979—; artist The Bradford Exchange, Niles, Ill., 1987—. Paintings used for America the Beautiful Series of Collector Plates sold throughthe Bradford Exchange, Niles, Ill., 1988-89; featured artist in U.S. Art Mag. Dec. 1988, Plate World Mag., Jan. 1989. Named in Top 100 Arts for the Parks Show, Nat. Parks Found., Jackson Hole, Wyo., displayed in Smithsonian, 1987; recipient award of Merit for Painting, Audubon Alaska Wildlife Art Show, Anchorage, 1987. Mem. Puget Sound Group Northwest Painters. Home: 20316 34th Ave S Seattle WA 98188

JOHNSON, HEIDI SMITH, educator; b. Mpls., June 1, 1946; d. Russell Ward and Eva Ninette (Holmquist) Smith; m. Alan C. Sweeney, Dec. 21, 1968 (div. 1977); m. Robert Allen Johnson, July 17, 1981. BA, U. Calif., Riverside, 1969. Park ranger U.S. Nat. Parks Svc., Pinnacles Nat. Monument, 1972-73; aide Petrified Forest Mus. Assn., Ariz., 1973-75; dispatcher police dept. U. Ariz., Tucson, 1975-76; communications operator II dept. ops. City of Tucson, 1976-78; dispatcher Tucson Police Dept., 1978-82, communications supr., 1982-85, communications coord., 1985; substitute tchr. Bisbee (Ariz.) Sch. Dist., 1985—; GED tchr. Cochise County Jail, 1988—. Mem. bd. trustees Bisbee Coun. on Arts & Humanities, 1986—; pres. Copper Queen Libr. Bd., Bisbee, 1988—; book sales chmn. Shattuck Libr., Bisbee Mining Mus., 1987—. Mem. Mid-Am. Paleontol. Soc., N.Mex. Geol. Soc., Ariz. Geol. Soc., Paleontol. Soc. So. Ariz., AAUW, Fed. Women's Clubs. Roman Catholic. Home: PO Box 1221 174 Quality Hill Bisbee AZ 85603

JOHNSON, HOWARD LESLIE, JR., computer company executive, consultant; b. Denver, Dec. 13, 1937; s. Howard Leslie and Bonita Delores (Fancher) J.; m. Sharyl Irene Woods, June 5, 1960; children: Karin Christine, Howard Leslie III, Michael Woods. Student, Stanford U., 1956-57; BS, Colo. State U., 1960; MS, San. Jose State U., 1963; postgrad., Calif. State U., Northridge, 1975-76, UCLA, 1977. Supr. Lockheed Missiles and Space, Sunnyvale, Calif., 1963-67; software systems engr. Aerospace Corp., El Segundo, Calif., 1967-72; tech. and advanced programs System Devel. Corp., Santa Monica, Calif., 1972-79; dir. applications and devel. Denelcor, Aurora, Colo., 1979-80; sr. mem. profl. staff Geodynamics Corp., Aurora, 1980-82; sr. computer scientist Computer Corp. Am., Littleton, Colo., 1982; pres., owner Info. Intelligence and Scis. Inc., Aurora, 1982—; cons. Computer Tech. Assocs., Colorado Springs, 1983—; dir. Colo. SuperNet, Denver, Coop. Inst. Geodata Mgmt., Golden, Colo.; mem. faculty, lectr., conductor seminars Univ. Coll., Denver, 1983—, U.S. Astronaut Program, Edwards AFB, Calif., 1965-66, Colo. Sch. of Mines, Golden, 1983-88, Denver U., 1986-87, U. Calif. Santa Cruz, 1986, U. Colo. at Denver, 1986-87, U. Colo., Colorado Springs, 1988, Colo. State U., Ft. Collins, 1988, Integrated Computer Systems, L.A., 1988—, Nat. Theol. U., Ft. Collins, 1989. Author: Assorted Annotated Poems, 1988, Guide to Vector and Parallel Processors, 1988; contbr. articles, papers to profl. jours. Tutorial chmn. Supercomputing '88, Orlando, Fla.; exhibits chmn. Supercomputing '89—, Reno, Dupercomputing '90, N.Y.C.; pres. Palos Verdes (Calif.) Jaycees, 1970. Maj. USAF, 1960-63. Named one of Outstanding Young Men of Am., Jaycees, 1970. Mem. IEEE, Assn. for Computing Machinery, Soc. for Indsl. and Applied Maths., Math. Assn. Am., Soc. for Computer Simulation (chmn. Multi and Array Processing Conf. 1988), Assn. Old Crows, Sigma Alpha Epsilon. Republican. Office: Info Intelligence Scis Inc 15694 E Chenango Aurora CO 80015

JOHNSON, HOYT CHARLES, publisher; b. Elmwood, Wis., Feb. 17, 1930; s. Hoyt Willard and Thelma Celia (Anderson) J.; m. Marcia Ruth Peterson, July 5, 1958; children: Tom, John, Hoyt III, Julie. BA, U. Wis., 1956; postgrad., Marquette U., 1961, Creighton U., 1961. Pub., editor

Cumberland (Wis.) Adv., 1973-78, The Rancher, Scottsdale, Ariz., 1979-83; founder, pub. Scottsdale Scene Mag., 1983—; pub., editor Sedona (Ariz.) Mag., 1986—; bd. dirs. Walter Cronkite Endowment Sch. of Journalism, Ariz. State U. Bd. trustees, sec. Scottsdale Meml. Health Found., 1985-87; mem. Fiesta Bowl Com., 1986—; gen. chmn. Scottsdale Disting. Citizen, 1987. Mem. U. Wis. Alumni Assn. (pres. 1986), Scottsdale C. of C. (bd. dirs.), Sedona C. of C., Gainey Ranch Golf Club, Oak Creek Country Club. Home: Box 4421 Scottsdale AZ 85261 Office: Scottsdale Scene Mag Box 4455 Scottsdale AZ 85261

JOHNSON, JACKSON MELVIN, computer company executive; b. Bemidji, Minn., Oct. 23, 1940; s. Melvin Sigurd and Margaret Marie (Hendershot) J.; m. Karen F. Winegartner, Aug. 15, 1981; children: D. Scott, Kim, Julia M., Lisa, Cyndra E. BS in Bus. Adminstrn., Wright State U., 1978; BS, U.S. Naval Acad., 1965; AS in Bus. Adminstrn. with honors, Sinclair Coll., 1974. CPA, Ohio. Dir. mgmt. info. systems United Aircraft Products, Dayton, Ohio, 1969-70; fin. EDP sales mgr. NCR, Los Angeles, 1970-77; regional sales mgr. Calcomp/Sanders, Dayton, 1977-82; v.p. sales Universal Data, Inc., Dayton, 1982-87; regional sales mgr. West Computer Identics, Orange, Calif., 1988—; assoc. prof. EDP Sinclair Coll. Served with USMC, 1958-67. Mem. Data Processing Mgmt. Assn., NCR Speakers' Bur. Republican. Lutheran. Home: 19532 Misty Ridge Ln Trabuco Canyon CA 92679

JOHNSON, JAMES DAVID, concert pianist, educator; b. Greenville, S.C., Aug. 7, 1948; s. Theron David and Lucile (Pearson) J.; m. Karen Elizabeth Jacobson, Feb. 1, 1975. MusB, U. Ariz., 1970, MusM, 1972, D of Mus. Arts, 1976; MusM, Westminster Choir Coll., 1986. Concert pianist, organist Pianists Found. Am., Boston Pops Orch., Royal Philharm., Victoria Symphony, others, 1961—; organist, choirmaster St. Paul's Episcopal Ch., Tucson, 1968-74, First United Meth. Ch., Fairbanks, Alaska, 1974-89; prof. music U. Alaska, Fairbanks, 1974—; Recordings: Moszkowski Etudes, 1973, Works of Chaminade/Dohnanyi, 1977, Mendelssohn Concerti, 1978, Beethoven First Concerto, 1980, Beethoven, Reiecke Ireland Trios with Alaska Chamber Ensemble, 1988. Recipient Record of Month award Mus. Heritage Soc., 1979, 80; finalist mus. amb. program USIA, 1983. Mem. Music Tchrs. Nat. Assn., Phi Kappa Phi, Pi Kappa Lambda. Episcopalian. Office: U Alaska-Fairbanks Dept Music Fairbanks AK 99775

JOHNSON, JAMES DOW, broadcast television executive; b. Beaumont, Tex., Nov. 20, 1934; s. Walter Alonzo and Mohnike (Wheeler) J.; m. Linda Lee Rideout, Aug. 23, 1958; children: Christopher, Karen. BA in English, Tex. A&M U., 1957, MBA, 1958. Pub. relations dir., announcer Sta. WTVC-TV, Chattanooga, Tenn., 1960-66; dir. advt. promotion publicity Sta. KTVI-TV, St. Louis, 1966-68, Sta. WLWT-TV, Cin., 1968-69; dir. info. svcs. Sta. KMOX-TV, St. Louis, 1969-71; exec. v.p., gen. mgr. NTV Network, Kearney, Nebr., 1971-80; pres., gen. mgr. Sta. KFTY-TV, Santa Rosa, Calif., 1980—. Vice-chmn. Nebr. Am. Bicentennial commn., Lincoln, 1972-78; chmn. Nebr. Ednl. TV commn., Lincoln, 1975-80; Nebr. del. to Rep. Nat. Conv., Detroit, 1980; pres., v.p., sec. Burbank (Calif.) Ctr. for Arts, 1983—; bd. dirs. United Way of North Bay, 1986—, Sonoma County Salvation Army. Served with USAR, 1958-66. Recipient Disting. Svc. award Nebr. N.G., 1973, Svc. award St. Louis Advt. Club, 1968. Mem. Nat. Assn. Broadcasters, Assn. Ind. TV Stas., Nat. Assn. TV Program Execs., Nat. Broadcast Editorial Assn. (founder 1971, treas. 1972-73, v.p. 1973-74), Calif. Broadcasters Assn. (bd. dirs. 1984—, v.p. legis. affairs), Nat. Acad. TV Arts and Scis. (pres. St. Louis chpt. 1970-71), Santa Rosa C. of C. (bd. dirs.), Empire Breakfast Club (pes. 1986), Rotary, Alpha Epsilon Rho. Office: Sta KFTY-TV 533 Mendocino Ave Santa Rosa CA 95401

JOHNSON, JAMES GIBSON, JR., recycling company executive; b. Flagstaff, Ariz., Feb. 26, 1938; s. James Gibson and Inga Anette J.; m. Faye Bodian, Aug. 23, 1973; children: Jill Johnson, Ginger Johnson, Jonathan Johnson. BA, U. Colo., 1960. Editor, pub. Town and Country Rev., Boulder, Colo., 1963-78; owner James G. Johnson and Assocs., Boulder, Colo., 1978-87; exec. dir. Eco Cycle Recycling, Boulder, Colo., 1987—. Mem. Open Space Bd. Trustees, Boulder, 1980-85, chmn. 1984-85; mem. Boulder County Pks. and Open Space Bd., 1985—, chmn 1986—. Democrat. Home: 630 Northstar Ct Boulder CO 80302 Office: Eco Cycle 5030 Pearl St Boulder CO 80302

JOHNSON, JANICE ELAINE, social worker; b. New Ulm, Minn., July 27, 1936; d. James Edward and Mathilda Marie (Nider) Honzay; m. Frank J. Johnson, Aug. 8, 1964 (div. Apr. 1982); children: Frank J. Jr., Kristin Marie. BA, St. Catherine Coll., St. Paul, 1958; postgrad., U. Minn., Mpls., 1961-63; MS in Social Adminstrn., Case Western Res. U., 1964. Caseworker Cath. Social Services, St. Paul, 1958-63; intern Kenny Rehab. Inst., Mpls., 1962-63, Cleve. Psychiat. Inst., 1963-64; social worker Family Service Assn., Cleve., 1964-66; parent facilitator San Diego City Schs., 1978; sr. social worker San Diego County Dept. Social Services, 1984—; Mem. Foster Parent Recruitment com., San Diego, 1985-87. Vol. Spl. Edn. Dept., San Diego, 1974-80, Spl. Olympics. Mem. Nat. Assn. Social Workers, AAUW, Parents of Lang. Disabled Children (treas. San Diego chpt. 1979-80), Assn. Retarded Citizens, VFW Aux. (sec. San Diego chpt. 1975-80), Phi Beta Kappa, Pi Gamma Mu. Office: 6950 Levant St San Diego CA 92111

JOHNSON, JEFFREY MICHAEL, aerospace engineer; b. Oregon City, Oreg., Aug. 21, 1962; s. Jesse Leroy and Linda Elisa (Beard) J.; m. Joann Lawrence, Dec. 17, 1988. BS in Math., Oreg. State U., 1984; MA in Applied Math., Calif. State U., Fullerton, 1989. Sr. engr. B-2 div. Northrop, Pico Rivera, Calif., 1984—. Mem. Beta Theta Pi. Republican. Home: 223 W Brookdale Pl Fullerton CA 92623 Office: Northrop B-2 Div 8900 E Washington Blvd Pico Rivera CA 90660

JOHNSON, JEROME BEN, research geophysicist; b. Ellensburg, Wash., Sept. 13, 1950; s. Ben Batchelor and Ann Carol (Bruketta) J.; m. Nancy Dean Hausle, Nov. 22, 1975; children: Nicole, Leah, Eric. BA in Physics and Math., Cen. Wash. State Coll., 1972; student, U. Alaska, 1973-74; PhD in Geophysics, U. Wash., 1978. Instr. Cen. Wash. State Coll., Ellensburg, 1978-79; sr. research engr. Oceanographic Services, Inc., Santa Barbara, Calif., 1979-80; research fellow Geophys. Inst., Fairbanks, Alaska, 1980-83; research geophysicist USA Cold Regions Research and Engring. Lab., Fairbanks, Alaska, 1983—; cons. State of Alaska, Shannon and Wilson Co., 1980-85; participant Properties of Snow Workshop, Alta, Utah, 1981; adm. assoc. prof. U. Alaska, Fairbanks, 1983—. Inventor in field; contbr. articles to profl. jours. Speaker N. Star Borough Sch. Dist., Fairbanks, 1986—. Mem. AAAS, Am. Geophys. Union, Internat. Glaciol. Soc., ASME (ice forces subcom. 1985-87). Office: USA CRREL 72 Lyme Rd Hanover NH 03755

JOHNSON, JERRY LEE, mathematics educator; b. Wilmar, Minn., July 28, 1948; s. Harry Reynolds and Mildred Bernice (Kendall) J.; m. Millie Jane Blehert, Aug. 7;, 1981; one child, Benjamin. BA Math. magna cum laude, Augsburg Coll., 1970; MS in Math., Calif. Inst. Tech., 1971; MA in Ednl. Rsch., UCLA, 1976; PhD in Math Edn., U. Wash., 1981. Tchr. math. Chadwick Sch., Palos Verdes, Calif., 1971-76, Bush Sch., Seattle, 1976-81; asst. prof. math. Seattle Pacific U., 1980-81, St. Olaf Coll., Northfield, Minn., 1981-82, U. Pacific, Stockton, Calif., 1982-84; assoc. prof. math. Western Wash. U., Bellingham, Wash., 1984—; coord., participant, presenter in numerous math. confs., task forces, insts., 1973—; cons. numerous math. projects. Author: Graphics Discoveries, Books I and II, 1984, Dr. Micro's Computer Teaching Kit: A Resource To Meet Individual Needs, 1984; contbg. editor Computing Tchr., 1983—; contbr. numerous articles to math. jours. Mem. Wash. State Math. Coun. (regional bd. dirs. 1985-88, editor Wash. Math.), Internat. Coun. for Computers in edn. (chmn. tech. liaison com. on math. 1981-83), Assn. for Computing Machinery, Nat. Consortium on Uses of Computer in Math.-Sci. Edn. (vice chmn.1982-83, mem. steering com. 1981-84), Nat. Coun. Suprs. Math., Rsch. Coun. for Diagnostic and Prescriptive Math., Internat. Group for Psychology Math. Edn., N.W. Coun. for Computers in Edn., Nat. Coun. Tchrs. Math., Oreg. Coun. for Tchr. Math., Western Wash. Math. Cons. Group, Am. Ednl. Rsch. Assn., Mu Alpha Theta (program com. nat. conv. 1987). Office: Western Wash U Dept Math Bellingham WA 98225

JOHNSON, JO M., petroleum accountant; b. Ranger, Tex., July 29, 1928; d. Joe Robert and Mary Louella (Gladden) McDougal; m. Wayne F. Johnson, May 11, 1966; children: Jim, Bob, Larry, Judy. BBA, N. Tex. State U., 1947. k. Owner Jo Johnson Petroleum Acct., Hobbs, N.Mex., 1957—; sec.-treas. Wayne F. Johnson, Inc., Hobbs, N.Mex., 1974—; ptnr. Wayne F. Johnson Co., Artesia, N.Mex., 1970—, Computer Programming Unltd., Hobbs, N.Mex., 1984—. Narrator Living Pictures of Easter, 1st Bapt. Ch., Hobbs, 1983-87. Recipient Yellow Rose of Tex., Gov. State of Tex., 1983. Mem. Hobbs C. of C. (ambassador 1988), Assn. Desk and Derrick Clubs (reg. dir. 1958), Internat. Tng. in Communication (named disting. communicator 1987, v.p. 1984-85), N.Mex. Petroleum Accts. Soc., Internat. Platform Soc., Hobbs Stock Club (pres. 1988). Democrat. Baptist. Home: 114 E Alto Hobbs NM 88240 Office: PO Box 2446 418 N Turner St Ste 300 Hobbs NM 88240

JOHNSON, JOHN CLARENCE BERTRAM, government executive; b. Monroe, La., Feb. 24, 1937; s. Clarence Bertram and Allie Belle (McDaniel) J.; m. Dolores Ann Gonzales, Aug. 25, 1957 (div. 1963); 1 child, Kelly; m. Mary Lorraine Buscher, July 22, 1963 (dec. 1973); children: Lisette, John W., Maria, Christopher, John E.B.; m. Raelene Lillian Reagan, Nov. 23, 1973; children: Michael, Randall, Patrick, Sean. BA in Pub. Adminstrn., La. State U., 1958. Personnel specialist Bur. Mines U.S. Dept. Interior, Bartlesville, Okla., 1958-60, Washington, 1961-63; sr. job analyst Phillips Petroleum Corp., Bartlesville, Okla., 1960-61; personnel specialist U. Calif., Davis, 1963-65; exec. dir. Nat. Found., New Orleans, 1965-67; personnel specialist Agy. for Internat. Devel. U.S. Dept. State, Wash., D.C., 1967-68; special asst. Office of Econ. Opportunity, Wash., D.C., 1968-69; personnel specialist USN, Port Hueneme, Calif., 1969-73; personnel officer USN, Mayport, Fla., 1977; personnel mgmt. supr. U.S. Dept. HHS, Wash., D.C., 1974-77; dir. adminstrv. svcs. U.S. Dept. HHS, San Francisco, 1977—. Served with USMCR, 1955-61. Episcopalian. Office: US Dept HHS 50 UN Plaza 413 San Francisco CA 94102

JOHNSON, JOHN PHILIP, geneticist, researcher; b. Wabash, Ind., June 6, 1949; s. Melvin Leroy and Cleo Pauline (Aldrich) J.; m. Sheryl Kay Kennedy, June 3, 1978; 1 child, Craig Eric. BS, U. Mich., 1971, MD, 1975. Diplomate Am. Bd. Pediatrics, Am. Bd. Med. Genetics. Intern, 2d-yr. resident Children's Hosp. Los Angeles, 1975-77; 3d yr. resident in pediatrics U. Utah, Salt Lake City, 1977-78, fellow in genetics, 1980-82, asst. prof. pediatrics, 1982-85; pediatrician Family Health Program, Salt Lake City, 1978-80; staff physician, geneticist Children's Hosp. Oakland, Calif., 1985—; clinic physician Utah State Tng. Sch., American Fork, 1982-85; attending and staff physician Primary Children's Med. Ctr., Salt Lake City, 1978-80. Contbr. articles to med. jours. Recipient William J. Branstrom award U. Mich., 1967. Fellow Am. Acad. Pediatrics; mem. Am. Soc. Human Genetics, Alpha Omega Alpha. Home: 1638 Harlan Dr Danville CA 94526 Office: Children's Hosp 747 52d St Oakland CA 94609

JOHNSON, KEVIN RAYMOND, lawyer, educator; b. Culver City, Calif., June 29, 1958; s. Kenneth R. Johnson and Angela J. (Gallardo) McEachron; m. Virginia Salazar, Oct. 17, 1987. AB in Econs. with great distinction, U. Calif., 1983; JD magna cum laude, Harvard U., 1983. Bar: Calif. 1985, U.S. Dist. Ct. (no., ea. and so. dists.) Calif. 1985, U.S. Ct. Appeals (9th cir.) 1985. Rsch asst. Harvard U., Cambridge, Mass., 1982-83, instr. legal writing, 1982; law clk. to presiding justice U.S. Ct. Appeals (9th cir.), L.A., 1983-84; assoc. Heller Ehrman White & McAuliffe, San Francisco, 1984-89; acting prof. of law U. Calif., Davis, 1989—; speaker Fed. Bar Assn., 1988; del. to El Salvador, 1987. Editor Harvard law rev., 1981-83, Asylum Laws; contbr. articles to profl. jours. Mem. ABA, Calif. Bar Assn., Bar Assn. San Francisco, Calif. Alumni Assn., Phi Beta Kappa. Democrat. Roman Catholic. Home: 756 Pierce St Albany CA 94706 Office: Heller Ehrman White & McAuliffe 333 Bush St San Francisco CA 94104

JOHNSON, LARRY ARTHUR, insurance company executive; b. Milaca, Minn., May 7, 1950; s. Leonard A. and Anna M. (Sageng) J.; m. Deborah R. Wiley, Sept. 12, 1981; children: Lance, Luke. BS in Indsl. Engring., St. Cloud State U., 1972; MBA in Fin., U. Oreg., 1977. Mgr. investments The Travelers Ins. Co., Seattle, 1978--. Council mem. Holy Cross Luth. Ch., Bellevue, Wash., 1987-88. Lt. USNR, 1973-76. Mem. Nat. Assn. Indsl. Office Parks, Am. Inst. Real Estate Appraisers. Republican. Home: 6010 147th Ave SE Bellevue WA 98006 Office: Travelers Ins Co 1111 3d Ave #1280 Seattle WA 98101

JOHNSON, LAWRENCE ALLAN, SR., chiropractic physician, restauranteur; b. Balt., Feb. 17, 1943; s. Harvey McMullen and Virginia Pauline (Thompson) J.; m. Sunny Lin Malone, Apr. 22, 1967; children: James, Melanie, Lawrence Jr., Jeff, Amanda, Amber, Susanne, Brittany, Courtney. BA magna cum laude, George Williams Coll., 1968; D in Chiropractic Medicine, Nat. Coll., Lombard, Ill., 1972. Pres. Chriopractic Clinics N.Mex., Los Lunas, Belen, Rio Rancho and Albuquerque, 1972—; pres. Ambulance Services N.Mex., Bernalillo and Valencia Counties, 1983-87, Lazy J Enterprises, Bernalillo and Valencia Counties, 1975—. Chmn. Rep. fin. com., Valencia County, 1983-84, 19th precinct chmn., 1985-87, vice chmn. 1980-84. Mem. N.Mex. Physicians of Chiropractic Medicine (charter, pres. 1986, chmn. bd. 1986—), N.Mex. Chiropractic Assn. (sec., treas. 1972-73, 81-82, bd. dirs. 1972-73, 79-83, editor jour. 1972-85, Nat. Excellence jour. award 1980, Outstanding Service 1972-82, founder, editor newsletter 1985—), Bernalillo County Chiropractic Assn. (charter, pres. 1972-74, 79-85, 88—), Nat. Coll. Alumni Assn. (field advisor 1983-86, bd. dirs. 1986—, Chiropractor of Yr. 1986, Outstanding Grad. 1982, bd. dirs. 1985—). Roman Catholic. Lodges: Lions (sec., treas. Los Lunas, N.Mex. club 1980, pres. 1981, 86, Lion of Yr. 1981, Outstanding E.M.S. award 1987), Masons, Moose. Home: 4203 Hwy 85 SW Los Lunas NM 87031 Office: Chiropractic Clinic NMex 4205 Hwy 85 SW Los Lunas NM 87031

JOHNSON, LAYMON, JR., budget analyst; b. Jackson, Miss., Sept. 1, 1948; s. Laymon and Bertha (Yarbrough) J.; m. Charlene J. Johnson, Nov. 13, 1982. B in Tech., U. Dayton, 1970; MS in Systems Mgmt., U. So. Calif., 1978. Mem. tech. staff Rockwell Internat., Canoga Park, Calif., 1975-77; sr. dynamics engr. Gen. Dynamics, Pomona, Calif., 1978-83; sr. budget analyst, budget mgr. Northrop Corp., Pico Rivera, Calif., 1983—. Served to lt. comdr. USNR, 1970—. Mem. U.S. Naval Inst., Naval Res. Assn., Res. Officers Assn. U.S., Assn. Mil. Surgeons U.S., Assn. Systems Mgmt., Ops. Research Soc. Am., Los Angeles County Mus. Art, Smithsonian Assos., Nat. Hist. Soc., Archimedes Circle, Tau Alpha Pi. Democrat. Roman Catholic.

JOHNSON, LEE CARROLL, electronics company executive; b. Monroe, Ind., Sept. 29, 1933; s. Thetus Jesse and Vida Louise (Ward) J.; m. Donna Lee Heald, Nov. 25, 1951; children: Marga Lynn Johnson Cullumber, Shelon Lee. BEE, Purdue U., 1953; LLB, LaSalle U., Chgo., 1966. V.p., dir. bus. devel. ITT Aerospace, Ft. Wayne, Ind., 1952-74; v.p., gen. mgr. govt. electronics group Motorola Corp., Scottsdale, Ariz., 1974-88; cons. Motorola Tng. and Edn. Ctr., Schaumburg, Ill. Patentee in field. Mem. fin. com. Devereux Found., Scottsdale, 1981-88. Mem. IEEE, Air Force Assn., Navy League, Assn. of U.S. Army, NRA (life), Aircraft Owners and Pilots Assn., Assn. Old Crows. Republican. Methodist. Home and Office: 9090 N 86th Pl Scottsdale AZ 85258

JOHNSON, LLOYD WALLACE, controller; b. Lincoln, Nebr., May 26, 1928; s. Walter Richard and Flora Ivy (Wallen) J.; m. Delores Fay Hudson; children: Wayne R., Ellen L. BS, Creighton U., 1953. CPA, Minn., Mont. With staff Arthur Andersen & Co., Omaha, 1953-57; controller Calandra Photo, Inc., Omaha, 1957-70; audit mgr. McGladry, Hendrickson, Mpls., 1970-73; controller Midland Foods, Inc., Billings, Mont., 1973-84, Western Plains Machinery Co., Billings, 1984—. Served with USN, 1944-46, PTO. Mem. Am. Inst. CPAs, Minn. Soc. CPAs, Billings Chpt. CPAs. Republican. Home: 3516 Ben Hogan Ln Billings MT 59106 Office: Western Plains Machinery Co 505 N 24th St Box 30438 Billings MT 59107

JOHNSON, LOIS JEAN, music educator; b. Los Angeles, Jan. 13, 1950; d. Kenneth Franklin and Iona Jean (Miller) J. BA, Brigham Young U., 1971, MusM, 1975. Grad. teaching asst. Brigham Young U., Provo, Utah, 1972-75, instr. voice, 1975—; instr. music study Vienna, Austria, 1978; chief registrar vital stas. City-County Health Dept., Provo, 1979-85; mus. dir. Utah Valley Choral Soc., Provo, 1980—, trustee, 1983—; mus. dir. Promised Valley Playhouse, Salt Lake City, 1984; dir. choral activities American Fork (Utah) High Sch., 1985—; vocal tchr., Provo, 1972—; mem., soloist Mormon Tabernacle Choir, Salt Lake City, 1972—. Mem. Am. Choral Dirs. Assn., Nat. Assn. Tchrs. Singing (v.p. local chpt. 1983-84), Assn. Profl. Vocal Ensembles, NEA, Utah Edn. Assn., Music Educator Nat. Conf., Utah Music Educators Assn. Republican. Mormon. Home: 835 North 750 West Provo UT 84604 Office: Am Fork High Sch 510 N 600 East American Fork UT 84003

JOHNSON, LYNN BARBARA, artist, civic worker; b. N.Y.C., Jan. 23, 1933; d. Carl Lincoln (stepfather) and Mary Catherine (Albert) Nelson; m. Frederick Hannan Johnson, Dec. 14, 1957; children: Christopher H., Laura B., Thor A. AA with honors, Stockton Jr. Coll., 1952; BFA, BA, U. Wash., 1954. Clk. Standard Oil Co., San Francisco, 1956-57; tchr. nursery sch., Menlo Park, Calif., 1957-58; pvt. tchr. art San Diego, 1968-69; art dealer Kenneth Behm Galleries, Seattle and Bellevue, Wash., 1981-84. One-woman shows include Hartford Conn. Amory Show, 1965, Converse Gallery Annual Show, 1965, San Diego Watercolor Annual, 1967, Northwest Watercolor Annual, 1972. Active numerous civic orgns.; founder Niantic (Conn.) Outdoor Art Show, 1962; co-founder Bellevue Jazz Festival, 1977; mem. Bellevue Sch. Dist. Citizens' Task Force, 1979-80, Wash. State Ad Hoc Com. on Arts, 1977-79; mem. Bellevue Centennial Steering Com., 1988; mem. citizens' coodinating com. King County Centennial, 1988; chmn. Bellevue City Arts Commn., 1980-81, 83; co-founder, pres. Seattle-King County Community Arts Network, 1986-87; co-founder Bellevue Allied Arts Coun., 1981; v.p. Found. for Internat. Understanding through Students, U. Wash., 1987-88; del. Wash. Rep. Com., 1987-88. Recipient numerous awards for watercolors, Calif., N.Y., Conn.; finalist Priz de Paris, Vogue mag., 1954; Nat. Assn. Fgn. Student Affairs travel grantee, 1987. Mem. AAUW (Wash. chpt. bd. dirs., past branch v.p.), San Diego Watercolor Soc. (profl.), Wash. Arts Alliance, Native Am. Studies Assn., Seattle Art Mus. (ethnic arts coun.), Bellevue Art Mus. (founding, docent coun. 1978, branch v.p.), Seattle Opera Guild, Nat. Mus. Women Arts (charter mem.), U. Wash. Alumni Assn. Home: 2202 102d Pl SE Bellevue WA 98004

JOHNSON, LYNN CRAVAT, senior financial consultant; b. Portland, Oreg., Dec. 14, 1953; s. Leland H. and Gray (Cravat) J.; m. Marian Kay Scott, May 27, 1978; 1 child, Rachel Star. BS in Econs., U.S. Internat. U., 1976; MS in Pub. Adminstrn., Lewis & Clark U., 1984. Asst. ops. officer United BAnk of Calif., Palm Springs, 1978-81; regional officer Oreg. Bank, Portland, 1981-84; sr. fin. cons. Merrill Lynch, Portland, 1984—. Team capt. Portland United Way, 1983. Named Worker of the Year Sports Car Club of Am., Portland, 1971. Clubs: Oswego Lake Country (Lake Oswego); Multnomah Athletic (Portland). Lodge: Kiwanis (Portland pres. 1982-83). Home: 18031 Meadowlake Ln Lake Oswego OR 97034 Office: Merrill Lynch 1211 SW 5th Ave Portland OR 97204

JOHNSON, LYNN RAYMOND, physical therapist; b. Nampa, Idaho, Aug. 27, 1952; s. Sumner Maurice and Betty Jean (Wisely) J.; m. Anita Louise Leccese, Aug. 31, 1980; children: Amelia Rose, Lucy Elizabeth. BS, U. Idaho, 1974; Cert. Phys. Therapy, Children's Hosp. L.A., 1976. Staff phys. therapist Kerlan-Jobe Clinic, Inglewood, Calif., 1976-78, R.S. Weber, Inc., Westlake Village, Calif., 1978; co-owner Ada Phys. Therapy, Boise, Idaho, 1978-79; dir. phys. therapy. Idaho Sports Medicine, Boise, 1979-80; owner, therapist The Therapy Source, P.A., Boise, 1981—; athletic trainer, Boise Blades Hockey Club, 1978-85, Bishop Kelly High Sch., Boise, 1984-88. Mem. Am. Phys. Therapy Assn., Idaho Phys. Therapy Assn. (legis. chmn. 1983—), Nat. Athletic Trainers Assn. Republican. Office: The Therapy Source PA 6110 Emerald St Boise ID 83704

JOHNSON, MAGIC See JOHNSON, EARVIN

JOHNSON, MARC, construction executive; b. Xenia, Ohio, Dec. 12, 1943; s. Carl Andrew and Gertrude Virginia (Moon) J. Student, Miami U., Oxford, Ohio, 1960, Cornell U., Ithaca, N.Y., 1961-63. Nat. mgr. sales Alpine div. Skyline Corp., Elkhart, Ind., 1969; plant mgr. Automated Structures, 1970-71; prin. The Store, Laramie, Wyo., 1971-83. Author (column) Housing in Hawaii, Hawaii Tribune-Herald. Com. chmn. Pres.'s Coun. on Housing, Washington, 1971. Ellsworth M. Statler scholar Cornell U., N.Y., 1961-63. Home and Office: 717 Hwy 11 Laramie WY 82070

JOHNSON, MARGARET JANE, brokerage house executive; b. Tucson, Mar. 3, 1939; d. Andrew Carlos and Helen Martha (Archibald) Larsen; m. Alfred Russell Johnson, June 28, 1958 (div. 1987); children: Diane Lynn, Mark Kevin. Grad. high sch., Whittier, Calif. Lic. stock broker, ins. broker, Ariz., Calif. and Co. Securities ops. mgr. The Advisors Inc., Phoenix, 1983-87; MAI Securities Corp., Phoenix, 1986; stock broker Value Equities Corp., San Diego, 1986-87; stock broker, exec. sales asst. Shearson Lehman Hutton, Sun City, Ariz., 1988-89; stock broker, ins. broker Fin. Discovery, Phoenix, 1989—; securities libr. Am. Network Securities, Sun City, Ariz., 1987-88. V.p., sec. Paradise Valley Spl. Edn. Parent Adv. Group, Phoenix, 1975-76; asst. Eisenhower-Nixon Campaign, 1952. Republican. Reorganized Ch. of Jesus Christ of Latter Day Saints. Home: 3028 E Dahlia Dr Phoenix AZ 85032 Office: Phoenix Office of Admissions 4811 N 7th St A-1 Phoenix AZ 85014

JOHNSON, MARK ALAN, antique dealer and importer; b. San Diego, July 11, 1952; s. Clyde B. and JoJean (McCall) J.; m. Kathy Mae Samuelson, Nov. 6, 1983; children: Alan Forrest, Aaron Kendal. Student, Mt. San Antonio Coll., 1970-72. Owner Mark A. Johnson Imports, Vista, Calif., 1979—. Mem. Textile Mus., 1983—, Seattle Art Mus., 1986—, Los Angeles County Mus. of Art, 1988—, Mingel Internat., 1987—. Mem. Antique Tribal Art Dealers Assn., San Diego Rug and Textiles Soc. (co-founder 1985), Rare Fruit Growers Club, Vista. Democrat. Office: Ethnic Arts of Asia 1745 E Vista Way #9 Vista CA 92084

JOHNSON, MARK HENRY, consumer electronics association executive; b. Worcester, Mass., Apr. 28, 1953; s. Henry Adolph and Julie rosella (Lofstedt) J.; m. Gayle Borderick, Aug. 1, 1981 (div. Apr. 1987). BS in Biology, Clark U., 1974; postgrad., Lowell U., 1977-78. Regional sales mgr. Volteck Inc., Lawrence, Mass., 1976-81; mgr. Ariz ops. Republic Packaging Corp., Chgo., 1981-82; v.p. ops. Am. Video Assn., Mesa, Ariz., 1983—. Mem. Internat. Soc. Cert. Electronics Technicians (cert.), Nat. Honor Soc., Latin Honor Soc. Home: 1570 N Pennington Dr Chandler AZ 85224 Office: Am Video Assn 557 E Juanita Ave Mesa AZ 85204

JOHNSON, MARQUES KEVIN, professional basketball player; b. Nachitoches, La., Feb. 8, 1956; s. Jeff David and Baasha Violet (Kessee) J.; 1 child, Kristaan Iman. B.A., UCLA, 1977. Mem. UCLA Varsity Basketball Team, 1973-77; mem. Milw. Bucks NBA, 1977-84, mem. L.A. Clippers, 1984-88. Producer, dir., editor: film Livin' for the Weekend, 1979; producer: TV film On the Road with the Milwaukee Bucks, 1984. Recipient Bob Hope Youth award, 1979, John W. Wooden sports award, 1977, Inspiration to Youth award, 1983; named Coll. Acad. All-Am., 1977, Coll. Player of Yr., 1977; named to Nat. Basketball Assn. All-Star Team, 1979, 80, 81, 83, 86, Nat. Basketball Assn. All-Pro 1st Team, 1979. Democrat. Baptist. Office: PO Box 2586 Inglewood CA 90305

JOHNSON, MARY LUCILE, writer; b. Salida, Colo., May 13, 1927; d. Russell Lyons and Lael Rose (Phippemy) Margrave; m. H. Bruce Johnson, Mar. 22. 1947; children: Laura Lael Johnson Reveles, Freya Eileen. AA, Pasadena City Jr. Coll., 1946. Dir. publicity Rep. Women, Merced, Calif., 1955-57; chairwoman 3rd dist. United Reps. Calif., Sacramento, 1963-65; dir. UROC press rooms Fresno, Bakersfield and Sacramento, 1963-65; writer publicity Splty. Publicity & Pub. Rels., Sacramento, 1964-68; writer Sacramento, 1964—; cons. real estate Country Inns, Grass Valley, Calif. and Neveda City, Calif., 1982-86; owner Inheritance Antiques, Carmichael, Calif., 1986—; publicity cons. Cushion Rail Internat., 1964-70; editor, lit. agt., 1976—. Author: Where Flies Don't Land, 1975, Big Girls Still Cry, 1988; assoc. editor The Sacramento Newsletter, 1963-65. Recipient Nat. Guideposts Writers Contest award, 1971. Mem. Nat. League Am. Penwomen, Authors Guild, Authors League Am. Presbyterian. Home: 5346 Kenneth Ave Carmichael CA 95608

JOHNSON, MAURICE VERNER, JR., agricultural research and development executive; b. Duluth, Minn., Sept. 13, 1925; s. Maurice Verner Sr. and Elvira Marie (Westberg) J.; m. Darlene Ruth Durand, June 23, 1944; children: Susan Kay, Steven Dale. BS, U. Calif., 1953. registered profl.

engr. From research engr. to dir. research and devel. Sunkist Growers, Ontario, Calif., 1953-84; v.p. research and devel. Sunkist Growers, Ontario, 1984—; v.p., dir. Calif. Citrus Quality Council, Claremont. Contbr. articles to profl. pubs.; patentee in field. Sgt. U.S. Army, 1944-46, ETO. Fellow Am. Soc. Agrl. Engrs. (dir. 1969-70); mem. ASME, Am. Inst. Indsl. Engrs., Am. Assn. Advancement Sci., Nat. Soc. Profl. Engrs., Tau Beta Pi. Republican. Home: 1344 Taylor Way Upland CA 91786 Office: Sunkist Growers 760 E Sunkist St PO Box 3720 Ontario CA 91761

JOHNSON, MELINDA See CUMMINGS, SPANGLER

JOHNSON, MICHAEL WILLIAM, talent casting agency director; b. Chgo., Oct. 26, 1953; s. Rudolph Eugene and Audrey Pauline (Demos) J. Announcer Sta. WLUV-AM, Rockford, Ill., 1973-75, Sta. WVVX-AM, Highland Park, Ill., 1975-76, Sta. WWMM-AM, Arlington Heights, Ill., 1976-78; dir. promotions Sta. WKKW-AM, Clarksburg, W.Va., 1978-81; dir. ops. Sta. WKUL-AM, Cullman, Ala., 1980-81; dir. spl. projects Sta. WAHR-AM, Huntsville, Ala., 1981-83; dir. ops. Johnson & Buckingham Nationwide Talent Casting, Hollywood, Calif., 1983—; owner Pacific Entertainment Group, Hollywood, 1987—. Mem. Mothers Against Drunk Drivers, Los Angeles, 1988; vol. Sta. KCET-TV Pub. TV, Los Angeles, 1986—. Mem. Hollywood C. of C. Democrat. Office: Johnson & Buckingham Nationwide Talent Casting 6362 Hollywood Blvd Ste 320 Hollywood CA 90028

JOHNSON, PATRICIA GAYLE, corporate communication executive, writer; b. Conway, Ark., Oct. 23, 1947; d. Rudolph and Frances Modene (Hayes) J. Student U. Calif., Irvine, 1965-68. Advance rep. Disney on Parade, Los Angeles, 1971-75; mktg. dir., dir. field ops. Am. Freedom Train, 1975-77; publ. rels. mgr. Six Flags, Inc., Los Angeles, 1977-81; mgr. corp. communications Playboy Enterprises, Inc., Los Angeles, 1981-82; external rels. mgr. Kal Kan Foods, Inc., Los Angeles, 1982-86; v.p. Daniel J. Edelman, Inc., 1986-88; sr. v.p. Amies Advt. and Pub. Rels., Irvine, 1988—; lectr. U. So. Calif., UCLA, Calif. State U., Northridge, Calif. State U., Dominguez Hills. Mem. Pub. Rels. Soc. Am. (past officer), Pub. Affairs Council, Delta Soc. (advisor). Mem. Foursquare Gospel Ch. Collaborator TV scripts; contbr. articles to various consumer and profl. mags. Office: Amies Advt & Pub Rels 19100 Von Karman Ave Irvine CA 91715

JOHNSON, PAUL ALFRED, utilities executive, engineer; b. Denver, Apr. 25, 1946; s. James William and Mary Ann (Potts) J.; m. Karen Blythe Jacobson, June 19, 1969; children: Lorelei Layne, Marc Raymond. BA in Electronic Engring., U. Colo., 1969, BA in Applied Math., 1969. Registered profl. engr., Minn. Ops. mgr. Magnavox Corp., Chgo., 1969-73; sr. exec. account mgr. Xerox Corp., Rockford, Ill., 1973-78; ptnr. Go-Rite Bus. Systems, Rockford, 1978-81; v.p. R & D Internat. Energy Masters, St. Paul, 1981-83; software engr. TSI, St. Paul, 1983-84; dir. devel. Asea Brown Boveri, St. Paul, 1984-87; engring. mgr. ESCA Corp., Bellevue, Wash., 1987—. Mem. IEEE. Office: ESCA Corp 13208 Northup Way Bellevue WA 98005

JOHNSON, PAUL LAWRENCE, electronic instrumentation technician; b. Superior, Wis., June 15, 1952; s. Lawrence Herman and Jessie Beth (Osborn) J.; m. Maria Magdelena Sanchez, Apr. 17, 1976; children: Amber Beth, Eve Denise. Student, Cen. Ariz. Coll., 1970-71, No. Ariz. U., 1976-78. Electrician Cyprus Pima Mining Co., Tucson, 1978-82, Cyprus Bagdad (Ariz.) Mining Co., 1982-83; instrument technician Round Mountain (Nev.) Gold Corp., 1984—; owner Heritage Merchandising, Paul's Appliance Svc. Sgt. USAF, 1971-75. Mem. Instrument Soc. Am., Ludwig Von Mises Assn. Home: PO Box 316 Round Mountain NV 89045 Office: Round Mountain Gold Corp PO Box 480 Round Mountain NV 89045

JOHNSON, PAUL MARTIN, medical center director; b. Flint, Mich., June 3, 1946; s. Willard Robert and Patricia Grayce (Martin) J.; m. Penelope Anne Lawson, Apr. 16, 1983; children: Melissa, Matthew. AA, Diablo Valley Coll., 1966; BA in Polit. Sci., Calif. State U., Hayward, 1978; MS in Health Svcs., St. Mary's Coll., 1986. Cert. radiologic technologist, Calif. Chief technologist Peralta Hosp., Oakland, Calif., 1972-82; mgr. radiation Peralta Hosp., Oakland, 1986-87; dir. radiation oncology Merritt-Peralta Med. Ctr., Oakland, 1987, asst. adminstr., 1987—; cons. Monterey Community Hosp., Monterey, Calif., 1988. Sec. Health Svcs. Agy., Alameda Contra Costa, Oakland, 1987; chmn. Child Health & Disability Prevention, Concord, 1983; mem. adv. com. San Francisco City Coll., 1989. With U.S. Army, 1969-72. Recipient Outstanding Service Plaque, Child Health & Disability Prevention, Concord, 1983, Health Svcs. Agy., Oakland, 1983. Mem. Am. Registry of Radiologic Technologists, Calif. Soc. Radiologic Technologists (chmn. 1982-87, pres. 1981-82, Past Pres. award, 1981, 82), No. Calif. Soc. Radiation Technologists (pres. 1981, com. mem. 1989), Am. Assn. Med. Dosimetrists, Am. Coll. Healthcare Execs., Sunny Hills Club (treas. 1976-79). Republican. Episcopalian. Office: Merritt Peralta Med Ctr 450 30th St Oakland CA 94609

JOHNSON, PHILIP BIESINGER, psycholotherapist; b. Salt Lake City, May 25, 1949; s. Glenn Henry and Helen (Biesinger) J.; m. Marsha Irene Ocamb, June 19, 1968; children: Matthew, Danielle. BS in Psychology, U. Utan, 1972; MS in Psychology, U. Bridgeport (Conn.), 1974; postgrad., Calif. Sch. Profl. Psychology, 1974. Therapist in drug rehab. Vitam Ctr., Stamford, Conn., 1972-73; program coordinator men's rehab. ctr. Salvation Army, San Diego, 1973-74, program coordinator social svcs., 1974-75; program coordinator Community Resource and Self Help, Inc., San Diego, 1975-79; psychologist Handicapped Children's Svc., Dept. Health, Ogden, Utah, 1979-88; pvt. practice Ctr. for Behavior Change, Ogden, 1982—; cons. psychologist No. Utah Maxillo-Facial Panel, Ogden, 1980-88; chmn. Marriage and Family Licensing Bd., State of Utah, 1988—. Contbg. author: Providers Manual for Marriage and Family Therapist, 1986. Mem. Am. Assn. Marriage and Family Therapists (clin. mem.), Utah Assn. Marriage and Family Therapy (clin. mem., co-chmn. ins. sub-com. 1986-88). Democrat. Office: Associated Therapist 425 E 5350 S #280 Ogden UT 84405

JOHNSON, PHYLLIS, retired engineering draftsman; b. Seneca, Kans., June 5, 1923; d. Paul Eugene and Emily (Burger) J. BA, U. Wash., 1950. With Boeing Airplane Co., Seattle, 1942—, jr. engr., 1945-51, drafter, 1951-88. Mem. Seattle Profl. Engring. Employees Assn., Boeing Employees Travel Club (sec. 1974-76). Republican. Home: 24525 13th Ave S Des Moines WA 98198

JOHNSON, QULAN ADRIAN, software engineer; b. Gt. Falls, Mont., Sept. 17, 1942; s. Raymond Eugene and Bertha Marie (Nagengast) J.; m. Helen Louise Pocha, July 24, 1965; children—Brenda Marie, Douglas Paul, Scot Paul, Mathew James. B.A. in Psychology, Coll. Gt. Falls, 1964. Lead operator 1st Computer Corp., Helena, Mont., 1966-67; v.p., sec.-treas. Computer Corp. of Mt., Great Falls, 1967-76, dir., 1971-76; sr. systems analyst Mont. Dept. Revenue, Helena, 1976-78; software engr. Mont. Systems Devel. Co., Helena, 1978-80; programmer/analyst III info. systems div. Mont. Dept. Adminstrn., Helena, 1980-82; systems analyst centralized services Dept. Social and Rehab. Services State of Mont., 1982-87, systems and programming mgr. info systems, Blue Cross and Blue Shield of Montana, Helena, 1987—. Mem. Assn. for Systems Mgmt., Mont. Data Processing Assn., Data Processing Mgmt. Assn., Mensa. Club: K.C. (rec. sec. 1975-76). Home: 2231 8th Ave Helena MT 59601 Office: Blue Cross & Blue Shield Info Systems 404 Fuller Ave Helena MT 59604-4309

JOHNSON, RALPH MAXWELL, lawyer; b. Sioux City, Iowa, Mar. 22, 1940; s. Ralph Mills and Bernice (Eastman) J.; m. Melissa Crowell, Sept. 1, 1985; 1 child, Andrew. B.A., Calif. State U.-Fullerton, 1967; J.D., U. Calif.-San Francisco, 1971. Bar: Calif. 1972, U.S. Dist. Ct. (no. dist.) Calif. 1972, U.S. Ct. Appeals (9th cir.) 1972, U.S. Supreme Ct. 1978. clk., assoc. Smith & Granberg, San Francisco, 1971-72, dep. atty. gen. Office of Atty. Gen., San Francisco, 1972—; mem. faculty, lectr. Adminstrv. Law Coll., Sacramento, 1979-82. Mem. Friends of San Francisco Symphony, 1985, Lawyers for San Francisco Conservatory of Music, 1984, Friends of San Francisco Conservatory of Music, 1988; Active San Francisco Symphony Found., 1988. Served with USN, 1958-62. Mem. Calif. State Bar, Bar Assn. of San Francisco, World Affairs Council No. Calif. Democrat. Avocation: running. Office: Calif Atty Gen's Office 350 McAllister 6th Fl San Francisco CA 94102

JOHNSON, RAYMOND W. (PADRE JOHNSON), artist, minister; b. Mpls., June 27, 1934; s. Raymond Wendell and Lorena Sylvia (Harbrecht) J.; divorced; children: Raymond, Richard. BA, Gustavus Adolphus Coll., 1956; MDiv., Luth. Sch. Theology, 1960; postgrad., U. Minn., 1971-72; D in Ministry, United Theol. Sem., 1978. Ordained to ministry Luth. Ch., 1960. Med. technician Pub. Hosp., Moline, Ill., 1956-58; campus pastor Middlebury (Vt.), Dartmouth (N.H.) Colls., 1960-66; chaplain USN, Charleston, S.C., 1966; chaplain, field med. officer Navy Spl. Forces, USN, Vietnam, 1967-68; chaplain Blue Angels flight squadron Navy Spl. Forces, USN, Pensacola, Fla., 1968-69; dir. devel. gov.'s crime commn. State of Minn., St. Paul, 1969-72; community devel. specialist Nat. Tech. Services Found., Mpls., 1972-74; resident minister Jonathan Ecumenical Community Ch., Mpls., 1974-79. Author: Postmark Mekong Delta, 1968; exhibits include Voyageur Art, Portrait of the Human Family; contbr. article to profl. jours. Served lt. USN, 1966-69, Vietnam; comdr. USNR, 1979—. Decorated Legion of Merit, Silver Star with oak leaf cluster, Cross of Gallantry, Purple Heart with oak leaf cluster. Recipinet Gold medal Internat. Art Honor Soc., 1984; named one of 10 Outstanding Young Men of Am. U.S. Jaycees. Avocation: sports, mountain climbing. Home and Office: PO Box 146 Cody WY 82414

JOHNSON, REID STUART, financial advisor; b. Pitts., July 22, 1951; s. Ross H. and Marjorie J. M in Fin. Services, Am. Coll. CLU, Cert. Fin. Planner, employee benefits specialist; chartered fin. cons.; registered health underwriter, investment advisor, gen. prin. Assoc. regional mgr. Old Heritage Life Ins. Co., Lincoln, Ill., 1972-74; regional v.p. Lincoln Heritage Life Ins. Co., Springfield, Ill., 1974-76; pres. First Line Brokerage Inc., Champaign, Ill., 1976-83, First Line Fin. Planning, Inc., Champaign, 1981—; fin. advisor Shearson Lehman Hutton Inc., Mesa, Az., 1986—; faculty council mem. Coll. Fin. Planning, Denver, Parkland Coll., Champaign; ednl. cons. Nat. Ctr. Fin. Edn., Inc., San Francisco. Conbtr. weekly articles on fin. planning and money mgmt. to area newspapers and profl. publs.; mem. rev. com. Longman Pub. Mem. Am. Soc. CLU's, Soc. Chartered Fin. Cons., Internat. Assn. Fin. Planners (registered), Eastern Ill. Estate Planning Council, Inst. Cert. Fin. Planners, Am. Assn. Fin. Planning. Home: 1055 W Baseline #1085 Mesa AZ 85210 Office: Shearson Lehman Hutton 1901 E University Dr Ste #100 Mesa AZ 85203

JOHNSON, RICHARD HARMON, animal scientist; b. Altadena, Calif., Jan. 4, 1931; s. Josiah Victor and Marcilest Rae (Mayhall) Johnson Harmon; m. Patricia Ann Coffey, May 30, 1959; children: Catherine Teresa, Deborah Lynne. BS with hons., Calif. State Poly. Coll., 1955; PhD, Iowa State U., 1959. Cons. Govt. Argentina, Buenos Aires, 1959; tech. svc. rep. Dawe's Labs., Chgo., 1960-63; dir. tech. svc. A.L. Gilbert Co., Oakdale, Calif., 1964-68, 1971—; asst. ext. prof. U. Ky., Bowling Green, 1968-71; adv. com. animal sci. dept. U. Calif., Davis, 1975-80; cons. in field. Contbr. articles to profl. jours.; patentee in field. Mem. Am. Feed Ind. Assn. (mem. nutrition coun. 1973-74), Calif. Grain and Feed Assn., Am. Dairy Sci. Assn., Am. Soc. Animal Sci., Am. Registry Profl. Animal Scientists (dir. 1987-89), Coun. for Agrl. Sci. and Tech., Calif. Animal Nutrition Coun., K.C. Republican. Roman Catholic. Home: 1257 W I St Oakdale CA 95361 Office: AL Gilbert Co 304 N Yosemite Ave PO Box 38 Oakdale CA 95361

JOHNSON, RICHARD KARL, hospitality company executive; b. Gaylord, Minn., May 27, 1947; s. Karl S. and Mildred (Tollefson) J.; m. Eva Margaret Wick, Oct. 12, 1973; children: Michelle, Richard, Ryan. BA, Gustavus Adolphus U., St. Peter, Minn., 1969. Gen. mgr. Green Giant Restaurants, Inc., Mpls., 1969-71, Mpls. Elks Club, Mpls., 1971-73; dir. concept devel. Internat. Multifoods, Mpls., 1972-75; v.p. concept devel. A&WFood Svcs. Can., North Vancouver, B.C., 1975-81; dir. food and beverages Ramada, Reno, 1981-82; pres., owner R.K. Johnson & Assoc., Reno, 1981—; asst. gen. mgr. Gold Dust West Casino, Reno, 1983-85; gen. mgr. P&W Corp., Reno, 1985-86; v.p. ops. C.P.S.W. Inc., Reno and Tempe, Ariz., 1986-87, Lincoln Fairview, Reno, 1987—. Mem. Aircraft Owners and Pilots Assn., Nat. Restaurant Assn., Nev. Bd. Realtors, Elks Club. Lutheran. Home: 825 Meadow Springs Dr Reno NV 89502 Office: RK Johnson & Assoc 825 Meadow Springs Dr Reno NV 89502

JOHNSON, RICHARD LLOYD, internist; b. Weaverville, Calif., Feb. 16, 1918; s. Lloyd Godfrey and Elizabeth (Henderson) J.; m. Muriel Cannon, Mar. 21, 1945 (div. Dec. 1966); children: Elizabeth, Ellen Norquist, Victoria Sulski, Caroline; m. Claire Morgan, July 19, 1987. AB, U. Calif., 1939; MD, U. Calif., San Francisco, 1942. Intern Sacramento (Calif.) County Hosp., 1942-43; resident in internal medicine Milw. County Hosp., 1946-48; sr. mem. staff Mercy Gen. Hosp., Sacramento, 1953—, Sutter Community Hosps., Sacramento, 1953—; chmn. dept. medicine Mercy Gen. Hosp., Sacramento, 1960; chief dept. medicine Sutter Community Hosps., Sacramento, 1964-65, 75-76, chmn. staff, 1966; pvt. practice Sacramento, 1949-88; med. dir. Pub. Health Div., Sacramento County Health Dept. Calif. del. White House Conf. Aging, 1961, 81; mem. Citizen's Adv. Com. Aging, Calif., 1958-65, state of Calif. Bd. Med. Examiners, 1965-69, New England Hist. Gen. Soc. Maj. Med. Corps., U.S. Army, 1943-46. Mem. AMA (alt. del. 1985—), Am. Geriatrics Sect. (trustee western sect. 1979-85), Calif. Med. Assn. (del. 1977—, chmn. editorial bd. assn. publ. 1987—, active various coms.), Calif. Soc. Internal Medicine (bd. trustees 1976-81, pres. 1980), Sacramento-El Dorado Med. Soc. (bd. dirs. 1955-59, 77-79, pres. 1978, editor soc. publ. 1955, 79—, Golden Stethoscope award 1986), Sons Am. Revolution, Mason, Shriners. Democrat. Episcopalian. Home: 1500 4th St Apt 16 Sacramento CA 95814 Office: 3701 Branch Center Rd Sacramento CA 95827

JOHNSON, RICHARD MILTON, finance executive; b. Denver, Nov. 29, 1940; s. Carl Milton and Alice Adeline (Sunblade) J.; m. Norma Sue Shelton, Sept. 1978. BS, Ariz. State U., 1968, MBA, 1970. Govt. programs adminstr. Blue Cross/Blue Shield Ariz., Phoenix, 1969-73; fiscal services dir. Walter O. Boswell Meml. Hosp., Sun City, Ariz., 1973-78; exec. v.p. Flagstaff (Ariz.) Health Mgmt. Corp., 1978—; bd. dirs. Ariz. Voluntary Hosp. Fedn., Ariz. Dept. Health Services. Fellow Healthcare Fin. Mgmt. Assn. (pres. 1986-87), Sigma Iota Epsilon. Republican. Lutheran. Office: Flagstaff Health Mgmt Corp 1200 N Beaver St Flagstaff AZ 86001

JOHNSON, ROBERT NEIL, pharmacist; b. Dallas, July 9, 1943; s. John Robert and Irene E. (Parent) J.; m. Marsha Childers, Dec. 1, 1984 (div. 1986). BS, Oreg. State U., 1966. Lic. pharmacist, Oreg., 1966, Calif. 1966. Pharmacist Stewart Drug, Inc., Taft, Calif., 1966-67, 72-73, Sav-On Drug, Inc., Bakersfield, Calif., 1973-79, San Joaquin Community Hosp., Bakersfield, 1979-; cons. Central Purchasing, Irvine, Calif., 1983-87, Community Dialysis Svcs., Bakersfield, 1986-88. Author, editor Pharmacy News, 1986-88. Pres. Park Stockdale Civic Assn., Bakersfield, 1980; chmn. Kern County CETA Audit Subcom., Bakersfield, 1977-83; active Kern County CETA Bd., Bakersfield, 1977-83. Capt. USAF, 1967-72, Vietnam. Decorated D.F.C. with two oak leaf clusters, Air medal with ten oak leaf c. Republican. Methodist. Office: San Joaquin Community Hosp 2615 Eye St Bakersfield CA 93303

JOHNSON, RODNEY DALE, protective services official, photographer; b. Montebello, Calif., May 14, 1944; s. Albert Gottfreid and Maxine Elliot (Rogers) J.; m. Karen Rae Van Antwerp, May 18, 1968; 1 child, Tiffany Nicole. AA, Ela Community Coll., 1973; postgrad. Law Enforcement Spl., FBI, Acad., 1976; BA, U. of La Verne, 1978. Cert. tchr. police sci., Calif. Dep., Los Angeles County Sheriff, 1969-75, dep. IV, 1976-78, sgt., 1978—; fire arms inst., Hacienda Heights, Calif., 1975—; photography instr., Hacienda Heights, 1983—; pres. Wheelhouse Enterprises, Inc., Whittier, 1971-86; instr. State Sheriff's Civil Procedural Sch. Los Medanos Coll., Concord, Calif., 1985-88. Creator and actor, Cap'n Andy, 1973-80; song writer for Cap'n Andy theme, 1972. Sgt. USMC, 1965-69, Vietnam, master sgt. Res., 1969—. Recipient Service award Trinity Broadcasting Network, 1979. Mem. Profl. Peace Officers Assn., Sheriff's Relief Assn., Assoc. Photographers Internat. Republican. Mem. Assembly of God. Club: Faithbuilders (pres. 1981-87), (Pomona).

JOHNSON, ROYAL M., retired civil service administrative officer, consultant; b. Spokane, Wash., May 31, 1944; s. Ward Willis and Juanita May (Whitmore) J.; m. Anne-Marie Marshall Seale, Feb. 4, 1965 (div. Sept. 1979); children: Veronica Anne, Chad Lewis, Dale Richard; m. Virginia Laverne Pelton, June 15, 1981; stepchildren: Cynthia Conner, David Conner, Debra Conner. AA, Ventura Community Coll., 1971; BA, LaVerne U., 1972; MA, Columbia Pacific U., 1986, postgrad., 1986—. Prodn. dispatcher Naval Missile Ctr., Pt. Mugu, Calif., 1969-71, adminstrv. asst., 1971-74, mgmt. analyst, 1974-75; adminstrv. officer Shasta Lake Ranger Dist., Redding, Calif., 1975-77; program mgr. Shasta-Trinity Nat. Forest, Redding, 1977-79; adminstrv. officer Tongass Nat. Forest, Ketchikan, Alaska, 1979-89; retired 1989; Bd. dirs. Royal Assocs., Ketchikan; pres. Opportunity Cons., Anderson, Calif., 1976-79. Author: (pamphlet) Handbook for Redi-Reminder Service, 1970, The Complete, Realistic Self-Hypnosis Program, 1982, The Royal Trust, 1984, (audio cassette) The Outside Assistance Program, 1982; (software) The Classified Connection, 1989. Served with U.S. Army, 1961-64, Korea. Home: PO Box 7158 Ketchikan AK 99901 Office: USDA Forest Svc Fed Bldg Ketchikan AK 99901

JOHNSON, RUTH ANNA, data processing company executive, consultant; b. Coeur D'Alene, Idaho, Jan. 21, 1950; d. Lowell Verne and Maurine Grace (Wert) Wallace; m. Thomas Bradley Johnson, May 21, 1970 (div. Dec. 1981); 1 child, Bradley Paul. Student, Antioch U. Exec. sec. Boeing Co., Seattle, 1970-71; exec. sec. Air Route Traffic Control Ctr., Auburn, Wash., 1972-73, dir. student svcs., 1982-83; bus. mgr. Collins Group, Seattle, 1983-84, v.p., 1985, also bd. dirs.; cons., ct.-apptd. spl. adv. Nat. CASA Assn., Seattle, 1986-88, Camp Fire, Inc., Kansas City, Mo., 1987—. Author: Running from a Secret, 1986; co-author: The Novice Notebook, 1988. Mem. community adv. bd. Valley Med. Ctr., Renton, Wash., 1984-86; spl. adv. King County Superior Ct., Seattle, 1984-88; chmn. S. King County Children's Sexual Assault Ctr. Task Force; chmn. program com. Computer and Ministry Conf., 1988; ex-officio Computer and Ministry Network, N.Y.C., 1988. Mem. Data Processing Mgrs. Assn., Wash. Software Assn. R:GANG (bd. dirs. 1987-88). Office: Collins Group 101 Stewart St Ste 840 Seattle WA 98101

JOHNSON, SHEILA DEANNA, small business owner; b. San Francisco, Jan. 17, 1938; d. Earl Lewis and Juanita Amy (Hearsum) J. AA, Ventura Coll., 1963; postgrad., Modesto Jr. Coll., 1965; BA, U. Calif.-Stanislaus, MA, 1976. Tchr. Oakdale (Calif.) elem. schs., 1965-75, compensatory edn. projects coordinator, 1975-76, prin., 1976-78; dir. Christian edn. St. James' Episcopal Ch., Sonora, Calif., 1978; dir. elem. and day care grog. St. Michael's Episcopal Schs., Sonora, 1978-82; adminstrv. asst. St. James Episcopal Ch., 1982-83; owner Sheila's Gifts, Sonora, 1987--. Author various ECE-Title I prog. booklets. Mem. various coms. Episcopal Ch. Mem. AAUW, Calif. Parent Tchrs. Assn., Delta Kappa Gamma, Phi Delta Kappa. Republican.

JOHNSON, SHERREL EDMUND, broadcasting company executive; b. Los Angeles, Nov. 9, 1945; s. Joseph Edmund and Miney Oleta (Stanley) J.; m. Dorothy B. Lopez, Nov. 12, 1966 (div. Apr. 1983); 1 child, Carl Edmund; m. Terry Ann Kimber, July 27, 1983 (div. Apr. 1987). Grad. high sch., Oakland, Calif. Staff technician overseas radio div. Am. Telephone and Telegraph, Oakland, 1963-68; staff engr. Sta. KGO-TV, San Francisco, 1968, mgr. R.F. facilities, 1984-86, dir. engring., 1986—; staff engr. Sta. KBHK-TV, San Francisco, 1968-69, various ABC TV and radio stas., San Francisco, 1969-77; chief engr. Sta. KSFX-FM, San Francisco, 1977-81, Sta. KGO-AM, San Francisco, 1981-82; chmn. bd. dirs., chief exec. officer Madzar Corp., Fremont, Calif., 1982-84; chmn. bd. dirs., chief exec. officer No. Calif. Frequency Coordinating Com. Inc., San Francisco, 1985—; asst. treas. Sutro Tower, Inc., San Francisco, 1986—. Served as sgt. USMCR, 1966-71. Mem. Soc. Motion Picture and TV Engrs., Soc. Broadcast Engrs., IEEE, Soc. Bay Area Broadcast Engrs. Republican. Lutheran. Office: Sta KGO-TV 900 Front St San Francisco CA 94111

JOHNSON, STEWART WILLARD, civil engineer; b. Mitchell, S.D., Aug. 17, 1933; s. James Elmer Johnson and Grace Mahala (Erwin) Johnson Parsons; m. Mary Anis Giddings, June 24, 1956; children: Janelle Chiemi, Gregory Stewart, Eric Willard. BSCE, S.D. State U., 1956; BA in Bus. Adminstrn. and Polit. Sci., U. Md., 1960; MSCE, PhD, U. Ill., 1964. Registered profl. engr., Ohio. Commd. 2d lt. USAF, 1956, advanced through grades to lt. col.; prof. mechs. and civil engring. Air Force Inst. Tech. USAF, Dayton, Ohio, 1964-75; dir. civil engring. USAF, Seoul, Republic of Korea, 1976-77; chief civil engring. research div. USAF, Kirtland AFB, N.Mex., 1977-80; ret. USAF, 1980; prin. engr. BDM Corp., Albuquerque, 1980—; cons. in space sci. and lunar basing to NASA, U. N.Mex., Los Alamos (N.Mex.) Nat. Labs., 1986—; adj. prof. civil engring. U. N.Mex., 1987—; prin. investigator devel. concepts for lunar astronomical observatories U. N.Mex., NASA, 1987—; tech. chmn. Space 88 Internat. Conf., 1988. Editor Engineering, Construction, and Operations in Space; contbr. articles to profl. jours. Pres. ch. council Ch. of Good Shepherd United Ch. Christ, Albuquerque, 1983-85. Fellow Nat. Acad. Scis. NRC, 1970-71. Mem. AIAA, AAAS, ASCE (chmn. exec. com. aerospace div. 1979, tech. activities com. 1984, nat. space policy com., 1988—, Aerospace and Tech. award 1985, Outstnding News Corr. award 1981), Am. Geophys. Union, Sigma Xi, Pi Sigma Alpha. Republican. Mem. United Ch. of Christ. Office: BDM Corp 1801 Randolph Rd SE Albuquerque NM 87106

JOHNSON, SUSANNE PEARL, nurse; b. Spokane, Wash., Aug. 6, 1946; d. Roy Sidney and Emily Pearl (Parkhurst) Kincaid; m. Robert Gerald Downer Johnson, Sept. 10, 1966; children: Jeri Lynn, Bobbi Ann. LPN, Big Bend Community Coll., 1977; RN, Spokane Community Coll., 1985. RN, Washington. Nurse Columbia Basin Hosp., Ephrata, Wash., 1977-82, Ephrata Med. Ctr., 1979-82, Stevens Meml. Hosp., Edmonds, Wash., 1982-83, Spokane Minor Emergency Ctrs., 1983, Manor Care, Spokane, 1983-85, Holy Family Hosp., Spokane, 1983-87, Sacred Heart Hosp., Spokane, 1987—. Author: Family Geneology, 1988. Mem. Wash. State Nurses Assn., YWCA. Methodist.

JOHNSON, SYLVIA SUE, university administrator, educator; b. Abiline, Tex., Aug. 10, 1940; d. SE Boyd and Margaret MacGilliuray (Withington) Smith; m. William Ruel Johnson; children: Margaret Ruth, Laura Jane, Catherine Withington. BA, U. Calif., Riverside, 1962; postgrad., U. Hawaii, 1963. Elem. edn. credential, 1962. mem. bd. regents U. Calif.-Riverside. Mem. steering com. Citizens University Com., chmn. 1978-79; bd. dirs., charter mem. U. Calif.-Riverside Found., chmn. nominating com., 1983—; charter mem. Affiliates of U. Calif.-Riverside, Friends of UCR Bot. Gardens; pres., bd. dirs. Friends of the Mission Inn, 1969-72, 73-76, Mission Inn Found., 1977—, Calif. Bapt. Coll. Citizens Com., 1980—; v.p. Riverside Community Hosp. Aux., Riversity Community Hosp. Founders Club; bd. dirs. Riverside Community Hosp., 1980—, Riverside Jr. league, 1976-77, Nat. Charity League, 1984-85, Riverside Art Alliance, 1968-69; mem. Riverside Com. to Rev. Sign Ordinance Moratorium, Com. to Rev. Mgmt. Structure of Mission Inn, Salvation Army Alternatives for Transient Housing, Riverside Art Ctr. Capitol Campaign Com.; co-chmn. Riverside Com. for Sign Control; mem. chancellors blue ribbon com., devel. com. Calif. Mus. Photography. Mem. U. Calif.-Riverside Alumni Assn. (bd. dirs. 1966-68, v.p. 1968-70).

JOHNSON, TOM See JOHNSON, WYATT THOMAS, JR.

JOHNSON, VERNON EUGENE, corporate lawyer; b. Omaha, Feb. 11, 1930; s. Eugene Howard and Thelma Kathleen (Carter) J.; m. Martha Alvo, Dec. 18, 1953; children: Pamela Robin Johnson Ackrich, Denise Gaye. Student, U. Nebr., Omaha, 1948-50; JD, Pepperdine U., 1969. Bar: Calif. 1970. Lather foreman W.F. Hayward Co., Inglewood, Calif., 1956-66; claims rep. United Pacific Ins. Co., Pasadena, Calif., 1966-70; atty. United Pacific Ins. Co., Los Angeles, 1970-73; atty., dept. mgr. Western Employers Ins., Fullerton, Calif., 1973—; arbitrator, judge pro tem Orange Co. Superior Ct., Santa Ana, 1981—; arbitrator Am. Arbitration Assn., Los Angeles, 1975—. Chmn. Ways and Means com. Western High Sch. Drill Team, Anaheim, Calif., 1973; served to cpl. U.S. Army, 1951-53. Mem. Orange County Bar Assn., Calif. Bar Assn., (conf. del. 1982, 83, 86), So. Calif. Rehab. Exchange. Republican. Protestant. Home: 4480 Guava Ave Seal Beach CA 90740 Office: Vernon E Johnson & Assoc 1400 N Harbor Blvd Fullerton CA 92635

JOHNSON, VIRGIL JAMES, chemist; b. Idaho Falls, Idaho, Apr. 7, 1948; s. James Eugene and Eva Faye (Izatt) J.; m. Kathern Crow, June 11, 1971;

children: Trevor, Kylee, Lindzie, Devvin. Student, Ricks Coll., 1966-67; BS, Brigham Young U., 1972, 75; MS, U. Idaho, 1985. Chem. analyst Allied Chem. Exxon Nuclear Corp., Idaho Falls, 1976-82; lab supr. Exxon-Westinghouse Idaho Nuclear Co., Idaho Falls, 1982—. Varsity coach Teton Peaks Coun. Boy Scouts Am., 1986—. Served to ensign USN, 1971-73. Mormon. Office: Analytical Chemistry PO Box 4000 MS-5113 Idaho Falls ID 83403-5113

JOHNSON, VIRGINIA MACPHERSON, educator; b. Washington, Feb. 23, 1923; d. Alfred Bradford and Margaret Edna (Breed) Macpherson; m. Robert Allen Johnson, Sept. 11, 1948; children: Ann Elizabeth, Constance Ellen. BS, Oreg. State, 1945. Tchr. secondary schs. Parkrose High Sch., Portland, Oreg., 1945-47, Redwood High Sch., San Mateo, Calif., 1947-48. Vol. food svcs., Kerr Children's Ctr., Portland, 1987-89; chmn., bd. dirs. Camp Fire Inc., Portland, 1967-70, Camp Fire (nat.), Kansas City, Mo., 1969-75; pres Highland Games (Scottish), Portland, 1978-79; sec. St. Andrews Soc. Oreg., 1980-88, chmn. coll. scholarship selection com., 1986-89. Mem. Alpha Chi Omega Alumnae (pres. 1971-72). Republican. Presbyterian. Club: Multnomah Athletic (Portland). Lodge: PEO. Home and Office: 8855 SW Birchwood Rd Portland OR 97225

JOHNSON, WALTER EARL, geophysicist; b. Denver, Dec. 16, 1942; s. Earl S. and Helen F. (Llewellyn) J.; Geophys. Engr., Colo. Sch. Mines, 1966; m. Ramey Kandice Kayes, Aug. 6, 1967; children—Gretchen, Roger, Aniela. Geophysicist, Pan. Am. Petroleum Corp., 1966-73; seismic processing supr. Amoco Prodn. Co., Denver, 1973-74, marine tech. supr., 1974-76, div. processing cons., 1976-79, geophys. supr. No. Thrust Belt, 1979-80; chief geophysicist Husky Oil Co., 1981-82, exploration mgr. Rocky Mountain and Gulf Coast div., 1982-84; geophys. mgr. ANR Prodn. Co., 1985—; pres. Sch. Lateral Ditch Co.; cons. engr. Bd. dirs. Rocky Mountain Residence, nursing home. Registered profl. engr., cert. geologist, Colo. Mem. Denver Geophys. Soc., Soc. Exploration Geophysicists. Republican. Baptist. Office: 600 17th St Ste 800 Denver CO 80202

JOHNSON, WAYNE HAROLD, librarian, state official; b. El Paso, Tex., May 2, 1942; s. Earl Harold and Cathryn Louise (Greeno) J.; m. Patricia Ann Froedge, June 15, 1973; children: Meredith Jessica (dec.), Alexandra Noëlle Victoria. B.S., Utah State U., 1968; M.P.A., U. Colo., 1970; M.L.S., U. Okla., 1972. Circulation librarian Utah State U., Logan, 1968, adminstrv. asst. librarian, 1969; research Okla. Mgmt. and Engring. Cons., Norman, 1972; chief adminstrv. services Wyo. State Library, Cheyenne, 1973-76, chief bus. officer library archives and hist. dept., 1976-78, state librarian, 1978—. Trustee Bibliog. Center for Research, Denver, pres., 1983, 84; Cheyenne dist. Longs Peak council Boy Scouts Am., 1982—; v.p. Cheyenne/Laramie County Airport Bd., 1980, pres., 1981-85, 87. Served with USCG, 1960-64. Mem. ALA, Wyo. Library Assn., Aircraft Owners and Pilots Assn., Cheyenne C. of C. (chmn. transp. com. 1982, 83). Republican. Presbyterian. Club: No. Colo. Yacht. Lodges: Masons, Kiwanis (bd. dirs. 1986, 87, Cheyenne Frontier Days 1975—). Office: Wyo State Libr Cheyenne WY 82002

JOHNSON, WAYNE LAVERNE, real estate broker; b. Inglewood, Calif., Sept. 17, 1928; s. Loren W. and Naomi (Moyer) J.; m. Carolyn Joyce, July 29, 1963; children: Jeffrey, Deborah, Shelley, Gregory. BA, Northwest Nazarene Coll., 1949. Ptnr. Olsen-Johnson, Eugene, Oreg., 1954-65; developer Foremost Systems, Inc., Eugene, 1965-75; v.p. Freedom TV, Inc., Eugene, 1987—, Phoenix One, Inc., Eugene, 1988—; sec., treas. Fone Am., Inc., Eugene, 1988—; owner, broker N.W. Systems, Eugene, 1975—. Capt. U.S. Army, 1952-54. Republican. Office: NW Systems 1700 Valley River Dr 4th Fl Eugene OR 97401

JOHNSON, WILLARD PARKER, physician, administrator; b. Mexia, Tex., June 26, 1927; s. John Edward and Mary Anna (Blasdel) J.; m. Elaine M. Carlock, July 31, 1949 (div. 1973); children—Stephen M., Kristin A., Katherine L., Matthew L.; m. 2d, Judy M. Ismach, Mar. 15, 1975. B.A., U. Calif.-Berkeley, 1948; M.D., U. Tex.-Galveston, 1953. Diplomate Am. Bd. Internal Medicine. Resident in internal medicine USPHS Hosp., S.I., N.Y., 1956-59; research fellow in cardiology U. Wash. Med. Ctr., Seattle, 1959-61; chief of research USPHS Hosp., Seattle, 1961-68, hosp. dir., 1968-71; regional program dir. Nat. Health Service Corps, Seattle, 1971-72; from instr. to assoc. prof. medicine U. Wash., 1961-73, also assoc. dean; med. dir. Seafarers Med. Ctr., San Francisco, 1973—. Med. cons. Cardio mag., 1983; contbr. articles to profl. jours. Served with USPHS, 1953-72. NIH grantee, 1961, 62, 63, 64-68. Fellow ACP; mem. USPHS Clin. Soc. (pres. 1967-68), Am. Fedn. Clin. Research, Am. Heart Assn., Physicians for Social Responsibility. Democrat. Home: 566 Kansas St San Francisco CA 94107 Office: Seafarers Med Ctr 40 Lansing St San Francisco CA 94105

JOHNSON, WILLIAM HUGH, JR., hospital administrator; b. N.Y.C., Oct. 29, 1935; s. William H. and Florence P. (Seinsoth) J.; m. Gloria C. Stube., Jan. 23, 1960; children: Karen A., William H. III. B.A., Hofstra U., 1957; M.Ed., U. Hawaii, 1969. Commd. 2d lt. U.S. Army, 1957, advanced through grades to lt. col., 1972, health adminstr., world wide, 1957-77, health adminstr., world wide, ret., 1977; chief exec. officer U. N. Mex. Hosp., Albuquerque, 1977—; asst. prof. U.S. Mil. Acad., West Point, N.Y., 1962-65; mem. clin. faculty U. Minn., Mpls., 1980-83; preceptor Ariz. State U., Tempe, 1982-83; pres. Albuquerque Area Hosp. Council, 1980. Vice pres. Vis Nurse Service, Albuquerque, 1979; mem. exec. bd., Albuquerque Com. on Devel. Decorated Army Commendation Medal with 2 oak leaf clusters, RVN, Legion of Merit. Mem. Am. Hosp. Assn. (governing bd. met. hosp. sect. 1982-86, chmn. com. AIDS, mem. regional policy bd. 1982-86, 88—), Am. Coll. Hosp. Adminstrs., Council Tchg. Hosps., N. Mex. Hosp. Assn. (bd. dirs. 1983, chmn.), Nat. Assn. Pub. Hosps., Coun. of Teaching Hosps. (bd. dirs.), Greater Albuquerque C. of C. (econ. planning council), N.Mex. Assn. Commerce and Industry, Albuquerque Conv. and Visitors Bur. (bd. dirs.). Roman Catholic. Home: 7920 Sartan Way NE Albuquerque NM 87109 Office: U NMex Hosp Office of Chief Exec Officer 2211 Lomas Blvd NE Albuquerque NM 87106

JOHNSON, WILLIAM POTTER, newspaper publisher; b. Peoria, Ill., May 4, 1935; s. William Zweigle and Helen Marr (Potter) J.; m. Pauline Ruth Rowe, May 18, 1968; children: Darragh Elizabeth, William Potter. AB, U. Mich., 1957. Gen. mgr. Bureau County Rep., Inc., Princeton, Ill., 1961-72; pres. Johnson Newspapers, Inc., Sebastopol, Calif., 1972-75, Evergreen, Colo., 1974-86, Canyon Commons Investment, Evergreen, 1974—; pres., chmn. bd. dirs. Johnson Media, Inc., Winter Park, Colo., 1987—. Author: How the Michigan Betas Built a $1,000,000 Chapter House in the '80s. Alt. del. Rep. Nat. Conv., 1968. Lt. USNR, 1958-61. Mem. Colo. Press Assn., Nat. Newspaper Assn., Suburban Newspapers Am., San Francisco Press Club, Hiwan Country Club, Oro Valley Country Club, Cañada Hills Country Club, Beta Theta Pi. Roman Catholic. Home: 445 W Rapa Pl Tucson AZ 85737 Office: PO Box 409 Winter Park CO 80482

JOHNSON, WILLIAM ROBERT, JR., management executive; b. Buffalo, Sept. 24, 1939; s. William Robert and Maxine Alberta (Patterson) J.; m. Lynn Charlene Johnson. BS in Material Sci. with honors, San Jose State Coll., Calif., 1964; MS in Material Sci., Stanford U., Palo Alto, Calif., 1967, PhD, 1969. Prodn. metallurgist Mare Island Naval Shipyard, Vallejo, Calif., 1964; lab. scientist St. Clair Field, Inc., Cupertino, Calif., 1969-70; assoc. scientist Gen. Atomics Inc., San Diego, 1970-71, staff assoc., 1971-72, sr. scientist, 1972-73, staff scientist, 1973-83; mgr., materials evaluation Gen. Atomics, Inc., San Diego, 1983—. Co-Editor, author: Chap. Book, Magnetism & Magnetic Materials Digest, 1965. Recipient Student award Am. Soc. for Testing & Materials, 1964. Mem. Am. Soc. Metals, Tau Beta Pi, Scripps Ranch Old Pros, Men's Athletic Club. Democrat. Home: 12243 Riesling Ct San Diego CA 92131 Office: Gen Atomics PO Box 85608 San Diego CA 92138

JOHNSON, WILLIAM STEWART, cultural arts administrator; b. Spring Lake, Mich., Jan. 3, 1933; s. Howard Kenneth Johnson and Dorothy Irene (Cooper) Van Den Heuvel; m. Luanna Hughes, Sept. 1, 1964. Student, Howe (Ind.) Mil. Sch., 1948-51; BA, Mich. State U., 1955. Dir. govt. rels. IBM Corp., Washington, 1978-88; chmn. Inst. Am.-Indian Arts, Santa Fe, 1988—. Bd. dirs. YMCA, Washington, 1980-82, Mary Baldwin Coll., Staunton, Va., 1980-86. 1st lt. U. S. Army, 1956-64. Mem. Am. Soc. Personnel Adminstrs. Home: 1852 S Sun Mountain Dr Santa Fe NM 87505 Office: Inst Am Indian Arts Cathedral Place Box 1836 Santa Fe NM 87504

JOHNSON, WYATT THOMAS, JR. (TOM JOHNSON), newspaper publisher; b. Macon, Ga., Sept. 30, 1941; s. Wyatt Thomas and Josephine Victoria (Brown) J.; m. Edwina Mac Chastain, Dec. 29, 1963; children: Wyatt Thomas III, Christa Farie. A.B. in Journalism, U. Ga., 1963; M.B.A., Harvard, 1965. Reporter, mgmt. trainee Macon Telegraph and News, 1957-65; White House fellow 1965-66; asst. press sec. to Pres. U.S., 1966, dep. press sec., 1967; spl. asst. to Pres., 1968, exec. asst., 1969-70; exec. v.p., dir. Tex. Broadcasting Corp., Sta. KTBC-AM-FM-TV, Austin, 1970-73; exec. editor, v.p., dir. Dallas Times Herald, 1973-75, publisher, 1975-77; pres. Los Angeles Times, 1977-80, publisher, 1980—, also chief exec. officer; Mem. Pres.'s Commn. on White House Fellows, 1979, Neiman Fellows Selection Com., Harvard U., 1977; Pres. adv. bd. Henry W. Grady Sch. Journalism, 1974-75. Co-author: Automating Newspaper Composition, 1965. Bd. dirs. Rockefeller Found., Trilateral Commn.; chmn. bd. Lyndon B. Johnson Found., John S. Knight/Stanford Profl. Journalism Fellows. Named Nat. Man of Year Sigma Nu, 1962, Outstanding Young Man of Ga. Jr. C. of C., 1967, One of Five Outstanding Young Texans Tex. Jaycees, 1969, One of 10 Outstanding Men of U.S., 1975. Mem. Am. Newspaper Pubs. Assn., Newspaper Advt. Bur. (dir.), Ga. Alumni Soc. (pres. 1979), Council on Fgn. Relations N.Y., Sphinx Soc., Young Pres.'s Orgn., Gridiron Soc. (Ga.), Sigma Delta Chi, Sigma Nu. Office: Los Angeles Times Times Mirror Sq Los Angeles CA 90053

JOHNSTON, BARBARA ANNE, veterinarian; b. Detroit, Dec. 26, 1958; d. Robert Garner and Dolores (Shyne) J. BS, U. Wash., 1981; DVM, Wash. State U., 1985. Head animal health resources Fred Hutchinson Cancer Research Ctr., Seattle, 1987—; cons. veterinarian Hope Heart Inst., Seattle, 1987—, chairwoman animal care com., 1988—. Nat. Merit scholar, 1976-81; NIH fellow, 1985-87. Mem. Am. Vet. Med. Assn., Wash. State Vet. Med. Assn., Am. Assn. Lab. Animal Sci., Wash. State Assn. Biomed. Research (bd. dirs. 1988—), Alpha Psi. Office: Fred Hutchinson Cancer Rsch Ctr 1124 Columbia Seattle WA 98104

JOHNSTON, BRUCE FREDRICK, real estate manager; b. Chapel Hill, N.C., May 22, 1957; s. Charles Louis and Marjorie Sarah (Hohenstein) J.; m. Carol Joanne Burns, Aug. 13, 1988. BA, U. N.C., 1979. Pvt. practice sales rep. Richmond, Va., 1979-82, Ziff-Davis Pub., Miami, Fla., 1982-84; leasing mgr. The MaceRich Co., Walnut Creek, Calif., 1985—. Mem. Internat. Coun. of Shopping Ctrs. Home: 550 Canyonwoods Circle #202 San Ramon CA 94583 Office: The MaceRich Co 1275 Broadway Pla Walnut Creek CA 94596

JOHNSTON, GAIL, health and fitness company executive; b. Boston, Aug. 23, 1951; d. William Leslie and Margaret (MacFarlane) J. BA, U. N.H., 1972. Owner, mgr. Diablo Prodns., Walnut Creek, Calif., 1982—, Symmetry Systems, Walnut Creek, 1984—, Curves Unltd., Phoenix, 1987—, Sports Resource Group, San Diego, 1987—; fitness cons. for eating disorders Eden Hosp., Castro Valley, Calif., 1985-88; tech. cons. Nat. Media Group, L.A., 1988; cons., tech. advisor Fit Video, Denver, 1988. Writer, producer fitness video. Mem. Aerobics and Fitness Assn. Am. (bd. mem. overweight fitness edn. 1983—, nat. lectr. 1983—, bd. cert. and tng. 1984—), Internat. Dance Exercise Assn., Am. Coll. Sprots Medicine (cert.).

JOHNSTON, GWINAVERE ADAMS, public relations consultant; b. Casper, Wyo., Jan. 6, 1943; d. Donald Milton Adams and Gwinavere Marie (Newell) Quillen; m. H.R. Johnston, Sept. 26, 1963 (div. 1973); children: Gwinavere G., Gabrielle Suzanne; m. Donald Charles Cannalte, Apr. 4, 1981. BS in Journalism, U. Wyo., 1966; postgrad., Denver U., 1968-69. Editor, reporter Laramie (Wyo.) Daily Boomerang, 1965-66; account exec. William Kostka Assocs., Denver, 1966-71, v.p., 1971-73; exec. v.p. Slottow, McKinlay & Johnston, Denver, 1973-74; pres. The Johnston Group, Denver, 1974—; bd. dirs. Designers Marketplace, Denver; mem. adj. faculty U. Colo. Sch. Journalism, 1988—. Bd. dirs. Leadership Denver Assn., 1975-77, 83-86, Mile High United Way, 1989—. Mem. Pub. Relations Soc. Am. (pres. Colo. chpt. 1978-79, bd. dirs. 1975-80, 83-86, nat. exec. com., counselor's acad. 1988—, profl. award), Colo. Women's Forum. Republican. Clubs: Denver Athletic, Denver Press, Com. of 200. Home: 717 Monaco Pkwy Denver CO 80220 Office: The Johnston Group 1512 Larimer St #720 Denver CO 80202

JOHNSTON, HUGH BAKER, internist; b. Bakersfield, Calif., June 30, 1933; s. Carl Winifred and Sarah (Long) J.; m. Janet Owens, June 17, 1957; children: Anne, William, Polly. AB, Stanford U., 1955, MD, 1958. Diplomate Am. Bd. Internal Medicine. Intern U. Oreg. Health Sci. Ctr., residency in hematology; resident Portland V.A. Hosp.; pvt. practice Eugene, Oreg., 1964—; pres. Oreg. Med. Found., Portland, 1974; mem. Oreg. Bd. Med. Examiners, 1985—. Mem. Eugene Budget Commn., 197l. Capt. M.C., USAF, 1959-6l. Fellow ACP (svc. award Oreg. chpt. 1987); mem. AMA, Oreg. Med. Assn. (pres. 1983), Lane County Med. Soc. (pres. 1976), North Pacific Soc. Internal Medicine, Oreg. Soc. Internal Medicine (pres. 1976). Republican. Episcopalian. Office: 633 E llth St Eugene OR 97401

JOHNSTON, KAREN QUEALLY, rehabilitation director; b. Yonkers, N.Y., Mar. 3, 1952; d. Terence Dennis and Ann S. Queally. BS in Phys. Therapy, NYU, 1974; MS Health Care Adminstrn., Iona Coll., 1983. Phys. therapist Burks Rehab. Ctr., White Plains, N.Y., 1974-79; phys. therapy dir. St. Patrick's Home, Bronx, N.Y., 1979-80; rehab. dir. Cabrini Nursing Home, Dobbs Ferry, N.Y., 1980-84; asst. adminstr. Met. Jewish Geriatric Ctr., Bklyn., 1984-85; rehab. dir. E. Bay Hillhaven, Alameda, Calif., 1985-86; regional rehab. dir. No. Calif. Hillhaven, Richmond, Calif., 1986-88; East Bay Area dir. No. Calif. Hillhaven, Richmond, 1988—; cons. in field; instr. at various univs. Recipient Robert B. Power Award for Excellence in Health Care Systems Mgmt., 1984. Mem. Am. Phys. Therapy Assn. (treas. 1988—). Home: 519 Santa Teresa Millbrae CA 94030 Office: Hillhaven 3030 Webster St Oakland CA 94609

JOHNSTON, KAY KILBURN, piano teacher; b. Ft. Collins, Colo., Sept. 12, 1943; d. Estes James and Winifred (Christie) Kilburn; m. Daniel Clement Johnston, Aug. 3, 1974; 1 child, Daniel Estes. BS, Colo. State U., 1966; MA, Wash. State U., 1984. Sec. Southwestern Pipe of Colo., Fort Collins, 1966-67, Colo. State U., Fort Collins, 1967-72; bus. edn. tchr. Dolores City High Sch., Dove Creek, Colo., 1973-74, Forsyth Community Coll., Winston-Salem, N.C., 1975-76; bus. edn. instr. Columbia Basin Coll., Pasco, Wash., 1986-87; pvt. practice piano tchr. Richland, Wash., 1978—; car instr. Richland Community Sch., 1989—. Mem. Free Meth. Ch. Home: 1471 Amon Ct Richland WA 99352

JOHNSTON, LAURENCE, medical entomologist, county government official; b. Huron, S.D., Nov. 29, 1931; s. Robert E. and Erma D. (Florence) J.; m. Gladys Elaine Mikkelson, July 31, 1955. BS, S.D. State U., 1954; MS, U. Md., 1961; PhD, Okla. State U., 1970. Commd. 2d lt. U.S. Army, 1955, advanced through grades to lt. comdr., 1969; entomologist U.S. Army, Republic of Korea, Socialist Republic of Vietnam, 1955-61; mgr. environ. health U.S. Army, Socialist Republic of Vietnam, Republic of Panama, 1961-78; ret. U.S. Army, 1978; dir. environ. health Larimer County Health Dept., Ft. Collins, Colo., 1978—. Contbr. articles to profl. publs. Active Boy Scouts Am., Calif., Okla, C.Z. and Colo., 1966-87. Decorated Bronze Star, Legion of Merit. Mem. Colo. Environ. Health Assn. (pres. 1983-84), Centennial Health Edn. Ctr. (pres. 1981-83), Nat. Environ. Health Assn., Entomol. Soc. Am., Am. Mosquito Control Assn., Sigma Xi, Phi Kappa Phi. Office: Larimer County Health Dept 363 Jefferson St Fort Collins CO 80524

JOHNSTON, MALCOLM ANDREW, educator; b. Winchester, Mass., Feb. 19, 1945; s. Malcolm George and Carolyn (Lumsden) J.; m. Christine Louise Ronay, Sept. 5, 1970; children: Alexander George, Emily Ronay. BA cum laude, Yale U., 1962; MA, Tufts U., 1973. Instr. history Choate Sch., Wallingford, Conn., 1968-71; instr. English Abbot Acad., Andover, Mass., 1971-73; chmn. dept. history Pingree Sch., Hamilton, Mass., 1973-86; dean faculty Pingree Sch., 1983-86, coll. counselor, 1984-86; instr. history St. Paul's Sch., Concord, N.H., 1970, 71, 80, Milton Acad., Milton, Mass., 1981, 82; headmaster Calasanetius Sch., Buffalo, 1986-88; dir upper sch. and acad. dean Town Sch. for Boys, San Francisco, 1988—. Organist First Ch., Wenham, Mass., deacon, 1977-86; organist Christ Presbyn. Ch., San Rafael, Calif., 1988—. Mem. Nat. Assn. Ind. Sch., Am. Guild Organists, Nat. Assn. Coll. Admissions Counselors, Nat. Mid. Sch. Assn. Presbyterian. Home: 365 Nova Albion Way San Rafael CA 94903 Office: Town School for Boys 2750 Jackson St San Francisco CA 94115

JOHNSTON, MARJORIE DIANE, computer programming executive, analyst; b. Fullerton, Calif., Sept. 19, 1943; d. Earl Lawrence and Ruth Junita (Long) Whipple; children: Stephen, Deborah. Grad computer programming LaSalle U., Chgo., 1973. Computer programmer Los Alamos (N.Mex.) Nat. Lab., 1972-81, sr. analyst, programmer, cons., 1989—; contract programmer Computer Assistance, Inc., Tulsa, 1981-82; profl. svcs. analyst Control Data Corp., Denver, 1982-84, Los Alamos, 1984-89. Mem. Rebekah, Order Eastern Star (past matron). Home: 950 Santa Clara Pl Los Alamos NM 87544

JOHNSTON, MAXENE, health facility administrator; b. Bethlehem, Pa., Aug. 26, 1943; d. Samuel and Betty (Kaplan) Pisaren; m. William Johnston, May 7, 1970; 1 child, Samara. BS, U. San Francisco, 1970; MA, Calif. State U.-L.A., 1977. Coordinator clin. svcs. L.A. County Med. Ctr.-U. So. Calif., 1970-74; mgr. ambulatory care Rancho Los Amigos Hosp., Downey, Calif., 1974-77; dir. profl. devel. dept. health svcs. L.A. County, 1977-78; asst. dir. hosp. ops. Children's Hosp., L.A., 1978-83; mgr. health svcs. L.A. Olympic Organizing Com., 1983-84; pres. Weingart Ctr. Assn., L.A., 1984—; instr. anthropology, health care, UCLA, 1978; lectr. Chgo. Rehab. Inst., 1979, 81; adj. asst. prof. Calif. State U., L.A., 1982; bd. dirs. Inner City Law Ctr., L.A., Pediatrics Projects, Inc., L.A. Contbr. articles to profl. pubs. Cons. March of Dimes, L.A., 1979; adv. bd. sta. KCET-TV Pub. Broadcasting, L.A.,1986—; appointed to Hollywood Redevel. Com., 1987—; mem. Town Hall L.A., 1986—, Mayor's L.A. 2000 Com., 1986—. W.K. Kellogg Found. fellow, 1986. Mem. So. Calif. Bus. Men's Assn., L. A. Area C. of C. Office: Weingart Ctr Assn 566 S San Pedro St Los Angeles CA 90013

JOHNSTON, RALPH THOMAS, museum director; b. Washington, Aug. 25, 1954; s. Ralph T. and Norma (Follin) J. Student, U. Md., 1975-79; M in Pub. and Pvt. Mgmt., Yale U., 1986. Mgr. theatre and planetarium ops. Nat. Air and Space Mus., Smithsonian Instn., Washington, 1975-84; dir. exhibits Mus. Flight, Seattle, 1886-87, dep. dir., 1987—; assessor Mus. Assessment Program Am. Assn. Mus., Washington, 1986-88. Home: 318 10th Ave E #C6 Seattle WA 98102 Office: Museum Flight 9400 E Marginal Way S Seattle WA 98108

JOHNSTON, VIRGINIA EVELYN, editor; b. Spokane, Wash., Apr. 26, 1933; d. Edwin and Emma Lucile (Munroe) Rowe; student Portland Community Coll., 1964, Portland State U., 1966, 78-79; m. Alan Paul Beckley, Dec. 26, 1974; children—Chris, Denise, Rex. Proofreader, The Oregonian, Portland, 1960-62, teletypesetter operator, 1962-66, operator Photon 200, 1966-68, copy editor, asst. women's editor, 1968-80, spl. sects. editor (UPDATE), 1981-83; editor FOODday, 1982—; pres. Matrix Assos., Inc., Portland, 1975—, chmn. bd., 1979—; cons. Democratic party Oreg., 1969, Portland Sch. Dist. No. 1, 1978. Mem. Women in Communications, Inc., Inst. Profl. and Managerial Women, Nat. Assn. Female Execs., Eating and Drinking Soc. Oreg. (pres.), We. Culinary Inst. (mem. adv. bd.), Portland Culinary Alliance (mem. adv. bd.). Democrat. Editor Principles of Computer Systems for Newspaper Mgmt., 1975-76. Home: 4140 NE 137th Ave Portland OR 97230 Office: 1320 SW Broadway Portland OR 97201

JOHNSTONE, IAIN MURRAY, statistician, consultant; b. Melbourne, Victoria, Australia, Dec. 10, 1956; s. Samuel Thomas Murray and Pamela Beatrice (Kriegel) J. BS with honors, Australian Nat. U., Canberra, 1978, MS, 1979; PhD, Cornell U., 1981. Asst. prof. stats. Stanford (Calif.) U., 1981-85, assoc prof. stats., 1986—; statis. cons. Stanford U. Med. Sch., 1986—. Assoc. editor (jours.) Annals of Stats., 1987—; contbr. articles to profl. jours. Alfred P. Sloan Rsch. fellow, 1988—; named Presdl. Young Investigator NSF, 1985—. Fellow Royal Statis. Soc., Inst. Math. Stats.; mem. Am. Statis. Assn., Am. Math. Soc., AAAS. Office: Stanford U Dept Stats Sequoia Hall Stanford CA 94305-4065

JOHNSTONE, KENNETH ERNEST, engineering executive; b. Los Angeles, Sept. 13, 1929; s. John Ernest and Lorena Hayes (Patterson) J.; m. Edna Mae Iverson, Aug. 20, 1950; children: Bruce, Kent, Anita, Christian, Daniel, Carol, Karen. BSEE, U. Wash., 1966. Registered profl. engr., Wash. Electronics technician The Boeing Co., Seattle, 1955-66, engr., 1966-75; engring. mgr. Boeing Aerosystems Internat., Seattle, 1975-85; ptnr. North Creek Engring., Lynnwood, Wash., 1985-87; pres. SensorLink Corp., Lynnwood, 1987—; internat. lectr. in field. Mem. IEEE (sr.), Tau Beta Pi. Home: 927 Duchess Rd Bothell WA 98012 Office: SensorLink Corp PO Box 6608 Lynnwood WA 98036

JOJOLA, THEODORE SYLVESTER, Native American educator and administrator; b. Isleta Pueblo, N.Mex., Nov. 19, 1951; s. Jose Levi and Juanita Bautista (Papuyo) J.; m. Adelamer Novino Alcantara, Jan. 4, 1980; 1 child, Manoa Alcantara. BArch, U. N.Mex., 1973; M. in City Planning, MIT, 1975; PhD in Polit. Sci., U. Hawaii., Manoa, 1982; cert. internat. human rights law U. Strasbourg, France, 1984. Intern planner Nat. Capital Planning Commn., Washington, 1973; legal/hist. researcher Inst. for Devel. of Indian Law, Washington, 1976; vis. rsch. assoc. Inst. Philippine Culture, Manila, 1977-78; vis. prof. urban planning UCLA, 1984; asst. prof. planning U. N.Mex., Albuquerque, 1982—, dir. Native Am. Studies, 1980—, coordinator Ethnic/Minority Dirs.' Coalition, 1983-85; assoc. faculty mem. U. N.Mex. Nat. Resource Ctr., 1987; Martin Luther-Cesar Chavez-Rosa Parks vis. prof. N. Mich. U., 1988; mem. chmns. adv. bd. Middle Rio Grande Conservancy Dist., 1987—; cons. Thurshun Consultants, Albuquerque, 1980—; postdoctoral fellow Am. Indian Studies, UCLA, 1984. Author: Memoirs of an American Indian House, 1976; contbr. articles to publs. Co-dir. sta. KOB-TV pub. issues prodns., Albuquerque, 1983-85; mem. U.S. organizing com. 9th Inter-Am. Indian Congress, Santa Fe, 1985; mem. adv. bd. N.Mex. Architecture Found., 1988—, United Way Project Blue Print, 1988-89, Zuni Tribal Mus., N.Mex., 1985—, edn. affairs office Apple Computer, Inc., 1986—, Mus. Indian Culture & Arts, Mus. N. Mex., Santa Fe, 1986—; sch. bd. dirs. Isleta (N.Mex.) Isleta Elem. Sch., 1985-86; chmn. JOM/Indian Edn. Parent's Com., Isleta Pueblo, N.Mex., 1985-86; adv. bd. KIMO Cultural Arts Theatre, 1983-85; assoc. Indigenous World: El Mundo Indigena, San Francisco, 1982-84; directorate of studies on indigenous peoples Internat. Inst. Human Rights, Strasbourg, 1984. Rsch. grantee, Lab. for Arch. and Planning, MIT, 1975, Inst. Am. Culture, UCLA, 1984; publ. grantee Atherton Trust, Honolulu, 1976; recipient Participant award, East-West Ctr., Honolulu, 1975-81. Mem. Native Am. Studies Assn. (coordinator Albuquerque 1980), N.Mex. 1st (hon), U. N.Mex. 21 Club. Roman Catholic. Home: Rte 6 Box 578 Albuquerque NM 87105 Office: U NMex Native Am Studies Albuquerque NM 87131

JOLLEY, RONALD SWAPP, religious organization executive; b. Ogden, Utah, Aug. 11, 1936; s. Leonard and Farris (Swapp) J.; m. Joette Fern Rogers, June 13, 1959; children: Jay Ronald, Jeffrey Leonard, Jon Rex, James Bruce. BS, Oreg. State U., 1962; JD, Willamette U., 1965; postgrad., Brigham Young U., 1970. Area coordinator ch. ednl. system Ch. of Jesus Christ of Latter-day Saints, Salem, Oreg., 1965-67; dist. coordinator cen. Oreg. Ch. of Jesus Christ of Latter-day Saints, Salem, 1967-68, area dir. Pacific northwest, 1968—; stake pres Ch. of Jesus Christ of Latter-day Saints, Salem, 1971-80, bd. dirs. social services, 1971—, regional rep., 1980-87; sealer Seattle Temple, 1984—. Exec. bd. Cascade Area council Boy Scouts Am., Salem, 1967-74, 83--; adv. bd., 1974-81, v.p., 1987--. Recipient Silver Beaver award, 1987, Scouter's tng. award, 1970. Mem. Assn. Mormon Counselors and Psychotherapists, Mormon History Assn. Republican. Home: 1696 Aerial Way SE Salem OR 97302 Office: Ch Ednl System 2110 State St Salem OR 97309-0967

JOLLIFF, DAVID EVERETT, chiropractor; b. Modesto, Calif., Aug. 16, 1951; s. Walter Washington and Evelyn Vera (Mogensen) J.; m. Suzanne Phillips, Mar. 16, 1973; children: Amy, Todd, Amanda. AA, Modesto Jr. Coll., 1972; BA, Calif. State U., Hayward, 1974; DChiropractic, Life Chiropractic Coll. West, 1983. Pvt. practice Modesto, 1983—; mem. extension faculty Life Chiropractic Coll. West, 1983—; regional dir. Kale Chiropractic Network, Spartanburg, S.C., 1986—; staff mem.-at-large Kale Chiropractic Hosp., Spartanburg, 1984—. Mem. Modesto Downtown Improvement Assn. Mem. Internat. Chiropractic Assn., Internat. Chiropractic

Assn. Calif., Calif. Chiropractic Assn. (pres. Stanislaus-San Joaquin chpt. 1988-89), Am. Guild Organists, Am. Pub. Health Assn., Modesto C. of C., Modesto Trade Club, Old Fisherman's Club, Rotary. Republican. Home and Office: 1218 13th St Modesto CA 95356

JOLLY, JAMES A., educator; b. Oceanside, Calif., Nov. 2, 1921; s. Peter Benjamine and Amelia (DeMuth) J.; BA, U. Pacific, 1951; MBA, U. Santa Clara, 1963, PhD, 1970; m. Rose Calvina Binkley, Jan. 14, 1945; children: Mayeve O. Jolly Tate, David O., Heidi O. Jolly Wolf. Rsch. physicist Eitel McCullough, San Bruno, Calif., 1951-54, prodn. engr., 1954-59, mgr. prodn. engring. and indsl. engring., 1959-60, mgr. advanced devel., 1960-64; mgr. indsl. microwave activity Varian Assocs., Palo Alto, Calif., 1964-69; assoc. prof. Naval Postgraduate Sch., Monterey, Calif., 1969-76; prof. Sch. Bus., Calif. State U., Sacramento, 1976—. Mem. IEEE (sr. life), Internat. Microwave Power Inst. (past pres.), Acad. Mgmt. Author: (with J.W. Creighton) Technology Transfer Process Model and Annotated Selected Bibliography, 1978. Editor: (with J.W. Creighton) Technology Transfer in Research and Development, 1975; assoc. editor Jour. Microwave Power, 1973-85; editor Jour. Tech. Transfer, 1976-88. Home: 510 Elmhurst Circle Sacramento CA 95825

JOLLY, PURSHOTAM LAL, computer scientist; b. Baroundi, Punjab, India, Mar. 7, 1949; s. Krishnan Dev and Shakuntla (Devi) J.; m. Nirmal Jolly; 1 child, Poonam. BS with honors, Punjab U., 1969, MS in Math., 1972; MS in Computer Sci., Kurukshetra (India) U., 1973; PhD in Ops. Research, Indian Inst. Tech. Kanpur, 1980. Rsch. instr. Indian Inst. Tech. Kanpur, 1977-80; asst. prof. computer sci. and math. SUNY, Binghamton, 1981-82; assoc. prof. computer sci. Calif. Poly. State U., Pomona, 1982-85; mem. research tech. staff Northrop Research and Tech. Ctr., Palos Verdes, Calif., 1985-88; cons. Abacus Programming Corp. & Rockwell Internat., Anaheim, Calif., 1984; cons. Odetics, Inc., Anaheim, Calif., 1988, cons. contracts, 1988—; instr. artificial intelligence UCLA, 1989—. Contbr. articles to profl. jours. Mem. Ops. Research Soc. Am., Assn. Computing Machinery, Am. Assn. Artificial Intelligence, IEEE. Home: 1241 E Tujunga Ave Burbank CA 91501

JOLLY, SIDNEY JOSEPH, electronics technician; b. Logansport, Ind., Aug. 22, 1946; s. Frank and Ruth Elizabeth (McClain) J. BS in Computer Sci., Chapman Coll., Orange, Calif., 1984; BS in Computer Electronics, Coleman Coll., La Mesa, Calif., 1988. With ITT Cable-Hydrospace, National City, Calif., 1973-74; oper. engr. KSDO Radio, San Diego, 1975-82; electronic tech. Cipher Data Products, San Diego, 1978-81, Sci. Atlanta Inc., San Diego, 1981-82, Bendix Energy Controls. Div., San Diego, 1982-83; freelance electronic tech. San Diego, 1983—; treas. AHIKS, 1985—. Precinct capt. Rep. Party, Chula Vista, Calif., 1986. With USN, 1968-73. Mem. Mensa (membership officer 1985-88), AHIKS (treas. 1985—). Home and Office: 1600 Stanton Pl #22 Long Beach CA 90804

JONAS, FRED MORGAN, military officer; b. Gallup, N.Mex., Feb. 18, 1948; s. Frederick Crawford and Betty Gene (Shackelford) J.; m. Janet Larraine Hein, June 4, 1970; children: Frederick Jonathan and Daniel Morgan. BS in Aero. Engring., USAF Acad., 1970; MS in Aero. and Astron., Stanford U., 1971; PhD, Air Force Inst. Tech., Wright-Patterson Air Force Base, Ohio, 1980. Registered Profl. Engr. Colo. Commd. 2d lt. USAF, 1970, advanced through grades to lt. col.; test dir. Arnold Engring. Devel. Ctr., Tullahoma, Tenn., 1971-74; instr. Dept. of Aeron., USAF Acad., Colo., 1974-76; engr. br. and sect. chief Aerodynamics and Performance Br. Aero. Systems Div., Wright-Patterson AFB, Ohio, 1979-81; assoc. prof. Dept. of Aero., USAF Acad., Colo., 1981-85; br. chief Tech. Br. Civil Engring. Research Div., Air Force Weapons Lab., N.Mex., 1985-88; div. chief Aircraft/Missiles Div., Air Force Weapons Lab., 1988—. Contbr. articles, test reports to profl. jours. Recipient Air Force Meritorious Svc. medal 1985, Air Force commendation medal with 2 oak leaf clusters. Named Disting. Grad. Air Force Inst. of Tech., Wright-Patterson AFB, Ohio 1980, Jr. Officer of Yr. Arnold Engring. Devel. Ctr., Tullahoma 1972. Mem. Soc. of Am. Mil. Engrs., Air Force Assn., Assn. of Grad. USAFA, Tau Beta Pi Assn. Republican. Protestant. Home: 1700 Georgia NE Albuquerque NM 87110

JONES, AMY JO, travel agency executive; b. Longview, Wash., June 21, 1950; d. Thomas Owen and Georgia Roberta (Smith) Mendenhall; m. Gerald Douglas Jones, Nov. 25, 1972; children: Andrew, Thomas. V.p. Travel Network, Inc., Bellevue, Wash., 1985—. Office: Travel Network Inc 13200 Northup Way Bellevue WA 98005

JONES, BARBARA CHRISTINE, educator, linguist, creative arts designer; b. Augsburg, Swabia, Bavaria, Fed. Republic Germany, Nov. 14, 1942; came to U.S., 1964, naturalized, 1971; d. Martin Walter and Margarete Katharina (Roth-Rommel) Schulz von Hammer-Parstein; m. Robert Edward Dickey, 1967 (div. 1980); m. Raymond Lee Jones, 1981. Student U. Munich, 1961, Philomatique de Bordeaux, France, 1962; BA in German, French, Speech, Calif. State U., Chico, 1969, MA in Comparative Internat. Edn., 1974. Cert. secondary tchr., community coll. instr., Calif. Fgn. lang. tchr. Gridley Union High Sch., Calif., 1970-80, home econs., decorative arts instr., cons., 1970-80, English study skills instr., 1974-80, ESL coordinator, instr. Punjabi, Mex. Ams., 1970-72, curriculum com. chmn., 1970-80; program devel. adviser Program Devel. Ctr. Supt. Schs. Butte County, Oroville, Calif., 1975-77; opportunity tchr. Esperanza High Sch., Gridley, 1980-81, Liberty High Sch., Lodi, Calif., 1981-82, resource specialist coordinator, 1981-82; Title I coordinator Bear Creek Ranch Sch., Lodi, 1981-82, instr., counselor, 1981-82; substitute tchr. Elk Grove (Calif.) Unified, 1982-84; freelance decorative arts and textiles designer, 1982—; internat. heritage and foods advisor AAUW, Chico, Calif., 1973-75; workshop dir. Creative Arts Ctr., Chico, 1972-73; workshop dir., advisor Bus. Profl. Women's Club of Gridley, 1972-74; v.p. Golden State Mobile Home League, Sacramento, 1980-82. Designer weavings-wallhangings (1st place 10 categories, Silver Dollar Fair, Chico, 1970). Mem. United European Am. Club, Am. Assn. German Tchrs., U.S. Army Res. Non-Commd. Officer's Assn. (ednl. adv. 1984-86), Kappa Delta Pi. Avocations: weaving, fiber designs, swimming, skiing, internat. travel and culture. Home: 2485 Viejo Dr Lake Havasu City AZ 86403

JONES, BOB GORDON, bishop; b. Paragould, Ark., Aug. 22, 1932; s. F.H. and Helen Truman (Ellis) J.; m. Judith Munroe, Feb. 22, 1963; children: Robert Gordon, Timothy Andrew. B.B.A., U. Miss., 1956; M.Div., Episcopal Sem. S.W., 1959, D.D. hon., 1978. Asst. to dean Trinity Cathedral, Little Rock, 1959-62; vicar St. George-in-Arctic, Kotzebue, Alaska, 1962-67; rector St. Christopher's Ch., Anchorage, 1967-77; bishop Episcopal Diocese Wyo., Laramie, 1977—; chmn. bd. Cathedral Home Children, Laramie, 1977—; mem. exec. com. Provence N.W., Helena, Mont., 1980-83, Coalition 14, Phoenix, 1982-84. Pres. Arctic Circle C. of C., Kotzebue, 1966; mem. exec. com. Alaska C. of C., Juneau, 1967; chmn. allocations com. United Way, Anchorage, 1973-75; pres. United Way Anchorage, 1975-76. Served with USN, 1950-55, Korea. Republican. Lodges: Lions; Elks. Home: 3207 Alta Vista Dr Laramie WY 82070 Office: Episcopal Diocese of Wyo 104 S 4th St Box 1007 Laramie WY 82070

JONES, CHARLES IRVING, bishop; b. El Paso, Tex., Sept. 13, 1943; s. Charles I. Jr. and Helen A. (Heyward) J.; m. Ashby MacArthur, June 18, 1966; children: Charles I. IV, Courtney M., Frederic M., Keith A. BS, The Citadel, 1965; MBA, U. N.C., 1966; MDiv., U. of the South, 1977. CPA. Pub. acctg. D.E. Gatewood and Co., Winston-Salem, N.C., 1966-72; dir. devel. Chatham (Va.) Hall, 1972-74; instr. acctg. U. of the South, Sewanee, Tenn., 1974-77; coll. chaplain Western Ky. U., Bowling Green, 1977-81; vicar Trinity Episcopal Ch., Russelville, Ky., 1977-85; archdeacon Diocese of Ky., Louisville, 1981-86; bishop Episcopal Diocese of Mont., Helena, 1986—; bd. dirs. New Directions Ministries, Inc., N.Y.C.; mem. Joint Commn. on Chs. in Small Communities, 1988—. Bd. editors Grass Roots, Luling, Tex., 1985—; contbr. articles to profl. jours. Founder Concerned Citizens for Children, Russelville, 1981; bd. dirs. St. Peter's Hosp., Helena, 1986—. With USMCR, 1961-65. Mem. Aircraft Owners and Pilots Assn. Office: Diocese Mont 515 N Park Ave Helena MT 59601

JONES, CHARLES J., consultant; b. Marshfield, Oreg., Jan. 29, 1940; s. Charles J. Cotter and Lois C. (Smith) Meltebeke; m. Carol S. Lund, Jan. 11, 1961 (div. 1966); children: April M., Autumn C.; m. Sharon S. Madsen, Mar. 29, 1969; children: Mary E., Judith A., Kari C. AS in Fire Sci. Tech., Portland Community Coll., 1974; BS in Fire Adminstrn., Eastern Oreg. State Coll., 1983; diploma, Nat. Fire Acad., 1983, 85; MPA, Lewis and Clark Coll., 1989. Cert. class VI fire officer, Oreg.; lic. real estate agt., Oreg. From firefighter to capt. Washington County Fire Dist., Aloha, Oreg., 1964-74, battalion chief, 1974-81, dir. research and devel., 1981-85, dir. strategic planning, 1986-88; cons. fire dept. mgmt. Washington County Fire Dist. (name changed to Tualatin Valley Fire & Rescue), Aloha, 1989—; pres., cons. Jones Internat.; cons. Washington County Consol. Communications Agy., 1983-86, chmn. mgmt. bd., 1982-83; mem. adv. bd. Washington County Emergency Med. Services, 1981-83;. Editor local newsletter Internat. Assn. Firefighters, 1970; contbr. articles on fire dept. mgmt. to jours. Active Community Planning Orgn., Washington County, 1979—, chmn. 1988-89. Servd with USAF, 1957-59. Mem. Oreg. Fire Chiefs Assn. (chmn. seminar com. 1982-83, 89, co-chmn. 1981, 84, 86, 87, 88). Republican. Congregationalist. Club: Pontiac (Portland). Office: Tualatin Valley Fire & Rescue 20665 SW Blanton Aloha OR 97007

JONES, CHARLES LEONARD (CHUCK JONES), religious organization administrator; b. Santa Monica, Calif., Mar. 30, 1949; s. Johnny W. and Alice Billie (Robinson) J.; m. Beth Ellen Brainerd, Oct. 12, 1986. BA in Humanities, U. So. Calif., 1971, MA in Drama and Cinema, 1973, MFA, 1974. Asst. mgr. The Wherehouse, Santa Monica/Westwood, Calif., 1972; press agt./act rep. Gene Shefrin Entertainment, Beverly Hills, Calif., 1973; dispatcher, supr. Yellow Cab Co., L.A., 1973-75; owner Express Transp. Svc., L.A., 1975-77; ops. mgr. Baggage Master Delivery, El Segundo, Calif., 1978; dir. communications United Ind. Taxi, Hollywood, Calif., 1979; gen. mgr. Extran Inc., Westchester, Calif., 1980-86; ind. ch. cons. L.A., 1987; exec. dir. So. Calif. Ecumenical Council, L.A., 1987—; bd. dirs. Gen. Bd. Discipleship United Meth. Ch., nat. chmn. Ummens div.; bd. dirs. Calif. Ch. Council, So. Calif. Interreligious Council. Mem. The Canterbury Trust Fund in Am., Washington, 1986—, The Williamsburg (Va.) Trust, 1987—; bd. dirs. Aids Interfaith Task Force, L.A., 1988, United Meth. Men's Found., 1988—, life mem., 1986; del. United Meth. Ch. Gen. Conf., 1988; active Boy Scouts Am. Named Layman of Yr. United Meth. Ch. Calif.-Pacific Ann. Conf., 1987, John Wesley fellow, 1988; recipient Torch award United Meth. Ch., 1986. Mem. Nat. Assn. United Meth. Scouters (bd. dirs. 1988—), U. So. Calif. Gen. Alumni Assn. (life), U.S.C. Cinema/TV Alumni Assn., Cinema Circulus, The Am. Film Inst., Alpha Phi Omega. Democrat. Home: 15917 Kittridge St Van Nuys CA 91406 Office: So Calif Ecumenical Coun 1010 S Flower St #500 Los Angeles CA 90015

JONES, CLARK DAVID, restaurant executive, accountant; b. Wells, Nev., May 12, 1935; s. Waldo LeRoy and Beatrice (Bollschweiler) J.; m. LaRue Morrison, Nov. 20, 1953 (div. 1985); children: Debra, Pam, David, Diane, Christy; m. Pam James. BS in Acctg., U. Nev., 1957; postgrad. U. Utah, 1964-65. CPA, Nev. Mgr., Al Huber, CPA, Elko, Nev., 1960-62; ptnr. Main Hurdman CPAs, Salt Lake City, 1962-70; v.p. fin. JB's Restaurants, Inc., Salt Lake City, 1970-81, pres., 1981—; bd. dirs. JB's Restaurant Inc., MDT Inc. 1st lt. U.S. Army, 1958-60. Mem. AICPA, Utah Soc. CPAs, Am. Mgmt. Assn., Nat. Restaurant Assn., Rotary. Republican. Mormon. Home: 9717 S Ruskin Circle Sandy UT 84092 Office: JB's Restaurants Inc 1010 W 2610 S Salt Lake City UT 84119

JONES, CLEON BOYD, flight control engineer; b. Norwalk, Calif., Nov. 9, 1961; s. Cleon Earl and Marjorie Helen (McDade) J. BS in Math., Biola U., 1983. Research librarian Christian Research Inst., San Juan Capistrano, Calif., 1981-84; flight control engineer Leading Systems, Inc., Irvine, Calif., 1984—. Mem. AIAA. Republican. Home: 1313 Memory Ln Apt 308 Santa Ana CA 92706

JONES, CLYDE TILLMAN, data processing official, consultant; b. Ogden, Utah, Mar. 11, 1948; s. Prentiss and Ruby J.; m. Esther Patricia Williams, July 31, 1970; children: Tillman, Elisabeth. BSBA, Weber State Coll., 1971. With U.S. Forest Service, various locations, 1966--; mgmt. analyst U.S. Forest Service, San Francisco, 1974-80, computer programmer analyst, 1980-87, computer systems analyst, 1987--, local area network mgr., 1986--; cons. Peter Pan Acads., Alameda, Calif., 1984--; developer software Dominos with Rodney, lang. arts curriculum. Vol. Oakland (Calif.) Pub. Schs.; dir. Sunday sch. Mt. Zion Bapt. Ch., Oakland. Recipient vol. service award Sherman Elem. Sch., Oakland, 1986, cert. of appreciation U.S. Forest Service, 1987. Democrat. Office: US Forest Svc 630 Sansome St San Francisco CA 94111

JONES, DAISY MARVEL, retired education educator; b. Brownsburg, Ind., Apr. 22, 1906; d. Harlen Harper and Nannie Bell (Mark) Marvel; m. Vivian L. Jones, Aug. 3, 1927 (dec. Mar. 1983). BS, Ind. State U., 1931, MS, 1933; EdD, Ind. U., 1947. Classroom tchr. Pub. Schs., Marion County, Ind., 1925-36; tchr. Cen. Normal Coll., Danville, Ind., 1936-42; supr. Muncie (Ind.) City Schs., 1942-46; dir. elem. edn. Richmond (Ind.) Community Schd., 1946-63; prof. edn. Ariz. State U., Tempe, 1963-73, prof. emeritus, 1973—; rep. Assn. for Supervision and Curriculum Devel. Washington, 1966-71; rep. Elem. English, Urbana, Ill., 1964-70; book reviewer Curriculum Adv. Service, Chgo., 1956—. Author: Teaching Children to Read, 1971, Curriculum Targets in Elementary School, 1977; co-author: Communication Skills in Elementary Schools, 1977, others; mem. editorial bd. Childhood Edn., 1954-68. Elder Community Christian Ch., Tempe, 1967; chmn. found. drive Ariz. State U., Tempe, 1986-87; bd. chmn. Friendship Village Found., Tempe, 1986—. Mem. AAUW (com. chmn.), Ariz. State Reading Council (pres. 1970), Octillo East Reading Council (pres. 1967). Democrat. Mem. Christian Ch. (Disciples of Christ). Home: 2625 E Southern Ave Cottage C-48 Tempe AZ 85282

JONES, DARYL EMRYS, college dean, English educator; b. Washington, July 26, 1946; s. William Emrys and Willa Jean (Hibbard) J.; m. Martha Ann Bilton, June 11, 1979. BA, Mich. State U., 1968, MA, 1970, PhD, 1974. Prof. English Tex. Tech U., Lubbock, 1973-86, chmn. English dept., 1982-86; prof. English, dean Coll. Arts and Scis. Boise (Idaho) State U., 1986—. Author: The Dime Novel Western, 1978; author numerous poems and book revs. Recipient fellowship NDEA, 1969-71, Creative Writing fellowship Nat. Endowment for Arts, 1985. Mem. Tex. Assn. Creative Writing Tchrs. (pres. 1984-86), Tex. Joint Coun. Tchrs. of English (pres. South Plains area coun. 1983-84), Coun. Colls. Arts and Scis., Internat. Coun. Fine Arts Deans, Phi Beta Kappa, Phi Kappa Phi. Home: 1375 E Monterey Dr Boise ID 83706 Office: Boise State U Coll Arts and Scis 1910 University Dr Boise ID 83725

JONES, DAVID B., venture capitalist, corporation executive; b. Jamestown, N.Y., Oct. 12, 1943; s. Gustav E. and Jeane Louise (Nord) J.; m. Cornelia Corson Morris, Sept. 3, 1966; children: Caroline Vaughan, David Kristofer. AB, Dartmouth Coll., 1965; MBA, U. So. Calif., 1967, JD, 1970. Bar: Calif. 1971. Assoc. firm Hufstedler, Miller, Carlson & Beardsley, L.A., 1970-72; v.p. Union Venture Corp., L.A., 1972-78; v.p. fin. Am. Tech., Inc., Northridge, Calif., 1978, The Tannery West Corp., San Francisco, 1978-79; pres. First Interstate Capital, Inc., First Interstate Equities Corp., L.A., 1979-85; gen. ptnr. InterVen Ptnrs., 1985—; pres. InterVen Ptnrs., Inc., 1985—; bd. dirs. The Birtcher Corp., Gigabit Logic, Internat. Furniture & Accessories Mart, Inc., Tiger Media, Inc. Mem. Am. Coun. Capital Formation (bd. dirs. 1987-88), Western Assn. Venture Capitalists (former v.p., dir.), So. Pacific Regional Assn. Small Bus. Investment Cos. (former pres.), Nat. Assn. Small Bus. Investment Cos. (chmn. 1987-88, bd. govs.) (exec. com.). Clubs: Jonathan; City (Bunker Hill). Office: 333 S Grand Ave Ste 4050 Los Angeles CA 90071

JONES, DAVID JOHN, aerospace executive; b. Pueblo, Colo., Jan. 21, 1934; s. David John and Clare Elizabeth (Bronish) J.; m. Margaret Alice Hoagland; children—David Robert, Pamela Ruth. A. Engring., Pueblo Jr. Coll., 1954; B.S. in Aero. Engring., U. Colo., 1956; Exec. Program, Stanford U., 1977. Engr., Ryan Aero., 1956-59; program mgr. Convair div. Gen. Dynamics Corp., 1959-71, program mgr. space, 1971-75, dir. conventional applications of Tomahawk Cruise Missile, 1975-79, dir. advanced space systems, 1979-80; dir. space techs. System Devel. Corp., Santa Monica, Calif., 1980-82, dep. gen. mgr. Space and Control Systems div., 1987, v.p., gen. mgr. Command and Control div., Camarillo, Calif., 1987—; mem. Joint NASA/Congl. Budget Com., 1964-65; mem. planning com. on space NASA, 1975-76. Cons. Jr. Achievement Project Bus., 1980—; mem. San Diego council Boy Scouts Am., 1967-70, San Diego Multiple Sclerosis Com., 1973; bd. dirs. Moorpark Coll., 1988—. Assoc. fellow AIAA (dir., Nat. Service award San Diego chpt. 1977, 80); mem. Aerospace Industries Assn., Nat. Mgmt. Assn., Assn. U.S. Army, Am. Def. Preparedness Assn., Assn. Unmanned Vehicle Systems, Porsche Club Am., Unisys Mgmt. Assn. Contbr. articles to profl. jours. Home: 1853 Via Montecito Camarillo CA 93010 Office: 5151 Camino Ruiz Camarillo CA 93010

JONES, DELORES SHIRLEY, environmental specialist; b. Little Rock, Aug. 6, 1935; d. Thomas and Della (Shelton) Brockington; m. Don Merle Jones, Apr. 3, 1963 (div. 1973); children: Phillip, Charles, Lincoln, Barry, Thomas, Marvin, Sorita, Rhonda, Wiley, Don Merle II. AA, Valley Coll., 1972; BA, Calif. State U., San Bernardino, 1975. Family housing rep. County of San Bernardino, Calif., 1973-74, 76, planner I, 1975-76, housing supr., 1976-82, environ. specialist, 1982—; lectr. in field. Editor: newsletter Recycling Register, 1987. Sustaining mem. YMCA, San Bernardino, 1989—; loaned exec. Arrowhead United Way, San Bernardino, 1988; co-chair Environ. Expo, San Bernardino, 1989—; treas. CampFire Inc., San Bernardino, 1989—. Recipient Meritorius award Consumers Credit, 1982, Clean Community award San Bernardino Bd. Suprs., 1988, Outstanding Svc. award San Bernardino Dept. Environ. Health, 1988. Mem. Mme. NAACP (housing com. 1980-83), Bus. and Profl. Women (recording sec. 1983), Lilly of the Valley, Social Lites (publicity chmn., pres.). Democrat. Baptist. Home: 2348 San Carlo San Bernardino CA 92405

JONES, DENNY ALAN, engineering educator; b. Port Angeles, Wash., Jan. 20, 1938; s. Lloyd Leo Jones and Alice Jean (Kendrick) Vines; m. Wanda Wallace, Dec. 30, 1962; children: Regina, Gillian, Michael, Bryce. BS, U. Nev., Reno, 1960; MS, U. Ariz., 1962; PhD, Rensselaer Poly., Troy, N.Y., 1966. Research chemist Kaiser Aluminum, Spokane, Wash., 1966-68; sr. research engr. Battelle-Northwest, Richland, Wash., 1968-70; asst. prof. U. Hawaii, Honolulu, 1970-74; sr. research engr. U.S. Steel Corp., Monroeville, Pa., 1974-79; prof. engring. U. Nev., Reno, 1979—, chmn. dept. chem. and metall. engring., 1984-87; cons. Electric Power research Inst., Palo Alto, Calif., 1980-85, Dept. Energy, Las Vegas, 1985-86. Contbr. articles to profl. jours. Grantee Am. Iron and Steel Inst., 1980-83, NSF, 1982-86, Electric Power Research Inst., 1985-86. Mem. Nat. Assn. Engrs. (cert. corrosion specialist), Nat. Assn. Corrosion Engrs., Am. Soc. Metals, ASTM. Republican. Mormon. Home: 1705 Plymouth Way Sparks NV 89431 Office: U Nev Dept Chem & Metall Engring Reno NV 89557 *

JONES, DONALD FORSYTH, corporation executive; b. Chgo., Mar. 28, 1942; s. H. Carter and Dorothy S. (Simons) J.; m. Jeri Lynn Riha, July 3, 1965; children: Marcus, David. BS in Indsl. Engring., Calif. State Poly. U., 1965. Test engr. Boeing Co., Seattle, 1965-70; plant mgr. Western Kraft Corp., Portland, Oreg., 1970-78; gen. mgr. Spear & Jackson, Ltd., Eugene, Oreg., 1978-80; pres. J.V. Northwest, Inc., Portland, 1980—. Contbr. articles to mags. Republican. Mem. Christian Ch. (Disciples of Christ). Home: 17405 SW Wren Ct Lake Oswego OR 97035 Office: JV Northwest Inc 28120 SW Boberg Rd Wilsonville OR 97070

JONES, DONALD RAY, entrepreneur; b. Phoenix, July 19, 1947. Student, Phoenix Coll., 1972-74. Sales rep. various cos. including Hills Bros. Coffee, Inc., Holly World Foods, Keebler Co., 1973-81; dir. mktg. Scott Toyota, 1983-84; founder, pres. DRJ & Assocs., Inc., Phoenix, 1984—. Mem. adv. bd. Sta. KPNX Broadcasting, South Mountain Community Coll., Foster Care Rev. Bd., edn. bd. Antioch Missionary Bapt. Ch. Served with U.S. Army, 1967-69, Vietnam. Office: DRJ & Assocs Box 2314 Phoenix AZ 85002

JONES, DONNA RUTH, librarian; b. Denver, June 23, 1948; d. Don and Ruth Virginia (Hampton) Lusk; 1 child, Matthew Trevor. BA, Ft. Hays State U., 1969; MLS, Emporia State U., 1972. Librarian, instr. Colby (Kans.) Community Coll., 1969-76; dir. library services Pioneer Meml. Library, Colby, 1976-85; dir. Ark. Valley Regional Library Service System, Pueblo, Colo., 1985—; adj. prof. library sci. Ft. Hays State U., 1972-73, 78-80; cons. N.W. Kans. Library System, 1970-71, 74, humanities cons., 1979—. Researcher: (movie and brochure) Country School Legacy: Humanities on the Frontier, 1980-82. Mem., chmn. Kans. Com. for Humanities, Topeka, 1979-85; pres. Thomas County Day Care, Colby, 1983-85; chmn. state steering com. Humanities in Pub. Libraries, 1980-85; active Colo. Endowment for the Humanities, Denver, 1986—. Recipient Jr. Mems. Round Table award 3-M, 1975, Young Alumni award Ft. Hays State U., 1979. Mem. ALA, Mountain Plains Library Assn. (pres. 1984-85), Colo. Library Assn. (v.p., pres. elect 1988—), Beta Sigma Phi (Sister of Yr.). Republican. Methodist. Lodge: Order of Eastern Star. Home: 2 Pedregal Ln Pueblo CO 81005 Office: Arkansas Valley Regional Libr Svc System 205 W Abriendo Pueblo CO 81004

JONES, DOROTHY CAMERON, language professional, educator; b. Detroit, Feb. 5, 1922; d. Vinton Ernest and Beatrice Olive (Cameron) J. B.A., Wayne State U., 1943, M.A., 1944; Ph.D., U. Colo., 1965. Attendance officer Detroit Bd. Edn., 1943-44; tchr. English Denby High Sch., Detroit, 1946-56, 57-58; exchange tchr. Honolulu, 1956-57; instr., asst. prof. English Colo. Women's Coll., Denver, 1962-66; mem. faculty U. No. Colo., Greeley, 1966—; prof. English U. No. Colo., 1974—. Contbr. articles to profl. lit. Served with WAVES USNR, 1944-46. Faculty research grantee, 1970, 76. Mem. Internat. Shakespeare Assn., Central States Renaissance Soc., Patristic, Medieval and Renaissance Conf., Rocky Mountain Medieval and Renaissance Soc., Rocky Mountain MLA, Delta Kappa Gamma, Pi Lambda Theta. Home: 1009 13th Ave Apt 312 Greeley CO 80631 Office: U No Colo Dept English 40 Michener Libr Greeley CO 80639

JONES, EARL, former college president, research specialist; b. Canton, Okla., Aug. 4, 1925; s. Hercel C. and Florence (Hill) L.; m. Eleanor Harriett Vance, July 15, 1951; children: Beverly Anne, Mark Earl, James Richard, Cindy Kay. B.S. Oreg. State U., 1949; M.S., Inter-Am. Inst. of OAS, Turrialba, Costa Rica, 1958; Ed.D., Mont. State U., 1962. Tchr. pub. schs. Ontario, Oreg., 1949-55; dir. rural programs Sta. KSRV, Ontario, 1955-56; dir. Sta. KSLM, Salem, Oreg., 1956; vocat. dir. Arcata Pub. Schs., Calif., 1956-57; instr. Inter-Am. Inst., 1957-58, asst. prof., 1960-62; assoc. prof. sociology UCLA, 1963-66; prof. sociology and edn., assoc. dean Tex. A&M U. Coll. Edn., 1967-71; pres. Incarnate Word Coll., San Antonio, 1971-73; sr. research specialist Devel. Assocs., San Francisco, 1974—; dir. research office Devel. Assocs., San Antonio, 1977—; prof. Antioch U., West San Antonio, 1977—; dir. research Caribbean Inst. Sociology and Anthropology, Caracas, Venezuela, 1963-65; chair prof. U. Chile Sch. Law, Santiago, Valparaiso, 1965-66; vis. prof. Royal Danish Acad., Copenhagen, 1955, U. P.R., Mayaguez, 1960, Cath. U., Caracas, 1963-65, U. Pacific, 1966, Calif. State Coll.-Los Angeles, Calif. State Coll.-San Francisco, 1968; prof. Antioch Coll., 1973—; cons. Mexican-Am. Cultural Ctr., San Antonio, 1973-75; mem. Gov.'s Com. on Confluence of Tex. Cultures, 1969-76, Gov's Com. to Reconstruct Tchr. Edn., 1969-72; cons. Cabinet Com. on Spanish Speaking Peoples, 1972-75. Author: Rural Youth in the Americas, 1960, Lideracao, 1961, A Study of the Costa Rican Extension Service, 1962, The Cooperative Extension Services of Jamaica, 1962, Supervision en Extension Agricola, 1963, Latin American Literature for Youth, 1968, Some Perspectives on the Americas, 1968, Self-Identification and the Americas, 1970, Social Atitudes of South Texas Primary Children, 1976, (with others) Teacher Classroom Behaviors, 1977, Case Studies in Educational Change, 1978, Client Satisfaction with Services to Limited and Non-English-Speaking Students In California, 1980, Study of Small Farmer Titling in Honduras, 1983, Supply and Demand of Professionals in Sri Lanka, 1984. Served with USMCR, 1943-46. Recipient Presdl. citation Republic of Guatemala, 1969; recipient Standard Oil Disting. Teaching Award, 1970. Mem. Am. Sociol Assn., Rural Sociol. Soc., Alpha Zeta, Phi Kappa Delta. Democrat. Roman Catholic. Lodge: Lions. Home: 2695 37th Ave San Francisco CA 94116 Office: 1475 N Broadway Ste 200 Walnut Creek CA 94596

JONES, EBON RICHARD, retail executive; b. Oak Park, Ill., Aug. 23, 1944; s. Ebon Clark and Marilyn B. (Dow) J.; m. Sally Samuelson, Jan. 27, 1968; children: Stephanie Blythe, Heather Denise. B.A., Priceton U., 1966; M.B.A., Stanford U., 1968. Adminstrv. asst. Nat. Air Pollution Control Adminstrn., Washington, 1968-70; cons. McKinsey & Co., San Francisco and Paris, 1970-83; exec. v.p. Safeway Stores Inc., Oakland, Calif., 1983-86, group v.p., 1986-88, exec. v.p., 1988—. Chmn. bd. San Francisco Zool. Soc., 1979-84, pres. 1985—; trustee San Francisco Trust; Crystal Springs Uplands Sch., 1986—; gov. Uniform Code Council, 1984—. Served to lt. USPHS,

1968-70. Mem. Phi Beta Kappa. Home: 58 Chester Way San Mateo CA 94402 Office: Safeway Stores Inc 201 4th St Oakland CA 94660

JONES, EDWARD LOUIS, historian, educator; b. Georgetown, Tex., Jan. 15, 1922; s. Henry Horace and Elizabeth (Steen) J.; m. Dorothy M. Showers, Mar. 1, 1952 (div. Sept. 1963); children: Cynthia, Frances, Edward Lawrence; Lynne Ann McGreevy, Oct. 7, 1963; children Christopher Louis, Teresa Lynne. BA in Philosophy, U. Wash., 1952, BA in Far East, 1952, BA in Speech, 1955, postgrad., 1952-54; JD, Gonzaga U., 1967. Social worker Los Angeles Pub. Assistance, 1956-57; producer, dir. Little Theatre, Hollywood, Calif. and Seattle, 1956-60; research analyst, cons. to Office of Atty. Gen., Olympia and Seattle, Wash., 1963-66; coordinator of counseling SOIC, Seattle, 1966-68; lectr., advisor, asst. to dean U. Wash., Seattle, 1968—; instr. Gonzaga U., Spokane, Wash., 1961-62, Seattle Community Coll., 1967-68; dir. drama workshop, Driftwood Players, Edmonds, Wash., 1975-76. Author: The Black Diaspora: Colonization of Colored People, 1988, Tutankhamon: Son of the Sun, King of Upper and Lower Egypt, 1978, Black Orators' Workbook, 1982, Black Zeus, 1972, Profiles in African Heritage, 1972; editor, pub. NACADA Jour. Nat. Acad. Advising Assn., 1981—, Afro-World Briefs newsletter, 1985—. V.p. Wash. Com. on Consumer Interests, Seattle, 1966-68. Served to 2d lt. Fr. Army, 1940-45. Recipient Outstanding Teaching award U. Wash., 1986, Tyee Inst. Yr. U. Wash., 1987, appreciation award Office Minority Affairs, 1987, acad. excellence award Nat. Soc. Black Engrs., 1987; Frederick Douglass scholar Nat. Council Black Studies, 1985, 86. Mem. Nat. Assn. Student Personnel Adminstrs., Smithsonian Inst. (assoc.), Am. Acad. Polit. and Social Sci., Nat. Acad. Advising Assn. (bd. dirs. 1979-82, Cert. of Appreciation 1982, editor Jour. 1981—, award for Excellence 1985), Western Polit. Sci. Assn. Democrat. Baptist. Office: U Wash Seattle WA 98195

JONES, FRANCIS CLARK, writer; b. Gregory, S.D., Sept. 4, 1933; s. Francis Leroy and Cornelia Clark (Smith) J.; m. Shirley A. Mader, Jan. 7, 1955 (div. Jan. 1984); children: Mark D., Deniece Jones Smith, Wendy M., Craig F. BA, Eastern Wash. State U., 1956; MEd, U. Idaho, 1966; DEd, Wash. Stsate U., 1979. Cert. tchr., prin., adminstr. Tchr., prin. various sch. dists., 1956-59, 60-65; radio announcer KGEE, Bakersfield, Calif., 1959-60; asst. dir. audio-visual dept. U. Idaho, Moscow, 1965-66; asst. supt. Othello (Wash.) Sch. Dist., 1966-69; jr. high prin. North Franklin Sch. Dist., Connell, Wash., 1969-71; lit. cons. Ednl. Cons., Inc., Edmonds, Wash., 1971-72; state coordinator adult edn. staff devel. Wash. State U., Pullman, 1972-74; asst. prof. U. Alaska, S.E., Juneau, 1974-75; supr. adult edn. Alaska Dept. Edn., Juneau, 1975-81; writer S.E. Regional Resource Ctr., Juneau, 1987—; Bd. mem. S.E. Rehab. Svcs., Juneau, 1987—; cons. State of Alaska, Juneau, 1987—. Editor Internat. Literacy Rsch. Jour., 1981-83, Rsch. Jour. U. Alaska., 1982, various newsletters, 1972-89; contbr articles to profl. jours. Campaign com. Sheffield & Cowper for Gov., S.E. Alaska, 1981, 86; scoutmaster, commr. Boy Scouts Am., Idaho, Wash., 1956-72; pres., v.p., bd. PTA, Idaho, Calif., Wash., 1956-72; coach, umpire Little League, Am. Softball Assn., Idaho, Wash., Alaska, 1960—. Univ. fellow U. Idaho, Wash. State U., 1966, 71-74; Region X Adult Edn. Consortium, Wash., Oreg., Idaho, Alaska, 1975-86 (chmn. bd. 1981, 83-85), Outstanding Adult Educator, S.E. Alaska Adult Edn. Program, 1987, Tribute to Clark Jones, Am. Coun. on Edn., Washington, 1987. Mem. Commn. on Adult Edn. (bd. dirs., pres. 1979-85, Nat. Adminstr. of Yr. 1987), Am. Asns. Adult and Continuing Edn., N.W. Adult Edn. Assn. (bd. dirs. 1972-74), Alaska Adult Edn. Assn. (pres. award for svc. 1979), Alaskan Soc. Curriculum Devel., Am. Fedn. Police, Turtles Internat. Home: PO Box 22234 Juneau AK 99802 Office: SE Regional Resource Ctr 210 Ferry Way Ste 200 Juneau AK 99801

JONES, GALEN RAY, physician assistant; b. Salt Lake City, Feb. 1, 1948; s. Leonard Ray and Veda (Whitehead) J.; m. Patricia Ann Poulson, Jan. 21, 1972; children: Brian, Marci, Natalie. Grad., Med. Field Svc. Sch. Ft. Sam Houston, San Antonio, 1971; BS, U. Utah, 1982. Missionary Ch. of Jesus Christ of Latter Day Saints, Alta., Sask., Can., 1967-69; asst. mgr. Cowan's Frostop Hamburger Stand, Salt Lake City, 1969-70; with Safeway Stores, Inc., Salt Lake City, 1970; o.r. tech. Latter Day Saint Hosp., Salt Lake City, 1973-75; physician asst. Lovell Clinic Inc., Lovell, Wyo., 1975-77, Family Health Care, Inc., Tooele, Utah, 1977-86, West Dermatology and Surgery Med. Grp., San Bernardino, Calif., 1986—; maturation lectr. Tooele Sch. Dist., Utah, 1978-86; course dir., instr. EMT for North Big Horn County Search and Rescue, 1976; instr. of E.M.T., Grantsville Ambulance Inc., 1979-85. Chmn. County Health Teen Pregnancy Prevention Project, Tooele, 1980-81; adv. bd. State Dept. Health-Rural Health Network, Salt Lake City, 1985-86; health lectr. County Health & Edn. Dept. Progs., Tooele, 1977-86; mormon bishop/pastor Lakeview Ward, Latter Day Saints Ch., Tooele, 1982-86; mem. Utah Acad. Physician Assts. (pres. 1980-81, editor newsletter 1979-80). With U.S. Army, 1971-73. U. Utah grantee, 1966, 67, 69. Fellow Am. Acad. Physician Assts., Calif. Acad. Physicians Assts.; mem. Moreno Valley C. of C. Republican. Mem. Ch. of Jesus Christ of Latter Day Saints Ch. Home: 101 Channing St Redlands CA 92373-4862

JONES, GARY LEE, surveyor, consultant; b. Clovis, N.Mex., Dec. 31, 1949; s. Herschel Lee and Bobbie June (Wilson) J.; m. Donna Lynn Clarke, Nov. 16, 1952; children: Curtis Lee, Casey Anne, Derek Austin. Student, N.Mex. State U., 1969-77. Registered profl. land surveyor, N.Mex. Ptnr. Gen. Surveying Co., Lovington, N.Mex., 1977-82; co-owner Gen. Hydrocarbons, Lovington, 1981-84, Enging. Services Ltd., Hobbs, N.Mex., 1983; owner The Surveying Co., Hobbs, 1984-85; supr. John West Engring. Co., Hobbs, 1985—. Area dir. Spl. Olympics, Lea County, 1988—. Mem. Nat. Soc. Profl. Surveyors. Republican. Methodist. Clubs: Hobbs Downtown (pres. elect). Lodge: Lions (Lion of Yr. 1986). Home: 904 W Lead Hobbs NM 88240 Office: John West Engring 412 N Dal Paso St Hobbs NM 88240

JONES, GERALD JOSEPH, former broadcasting executive; b. Saginaw, Mich., May 22, 1920; s. LaVern Pierce and Yvonne Maria (Berthaud) J.; student Los Angeles Jr. Coll., 1939; m. Madelyn Fio Rito, Nov. 15, 1970; children by previous marriage—Jennifer Jones Batteau, Steven G. Account exec. Murray Dymock, 1946, West-Holliday, 1947-50, The Katz Agy., Inc., 1950-60, v.p., 1967-78, West Coast mgr., 1977-78, v.p. sta. and industry relations, 1978-80. Served to flight lt. RCAF, 1941-45. Decorated D.F.C.; col. Staff of Gov. John McKeithen, La., 1971. Mem. Pacific Pioneer Broadcasters, So Calif. Advt. Golfers Assn. Republican. Clubs: Bel Air, Woburn Golf and Country (Milton Keynes, Eng.), Milline (sec. 1963-66); Thunderbird Country. Home: 10690 Somma Way Los Angeles CA 90077

JONES, HARVEY ROYDEN, III, computer science educator, consultant; b. Phila., Feb. 7, 1963; s. Harvey Royden and Mary Elizabeth (Norman) J. BA in History, Stanford U., 1985, MS in Computer Sci., 1986. Teaching asst. Stanford (Calif.) U., 1984-85, teaching fellow, 1985-86, lectr. computer sci., 1986—, asst. chmn. dept. computer sci., 1987-88; cons. Lahey Clinic Med. Ctr., Burlington, Mass., 1981—, Warthman Assocs., Palo Alto, Calif., 1982-88; instr. Prime Computer, Natick, Mass., 1986; with 4th Connection Cons., Inc., 1988—. Mem. Am. Assn. Artificial Intelligence, Assn. Computing Machinists. Republican. Home: PO Box 4504 Stanford CA 94309 Office: Stanford U Tresidder Rm 101 Stanford CA 94305

JONES, HENRY ALPHONSO, teacher; b. Jacksonville, Fla., May 20, 1936; s. Harold Wilbur and Lula (Mack) J.; m. Mattie Lee Hite, June 30, 1973; children: Muszetta, Heneliaka. BA, Morris Brown U., 1959. Cert. Tchr., Calif. Secondary sch. tchr. San Francisco Unified Sch. Dist., 1968—; bldg. rep. Am. Fedn. Tchrs., San Francisco, 1979-89. Author: Thy Kingdom Come, 1987. Mem. Jones Meth. Ch. (pres. 1979—) adult Sunday sch. tchr.; pres. United Meth. Men. Named Tchr. of the Year Tex. Coll., 1985. Mem. Bay Area Pan Hellenic Coun. (pres. 1986-88), Omega Psi Phi. Methodist. Home: 269 Dennis Dr Daly City CA 94015

JONES, J. GILBERT, research consultant; b. San Francisco, June 1, 1922; s. Enoch Roscoe L. Sr. and Remedios (Ponce de Leon) J.; student U.S. Mcht. Marine Acad., 1942-44, San Francisco City Coll., 1942-44, 46-47; AB, U. Calif., Berkeley, 1949, MA, 1952. Ins. insp. Ins. Cos. Insp. Bur., San Francisco, 1959-62; pub. rels. cons., San Francisco, 1962-67; ins. insp. Am. Svc. Bur., San Francisco, 1967-72; propr., mgr. Dawn Universal Internat. San Francisco, 1972—, Dawn Universal Security Svc., San Francisco, 1983—. Mem. Calif. Rep. Assembly, 1978—, sponsor Nat. Rep. Congl. Com. Mem. SAR, Sons Spanish-Am. War Vets., U. Calif. Alumni Assn. Office: PO Box 4239 San Francisco CA 94101

JONES, JAMES THOMAS, state official; b. Twin Falls, Idaho, May 13, 1942; s. Henry C. and Eunice Irene (Martens) J.; m. Nancy June Babson, Nov. 25, 1972; 1 dau., Katherine A. Student, Idaho State U., 1960-61; BA, U. Oreg., 1964; JD, Northwestern U., 1967. Bar: Idaho 1967. Legis. asst. to U.S. Senator, Washington, 1970-72; law practice Jerome, Idaho, 1973-82; atty. gen. State of Idaho, Boise, 1973—. Capt. U.S. Army, 1967-79, Vietnam. Decorated Bronze Star; decorated Air medal with 4 oak leaf clusters, Cross of Gallantry (Vietnam), Army Commendation medal. Mem. Idaho Bar Assn., Am. Legion, VFW. Republican. Lutheran. Office: Office Atty Gen Statehouse Rm 210 Boise ID 83720

JONES, JANICE CARLA, day care administrator; b. Pine Bluff, Ark., July 19, 1953; d. Walter Calvin and Mittie Lee (Gordon) Davis; m. Edward Carroll Jones, June 10, 1972; children: Janine Antoinette, Janae Michelle. Student, U. So. Calif., 1972; BS, Calif. State U., Hayward, 1976. Lic. family day care provider, Calif. Claims examiner Blue Shield, San Francisco, 1973-74; receptionist Kaiser Hosp., Hayward, 1976-79; business auditer Kaiser Hosp., Oakland, Calif., 1979-80; prin. Wee Care Day Care, San Leandro, Calif., 1980—; Sec. Western Regional Family Day Care, Reno, Nev., 1986-87; day care rep. Bldg. Quality Child Care, Hayward, 1985-86; planner So. Alameda County Day Care, San Leandro, 1985—. Planning com. Library Books to Home Care Providers, So. Alameda County, 1988; participant workshop Dept. Social Services, Emeryville, Calif., 1988; active Senate Task Force on Child Care, Sacramento, 1987; troup mother Oakland counsel Girl Scouts U.S., 1980-86; fundraiser United Way, Hayward, 1976-79. Mem. So. Alameda County Day Care Assn. (pres. 1985), Family Day Care Assn. of Calif. (rec. sec.), Nat. Assn. Family Day Care, Internat. Family Day Care. Democrat. Baptist. Home and Office: Wee Care Day Care 357 Durant Ave Oakland CA 94577

JONES, JEFFREY THOMAS, dentist; b. Long Beach, Calif., Sept. 28, 1952; s. Thomas Arthur and Jacqueline Ann (Walker) J.; m. Dru Mason, Aug. 14, 1982. BS in Biology, U. Calif., Irvine, 1976; MS in Biochemistry, Loma Linda U., 1978, DDS, 1984. Pvt. practice Santa Ana, Calif., 1985--. V. p. Garden Grove Youth Council, Calif., 1970. Served with USN, 1971-73. Mem. ADA, Calif. Dental Assn., Orange County Dental Soc. Home: 2138 S Atlanta St Anaheim CA 92802

JONES, JEREMY, architect, author; b. Spokane, Oct. 14, 1944; s. Alan Hubert and Helen Sylvia (Fairbrook) J.; m. Barbara La Dean Steward, Sept. 14, 1968; children: Allysen Steward, Braden Lloyd. B.Arch., U. Wash., 1968. Registered architect, Wash., Ariz., Colo. Designer DAF Co., Seattle, 1968-72, M & K Goodwin, Ltd., Tempe, Ariz., 1972-73; dir. design PA Lendrum Assocs., Phoenix, 1973-77; designer WMFL, Spokane, 1978-79; ptnr. Design Concept Assocs., Spokane, 1979-82; designer, assoc. v.p. Rogers Nagel Langhart, Inc., Denver, 1982-86; dir. design, DMJM, Phoenix, 1986—. Author: Homes In The Earth, 1980; Homes for Creative Living, 1984. Recipient Design award Portland Cement Assn., 1978, Regional Merit award AIA, 1979, award Seattle Art of Urban Housing Nat. Design Competition, 1988. Office: DMJM 300 W Clarendon Phoenix AZ 85013

JONES, KENNETH ALAN, psychologist; b. Leominster, Mass., June 30, 1944; s. Robert William and Eleanor (DiMarzio) J. BS in Edn., Mass. State Coll., 1966; MA in Psychology, Calif. State U., Northridge, 1974. Lic. sch. psychologist, Calif. Tchr. Los Angeles Unified, 1966-75, social worker, 1975-84; master tchr. Calif. State U., Northridge, 1968-71, U. So. Calif., Los Angeles, 1972-74; eligibility specialist for educationally and physically handicapped progrms State of Calif., Los Angeles, 1979-81; ct. liaison juvenile div. Superior Ct., City of Los Angeles, 1984—; mem. Educare Sch. of Edn. U. So. Calif., Los Angeles, 1980—. Mem. Mass. State U. Alumni Assn., Calif. State U. Alumni Assn., Kappa Delta Phi. Democrat. Roman Catholic. Home: 8127 McKim Ct Los Angeles CA 90046-1516 Office: Superior Ct Sylmar Juvenile 16350 Filbert St Sylmar CA 91342

JONES, LAWRENCE DONALD, economics educator; b. Columbus, Ohio, Apr. 24, 1931; s. Lawrence Donald and Alice Bradford (Colton) J.; m. Sheila Ann Conlin, June 30, 1962; children: Thomas Conlin, David Lawrence. BA in Math., Ohio State U., 1953, MA in Econs., 1954; PhD in Econs., Harvard U., 1959. Instr. econs. Harvard U., Cambridge, Mass., 1959-62; asst. prof. Wesleyan U., Middletown, Conn., 1962-66; assoc. prof. Ind. U., Bloomington, 1966-69; assoc. dir. SEC, Washington, 1969-70; assoc. prof. U. Pa., Phila., 1969-76, U. B.C., Vancouver, Can., 1976—; vis. prof. U. Calif. Berkeley, 1986-87. Author: Investment Policies of Life Insurance Companies, 1968 (Clarence Arthur Kulp award). Contbr. articles to profl. jours. Mem. Am. Econ. Assn., Am. Fin. Assn., Am. Real Estate and Urban Econs. Assn. Home: 4263 W 14th Ave, Vancouver, BC Canada V6R 2X7 Office: U BC Faculty Commerce & Bus Adminstrn, 2053 Main Mall, Vancouver, BC Canada V6T 1Y8

JONES, LEON BRUCE, research gemologist; b. Seattle, May 14, 1956; s. John Paul and Nola (DeLong) J.; divorced; children: L. Brandon, Devon Danielle. BA in Geology, Trinity U., 1978; grad., Gemmol. Inst. Am., 1978; postgrad., U. Wash., 1982-83. Pres. Pacific Gemological Services, Seattle, 1979-83; v.p., dir. of research and edn. Am. Gem Market System, Lafayette, Calif., 1984-85; sr. research gemologist Am. Gem Market System, Moraga, Calif., 1985; cons. Seattle, 1986—; gemologist Deutsche Gemolis Gesselschaft, Fed. Republic Germany, 1982. Contbr. articles to profl. jours. Fellow Gemological Assn. Gt. Britain; mem. Gemological Assn. of Australia, Mineral. Soc. of Am., Nat. Assoc. Jewelry Appraisers (sr.),Pacific N.W. Gemological Assn. (founder, past pres.). Home and Office: 201 E Park Dr Anacortes WA 98221

JONES, LEON LAMONT, psychotherapist, social worker, consultant; b. Glendale, Calif., Mar. 14, 1930; s. Deorval Herbert and Dana Ruth (Field) J.; m. Kathryn Duff, Apr. 3, 1964; children: James Murphy, Lisa Murphy, Christina Murphy, Steven, Nicholas. BA in Psychology, Calif. State U., 1955; postgrad., U. So. Calif., 1961-64; MSW, San Diego State U., 1967. Social worker Dept. Pub. Social Svcs., L.A. County, 1962-66, ct. dependency supr., child welfare div., 1967-68; psychiat. social worker L.A. County, U. So. Calif. Med. Ctr., 1968-69; psychiat. social worker San Gabriel Valley Mental Health Svc., 1969-70, supr., 1970-73; chief psychiat. social worker adult svc. div. Pasadena (Calif.) Guidance Clinic, 1973-77; pvt. practice Pasadena, 1977—; part-time psychotherapist Gilfillan Clinic, 1967-70; clin. instr. Sch. Social Welfare UCLA, 1972-73, Sch. Edn. U. So. Calif., 1973-74, Sch. Social Work, 1974-76, Sch. Nursing Calif. State U., L.A., 1975-76; clin. instr., clin. field cons. Sch. Social Work U. So. Calif., 1976-77; cons. Pasadena Community Hosp. Alcoholic Rehab. Unit, 1975-76, Huntington Meml. Hosp., 1977—, Foothill Family Svc., 1978-80. Cpl. U.S. Army, 1952-54, Korea. Mem. Phi Delta Kappa. Office: 547 Union St Pasadena CA 91101

JONES, LINDA LEE, health facility administrator; b. Havana, Ill., July 25, 1959; d. George Mathew and Juanita Jean (Tyler) Pintar; m. Duane Gilbert Jones, June 29, 1985. BS, Western Ill. U., 1981; MS, Tex. Women's U., 1983. Registered dietician. Clin. dietician U. Med. Ctr., Tucson, 1983-87, Med. Personnel Pool, Tucson, 1987—; dir. health promotion Univ. Physicians, Tucson, 1987—; nutrition counselor Canyon Ranch Health Resort, Tucson, 1985—, Assocs. in Profl. Nutrition Counseling, Tucson, 1985-87. Author nutrition edn. booklets. Mem. So. Ariz. Dist. Dietitic Assn. (pres. 1987-88), Tucson Diabetic Educators (v.p. 1984-85), Ariz. Diabetic Assn. (bd. dirs.), Am. Dietitic Assn. (pub. com. chairperson 1986-87). Methodist. Home: 2625 E Sylvia Tucson AZ 85716 Office: Univ Physicians 2028 E Prince Rd Tucson AZ 85719

JONES, LOUISA ELSA, medical association executive; b. Watertown, N.Y., Nov. 18, 1940; d. Emlen Howell and Elsa (Singer) J. BS, Fordham U., 1962. Programmer Dillon Read & Co., N.Y.C., 1965-67; editor research publs. dept. anesthesiology U. Wash., Seattle, 1968-82; exec. officer Internat. Assn. for the Study of Pain, Seattle, 1978—; sec./treas., bd. dirs. Internat. Pain Found., Seattle, 1986—. Mem. Am. Soc. Assn. Execs., Am. Pain Soc. Democrat. Roman Catholic. Office: Internat Assn for the Study of Pain 909 NE 43d St Ste 306 Seattle WA 98105

JONES, MALCOLM MURRAY, banker; b. Scarsdale, N.Y., Oct. 24, 1935; s. Samuel Murray and Norma Joy (Hopson) J.; m. Lesly Sheldon Weaver, June 18, 1966; children: Oliver Neville, Marbury Joy. BS, MIT, 1957, MS, 1958, PhD, 1967. Lectr. Sloan Sch. Mgmt., MIT, Cambridge, 1967-74; asst. prof. Sloan Sch. Mgmt., MIT, 1965-67, asst. dir. project MAC, 1967-71; v.p. lst of Denver Bank, 1975-82, United Bank Svc. Co., Denver, 1974-75; pres. Minibank Switch Network, Denver, 1982—; chmn. bd. dirs. Unique Industries, Denver, 1989—; lectr. Sr. Seminar on Fgn. Policy, U.S. Dept. State, 1970-73, U.S. CSC, 1970-73; cons. data processing div. Fed. Res. Bd., 1971-73. Co-author: On Line Computation and Simulation: The OPS-3 System, 1965. Treas. Denver Civic Ballet, 1977-80; pres. Mens Orgn. for Denver Symphony, 1980-81; bd. dirs. Denver chpt. Young Audiences, 1985-87, Denver Ctr. for Performing Arts, Denver Mus. Natural History, Denver Art Mus. Capt. USAF, 1958-62; pres. Silverado II Homeowners Assn., Winter Park, Colo., 1983—. Recipient various outstanding svc. awards, 1958-62. Mem. Ancient and Hon. Arty. Co. Mass., Soc. Colonial Wars, Nat. Huguenot Soc., Hereditary Order Colonial Govs., Flagon and Trencher, Ams. Armorial Ancestry, Nat. Soc. Old Plymouth Colony Desc., Knights Most Noble Order of Garter, Jacques Cousteau Soc., Ends of Earth Soc., Newcomen Soc., Heather Ridge Country Club, Colo. Arlberg Club, Osiris, Tau Beta Pi, Sigma Chi. Home: 2623 S Vaughn Way Aurora CO 80014 Office: 2696 S Colorado Blvd Ste 420 Denver CO 80222

JONES, MARIAN ILENE, educator; b. Hawarden, Iowa, Oct. 3, 1929; d. Henry Richard and Wilhelmina Anna (Schmidt) Stoltenberg; m. Paul Irving Jones, June 14, 1958 (dec. Feb. 1985). BA, La Verne Coll., 1959; MA, Claremont Grad. Sch., 1962; PhD, Ariz. State U., 197l. Cert. tchr., Iowa, Calif. Elem. tchr. Cherokee (Iowa) Sch. Dist., 1949-52, Sioux City (Iowa) Sch. Dist., 1952-56, Ontario (Calif.) Pub. Schs., 1956-6l, Reed Union Sch. Dist., Belvedere-Tiburon, Calif., 1962-65, Columbia (Calif.) Union Sch. Dist., 1965-68; prof. edn. Calif. State U., Chico, 1972—. Contbr. articles to profl. jours. Mem. Internat. Reading Assn., AAUW, Phi Delta Kappa, Delta Kappa Gamma. Home: 1675 Manzanita Ave Apt l4 Chico CA 95926 Office: Calif State U Dept Edn Chico CA 95929

JONES, MARY DAILEY (MRS. HARVEY BRADLEY JONES), civic worker; b. Billings, Mont.; d. Leroy Nathaniel and Janet (Currie) Dailey; m. Harvey Bradley Jones, Nov. 15, 1952; children: Dailey, Janet Currie, Ellis Bradley. Student, Carleton Coll., 1943-44, U. Mont., 1944-46, UCLA, 1959. Owner Mary Jones Interiors. Founder, treas. Jr. Art Council, Los Angeles County Mus., 1953-55, v.p., 1955-56; mem. costume council Pasadena (Calif.) Philharm.; co-founder Art Rental Gallery, 1953, chmn. art and architecture tour, 1955; founding mem., sec. Art Alliance, Pasadena Art Mus., 1955-56; benefit chmn. Pasadena Girls Club, 1959, bd. dirs., 1958-60; chmn. Los Angeles Tennis Patron's Assn. Benefit, 1965; sustaining Jr. League Pasadena; mem. docent council Los Angeles County Mus.; mem. costume council Los Angeles County Mus. Art, program chmn. 20th Century Greatest Designers; mem. blue ribbon com. Los Angeles Music Center; benefit chmn. Venice com. Internat. Fund for Monuments, 1971; bd. dirs. Art Ctr. 100, Pasadena, 1988—; co-chmn. benefit Harvard Coll. Scholarship Fund, 1974, steering com. benefit, 1987, Otis Art Inst., 1975; mem. Harvard-Radcliffe scholarship dinner com., 1985; mem. adv. bd. Estelle Doheny Eye Found., 1976, chmn. benefit, 1980; adv. bd. Loyola U. Sch. Fine Arts, Los Angeles, Art Ctr. Sch. Design, Pasadena, Calif., 1987—; patron chmn. Benefit Achievement Rewards for Coll. Scientists, 1988; chmn. com. Sch. Am. Ballet Benefit, 1988, N.Y.C.; bd. dirs. Founders Music Center, Los Angeles, 1977-81; mem. nat. adv. council Sch. Am. Ballet, N.Y.C., nat. co-chmn. gala, 1980; adv. council on fine arts Loyola-Marymount U.; mem. Los Angeles Olympic Com., 1984, The Colleagues; founding mem. Mus. Contemporary Art, 1986. Mem. Kappa Alpha Theta. Clubs: Valley Hunt (Pasadena); Calif. (Los Angeles). Home: 10375 Wilshire Blvd Apt 8B Los Angeles CA 90024

JONES, MICHAEL HAROLD, veterinarian; b. Tacoma, July 18, 1947; s. Marlowe Harold and Helen Jean Jones; m. Amy Diane Shemet, June 1972 (div. Mar. 1979); m. Mary Byers, Sept. 28, 1985; 1 child, Alexandra Michelle. BS, Wash. State U., Pullman, 1969, DVM, 1973. Veterinarian Jones Animal Hosp., Tacoma, 1973—, owner, 1979—; vet. cons. Point Defiance Zoo and Aquarium, Tacoma, 1973—, NW Trek Wildlife Park, Eatonville, Wash., 1974-79; dir. Pierce County Animal Emergency Clinic, Tacoma, 1987—. Contbr. articles on exotic animals to profl. jours. Pres. Tacoma Community Coll. Found., 1987-88; vice-chmn. activities council Tacoma Art Mus., 1986—; chmn. Tacoma Wine Festival 1984-86, Tacoma Visitor and Conv. Bur., 1984. Mem. Am. Animal Hosp. Assn., South Puget Sound Vet. Med. Assn. (pres. 1985-86), Am. Vet. Med. Assn., Internat. Assn. Aquatic Animal Life Medicine, Am. Assn. Zoo Veterinarians, Assn. Avian Veterinarians, Tacoma C. of C. (bd. dirs. 1980-86), Tacoma Zool. Soc. (pres. 1978-79, v.p. 1988—), Alpha Psi. Lodges: Kiwanis (pres. local club 1978), Rotary (bd. dirs. 1987—), Elks, Masons. Office: Jones Animal Hosp Inc P/S 3322 S Union Tacoma WA 98409

JONES, NANCY C., construction executive; b. Cody, Wyo., Mar. 16, 1942; d. John Carl and Catherine (Schaff) Buckingham; m. William D. Norman, Feb. 5, 1965 (div. 1972); 1 child, Kelly Blue; m. Raymond M. Jones, May 31, 1974; children: Dan, Stephen, Renee, Kelly, Susie. Student, Colo. State U., 1963-65. Owner J.B. Blue Restaurant, Gillette, Wyo., 1968-74; pres. WoodBuck, Inc., Sheridan, Wyo., 1973—; bd. dirs. Shayne and Shortco, Inc., Belen, N.Mex., 1983—. Republican. Roman Catholic. Home: 1415 Easy St Sheridan WY 82801 Office: Shayne & Shortco Inc 385 Rio Communities Belen NM 87002

JONES, OGDEN STERLING, aerospace and astonautical engineer; b. Lawrence, Kans., July 31, 1962; s. Ogden Sherman Jr. and Jean (Murray) J.; m. Jennifer Huei Lin, Dec. 27, 1986. BS in Aerospace and Astronautical Engring., MIT, 1985; MS in Aerospace and Astronautical Engring., U. Mich., 1985. Propulsion engr. Boeing Aerospace Co., Kent, Wash., 1985—. Mem. AIAA. Home: 1529 29th Ave Seattle WA 98122

JONES, PAUL MAX, chemist; b. Paterson, N.J., Apr. 3, 1955; s. Paul Gibson and Violet Yolanda (Orsi) J.; m. Cecilia Annete Sack, Mar. 1, 1980; 1 child, Ryan Kyle. BA, SUNY, Binghamton, 1982; student, Stanford U., 1982—. Research asst. SUNY, Binghamton, 1980-82; assoc. scientist IBM Instruments, Danbury, Conn., 1982-85; sr. assoc. scientist IBM Gen. Products Div., San Jose, 1985—. Contbr. articles to profl. jours. Mem. ACS, Sigma Xi. Office: Stanford University Chemistry Dept. Stanford CA 94305

JONES, RALPH DARRELL, manufacturing executive; b. Cogur d'Alene, Idaho, Apr. 17, 1936; s. Rollen Thurbert and Florence Caroline (Tapley) J.; m. Beatrice Darlene Blehm, Nov. 27, 1955; children: Delvin Ralph, Darrell Darwin, Della Darlene. Student, Walla Wallege Coll., 1954-55; AA in Mgmt., Portland Community Coll., Portland, Oreg., 1971. Plant mgr. Woodfold-Marco, Forest Grove, Oreg., 1958—; instr. Portland Community Coll., 1977—. Bd. dirs. Tualatin Valley Jr. Acad., Beaverton, Oreg., 1973-85, chmn. bd., 1980-82. Mem. Forest Grove C. of C. (bd. dirs. 1970-74, pres. 1974). Home: Rte 3 Box 614 Cornelius OR 97113 Office: Woodfold-Marco Mfg Inc PO Box 346 1811 18th St Forest Grove OR 97116

JONES, REINOLD JOSEPH, thoracic surgeon; b. San Francisco, Nov. 3, 1925; s. Reinold Joseph and Mary C. (Ward) J.; m. Marjorie Ann Smith, June 23, 1964; children: Trish, Ron. B in Mech. Engring., U. Minn., 1946; MD, Creighton U., 1953. Diplomate Am. Bd. Surgery, Am. Bd. Thoracic Surgery. Assoc. clin. prof. surgery U. Calif. Med. Sch., San Francisco, 1970-88; chief of staff Seton Med. Ctr., Daley City, Calif., 1975-76, chmn. dept. surgery, 1987—; chmn. dept. surgery St. Mary's Hosp., San Francisco, 1984-87. Served to lt. USN, 1953-55. Fellow ACS; mem. Soc. Thoracic Surgeons, Western Thoracic Surg. Assn. (founding mem.), San Francisco Surg. Soc. (councilor 1984-88). Roman Catholic. Club: Olympic (San Francisco). Office: 2645 Ocean Ave San Francisco CA 94132

JONES, ROBERT ALONZO, economist; b. Evanston, Ill., Mar. 15, 1937; s. Robert Vernon and Elsie Pierce (Brown) J.; m. Kathleen Mary Bush, Aug. 16, 1958; children: Lindsay Rae, Robert Pierce, Gregory Alan, William Kenneth. AB, Middlebury Coll., 1959; MBA, Northwestern U., 1961. Sr. research officer Bank of Am., San Francisco, 1969-74; v.p., dir. fin. forecasting Chase Econometrics, San Francisco, 1974-76; chmn. bd. Money Market Services, Inc., Belmont, Calif., 1974-86; chmn. bd. MMS Internat., Redwood City, Calif., 1986-89, Market News Service, Inc., N.Y.C., 1987-89;

dir. Money Market Services, Ltd., London, 1981-85, Money Market Services, Ltd., Hong Kong, 1982-85; chmn. bd. trustees GeonomicsInst. Econ. 1986—; chmn. bd. Jones Internat., 1989—; instr. money and banking, Am. Inst. Banking, San Francisco, 1971, 72. Councilman, City of Belmont (Calif.), 1970-77, mayor, 1971, 72, 75, 76; dir. San Mateo County Transit Dist., 1975-77; chmn. San Mateo County Council of Mayors, 1975-76; trustee Incline Village Gen. Improvement Dist., 1984-85. Author: U.S. Financial System and the Federal Reserve, 1974, Power of Coinage, 1987. Named Hon. Life Mem. Calif. PTA, ordo honorum Kappa Delta Rho Nat. Fraternity. Mem. Nat. Assn. Bus. Economists, San Francisco Bond Club. Republican. Methodist.

JONES, ROBERT EDWARD, justice state supreme court; b. Portland, Oreg., July 5, 1927; s. Howard C. and Leita (Hendricks) J.; m. Pearl F. Jensen, May 29, 1948; children—Jeffrey Scott, Julie Lynn. B.A., U. Hawaii, 1949; J.D., Lewis and Clark Coll., 1953; LL.D. (hon.), City U., Seattle, 1984. Bar: Oreg. 1953. Trial atty. Portland, Oreg., 1953-63; judge Oreg. Circuit Ct., Portland, 1963-83; justice Oreg. Supreme Ct., Salem, 1983—; adj. prof. Willamette Univ. Law Sch., Salem, Oreg., 1989—; mem. faculty Nat. Jud. Coll., Am. Acad. Jud. Edn.; pres. Oreg. Circuit Judges Assn., 1967—, Oreg. Trial Lawyers Assn., 1959; former mem. Oreg. Evidence Revision Commn., Oreg. Ho. of Reps.; former chair Oreg. Commn. Prison Terms and Parole Standards; adj. prof. Northwestern Sch. Law, Lewis and Clark Coll. 1963—. Bd. overseers Lewis and Clark Coll. Served to capt. JAGC, USNR. Recipient merit award Multnomah Bar Assn., 1979; Citizen award NCCJ, Legal Citizen of the Yr. award Law Related Edn. Project, 1988; Service to Mankind award Sertoma Club Oreg.; James Madison award Sigma Delta Chi; named Disting. Grad., Northwestern Sch. Law. Mem. State Bar Oreg. (former chmn. continuing legal edn. com.). Office: Oreg Supreme Ct Supreme Ct Bldg Salem OR 97310

JONES, ROBERT EUGENE, systems engineering executive; b. St. Paul, Dec. 16, 1923; s. Keith Andrew and Gertrude Mabel (Colwell) J.; m. Barbara Mason, June 6, 1944 (div. 1963); children: Douglas; m. Joy Hewins, Dec. 28, 1964; children: Keith, Christopher, David. BA, U. N.C., 1948; MA, U. Colo., Boulder, 1962, PhD, 1966. Asst. dir. US Bi-Nat. Ctr., San Jose, Costa Rica, 1948-50; prodn. control mgr. Brown Brockmeyer Electric Mfg., Dayton, Ohio, 1950-51; systems analyst Wright Patterson AFB, Dayton, 1951-52; chief mgmt. engring. br. Air Def. Command, Colorado Springs, Colo., 1952-60; dir. systems evaluation N. Am. Aerospace Def. and Space Command, Colorado Springs, 1960-84; asst. to v.p. Teledyne Brown Engring., Colorado Springs, 1984-86; project mgr., Rockwell Internat., 1986—; lectr. U. Colo., Colorado Springs, 1966-72. Contbr. in field. Chmn. dist. com. Pikes Peak coun.l Boy Scouts Am., Colorado Springs, 1960-74; bd. dirs. Broadmoor Ski Racing Acad., Colorado Springs, 1981-84; vice chmn. Com. to Elect W.W. Cogswell III, Colorado Springs, 1983. With U.S. Army, 1943-46. Recipient Meritorious Civilian Svc. award Sec. of the Air Force, 1973, Exceptional Civilian Svc. award, Sec. of Air Force, 1983. Mem. N.Y. Acad. Sci., Ops. Rsch. Soc. Am., Am. Econ. Assn., AAAS. Episcopalian. Office: Rockwell Internat 1250 Academy Park Loop Colorado Springs CO 80910

JONES, ROBERT THOMAS, management executive; b. Cleburne, Tex., Dec. 10, 1947; s. A. V. and Eliza Lorene (Bracken) J.; m. Diana Lynn Turley, May 23, 1970; children: Matthew Aaron, Andrew Harold. BS, U. Ariz., 1970, MS, 1985. Cert. secondary tchr., Ariz. Tchr. Bowie (Ariz.) Pub. Schs., 1971-73, Marana (Ariz.) Pub. Schs., 1973-84; instr. Pima Community Coll., Tucson, Ariz., 1975-79; dir. U. Ariz., Tucson, 1984-86; coord. Pima Community Coll., Tucson, 1986-88; owner RTJ Enterprises, Marana, 1986—; dir. Ariz. Nat. Livestock Show, Phoenix, 1988—; mem. regional coun. Pima Assn. Govts., Tucson, 1987-89. Contbr. articles to profl. jours. Councilman Town of Marana (Ariz.), 1982-89, mayor, 1987-89. With U.S. Army Nat. Guard, 1970-76. Mem. Nat. Vocat. Agrl. Tchrs. Assn. (life, pres. 1981-82), Ariz. Fairs Assn. Democrat. Office: Ariz Nat Livestock Show 1826 W McDowell Phoenix AZ 85007

JONES, ROBIN, city planner; b. Los Angeles, Sept. 15, 1949; d. Walter Alfred and Caroline (Nemcic) J.; m. Martin G. Gellen, March 21, 1981. BA, UCLA, 1971; MA in City Planning, Harvard U., 1974. Planner city planning dept., City of San Francisco, 1974-87; dir. capital planning U. Calif., San Francisco, 1987—. Mem. Am. Planning Assn. Democrat. Office: U Calif PO Box 0286 San Francisco CA 94143

JONES, ROGER CLYDE, electrical engineer, educator; b. Lake Andes, S.D., Aug. 17, 1919; s. Robert Clyde and Martha (Albertson) J.; m. Katherine M. Tucker, June 7, 1952; children: Linda Lee, Vonnie Lynette. B.S., U. Nebr., 1949; M.S., U. Md., 1953; Ph.D. U. Md., 1963. With U.S. Naval Research Lab., Washington, 1949-57; staff sr. engr. to chief engr. Melpar, Inc., Falls Church, Va., 1957-58; cons. project engr. Melpar, Inc., 1958-59, sect. head physics, 1959-64, chief scientist for physics, 1964; prof. dept. elec. engring. U. Ariz., Tucson, 1964—; dir. quantum electronics lab. U. Ariz., 1968-88, adj. prof. radiology, 1978-86, adj. prof. radiation-oncology, 1986-88, prof. of radiation-oncology, 1988—; guest prof. in exptl. oncology Inst. Cancer Research, Aarhus, Denmark, 1982-83. Patentee in field. Served with AUS, 1942-45. Mem. Am. Phys. Soc., Optical Soc. Am., Bioelectromagnetics Soc., IEEE, AAAS, NSPE, Am. Congress on Surveying and Mapping, Eta Kappa Nu, Pi Mu Epsilon. Home: 5809 E 3d St Tucson AZ 85711 Office: U Ariz Dept Elec and Computer Engring Tucson AZ 85711

JONES, RONALD H., computer information systems executive; b. San Diego, Feb. 11, 1938; s. Henry G. and Geneva H. (Hodges) J.; m. Carol Sue Carmichael, Dec. 9, 1967. BS, San Diego State Coll., 1959, MS, 1961. Project mgr. UNIVAC, San Diego, 1961-67, Computer Scis. Corp., San Diego, 1967-75; v.p. Interactive, Inc., San Diego, 1975—; also bd. dirs. Contbr. articles to profl. jours. Advisor San Diego State Coll.; Rep. nat. committeeman, 1979—. Mem. Am. Prodn. & Inventory Control Soc., Assn. Computing Machinery. Presbyterian. Home: 2484 Pine St San Diego CA 92103 Office: Interactive Inc 5095 Murphy Canyon Rd San Diego CA 92123

JONES, RONALD ROBERT, neurological surgeon, educator; b. Lorain, Ohio, Nov. 26, 1937; s. Earle R. and Elizabeth T. (Marshall) J.; m. Phyllis D. Strauser, 1958 (div. 1985); children: Rhonda, Jacqueline, Jennifer. Student, St. Meinrad Coll., 1955-56, John Carroll U., 1956-57; BS, Ohio State U., 1959, MD, 1963. Diplomate Am. Bd. Neurosurgery. Intern Chgo. Wesley Meml. Hosp., 1963-64, resident in gen. surgery, 1964-65, asst. resident in neurosurgery, 1965-66, sr. resident, 1967-68; resident in neuropathology Northwestern U. Med. Sch., Chgo., 1965-66, assoc. div. neurosurgery, 1971—; fellow in neurology State U. Iowa, 1966-67; asst. resident in neurosurgery Children's Meml. Hosp., Chgo., 1967; chief resident, clin. instr. neur. surgery VA Rsch. Hosp., Chgo., 1967-68; pvt. practice Oak Lawn, Ill., 1974—, Hobbs, N.Mex., 1987—; assoc. attending Little Company of Mary Hosp., Evergreen Park, Ill., 1973-80, Palos Community Hosp., Palos Heights, Ill., 1975—, St. Francis Hosp., Blue Island, Ill., 1977—; sr. staff, div. head neur. surgery Christ Hosp and Med. Ctr., Oak Lawn, Ill., 1974—, Lea Regional Hosp., 1987—; presenter in field. Contbr. articles to med. jours. Comdr. USN, 1969-71. Mem. AMA, AAAS, Internat. Soc. Pediatric Neurosurgeons, Congress Neur. Surgeons, Am. Acad. Neur. and Orthopaedic Surgeons, Cen. Neurosurg. Soc., Soc. Mil. Surgeons U.S., Ill. Med. Soc., Chgo. Med. Soc., Chgo. Neur. Soc., Interurban Neur. Soc., Inst. Medicine, Hobbs C. of C., Hobbs Country Club, Midlothian Country Club (Chgo.). Republican. Roman Catholic. Office: Neurosurg Cons 5419 N Lovington Hwy Ste 21 Hobbs NM 88240

JONES, RONNIE K., infosystems executive; b. Ft. Worth, Jan. 8, 1943; s. Louis Wyman and Gwendolyn F. (Littlefield) J.; m. Mary Ann Warren, Apt. 19, 1963. AA, Cen. Tex. Coll., 1973; B Gen. Studies, U. Nebr., Omaha, 1974; MBA, Ariz. State U., 1977. Ops. trainee, systems analyst First Western Bank & Trust, L.A., 1963-66; budget analyst City of Tempe (Ariz.), 1974-79; asst. dir. Office Mgmt. and Budget, Phoenix, 1979-83; pres. Mgmt. Decision Systems, Inc., Tempe, 1983—; instr. Mesa (Ariz.) Community Coll., 1975-76; lectr. pub. affairs Ariz. State U., Tempe, 1978, Nat. Jud. Coll., Reno, 1985-86. Bd. dirs. fund raising Boy Scouts Am., Tempe, 1978; sec. Rep. Men's Club, Tempe, 1976. Capt. U.S. Army, 1966-73. Mem. Personal Computer Users Group, DBase Users Group, Ventura Users Group, Automated Acctg. Users Group. Office: Mgmt Decision Systems 1109 E Carmen St Tempe AZ 85283

JONES, RUSSELL DEAN, real estate developer; b. L.A., Aug. 17, 1933; s. Fred S. and Rose Marie (Mauler) J.; m. Hae Young Lee; children: Kellianne P. Jones Wilder, Katelyn M. BBA, Loyola U., L.A., 1954; JD, Loyola U., 1957. Bar: Calif.; lic. real estate broker, Calif. Asst. city adminstr. City of Culver City, Calif., 1958-60; sr. asst. city mgr. City of Santa Monica, Calif., 1960-64; city adminstr. City of Placentia, Calif., 1964-67; asst. dir. Calif. Dept. Housing & Community Devel., Sacramento, 1967-68; v.p. Boise Cascade Bldg. Co., L.A., 1968-72; pres. Russell D. Jones Group, L.A., 1972-81; v.p. hotel devel. Marriott Corp., L.A., 1981—; lectr. in field. Mem. Gov.'s Adv. Com. on Factory Built Housing, Sacramento, 1969-72; mem. subdivision adv. com. Dept. Real Estate, Sacramento, 1968-71. Named Alumnus of the Yr., Alpha Delta Gamma, 1964. Mem. State Bar of Calif., Internat. City Mgmt. Assn., We. Govtl. Research Assn., Loyola Marymount U. Alumni Assn. (bd. dirs. 1981-84), Bldg. Industry Assn. Calif. (v.p. 1971-72), Alpha Delta Gamma (nat. pres. 1956-57). Republican. Roman Catholic. Home: 4129 Admirable Dr Rancho Palos Verdes CA 90274

JONES, THOMAS EBERLE, small business owner; b. Tucson, Aug. 17, 1923; s. John Willard and Elsie (Eberle) J.; m. Nance, 1959 (div. 1964); children: Thomas Eberle Jr., Deborah Leigh. Student, U. Ariz., 1946-54. Owner, operator Rubitom's, Tucson, 1953—. With USN, 1941-46. Roman Catholic. Home: 5721 E Camden Tucson AZ 85712 Office: Rubitoms 5334 S Nogales Hwy Tucson AZ 85706

JONES, THOMAS ROBERT, social worker; b. Escanaba, Mich., Jan. 3, 1950; s. Gene Milton and Alica Una (Mattson) J.; m. Joy Sedlock. BA, U. Laverne, 1977; MSW, U. Hawaii, 1979. Social work assoc. Continuing Care Services, Camarillo, Calif., 1973-78; psychiat. social worker Camarillo State Hosp., 1980-84; psychotherapist Terkensha Child Treatment Ctr., Sacramento, Calif., 1984-86; psychiat. social worker Napa (Calif.) State Hosp., 1986-87, Vets. Home Calif., Yountville, 1987—. Mem. Nat. Assn. Social Workers, Soc. Clin. Social Work, Am. Orthopsychiat. Assn., Acad. Cert. Social Workers, Assn. for Advancement Behavior Therapy. Home: PO Box 1095 Yountville CA 94599 Office: Veterans Home of Calif Yountville CA 94599

JONES, THOMAS VICTOR, aerospace company executive; b. Pomona, Calif., July 21, 1920; s. Victor March and Elizabeth (Brettelle) J.; m. Ruth Nagel, Aug. 10, 1946; children: Ruth Marilyn, Peter Thomas. Student, Pomona Jr. Coll., 1938-40; BA with distinction, Stanford U., 1942; LLD (hon.), George Washington U., 1967. Engr. El Segundo div. Douglas Aircraft Co., 1941-47; tech. adviser Brazilian Air Ministry, 1947-51; prof., head dept. Brazilian Inst. Tech., 1947-51; staff cons. Air Staff of USAF, Rand Corp., 1951-53; asst. to chief engr. Northrop Corp., Los Angeles, 1953, dep. chief engr., 1954-56, dir. devel. planning, 1956-57, corp. v.p., 1957, sr. v.p., 1958-59, pres., 1959-76, chief exec. officer, 1960—, chmn. bd., 1963—; bd. dirs. MCA Inc., Universal City, Calif. Author: Capabilities and Operating Costs of Possible Future Transport Airplanes, 1953. Bd. dirs. Los Angeles World Affairs Council, Calif. Nature Conservancy; trustee Inst. for Strategic Studies, London. Fellow AIAA (hon.); mem. Los Angeles C. of C., Navy League U.S. (life), Aerospace Industries Assn., U. So. Calif. Assocs., Town Hall, Nat. Acad. Engring. Clubs: California; The Beach (Santa Monica); Georgetown, California Yacht, Bohemian. Home: 1050 Moraga Dr Los Angeles CA 90049 Office: Northrop Corp 1840 Century Park E Century City Los Angeles CA 90067 *

JONES, THORNTON KEITH, research chemist; b. Brawley, Calif., Dec. 17, 1923; s. Alfred George and Madge Jones; m. Evalee Vestal, July 4, 1965; children: Brian Keith, Donna Eileen. BS, U. Calif., Berkeley, 1949, postgrad., 1951-52. Research chemist Griffin Chem. Co., Richmond, Calif., 1949-55; western product devel. and improvement mgr. Nopco Chem. Co., Richmond, Calif., 1955; research chemist Chevron Research Co., Richmond, 1956-65, research chemist in spl. products research and devel., 1965-1982; product quality mgr. Chevron USA, Inc., San Francisco, 1982-87, ret. Patentee in field. Vol. fireman and officer, Terra Linda, Calif., 1957-64; mem. adv. com. Terra Linda Dixie Elem. Sch. Dist., 1960-64. Served with Signal Corps, U.S. Army, 1943-46. Mem. Am. Chem. Soc., Forest Products Research Soc., Am. Wood Preservers Assn., Alpha Chi Sigma. Republican. Presbyterian.

JONES, TOM D., software company executive; b. Hillsdale, Mich., Nov. 13, 1939; s. Harry D. and Melissa Ann (Martin) J.; m. Angela S. Wurl, June 22, 1963; children: Todd R., Michelle N. BS, MS in Math., Mich. State U., East Lansing, 1962; MS in Computer Engring, U. Mich., 1968. Mathematician Honeywell, Inc., Mpls., 1963-67; mgr. software devel. Com-Share, Inc., Ann Arbor, Mich., 1968-71; cons. K@ Systems, Inc., Portland, Oreg., 1971-78; sr. systems analyst Computer Mgmt. Systems, Inc., Portland, 1978-83; v.p. engring. Tri-Com Systems, Inc., Portland, 1983-88, also bd. dirs.; bd. dirs. The Metier Group, Seattle. bd. dirs. Portland Mountain Rescue, 1985-88. Mem. Mazamas Club (Portland). Avocations: mountain climbing, golf, photography. Home: 6980 SW Bancroft Way Portland OR 97225 Office: Tri-Com Systems 6443 SW Beau-Hills Hwy Portland OR 97221

JONES, VERNON QUENTIN, surveyor; b. Sioux City, Iowa, May 6, 1930; s. Vernon Boyd and Winnifred Rhoda (Bremmer) J.; student UCLA, 1948-50; m. Rebeca Buckovecz, Oct. 1981; children:Steven Vernon, Gregory Richard, Stanley Alan. Draftsman III Pasadena (Calif.) city engr., 1950-53; sr. civil engring. asst. L.A. County engr., L.A., 1953-55; v.p. Treadwell Engring. Corp., Arcadia, Calif., 1955-61, pres., 1961-64; pres. Hillcrest Engring. Corp., Arcadia, 1961-64; dep. county surveyor, Ventura, Calif., 1964-78; propr. Vernon Jones Land Surveyor, Riviera, Ariz., 1978—; city engr. Needles (Calif.), 1980-87; instr. Mohave Community Coll., 1987—. Chmn. graphic tech. com. Ventura Unified Sch. Dist., 1972-78, mem. career adv. com., 1972-74; mem. engring. adv. com. Pierce Coll., 1973; pres. Mgmt. Employees of Ventura County, 1974. V.p. Young Reps. of Ventura County, 1965. Pres., Marina Pacifica Homeowners Assn., 1973. Mem. League Calif. Surveying Orgns. (pres. 1975), Am. Congress on Surveying and Mapping (chmn. So. Calif. sect. 1976), Am. Soc. Photogrammetry, Am. Pub. Works Assn., County Engr. Assn. Calif. Home: 913E San Juan Ct Riviera AZ 86442

JONES, VICTOR CRAIG, computer company executive; b. Ft. Worth, Mar. 21, 1955; s. Reeder Putman and Rebecca Broucious (Daniels) J.; m. Patricia Kay Halloran; children: Tyler Craig, Justin Lee. Student, U. Ariz., 1973-74. Asst. mgr. Marie Callanders Restaurants, Buena Park, Calif., 1974-79; life underwriter Prudential Ins., Riverside, Calif., 1979-80; mgr. Cracker Barrel Restaurants, Anaheim, Calif., 1980-83; sales rep. Database/Computerland, Phoenix, 1983-84; dir. ops. Dataphaz/Computerland, Phoenix, 1984-87, facilities planning mgr., 1987-89, mgr. info. systems, 1989—. Cubmaster Cub Scouts Am. Mem. Am. Mgmt. Assn. Republican. Baptist. Office: Dataphaz/Computerland 15002 N 25th Dr Phoenix AZ 85023

JONES, WARREN WILL, publisher, consultant; b. Seattle, Feb. 4, 1929; s. J. Will and Ethel H. (Scott) J.; m. Ning-Su Ong, May 13, 1965 (div. 1985); 1 child, Ling-Yen. BA, U. Wash., Seattle, 1951; M in City Planning, U. Calif., Berkeley, 1957. Prin. Duncan & Jones, Berkeley, 1965-78; chmn. dept. continuing edn. in environ. design U. Calif., Berkeley, 1972-86, lectr. in city planning, 1978-87; owner, chief adminstrv. officer Solano Press, Point Arena, Calif., 1984—; cons., tchr. U. Calif. Extension, Berkeley and Irvine, Calif., 1980-86. Author: (with others) What Do I Do Next?, 1980. Cpl. U.S. Army, 1953-55, CBI. Mem. Am. Planning Assn. (sec., treas. Calif. chpt. 1965-67). Democrat. Office: Solano Press PO Box 773 Point Arena CA 95468

JONES, WYMAN H., librarian; b. St. Louis, Dec. 17, 1929; s. Jay Hugh and Nina Marie (Dallas) J.; children—Gregory Foster, Mark Jay, Manson Matthew, Ross Christopher. Student, So. Ill. U., 1945-47, Washington U., St. Louis, 1948-50; B.A., Adams State Coll., Alamosa, Colo., 1956; postgrad., U. Iowa, 1956-57; M.S. in L.S, U. Tex., 1958. Head sci. and industry div. Dallas Pub. Library, 1958-60, chief br. services, 1960-64; dir. Ft. Worth Pub. Library, 1964-70; city librarian Los Angeles Pub. Library, 1970—; cons. library bldg. and site selections, 1962—; Mem. Gov. Tex. Adv. Bd., 1969-70, Calif. Bd. Library Examiners, 1970—. Author: (with E. Castagna) The Library Reaches Out, 1964; also articles. Bd. dirs. Young Symphony Orch., Ft. Worth, 1967-69. Served with USAF, 1951-55. Mem. ALA (legis. com. 1974-78), S.W. Libr. Assn. (pres.-elect 1967), Tex. Libr.Assn. (pres. pub. libr. div. 1966), Calif. Libr. Assn. (coun. 1972—), L.A. Pub. Libr. Office: LA Pub Libr 630 W 5th St Los Angeles CA 90017

JONGEWARD, GEORGE RONALD, systems analyst; b. Yakima, Wash., Aug. 9, 1934; s. George Ira and Dorothy Marie (Cronk) J.; m. Janet Jeanne Williams, July 15, 1955; children: Mary Jeanne, Dona Lee, Karen Anne. BA, Whitworth Coll., 1957; postgrad., Utah State U., 1961. Sr. systems analyst Computer Scis. Corp., Honolulu, 1969-71; cons. in field Honolulu, 1972-76; prin. The Hobby Co., Honolulu, 1977-81; sr. systems analyst Computer Systems Internat., Honolulu, 1981—; instr. EDP Hawaii Pacific Coll., Honolulu, 1982—. Mem. car show com. Easter Seal Soc., Honolulu. 1977-82; active Variety Club, Honolulu. Mem. Mensa (local pres. 1967-69). Republican. Presbyterian. Club: Triple-9. Home: 400 Hobron Ln #2611 Honolulu HI 96815 Office: Computer Systems Internat 841 Bishop St #501 Honolulu HI 96813

JONKER, PETER EMILE, gas company executive; b. The Hague, The Netherlands, Sept. 15, 1948; came to U.S., 1966, naturalized, 1985; s. Jacob and Jurrina (Wories) J.; m. Janet Lynn Gotfredson, Sept. 6, 1974; children: Jeffrey, Annelies. BSChemE cum laude, U. So. Calif., 1971, MSChemE, 1972; JD with honors, Western State U., Fullerton, Calif., 1979. Bar: Calif. 1979. Research engr. Union Oil Co., Los Angeles, 1972-75, regulations coordinator, 1975-79, atty., 1979; mgr. govtl. and pub. affairs Western Liquefied Nat. Gas, Los Angeles, 1979-81; mgr. environ. permitting Tosco Corp., Los Angeles, 1981-83; mgr. regional pub. affairs So. Calif. Gas. Co., Los Angeles, 1983-85, mgr. rate design, demand forecast and analysis, 1986-88, mgr. fed. energy affairs, 1988—; mem. So. Coast Air Quality Mgmt. Dist. Adv. Council, Los Angeles, 1983-85. Editor Western State Law Rev., 1976-79; contbr. articles to profl. jours. Trustee, deacon San Marino (Calif.) Presbyn. Community Ch., 1980—; councilman U. So. Calif. Engring. Student Council, Los Angeles, 1971-72, dir. Engring. Alumni Assn., 1971-72; fgn. del. White House Conf., Washington, 1971. Mem. Am. Gas Assn., Air Pollution Control Assn. (v.p. West coast chpt. 1984, 85), Fed. Energy Bar Assn., Pacific Coast Gas Assn., Tau Beta Pi (pres., v.p. Calif. Delta chpt. 1970-71). Republican. Home: 2450 Melville San Marino CA 91108 Office: So Calif Gas Co 810 S Flower St ML 108T Los Angeles CA 90017

JONSEN, RICHARD WILIAM, educational administrator; b. San Francisco, Mar. 29, 1934; s. Albert Rupert and Helen Catherine (Sweigert) J.; m. Ann Margaret Parsons, Nov. 22, 1955; children: Marie, Eric, Gregory, Stephen, Matthew. BA, U. Santa Clara, 1955; MA, San Jose (Calif.) State U., 1970; PhD, Stanford U., 1973. Pub.'s rep. Hearst Advt. Service, San Francisco, 1955-58; alumni dir. U. Santa Clara, Calif., 1958-70; dir. admissions, asst. dean. Sch. Edn. Syracuse (N.Y.) U., 1972-76; project dir. Edn. Commn. States, Denver, 1976-77; project dir. Western Interstate Commn. Higher Edn., Boulder, Colo., 1977-79, dep. dir., 1979—. Author: State Policy and Independent Higher Education, 1975, Small Liberal Arts Colleges, 1978; editor: Higher Education Policies in the Information Age, 1987. Roman Catholic. Home: 4181 S Pontiac St Denver CO 80237 Office: Western Interstate Commn Higher Edn PO Drawer P Boulder CO 80302

JONTRY, RICHARD, psychologist; b. Bklyn., May 5, 1942; s. Henry and Esther (Schor) J.; BA, City U. N.Y., 1964; MA, New Sch., 1966; PhD, Ind. No. U., 1973; m. Sharon Gladson; children: Brie, Ari. Clin. psychology intern N.J. Neuro-Psychiat. Inst., Princeton, 1966-67, research scientist bur. research in neurology and psychiatry, 1967-73; dir. Center Family Interaction, Hatboro, Pa., 1972-74; dir. tng. and edn. bur. substance abuse, div. mental health Del. Dept. Health and Social Services, New Castle, 1974-79; dir. Intercept, Oxford, Pa., 1981—; clin. supr. ARC Counseling Services, So. Chester County Med. Ctr., West Grove, Pa.; adj. prof. Washington Coll., Chestertown, Md., 1980—; cons. Four Winds Alcoholism Rehab. Ctr., N.Mex., 1986—, Family Crises Ctr.; condr. tng. seminars for mental health profls.; mem. Cecil County (Md.) Mental Health and Addictions Adv. Bd., 1970-81, Cecil County Anti-Drug Abuse Action Com., 1980-82, Talbot County (Md.) Sch. Health Curriculum Adv. Com., 1980-82; adv. bd. Lincoln (Pa.) U., 1975-79, NE Regional Support Center, New Haven, 1976-79, Eastern Area Alcohol Tng. Program, Bloomfield, Conn., 1976-79, Johns Hopkins U. Tng. Inst. Alcoholism Counselors, 1976-79; cons. in field. Mem. Internat. Imagery Assn., Assn. Specialists Group Works, Assn. Labor Mgmt. Adminstrs. and Cons. on Alcoholism, Am. Personnel and Guidance Assn., N.Y. Inst. Gestalt Therapy, Psi Chi. Home: 3413 Monterey Cir Farmington NM 87401 Office: Four Winds Addiction Recovery Ctr 1313 Mission Ave Box 736 Farmington NM 87499

JORDAN, BONITA ADELE, television producer; b. Dayton, Ohio, Mar. 9, 1948; d. Theodore and Faye Annette (Fields) Sampson; divorced; 1 son, Brett Anthony. Student, Habor Jr. Coll., Wilmington, Calif., 1966-68. Assoc. producer Dick Clark Prodns., Hollywood, Calif., 1972-73, Sta. KNBC-TV, L.A., 1973-75; account exec. Ameron co., Monterey Park, Calif., 1976; prodn. coordinator Movie of the Week for CBS, Paramount Studios, Hollywood, 1977-78; asst. to producer Glen Larson Prodns., Film TV Devel. and Casting, 20th Century Fox, Beverly Hills, Calif., 1978-84; prodn. coordinator Universal Studios, 1986; prodn. coordinator Rags to Riches, 1st season Len Hill Films/New World Television, 1986-87; prodn. coordinator Sledge Hammer, 2d season, The Incredible Hulk Returns New World TV, 1987—. Exec. producer Calif. Magic at the Hollywood Palace, for Jesse Jackson campaign, 1988; prodn. coord. "Cindy" CBS-TV Paramount Studios, 1977-78, "The Ultimate Adventure Company" NBC-TV Universal Studios, 1986, "Rags to Riches" NBC-TV and New World Television, 1986-87, "Circus" ABC-TV, Phoenix Entertainment and New World Television, 1987, "Sledge Hammer" ABC-TV, 1987, "The Incredible Hulk Returns" NBC-TV, 1987—. Co-chmn., asst. to producer telethon United High Blood Pressure Found., 1977, mem. exec. bd., 1975-78, treas., 1977. Recipient cert. achievement City of Los Angeles and UCLA Mardi Gras, 1974. Mem. Women in Film, Nat. Assn. Media Women (corr. rec. sec. 1974-75). Home: 14215 Calvert St #4 Van Nuys CA 91401 Office: New World TV 1440 Sepulveda Blvd Los Angeles CA 90025

JORDAN, DARRYL FRANKLIN, civil engineer; b. Glenallen, Alaska, June 14, 1955; s. Franklin Jordan and Joyce Mae (Ewan) Kallander; m. Leigh Andrea Slaughter, June 30, 1979 (div. 1981); m. Cherie Jean Cottrill, Apr. 21, 1982. B.S., MIT, 1977, M.S., 1978. Staff engr. R&M Cons., Anchorage, 1979-80; sr. project engr. ARCO Oil & Gas Co., Anchorage, 1980—. Editor: Cold Region Construction, 1983. Mem. microcomputer com. Anchorage Sch. Dist., 1983, Anchorage Sch. Bd., 1986—, Anchorage Sch. Dist. Citizen Adv. Concerns Com., 1985-86, Anchorage Sch. Dist. Transp. Task Force, 1985-86, Alaska Hist. Commn., 1986—, Hugh O'Brien Youth Adv. Bd., 1986— ARCO Dependent Child Care Task Force, 1986—; bd. dirs. Anchorage Ctr. for Families, 1986—, Musk Ox Devel. Bd., 1986—, Cook Inlet Native Assn., 1985-86, Anchorage Community Theater, 1988—. Served to 1st lt. USAR, 1977-86. Mem. ASCE, Tech. Council on Cold Region Engring., Alaska Soc. Civil Engrs., Rotary. Office: ARCO Oil & Gas Co 700 G St PO Box 100360 Anchorage AK 99510-0360

JORDAN, DAWSON CLANDE, animal science educator; b. Horace, Kans., Jan. 11, 1935; s. Nestor Wallace and Shirley Erleen (Huddleston) J.; m. Glenna Vale Duren, Sept. 5, 1953 (div. Mar. 1966); children: Claudia E., Kerry Lee, B. Scott, Leila Ann, Melande C.; m. Doreen E. Parish, Dec. 21, 1967. AA, Pueblo (Colo.) Jr. Coll., 1955; BS, Colo. State U., 1958. Millright, helper Colo. Fuel & Iron Corp., Pueblo, 1955-56; mgr. San-Mor Guernsey Farms, Maume, Ohio, 1958-59; with Colo. State U., Ft. Collins, 1959—, asst. dairyman, 1960-62, dairyman, 1962-68, extension animal scientist-dairy, 1968—, assoc. prof., 1976-81, prof., 1981—; cons., mgr. Ft. Collins Milk Producers, Inc., 1966; cons. Colo. Dairy Youth Found., Ft. Collins, 1972—; ofcl. dairy cattle judge; sec.-treas. Western Dairy Conf., 1973-74, 82-83. Contbr. articles to profl. and popular publs. Dairy supt. Colo. State Fair, Pueblo, 1959-86; ruling elder La Porte (Colo.) Presbyn. Ch., 1970-78. Recipient F.A. Anderson Disting. Svc. award Colo. State U., 1975. Mem. Am. Dairy Sci. Assn. (com. chmn. 1963-67, 68-71, 81-83, 87-88, nat. award 1988), Colo. Dairy Herd Improvement (sec.-treas. 1967—), Brown Swiss Cattle Breeders Assn. U.S. (classifier 1972-86), Colo. Dairy Youth Found.

(life), Dairy Shrine Club (life), Alpha Zeta (Outstanding Tchr. award Colo. State U. chpt. 1980), Gamma Sigma Delta, Epsilon Sigma Phi. Republican. Home: 8529 Cherokee Park Rd Box 98 Livermore CO 80536 Office: Colo State U Animal Sci Dept Rm 13B Fort Collins CO 80523

JORDAN, FRANK M., protective services official. Chief of police, San Francisco. Office: San Francisco Police Dept Chief's Office 850 Bryant St San Francisco CA 94103 *

JORDAN, J. PETER, architect, educator; b. Corpus Christi, Tex., Nov. 16, 1948; s. James M. and Ann (Key) J.; m. Carolyn L. Stapleton, May 18, 1973. BA, Rice U., 1971, BArch, 1971; MBA, Ga. State U., 1978; postgrad., Princeton Theological Sem., 1971-72. Draftsman various firms, Corpus Christi, 1973-74; draftsman various firms, Atlanta, 1974-75, architect, 1975-77; architect FABRAP, Atlanta, 1977-78; architect Media Five Ltd., Honolulu, 1978-80, assoc., 1980-84, sr. assoc., 1984-86; assoc. prof. sch. architecture U. Hawaii, Honolulu, 1986—. Contbr. articles to profl. jours. Mem. AIA (Hawaiian soc.), Construction Specifications Inst. (Honolulu chpt.). Democrat. Methodist. Office: U Hawaii at Manoa Sch of Architecture 2560 Campus Rd George Annex B-3 Honolulu HI 96822

JORDAN, JIM, artist, Buddhist priest; b. Memphis, Nov. 27, 1940; s. H.T. and Avium Dupree (Sharpe) J.; m. Louise Correll, June 10, 1962 (div. 1970); 1 child: Strider Donovan; m. Barbara Kohn, Nov. 13, 1979. BFA, U. Tex., 1963; MFA, U. Ill., 1965, MA, 1965; ABD, Harvard U., 1967; PhD in Psychology, Saybrook Inst., San Francisco, 1984. Art prof. Antioch Coll., Yellow Springs, Ohio, 1967-80; art dept. chmn. S.D. State U., 1981-84; vis. prof. John F. Kennedy U., Orinda, Calif., 1984-87; co-chmn. exptl. arts San Francisco State U., 1985-87; vis. prof. in psychology Calif. Sch. Profl. Psychology, Berkeley, 1985-87; priest Zen Ctr., San Francisco, 1987-88; vis. prof. U. So. Calif., Los Angeles, 1975; art cons. Avco Corp., Washington, D.C., 1976; lectr. San Francisco Art Inst., 1985-87, Calif. Coll. Arts and Crafts, Berkeley, 1985-87. Author: (with others) The New Teachers, 1971, Light Years: The Photography of Morley Baer, 1988; contbr. essays to profl. jours.; co-editor: Antioch Review, 1971-80, Artweek, 1984—, Express, 1984—, Bay Guardian, 1984—. Grantee Kress Found., 1967, Ford Found., 1969-72, Nat. Endowment for the Arts, 1982-84. Mem. Assn. Internat. Critics D'Art, Coll. Art Assn. Am. Democrat. Buddhist. Home: Green Gulch Farm State Rte 1 Sausalito CA 94965

JORDAN, JOHN MOYER, transportation executive; b. San Marino, Calif., Sept. 25, 1942; s. Fred Moyer Jordan and Elisabeth (Shuler) Jarecki; m. Christina Louise Holmes, June 21, 1969. BSEE, Stanford U., 1964, MSIE, 1967. Ops. rsch. analyst Ford Motor Co., Dearborn, Mich., 1967-69; supr. capital budgeting Ford Motor Co., Ypsilanti, Mich., 1969-72; dir. operational planning IU Internat. Corp., Phila., 1972-76; sr. dir. planning Gotaas-Larsen, Inc., N.Y.C., 1976-79; v.p. corp. planning Gotaas-Larsen Ltd., London, 1979-82; v.p. fin. Interpool Ltd., N.Y.C., 1982-86; cons. Marine Med. Svcs., Inc., Solana Beach, Calif., 1986-87; dir. fin. planning and reporting Am. Pres. Cos., Ltd., Oakland, Calif., 1988—. Republican. Home: 7036 Shirley Dr Oakland CA 94611 Office: Am Pres Cos Ltd 1800 Harrison St Oakland CA 94612

JORDAN, LOIS HEYWOOD, real estate developer; b. Salem, Oreg., Apr. 22, 1913; d. Frank Hall and Winnifred (Heywood) Reeves; m. Edmund A. Jordan, Nov. 19, 1936 (dec. Dec. 1982); children: Jennifer, Jolie J. Stricklin, E. Andrew. Student, Oreg. State U., 1931-36, N.W. Sch. of Art, Portland, Oreg. Dress designer Portland, 1933-36, real estate developer, 1955—; pres. Jordan Developers, Portland, 1987—. Pres. Alameda Sch. PTA, Portland, 1958; v.p. Ainsworth Sch. PTA, Portland, 1964; pres. Alameda Garden Club, Portland, 1956, Women's Convalescent Home, Portland, 1957; v.p. sec. SW Hills Residential League, Portland, 1968; v.p. Friends Marquam Ravine, Portland, 1976; bd. dirs. Friendly House, Portland, 1986. Mem. Multnomah Athletic Club, Pi Beta Phi (mgr. Oreg. State chpt. 1932-33). Republican. Prebyterian. Office: Jordan Developers 1650 NW 113th Portland OR 97229

JORDAN, RAYMOND BRUCE, health services consultant; b. Holland, Mich., Mar. 10, 1912; s. Albert Raymond and Aimee (Best) J.; m. Dorothy Caig, June 6, 1942. B.A., Sacramento State Coll., 1952; M.B.A., Stanford U., 1959. Pub. acct., Calif. Acct., auditor State Bd. Equalization, Calif. Dept. Employment, 1947-48, mgmt. analyst, 1948-52, chief analyst, 1952-59; chief mgmt. analyst Hdqrs. Office, Calif. Dept. Mental Hygiene, 1959-63; bus. adminstr. Atascadero State Hosp., 1963-68, Patton State Hosp., San Bernardino, Calif., 1968-70; mgmt. cons. hosps., Victoria, B.C., Can., 1970-72; instr. Sacramento City Coll., 1951-62; cons. Govt. Iran, faculty, U. Tehran, 1956; instr. U. Calif.-Davis, 1963, Cuesta Coll., San Luis Obispo, 1967-68, Monterey Peninsula Coll., 1974-76; adj. prof. Golden Gate U., Monterey and San Francisco Campus, 1974-84; chmn. grievance rev. bd. Monterey Peninsula Unified Sch. Dist., 1976. Pres., Monterey County Ombudsman Program, 1976-79; founder, adv. bd. mem. Monterey County Sr. Hearing Ctr., 1977-78; treas. Experience, Inc., 1973-78; bd. dirs. Monterey County Sr. Aide Program, 1976-78; mem. adv. bd. Alliance on Aging, 1976-78; founder, pres. Concerned Sr. Citizens, Monterey Peninsula Club, 1974-77; mem. adv. group Monterey Sr. Day Care Ctr., 1977-78. Recipient Bronze Achievement award Mental Hosp. Service, 1963. Served with U.S. Army, 1943-46. Club: Toastmasters. Author: Management Analysis in Health Services, 1982; Supervision—Effective Management, 1982; contbr. articles to profl. jours. Home: 33 Linda Ave Apt 1908 Oakland CA 94611

JORDAN, RICHARD CHARLES, engineering executive; b. Mpls., Apr. 16, 1909; s. C. and Estelle R. (Martin) J.; m. Freda M. Laudon, Aug. 10, 1935; children: Mary Ann, Carol Lynn, Linda Lee. B. Aero. Engring., U. Minn., 1931, M.S., 1933, Ph.D., 1940. In charge air conditioning div. Mpls. br. Am. Radiator & Standard San. Corp., 1933-36; instr. petroleum engring. U. Tulsa, 1936-37; instr. engring. expt. sta. U. Minn., Mpls., 1937-41, asst. dir., 1941-44, assoc. prof., 1944-45, prof., asst. head mech. engring. dept., 1946-49, prof., head dept. mech. engring., 1950-77, prof., head Sch. Mech. and Aero. Engring., 1966-77, acting assoc. dean Inst. Tech., 1977-78, assoc. dean, 1978-85; pres. Jordan Assocs., 1985—; dir. Onan Corp. of McGraw-Edison; cons. various refrigeration and air conditioning cos., 1937—; cons. NSF, U.S. Dept. State, Control Data Corp., others.; Mem. engring. sci. adv. panel NSF, 1954-57, chmn., 1957; mem. div. engring. and indsl. research NRC, mem. exec. com., 1957-69, chmn., 1962-65; del. OAS Conf. on Strategy for Tech. Devel. Latin Am., Chile, 1969; chmn. U.S.-Brazil Sci. Coop. Program Com. on Indsl. Research, Rio de Janeiro, 1967, Washington, 1967, Belo Horizonte, 1968, Houston, 1968; del. World Power Conf., Melbourne, 1962; v.p. sci. council Internat. Institut de du Froid, 1967-71; cons. to World Bank on alternative energy for Northeastern Brazil, 1976. Author: (with Priester) Refrigeration and Air Conditioning, 1948, rev. edit., 1956, also numerous publs. on mech. engring., environ. control, solar energy, energy resources, engring. edn., tech. transfer.; Contbr. Mech. Engring. Recipient F. Paul Anderson medal ASHRAE, 1966, E.K. Campbell award, 1966, Outstanding Publs. Golden Key award, 1949; Outstanding Achievement award U. Minn., 1979; elected to Solar Energy Hall of Fame, 1980. Fellow ASME, AAAS, ASHRAE (presdl. mem.); mem. Nat. Acad. Engring., Assn. Applied Solar Energy (adv. council 1958-61), Am. Soc. Refrigerating Engrs. (1st v.p. 1952, pres. 1953, dir., council mem. 1946-53), Am. Soc. Engring. Edn., AAAS, Nat., Minn. (Engr. of Yr. award 1972), socs. profl. engrs., Internat. Inst. Refrigeration (hon. mem., del. NRC to exec. com. 1957-76, v.p. exec. com. 1959-63, v.p. sci. council 1963-71), Engr. Council Profl. Devel. (chmn. regional edn. and accreditation com.), Sigma Xi, Tau Beta Pi, Pi Tau Sigma, Sigma Chi. Club: Campus. Home: 18418 Horseshoe Circle PO Box 2101 Rio Verde AZ 85255

JORDAN, RICHARD PHILLIP, JR., accountant, financial executive; b. Denver, June 22, 1954; s. Richard Phillip and Anne Marie (Oberst) J.; m. Lorraine Mary Lawson, Dec. 30, 1977; children: Kevin Richard, Mark Gerald, Julianne Elaine. BS, U. No. Colo., 1976; postgrad., Met. State Coll., Denver, 1983-84. CPA, Colo. Loan officer lst Nat. Bank, Englewood, Colo., 1977-78; internat. auditor United Banks Colo., Denver, 1978-82; asst. auditor Jefferson Bank & Trust, Lakewood, Colo., 1982-84; audit dir. lst Golden (Colo) Bancorp/lst Interstate Banks, 1984-88; cost mgr. Martin Marietta Astronautics, Denver, 1988-. Fundraiser Easter Seals Found., Denver, 1985-; head coach Columbine Sports Assn., Littleton, Colo., 1986-, bd. dirs., 1988-. Fellow Colo. Soc. CPA's; mem. AICPA. Roman Catholic. Office: Martin Marietta Astronautics PO Box 179 Denver CO 80201

JORDAN, ROGER LYNN, optometrist; b. Livingston, Mont., Dec. 6, 1953; s. Russell Leroy and Marlys Mae (Seeback) J.; m. Peggy Jo Keck, Feb. 25, 1984; children: Darcy, Kelsey, Barret. BS with honors, Mont. State U., 1976; OD magna cum laude, So. Calif. Coll. Optometry, 1980. Asst. mgr. Safeway, Livingston, Mont., 1967-76; optometrist, owner Gillette (Wyo.) Optometric Clinic, 1980—; visual cons. N.E. Wyo. Bd. Coop. Ednl. Svcs., Gillette, 1987—. Bd. trustees Prince of Peace Luth. Ch., Gillette, 1981-85, 89—; mem. Gillette Leadership Inst., 1986-87; pres. Razor City Football League, Gillette, 1985-89. Recipient Charles Kulp Jr. award U.S. Jaycees, Gillette, 1985, U.S. Ambassadorship, 1987, Ben Mott Meml. award Wyo. Jaycees, Gillette, 1985. Fellow Am. Acad. Optometry; mem. Am. Otpometric Assn. (Wyo. keyperson 1987-89), Wyo. Optometric Assn. (bd. dirs. 1985-87, state sec. 1988-89), Gillette Jaycees (chmn. bd. 1985-86), Wyo. Jaycees (exec. v.p. 1985-86), Rotary (chmn. Rula program and scholarship program), Omega Epsilon Phi, Beta Sigma Kappa. Republican. Lutheran. Home: 604 Clarion Gillette WY 82716 Office: Gillette Optometric Clinic 706 W 8th St Gillette WY 82716

JORDAN, THOMAS FRANCIS, academic administrator, consultant; b. Indpls., Jan. 18, 1926; s. Walter Thomas and Bertha (Greiner) J.; m. Ann Marie Joyce, Dec. 31, 1957; children: Mary, Daniel, Cecily, Sean. BS, St. Louis U., 1949. Dir. Cath. Youth Orgn., 1950-53; exec. asst. to pres. and sr. campaign dir. Lawson Assocs., Rockville Ctr., N.Y., 1953-57; v.p. St. Louis U., 1957-59, U. San Francisco, 1960-68, Grad. Theol. Union, Berkeley, Calif., 1968-74, Coll. of Notre Dame, Belmont, Calif., 1974—; cons. Nat. Judicial Coll., Reno, Am. Ireland Fund, Boston; U. of San Francisco Sch. of Law; St. Mary's Coll. High Sch., Berkeley. Author articles on fund raising. Appointed Knight of Malta 1987; Disting. Service Award, U. of San Francisco Sch. of Law 1987; Council for Advancement & Support of Edu. Tribute Award 1987. Home: 2111 Hyde St #306 San Francisco CA 94109 Office: Coll Notre Dame 1500 Ralston Ave Belmont CA 94002

JORGENSEN, BRIAN KENT, lawyer, financial planner; b. Santa Rosa, Calif., Aug. 26, 1958; s. Jerry L. and LaRae (Watkins) J. BA in Fin., U. Utah, 1981, MBA, 1982; JD, Brigham Young U., 1985. Bar: Utah. 1985, U.S. Dist. Ct. Utah 1985, Ariz. 1986, U.S. Dist. Ct. Ariz. 1986. Judicial clk. U.S. Dist. Ct. Nev., Las Vegas, 1985-86; assoc. atty. Evans, Kitchel & Jenckes PC, Phoenix, 1986-87; mgr., fin. planner Sterling Wentworth Corp., Salt Lake City, 1987—. Contbg. article to Brigham Young U. Law Rev., 1985. Del. to Rep. Party Salt Lake County (Utah) Convention, 1988. Mem. Order of the Coif, Phi Beta Kappa, Beta Gamma Sigma, Phi Kappa Phi. Home: 7805 Dolphin Circle Salt Lake City UT 84121 Office: Sterling Wentworth Corp 2319 S Foothill Dr Ste 290 Salt Lake City UT 84109

JORGENSEN, ERIK HOLGER, lawyer; b. Copenhagen, July 18, 1916; s. Holger and Karla (Andersen) J.; children—Jette Friis, Lone Olesen, John, Jean Ann. J.D., San Francisco Law Sch., 1960. Bar: Calif. 1961. Pvt. practice law, 1961-70; ptnr. Hersh, Hadfield, Jorgensen & Fried, San Francisco, 1970-76, Hadfield & Jorgensen, San Francisco, 1976-88 . Pres. Aldersly, Danish Retirement Home, San Rafael, Calif., 1974-77, Rebild Park Soc. Bay Area chpt., 1974-77. Fellow Scandinavian Am. Found. (hon.); mem. ABA, Assn. Trial Lawyers Am., San Francisco Lawyers Club, Bar Assn. of San Francisco, Calif. Assn. Realtors (hon. life bd. dirs.). Author: Master Forms Guide for Successful Real Estate Agreements, Successful Real Estate Sales Agreements, 1988; contbr. articles on law and real estate law to profl. jours. Office: 350 California St San Francisco CA 94104

JORGENSEN, GORDON DAVID, engineering company executive; b. Chgo., Apr. 29, 1921; s. Jacob and Marie (Jensen) J.; B.S. in Elec. Engring., U. Wash., 1948, postgrad. in bus. and mgmt., 1956-59; m. Nadina Anita Peters, Dec. 17, 1948 (div. Aug. 1971); children—Karen Ann, David William, Susan Marie; m. 2d, Barbara Noel, Feb. 10, 1972 (div. July 1976). With R.W. Beck & Assos., Cons. Engrs., Phoenix, 1948—, ptnr., 1954-86; pres. Beck Internat., Phoenix, 1971—. Served to lt. (j.g.) U.S. Maritime Service, 1942-45. Recipient Outstanding Service award Phoenix Tennis Assn., 1967; Commendation, Govt. Honduras, 1970. Registered profl. engr., Alaska, Ariz., Calif., Colo., Nev., N.Mex., N.D., Utah, Wash., Wyo. Mem. IEEE (chmn. Wash.-Alaska sect. 1959-60), Nat. Soc. Profl. Engrs., Am. Soc. Appraisers (sr. mem.), Ariz. Cons. Engrs. Assn., Ariz. Soc. Profl. Engrs., Internat. Assn. Assessing Officers, Southwestern Tennis Assn. (past pres.), U.S. Tennis Assn. (pres. 1987-88, chmn. U.S. Open com.); chmn. U.S. Davis Cup com.; chmn. Internat. Tennis Fed., Davis Cup com. Presbyterian (elder). Project mgr. for mgmt., operation studies and reorgn. study Honduras power system, 1969-70. Home: 5329 N 25th St Phoenix AZ 85016 Office: RW Beck & Assocs 3003 N Central Phoenix AZ 85012

JORGENSEN, JUDITH ANN, psychiatrist; b. Parris Island, S.C.; d. George Emil and Margaret Georgia Jorgensen; B.A., Stanford U., 1963; M.D., U. Calif., 1968; m. Ronald Francis Crown, July 11, 1970. Intern, Meml. Hosp., Long Beach, 1969-70; resident County Mental Health Services, San Diego, 1970-73; staff psychiatrist Children and Adolescent Services, San Diego, 1973-78; practice medicine specializing in psychiatry, La Jolla, Calif., 1973—; staff psychiatrist County Mental Health Services of San Diego, 1973-78, San Diego State U. Health Services, 1985-87; psychiat. cons. San Diego City Coll., 1973-78, 85-86; asst. prof. dept. psychiatry U. Calif., 1978—; chmn. med. quality rev. com. Dist. XIV, State of Calif., 1982-83. Mem. Am. Psychiat. Assn., San Diego Soc. Psychiat. Physicians (chmn. membership com. 1976-78, v.p. 1978-80, fed. legis. rep. 1985-87), Am. Soc. Adolescent Psychiatry, San Diego Soc. Adolescent Psychiatry (pres. 1981-82), Calif. Med. Assn. (alternate del.), Soc. Sci. Study of Sex, San Diego Soc. Sex Therapy and Edn., San Diego County Med. Soc. (credentials com. 1982-84). Club: Rowing. Office: 470 Nautilus St Suite 211 La Jolla CA 92037

JORGENSEN, LENNART ANDREW, utility company executive, security company executive; b. Great Falls, Mont., Apr. 17, 1947; s. Lennart Gustave and Thelma Marguerite (Loberg) J.; m. Georgielea Ann Weisgerber, July 22, 1967; children: Eric, Kristopher. Diploma, U.S. Army Air Def. Sch., El Paso, Tex., 1971, 74, U.S. Army Adjutant Gens.' Sch., Indpls., 1972. Engr. Nebr. Pub. Power Dist., Columbus, 1976-80; dir. power City of Colby, Kans., 1980-82; asst. gen. mgr. Clatskanie (Oreg.) People's Utility Dist., 1982—; pres. Oreg. Security and Investigation, Clatskanie, 1988—; v.p. Quincy Water Assn., Clatskanie, 1985-87, pres., 1987—, bd. dirs. Mem. Colby Energy Bd., 1981-82, pres., 1982; mem. Colby Drug and Alcohol Abuse Coun., 1982; cubmaster Boy Scouts Am., Clatskanie, 1983; tng. mgr. USAF MARS Region 5, 1986, emergency coordinator, 1988—; served as staff sgt. U.S. Army, 1966-76. Mem. Am. Pub. Power Assn. (energy services plan com. 1981-82, rates load research com. 1983—, human resources com. 1983—), N.W. Pub. Power Assn. (mem. rates com. 1982—), Am. Soc. Pub. Adminstrn., Am. Radio Relay League (emergency coordinator 1976, 85—, 2 Pub. Service awards, 1964, 65, phone activities mgr. 1978), VFW (life, dist. adjutant Columbus, Nebr. Post 1979-80), Am. Legion, NRA, Citizens Com. for Right to Keep and Bear Arms (nat. adv. council, citizen of Yr. 1986), Oreg. Mcpl. Fin. Officer's Assn., Internat. Platform Assn., Internat. Security and Detective Alliance (chartered investigator, commissioned col.), Oreg. State Sheriff's Assn., Second Amendment Found. Club: North American Hunting. Lodge: Kiwanis (bd. dirs. Clatskanie club 1983-84). Home: 20109 Ilmari Rd Clatskanie OR 97016 Office: Clatskanie People's Utility Dist PO Box 216 Clatskanie OR 97016-0216 also: Oreg Security and Investigation PO Box 1197 Clatskanie OR 97016-1197

JORGENSEN, LOU ANN BIRKBECK, social worker; b. Park City, Utah, May 14, 1931; d. Robert John and Lillian Pearl (Langford) Birkbeck; student Westminster Coll., 1949-51; B.S., U. Utah, 1953, M.S.W., 1972, D.S.W., 1979; grad. Harvard Inst. Ednl. Mgmt., 1983; m. Howard Arnold Jorgensen, June 9, 1954; children—Gregory Arnold, Blake John, Paul Clayton. Social work adminstr. nursing home demonstration project, dept. family and community medicine U. Utah Med. Center, Salt Lake City, 1972-74; mental health ednl. specialist Grad. Sch. Social Work, U. Utah, 1974-77, 77-80, asst. prof., 1974-80, assoc. prof., 1980—, dir. doctoral program, 1984—, assoc. dean, 1986—; regional mental health cons. Bd. dirs. Info. and Referral Center, 1975-82, United Way of Utah, 1976-82, Pioneer Trail Parks, 1977-83, Rowland Hall-St. Marks Sch., 1980-86; Salt Lake County housing commr., 1980-86; pres. Human Services Conf. for Utah, 1979-80. Mem. Council on Social Work Edn., Nat. Assn. Social Workers (pres. Utah chpt. 1978-79), Adminstrs. of Public Agys. Assn., Human Services Assn. Utah, Jr. League of Salt Lake City, Phi Kappa Phi. Republican. Episcopalian. Clubs: Town, Eastern Star. Author: Explorations in Living, 1978; Social Work in Business and Industry, 1979; Handbook of the Social Services, 1981; contbr. articles to profl. jours. Home: 3442 East Oaks Dr Salt Lake City UT 84124 Office: U Utah Grad Sch Social Work Salt Lake City UT 84112

JORNALES, ROBERT ARNALDO, electronics engineer; b. General Trias, Cavite, Philippines, May 10, 1945; came to U.S. 1958; s. Felipe Buhain Jornales and Rosa Grepo Arnaldo; m. Hanh Thi Nguyen, Mar. 7, 1981;l children: Phuong, Kim, Darrius, Rose, Philip, Mary. BS in Engring., UCLA, 1966; MSEE, U. So. Calif., 1971. Electronics engr. Naval Weapons Ctr., China Lake, Calif., 1967—. Mem. IEEE.

JORTNER, JULIUS, materials engineer, consultant; b. Cernauti, Rumania, Mar. 3, 1936; came to U.S, 1946; s. Michael Maria (Spielvogel) J.; m. Carolee June Robbins, May 25, 1975. B in Mech. Engring., Cooper Union, 1956; MS in Engring., UCLA, 1968. Research engr. Rocketdyne div. North Am. Aviation, Canoga Park, Calif., 1956-68, McDonnell Douglas Astronautics Co., Huntington Beach, Calif., 1968-79, Sci. Applications, Inc., Irvine, Calif., 1979-82; pres. Jortner Research and Engring., Inc., Costa Mesa, Calif., 1982—; lectr. in field, 1983—. Editor: Thermomechanical Behavior of High-Temperature Composites, 1982, Thermostructural Behavior of Carbon-Carbon Composites, 1986; contbr. articles to profl. jours. Mem. ASME (mem. structure & materials com., 1979—), ASTM (mem. com. D-30 on advanced composites, 1969—), Am. Carbon Soc. (Graffin lectureship, 1988), Am. Ceramic Soc. Office: Jortner Rsch & Engring Inc PO Box 2825 Costa Mesa CA 92628

JOSEFOWITZ, NATASHA, sydicated columnist; b. Paris, Oct. 31, 1926; d. Myron T. and Tamara (Fradkin) Chapro; m. Sam Josefowitz, May 15, 1949; children: Nina, Paul. MSW, Columbia Sch. Social Work, 1965; Doctorans, Lausanne U., Switzerland, 1974; PhD, Sussex Coll., Eng., 1977. Prof. social work Lausanne U. Child Guidance Clinic, Switzerland, 1965-74; lectr., psychologist Lausanne U., Switzerland, 1972-74; prof. mgmt. U. N.H., 1974-80, Coll. Bus., San Diego State U., 1980-84; syndicated columnist 1985—. Author: Paths to Power, 1980, Is This Where I Was Going?, 1983, You're the Boss, 1985, Natasha's Words for Friends, Families, and Lovers, 1986, How to Get a Good Start in Your New Job, 1988, 100 Scoops of Ice Cream: Tiny Tales for Children, 1988. Named Woman of Yr., Women in Mgmt. Assn., 1988. Mem. Organized Devel. Network, Nat. Tng. Lab. (emeritus 1985), Rotary. Home and Office: 2235 Calle Guaymas La Jolla CA 92037

JOSEPH, EZEKIEL (ED JOSEPH), manufacturing company executive; b. Rangoon, Burma, June 24, 1938; s. Joe E. Joseph and Rachel Levi; m. Sheila G. Rabinovitch, Feb. 17, 1963; children: Renah, Heather, Jerald. Mktg. mgr. Gen. Electric Corp., Waynesboro, Va., 1964-75; dir. Actron div. McDonnell Douglas Corp., Monrovia, Calif., 1975-78; pres. Joseph Machinery Inc., Huntington Beach, Calif., 1978-83; prin. Computer and Software Solutions, Huntington Beach, 1983—; pres. Tangent Inds. Inc. (now Xtalite Display Systems Inc.), Huntington Beach, 1985—; pres. Retract-a-Roof Inc., Huntington Beach. V.p. Temple Beth David, Huntington Beach, 1975—. Mem. Austin Healey Assoc. Democrat. Home: 16242 Typhoon Ln Huntington Beach CA 92649 Office: Retract-A-Roof Inc 17632 Metzler Ln Huntington Beach CA 92647

JOSEPH, GEORGE MANLEY, chief judge; b. Caldwell, Idaho, Aug. 31, 1930; s. Ben Manley and Mabel Gertrude (Newburn) J.; m. Elizabeth Lyle Starr, dec. 21, 1954; children: Sarah Katherine, Amy Elizabeth, Abigail Serena, Benjamin Manley, Jonathan Lyle. BA, Reed Coll., 1952; JD, U. Chgo., 1955; LLM, NYU, 1959. Law clk. Oreg. Supreme Ct., Salem, Oreg., 1955-56; law prof. Ohio No. U., Dickinson Sch. Law, U. Ark., 1956-63; dep. dist. atty. Multnomah County, Portland, Oreg., 1963-66; pvt. practice Portland, 1966-74; county counsel Multnomah County, Portland, 1975-77; judge State of Oreg., Salem, 1977-80, chief judge, 1981—; chmn. Council Chief Judges of Cts. Appeal Edn. Standards Com., 1988. Alumni trustee Reed Coll., Portland, 1972-75; trustee Reed Coll., Portland, 1975-80; chmn. City-County Charter Commn., Portland, 1971-74; bd. visitors Willamette U. Sch. Law, Salem, 1980—; visiting com. mem. Oriental Inst. U. Chgo., 1986—. Mem. Oreg. State Bar Assn., ABA, Multnomah Bar Assn., Council of Chief Judges (exec. com. vice-chmn. 1983-84, chmn. 1984-85). Home: 7110 SE 29th Portland OR 97202 Office: Ct Appeals Third Floor Justice Bldg Salem OR 97310

JOSEPH-RICHARDSON, RUTH, dean of students; b. National City, Calif., Apr. 15, 1947; d. Warren G. and Mabel Virginia (Nelson) B.; m. Eddie Joseph Jr., Jan. 22, 1968 (div. May 1981); children: Robert, Stacey, Cynthia; m. Samuel Wilson Richardson, Aug. 14, 1983. BA, U. Nev., 1980, MA, 1985. Tchr. Clark County Sch. Dist., Las Vegas, Nev., 1981-88; dean of students Clark County Sch. Dist., 1988—; Congl. dist. coord. Ctr. for Civic Edn., Calabasas, Calif., 1987—. Mem. Democratic Cen. Com., Clark County, Nev., 1988-89; dep. registrar Clark County Election Dept., 1984—; del. County, State Dem. Convs., Clark County, 1988; mem. Allied Arts Coun., Las Vegas, 1988—. Alumni scholar U. Nev. Las Vegas Alumni Assn., 1982; recipient Project TEE award Nev. Coun. on Econ. Edn., 1988. Mem. Nat. Coun. for Social Studies, Assn. for Supervision & Curriculum Devel., Calif. Scholarship Fedn. (life), Alpha Kappa Gamma, Phi Kappa Phi. Democrat. Office: Hyde Park Jr High School 900 Hinson St Las Vegas NV 89107

JOSEPHSON, HAROLD ALLAN, real estate developer; b. Montreal, Que., Can., July 21, 1944; s. Joseph and Edith (Marco) J.; m. Sheila Gloria Laing, July 4, 1966 (div. July 1976); children: Daniel, Robert.; MBA with distinction, Harvard U., 1971. V.p. Marcil Mortgage Corp., Montreal, 1976-78; prin. Josephson Properties, Montreal, 1978-83, Los Angeles, 1983—. Mem. Urban Land Inst., Nat. Assn. Indsl. and Office Parks, Internat. Council Shopping Ctrs. Jewish. Club: Beverly Hills Country (Los Angeles), Regency (Los Angeles). Office: 2029 Century Park E #1200 Los Angeles CA 90067

JOSEPHSON, JOSEPH PAUL, lawyer; b. Trenton, N.J., June 3, 1933; s. David S. and Jenny (Randelman) J.; m. Virginia McKinney; children: Peter, Andrew, Sarah, Anna, Amelia. BA, U. Chgo., 1953; JD, Cath. U. Am., 1960. Bar: Alaska 1961. Since practiced in Anchorage; legis. asst. to territorial del. and U.S. Senator from Alaska 1957-60; mem. Alaska Ho. of Reps., Juneau, 1963-67; acting mayor Anchorage, 1968; mem. Alaska Senate, 1969-72, 83-89, chmn. senate majority caucus, chmn. com. on health, edn. and social svcs., 1983-85; co-chmn. Joint Fed.-State Land Use Planning Commn. for Alaska, 1972-74; assemblyman Municipality of Anchorage, 1980-82; lectr. Alaska Pacific U., 1983, 88. Editorial bd.: Cath. U. Am. Law Rev, 1959-60; columnist: Anchorage Daily News, 1976-79; contbg. editor: Alaska Bar Assn. Newspaper. Chmn. S. Cen. Alaska ARC, 1964-65; Candidate U.S. Senate, 1970; mem., dep. chmn. Greater Anchorage Charter Commn., 1975-76. Served with AUS, 1955-57. Mem. Am., Alaska, Anchorage bar assns., Am. Arbitration Assn. (arbitrator 1977—). Democrat. Home: 1526 F St Anchorage AK 99501 Office: 840 K St Ste 100 Anchorage AK 99503

JOSEPHSON, KRYSTINE KNIGHT, youth counselor; b. Delta, Utah, Jan. 11, 1952; d. Newel Wesley and Venice Ruth (Cropper) Knight; m. David W. Josephson, Dec. 10, 1982. BA, Weber State Coll., 1974; M Ednl. Psychology, Brigham Young U., 1987. Supr. locomotives for mech. dept. Union Pacific RR, various locations, Utah, Nebr., 1979-81; office mgr. Bennett & Knight Constrn., Delta, Utah, 1981-82; sec. Weyher Constrn. Co., Delta, 1982, Bechtel Corp., Delta, 1982; exec. sec. Weber County Commr., Ogden, Utah, 1983; receptionist Job Svc., Ogden, 1983-84; receptionist to atty. of pvt. practice Ogden, 1985-87; intake officer Moweda Youth Home, Roy, Utah, 1987; sch. counselor Ogden City Sch. Dist., 1987—; mem. Sch. Counselors Com., Testing Com., Interagy. Com., all Ogden, 1987—; presenter workshops. Mem. Utah Sch. Counseling and Vocat. Guidance Assn., Utah Ednl. Assn., NEA, NAFE, Women's Internat. Bowling Congress, UACO. Democrat.

JOSHI, CHANDRASHEKHAR JANARDAN, physics educator; b. Wai, India, July 22, 1953; came to U.S., 1981; s. Janardan Digambar and Ramabai (Kirpekar) J.; m. Asha Bhatt, Jan. 18, 1982. BS, London U., 1974; PhD, Hull U., U.K., 1978. Research assoc. Nat. Research Council, Can., 1978-81; research engr. UCLA, 1981-83, adj. assoc. prof., 1983-86, assoc. prof.-in-residence, 1986-87, assoc. prof., 1987-88, prof. elec. engring., 1988—; cons. Lawrence Livermore (Calif.) Nat. Lab., 1984, Los Alamos (N.Mex.) Nat. Lab., 1985—. Editor: Laser Acceleration of Particles, 1985, Advanced Acceleration Concepts, 1989; contbr. articles to profl. jours. Grantee NSF, U.S. Dept. Energy; recipient Queen Mary Prize, Inst. Nuclear Engring., 1974. Mem. AAAS, IEEE, Am. Phys. Soc., N.Y. Acad. Scis. Home: 2004 Pier Ave Santa Monica CA 90405 Office: UCLA 405 Hilgard Ave Los Angeles CA 90024

JOSHI, SATYAPRIY, engineer; b. Indore, M.P., India, Aug. 21, 1951; s. Dayashankar and Shanti (Joshi) J.; m. Nisha, May 15, 1978; 1 child, Sonal. MS, U. Indore, 1975; MT, Indian Inst. Tech., 1977; diploma, Inst. Mgmt. Studies, New Delhi, India, 1983. Technologist Cen. Electronics Ltd., New Delhi, 1977-80, asst. technical mgr., 1980-86; sr. process engr. Nat. Semiconductor Corp., Puyallup, Wash., 1987—; cons. Jet Propulsion Lab., Pasadena, Calif., 1982. Contbr. articles to profl. jours. Recipient Membership award Electrochem. Soc., 1985, Scholarship award Am. Vacuum Soc., 1984. Mem. IEEE. Hindu. Office: Nat Semiconductor Corp 1111 39th Ave SE Puyallup WA 98374

JOSHUA, AARON, investment company executive; b. Los Angeles, Aug. 26, 1957; s. Elmo and Pineniece Penny (Starks) J.; m. Valeri Janien. B.A. in Bus. Adminstrn., Whittier Coll., 1978, M.B.A., 1980. Life ins. agt. ITT Ins. Corp., Marina del Rey, Calif., 1977; pres., chmn. bd. Joshua's Restaurant Inc., Inglewood, Calif., 1980—; gen. ptnr. Internat. Mgmt. Assocs., fin. planning and asset mgmt., Beverly Hills, Calif., 1980—; SEC investment adviser. Mem. Am. Mgmt. Assn., Beverly Hills C. of C. (edn. com.), Inglewood C. of C., Internat. Assn. Fin. Planning. Republican. Baptist. Club: Inglewood Rotary. Office: 3216 W Manchester Blvd Inglewood CA 90305

JOSS, JUDY HARUE, lawyer; b. Columbus, Ohio, Mar. 1, 1953; d. Leon Kurtz and Sadae (Yamamoto) Walters; m. David Robert Joss, Jan. 18, 1989. Student, Princeton U., 1971-73, 74-75; AB, U. Calif., Berkeley, 1977; JD, Harvard U., 1981. Bar: Calif. 1981, U.S. Dist. Ct. (cen. dist.) Calif. 1981. Assoc. Sheppard, Mullin, Richter & Hampton, L.A., 1981-87, Paul, Hastings, Janofsky & Walker, Santa Monica, Calif., 1987-89, McDermott, Will & Emery, Newport Beach, Calif., 1989—. Nat. Merit scholar, 1971. Mem. ABA, L.A. County Bar Assn., Women Lawyers Assn. of L.A., Princeton Profl. Women, Assn. Real Estate Attys., Phi Beta Kappa. Democrat. Office: McDermott Will & Emery 1301 Dove St Ste 500 Newport Beach CA 92660

JOVE, STEPHEN ALAN, electrical engineer, instructor; b. Pitts., Sept. 2, 1952; s. Stephen and Clara (Briola) J. AA, Coll. of San Mateo, Calif., 1977; BSEE, San Jose (Calif.) State U., 1979; MSEE, U. Santa Clara, Calif., 1984, postgrad., 1984-86. Asst. product engr. Nat. Semiconductor, Inc., Santa Clara, 1978-79; adv. engr. IBM Corp., San Jose, 1979—; instr. Vietnamese Voluntary Orgn., Santa Clara, 1980; candidate for prof. San Jose State U., 1989. Inventor PSK modulation in AC bias data recording, amplification of signals produced by magnetic sensor, frequency response compensation cir., voltage-biased dR/R detection of signals in magnetic resistive device; contbr. articles to profl. jours. Republican. Roman Catholic. Office: IBM Corp 5600 Cottle Rd San Jose CA 95193

JOY, CARLA MARIE, educator; b. Denver, Sept. 5, 1945; d. Carl P. and Theresa M. (Lotito) J. AB cum laude, Loretto Heights Coll., 1967; MA (Ford Found. fellow), U. Denver, 1969, postgrad., 1984—. Instr. history Community Coll. Denver; prof. history Red Rocks Community Coll., Lakewood, Colo., 1970—; cons. for innovative ednl. programs; reviewer fed. grants; mem. adv. panel Colo. Endowment for Humanities, 1985—. Contbr. articles to profl. publs. Instr. vocat. edn. Mile High United Way, Jefferson County, 1975; participant Jefferson County Sch. System R-1 Dist., 1983—; active Red Rocks Community Coll. Speakers Bur., 1972—; chair history discipline The Colo. Core Transfer Consortium Project, 1986—. Cert. in vocat. edn. Colo. State Bd. Community Colls. and Occupational Edn. Recipient cert. of appreciation Kiwanis Club, 1981; Master Tchr. award U. Tex. at Austin, 1982. Mem. Am. Hist. Assn., Nat. Council for Social Studies, Nat. Geog. Soc., Inst. Early Am. History and Culture, Colo. Council for Social Studies, Community Coll. Humanities Assn., Orgn. Am. Historians, The Colo. Hist. Soc., Am. Soc. Profl. and Exec. Women, Phi Alpha Theta. Democrat. Episcopalian. Home: 1849 S Lee St Apt D Lakewood CO 80226 Office: Red Rocks Community Coll 12600 W 6th Ave Golden CO 80401

JOY, FREDERIC CHARLES, photographic artist; b. Salt Lake City, Oct. 5, 1949; s. Charles Forbes and Clare (Pack) J.; m. Devon Denny, Sept. 5, 1970 (div. 1972); m. Diana Murri, July 30, 1974; children: Heather, Kristen, Charles. BS, Utah State U., 1974; BA in Profl. Photography, Brooks Inst. Photography, Santa Barbara, Calif., 1977. Owner, mgr. Eagle Photographics-A Frederick Joy Gallery, Jackson Hole, Wyo., 1978—. Editor, curator: The C.L. Joy Collection, 1986; photographs have appeared in Teton, Sierra, Atlantic, Outdoor Photographer mags.; represented in numerous corp. offices and pvt. collections. Named Comml. Photographer of Yr., Wyo. Profl. Photographers Assn. Mem. Am. Soc. Mag. Photographers, Wilderness Soc., Rotary. Office: Eagle Photographics 35 E Deloney St Box 168l Jackson WY 83001

JOYCE, KATHERINE H., computer technology executive; b. N.Y.C., July 7, 1938; d. Fred John and Helen Dorothy (Brockmann) Krauer. BA in Math., San Diego State U., 1959; MA in Math., UCLA, 1964; MBA, Calif. Coast U., Santa Ana, 1984, PhD in Mgmt., 1986. Programmer brain rsch. inst. UCLA, 1964-65; programming analyst System Devel. Corp., L.A., 1965-72; sr. analyst Computer Software Analysts, L.A., 1972-78; mag. pub. Energy Unltd., Los Lunas, N.Mex., 1978-83; project mgr. Evans, Neal & Assocs., Albuquerque, 1981; computer systems specialist System Devel. Corp., Albuquerque, 1981-83; sci. programmer Mgmt. Scis., Albuquerque, 1984; mgr. Albuquerque ops., chief scientist Applications Rsch. Corp., 1984-88; dir. new bus., sr. scientist Applied Tech. Assocs., Albuquerque, 1988; pres. Halcyon, Inc., Los Lunas, N.Mex., 1987—. Editor jour. Energy Unltd., 1978-83; contbr. articles to profl. jours. Bd. dirs. Coop. Edn. Adv. Bd., Albuquerque, 1987-88. Small Bus. Innovative Rsch. grantee USAF, 1985, Strategic Def. Initiative Orgn., 1985, NASA, 1986, R.I.P.E. grantee ARC, 1986. Mem. NAFE, U.S. Psychotronics Assn. (bd. dirs. 1983-86, 2d v.p. 1978-79), Data Processing Mgrs. Assn. (bd. dirs. 1986, 87), N.Mex. Entrepreneurs Assn. (com. chairperson 1986), Am. Assn. Artificial Intelligence. Home: 64 Fire Station Rd Los Lunas NM 87031

JOYNER, ROBERT CARTER, healthcare lawyer; b. Pensacola, Fla., July 30, 1947; s. William Carter and Mary Yvonne (Hassell) J.; m. Genevieve Czepiel, June 20, 1970; children: Robert Jr., Mary Genevieve. AA, Pensacola Jr. Coll., 1967; Bachelors, U. Fla., 1969, JD, 1972. Bar: Fla. 1972, Calif. 1984. Tax acct. Arthur Anderson & Co., Tampa, Fla., 1972-73; atty. Ruttenberg Corp., St. Petersburg, Fla., 1973-76; asst. gen. counsel Nat. Med. Enterprise, L.A., 1976-86; v.p., gen. counsel Paracelsus Healthcare Corp., Pasadena, Calif., 1986—; bd. dirs. Bellwood Gen. Hosp., Bellwood Health Ctr., Buena Park Community Hosp., Chico Community Hosp., Doctors Hosp. Lodi, Hollywood Community Hosp., Lancaster Community Hosp., L.A. Community Hosp., Monrovia Community Hosp., Norwalk Communiyt Hosp., Van Nuys Community Hosp., West Corvia Hosp., West Hollywood Hosp., Women's Hosp., Bledsoe County Gen. Hosp., Clay County Hosp., Fentress County Gen. Hosp., Macon County Med. Ctr., Peninsula Med. Ctr., Senatobia Community Hosp. and Women's Hosp. Mem. ABA, Nat. Assn. Healthcare, North Ranch Tennis Club (bd. dirs. 1985-86), North Ranch Country Club, Marina Sailing Club. Republican. Baptist. Home: 1562 Wynnefield Westlake Village CA 91362 Office: Paracelsus Healthcare Corp 155 N Lake Ave Pasadena CA 91101

JUAREZ, LONNIE G., management consultant; b. Belen, N.Mex., Feb. 9, 1947; s. Lonnie G. and Refugio (Valencia) J.; m. Sarah E. Gutierrez, June 26, 1969 (div. Aug. 1978); children: Andrea, Bernadette; m. Colleen M. Schiendler, Sept. 21, 1984; children: Kara, Nancy. BS, U. N.Mex., 1970; MA, U. Colo., 1974; postgrad., U. Wash., 1978. Dir. Salt Lake Valley Bilingual Bicultural Consortium, 1974-75; coord. Yakima (Wash.) Valley Bilingual Bicultural Project, 1975-76; interim dir. Nat. Bilingual Tng. Resource Ctr., Seattle, 1976-77; coord. Eastern Valencia County Resident Ctr., Albuquerque, 1978-80; cons., proposal reader U.S. Dept. of Edn., Washington, 1980; program specialist Cultural Awareness Ctr. U. N.Mex., Albuquerque, 1980-81; dir. Multicultural Edn. Ctr. U. N.Mex, Albuquerque, 1981-84; pres. Computers Communication Analysis Resource Mgmt Corp., Santa Fe, 1987—; chmn. 1st Annual Conf. on Ednl. Equity, Nat. State and Local Partnership; instr. N.Mex. Highlands U., 1987—, CTL 900 Grad. Extension Course, U. N.D., Grand Forks, 1984, Socio-Cultural Perspectives of Bilingual Edn.-Socio Founds. of Edn., U. N.Mex., 1983, Dept. of Edn., U. Utah, 1974-75. Contbr. articles to profl. jours. Chmn. search com. Am. Indian Bilingual Edn. Ctr. Dir., 1981, search com. Cultural Awareness Bilingual Asst. Ctr. Dir. 1982; assessment evaluation specialist Am. Indian Bilingual Edn. Ctr., 1981. Mem. Santa Fe C. of C., Albuquerque C. of C., The Ctr. for Entrepreneurial Mgmt., Assn. of Computer Users, Kiwanis Internat., Rio Rancho TIPS, Am. Assn. of Profl. Cons., Am. Mgmt. Assn., Assn. for Supervision and Curriculum Devel., N.D. Assn. for Supervision and Curriculum Devel., N.Mex. Assn. Bilingual Edn. (chmn nomination election com. 1981-84, bd. dirs. 1981-84), Nat. Assn. for Bilingual Edn. Democrat. Roman Catholic. Home: 1903 Camino Lumbre Santa Fe NM 87505 Office: CARM Corp 1911 5th St Ste 209 Santa Fe NM 87501

JUAREZ, MARETTA LÍYA CALIMPONG, social worker; b. Gilroy, Calif., Feb. 14, 1958; d. Sulpicio Magsalay and Pelagia Lagotom (Viacrusis) Calimpong; m. Henry Juarez, Mar. 24, 1984. BA, U. Calif., Berkeley, 1979; MSW, San Jose State U., 1983. Lic. clin. social worker. Mgr. Pacific Bell, San Jose, Calif., 1983-84; revenue officer IRS, Salinas, Calif., 1984-85; social worker Santa Cruz (Calif.) County, 1985, Santa Clara County, San Jose, 1985—. Recipient award Am. Legion, 1972. Mem. NOW, Nat. Assn. Social Workers, Nat. Council on Alcoholism. Democrat. Roman Catholic.

JUBANY, HELENA LIN, architect; b. Thou-Fun, Taiwan, May 8, 1960; d. Yu Yuan and Su Tsuen (Tun) L.; m. Luis Jubany. BA, U. São Paulo, Brazil, 1982; MA, Calif. Poly. State U., 1985. Draftsperson C & C Architects, San Marino, Calif., 1985-86; project mgr. J.R. Grimsgaard, Pasadena, Calif., 1986—; pres. Jubany Deve., Chino Hills, Chino Hills, Calif., 1986-88. Home: 12877 Homeridge Ln Chino Hills CA 91710 Office: JR Grimsgaard 283 S Lake Ave Pasadena CA 91101

JUDD, BARRY GENE, sales executive; b. L.A., Dec. 14, 1946; s. Gene and Meriehilda (Downs) J.; m. Dee Ann Sanders, July 7, 1968; children: Derrick Quinn, Dustin Ian. BSME, Utah State U., Logan, 1971; MS in Human Resource Mgmt, U. Utah, 1979. Engr. trainee Northrop Corp., Hawthorne, Calif., 1965-69 summers; process engr. Morton Thiokol, Brigham City, Utah, 1974-78; mech. systems engr. Eaton-Kenway, Salt Lake City, 1978-81; project mgr. Eaton-Kenway, 1981-84, prog. mgr., 1984-86; prog. mgr. Harnischfeger Engring. Inc., Salt Lake City, 1987-88; sales mgr. Eaton Kenway, Salt Lake City, 1988—. Capt. U.S. Army, 1971-74. Named Engr. of the Mo., Eaton-Kenway, 1980; decorated Army Commendation medal. Mem. ASME. Republican. Mem. Ch. of Jesus Christ of Latter Day Saints. Home: 2062 N 2200 E Layton UT 84040 Office: 515 E 100 S Salt Lake City UT 84102

JUDD, DAVID THOMAS, educator; b. Tacoma, July 5, 1941; s. T. Frank and Georgianna (Tweter) J.; m. Kay Reese, Mar. 7, 1962; children: Jennifer Sant, Heather Stewart, Jon Thomas, Amy. BS, Brigham Young U., 1964, postgrad., 1984—; MS, U. Utah, 1975. Tchr. Jordan Sch. Dist., Sandy, Utah, 1964-86; chmn. English dept. Jordan Sch. Dist., Sandy, 1979-86, fine arts cons., 1986—; talent coord. World Conf., Gifted and Talented, Salt Lake City, 1986. Editor: (newsletters) The Share, 1975-86, Good Cents, 1979—; mem. editorial bd. Contemporary Issues in Reading, 1987—; contbr. articles to profl. jours. Mem. Bus. Edn. Alliance Com., Salt Lake City, 1985; leader Latter Day Saints Ch., Salt Lake City, 1970—; writer, contbr. Latter Day Saints mags./manuals, 1979-84. Mem. Nat. Coun. of Tchrs. of English, Utah Coun. of Tchrs. of English, Nat. Music Educators, Utah Music Educators. Democrat. Mormon. Home: 7493 Brighton Way Salt Lake City UT 84121 Office: Jordan Sch Dist 9361 S 300 East Sandy UT 84070-2998

JUDD, PATRICIA HOFFMAN, social worker; b. Pitts., June 22, 1946; d. Joseph Andrew and Irene Patricia (Bednar) Hoffman; m. Lewis Lund Judd, Jan. 26, 1974. BA, Marquette U., 1968; MSW., San Diego State U., 1970; PhD Calif. Sch. Profl. Psychology, 1989.Dir. treatment services DEFY, Health Care Agy. of San Diego County, San Diego, 1973-75; coordinator emergency psychiat. services U. Calif. Med. Ctr., San Diego, 1975-77, mem. attending staff, 1975-85; clin. coordinator crisis and brief treatment service Gifford Mental Health Clinic, U. Calif.-San Diego, 1975-79, coordinator clin. services, 1979-82, asst. dir., 1983—; clin. instr. dept. psychiatry U. Calif.-San Diego Sch. Medicine, 1976—; field instr. Sch. Social Work, San Diego State U., 1970—, lectr., 1978-80; pvt. practice psychotherapy, San Diego, 1979—; rsch. assoc. Chestnut Lodge Rsch. Inst., Rockville, Md., 1988-90, asst. prof. Sch. of Social Work, U. Md., 1988-90, coord. Shady Grove program. Mem. Nat. Assn. Social Workers, Acad. Cert. Social Workers, Soc. Clin. Social Workers. Office: 500 W Montgomery Ave Rockville MD 20850

JUDD, THOMAS ELI, electrical engineer; b. Salt Lake City, Apr. 12, 1927; s. Henry Eli Judd and Jennie Meibos; m. Mary Lu Edman, June 2l, 1948; children: Shauna, Kirk E., Blake E., Lisa. BSEE, U. Utah, 1950. Registered profl. engr., Utah. Mech. engr. Utah Power & Light Co., Salt Lake City, 1950-55; chief engr. Electronic Motor Car Corp., Salt Lake City, 1955-56, Equi-Tech Corp., Salt Lake City, 1978-79; hydraulic devel. engr. Galigher Co., Salt Lake City, 1956-58; pres. Toran Corp., Salt Lake City, 1958-7l, T M Industries, Salt Lake City, 197l-78; chief exec. officer, mgr. Ramos Corp., Salt Lake City, 1979—; project cons. Eimco Corp., Salt Lake City, 1966; design cons. to tech. cos. Patentee in field in U.S. and fgn. countries; contbr. editor U.S. Rail News, 1982—. Cons. Nat. Fedn. Ind. Bus., 1983—. With USNR, 1945-46, PTO. Mem. Tau Beta Pi. Republican. Mormon. Home: l29 W Harris Ave Salt Lake City UT 84115 Office: Ramos Corp 125 W Harris Ave Salt Lake City UT 84115

JUDGE, JAMES CARL, engineering technician; b. Casper, Wyo., Aug. 26, 1945; s. Herbert B. and E. Francis (Sheehan) J.; m. Judith Karen Stillwell, May 15, 1971; children: Tracy Michelle, Eric James Michael, Casey McKay. Micrographics technician Chevron Oil Co., Denver, 1969-77; mgr. micro-image processing EG&G Idaho Inc., Idaho Falls, 1977-81; engring. assoc. Lawrence Livermore Calif.) Nat. Lab., 1981—. Editor newsletter Hard Copy, 1977. Mem. adv. com. Community Coll. Denver, 1976. With U.S. Army, 1965-69. Mem. Nat. Micrographics Assn. (chmn. edn. com. Rocky Mountain chpt. 1974-75, Mem. of Yr. award 1977), Contractors Micrographics and Info. Mgmt. Assn. (conf. host 1986, mem. exec. com. 1984—, vice chmn. 1985-86, chmn. 1986-87), Assn. Info. and Image Mgmt. Republican. Roman Catholic. Home: 961 Hazel St Livermore CA 94550 Office: Lawrence Livermore Nat Lab PO Box 808 Livermore CA 94550

JUDSON, FRANKLYN NEVIN, physician, educator; b. Cleve., Apr. 14, 1942; s. Franklyn S. and Nancy Elizabeth (Nevin) J.; m. Kathleen A. Thompson, June 24, 1972 (div. 1977); m. Marti J. Sachse, Dec. 10, 1981; children: Jennifer, Rachel. BA, Wesleyan U., 1964; MD, U. Pa., 1968. Intern U. Wis. Hosps., Madison, 1968-69, resident, 1969-70; epidemic intelligence svc. officer Ctrs. Disease Control, Atlanta, 1970-72; fellow in infectious diseases U. Colo., Denver, 1972-74, from asst. prof. to assoc. prof. depts. medicine and preventive medicine, 1976-87, prof., 1987—; dir. Denver Disease Control Service, 1976-86; chief infectious disease service Denver Gen. Hosp., 1974—; dir. Dept. Pub. Health City of Denver, 1986—. Editor: Diagnosis of Sexually Transmitted Diseases, 1985; assoc. editor Sexually Transmitted Diseases, 1988—; mem. editorial bd. Genitourinary Medicine, 1984—; contbr. articles to profl. jours. Pres. met. council Colo. chpt. Am. Lung Assn., Denver, 1988—, bd. dirs. Mem. Am. Veneral Disease Assn. (bd. dirs. 1981—, pres. 1983-85, Outstanding Investigator 1980), Am. Social Health Assn. (bd. dirs. 1983—, v.p. 1987), Group Against Smokers' Pollution (bd. dirs., v.p. Colo. chpt. 1982—). Soc. of Friends. Home: 662 Josephine Denver CO 80206

JUKKOLA, GEORGE DUANE, obstetrician-gynecologist; b. Aliquippa, Pa., Feb. 28, 1945; s. Waino Helmer and Bedelia (Pyle) J.; m. Gretchen Louise Strom, Feb. 14, 1970 (div. 1985); children: David, Jeffrey; m. Wendee Leigh Bookhart, Apr. 23, 1988. BA in Psychology, U. Calif., Berkeley, 1970; MD, U. Pitts., 1975. Diplomate, Am. Bd. Ob.-Gyn. Caseworker Pa. Dept. Welfare, Rochester, 1971; resident in ob.-gyn. Akron (Ohio) Med. Ctr., 1975-78; pvt. practice Riverside, Calif., 1978—; co-founder, Family Birthing Ctr. Riverside, 1981-87; mng. ptnr. Parkview Profl. Ctr., Riverside, 1984—; chief dept. ob.-gyn., Parkview Community Hosp., Riverside, 1986—; guest lectr., Riverside Community Coll., 1984, 85. With USAF, 1965-69. Decorated Air medal with 4 oak leaf clusters. Fellow Am. Coll. Ob.-Gyn.; mem. AMA, Calif. Med. Assn., Riverside County Med. Assn., Am. Assn. Individual Investors, Victoria Club Riverside, Inland Physicians Med. Group (v.p. 1987-88), Mensa. Republican. Unitarian-Universalist. Home: 10252 Victoria Ave Riverside CA 92503-6100 Office: Ste G 3900 Sherman Dr Riverside CA 92503-4062

JULIUSSEN, KAREN, computer company executive; b. Chgo., Apr. 16, 1948; d. Adolph Vernon Petska and Jean (Hebert) Leyendecker; divorced; children: Lisa, Krista; m. Egil Juliussen, Jan. 1, 1987; 1 child, Jon. Grad. high sch., Manitowoc, Wis. Adminstrv. asst. Future Computing Inc., Dallas, 1982-86; mgr. market devel. StoreBoard Inc., Dallas, 1986, also bd. dirs.; v.p. mktg. Worksta. Labs., Inc., Dallas, 1987; pres. Savantek, Inc., Incline Village, Nev., 1987—; chmn. Computer Industry Almanac, Inc., Incline Village, 1988—. Editor: Computer Industry Almanac, 1988. Home and Office: 737 Allison Dr Incline Village NV 89451

JULLE, KEITH LEROY, oil executive; b. Lagrand, Oreg., May 13, 1939; s. William Leroy and Eleta Catherine (Spangler) J.; m. Marilyn Jean Biekofsky, Aug. 14, 1965; children: Pamela J., Kevin L. BS, S.W. Mo. State U., 1966; MBA, Pepperdine U., 1979. With sales dept. Shell Oil Co., St. Louis, 1966-72; with sales and mgmt. dept. Shell Oil Co., Chgo., 1972-73, L.A., 1973-77; with mgmt. Shell Oil Co., Houston, 1977-79; pres. Mohave Oil Co., Kingman, Ariz., 1979—; mem. adv. bd. Valley Nat. Bank, Kingman, 1986—. Pres. 2005 Indsl. Devel., Kingman, 1986, Kingsmen Promotional Group, Kingman, 1986. With USN, 1960-64. Mem. Kingman Area C. of C. (bd. dirs. 1982-88, pres. 1986-87), Rotary, Elks (all chairs exalted ruler 1987-88). Republican. Lutheran. Home: 3768 Stirrup Dr Kingman AZ 86401

JUMAO-AS, ALEX BARONDA, engineer; b. Surigao City, Philippines, June 12, 1961; came to U.S., 1982; s. Gaudencio Tamosa and Adelaida (Baronda) J.; m. Remedios Panoncillo, Jan. 28, 1981; 1 child, Real James. BS in Indsl. Engring. with high honors, U. San Jose Recoletos, Cebu City, Philippines, 1982; grad. mech. and elec. tech. with high honors, U. Alaska, 1988, AAS in Archtl. and Engring. with honors, 1989. Drafter Dept. Interior Bur. Land Mgmt., Anchorage, 1983-84, Raj Bhargava Assocs., Anchorage, 1984; asst. engr., drafter Unicom, Inc., Anchorage, 1984—; v.p. Unicom, Inc. Anchorage Employee Svc. Assn., 1985-86. Mem. Metro Cebu Jr. Jaycees, Am. Inst. Design and Drafting. Roman Catholic. Home: 701 S Klevin St Sp 31-A Anchorage AK 99508 Office: Unicom Inc 5450 A St Anchorage AK 99518

JUMP, LEWIS HOWARD, forester; b. Newton, N.J., Nov. 2, 1946; s. Howard Ingalls and Audrey (Cooper) J.; m. Lillian Grace Sinquah, July 8, 1967; children: Valerie, Glen, Lila. BS in Forestry, No. Ariz. U., 1971. Asst. dist. forester N.Mex. Dept. Forestry, Magdalena, 1971-72; soil conservationist USDA Soil Conservation Svc., various locations, 1972-76; forester USDA Forest Svc., Fredonia, Ariz., 1976-79; forest silviculturist USDA Forest Svc., Cedar City, Utah, 1979-85; dist. silviculturist USDA Forest Svc., Bakersfield, Calif., 1985-88; asst. forest planner USDA Forest Svc., Porterville, Calif., 1988—. Contbr. to USDA publs. Mem. Soc. Am. Foresters. Home: 2330 Kings Cross Way Porterville CA 93257 Office: Sequoia Nat Forest 900 W Grand Ave Porterville CA 93257

JUMP, MARGARET PATRICIA, real estate investment specialist; b. N.Y.C., Feb. 13, 1934; d. Albert and Margaret (Fitzgerald) Stewart; m. Richard Wolfe Schiller, July, 1951 (div. 1958); 1 child, Leslie Schiller Hooker; m. John Wilkes Jump; children: Jeffrey Walter, Monica Stewart, John Albert. AS in Real Estate, Ventura Coll. Sales rep. House and Home Real Estate, Ventura, Calif., 1960-64; real estate assoc. Pat Jump & Assocs., Ventura, 1964-71, Red Carpet Real Estate, Ventura, 1971-74; pvt. practice Ventura, 1974—. Mem. Ventura Bd. Realtors, Ventura C. of C., Sierra, 50th. Home and Office: 1740 Miramar St Ventura CA 93001

JUNCHEN, DAVID LAWRENCE, pipe organ manufacturing company executive; b. Rock Island, Ill., Feb. 23, 1946; s. Lawrence Ernest and Lucy Mae (Ditto) J.; B.S. in Elec. Engring. with highest honors, U. Ill., 1968. Founder, owner Junchen Pipe Organ Service, Sherrard, Ill., 1968—; co-owner Junchen-Collins Organ Corp., Woodstock, Ill., 1975-80; mng. dir. Baranger Studios, South Pasadena, Calif., 1980-81. Named Outstanding Freshman in Engring. U. Ill., 1963-64. Mem. Am. Inst. Organbuilders (bd. dirs. 1986—), Am. Theatre Organ Soc. (Tech. Excellence award 1986), Mus. Box Soc., Automatic Mus. Instrument Collectors Assn., Tau Beta Pi, Sigma Tau, Eta Kappa Nu. Author: Encyclopedia of American Theatre Organs; contbr. to Ency. Automatic Mus. Instruments; composer, arranger over 100 music rolls for self-playing mus. instruments. Office: 280 E Del Mar Ste 311 Pasadena CA 91101

JUNE, ROY ETHIEL, lawyer; b. Forsyth, Mont., Aug. 12, 1922; s. Charles E. and Elizabeth F. (Newnes) J.; m. Laura Brautigam, June 20, 1949; children—Patricia June, Richard Tyler. B.A., U. Mont., 1948, B.A. in Law, 1951, LL.B., 1952. Bar: Mont. 1952, Calif. 1961. Sole practice, Billings, Mont., 1952-57, Sanders and June, 1953-57; real estate developer, Orange County, Calif., 1957-61; ptnr. Dugan, Tobias, Tornay & June, Costa Mesa, Calif., 1961-62; city prosecutor, Costa Mesa, 1962-63, asst. city atty., 1963-67, city atty., 1967-78; sole practice, Costa Mesa, 1962—. Atty. Costa Mesa Hist. Soc., Costa Mesa Playhouse Patron's Assn., Red Barons Orange County, Costa Mesa Meml. Hosp. Aux., Harbc. Key, Child Guidance Ctr. Orange County, Fairview State Hosp. Therapeutic Pool Vols., Inc.; active Eagle Scout evaluation team, Harbor Area Boy Scouts Am., YMCA; atty. United Fund/Community Chest Costa Mesa and Newport Beach; bd. dirs. Boys' Club Harbor Area, bd. dirs. Mardan Ctr. Ednl. Therapy, United Cerebral Palsy Found. Orange County. Served with USAF, World War II. Decorated Air medal with oak leaf cluster, D.F.C. Mem. Mont. Bar Assn., Calif. Bar Assn., Orange County Bar Assn., Harbor Bar Assn., Costa Mesa C. of C. (bd. dirs.). Clubs: Masons, Scottish Rite, Shriners, Santa Ana Country, Amigos Viejos, Los Fiestadores. Office: 2970 Harbor Blvd Ste 211 PO Box 3050 Costa Mesa CA 92626

JUNEJA, BACHITTAR SINGH, mechanical engineer, consultant; b. Hoshiarpur, Punjab, India, Sept. 3, 1947; came to U.S., 1973; s. Jiwan Mal and Kartar (Devi) J.; m. Anju Bala, Mar. 30, 1987; 1 son, Christopher Mayur. BS in Mech. engring., Birla Inst. Tech. and Sci., 1970. Design engr. Asiatic Inc., New Delhi, India, 1970-73; sr. field engr. Logicon Inc., Fairfax, Va., 1973-76; tech. staff engr. U.S. Postal Svc., Los Angeles, 1976-81; sr. maintenance engr. regional hdqrs. U.S. Postal Svc., San Bruno, Calif., 1981-86; mgr. maintenance engring. support U.S. Postal Svc., Los Angeles, 1986—. Home: 10404 Morning Glory Ave Fountain Valley CA 92708 Office: US Postal Svc 7001 S Central Ave Los Angeles CA 90052-9341

JUNG, EDMUND DIXON, physician; b. Hanford, Calif., June 29, 1914; s. Ming Stanley and Mabel (Wye) J.; m. Haw Chan, Jan. 28, 1950. AB, Stanford U., 1938; MS, U. Calif., San Francisco, 1941, MD, 1944. Diplomate Am. Bd. Internal Medicine. Staff physician, chief allergy sect. VA Med. Ctr., Oakland, Martinez, Calif., 1951-82; assoc. clin. prof. medicine U. Calif., San Francisco, 1982—; cons. allergy VA Regional Office, San Francisco, 1961-66; asst. clin. prof. U. Calif., San Francisco, 1974-84, assoc. clin. prof., 1984—. Bd. dirs. Chinese Hist. Soc. Am., San Francisco, 1986—. Capt. M.C., U.S. Army, 1945-47, PTO. Fellow ACP; mem. Am. Acad. Allergy and Clin. Immunology, Am. Soc. Clin. Hypnosis.

JUNG, HENRY HUNG, mechanical engineer; b. Hong Kong, Aug. 3, 1957; s. Cheuk-Sun and Siu-Kuen (Ma) J.; m. Mi-Ying Miranda, Mar. 28, 1986. BS MechE, Ariz. State U., 1980; MS MechE, U. Ill., 1983. Engr. Lockheed Aircraft, Burbank, Calif., 1981-82; researcher U. Ill., Champaign-

Urbana, 1982-83; engr. Pratt & Whitney Aircraft, West Palm Beach, Fla., 1983-84; sr. scientist Lockheed Missiles & Space Co., Palo Alto, Calif., 1984—. Mem. ASME, AIAA, N.Y. Acad. Scis., Sigma Xi, Tau Beta Pi, Pi Tau Sigma. Home: 21486 Holly Oak Dr Cupertino CA 95014

JUNG, SAMSON PANG, computer analyst, investment company executive; b. Hong Kong, Sept. 28, 1963; came to U.S. 1978; s. Fook Leugn and Mee Yung (Lee) J. AA, City Coll., San Francisco, 1983; BA, San Francisco State U., 1988. Cert. Chineses and holistic medicine. Computer cons. Brasswork, San Francisco, 1981-82; dir. Inst. Sef Improvement, San Francisco, 1983-88; v.p. Eagle Investment Co., San Francisco, 1985—; computer analyst D.W. Smith & Assoc., Foster City, Calif., 1987—; healer, counselor Wole Life Expn., San Francisco, 1981-83; cons. Mind, Body and Spirit Fair, San Francisco, 1982. Author: Holistic Enlightment Learning Process, 1985; inventor acupuncture probe. Counselor Ctr. for Instnl. Change, San Francisco, 1986. Mem. Computer Learning Ctr., Golden Key (life). Home: 3529 Anza St San Francisco CA 94121

JUNG, TIMOTHY TAE KUN, otolaryngologist; b. Seoul, Korea, Dec. 1, 1943; came to U.S., 1969; s. Yoon Yong and Helen Chung-Hyuk (Im) J.; m. Lucy Moon Young, Sept. 10, 1972; children: David, Michael, Karen. BS, Seoul Nat. U., 1966, Loma Linda U., 1971; MD, Loma Linda U., 1974; PhD, U. Minn., 1980. Diplomate, Am. Bd. Otolaryngology. Med. intern Loma Linda (Calif.) U. Med. Ctr., 1974-75; fellow in surgery U. Minn. Med. Sch., Mpls., 1975-76; fellow in otolaryngology U. Minn. Med. Sch., 1976-80, asst. prof. otolaryngology, 1980-84, clin. asst. prof., dir. prostaglandin lab., 1984-85; assoc. prof., dir. otolaryngology rsch. Loma Linda U., 1985—; cons., Otitis Media Rsch. Ctr., Mpls., 1985—. Contbr. chpts. to 18 med. books, over 60 articles and abstracts to med. jours. Sgt. Korean army, 1966-69. Fellow The Triological Soc., Am. Acad. Otolaryngology; mem. AMA, Soc. Univ. Otolaryngologists, Assn. Rsch. in Otolaryngology. Seventh-day Adventist. Home: 11790 Pecan Way Loma Linda CA 92354 Office: Loma Linda U Med Ctr Loma Linda CA 92354

JUNGBLUTH, CONNIE CARLSON, investment banker; b. Cheyenne, Wyo., June 20, 1955; d. Charles Marion and Janice Yvonne (Keldsen) Carlson; m. Kirk E. Jungbluth, Feb. 5, 1977; 1 child, Tyler. BS, Colo. State U., 1976. CPA, Colo. Sr. acct. Rhode Scripter & Assoc., Boulder, Colo., 1977-81; mng. acct. Arthur Young, Denver, 1981-85; asst. v.p. Dain Bosworth, Denver, 1985-87, George K. Baum & Assocs., Denver, 1987—; bd. dirs. Security Diamond Exchange, Denver. mem. Denver Estate Planning Council, 1981-85, organizer Little People Am., Rocky Mountain Med. Clinic and Symposium, Denver, 1986; adv. bd. Children's Home Health, Denver, 1986—; fin. adv. bd. Gail Shoettler for State Treas., Denver, 1986; bd. advisors U. Denver Sch. Accountancy, 1986-89; campaign chmn. Kathi Williams for Colo. State Legis., 1986. Named one of 50 to watch, Denver mag., 1988. Mem. AICPA, Colo. Soc. CPAs (strategic planning com. 1987-89, instr. bank 1983, trustee 1984-87, pres. bd. trustees, 1986-87, bd. dirs. 1987-89, Pub. Svc. award 1985-87, chmn. career edn. com. 1982-83), Colo. Mcpl. Bond Dealers, MetroNorth C. of C. (bd. dirs. 1987—), Pi Beta Phi. Club: Denver City (bd. dirs. 1987-88).

JUNGBLUTH, KIRK E., mortgage banking executive; b. Lima, Ohio, Apr. 5, 1949; s. Harold A. and Marjorie J. (Brown) J.; m. Connie Carlson, Feb. 5, 1977; 1 child, Tyler. Student, Mesa Coll., Grand Junction, Colo., 1967-69, Regis Coll., Denver, 1987—. Lic. real estate broker, Colo. Loan officer, real estate appraiser Home Fed. Savs. & Loan, Ft. Collins, Colo., 1973-76; real estate appraiser Jungbluth & Assocs., Ft. Collins, 1976-83; pres., bd. dirs. Security Diamond Corp., Denver, 1982—; nat. sales dir. InfoAm. Computers, Denver, 1983-85; chmn. bd. dirs., chief exec. officer U.S. Capital Lending Corp., Denver, 1987—, U.S. Capital Corp., Denver, 1987—, Capital Real Estate & Devel. Corp., Denver, 1988—. Sec.-treas. St. Peters Luth. Ch., Ft. Collins, Colo., 1980-81, pres., 1982-84. Sgt. USMC, 1969-71. Republican. Office: US Capital Lending Corp 360 S Monroe Ste 210 Denver CO 80209

JUNKIN, ELIZABETH DARBY, editor; b. Denver, Dec. 7, 1958; d. H.L. Junkin Jr. and Merrie Lynn (Knott) McNabb; m. Cameron Shaw, Aug. 1988. BA cum laude, Barnard Coll., 1980; student, Paris Am. Acad., France, 1977. Reporter Gemini News Svc./United Nations, N.Y.C., 1978-81; statehouse corr. Sta. KCFR-FM/Nat. Pub. Radio, Denver, 1981-82; We. corr. Nat. Pub. Radio, Denver, 1981-82; staff reporter Newsweek mag., Denver, 1982-84, 1985, acting bur. chief, 1984; writer Newsweek mag., Denver, Paris, S. Africa, 1986-88; assoc. pub. Fulcrum Press, Golden, Colo., 1987-88; mng. editor BUZZWORM mag., Boulder, Colo., 1989—; freelance writer N.Y. Times, Newsweek, French Geo, 1986—; chief press aide, 4th World Wilderness Congress, Colo., 1987; speaker Colo. U. Law Sch. seminar on pub. lands, Boulder, Colo., 1986, Women's Press Club, Denver, 1986, Polit. Economy Rsch. Ctr., Bozeman, Mont., 1986, Internat. Wilderness Leadership Sch., Durban, 1988. Author: Lands of Brighter Destiny, 1986; editor: Of Destiny & Discovery, 1986, South African Passage, 1987; contbr. numerous articles publs. Democrat. Episcopalian. Office: BUZZWORM Mag 1818 16th St Boulder CO 80302

JUNKIN, WILLIAM WAKEMAN, advertising agency executive; b. N.Y.C., July 13, 1943; s. George de Forest and Alice Gertrude Maslin J.; m. Janet Grace Blass, Feb. 28, 1968 (div. May 1973); children: Jennifer Noel, Drew deForest; m. Pamela Brewer, June 21, 1981; children: Devon deForrest, Trent Brewer. BS, Fordham U., 1965. Asst. mgr. customer relations Hertz Corp., N.Y.C., 1965-67; advt. mgr. Diners Club, N.Y.C., 1967-70; acct. supr. N.W. Ayer Co., N.Y.C., 1970-75; v.p. mktg. Cally Curtis Co., Hollywood, Calif., 1975-78; sr. v.p., mgmt. supr. Cochran Chase Livingston, Newport Beach, Calif., 1978-81; exec. v.p. Gillen Stone, Newport Beach, 1981—; pres. Wakeman & deForrest, Newport Beach, 1981—. Mem. Calif. Rep. Assembly, Newport Beach. Served to lt. USMC, 1962-68. Mem. Direct Mktg. Assn. Roman Catholic. Office: Wakeman & deForrest 2601 Main St Irvine CA 92714

JUPIN, LAWRENCE EARL, special educator; b. Centralia, Ill., July 11, 1939; s. Earl Cranston and Laura Lorraine (Rose) J.; m. Jackie Scuccimarri, July 18, 1981 (div. 1986); m. Deborah Huang, June 27, 1987. BS, Southern Ill. U., 1962, MS, 1972; tchr. cert., Western Mich. U., 1964; postgrad., UCLA, 1972-74. Cert. spl. edn. tchr., Calif. Spl. edn. tchr. Centralia City Schs., 1968-71, Rialto (Calif.) Sch. Dsit., 1972-73; Spl. edn. tchr. Riverside (Calif.) County Schs., 1974-79, lead tchr., 1979-81; spl. edn. tchr. L.A. County Schs., 1984—; auxiliary speech clinician UCLA Speech Clinic, 1973-75; pvt. speech therapist, Palm Springs, Calif., 1978-83; cons. Nat. Stuttering Project, Huntington Beach, Calif., 1984-86. Co-author: That's Easy for You to Say!, 1985; author: The Brother's Keeper, 1989, Reunion, 1989. Mem. Spl. Edn. Parents' Group, Centralia, 1968-71; fundraiser Mar. of Dimes, Palm Springs, Calif., 1978-80. Tchr. scholar, State of Ill., 1970. Mem. L.A. County Tchrs. Assn., Calif. Tchrs. Assn., NEA, Elks. Republican. Home: 22332-5 Harbor Ridge Ln Torrance CA 90502

JURECKI, CASIMER JOHN JOSEPH, financial analyst; b. Cleve., Apr. 5, 1952; s. Casimer Joseph and Helen Ann (Hertvik) J.; m. Marcella Loubet, July 16, 1988. BA, Cleve. State U., 1976; MBA, Calif. State U.-L.A., 1984. Accounts analyst Am. Greetings Corp., Cleve., 1977-79; regional credit mgr. Carnation Co., L.A., 1979-84; fin. analyst Carnation Co., 1984-86, sr. fin. analyst, 1986--. Mem. So. Calif. Food Mfrs. Credit Assn. (v.p. 1978-79), Santa Anita Catholic Singles (pres.'s award 1987), U.S. Assn. Evening Students (Roy J. Barry award 1981), Assn. MBA Execs., Choice L.A. Retreat Program. Republican. Roman Catholic. Home: 5858 Coldwater Canyon Ave Apt 3 North Hollywood CA 91607 Office: Carnation Corp Office 5045 Wilshire Blvd Los Angeles CA 90036

JUREWICZ, THOMAS, pilot; b. Amittyville, N.Y., Nov. 24, 1958; s. Richard A. and Marion (Ortowski) J.; m. Nedra O'Bryant, Nov. 14, 1987. AS in Pre Architecture, Moorpark (Calif.) Jr. Coll., 1978; BS in Aero. Tech., Ariz. State U., 1983. With Sears, Roebuck & Co., Thousand Oaks, Calif., 1976-77; salesperson Broadway Dept. Stores, Thousand Oaks, 1977-78; with Continental Cyclery, Thousand Oaks, 1978, Tempe (Ariz.) Bicycle Shop, 1979; flight instr. Superstition Air Svc., Mesa, Ariz., 1979-83, Channel Islands Aviation, Camarillo, Calif., 1983-84; pilot Westair Industries, Chico, Calif., 1984, Comair, Inc., Cin., 1985-87, U.S. Air, Inc., Washington, 1987—. Mem. Air Line Pilots Assn., Aircraft Owners and Pilots Assn., Air and Space Smithsonian, Kappa Sigma. Republican. Roman Catholic. Home: 2629 E Aldine St Phoenix AZ 85032

JURSCHAK, JAY ALOYSIUS, company executive; b. Council Bluffs, Iowa, Nov. 21, 1952; s. Mary Ann (Kirschbaum) Schwinderman. Student, U. Iowa, 1973-75; BS, U. Nev., 1981. Sales mgr. Manpower Temporary Svcs., Reno, 1978-81; sales rep. Burroughs Wellcome Co., Research Triangle Park, Nev., 1981-84; investment officer Crocker Bank/Wells Fargo Bank, L.A., 1984-86; 2nd v.p. Chase Manhattan Bank, L.A., 1986-87; pres. Pacific Temporary Svc., Inc., Sacramento, Calif., 1987—; hon. bd. dirs. Skills & Bus. Edn. Ctr., Sacramento, 1988—. Mem. bus. jour. John Entrepreneaur, Jurschak takes Byte out of. Vol. Ronald Reagan for Pres., L.A., 1984, Brunic for U.S. senate. Mem. Sacramento Metro C. of C., Roseville C. of C., Rancho Cordova C. ofC. Republican Catholic. Office: Pacific Temporary Svcs 911 Howe Ave Sacramento CA 95825

JUST, KEVIN L., accountant; b. Santa Monica, Calif., May 4, 1956; s. Virgil Louis and Joyce (Jopp) J.; m. Cheryl Martin, Dec. 31, 1979; children: Trevor Lee, Brett Richard. AS, Cabrillo Coll., 1977; BS in Acctg., San Jose State U., 1979. CPA, Calif. Tax mgr. Armstrong, Bastow & Potter (Peat Marwick & Mitchell), San Jose, Calif., 1979-86; ptnr. Powell & Just Accountancy Corp, Campbell, Calif., 1987—. Office: Powell & Just Accountancy Corp 1550 S Bascom Ave #380 Campbell CA 95008

JUSTESEN, BRYCE EVERETT, dentist; b. Utah, Feb. 25, 1953; s. Donald Jay and Carol Starr (Cromar) J.; m. Annette James, July 7, 1976; children: Jason Bryce, Holly Ann, Sarah Dawn, Jamie Starr. BS, Brigham Young U., 1977; DDS, Northwestern U., 1981. Pvt. practice Mesa, Ariz., 1981--. Scoutmaster Boy Scouts Am., Chgo. and Mesa, 1980--. Recipient Wood Badge award Boy Scouts Am., 1988. Mem. ADA, Ariz. State Dental Assn. Mormon. Office: 1150 N Country Club St Ste 9 Mesa AZ 85201

JUSTIN, JOSEPH EUGENE, military officer; b. Orange, N.J., June 3, 1945; s. James Fredrick and Elizabeth Ann (McCartney) J.; children: James Kenneth, Joseph Patrick. BS, USAF Acad., 1969; MS, Ohio State U., 1973; MA, U. So. Calif., 1980. Commd. 2d lt. USAF, 1969, advanced through grades to maj., 1980; lead project engr. USAF Avionics Lab. USAF, Wright-Patterson AFB, Ohio, 1970-74; exchange officer USAF Systems Commd. USAF, F.E. Warren AFB, Cheyenne, Wyo., 1974; mgr. guidance improvement program USAF Ballistic Missiles Office, Norton AFB, Calif., 1975-77, chief flight test integration div., 1985—; asst. prof. astronautics USAF Acad., Colorado Springs, Colo., 1977-81; research fellow USAF Hdqrs.-Rand Corp., Santa Monica, Calif., 1981-82; dir. space system studies Hdqrs. USAF, Washington, 1982-85. Mem. AIAA (sr.), Air Force Assn. (life), Air Force War Coll. Assn. (life), USAF Acad. Assn. Grads. (life), Ohio State U. Alumni Assn. (life), USAF Research Assocs. Assn., Naval Inst. Office: USAF Ballistic Missile Office Norton AFB CA 92409

JUVET, RICHARD SPALDING, JR., chemistry educator; b. Los Angeles, Aug. 8, 1930; s. Richard Spalding and Marion Elizabeth (Dalton) J.; m. Martha Joy Myers, Jan. 29, 1955 (div. Nov. 1978); children: Victoria, David, Stephen, Richard P.; m. Evelyn Raeburn Elthon, July 1, 1984. B.S., UCLA, 1952, Ph.D., 1955. Research chemist Dupont, 1955; instr. U. Ill., 1955-57, asst. prof., 1957-61, assoc. prof., 1961-70; prof. analytical chemistry Ariz. State U., Tempe, 1970—; researcher on gas and liquid chromatography, instrumental analysis, computer interfacing; vis. prof. UCLA, 1960, U. Cambridge, Eng., 1964-65, Nat. Taiwan U., 1968, Ecole Polytechnique, France, 1976-77, U. Vienna, Austria, 1989—; mem. air pollution chemistry and physics adv. com. EPA, HEW, 1969-72; cons. R.J. Reynolds Industries, 1966-72; mem. adv. panel on advanced chem. alarm tech., devel. and engring. directorate Def. Systems div. Edgewood Arsenal, 1975. Author: Gas-Liquid Chromatography, Theory and Practice, 1962; Editorial advisor to: Jour. Chromatographic Sci., 1969-85, Jour. Gas Chromatography, 1963-68, Analytica Chimica Acta, 1972-74, Analytical Chemistry, 1974-77, biennial reviewer in, 1962-76. NSF sr. postdoctoral fellow, 1964-65; recipient Sci. Exchange Agreement award Czechoslovakia, Hungary, Romania and Yugoslavia, 1977. Fellow Am. Inst. Chemists; mem. Am. Chem. Soc. (nat. chmn. div. analytical chemistry 1972-73, nat. sec.-treas. div. analytical chemistry 1969-71, councilor 1978-89, coun. com. analytical reagents 1985—, chmn. U. Ill. sect. 1968-69, sec. 1962-63, co-author Reagent Chemicals 7th edit., 1986, directorate div. officers' caucus 1987—), AAAS, Internat. Platform Assn., Internat. Union of Pure and Applied Chemistry, Am. Radio Relay League, Sigma Xi, Phi Lambda Upsilon, Alpha Chi Sigma (profl. rep.-at-large 1989—). Presbyn. (deacon 1960—, ruling elder 1972—, commr. Grand Canyon Presbytery 1974-76). Home: 4821 E Calle Tuberia Phoenix AZ 85018 Office: Ariz State U Dept Chemistry Tempe AZ 85287-1604

KAAKE, RICHARD HOWARD, lawyer; b. Long Beach, Calif., Sept. 2, 1948; s. Richard Harold and Nancy Ann (Tierney) K.; m. Joan Lynn Nilson, July 31, 1970; children: Steven Terrill, Richard Heyden, Jennifer Renee. BA, Calif. State U., Long Beach, 1970; MA in Edn., East Carolina U., Greenville, N.C., 1974; JD, Calif. Western Sch. Law, 1977; postgrad., Georgetown U., 1978-80. Bar: Calif., Colo., D.C., U.S. Ct. Mil. Appeals, 1978, U.S. Dist. Ct. (so. dist.) Calif. 1978, U.S. Dist. Ct., D.C. 1978, U.S Ct. Appeals (D.C. cir.) 1978, U.S. Ct. Appeals, D.C. 1978, U.S. Supreme Ct., Calif. 1978, U.S. Ct. Appeals (9th cir.) 1979, U.S. Claims Ct. 1979, U.S. Tax Ct. 1979, U.S. Supreme Ct. 1981, U.S. Ct. Appeals (fed. cir.), 1983, U.S. Supreme Ct., Colo. 1988. Atty.-advisor Def. Logistics Agy., Washington, 1977-79; chief counsel Def. Logistics Agy., Tracy, Calif., 1979-84; assoc. counsel Def. Logistics Agy., Washington, 1984-85; sr. atty. aeronutronic div. Ford Aerospace Corp., Newport Beach, Calif., 1985-88; div. counsel Ford Aerospace Corp., Colorado Springs, Colo., 1988—; counsel Ford Microelectronics, Inc., Colorado Springs, 1989—. Capt. USMC, 1970-74. Mem. El Paso County Bar Assn., Soccer Orgn. of Colorado Springs, Phi Alpha Delta, Pi Sigma Alpha, Kappa Delta Pi. Office: Ford Aerospace Corp Div Counsel 9970 Federal Dr Colorado Springs CO 80921-3603

KABAT, HUGH, pharmacy educator; b. Manitowoc, Wis., Oct. 3, 1932; s. Frank William and Norene Mary (McCorkle) K.; m. Rita Catherine Laboe, Sept. 15, 1956 (div. Oct. 1977); children: Edward Michael, Patrick William, James Robert; m. Sally Phoebe Gutteridge, Aug. 16, 1980. BS in Pharmacy, U. Mich., 1954, MS in Hosp. Pharmacy, 1956; PhD in Pharm. Adminstrn., U. Colo., 1961. Cert. pharmacist, Mich., N.Mex. Instr. U. Colo., Boulder, 1959-61; from asst. prof. to assoc. dean U. Minn., Mpls., 1961-86; prof. U. N.Mex., Albuquerque, 1984—; cons. Med. Pharm. Industry Inc., Deltona, Fla., 1985—, AID/USPHS, 1984—. Author: Drug-Induced, 1968, Hospital Pharmaceutical Handbook, 1968. Served to capt. USPHS, 1956-58. Fellow Acad. Pharm. Scis., 1974; recipient disting. service award, Minn. Epilepsy League, 1971; Hallie Bruce Meml. lectr., Minn. Soc. Hosp. Pharmacists, 1969; Fulbright scholar, 1977. Fellow Am. Pharm. Assn., 1953—; mem. Am. Assn. Colls. Pharmacy, Am. Soc. Hosp. Pharmacists, Am. Assn. Pharm. Scis., Fulbright Assn. Roman Catholic. Office: U NMex Coll Pharmacy Albuquerque NM 87131

KACI, JUDITH ARLENE, criminal justice educator; b. San Francisco, Sept. 22, 1945; d. Harry William and Mae Alice (Pate) Hails; m. Ahmed Kaci, July 28, 1979; children: Miriam E., Kahina K. BS, Loma Linda U., 1968; MS, Calif. State U., Long Beach, 1972; JD, Southwestern U., L.A., 1976; LLM, NYU, 1979. Dep. sheriff L.A. Sheriff's Dept., 1968-72, sgt., 1972-73; asst. prof. Calif. State U., Long Beach, 1972-76, assoc. prof., 1976—, chmn. dept. criminal justice, 1985—; adj. prof. John Jay Coll., N.Y.C., 1978-80; vis. prof. Ill. State U., Normal, 1981-83. Contbr. numerous articles on criminal law and domestic violence to profl. jours. Commr. Orange County (Calif.) Commn. on Status of Women, 1986—; mem. Orange County Coalition Against Domestic Violence, 1987—. Named Prof. of Yr., Calif. State U., Long Beach, 1974-75; Judge Jacob Fuchsburg fellow NYU, 1978-79. Mem. Calif. Assn. Adminstrn. Justice Educators (pres. 1987-88), Western & Pacific Assn. Criminal Justice Educators (v.p. 1987-88, pres. 1988-89), Acad. Criminal Justice Scis. (trustee 1986-89). Republican. Seventh-Day Adventist. Office: Calif State U 1250 Bellflower Blvd Long Beach CA 90840

KADELL, KATHERINE, artist, printmaker; b. Vienna, Austria; came to U.S., 1938, naturalized, 1943; d. Leopold and and Lina (Wohl) Kuert; m. Rudolph Kadelburg, March 8, 1938 (dec. Jan. 1960); 1 child, Anthony Kadell. Student, Chgo. Art Inst., 1946-47, Otis Art Inst., 1956-57, UCLA, 1960-61; BA, UCLA, 1979. Conducted sculpture workshops L.A., 1975-80; sculpture faculty tchr. U. Judaism, L.A., 1977-79. One-woman shows include Paideia Gallery, L.A., 1964, Brand Art Gallery, Glendale, Calif., 1967, Inglewood (Calif.) main library, Sr. Eye Gallery, Longbeach, Calif., 1981, 1986-87, Goethe Inst., L.A., 1988; exhibited in group shows at De Young Mus., San Francisco, ART U.S.A., N.Y.C., Downey Mus., Calif., Long Beach Mus.; represented in permanent collections Beverly Hills library, Edgar G. Robinson, Beverly Hills, Judge Leonard Wolf, Beverly Hills, Paul Lampl architect, N.Y.C., Skirball Mus., L.A. Mem. Artists Equity Assn. (L.A. chpt. membership chmn. 1975-76), L.A. Art Assn., Women's Caucus for Art, Nat. Water Color Soc. (assoc.), Women Painters West, Artist for Econ. Action, Beverly Hills Arts League. Home and Office: 1344 Londondery Pl Los Angeles CA 90069

KADEN, RICHARD ARTHUR, civil engineer; b. Coulee Dam, Wash., May 10, 1939; s. Fred Arthur and Kathryn Marie (Kellerman) K.; m. Olive Anne Mangus, Sept. 9, 1961; children: Todd Alan, Scott Alan, JoEllen Alene. BS, Wash. State U., 1963; MS, U. Calif., Berkeley, 1968; postgrad., U. Wash., 1988. Registered profl. engr., Wash. Asst. chief Corps of Engrs., Walla Walla (Wash.), 1977-79; exec. devel. assn. Corps of Engrs., Walla Walla, Washington, 1979; chief materials sect. Corps of Engrs., Walla Walla (Wash.), 1979-84, asst. chief design br., 1984-85, acting chief, 1985-86, mgr. mil. project, 1986-88, chief geology sect., 1988—; cons. Cargill, Inc.. Seattle, 1976, Walla Walla Grain Growers, 1976, cons. in field, Walla Walla, 1976-83. Contbr. articles to profl. jours. Mem. ASCE (Rsch. and Devel. Achievement award 1976), Soc. Am. Mil. Engrs. (v.p. 1985, Recruiting award 1984), Am. Concrete Inst. (com. chmn. 1982, editor Lunar Concrete). Democrat. Roman Catholic. Lodge: Elks. Home: 1936 Howard St Walla Walla WA 99362 Office: US Army Corps Engrs City-County Airport Bldg 602 Walla Walla WA 99362-9265

KADERLAN, ALICE, video producer; b. Atlantic City, Mar. 29, 1947; d. Sol and Shirley (Sussman) Youngerman; m. Norman Stanley Kaderlan, Dec. 28, 1969 (div.); m. Stephen Mark Goldman, Apr. 11, 1987. BA in English, George Washington U., 1969; postgrad., U. Wis., 1969-70. Reporter, producer Sta. WAMU-FM, Washington, 1977-80; reporter, sr. producer Nebr. Ednl. TV Network, Lincoln, 1980-84; producer Sta. KCNC-TV, Denver, 1984-86; pvt. practice pub. affairs media cons. Denver, 1986—; freelance reporter Nat. Pub. Radio, newspapers, Washington, 1977-80; part-time dance critic, various newspapers and radio stas., 1977-87. Mem. program panels Nebr. Arts Council, 1981-84; dir. pub. awareness, Colo. Seat Belt Network, Denver, 1986-88; asst. press sec. Dukakis-Bentsen Campaign, Colo.,1988; mem. Denver Dem. Com., 1988; mem. media task force Anti-Defamation League, Denver, 1987-88; co-chmn. emergency med. svcs. council, City of Denver, 1988—; bd. dirs. Am Jewish Com., Denver. Named One of 50 People to Watch in 1987 Denver Mag., 1986, One of 25 People to Watch in 1981 Omaha Mag., 1980. Mem. Am. Mktg. Assn. (Peak award 1988). Office: Bus Video Prodns 5808 S Rapp St Ste 100 Littleton CO 80120

KADEY, FREDERIC LIONEL, JR., geological consultant; b. Toronto, Ont., Can., June 21, 1918; came to U.S., 1925; s. Frederic Lionel and Catherine Amelia (Davies) K.; m. Brenda Boocook, Oct. 7, 1950; children—Brenda Catherine Kadey King. Frederic Lionel III. BSc, Rutgers U., 1941; MA, Harvard U., 1947. Lic. profl. geologist, Fla. Teaching fellow Harvard U., 1946-47; field geol. asst. Sinclair Oil Co., Casper, Wyo.; petrographer, rsch./devel. dept. U.S. Steel Corp., Pitts., 1947-51; mineralogist Manville Corp., N.J., 1951-66, sect. chief fillers, 1966-71, exploration mgr., Denver, 1972-83; cons. indsl. minerals, Englewood, Colo., 1983—; nat. def. exec. reservist, metals and minerals br. U.S. Dept. Interior, Washington, 1972—. Contbr. chpt. to book, numerous articles in field to profl. jours. Patentee indirect perlite expander. Pres., Chester Twp. Taxpayers Assn., N.J., 1957-61, Chester Twp. Bd. Edn., 1961-68. With AUS, 1941-45. Decorated Croix de Guerre (France). Recipient Hal Williams Hardinge award, 1986. Fellow AAAS; mem. Mineral Soc. Am., AIME (Disting. mem. 1981 Soc. Mining Engrs., soc. program chmn. 1981, soc. pres. 1984), Am. Inst. Profl. Geologists (charter, pres. N.Y. State sect. 1967-68), Sigma Xi, Alpha Sigma Phi. Republican. Episcopalian. Home: 7653 S Rosemary Circle Englewood CO 80112

KADISH, AVNI SAMUEL, clinical physician; b. Passaic, N.J., Jan. 2, 1954; s. Ben-Ami and Doris (Liepold) K. BA in Biology and Chemistry, Montclair State Coll., 1975; ND with high honors, John Bastyr Coll. Naturopathic Medicine, 1983. Teaching asst. minor surgery Pacific Coll. Naturopathic Medicine, San Rafael, Calif., 1981; lectr. nutrition T.T. Minor Sch., Seattle, 1983, Sierra Heights Elem. Sch., Renton, Wash., 1983, on Alzheimers, Rogue Valley Hosp., Medford, Oreg., 1983, nutrition and clin. ecology Vols. Unltd., Medford, 1983, Adopted Childrens Soc.; dir., clin. physician Ctr. of Health, Medford, 1983—; dir. Laser Acupuncture Project, 1981; USDA class A dealer exotic animals. Editor: Life Extension Handbook, 1979. Mem. Oreg. Assn. Naturopathic Physicians, Rogue Valley Naturopathic Physicians Assn., So. Oreg. Soc. Preventive Medicine, LIOC, SOAR. Home and Office: Ctr of Health 1012 E Jackson St Medford OR 97504

KADLEC, ROBERT MILTON, city official; b. San Diego, Feb. 6, 1953; s. Milton J. and Marilyn M. (Wertz) K. BA in Polit. Sci., U. Cin., 1975, MPA, 1978. Devel. officer I & II City of Cin., 1978-81, acting div. head devel. dept. neighborhood housing, 1981-82, devel. officer III dept. econ. devel., 1982-84; devel. asst. Baltimore County Econ. Devel., Towson, Md., 1984-86; project coord. redevel. agy. City of Oceanside, Calif., 1987-88, asst. dir. redevel. agy., 1988-89; mgr. redevel. projects City of Riverside, Calif., 1989—. Mem. Internat. City Mgmt. Assn. (assoc.), Am. Soc. Pub. Adminstrn., Am. Planning Assn., U. Cin. Alumni Assn. Home: 8918 Paddington Dr Riverside CA 92503 Office: 3900 Main St 5th Fl Riverside CA 92522

KADNER, CARL GEORGE, biology educator emeritus; b. Oakland, Calif., May 23, 1911; s. Adolph L. and Otilia (Pecht) K.; m. Mary Elizabeth Moran, June 24, 1939; children: Robert, Grace Wickersham, Carl L. BS, U. San Francisco, 1933; MS, U. Calif., Berkeley, 1936, PhD, 1941. Prof. biology Loyola Marymount U., Los Angeles, 1936-78, prof. emeritus, 1978—; trustee Loyola U., Los Angeles, 1970-73. Served to maj. U.S. Army, 1943-46. Mem. Entomol. Soc. Am. (emeritus), Sigma Xi, Alpha Sigma Nu. Republican. Roman Catholic. Home: 8100 Loyola Blvd Los Angeles CA 90045

KADTKE, JAMES BERNARD, physicist; b. Wilkes-Barre, Pa., May 28, 1957; s. Bernard C. and Irene (Domashinski) K. BSc in Physics, Pa. State U., State College, 1979, BSc in Math., 1979; MSc in Physics, Brown U., 1983, PhD in Physics, 1987. Grad. rsch. asst. Brown U., Providence, 1981-85; rsch. fellow Los Alamos (N.Mex.) Nat. Lab., 1985-87; postdoctoral rsch. fellow Inst. Non-Linear Sci., U. Calif.-San Diego, La Jolla, 1987-88, rsch. physicist, 1988—; cons. SAIC Corp., La Jolla, 1988—. Contbr. articles to profl. jours. Air Force Office Sci. Rsch. rsch. grantee, Bolling AFB, 1988-89. Mem. Am. Phys. Soc., Sigma Xi. Republican. Roman Catholic. Home: 8949 Lombard Pl Ste 401 San Diego CA 92122 Office: Inst Non-Linear Sci U Calif R-002 La Jolla CA 92093

KAEHLER, WILLIAM BRYANT, auditor, bank executive; b. Oak Park, Ill., May 23, 1947; s. William Joachim and Roselle I. (Peterson) K.; m. Robin Elaine Dicken, July 12, 1975; children: Larissa, Bryant. AA, Phoenix Coll., 1968; BA, U. Ariz., 1971. Asst., auditor The Ariz. Bank, Phoenix, 1972-75; dep. auditor United Bank Ariz., Phoenix, 1975-79; dir. audit Am. Fed. Savs., Salem, Oreg., 1979-82; v.p. audit Pima Savs., Tucson, 1982—. Asst. mgr. Little League Baseball, Tempe, Ariz., 1976. Mem. Fin. Mgrs. Soc., Inst. Internal Auditors (cert. internal auditor). Republican. Lutheran. Club: Ventana Tennis (Tucson). Home: 8218 E Bighorn Tr Tucson AZ 85715 Office: Pima Savs 4801 E Broadway Blvd Tucson AZ 85732

KAFER, MARGARET, realtor, appraiser; b. San Jose, Calif., Dec. 19, 1951; d. Joaquin Albert and Caroline (Machado) Chavez; m. William Harold Kafer, Mar. 1, 1975; children: Nicole, Brooke. BA, San Jose (Calif.) State U., 1974. Cert. realtor, Calif. Social worker Sonoma County, Santa Rosa, Calif., 1976-78; ednl. cons. Rohnert Park, Calif., 1981-84; co-mgr., dir. G. Caravan Ensemble, Sebastopol, Calif., 1978-88; apparaisor Rose Appraisals, Cotati, Calif., 1986-88; mktg. adminstr. Team for Fin. Planning, Santa Rosa, 1984-86; realtor Plaza Realty and Investments, Kohnert Park, 1985-88.

Clergy and Laity Concerned, 1987. Mem. Sonoma County Bd. Realtors, Redwood Union, Multiple Listing Service, Calif. Assn. Realtors, Women's Council of Realtors. Democrat. Roman Catholic. Home: 331 Alma Ave Rohnert Park CA 94928 Office: Plaza Realty & Investments 5959 Commerce Blvd #14 Rohnert Park CA 94928

KAGAWA, KATHLEEN HATSUYO, entrepreneur; b. Honolulu, June 9, 1952; d. Shinso and Jane Fumiko (Murata) K.; m. Masamichi Irimajiri (div. 1977). Student, U. Hawaii, Honolulu, 1970-73, Sophia U., Tokyo, 1973; BSBA, U. Beverly Hills, 1977, MBA, 1979, PhD in Internat. Bus., 1982. Mgr. Flipside Record Shop, Honolulu, 1969-70; producer, singer Victor Records, Tokyo, 1973-76; actress Hawaii Five-O, Honolulu, 1976; co-owner Images Internat. of Hawaii, Honolulu, 1976-79; v.p., sec., hostess East-West Connection TV Show, L.A., 1980-81; dir. pub. rels. Fendi, Beverly Hills, 1981-82; pres. Sky Prodns., Inc., Honolulu, 1982-86; v.p., treas. Born Internat., Inc., Honolulu, 1986—; cons. Schlossberg-Cassidy and Assoc., Washington, 1983-86, Yamada Group, Japan and U.S.A., 1987—; sponsor State of Hawaii Nat. Aquaculture Assn., Washington, 1983-86; admissions counselor U. Beverly Hills, Honolulu, 1984-86; adminstrv. exec., corp. sec. New Tokyo-Hawaii Restaurant Co, Ltd., 1981—; pres. K & H Devel. Co., Ltd.; realtor Diamond Head Group subs. New Tokyo Restaurant, 1986, bd. dirs; sec.-treas. Azabu Enterprises Ltd., 1989—, bd. dirs. Named Best in Backstroke, State of Hawaii Swim Competition, 1968. Mem. Gemological Inst. Am. Alumni Assn., Japan-Am. Soc. of Honolulu, Honolulu Bd. Realtors, Mortgage Broker Assn., Pacific and Asian Affairs Coun., Punahou Alumni Assn., Oahu Country Club. Baptist. Club: Oahu Country (Hawaii). Home: 3215 Kaohinani Dr Honolulu HI 96817

KAHAN, JAMES PAUL, psychologist; b. N.Y.C., Oct. 15, 1942; s. Robert Helmen Kahan and Janet (Rieders) Pressman; m. Edith Jane Lester, Dec. 27, 1970 (div. 1983); m. Elaine Marie Engman, June 29, 1984;. BA in Psychology, Reed Coll., 1964; PhD in Psychology, U. N.C., 1968. Asst. to assoc. prof. U. So. Calif., L.A., 1970-80; scientist to sr. scientist The RAND Corp., Santa Monica, Calif., 1981—; prof. RAND Grad. Sch., Santa Monica, 1983—; vis. prof. U. Haifa (Israel), 1980-81. Author: Theories of Coalition Formation, 1984; contbr. articles toprofl. jours. Instr. Skamdia Folk Dance Club, L.A., 1984—. Fellow Am. Psychol. Assn., Soc. Psychol. Study Social. Office: The RAND Corp 1700 Main St Santa Monica CA 90406

KAHAN, SHELDON JEREMIAH, musician, singer; b. Honolulu, Mar. 5, 1948; s. Aaron Kahan and Marianne (Royjiczek) Sann. Student, Tel Aviv U., 1967-69, Merritt Coll., 1972-74. Guitarist The Grim Reapers, Miami Beach, Fla., 1965-66; bassist The Electric Stage, Jerusalem, 1969-71; music dir., musician Fanfare, Los Angeles, 1974-75, Jean Paul Vignon & 1st Love, Los Angeles, 1975-76; musician Jenny Jones & Co., Los Angeles, 1976; musician, vocalist Fantasy, Los Angeles, 1977-79; leader, musician, vocalist Fortune, Los Angeles, 1980-83; bassist Johnny Tillotson Show, Nev., 1983; ptnr., musician, vocalist Heartlight, Los Angeles, 1983-84; leader, musician, vocalist The Boogie Bros., Los Angeles, 1984—; arranger, conductor L.A. Rock Chorus, 1988; musician, vocalist Jeremiah Kahan, L.A., 1988; spokesman Moore Oldsmobile & Cadillac, Valencia, Calif., 1987. compiler musical work copyrighted in Library of Congress: "Sheldon Jeremiah Kahan The Early Years-Vol.I". Mem. AFTRA, Am. Fedn. Musicians. Democrat. Jewish. Home: 3915 1/2 Fredonia Dr Los Angeles CA 90068

KAHLER, CHUCK, engineer, manufacturing executive; b. Youngstown, Ohio, Oct. 12, 1942; s. Gerhard and Mary Edith (Schweinberg) K; m. Geri Mauser, May 29, 1965; children: Charles, Michael, Kara Lee. BSME, William Rayen Sch. Engring., 1966; MBA, U. Wash., 1986. Mgr. PP&S-BCA Boeing Co., Seattle, 1976-82, sr. mgr., 1982-85, chief engr., 1985-88, gen. mgr., 1988—. Patentee thrust reversing device, thrust control apparatus. Roman Catholic. Home: 18008 176th NE Woodinville WA 98072 Office: Boeing PO Box 3707 Mail Stop 3K-11 Seattle WA 98124-2207

KAHN, DANIEL JEAN, small business owner; b. Fontaine L'Eveque, Belgium, Mar. 8, 1942; came to U.S., 1949; s. Michel and Anna Marie (Poncelet) K.; m. M. Reneé Dansker, June 7, 1964; children: Donna Michelle Johnson, Nicole Yvonne. BSME, Kansas U., 1965. CLU. Design engr. Internat. Harvester, Ft. Wayne, Ind., 1965-68, Western Gear, Belmont, Calif., 1968; indsl. salesman Shell Oil Co., L.A., 1968-71; ins. salesman Mass. Mutual, Newport Beach, Calif., 1971-74; salesman Prentice Hall Pub., So. Calif., 1974-77, Nat. Buyers Assn., Orange, Calif., 1977-79, Anthony Pools, Lguna Hills, Calif., 1979; owner Valley Advt., Fountain Valley, Calif., 1980—. Recipient Nat. Quality award, Am. Life Underwrtiters Assn., Santa Ana, Calif. 1973-75. Mem. Specialty Advt. Assn. Internat., Los Caballeros Sports Club. Democrat. Home: 17158 Buttonwood Fountain Valley CA 92708 Office: Valley Advt 17227 Newhope #8093 Fountain Valley CA 92708

KAHN, DOUGLAS GERARD, psychiatrist; b. Bklyn., July 22, 1946; s. Donald David and Diane Lilyan (Shankin) K.; m. Carol Janette Casserly, Aug. 12, 1983. BA cum laude, Tulane U., 1968; MD, U. Miami (Fla.), 1972. Diplomate Am. Bd. Psychiatry and Neurology. Intern medicine Jackson Meml. Hosp., Miami, 1972-73; resident psychiatry Inst. of Living, Hartford, Conn., 1973-75, chief resident psychiatry, 1975-76, staff psychiatrist, 1976-77; pvt. practice Newport Beach, Calif., 1977—; med. dir. mental health unit Hoag Hosp., Newport Beach, 1982-83, chmn. dept. psychiatry, 1983-85; asst. clin. prof. dept. psychiatry U. Calif.-Irvine Sch. Medicine, 1979—, assoc. clin. prof. dept. psychiatry U. Calif.-Irvine Sch. Medicine, 1988—; pres. med. staff Santa Ana (Calif.) Psychiat. Hosp., 1980. Fellow Am. Psychiat. Assn. (Falk fellow 1975-76); mem. Am. Soc. Clin. Hypnosis, Am. Acad. Med. Dirs., Am. Soc. Adolescent Psychiatry, Calif. Med. Assn., Calif. Psychiat. Assn. (mem. jud. com. 1988—), Orange County Psychiat. Soc. (pres. 1986-88), Phi Beta Kappa. Democrat. Jewish. Office: 400 Newport Ctr Dr Ste 706 Newport Beach CA 92660

KAHN, EARL LESTER, market research executive; b. Kansas City, Mo., May 30, 1919; s. Samuel and Sarah (Kaufman) K. BA, Harvard U., 1940; MA, U. Chgo., 1947. Pres. Social Research, Inc., Chgo., 1946-74; chmn. bd. KPR Assocs., Inc., Scottsdale, Ariz., 1974-88. Contbr. articles to profl. jour. Served to capt. USAF, 1942-46. Mem. Am. Mktg. Assn, Am. Sociol. Assn. Home: 5608 N Scottsdale Rd Scottsdale AZ 85253

KAHN, EDWIN WALTER, construction company executive, engineer; b. Pitts., June 3, 1922; s. Theodore and Helen Henrietta (Meyers) K.; m. Arleen Barbara Rudolph, Dec. 23, 1951 (div.); children: Gregory, Julie, David; m. Sandra Swartz, Aug. 10, 1985. BSCE, U. Calif., Berkeley, 1948. Registered profl. engr., Calif.; lic. gen. contractor, Calif. Civil engr. Gen. Engring. Svc. Co., L.A., 1948-50, chief structural designer, 1950-54; ptnr. Pollack-Kahn & Assocs., L.A., 1954-56, Mogil-Kahn Constrn. Co., L.A., 1956-60; pres. Kahn Constrn. Co., L.A., 1960—. With USAAF, 1942-45. Mem. ASCE, Am. Concrete Inst., L.A. World Affairs Coun., Town Hall Calif., Varsity Club (UCLA), Masons, Shriners. Democrat. Jewish. Home: 13029 Mindanao Way Apt 3 Marina Del Rey CA 90292 Office: 100 W Imperial Ave Ste K El Segundo CA 90245

KAHN, FREDRICK HENRY, internist; b. L.A., Aug. 26, 1925; s. Julius and Josephine Leone (Langdon) K.; m. Barbara Ruth Visscher, Feb. 14, 1988; children: Susan, Kathryn, William. AB, Stanford U., 1947, MD, 1951. Diplomate Am. Bd. Internal Medicine. Rotating intern San Francisco Gen. Hosp., 1950-51, fellow pathology, 1951-52; resident medicine Los Angeles VA Hosp., 1954-57, sr. resident, 1956-57; asst. clin. prof. medicine UCLA Sch. Medicine, 1957—; attending physician Cedars Sinai Med. Ctr., Los Angeles, 1957—; med. advisor Vis. Nurse Assn., Los Angeles, 1957-87. Contbr. articles to med. jours. Served with USNR, 1943-46; lt. (M.C.), USNR, 1952-54. Fellow ACP; mem. AMA, Los Angeles County Internal Medicine Soc., Am. Handel Soc. Home: 3309 Corinth Ave Los Angeles CA 90066 Office: Shapiro Lipkis Kahn Med Group 6221 Wilshire Blvd Los Angeles CA 90048

KAHN, IRWIN WILLIAM, industrial engineer; b. N.Y.C., Feb. 3, 1923; s. Milton and Clara (Clark) K.; B.S., U. Calif.-Berkeley, 1949; student Cath. U., 1943-44; m. Mildred Cross, May 14, 1946 (dec. May 1966); children: Steven Edward, Michael William, Evelyn Ruth, Joanne Susan; m. 2d, Marajayne Smith, Oct. 9, 1979. Chief indsl. engr. Malsbary Mfg. Co., Oakland, Calif., 1953-57, Yale & Towne Mfg. Co., San Leandro, Calif., 1957-60; sr. indsl. engr. Eitel McCulloch, San Carlos, Calif., 1961-62, Lockheed, Sunnyvale, Calif., 1962-69; v.p. Performance Investors, Inc., Palo Alto, 1969-74; with Kaiser-Permanente Services, Oakland, 1974-76; nat. mgr. material handling Cutter Labs., Berkeley, Calif., 1976-83; sr. mgmt. engr. Children's Hosp. Med. Ctr., Oakland, 1983; sr. indsl. engr. Naval Air Rework Facility, Alameda, Calif., 1983-85, Naval Supply Ctr., Oakland, 1985-88; vis. lectr. U. Calif., Berkeley, 1986; tchr. indsl. engring. Laney Coll., Oakland, 1967—, Chabot Coll., Hayward, Calif. Chmn. Alameda County Library Adv. Commn., 1965—. Served with AUS, 1943-46. Registered profl. engr., Calif. Mem. Am. Inst. Indsl. Engrs. (chpt. pres. 1963-64, chmn. conf. 1967 nat. publ. dir. aerospace div. 1968-69), Calif. Soc. Profl. Engrs. (pres. chpt.). Club: Toastmasters (dist. gov. 1960-61).

KAHN, LEOPOLDO DAVID, business executive; b. Huancayo, Peru, Aug. 8, 1943; came to the U.S., 1988; s. Max and Thea (Hirsch) K.; m. Marilyn Tepperman, Feb. 25, 1967. Grad., U. Ingenieria, 1965. Engr. Cosmana Siemens Div., Lima, Peru, 1965-66; project mgr. Fabrica Papeles Paracas, Lima, 1967-68; asst. engr. Marco Peruana, Lima, 1968-69, chief engr., 1970-71, chief engr., prodn. mgr., 1971-72, asst. mgr., 1973-74, mng. dir., 1973-88; gen. mgr. Marco Marine, San Diego, 1988—. Pres. Jewish Community, 1975-79, 82-84, Peruvian Conservative Jewish. Mem. Rotary. Office: Marico Marine 600 E Harbor Dr San Diego CA 92101

KAHN, LINDA MCCLURE, maritime industry executive; b. Jacksonville, Fla.; d. George Calvin and Myrtice Louise (Boggs) McClure; m. Paul Markham Kahn, May 20, 1968. B.S. with high honors, U. Fla.; M.S., U. Mich., 1964. Actuarial trainee N.Y. Life Ins. Co., N.Y.C., 1964-66, actuarial asst., 1966-69, asst. actuary, 1969-71; v.p., actuary US Life Ins., Pasadena, Calif., 1972-74; mgr. Coopers & Lybrand, Los Angeles, 1974-76, sr. cons., San Francisco, 1976-82; dir. program mgmt. Pacific Maritime Assn., San Francisco, 1982—. Sec.-Bd. dirs. Pacific Heights Residents Assn., sec.-treas., 1981; trustee ILWU-PMA Welfare Plan, SIU-PD-PMA Pension and Supplemental Benefits Plans, Seafarers Med. Ctr., others. Fellow Soc. Actuaries, Conf. Actuaries in Pub. Practice; mem. Internat. Actuarial Assn., Internat. Assn. Cons. Actuaries, Actuarial Studies Non-Life Ins., Am. Acad. Actuaries, Western Pension Conf. (newsletter editor 1983-85, sec. 1985—), Actuarial Club Pacific States, San Francisco Actuarial Club (pres. 1981). Clubs: Metropolitan Soroptimist (v.p. 1973-74), Commonwealth. Home: 2430 Pacific Ave San Francisco CA 94115 Office: Pacific Maritime Assn 635 Sacramento St San Francisco CA 94111

KAHN, MARVIN WILLIAM, psychology educator; b. Cleve., Feb. 1, 1926; s. Alexander and Ida (Solowitz) K.; m. Gale C. Carroll, Sept. 10, 1982; children: Karen V. Kahn Dotson, David B. PhD, Pa. State U., 1952. Diplomate Am. Bd. Profl. Psychology; cert. psychologist., Ariz. Instr., asst. prof. Yale U., New Haven, 1952-54; asst. prof., assoc. prof. U. Colo. Sch. Medicine, Denver, 1954-64; prof. Ohio U., Athens, 1964-69; prof. psychology U. Ariz., Tucson, 1969—. Office: U Ariz Dept Psychology Tucson AZ 85721

KAHN, PAUL MARKHAM, actuary; b. San Francisco, May 8, 1935; s. Sigmund Max and Alexandrina K. (Strauch) K.; m. Linda P. McClure, May 20, 1968. BS, Stanford U., 1956; MA, U. Mich., 1957, PhD, 1961. Asst. actuary Equitable Life Assurance Soc., N.Y.C., 1961-71; v.p., life actuary Beneficial Standard Life, Los Angeles, 1971-75; v.p., actuary Am. Express Life Ins. Co., San Rafael, Calif., 1975-77, P.M. Kahn & Assocs., 1977-. Editor Dictionary of Actuarial and Life Ins. Terms, 1972, 2d edit., 1983, Credibility: Theory and Practice, 1975, Computational Probability, 1980. Fellow Soc. Actuaries (Triennial prize 1961-64), Can. Inst. Actuaries, Conf. Actuaries in Pub. Practice; mem. Am. Acad. Actuaries, Internat. Actuarial Assn., Inst. Actuaries (Eng.), Spanish Actuarial Assn., Swiss Actuarial Assn., German Actuarial Assn., Italian Actuarial Assn., Am. Antiquarian Soc. Clubs: Zamorano (Los Angeles); Roxburghe; Concordia-Argonaut, Comml. (San Francisco); Pacific, Waikiki Yacht (Honolulu). Address: 2430 Pacific Ave San Francisco CA 94115

KAHN, TED STEWART, clinical psychotherapist; b. N.Y.C., July 31, 1933; s. Hubert Kahn and Martha (Kamena) Blount; m. Ronnye Sue Yarbrough, Sept. 20, 1985; children by previous marriage: Martha, Suzy, Teddy. AA in Psychology, Scottsdale Community Coll., 1974; BA in Behavioral Sci., Grand Canyon Coll., 1976; MA in Clin. Psychology, Goddard Coll., 1977; PhD in Clin. Psychology, Calif. Western U., 1978, CAlif. Coast U., 1985. Cert. Am. Bd. Med. Psychotherapists; diplomate Am. Bd. Sexology. Enlisted USAF, 1952; resigned 1962; intern Ariz. State Hosp., 1973-76; dir. Westside Ctr. Psychotherapy and Counseling, Phoenix, 1976—, adminstrv. dir., 1977—; researcher in field of schizophrenia. Mem. Am. Psychol. Assn., Western Psychol. Assn, AAUP, Am. Assn. Sex Educators, Counselors and Therapists, Am. Assn. Profl. Hypnotists, Mensa. Office: 4225 W Glendale Ave Phoenix AZ 85052

KAHNE, STEPHEN JAMES, systems engineer, educator, administrator; b. N.Y.C., Apr. 5, 1937; s. Arnold W. and Janet (Weatherlow) K.; m. Irena Nowacka, Dec. 11, 1970; children: Christopher, Katarzyna. B.E.E., Cornell U., 1960; M.S., U. Ill., 1961, Ph.D., 1963. Asst. prof. elec. engring. U. Minn., Mpls., 1966-69; assoc. prof. U. Minn., 1969-76; dir. Hybrid Computer Lab., 1968-76; founder, dir., cons. InterDesign Inc., Mpls., 1968-76; prof. dept. systems engring. Case Western Res. U., Cleve., 1976-83; chmn. dept. Case Western Res. U., 1976-80; dir. div. elec., computer and systems engring. NSF, Washington, 1980-82; prof. Poly Inst. N.Y., 1983-85, dean engring., 1983-84; prof. Oreg. Grad. Ctr., Beaverton, 1985—, pres., 1985-86, prof. dept. applied physics and elec. engring., 1985—; cons. in field; exchange scientist Nat. Acad. Scis., 1968, 75. Editor: IEEE Transactions on Automatic Control, 1975-79; hon. editor: Internat. Fedn. of Automatic Control, 1975-81, dep. chmn. mng. bd. publs., 1976-87, v.p. 1987-90; editorial bd.: IEEE Spectrum, 1979-82; dep. chmn. editorial bd.: Automatica, 1976-82; contbr. articles to sci. jours. Active Mpls. Citizens League, 1968-75; regent L.I. Coll. Hosp., Bklyn., 1984-85; chmn. Beaverton Sister Cities Found., 1986-87. Served with USAF, 1963-66. Recipient Amicus Poloniae award POLAND Mag., 1975, John A. Curtis award Am. Soc. Engring. Edn.; Case Centennial scholar, 1980. Fellow AAAS, IEEE (pres. Control Systems Soc. 1981, bd. dirs. 1982-86, v.p. tech. activities 1984-85, Centennial medal 1984, Disting. Mem. award 1983). Office: Oreg Grad Ctr 19600 NW Von Neumann Dr Beaverton OR 97006

KAIGHN, JAMES MCELROY, industrial relations arbitrator and consultant; b. Eureka, Utah, Feb. 9, 1927; s. Merrill McElroy and Goldie Anna (Crooks) K.; m. Julia Francis Softchin, Mar. 14, 1959; 1 child, Kelly Pauline. Student, Utah State U., 1943, Weber State Coll., 1943, Calif. Maritime Acad., 1943; JD, Harvard Coll., 1968. Advisor cons. Am. Bankers Assoc., Washington, 1966-68; resident spats engr. H.K. Ferguson Co., Cleve., 1968; area labor rels. mgr. Arthur G McKee & Co., Cleve., N.Y., Chgo. and San Francisco; advisor cons. Internat. Teamsters, Washington, 1969, Internat. IndustrialSafety, Washington. Chmn. Labor and Mgmt. Adv. Bd. Lt. U.S. Mcht. Marine, World War II. Mem. Am. Arbitration Assn., Am. Savs. and Loan Inst., Nat. Panel Arbitrators, Cleve. Engring. Soc. Home: 820 Ave A #21 Boulder City NV 89005

KAIL, JOSEPH GERARD, computer sales executive; b. Cin., Dec. 23, 1946; s. Henry Thomas and Cosma (Contadino) K.; m. Patricia Lynne Riedel, June 28, 1969; children: Robert, Daniel, Joseph. BS, Xavier U., Cin., 1969, MEd, 1973. Tchr., athletic coach Alter High Sch., Kettering, Ohio, 1969-77; sales rep. Philips Bus. Systems, Inc., Cin., 1977-78, Hewlett-Packard Co., Dayton, 1978-81; dist. sales mgr. Hewlett-Packard Co., Pitts., 1981-83; sales mgr. Rocky Mountain area Hewlett-Packard Co., Denver, 1983-87, western regional sales mgr. bus. computer systems, 1988--. Com. mem. troop 986, Boy Scouts Am., Denver, 1984-88, Highlands Ranch High Sch. Boosters, Denver, 1988. Republican. Roman Catholic. Office: Hewlett-Packard Co 24 Inverness Dr E Englewood CO 80112

KAILASAM, VELUSAMY, immunologist; b. Namakkal, India, Dec. 19, 1951; came to U.S., 1979; s. Velu and Sellammal K.; m. Kalaiselvi Nalluswami, Aug. 21, 1978; children: Vani, Kavitha, Vijay. MB, BS, Madras (India) U., 1975, Diploma in Dermatology, 1978. Cert. Bd. Internal Medicine, Bd. Allergy and Immunology. Resident in dermatology Govt. Gen. Hosp., Madras, 1976-77; physician Norwich (Conn.) State Hosp., 1979-80; resident in internal medicine Hurley Med. Ctr., Flint, Mich., 1980-83; fellow in allergy and immunology U. Mich. Hosp., Ann Arbor, 1983-85; cons. allergy and immunology No. Colo. Allergy and Asthma Clin., Greeley, 1985—; mem. John Sheldon Allergy Soc., 1985—. Contbr. articles to profl. jours. Mem. Am. Coll. Physicians, Am. Acad. Allergy and Immunology, Colo. Med. Soc. Home: 4204 21st St Rd Greeley CO 80634 Office: No Colo Allergy & Asthma Clin 1018 14th St Greeley CO 80631

KAISSE, ELLEN MAUD, linguistics educator; b. Montreal, Que., Can., June 29, 1949; came to U.S., 1950; d. Clifton and Lois Naomi (Simand) K. BA, U. Chgo., 1971; PhD, Harvard U., 1977. Asst. prof. dept. linguistics U. Wash., Seattle, 1976-83, assoc. prof., 1983—, chmn. dept., 1985—; mem. rev. bd. Language, 1988. Author: Connected Speech, 1985; editor Phonology, 1984—; contbr. articles to profl. jours. Mem. Linguistics Soc. Am. Office: U Wash Dept Linguistics GN-40 Seattle WA 98195

KAITSCHUK, ROBERT CHARLES, psychologist, travel agency executive; b. Oak Park, Ill., Sept. 28, 1934; s. Oscar C. and Victoria Marguerite (Schmaus) K.; B.A., Wittenberg U., 1956; M.A., Pepperdine U., 1967. Tchr., Henry Ford II Sch., Chicago Ridge, Ill., 1961-64; counselor, psychologist, div. vocat. edn. West Covina (Calif.) Unified Sch. Dist., 1966-70; prin. Renaissance High Sch., Santa Paula, Calif., 1970-72; personnel mgmt. specialist Ventura County Personnel Dept., Ventura, Calif., 1972-73; vocat. psychologist Calif. Dept. Rehab., Bakersfield dist., 1974-76; psychologist, account exec. Dean Witter & Co., Inc., 1976-77; owner, pres. Elegant Travel, Inc., Mission Viejo, Calif., 1977—; mem. pres. adv. bd. Mission Viejo Nat. Bank, 1982—; mem. Saddleback Community Hosp. Assocs., Laguna Hills, Calif., 1986—. Bd. convocators Calif. Luth. Coll., Thousand Oaks, 1969-77; bd. dirs. Santa Paula Boys Club, 1971-74, Kern County Campfire Girls, 1976-77; v.p. Orange County Assn. for Retarded Citizens, 1978-79. HEW grantee, 1970. Mem. Am. Psychol. Assn., Western Psychol. Assn., Calif. Psychol. Assn., Assn. Retail Travel Agts., Am. Soc. Travel Agts., Soc. Advancement Travel Handicapped. Assn. Calif. Sch. Adminstrs., Benjamin Prince Soc. Wittenberg U. (life), Phi Kappa Psi, Theta Alpha Phi. Republican. Lutheran. Clubs: Rotary (sec. 1978-79, v.p. 1979-80, pres. 1980-81) (Mission Viejo), Mission Viejo Country; Town Hall of Calif. Home: 25751 Knotty Pine Laguna Hills CA 92653 Office: Gateway Ctr 24000 Alicia Pkwy Ste 16 Mission Viejo CA 92691

KALAFUS, RUDOLPH MORTON, manufacturing executive; b. Jackson, Mich., Dec. 17, 1937; s. William Robert and Beulah Ida (Morton) K.; m. Lois Eleanor Aptekar, Jan. 30, 1965; children: Daniel Paul, Alexander Aptekar. BEE, U. Mich., 1960, MEE, 1962, PhD, 1966. Electronics engr. electronics res. ctr. NASA, Cambridge, Mass., 1967-70; head satellite navigation group transp. systems ctr. U.S. Dept. Transp., Cambridge, 1970-88; dir. engring. navigation div. Tau Corp., Los Gatos, Calif., 1988; dir. engring. Taunav div. Trimble Navigation Ltd., Sunnyvale, Calif., 1988—; chmn. spl. com. 104 Radio Tech. Commn. for Maritime Svcs., Washington, 1984—. Editor: Special Issue on the Global Positioning System, Vol. III, 1986; contbr. articles to profl. jours.; inventor VHF radio/radar collision avoidance aid. Mem. IEEE, Inst. Navigation, Tau Beta Pi. Office: Trimble Navigation Ltd 585 N Mary Ave Sunnyvale CA 94086

KALAN, JONATHAN RUSSEL, marketing executive; b. N.Y.C.. BS, U. Ill., 1972; MBA, Boston U., 1978. Asst. dir. ops. Decision Research Corp., Wellesley, Mass., 1971-73; research analyst personal care div. Gillette Co., Boston, 1973-75, sr. analyst, 1975-77, research supr., 1977-78, research mgr., 1978-80; group research mgr. Clorox Co., Oakland, Calif., 1980-87, assoc. dir. mktg. research, 1987--; guest lectr. Stanford U., San Francisco State U. Mem. Am. Mktg. Assn. (exec.). Home: 1029 Rudgear Rd Walnut Creek CA 94596 Office: Clorox Co 1221 Broadway Ave Oakland CA 94612

KALB, BENJAMIN STUART, television producer, director; b. Los Angeles, Mar. 17, 1948; s. Marcus and Charlotte K. B.S. in Journalism, U. Oreg., 1969. Sportswriter, Honolulu Advertiser, 1971-76; traveled with tennis profl. Ilie Nastase; contbr. articles N.Y. Times, Sport Mag. and Tennis U.S.A., 1976; editor Racquetball Illustrated, 1978-82; segment producer PM Mag. and Hollywood Close-Up, 1983-86; exec. producer Delicious Prodns., 1986—; instr. sports in soc. U. Hawaii, 1974-75. Producer (video) The Natural Way to Meet the Right Person, 1987; producer, dir.: (video) Casting Call: Director's Choice, 1987, (TV pilot and home video) Bizarro, 1988; producer, host (cable TV show) Delicious Sports, 1987-88. Served with Hawaii Army N.G., 1970-75. Named Outstanding Male Grad. in Journalism, U. Oreg., 1969. Mem. Sigma Delta Chi (chpt. pres. 1968). Democrat. Jewish. Contbr. articles to mags. and newspapers. Home: 605 San Vicente Blvd Apt 104 Santa Monica CA 90402

KALEJS, KARLIS, aerospace engineer; b. Tukums, Latvia, June 23, 1926; came to U.S., 1949, naturalized 1955; s. Janis and Olga (Smits) K.; m. Klitija Pilmanis, Apr. 5, 1953; children—Lija, Nora, Valdis. A.A., Los Angeles City Coll., 1952; B.S., U. So. Calif., 1962, M.S., 1965. Registered profl. mech. engr., Calif. Design engr. Weber Aircraft Co., Burbank, Calif., 1955-59; design engr. Marquardt Aircraft Corp., Van Nuys, Calif., 1959, N.Am. Aviation, Canoga Park, Calif., 1959-61; sr. design engr. Rocketdyne div. N.Am. Rockwell, 1961-65; mem. tech. staff Rocketdyne div. Rockwell Internat., 1965—. Pres. Peace Luth. Ch. of Los Angeles, 1969-72; v.p. Latvian Welfare Assn. So. Calif., 1970—; chmn. bd. Latvian Community Ctr. So. Calif., 1978—; bd. dirs. Baltic Am. Freedom League, 1981—. Served with USAF, 1948-49. Recipient Apollo Achievement award NASA, 1969; cert. of appreciation of contbn. to Apollo II, NASA and Rocketdyne, 1969; tech. utilization cert. George Marshall Space Ctr., 1972. Mem. AIAA, Latvian Engrs. Assn., Soc. Profl. Indsl. Engrs., Deutsche Gesellschaft fur Luft- und Raumfahrt. Club: Latvian Community. Home: 3822 Markridge Road La Crescenta CA 91214 Office: 6633 Canoga Ave Apt FA 30 Canoga Park CA 91304

KALENSCHER, ALAN JAY, surgeon; b. Bklyn., July 9, 1926; s. Abraham and Julia (Horwitz) K.; BS, Union Coll., Schenectady, 1945; MD, N.Y. U., 1949; m. Hannah Blaufox, June 18, 1949; children: Judith Lynne, Mark Robert. Intern Morrisania City Hosp., N.Y.C., 1949-50; surg. resident Maimonides Med. Ctr., Bklyn., 1950-51, 54; asst., then chief resident Bronx Mcpl. Hosp. Ctr., 1954-56; mem. faculty surgery dept. Albert Einstein Coll. Medicine, 1956-59; practice medicine specializing in surgery, Sacramento, 1959-84; chief med. cons. Disability Evaluation Div. Calif. State Dept. Soc. Svcs., 1984—; attending surgeon Sacramento Med. Ctr.; commr. Bd. Med. Quality Assurance Calif.; clin. faculty dept. surgery U. Calif. Coll. Medicine, Davis, 1970-75 . Served with USNR, 1943-45, 51-53; ETO, Korea. Recipient citation N.Y.C. Cancer Com., 1959. Diplomate Am. Bd. Surgery, Nat. Bd. Med. Examiners (examiner 1957-59). Fellow Am. Soc. Contemporary Medicine and Surgery; mem. AAAS, Calif. Med. Assn., Sacramento County Med. Soc., Am. Diabetes Assn., Am. Mensa Ltd.

KALIHER, LARKIN LEWIS, retail building material executive; b. Pelican Rapids, Minn., Jan. 25, 1947; s. Howard Kenneth and Muriel Jannet (Schermer) K.; m. Ann Tucker, Oct. 6, 1972; children: Vicki, Lisa, Lori. BS, Lewis and Clark Coll., 1969. Food svc. mgr. Saga Food Svc., Sewanee, Tenn., 1970-72; owner Newport Bldg. Supply Co./Larkin Lumber, Newport, Oreg., 1973—; bd. dirs., treas., v.p., chmn. bd. No. Yards Inc., Portland, Oreg., 1978—. Recipient community svc. award Newport C. of C., 1978. Mem. Pacific Northwest Hardware and Implement Assn. (dir. 1982, v.p. 1987, pres. 1988), Nat. Retail Hardware Assn. (nat. dir. 1988—), Rotary, Elks. Republican. Home: 106 SE Elder St Toledo OR 97391 Office: Larkins Lumber 615 N Coast Hwy Newport OR 97365

KALIHER, MICHAEL DENNIS, historian; b. Santa Monica, Calif., Nov. 7, 1947; s. Eugene Charles and Phyllis Marie (McCrary) K. Studnet, U. Ariz., 1987—. pres. Klamath Country Hist. Soc., Klamath Falls, Oreg., 1985. Contbr. articles to Jour. of the Shaw Hist. Libr., 1986, Curry County Echoes, 1986, Northwest Rev., 1986. Mem. Pi Lambda Theta. Roman Catholic. Office: Hist Rsch PO Box 50521 Tucson AZ 85703

KALLAY, MICHAEL FRANK, II, medical devices company official; b. Painesville, Ohio, Aug. 24, 1944; s. Michael Frank and Marie Francis (Sage) K.; BBA, Ohio U., 1967; m. Irma Yolanda Corona, Aug. 30, 1975; 1 son, William Albert. Salesman, Howmedica, Inc., Rutherford, N.J., 1972-75, Biochem. Procedures/Metpath, North Hollywood, Calif., 1975-76; surg. specialist USCI div. C. R. Bard, Inc., Billerica, Mass., 1976-78; western and central regional mgr. ARCO Med. Products Co., Phila., 1978-80; Midwest regional mgr. Intermedics, Inc., Freeport, Tex., 1980-82; Western U.S. mgr. Renal Systems, Inc., Mpls., 1982—; pres. Kall-Med, Inc., Anaheim Hills, Calif., 1982—. Mem. Am. Mgmt. Assn., Phi Kappa Sigma. Home and Office: 6515 Marengo Dr PO Box 17248 Anaheim Hills CA 92817-7248

KALLENBERG, JOHN KENNETH, librarian; b. Anderson, Ind., June 10, 1942; s. Herbert A. and Helen S. K.; m. Ruth Barrett, Aug. 19, 1965; children—Jennifer Anne, Gregory John. A.B., Ind. U., 1964, M.L.S., 1969. With Fresno County Library, Fresno, Calif., 1965-70, dir., 1976—; librarian Fig Garden Pub. Library br., 1968-70; asst. dir. Santa Barbara (Calif.) Pub. Library, 1970-76. Mem. Calif. Library Assn. (councilor 1976-77, v.p., pres. 1987), Calif. County Librarians Assn. (pres. 1977), Calif. Library Authority for Systems and Services (chmn. authority adv. council 1978-80), Kiwanis (pres. Fresno 1981-2). Presbyterian. Office: Fresno County Free Libr 2420 Mariposa St Fresno CA 93721-2285

KALLGREN, JOYCE KISLITZIN, political science educator; b. San Francisco, Apr. 17, 1930; d. Alexander and Dorothea (Willett) K.; m. Edward E. Kallgren, Feb. 8, 1953; children: Virginia, Charles. BA, U. Calif., Berkeley, 1953, MA, 1955; PhD, Harvard U., 1968. Jr. researcher to asst. researcher Ctr. Chinese Studies U. Calif., Berkeley, 1961-65, research assoc., 1965—, chair, 1983-88; assoc. dir. Inst. of East Asian Studies, Berkeley, 1987—; from lectr. to prof. polit. sci. U. Calif., Davis, 1965—; cons. in field. Contbg. editor: China After Thirty Years, 1979, Academic Exchanges: Essays on the Sino-American Experience; editor, Jour. Asian Studies, 1980-83; mem. editorial bd. Asian Survey, World Affairs; contbr. articles to profl. jours., chpts. to books. Ford Found. awardee, 1978-79. Mem. Am. Polit. Sci. Assn., Assn. Asian Studies, China Council, Nat. Com. U.S./China Relations. Home: 28 Hillcrest Rd Berkeley CA 94705 Office: U Calif Inst East Asian Studies Berkeley CA 94720

KALMAN, ANN ELIZABETH, marketing, advertising executive; b. Champaign, Ill., Nov. 27, 1941; d. George Hamption and Freida Irene (Harshbarger) Hyde; m. Jerry Lee Kalman, Aug. 19, 1961; children: Wendy, David. BS, U. Ill., 1963; postgrad., Ariz. State U., 1974-76. Assoc. media dir. McCann-Erickson Advt. Agy., L.A., 1964-70; asst. advt. mgr. Haggarty's, L.A., 1964; account exec. Max Goldberg Advt. Agy., Denver, 1963-64; teaching asst. Ariz. State U., Tempe, 1974-76; advt. and pub. rels. dir. Ariz. Biltmore, Phoenix, 1977-78; media supr. Foote, Cone and Belding Advt. Agy., L.A., 1978—; account supr. Dalla Femina and Travisano Advt. Agy., L.A., 1978-81; v.p. media svcs. CBS Entertainment div., L.A., 1981-87; sr. v.p.media dir. Della Femina, McNamee, WCRS, L.A., 1987—. Mem. Broadcast Mktg. Promotion Execs., L.A. Advt. Club.

KALODNER, JOHN DAVID, recording company executive; b. Phila., Dec. 10, 1949; s. Alfred Leonard and Corinne (Feinberg) K. Student, George Washington U., 1967-69, U. Pa., 1971-72. Music writer Phila. Inquirer, 1971-74; mgr. artists and repertoire Atlantic Records, N.Y.C., 1974-76; dir. artists and repertoire Atlantic Records, L.A., 1976-80; v.p. artists and repertoire Geffen Records, L.A., 1980—. Named Nat. Record Exec. of Yr., Phila. Music Found., 1987. Mem. NARAS. Office: Geffen Records 9130 Sunset Blvd Los Angeles CA 90069

KAM, IVAN LOY, data processing executive; b. Honolulu, Aug. 24, 1943; s. Alfred Y. H. and Mildred Oi (Ching) K.; m. Anne Barnes, May. Student, U. Hawaii, 1961-65. V.p., mgr. Hotel Grant Ave., San Francisco, 1965-66; owner Internat. Fine Arts Gallery, Berkeley, Calif., 1967-68; v.p. systems Crocker Nat. Bank, San Francisco, 1968-80, Bank of Am., San Francisco, 1980-81; cons. Knowlegeworks, Honolulu, 1982; systems analyst Visa Internat., San Mateo, Calif., 1983-84; mgr. systems planning Wells Fargo Bank, San Francisco, 1984-89. Author, artist: Pen and Ink Sketch Book, 1981. Mem. AIAA, NRA, Explorer Club. Republican.

KAMADA, RODNEY THOMAS, transportation executive; b. Honolulu, July 7, 1957; s. Thomas Takeshi and Karen (Fujita) K.; m. Kaylene Kau Sinn Chun, May 2, 1981; 1 child, Stacie Leigh. AS, Honolulu Community Coll., 1978. Helicopter mechanic Air Service Corp., Honolulu, 1978-85; line supr. Associated Aviation, Honolulu, 1983-86; mgr. Mid Pacific Airlines, Honolulu, 1985-86; supr. Continental Airlines, Honolulu, 1986—.

KAMALESON, SAMUEL THEODORE, religious organization administrator; b. Vellore, Madras, India, Nov. 18, 1930; came to U.S., 1974; s. Job and Lily Sundaresan; m. Adela Balraj, May 27, 1953; children: Sunderraj Mark, Nirmala Ruth, Manoharan Paul. BVSci., U. Madras, India, 1957; M in Divinity, Asbury Sem., Wilmore, Ky., 1960, ThM, 1971, DD, 1971; STD, Emory U., Atlanta, 1971. Pastor Emmanuel Meth. Ch., Madras, 1961-68, 1971-74; evangelist-at-large Meth. Ch. So. Asia, India, 1963-74; v.p. at large World Vision Internat., Monrovia, Calif., 1974-79, v.p. pastor's conf., 1980-84, v.p. evangelism/leadership, 1985—; pres. Bethel Agrl. Fellowship, Salem, South India, 1961—, Friends Missionary Prayer Band Hqtrs., Madras, India, 1961—; adj. prof. Fuller Theol. Sem., Pasadena, Calif., 1979; Staley lectr. Asbury Theol. Sem., 1983, bd. dirs.; mem. council Azuza Pacific U. Sch. Theology, 1983. Author: Christ Alive is Man Alive, 1973, Happy: Married or Single, 1975, Transforming Power of Jesus, 1980. Recipient Philip award Nat. Assn. United Meths. Fla., 1980. Mem. Theta Phi. Office: World Vision Internat 919 W Huntington Dr Monrovia CA 91016

KAMDEN, IRENE BLANCHE, writer; b. Bklyn., Apr. 18, 1922; d. Jack and Mary (Harris) Trepel; 1 child, Christine. BA in Journalism, U. Wis., 1943. Author: Life Without George, 1961, We That Are Left, 1962, The Ziegfelds' Girl, 1964, Europe Without George, 1965, Last Year At Sugarbush, 1966, Her Comes The Bride There Goes Mother, 1967, Due To Lack of Interest Tomorrow Has Been Canceled, 1969, Are You Carrying Any Gold or Living Relatives, 1970, Nobody Calls At This Hour Just To Say Hello, 1975, Fear Without Childbirth, 1978; contbr. numerous articles to mags. Fellow MacDowell Colony. Mem. Author's Guild Am.

KAMERMAN, KENNETH M., state senator, real estate agent; b. N.Y.C., June 21, 1931; m. Pati Kleinhein, Dec. 21, 1957; children: Kim Patrice, Brett Padraic, Trent Irving. BS in Textile Engring., U. Lowell, 1953; MBA, U. N.Mex., 1970. Mgr. customer rels. Lytle Corp., Albuquerque, 1956-61; bus. mgr. Teaching Machines Inc., Albuquerque, 1961-65; adminstrv. mgr. Westinghouse Learning Corp., Albuquerque, 1965-71; mgr. pers. and adminstrv. svcs. Bellamah Corp., Albuquerque, 1972-78; v.p. Honor Corp., Albuquerque, 1979-81; firm adminstr. Rogoff, Diamond & Walker, Albuquerque, 1981-82; v.p. Battery Power Specialists, Albuquerque, 1982-87; assoc. Lee A. Welsh Real Estate Inc., Albuquerque, 1987—; bd. dirs. Design Products Inc., Learning Mgmt. Corp. Vice chmn. Rep. Cen. Com., Bernalillo County, N.Mex., 1978-81, mem. 1976—; state senator, 1986—; chmn. Police Adv. Bd., Albuquerque, 1978-80; sec. bd. trustees Bernalillo County Mental Health/Mental Retardation Ctr., 1981-86, v.p. 1984, pres. 1985; treas. N.Mex. Rep. Legis. Campaign Com., 1987—. USN, 1953-56. Home: 3305 Utah St NE Albuquerque NM 87110 Office: 4210 Louisiana Blvd NE Albuquerque NM 87109

KAMINE, BERNARD SAMUEL, lawyer; b. Oklahoma City, Dec. 5, 1943; s. Martin and Mildred Esther Kamine; m. Marcia Phyllis Haber, Sept. 9, 1982; children: Jorge Hershel, Benjamin Haber, Tovy Haber. BA, U. Denver, 1965; JD, Harvard U., 1968. Bar: Calif. 1969, Colo. 1969, U.S. Supreme Ct. 1973. Dep. atty. gen. Calif. Dept. Justice, Los Angeles, 1969-72; asst. atty. gen. Colo. Dept. Law, Denver, 1972-74; ptnr. Kamine, Steiner & Ungerer (and predecessor firms), L.A., Calif., 1976—; instr. Glendale (Calif.) U. Coll. Law, 1971-72; judge pro tem Mcpl. Ct., 1974-89; mem. adv. com. legal forms Calif. Jud. Council, 1978-82; lectr. Calif. Continuing Edn. of the Bar Programs, 1979-85. Mem. L.A. County Dem. Cen. Com., 1982-85; mem. exec. ocm. Pacific S.W. Region Anti-Defamation League. Served to maj., inf. USAR, 1969—. Mem. ABA, Calif. State Bar Assn. (conf. dels. calendar coordinating com. 1987—), L.A. County Bar Assn. (chmn. Superior Cts. com. 1977-79, del. state bar conf. 1978-89, chmn. constrn. law subsect. of real property sect. 1981-83), Engring. Contractors' Assn. (bd. dirs. 1985—, rep. APWA-AGC joint coop. com. standard specifications for pub. works constrn. 1984—), Am. Arbitration Assn. (panel of arbitrators 1976—, mem. regional constrn. industry arbitration adv. com. 1987—), Res. Officers Assn. (pres. chpt. 1977-78), Assoc. Gen. Contractors (legal adv. com. 1982—), Omicron Delta Kappa. Contbr. chpts. to legal texts, articles to profl. jours. Office: Kamine Steiner & Ungerer 350 S Figueroa St Ste 250 Los Angeles CA 90071

KAMINSKY, GLENN FRANCIS, deputy chief of police, business owner, teacher; b. Passaic, N.J., Apr. 29, 1934; s. Francis Gustave and Leona Regina (Tubach) K.; m. Janet Lindesay Strachan (div. June 1985); children: Lindesay Anne, Jon Francis; m. Melanie Sue Rhamey, Mar. 1, 1989. BS in Police Sci., San Jose (Calif.) State Coll., 1958; MS in Adminstrn., San Jose State U., 1975. Cert. tchr. Police officer San Jose Police Dept., 1957-65, sgt., 1965-75, lt., 1975-81; dep. chief Boulder (Colo.) Police Dept., 1981—; pres. Kaminsky & Assocs., Inc., Longmont, Colo. 1981—. Author, editor: textbook Implementing the FTO Program, 1981—; contbr. articles to profl. jours. Sgt. U.S. Army, 1957-61, Korea. Mem. Police Mgmt. Assn. (sec. 1983—), Calif. Assn. Police Tng. Officers, Internat. Assn. Women Police, Calif. Assn. Adminstrn. of Justice Educators, Internat. Assn. Chiefs of Police (use of deadly force com.). Republican. Episcopalian. Home: 7616 Estate Circle Longmont CO 80501 Office: Boulder Police Dept 1777 6th St Boulder CO 80302

KAMMER, THOMAS EVERS, dentist; b. Cin., July 12, 1956; s. Robert John and Mary Adelaide (Evers) K. BS in Biology and Chemistry, Regis Coll., 1978; DDS, U. Iowa, 1982. Co-owner Kammer & Kammer, Boulder, Colo., 1982—; cons. Boulder MEml. Hosp. Eating Disorder Clinic, 1983-84; bd. dirs. dental div. U. Colo. Sports and Medicine, Boulder. Mem. ADA, Acad. Gen. Dentistry, Am. Acad. Sports Dentistry. Club: Flatirons Athletic (Boulder). Office: Kammer & Kammer 1440m 28th St Boulder CO 80303

KAMP, CHRISTOPHER WAYNE, structural engineer; b. Burbank, Calif., Mar. 20, 1954; s. William Paul and Beverly June (Snell) K.; m. Stephanie Lynne Dukin, Oct. 11, 1980; children: Alexis Anne, William Christopher. BCE, San Diego State U., 1977, MCE, 1984. Reg. profl. engr., Calif. Staff engr. Alvarado Engring., La Mesa, Calif., 1977-80; structural engr. Blaylock, Willis & Assocs., San Diego, 1980--; com. mem. Calif. Structural Engring. Registration Exam, 1987-88. Mem. Structural Engrs. Assn., San Diego. Democrat. Methodist. Office: Blaylock Willis & Assocs 1899 McKee St 2d Fl San Diego CA 92110

KAMPEN, IRENE BLANCHE, writer; b. Bklyn., Apr. 18, 1922; d. Jack and Mary (Harris) Trepel; 1 child, Christine. BA in Journalism, U. Wis., 1943. Author: Fear Without Childbirth, 1978, Nobody Calls At This Hour Just To Say Hello, 1975, Are You Carrying Any Gold or Living Relatives, 1970, Due To Lack of Interest Tomorrow Has Been Canceled, 1969, Here Comes The Bride There Goes Mother, 1967, Last Year At Sugarbush, 1966, Europe Without George, 1965, The Ziegfelds' Girl, 1964, We That Are Left, 1963, Life Without George, 1961; contbr. numerous articles to mags. Fellow MacDowell Colony; mem. Author's Guild Am. Home: 4862 Galicia Way Ocean Hills CA 92056

KAMPS, ROLAND MAURICE, teacher; b. Hudsonville, Mich., May 30, 1927; s. Jacob and Isabel (Everse) K.; m. Ruth Elizabeth Poppen, Aug. 4, 1950; children: Linda, Randall, Ken, Lori. AB, Calvin Coll., Grand Rapids, Mich., 1949; MA, No. Ariz. U., 1965. Tchr. Rehoboth (N.Mex.) Missions Sch., 1949-64, supt. edn., 1964-66; prin. Zuni Sec. Sch., 1966-68, Ripon (Calif.) Christian High Sch., 1968-71; councilor Bellflower (Calif.) Christian High Sch., 1971-75; tchr. Gallup (N.Mex.) McKinly Schs., 1975—. With USN, 1945-46. Mem. So. Calif. World Home Bible League (dir. 1971-75). Christian Ref. Ch. Home: PO Box 42 Rehoboth NM 87322

KAN, JOSEPH RUCE, geophysicist, educator; b. Shanghai, China, Feb. 10, 1938; s. John H. S. and Mary A. (Chen) K.; m. Rosalind J. Chen; children—Christina, Deborah, Steven. Ph.D., U. Calif.-San Diego, 1969. Asst. prof. U. Alaska, Fairbanks, 1972-76, assoc. prof., 1976-81, prof. geophysics, 1981—. Grantee NSF, NASA, Air Force Geophysics Lab., 1974—. Mem. Am. Geophys. Union, Am. Phys. Soc., AAAS. Contbr. papers to profl. publs. including: Jour. Geophysical Research, Jour. Plasma Physics, Solar Physics, Planetary and Space Sci., Geophysical Research Letters, Rev. of Space Physics. Office: U Alaska Geophysical Inst Fairbanks AK 99701

KANAGAWA, ROBERT KIYOSHI, citrus company executive; b. Sanger, Calif., Sept. 10, 1917; s. Yasoichi T. and Jitsuyo (Sumii) K.; B.B.A., Central Calif. Comml. Coll., 1939; m. Yukiye Nakamura, Feb. 12, 1944; children—Rodney M., Floyd A., Dallas W. Vice pres., treas. Kanagawa Citrus Co., Sanger, 1939-65, pres., 1965—; charter dir. Sequoia Community Bank, 1980—, chmn. bd., 1981—; bd. chmn. Agrl Export Calif., Inc., 1985—. Chmn. Agrl. Exhibit, Fresno Dist. Fair, 1953-58, Nations Christmas Tree Festival, Sanger, 1959, Sanger Grape Bowl Festival, 1964-74; bd. dirs. Valley Children's Hosp., 1968-72; bd. trustees St. Agnes Hosp., 1972-86, v.p., 1979; bd. trustees Fairmont Elem. Sch., 1954-58, Sanger Union High Sch., 1958-65, Sanger Unified Sch. Dist., 1965-69, Sanger Parks and Recreation Commn., 1963-73, Sanger Sr. Citizens Commn., 1975-79; mem. Republican State Central Com., 1972-76; bd. dirs. 21st Dist. Agrl. Assn., 1970-79, pres., 1977; exec. bd. Sequoia council Boy Scouts Am., 1971-84 , v.p., 1979; mem. Calif. Council Humanities in Public Policy, 1977-82; campaign chmn. Am. Heart Assn., 1981-82, v.p. Central Valley chpt., 1984-85, pres., 1985-86; bd. dirs., treas. Calif. Agrl. Mus., 1980-85 . Named Man of Yr., Sanger Dist. C. of C., 1968; recipient Golden Apple award Fresno County Sch. Adminstrs., 1976. Mem. Sanger Citrus Assn. (dir. 1961-72, pres. 1972), Orange Cove-Sanger Citrus Assn. (dir., v.p. 1973—), Sanger Japanese Am. Citizens League (charter, charter pres., dist. gov. 1977-78). Republican. Methodist. Club: Rotary of Sanger (pres. 1970-71, dist. gov. internat. 1974-75). Home: 16156 E McKinley Ave Sanger CA 93657 Office: 2720 Jensen Ave Sanger CA 93657

KANDELL, MARSHALL JAY, public relations counselor; b. Bklyn., Dec. 5, 1937; s. Harry and Mollie Rebecca (Remstein) K.; m. Judith Ann Zeve, May 28, 1961; children: Paul Bryon, Robin Pilar. AA in Journalism, Los Angeles City Coll., 1958; student Calif. State U., Los Angeles, 1963-65. Cert. tchr. community colls., Calif. Pub. relations staff City of Hope (Calif.) Nat. Med. Ctr., 1966-68; v.p. Roger Beck Pub. Relations, Sherman Oaks, Calif., 1968-71; account supr. Laurence Laurie & Assoc., Los Angeles, 1971-72; community relations dir. St. Mary Med. Ctr., Long Beach, Calif., 1972-75; dir. pub. relations Cedars-Sinai Med. Ctr., Los Angeles, 1975; founder Marshall Jay Kandell Pub. Relations, Huntington Beach, Calif., 1976—; vis. faculty mem. Calif. State U., Long Beach; mem. founding faculty Coastline Community Coll. Pres. Encino Jaycees, 1970-71; pres. Community Vol. Office, Long Beach, 1975-76; bd. dirs. Long Beach chpt. ARC, 1974-75, Civic Ctr. Barrio Housing Corp., Santa Ana, Calif.; mem. Citizen's Adv. Commn. 1984 Olympic Games, adv. panel Jewish Family Service of Orange County, Calif.; v.p. Irvine Jewish Community, 1973; founding mem., v.p. Congregation B'nai Tzedek, Fountain Valley, Calif., 1976. Served in USAF, 1958-63. Recipient Disting. Service award Encino Jaycees, 1972; MacEachern award Acad. Hosp. Pub. Relations, 1973-74; Best written story award Press Club Greater Los Angeles, 1965. Mem. Pub. Relations Soc. Am. Democrat. Jewish. Home: 18882 Deodar St Fountain Valley CA 92708 Office: PO Box 9200-322 Fountain Valley CA 92728

KANDO, THOMAS MATHEW, sociology educator, author; b. Budapest, Hungary, Apr. 8, 1941; came to U.S., 1965; s. Jules and Ata Edith (Gorog) K.; m. Anita Chris Costa, June 30, 1973; children—Danielle, Leah. Student Union Coll., 1960-61; B.S., U. Amsterdam (Netherlands), 1965; M.A., U. Minn., 1967, Ph.D., 1969. Asst. prof. sociology U. Wis.-Stout, Menomonie, 1968-69; cons. Calif. Dept. Parks and Recreation, Sacramento, 1969-70; asst. prof. Calif. State U.-Sacramento, 1969-72, U. Calif.-Riverside, 1972-73; assoc. prof. Calif. State U.-Sacramento, 1973-77; assoc. prof. recreation and parks Pa. State U., 1978-79; prof. sociology and criminal justice Calif. State U.-Sacramento, 1979—. U. Amsterdam fellow, 1962-65; U. Minn. fellow, 1967; Fulbright fellow, 1960-61. Mem. AAUP (pres. local chpt. 1974—, pres. statewide 1976-78), Am. Sociol Assn., Internat. Sociol. Assn., Internat. Com. Leisure Research, Nat. Recreation and Parks Assn., Pacific Sociol. Assn., Popular Culture Assn., Internat. Com. on Sports Sociology, Athletic Congress, Phi Sigma Kappa. Republican. Author: Sex Change: The Achievement of Gender Identity Among Feminized Transsexuals, 1973; Leisure and Popular Culture in Transition, 1975, 80; Social Interaction, 1977; Sexual Behavior and Family Life in Transition, 1978; assoc. editor Pacific Sociol. Rev., 1973-78; Contemporary Sociology, 1975-79; contbr. numerous articles to profl. jours, popular mags. Home: 8267 Caribbean Way Sacramento CA 95826 Office: Calif State U Dept Sociology 6000 Jay St Sacramento CA 95819

KANE, BARTHOLOMEW ALOYSIUS, state librarian; b. Pitts., Nov. 2, 1945; s. Bartholomew A. and Ruth M. (Loerlein) K.; m. Kathleen Osborne, Aug. 7, 1967 (div.); 1 child, Leah. B.A. in Journalism, Pa. State U., 1967; M.L.S., U. Pitts., 1971. Dir. Bradford Meml. Library, El Dorado, Kans., 1972-74; researcher Hawaii Dept. Planning and Econ. Devel., Honolulu, 1974-75, state librarian, 1982—; librarian Hawaii State Library System, Lanai City, 1975-79, Honolulu, 1979-82; adj. faulty mem. U. Hawaii, Manoa, 1986, 88. Founder Lanai Community Services Council, 1976-79; founder Hawaii Visual Arts Consortium Inc., Honolulu, 1976-81; mem. Hawaii Literacy Inc., 1982—; mem. Hawaii Commn. for Humanities, 1984—. Hazel McCoy fellow Friends of Library of Hawaii, 1971. Mem. ALA, Hawaii Library Assn., Librarians Assn. Hawaii (v.p. 1982), Hawaii Commn. for Humanities. Democrat. Home: 60 N Kuakini St #2H Honolulu HI 96817 Office: Hawaii State Pub Libr System Dept Edn 465 S King St B-1 Honolulu HI 96813

KANE, CHARLES A., academic administrator. BS, Pepperdine U.; MS, U. So. Calif., EdD. Instr., dean, v.p. Long Beach (Calif.) City Coll., 1964-78; pres., supt. Riverside (Calif.) Community Coll. Dist., 1978—; coach basketball, student activities dir. Dominguez High Sch., Compton, Calif., 1957-64. Mem. Inland Empire Higher Edn. Council; bd. dirs. Community Health Corp., Riverside Community Hosp. Served with U.S. Army, 1954-56. Presented with Key to City, Long Beach, Calif. Mem. Calif. Assn. Community Colls. (chmn. commn. on athletics), Assn. Calif. Community Coll. Adminstrs., Calif. Community Coll. Chief Exec. Officers Assn., So. Calif. Interscholastic Basketball Coaches Assn. (life), Riverside City Coll. Alumni Assn. Office: Riverside Community Coll 4800 Magnolia Ave Riverside CA 92506

KANE, ELIZABETH ANN, art educator; b. Napa, Calif., Aug. 12, 1937; d. Vernon Delbert and Reba Elizabeth (Graves) Van Sant; m. William E. Kane, Dec. 31, 1967 (div.); 1 child, Valerie Ann. AA, Napa (Calif.) Coll., Napa, 1957; BA, San Jose State U., 1959; MA, U. San Francisco, 1988. Tchr. Moreland Sch. Dist., San Jose, Calif., 1959-62, tchr., chair. art dept., art mentor, 1963—; tchr. U.S. Air Force in Europe, England, 1962-63; trainer visual and performing arts staff Devel. Inst.; presenter visual and performing arts Calif. State Dept. Edn. Mem. Women Leaders in Edn., Nat. Art Educator Assn., Calif. Art Educator Assn., Calif. Assn. Supervision and Cirriculum Devel., AAUW, Moreland Tchrs. Assn. (mem. negotiation team 2988—, chmn. profl. growth sect. 1977-84), various nat. mus. socs. Lodge: Masons (grand officer.). Home: 408 Clear View Dr Los Gatos CA 95030

KANE, JAMES PATRICK, utility company manager; b. Rahway, N.J., Nov. 16, 1946; s. John Francis and Marcella Ann (Moore) K.; m. Su Ann Roberts, June 1, 1968; children: Jennifer Jill, Christopher Matthew. BA in Edn., Ariz. State U., 1969, postgrad. sch. mgmt., 1986—. Groundman Ariz. Pub. Service, Phoenix, 1970-72, assoc. engr., 1972-75; supt. Vanguard Concrete, Edmonton, Alta., Can., 1975-77; mktg. rep. Ariz. Pub. Service, Flagstaff, 1977-80; mktg. supr. Ariz. Pub. Service, Phoenix, 1981-82; dist. mgr. Ariz. Pub. Service, Yuma, 1982-84; gen. mgr. S.W. Gas Corp., Phoenix, 1984—; expert witness Ariz. Corp. Commn., Phoenix, 1985, 87. Bd. dirs. Phoenix Urban League, 1987—, Ariz. State U. West, Phoenix, 1987—; grad. Valley Leadership Orgn., Phoenix, 1986—. Served with U.S. Army, 1968-70. Named Football All-American, UPI, Tempe, 1968. Mem. Am. Gas Assn., Pacific Gas Assn. Republican. Club: Ariz. State U. Lettermans. Home: 6332 W Cortez Glendale AZ 85304 Office: SW Gas Corp 10851 N Black Canyon Hwy Phoenix AZ 85029

KANEFSKY, IRWIN HILLARD, service industry executive; b. Chgo., June 30, 1943; s. Louis Sam and Celia (Rifkin) K.; m. Sharon Phillips, Aug. 29, 1965; children:Steven, Lawrence. BS in Acctg., U. Ill., 1965; MBA, Roosevelt U., 1970. CPA, Ill.; lic. nursery home adminstr. Ill., Ariz. Staff acct. Lester White & Co., Chgo., 1965; adminstr. Eden View Convalescent Ctr., Northbrook, Ill., 1965-71; staff acct. Seymour Rose & Co., Chgo., 1971-72; comptroller, ptnr. Lake Shore Nursing Ctr., Chgo., 1972-86; pres., chief fin. officer Inter Plan Design Group, Inc., Scottsdale, Ariz., 1987—; bd. dirs. Lake Shore Nursing Ctr., Chgo., Lake Bluff (Ill.) Health Care Ctr. Mem. Am. Coll. of Health Care Adminstrs. Jewish. Home: 10673 E Terra Dr Scottsdale AZ 85258 Office: Inter Plan Design Group Inc 4147 N 70th St Scottsdale AZ 85258

KANELLAKIS, NICHOLAS ALEXANDER, marketing executive; b. Athens, Greece, Sept. 9, 1963; came to U.S., 1978; s. Alexander and Evangelia (Sakellariou) K. BEE, Sacramento State U., 1986. Gen. mgr. Lynn Mktg., Concord, Calif., 1985—. Democrat. Greek Orthodox. Home: 5100-1B Clayton Rd #244 Concord CA 94521

KANEPS, ANDRIS JANIS, veterinarian; b. St. Paul, July 17, 1953; s. Janis Kaneps and Vera Ziverts. BS, U. Minn., 1976, DVM, 1978; MS, Ohio State U., 1981. Intern Colo. State U., Ft. Collins, 1978-79; resident Ohio State U., Columbus, 1979-81; staff veterinarian Equine Med. Ctr., Kaleville, Minn., 1981, Alamo Pintado Equine Med. Ctr., Los Olivos, Calif., 1988, North State Equine Vet. Hosp., Pleasanton, Calif., 1988—; asst. prof. Coll. Vet. Medicine Oreg. State U., Corvallis, 1981-87; faculty adviser student chpt. Am. Vet. Medicine Assn. Oreg. State U., 1985-87. Contbr. articles to vet. jours. Mem. Am. Vet. Med. Assn., Am. Assn. Equine Practitioners. Democrat. Lutheran. Home: 3835 Harvard Way Livermore CA 94550 Office: North State Equine Vet Hosp PO Box 1715 Pleasanton CA 94566

KANIECKI, MICHAEL JOSEPH, bishop; b. Detroit, Apr. 13, 1935; s. Stanley Joseph and Julia Marie (Konjora) K. BA, Gonzaga U., 1958, MA in Philosophy, 1960; MA in Theology, St. Mary's, Halifax, Can., 1966. Ordained priest, 1965; consecrated bishop, 1984. Missionary Alaska, 1960-83; coadjutor bishop Diocese of Fairbanks, Alaska, 1984-85, bishop, 1985—. Address: 1316 Peger Rd Fairbanks AK 99709

KANJI, JENNY, librarian; b. Kampala, Uganda, Africa, Mar. 22, 1945; came to U.S, 1977; d. Gulamhusein and Dolat Pirbhai; m. Amir Kanji, Sept 3, 1968; children: Shari, Aliya. BA, Am. U. of Beirut, 1965; BLS, U. BC., Vancouver, 1969, MLS, 1983. Libr. Vancouver Pub. Lib., B.C., 1972-80; law libr. U. San Diego, 1983-86; sr. acct. rep. Mead Data Cen., San Diego, 1986—. Nat. mem. Agakhan Found., 1987-88. Mem. Spl. Libr. Assn. (dir. 1986-87), Am. Assn. of Law Librs., San Diego on Line Users Group. Office: Mead Data Cen 701 B St Ste 1300 San Diego CA 92101

KANNAPELL, JOHN TROUY, mechanical engineer; b. St. Louis, Dec. 5, 1957; s. Paul Albert and Helen Frances (Williams) K. Student, U. Ill., 1976-79; BSMe, U. Mo., 1981. Engr. Northrop Aircraft Div., Hawthorne, Calif., 1981-83; sr. engr. hydromech. Northrop B-2 Div., Pico Rivera, Calif., 1983—. Patentee in field. Charter mem. St. Louis Symphony Youth Orch., 1971-76; vol., fundraiser Am. Diabetes Assn., L.A., 1987—. U. Mo. scholar, 1979-81. Mem. ASME, AIAA, Pi Tau Sigma, Phi Theta Kappa, Tau Beta Pi, Lambda Chi Alpha.

KANNEL, ALAN HOWARD, marketing and administrative services specialist; b. L.A., Feb. 9, 1960; s. Melvin Jules and Geri Harriet (Davis) K.; m. Julia Marie Greenwald, June 22, 1986; 1 child, Alexandria Nicole. BS in Geology, U. Ariz., 1983. Mktg. rep. Executone, Atlantic, Inc., Fairfax, Va., 1981-82; asst. The JNC Companies, Tucson, 1983-85; mktg. coord. Dooley Jones & Assoc., Tucson, 1986-87; mgr. proposal svcs. & mktg. Cella Barr Assoc., Tucson, 1987-89, mgr. of adminstrn., 1989—; prin. A&K Mktg., Tucson, 1986—. Vol. Reagan for Pres., Tucson, 1984, Bush for Pres., Tucson, 1988; bd. dirs. vol. ctr. of Tucson, 1986—, So. Ariz. Coun. of Campfire Girls, Tucson, 1987—. Mem. Am. Mktg. Assn. (v.p.), Am. Mgmt. Assn., Am. Soc. Petroleum Engrs., Profl. Assn. Diving Instrs., Am. Records Mgmt. Assn., Bether World Soc., Nature Conservancy, Cousteau Soc., Casa Adobes Rotary. Office: Cella Barr Assoc 2075 N 6th Ave Tucson AZ 85705

KANOFSKY, MYRON ROSS, physician; b. Waterloo, Iowa, Sept. 14, 1952; s. Herbert Bernard and Sylvia Reva (Widerschein) K.; m. Carol Susan Brody, June 16, 1974; children: Sarah Joanne, Megan Ann. BS, U. Wis., 1974; MD, U. Iowa, 1977. Diplomate Am. Bd. Ob-Gyn. Intern U. Wis. Hosps., Madison, 1977-79; resident in ob-gyn Hershey (Pa.) Med. Ctr., 1979-81; physician Arcadia (Calif.) Ob.-Gyn. Med. Group, 1981-82; physician Cigna Healthplans, Orange, Calif., 1982-87, Irvine, Calif., 1987-88; pvt. practice ob-gyn Orange, 1988—. Fellow Am. Coll. Ob.-Gyn.; mem. Orange County Med. Assn., Orange County Ob.-Gyn. Soc., Am. Fertility Soc. Office: 805 W La Veta Ave Ste 200 Orange CA 92668

KANTER, JAY, film company executive; b. Dec. 12, 1926. Began career with MCA, Inc.; then pres. First Artists Prodn. Co., Ltd.; v.p. prodn. 20th Century-Fox, 1975-76, sr. v.p. worldwide prodns., 1976-79; v.p. The Ladd Co., 1979-84; pres. worldwide prodns. motion picture div. MGM-United Artists Entertainment Co., 1984-85; pres. worldwide prodns. United Artists Corp., 1985; pres. Worldwide Prodn. MGM Pictures, Inc., Culver City, Calif., 1986-89; pres. prodn. Pathé Entertainment Co., Beverly Hills, Calif., 1989—. Office: Pathe Entertainment Inc 640 So San Vicente Blvd Los Angeles CA 90048

KANTER, STEPHEN, dean, law educator; b. Cin., June 30, 1946; s. Aaron J. and Edythe (Kasfir) K.; m. Dory Jean Poduska, June 24, 1972; children: Jordan Alexander, Laura Elizabeth. BS in Math., MIT, 1968; JD, Yale U., 1971. Spl. asst. Portland (Oreg.) City Commr., 1971-72; from staff atty. to asst. dir. Met. Pub. Defender, Portland, 1972-77; successively law prof., assoc. dean, acting dean sch. law Lewis and Clark Coll., Portland, 1977—; dean sch. law Lewis and Clark Coll., 1986—; Fulbright prof. law Nanjing (People's Republic of China) U., 1984-85; exec. com. Portland Am. Inns of Ct. Contbr. articles to profl. jours. Mem. bd. overseers World Affairs Council Oreg., Portland, 1986—; mem. Oreg. Criminal Justice Council, Salem, 1987—, Oreg. Bicentennial Commn., Portland, 1986—. Named one of Ten Great Portlanders, Willamette Week Newspaper, Portland, 1980. Mem. ACLU (bd. dirs. Oreg. chpt., 1976-82, pres. 1979-81, lawyers com. 1976—), Oreg. State Bar Assn., Am. Law Inst. (ex-officio), Fulbright Alumni Assn. (bd. dirs. 1986—), Rotary. Office: Lewis & Clark Coll Northwestern Sch Law 10015 SW Terwilliger Blvd Portland OR 97219

KAO, CHENG CHI, electronics executive; b. Taipei, Taiwan, Republic of China, Aug. 3, 1941; s. Chin Wu and Su Chin (Wu) K.; m. Susan Lin, July 4, 1970; children: Antonia Hueilan, Albert Chengwei, Helen Siaolan. BS, Taiwan U., 1963; AM, Harvard U., 1965, PhD, 1969. Research fellow Harvard U., Cambridge, Mass., 1969-70; scientist Xerox Corp., Webster, N.Y., 1970-75; mgr. Internat. Materials Research, Inc., Santa Clara, Calif., 1976-78; exec. v.p. President Enterprises Corp., Tainan, Taiwan, 1979-85; pres. Kolyn Enterprises Corp., Los Altos, Calif., 1979—. Contbr. articles to profl. jours. Bd. dirs. Taipei Am. Sch., 1980-82. Mem. IEEE, Chinese Inst. Elec. Engring. (bd. dirs. 1982-85), Sigma Xi. Club: Am. in China (Taipei), Palo Alto Hills Golf and Country. Office: Kolyn Enterprises Corp 4962 El Camino Real Ste 119 Los Altos CA 94022

KAPLAN, CAROL BLAKELY, communications executive; b. Oak Ridge, Tenn., Sept. 17, 1945; d. John Paul and Tinque June (Spann) Blakely; m. Jonathan Wall Kaplan, July 29, 1967 (div. 1976). BA, Swarthmore (Pa.) Coll., 1967; MS, U. Pa., 1971. Tchr. Sch. Dist. of Phila., 1967-68, 69-70, Monona (Wis.) pub. schs., 1968-69, Prince Georges Co. pub. schs., Upper Marlboro, Md., 1971-74; assoc. rsch. scientist Am. Inst. Rsch., Palo Alto, Calif., 1974-82; dir. corp. communications Boole & Babbage, Sunnyvale, Calif., 1982—. Editor BooleanWorld, 1986-88, Info. Exec., 1983, Jour. of Capacity Mgmt., 1982-83, Inside Software Engring., 1982-84. Coordinator United Way campaign, Sunnyvale, 1984-87. Mem. AAUW, Mt. View Tennis Club (pres. 1987). Democrat. Office: Boole & Babbage 510 Oakmead Pkwy Sunnyvale CA 94086

KAPLAN, DONALD SHELDON, real estate developer and rehabilitator, property management company executive; b. L.A., Aug. 1, 1938; s. Adolph Iven and Ruth Janet (Rose) K.; m. Marsha Lynn Le Van, June 12, 1960 (div. July 1980); children: Lisa Ann, Drew Jason; m. Joanne Natalie Cossu, Apr. 19, 1981; children: Alyson Ilene, Tara Ruth. Student, L.A. City Coll., Pacific State U. Pres. DSK Devel. Co., Inc., 1964--, Assured Maintenance Corp., Inc., 1974--, DSK Mgmt. Co., Inc., 1983--, New Renaissance Investments, Inc., 1986--, Kaplan Enterprises, Inc., L.A., 1986--. Home: 5699 Kanan Rd Apt 234 Agoura Hills CA 91301 Office: Kaplan Enterprises Inc 621 S Gramercy Pl Los Angeles CA 90005

KAPLAN, GARY, executive recruiter; b. Phila., Aug. 14, 1939; s. Morris and Minnie (Leve) K.; m. Linda Ann Wilson, May 30, 1968; children: Michael Warren, Marc Jonathan, Jeffrey Russell. B.A. in Polit. Sci., Pa. State U., 1961. Tchr. biology N.E. High Sch., Phila., 1962-63; coll. employment rep. Bell Telephone Labs., Murray Hill, N.J., 1966-67; supr. recruitment and placement Unisys, Blue Bell, Pa., 1967-69; pres. Electronic Systems Personnel, Phila., 1969-70; staff selection rep. Booz, Allen & Hamilton, N.Y.C., 1970-72; mgr. exec. recruitment M&T Chems., Rahway, N.J., 1972-74; dir. exec. recruitment IU Internat. Mgmt. Corp., Phila., 1974-78; v.p. personnel Crocker Bank, Los Angeles, 1978-79; mng. v.p. ptnr. western region Korn-Ferry Internat., Los Angeles, 1979-85; pres. Gary Kaplan & Assocs., Pasadena, Calif., 1985—. Mgmt. columnist, Radio and Records newspaper, 1984-85. Chmn. bd. dirs. Vis. Nurse Assn., L.A., 1985-87. Capt. Adj. Gen. Corps., U.S. Army, 1963-66. Mem. Employment Mgmt. Assn., Calif. Exec. Recruiters Assn., Am. Soc. Personal Adminstrn., Am. Compensation Assn. Home: 1735 Fairmount Ave La Canada CA 91011 Office: Gary Kaplan & Assocs 201 S Lake Ave Pasadena CA 91101

KAPLAN, IRVING EUGENE, human ecologist, psychologist; b. Phila., May 1, 1926; s. Abraham and Bertha (Posner) K.; m. Harriet Bromberg, Sept. 29, 1951; children: Addie Eve, Meryl Denise. BS, L.I. U., 1950; MA, New Sch. Social Rsch., 1953; PhD, U.S. Internat. U., 1971. Lic. psychologist, Calif. Depth interviewer Dr. Ernest Dichter, N.Y.C., 1950-52; employment interviewer N.Y. State Employment Svc., N.Y.C., 1952-56; rsch., program dir. U.S. Naval Personnel Rsch. Activity, San Diego, 1957-66; cons. psychologist San Diego, 1957—, human ecologist, designer, 1962—; cons., writer Ctr. for Study Dem. Instns., Santa Barbara, Calif., 1964-78, UN Law of Sea, N.Y.C. and Jamaica, N.Y., 1970—, Found. Reshaping the Internat. Order, Rotterdam, The Netherlands, 1980-82, UN Commn. Peaceful Uses of Outer Space, N.Y.C. and Vienna, Austria, 1982, Sri Lanka Inst. Advanced Study, 1982; designer in field. Contbr. articles to profl. jours. Served with USN, 1944-46. Mem. AAAS, Am. Geophys. Union, Am. Psychol. Assn. Home and Office: 3121 Beech St San Diego CA 92102

KAPLAN, MICHAEL AARON, aerospace engineer; b. Glendale, Calif., Apr. 13, 1944; s. Abraham Moses and Edda (Lillian) K.; m. Terry Ann Winfield, Dec. 18, 1965; children: Lisa, Stephen. BS, UCLA, 1966; MS, U. So. Calif., 1970. Registered profl. engr., Calif. Chief of stress Strato Engring. Co., Burbank, Calif., 1966-70, ATS, Van Nuys, Calif., 1972-74; flight test analyst Lockheed Corp., Palmdale, Calif., 1970-72; chief engr. Am. Jet Co., Van Nuys, 1974-76; pres. Cons. Aerospace Engrs., Van Nuys, 1976—. Office: Cons Aerospace Engrs 16123 Covello St Van Nuys CA 91324

KAPLAN, MIKE, film producer, independent film and video distributor; b. Providence, Mar. 16, 1943; s. Julius and Ida (Rabinowitz) K. BA, U. R.I., 1964. Assoc. editor Ind. Film Jour., N.Y.C., 1964-65; publicist MGM, N.Y.C., 1965-68, publicity coord., 1968, nat. publicity dir., 1968-71; v.p.Polaris Prodn. Stanley Kubrick, London, 1971-73; internat mkgt. exec. Warner Bros., L.A., London, 1973-74; pres. Circle Assocs. Ltd., U.S., London, 1973—; v.p. mktg. Northstar Internat., Hal Ashby, L.A., 1981-83; pres. mktg. Alive Films, L.A., 1985-87; producer, pres. Circle Assoc. Ltd., L.A., 1988—. Producer: (film) The Whales of August, 1987; viedo Oak Grove Sch., 1988; actor: Buffalo Bill And The Indians, Welcome To L.A., Choose Me. Recipient Owl award Retirement Rsch. Found., 1987, Key Art award Hollywood Reporter, 1976, 87. Mem. Acad. Motion Picture Arts and Scis., Screen Actors Guild, Publicists Guild. Office: Cir Assocs PO Box 5730 Santa Monica CA 90405

KAPLAN, ROBERT B., linguistics educator, consultant, researcher; b. N.Y.C., Sept. 20, 1929; s. Emanuel B. and Natalie K.; m. Audrey A. Lien, Apr. 21, 1951; children—Robin Ann Kaplan Gibson, Lisa Kaplan Morris, Robert Allen. Student, Champlain Coll., 1947-48, Syracuse U., 1948-49; B.A., Willamette U., 1952; M.A., U. So. Calif., 1957, Ph.D., 1962. Teaching asst. U. So. Calif., Los Angeles, 1955-57, instr. coordinator, asst. prof. English communication program for fgn. students, 1965-72, assoc. prof., dir. English communication program for fgn. students, 1972-76, assoc. dean continuing edn., prof. applied linguistics, 1976—, dir. Am. Lang. Inst., 1986—; instr. U. Oreg., 1957-60; cons. field service program Nat. Assn. Fgn. Student Affairs, 1964-84; pres.-elect faculty senate U. So. Calif., 1988-89, pres., 1989-90; adv. bd. internat. comparability study of standardized lang. exams. U. Cambridge Local Exams. Syndicate. Author: Reading and Rhetoric: A Reader, 1963; (with V. Tufte, P. Cook and J. Aurbach) Transformational Grammar: A Guide for Teachers, 1968; (with R.D. Schoesler) Learning English Through Typewriting, 1969; The Anatomy of Rhetoric: Prolegomena to a Functional Theory of Rhetoric, 1971; On the Scope of Applied Linguistics, 1980; The Language Needs of Migrant Workers, 1980; (with P. Shaw) Exploring Academic English, 1984; (with U. Connor) Writing Across Languages: Analysis of L2 Text, 1987; editorial bd. Standpoints, Jour. Pacific Rim Communication; contbr. articles to profl. jours., U.S. Australia, Brazil, Can., Germany, Holland, Japan, Mexico, N.Z., Philippines and Singapore; edit. bd. Oxford Internat. Encyclopedia Linguistics; contbr. notes, revs. to profl. jours. U.S. and abroad. Editor-in-chief Ann. Rev. Applied Linguistics, 1980—. Bd. dirs. Internat. Bilingual Sch. L.A., 1986—, Internat. Edn. Research Found., 1986—. Served with inf. U.S. Army, Korea. Fulbright sr. scholar, Australia, 1978, Hong Kong, 1986. Mem. Am. Anthrop. Assn., AAAS, Am. Assn. Applied Linguistics, AAUP, Assn. Internationale de Linguistique Applique, Assn. Internationale Pour La Researche et La Diffusion Des Methodes Audio-Visuelles et Structuro-Globales, Assn. Tchrs. English as Second Lang., Calif. Assn. Tchrs. English to Speakers Other Langs., Can. Council Tchrs. English, Nat. Assn. Fgn. Student Affairs (nat. pres. 1983-84), Linguistics Soc. Am., Tchrs. English to Speakers of Other Langs. (1st v.p., pres.-elect 1989-90, pres. 1990-91). Office: U So Calif Dept Linguistics Los Angeles CA 90089-1693

KAPLAN, ROBERT MARSHALL, investment company executive; b. Montreal, Que., Can., Nov. 11, 1936; came to U.S., 1959; s. Albert Oscar and Alice Lillian (Westbury) K.; m. Candace Kay Holt, June 12, 1981; children: Matthew Dana, Meredith Leigh. MBA, Harvard U., 1961; PhD, Mich. State U., 1967. Prof. U. No. Iowa, Cedar Falls, 1971-76, U. Vermont, Burlington, 1976-80; 2nd v.p. Shearson Lehman Hutton, Phoenix, 1981-86; sr. v.p. Drexel Burnham Lambert, Phoenix, 1986—. Author: (books) Marketing Concept in Action, 1964, Salesmanship, 1968; contbr. articles to profl. jours. Bd. dirs. Sun Angel Found., Phoenix, men's league Scottsdale Ctr. for the Arts. Home: 5546 E Sanna St Scottsdale AZ 85253 Office: Drexel Burnham Lambert 6991 E Camelback Rd Scottsdale AZ 85251

KAPLAN, SAMUEL SIMON, orthopedic surgeon; b. N.Y.C., Aug. 31, 1939; s. Arthur Murray and Gertrude K.; m. Brenda Joan, June 10, 1962; children: Kenneth, Karen. AB, N.Y.U., 1961, MD, 1965. Diplomate Am. Bd. Orthopedic Surgery. Intern Kings County Hosp., Bklyn., 1965-66; sugrical resident Albert Einstein Coll. Medicine, Bronx, N.Y., 1966-67; chief surg. services 328th Air Force Base Hosp., Grandview, Mo., 1967-69; resident orthopedic Kans. U. Med. Ctr., Kansas City, 1969-72; pres. Orthopedists Ltd., Scottsdale, Ariz., 1972—; tchr. Maricopa County Med. Ctr., Phoenix, 1986—. Reviewer: Jour. Bone and Joint Surgery 1986—; conbtr. articles to profl. jours. Fellow Am. Acad. Orthopedic Surgeon; mem. Western Orthopedic Assn., Ariz. Orthopedic Assn., Maricopa County Med. Soc., Ariz. Med. Soc. Club: Road Runners M.D. (Scottsdale). Office: Orthopedists Ltd 1402 N Miller Rd Scottsdale AZ 85257

KAPLAN, SANFORD SANDY, geologist; b. N.Y.C., Oct. 2, 1950; s. Lawrence J. and Jerome (Leon) K.; m. Joanne Mandel Kaplan, June 5, 1975 (dec. Sept. 1985); children: Micah, Elicia Anne, Shira Frieda; m. Connie Clarke Kaplan, Jan. 19, 1989; stepchildren: Todd, Wendi, Bryan. AB, Lafayette Coll., Easton, Pa., 1971; MS, Lehigh U., 1976; postgrad., U. Nebr., 1976-79; MA in Internat. Rels., Salve Regina Coll.; PhD, U. Pitts., 1980; postgrad., U.S. Naval War Coll., 1986-87. Teaching asst. Lehigh U., Bethlehem, Pa., 1975-76; engr. U.S. Steel Corp., Monroeville, Pa., 1976; vis. instr. U. Nebr., Lincoln, 1976-80; vis. prof. U. Pitts., 1980; geologist U.S. Dept. Energy, Breeceton, Pa., 1979-80; geol. specialist Pennzoil Exploration, Denver, 1980-86; pvt. practice geology Denver, 1987—; pres. KF Energy, Denver, 1987—. Editor Cenzoic Paleogeography of West Central U.S., 1985; composer Trio Medieval Fantasy, 1979, Short Trio; contbr. articles to profl. jours. Chmn. Citizens Against Jewell Ave Overpass, Aurora, Colo., 1983-84; mem. Adoptive Families of Denver. Recipient Silver Acorn award Boy Scouts Am., 1986; James L. Dyson scholar Lafayette Coll., 1970; rsch. grantee NSF, 1970, Sigma Xi, 1978. Mem. Am. Econ. Assn., Am. Assn. Petroleum Geologists, Geol. Soc. Am. Soc. Econ. Paleontologists and Mineralogists (editor 1982-84), Rocky Mountain Assn. Geologists. Jewish. Home: 11761 E Asbury Pl Aurora CO 80014 Office: KF Energy 2201 Stout St Denver CO 86205

KAPLAN, SHELBY JEAN, real estate syndications and investment company executive; b. Quantico, Va., May 2, 1947; d. James Sharpe and Jean Rita (Catusco) William; m. David Kaplan (div.); children: James David, Jeannie Louise; m. Sheldon H. Sloan, Mar. 6, 1988. BS, UCLA; MBA summa cum laude, Pepperdine U., 1976. Exec. v.p. Nat. Investment Devel. Corp., L.A., 1976-85; pres., chief exec. officer Securities Placements, Inc., L.A., 1981—; pres., cheif exec. officer Tricap Corp., L.A., 1984—; guest lectr. on real estate tax shelter programs to CPA socs. and Internat. Assn. Cert. Fin. Planners, on real estate syndication and investments on local TV and radio programs. Mem. women's coun. Dem. Nat. Com., 1984; mem. exec. com. Friends of Van de Kamp, L.A., 1987—; founder, chmn. bd. trustees L.A. Theatre Ctr., 1989; mem. Blue Ribbon of Music Ctr.of L.A., 1989. Mem. Nat. Assn. Pvt. Placements, Greater L.A. Zoo Assn. (bd. trustees 1989), Real Estate Securities and Syndication Inst., West L.A. C. of C. (fin. coun. 1982—), Riviera Tennis Club, Hillcrest Country Club, Regency Club. Home: 2 Latimer Rd Santa Monica CA 90402 Office: Tricap Corp 1801 Ave of the Stars Ste 727 Los Angeles CA 90067

KAPLAN, ZACHARY, dentist; b. Los Angeles, Nov. 11, 1939; s. Harry and Tillie (Cohen) K.; m. Peggy Jean Knibb, June 25, 1966; childen: Scott Matthew, Alison Jean. Student, U. Calif., Santa Barbara, 1957-61; DDS, St. Louis U., 1965. Gen. practice dentistry Ft. Collins, Colo., 1967—; asst. clin. prof. U. Colo., Denver, 1983—. Served to lt. comdr. USN, 1965-67. Mem. ADA, Colo. Dental Assn., Larimer County Dental Soc. (peer rev. com., 1983—, community resource com. 1985—). Democrat. Jewish. Office: 373 W Drake Rd Fort Collins CO 80526

KAPLANSKY, IRVING, mathematician, educator, research institute director; b. Toronto, Ont., Can., Mar. 22, 1917; came to U.S., 1940, naturalized, 1955; s. Samuel and Anna (Zuckerman) K.; m. Rachelle Brenner, Mar. 16, 1951; children—Steven, Daniel, Lucille. B.A., U. Toronto, 1938, M.A., 1939; Ph.D., Harvard, 1941; LL.D. (hon.), Queen's U., 1969. Instr. math. Harvard, 1941-44; mem. faculty U. Chgo., 1945-84, prof. math., 1956-84, chmn. dept., 1962-67, George Herbert Mead Distinguished Service prof. math., 1969-84; dir. Math. Scis. Research Inst., Berkeley, Calif., 1984—; Mem. exec. com. div. math. NRC, 1959-62. Author books, tech. papers. Mem. Nat. Acad. Scis., Am. Math. Soc. (pres. 1985-86). Office: Math Scis Rsch Inst 1000 Centennial Dr Berkeley CA 94720

KAPOOR, ASHOK KUMAR, engineer; b. Allahabad, Uttar Pradesh, India, Feb. 7, 1952; s. Ram Nath and Sarla Kapoor; m. Nisha Malhotra, May 9, 1984; 1 child, Shweta. BTech, Indian Inst. Tech., 1973; MS, U. Cin., 1979, PhD, 1981. Illumination engr. Philips India Ltd., Bombay, 1973-76; mem. research staff Fairchild Rsch. Ctr., Palo Alto, Calif., 1981-86; mgr. device modeling and bipolar research Fairchild Research Ctr., Palo Alto, Calif., 1986-87; mgr. tech. devel. ASIC div. Nat. Semicondr., Santa Clara, Calif., 1987-88; mgr. HP Labs., Palo Alto, 1988—. Editor: Polysilicon Bipolar Transistors; contbr. tech. articles to profl. jours.; patentee in field. Mem. IEEE (working com., electron devices soc. Santa Clara Valley chpt.), Sigma Xi. Hindu. Home: 1056 Amarillo Ave Palo Alto CA 94303

KAPPES, GEORGE, JR., insurance agency executive; b. Milw., May 2, 1928; s. George William and Anna Gertrude (Von Nimitz) K.; m. Roberta G. Baldwin, May 27, 1958; children: George III, Margaret Ann. BA, U. Wis., 1950. Underwriter Continental Casualty Co., 1950-53; supr. underwriting Marketments Mutual, Milw., 1953-56, Ohio Casualty Co., Hamilton, 1956-64; regional mgr. underwriting Utica Mut., Alhambra, Calif. and Waltham, Mass., 1964-72; v.p. Medallion Ins. Group, Kansas City, Mo., 1972-74, Cal Surance Assocs., Torrance, Calif., 1974-75; pres. Ins. Mktg., Torrance, 1975-77, Kappes-Coombe Ins. Svc., Redondo Beach, Calif., 1977-80, Am. Facilities Ins. Agy., Ft. Bragg, Calif., 1980—. Founder Greater Hamilton (Ohio) Civic Theatre, 1958-61; pres. Ocean Lake Park Homowners Assn., Ft. Bragg, 1988—. Mem. Profl. Ins. Agts., Ins. Inst. Am. (diplomate in mgmt.), Am. Security Coun., King Harbor Yacht Club, Rotary (chmn., dir. scholarship com. Ft. Bragg 1988—). Home: 1184 N Main St Fort Bragg CA 95437 Office: Am Facilities Ins Agy 101 Cypress St Fort Bragg CA 95437

KAPPHAHN, ERNEST L., small business owner; b. Salem, Oreg., Oct. 18, 1946; s. Willard L. and Cleo (Sanders) K.; m. Carole Lynn Stiefel, Sept. 9, 1967; 1 child, James E. BA in English, Calif. Poly. U., 1970. Police officer City of Santa Monica, Calif., 1968-69, City of Pismo Beach, Calif., 1969-70; police officer, detective City of Santa Maria, Calif., 1970-79; owner, operator Capitol News Ctr., Salem, 1979-83, Cambridge Bookstore, Salem, 1980-83; owner, operator Books West, Arroyo Grande, Calif., 1982—, Lompoc, Calif., 1985—, San Luis Obispo, Calif., 1985—, Bakersfield, Calif., 1986—; pres. Laguna Merchants Assn., San Luis Obispo, 1985-87, bd. dirs. Civil def. radio officer City of Santa Maria, 1972-79; active San Luis Obispo County Band. Mem. Am. Booksellers Assn., Am. Radio Relay League (chmn. southwestern div. conv. 1978, 84, pub. service award 1965), No. Calif. Booksellers Assn., So. Calif. Booksellers Assn., Satellite Amateur Radio Club. Republican. Methodist. Office: Books West 1420 Grand Ave Arroyo Grande CA 93420

KAPUR, KRISHAN KISHORE, health facility administrator, educator; b. Jullundur, Punjab, India, Mar. 14, 1930; s. Des Raj and Pritam Devi (Sodhi) K.; m. Althea Uher, Dec. 31, 1957; children: Raj Paul, Aneal Kumar, Leela Ann. BS, Pujab U., 1948; BDS, Bombay U., 1954; MS, Tufts U., 1956, D in Med. Dentistry, 1958. Diplomate Am. Bd. Prosthodontics. Asst. prof. prosthetic dentistry Tufts U., Boston, 1960-61, assoc. prof. dental sci., 1961-62; prof., chmn. oral biology sch. dentistry U. Detroit, 1964-67; chief dental svcs. VA Outpatient Clinic, Boston, 1967-71; chief dental svcs. VA Med. Ctr., West Roxbury, Mass., 1971-75, chief dental svcs., dir. dental geriatric fellowship program, 1975-88; chief dental svcs. VA Med. Ctr., West L.A., Calif., 1988—; prof. removable prosthodontics sch. dentistry UCLA, 1975—; cons. Commn. on Dental Accreditation. Editorial bd. Jour. Gerontology, 1983-87; contbr. over 65 articles to profl. jours. Recipient Carl A. Schlack award Assn. Mil. Surgeons U.S., 1986. Fellow Internat. Coll. Dentists, Am. Acad. Denture Prosthetics; mem. ADA, Internat. Assn. Dental Research (Sci. award 1974), Gerontology Soc. Am. Hindu. Home: 3935 Bon Homme Rd Woodland Hills CA 91364 Office: VA Med Ctr 16111 Plummer St Sepulveda CA 91364

KARABEL, JEROME BERNARD, sociologist, educator; b. Phila., May 20, 1950; s. Henry Leon and Dorothy (Forstein) K. BA, Harvard U., 1972, PhD, 1977; postgrad., Nuffield Coll., Oxford, Eng., 1972-73, Ecole Pratique des Hautes Etudes, Paris, 1974-75. Sr. research assoc. Huron Inst., Cambridge, Mass., 1977-84; asst. prof. sociology U. Calif., Berkeley, 1984-86, assoc. prof., 1986—; cons. Nat. Inst. Edn., Washington, 1976-80. Co-author and co-editor: Power and Ideology in Education, 1977; co-author: The Diverted Dream: Community Colleges and the Promise of Educational Opportunity in America, 1900-1985, 1989; editorial cons. Oxford U. Press, N.Y.C., 1977—; sr. editor: Theory and Society, 1978—; assoc. editor: Sociology of Edn., 1982-85; contbr. articles to profl. jours. Grantee Nat. Inst. Edn., 1977-81, NSF, 1972-75, 81-87, Ford Found., 1981-83. Mem. Am. Sociol. Assn. (council mem. soc. edn. sect. 1984-87), Soc. Study Social Problems, Phi Beta Kappa. Home: 2732 Stuart St Berkeley CA 94705 Office: U Calif Dept Sociology Berkeley CA 94720

KARAKEY, SHERRY JOANNE, financial and real estate investment company executive, interior designer; b. Wendall, Idaho, Apr. 16, 1942; d. John Donald and Vera Ella (Frost) Kingery; divorced; children: Artist Roxanne, Buddy (George II), Kami JoAnne, Launi JoElla. Student, Ariz. State U., 1960. Corp. sec., treas. Karbel Metals Co., Phoenix, 1963-67; sec. to pub. Scottsdale (Ariz.) Daily Progress, 1969-72; with D-Velco Mfg. of Ariz., Phoenix, 1959-62, dir., exec. v.p., sec., treas., 1972-87; mng. ptnr. Karitage, Ltd., Scottsdale, 1987—. Mem. Nat. Rep. Com.

KARAMITAS, MICHALIS GEORGE, accountant; b. Benoni, Transvaal, South Africa, Dec. 5, 1951; came to U.S., 1986; s. George and Irene Daphne Agnes (Faulkner) K.; m. Karin Penelope Klopper, Nov. 27, 1982. CTA, Witwatersrand U., Johannesburg, 1978. cert. chartered acct. 1981, South Africa. Sr. auditor Sussman Goddard and Co., Johannesburg, 1970-76, Arthur Young and Co., Johannesburg, 1976-78; fin. acct. Gallic Construction, Johannesburg, 1978-79; group fin. dir. National Machinery, Johannesburg, 1979-82; group mgmt. acct. Russell Holdings Ltd., Johannesburg, 1983-84; computer applications spec. McCormack and Dodge, Johannesburg, 1984-86; computer applications cons. McCormack and Dodge, San Francisco, 1986—. Served as air mechanic, South African Air Force, 1969. Mem. South African Inst. Chartered Accts. Anglican. Office: McCormack & Dodge 1450 Fashion Island Blvd Ste 500 San Mateo CA 94404

KARBY, MICHAEL EDWARD, architect, planner; b. San Francisco, June 20, 1956; s. Warren Edward and Marie Etoyal (Stoddart) K.; divorced; 1 child, Evelyn Amelia. AA, Fresno City Coll., 1978; student, Calif. Poly. Inst., Pomona, 1978; BA in Indsl. Arts, Architecture, Calif. State U., Fresno, 1980, MCRP in City and Regional Planning, 1983. Draftsman L. Gene Zellmer AIA, Fresno, 1977-80; designer Armen Dervishian AIA, Fresno, 1981-84; prin. Meka Architecture/Planning, Fresno, 1984—; design cons. Taylor Group Architects, Fresno, 1987—, Stan Stanovich AIA, Orinda, Calif., 1985, Richard Marshall FAIA, San Francisco, 1985. Prin. works include Prototypical Community, Los Cielo, Calif., New Millerton, Calif., China Bay, Calif. Mem. AIA, Am. Mensa Ltd., Am. Planning Assn., Architects, Designers, Planners for Social Responsibility. Home: 1445 E Bulldog Ln #201 Fresno CA 93710 Office: 1195 W Shaw Ave Ste A Fresno CA 93711

KAREL, STEPHEN GERARD, health services administrator; b. Louisville, Apr. 4, 1951; s. John Jeroslav and Beatrice (Bryan) K.; m. Harumi Sasaki. BS in Edn., U. Mo., 1973; MPH, U. Hawaii, 1982. Profl. rels. cons. H.M.S.A., Honolulu, 1982-83; health officer East-West Ctr., Honolulu, 1983—; bd. dirs. Omega Rose Found. Contbr. articles to profl. jours. Named one of Outstanding Young Men of Am., 1985. Mem. Am. Pub. Health Assn., Hawaii Pub. Health Assn., Am. Coll. Health. Home: PO Box 22182 Honolulu HI 96822

KARGUL, MARK CRAIG, airline pilot; b. Alameda, Calif., July 2, 1954; s. Frank Stanley and Edna Lois (Wyrick) K. BS in Aero. Engring., U.S. Air Force Acad., 1978. Commd. 2d lt. USAF, 1978, advanced through grades to capt., 1982; instr. pilot USAF, Kadena Air Base, Japan, 1980-81, Bergstrom AFB, Tex., 1981-84; instr. pilot U.S. Air Force Acad., Colorado Springs, Colo., 1985-86; resigned USAF, 1986; pilot Am. Airlines, L.A., 1986—. Republican. Home: 20341 Bluffside Cir Apt 306 Huntington Beach CA 92646

KARL, GREGORY PAUL, accountant, financial executive; b. Saginaw, Mich., Feb. 7, 1950; s. Harry Frederick and Mary Elizabeth (Knox) K.; m. Mary Rose Capizzo, July 15, 1972 (div. 1983); children: Sheri Lynn, Matthew John, Joseph Harry; m. Elizabeth T. Kenzelmann, Dec. 31, 1983. BS in Acctg., U. Detroit, 1971. CPA, Mich. Sr. acct. Ernst and Whinney, Saginaw, 1969-74; controller Blount Materials Inc., Saginaw, 1974-79; adminstr. Gen. Motors Corp., Detroit, 1979-80; controller Wickes Engineered Materials, Saginaw, 1980-83; dir. Wickes Cos. Inc., Santa Monica, Calif., 1983-84; v.p. fin. Primarius Assocs., San Diego, 1984-88; chief fin. officer Celltronics, Inc., San Diego, Calif., 1989—. Mem. curriculum adv. bd. Delta Coll., Saginaw, 1982-83. Mem. AICPA, Mich. Soc. CPAs, Am. Mgmt. Assn. Home: 1460 Santa Luisa Solana Beach CA 92075 Office: Celltronics Inc 10040 Mesa Rim Rd San Diego CA 92121

KARLEN, ROBERT EDWIN, sales executive; b. Aberdeen, S.D., Feb. 23, 1947; s. Albert Edwin and Rhea (Christen) K.; m. Judith Ann Langemeier, June 30, 1972 (div. 1977). BA in Econs., U. S.D., 1969, MA in Pub. Adminstrn., 1970. Owner, ptnr. Hanco Imports/Sports, Anchorage, 1978—. Bd. dirs. Anchorage Boys and Girls Clubs, 1985—; Alaska Sports Ofcls. Assn., Anchorage, 1973—. Capt. U.S. Army, 1971-76; lt. col. Alaskan N.G., 1976—. Mem. Army N.G. Assn., Nat. Sporting Goods Assn., Lambda Chi Alpha (pres.). Republican. Lutheran. Lodge: Elks. Home: 6262 E 41st Ct Anchorage AK 99504 Office: Hanco Imports/Sports 5531 Arctic Blvd Anchorage AK 99518

KARLESKINT, BARRY MICHAEL, retail store executive, landscape contractor; b. Santa Maria, Calif., May 25, 1941; s. John Peter and Mary Alward (Fitzgerald) K.; student Calif. State Poly. U., 1959-62; m. Brenda Signorelli, July 20, 1963; children: Kenneth Brian, Robert Jasen, Ann Marie. Foreman, Landscape Dept., Karleskint's Florist & Nursery, San Luis Obispo, 1962-67; gen. mgr. Landscape Dept., Karleskint-Crum, Inc., San Luis Obispo, Calif., 1969, v.p., 1969, 85—, v.p., retail gen. mgr., 1975, pres., 1980-85, dir., 1967—; pres., dir. Canyon Leasing Co., 1984—; pres. KC Stores Inc., San Luis Obispo, 1985—, also bd. dirs.; instr. San Luis Coastal Sch. Dist. Adult Sch., 1977-78; gen. ptnr. Suburban Assocs.; cons. in field. Mem. organizing com. Obispo Beautiful Assn., 1970; mem. San Luis Obispo City Joint Use Adv. Com., 1985-89; pres. Mission-Nativity Parents Assn., 1974-76, mem. sch. bd., 1974-76; pres. Nativity of Our Lady Cath. Ch. Council, 1977; mem. San Luis Obispo City Parks and Recreation Commn., 1981-89; com. chmn. 1987-89; mem. San Luis Obispo City Tree Com., 1981-84; mem. San Luis City Planning Commn., 1989—. Served with U.S. Army, 1962, USAR, 1962-66, USNG, 1966-68. Cert. nurseryman, Calif. Mem. Calif. Assn. Nurserymen (chpt. dir. 1978-80), Calif. Landscape Contractor's Assn. (chpt. dir. 1964-66), Calif. Assn. Park and Recreation Commrs. and Bd. Mems., Calif. State Sheriff's Assn., Controller's Roundtable San Luis Obispo, Alpha-Micro Users Soc., Roman Catholic. Clubs: San Luis Obispo Swim (pres. 1977-78); KC, Old Mission Sch. Booster (sec. 1961-63). Lodge: Rotary. Home: 623 Jeffrey Dr San Luis Obispo CA 93401 Office: 225 Suburban Rd San Luis Obispo CA 93401

KARLIN, SAMUEL, mathematics educator, researcher; b. Yonova, Poland, June 8, 1924; s. Morris K.; m. Elsie (div.); children—Kenneth, Manuel, Anna. B.S. in Math., Ill. Inst. Tech., 1944; Ph.D. in Math., Princeton U., 1947; D.Sc. (hon.), Technion-Israel Inst. Tech., Haifa, 1985. Instr. math. Calif. Inst. Tech., Pasadena, 1948-49; asst. prof. Calif. Inst. Tech., 1949-52, assoc. prof., 1952-55, prof., 1955-56; vis. asst. prof. Princeton U., N.J., 1950-51; prof. Stanford U., Calif., 1956—; Andrew D. White prof.-at-large Cornell U., 1975-81; Wilks lectr. Princeton U., 1977; pres. Inst. Math. Stats., 1978-79; Commonwealth lectr. U. Mass., 1980; 1st Mahalanobis Meml. Lectr., Indian Statis. Inst., 1983; prin. invited speaker XII Internat. Biometics Meeting, Japan; prin. lectr. Quebec Math. Soc., 1984; adv. dean math. dept. Weizmann Inst. Sci., Israel, 1970-77. Author: Mathematical Methods and Theory in Games, Programming, Economics, Vol. I: Matrix Games, Programming and Mathematical Economics, 1959, Mathematical Methods and Theory in Games, Programming, Economics, Vol. II: The Theory of Infinite Games, 1959, A First Course in Stochastic Processes, 1966, Total Positivity Vol. I, 1968; (with K. Arrow and H. Scarf) Studies in the Mathematical Theory of Inventory and Production, 1958; (with W.J. Sudden) Tchebycheff Systems: With Applications in Analysis and Statistics, 1966; (with H. Taylor) A First Course in Stochastic Processes, 2d edit., 1975, A Second Course in Stochastic Processes, 1980, An Introduction to Stochastic Modeling, 1984; (with C.A. Micchelli, A. Pinkus, I.I. Schoenberg) Studies in Spline Functions and Approximation Theory, 1976; editor: (with E. Nevo) Population Genetics and Ecology, 1976; (with T. Amemiya and L.A. Goodman) Studies in Econometric, Time Series, and Multivariate Statistics, 1983; (with K. Arrow and P. Suppes) Contributions to Mathematical Methods in the Social Sciences, 1960; (with K. Arrow and H. Scarf) Studies in Applied Probability and Management Sciences, 1962; (with S. Lessard) Theoretical Studies on Sex Ratio Evolution, 1986; editor: (with E. Nevo) Evolutionary Processes and Theory, 1986; sr. editor Theoretical Population Biology, Jour. D'Analyse; assoc. editor Jour. Math. Analysis, Lecture Notes in Biomath., Jour. Applied Probability, Jour. Multivariate Analysis, Jour. Approximation Theory, SIAM Jour. Math. Analysis, Jour. Linear Algebra, Computers and Math. with Applications, Ency. of Math. and Its Applications, Advanced in Applied Math.; contbr. articles to profl. jours. Recipient Lester R. Ford award Am. Math. Monthly, 1973, Robert Grimmett Chair Math., Stanford U., 1978, The John Von Neumann Theory prize, 1987; Proctor fellow, 1945, Bateman Research fellow, 1947-48; fellow Guggenheim Found., 1959-60, NSF, 1960-61; Wald lectr., 1957. Fellow Internat. Statis. Inst., Inst. Math. Stats., AAAS; mem. Am. Math. Soc., Am. Acad. Arts and Scis., Nat. Acad. Scis. (award in applied math. 1973), Am. Soc. Human Genetics, Genetic Soc. Am., Am. Naturalist Soc. Office: Stanford U Bldg 380 Stanford CA 94305

KARLSSON, ERIC ALLAN, electronics engineer; b. San Francisco, Dec. 3, 1950; s. Jon Love and Lura Lee (Lincicum) K. BS in Physics, U. Calif., Davis, 1973; MS in Physics, San Francisco State U., 1980. Process engr. Fairchild, San Rafael, Calif., 1977-79, sr. engr., 1981-83; rsch. engr. Lawrence Berkeley Labs., Calif., 1979-80; sr. engr. Allen-Bradley, Torrance, Calif., 1983-84; project engr. Burroughs Corp., Carlsbad, Calif., 1984-85; cons. semicondr. devices Allen-Bradley, 1984-85; engring. mgr. TAG Semiconductor, Zurich, Switzerland, 1985-86; dir. rsch. and engring., Zurich, 1986-88; sr. rsch. scientist Raytheon Rsch., Lexington, Mass., 1988-89; engring. mgr., cons. Microsemi PTC, Torrance, Calif., 1989—. Home: 1380 Thompson Ave Napa CA 94558 Office: 23201 S Normandie Ave Torrance CA 90501

KARLTON, LAWRENCE K., federal judge; b. Bklyn., May 28, 1935; s. Aaron Katz and Sylvia (Meltzer) K.; m. Mychelle Stiebel, Sept. 7, 1958. Student, Washington Sq. Coll.; LL.B., Columbia U., 1958. Bar: Fla. 1958, Calif. 1962. Acting legal officer Sacramento Army Depot, Dept. Army, Sacramento, 1959-60; civilian legal officer Sacramento Army Depot, Dept. Army, 1960-62; individual practice law Sacramento, 1962-64; mem. firm Abbott, Karlton & White, 1964, Karlton & Blease, until 1971, Karlton, Blease & Vanderlaan, 1971-76; judge Calif. Superior Ct. for Sacramento County, 1976-79; judge U.S. Dist. Ct., Sacramento, 1979—, now chief judge. Co-chmn. Central Calif. council B'nai B'rith Anit-Defamation League Commn., 1964-65; treas. Sacramento Jewish Community Relations Council, chmn., 1967-68. Mem. Am. Bar Assn., Sacramento County Bar Assn. Club: B'nai B'rith (past pres.). Office: US Dist Ct 2012 US Courthouse 650 Capitol Mall Sacramento CA 95814

KARO, ARNOLD MITCHELL, physicist; b. Wayne, Nebr., May 14, 1928; s. Henry Arnold and Ethel Leila (Mitchell) Maynard; m. Daniella Thea Cassvan, July 1, 1966; children: Barbara Melissa, Stephen Arnold. BS in Chemistry, Stanford U., 1949, BS in Physics, 1949; PhD in Chem. Physics, MIT, 1953. Teaching fellow MIT, Cambridge, 1949-51; staff physicist Lincoln Lab., Lexington, Mass., 1952; teaching assoc. dept. chemistry U. Utah, Salt Lake City, 1953-54; research assoc. Solid State and Molecular Theory Group, MIT, Cambridge, 1955-58; vis. research scientist European Ctr. Atomic and Molecular Theory U. Paris, Orsay, France, 1975; sr. scientist U. Calif. Lawrence Livermore Nat. Lab., 1958—; cons. in field. Author: (with others) The Lattice Dynamics and Statics of Alkali Halide Crystals, 1979. Contbr. articles to profl. jours. Mem. rev. com. City Pleasanton, Calif., 1973-74. Served with Chem. Corps AUS, 1953-55. Nat. Coffin fellow Gen. Electric Co., 1951-52. Fellow Am. Phys. Soc., AAAS, Am. Inst. Chemistry, N.Y. Acad. Scis.; mem. Calif. Inst. Chemists, (charter), Calif. Acad. Scis., Am. Chem. Soc., Commonwealth Club of Calif., Phi Theta Kappa, Phi Lambda Upsilon, Sigma Xi. Presbyterian.

KARP, JERRY STEVEN, sales executive; b. Bklyn., Mar. 23, 1944; s. Albert and Florence (Kaplan) K.; m. Sylvia Slodzina, Sept. 1, 1965 (div. 1977); 1 child, Brian Scott; m. Cheryl Gail Briendel, Sept. 2, 1984; 1 child, Justin Samuel. Student, Bklyn. Coll., 1961-63, Queens Coll., 1963-64. Claims adjuster Consolidated Mutual Ins. Co., Bklyn., 1963-65; sr. claims adjuster Firemans Fund Ins. Co., N.Y.C., 1965-66; sales mgr. Woodlin Shirt Co., N.Y.C., 1966-68; gen. mgr. Albert Weiss & Sons, N.Y.C., 1968-71; sales rep. Marshall Industries, Sunnyvale, Calif., 1972-74; reg. sales mgr. Prodn. Tech., Santa Clara, Calif., 1974-79; pres. JSK Assocs., Santa Clara, Calif., 1979—. Steering com. Am. Heart Assn. Tennis Tournament, Santa Clara, 1983. Mem. Surface Mount Tech. Assn. (sec. 1988—), Porsche Club of Am., Decathlon, Kiwanis. Democrat. Jewish. Office: JSK Associates 3080 Olcott St Santa Clara CA 95054

KARPAN, KATHLEEN MARIE, state official, lawyer, journalist; b. Rock Springs, Wyo., Sept. 1, 1942; d. Thomas Michael and Pauline Ann (Taucher) K. B.S. in Journalism, U. Wyo., 1964, M.A. in Am. Studies, 1975; J.D., U. Oreg., 1978. Bar: D.C. 1979, Wyo. 1983, U.S. Dist. Ct. Wyo., U.S. Ct. Appeals (D.C. and 10th cirs.). Editor Cody Enterprise, Wyo., 1964; press asst. to U.S. Congressman Teno Roncalio U.S. Ho. of Reps., Washington, 1965-67, 71-72, adminstrv. asst., 1973-74; asst. news editor Wyo. Eagle, Cheyenne, 1967; free-lance writer 1968; teaching asst. dept. history U. Wyo., 1969-70; desk editor Canberra Times, Australia, 1970; dep. dir. Office Congl. Relations, Econ. Devel. Adminstrn. U.S. Dept. Commerce, Washington, 1979-80, atty. advisor Office of Chief Counsel, Econ. Devel. Adminstrn., 1980-81; campaign mgr. Rodger McDaniel for U.S. Senator, Wyo., 1981-82; asst. atty. gen. State of Wyo., Cheyenne, 1983-84, dir. Dept. Health and Social Services, 1984-86, sec. of state, 1987—. Del. Democratic Nat. Conv., San Francisco, 1984, Atlanta, 1988; del., chmn. platform com. Dem. State Conv., Douglas, Wyo., 1984. W.R. Coe fellow, 1969. Mem. D.C. Bar Assn., Wyo. Bar Assn., Nat. Assn. Secs. State, Bus. and Profl. Women, Women Execs. in State Govt., Am. Pub. Welfare Assn., Nat. Assn. Lt. Govs., Nat. Assn. Secs. of State. Roman Catholic. Lodge: Zonta. Home: 410 W 2d Ave Cheyenne WY 82001 Office: Wyo Sec of State State Capitol Cheyenne WY 82002

KARPENKO, VICTOR NICHOLAS, mechanical engineer; b. Harbin, China, Jan. 23, 1922; s. Nicholas Stephan and Sophia Andrea (Kootas) K.; came to U.S., 1941, naturalized, 1943; student San Francisco State Coll., 1941-42, Oreg. State Coll., 1943; B.S. in Mech. Engring., U. Calif., Berkeley, 1948; m. Lydia Kamotsky, June 23, 1950; children—Victor, Mark, Alexandra. Staff engr. Atomic Products Equipment div. Gen. Electric Co., San Jose, Calif., 1956-57; project engr. nuclear explosives engring. Lawrence Livermore (Calif.) Lab., 1957-65, sect. leader nuclear explosives engring., 1965-66, div. leader Nuclear Test Engring. div., 1966-76, project mgr. Mirror Fusion Test Facility, 1976-85; div. head Magnet System Superconducting Super Collider, Univ. Research Assn., Berkeley, Calif., 1986-87, cons., 1987—; mem. fusion reactor safety com. Dept. Energy; mem. Containment Evaluation Panel, ERDA; cons. undergrounding of nuclear reactors. Dist. chmn. U. Calif. Alumni Scholarship Program, 1976—; com. mem. U. Calif. Alumni Scholarship Program, 1972-76; com. mem. San Ramon High Sch. Boosters, 1969; pres. San Ramon AAU Swim Club, 1964. Served with AUS, 1943-46. Registered profl. mech. and nuclear engr., Calif. Mem. Am. Nuclear Soc., Calif. Alumni Assn. Republican. Greek Orthodox. Home: 613 Bradford Pl Danville CA 94526 Office: Univ Rsch Assn Cyclotron Rd Berkeley CA 94720

KARPILOW, CRAIG, physician; b. San Francisco, Oct. 23, 1947; s. David and Babette (David) K.; B.Sc., U. Alta. (Can.), 1967; M.A., U. So. Calif., 1970; M.D., Dalhousie U., 1974. Intern, Dalhousie U., Halifax, N.S., Can., 1974-75; resident in family practice medicine Meml. U. Nfld., St. John's, 1975-77; practice medicine specializing in family medicine and occupational medicine, 1978-81; practice occupational medicine, Snohomish, Wash., 1981-83; med. health officer Storey County, Nev., 1978-80; med. dir. Med. Center, Dayton, 1978-81; pres. Internat. Profl. Assocs. Ltd., 1979—; med. dir./clin. N.W. Occupational Health Ctrs., Seattle, 1983-84; ptnr. physician, co-dir. CHEC Med. Ctr., Seattle, 1984-85; head dept. occupational and diagnostic medicine St. Cabrini Hosp., Seattle, 1984-86; med. dir. N.W. Indsl. Services, 1985-86, Queen Anne Med. Ctr., Seattle, 1985—, Travelers Med. and Immunization Clinic of Seattle, 1986—. Diplomate Am. Bd. Family Practice; licenciate Med. Coll. Can. Fellow Am. Acad. Family Practice, Am. Coll. Occupational Medicine, Royal Soc. Tropical Medicine, Am. Coll. Occupational Medicine; mem. AMA, Am. Soc. Tropical Medicine and Hygiene, Wash. State Med. Assn. King County Med. Soc., Wash. Acad. Family Physicians (research collaborative, dir. Commn. on Research), Coll. Can. Med. Assn., Am. Occupational Med. Assn. (chmn. internat. occupational medicine sect.), N.W. Occupational Med. Assn. (bd. dirs. 1985—), Marimed Found. Pacific N.W. (adv. bd.) Seattle Swiss Soc., Finnish Soc., Corinthian Yacht Club, Mountaineers, Nature Conservancy Club, Rotary (bd. dirs., chmn. internat. rels. com., US Hepatis Project), Kappa Sigma. Office: 509 Olive Way #1201 Seattle WA 98101

KARPMAN, HAROLD LEW, cardiologist, educator, author; b. Belvedere, Calif., Aug. 23, 1927; s. Samuel and Dora (Kastleman) K.; m. Molinda Karpman. Student, UCLA, 1945-46; BA, U. Calif., Berkeley, 1950; MD, U. Calif., San Francisco, 1954. Diplomate Am. Bd. Internal Medicine. Rotating intern L.A. County Gen. Hosp., L.A., 1954-55; cardiovascular trainee Nat. Heart Inst., L.A., 1957-58; asst. resident Beth Israel Hosp., Boston, 1955-57; fellow Wyley Winsor Rsch. Found., L.A., 1958-59; pvt. practice Beverly Hills, Calif., 1958—; instr. medicine Harvard U., Boston, 1955-57; clin. instr. medicine U. So. Calif., L.A., 1958-64, asst. clin. prof., 1964-72, assoc. clin. prof., 1971-72; assoc. clin. prof. medicine UCLA Sch. Medicine, 1972—; attending physician Cedars-Sinai Med. Ctr., L.A., UCLA Med. Ctr., Westside Hosp., L.A., Brotman Med. Ctr., Culver City, Calif.; cons. in cardiology Wadsworth VA Hosp., L.A.; examiner in cardiovascular diseases Calif. Indsl. Accident Commn., Calif. Dept. Vocat. Rehab.; founder, bd. dirs., chmn. bd. Cardio-Dynamics Labs., Inc., 1969-82; gen. ptnr. Camden Med. Bldg., L.A., 1970—; bd. dirs. Mcht. Bank Calif.; dir. med. rsch. Faberge, Inc., N.Y.C., 1980-84. Contbr. numerous articles to med. jours. Fellow ACP, Am. Coll. Cardiology, Am. Coll. Chest Physicians, Internat. Cardiovascular Soc., Am. Coll. Angiology, Internat. Coll. Angiology, Am. Thermographic Soc. (charter, pres. 1971-72), Am. Acad. Thermology (exec. com. 1984--, bd. editors Thermology); mem. AMA, Calif. Med. Assn., Los Angeles Med. Assn., Am. Soc. Internal Medicine, Calif. Soc. Internal Medicine, Am. Heart Assn., Calif. Heart Assn., Los Angeles County Heart Assn. Office: 414 N Camden Dr Beverly Hills CA 90210

KARR, CHERYL LOFGREEN, producer, consultant; b. Norco, Calif., Oct. 6, 1954; d. Ted Lee and Charlotte Dorae (Mackinga) Lofgreen; m. Paul Michael James Karr, Apr. 21, 1977. AA, Brigham Young U., 1975, BA, 1978, MA, 1983. Instr. radio and TV prodn. Brigham Young U., Provo, Utah, 1976-77; writer, dir. Paul S. Karr Prodns., Phoenix, 1978-80; mng. editor Weeknight TV News Mag., Provo, 1981-82; gen. mgr. CCN Cable Network, Provo, 1982-83; news reporter The Daily Herald, Provo, 1984; v.p. prodn. Alpine Film and Video Exchange, Inc., Orem, Utah, 1984-86; producer, dir. Sta. KBYU-TV, Provo, 1984—; instr. English, Utah Valley Community Coll., Orem, 1986—; pres. SEEN-BY-SCENE PRODNS., Orem, 1987—; cons. Film Video Services, Phoenix, 1985-87, Producers Consortium, Orem, 1986—, Skaggs Retail Inst., Provo, 1987—. Writer (documentary) Escape from Ground Zero, 1983; producer, writer (documentary) Tonga: A King and Its People, 1987; writer Yue-Sai Kan, Inc. CCTV, 1986—. Recipient Prodn. Excellence award Phototec, 1978, Nat. TV award Women in Communications, 1983, Golden Microphone award Brigham Young U., 1984, Cine Golden Eagle Gold Camera award. Mem. Am. Film Inst. Republican. Mormon. Home: 1045 N 300 E Orem UT 84057 Office: Seen-By-Scene Prodns 1363 W 1600 N Orem UT 84057

KARR, DANIEL JOHN, ophthalmologist, educator; b. Albany, N.Y., Aug. 29, 1946; s. William Karashopoff and Beda Evangeline (Addy) Dick; m. Susan Jo Jett, Jan. 2, 1971; children: Emilia, Eli. BA, Fla. Presbyn. Coll. (formerly Eckerd Coll.), 1968; MD, U. Miami, 1978. Diplomate Am. Bd. Ophthalmology, Nat. Bd. Med. Examiners. Vol. Peace Corps, Nepal, 1968-70; resident in pediatrics U. Wash.-Children's Hosp. and Med. Ctr., Seattle, 1978-81, resident in ophthalmology, 1981-84, asst. prof. ophthalmology, 1986—, adj. asst. prof. pediatrics, 1986—, chief pediatric ophthalmology, 1986—. Contbr. articles to med. jours. K.T. Eye Found. grantee, 1987-88. Fellow Am. Acad. Ophthalmology; mem. Am. Assn. Pediatric Ophthalmology and Strabismus, Assn. for Rsch. in Vision and Ophthalmology, AMA, Wash. State Acad. Ophthalmology, Wash. State Soc. Pediatrics. Office: Children's Hosp & Med Ctr 4800 Sandpoint Way NE Seattle WA 98105

KARR, DAY PAYNE, lawyer; b. Feb. 15, 1909; s. Earnest Day and Jessie G. (Payne) K.; m. Susan Fitch, Feb. 2, 1933; children: Susan Karr Kuebler, Robert Payne, William Thomas, Cynthia Karr Feerick. BA, U. Wash., 1929; LLB, George Washington U., Washington, 1932. Bar: Wash. 1932, U.S. Dist. Ct. Wash. 1932, U.S. Supreme Ct. 1939. With Selective Svc. System, 1941-45, Seattle Transit System, 1943-49; pres. World Affairs Coun., 1960-62; ptnr. Karr, Tuttle, Campbell, Seattle. Mem. Am. Coll. Trial Lawyers, Wash. State Bar Assn. (past pres.), Seattle C. of C. (past. pres.). Republican. Office: Karr Tuttle Campbell 1201 3d Ave Ste 2900 Seattle WA 98101

KARRAS, DONALD GEORGE, tax administrator; b. Sioux City, Iowa, Dec. 23, 1953; s. George D. and Mary T. (Kyriakos) K.; m. Donna Lynn Ciripompa, Mar. 6, 1982; children: Dane Anthony, Dillon James. BA, Augustana Coll., 1977; MBA, U. S.D., 1980, JD, 1981. CPA, S.D. Bar: S.D. 1981. Legal intern Strange & Strange, Sioux Falls, S.D., 1980; instr. U. S.D. Sch. Bus., Vermillion, 1980-81; tax sr. acct. Deloitte Haskins & Sells, Denver, 1981-84; tax mgr. The Anschutz Corp., Denver, 1984-87; dir. taxes BP Minerals Am., Salt Lake City, 1988—. Advisor Denver Area Jr. Achievement, 1982, Salt Lake Area Jr. Achievement, 1988-89; coach YMCA Tri-Y Basketball, Denver, 1984-85; mem. Vermillion Area Jaycees, 1977. Mem. S.D. Bar Assn., ABA, Am. Hellenic Ednl. Progressive Assn., Tax Execs. Inst., Inc. (Rocky Mountain chpt.), Am. Mining Congress (tax com.). Republican. Greek Orthodox. Home: 590 W Eastborne Ct Farmington UT 84025 Office: BP Minerals Am 10 E South Temple Salt Lake City UT 84147

KARSH, PHILIP HOWARD, advertising executive; b. Salt Lake City, Sept. 19, 1935; s. Sol and Ruth (Marks) K.; m. Carol Hyman, July 3, 1962 (div. Sept. 1973); children: Michael David, Jill Ann; m. Linda Love, Sept. 7, 1984. BA, U. Colo., 1957. Account exec. Ted Levy/Richard Lane & Co., Denver, 1957-59; v.p. Jerome/Philip Advt., Denver, 1959-62, pres., 1962-65; v.p. Frye Sills Advt., Denver, 1966-77; pres. Karsh & Hagan Advt. Inc., Denver, 1977-85, co-chmn., 1985—. Trustee Nat. Jewish Ctr. Immunology and Respiratory Medicine, Denver, 1963—, Kern Research Found., Denver, 1984—, Mile High United Way, Denver, 1986—. Mem. Affiliated Advt. Agys. Internat. (internat. chmn. 1986-87), Denver Advt. Fedn. (bd. dirs. 1967-69, 87—), Rotary (pres. S.E. Denver club 1989—). Republican. Jewish. Home: 12933 E Cornell Aurora CO 80014 Office: Karsh & Hagan Advt Inc 5500 Greenwood Plaza Blvd Englewood CO 80111

KARSTEN, ERNIE, educator, consultant, poet; b. L.A., Sept. 18, 1933; s. Ernest Everett and Marie Margaret (Chovan) K. BA, U. Calif., Berkeley, 1955, MA, 1960. Gen. secondary life diploma, Calif. Instr. Contra Costa Coll., San Pablo, Calif., 1960-61; tchr. Latin and English, Castlemont High Sch., Oakland, Calif., 1961-76, Skyline High Sch., Oakland, 1976—; reader Ednl. Testing Svc., Emeryville, Calif., 1978—. Editor: The Asilomar Papers; contbr. articles and poems to various publs. With U.S. Army, 1955-57. Mem. Nat. Coun. Tchrs. English, Am. Classical League, Calif. Assn. Tchrs. English, Cen. Calif. Coun. Tchrs. English (exec. bd. 1987—, chmn. curriculum study commn. 1987—), Phi Beta Kappa. Office: Skyline High School 12250 Skyline Blvd Oakland CA 94619

KASARI, LEONARD SAMUEL, quality control professional; b. Los Angeles, Sept. 22, 1924; s. Kustaa Adolph and Impi (Sikio) K.; m. Elizabeth P. Keplinger, Aug. 25, 1956; children: Lorraine Carol, Lance Eric. Student, Compton Coll., 1942-43, UCLA, 1964-70. Registered profl. engr., Calif. Gen. construction Los Angeles, 1946-61; supr. inspection service Osborne Labs., Los Angeles, 1961-64; mgr. customer service Lightweight Processing, Los Angeles, 1965-77; dir. tech. service Crestlite Aggregates, San Clemente, Calif., 1977-78; quality control mgr. Standard Concrete, Santa Ana, Calif., 1978—. Camp dir. Torrance YMCA, High Sierras, Calif., 1969-80, mem. bd. mgrs., 1970—. Served with USN, 1943-46. Named Hon. Life Mem. Calif. PTA, 1983. Mem. Am. Concrete Inst., So. Calif. Structural Engrs. Assn. Democrat. Lutheran. Home: 2450 W 233 St Torrance CA 90501 Office: Standard Concrete Products 117 W 4th St Santa Ana CA 92701

KASARJIAN, JACK ALBERT, real estate developer; b. Boston, May 3, 1951; s. Albert Sarkis and Helen Jane (Moranian) K.; m. Beverlee Ann Cox, Nov. 27, 1977; children: Jake, Kris. BS, Union Coll., Schenectady, N.Y., 1972; MS, Boston U., 1973; PhD, MD, Harvard U., 1976; JD, Southwestern U., L.A., 1983. Research fellow Montreal (Que., Can.) Gen. Hosp., 1976-77; pres. Pan African Devel. Inc., Ottawa, Ont., Can., 1976—, EuroWest, Westlake Village, Calif., 1977—, Triple K Investments Inc., Westlake Village, 1983—, Forkay Devel. Inc., Westlake Village, 1986—. Office: Forkay Devel Inc 660 Hampshire Rd Ste 110 Westlake Village CA 91361

KASEMAN, JAMES, aircraft company official; b. Woodland, Calif., Mar. 20, 1964; s. Arthur and Margery (Oehlman) K. Student, Sacramento City Coll., 1982-84. Mechanic Timaire Aircraft Maintenance Co., Paso Robles, Calif., 1984-86; insp. Wings West-Am. Eagle, San Luis Obispo, Calif., 1986—. Office: Wings West-Am Eagle 835 Airport Dr San Luis Obispo CA 93403-8115

KASSMAN, ANDREW LANCE, orthodontist; b. N.Y.C., Nov. 14, 1950; s. David and Phyllis Ivy (Einhorn) K.; m. Terry Jean Morf, Aug. 8, 1982; children: Stacey Arielle, Alexandria Devin. BS in Engring., Tulane U., 1972; DMD, Tufts U., 1975; cert. orthodontics, Columbia U., 1978. Lab. technician Tufts Med. Ctr., Boston, 1973-75; resident VA Hosp., Northport, N.Y., 1975-76; pvt. practice Astoria, N.Y., 1976-78, Phila., 1978-79, East Pathogue, N.Y., 1979-80; pvt. practice dentistry specializing in orthodontics Tucson, 1980—; chief orthodontist Crippled Children's Ctr., Tucson, 1980—; assoc. staff Tucson Med. Ctr., 1980—. Bd. dirs. Comstock Found., Tucson, 1980--; active Temple Emanu-El, Tucson, 1988, Shadow Hill Assn., Tucson, 1988, Tucson Boys Club, 1988, Jewish Community Ctr., Tucson, 1988. Mem. ADA, Am. Assn. Orthodontists, Pacific Coast Soc. Orthodontists, Tucson Orthodontist Soc., Tucson C. of C. Democrat. Home: 7601 N Calle Sin Envidia #8 Tucson AZ 85718 Office: 6700 N Oracle Rd Ste 327 Tucson AZ 85704

KASSNER, MICHAEL ERNEST, materials science researcher, educator; b. Osaka, Japan, Nov. 22, 1950; (parents Am. citizens); s. Ernest and Clara (Christa) K.; m. Marcia J. Wright, Aug. 19, 1972 (div. Dec. 1976). BS, Northwestern U., 1972; MS, Stanford U., 1979, PhD, 1981. Metallurgist Lawrence Livermore (Calif.) Nat. Lab., 1981—, head phys. metallurgy and joining sect., 1988—; prof. Naval Postgrad. Sch., Monterey, Calif., 1984-86. Editor various scientific jours. Served to lt. USN, 1972-76. Fulbright scholar Council for Internat. Exchange of scholars, Netherlands, 1983-84. Mem. Am. Soc. Metals, Materials Research Soc., Sigma Xi. Roman Catholic. Home: 311 Cedar Pacific Grove CA 93950

KASTENS, SAMUEL RAHE, medical technologist; b. Kiowa, Kans., June 22, 1943; s. Elmer and Pauline (Crum) K.; m. Janice Marie Miller, Nov. 30, 1968; children: Stephen Rahe, Sherri Lynn. Student, Kans. State U., 1961-63; BS, Northwestern Okla. State U., 1967. Cert. med. technologist. Med. technologist St. John's Hosp., Salina, Kans., 1967-70; chief med. technologist, lab. supr. St. Catherine Hosp., Garden City, Kans., 1970-77; gen. supr. chem. lab. Nat. Health Labs., Englewood, Colo., 1977-78; lab. supr. DTC Med. Ctr. Lab. Swedish Med. Ctr., Englewood, 1980-86, Arvada (Colo.) Med. Clinic, 1986-89, Western Arthritis Clinic, Wheatridge, Colo., 1989—. Inventor anaerobic role tube innoculator. Mem. Kanorado Touring Club (pres. 1985-88), Rocky Mountain Venture Touring Club, Phi Kappa Theta. Roman Catholic.

KASZNIAK, ALFRED WAYNE, neuropsychologist; b. Chgo., June 2, 1949; s. Alfred H. and Ann Virginia (Simonsen) K.; B.S. with honors, U. Ill., 1970, M.A., 1973, Ph.D., 1976; m. Mary Ellen Beaurain, Aug. 26, 1973; children—Jesse, Elizabeth. Instr. dept. psychology Rush Med. Coll., Chgo., 1974-76, asst. prof. dept. psychology, 1976-79; from asst. prof. to assoc. prof. dept. psychiatry U. Ariz. Coll. Medicine, Tucson, 1979-82, assoc. prof. dept. psychology and psychiatry, 1982-87; prof. depts. psychology and psychiatry, 1987—; staff psychologist Presbyn.-St. Luke's Hosp., Chgo., 1976-79; mem. human devel. and aging study sect. div. research grants NIH, 1981-86. Trustee So. Ariz. chpt. Nat. Multiple Sclerosis Soc., 1980-82; mem. med. and sci. adv. bd. Nat. Alzheimer's Disease and Related Disorders Assn., 1981-84; mem. med. adv. bd. Fan Kane Fund for Brain-Injured Children, Tucson, 1980—. Grantee Nat. Inst. Aging, 1978-83, NIMH, 1984—, Robert Wood Johnson Found., 1986—. Mem. Am. Psychol. Assn. (Disting. Contbr. award div. 20 1978), Internat. Neuropsychol. Soc., Soc. for Neurosci., Gerontol. Soc. (research fellow 1980), AAAS, Editorial cons. Jour. Gerontology,

1979—; mem. editorial bd. Psychology and Aging, 1984-87; The Clin. Neuropsychologist, 1986—, Jour. Clin. and Exp. Neuropsychol., 1987—, Jour Gerontology, 1988—; contbr. articles to profl. jours. Home: 2327 E Hawthorne St Tucson AZ 85719 Office: U Ariz Dept Psychology Tucson AZ 85721

KATAGUE, DAVID BALLEZA, analytical chemist, consultant; b. Iloilo City, Philippines, Dec. 20, 1934; came to U.S., 1959, naturalized, 1971; s. David J. Katague Sr. and Paz (Barrido) Balleza; m. Macrine Nieva Jambalos, May 8, 1957; children: Diosdado Dodie, Dinah E., David E., Ditas M. BS in Chemistry, U. Philippines, 1955; MS in Chemistry, U. Ill., Chgo., 1962, PhD in Chemistry, 1964. Instr. chemistry U. Philippines, 1955-59; instr. chemistry U. Ill., Chgo., 1962-64, teaching asst., 1959-62; chemist Mobay Chems., Kansas City, Mo., 1964-69; prin. research chemist Stauffer Chem. Co., Richmond, Calif., 1974-85; research chemist Shell Devel. Co., Modesto, Calif., 1969-74, Chevron Chem. Co., Richmond, 1986—; cons. United Nations Tokten Project, Diliman, U.P., Philippines, 1985—. Fellow Am. Inst. Chemists; mem. Am. Chem. Soc., Philippine Am. Acad. Sci. and Engring. (founding mem.), U. Philippines Alumni Assn. (pres. Berkeley chpt. 1989). Home: 2638 Silvercrest St Pinole CA 94564 Office: Chevron Chem Co 15049 San Pablo Ave Richmond CA 94804

KATAKKAR, SURESH B., hematologist, oncologist; b. Poona, India, Feb. 9, 1944; s. Balaji Vasudeo Katakkar and Padmauate (Gangadhar) Varavadakar; m. Sunila Mohehe; children: Smita, Sucheta, Swati. MB, BS, Poona U., India, 1969. Diplomate Am. Bd. Internal Medicine, Am. Bd. Oncology. Intern the resident St. Paul's Hosp., Saskatoon, 1969-71; resident U. Hosp., Saskatoon, 1971-72; resident clin. hematology Gen. Hosp., Ottawa, 1973-74; sr. cancer clin. assoc. Sasketchewan Cancer Commn., 1975-78; clin. investigator NCI, USA, 1975—; med. oncologist Madigan Army Med. Ctr., 1978-80; pvt. practice Tucson, Ariz., 1980—; chmn. tumor bd. St. Mary's Hosp., Tucson, 1981-83, chmn. transfusion com., 1982—; chmn. dept. med. Northwest Hosp., 1983-84, chief of staff, 1984-86, bd. trustees, 1984—. Contbr. articles to profl. jours. W.W. Cross Cancer Inst. fellow, 1974-75. Fellow Royal Coll. Physicians, Am. Coll. Physicians; mem. Am. Soc. Clin. Oncology, AMA, Internat. Soc. Preventative Oncology, Am. Geriatrics Soc., N.Y. Acad. Scis., Am. Hosp. Assn., Am. Assn. Blood Banks, Am. Bd. Med. Dirs. Home: 1391 E Placita Mapache Tucson AZ 85718 Office: NW Hosp Med Pla 1980 W Hospital Dr Ste 301 Tucson AZ 85705

KATAYAMA, TAMIO, travel company executive, management consultant; b. Fujisawa, Japan, July 8, 1928; came to U.S., 1963; s. Tetsu and Kikue (Shimizu) K.; m. Miyoko Shimura, Sept. 30, 1961. BA, Nihon U., Tokyo, 1950, Calif. State U., San Francisco, 1951; postgrad., U. Calif., Berkeley, 1952. Mem. staff Japan Airlines, Tokyo, 1952-62; pres. Orient Pacific, Inc., L.A., 1963—, I.K., Inc., L.A., 1978—. Contbr. essays to econs. publs. Mem. L.A. Jaycees. Home: 12004 Kling St North Hollywood CA 91607 Office: IK Inc 6350 Laurel Canyon Blvd Ste 370 North Hollywood CA 91606

KATERSKY, HAROLD ALAN, shopping center executive; b. Fall River, Mass., Oct. 24, 1942; s. Morton and Evelyn (Mines) K.; m. Ileen Miller, June 10, 1966 (div. 1980); m. Klara Sendowski, Sept. 3, 1981 (div. 1989); children: Andrew, Robin, Jeffrey. BS, U. R.I., 1964; MBA with honors, Boston U., 1966. Ptnr. Touche Ross & Co., Detroit, 1968-78; sr. v.p., chief exec. officer Taubman Co., Bloomfield Hills, Mich., 1978-81, R&B Enterprises, L.A., 1981-82; pres., chief exec. officer Katersky Fin., Woodland Hills, Calif., 1982--. Author: There's No Free Lunch, 1986, Real Estate Limited Partnerships, 1988. Vice chmn. Los Angeles County Republican. Fin. Com., 1987. 1st lt. U.S. Army, 1966-68. Jewish. Home: 555 S Barrington Ave Los Angeles CA 90049 Office: 21800 Oxnard St Ste 480 Woodland Hills CA 91367

KATHER, GERHARD, air force base administrator; b. Allenstein, Germany, Jan. 30, 1939; came to U.S., 1952, naturalized, 1959; s. Ernst and Maria (Kempa) K.; m. Carol Anne Knutsen, Aug. 18, 1962; children—Scott T., Cynthia M., Tracey S., Chris A.; m. Mary Elsie Frank, Oct. 25, 1980. B.A. in Govt., U. Ariz., 1964; M.P.A., U. So. Calif., 1971; cert. in personnel adminstrn., U. N.Mex., 1987. Tchr. social studies, Covina, Calif., 1965-67; tng. officer Civil Personnel, Ft. MacArthur, Calif., 1967-70; chief employee tng. and devel. Corps Engrs., Los Angeles, 1970-72; chief employee tng. and devel. Frankfurt Area Army Personnel Office, 1972-73; chief employee relations and tng. brs. Corps Engrs., Los Angeles, 1973-74; chief employee devel. and tng. Kirtland AFB, N.Mex., 1974-87; labor relations officer, Kirtland AFB and detachments in 13 U.S. cities, 1987—. Mem. adv. com. Albuquerque Tech.-Vocat. Inst., 1982—, U. N.Mex. Valencia Campus, 1985—. Served with USAF, 1958-64. Named Prominent Tng. and Devel. Profl., H. Whitney McMillan Co., 1984; Outstanding Handicapped Fed. Employee of Yr., all fed. agys., 1984; recipient Govt. Employees Ins. Co. GEICO Pub. Svc. award for work in phys. rehab., 1988. Mem. Am. Soc. Tng. and Devel. (treas. chpt. 1984-85), Paralyzed Vets. Am. (bd. dirs. 1986-87, pres. local chpt. 1986-87), Toastmasters Internat. (chpt. treas., v.p., pres. 1967-70), Phi Delta Kappa. Democrat. Roman Catholic. Office: 1606 MSSQ/MSCEL Kirtland AFB NM 87117

KATHKA, DAVID ARLIN, state archives and historical administrator; b. Columbus, Nebr.; s. Arlin Arthur and Edith Ferne (Wilcox) K.; m. Anne Condon Butler, Aug. 15, 1965. BA, Wayne (Nebr.) State Coll., 1964, MA, 1966; PhD in History, U. Mo., 1976. Tchr. Ravenna (Nebr.) Pub. Schs., 1964-65; instr. Midwestern Coll., Denison, Iowa, 1966-68; prof. history Western Wyo. Coll., Rock Springs, 1972-87, dean acad. affairs, 1980-84, interim pres., 1984-85, v.p. acad. affairs, 1985-87; dir. State Hist. Preservation Office Wyo. State Archives, Mus. and Hist. Dept., Cheyenne, 1987—; adj. prof. U. Wyo., Laramie, 1976-88; vis. instr. U. Mo., St. Louis, 1971-72; cons. various Wyo. govt. agys. Author hist. papers; contbr. hist. articles to mags. Mem. Wyo. Centennial Commn., 1986-87, Rock Springs Library Bd., 1984-87, Gov.'s Com. on Hist. Preservation, 1982; v.p. Rocky Mountain Region Kidney Found., Denver, 1976-77. Mem. Orgn. Am. Historians, Am. Assn. State and Local History (Commendation 1982), Western History Assn., Wyo. State Hist. Soc. (pres. 1984-85), Kiwanis. Democrat. Office: Wyo State Mus/AMH Dept Barrett Bldg 2301 Central Ave Cheyenne WY 82002

KATHOL, ANTHONY LOUIS, railway official; b. San Diego, June 12, 1964; s. Cletus Louis and Regina Antoinette (Ellrott) K.; m. Kathleen Marie Moore, Jan. 23, 1988. BS, U. So. Calif., 1986; MBA, U. San Diego, 1988. Fin. aid analyst U. San Diego, 1986-87; bookkeeper Golden Lion Tavern, San Diego, 1987-88; fin. and budget coord. Santa Fe Pacific Realty Corp., Brea, Calif., 1988—. Calif. Bldg. Industry Assn. fellow, 1986, U. San Diego fellow, 1987. Mem. U. San Diego Grad. Bus. Students Assn., KC, Tau Kappa Epsilon. Republican. Roman Catholic. Home: 11370 Millstone Ln Pomona CA 91766 Office: Santa Fe Pacific Realty Corp 3230 E Imperial Hwy Ste 100 Brea CA 92621

KATONA, CYNTHIA LEE, journalism and desktop publishing educator; b. Stockton, Calif., June 4, 1947; d. Richard Lee and Catherine Louise (Doll) Davies; m. Dennis Charles Katona, July 22, 1967 (div. 1985). BA in English, Calif. State U., Hayward, 1969; MA in English, Calif. State U., 1972. Asst. librarian Alameda County Library, Hayward, 1969-71; lectr., instr., asst. prof., assoc. prof. English Calif. State U., Hayward, 1971-83; from instr. to prof. English, journalism, photography Ohlone Coll., Fremont, Calif., 1975—; mem., faculty senate Ohlone Coll., Fremont, 1980—, pres., senate, 1982-83, 86-87; owner, cons. Word Mcht., Fremont, 1984—. Contbr. articles, revs. and essays to various publs. Recipient award Columbia Scholastic Press Assn., 1976—; 1st place gen. excellence award Journalism Assn. Community Colls., 1978; State of Calif. desktop pub. grantee, 1988. Mem. Nat. Coun. Tchrs. English, Calif. Community Coll. Tchrs. English, Nat. Women's Studies Assn., Calif. Assn. Tchrs. English. Republican. Roman Catholic. Office: Ohlone College 43600 Mission Blvd Fremont CA 94539

KATSARIS, ROBERT JACK, real estate developer; b. Canton, Ohio, Dec. 7, 1943; s. Nick Anthony and Ruth E. (Pitts) K.; m. Lynn Parker, Sept. 2, 1960; children: Judith, Robert, Steven. Restaurateur Orange County, Calif., 1960-76; constrn. co. Palm Springs, Calif., 1960-81; real estate broker Lake Havasu City, Ariz., 1981—; gen. contractor, developer Lake Havasu City, 1981—.

KATSAROS, KRISTINA BARBRO, atmospheric sciences educator; b. Goteborg, Sweden, July 24, 1938; came to U.S., 1957; d. Gustav Adolf Olof and Ester Aurora (Sundstrom) Sander; m. Michael Anthony Katsaros, June 20, 1959; children—Anthony Olof, Ester Sofia. BSc in Atmospheric Scis., U. Wash., 1960, PhD, 1969; postgrad. in astronomy U. Goteborg, 1961. Rsch. asst., dept. atmospheric scis. U. Wash., Seattle, 1962-69, nat. def. edn. act title IV fellow, 1963-65, rsch. assoc., 1969-74, rsch. asst. prof., 1974-77, rsch. assoc. prof., 1977-83, assoc. prof., 1983—; mem. NASA Com. on Satellite Surface Stress, 1981-84, NASA Sci. Working Group on Ocean Energetics, 1984—; vis. scientist Riso Nat. Lab., Denmark, 1980; NSF vis. prof. for women Naval Postgrad. Sch., Monterey, Calif., 1983-85; vis. scientist Royal Dutch Met. Inst., 1984; vis. scientist U. Paris, 1987; participant numerous workshops, colloquia and confs. Assoc. editor Weatherwise, 1980—, Jour. Geophys. Rsch.-Oceans, 1983—; reviewer and contbr. articles to tech. jours. Fellow Am. Meteorol. Soc. (chpt. sec. 1974-75, mem. nat. com. on interactions sea and air 1974-80, 84-86, chmn. 1978-80, mem. nominating com. 1981-84, nominating com. for fellows, 1987, chair 1989, councilor 1990—); mem. Am. Geophys. Union (pres. coun. Pacific NW region 1972-73, mem. nat. com. on constn. and by-laws 1974-78), AAAS (mem. nominating com. 1979-82), AAUP, Swedish Geophys. Soc., European Geophys. Soc., Sigma Xi, Zeta Mu Tau. Home: 3151 E Laurelhurst Dr NE Seattle WA 98105 Office: U Wash Dept Atmospheric Scis AK-40 Seattle WA 98195

KATSURA, KOTARO, dentist; b. Paia, Hawaii, Nov. 11, 1912; s. Kumanoshin and Samu K.; m. Kyoko Someya, Oct. 26, 1973. DDS, U. Mo., Kansas City, 1947. Dental officer City of Honolulu, 1947-50; pvt. practice gen. dentistry Kailua, Hawaii, 1953—. Capt. U.S. Army, 1951-53. Fellow Honolulu County Dental Soc.; mem. ADA, Hawaii Dental Soc., Kiwanis, Omicron Kappa Upsilon. Home: 458 Ka-Awakea Rd Kailua HI 96734 Office: PO Box 794 Kaneohe HI 96744

KATTELMANN, HARRY RICHARD, mechanical engineering consultant; b. San Francisco, Nov. 23, 1920; s. Harry Henry and Mildred Elizabeth Doepfner K.; m. Jeanette M. Landgren, Aug. 24, 1943 (div. 1982); 1 child, Richard; m. Doris Maud Griffin, May 5, 1984; children: Gregory, Patricia. BME, Poly. Coll. Engring., 1942; Cert. in Bus. and Mgmt., U. Calif. Berkeley, 1971. Reg. profl. engr., Calif., N.J. Design engr. Marchant Calculating Machine Co., Oakland, Calif., 1944-48; div. mgr. Container Labs, Inc., San Francisco, 1948-57; mgr. product engring. and engring. adminstrn. SCM Corp., Oakland, Calif., 1957-67; tech. dir. Fabricated Metals, Inc., San Leandro, Calif., 1967-87; cons. engr. Alameda, Calif., 1987--. Patentee tape reader, volumetric feeder, other devices; contbr. articles to tech. publs. Dist. commr. Oakland area Boy Scouts Am., 1944-46; dist. chmn. Oakland Master P lan Com., 1960; v.p. Woodgate Homeowners Assn., San Leandro, 1985-86; instr., counselor tax aid program Am. Assn. Retired Persons, San Leandro, 1987-88. Served to 2nd lt. CE, U.S. Army, 1943-44. Recipient Archimedes Engring. Achievement award, Calif. Soc. Profl. Engrs., 1979. Mem. Am. Soc. Mech. Engrs. (chmn. San Francisco sect. 1967), Bay Area Engring. Council (chmn. career guidance com. 1977-79, engrs. week com. 1979). Republican. Home and office: 139 Justin Circle Alameda CA 94501

KATTLOVE, ROSE WEINER, information management company executive; b. Chgo., Nov. 30, 1938; d. Nathan and Bessie (Ostrofsky) Weiner; m. Herman E. Kattlove, July 3, 1960; children: Susan, Rachel, Jennifer. AB, U. Chgo., 1960; MLS, U. So. Calif., 1973. Libr. Info. Scis. Inst., Marina Del Rey, Calif., 1972-77, Ernst & Whinney, Los Angeles, 1977-79; info. mgr. Xerox Corp., El Segundo, Calif., 1979-82; dir. Savage Info. Svcs., Rancho Palos Verdes, Calif., 1982-83; pres., owner Kattlove & Assocs., Inc., Rancho Palos Verdes, Calif., 1984—. Mem. Am. Soc. for Info. Sci., Spl. Librs. Assn., Assn. Records Mgrs. and Adminstrs. Office: 30405 Via Victoria Rancho Palos Verdes CA 90274

KATZ, JOHN W., lawyer, state official; b. Balt., June 3, 1943; s. Leonard Wallach and Jean W. (Kane) K.; m. Joan Katz, June 11, 1969 (div. 1982); 1 child, Kimberly Erin. BA, Johns Hopkins U., 1965; JD, U. Calif., Berkeley, 1969. Bar: Alaska, Pa., U.S. Dist. Ct. D.C. 1971, U.S. Ct. Appeals (D.C. cir.), U.S. Tax Ct., U.S. Ct. Claims, U.S. Ct. Mil. Justice, U.S. Supreme Ct. Legis. and adminstrv. asst. to Congressman Howard W. Pollock of Alaska, Washington, 1969-70; legis. asst. to U.S. Senator Ted Stevens of Alaska, Washington, 1971; assoc. McGrath and Flint, Anchorage, 1972; gen. counsel Joint Fed. State Land Use Planning Commn. for Alaska, Anchorage, 1972-79; spl. counsel to Gov. Jay S. Hammond of Alaska, Anchorage and Washington, 1979-81; commr. Alaska Dept. Natural Resources, Juneau, 1981-83; dir. state fed. relations and spl. counsel to Gov. Bill Sheffield of Alaska, Washington and Juneau, 1983-86; dir. state-fed. relations, spl. counsel to Gov. Steve Cowper of Alaska, Washington, 1986—; mem. Alaska Power Survey Exec. Adv. Com. of FPC, Anchorage, 1972-74; mem. spl. com. hard rock minerals Govs. Council of Sci. and Tech., Anchorage, 1979-80; guest lectr. on natural resources U. Alaska, U. Denver. Contbr. articles to profl. jours.; columnist Anchorage Times. Acad. supr. Alaska Externship Program, U. Denver Coll. Law, 1976-79; mem. Reagan-Bush transition team for U.S. Dept. Justice, 1980. Recipient Superior Sustained Performance award Joint Fed. State Land Use Planning Commn. for Alaska, 1978. Republican. Office: State of Alaska Office of Gov 444 N Capitol St NW #518 Washington DC 20001

KATZ, PERRY MARC, motion picture company executive; b. N.Y.C., Aug. 31, 1951; s. Arthur E. and Shirley (Cohen) K. BA in Psychology with honors, CUNY, 1974; MBA, NYU, 1976. Project mgr. Eric Marder and Assocs., N.Y.C., 1975-78; sr. rsch. exec. Grey Advt., N.Y.C., 1978-80; dir. rsch. Columbia Pictures Industries, L.A., 1980-82; pres. Creative Mktg. Assocs., L.A., 1982-83; v.p. rsch. Metro-Goldwyn-Mayer/United Artists, L.A., 1983-87; sr. v.p. mktg. MCA/Universal Pictures, L.A., 1987—. Mem. Acad. Motion Picture Arts and Scis., Motion Picture Assn. Am. (rsch. com.), Am. Film Inst., So. Calif. Rsch. Soc., Film Info. Council. Office: MCA/Universal Pictures 100 Universal City Pla University City CA 91608

KATZ, SOLOMON STUART, geologist; b. Uppsala, Sweden, Aug. 3, 1947; s. Moses David and Rachel (Szykman) K.; m. Hedy Dale Prusin, Oct. 11, 1969; 1 child, Shanna Raquel. BS in Geology, Bklyn. Coll., 1971, MA in Geology, 1975; postgrad., U. Denver, 1989. Cert. sci. tchr., N.Y. Tchr. N.Y.C. Bd. Edn., 1973-75; geologist Bur. Land Mgmt., Socorro, N.Mex., 1976-77, environ. specialist, 1977-79; geologist Bur. Land Mgmt., Phoenix, 1979-80, land use planner, 1980-82; geologist Bur. Land Mgmt., Washington, 1982-85; geographic info. system specialist Bur. Land Mgmt., Denver, 1985-88, quality assurance mgr., 1988—. Contbr. articles to profl. publs. Sgt. USAF, 1965-69. Mem. Computer Oriented Geol. Soc., Geotech (chmn. 1988—), Colo. Commodore Computer Club. Jewish. Office: Bur Land Mgmt SC344 Denver Fed Ctr Denver CO 80225-0047

KATZMANN, BARRY A., writer; b. Mpls., May 18, 1951; s. Frank Alfred and Geraldine (Lipstein) K.; m. Pat Kovachevich, Oct. 21, 1985. BA in Journalism, U. Wis., 1973. Writer Harcourt Brace and Jovanivich, Chgo., 1974-75, Griswold-Eshleman/Chgo., 1976-79, Wilk & Brichta Advt., Chgo., 1979-81, Campbell-Mithun/Chgo., 1981-83; assoc. creative dir. Chase/Ehrenberg and Rosene, Chgo., 1983-84; sr. writer San Francisco Newspaper Agy., 1985—; free-lance writer, 1984—. Writer/producer radio comml. 1984-88 (Addy award 1988). Mem. Comedy/Humor Writers Assn. Office: San Francisco Newspaper Agy 925 Mission St San Francisco CA 94103

KATZOWICZ, HILLEL, data processing executive; b. Kfar-Saba, Israel, Jan. 20, 1959; came to U.S., 1962; s. Max and Lisa (Sajevich) K.; m. Jeanne L. Pratuch, May 17, 1980; children: Hilary J., James H. Student, Rochester Inst. Tech., 1976-80. Systems mgr. Western N.Y. Computing, Penfield, 1974-79; tech. rep. Info. Assocs., Rochester, N.Y., 1979-80; dir. Mitchellmatix, Inc., San Diego, 1981—. Patentee in field. Mem. Assn. for Computing Machinery. Office: Mitchellmatix Inc 9889 Willow Creek Rd San Diego CA 92126

KAUAHIKAUA, JAMES PUUPAI, geophysicist; b. Honolulu, Aug. 1, 1951; s. Ben and Aileen (Spillner) K.; 1 child, Lilinoe Yael Beatrice. BA, Pomona Coll., 1973; MS, U. Hawaii, 1976, PhD, 1982. Geophysicist U.S. Geol. Survey, Hawaii, 1978—. Mem. Soc. Exploration Geophysicists, Am. Geophys. Union. Home: 1706 Wailuku Dr Hilo HI 96720 Office: US Geol Survey Hawaii Volcano Obs Hawaii National Park HI 96718

KAUB, GEORGE HUBERT, manufacturer's representative; b. Boulder, Colo., Mar. 31, 1924; s. Hubert and Ruth Bixby (Warren) K.; m. Roberta Helen Lehman, June 14, 1947; children: George Kristopher, Germaine, Lisa. BA, U. Colo., 1947. Lic. geologist, Colo. Geologist Anglo Saxon Mine, Georgetown, Colo., 1947; ptnr. Hubert Kaub & Co., Englewood, Colo., 1948--. Pres., chmn. bd. dirs. Pride Programs, Inc., Denver, 1986. Sgt. USAF, 1942-45, ETO. Mem. Rocky Mountain Electronics Mfr. Rep. Club (pres. Denver chpt. 1960), Cherry Creek Optimist Club, Cherry Creek Civ. Club, Denver Athletic Club, Phi Delta Theta. Republican. Home: 900 S Elizabeth St Denver CO 80209 Office: Hubert Kaub & Co 2721 W Oxford Ave Englewood CO 80110

KAUFER, SCOTT AUSTIN, television executive; b. L.A., Mar. 15, 1953; s. Maxwell and Jeanne Carol (Austin) K. BA, Harvard U., 1976. Editorial positions with various mags., 1976-81; sr. editor Calif. mag., L.A., 1981, exec. editor, 1982, editor, 1982-84; v.p. comedy devel. Warner Bros. TV, L.A., 1985—. Contbr. articles to numerous mags. Mem. Claw League (life commr. L.A. chpt. 1984—). Office: Warner Bros 4000 Warner Blvd Burbank CA 91522

KAUFFMAN, DONALD GOODWIN, food products company executive; b. Hillsboro, Wis., Jan. 13, 1918; s. Jesse and Grace (Goodwin) K.; m. Ethelynn Helen Bays, Feb. 22, 1942; children—Camille Taylor, Donald G., Patrick Taylor, Thomas W.; m. 2d, Marilyn Jean Miller Taylor, Dec. 2, 1960; Ph.B., U. Wis., 1940. Salesman, food brokerage co., Portland, Oreg., 1946-47; owner D.G. Kauffman Co., 1947-48; pres., gen. mgr. Stater-Kauffman Co., Portland, Oreg., 1948-61, Edwards/Kauffman Co., Portland, 1961-79; pres. Erlandson-Kauffman, Seattle, 1965-80; sr. v.p. charge corp. devel. Bromar, Inc., Newport Beach, Calif., 1979—, dir., 1980—. Dir. ops. and tng. Oreg. Air N.G., 1946-50; past chmn. food div. Multonomah County ARC, United Fund Drive; bd. deacons St. Andrews United Presbyn. Ch., 1959-62; v.p. USO for Oreg., 1977-80, bd. dirs., 1978-80. Served to maj. USAAF, 1941-45. Mem. Portland Food Brokers Assn. (past pres.), Nat. Food Brokers Assn. (regional dir. 1965-66), Republican. Presbyterian. Clubs: Multnomah Athletic, Waverley Country, Eldorado Country, Arlington (Portland), Rotary (pres. 1975-76). Home: 4014 SW 36th Pl Portland OR 97221 Office: 1900 SE Milport Rd Portland OR 97222

KAUFFMAN, ERLE GALEN, geologist, educator; b. Washington, Feb. 9, 1933; s. Erle Benton and Paula Virginia (Graff) K.; children: Donald Erle, Robin Lyn, Erica Jean. BS, U. Mich., 1955, MS, 1956, PhD, 1961; MSc (hon.), Oxford (Eng.) U., 1970; DSc (hon.), U. Göttingen, Fed. Republic of Germany, 1987. Teaching fellow, instr. U. Mich., Ann Arbor, 1956-60; from asst. to full curator paleobiology Mus. Natural History Smithsonian Inst., Washington, 1960-80; prof. geology, chmn. U. Colo., Boulder, 1980—; adj. prof. geology George Washington U., Washington, 1962-80; cons. geologist, Boulder, 1980—. Author/editor: Cretaceous Facies, Faunas and Paleoenvironments Across the Cretaceous Western Interior Basin, 1977; contbg. editor: Concepts and Methods of Biostratigraphy, 1977, Fine-grained Deposits and Biofacies of the Cretaceous Western Seaway, 1985, High-Resolution Event Stratigraphy, 1988; contbr. articles to profl. jours. Recipient U.S. Govt. Spl. Service award, 1969, NSF Best Tchr. award, U. Colo., 1985; named Disting. Lectr. Am. Geol. Inst., 1963-64, Am. Assn. Petroleum Geologist, 1984, 85; Fullbright fellow, Australia, 1986. Fellow Geol. Soc. Am., AAAS; mem. Paleontol. Soc. (councilor under 40, pres. elect 1981, pres. 1982, 83, chmn. 5 coms., rep. and mem. NRC, Palaeontol. Assn., Internat. Paleontol. Assn. (v.p. 1982—), Paleontol. Research Instn., Internat. Malacological Union, Malacological Soc. London, Soc. Econ. Paleontologists and Mineralogists (com. mem.) (Spl. Service award 1985, Best Paper award 1985), Rocky Mountain Assn. Geologists (project chief) (Scientist of Yr. 1977), Paleontol. Soc. Wash. (pres., sec., treas.), Geol. Soc. Wash. (councilor), Colo.-Wyo. Paleontol. Soc., Four Corners Geol. Soc., Saskatchewan Geol. Soc., Md. Acad. Scis. (hon. Paleontology sect.), Sigma Xi, Phi Kappa Phi, Sigma Gamma Epsilon. Democrat. Home: 3555 Bison Dr Boulder CO 80302 Office: U Colo Dept Geol Scis Campus Box 250 Boulder CO 80309

KAUFMAN, HAROLD RICHARD, mechanical engineer and physics educator; b. Audubon, Iowa, Nov. 24, 1926; s. Walter Richard and Hazel (Steere) K.; m. Elinor Mae Wheat, June 25, 1948; children: Brian, Karin, Bruce, Cynthia. Student, Evanston Community Coll., 1947-49; B.S.M.E., Northwestern U., 1951; Ph.D., Colo. State U., 1971. Researcher in aerospace propulsion NACA, Cleve., 1951-58; mgr. space propulsion research NASA, Cleve., 1958-74; prof. physics and mech. engring. Colo. State U., Ft. Collins, 1974-84; prof. emeritus Colo. State U., 1984—, chmn. dept. physics, 1979-84; pres. Front Range Research, Ft. Collins, 1984—; v.p. R&D Commonwealth Sci. Corp., Alexandria, Va., 1984—; pioneer in field of electron bombardment ion thruster, 1960; cons. ion source design and applications. Served with USNR, 1944-46. Recipient James H. Wyld Propulsion award AIAA, 1969; NASA medal for exceptional sci. achievement, 1971. Asso. fellow AIAA; mem. Tau Beta Pi, Pi Tau Sigma. Office: Front Range Rsch 1306 Blue Spruce Ste A-2 Fort Collins CO 80524

KAUFMAN, HERBERT MARK, educator; b. Bronx, N.Y., Jan. 1, 1946; s. Henry and Betty (Fried) K.; m. Helen Laurie Fox, July 23, 1967; 1 child, Jonathan Hart. BA, SUNY, Binghamton, 1967; PhD, Pa. State U., 1972. Economist Fed. Nat. Mortgage Assn., Washington, 1972-73; asst. prof. Ariz. State U., Tempe, 1973-76; econs. prof. Ariz. State U., 1980-88, fin. prof., 1988—, dir. Ctr. for Fin. System Research, 1988—; cons. World Bank, Washington, 1985-86, Gen. Acctg. Office, Washington, 1985, Congl. Budget Office, Washington, 1980, MERABANK, Pheonix, 1981—. Author: Financial Markets, Financial Institutions and Money, 1983; (withothers) The Political Economy of Policy Making, 1979; contbr. articles to profl. jours. Mem. Am. Econ. Assn., Am. Fin. Assn., Nat. Assn. of Bus. Economists. Home: 1847 E Calle De Caballos Tempe AZ 85284 Office: Ariz State U Ctr for Fin System Rsch Tempe AZ 85287

KAUFMAN, IRWIN, civil engineer; b. N.Y.C., June 14, 1936; s. Morris and Rose (Gold) K.; m. Barbara Jane Beneckc, Nov. 25, 1972 (div. 1982); m. Rhonda Grace Raymond, Sept. 24, 1983; 1 child, Rebecca Rose. BCE, CUNY, 1958, MCE, 1962. Lic. profl. engr., Nev., N.Y. Chief plan examiner City of N.Y., 1958-67; resident engr. A.S. Malkiel, Inc., N.Y.C., 1967-70, Secyle, Stevenson, Valve & Knecht, N.Y.C., 1970-73; project engr. Ray Tech. Inc., N.Y.C., 1973-76, Holmes & Narver, Inc., Las Vegas, Nev., 1976-80; project mgr. Nev. Power Co., Las Vegas, 1980—. Mem. Rep. Cen. Com., Las Vegas, 1980-82. Mem. NSPE (pres. Nev. br. 1988—), ASCE, Profl. Engrs. in Constrn. (pres. Nev. div. 1985—), Am. Constrn. Inst., Am. Arbitration Assn. (panel mem.), Clark County C. of C. (adv. com.), B'nai Brith (v.p. local chpt. 1978-80). Jewish. Home: 5576 W Rochelle Ave 33B Las Vegas NV 89103 Office: Nev Power Co 6226 W Sahara Ave Las Vegas NV 85102

KAUFMAN, LEONARD LEE, lawyer; b. Butte, Mont., May 8, 1939; s. Leonard Carl and Medeline (Marx) K.; m. Mary F. Culleton; children: Jennifer Lee, Julie Lee, Jody Lee. BA, Middlebury Coll., 1961; JD, U. Mont., 1964; LLM in Taxation, Denver U., 1976. Bar: Mont. Trial atty. Mont. Dept. Hwys., Helena, 1967-69; asst. county atty. County of Lincoln, Mont., 1969-72; ptnr. Murray, Kaufman, Vidal, Gordon & Ogle, Kalispell, Mont., 1972—. Contbr. articles to agrl. publs. Pres., bd. dirs. Flathead Valley Ski Found., Kalispell, 1978—. Capt. U.S. Army, 1964-66. Mem. Northwest Mont. Bar Assn. (pres. 1978), U.S. Ski Assn. (cert. ofcl.), No. Div. Ski Assn. (v.p. 1988-89). Republican. Office: Murray Kaufman Vidal et al 222d Ave W kalispell MT 59903

KAUFMAN, MICHAEL DAVID, management executive; b. Bklyn., Apr. 7, 1941; s. Abraham and Shirley (Blank) K.; m. Susan Gail Zipkis, June 30, 1962; children—Robert Jay, Craig Douglas. B.S.M.E., Poly. Inst. Bklyn., 1962, M.S. in Indsl. Mgmt, 1967. With Xerox Corp., Stamford, Conn., 1967-80; dir. corp. fin. planning Xerox Corp., 1980-81; pres., chief operating officer Centronics Data Computer Corp., Hudson, N.H., 1980-81; partner Oak Mgmt. Corp., Westport, Conn., 1981-87; pres., chief exec. officer M.K. Global Ventures, Palo Alto, Calif., 1987—; bd. dirs. Businessland, Ekco Group, Clustrix, Davox Corp., Document Techs.; instr. M.B.A. program U. Conn., 1977-78; mem. adv. bd. Imaging Scis. Inst., Poly. Inst. N.Y., 1980—. Bd. dirs. So. N.H. Bd. Commerce and Industry, 1980-81. Recipient award of distinction Poly. Inst. Bklyn., 1980. Mem. Am. Inst. Indsl. Engrs.,

ASME, Nat. Soc. Profl. Engrs., Poly. Inst. Bklyn. Alumni Assn. (dir.). Office: MK Global Ventures 2471 E Bayshore Rd Ste 520 Palo Alto CA 94303

KAUFMANN, THOMAS ARTHUR, investment advisor broker, newsletter publisher; b. Aurora, Ill., May 12, 1954; s. Carl Joseph and Barbra (Weil) K.; m. Linda Brehmer, Aug. 30, 1980; children: Kristina, Coco, Melissa, Chase, Jordan. BSME, Colo. State U., 1976; MBA in Finance, U. Denver, 1980. Engr. Teledyne Water Pik, Fort Collins, Colo., 1976-78; v.p., sales mgr. N. Donald & Co., Denver, 1980-84, Nieson & Clark, Denver, 1984-85, R. B. Marich, Inc., Denver, 1985—; pres. The Dynasty Report (Newsletter), Denver, —, Compubrokes-Software & Financial P.R., Denver, —. Editor: The Dynasty Report, 1983-88; publisher Compubroke-Financial Software and P.R., 1980-88; contbr. articles to profl. jours. Organizer United Way of Colo. (recipient outstanding vol. award), Denver, 1988. Mem. Internat. Soc. of Fin. Planners. Home and Office: 3465 S Columbine Circle Englewood CO 80110

KAUFMANN, THOMAS DAVID, economist, educator; b. Rye, N.Y., July 23, 1922; s. Fritz and Irma (Heiden) K.; B.A., Oberlin Coll., 1943; M.P.A., Harvard U., 1947, M.A., 1947, Ph.D., 1949; m. Maureen Liebl, June 4, 1983; children—Peter F., David T. Economist, U.S. del. NATO and OEEC, Paris, 1949-56; dir. new bus. Amax, Inc., N.Y.C., 1956-67; v.p. Alumax, Inc., Greenwich, Conn., 1967-69; dir. bus. planning Hunter-Douglas, London, 1969-75; trader Asoma, N.Y.C., 1975-77; cons. Daniel K. Ludwig, N.Y.C., 1977-82; prof. mineral econs. Colo. Sch. Mines, Golden, 1982—. Contbr. articles to profl. jours. Served with U.S. Army, 1943-46. Mem. Am. Econ. Assn., Phi Beta Kappa. Jewish. Home: 1966 Mount Zion Dr Golden CO 80401 Office: Colo Sch Mines Golden CO 80401

KAUNDART, STEPHEN RAY, commercial laundry service executive; b. Martinez, Calif., June 30, 1952; s. Ray Junior Kaundart and Dawn E. (Grummett) O'Neill. Grad. high sch., San Diego. Svc. technician, grounds keeper Christa's Wash, San Diego, 1979-81; sr. technician Comml. Laundry Sales, San Diego, 1982-87; owner, operator Kaundart's Laundry Svc., San Diego, 1987--. Chmn. Nat. Alliance Alcoholism Prevention and Treatment, San Diego, 1976. With U.S. Army, 1972-78. Democrat. Home and Office: 3851 Bernice Dr San Diego CA 92107

KAUNE, JAMES EDWARD, ship repair company executive, former naval officer; b. Santa Fe, N.Mex., Mar. 4, 1927; s. Henry Eugene and Lucile (Carter) K.; B.S., U.S. Naval Acad., 1950; Naval Engr. degree Mass. Inst. Tech., 1955; B.S. in Metallurgy, Carnegie-Mellon U., 1960; m. Pauline Stamatos, June 24, 1956; children—Bradford Scott, Audrey Lynn, Jason Douglas. Commd. ensign U.S. Navy, 1950, advanced through grades to capt., 1970; asst. gunnery officer U.S.S. Floyd B. Parks, 1950-52; project officer U.S.S. Gyatt, Boston Naval Shipyard, 1955-57; main propulsion officer U.S.S. Tarawa, 1957-58; asst. planning officer Her Majesty's Canadian Dockyard, Halifax, N.S., Can., 1960-62; repair officer U.S.S. Cadmus, 1962-64; fleet maintenance officer Naval Boiler and Turbine Lab., 1964-68; various shipyard assignments, 1968-70, material staff officer U.S. Naval Air Forces Atlantic Fleet, 1971-74; production officer Phila. Naval Shipyard, 1974-79; comdr. Long Beach Naval Shipyard, Calif.; exec. v.p. Am. Metal Bearing Co., Garden Grove, Calif., from 1979; gen. mgr. San Francisco div. Topp Shipyards, Alameda, Calif., v.p. engring. Point Richmond Shipyard (Calif.); v.p. engring., mktg. Service Engring. Corp, San Francisco. Mem. Am. Soc. Naval Engrs., Am. Soc. Quality Control, Soc. Naval Architects and Marine Engrs., U.S. Naval Inst., Am. Soc. Metals. Episcopalian. Club: Masons. Contbr. articles to profl. jours. Home: 403 Camino Sobrante Orinda CA 94563 Office: Svc Engring Corp Pier 38 San Francisco CA 94107

KAUS, OTTO MICHAEL, lawyer; b. Vienna, Austria, Jan. 7, 1920; came to U.S., 1939, naturalized, 1942; s. Otto F. and Gina (Wiener) K.; m. Peggy A. Huttenback, Jan. 12, 1943; children: Stephen D., Robert M. B.A., UCLA, 1942; LL.B., Loyola U., Los Angeles, 1949. Bar: Calif. 1949. Pvt. practice Los Angeles, 1949-61; judge Superior Ct. Calif., 1961-64; assoc. justice Calif. Ct. Appeal (2d appellate dist., div. 3), Los Angeles, 1965-66; presiding justice Calif. Ct. Appeal (div. 5), 1966-81; assoc. justice Supreme Ct. Calif., San Francisco, 1981-85; ptnr. Hufstedler, Miller, Kaus & Beardsley, Los Angeles, 1986—; mem. faculty Loyola U. Law Sch., 1950-75, U. So. Calif., 1974-76. Served with U.S. Army, 1942-45. Mem. Am. Law Inst., Phi Beta Kappa, Order of Coif. Office: Hufstedler Miller Kaus & Beardsley 355 S Grand Ave 45th Fl Los Angeles CA 90071

KAUS, PETER EDWARD, physicist, educator; b. Vienna, Austria, Oct. 9, 1924; came to U.S., 1939; s. Otto and Gina (Wiener) K.; m. Eva Lewy, Sept. 10, 1950; children: Antonia, Nicola, Andrea. BS, UCLA, 1946, PhD, 1954. Rsch. physicist RCA Lab., Princeton, N.J., 1954-58; asst. prof. U. So. Calif., L.A., 1958-62; assoc. U. Calif., Riverside, 1962-64, prof., 1964—; pres. Aspen (Colo.) Ctr. for Physics, 1982-85; cons. in field. Contbr. articles to profl. publs.; patentee in field. With U.S. Army, 1944-45, ATO. Recipient Sarnof Achievement medal, 1956, Fulbright award, 1965. Fellow Am. Phys. Soc.; mem. Sierra Club. Home: 2825 Maude St Riverside CA 92506 Office: U Calif Physics Dept Riverside CA 92521

KAVADAS, PAUL PETER, real estate county manager; b. DeKalb, Ill., May 9, 1927; s. Peter Samuel and Maude Alice (Frost) K.; m. Janet Dana Head, Nov. 11, 1982. BS in Edn., No. Ill. U., 1948; BS in Ceramic Engring., U. Wash., 1959, MS in Ceramic Engring., 1966. Notary pub.; cert. rev. appraiser; arbitrator. Secondary sch. tchr. various schs., 1948-53; engr. Gen. Dynamics/Astronautics, San Diego, 1959-60, Boeing Co., Seattle, 1961-68; lead engr. Boeing Co., Renton, Wash., 1968-70; right of way agt. Wash. Dept. Transp., Bellevue, 1971-72; mgmt. analyst, editor Wash. Dept. Transp., Olympia, 1972-76; mgmt. analyst, auditor Dept. Social & Health Svcs., Olympia, 1976-78; supr. project support Wash. Dept. Transp., Olympia, 1978-82; chief right of way agt. Snohomish County Pub. Works, Everett, Wash., 1982—; founder Pacific Northwest Regional Right of Way Workshop, various cities, 1986—. Author, editor: Book Right of Way Manual, 1975; contbr. articles to profl. jours. Judge Sci. Olympics, Everett, 1989; panelist high sch. DARE program, Everett, 1989; track and field official U.S. Am./The Athletic Congress, Pacific N.W. Athletic Congress, Seattle, 1989; com. mem. Footballs & Baseballs Race, Everett, 1989—, YMCA. Recipient gold medal 5K racewalk Can. Nat. Masters Track & Field, Vancouver, 1987, bronze medal 5K racewalk U.S. Nat. Masters Track & Field, Eugene, Oreg., 1987, silver medal 20K racewalk U.S. Nat. Masters Track & Field, Eugene, 1987. Mem. Internat. Right of Way Assn. (sr. mem., treas., award 1981), Am. Arbitration Assn. (panel mem.), Nat. Assn. Review Appraisers & Mortgage Underwriters (sr. mem., Cert. Rev. award 1989), Athletics Congress, Pacific Northwest Athletics Congress, Pacific Pacers, Elks. Greek Orthodox. Home: 217 Alder St 305 Edmonds WA 98020 Office: Snohomish County Pub Works County Adminstrn Bldg Everett WA 98201

KAVAYA, MICHAEL JOSEPH, research and development company executive; b. Montebello, Calif., June 16, 1951; s. Dan Kavaya and Marilyn Joyce (McMinn) Leone; m. Janet Elaine Potter, Aug. 27, 1978; children: Sarah Elizabeth, Anna Catherine. BSEE, Purdue U., 1974; MSEE, Calif. Inst. Tech., 1975, PhDEE, 1982, engr. mgmt. cert., 1984. Elec. engr. Continental Can Co., Chgo., 1970-73; mem. tech. staff Jet Propulsion Lab (NASA), Pasadena, Calif., 1975-85; v.p., chief scientist Coherent Techs., Inc., Boulder, Colo., 1985—; program chmn. Third NASA/NOAA Infared Backscatter Workshop, 1985. Contbr. aticles to profl. jours.; patentee in field. Mem. IEEE, Am. Metorol. Soc., Optical Soc. Am., Tau Beta Pi, Eta kKappa Nu. Republican. Office: Coherent Techs Inc 3300 Mitchell Ln Ste 330 Boulder CO 80301-2272

KAVIN, REBECCA JEAN, health science executive; b. Dodge, Nebr., June 29, 1946; d. William Wilber Walsh and Dorothy Eleanor (Watson) Williams; m. Paul Babcock, May 15, 1965 (div. Sept. 1976); m. E. Iraj Kavin, Apr. 23, 1977; children: Mark Bijan, Seana Shereen. Cert., Ohio U., 1963. Claims adjuster San Found. for Med. Care, San Diego, 1968-70; adminstrv. asst. Friendly Hills Med. Group, La Habra, Calif., 1971-77; office mgr. Robert M. Peck and Sergio Blesa, M.D., Pasadena, Calif., 1978-81; pres. Provider Mgmt. Assocs., La Canada, Calif., 1981—; speaker Continuing Edn. Dept. UCLA, 1985, Hosp. Council of So. Calif., Los Angeles, 1986, Am. Acad. Med. Preventics, Los Angeles, 1986. Contbr. articles to profl. jours. Mem. Am. Guild Patient Account Mgrs. (speaker Los Angeles chpt. 1986). Republican. Presbyterian. Office: Provider Mgmt Assocs 2418 Honolulu Ave Montrose CA 91020

KAWAMURA, SUSUMU, consulting engineering company executive, lecturer; b. Kobe, Hyogo, Japan, Sept. 25, 1929; came U.S., 1959, naturalized, 1979; s. Akira and Yuri (Itoh) K.; m. Reiko Fujiwara, Apr. 8, 1957; children: Midori, Mika Kawamura Firestone. BCE, Kobe U., Japan, 1949; MS, Ohio State U., 1961; PhD, Kyoto U., 1979. Project engr. Mcpl. Water Dist. of Hanshin, Kobe, Japan, 1950-59, Burgess & Niple, Cons. Engrs. Ltd., Columbus, Ohio, 1966-69; rsch. asst. Ohio State U., Columbus, 1965-66; technical dir., v.p. James M. Montgomery Cons. Engrs. Inc., Pasadena, Calif., 1969—; project engr. James M. Montgomery Cons. Engrs. Inc., 1969-74, v.p., 1975; lectr. U. So. Calif., L.A., 1981—. Recipient Disting. Svc. award MWD of Hanshin, Kobe, Japan, 1958. Mem. Am. Water Works Assn., Am. Acad. Environ. Engrs. (diplomate), Australian Water and Wastewater Assn., Internat. Water Supply Assn., Japan Water Works Assn. (recipient Yuko prize 1959). Office: James M Montgomery Cons Engrs Inc 250 N Madison Pasadena CA 91109

KAY, ALAN COOKE, federal judge; b. Honolulu, July 5, 1932; s. Harold Thomas and Ann (Cooke) K.; m. Patricia Patmont; children: Peter, Anna, David. BA, Princeton U., 1957; LLB, U. Calif., Berkeley, 1960. Assoc. Case, Kay & Lynch, Honolulu, 1960-64, ptnr., 1965-86; judge U.S. Dist. Ct. Hawaii, Honolulu, 1987—. Mem. steering com. Fuller Theol. Sem. Hawaii, 1985-86; pres., trustee Hawaii Mission Children's Soc., Honolulu, 1980-86; bd. dirs. Good News Mission, 1980-86, Econ. Devel. Corp. Honolulu, 1985-86, Legal Aid Soc., Honolulu, 1968-71. Mem. ABA, Am. Inn Ct. (counselor Aloha Inn 1987-88), Hawaii Bar Assn. (exec. com. 1972-73, bd. dirs. real estate sect. 1983-86), 9th Cir. Dist. Ct. Judges Assn, Pacific Club, Honolulu Club. Republican. Office: US Dist Ct PO Box 50128 Honolulu HI 96850

KAY, ELIZABETH ALISON, zoology educator; b. Kauai, Hawaii, Sept. 27, 1928; d. Robert Buttercase and Jessie Dowie (McConnachie) K. BA, Mills Coll., 1950, Cambridge U., Eng., 1952; MA, Cambridge U., Eng., 1956; PhD, U. Hawaii, 1957. From asst. prof. to prof. zoology U. Hawaii, Honolulu, 1957-62, assoc. prof., 1962-67, prof., 1967—; research assoc. Bishop Mus., Honolulu, 1968—. Author: Hawaiian Marine Mollusks, 1979; editor: A Natural History of The Hawaiian Islands, 1972. Chmn. Animal Species Adv. Commn., Honolulu, 1983-87; v.p. Save Diamond Head Assn., Honolulu, 1968-87, pres., 1987—; trustee B.P. Bishop Mus., Honolulu, 1983-88. Fellow Linnean Soc., AAAS; mem. Marine Biol. Assn. (Eng.), Australian Malacol. Soc. Episcopalian. Office: U Hawaii Manoa Dept Zoology 2538 The Mall Honolulu HI 96822

KAY, JEROME HAROLD, cardiac surgeon; b. St. Cloud, Minn., Mar. 17, 1921; m. Adrienne Levin, June 15, 1950; children: Gregory Louis, Stephen Paul, Karen Lynne, Cathy Ann, Robert Michael, Richard Keith. A.A., UCLA, 1941; A.B., U. Calif., San Francisco, 1943, M.D., 1945. Diplomate: Am. Bd. Surgery, Am. Bd. Thoracic Surgery. Intern San Francisco County Hosp., 1945-46; asst. resident surgeon VA Hosp., McKinney, Tex., 1946-49; resident surgeon VA Hosp., 1949-50; fellow in surgery Johns Hopkins Sch. Medicine, Balt., 1950-52; asst. resident surgeon Johns Hopkins Sch. Medicine, 1952-53, resident surgeon, 1953-54, instr., 1953-54; instr. surgery U. So. Calif. Sch. Medicine, Los Angeles, 1956; asst. clin. prof. U. So. Calif. Sch. Medicine, 1958, asso. prof. surgery, 1958-80, clin. prof., 1982—; prof. surgery Charles R. Drew Postgrad. Med. Sch., 1982—. Producer of 9 motion pictures in field of open heart surgery; co-author 15 chpts. in med. textbooks; contbr. over 146 articles to med. jours in field of cardiopulmonary diseases and surgery; inventor Kay-Anderson Heart Lung Machine, 1958, Kay-Shiley disc valve, 1965, Kay muscle guard, 1967. Trustee Heart Inst. Hosp. of Good Samaritan, 1986—. Served to maj. USPHS, 1954-56. Recipient 1st ann. Heart Research award Children's Heart Found. So. Calif., 1966. Fellow A.C.S., Am. Coll. Cardiology, Am. Coll. Angiology, Am. Heart Assn.; mem. Am. Assn. Thoracic Surgery, AMA, Los Angeles County Med. Assn., Pan Pacific Surg. Assn. (v.p. 1975-78), Am. Fedn. Clin. Research, Assn. Advancement Med. Instrumentation, Am. Coll. Chest Physicians (gov. So. Calif. area 1970-73), Internat. Cardiovascular Soc., Soc. Thoracic Surgeons (founding mem.), Soc. Univ. Surgeons, John Paul North Surg. Soc. (past pres.), Los Angeles County Heart Assn., Med. Research Assn. Calif. (past v.p., dir.), numerous others. Office: 123 S Alvarado St Los Angeles CA 90057

KAY, JOHN CHESTER, educator; b. Chgo., May 29, 1937; s. John Chester Sr. and Adelaide Martha (Krutsch) K.; m. Violet, Oct. 17, 1961 (dec. 1988); children: Constance, Marlene, Susan, Ke Lin. BS in Biology, Carthage (Ill.) Coll., 1959; MS in Marine Biology, U. Hawaii, 1963; MA in Botany, U. Oreg., 1971. Teaching asst. dept. marine biology U. Hawaii, Honolulu, 1959-60; tchr. sci. Iolani Sch., Honolulu, 1962-65; tchr. biology Iolani Sch., 1966—, dept. chair, 1974-85; bowling coach Iolani Sch., 1982—; invited to teach Ctr. Talented Youth, johns Hopkins U., 1987-88. Contbr. articles to profl. jours. Chmn., sec., bd. dirs. Makana Found., 1980-83; appt. by Pres. Reagan to Selective Svc. Local Bd. No. 2, Hawaii, 1982—; bd. dirs. Lyon Aboretum, U. Hawaii, 1984. Recipient Outstanding Sci. Tchr. Hawaii award Serteens of Hawaii, 1983, Outstanding Biology Tchr., Nat. Assn. Biology Tchrs., 1973; NSF grantee, 1970-71. Mem. N.Y. Acad. Sci. Nat. Sci. Tchrs. assn., Am. Biology Tchrs. assn., Audubon Soc., Nat. Acad. Scis., Smithsonian Instn., Natural History, Nat. Assn. Secondary Sch. Prins., Assn. Biology Lab. Edn., Lions International (Pres. award 1983, Lion of Yr. award 1984), Key Club, Cum Laude Soc., Beta Beta Beta. Home: 583 Kamoku St 407 Honolulu HI 96826 Office: Iolani Sch 563 Kamoku St Honolulu HI 96826

KAYA, ROBERT MASAYOSHI, contractor; b. Waialua, Oahu, Hawaii, Feb. 3, 1914; s. Jinhichi and Aki (Tanimoto) K.; student pub. schs.; m. Florence Shinayo Okinaka, Mar. 15, 1939; children—Kathleen Tatsue, Merle Nobue, Virginia Sachie, Winifred Fumie. Carpenter, Hawaiian Contracting Co., 1935, carpenter, foreman D. Orita, contractor, 1936-37; owner contracting bus., Honolulu, 1937—; dir. City Bank Honolulu. Active YMCA; bd. dirs. Kuakini Med. Ctr. Mem. Gen. Contractors Assn. Hawaii, Oahu Contractors Assn. (pres. 1954-55), Building Industry Assn. Hawaii (pres. 1956), Honolulu C. of C., Honolulu Japanese C. of C. (pres. 1974-75), Nat. Assn. Home Builders (life dir. 1976—), Nat. Fedn. Ind. Bus., Japan Am. Soc. Honolulu, Bishop Museum Assn., U.S. Army Museum, U. Hawaii Found. Buddhist (pres. Zen sect. Soto Mission 1973-74). Clubs: Lions (dist. gov. Hawaii 1964-65, pres. 1955-56; life mem., Melvin Jones fellow), 200 (Honolulu). Home: 2380 Beckwith St Honolulu HI 96822 Office: 525 Kokea St #B3 Honolulu HI 96817

KAYE, LESLIE, film and video editor, director; b. N.Y.C., June 3, 1952; s. Isaac and Esther (Szear) Kozlowski. BA, CUNY, 1973. News asst., assignment editor, writer WNBC-TV News, NBC News, N.Y.C., 1972-77; trailer editor Universal Studios, L.A., 1979-85; asst. editor 8 Million Ways to Die, L.A., 1985; 2nd editor Fame MGM TV, Culver City, Calif., 1985; editor (TV series) PeeWees's Playhouse Broadcast Arts, N.Y.C., 1986; freelance video editor L.A., 1987—; editor, writer TV show-Who Murdered JFK Barbour/Langley, Marina Del Rey, Calif., 1988. Recipient Daytime Emmy award NATAS, 1987, Monitor award Internat. Teleprodn. Soc. N.Y. Mem. NATAS. Democrat. Jewish. Office: Creative Accounts PO Box 1378 Venice CA 90294

KAYFETZ, VICTOR JOEL, journalist, editor, translator; b. N.Y.C., July 20, 1945; s. Daniel Osler and Selma Harriet (Walowitz) K.; B.A., Columbia U., 1966; postgrad. U. Stockholm (Sweden), 1966-67; M.A. in History, U. Calif.-Berkeley, 1969. Teaching asst. in Swedish, U. Calif., Berkeley, 1969-70; tchr., adminstr. Dalaro Folk Coll., Sweden, 1970-71, Visingso Folk Coll., Sweden, 1972-73; head tchr. English, Studieframjandet Adult Sch., Stockholm, 1973-74, sec. head, 1974-75; corr. Reuters, Stockholm, 1975-78; sub-editor Reuters World Ser., London, 1978; corr. London Fin. Times, Stockholm, 1979-80; copy editor, translator Scandinavian Bus. World, 1981-82; free lance translator Swedish, Danish, Norwegian, 1967—; free lance journalist, editor Swedish and Am. mags., Stockholm, 1979-80, San Francisco, 1980—. Henry Evans traveling fellow, 1966-67; Nat. Def. Fgn. Lang. fellow, 1967-69; Thord Gray fellow Am.-Scandinavian Found., 1970. Mem. Swedish Am. C. of C. (bd. dirs., Swedish Bus. and Soc. Research Inst., Soc. Advancement Scandinavian Study, Am. Scandinavian Found., World Affairs Council No. Calif., Sierra Club, Phi Beta Kappa. Author: Sweden in Brief, 1974, 2d edit., 1977; Invest in Sweden, 1984, Skanska, the First Century, 1987; editor, translator numerous books and articles Swedish Inst., 1971—; editor, translator Fed. Swedish Industries, 1977—, Swedish Industry Faces the 80s, 1981; translator ann. reports Swedish indsl. corps., banks, 1977—; others. Office: Scan Edit 870 Market St Ste 1284 San Francisco CA 94102

KAYLAN, HOWARD LAWRENCE, musical entertainer, composer; b. N.Y.C., June 22, 1947; s. Sidney and Sally Joyce (Berlin) K.; m. Mary Melita Pepper, June 10, 1967 (div. Sept. 1971); 1 child, Emily Anne; m. Susan Karen Olsen, Apr. 18, 1982; 1 child, Alexandra Leigh. Grad. high sch., Los Angeles. Lead singer rock group The Turtles, Los Angeles, 1965-70, Mothers of Invention, Los Angeles, 1970-72; radio, TV, recording entertainer various broadcast organizations, Los Angeles, 1972—; screenwriter Larry Gelbart, Carl Gotleib prodns., Los Angeles, 1979-85; producer children's records Kidstuff Records, Hollywood, Fla., 1980—; singer, producer rock band Flo and Eddie, Los Angeles, 1976—; singer, producer The Turtles (reunion of original band), Los Angeles, 1980—; actor, TV and film Screen Actors Guild, Los Angeles, 1983—; v.p. Flo and Eddie, Inc., Los Angeles, 1972—; background vocalist various albums for Bruce Springsteen, T. Rex, Blondie, Andy Taylor, Psychedelic Furs, John Lennon, Ozzy Osbourne; syndicated radio talk show host Transtar Radio Network, 1989—. Contbr. articles to Creem Magazine, Los Angeles Free Press, Rockit Magazine, Phonograph Record; screenwriter motion picture Death Masque, 1985; actor motion picture Get Crazy, 1985; performed at the White House, 1970. Recipient 6 gold and platinum LP album awards while lead singer, 1965—, cert. achievement State of Calif., 1982, Fine Arts award Bank of Am., Los Angeles, 1965; achieved numerous Top Ten hit songs during the sixties with the Turtles. Mem. AFTRA, Screen Actors Guild, Am. Fedn. Musicians, AGVA. Democrat.

KAYLOR, ANDREA LYNN, educator; b. L.A., May 19, 1946; d. Kenneth D. and Florence R. (Berkman) Cooper; m. Stephan A. Kaylor, Dec. 4, 1983; children: Gavin Chandler, Kiley Chandler. AA, Diablo Valley Coll., Pleasant Hill, Calif., 1971; BS, U. Nev., Reno, 1983. Cert. dental hygiene, teaching cert. Registered dental hygienist Davis, Calif., 1971-73, L.A., 1973-78, Reno, 1978-80; elem. tchr. Rita Cannon Sch., Reno, 1984-88, Alice Maxwell Sch., Sparks, Nev., 1989; tchr. trainer Math Cadre Washoe County Sch. Dist., Reno, 1987-89; presenter WC Math Assn. Biannual Conf., Reno, 1985-89. Del. Democratic County Conv., Reno, 1988; campaign mgr. Mcpl. Judge Race, Reno, 1980; treas., state conv. del. PTA, Reno, 1985-89; tchr. rep. Alice Maxwell PTA, Sparks, 1989—. Recipient Nat. Sallie Mae Tchr. Award for Outstanding 1st Yr. Tchrs., Sallie Mae Found., 1985; Mary Sartor Meml. scholar for acad. excellence, Dept. Edn. U. Nev. Reno, 1982. Mem. Nev. State Edn. Assn., Washoe County Greater Area Counselors, NEA, Calif. Math. Coun. Democrat. Home: PO Box 696 Verdi NV 89439

KAYS, RANDY LEE, physicist; b. Three Rivers, Mich., Jan. 27, 1955; s. George Fredric and Martha M. (McCourt) K. BS, Western Mich. U., 1978; postgrad., N.Mex. State U., 1980-89. Scientist Lockheed Engring. and Sci. Co., Las Cruces, N.Mex., 1984—. Vol. Peace Corps, Cameroon, Africa, 1978-80. Mem. Am. Geophys. Union, AIAA. Democrat. Methodist. Home: 1425 Monte Vista #5 Las Cruces NM 88001 Office: Lockheed Engring & Sci Co NASA-WSTF Po Drawer MM Las Cruces NM 88004

KAYSER, DONALD ROBERT, financial executive; b. Chgo., Oct. 7, 1930; s. Harold William and Catherine (Spillane) K.; m. Mary King, Oct. 13, 1956; children—Catherine E. Blazer, D. Robert, Kevin C., Jean K., William H., Christopher J. B.S.E.E., Fournier Inst. Tech., 1952; M.B.A., Harvard U., 1956. V.p., gen. mgr. southern ops. La.-Pacific Corp., Portland, Oreg., 1972-73, Vice pres., chief fin. officer, 1973-82, dir., 1972—; sr. v.p., chief fin. officer Bendix Corp., Southfield, Mich., 1982-83; v.p. fin. Allied Corp., Morristown, N.J., 1983-84; sr. v.p., chief fin. officer Allied-Signal Inc., Morristown, N.J., 1984-88; exec. v.p., chief fin. officer Morrison Knudsen Corp., Boise, Idaho, 1988—, also bd. dirs.; Bd. dirs. La. Pacific Corp. With Signal Corps, U.S. Army, 1952-54. Baker scholar, Harvard U., 1956. Mem. Nat. Assn. Mfrs. (bd. dirs. 1986—). Roman Catholic. Office: Morrison Knudsen Corp Box 73 Boise ID 83707

KAYTON, HOWARD H., actuary; b. N.Y.C., Nov. 19, 1936; s. Albert Louis and Rae (Danoff) K.; m. Marilyn Simmons, June 20, 1957 (div. 1968); children: Bruce Charles, David Lawrence; m. Myrna Sue Blum, Dec. 28, 1975. BBA magna cum laude, CCNY, 1958; postgrad., U. So. Calif., 1970-72. Asst. actuary N.Y. Life Ins. Co., N.Y.C., 1958-67; assoc. actuary Pacific Mutual Life Ins. Co., L.A., 1967-71; cons. actuary, prin. Milliman & Robertson Inc., L.A., 1971-77; exec. v.p., chief actuary Security First Life Ins. Co., L.A., 1977—. Contbr. articles to profl. jours. Fellow Soc. Actuaries, Casualty Actuarial Soc., Conf. Actuaries in Pub. Practice; mem. Am. Acad. Actuaries, Am. Risk and Ins. Assn., L.A. Actuarial Club (pres. 1976-77), Actuarial Club Pacific States, So. Calif. Actuarial Club., Sierra Club. Office: Security First Life Ins Co 11365 W Olympic Blvd Los Angeles CA 90064

KAYTON, MYRON, engineering company executive; b. N.Y.C., Apr. 26, 1934; s. Albert Louis and Rae (Danoff) K.; m. Paula Erde, Sept. 5, 1954; children: Elizabeth Kayton Kerns, Susan Kayton Barclay. BS, The Cooper Union, 1955; MS, Harvard U., 1956; PhD, MIT, 1960. Registered engr., Calif. Sect. head Litton Industries, Woodland Hills, Calif., 1960-65; dep. mgr. NASA, Houston, 1965-69; mem. sr. staff TRW, Inc., Redondo Beach, Calif., 1969-81; pres. Kayton Engring. Co., Inc., Santa Monica, Calif., 1981—; bd. dirs. WINCON Conf., Los Angeles, 1985—; founding dir. Caltech-MIT Enterprise Forum, Pasadena, Calif., 1984—. Author: Avionic Navigation Systems, 1966, Navigation: Land, Sea, Aerial Space, 1989; contbr. numerous articles on engring., econs. and other profl. subjects. Founding dir. UCLA Friends of Humanities, 1971-75; West coast chmn. Cooper Union Fund Campaign, 1989—. Fellow NSF, Washington, 1956-57, 58-60; recipient Gano Dunn medal The Cooper Union, N.Y.C., 1975. Fellow IEEE (nat. v.p. tech. ops, 1988—, nat. v.p. mem. affairs 1986-87, nat. bd. govs. 1983—); mem. ASME, Harvard Grad. Soc. Clubs: Harvard (So. Calif.) (pres. 1979-80); MIT (Los Angeles). Office: Kayton Engring Co PO Box 802 Santa Monica CA 90406

KAZANTZIS, KENTIA ANN, freelance writer, music composer; b. Los Angeles, Sept. 2, 1962; d. Alexander John and Kaayane (Tatar) K. BS in Bus., U. So. Calif., 1985. Owner New Salon Contemporary Fine Art, Venice, Calif., 1987-88; freelance writer, music composer Los Angeles, 1988—. Mem. Women's Referral Service, U. So. Calif. Alumni Assn.

KAZLE, ELYNMARIE, production stage manager, producer; b. St. Paul, June 22, 1958; d. Victor Anton and Marylu (Gardner) K. BFA, U. Minn., Duluth, 1982; MFA, Ohio U., 1984. Prodn. mgr. Great Lakes Shakespeare, Cleve., 1983; prodn. stage mgr. San Diego (Calif.) Opera, 1984, PCPA Theaterfest, Santa Maria, Calif., 1986-87; stage mgr. Bklyn. Acad. Music, 1987; assoc. producer Am. Theater Actors, N.Y.C., 1988—; prodn. stage mgr. Time Flies When You're Alive, West Hollywood, Calif., 1988—; assoc. producer Paulmark Prodns., L.A., 1988—; asst. advt. display Wall St. Jour., L.A., 1988-89. Editor, pub.: (newsletter) The Ohio Network, 1984—; producer Santa Monica Playhouse, 1989—. Mem. Stage Mgrs. Assn., Stage Mgrs. Assn. Los Angeles (assoc. dir.), U.S. Inst. Theatre Tech., Actors Equity Assn., Phi Kappa Phi, Delta Chi Omega (past pres. 1978). Home: 6075 Franklin #360 Los Angeles CA 90028 Office: Santa Monica Playhouse 1211 4th St Santa Monica CA 90401

KAZOR, WALTER ROBERT, statistical process control and quality assurance consultant; b. Avonmore, Pa., Apr. 16, 1922; s. Steven Stanley and Josephine (Lestic) K.; B.S. in Mech. Engring., Pa. State U., 1943; M.S., U. Pitts., 1953, M.Letters in Econs. and Indsl. Mgmt., 1957; m. Gloria Rosalind Roma, Aug. 10, 1946; children—Steven Edward, Christopher Paul, Kathleen Mary Jo. Research engr. Gulf Oil Corp., Pitts., 1946-57; with Westinghouse Electric Corp., 1957-84, quality assurance mgr. breeder reactor components project, Tampa, Fla., 1977-81, mgr. nuclear service center, Tampa, 1981-84; pres. Integrated Quality Systems Corp., Mgmt. Quality Assurance Cons., St. Petersburg, Fla., 1984-86; quality assurance specialist in nuclear waste mgmt. Sci. Applications Internat. Corp., Las Vegas, 1986-88; sr. cons. statis. process control and quality assurance Fischbach Tech. Svcs., Inc., Dallas,

1988—; cons., guest lectr. in field. Bd. dirs. New Kensington (Pa.) council Boy Scouts Am., 1958-62. Served with USNR, 1944-46. Registered profl. engr., Pa. Mem. ASME, Am. Soc. Quality Control. Republican. Roman Catholic. Club: Lions (past pres. clubs). Author, patentee in field.

KEACH, KENNETH LOWELL, banker; b. Fond du Lac, Wis., July 9, 1946; s. Lowell James and Gladys May (Trezona) K.; m. Janet Connant Meredith, May 13, 1980; children: Andrew, Elizabeth. BBA, U. Wis., 1969; MBA, Seattle U., 1979. Asst. mgr. Continental Ill. Bank, Chgo., 1969-76; v.p., mgr. Hong Kong and Shanghai Bank, Seattle, 1976-79, Rainier Bank, Seattle, 1979-85, Barclay's Bank PLC, Seattle, 1985—; bd. dirs. Kether Corp., Wash., Seahaven Inc., Wash.; mem. faculty Seattle U., 1978-80, U. Puget Sound, 1977-85. Author: SBA Programs and Procedures, 1971International TRade Finance, 1982; contbr. articles to profl. jours. Chmn. Pacific NW Internat. Trade Conf. and Western Gov's. Meeting, Tacoma, 1984, Export Assistance Ctr., Seattle, 1983; dir. adv. bd. Dept. Agr., Olympia, 1982. Fellow Royal Asiatic Soc., Royal African Soc., Brit. Mgmt. Assn.; mem. RMA, Wash. Bankers Assn. (chmn. 1982), Seattle C. of C., Masons, Shriners, Wash. Athletic Club, Kobe Club. Home: 13200 Phelps Rd NE Bainbridge WA 98110 Office: Barclays Bank PLC 600 University St Seattle WA 98101

KEALIHER, CAROLYN LOUISE, human resources executive; b. Helena, Okla., Jan. 19, 1926; d. Amos R. and Martha Louise (Werner) K. BA, Colo. State U., 1974. Employment interviewer Martin Marietta Corp., Denver, 1957-64; employment mgr. 1st of Denver, 1965-67, asst. v.p., 1967-78; sr. v.p. 1st Nat. Service Corp., Denver, 1978—; bd. dirs. Francis Heights, Denver, Clare Gardens, Denver. Mem. Colo. Soc. for Personnel Adminstrn. (Personnel Adminstr. of Yr. 1972), Womens Forum. Democrat. Roman Catholic. Office: 1st Nat Service Corp 3910 Buchtel Blvd Denver CO 80210

KEANE, DANIEL JAY, hair salon executive; b. Butte, Mont., July 24, 1958; s. Jeremiah Joseph and Barbara Rose (Downey) K.; m. Melinda Lee Minice, Sept 8, 1979; children: Adam Riley, Andrew Jacob. Student, Wash. State U., 1976-78; grad., Highline Beauty Sch., Burien, Wash., 1980. Designer, mgr. Rosalie Cantrell, Seattle, 1980-83; owner, mgr., motivational lectr. Market Place Salon, Seattle, 1983—; platform artist Lansa, Seattle, 1987—; nat. educator Aveda Indra Cosmetics, 1988-89. Contbr. articles to trade jours. Coordinator vol. hairstylists Harborview Hosp., Seattle, 1987-88; master ceremonies Auditions '87 Seattle Trade Ctr., 1987; co-chmn. Rainbow Montessori Ann. Auction, Seattle, 1988. Office: Market Pl Salon 2001 1st Ave Seattle WA 98121

KEANINI, RUSSELL GUY, researcher; b. Denver, June 29, 1959; s. Russell Eldridge and Patricia Ann (Regan) K.; m. Yvette Michelle. BS, Colo. Sch. of Mines, Golden, 1983; MS, U. Colo., Boulder, 1987; postgrad., U. Calif., Berkeley, 1987—. Bldg. specialist Nicor Exploration, Golden, 1984-85; structural designer Commerce City Supply, 1985-86; grad. rsch. asst. U. of Colo. Dept. of Mech. Engr., Denver, 1985-87; grad. teaching asst. U. of Calif., Berkeley, Calif., 1987-88; grad. student researcher NASA Ames Rsch. Cntr., Moffett Field, Calif., 1988—. Contbr. articles to profl. jours. Colo. Sch. of Mines scholar, 1982-83. Mem. AIAA, Soc. of Indsl. and Applied Math., Tau Beta Pi. Home: 1113 9th H31 Albany CA 94710 Office: NASA Ames Research Ctr Mail Stop 229-1 Moffett Field CA 94035

KEARNEY, PAUL LOUIS, aerospace company executive; b. Phila., Nov. 20, 1934; s. Louis Edward and Eunice Mary (Caffery) K.; m. Mary Margaret Dahm, July 27, 1957; children: Michael, Kathryn, Timothy, Margaret, Joseph. BS in Physics, U. Notre Dame, 1956; JD, Loyola U., Chgo., 1966. Bar: Ill. 1967, Wis. 1968. Contract adminstr. Cook Electric Co., Morton Grove, Ill., 1959-67; atty. legal dept. Ft. Howard Paper Co., Green Bay, Wis., 1967-69; mgr. contract adminstrn. Grumman Corp., Bethpage, N.Y., 1969-73; mgr. and dir. contracts Garrett Corp., L.A., 1973-87; dir. contracts Allied Signal Aerospace Co., Torrance, Calif., 1987—. Lt. USN, 1956-59. Mem. Nat. Contract Mgmt. Assn. (advisor 1984-87), ABA, Ill. State Bar Assn., Wis. State Bar Assn., Proprietary Industries Assn. (bd. dirs. 1986—), Notre Dame Club L.A. Republican. Roman Catholic. Home: 28435 Covecrest Dr Rancho Palos Verdes CA 90274 Office: Allied Signal Aerospace Co 2525 W 190th St Torrance CA 90509

KEARNEY, ROBERT EDWARD, advertising executive; b. Mankato, Minn., Mar. 18, 1958; s. Rochfort Wynn and Elizabeth (McLean) K. BA with honors Economics, Carleton Coll., 1980; MBA, Harvard U., 1984. Lending officer 1st Bank St. Paul, 1980-82; dir. mktg. PACE Membership Warehouse, Denver, 1984-86; mgmt. cons. Fails Mgmt. Inst., Denver, 1987-88; mng. dir. Krupp Taylor USA, Denver, 1988—; pres. Ind. Mgmt. Services, Denver, 1988--. Editor: Do-It-Yourself Personnel Manager, 1988. Mem. Rocky Mountain Direct Mktg. Assn. Episcopalian. Office: Krupp Taylor USA 1241 S Parker Rd Ste 203 Denver CO 80231

KEATING, CHARLES H., JR., construction company executive; b. 1923. J.D., U. Cin., 1948. Formerly with firm, ptnr. Keating Muething & Klekamp; now chmn., chief exec. officer Am. Continental Corp., Phoenix, Ariz. Office: Am Continental Corp 2735 E Camelback Rd Phoenix AZ 80516 *

KEATING, JOY MARIE, hospital administrator; b. Seattle, Oct. 4, 1944; d. Albert Franklin Amundsen and Wilma Ruth (Radley) Haughn; m. Richard William Nyholm, Apr. 23, 1963 (div. July 1975); children: John Derek, Troy David, Allison Joy; m. Douglas Arthur Keating, May 8, 1976. ADN, U. Alaska, 1976; BS in Pub. Adminstrn., Kennedy-Western U., 1986, MS in Pub. Adminstrn., 1988. RN Cen. Peninsula Hosp. Soldotna (Alaska)/Luth. Hosp. and Homes Soc., 1976-77; nurse counselor and bush nurse Kenai Peninsula Borough Sch. Dist., Soldotna, 1979-83; nurse supr. dept. corrections State of Alaska, Kenai, 1983-87; hosp. adminstr. Valdez Community Hosp. Valdez (Alaska) Community Hosp/Luth. Health Systems Mgmt. Co., 1987—; home health nurse State of Alaska, Soldotna, 1979-80; cons., speaker in field. Author sch. health curriculum and correctional healthcare programs; contbr. articles on Exxon oil spill's impact on healthcare to AP, Los Angeles Times, EMS Jour. Pres. bd. dirs. Emergency Assistance of Valdez, Alaska, 1987-89; mem. Care Providers, Valdez, 1987-89. Mem. Health Assn. Alaska (bd. dirs. 1987-89, mem. legis. affairs com. 1987-89), Am. Hosp. Assn., Am. Correctional Health Assn., Rotary (sec. 1988-89). Home: PO Box 1658 Valdez AK 99686 Office: Valdez Community Hosp Luth Health Systems Mgmt Co PO Box 550 Valdez AK 99686

KEATING, LARRY GRANT, electrical engineer, educator; b. Omaha, Jan. 15, 1944; s. Grant Morris and Dorothy Ann (Kauffold) K.; m. Barbara Jean Merley, Dec. 21, 1968. LLB, Blackstone Sch. Law, 1968; BS, U. Nebr., 1969; BS summa cum laude, Met. State Coll., 1971; MS, U. Colo., Denver, 1978. Chief engr. broadcast electronics 3 radio stas., 1965-69; coord. engring. reliability Cobe Labs., Lakewood, Colo., 1972-74; quality engr. Statitrol Corp., Lakewood, Colo., 1974-76; instr. electrical engring. U. Colo., Denver, 1976-78; from asst. prof. to prof. Met. State Coll., Denver, 1978—, chmn. dept., 1984—; cons. Transplan Assocs., Boulder, Colo., 1983-84. Co-author: (book) South Santa Fe Corridor, 1985. 1st lt. U.S. Army, 1962-70. Recipient Outstanding Faculty award U. Colo., Denver, 1980, Outstanding Alumnus award Met. State Coll., 1985. Mem. IEEE (sr.), Instrument Soc. Am. (sr.), Robotics Internat. (sr.), Am. Soc. Engring. Edn., Nat. Assn. Radio and Telecommunications Engrs. (cert. 1st class)., Eta Kappa Nu, Tau Alpha Pi, Chi Epsilon. Home: 6455 E Bates Ave 4-108 Denver CO 80222 Office: Met State Coll 1006 11th St Campus Box 29 Denver CO 80204

KEATOR, CAROL LYNNE, library director; b. Annapolis, Md., Aug. 9, 1945; d. Lyle H. and Juanita F (Waits) K. BA, Syracuse U., 1967; MS, Simmons Coll., 1968. Librarian Bristol (Conn.) Pub. Sch.s, 1968-69, MIT, Cambridge, 1969-72; librarian Santa Barbara (Calif.) PUb. Library, 1972-77, br. supr., 1977-81, prin. librarian, 1981-88, library dir., 1988—. Mem. ALA, Calif. Library Assn. Unitarian. Office: Santa Barbara Pub Libr 40 E Anapamu St Santa Barbara CA 93101

KEATS, FRANK JOSEPH, sales executive, sales and management consultant; b. Chgo., Nov. 3, 1950; s. Joseph Keats and Myrtle (Garman) Delaney; m. Linda Marie Rensen, Aug. 30, 1986; 1 child, Phillip Jay. AS in Bus., Loop Jr. Coll., Chgo., 1971. Gen. mgr. Florsheim Shoe Co., Chgo., 1971-76; regional mgr. Emmissary Wines, Chgo., 1976-85; regional v.p. sales Nat. Reading Devel. Inst., Garden Grove, Calif., 1986—; cons. Wine Masters Inc., City of Commerce, Calif., 1985-86, Tel-A-Sign Corp., Garden Grove, 1985. Named Vol. Worker of Yr., Safer Found., Chgo., 1973. Mem. Am. Mgmt. Assn., Direct Selling Assn. Republican. Home: 14346 Baker St Westminster CA 92683 Office: Nat Reading Devel Inst 12792 Valley View St Garden Grove CA 92045

KECK, BARBARA ANNE, management consulting company executive; b. Goshen, Ind., Aug. 10, 1946; d. Howard and Mary Elizabeth (Taylor) Brumbaugh; m. Gerald Nadel, June, 1966 (div. 1972); Chad Whitney Keck, May 16, 1976; children: Martin Whitney, Matthew James Howard. BA cum laude, Rutgers U., 1968; MBA, Harvard U., 1976. Communications specialist U.S. Dept. Agrl., New Brunswick, N.Y., 1968-71; asst. dir. pub. relations dept. Hill & Holliday, Boston, 1971-73; dir. advt. and pub. relations Paperback Booksmith, Boston, 1973-74; mktg. mgr. food packaging Continental Can Co. Hdqrs., Stamford, Conn., 1976-79; chmn., chief exec. officer Keck & Co. Bus. Cons. Inc., N.Y.C., 1979-85; pres. Keck & Co. Bus. Cons., Atherton, Calif., 1985—. Sec. N.J. Tenants Assn., 1969-70; bd. dirs. Puppetry Guild Greater N.Y., N.Y.C., 1981-84. Mem. Assn. Mgmt. Cons., Women in Mgmt. (founder 1978, pres. 1979-80). Episcopalian. Club: Harvard Bus. Sch. (San Francisco). Home and Office: 410 Walsh Rd Atherton CA 94025

KECK, CAROLYN ANNE, software executive; b. Corvalis, Oreg., Nov. 9, 1940; d. Dennis Clifford and Margaret May (Brown) K. BA in Math., Philosophy, Pacific Luth. U., 1962. Asst. engring. Nuclear Energy Div. Gen. Electric, San Jose, Calif., 1963-64; programmer Gen. Electric, San Jose, 1964-66, numerical analyst, 1966-68; prin., chief programmer ACD Software (formerly Uhalu Dancers), San Jose, 1968—. Treas. Holy Redeemer Luth. Ch., San Jose, 1983-86, v.p., 1987-88, pres., 1988-89. Republican. Home: 116 N 13th St San Jose CA 95112

KEDDIE, CLIFFORD MELVILLE, SR., entrepreneur; b. Chgo., Oct. 7, 1925; s. Clifford M. and Florence (Sugrue) K.; m. Lerna Shanley, Nov. 5, 1945; children: Joyce Carol, Clifford M., Barbara Jo, Kaye Ellen. BA, Western Mich. U., 1947. Tchr. various schs., Mich., Ill., 1947-59; computer salesman Honeywell, Chgo., 1959-64; v.p. mktg. Honeywell, Tex., Calif., 1968-72; dist. mgr. Control Data Corp., Houston, 1964-67; pvt. practice as computer cons. Calif., 1973-74; chief exec. officer Keddie Kreations of Calif., Rancho Cordova, Calif., 1975—; with Vision Mortgage, Sacramento, 1987—. Author: Beating the Odds in Love & War, 1988. Bd. dirs. Mathiot Boys Homes, Sacramento, 1988, edn. dir., 1988. Cpl. USMC, 1943-46. Mem. Sacramento PC Users Group, Elks. Republican. Home: 11447 Fortyniner Circle Gold River CA 95670 Office: Keddie Kreations Inc 11367 Sunrise Gold Circle Rancho Cordova CA 95742

KEDER, JANICE KRENZER, librarian; b. Fremont, Nebr., Dec. 22, 1930; d. Wilson Mason and Carolyn M. (Bowman) Krenzer; m. Wilbert Eugene Keder, Feb. 9, 1951; children: Nancy, John, Lisa, Martha. AA, Glendale Coll., 1951; BA, U. Pitts., 1975, MLS, 1976. Reference librarian U. Pitts., Bradford, Pa., 1976-86, Colo. Coll. Tutt Library, Colorado Springs, 1986—. Mem. ALA, Colo. Library Assn., Assn. Coll. and Research Libraries (sec. 1987-88), Beta Phi Mu. Home: 971 Terrace Circle Colorado Springs CO 80904 Office: Tutt Libr 1021 N Cascade Colorado Springs CO 80903

KEDING, ANN CLYRENE, free-lance copywriter; b. Ft. Benning, Ga., Aug. 31, 1944; d. Porter Bill and Clyrene (Stull) Maxwell; children from previous marriage: Robert, Jeff. BA in Psychology, Calif. State U., Fullerton, 1973, MA in Psychology, 1975; postgrad., U. So. Calif., 1980-83. Instr. psychology Calif. State U., Fullerton, 1974-76, Golden West Coll., Huntington Beach, Calif., 1976-78; mktg. research project dir. Foote, Cone & Belding, Los Angeles, 1978-80; copywriter Yuguchi & Krogstad, Los Angeles, 1980-82, Hamilton Advt., Los Angeles, 1982-84, Grey Advt., Los Angeles, 1984-85; freelance copywriter Los Angeles, Eugene, Calif., Oreg., 1985—; asst. prof. U. Oreg., Eugene, 1986—. Writer TV commls, advt. campaigns, brochures. Mem. adv. council Los Angeles Commn. on Assaults Against Women, 1985—. Recipient Pub. Citation Govt. Calif., 1985, Humanitarian award Los Angeles Commn. Assaults Against Women, 1986; Gannett fellow, Ind. U., 1987, 88. Mem. Am. Acad. Advt., Calif. State U. Fullerton Alumni Assn., Phi Kappa Phi (bd. dirs. 1974-75). Office: U Oreg Sch Journalism Eugene OR 97403

KEENAN, EDWARD JOSEPH, management consultant; b. N.Y.C., Oct. 3, 1932; s. Edward Joseph and Leona (Tansey) K.; married; 2 children. BA, U. Minn., 1967; MA in Edn., Chapman Coll., 1977; MBA, Pepperdine U., 1984; PhD in Bus. Adminstrn., Kensington U., 1989. Served with U.S. Air Force, 1951-71; ptnr. Edman-Keenan & Assocs., San Bernardino, Calif., 1971-73; adminstr. for pvt. law firms, Los Angeles and Beverly Hills, Calif., 1973-78; cons. to law firms, small bus., and hosps., 1978—; instr. law office mgmt. U. So. Calif., U. West Los Angeles, Calif. State U., Long Beach; cons. in field. Mem. Am. Inst. Indsl. Engrs., Assn. Legal Adminstrs. (charter; pres. Beverly Hills chpt. 1977-78), Hosp. Mgmt. Systems Soc. Republican. Lodges: Elks, Moose, K.C. Office: 1334 Park View Ave Manhattan Beach CA 90266

KEENAN, MARY ANN, orthopaedic surgeon, researcher; b. Phila., Aug. 14, 1950; d. William Joseph and Irene Agnes (Obara) K. A.B., U. Pa., 1971; M.D., Med. Coll. Pa., 1976. Diplomate Am. Bd. Med. Examiners, Am. Bd. Orthopedic Surgery. Orthopaedic resident Albert Einstein Med. Ctr., Phila., 1976-81; fellow rehab. Rancho Los Amigos Hosp., Downey, Calif., 1981-82, research dir. Head Trauma Service, 1982-87, chief, 1987— ; orthopaedic surgeon, chmn. rehab. team Kaiser Found. Hosp., Bellflower, Calif., 1982-87, regional rehab. cons., 1987—; asst. prof. orthopaedics U. So. Calif. Med. Sch., Los Angeles, 1982—. Contbr. articles in field to profl. jours. Recipient Annual Radiology prize Albert Einstein Med. Ctr., 1977, 78, 79, First Prize in research competition, 1980. Mem. Am. Congress Rehab. Med., AMA, Am. Acad. Orthopedic Surgeons, Am. Med. Women's Assn., Ruth Jackson Orthopaedic Soc. (bd. dirs.), Am. Congress of Rehab. Medicine, Profl. Staff Assn. Rancho Los Amigos Hosp., Alumnae Assn. Med. Coll. Pa. Democrat. Office: Dept Orthopaedic Surgery 9400 E Rosecrans Ave Bellflower CA 90706

KEENAN, NANCY A., state agency administrator. BA in Elem. and Spl. Edn., Mont. Coll., 1974. Tchr. Yellowstone Boys' Ranch, 1974-75; tchr. spl. edn. Anaconda, Mont., 1975-88; mem. Mont. Ho. of Reps., 1982-88; supt. of pub. instrn. State of Mont., 1988—; mem. taxation, edn., local govt. and revenue oversight coms., 1982-84; chmn. ho. human svcs. and aging com.; asst. Dem. whip. Active Anaconda Local Devel. Corp.; past pres. A.W.A.R.E.; bd. dirs. Deer Lodge County Hospice; mem. Mont. Coun. for Exceptional Children. Recipient Pub. Svc. award Mont. Coun. for Exceptional Children, 1981. Mem. AAUW. Office: Pub Instrn Office Rm 106 State Capitol Helena MT 59620

KEENAN, RETHA VORNHOLT, nurse, educator; b. Solon, Iowa, Aug. 15, 1934; d. Charles Elias and Helen Maurine (Konicek) V.; BSN, State U. Iowa, 1955; MSN, Calif. State U., Long Beach, 1978; m. Roy Vincent Keenan, Jan. 5, 1980; children from previous marriage: Scott Iverson, Craig Iverson. Publ. health nurse City of Long Beach, 1970-73, Hosp. Home Care, Torrance, Calif., 1973-75; patient care coord. Hillhaven, L.A., 1975-76; mental health cons. InterCity Home Health, L.A., 1978-79; instr. Community Coll. Dist., L.A., 1979-87; instr. nursing El Camino Coll., Torrance, 1981-86, NIMH grantee, 1977-78; instr. nursing Chapman Coll., Orange, Calif., 1982, Mt. Saint Mary's Coll., 1986-87. Contbg. author: American Journal of Nursing Question and Answer Book for Nursing Boards Review, 1984, Nursing Care Planning Guides for Psychiatric and Mental Health Care, 1987-88, Nursing Care Planning Guides for Children, 1987, Nursing Care Planning Guides for Adults, 1988, Nursing Care Planning Guides for Critically Ill Adults, 1988. Cert. nurse practitioner adult and mental health, 1979; mem. Assistance League of San Pedro, Palos Verdes, Calif. Bd. dirs. Luth. Ch. Mem. Am. Nurses Assn., Calif. Nurses Assn., AAUW, Am. Nurses Assn. Council on Psychiatric and Mental Health Nursing, Phi Delta Gamma, Sigma Theta Tau, Phi Kappa Phi, Delta Zeta (bd. dirs.). Home: 27849 Longhill Dr Rancho Palos Verdes CA 90274

KEENAN, ROBERT, architect; b. Rochester, N.Y., Jan. 8, 1950; s. John Lawrence and Frances (Hartigan) K.; m. Marianne Julia Janko, Sept. 9, 1989. BA, Fordham U., 1971; MArch, Harvard U., 1976. Registered architect, Mass., Calif.; cert. nat. coun. archtl. registration bds. Architect Archtl. Resources Cambridge Inc., Cambridge, Mass., 1977-79, Hoskins, Scott, Taylor & Ptnrs., Boston, 1979-81; architect Harry Weese & Assocs., Chgo., 1981—, v.p., 1983-89; v.p. Architect, Bechtel Civil, Inc., San Francisco, 1989—; speaker, session chmn. Internat. Conf. on Tall Bldgs, Singapore, 1984. Prin. works include Regis Coll. Athletic Facility, Weston, Mass., Singapore Mass Rapid Transit System, So. Calif. Metro Rail Project, Bay Area Rapid Transit Systems, San Francisco. Mem. AIA. Republican. Roman Catholic. Clubs: So. Calif. Harvard/Radcliffe, Los Angeles Athletic. Office: Bechtel Civil Inc PO Box 3965 50th Beale St San Francisco CA 94119

KEENBERG, SUSAN CAROL, franchise company executive; b. Bklyn., Apr. 20, 1947; d. William and Roslyn (Silberstein) Orenstein; m. Steven H. Keenberg, Apr. 6, 1968; 1 child, Michael Aaron. Diploma, W.C. Mepham Sch., Bellmore, N.Y., 1965. Mng. ptnr. Steven H. Keenberg, P.A., Miami, 1970-85; owner, prin. SGO Custon Glassworks, Miami, 1985-88; v.p., bd. dirs. Stained Glass Overlay, Inc., Irvine, Calif., 1988-89; pres. Creative Curb, Inc., Tustin, Calif., 1989—. Recipient Franny award Internat. Franchise Assn., 1987. Mem. Am. Soc. Interior Designers. Office: Creative Curb Inc 3002 Dow Ave #420 Tustin CA 92680

KEESLING, HENRY STEBBINS, archaeologist, photographer; b. Palo Alto, Calif., June 4, 1944; s. James C. and Amelia (Stebbins) K. BA, Calif. State U., Sacramento, 1974; MA, Calif. State U., 1976. Crew chief Bur. Indian Affairs, Albuquerque, 1978-81; area archaeologist Bur. Land Mgmt., Craig, Colo., 1981-88, archaelogist Craig dist., 1988—; cons. archaeologist Archaeol. Study Ctr., Sacramento, 1974-76. Photographs exhibited, 1983. With U.S. Army, 1968-72. Mem. Soc. Am. Archaeology, Smithsonian Assn. Republican. Home: PO Box 131 Craig CO 81626 Office: Bur Land Mgmt 1280 Industrial Ave Craig CO 81625

KEESLING, THOMAS MARION, travel agent; b. San Mateo, Calif., Sept. 14, 1932; s. Hector Victor Joseph and Margaret (Downing) K.; m. Ruth Louise Morris, June 30, 1956; children: Thomas Mark, James H., Frank M. BSBA, U. Colo., 1959. Pres., travel agt. Travel Assocs., Inc., Denver, 1960—; cons. World Bank, Addis Ababa, Ethiopia, 1972-73, China Internat. Travel Svc., Beijing, 1978-85. Presdl. appointee, Nat. Tourism Rev. Commn., Washington, 1971. 1st lt. USAF, 1952-57. Named hon. ambassador, City of Chgo., 1971; recipient medal of recognition, French Nat. Tourist Orgn., Paris, 1972; knight, Order of Cedars of Lebanon. Mem. Am. Soc. Travel Agts. (pres. 1971-73, creator agt. proficiency program, founder travel hall of fame), Pacific Asia Travel Assn. (bd. dirs. 1974-76). Republican. Office: Travel Assocs Inc 7007 E Hampden Ave Denver CO 80224

KEGLEY, JACQUELYN ANN, philosophy educator; b. Conneaut, Ohio, July 18, 1938; d. Steven Paul and Gertrude Evelyn (Frank) Kovacevic; m. Charles William Kegley, June 12, 1964; children: Jacquelyn Ann, Stephen Lincoln Luther. BA cum laude, Allegheny Coll., 1960; MA summa cum laude, Rice U., 1964; PhD, Columbia U., 1971. Asst. prof. philosophy Calif. State U., Bakersfield, 1973-77, assoc. prof., 1977-81, prof., 1981—; vis. prof. U. Philippines, Quezon City, 1966-68; grant project dir. Calif. Council Humanities, 1977, project dir. 1980, 82; mem. work group on ethics Am. Colls. of Nursing, Washington, 1984-86. Author: Introduction to Logic, 1978; editor: Humanistic Delivery of Services to Families, 1982, Education for the Handicapped, 1982; mem. editorial bd. Jour. Philosophy in Lit., 1979-84; contbr. articles to profl. jours. Bd. dirs. Bakersfield Mental Health Assn., 1982-84. Mem. N.Y. Acad. Scis., Philosophy of Sci. Assn., Soc. Advancement Am. Phil. soc. (chmn. Pacific div. 1979-83, nat. exec. com. 1974-79), Philosophy Soc., Soc. Interdisciplinary Study of Mind, Am. Philosophical Assn., Dorian Soc., Phi Beta Kappa. Democrat. Lutheran. Home: 7312 Kroll Way Bakersfield CA 93309 Office: Calif State U Dept Philosophy & Religious Studies Bakersfield CA 93309

KEHLMANN, ROBERT, artist, critic; b. Bklyn., Mar. 9, 1942. BA, Antioch Coll., 1963; MA, U. Calif., Berkeley, 1966. One-man shows include: Richmond Art Ctr., Calif., 1976, William Sawyer Gallery, San Francisco, 1978, 82, 86, Galerie M, Kassel, Fed. Republic Germany, 1985, Anne O'Brien Gallery, Washington, 1988; group shows include: Am. Craft Mus., N.Y.C., 1978, 86, Corning (N.Y.) Mus. Glass, 1979, Tucson Mus. of Art, 1983, Kulturhuset, Stockholm, Sweden, 1985; represented in permanent collections at Corning Mus. Glass, Leigh Yawkey Woodson Art Mus., Hessisches Landes Mus., W.Ger., Bank of Am. World Hdqrs., San Francisco, Hokkaido Mus. Modern Art, Sapporo, Japan, Huntington Mus. of Art, W.Va., Am. Craft Mus., N.Y.C., Musée des Arts Décoratifs, Lausanne, Switzerland; instr. glass design Calif. Coll. Arts and Crafts, Oakland, 1978-80, Pilchuck Glass Ctr., Stanwood, Wash., 1978-80; contbg. editor New Glass Work mag.; editor Glass Art Soc. Jour.,1981-84. Nat. Endowment Arts grantee, 1977-78. Mem. Glass Art Soc. (bd. dirs. 1980-84, 89—). Office: William Sawyer Gallery 3045 Clay St San Francisco CA 94115

KEHOE, VINCENT JEFFRÉ-ROUX, photographer, author, cosmetic company executive; b. Bklyn., N.Y., Sept. 12, 1921; s. John James and Bertha Florence (Roux) K.; m. Gena Irene Marino, Nov. 2, 1966. Student, MIT, 1940-41, Lowell Technol. Inst., 1941-42, Boston U., 1942; BFA in Motion Picture and TV Prodn., Columbia U., 1957. Dir. make-up dept. CBS-TV, N.Y.C., 1948-49, NBC Hallmark Hall of Fame series, 1951-53; make-up artist in charge of make-up for numerous film, TV and stage prodns., 1942—; dir. make-up Turner Hall Corp., 1959-61, Internat. Beauty Show, 1962-66; pres., dir. research Research Council of Make-up Artists, Inc., 1963—; chief press officer at Spanish Pavilion, N.Y. World's Fair, 1965; free-lance photographer, 1956—. Contbr. photographs to numerous mags. including Time, Life, Sports Illustrated, Argosy, Popular Photography; author: The Technique of Film and Television Make-up for Color, 1970, The Make-up Artist in the Beauty Salon, 1969, We Were There: April 19, 1775, 1975, The Military Guide, 1975, The Technique of the Professional Makeup Artist, 1985; author-photographer bullfighting books: Aficionado! (N.Y. Art Dirs. Club award 1960), Wine, Women and Toros (N.Y. Art Dirs. award 1962); producer: (documentary color film) Matador de Toros, 1959. Served with inf. U.S. Army, World War II, ETO. Decorated Purple Heart, Bronze Star; recipient Torch award Council of 13 Original States, 1979. Fellow Co. Mil. Historians; mem. Soc. for Preservation of Colonial Culture (curator), Tenth Foot Royal Lincolnshire Regimental Assn. (life; Hon. Col. 1968), Soc. Motion Picture and TV Engrs. (life), Acad. TV Arts and Scis., Soc. for Army Hist. Research (Eng.) (life), Brit. Officers Club New England (life), 10th Mountain Div. Assn., DAV (life), Nat. Rifle Assn. (life). Home and Office: PO Box 850 Somis CA 93066

KEIL, CHARLES CHEUVRONT, III, real estate syndicator, developer; b. Lima, Ohio, Nov. 1, 1944; s. Charles Cheuvront II and Clara Charlotte (Fouts) K.; m. Judith Ann Schott, Sept. 8, 1964 (div. Mar. 1975); m. Nancy Lou Wimmer, Mar. 28, 1981. BS, Ohio State U., 1970. Registered investment advisor, Colo. Salesman ProMed Co., Santa Fe Springs, Calif., 1971-78; pres. Cen. Fin. Planning Keil Cos., Inc., Ft. Collins, Colo., 1978—. Mem. Larimer County Sheriff's Posse, Ft. Collins, 1984-87. With USNG, 1965-71. Republican. Home: 551 Spindrift Ct Fort Collins CO 80525

KEIL, ELLSWORTH CARLYLE, psychologist; b. Thompson, Iowa, Sept. 30, 1930; m. Maureen Jensen Keil, Aug. 30, 1957; children: Jeffrey, Timothy. AB, Luther Coll., 1952; MA, U. Minn., 1956; EdD, Boston U., 1968. Lic. psychologist, Colo. Instr. Iowa State U., Ames, 1956-57, Boston U., 1957-62; asst. dean Tufts U., Medford, Mass., 1962-66; asst. prof. psychology Colo. State U., Ft. Collins, 1966-72; cons. Denver, 1973—. Author: Performance Appraisal, 1978, Assessment Centers, 1982; contbr. articles to profl. jours. Pres. Homeowner's Assn., Denver, 1983—. Served to cpl. U.S. Army, 1952-54. Mem. Am. Psychol. Assn., Colo. Psychol. Assn. Home: 1683 S Uinta Way Denver CO 80231 Office: 3601 S Clarkson St Ste 540 Englewood CO 80110

KEIL, KLAUS, geology educator, consultant; b. Hamburg, Germany, Nov. 15, 1934; s. Walter and Elsbeth K.; m. Rosemarie, Mar. 30, 1961; children: Kathrin R., Mark K.; m. Linde, Jan. 28, 1984. M.S., Schiller U., Jena, Germany, 1958; Ph.D., Gutenberg U., Mainz, Fed. Republic Germany, 1961. Research assoc. Mineral. Inst., Jena, 1958-60, Max Planck-Inst. Chemistry,

Mainz, 1961, U. Calif., San Diego, 1961-63; research scientist Ames Research Center NASA, Moffett Field, Calif., 1964-68; prof. geology, dir. Inst. Meteoritics, U. N.Mex., Albuquerque, 1968—; pres. prof. U. N.Mex., 1985—; chmn. dept. of geology U. N.Mex., Albuquerque, 1986—; cons. Sandia Labs., others. Contbr. over 400 articles to sci. jours. Recipient Apollo Achievement award NASA, 1970; recipient George P. Merrill medal Nat. Acad. Scis., 1970, Exceptional Sci. Achievement medal NASA, 1977, Regents Meritorious Service medal U. N.Mex., 1983, Leonard medal Meteoritical Soc., 1988, Zimmerman award U. N.Mex., 1988, numerous others. Fellow Meteoritical Soc., AAAS, Mineral. Soc. Am.; mem. Am. Geophys. Union, German Mineral. Soc., others. Office: U NMex Dept Geology Albuquerque NM 87131

KEIL, ROBERT ALVIN, operations research analyst; b. Chgo., Sept. 9, 1919; s. Walter Alvin and Della Sophia (Danielson) K.; BS in Bus. (fellowship), U. Richmond, 1941; MA, U. Hawaii, 1963; m. Betsy Tingle Breece, Feb. 21, 1945 (dec.); m. Louise Victoria Wigchert, Apr. 25, 1981. Exec. trainee C & P Telephone Co. of Va., 1941-42; assoc. Planning rsch. Corp., Honolulu, San Diego, 1964-67; ops. rsch. analyst Naval Ocean Systems Ctr., San Diego, 1967-80, scientist, 1980-85, emeritus, 1985-88. Pres., Coronado Residential Assn., 1968-71; chmn. Coronado Planning Commn., 1975, 77, 78, commr., 1972-78. With USN, 1942-64. Mem. U.S. Naval Inst., Rotary, Phi Beta Kappa, Omicron Delta Kappa, Phi Kappa Sigma. Episcopalian. Contbr. tech. research papers. Home: 110 Carob Way Coronado CA 92118

KEILHOLZ, CHERYL ANN, service executive; b. Boston, May 10, 1956; d. Albert Bernard and Maureen Theresa (Mack) Gallant; m. Steven Paul Keilholz, June 28, 1980 (dec. 1986); 1 stepchild, Steven Sean. Cert. completion, U.S. Grant Vocat. Sch., Bethel, Ohio, 1985; cert. completion, Nat. Seminars, Inc., Tucson, 1987. Press operator H.S. Crocker Co., Inc., Cin., 1975-83; supr. Holiday Inn Hotel, Cin., 1984-86; owner, operator Tranquility Foods, Hamersville, Ohio, 1984-85; banquet server, trainer Doubletree Hotels, Tucson, 1986; banquet capt. Hilton Hotel, Tucson, 1986-87; owner, operator Creative Domestics, Tucson, 1988—. Mem. So. Ariz. Hiking Club. Republican. Mem. Christian Ch. Office: 4325 E Grant Rd Tucson AZ 85712

KEIM, EARL GEORGE, real estate consulting; b. Dearborn, Mich., Feb. 26, 1927; s. Earl and Gladys (Bourassa) K.; m. Sharron Tyler,Dec. 24, 1971; children: Musette, Melissa, Susan, Allison, Ruth. BS, U. Mich., 1952. Salesman West Dearborn (Mich.) Realty, 1952-55, sales mgr., 1955-58; owner, mgr. Earl Keim Realty, Dearborn, 1958-84, Keim Group, Southfield, Mich., 1975-84; sr. v.p. Coldwell Banker, Morristown, N.J., 1984-86, Mauna Lani Resort, Inc., Kawaihae, Hawaii, 1986-87; cons. Kawaihae, Hawaii, 1988—; co-founder, 2d chmn. Metro Detroit Coun. Bd. Realtors. Chmn. Dearborn YMCA, 1969; active Centurions, Dearborn, 1972-84. Mem. Nat. Assn. Realtors (bd. dirs.), Mich. Assn. Realtors (pres. 1972), Kona Bd. Realtors. Republican. Methodist. Home: Mauna Lani Terr C302 Kawaihae HI 96743

KEIM, MICHAEL RAY, dentist; b. Sabetha, Kans., June 8, 1951; s. Milton Leroy and Dorothy Juanita (Stover) K.; m. Christine Anne Lorenzen, Nov. 20, 1971; children: Michael Scott, Dawn Marie, Erik Alan. Student, U. Utah, 1969-72; DDS, Creighton U., 1976. Pvt. practice Casper, Wyo., 1976—. Organizing bd. dirs. Cen. Wyo. Soccer Assn., 1976-77; mem. Casper Mountain Ski Patrol Nat. Ski Patrol System, 1980—; bd. dirs. and dep. commr. for fast pitch Wyo. Amateur Softball Assn., 1980-84; bd. dirs. Cen. Wyo. Softball Assn., 1980-84. Mem. ADA, Fedn. Dentaire Internat., Wyo. Acad. Gen. Dentistry (sec.-treas. 1980-82, pres. 1982-87), Wyo. Dental Assn., Wyo. Dental Polit. Action Com. (sec.-treas. 1985—), Cen. Wyo. Dental Assn. (sec.-treas. 1981-82, pres. 1982-83), Wyo. Dental Hist. Assn. (bd. dirs. 1989—), Kiwanis (v.p. Casper club 1988-89, bd. dirs. 1986—, pres.-elect 1989—, internat. del. 1989), Creighton Club (pres. 1982-84). Methodist. Home: 58 Jonquil Casper WY 82604 Office: 1749 S Boxelder Casper WY 82604

KEIM, PAUL FERDINAND, civil engineer, educator; b. Falls City, Nebr., Apr. 22, 1902; s. Will Seward and Fernande Rose (Godfirnon) K.; m. Marjorie Little, Dec. 31, 1927 (dec. Dec. 1982); children: Seward Russell (dec.), Charles Bruce. BSc, U. Calif., Berkeley, 1925; MSc in C.E., U. Nebr., 1932. Registered profl. engr., Calif., Oreg., Wash. Engr. contracting co., Los Angeles, 1925-26; instr. civil engring. U. Nebr., 1926-32; cons. Platte Valley Pub. Power and Irrigation Dist. Nebr., 1933-36, Calif. Hwy. div., Marysville, 1936-37; hydraulic engr. Los Angeles County Flood Control Dist., 1937-39; prin. engr. FPC, Washington, 1939-41, 46; pub. works officer, damage control officer Midway Islands, 1942; pub. works and constrn. officer Whidbey Island Naval Air Sta., 1943; staff civil engring. officer 13th Naval dist. Naval Air Command, 1944-46; mem. res. 1946—; cons. transp. and water supply U.S. Dept. State Econ. Mission to Liberia, 1947-48; assoc. Tippets, Abbett, McCarthy, Stratton, Engrs., N.Y.C., 1948-52; ops. Greece, Turkey, Alaksa, throughout U.S., 1948-52; prof. civil engring. U. Calif., Berkeley, 1952-69, prof. emeritus, 1970—; on leave cons. ports Taiwan, 1957; adv. to dir. U.S. Ops. Mission Egypt, tchr. U. Cairo Grad. Sch., 1959-61; cons. Calif. Joint Senate-House com. Water Resources, various times, 1952-59; chief staff civil engr. Ralph M. Parsons Co., Pasadena, Calif., Peru, Greece, Argentina, Mex., Tunisia, Morocco, 1968-71; cons. Internat. Exec. Service Corps, N.Y.C.; port cons., Taiwan, 1975; OAS cons., Brazil, 1971; FMC cons., Rumania, 1972. Contbr. articles to profl. jours. Recipient citation for disting. profl. conduct during Battle of Midway, 1942. Mem. ASCE (permanent del. to Los Angeles Council Engring. and Sci., mem. profl. practice com. 1984-89, continuing cons. and expert witness Los Angeles cts., 1984-88), Los Angeles Council Engrs. and Scientists (pres. 1979-81), Inst. Advancement Engring. (pres.-elect 1981, emeritus dir. 1983-84, award of merit 1982), Am. Soc. Engring. Edn., Nat. Reclamation Assn., Am. Geophys. Union, Soc. Mil. Engrs., Chi Epsilon, Tau Beta Pi. Clubs: Town Hall of Calif., Los Angeles Breakfast. Lodge: Lions. Address: 4552 Fountain Ave Apt 2 Los Angeles CA 90029

KEIRN, RICHARD DUANE, communications company executive; b. Blackwell, Okla., Jan. 7, 1944; s. William Julius and Doris Avanelle (Young) K.; m. Hue Thi Danh, Sept. 22, 1973. BS, Pacific Western U., 1987. Supr. U.S. Army Engrs., 1961-81; material specialist Todd Pacific Shipyards, L.A., 1981-87; asst. mgr. Ken Cranes, Hawthorne, Calif., 1988; supr. Standard Communications Corp., Carson, Calif., 1988—. Lt. col. State Mil. Forces Calif. State Mil. Dep. NG Res., 1982—. Recipient Gill Robb Wilson award CAP, Maxwell AFB, Ala., 1984. Mem. Soc. Logistical Engrs., Am. Prodn. and Inventory Control Soc., Mil. Order of Purple Heart, VFW, State Def. Force Assn. U.S., Nat. Guard Assn., British-U.S. Club (Glendale, Calif.), Masons (sr. deacon 1987-88). Democrat. Methodist. Home: 2404 Cabrillo Ave Apt C San Pedro CA 90731 Office: Standard Communications Corp PO Box 92151 Los Angeles CA 90009-2151

KEITH, BRUCE EDGAR, political analyst, genealogist; b. Curtis, Nebr., Feb. 17, 1918; s. Edgar L. and Corinne E. (Marsteller) K.; m. Evelyn E. Johnston, Oct. 29, 1944; children—Mona Louise, Kent Marsteller, Melanie Ann. A.B. with high distinction, Nebr. Wesleyan U., 1940; M.A., Stanford U., 1952; grad. Command and Staff, Marine Corps Schs., 1958, Sr. Resident Sch., Naval War Coll., 1962; Ph.D., U. Calif.-Berkeley, 1982. Commd. 2d lt. U.S. Marine Corps, 1942, advanced through grades to col., 1962, ret., 1971, comdg. officer 3d Bn., 11th Marines, 1958-59, ops. officer, Pres. Dwight D. Eisenhower visit to Okinawa, 1960, G-3 ops. officer Fleet Marine Force, Pacific, Cuban Missile Crisis, 1962, mem. U.S. del. SEATO, Planning Conf., Bangkok, Thailand, 1964, G-3, Fleet Marine Force, Pacific, 1964-65, head Strategic Planning Study Dept., Naval War Coll., 1966-68, genealogist, 1967—, exec. officer Hdqrs. Marine Corps programs, Washington, 1968-71; election analyst Inst. Govtl. Studies, U. Calif.-Berkeley, 1974-86, polit. analyst, 1986—; teaching asst. U. Calif.-Berkeley, 1973-74. Bd. dirs., Bay Area Funeral Soc., 1980-83, v.p., 1981-83. Decorated Bronze Star, Navy Commendation medal, Presdl. Unit citation with 3 bronze stars. Recipient Phi Kappa Phi Silver medal Nebr. Wesleyan U., 1940, Alumni award, 1964. Mem. Am. Polit. Sci. Assn., Acad. Polit. Sci., Am. Acad. Polit. and Social Sci., Marine Corps Assn., Ret. Officers Assn. Phi Kappa Phi, Pi Gamma Mu. Republican. Unitarian. Clubs: Commonwealth of Calif. (San Francisco), Marines' Meml. (San Francisco). Lodge: Masons. Contbg. author: The Descendants of Daniel and Elizabeth (Disbrow) Keith, 1979-81; History of Curtis, Nebraska-The First Hundred Years, 1984; author: A Comparison of the House Armed Services Coms. in the 91st and 94th Congresses: How They Differed and Why, 1982; The Johnstons of Morning Sun, 1979; The Marstellers of Arrellton, 1978; The Morris Family of Brookville, 1977; Japan-the Key to America's Future in the Far East, 1962; A United States General Staff: A Must or a Monster?, 1950; co-author: California Votes, 1960-72, 1974; The Myth of the Independent Voter, 1977; Further Evidence on the Partisan Affinities of Independent " Leaners" , 1983. Address: PO Box 156 El Cerrito CA 94530

KEITH, DAVID, symphony orchestra conductor; b. Tacoma, Oct. 9, 1930; s. David and Barbara (Ferry) K.; m. Ginni Paynton, July 5, 1972. Student, San Francisco Conservatory of Music, 1948-50; studied with, Dr. Stanley Chapple, U. Wash., 1968-72. Assoc. conductor Bellevue (Wash.) Philharm. Orch., 1968-70; conductor, music dir. Seattle Concert Orch., 1970-73; founder, conductor, dir. Los Angeles Mozart Orch., 1974—, also trustee, 1974—. Mem. Musicians' Union.

KEITH, DONALD BUEL, military flight instructor, protective services official; b. Houston, Jan. 4, 1943; s. Albert Buel and Helen (Koehn) K.; m. Linda Ashford, May 6, 1967 (div. Apr. 7, 1988); children: Donald Lee, John David. BA in Psychology, St. Martins Coll., Olympia, Wash., 1975; MPA in Mgmt., Golden Gate U., 1988. Patrolman Tex. Dept. Pub. Safety, Austin, 1964-71; flight instr. U.S. Army, Ft. Lewis, Wash., 1972-76, Korea, 1976-77, Ft. Polk, La., 1977-80, Panama, 1980-83, Ft. Polk, 1983-87, Ft. Irwin, Calif., 987—. Transp. coordinator Silver Valley High Sch. Booster Club, Ft. Irwin. Served with USMC, 1961-64. Mem. Army Aviation Assn, Tex. Sheriffs Assn. Republican. Presbyn. Home: 13 Little Big Horn Fort Irwin CA 92310 Office: US Army D Co 177 FSB Fort Irwin CA 92310

KEITH, GORDON, publisher; b. Kent, Wash., Aug. 27, 1913; s. John Albert and Grace (Calkins) K.; student San Jose State Coll., 1938-39, U. Calif. at Oakland, 1940; m. Barbara Louise Henson, Sept. 4, 1953 (div. Apr. 1979); 1 dau., Michelle Louise. Operator several small chain dance schs. No. Calif., 1933-42; free lance writer, 1945-50; pub., editor Dance Digest, 1951-62; pub., printer Personnel Improvement Booklets, also specialized greeting cards, note paper, San Jose, Calif., 1962—; feature writer Island Sounder newspaper, San Juan, 1971—; mng. editor Pub. Forum of San Juan County, 1983—. Served with AUS, 1942-45. Mem. Dance Masters Am. (past pres. Calif., dir.). Lion (sec. 1972). Author: (booklets) A Special 48-State Survey on Examining and Licensing of Dance Teachers in America, 1958; Why You Should Belong to an Accredited Dance Teachers' Organization, 1958; Private Dance Schools vs. Recreation Departments, 1960; (books) (with Roderic Marble Olzendam) Liberty's Grandson, An Unconventional Autobiography, 1977, It Came to Pass in the San Juan Islands, 1978; Green Gold for America, 1981; Voices from the Islands, 1982; The Ferryboat Islands: A Practical Guide to Washington State's San Juan Islands, 1989. compiler, editor The James Francis Tulloch Diary 1875-1910, 1978. Home and Office: PO Box 280 Eastsound Orcas Island WA 98245

KEITH, KENT MARSTELLER, corporate executive, lawyer; b. N.Y.C., May 22, 1948; s. Bruce Edgar and Evelyn E. (Johnston) K.; m. Elizabeth Misao Carlson, Aug. 22, 1976. BA in Govt., Harvard U., 1970; BA in Politics and Philosophy, Oxford U., Eng., 1972, MA, 1977; JD, U. Hawaii, 1977. Bar: Hawaii 1977, D.C. 1979. Assoc. Cades, Schutte, Fleming & Wright, Honolulu, 1977-79; coordinator Hawaii Dept. Planning and Econ. Devel., Honolulu, 1979-81, dep. dir., 1981-83, dir., 1983-86; energy resources coordinator State of Hawaii, Honolulu, 1983-86, chmn. State Policy Council, 1983-86; chmn. Aloha Tower Devel. Corp., 1983-86; project mgr. Mililani Tech. Park Oceanic Properties Inc. 1986-88, v.p. pub. relations and bus. devel., 1988-89, pres. Chaminade U. Honolulu, 1989—. Author: Hawaii: Looking Back from the Year 2050, 1987; contbr. articles on ocean law to law jours. Pres. Manoa Valley Ch., Honolulu, 1976-78; mem. platform com., Hawaii Dem. Conv., 1982, 84, 86; trustee Hawaii Loa Coll., 1986—, vice chmn. 1987—. Rhodes scholar, 1970; named one of 10 Outstanding Young Men of Am., U.S. Jaycees, 1984. Mem. Am. Assn. Rhodes Scholars, Internat. House of Japan, Nature Conservancy. Clubs: Plaza, Harvard of Hawaii (Honolulu) (bd. dirs. 1974-78, sec. 1974-76). Home: 2626 Hillside Ave Honolulu HI 96822 Office: Chamirade U Honolulu 3140 Waialae Ave Honolulu HI 96816-1578

KEITH, NORMAN THOMAS, engineering company administrator, management specialist; b. Antioch, Calif., Jan. 12, 1936; s. Dean Theodore and Edna Margaret (Doty) K.; m. Marla Mildred Osten, Sept. 9, 1962. B of Tech., Tex. State Tech. Inst. Cert. profl. mgr. Field service engr. Gen. Dynamics Corp., San Diego, 1955-66, supr. Data Ctr., 1966-76, chief data systems, 1976-81, chief property adminstrn., 1981-83, motivational mgr., 1983-86, program adminstr., 1986—. Contbr. articles to profl. jours. Mem. mil. adv. bd. congressman Ron Packard, 1983-86; sgt. Res. Dep. Sheriff's Office, San Diego County; bd. dirs. San Dieguito Boys/Girls Clubs, Encinitas, 1966-69; loaned exec. United Way, San Diego, 1980-81. Mem. Nat. Mgmt. Assn. (bd. dirs., pres.), Nat. U. Alumni Assn. (life), Woodbury Coll. Alumni Assn., San Diego State U. Alumni Assn., Hon. Dep. Sheriff's Assn. (bd. dirs.). Republican. Lutheran. Lodges: Lions (sec. 1962-63), Elks. Home: 620 E St Encinitas CA 92024 Office: Gen Dynamics Convair Div 5001 Kearny Villa Rd San Diego CA 92138

KEITH, PAULINE MARY, artist, illustrator, writer; b. Fairfield, Nebr., July 21, 1924; d. Siebelt Ralph and Pauline Alethia (Garrison) Goldenstein; m. Everett B. Keith, Feb. 14, 1957; 1 child, Nathan Ralph. Student, George Fox Coll., 1947-48, Oreg. State U., 1955. Illustrator Merlin Press, San Jose, Calif., 1980-81; artist, illustrator, watercolorist Corvallis, Oreg., 1980—. Author 5 chapbooks, 1980-85; editor: Four Generations of Verse, 1979; illustrator Sagebrush Girl, 1981; contbr. poetry to anthologies and mags.; one-woman show Roger's Meml. Library, Forest Grove, Oreg., 1959, Corvallis Art Ctr., 1960, Human Resources Bldg., Corvallis, 1976; exhibited in group shows Nolan's Dept. Store, Corvallis, 1959-61, Hewlett-Packard Co., Corvallis, 1984, 85. Co-elder First Christian Ch. (Disciples of Christ), Corvallis, 1988-89, co-deacon, 1980-83; sec. Chintimmini Sr. Ctr., Corvallis, 1987, pres. Hostess Club, 1988-89. Recipient lst prize Benton County Fair, 1982, 83, 3d prize, 1984, 2d prize, 1987. Mem. Oreg. Assn. Christian Writers, Internat. Assn. Women Mins., Linn-Benton Diabetes Assn., Am. Legion Aux., Corvallis Art Guild, Chintimmini Artists, Chintimmini Writers. Republican. Office: PO Box 825 Corvallis OR 97339

KEITH, ROBERT ALLEN, psychology educator; b. Brea, Calif., Mar. 16, 1924; s. Albert Henry Keith and Delphene Ruth (Morgan) Parker;m. Nanette Hardesty, Sept. 1, 1949; children: Leslie Susan Keith Berclaz, Claudia Lynn Keith Lorenzana. BA, U. Calif., L.A., 1948, MA, 1951, PhD, 1953. Lic. psychologist, Calif.; diplomate in clin. psychology. Clin. psychology intern L.A. Psychiat. Svcs., 1950-53; dir. counseling svcs. Claremont (Calif.) Coll., 1953-59; from asst. to assoc. prof. psychology Claremont Grad. Sch., 1953—; bd. dirs. rsch. div. Casa Colina Hosp., Pomona, Calif., 1968--. Contbr. articles related to med. rehab. to profl. jours. Lt. USNR, 1943-46, PTO. Harvard U. fellow, 1960-61; Rehab. Psychol. fellow, 1984, World Rehab. Fund of London fellow, 1987. Fellow Am. Psych. Assn., Am. Assn. U. Profs., Am. Congress Rehab. Medicine, Assn. for Health Svcs. Rsch., Am. Pub. Health Assn.

KELEN, JOYCE ARLENE, social worker; b. N.Y.C., Dec. 5, 1949; d. Samuel and Rebecca (Rothman) Green; m. Leslie George Kelen, Jan. 31, 1971; children: David, Jonathan. BA, Lehman Coll., 1970; MSW, Univ. Utah, 1974, DSW, 1980. Recreation dir. N.Y.C. Housing Authority, Bronx, 1970-72; cottage supr. Kennedy Home, Bronx, 1974; sch. social worker Davis County Sch. Dist., Farmington, Utah, 1976-86; clin. asst. prof. U. Utah., Salt Lake City, 1976—; sch. social worker Salt Lake City Sch. Dist., 1986—; cons. in field, Salt Lake City, 1981—. Editor: To Whom Are We Beautiful As We Go?, 1979; contbr. articles to profl. jours. Utah Coll. of Nursing grantee, 1985. Mem. Nat. Assn. Social Workers (chairperson Gerontology Council, 1983-84, Utah Sch. Social Worker of Yr., 1977), NEA, Utah Edn. Assn., Davis Edn. Assn. Democrat. Jewish. Home: 128 M St Salt Lake City UT 84103 Office: Franklin Elem Sch 1100 W 400 S Salt Lake City UT 84104

KELESIS, ANGELA MICHELE, real estate broker; b. San Francisco, Feb. 7, 1960; d. Jesse Garland and Jenny Angela (Mikulewicz) Touhey; m. George Peter Kelesis, Nov. 7, 1982. Student in engring., U. Nev., 1983-85. Exec. sec. Calif. Cen. Bank, San Francisco, 1978-79, graphics asst., 1979-81, money market trader, 1981-82; comml. real estate broker Jack Matthews & Co., Las Vegas, Nev., 1985—. Contbr. articles to realtor publs. Mem. Las Vegas Allied Arts Coun., 1986—. Mem. Nat. Coun. Exchangers, Soc. Las Vegas Exchangers (pres.-elect 1987—), Las Vegas Bd. Realtors (chairwoman comml. investment div. 1987—), Soc. Cert. Comml. Investment Mems. (bd. dirs. So. Nev. chpt. 1988—). Republican. Greek Orthodox. Office: Jack Matthews & Co 3120 S Valley View Las Vegas NV 89101

KELL, ERNEST EUGENE, JR., mayor, contractor; b. N.D., July 5, 1928; s. Ernest Eugene and Katherine (Moynier) K.; m. Jacqueline; children: Julie, Brian. Owner, operator Western Detailing Service, Inc., Anaheim, Calif., 1955-71; gen. contractor Long Beach, Calif., 1971—; councilman 5th dist. City Long Beach, Calif., 1975—, mayor, 1984—. Commr. Los Angeles County Transp. Commn., 1982-84; trustee Mosquito Abatement Dist., Los Angeles County, 1977—; chmn. Californians for Consumers No-Fault. Mem. Calif. Steel Detailers Assn. (pres.). League of Calif. Cities. Democrat. Lodge: Lions. Home: 3471 Marna Ave Long Beach CA 90808 Office: City of Long Beach 333 W Ocean Blvd Long Beach CA 90802 *

KELLEHER, JOHN, foundation administrator; b. L.A., July 21, 1949; s. James Thomas and Mary Louise (Murphy) K.; m. Cathy Sue Perry, Dec. 22, 1978 (div. July 1987); 1 child, Kevin Todd. AA, Glendale Community Coll., 1970; BA in Polit. Sci., Calif. State U., L.A., 1971. Council aide City of Los Angeles, 1977-81; dir. youth activities First Christian Ch. of No. Hollywood, Calif., 1981-82; dir. L.A. area ALSAC/St. Jude Children's Rsch. Hosp., L.A., 1982-84; exec. dir. devel. Holy Cross Med. Ctr., Mission Hills, Calif., 1984-89. Mem. spl. task force Am. Cancer Soc., 1987—; mem. steering com., superwalk March of Dimes, 1977-79; active Jaycees; bd. dirs., fund raising adv. com. John Rossi Youth Found. Served with USMC, 1970. Named one of Outstanding Young Men Am., 1975-85; recipient numerous civic awards. Mem. Glendale Community Coll. Alumni Assn., NRA, Nat. Soc. Fund Raising Execs. (cert.), So. Calif. Assn. Hosp. Devel., Nat. Assn. Hosp. Devel. (cert.), Calif. Notary Public, KC, Optimist, Greater Van Nuys C. of C., Canyon Country C. of C., Kiwanis, Century Club. Home: 15240 Lotusgarden Dr Canyon Country CA 91351

KELLEHER, ROBERT JOSEPH, judge; b. N.Y.C., Mar. 5, 1913; s. Frank and Mary (Donovan) K.; m. Gracyn W. Wheeler, Aug. 14, 1940; children: R. Jeffrey, Karen Kathleen. A.B., Williams Coll., 1935; LL.B., Harvard U., 1938. Bar: N.Y. 1939, Calif. 1942, U.S. Supreme Ct 1954. Atty. War Dept., 1941-43; Asst. U.S. atty. So. Dist. Calif., 1948-50; pvt. practice Beverly Hills, 1951-71; U.S. dist. judge 1971—. Mem. So. Calif. Com. Olympic Games, 1964; capt. U.S. Davis Cup Team, 1962-63; treas. Youth Tennis Found. So. Calif., 1961-64. Served to lt. USNR, 1942-45. Mem. So. Calif. Tennis Assn. (v.p. 1958-64, pres. 1983-85), U.S. Lawn Tennis Assn. (pres. 1967-68), Delta Kappa Epsilon, Harvard of So. Calif., Williams (N.Y.C.). Clubs: All Eng. Lawn Tennis and Croquet (Wimbeldon); Internat. Lawn Tennis of USA; Internat. Lawn Tennis of Gt. Britain; Internat. Lawn Tennis of France; Internat. Lawn Tennis of Can.; Internat. Lawn Tennis of Mex.; Internat. Lawn Tennis of Australia; Internat. Lawn Tennis of India; Internat. Lawn Tennis of Israel; Los Angeles Country; Harvard (New York). Home: 15 St Malo Oceanside CA 92054 Office: US Dist Ct 312 N Spring St Los Angeles CA 90012

KELLEHER, ROBERT NEAL, chemist, chemical engineer; b. Teaneck, N.J., June 26, 1943; s. Vincent J. and Gladys A. (Storms) K.; m. Sandra A. Martin, Dec. 27, 1969 (div. Jan. 1986); children: Scott V., Kristen A. Student, Grove City Coll., 1961-62, Fairleigh Dickenson U., 1962-64; BSChemE, U. Eastern Fla., 1965; cert. pharmacist, USAF Med. Coll., 1966; cert. bus. mgmt., Rutgers U., 1971-72; cert. indsl. safety and hygeine, U. N.C., 1976. Chief control chemist Washine-Intex Chem., Lodi, N.J., 1962-64; asst. city chemist City of Ft. Lauderdale, Fla., 1965; asst. research and devel. chemist Amerace-Esna Corp., Tenafly, N.J., 1965-66, 67-68, terminal supr., 1968-69; ops. coordinator Jefferson Chem. Co., N.Y.C., 1969-71; gen. mgr. Ajax Chem. div. Biscayne Chem. Corp., Miami, Fla., 1971-79; v.p./mgr. Trojan Chem., Newbury Park, Calif., 1979-81; mgr. west coast ops. Cyclo Chem., Los Angeles, 1981-84; plant mgr. Chemron Corp., Paso Robles, Calif., 1984-85; pres., chief exec. officer Clean-Agri Fruit Chemicals, Inc. div. R&D Enterprises, Tulare, Calif., 1985—; chem. and engring. cons. R&D Enterprises, Lindsay, 1984—. Patentee in field. Bd. youth advisor Melrose Park Meth. Ch., Ft. Lauderdale, 1965; pres. coll. youth fellowship Good Shepard Meth. Ch., Bergenfield, N.J., 1964-65; co-chmn. PTO Valle Lindo Sch. Camarillo, Calif., 1980-82; div. dir. Am. Youth Soccer, Camarillo, 1982-84. Served with USAF, 1966-67. Mem. Pa. Soc. Profl. Engrs., Am. Chem. Soc., AAAS, Am. Inst. Plant Engrs., Chem. Week Adv. Panel. Republican. Home: PO Box 2011 Tulare CA 93274-2011 Office: Clean Agrl Fruit Chems PO Box 2011 Tulare CA 93275

KELLER, ARTHUR MICHAEL, computer science educator; b. N.Y.C., Jan. 14, 1957; s. David and Luba K. BS summa cum laude, Bklyn. Coll., 1977; MS, Stanford U., 1979, PhD, 1985. Instr. computer sci. Stanford (Calif.) U., 1979-81, rsch. asst., 1977-85, acting asst. chmn. dept. computer sci., 1982, rsch. assoc., 1985, vis. asst. prof., 1987—; systems analyst Bklyn. Coll. Computer Ctr., 1974-77; summer rsch. asst. IBM, Thomas J. Watson Rsch. Ctr., Yorktown Heights, N.Y., 1980; acad. assoc. San Jose Rsch. Lab., 1981; asst. prof. U. Tex., Austin, 1985-87, adjunct asst. prof., 1987—; mem. program com. Internat. Conf. on Data Engring., L.A., 1986, 87, 89, Internat. Conf. on Very Large Data Bases, Amsterdam, The Netherlands, 1989. Author: A First Course in Computer Programming Using Pascal, 1982. Mem. IEEE, (vice-chmn. com. database engring. computer soc. 1986-87), Assn. Computing Machinery, T&X Users Group (fin. com. 1983-85, internat. coord. 1985-87), Chai Soc. (communications officer 1987-89, v.p. publicity 1989—). Home: 3881 Corina Way Palo Alto CA 94303-4507 Office: Stanford U Dept Computer Sci Stanford CA 94305-2140

KELLER, GEORGE HENRIK, marine geologist; b. Hartford, Conn., Sept. 9, 1931; s. George and Eva (Damschneider) K.; m. Suzanne Bray, Sept. 10, 1955; children: Mark, Lauri. AB, U. Conn., 1954; MS, U. Utah, 1956; PhD, U. Ill., 1966. Marine geologist USN, Washington, 1959-64; dir. marine G&G Lab. NOAA-AOML, Miami, Fla., 1966-75; assoc. dean oceanography Oreg. State U., Corvallis, 1975-82; rep. Oreg. State U. Univ. Corp. Atmospheric Rsch., Boulder, Colo., 1982—; acting dean oceanography Oreg. State U., Corvallis, 1978-80, acting dean research, 1981-82,, dean research, 1982-84, 1984-87, v.p. rsch., grad. studies, internat. programs, 1987—; bd. dirs. Nat. Assoc. State Univs. and Land Grant Colls. Marine div., Washington, 1984-86, Oreg. Resource and Tech. Devel. Corp., 1986—; council mem. Ctr. for Research Libraries, Chgo., 1984—. Editorial bd. mem. Marine Geotechnology, 1974—; vice chair consortium for internat. devel., 1988—; contbr. articles to profl. jours. Recipient C.A. Hogentoler award ASCE. Fellow Geol. Soc. Am.; mem. AAAS, Am. Geophys. Union, Internat. Sedimentol. Soc., Soc. Sigma Xi. Home: 3360 NW Witham Hill Dr Corvallis OR 97330 Office: Oreg State U Rsch Office Corvallis OR 97331

KELLER, GEORGE MATTHEW, oil company executive; b. Kansas City, Mo., Dec. 3, 1923; s. George Matthew and Edna Louise (Mathews) K.; m. Adelaide McCague, Dec. 27, 1946; children: William G., Robert A., Barry R. BS in Chem. Engring., MIT, 1948. Engr. Standard Oil Calif. (now Chevron Corp.), San Francisco, 1948-63, fgn. ops. staff, 1963-67, asst. v.p., asst. to pres., 1967-69, v.p., 1969-74, dir., 1970—, vice-chmn., 1974-81, chmn., chief exec. officer, 1981-88; bd. dirs. First Interstate Bancorp., First Interstate Bank Calif., Boeing Co., McKesson Corp., SRI Internat., Met. Life Ins. Co. Trustee Notre Dame Coll., Belmont, Calif. Served to 1st lt. USAAF, 1943-46. Mem. Bus. Council, Trilateral Commn., Coun. Fgn. Rels. Office: Chevron Corp 555 Market St San Francisco CA 94105

KELLER, J(AMES) WESLEY, credit union executive; b. Jonesboro, Ark., Jan. 6, 1958; s. Norman Grady and Norma Lee (Ridgeway) Patrick; m. Patricia Maria Delavan, July 7, 1979. Student, U. Miss., 1976-78, Redlands (Calif.) U. Sr. collector Rodkwell Fed. Credit Union, Downey, Calif., 1978-79; acct. Lucky Fed. Credit Union, Buena Park, Calif., 1979-84; pres., chief exec. officer Long Beach (Calif.) State Employees Credit Union, 1984—. Mem. Credit Union Exec. Soc., Calif. Credit Union League (bd. govs. Long Beach chpt., treas. 1985-86), So. Calif. Credit Union Mgr.s Assn. Republican. Baptist. Home: 1261 Cambridge La Habra CA 90631 Office: Long

Beach State Employees Credit Union 150 W Wardlow Rd Long Beach CA 90807

KELLER, KENNETH JOHN, PHD., psychologist, consultant; b. Portland, Oreg., Oct. 23, 1950; s. Karl William and Gerda (Menke) K. BS in Psychology, U. Oreg., 1979; PhD. in Psychology, Calif. Sch. Profl. Psychology, San Diego, 1986. Lic. clinical psychologist. Psychology Assoc. Weinberger Hall & Assocs., Houston, 1986-87; psychologist Fresno County Dept. of Health, Fresno, Calif., 1987-88; psychologist/program Coordinator Portland Adventist Med. Ctr., Portland, Oreg., 1988-89; psychologist Pvt. Practice, Portland, 1988—, United Behavioral Clinics, Portland, 1989—; Cert. trainer Suicide Intervention and Prevention Workshops, various locations, 1987—. Mem. Am. Psychological Assn. Democrat. Lutheran. Office: Kenneth John Keller PhD 10163 S E Sunnyside Rd Ste 495 Clackauras OR 97015

KELLER, L(YNN) ROBIN, management educator; b. Pasadena, Calif., Oct. 25, 1952; d. Robert Phillips and Colleen Ann (Putnam) K.; m. Henry Mark McMillan, Oct. 11,1987. BA, UCLA, 1974, MBA, 1976, PhD, 1982. Asst. prof. Grad. Sch. Mgmt. U. Calif.-Irvine, 1982--, dir. doctoral program in mgmt., 1985-86, asst. prof. Sch. Social Scis., 1987--; vis. asst. rsch. prof. Fuqua Sch. Bus., Duke U., Durham, N.C., 1987. Contbr. articles to profl. jours. Program dir. UniCamp, 1982; assoc. dir. mgmt. sci. program Nat. Sci. Found's. Decision. Mem. Ops. Rsch. Soc. Am. (steering com. Orange County joint chpt. 1982-83; paper competition chmn. decision analysis spl. interest group 1986-87, coun. 1986—), Inst. Mgmt. Scis. (chmn. conf. employment 1986), Inst. Mgmt. Scis., Beta Gamma Sigma, Alpha Phi (v.p. South Orange County chpt. 1985-86, adviser Eta Kappa chpt. 1988—). Office: U Calif Grad Sch Mgmt Irvine CA 92717

KELLER, MARVIN ANTHONY, geologist; b. Seward, Kans., May 14, 1931; s. Charles L. and Lucile M. (Duddy) K.; m. Jerene Helen Fleck, July 16, 1960; children: Constance L., Margaret J., Denise A. BS in Geology, U. Kans., 1956; MA in Geology, U. Wyo., 1958. Geologist Conoco, Inc., Durango, Colo., 1958-67, Ventura, Calif., 1967-68; sr. geologist Superior Oil Co., Casper, Wyo., 1968-69; exec. v.p. Rainbow Resources Inc., Casper, 1969-79; free lance geologist Casper, 1979—; bd. dirs. Mustang Cos., Great Bend, Kans., Wyo. Nat. Bank, Casper. Bd. dirs. Casper YMCA, 1982-84; mem. Wyo. Oil and Gas Commn., Casper, 1984-88. Mem. Am. Assn. Petroleum Geologists, Wyo. Petroleum Assn. (treas. 1986-89, award 1972), Rocky Mountain Oil and Gas Assn. (asst. sec.-treas. 1988—), Casper Country Club. Republican. Roman Catholic.

KELLER, ROBERT SCOTT, writer; b. Portland, Oreg., June 5, 1945; s. Stuart Robert and Royce Myrtle (Latham) K.; m. Tana Nancy Thiele, Dec. 15, 1986; 1 child, Aaron Charles. BA in Molecular Biology, Harvard U., 1967. Tchr. Peace Corps, Monrovia, Liberia, 1967-69, Washington Pub. Sch., 1970-71; musician various orgns., Washington, 1971-80, Eugene, Oreg., 1971-80; tchr. Willamette Sci. & Tech. Ctr., Eugene, 1981-82; editor Home Computer Mag., Eugene, 1983-86, Programmer's Jour., Eugene, 1986-87; pres. Spirit Software, Eugene, 1988—. Contbr. articles profl. jours.; author software. NSF grantee, 1966. Home: 2920 Jefferson Eugene OR 97405 Office: Spirit Software 357 E 15th Eugene OR 97401

KELLER, SUSAN AGNES, insurance officer; b. Moline, Ill., July 12, 1952; d. Kenneth Francis and Ethel Louise (Odendahl) Hulsbrink; m. Kevin Eugene Keller, June 20, 1981; 1 child, Dawn Marie. Grad. in Pub. Relations, Patricia Stevens Career Coll., 1971; grad. in Gen. Ins., Ins. Inst. Am., 1986. CPCU. Comml. lines rater Bitiminous Casualty Corp., Rock Island, Ill., 1973-78; with Roadway Express, Inc., Rock Island, 1978-81; front line supr. Yellow Freight System, Inc., Denver, 1982-83; supr. plumbing and sheet metal prodn. Bell Plumbing and Heating, Denver, 1983-84; underwriter Golden Eagle Ins. Co., San Diego, 1985—; cons. real estate foreclosure County Records Service, San Diego, 1986—. Vol. DAV, San Diego, 1985—. Mem. Soc. Chartered Property and Casualty Underwriters, Profl. Women in Ins., Nat. Assn. Female Execs. Roman Catholic. Home: 449 Jamul Ct Chula Vista CA 92001 Office: Golden Eagle Ins Co 7175 Navajo Rd San Diego CA 92119

KELLERMAN, FAYE MARDER, novelist, dentist; b. St. Louis, July 31, 1952; d. Oscar and Anne (Steinberg) Marder; m. Jonathan Seth Kellerman, July 23, 1972; children: Jesse Oren, Rachel Diana, Ilana Judith. AB in Math, UCLA, 1974, DDS, 1978. Author: The Ritual Bath, 1986 (Macavity award best 1st novel 1986), Sacred & Profane, 1987, The Quality of Mercy, 1989. UCLA rsch. fellow, 1978. Mem. Mystery Writers of Am., Womens' Israeli Polit. Action Com., Sisters in Crime. Jewish.

KELLEY, BRIDGET ANN (NAOMI V.), artist; b. Hemet, Calif., May 25, 1955; d. David Gerald and Brigitte Marie (Frey) K.; m. A. Thomas Stoeckl, Oct. 5, 1976 (div. Aug. 1982); children: Tarja, Samuel. AA, Balin Inst. Tech., 1986; BA in Music, Mills Coll., 1988. Freelance artist Freiburg, Fed. Republic Germany, 1976-83; archtl. designer James Calkins AIA, Hemet, 1987, Rudd Gast A.R.A., Alameda, Calif., 1987—. Recipient Diplom D'Honneur, Salon Internat. De Bourgogne Et Franche-Comte, 1978, Gold medal Vanvitelli Assn., 1978, Diplom De Selection Palme D'Or Des Beaux-aArts, 1977. Home: 44381 Bautista Canyon Rd Hemet CA 92344

KELLEY, GREGORY MICHAEL, high vacuum technologist; b. Boston, Nov. 18, 1933; s. Bernard Thomas and Anne (Sweeney) K.; m. Ann Marshall Price, 1962 (div. 1975); children: Gregory, Michael; m. Sandra Dee Kachelhoffer, Aug. 16, 1975. AS in Engring., Wentworth Inst., 1958, 65; BS, Coll. Santa Fe, 1985. Supr. Tenco Electronics, Inc., Boston, 1959-60; sr. technician Avco-Everett (Mass.) Rsch. Lab., 1961-66; sr. technologist Los Alamos (N.Mex.) Nat. Lab., 1966—, mem. pressure, vacuum com., 1975—; instr. high vacuum tech., U. N.Mex., Los Alamos, 1983—. Contbr. papers to sci. publs. Vice-comdr., USCG Aux., Rio Rancho, N.Mex., 1988. Sgt. U.S. Army, 1953-56. Mem. Am. Vacuum Soc., Am. Chem. Soc., Los Alamos Hist. Soc. (pres. 1968), Los Alamos Figure Skating Club (pres. 1967-70), Elks. Unitarian-Universalist. Home: 1710 37th St Los Alamos NM 87544 Office: Los Alamos Nat Lab PO Box 1663 MSJ 514 Los Alamos NM 87545

KELLEY, JACQUELYN FRANCES, gerontologist; b. Palo Alto, Calif., Oct. 28, 1945; d. John Monroe and Glendora Drusilla (Sampson) Larson; m. Stephen Earl Kelley, Dec. 24, 1963; children: Kristina Leona Jane, Stephenie Victoria. AA, Coll. San Mateo, 1974; BS summa cum laude, Coll. Notre Dame, Belmont, Calif., 1980; postgrad., San Francisco State U., 1980-82. ESL aide Cabrillo Unified Sch. Dist., Half Moon Bay, Calif., 1975-76; community services specialist Ret. Sr. Vol. Program, Menlo Park, Calif., 1980-82, dir., 1982-83; dir. vol. services Vis. Nurse Assn. San Francisco, 1983-85; gerontology specialist San Jose (Calif.) Office on Aging, 1986—; cons., trainer, mgmt., aging and retirement, 1981—. Founder Ocean Shore Resident's Assn., Half Moon Bay, 1976; founder Friends of RSVP Inc., Redwood City, Calif., 1983. Mem. Internat. Soc. Preretirement Planners (chpt. pres., bd. dirs. 1985—), Nat. Coun. Aging, Am. Soc. on Aging (com. chmn. 1984-87, chmn. retirement program planning com. 1988—), Assn. Profl. Vol. Mgrs. (founder, chmn. 1984-87, trainer), Calif. Parks and Recreation Soc. (bd. dirs., founder, pres. aging sect. 1984—), Alpha Gamma Sigma, Delta Epsilon Sigma, Kappa Gamma Pi. Republican. Lutheran. Home: 339 Grand Blvd Half Moon Bay CA 94019

KELLEY, JOHN JAMES, neurosurgeon; b. Stoughton, Mass., June 15, 1930; s. Timothy Francis and Agnes Josephine (O'Halloran) K.; m. Patricia Ann Stone, Aug. 13, 1960; children: James Matthew, Michael John. BS, Stonehill Coll., 1952; MS, Boston Coll., 1954; MD, Georgetown U., 1958; MBA, U. Phoenix, 1986. Diplomate, Am. Bd. Neurol. Surgery. Intern William Beaumont Gen. Hosp., El Paso, Tex., 1958-59; resident in neurology Walter Reed Gen. Hosp., Washington, 1959-60; resident, neurosurgeon Mayo Clinic, Rochester, Minn., 1962-66; assoc. cons. Mayo Clinic, Rochester, 1967-68; pvt. practice Fresno, Calif., 1966-67, Phoenix, 1968—; assoc., Med. Mgmt. Analysis, Inc., Auburn, Calif., 1986—; bd. dirs. Mut. Ins. C. Ariz., Phoenix, Phoenix Bapt. Hosp. and Health Systems, Greater PhoenixAffordable Health Care Found. Contbr. articles to profl. jours. Capt. U.S. Army, 1957-62. Fellow ACS; mem. AMA, Am. Assn. Neurol. Surgeons, Am. Judicature Soc., Maricopa County Med. Soc. (pres. 1987). Republican. Roman Catholic. Office: Ste 505 6036 N 19th Ave Phoenix AZ 85015

KELLEY, KEVIN PATRICK, security, safety administrator; b. Indpls., Apr. 21, 1954; s. Everett Lee and Emily Louise (Bottoms) K.; m. Kathie Jo Fluegeman, Oct. 13, 1984. BS, Calif. State U., Long Beach, 1984; cert. mgmt. supervision, UCLA, 1984. Mgmt. asst. FBI, Los Angeles, 1973-79; security supr. UCLA, 1979-82; security, safety adminstr. Micom Systems, Inc., Chatsworth, Calif., 1982-83; loss prevention, safety auditor Joseph Magnin, Inc., San Francisco, 1983-84; loss prevention, safety adminstr. Wherehouse Entertainment, Inc., Gardena, Calif., 1984-86; risk control cons. Indsl. Indemnity Co., Los Angeles, 1986-87, Kemper Group, City of Industry, Calif., 1987—; commr. pub. safety City of Norwalk, Calif., 1984-86. Mem. security com. Los Angeles Olympic Organizing Com., 1984. Mem. Am. Soc. Indsl. Security (cert., Peter Updike Meml. scholar 1985), Am. Soc. Safety Engrs., Chief Spl. Agts. Assn., Risk Ins. Mgmt. Soc., Nat. Safety Mgmt. Soc. (sec. 1985-86), Am. Heart Assn. (governing bd. chmn. 1986-88), Ins. Inst. Am. (cert.). Republican. Roman Catholic. Lodges: Rotary, Kiwanis. Home: 5930 Via Santana Yorba Linda CA 92686 Office: Kemper Group 17800 Castleton Ave City of Industry CA 91748

KELLEY, LOUANNA ELAINE, newspaper columnist, researcher; b. Denver, Oct. 17, 1920; d. John Earl and Violet May (Griffin) Richards; m. George Vanstavoren Kelley, Dec. 1942 (dec. Oct. 1975); children: William Richard, John Henry; m. Glen Russell Fenicle, Jan. 1984. Student in Dental Tng., Emily Griffith Sch., 1960-61; Student in Bus., Red Rocks Coll., 1976-77. Dental asst. Colo. Dental, Denver, 1961-70; columnist Front Range Jour., Idaho Springs, Colo., 1975-80; reporter Colo. Transcript, Golden, Colo., 1975-82; columnist, reporter Clear Creek Courant, Idaho Springs, Colo., 1980—; researcher Nat. Mining Hall of Fame, Leadville, Colo. 1987—, lectr. Colo. Sch. Mines, Golden, 1977, Jefferson County Schs., Golden, 1975-84; bd. dirs. Vetco Credit Union, Denver. Author: Take Your Pick And Strike It Rich, 1988; contbr. articles to profl. jours. Mem. Social Ethics (v.p. 1986—), Colo. Fedn. Women's. Republican. Lutheran. Home: 303 Iowa Dr Golden CO 80403 Office: Clear Creek Courant 1514 Miner Idaho Springs CO 80452

KELLEY, NEIL DAVIS, meteorologist; b. St. Louis, Jan. 8, 1942; s. Davis Franklin and Louise Minnie (Zager) K. BS in Meteorology, St. Louis U., 1963; MS in Meteorology, Pa. State U., 1968, postgrad. studies, 1970-71. Meteorologist Meteorology Rsch. Inc., Altadena, Calif., 1963-66; instr. Pa. State U., State College, 1968-71; chief devel. Rsch. Aviation, NCAR, Boulder, Colo., 1972-77; prin. scientist Solar Energy Rsch. Inst., Golden, Colo., 1977—. Mem. Inst. for Environ. Sci. (sr. mem.), Instrument Soc. Am. (sr. mem.), AIAA, AAAS, Am. Meteorol. Soc., Torch Club (Boulder), Elks (Boulder), Sigma Xi. Office: Solar Energy Rsch Inst 1617 Cole Blvd Golden CO 80401

KELLEY, NILES ELMER, graphics designer; b. Ft. Dodge, Iowa, June 15, 1916; s. Niles E. and Mabel (Severson) K.; m. Joyce Ordell Gjerde, mar. 13, 1941; children: Amanda O., Martha Anne, Robert N., Ellen N. Student, U. Wash., 1934-38, Cornish Art Sch., 1940-43. Illustrator Boeing Co., Seattle, 1943-45; free lances artist Niles Kelley, Inc., Seattle, 1945-50, free lance art dir., 1956-58; creative visual dir. Cole & Weber, Inc., Seattle, 1950-56; chmn. bd. dirs. Western Graphics, Inc., Seattle, 1958—; cons. art dir. Sta. KOMO-TV, Seattle, 1952-75, McCann-Erickson, Seattle, 1956-57, Fiberbd. Products, Seattle, 1946-50; instr. U. Wash., 1952-55; portrait artists, lanscape artists. Mem. Puget Sound Group of NW Painters (life), Soc. Profl. Graphic Artists. Club: Seattle Tennis, Swedish. Home: 3849-42 NE Seattle WA 98105

KELLEY, NORMAN RAY, pediatrician; b. Chgo., July 30, 1942; s. Ray Hansen and Eleonora Julia (Norling) K.; m. Yoko Mori, July 15, 1975. BS in Letters & Sci., U. Idaho, 1964; MD, Northwestern U., 1968. Asst. prof. pediatrics U. Hawaii Sch. Med., Okinawa, Japan, 1973-76; dir. emergency room Kauikeolani Childrens' Hosp., Honolulu, 1976-77; pvt. practice pediatrics Waianae (Hawaii) Pediatrics Inc., 1977—; owner Smart Chart Med. Record Systems, Honolulu, 1981—, Internat. Med. Systems, Honolulu, 1984—, Maili Point Studio, Waianae, Hawaii, 1988—. Illustrator: Synopsis of Anatomy, 1970. Maj. U.S. Army, 1971-73. Mem. Hawaiian Fed. of Physicians and Dentists, Hawaiian Watercolor Soc., Midwest Watercolor Soc., Pa. Watercolor Soc. Office: Waianae Pediatrics Inc 85-910 Farrington Hwy Waianae HI 96792-2605

KELLEY, RICHARD ALLEN, JR., software engineer; b. San Diego, Sept. 16, 1954; s. Richard Allen and Hilja Jean (Cooke) K.; m. Laura Jean Carlson, Mar. 20, 1976. BS in Math., U. Wash., 1979. Software engr. Boeing Aerospace, Seattle, 1980—. Newsletter editor Friends of Snoqualmie Valley, Snoqualmie, Wash., 1987—. With U.S. Army, 1973-75. Mem. Assn. for Computing Machinery, IEEE Computer Soc. (affiliate mem.). Lutheran. Home: 35805 SE 89th Pl Snoqualmie WA 98065

KELLEY, RICHARD ROY, hotel executive; b. Honolulu, Dec. 28, 1923; s. Roy Cecil and Estelle Louise (Foote) K.; m. Jane Zieber, June 21, 1955 (dec. 1978); children: Elizabeth, Kathryn, Charles, Linda J., Mary Colleen; m. Linda Van Gilder, June 23, 1979; children: Christopher Van Gilder, Anne Marie. BA, Stanford U., 1955; MD, Harvard U., 1960. Pathologist Queen's Med. Ctr., Honolulu, 1962-70, Kapiolani Maternity Hosp., Honolulu, 1961-70; asst. prof. pathology John A. Burns Med. Sch., U. Hawaii, Honolulu, 1968-70; chmn., chief exec. officer Outrigger Hotels Hawaii, Honolulu, 1970-88; bd. dirs. Econ. Devel. Corp., 1st Hawaiian Bank. Bd. dirs. Straub Med. Rsch. and Edn. Found., Assets Sch., Hawaii Conv. Park Coun., Hawaii Visitors Bur.; trustee Punahou Sch.; bd. govs. Ctr. for Internat. Comml. Dispute Resolution. Named Marketer of Yr., Am. Mktg. Assn., 1985, Communicator of Yr., Internat. Assn. Bus. Communicators, 1987. Mem. Am. Cancer Soc. (chmn., bd. councilors Hawaii Pacific div.), Hawaii Hotel Assn., Hawaii Bus. Roundtable, Waikiki Beach Operators Assn., Waikiki Improvement Assn., Chief Execs. Orgn., Oahu Country Club, Waialae Country Club. Office: Outrigger Hotels Hawaii 2375 Kuhio Ave Honolulu HI 96815

KELLEY, ROBERT EDWARD, JR., nuclear engineer; b. Chgo., Feb. 16, 1947; s. Robert Edward and Leona Elizabeth Kelley; m. Mary Ann Rath, Aug. 8, 1968 (div. 1987); 1 child, Christine E. BS in Physics, Harvey Mudd Coll., 1967; MS in Nuclear Engring., U. Mo., 1968. Registered profl. engr., Calif. Reactor supr. Lawrence Radiation Lab., Mercury, Nev., 1968-73; metallurgy group leader Lawrence Livermore Lab., Calif., 1973-80; systems tech. group leader Los Alamos (N.Mex.) Nat. Lab., 1980—; examiner Calif. Bd. Profl. Engrs., 1976. V.p. Flying Particles Inc., Livermore, Calif., 1974-79. Republican. Home: 4081 B Ridgeway Dr Los Alamos NM 87544 Office: Los Alamos Nat Lab PO Box 1663 Los Alamos NM 87545

KELLEY, ROBERT PAUL, JR., management consultation executive; b. Mansfield, Ohio, Mar. 27, 1942; s. Robert Paul and Rachel Marie Kelley; BBA, Notre Dame U., 1964; MBA, Harvard U., 1969; m. Mimi Grant, June 15, 1975; children: Robert, Laura, Elizabeth. Mktg. cons., supr. Laventhol & Horwath, Los Angeles, 1972-73; dir. mktg., entertainment and mdsg. Knott's Berry Farm, Buena Park, Calif., 1974-76; sr. v.p. mktg. Am. Warranty Corp., Los Angeles, 1978-80; chief exec. officer Strategy Network Corp. Dirs., Inc., 1976—; exec. program dir. So. Calif. Tech. Execs. Network, 1984; dir. Orange County sect. So. Calif. Tech. Exec.'s Network, 1984-85, pres., chief exec. officer, 1985—. Author: The Board of Directors and its Role in Growing Companies, 1984. Served with USNR, 1964-67. Home: 13992 Malena Dr Tustin CA 92680 Office: 4667 MacArthur Blvd Ste 200 Newport Beach CA 92660

KELLING, BRUCE DANA, architectural draftman; b. Denver, Dec. 29, 1957; s. Ralph Victor and Shirley Ruth (Rymer) K. Student, Mesa Coll., 1982-84, Wash. State U., 1985—. Draftsman J. Fredrick Fleenor P.A., Phoenix, 1978-80, Anderson & Boone Architiects, Olympia, Wash., 1987, Design Works N.W., Pullman, Wash., 1988—. Past Master Councillor Order of DeMolay, Montrose, Colo., 1975; mem. Amnesty Internat., Pullman, 1988. Recipient first place design award Mason Contractors' Assn. Spokane Inc., 1987. Mem. Am. Inst. Archtl. Students., Nat. Engring. Honor Soc., Tau Beta Pi.

KELLNER, DAVID LEE, data processing executive; b. Puyallup, Wash., Oct. 8, 1943; s. Kenneth and Gertrude (Niemi) K.; m. Gloria J. Ranallo, Oct. 22, 1977; children: Scott D., Robin B. Student, Northrop U., Inglewood, Calif., 1965, Orange Coast Coll., 1971-75. Sr. programmer, project leader Western Airlines, L.A., 1965-74; MIS mgr. Avco Fin. Svcs., Newport Beach, Calif., 1974-79; project mgr. Taco Bell, Irvine, Calif., 1979-80; asst. v.p., mgr. data processing Sperry & Hutchinson Ins. Co., San Diego, 1980-81; cons. PDC Systems, Inc., San Diego, 1981-82; product mgr. Home Fed. Savs. & Loan, San Diego, 1982-84; asst. v.p., S & P supr. Home Savs. Am., North Hollywood, Calif., 1984—. With USN, 1961-64. Republican. Epispcopalian. Home: 5500 Via Sepulveda Yorba Linda CA 92686 Office: Home Savs Am 4900 Rivergrade Rd Irwindale CA 91706

KELLNER, ROBERT ALLEN, epidemiologist; b. Burbank, Calif., Oct. 18, 1948; s. Hank and Iola (Heffernan) k.; m. Nancy Holte, Aug. 4, 1973 (div. 1982); children: James R., Olivia A. BA, Rockhurst Coll., 1976; AA, Penn Valley Community Coll., 1972. Public health advisor Kansas City Health Dept., Mo., 1977-80; disease control spec. Colo. Dept. Health, Pueblo, 1980—; Colo. State Hosp. (infection control comm.), Pueblo, 1987-88; lectr. in field. contbr. articles to profl. jours. Scout master Boy Scouts Am., Kansas City, 1975-77, Pueblo West, Colo., 1986-87. With USN and USNR (numerous awards), 1966-76. Recipient Leadership award Pueblo C. of C., 1988. Fellow of CORO Found., 1976—. Republican. Roman Catholic. Club: Optimists, Pueblo. Office: Colo Dept Health 720 N Main St Ste 300 Pueblo CO 81001

KELLOGG, BRUCE MICHAEL, real estate investor, agent; b. Buffalo, Jan. 3, 1947; s. Harlan Wood and Hilma Moore (Yarrington) K.; m. Diane Linda Mancuso, Dec. 25, 1979; children: Jeremy, Catherine, Michael, Elizabeth, David, Allison. BSEE, Rutgers U., 1969; MBA, Golden Gate U., 1976, Securities investor, Wilmington, N.C., 1970-73; real estate investor, San Jose, Calif., 1973—; assoc. ERA Hill and Assocs., San Jose, 1987—. Mem. Tri-County Apt. Assn., Calif. Apt. Assn. Nat. Apt. Assn., San Jose Bd. Realtors, Calif. Assn. Realtors, Nat. Assn. Realtors, Republican. Roman Catholic. Contbr. articles to profl. jours. Office: 1510 Parkmoor Ave San Jose CA 95128

KELLOGG, DAVID LARKE, real estate broker, construction company executive; b. Denver, Mar. 31, 1958; s. John Scott and Margaret Elaine (Pietz) K.; m. Kimberly Ann Thurman, May 20, 1987. Student, Cen. Mich. U., 1979-80; grad., Real Estate Inst., 1986. Cert. residential specialist, broker assoc., real estate appraiser. Pres. Blue River Constrn., Inc., Denver, 1980—; broker assoc. Coldwell Banker-Residential, Lakewood, Colo., 1984-88, Re/Max Profls., Inc., Lakewood, 1988—. Mem. Nat. Bd. Realtor, Jefferson County Realtors (guest speaker 1987), Evergreen Bd. Realtors, Hiwan Country Club, Rotary. Republican. Presbyterian. Home: 2334 El Dorado Ln Evergreen CO 80439 Office: Re/Max Profls Inc 390 Union Blvd Ste 100 Lakewood CO 80228 also: Blue River Constrn Co Inc 4704 Harlan St #300 Lakeside National Bank Bldg Denver CO 80212

KELLOGG, FREDERICK, historian; b. Boston, Dec. 9, 1929; s. Frederick Floyd and Stella Harriet (Plummer) K.; A.B., Stanford U., 1952; M.A., U. So. Calif., 1958; Ph.D., Ind. U., 1969; m. Patricia Kay Hanbery, Aug. 21, 1954 (dec. 1975); 1 dau., Kristine Marie Calvert. Instr., Boise State U., 1962-64, asst. prof., 1964-65; vis. asst. prof. U. Idaho, 1965; asso. prof. Boise State U., 1966-67; instr. history U. Ariz., 1967-68, asst. prof., 1968-71, asso. prof., 1971—. Founder, chmn. Idaho Hist. Conf., 1964. U.S.-Romania Cultural Exchange Research scholar, 1960-61; Sr. Fulbright-Hays Research scholar, Romania, 1969-70. Recipient Am. Council Learned Socs. Research grant, 1970-71; Internat. Research and Exchanges Bd. Sr. Research grant, 1973-74. Mem. Am. Hist. Assn., Am. Assn. Advancement Slavic Studies, Am. Assn. Southeast European Studies. Mng. editor Southeastern Europe, 1974—; contbr. articles to academic publs. Office: U Ariz Dept History Tucson AZ 85721

KELLOGG, JOHN WELLINGTON, accountant; b. Englewood, Colo., June 6, 1964; s. Charles Wellington and Bonnie (Wickens) K. BS, U. Colo., 1986. CPA, Colo. Sr. acct. Arthur Andersen & Co., Denver, 1986—. Vol. Big Brothers of Colo., Denver, 1987—. Republican. Office: Arthur Andersen & Co 717 17th St #1900 Denver CO 80202

KELLOGG, LILLIAN RENEE, electronics executive; b. San Antonio, July 2, 1953; d. Vincent S. and Olympia T. (Pinto) Maggiore; m. Geoffrey Edward Kellogg, July 4, 1981; 1 child, Geoffrey Max. BA, Kean Coll., 1974. Sales sec. Tex. Instruments Inc., San Francisco, 1974-76, sales rep., 1976-78; v.p. United Components Inc., Santa Clara, Calif., 1978-82; exec. v.p. No. Specialty Sales, Portland, Oreg., 1982-84; pres. ERA Computers and Electronics, Los Altos, Calif., 1984—; mem. Hewlett Packard Dealer Adv. Council, 1988—. Democrat. Roman Catholic. Club: Decathalon (Santa Clara). Office: ERA Computers & Electronics 4546 El Camino Real Los Altos CA 94022

KELLOGG, WILLIAM WELCH, meteorologist; b. New York Mills, N.Y., Feb. 14, 1917; s. Frederick S. and Elizabeth (Walcott) K.; m. Elizabeth Thorson, Feb. 14, 1942; children: Karl S., Judith K. Liebert, Joseph W., Jane K. Holien, Thomas W. B.A., Yale U., 1939; M.A., UCLA, 1942, Ph.D., 1949. With Inst. Geophysics UCLA, L.A., 1946-52, asst. prof., 1950-52; scientist Rand Corp., Santa Monica, Calif., 1947-59, head planetary scis. dept., 1959-64; assoc. dir. Nat. Ctr. Atmospheric Research, Boulder, Colo., also dir. lab. atmospheric scis., 1964-73, sr. scientist, 1973-87; Mem. earth satellite panel IGY, 1956-59; mem. space sci. bd. Nat. Acad. Scis., 1959-68, mem. com. meteorol. aspects of effects of atomic radiation, 1956-58, mem. com. atmospheric scis., 1966-72, mem. polar research bd., 1972-77; mem. Rocket and Satellite Research Panel, 1957-62; mem. adv. group supporting tech. for operational meteorol. satellites NASA-NOAA, 1964-72; rapporteur meteorology of high atmosphere, commn. aerology World Meteorol. Orgn., 1965-71; chmn. internat. commn. meteorology upper atmosphere Internat. Union Geodesy and Geophysics, 1960-67, mem., 1967-75; mem. internat. com. climate Internat. Assn. Meteorology and Atmospheric Physics, 1978-87; mem. sci. adv. bd. USAF, 1956-65; chmn. meteorol. satellite com. Advanced Research Projects Agy., 1958-59; mem. panel on environment President's Sci. Adv. Com., 1968-72; mem. space program adv. council NASA, 1976-77; chmn. meteorol. adv. com. EPA, 1970-74, mem. nat. air quality criteria adv. com., 1975-76, air pollution transport and transformation adv. com., 1976-78; mem. council on carbon dioxide environ. assessment Dept. Energy, 1976-78; adv. to sec. gen. on World Climate Program, World Meteorol. Orgn., 1978-79; dir. research Naval Environ. Prediction Research Facility, Monterey, Calif., 1983-84; chmn. adv. com. Div. Polar Programs NSF, 1983-86; researcher on meteorology, dynamics and turbulence of upper atmosphere, prediction radioactive fallout and dispersal, applications of infrared techniques, atmospheres of Mars and Venus, theory of climate and causes of climate change. Served as pilot-weather officer USAAF, 1941-46. Co-recipient spl. award pioneering work in planning meteorol. satellite Am. Meteorol. Soc., 1961; recipient Risseca award contbn. human relations in scis. Jewish War Vets. U.S.A., 1962-63, Exceptional Civilian Service award Dept. Air Force, 1966, Spl. award for pioneering meteorol. satellites Dept. Commerce, 1985, Spl. Citation award for atmospheric conservation Garden Club of Am., 1988. Fellow Am. Geophys. Union (pres, meteorol. sect. 1972-74), Am. Meteorol. Soc. (council 1960-63, pres. 1973-74), AAAS (chmn. atmospheric and hydrospheric sect. 1984); mem. Internat. Acad. Astronautics, Sigma Xi. Club: Cosmos (Washington). Home: 445 College Ave Boulder CO 80302 Office: Adjunct/Nat Ctr Atmospheric Rsch Boulder CO 80307

KELLY, BRENDAN JOHN, account marketing representative; b. Davenport, IA, Mar. 25, 1962; s. James John and Elizabeth Ann (Loosbrock) K. BS, U. Ariz., 1984. Mktg. trainee IBM, Tucson, 1984-85; mktg. rep. IBM, 1985-88, acct. mktg. rep., 1988—. Pres. Active 20-30 Club, Tucson, 1987-88. Mem. Ariz. Acad., Phi Gamma Delta. Democrat. Roman Catholic. Home: 6702 E Brooks Dr Tucson AZ 85730 Office: IBM 5255 E Williams Circle Tucson AZ 85711

KELLY, BRIAN MATTHEW, industrial hygienist; b. Ogdensburg, N.Y., June 16, 1956; s. Lauris F. and Catherine M. (McEvoy) K. BA, SUNY, Oswego, 1978; BS, Clarkson U., 1981. Cert. indsl. toxicologist. Maintenance engr. Kelly Sales Corp., Madrid, N.Y., 1978-80, carpenter,

1981-82; hygienist indsl. hygiene and toxicology div. Sandia Nat. Labs., Albuquerque, 1983—. Mem. Air Pollution and Hazerdous Waste Mgmt. Assn., Am. Chem. Soc. (div. chem. health and safety), Am. Inst. Chemists, Am. Indsl. Hygienists Assn., N.Y. Acad. Scis., Am. Soc. Safety Engrs., Am. Welding Soc., Gamma Sigma Epsilon, Phi Kappa Phi. Republican. Roman Catholic. Home: 1570 W Bosque Loop Bosque Farms NM 87068 Office: Sandia Nat Labs Div Indsl Hygiene & Toxicology PO Box 5800 Orgn 3311 Albuquerque NM 87185

KELLY, CHERYL ANN, social service administrator; b. Bay City, Mich., July 28, 1956; d. Frederick Joseph and Julie Frances (Filary) Budzinski; m. Hugh Paul Kelly, Aug. 3, 1979; 1 child, Jenna Ann. BS, U. Mich., 1977; MS, U. Ariz., 1981, MBA, 1988. Cert. rehab. counselor. Tchr. Northview Pub. Schs., Grand Rapids, Mich., 1977-78; rehab. counselor St. Mary's Hosp., Tucson, 1980-81; mgr. Jewish Family Service, Tucson, 1981-82; service coordinator Pima County, Tucson, 1982-86; bus. devel. officer Western Savs. and Loan, Tucson, 1986-88; dir. social services Carondelet Holy Family Ctr., Tucson, 1988—; cons. Tucson Australian Shepard Club, Tucson, 1987-88. Bd. dirs. Tucson Old Pueblo Exchange, 1987. Mem. Am. Mktg. Assn., Nat. Orgn. Female Execs. Republican. Roman Catholic.

KELLY, DAVID RICHARD, accountant; b. Oakland, Calif., June 9, 1940; s. David Philip and Annetta Marie K.; m. Margo Ann Lourdeaux, May 9, 1964; children: Brian D., Timothy A. BS in Econs., Bus. Adminstrn., St. Mary's Coll., Moraga, Calif., 1962; MBA, U. Calif., Berkeley, 1971. CPA, Calif. Staff acct. Price Waterhouse, San Francisco, 1962-65, Victor Equipment Co., San Francisco, 1965-66; staff acct., mgr. taxes Hood & Strong, San Francisco, 1966-69; pvt. practice acctg. Walnut Creek, Calif., 1970-74; officer Kelly Tama Shiffman, Inc., CPA's, Walnut Creek, 1974—. Chmn. CPA com. Children's Hosp. Med. Ctr. Found., 1981-82, 87-88, dir. 1988—; bd. dirs. (hon.) Contra Costa County Dist. Council Soc. St. Vincent de Paul, Children's Hosp. Med. Ctr. Found., 1988—; alumni ex-officio mem. Bd. Regents, bd. trustees St. Mary's Coll., 1979-80; treas. St. Mary's East Bay Scholarship Fund, Inc.; mem. budget and fin. coms. Mt. Diablo Family YMCA, 1982-84, bishop's com. for charity Roman Catholic Diocese Oakland, Calif.; past treas. Easter Seal Soc. Contra Costa County; past bd. dirs. Diablo Valley Estate Planning Council; mem. bd. regents St. Mary's Coll. High Sch., Berkeley, Calif., 1988—. Mem. Am. Inst. CPA's, Calif. Soc. CPA's (statewide dir. 1977-80, pres. East Bay chpt. 1978-79, task force for community service, 1982, task force CPA requirements 1985), St. Mary's Coll. Nat. Alumni Assn. (bd. dirs. 1972—, pres. 1979-80). Democrat. Roman Catholic. Office: Kelly Tama Shiffman Inc 2121 N California Blvd Ste 900 Walnut Creek CA 94596

KELLY, DEBORAH GAIL TITUS, teacher; b. Great Falls, Mont., June 1, 1954; d. Walter Leonard and Katherine Louise (Sim) Titus; m. David Wayne Kelly, June 11, 1977; children: Brian Douglas, Daniel David. BS, Mont. State U., 1976. Tutor math. Sch. Dist. #1, Great Falls, 1976-78, substitute tchr., 1978-85, tchr. elem. sch., 1985—. Mem. AAUW. Home: 320 Riverview 6W Great Falls MT 59404

KELLY, DENNIS RAY, sales executive; b. Olympia, Wash., Aug. 20, 1948; s. William E. and Irene (Lewis) K.; m. Pamela Jo Kresevich, Mar. 16, 1974. BA, Cen. Wash. U., 1972; postgrad., U. Wash., 1977-78. Sales rep. Bumble Bee Sea Foods, Seattle, 1972-74; retail sales mgr. Pacific Pearl Sea Foods, Seattle, 1974-76; regional sales mgr. Castle & Cooke Foods, Seattle, Phila., and N.Y.C., 1976-80; v.p. sales mktg. Frances Andrew Ltd., Seattle, 1980-82; regional sales mgr. Tenneco West, Seattle, 1982-85; sales and mktg. mgr. for western U.S. David Oppenheimer, Seattle, 1985—. Alumni advisor Cen. Wash. U., Ellensburg, 1979-87, alumni bd. dirs., 1986—, fund drive chmn., 1988, mem. sch. community group bd.; mem. Statue of Liberty Ellis Island Found.; chmn. annual fund drive Cen. Wash. U. Mem. New Zealand-Am. Soc., Mfrs. Reps. Club Wash. Republican. Home: 2821 2d Ave Ste 1204 Seattle WA 98121

KELLY, DONALD ANDREW, engineer; b. Orlando, Fla., Sept. 12, 1957; s. Donald Arthur and Katherine (Harding) K.; m. Joy Hilty, Dec. 16, 1979. BSEE, U.S. Mil. Acad., 1979; MSEE, U. Colo., 1986; postgrad., Colo. State U., 1986—. Commd. 2d lt. U.S. Army, 1979, advanced through grades to capt., 1982; electronics officer U.S. Army, Ft. Carson, Colo., 1979-82; satellite systems engr. USAF, Aurora, Colo., 1982-86, resigned, 1986; staff engr. Hughes Aircraft Co., Englewood, Colo., 1986—. Mem. IEEE, AIAA, U.S. Racquetball Assn., U.S. Squash Racquets Assn. Republican. Presbyterian. Home: 8817 W Glasgow Pl Littleton CO 80123 Office: Hughes Aircraft Co Center Tech Pkwy Aurora CO 80011

KELLY, DONALD HORTON, visual scientist; b. Erie, Pa., May 6, 1923; s. George Luther and Gladys Esther (Short) K.; m. Jessie Helen Wells, June 18, 1950; 1 child, George Bradner. B.S., U. Rochester, 1944; postgrad. U. So. Calif., 1947-49; Ph.D., UCLA, 1960. Research scientist Technicolor Corp., Hollywood, Calif., 1946-61, Itek Corp., Lexington, Mass., Palo Alto, Calif., 1961-66; staff scientist SRI Internat., Menlo Park, Calif., 1966—; vis. prof. optics and visual sci. U. Rochester, N.Y., 1971-72; mem. Nat. Acad. Sci.-NRC Com. on Vision; mem. visual scis. B study sect. NIH, 1973-77. Contbr. articles to sci. jours., chpts. to books. Patentee in field. Served to lt. (j.g.) USN, 1944-46. NIH spl. fellow, 1971-72. Fellow Optical Soc. Am. (chmn. vision tech. group 1978-79, Edgar D. Tillyer award 1986); mem. Assn. Research in Vision and Ophthalmology, AAAS, Phi Beta Kappa, Sigma Xi. Home: 24143 Hillview Rd Los Altos Hills CA 94022 Office: SRI Internat 333 Ravenswood Ave Menlo Park CA 94025

KELLY, ERIC DAMIAN, lawyer; b. Pueblo, Colo., Mar. 16, 1947; s. William Bret and Patricia Ruth (Ducy) K.; m. Viana Eileen Rockel, 1980; children: Damian Charles, Eliza Jane, Valissitie Christina Heeren, Douglas Ray Heeren. BA, Williams Coll., 1969; JD, U. Pa., 1975, M of City Planning, 1975. Bar: Colo. 1975, U.S. Dist. Ct. 1976, U.S. Tax Ct. 1976, U.S. Ct. Appeals (10th cir.) 1986. Chief citizens' participation unit EPA, Region III, Phila., 1971-72; project planner Beckett New Town, N.J., 1972-73; v.p., project mgr. Rahenkamp Sachs Wells & Assocs., Inc., Denver and Phila., 1973-76; sole practice, Pueblo, 1976-83; pres. Kelly & Potter, P.C., Pueblo, Albuquerque and Santa Fe, 1983—; adj. assoc. prof. U. Colo. Coll. Architecture and Planning, 1976—, land use seminars Fed. Publs., Inc., 1976-84; adj. asst. prof. grad. sch. bus. U. So. Colo., 1986—; pres. Color Radio, Ltd., 1979—; sec., bd. dirs. Lodging Svc. Corp., 1980—; bd. dirs. Mar Tec Broadcasting Corp., Pueblo Growth Corp., Wildflower, Inc. Author: Land Use Controls, 1976-80, 82; editor, prin. author: The Roadtripper, 1969; contbr. articles to profl. planning and legal jours. Mem. adv. bd. Mcpl. Legal Studies Ctr., S.W. Legal Found., 1989—; bd. dirs. Broadway Theatre League, Pueblo, 1976-77, Pueblo Beautiful Assn., 1978-82, Better Bus. Bur., 1988; trustee Sangre de Cristo Arts and Conf. Ctr., 1981—, chmn. 1986; trustee Christ Congl. Ch., 1982-83. Served with U.S. Army, 1969-71. Named Outstanding Student, Am. Inst. Planners, 1976. Mem. ABA, APA (Amicus Curiac com. 1988—), Am. Inst. Cert. Planners (charter), Am. Planning Assn., Colo. Bar Assn., Denver Bar Assn., Pueblo County Bar Assn., Williams Coll. Alumni Assn. (class sec. 1969-74, regional sec. 1980-82, class agt. 1985—), Pueblo Country Club, Rotary (local dir. 1988, dir., pres. Pueblo Rotary Found. 1988—, v.p. 1988—, pres. 1989—). Democrat. Office: 200 E Abriendo Ave Pueblo CO 81004

KELLY, FRANK JOSEPH, construction and contracting company executive; b. Oakland, Calif., Nov. 23, 1921; s. Francis Joseph ad Jule Frances (Gilissman) K.; m. Eleanor Jane Mason, Oct. 11, 1947; children: Maureen, Stephen, Barbara, Susan, James. BS, U.S. Naval Acad., 1943. Cert. cost engr. Cost engr. Barrett & Hilp and Barrett Constrn. Co., San Francisco, 1947-66; chief estimator, sr. v.p. Stone, Marraccini & Patterson, San Francisco, 1966-82; v.p. mktg. Rudolph & Sletten, Inc., Foster City, Calif., 1982--. Comdr. USN, 1939-57, PTO. Fellow Am. Assn. Cost Engrs. (pres. 1977-78, Merit award 1981). Republican. Roman Catholic. Home: 45 Alannah Ct Palo Alto CA 94303 Office: Rudolph & Sletten Inc 989 E Hillsdale Blvd Foster City CA 94404

KELLY, FRANK KING, foundation administrator; b. Kansas City, Mo., June 12, 1914; s. Francis Michael and Martha Oneita (King) K.; m. Barbara Allen Mandigo, Dec. 5, 1941; children: Terence F., Stephen D. AB, U. Mo., Kansas City, 1937. Reporter, editor The Kansas City Star, 1937-41; editor, feature writer AP, N.Y.C., 1941-46; info. specialist Nat. Housing Agy., N.Y.C., 1946-47; speech writer Pres. Harry S. Truman, Washington, 1948; asst. dir. research div. Dem. Nat. Com., Washington, 1948; prof. Boston U., 1948; asst. to U.S. senate majority leader, dir. Senate Majority Policy Com., Washington, 1949-52; U.S. dir. Internat. Press Inst., N.Y.C., 1952-53; v.p. Fund for Republic and Ctr. for Study Dem. Instns., Santa Barbara, Calif., 1956-75; sr. v.p. Nuclear Age Peace Found., Santa Barbara, 1982—; advisor Acad. World Studies, San Francisco; cons. Santa Barbara Community Coll.; hon. chmn. Univ. Religious Ctr., U. Calif.-Santa Barbara; participant White House Conf. Internat. Coop., Washington, 1965. Author: An Edge of Light, 1949, Reporters Around the World, 1957, Your Freedoms: The Bill of Rights, 1964, The Martyred Presidents, 1967, Your Laws, 1970, The Fight for the White House, 1961, Court of Reason, 1981, The 100% Challenge: The United States Academy of Peace, 1983, Searching for a President in a Nuclear Age, 1988, Star Ship Invincible, 1979, Waging Peace in a Nuclear Age, 1988. Dir. Harriman for Pres. Com., Washington, 1952, Work Tng. Program, Santa Barbara, 1964—, UN Assn., Santa Barbara, 1980—, Calif. Council, UN U., 1987—; bd. dirs. Nat. Peace Acad. Campaign., 1978-84; past pres. Cath. Social Services, Santa Barbara. Served with U.S. Army, 1943-45. Nieman fellow Harvard U., 1942-43. Democrat. Roman Catholic. Clubs: Harvard, Channel City (Santa Barbara). Home: 34 E Padre St Santa Barbara CA 93105 Office: Nuclear Age Peace Found 1187 Coast Village Rd Ste 123 Santa Barbara CA 93108

KELLY, GEORGE THOMAS, law firm administrator, consultant; b. Malden, Mass., June 24, 1941; s. Thomas Patrick and Eunice Estelle (Hinckley) K.; m. Jo Ann D'Agostino, July 4, 1964; children: Denise, Richard, George Jr., Steven. BS, N.H. Coll., 1976. Personnal adminstr. USMC, 1961-83; adminstrv. svcs. mgr. Gray, Cary, Ames & Frye, San Diego, 1983-86; adminstr. Corona & Prager, San Diego, 1986-87, Solomon, Ward, Seidenwurm & Smith, San Diego, 1987—; cons. San Diego, 1983—. Mem. Assn. Legal Adminstrs. (chair, survey com. 1988), Friendly Sons of St. Patrick. Roman Catholic.

KELLY, JAMES FRANCIS, department store executive; b. Mt. Vernon, N.Y., Nov. 7, 1906; s. Hugh and Elizabeth (Dunne) K.; m. Ruth Wellington Dee, Oct. 19, 1935; children—Barbara (Mrs. John G. Ryden), Hampton Merrill (stepson). LL.B., St. John's U., 1930. Bar: N.Y. bar 1940. With Assoc. Dry Goods Corp., 1934-72, sec., 1956-71, also v.p., dir. Club: Dunes Golf (Myrtle Beach, S.C.). Home: 310 73d Ave #3A Myrtle Beach SC 29577

KELLY, JOHN, industrial engineer; b. N.Y.C., Feb. 3, 1940; s. John and Laura (Finner) K.; m. Barbara Jean Childress, June, 1965 (div. June 1980); 1 child, Cassandra B.; m. Gail Vanessa Wilkerson, Jan. 17, 1981; children: John Ashley III, Jame Augustina. BS in Indsl. Adminstrn., U. Calif., San Jose, 1972. Indsl. engr. Colgate Palmolive, Berkeley, Calif., 1972-74; sr. indsl. engr. Crown Zellerbach, Oakland, Calif., 1974-80, C&H Sugar, Crockett, Calif., 1980-82; distribution mgr. USN Dept., Oakland, 1982-83; project engr. Fed. Express, Redmond, Wash., 1983—; cons. math. and engring. sci., San Francisco, 1981-82, Portland, Oreg., 1986—. With USAF, 1958-62. Mem. Black Am. Polit. Assn. Calif., Urban League (Meritorious Achievement award 1975-80), Am. Inst. Indsl. Engrs., Indsl. Adminstrn. Soc., Am. Soc. Plastics Engrs. Democrat.

KELLY, KATHLEEN DIANNE, real estate salesperson; b. Oceanside, Calif., Sept. 16, 1956; d. Marcus and Dianna Mae (Shultz) Cook; m. Ralph Edward Kelly, Nov. 10, 1979; 1 child, Megan Kathleen. BS, Woodbury U., 1977. Exec. sec. Ind. Colls. of So. Calif. Inc., Los Angeles, 1975-78; adminstrv. asst. Barry and Co., Los Angeles, 1978-79; tech. services asst. Assn. Adminstrs. and Cons. Inc., Irvine, Calif., 1979-80; adminstrv. mgr. CFS Bakeries, Inc., Ont., Calif., 1980-83; asst. property mgr. Century 21 Golden West Realtors, Lake Elsinore, Calif., 1984-86; regional sales mgr. South Shores Sales, Inc., Arcadia, Calif., 1987—; advisor Calif. State Polytech. U., Pomona. Tchr. St. Matthew's Ch., Corona, Calif., 1987, 88. Mem. Zeta Tau Alpha (pres. 1987). Republican. Roman Catholic. Home: 1449 Moore Cir Corona CA 91720 Office: South Shores Sales Inc 315 Vaquero Rd Arcadia CA 91006

KELLY, KEVIN RICHARD, banker, economist; b. The Dalles, Oreg., Sept. 17, 1949; s. James Edward and Mercedes (Foley) K.; m. Karen Ann Lillegard, Oct. 25, 1975; children: Ian Patrick, Conor Michael, Patrick James. BA, Santa Clara U., 1971; MA, U. Oreg., 1973, PhD in Econs., 1974. Instr. U. Oreg., Eugene, 1974; asst. prof. Reed Coll., Portland, Oreg., 1974-76, Lewis and Clark Coll., Portland, 1976-78; chief economist U.S. Bancorp., Portland, 1978-80, mgr. corp. devel. and strategic planning, 1980-86, mgr. investment svcs., 1986-87; pres. U.S. Bank Oreg., Portland, 1987—; bd. dirs. Sci. Advances Inc., Columbis, Ohio; mem. faculty Pacific Coast Banking Sch., Seattle, 1982-84. Editor Oreg. Bus. Barometer, 1978-83; weekly columnist UPI, 1983-85; contbr. articles to profl. publs. Mem. Oreg. Gov.'s Panel on Econ. Devel., 1981-82, Portland Planning Commn., 1986-87; vice-chmn. Oreg. Gov.'s Econ. Advisors, 1982-84; trustee Sisters of Providence Pension Plan, Seattle, 1986—, U. Portland, 1988—. Basketball scholar Santa Clara U., 1967; Northwest Area Found. grantee, 1976. Mem. Res. City Bankers, Oreg. Council for Econ. Edn. (bd. dirs.), Nat. Assn. Bus. Economists (pres. Portland chpt. 1982), Multnomah Athletic Club, Waverley Golf Club. Republican. Roman Catholic. Office: US Bank Oreg PO Box 4412 Portland OR 97208

KELLY, LEONTINE T. C., clergywoman; b. Washington; d. David D. and Ila M. Turpeau; m. Gloster Current (div.); children: Angella, Gloster Jr., John David; m. James David Kelly (dec.); 1 child, Pamela (adopted). Student W.Va. State Coll.; grad. Va. Union U., 1960; M.Div., Union Theol. Sem., Richmond, Va., 1969. Formerly sch. tchr.; former pastor Galilee United Meth. Ch., Edwardsville, Va.; later mem. staff Va. Conf. Council on Ministries; pastor Asbury United Meth. Ch., Richmond, 1976-83; mem. nat. staff United Meth. Ch., Nashville, 1983-84; bishop Calif.-Nev. Conf., San Francisco, 1984-88. Vis. prof. evangelism and witness Pacific Sch. Religion, Berkeley, Calif., 1988—. Office: 316 N El Camino Real #112 San Mateo CA 94401

KELLY, NANCY LEE, sales and marketing executive, video producer; b. Wyandotte, Mich., Mar. 26, 1942; d. Adhemar Howard and Bertha Elizabeth (Loosli) Stults; m. Terence James Kelly, June 5, 1965 (div. Mar. 198l); children: Eron Stults, Ty Calvin. BA, Mich. State U., 1964; MA, U. Wash., 197l. Instr. spl. edn. U. Mich., Ann Arbor, 1964-65; tchr. math. U.S. Army Sch., Wertheim, Fed. Republic Germany, 1966; tchr. spl. edn. Seattle Area Pub. Schs., 1968-71; tchr. State Hosp., Traverse City, Mich., 1968; owner, mgr. N.W. Health Ctr., Woodinville, Wash., 1978-81; saleswoman, facilitator Stonebridge Inst., Seattle and Denver, 1981-86; saleswoman Krause & Assocs., Denver, 1986-88; assoc. video producer Crest Group, Denver, 1987—. Founder Woodinville Slough Run, 1978-84; pres. La Crosse Club, Colorado Springs, Colo., 1986-88. Mem. Am. Soc. for Tng. and Devel. Republican. Home: 1029 War Eagle Dr N Colorado Springs CO 80919 Office: Crest Group 1750 E Hampden Denver CO 80224

KELLY, ROBERT EDWARD, realtor; b. Denver, June 19, 1953; s. Robert Hugh and Donna Rae (Williams) K.; m. May Kay Crabtree, Aug. 21, 1976; children: Robert Brian, Sean Patrick, Brenden Michael, Scott Joseph. BS in Bus., U. Colo., 1978. Real estate agt. Kelly Realty, Denver, 1978-80, Moore & Co. Realtors, Lakewood, Colo., 1980—. Mem. Nat. Assn. Realtors, Colo. Assn. Realtors, Jeffco Bd. Realtors. Home: 4663 W Oberlin Pl Denver CO 80236 Office: Moore & Co 3199 S Wadsworth Blvd Lakewood CO 80227

KELLY, ROBERT JEROME, public relations executive; b. Anaconda, Mont., Aug. 27, 1946; s. Robert J. and Mary Catherine (Cunningham) K.; m. Sandra Jean Jensen, Nov. 22, 1974. B.S. in Biology, U. Mont., 1969; M.P.H., U. Minn., 1972. Aide to U.S. Congressman Shoup, Washington, 1972-74; mgr. Ecol. Cons., Helena, Mont., 1974-75; dir. air, water and reclamation The Anaconda Co., Mont., 1975-76; pub. affairs mgr. Champion Internat. Corp., Missoula, Mont., 1976-87; pres. INTERTEC, 1987—; pres. Mont. Internat. Trade Commn., 1984—; mem. Sec. of Agr.'s Nat. Scenic Trail Adv. Com., Denver, 1981.Trustee, U. Mont., Missoula, 1983-88, pres., 1988—; pres. Mont. Council on Econ. Edn., 1984, U. Mont. Athletic Assn., 1984. Served to 1st lt. USN, 1969-71. USPHS grantee, 1971. Roman Catholic. Lodge: Rotary (pres. 1984-85). Office: Intertec 619 SW Higgins Ave Ste O Missoula MT 59803

KELLY, TIM DONAHUE, state senator; b. Sacramento, Aug. 15, 1944. Former legis. aide to Calif. and Nev. Legislatures; mortgage banker; mem. Alaska Ho. of Reps., 1976-78, Alaska Senate, 1978—, senate pres., 1989-90. With USMC, Alaska Air NG. Office: Pouch V Juneau AK 99811

KELLY, TIMOTHY MICHAEL, newspaper editor; b. Ashland, Ky., Nov. 28, 1947; s. Robert John and Pauline Elizabeth (Henneman) K.; m. Carol Ann Knight, Aug. 2, 1969; children—Kimberly, Kevin. B.A., U. Miami, Fla., 1970. Sports copy editor, writer The Courier-Jour., Louisville, 1970-71; exec. sports editor The Phila. Inquirer, 1971-75; dep. mng. editor Dallas Times Herald, 1975-81; mng. editor The Denver Post, 1981-84; exec. editor Dallas Times Herald, 1984; editor Daily News, Los Angeles, 1984-87; mng. editor The Orange County Register, Santa Ana, Calif., 1987—. Mem. Am. Soc. Newspaper Editors, Sigma Delta Chi. Roman Catholic. Office: Orange County Register 625 N Grand Ave Santa Ana CA 92701

KELLY, WILLIAM BRET, insurance executive; b. Rocky Ford, Colo., Sept. 28, 1922; s. William Andrew and Florence Gail (Yant) K.; B.A. cum laude, U. Colo., 1947; m. Patricia Ruth Ducy, Mar. 25, 1944; children: Eric Damian, Kathryn Gail Kelly Schweitzer. With Steel City Agencies, Inc., and predecessor, Pueblo, Colo., 1946—, pres., 1961-76, chmn. bd., 1977—; dir. United Bank Pueblo, 1963—, chmn. bd., 1983-88; mem. Pub. Expenditure Coun., 1984—; v.p. Colo. Ins. Edn. Found., 1981, pres., 1982. Mem. Pueblo Area Council Govts., 1971-73, Colo. Forum 1985—, trustee Pueblo Bd. Water Works, 1966-80, pres., 1970-71; pres. Pueblo Single Fund Plan, 1960-61, Pueblo Heart Council, 1962, Family Service Soc. Pueblo, 1963; mem. 10th Jud. Dist. Nominating Com., 1967-71; trustee U. So. Colo. Found., 1967—, Jackson Found., 1972—, Farley Found., 1979—, Roselawn Cemetery Assn., 1982—; Kelly-Ducy Found., 1983—. Served with inf. AUS, 1943-45. Decorated Silver Star, Bronze Star with oak leaf cluster, Purple Heart with oak leaf cluster; C.P.C.U. Mem. Soc. C.P.C.U.'s, Pueblo C. of C. (past pres.), Pueblo Kiwanis (past pres.), Pueblo Country Club (treas. 1964-66), Phi Beta Kappa. Democrat. Home: 264 Sifford Ct Pueblo West CO 81007 Office: 1414 W 4th St Pueblo CO 81004

KELSEY, EDITH JEANINE, psychotherapist, consultant; b. Freeport, Ill., Oct. 15, 1937; d. John Melvin and Florence Lucille (Ewald) Anderson; m. Craig Ken Kelsey, Dec. 12, 1960; children: Steven Craig, Kevin John. Student, Pasadena Coll., 1955-58; BA in Psychology, Calif. State U., San Jose, 1980; MA in Counseling Psychology, Santa Clara U., 1984. Lic. marriage, family and child counselor. Counselor, cons. Omega Assocs. Santa Clara (Calif.) U., 1981-85, dir. research, 1982-84; intern in counseling Sr. Residential Services, San Jose, 1983-84; psychotherapist Process Therapy Inst., Los Gatos, Calif., 1983-86, Sexual Abuse Treatment Ctr., San Jose, 1984-87; cons. in field, Santa Clara Valley, 1982—; trainer, cons. Omega Assoc., 1987-88; teaching asst. Santa Clara U., 1987-88. Contbr. articles to profl. jours. Vol. Parental Stress Hotline, Palo Alto, Calif., 1980-85. Mem. Am. Assn. Marriage and Family Therapists, Calif. Assn. Marriage and Family Therapists (clin.), Sierra Club. Republican. Presbyterian. Home: 4250 El Camino Real C328 Palo Alto CA 94306 Office: 4250 El Camino Real D229 Palo Alto CA 94306

KELSEY, FLOYD LAMAR, JR., architect; b. Colorado Springs, Colo., Jan. 2, 1925; s. Floyd Lamar and Myrtice (Graves) K.; m. Ruth Ann Witty, June 22, 1946; children—Patricia Ann, Carol Susan. Student, Colo. Coll., 1942-44; B.S. in Architecture with honors, U. Ill., 1947. Partner Bunts & Kelsey (architects), Colorado Springs, 1952-66; pres. Lamar Kelsey Assos., 1966-85, The LKA Ptnrs. Inc., 1985-88; cons. in arch. and planning Colorado Springs, 1989—; cons. design rev. bd. U. Colo., 1969-70, 86—; adv. panel, region 8 Gen. Services Adminstrn., 1969-70; vis. lectr. U. Colo., 1960, U. Denver, 1958. Author: Schools for America, 1967, Open Space Schools, 1971; Contbr. to profl. jours. Recipient design awards AIA, design awards Am. Inst. Steel Constrn., design awards Am. Assn. Sch. Adminstrs., design awards Nation's Schs. mag. Fellow AIA (former mem. nat. coms. on ednl. facilities, edn., architecture for arts and recreation); mem. Colorado Springs C. of C. (past dir.), Broadmoor Golf Club, Winter Night Club (pres. 1976), Gargoyle Archtl. Hon. Soc., Phi Delta Theta. Methodist. Home: 10 Briarcrest Pl Colorado Springs CO 80906 Office: 10012 E Purdue Ave Scottsdale AZ 85258

KELTON, ARTHUR MARVIN, JR., real estate developer; b. Bennington, Vt., Sept. 12, 1939; s. Arthur Marvin and Lorraine (Millington) K.; m. Elaine White, Nov. 1, 1986; 1 child, Ashley. BA, Dartmouth Coll., 1961. Ptnr. Kelton and Assocs., Vail, Colo., 1966-77; pres. Kelton, Garton and Assocs. Inc., Vail, 1977-84, Kelton, Garton, Kendall, Vail, 1984—. Head agt. Dartmouth Alumni Fund, Hanover, N.H., 1985—. With U.S. Army, 1966-69. Republican. Congregationalist. Home: 1034 Homestake Cir Vail CO 81657 Office: Kelton Garton Kendall 288 Bridge St Vail CO 81657

KEMBLE, STEPHEN BROOKS, psychiatrist; b. Boston, May 19, 1947; s. Robert Day Kemble and Virginia Elizabeth (Owens) Fine; m. Naomi Shimoda, June 19, 1973; children: Sarah, Anne. BA, Reed Coll., 1969; MD, Harvard U., 1973. Intern in internal medicine The Queen's Med. Ctr., Honolulu, 1973-74; resident internal medicine U. Hawaii, Honolulu, 1975-76; resident in psychiatry Cambridge (Mass.) Hosp., 1976-79, fellow in psychiatry, consultation liaison, 1979-80; pvt. practice in psychiatry Honolulu, 1985—. Mem. ACP, AMA, Hawaii Med. Assn., Am. Psychiatric Assn., Hawaii Psychiatric Soc. Office: 600 Kapiolani Blvd Ste 211 Honolulu HI 90813

KEMMERLY, JACK DALE, state official; b. El Dorado, Kans., Sept. 17, 1936; s. Arthur Allen and Eythel Louise (Throckmorton) K.; m. Frances Cecile Gregorio, June 22, 1958; children: Jack Dale Jr., Kathleen Frances, Grant Lee. BA, San Jose State U., 1962; cert. in real estate, UCLA, 1970; MPA, Golden Gate U., 1973; cert. labor-mgmt. rels., U. Calif., Davis, 1978. Right of way agt. Calif. Div. Hwys., Marysville, 1962-7l; adminstrv. officer Calif. Dept. Transp., Sacramento, 197l-82; dist. dir. Calif. Dept. Transp., Redding, 1982-83; chief aeros. Calif. Dept. Transp., Sacramento, 1984—; mgmt. cons. U.S. Dept. Transp., Riyadh, Saudi Arabia, 1983-84; mem. Calif. Commn. on Aviation and Airports, 1987—. Bd. dirs. Yuba-Sutter Campfire Girls, 1972-73. With USN, 1954-57. Recipient superior accomplishment award Calif. Dept. Transp., 198l. Mem. Nat. Assn. State Aviation Ofcls. (nat. pres. 1989—), Am. Assn. State Hwy. and Transp. Ofcls. (aviation com. 1985—), Calif. Assn. Aerospace Educators (adv. bd. 1984—), Calif. Assn. Airport Execs., Calif. Aviation Coun., Aircraft Owners and Pilots Assn., Elks (exalted ruler Marysville, Calif. 1974-75). Republican. Roman Catholic. Office: Calif Div Transp-Aeros PO Box 942874 Sacramento CA 94274-0001

KEMP, DAVID WESTLEY, communications executive, police officer; b. San Diego, Dec. 10, 1958; s. George Washington and Marjorie Jean (Erickson) K. BBA, San Diego State U., 1981; AA in Criminal Justice, Rancho Santiago Coll., 1982. Owner Countryside Landscaping, Santa Ana, Calif., 1976-78; dep. sheriff Orange County, Santa Ana, 1977—; technician Motorola MSS, Westminster, Calif., 1979-81, Santa Ana, 1981-82; pres. internat. radiotelephone AT&T, Santa Ana, 1981-85; pres. Internat. Satellite, Santa Ana, 1982—; mgr. Western Mobile Telephone, Anaheim, Calif., 1987-88; supr., tech. svc. Global Telecommunications, PAC-TEL Cellular, Anaheim, 1988—; cable TV cons. Internat. Satellite, 1982—. Patentee multi plexor systems for satellite and cable TV. Mem. Nat. Assn. Bus. Radio Users, Orange County Dep. Sheriff's Assn. (mem. adv. com., youth com. 1989—). Republican. Office: Global Telecommunications 1990 S Anaheim Blvd Anaheim CA 92805

KEMP, JAMES P., clinical immunologist, pediatric allergist; b. Charleston, W.Va., June 18, 1936; s. James P. Kemp; m. Judith A. Kemp. BA in Biology, U. Va., 1958, MD, 1962. Diplomate Am. Bd. Pediatrics, Sub-bd. Pediatric Allergy, Am. Bd. Allergy and Immunology. Intern in pediatrics U. Fla., Gainesville, 1962-63; resident in pediatrics Emory U. Grady Meml. Hosp., Atlanta, 1964-65; staff pediatrician U.S. Naval Hosp., San Diego, 1965-67; fellow pediatric allergy and clin. immunology U. Calif., San Francisco, 1967-69; co-dir. pediatric allergy and immunology tng. prog. U. Calif., San Diego, 1969-76; pvt. practice pediatric allergy San Diego, 1969—; mem. med. staff U. Hosp., Mercy Hosp., Chilren's Hosp. and Health Ctr., Grossmont Hosp., Sharp's Meml. Hosp., all in San Diego; presenter numerous research papers in field. Mem. editorial bd. Respiratory Medicine

Today, 1985—; editorial adv. bd. Clin. Advances in Treatment of Allergic Reactions, 1987—, Am. Jour. Asthma and Allergy for Pediatricians, 1987—; contbr. 88 articles to med. jours. Fellow Am. Acad. Allergy and Immunology (Bronchopulmonary com. 1982, com. on drugs 1970—, Asthma Mortality Task Force 1986—, Research Council 1987—), Am. Acad. Pediatrics (exec. com. allergy and immunology sect. 1982—), Am. Assn. Cert. Allergists, Am. Coll. Chest Physicians (steering com. sect. on allergy and clin. immunology 1988); mem. AMA (drug evaluations cons. 1986), Am. Thoracic Soc., Assn. for the Care of Asthma, Western Soc. Allergy and Immunology, Calif. Med. Assn., Calif. Soc. Allergy and Clin. Immunology, San Diego County Med. Soc., San Diego Allergy Soc. (pres. 1971), Asthma and Allergy Found. Am. (pres. 1980). Republican. Home: 3264 Curlew San Diego CA 92103 Office: Allergy and Asthma Med Group 3444 Kearny Villa Rd Suite 100 San Diego CA 92123

KEMP, JEANNE FRANCES, office manager; b. L.A., Dec. 8, 1942; d. Damian Thomas and Helen Catherine (Bohin) Hanife; m. Don H. Kemp, Dec. 16, 1966 (div. 1972). AB, San Francisco State U., 1965. Food svc. technician United Air Lines, San Francisco, 1961-65; clk. N.Y. Life Ins., San Francisco, 1965-66; inventory clk. Ingersoll-Rand, San Francisco, 1966; advt./order clk. Patrick's Stationers, San Francisco, 1966-67; sec. Dartmouth Travel, Hanover, N.H., 1967-68, Olsten Temp. Svcs., N.Y.C., 1968-70; mgr. office Brown U. Devel., N.Y.C., 1970-73; asst. dir. Cen. Opera Svc., N.Y.C., 1974-85; office mgr., sec. Payne, Thompson, Walker & Taaffe, San Francisco, 1986—. Editor: Career Guide...Singers, 1985, Operas...for Children, 1985; asst. editor COS Bull., 1976-85; editorial asst.: Who's Who in Opera, 1975. Democrat. Roman Catholic. Office: Payne Thompson Walker & Taaffe 235 Montgomery Ste 760 San Francisco CA 94104

KEMP, LOUISA RUTH, nurse, firefighter; b. Pitts., Oct. 31, 1930; d. Albert Leonard and Bertha Christina (Birch) Huber; m. William Norman Kemp, May 27, 1950 (div. 1975); children: Janyce Louise Kemp Lipson, Barbra Lea Kemp Bilharz, Robert William, Paul Lee, Charles Albert. Diploma in nursing, San Bernardino Community Coll., Needles, Calif., 1983. Office nurse Santa Fe Clinic, Needles, 1953-57; spl. duty nurse Needles Communities Hosp., 1957-62; nurse supr. Santa Fe Clinic, 1962-79; staff nurse in surgery Needles Desert Communities Hosp., 1979—; CPR instr. Needles Desert Communities Hosp., 1987—; med. officer San Bernadino County Fire Dept., Needles, 1980-83, pub. info. officer 1983—. Mem. Calif. State Fireman Assn., Needles Firefighters Assn. (treas. 1987, 88), Beta Sigma Phi-Zeta Gamma (treas. 1966, sec. 1967, v.p. 1968, pres. 1969 named Sweetheart Queen 1969), Order of Rose (life). Office: Needles Desert Communities Hosp 1401 Bailey Ave Needles CA 92363

KEMP, NANCY PRIBANICH, educational and marketing consultant; b. Rochester, N.Y., Feb. 5, 1949; d. Andrew F. Prib and Ruth (Rymond) Jones; m. David S. Kemp, Dec. 26, 1967 (div. Oct. 1972): 1 child, Nolan Christopher. Student, Rochester Inst. Tech., 1967, Bay Park Jr. Coll., 1967-68, Dartmouth Coll., 1968-69, Brown U., 1971. Bus. columnist, photograher, classified sales rep. Conn. Valley Times Reporter, Springfield, Vt., 1970-71; salesman pub. Phoenix Times Pub. Co, Bristol, R.I., 1972-73; sales dir. Sentinel Newspapers, Denver, 1973-80; gen. mgr. Titsch Pub. Co., Denver, 1980-82; mtkg. dir. Scripps Howard Bus. Jours., Denver, 1982-86; cons. Kemp Mktg. & Cons., Denver, 1986—; pres. adv. com. Women'sCtr., Front Range Community Coll., Westminister, Colo., 1988. Mem. NAFE, Golden (Colo.) C. of C., Press Assn. Democrat. Lutheran. Home and Office: 618 Kinnikinnik Hill Golden CO 80401

KEMPF, GEORGE LEONARD, management executive; b. Chgo., Jan. 8, 1939; s. Jacob Andrew and June Viola (Lucht) K.; m. Bonnie Charlene Daulton, June 8, 1960 (div. 1971); m. Sally Jo Gunsaulies; children: Hayley Beth, Joseph Michael. Student, Wright State U., 1971, U. Wash., 1986-87. Cert. in Prodn. and Mgmt. Drafter Grimes Mfg. Co., Urbana, Ohio, 1958-66; designer Systems Rsch. Labs., Dayton, Ohio, 1966-68; devel. engr. Grimes Mfg. Co., Urbana, Ohio, 1968-77, sr. engr. Midland Ross div., 1977-80, mgr., electroluminescent engring., 1980-82, design mgr., 1982-83; engring mgr. Bell Industries IDD, Redmond, Wash., 1983—. Cubmaster Pack 553 Boy Scouts Am., Woodinville, Wash., 1985-88. Mem. Am. Prodn. & Inventory Control Soc., Soc. Automotive Engring., Soc. Advancement Material & Process Engring, Redmond C. of C., Lions (pres. 1987-88, sec. 1988—). Republican. Presbyterian. Home: 19225 NE 202 St Woodinville WA 98072 Office: Bell Industries IDD 18225 NE 76th St Redmond WA 98052

KEMPF, MARTINE, voice control device manufacturing company executive; b. Strasbourg, France, Dec. 9, 1958; came to U.S., 1985; d. Jean-Pierre and Brigitte Marguerite (Klockenbring) K. Student in Astronomy, Friedrich Wilhelm U., Bonn, Fed. Republic of Germany, 1981-83. Owner, mgr. Kempf, Sunnyvale, Calif., 1985—. Inventor Comeldir Multiplex Handicapped Driving Systems (Goldenes Lenkrad Axel Springer Verlag 1981), Katalavox speech recognition control system (Oscar, World Almanac Inventions 1984, Prix Grand Siecle, Comite Couronne Francaise 1985). Recipient Medal for Service to Humanity Spinal Cord Soc., 1986; street named in honor in Dossenheim-Kochersberg, Alsace, France, 1987; named Citizen of Honor City of Dossenheim-Kochersberg, 1985. Home: 730 E Evelyn Sunnyvale CA 94086 Office: Kempf 1080 E Duane Ave Ste E Sunnyvale CA 94086

KEMPNER, KENNETH MARC, educator; b. N.Y.C., Aug. 7, 1947; s. Jack J. and Marjorie Harriet (Wasserthal) K.; m. Cheryl Lou Ouse, Nov. 20, 1971; children: Brandon, Jessica. BA, U. Mont., 1969; MA, U. Colo., 1974; PhD, U. Oreg., 1979. Dir. info. Barton Community Coll., Great Bend, Kans., 1974-76; research asst. U. Oreg., Eugene, 1976-79, asst. prof. higher edn. and research, 1986—; research assoc. Portland (Oreg.) State U., 1979-82, asst. prof., 1982-86; cons. Oreg. State Dept. Edn., Northwest Regional Edn. Lab., U. Portland, Portland Pub. Schs., Eugene Schs., Lane Community Coll., Outward Bound, Evergreen Coll., Bur. Land Mgmt. Author: (with others) Sex Equity in Educational Leadership, 1980; contbr. articles to profl. jours. Cons. Gov.'s Commn. Student Retention Community Coll. Subcom., Salem, Oreg., 1988; bd. dirs. Willamette Valley Racial Consortium, Portland, 1985-87. Fulbright scholar, Brazil, 1985. Mem. Am. Edn. Research Assn., Am. Assn. Community and Jr. Colls., Council Univs. and Colls., Am. Edn. Studies Assn. Democrat. Office: U Oreg Div Edn Policy and Mgmt Eugene OR 97403

KEMPTHORNE, DIRK ARTHUR, mayor; b. San Diego, Oct. 29, 1951; s. James Henry and Maxine Jesse (Gustason) K.; m. Patricia Jean Merrill, Sept. 18, 1977; children: Heather Patricia, Jeffrey Dirk. BS in Polit. Sci., U. Idaho, 1975. Exec. asst. to dir. Idaho Dept. Lands, Boise, 1975-78; exec. v.p. Idaho Home Builders Assn., Boise, 1978-80; campaign mgr. Batt for Gov., Boise, 1980-82; lic. securities rep. Swanson Investments, Boise, 1983; Idaho pub. affairs mgr. FMC Corp., Boise, 1983-86; mayor Boise, 1986—. Pres. Assn. Students U. Idaho, Moscow, 1975; chmn. bd. dirs. Wesleyan Presch., Boise, 1982-85; mem. magistrate commn. 4th Jud. Dist., Boise, 1986—. Republican. Methodist. Home: 2211 Cornwale Ct Boise ID 83706 Office: Office of the Mayor PO Box 500 Boise ID 83701 *

KENAGY, JOHN WARNER, surgeon; b. Lincoln, Nebr., May 28, 1945; s. Wyman Black and Sylvia (Adams) K.; m. Barbara Penterman, Feb. 1968 (div. 1975); 1 child, Jennifer; m. Jonell Day, Apr. 21, 1978; children: Susanne, Emma, John Wyman. BS, U. Nebr., 1967, MD, U. Nebr., Omaha, 1971. Diplomate Am. Bd. Surgery; splty. cert. in gen. vascular surgery. Intern, Hosps. of U. Wash., Seattle, 1971-72, resident in surgery, 1971-76; surgeon Longview Gen. & Thoracic Surgery, Longview, Wash., 1976—; clin. instr. surgery U. Wash., Seattle, 1979-82, clin. asst. prof. surgery, 1982—; dir. peripheral vascular services St. Johns Hosp., Longview, 1979-88, chmn. credentials com., 1989-90; editor current concepts in vascular diagnosis St. Johns Vascular Lab., Longview, 1979-88. Contbr. articles to profl. jours. Chmn. bd. dirs. Cowlitz Med. Service, Longview, 1985-86. Regents scholar U. Nebr., Lincoln, 1963-67. Fellow ACS, Henry Harkins Surg. Soc. (trustee 1983-84), Seattle Surg. Soc.; mem. Internat. Cardiovascular Soc., Pacific N.W. Vascular Soc. (pres.-elect 1986-87, pres. 1987-88), Alpha Omega Alpha, Theta Nu, Phi Gamma Delta. Republican. Office: Longview Gen & Thoracic Surgery 900 Fir St Ste 1-J Longview WA 98632

KENDALL, THOMAS LEE, engineering executive; b. Long Beach, Calif., Aug. 23, 1946; s. Albert Russell and Constance Mary (Thady) K.; m. Kathryn Ann Delperdang, Jan. 29, 1966; children: Shalimar Anne, Scott Alexander. AA, Pasadena City Coll., 1967; Bachelors, Calif. State U., Los Angeles, 1973; MBA, Nat. U., Vista, Calif., 1987. Engr. The Digitran Co., Pasadena, Calif., 1968-73; mgr. electronics The Toro Co., Riverside, Calif., 1973-79; mgr. engring. Electro-Static Sound Systems, Sacramento, 1979-81; supr. design services Gen. Electric Med. Systems, Sacramento, 1981-84; mgr. mfg. material control Dynatech Fluid Tech. Corp., Sacramento, 1984-85; mgr. engring. Advanced Structures, San Marcos, Calif., 1985-88; engring. analyst Fujitsu Systems Am., Inc., San Diego, 1988—; mem. Modern Plastics Mgmt. Adv. Council, 1981-82. Contbr. articles to profl. jours.; patentee in field. Res. dep. San Bernardino County Sheriff's Office, Big Bear Lake, 1974-79, comdr. res. unit, 1976-78. Recipient Letter of Commendation San Bernardino County Sheriff's Office. Mem. ASME, Soc. Mfg. Engrs., Am. Soc. Metals, Am. Production and Inventory Countrol Soc., Nat. Mgmt. Assn. Republican. Methodist. Home: 1019 Partridge Ct San Marcos CA 92069 Office: 12670 High Bluff Dr San Diego CA 92130

KENDIG, MARTIN WILLIAM, chemist; b. Danville, Pa., Oct. 20, 1945; s. Paul Miller and Adelaide Anna Augusta (Hagerty) K.; m. Michele Lynne Mulligan, Feb. 19, 1969; children: Rebecca, Jamie. AB, Franklin and Marshall Coll., 1967; PhD, Brown U., 1974. Rsch. assoc. Lehigh U., Bethlehem, Pa., 1973-76; assoc. chemist Brookhaven Nat. Lab., Upton, N.Y., 1976-80; with tech. staff Rockwell Internat., Thousand Oaks, Calif., 1980—. Mem. Electrochem. Soc. (exec. com. corrosion div. 1987—), Nat. Assn. Corrsion Engrs. (chmn. task group 1986-89, chmn. corrosion aerospace structural materials 1989—), ASTM, Sigma Xi (v.p. Rockwell chpt. 1988-89, pres. 1989—). Office: Rockwell Internat Sci Ctr 1049 Camino dos Rios Thousand Oaks CA 91360

KENDLE, NICK WARREN, marketing professional; b. Perry, Okla., Mar. 30, 1950; s. Howard Warren and Glenda Francis (Webb) K.; m. Debra Elaine Ram, Jan. 24, 1971 (div. Aug. 1988). Student, Phoenix Coll., 1968-69, Cen. Ariz. Coll., Coolidge, 1969-70, Ariz. State, Tempe, 1970-71. Engring. rep. Southwest Gas Corp., Casa Grande, Ariz., 1974-79; v.p. sales Metasoft Corp., Chandler, Ariz., 1979-84; supr. mktg. svcs. Southwest Gas Corp., Las Vegas, Nev., 1984-88; v.p. mktg. Enercom/Equifax, Tempe, Ariz., 1988—. Sustaining mem. Republican Nat. Com., Phoenix, 1987-89; mem. The 1988 Presidential Trust, Phoenix, 1988. Mem. Pacific Coast Gas Assn., Am. Mgmt. Assn., So. Ariz. Assn. of Tele-Profls., Am. Gas Assn. (Mktg. Program awards 1984, 86), Pachyderms (second v.p. 1988). Republican. Roman Catholic. Home: 1119 E Ninth St Casa Grande AZ 85222 Office: Enercom/Equifax 6115 S Kyrene Rd Tempe AZ 85283

KENDRICK, WILLIAM MARVIN, school system administrator. m. Carol Kendrick; children: Julie, Jeffrey, Jay. BA, Western Wash. U., 1953; MA, UCLA, 1960; postgrad., San Diego State Coll., 1965, Northwestern U., 1968. Supt. Seattle Pub. Schs. Office: Seattle Pub Schs 815 4th Ave N Seattle WA 98109

KENDRO, ROBERT LOUIS, financial executive; b. Canton, Ohio, Sept. 5, 1934; s. Joseph F. and Anna M (Kvasnick) K.; m. Nancy A. Holeski, Dec. 28, 1963; children: Lisa, Stephen. BS, Kent State U., 1968. Asst. supt. Wickliffe (Ohio) City Schs., 1964-69; asst. to fin. dir. City of Newport Beach, Calif., 1969-71; dir. finance City of Upland, Calif., 1971-76, City of Reno, Nev., 1976-78; dir. property and fin. Airport Authority of Washoe County, Reno, 1978-84; controller EPCO, Reno, 1984-85; fin. mgr. Tucson Airport Authority, 1986—. Bus. adv. council mem. Tucson Unified Sch. Dist., 1988-89. Mem. Ariz. Airports Assn., Calif. Assn. Airport Execs., Airport Operations Council, Gov. Fin. Officers Assn., Catalina Rotary, Reno S. Rotary, Upland Rotary. Roman Catholic. Home: 3202 N Placita Brazos Tucson AZ 85715 Office: Tucson Airport Authority 7005 S Plumer Tucson AZ 85706

KENEMORE, LAWRENCE D., JR., insurance executive; b. Bakersfield, Calif., May 18, 1944; s. Lawrence D. and Dorothy (Frick) K.; m. Carol McEntire (div.); m. Sherlyn Denice Hill; children: Joseph, Craig, Larry III, Brent, Matthew. Dist. mgr. Fuller Brush Co., Whittier, Calif., 1967-70; v.p. AIS Ins., Anaheim, Calif., 1970-75; pres. Countywide Inc., Bolivar, Mo., 1975-79; paramedic City of San Diego, 1980-85; v.p. Unico Ins. Agy., Cerritos, Calif., 1980-87; pres. Bestland Ins. Agy., Brea, Calif., 1987—; instr. Southwest Baptist U., Bolivar, Mo., 1975-79; pres. Mo. Assn. EMT Paramedics, 1976-79; bd. dirs., founder Nat. Assn. EMT Paramedics, Braintree, Mass., 1976-79. Pres. Fullerton (Calif.) Pop-Warner Football League, 1985—. Served with USN, 1964-66. Mem. Profl. Ins. Agts. Assn. Republican. Mem. Church of the Brethren. Home: 637 El Mirador Dr Fullerton CA 92635

KENISON, LYNN T., chemist; b. Provo, Utah, Feb. 20, 1943; s. John Silves and Grace (Thacker) K.; m. Daralyn Wold, June 10, 1969; children: Marlene, Mark, Evan, Guy, Amy, Suzanne. BS in Chemistry, Brigham Young U., 1968, MS in Chemistry, 1971. Tchr. Weber County Sch. Dist., Ogden, Utah, 1968-69; chemist Salt Lake City County Health Dept., 1971-74, U.S. Dept. Labor OSHA Lab., Salt Lake City, 1974—; bench chemist (drugs) Salt Lake City County Health Dept., 1971-74, U.S. Dept. Labor OSHA lab., Salt Lake City, 1974-77; supr., branch chief U.S. Dept. Labor OSHA Lab., Salt Lake City, 1977-84, sr. chemist, 1984—. Editor, Review Methods Before Publication, 1984—. City councilman West Bountiful City, Utah, 1980-83, 85—; area scouting coord. Boy Scouts Am.; full time missionary for church in Ark., Mo., Ill., 1962-64. Mem. Am. Idsl. Hygiene Assn., Fed. Exec. Assn. (Disting. Svc. award, Jr. Award for Outstanding Fed. & Community Svc.), Toastmasters Internat. (treas. Salt Lake City 1987-88). Mormon. Home: 1745 N 600 West Bountiful UT 84087

KENISON, ROBERT JOHN, financial executive; b. Dillon, Mont., Oct. 9, 1948; s. Floyd Sanders and Norlene (Buchmiller) K.; m. Helen Hayes, Dec. 25, 1968 (div. 1976); children: Erika Renate, Michael Hayes, Wendy Claire; Eugenie Annette Veers, May 6, 1988; 1 child, Aimee Marie. AA, Phoenix Coll., 1971; BS, Ariz. State U., 1974. Accredited Bus. Credit Exec. Dept. mgr. J.C. Penney, Vallejo, Calif., 1968-70; credit analyst Am. Express, Phoenix, 1970-71; br. mgr. Security Pacific, Tucson, Yuma, Ariz., 1975-79; consumer lending mgr. SW Savs., Phoenix, 1979-80; credit mgr. The Tanner Cos., Phoenix, 1980-88; fin. mgr. York Internat., Phoenix, 1988; credit mgr. Penn. Athletic Products, Phoenix, 1988—; pres. Tanner Employees Credit Union, Phoenix, 1984-86, Mesa (Ariz.) Bd. Adjustment, 1988—. Chmn. Mesa Design Rev. Bd., 1986-88, Mesa Crime Prevention Bd., 1984-86; com. chmn. Gov.'s Council Devel. Disabilities, Phoenix, 1986-88; bd. dirs. Mesa Assn. Retarded Citizens. Fellow Nat. Inst. Credit; mem. Credit Reseach Found., Nat. Assn. Credit Mgrs. (bd. dirs. 1988—), Ariz. State U. Alumni Assn. (bd. dirs. 1974-75), Yuma Jaycees (pres. 1977-79), Dons Club. Republican. Mormon. Office: Penn Athletic Products 306 S 45th Ave Phoenix AZ 85043

KENNALEY, MICHAEL THOMAS, construction company executive; b. Oakland, Calif., June 30, 1950; s. Thomas H. Kennaley and Joyce Edna (Poli) Luttrell, m. Linda Louise, Feb. 6, 1970 (div. 1985); children: Heather, Tawnya. BS in Criminology, Modesto (Calif.) Jr. Coll., 1975. Chief draftsman Varco-Pruden, Inc., Turlock, Calif., 1970-74; officer Modesto Police Dept., Turlock, 1971-76; designer, draftsman Hogan Mfg. Co., Escalon, Calif., 1976-78; estimator, projects mgr. H.L. Hegstedd, Belmont, Calif., 1978-80; project mgr. H.H. Robertson, Stockton, Calif., 1980-84; ops. mgr. Gen. Am. Window Co., Stockton, Calif., 1984-87; estimator Cobbledick-Kibbe Glass Co., Alameda, Calif., 1987-88; estimator, regional mgr. Bello Glass Co., San Francisco, 1988—; owner MTK Exports, Modesto, 1988—, MTK Constrn., Modesto, 1988—; cons. in field. Res. police officer Modesto Police Dept., 1971-76. With USN, 1968-70. Democrat. Roman Catholic. Home: 3200 Hahn Dr Apt B Modesto CA 95356 Office: Bello Glass Co 4861 Mission St San Francisco CA 94112

KENNEDY, BETH BLUMENREICH, film studio executive; b. Detroit, Mar. 11, 1950; d. Leonard and Bernice Blumenreich; m. Michael F. Kennedy; 1 child, Joshua Hayes. BA, U. Mich., 1971; MA, UCLA, 1974; JD, Southwestern U., 1984. Mgr. sensurround dept. Universal Studios, Universal City, Calif., 1975; asst. to studio mgr. Universal Studios, Universal City, 1977, adminstr. transp. dept., 1978, dir. infor systems TV & UP, 1980; dir. corp. int. mgmt. MCA Inc., Universal City, 1982-87; v.p. planning and adminstrn. Universal Studios, Universal City, 1987, sr. v.p. planning and adminstrn., 1989—. Contbr. articles to profl. jour. Mem. legal com. The Nurtury, Sherman Oaks, Calif., 1988—. Named one of Outstanding Young Women of Am., Outstanding Young Women of Am. awards program, 1980. Mem. ABA, Women in Bus. (mem. com. 1985-88), Orgn. of Women Execs. (chair membership com. 1989, bd. dirs.), NAFE, Women's Referral Svc., Inc, Women in Film, Beverly Hills Bar Assn., L.A. County Bar Assn. Office: Universal City Studios 100 Universal City Pla Universal City CA 91608

KENNEDY, DAVID MICHAEL, historian, educator; b. Seattle, July 22, 1941; s. Albert John and Mary Ellen (Caufield) K.; m. Judith Ann Osborne, Mar. 14, 1970; children: Ben Caufield, Elizabeth Margaret, Thomas Osborne. B.A., Stanford U., 1963; M.A., Yale U., 1964, Ph.D., 1968. Asst. prof. history Stanford (Calif.) U., 1967-72, assoc. prof., 1972-80, prof., 1980—, William Robertson Coe prof. history and Am. studies, 1987—, chmn. program in internat. relations, 1977-80, assoc. dean Sch. Humanities and Scis., 1981-85; William Robertson Coe prof. History and Am. Studies, 1987—; vis. prof. U. Florence, Italy, 1976-77; lectr. Internat. Communications Agy., Denmark, Finland, Turkey, Italy, 1976-77, Ireland, 1980. Author: Birth Control in America: The Career of Margaret Sanger, 1970, Over Here: The First World War and American Society, 1980, (with Thomas A. Bailey) The American Pageant: A History of the Republic, 8th edit, 1987, Power and Responsibility: Case Studies in American Leadership, 1986; mem. adv. bd. (TV program) The American Experience, Sta. WGBH, 1986—. Mem. nat. planning group Am. Issues Forum, 1974-75; bd. dirs. CORO Found., 1981-87, Environ. Traveling Companions, 1986—. Recipient Bancroft prize, 1971, John Gilmary Shea prize, 1970, Richard W. Lyman award Stanford U. Alumni Assn., 1989; fellow Am. Council Learned Socs., 1971-72, John Simon Guggenheim Meml. Found., 75-76, Ctr. for Advanced Study in Behavioral Scis., 1986-87. Mem. Am. Hist. Assn., Orgn. Am. Historians, Soc. Am. Historians, Am. Studies Assn. Democrat. Roman Catholic. Office: Stanford U Dept History Stanford CA 94305-2024

KENNEDY, DEBRA JOYCE, marketing professional; b. Covina, Calif., July 9, 1955; d. John Nathan and Drea Hannah (Lancaster) Ward; m. John William Kennedy, Sept. 3, 1977 (div.); children: Drea, Noelle. B.S. in Communications, Calif. State Poly. U., 1977. Pub. relations coordinator Whittier (Calif.) Hosp., 1978-79, pub. relations mgr., 1980; pub. relations dir. San Clemente (Calif.) Hosp., 1979-80; dir. pub. relations Garfield Med. Ctr., Monterey Park, Calif., 1980-82; dir. mktg. and community relations Charter Oak Hosp., Covina, 1983-85; mktg. dir. CPC Horizon Hosp., Pomona, 1985—. Mem. Am. Soc. Hosp. Pub. Relations, Healthcare Mktg. Assn., Healthcare Pub. Relations and Mktg. Assn., Covina and Covina West C. of C., West Covina Jaycees. Republican. Methodist. Club: Soroptimists (coord. council Pomona chpt.). Contbr. articles to profl. jours.

KENNEDY, DONALD, university president; b. N.Y.C., Aug. 18, 1931; s. William Dorsey and Barbara (Bean) K.; children: Laura Page, Julia Hale; m. Robin Beth Wiseman, Nov. 27, 1987; stepchildren: Cameron Rachel, Jamie Christopher. AB, Harvard U., 1952, AM, 1954, PhD, 1956; DSc (hon.), Columbia U., Williams Coll., U. Mich., U. Ariz., U. Rochester, Reed Coll. Mem. faculty Syracuse U., 1956-60; mem. faculty Stanford U., 1960-77, prof. biol. scis., 1965-77, chmn. dept., 1965-72; sr. cons. Office Sci. and Tech. Policy, Exec. Office of Pres., 1976; commr. FDA, 1977-79; v.p., provost Stanford U., 1979-80, pres., 1980—; bd. overseers Harvard U., 1970-76; bd. dirs. Health Effects Inst., Clean Sites Inc., Calif. Nature Conservancy, Nat. Commn. on Pub. Svc. Author: (with W. H. Telfer) The Biology of Organisms, 1965; also articles.; editor: The Living Cell, 1966, From Cell to Organism, 1967; editorial bd. Jour. Exptl. Zoology, 1965-71, Jour. Comparative Physiology, 1965-76, Jour. Neurophysiology, 1969-75, Science, 1973-77. Fellow Am. Acad. Arts and Scis., AAAS; mem. Nat. Acad. Scis., Am. Philos. Soc. Office: Stanford U Office of Pres Stanford CA 94305

KENNEDY, DONALD REID, engineer; b. San Diego, Dec. 7, 1922; s. James Royce and Berniece Estelle (McMakin) K.; m. Jacqueline Marie Harbarger, Aug. 1949 (div. 1965); children: Michael, Robert, Laurie, Paul; m. Wilma LaJune Relaford, Sept. 3, 1966; 1 child, Kathryn. BA in Gen. Engring. with hons., San Diego State U., 1948. Analyst missile flight test Convair, San Diego, 1948-49; scientific staff asst., ordnance engr. USN Ordnance Test Sta., China Lake, Calif., 1949-53; tech. specialist, tech. asst. to mgr. ordnance div. Aerojet Gen. Corp., Azusa, Downey, Glendale, Calif., 1953-65; sr. tech. specialist Def. Tech. Labs. FMC Corp., Santa Clara, Calif., 1965-75; sr. rsch. specialist Shock Hydrodynamics div. Whittaker Corp., Los Altos, Calif., 1975-76; ordnance engr., cons. Setter Assocs., Inc., Menlo Park, Calif., 1976-78; pres. D.R. Kennedy & Assocs., Inc., Los Altos, Calif., 1978—; cons. terminal ballistician.; researcher in field. Contbr. articles to profl. jours.; patentee in ballistics. Served with U.S. Army, 1940-43. Named to Order of St. Barbara U.S. Army Artillery Ctr., 1983. Mem. Am. Def. Preparedness Assn. (life, recipient Bronze medal 1983, ADPA award 1989), U.S. Armor Assn. (winner tank design contest. 1962), Royal Philatelic Soc. (London), Pearl Harbor Survivors Assn., Am. Philatelic Soc., Friends of the Western Philatelic Library, Sigma Xi, Sigma Pi Sigma. Republican. Lutheran. Home: 1470 Montclair Pl Los Altos CA 94022 Office: PO Box 4003 Mountain View CA 94040

KENNEDY, ELGIN KEITH, gastroenterologist; b. Glendale, Calif., Nov. 7, 1940; s. William Elgin and Claribel (Keith) K.; m. Anne Catherine Male, Mar. 7, 1981; children: Keith Elgin, Catherine Clare. BA in History, U. Calif., Berkeley, 1962; MD, Stanford U., 1967. Diplomate Am. Bd. Internal Medicine in medicine and gastroenterology. Pracitce medicine specializing in gastroenterology San Mateo, Calif., 1975—; asst. clin. prof. U. Calif. Sch. Medicine, San Francisco, 1976-84, assoc. clin. prof., 1984—. Bd. dirs. Pacific Peer Review, Inc., Oakland, Calif., 1985—. Lt. comdr. USPHS, 1970-72. Mem. AMA, ACP, Calif. Med. Assn., Am. Soc. Internal Medicine. Office: 109 St Matthews Ave San Mateo CA 94401

KENNEDY, GEORGE HUNT, chemistry educator; b. Seattle, Apr. 24, 1936; s. George Francis and Frances (Huse) K.; m. Kay Rife, Sept. 1, 1961; children: Joseph, Jill. BS in Chemistry, U. Oreg., 1959; MS in Chemistry, Oreg. State U., 1962, PhD in Phys. Chemistry, 1966. Chemist Borden Chem. Co., Springfield, Oreg., 1957-58; rsch. chemist Chevron Rsch. Corp., Richmond, Calif., 1961-62; prof. chemistry Colo. Sch. Mines, Golden, 1965—. Contbr. articles to profl. jours. With USNR, 1954-62. Mem. Am. Chem. Soc., Internat. Oceanographic Found., Sigma Xi, Phi Lambda Upsilon. Democrat. Office: Colo Sch Mines Chemistry Dept Golden CO 80401

KENNEDY, JAMES CLELLAN, infosystems specialist; b. Louisville, Feb. 11, 1952; s. John Leslie and Leola (Miller) K.; m. Colleen Marie O'Connell, June 28, 1980; children: Kelly Jacqueline, James Alexander II, Katherine Marie. BA, Coll. William and Mary, 1974, MBA, 1976. Mgmt. cons. Arthur Andersen & Co., Washington, 1976-79; project mgr. Info. Svcs. Group, Mars, Inc., Randolph, N.J., 1979-80; systems and programming mgr. Info. Svcs. Group, Mars, Inc., 1980-82; dir. systems devel. Fluor Corp., Irvine, Calif., 1982-84; mgr. info. systems Fluor Corp., 1984-86; v.p. systems devel. First Capital Life Ins. Co., San Diego, 1986—. Vol. exec. San Diego campaign United Way, 1987--. Baptist. Home: 3971 Tynebourne Cir San Diego CA 92130 Office: First Capital Life Ins Co 10241 Wateridge Cir San Diego CA 92121-2733

KENNEDY, JOHN HARVEY, chemistry educator; b. Oak Park, Ill., Apr. 24, 1933; s. John Harvey and Margaret Helen (Drenthe) K.; m. Joan Corinne Hipsky, June 9, 1956 (div. Mar. 1969); children: Bruce Laurence, Bryan Donald, Brent Peter, Jill Amy.; m. Victoria Jane Matthew, July 2, 1970; 1 child, Karen Anne. BS, UCLA, 1954; AM, Harvard U., 1956, PhD, 1957. Sr. research chemist E.I. du Pont de Nemours, Wilmington, Del., 1957-61; asst. prof. chemistry U. Calif., Santa Barbara, 1961-63, prof., 1967—, chmn. dept., 1982-85; assoc. prof. Boston Coll., Chestnut Hill, 1963-64; head inorganic chemistry Gen. Motors, Santa Barbara, 1964-67; cons. Union Carbide Corp., Cleve., 1983—; vis. prof. U. N.C., Chapel Hill, 1980-81, Japan Soc. Promotion of Sci., Nagoya, 1984-85. Author: Analytical Chemistry, Principles, 1984, Analytical Chemistry, Practice, 1984; contbr. articles to profl. jours; patentee in field. Mus. dir. Christ the King Episcopal Ch., Santa Barbara, 1982—. Mem. Am. Chem. Soc., Electrochem. Soc. Democrat. Home: 5357 Agana Dr Santa Barbara CA 93111 Office: U Calif Dept Chemistry Santa Barbara CA 93106

KENNEDY, L. THOMAS, restaurateur and developer; b. Metropolis, Ill., Oct. 5, 1934; s. Nellis Lowell and Dora Esther (Womack) K.; m. Binni Jo Lewis, June 10, 1955; children: Lori Ann, Scott Thomas. Owner Kennedy's Kwik Inn, Colorado Springs, Colo., 1956—, A&W Drive-In, Security, Colo., 1959-77; developer Security (Colo.) Shoppette, 1983-84, Ivywild Plaza, Colorado Springs, 1986—. Treas. Ch. Christ, Security, 1965-77; cons. Widefield High Sch. Adv. Council, Security, 1974-76. Mem. Colo. A&W Operators Assn. (bd. dirs., v.p. 1970-75, pres. 1974-75), Security Businessmen's Assn. (pres. 1969-70). Republican. Clubs: Broadmoor Figure Skating (bd. dirs. 1968-72); Adaman (Colorado Springs) (named Mem. of Year 1979). Home: 2607 Leo Dr Colorado Springs CO 80906 Office: Kwik Inn 385 Main St Colorado Springs CO 80911

KENNEDY, LINDA FRANCIS, public relations executive. Pres. NASA Facts, 1980—, Bobby Curtola, Inc., 1981—; protocal, pub. rels. liaison The Great Space Shuttle Exhibition of Japan, 1982-84; care Cernan Corp.-USA; cons. in field; exhibitor liaison Air/Space Am., Mil. Base Air Shows, 1980—; prin. investigator NASA Space Adaptation Rsch. Program, 1986. Author, pub. Space is the Place, 1987. Mem. RFK Meml. Found. Mem. Hon. Fellows of the JFK Library (hon. life mem., founding mem.), Smithsonian Inst. (air, space mus.), Aircraft Owners and Pilots Assn., Kans. Cosmosphere & Space Ctr. Democrat. Roman Catholic.

KENNEDY, ORIN, film company executive; b. N.Y.C., May 24, 1939; s. Solomon Fuchs and Gertrude Krex. BFA, N.Y. Sch. Interior Design, 1963. Prodn. assoc. Fries Entertainment, Los Angeles, 1976-84; exec. location mgr. Metro-Goldwyn-Mayer subs. United Artists Entertainment, Culver City, Calif., 1984-85; exec. location mgr. The Twilight Zone TV series CBS Entertainment, Los Angeles, 1985-86; exec. location mgr. LA Law TV series 20th Century Fox Film Corp., Los Angeles, 1986—.

KENNEDY, RAYMOND MCCORMICK, JR., interior designer; b. Glendale, Calif., Sept. 19, 1930; s. Raymond McCormick and June (Sparks) K.; adopted son Myrtle Abrahamson Kennedy. BA in Architecture, U. Calif.-Berkeley, 1956. Draftsman, Bechtel Corp., San Francisco, 1956-58; draftsman/designer Maher & Martens, Architects, San Francisco, 1956; free lance designer, San Francisco, 1966-67; designer Bernard J. Block, Architect, San Francisco, 1967-69; v.p. Rodgers Assocs., San Francisco, 1969-77; pres. RMK Design, Inc., San Francisco, 1977-83; pres. Kennedy-Bowen Assocs., Inc., San Francisco, 1983—; mem. faculty Acad. of Art Coll., San Francisco, 1982-86. Bd. dirs. San Francisco Easter Seals Soc., 1974-79; bd. dirs., pres. Design Found., Inc., 1986-87. Served with U.S. Army, 1952-54. Mem. Golden Gate U. Assocs., Am. Soc. Interior Designers (dir., v.p. No. Calif. chpt. 1983, sec. bd. 1984, pres. 1987-88, nat. bd. dirs. 1989—), Nat. Trust for Hist. Preservation, Assocs. for San Francisco's Archtl. Heritage. Presbyterian. Clubs: Commonwealth, Press (San Francisco). Office: Kennedy-Bowen Assocs Inc 930 Lombard St San Francisco CA 94133

KENNEDY, RICHARD CORRINGTON, JR., accountant; b. Denver, Oct. 14, 1964; s. Richard Corrington and Sharon Lynn (Calomino) K. BBA, U. Notre Dame. CPA. Research asst. U. Notre Dame, South Bend, Ind., 1986-87; staff acct. Ernst and Whinney, Denver, 1987—. Hockey Coach Cherry Creek High Sch., Littleton, Colo., 1987. Home: 4938 E Lake Ave Littleton CO 80121 Office: Ernst and Whinney 4300 Republic Pla Denver CO 80202

KENNEDY, SHEILA GRACE, medical social worker; b. San Jose, Calif., May 17, 1949; d. Irwin Thomas and Martha Ruth (Markey) O'Connell; m. Timothy Anthony Kennedy, Apr. 4, 1975; children: Maureen, Timmy, Patrick. BA in Social Work, Coll. Notre Dame, 1971; MA in Counseling Psychology, U. Santa Clara, 1977. Elem. sch. tchr. St. Louise de Marrillac Sch., Covina, Calif., 1971-72; dir. social services and hospice Sequoia Hosp., Redwood City, Calif., 1972—. Mem. adv. bd. peer counseling for srs. San Carlos (Calif.) Sr. Ctr., 1986-88; bd. dirs. San Mateo (Calif.) County com. on child abuse, 1981-83, Parish bd. edn., Nativity Ch., 1984—, pres. 1988; v.p. bd. dirs. Am. Cancer Soc., San Mateo County, Burlingame, Calif., 1983-85, pres. bd. dirs., 1985-87. Named Woman of Yr. Notre Dame High Sch., San Jose, 1989. Mem. Nat. Assn. Social Workers, Am. Hosp. Assn., Hosp. Social Work Dirs. Democrat. Roman Catholic. Home: 67 Lorelei Ln Menlo Park CA 94025 Office: Sequoia Hosp Whipple and Alameda Redwood City CA 94062

KENNEDY, SUSAN CICCARELLI, financial planner, nurse; b. L.A., Nov. 12, 1953; d. Vincent James and Alberta (Bennett) Ciccarelli; m. J. Rodney Kennedy (div. Feb. 1989). BSN, Loma Linda U., 1975, cert. pediatric nurse, 1976, MPH, 1979. RN, Calif. Nurse coord. St. Helena Hosp. and Health Ctr., Deer Park, Calif., 1979-84; critical care home care nurse Queen of Valley Hosp., Napa, Calif., 1984-85; fin. planner Kennedy Fin. Mgmt., Napa, 1985—; chmn. Valley Investment Ptnrs., St. Helena, Calif., 1985-88. Bd. dirs. Planned Parenthood, Contra Costa County, Calif., 1989—. Mem. Napa Valley Tennis Assn. (bd. dirs.), Soroptimists. Republican. Adventist. Office: 1001 2d St Ste 295 Napa CA 94559

KENNEDY-MINOTT, RODNEY, international relations educator, former ambassador; b. Portland, Oreg.; s. Joseph Albert and Gainor (Baird) Minott; children: Katharine Pardow, Rodney Glisan, Polly Berry. AB, Stanford U., 1953, MA, 1956, PhD, 1960. Instr. history Stanford U., 1960-61, asst. prof., asst. dir. history of western civilization program, 1961-62, asst. dir. summer session, 1962-63, dir. summer session, 1963-65; assoc. prof. Portland State U., 1965-66; assoc. prof., assoc. dean instrn. Calif. State U., Hayward, 1966-67, prof., 1967-77, head div. humanities, 1967-69; ambassador to Sweden and chmn. Swedish Fulbright Com. 1977-80; adj. prof. Monterey Inst. Internat. Studies, Calif., 1981; exec. v.p. Direction Internat., Washington, 1982-83; sr. research fellow Hoover Instn., 1981-82, 85—; chmn. Alpha Internat., Washington, 1983-85; congl. staff mem., 1965-66; sr. fellow Ctr. Internat. and Strategic Affairs, UCLA, 1986—; lectr. in field. Author: Peerless Patriots: The Organized Veterans and the Spirit of Americanism, 1962; The Fortress That Never Was: The Myth of Hitler's Bavarian Stronghold, 1964; The Sinking of the Lollipop: Shirley Temple v. Pete McCloskey, 1968, Regional Force Application: The Maritime Strategy and Its Affect on Nordic Stability, 1988, Regional Power Projection: The U.S. Forward Maritime Strategy and Scandinavia, 1988, The Far North: Tension Point, 1989. Mem. citizen's adv. council Dominican Coll.; mem. adv. council Pacific Rim Studies, Dominican Coll., San Rafael, Calif.; bd. dirs. Inst. Internat. Studies; adv. bd. Ctr. for the Pacific Rim U. San Francisco, 1988—. Served with U.S. Army, 1950-52. Mem. Am. Hist. Assn., Orgn. Am. Historians, World Affairs Council No. Calif., Internat. Studies Assn., Am. Fgn. Service Assn. (assoc.), Internat. Inst. for Strategic Studies, Swedish-Am. C. of C. Clubs: Marines Meml. Assn. (San Francisco), Multnomah Athletic (Portland, Oreg.). Office: Stanford U The Hoover Instn RM231 LHH Stanford CA 94305

KENNERLY, ROBERT WILSON, financial executive; b. Detroit, Feb. 13, 1931; s. Samuel Wilson and Margaret Claire (Kelley) K.; m. Jeannette Wade, June 14, 1947; children: Kathryn, Carol, Margaret, Robin. With Superlite Builders Supply, Yuma, Ariz., 1948-56; purchasing agt. Holiday Homes, Yuma, 1957-60; v.p. Nixon Homes, Yuma, 1960-63; sec./treas. West Ariz Coun. Grants, Yuma, 1969-74; exec. dir. Rain Forest, Yuma, 1974—; bd. dirs. So. Ariz. Bank, Yuma, Cocopah Devel. Corp., Yuma, Sunset Vista Cemetary & Mortuary, Yuma. Councilman City of Yuma, 1962-66; county supr. County of Yuma, 1976-84; mem. Ariz. Parole Bd., Phoenix, 1984-88. Mem. Rotary (charter mem. Yuma chpt., chpt. pres. 1965). Home: 608 2nd Ave Yuma AZ 85364 Office: Rain Forest 608 2nd Ave Yuma AZ 85364

KENNEY, JACK STEPHEN, management consultant; b. Bainbridge, N.Y., Sept. 29, 1942; s. Eugene John and Myra Betty (Harned) K.; m. Nancy Lee Rahke, Aug. 7, 1965 (div. Sept. 1986); children: Patricia, Steven. AAS, Broome Coll, Binghamton, N.Y., 1962; BSBA, U. Denver, 1964. Analyst IBM, Poughkeepsie, N.Y.; materials mgr. Honeywell, Inc., Littleton, Colo., Digital Equipment Corp., Phoenix; dir. mfg. Dataproducts Corp., San Jose, Calif.; v.p., gen. mgr. Memorex Corp., Santa Clara, Calif.; prin. Task Internat., Los Gatos, Calif.; assoc. Regent Pacific Mgmt. Corp., Cupertino, Calif. Republican. Office: Regent Pacific Mgmt Corp 10600 N Deanza Blvd Cupertino CA 95014

KENNEY, JOHN WILLIAM, III, chemistry educator; b. Long Beach, Calif., Aug. 15, 1950; s. John William Jr. and Janice (Kendrick) K.; m. M. Inga Samuelsen, Sept. 11, 1982. BS in Chemistry, U. Nev., 1972; PhD in Chemistry, U. Utah, 1979. Postdoctoral assoc. in chem. physics Wash. State U., Pullman, 1979-81; asst. prof. chemistry Eastern N.Mex. U., Portales, 1982—. Contbr. articles to profl. jours. Troop leader Sangre de Cristo council Girl Scouts U.S., 1985—, mem. cadette/sr. planning bd. advisers, 1988—; adviser Ea. N.Mex. U. chpt. Alpha Lambda Delta, 1988—. Recipient Teola Artman award Sangre de Cristo council Girl Scouts U.S., 1988, Outstanding Vol. award, 1988; named one of Outstanding Young Men of Am., 1982-84; grantee Universal Energy Systems/USAF Office of Sci. Research, 1987—. Mem. AAAS, Am. Vacuum Soc. (research award 1986, 87, 88), Am. Chem. Soc. (co-chmn. South Plains sect., 1989—, research award 1984), Am. Phys. Soc., Sigma Xi (research award 1986), Phi Kappa Phi (sec. Ea. N.Mex. U. chpt. 1988—). Democrat. Lutheran. Home: 1112 Leo Dr Portales NM 88130

KENNEY, WILLIAM FITZGERALD, lawyer; b. San Francisco, Nov. 4, 1935; s. Lionel Fitzgerald and Ethel Constance (Brennan) K.; m. Susan Elizabeth Langfitt, May 5, 1962; children—Anne, Carol, James. BA, U. Calif.-Berkeley, 1957, JD, 1960. Bar: Calif. 1961. Assoc. Miller, Osborne Miller & Bartlett, San Mateo, Calif., 1962-64; ptnr. Tormey, Kenney & Cotchett, San Mateo, 1965-67; pres. William F. Kenney, Inc., San Mateo, 1968—; gen. ptnr. All-Am. Self Storage, 1985—. Trustee San Mateo City Sch. Dist., 1971-79, pres., 1972-74; pres. March of Dimes, 1972-73; bd. dirs. Boys Club of San Mateo, 1972—. With U.S. Army, 1960-62. Mem. State Bar of Calif. (taxation com. 1973-76), San Mateo County Bar Assn. (bd. dir. 1973-75), Calif. Assn. Realtors (legal affairs com. 1978—), San Mateo C. of C. (bd. dirs. 1987—), Self Svc. Storage Assn. (bd. dirs. western region 1987—, pres. 1989—). Republican. Roman Catholic. Club: Rotary (pres. 1978-79). Lodge: Elks (exalted ruler 1974-75). Home: 221 Clark Dr San Mateo CA 94402 Office: William F Kenney Inc 120 N El Camino Real San Mateo CA 94401

KENNICOTT, JAMES W., lawyer; b. Latrobe, Pa., Feb. 14, 1945; s. W.L. and Alice (Hayes) K.; m. Margot Barnes, Aug. 19, 1975 (div. Oct. 1977); m. Lynne Dratler Finney, July 1, 1984. AB, Syracuse (N.Y.) U., 1967; JD, U. Wyo., 1979. Bar: Utah 1979. Prin. Ski Cons., Park City, Utah, 1969—; pvt. practice Park City, 1979-87, 89—; ptnr. Kennicott & Finney, Park City, 1987-89; cons. Destination Sports Specialists, Park City, 1984—; judge Utah 3d Cir. Ct., Park City, 1988—. Chmn. Park City Library Bd., 1987; bd. dirs. Park City Library, 1985—, Park City Handicapped Sports, 1988—. Mem. ABA, Internat. Platform Assn., Utah Bar Assn., Am. Library Assn., Utah Library Assn., Am. Arbitration Assn. Home: PO Box 2339 Park City UT 84060 Office: Kennicott & Finney PO Box 2339 Park City UT 84060

KENNY, KARL ANDREW, computer company executive; b. St. John's, Nfld., Can., Apr. 14, 1960; came to U.S., 1982; s. Albert William and Marion (Daly) K.; m. Dee Gail Parker, June 19, 1982 (div. Jan. 1988); 1 child, Samantha. Student, Naval Coll., Victoria, B.B., Can., 1977-80, Naval Coll., Halifax, N.S., Can., 1980. Air traffic controller Pan-Arctic Oils, N.W.T., Can., 1981-82; pres. Brukar Industries, Inc., Arlington, Wash., 1982—; cons. SMS Group, Taipei, Taiwan, 1987—; bd. dirs. Austrian Cons. Svc., Vienna, 1987—. Author: Coastal Navigation, 1980. Served to lt. Royal Can. Navy, 1977-81. Roman Catholic. Office: Brukar Industries Inc 5917 195th NE #15 Arlington WA 98223

KENNY, MICHAEL H., bishop; b. Hollywood, Calif., June 26, 1937. Ed., St. Joseph Coll., Mountain View, Calif., St. Patrick's Sem., Menlo Park, Calif., Cath. U. Am. Ordained priest Roman Cath. Ch., 1963; ordained bishop of Juneau, Alaska, 1979—. Office: Diocese of Juneau 419 6th St Juneau AK 99801 *

KENT, JAMES GUY, health care executive; b. Jacksonville, N.C., Nov. 8, 1952; s. David Wolfe and Lucille (Epstein) K.; m. Rochelle Sue Halfon, June 16, 1979; children: Ashley, Jason, Bryan. BA, Calif. State U., Northridge, 1974; MS, UCLA, 1979; PhD, Pacific Western U., L.A., 1982. Dir. Wilshire Phys. Therapy, L.A., 1977-80; pres., founder Integrated Rehab. Corp. and predecessor cos., Marina Del Rey, Calif., 1980—; clin. assoc. prof. Calif. Coll. Podiatric Medicine L.A. County/So. Calif. U. Med. Ctr., L.A., 1984-85, clin. instr., 1983-84. Editorial bd. Sports Medicine Digest, 1981-86. Sponsor Student Internships, UCLA, 1979-84; bd. dirs. Switzer Ctr. for Children, Torrance, Calif., 1988—. Mem. Am. Coll. Sports Medicine, Nat. Assn. Rehab. Facilities. Republican. Office: Integrated Rehab Corp 4640 Admiralty Way #402 Marina Del Rey CA 90292

KENT, PAUL BRYANT, computer company executive; b. Bklyn., Oct. 12, 1962; s. Richard Stephen and Susan Jane (Silver) K.; m. Terrie Jo Steck, Apr. 19, 1986; 1 child, Stephanie Marie. Grad. high sch. Sales rep. Computer Insights, Fremont, Calif., 1984-85; cons. DLM Cons., Inc., Sunnyvale, Calif., 1985-86; pres. Winehouse Computer Co., San Jose, Calif., 1986—. Democrat. Jewish. Office: Winehouse Computer Co 1735 N 1st St Ste 303 San Jose CA 95412

KENT, RANDALL S., manager; b. Chgo., Aug. 11, 1946; m. Amelia-Louise Bissell, Oct. 8, 1971; children: Elizabeth Brooks, Margarite Wills, Phillip Dale. BS in Biology, NE Mo. State U., 1969. Cert. bus. mgr. Sr. technologist Bio Labs, Northbrook, Ill., 1970-73; vaccine supr. Am. Scientific/Schering Plough, Madison, Wis., 1973-76; prodn. supr. Armour Pharm., Kankakee, Ill., 1977-80; product devel. Armour Pharm., Kankakee, 1980-81, tech. svc. mgr., 1981-83; biolog. prodn. mgr. Ortho Diagnostics, Carpenteria, Calif., 1983-84; process devel. mgr. Alpha Therapeutic, L.A., 1984-88; scale-up mgr. parenteral Syntex, Palo Alto, Calif., 1988—. Mem. Am. Filtration Soc. (sec. 1987-88), Tissue Culture Assn., Parenteral Drug Assn., Am. Prodn. and Inventory. Home: 3555 Ballantyne Pleasanton CA 94566

KENT, RODERICK SIDNEY, opthalmologist; b. Newark, Dec. 11, 1946; s. Sidney Joseph and Dorothy Bertha (Matheke) K.; m. Carolyn Marie Mullinix, June, 1969; children: Crystal, Roderick S. II, Roland, Elizabeth, Carrie. BS in Chemistry, UCLA; MD, St. Louis U. Diplomate Am. Bd. Med. Examiners, Am. Bd. Ophthalmology. Rotating surg. intern Nat. Naval Med. Ctr., Bethesda, Md., 1972-73; flight surgeon 3d Marine Air Wing, El Toro, Calif., 1974-76; resident in ophthalmology Naval Regional Med. Ctr., Oakland, Calif., 1976-79; chief of ophthalmology Naval Regional Med. Ctr., Phila., 1979-81; pvt. practice Coeur d'Alene (Idaho) Eye Clinic, 1981—. Comdr. USNR, 1971-88. Fellow Am. Acad. Ophthalmology, ACS. Mormon. Office: Coeur d'Alene Eye Clinic 1814 Lincoln Way Coeur d'Alene ID 83814

KENT, THEODORE CHARLES, psychologist; m. Shirley, June 7, 1948; children: Donald, Susan, Steven. PhD, U. So. Calif., 1951; Dr. Rerum Naturalium, Johannes Gutenberg U., Mainz, Germany, 1960. Diplomate in clin. psychology. Commd. col., clin. psychologist, behavioral scientist USAF, 1951-65; chief psychologist USAF, Europe, 1956-60; head dept. behavioral sci. U. So. Colo., Pueblo, 1965-78, emeritus, 1978—; staff psychologist Yuma Behavioral Health, Ariz., 1978-82, chief profl. svcs., 1982-83; dir. psychol. svcs. Rio Colo. Health Systems, Yuma, 1983-85; clin psychologist, dir. mental health Ft. Yuma (Calif.) Indian Health Svc., USPHS, 1985-88; exec. dir. Human Sci. Ctr., Yuma, 1982—. Columnist Yuma Daily Sun, 1982-86. Author (tests) non-verbal test of suffering, 1982; (books) Skills in Living Together, 1983, Conflict Resolution, 1986, A Psychologist Answers Your Questions, 1987. Named Outstanding prof. U. So. Colo., 1977. Fellow Am. Psychol. Assn. (disting. visitor undergrad. edn. program).

KENTRA-GOREY, ELIZABETH RENEE, physician; b. Oak Lawn, Ill., Oct. 8, 1961; d. Edward Joseph and Joyce Leigh (Metz) Kentra; m. Rian Mark Gorey, Dec. 30, 1984. BA, St. Mary's Coll., Notre Dame, Ind., 1983; MD, Loyola U., 1987. Researcher, author Loyola U., Chgo., 1986-87; med. doctor, researcher U. So. Calif., Los Angeles, 1987—. Author: (with others) What I Believe, 1985; contbr. articles to profl. jours. Mem. AMA, Ill. Med. Assn., Chgo. Med. Assn., Am. Med. Students Assn. (v.p. 1984-85), Nat. Assn. Residents and Interns. Republican. Roman Catholic.

KENYON, KENNETH JAMES, research librarian; b. Phila., Oct. 30, 1930; s. H. Edison and Astrid (Sorensen) K.; m. Mary Ann Strong, Mar. 28, 1959; children—Kenneth, Jr., Norman. A.A., Los Angeles City Coll., 1961; student Santa Ana Coll., 1963, UCLA, 1964. Record librarian ABC, Hollywood, Calif., 1953-55; with camera dept. Walt Disney Prodns., 1955-56; research librarian 20th Century Fox Film Corp., Beverly Hills, Calif., 1957-70, head research dept., 1970—. Served with USMC, 1948-52. Mem. Spl. Libraries Assn., Acad. Motion Picture Arts and Scis., TV Acad. Arts and Scis., Am. Film Inst., Am. Legion, USMC Combat Corrs. Assn. Lodges: Masons, VASA. Office: 20th Century Fox Rsch Libr PO Box 900 Beverly Hills CA 90213

KEOWN, LAURISTON LIVINGSTON, JR., transportation executive; b. Balt., Feb. 24, 1942; s. Lauriston Livingston and Gladys May (Dykes) K.; m. Patje Alexandra Susemihl, Aug. 7, 1962 (div. 1977); children: Christina, Cassandra, Lauriston, Clayton; m. Nancy Ann Hastie, Mar. 18, 1978. BA cum laude, U. Balt., 1965; MS, U. Alta., 1970, PhD, 1977. Chartered psychologist, Alta. Lectr. Nippissing Coll., Laurentian U., North Bay, Ont., Can., 1968-69; chief systems analyst Dept. Youth, Edmonton, Alta., Can., 1969-71, research dir., 1971-72; dir. planning and research Dept. Culture, Youth and Recreation, Alta., 1972-74; dir. planning and devel. Dept. Recreation, Parks and Wildlife, Alta., Edmonton, 1974-75; asst. dir. Transp. Safety Alta. Transp. Dept., 1975-87; dir. Motor Transp. Planning and Bus. Analysis, Alta. Transp. and Utilities, 1987—; cons. R. Dehaas Assocs., Edmonton, 1979-80, Draherin Group, Edmonton, 1980-82. Author: (with others) Evaluation of Traffic Safety Programs, 1980; contbr. articles to profl. jours. Mem. Alta. Planning Bd., 1974-82, bd. dirs. Alta. Royal Can. Mounted Police Hist. Celebrations Commn., 1974-75; exec. bd. Traffic Records Commn., Nat. Safety Council, 1978—. Indsl. psychology scholar Lamond Dewhurst & Assocs., U. Alta., 1966. Mem. Am. Assn. Motor Vehicle Adminstr., Can. Conf. Motor Transp. Adminstrs., Alta. Psychologists Assn. Episcopalian. Home: PO Box 148, Bon Accord, AB Canada T0A 0K0 Office: AB Transp, Twin Atria Bldg, 4999-98 Ave, Edmonton, AB Canada T6B X3

KEPROS, JOHN GEORGE, physicist; b. Salt Lake City, Jan. 6, 1941; s. George Nicholas and Maria (Deliazas) K.; m. Karen Sue Scholl, Sept. 23, 1974 (div. July 1977). BS in Physics, U. Utah, 1963, PhD in Physics, 1971. Teaching/rsch. assoc. dept. physics U. Utah, Salt Lake City, 1963-71, postdoctoral rsch. assoc. depts. physics and chemistry, 1971-73; rsch. physicist Hercules, Inc., Magna, Utah, 1973-75; sr. postdoctoral rsch. assoc. dept. elec. engring. U. Utah, Salt Lake City, 1975-77; sr. engr. Morton Thiokol, Brigham City, Utah, 1977-79; staff scientist Gen. Dynamics-Conair, San Diego, 1979-81; rsch. scientist Lockheed Missiles & Space Co., Sunnyvale, Calif., 1981—. Patentee in field. Mem. Optical Soc. Am., Soc. Photo-Optical Instrumentation, Optical Soc. No. Calif. (bd., pres. 1982-85), Optical Soc. San Diego (sec. 1980-81), Democritos Soc. West (treas. 1985-86), ASTM (sci. standard com.), Sigma Xi. Democrat. Greek Orthodox. Home: 450 N Mathilda Ave #201 Sunnyvale CA 94086 Office: Lockheed Missiles & Space 1111 Lockheed Way 0/62-92 B/564 Sunnyvale CA 94086

KERCHEVAL, RONALD LYNN, marketing professional; b. Pullman, Wash., Nov. 5, 1951; s. Ronald Lynn Kercheval Sr. and Ruth Elaine (Parker) Wylie; m. Debra Lassen, Sept. 25, 1975 (div. June 1978); m. Denise Marie Van Royan, June 27, 1982; children: Kent Robert, Karly Marie. BA, Washington State, 1974; MBA, Ind. U., 1976. Product mgr. Richardson-Merrell, Cin., 1976-77, mktg. svcs. mgr., 1978-79; new products mgr. Armour-Dial Co., Phoenix, 1979-81; mgr. fin., adminstrn. Taggares Co., Prosser, Wash., 1981-82; new and existing brand mgr. John Labatt Foods, Eugene, Oreg., 1982-85; v.p. Moskowitz and Jacobs Inc., Valhalla, N.Y., 1985-86; pres. Endeavour, Ltd., Eugene, 1986—. Republican. Roman Catholic. Home: 2884 Spring Blvd Eugene OR 97401 Office: Endeavour Ltd 944 W 5th Eugene OR 97402

KERKORIAN, KIRK, motion picture company executive, consultant; b. Fresno, Calif., June 6, 1917; s. Ahron and Lily K.; m. Hilda Schmidt, Jan. 24, 1942 (div. 1951); m. Jane Maree Hardy, Dec. 5, 1954; children: Tracy, Linda. Student pub. schs., Los Angeles. Comml. airline pilot from 1940; founder Los Angeles Air Service (later Trans Internat. Airlines Corp.), 1948, Internat. Leisure Corp., 1968; controlling stockholder Western Airlines, 1970; chief exec. officer Metro-Goldwyn-Mayer, Inc., Culver City, Calif., 1973-74; chmn. exec. com., vice-chmn. bd. Metro-Goldwyn-Mayer, Inc., 1974-79; controlling stockholder MGM/UA Communications Co.; cons. 1979—. Served as capt. Transport Command RAF, 1942-44. Office: MGM/UA Communications Co 450 N Roxbury Dr Beverly Hills CA 90210 *

KERMAN, BARRY MARTIN, ophthalmologist, educator; b. Chgo., Mar. 31, 1945; s. Harvey Nathan and Evelyn (Bialis) K.; B.S., U. Ill., 1967, M.D. with high honors, 1970; m. Pamela Renee Berliant, Aug. 18, 1968; children—Gregory Jason, Jeremy Adam. Intern in medicine Harbor Gen. Hosp., Torrance, Calif., 1970-71; resident in ophthalmology Wadsworth VA Hosp., Los Angeles, 1971-74; fellow in diseases of the retina, vitreous and choroid Jules Stein Eye Inst. UCLA, 1974-75; fellow in ophthalmic ultrasonography Edward S. Harkness Eye Inst., Columbia U., N.Y.C. and U. Iowa Hosps., Iowa City, 1975; asst. prof. ophthalmology UCLA, 1976-78, Harbor Gen. Hosp., 1976-78; asst. clin. prof. ophthalmology UCLA, 1978-83, assoc. clin. prof., 1983—, dir. ophthalmic ultrasonography lab., 1976—; cons. ophthalmologist, Los Angeles, 1976—; mem. exec. bd. Am. Registry Diagnostic Med. Sonographers, 1981-87. Served with USAFR, 1971-77. Diplomate Am. Bd. Ophthalmology. Fellow Am. Acad. Ophthalmology; mem. Calif. Med. Assn., Los Angeles County Med. Assn., Los Angeles Soc. Ophthalmology, Am. Inst. Ultrasound in Medicine, Am. Soc. Ophthalmic Ultrasound, Am. Assn. Ophthalmic Standardized Echography, Societas Internationalis Pro Diagnostica Ultrasonica in Opthalmic. Contbr. articles to profl. jours. Office: 2080 Century Park E Ste 800 Los Angeles CA 90067

KERMES, CHARLES WALTER, state agency official; b. Syracuse, N.Y., Sept. 7, 1952; s. Charles August and Doris Anne (Halbe) K.; m. Fredda Jean Parkhill,. BA in Sociology, SUNY, Buffalo, 1976; MS, U. Syracuse, 1978. Rehab. coord. City of Syracuse, N.Y., 1977-79, Phoenix South Community Mental Health Ctr., 1979-82; rehab. rep. State Workers Compensation Fund, Phoenix, Ariz., 1982-84, Ariz. Economic Security, Show Low, 1984—; mem. sociology faculty Northland Pioneer Coll., 1986—; cons. Contact Inc. Sec. treas. Navajo County Pvt. Industry Coun., Holbrook, Ariz. Repubilcan. Espiscopalian. Office: Dept Economic Security 40 S 11 St Show Low AZ 85901

KERN, DAVID JEFFREY, film editor; b. Phila., Feb. 21, 1950; s. William Bliem and Helen Elizabeth (Kennedy) K.; m. Stephanie Jean Schulz, May6, 1978; children: Autumn Elizabeth, Kristin Janine. BS in Art Edn., Kutztown U., 1971. Film editor L.A., 1981—. Works edited include: Americana, 1981, Q, 1982, Las Vegas Weekend, 1984, Island of the Alive, 1985, Maniac Cop, 1986, Hit List, 1987, Wicked Stepmother, 1988, Relentless, 1988, Spontaneous Combustion, 1989. Mem. Motion Picture Editors Guild. Democrat. Home: 880 Camino Calibri St Calabasas CA 91302 Office: 724 S Victory Blvd Burbank CA 91505

KERN, DONALD MICHAEL, internist; b. Belleville, Ill., Nov. 21, 1951; s. Donald Milton Kern and Dolores Olivia (Rust) Cohoon. BS in Biology, Tulane U., 1973; MD magna cum laude, U. Brussels, 1983. ECFMG cert.; lic. Calif. Intern in surgery Berkshire Med. Ctr., Pittsfield, Mass., 1983-84; intern in psychiatry Tufts New England Med. Ctr., Boston, 1984-85; resident in internal medicine Kaiser Found. Hosp., San Francisco, 1985-87; with assoc. staff internal medicine Kaiser Permanente Med. Group, Inc., San Francisco, 1987—; assoc. investigator AIDS Clin. Trial Unit Kaiser Permanente Med. Ctr., Stanford U., Nat. Inst. Allergy & Infectious Disease, San Francisco, 1988—. Mem. Mass. Med. Soc., Am. Coll. Physicians (assoc.), Calif. Med. Assn., San Francisco Med. Soc., Pacific Heights Health Club. Republican. Roman Catholic. Home: 3080 Jackson St 4 San Francisco CA 94115 Office: Kaiser Permanente Med Group Inc 2200 O Farrell San Francisco CA 94115

KERN, GERALD NEIL, chemical company executive; b. Bklyn., Mar. 24, 1938; s. Harry and Rose (Greenfield) K.; m. Judith Miller, July 17, 1956 (div. Feb. 1982); children: Robert, Howard, Steven, Randi Anne; m. Cynthia Chapman, June 12, 1982. Student Bklyn. Coll., 1959-61. Dist. mgr. Pet, Inc., St. Louis, 1960-67; v.p., gen. mgr. Internat. Playtex, N.Y.C., 1967-77; exec. v.p. Max Factor & Co. div. NSI, Inc., Hollywood, Calif., 1977-80; pres. Parfums Lamborghini, N.Y.C., 1980-81, pres., chief exec. officer Meditech

Pharm. Inc., Encino Calif., 1981—.Patentee treatments of viral and bacterial infections, 1988. Exec. councilman, LAPD Police Dept. Crime Prevention Adv. Com., 1984—. Lt. (j.g.) USN, 1955-59. Republican. Jewish. Hon. chief, LAPD, 1985. Avocation: golf. Home: 4631 Louise Ave Encino CA 91316

KERN, HAROLD SKIP, investment advisor, tax consultant; b. Ashland, Ky., Mar. 9, 1951; s. Harold G. Kern and Jane C. (Crist) McIssac; m. A. Edith Kern, Apr. 12, 1980; 1 child, Phillip Tyler, Patrick-Lee. Cert. fin. planner; registered investment adviser, real estate broker. Real estate sales rep. San Jose, Calif., 1977—; tax adviser ETS & Assocs., San Jose, 1984-85; ins. sales rep. Provident Mutual, San Jose, 1985-88; fin. planner, investment advisor Integrated Resources, San Jose, 1988—; tax preparer, cons. San Jose, 1984—. Mem. Inst. for Cert. Fin. Planners, Internat. Assn. for Fin. Planners. Republican. Office: Integrated Resources 888 Saratoga Ave #2 San Jose CA 95129

KERN, LYNN RUSSELL, electronic engineer; b. Herrin, Ill., July 24, 1958; s. Bobby Gene and LaDonna Sue (Morgan) K.; m. Mary Elizabeth Swalls, Nov. 11, 1977 (div. 1983); 1 child, Jason Alan; m. Joyce Lynn Bailey, May 12, 1984 (div. 1988); children: Anna Pauline, Daniel Morgan; m. Tamie Ann Watts, Mar. 27, 1988; children: John Alan, Nichole Marie. BSEE, So. Ill. U., 1984. Registered profl. engr., Calif. Teaching asst. So. Ill. U., Carbondale, 1982-84; elect. engr. Naval Weapons Ctr. 3112, China Lake, Calif., 1984-85; systems engr. various programs Naval Weapons Ctr. 6133, China Lake, 1985-86; prin. investigator Naval Weapons Ctr. Code 3311, China Lake, 1986-88, Naval Weapons Ctr. Code 3926, China Lake, 1988—. Co-author (book): A Guide to CMS, 1982. Mem. Midwest Assn. Electrical Contractors, Tau Beta Pi. Office: Naval Weapons Ctr Code 3926 China Lake CA 93555

KERN, PAUL ALFRED, advertising executive, research consultant, realtor; b. Hackensack, N.J., Mar. 17, 1958; s. Paul Julian and Edith Helen (Colten) K. BS in Commerce, U. Va., 1980; MBA, U. So. Calif., 1983. Sales rep. Procter and Gamble, Cin., 1980-81; research services mgr. Opinion Research, Long Beach, Calif., 1984; consumer planning supr. Dentsu, Young and Rubicam, Los Angeles, 1984-85; research executive DJMC Advt., Inc., Los Angeles, 1986; realtors assoc. Tarbell Realtors, Santa Ana, Calif., 1988—; bd. dirs. Applicon, Inc., Hillsdale, N.J., Kernakopia, Hillsdale; cons. Venture Six Enterprises, Encino, Calif., 1985—, DFS/Dorland, Torrance, Calif., 1986, IMI Machinery Inc., Charleston, S.C., 1987—. Coach, supr. Little League Football, Alexandria, Va., 1981; active Surf and Sun Softball League (1987 champions). Recipient Most Calls Per Day award Procter and Gamble, 1980. Mem. Profl. Research Assn., Am. Mktg. Assn., Am. Film Inst., Internat. Platform Assn., U.S. Tennis Assn. (Michelob Light 4.5 Team Championship 1982), U. Va. Alumni Assn, Nat. Assn. Realtors, Calif. Assn. of Realtors, S. Bay Rd. of Realtors (Torrance-Lomita), Carson Bd. of Realtors. Club: Alta Vista Racquet. Home: 516 S Irena Redondo Beach CA 90277 Office: Tarbell Realtors 1774 S Pacific Coast Hwy Redondo Beach CA 90277

KERNEN, JULES ALFRED, pathologist; b. St. Louis, July 23, 1929; s. Jules Henri and Edna Lina (Aigler) K.; m. Rita Dennehy, Oct. 25, 1981. AB, Harvard U., 1951; MD, Wash. U. Sch. of Medicine, 1955. Diplomate Am. Bd. Path. Intern Barnes Hosp., St. Louis, 1955-56; asst. resident Ind. U. Med. Ctr., Indpls., 1956-58; resident Barnes Hosp., St. Louis, 1958-59, Hosp. U. Pa., Phila., 1959-60; chief of pathology 5th Army Med. Lab., St. Louis, 1960-62; pathologist St. Vincent Hosp., Birmingham, Ala., 1962-63, Hosp. of the Good Samaritan, Los Angeles, 1964—; pathologist, ptnr. Clin. Lab Med. Group, Los Angeles, 1964-87; v.p. CLMG Inc., Los Angeles, 1972-84; clin. prof. pathology, U. So. Calif. Sch. of Medicine, Los Angeles, 1965—. Author of numerous published articles in field. Served to capt. U.S. Army, 1960-62. Mem. Los Angeles Soc. of Pathologists (pres. 1979), Coll. of Am. Pathologists, Am. Soc. of Clin. Pathologists, Internat. Acad. of Pathology, Calif. Soc. of Pathologists, Phi Beta Kappa, Alpha Omega Alpha. Republican. Club: Harvard of So. Calif. Home: 1000 Principia Dr Glendale CA 91206

KERNODLE, UNA MAE, teacher; b. Jackson, Tenn., Mar. 4, 1947; d. James G. and Mary E. (McLemore) Sikes. B.S. in Home Econs., U. Tenn., 1969; M.Edn., U. Alaska, 1974. Tchr., head dept. vocat. edn. and electives Chugiak High Sch., Anchorage; edn. cons. State of Alaska, Anchorage Talent Bank; presenter Gov.'s Conf. on Child Abuse, Alaska Vocat. Edn. Assn. Conf., Alaska Home Econs. Inst., 1989; state officer Alaska Home Econs. Recipient Gruening award, 1989. Mem. Am. Home Econs. Assn., Anchorage Assn. Edn. Young Children, NEA, Am. Vocat. Assn. Democrat. Baptist. Office: Chugiak High Sch PO Box 218 Eagle River AK 99577

KERNS, JOANNA DE VARONA, actress, writer; b. San Francisco, Feb. 12, 1953; d. David Thomas and Martha Louise (Smith) de V.; m. Richard Martin Kerns, Dec. 11, 1976 (div. Dec. 1986); 1 child, Ashley Cooper. Student, UCLA, 1970-71. TV series include The Four Seasons, 1984; movies include Cross My Heart, 1986. Democrat.

KERR, C. DUANE, physician occupational medicine; b. Tremonton, Utah, Aug. 21, 1933; s. Clifton George Mercer and Irene (Pack) K.; m. Carrie Kathryn Calder, July 8, 1958; children: Darin Duane, Brian Calder, Kaleen Irene, Kimberly, Cameron, Karalee. Student, Brigham Young U., 1951-53; BS, Utah State U., 1957; MD, U. Utah, 1960. Intern Dee Hosp., Ogen, Utah, 1960-61; pvt. practice Tremonton, 1961-85; med. dir. Morton Thiokol, Brigham City, Utah, 1985—; governing bd. mem. Bear River Valley Hosp., Tremonton, 1984—. Recipient Award of Merit Boy Scouts Am., Ogden, Utah, 1987. Mem. AMA, Utah State Med. Assn., Box Elder County Med. Soc. (pres. 1976). Republican. Mormon. Home: 725 West 10th St N Tremonton UT 84337 Office: Morton Thiokol Inc Box 524 Mail Stop 003 Brigham City UT 84302

KERR, CHARLES MORGAN, psychiatrist, educator; b. Perry, Okla., Feb. 14, 1935; s. John Bradley and Eddith Geneva (Thompson) K.; m. Esther Elizabeth Vargo, Oct. 21, 1957 (div. Dec. 1986); children: Charles Morgan II, John Timothy, Christopher Scott, Erik Bradley. BA, Yale U., 1957; MD, Baylor Coll. Medicine, 1963. Diplomate Am. Bd. Psychiatry and Neurology. Rotating intern U.S. Naval Hosp., Portsmouth, Va., 1963-64; resident in psychiatry U. Rochester (N.Y.) and Strong Meml. Hosp., 1967-70, clin. instr., 1970; asst. prof. psychiatry U. Ariz. Coll. Medicine, Tucson, 1970-75, sr. lectr., 1975—; pvt. practice Tucson, 1975—; cons. So. Ariz. Mental Health Ctr., Tucson, 1970-76, U.S. Indian Health Svc., Tucson, 1971-73, Ariz. Dept. Corrections, Tucson, 1972-76. Bd. dirs., v.p. Tucson South Community Mental Health Ctr., Tucson, 1971-74; sustaining fund drive chmn., committeeman troop 166, Boy Scouts Am., Tucson, 1972; chmn. edn. com. Ariz. Gov.'s Coun. on Health and Fitness, Phoenix, 1980-82; mem. ad hoc com. for gen. budgets Tucson Community Coun., 1982. Lt. M.C., USN, 1963-67. Named torchbearer for opening ceremonies Winter Olympics, Lake Placid, N.Y., 1980; recipient award for excellence in teaching U. Ariz. Med. Ctr., 1984; Dr. Charles Kerr Day proclaimed by City of Tucson, May 19, 1980. Fellow Am. Psychiat Assn. (pres. Tucson 1982-83); mem. AMA, Ariz. Med. Assn., Pima County Med. Soc., Am. Group Psychotherapy Assn., Am. Coll. Sports Medicine, Am. Orthopsychiat. Assn., Am. Assn. Sex Educators, Counselors and Therapists (cert. educator and therapist), So. Ariz. Roadrunners Assn. (Outstanding Mem. award 1978), Yale U. Alumni Assn. (rep. 1982-85), Yale Club (pres. 1986). Republican. Episcopalian. Office: 8230 E Broadway Ste W-2 Tucson AZ 85710

KERR, EWING THOMAS, judge; b. Bowie, Tex., Jan. 21, 1900; s. George N. and Ellen H. (Wisdom) K.; m. Ellen Irene Peterson, Feb. 22, 1933; children—Hugh Neal, Judith Ann. B.A., U. Okla., 1923; B.S., Central Coll., Okla., 1923; postgrad., U. Colo., 1925; LLD (hon.), U. Wyo., 1987. Bar: Wyo. bar 1927. Prin. jr. high sch. Hominy, Okla., 1923-25, Cheyenne Pub. Schs., 1925-27; practice at Cheyenne, 1927-29; asst. U.S. dist. atty. for Wyo., 1930-33, atty. gen., 1939-43; atty. for Wyo. Senate, 1943; U.S. dist. judge Dist. Wyo., Cheyenne, 1955—. Served as maj. AUS; with Allied Commn. in Italy; head legal div. in area reorganized civilian cts. in 1945, Austria. Recipient Herbert Harley award, 1987. Mem. Wyo. Bar Assn., Cheyenne C. of C. Republican. Presbyn. Clubs: Mason (past master lodge, past grand master lodge, 33 deg.), Rotarian. Home: 2951 Spruce Dr Cheyenne WY 82001 Office: US Dist Ct PO Box 888 Cheyenne WY 82001

KERR, JAMES WILFRID, artist; b. N.Y.C., Aug. 7, 1897; s. James Fairbairn and Leah M. (Galer) K.; grad. Poppenhusen Inst., 1914, N.Y. Sch. Fine and Applied Arts, 1923; m. Rose R. Netzorg, June 24, 1922; children: Andra Gail (dec.), Paul F. (adopted). Dir., Art Summer Sch., Detroit, 1923-24; artist, lectr., art adminstr., 1923—; painter in oils, tchr.; one-man and group shows include: Galeria Del Sol, Allied Artists Am., NAD, Am. Vets. Soc., N.J. Painters and Sculptors Soc., Carnegie Inst. Pitts., 1949 (by invitation), Conn. Acad. Fine Arts, Davenport (Iowa) Mus., Houston Mus., Irvington (N.J.) Mus., Norfolk Mus. Arts and Scis., Dialists Exhibit, N.J. Artists, Newark Mus., Ridgewood, N.J., Salmagundi Club, N.Y.C., Delgado Mus., New Orleans, Art U.S.A., Madison Sq. Garden, N.Y.C., 1958, Richmond Mus., Artists Equity Assn. show Botts Meml. Hall, Albuquerque, 48th-50th Fiesta shows at Mus. Fine Arts, Santa Fe, Springville, Utah, 1962-63, 1st Air Force Acad. Exhbn., 1962-63, Juried Arts Nat. Exhbn., Tyler, Tex., 1963, Western Mich. U., Kalamazoo, 1983; represented in permanent collections: Mus. City N.Y., Joslyn Art Mus., Omaha, Newark Mus., Mus. Albuquerque, Fla. So. Coll., Lakeland, N.Mex. State Fair, Fergusson Library, Albuquerque, Waldwick (N.J.) Elem. Sch., Western Mich. U. Trustee, Mus. Albuquerque. Recipient awards, prizes N.J. State Exhibit, Montclair, 1943 (hon. award); NAD, 1945 (1st Altman prize); Plainfield (N.J.) Art Assn. (hon. award), 1946; prize Oil, Morristown (N.J.) Art Assn.; Irvington Art and Mus. Assn., 1st prize in Oil, 1948, 49; Ridgewood (N.J.) Art Assn., 1st prize Oil, 1948; Art Council N.J., 2d Oil prize, 1948; Am. Vets. Soc. Artists purchase award, 1951; Ridgewood (N.J.) Art Assn. (hon. award), 1952; citation Fla. So. Coll., Lakeland, 1952; 1st prize 50th Fiesta Show, Mus. N.Mex., 1963; purchase prize N.Mex. State Fair, 1963, grand award, 1964; silver medal Am. Vets. Soc. Artists, 1963; prizes Ouray County Ann. Exhbn., 1964, State Fair, 1966; The Rose M. Kerr and James W. Kerr Found. named in his honor at Western Mich. U. Served with USN, World War I. Mem. Allied Artists Am. (treas. 1952, mem. jury awards oil painting 1958, dir. 1955, chmn. membership com. 1955), Internat. Assn. Plastic Arts (Joint com. for Am. participation), Assn. Artists N.J. (dir.), Artists Equity Assn. (chmn. nat. mus. com., co-chmn. nat. artists-museums com. 1958, nat. treas. 1959), Dialists (N.J.), Grand Central Galleries (artist-mem.), Irvington (N.J.) Art and Mus. Assn. (artist mem.), N.J. Soc. Painters and Sculptors, New Mexican Art League (dir. 1966), Ridgewood Art Center (past pres.), Salmagundi Club (artist mem.), Art Assn. New Orleans, Artists Equity Assn. (nat. treas. 1952-55), Am. Vets. Soc. Artists (pres. 1958-60), Albuquerque Mus. Assn. (pres. 1967-68, dir.), Smithsonian Instn. Archives Am. Art, Pres.'s Club Western Mich. U. Co-artist, author: Historic Design for Modern Use; also articles on art for School Arts mag. and Everyday Art mag. Lectr. women's clubs, high schs., colls., univs., art clubs and assns. on painting, graphic arts, modern movements in arts, and psychology related to art, radio and TV. Address: 7017 Bellrose Ave NE Albuquerque NM 87110

KERR, KENNETH GORDON, producer; b. Pittsburg, Calif., Nov. 25, 1951; s. Jack C. and Peggy Louise (Meacham) K.; m. Vicki June Jimmerson, June 25, 1970 (div. 1972); 1 child, Amy Marie; m. Kerry Jean Bedortha, Jan. 25, 1975; 1 child, Talla Leanne. AS in Indsl. Tech., Cen. Oreg. Community Coll., 1982. Apprentice plumber Del's Plumbing, Ontario, Oreg., 1976-80; mgr. Triple K Plumbing, Prineville, Oreg., 1980-83; pres. Western Experience, Inc., Prineville, 1983—; cons., producer TV Sta., Powell Butte, Oreg., 1989—. Pub. The Songwriter, 1981, Teardrops and Footprints, 1983; producer, writer record videos including Sing Me Willie Nelson, 1989, Guitar for Fun, 1989. Active apprentice tng. com. State of Oreg., 1986-88; chmn. Instruments for Kids, Bend, Oreg., 1989—, Words and Music Sch. Program, Bend, 1989—; pres., bd. dirs. Cen. Oreg. Parks Concert Series, 1988—. With U.S. Army, 1971-74. Mem. Songwriters Inc. of Nashville, Am. Soc. Composers, Authors and Poets, Nashville Songwriters Assn. Internat., Cen. Oreg. Singers, Songwriters and Musicians Assn. (pres. 1988—, bd. dirs. 1988—). Democrat.

KERR, KLEON HARDING, state senator, educator; b. Plain City, Utah, Apr. 26, 1911; s. William A. and Rosemond (Harding) K.; m. Katherine Abbott, Mar. 15, 1941; children: Kathleen, William A., Rebecca Rae. AS, Weber Coll., 1936; BA, George Washington U., 1939; MS, Utah State U., Logan, 1946. Tchr., Bear River High Sch., Tremonton, Utah, 1940-56, prin. jr. high sch., 1956-60, prin. Bear River High Sch., 1960-71; city justice Tremonton, 1941-46; sec. to Senator Arthur V. Watkins, 1947. Mayor, Tremonton City, 1948-53; mem. Utah Local Govt. Survey Commn., 1954-55; mem. Utah Ho. of Reps., 1953-56; mem. Utah State Senate, 1957-64, chmn. appropriation com., 1959—, majority leader, 1963; mem. Utah Legis. Council. Dist. dir. vocat. edn. Box Elder Sch. Dist. Recipient Alpha Delta Kappa award for outstanding contbn. to edn., 1982, award for outstanding contbrs. to edn. and govt. Theta Chpt. Alpha Beta Kappa, 1982, Excellence Achieved in Promotion of Tourism award, Allied Category award Utah Travel Counc., 1988; named Tourism Ambassador of Month, 1986. Mem. NEA, Utah, Box Elder edn. assns., Nat., Utah secondary schs. prins. assns., Bear River Valley. C. of C. (sec., mgr. 1955-58), Phi Delta Kappa. Mem. Ch. of Jesus Christ of Latter-day Saints. Lion, Kiwanian. Author: (poetry) Open My Eyes 1983, Trouble In the Amen Corner, 1985, Past Imperfect, 1988; We Remember, 1983; (history) Those Who Served Box Elder County, 1984, Those Who Served Tremonton City, 1985, Diamonds in the Rough, 1987, Facts of Life, 1987. Home: Box 246 Tremonton UT 84337

KERR, ROBERT ALEXANDER, data processing executive, lawyer; b. L.A., Nov. 12, 1940; s. Robert McCombs and Adelaide (Fielding) K.; m. Ilona Kerr. BS, Calif. State U., Northridge, 1980; JD, U. La Verne, 1988. Bar: Calif. 1988. Computer analyst various cos., 1962-77, Getty Oil Co., L.A., 1977-83; sr. programmer, analyst Jet Propulsion Lab., Pasadena, Calif., 1983—. Mem. Calif. Trial Lawyers Assn. Democrat. Home and Office: 4015 Clayton Ave Los Angeles CA 90027

KERSEY, TERRY L(EE), astronautical engineer; b. San Francisco, June 9, 1947; s. Ida Helen (Schmeichel) K. Houseman, orderly Mills Meml. Hosp., San Mateo, Calif., 1965-68; security guard Lawrence Security, San Francisco, 1973-74; electronic engr. and technician engring. research and devel. dept. McCulloch Corp., Los Angeles, 1977; warehouseman C.C.H. Computax Co., Redondo Beach, Calif., 1977-78; with material ops. and planning customer support dept. Allied-Signal Aerospace Co., Torrance, Calif., 1978—. Participant 9th Space Simulation conf., Los Angeles, 1977, 31st Internat. Astronautical Fedn. Congress., Tokyo, 1980, Unispace 1982 for the U.N., Vienna. Served to sgt. USAF, 1968-72, Vietnam. Decorated Vietnam Service medal with 2 bronze stars, Republic of Vietnam Campaign medal, Air Force aommendation medal for Vietnam campign Service.. Mem. AAAS, AIAA (mem. space systems tech. com. 1981—, mem. aerodynamics com. 1980—, Wright Flyer Project Aerodynamics com. 1980—), Nat. Space Inst., Am. Astronautical Soc., The Planetary Soc., Internat. L5 Soc., Ind. Space Research Group, IEEE Computer Soc. Zen Buddhist.

KERSTEN, TIMOTHY WAYNE, economics educator, consultant; b. Algona, Iowa, Nov. 18, 1944; s. Harold Arthur and Marcella (Heger) K.; m. Carol Ann Oliver, Dec. 22, 1967; one child, Jeffrey Alexander. BA, Calif. State U., Sacramento, 1967; MA, U. Oreg., 1971, PhD, 1973. Asst. prof. econs. Calif. Poly. State U., San Luis Obispo, 1971-75, assoc. prof., 1976-80, prof., 1981—; chmn. Calif. State U. Acad. Senate, San Luis Obispo, 1980-82; mem. Calif. State U. state-wide Acad. Senate, 1983—, chmn. faculty affairs com., 1984-86, govtl. affairs com., 1986—. Author: Instructors Guide to Accompany Contemporary Economics, 1975. Mem. citizens adv. com. San Luis Obispo City Council, 1976-77. Fellow U.S. Govt., 1969-71. Mem. Am. Econ. Assn., Western Social Sci. Assn., Omicron Delta Epsilon, Phi Mu Alpha Sinfonia. Office: Calif State Poly U Dept Econs San Luis Obispo CA 93407

KERSTETTER, MICHAEL JAMES, manufacturing company executive; b. Spokane, Wash., Sept. 3, 1936; s. James B. and Ruth (Marquardt) K.; m. Eileen Virginia Behm, June 26, 1955; children: Michael Stuart, Steven Douglas. AA, Long Beach (Calif.) City Coll., 1957; BSCE, Calif. State U., Long Beach, 1962, MSCE, 1968. Registered structural engr., Ca., civil engr., Ca. Process engr. Aerojet-Gen., Downey, Calif., 1955-62; design engr.Aetron div. Aerojet-Gen., Covina, Calif., 1962-64; structural engr. C.F. Braun & Co., Alhambra, Calif., 1964-69, structural engring. section head, 1969-70; engr. Conrock Co., Los Angeles, 1970-72, asst. prodn. mgr., 1972-75, ops. mgr., 1975-79, v.p., 1979-84; exec. v.p., gen. mgr. ConAgg div. CalMat Co. (formerly Conrock Co.), Los Angeles, 1984—. Pack master Cub Scouts Am., West Covina, Calif., 1976; steering com. Boy Scouts Am. Troop 443, West Covina, 1977-79. Fellow Am. Concrete Inst. (pres. So. Calif. chpt. 1984-85), Inst. Advancement Engring.; mem. Structural Engrs. Assn. So. Calif. (sec. 1979-80), Nat. Ready Mixed Concrete Assn. (bd. dirs. 1985—), So. Calif. Rock Products Assn. (chmn. 1987—). Clubs: Jonathan (Los Angeles); Glendora (Calif.) Country. Office: CalMat Co 3200 San Fernando Rd Los Angeles CA 90065

KERSTITCH, ALEX, teacher, marine biologist; b. Nice, France, Sept. 9, 1945; came to U.S., 1951; m. Myra Lee Muramoto, May 26, 1986. BFA, U. Ariz., 1966; postgrad., Stanford U., 1967. Cert. sec. tchr., Ariz. Marine tech. U. Ariz., Tucson, 1966-70, rsch. assoc., 1970—; tchr. Sabino High Sch., Tucson, 1972—. Contbg. editor: Fresh/Marine Aquarium Mag., 1980—, Marine Fish Monthly Mag., 1987—; co-author, illustrator: (book) Reef Fishes of Sea of Cortez, 1979; author, photographer: (book) Marine Invertebrates of Sea of Cortez, 1989; contbr. articles to profl. jours.; discoverer of six new species of marine animals, 1980-88. Recipient 1st place awards, photo competitions, Nat. History Maga., 1979, 80, Nat. Wildlife Mag., 1982, Ariz. Biolog. Photo Assn., 1982. Mem. Profl. Photographers of Am., Outdoor Writer's Assn. of Am. (featured artist 1985), Desert Dolphins, Desert Aquarist Soc. Home: 10700 Calle Vaqueros Tucson AZ 85749 Office: Sabino High Sch 5000 N Bowes Rd Tucson AZ 85749

KERSZENBAUM, ISIDORO, electrical engineer, educator; b. Buenos Aires, Nov. 11, 1949; came to U.S., 1985; s. Abraham and Rosa (Eikeres) K.; m. Jacqueline Hirsch, May 10, 1974; children: Livnat, Yigal. BSEE, Inst. of Tech., Haifa, Israel, 1978; GDE, Witwatersrand U., Johannesburg, Republic of South Africa, 1982, PhD in Elec. Engring., 1984. Registered profl. engr., Calif. H.V. protection engr. Israel Elec. Corp., Haifa, 1978-79, ESCOM, Johannesburg, 1979-80; engr. rsch. and devel. design G.E.C. Large Machines, Johannesburg, 1980-84; elec. engr. Gazit, Israel, 1984-85; mgr. rsch. and devel. Internat. Transfer Corp., Montebello, Calif., 1985-89; lectr. Dept. Elec. Engring. Calif. State U., Long Beach, 1988—. Author, co-author several tech. papers (Inst. Premium award, Republic of South Africa, 1983, South African Transport Svcs. award, 1986, IEEE Com. Prize Paper award, 1987). Served with armed services, 1971-74, Israel. South African Coun. for Sci. Indsl. Rsch. grantee, Johannesburg, 1982-83. Mem. IEEE (sr.), Nat. Assn. Profl. Engrs., South African Assn. Profl. Engrs. Home: 1 Echo Run Irvine CA 92714

KERZIE, TED L., JR., fine arts educator; b. Tacoma, May 10, 1943; s. Ted L. Sr. and Frances (Chesky) K.; m. Diane Vines; children: Kristin, Jennifer, Michael. BA, Wash. State U., 1966; MFA with honors, Claremont Grad. Sch., 1972. Asst. prof. fine arts Claremont (Calif.) Grad. Sch., 1973-76; assoc. prof. Calif. State U., Bakersfield, 1976-86, prof., 1986—; artist Cirrus Gallery, Los Angeles, 1980—; pres. Info-Sell, Los Angeles, 1986—. Served to capt. USAF, 1966-70;. Home: 2606 Purdue Los Angeles CA 90064

KESNER, SOCORRO, realtor; b. Ojinaga, Chihuahua, Mex., May 13, 1945; came to U.S., 1954.; d. Alejo E. and Margarita (Morales) Valenzuela; m. Elias Garcia, Jr., Dec. 19, 1968 (div. Feb. 1975); children: Lori, Chris; m. Elton M. Kesner, Nov. 19, 1979; children: Eva Wheeler, Guy Kesner. Grad. high sch., 1972. Lic. real estate, N. Mex. Various positions First Nat. Bank, Hobbs, N.Mex., 1975-81; realtor First Equity Realtors, Hobbs, 1982—; Active in Women's Council of Realtors, Hobbs (pres. 1987). Mem. Dem. Women; bd. dirs. Children's Home for Abused/Neglected; chmn. advt. campaign for city, Hobbs. Mem. Ambassador Hobbs C. of C. Democrat. Episcopalian. Office: First Equity Realtors 1819 N Turner Hobbs NM 88240

KESSARIS, ELIZABETH JOLLEY, social worker; b. Mexico, Mo., Dec. 9, 1916; d. James Frank and Florence Leola (York) Jolley; m. Constantine Kessaris, May 18, 1961. AB, Lindenwood Coll., 1938; MSW, Smith Coll., 1947. Psychiat. social worker VA Hosp., Topeka, Kans., 1947-49; caseworker family service bur. Salvation Army, Bklyn., 1949-51; sr. caseworker Youth Consultation Service, Newark, 1951-52; supr. student unit Office of Commnr. of Welfare, Hartford, Conn., 1952-54; dist. rep., child welfare worker Alaska Dept. Pub. Welfare, Juneau, 1954-57; supr. social work Beth El Hosp., Bklyn., 1957; sr. psychiat. social worker N.Y. State Dept. Mental Hygiene, 1957-63, Calif. State Dept. Mental Hygiene, Oakland, 1963-64; asst. dir. Contra Costa County Social Services, Concord, Calif., 1966-76; child welfare specialist Eastern Nev. Tribal Social Service, Elko, 1976-78; child welfare worker Jewish Family and Children's Services, Phenix, 1979; social worker Bur. Indian Affairs, Carson City, Nev., 1979-89, ret., 1989. Mem. ACLU. Club: Am. Duplicate Bridge (Reno). Home: 330 W Nye Ln #40 Carson City NV 89701

KESSLER, A. D., business, financial, investment and real estate advisor, consultant, educator, lecturer, author; b. N.Y.C., May 1, 1923; s. Morris William and Belle Miriam (Pastor) K.; m. Ruth Schwartz, Nov. 20, 1944; children: Brian Lloyd, Judd Stuart, Earl Vaughn. Student U. Newark, 1940-41, Rutgers U., 1941-42, 46, Albright Coll., 1942, Newark Coll. Engring., 1946; MBA, Kensington U., 1976, PhD in Mgmt. and Behavioral Psychology, 1977. Sr. cert. rev. appraiser (CRA), cert. exchangor (CE); registered mortgage underwriter (RMU); registered investment advisor (RIA). Pvt. practice real estate, ins. and bus. brokerage, N.J., Pa., Fla., N.Y., Nev., Calif., Hong Kong, 1946—; pres. Armor Corp., 1947-68; pres. Folding Carton Corp., Am., N.Y.C., 1958-68; exec. v.p. Henry Schindall Assocs., N.Y.C., 1966-67; tax rep. Calif. State Bd. Equalization, 1968-69; aviation cons. transp. div. Calif., Dept. Aeros., also pub. info. officer; 1969-71; FAA Gen. Aviation Safety Counselor; broker, mgr. La Costa (Calif.) Sales Corp., 1971-75; chmn. bd. Profl. Ednl. Found., 1975—, Timeshare Resorts Internat., 1975—, Interex, Leucadia, Calif., 1975-82, The Kessler Orgn., Rancho Santa Fe, Calif., 1975—, The Kessler Fin. Group, Fin. Ind. Inst., 1977—; pres. Ednl. Video Inst., 1978—, Fin. Planning Inst., 1975—, Rancho Santa Fe Real Estate & Land, Inc., 1975—; treas., exec. bd. dirs. Nat. Challenge Com. on Disability, 1983—; dir. Practice Mgmt. Cons. Abacus Data Systems, 1984—; broker mgr. Rancho Sante Fe Acreage & Homes, Inc., 1987—; mktg. dir. Commercial Real Estate Services, Rancho Sante Fe, 1987—; cons. broker Glenct. Properties Ptnrs., 1989—; publisher, editor in chief Creative Real Estate Mag., 1975—; publisher Creative Real Estate Mag. of Australia and New Zealand; founder, editor Moderator of Tape of the Month Club; founder, producer, chmn. Internat. Real Estate Expo; chmn. bd. The Brain Trust, Rancho Santa Fe, Calif., 1977—; fin. lectr. for Internat. Cruise Ships, Cunard Line, Norwegian Am. Cruises, others; lectr. life enrichment and stress mgmt. Internat. Cruise Ships; Calif. adj. faculty, prof. fin. Clayton U., St. Louis. Scoutmaster Orange Mountain council Boy Scouts Am., 1955-62; harbor master N.J. Marine Patrol, 1958-67; dep. sheriff, Essex County, N.J., 1951-65. Served with USAF, 1942-45. Decorated D.F.C., Air medal, Purple Heart; named to French Legion of Honor, Order of Lafayette. Mem. Am. Soc. Editors and Publishers, Author's Guild, Internat. Platform Assn., Nat. Speakers Assn., Nat. Press Photographers Assn., Guild Assn. Airport Execs., Aviation and Space Writers Assn., Nat. Assn. of Real Estate Editors (NAAREE), Internat. Exchangors Assn. (founder), Nat. Press Club, Overseas Press Club. Clubs: La Costa Country, Cuyamaca, Rancho Santa Fe Country, Passport. Lodges: Masons, Shriners. Author: A Fortune At Your Feet, 1981, How You Can Get Rich, Stay Rich and Enjoy Being Rich, 1981, Financial Independence, 1987, The Profit, 1987; author and inst. "Your Key to Success" seminar, 1988; editor: The Real Estate News Observer, 1975—; fin. editor API, 1978—; fin. columnist Money Matters, 1986—; syndicated columnist, radio and tv host of "Money Making Ideas," 1977—; songwriter: Only You, 1939, If I'm Not Home For Christmas, 1940, Franny, 1940, Flajaloppa, 1940, They've Nothing More Dear Only They've Got It Here, 1941, The Summer of Life, 1956; producer (movies) The Flight of the Cobra, Rena, We Have Your Daughters, Music Row; speaker for radio and TV as The Real Estate Answerman, 1975—; host (radio and TV show) Ask Mr. Money. Inventor swivel seat, siptop, inflatumbrella. Home: Box 1144 Rancho Santa Fe CA 92067

KESSLER, JASCHA, English educator; b. N.Y.C., Nov. 27, 1929; s. Hyman and Rose (Bronsweig) K.; m. Julia Braun, July 19, 1950; children: Margot Lucia Braun, Adam Theodore Braun, Alessandro Braun. BA, NYU, 1950; MA, U. Mich., 1951, PhD, 1955. Prof. English U. Mich., 1951-54, NYU, 1954-55, Hunter Coll., 1955-56, Hamilton Coll., 1957-61, UCLA, 1961—; asst. dir. curriculum rsch., Harcourt, Brace & Co., N.Y.C., 1956-57; dir. Am. Studies Seminar, Rome, 1970; lectr., NEH, Western U.S., 1973-74, USIA, Brussels, Hungary, Iran, 1974; panelist, judge profl. meetings;

presenter poetry readings. Author: (fiction) An Egyptian Bondage and Other Stories, Bearing Gifts, Death Comes for the Behaviorist, Classical Illusions, Transmigrations; (poetry) Whatever Love Declares, After the Armies Have Passed, In Memory of the Future; translator works of Geza Csath, Forugh Farrokhzad, Miklos Radnoti, Nikolai Kantchev, Sándor Rákos, Ottó Orbium, Kirsti Sinodnsurri, others; (opera) The Cave. Recipient numerous poetry awards; writing fellow, Yaddo, Saratoga Springs, N.Y., 1958, Danforth Found., 1960, Helene Wurlitzer Found. of Taos, N.Mex., 1961, others; visiting poet, Israel, 1964; Fulbright fellow, Italy, 1963-64; sr. Fulbright prof. Am. lit., Rome, 1970; writer-in-residence, The Jerusalem Found., 1985; recipient Corvina Press Translation prize, Budapest, Hungary, 1987. Mem. PEN Am. Ctr. (winner numerous awards), ASCAP, Poetry Soc. Am., N.Y.C. Translation Ctr. Home: 218 16th St Santa Monica CA 90402 Office: Dept English UCLA 405 Hilgard Ave Los Angeles CA 90024

KESSLER, MICHAEL, computer scientist; b. Whitestone, N.Y., June 11, 1964; s. Klaus and Sonia Frieda (Kamm) K. BA in Computer Sci., Queens Coll., 1986. Computer salesman Mitchel Field Navy Exch., Garden City, N.Y., 1985-86; tchr. computer edn. Ces Computech, Inc., Glendale, N.Y., 1986-87; data entry clk. Univ. Med. Ctr., Tucson, 1987; computer operator, analyst Bell Tech. Ops., Fort Huachuca, Ariz., 1987-88; instr. math. and computers Chaparral Career Coll., Tucson, 1988; computer programmer Morrison-Knudsen Svcs., Inc., Fort Huachuca, 1988—, Planning Rsch. Corp., Sierra Vista, Ariz., 1988—; computer cons. MKCIC, Bayside N.Y. 1985-87. Vol. Tucson chpt. Leukemia Soc. Am., 1987—. Home and Office: 743 E Fry Blvd #72 Sierra Vista AZ 85635

KESSLER, NEIL JAY, electrical engineer; b. St. Louis, Feb. 6, 1938; s. Maury and Mollie (Schwartz) K.; m. Diane G. Schachter, Nov. 5, 1961; 1 child, Robert. BSEE, Washington U., St. Louis, 1959, MSEE, 1961. Instr. elec. engring. Washington U., St. Louis, 1959-61, 63-66; rsch. engr. Autonetics, N.Am. Rockwell, Anaheim, Calif., 1961-63; sr. engr. McDonnell Astronautics, St. Louis, 1963-66; group engr. Emerson Electric, St. Louis, 1966-70; sect. chief McDonnell Aircraft Co., St. Louis, 1970-83; avionics mgr. Northrop Ventura, Newbury Park, Calif., 1983-84, Northrup Aircraft, Hawthorne, Calif., 1984—. With USNR, 1955-63. Recipient Teammate of Distinction Commendation, McDonnell Aircraft, 1982. Mem. Am. Def. Preparedness Assn. (session chmn. 1980-82), Sigma Xi, Tau Beta Pi, Eta Kappa Nu. Home: 3107 Corte Portofino Newport Beach CA 92660 Office: Northrop Aircraft 1 Northrop Ave Hawthorne CA 90250

KESSLER, ROBERT ALLEN, data processing executive; b. N.Y.C., Feb. 2, 1940; s. Henry and Caroline Catherine (Axinger) K.; m. Marie Therese Anton, Mar. 17, 1967; children: Susanne, Mark. BA in Math., CUNY, 1961; postgrad., UCLA, 1963-64. EDP analyst Boeing Aircraft, Seattle, 1961-62; computer specialist System Devel. Corp., Santa Monica, Calif., 1962-66; mem. tech. staff Computer Scis. Corp., El Segundo, Calif., 1966-67, sr. mem. tech. staff, 1971-72, computer scientist, 1974-81; systems mgr. Xerox Data Systems, L.A., 1967-71; prin. scientist Digital Resources, Algiers, Algeria, 1972-74; sr. systems cons. Atlantic Richfield, L.A., 1981—. Mem. Big. Bros. L.A., 1962-66; precinct cpat. Goldwater for Pres., Santa Monica, 1964; mem. L.A. Conservacy, 1987. Mem. Assn. Computing Machinery. Home: 6138 W 75th Pl Los Angeles CA 90045 Office: ARCO 515 S Flower Los Angeles CA 90071

KESSLER, WALTER ARNOLD, food products executive; b. San Jose, Calif., Aug. 24, 1953; s. W. Arnold and Elizabeth (Waspi) K. AA, San Joaquin Delta Coll., 1973; BS, Fresno State Coll., 1973. Ptnr. Bay Meadow Farms, Galt, Calif., 1986—; bd. dirs., pres. 1980-81. Bd. dirs., pres. Barnyard Olympics, Galt, 1980—, Galt Community Coun., 1984—, chmn. 1985-86. Recipient Am. Farmer award Future Famers Am., 1973; named Outstanding Guernsey Young Breeder Calif., 1984. Mem. Am. Guernsey Assn. (bd. dirs.-at-large 1985), Calif. Guernsey Cattle Club (bd. dirs. 1983—, pres. 1981—), Western Guernsey Sires 1983— (pres. 1988—, rep.), Western United Dairymen , Calif. Tax Reduction Movement.

KETCHERSID, WAYNE LESTER, JR., medical technologist; b. Seattle, Oct. 16, 1946; s. Wayne Lester and Hazel May (Greene) K.; m. Wilette LaVerne Mautz, Oct. 6, 1972; 1 son, William Les. BS in Biology Pacific Luth. U., 1976, BS in Med. Tech., 1978, MS in Adminstrn. Cen. Mich. U., 1989. Cert. med. technologist. Staff technologist Tacoma Gen. Hosp., 1978-79, chemistry supr., 1979-81, head chemistry, 1981-83; head chemistry Multicare Med. Ctr., 1984-86, mgr., 1986—. Mem. Nat. Rep. Com. Served with U.S. Army, 1966-68. William E. Slaughter Found. scholar, 1975-76. Mem. Am. Assn. Clin. Chemistry, Am. Hosp. Assn., Am. Soc. Med. Tech. (cert., chmn. region IX adminstrn. 1984—, nat. del. 1984—), Wash. State Soc. Med. Tech. (chmn. biochemistry sect. 1983-86 dist. pres. 1986—, cert. merit 1983, 84, 86, 88, pres. 1988-89, pres. 1989—), Am. Soc. Clin. Pathologists (med. technolgist), N.W. Med. lab. Symposium (chmn. 1986-88, 90), Internat. Platform Assn. Lutheran. Contbr. articles to profl. jours. Office: Multicare Med Ctr 315 S K St Tacoma WA 98405

KETCHUM, MILO SMITH, civil engineer; b. Denver, Mar. 8, 1910; s. Milo Smith and Esther (Beatty) K.; m. Gretchen Allenbach, Feb. 28, 1944; children: David Milo, Marcia Anne, Matthew Phillip, Mark Allen. B.S., U. Ill., 1931, M.S., 1932; D.Sc. (hon.), U. Colo., 1976. Asst. prof. Case Sch. Applied Sci., Cleve., 1937-44; engr. F.G. Browne, Marion, Ohio, 1944-45; owner, operator Milo S. Ketchum, Cons. Engrs., Denver, 1945-52; partner, prin. Ketchum, Konkel, Barrett, Nickel & Austin, Cons. Engrs. and predecessor firm, Denver, 1952—; prof. civil engring. U. Conn., Storrs, 1967-78; emeritus U. Conn., 1978—; mem. Progressive Architecture Design Awards Jury, 1958, Am. Inst. Steel Constrn. Design Awards Jury, 1975, James F. Lincoln Arc Welding Found. Design Awards Jury, 1977; Stanton Walker lectr. U. Md., 1966. Author: Handbook of Standard Structural Details for Buildings, 1956; editor-in-chief Structural Engineering Practice, 1981-84; contbr. engring. articles to tech. mags. and jours. Recipient Disting. Alumnus award U. Ill., 1979. Mem. Am. Concrete Inst. (hon.; dir., Turner medal 1966), ASCE (pres. Colo. sect., hon.), Am. Cons. Engrs. Coun., Nat. Acad. Engring., Am. Soc. Engring. Edn., Internat. Assn. Shell and Space Structures, Structural Engrs. Assn. Colo. (pres.), Cons. Engrs. Coun. Colo. (pres.), Sigma Xi, Tau Beta Pi, Chi Epsilon, Phi Kappa Phi, Alpha Delta Phi.

KETTEL, EDWARD JOSEPH, oil company executive; b. N.Y.C., Sept. 13, 1925; s. Harold J. and Evelyn M. (Melbourne) K.; student St. John's U., 1943; BA, St. Francis Coll., 1949; MA, Columbia U., 1953; m. Janet M. Johnson, Nov. 27, 1952; children: Dorothy A., David A. Ins. mgr. Arabian Am. Oil Co., 1950-56, Ethyl Corp., 1956-65; asst. treas. Atlantic Richfield Co., L.A., 1965-85, asst. treas., Chevron Corp., San Francisco, 1985—; chmn. bd. Oil Ins., Ltd.; pres. Greater Pacific, Ltd.; dir. Am. S.S. Owners Mut. Protection and Indemnity Assn., Inc., Internat. Tanker Indemnity Assn., Ltd. With inf. AUS, 1943-46. Decorated Bronze Star, Purple Heart with oak leaf cluster. Mem. Am. Petroleum Inst., Mfrs. Chem. Assn., Nat. Fire Protection Assn., Risk and Ins. Mgmt. Soc., N.Y. Athletic Club, L.A. Athletic Club, Palos Verdes Country Club, Jonathan Club, Comml. Club, Colony Golf Club. Office: 225 Bush St San Francisco CA 94104

KETTLEWELL, JEANNE KAY, marketing executive; b. Lafayette, Ind., June 15, 1955; d. John and Norma (Henry) K. BS in Microbiology and Chemistry, Ohio State U., 1977. Sales rep. Sargent-Welch Sci., Dallas, 1977-81, Organon Diagnostics, Dallas, 1979-81, Am. Sci. Products, Dallas, 1981-82; mgr. mktg. Am. Sci. Products, Chgo., 1982-83; mgr. regional sales Am. Sci. Products, Irvine, Calif., 1983-87; v.p. sales and mktg. Pacific Biotech, Inc., San Diego, 1987—. Mem. Clin. Lab. Mgrs. Assn. (pres. 1988-89), Nat. Assn. Female Execs., Nat. Assn. Profl. Saleswomen, Am. Soc. Microbiology, Med. Mktg. Assn., Biomedical Mktg. Assn. Republican. Episcopalian. Office: Pacific Biotech 9050 Camino Santa Fe San Diego CA 92121

KETTLEWELL, NEIL MACKEWAN, neuroscience educator, researcher, sculptor; b. Evanston, Ill., May 27, 1938; s. George Edward and Barbara Sidney (Kidde) K.; m. Phyllis Ann Miller, Jan. 30, 1965 (div. Sept. 1976); 1 son, Brant Regnar; m. Toni Ann Gianoulias, June 2, 1978. B.S., Kent State U., 1962; M.A., U. Mich., 1965, Ph.D., 1969. Research asst. in psychology U. Mich., 1963-69, programmer, 1966-69, systems analyst time scheduling office, 1967-69; lectr. U. Mont., 1969-70, asst. prof. psychology, 1970-75, assoc. prof., 1976—; cons. in field; sculptor, exhibited numerous nat. galleries; sculptural commns. Franklin Mint, 1981, 82, Cin. Reds, 1981, others; cons. in art mktg. Served with USAR, 1958-66. U. Mich. Presdl. scholar, 1964. Mem. Soc. Neurosci., N.Y. Acad. Scis., Sculptors Internat., Pi Mu Epsilon, Psi Chi, Phi Eta Sigma. Subspecialties: Neuropsychology; Molecular biology. Current work: Ultrastructural synaptic changes in brain as result of experience. Home: 172 Fairway Dr Missoula MT 59803 Office: Dept Psychology U Mont Missoula MT 59801

KEVINS, DAVID VINCENT, financial investment consultant; b. Toronto, Ont., Can., Apr. 5, 1954; came to U.S., 1956; s. Francis and Edith Kathleen (O'Hara) K.; m. Karen Alice Millar, Aug. 9, 1986. BS, U. So. Calif., 1976, PharmD, 1981. Profl. harness racing driver, trainer U.S. Trotting Assn., Columbus, Ohio, 1977-83; pharmacy mgmt. Better Drugs of Calif., Inc., Glendale, 1983-86; chief exec. officer D&K Inc., L.A., 1986—; cons. Aversa & Uversa Ltd, Monterey Park, Calif., 1985—; owner, chief exec. officer D&K Inc., Hermosa Beach, Calif., 1986—. Vol. L.A. Mission, 1984—; contbr. Christian Childrens Fund, Richmond, Va., 1982—. Recipient Attridge award for musical performance, U. So. Calif. Sch. Music, 1972; Calif. State U. scholar. Mem. Am. Assn. Investors., Sports Connection, Manhattan Beach. Democrat. Roman Catholic. Home and Office: 72 The Strand #2 Hermosa Beach CA 90254

KEVLES, DANIEL JEROME, history educator, writer; b. Phila., Mar. 2, 1939; s. David and Anne (Rothstein) K.; m. Bettyann Holtzmann, May 18, 1961; children: Beth Carolyn, Jonathan David. BA in Physics, Princeton U., 1960; postgrad., Oxford U., 1960-61; PhD in History, Princeton U., 1964. From asst. to full prof. of history Calif. Inst. Tech., Pasadena, 1964-86, Koepfli prof. humanities, 1986—; vis. rsch. fellow U. Sussex, Brighton, Eng., 1976; vis. prof. U. Pa., Phila., 1979. Author: The Physicists, 1978 (Nat. Hist. Soc. prize 1979), In the Name of Eugenics, 1985; (mag. series) Annals of Eugenics (Page One award 1985); contbr. articles to The New Yorker, other mags. Charles Warren fellow Harvard U., 1981-82, Ctr. for Advanced Study Behavorial Scis. fellow, 1986-87, Nat. Endowment for Humanities sr. fellow, 1981-82, Guggenheim fellow, 1983. Mem. PEN, Author's Guild, Orgn. Am. Historians, Am. Hist. Assn., AAAS (chmn. sect. L 1983-85), History Sci. Soc. (coun. 1980-82, com. publ. 1984-88, Sarton lectr. 1985), Phi Beta Kappa. Democrat. Club: Princeton of N.Y. Office: Calif Inst Tech 1201 E California Blvd Pasadena CA 91125

KEY, CHARLES CHRISTOPHER, writer, photographer, producer; b. San Francisco, Oct. 20, 1948; s. Dudley and Lois Dowd (Wilson) K.; m. Lynne Kay Stevens, Nov. 1, 1978 (div. Mar., 1984); children: Bonnie Lynne, Brenda Kay. BA, Western Carolina U., 1969; MA, U. N.C., 1974. Anchorman, producer Sta. WTVD-TV, Durham, N.C., 1972-74; advt. mgr. Minnick Realtors, Bainbridge Island, Wash., 1975-77; gen. mgr. Anchor Excursions, Bainbridge Island, 1977-79; legis. reporter Sta. KTOO-TV, Juneau, Alaska, 1979-80; mgr. Sta. KTOO-FM, Juneau, 1980-81; mgr. broadcast services Sta. KTOO-FM, TV, Juneau, 1981-82; prod. dir. Sta. KHNS-FM, Haines, Alaska, 1982-83; gen. mgr. Bainbridge Island (Wash.) Broadcasting, 1984-88; freelance writer, photographer, 1974—; cons. Tekakwitha Conf. Gr. Falls, Mont., 1985-88. Author: Scotch Broom Chronicles, 1985, Last Voyage of Spokane, 1987, and various poems. Founder Oktoberfest, Bainbridge Island Broadcasting; cons. Winter Festival; lay minister Holy Spirit Episcopal Ch. Recipient Best Radio Commentary and Best Breaking News awards, Alaska Press Club. Mem. Sigma Delta Chi. Home and Office: Rt 2 PO Box 426-C Vashon WA 98070

KEY, EDWIN REES, human resources director; b. Anderson, Ind., June 29, 1941; s. Don Ellis and Delores (Rees) K.; m. Rae Anne Trainer, Dec. 26, 1965; 1 child, David Scott. BS, Purdue U., 1964; MA, Ball State U., 1965. Recruiter United Airlines, San Francisco, 1966-71; employment mgr. Applied Tech., Sunnyvale, Calif., 1971-73; personnel dir. NDA Search, Santa Clara, 1974; personnel mgr. Dalmo Victor, Belmont, 1975; personnel dir. Wadsworth, 1976-85; personnel mgr. Goodwill Industries, Oakland, 1986-87; dir. human resources Free-Flow Packaging Corp., Redwood City, 1987—. Active Boy Scouts Am.., San Mateo (Father of the Yr. 1979). With U.S. Army, 1964. Mem. Calif. Human Resources Council, Santa Clara Valley Personnel Assn., Belmont C. of C. (pres. 1982-83). Home: 1501 Maple St San Mateo CA 94402 Office: Free-Flow Packaging Corp 1093 Charter St Redwood City CA 94063

KEY, RAMONA THORNTON, health facility administrator; b. Little Rock, Ark., Dec. 13, 1939; d. J.P. and H. Belle (Jones) T.; m. Charles E. Winters, Jan. 21, 1961 (dec. Dec. 1965); children: Lesa Trujillo, Kellie Scarpa, Dale Winters; m. George Trujillo, May 24, 1970 (dec. July 1977); 1 child, Melinda Trujillo; m. Dennis Russell Key, May 15, 1982 (div. Feb. 1988). BS in Psychology, Southwestern Coll., 1963; cert. coronary intensive care, U. Tenn., 1973; postgrad., Memphis State U., 1979-81. Nurse various hosps., 1961-72; dir. personal adjustment ctr. Mental Health and Retardation Ctr., Oxford, Miss., 1972-75; cons. Interagy. Commn.'s Devel. Disabilities Tng. program State of Miss., 1974-75; coordinator for adult acute psychiat. services, liaison with local mental health ctr. Boulder (Colo.) Psychiat. Inst., 1975-77; head nurse behavior modification VA Hosp., Memphis, 1978-81; hosp. supr. Vista Sandia Psychiat. Hosp., Albuquerque, 1981-85, dir. nursing services, 1985-88; leader health workshops, Miss., 1974; bd. dirs. Nurse Profl. Standards Bd., VA Med. Ctr., Memphis, 1979-81; mem. faculty U. N.Mex. Coll. Nursing, 1986—. Mem. Am. Nurses Assn., N.Mex. Nurses Assn. (CEU com. 1986—), N.Mex. Orgn. Nurse Execs. (program chairperson 1987-88). Democrat. Methodist. Home: 3702 Rose Circle SE Rio Rancho NM 87124 Office: U NMex Mental Health Ctr Dir Nursing Svc 2600 Marble NE Albuquerque NM 87106

KEYES, DARLYNN LADD, real estate executive; b. Denver, Apr. 14, 1948; d. Ernest Victor and Mary Louise (Webb) K. BS, U. Wyo., 1971. Lic. in real estate, Fla.; cert. real estate broker, Colo. Dir. mktg., ski instr., ski patrol Geneva Basin, Grant, Colo., 1972-78; gen. mgr. Tumbling River Guest Ranch, Grant, 1974-76; owner Above Timberline Outfitters, Grant, 1974—, Keyes Real Estate and Investment Co., Vail, Colo., 1979—; comml. and residential real estate salesperson 1977-79; interval owner in real estate Streamside of Vail, 1979-80; project dir. real estate Brewster Green, Cape Cod, Mass., 1981-82, Vallarta Torrs, Puerta Vallarta, Mex., 1983-84; real estate salesperson Clube Praia de Ora, Algarve, Portugal, 1984; project dir. real estate Sandstone Creek Club, Vail, 1985-87; sales dir. Gold Point Condos, Breckenridge, Colo., 1987-88; sales mgr. Torres Mazattan, Mexico, 1989—; sec., treas. Viking Vacation Internat., Brewster, 1982-83. Mem. Nat. Assn. Exec. Women, Colo. Bd. Realtors, Vail Bd. Realtors, Colo. Cattleman's Assn., Nat. Bd. Realtors, Colo. Wool Growers Assn., Nat. Dude Ranch Assn. (bd. dirs. 1975, Washington rep.), Am. Resort and Residential Devel. Assn., Profl. Assn. Diving Instrs. Clubs: Alpine Garden, Beaver Scuba Divers (Vail); London (Eng.) Gliding. Home and Office: PO Box 1952 Vail CO 81657

KEYES, JAMES BONDURANT, business consultant; b. Des Moines, May 22, 1927; s. Arthur Hyde and Dorothy (Bondurant) K.; BS, Iowa State U., 1950; MBA, Northwestern U., 1951; m. Mary Jane McAfee, July 26, 1957; children—Edward, Jason. Asst. cashier Bank of Am., L.A., 1952-57; profl. bus. cons. Dental Bus. Adminstrn., Laguna Beach, Calif., 1957—. Prof. clin. dentistry and dir. of advanced studies in gen. dentistry U. So. Claif., 1989—; pres. Laguna Beach Community Chest, 1961-62; treas. Orange County (Calif.) United Way, 1972-74. Treas. Orange County Rep. Cen. Com., 1960-62; pres. Young Reps., 1960-61. With AUS, 1945-46. Mem. Acad. Prof. Bus. Cons.'s (pres. 1974-75, 85-87), Soc. Profl. Bus. Cons.'s (pres. 1974-75), Inst. Cert. Profl. Bus. Cons.'s, Inst. Cert. Fin. Planners, Internat. Assn. Fin. Planning, Ankylosing Spondylitis Assn. U.S.A. (v.p. 1986—), Ankylosing Spondylitis Internat. (councillor 1988), Delta Upsilon. Episcopalian. Editorial cons. Dental Mgmt. Mag., 1972-80, Dental Econ. Mag., 1980-83. Address: 1125 Emerald Bay Laguna Beach CA 92651

KEYES, JUDITH DROZ, lawyer; b. Pitts., Jan. 16, 1946; d. Blair Guthrie Huddart and Barbara Jane (Tilden) McCoy; m. Donald Glenn Droz, May 25, 1968 (dec. Apr. 12, 1969); 1 child, Tracy Tilden Droz; m. David Phillip Keyes, June 6, 1970. BS, Pa. State U., 1966; MA in Linguistics, U. Mo., 1970; JD, U. Calif., Berkeley, 1975. Bar: Calif. 1975, U.S. Dist. Ct. (no. and ea. dists.) Calif. 1975. Tchr. Chgo. Pub. High Sch. System, 1966-67; field atty. NLRB, San Francisco, 1975-76; ptnr. Corbett & Kane, Oakland, Calif., 1976—; vis. assoc. prof. Suffolk U. Law Sch., Boston, 1986-87; bd. dirs. Calif.-Nev. Meth. Homes, Oakland, Calif. Mem. ABA, Calif. Bar Assn., San Francisco Bar Assn., Alameda County Bar Assn., Order of the Coif. Democrat. Unitarian Universalist. Office: Corbett & Kane 2000 Powell St Ste 1450 Emeryville CA 94608

KEYES, ROBERT JAMES, lawyer; b. New Brunswick, N.J., Aug. 11, 1952; s. William A. Sr. and Betsy (Ross) K. BA in Philosophy, St. Mary's Sem., Balt., 1974; MDiv, U. St. Michael's Coll., Toronto, 1977; JD, Georgetown U., 1986. Bar: Calif. 1986, D.C. 1989. Former Roman Catholic priest Diocese of Richmond, Richmond, Va., 1978-80; assoc. Pettit & Martin, San Francisco, 1986—. Mem. Bay Area Lawyers for Individual Freedom. Democrat. Roman Catholic. Home: 111 Corwin St #9 San Francisco CA 94114 Office: Pettit & Martin 101 California St 35th Fl San Francisco CA 94111

KEYSER, JAMES DAVID, archaeologist, researcher; b. Ft. Collins, Colo., Mar. 3, 1950; s. Raymond Clyde and Mina Marie (Hawthorne) K. BA, U. Mont., 1972, MA, 1974; PhD, U. Oreg., 1977. Rsch. archaeologist U. Mont., Missoula, 1973-76; teaching asst. U. Oreg., Eugene, 1976; pvt. rsch. archaeologist Missoula, 1976; asst. prof. archaeology SUNY, Buffalo, 1976-77, U. Tulsa, 1977-78; archaeologist U.S. Forest Svc., Billings, Mont., 1978-80; regional archaeologist U.S. Forest Svc., Portland, Oreg., 1980—. Contbr. articles to profl. jours. Bd. dirs. Cultural Heritage Found., Portland, 1986—; pres., bd. dirs. Stephanie Terr. Homeowners Assn., Portland, 1986-87. NEH travel grantee, 1987-88. Mem. Plains Anthrop. Soc. (bd. dirs. 1985-88), Amici d'Italia (v.p. Portland 1987). Republican. Episcopalian. Office: US Forest Svc 319 SW Pine St Portland OR 97208

KEYSER, RICHARD LEE, hospital executive; b. Gary, Ind., Nov. 4, 1941; s. Edward Arnold and Mildred Lee (Hernly) K.; m. Joan Carolyn Whitson, Apr. 2, 1967; children: Brian Lester, Lauren Elizabeth. B.Acctg., U. Ill, 1963, M.Acctg., 1964. Mgr. Arthur Andersen & Co., San Francisco, 1965-71; health services coordinator Sisters of Mercy, Burlingame, Calif., 1971-76; v.p. ops. Health Care Devel., Newport Beach, Calif., 1976-77; sr. v.p. Amherst Assocs., Walnut Creek, Calif., 1977-83; pres. Mercy Hosp. and Med. Ctr., San Diego, 1983—; bd. dirs. Community Care Network, San Diego, 1984-88. Mem. budget panel United Bay Area Crusade, San Francisco, 1972-73. Mem. Am. Coll. Hosp. Adminstrs., Am. Hosp. Assn., Calif. Hosp. Assn., Calif. Assn. Hosps. and Health Systems (bd. dirs. 1987—), Calif. Assn. Cath. Hosps. (bd. dirs. 1984—), Hosp. Council San Diego/Imperial Counties (trustee 1985—). Republican. Presbyterian. Lodge: Rotary. Office: Mercy Hosp and Med Ctr 4077 5th Ave San Diego CA 92103-2180

KEYSTON, STEPHANI ANN, small business owner; b. Baytown, Tex., Aug. 6, 1955; d. Herbert Howard and Janice Faye (Stowe) Cruickshank; m. George Keyston III, Oct. 8, 1983; 1 child, Jeremy George. AA with honors, Merced Coll., Merced, Calif., 1975; BA in Journalism with distinction, San Jose State U., 1976. Reporter, Fresno (Calif.) Bee, 1974-75; reporter, photographer Merced (Calif.) Sun-Star, 1974-77; pub. info. officer Fresno City Coll. (Calif.), 1977-80; dir. communications Aerojet Tactical Systems Co., Sacramento, 1980-83; co-owner, v.p. Keyco Landscape Contractor Inc., Auburn, Calif., 1984—. Co.-coordinator Aerojet United Way Campaign, 1981; Aerojet Tactical Systems Co. coordinator West Coast Nat. Derby Rallies, 1981-83. Mem. Internat. Assn. Bus. Communicators (dir. Sacramento chpt. 1983), Citrus Heights C. of C. (v.p. 1983). Republican. Home: 13399 Lakeview Pl Auburn CA 95603 Office: Keyco Landscape Contractor Inc 10594 Combie Rd Ste 6476 Auburn CA 95603

KHADAVI, KAMRAN RON, electronics engineer; b. Tehran, Iran, Oct. 30, 1948; came to U.S., 1979; s. Sion Nissan and Touran (Kalimian) K; m. Dina Falakasa, Nov. 23, 1978; children: Natalie, Nicole. BSEE, Arya Mehr U., Tehran, 1972; PhD in Elec. Engring., U. Rennes, Rennes, France, 1977. Engr. Ctr. Commun d'Etudes de TV et Télécommunications, 1975-77; staff engr. Nat. Iranian Radio & TV, Tehran, 1977-78, Magnavox Research Operation, Torrance, Calif., 1979-81; sr. engr. VG Systems, Inc., Woodland Hills, Calif., 1982-85, Edwards CPE, Inc., San Fernando, Calif., 1986-88; prin. engr. Micropolis Corp., Chatsworth, Calif., 1989—; cons. Edwards-CPE, Inc., San Fernando, 1988-89, Hubbard's Consultants, Camarillo, Calif., 1987-89. Inventor noise reduction on TV invention. Post-grad. scholar Govt. of France, 1974-77. Mem. IEEE. Republican. Jewish. Home: 24115 Hatteras St Woodland Hills CA 91367

KHALID, AMIR A. R., insurance broker; b. Pickens, Miss., Feb. 24, 1941; s. Jessie Nick and Hattie Jane (Simpson) Brim; m. Garnell Pierce (div.); children: Earl M., Marcus L., Na'im A., Maiya, Janan. EdB cum laude, U. Mich., 1975; BBA magna cum laude, Shaw Coll., 1976; teaching fellow, U. Mich., 1976-77. Cert. tchr., FCC operators permit ins. broker. Program supr. Project Community, Ann Arbor, Mich., 1977-78; tchr. Huron Valley Pub. Schs., New Boston, Mich., 1978-80, Detroit Pub. Schs., 1980-81; dist. mgr. Learning Well Inc., Glendale, Ariz., 1981-83; account supr. Creative Mktg. Concepts, La Mesa, Calif., 1983-85; sales rep. Studio Security Co., Burbank, Calif., 1985-86; fin. svc. rep. John Hancock Ins. Co., Canoga Park, Calif., 1986-87; broker Equitable Fin. Co., N.Y.C., 1987—. Author: (anthology of poems) Never to Much, 1989. With USAF, 1959-67. Teaching fellow U. Mich., 1976. Mem. Kiwanis, Toastmasters, NAACP. Democrat. Muslem. Home: 22968 Victory Blvd Woodland Hills CA 91367

KHAN, SARBULAND BILL, inventor, entrepreneur, consultant; b. Zanzibar, E. Africa, Apr. 11, 1951; came to U.S., 1984; s. Gulkhan Yusufzai and Sarfiraz (Abdulhakim) Awan; m. Stella Conner, May 12, 1979; 1 child, Zenobia. Cert. telecommunications, Garrettesgreen Tech. Coll., Birmingham, Eng., 1969; cert. advanced level physics, Handsworth Tech. Coll., Birmingham, 1973. Telecommunications technician G.P.O. (name now Brit. Telecom), W. Midlands, Eng., 1968-71; sr. instr., co-owner Aston Martial Arts Centre, Birmingham, 1972-75; exec. dir. Dianetics & Scientology Centre, Birmingham, 1976-82, Am. Sun Solar, Inc., Redondo Beach, Calif., 1984-86; Hubbard adminstrv. tech. instr., supr. Singer Consultants, Beverly Hills, Calif., 1985-86; bus. cons., supr. W.I.S.E. Corp., L.A., 1986-88; pvt. rsch. and discovery and mktg. L.A., 1987—. Inventor international patent disposable diaper. Dancer Ballroom and Latin Am. Gold Medalist, 1970-71. Home and Office: 1539 N Alexandria Ave Los Angeles CA 90027

KHANDPUR, ROSHAN L., import company executive; b. Gujranwala, Delhi, India, Mar. 6, 1946; came to U.S., 1980; s. Harbans Singh and Kartar (Devi) K.; m. Dec. 1972 (div. Mar. 1979); children: Amitesh, Madhu Bala; m. Kulwant K., Oct. 10, 1979; children: Ritika, Krishan G. BA, Dayal Singh Coll., New Delhi. Sales rep. Metro. Ins. Co., L.A., 1982-83; pres. Radhika Imports Inc., L.A., 1984—. Office: Radhika Imports Inc 1018-A So Los Angeles St Los Angeles CA 90015

KHAW, NOELINE, pediatrician, navy officer; b. Bhamo, Kachin, Burma, Dec. 25, 1944; came to U.S., 1969; d. Thai Pek and Li-Chen (Wu) K. MB, BS, U. Rangoon, 1968. Diplomate Am. Bd. Pediatrics. Rotating intern Rangoon (Burma) Gen. Hosp., 1968-69, Providence Hosp., Portland, Oreg., 1970-71; resident in pediatrics Maricopa County Gen. Hosp., Phoenix, 1971-73; sr. resident in pediatrics Kauikeolani Children's Hosp., Honolulu, 1973-74; commd. lt. comdr. USN, 1975, advanced through grades to comdr., 1979; staff pediatrician Naval Regional Med. Ctr., Long Beach, Calif., 1975-82; chief pediatrics U.S. Naval Hosp., Oak Harbor, Wash., 1982-85; staff pediatrician U.S. Naval Hosp., Long Beach, 185-87, 88—, asst. chief, 1985-87; staff pediatrician Mullikin Med. Group, Artesia, Calif., 1987-88. Fellow Am. Acad. Pediatrics; mem. Am. Women Physicians Assn., Assn. Mil. Surgeons U.S., Wilderness Soc., Bread for World Assn., Uniformed Svcs. AAP (chpt. west), Orange County Pediatric Soc. Methodist. Office: Naval Hosp Pediatric Clinic 7500 E Carson St Long Beach CA 90822

KHEIFETS, SEMYON ABRAHAM (SAM KHEIFETS), physicist; b. Minsk, USSR, Apr. 17, 1928; came to U.S., 1977; s. Abraham Hilel and Emma (Pinhas) K.; m. Julia Entin, July 10, 1952; 1 child, Leeka. M in Physics, Moscow U., 1952; PhD, Inst. Theoretical and Exptl. Physics, Moscow, 1961. Physicist Yerevan (USSR) Phys. Inst., 1952-75, Deutsches Electric Synchrotron, Hamburg, Fed. Republic Germany, 1975-77, Stanford U., Palo Alto, Calif., 1978—. Author: Electron Synchrotron, 1963; contbr.

articles to jours. Mem. Am. Phys. Soc. Republican. Home: 2389 Sharon Rd Menlo Park CA 94025 Office: Stanford U 2575 Sand Hill Rd SLAC Bin 26 Menlo Park CA 94025

KHISTY, C. JOTIN, civil engineer, educator; b. Nagpur, India, July 4, 1928; m. Lena Licon, June 21, 1981. MSCE, U. Cin., 1970, MCP, 1973; PhD, The Ohio State U., 1977. Profl. engr., Ohio, Wash. Civil engr. Pub. Works Dept., India Govt., 1948-50, Electricity Dept., India Govt., 1951-57; asst. prof. Edn. Dept., India Govt., 1957-65; dep. dir. Tech. Edn., India Govt., 1965-69; transport and traffic engr. Metro Planning Orgns., Ohio, 1971-77; civil engring. prof. Wash. State U., Pullman, Wash., 1978—; cons. in field; mem. Wash. State Transp. Research Ctr., 1980—. Author: Transportation Engineering, 1989. Recipient Nicolaides Prize & Award, Inst. Engring., 1965. Mem. ASCE, Am. Inst. Transport Engrs., Am. Planning Assn., Am. Artificial Intelligence Soc. Home: 1215 Myrtle St Pullman WA 99163 Office: Washington State U Dept Civil Engring Pullman WA 99164-2910

KHOO, STANLEY SOO AUN, transportation executive; b. Rangoon, Burma, Feb. 7, 1945; came to U.S., 1977; s. Teng Sum and Leng Sim (Oei) K.; m. Sheila Su Lee Yeap, Feb. 18, 1977; children: Arthur K. H., Cyril K.S. Chief cadet officer Burma Five Star Line, Rangoon, 1966-76; supt. Marine Terminals Corp., San Francisco, 1977-80, div. supt., 1980-83, div. mgr., 1983—. Mem. Chinese Am. Polit. Assn., Star of Burma, Theravada Buddhist Soc. Am. (sec. 1986-87, pres. 1988—). Home: 4549 Marsh Meadow Way Concord CA 94521 Office: Marine Terminals Corp 5190 7th St Oakland CA 94607

KHOSLA, VED MITTER, oral and maxillofacial surgeon, educator; b. Nairobi, Kenya, Jan. 13, 1926; s. Jagdish Rai and Tara V. K.; m. Santosh Ved Chabra, Oct. 11, 1952; children: Ashok M., Siddarth M. Student, U. Cambridge, 1945; L.D.S., Edinburgh Dental Hosp. and Sch., 1950, Coll. Dental Surgeons, Sask., Can., 1962. Prof. oral surgery, dir. postdoctoral studies in oral surgery U. Calif. Sch. Dentistry, San Francisco, 1968—; chief oral surgery San Francisco Gen. Hosp.; lectr. oral surgery U. of Pacific, VA Hosp.; vis. cons. Fresno County Hosp. Dental Clinic.; Mem. planning com., exec. med. com. San Francisco Gen. Hosp. Contbr. articles to profl. jours. Examiner in photography and gardening Boy Scouts Am., 1971-73, Guatemala Clinic, 1972. Granted personal coat of arms by H.M. Queen Elizabeth II, 1959. Fellow Royal Coll. Surgeons (Edinburgh), Internat. Assn. Oral Surgeons, Internat. Coll. Applied Nutrition, Internat. Coll. Dentists, Royal Soc. Health, AAAS, Am. Coll. Dentists; mem. Brit. Assn. Oral Surgeons, Am. Soc. Oral Surgeons, Am. Dental Soc. Anesthesiology, Am. Acad. Dental Radiology, Omicron Kappa Upsilon. Club: Masons. Home: 1525 Lakeview Dr Hillsborough CA 94010 Office: U Calif Sch Dentistry Oral Surgery Div 3rd & Parnassus Aves San Francisco CA 94122

KHOUGAZ, SHELDON ERNEST, manufacturing engineering; b. Hamilton AFB, Calif., Jan. 19, 1952; s. James Norman Khougaz and Corky (Hoffman) Johnson; m. Sue Ellen Murphy, Jan. 8, 1988. Student, Calif. State U., Northridge, 1970, 74-76, USAF Acad., 1971-73. Project engr. Composite Tech.-KDI, L.A., 1978-82; mfg. engr. Hydro-Mill Co., L.A., 1982-. Mem. Soc. Mfg. Engrs., Am. Welding Soc. Republican. Roman Catholic. Home: 8157 Rhea Ave Reseda CA 91335 Office: Hydro-Mill Co 9301 Mason Ave Chatsworth CA 91311

KIANG, ASSUMPTA, (AMY KIANG), brokerage house executive; b. Bejing, Aug. 15, 1939; came to U.S., 1962; d. Pei-yu and Yu-Jean (Liu) Chao; m. Wan-lin Kiang, Aug. 14, 1965; 1 child, Eliot Y. BA, Nat. Taiwan U., 1960; MS, Marywood Coll., Scranton, Pa., 1964; MBA, Calif. State U., Long Beach, 1977. Data programmer IBM World Trade, N.Y.C., 1963; libr. East Cleve. Pub. Libr., 1964-68; lectr. Nat. Taiwan U., Taipei, 1971-73; with reference dept. U.S. Info. Svc., Taipei, 1971-74; asst v.p. Merrill Lynch, Sanata Ana, Calif., 1977—. Founder Pan Pacific Performing Arts Inc., Orange County, Calif., 1987; treas. women league Calif. State. U., Long Beach, 1980-82. Mem. Chineses Bus. Assn. So. Calif. (chmn. 1987—, v.p. 1986-87), Chancellor's Club, Old Ranch Country Club. Democrat. Roman Catholic. Office: Merrill Lynch 2670 N Main St Santa Ana CA 92702

KIDD, GERALD STEELE, II, endocrinologist; b. Phoenix, Jan. 27, 1945; s. Gerald Steele and Edith Belle (King) K.; children: Gerald III, Lindsey, Jaime. BA, U. Tex., Austin, 1967; MD, U. Tex., Galveston, 1971. Diplomate Am. Bd. Internal Medicine and Endocrinology and Metabolism. Commd. 2nd lt. U.S. Army, 1972, advanced through grades to col., 1986; gen. med. officer U.S. Army MEDDAC, Ft. Sill, Okla., 1972-73; resident medicine Fitzsimons Army Med. Ctr., Aurora, Colo., 1973-75; internist Ft. Belvoir (Va.) MEDDAC, 1975-76; fellow endocrinology Walter Reed Army Med. Ctr., Washington, 1976-78; endocrinologist William Beaumont Army Med. Ctr., El Paso, Tex., 1978-79; chief thyroid sect. Fitzsimmons Army Med. Ctr., Aurora, 1979-81, asst. chief endocrinology, 1981-84, chief endocrinology, dir. fellowship program, 1984—; asst. prof. Tex. Tech. Med. Sch., El Paso, 1978-79; asst. prof. U. Colo. Health Scis. Ctr., Denver, 1980-84, assoc. clin. prof., 1984—. Contbr. articles to med. jours. Fellow ACP; mem. Endocrine Soc., Am. Thyroid Assn., Am. Diabetes Assn., Am. Fedn. Clin. Rsch., Am. Soc. Bone and Mineral Rsch., Phi Beta Kappa, Mu Delta, Alpha Omega Alpha. Office: Endocrine Svc Fitzsimmons Army Med Ctr Aurora CO 80045-5001

KIDD, REUBEN PROCTOR, management engineer; b. Bedford, Va., Feb. 18, 1913; s. Oscar Kibbler and Estelle (Johnson) K.; B.S., Va. Poly. Inst., 1936; m. Margaret Jerome, June 23, 1952. Pres., Frito Corp. of Roanoke (Va.), 1947-49; indsl. engr. USAF, Sacramento, 1956-73; chmn. bd. USDR, Inc., Sacramento, 1961-69, MEN Internat., Inc., Mpls., 1977—; owner The Kidd Cos., operator Precision Tune-Up, Sacramento, 1974—. Served to capt. U.S. Army, 1942-46, to maj., 1949-51. Decorated Silver Star; registered profl. engr., Calif. Republican. Presbyterian. Home: 5809 Northgrove Way Citrus Heights CA 95610 Office: Precision Tune-Up 6241 Spruce Ave Sacramento CA 95841

KIDD, SHARON LAYNE, sales representative; b. Denver, June 25, 1941; d. O.W. and Marcella Winona (Piper) Nelson; m. Joseph Henry Kidd (div. Dec. 1980); children: Kimberlee Kae, Kelly Jo; m. William Joseph Walters, Sept. 12, 1986. Student, Colo. State U., 1959-60. Co-owner Am. Warehouse Co., Denver, 1963-80; property mgr. Am. Fin. Devel., Los Angeles, 1980-82; sales rep. Columbine Mech., Denver, 1982-84, Tolin Mech. Systems, Denver, 1984—. Printer Denver Post, Rocky Mountain News. Mem. Bldg. Owners and Mgrs. Assn. (vice-chair 1987, chair, bd. dirs. 1988—, chair golf tournaments 1988—, printer newsletter 1989, Allied Mem. of Yr. 1987). Lutheran. Club: Willow Springs Country (Golden, Colo.). Office: Tolin Mech Systems 450 W 42d Ave Denver CO 80226

KIDDER, THOMAS VERNON, financial executive; b. Eugene, Oreg., Nov. 1, 1951; s. Thomas Ellsworth and Eileen Louise (Smith) K.; m. Mary Colleen LeMoigne, Aug. 18, 1973; children: Thomas Tyson, Tiffany Hope, Drew Joshua. Student, Lane County Coll., Eugene, 1969-70, U. Md., Bremmerhaven, Fed. Republic Germany, 1971-72. Dir. co. store ops. Stretch & Sew, Inc., Eugene, 1973-81; chmn. bd. dirs. Bankers Land Corp., Eugene, 1981-83; pres., chief exec. officer Deltatek, Inc., Eugene, 1984-86; pres. Kidder Trust, Inc., Eugene, 1986—; fin. cons., Kidder,Kidder & Assocs., Eugene, 1976—. Treas., Lane County Commr. Campaign, Eugene, 1986; active state polit. campaigns. Sgt. U.S. Army, 1970-72. Decorated Nat. Def. medal. Mem. Nat. Fedn. Ind. Bus., Elks. Republican. Lutheran. Home and Office: 827 Spyglass Dr Eugene OR 97401

KIDWELL, MICHAEL W., packaging supply company executive; b. Phoenix, Dec. 17, 1949; s. Walter and Betty (Snyder) K.; m. Gay L. Boggess, Dec. 2, 1972; children: Christy, Sharon, Jeff. AA in Bus. Adminstrn., El Camino Coll., 1972; BS in Manpower Mgmt., Calif. State U., Long Beach, BS in Bus. Mgmt. Ter. rep. Instapak Corp., Denver, 1974-76; sales rep. Sealed Air Corp., Denver, 1977-78; pres. Midland Packaging-Supply Co., Littleton, Colo., 1979-, Foamtech Corp., Littleton, Colo., 1986-. With USMC, 1968-70. Alpha Kappa Psi. Office: Midland Packaging Supply Co 7561 S Grant St Bldg A-4 Littleton CO 80122

KIECKHAEFER, WILLIAM FREDERICK, psychologist; b. Meridian, Miss., June 29, 1950; s. Robert Victor and Thelma (Sledge) K.; m. Patricia Anne Mitchell, Aug. 7, 1982 ; 1 child: Jenna Mitchell. BA in Psychology, UCLA, 1972; MS in Indsl. Psychology, Calif. State U., San Diego, 1976. Data analyst San Diego State U. Found., 1973-74; personnel research psychologist Navy Personnel Research and Devel. Ctr., San Diego, 1974-76; mgmt. cons. Hooper, Goode, Inc., La Jolla, Calif., 1976-82; personnel research psychologist RGI, Inc., La Jolla, 1982-85, project mgr./sr. scientist, 1985--; v.p. personnel systems, 1988--; cons. in field. Author: tng. workbook: Communication Skills Guidebook, 1985; contbr. articles toprofl. publs. Research garantee Army Research Inst. 1980, 85, Navy Personnel Research and Devel. Ctr., 1985, 87, Personnel Security Research and Edn. Ctr., 1987. Mem. Personnel Testing Council, San Diego (pres. 1985-86, v.p. programs, 1986-87, treas. 1987-). Democrat. Home: 7585 Eads Ave Unit H La Jolla CA 92037 Office: RGI Inc 591 Camino Del L Reina Ste 917 San Diego CA 92108

KIEFF, JAMES RICHARD, marketing executive; b. Syracuse, N.Y., Jan. 11, 1941; s. James Richard Kieff and Jane Elizabeth (Bednarski) Womack; m. Priscilla Ann Muller, Sept. 4, 1965; children: Kristina, Timothy. BS, Syracuse U., 1962; MBA, U. Hawaii, 1963; postgrad., Columbia U., 1964, NYU, 1965-69. Mktg. economist Shell Oil Co., N.Y.C., 1964-66; instr. Hofstra U., Hempstead, N.Y., 1966-70; mktg. strategist Avon Products, N.Y.C., 1970-73; v.p. various mktg. positions Am. Express Co., N.Y.C., 1973-78; dir. mktg. Comml. Credit Co., Balt., 1978-81; v.p. market, product mgmt. Bankers Trust Co., N.Y.C., 1981-83; sr. v.p., dir. research BBDO Inc., N.Y.C., 1983-85; pres. Inst. Strategy Devel., New Canaan, Conn., 1985-86, Hillsborough, Calif., 1988—; v.p. product devel. VISA USA, San Mateo, Calif., 1986-88. Author: (with others) Media Trends '86, 1986. Pres. Ea. Property Owners Assn., Garden City, N.Y., 1971, v.p. 1970, bd. dirs., 1967; vice chmn. fin. svcs. coun. Advt. Rsch. Found., 1986-88. Recipient Trustee scholar Syracuse U., 1960-62, grad. Teching fellow U. Hawaii, 1962-63, Grad. Scholar Columbia U., 1963-64. Mem. Am. Mktg. Assn. (Exec. fellow 1986-87). Office: Inst Strategy Devel 90 Woodridge Rd Hillsborough CA 94010

KIEHN, MOGENS HANS, aviation engineer, consultant; b. Copenhagen, July 30, 1918; came to U.S., 1957; s. Hans-Christian and Lydia-Thea (Theillx Burban de Parmer) K.; m. Ase Rasmusen, Apr. 28, 1942; children: Marianne, Hans, Lars. BSME, U. Tech. Engring., Copenhagen, 1941; MS, Copenhagen U., 1942; degree in Army Intelligence, Def. Indsl. Security Inst., 1972. Profl. engr. Pres. Hamo Engring., Copenhagen, 1939-49, Evanston, Ill., 1958-78; engr. Sondstrand, Rockford, Ill., 1957-58; pres. Kiehn Internat. Engring., Phoenix, 1980—; chmn., pres. ETO Internat. Engring., Phoenix, 1985—; tech. engring. cons. Scandinavian Airlines, Sundstrand Engring., McDonnell Douglas, Ford, GM, Chrysler, Honeywell, Motorola, Gen. Electric, Hughes Aircraft. Patents include Rehab. Hosp. Lighting for Highmast, Drafting Machine, Tooling Machinery, Parts for Aircraft, Garbage and Pollution Burnemachine Optical Coupler. Served Finnish war, 1939, Danish Undergrav War, 1940-45, Morocco French Fgn. Legion, Vietnam, 1948-53. Mem. AIAA, Nat. Soc. Profl. Engring., Illuminating Engring. Soc. Engring., Nat. Geographic Soc., The Adventures Club of Denmark, Honors Club Internat., East Africa Wildlife Soc., Internat. Intelligence and Organized Crime Orgn.

KIELHORN, RICHARD WERNER, chemist; b. Berlin, Germany, June 17, 1931; s. Richard H. and Auguste (Lammek) K.; m. Anneliese Heinrich, Aug. 9, 1952; children: Anita, Margit. BS, Chem. Tech. Sch., Berlin, 1953. Lab. tech. Zoellner Werke, Berlin, 1950-57, Montrose Chem. Corp., Henderson, Nev., 1957-78; chief chemist Stauffer Chem. Corp., Henderson, 1978-88, Pioneer Chlor Alkali Co., Henderson, 1988—; tax cons. H&R Block, Las Vegas, Nev., 1972—, instr, 1978—. Mem. ASTM, Am. Chem. Soc., Am. Mgmt. Assn., Nev. Soc. Tax Cons. (v.p.), Am. Soc. Quality Control, Am. Water Works Assn. Home: 1047 Westminster Ave Las Vegas NV 89119 Office: Pioneer Chlor Alkali Co Lake Mead Dr Henderson NV 89015

KIELSKY, MICHAEL GERD, software engineer; b. Heidelberg, W. Germany, Sept. 14, 1964; came to U.S., 1978; s. Joseph and Vera Emuna (Landshut) K.; m. Jodi Michele Lewkowitz, Jan. 4, 1987. BS in Computer Sci., Grand Canyon Coll., 1984; MS in Computer Sci., Ariz. State U., 1989. Program intern Goodyear Aerospace, Litchfield, Ariz., 1984; teaching asst. Ariz. State U., Tempe, 1984-85; systems analyst Durham Communications, Mesa, Ariz., 1985-86; cons. Phoenix, 1986-87; sr. software engr. Tag Software, Glendale, Ariz., 1987-88; contract engr. McDonnell Douglas Helicopter Co., Mesa, 1988-89, Honeywell Comml. Flight Systems, Phoenix, 1989—; pres. WCI, Inc., Phoenix, 1986—. Mem. Assn. Computing Machinery, IEEE Computer Soc., Digital Equipment Computer Users Soc. Republican. Jewish. Home: 1902 E St Catherine Ave Phoenix AZ 85040

KIELSMEIER, CATHERINE JANE, school system administrator; b. San Jose, Calif; d. Frank Delos and Catherine Doris (Sellar) MacGowan; M.S., U. So. Calif., 1964, Ph.D., 1971; m. Milton Kielsmeier; children—Catherine Louise, Barry Delos. Tchr. pub. schs. Maricopa, Calif.; sch. psychologist Campbell (Calif.) Union Sch Dist., 1961-66; asst. prof. edn. and psychology Western Oreg. State Coll., Monmouth, 1966-67, 70; asst. research prof. Oreg. System Higher Edn., Monmouth, 1967-70; dir. spl. services Pub. Schs., Santa Rosa, Calif., 1972—. Mem. Sonoma County Council Community Services, 1976—, Sonoma County Orgn. for Retarded/Becoming Independent, 1978—. Mem. Council for Exceptional Children. Club: Commonwealth of Calif. Home: 7495 Poplar Dr Forestville CA 95436 Office: 211 Ridgeway Ave Santa Rosa CA 95402

KIENHOLZ, LYN SHEARER, arts projects coordinator; b. Chgo.; d. Mitchell W. and Lucille M. (Hock) Shearer; student Sullins Coll., Md. Coll. Women. Assoc. producer Kurt Simon Prodns., Beverly Hills, Calif., 1963-65; owner, mgr. Vuokko Boutique, Beverly Hills, 1969-75; bd. dirs. Los Angeles Inst. Contemporary Art, 1976-79, Fellows of Contemporary Art, 1977-79, Internat. Network for Arts, 1979-89, Los Angeles Contemporary Exhbns., 1980-82; exec. sec., bd. dirs. Beaubourg Found. (now George Pompidou Art and Culture Found.), 1977-81; visual arts adv. Performing Arts Council, Los Angeles Music Center, 1980-89; bd. govs. Calif. Inst. Tech. Baxter Art Gallery, 1980-85; adv. bd. dirs. Fine Arts Communications, pub. Images & Issues mag., 1981-85; founder, pres. bd. dirs. Calif./Internat. Arts Found., 1981—; bd. dirs., western chmn. ArtTable 1983-89; exec. bd. Sovereign Fund, 1981—; exec. bd. dirs. Scandinavia Today, 1982-83, Arts, Inc., 1987—, Art L.A./87, 1987, Art L.A., 1988; mem. adv. bd. Otis/Parsons Sch. Design, 1983-85, U. So. Calif. dept. fine arts, 1983-85; bd. dirs. UK/LA Festival of Britain, 1986-88; hon. bd. dirs. L'Ensemble des Deux Mondes, Paris, 1986—; mem. Comité International pour les Musées d'Art Moderne, 1985—. Bd. dirs. Arts, Inc., 1987-89. Co-host radio program ARTS/L.A., 1987—; contbg. editor Calif. mag., 1984-89 Address: 2737 Outpost Dr Los Angeles CA 90068

KIERNAN, ELAINE RUTH, financial analyst; b. Portland, Oreg., Feb. 27, 1947; d. Merle and Margaret (Nielsen) Schevenius; m. Walter R. Kiernan Jr.; children: Walter, Michael, Patty, Lexie. BS in Human Relations, U. San Francisco, 1984. Registered investment advisor. Account exec. P.H.H., Balt., 1970-80; nat. account mgr. Diasonics, Milpitas, Calif., 1980-82; pvt. practice fin. planning Fremont, Calif., 1982—. Editor: newsletter The Financial Informer. Active pub. affairs com. Fremont City Council. Mem. Internat. Order Fin. Planners, Palo Alto Fin. Planning Forum, Am. Bus. Women's Assn. Republican. Lutheran. Home: 44959 Washo Ct Fremont CA 94539 Office: N Am Securities 43255 Mission Blvd Fremont CA 94539

KIERSCH, GEORGE ALFRED, geological consultant, emeritus educator; b. Lodi, Calif., Apr. 15, 1918; s. Adolph Theodore and Viola Elizabeth (Bahmeier) K.; m. Jane J. Keith, Nov. 29, 1942; children—Dana Elizabeth Kiersch Haycock, Mary Annan, George Keith, Nancy McCandless Kiersch Bohnett. Student, Modesto Jr. Coll., 1936-37; B.S. in Geol. Engring., Colo. Sch. Mines, 1942; Ph.D. in Geology, U. Ariz., 1947. Geologist 79 Mining Co., Ariz., 1946-47; geologist underground explosion tests and Folsom Dam-Reservoir Project U.S. C.E., Calif., 1948-50; supervising geologist Internat. Boundary and Water Commn., U.S.-Mex., 1950-51; asst. prof. geology U. Ariz., Tucson, 1951-55; dir. Mineral Resources Survey Navajo-Hopi Indian Reservations, 1952-55; exploration mgr. resources survey So. Pacific Co., San Francisco, 1955-60; assoc. prof. geol. sci. Cornell U., Ithaca, N.Y., 1960-63, prof., 1963-78, prof. emeritus, 1978—, chmn. dept. geol. scis., 1965-71; geol. cons., Ithaca, 1960-78, Tucson, 1978—; chmn. coordinating com. on environment and natural hazards, Internat. Lithosphere Program, 1986-1991. Author: Engineering Geology, 1955, Mineral Resources of Navajo-Hopi Indian Reservations, 3 vols., 1955, Geothermal Steam-A World Wide Assessment, 1964; editor/author: Heritage of Engineering Geology--First Hundred Years 1888-1988 (vol. of Geol. Soc. Am.), 1989; editor: Case Histories in Engineering Geology, 4 vols., 1963-69; mem. editorial bd. Engring. Geology/Amsterdam. Mem. adv. council to bd. trustees Colo. Sch. Mines, 1962-71; mem. coms. Nat. Acad. Engring./Nat. Acad. Scis., 1966—; reporter coordinating com. 1 CC1 Nat. Hazards U.S. GeoDynamics Com., 1985—. Capt. C.E., U.S. Army, 1942-45. Recipient award for best articles Indsl. Mktg. Mag., 1964; NSF sr. postdoctoral fellow Tech. U. Vienna, 1963-64. Fellow Geol. Soc. Am. (chmn. div. engring. geology 1960-61, mem. U.S. nat. com. on rock mechanics 1980-86, Disting. Practice award 1986, Meritorious Svc. award 1989), ASCE; mem. Soc. Econ. Geologists, U.S. Com. on Large Dams, Internat. Soc. Rock Mechanics, Internat. Assn. Engring. Geologists (U.S. com. 1980-86, chmn. com. 1983-87, v.p. N.Am. 1986—), Assn. Engring. Geologists (1st recipient Claire P. Holdredge award 1965, hon. mem. 1985, Presdl. Cert. of Appreciation, 1986). Republican. Episcopalian. Clubs: Cornell (N.Y.C.); Statler, Tower (Ithaca); Mining of Southwest (Tucson). Home and Office: 4750 N Camino Luz Tucson AZ 85718

KIERSCH, THEODORE ALAN, oral surgeon; b. Temple, Tex., Nov. 25, 1943; s. Theodore Alexander and Mary (Omel) K.; Malinda Kay Masterson, Aug. 23, 1953; children: Deborah, Tanner, Tiffany. BS, U. Ill., Urbana, 1966; DDS, Chgo. Coll. Dental Surgery, 1970. Diplomate Am. Bd. Oral and Maxillofacial Surgery. Chief dept. oral surgery El Dorado Med. Ctr., Tucson, 1985-87; practice dentistry specializing in oral and maxillofacial surgery Tucson Med. Ctr., St. Joseph's Hosp., Tucson; assoc. prof. of surgery U. Ariz. Med. Sch., Tucson; med. staff mem. Tucson Crippled Children's Clinic; cons. Vets. Hosp., Tucson; assoc. prof. U. Ariz. Med. Ctr. Hosp., Tucson. Contbr. scholarly articles to profl. jours. Fellow Am. Coll. Oral and Maxillofacial Surgeons, Internat. Assn. Oral and Maxillofacial Surgeons; mem. Am. Assn. Oral and Maxillofacial Surgeons, Ariz. Soc. Oral and Maxillofacial Surgeons (pres. 1981-83), ALA, So. Ariz. Dental Soc., Western Soc. Oral and Maxillofacial Surgeons, Rocky Mountain Soc. Oral Surgeons, Alpha Delta Phi, Xi Psi Phi. Office: 801 N Wilmot Rd Tucson AZ 85711

KIERULFF, CHARLES TAYLOR (CAP KIERULFF), retired electrical engineer; b. Los Angeles, Mar. 5, 1919; s. Charles Rogers and Barbara Claire (Taylor) Kjerulf; m. Barbara Philips Smith, Sept. 21, 1940; children: Stephen Charles, William Douglas, Nancy Christine. BEE, U. Calif., Berkeley, 1941; postgrad., Harvard U., MIT, 1942. Jr. engr. So. Calif. Gas Co., L.A., 1942-43; owner, pres. Kierulff Sound Corp., L.A., 1946-50, Kierulff Electronics, Inc., L.A., 1951-61; v.p. Ducommun, Inc., L.A., 1961-65, The Federated Group, L.A., 1967-82; ret 1982. Author: Twentieth Century Kjaerulfs, 1986. Bd. dirs. Children's Bur., L.A., 1950-57, 75-82; organizer, vol. L.A. Stereo Music Show, 1950, 51, 52. Capt. U.S. Army, 1942-46. Mem. Radio Pioneers So. Calif., Young Pres.' Orgn. Grads. Address: 358 S Bentley Ave Los Angeles CA 90049

KIESLING, ROY ADOLPH, JR., consumer affairs consultant, writer, land developer; b. Houston, Mar. 11, 1934; s. Roy Adolph and Ninon (Collins) K.; B.A., Yale U., 1955; J.D., U. Tex., 1959; B.A., San Jose State Coll., 1966; m. Nancy Lou Hunt, Dec. 22, 1955 (div. 1975); children—Eugenia Collins, John Brady, Stephen Howard, Roy Adolph; m. Ann Adrian, Aug. 7, 1980 (div. 1984). Research contract adminstr. Lockheed Missiles & Space Co., Sunnyvale, Calif., 1960-62, systems test engr., 1966-69; staff mem. Zero Population Growth, Los Altos, Calif., 1969-70; cons. environ. and consumer affairs, Palo Alto, Calif., 1970—. Past pres. Consumer Fedn. Calif., Consumers Co-op Palo Alto; adv. bd. Calif. Bur. Automotive Repair, chmn., 1978-84. Lic. real estate broker, Calif. Mem. Tex. Bar Assn. Address: 502 Woodhaven Ct Aptos CA 95003

KIEST, ALAN SCOTT, social services administrator; b. Portland, Oreg., May 14, 1949; s. Roger M. and Ellen K.; 1 child, Jennifer S. BA in Polit. Sci., U. Puget Sound, Tacoma, 1970; MPA, U. Wash., 1979. Welfare eligibility examiner Wash. Dept. Social and Health Services, Seattle, 1970-72, caseworker, 1972-76, service delivery coordinator, 1976-82, community services office adminstr., 1982—; planning commr. City of Lake Forest Park, 1989—. Home: 18810 26th Ave NE Seattle WA 98155 Office: Wash Dept Social and Health Svcs 907 NW Ballard Way Seattle WA 98107

KIEVIT, KAREN-ANN, educator, researcher; b. Dayton, Ohio; d. George and Kathleen K. BS, Butler U., 1967; MS, Ind. U., 1969; PhD, Fla. State U., 1975, MBA, 1983. Mem. bd. of regents Dept. Gen. Svcs. and Dept. Adminstrn. State of Fla., Tallahassee, 1973-83; rsch. assoc. U. So. Calif., L.A., 1983-84; fin. analyst Hughes Helicopters, Culver City, Calif., 1984-85; asst. prof. Calif. State U., Long Beach, 1985—. Contbr. articles to profl. jours. Mem. Info. Systems Security Assn. (rec. sec. 1987-88, v.p. 1988—), Inst. Internal Auditors, Assn. Computing Machinery, Data Processing Mgmt. Assn., Sierra Club (ski coord.). Office: Calif State U Long Beach Dept Mgmt Info Systems Los Angeles CA 90840

KIGER, RONALD LEE, price analyst; b. Pasadena, Calif., Dec. 30, 1940; s. Wallace Lee and Ilo Marie (Smith) K.; m. Carole Ann Bates, Apr. 10, 1965 (div. Dec. 1978); children: Darren Lee, Lorene Elizabeth. Student, U. Calif., Berkeley, 1958-62; BBA, Armstrong Coll., 1964. Auditor GAO, San Francisco, 1964-66; sr. auditor Def. Contract Audit Agy., San Francisco, 1966-84; material price analyst Lockheed Missiles and Space Co., Sunnyvale, Calif., 1984—. State dir. U.S. Jaycees, Castro Valley, Calif., 1968, pres., 1969, dist. lt. gov., Alameda County, Calif., 1970, state credentials chmn., Calif., 1970. Mem. Assn. Govt. Accts. (sec. 1968, spl. activities dir. 1982-83, pres. 1983-84, newsletter editor 1984-85, nat. chpt. recognition com. 1985-87, regional v.p. western region, 1988-89). Democrat. Mem. Christian Ch. Home: 1975-U Barrymore Common Fremont CA 94538

KIHARA, VICTOR HIROSHI, import-export trading company executive; b. Seattle, Dec. 13, 1937; s. Ray Iwao and Jane Mitsuko (Funai) K.; m. Patti Emiko Takahashi, June 26, 1966; childen: Michael, David. BA in Polit. Sci., Whitman Coll., 1960. Sales mgr. Main Fish Co., Seattle, 1961-70; v.p., gen. mgr. Security Control Systems, Inc., Seattle, 1970-73; v.p. ops. United Devel. Corp., Seattle, 1973-78; foreign trade cons. Calista Corp., Anchorage, 1983-85; ptnr. C. T. Takahashi & Assocs. (now C. T. Takahashi & Co., Inc.), Seattle, 1979-83, v.p., corp. dir., 1986—; ptnr. Pacrim Assocs., Bellevue, Wash., 1983—. Co-founder Mill Creek (Wash.) Community Assn., 1974. With USAR, 1961-62. Mem. Corinthian Yacht Club (trustee 1987—). Democrat. Home: 10230 SE 21st St Bellevue WA 98004 Office: CT Takahashi & Co Inc 2815 2d Ave Ste 230 Seattle WA 98121

KIKAWADA, ISAAC MITZURU, teacher, priest; b. Sendai, Miyagi, Japan, Apr. 16, 1936; came to U.S., 1956; s. John Seiki and Sarah Katsuko (Ito) K. BS, Baldwin-Wallace Coll., 1962; BD, Kenyon Coll., 1965; PhD, U. Calif., Berkeley, 1979. Cert. secondary tchr., Ohio; ordained to minister Episcopal Ch., 1966. Tchr. Cain Pk. Youtheatre, Cleveland Heights, Ohio, 1958-59; chaplain, tchr. St. Ann's Sch. for Girls, Boca Raton, Fla., 1965-66; dir. summer sch. St. James Episcopal Ch., Painesville, Ohio, 1967-68; instr. Near Eastern studies U. Calif., Berkeley, 1972-84, vis. lectr., 1985—; vis. assoc. prof. Oriental studies U. Ariz., Tucson, 1984-85; cons. LENANTE, Inc., Osaka, Japan, 1983—. Co-author: Before Abraham Was, 1985; contbr. articles to profl. jours. Advisor St. Luke's Ch., Osaka, 1969—. Baldwin-Wallace scholar, 1959-62, Firestone scholar Kenyon Coll., 1962-65, Grad. Theol. Union scholar, 1968-69; Ford grantee U. Calif.-Berkeley, 1972-73. Mem. Am. Oriental Soc. (exec. com. 1976-80), Soc. Biblical Lit. (Pres. West Coast chpt. 1984-85), Soc. of Palaeology Japan, Japanese Biblical Inst. (contbg. mem.), World Union Jewish Studies of Jerualem, San Francisco Mycological Soc. Episcopalian. Home: 1787 Sonoma Ave Berkeley CA 94707 Office: U Calif Dept Near Ea Studies Berkeley CA 94720

KILBY, DAVE, chamber of commerce executive. Exec. v.p. Modesto (Calif.) C. of C., until 1988; v.p. Calif. C. of C., Sacramento, 1989—. Office: Calif C of C PO Box 1736 Sacramento CA 95812-1736 *

KILE, RAYMOND LAWRENCE, aerospace project manager, consultant; b. Tucson, Oct. 3, 1946; s. Roddie Lloyd and Polly Ann (Vardalakes) K.; m. Sharon Kate Durham, June 5, 1969; 1 child, Kasey Sheridan. BSEE, U.S. Air Force Acad., 1969; MSEE, U. Mo., 1972. Commd. 2d lt. USAF, 1969, advanced thorugh grades to capt., engr., 1969-78; maj. USAR, 1986—; software developer Westinghouse Hanford, Richland, Wash., 1978-79; communications mgr. Wash. Pub. Power Supply System, Richland, 1980-82; dir. projects Contel Info. Systems, Denver, 1982-86; project mgr. Hughes Aircraft Co., Aurora, Colo., 1986—; software cons. USAFR, Contract Mgmt. Div., 1978—, pvt. practice, 1988—; guest lectr. USAF Software Devel. Courses, 1987—, Chapman Coll., Colo. Springs, Colo., 1988. Author: (Software) REVIC (cost estimating program), 1986, '87, '88. Mem. Reserve Officers' Assn., Assn. Grads. USAF Acad., Air Force Assn., Internat. Soc. Parametrics Analysts, BMW Motor Owners of Am., Airplane Owners and Pilots Assn. Republican. Home: 1539 E Nichols Circle Littleton CO 80122 Office: Hughes Aircraft Co 16800 E Centretech Pkwy Aurora CO 80011

KILEY, LANCE JAMES, land management executive, lawyer; b. Peoria, Ill., Aug. 16, 1942; s. Louis Joseph and Elaine (Kalberg) K.; children: Dawn Louise, Wendy Elaine; m. Lizabeth Ann Rasmussen, Feb. 12, 1977; 1 child, Caitlin Siobhan. AA, Am. River Coll., Sacramento, 1973; student, Calif. State U., 1973-76; JD, Lincoln Law Sch., Sacramento, 1980. Bar: Calif. 1980; registered profl. engr., Calif.; registered land surveyor, 1970. Hwy. engrng. tech. Caltrans, Sacramento, 1960-73; boundary determination officer Calif. State Lands Commn., Sacramento, 1973-80, staff counsel, 1980-82, chief div. land mgmt., 1982—. Mem. Calif. Bar Assn., E Clampus Vitus. Democrat. Lutheran. Office: Calif State Lands Commn 1807 13th St Sacramento CA 95814

KILGORE, GARY ALLEN, educator; b. Napa, Calif., Nov. 6, 1945; s. Ira Samuel and Margret Edwina (Paterson) K.; children: Heather Anne Kilgore Amari, Nicole Michelle. BA in History, Humboldt State Coll., 1967; MA in Theatre, Humboldt State U., 1974, MFA in Theatre, 1979; PhD in Edn., U. Wash., 1987. Commd. 2d lt. U.S. Army, 1967, advance through grades to capt., 1969; theatre cons. Arcata, Calif., 1972-76; assoc. dir. IDMS Humboldt State U., Arcata, 1976-86; ednl. cons. Tacoma, Wash., 1986-87; asst. prof. mil. sci. U. Wash., Seattle, 1987—. With USAR, 1972—. Home: PO Box 95712 Seattle WA 98145 Office: Dept Military Science 104 Clark Hall Du-20 Seattle WA 98195

KILLAM, JAMES F., systems analyst, consultant; b. Springfield, Mass, Apr. 24, 1951; s. James F. and Jane L. (Eldridge) K. A of Tech. Arts, Olympic Coll., Bremerton, Wash., 1979. Systems mgr. Kitsap County, Port Orchard, Wash., 1978-87; mgr. tech. services Imacs Systems Corp., Marina del Rey, Calif., 1987—. Served to staff sgt. USAF, 1971-77. Mem. INTEREX, Super Group. Office: 2825 East Lake Ave E Ste 107 Seattle WA 98102 Office: Imacs Systems Corp 4676 Admiralty Way #516 Marina del Rey CA 90292

KILLEN, JOEL DAVIS, psychologist; b. Reno, July 16, 1950; s. Claude Louis and Helen Kathleen (Davis) K.; m. Diana Li Templeton, June 16, 1972. BA, U. Calif., Davis, 1972; PhD, Stanford U., 1982. Lic. psychologist, Calif. Fellow Stanford (Calif.) U. Med. Sch., 1982-84, research assoc., 1984-87, sr. research assoc., 1987—. Author: Medical Psychology Contributions to Behaviroal Medicine, 1982, Promoting Adolescent Health, 1982, New Developments in Behavior Ttherapy, 1984, Review of Research in Education, 1988; contbr. articles to profl. jours. Fellow Am. Heart Assn.; mem. Am. Psychol. Assn., Am. Pub. Health Assn., Soc. Behavioral Medicine. Home: 136 Lowell St Redwood City CA 94062 Office: Stanford Med Sch 1000 Welch Rd Stanford CA 94304

KILLIAN, DANIEL MARK, sales executive; b. Rock Springs, Wyo., Dec. 29, 1953; s. Daniel William and Mary (Gosar) K.; m. Gayle Ann Brown, May 29, 1976; children: Daniel Michael, Kevin Patrick. BS, U. Wyo., 1976. Warehouseman Nat. Supply Co., Casper, Wyo., 1976-77; inside salesman Nat. Supply Co., Evanston, Wyo., 1977-79, store mgr., 1979-81; salesman Oncor Corp., Evanston, Wyo., 1981-83, dist. sales mgr., 1983-85; dist. mgr. Houston Engrs., Inc., Evanston, Wyo., 1985-86, 88--; area mgr. Houston Engrs. and Wilson Downhole, Evanston, Wyo., 1986-88. Council pres. St. Mary Magdalen Ch., Evanston, 1984. Mem. Soc. Petroleum Engrs., Evanston C. of C. (pres. 1981), Elks, KC, Beta Gamma Sigma, Alpha Kappa Psi. Democrat. Roman Catholic. Home: 1900 W Center St Evanston WY 82930 Office: Houston Engrs Inc 64 Imperial Dr Ste A Evanston WY 82930

KILLIAN, RICHARD M., library director; b. Buffalo, Jan. 13, 1942; m. Nancy Killian; children from previous marriage: Tessa, Lee Ann. BA, SUNY, Buffalo, 1964; MA, Western Mich. U., 1965; grad. advanced mgmt. library adminstrn., Miami U., Oxford, Ohio, 1981; grad. library adminstrn. devel. program, U. Md., 1985. Various positions Buffalo and Erie County Pub. Libraries, 1963-74, asst. dep. dir., personnel officer, 1979-80; dir. Town of Tonawanda (N.Y.) Pub. Library, 1974-78; asst. city librarian, dir. pub. svcs. Denver Pub. Library, 1978-79; exec. dir. Nioga Library System, Buffalo, 1980-87; library dir. Sacramento (Calif.) Pub. Library, 1987—. Mem. ALA, Calif. Library Assn., Rotary. Home: 1190 Cedar Tree Way Sacramento CA 95831 Office: Sacramento Pub Libr 1010 8th St Sacramento CA 95814-3576

KILLION, FREDERICK JOHN, postmaster; b. Burbank, Calif., July 7, 1951; s. Jack Charles and Elisabeth (Horn) K.; m. Barbara Elaine McConathy, Sept. 29, 1973; children: Brenda Elaine, Rhonda Elaine. AA, Moorpark Coll., 1972. Letter carrier U.S. Post Office, N. Hollywood, Calif., 1973-79; clerk U.S. Post Office, Porterville, Calif., 1979-83; postmaster U.S. Post Office, New Cuyama, Calif., 1983—; pres. Local #636 Am. Postal Workers Union, Porterville, Calif., 1980-82. Mem. Nat. Assn. Postmasters, Nat. League Postmasters (effective svc. com. 1984-86), Exch. Club (treas. 1985-86, v.p. 1986-87, pres. 1987-88). Lutheran. Home: 4707 Morales St New Cuyama CA 93254 Office: US Post Office 4855 Primero St New Cuyama CA 93254

KILLION, JACK CHARLES, newspaper columnist; b. L.A., Aug. 21, 1921; s. Roger William and Anna Virginia (Moser) K.; m. Elisabeth Horn, June 29, 1947; children: Joanna Barbara, Heidi Anna, Frederick John. Student, L.A. City Coll., 1940-42. Chief of spl. branch U.S. Army Mil. Govt., Bruchsal, Baden, Germany, 1945-47; sports editor Van Nuys News, Van Nuys, Calif., 1947-48; repair supr. L.A. Dept. Water & Power, 1948-81; columnist Simi Valley Enterprise, Simi Valley, Calif., 1986—, L.A. Daily News, 1989—. Sgt. U.S. Army, 1942-45, ETO. Decorated Hon. Membership German Severely Wounded War Vets., Pacific Battle Star, European Battle Star; Commendation for work as Chief of Spl. Branch and Denazification, Bruchsal, Baden, Germany. Republican. Lutheran. Home: 2403 Lukens St Simi Valley CA 93065

KILLOUGH, JACK CHRISTOPHER, security company executive; b. San Antonio, Sept. 8, 1948; s. Joe and Mary Dixon (Henry) K.; m. Caroline Parmelee, Apr. 12, 1964. BA, Lone Mountain Coll., 1974; postgrad., Sonoma Coll., 1976-77, Golden Gate U., 1978-80. Asst. to pres. John F. Kennedy U., Orinda, Calif., 1974-76; res. dep. sheriff Contra Costa County Sheriff's Dept., Martinez, Calif., 1975-78; correctional officer San Quentin (Calif.) State Prison, 1977-80; chief exec. officer Phoenix Ops. Inc., San Francisco, 1986—; police officer San Francisco Police Dept., 1980—. Active World Affairs Coun., San Francisco.. Named one of Outstanding Young Men Am. U.S. Jaycees, 1975; recipient Proclamation Mayor Dianne Feinstein of San Francisco, 1985, Outstanding Police Work Commendation San Francisco Police Commn., 1985. Mem. Calif. Assn. Lic. Investigators, Scottish Assn., San Francisco C. of C., Commonwealth Club.

KILMER, JOYCE CARL, real estate company executive; b. Malmo, Minn., Aug. 29, 1924; s. Carl William and Anna Christine (Ostermann) K.; m. Ione Bernice Hust, Jan. 3, 1953; children—Jeffrey K., Jana Lee Kilmer Wallace. Student, U. Minn., 1944-45, Colo. U., 1967-68; cert. in real estate sales Regis Coll., 1981. Lineman Mountain Bell Telephone Co., Denver, 1947-50, recordman, 1950-53, right-of-way engr., Denver, 1953-55, right-of-way agent, 1955-83; field supr. U.S. Telecommunications, Kansas City, Kans., 1985-86; project supt. acquisitions, Williams Telecommunications Co., Tulsa, 1986—; real estate cons., Livingston, Mont., 1983-84, GTE-Sprint, Orlando, Fla., 1984—, Mountain Bell Telephone Co., Grand Junction, Colo., 1984—, City of Grand Junction, 1984—, Butler Service Group, Durango, Colo. and Orlando, Fla., 1983-84; right-of-way cons. U.S. Telecom, Inc., 1985-86, Wiltel, Inc., 1986; cons. and supr. United Telephone Co. of Ohio, 1986; right-of-way sr. project engr. Ill. Bell Telphone Co., Peoria, 1988. Active Boy Scouts Am., Denver, 1954, 61-78; vice commdr. USCG Aux., Grand Junction, 1975-76, flotilla commdr., 1976-78. Served with U.S. Army, 1943-43. Sr. mem. Internat. Right-of-Way Assn. (pres. Colo. West chpt. 70, 1978, dir. Rocky Mountain region 1982, Profl. of Yr. 1982, 83, Frank C. Balfour award finalist, 1983, 85); mem. Nat. Assn. Ind. Appraisers, Am. Legion. Republican. Methodist.

KILMER, MAURICE DOUGLAS, real estate company executive; b. Flint, Mich., Sept. 14, 1928; s. John Jennings and Eleanor Minnie (Gerholz) K.; m. Vera May Passino; children: Brad Douglas, Mark David, Brian John, David Scott, Karen Sue. B of Indsl. Engring., Gen. Motors Inst., 1951; MBA, U. Minn., 1969. Quality svcs. mgr. ordnance div. Honeywell, Hopkins, Minn., 1964-69; product assurance dir. peripheral ops. Honeywell, San Diego, 1969-71; pres. Convenience Systems, Inc., San Diego, 1972-75; salesman real estate Forest E. Olson Coldwell Banker, La Mesa, Calif., 1976-77; resident mgr. Forest E. Olson Coldwell Banker, Huntington Beach, Calif., 1977-78; mgmt. cons. Century 21 of the Pacific, Santa Ana, Calif., 1978-83; dir. broker svcs. Century 21 of the Pacific, Anaheim, Calif., 1983-85; exec. dir. Century 21 of S.W., Phoenix, 1985-86; mgr. Century 21 Rattan Realtors, San Diego, 1986—. With U.S. Army, 1951-52. Mem. Am. Soc. for Quality Control, San Diego Bd. Realtors. Republican. Lutheran. Home: 2634 Cove Ct Vista CA 92083-8974 Office: Century 21 Rattan Realtors 8655 Navajo Rd San Diego CA 92119

KILTS, CLAIR THEODORE, teacher; b. Ogden, Utah, Sept. 13, 1930; s. William Theodore and Alice Elnora (Simpson) K.; m. Liliane Lucie Burgat, Apr. 29, 1954; children: Jeffery, Timothy, Mark, Rebecca, Matthew. AS, Weber State Coll., 1950; BA, Brigham Young U., 1957, MA, 1959. Cert. secondary tchr., Utah. Tchr. Ogden City Schs., 1959—; instr. night sch. Weber State Coll., Ogden, 1960-63, Brigham Young U., Ogden, 1964-68. Author: Utah Territorial Court Conflict 1850-1874, 1959. Trustee Hooper (Utah) Water Improvement Dist., 1968-87; mem. council advancement com. Lake Bonneville Council Boy Scouts Am., 1980-82. Served with M.I. Corps, U.S. Army, 1954-56. Recipient Award of merit Boy Scouts Am., 1967, Silver Beaver award Boy Scouts Am., 1969, Outstanding Tchr. award Utah State Hist. Soc., 1978, Liberty Bell award Utah State Bar Assn., 1980, Disting. Service award Hooper Water Improvement Dist., 1987. Mem. NEA, Utah Edn. Assn., Ogden Edn. Assn. (pres. 1974, 80, 85, Award of Honor, 1980), Phi Delta Kappa, Phi Alpha Theta. Democrat. Mormon. Home: 6008 W 5500 S Hooper UT 84315 Office: Mt Ogden Middle Sch 3260 Harrison Blvd Ogden UT 84403

KIM, DEWEY HONGWOO, public service consultant; b. Washington, July 4, 1928; s. Henry Cu and Edith (Ahn) K.; B.A. with honors, U. Hawaii, 1950; M.P.A. with highest distinction (Hugh D. Ingersol Outstanding Grad. award), Maxwell Sch., Syracuse (N.Y.) U., 1961; LL.D. (hon.), Myong Ji U., Seoul, Korea, 1981; m. Lila Lee, Mar. 10, 1951; children—Melissa, Dewey Hongwoo, Michael. Personnel officer 14th Coast Guard Dist., 1953-54; with IRS, 1956-68, dir. mgmt. tng., 1966-68; assoc. dean Coll. Continuing Edn., U. Hawaii, 1968-70, asst. v.p. acad. affairs, 1970-78, vice-chancellor for community colls., 1978-80, chancellor community colls., 1980-83, chancellor emeritus, 1983—; dir. Pacific and Asian affairs Pub. Adminstrn. Service, 1983-86; mgmt. cons., 1960—; dir. 1st Fed. Savs. & Loan Assn., Firstfed of Am., Inc.; pres. Friends of the Ctr. for Korean Studies U. Hawaii, 1987—. Exec. asst. Honolulu Fed. Exec. Bd., 1967; chmn. Hawaii Task Force Police and Pub. Protection, 1970-74; commr. Accrediting Commn. Jr. and Community Colls. Trustee U. Hawaii Found., 1972-82; co-sponsor Dewey and Lila Kim fellowship for univ. faculty in English from Korea to study in U.S.; chmn. adv. council Kapiolani Community Coll., 1985—. Recipient awards IRS, 1958, 59, 67, 68; William E. Mosher fellow, 1960-61. Mem. Am. Soc. Pub. Adminstrn. (pres. Honolulu 1959), Honolulu Fed. Businessmen's Assn., Western Assn. Schs. and Colls. (chmn. and pres. 1981-83), Soc. Fellow Syracuse U. (founding mem. 1986), Phi Kappa Phi.

KIM, EDWARD WILLIAM, ophthalmic surgeon; b. Seoul, Korea, Nov. 25, 1949; came to U.S., 1957; s. Shoon Kul and Pok Chu (Kim) K.; m. Carole Sachi Takemoto, July 24, 1976; children:Brian, Ashley. BA, Occidental Coll., Los Angeles, 1971; postgrad. Calif. Inst. Tech., 1971; MD, U. Calif.-San Francisco, 1975; MPH, U. Calif.-Berkley, 1975. Diplomate Nat. Bd. Med. Examiners, Am. Bd. Ophthalmology. Intern, San Francisco Gen. Hosp., 1975-76; resident in ophthalmology Harvard U.-Mass. Eye and Ear Infirmary, Boston, 1977-79; clin. fellow in ophthalmology Harvard U., 1977-79; clin. fellow in retina Harvard, 1980; practice medicine in ophthalmic surgery, South Laguna and San Clemente, Calif., 1980—; vol. ophthalmologist Eye Care Inc., Ecole St. Vincent's, Haiti, 1980; core investigator Staar Surg., Monrovia, Calif., 1984-87; chief of staff, South Coast Med. Ctr., 1988-89; asst. clin. prof. dept. ophthalmology, U. Calif., Irvine. Founding mem. Orange County Ctr. for Performing Arts, Calif., 1982; pres. Laguna Beach Summer Music Festival, Calif., 1984. Reinhart scholar U. Calif.-San Francisco, 1972-73; R. Taussig scholar, 1974-75. Fellow ACS, Am. Acad. Ophthalmology, Internat. Coll. Surgeons; mem. Calif. Med. Assn., Keratorefractive Soc., Orange County Med. Assn., Mensa, Expts. in Art and Tech. Office: Harvard Eye Assocs 665 Camino De Los Mares Ste 102 San Clemente CA 92672

KIM, JAI CHOON, nurse; b. Kyung Nam, Republic of Korea, Oct. 3, 1950; came to U.S., 1974; d. Taek Hwan Kim and Jung Sook Shin. Grad., Gospel Sch. Nursing, Busan, Republic of Korea, 1972; student, Seoul Nat. U., Republic of Korea, 1974. RN. Nurse Germantown Hosp., Phila., 1974-76, Roosevelt Meml. Hosp., Chgo., 1976-78, Oak Park (Ill.) Hosp., 1978-81, Hines (Ill.) VA Hosp., 1981-86, Washoe Med. Ctr., Reno, 1986—. Home: 400 Douglas Fir Dr Reno NV 89511

KIM, LEO, oil executive; b. Reedley, Calif., Oct. 3, 1942; s. M.I. and Eva (Kim) K.; m. June M. Makata, Dec. 4, 1963; children: Kerry Justin, Corinne Kara. AA, Reedley Coll., 1962; BS, Fresno (Calif.) State Coll., 1964; PhD, U. Kans., 1967; postdoctoral, MIT, 1968. With Shell Devel., 1968-86; mgr. Shell Devel., Modesto, Calif., 1979-80, prin. scientist, 1983-86; with spl. assignment div. Royal Dutch Shell, Sittingbourough, Eng., 1978-79; dir. Interferon R & D Shell Oil, Berkeley, Calif., 1981-82, dir. biomed. R & D, 1982-83; chief tech. officer, v.p. rsch. dept. Mycogen Corp., San Diego, 1986—; bd. dirs. indsl. biotech. com. U. Calif., San Diego, 1988—. Contbr. articles to profl. jours. Mem. Indsl. Biotech. Assn. Office: Mycogen Corp 5451 Oberlin Dr San Diego CA 92121

KIM, MATTHEW YOUNG, dentist; b. Seoul, Republic of Korea, Sept. 27, 1959; came to U.S., 1962; s. Chisu and Cecilia K. BS, Calif. Poly. State U., 1982; DDS, UCLA, 1986. Extern in oral surgery VA Hosp., Phoenix, 1986; chief dental svc. Daniel Reeves, DDS, San Luis Obispo, Calif., 1986—; rotating dentist VA Hosp. Wadsworth, L.A., VA Hosp., Supulveda, Calif., Pediatric Downtown Clinic, L.A., Venice (Calif.) Dental Clinic. Nat. Cancer Inst. fellow, USPHS, 1983. Mem. ADA, Calif. Dental Assn., Cen. Coast Dental Soc. (dental health chmn. 1986—). Republican. Roman Catholic. Office: 1370 Chorro St San Luis Obispo CA 93401

KIM, MIN GYUN, business owner, real estate broker; b. Seoul, Korea, Apr. 1, 1964; came to U.S., 1979; d. Joo Hyung and Yung Sook (Lee) K. Student, L.A. Community Coll., 1982-83, Glendale (Calif.) Coll., 1983-84; BSEE, U. So. Calif., L.A., 1988. Owner Car Stereo & Alarm, L.A., 1988—. Mem. U. So. Calif. Gen. Alumni Assn. Republican. Office: 3440 S Broadway Los Angeles CA 90007

KIM, VICKIE IWALANI, information specialist; b. Honolulu. BS in Journalism, Pacific U., 1966. Pub. rels. asst. The Queen's Med. Ctr., Honolulu, 1966-69; publs. editor U. Hawaii, Honolulu, 1969-70; info. specialist Hawaii Dept. Transp., Honolulu, 1970-71, Hawaii Dept. Bus. and Econ. Devel., Honolulu, 1971—. Home: 1541 Dominis St Honolulu HI 96822 Office: Hawaii Dept Bus Devel PO Box 2359 Honolulu HI 96804

KIMBALL, BRUCE ARNOLD, soil scientist; b. Aitkin, Minn., Sept. 27, 1941; s. Robert Clinton and Rica (Barneveld) K.; m. Laurel Sue Hanway, Aug. 20, 1966; children: Britt, Rica, Megan. BS, U. Minn., 1963; MS, Iowa State U., 1965; PhD, Cornell U., 1970. Soil scientist USDA-Agrl. Research Service U.S. Water Conservation Lab., Phoenix, 1969—. Co-editor: CO2 Enrichment of GreenHouse Crops, 1986; contbr. articles to profl. jours. Mem. AAAS, Am. Soc. Agronomy (fellow 1988 div. A3 program chmn., assoc. editor 1988—), Soil Sci. Soc. Am. (assoc. editor, 1977-83, fellow), Internat. Solar Energy Soc. Office: US Water Conservation Lab 4331 E Broadway Phoenix AZ 85040

KIMBALL, DONALD W., electric utility corporate executive; b. Deadwood, S.D., Apr. 17, 1947; s. Garrett J. and Marietta (Alexander) K.; m. A. Susan Eide, Sept. 19, 1964; children: Lisa Gray, Tammi Bymers. BSEE, Colo. State U., 1974. Lineman Butte Electric Corp., Newell, S.D., 1965-68; journeyman linman Pourdre Valley Rural Electric, F. Collins, Colo., 1968-69, engr., 1969-74; systems engr. Grand Valley Rural Power Lines, Grand Junction, Colo., 1974-76, Heartland Consumers Power Dist., Madison, S.D., 1976-77; spl. projects enrg. East River Electric Power Corp., Madison, S.D., 1977-78; mgr. Union County Electric, Elk Point, S.D., 1984-88, Clay Union Electric Corp., Kermillion, S.D., 1978-88; exec. v.p., gen. mgr. Ariz. Electric Power Corp., Benson, Ariz., 1988—; dir. officer, Heartland Consumers Power, Madison, S.D., 1979-88; cons. City of Elk Point, S.D., 1984-88; dir. Ariz. Power Pooling Assoc., Phoenix, 1988—, Colo. River Energy Distrbn. Assn., Phoenix, 1988—. Dir. Vermillion (S.D.) Devel. Corp., 1984-86; mem. Govs. Rural Econ. Devel. Task Forse, Phoenix, 1989. Named Outstanding Chairperson, Vermillion C. of C., 1985. Mem. Vermillion Golf. Democrat. Lutheran. Home: 6828 Calle Luciente Tucson AZ 85715 Office: Ariz Electric Power Corp PO Box 670 Benson AZ 85602-0670

KIMBALL, GAYLE HALLIE, sociologist, educator; b. L.A., June 12, 1943; d. Thomas R. and Barbara L. (Stamps) K.; 1 child, Jed. BA, U. Calif., Berkeley, 1964; MA, U. Calif., L.A., 1967, U. Calif., Santa Barbara, 1971; PhD, U. Calif., Santa Barbara, 1976. Tchr. L.A. City Schs., 1965-70; prof. Calif. State U., Chico, 1972—. Author: Women's Culture, 1981, Religious Ideas of Harriet Beecher Stowe, 1982, 50/50 Marriage, 1983, 50/50 Parenting, 1988; producer instructional videotapes on gender and family. Office: Calif State U Ethnic & Women's Studies #445 Chico CA 95929

KIMBALL, REID ROBERTS, psychiatrist; b. Draper, Utah, June 29, 1926; s. Crozier and Mary Lenore (Roberts) K.; B.S., Brigham Young U., 1949; M.D., U. Utah, 1951; m. Barbara Joy Radmore, Aug. 3, 1962; children—Valery, Michael, Pauline, Karen, Kay. Intern, Thomas D. Dee Hosp., Ogden, Utah, 1951-52; resident Norristown (Pa.) State Hosp., 1952-53, Oreg. State Hosp., Salem, 1953-55, Palo Alto (Calif.) VA Hosp., 1956; practice medicine specializing in psychiatry, Eugene, Oreg., 1957-60, Salem, Oreg., 1960-72, Portland, Oreg., 1972-77; dir. Out-patient Clinic Oreg. State Hosp., Salem, 1956-57; mem. staff Sacred Heart Hosp., Eugene, consultation/liaison psychiatry, 1977—; asst. prof. psychology U. Oreg., Eugene, 1957-65, prof., 1977—; dir. med. edn. Oreg. State Hosp., Salem, 1984—; asst. prof. psychiatry U. Oreg., Portland, 1965, adj. asst. prof., 1982—. Mem. Lane County Community Mental Health Adv. Bd., 1980-81. Served with USN, 1943-45. Mem. Am., Oreg. (chmn. psychiatry sect. 1973-74) med. assns., Lane County Med. Soc., Am. (pres. Oreg. dist. br. 1973-74), North Pacific Psychiat. Assn. (pres. 1988—), Lane County (pres. 1979-80) Psychiat. Assn. (pres. 1979-80), Am. Gerontology Soc. Home: 1963 Stone Crest Dr Eugene OR 97401 Office: 132 E Broadway Ste 303 Eugene OR 97401

KIMBALL, ROGER STANLEY, physician, internist; b. Portland, Oreg., May 18, 1935; s. Stanley M. and Sylvia M. (Seymour) K.; BA, Stanford U., 1957; MA, U. Calif., Berkeley, 1958; MD, Albany Med. Coll., 1962; m. Patricia M. Wadsworth, Apr. 11, 1970; children: Keri Ann, Dyana Jean. Intern, Highland Hosp., Oakland, Calif., 1962-63; resident U. Calif Med. Ctr., San Francisco, 1963-67; pvt. practice, San Francisco, 1969—; mem. staffs U. Calif. Hosps., Ralph K. Davies Med. Ctr. Hosp.; fellow in cardiology, dept. medicine Stanford U., 1965; assoc. clin. prof. medicine Sch. Medicine, U. Calif., San Francisco. Mem. AMA, Am. Soc. Internal Medicine, Calif. Med. Soc. Presbyterian. Home: 183 Los Robles Dr Burlingame CA 94010 Office: 350 Parnassus Ave San Francisco CA 94117

KIMBELL, MARION JOEL, retired engineer; b. McDonough, Ga., Sept. 7, 1923; s. Charles Marvin and Mary (McMillian) K.; B.S. in Civil Engring., U. Houston, 1949, M.Chem. Engring., 1953; m. Judy Weidner, Dec. 18, 1946; children—Nancy, Susan, Candice. Civil engr. U.S. Dept. Interior, Lemmon, S.D., 1954; chief piping engr. M.W. Kellog Co., Paducah, Ky., 1955; nuclear engr. Westinghouse Atomic Power Div., Pitts., 1956-59; control systems prin. engr. Kaiser Engrs., Oakland, Calif., 1959-80; control systems supervising engr. Bechtel Inc., San Francisco, 1980—; control systems tchr. Laney Coll. cons. engr. NASA, Gen. Atomic Co.; advisory bd. Chabot College on radiation tech. Served as sgt. U.S. Army, 1943-46. Registered profl. nuclear engr., Calif.; control systems engr., Calif. Mem. Instrument Soc. of Am. (sr. mem. exec. com.). Clubs: Moose. Contbr. articles to profl. jours. Home: 22324 Ralston Ct Hayward CA 94541

KIMBERLEY, A. G., JR., management executive; b. Portland, Oreg., Oct. 29, 1939; s. A. Gurney and Meta (Horgan) K.; m. M. Susan Solie, Sept. 15, 1949 (div.); children: John Langton, Thea Ness; m. Roxanne Johannesen, Mar. 26, 1952. BS, Lewis & Clark Coll., 1959-62; student, U. Oreg., 1963. Mgr. meat and dairy div. Hudson House Co., Portland, 1963-64; pres. Wall-Western Inc., Portland, 1964—; v.p. Kimberley Indsl., Portland, 1982—; owner Kimberley Boxwood Farm, Wilsonville, Oreg., 1987—. Republican. Episcopalian. Home: 16720 SW Wilsonville Rd Wilsonville OR 97070

KIMBRELL, GRADY NED, author, retired educator; b. Tallant, Okla., Apr. 6, 1933; s. Virgil Leroy Kimbrell and La Veria Dee Underwood; m. Marilyn Louise King, May 30, 1953 (div.); m. Mary Ellen Cunningham, Apr. 11, 1973; children: Mark Leroy, Lisa Christine, Joni Lynne. BA, Southwestern Coll., Winfield, Kans., 1956; MA, Colo. State Coll., 1958. Cert. tchr. (life), Calif., Colo.; cert. adminstr., Calif. Bus. tchr. Peabody (Kans.) High Sch., 1956-58; bus. tchr. Santa Barbara (Calif.) High Sch., 1958-65, coordinator work edn., 1965-75, dir. research and evaluation, 1975-88; cons., textbook researcher and author. Author: Introduction to Business and Office Careers, 1974, The World of Work Career Interest Survey, 1986, The Testmaker for Succeeding in the World of Work, 1986; co-author: Succeeding in the World of Work, 1970, 4th rev. edit., 1986, Entering the World of Work, 1978, 3d rev. edit., 1989, Independent Study for the World of Work, 1974, 4th rev. edit., 1989, The Savvy Consumer, 1984. Served as cpl. U.S. Army, 1953-55. Mem. NEA, Calif. Assn. Work Experience Educators (life, v.p. 1968-70), Nat. Work Experience Edn. Assn., Calif. Tchrs. Assn., Coop. Work Experience Assn. Republican. Lodge: Kiwanis (sec. local chpt. 1968-70).

KIMME, ERNEST GODFREY, communications engineer; b. Long Beach, Calif., June 7, 1929; s. Ernest Godfrey and Lura Elizabeth (Dake) K.; B.A. magna cum laude, Pomona Coll., 1952; M.A., U. Minn., 1954, Ph.D., 1955; m. Margaret Jeanne Bolen, Dec. 10, 1978; children by previous marriage—Ernest G., Elizabeth E., Karl Frederick. Mem. grad. faculty Oreg. State U., Corvallis, 1955-57; mem. tech. staff Bell Telephone Labs., Murray Hill, N.J., 1957-65, supr. mobile radio research lab., 1962-65; head applied sci. dept. Collins Radio Co., Newport Beach, Calif., 1965-72; research engr. Northrop Electronics, Hawthorne, Calif., 1972-74; sr. staff engr. Interstate Electronics Corp., Anaheim, Calif., 1974-79; dir. advanced systems, dir. advanced communications systems, tech. dir. spl. communications programs Gould Navcomm Systems, El Monte, Calif., 1979-82; pres. Cobit, Inc, 1982-84; tech. staff Gen. Research Corp., Santa Barbara, 1984-87; v.p. engring. Starfind, Inc., Laguna Niguel, Calif., 1987-88; dir. engring. R & D Unit Instruments, Orange, Calif., 1988-89; prin. assoc. Ameta Cons. Technologists; v.p. A.S. Johnston Drilling Corp., Woodland Hills, Calif. Mem. AAAS, IEEE, Soc. Indsl. and Applied Math., Aircraft Owners and Pilots Assn., Phi Beta Kappa, Sigma Xi. Contbr. articles to profl. jours. Home: 301 Starfire St Anaheim CA 92807

KIMMERLE, GERALD WILLIAM, insurance company executive; b. Seattle, Dec. 11, 1928; s. John William and Elsie Evelyn (Gustafson) K.; m. Joan Beverly Hinxman, Sept. 11, 1953; 1 child, Susan D. Foltz. BA in Econs., U. Wash., 1951; postgrad., Stanford U., 1978. Broker Wash. Union

Group, Seattle, 1956-59; group field rep. Pacific Mut. Life Ins. Co., Seattle, 1955-56, pension specialist, 1959-60, mgr., 1960-62; regional dir. Pacific Mut. Life Ins. Co., Los Angeles, 1962-71, asst. v.p., 1971-72; from v.p. to exec. v.p. Pacific Mut. Life Ins. Co. (name now PM Group Life Ins. Co.), Fountain Valley, Calif., 1972—; bd. dirs. Life Ins. Mktg. Research Assn., Farmington, Conn., CaPP Care, Inc. ; chmn. bd. dirs. Imperial Industries, Pacific Fin. HMO Holding Co.; chmn. bd. dirs., chief exec. officer Group Holding Co., Pacific Fin. Life Ins. Co. Bd. dirs. Pacific Mut. Polit. Action Com., Newport Beach, 1985. Mem. Health Ins. Assn. Am. (corr. officer). Republican. Lutheran. Office: PM Group Life Ins Co 17360 Brookhurst St Fountain Valley CA 92708

KIMSEY, RUSTIN RAY, bishop. s. Lauren Chamness K.; m. Gretchen Beck Rinehart, 1961; 2 children. BS U. Oreg., 1957, BD Episcopal Theol. Sem., 1960. Ordained priest, Episcopal Ch., 1960; vicar, St. John Ch., Hermiston, 1960-61; priest in charge, St. Paul NYSSA, 1961; vicar, St. Albany, 1961-67; rector, St. Stephen, Baker, 1967-71, St. Paul, the Dalles, 1971-80; consecrated bishop of Eastern Oreg., 1980; bishop, Episcopal Diocese Eastern Oreg., The Dalles. Office: Episcopal Diocese Ea Oreg PO Box 620 The Dalles OR 97058 *

KINARD, J. SPENCER, television news executive; b. Long Beach, Calif., Aug. 29, 1940. BS in Speech and Journalism, U. Utah, 1966. Writer, producer CBS News, N.Y.C., 1970; corr. Salt Lake (City) Tribune; staff photographer Ogden (Utah) Standard Examiner; radio announcer Centerville, Utah; news dir., anchorman KSL-TV, Salt Lake City; account exec. Sta. KSL-TV, Salt Lake City, 1979-80, news dir., 1980-81; v.p., TV news dir. KSL-TV, Salt Lake City, 1981—. Announcer Mormon Tabernacle Choir, LDS Ch., Salt Lake City, Spoken Word program host, 1972—; past moderator Humana Hosp. Davis No.; past founding bd. mem. Children's Mus. of Utah. CBS fellow Columbia U., 1968. Mem. Nat. Radio-TV News Dirs. Assn. (past pres.). Office: Sta KSL TV Broadcast House 55 North 3d W Salt Lake City UT 84110

KINCAID, ROBIN LEE, nurse; b. Worcester, Mass., Jan. 12, 1963; d. Robert Carl and Ellen (Lehto) K.; m. John Henry Hearne Jr., 1988. BS, U. Maine, 1985; postgrad., U. Calif., San Francisco, 1988—. RN, Ca. and Mass, cert. critical care RN. Nurse Worcester Meml. Hosp., 1985-86; commd. USNR, Oakland, Calif., 1986, advanced through grades to lt. (j.g.), 1988, nurse, officer, 1986—. Mem. Am. Assn. Critical Care Nurses, Alpha Phi (pres. 1984-85). Home: 1434 9th St Alameda CA 94501

KINCAID, WILLIAM KEITH, JR., marketing executive; b. Montgomery, Ala., Dec. 27, 1940; s. Col. William Keith and Marjorie Louise (Brown) K.; m. Susan Jane Moran, July 24, 1971; children: Karen Lynn , Kathryn Glenn. BA in Aeronautical Engring., U. Va., 1963, MA in Aerospace Engring., 1966; Exec. Mgmt. Prog. (hon.), Columbia U., 1986, Santa Clara U., 1984. System engr. Lockheed M & S Co., Sunnyvale, Calif., 1965-76; adv. sys. mgr. Lockheed M & S Co., Sunnyvale, 1978-82, strategic plan dir., 1982-84, adv. sys. mktg. mgr., 1984-87; dir. mktg. ESL, Inc., Sunnyvale, 1987—; chmn. Strategic Mgmt. of Rsch. & Devel. Symposium, Santa Clara, Calif. 1988. Contbr. articles to profl. jours. Dir. Comm. for Restoration Mission San Jose, Fremont, Calif. 1987—. Recipient Rsch. Asst. U. Va. Charlottesville, Va. 1963-65. Mem. AIAA (assoc., mem. future concepts panel 1983-85), Assn. of Old Crows (Armed Forces Commn., assoc.), Security Affiars Support Assn., Aerospace Planners (AIA Subcommittee), Sigma XI, Theta Tau. Republican. Roman Catholic. Office: ESL Inc 495 Java Dr Sunnyvale CA 94088

KINCHELOE, LAWRENCE RAY, state official; b. Twin Falls, Idaho, Jan. 1, 1941; s. Kenneth Kincheloe and Wilma Gladys (Barnett) Routt; m. Sharon Kathleen Moseley, July 14, 1964; children—Gerry, Corey, Michelle, Lawrence, Jeffrey. BA, Mont. State U., 1963; MA, Pacific Luth. U., 1978. Assoc. supt. Dept. Corrections, Wash. State Penitentiary, Walla Walla, 1978-82, warden, 1982-89; dir. Div. of Prisons, Olympia, Wash., 1989—. Served to maj. U.S. Army, 1963-78. Decorated Silver Star, Bronze Star with oak leaf cluster, Legion of Merit, Air medal with oak leaf cluster, Army Commendation medal (2); Vietnamese Cross of Gallantry (3). Mem. Am. Corrections Assn., N.Am. Assn. Wardens, West Cen. Wardens and Supts. Assn. Home: E 6111 Sarazan Olympia WA 98503 Office: Wash Dept Corrections Div Prisons PO Box 9699 FN-61 Olympia WA 98504

KIND, KENNETH WAYNE, lawyer, real estate broker; b. Missoula, Mont., Apr. 1, 1948; s. Joseph Bruce and Elinor Joy (Smith) K.; m. Diane Lucille Jozaitis, Aug. 28, 1971; children: Kirstin Amber, Kenneth Warner. B.A., Calif. State U.-Northridge, 1973; J.D., Calif. Western U., 1976. Bar: Calif. 1976, U.S. Dist. Ct. (ea., so., no. dists.) Calif., 1976, U.S. Cir. Ct. Appeals (9th cir.). Mem. celebrity security staff Brownstone Am., Beverly Hills, Calif., 1970-76; tchr. Army and Navy Acad., Carlsbad, Calif., 1975-76; real estate broker, Bakersfield, Calif., 1978—; sole practice, Bakersfield, 1976—; lectr. mechanic's lien laws, Calif., 1983—. Staff writer Calif. Western Law Jour., 1975. Served as sgt. U.S. Army, 1967-70. Mem. ABA, VFW, Nat. Order Barristers. Libertarian. Office: 1715 Chester Ave Ste 300 Bakersfield CA 93301

KINDLER, ARTHUR, teacher; b. Jacksonville, Fla., Mar. 3, 1942; s. Arthur and Mary Ann (Bennett) Sheppard K.; m. Lucia De. Hernandez, Dec. 23, 1983: stepchildren: Ruth, Brenda, Tony, Nora. BA in Edn., U. Ariz., 1976, MEd, 1980. Enlisted USAF, 1961, advanced through grades to staff sgt., 1961-71, ret., 1971; tchr. Tucson Unified Sch. Dist., 1977—. Bd. dirs. Ariz. Div. of UN, Phoenix, 1984-85. Mem. Phi Lambda Theta, NEA (chairperson standing com. on benefits 1987-89, dir. Ariz. chpt. 1985—), Ariz. Edn. Assn., Tucson Edn. Assn. Democrat. Home: 4771 W Ferret Dr Tucson AZ 85741 Office: 725 E Fair St Tucson AZ 85714

KINDQUIST, CATHY ELSA, historical geographer; b. N.Y.C., June 28, 1956; d. Eric Birger Tage and Carol (Simon) K. BA, Colby Coll., 1978; MA, U. Colo., 1986. Teaching asst. U. Colo., Boulder, 1983-85; ind. researcher Nederland, Colo., 1984-86; grad. asst. Queens U., Kingston, Ont., Can., 1986-87; lectr. U. Colo., Boulder, 1987-88; grad. asst. U. of B.C., Vancouver, 1988—. Author: Stony Pass: The Tumbling and Impetuous Trail, 1987. Student rep. Hist. Geography Specialty Group. Recipient R.S. McLaughlin fellowship Queen's U., Kingston, Ont., 1986-87. Mem. Am. Soc. of Photogrammetry and Remote Sensing, Can. Assn. of Geographers, Assn. of Am. Geographers. Home: 2392 Haywood Ave, West Vancouver, BC Canada V7V 1X7 Office: U BC Dept Geography, 217-1984 West Mall, Vancouver, BC Canada V6T 1W5

KING, ALEXANDER VERNON, film producer; b. Hollywood, Calif., May 20, 1956; s. James Vernon and Vera Mae (Torres) K. BA in Communications, U. Calif., Santa Cruz, 1977; MFA in Film Prodn., U. So. Calif., 1981. Adminstr. bus. affairs Walt Disney Pictures, Burbank, Calif., 1983-84; freelance producer and writer Hollywood, 1985—; producer of animated episode for TV series Amblin' Entertainment & Universal TV, L.A., 1986-87.

KING, BUCKY, rancher, writer, educator, artist; b. Pitts., Aug. 9, 1929; d. John Vastine and Josephine (Heckel) K.; (dec. Oct. 1985); 1 child, John Alexander. BA, Penn. Coll. for Women, 1948. tchr. Pitts. Ctr. for the Arts, 1961-71, various schs. and colls. Author: Creative Canvas Embroidery, 1962, The Dude Connection, 1983, Big Horn Polo, 1987; author: (with Lillian Freehof) Embroidery & Fabrics for the Synagogue & Home, 1967, (with Jude Martin) Ecclesiastical Crafts, 1976; exhibited in Brussels Lace Internat. Show. Mem. Nat. Standards Counsel Am. Embroidery, Embroiderers Guild of Am. Republican. Episcopalian. Clubs: Fox Chapel Gold (Pitts.), Pen & Brush (N.Y.C.). Home: 3102 Hwy 87 Sheridan WY 82801

KING, CARY JUDSON, III, chemical engineer, educator, university official; b. Ft. Monmouth, N.J., Sept. 27, 1934; s. Cary Judson and Mary Margaret (Forbes) K., Jr.; m. Jeanne Antoinette Yorke, June 22, 1957; children: Mary Elizabeth, Cary Judson IV, Catherine Jeanne. B. Engring., Yale, 1956; S.M., Mass. Inst. Tech., 1958, Sc.D., 1960. Asst. prof. chem. engring. MIT, Cambridge, 1959-63; dir. Bayway Sta. Sch. Chem. Engring. Practice, Linden, N.J., 1959-61; asst. prof. chem. engring. U. Calif. at Berkeley, 1963-66, assoc. prof., 1966-69, prof., 1969—, vice chmn. dept. chem. engring., 1967-72, chmn., 1972-81, dean Coll. Chemistry, 1981-87, provost profl. schs. and colls., 1987—; cons. Procter & Gamble Co., 1969—; bd. dirs. Coun. for Chem. Rsrch., chmn., 1989. Author: Separation Processes, 1971, 80, Freeze Drying of Foods, 1971; contbr. numerous articles to profl. jours.; patentee in field. Active Boy Scouts Am., 1947—; pres. Kensington Community Council, 1972-73, dir., 1970-73. Fellow Am. Inst. Chem. Engrs. (Inst. lectr. 1973, Food, Pharm. and Bioengring. Div. award 1975, William H. Walker award 1976, bd. dirs. 1987-89); mem. Nat. Acad. Engring., Am. Soc. Engring. Edn. (George Westinghouse award 1978), Am. Chem. Soc., AAAS. Home: 7 Kensington Ct Kensington CA 94707 Office: U Calif Office of Chancellor 200 California Hall Berkeley CA 94720

KING, CHAROLETTE ELAINE, infosystems specialist; b. Baker, Oreg., Apr. 10, 1945; d. Melvin Howard and Rella Maxine (Gwilliam) Wright; m. Craig Seldon King, April 14, 1965; children: Andrea Karen, Diana Susan. Clerical positions various firms, Idaho, Va., Conn., 1964-71; nursing sec. VA, San Diego, 1974-77; sec. USN, Agana, Guam, 1972-73; procurement clk. USN, Bremerton, Wash., 1977-80; procurement clk. USN, San Diego, 1980, support svcs. supr., 1980-83, div. dir., 1983-87, program analyst, 1987—. Recipient Model Agy. cup USN, San Diego, 1986. Republican. Office: USN Pub Works Ctr Code 120C Box 113 Naval Sta San Diego CA 92136

KING, DANA LELAND, marketing executive; b. Hollywood, Calif., Mar. 15, 1955; s. Ernest Leland and Arline Evelyn (Halvorson) Gillespie K.; m. Nancy McDaniel, Apr. 30, 1988. BA in Econs., U. Calif., Santa Barbara, 1977; MBA, UCLA, 1980. Cert. in mktg. rsch., planning and mgmt. Dir. campus residence halls, dean student residents U. Calif., Santa Barbara, 1977-78; mktg. analyst Atlantic Richfield Co., L.A., 1979-80; sr. corp. planning analyst Continental Airlines, L.A., 1980-82, strategic planning mgr., 1982-83; mgr. mktg. programs, sales devel. Pacific S.W. Airlines, San Diego, 1983-85, asst. sales, dir., 1985-86; dir. PSA Learning Systems, Inc., San Diego, 1986-88; v.p. mktg. PEPP Inc., Long Beach, Calif., 1988—; advt. cons. Dataquick Inc., San Diego, 1988—; mgmt. cons. Middlebrook Group, Wilton, Conn., 1988—. Mem. Nature Conservancy, Calif. chpt., 1978—, San Diego Zool. Soc., 1986—, U.S. Olympic Team Found., 1987—, Cardiff Towne Coun., 1988—; bd. dirs. Incredible Journeys Travel Inc., 1988. Named Businessman of the Yr., Alpha Kappa Psi, 1986. Mem. Direct Mktg. Club San Diego, UCLA Anderson Sch. Mgmt. Alumni Assn., Audobon Soc., Alpha Epsilon. Republican. Home: 2011 Glasgow Ave Cardiff CA 92007

KING, ELLEN AUDREY, home economics educator, nutritionist; b. Halifax, Va., Mar. 26, 1951; d. Robert Earl and Catherine (Bailey) Childress; m. Johnny King, Sept. 5, 1970; children: Sherita, Demetrius. BS, Norfolk (Va.) State U., 1975, AS, 1977, MA, 1981. Cert. tchr., Wash., Ohio. Dietary supr. Norfolk State U., 1976-78; tchr. home econs. Virginia Beach Pub. Sch., 1978-80; with home econs., food service dept. Norfolk Pub. Sch. Dist., 1981; program coordinator Pasco (Wash.) Sch. Dist., 1982, Nat Jackson & Assocs., Pasco, 1983—. Com. Chairperson Cameo Women's Ctr., Kennewick, Wash., 1985—; employment chmn. NAACP, Kennewick, 1987—; sec. Tri-Cities Scholarship Pageant, Pasco, 1981-82, pres., 1983-84; pres. Tri-Cities Women Caucus, Kennewick, 1983-85; pub. relations liaision Martin Luther King Monument Com., Pasco, 1986—, Benton County Dem. Cen. com., Richland, Wash., 1988—; active Benton Franklin Council Children and Youth. Mem. Home Econs. Assn. (plaque 1976), Bus. and Profl. Women Assn., Nat. Panel Consumer Arbitrators (cert. 1981), Delta Sigma Theta (chmn. 1979-80, cert. 1980). Methodist. Lodges: Eastern Star, Daus. of Elks. Home: 6610 W Arrowhead Kennewick WA 99336

KING, FRANK, investment company executive; b. Redcliff, Alta., Can.; married; 4 children. BSChemE, U. Alta., 1958; LLD (hon.), U. Calgary, 1988. Pres. Met. Investment Corp.; also bd. dirs. other cos., Can. Chmn., chief exec. officer XV Olympic Winter Games Organizing Com.; bd. dirs. Calgary Olympic Devel. Assn.; mem. Calgary Econ. Devel. Authority; bd. govs. Olympic Trust; mem. adv. bd. Nat. Census; active many community/sports programs. Decorated Officer Order of Can., Olympic Order in gold; recipient Air Can. Amateur Sports award, Premier's Award of Excellence, 1981, Champion d'Afrique Gold medal. Mem. Assn. Profl. Engrs., Geologists and Geophysicists of Alta., Calgary C. of C. (bd. dirs.), Young Pres.' Orgn., Calgary Booster Club (hon., life), Calgary Stampeders Football Club (bd. dirs.). Club: Men's Can. (hon. life). Lodge: Lions (hon. life). Office: 909 Fifth Ave SW, Calgary, AB Canada T2P 3G5

KING, FRANK WILLIAM, public relations writer; b. Port Huron, Mich., Oct. 1, 1922; s. William Ernest and Catherine Theresa (Smith) K.; student U. Utah, 1963-65, Santa Monica City Coll., 1941, 48-49; B.A., Marylhurst Coll., 1979; M.A., U. Portland, 1982; m. Carma Morrison Sellers, Sept. 16, 1961; children—Rosanne, Jeanine Nell, Melanie, Lisa June; one stepson, Michael Sellers. Air traffic controller FAA, Salt Lake City, Albuquerque and Boise, Idaho; 1949-65, info. officer Western Region, Los Angeles, 1965-68; pub. affairs officer Los Angeles Dist. C.E., U.S. Army, 1968-69, Walla Walla (Wash.), 1969-77, N. Pacific div., Portland, Oreg., 1977-79; dir. pub. relations U. Portland, 1979-80; adj. asst. prof. communications U. Portland, 1982-83; instr. Portland Community Coll., 1980—; freelance writer, 1980—. Exec. asst. Los Angeles Fed. Exec. Bd., 1965-67; chmn. Walla Walla County Alcoholism Adminstrv. Bd., 1974-75; vice-chmn. Walla Walla County Human Services Adminstrv. Bd., 1976-78, chmn., 1977-78. Served with USMCR, 1942-45. Decorated Air medal; William Randolph Hearst scholar, 1965. Mem. Soc. Profl. Journalists, Pub. Relations Soc. Am. (accredited), Kappa Tau Alpha. Democrat. Roman Catholic. Home and Office: 1570 B SE 51st St #B Lincoln City OR 97367

KING, FREDERIC, health services management executive, educator; b. N.Y.C., N.Y., May 9, 1937; s. Benjamin and Jeanne (Fritz) K.; m. Linda Ann Udell, Mar. 17, 1976; children by previous marriage—Coby Allen, Allison Beth, Lisa Robyn, Daniel Seth. B.B.A. cum laude, Bernard M. Baruch Sch. Bus. and Public Adminstrn., CUNY, 1958. Dir. adminstrn. Albert Einstein Coll. Medicine, Bronx, N.Y., 1970-72; assoc. v.p. health affairs Tulane Med. Ctr., New Orleans, 1972-77; dir. fin. Mt. Sinai Med. Ctr., N.Y.C., 1977-78; v.p. fin. Cedars-Sinai Med. Ctr., Los Angeles, 1978-82; pres. Vascular Diagnostic Services, Inc., Woodland Hills, Calif., 1982-84; exec. dir. South Bay Ind. Physicians Med. Group Inc., Torrance, Calif., 1984—; ptnr. Health Ventures, San Rafael, Calif., 1984—; assoc. adj. prof. Tulane U. Sch. Pub. Health; asst. prof. Mt. Sinai Med. Ctr.; instr. Pierce Coll., Los Angeles. Served with U.S. Army, 1959-62. Mem. Am. Pub. Health Assn., Healthcare Forum, Am. Hosp. Assn., Soc. Ambulatory Care Profls., Internat. Platform Assn., Calif. Assn. Hosps. and Health Systems. Republican. Jewish. Home: 1116 Rose Ave Venice CA 90291 Office: 23505 Crenshaw Blvd Ste 132 Torrance CA 90505

KING, GORDON DARROW, commercial real estate broker; b. Renton, Wash., June 26, 1951; s. Gordon John and Dara Clarice (Wilson)K.; m. Jeanne Marie Kendrick, June 8, 1974; children: Heather Marie, Rachel Suzanne, Andrew Gordon, Abigail June. BS, U. Oreg., 1974; JD, Lewis & Clark Coll., 1983. Asst. buyer Meier & Frank Co., Portland, Oreg., 1977-78; claims examiner Std. Ins. Co., Portland, 1978-83; comml. real estate broker Norris, Beggs & Simpson, Portland, 1983-85, Cushman & Wakefield of Oreg., Portland, 1985—; leasing rep. Kruse Woods Office Pk., Lake Oswego, Oreg., 1985—; cons. City of Gresham, Oreg., 1987; tenant rep. Portland Tchrs. Credit Union, 1987—; cons. Willamette Falls Hosp., Oregon City, 1987—. Mem. Realtors Nat. Mktg. Inst., Nat. Assn. Realtors, Bldg. Owners and Mgrs. Assn. Home: 4214 SW 51st Pl Portland OR 97221 Office: Cushman & Wakefield of Oreg 111 SW 5th Ave #2400 Portland OR 97204

KING, HARRY ROBERT, electronics technician; b. Connellsville, Pa., June 26, 1936; s. Verner Hugh and Florence Jennette (Sheetz) K.; m. Barbara Jane Hout, July 1, 1958; 1 child, Kevin Ray. AA in Gen. Studies, Pines Peak Community Coll., Colorado Springs, Colo., 1979, AAS in Elec. Tech., 1981. Commd. 2d lt. U.S. Army, 1955, advance through grades to maj., 1974, ret., 1978; with Vitro Corp., Wheaton, Md., 1958-59, Norge Range & Dryer, Effingham, Ill., 1959-60; attendant Imperial Oil Co., Flora, Ill., 1960; tire customizing specialist Tire Magic of Colo., Colorado Springs, 1978-81; sr. electronics technician Data Gen. Corp., Fountain, Colo., 1981-89. With U.S. Army, 1955-58, 60-78. Mem. Rocky Mountain Cloggers (pres., treas. Colorado Springs chpt.). Avocations: clog dancing, fishing, camping, hunting.

KING, HEATHER GAGE LITTLE, marketing executive; b. Wellesley, Mass., Mar. 17, 1959; d. Dennis Gage and Susan Gage (Walker) Little; m. Wade Hampton King, Sept. 10, 1988. BA, Dartmouth Coll., 1981; MBA, U. N.H., Dartmouth, 1986. Analyst Sutro & Co., 1984-85; with Apple Computer, Cupertino, Calif., 1985—; market mgr. Apple Computer, 1985—. Republican. Home: 1918 Pierce St San Francisco CA 94115

KING, JAMES LAWRENCE, JR., mathematics educator, education administrator; b. Detroit, Mar. 20, 1935; s. James Lawrence and Olive Lenore (Vibbard) K.; m. Gloria Herrera; 1 child, Gloria Lynn. BS in Physics, Wayne State U., 1960, BS in Math., 1962, MA in Math. Stats., 1965, postgrad. First aid medic Great Lakes Steel, Ecorse, Mich., 1956-65; instr. Wayne State U., Detroit, 1960-62, 65; sci., math. tchr. Yeshivath Beth Yehudah Schs., 1960-65; sr. mathematician Gen. Motors Corp., Warren, Mich., 1965-67; tchr. math., sci. Los Angeles Unified Schs., 1967-68; prof. math., student advisor Los Angeles S.W. Coll., 1968—, math. tech., engring. dept. chmn.; numismatist, 1974—. Bass-baritone concert choir Wayne State U., 1956-64. Served with USN, 1952-56, USNR, 1956-64. Grantee NSF, 1969. Mem. Am. Numismatic Assn. (cert.), Nat. Geographic Soc., Math. Assn. Am. Republican. Club: Interval Internat. Time Share. Office: Los Angeles SW Coll 1600 W Imperial Hwy Los Angeles CA 90047

KING, JEFFREY NORMAN, insurance agency executive; b. Lebanon, Oreg., Nov. 19, 1953; s. Roland Norman and Patricia Laverne (Reeves) K.; m. Edda Jean Zerkel, Dec. 27, 1981; 2 children: Ryan Reeves, Wyatt Scott. BS, U. Oreg., 1976. Agt. Roland King Ins., Lebanon, Oreg., 1976-81, v.p., 1981-84, pres., owner, 1984—. Contbr. articles to profl. jours. Vice pres., dir. Lebanon Boys/Girls Club, 1984-85. Mem. Soc. Cert. Ins. counselors (edn. com. 1987—), Lebanon C. of C. (dir. 1986-87), Linn-Benton Agts. Assn. (pres. 1988), Oreg. Ind. Agts. Assn. (legis. award 1987), Pineway Men's (dir. 1986—), Elks.

KING, JOHN ANDERSON, engineer; b. Detroit, Apr. 30, 1951; s. John L. and Eileen E. (Anderson) K.; m. Joan R. Cantwell, Aug. 7, 1971; children: Melissa, Joel. BS, Ariz. State U., 1974. Operating engr. Concrete Placement Co., Tempe, Ariz., 1971-76; engr. Accessible Products Co., Tempe, 1976—. Inventor insulation jacket, 1987. Mem. Indsl. Fabrics Assn., Soc. Plastic Engrs., Soc. Mfg. Engrs. Republican. Baptist. Office: Accessible Products Co 2122 W 5th Pl Tempe AZ 85281

KING, JOSEPH CLEMENT, physician; b. Colorado Springs, Colo., Aug. 20, 1922; s. Charles Clement and Gladys (Ascher) K.; BS Tulane U., 1944, MD, 1946; m. Margie Freudenthal Leopold, Apr. 2, 1947; children: Leopold Ascher, Jocelyn King Tobias. Instr. zoology Tulane U., 1941-42; rotating intern Michael Reese Hosp., Chgo., 1946-47, resident in internal medicine, 1947-50; assoc. with Dr. Sidney Portis, Chgo., 1950-51; practice medicine specializing in internal medicine, Chgo., 1953-77, Palm Springs, Calif., 1977-79; attending staff Louis A. Weiss Hosp., Chgo., 1953-77, hon. staff, 1979—; attending staff Desert Hosp., 1977-79, 89—; med. dir. Life Extension Inst., Chgo., 1979-80; dir. employee health svcs. Continental Ill. Nat. Bank, Chgo., 1980-87; exec. cons. health care mgmt. Coopers & Lybrand, Chgo., 1987-88; asst. to assoc. clin. prof. internal medicine Northwestern U. Med. Sch., Chgo., 1954-67; clin. asst. prof. medicine Abraham Lincoln Sch. Medicine U. Ill., 1973-77; clin. asst. prof. preventive medicine and community health Northwestern U. Med. Sch., 1980-88 ; asst. prof. preventive medicine Rush Med. Coll., 1986-88. Capt. M.C., AUS, 1944-46, 1951-53. Diplomate Am. Bd. Internal Medicine. Fellow ACP, Am. Coll. Occupational Med.; mem. Chgo. Soc. Internal Medicine, Chgo. Med. Soc., AMA, Ill., Riverside County, Calif. med. assns., Am. Heart Assn., Chgo. Heart Assn. (past bd. govs.), Am. Rheumatism Assn., Assn. Bank Med. Dirs., Am. Cancer Soc. (v.p. Chgo. unit), Cen. States Assn. Occupational Medicine, Tulane Med. Alumni Assn. (past dir.), Medic Alert (past mem. midwest adv. bd.), Chgo. Assn. Commerce and Industry (past mem. occupational medicine com.), Med. Dirs. Club Chgo. (past pres.), Phi Beta Kappa, Beta Mu, Alpha Omega Alpha. Contbr. numerous articles in field to med. jours. Office: 555 Tachevah Dr Ste 1E-201 Palm Springs CA 92262

KING, JOSEPH JERONE, association executive; b. Spokane, Wash., Sept. 27, 1910; s. Joseph Jerone and Alice (Halferty) K.; B.A. with gt. distinction, Stanford U., 1935; M.A., Duke U., 1937; m. Irma Kathleen Martin, Aug. 22, 1937; children—Sally Jo (Mrs. John S. Thompson), Nikki Sue (Mrs. Dennis Ring), Cindy Lou (Mrs. Richard Mullen). Instr. econs. Black Mountain Coll., 1937-38; numerous adminstrv. positions Farm Security Adminstrn., U.S. Dept. Agriculture, Portland, 1939-51; Oreg. state dir. Christian Rural Overseas Program, 1950-51; sr. civilian for indsl. relations Puget Sound Naval Shipyard, 1951-58; public affairs dir. Assn. Wash. Industries, Olympia, 1958-78, exec. cons., 1978—; Western mgr. Inst. Applied Econs., 1981—. Mem. President's Assos., Central Wash. U., mem. Gov.'s Council for Reorg. Wash. State Govt.; mem. adv. council Coll. Edn. Washington State U.; dir. manpower Statewide Public Edn. Mgmt. Survey; mem. Gov.'s Commn. on Employment of Physically Handicapped; mem. adv. council, dept. econs. and bus. adminstrn. Central Wash. U., 1973—, Coll. of Edn., mem. exec. com. Rural Edn. Ctr.; mem. profl. edn. adv. council Wash. State Dept. Public Instrn., 1977—, chmn. community edn. adv. council, 1981—; chmn. adv. com. for Anderson Landing Wildlife Project, Kitsap County (Wash.) Bd. Commrs.; pres. bd. State-Wide Project Bus. Liaison with Edn.; mem. Spokane Bd. Scholastic Excellence; bd. dirs. Paul Linder Found. for Edn. in Cen. Kitsap, Spokane Bus. Assisting Scholastic Excellence, Moses Lake Agrl. Edn. Found. Served with USAAF, 1944. Recipient Outstanding Service awards DAV, Assn. Wash. Bus., Golden Bell award Washington Assn. Sch. Adminstrs., Disting. Achievement award U.S. Basic Skills Investment Corp., 1988; named hon. citizen City of Vancouver (Wash.), hon. Wash. adm., hon. Wash. gen. Mem. Am. Soc. Pub. Adminstrn., Am. Legion (hon. life mem.), Phi Beta Kappa, Pi Gamma Mu. Clubs: Washington Athletic, Kitsap Country, Elks, Masons (Shriner). Author: Winning, Printings, 1961. Home: Ioka Beach-Hood Canal 11655 Ioka Way NW Silverdale WA 98383

KING, JOY KERLER, classics educator; b. Glencoe, Ill., Mar. 6, 1926; d. William J. and June (Bennett) K.; m. Edward Louis King, Dec. 20, 1952; children: Paul Gregory, Marcia (dec.). BA in Classical Langs., Knox Coll., 1947; MA in Latin, U. Wis., 1952; PhD in Classics, U. Colo., 1969. Assoc. prof. classics U. Colo., Boulder, 1968—, chmn. dept., 1982-86. Editor Colo. Classics: A Newsletter, 1979-88. Author articles on Latin poetry. Recipient Student-Alumni award U. Colo., 1974. Mem. Am. Philol. Assn., Classical Assn. Middle West and South (promotion of Latin com. 1982-85), Women's Classical Caucus (co-chair 1983-84), Rocky Mountain Modern Lang. Assn., Phi Beta Kappa. Office: U Colo Box 248 Boulder CO 80309

KING, KATHLEEN ANNE, nurse; b. L.A., Oct. 28, 1947; d. Gilbert Howard and Dorothy Anne (Davis) Gaal; m. William C. Guard, Mar. 6, 1967 (wid. Apr. 1969); 1 child, William L. King; m. Jerry Lee King, Aug. 14, 1969; 1 child, Lisa L. AA, Cerritos Jr. Coll., Norwalk, Calif., 1968; BS, Fullerton Calif. State Coll., 1988. Office nurse, surgery Gallatin Med. Group, Downey, Calif., 1967-69; asst. head nurse, nurse orthopedics Presbyn. Intercommunity Hosp., Whittier, Calif., 1969-72; staff nurse, orthopedics Presbyn. Intercommunity Hosp., Whittier, 1976—; instr. Downey Union Sch. Dist., Downey, 1973-75. Mem. Calif. Nursing Assn., Alumni Assn. Calif. State, Fullerton, Nat. Assn. Orthopedic Nurses. Democrat.

KING, KATHLEEN MARIE, English educator; b. Wabasha, Minn., Nov. 27, 1948; d. Arthur Edward and Elizabeth Mary (Clowry) K.; m. Winslow R. Hunt; 1 child, Randall Wooldridge. BA in Environs., Sangamon State U., 1979, MA in Lit., 1980; PhD in English, U. Nebr., 1984. Instr. English U. Nebr., Lincoln, 1981-84; asst. prof. dept. English and philosophy Idaho State U., Pocatello, 1984—, dir. Idaho writing project, 1985—, adminstrv. intern office v.p. acad. affairs, 1987—, assoc. prof., 1989—; presenter in field. Author: Cricket Sings, A Novel of Pre-Columbian Cahokia, 1983 (Fiction award Alchemist Rev. 1980); contbr. poetry and fiction to lit. publs. Mem. forum for U.S.-Soviet Dialogue. Recipient Outstanding Alumni Achievement award, Sangamon State U., 1989. Mem. Rocky Mountain MLA (chmn. creative writing sect. 1986-87), Acad. Poets, Nat. Coun. Tchrs. English, Am. Culture Assn., Idaho State U. Profl. Women. Office: Idaho State U Campus Box 8266 Pocatello ID 83209

KING, KENNETH PAUL, financial planning consultant; b. Borger, Tex., July 9, 1938; s. Roy Edwin and Cornelia (Shell) K.; m. Sheryl Smith, Dec. 20, 1961; children: Barbara Shell, Julanne Elizabeth. BSCE, Stanford (Calif.) U., 1960, MBA in Fin., 1963. Fin. analyst Amoco Oil Co., Chgo., 1963-68; sr. fin. analyst Signal Oil & Gas Co., L.A., 1968-71; mgr. planning and econ. dept. Signal Cos., Inc., Beverly Hills, Calif., 1971-75, asst. controller, 1975-83; dir. mergers and acquisitions dept. Signal Cos., Inc., San Diego, 1983-85; dir. planning and fin. analysis Allied-Signal Internat., San Diego, 1985-88; cons. Kenneth P. King Cons., San Diego, 1988—. Pres. La Jolla (Calif.) Town Coun., 1984-86; v.p. bd. dirs. Bishop's Sch., La Jolla, 1986—. Mem. Planning Forum, Fin. Execs. Inst. (v.p. 1982-84), La Jolla Beach and Tennis Club. Republican. Presbyterian. Office: 11255 N Torrey Pines Rd La Jolla CA 92037

KING, MANUELA ANNE, landscape architect, horticulturist; b. Butler, Pa., May 16, 1956; d. Bartolome B. and Eugenia (Zavacky) K. BS, Pa. State U., 1978; B in Landscape Architecture, U. Oreg., 1985, M in Landscape Architecture, 1988. Teaching fellow U. Oreg., Eugene, 1983-85; landscape architect SWA Group, Sausalito, Calif., 1984, Royston, Hanamoto, Alley & Abey, Mill Valley, Calif., 1985—; cons. Ortho Info. Services; instr. U. Calif., Berkeley. Co-author: Creative Home Landscaping, 1988; cons. (video) Gardening With Color, 1989. Mem. Am. Soc. Landscape Architects, MENSA (mem. dept. landscape architecture extension).

KING, MARCIA, library director; b. Lewiston, Maine, Aug. 4, 1940; d. Daniel Alden and Clarice Evelyn (Curtis) Barrell; m. Howard P. Lowell, Feb. 15, 1969 (div. 1980); m. Richard G. King Jr., Aug., 1980. BS, U. Maine, 1965; MSLS, Simmons Coll., 1967. Reference, field advisory and bookmobile librarian Maine State Library, Augusta, 1965-69; dir. Lithgow Pub. Library, Augusta, 1969-72; exec. sec. Maine Library Adv. Com., Maine State Library, 1972-73; dir. Wayland (Mass.) Free Pub. Library, 1973-76; state librarian State of Oreg., Salem, 1976-82; dir. Tucson Pub. Library, 1982—. Chmn. bd. dirs. Tucson United Way; mem. adv. bd. com. Sta. KUAT (PBS-TV and Radio); mem. adv. bd. Resources for Women, Inc. Mem. ALA, Pub. Library Assn., Ariz. State Library Assn., AAUW, Assn. Specialized and Coop. Library Agys., Exec. Women's Council So. Ariz., Resources for Women Inc. (adv. bd.). Unitarian. Office: Tucson Pub Libr 110 E Pennington PO Box 27470 Tucson AZ 85726-7470

KING, MARILYN JEANNE, nurse; b. Salt Lake City, June 15, 1954; d. James Keith and Reva (Thorne) Parker; m. Roderick Leon King, Dec. 1, 1986; 1 child, Amy. AA, Brigham Young U., 1975. R.N., Utah, Idaho. Staff nurse Latter Day Saints Hosp., Salt Lake City, 1975-76, 79-82, Magic Valley Regional Med. Ctr., Twin Falls, Idaho, 1976-77, Utah Valley Regional Med. Ctr., Provo, Utah, 1977-79, Cassia Meml. Hosp., Barley, Idaho, 1982-83; mgr. ICU Cassia Meml. Hosp., 1983—. Mormon. Home: Rte 1 Box 64 Oakley ID 83346 Office: Cassia Meml Hosp 2303 Park Ave Burley ID 83318

KING, MICHAEL HENRY, county administrative support manager; b. Jerome, Ariz., Dec. 20, 1935; s. Raymond M. and Grace (Young) K. BS in Acctg., No. Ariz. U., 1957. Support svcs. mgr. Maricopa County Civil Defense, Phoenix, 1964-70; adminstrv. support mgr. Maricopa County Parks & Recreation, Phoenix, 1970—. With U.S. Army, 1957-60. Mem. Am. Soc. for Pub. Adminstrn., Nat. Assn. Accts., Assn. Govt. Accts., Nat. Park & Recreation Assn., Ariz. Park & Recreation Assn. Democrat. Methodist. Office: Maricopa County Parks and Recreation 3355 W Durango Phoenix AZ 85009

KING, NANCY EVANS-RUIZ, teacher; b. Great Bend, Kans., June 25, 1946; d. Dick Blaine and Chrissie Leona (Roe) Evans; m. Jorge L. Ruiz, Aug. 16, 1969 (div. Oct. 1976); m. Eddie King Jr., Sept. 17, 1987. BSE in Home Econs., Emporia State U., 1968; MS in Consumer Edn. and Econs., Kans. State U., 1975; postgrad., Colo. State U., 1978, Lesley Coll., 1989—. Grad. asst. Kans. State U., Manhattan, 1968-69; substitute tchr. L.A. pub. schs., 1969-71; tchr. food mgmt. Denver pub. schs., 1971—, Kunsmiller Mid. Sch., Denver, 1971—; v.p. Basic. Systems Group, Ltd., Lakewood, Colo., 1987. Mem. NEA (pro-coun. del.), Colo. Edn. Assn. (del. state conv.), Denver Classroom Tchrs. Assn. (area dir. 1988—, bd. dirs 1988—, v.p. exec. com., chair person), Order Ea. Star, Delta Kappa Gamma, Delta Zeta. Office: Kunsmiller Mid Sch 2250 S Quitman St Denver CO 80219

KING, RICHARD S., insurance company executive; b. San Francisco, Feb. 14, 1925; s. Sidney Scott and Hazel Clara (Froom) K.; m. Dorothy Lenore Powell, July 24, 1954 (div. 1978); children: David Scott, Denise Lynn Case. BS, U. San Francisco, 1948. Claim supt. Traders & Gen. Ins. Co., San Francisco, 1950-56; claim supr. Am. Ins. Co., San Francisco, 1956-57; litigation supr. Zurich Ins. Co., San Francisco, 1957-61; asst. claim mgr. Crum & Forster Ins. Group, San Francisco, 1961-69; v.p. Yosemite Ins. Co., San Francisco, 1969-72; exec. v.p. Ins. Co. The West, San Diego, 1972—; pres. Risk Ins. Brokers, San Diego, 1985—; pres., chmn. Canadian Am. Reinsurance Co., Ltd., Hamilton, Bermuda, 1985—; pres. San Diego Chap., Soc. Chartered Property & Casualty Underwriters,. Author: Pub. article in jour., 1978. With U.S. Navy 1943-46. Mem. Soc. Chartered Property & Casualty Underwriters (Nat. Dir. 1982-85,. Democrat. Methodist. Home: 4775 Valdina Way San Diego CA 92124 Office: Ins Co of the West 10140 Campus Point Dr San Diego CA 92121

KING, ROBERT EUGENE, sales representative; b. Pendleton, Oreg., Nov. 21, 1940; s. Everett Eugene King and Vaunda Eileen (Gilchrist) King Haller; m. Ellen Noreen Wismer, June 17, 1967; children: Darren Louis, Gretchen Rae. BS, Ariz. State U., 1963. Salesman Firestone Tire & Rubber Co., Mesa, Ariz., 1963-64, Albuquerque, 1964-65, El Centro, Calif., 1965; rep. med. sales McNeil Labs., Tucson, 1965-70, Norwich Eaton Pharm., Phoenix, 1970—. Mem. Ariz. Pharm. Reps. Assn. (pres. 1981), Pi Sigma Epsilon. Republican. Lutheran. Home: 14420 N 66 Dr Glendale CA 85306

KING, ROSALIE ROSSO, costume designer, educator; b. Tacoma, May 22, 1938; d. Stanley and Gertrude Emma (Conrad) Rosso; BS, U. Wash., 1960, PhD, 1975; MEd, Mass. State Coll., Framingham, 1965; m. Indle Gifford King, Sept. 10, 1960; children—Indle Gifford, Paige Phyllis. Product developer Lyndens (Wash.) State Coop., 1960; home economist Seattle Times, 1961; acad. adv. U. Wash., Seattle, 1965-67, assoc. and lectr., 1967-75, chmn. div. textile sci. and costume studies, 1975-83; chmn. dept. home econs., Ctr. Apparel Design and Internat. Fashion Mktg. and Western Wash. State Coll., Bellingham, 1983—; mem. flammable fabrics adv. com. Consumer Product Safety Commn., 1977-79; cons. textile flammability litigation. Pres., Mercer Island Sch. PTA, 1972-73; active Cub Scouts, Girl Scouts. Denney fellow, 1973-74. Mem. Am. Assn. Textile Chemists and Colorists, ASTM, Am. Chem. Soc., Nat. Assn. Coll. Profs. Textiles and Clothing, Fashion Group, Women's Univ. Club, U. Wash. Faculty (dir.), Pi Beta Phi, Omicron Nu (nat. v.p. 1978-80, nat. pres. 1981-83), Author reference books in field; contbr. articles to profl. jours.; participant fiber art exhbns. Home: 16 Brook Bay Mercer Island WA 98040 Office: Western Wash U 560 Old Main Bellingham WA 98225

KING, SHELDON SELIG, medical center administrator, educator; b. N.Y.C., Aug. 28, 1931; s. Benjamin and Jeanne (Fritz) K.; m. Ruth Arden Zeller, June 26, 1955 (div. 1987); children: Tracy Elizabeth, Meredith Ellen, Adam Bradley; m. Xenia Tonesk, 1988. A.B., NYU, 1952; M.S., Yale U., 1957. Adminstrv. intern Montefiore Hosp., N.Y.C., 1952, 55; adminstrv. asst. Mt. Sinai Hosp., N.Y.C., 1957-60; asst. dir. Mt. Sinai Hosp., 1960-66, dir. planning, 1966-68; exec. dir. Albert Einstein Coll. Medicine-Bronx Mcpl. Hosp. Ctr., Bronx, N.Y., 1968-72; exec. dir. Albert Einstein Coll. Medicine, N.Y.C., 1968-72; dir. hosps. and clinics Univ. Hosp., assoc. clin. prof. U. Calif., San Diego, 1972-81; acting head div. health care scis., dept. community medicine U. Calif. (Sch. Medicine), 1978-81; assoc. v.p. Stanford U., 1981-85, clin. assoc. prof. dept. community, family and preventive medicine; exec. v.p. Stanford U. Hosp., 1981-85, pres., 1986-87; pres. Cedars-Sinai Med. Ctr., L.A., 1989—; mem. adminstrv. bd. coun. teaching hosps., 1981-86, chmn. adminstrv. bd., 1985; preceptor George Washington U., Ithaca Coll., Yale, U. Mo., CUNY; chmn. health care com. San Diego County Immigration Coun., 1974-77; adv. coun. Calif. Health Facilities Commn., 1977-82; chmn. ad hoc bd. advs. Am. Bd. Internal Medicine, 1985—. Mem. editorial adv. bd.: Who's Who in Health Care, 1977; mem. editorial bd. Jour. Med. Edn, 1979-84. Bd. dirs. hosp. coun. San Diego and Imperial Counties, 1974-77, treas., 1976, pres., 1977; bd. dirs. United Way San Diego, 1975-80, Brith Milah Bd.; active Accreditation Coun. for grad. med. edn., 1987—, Prospective Payment Assessment Commn., 1987—, Inst. of Medicine, 1988—; bd. dirs. Am. Health Properties, 1988—. With AUS, 1952-55. Fellow Am. Coll. Health Care Execs., Am. Pub. Health Assn., Royal Soc. Health; mem. Am. Hosp. Assn. (gov. coun. Met. sect. 1983-86, coun. on fin. 1987, house of dels. 1987—), Calif. Hosp. Assn. (trustee 1978-81), Am. Podiatric Med. Assn.(Project Coun. 2000 1985-86), Hosp. Rsch. and Devel. Inst. Inc., Assn. Am. Med. Coll. Home: 330 S Reeves Dr #103 Beverly Hills CA 90212 Office: Cedars Sinai Med Ctr Pla 2622 8700 Beverly Blvd Los Angeles CA 90048

KING, WILLIAM CURTIS, educator; b. Hobbs, N.Mex., Aug. 18, 1933; s. William Hugh and Minnie Pearl (Warlick) K.; m. Patsy Ruth Crow, Mar. 26, 1961; children: William Frederick, Blanch Annette. B Music Edn., U. Denver, 1956; MA, N.Mex. State U., 1959. Band dir. Alameda Jr. High Sch., Las Cruces, N.Mex., 1956-63, Carlsbad (N.Mex.) High Sch., 1963-71, Gadsden High Sch., Anthony, N.Mex., 1971—. Officer bd. trustees, Anthony Ind. Sch. Dist., Anthony, Tex., 1983—. With U.S. Army, 1953-55. Mem. Am. Sch. Band Dirs. Assn., Music Educators Nat. Conf., Am. Fedn. Tchrs., Am. Legion, Lions, Phi Beta Mu, Phi Mu Alpha. Democrat. Methodist. Home: PO Drawer 1778 Anthony NM 88021 Office: Gadsden High Sch Rte 1 Box 268 Anthony NM 88021

KING, WILLIAM HOWARD, home decorating products company executive; b. L.A., Apr. 29, 1943; s. Charles Alexander and Irene Selma (Hofmann) K.; m. Barbara Jean Witt, May 15, 1964 (div. 1978); m. Trisha Ann Gillow, June 29, 1978. V.p. Howard's Lumber Inc., Bishop, Calif., 1970-75; gen. ptnr. King's Paint and Paper, Soquel, Calif., 1976-87, pres., 1987—; chmn. Western Decorating Products Show, 1988. Mem. Western Decorating Products Assn. (bd. dirs. 1985—, v.p. 1988—), No. Calif. Decorating Products Assn. (bd. dirs. 1980-84, pres. 1985). Democrat. Episcopalian. Home: 209 Jolon Dr Watsonville CA 95076 Office: King's Paint & Paper Inc 2851 41st Ave Soquel CA 95073

KING, WILLIAM JOHN, real estate investment company executive; b. Phila., Mar. 23, 1947; s. Thomas Graham and Annie Lee (Kilburn) K.; m. Marcia Joanna Miller, Sept. 7, 1968 (div. 1975); 1 child, Eliza; m. Patricia Susan Radez, July 12, 1980; children: Michael, Toby. BA, Carleton Coll., 1969; M in Urban Planning, U. Wash., 1978; M in Pub. and Pvt. Mgmt., Yale U., 1980. Prin., founder Community Futures Assocs., Seattle, 1976-80; v.p. Century Ptnrs., San Mateo, Calif., 1980-83; exec. v.p. Wingfield Cos., San Francisco, 1983-88; chmn., chief exec. King & Co., San Francisco, 1988—; cons. U. Wash., Seattle, 1977, Seattle U., 1977, Tulalip Tribes, Inc., Marysville, Wash., 1977, City of Phila., 1980. Yale Sch. Mgmt. fellow, 1978-80, HEW fellow, 1979-80. Mem. Urban Land Inst., Real Estate Securities and Syndication Inst., Nat. Trust for Hist. Preservation.

KING, WILLIAM TRAVIS, radiologist; b. Vicksburg, Miss., June 11, 1947; s. Travis Menton and Mary Cecile (Dornbusch) K. BS in Pharmacy, U. Miss., 1970; MD, U. Miss., Jackson, 1974. Pharmacy research asst. U. Miss., University, 1965-70; resident in radiology U. Tenn., Memphis, 1975-78; pharmacist Doctors Hosp., Jackson, 1970-74; staff physician U. Ariz., Tucson, 1978-79, radiology fellow, 1978-79; radiologist Phoenix Radiology Assts. Ltd., 1980—; dir. CAT scanning, ultrasound and thermography St. Luke's Hosp., Phoenix, 1983—. Contbr. articles to profl. jours. Mem. AMA, Ariz. Med. Assn., Phoenix Radiol. Soc., Am. Pharm. Assn., Multiple Sclerosis Soc., Sigma Xi, Omicron Delta Kappa, Rho Chi, Alpha Tau Omega, Kappa Psi (pres. 1968-69). Democrat. Methodist. Home: 1602 E Weahtervane Tempe AZ 85283 Office: St Luke's Hosp 1800 E Van Buren Phoenix AZ 85006

KINGMAN, ELIZABETH YELM, anthropologist; b. Lafayette, Ind., Oct. 15, 1911; d. Charles Walter and Mary Irene (Weakley) Yelm; m. Eugene Kingman, June 10, 1939; children—Mixie Kingman Eddy, Elizabeth Anne Kingman. BA U. Denver, 1933, MA, 1935. Asst. in anthropology U. Denver, 1932-34; mus. asst. Ranger Naturalist Force, Mesa Verde Nat. Park, Colo., 1934-38; asst. to husband in curatorial work, Indian art exhibits Philbrook Art Ctr., Tulsa, 1939-42, Joslyn Art Mus., Omaha, 1947-69; tutor humanities dept. U. Omaha, 1947-50; asst. to husband in exhibit design mus. of Tex. Tech. U., 1970-75, bibliographer Internat. Ctr. Arid and Semi-Arid Land Studies, 1974-75; librarian Sch. Am. Research, Santa Fe, 1978-86; research assoc., 1986—; v.p. Santa Fe Corral of the Westerners, 1985-86. Mem. Archeol. Inst. Am. (v.p. Santa Fe chpt. 1981-83), LWV, Santa Fe Hist. Soc. (sec. 1981-83). Presbyterian. Home: 604 Sunset St Santa Fe NM 87501-1118 Office: Sch Am Rsch 660 Garcia St Santa Fe NM 87501-1118

KINGSBURY, CAROLYN ANN, software systems engineer; b. Newark, Ohio, Aug. 4, 1938; d. Cecil C. Layman and Orpha Edith (Hisey) Layman Dick; m. L.C. James Kingsbury, Apr. 25, 1959; children—Donald Lynn, Kenneth James. B.S. in Math., B.S. in Info. and Computer Scis., U. Calif.-Irvine, 1979; postgrad. West Coast U., 1982-84. Integrated test engr. Rockwell Internat., Downey, Calif., 1979-82, system engr., analyst, 1982-84; software test engr. Northrop Corp., Pico Rivera, Calif., 1984-87, software systems engr., 1987—. Pres., PTA, Manhattan Beach, Calif., 1971-73; Cub Scout den mother Boy Scouts Am., Manhattan Beach, 1972-73. Recipient Service award Calif. Congress Parents and Tchrs., 1973, Leadership Achievement award YWCA, Los Angeles, 1980, 84, NASA Achievement awards, 1983. Mem. Nat. Assn. Female Execs., Nat. Mgmt. Assn., AAUW. Republican. Club: Newtowners (pres. 1962). Home: 11392 Stonecress Ave Fountain Valley CA 92708 Office: Northrop Corp 8900 E Washington Blvd Pico Rivera CA 90660

KINGSBURY, SUSAN NIEMCZYK, medical record consultant; b. Detroit, Nov. 17, 1952; d. Steve and Eleanor Kusz Niemczyk; m. John Gordon Kingsbury, July 11, 1981. BS Med. Record Adminstrn., Mercy Coll., Detroit, 1974; MPH Health Info. Systems, UCLA, 1980. Registered record adminstr. Hosp. rep. Commn. onProfl. 7 Hosp. Activities, Ann Arbor, Mich., 1974-78; quality assurance mgr. Area 18 PSRO, Pasadena, Calif., 1978-79; cons. health planning Coopers & Lybrand, L.A., 1980-81; mgr. consulting Ernst & Whinney, 1981-85; med. record cons. Am. Med. Internat., Brea, Calif., 1985-86, Marina Del Rey, Calif., 1986—. Mem. Southern Calif. Med. Records Assn. (sec. 1987-88); Calif. Med. Record Assn. (bd. dirs. 1988-90. Roman Catholic. Office: Am Med Internat 12960 Coral Tree Pl Los Angeles CA 90066

KINGSLEY, LAWRENCE SCOTT, military officer; b. Carlsbad, N.Mex., Oct. 30, 1955; s. Joe David Kingsley and Patricia (Byrnes) Swartz; m. Cynthia Beacham, Oct. 3, 1978; children: Nathan Scott, Emily Ann, Peter Lawrence, Leeann Marie, Andrew Joseph, Benjamin Paul. BS, Utah State U., 1977; MA, Cen. Mo. State U., 1983. Commd. 2nd lt. USAF, 1978; advanced through grades to maj. 1982; missile combat crew comdr. 351 Strategic Missile Wing, Knob Noster, Mo., 1978-82; maintenance control officer 41 Consol. Aircraft Squadron, Sacramento, 1982-85; maintenance plans officer 21 Tactical Fighter Wing, Anchorage, 1985-88; maintenance ops. officer 343 Tactical Fighter Wing, Fairbanks, Alaska, 1988—; aircraft accident investigator 21 Tactical Fighter Wing, Elmendorf AFB, 1985-88. Exec. bd. PTA, Elmendorf AFB, 1987-88; USAF rep. Elmendorf Speakers Bur., 1985-88; active Boy Scouts Am., Anchorage, 1985-88. Named one of Outstanding Young Men of Am., Jaycees, 1987. Mem. Air Force Assn. (life). Republican. Mormon. Home: 5275 G Broadway Eielson AFB AK 99702 Office: 343 Tactical Fighter Wing Eielson AFB AK 99702

KINGSLEY, PATRICIA, public relations executive; b. Gastonia, N.C., May 7, 1932; d. Robert Henry and Marjorie (Norment) Ratchford; m. Walter Kingsley, Apr. 1, 1966 (div. 1978); 1 child, Janis Susan. Student, Winthrop Coll., 1950-51. Publicist Fountainebleau Hotel, Miami Beach, Fla., 1952; exec. asst. ZIV TV, N.Y.C., 1953-58; publicist Rogers & Cowan, L.A. and N.Y.C., 1960-71; ptnr. Pickwick Pub. Relations, L.A., 1971-80, PMK Pub. Relations, L.A., 1980—; adv. com. Women's Action for Nuclear Disarmament, Arlington, Mass., 1983—. Democrat. Office: PMK Pub Relations Inc 8436 W 3rd St Los Angeles CA 90048

KINGSLEY, SHERWOOD CLARK, accountant; b. Los Angeles, July 5, 1939; s. William Jackson and Eleanor Nevin (Veale) K.; m. Rona Toby Fretter, Nov. 8, 1980; 1 son, Aron Sherwood. Staff acct. Arthur Young & Co., Los Angeles, 1965-66; supr. accounts payable Interpace Co., Los Angeles, 1966-67; controller Illig Constrn. Co., Los Angeles, 1967-73; supr. John F. Forbes Co., Los Angeles, 1974; practice public acctg., Los Angeles, 1975—. Organizer alumni fund raising orgn. Webb Sch. C.P.A., Calif. Mem. Am. Inst. C.P.A.s, Calif. Soc. C.P.A.s, SAR. Republican. Congregationalist. Clubs: Lions (pres. 1981-82), Masons (master 1976). Home: 4159 Keystone Ave Culver City CA 90232

KINKADE, KATE, publishing executive, magazine editor, insurance executive; b. N.Y.C., Jan. 22, 1951; d. Joel M. and Peeta S. (Sherman) Sandleman; m. Patrick Ramsey, June 27, 1981; children: Jamaa Ramsey, Kikanza Ramsey. BS in Speech, Emerson Coll., Boston, 1972; postgrad., Am. Coll., Bryn Mawr, Pa. CLU. Agt. Equitable Life Ins., Los Angeles, 1973-75, mgr., 1975-77; v.p. Lincoln Nat. Life Ins., Tarzana, Calif., 1977-80; pres. TIME Ins., Encino, Calif., 1980—; mng. editor McGee Pub., Burbank, Calif., 1983—; exec. v.p. Life Underwriters Assn., Encino, 1978-81. Contbr. articles to profl. jours. Mem. steering com. nat. office Beyond War, Palo Alto, Calif., also Los Angeles regional fin. support and chairperson local chpt., Burbank, Calif., 1984—. Recipient Asst. Prodn. awards Equitable Life, 1973, 77, Lincoln Nat. Life, 1978, 80, Pacific Mut. Life, 1983. Mem. Assn. CLU's. Democrat. Jewish. also: 18107 Sherman Way #205 Reseda CA 91335-4564

KINNEBREW, JOSEPH E., IV, designer, artist; b. Tacoma, Wash., Oct. 12, 1942; s. Joseph E. Kinnebrew III and Elaine (Montgomery) Dexter; m. Ellen Carol McKittrick, June 28, 1970; children: Alexis Heather, Peter Joseph Tobias. BA, Syracuse U., 1964; MFA, Mich. State U., 1970; postgrad., Inst. Study Instructional Devel. and Tech., 1969-70. Prin. The Kinnebrew Design Collaborative, Clinton, Wash., 1976-85; mng. dir. Jacquot Ltd., St. Lucia, West Indies, 1981-85; dir. Ojé Internat., Sun Valley, Idaho, 1986-87, Ojé, Ketchum, Idaho, 1987—; artist in residence NEA, Mich. State U. Sch. Packaging, Sch. of Human Ecology; cons. Mich. Joint Legis. Com. Arts, Mich. Council for Arts, McMillan, Palmer, Fritz & Assocs., WBDC Inc. Architects, Wayne State U. Sch. Edn., others; pres. LMD Inc. Ojé Gallery; sec., treas. Ojé Internat., Inc. Represented in permanent collections Nat. Collection Fine Arts, The Art Inst. Chgo., Walker Art Ctr., Mpls., The Guggenheim Mus., The Met. Mus. Art, Mus. Modern Art, Library of Congress, Bkln. Mus., The Montreal Mus. Fine Arts, Detroit Inst. Art, Phila. Mus. Art, Atkins Mus. Fine Arts, Kansas City, The Houghton Library, Harvard U., New Orleans Mus. Art, The Mpls. Inst. Arts, Honolulu Acad. Arts, Flint Inst. Arts, Swedish Hosp., Seattle, others; works pub. in various mags. including Fortune mag., Art Forum, Saturday Rev., AIA Jour., Sports Illustrated, Esquire, Accent mag., Interior Design, numerous others; patentee in field. Recipient Mich. Product of Yr. award, 1979, Nat. Design award Indsl. Design Soc. Am., 1980, First Honor award Mich. Soc. Landscape Architecture, 1983; grantee NEA, Mich. Council Arts, Mich. State U. Communications Inst., Assoc. Truck Lines Found., Wis. State Arts Council, Thomas Erler Seidman Found., Dexter Charitable Trust. Mem. Indsl. Des Soc. of Am. Home: PO 2923 Ketchum ID 83340 Office: Ojé Internat Inc PO Box 2840 Sun Valley ID 83353

KINNEY, HARRY EDWIN, mechanical engineer; b. Trinidad, Colo., June 7, 1924; s. Oliver Earl and Opal (Sanger) K.; m. Carol N. Roberts, Aug. 30, 1970; children: Charlotte Jean, Donald Bruce. B.S. in Mech. Engring., U. N.Mex., 1945; hon. degree in pub. adminstrn., U. Albuquerque, 1985. Staff mem. Sandia Labs., 1956-73; commr. City of Albuquerque, 1966-73, vice chmn. City Commn., 1970-71, chmn., 1971-73, mayor, 1974-77, 81-85; gen. contractor, residential constrn. 1977-81; bldg. contractor, dir. bus. devel. Jacobs Engring. Group, Inc., Albuquerque, 1981-88; pvt. bldg. contractor Albuquerque, 1988—; commr. Bernalillo County, N.Mex., 1956-58, 61-65; mem. adv. panel on infrastructure to U.S. Senate budget com., 1985-86; mem. mgmt. adv. group for constrn. grants EPA, 1982-86. Chmn. Middle Rio Grande Council Govts. of N.Mex., 1970-72; mem. U.S. Adv. Commn. on Intergovtl. Relations, 1975-77; mem. adv. bd. U.S. Conf. Mayors, 1975-77, 82-85, chmn., 1977; Pres. Albuquerque-Bernalillo County Econ. Opportunity Bd., 1964-66; pres. N.Mex. Council Social Welfare, 1965-67; chmn. City-County Joint Alcoholism Bd., 1969-72; pres. Ams. for Rational Energy Alternatives, 1980-84, 85—; v.p. Chapparal council Girl Scouts U.S.A., 1978-81; bd. dirs. Met. YMCA, 1977-81; bd. dirs. Lovelace Med. Ctr. Health Plan, 1985—; spl. asst. to U.S. senator, 1973-74. Served with USNR, 1943-46, 50-52. Mem. ASME (Pub. Service award Region VIII, 1977, 84), Naval Res. Assn., Kappa Sigma. Episcopalian. Address: 801 Piedra Larga NE Albuquerque NM 87123

KINNEY, LISA FRANCES, state senator; b. Laramie, Wyo., Mar. 13, 1951; d. Irvin Wayne and Phyllis (Poe) K.; m. Rodney Philip Lang, Feb. 5, 1971; children: Cambria Helen, Shelby Robert. BA, U. Wyo., 1973, JD, 1986; MLS, U. Oreg., 1975. Reference librarian U. Wyo. Sci. Library, Laramie, 1975-76; outreach dir. Albany County Library, Laramie, 1975-76, dir., 1977-83; mem. Wyo. State Senate, Laramie, 1985—. Author: (with Rodney Lang) Civil Rights of the Developmentally Disabled, 1986; (with Rodney Lang and Phyllis Kinney) Manual For Families with Emotionally Disturbed and Mentally Ill Relatives, 1988; contbr. articles to profl. jours; editor, compiler pub. relations directory for ALA, 1982. Bd. dirs. Big Bros./Big Sisters, Laramie, 1980-83. Recipient Beginning Young Profl. award Mt. Plains Library Assn., 1980; named Outstanding Wyo. Librarian Wyo. Library Assn., 1977, Outstanding Young Woman State of Wyo., 1980. Mem. ABA , Nat. Confs. of State Legislatures (various coms.), LWV, Laramie C. of C. Democrat. Club: Snowy Range Internat. Folk Dance (pres. 1980-87). Lodges: Zonta Internat., Gem City Lioness. Avocations: photography, dance, reading, travel, languages. Home: 603 Spring Creek Laramie WY 82070

KINNEY, RALEIGH EARL, artist; b. Brainerd, Minn., Mar. 11, 1938; s. Earl Martin and Nancy Ann (Wolleat) K.; m. Darlene Joyce Fox, Sept. 12, 1964; children: Rodney Eric, Aaron Weston. BS, St. Cloud (Minn.) State U., 1965, MA, 1968. Cert. tchr. Art tchr. St. Cloud Jr. High Sch., 1965-70; art tchr., dept. chmn. St. Cloud Sr. High Sch., 1970-80; ind. instr. watercolor workshop 1980—. Served with USN, 1957-61. Named Artist of Yr. Phoenix C. of C., 1987. Mem. Ariz. Watercolor Soc. (signature), Midwest Watercolor Soc. (v.p. 1976-77, signature). Republican. Home: 1947 E ManhattanDr Tempe AZ 85282

KINNISON, HARRY AUSTIN, transportation engineer; b. Springfield, Ohio, Oct. 2, 1935; s. Errett Lowell and Audrey Muriel (Smith) K. BSEE, U. Wyo., 1964; M. in Transp. Engring., Seattle U., 1983; PhD in Civil Engring., U. Tenn., 1987. Enlisted USAF, 1958, commd. 2d lt., 1964, advanced through grades to capt., 1968, released from active duty, 1968; electronics engr. 1939 Electronics Installing Group, Keesler AFB, Biloxi, Miss., 1972-77; staff engr. Casper (Wyo.) Air Facilities Sector FAA, 1977; test engr. Boeing Aerospace Co., Seattle, 1977-81; avionics engr. Boeing Comml. Airplane Co., Seattle, 1981-83, 87—; grad. rsch. engr. U. Tenn. Transp. Ctr., Knoxville, 1983-87. Mem. Inst. Transp. Engrs. (assoc.), Transp. Rsch. Bd. (assoc.). Republican. Mem. Christian Ch. Home: 3020 118th Ave SE Apt B102 Bellevue WA 98005 Office: Boeing Comml Planes PO Box 3707 M/A 2J03 Seattle WA 98124

KINNISON, ROBERT RAY, statistician; b. L.A., Sept. 10, 1934; s. Ray Hiram and Helen Louise (Krozek) K.; m. Karne Dale Wingo, July 10, 1959; children: Sharon Dale, Donald Ray. BA, Pomona Coll., 1956; PhD, UCLA, 1971. Pharmacologist Rexall Drug & Chem. Co., L.A., 1960-68; rsch. statistician U. Calif., San Francisco, 1971-72; statistician U.S. EPA, Las Vegas, Nev., 1972-79, Battelle Pacific N.W. Labs., Richland, Wash., 1979-85; sr. statistician Desert Rshc. Inst., Las Vegas, 1985—; adj. assoc. prof. math. U. Nev., Las Vegas; assoc. editor Environ. Monitoring and Assessment, 1985—. Assoc. editor jour. Simulation, 1972—. Mem. Am. Statis. Assn., Biometric Soc., AAAS, Simulation Soc., Masons, Sigma Xi. Democrat. Methodist. Home: 846 E Pescados Dr Las Vegas NV 89123 Office: Desert Research Inst Water Resources Ctr 2305 Chandler Ave 1 Las Vegas NV 89120

KINNISON, ROBERT WHEELOCK, certified public accountant; b. Des Moines, Sept. 17, 1914; s. Virgil R. and Sopha J. (Jackson) K.; m. Randi

Hjelle, Oct. 28, 1971; children—Paul F., Hazel Jo Huff. B.S. in Acctg., U. Wyo., 1940. C.P.A., Wyo., Colo. Ptnr. 24 hour auto service, Laramie, Wyo., 1945-59; pvt. practice acctg., Laramie, Wyo., 1963-71, Las Vegas, Nev., 1972-74, Westminster, Colo., 1974-76, Ft. Collins, Colo., 1976—. Served with U.S. Army, 1941-45; PTO. Mem. Am. Soc. C.P.A.s, Wyo. Soc. C.P.A.s, Am. Legion (past comdr.), Laramie Soc. C.P.A.s (pres. 1966), VFW. Clubs: Laramie Optimist (pres. 1950), Sertoma. Home: PO Box 168 Fort Collins CO 80522 Office: 2050 Airway Ave Fort Collins CO 80524

KINSEY, LOU ANNA, speech and language pathologist; b. Watsonville, Calif., Nov. 12, 1954; d. William Ronald and Wilma Jane (Baker) George. BA, Humboldt State U., 1975, MA, 1982. Lic. speech pathologist, Calif. Speech therapist Redwoods United, Inc., Eureka, Calif., 1978-80; outreach worker Humboldt Child Care Council, Eureka, 1980-81; spl. edn. tchr. South Humboldt Unified, Garberville, Calif., 1981-84; speech and lang. therapist Arcata (Calif.) Elem., 1984—; pvt. practice speech and lang. pathology Arcata, 1984—; speech pathologist Redwood Coast Regional Ctr., Eureka, 1984—. Bd. dirs. Arcata-McKinleyville Children's Ctr., Minor Theatre Co., Arcata. Mem. Calif. Tchrs. Assn., Calif. Speech and Hearing Assn., North Country Speech and Lang. Pathologists, Eureka (co-pres. 1987—), Arcata Elem. Tchrs. Assn. (v.p. 1988—). Democrat. Office: Arcata Sch Dist 1125 16th St Ste 201 Arcata CA 95521

KINSKY, IVAN, electronics engineer; b. Temesvar, Romania, Apr. 24, 1947; came to Israel, 1962, U.S., 1984.; s. Stefan and Margareta (Reiter) K.; m. Yael Grynberg, Aug. 12, 1970; children: Danna, Gilly. BSEE, Technion, Israel, 1969, MSEE, 1973. Project mgr. Tamam Israel Aircraft Industries, Tel Aviv, 1975-81, program mgr., 1981-82; dep. div. mgr. Elco Ltd., Tel Aviv, 1982-83, div. mgr., 1983-84; prin. Quad Inc., Canoga Park, Calif., 1985—; cons. Elco Ltd., 1984-85, FMC, San Jose, Calif., 1985—, Condor Pacific, Canoga Park, 1984—. Served to capt. Israel Army, 1979. Mem. Inst. Navigation, Royal Inst. Navigation (Eng.). Home and Office: Quad Inc 5080 Campo Dr Woodland Hills CA 91364

KINSLER, BRUCE WHITNEY, air traffic controller; b. Ukiah, Calif., Jan. 11, 1947; s. John Arthur and Mary Helen (Hudson) K.; m. Mickey Kinsler, Apr. 1, 1969 (div. Nov. 1976); 1 child, Arthur Todd; m. Segundina L. Pangilinan, May 27, 1978; 1 stepchild, Stephanie Camalig. AA, El Camino Coll., 1979; BA, Calif. State U., Long Beach, 1984. Air traffic controller FAA, various locations, 1971-81; cen. sta. mgr. Times Mirror Security Communications, Irvine, Calif., 1982-84; supr. office services Law Offices Paul, Hastings, Janofsky & Walker, L.A., 1984-85; air traffic control cons. to Hughes Aircraft Corp. Fullerton, Calif., 1985—; with Fortier and Assocs., Fullerton; mem. citizens adv. com. Calif. Dept. Transp., Sacramento, 1982—. Author air traffic control tng. manuals. With USNR, 1986—. Mem. Air Traffic Control Assn., Aircraft Owners and Pilots Assn., U.S. Naval Inst., Internat. Platform Assn. Democrat. Home: 335 Mountain Ct Brea CA 92621

KINSMAN, ROBERT PRESTON, biomedical plastics engineer; b. Cambridge, Mass., July 25, 1949; s. Fred Nelson and Myra Roxanne (Preston) K. BS in Plastics Engring., U. Lowell, 1971; MBA, Pepperdine U., 1982. Cert. biomedical engr., Calif. Product devel. engr., plastics div. Gen. Tire Corp., Lawrence, Mass., 1976-77; mfg. engr. Edwards Labs. subs. Am. Hosp. Supply Corp., Irvine, Calif., 1978-80, sr. engr., 1981-82; mfg. engr. mgr. Edwards Labs. subs. Am. Hosp. Supply Corp., Añasco, P.R., 1983; project mgr. Baxter Edwards Critical Care div. Baxter Healthcare Corp., Irvine, 1984-87, engring. and prodn. mgr., 1987—; mem. mgmt. adv. panel Modern Plastics mag., N.Y.C., 1979-80. First aid instr. ARC, N.O., Mass., Calif., 1971—; vol. worker VA, Bedford, Mass., 1967-71 (Cert. of Appreciation award 1971); pres., bd. dirs. Lake Homeowners Assn., Irvine, 1985—; bd. dirs. Paradise Park Owners Assn., Las Vegas, 1988—. Capt. USAF, 1971-75. Mem. Soc. Plastics Engrs., Am. Mgmt. Assn., Plastics Acad., Mensa, Nat. Honor Soc., VFW, Am. Legion, Elks. Office: Baxter Edwards Critical Care 17221 Red Hill Ave Irvine CA 92714

KIPP, JUNE CAROL, health science facility administrator; b. Johnstown, Penn., Apr. 11, 1932; d. John Claude and Margaretta Olive (Firth) Saylor; m. David Franklin Kipp Sr., Aug. 18, 1951; children: Peggy Carol, David Franklin Jr., Matthew. AA, Lamar (Colo.) Coll., 1974; postgrad., U. Colo., Denver, 1978. Rsch. tech. Eli Lilly Co., Indpls., 1950-51; blood bank tech. Charleroi-Monessen Hosp., Penn., 1957-60; cheif tech. Windber Hosp., Penn., 1960-70; technologist Nuclear Test Site, Mercury, Nev., 1970-71; blood bank tech ARC, Johnstown, Penn., 1971-72; chief tech. S.E. Colo. Hosp., Springfield, 1972-76; lab. supr. Smith Kline Clin. Labs., Denver, 1976-81, Indian Pub. Health Svc., Chinle, Ariz., 1982—. Mem. Am. Med. Tech. Assn., Colo. Med. Tech. Assn. (sec. 1977-81), Ariz. Med. Tech. Assn. Republican. Mem. Ch. of the Brethren. Office: Indian Pub Health Svc PO Drawer Chinle AZ 86503

KIPP, THOMAS H., service contract manager; b. Pitts., Aug. 9, 1922; m. Naida Joan Curtis, Apr. 30, 1955. BA, U. So. Calif., 1948, MS, 1949. News and spl. events dir. Don Lee Mutual Broadcasting, Hollywood, Calif., 1955-62; mktg. mgr. Kipp Ind. Sales., Pasadena, Calif., 1955-62; pres. 49'er Industries, Oakland, Calif., 1962-69; founder, pres. NCD Assocs., Oakland, 1969-88. Home: PO Box 1192 Middletown CA 95461

KIPPING, VERNON LOUIS, film consultant, marine scientist; b. Cape Girardeau, Mo., Oct. 19, 1921; s. Theodore Frederick and Augusta (Meyer) K.; m. Anna Ruth Uelsmann, Mar. 26, 1944; children: Theodore Paul, John Louis, Douglas Kim. Student, S.E. Mo. State U., 1940-41; AA, Multnomah Coll., 1948; JD, U. San Francisco, 1951. Fingerprint examiner FBI, Washington, 1941-43; with radio communications FBI, Portland, Oreg., 1943-44; spl. employee FBI, Portland, 1946-48; spl. employee San Francisco, 1948-71, 72-76, Chgo., 1971-72; freelance film cons. San Francisco, 1976—; testified as expert witness Patricia Hearst trial. Owner 19 U.S. and fgn. patents motion picture tech., marine sci.; invented means to convert still photos of Patricia Hearsts bank robbery into motion picture for use at trial. Sgt. USAAF, 1944-46, PTO. Recipient Spl. prize San Francisco Film Festival, 1957. Mem. Soc. Motion Picture and TV Engrs. (program chmn. 1977-79, mgr. 1979-81, membership chmn. 1981-85, spl. events chmn. 1985-88, sec./treas. 1988—, past audio-visual conf. chmn., Citation for Outstanding Svc. 1986). Republican. Club: No. Calif. Imperial Owners (San Francisco) (v.p. 1979-83, pres. 1983-87). Home and Office: 540 Melrode Ave San Francisco CA 94127

KIRBY, KEVIN ARTHUR, podiatrist, educator; b. Danville, Va., Jan. 30, 1957; s. James Clyde and Dorothy Annette (Skeen) K.; m. Pamela Joy Pearce, May 31, 1980; children: Keegan James, Cameron Lee. BS, U. Calif., Davis, 1979; D, Calif. Coll. Podiatric Medicine, 1983, MS, 1985. Resident in podiatry VA Med. Ctr., Palo Alto, Calif., 1983-84; fellow in podiatry Calif. Coll. Podiatric Medicine, San Francisco, 1984-85, asst. prof. dept. biomechanics, 1985—; podiatrist Pacific Health Ctr., Sacramento, 1985—; dir. clin. biomechanics Precision Intricast Co., Lodi, Calif., 1985—, Kaiser Hosp., Sacramento, 1985—; tchr. Internat. Biomechanics Found., Auburn, Calif., 1985—. Contbr. articles to jours. Mem. Am. Podiatric Med. Assn., Calif. Podiatric Med. Assn., Am. Coll. Foot Surgeons, Am. Acad. Podiatric Sports Medicine. Democrat. Baptist. Office: Pacific Health Ctr 1675 Alhambra Blvd Sacramento CA 95816

KIRBY, RONALD EUGENE, fish and wildlife biologist; b. Angola, Ind., Nov. 26, 1947; s. Robert Waye and Lorraine Alice (Hoag) K.; m. Kristina Moeller Hokanson, Sept. 5, 1970; children: Cyrus Robert, William Emil, Peter Waye. BS, Duke U., 1969; MA, So. Ill. U., 1973; PhD, U. Minn., 1976. Staff biologist Coop. Wildlife Rsch. Lab., So. Ill. U., Carbondale, 1969-72; collaborating biologist U.S. Forest Svc., St. Paul and Cass Lake, Minn., 1970-72; rsch. biologist Antarctic Rsch. Program NSF, McMurdo Station, Antarctica, 1974; NIH rsch. trainee dept. ecology and behavioral biology U. Minn., Mpls., 1972-76; wildlife biologist, Patuxent Wildlife Rsch. Ctr. U.S. Fish and Wildlife Svc., Laurel, Md., 1976-80; population mgmt. specialist div. refuge mgmt. U.S. Fish and Wildlife Svc., Washington, 1980-82, rsch. coord. Nat. Wildlife Refuge System, 1982-83; regional assistance biologist, office info. transfer U.S. Fish and Wildlife Svc., Ft. Collins, Colo., 1983-88; leader info. transfer sect. U.S. Fish and Wildlife Svc., Ft. Collins, 1988—; mem. waterfowl adv. com., Minn. Dept. Natural Resources, St. Paul, 1970-72; mem. black duck subcom., Atlantic Flyway Coun., 1976-80; course dir., continuing edn., U.S. Fish and Wildlife Svc. R & D, Jamestown, N.D., 1988—. Contbr. to numerous profl. publs; editorial referee, sci. jours. and profl. reports. Active, Boy Scouts Am., Ft. Collins, 1984—. Grantee, AEC, 1972-76. Mem. The Wildlife Soc., Am. Ornithologists Union, Lambda Chi Alpha. Office: US Fish Wildlife Svc 1025 Pennock Pl Ste 212 Fort Collins CO 80524

KIRK, CARMEN ZETLER, data processing executive; b. Altoona, Pa., May 22, 1941; d. Paul Alan and Mary Evelyn (Pearce) Zetler. BA, Pa. State U., 1959-63; MBA, St. Mary's Coll. Calif., 1977. Cert. in data processing. Pub. sch. tchr. State Ga., 1965-66; systems analyst U.S. Govt. Dept. Army, Oakland, Calif., 1967-70; programmer analyst Contra Costa County, Martinez, Calif., 1970-76; applications mgr. Stanford (Calif.) U., 1976-79; pres. Zetler Assocs., Inc., Palo Alto, Calif., 1979—; cons. State Calif., Sacramento, 1985—. Author: (tech. manuals) Comparex, 1982-83. Vol. Stanford Med. Ctr. Aux., 1985—. Office: Zetler Assocs Inc PO Box 50395 Palo Alto CA 94303

KIRK, CASSIUS LAMB, JR., lawyer, investor; b. Bozeman, Mont., June 8, 1929; s. Cassius Lamb and Gertrude Violet (McCarthy) K.; A.B., Stanford U., 1951; J.D., U. Calif., Berkeley, 1954. Bar: Calif. 1955; lic. real estate broker. Assoc. firm Cooley, Godward, Castro, Huddleson & Tatum, San Francisco, 1956-60; staff counsel for bus. affairs Stanford U., 1960-78; chief bus. officer, staff counsel Menlo Sch. and Coll., Redwood City, Calif., 1978-81; pres. Eberli-Kirk Properties, Inc., Menlo Park, 1981—; mem. faculty Coll. Bus. Adminstrn. U. Calif., Santa Barbara, 1967-73; bd. dirs. Just Closets, Inc., San Rafael, Calif.; bd. dirs. San Francisco Pocket Opera; mem. adv. bd. Allied Arts Guild, Menlo Park. With U.S. Army, 1954-56. Mem. Calif. Bar Assn., Stanford Assocs., Order of Coif, Phi Alpha Delta. Republican. Club: Stanford Faculty. Home: 1330 University Dr Apt 52 Menlo Park CA 94025 Office: 3551-N Haven Ave Menlo Park CA 94025

KIRK, DUDLEY, sociologist, educator; b. Rochester, N.Y., Oct. 6, 1913; s. William and Margaret Louise (Dudley) K.; m. Ruth Louise Avelar, Nov. 21, 1947; children: Margaret Louise, John Dudley, Deborah Avelar. B.A., Pomona Coll., 1934; M.A., Fletcher Sch. Law and Diplomacy, Tufts U., 1935, Harvard U., 1938; Ph.D., Harvard U., 1946; student, U. Mexico, 1930, London Sch. Econ. and Polit. Sci., 1936. Tutor sociology Harvard U., 1937-39; research asst., later research asso. Office Population Research, Princeton U., 1939-47, asst. prof. sociology at univ., 1945-47; demographer Office Intelligence Research, State Dept., 1947-51; chief div. research Office Intelligence Research, State Dept., Near East, South Asia and Africa, 1952; chief planning staff for research and intelligence Office Intelligence Research, State Dept., 1952-54; staff mem. Pres.'s Com. Immigration and Naturalization, 1951; demographic dir. Population Council, N.Y.C., 1954-67; prof. demography Food Research Inst. and dept. sociology Stanford U., from 1967, Morrison prof. population studies, from 1971, chmn. dept. sociology, 1975-76; vis. sr. research demographer Princeton U., 1978; coordinator Courses by Newspaper, NEH, 1981-82; mem. U.S. Nat. Com. on Health and Vital Stats., 1961-65; mem. research adv. com. AID, 1968-72. Author: (with others) The Future Population of Europe and the Soviet Union, 1944, Europe's Population in the Interwar Years, 1946, The Principles of Political Geography, 1957, (with Ellen K. Eliason) Food and People, 1982. Fellow Center Advanced Study in the Behavioral Scis., 1964-65. Fellow AAAS, Am. Sociol. Assn., Am. Statis. Assn., Inter-Am. Statis. Inst., Am. Pub. Health Assn.; mem. Am. Soc. Study Social Biology (dir., chmn. editorial bd. Social Biology, pres. 1969-72), Am. Acad. Polit. and Social Sci., Internat. Union Sci. Study Population, Population Assn. Am. (pres. 1959-60), Sociol. Research Assn. Home: 53 Peter Coutts Circle Stanford CA 94305 *

KIRK, JUDD, real estate development executive; b. Salt Lake City, Apr. 29, 1945; s. George and Mary (Foster) K.; m. Barbara Sharon Almrig, June 15, 1968; children: Lisa, Jon. BA in Fin., U. Wash., 1967; JD, Harvard U., 1970. Bar: Wash. 1970. Ptnr. Davis, Wright & Jones, Seattle, 1970-86; pres. Skinner Devel. Co., Seattle, 1986—. Vestryman, treas., St. Stephens Ch., Seattle, 1983-86; pres. bd. dirs., Epiphany Sch., Seattle, 1984-86. Mem. ABA, Wash. State Bar Assn. (chmn. real property, probate and trust sect. 1980-81), Urban Land Inst., Nat. Assn. Indsl. and Office Parks, Am. Coll. Real Estate Lawyers, Kirkland C. of C. (bd. dirs. 1987—). Office: Skinner Devel Co 5305 Lake Washington Blvd NE Kirkland WA 98033

KIRK, RANDOLPH WILLIAM, manufacturing executive; b. St. Louis, Mar. 16, 1948; s. Robert Charles and Phyllis Ann (Plummer) K.; m. Christy Lynn Stock, Sept. 6, 1969 (div. 1986); m. Pamela Lynn Thornbrugh, Dec. 27, 1987; children: Christian Kirk, Ann Wood, Brandy Lynn Ploeger. BA, UCLA, 1970, JD, 1975. V.p. Abus Security Locks, Huntington Beach, Calif., 1971-79; pres. Atlas Lock Co., Torrance, Calif., 1979-83; v.p. Nat. Sales Hdqrs., Santa Fe Springs, Calif., 1980—; pres. AC Internat., Santa Fe Springs, 1981—, Reliance Security Inc., Santa Fe Springs, 1985—; v.p. Kreger Design Co., Santa Fe Springs, 1986—. Author: Principles of Bicycle Retailing, 1982, 87, Getting Rich in the Recession, 1989; patentee in field; contbr. articles to profl. jours. Pres., founder Citizens Against Diamond Lanes, Culver City, Calif., 1977. Republican. Lodge: Optimists (pres. Santa Monica Sunrise chpt., lt. gov. internat. chpt., Los Angeles, 1982). Home: 6541 Copperwood Ave LaderaHeights CA 90302 Office: AC Internat 11911 Hamden Pl Santa Fe Springs CA 90670

KIRK, REA HELENE (REA HELENE GLAZER), social services administrator, educator; b. N.Y.C., Nov. 17, 1944; d. Benjamin and Lillian (Kellis) Glazer; 3 stepdaughters. B.A., UCLA, 1966; M.A., Eastern Mont. Coll., 1981. Life cert. spl. edn. tchr., Calif., Mont. Spl. edn. tchr., Los Angeles, 1966-73; clin. sec. speech and lang. clinic, Missoula, Mont., 1973-75; spl. edn. tchr., Missoula and Gt. Falls, Mont., 1975-82; br. mgr., bd. dirs. YWCA of L.A., Beverly Hills, Calif., 1989; dir. Woman's Resource Ctr., Gt. Falls, Mont., 1981-82; dir. Battered Woman's Shelter, Rock Springs, Wyo., 1982-84; dir. Battered Victims Program Sweetwater County, Wyo., 1984—, Battered Woman's Program, San Gabriel Valley, Calif., 1988; mem. Wyo. Commn. on Aging, Rock Springs. Pres. bd. dirs. battered woman's shelter, Gt. Falls, Woman's Resource Ctr., Gt. Falls; founder, advisor Rape Action Line, Gt. Falls; founder Jewish religious services, Missoula; 4-H leader; hostess Friendship Force; Friendship Force ambassador from Wyo. to W. Germany; mem. YMCA Mont. and Wyo. Recipient honors Missoula 4-H; recognized as significant Wyo. woman as social justice reformer and peace activist Sweetwater County, Wyo.; nominated Wyo. Woman of the Yr. Mem. Council for Exceptional Children (v.p. Gt. Falls 1981-82), Assn. for Children with Learning Disabilities (Named Oustanding Mem.), Delta Kappa Gamma, Psi Chi. Democrat. Jewish.

KIRK, WILLIAM LAWRENCE, casket company executive; b. Kansas City, Mo., Nov. 30, 1950; s. Robert Leland and Wilma Louise (Bicknell) K.; m. Nancy Rae Collier, Apr. 3, 1971; children: Jonathan Andrew, Eric Randall. Student, North Tex. State U., 1972, Dallas Inst. Mortuary Sci., 1973. Lic. funeral dir., Tex.; lic. embalmer, Tex., Calif. Funeral dir. Restland Funeral Home, Dallas, 1972-80; prin. Kirk Casket Co., Dallas, 1978-80; sales rep. No. Calif. Batesville Casket Co./Hillenbrand Industries, Denver, 1980-82, mgr. Western U.S. region, 1982—. Office: Batesville Casket Co Ste D 11333 E 55th Ave Denver CO 80239

KIRKBRIDE, RAELENE JOYCE, financial manager; b. Rudyard, Mich., June 15, 1940; d. Jacob and Johanna (Besteman) Folkersma; m. Richard James Kirkbride, Apr. 28, 1960; 1 child, Robert James. BS in Acctg., U. LaVerne, 1984. Acct. Simplex Industries, Adrian, Mich., 1972-73; bookkeeper Westview Leasing, Balt., 1973-74; sec. Olin Am. Homes, Balt., 1974-75; bookkeeper Resources Mgmt., Glen Burnie, Md., 1975-76, Hoye, Graves, Bailey & Assocs., Glen Burnie, 1976-79; acct. Soares, Sandall, Bernacchi & Petrovich, Oxnard, Calif., 1979-81; office mgr. Lindsay & O'Kelley, CPA's, Ventura, Calif., 1981-83; bus. office coordinator T.M.C. Communications Inc., Ventura, 1984-85; fin. mgr. Am. Pacific Ins. Brokers, Westlake Village, Calif., 1985—. Mem. AAUW, NOW, Am. Soc. Women Accts., Nat. Assn. Female Execs., Oxnard Jaycee Women (pres. 1981-82, nat. award congress 1984), Glen Burnie C. of C. (sec. 1979, v.p. 1980, presdl. award 1976). Democrat. Clubs: New in Town (Simi Valley) (auditor 1988-89), Jack and Jills. Home: 3440 Leora Simi Valley CA 93063 Office: Am Pacific Ins Brokers 31255 Cedar Valley Dr #224 Westlake Village CA 91362

KIRKENDALL, JEFFREY LAWRENCE, real estate executive; b. Lynwood, Calif., Feb. 20, 1954; s. Richard S. and Marilyn E. Kirkendall; m. Charlotte A. Kirkendall. BS in Bus. Adminstrn. Mktg., San Diego State U., 1976. Broker assoc. Grubb & Ellis Comml. Brokerage, San Diego, 1976-80; v.p., regional mgr. Meyer Investment Properties, Denver, 1980-85; pres. Moore & Co. Comml., Denver, currently, also bd. dirs.; pres. Moore Asset Mgmt., Inc., Denver, currently. Bd. dirs. Aspen Child Devel. Ctrs. Englewood, Colo.; mem. econ. devel. adv. com. Denver Partnership; mem. mktg. com. Metro Denver Network; legis. chmn. Denver Bd. Realtors. Comml. Div.; legis. co-chmn. Internat. Coun. Shopping Ctrs., Colo. Mem. Bldg. owners & Mgrs. Assn., Urban Land Inst., Denver Athletic Club. Office: Moore Comml 370 17th St Ste 3600 Denver CO 80202

KIRKENDOLL, ROY NATHAN, JR., real estate broker, educator; b. Joplin, Mo., June 22, 1950; s. Roy Nathan Sr. and Ruth Mae (King) K.; m. Diana Lucille Brown, Aug. 7, 1971 (div. apr. 1975); 1 child, Christopher Michael. BA in English, U. Kans., 1972. Salesman Mayer-Rossberg Realtors, Overland Park, Kans., 1972-74; mgr. Kroh Bros. Realty, Kansas City, Mo., 1974-75; salesman Coldwell Banker, La Jolla, Calif., 1975-81; pres. Kirkendoll Co., Malibu, Calif., 1981—; broker, gen. mgr. Better Homes Realty, Dublin, Calif., 1985-87; pres. The Kirkendoll Co., 1987—; sponsor Dept. Real Estate, Sacramento, 1981—. Author: California Escrow Guide, 1985, Keys to Success, 1986, Negotiation, The Power of Effective Listening, Beyond Conventional Selling, 1988, Expose Yourself With Dignity, 1988, various ednl. video tapes. Recipient Outstanding Sales Achievement award Coldwell Banker, 1975-80. Mem. Nat. Inst. Real Estate Sales Counselors (founder 1987), Internat. Platform Assn., Phi Beta Kappa, Delta Chi. Office: 245 Upper Terr San Francisco CA 94117

KIRKER, JACK M., telecommunications company executive. Former pres. GTE Automatic Electric Inc., Northlake, Ill.; now pres. AG Communications Systems Corp. (formerly GTE Communicaiton Systems Corp.), Phoenix. Office: AG Communications Systems 2500 W Utopia Rd Phoenix AZ 85027 *

KIRKHART, BARBARA JEAN, mechanical engineer; b. Madison, Wis., July 22, 1960; d. Robert William and Barbara Delores (Fuhr) Schumann; m. Mark Robert Kirkhart, Feb. 22, 1988. BSME, U. Wis., 1987. Cert. quality engr. Design engr. Motorola, Inc., Schaumburg, Ill., 1983-86; mfg. engr. Advanced Tech. Labs., Bothell, Wash., 1986-88, quality engr., 1988, procurement engr., 1989—. Leader 4-H Club, Madison, 1980. Mem. Am. Soc. Quality Control, Internat. Soc. Hybrid Microelectronics. Office: Advanced Tech Labs PO Box 3003 Bothell WA 98041

KIRKLAND, BERTHA THERESA (MRS. THORNTON CROWNS KIRKLAND, JR.), engineer; b. San Francisco, May 16, 1916; d. Lawrence and Theresa (Kanzler) Schmelzer; m. Thornton Crowns Kirkland, Jr., Dec. 27, 1937 (dec. July 1971); children: Kathryn Elizabeth, Francis Charles. Supr. hosp. ops. Am. Potash & Chem. Corp., Trona, Calif., 1953-54; office mgr., T.C. Kirkland, elec. contractor, 1954-56; sec.-treas., bd. dirs. T.C. Kirkland, Inc., San Bernardino, Calif., 1958-74; design-install estimator Add-M Electric, Inc., 1972-82, v.p., 1974-82; estimator, engr. Corona Indsl. Electric, Inc. (Calif.), 1982-83; asst. project engr. Fischbach and Moore, Inc., Los Angeles, 1984—. Episcopalian. Club: Arrowhead Country (San Bernardino). Home: 526 E Sonora St San Bernardino CA 92404 Office: Fischbach & Moore Inc 4932 Worth St Los Angeles CA 90063

KIRKORIAN, DONALD GEORGE, college official, management consultant; b. San Mateo, Calif., Nov. 30, 1938; s. George and Alice (Sergius) K. BA, San Jose State U., 1961, MA, 1966, postgrad., 1968; postgrad., Stanford U., 1961, U. So. Calif., 1966; PhD, Northwestern U., 1972. Producer Sta. KNTV, San Jose, Calif., 1961; tchr. L.A. City Schs., 1963; instrnl. TV coord. Fremont Union High Sch. Dist., Sunnyvale, Calif., 1963-73; assoc. dean instrn. learning resources Solano Community Coll., Suisun City, Calif., 1973-85, dean instrnl. services, 1985—; owner, pres. Kirkorian and Assocs., Suisun City; field cons. Nat. Assn. Edn. Broadcasters, 1966-68; extension faculty San Jose State U., 1968-69, U. Calif. Santa Cruz, 1970-73, U. Calif. Davis, 1973-76; chmn. Bay Area TV Consortium, 1976-77, 86-87; mem. adv. panel Speech Communication Assn./Am. Theater Assn. tchr. preparation in speech, communication, theater and media, N.Y.C., 1973-77. Editor: Media Memo, 1973-80, Intercom: The Newsletter for Calif. Community Coll. Librarians, 1974-75, Update, 1980—, Exploring the Benicia State Recreation Area, 1977, California History Resource Materials, 1977, Time Management, 1980; contbr. articles to profl. jours. chmn. Solano County Media Adv. Com., 1974-76; bd. dirs. Napa-Solano United Way, 1980-82; mem. adv. bd. Calif. Youth Authority, 1986—. Mem. Nat. Assn. Ednl. Broadcasters, Assn. for Edn. Communications and Tech., Broadcast Edn. Assn., Calif. Assn. Ednl. Media and Tech. (treas.), Western Ednl. Soc. for Telecommunications (bd. dirs. 1973-75, pres. 1976-77, State Chancellor's com. on Telecommunications 1982-86), Learning Resources Assn. Calif. Community Colls. (exec. dir. 1976—, sec.-treas.), Assn. Calif. Community Coll. Adminstrs. (bd. dirs. 1985—), Phi Delta Kappa. Home: 1655 Rockville Rd Suisun City CA 94585 Office: Solano Community Coll 4000 Suisun Valley Rd Suisun City CA 94585

KIRKPATRICK, MARGARET ANN, school system administrator, consultant; b. Orange, Tex., Aug. 4, 1946; d. J.D. and Emma Louise (Walker) Heard; m. Michael A. Kirkpatrick, Mar. 23, 1968; children: Melanie Louise, Glen Alfred. BA, U. Okla., 1968, MA, 1970. Tchr. Ark. State U., Beebe, 1978-79; asst. program mgr. Columbia Coll., San Francisco, 1979-81; tchr. Merced (Calif.) Adult Sch. Merced Coll., 1981-85; vice prin. Merced Union High Sch. Dist., 1985—; cons. State Dept. of Edn., Adult Edn., Sacramento, 1985—, Comprehensive Adult and Student Assessment System, San Diego, 1985—, Vocat. Occupational Info. Educators, 1985—. Mem. Refugee Svcs. Adv. Com., Merced, 1986-88. Recipient Supt. Sch. Recognition award, 1988. Office: Merced Adult Sch 50 E 20th St Merced CA 95340

KIRKPATRICK, RICHARD ALAN, internist; b. Rochester, Minn., Jan. 17, 1947; s. Neal R. and Ethel C. (Hull) K.; m. Susan Baxter; children: James N., Ronald S., David B., Mary J. B.A. in Chemistry with honors, U. Wash., 1968, B.S. in Psychology, 1968, M.D., 1972. Intern, resident in internal medicine Mayo Grad. Sch., Rochester, 1972-76, spl. resident in biomed. communications, 1974-75; practice medicine specializing in internal medicine, Longview, Wash., 1976—; sr. ptnr. Internal Medicine Clinic of Longview; mem. clin. faculty U. Wash.; dir. cardiac rehab. program St. John's Hosp. Mem. City Council, Longview; mem. SW Wash. Symphony; bd. dirs. SW Wash. Youth Symphony; pres., bd. dirs. Sta. KLTV. Diplomate Am. Bd. Internal Medicine. Fellow ACP; mem. Wash. State Soc. Internal Medicine (trustee, past pres.), Am. Geriatrics Soc., Am. Soc. Echocardiography, Am. Soc. Internal Medicine, Wash. Med. Assn. (council med. service), Am. Cancer Soc. (local bd. dirs.), Am. Soc. Clin. Oncology, AMA, Am. Med. Writers Assn. Editor: Drug Therapy Abstracts, Wash. Internists; mem. editorial adv. bd. Your Patient and Cancer, Primary Care and Cancer; weekly med. TV talk show host, 1978—; contbr. articles to med. jours. Office: PO Box 578 748 14th Ave Longview WA 98632

KIRKPATRICK, RONALD LEE, food company executive; b. Rapid City, S.D., June 2, 1950; s. Archibald Thomas and Genevieve (Mae) K.; m. Linda Lee Steinmetz, Sept. 20, 1981; 1 child, Grant Michael. BA in Journalism, Calif. State U., Fullerton. Staff writer Register newspaper, Santa Ana, Calif., 1977-78; pub. info. officer Santa Ana Coll., 1978-79; account supr. Bob Thomas and Assocs., Redondo Beach, Calif., 1979-82; area pub. relations mgr. Adolph Coors Co., Lakewood, Calif., 1982-84; community relations regional mgr. Adolph Coors Co., Cerritos, Calif., 1984—; planner Adolph Coors Black Fair Share Agreement, Los Angeles and Golden, Colo., 1984. Recipient Lulu award, Los Angeles Ad Club, 1981. Mem. Pub. Relations Soc. Am., Publicity Club of Los Angeles, Orange County Press Club (v.p. 1977, bd. dirs. 1978, Best Story on Fire Prevention, 1975, 76). Office: Coors Community Rels 10900 183rd St #390 Cerritos CA 90701

KIRLIKOVALI, ERGUN, manufacturing company executive; b. Izmir, Turkey, Oct. 31, 1952; came to U.S. 1978; s. Ratip and Munire K.; m. Juliana M. Kirlikovali, Apr. 22, 1978. BS in Chemistry, Bogazici U., Istanbul, Turkey, 1974; MS in Poly. Sci., U. Manchester, Eng., 1975. Product devel. chemist Adhesive Enging. Co., San Carlos, Calif., 1978-81, Narmco/Celanese, Costa Mesa, Calif., 1981-82; chief chemist Belzona Molecular, Inc., Uniondale, N.Y., 1982-83; v.p. Belzona Molecular, Inc., 1983-85; pres. Integrated Polymer Ind., Santa Ana, Calif., 1985—. Contbr. articles to profl.

jours. Mem. Soc. Plastics Engrs. (epoxy formulators div.), ASTM, Adhesives & Sealants Council, Am. Turkish Assn. So. Calif. (Named Turkish-Am. of the Year 1988), Fedn. Turkish Am. Soc. (Disting. svc. award 1984), Assembly of Turkish Am. Assns. Republican. Office: Integrated Polymer Ind 1430P Village Way Santa Ana CA 92705

KIRLIN, JOHN JOSEPH, public administration educator; b. Louisville, Sept. 1, 1941; s. John Clement and Hazel Rose (Van Tuyl) K.; m. Anne Marget Gullickson, Aug. 18, 1968; children: Kristin, Heather. BA, U. Notre Dame, 1963; MPA, UCLA, 1966, PhD, 1969. Vol. Peace Corps, Chile, 1963-65; asst. prof. pub. adminstrn. U. So. Calif., L.A., 1969-73, assoc. prof., 1973-80, assoc. dean, 1974-75, interim dean, 1975-76, prof., 1980—; Olson prof. pub.-pvt. entrepreneurship U. So. Calif., Sacramento, 1985—; cons.to com. on 21 League of Calif. Cities, Sacramento, 1986—; cons. Kidder-Peabody, San Francisco, 1986-87, Wells Fargo, San Francisco, 1986-87; mem. bd. economists Calif. Bus. mag., L.A., 1987—. Author: Political Economy of Land Use, 1982, (with others) How Cities Produce Services, 1974; author, co-editor: (ann. book series) California Policy Choices, 1984-85, 87-88. Mem. select com. on jails County of Napa, Calif., 1987, Napa County Grand Jury, 1985-86; chmn. Gov's. Com. on Govtl. Reform, Sacramento, 1978-79. Grantee William and Flora Hewlett Found., 1984—, NSF, 1971-73, U.S. Dept. Housing and Urban Devel., 1978-79; fellow in internat. devel. Ford Found., 1965-66. Mem. Nat. Acad. of Pub. Adminstrn., Am. Soc. for Pub. Adminstrn., Am. Polit. Sci. Assn., Napa Valley Vintners Assn. (fin. com. 1987, bd. dirs. 1989—), The Wine Inst., Napa Valley Country Club, Commonwealth Club. Democrat. Roman Catholic. Office: U So Calif 1201 J St Sacramento CA 95814

KIRMSER, LAWRENCE PHILIP, musician, educator, writer; b. St. Paul, Oct. 6, 1945; s. Philip George and Jeune Ethel (Blomquist) K.; m. Sally Ann Deetjen, Sept. 3, 1971 (div. 1977); 1 child, Philip James. Student, Kans. State U., 1971. Quality control supr. W.T. Armstrong, Elkhart, Ind., 1971-73; pres. Mus. Inst. Techs., Inc., South Bend, Ind., 1973-77; pub., pres. Nat. Assn. Instrument Techs. Jour., South Bend, 1977-79; instr. Renton (Wash.) Vocat. Tech. Inst., 1979--; nat. svc. rep. Yamaha Mus. Inst. Corp., Grand Rapids, Mich. Contbr. numerous articles regarding mus. instrument tech. and maintenance; author: A Business Guide to the Operations & Management of the Musical Instrument Repair Facility, 1987. With USN, 1963-68. Recipient Vietnam Svc. medal USN, 1964, Vietnam Expdn. medal, 1964, Good Conduct medal, 1967. Mem. Guild Am. Luthiers, Gatgut Acoustical Soc., Internat. Double Reed Soc., Nat. Flute Soc. (pres., founder), Nat. Assn. Mus. Instrument Tech. Unitarian. Home: 42755 SE 172d Pl North Bend WA 98045 Office: Renton Vocat Tech Inst 3000 NE 4th St Renton WA 98056

KIRNAN, COLEEN LORENA, commercial development leasing agent; b. L.A., Aug. 23, 1962; d. Thomas Leo and Jean Elizabeth (Bender) K. BS in Cadiac Rehab., U. London, 1986, Calif. State U., Northridge, 1985. Cardiac technician Kensington Hosp., London, 1985-86; leasing agt. Riley/Pearlman Co., L.A., 1986—; bd. dirs., co-founder Women in Retail Estate, L.A. Participant SD Half Marathon, San Diego, 1987, 50 Mile Rosarito-Ensendada Bike Ride, Mex., 1984-89; mem. Granada Hills (Calif.) C. of C., 1985, Palos Verdes (Calif.) C. of C., 1986-87, Big Sisters L.A. Mem. Internat. Coun. Shopping Ctrs., Nat. Assn. Working Women, Scuba Club. Roman Catholic. Home: 2437 Corinth 111 West Los Angeles CA 90064 Office: Riley Pearlman Co 11640 San Vicente Blvd 202 Los Angeles CA 90064

KIRONDE-KIGOZI, SAMS SENDAWULA, data processing executive; b. Mityana, Uganda, Oct. 17, 1943; s. Samson Kironde and Solome (Nalukwago) Birabwa; m. Alice Norah, Jan. 18, 1970 (dec. June 1975); children: Solome Nampala, Don Wassanyi; m. Flavia Nakawombe, Feb. 25, 1984; children: Andrew Joseph Sempala, Isaac Philip Kisitu. Cert. edn., Makerere U., Kampala, Uganda; Dip. TH candidate, Trinity Coll., Bristol, Eng.; MABS, Covenant Sem., St. Louis, 1980; D of Theology, Internat. Seminary, Orlando, Fla., 1989. Tchr. Namutamba Sch., Kampala, Uganda, 1966; depot mgr. Brooke Bond Ltd., Kamuli, Uganda, 1966-71; ter. mgr. Wrigley Co. E.A., Kampala, 1971-72; asst. pastor Redeemed Ch., Kampala, 1971-73; computer operator Sauer Computers, St. Louis, 1977-79; data processing mgr. Anheuser-Busch, Inc., Sylmar, Calif., 1980—. Exec. sec. Com. on Uganda, Inc., Van Nuys, Calif. 1978—; sec. Uganda Human Rights League, Washington, 1982-83; chmn. Ugandan Com. Dem. Assn., Los Angeles, 1982-84. Home: 6541 Kester Ave Van Nuys CA 91411 Office: Anheuser Busch 15420 Cobalt Sylmar CA 91342

KIRSCH, RALPH M., oil company executive; b. Burton, Nebr., Nov. 15, 1928; s. George J. Kirsch and Gladys Hudson; m. Delores M. Birkel, Feb. 3, 1952; children: Michael, Alan. BS in Edn., U. Nebr.-Lincoln, 1953; JD, U. Wyo., 1956. Bar: Wyo. 1956, Utah 1961. Spl. asst. to atty. gen. State of Wyo., Cheyenne, 1957-59; legal dept. Mountain Fuel Supply, Salt Lake City, 1959-74, mgr. contracts, lands, 1974-79; exec. v.p. Wexpro Co., Salt Lake City, 1977-80, pres., chief exec. officer, 1980—; pres., chief exec. officer Celsius Energy Co., Salt Lake City, 1982—, also dir., 1982—; dir. Entrada Industries, Inc., Salt Lake City, 1982—, Wexpro Co., 1976—; pres., chief exec. officer Universal Resources Corp., 1988—. Served with USN, 1945-47, 50-51, PTO. Mem. Ind. Petroleum Assn. Am., Rocky Mountain Oil and Gas Assn., Rocky Mountain Mineral Law Found., Utah Petroleum Assn., Domestic Petroleum Council, Utah State Bar Assn., Wyo. State Bar Assn. Office: Wexpro Co 79 S State St Salt Lake City UT 84111

KIRSCH, WARAND RICHARD, industrial designer; b. Duluth, Minn., June 22, 1929; s. Edgar William John and Margaret Erna Marie (Zimmerman) K.; m. Romayne Joyce Spindler, Sept. 11, 1953; children: Sandra Marie, Laurie Jean. Engr. design Brewmatic Div. Farmer Bros. Co., Los Angeles, 1956-70; engr. project Swimquip Inc., El Monte, Calif., 1970-73; pres. Rookey Transfer Co., Superior, Wis., 1974-84; mgr. engring. Brewmatic Div. Farmer Bros. Co., Los Angeles, 1984—. Patentee in field. Served to sgt. USMC, 1950-52, Korea. Mem. Chosin Few. Republican. Lutheran. Home: 15899 Indies Ct Fountain Valley CA 92708 Office: Brewmatic Div Farmer Bros Co 3828 S Main St Los Angeles CA 90037

KIRSCHBAUM, JAMES LOUIS, mortgage banker; b. Missoula, Mont., Oct. 19, 1940; s. Louis Elsworth and Margaret Marie (Lloyd) K.; m. Marilyn Jean McCann, Sept. 5, 1964; children—Kristyn Marie, Heidi Maureen. Student Eastern Wash. U., 1958-61, Whitworth Coll., 1963-65. Vice pres. Far West Securities, Spokane, 1963-73; v.p. Columbia Mortgage, Spokane and Portland, Oreg., 1973-75; regional v.p. Sherwood & Roberts, Spokane, 1975-80; pres., chief exec. officer Bancshares Mortgage, Spokane, 1980-86; exec. v.p. Seafirst Bank, Seattle, 1986—; chmn. Housing Fin. Commn. State of Wash., Seattle, 1983-87. Trustee Eastern Wash. U. Found., Cheney, 1987—; chmn. Leadership Spokane, 1983; pres. United Way, Spokane County, 1984. Served to 1st lt. USAR, 1961-63. Mem. Wash. Mortgage Bankers (pres. 1982-83), Broadmoor Golf Club. Republican. Lutheran. Home: 5819 SW Horton St Seattle WA 98116 Office: Columbia Seafirst Ctr-56 701 5th Ave Seattle WA 98104

KIRSCHNER, RICHARD MICHAEL, naturopathic physician, speaker; b. Cin., Sept. 27, 1949; s. Alan George and Lois (Dickey) K.; 1 child, Aden Netanya. BS in Human Biology, Kans. Newman Coll., 1979; degree in naturopathy, Nat. Coll. Naturopathic Medicine, 198l. Vice pres. D. Kirschner & Son, Inc., Newport, Ky., 1974-77; co-owner, mgr. Sunshine Ranch Arabian Horses, Melbourne, Ky., 1975-77; pvt. practice Portland, Oreg., 198l-83, Ashland, Oreg., 1983—; seminar leader, trainer Inst. for Meta-Linguistics, Portland, 198l-84; speaker, trainer R & R Co. Educating thru Entertainment, Ashland, 1984—, Careertrack Seminars, Boulder, Colo., 1986—; cons. Nat. Elec. Contractors Assn., So. Oreg., 1985, 86, United Telephone N.W., 1986; speaker Ford Motor Co., Blue Cross-Blue Shield, Balfour Corp., Mich. Edn. Assn., Nat. Edn. Assn., Supercuts, 1986-88. Co-author audio tape seminar How To Deal with Difficult People, 1987, video tape seminar, 1988; author audio tape seminar How To Find and Keep a Mate, 1988. Spokesman Rogue Valley PBS, 1986, 87; active Jeff Golden's County Commr. Campaign, 1986. Mem. Am. Assn. Naturopathic Physicians, Wilderness Soc., Postal Commemorative Soc. Republican. Office: R&R Seminars PO Box 896 Ashland OR 97520

KIRSHBAUM, HOWARD M., judge; b. Oberlin, Ohio, Sept. 19, 1938; s. Joseph and Gertrude (Morris) K.; m. Priscilla Joy Parmakian, Aug. 15, 1964; children—Audra Lee, Andrew William. B.A., Yale U., 1960; A.B., Cambridge U., 1962, M.A., 1966; LL.B., Harvard U., 1965. Ptnr. Zarlengo and Kirshbaum, Denver, 1969-75; judge Denver Dist. Ct., Denver, 1975-80, Colo. Ct. Appeals, Denver, 1980-83; justice Colo. Supreme Ct., Denver, 1983—; adj. prof. law U. Denver, 1972—; dir. Colo. Jud. Inst., Denver, Am. Law Inst. Phila., Am. Judicature Soc., Chgo., 1983-85; pres. Colo. Legal Care Soc., Denver, 1974-75. Bd. dirs. Young Artists Orch., Denver, 1976-85; pres. Community Arts Symphony, Englewood, Colo., 1972-74; dir. Denver Opportunity, Inc., Denver, 1972-74; vice-chmn. Denver Council on Arts and Humanities, 1969. Mem. ABA, Denver Bar Assn. (trustee 1981-83), Colo. Bar Assn., Am. Judicature Soc. Office: Colo Supreme Ct 2 E 14th Ave Denver CO 80203

KIRSHNER, EDWARD, urban planner; b. N.Y.C, Aug. 14, 1940; s. Morris N. and Helen S. (Berman) K.; m. Joan P. Scheiman, 1960 (div. 1963); m. Elisabeth Gruber, Dec. 28, 1967 (div. 1977); 1 child, Orin Tove. BArch, U. Calif., Berkeley, 1966; M in City Planning, U. Calif., 1971. Archtl. planner Rouse Co., Columbia, Md., 1966-68; urban and econ. planner Cambridge (Mass) Policy Studies Inst. Ctr. Community Econ. Devel, 1971-72; housing and econ. planner Nat. Housing and Econ. Devel. Law Project, Berkeley, 1972; urban planner Sedway Cooke & Assoc., San Francisco, 1971-72; exec. dir. Community Econs., Inc., Oakland, Calif., 1972-80; dir. housing programs Nat. Consumers' Coop. Bank, Washington, 1980-81; assoc. dir. housing and constrn. Century Freeway Housing Program, Calif. Dept. Housing and Community Devel., Inglewood, Calif., 1982-83; dir. housing and redevel. City of Berkeley, 1986-87; v.p. Affirmative Investments, Inc., San Francisco, Boston, 1983—; vis. lectr. U. Calif. Berkeley, L.A., Santa Barbara, Davis, 1977—; vis. instr. Antioch Coll. W., San Francisco, 1977-80, Lone Mountain Coll. San Francisco, 1977-78; commr., vice-chmn. Santa Monica City Planning Commn., 1984-86. Co-author: The Cities' Wealth, 1976. Bd. alternate Consumers' Corp. Berkeley, 1977; mem. Gov.'s Small Farm Fin. Viability Task Force, Sacramento, 1977; bd. dirs. Oakland Citizens' Com. Urban Renewal, 1979-80; mem. steering com. Santa Monicans for Renters' Rights, 1985-86. Mem. Am. Planning Assn., Social Investment Forum, Planners' Network, Bay Area Socially Responsible Investment Profls. Assn. Democrat. Home: 1539 Shrader San Francisco CA 94117-4235 Office: Affirmative Investments Inc 605 Market St #1111 San Francisco CA 94105-3213

KIRST, WILLIAM JAMES, JR., geophysicist; b. Kenmore, N.Y., June 3, 1923; s. William James and Barbara Louise (Wagner) K.; B.S., Yale U., 1947; postgrad. Casper (Wyo.) Jr. Coll., 1954, Santa Barbara Jr. Coll., 1955, U. Alta., 1960, 67, U. Calgary, 1966, So. Alta. Inst. Tech., 1977, Mt. Royal Coll., Calgary, 1979; m. Frances Patricia Borders, Nov. 19, 1948; children—Dubhe, Heidi, William James, Joshua, Forest, Tracy, Alexander, Whitehorn. Party mgr., party chief, computer Western Geophys. Co., Wyo., Utah, Colo., N.D., Mont., Calif., 1948-55, Alta., B.C., N.W.T., Can., Arctic, 1955-66; No. dist. physicist Canadian Pacific Oil and Gas Co. Ltd., Calgary, Alta., Can., 1966-67; geophys. cons. Kirst Exploration, Calgary, 1967—, Voyager Energy Co., 1985-86, Virago Energy Corp., 1986-87; pres., chmn. bd. Marazan Petroleums Ltd., Marazan Petroleums Inc., Lochfayne Resources Inc., 1983—; dir. cable TV show; photographer, owner Kirst Photographers studio; photographer Calgary Real Estate Bd.; pres. 267313 Atla. Ltd.; dir. Take 5 Graphic Arts Ltd. Voluntary resource person, bd. dirs. Calgary Drug Info. Centre, 1970-81; pres. Southwood Community Assn., 1962, 63; pres. Calgary Boys and Girls Band and Baton Corps, 1966-67; chmn. bd. dirs. Calgary Distress Centre/Drug Centre, 1980-81. Served with USMC, 1943-46. Registered profl. engr., Alta.; profl. geophysicist, Alta.; geophysicist, Calif.; pvt. pilot. Mem. Can. Soc. Exploration Geophysicists, Yale Football Y Assn., Nat. Football Found. and Hall of Fame, Yale Sci. and Engring. Assn., Calgary Flying Club, Can. Owners and Pilots Assn., Am. Yankee Assn., St. Elmo Soc., Soc. Exploration Geophysicists, Alta. Aviation Council, Can. C. of C. Attempted circumnavigation of Banks Island, Arctic Ocean, in kayak with son, 1971. Home: 3809 Elbow Dr SW, Calgary, AB Canada T2S 2J9

KIRTLEY, ROBERT BASSETT, computer software company executive; b. Oklahoma City, Apr. 22, 1949; s. Bayless Edward and Verlyne Imojean (Bassett) K.; m. Deidre Sue Zaffos, May l, 1970 (div. Apr. 1974); m. Pamela Lynne Copper, Sept. 22, 1984. BA, Okla. State U., 197l. Sales rep., buyer Am. Timber Products Co., Oklahoma City, 197l-76; regional mgr. Synflex, Inc., Oklahoma City, 1977-78; v.p. sales and mktg. Kirtley Systems, Oklahoma City, 1979-83, Digital Software Corp., Inc., Wichita, Kans., 1984-87, Am. Fundware, Inc., Steamboat Springs, Colo., 1988—. Contbr. articles to profl. jours. Ofcl. Okla. Secondary Athletic Assn., 1974-79; umpire Amateur Softball Umpires Assn., 1985-87. Mem. N.Am. Data Gen. Users Group. Democrat. Baptist. Home: PO Box 880128 Steamboat Springs CO 80488 Office: Am Fundware Inc PO Box 773028 Steamboat Springs CO 80477

KIRTS, WAYNE CHARLES, interior designer; b. Terre Haute, Ind., Aug. 9, 1934; s. Harold Murray and Juanita June (DuChane) K.; m. Melinda Suzanne Peacock, Jan. 18, 1959 (div. 1963); children: Daren Arthur Laurence. Student, Ind. State U., 1952-54; student, U. Cin., 1954-55; BA, UCLA, 1957. Interior designer Adele Faulkner, FASID, Inc., L.A., 1957-67; interior designer Arthur Elrod, AID, Inc., Palm Springs, Calif., 1957-67, Virginia Douglas, AID, Inc., Bel Air, Calif., 1967-81, Kirts Assocs., Beverly Hills, Calif., 1967-81; owner, interior designer Kirts Assocs., Scottsdale, Ariz., 1981-86, San Diego, 1986—; instr. interior design UCLA, 1973-81, Mesa Community Coll., San Diego, 1987—, Scottsdale (Ariz.) Community Coll., 1983-86. Contbr. articles to profl. jours. Mem. Am. Soc. Interior Designers (chpt. v.p. 1969-71, 1st v.p. 1987-88, pres. 1989).

KIRWIN, JACQUELINE MARIE, rates analyst; b. Newport, R.I., Feb. 27, 1965; d. Edward Francis and Joanne Marie (Glynn) K. BA, Smith Coll., 1987. Rates analyst Pacific Gas and Electric Co., San Francisco, 1987—. Mem. NAFE, Pacific Svcs. Employees Assn., Pacific Coast Elec. Assn., Smith Coll. Alumnae Assn., Smith Coll. Club San Francisco and Marin Counties, Sigma Xi. Roman Catholic. Office: Pacific Gas & Electric Co 77 Beale St Rm 901 San Francisco CA 94106

KISER, ELLIS EUGENE, police chief; b. North Platte, Nebr., Feb. 22, 1936; s. Coy D. and Dorthy M. (Todd) K.; m. LuElla M. Faught, June 7, 1958; 1 son, Tim E. Student Eastern Mont. Coll., 1955-59. With Billings (Mont.) Police Dept., 1961—, chief of police, 1977—. Bd. dirs. Mont. Bd. Crime Control, 1981—. Mem. Internat. Assn. Chiefs of Police, Mont. Police Chiefs Assn. Baptist. Club: Exchange. Office: Billings Police Dept PO Box 1554 Billings MT 59101 *

KISER, NAGIKO SATO, librarian; b. Taipei, Republic of China, Aug. 7, 1923; came to U.S., 1950; d. Takeichi and Kinue (Sooma) Sato; m. Virgil Kiser, Dec. 4, 1979 (dec. Mar. 1981). Secondary teaching credential, Tsuda Coll., Tokyo, 1945; BA in Journalism, Trinity U., 1953; BFA, Ohio State U., 1956, MA in Art History, 1959; MLS, cert. in library media, SUNY, Albany, 1974. Cert. community coll. librarian, Calif., cert. jr. coll. tchr., Calif., cert. secondary edn. tchr., Calif., cert. tchr. library media specialist and art, N.Y. Pub. relations reporter The Mainichi Newspapers, Osaka, Japan, 1945-50; contract interpreter U.S. Dept. State, Washington, 1956-58, 66-67; resource specialist Richmond (Calif.) Unified Sch. Dist., 1968-69; editing supr. CTB/McGraw-Hill, Monterey, Calif., 1969-71; multi-media specialist Monterey Peninsula Unified Sch. Dist., 1975-77; librarian Nishimachi International Sch., Tokyo, 1979-80, Sacramento City Unified Sch. Dist., 1977-79, 81-85; sr. librarian Camarillo (Calif.) State Hosp., 1985—. Editor: Short Form Test of Academic Aptitude, 1970, Prescriptive Mathematics Inventory, 1970, Tests of Basic Experience, 1970. Mem. Calif. State Supt.'s Regional Council on Asian Pacific Affairs, Sacramento, 1984—. Library Media Specialist Tng. Program scholar U.S. Office Edn., 1974. Fellow Internat. Biographical Assn. (life); mem. ALA, AAUW, Calif. Library Assn., Calif. Media and Library Educators Assn., Asunaro Shoogai Kyooiku Kondankai (Lifetime Edn. Promoting Assn.) (Japan), The Mus. Soc., Internat. House of Japan, Matsuyama Sacramento Sister City Corp., Japanese Am. Citizens League, UN Assn. U.S., Ikenoboo Ikebana Soc. Am., Los Angeles Hototogisu Haiku Assn., Ventura County Archeol. Soc. Mem. Christian Science Ch. Office: Camarillo State Hosp Profl Libr Box A 1878 S Lewis Rd Camarillo CA 93011-1350

KISER, ROBERTA KATHERINE, daycare administrator; b. Alton, Ill., Aug. 13, 1938; d. Stephen Robert and Virginia Elizabeth (Lasher) Golden; m. James Robert Crisman, sept. 6, 1958 (div. May 1971); 1 child, Robert Glenn; m. James Earl Kiser, Dec. 19, 1971; 1 child, James Jacob. BEd, So. Ill. U., 1960. Cert. tchr., Ill., Calif. Librarian Oaklawn (Ill.) Elem. Sch., 1960-62, Alsip (Ill.) Elem. Sch., 1966-69; tchr. Desert Sands Unified Sch. Dist., Indio, Calif., 1969-79; prin. Mothercare Infant Sch., Rancho Mirage, Calif., 1980—. V.p. Palm Desert (Calif.) Community Ch. Montessori Sch. Bd., 1982—85. Republican. Presbyterian. Home and Office: Mothercare Infant Sch 39-575 Keenan Dr Rancho Mirage CA 92270

KISHIYAMA, CRAIG AKIRA, orthodontist; b. Inglewood, Calif., Apr. 17, 1958; s. Hare Takashi and Meriko (Miyagishima) K.; m. Janice Michiko Arita, May 18, 1985. BS, U. So. Calif., 1980, DDS, 1984; MS in Dentistry, Case Western Res. U., 1987. Gen. practice dentistry, Los Angeles, 1984-85; practice dentistry specializing in orthodontics, Anaheim, Calif., 1987—; instr. periodontology U. So. Calif., Los Angeles, 1984-85; instr. orthodontic lab. Case Western Res. U., Cleve., 1986-87. Mem. ADA, Am. Assn. Orthodontists, Pacific Coast Soc. Orthodontists (assoc.). Baptist. Office: 1314 S Euclid Ste 2 Anaheim CA 92802

KISSEE, CHARLES NORMAN, aerospace engineer, computer programmer; b. Concord, Calif., July 6, 1958; s. Marvin E. and Mildred A. (Poelke) K.; m. Barbara A. Latty, Sept. 15, 1984; children: Andrew, Charles. Student, Calif. Poly. State U., 1983-84; AS in Engring. and Computer Sci. with honors, Sierra Community Coll., 1984; BS in Aerospace Engring., U. So. Calif., 1987. Maintenance man Driftwood Village Apts., Auburn, Calif., 1981-82; tchr.'s aide Sierra Community Coll., Rocklin, Calif., 1982-83; carpenter Al J. Patrick, Auburn, 1983; engr. Northrop Co., L.A., 1984-87; rsch. engr., sr. assoc. engr. Lockheed Missiles & Space Co., Sunnyvale, Calif., 1987—; owner Chuck's Handyman Svc., Sunnyvale, 1988—. Sgt. USAF, 1976-80. Mem. Nat. Mgmt. Assn., Sigma Gamma Tau. Republican. Office: Lockheed Missiles & Space Co 1111 Lockheed Way Box 504 0/81-15 B/157-5E Sunnyvale CA 94088

KISSEL, PHILLIP, neurosurgeon; b. Chgo., Jan. 18, 1954; s. Edwin and Hilda (Bock) K.; m. Janice E. Blair, June, 1984; children: Bianca Elizabeth, Marguerite Blair. BA, U. Calif., 1976; MD, U. Chgo., 1983. Diplomate Am. Bd. Neurol. Surgery. Intern Harbor Gen. Hosp., Los Angeles, 1983-84; resident in neurol. surgery U. Calif., Sacramento, 1984-89, chief resident neurol. surgery, 1988-89. Contbr. articles on stroke research to profl. jours. Mem. Physicians for Social Responsibilities, 1987—. Mem. AMA, Am. Coll. Surgeons, Assn. Neurol. Surgeons, Calif. Assn. Neurol. Surgeons. Office: U Calif Davis 4301 X St Sacramento CA 95817

KISSNER, JON ANDREW, city official, international trade consultant; b. Delaware, Ohio, July 22, 1952; s. Paul Dewitt and Lois (Ahlman) K.; m. Debbie Anne Neel, July 25, 1987; 1 child, Jessica Anne. BS in Polit. Sci., Ariz. State U., 1974. Vice pres. spl. projects Mont. Internat. Trade Commn., Butte and Helena, 1974-79; pres. Mont. Export Co., Great Falls, 1979-84; exec. dir. Las Cruces (N. Mex.) Econ. Devel. Coun., 1985--; mem. dist. export coun. U.S. Dept. Commerce, 1985--; co-chmn. tech. resources group N. Mex. Border Commn. Organizing mem. Las Cruces Forum, 1985. Recipient Spl. Achievement award Office Mont. Gov., 1978. Mem. N.Mex. Indsl. Devel. Execs. Assn. (bd. dirs. 1985--), El Paso Fgn. Trade Assn. (ex-officio bd. 1985--). Methodist. Home: 1945 N Alameda Las Cruces NM 88005 Office: Las Cruces Econs Devel Coun 400 S Main St Las Cruces NM 88005

KITADA, SHINICHI, biochemist; b. Osaka, Japan, Dec. 9, 1948; came to U.S., 1975; s. Koichi and Asako Kitada; MD, Kyoto U., 1973; MS in Biol. Chemistry (Japan Soc. Promotion Sci. fellow 1975-76), UCLA, 1977, PhD, 1979. Intern, Kyoto U. Hosp., 1973-74, resident physician Chest Disease Research Inst., 1974-75; research scholar lab. nuclear medicine and radiation biology UCLA, 1979-87, Jules Stein Eye Inst. UCLA, 1988—. Mem. Am. Oil Chemists Soc., N.Y. Acad. Scis., Sigma Xi. Author papers in field. Home: 478 Landfair Ave Apt 5 Los Angeles CA 90024 Office: UCLA Jules Stein Eye Inst 800 Westwood Pla Los Angeles CA 90024

KITCHEN, LAWRENCE OSCAR, aircraft/aerospace corporation executive; b. Ft. Mill, S.C., June 8, 1923; s. Samuel Sumpter and Ruby Azalee (Grigg) K.; m. Brenda Lenhart, Nov. 25, 1978; children by previous marriage: Brenda, Alan, Janet. Ed., Foothill Coll. Aero. engr. U.S. Navy Bur. Aeronautics, Washington, 1946-58; staff asst. to asst. chief bur. U.S. Navy Bur. Aeronautics, 1958; with Lockheed Missiles & Space Co., Sunnyvale, Calif., 1958-70; mgr. product support logistics Lockheed Missiles & Space Co., 1964-68, dir. fin. controls, 1968-70; v.p.-fin. Lockheed-Ga. Co., Marietta, 1970-71; pres. Lockheed-Ga. Co., 1971-75; pres. Lockheed Corp., Burbank, Calif., 1975-76, pres., chief operating officer, 1976-85, chmn. bd. dirs., chief exec. officer, 1986-88, chmn. exec. com., also bd. dirs., 1989—; bd. dirs. Security Pacific Corp. Mem. nominating com. Aviation Hall of Fame. With USMC, 1942-46. Mem. Nat. Def. Transp. Assn., AIAA, Navy League, Soc. Logistics Engrs., Air Force Assn., Assn. U.S. Army. Clubs: North Ranch, Lakeside Golf. Office: Lockheed Corp 4500 Park Granada Blvd Calabasas CA 91399

KITTEL, PETER, research scientist; b. Fairfax, Va., Mar. 23, 1945; s. Charles and Muriel (Lister) K.; m. Mary Ellen Murchio, Aug. 12, 1972; 1 child, Katherine. BS, U. Calif., Berkeley, 1967; MS, U. Calif., La Jolla, 1969; PhD, Oxford U., 1974. Res. asst. U. Calif., La Jolla, 1967-69, Oxford (Eng.) U., 1969-74; res. assoc., adj. assoc. prof. U. Oreg., Eugene, 1974-78; res. assoc. Stanford (Calif.) U., 1978; res. assoc. Nat. Res. Council Ames Res. Ctr. NASA, Moffett Field, Calif., 1978-80, res. scientist, 1980—; dir. Cryogenic Engring. Conf., 1983-89. Contbr. articles to profl. jours. Nat. Res. Council fellow, 1978-80, Oxford U. fellow, 1972-74. Mem. Am. Phys. Soc., AAAS. Home: 3132 Morris Dr Palo Alto CA 94303 Office: NASA 244-10 Ames Research Ctr Moffett Field CA 94035

KITTELL, ROBERT STANTON, security services executive; b. Beaumont, Tex., July 30, 1943; s. Robert Dale and Wylie Elizabeth (Stanton) K.; m. Mary Elizabeth Panek, Aug. 17, 1963; children: Kristine Anne Costello, Debra Kay. BA, U. Nebr., 1972, MS, 1977. Cert. protection profl. Enlisted USAF, 1961, advanced through grades to major, 1961-86; ret. 1986; security analyst Trident Data Systems, Los Angeles, 1986—; cons. New Dimensions Internat., Rockville, Md., 1987—; cons. Albuquerque Police Dept., 1984-86. Contbr. articles to profl. jours.; speaker in field. Mem. Am. Soc. Indsl. Security, Am. Def. Preparedness Assn., Air Force Assn. (life), Phi Alpha Theta. Republican. Lutheran. Office: Trident Data Systems 5933 W Century Blvd Ste 700 Los Angeles CA 90045

KITTO, FRANKLIN CURTIS, computer systems specialist; b. Salt Lake City, Nov. 18, 1954; s. Curtis Eugene and Margaret (Ipson) K.; m. Collette Madsen, Sept. 16, 1982; children: Melissa Erin, Heather Elise. BA, Brigham Young U., 1978, MA, 1980. Tv sta. operator Sta. KBYU-TV, Provo, Utah, 1973-78; cable TV system operator Instructional Media U. Utah, Salt Lake City, 1980-82, data processing mgr., 1982-83, media supr., 1983-85, bus. mgr., 1985-87; dir. computer systems tng. MegaWest Systems, Inc., Salt Lake City, 1987—. Recipient Kiwanis Freedom Leadership award, Salt Lake City, 1970, Golden Microphone award Brigham Young U., 1978. Mem. Assn. Ednl. Communications and Tech., Utah Pick Users Group (sec. 1983—87, pres. 1987-89, treas. 1989—), Am. Soc. Tng. and Devel., Phi Eta Sigma, Kappa Tau Alpha. Mormon. Home: 8892 Flatiron Dr Sandy UT 84093 Office: MegaWest Systems Inc 345 Bearcat Dr Salt Lake City UT 84115

KITZHABER, JOHN ALBERT, physician, state senator; b. Colfax, Wash., Mar. 5, 1947; s. Albert Raymond and Annabel Reed (Wetzel) K. BA, Dartmouth Coll., 1969; MD, U. Oreg., 1973. Intern Gen. Rose Meml. Hosp., Denver, 1976-77; Emergency physician Mercy Hosp., Roseburg, Oreg., 1974-75; mem. Oreg. Ho. of Reps., 1979-81; mem. Oreg. Senate, 1981—, pres., 1985—; assoc. prof. Oreg. Health Sci. U., 1986—. Mem. Am. Coll. Emergency Physicians, Douglas County Med. Soc., Physicians for Social Responsibility, Am. Council Young Polit. Leaders, Oreg. Trout. Democrat. Home: 1033 W Brown Roseburg OR 97470 Office: Senate Pres S-203 State Capitol Salem OR 97310

KIUCHI, TAKASHI, electronics company executive; b. Hamburg, Fed. Republic Germany, Jan. 6, 1935; s. Nobutane and Tayo (Shidachi) K.; m. Kyoko Tsutsumi, Aug. 3, 1965; children: Shintaro, Reijiro, Eriko, Junzaburo. BA, Keio U, Tokyo, 1958; MA, U. B.C., Vancouver, Can., 1960; program for sr. execs., MIT, 1980. Exec. v.p. Mitsubishi Electric Am., L.A., 1974-76; pres., chmn. Mitsubishi Electric Am., Cypress, Calif., 1988—; gen. mgr. Mitsubishi Electric Corp., Tokyo, 1981-87. Co-author: Management Challenge, 1985. Home: 17 Hilltop Circle Rancho Palos Verdes CA 90274 Office: Mitsubishi Electric Am 5757 Plaza Dr Cypress CA 90630

KIVELSON, MARGARET GALLAND, physicist; b. N.Y.C., Oct. 21, 1928; d. Walter Isaac and Madeleine (Wiener) Galland; m. Daniel Kivelson, Aug. 15, 1949; children: Steven Allan, Valerie Ann. AB, Radcliffe Coll., 1950, AM, 1951, PhD, 1957. Cons. Rand Corp., Santa Monica, Calif., 1956-69; asst. to geophysicist UCLA, 1967-83, prof., 1983—, also chmn. dept. earth and space scis., 1984-87; prin. investigator of magnetometer, Galileo Mission, Jet Propulsion Lab., Pasadena, Calif., 1977—; overseer Harvard Coll., 1977-83; mem. adv. council NASA, 1987-89; chair adv. com. NSF, Com. Solar and Space Physics, 1977-86, com. planetary exploration, 1986-87. Editor: The Solar System: Observations and Interpretations, 1986; contbr. articles to profl. jours. Named Woman of Yr., Los Angeles Mus. Sci. and Industry, 1979, Woman of Sci., UCLA, 1984; recipient Grad. Soc. medal Radcliffe Coll., 1983, 350th Anniversary Alumni medal Harvard U. Mem. Am. Geophysics Union, Am. Phys. Soc., Am. Astron. Soc.; fellow AAAS. Office: UCLA Dept Earth & Space Scis 6843 Slichter Los Angeles CA 90024

KJOME, NORMAN T., atmospheric physics researcher; b. Spring Grove, Minn., Nov. 24, 1944; m. Peny Goodson-Kjome. BA, St. Olaf Coll., 1966. Research asst. U. Minn., Mpls., 1967-69; research assoc. U. Wyo., Laramie, 1969--. Patentee in field. Office: U Wyo Dept Physics and Astronomy Laramie WY 82071

KJOS, VICTORIA ANN, lawyer; b. Fargo, N.D., Sept. 17, 1953; d. Orville I. and Annie J. (Tanberg) K. BA, Minot State U., 1974; JD, U. N.D., 1977. Bar: Ariz. 1978. Assoc. Jack E. Evans, Ltd., Phoenix, 1977-78, pension and ins. cons., 1978-79; dep. state treas. State of N.D., Bismarck, 1979-80; free-lance cons. Phoenix, 1980-81, Anchorage, 1981-82; asst. v.p., v.p., mgr. trust dept. Great Western Bank, Phoenix, 1982-84; assoc. Robert A. Jensen P.C., Phoenix, 1984-86; ptnr. Jensen & Kjos, P.C., Phoenix, 1986-89; assoc. Allen, Kimerer & LaVelle, Phoenix, 1989—; lectr. in domestic relations. Contbr. articles to profl. jours. Mem. Ariz. Dem. Coun., Western Pension Conf.; bd. dirs. Arthritis Found., Phoenix, 1986-89, v.p. for chpt. devel., 1988-89. Mem. ABA, Ariz. Bar Assn. (exec. coun. family law sect.), Maricopa Bar Assn. (family law com 1988-89, pres. 1989—), Assn. Trial Lawyers Am., Ariz. Trial Lawyers Assn., Ariz. Women's Lawyers Assn., NOW, Phi Delta Phi. Office: Allen Kimerer & LaVelle 2715 N 3rd St Phoenix AZ 85004

KLAAR, RICHARD, aerospace engineer; b. Novi Vrbas, Vodjvodina, Yugoslavia, Oct. 6, 1941; s. Richard and Katharina (Greiling) K.; m. Kay Murray, Apr. 26, 1964; children: Richard Raymond, Raymond Richard. Diploma, Metals Engring. Inst., 1986. Welding technician Sea-train Shipbldg., N.Y.C., 1973-75; foreman welding Nat. Steel & Shipbldg. Co., San Diego, 1975-76, gen. foreman welding, 1976-77, welding engr., 1977-82, welding engr. sr., 1982-87; mfg. tech. engr. Gen. Dynamics space systems div., San Diego, 1987-88, mfg. engring. specialist, 1988—. Mem. welding adv. bd. San Diego Community Coll., 1980-89. Mem. Am. Soc. Nondestructive Testing, Am. Soc. Metals, Am. Welding Soc., Nat. Mgmt. Assn. Republican. Home: 10962 Columbus St Santee CA 92071

KLAD, JEFFREY SANFORD, lawyer, accountant; b. Cleve., May 17, 1949; s. Jack and Pauline (Kessler) K. BBA cum laude, Boston U., 1971; MBA, Northwestern U., 1972; JD, Cleve. State U., 1977. Bar: Ill. 1977, U.S. Dist. Ct. (no. dist.) Ill. 1977. Tax atty. Kraft, Inc., Glenview, Ill., 1977-80, Internat. Harvester, Chgo., 1980-82; asst. treas., legal counsel G-R-I Corp., Chgo., 1982-84; tax mgr. Chgo. Tribune, 1984-87; pvt. practice tax atty., Beverly Hills, Calif., 1987-89, Santa Monica, Calif., 1989—. Mem., adviser HB Meml. Clinic, Chgo., 1982-86; active worker Democratic Party, Chgo., 1984. Mem. ABA, Am. Inst. CPAs, Chgo. Bar Assn., Calif. Bar Assn., Calif. CPA Soc., L.A. Bus. & Profl. League, LA. Club. Jewish. Avocations: theatre, travel, vintage cars. Home and Office: 1940 N Highland #21 Hollywood CA 90068

KLAISNER, LOWELL ALAN, engineer consultant; b. San Francisco, Dec. 30, 1938; s. William and Clara Elizabeth (Gray) K.; m. Sharon Louise Burkitt. BSEE, Stanford U., 1960; MSEE, Standard U., 1961; MBA, U. Wash., 1989. Registered profl. engr., Wash. Electronic engr. Argonne (Ill.) Nat. Lab., 1961-68; chief engr. Fermilab, Batavia, Ill., 1968-72; v.p. Kinetic Systems Corp., Lockport, Ill., 1972-77; group mgr. Eldec Corp., Lynnwood, Wash., 1977-80; v.p. Intermec Corp., Lynnwood, 1980-88; cons. Lowell A. Klaisner & Assoc., Bothell, Wash., 1988-89; head. electronics dept. Stanford (Calif.) Linear Accelerator Ctr., 1989—. Mem. Instrument Soc. Am., Computer and Automated Systems Assn. SME,Soc. Mfg. Engrs., Nat. Bus. Honor Soc., IEEE, Beta Gamma Sigma. Office: SLAC PO Box 4349 Stanford CA 94309

KLAKEG, CLAYTON HAROLD, cardiologist; b. Big Woods, Minn., Mar. 31, 1920; s. Knute O. and Agnes (Folvik) K.; student Concordia Coll., Moorhead, Minn., 1938-40; B.S., N.D. State U., 1942; B.S. in Medicine, N.D. U., 1943; M.D., Temple U., 1945; M.S. in Medicine and Physiology, U. Minn.-Mayo Found., 1954; children—Julie Ann, Robert Clayton, Richard Scott. Intern, Med. Center, Jersey City, 1945-46; mem. staff VA Hosp., Fargo, N.D., 1948-51; fellow in medicine and cardiology Mayo Found., Rochester, Minn., 1951-55; internist, cardiologist Sansum Med. Clinic Inc., Santa Barbara, Calif., 1955—; mem. staff Cottage Hosp., St. Francis Hosp. Bd. dirs. Sansum Med. Research Found. Served to capt. M.C., USAF, 1946-48. Diplomate Am. Bd. Internal Medicine. Fellow ACP, Am. Coll. Cardiology, Am. Coll. Chest Physicians, Am. Heart Assn. (mem. council on clin. cardiology); mem. Calif. Heart Assn. (pres. 1971-72, Meritorious Service award 1968, Disting. Service award 1972, Disting. Achievement award 1975), Santa Barbara County Heart Assn. (pres. 1959-60, Disting. Service award 1958, Disting. Achievement award 1971), Calif. Med. Assn., Los Angeles Acad. Medicine, Santa Barbara County Med. Assn., Mayo Clinic Alumni Assn., Santa Barbara Soc. Internal Medicine (pres. 1963), Sigma Xi, Phi Beta Pi. Republican. Lutheran. Club: Channel City. Contbr. articles to profl. jours. Home: 5956 Trudi Dr Goleta CA 93117 Office: Sansum Med Clinic Inc 317 W Pueblo St Santa Barbara CA 93102

KLAMMER, JOSEPH FRANCIS, management consultant; b. Omaha, Mar. 25, 1925; s. Aloys Arcadius and Sophie (Nadolny) K.; B.S., Creighton U., 1948; M.B.A., Stanford, 1950; cert. in polit. econs. Grad. Inst. Internat. Studies, U. Geneva, 1951. Adminstrv. analyst Chevron Corp. (formerly Standard Oil Co. Calif.), San Francisco, 1952-53; staff asst. Enron Corp. (formerly Internorth, Inc.), Omaha, 1953-57; mgmt. cons. Cresap, McCormick and Paget, Inc., San Francisco, 1957-75, v.p., mgr. San Francisco office; mgmt. cons., prin. J.F. Klammer Assocs., San Francisco, 1975—. Served to 1st lt. USAAF, 1943-46; lt. col. USAFR (ret.). Rotary Found. fellow, 1950-51. Republican. Roman Catholic. Clubs: Univ. Home: 1998 Broadway San Francisco CA 94109 Office: 1 Market Pla San Francisco CA 94105

KLAPKA, EDWARD JOHN, JR. (TED KLAPKA), naval officer, space systems and satellite navigation specialist; b. N.Y.C., Apr. 2, 1956; s. Edward John and June Gwendolyn (Cooke) K.; m. Patti Jean Andrews, Dec. 28, 1982 (div. May 1986); m. Miriam Anderson Cox, Nov. 23, 1988. BS, U. Ill., 1978; MS, Naval Postgrad. Sch., 1988. Commd. ensign USN, 1978, advanced through grades to lt. cmdr., 1988, ships navigator U.S.S. Berkeley, San Diego, 1978-81, grad. flight sch., Pensacola, Fla., 1982-83, avionics officer, mission comdr., Patrol Squadron 49, Jacksonville, Fla., 1983-86; mrg. NAVSTAR Global Positioning System Air Integration project Space and Naval Warfare Systems Command, Washington, 1988—. Contbr. articles to profl. jours. Mem. AIAA, Assn. Naval Aviation (life), U.S. Naval Inst.

KLASSEN, PETER JAMES, academic administrator, history educator; b. Crowfoot, Alta., Can., Dec. 18, 1930; came to U.S., 1955; s. John C. and Elizabeth (Martens) K.; m. Nancy Jo Cooprider, Aug. 1, 1959; children: Kenton, Kevin, Bryan. BA, also cert., U. B.C., Can., 1955; MA, U. So. Calif., 1958, PhD, 1962. Cert. secondary tchr. Lectr. U. So. Calif., Los Angeles, 1957-62; prof. history Fresno (Calif.) Pacific Coll., 1962-66; prof. history Calif. State U., Fresno, 1966—, dean sch. social scis., 1979—. Author: The Economics of Anabaptism, 1964, Europe in the Reformation, 1979, Reformation: Change and Stability, 1980; contbr. articles to jours. Pres. West Fresno Home Improvement Assn. 1966-70; pres. Fresno Sister Cities Council, 1987—; mem. Calif. Council for the Humanities, 1987—. Research grantee Deutscher Akademischer Austauschdienst, 1975. Mem. Am. Hist. Assn., Am. Soc. Ch. History, Fresno City and County Hist. Soc. (pres. 1983-85), Soc. Reformation Research, German Studies Assn., Assn. Advancement Slavic Studies, Phi Alpha Theta, Phi Kappa Phi. Home: 1838 S Bundy Dr Fresno CA 93727 Office: Calif State U Sch Social Scis Fresno CA 93740

KLATT, GORDON ROY, surgeon, army reserve officer; b. St. Paul, Dec. 1, 1942; s. Roy Paul and Elizabeth (Gartner) K.; m. Trudy Faye Welander, Aug. 28, 1965; children: Lisa Mary, Julie Ann, David Christopher. BS in Biolog, Coll. of St. Thomas, St. Paul, 1964; MD, U. Minn., 1968. Diplomate Am. Bd. of Surgery, Am. Bd. Colon and Rectal Surgery. Commd. 2d lt. U.S. Army, 1966, advanced through grades to lt. col., off active duty, 1976; intern Fitzsimons Army Med. Ctr., Denver, 1968-69; resident in gen. surgery Madigan Army Med. Ctr., Tacoma, 1969-73; gen. surgeon Madigan Army Med. Ctr./U.S. Army, Okinawa, Japan, 1969-76; fellow colorectal surgery U. Minn., Mpls., 1977-78; pvt. practice Tacoma, 1978—; commdr. 6250th U.S. Army Hosp., 1985-87, 50th Gen. Hosp., 1987—; chmn. Coalition for a Tobacco-Free Pierce County, Tacoma, 1988—; co-chmn. tobacco addiction coordinating coun. State of Wash., Olympia, 1988—. Bd. dirs. Tacoma Philharmonic, 1979-81, A. Cancer Soc., Pierce County unit, Tacoma, 1978—, Wash., 1980—, pres., 1985-87, chmn. tobacco free Wash. com., Seattle, 1986—; originator, coord. 24 Hour Run Against Cancer, 1985—. Fellow ACS, Am. Soc. Colon and Rectal Surgeons; mem. AMA, Wash. State Med. Assn., Pierce County Med. Soc., N. Pacific Surg. Assn., Pan Pacific Surg. Assn., Kiwanis. Roman Catholic. Home: 4812 Browns Point Blvd Tacoma WA 98422 Office: Mt Rainier Surg Assocs 902 S L St Ste 202 Tacoma WA 98405

KLEBOW, NORA RUTH, architect; b. Medina, Ohio, May 10, 1958; d. Guenter Werner Heinz and Ruth Anna (Gebhardt) K. BS, Kent State U., 1980, BArch, 1981; MBA, MArch, Washington U., 1985. CADD standards asst. Hellmuth, Obata & Kassabaum, Inc., St. Louis, 1984-85, CADD standards Coordinator, 1985-86, intern architect, 1986; computer site mgr. Hellmuth, Obata & Kassabaum, Inc., San Francisco, 1986-88; architect Skidmore, Owings & Merrill, San Francisco, 1988—; Mem. Nat. Archtl. Accrediting Bd., 1982-84. Mem. AIA (co-chairperson Women Architecture Task Force, 1986, assoc. dir., 1988-89), ASC/AIA (v.p.). Lutheran. Home: 101 Cervantes Blvd San Francisco CA 94123 Office: Skidmore Owings & Merrill 333 Bush St San Francisco CA 94104

KLEEMAN, NANCY GRAY ERVIN, teacher; b. Boston, Feb. 19, 1946; d. John Wesley and Harriet Elizabeth (Teuchert) Ervin; m. Brian Carlton Kleeman, June 27, 1969. BA, Calif. State U., Northridge, 1969; cert. elem. edn., Calif. State U., Long Beach, 1974, MS, 1976, cert. resource specialist, 1982. Cert. spl. edn., learning disabilities and resource specialist tchr., Calif. Tchr. spl. edn., resource specialist Downey (Calif.) Unified Sch. Dist., 1972-86; tchr. spl. day class Irvine (Calif.) Sch. Dist., 1986—; tutor in field; speaker Commn. for Handicapped, L.A., 1975; advisor Com. to Downey Unified Sch. Dist., 1976-82. Sec. UN, L.A., 1980-83; vol. coord., art dir, educator Sierra Vista Mid. Sch., Irvine, 1986-88; liaison Tustin (Calif.) Manor Convalescent Home and Regents Point Retirement Home, Irvine, 1986-88. Named Tchr. Yr. Sierra Vista Middle Sch., 1988. Mem. Irvine Tchrs. Assn., Calif. Tchrs. Assn., NEA, Nat. Carousel Assn., Am. Carousel Assn. Office: Irvine Unified Sch Dist 2 Liberty Irvine CA 92720

KLEEMANN, GARY LEWIS, educational program administrator; b. Pasadena, Calif., June 8, 1945; s. Ernest W. Kleemann and Martha May (Lewis) Grant; m. Balvina Sotelo, Sept. 12, 1970; children: Robert Franklin, Michael Patrick. BA, San Jose (Calif.) State U., 1968; MS, Oreg. State U., 1973; PhD, Ariz. State U., 1984. Dir. student activities Boise (Idaho) State U., 1970-72; asst. dean U. Calif., Irvine, 1973-74; dir. univ. ctr. U. of the Pacific, Stockton, Calif., 1974-79; exec. coord. assoc. students program Ariz. State U., Tempe, 1979—; pres. GarVi Assocs., Inc., Tempe, 1982—. Contbr. numerous articles to profl. jours. Lt. USN, 1968-70, Vietnam. Calif. State scholar, 1963-67; recipient La Torre Svc. award, 1966. Mem. Am. Assn. Higher Edn., Am. Coll. Personnel Assn., Am. Ednl. Rsch. Assn., Am. Assn. for Counseling and Devel., Ariz. Coll. Personnel Assn., Assn. for the Study Higher Edn., Assn. Coll. Unions Internat., Nat. Assn. Student Personnel Adminstrs. (exec. com. Ariz. chpt.), Blue Key Honor Soc. Home: 1831 E Cornell Dr Tempe AZ 85283 Office: Ariz State U Mail Code QAS Tempe AZ 85287-1001

KLEHS, HENRY JOHN WILHELM, civil engineer; b. Dornbusch bez Stade, Germany, Dec. 7, 1910; s. Frederick and Anna (Mahler) K.; B.S., U. Calif., 1935; m. Clodell Peters, July 17, 1948; came to U.S., 1920, naturalized through father, 1922. Engr. So. Pacific Transp. Co., 1936-75, supr. hazardous materials control, until 1975; ret., 1975. Mem. Calif. Fire Chiefs Assn., Internat. Assn. Fire Chiefs, Steuben Soc. Am., Am. Ry. Engring Assn., ASCE. Home: 604 Glenwood Isle Alameda CA 94501

KLEIMAN, GEORGE LAWRENCE, artist; b. N.Y.C., Aug. 29, 1946; s. Irving and Beatrice K.; m. Mary Ann Paigen, Apr. 8, 1984. Student architecture, CCNY, 1964-67; BA in Art, Calif. State U., San Jose, 1970. Works exhibited: Shippee Gallery, N.Y.C., 1985-89, Phyllis Needlman Gallery, Chgo., 1982-83, Tom Luttrell Gallery, San Francisco, 1981, Mirage Gallery, L.A., 1981; permanent collections: Atlantic Richfield Co., Citicorp, Gen. Mills Corp., Itel Corp., Mobil Oil Co., Pepisco Inc., Security Pacific Nat. Bank, Shearson Lehman Hutton, U. So. Calif. Studio: 1650 N Cosmo St Hollywood CA 90028

KLEIMAN, HARLAN PHILIP, film company executive; b. N.Y.C., Nov. 9, 1940; s. Ira Arthur Kleiman and Dorothy Rosen; m. Sondra Lee (divorced); m. Sandy Charles, May 12, 1984. BA, Hunter Coll., 1962; MS in Indsl. adminstrn., Yale U., 1964. Founder, exec. dir. Long Wharf Theater, New Haven, Conn., 1964-68; producer Off Broadway, N.Y.C., 1968-72; v.p. Video Corp. Am., N.Y.C., 1972-74, HBO, N.Y.C., 1974-76; sr. v.p. cable div. Warner Communications, N.Y.C., 1976-79; pres. Harlan Kleiman Co., L.A., 1979-87; chmn. bd. dirs. Filmstar Inc., L.A., 1987—. Recipient ACE award Best Dramatic TV Spl., Nat. Cable TV Assn., 1984. Mem. Hollywood Radio & TV Soc. Home: 15710 Dicken St Encino CA 91436 Office: Filmstar Inc 12301 Wilshire Blvd Los Angeles CA 90025

KLEIMAN, MELODIE YVONNE, chief assistant county counsel; b. La Porte, Ind., Oct. 12, 1945; d. John and Edna Mae (Printup) McLennan; m. Theodore William Kleiman, Oct. 22, 1972; children—Marjorie T'Anne, Sarah Margaret, Alexis Leah. A.B., U. So. Calif., 1968; J.D., Stanford U., 1971. Bar: Calif. 1972. In-house counsel Atlantic Richfield Co., Los Angeles, 1971-74; sole practice, Ventura, Calif., 1974-83; asst. county counsel County Ventura, Calif., 1983-85, chief asst. county counsel, 1985—; pres. Calif. Women Lawyers, 1978-79. Mem. Calif. State Bar. Democrat. Jewish. Office: Office of County Counsel 800 S Victoria Ave Ventura CA 93009

KLEIN, ARNOLD WILLIAM, dermatologist; b. Mt. Clemens, Mich., Feb. 27, 1945; m. Malvina Kraemer. BA, U. Pa., 1967, MD, 1971. Intern Cedars-Sinai Med. Ctr., Los Angeles, 1971-72; resident in dermatology Hosp. U. Pa., Phila., 1972-73, U. Calif., Los Angeles, 1973-75; pvt. practice dermatology Beverly Hills, Calif., 1975—; mem. med. staff Cedars-Sinai Med. Ctr., U. Calif. Ctr. for the Health Scis., Los Angeles, Stanford (Calif.) U. Hosp.; asst. clin. prof. dermatology/medicine, U. Calif., Los Angeles; asst. prof. dermatology, Stanford U. Sch. Medicine; Calif. state commr. Malpractice Adv. Commn.; med. adv. bd. Skin Cancer Found., Lupus Found. Am., Collagen Corp.; presenter seminars in field. Reviewer Jour. Dermatologic Surgery and Oncology, Jour. Sexually Transmitted Diseases; editorial bd. Men's Fitness mag., Shape mag.; contbr. numerous articles to med. jours. Mem. AMA, Calif. Med. Assn., Am. Soc. Dermatologic Surgery, Internat. Soc. Dermatologic Surgery, Calif. Soc. Specialty Plastic Surgery, Am. Assn. Cosmetic Surgeons, Assn. Sci. Advosors, Los Angeles Med. Assn., Am. Coll. Chemosurgery, Met. Dermatology Soc., Am. Acad. Dermatology, Dermatology Found., Scleroderma Found., Internat. Psoriasis Found., Lupus Found., Am. Venereal Disease Assn., Soc. Cosmetic Chemists, AFTRA, Los Angeles Mus. Contemporary Art (founder), Dance Gallery Los Angeles (founder), Am. Found. AIDS Research (founder, dir.), Friars Club, Phi Beta Kappa, Sigma Tau Sigma, Delphos. Office: 435 N Roxbury Dr Ste 204 Beverly Hills CA 90210

KLEIN, CHERYL GOODRICH, audit manager; b. Phoenix, Sept. 9, 1963; d. Robert Lee and Sue (Tautfest) G.; m. Philip John Klein, Nov. 14, 1987. BS in Acctg., Portland (Oreg.) State U., 1985. Staff acct. Ernst and Whinney, Portland, 1985-86, Nygaard, Mims and Hoffman CPA's, Portland, 1986-87; internal auditor Fred Meyer, Inc., Portland, 1987—; computer cons. Emanual Hosp., Portland, 1984—. Bd. dirs., fin. advisor Cath. Youth Orgn., Portland, 1988; active fin. com. Rose Festival, Portland, 1988. Mem. Electronic Data Processing Auditing Assn. Republican. Office: Fred Meyer Inc 3800 SE 22d Ave Portland OR 97232

KLEIN, DIANNE CURTIS, media representative; b. South Bend, Ind., Nov. 3, 1949; d. George Eugene and Mary (Pawlowski) Curtis; m. Thomas G. Klein, Nov. 2, 1988. Horse trainer various ranches Wis., 1966-69; playboy bunny Playboy Club, Lake Geneva, Wis., 1969-72; owner, pub. Pace Mag., Lake Geneva, 1973-75; advt. sales Pioneer Press, Wilmette, Ill., 1975-78; mktg. dir. Classic Motor Carriages, Miami, Fla., 1978-83; with sales advt. peterson Publ., L.A., 1983—; media rep. Curtis Ltd., Mesa, Ariz., 1986—. Home: 2632 W Loughlin Dr Chandler AZ 85224 Office: Curtis Ltd PO Box 17729 Mesa AZ 85212

KLEIN, (MARY) ELEANOR, retired clinical social worker; b. Luzon, Philippines, Dec. 13, 1919; came to U.S., 1921; (parents Am. citizens); d. Roy Edgar and Edith Lillian (Dransfield) Hay; m. Edward George Klein, June 24, 1955. BA, Pacific Union Coll., 1946; MSW, U. So. Calif., 1953. Lic. clin. social worker. Social worker White Meml. Hosp., Los Angeles, 1948-56; clin. social worker UCLA Hosp. Clinics, 1956-65, supr. social worker, 1965-67, assoc. dir., 1967-73, dir., 1973-82; mem. vol. bd. Calif. div., 1964—, Am. Cancer Soc., del., nat. dir., 1980-84, chmn. Residential Crusade for Orange County (Calif.) Unit, 1985-86. Bd. dirs., treas. Los Amigos de la Humanidad, U. So. Calif. Sch. Social Work, Calif. div. Am. Cancer Soc., also life mem.; bd. dirs. Vol. Ctr. Orange County West, 1988—, also hon. life mem. Recipient Disting. Alumni award Los Amigos de la Humanidad, 1984, Outstanding Performance award UCLA Hosp., 1968, various service awards Am. Cancer Soc., 1972-88. Fellow Soc. Clin. Social Work; mem. Nat. Assn. Soc. Workers (charter), Am. Hosp. Assn., Soc. Hosp. Social Work Dirs. of Am. Hosp. Assn. (nat. pres. 1981, bd. dirs. 1978-82, life mem. local chpt.), Am. Pub. Health Assn. Democrat. Adventist. Home: 1661 Texas Circle Costa Mesa CA 92626

KLEIN, FREDERICK TIMOTHY, marketing professional; b. N.Y.C., Apr. 19, 1940; s. Ernest Donald and Demetria Ann (Aaglan) K.; m. Mary Kay Casey, Oct. 3., 1964; children: Christine, Cecilia. Student, NYU, 1957-58, U. Colo., 1958-61; grad. summa cum laude, U.S. Army Intelligence Sch., 1962; BA in Human Behavior, Newport U., 1988. Machine acct. Haskins & Sells, N.Y.C., 1957-65; methods analyst Ford Motor Co., Newark, 1965-68; div. supr. Thiokol Chem. Co., Trenton, N.J., 1968-72; br. mgr. McDonnell Douglas Automation Co., Denver, 1972-79; dist. mgr. United Info. Systems, Englewood, Colo., 1979-81; pres. Nat. Resources Cos., Englewood, Colo., 1981-83; mktg. mgr. Analysts Internat. Corp., Englewood, 1983—; publ. critic computer scis. dept. U. Minn., 1986-88. Author: (manual) Div. Policy and Procedures, 1971. Chmn. Littleton (Colo.) Leadership Retreat, 1986-88; com. chmn. Colo. Centennial Conf., Denver, 1987-88; precinct capt. Colo. Operation ID, Littleton, 1983—; mem. Statue of Liberty Found., N.Y.C., 1985—, U.S. Olympic Com., 1968. Served in U.S. Army, 1962-64. Recipient Humanitarian award N.J. Sch. for the Deaf, 1971, Outstanding Service award Nat. Security Agy., 1964. Mem. Am. Mgmt. Assn. (mem. com. 1968-72), Soc. for Info. Mgmt. (chmn. 1985-86, Outstanding Mem. 1984), Data Processing Mgmt. Assn. (program chmn. 1971). Roman Catholic. Clubs: Summit (pres. 1988), Highline Athletic (Littleton), Pres.' (Denver). Home: 7139 S Curtice Littleton CO 80120 Office: Analysts Internat Corp 14 Inverness Dr E Englewood CO 80112

KLEIN, HAROLD PAUL, microbiologist; b. N.Y.C., Apr. 1, 1921; Alexander and and Lillyan (Pal) K.; m. Gloria Nancy Dolgov, Nov. 14, 1942; children—Susan Ann, Judith Ellen. B.A., Bklyn. Coll., 1942; Ph.D., U. Calif., Berkeley, 1950. Am. Cancer Soc. fellow Mass. Gen. Hosp., Boston, 1950-51; instr. microbiology U. Wash., Seattle, 1951-54; asst. prof. U. Wash., 1954-55; asst. prof. biology Brandeis U., Waltham, Mass., 1955-56; assoc. prof. Brandeis U., 1956-60, prof., 1960-63, chmn. dept. biology, 1956-63; vis. prof. bacteriology U. Calif., Berkeley, 1960-61; div. chief exobiology, dir. life scis. Ames Research Center, NASA, Mountain View, Calif., 1963-84; scientist-in-residence Santa Clara U., Calif., 1984—; mem. U.S.-USSR Working Group in Space Biology and Medicine, 1971-84; leader biology team Viking Mars Mission, 1976; mem. space sci. bd. Nat. Acad. Scis., 1984-89. Mem. editorial bd. Origins of Life, 1970-89. Served with U.S. Army, 1943-46. NSF Sr. Postdoctoral fellow, 1963; grantee NIH, 1955-63; NSF, 1957-63. Mem. Interat. Soc. Study Origin of Life, Am. Soc. Biol. Chemists, Internat. Astronautical Fedn., Phi Beta Kappa. Home: 1022 N California Ave Palo Alto CA 94303 Office: Santa Clara U Dept Biology Santa Clara CA 95053

KLEIN, HENRY, lawyer; b. N.Y.C., Oct. 6, 1949; s. Leo Herman and Florence (Silver) K.; m. Ann Laura Hallasey, July 30, 1972; children: Lauren Jennifer, Benjamin Jason. BA, SUNY, Albany, 1971; JD, U. San Diego, 1975. Bar: Calif. 1975, U.S. Ct. Customs and Patent Appeals 1976, U.S. Ct. Appeals (Fed. cir.) 1985, U.S. Dist. Ct. (cen. dist.) Calif. 1986. Trademark atty. U.S. Patent Office, Washington, 1975-77; ptnr. Ladas & Parry, Los Angeles, 1978—. Mem. San Diego Law Rev., 1974-75; editor-in-chief Trademark Soc. Newsletter, 1977. Mem. U. San Diego Civil Legal Clinic, 1974, Civil Rights Research Council, San Diego, 1974, Calif. Pub. Interest Research Group, San Diego, 1975. N.Y. State scholar, 1967-71; Tex. State legal scholar State of Tex., 1972; recipient Am. Jurisprudence award Bancroft-Whitney Co. and Lawyer Co-Op. Pub. Co., Lubbock, Tex., 1972; Patent Trademark Spl. Achievement awards U.S. Dept. Commerce, Washington, 1976, 77. Mem. U.S. Trademark Assn. (v.p. 1976, pres., chmn. 1977), Los Angeles Patent Law Assn., Phi Delta Phi. Republican. Jewish. Home: 6134 Cabrillo Ct Alta Loma CA 91701

KLEIN, HENRY F., art educator; b. Newark, N.J., Jan. 5, 1943; s. Philip and Anne (Adickman) K.; m. Cecelia Jane Fore, July 22, 1966 (div. 1987); children: Stefyn Mikaela, Sacha Mareka. BA, Oberlin Coll., 1965; MFA, Ohio State U., 1968. Exhibition preparator U. Mus. U. Mich., Ann Arbor, 1968-69; instr., asst. prof. Grinnell (Iowa) Coll., 1969-72; prodn. mgr., v.p. Peace Press, Culver City, Calif., 1976-79; chairperson, prof. art dept. L.A. Valley Coll., Van Nuys, Calif., 1977—; asst. prof. Henry Ford Community Coll., 1973-76; instr. C. S. Mott Community Coll., Flint, Mich., 1972-75, Wayne County Community Coll., Detroit, 1973-74. Contbr. articles to profl. jours. Adv. bd. Book Arts Cert. Program, UCLA extension, 1981-82; adv. com. Hillel Mawr Multi Campaign, 1985-87. Recipient Purchase prize Smithsonian Inst., 1978, Purchase award Minot State Coll., 1985. Mem. L.A. Pritmaking Soc. (v.p. 1988—), Am. Fedn. Tchr. Coll. Guild (exec. bd. 1986—), Visual Arts Assn. Calif. (bd. dirs. 1982-84), Coll. Art Assn. Am. Democratic. Home: 4942 Paso Robles Ave Encino CA 91316 Office: LA Valley Coll Art Dept 5800 Fulton Ave Van Nuys CA 91401

KLEIN, HERBERT GEORGE, newspaper editor; b. Los Angeles, Apr. 1, 1918; s. George and Amy (Cordes) K.; m. Marjorie G. Galbraith, Nov. 1, 1941; children—Joanne L. (Mrs. Robert Mayne), Patricia A. (Mrs. John Root). AB, U. So. Calif., 1940; Hon. Doctorate, U. San Diego, 1989. Reporter Alhambra (Calif.) Post-Advocate, 1940-42, news editor, 1946-50; spl. corr. Copley Newspapers, 1946-50, Washington corr., 1950; with San Diego Union, 1950-68, editorial writer, 1950-52, editorial page editor, 1952-56, assoc. editor, 1956-57, exec. editor, 1957-58, editor, 1959-68; mgr. communications Nixon for Pres. Campaign, 1968-69; dir. communications Exec. Br., U.S. Govt., 1969-73; v.p. corp. relations Metromedia, Inc., 1973-77; media cons. 1977-80; editor-in-chief, v.p. Copley Newspapers, Inc., San Diego, 1980—; publicity dir. Eisenhower-Nixon campaign in Calif., 1952; asst. press sec. Vice Pres. Nixon Campaign, 1956; press sec. Nixon inaugural, 1957, Nixon campaign, 1958; spl. asst., press sec. to Nixon, 1959-61; press sec. Nixon Gov. Campaign, 1962; dir. communications Nixon presdl. campaign, 1968; mem. Advt. Council, N.Y. Trustee U. So. Calif.; chmn. Holiday Bowl; bd. dirs. Clair Burgener Found., Greater San Diego Sports Assn.; mem. exec. com. San Diego unit Am. Cancer Soc., Super Bowl XXII, Olympic Tng. Site com.; bd. dirs. San Diego Econ. Devel. Com. Served with USNR, 1942-46; comdr. Res. Recipient Fourth Estate award U. So. Calif., 1947, Alumnus of Yr. award U. So. Calif., 1971, Gen. Alumni Merit award, 1977, Spl. Service to Journalism award, 1969; Headliner of Yr. award Greater Los Angeles Press Club, 1971, San Diego State Univ.'s First Fourth Estate Award, 1986. Mem. Am. Soc. Newspaper Editors (past dir.), Calif. Press Assn., Pub. Relations seminar, Gen. Alumni U. So. Calif. (past pres.), Alhambra Jr. C. of C. (past pres.), Greater San Diego C. of C. (exec. com.), Sigma Delta Chi (nat. com. chmn., gen. activities chmn. nat. conv. 1958), Delta Chi. Presbyn. Clubs: Commonwealth, Bohemian, Fairbanks Country. Lodges: Kiwanis, Rotary (hon.). Home: 5110 Saddlery Sq PO Box 8935 Rancho Santa Fe CA 92067

KLEIN, JACK, Canadian provincial government official. Mem. Province of Sask. Legis. Assembly; former minister of tourism and small bus., now minister of urban affairs. Office: Cabinet of Sask, Legislative Bldg, Regina, SK Canada S4S 0B3

KLEIN, JAMES EDWIN, minister; b. Oakes, N.D., Jan. 11, 1951; s. Albert Franklin and Frances (Long) K.; m. Patricia Renee, Aug. 10, 1974; children: Jason, Katrina. BA, Vennard Coll., University Park, Iowa, 1973. Ordained elder in the Ch. of the Nazarene. Assoc. minister Evang. Meth. Ch., Cudahy, Calif., 1973-75; sr. pastor Evang. Meth. Ch., Lake Elsinore, Calif., 1975-79; asst. to the pres. World Gospel Crusades, Upland, Calif., 1979-80; field coordinator Energy Mktg., Inc., Tustin, Calif., 1981; regional v.p. A.L. Williams, Garden Grove, Calif., 1982—; minister Ch. of the Nazarene, Anaheim, Calif., 1985-89; asst. dist. supt. Evang. Meth. Ch., Stockton, Calif., 1979-81; bd. dirs. Azusa Pacific U. Scoutmaster Boy Scouts of Am., Garden Grove, Calif., 1983-85, com. chmn. Troop 1340, Anaheim, 1987—; named Eagle Scout, 1969. Republican. Club: Rotary. Home: 306 N Harrington Dr Fullerton CA 92631 Office: First Church of the Nazarene 1340 N Candlewood St Anaheim CA 92805

KLEIN, JAMES MIKEL, music educator; b. Greenville, S.C., Aug. 27, 1953; s. Rubin Harry Klein and Billie (Mikel) Newton. BM, U. Tex., 1975, MM, 1977; MusD, U. Cincinnati, 1981. Prin. trombone player Austin (Tex.) Symphony Orch., 1973-77; conducting asst. U. Tex., Austin, 1975-77, U. Cin., 1977-78; dir. instrumental music Valparaiso (Ind.) U., 1978-84; prof. music Calif. State U. Stanislaus, Turlock, 1984—; mem. faculty Nat. Luth. Music Camp, Lincoln, Nebr., 1985—; guest conductor, clinician, adjudicator various states, 1978—; trombone player Modesto (Calif.) Symphony Orch., 1984—; conductor Stanislaus Youth Symphony, Modesto, 1985, Modesto Symphony Youth Orchestra, 1986—; site adminstr. Nat. Honors Orch., Anaheim, Calif., 1986, Indpls. 88; faculty, coordinator instrumental music Calif. State Summer Sch. of Arts, 1987—. Pres. Turlock Arts Fund for Youth, 1986-88. Recipient Meritorious Prof. award Calif. State U., Stanislaus, 1988. Mem. Music Educators Nat. Assn., Nat. Sch. Orch. Assn., Am. Fedn. Musicians (Local 1), Condrs. Guild, Am. Symphony Orch. League, Calif. Orchestra Dir.'s Assn. (pres. elect 1988—). Home: 840 Georgetown Ave Turlock CA 95380 Office: Calif State U Dept Music 801 W Monte Vista Ave Turlock CA 95380

KLEIN, MICHAEL STEVEN, lawyer; b. Portsmouth, Ohio, July 7, 1952; s. Robert Ernest and Dorothy (Goldish) K. BA in Psychology, Ind. U., 1973; JD, Yale U., 1976. Bar: Calif. 1976; lic. real estate broker, Calif. Assoc. Greenberg & Glusker, L.A., 1976-80; pvt. practice L.A., 1981-85; ptnr. Klein & Stein, L.A., 1985—. Contbr. to profl. publs. Mem. State Bar Calif., L.A. County Bar Assn., Beverly Hills Bar Assn. (bd. govs. 1984—, chmn. real estate com. 1986-89), ACLU (bd. dirs. So. Calif. chpt. 1978—, chmn. free speech com. 1982—, pres. chpt. coun. 1980-82), Yale Club So. Calif. (bd. dirs. 1983—), New Democratic Channel (bd. dirs. So. Calif. chpt. 1981—), Internat. Jugglers' Assn. Jewish. Office: Klein & Stein Ste 600 2029 Century Park E Los Angeles CA 90067

KLEIN, RALPH, provincial legislator, former city mayor; b. Calgary, Alta., Can.; m. 2nd, Colleen, 1972; 5 children; dir. public relations, Alta. div. Red Cross; dir. public relations, Calgary United Way Fund, 1966-69; with CFCN, 1969-80, newsreader radio div., later television reporter; mayor, city of Calgary, 1980-89; elected to Alta. Legislature 1989 from Calgary-Elbow constituency, minister of environment. Office: Alta Legislature, Legislature Bldg, Edmonton, AB Canada T5K 2B6 *

KLEIN, ROBERT MARTIN, utilities executive; b. San Francisco, Sept. 6, 1944; s. Julius Oscar and Carmen Pauline (Aguirre) K.; m. Voni Janeen Pruett, Jan. 2, 1980 (div. Apr. 1983). BA, U. Calif., Davis, 1966; MBA, U. Calif., Berkeley, 1970. Mgr. Pacific Telephone, San Francisco, 1969-80, Nev. Bell, Reno, 1981-83, AT&T, Reno, 1984—; pres. Golden State Ltd., Verdi, Nev., 1981—. Capt. U.S. Army, 1966-69, Vietnam. Decorated Bronze Star with clusters, Purple Heart. Mem. Sierra Club, Olympic Club (San Francisco), Basque Club (Reno). Roman Catholic. Home: PO Box 703 Verdi NV 89439 Office: AT&T 220 Edison Way #200 Reno NV 89502

KLEIN, SNIRA L(UBOVSKY), Hebrew language and literature educator. came to U.S., 1959, naturalized, 1974; d. Avraham and Devora (Unger) Lubovsky; m. Earl H. Klein, Dec. 25, 1975. Tchr. cert., Tchrs. Seminar, Netanya, Israel, 1956; B. Rel. Edn., U. Judaism, 1961, M in Hebrew Lit., 1963; BA, Calif. State U., Northridge, 1966; MA, UCLA, 1971, PhD, 1983. Teaching asst. UCLA, 1969-71, vis. lectr., 1985-87; instr., continuing edn. U. Judaism, Los Angeles, 1971-76, instr., 1975—. Mem. Assn. for Jewish Studies, Nat. Assn. of Profs. of Hebrew, World Union of Jewish Studies. Jewish. Office: U Judaism 15600 Mulholland Dr Los Angeles CA 90077

KLEIN, STEPHEN ALLAN, solid and hazardous waste management consultant; b. Balt., Nov. 26, 1943; s. Earl Louis Klein and Phyllis (Snyder) Kane; m. Sandra Ruth Harp, Dec. 10, 1978; 1 child, Jonathan Allan. BS, U. Md., 1976. Cert. hazardous waste mgmt., Calif.; registered hazardous waste assessor. With Scrap Corp. of Am., 1966-75; plant supt. Englehard Minerals & Chemicals, 1975-77; dir. mktg. Riverside Scrap Iron and Metal Inc., 1977-82; chief operating officer Weiner Metals, Inc., 1982; pres. Extra Energy Resources, Corona, Calif., 1982—; chief executive officer Environet Inc., Corona, 1982—; mktg. Aluminum Alloy Metals, L.A., 1988—; mgmt. Harris Group rep., World Leader in Scrap Processing and Material Equipment, Ecology Recycling, Huntington Beach, Calif., 1988—; cons. Non-Ferrous Metal Smelting. Mem. Citizens for Growth, Corona, 1988. With USAF (ROTC), 1962. Mem. Corona C. of C., Masons. Democrat. Jewish. Home: 2932 Sonrisa Dr Corona CA 91719

KLEINBERG, DIANA LOUISE, owner, designer; b. San Antonio, Apr. 23, 1946; d. Jermone Edwin and Emily (Quinones) K.; m. Gary Lee Clendenin, Apr. 25, 1970; children: David Michael, Chelsea Ann. BS, NYU. Owner, operator Austin Now, Inc. Mem. Phi Theta Kappa. Office: PO Box 2855 Granite Bay CA 95746

KLEINER, RICHARD AARON, management consultant; b. Pomona, Calif., Dec. 14, 1952; s. Albert Abraham and Cora (Young) K. BS, U. Calif., Santa Cruz, 1975; MA, U. Calif., Los Angeles, 1985. Research assoc. Ctr. for Pacific Studies U. Calif., Santa Cruz, 1975-77; market analyst Norfolk Island (South Pacific) Tourist Bur., 1977-78; owner, operator Kleiner Inventories, Los Angeles, 1979-83; project planner Jet Propulsion Lab., Pasadena, Calif., 1984-87; prin. Richard Kleiner and Assocs., Los Angeles, 1987—. Contbr. articles to profl. jours. and newspapers. Mem. AIAA, Am. Mgmt. Assn., Project Mgmt. Inst. Home: 519 Hill St Santa Monica CA 90405 Office: Richard Kleiner & Assocs 628 Lincoln Blvd Ste 3 Santa Monica CA 90402

KLEINROCK, LEONARD, computer scientist; b. N.Y.C., June 13, 1934; s. Bernard and Anne (Schoenfeld) K.; m. Stella Schuler, Dec. 1, 1967; children—Nancy S., Martin C. BEE, CCNY, 1957; M.S., MIT, 1959, Ph.D., 1963. Asst. elec. engr. Photobell Co. Inc., 1951-57; research engr. Lincoln Labs., M.I.T., 1957-63; mem. faculty UCLA, 1963—, prof. computer sci., 1970—; pres. Linkabit Corp., 1968-69; chief exec. officer Tech. Transfer Inst., 1976—; cons. in field, prin. investigator govt. contracts. Author: Queueing Systems, Vol. I, 1975, Vol. II, 1976, Communication Nets: Stochastic Message Flow and Delay, 1964, Solutions Manual for Queueing Systems, Vol. I, 1982, Vol. II, 1986; also articles. Recipient Paper award ICC, 1978, Leonard G. Abraham paper award Communications Soc., 1975, Outstanding Faculty Mem. award UCLA Engring. Grad. Students Assn., 1966, Townsend Harris medal CCNY, 1982, L.M. Ericsson Prize Sweden, 1982, 12th Marconi award, 1986; Guggenheim fellow, 1971-72. Fellow IEEE (disting. lectr. 1973, 76); mem. Nat. Acad. Engring., Ops. Research Soc. Am. (Lanchester prize 1976), Assn. Computing Machinery, Internat. Fedn. Info. Processes Systems, Amateur Athletic Union. Jewish. Home: 801 N Kenter Ave Los Angeles CA 90049 Office: UCLA Dept Computer Sci 405 Hilgard Ave Boelter Hall Los Angeles CA 90024-1596

KLEINSMITH, GENE, artist; b. Madison, Wis., Feb. 22, 1942; BA, Augustana Coll., Sioux Falls, S.D., 1963; MA, U. No. Ariz., Flagstaff, 1969; children: Jon Darin, Paul, Christin. Tchr. art high schs. in S.D., Colo., Minn. and Calif., 1963-71; mem. faculty San Bernardino Valley Coll., eves. 1967-71; instr. ceramics Victor Valley Coll., Victorville, Calif., 1971—, chmn. art dept., also coordinator artist-in-residence programs; lectr., condr. workshops in field; Keynote presenter Clay Today, 1987, Nat. Council on Edn. Ceramic Arts, Boston, 1984; presenter Nat. Council on Edn. for Ceramic Arts, Atlanta, 1983. One-man shows include U. Minn., Mankato, 1967, U. Calif., Riverside, 1969, U. S.D., 1976, No. Ariz. U., 1980, Olive Tree Gallery, Ft. Collins, Colo., 1966, Yavapai Coll., Prescott, Ariz., 1976, Apple Valley, Calif., 1977, Hi-Desert Symphony, Victor Valley, 1979, The Gallery in Flagstaff, Ariz., 1986; group and invitational exhbns. include Gallery II, Charlottesville, Va., 1983, Gallery II, St. George, Utah, 1984, Nat. Council on Edn. for Ceramic Arts, Atlanta, 1983; represented in permanent collections Mpls. Art Inst., Valparaiso (Ind.) U., Gustavus Adolphus Coll., St. Peter, Minn., No. Ariz. U., Ariz. Western Coll., Yuma, U. S.D., U. Minn., Mankato, Miami-Dade Community Coll., Gallery II, West Charlottesville, Va., Gallery II West, Beverly Hills, Calif., Rodell Gallery, Los Angeles, Pompidou Ctr., Paris, Topkapi Palace, Istanbul, Turkey; one man show Art of the Olympiad at Marcia Rodell Gallery, Los Angeles, 1984; also pvt. collections; feature artist La Ceramique Moderne, Paris, 1985; presenter workshops; internat. lectr. Faculty fellow Victor Valley Coll., 1973; keynote speaker Internat. Identitic Ceramique, Auxerre, France, 1985. Mem. Nat. Council Art Adminstrs., Nat. Council Edn. for Ceramic Arts (mem. exhbns.), Am. Crafts Council, Calif. Art Italy, Paris, Inst. Ceramic History (lectr. 1987), Athens, Greece. Art Mus., Phi Delta Kappa, Kappa Delta Pi. Author: Earth, Fire, Air and Water, 1974, Clay's The Way, 3d edit., 1988; writer Ceramics monthly mag.; contbg. writer TV series Search, Humanities Through The Arts; internat. presenter in field; contbr. articles to profl. jours. Office: 13624 Quapaw Apple Valley CA 92308

KLEIST, DOUGLAS D., banker; b. La Crosse, Wis., July 7, 1931; s. August Herman and Grace E. (Olson) K.; m. Doreen Michael Patakas, Sept. 5, 1959; children: Michael, Mary, Janine, Lisa, David. AA, Peirce Jr. Coll., 1953; BS, Fresno State U., 1955; MEd, U. Calif., Davis, 1959; lender cert., So. Meth. U., 1981. Tchr. vocat. agr. Livingston (Calif.) High Sch., 1960-64; assoc. prof. Fresno (Calif.) State U., 1966-67; assoc. v.p. loans Crocker-Citizens Nat. Bank, Fresno, 1964-71; v.p. loan adminstrn. Nat. Bank of Agr., Fresno, 1971-73, Centinela Bank, Inglewood, Calif., 1973-75; corp. v.p., treas. Bev Mar Food Corp., Torrance, Calif., 1975-77; v.p. loan adminstrn. Calif. Republic Bank, Bakersfield, 1977-79; pres., chief fin. officer The Service Bank of Tonkawa, Okla., 1979-85; v.p., sr. loan officer Upland (Calif.) Nat. Bank, 1985—; treas. Calif. Farm Bur. Credit Union, Fresno, 1965-69. Author: How Fertilizer Dealers Affect Fertilizer Use, 1959. Committeeman Fresno Dist. Fair-Livestock Show, 1966; chmn. Kay County Reps., Tonkawa, 1982. Served with USN, 1950-58. Recipient Stokoyke award Am. Inst. Cooperatives, 1959. Mem. Am. Inst. Banking (instr.), Calif. Bankers Assn., Okla. Bankers Assn., Calif. Sheriff's Assn. (assoc.). Lutheran. Lodge: Lions (dist. gov. Bakersfield club 1978-79, Tonkawa club 1983-84). Office: Upland Nat Bank 100 N Euclid Ave Upland CA 91786

KLEM, ROBERT BRUCE, geologist, geochemist; b. Denver, Mar. 31, 1953; s. Charles Richard and Laura (Prokopek) K. AA, Menlo Coll., Calif., 1973; BS in Psychology, U. Oreg., 1975; BA in Geology, U. Colo., 1982; MS in Geology, Colo. State U., 1985. Cons. TransCentury Corp., Washington, 1977-78; geochemist Atlantic Richfield Corp., Denver, 1979-85; software engr. ITT Fedl. Electric Corp., Vandenberg AFB, Calif., 1986—; pres., chief exec. officer Discovery Internat. Corp., Denver, 1985—. Mem. Assn. Exploration Geochemists. Digital Equipment Computer Users Soc., Aircraft Owners and Pilots Assn. Home: 402-A N I St Lompoc CA 93436 Office: ITT Fedl Electric Corp PO Box 5728 Vandenberg AFB CA 93437

KLEMM, RICHARD LEE, agricultural association official; b. Erie, Pa., Dec. 3, 1942; s. Herbert Charles and Margaret Jane (Lambert) K.; m. E. Barbara Cockcroft, Sept. 22, 1964. Student, Ohio Wesleyan U., 1960-63; BA, U. Hawaii, 1970, MA, 1972. Tchr. St. Francis High Sch., Honolulu, 1972-75; lectr. U. Hawaii, Honolulu, 1975-78, 80-81; dist. exec. Aloha Coun. Boy Scouts Am., Honolulu, 1978-79; communicator sea grant U. Hawaii, 1981-87; pub. rels. rep. Hawaiian Sugar Planters Assn., Aiea, Hawaii, 1988—. Author, editor: Big Island Recreational and Weather Guide, 1986; compiler Directory of Marine Resources for Secondary Educators in Hawaii. Vice-chair pub. rels. Hawaii Heart Assn., 1978-81; chmn. Carole Kai Bed Race, Honolulu, 1984—. With USMC, 1964-67. Mem. Hawaiian Acad. Sci., Nat. Assn. Sci. Writers, Internat. TV Assn., Pub. Rels. Soc. Am. Democrat. Lutheran. Club: Hawaii Divers. Lodge: Masons. Home: 227 Uilama St Kailua HI 96734 Office: Hawaiian Sugar Planters Assn PO Box 1057 Aiea HI 96701

KLEPINGER, JOHN WILLIAM, trailer manufacturing company executive; b. Lafayette, Ind., Feb. 7, 1945; s. John Franklin and R. Wanda (North) K.; m. Mary Patricia Duffy, May 1, 1976; 1 child, Nicholas Patrick. BS, Ball State U., 1967, MA, 1968. Sales engr. CTS Corp., Elkhart, Ind., 1969-70; exec. v.p. Woodlawn Products Corp., Elkhart, 1970-78; v.p. Period Ind., Henderson, Ky., 1976-78, Sotebeer Constrn. Co., Inc., Elkhart, 1978-81; gen. mgr. Wells Industries Inc., Ogden, Utah, 1981—; regional dir. Zion's First Nat. Bank, Ogden, 1986—. Bd. dirs. St. Benedict's Hosp., Ogden, 1986—, chmn. 1987—. Named Ogden Bus. Man of Yr., Weber County Sch. Dist., 1984. Mem. Weber County Prodn. Mgrs. Assn. (pres. 1984-85), Weber County Indsl. Devel. Corp. (bd. dirs. 1984—), Weber/Morgan Pvt. Industry Council, Nat. Assn. Pvt. Industry Councils (pres., bd. dirs. 1986—), Nat. Job Tng. Ptnrship Inc. (bd. dirs. 1986—), Nat. Alliance Bus. (bd. dirs. 1987—), Ogden Area C. of C. (bd. dirs., treas. 1986—). Roman Catholic. Club: Exchange (Ogden) (bd. dirs. 1984-86). Home: 5181 Aztec Dr Ogden UT 84403 Office: Wells Industries Inc PO Box 1619 Ogden UT 84402

KLEPPER, ELIZABETH LEE, physiologist; b. Memphis, Mar. 8, 1936; d. George Madden and Margaret Elizabeth (Lee) K. BA, Vanderbilt U., 1958; MA, Duke U., 1963, PhD, 1966. Research scientist Commonwealth Sci. and Indsl. Research Orgn., Griffith, Australia, 1966-68, Battelle Northwest Lab., Richland, Wash., 1972-76; asst. prof. Auburn (Ala.) U., 1968-72; Plant physiologist USDA Agrl. Research Service, Pendleton, Oreg., 1976-85, research leader, 1985—. Assoc. editor Crop Sci., 1977-80, 88—; mem. editorial bd. Plant Physiology, 1977—; mem. editorial adv. bd. Field Crops Research, 1983—; mem. editorial bd. Irrigation Sci., 1987—; contbr. chpts. to books and articles to jours. Marshall scholar British Govt., 1958-59; NSF fellow, 1964-66. Mem. AAAS, Am. Soc. Plant Physiologists, Crop Sci. Soc. Am., Soil Sci. Soc. Am. (Fellows com. 1986—), Am. Soc. Agronomy (monograph com. 1983—), Sigma Xi. Home: 1454 SW 45th Pendleton OR 98701 Office: USDA Argl Rsch Svc PO Box 370 Pendleton OR 98701

KLESTADT, BERNARD, aerospace scientist; b. Buren, Germany, Jan. 31, 1925; came to U.S., 1938; s. Rudolf and Ida (Alexander) K.; m. Bernice Florence Hersch, July 5, 1956; 1 child, Ralph. BSEE, Columbia U., 1949, MSEE, 1950; PhD, U. Southern Calif., 1958. Registered profl. engr., Calif. Elec. engr. Wright Air Devel. Ctr., Dayton, Ohio, 1949; asst. project engr. Sperry Gyroscope Co., Lake Success, N.Y., 1950; with Hughes Aircraft Co., various locations, 1950—; program mgr. space and comm. group Hughes Aircraft Co., El Segundo, Calif., 1970-76; program mgr. advanced missile systems div. Hughes Aircraft Co., Canoga Park, Calif., 1977-82, chief scientist missile devel. div., 1983-87, program mgr. automotive controls engring. div., 1987—; lectr. U. So. Calif., 1956-58; mem. panel on rsch. associateships NRC, Washington, 1975-79. Patentee electrical devices. With U.S. Army, 1943-46. Howard Hughes doctoral fellow, 1956. Mem. N.Y. Acad. Scis., Sigma Xi. Home: 16821 Ivyside Pl Encino CA 91436 Office: Hughes Aircraft Co 8433 Fallbrook Ave Canoga Park CA 91304

KLESTADT, RALPH HOWARD, aerodynamics design engineer; b. L.A., Aug. 31, 1960; s. Bernard and Bernice Florence (Hersch) K. BS in Aerospace Engring., UCLA, 1982; MS in Aerospace Engring., U. So. Calif., 1985. Mem. tech. staff Missile Systems Group Hughes Aircraft Co., L.A., 1983-88, project engr., 1988—. Mem. Nat. Corvette Restorers Soc., Tau Beta Pi. Office: Hughes Aircraft Co MSG 8433 Fallbrook Ave Canoga Park CA 91304

KLIEM, RALPH LEONARD, infosystems professional; b. Honolulu, Nov. 26, 1951; m. Priscilla Alvidrez, Jan. 3, 1981; 1 child, Tonia Elizabeth. BA in Polit. Sci., U. Idaho, 1974; MA in Polit. Sci., Wash. State U., 1980. Methods analyst Safeco Ins. Co., Seattle, Wash.; sr. tech. writer Sci. Info. Assocs., Seattle, 1984; program planner Boeing Computer Svcs., Seattle, 1985-86, tng. specialist, 1986—. Author: The Secrets of Successful Project Management, 1986. Capt. U.S. Army, 1974-78. Mem. Project Mgmt. Inst., Toastmasters, KC. Republican. Roman Catholic. Home: 8113 NE 158th Bothell WA 98011

KLIEN, WOLFGANG JOSEF, architect; b. Hollabrunn, Austria, Sept. 29, 1942; s. Josef and Maria (Kainz) K.; Dipl. Ing., Vienna Tech. U., 1967; m. Charlotte Olga Kutscherer, Aug. 14, 1968; children—Christina Olga, Angelika Maria. Designer, E. Donau, Architect, Vienna, 1968; with C. Nitschke & Assos., Architects, Columbus, Ohio, 1968-71; project architect GSAS Architects, Phoenix, 1971-75, 77-78; prodn. architect Harry Glueck, Vienna, 1976-77; v.p. architecture Am. Indian Engring. Inc., Phoenix, 1978-81; pres. S.W. Estate Group, Inc., real estate devel., San Diego, 1980-82; pres., tech. dir., branch mgr. Ariz. br. office SEG-S.W. Estate Group, Inc., Phoenix, 1982-86; prin. Klien & Assoc., Architecture, Planning, Devel. Cons., Phoenix, 1986-88, Atlantic-Pacific Trading Corp., Internat. Trade, Phoenix, 1986-88; pres., gen. mgr. Polybau, Inc., Hayward, Calif., 1988—. Mem. AIA, Austro-Am. Council West, Austrian Soc. Ariz. (founder 1985, v.p. 1985-86, pres. 1987—). Roman Catholic. Home: 214 E Griswold Rd Phoenix AZ 85020 Office: 4501 N 22d St Phoenix AZ 85016

KLIMBAL, PHILIP JOHN, computer/infosystems engineer; b. Redford Twp., Mich., July 13, 1963; s. Roy Mark and Florence Mary (Saja) K. BS, Purdue U., 1985. Programmer Digital Svc. Maintenance, Purdue U., West Lafayette, Ind., 1984-85; system software engr. Engring. Computer Network, Purdue U., West Lafayette, 1985-87; rsch. assoc. Rsch. Inst. for Advanced Computer Sci., Moffett Field, Calif., 1987—. Mem. IEEE, Assn. for Computing Machinery, Usenix Assn. Republican. Roman Catholic. Home: 135 Belcrest Dr Los Gatos CA 95032 Office: Rsch Inst Adv Computer Sci NASA Ames Rsch Ctr Moffett Field CA 94035

KLIMSTRA, KERRI LUANN, fast food executive; b. Litchfield, Minn., Sept. 20, 1962; d. Larry Duane and Deanna Ione (Lofquist) K. BA, St. Cloud State U., 1984. Specialist internat. Dairy Queen, Mpls., 1984-85, dist. mgr., 1985-86, sr. dist. mgr., 1986-87; regional mgr. Dairy Queen, Westminster, Colo., 1987—. Mem. NAFE, Sigma Alpha Iota. Republican. Lutheran. Home: 11373 Albion St Thornton CO 80233

KLINE, CARL GEORGE, consulting referral company executive; b. La Harpe, Ill., Sept. 5, 1935; s. Davis Carl and Helen Harriet (Gillette) K.; m. Nancy Truran (div. 1971); children: Stephen, Douglas, Dana; m. Leona Tompkins, Nov. 26, 1988. BS, Cen. Mo. State U., 1959; MBA, Ohio U., 1983. Regional rep. Gillette Co., Boston, 1960-64; mgr. human resources Magnavox Co., Ft. Wayne, Iowa, 1964-67; dir. personnel Emerson Elec. Co., St. Louis, 1967-70; pres. Kline Co., Dayton, Ohio, 1970-77; mgr. manpower NCR, Cambridge, Ohio, 1977-82, product mgr., 1982-84; pres. Nat. Cons. Referrals, Inc., San Diego, 1984—. Author: College Recruiting, 1983, How To Select Computer Hardware and Software, 1984, Practical Tools of Consulting, 1987. Pres., founder Cambridge Dem. Soc., 1982; v.p. Cambridge C. of C., 1982; pres. Guernsey County (Ohio) Bd. Health, 1983; trustee 6 County Mental Health, Zanesville, Ohio, 1983. With U.S. Army, 1954-56. Recipient plaque Guernsey County Bd. Health, 1983, 6 County Mental Health, 1983. Office: Nat Cons Referrals Inc 8445 Camino Santa Fe 207 San Diego CA 92121

KLINE, ELLIOT HOWARD, university dean, business educator; b. Denver, July 16, 1940; s. Morris and Sadie (Uswalk) K.; m. Linda Sue Newman, May 18, 1964; children: James, Edward. B.A., U. Colo., 1963, M.P.A., 1966, Ph.D., 1971. Instr. Tex. A&M U., College Station, 1966-67; lectr. U. Colo., Colorado Springs, 1968-69; asst. prof. U. Denver, 1968-70; dir., assoc. prof. Inst. Public Affairs and Adminstrn. Drake U., Des Moines, 1970-77; dean, prof. Sch. Bus. and Pub. Adminstrn. U. Pacific, Stockton, Calif., 1977-87; dean, prof. Coll. Bus. Adminstrn. U. Denver, Denver, 1987—; planning cons. State Savs. and Loan Assn., Stockton, 1979; dir. adminstrv. analysis Office City Clk., Indianola, Iowa, 1975; lectr. Brookings Instn., 1982, 83; vis. lectr. Washington Sem. Program, Am. U., 1982; cons. various orgns., 1973—. Guest editor: The Stockton Record, 1980—; contbr. articles to various publs. Served with USCGR, 1960-65. Recipient Grad. Sch. Research grants Drake Univ., 1972, 74. Mem. C. of C., Acad. Mgmt., Am. Assn. Higher Edn., Am. Mgmt. Assn., Am. Soc. Public Adminstrn. (mem. nat. council 1976-79), Calif. Assn. Public Adminstrn., Edn., Internat. Personnel Mgmt. Assn., No. Calif. Polit. Sci. Assn. (mem. exec. bd. 1981—), Western Govtl. Research Assn. (exec. com. 1981—), Western Assn. Collegiate Schs. Bus. (exec. bd. 1981—, pres. 1985-86). Office: U Denver Coll Bus Adminstrn Denver CO 80208

KLINE, FRANK MENEFEE, psychiatrist; b. Cumberland, Md., May 14, 1928; s. Frank Huber and Margaret (Menefee) K.; m. Shirley Steinmetz, June 27, 1953; children: Frank F., Margaret L. BS, U. Md., 1950, MD, 1952; PhD, So. Calif. Psychoanalytic Ins., 1977. Diplomate Am. Bd. Psychiatry and Neurology (examiner 1970-88). Intern Cin. Gen. Hosp., 1952-53; resident Brentwood VA Med. Ctr., West L.A., 1955-58; Regional chief West Cen. Mental Svc., L.A. County Dept. Mental Health, L.A., 1967-68; assoc. dir. adult psychiatry out-patient dept. L.A. County, U. So. Calif. Med. Ctr., 1968-77, acting dir. adult psychiatric dept., 1977-78; chief psychiatry VA Med. Ctr., Long Beach, Calif., 1977--; reviewer Hosp. Community Psychiatry, 1978-88, Am. Jour. Psychiatry, 1978-88. Editor: A Handbook of Group Psychotherapy, 1983. 1st lt. M.C., U.S. Army, 1953-55. Mem. Nat. Assn. VA Chiefs Psychiatry, Nat. Assn. VA Physicians, Jack Kramer Tennis (Rolling Hills Estates, Calif.). Office: VA Med Ctr 5901 E 7th St Long Beach CA 90822

KLINE, FRED WALTER, communications company executive; b. Oakland, Calif., May 17, 1918; s. Walter E. and Jean M. Kline; m. Verna Marie Taylor, Dec. 27, 1952; children—Kathleen, Nora, Fred Walter. B.A. in Calif. History, U. Calif.-Berkeley, 1940. With Walter E. Kline & Assocs. and successor Fred Kline Agy., Inc., from 1937; chmn. bd., pres. Kline Communications Corp., Los Angeles, 1956—; pres. Capitol News Service. Commr. Los Angeles County Fire Services Commn., Calif. Motion Picture Devel. Council; cons., advisor Calif. Film Commn.; former fed. civil def. liaison; developer state-wide paramedic rescue program; Calif. chmn. Office of Asst. Sec. Def.; mem. Calif. Com. for Employer Support of Guard and Res.; mem. Los Angeles Film Com. Served with USAAF, World War II; brig. gen. Calif. Mil. Dept. Recipient Inter-Racial award City of Los Angeles, 1963, named Man of Yr., 1964. Mem. Acad. Motion Picture Arts and Scis., Radio and TV News Assn. So. Calif., Pub. Relations Soc. Am., Calif. Newspaper Pubs. Assn., Cath. Press Council (founding mem.), Pacific Pioneer Broadcasters, Footprinters Internat., Am. Mil. Govt. Assn. (past pres.), Navy League, Calif. State Police Officers Assn., Internat. Assn. Profl. Firefighters (hon. life), Peace Officers Assn. Los Angeles County (life), Internat. Assn. Chiefs of Police, Internat. Assn. Fire Chiefs, Calif. Fire Chiefs Assn., Fire Marshals Assn. N.Am., Nat. Fire Protection Assn., Nat. Fin. Writers Assn., Hollywood C. of C., Nat. Fire Sci. Acad., Calif. State Mil. Forces, Calif. Pubs. Assn., So. Calif. Cable Club. Sigma Delta Chi. Clubs: Greater Los Angeles Press, Media (Los Angeles), Sacramento Press. Columnist Calif. newspapers. Office: 6340 Bryn Mawr Dr Los Angeles CA 90068

KLINE, PAMELA IRIS, consulting company executive; b. Pitts., Aug. 23, 1958; d. Robert Edward and Rae K. Cert., U. Paris, Sorbonne, 1979; AB magna cum laude, Harvard U., 1980, MBA, 1984. Asst. staff mgr. Bell of Pa., Phila., 1980-82; product mgr. Visa Internat., San Francisco, 1983; v.p. Prognostics, Palo Alto, Calif., 1984—. Vol. San Jose Civic Lights, 1987; dir. Harvard/Radcliff Fundraising, Boston, 1980—; chmn. Harvard/Radcli Schs. com., San Mateo County, 1985—. Mem. Young Profl. Woman Assn., Assn. Field Svc. Mgrs., Radcli Club (dir. 1987—), Harvard Club. Republican. Home: 2321 Sharon Rd Menlo Park CA 94025 Office: Prognostics 550 California Ave #300 Palo Alto CA 94306

KLINGEL, JOAN ELIZABETH, English educator; b. N.Y.C., Dec. 8, 1950; d. Frank Raymond and Jean Elizabeth (Pottebaum) K.; m. Robert D. Ray., June 4, 1988. BA, SUNY-Stony Brook, 1972; AM, Brown U., 1973, PhD in English, 1977, cert. Harvard U., 1987. Asst. prof. English, U. Colo., Colorado Springs, 1978-84, assoc. prof., 1984—, chmn. Enlish dept., 1980-83, asst. dean Coll. Letters, Arts, Scis., 1983-85, assoc. dean. 1985-86, interim vice chancellor for acad. affairs, UCCS, 1986-88; panelist div. edn. and research NEH, project dir. Humanities Enrichment at a Technically Oriented Campus, 1983-86; cons., evaluator NCA, 1987—. Assoc. editor: Letters of Hester Piozzi, 1987. Contbr. articles to profl. jours. Lector Grace Episcopal Ch., Colorado Springs. Brown U. fellow, 1972-73, Am. Council Learned Socs. grantee-in-aid, N.Y.C., 1979, U. Colo. Grad. Sch. research grantee, 1978, 79; recipient Chancellor's award U. Colo., Colorado Springs, 1983. Mem. MLA. Democrat. Office: U Colo PO Box 7150 Colorado Springs CO 80933

KLINGENSMITH, ARTHUR PAUL, relocation and redevelopment executive, consultant; b. L.A., May 23, 1949; s. Paul Arthur and Hermine Elinore (Wacek) K.; m. Donna J. Bellucci, Apr. 26, 1976 (div. Jan. 1981). AA in Social Sci., Indian Valley Jr. Coll., 1976; BA in Indsl. Psychology, San Francisco State U., 1979; MA in Indsl. Psychology, Columbia Pacific U., 1980. Enlisted USAF, Biloxi, Miss.; advanced through grades to staff sgt. USAF; instr. radio ops. USAF, Biloxi, 1968-72; air traffic control operator USAF, Hamilton AFB Novato, Calif., 1972-74; resigned USAF, 1974; elec. technician Calif. Dept. Transp., Oakland, 1975-78; right of way agt. Calif. Dept. Transp., San Francisco, 1978-85; sr. right of way agt. Calif. Dept. Transp., Sacramento, 1985-87, computer researcher, 1985-87; pres., cons. Associated Right of Way Svcs., Inc.; Please give current office address and date of current position. Bd. dirs. Kentfield Med. Found. Mem. Internat. Right of Way Assn. (instr. 1982—), Am. Arbitration Assn., Marin County Bd. Realtors, Assn. Humanistic Psychology, Nat. Assn. Housing and Redevel. Ofcls., Inst. Noetic Sci., Am. Mgmt. Assn. Republican. Office: APK Enterprises PO Box 574 Sausalito CA 94966

KLINHORMHUAL, EVERLIDA LLAMAS, clothing manufacturing company executive; b. The Philippines, July 7, 1950; came to U.S., 1974; d. Honesto S. and Carolina (Pastores) Llamas; m. Prapassorn Klinhormhual, Dec. 16, 1978. BS in Commerce, Philippine Coll. Commerce, 1972; MBA, Lincoln U., San Francisco, 1977. Loan clk. Great Pacific Life Ins. Co., Makati, Philippines, 1971-74; acctg. clk. Goodwill Industries East Bay, Oakland, Calif., 1976-77, office mgr., 1977-78; acctg. clk. Levi Strauss and Co., San Francisco, 1980-83, office mgr., 1983—. Mem. NAFE, Nat. Notary Assn., CIT. Office: Levi Strauss & Co 250 Valencia St San Francisco CA 94103

KLINNER, ALVIN RICHARD, financial executive; b. Glen Ullin, N.D., Jan. 28, 1930; s. Herman Joseph and Elizabeth Magdelan (Hoerner) K.; m. Chestine Wanda Smith, Dec. 31, 1956 (div. May 1976); children: Devnee, Bobbi, Steven; m. Patricia Ann Krueger, July 22, 1978 (div. Feb. 1989). AAS, Yakima Valley Jr. Coll., 1955; BBA, U. Wash., 1957, MBA, 1971. Cert. systems profl. Inst. Cert. Computer Profls. Mgr. gen. and cost acctg. Gen. Electric Co., Richland, Wash., 1957-64; mgr. adminstrn. Battelle-N.W., Richland, 1965-81; mgr. fin. svcs. Wash. Pub. Power Supply System, Richland, 1981—. Treas. Gesa Fed. Credit Union, Richland, 1968-74, pres., 1975; bd. dirs. Cerondelet Psychiatric Care Ctr. (formerly Mid Columbia Mental Health and Psychiat. Hosp.), Richland, 1985—. With U.S. Army, 1950-53, Korea. Mem. Assn. Systems Mgmt. (div. dir. 1983-85, div. 20 chmn. 1984-85, Columbia chpt. pres. 1985-86), Inst. for Cert. of Computer Profl. (cert.). Office: WPPSS MD 065 PO Box 968 Richland WA 99352

KLIPPERT, RICHARD HOBDELL, JR., engineering executive; b. Oakland, Calif., Jan. 25, 1940; s. Richard Hobdell and Carol Ione (Knight) K.; m. Penelope Ann Barker, Sept. 5, 1979; children—David, Deborah, Candice, Kristina. BS in Bus., Oreg. State U., 1962; postgrad. in polit. sci. U. Calif.-Berkeley, 1968-69, in polit. sci. and mgmt. George Washington U., 1972-73; grad. Naval War Coll., 1973. Commd. ensign USN, 1962, advanced through grades to comdr., 1971, ret., 1982, expert: Antisubmarine Warfare; mem. Combat Search and Rescue, Southeast Asia, 1964-67; exec. officer H.S. Squadron, 1974; mem. Flag Staff, 1974-79; chief engr. Light Airborne Multipurpose System MK-III, Washington, 1979-82; sr. engr., mgr. IBM, Boulder, Colo., 1982-83, engring. mgr., 1983-84, mgr. HH-60 systems engring., 1984-85, mgr. V-22 engring., 1985-88, program mgr. Document Mgmt. Systems Integration, 1988—. Author: The Moon Book, 1971. Contbr. papers to tech. lit. Decorated Silver Star, Navy Commendation; recipient Outstanding Achievement and Golden Circle awards IBM, 1986. Mem. Soc. Naval Engrs., Soc. Automotive Engrs., Naval Inst., Sigma Chi. Republican. Avocations: golf, tennis, photography, bridge. Home: Box 615 Niwot CO 80544-0615 Office: IBM Diagonal Hwy Boulder CO 80301

KLIPSCH, LEONA KATHERINE, retired newspaper publisher and editor; b. Vancouver, Wash., Feb. 24, 1914; d. Louis John and Marie Rosetta (Debitt) Hinkel; A.B., Smith Coll., 1935; student Sorbonne, Paris, 1934, Columbia U. Grad. Sch. Library Service, summers 1942-44; m. Robert Darius Klipsch, Nov. 25, 1937; children—Phyllis Marie Klipsch Smith, Katharine Klipsch Abbott, Marjorie Klipsch McCracken. Tchr. French and library sci. Marshall U., Huntington, W.Va., 1949-54; br. librarian Albuquerque Public Library, 1955-56; high sch. librarian, Gallup, N.Mex., 1963-65; co-owner, editor Defensor Chieftain, Socorro, N.Mex., 1965-82, pub., 1980-82. Bd. dirs. Socorro Gen. Hosp. Mem. AAUW, PEO, Sigma Delta Chi. Republican. Presbyterian. Author: Treasure Your Love (Librarian prize for jr. novel 1958); (as Jean Kirby) A Very Special Girl, 1963. Home: 1304 Kitt Pl PO Box V Socorro NM 87801

KLOBE, TOM, art gallery director; b. Mpls., Nov. 26, 1940; s. Charles S. and Lorna (Effertz) K.; m. Delmarie Pauline Motta, June 21, 1975. BFA, U. Hawaii, 1964, MFA, 1968; postgrad., UCLA, 1972-73. Vol. peace corps Alang, Iran, 1964-66; tchr. Calif. State U., Fullerton, 1969-72, Santa Ana (Calif.) Coll., 1972-77, Orange Coast Coll., Costa Mesa, Calif., 1974-77, Golden West Coll., Huntington Beach, Calif., 1976-77; art gallery dir. U. Hawaii, Honolulu, 1977—; acting dir. Downey (Calif.) Mus. Art, 1976; cons. Judiciary Mus., Honolulu, 1982—, Visual and Performing Arts Ctr., Maui, Hawaii, 1984—; exhibit designer Inst. for Astronomy, Honolulu, 1983-86; juror Print Casebooks. Recipient Best in Exhbn. Design award Print Casebooks, 1984, 86, Vol. Service award City of Downey, 1977; Exhbn. grantee NEA, 1979—, State Found. Culture and the Arts, 1977—. Mem. Hawaii Mus. Assn., Art Mus. Assn. Roman Catholic. Office: U Hawaii Art Gallery 2535 The Mall Honolulu HI 96822

KLOBUCHER, JOHN MARCELLUS, judge; b. Spokane, Wash., July 12, 1932; m. Virginia Rose Nilles; children—Marcella Marie, John Marcellus II, Christopher. Student Wash. State U., 1952; student Gonzaga U., 1954-57, J.D., 1960. Bar: Wash. 1960, U.S. Dist. Ct. (ea. dist.) Wash. 1961, U.S. Ct. Appeals (9th cir.) 1972. Law clk. to judge U.S. Dist. Ct. (ea. dist.) Wash., 1960-61; dep. pros. atty. criminal div. Spokane County Pros. Atty.'s Office, 1961-63; ptnr. Ennis & Klobucher, Spokane, 1963-78, Murphy, Bantz, Jansen, Klobucher, Clemens & Bury, Spokane, 1981; U.S. bankruptcy judge Eastern Dist. Wash., Spokane, 1981—. Served with U.S. Army, 1953-54. Mem. Wash. State Bar Assn., Spokane County Bar Assn. (pres. 1981), Inland Empire Fly Fishing (pres. 1977). Home: E 11320 17th Spokane WA 99206 Office: US Bankruptcy Ct PO Box 2164 Spokane WA 99210

KLUBER, BERNICE HERRIG, early childhood educator; b. La Motte, Iowa, Feb. 24, 1923; d. William P. and Mary (Schons) Herrig; m. Robert E. Kluber, Oct. 7, 1944; children: Robert E. Jr., Frank J., William P., Mary Ann Kreider, James V., Lisa H., Thomas L., Jeffrey A. BS, Iowa State U., 1944; MS, Portland State U., 1975. Cert. elem. tchr., Oreg., Calif. Instr. Portland (Oreg.) Community Coll., 1972-77; head tchr. Northridge (Calif.) Children's Ctr., 1977-79; tchr. Portland Pub. Schs., 1981—. Mem. Nat. Assn. for the Edn. of Young Children, Portland Assn. for the Edn. of Young Children. Republican. Roman Catholic. Office: Boise-Eliot Early 620 N Fremont Portland OR 97227

KLUCK, CLARENCE JOSEPH, physician; b. Stevens Point, Wis., June 20, 1929; s. Joseph Bernard and Mildred Lorraine (Helminiak) K.; divorced; children: Paul Bernard, Annette Louise Kluck Winston, David John, Maureen Ellen. BS in Med. Sci., U. Wis., 1951, MD, 1954. Resident San Joaquin Hosp., French Camp, Calif., 1955-56; asst. instr. medicine Ohio State U., Columbus, 1958-60; physician, chief of medicine Redford Med. Ctr., Detroit, 1960-69; practice medicine specializing in internal medicine Denver, 1969-83; med. dir. Atlantic Richfield Co., Denver, 1983-85; corp. med. dir. Cyprus Minerals Co., Englewood, Colo., 1985—; bd. dirs. Climbo Catering, Detroit, 1967-69, Met. Labs., Denver, 1970-81, Provest, Inc.; pres., bd. dirs. Pack Investments, Inc., Denver, 1985—. Contbr. articles to profl. jours. Served to capt. U.S. Army, 1956-58. Recipient Century Club award Boy Scouts Am., 1972. Fellow Am. Occupational Med. Assn., Am. Coll. Occupational Medicine; mem. Am. Acad. Occupational Medicine, Rocky Mountain Acad. Occupational Medicine (bd. dirs. 1985-88), Arapahoe County Med. Soc., Denver Med. Soc. (bd. dirs. 1973-74, council mem. 1981-87), Colo. Med. Soc. (del. 1973-74, 81-87), Am. Mining Congress Health Commn., Am. Soc. Internal Medicine, Colo. Soc. Internal Medicine. Roman Catholic. Clubs: Flatirons (Boulder, Colo.); Metropolitan. Home: 5245 E Oxford Ave PO Box 5277 Englewood CO 80155-5277 Office: Cyprus Minerals Co 9100 E Mineral Circle Englewood CO 80112

KMACK, GERALD ALLEN, computer consultant; b. Buffalo, Dec. 12, 1950; s. Chester A. and Ingrid W. (Reiner) K.; m. Marcia E. Hamm, Aug. 12, 1972; children: Steven, Ellen, Daniel. BS, SUNY, Stony Brook, 1972; postgrad., Ind. U., 1972-74. Mgr. digital dept. Data Indexing Systems Corp., Bloomington, Ind., 1974-75; MIS mgr. Vogt, Sage & Pflum Cons., Indpls., 1975-77; mgr. systems group Micor Internat., Phoenix, 1977-79; sr. software engr. Terak Corp., Scottsdale, Ariz., 1979-81; ptnr. Hirschi-Kmack & Assocs., Phoenix, 1981-85; owner, pres. Software Svcs. Group, Scottsdale, 1985—. Republican. Office: Software Svcs Group 14901 N Scottsdale Rd 302 Scottsdale AZ 85254

KNABENBAUER, ALAN LEE, stenciling company executive, security specialist; b. Neenah, Wis., Nov. 7, 1952; s. Jerome Joseph and Lucille Barbarra (Ulrich) K.; m. Yolanda Maria Peters, Dec. 15, 1952; children: Kassandra Rene, Rebecca Lee. Student, Central Tex. Coll., 1984. Security guard Civil Police Ltd. Inc., Appleton, Wis., 1968-71; correctional officer Fed. Dept. Corrections, Washington, 1975-77; forms insp. Neenah Foundry, 1977-79; correctional officer Ariz. Dept. Corrections, Tucson, 1986-88; exec. officer Am. Stenciling Co., Tucson, 1988-89, Knabenbauer Plastics Co., Tucson, 1989—, Alk Programs Co., Tucson, 1989—. Author: One Man's Thoughts, 1973, Origins of Catholicism, 1986; inventor aquarium vacuum. Sec., bd. dirs., cons. Christian Awareness Fellowship, Tucson, 1986—. With U.S. Army, 1972-74, 79-85. Republican. Baptist. Home and Office: 2384 W Diamond St 39 Tucson AZ 85705

KNAEBEL, JOHN BALLANTINE, mining consulant; b. Denver, Jan. 1, 1906; s. Ernest and Cornelia (Park) K.; student Cornell U., 1924-28; field geology Northwestern U., summer 1928; B.S. in Engring., Stanford U., 1929, E.M., 1930; m. Joy James, 1931 (div. May 1956); children—Jeffrey James, Stephen Park; m. 2d, Nelle M. McNulty, Mar. 14, 1958; 1 stepson, Terrence Patrick McNulty. Mining engr. Cananea Consol. Copper Co., Mexico, summer 1929; with U.S. Bur. Mines, 1930-33; mgr. East Mindanao Mining Co., Philippines, 1933-36; cons. engr., Western U.S., Can., C.Am., Mex., 1937-38; mng. dir. Amparo Mining Co., Ltd., Can., 1938-40; successively supt., asst. mgr., asst. to v.p., asst. mgr. Western Mines, U.S. Smelting, Refining & Mining Co., N.Mex., Utah, Western U.S., 1940-46; engr.-in-charge Anaconda Brit. Guiana Mines, Ltd., also mng. dir. Mineração Gurupi. S.A., Brasil (Anaconda Copper Mining Co. subs), 1946-50; gen. mgr. N.Mex. ops. Anaconda Co., 1951-56, Anaconda Co., 1955—, asst. to v.p.-in-charge mining ops., 1956-58; cons. engr., 1958; pres., mng. dir. Anaconda Iron Ore (Ont.) Ltd., Can., 1959-71; v.p., gen. mgr. Anaconda Co. (Can.), Ltd., Western div., 1962-71; v.p. Anaconda Am. Brass, Ltd., Western Exploration div., 1963-71; gen mgr. new mines dept. Anaconda Co., 1963-71, v.p., 1964-71; mining cons., 1971—. Named Mining Man of Yr., Mining World mag., 1956; recipient William Lawrence Saunders Gold medal for disting. achievement in mining AIME, 1959; Daniel C. Jackling award Soc. Mining Engrs.-Am. Inst. Mining Engrs., 1972. Mem. N.W., N.Mex. (dir. 1952-57, pres. 1956), Colo., Ariz. mining assns., Am. Mining Congress (Western bd. govs. 1955-57), Geol. and Mining Soc., AIME (Disting. Mem. 1975), Soc. Econ. Geologists, Tucson C. of C. (dir., mem. exec. com. 1964), Ariz. Acad. Public Affairs, Can. Inst. Mining and Metallurgy, Assn. Profl. Engrs. B.C., Assn. Profl. Engrs. Ont., Am. Forestry Assn., Nat. Geog. Soc., Nat. Wildlife Fedn., Aircraft Owners and Pilots Assn., Quiet Birdmen, Internat. Wood Collectors Soc., Sigma Xi, Sigma Gamma Epsilon. Contbr. articles and papers on mining to profl. publs. Home and Office: PO Box 1329 Winston OR 97496

KNAEPS, MARK JOZEF, marketing professional; b. Schoten, Belgium, June 13, 1958; came to U.S., 1980; s. Hugo Jan and Lea (Oste) K. Degree in Comml. Engring., U. Louvain, Belgium, 1980; MBA, U. Chgo., 1981. Mgr. new bus. W.R. Grace Co., Cin., 1981-82; mgr. internat. bus. planning Thyssen-Bornemisa div. Sterling Fluid Products Co., L.A., 1983; exec. asst. to gen. mgr. ITT Corp., Santa Ana, Calif., 1983—. Fulbright Commn. grantee, 1980, 81; recipient Procter & Gamble award, 1980. Mem. Eurocal Club. Home: 309 E 19th St Costa Mesa CA 92627 Office: ITT EMC Worldwide Group 1851 E Deere Ave Santa Ana CA 92705

KNAKE, BARRY EDWARD, management consulting executive, industrial psychologist; b. Chgo., Oct. 1, 1946; s. Louis Edward and Betty (Ryden) K.; m. Rita Kaye Watson, Feb. 7, 1967; children: Sean, Ryan, Julene. BA, Eastern Wash. U., 1969, MS, 1971. Grad. teaching fellow Eastern Wash. U., Cheney, 1969-70; personnel analyst City of Seattle, 1972-74; psychology instr. So. Seattle Community Coll., 1973; personnel psychologist U.S. Office Personnel Mgmt., Seattle, 1974-81; pres. KMB Assocs., Seattle, 1981—; rsch. bd. advisors Am. Biog. Inst., Inc., Raleigh, N.C., 1988—; v.p. rsch. and devel., advisor, bd. dirs. Nat. Compu Screen, Inc., Tualatin, Oreg., 1988—. Contbr. articles on personnel mgmt., testing, job analysis, affirmative action, job element testing to profl. jours. Mem. Seattle Urban League Employment Com., Seattle, 1983—; mem. Gov.'s Com. on Disability Issues and Employment, Olympia, 1980—. Mem. AAAS, Am. Psychol. Assn. (assoc.). Home and Office: 6730 13th Ave SW Seattle WA 98106

KNAPLUND, JUSTIN KING, military officer; b. Bronxville, N.Y., July 23, 1960; s. Paul William and Virginia (Samp) K.; m. Janet Lee Maykus, Mar. 2, 1985. BS in Astronautical Engring., USAF Acad., 1982. Commd. 2nd lt. USAF, 1982, advanced through grades to capt., 1986; student pilot Sheppard AFB, Wichita Falls, Tex., 1982-83; F-4E fighter pilot Seymour-Johnson AFB, Goldsboro, N.C., 1984-87; F-4E instr. pilot, safety officer, investigator George AFB, Victorville, Calif., 1988—. Office: 21 TFTS George AFB CA 92394

KNAPP, CLEON TALBOYS, publisher; b. Los Angeles, Apr. 28, 1937; s. Cleon T. and Sally (Brasfield) K.; m. Elizabeth Ann Wood, Mar. 17, 1979; children: Jeffrey James, Brian Patrick, Aaron Bradley, Laura Ann. Student, UCLA, 1955-58. With John C. Brasfield Pub. Corp. (purchased co. in 1965, changed name to Knapp Communications Corp. 1977); now pub. Bon Appetit mag., Archtl. Digest, Home mag., Los Angeles, 1958—; chief exec. officer Bon Appetit mag., Archtl. Digest, Home mag., 1965—, chmn. bd.; chmn. Knapp Press, Rosebud Press; owner Wilshire Mktg. Corp., Wood Knapp Home Video. Trustee UCLA Found.; bd. dirs. Damon Runyon-Walter Winchell Cancer Fund. Mem. Mag. Pubs. Assn. (bd. dirs.). Office: Knapp Communications Corp 5900 Wilshire Blvd Los Angeles CA 90036

KNAPP, EBER GUY, accountant; b. Seattle, Sept. 18, 1916; s. Eber G. and Ernestine C. (Venter) K.; student Wilson's Bus. Coll., 1938-39, U. So. Calif., 1946-47; m. M. Lorraine Knapp, July 2, 1947; children—Candyce Lorraine, Ardyce Christine, Carol Lynn. Cert. acct. Owner, Knapp's Tax & Bus. Service, Westminster, Calif., 1959—; overall coordinator Orange County (Calif.) Am. Assn. Ret. Persons Tax-Aide Program, 1979-88. Mem. Vice chmn. Mobile Home Commn., Westminster, Calif. Served with U.S. Army, 1941-45. Mem. Inland Soc. Tax Cons., Assn. Bus. and Tax Cons. Orange County (v.p.), Am. Legion, Calif. Assn. Ind. Accts. (charter), Nat. Assn. Pub. Accts., VFW. Republican. Mem. Christian Ch. Author: Groom's Survival Handbook, or How to Teach Your Bride to Cook, 1982. Home: 7152 Santee Ave PO Box 1 Westminster CA 92684

KNAPP, JOHN FREDERICK, publishing executive; b. Sacramento, Nov. 25, 1935; s. Eugene Russell and Ella Lucy (Long) K.; m. Suzanne Louise Small, Jan. 31, 1959; children: Jennifer Louise, Lucy Catherine. AB, U. Calif., Berkeley, 1959, MLS, 1966; MA, UCLA, 1961. Systems rsch. libr. Libr. of Congress, Washington, 1966-69; head libr. systems devel. U. Calif., Santa Cruz and Berkeley, Calif., 1969-72; mgr. systems devel. Richard Abel Co., Portland, Oreg., 1972-74; v.p. systems Rsch. Librs. Group, Branford, Conn., 1975-78; v.p. new products Blackwell N.Am., Portland, 1979-81; v.p. Ringgold Mgmt. Systems, Portland, 1982-84; gen. mgr. Internat. Specialized Book Svc., Portland, 1985—. With U.S. Army, 1956-57, Korea. Office: Internat Specialized Book 5602 NE Hassalo St Portland OR 97213

KNAPP, STUART EUGENE, computer consultant; b. Indpls., Jan. 30, 1933; s. Cecil Wayne and Mabel Pauline (Israel) K.; m. Mary Olive Phelps, Jan. 16, 1972; children by previous marriage; Kathleen Adele, Charles David, Steven Eugene, Dorothy Lorena. BSME, U. Denver, 1955. Cert. sys. profl.; cert. data processor. Wt. analyst Lockheed Aircraft Co., Burbank, Calif., 1955-56, Radioplane Co., Van Nuys, Calif., 1956; traffic engr. asst. City of Los Angeles, 1957-58; traffic engr. City of Anchorage, 1959-63; computer sys. programmer So. Pacific Co., San Francisco, 1964-69; sr. cons. Ernst & Ernst, San Francisco, 1970-71; sys. programmer III, sys. programmer supr. State of Nev., Carson City, 1973-76, 86-88; cons.,pres. Applied Sys., Inc., Carson City, 1977-85; cons., pres. Applied Sys., Inc., 1988—. Pres. bd. trustees Family Counseling Svc., Reno, 1973-74. Mem. Assn. Sys. Mgmt., C. of C. of Carson City, Kiwanis (pres. 1985). Methodist. Home: 310 Arrowhead Dr Carson City NV 98706 Office: Applied Systems Inc 202 S Pratt Ave Carson City NV 89701

KNAPP, THOMAS EDWIN, sculptor, painter; b. Gillette, Wyo., Sept. 28, 1925; s. Chester M. and Georgia Mabel (Blankenship) K.; m. Dorothy Wellborn; children: Gordon, Kathy, Dan, Kent, Keith. Student, Santa Rosa Jr. Coll., 1952-53; A.A., Calif. Coll. Arts and Crafts, 1953-54; student, Art Ctr. Sch., Los Angeles, 1954-55. Animation artist Walt Disney Studios, Burbank, Calif., 1954-56, Portrait & Hobby Camera Shops, WyoFoto Studies, Cody, Wyo., 1956-64; owner Rocky Mountain Land Devel. Corp., Cody, Wyo., 1965-66; comml. artist Mountain States Telephone Co., Albuquerque, 1966-69; lectr. at art seminars. Exhibited one-man shows, Cody County Art League, 1968, Jamison Gallery, Santa Fe, 1969, Mesilla Gallery, 1971, Inn of Mountain Gods, Mescalero Apache Reservations, N.Mex., 1978, Mountain Oyster Club, Tucson, 1978, Dos Pajaros Gallery, El Paso, 1978, (with Dorothy Wellborn) joint shows, Rosquist Gallery, Tucson, 1975, 77, Colony House, Roswell, N.Mex., 1974, 75, (with Michael Coleman), Zantman Gallery, Palm Desert Calif., 1977; one and two person shows nationally with Dorothy Bell Knapp through 1988; group shows, Saddleback Inn, Santa Ana, Calif., 1968-77, Zantman Gallery, Carmel, Calif., 1975, 76, 77, Borglum Meml. Sculpture Exhbn. Nat. Cowboy Hall of Fame, Oklahoma City, 1975-76, Maxwell Gallery, San Francisco, 1975; represented permanent collections, Whitney Gallery Western Art, Cody, Senator Quinn Meml. Auditorium, Spencer, Mass., Heritage Mus., Anchorage, Indpls. Mus. Art, Mescalero Tribe, N.Mex.; works include Dance of the Mountain Spirits (Blue Ribbon award 1976), Laguna Eagle dancer (spl. award 1974, Blue Ribbon Los Angeles Indian Art Show, 1975-76), Santa Clara Buffalo dancer (Spl. award San Antonio Indian Nat. show 1974, Spl. award Los Angeles Indian show 1976), Mandan chieftan (Spl. award San Diego Indian show 1974, Spl. award Los Angeles Indian show 1976); commd. to sculpt bronze statue of Tex. ranger Capt. Bill McMurrey, now in Tex. Ranger Mus., San Antonio, bronze Giant Galapagos Tortoise in collection of Gladys Porter Zoo, Brownsville, Tex., El Paso Mus. of Art, Mus. of Native Am. Cultures, Spokane, Wash., Cherokee Nat. Hist. Mus., Talequah, Okla., Diamond M. Found. Mus., Snyder, Tex., Buffalo Bill Hist. Ctr., Cody, Wyoming. Active Boy Scouts Am., 1947-68, World Wildlife Fund. Served with USN, World War II, Korea. Decorated Air medal; recipient Order Arrow award Boy Scout Am., 1968. Mem. N.Mex. Amigos, Mensa, New York Zool. Soc. Home and Office: PO Box 510 Ruidoso Downs NM 88346

KNAUB, GEORGIE ANN, nurse; b. Scottsbluff, Nebr., Nov. 9, 1955; d. George Jacob and Violet (Eskam) K.; m. James J. Jones, June 12, 1976 (div. May 1985). BS in Nursing, U. No. Colo., 1988; postgrad., U. Colo., 1988—. RN. With fire div. State Farm Ins., Greeley, Colo., 1979-81; data processor, bookkeeper Continental Emsco Co. div. LTV Corp., Dickinson, N.D., 1981-82, Berger Electric, Inc., Dickinson, 1982-83, MAC Devel. Inc., Cody, Wyo., 1983-85; data processor, coder Greeley (Colo.) Med. Clinic, P.C., 1985—; with neurosci. unit Poudre Valley Hosp. Vol. United Way Weld County, Greeley, Colo., 1979-81. Mem. Nat. Student Nurses Assn., Golden Key, Sigma Theta Tau (Drennan award 1988), Lambda Sigma Tau. Lutheran. Home: 1720 Kirkwood Dr Apt O #4 Fort Collins CO 80525 Office: Poudre Valley Hosp 1024 Lemay Ave Fort Collins CO 80525

KNAUER, KAREN LEE, contractor; b. San Diego, Jan. 30, 1960; d. William Edward and Alta Jean (Hendricks) K.; m. Brent Allan Anderson, Mar. 22, 1986. Grad. high sch., El Cajon, Calif. Sec. Accent Gen., Inc., Santee, Calif., 1981-82, Jean-Beck & Assocs., San Diego, 1982-84, Kertzman Contracting, Spring Valley, Calif., 1984-86; owner Karen Knauer Gen. Contractors, El Cajon, 1986—. Mem. Assn. Builders & Contractors, Women Constrn. Owners & Execs., Am. Gen. Contractors, NAFE. Republican. Office: 790 E Washington Ave Ste F El Cajon CA 92020

KNECHT, BEN HARROLD, surgeon; b. Rapid City, S.D., May 3, 1938; s. Ben and Ona K.; m. Jane Bowles, Aug. 27, 1961; children: John, Janelle. BA, U. S.D., 1960; MD, U. Iowa, 1964. Diplomate Am. Bd. Surgery. Intern Los Angeles County Gen. Hosp., 1964-65; resident in surgery U. Iowa Sch. Medicine, Iowa City, 1968-72; surgeon Wenatchee (Wash.) Valley Clinic, 1972—; dir. emergency room Cen. Wash. Hosp., Wenatchee, 1972-79, chief surgery, 1983-86; chmn. claims rev. panel Wash. State Med. Assn., Seattle, 1979—, profl. liability com. risk mgmt., 1985—; clin. assoc. prof. surgery U. Wash. Fundraiser Cen. Wash. Hosp. Found., 1987. Lt. commdr. USN, 1965-68, Vietnam. Mem. AMA (alt. del. 1985-87, del. 1988-90), Am. Coll. Surgeons (bd. dirs. Wash. chpt. 1981-84), Am. Soc. Bariatric Surgery, North Pacific Surg. Assn., Washington State Med. Assn. (trustee 1980—), Chelan-Douglas County Med. Soc. Lodge: Rotary (chmn. youth com. 1976-78). Office: Wenatchee Valley Clinic 820 N Chelan Ave Wenatchee WA 98801

KNECHT, ROBERT DOUGLAS, chemical engineer; b. Denver, Mar. 12, 1947; s. Robert Albert and Dorris Marie (Schneider) K.; m. Joan Elizabeth Lombardi, Aug. 22, 1970; children: Nathan L., Daniel L. ME, Colo. Sch. Mines, 1970, MS, 1976, PhD, 1978. Jr. engr. Amax Co., Golden, Colo., 1970, rsch. engr., 1970-76; project engr. Earth Sci., Inc., Golden, 1979-80; project mgr. ESI, Golden, 1980-81; mgr. Sci. Applications Internat., Golden, 1981—; adj. prof. Colo. Sch. Mines, Golden, 1979—. Rep. White House Children and Youth Conf., Washington, 1970. Mem. Internat. Soc. for Teaching Alternatives. Office: Sci Applications Internat 1626 Cole Blvd Lakewood CO 80401

KNEE, STEVEN THOMAS, psychiatrist; b. Lincoln, Nebr., Sept. 16, 1942; s. William Rex and Katherine Marion (Larson) K.; m. Jacquelyn Sue Kinavey, Oct. 14, 1986; children: Jessica, Alexis, Patrick, Olivia. BS, U. Nebr., 1964, MD, 1968. Intern U.S. Naval Hosp., San Diego, 1968-69; resident LAC-USC Med. Ctr., L.A., 1972-75; med. dir. Crossroads Hosp., Van Nuys, Calif., 1977-82, Child & Adolescent Treatment Ctr., Pueblo, Colo., 1982-85; v.p. med. svcs. Colo. Boys' Ranch Found., La Junta, 1985-87; program dir. VA Med. Ctr., Ft. Lyon, Colo., 1987; med. dir. Sangre de Cristo Community Mental Health Ctr., Santa Fe, 1987-88, Pinon Hills Hosp., Santa Fe, 1989—. Lt. comdr. USN, 1968-72. Mem. Am. Psychiatric Assn., Am. Soc. Adolescent Psychiatry, Am. Med. Soc. for Addictive and Other Drug Dependencies, Sigma Xi. Office: Pinon Hills Hosp 313 Camino Alire Santa Fe NM 87501

KNEELAND, DAVID TIMOTHY, management executive; b. Shelton, Wash., Feb. 22, 1945; s. David Tollefson and Elsie Margaret (Smith) K.; m. Mary Elizabeth Bowman, June 27, 1970; 1 child, David Thomas. BA, Ea. Wash. U., 1976; postgrad., U. Minn., 1976-77. Laborer Simpson Timber Co., Shelton, Wash., 1963-65; sales assoc. Northgate Homes, Seattle, 1970-71; dir. Inst. for Survival Edn., Seattle, 1971-76; teaching asst. U. Minn., Mpls., 1976-77; mgmt. devel. specialist Medtronic Inc., Mpls., 1977-80; dir. Inst. for Survival Edn., Mpls., 1979-83; pres. Tim Kneeland & Assocs. Inc., Seattle, 1983—. Loaned exec. United Way, Mpls., 1978, mem. campaign cabinet, 1979; nat. cons. Am. Lung Assn., N.Y.C., 1981—. Served with USAF, 1965-69. Democrat. Home: 317 NE 58th St Seattle WA 98105-2714 Office: Tim Kneeland & Assocs Inc 2603 3d Ave Ste 101 Seattle WA 98121-1213

KNELL-JONES, LYNN, teacher; b. Spokane, Wash., Nov. 25, 1944; d. John Klein and Emma Ellen (Fortner) Brackin; m. William G. Knell, June 9, 1967 (div. 1981); m. Lemanuel Jones, Apr. 6, 1983. BA in Art Edn., U. Wash., 1967; postgrad., Cen. Wash. U., 1968, Western Wash. U., 1970, Seattle Pacific U., 1970--. Cert. tchr., Wash. Tchr. art Univ. Place Sch. Dist., Tacoma, Wash., 1967-69; tchr. art Seattle Pub. Schs., 1969—, coordinator multi arts option, 1978--; grant planner Fed. Grant Magnet Program, Seattle, 1976-77. Scholarship com. Music and Art Found., Seattle, 1981-83; art dir. sch. earthquake safety edn. project U. Wash., 1985-86; activity planner for handicapped S.K.Y. Club, Seattle, 1980-87. Recipient award for acad. excellenc Citizens Com. for Acad. Excellence, Seattle, 1979-81, Tchr. of Yr. award Lincoln High Sch., Seattle, 1980, Golden Acord award Wash. PTA, 1987, Excellence in Edn. Com. for Excellence in Edn., Seattle, 1988, award for profl. excellence Western Wash. U. Sch. Edn., 1988. Mem. NEA, Wash. Edn. Assn., Seattle Educators Alliance, Seattle Parent, Tchr. and Student Assn., NAACP (art coach Seattle chpt. 1977-80, 81, 88). Democrat. Episcopalian. Home: 22612 4th Ave SE Bothell WA 98021 Office: Franklin High Sch 3013 S Mount Baker Blvd Seattle WA 98144

KNIERIM, KIM PHILLIP, lawyer; b. Tacoma, Nov. 18, 1945; s. Oscar Fitzpatrick and Dorothy Margaret (King) K.; m. Pamela Gail Waller. B.S. in Sociology, U. Wash., Seattle, 1968; J.D., Columbia U., 1974. Dir. human resources planning N.Y. Telephone Co., 1969-71; atty. Pillsbury, Madison & Sutro, San Francisco, 1974-76, Fulop, Polston, Burns & McKittrick, Beverly Hills, Calif., 1976-81, Gordon, Weinberg & Zipser, Los Angeles, 1982-84, Wood, Lucksinger & Epstein, Los Angeles, 1984-85; sole practice Los Angeles, 1985—; judge pro tem Beverly Hills Mcpl. Ct., 1979-87, Los Angeles Mcpl. Ct., 1985—; guest lectr. Pepperdine U. Law Sch., Los Angeles, 1981; mem. Los Angeles City Atty.'s Regulatory Reform Task Force, 1982-86; mem. U.S. Army War Coll. Nat. Security Seminar, 1984. Legal editor: Century 21 Brokers Guide to Working With Developers, 1988—. Chmn. pub. affairs Planned Parenthood N.Y.C., 1971-74; gen. counsel Los Angeles Ballet, 1979-80; chmn. bd. Bethune Ballet, 1981-82, pres., 1982-83, bd. dirs., 1983—. Served with RNSC, 1957-63; with USNR, 1969. Decorated Nat. Def. Service medal; Order Hosp. St. John Jerusalem (Anglican); Harlan Fiske Stone scholar, 1971-72, James Kent scholar 1972-74; teaching fellow Columbia U., 1973-74. Mem. ABA (vice chmn. young lawyers div. com. jud. tenure, selection and performance 1980-81), Calif. State Bar (del. 1980-87), Los Angeles County Bar Assn. (arbitrator 1979-88), Beverly Hills Bar Assn. (chmn. environ. law com. 1979-82, vice chmn. resolutions com. 1983-86), Pasadena Bar Assn., Beverly Hills Barristers (gov. 1979-81), U.S. Combined Tng. Assn. Anglican. Clubs: West Hills Hunt (hon. sec. 1988-89, dir. 1989—); Brit. United Services, Paddock Riding, University (Pasadena). Home: 279 Camino Del Sol South Pasadena CA 91030 Office: Wells Fargo Ctr 355 S Grand Ave Ste 3788 Los Angeles CA 90071-3101

KNIERIM, ROBERT VALENTINE, electrical engineer, consultant; b. Oakland, Calif., Sept. 27, 1916; s. Otto Valentine and Edith May (Bell) K.; m. Esther Perry Bateman, July 10, 1954; children: Kathleen Dianne, David Lyell, Daniel Goddard. BS, U. Calif., Berkeley, 1941; postgrad., U. Pitts., 1942, U. Colo., 1944-45, Raytheon Field Engring Sch, 1945. Registered profl. elec. engr., Calif. Student engr. Westinghouse Corp., East Pittsburgh, Pa., 1942; marine elec. engr. U.S. Maritime Commn., Oakland, 1943-44; elec. engr. U.S. Bur. Reclamation, Denver, 1944-45, Sacramento, 1945-48; field engr. Raytheon Corp., Waltham, Mass., 1945; electronics engr. Sacramento Signal Depot, 1948-49; assoc. elec. engr. Calif. Office Architecture and Constrn., 1949-57, sr. elec. engr., 1957-76; cons. engring. 1976. Mem. Century Club of Golden Empire Council Boy Scouts Am., 1969—, instnl. rep., 1948-54, dist. chmn. camping and activities com., 1951-54. Mem. Sacramento Engrs. Club (charter), IEEE (sr., life), Nat. Rifle Assn. (life), Sierra Club (life, chpt. treas. 1962-65), Nat. Assn. Corrosion Engrs. (life), Calif. Alumni Assn. (life), Eta Kappa Nu, Alpha Phi Omega (life). Republican. Congregationalist. Lodge: Masons. Home and Office: Cons Elec Engring 10325 SW Ashton Circle Wilsonville OR 97070

KNIGHT, BARRY ALLAN, accountant, educator; b. Webster City, Iowa, May 17, 1937; s. Allan Herbert and Beverly Eugene (Compton) K.; m. Joyce Irene Graham, June 13, 1959; children: Laurie Denise, Leslie Patricia, LeiAn Irene. BS, UCLA, 1960; MBA, U. So. Calif., 1971, DBA, 1976. CPA, N.Mex., Okla., Calif. Sr. acct. Coopers & Lybrand, L.A., 1961-64; prof. acctg. Calif. State Poly. U., Pomona, 1964-79; v.p. fin. TOTCO, Baker Internat., Norman, Okla., 1979-86; dean coll. bus. Ea. N.Mex. U., Portales, 1986—. Mem. Am. Inst. CPA's, Am. Acctg. Assn., Am. Soc. Personnel Adminstrs., N.Mex. Soc. CPA's, Rotary. Office: Ea NMex U Coll Bus Sta 49 Portales NM 88130

KNIGHT, CHARLES HENRY, JR., engineer; b. L.A., Nov. 26, 1924; s. Charles Henry and Lucile Marie (Darton) K.; m. Ruth Aileen Boyd, Apr. 17, 1945; children: Richard, Marilyn Knight McDougall, Robert. BS, Calif. Inst. Tech., 1949. Assoc. bridge engr. Calif. Div. Hwys., L.A., 1949-54; chief engr. NIGG Engring. Corp., Covina, Calif., 1954-56; field engr. Portland Cement Assn., L.A., 1956-60; dist. engr. Portland Cement Assn., Seattle, 1960-66; v.p., div. mgr. Portland Cement Assn., Skokie, Ill., 1966-70; v.p. mktg. Concrete Tech. Corp., Tacoma, 1970-77, pres., chief exec. officer, 1977—; bd. dirs. United Bank, Tacoma, ABAM Engrs., Inc., Fed. Way, Wash., Prestressed Concrete Inst., Chgo., pres., 1980. Cpl. USAAF, 1944-46. Fellow ASCE, Am. Concrete Inst.; mem. Seattle Tennis Club, Rotary. Home: 807 Hillside Dr E Seattle WA 98112 Office: Concrete Tech Corp 1123 Port of Tacoma Rd Tacoma WA 98421

KNIGHT, HELENKA STRETESKY, advertising agency executive; b. Tipton, Okla., Feb. 26, 1944; d. Frank and Rose (Serak) Stretesky; m Lynn B. Knight, Jr., Oct. 17, 1981; 1 child, Peter Joseph Stretesky. BFA, U. Okla., 1967; postgrad., Art Ctr. L.A., 1971-73, U. Calif., Irvine, 1976. Designer Bloom Advt., Dallas, 1967-69, Gaynor & Ducas Advt., Century City and L.A., 1969-71; creative dir. Bozell & Jacobs, Phoenix, 1973-74, Richard Holmes Design, Laguna Beach, Calif., 1974-76, King Advt., Newport Beach, Calif., 1976-80; owner, chief exec. officer Helegraphics, Laguna Niguel, Calif., 1980-88; owner, mgr., creative dir. HMS Knight Advt., Phoenix, 1988—; v.p., creative dir. mktg. Knight Lithograph, Inc., Phoenix, 1988—; cons. Saber Communications, Laguna Beach, 1976-85. Pres. Monarch Beach Homeowners Assn., Laguna Niguel and Monarch Beach, Calif., 1982-84. Mem. Women in Advt. (v.p. L.A. 1982), Laguna Niguel Bus. Assn. (mktg. rep.). Republican. Office: 3540E Corona Ave Phoenix AZ 85040

KNIGHT, JEFFREY RICHARD, systems requirements analyst; b. Salt Lake City, Apr. 2, 1962; s. Richard M. and Donna H. (Hallman) K. BBA, Calif. State Poly. Inst. U., 1984, MBA, 1986. Systems requirement analyst System Devel. Corp., Camarillo, Calif., 1985—; treas. Co. Activities Coordinating Com., Camarillo. Mem. Co. Mgmt. Assn., Rose Float Alumni Assn. (treas. 1985-86, bd. dirs. 1987-88). Republican. Home: 1857 Chickasaw Ave Apt #2 Los Angeles CA 90041 Office: Unisys 5151 Camino Ruiz Camarillo CA 93001-6004

KNIGHT, JOSEPH ADAMS, pathologist; b. Provo, Utah, Dec. 22, 1930; s. John Clarence and Martha Maude (Adams) K.; m. Pauline Brown, Oct. 18, 1949; children: David Paul, Leigh Knight Smith. BS in Chemistry, Brigham Young U., 1955, MS in Organic Chemistry, 1957; MD, U. Utah, 1963. Diplomate Am. Bd. Pathology; lic. Utah, Calif., Nev., Tex. Intern U. Utah Hosp., Salt Lake City, 1963-64, residency in pathology, 1964-67; instr. pathology Sch. Medicine U. Utah, Salt Lake City, 1966-67, clin. instr. pathology, 1967-70; assoc. pathologist Holy Cross Hosp., Salt Lake City, 1967-70; asst. clin. prof. pathology Sch. Medicine U. Utah, Salt Lake City, 1970-75; assoc. Health Svcs. Corp., Salt Lake City, 1969-75; assoc. pathologist Santa Rosa Med. Ctr., San Antonio, 1975-76; assoc. clin. prof. pathology Sch. Medicine U. Tex., San Antonio, 1975-76; dir. clin. labs. Primary Children's Med. Ctr., Salt Lake City, 1976-79; assoc. clin. prof. Sch. Medicine U. Utah, Salt Lake City, 1977-79, assoc. prof. pathology, 1979-88, assoc. chmn. pathology, head div. clin. pathology, 1979-85; assoc. chmn. pathology, head dir. edn., dir. clin. labs. and clin. chemistry VAMC, Salt Lake City, 1986—; prof. pathology Sch. Medicine U. Utah, Salt Lake City, 1988—; vis. prof. pathology Sch. Medicine U. Conn., Farmington, 1985-86; mem. admissions com. Sch. Medicine U. Utah, 1981-82, chmn. pathology residency com., 1980-85, co-chmn. pathology residency com., 1987—, mem. grad. sch. com. Sch. Med. Technologists U. Utah, 981-85. Author: (with others) Laboratory Examination of Cerebrospinal, Synovial and Serous Fluids: A Textbook Atlas, 1982, Body Fluids: A Textbook Atlas, 2nd ed., 1986 ; reviewer Clin. Chemistry, 1971, 77, 84, 86—; contrbr. articles to profl. jours. Served with U.S. Navy, 1948-52, Korea. Fellow Am. Soc. Clin. Pathologists, Coll. Am. Pathologists, Nat. Acad. Clin. Biochem.; mem. AMA, Am. Assn. Clin. Chemists, Utah Soc. Pathologists (pres. 1968-70, 79-80), Utah Med. Assn. (del. 1981-85), Am. Bd. Pathology (test com. 1987—), Am. Soc. Clin. Pathology (editorial rev. bd. 1987—, numerous others com.), Assn. Clin. Scientists (mem. com. 1985—), Coll. Am. Pathologists (inspector 1978—), Internat. Soc. Clin. Enzymology, Alpha Omega Alpha. Republican. Mormon. Office: U Utah Sch Medicine Dept Pathology 50 N Medical Dr Salt Lake City UT 84132

KNIGHT, PHILIP H(AMPSON), shoe manufacturing company executive; b. Portland, Oreg., Feb. 24, 1938; s. William W. and Lota (Hatfield) K.; m. Penelope Parks, Sept. 13, 1968; children: Matthew, Travis. B.B.A., U. Oreg.; M.B.A., Stanford U. C.P.A., Oreg. Chmn., pres., chief exec. officer Nike, Inc., Beaverton, Oreg., 1967—; dir. Metheus Corp. Trustee Reed Coll., Portland; mem. adv. council Stanford U. Grad. Sch.; bd. dirs. U.S.-Asian Bus. Council, Washington. Served to 1st lt. AUS, 1959-60. Named Oreg. Businessman of Yr., 1982. Mem. Am. Inst. C.P.A.s. Republican. Episcopalian. Office: Nike Inc 3900 SW Murray Blvd Beaverton OR 97005 *

KNIGHT, THOMAS J., JR., air force officer; b. San Antonio, Oct. 21, 1955; s. Thomas Jefferson and Martha Lena (Craig) K.; m. Lois Ann Simmons, July 13, 1985; 1 child, Thomas Jefferson III. BS, Baylor U., 1978; M. Pub. Adminstrn., Golden Gate U., 1988. Commd. 2d lt. USAF, 1978, advanced thru grades to capt., 1988; chief of adminstrn. USAF 780th Radar Squadron, Fortuna AFB, N.D., 1978-79; squadron sect. comdr. USAF 325th Component Repair Squadron, Tyndall AFB, Fla., 1979-82; protocol officer USAF HQ Tactical Air Command, Langley AFB, Va., 1982-85; exec. officer USAF 487th Tactical Missile Wing, Comiso AS, Italy, 1985-86, USAF 57th Fighter Weapons Wing, Nellis AFB, Nev., 1986—. Local commr. Panama City (Fla.) Boy Scouts Am., 1979-80. Mem. Air Force Assn. Presbyterian. Office: 57 FWW/CCE Nellis AFB NV 89191

KNIGHT, VICK (RALPH), JR., fundraising counselor; b. Lakewood, Ohio, Apr. 6, 1928; s. Vick Ralph and Janice (Higgins) K.; B.S., U. So. Calif., 1952; M.A., Los Angeles State Coll., 1956; postgrad. Whittier Coll., 1959-61, Long Beach State Coll., 1960-61, Calif. State Coll.-Fullerton, 1961-64, Claremont Grad. Sch., 1963-65; Ed.D., Calif. Coast U., 1989; m. Beverly Joyce McKeighan, Apr. 14, 1949 (div. 1973); children: Stephen Foster, Mary Ann; m. 2d, Carolyn Schlee, June 6, 1981. Producer-dir. Here Comes Tom Harmon radio series ABC, Hollywood, Calif., 1947-50; tchr., vice-prin. Ranchito Sch. Dist., Pico Rivera, Calif., 1952-59; prin. Kraemer Intermediate Sch., Placentia, Calif., 1959-64; dir. instructional services Placentia Unified Sch. Dist., 1964-65, asst. supt., 1965-71; program dir. World Vista Travel Service, 1970-72; dir. grad. extension La Verne Coll., 1971-73; v.p. Nat. Gen. West Investments, 1971-74; dir. community relations and devel. Childrens Hosp. of Orange County (Calif.), 1974-84; sr. dir. curriculum and edn. services Elsinore Union High Sch. Dist., Lake Elsinore, Calif., 1985-88; exec. dir. Elsinore valley Community Devel. corp., 1989—; exec. dir. Elsinore Valley Community Devel. Corp., 1989—; pres. Aristan Assocs.; dir. Key Records, Hollywood. Dist. chmn. Valencia council Boy Scouts Am.; chmn. Cancer Soc. Partners of Ams., also chmn. Sister City Com.; chmn. of Community Chest Drives; chmn. adv. com. Esperenza Hosp.; mem. Educare; hon. life mem. Calif. PTA. Bd. dirs. U. Calif.-Irvine Friends of Library, pres., 1975-77; bd. dirs. Muckenthaler Cultural Groups Found.; chmn. bd. William Claude Fields Found. Served with USN, 1946-48. Named One of Five Outstanding Young Men, Calif. Jr. C. of C., 1959; recipient Distinguished Citizen award Whittier Coll., 1960; Educator of Yr. award Orange County Press Club, 1971; Author and Book award U. Calif., 1973; Children's Lit. award Calif. State U.-Fullerton, 1979; Bronze Pelican award Boy Scouts Am. Mem. Nat. Sch. Pub. Relations Assn. (regional v.p.), U.S. (dir.), Calif. (state v.p.), Pico Rivera (pres.) jr. chambers commerce, Audubon Soc., Western Soc. Naturalists, Calif. Tchrs. Assn., NEA, Internat. Platform Assn., ASCAP, Soc. Children's Book Writers, Authors Guild, Authors League Am., Anti-Slubberdegullion Soc., Bank Dicks, Assn. Hosp. Devel., Art Experience, Good Bears of World, Los Compadres con Libros, Blue Key, Skull and Dagger, Les Amis du Vin, Phi Sigma Kappa, Alpha Delta Sigma, E Clampus Vitus, Theta Nu Epsilon. Kiwanian (pres.), Mason. Club: Canyon Lake Home Owners (pres. 1989—), West Atwood Yacht (commodore). Writer weekly Nature Notebook newspaper columns, 1957—; fine arts editor Placentia Courier. Editor curriculum guides: New Math., Lang. Arts, Social Scis., Pub. Relations, Biol. Sci. Substitute Tchrs. Author: (ecology textbooks) It's Our World; It's Our Future; It's Our Choice; Snakes of Hawaii; Earle the Squirrel; Night the Crayons Talked; My Word!; Send for Haym Salomon!; Joby and the Wishing Well; Twilight of the Animal Kingdom; A Tale of Twos; Who's Zoo; A Navel Salute; Friend or Enema?; also math. instrn. units; contbr. articles to various jours. Home: PO Box 4664 Canyon Lake CA 92380

KNIGHTON, ROBERT SYRON, neurosurgeon, educator; b. Vallejo, Calif., Aug. 17, 1914; s. David William and Mae Virginia (Clauson) K.; m. Cora Louise Taylor, Sept. 9, 1939; children—Robert W., George L., James E., Joan L., Thomas D. B.S., Pacific Union Coll., 1939; M.D., Loma Linda U., 1942. Diplomate Am. Bd. Neurol. Surgery. Intern Los Angeles County Hosp., 1942-43; resident in neurosurgery White Meml. Hosp., Los Angeles, 1943-44, 46-47; NRC fellow Montreal Neurol. Inst., Que., Can., 1947-48; chief div. neurosurgery Henry Ford Hosp., Detroit, 1952-71, chmn. dept. neurology and neurosurgery, 1971-79, emeritus chmn. dept. neurology and neurosurgery, cons., 1979—; prof. neurosurgery, chmn. div. neurosurgery Loma Linda U., Calif., 1981—; chief neurosurgeon Jerry L. Pettis VA Hosp., Loma Linda, Calif., 1982—; clin. prof. surgery U. Mich., Ann Arbor, 1971-79. Editor: Reticular Formations of Brain, 1957, Pain, 1966; contbr. papers to profl. publs. Served to capt. U.S. Army, 1944-46; ETO. Fellow ACS; mem. Soc. Neurol. Surgeons, Am. Assn. Neurol. Surgeons, Am. Acad. Neurol. Surgeons (v.p. 1977), Neurosurg. Soc. Am. (pres. 1975), Calif. Med. Assn., San Bernardino County Med. Soc. Home: 9388 Avenida San Timoteo Cherry Valley CA 92223 Office: Loma Linda U Div Neurol Surgery 11234 Anderson Loma Linda CA 92354

KNILL, KEEFER LESLIE, company executive; b. Frederick, Md., Aug. 5, 1949; s. Elbert Keefer and Peggy Ann (Walkinshaw) K.; m. Patricia Ann Bullinger, May 19, 1976; 1 child, Amy Ann. BBA, Nat. U., San Diego, 1986, MBA, 1988. Cryptanalyst Naval Security Group Activity, Okinawa, Japan, 1970-71, Nat. Security Agy., Ft. Meade, Md., 1973-76; analyst First Radio Bn., Kaneohe, Hawaii, 1976-79; basic course mgr. Naval Tech. Tng. Ctr., Pensacola, Fla., 1979-83; ops. mgr. XonTech, Inc., L.A., 1987—. Mem. sch. bd. Liberty Christian Schs., Huntington Beach, Calif., 1984-88; lay pastor Saddleback Valley Community Ch., Mission Viejo, Calif., 1989—. Master sgt. USMC, 1983-87. Mem. Armed Forces Communications & Electronics Assn., Am. Soc. Indsl. Security, Nat. Classification Mgmt. Soc. Republican. Baptist. Office: XonTech Inc 6151 W Century Blvd Ste 600 Los Angeles CA 92691

KNISELY, JAY WALLACE, plastics company executive; b. Casper, Wyo., Apr. 2, 1947; s. Vernon Howard and Jean E. Knisely; m. Maryann Jakopic, June 7, 1975; children: Ryan, Collin, Jennell. BSBA, U. Wyo., 1971; postgrad. in pub. rels., Stanford U., 1972-73. Adminstrv. asst. to Senator Clifford P. Hansen, U.S. Senate, Washington, 1970-72; ptnr., owner Knisely Moore Co., stock and bond investment co., Denver, 1975—; pres. Oakley Knisely Trucking Co., Denver, 1978-81, Terra Alta Corp., 1978-86; with ops. mgmt. dept. P.I.C. Plastics Inc., Denver, 1981—. Pres. Wyo. Young Reps., 1969; active Boy Scouts Am., Denver, 1988. Roman Catholic. Office: PIC Plastics Inc 1853 S Ivy St Denver CO 80224

KNITTLE, WILLIAM JOSEPH, JR., media executive, psychologist; b. Santa Monica, Calif., June 11, 1945; s. William Joseph Knittle and Lahlee (Duggins) Morrell; m. Linda Catherine Black, Apr. 19, 1969 (div. Aug. 1977); 1 child, Kristen Elizabeth; m. Alexis Carrell Upton, Sept. 30, 1977; 1 child, Jonathan Kynan. BA in English, Loyola U., Los Angeles, 1966, MA in Communication Arts, 1970, MA in Counseling Psychology, 1973; PhD in Communication Theory and Social Psychology, Lawrence U., Santa Barbara, Calif., 1976; D of Dharma in Asian Religion and Philosophy, U. Oriental Studies, 1980; MBA, U. La Verne, 1983. Assoc. editor Black Belt mag., 1960-65; asst. news dir. Sta. KHJ-TV, Los Angeles, 1966-67; news editor Sta. KFWB Radio, Los Angeles, 1967-69; dir. news and pub. info. Loyola Marymount U., Los Angeles, 1969-75; gen. mgr. Media Five, Los Angeles, 1976-79, v.p., 1981-83; assoc. dir. div. of continuing edn. U. La Verne, Calif., 1979-81; pres. Western News Assocs., Los Angeles, 1983—; asst. to dean UCLA Sch. Medicine, 1985—. Author: Survival Strategies for the Classroom Teacher, 1982; columnist various newspapers, mags., 1970—; contbr. articles to profl. jours. Asst. abbot Internat. Buddhist Med. Ctr., Los Angeles, 1976-81; assoc. dir. Pasadena/San Gabriel Valley Counseling Ctr., 1973. Recipient Martial Arts Pioneer award Am. Tae Kwon Do-Kung Fu Assn., 1976, Nat. Headliners award Wash. Press Club, 1968, Internat. Journalism award Sigma Delta Chi, 1968. Mem. AAAS, Assn. for Transpersonal Psychology, Inst. for Holistic Edn., Soc. Interdisciplinary Study of Mind, Internat. Brotherhood of Magicians, Internat. Imagery Assn., Am. Soc. Tng. and Devel., Nat. Book Critics Circle, Investigative Reporters and Editors, Am. Fedn. Police (chaplain 1985—), Nat. Police Acad. Home and Office: Western News Assocs PO Box 241778 Los Angeles CA 90024-9578

KNORR, WILBUR RICHARD, JR., philosophy and classics educator; b. Bklyn., Aug. 29, 1945; s. Wilbur Richard Sr. and Dorothy Louise (Keifer) K. BA, Harvard U., 1966, AM, 1968, PhD, 1973. Asst. prof. U. Calif., Berkeley, 1971-73, CUNY, Bklyn., 1975-79; asst. prof. Stanford (Calif.) U., 1979-84, assoc. prof., 1984—. Author: Evolution of the Euclidean Elements, 1975, Ancient Sources of Medieval Tradition of Mechanics, 1982, Ancient Tradition of Geometric Problems, 1986. postdoctoral fellow Inst. Advanced Study, 1978-79, Am. Council Learned Socs., 1978-79; rsch. grantee NSF, 1973-74, 79-80. Office: Stanford U History of Sci Program Stanford CA 94305

KNOTT, FRANK C., small business owner; b. Spokane, Wash., June 14, 1942; s. William Ernest and Dorothy Marie (Menger) K.; m. Vivienne Joy Adams, Dec. 17, 1982; children: Ronald, Jody. BA, Whitworth Coll., 1964. Tchr. Palmer (Alaska) Sch. Dist., 1964-67, Selkirk Schs., Metaline, Wash., 1967-69; with sales R.M. Wade Co., Beaverton, Oreg., 1969-72; owner, mgr. Saunders and Ott Inc., Fairfield, Wash., 1972—. Mem. adv. com. Mead (Wash.) Vocat. Dept., 1972-76, Fairfield City Council, 1973-87, steering com. Liberty Sch., Fairfield, 1983-87. Mem. Pacific Hardware and Implement Assn., Spokane Club, Elks, Moose. Presbyterian. Home: PO Box 247 410 W Hamilton Fairfield WA 99012 Office: Saunders and Ott Box 327 1st and Carlton Fairfield WA 99012

KNOTT, SYDNEY SULLIVAN, public relations executive; b. Santa Barbara, Calif., Oct. 16, 1956; d. Warren Arthur and Thelma Nadine (Adkins) Sullivan; m. Martin R. Wilson, Aug. 18, 1979 (div. July 1986); m. John T. Knott II, Sept. 4, 1988. AB in Pub. Relations, U. So. Calif., 1978. Mgr. dept. May Co., San Diego, 1979-80; acct. exec. Stoorza, Ziegaus & Metzger, San Diego, 1980-82, Braun & Co., Los Angeles, 1984-85; specialist pub. relations U.S. Dept. Treasury, Washington, 1983-84; dir. fin. Calif. Repub. Com., Burbank, Calif., 1985-86; dir. pub. relations Katersky Fin., Woodland Hills, Calif., 1987; mng. assoc. Casey & Sayre, Inc., Malibu, Calif., 1987—; cons. Knott Communications, Los Angeles, 1987. Coord. campaign Gibson for Assembly, Huntington Beach, Calif., 1978; press asst. Pete Wilson for U.S. Senate, San Diego, 1982; network liaison Reagan for Pres. GOP Conv., Dallas, 1984. Mem. Pub. Relations Soc. Am. (La. chpt. PRISM award for outstanding community rels. program 1988), Nat. Assn. Real Estate Editors (assoc.), Jr. League (bd. dirs. 1986-87). Congregationalist. Office: Casey & Sayre Inc 29350 Pacific Coast Hwy Malibu CA 90265

KNOTT, WILLIAM ALAN, library director, library management and building consultant; b. Muscatine, Iowa, Oct. 4, 1942; s. Edward Marlan and Dorothy Mae (Holzhauer) K.; m. Mary Farrell, Aug. 23, 1969; children—Andrew Jerome, Sarah Louise. B.A. in English, U. Iowa, 1967, M.A. in L.S., 1968. Asst. dir. Ottumwa (Iowa) Pub. Library, 1968-69; library cons. Iowa State Library, Des Moines, 1968-69; dir. Hutchinson (Kans.) Pub. Library and S. Central Kans. Library System, Hutchinson, 1969-71; dir. Jefferson County Pub. Library, Lakewood, Colo., 1971—. Served with U.S. Army, 1965-67. Mem. Colo. Library Assn. Author: Books by Mail: A Guide, 1973; co-author: A Phased Approach to Library Automation, 1969; editor: Conservation Catalog, 1982. Office: Jefferson County Pub Libr 10200 W 20th Ave Lakewood CO 80215

KNOTTER, LUCIEN THEODORE, III, sales executive; b. Pitts., Feb. 11, 1948; s. Lucien Theodore Jr. and Anne (Malaga) K.; m. Julie Marguerite Fischer, May 25, 1984; children: Lucien Theodore IV, Tessa Christine. BSCE, Ariz. State U., 1973. Civil engr. City of Phoenix, 1973-75; sales rep. Hewlett Packard Co., Fullerton, Calif., 1975-78, 1981-83; dist. sales mgr. Hewlett Packard Co., Rolling Meadows, Ill, 1978-80; assoc. dir. Engring. Career ASsocs., Newport Beach, Calif., 1980-81; sales rep. Group III Electronics, Irvine, Calif., 1983-85; sr. account mgr. Texas Instruments, Torrance, Calif., 1985-88; sales mgr. Pyramid Tech. Corp., Irvine, 1988—. Republican. Presbyterian. Office: Pyramid Tech Corp 18662 MacArthur Blvd Suite 200 Irvine CA 92715

KNOWLES, PAUL WESLEY, banker; b. Stillwater, Minn., Apr. 25, 1924; s. Elmer David and Lulu May (Brown) K.; m. Helen Virginia Shepherd, Jan. 20, 1946; children: Suzanne Knowles Curtis, Deborah Blair, Paul W. Jr. BS in Commerce, State U. Iowa, 1949; postgrad., Harvard U., 1972. Gen. agt. Nat. Life of Vt., Davenport, Iowa, 1949-61; owner, mgr. Sta. KSGT Radio, Jackson, Wyo., 1966-75, Sta. KAPR Radio, Douglas, Ariz., 1973-78; bank trust exec. Valley Nat. Bank of Ariz., Tuscon and Phoenix, 1979-89, ret., 1989. State rep. Iowa Ho. of Reps., Des Moines, 1960-64. Lt. USAAF, 1943-45. Mem. Am. Soc. CLUs, Am. Soc. Appraisers (cert.), Masons, Shriners. Republican. Episcopalian. Home and Office: 2323 N Central #402 Phoenix AZ 85004

KNOWLES, TONY, restaurant operator, former mayor; b. Tulsa, Jan. 1, 1943; m. Susan Knowles; children: Devon, Lucas. BA in Econs., Yale U., 1968. Owner, mgr. The Works, Anchorage, 1968—, Downtown Deli, Anchorage, 1978—; mayor Municipality of Anchorage, 1981-87. Mem. citizen's com. to develop comprehensive plan for growth and devel., Anchorage, 1972; mem. Borough Assembly, Anchorage, 1975-79; bd. dirs. Fairview Community Ctr., March of Dimes, Pub. TV Sta. KAKM, numerous sports facilities coms. Served with U.S. Army, Vietnam. Mem. Anchorage C. of C. (bd. dirs.). Office: Downtown Deli 525 W 4th Ave Anchorage AK 99501 *

KNOX, CARL BRADFORD, JR., operations and engineering company executive; b. Huntington Park, Calif., Sept. 11, 1931; s. Carl Bradford and Leila Marie (Maggard) K.; m. Liane Arlene Griffiths, March 5, 1954; children: Janice Susan, Gary Stephen. Student, Fullerton Coll., 1956-58, Orange Coast Coll., 1958-59, West Coast U., 1966, Century U., L.A., 1982—. Mgr. specifications engring. Babcock Relays Inc., Costa Mesa, Calif., 1960-68; dir. ops. and spl. projects mgr. Babcock Inc., Orange, Calif., 1982-86; mgr. mfg., engring. and quality Kratos Precision Products, Inc., L.A., 1968-69; engr., scientist specialist McDonnell Douglass, Inc., Huntington Beach, Calif., 1969-73; v.p. engring. Electronic Applications, Inc., El Monte, Calif., 1973; v.p. ops. Q Tron, Inc., Santa Ana, Calif., 1973-76; plant mgr., chief plant operating officer AMF Potter and Brumfield, San Juan Capistrano, Calif., 1976-82; dir. engring. and quality Leach Corp., L.A., 1986-88; pvt. practice cons. Costa Mesa, 1988—; cons. Struthers-Dunn, Inc., Pitman, N.J., 1988—; guest lectr. Purdue U., 1967. Contbg. author: Engineers Relay Handbook (3 vols.); contbr. numerous papers to profl. jours. Regional dir., US Naval Sea Cadet Corps, Calif., 1978—. With USNR, 1951-53. Mem. Nat. Assn. Relay Mfrs. (rep. 1980-88, v.p. 1908-86, svc. tech. affairs com. 1983, v.p. tech. affairs 1980-86), Toastmasters (pres. 1967). Republican. Presbyterian. Home and Office: 1112 Corona Ln Costa Mesa CA 92626

KNOX, CHARLES ROBERT, professional football coach; b. Sewickley, Pa., Apr. 27, 1932; s. Charles McMeehan and Helen (Keith) K.; m. Shirley Ann Rhine, Aug. 2, 1952; children: Christeen, Kathy, Colleen, Chuck. BA, Juniata Coll., 1954; postgrad., Pa. State U., 1955. Asst. football coach Wake Forest Coll., 1959-60, U. Ky., 1961-62, N.Y. Jets, 1963-66, Detroit Lions, 1967-72; head football coach Los Angeles Rams, 1973-78; head football coach, v.p. football ops. Buffalo Bills, 1978-82; head football coach Seattle Seahawks, 1983—. Named NFL Coach of Yr., Sporting News, 1973, 80, NFL Coach of Yr., Seattle Gold Helmet Com., 1983, 84. Lutheran. Club: Big Canyon Country. Office: care Seattle Seahawks 11220 NE 53rd St Kirkland WA 98033 *

KNOX, DAVID GLEN, emergency physician; b. Pullman, Wash., Apr. 12, 1950; s. Richard Franklin and Helen Edith (Price) Knox; m. Janice Marie Vaughn, May 27, 1977; children: Zachary Aaron, Rachel Melissa, Jessica Brittany. BS, U. Wash., 1973, MD, 1977. Cert. AM. Bd. of Emergency Med. Intern San Francisco Gen. Hosp., 1977-78; emergency physician Emergency Med. Systems Inc., San Francisco, 1978-80, Providence Milwaukie (Oreg.) Hosp., 1980—. Mem. Am. Coll. of Emergency Physicians. Christian. Home: 1942 Sunburst Terr West Linn OR 97068 Office: Providence Milwaukie Hosp 10150 SE 32d Ave Milwaukie OR 97222

KNOX, HELENE MARGRETHE, writer; b. Sacramento, Calif., May 1, 1943; d. James Dale and Helen Margrete (Clemens) K. BA with honors, U. Calif., Berkeley, 1965, MA, 1968, PhD, 1979. Assoc., instr., sect. leader dept. English U. Calif., Berkeley, 1972-74, 77-78; Fulbright lectr. in Am. studies U. Perpignan, France, 1972-73, U. Augsburg, Fed. Republic Germany, 1980-81; lectr. English U. San Francisco, 1979; vis. asst. prof. English Drexel U., Phila., 1981-82; asst. prof. English and creative writing Muhlenberg Coll., Allentown, Pa., 1982-86; ind. poet, novelist, scholar, editor, interviewer Oakland, Calif., 1986—; presenter pub. readings of original poetry, U.S., Europe and Tunisia, 1970—; lectr. on lit., U.S. and Europe, 1972-89; presenter papers at profl. meetings. Contbr. poetry to lit. mags. and anthologies; contbr. stories, scholarly articles to various publs. Campaign worker, Jesse Jackson for Pres., Calif., 1988. Mem. MLA, NOW. Democrat. Unitarian-Universalist. Home: 331 62d St Oakland CA 94618

KNOX, JEFFEREY FRANKLYN, architectural engineer; b. Fredricksburg, Va., June 17, 1960; s. Ronald Onzalo and Yvonne (Zitzman) K. BS in Archtl. Engring., U. Colo., 1985. Bookkeeper Dunhill of Boulder, Inc., Colo., 1976-85; asst. to pres. Boulder Valley Orchids, Ltd., 1978-85; lectr. N.Y.U., N.Y.C., 1986-87; intermediate engr. Syska & Hennessy, Inc., N.Y.C., 1985-87; designer Patrick B. Quigley & Assoc., Torrance, Calif., 1987—; v.p., mem. bd. dirs. Dunhill of Boulder, Inc., 1982—. Mem. Internat. Assn. Lighting Designers, Illuminating Engring. Soc., Am. Orchid Soc. Republican. Office: Patrick B Quigley & Assoc 2340 Plaza Dec Amo Ste 125 Torrance CA 90501

KNOX, JOHN T., lawyer; b. Reno, Nev., Sept. 30, 1924; s. Ernest Botte and Jean Bolarne (Monat) K.; m. Margaret Jean Henderson, Dec. 27, 1949; children: John, Charlotte, Mary. AB, Occidental Coll., 1949; JD, Hastings Coll. of Law, 1952. Pvt. practice Richmond, Calif., 1953-65; ptnr. Knox and Herron, Richmond, 1965-80, Nossaman, Guthner, Knox and Elliott, San Francisco, 1980—; mem. Calif. State Assembly, Sacramento, 1960-80; gen. ptnr. United Enterprises, Ltd., San Diego, 1987—; trustee, Occidental Coll., L.A., 1975—; bd. dirs. Hastings Coll. of Law, San Francisco, 1981—. Author numerous pieces legis. Mem. steering com. San Francisco Bay Area Council, 1980—; bd. dirs. Calif. Council for Environ. and Econ. Balance, Sacramento, 1982—; pres. Calif. Found. for Environ. and Econs., San Francisco, 1987—. Sgt. USAF, 1943-45. Recipient Environ. award, San Francisco Bay Area Council, 1970. Mem. Pt. Pinale Lodge F&AM, Calif. State Bar Assn., ABA, Contra Costa Bar Assn., Am. Club, City Club. Democrat. Home: 229 Bishop Ave Richmond CA 94801 Office: Nossaman Guthner Knox et al 50 California St San Francisco CA 94111

KNOX, KEVIN BRADFORD, real estate company executive; b. Chgo., Oct. 17, 1957; s. James George and Jacquline (Cook) K.; m. Janet Lynn Nelson, Aug. 24, 1985. BS, Calif. Poly., Pomona, Calif., 1980. Regional planner County of Los Angeles, 1980; asst. dir. community planning RBF & Assocs. Inc., Newport Beach, Calif., 1980-82; principal The Fifth Day, Orange, Calif., 1982-87; sr. architect Milestone Builders Inc., Anaheim, Calif., 1987-89; v.p. Erin-Madison Ltd., Newport Beach, Calif., 1989—. Mem. Assn. Environ. Profls. (treas. 1983-86), Am. Planning Assn., Am. Inst. of Cert. Planners. Republican. Presbyterian. HOme: 25660 Cross Creek Road #C Yorba Linda CA 92686 Office: Erin Madison Ltd 2424 SE Bristol St Ste 220 Newport Beach CA 92658

KNOX, ROBERT LEE, educator; b. Enid, Okla., Jan. 15, 1932; s. Beryl Leroy and Doris Ethel (Ulrey) K.; m. Mary Frances Kern, Aug. 16, 1958; children: Shelly L., Cynthia C. BS in Commerce, Okla. State U., 1954, MS in Econs., 1958; PhD in Econs., U. N.C., 1963. Asst. prof. econs. Coll. William and Mary, Williamsburg, Pa., 1961-63; asst. prof. econs. Ariz. State U., Tempe, 1963-66, assoc. prof. econs., 1966-71, prof. econs., 1971—; cons. antitrust econs., 1971—. Contbr. articles to profl. jours. Chmn. Ariz. Health Planning Council, 1973-75. Capt. USAF, 1954-57. Mem. Am. Econs. Assn. Home: 46 W Caroline Ln Tempe AZ 85284 Office: Ariz State U Dept Econs Tempe AZ 85287

KNUDSEN, CONRAD CALVERT, corporate lawyer; b. Tacoma, Oct. 3, 1923; s. Conrad and Annabelle (Callison) K.; m. Julia Lee Roderick, Nov. 22, 1950; children: Calvert Jr., Elizabeth Page, Colin Roderick, David Callison. BA, U. Wash., 1948, LLB, 1950. From assoc. to ptnr. Bogle, Bogle & Gates, Seattle, 1951-61; exec. v.p., dir. Aberdeen Plywood & Veneer Inc., Aberdeen, Oreg., 1961-63; pres., chief adminstrv. officer, vice chmn. Evans Products Co., Portland, Oreg., 1963-68; sr. v.p. corp. growth Weyerhaeuser Co., Tacoma, 1969-76; pres., chief exec. officer, dir. MacMillan Bloedel Ltd., Vancouver, B.C., Can., 1976-80; chmn., chief exec. officer, dir. MacMillan Bloedel Ltd., 1980-83, vice-chmn., 1983—; bd. dirs. Cascade Corp., Portland Gen. Corp./Portland Gen. Electric, Portland Penwest Ltd., Security Pacific Bank of Washington, Safeco Ins. Co., Seattle Security Pacific Corp., Security Pacific Bank, L.A. West Fraser Timber Co. Ltd., MacMillan Bloedel Ltd., Vancouver, B.C., Can. Imperial Bank of Commerce, Toronto, Can. Chmn. Seattle Art Mus.; bd. dirs. Assocs. Harvard U., Boston. With U.S. Army 1942-46. Fellow in law Columbia U., 1951. Mem. ABA, Wash. State Bar Assn., Columbia Law Sch. Alumni Assn., Confrerie des Chevaliers du Tastevin (wine), Enological Soc. of the Pacific Northwest, U. Wash. Alumni Assn., Bohemian Club, Univ. Club, Rainier Club, Seattle Tennis Club, Seattle Arlington Club, Multnomah Athletic, Racquet Club Portland. Home: 602 36th Ave East Seattle WA 98112 Office: MacMillan Bloedel Ltd, 1075 W Georgia St, Vancouver, BC Canada V6E 3R9

KNUDSEN, ERIC INGVALD, neuroscientist; b. Palo Alto, Calif., Oct. 7, 1949. BA, U. Calif., Santa Barbara, 1971; MA, U. Calif., 1973; PhD in Neuroscience, U. Calif., San Diego, 1976. Rsch. fellow in neuroscience Calif. Inst. Tech., 1976-80; mem. faculty dept. neuroscience Stanford Sch. Med., 1980—; now assoc. prof. Recipient Troland Rsch. award Nat. Acad. Scis. Office: Stanford U Sch Medicine Dept Neurobiology 300 Pasteur Dr Stanford CA 94305 *

KNUDSEN, LISA LEE, computer consultant; b. Inglewood, Calif., Nov. 14, 1959; d. Thomas Carl and Belle Marie (Lillard) Duke; m. John Frank Knudsen, Dec. 29, 1984; children: Johanna Joy, John Christian. Asst. mgr. Morse Shoes, Nashville, 1976-78; bookkeeper Culver Fed. Savs. and Loan, Manhattan Beach, Calif., 1978-80; assoc. tech. staff The Aerospace Corp., El Segundo, Calif., 1980—; notary pub. Culver Fed. Savs. and Loan, Manhattan Beach and Redondo Beach, Calif., 1978-82; cons. mem. Microsoft Corp., N.Y., 1986-87. Precinct worker State of Calif., Redondo Beach, 1988. Republican. Office: Aerospace Corp M2-244 2350 E El Segundo El Segundo CA 90254

KNUDSEN, ROBERT THEODORE, sales executive; b. East Grand Rapids, Mich., Apr. 29, 1937; s. LeRoy Bjarne and Florence Isabelle (Haberkorn) K.; m. Danene Lynn Schoessler, Aug. 6, 1965; children: Michelle J., Kristine L. BS in Elem. Edn., Rocky Mountain Coll., Billings, Mont., 1965. Food svc. dir. Saga Food Svc., 1965-73; sales mgr. C.F.S. Continental, Yakima, Wash., 1973-77; v.p., gen. mgr., ptnr. Gen. Supply, Inc., Yakima, 1977-83; gen. mgr., sale mgr. Care Group, Yakima, 1983—. Bd. dirs. Campfire Girls Coun., Yakima, 1975-79, Yakima Valley Coll. Concert Series, 1976-78. Paul Harris fellow, 1980. Mem. Wash. Interment Assn. (bd. dirs. 1988—), Am. Cemetery Assn., Rocky Mountain Coll. Alumni Assn. (bd. dirs. 1975-80), Rotary (pres. Yakima chpt. 1979, award 1982). Republican. Methodist. Home: 6907 Alpine Way Yakima WA 98908

KNUDSON, MELVIN ROBERT, management consultant, business executive; b. Libby, Mont., Oct. 27, 1917; s. John and Serina (Bakken) K.; B.S. in Wood Chemistry, Oreg. State U., 1942; m. Melba Irene Joice, Mar. 5, 1946; children—Mark Bradley, Kevin Marie, Kari Lynne. Mgr. quality control J. Neils Lumber Co., Libby, Mont., 1946-55; mgr. research and devel. St. Regis Paper Co., Libby, 1955-65, div. dir. tech. devel., Tacoma, Wash., 1965-69, div. dir. short and long-range planning, 1969-70; exec. v.p. Property Holding and Devel. Co., Tacoma, 1970-75; exec. v.p. and gen. mgr. U.S. Computers, Inc., Tacoma, 1975-79; corp. mgmt., orgn., univ. governance and adminstrn. cons., 1979—; owner Knudson Travel, Tacoma, 1981—; pres., incorporator, Larex Internat. Corp.; dir. Property Holding and Devel. Co., U.S. Computers; adv. bd. Coll. Engring., Wash. State U., 1967—, chmn., 1971-73. Trustee 1st Luth. Ch., Libby, 1948-56, chmn., 1954-56; trustee Sch. Dist. #4, Libby, 1964-65; trustee Christ Luth. Ch., Tacoma, 1966-71, com. chmn.; trustee Greater Lakes Mental Health Clinic, 1969-73, com. chmn., 1970-73; bd. regents Pacific Luth. U., Tacoma, 1969—, chmn., 1976-81; mem. Steilacoom Improvement Com., 1971-73; chmn. Pacific Luth. U. Pres. Search Com., 1974-75; dir. Wauna Dance Club, 1976-79; dir. Pacific Luth. Univ. "Q" Club, 1976—; bd. dirs. Tenzler Library, Tacoma, 1980-83, Crime Stoppers, 1981-84. Served to lt. col. F.A., Paratroops, U.S. Army, 1941-46. Recipient Disting. Service award Pacific Luth. U., 1986. Mem. Wash. Realtors Assn., Wash. Securities Sales, Am. Governing Bds., Center for Study of Democratic Institutions. Republican. Clubs: Tacoma Country and Golf, Normana Male Chorus (Norwegian Singers Assn. Am.). Patentee high-temperature wood-drying process; developer domestic natural gum. Home: 6928 100th St SW Tacoma WA 98499 Office: 1103 A St Ste 200 Tacoma WA 98402

KNUDSON, RONALD JOEL, physician, educator; b. Chgo., Feb. 22, 1932; s. Joel William and Helga Louise (Anderson) K.; m. Dwyn Elise Boulanger, July 15, 1971. BS, Yale U., 1953; MD, Northwestern U., Chgo., 1957. Intern Chgo. Wesley Meml. Hosp., 1957-58; resident Ochsner Found. Hosp., New Orleans, 1959-63, Overholt Thoracic Clinic, Boston, 1963-64; fellow thoracic svcs. Boston U. Med. Sch., 1964-66, Harvard U. Sch. Pub. Health, 1966-68; asst. prof. internal medicine Yale U., New Haven, 1968-70, assoc. prof. internal medicine, 1970-75; prof. internal medicine Coll. Medicine U. Ariz., Tucson, 1975—; assoc. dir. Div. Respiratory Scis. U. Ariz., Tucson, 1975—. Contbr. articles to profl. jours. Fellow NIH, 1979-80. Mem. ACCP, Am. Physiol. Soc., Am. Thoracic Soc., Soc. European Physiol. Clin. Respiratory Physicians, AAAS, N.Y. Acad. Sci. Office: U Ariz Coll Medicine Div Respiratory Scis Tucson AZ 85724

KNUTESON, HAROLD DOUGLAS, electronic design and fabrication company executive; b. Spanish Fork, Utah, June 19, 1953; s. Harold and Donna Faye (Gardner) K.; m. Debra Ann Reed, 1972 (div. 1978); 1 child, Joey; m. Eileen Farley, Nov. 23, 1979; children: Cory, Kiel, Kira. AS, Utah Tech. Coll., 1978. Cert. IGDS, IEDS, DBMS, Intergraph. Electronics designer Tex. Instruments, Ridgecrest, Calif., 1978-81; mgr. Rocky Mountain Engring., Salt Lake City, 1981; sr. designer Computer Video Systems, Inc., Salt Lake City, 1981-82; sr. designer, computer cons. Eaton Corp., Salt Lake City, 1980-86; pres., chief exec. officer Artwerk Specialties, Salt Lake City, 1981—; exec. v.p. Cimsoft, Salt Lake City, 1984-86; regional mgr. Chinook Tech., Salt Lake City, 1987-89; cons. Ashworth Acctg., Salt Lake City, 1987—, Mountain Tech., West Valley, Utah, 1987—. Author: I Have Two Hearts, 1987; inventor IC Spacesaver, 1984, Surface Mount Electronic Library, 1985. Mem. Blue Chips, Salt Lake Practical Shooters. Republican. Mormon. Home: 13201 S 3300 W Riverton UT 84065 Office: Artwerk Specialties PO Box 897 Riverton UT 84065

KNUTESON, KNUT JEFFERY, computer engineer; b. Spanish Fork, Utah, Nov. 1, 1949; s. Harold and Donna Fay (Gardner) K.; m. Kirsti Krogvik, Aug. 25, 1971 (div. Oct. 1988); children: Kathrine, Knut-Sigurd, Joshua, Kristian, Harold, Marie Elizabeth. Student, Brigham Young U., 1967-72; A in Electronics Tech., Utah Tech. Coll., 1979. Electronics monitor Amund Clausen A/S, Porsgrunn, Norway, 1972-73; electronics technician, libr. Orem (Utah) City Pub. Libr., 1977-79; electronics test and lab. technician Gen. Products div. IBM Corp., Tucson, 1979-82; computer systems technician and asst. programmer OmniSoft Corp., Salt Lake City, 1982-83; computer systems technician and cons. World Industries Cons., Inc., Tacoma, 1983-84; engr.-in-charge customer engring. KET Svc., Inc., Tooele, Utah and Minnetonka, Minn., 1984-88, Que Internat., Colonia LeBaron, Galeana, Mex., 1988—; bd. dirs. OmniSoft, A.M.S. ; cons. engr. Collier's Pub., 1980-88; researcher, compiler Mormon genetic materials. Author religious booklets; compiler indices to Mormon scholarly books. Mem. Brotherhood of Liberty and Peace, Mex., 1988—, fine arts com. chmn., 1989—; sr. advisor Coll. Reps. Nat. com., 1987—; active neighborhood Crime Watch Pima County Sheriff's Dept., Tucson, 1980-82. Recipient Disting. Leadership award Am. Biog. Inst., 1988, Cert. of Appreciation 2d Amendment Found., 1985-87. Mem. Second Amendment Found. (nat. bd. advisors 1986—), Citizen's Com. for the Right to Keep and Bear Arms (nat. adv. coun. 1987—, Citizen of Yr. award 1982-87). Libertarian. Mormon. Mailing Address: Domocilio Conocido, Colonia LeBaron, 31870 Galeana Chihuahua, Mexico

KNUTSON, MARTIN ARTHUR, aerospace engineer; b. Mpls., May 31, 1930; s. Martin Arthur and Bessie Caroline (Kruse) K.; m. Jeanine Danielle Lucas, Dec. 17, 1955; children: Martin Arthur Jr., Eric Danny, Kristin Anne, Robin Leslie. Student, U. Minn., 1948-50; AA, De Anza Coll., 1981. Enlisted man U.S. Air Force, 1950, advanced through grades to lt. col., 1968, ret., 1970; v.p. Farm Air Svc., Nome, Tex., 1968-73; with Ames Rsch. Ctr., NASA, Mountain View, Calif., 1971--, chief airborne missions applications div., 1976-84, dir. flight ops. and rsch., site mgr. Dryden Flight Rsch. Facility, 1984--; active Sr. Exec. Svc. Decorated DFC; recipient Intelligence Star, CIA, 1965-73, Outstanding Leadership medal NASA, 1983. Fellow Soc. Exptl. Test Pilots (assoc.). Republican. Methodist. Home: 27999 Via Ventana Los Altos Hills CA 94022 Office: NASA Ames Rsch Ctr Moffett Field Mountain View CA 94035

KNYCHA, JOSEF ROBERT, journalist; b. Summerside, P.E.I., Can., Apr. 19, 1953; s. Michael Stanley and Marjorie Mary (Gallant) K. Student pub. schs., Auburn, N.S., Can. Reporter Halifax Herald Ltd., N.S., 1971-81; editor The Mirror, Cameron Publs., Kentville, N.S., 1981-82, editor The Register, 1982-84; bus./markets/automotive editor Star-Phoenix, Saskatoon, Sask., Can., 1984—. Southam fellow U. Toronto. Mem. Sask. Farm Writers' Assn. (bd. dirs.), Can. Farm Writers' Fedn. Home: 1361 Sixth St, Brandon, MB Canada R7A 3R7 Office: The Star-Phoenix, 204 5th Ave N, Saskatoon, SK Canada S7K 2P1

KO, ALLEN HIU-CHING, orthodontist; b. Hanzhow, Chekiang, China, Jan. 27, 1953; came to U.S., 1972; s. Ki Chung and Yu Chung (Lee) K.; m. Annie Sze-han Yang, Dec. 20, 1983; children: Christopher, Elizabeth. DDS, Loyola U. Sch. of Dentistry, Maywood, Ill., 1979, cert. of specialty, 1981. Cert. Am. Bd. Orthodontists, dentist, orthodontist, Ill. Orthodontist Old Town Dental Ctr., Chgo., 1980—; commodity trading advisor, Chgo., 1984—. Mem. Am. Dental Soc., Chgo. Dental Soc., Ill. State Dental Soc., Phi Kappa Phi.

KOBAYASHI, YUMI, financial analyst; b. Tokyo, Apr. 19, 1951; came to U.S., 1980; d. Jin and Katsuko (Sato) K.; m. Masahiro Murakami, Apr. 4, 1977 (div. 1982); m. James W.G. Sagin, Jan. 23, 1984. BA in Econs., Tokyo U., 1975; MBA, Stanford U., 1982. Chartered fin. analyst. Industry analyst The Long-Term Credit Bank Japan, Tokyo, 1975-80; security analyst Paine Webber Mitchell Hutchins, N.Y.C., 1982-84; ptnr. James Sagin Assocs., San Francisco, 1984—; bd. dirs. Sakura Color Products Corp., Union City, Calif. Author: Economic History of the Showa Era, 1988, Medical Industry in Japan, 1980, Survey of the Future Growth of the Electronics Industry, 1978, The Changing Structure of Japanese Industry, 1978. Mem. Akamonkai, San Francisco, 1984—, Gakushikai, Tokyo, 1975—. Mem. Inst. Chartered Fin. Analysts, N.Y. Soc. Security Analysts. Office: James Sagin Assocs 150 Beach Park Blvd Foster City CA 94404

KOBER, CARL LEOPOLD, exploration company executive; b. Vienna, Austria, Nov. 22, 1913; s. Leopold and Maria Gertrud (Cremer) K.; m. Christiana Futschig, Mar. 26, 1942; children: Wolfgang, Peter Christian. PhD in Physics, U. Vienna, Austria, 1935; PhD in Electronics, Tech. U., 1939. Dir. GEMA G.M.B.H., Berlin, Germany, 1940-45; cons. armament lab. USAF, Wright Patterson AFB, 1949-55; v.p. electronics div. AVCO Corp., Cin., 1958-61; dir. Martin Marietta, Denver, 1961-74; pres. DEMEX Mineral Exploration Co., Denver, 1974—; prof. Colo. State U., Ft. Collins, 1968-79. Patentee in field. Fellow IEEE (life), AAAS, Explorer Club. Club: Columbine Country (Littleton). Home: 605 Front Range Rd Littleton CO 80120 Office: DEMEX Denver Mineral Exploration Co PO Box 4206 Highlands Ranch CO 80126

KOBERSTEIN, GARY RICHARD, aerospace engineer; b. Lewellen, Nebr., June 14, 1933; s. Fred and Mae (McCormick) K.; m. Kay Yvonne Hobson-Percell, Feb. 25, 1984. BSEE, U. Nebr., 1956. Engr. N.Am. Aviation, Anaheim, Calif., 1959-70; mgr. N.Am. Rockwell, Anaheim, 1970-86; chief systems engr. Rockwell Internat., Anaheim, 1987—. Capt. USAF, 1956-59. Mem. AIEE, Sigma Xi, Sigma Tau, Eta Kappa Nu, Pi Mu Epsilon. Republican. Methodist. Home: 620 Inverness Ct Fullerton CA 92635 Office: Autonetics ILBM Systems Div 3370 Miraloma St Anaheim CA 92803

KOBLIN, RONALD LEE, business management, real estate development consultant; b. Santa Monica, Calif., Nov. 28, 1946; s. Bernard Lewis and Sadie Irene K.; student U. Oreg., 1965, U. Ariz., 1967; B.A., Calif. State U., Northridge, 1969, postgrad., 1970-71; postgrad. U. So. Calif., 1971. Field advt. rep. Procter & Gamble, 1969; urban planner cities of Compton and Simi Valley, Calif., 1970-72; dir. planning and constrn. Nat. Med. Enterprises, Beverly Hills, Calif., 1972-74; dir. planning and devel. Am. Nat. Group, Beverly Hills, 1974-75, v.p./cons. planning and devel.; founder, pres., vice chmn. bd. dirs. Art Showcases, Inc., Glendale, Calif., 1976-82; founder, owner Firstworld Travel of Century City, Inc., 1982—; gen. ptnr. various Calif. business and real estate ltd. ptnrships.; cons. in bus. devel., mgmt. and sales; founder, pres. The Concept Implementation Co., 1982—. Mem. Am. Planners Assn., Am. Mgmt. Assn., Urban Land Inst. Office: PO Box 115 La Canada-Flintridge CA 91012

KOBRIN, TANNIS CLAIRE, writer, exercise educator; b. Winnipeg, Man., Can., Nov. 27, 1953; came to U.S., 1962; d. Morris Tubber and Wilman Graham (Davison) Kobrinsky; m. Bruce Raymond Cervi, Oct. 9, 1976 (div. 1980). Student, theatre, Santa Barbara City Coll., 1972-73; student acting writing, Daniel Mann Workshop, Los Angeles, 1984-86; student writing, UCLA, 1987. Pres., tchr. owner Home Stretch Exercise, Los Angeles, 1980—; agt.'s asst. Sheri Mann Agy., Los Angeles, 1984-86; writer Sascha Schneider Prodns., Los Angeles, 1985—; Astral Prodns./Lorimar Video, Montreal & Los Angeles, 1986—; exercise cons., Weider Body and Fitness, Los Angeles 1987—; choreographer, Wonderworks, Los Angeles, 1987. Author: (screenplays) Ballerina and the Blues, 1986, Midnight Magic, 1987. Recipient actress award Drama Logue, 1977. Mem. Women in Film, Screen Actors Guild, Alliance Can. Cinema, TV and Radio Artists, Acad. Can. Cinema and TV, Nat. Assn. Female Execs. Home: 2326 Sunset Heights Dr Los Angeles CA 90046

KOBUS, PAUL, JR., manufacturing control systems consultant; b. Chgo., Dec. 6, 1941; s. Paul and Margaret (Ackerman) K.; m. Nancy Ann Fircz, Oct. 12, 1963 (div.). Mgr. package devel. Cen. Data Systems, Brook Park, Ohio, 1967-69; dir. systems Cook United, Maple Heights, Ohio, 1970-71; controller Nat. Solvents, Medina, Ohio, 1971-72; dir. MIS Internat. Chem. and Nuclear Co., Solon, Ohio, 1973-74, Highland Mfg. Co., Cleve., 1974-75; prin. Legal Data Systems, Cleve., 1976-77; founder, owner, pres. CDSM, Inc. of Ohio, Brecksville, 1977-84; pres., chief operating officer CDSM, Inc. of Ariz., Phoenix, 1984-86; pres. C-Guard Labs., Inc., Phoenix, 1986—. Patentee in field. Republican. Lutheran. Home: 1232 E Townley Ave Phoenix AZ 85020 Office: C Guard Labs Inc PO Box 26508 Phoenix AZ 85068

KOBZA, DENNIS JEROME, architect; b. Ullysses, Nebr., Sept. 30, 1933; s. Jerry Frank and Agnes Elizabeth (Lavicky) K.; B.S., Healds Archtl. Engring., 1959; m. Doris Mae Riemann, Dec. 26, 1953; children—Dennis Jerome, Diana Jill, David John. Draftsman, designer B.L. Schroder, Palo Alto, Calif., 1959-60; sr. draftsman, designer Ned Abrams, Architect, Sunnyvale, Calif., 1960-61, Kenneth Elvin, Architect, Los Altos, Calif., 1961-62; partner B.L. Schroder, Architect, Palo Alto, 1962-66; pvt. practice architecture, Mountain View, Calif., 1966—. Served with USAF, 1952-56. Recipient Solar PAL award, Palo Alto, 1983, Mountain View Mayoral award, 1979. Mem. C. of C. (dir. 1977-79, Archtl. Excellence award Hayward chpt. 1985, Outstanding Indsl. Devel. award Sacramento chpt., 1980) , AIA (chpt. dir. 1973), Constrn. Specifications Inst. (dir. 1967-68), Am. Inst. Plant Engrs., Nat. Fedn. Ind. Bus. Orgn. Club: Rotary (dir. 1978-79, pres. 1986-87). Home: 3840 May Ct Palo Alto CA 94303 Office: 2083 Old Middlefield Way Mountain View CA 94043

KOCAOGLU, DUNDAR F., industrial engineer, educator; b. Turkey, June 1, 1939; came to U.S., 1960; s. Irfan and Meliha (Uzay) K.; m. Alev Baysak, Oct. 17, 1968; 1 child, Timur. BSCE, Robert Coll., Istanbul, Turkey, 1960; MSCE, Lehigh U., 1962; MS in Indsl. Engring., U. Pitts., 1972, PhD in Ops. Rsch., 1976. Registered profl. engr., Pa., Oreg. Design engr. Modjeski & Masters, Harrisburg, Pa., 1962-64; ptnr. TEKSER Engring. Co., Istanbul, 1966-69; project engr. United Engrs., Phila., 1964-71; rsch. asst. U. Pitts., 1972-74, vis. asst. prof., 1974-76, assoc. prof. indsl. engring., dir. engring. mgmt., 1976-87; prof., dir. engring. mgmt. program, Portland State U., 1987—; pres. TMA-Tech. Mgmt. Assocs., Portland, Oreg., 1973—. Author: Engineering Management, 1981, Management of R&D and Engineering, 1989, Handbook of Technology Management, 1989; series editor Wiley Series in Engring. Mgmt.; editor-in-chief IEEE Transactions on Engring. Mgmt.; contbr. articles on tech. mgmt. to profl. jours. Lt. C.E., Turkish Army, 1966-68. Recipient Centennial medal IEEE, 1984. Mem. Inst. Mgmt. Scis. (pres. Coll. Engring. Mgmt. 1979-81), Am. Soc. Engring. Edn. (chmn. engring. mgmt. div. 1982-83), IEEE Engring. Mgmt. Soc. (sr., publs. dir. 1982-85), ASCE (mem. engring. mgmt. adminstrv. coun. 1988—), MIM Soc. Turkish Engrs. and Scientists (hon.), Am. Soc. Engring. Mgmt. (dir. 1981-86), Omega Rho (pres. 1984-86).

KOCH, GERALD LYNN, computer company executive; b. Denver, Dec. 11, 1940; s. Alfred Fredrick and Anna (Meier) K.; m. Janet Burton, Sept. 10, 1977; children: Ryan, Eric. Student, Colo. Sch. Mines, 1958-62; AA, Canada Coll., Redwood City, Calif., 1969; BSBA, U. Phoenix, 1985, MS in Bus. Adminstrn., 1987. Estimator Bartlett Snow Pacific, San Francisco, 1965-68; sr. rsch. and devel. technician Varian Vacuum Co., Palo Alto, Calif., 1968-72; coord. quality assurance Lockheed Missiles and Space Co., Sunnyvale, Calif., 1972-77, sr. mfg. engr., 1982-84; head swim coach Republic of China, Kaoshiung, 1977; mgr. quality engring. Dyna Craft, Santa Clara, Calif., 1978-79; sr. packaging engr. Nat. Semicondr. Co., Santa Clara, 1979-82; mgr. mfg. engring. Tandem Computers, Cupertino, Calif., 1984—; project mgr. Australian Terminal Project, Melborne. Democrat. Lutheran. Home: 417 Lock Dr Aptos CA 95003 Office: Tandem Computers 130 Hanger Way Watsonville CA 95076

KOCH, JAMES VERCH, economist; b. Springfield, Ill., Oct. 7, 1942; s. Elmer O. and Wilma L. K.; m. Donna L. Stickling, Aug. 20, 1967; children: Elizabeth, Mark. B.A., Ill. State U., 1964; Ph.D., Northwestern U., 1968. Research economist Harris Trust Bank, Chgo., 1966; from asst. prof. to prof. econs. Ill. State U., 1967-78, chmn. dept., 1972-78; dean Faculty Arts and Scis., R.I. Coll., Providence, 1978-80; prof. econs., provost, v.p. acad. affairs Ball State U., Muncie, Ind., 1980-86; pres. U. Mont., Missoula, 1986—. Author: Industrial Organization and Prices, 2d edit, 1980, Microeconomic Theory and Applications, 1976, The Economics of Affirmative Action, 1976,

Introduction to Mathematical Economics, 1979. Mem. Am. Econ. Assn., Econometric Soc., Am. Assn. Higher Edn., AAUP. Lutheran. Home: 1325 Gerald Ave Missoula MT 59801 Office: U Mont Office of Pres Missoula MT 59812

KOCH, JOSEPH WILLIAM, JR., marine and mechanical engineer; b. Balt., Feb. 17, 1936; s. Joseph William and Alberta Son (Goldsmith) K.; m. Ellen L. Ginns, Oct. 6,. BS in Engring., U.S. Naval Acad., 1957; MME, U.S. Naval Postgrad. Sch., 1966. Staff engr. Kaiser Aluminum Co., Oakland, Calif., 1967-70; staff marine engr. Marcona Corp., San Francisco, 1970-74, mgr. spl. projects, 1974-77; -gr. marine ops. So. Calif. Gas Co., Los Angeles, 1977-83, project mgr., 1983--. Contbr. articles to profl. jours. Adult leader Boy Scouts Am., Oakland, 1972-77, Fullerton, Calif., 1977--; bd. Recipient dist. award of merit Boy Scouts Am., 1980, Silver Beaver Award, 1983. Mem. Soc. Naval Architects and Marine Engrs. (chmn. fund raising 1980-84), Am. Soc. Naval Engrs. (sect. chmn. 1976-77), ASME. Republican. Jewish. Office: So Calif Gas Co 810 S Flower St Los Angeles CA 90017

KOCH, KEVIN A., priest, teacher; b. Lincoln, Nebr., Sept. 23, 1958; s. Cornelius Michael and Ida Jane (Wirges) K. BA in Social Sci., Conception Sem. Coll., 1977-81; M of Divinity, St. Thomas Theol. Sem., 1981-85. Assoc. pastor St. Mathew's Ch., Gilictte, Wyo., 1985-86, St. Mary's Cathedral, Cheyenne, Wyo., 1986—; instr. religion and morality Seton Cath. High Sch., Cheyenne, Wyo., 1986—; assc. pastor Cathedral of St. Mary, Cheyenne, 1986—, child care worker St. Joseph's Children's Home, Torrington, Wyo., 1981-82, chaplain asst. Fed. Correction Instn., Englewood, Colo., 1982-83, hosp. chaplain trainee W. Nebr. Gen. Hosp., Scottsbluff, 1984. Mem. Nat. Cath. Edn. Assn. Home: 100 W 21st Cheyenne WY 82003-1268 Office: St Mary's Cathedral PO Box 1268 Cheyenne WY 82003-1268

KOCH, RUSSELL GORDON, securities trader; b. Wenatchee, Wash., July 28, 1954; s. Gerald Eugene and Ann Jeanette (Gruenberg) K.; m. Pennie Elaine Hotchkins, Oct. 5, 1983; children: Christjohn Russell, Kelsey Ann. AA, Wenatchee Valley Coll., 1977. Securities broker Southmark Fin. Services, Seattle, 1986; br. mgr. Pan Oceanic Investments, Seattle, 1987-88; pres. Koch Trading Corp., Federal Way, Wash., 1981—; pres., owner, gen. prin. Kochcapital, Bellevue, Wash., 1988—; pres. C.C.I., Inc., U.S. Petrol, Seattle; bd. dirs. Winchester Gold, Spokane, Wash; mem. Spokane Stock Exch. Served to cpl. USMC, 1973-75. Mem. Nat. Assn. Securities Dealers, Mensa. Office: Kochcapital PO Box 3347 1300 114th Ave SE #232 Bellevue WA 98009

KOCHMAN, CARL JESSEE, media executive, consultant, educator; b. Conrad, Mont., Aug. 14, 1948; s. George Francis and Margaret Claire (Miller) K.; m. Margaret MacIntyre Warden, Nov. 21, 1974; 1 child, Aaron Jessee. Student, Carroll Coll., 1966-68; BS in Film and TV Prodn., Mont. State U., 1970. Dir. prodn. Sta. KXLF TV, Butte, Mont., 1970-72, Great Falls, Mont., 1972-74; mgr. prodn. Garryowen Broadcasting, Great Falls, 1974-78; v.p., owner North County Media Group, Great Falls, 1978—. Bd. dirs. Crimestoppers, Great Falls, 1984, Symphony Assn., Great Falls, 1988—; with publicity com. Meml. Youth Ctr., Great Falls, 1988. Recipient Greater Mont. Found. scholarship, 1969, Mont. Ad award Mont. Advt. Fedn., 1978-88; named Best in the West, Regional Advt. Fedn., 1980. Mem. Am. Film Inst., Washington Film and Video Assn., Internat. TV Soc., Mont. State U. Alumni Assn., Electric City Divers Club (Great Falls). Roman Catholic. Office: North County Media Group 721 2d St S Great Falls MT 59404

KOCIS, THOMAS JOSEPH, electronics engineer; b. Detroit, Dec. 8, 1961; s. Andrew J. and Rita Margaret (Knoebel) K.; m. Susana Santos, Aug. 1, 1981. BSEE, Mich. State U., 1984. Engr. IBM, Boca Raton, Fla., 1984-85, assoc. engr., 1985-87; sr. assoc. engr. IBM, Colorado Springs, Colo., 1987—. Mem. IEEE, Eta Kappa Nu, Tau Beta Pi. Roman Catholic. Home: 7740 Montane Dr Colorado Springs CO 80920 Office: IBM 4678 Alpine Meadows Ln Colorado Springs CO 80919

KOCOL, HENRY, health physicist; b. Chgo., July 16, 1937; s. Henry Frances and Mary Barbara (Strumidlowska) K.; m. Cleo Florence Fellers, Jan. 8, 1971; children: Steven Ray, Henry Peter. BS in Chemistry, Loyola U., 1958; MS in Chemistry, Purdue U., 1961. Cert. hazard control mgr. Radiochemist Nat. Bureau Standards, Washington, 1961-64; radiochemist U.S. Pub. Health Service, Las Vegas, Nev., 1964-71; chemist FDA, Rockville, Md., 1971-73; radiation control officer FDA, Phila., 1973-77, radiol. health rep., 1977-79; mgr. Wash. State Dept. Social & Health Services, Seattle, 1979-82; fed.-state liaison FDA, Seattle, 1982—; cons. in field; lectr. various colls. and univs. Contbr. articles to profl. jours. Mem. Health Physics Soc. (Cascade chpt. pres. 1983-85, mem. com. 1980-83), Conf. Radiation Control Dirs. (mem. com. 1976-82). Office: FDA 22201 23d Dr SE Bothell WA 98021

KODIS, MARY CAROLINE, marketing consultant; b. Chgo., Dec. 17, 1927; d. Anthony John and Callis Ferebee (Old) K.; student San Diego State Coll., 1945-47, Latin Am. Inst., 1948. Controller, div. adminstrv. mgr. Fed. Mart Stores, 1957-65; controller, adminstrv. mgr. Gulf Mart Stores, 1965-67; budget dir., adminstrv. mgr. Diana Stores, 1967-68; founder, treas., controller Handy Dan Stores, 1968-72; founder, v.p., treas. Handy City Stores, 1972-76; sr. v.p., treas. Handy City div. W.R. Grace & Co., Atlanta, 1976-79; founder, pres. Hal's Hardware and Lumber Stores, 1982-84; retail and restaurant cons., 1979—. Treas., bd. dirs. YWCA Watsonville,1981-84, 85-87; mem. Santa Cruz County Grand Jury, 1984-85. Recipient 1st Tribute to Women in Internat. Industry, 1978; named Woman of the Yr., 1986. Mem. Ducks Unltd. (treas. Watsonville chpt. 1981—). Republican. Home and Office: 302 Wheelock Rd Watsonville CA 95076

KODMAN, DENNIS PAUL, aerospace engineer; b. Hamilton, Ont., Can., May 25, 1946; came to U.S. in 1965; s. Stephen Julius and Juliana Margaret (Andrews) K.; m. Pauline Vivian Lefebvre, Sept. 4, 1971; children: Jeffrey, Allan. AAS, Rio Salado Community Coll., 1983; BS in Bus. Adminstrn., U. Phoenix, 1986. Prodn. engr. Garrett Turbine Engine Co., Phoenix, 1979-84; rework tech. engr. Garrett Gen. Aviation Services Co., Phoenix, 1984-86, mfg. engr., 1986-88; mfg. engr. Allied-Signal Aerospace Co., Tempe, Ariz., 1988-89; prodn. support engr. Garrett Fluid Systems Div.- Allied Signal Aerospace Co., Tempe, 1989—. Author/editor (procedures Manual, 1986; editor Prodn. Engring. Handbook, 1984. Served as sgt. U.S. Army, 1967-70. Mem. Internat. Platform Assn. Office: Garrett Gen Aviation Svcs Co Fluid Systems Div PO Box 22200 Tempe AZ 85282

KOECHLEIN, KEVIN BARRY, borough official; b. Ridgewood, N.J., Nov. 21, 1953; s. George John Koechlein and Barbara Elkan; m. Beth Ellen Koechlein, June 10, 1979; 1 child, Alyssa Claire. Student, Colo. State U., 1971-74; cert. peace officer, Aim Community Coll., Greeley, Colo., 1975; cert. parmedic, Swedish Med. Ctr., Englewood, Colo., 1977; student fire adminstrn., Western Oreg. State U., 1988—. Cert. mobile intensive care paramedic, emergency med. svc instr., Colo., Alaska. Mission leader, mem. dive team Larimer County Sheriff's Dept., Ft. Collins, Colo., 1972-77, dep. sheriff, 1974-75; paramedic, supr. Poudre Valley Hosp., Ft. Collins, 1975-79; paramedic Anchorage Fire Dept., 1979-82; coord. emergency med. svcs. Matanuska-Susitna Borough, Palmer, Alaska, 1982—; bd. dirs. So. Region Emergency Med. Svcs. Coun., Anchorage, 1982—. Mem. Nat. Assn. Emergency Med. Technicians, Internat. Fire Chiefs Assn., ASTM (emergency med. svcs. com.), Am. Heart Assn. Office: Matanuska-Susitna Borough PO Box 1608 Palmer AK 99645

KOEDYKER, BRENDA BASHAM, banker; b. Harned, Ky., Apr. 5, 1942; d. Millis and Mildred Catherine (Henning) Basham; m. James L. Futrell (dec. May 1963); 1 child, Robin Lynn Chen. Student banking, So. Meth. U., 1987. Adminstr. asst. to pres. Owensboro (Ky.) Nat. Bank, 1968-69; various positions Valley Nat. Bank, Tucson, 1969-74, asst. mgr., 1975-78, comml. loan officer, 1978-84, asst. v.p., 1978-82, v.p., 1982—, mgr. priority banking group, 1984—. Mem. adv. bd. Ariz. Theatre Co., Tucson; bd. dirs. Invisible Theatre, Tucson; trustee 2d Century Found., St. Mary's Hosp., Tucson, 1985—, pres., 1988-89. Recipient citation of merit Jr. Achievement, Tucson, 1973, cert. of appreciation Tucson C. of C., 1976, award of merit Tucson Met. C. of C., 1976-82, Woman on Move award YWCA, Tucson, 1983. Mem. Nat. Assn. Bank Women (pres. So. Ariz. chpt. 1980-81, state pres. 1982-83), Robert Morris Assocs., Resources for Women (adv. bd. 1987-89), Execs. Women's Coun. So. Ariz., Exec. Women Internat. (sec. 1979, chmn. various coms.), Soroptimist (v.p. Tucson 1975-76). Democrat. Methodist. Office: Valley Nat Bank PO Box 13767 Tucson AZ 85732

KOEHLER, CONSTANCE LYNCH, political economist, aerospace business development planner; b. Newark, Mar. 3, 1953; d. Robert John and Dorothy Helen (Jano) Lynch; m. Jeffrey Darrell Koehler, Dec. 5, 1987. BA in Polit. Sci. cum laude, UCLA, 1974; MA in Internal. Relations, U. So. Calif., 1977, postgrad. Sr. lectr. Sch. Internat. Relations U. So. Calif., Los Angeles, 1978-81, Dept. Polit. Sci. Calif. State U., Carson, 1980-81; cons. Polit. Sci. Dept. RAND Corp., Santa Monica, Calif., 1981-82; sr. rsch. analyst Fgn. Assessments Northrop Corp., Hawthorne, Calif., 1983-86, Def. Research and Analysis Northrop Corp., Hawthorne, 1983-86; dir. mkt. research and analysis Bus. Devel. Northrop Corp., Hawthorne, 1987-88, dir. advanced planning and analysis, 1988—. Herman fellow, 1976-77, U. So. Calif., 1978-79. Mem. Los Angeles World Affairs Council, Seminar Internat. Relations and Fgn. Policy, Internat. Inst. Strategic Studies, UCLA Ctr. Internat. and Strategic Affairs (assoc.). Office: Northrop Corp Aircraft Div 1 Northrop Ave 2310/31 Hawthorne CA 90250-3277

KOEHNEN, MARK FRANS, telecommunications company executive; b. Snoqualmie, Wash., Apr. 11, 1951; s. Robert and Marilyn (Miller) K.; m. Gwendolyn Vaughn, Aug. 19, 1972; children: Erick Don, Chance Wolf, Jacob Vaughn, Sean Miller. Student, Devry Inst. Tech., Chgo., 1975; A.Elec.Tech., Columbia Basin Coll., 1976. Quality engring. tech. Mannesmann/Tally, Kent, Wash., 1976-81; quality control supr. Mannesmann/Tally, Kent, 1981-82; quality assurance engr. Tone Commander Systems, Redmond, Wash., 1982-84; quality assurance dir. Tone Commander Systems, Redmond, 1984—; speaker Am. Soc. Quality Control, Bellevue, Wash., 1988, Nat. Quality Mgmt. Conf., Nashville, 1989. Lt. Snoqualnie Vol. Fire Dept., 1981—. With USAF, 1971-75. Recipient Community Svc. award City of Snoqualmie, 1983, 88. Mem. Am. Soc. Quality Control (telecommunications div., newsletter editor). Office: Tone Comdr Systems Inc 4320 150th Ave NE Redmond WA 98073-9739

KOELBL, JOSEF, real estate broker, stockbroker; b. Brandten, Fed. Republic Germany, Jan. 15, 1947; came to U.S., 1974; BS in Bus. and Econs., U. Regensburg, 1974; MA in Econs., U. Colo., 1975. Owner Accent Realty & Mgmt., Lakewood, Colo., 1980—, Accent Disposal, Lakewood, 1987—; pres. Accent Transports, Inc., Lakewood, 1988—. Office: Accent Realty & Mmgt 567 S Fairfax Glendale CO 80222

KOELMEL, LORNA LEE, data processing executive; b. Denver, May 15, 1936; d. George Bannister and Gladys Lee (Henshall) Steuart; m. Herbert Howard Nelson, Sept. 9, 1956 (div. Mar. 1967); children: Karen Dianne, Phillip Dean, Lois Lynn; m. Robert Darrel Koelmel, May 12, 1981; stepchildren: Kim, Cheryl, Dawn, Debbie. BA in English, U. Colo., 1967. Cert. secondary English tchr. Substitute English tchr. Jefferson County Schs., Lakewood, Colo., 1967-68; sec. specialist IBM Corp., Denver, 1968-75, personnel adminstr., 1975-82, asst. ctr. coordinator, 1982-85, office systems specialist, 1985-87, backup computer operator, 1987—; computer instr. Barnes Bus. Coll., Denver, 1987—; owner, mgr. Lorna's Precision Word Processing and Desktop Pub., Denver, 1987—. Organist Christian Sci. Soc., Buena Vista, Colo., 1963-66, chmn. bd. dirs.,Thornton, Colo., 1979-80. Mem. NAFE, Nat. Secs. Assn. (retirement ctr. chair 1977-78, newsletter chair 1979-80, v.p. 1980-81), U. Colo. Alumni Assn., Alpha Chi Omega (publicity com. 1986-88). Republican. Club: Nat. Writers. Lodge: Job's Daus. (recorder 1953-54).

KOELSCH, M. OLIVER, federal judge; b. Boise, Idaho, Mar. 5, 1912; m. Virginia Lee Daley, Oct. 30, 1937; children—Katherine, John, Jane (Mrs. Dennis P. Houghton). B.A., U. Wash., LL.B., 1935. Judge U.S. Ct. Appeals, San Francisco; now sr. judge 9th Circuit, Seattle. Office: US Ct Appeals 816 US Courthouse 1010 5th Ave Seattle WA 98104

KOELSCH, THEODORE ALLEN, geoscientist; b. Fairfield, Ill., Apr. 12, 1951; s. Emery Frederick and Kathryn Lucille (Koontz) K.; m. Jean Bryna Kulla, July 3, 1975. BA, Occidental Coll., 1973; MS, U. Ill., Urbana, 1977, PhD, 1979. Rsch. geologist Exxon Prodn. Rsch. Co., Houston, 1979-81, sr. rsch. geologist, 1981-84; res. experimental officer Australian Antarctic Expedition, 1985; sr. project geologist Earth Tech. Corp., Long Beach, Calif., 1986-88; coord. rsch. and devel. Earth Tech. Corp., Long Beach, 1987, mgr. geomechanical testing, 1988; cons. San Diego, 1988—. Mem. Am. Geological Inst., Am. Geophysical Union, Am. Assn. of Petroleum Geologists, Am. Soc. for Testing and Materials (com. mem. 1988—), Internat. Soc. Rock Mechanics. Democrat. Home and Office: 2972 Caminito Niquel San Diego CA 92117

KOEPPEL, GARY MERLE, writer, publisher, art gallery owner; b. Albany, Oreg., Jan 20, 1938; s. Carl Melvin and Barbara Emma (Adams) K.; m. Emma Katerina Koeppel, May 20, 1984. BA, Portland State U., 1961; MFA, State U. Iowa, 1963. Writing instr. State U. Iowa, Iowa City, 1963-64; guest prof. English, U. P.R. San Juan, 1964-65; assoc. prof. creative writing Portland (Oreg.) State U., 1965-68; owner, operator Coast Gallery, Big Sur, 1971—, Pebble Beach, Calif., 1986—, Maui, Hawaii, 1985—; owner Coast Pub. Co.; editor, pub. Big Sur Gazette, 1978-81; producer, sponsor Maui Marine Art Expo., Monterey Marine Art Expo. Author: Sculptured Sandcast Candles, 1974. Founder Big Sur Vol. Fire Brigade, 1975; chmn. coordinating com. Big Sur Area Planning, 1972-75; chmn. Big Sur Citizens Adv. Com., 1975-78. Mem. Big Sur C. of C. (pres. 1974-75, 82-84), Big Sur Grange, Audubon Soc., Cousteau Soc., Phi Gamma Delta, Alpha Delta Sigma. Address: Coast Gallery PO Box 1501 Pebble Beach CA 93953

KOERT, DOROTHY LUCILE, author, writing educator; b. Lynden, Wash., Aug. 12, 1908; d. Erick John and Emma (Kilcup) Grandquist; m. Peter Koert (dec. 1965); children: Murella, Peter. BA in English, Western Wash. U., 1972, MA, 1975. Announcer KPUG Radio, Bellingham, Wash., 1948-66; reporter, feature writer, columnist Lynden (Wash.) Tribune, 1949-52; instr., dir. Fourth Corner Registry, Bellingham, 1978—. Author: Portrait of Lynden, 1976, Entering Vividly into Life, 1980, History of Whatcom Theaters, 1979, Walk in the Spirit, 1978, Morning Thoughts, 1979, Christian Writer, 1980, Beyond the Veil, 1981, Looking Back, (vol. 1, 1980, 3rd ed. 1985, vol. 11, 1982), The Sue Boynton Story, 1982, The Lyric Singer, 1985, Days of Our Years, 1989; editor: Spoken in Due Season, 1979, Whatcom Scenes, 1981, Whatcom Images, 1982, The Wilderness Days, 1989. Mem. AAUW (historian 1983-87), Bellingham Music Club, Aftermath. Home: Riptide 301 600 S State Bellingham WA 98225

KOESTER, BERTHOLD KARL, lawyer, honorary consul Federal Republic of Germany; b. Aachen, Germany, June 30, 1931; s. Wilhelm P. and Margarethe A. (Witteler) K.; m. Hildegard Maria Buettner, June 30, 1961; children: Georg W., Wolfgang J., Reinhard B. JD, U. Muenster, Fed. Republic Germany, 1957. Cert. Real Estate Agt., Ariz. Asst. prof. civil and internat. law U. Muenster, 1957-60; atty. Cts. of Duesseldorf, Fed. Republic Germany, 1960-82; v.p. Bank J. H. Vogeler & Co., Duesseldorf, 1960-64; pres. Bremer Tank-u. Kuehlschifahrts Gesellschaft, Bremen, Fed. Republic Germany, 1964-72; atty., trustee internat. corps., Duesseldorf and Phoenix, 1973-82, Phoenix, 1983—; of counsel Tancer Law Offices, Phoenix, 1978-86; prof. internat. bus. law Am. Grad. Sch. Internat. Mgmt., Glendale, Ariz., 1978-81; with Applewhite, Laflin & Lewis, Real Estate Investments, Phoenix, 1981-86, ptnr., 1982-86, Beucler Real Estate Investments, 1986-88, Scottsdale, Ariz.; hon. consul Fed. Republic of Germany for Ariz., 1982—; chmn., chief exec. officer Arimpex Hi-Tec, Inc., Phoenix, 1981—. Contbr. articles to profl. jours. Pres. Parents Assn. Humboldt Gymnasium, Duesseldorf, 1971-78; active German Red Cross, from 1977. Mem. Duesseldorf Chamber of Lawyers, Bochum (Fed. Republic Germany) Assn. Tax Lawyers, Bonn German-Saudi Arabian Assn. (pres. 1976-79), Bonn German-Korean Assn., Assn. for German-Korean Econ. Devel. (pres. 1974-78), Ariz. Consular Corps, German-Am. C. of C., Phoenix Met. C. of C. Club: Rotary (Scottsdale, Ariz.). Home: 6201 E Cactus Rd Scottsdale AZ 85254

KOFF, ROBERT LOUIS, insurance executive; b. Phila., Nov. 5, 1943; s. Harry Nathaniel and Ida Sarah (Lurge) K.; m. Lynn Dane, Sept. 2, 1984; children: Betsy, Richard, Alexa Lynsay. BA in English, Calif. State U., Northridge, 1966; postgrad., U. San Fernando, 1966-68. Registered health underwriter. Mgr. Harry N. Koff Agy. Inc., L.A., 1966-68, v.p., 1968-78, pres., chief exec. officer, 1978—; chmn. nat. adv. coun. Mass. Casualty Ins. Co., Boston, 1986-87; mem. faculty Davidson Ctr. for Continuing Edn. U. So. Calif.; appointee Senate Adv. Commn. on Life and Health Ins., Calif., 1989—. Mem. Starlight Found., L.A., 1987—; bd. dirs. United Cerebral Palsy, L.A., 1974-79, L.A. Children's Film Inst., 1983. Mem. Internat. Assn. Health Underwriters (Health Ins. Quality award 1978), Internat. Assn. Fin. Planners, Variety Club Internat. Republican. Jewish. Office: Harry N Koff Agy Inc 23603 Park Sorrento #104 Calabasas CA 91302

KOFF, THEODORE H., researcher, educator; b. Phila., July 9, 1928; s. Harry and Yetta (Bernstein) K.; m. Nancy Koff; children: Louis, Susan, David. BS in Psychology, CCNY, 1950; MSW, Columbia U., 1953; EdD in Rehab. Adminstrn., U. Ariz., 1971. Program asst. Jewish Community Ctr., Houston, 1953-56; program dir. Jewish Community Ctr., Dallas, 1956-60; asst. exec. dir. Dallas Home for Jewish Aged, 1960-62; exec. dir. Handmaker Jewish Nursing Home for the Aged, 1962-73, exec. dir. Community Mental Health Services Adult Day Health Program, 1962-73; prof. mgmt. and policy Coll. Bus. and Pub. Adminstrn. U. Ariz., Tucson, 1973—, dir. Ariz. Long Term Care Gerontology Ctr., 1973—, dir. pub. sector programs, 1986-88. Author: Hospice: A Caring Community, 1980, Long Term Care: An Approach to Serving the Frail Elderly, 1982, New Approaches to Health Care for an Aging Population: Developing a Continuum of Chronic Care Services, 1988, Services for the Dying (chpt. in Handbook of Gerontological Services), 1989; contbr. articles to profl. jours. Recipient Research award, Am. Coll. Health Care Adminstrs., 1986, Outstanding Gerontologist award, Western Gerontol. Soc., 1984, Outstanding Gerontol. Educator, Weber State Coll., 1982, Outstanding Leadership and Dedicated Service award, Tucson Community Council, 1972, Outstanding Citizen of Tucson award, 1972, Profl. Service award, Tucson Jewish Community Council, 1967. Fellow Gerontol. Soc. (chmn. edn. com.); mem. Nat. Assn. Long Term Care Gerontology Ctrs. (pres. 1986-88), Ariz. License Bd. for Nursing Home Adminstrs., Am. Soc. Aging, Tex. Assn. Homes for the Ages, Pima Council on Aging, Am. Hosp. Assn. Council on Long Term Care (Assembly on Long Term Care), Sr. Now Generation (treas.), Am. Assn. Homes for the Aged. Am. Pub. Health Assn. (bd. govs. Gerontol. Health sect.), Am. Coll. Nursing Home Adminstrs., Nat. Hospice Orgn., Am. Soc. Pub. Adminstrs., Nat. Assn. Social Workers, Acad. Cert. Social Workers, Nat. Coun. on Aging (bd. dirs.). Home: 5209 E Woodspring Dr Tucson AZ 85712 Office: Ariz Long Term Care Gerontology Ctr 1807 E Elm Tucson AZ 85719

KOFFLER, HENRY, university president; b. Vienna, Austria, Sept. 17, 1922; naturalized U.S. citizen, 1945.; BS, U. Ariz., 1943; MS, U. Wis., 1944, PhD, 1947; DSc (hon.), Purdue U., 1977, U. Ariz., 1981; LLD (hon.), Amherst Coll., 1981. From asst. prof. to prof. bacteriology Purdue U., West Lafayette, Ind., 1947-52, coodinator research, 1949-59, prof. biology, 1952-74, asst. to dean Grad. Sch., 1957-59, asst. dean, 1959-60, head dept. biol. sci., 1959-75, F. L. Hovde Disting. prof., 1974-75; prof. biochemistry and microbiology, v.p. acad. affairs U. Minn., Mpls., 1975-79; prof. biochemistry and microbiology, chancellor U. Mass., Amherst, 1979-82; prof. biochemistry, molecular and cell biology, microbiology and immunology, pres. U. Ariz., Tucson, 1982—; cons. in field; mem. Commn. Undergrad. Edn. in Biol. Sci., 1966-69, vice chmn., 1966-67, chmn., 1967-69; mem. Purdue Research Found., 1967—; cons., examiner North Central Assn. Colls., 1967—; mem. numerous internat. congresses and symposia, Athens, Birmingham, Eng., Boston, Brussels, Cambridge, Eng., Cambridge, Mass., Canberra, Australia, Jerusalem, Mexico City, Montreal, Que., Can., Moscow, Paris, Phila., Rome, Salamanca, Seattle, Stockholm, Tokyo, Vienna, Washington; mem. med. scientists tng. com. Nat. Inst. Gen. Med. Scis., 1972-75; bd. dirs. Minn. Ednl. Computing Consortium, 1975-79; mem. policy bd. Planning Council on Computing in Edn. and Research, 1976-79; mem. U.S. Dept. Def. Univ. Forum Adv. Com., 1985—; trustee Univs. Research Assn., 1976-79, 88—, exec. com. council pres., 1985-88, vice chmn., council pres., 1987; trustee Argonne Univs. Assn., 1978-81; mem Tucson Airport Authority, 1983—, adv. coun. office of tech. assessment U.S. Congress, 1988—, Ariz. commn. postsecondary edn., 1988—; author and lectr. in field. Mem. adv. bd. Quar. Rev. Biology, 1968-75. Bd. dirs. U. Minn. Found., 1977-79, U. Mass. Found., 1979-82, 5 Colls. Inc., 1979-82, Hampshire Coll., 1978-82, United Way Tucson, 1982-84, Tucson Tomorrow, 1982-88, U. Ariz. Found., 1982—, Ariz. Acad., 1982—, Tucson Tomorrow, 1982—, Tucson Econ. Devel. Corp., 1982—, U. Med. Ctr. Corp., 1984—, Up With People, 1984—, Assoc. Am. Coll., 1988—. Named to Ordre dès Palmes Académiques, 1977; recipient Citation, U. Minn., 1979, Citation, U. Mass., 1982; Wis. Alumni Research Found. fellow, 1943-46; Nat. Research Council fellow, 1946-47; Guggenheim fellow Sch. Medicine, Case Western Res. U., 1953-54; recipient Eli Lilly award, 1957. Fellow Am. Acad. Microbiology (bd. govs. 1969-72, vice chmn. 1971-72), AAAS; mem. Am. Soc. Biol. Chemists, Biophys. Soc., Am. Soc. Microbiology, Am. Soc. Cell Biologists, Am. Assn. Univ. Profs., Am. Chem. Soc., Biophysical Soc., U. Mass. Assoc. Alumni (bd. dirs. 1979-82, hon. alumnus 1982), U. Ariz. Alumni Assn. (bd. dirs. 1982—), Phi Beta Kappa, Alpha Epsilon Delta, Alpha Lambda Delta, Alpha Zeta, Gamma Alpha, Phi Kappa Phi, Phi Lamba Upsilon, Phi Sigma, Sigma Pi, Sigma, Sigma Xi. Office: U Ariz Office of Pres Tucson AZ 85721

KOFFORD, KAY G., corporate executive; b. Price, Utah, Feb. 28, 1948; d. Don B. and Lylas (Grange) K.; m. Florence Swapp, Mar. 8, 1969; children: Steven K., Shannon, Brian S. Student, No. Ariz. U., 1967; BS in Polit. Sci./Pub. Safety Adminstrn., Ariz. State U., 1975. Supr. communications Ariz. Dept. of Pub. Safety, Phoenix, 1974-75; dir. safety and tng. Plateau Mining UNC, Price, 1976-79; mgr. safety Mining and Milling UNC, Albuquerque, 1979-80; various managerial positions Occidental Oil Shale, Inc., Grand Junction, Colo., 1980-86; pres. EMRx Corp., Palisade, Colo., 1986—. Chmn. Mining Adv. Council, Price, 1978-79; dir. Utah Assn. of Emergency Med. Technicians, Salt Lake City, 1977-79; mem. Gov.'s Com. Vocational Edn., 1978. Served with USAF, 1967-71. Mem. Colo. Mining Assn., Nat. Fedn. Ind. Bus. Republican. Mormon. Office: EMRx Corp 528 S Iowa Ave Palisade CO 81526

KOGA, ROKUTARO, astrophysicist; b. Nagoya, Japan, Aug. 18, 1942; came to U.S., 1961, naturalized, 1966; s. Toyoki and Emiko (Shinra) K.; m. Cordula Rosow, May 5, 1981; children: Evan A., Nicole A. B.A., U. Calif.-Berkeley, 1966; Ph.D., U. Calif.-Riverside, 1974. Research fellow U. Calif.-Riverside, 1974-75; research physicist Case Western Res U., Cleve., 1975-79, asst. prof., 1979-81; physicist Aerospace Corp., Los Angeles, 1981—. Mem. Am. Phys. Soc., Am. Geophys. Union, IEEE, N.Y. Acad. Scis., Sigma Xi. Contbr. articles to profl. confs.; research on gamma-ray astronomy, solar neutron observation, space scis., charged particles in space and the effect of cosmic rays on microcircuits in space. Home: 7325 Ogelsby Ave Los Angeles CA 90045 Office: Aerospace Corp Space Scis Labs PO Box 92957 Los Angeles CA 90009

KOGAN, ALMA ESTELLE, educator; b. N.Y.C., Feb. 12, 1924; d. Joseph Michael and Margaret Cecilia (Biss) Maytene; m. Al Kogan, Mar. 3, 1945 (div. July 1976); children: Michael Joseph, Edward Charles, Robert Linn. BA, Calif. State U., Northridge, 1963, MA, 1970; counseling credential, U. Calif., L.A., 1973. Cert. secondary tchr., counseling, Calif. History tchr. L.A. Unified Sch. Dist., 1965—; faculty coun. pres. Nobel Jr. High Sch., L.A., 1976-78, tchr., coord., 1965—, history dept. chairperson, 1981-84; mentor selection com. L.A. Sch. Dist. Region F, 1984-86; gifted coord. Nobel Jr. High Sch., L.A., 1986—. Assoc. Constitutional Rights Found., 1976-89. Hays-Fulbright grantee, U. So. Calif., People's Rep. China, 1986. Mem. Calif. Humanities Assn. (bd. govs., at large 1980-86, v.p. 1987-88, pres. 1988-89, Achievement award 1988), So. Calif. Social Studies Assn., Calif. Assn. for Gifted, UCLA Alumni Assn. Democrat. Roman Catholic. Office: LA Sch Dist/Nobel Jr High 9950 Tampa Ave Northridge CA 91324

KOGER, THOMAS HARLAN, military officer; b. Ontario, Oreg., Apr. 12, 1951; s. Lavon Marion and Kathleen (Conklin) K. BS, U. Wash., 1973; MA, Webster U., 1982. Commd. 2d lt. USN, 1973, advanced to maj.; Squadron pilot, asst. div. officer VMAQ-2 MAG-14 2nd Marine Aircraft Wing, Cherry Point, N.C., 1976-80; flight instructor, asst. maintenance officer VT-24 Naval Air Tng. Command, Beeville, Tex., 1980-82; asst. to dir. for officer procurement 12th Marine Corps Dist., San Francisco, 1982-85; maintenance officer, detachment exec. officer VMAQ-2 MAG-14 2nd Marine

Aircraft Wing, Cherry Point, 1985-88; exchange officer Norwegian Army Command and Staff Coll., Oslo, 1988—. Decorated Navy Achievement medal, Navy Commendation medal. Mem. Sierra Club, Dolphin Club. Home and Office: US Embassy Oslo USDAO APO New York NY 09085

KOHAN, DAVOOD, real estate developer; b. Teheran, Iran, Dec. 18, 1946; came to U.S., 1965; s. Mousa and Rouhanguiz (Moradzadeh) Kohanzadeh; div. 1977; 1 child, Soraya. BSBA, U. Calif., Berkeley, 1971. Owner Cheese Unlimited, Mill Valley, Calif., 1971-76, Davood's Restaurant, Mill Valley, Calif., 1973-80, Davood's Internat. Investments, Mill Valley, Calif., 1976-87; chief exec. officer LandVest, San Rafael, Calif., 1987—. Mem. Internat. Assn. Fin. Planners, Marin County C. of C. Republican. Jewish. Office: LandVest 700 Irwin St Ste 300 San Rafael CA 94901

KOHAN, DENNIS LYNN, banker, consultant; b. Kankakee, Ill., Nov. 22, 1945; s. Leon Stanley and Nellie (Foster) K.; m. Julianne Johnson, Feb. 14, 1976 (dec. Sept. 1985); children: Toni, Bart, Elyse; m. Betsy Burns, Mar. 8, 1986; 1 child, David. BA, Ill. Wesleyan U., 1967; MPA, Gov.'s State U., 1975; postgrad., John. Marshall Law Sch., 1971-74. Police officer Kankakee County, 1967-75; loan counselor, security officer Kankakee Fed. Savs. & Loan, Kankakee, 1975-76; mgr. Bank of Western, Denver, 1976-85; mgr. real estate lending dept. Cen. Savs., San Diego, 1985-87; maj. loan work-out officer Imperial Savs., San Diego, 1987-88; cons. Equity Assurance Holding Corp., Newport Beach, Calif., 1987-88; compliance officer Am. Real Estate Group and New West Fed. Savs. and Loan, Irvine, Calif., 1988—; instr. U. No. Colo. Coll. of Bus., Greeley, 1981-85; chmn. bd. N. Colo. Med. Ctr., Greeley, 1983-85; pres. bd. Normedco, Greeley, 1984-85. Vol. cons., chmn. ARC, Colo., 1979-85; campaign mgr. Donley Senatorial campaign, Colo., 1982, Kinkade City Coun. campaign, Colo., 1983; chmn. Weld County Housing Authority, 1981. Staff sgt. U.S. Army, 1969-71, Vietnam. Mem. Nat. Assn. Realtors, Shriners, Kiwanis. Office: Am Real Estate Group 2500 Michelson Ste 300 Irvine CA 92715

KOHAN, RONALD MARK, public relations executive; b. Youngstown, Ohio, May 23, 1951; s. David Michael and Audrey Marion (Gurss) K.; m. Deborah Ann Tibbets. BA in Mktg., Acctg., Pa. State U., 1973; postgrad, Hillsboro Community Coll., Tampa, Fla. Lic. real estate broker. Mktg. dir. Tomac Services, Ft. Lauderdale, Fla., 1973-75; real estate agt. Delta-Century 21, Coral Springs, Fla., 1975-80; owner Pro-Ad Services, Ft. Lauderdale, 1975-80; broker Pro-Ad Real Estate Co., Tampa, Fla., 1980-83; pres. automobile service assn. Pro-Ad, Inc., Tampa, 1980-86; pub. relations animal welfare Living Free Animal Sanctuary, Mountain Ctr., Calif., 1986—; cons. Profl. Sales Group, Tampa, Fla., 1985; adv. Georesco Social Systems, Tampa, 1985; artist, mktg. dir. Lilies Wearable Art of Palm Desert. Mem. needy ministry Calvary Ch., Tampa, 1985. Named one of Outstanding Young Men of Am., 1986. Mem. Sertoma Club, Delta Soc. Animal Human Bond.

KOHL, RICHARD MCCLURE, music educator; b. ColoradoSprings, Colo., Oct. 13, 1940; s. Alfred John Wilhelm and Pauline Louise (McClure) K.; m. Janet Dorthea Kibben, Sept. 7, 1963 (div. 1980); children: Richard W., Alfred John III; m. Bonnie Rose Colescott, July 28, 1981. BA, U. No. Colo., 1963. Chorus soloist Central City (Colo.) Opera Assn., 1960-63; tchr. Culbertson (Nebr.) Pub. Schs., 1963-65, Wild County Schs., Johnstown, Colo., 1965-67, St. Urain Valley Schs., Longmont, Colo., 1967—; dir., Longmont Choral Soc., 1968, Oratorio Soc., Estes Park, Colo., 1988. Participant tchrs. performance inst., Ford Found., Oberlin, Ohio, 1968. Mem. NEA, Colo. Edn. Assn., Music Educators Nat. Conf., Nat. Jazz Educators Assn., Saint Vrain Valley Een. Assn., Am. Guild Mus. Artist. Republican. Presbyterian. Home: 96 Taylor Rd Box 91 Lyons CO 80540-0091 Office: Lyons High Sch PO Box 619 Lyons CO 80540-0619

KOHLER, PETER OGDEN, physician, educator, university president; b. Bklyn., July 18, 1938; s. Dayton McCue and Jean Stewart (Ogden) K.; m. Judy Lynn Baker, Dec. 26, 1959; children: Brooke Culp, Stephen Edwin, Todd Randolph, Adam Stewart. B.A., U. Va., 1959; M.D., Duke U., 1963. Diplomate Am. Bd. Internal Medicine, Am. Bd. Endocrinology. Intern Duke U. Hosp., Durham, N.C., 1963-64, fellow, 1964-65; clin. assoc. Nat Cancer Inst., Nat Inst. Child Health and Human Devel., NIH, Bethesda, Md., 1965-67, sr. investigator, 1968-73, head endocrinology service, 1972-73; resident in medicine Georgetown U. Hosp., Washington, 1969-70; prof. medicine and cell biology Baylor Coll. Medicine, Houston, 1973-77; chief endocrinology div. and med. service, prof., chmn. dept. medicine U. Ark., 1977-86, interim dean, 1985-86; chmn. Hosp. Med. Bd., 1980-82, chmn. council dept. chmn., 1979-80; prof., dean Sch. Medicine, U. Tex., San Antonio, 1986-88; pres. Oreg. Health Scis. U., Portland, 1988—; cons. endrocrinology merit rev. bd. VA, 1985—; mem. endocrinology study sect. NIH, 1981-85, chmn., 1984-85; mem. bd. sci. counsellors NICHP, 1987—. Editor: (with G.T. Ross) Diagnosis and Treatment of Pituitary Tumors, 1973, Clinical Endocrinology, 1986; assoc. editor: Internal Medicine, 1983, 87; contbr. articles to profl. jours. Served with USPHS, 1965-68. NIH grantee, 1973—; Howard Hughes Med. Investigator, 1976-77; recipient NIH Quality awards, 1969, 71. Fellow ACP; mem. Am. Soc. Clin. Investigation, Am. Fedn. Clin. Research (mem. nat. council 1977-78, pres. so. sect. 1976), So. Soc. Clin. Investigation (council 1979-82, pres. 1983, Founder's Medal 1987), AMA (William Beaumont award 1988), Am. Bd. Endocrinology (chmn., mem. bd. govs. ABIM 1987—), Tex. Med. Assn., Bexar County Med. Assn., Am. Soc. Cell Biology, Assn. Am. Physicians, Am. Diabetes Assn., Endocrine Soc., Raven Soc., Sigma Xi, Alpha Omega Alpha, Phi Beta Kappa, Omicron Delta Kappa, Phi Eta Sigma. Methodist. Office: Oreg Health Scis U Office of Pres Portland OR 97201

KOHLER, WILLIAM CHARLES, life insurance agency executive, business consultant; b. Buffalo, Nov. 4, 1929; s. William David and Elizabeth (Barnes) K.; m. Mary Lou Sublett, Feb. 7, 1970; 1 child, Elizabeth Marie. BA, U. Buffalo, 1956; postgrad., Santa Ana Coll., 1964-65, Saddleback Coll., 1966-68. Enlisted USMC, 1948, advanced through grades to capt., 1967, assignments in Korea, Japan, Vietnam, The Philippines, ret., 1973; advt. sales rep. Golden West Pub. Co., Mission Viejo, Calif., 1973-74; agt. Penn. Mut. Life Ins. Co., Irvine, Calif., 1974-80, Mut. Trust Life Ins. Co., Tustin, Calif., 1980-83; ind. life ins. agt. Tustin, 1983; supr. agy. Transam. Life Cos., El Toro, Calif., 1983—; v.p., treas. Pro Futures Inc. Bd. dirs. Saddleback Valley YMCA, 1971-73; mem., pres. Saddleback Valley Unified Sch. Dist. Bd. Edn., Mission Viejo, 1975-81; pres., trustee Coastline Regional Occupational Program, Costa Mesa, Calif., 1976-82. Recipient Merit award Orange County Sch. Bd. Assn., 1980; named Man of Yr. Saddleback Valley YMCA Men's Club. Mem. M.C. League Assn., Ret. Officers Assn., Exch. Club (charter, pres. Saddleback Valley 1972-73, area gov. Calif. 1973-75, dist. dir. 1975-80, chmn. membership expansion 1974-75, 80-81, pres. Calif.-Nev. dist. 1981-82, Pub. Rels. award 1971-73, 79, nat. bd. dirs. 1983-85, regional nat. v.p. 1985-87, pres., bd. dirs. Child Abuse Prevention Ctrs. 1983—, Golden award San Bernardino, Calif. 1986), Saddleback Valley Hi-12 Club, Masons. Republican. Home: 25212 Pike Rd Laguna Hills CA 92653

KOHL MAXWELL, LOIS, marketing professional; b. Balt., Mar. 28, 1952; d. Morton Barnard and Gwen (Caplan) Cole; m. Michael Kim Maxwell, July 11, 1980. BA, U. Colo., 1975. V.p. Mill Valley (Calif.) Film Festival, 1977-80; prin. Lois Cole Designs, Fairfax, Calif., 1978-82; asst. v.p. advt. Fireman's Fund Ins., Novato, Calif., 1982-86; gen. mgr. corp. mktg. Hornblower Yachts, Inc., San Francisco, 1986—. Author Innkeeper Newsletter advt. column, 1984. Mem. San Francisco Advt. Club. Democrat. Home: 500 Pinewood Dr San Rafael CA 94903

KOHN, GERHARD, psychologist, educator; b. Neisse, Germany, Nov. 18, 1921; s. Erich and Marie (Prager) K.; m. Irene M. Billinger, Feb. 9, 1947; children—Mary, Eric. B.S., Northwestern U., 1948, M.A., 1949, Ph.D., 1952; postgrad. U. So. Calif., 1960. Instr., Northwestern U., 1947-49; instr., counselor, dir. pub. relations Kendall Coll., Evanston, Ill., 1947-51; psychologist, counselor Jewish Vocat. Services, Los Angeles, 1951-53, Long Beach Unified Sch. Dist., Calif., 1953-61; instr. Long Beach City Coll., 1955-61; asst. prof. psychology Long Beach State U., 1955-56; counselor, instr. Santa Ana Coll., Calif., 1961-65; prof. Calif. State U., Fullerton, 1971-72; lectr. Orange Coast Coll., 1972-75; asst. clin. prof. psychiatry U. Calif.-Irvine; dir. Reading Devel. Ctr., Long Beach, 1958—, Gerhard Kohn Sch. Ednl. Therapy, 1967-85 ; exec. dir. Young Horizons; pvt. practice psychology, 1958—; cons. HEW, Bur. Hearing and Appeals, Social Security Adminstrn., Long Beach/Orange County B'nai B'rith Career and Counseling Services (cons. to Long Beach Coun.), Long Beach Coun. of Parent Coop. Nursery Sch., Orange County Headstart, Orange County Coop. Pre-Schs. With AUS, 1942-47. Mem. NEA, Am. Pers. and Guidance Assn., Nat. Vocat. Guidance Assn., Am. Psychol. Assn., Calif. Psychol. Assn. (dir. 1976-79, sec. 1980-81), Orange County Psychol. Assn. (dir., pres. 1974), Long Beach Psychol. Assn. (pres. 1985, 86, sec. 1989), L.A. County Psychol. Assn. (treas., sec.), Calif. Assn. Sch. Psychologists, Elks, Phi Delta Kappa, Psi Chi. Office: 5479 Abbeyfield St Long Beach CA 90815

KOHN, LARRY NICKOLAS, insurance executive; b. Merced, Calif., Feb. 14, 1942; s. Robert Jacob and Pauline Ema (Gasper) K.; m. Mary Patricia Walsh, June 4, 1966; 1 child, Deanna Marie. Student, U. Colo., 1962-64, U. Wis., Milw., 1978; BBA, U. Portland, 1985; postgrad., Am. Coll., Bryn Mawr, Pa., 1987—. Asst. parts mgr. Scarborough Implement Co., Merced, 1958-61; mgr. Tektronix, Inc., Beaverton, Oreg., 1968-86; spl. agt. Northwestern Mut. Life Ins. Co., Portland, Oreg., 1986—; registered rep. NML Equity Services, Inc., Portland, 1988—. Active Aloha (Oreg.) High Sch. Band Boosters, 1986—; chmn. St. Elizabeth Ann Seton Adminstrv. Council, Aloha, 1989—. With USN, 1961-68. Mem. Elks. Roman Catholic.

KOHN, ROBERT SAMUEL, JR., real estate investment consultant; b. Denver, Jan. 7, 1949; s. Robert Samuel and Miriam Lackner (Neusteter) K.; BS, U. Ariz., 1971; m., Eleanor B. Kohn; children: Joseph Robert, Randall Stanton, Andrea Rene. Asst. buyer Robinson's Dept. Store, L.A., 1971; agt. Neusteter Realty Co., Denver, 1972-73, exec. v.p., 1973-76; pres. Project Devel. Svcs., Denver, 1976-78, pres., chief exec. officer, 1978-83; pres. Kohn and Assos., Inc., 1979-83, The Burke Co., Inc., Irvine, Calif., 1983-84, ptnr. 1984—. Mem. Bldg. Owners and Mgrs. Assn. (pres. 1977-78, dir. 1972-78, dir. S.W. Conf. Bd. 1977-78), Denver Art Mus., Denver U. Library Assn., Central City Opera House Assn., Inst. Real Estate Mgmt., Newport Beach Tennis Club. Republican. Jewish. Home: 10 Skysail Dr Corona Del Mar CA 92625 Office: The Burke Co Inc 2111 Business Center Dr Irvine CA 92715

KOJIAN, VARUJAN HAIG, conductor; b. Beirut, Mar. 12, 1935; came to U.S., 1956, naturalized, 1965; s. Haig Awak and Anouche (Der-Parseghian) K. Student (1st prize), Paris Nat. Conservatory, 1947-50; diploma, Curtis Inst. Music, 1959; student, U. So. Calif., 1964. Asst. concertmaster and asst. condr. Los Angeles Philharm., 1965-71; assoc. condr. Seattle Symphony, 1972-75; prin. guest condr. Royal Opera, Stockholm, 1973-80; music dir. Utah Symphony, Salt Lake City, 1980-83, Chautauqua (N.Y.) Symphony, 1981-84, Ballet West, Salt Lake City, 1984—, Santa Barbara (Calif.) Symphony, 1985—; faculty dept. music U. Utah, Salt Lake City, 1980-83; music dir. Santa Barbara Sympnony, 1985—. Recipient 1st prize Internat. Conducting Competition, Sorrento, Italy, 1972; decorated Order of Lion Finland, 1975, Order of Lion also by govts. Greece, 1956, Iran, 1955, Lebanon, 1956. Home: 4455 J Carpinteria Ave Carpinteria CA 93013 Office: Santa Barbara Symphony 214 E Victoria Santa Barbara CA 93101

KOKICH, VINCENT GEORGE, orthodontist; b. Tacoma, Wash., Sept. 17, 1944; s. Obren and Helen Margaret (Lisicich) K.; m. Marilyn Frances Vukovich, Dec. 21, 1968; children: Vincent, Mary, Obren, Marija. BS, U. Puget Sound, 1966; DDS, U. Wash., 1971, MS in Dentistry, 1974. Diplomate Am. Bd. Orthodontists. Dental intern VA Hosp., Palo Alto, Calif., 1971-72; rsch. assoc. U. Wash., Seattle, 1974-77, rsch. asst. prof., 1977-79, asst. prof., 1979-81, assoc. prof., 1981-86, prof. orthodontics, 1986—; pvt. practice Tacoma, 1974—; cons. Pierce County Cleft Palate Bd., Tacoma, 1975—, U.S. Army Dental Corps, 1977—; bd. dirs. Grad. Orthodontic Rsch., Seattle, 1980—; mem. cons. staff Mary Bridge Children's Hosp., Tacoma, 1975—, Madigan Army Hosp., Tacoma, 1975—; examiner B.C. Orthodontic Specialty Exam. Editor Pacific Coast Orthodontic Jour., 1977-87; reviewer Am. Jour. Orthodontics; contbr. articles to profl. jours., chpt. to books. Bd. dirs. Slavonian Am. Benevolent Soc., 1979-83; lector St. Rita's Cath. Ch., Tacoma, 1984—. Mem. ADA, Am. Acad. Esthetic Dentistry, Am. Assn. Dental Rsch., Am. Assn. Orthodontists (award 1975), Am. Cleft Palate Assn., Edward H. Angle Soc. Orthodontists, Internat. Assn. Dental Rsch., Pacific Coast Soc. Orthodontists, Wash. State Assn. Orthodontists, Wash. State Dental Assn. (award 1971), Pierce County Dental Soc. Home: 1018 Corona Dr Tacoma WA 98466 Office: U Wash Sch Dentistry Dept Orthodontics Tacoma WA 98195

KOLANOSKI, THOMAS EDWIN, financial company executive; b. San Francisco, Mar. 1, 1937; s. Theodore Thaddeus and Mary J. (Luczynski) K.; m. Sheila O'Brien, Dec. 26, 1960; children: Kenneth John, Thomas Patrick, Michael Sean. BS, U. San Francisco, 1959, MA, 1965. Cert. fin. planner. Educator, counselor, administr. San Francisco Unified Sch. Dist., 1960-79; adminstr. Huntington Beach (Calif.) Union, 1969-79; v.p. fin. svcs. Waddell & Reed, Inc., Ariz., Nev., Utah, So. Calif., 1969—. Fellow NDEA, 1965. Mem. Nat. Assn. Secondary Sch. Prins., Internat. Assn. of Fin. Planners, Nat. Assn. Securities Dealers. Republican. Roman Catholic. Home: 1783 Pany Circle Costa Mesa CA 92626 also: 10218 N Central Phoenix AZ 85021

KOLBE, JAMES THOMAS, congressman; b. Evanston, Ill., June 28, 1942; s. Walter William and Helen (Reed) K.; m. Sarah Marjorie Dinham, Apr. 16, 1977. B.A. in Polit. Sci., Northwestern U., 1965; M.B.A. in Econs., Stanford U., 1967. Asst. to coordinating architect Ill. Bldg. Authority, Chgo., 1970-72; spl. asst. to Gov. Richard Ogilvie Chgo., 1972-73; v.p. Wood Canyon Corp., Tucson, 1973—; mem. Ariz. Senate, 1977-83, majority whip, 1979-81; cons. Tucson, 1983-85; mem. 99th-101st Congresses, 1985—; mem. appropriations com. 1985-87. Trustee Embry-Riddle Aero. U., Daytona Beach, Fla.; bd. dirs. Community Food Bank, Tucson, Casa de los Niños Crisis Nursery, Tucson; Republican precinct committeeman, Tucson, 1974—. Served as lt. USNR, 1977-79, Vietnam. Mem. Am. Legion, VFW. Republican. Methodist. Office: 5th Dist Congl Office 1661 N Swan Rd Ste 116 Tucson AZ 85712 also: Office of House Members care The Postmaster Washington DC 20515

KOLBET, LE ANN, nurse; b. Hastings, Nebr., Mar. 3, 1963; d. Jerome William and Agnes Ann K. Assoc. in Nursing, U Nebr., 1983-85, BS in Nursing, 1985-87. Relief nursing supr. Tasitha Home, Lincoln, Nebr., 1986-88; charge nurse Holy Rosary Med. Ctr., Ontario, Oreg., 1988. Mem. Sigma Theta Tau Nat. Honor Soc. of Nursing, Golden Key Nat. Honor Soc., YMCA. Roman Catholic.

KOLKER, HAL, entertainment arena executive, sports marketing executive; b. Buffalo, Oct. 4, 1949; s. Benjamin and Rose (Lippes) K.; student U. So. Caliif., 1969-72. Exec. asst. Neil Diamond, Los Angeles, 1972-74; cons. Norman Lear Tandem Prodns., Los Angeles, 1974-76; pres. Century City Sound, Los Angeles, 1976-77; pres. Budget Rent-A-Car, San Diego, 1976-78; v.p. San Diego Clippers NBA Basketball Club, Inc., 1978-80; v.p. San Diego Entertainment Inc., operator San Diego Sports Arena, 1980—; pres. Spectator Collegiate Mktg. Corp., San Diego, 1983-88, pres., chief exec. officer, 1988—, Innovative Electronics, Inc. 1988—; pres. Edwin Schlossberg Prodns., 1987—; exec. v.p. Internat. Action Pack, Inc., 1988—; pres., chief ops. officer Miletus Rsch. corp., 1989—; cons. Paramount Pictures Corp.; Bob Speck Sports Prodns.; exec. producer Bill Walton Show, 1979-80. Campaign chmn. George C. Hardie for 46th Dist. Assembly Calif., 1976. Mem. Am. Mgmt. Assn., Am. Mktg. Assn. Office: 1250 Prospect Pl Ste 202 La Jolla CA 92037

KOLKEY, DANIEL MILES, lawyer; b. Chgo., Apr. 21, 1952; s. Eugene Louis and Gilda Penelope (Cowan) K.; m. Donna Lynn Christie, May 15, 1982; children: Eugene, William, Christopher, Jonathan. BA, Stanford U., 1974; JD, Harvard U., 1977. Bar: Calif. 1977, U.S. Dist. Ct. (cen., no., ea. dists.) Calif., U.S. Ct. Appeals (9th cir.) 1979, U.S. Supreme Ct., 1983. Law clk. U.S. Dist. Ct. judge, N.Y.C., 1977-78; ptnr. Gibson Dunn & Crutcher, Los Angeles, 1978—. Contbr. articles to profl. publs. Co-chmn. internat. relations sect. Town Hall of Calif., Los Angeles, 1981—; chmn. internat. trade legis. subcom., internat. commerce steering com. Los Angeles Area C. of C., 1983—; mem. adv. council Asia Pacific Ctr. for Resolution of Internat. Bus. Disputes; bd. dirs., v.p., treas. Los Angeles Ctr. for Internat. Comml. Arbitration, 1986—, v.p. 1988—; assoc. mem. central com. Calif. Rep. Party, 1983—; mem. Los Angeles Com. on Fgn. Relations, 1983—; mem. Los Angeles World Affairs Council, Rep. Assocs. Mem. ABA, Internat. Bar Assn., Los Angeles County Bar Assn. (exec. com. internat. law sect. 1987—, vice chmn. 1989—), Chartered Inst. Arbitrators, London (assoc.), Cour Pour L'Arbitrage Internat. en Matiere de Commerce et D'Industrie (Geneva), Wilton Park Alumni of So. Calif. (chmn. exec. com.). Jewish. Office: Gibson Dunn & Crutcher 333 S Grand Ave Los Angeles CA 90071

KOLKMEYER, ALEXANDRA, principal; b. St. Louis, Apr. 22, 1953; s. James and Alice (Lehky) Valestin; m. John Kolkmeyer, June 21, 1981; children: Anton, Maxwell. BA in Edn., Goddard U., 1975; M in Curriculum, U. N.Mex., 1977. Cert. elem., sec. educator. Youth dept. head St. Jude's Hosp., Austin, Tex., 1975-79; publisher Insight Press, Santa Fe, N.Mex., 1980—; dir. Insight Child Devel. Ctr., Santa Fe, 1981-84; prin., owner Sequoia Prep. Sch., Santa Fe, 1984—. Author: Clear Red Stone, 1976, Reading Assessment, 1978, Modern Woman's Herbal, 1979, Math Assessment, 1980. Recipient Outstanding Service award United Way Tex., Austin, 1976, Gov.'s award State N.Mex., Santa Fe, 1988. Mem. Nat. Edn. Agy. Syda. Office: Sequoia Sch 1989 Siringo Rd Santa Fe NM 87505

KOLKO, PHILIP, manufacturing executive; b. N.Y.C., Aug. 5, 1935; s. David and Rose (Suchenky) K.; m. Arleen Powdermaker, June 5, 1957 (div. 1975); children: Richard, David, Beth; m. Yuriko Tanabe, Oct. 26, 1986. BA, Duke U., 1956. Mgr. software devel. IBM Corp., Kingston, N.Y., 1960-80; mgr. network svcs. IBM Corp., White Plains, N.Y., 1981-83; mgr. communications strategy Asia Pacific group IBM Corp., Tokyo, 1983-87; mgr. network svcs. Hawaiian Airlines, Honolulu, 1988-89; dir. mgmt. info. Verifone Inc., Costa Mesa, Calif., 1989—; chmn., bd. dirs. Trans Pacific Mgmt. Corp., Denver, 1986—; prin. P. Kolko Cons., Honolulu, 1987—; sec. Hawaii High Tech. Adv. Com., 1988—. Contbr. articles to profl. jours. Active Pres. Coun. U. Fla., Gainesville, 1986—; bd. dirs. Mid Hudson Sci. Ctr., Poughkeepsie, N.Y., 1985-86; chmn. Boy Scout com., Poughkeepsie, 1983-84; v.p. Hale Kaheka Assn., Honolulu, 1988—. Lt. USN, 1957-61. Mem. Honolulu Telecommunications Assn., Japan Am. Soc., Duke U. Alumni Assn., Tokyo Am. Club, Masons. Democrat. Home: 78 Stanford Irvine CA 92715

KOLKOWICZ, ROMAN, political science educator, academic administrator, consultant; b. Poland, Nov. 15, 1929; came to U.S., 1949, naturalized, 1955; s. William and Edwarda (Goldberg) K.; children—Susan, Lisa, Gabriella. B.A., U. Buffalo, 1954; M.A., U. Chgo., 1958, Ph.D., 1964. Sr. staff mem. Rand Corp., Santa Monica, Calif., 1961-66, Inst. Def. analysis, Washington, 1966-70; prof. polit. sci. UCLA, 1970—, dir. Ctr. Internat. Strategic Affairs, 1974-82; co-dir. Project on Arms Control, 1983-85; dir. Project on Politics and War, 1985—; cons. to govt., others. Chmn. fgn. policy platform Calif. Dem. Party, 1972, 76. Served with U.S. Army, 1954-56. Ford Found. grantee, 1975-83; Rockefeller Found. grantee, 1975-77. Mem. Am. Polit. Sci. Assn., Internat. Sociol. Assn., Internat. Polit. Sci. Assn. Author: Soviet Military-Communist Party, 1967; Soldiers, Peasants, Bureaucrats, 1982; National Security and International Stability, 1983; Arms Control and International Security, 1983; Soviet Calculus of War, 1983, Logic of Nuclear Terror, 1987, Dilemmas of Nuclear Deterrence, 1987. Home: 21310 Bellini Dr Topanga CA 90290 Office: UCLA Dept Polit Sci Los Angeles CA 90024

KOLLER, BRANT WILLIAM, manufacturing company executive; b. Albuquerque, Sept. 2, 1943; s. Ernest Herman and Elizabeth Virginia (Phillips) K.; m. Carol Jean Miller, Sept. 4, 1965; children: Jennifer Jean, Heather Elizabeth. BA, Wash. State U., 1966. Gen. mgr. Cheny Weeder div. Chinook Pontoon Boats, Spokane, Wash., 1970-77, 78—; owner, mgr. N.W. Floor Covering Co., Spokane, Wash., 1977-78. Co-founder Ronald McDonald House, Spokane, 1981-85; trustee Ag Trade Ctr., Spokane, 1985-87; pres. Ag Expo, Spokane, 1986-87. Mem. Spokane Area C. of C. (trustee 1985--), Small Bus. Coun. (advisor 1985), Armed Forces Coun. Office: Cheney Weeder Box 232 Spokane WA 99210

KOLONEL, LAURENCE NORMAN, epidemiologist, public health educator; b. Corner Brook, Can., Apr. 29, 1942; came to U.S., 1958; s. Arthur and Reta (Marshall) K. BA magna cum laude, Williams Coll., 1964; MD, Harvard U., 1968; MPH, U. Calif., Berkeley, 1970, PhD, 1972. Lic. physician, Calif.; diplomate Am. Bd. Gen. Preventive Medicine. Assoc. epidemiologist Cancer Research Ctr. U. Hawaii, Honolulu, 1974-76, dir. epidemiology program Cancer Research Ctr., 1977—, acting exec. dir., 1984-85, assoc. prof. epidemiology Sch. Pub. Health, 1976-81, prof. Sch. Pub. Health, 1981—; vis. prof. Stanford (Calif.) U. Med. Ctr., 1986. Assoc. editor Jour. Nutrition and Cancer, (jour.) Cancer Research, 1987—; contbr. articles to profl. jours. Served to maj. USAF, 1972-74. Grantee Nat. Cancer Inst., 1977—. Mem. AAAS, Nat. Cancer Inst. (bd. sci. counselors 1982-86), Nat. Acad. Sci. (diet and health com. 1986—, nutrition and cancer com. 1980-83, food and nutrition bd. 1988—), Am. Pub. Health Assn., Soc. Epidemiol. Research, Am. Assn. Cancer Research, Am. Epidemiological Soc., Phi Beta Kappa, Delta Omega. Democrat. Office: U Hawaii Cancer Rsch Ctr 1236 Lauhala St Honolulu HI 96813

KOLSRUD, HENRY GERALD, dentist; b. Minnewaukan, N.D., Aug. 12, 1923; s. Henry G. and Anna Naomi (Moen) K.; m. Loretta Dorothy Cooper, Sept. 3, 1945; children—Gerald Roger, Charles Cooper. Student Concordia Coll., 1941-44; DDS, U. Minn., 1947. Gen. practice dentistry, Spokane, Wash., 1953—. Bd. dirs. Spokane County Rep. Com., United Crusade, Spokane. Capt. USAF, 1950-52. Mem. ADA, Wash. State Dental Assn., Spokane Dist. Dental Soc. Lutheran. Clubs: Spokane Country, Spokane, Empire. Lodges: Masons, Shriners. Home: 2107 Waikiki Rd Spokane WA 99218 Office: 3718 N Monroe St Spokane WA 99218

KOLSTAD, ALLEN C., state official; b. Chester, Mont., Dec. 24, 1931; s. Henry B. & Mabel (Webb) K.; m. Iva Matteson, 1951; children: Cedric A., Chris A., Cheryl D., Corrine F. Student, Concordia Coll., Moorhead, Minn. Mont. state rep., dist. 19, 1969-75, state senator, dist. 5,, 1975-88, pres. pro tem. 1979-84, lt. gov., 1989—; precinct committeeman, 1962-66; chmn. Liberty County Rep. Com., 1967-68. Mem. Jaycees, Shriners, Masons. Republican. Lutheran. Office: Office of Lt Gov Capitol Sta Rm 207 Helena MT 59620 *

KOLTAI, STEPHEN MIKLOS, mechanical engineer, consultant, economist; b. Ujpest, Hungary, Nov. 5, 1922; came to U.S., 1963; s. Maximilian and Elisabeth (Rado) K.; m. Franciska Gabor, Sept. 14, 1948; children: Eva, Susy. MS in Mech. Engring., U. Budapest, Hungary, 1948, MS in Econs., MS, BA, 1955. Engr. Hungarian Govt., 1943-49; cons. engr. and diplomatic service various European countries, 1950-62; cons. engr. Pan Bus. Cons. Corp., Switzerland and U.S., 1963-77, Palm Springs, Calif., 1977—. Patentee in field. Charter mem. Rep. Presdl. task force, Washington, 1984—.

KOLTS, RICHARD BRUCE, mortgage banking executive. BA in Fin., U. Wash., Seattle, 1969; MBA, Pepperdine U., 1981. Bus. mgr. Browning-Ferris Industries, Pt. Richmond, Calif., 1974-81; loan officer Seafirst Mortgage, Pleasant Hill, Calif., 1981-82; asst. v.p. I.M.I., San Bruno, Calif., 1982-84; account exec. RMIC/West, Danville, Calif., 1984-86; br. mgr. Colwell Fin. Corp., Sacramento, 1986-88; asst. v.p. ARCS Mortgage Inc., Citrus Heights, Calif., 1988—. Served to lt. (j.g.) USN, 1970-72. Mem. Mortgage Bankers Sacramento (pres. 1988—). Office: ARCS Mortgage 7919 Pebble Beach Dr Suite 106 Citrus Heights CA 95610

KOMDAT, JOHN RAYMOND, data processing consultant; b. Brownsville, Tex., Apr. 29, 1943; s. John William and Sara Grace (Williams) K.; m. Linda Jean Garrette, Aug. 26, 1965 (div.); m. Barbara Milroy O'Cain, Sept. 27, 1986; 1 child, Philip August. Student U. Tex., 1961-65. Sr. systems analyst Mass. Blue Cross, Boston, 1970-74; pvt. practice data processing cons., San Francisco, 1974-80, Denver, 1981—; prin. systems analyst mgmt. info. services div. Dept. of Revenue, State of Colo., 1986-89; prin. systems analyst Dept. Adminstrn. State Colo., 1989—; mem. CODASYL End User Facilities Com., 1974-76, allocation com. Mile High United Way. Served with U.S. Army, 1966-70. Mem. AAAS, Assn. Computing Machinery, Denver Downtown Dem. Forum (mem. exec. com.), Mus. Modern Art, Denver Art Mus., Friend of Pub. Radio, Friend of Denver Pub. Library, Colo. State Mgrs. Assn. Democrat. Office: PO Box 10666 Denver CO 80210

KOMENICH, KIM, photographer; b. Laramie, Wyo., Oct. 15, 1956; s. Milo and Juanita Mary (Beggs) K. BA in Journalism, San Jose State U., 1979. Photographer Forbis Studio, Modesto, Calif., 1973-76; reporter/photographer Manteca (Calif.) Bulletin, 1976-77; staff photographer Contra Costa Times, Walnut Creek, Calif., 1979-82, San Francisco Examiner, 1982—; lectr. San Francisco Acad. Art. Recipient 1st Pl. award UPI, 1982, 85, Nat. Headliner award, 1983, 88, 87 1st Pl. award World Press Photo Awards, 1983, 1st Pl. award AP, 1985, 87, Pulitzer Prize, 1987, others. Mem. Nat. Press Photographers Assn. (2d Pl. award 1982), San Francisco Bay Area Press Photographers Assn. (Photographer of Yr. award 1982, 84), Sigma Delta Chi (Disting. Service award 1986). Office: San Francisco Examiner 110 5th St San Francisco CA 94103

KOMILI, OMER, data processing company executive; b. Istanbul, Turkey, Mar. 30, 1952; parents: Faruk and Mufide (Anar) K. Baccalaureat C, Esenis Lisesi, France, 1972; MS in Computer Sci., U. Nancy (France) 2, 1977. Programmer, analyst Ctr. of Preventive Medicine, Nancy, 1976-80; analyst, system mgr. Transco Ins., Solvang, Calif., 1980-82; network specialist Hewlett-Packard, L.A., 1982-84; pres. Komdata, Inc., Santa Barbara, Calif., 1984—; cons. Transco Ins., 1983-84, Premium Computer Co., Istanbul, 1987-88. Contbr. articles to profl. jours. Mem. European Computer Profls., Rotary Internat., Galatasaray Alumni. Office: Komdata Inc 350 S Hope #A-225 Santa Barbara CA 93105

KOMPALA, DHINAKAR SATHYANATHAN, chemical engineering educator, biochemical engineering researcher; b. Madras, India, Nov. 20, 1958; came to U.S., 1979; s. Sathyanathan and Sulochana K.; m. Sushila Viswamurthy Rudramuniappa, Nov. 18, 1983. BTech., Indian Inst. Tech., Madras, 1979; MS, Purdue U., 1982, PhD, 1984. Asst. prof. chem. engring. U. Colo., Boulder, 1985—. Contbr. articles to profl. jours. Recipient NSF Presdl. Young Investigators award, 1988—; council Rsch. and Creative Work grantee, 1985, NIH rsch. grantee, 1985, Solar Energy Rsch. Inst., 1986, NSF Biotech. Rsch. grantee 1986-89, Dept. Commerce Rsch. grantee, 1988. Mem. Soc. Indsl. Microbiology, N.Y. Acad. Scis., Am. Soc. Engring. Edn., Am. Inst. Chem. Engrs., Am. Chem Soc., AAS. Hindu. Office: U Colo PO Box 424 Boulder CO 80309

KONDO, SADAO, trading company executive; b. Hirosakishi, Japan, Sept. 9, 1980; came to U.S. , 1968; s. Saikichi and Shino (Yannai) K.; m. Setsuko Itoh, May 27, 1943; 1 child, Michiko. Grad., Communication Acad., Japan, 1942. Mem. staff Ministry Communications, Japan, 1942-45; with J. Osawa Co., Tokyo, 1956-69; mgr. J. Osawa Co., L.A., 1969, Nihon Seimitxu Sokki, K.K., L.A., 1970-74; v.p. JPI, Santa Monica, Calif., 1974-76; pres. JPI, Santa Monica, 1976—; also bd. dirs. JPI. Home and Office: 1507 San Vicente Blvd Santa Monica CA 90402

KONICEK, VINCE, educational specialist; b. Racine, Wis., Jan. 6, 1935; s. V.J. and Helen (Kuzela) K.; divorced 1973; m. Nancy Ann Barrett, Aug. 25, 1984; children: Steve, Kathy, Sue, Nancy, Vikki. B in Edn., Dominican Coll., 1960; MA, U. Calif., Riverside, 1977. Tchr. various pub. and pvt. elem. schs., Wis., 1960-72; tchr. spl. edn. Riverside County Office of Edn., 1977-84; tchr. Court Schs., Riverside, 1984—; negotiator Riverside County Office Tchrs. Assn., 1987—; lectr. coalition for ednl. reform, Madison, Wis., 1969-72. Served as sgt. USAF, 1955-58. Home: PO Box 761 Lake Arrowhead CA 92352 Office: Court Schs W 3933 Harrison St Riverside CA 92503

KONKEL, PAUL EDWARD, chemical company executive; b. Phila., June 11, 1933; s. Paul Leo and Anna Marie (McCreery) K.; m. Patricia Marion Genthert, Sept. 17, 1955; children: Patricia Ann, Kenneth Paul, Timothy, Terrance. BS in Commerce, Engring., Drexel U., 1956, MBA, 1959; MS, U. Pa., 1958. Nat. systems mgr. RCA, Cherry Hill, N.J., 1952-65; mng. assoc. Arthur Young & Co., Chgo., 1965-67; v.p., gen. mgr. Nat.Liberty Corp., Valley Forge, Pa., 1967-71; v.p., mgr. Bechtel Corp., San Francisco, 1971-77; v.p., div. mgr. Daniel, Mann, Johnston & Mendenhall, L.A., 1977-81; dir. gen. Saudi Arabia Basic Industries Corp., Riyadh, 1981-88; cons. Saudi Arabia Basic Industries Corp., 1988—; cons. in mgmt. and bus. Author: Computer Management, 1962, Construction Management, 1982, Operations Reporting, 1988. Pres., Voge Boys Club, Phila., 1960; mayor, City of Cinamisson, N.J., 1964; pres. Rheem Valley Homeowners, Moraga, Calif., 1976. Mem. Phi Kappa Phi. Republican. Home: 26581 Royale Dr San Juan Capistrano CA 92675 Office: SABIL, PO Box 5101, Riyadh 11422, Saudi Arabia

KONNICK, RONALD JOHN, data processing executive, consultant; b. East Chicago, Ind., May 18, 1943; s. Michael and Sophie (Kostrubala) K.; m. Marie Anne Kwiecien, Dec. 9, 1972; children: Eric, Bryan. BSEE, Carnegie-Mellon U., 1966; MS in Indsl. Engring., Wayne State U., 1972; MBA, Calif. Poly. State U., 1974. Indsl. engr. Carrier Corp., LaPuente, Calif., 1973-76; sr. indsl. engr. Harris Corp., Quincy, Ill., 1976-78; dir. mgmt. info. service IML Freight, Salt Lake City, 1978-84; site mgr. data ctr. Sun Carriers, Salt Lake City, 1985—; instr. data processing, U. Phoenix, Salt Lake City, 1974—. Chmn. 4th of July com. City of Sandy, Utah, 1980-81. Mem. Data Processing Mgmt. Assn. (bd. dirs. 1974—), Inst. Cert. Computer Profls. (cert., award for excellence 1979). Roman Catholic. Home: 9513 Buttonwood Dr Sandy UT 84092 Office: Sun Carriers Systems Inc 275 W 2755 S Salt Lake City UT 84115

KONNYU, ERNEST LESLIE, former congressman; b. Tamasi, Hungary, May 17, 1937; came to U.S., 1949; s. Leslie and Elizabeth Konnyu; m. Lillian Muenks, Nov. 25, 1959; children: Carol, Renata, Lisa, Victoria. Student, U. Md., 1960-62; BS in Acctg., Ohio State U., 1965. Mem. Calif. Assembly, Sacramento, 1980-86, 100th Congress from 12th Calif. dist., 1987-89; chmn. Assembly Rep. Caucus, Sacramento, 1985-86; vice chmn. Assembly Human Services, Sacramento, 1980-86; vice chmn. Policy Research Com., Sacramento, 1985-86. Mem. Rep. State Cen. Com., Calif., 1977-88, Rep. Cen. Com., Santa Clara County, Calif., 1980-86; mem. adv. bd. El Camino Hosp., Mountain View, Calif., 1987. Served to maj. USAF, 1959-69. Recipient Nat. Def. Medal, 1968, Disting. Service award U.S. Jaycees, 1969, Nat. Security award Am. Security Council Found., 1987; named lifetime senator U.S. Jaycees, 1977. Republican. Roman Catholic.

KONOTCHICK, JOHN ANDREW, corporate professionl, consultant; b. Dover, N.J., Aug. 26, 1942; s. John Andrew Sr. and Florence Regina (Kelly) K.; m. Susan M. Stevens, Sept. 11, 1965 (div. 1977); children: Kristi Ann, Karin Jean, Kim Marie; m. Barbara Jane Sweetman, Nov. 7, 1979; children: Talina Helen, Anna Nelmore. BS, Northeastern U., 1966, MS, 1970. Registered profl. engr. Engring. trainee Picatinny Arsenal, Dover, N.J., 1961-66; systems engr. Sanders Assoc., Nashua, Mass., 1966-69; with The MITRE Corp., Bedford, Mass., 1969-87; pres., dir. KAB Labs, Inc., San Diego, 1987—; cons. Sanders Assoc., Nashua, N.H., PAR Technology Corp., New Hartford, N.Y., PSC Corp., Fairfax, Va., 1987—. Patentee in field. Dir. N.H. Clean Air Alliance; friend of library U. Calif., San Diego; donor Pub. Radio Service. Mem. Assn. Old Crows, Armed Forces Comm. and Elec. Assn., Naval Inst., Aircraft Owners and Pilots Assn., Navy League U.S. Roman Catholic.

KONTNY, VINCENT LAWRENCE, engineering and construction company executive; b. Chappell, Nebr., July 19, 1937; s. Edward James and Ruth Regina (Schumann) K.; m. Joan Dashwood FitzGibbon, Feb. 20, 1970; children: Natascha Marie, Michael Christian, Amber Brooke. BSCE, U. Colo., 1958. Operator heavy equipment, grade foreman Peter Kiewit Son's Co., Denver, 1958-59; project mgr. Utah Constrn. and Mining Co., Western Australia, 1965-69, Fluor Australia, Queensland, Australia, 1969-72; sr. project mgr. Fluor Utah, San Mateo, Calif., 1972-73; sr. v.p. Holmes & Narver, Inc., Orange, Calif., 1973-79; mng. dir. Fluor Australia, Melbourne, 1979-82; group v.p. Fluor Engrs., Inc., Irvine, Calif., 1982-85, pres., chief exec. officer, 1985-87; group pres. Fluor Daniel, Irvine, Calif., 1987-88, pres., chief exec. officer, 1988—. Contbr. articles to profl. jours. Mem. engring. devel. council, U. Colo. Lt. USN, 1959-65. Mem. AIME (soc. mining engrs.), Am. Assn. Cost Engrs., Australian Assn. Engrs., Am. Petroleum Inst. Republican. Roman Catholic. Club: Cet. (Costa Mesa, Calif.). Home: 10255 Overhill Dr Santa Ana CA 92705 Office: Fluor Corp 3333 Michelson Dr Irvine CA 92730

KOO, JOHN, linguistics educator; b. Seoul, Feb. 1, 1932; came to U.S., 1963; m. Sandra B. Koo; children: Willie, Charlie, Sarah. MA, U. Tex., 1965; PhD, Ind. U., 1970. Asst. prof. U. Alaska, Fairbanks, 1969-75, assoc. prof., 1975-82, head dept. lingustics and fgn. lang., 1976-80, 85-86, prof. linguistics, 1982—, dir. Korean Studies Program, 1986—; vis. prof. Western Mich. U., Kalmazoo, 1973, 76, Soong Jun U., Seoul, 1983; prin investigator in Eskimo rsch., U. Alaska, 1973-75; chmn. Internat. Exchange Program, U. Alaska, 1982-85, Internat. Conf. on Cross Cultural Communication, Seoul, 1985. Author: A Basic Conversational Eskimo: Yuk, 1975, Alaska: The Land of Boundless Potentiality, 1985, Let's Speak Korean, 1987; (co-author) Daremo Kakanakatta Arasuka, Sankei Shuppan, 1980. Bd. dirs. Adult Learning Program of Alaska, 1981-88; cons. bilingual program, Fairbanks Sch. Dist., 1977-80. Lingistic rsch. grantee NSF, 1973-75, Rsch. grantee Am. Council Learned Soc., 1971, 72, Korean Studies program grantee Korea Rsch. Found., 1988; Rsch. fellow, 1980. Mem. Linguistic Soc. Am., Assn. for Asian Studies, Internat. Assn. for Korean Lang. Edn., Korean Assn. of Fairbanks (pres. 1980-82), Rotary (chmn. internat. svc. 1978-79), Internat. Circle of Korean Linguistics (pres. 1984-86, advisor), Elks. Home: 4870 Palo Verde Fairbanks AK 99709 Office: U Alaska-Fairbanks Dept Linguistics Fairbanks AK 99775

KOOGLER, RUSSELL LEWIS, security specialist; b. Zanesville, Ohio, Sept. 12, 1938; s. Emerson L. and Betty J. (DeSantel) King; student Sacramento Jr. Coll., 1972-74; B.Police Sci. and Bus., Fullerton Coll., 1975; grad. in interview and interrogation technique, Reid Coll., 1987. m. Sue Ann Hicks, Dec. 10, 1982; 1 child, Malissa Sue; 1 child by previous marriage, Patricia Louise. Fed. police officer U.S. Postal Inspectors, Los Angeles, 1967-77; loss prevention dist. mgr. K-Mart Corp., Covina, Calif. Tchr., instr. CPR and first aid and disaster courses ARC, Santa Ana, Calif., 1971-78, disaster chmn., 1976-78; owner Koogler & Assocs., P.I. Svc., Citrus Heights, Calif., 1989—.b. Served with Signal Corps, U.S. Army, 1961-64. Recipient awards, ARC 1973, 74, 75, Freedom Train award, 1976. Mem. Nat. Assn. Chiefs of Police, Internat. Narcotic Enforcement Officers Assn., Nat. Assn. Investigators and Spl. Police, No. Calif. Retail Investigators Assn., , Am. Soc. Indsl. Security, No. Calif. Robbery Investigations Assn., Alpha Gamma Sigma. Lodge: Elks. Am. Legion.Contbr. articles to profl. jours. Address: 7202 LaLuna Ct Citrus Heights CA 95621 Address: PO Box 684 Citrus Heights CA 95611-0684

KOOKEN, JOHN FREDERICK, bank holding company executive; b. Denver, Nov. 1, 1931; s. Duff A. and Frances C. K.; m. Emily Howe, Sept. 18, 1954; children: Diane, Carolyn. M.S., Stanford U., 1954, Ph.D., 1961. With Security Pacific Nat. Bank-Security Pacific Corp., Los Angeles, 1960—; exec. v.p. Security Pacific Corp., Los Angeles, 1981-87, chief fin. officer, 1984—, vice chmn., 1987—; bd. dirs. U.S. Facilities Corp.; lectr. Grad. Sch. Bus., U. So. Calif., 1962-67. Pres. bd. dirs. Children's Bur. Los Angeles, 1981-84; bd. dirs. United Way Los Angeles, 1982—, Huntington Meml. Hosp., Pasadena, 1985—. Served to lt. (j.g.) USNR, 1954-57. Mem. Fin. Execs. Inst. (pres. Los Angeles chpt. 1979-80, dir. 1981-84). Office: Security Pacific Corp 333 S Hope St Los Angeles CA 90071

KOON, RAY HAROLD, management consultant; b. Little Mountain, S.C., Nov. 19, 1934; s. Harold Clay and Jessie Rae (Epting) K.; m. Bertha Mae Gardner, Aug. 19, 1958; children: Shari Madilyn Koon Goode, Schyler Michele, Kamela Suzanne. BSBA, Old Dominion U., 1957; postgrad., Columbia (S.C.) Coll., 1957-58. Lic. pvt. pilot. Office services supr. FBI, Norfolk, Va., 1953-60, Las Vegas, 1961-62; agt. State Gaming Control Bd., Carson City, Nev., 1962-64, coord., 1967-80, chief of investigations, 1980-83; prodn. control mgr. Colite Industries, Inc., West Columbia, S.C., 1964-67; pres., bd. dirs. Global Advisors, Ltd., Carson City, 1983; dir. gaming and surveillance Hilton Hotels Corp., Beverly Hills, Calif., 1983-86; pres., bd. dirs. JRJ Enterprises, Las Vegas, 1986-88; pres. Assoc. Cons. Enterprises, Las Vegas, 1983—; bd. dirs. Sta. KNIS-FM Radio, Carson City, 1968-84, also sec. Editor, pub. Ray Koon's Gaming Gram, 1986. Chief vols. Warren Engine Co. 1, Carson City Fire Dept., 1962-83; mem. Carson City Sheriff's Aero Squadron, 1983—, past comdr.; mem. exec. bd. Nev. Bapt. Conv. With U.S. Army, 1957-59. Mem. Nev. Arbitration Assn. (bd. dirs. 1986—), Las Vegas C. of C. (mem. commerce crime prevention and legis. action coms.), Zelzah Shrine Aviation Club, Toastmasters, Masons. Republican. Office: Assoc Cons Enterprises 2324 S Highland Ste 10 Las Vegas NV 89102-4806

KOONTZ, JAMES ALAN, manufacturing executive; b. Port Townsend, Wash., July 4, 1949; s. Darrell Dwain and Joyce (Bean) K.; 1 child, Brianna Joyce. BA, San Diego State U., 1975, MPA, 1978; BS, Coleman Coll., 1980. Adminstrv. asst. County of San Diego, 1976-83; regional chief planning and system mgmt. Inland Counties Emergency Med. Authority, San Bernardino, Calif., 1983-84; asst. to mayor intergovtl. rels. City of San Bernardino, 1984-85; inventory specialist product maintenance div. Anacomp, San Diego, 1985-89; mgr. inventory/warehouse Bluebird Systems, Carlsbad, Calif., 1989—; instr. San Diego City Coll., 1982-83. Author: Public Manager's Guide to Collective Bargaining, 1978. Bd. dirs. Casa de San Bernardino, Heartland Paramedic Dist./San Diegiuto Paramedic Dist., San Diego, 1983. Lt. USMC, 1969-74, major Calif. Army Nat. Guard, 1975—. Mem. Am. Prodn. and Inventory Control Soc., Soc. Logistics Engrs., Am. Soc. for Pub. Adminstrn. (chpt. pres. 1982), Sitzmarkers Ski Club (v.p. 1984-85), Pi Alpha Alpha, Pi Kappa Alpha. Republican. Episcopalian. Home: 9008 Pelton Ct San Diego CA 92126-1537 Office: Bluebird Systems 5900 LaPlace Ct Carlsbad CA 92008

KOOP, KENNETH DALE, retail executive; b. Bakersfield, Calif., Oct. 21, 1953; s. Walter and Rayetta (Kroeker) K.; m. Carol Lee Siebert (div.); m. Patricia Ann Burgi, June 27, 1953; 1 child, Brittany Casey. Grad., Highland High Sch., 1972. Ptnr. Clovis Tractor Co., Calif., 1973-76; chief exec. officer, pres. KCK Enterprises, Inc., Bakersfield, 1976—. Mem. Calif. Rental Assn. (pres. local chpt. 1984-85), Bakersfield Trade Club (bd. dirs. 1980), Rotary. Republican. Home: 2231 B St Bakersfield CA 93301 Office: KCK Enterprises Inc 516 Golden State Bakersfield CA 93301

KOPELMAN, JEROME N., perinatologist; b. Bronx, N.Y., June 3, 1952; s. Joseph and Edith Dina (Neulander) K.; m. Barbara Joan Harlin, Sept. 16, 1979; children: Sarah Dora, Rachel Elizabeth. BA, Queens Coll., CUNY, Flushing, 1974; MD, New York Med. Coll., Valhalla, 1978. Diplomte Am. Bd. Ob-Gyn. Ob-gyn. intern Brooke Army Med. Ctr., San Antonio, 1978-79, resident in ob-gyn., 1979-82; attending ob-gyn. Ireland Army Community Hosp., Ft. Knox, Ky., 1982-83, asst. chief ob-gyn., 1983-84, chief ob-gyn., 1984; fellow in maternal fetal medicine Madigan Army Med. Ctr., Tacoma, 1984-86; chief maternal fetal medicine service Tripler Army Med. Ctr., Honolulu, 1986—. Contbr. articles to ob-gyn. jours. Fellow Am. Coll. Ob-Gyn.; mem. Assn. Mil. Perinatologists of U.S. (founding mem.), Soc. Perinatal Obstericians (assoc.), AMA, AAAS, Phi Beta Kappa, Alpha Omega Alpha. Democrat. Jewish. Office: Tripler Army Med Ctr Honolulu HI 96759

KOPENHAVER, JOSEPHINE YOUNG, painter, educator; b. Seattle, June 9, 1908; d. George Samuel and Blanche Cecilia (Castle) Young; A.B., U. Calif., 1928; M.F.A. (scholar 1936-37), U. So. Calif., 1937; spl. student Claremont Grad. Sch., 1951, 67, Chouinard Art Inst., 1946-47, Otis Art Inst., 1954-55; m. Ralph Witmer Kopenhaver, Apr. 11, 1931. Prof. art Chaffee Jr. Coll., Ontario, Calif., 1946-47, Los Angeles City Coll., 1948-73, Woodbury U., Los Angeles, 1973-76, summer sessions Calif. State U., Los Angeles, 1950, Pasadena City Coll., 1949, Otis Art Inst., Los Angeles, 1959, Pasadena Art Inst., 1948; profl. painter, exhibiting artist, 1933—; work included in exhibits mus. and pvt. galleries U.S. and Mex., 1933—, including Hatfield Galleries, Los Angeles; art juror; represented Archives of Am. Art Oakland (Calif.) Art Mus. Winner first award in oil Los Angeles Art Festival, 1936, various art awards. Mem. Los Angeles Art Assn. (bd. dirs.), Nat. Watercolor Soc. (sec.), Audubon Artists, Artists for Econ. Action, Calif. Tchrs. Assn. Clubs: Los Angeles Athletic, Zeta Tau Alpha. Office: PO Box 10666 Glendale CA 91209

KOPENNY, LOUIS CLARENCE, lawyer, consultant, industrial engineer; b. Chgo., Mar. 31, 1926; s. Louis Joseph and Caroline (Zapfel) K.; m. Elizabeth Marie Macaluso, Nov. 23, 1946; children: Betty Lou, William James, Carol Anne, June Ellen, Robert Louis. PhB, Northwestern U., 1951; MBA, Calif. Stat U., Fullerton, 1970; JD, Western State U., 1980. Bar: Calif., registered profl. engr. Calif., cert. tchr. jr. coll., Calif. Indsl. engr. Motorola, Inc., Chgo., Toronto, 1951-55; chief indsl. engr. Westinghouse Radio TV Div., Metuchen, N.J., 1955-57; mng. assoc. Arthur Young & Co. Mgmt Svcs., L.A., N.Y., 1957-61; mgmt. cons. pvt. practice Sepulveda, Calif., 1961-62; asst. to v.p. ops. Rockwell Internat. Autonetics Div., Anaheim, Calif., 1962-70; prin. Arthur Young & Co., Santa Ana, Calif., 1970-75; indsl. engr., plant mgr. Knotts Berry Farm, Buena Park, Calif., 1975-82; atty. pvt. practice, Santa Ana, Calif., 1982-83; internal cons. and corp records mgr. MCA, inc., Universal City, Calif., 1983-88; atty. pvt. practice El Toro, Calif., 1988—; Instr. U. Calif., Irvine, 1969-73; adjunct prof. Nat. U., Orange County, Calif., 1982-83, Western State U. Coll of Law, Fullerton, Calif., 1989—. Cub Scoutmaster, Boy Scouts Am., New Shrewsbury, N.J., 1959-60; dir. Orange County Neighborhood Edn. Operating Ctrs., Fullerton, Calif., 1964-66; pres. of congregation, Redeemer Luth. Ch., Placentia, Calif., 1968-69. Recipient Am. Jurisprudence award Constitutional Law, 1979. Mem. Inst. Indsl. Engrs. (program dir. 1968-69), VFW, Am. Legion, Phoenix Club, Masons, Beta Gamma Sigma. Republican. Home & Office: 24921 Muirlands Blvd #285 El Toro CA 92630

KOPER, ALEX, dentist, educator; b. St. Louis, Nov. 15, 1917; s. Abram and Miriam Koper; m. Corrine Meta Nagin, Aug. 29, 1948; children: Alex II, Lisa R., Claudia J. BS, U. So. Calif., L.A., 1942, DDS, 1942. Diplomate Am. Bd. Prosthodontics. Pvt. practice prosthodontics 1946—; prof. dentistry U. So. Calif., L.A., 1966—; cons. USAF, 1981-85; lectr. in field. Contbr. articles to profl. jours. Capt. USAF, 1942-46. Fellow Am. Coll. Prosthodontics (past pres.), Am. Coll. Dentists, Acad. Denture Prosthetics, Internat. Coll. Dentists, Am. Acad. Crown & Bridge Prosthetics; mem. Pacific Coast Prosthodontists (past pres.), Fedn. Prosthodontic Orgns. (past pres.). Home: 520 N Bristol Ave Los Angeles CA 90049 Office: 11645 Wilshire Blvd Ste 1158 Los Angeles CA 90025

KOPFF, E(DWARD) CHRISTIAN, classical philology educator; b. Bklyn., Nov. 22, 1946; s. Frederick Louis and Willie Maude (Compton) K. BA summa cum laude, Haverford Coll., 1968; PhD in Classics, U. N.C., 1974. Asst. instr. Intercollegiate Ctr., Rome, 1972-73; asst. prof. dept. classics U. Colo., Boulder, 1973-77, assoc. prof., 1977—. Book rev. editor The Classical Jour., 1977-87; Am. editor Quaderni di Storia, Bari, Italy, 1982—; editor critical edit. Euripides' Bacchae, 1982. Contbg. editor chronicles, 1985—; contbr. articles and book revs. to Classics. Pres., Friends of Library, Boulder, 1984-86. Prix de Rome fellow Am. Acad. in Rome, 1978; U. Colo. faculty fellow, 1978, 86. Fellow Nat. Assn. Scholars; mem. Am. Philol. Assn., Classical Assn. Middle West and South, Assn. Ancient Historians. Republican. Lutheran. Home: 3800 Carlock Dr Boulder CO 80303 Office: U Colo Dept Classics Campus Box 248 Boulder CO 80309

KOPILOFF, GEORGE, psychiatrist; b. Buenos Aires, Argentina, Jan. 20, 1939; arrived in U.S., 1975; s. Gregorio (dec.) and Matilde (Garcia) K.; m. Nelly Caceres, Apr. 19, 1964; children: Araceli, George. BA, Vasquez Acevedo Inst., Montevideo, Uruguay, 1958; MD, Facultad de Medicina, Montevideo, Uruguay, 1969. Diplomate Internal Medicine Acad. Uruguay, diplomate Am. Bd. Psychiatry and Neurology. Intern and resident in internal medicine Montevideo, 1969-74; resident in internal medicine Northeastern Ohio U. and Youngstown (Ohio) Hosp. Assn., 1975-76; resident in psychiatry Temple U. and Ancora Psychiat. Hosp., Phila., 1976-77; resident in psychiatry Loma Linda (Calif.) U. Sch. Medicine, 1978-79, asst. prof. psychiatry, 1979—; pvt. practice specializing in internal medicine Uruguay, 1969-75; staff psychiatrist Hemet (Calif.) Valley Hosp., 1978—, med. dir. mental health svcs., 1986—; chief Triage Psychiat. Clinic Jerry L. Pettis Meml. VA Hosp., Loma Linda, 1979-83, chief day treatment ctr., 1983—; staff psychiatrist Kellogg Psychiat. Hosp., Corona, Calif., 1979-83, Riverside (Calif.) Gen. Hosp., 1979-87; psychiatrist Continuing Community Care Program, Riverside, 1979-87. Fellow Interam. Coll. Physicians and Surgeons, Am. Psychiat. Assn., Nat. Assn. VA Physicians, Am. Assn. Geriatric Psychiatry, World Fedn. Mental Health, So. Calif. Psychiat. Soc. (sec. 1982-83, pres. 1984-85). Republican. Seventh Day Adventist. Home: 25110 Tulip Ave Loma Linda CA 92354 Office: 1117 E Devonshire Ave Hemet CA 92343

KOPLIN, DONALD LEROY, health products executive; b. Greenleaf, Kans., Dec. 31, 1932; s. Henry G. Koplin and Edith Mary Stevens; m. Patricia Joynes, June 2, 1962 (div. Aug. 1974); children: Marie Claire, Marie Joelle (adopted). Student, U. San Diego, 1957-59, 67-68. Electronics test insp. Gen. Dynamics, San Diego, 1956-59; cryptographer Dept. of State, Washington, 1959-67; communications programs office fgn. office Dept. of State, France, Angola, Madagascar, Qatar, India, Oman, Bennin and the Bahamas, 1977-86; tech. writer Ryan Aero. Corp., San Francisco, 1967-68; comml. dir., tech. advisor, pub. rels. officer Societe AGM, San Francisco, Athens, Greece, Antananarivo and Morondava, Democratic Republic of Madagascar, 1968-72; founder, dir. Societe BECA, Antananarivo, 1972-74; founder, ptnr., assoc. editor, corr., polit. reporter Angola Report, Luanda, 1974-76; supr. Tex. Instruments, Lubbock, 1976-77; exec. Dial A Contact Lens, Inc., La'Jolla, Calif., 1986—. With USN, 1951-55, Korea. Republican. Roman Catholic. Home: 436 Rosemont La Jolla CA 92037 Office: Dial A Contact Lens Inc 470 Nautilus Ste 209 La Jolla CA 92037

KOPLITZ, EUGENE DEVERE, psychologist, educator; b. Wis., Apr. 30, 1926; s. Henry Lee and Lillian Mae (Chase) K.; m. Betty Theiles, June 25, 1953; children: Stephanie, Pamela (dec.), David. BS, U. Wis., Eau Claire, 1950; MS, U. Wis., 1955, PhD, 1958; postdoctoral studies, Harvard U., 1963. Tchr. Barron (Wis.) Sr. High Sch., 1950-52; instr. Artillery Sch. Command, Ft. Sill., Okla., 1952-54; rsch. asst. U. Wis., Madison, 1956-58; asst. prof. psychology U. No. Colo., Greeley, 1958-62, assoc. prof., 1962-66, prof., assoc. dean honors program, 1966-72, prof. ednl. psychology, 1972—. Author: Guidance in the Elementary School, 1978. Mem. Am. Psychol. Assn., Am. Assn. Counseling Devel., Am. Humanistic Edn. and Devel., Colo. Personnel and Guidance Assn. Republican. Lodge: Mason. Home: 1960 26th Ave Pl Greeley CO 80631 Office: U No Colo McKee Hall Greeley CO 80631

KOPP, CAROLYN SUE, nonprofit foundation executive; b. Lafayette, Ind., Feb. 22, 1940; d. William Edward and Josephine Laverne (Morrow) White; m. Mervyn Kopp, Mar. 19, 1967; children: Liesel Ayn, Kerry Jasyn. BS, Purdue U., 1963; Postgrad., Loyola U., L.A., 1965-68. Tchr. L.A. Unified Sch. Dist., 1963-71; pres., exec. officer Conejo Future Found., Thousand Oaks, Calif., 1987—; creator, ldr. workshops in field. Mem. sch. bd. Conejo Valley Unified Sch. Dist., 1981-83; chmn. affirmative action adv. com. Ventura county, 1986-88. Named Ventura County Woman of Yr., 1988. Mem. LWV, AAUW (br. pres. 1985-86, Calif. div. exec. coun. communications chair 1988—, Gift Honoree 1986). Home: 3488 Avenida Ladera Thousand Oaks CA 91362

KOPP, DAVID EUGENE, manufacturing company executive; b. St. Louis, Apr. 21, 1951; s. Doyle Eugene and Irene Audrey (Gloyeske) K. BA in English, U. South Fla., 1975. Supr. Titleist Golf Co., Escondido, Calif., 1979-80; supr. Imed Corp., San Diego, 1980-82, process engr., 1982-83, sr. process engr., 1983-85; area mgr. Husky Injection Molding Systems Inc., Newport Beach, Calif., 1985—. Mem. Soc. Plastic Engrs. (affiliate; bd. dirs., student liaison person Canoga Park, 1985—). Republican. Roman Catholic. Home: 21286 Beach Blvd #106 Huntington Beach CA 92648 Office: Husky Injection Molding Systems Inc 3701 Birch St 2d Fl Newport Beach CA 92660

KOPP, DAVID JAMES, accountant; b. San Francisco, Apr. 19, 1943; s. Alvin and Lorraine (Perry) K.; divorced; children: Anthony R., Randall A. BS, U. San Francisco, 1964; MBA, Golden Gate U., 1968. CPA, Calif. Ptnr. Pannell, Kerr, Forster and Co., San Francisco, 1966-80, Stanwood and Kopp CPAs, Zephyr Cove, N.Y., 1980-81; v.p. Internat. Innkeepers, South Laguna, Calif., 1981-88; prin. The Kopp Group, Cons., South Laguna, Calif., 1988—. Mem. Olympic Club. Republican. Home: 24731 La Plata Laguna Niguel CA 92677 Office: The Kopp Group PO Box 6892 Laguna Niguel CA 92677

KOPPULA, MOREEN, physician; b. Kurnool, India, Oct. 11, 1950; came to U.S. 1977; d. James and Kamala (Kandukuri) R; m. Sampurnarao Koppula, Dec. 29, 1973; children: Patrick, Anthony. MBBS, Gunter Med. Coll., India, 1973. Diplomate Am. Bd. of Anesthesiology. Intership Govt. Gen.

Hosp., Guntur, 1973-75; sr. house officer in anesthesia East Birmingham (U.K.) Hosp., 1976-77, Worthing (U.K.) Hosp., 1977; resident Hahnemann Med. Coll. and Hosp., Phila., 1978-79, Children's Hosp. of Phila., 1979; resident in pediatrics Cooper Med. Ctr., Camden, N.J., 1979-80; chief resident in anesthesia Hahnemann Med. Coll. and Hosp., Phila., 1980-81; fellow in anesthesia Childrens Hosp. of Phila., 1981; mem. staff anesthesiologist Our Lady Of Lourdes Hosp., Camden, 1981-82; mem. staff in anesthesiologist Maricopa Med. Ctr., Phoenix, 1982—, Good Samaritan Med. Ctr., Phoenix, 1983—, St. Joseph's Hosp., Phoenix, 1983—, Phoenix Meml. Hosp., 1983—, Thuderbird Samaritan Hosp., Glendale, Ariz., 1983—, St. Luke's Hosp., Phoenix, 1983—, Tempe (Ariz.) St. Luke's Hosp., 1983—; dir. of obstetrical anesthesia Desert Samaritan Hosp., Mesa, Ariz., 1988—. Mem. Am. Soc. of Anesthesiologist, Ariz. Soc. of Anesthesiologist, Maricopa County Soc. of Anesthesiologist. Republican. Lutheran. Home: 913 N 85th Pl Scottsdale AZ 85257 Office: Spring Group PO Box 60070 Phoenix AZ 85082

KORANDA, DAVID EDWARD, advertising executive; b. Fort Wayne, Ind., June 17, 1947; s. Leroy Fredrick and Jean Ester (Weil) K.; m. Laura Jo Golden, Mar. 18, 1978; 1 child, Julianne Yumiko. BA in Bus., Wilkes Coll., 1970; BS in Journalism, U. Oreg., 1978. Media buyer Jim Cox Advt., Eugene, Oreg., 1978-80; media dir. Advt. Svcs. Cappelli Miles & Wiltz, Eugene, 1980-84; media dir., pres. Koranda Communications, Eugene, 1984—; media dir., v.p. Baden & Co., Eugene, 1984—; vice-chmn. adv. bd. KLCC, Eugene, 1985-89, chair, 1989—; cons. Sta. KUGN Radio, Eugene, 1985—, U. Oreg. admissions, Eugene, 1985—. Pub. rels., bd. dirs. Boy Scouts Am. (Cub Scouts), Eugene, 1983; bd. dirs. Easter Seals, Eugene, 1983-84; adv. bd. YMCA, Eugene, 1984-85. Mem. Mid-Oreg. Ad Club (excellence award 1988). Democrat. Buddhist. Office: Baden & Co/ Koranda Communications 296 E Fifth NBU 9-4 Eugene OR 97401

KORB, LAWRENCE JOHN, metallurgist; b. Warren, Pa., Apr. 28, 1930; s. Stanley Curtis and Dagna (Pedersen) K.; B.Chem.Engring., Rensselaer Poly. Inst., Troy, N.Y., 1952; m. Janet Davis, Mar. 30, 1957; children—James, William, Jeanine. Sales engr. Alcoa, Buffalo, 1955-59; metall. engr. N. Am. Rockwell Co., Downey, Calif., 1959-62; engring. supr. metallurgy Apollo program Rockwell Internat. Co., Downey, 1962-66, engring. supr. advanced materials, 1966-72, engring. supr. metals and ceramics space shuttle program, 1972-86; cons., 1988—; mem. tech. adv. com. metallurgy Cerritos Coll., 1969-74. Served with USNR, 1952-55. Registered profl. engr., Calif. Mem. Am. Soc. Metals (chmn. aerospace activity com. 1971-76; judge materials application competition 1969, handbook com. 1978-83, chmn. handbook com. 1983, chmn. publs. council 1984). Republican. Author articles, chpts. in books. Home: 251 Violet Ln Orange CA 92669 Office: 12214 Lakewood Blvd Downey CA 90241

KORBULY, CHARLES GABOR, communications company executive; b. Budapest, Hungary, Mar. 5, 1938; came to U.S., 1956; s. Laszlo and Gabriella (Gerloczy) K.; m. Dorothy Katherine Walsh, Dec. 29, 1962. BSBA with distinction, U. Redlands, 1983. Draftsman Howard, Needles, Tammen & Bergendof Consulting Engrs., Boston, 1957, Charles W. Cole & Sons, Inc., Engrs. and Architects, South Bend, Ind., 1959-60; detail engr. Calif. Water and Telephone Co., Monrovia, 1961-70; cost acctg. supr. Gen. Telephone Co. Calif., Santa Monica, 1971-77, budget mgr., 1978-83; dir. customer acctg. GTE Svc. Corp., Thousand Oaks, Calif., 1984—. Bd. dirs., Santa Anita Dist. YMCA, Monrovia, 1969, pres. Monrovia Y's Men's Club, 1969-70; v.p. Tri-Gentel Fed. Credit Union, Monrovia,1969-70. Mem. Topanga C. of C., GTE Cen. Area Mgmt. Club (v.p. 1968-70), Good Govt. Club. Democrat. Roman Catholic. Home: 1126 S Parkway Trail Topanga CA 90290 Office: GTE Svc Corp 1 GTE Pl Thousand Oaks CA 91362-3811

KORDUCKI, BARBARA JOAN, orchestra executive, educator; b. Milw., May 2, 1956; d. Edward and Rita Korducki. BA in Mass Communication, U. Wis., Milw., 1980; MPA, Seattle U., 1986. News reporter, pub. affairs producer Sta. WUWM, Milw., 1979-81; cons. Adams & Assocs., Seattle, 1981-82; pub. rels. and projects coord. Nat. Multiple Sclerosis Soc., Seattle, 1982-85; pub. rels. and mktg. specialist Planned Parenthood of Seattle-King County, Seattle, 1985-87; mng. dir. Northwest Chamber Orch., Seattle, 1987—; adj. lectr. journalism Seattle U., 1989—. Pub. rels. cons. Seattle Urban League/King County Coalition on Teen Pregnancy, 1985-87; bd. dirs. Wash. Literacy, 1982-85; spl. events com. Nat. Multiple Sclerosis Soc., Seattle, 1987-88; panelist Puget Power Blue Ribbon Commn., 1986-87; project advisor Leadership Tomorrow, Seattle, 1986. Mem. N.W. Devel. Officers Assn., Pub. Rels. Soc. Am. (cert., chair Wash. awards 1987—, co-chair Totem awards 1984-86), Seattle Sailing Club (bd. dirs. 1986-87), Seattle Women's Sailing Assn. Democrat. Office: NW Chamber Orch 1305 4th Ave Ste 522 Seattle WA 98101

KORF, MARVIN EUGENE, financial services executive; b. Ft. Dodge, Iowa, July 13, 1942; s. Norman Edward Korf and Eleanor Margaret Schroeder; m. Patricia Cozad, Nov. 16, 1979. BSBA, Drake U., 1965. CPA, Colo. With Deloitte Haskins & Sells, Denver, 1966-68; head tax dept. Deloitte Haskins & Sells, Colorado Springs, Colo., 1968-82, ptnr., 1977-82, nat. tax coord. real estate industry, 1980-82; founder Highland Properties, Inc., Colorado Springs, 1982—. Mem. Estate Planning Coun. Colorado Springs; bd. dirs. YMCA, Jr. Achievement Colorado Springs, U. Colo. Found., Inc., U. Colorado, Colorado Springs; chmn. fin. and budget com. Pikes Peak Apt. Assn., 1979-80. Mem. AICPA, Colo. Soc. CPAs (bd. dirs. 1980-82, chmn. taxation com. 1978-80), Builders Assn. Colorado Springs (2d v.p. 1982, exec. com. 1982, bd. dirs. 1980-82).

KORMAN, MARK DOUGLAS, lawyer; b. Greeley, Colo., Aug. 14, 1957; s. Julius A. and Mary D. Korman. BS in Journalism, U. Colo., 1979; JD, U. Denver, 1984. Bar: Colo. 1984, U.S. Dist. Ct. Colo. 1984, U.S. Ct. Appeals (10th cir) 1984. Assoc. Irelana, Stapleton, Pryor and Pascoe, P.C., Denver, 1984-85, Deisch, Marion and Breslar P.C., Denver, 1985—. Staff mem. Denver U. Law Jour., 1983-84. Mem. ABA, Colo. Bar Assn., Denver Bar Assn., Colo. Def. Lawyers Assn., Denver Forum, Denver Art Mus., Denver Law Club, U. Colo. Alumni Assn., Kappa Sigma. Office: Deisch Marion & Breslar 851 Clarkson St Denver CO 80218

KORMAN, NATHANIEL IRVING, research and development company executive; b. Providence, Feb. 23, 1916; s. William and Tillie (Jacobs) K.; m. Ruth C. Kaplan, Apr. 6, 1941; children—Michael, Robert. B.S. summa cum laude, Worcester Poly. Inst., 1937; M.S. (Coffin fellow), M.I.T., 1938; Ph.D., U. Pa., 1958. Dir. advance mil. systems RCA Corp., 1958-67; pres., chief exec. officer Ventures Research and Devel. Group, Albuquerque, 1968—; chmn. radar panel U.S. Research and Devel. Bd., 1948-56; lectr. U. Pa. Evening Grad. Sch., 1967-68; cons. in field Color Sci. Patentee in field. Mem. Citizens Com. for Better Schs., Moorestown, N.J., 1958. Recipient Award of Merit RCA, 1951. Fellow IEEE; mem. Sigma Xi. Home and Office: 108 Yucca Ln Placitas NM 87043

KORMONDY, EDWARD JOHN, university official, biology educator; b. Beacon, N.Y., June 10, 1926; s. Anthony and Frances (Glover) K.; m. Peggy Virginia Hedrick, June 5, 1950 (div. 1989); children: Lynn Ellen, Eric Paul, Mark Hedrick. BA in Biology summa cum laude, Tusculum Coll., 1950; MS in Zoology, U. Mich., 1951, PhD in Zoology, 1955. Teaching fellow U. Mich., 1952-55; instr. zoology, curator insects Mus. Zoology, 1955-57; asst. prof. Oberlin (Ohio) Coll., 1957-63, assoc. prof., 1963-67, prof., 1967-69, acting assoc. dean, 1966-67; dir. Commn. Undergrad. Edn. in Biol. Scis., Washington, 1968-72; dir. Office Biol. Edn., Am. Inst. Biol. Scis., Washington, 1968-71; mem. faculty Evergreen State Coll., Olympia, Wash., 1971-79, interim acting dean, 1972-73, v.p., provost, 1973-78; sr. profl. assoc., directorate sci. edn. NSF, 1979; provost, prof. biology U. So. Maine, Portland, 1979-82; v.p. acad. affairs, prof. biology Calif. State U., Los Angeles, 1982-86; chancellor, prof. biology U. Hawaii, West Oahu, 1986—. Author: Concepts of Ecology, 1969, 76, 83, General Biology: The Integrity and Natural History of Organisms, 1977, Handbook of Contemporary World Developments in Ecology, 1981; high school textbook Biology, 1984, 88, International Handbook of Pollution Control, 1989; contbr. articles to profl. jours. Served with USN, 1944-46. U. Ga. postdoctoral fellow radiation ecology, 1963-64; vis. research fellow Center for Bioethics, Georgetown U., 1978-79; research grantee Nat. Acad. Scis., Am. Philos. Soc., NSF, Sigma Xi. Mem. AAAS, Ecol. Soc. Am. (sec. 1976-78), Nat. Assn. Biology Tchrs. (pres. 1981), Nat. Sci. Tchrs. Assn., So. Calif. Acad. Scis. (bd. dirs. 1985-86), Sigma Xi. Home: 1053 Olioli Way Hilo HI 96720 Office: U Hawaii-Hilo Office of Chancellor Hilo HI 96720

KORN, GRANINO ARTHUR, engineer; b. Berlin, Germany, May 7, 1922; came to U.S., 1939; s. Arthur and Elizabeth Korn; m. Theresa M. McLaughlin, Sept. 3, 1948; children: Anne Marie, John McLaughlin. BA, Brown U., 1942, PhD, 1948; MA, Columbia U., 1943. Project engr. Sperry Gyroscope Co., Garden City, N.Y., 1946-48; head analysis group Curtiss-Wright Corp., Columbus, Ohio, 1948-49; staff engr. Lockheed Aircraft Co., Burbank, Calif., 1949-53; pvt. practice L.A., 1953-57; prof. elec. engring. U. Ariz., Tucson, 1957-83; prin. G.A. and T.M. Korn Indsl. Cons., Tucson, 1983—. Author numerous engring. texts and handbooks, 1952—; editor: Digital Computer User's Handbook, 1962; editorial bd.: Simulation, 1958—, Mathematics and Computers in Simulation, 1962-84. With USN, 1944-46. Recipient Sr. Scientific award Simulation Councils, 1958, Alexander von Humboldt Found. Prize, 1976. Fellow IEEE; mem. Soc. for Computer Simulation (life, tech. excellence award 1988), Internat. Assn. for Mathematics and Computers in Simulations, Sigma Xi. Office: GA and TM Korn Indsl Cons 6801 Opatas St Tucson AZ 85715

KORN, WALTER, writer; b. Prague, Czechoslovakia, May 22, 1908; came to U.S., 1950, naturalized, 1956; s. Bernard and Clara (Deutsch) K.; m. Herta Klemperer, Dec. 24, 1933. Dr.Comm., Charles U., Prague, 1938; postgrad. London Sch. Econs., 1949-50; cert. systems and procedures Wayne State U., 1957; cert. polit. sci. New Sch., N.Y.C., 1972-73. Dir. mktg. Kosmos Works, Prague, 1934-39; contract mgr. Cantie Switches, Chester, Eng., 1941-44; dir. UNRRA, U.S. Zone Occupation, Germany, 1945-47; country dir. Orgn. for Rehab. and Vocational Tng., Geneva, 1948; contract mgr. Royal Metal Mfg. Co., N.Y.C., 1951-55; bus. mgr. J. Community Ctr., Detroit, 1956-59; dir. admintrn. joint distbn. com. United Jewish Appeal, Tel Aviv, 1960-64; exec. asst. Self Help/United Help, N.Y.C., 1965-69; housing mgmt. cons. Exec. Dept./Div. Housing and Community Renewal, State N.Y., N.Y.C., 1970-76; lectr. housing for aged and housing fin., 1958-74; lectr. Brit. Allied Council, Liverpool, Eng., 1942-44. Nat. field rep. United Jewish Appeal, 1968—; mem. Vols. for Internat. Tech. Assistance, 1968-71. Served to capt. Czechoslovakian Army, 1938. Mem. Acad. Polit. Sci., Acad. Polit and Social Sci., Am. Judicature Soc., Amnesty Internat. Clubs: Princeton of N.Y.; Commonwealth of Calif.; Press (San Francisco); Masons. Author: On Hobbies, 1936; Earn as You Learn, 1948; The Brilliant Touch, 1950; Modern Chess Openings, 13th edit., 1989; America's Chess Heritage, 1978, American Chess Art, 1975; Moderne Schach Eroeffnungen I and II, 1968, 75; contbr. essay on chess to Ency. Brit.

KORNBERG, ARTHUR, biochemist; b. N.Y.C., Mar. 3, 1918; s. Joseph and Lena (Katz) K.; m. Sylvy R. Levy, Nov. 21, 1943; children: Roger, Thomas Bill, Kenneth Andrew. BS (N.Y. State scholar), CCNY, 1937, LLD (hon.), 1960; MD (Buswell scholar), U. Rochester, 1941, DSc (hon.), 1962; DSc (hon.), U. Pa., U. Notre Dame, 1965, Washington U., 1968, Princeton U., 1970, Colby Coll., 1970; LHD (hon.), Yeshiva U., 1963; MD honoris causa, U. Barcelona, Italy, 1970. Intern in medicine Strong Meml. Hosp., Rochester, N.Y., 1941-42; commd. officer USPHS, 1942, advanced through grades to med. dir., 1951; mem. staff NIH, Bethesda, Md., 1942-52, nutrition sect., div. physiology, 1942-45; chief sect. enzymes and metabolism Nat. Inst. Arthritis and Metabolic Diseases, 1947-52; guest research worker depts. chemistry and pharmacology coll. medicine NYU, 1946; dept. biol. chemistry med. sch. Washington U., 1947; dept. plant biochemistry U. Calif., 1951; prof., head dept. microbiology, med. sch. Washington U., St. Louis, 1953-59; prof. biochemistry Stanford U. Sch. Medicine, 1959—, chmn. dept., 1959-69; Mem. sci. adv. bd. Mass. Gen. Hosp., 1964-67; bd. govs. Weizmann Inst., Israel. Author: For the Love of Enzymes, 1989; contbr. sci. articles to profl. jours. Served lt. (j.g.), med. officer USCGR, 1942. Recipient Paul-Lewis award in enzyme chemistry, 1951; co-recipient of Nobel prize in medicine, 1959; Max Berg award prolonging human life, 1968; Sci. Achievement award AMA, 1968; Lucy Wortham James award James Ewing Soc., 1968; Borden award Am. Assn. Med. Colls., 1968. Mem. Am. Soc. Biol. Chemists (pres. 1965), Am. Chem. Soc., Harvey Soc., Am. Acad. Arts and Scis., Royal Soc., Nat. Acad. Scis. (mem. council 1963-66), Am. Philos. Soc., Phi Beta Kappa, Sigma Xi, Alpha Omega Alpha. Office: Stanford U Med Ctr Dept Biochemistry Stanford CA 94305 *

KOSAVEACH, JOAN STEEVER, educational administrator; b. Jersey City, July 12, 1947; d. Walter Robert and Ruth Mabel (Durr) Steever; m. Bruce Edward Kosaveach, Oct. 5, 1979. BA in Edn., U. Mass., 1969; postgrad., West L.A. Coll., 1980-86. Cert. elem. tchr. Tchr. Bloomfield (N.J.) Bd. of Edn., 1969-74; asst. sec. Nat. Elec. Contractors Assn., Fairfield, Conn., 1974-75; policy owner service sec. INA Life INs. Co., L.A., 1975-77; account exec. sec. E. L. Kozberg & Sons Inc., L.A., 1976-77; underwriting asst. Teledyne Life Ins. Co., L.A., 1977-78; mgmt. intern L.A. community coll. dist., 1978-80; budget analyst L.A. Community Coll. Dist., 1980-87, instr., 1986—, sr. fiscal analyst, 1987—, also bd. dirs., 1985-86; treas. Dist. Mgmt. Assn., L.A., 1986-88. Vol. St. John's Ch., West L.A., 1981—. Mem. Am. Assn. Univ. Women, U. Mass Alumni Assn. Office: Los Angeles Community Coll Dist 617 W 7th St Los Angeles CA 90017

KOSECOFF, JACQUELINE BARBARA, health services administrator; b. Los Angeles, June 15, 1949; d. Herman Plaut and Betty (Bass) Hamburger; m. Robert Henry Brook, Jan. 17, 1982; children: Rachel Brook, Davida Brook. BA, UCLA, 1970; MS, Brown U., 1971; PhD, UCLA, 1973. Adj. assoc. prof. medicine and pub. health UCLA, 1976—; sr. v.p. Value Health Scis., Santa Monica, Calif., 1988—; chief exec. officer Chassin and Kosecoff Med. Systems, Santa Monica, 1988—. Author: An Evaluation Primer, 1978, How to Evaluate Education Programs, 1980, Evaluation Basics, 1982, How to Conduct Surveys, 1985; contbr. numerous articles to profl. publs. Regents scholar UCLA, 1967-71; NSF fellow, 1971-72. Mem. Am. Pub. Health Assn., Assn. for Health Services Research. Democrat. Jewish. Home: 1278 Norman Pl Los Angeles CA 90049

KOSHLAND, DANIEL EDWARD, JR., biochemist, educator; b. N.Y.C., Mar. 30, 1920; s. Daniel Edward and Eleanor (Haas) K.; m. Marian Elliott, May 25, 1945; children: Ellen, Phyllis, James, Gail, Douglas. BS, U. Calif., Berkeley, 1941; PhD, U. Chgo., 1949; PhD (hon.), Weizmann Inst. Sci., 1984; ScD (hon.), Carnegie Mellon U., 1985; LLD (hon.), Simon Fraser U., 1986. Chemist Shell Chem. Co., Martinez, 1941-42; research asso. Manhattan Dist. U. Chgo., 1942-44; group leader Oak Ridge Nat. Labs., 1944-46; postdoctoral fellow Harvard, 1949-51; staff Brookhaven Nat. Lab., Upton, N.Y., 1951-65; affiliate Rockefeller Inst., N.Y.C., 1958-65; prof. biochemistry U. Calif. at Berkeley, 1965—, chmn. dept., 1973-78; Harvey lectr., 1969; fellow All Souls, Oxford U., 1972; Phi Beta Kappa lectr., 1976; John Edsall lectr. Harvard U., 1980; William H. Stein lectr., Rockefeller U., 1985; Robert Woodward vis. prof. Harvard U., 1986. Author: Bacterial Chemotaxis as A Model Behavioral System, 1980; mem. editorial bds.: jour. Accounts Chem. Research; editor: jour. Procs. Nat. Acad. Scis, 1980-85; editor Sci. mag., 1985—. Recipient T. Duckett Jones award Helen Hay Whitney Found., 1977; Guggenheim fellow, 1972; delivered Rudin Lectures, Columbia U., 1985. Mem. Nat. Acad. Scis., Am. Chem. Soc. (Edgar Fahs Smith award 1979, Pauling award 1979, Rosenstiel award 1984, Waterford prize 1984), Am. Philos. Soc., Am. Soc. Biol. Chemists (pres.), Am. Acad. Arts and Scis. (council), Academy Forum (chmn.), Japanese Biochem. Soc. (hon.), Royal Swedish Acad. Scis. (hon.), Alpha Omega Aplha. Home: 3991 Happy Valley Rd Lafayette CA 94549 Office: U Calif Biochemistry Dept Berkeley CA 94720

KOSHLAND, MARIAN ELLIOTT, immunologist, educator; b. New Haven, Oct. 25, 1921; d. Waller Watkins and Margaret Ann (Smith) Elliott; m. Daniel Edward Koshland, Jr., May 25, 1945; children—Ellen R., Phyllis A., James M., Gail F., Douglas E. B.A., Vassar Coll., 1942, M.S., 1943; Ph.D., U. Chgo., 1949. Research asst. Manhattan Dist. Atomic Bomb Project, 1945-46; fellow dept. bacteriology Harvard Med. Sch., 1949-51; asso. bacteriologist biology dept. Brookhaven Nat. Lab., 1952-62, bacteriologist, 1963-65; assoc. research immunologist virus lab. U. Calif., Berkeley, 1965-69, lectr. dept. molecular biology, 1966-70, prof. dept. microbiology and immunology, 1970-89, chmn. dept., 1982-89, prof. dept. molecular and cell biology, 1989—; mem. Nat. Sci. Bd., 1976-82; mem. adv. com. to dir. NIH, 1972-75. Contbr. articles to profl. jours. Mem. Nat. Acad. Scis., Am. Acad. Microbiology, Am. Assn. Immunologists (pres. 1982-1983), Am. Soc. Biol. Chemists, Phi Beta Kappa, Sigma Xi. Office: U Calif Dept Molecular & Cell Biology LSA 439 Berkeley CA 94720

KOSINSKI, PATRICIA DIANE, nurse; b. San Diego, Feb. 19, 1945; d. Stanely William and Julia Antionette (Slania) K. BSN, Calif. State U., 1969, MSN, 1989. RN, Calif.; cert. tchr., Calif. Team leader Kaiser Hosp., Bellflower, Calif., 1966-69; orthopedic clinic supr. U. So. Calif. Med. Ctr., L.A., 1969-74; pub. health nurse San Gabriel Valley Health Dept., Monrovia, Calif., 1974-77; supr. maternal and child health clinic Aramco, Saudi Arabia, 1977-80; staff devel. dir. Everhealth Found., Whittier, Calif., 1980-84; rehab. nurse Intracorp., L.A., 1984-86, sr. rehab. nurse, 1986-87, rehab. unit supr., 1987-88, med. unit mgr., 1988, sr. specialist, supr., 1988—. Vol. nurse ARC, Whittier, 1986-87. Mem. Rehab. Nurses Soc., So. Calif. Rehab. Exch., Alpha Tau Delta. Democrat. Roman Catholic. Office: Intracorp 3711 Long Beach Blvd #401 Long Beach CA 90807

KOSKEY, B. EUGENE, real estate executive, instructional developer; b. Bessemer, Mich., Dec. 25, 1930; s. Bernard Waldo and Edith Christina (Hokanson) K.; m. Janice Ethel Berg, July 28, 1962; children: Allyson Marie, Brenda Jean, Christopher Allan. BA, Augustana Coll., Rock Island, Ill., 1953; MS in Edn., Ind. U., 1963, EdD, 1972. Tchr. music pub. schs. N.Y., 1957-62; dir. radio and TV No. Ill. U., DeKalb, 1963-66; asst. prof. edn. and library sci. U. Wis., Milw., 1966-71; asst. prof., dir. learning material ctr. U. N.Mex., Albuquerque, 1971-72; assoc. prof., dir. Ctr. Learning & Info. Resources U. N.Mex., 1972-73; dir. Office Instructional Devel., U. Wis. Ctr. System, Madison, 1973-76; sales mgr./trainer RECA and Continental Realty Cons., Albuquerque, 1978-80; dir. adminstrn. Albuquerque Bd. Realtors, 1980-81; owner/mgr. Real Estate Svcs., 1981—; cons. sys. tech. Tech. Cons. Inst., Albuquerque, 1988—; cons. ednl. media various univ. and sch. sys., Milw. and Albuquerque, 1966-73; tng. analyst Allan Corp of Am., 1988—. Author: What's Really Wrong with American Education and How to Fix It, 1987; author/developer music edn. films; composer songs/music; contbr. articles to profl. jours. Mem. Mayor's Kitchen Cabinet Devel. Com., Albuquerque, 1987. With U.S. Army, 1953-55. Mem. Tech. Cons. Inst. Democrat. Lutheran. Office: Allen Corp 317 Commercial NE Albuquerque NM 87102

KOSKI, ELSA LAVERNE, nurse, educator; b. Red Lodge, Mont., Feb. 23, 1929; d. Edgar Max and Elma Matilda (Prinkki) Gruel; m. Walfred Conrad Koski; children: Mark, Maureen. Nursing diploma, Carroll Coll., 1950; BS cum laude in Gen. Studies, So. Oreg. State Coll., 1976. Pediatric supr. St. James Hosp., Butte, Mont., 1951; night supr. Barrett Hosp., Dillon, Mont., 1951; asst. hosp. adminstr. Stillwater Meml. Hosp., 1952; pvt. duty nurse Josephine Meml. Hosp., Grants Pass, Oreg., 1952-53; clinic staff nurse ob-gyn Grants Pass Clinic, 1953-65; health tchr. Grants Pass High Sch., 1967—; adv. Future Med. Workers Club; adolescent pregnancy cons.; dir. Model H.H.E.Y. Project, Am. Heart Assn., 1983-86; guest lectr. local confs., 1975—. Task force mem. health edn., home econs. edn. Seaside Health Team, Heart Health Edn.; bd. dirs. Josephine County March of Dimes, Am. Cancer Soc.; project dir. Oreg. affiliate Josephine County unit Am. Heart Assn., 1984—; vital signs nurse instr. ARC; elder Bethany Presbyterian Ch. Recipient Conf. Coordinator Regional award March of Dimes, 1971, Health Educator Oreg., 1985. Assn., Oreg. Edn. Assn., NEA, Phi Delta Kappa, Delta Kappa Gamma. Democrat. Lodge: P.E.O., Daughters of the Nile. Office: Grants Pass High Sch 522 NE Olive St Grants Pass OR 97526

KOSKINEN, SULO MATIAS, electronics company executive b. Vaasa, Finland, Sept 15, 1922; s. William and Emma (Ollus) K.; student Kansan Valistus Seura Inst., 1941-45, Cleve. Inst. Radio Electronics, 1949-51; m. Anna Miriam Linnakallio, Aug. 4, 1946; children—Jarmo, Pirjo, Ellen; came to Can., 1951, naturalized, 1956. Product mgr. Chisholm Industries, 1952-56; dir. engring. Anaconda Electronics Ltd. (formerly Tele Signal Electronics), Vancouver, B.C., Can., 1956-75, also dir.; pres. Koskinen Electronic Lab., Ltd. Pres., Finnish Can. Rest Home Assn., 1964—, Finnish Kalevava Bros., Vancouver, 1964—; treas. Loyal Finns in Can., 1962-75. Served with Finnish Air Force, 1941-44. Mem. IEEE, Soc. Cable TV Engrs., Internat. Soc. Hybrid Microelectronics. Club: Finlandia (pres. 1978-79) (Vancouver). Contbr. articles to tech. jours. Patentee in field (3). Home: 5390 Frances St, Burnaby, BC Canada V5B 1T5

KOSMALSKI, RUTH GODTLAND, dentist; b. Butte, Mont., Dec. 19, 1958; d. Harold and Carol Faith (Christman) Godtland; m. Thomas Joseph Kosmalski, July 13, 1985. BA, Carroll Coll., Helena, Mont., 1981; DDS, U. Minn., 1985. Dentist Dental Office, Portland, Oreg., 1986-87, Powell Vista Dental Clinic, Gresham, Oreg., 1987—, Viewpoint Dental Clinic, Estacoda, Oreg., 1987—; sch. dental cons. Mem. ADA, Acad. Gen. Dentistry, Gresham C. of C. Office: Powell Vista Dental Clinic 4255 SE 182d St Gresham OR 97030

KOSSOFF, LESLIE LYNN, quality improvement professional; b. Los Angeles, Nov. 15, 1954; d. Leon and Harriet (Klass) K. BA, San Francisco State U., 1977, MA, 1980; MS, U. Oreg., 1983. Instr. U. Oreg., Eugene, 1979-81; cons. City of Eugene and Lane County, Oreg., 1981-82, L.A. Dept. Beaches and Harbors, 1985; mgr. productivity, quality improvement Hughes Aircraft Co., El Segundo, Calif., 1983-88; dir. total quality operation Kendall McGaw Labs.Inc., Irvine, CA, 1989—; instr., U. So. Calif., L.A., 1987—; prof. Loyola Marymount U., L.A., 1988—. Contbr. articles to profl. publs. Mem. San Francisco Symphony chorus, 1974-78. Mem. NAFE. Office: Kendall McGaw Labs Inc 2525 McGaw Ave Irvine CA 92714

KOST, GERALD JOSEPH, pathologist; b. Sacramento, July 12, 1945; s. Edward William and Ora Imogene (Casey) K.; m. Angela Louise Baldo, Sept. 9, 1972; children: Christopher Murray, Laurie Elizabeth. BS in Engring., Stanford U., 1967, MS in Engring., 1968; PhD in Bioengring., U. Calif., San Diego, 1977; MD, U. Calif., San Francisco, 1978. Diplomate Nat. Bd. Med. Examiners, Am. Bd. Pathology. Resident dept. medicine UCLA, 1978-79, resident dept. neurology, 1979-80; resident dept. lab. medicine U. Wash., Seattle, 1980-81, chief resident dept. lab. medicine, 1981-82, cardiopulmonary-bioengring. and clin. chemistry researcher, 1982-83; asst. prof. pathology U. Calif., Davis, 1983-87, assoc. prof., dir. clin. chemistry, faculty biomed. engring., 1987—; numerous sci. cons., nat. and internat. speaker, invited lectr. Author: Medial Gastrocnemius and Soleus Muscle in vivo Responses to Arterial Ischemia, Hemorrhagic Shock, and Catecholamine Infusions: Muscle Surface pH, Membrane Potential, and Histochemistry Studies, 1977; also author monographs; contbr. numerous articles to profl. and sci. jours.; various video productions. Recipient over 40 awards, honors and research grants including Bank Am. Fine Arts award 1963, Millberry Art award, 1970, Nat. Research Service award Nat. Heart, Lung and Blood Inst., U. Calif. San Diego, 1972-77, Young Investigator award Acad. Clin. Lab. Physicians and Scientists, 1982, 83, Nuclear Magnetic Resonance award U. Calif., Davis, 1984-88; S.A. Pepper Collegiate scholar, 1963; Fellow Stanford U., 1967-68, Internat. scholar MOP, Venezuela, 1967, NIH, 1970, Highest Honor Calif. Scholarship Fedn.; grantee Am. Heart Assn./U. Calif., Davis, 1983—, others. Mem. AAAS, Am. Assn. Clin. Chemistry, Acad. Clin. Lab. Physicians and Scientists, Am. Heart Assn., Biomed. Engring. Soc., Am. Soc. Testing Materials (hon.), Soc. Magnetic Resonance Imaging, Soc. Magnetic Resonance in Medicine, Sigma Xi, Phi Kappa Phi.

KOST, RICHARD STEPHEN, SR., aviation foundation executive; b. San Diego, Oct. 18, 1947; s. Ned Franklin and Helen Lucille (Mahaffey) K.; m. Crystal Dee Carter, Aug. 5, 1968 (div. July, 1975); m. Jennifer Edna Smith, Aug. 12, 1975 (div. Sept. 1979); children: Jaylene Elaine, Richard Stephen Jr. Student, U. Wyo., 1965-66, 67-68, NW Community Coll., 1967. V.p. Slyko Laramie, Wyo., 1969-70; pres. Unico, Laramie, 1970-71; editor Berthoud (Colo.) Bull. Newspapers, 1971-72; v.p. Aviation Maintenance Pubs., Basin, Wyo., 1973-78, pres. Aviation Maintenance Found., 1972—; also Aviation Maintenance Found. Internat. Aviation Maintenance Pubs., Redmond, Wash.; exec. v.p. Aviation Maintenance Pubs., Riverton, Wyo., 1982-84; pres. Bus. Computer Network, Riverton, 1983-85; cons. Midway Airlines, Chgo., 1981, Frontier Services Co., Denver, 1982, Ethiopian Airlines, Addis Ababa, 1983; exec. bd. dirs., cons. Aviation Maintenance Edn. Fund, Redmond, 1974—; gen. ptnr. Factory Showroom, Basin, 1981-82; chmn. and chief exec. officer Space Tng. Applications and Research Corp., Redmond, Wash., 1986—; founder, pres. Star Pub., Inc., Redmond Wash., 1987—; leader People-to-People Aviation Maintenance Delegation to People's Republic China, 1988, USSR, 1989. Contbr. articles to profl. jours.

Treas. Big Horn County (Wyo.) Rep. Cen. Com., 1976, chmn., 1978-82; bd. dirs. Wyo. State Rep. Cen. Com., 1976-82. Recipient Achievement award Aviation Technician Edn. Com., 1982. Lodge: Elks. Office: Aviation Maintenance Found Internat PO Box 2826 Redmond WA 98073

KOSTEK, PAUL JOHN, electrical engineer; b. Fall River, Mass., May 29, 1957; s. John Michael and Doris Claudette (Levesque) K. ASEE, Bristol Community Coll., 1977; BSEE, Southeastern Mass. U., 1979. Design engr. Grumman Aerospace Corp., Bethpage, N.Y., 1979-81, Boeing Co., Seattle, 1981—; pres., cons. Personal Systems Inc., Seattle, 1984-89, Sundstrand Data Control, Inc., Redmond, 1989—; mem. adv. bd. for Electronics Engring. Tech. Program Cen. Washington U., 1987—; session chmn. organizer Northcon, 1988—; facilitator engring. careers Phase II Workshop. Vol. Seattle Pub. Library, 1982—; vol. coordinator Spl. Olympics, Wash., 1983—. Mem. IEEE (chmn. profl. activities com. for engrs. 1984-88, mem. pensions and manpower coms., sec. Seattle sect., 1988-89, vice chmn. sect. 1989-90), Seattle Profl. Engring. Employees Assn. (sec. 1984-87). Democrat. Roman Catholic. Home: 13517 Empire Way S #406H Seattle WA 98178 Office: Boeing Aerospace Co PO Box 3999 M/S 2F-60 Seattle WA 98124

KOSTELECKY, WILLIAM LEE, dentist; b. Dickinson, N.D., Dec. 8, 1914; s. William and Harriet Kellogg (Lee) K.; m. Beatrice Barnard; children: Robert Barnard, Linda Lee Kostelecky Strauss. Student, Dickinson Coll., 1932-34; BS, DDS, Northwestern U., 1938. Pvt. practice dentistry Fargo, N.D., 1938-53, LaJolla, Calif., 1955—. Served to comdr. USN, 1953-55. Recipient 5 State Championship awards for golf. Mem. LaJolla Country Club, Elks. Republican. Episcopalian. Home: 1833 Puente Dr La Jolla CA 92037

KOSTENBAUER, JOHN HARRY, personnel director; b. Sheridan, Wyo., June 15, 1946; s. John and Jean (Babcock) K.; divorced; children: Brian John, Stacy Annette. BS, U. Md., 1970; MS, U. Oreg., 1984. Community dir. U.S. Army Health Svc., 1970-75; supr. pub. health State of Wyo., Cheyenne, 1975-77; mgr. preventive health County of Lane, Eugene, Oreg., 1977-80, pers. analyst, chmn. compensation/classification com., 1981-83, dir. health and human svcs., 1984-87; pers. mgr. Atlas Cylinder div. Parker Hannifin Corp., Eugene, 1987—. Mem. Springfield (Oreg.) Budget Com., 1987-88, City of Eugene Parks and Recreation Bd., 1981-87, Applied Tech. Adv. Bd., Eugene, 1988—; active Human Svcs. Planning Project, Eugene, 1985-87; pres. Springfield Booster Club, 1986-88; commr. Am. Youth Soccer, 1983-85; referee U.S. Soccer Fedn., 1980—. Capt. U.S. Army, 1970-75. Mem. Pers. Mgmt. Assn., Am. Soc. for Pers. Adminstrn., Oreg. Nurses Assn. Home: 1500 Norkenzie #15 Eugene OR 97401

KOSTIUK, DONNA MARIE, quality manager; b. Dearborn, Mich., Oct. 29, 1956; d. Harry and Mary (Boroskevych) K. B Indsl. Adminstrn., Gen. Motors Inst., 1979; MBA, U. Chgo., 1981. Statistician Gen. Motors Corp., Detroit, 1981-83; sr. quality engr. Gen. Motors Corp., Warren, Mich, 1983-84; quality mgr. Gencorp., Phoenix, 1984-85, Oreg. Steel Mills, Portland, 1985--. Mem. adv. bd. Chemeketa Community Coll., Salem, Oreg., 1987--. Mem. Am. Soc. Quality Control (chmn. Portland sect. 1988-89), Inst. Indsl. Republican. Office: Oreg Steel Mills 14400 N Rivergate Blvd Portland OR 97203

KOSTOULAS, IOANNIS GEORGIOU, physicist; b. Petra, Pierias, Greece, Sept. 12, 1936; came to U.S., 1965, naturalized, 1984; s. Georgios Ioannou and Panagiota (Zarogiannis) K.; m. Katina Sioras Kay, June 23, 1979; 1 child, Alexandra. Diploma in Physics U. Thessoloniki, Greece, 1963; MA, U. Rochester, 1969, PhD, 1972; MS, U. Ala., 1977, Instr. U. Thessaloniki, 1963-65; teaching asst. U. Ala., 1966-67, U. Rochester, 1967-68; guest jr. research assoc. Brookhaven Nat. Lab., Upton, N.Y., 1968-72; research physicist, lectr. UCLA, U. Calif.-San Diego, 1972-76; sr. research assoc. Mich. State U., East Lansing, 1976-78, Fermi Nat. Accelerator Lab., Betavia, Ill., 1976-78; research staff mem. MIT, Cambridge, 1978-80; sr. system engr., physicist Hughes Aircraft Co., El Segundo, Calif., 1980-86; sr. physicist electro-optics and space sensors Rockwell Internat. Corp., Downey, Calif., 1986—. Contbr. articles to profl. jours. Served with Greek Army, 1961-63. Research grantee U. Rochester, 1968-72. Mem. Am. Phys. Soc., Los Alamos Sci. Lab. Exptl. Users Group, Fermi Nat. Accelerator Lab. Users Group, High Energy Discussion Group of Brookhaven Nat. Lab., Pan Macedonian Assn., Save Cyprus Council Los Angeles, Sigma Pi Sigma. Club: Hellenic U. Lodge: Ahepa. Home: 2404 Marshall Field Ln #B Redondo Beach CA 90278 Office: Rockwell Internat Co MC EA20 Space Transp System Div 12214 Lakewood Blvd Downey CA 90241

KOSTRACH, PAUL LEONARD, motion control product manager; b. Hollywood, Calif., Apr. 26, 1951; s. Leonard Howard and Janet Louise (Foote) K.; m. Rebecca Sue Rankin, May 30, 1987; 1 child, Maxwell Robert. Student, UCLA, Westwood, 1969-71. Musician, producer L.A., 1971-78; repair supr. Pacific Telephone, N. Hollywood, Calif., 1978-80; sales engr. Motion Tech., Inc., Chatsworth, Calif., 1980-87; mgr. motion control Minarik Electrik Co., Glendale, Calif., 1987—. Writer, musician (record) Ice Nine, 1985. Mem. Acad. Magical Arts. Republican. Office: Minarik Electric Co 905 E Thompson Ave Glendale CA 91201

KOSTY, MICHAEL PAUL, naval officer, physician; b. South Bend, Ind., Sept. 17, 1950; s. Michael Peter and Irene Wanda (Czaskowski) K.; m. Antonette Christine Leone, May 18, 1980; children: Michael Phillip, Allison Elizabeth. BS, U. Calif., Berkeley, 1972, MA, 1975; MD, George Washington U., 1979. Commd. ensign USN, 1979, advanced through grades to commdr., 1988; intern U.S. Naval Hosp., San Diego, 1979-80, resident in internal medicine, 1981-83, fellow div. hematology/oncology, 1983-86, asst. head div. hematology/oncology, 1986—; med. officer USS Belleau Wood, 1980-81; clin. investigator Cancer and Leukemia Group B, San Diego, 1988, clin. instr. U. Calif. Dept. Internal Medicine, San Diego, 1986—. Contbr. articles to profl. jours. Mem. ACP, Am. Soc. Clin. Oncology, Phi Beta Kapa, Tau Beta Pi. Democrat. Office: US Naval Hosp Div Hematology/Oncology San Diego CA 92134-5000

KOSUT, LINDA RUTH, management consulting company manager; b. Bronx, Mar. 21, 1946; d. David and Marion (Zucker) K. BS in Maths., CCNY, 1968. With Audits & Surveys Co., N.Y.C., 1964-76; sr. project dir., dir. corp. communications Meyers Rsch. Co., N.Y.C., 1976-78; pvt. practice N.Y.C., 1978-83; dir. mktg. Braff & Assoc., N.Y.C., 1985-86; fin. mgr. Breakthrough Found., San Francisco, 1986-87; conf. and spl. events mgr. Transformational Tech., Greenbrae, Calif., 1987--. Mem. Am. Mktg. Assn. (chmn. membership com. N.Y. chpt. 1985-86). Democrat. Jewish.

KOTHARI, SAMIR PRABODHCHANDRA, computer systems executive; b. Ahmedabad, Gujarat, India, Dec. 3, 1954; came to U.S., 1976; s. Prabodh M. and Kunjbala P. Kothari; m. Sadhana S. Shah, Jan. 19, 1980; 1 chil, Neel. BS in Engring., M.S. U., Baroda, India, 1976; MSChemE, U. Cin., 1978; postgrad., Stevens Inst. Tech., Hoboken, N.J., 1982-83. Registered profl. engr., Fla. Project engr. Pedco Environ. Inc., Cin., 1978-80; design engr. Henningson, Durham & Richardson, Pensacola, Fla., 1980-81; engring. supr., design engr. Hoffman-La Roche, Nutley, N.J, 1981-84; systems engr. Procter and Gamble, Sacramento, 1984—; tchr. lang. Berlitz Inst., Cin., 1979. Contbr. articles to profl. jours. Mem. Am. Inst. Chem. Engrs. (Cert. Profl. Devel. Recognition, 1981). Club: Toastmasters (Cin.) (v.p. 1979-80). Office: Procter & Gamble 8201 Fruitridge Rd Sacramento CA 95825

KOTICK, JOHN ALEXANDER, association administrator; b. L.A., Aug. 28, 1947; s. Alexander Aaron Paul and Lucille Antoinette (Valentine) K.; m. Catherine Anne Hart Sowder, May 1, 1974; children: Jedediah Michael Sowder, Aaron Jesse Apodaca-Kotick, Daniel John Apodaca-Kotick. AA, East L.A. Coll., 1967; BA in Polit. Sci., U. So. Calif., L.A., 1969, JD, 1972. Exec. dir. community Bilingual Home Health Program, San Gabriel, Calif., 1975-78; asst. dir. Sr. Care Action Network, Long Beach, Calif., 1978-83; v.p. Human Svc. Cons., L.A. and Sacramento, 1983; v.p. community programs Am. Heart Assn., L.A., 1983-87; mgmt. cons., assoc. exec. dir. Assn. for Retarded Citizens, SE L.A., 1988—; bd. dirs. Self-Help Graphics & Art, Inc., L.A. Active L.A. County Health Rights Orgn., 1972; co-organizer Blind, Aged and Disabled Action Coalition, L.A., 1973; chairperson profl. adv. coun. Easter Seals, L.A., 1977; del. Calif. Conf. on Handicapped Individuals, 1977, Calif. State House Conf. on Aging, 1980; mem. long term care subcom. Calif. Health Facilites Commn., 1983-85. Mem. Nat. Hispanic Coun. on Aging, Calif. Assn. for Bilingual Edn. Democrat. Home: 1145 N Virgil Ave Los Angeles CA 90029

KOTINAS, DEMETRA, educator; b. Chgo., Mar. 4, 1942; d. Festus A. Johnson and Georgia (Filler) Kotinas. BEd, Nat. Coll. Edn., 1966; postgrad., No. Ariz. U., 1980-82. Cert. tchr., Ill., Ariz. Exec. sec. World Book Encyclopedia, Chgo., 1961-62; advt. asst. Norge Sales Corp., Chgo., 1963-66; tchr. Arlington Heights (Ill.) Jr. High Sch., 1966-68, Chgo. Pub. Schs., 1968-78, Phoenix Indian High Sch., 1978-79; tchr. dist. 1 Phoenix Elem Schs., 1979—, cons., 1984—. Author: All About Love, 1984; editor Pet Talk newsletter, 1986—. Adv. Maricopa County Rabies Animal Control, 1984—, Phoenix City Council, 1987—. Recipient Golden Bell award Ariz. Sch. Bd. Assn., 1985; grants for pet edn., 1987. Mem. Humane Soc. U.S., Animals Benefit Club Ariz. (founder/pres. 1984—), People for Ethical Treatment Animals, Soc. Prevention Cruelty to Animals, Cousteau Soc., Delta Soc. Home: 1226 E Seldon Ln Phoenix AZ 85020 Office: Animals Benefit Club Ariz 3111 E St John Rd Phoenix AZ 85032

KOTT, STANLEY PAUL, II, chemist, zoologist; b. Riverside, N.J., Sept. 18, 1957; s. Stanley Paul and Catherine (Fredrick) K. BS, Marshall U., 1981. Technician Littion Bionetics, Kensington, Md., 1981-82; biologist Microbiol. Assoc., Bethesda, Md., 1982-84; chemist Caleb Brett, U.S.A., Signal Hill, Calif., 1984-85; insp. ARCO Petroleum Products, Carson, Calif., 1985-86; chemist UNOCAL Corp., Rodeo, Calif., 1986—; cons. Caleb Brett, U.S.A., Signal Hill, 1985-86. Home: 413 Kitty Hawk Rd Alameda CA 94501 Office: UNOCAL San Francisco Rodeo CA 94572

KOTTKE, DANIEL GORDON, JR., electronics engineer; b. Bronxville, N.Y., Apr. 4, 1954; s. Daniel Gordon and Joanne Vernon (Lawrence) K. BA in Mus., Columbia Coll., 1977; student, Reed Coll., Portland, Oreg., 72-74. Technician Apple Computer, Inc., Cupertino, Calif., 1977-81; mem. tech. staff Apple Computer, Inc., 1981-84; elec. engring. cons. Palo Alto, Calif., 1985-88; engring. mgr. Kennect Tech., Inc., Campbell, Calif., 1989—; cons. in field; mem. Macintosh design team, 1981-84. Mem. Bay Area Siggraph. Libertarian. Home: 235 Embarcadero Rd Palo Alto CA 94301 Office: Kennect Tech Inc 120A Albright Way Los Gatos CA 95030

KOTTKE, FREDERICK EDWARD, economics educator; b. Menominee, Mich., Sept. 6, 1926; s. Edward Frederick and M. Marie (Braun) K.; B.S., Pepperdine U., 1950; postgrad, U. Wis., 1950-52; M.A., U. So. Calif., 1957, Ph.D., 1960; m. Lillian Dorathy Larson, Aug. 27, 1950; children—Karin Lee, Kurt Edward. Lectr., Pepperdine U., 1952-53; asst. prof. U. So. Calif., 1956-63; assoc. prof. econs., chmn. dept., speaker of gen. faculty Stanislaus State Coll., Turlock, Calif., 1963-68, prof., also chmn. div. arts and scis., 1968—; pres. KK Economic Consultants, Inc.; independent tax adviser, managerial adviser, 1960—. Chmn., Stanislaus County United Crusade, 1964-65; pres., Stanislaus State Coll. Found., 1972; trustee Emanuel Med. Center, 1974—; v.p. Good Shepherd Lutheran Ch. Served with USNR. 1943-46. Recipient Pologrammatic award Pepperdine Coll., 1952, Outstanding Prof. award Calif. State U., Stanislaus, 1987-88. Haynes Found. Postgrad. Research award U. So. Calif., 1959. Mem. Am., Western econ. assns., Nat. Tax Assn., Am. Finance Assn., C. of C., Omicron Delta Epsilon. Lodge: Kiwanis. Author: An Economic Analysis of Toll-Highway Finance, 1956, An Economic Analysis of Financing an Interstate Highway System, 1959. Home: 1890 N Denair Ave Turlock CA 95380 Office: Calif State Coll Stanislaus 801 W Monte Vista Ave Turlock CA 95380

KOTTLOWSKI, FRANK EDWARD, mineralogist; b. Indpls., Apr. 11, 1921; s. Frank Charles and Adella (Markworth) K.; m. Florence Jean Chriscoe, Sept. 15, 1945; children: Karen, Janet, Diane. Student, Butler U., 1939-42; A.B., Ind. U., 1947, M.A., 1949, Ph.D., 1951. Party chief Ind. Geology Survey, Bloomington, summers 1948-50; fellow Ind. U., 1947-51, instr. geology, 1950; adj. prof. N.Mex. Inst. Mining and Tech., Socorro, 1970—; econ. geologist N.Mex. Bur. Mines and Mineral Resources, 1951-66, asst. dir., 1966-68, 70-74, acting dir., 1968-70, dir., 1974—; geologic cons. Sandia Corp., 1966-72. Contbr. articles on mineral resources, stratigraphy and areal geology to tech. jours. Mem. Planning Commn. Socorro, 1960-68, 71-78, chmn. 86—; mem. N.Mex. Energy Resources Bd.; chmn. N.Mex. Coal Surface Mining Commn.; sec. Socorro County Democratic party, 1964-68. Served to 1st lt. USAAF, 1942-45. Decorated D.F.C.; decorated Air medal; recipient Richard Owen Disting. Alumni award in Govt. and Industry U. Ind., 1987. Fellow Geol. Soc. Am. (councilor 1980-82, exec. com. 1981-82); mem. Am. Assn. Petroleum Geologists (hon. mem., dist. rep. 1965-68, Disting. Service award, editor 1971-75, pres. energy minerals div. 1987-88), Assn. Am. State Geologists (pres. 1985-86), Soc. Econ. Geologists, AAAS, AIME, Am. Inst. Profl. Geologists (Pub. Service award 1986), Am. Commn. Stratigraphic Nomenclature (sec. 1964-68, chmn. 1968-70), Sigma Xi. Home: 703 Sunset Dr Socorro NM 87801 Office: NMex Bur Mines NMex Tech Socorro NM 87801

KOTYK, JOANN THERESA, small business owner; b. Detroit, Apr. 24, 1952; d. Frank and Mary Theresa (Assenmacher) K. BA, Kendall Sch. Design, Grand Rapids, Mich., 1974. Interior designer Gorman's Gallery, Southfield, Mich., 1975; typesetter, form designer Bus. Forms Design, Southfield, Mich., 1976-78; owner, v.p. Composing Arts Inc., Southfield, Birmingham, Mich., 1979-87; owner, pres. Composing Arts Inc., Scottsdale, Ariz., 1986—; art dir. VMEbus. mag., Phoenix, 1987—. Mem. Al Collins Graphic Design Sch. adv. bd., 1989—. Mem. Scottsdale C. of C. Office: Composing Arts Inc 13402 N Scottsdale Rd Ste A 100 Scottsdale AZ 85254-4041

KOURIS, PETER CONSTANTINE, television producer, director; b. Sioux City, Iowa, Aug. 19, 1928; s. Gus Constantine and Archonto Tula (Kostopoulos) K.; m. Elaine Carroll Nelson, May 8, 1955 (div. 1975); children: Steve, Kathy. Grad. high sch., SiouxCity. Dir. Sta. KETV, Sioux City, 1953-55; producer, dir. Sta. WFLA-TV, Tampa, Fla., 1955-60, Sta. WFIL-TV, Phila., 1964-70, Charles Fuller Prodns., Tampa, 1970-78, Good Morning Am., ABC-TV, Atlanta, 1980-85; prodn. mgr. Sta. KMBC-TV, Kansas City, Mo., 1960-62; ops. mgr. Sta. KETV, Omaha, 1962-64; co-founder, developer The Weather Channel, Chgo. and Atlanta, 1978-82; pres. Electroic Yearbook Photography Co. Am., San Francisco, 1985—. Active Boy Scouts Am., Phila., 1964. Recipient TV award Freedoms Found., 1967. Mem. Dirs. Guild Am. (TV prodn. cert.), Sons Pericles, Ahepa. Republican. Greek Orthodox. Address: 620 Jones St San Francisco CA 94102

KOUYMJIAN, DICKRAN, art historian, educator; b. Tulcea, Romania, June 6, 1934; came to U.S. (parents Am. citizens), 1939; s. Toros S. and Zabelle I. (Calusdian) K.; m. Angèle Kapoïan, Sept. 16, 1967. BS in European Cultural History, U. Wis., 1957; MA in Arab Studies, Am. U., Beirut, 1961; PhD in Near East Lang. and Culture, Columbia U., 1969. Instr. English Columbia U., N.Y.C., 1961-64; dir. Am. Authors, Inc., N.Y.C., 1965-67; asst. prof. and asst. dir. Ctr. for Arabic Studies Am. U., Cairo, 1967-71; assoc. prof. history Am. U. Beirut, 1971-75; prof. art history Am. Coll., Paris, 1976-77; prof. history and art, dir. Armenian Studies program Calif. State U., Fresno, 1977—; Fulbright disting. lectr., prof. Armenian and Am. Lit., Yerevan (Armenia, USSR), 1987; 1st incumbent Haig & Isabel Berberian endowed chair Armenian Studies Calif. State U., Fresno 1989—; cons. archaeology UNESCO, Paris, 1976. Author: Index of Armenian Art, part I, 1977, part II, 1979, The Armenian History of Ghazar P'arpetzi, 1986; co-author: (with A. Kapoïan) The Splendor of Egypt, 1975; author and editor: William Saroyan: An Armenian Trilogy, 1986; editor: (books) Near Eastern Numismatics, Iconography, Epigraphy and History, 1974, Essays in Armenian Numismatics in Honor of C. Sibilian, 1981, Armenian Studies: In Memoriam Haïg Berbérian, 1986; editorial bd. Armenian Rev., 1974—, Ararat Lit. mag., 1975—, Revue des Etudes Arméniennes, 1978—, NAASR Jour. Armenian Studies; contbr. articles to profl. jours. Served with U.S. Army, 1957. Recipient Outstanding Prof. award Am. U., Cairo, 1968-69, 69-70, Outstanding Prof. of Yr. faculty award Calif. State U., 1985-86, Hagop Kevorkian Disting. Lectureship in Near Eastern Art and Civilization, NYU, 1979; Fulbright fellow, USSR, 1986-87; grantee NEH, Paris, 1980-81. Mem. Am. Oriental Soc., Am. Numismatic Soc., Middle East Studies Assn. (charter), Coll. Arts Assn., Soc. Armenian Studies (charter, pres. 1985-86), Société Asiatique, Medieval Acad., other orgns. Home: 30 rue Chevert, 75007 Paris France Office: Calif State U Armenian Studies Program Fresno CA 93740

KOVAL, CHARLES, teacher; b. Gary, Ind., May 27, 1931; s. Wassol and Mary (Molchan) K.; m. Erlene Annette Nelson, Aug. 12, 1955; children: Richard Charles, Geri Lyn, Jeffrey Alan. BA, Idaho State U., 1955. Cert. secondary edn. tchr., Idaho. Tchr. art, athletic coach Froebel High Sch., Gary, 1957-59; mgr., youth bowling coach Karen Bowling Lanes, Pocatello, 1959-69; art educator, track coach Franklin Jr. High Sch., Pocatello; wildlife artist. Served with U.S. Army, 1955-57. Recipient Disting. Profl. Achievement Idaho State U., 1973, Commendation Mayor's Com., 1975, Gov's Com., 1981, Silver Triangle cert. Tau Kappa Epsilon, 1981. Mem. NEA, Lions, Elks. Democrat. Roman Catholic. Home: 833 Victor St Pocatello ID 83202 Office: Franklin Jr High Sch 2172 E Terry Pocatello ID 83201

KOVAR, FREDERICK RICHARD, physicist, researcher; b. Cleve., Sept. 20, 1933; s. Jaro Harold and Susan Appolonia (Brozowski) K.; m. Margaret Ann Wright, Aug. 11, 1962; children: Kathleen, Karen, Frederick Richard, Christine. BS, John Carroll U., 1955; MA, Washington U., St. Louis, 1958, PhD, 1963. Instr. St. Bonaventure U., Olean, N.Y., 1959-61; physicist Lawrence Livermore (Calif.) Nat. Lab., 1963-73, project leader, 1973-80, 86—, group leader, 1980-84; spl. sci. advisor Dept. Def., Washington, 1984-86; cons. Bradford Components, Salamanca, N.Y., 1959-61. Mem., pres. Mt. Diablo chpt. Calif. Assn. for Neurologically Handicapped Children, 1967-70, Walnut Creek (Calif.) Dem. Club, 1970-73. NSF fellow, 1961-63. Mem. AAAS, Am. Def. Preparedness Assn., Am. Phys. Soc., Calif. Acad. Scis. Roman Catholic. Home: 1078 Hacienda Dr Walnut Creek CA 94598 Office: Lawrence Livermore Nat Lab East Ave Livermore CA 94550

KOVTYNOVICH, DAN, civil engineer; b. Eugene, Oreg., May 17, 1952; s. John and Elva Lano (Robie) K. BCE, Oreg. State U., 1975, BBA, 1976. Registered profl. engr., Calif., Oreg. V.p. Kovtynovich, Inc., Contractors and Engrs., Eugene, 1976-80, pres., 1980—. Mem. ASCE, Am. Arbitration Assn. (arbitrator 1979—), N.W. China Coun., Navy League of U.S., Eugene Asian Coun. Republican. Office: Kovtynovich Inc 1595 Skyline Park Loop Eugene OR 97405

KOWITZ, CLAUDIA THEODORA, retail executive, consultant; b. Detroit, May 23, 1943; d. Charles Stanley and Hattie Theresa (Pendracki) Nowak; m. Gerald Jon Kowitz, Aug. 30, 1968; children: Michael, Paul. BS in Edn., Ariz. State U., 1966; MS in Edn., No. Ariz. U., 1968. Tchr. jr. high sch. Deer Valley Sch. Dist., Phoenix, 1966-68; chief fin. officer Jerry's Audio-Video, Phoenix, 1970—; speaker, chmn. SBA seminars, Phoenix, 1985—; speaker Consortium for Women Entrepreneurs, Phoenix, 1987—. Cons., tchr. sr. econs. Jr. Achievement, 1989—. Mem. Profl. Audio-Video Retailers, Am. Soc. Women Accts. (pres. 1989—), Ariz. Audio Dealers Assn., Retail Fin. Execs., Profl. Referral Orgn. Republican. Roman Catholic. Office: Jerry's Audio-Video 334 E Camelback Rd Phoenix AZ 85012

KOZAK, ALFRED WALDEMAR, lawyer, consultant; b. Camden, N.J., Dec. 13, 1922; s. Walter Peter and Laura (Swiecicka) K.; m. Maxine Louise Lawrence, Sept. 14, 1957; 1 child, Lael. BSEE, U. Pa., 1943, LLB, 1951. Bar: U.S. Patent Office. Adminstr. patents and licensing Leeds & Northrup Co., Phila., 1951-53, product engr., 1960-63; cons. Camden, 1953-56; tng. and edn. rsch. cons. Hubbard Rsch. Found., Washington, 1956-60; patent and licensing adminstr. Am. Chain & Cable Co., Waterbury, Conn., 1964-67; contract engr. Gen. Dynamics Corp., Rochester, N.Y., 1968-69; patent ops. mgr. Nat. Cash Register Co., San Diego, 1970-73; patent counsel Singer Bus. Machines Co., San Leandro, Calif., 1973-75, Unisys Corp., San Diego, 1975--. Patentee calibrating measuring system, 1950. 1st lt. signal corps U.S. Army, 1943-46. Mem. L.A. Patent Law Assn., Tau Beta Pi (past pres. Phila. chpt.), Eta Kappa Nu. Home: 6514 Muirlands Dr La Jolla CA 92037 Office: Unisys Corp 10850 Via Frontera-MS1000 San Diego CA 92127

KOZAK, MICHAEL, real estate counselor, seminar instructor; b. N.Y.C., Sept. 27, 1947; s. Michael and Sophie (Astashonak) K.; m. Alison Anne Clough Kozak, Nov. 19, 1982; 1 child, Marisa Anne. BS, Rensselaer Poly. Inst., 1969, BArch, 1970; MArch, U. Oreg., 1972. Design assoc. Art Larsen Architect, Bend, Oreg., 1973-74; owner and mgr. Palace Tavern, Bend, 1974-78; crew leader Food Devel. Corp., Pasco, Wash., 1978; assoc. broker Duke Warner Realty, Bend, 1979-82; broker Michael Kozak & Assocs., Inc., Bend, 1982—. Trustee Oreg. Realtors Polit. Action Com., Salem, 1984-87; commr. City of Bend, 1984—, mayor protem, 1988, mayor, 1989; adv. bd. Cen. Oreg. Econ. Devel. Council, Bend, 1987-88; mem. Cen. Oreg. Intergovtl. Council, Redmond, Oreg., 1988, Den. Oreg. Air Svcs. Task Force, 1989. Named Realtor of Yr. Cen. Oreg. Bd. Realtors, Bend, 1987. Mem. Oreg. Assn. Realtors (bd. dirs. dist. v.p.), Cert. Comml. Investment Mem., Comm.. Investment Div. (v.p. 1986-87). Republican. Lodges: Elks, Optimists. Home: 2170 NE 8th Bend OR 97701

KOZIK, FRANKLIN E., travel company executive; b. Orient, Pa., Aug. 1, 1913; s. George A. and Anna Theresa (Sobansky) K.; m. Myriam Mackay Searle, Dec. 27, 1952; children: Robert L., Christine A. Student, U. Hawaii, Rutgers, U. Calif., Berkeley; PhD (hon.), U. Mex., 1944. Instr. English Mil. Coll., Mexico City, 1942; official UN, N.Y.C., 1946-56, 58-73; press officer 11th-13th sessions UN Gen. Assemblies, N.Y.C., 1956-58; owner San Luis Obispo (Calif.) Motel, 1973-75; pres. Choice Travel, Inc., Solana Beach, Calif., 1978—; lectr., 1975-77. Author: Contemporary Mexican Poets, 1942, Literary Vision of Francisco de Miranda: Precursor of Latin American Independence, 1944; contbr. United Nations Rev.; author various UN publications and pamphlets; editor: United Nations Stamps, co-editor: Yearbook of the United Nations. Mem. Kappa Epsilon Theta (founder Honolulu chpt. 1937). Roman Catholic. Home: 1056 Newkirk Dr La Jolla CA 92037 Office: 911 Lomas Santa Fe Dr Solana Beach CA 92075

KOZOWSKI, LUCY MARIE, nurse; b. Seattle, May 12, 1953; d. Charles E. and Geneva M. (Holt) Ulbrickson; m. George E. Kozowski, June 17, 1987. BS in Nursing, Biola U., 1979; postgrad., M.N. Univ., Washinton, 1989. RN, Wash., Oreg. Staff nurse Va. Mason Hosp., Seattle, 1979-80; camp nurse Flying Horseshoe Ranch, Cle Elum, Wash., 1980; staff nurse Cabrini Hosp., Seattle, 1981-82; staff nurse intensive care unit Harborview Med. Ctr., Seattle, 1982-83; staff nurse Ocean Beach Hosp., Ilwaco, Wash., 1983-85; charge nurse Ocean View Convalescent Ctr., Long Beach, Wash., 1985-86, New Seaera Convalescent Home, Long Beach, 1986; staff nurse Univ. Hosp., Seattle, 1986-88; psychological nurse N.W. Evaluation and Treatment Ctr., Seattle, 1988—. ADAMHA grantee, 1986-87. Mem. N.W. Assn. Clin. Specialists in Psychosocial Nursing, Sigma Theta Tau. Home: 705 E Thomas St #103 Seattle WA 98102

KRAEMER, KENNETH LEO, urban planner, educator; b. Plain, Wis., Oct. 29, 1936; s. Leo Adam and Lucy Rose (Bauer) K.; m. Norine Florence, June 13, 1959; children: Kurt Randall, Kim Rene. BA, U. Notre Dame, 1959; MS in City and Regional Planning, U. So. Calif., 1964, M of Pub. Adminstrn., 1965, PhD, 1967. From instr. to asst. prof. U. So. Calif., Los Angeles, 1965-67; asst. prof. U. Calif., Irvine, 1967-71, assoc. prof., 1971-78, prof., 1978—, dir. Pub. Policy Research Orgn., 1974—; cons. Office of Tech. Assessment, Washington, 1980, 84-85; pres. Irvine Research Corp., 1978—. Author: Computers and Politics, 1982, Dynamics of Computing, 1983, People and Computers, 1985, Data Wars, 1987. Mem. Blue Ribbon Data Processing Com., Orange County, Calif., 1973, 79-80, Telecommunications Adv. Bd., Sacramento, 1987—. Lt. USAF, 1959-62, capt. Res. Mem. Am. Soc. for Pub. Adminstrn. (Disting. Research award 1985), Internat. Conf. on Info. Systems, Am. Planning Assn., Assn. for Computing Machinery. Democrat. Roman Catholic. Club: Notre Dame. Office: U Calif Pub Policy Rsch Orgn Irvine CA 92717

KRAEMER, ROBERT RICHARD, communications company executive; b. Tacoma, Wash., May 4, 1945; s. Robert Richard and Betty Jean (Dahl) K.; m. Mary Lisa Kupias, Mar. 28, 1981; children: William Johns, Ervin Michael, Edwin Shayne. Credit mgr. Alcoa Aluminum Credit Div., Sacramento, 1967-68; sr. credit mgr. Westinghouse Corp., Sacramento, 1968-71; fire fighter, paramedic Tumwater (Wash.) Fire Dept., 1971-75; sr. dispatcher Thurston County Dept. Communications, Olympia, Wash., 1975-81; owner, dir. prodns. Mediaworks/PSM, Tumwater, 1981--; mem. bd. appeals Thurston County Community Access TV, Olympia. Producer, dir., editor video presentations. Mem. Wash. Trial Lawyers Assn., Human Factors Soc. (tech. div.). Office: Mediaworks/PSM 6845 6th Ave SW Tumwater WA 98501

KRAEMER, ROGER BRUCE, marketing professional; b. East Orange, N.J., Oct. 10, 1954; s. Kenneth Philip and Beverly Arline (Leopold) K.; m. Giulii Marie Shambaugh, Nov. 19, 1983; children: Geoffrey Alan, Garrett Edward. BA in English, Calif. State U., Fullerton, 1982. Account exec. CPM Research West, Inc., Anaheim, Calif., 1981-84; dir., credit mktg. May Co., North Hollywood, Calif., 1984-86; regional v.p. Account Devel. Svcs., Whittier, Calif., 1986-89, pres., 1989—. Vol. Big Bros./Big Sisters of Orange County, Fullerton, 1981-84. Republican. Home: 1123 Grand Canyon Way Brea CA 92621 Office: Account Development Svcs 7931 S Painter Ave Whittier CA 90602

KRAFT, DONALD BOWMAN, advertising agency executive; b. Seattle, Mar. 20, 1927; s. Warren E. and Beulah (Bowman) K.; m. Mary Jo Erickson, Dec. 20, 1973; children: Daniel, Karen Kraft VanderHoek, Berkeley, Erika. BA, U. Wash., 1948. Pres. Kraft Advt., Seattle, 1948-54; v.p. Honig Cooper, Seattle, 1954-59; pres., chief exec. officer Kraft Smith Advt., Seattle, 1959-84, Evans, Kraft Advt., Seattle, 1984-87; chmn., chief exec. officer Evans, Kraft Alaska Advt., Seattle, 1987—; vice chmn. Evans Communications, Inc., Salt Lake City, 1984—; chmn. Evans, Kraft Bean Pub. Relations, Anchorage and Seattle, 1986—, Evans, Kraft Advt., Portland, Oreg., 1985—, Evans, Kraft Advt., Anchorage, 1986—. Bd. dirs. KCTS Assn., Public TV, Seattle. Served with USN, 1945-46. Recipient Man and Boy award Boys Club Am., 1960; named Young Man of Yr., Seattle Jaycees, 1962. Mem. Am. Assn. Advt. Agys. (chmn. we. region 1962-64, nat. sec.-treas. 1970-71, mem. nat. govt. relations com. 1983-86), Affiliated Advt. Agys. Internat. (internat. pres. 1967-68, Albert Emery Mgmt. Excellence award 1984), Young Pres.'s Orgn Alumni (chmn. Pacific NW chpt. 1980-81), Greater Seattle C. of C. (bd. dirs.). Republican. Methodist. Clubs: Wash. Athletic (pres. 1987-88), Rainier (trustee 1975), Seattle Tennis, Broadmoor Golf, Rotary Seattle (pres. 1973-74, Paul Harris fellow 1974). Home: 1569 Parkside Dr E Seattle WA 98112 Office: Evans/Kraft Inc 190 Queen Anne N Seattle WA 98109

KRAGULAC, OLGA GOLUBOVICH, interior designer; b. St. Louis, Nov. 27, 1937; d. Jovica Todor and Milka (Slijepcevich) Golubovich; A.A., U. Mo., 1958; cert. interior design UCLA, 1979. Interior designer William L. Pereira Assocs., Los Angeles, 1977-80; assoc. Reel/Grobman Assocs., Los Angeles, 1980-81; project mgr. Kaneko/Laff Assocs., Los Angeles, 1982; project mgr. Stuart Laff Assocs., Los Angeles, 1983-85; restaurateur The Edge, St. Louis, 1983-84; pvt. practice comml. interior design, Los Angeles, 1981—. Mem. invitation and ticket com. Calif. Chamber Symphony Soc., 1980-81; vol. Westside Rep. Council, Proposition 1, 1971; asst. inaugural presentation Mus. of Childhood, Los Angeles, 1985. Recipient Carole Eichen design award U. Calif., 1979. Mem. Am. Soc. Interior Designers, Inst. Bus. Designers, Phi Chi Theta, Beta Sigma Phi. Republican. Serbian Orthodox. Home and Office: 700 Levering #4 Los Angeles CA 90024

KRAHAM, GENE STANLEY, health care administrator; b. Bklyn., Jan. 15, 1953; s. Martin and Deborah (Ettinger) K.; m. Kathleen Clare Eckroth, Sept. 25, 1976; children: Martin, Paul, Joseph, James, Daniel. BA, U. Calif., Santa Cruz, 1975; BHS Physician Asst., Wichita State U., 1979; AA in Psychology, San Joaquin Delta Coll., 1981. Cert. Physician Asst., 1980. Physician asst. Drs. J. Berklett, I.A. Rishwain, MDS, Stockton, Calif., 1979-83; pres. Calif. Family Med. Group, Inc., Stockton, Calif., 1983—; cons. prin. Kraham & Assoc., Lodi, Calif., 1984—. Bd. dirs. San Joaquin Local Health Dist., Stockton, Calif., 1987. Chief Warrant Officer U.S. Army, 1980-85. Fellow Am. Acad. Physician Assts., Calif. Acad. Physician Assts. Republican. Jewish. Home: 201 Mokelumne River Dr Lodi CA 95240 Office: Calif Family Med Group Inc 1721 E Hummer Ln Ste A Stockton CA 95210

KRALLINGER, JOSEPH CHARLES, entrepreneur, business advisor, author; b. Lancaster, Pa., May 29, 1931; s. Ferdinand and Mathilde (Meyer) K.; m. Hilde Eisenhauer, Oct. 1, 1955; children—Joanne, Diane, Robert. B.S. in Econs. cum laude, Franklin and Marshall Coll., 1953. C.P.A. Auditor GAO, Denver, 1953; auditor Army Audit Agy., 1953-55; ptnr. Arthur Andersen & Co., Phila., 1955-76; v.p. strategic planning and acquisitions, chief fin. officer Berwind Corp., Phila., 1976-88; cons. Palm Desert, Calif., 1988—; dir., bus. advisor and investor various indsl. and health care cos., 1976—; cons. in field. Author: An Auditor's Approach to Statistical Sampling, 5 vols., 1967-72, Strategic Planning Workbook, 1988; contbr. articles to profl. jours. Bd. dirs. alumni coun. Franklin and Marshall Coll., Lancaster, 1969-75; pres., tchr. religious edn. St. Genevieve Cath. Ch., Flourtown, Pa., 1971-76; bd. dirs. Whitemarsh Twp. Citizens Coun., Plymouth Meeting, Pa., 1972-75, Ironwood Property Assn.; hon. life mem., former chmn. bd. Phila. div. Am. Cancer Soc. Recipient Nat. Vol. award Am. Cancer Soc., 1985, Crusade award Am. Cancer Soc., 1985, Teaching award St. Genevieve Ch., 1985. Mem. AICPA, (statis. sampling com.), Pa. Inst. CPA's, Assn. for Corp. Growth, Nat. Assn. Corp. Dirs., Nat. Assn. Accts. (pres. Phila. chpt.), Planning Execs. Inst. (pres. Phila. chpt.), Authors Guild, Ironwood Country Club. Home and Office: 48-872 Mariposa Dr Palm Desert CA 92260

KRALS, PATRICIA GEORGE, real estate associate; b. N.Y.C., June 4, 1945; d. Paul Thomas and Josephine Rosalyn (Czyzewski) George; m. Leon Eric Krals, June 29, 1968; 1 child, Andrew. BA in English, U. Mass., Amherst, 1967. Flight attendant Trans World Airlines, N.Y.C., 1967; tchr. Oxford (Mass.) High Sch., 1968-69, Tolland (Conn.) High Sch., 1970-71; real estate assoc. Coldwell Banker Real Estate, Scottsdale, Ariz., 1985-87, Ranch Realty, Scottsdale, 1987—. V.p. Sky Harbor Airport Aux., Phoenix, 1983-85. Mem. Scottsdale Bd. Realtors. Clubs: TWA Clipped Wings (Phoenix); Scotts Jr. Women's (internat. chmn. 1977-78). Home: 7960 N Hayden Rd C104 Scottsdale AZ 85258 Office: Cliff Winn Realtors 9719 N Hayden Rd Scottsdale AZ 85258

KRAMER, ANNE PEARCE, writer, communications and film executive, educator, research psychoanalyst; m. Stanley Kramer (div.); children: Larry David, Casey Lise. BA magna cum laude, U. So. Calif., MA, 1965, PhD, 1972. Gen. exec. asst. to producer/dir. Stanley Kramer Prodns., also prodn. exec., assoc. producer, story editor, casting dir., dialogue dir.; sr. lectr. cinema and comparative lit. U. So. Calif., Los Angeles; acting asst. prof. comparative lit. and film Calif. State U., Long Beach; pres. Cathexis 3, Los Angeles; story editor, v.p. creative affairs Castle Hill Prodns., Inc., Los Angeles, 1978-80; story editor Columbia Pictures, 1981-83, exec. story editor, exec. creative dir. 1983-86, creative cons. to the chmn., 1987; free-lance cons. film prodn. and editorial pub., 1986—; creative collaborator Clifton Fadiman, Ency. Brit. Films; judge Focus Award for Screenwriting; cons. communications Sta. KPFK-Radio, govt., others. Author: (with others) Directors at Work, 1970, Neo-Metamorphoses-A Cyclical Study, Comparative Transformations in Ovidian Myth and Modern Literature, 1972, Interview with Elia Kazan, 1974, Focus on Film and Theatre. Bd. dirs. Model UN; expert witness on censorship for Los Angeles Dist. Atty.; nurses aide ARC, Children's Hosp.; former pres. Recovery Found. for Disturbed Children; former ednl. cons., instr. Camarillo State Mental Hosp.; mem. Psychoanalytic Ctr. Calif. (affiliate). Mem. MLA, AAUP, Women in Film, Delta Kappa Alpha, Phi Kappa Phi, Pi Beta Phi.

KRAMER, BARRY ALAN, psychiatrist; b. Phila., Sept. 9, 1948; s. Morris and Harriet (Greenberg) K.; m. Paulie Hoffman, June 9, 1974; children—Daniel Mark, Steven Philip. B.A. in Chemistry, NYU, 1970; M.D., Hahnemann Med. Coll., 1974. Resident in psychiatry Montefiore Hosp. and Med. Ctr., Bronx, N.Y., 1974-77; practice medicine specializing in psychiatry, N.Y.C., 1977-82; staff psychiatrist L.I. Jewish-Hillside Med. Ctr., Glen Oaks, N.Y., 1977-82; asst. prof. SUNY, Stony Brook, 1978-82; practice medicine specializing in psychiatry, Los Angeles, 1982—; asst. prof. psychiatry U. So. Calif., 1982-89, assoc. prof. clin. psychiatry, 1989—; ward chief Los Angeles County/U. So. Calif. Med. Ctr., 1982—; mem. med. staff Brotman Hosp., Cedars Sinai Hosp.; cons. Little Neck Nursing Home (N.Y.), 1979-82, L.I. Nursing Home, 1980-82. Reviewer, Am. Jour. Psychiatry, Convulsive Therapy Jour., Hospital and Community Psychiatry; contbr. articles to profl. jours., papers to sci. meetings. NIMH grantee, 1979-80; fellow UCLA/U. So. Calif. Long-Term Gerontology Ctr., 1985-86. Mem. AMA, Am. Psychiat. Assn., AAAS, Internat. Soc. Chronobiology, Internat. Psychiat. Assn. for Advancement of Electrotherapy, Soc. Biol. Psychiatry, Calif. Med. Assn., Los Angeles Med. Assn., Am. Assn. Geriatric Psychiatry, Gerontol. Soc. Am. Jewish. Office: Los Angeles County-U So Calif Med Ctr 1934 Hospital Pl Los Angeles CA 90033 also: PO Box 2681 Beverly Hills CA 90213

KRAMER, GORDON, mechanical engineer; b. Bklyn., Aug. 1937; s. Joseph and Etta (Grossberg) K.; m. Ruth Ellen Harter, Mar. 5, 1967 (div. June 1986); children: Samuel Maurice, Leah Marie; m. Eve Burstein, Dec. 17, 1988. BS Cooper Union, 1959; MS, Calif. Inst. Tech., 1960. With Hughes Aircraft Co., Malibu, Calif., 1959-63; sr. scientist Avco Corp., Norman, Okla., 1963-64; asst. div. head Batelle Meml. Inst., Columbus, Ohio, 1964-67; sr. scientist Aerojet Electrosystems, Azusa, Calif., 1967-75; chief engr. Beckman Instrument Co., Fullerton, Calif., 1975-82; prin. scientist McDonnell Douglas Microelectronics Co., 1982-83, Kramer and Assocs., 1983-85; program mgr. Hughes Aircraft Co., 1985—; cons. Korea Inst. Tech. NSF fellow, 1959-60. Mem. IEEE. Democrat. Jewish. Home: 16141 Malaga Ln Huntington Beach CA 92647 Office: 16141 Malaga Ln Huntington Beach CA 92647

KRAMER, GORDON EDWARD, manufacturing executive; b. San Mateo, Calif., June 22, 1946; s. Roy Charles and Bernice Jeanne (Rones) K.; BS in Aero. Engring., San Jose State Coll., 1970; m. Christina Hodges, Feb. 14, 1970; children—Roy Charles, Charlena. Purchasing agent Am. Racing Equipment, Brisbane, Calif., 1970-71, asst. to v.p. mktg., 1971-72; founder, pres. Safety Direct Inc., hearing protection equipment, Sparks, Nev., 1972—; dir. Hodges Transp., Condor Inc. Named Nev. Small Businessperson of the Year, Nev. Small Bus. Adminstrn., 1987, Bus. Person of Yr. Sparks Community C. of C., 1987. Mem. Am. Soc. Safety Engrs., Safety Equipment Distributors Assn., Indsl. Safety Equipment Assn., Nat. Assn. Sporting Goods Wholesalers, Nat. Sporting Goods Assn., Nev. State Amature Trapshooting Assn. (dir. 1978-79), Pacific Internat. Trapshooting Assn. (Nev. pres. 1979-80, 80-81), Advanced Soccer Club (pres.1985-86). Republican. Methodist. Rotary Club (pres. Spark Club 1988-89). Office: Safety Direct Inc 23 Snider Way Sparks NV 89431

KRAMER, LAWRENCE STEPHEN, journalist; b. Hackensack, N.J., Apr. 24, 1950; s. Abraham and Ann Eve (Glasser) K.; m. Myla F. Lerner, Sept. 3, 1978; children: Matthew Lerner, Erika. B.S. in Journalism, Syracuse U., 1972; M.B.A., Harvard U., 1974. Reporter San Francisco Examiner, 1974-77; reporter Washington Post, 1977-80; exec. editor Trenton Times, N.J., 1980-82; asst. to exec. editor Washington Post, 1982, asst. mng. editor, 1982-86; exec. editor San Francisco Examiner, 1986—. Recipient W.R. Hearst Found. award 1971-72. Mem. Soc. Profl. Journalists. Home: 8 Auburn Ct Tiburon CA 94920 Office: San Francisco Examiner 110 Fifth St San Francisco CA 94103 *

KRAMER, MARVIN LEWIS, corporate executive, communications and computers consultant; b. Cleve., Jan. 16, 1931; s. Edward Aaron and Alma Zoe (Gaskill) K.; m. Edith Mae Nash, Nov. 25, 1949; children: Stuart C., Gregory B., Mark H. BS in Chemistry, George Washington U., 1951, post-grad., 1951-52; MEE, U. Ill., 1963. Lic. comml. balloon pilot, FAA. Commd. lt. U.S. Air Force, 1952; advanced through grades to col., 1972; dep. dir. communications SAC, Offutt AFB, Nebr., 1973-75; vice comdr. Strategic Communication Area, Offutt AFB, 1975-77; dir. communications NORAD, Peterson AFB, Colo., 1977-79, dep. comdr. for strategic def. forces, 1979-80; ret., 1980; pvt. practice communication, computer, command and control cons., Colorado Springs, Colo., 1980—; pres. M.E.K., Ltd. Decorated Bronze Star, Meritorious Service medal, Legion of Merit with oak leaf cluster. Mem. IEEE, Armed Forces Comm. Elec. Assn., Assn. Computing Machinery, Eta Kappa Nu, Alpha Chi Sigma. Jewish. Lodge: Elks. Home and Office: 1030 Doyle Pl Colorado Springs CO 80915

KRAMER, REMI THOMAS, film director; b. L.A., Mar. 7, 1935; s. Justina Magdelene Kramer; m. Agnes Marie Gallagher, Feb. 1, 1969; children: Matthew, Christiana, Timothy, Ian, Vincent, Brigitte, Danika. BA, UCLA, 1956; MA, Calif. State U., L.A., 1963. Art dir. Doyle, Dane, Bernbach Advt., L.A., 1965-66, N.W. Ayer Advt., N.Y.C., 1966-67; dir. John Urie & Assocs. Haboush Co., Hollywood, Calif., 1967-69, Columbia-Screen Gems, Hollywood, 1969-76, 79-81, 1st Asian Films, Hollywood and Manila, 1976-77, Peterson Co., Hollywood, 1977-79; freelance film dir. Hollywood, 1981-85; v.p. Oz Enterprises, Inc., Sandpoint, Idaho, 1985—. Author: The Legend of Lonestar Bear, 1988; writer, dir. film High Velocity, 1976; patentee children's pacifier toy. With U.S. Army, 1958-60. Recipient Clio award, 1971, 1st Internat. Broadcast awards, 1973, Cine Golden Eagle award, 1976. Mem. Dirs. Guild Am., Writers Guild Am. Roman Catholic. Office: 800 Thompson Rd Sandpoint ID 83864

KRAMER, RICHARD JAY, gastroenterologist; b. Morristown, N.J., Mar. 31, 1947; s. Bernard and Estelle (Mishkin) K.; m. Leslie Fay Davis, June 28, 1970; children: Bryan Jeffrey, Erik Seth Davis. Student, UCLA, 1965-68; MD, U. Calif., Irvine, 1972. Diplomate Am. Bd. Internat. Med., Am. Bd. Gastroenterology. Intern Los Angeles County Harbor Gen. Hosp., Torrance, Calif., 1972-73; resident Santa Clara Valley Med. Ctr., San Jose, Calif., 1973-76; fellow gastroent. Stanford (Calif.) U. Hosp., 1976-78; pvt. practice, San Jose, 1978—; asst. prof. clin. medicine Stanford (Calif.) U., 1984—; chmn. med. dept. Good Samaritan Hosp., San Jose, 1988. Pres. Jewish Family Service Bd., San Jose, 1974. Recipient Mosby Book award, Mosby books, Inc., Irvine, Calif., 1972. Mem. Am. Coll. Physicians, Calif. Med. Soc., Santa Clara County Med. Soc., No. Calif. Soc. Clin. Gastroenterologists, Internat. Brotherhood Magicians, Mystic 13 (pres. 1986-87, San Jose), Masons, Alpha Omega Alpha. Democrat. Jewish. Office: 2512 Samaritan Ct Apt G San Jose CA 95124

KRASNER, OSCAR JAY, business educator; b. St. Louis, Dec. 3, 1922; s. Benjamin and Rose (Persov) K.; BS in Pub. Adminstrn., Washington U., St. Louis, 1943; MA in Mgmt. with honors, U. Chgo., 1950; MS in Quantitative Bus. Analysis, U. So. Calif., 1965, DBA in Mgmt., 1969; m. Bonnie Kidder, June 4, 1944; children: Bruce Howard, Glenn Evan, Scott Allan, Steve Leland, Michael Shawn, Bettina Jeanine. Mem. staff Exec. Office of Sec., U.S. Dept. Navy, 1944-56; supervising cons. Bus. Research Corp., Chgo., 1956-57; mem. staff flight propulsion div. Gen. Electric Co., Cin., 1957-61, mgr. VTOL project planning, 1959-61; exec. adviser long range planning space div. N.Am. Rockwell Corp., Downey, Calif., 1962-64, dir. tech. resources analysis exec. offices, 1964-70; pres. Solid State Tech. Corp. Calif., 1968-71; prof. mgmt. Pepperdine U., Los Angeles, 1970—; pres. Rensark Assocs., 1976—; dir. U.S. Innovative Products Corp., Quadrant Tech. Corp. Active community orgns.; mem. nat. adv. bd. Nat. Congress Inventor Orgns., 1983-84; bd. dirs. Long Beach (Calif.) JCC, 1969-70; mem. adv. bd. Internat. Bus. Devel. Corp.; del. People-to-People Delegation to Peoples' Republic China, 1987. Served with Anti-Aircraft, AUS, 1942-44. Mem. Am. Acad. Mgmt., MBA Internat. (chmn. 1976-77), AIAA, AAAS, World Future Soc., Beta Gamma Sigma. Home: 4709 Autry Ave Long Beach CA 90808 Office: 2151 Michelson Ave Irvine CA 92715

KRASNYANSKY, ANATOLE LVOVICH, artist, architect; b. Kiev, Ukrain, USSR, Feb. 26, 1930; came to U.S., 1975; s. Leo Meer and Rose Boris (Landa) K.; m. Nelia Naum Koshevatsky, Aug. 29, 1957; 1 child, Rimma A. Kranet. MArch, Kiev State Art Inst., 1953. Registered architect, USSR. Archtl. designer Kiev State Project Inst., 1953-68; prin. architect, designer Kiev Branch Moscow State Project and Sci. Inst. Tech. Aesthetics, 1968-74; scenic artist ABC TV and NBC TV Studios, Hollywood, Calif., 1975-77; set designer Universal Studios, MGM, Studio Ctr., Universal City, Calif., 1977-84; art dir. State Odyssey Theatre Ensemble, L.A., 1981; artist Santa Monica, 1975—; archtl. cons. UCLA, 1983—; dir. archtl. and indsl. design, prodn. designer Renaissance Guild Inc., 1984—. Scenic art credits include General Hosp., Frank Sinatra Spl., John Denver, Bette Davis Spl., George Burns Spl., Olivia Newton-John Spl., Acad. Awards 1976 and 1977; set design credits include Coal Miner's Daughter, Beatles Forever, The Blues Brothers, Airport 79, Gilligan's Island, Dallas, 2010, Falcon Crest, others; prin. archtl. works include French Pavilion Disney World, others; exhibited in shows at Heritage Gallery, L.A., Gallery One, San Francisco, Los Gatos (Calif.) Mus., Sloan Gallery, Denver, Nakhamkin Fine Art, N.Y.C., Hishong, Gallery, Dallas, Stanford (Calif.) U., Dyansen Galleries, N.Y.C., Boston, San Francisco, Beverly Hills, Calif., New Orleans, Maui, Hawaii, Carmel, Calif., San Diego, Dalzell Hatfield Galleries, L.A., numerous others in Europe, Republic South Africa, Republic of Germany and U.S. Recipient 1st prize for Subway Sta. "Poly. Inst.," USSR, House of Lit., Alexandria, USSR; 2d prize Triumphal Arch of 300 Yrs. Union of Ukraine with Russia, Potemkin Monument in Odessa, USSR; 3d prize Bldg. Archtl. Guild, Kiev, Pantheon in Moscow Stalin's Tomb and Mausoleum of Famous People. Mem. Internat. Alliance Theatrical Stage Employees. Republican.

KRAUS, G. THOMAS, physician; b. Kansas City, Mo., Aug. 7, 1945; s. Alfred Paul and Lorraine (Marquardt) K.; m. Judy Kay Burks, 1970 (div. 1973); 1 child, Douglas William; m. Emily Anne Distler, Sept. 3, 1977. BA in Philosophy/Theology, Christian Bros. Coll., Memphis, 1967; MD, U. Tenn., 1971. Intern in internal medicine U. Ark., Little Rock, 1973; resident in internal medicine U. Minn., Mpls., 1975-77; lectr. U.S. Peace Corps, Kenya, 1977-79; pvt. practice Kremmling Med. Surg. Assn., Colo., 1980-81, Family Med. Clinic, Estes Park, Colo., 1981-88; med. dir. Skilled Nursing Facility, Estes Park, Colo., 1983-84, 86-88, Cardiac Rehab., Estes Park, Colo., 1983-88; chief staff Estes Park Med. Ctr., 1984-86, Kremmling Meml. Hosp., 1980-81, Fitzsimmons Army Med. Ctr., Aurora, Colo., 1988—. Founding bd. dirs. Estes Pk. Handicapped Ski Program, 1987-88. With USPHS, 1973-74. Mem. AMA, Larimer County Med. Soc. (pres. 1986-88, exec. com. 1985-88), Aurora-Adams County Med. Soc., Am. Geriatric Soc., Am. Soc. Internal Medicine, Colo. Soc. Internal Medicine, Colo. Med. Soc. (del. 1984—), Estes Park C. of C., Rotary. Democrat. Home: 16373 E Rice Pl #A Aurora CO 80015 Office: Fitzsimmons Army Med Ctr Aurora CO 80045

KRAUS, JEROME HILBERT, human resources and organization development consultant; b. Geneva, N.Y., Apr. 13, 1957; s. Francis Joseph and Joyce Lorraine (Hilbert) K.; m. Lori Jean DeYoung, Aug. 28, 1982; 1 child, Jeremy Wainwright. BA in Psychology, Hobart Coll., Geneva, 1979. Mgmt. devel. rep. Northrop Electronics Div., Hawthorne, Calif., 1985-86; salesperson Auto Ins. Specialists, Santa Monica, Calif., 1986; mgmt. devel. rep. quality circle facilitator, labor rels., prodn. control coord. McDonnell Douglas Corp., Long Beach, Calif., 1979-85, internal cons. human resources and orgn. devel., 1986—. Mem. Symlog Inst., Am. Soc. Tng. and Devel., Orange County Lacrosse Club, U.S. Intercollegiate Lacrosse Officials Assn. Home: 11612 MacMurray St Garden Grove CA 92641 Office: McDonnell Douglas Corp 3855 Lakewood Blvd M/C 204-11 Long Beach CA 90846

KRAUS, JOHN WALTER, aerospace engineering company executive; b. N.Y.C., Feb. 5, 1918; s. Walter Max Kraus and Marian Florance (Nathan) Sandor; m. Janice Edna Utter, June 21, 1947 (dec. Feb. 1981); children: Melinda Jean Kraus Peters, Kim Kohl Kraus Odgers; m. Jean Curtis, Aug. 27, 1983. BS, MIT, 1941; MBA, U. So. Calif., 1972. Registered indsl. engr., Ohio, Calif. From indsl. engr. to indsl. engring. mgr. TRW, Inc., Cleve., 1941-61; spl. asst. Atomics Internat., Chatsworth, Calif., 1961-65; br. chief McDonnell Douglas Astronautics Co., Huntington Beach, Calif., 1966-74; sr. mgr. McDonnell Douglas Space Systems Co., Huntington Beach, Calif., 1983—; pres. Kraus and DuVall, Inc., Santa Ana, Calif., 1975-83; cons. Tech. Assocs. So. Calif., Santa Ana, 1974-75. Author: (handbook) Handbook of Reliability Engineering and Management, 1988. Mem. Am. Soc. Quality Control (sr.), Am. Def. Preparedness Assn. (life, chmn. tech. div. 1954-57). Republican. Home: 2001 Commodore Rd Newport Beach CA 92660 Office: McDonnell Douglas Space Systems Co 5301 Bolsa Ave Huntington Beach CA 92467

KRAUS, PANSY DAEGLING, gemology consultant, editor; b. Santa Paula, Calif., Sept. 21, 1916; d. Arthur David and Elsie (Pardee) Daegling; m. Charles Frederick Kraus, Mar. 1, 1941 (div. Nov. 1961). AA, San Bernardino Valley Jr. Coll., 1938; student Longmeyer's Bus. Coll., 1940; grad. gemologist diploma Gemological Assn. Gt. Britain, 1960, Gemological Inst. Am., 1966. Clk. Convair, San Diego, 1943-48; clk. San Diego County Schs. Publs., 1948-57; mgr. Rogers and Boblet Art-Craft, San Diego, 1958-64; part-time editorial asst. Lapidary Jour., San Diego, 1963-64, assoc. editor, 1964-69, editor, 1970—, sr. editor, 1984-85; pvt. practice cons., San Diego, 1985—; lectr. gems, gemology local gem, mineral groups; gem & mineral club bull. editor groups. Mem. San Diego Mineral & Gem Soc., Gemol. Soc. San Diego, Gemol. Assn. Great Britain, Mineral. Soc. Am., Epsilon Sigma Alpha. Author: Introduction to Lapidary, 1987; editor, layout dir.: Gem. Cutting Shop Helps, 1964, The Fundamentals of Gemstone Carving, 1967, Appalachian Mineral and Gem Trails, 1968, Practical Gem Knowledge for the Amateur, 1969, Southwest Mineral and Gem Trails, 1972, revision editor Gemcraft (Quick and Leiper), 1977; contbr. articles to Lapidary jour., Keystone Mktg. catalog. Home and Office: PO Box 20908 San Diego CA 92120

KRAUS, RICHARD, marketing professional; b. L.A., Nov. 27, 1959; s. Stephen and Roslyn K. BS in Mktg., Calif. State U., Northridge, 1981; MBA, U. Tex., 1983. Mktg. rep. Xerox Corp., Dallas, 1983; sr. mktg. rep. Xerox Corp., Orange, Calif., 1984-85; acct. mgr. Xerox Corp., Costa Mesa, Calif., 1986-87; mgr. comml. markets Kinko's Copies, Ventura, Calif., 1987—, mgr. campus markets, 1988—; pvt. practice sales, cons. Santa Barbara, Calif., 1987—. Scholar U. Tex., 1984. Mem. Am. Mktg. Assn. Home: 1235-B Stonecreek Rd Santa Barbara CA 93109 Office: Kinko's Svc Corp 255 W Stanley Ventura CA 93001

KRAUSE, BEVERLY ANN, nurse; b. Silverton, Oreg., Sept. 13, 1933; d. Harold Laverne and Juanita Olive (Kuenzi) Sinclair; m. Norman Evan Krause, Aug. 13, 1955; children: Valli, Pella, Terry. Student, Providence Hosp. Sch. Nursing, 1955. RN. Staff nurse, asst. dir. Okla., 1955-58; asst. head nurse Providence Hosp., Portland, 1959-60, Victoria Nursing Home, Portland, 1960-63; staff nurse Portland Med. Ctr. Hosp., 1963-68; staff nurse Portland Indsl. Clinic, 1968-78, co-head nurse, 1978—. Home: 6541 SE 91st Portland OR 97266

KRAUSE, DAVID J., aerospace engineer; b. Beaver Dam, Wis., Jan. 4, 1956; s. Edward N. and Lucille (Hoinacki) K.; m. Catherine Piercecchi, Mar. 2, 1987. BS in Engring. Mechanics, U. Wis., 1987. Comml. diver Oceaneering Internat., Morgan City, La., 1978-81; aerospace engr. Space Data Corp., Tempe, Ariz., 1987—; project engr. Space Data Corp., Tempe, 1988—. With USAF, 1975-77. Mem. AIAA, SAE. Office: Space Data Corp 1333 W 21st St Tempe AZ 85282

KRAUSE, HAROLD A., company executive; b. Sterling, Colo., Mar. 22, 1940; s. Harold B. Krause and Marie (Sherwin) Egner; m. Lucinda Elaine Moore, July 2, 1965; children: Kara, Kammy, Kelly, Kevin. Student, U. Wyo., 1958-62, George Washington U., 1963-64. Chief exec. officer, founder Am. Salesmasters, Inc., Denver, 1964-80, Crest Group, Ltd., Denver, 1987—. Author audio and written training materials. Mem. Rep. Nat. Com., Colo., 1982-86; candidate U.S. Ho. Reps., 1986; founder speaking competition for high sch. students Land of Opportunity, 1984. With USNG, 1962-68. Mem. Am. Soc. Tng. and Devel., Nat. Speakers' Assn., Denver C. of C. Baptist. Office: Crest Group Ltd 7150 E Hampden Ave #304 Denver CO 80224

KRAUSE, LAWRENCE ALLEN, financial adviser, financial planner; b. Chgo., Oct. 28, 1939; s. Leo and Sylvia Harriet (Bergman) K.; m. Donna Lee Ferkel, Aug. 14, 1971; children—Danielle, Alexis. B.A., State U. Iowa, 1961. Cert. fin. planner. Exec. v.p. Jobs, Inc., Waukegan, Ill., 1961-62; pres. Inventory and Bus. Controls, Waukegan, 1963-66; broker real estate Shoen Realtors, Rockford, Ill., 1967-69; registered rep. Reynolds & Co., San Francisco, 1970-75; dir. fin. planning Sutro & Co., Inc., San Francisco, 1975-79; chmn., pres. Lawrence A. Krause & Assocs., Inc., San Francisco, 1979—; pres. KW Securities Corp., San Francisco, 1979—; adj. prof. fin. planning San Francisco State U., 1982-86; mem. adv. com. on fin. planning Golden Gate U., San Francisco, 1982—; mem. faculty U. So. Calif., Los Angeles, 1984; mem. adv. bd. Stanger Register, 1986—. Author: The Money-Go-Round, Sleep-Tight Money; (co-author) Marketing Your Financial Planning Practice; contbr. chpts. to books, articles to profl. jours.; contbg. columnist Los Angeles Times, ABA Jour.; monthly columnist Calif. Bus. mag. Bd. dirs. Am. Cancer Soc., San Francisco, 1980—; bd. govs., bd. dirs. NTL Ctr. Fin. Edn., San Francisco, 1982—. Recipient Fin. Writer's award Fin. Planner mag., 1981; named Nation's Outstanding Fin. Planner for 1980's. Mem. Registry Fin. Planning Practitioners, Internat. Assn. Fin. Planners (San Francisco Fin. Planner of Yr. award 1982, pres. 1980-82, chmn. 1982-83), Inst. Cert. Fin. Planners. Republican. Jewish. Club: Concordia-Argonaut (San Francisco). Office: Lawrence A Krause & Assocs Inc 500 Washington St Ste 750 San Francisco CA 94111 *

KRAUSS, GEORGE, metallurgist; b. Phila., May 14, 1933; s. George and Berta (Reichelt) K.; m. Ruth A. Oeste, Sept. 10, 1960; children: Matthew, Jonathan, Benjamin, Thomas. B.S. in Metall. Engring., Lehigh U., 1955; M.S., MIT, 1958, Sc.D., 1961. Registered profl. engr., Colo., Pa. Devel. metallurgist Superior Tube Co., Collegeville, Pa., 1955-56; prof. Lehigh U., Bethlehem, Pa., 1963-75, Colo. Sch. Mines, Golden, 1975—; dir. Advanced Steel Processing and Products Research Ctr., 1984—; cons. Colo. Sch. Mines, Golden, 1964—; Amax Found. prof. 1975—. Author: Principles of Heat Treatment of Steel, 1980; editor: Deformation Processing and Structure, 1984, Jour. Heat Treating, 1978-82; co-editor Fundamentals of Microalloying Forging Steels, 1987; contbr. articles profl. jours. NSF fellow Max Planck Inst. fur Eisenforschung, 1962-63. Fellow Am. Soc. Metals; mem. AIME, Am. Soc. Metals Internat., Internat. Fedn. Heat Treatment (pres. 1989—), Electron Microscope Soc. Am., Sigma Xi. Home: 3807 S Ridge Rd Evergreen CO 80439 Office: Colo Sch Mines Dept Metall Engring Golden CO 80401

KRAUSS, MICHAEL EDWARD, linguist; b. Cleve., Aug. 15, 1934; s. Lester William and Ethel (Sklarsky) K.; m. Jane Lowell, Feb. 16, 1962; children: Marcus Feder, Stephen Feder, Ethan, Alexandra, Isaac. Bacc. Phil. Islandicae, U. Iceland; BA, U. Chgo., 1953, Western Res. U., 1954; MA, Columbia U., 1955; Cert. d'études supérieures, U. Paris, 1956; PhD, Harvard U., 1959. Postdoctoral fellow U. Iceland, Reykjavik, 1958-60; rsch. fellow Dublin Inst. Advanced Studies, Ireland, 1956-57; vis. prof. MIT, Cambridge, 1969-70; prof. linguistics Alaska Native Lang. Ctr., U. Alaska, Fairbanks, 1960—, dir., 1972—, head Alaska native lang. program, 1972—; panel mem. linguistics NSF. Author: Eyak Dictionary, 1970, Eyak Texts, 1970, Alaska Native Languages: Past, Present and Future, 1980; editor: In Honor of Eyak: The Art of Anna Nelson Harry, 1982, Yupik Eskimo Prosodic Systems, 1985; mem. editorial bd.: Internat. Jour. Am. Linguistics; editor: dictionaries and books in Alaska Eskimo and Indian Langs. Halldór Kiljan Laxness fellow Scandinavian-Am. Found. Iceland, 1958-60; Fulbright study grantee Iceland, 1958-60; grantee NEH and NSF, 1978—; recipient Humanist of Yr. award Alaska Humanities Forum, 1981, Athabaskan and Eyak research award NSF, 1961—. Mem. Linguistics Soc. Am., Am. Anthropol. Assn. Jewish. Office: U Alaska Alaska Native Lang Ctr PO Box 111 Fairbanks AK 99775-0120

KRAUSS, RUTH HELEN, physician; b. N.Y.C., Jan. 31, 1941; d. Abraham and Sarah (Oken) K. Student, Cornell U., 1958-61; MD, N.Y.U., 1965. Intern King County Hosp., Seattle, 1965-66; resident in ob-gyn U. Wash., 1966-70; med. dir. Planned Parenthood of Seattle, 1970-73; staff physician Group Health Cooperative of Puget Sound, Seattle, 1970—, cen. region chief of specialty services, 1979-83, cen. region chief of hosp. services, 1986-88, cen. region chief dept. ob-gyn, 1988—; clin. assoc. prof. ob-gyn dept. U. Wash., Seattle, 1980—. Bd. dirs. Seattle Music Festival, 1982-88. Fellow Am. Coll. Obstetricians and Gynecologists; mem. Planned Parenthood (Nat. Med. Com.), Seattle Gynecological Soc. (pres. 1988). Democrat. Office: Group Health Coop Puget Sound 200 15th Ave E Seattle WA 98112

KRAUTBLATT, CHARLES JOHN, electrical engineer; b. College Point, N.Y., Sept. 28, 1950; s. Jack Charles and Catherine (DiDio) K.; m. Ann Florczak, Oct. 12, 1974; 1 child, Kristina Ann. BSEE, DeVry Inst. Tech., Phoenix, 1979. Mem. tech. staff TRW Def. and Space Corp., Los Angeles, 1979-81; dept. mgr. Kyocera Internat., San Diego, 1981-82; pres., tech. dir. EVS Engring., San Diego, 1982-84; cons. San Diego, 1983—. Served as cpl. with USMC, 1967-71. Mem. IEEE, Armed Forces Communications and Electronics Assn., Internat. Computer Cons. of Am. (nominating com. 1986), Calif. Chpt. Internat. Computer Cons. of Am., Air Force Assn., Scripps SR Club, Scripps Civic Assn. Home: 11826 Semillon Blvd San Diego CA 92131 Office: 9842 Herbert St Ste 256 San Diego CA 92131

KRAVER, THEODORE CHARLES, entrepreneur; b. Lodi, Ohio, May 14, 1938; s. Erwin Foskett and Elizabeth Gaite (Urch) K.; m. Barbara G. Halley, Jan. 1960 (div. 1970); children: Cynthia Anne, Charles Wells; m. Cathrine Adams, June 26, 1970 (div. 1978); 1 child, Adam; m. Barbara Alice Taubert, Jan. 1, 1979. BS, MIT, 1961, MS, 1961; MBA, UCLA, 1979. Sr. engr. specialist Garrett Corp., Phoenix, 1961-70; v.p. Burn Treatment Skin Bank Inc., Phoenix, 1970-77; strategic planner Garrett Turbine Engine Co., Phoenix, 1979-82; pres. Sendero Corp., Phoenix, 1982-84, bd. dirs.; bd. dirs. Strategic Planning Cons., Phoenix, 1982—; v.p. Kurta Corp., Phoenix, 1985-87; pres., bd. dirs. Kumm Industries Inc., Phoenix, 1984—; founding bd. dirs. Enterprises Network, Phoenix, 1985—, pres., 1988-89. Patentee in field. Founding v.p. Desert Alpine Res. Emergency Services, Phoenix, 1962-65; mem. Ariz. Spl. Edn. Adv. Com., 1978-83; founding pres. Tempe Parents for Gifted, 1977, Gifted Advocacy Info. Network, Phoenix, 1980-84. Mem. Assn. for Corp. growth, Planning Forum (v.p. 1983-84), Physicians for Social Responsibility (editor 1983-87), Phoenix Future Forum, Model Navy Carrier Assn. (found. pres. Tempe 1978).

KRAVETZ, ROBERT ELLIOT, physician; b. New York City, Jan. 15, 1934; s. Max and Dorothy K.; m. Nancy Wein, Dec. 22, 1958; children: Michael, Jeffrey, David. MD, N.Y. U., 1958. Intern Phila. Gen. Hosp., 1958-59; resident in internal medicine VA Hosp., Bklyn., 1959-61; fellow in gastroenterology Yale New Haven Med. Ctr., 1963-65; dir. alcholism unit Maricopa County Gen. Hosp., Phoenix, 1967-69; gen. practice medicine 1965—; curator med. mus. Bapt. Hosp. and Health Systems, 1981—. Served to srugeon USPHS, 1961-63. Republican. Jewish. Office: 6707 N 19th Ave #101 Phoenix AZ 85015

KRAVITZ, ELLEN KING, musicologist, educator; b. Fords, N.J., May 25, 1929; d. Walter J. and Frances M. (Prybylowski) Kokowicz; m. Hilard L. Kravitz, Jan. 9, 1972; 1 child, Julie Frances; stepchildren—Kent, Kerry, Jay. B.A., Georgian Ct. Coll., 1964; M.M., U. So. Calif., 1966, Ph.D., 1970. Tchr. 7th and 8th grade music Mt. St. Mary Acad., North Plainfield, N.J., 1949-50; cloistered nun Carmelite Monastery, Lafayette, La., 1950-61; instr. Loyola U., Los Angeles, 1967; asst. prof. music Calif. State U., Los Angeles, 1967-71; asso. prof. 1971-74, prof., 1974—; founder Friends of Music, 1976. Editorial bd.: Jour. Arnold Schoenberg Inst, Los Angeles; jour. editor Vol. I, No. 3, 1977, Vol. II, No. 3, 1978; author: (with others) Catalog of Schoenberg's Paintings, Drawings and Sketches. Mem. Schoenberg Centennial Com., 1974, guest lectr., 1969—. Recipient award for masters thesis U. So. Calif., 1966. Mem. Am. Musicol. Soc., Los Angeles County Mus. Art, Mu Phi Epsilon, Phi Kappa Lambda. Home: 402 Doheny Rd Beverly Hills CA 90210 Office: Calif State U 5151 State University Dr Los Angeles CA 90032

KRAVITZ, HILARD L(EONARD), physician; b. Dayton, Ohio, June 26, 1917; s. Philip and Elizabeth (Charek) K.; divorced; children: Kent C., Kerry, Jay; m. Ellen King, Jan. 9, 1972; 1 child, Julie Frances. BA, U. Cin., 1939, MD, 1943. Lic. physician, Calif., Ohio. Resident in internal medicine Miami Valley Hosp., VA Hosp., Dayton, 1946-49; practice medicine specializing in internal medicine Dayton, 1950-54, Beverly Hills and Los Angeles, Calif., 1955—; practice medicine specializing in internal medicine and cardiology Los Angeles, 1955—; attending physician Cedars-Sinai Med. Ctr., 1955—; cons., med. dir. Adolph's Ltd., Los Angeles, 1955-74; mem. exec. com. Reiss-Davis Clinic, Los Angeles, 1966-70; chmn. pharmacy and therapeutic com. Cent City Hosp., Los Angeles, 1974-79; mem. pain commn. service Dept. Health and Human Services, Washington, 1985-86. Patentee sugar substitute, 1959, mineral-based salt, 1978. V.p. Friends of Music Calif. State U., Los Angeles, 1979-81. Served to capt. U.S. Army, 1944-46, ETO. Decorated Bronze Star with oak leaf cluster; Fourragere (France). Mem. AMA, Calif. Med. Assn., Los Angeles County Med. Assn., Am. Soc. Internal Medicine, Calif. Soc. Internal Medicine (del. 1974). Jewish. Office: 2080 Century Park E Los Angeles CA 90067

KRAVITZ, KAREN GLASER, advertising executive; b. N.Y.C., Mar. 4, 1958; d. David and Alice Joan (Michaels) Glaser; m. Kenneth Lee Kravitz, Mar. 6, 1982. BA, SUNY, Binghamton, 1979. Asst. account exec. Backer and Spielvogel, N.Y.C., 1980-82; media planner Hill, Holiday, Connors & Cosmopulos, Boston, Mass., 1982-83; pres., owner Commotion Promotions, Ltd., Phoenix, 1983—; bd. dirs. Specialty Advt. Assn. of Ariz. Democrat. Office: Commotion Promotions Ltd 4648 E Shea Blvd Suite A-290 Phoenix AZ 85028

KRAW, GEORGE MARTIN, lawyer; b. Oakland, Calif., June 17, 1949; s. George and Pauline Dorothy (Herceg) K.; m. Sarah Lee Kenyon, Sept. 3, 1983. BA, U. Calif.-Santa Cruz, 1971; student, Lenin Inst., Moscow, 1971; MA, U. Calif.-Berkeley, 1974, JD, 1976. Bar: Calif. 1976, U.S. Dist. Ct. (no. dist.) Calif. 1976, U.S. Supreme Ct. 1980. Assoc. Bachan, Skillicorn, Watsonville, Calif., 1976-79, Trepel & Clark, San Jose, Calif., 1979-81; ptnr. Mount, Kraw & Stoelker, San Jose, 1981-88, Kraw & Kraw, San Jose, 1988—; asst. sec. Sysgen, Inc., Fremont, Calif., 1982—. Mem. ABA, Inter-Am. Bar Assn. Clubs: Metropolitan, University (San Jose). Office: Kraw & Kraw 333 W San Carlos Ste 1050 San Jose CA 95110

KREBS, ROGER DONAVON, architect; b. Waverly, Iowa, Nov. 22, 1949; s. Martin Andrew and Ruby Lilas (Homan) K.; m. Deborah Lynn Homerstad; children: Gretchen Marie, Emma Louise. BA, Rice U., 1973, BArch, 1974. Registered architect, Wyo. Archtl. designer John F. Houchins, Houston, 1974-77; archtl. designer Gorder South Group, Casper, Wyo., 1977-78, project architect, 1978-83; architect VA Med. Ctr., Salt Lake City, 1984-85, supervisory architect, 1985—. Prin. works include Wyo. Womens Ctr., Casper Events Ctr.

KREGER, MELVIN JOSEPH, lawyer; b. Buffalo, Feb. 21, 1937; s. Philip and Bernice (Gerstman) K.; m. Patricia Anderson, July 1, 1955 (div. 1963), children: Beth Barbour, Arlene Roux; m. Renate Hochleitner, Aug. 15, 1975. JD, Mid-valley Coll. Law, 1978; LLM in Taxation, U. San Diego, 1988. Bar: Calif. 1978, U.S. Dist. Ct. (cen. dist.) Calif. 1979, U.S. Tax Ct. 1979. Life underwriter Met. Life Ins. Co., Buffalo, 1958-63; bus. mgr. M. Kreger Bus. Mgmt., Sherman Oaks, Calif., 1963-78, enrolled agt., 1971-78; sole practice North Hollywood, Calif., 1978—. Mem. Nat. Assn. Enrolled Agts. (pres. Los Angeles chpt. 1980-81, chmn. legal com. 1983-86), San Fernando Valley Estate Planning Council, State Bar of Calif., Los Angeles Bar Assn., San Fernando Valley Bar Assn. (probate sect.),, Calif. Soc. Enrolled Agts. Jewish. Office: 11424 Burbank Blvd North Hollywood CA 91601

KREHBIEL, TY DENE, resort official; b. Dodge City, Kans., May 24, 1969; s. Roger Dean and Sally Ailene (Law) K. Student, Mesa Community Coll., 1987-88. Supr. Lakewood Country Club, Hutchinson, Kans., 1985-86; owner, operator Custom Stereo Installations, Mesa, Ariz., 1987-88; asst. mgr. dining room Los Abrigados Resort, Sedona, Ariz., 1988-89; dining room mgr. L'Augerge de Sedona Resort, 1989—. Maricopa County Bd. Edn. Pres.'s scholar, 1987. Mem. Nat. Restaurant Assn., Nat. Honor Soc. Home: PO Box 2373 Sedona AZ 86336 Office: 301 Little Ln Sedona AZ 86336

KREINER, PETER WARREN, organization researcher; b. Hartford, Conn., Feb. 15, 1948; s. William Warren and Mae Phyllis (Zakszewska) K.; m. Carol Anne Marsh, Apr. 17, 1983. BA in Philosophy, Princeton U., 1970; PhD in Bus. Adminstrn., U. So. Calif., 1989. Research assoc. Yale Sch. Medicine, New Haven, 1971-73; teaching asst. UCLA, 1974-77; proprietor Peter Kreiner Wood Finishing, Los Angeles, 1981-86; research asst. Ctr. for Effective Orgns., Los Angeles, 1986--; instr. U. So. Calif., Los Angeles, 1988--. Contbr. articles in field to profl. jours. U. So. Calif. doctoral fellow, 1985-89. Mem. Acad. Mgmt. (best papers proceedings 1988). Office: U So Calif Bridge Hall 306 Los Angeles CA 90089-1421

KREISEL, HENRY, university administrator; b. Vienna, Austria, June 5, 1922; s. David Leo and Helene (Schreier) K.; m. Esther Lazerson, June 22, 1947; 1 child, Philip. B.A., U. Toronto, 1946, M.A., 1947; Ph.D., U. London, 1954. With dept. English U. Alta., 1947—, prof., 1959—, head dept., 1961-67, asso. dean Grad. studies, 1967-69, acting dean grad. studies, 1969-70, acad. v.p., 1970-75, Univ. prof., 1975—, chmn. Can. studies program, 1979-82; vis. fellow Wolfson Coll., Cambridge U., 1975-76; Chmn. English lit. Can. Council Fellowship Com., 1963-65, Gov.-Gen.'s Jury for Lit., 1966-69; v.p. Edmonton Art Gallery, 1969-70. Author: The Rich Man, 1948, The Betrayal, 1964, The Almost Meeting, 1981, Another Country, 1985, (play) The Rich Man, 1987. Contbr.: numerous short stories, anthologies to mags., books, including Best American Short Stories, 1966, A Book of Canadian Stories, 1962. Author: plays for radio and TV, including Bob Hope Theatre, 1965, The Rich Man, 1987. Bd. govs. U. Alta., 1966-69; v.p. Edmonton Chamber Music Soc., 1978-80, pres., 1980-83; advisor to Sec. of State for Multiculturalism, 1987. Recipient U. Western Ont. President's medal, 1960; J. I. Segal Found. award lit., 1983; Rutherford award for excellence in teaching U. Alba., 1986, Sir Frederick Haultain prize Govt. Alta., 1986, Order of Can., 1988; Reuben Wells Leonard fellow U. Toronto, 1946-47; Royal Soc. Can. Travelling fellow, 1953-54. Fellow Royal Soc. Arts (London), Internat. Inst. Arts and Letters (Geneva); mem. Assn. Can. U. Tchrs. English (pres. 1962-63). Home: 12516 66th Ave, Edmonton, AB Canada T5B 1K5

KREITLER, RICHARD ROGERS, company executive; b. Summit, N.J., Nov. 15, 1942; s. Carl John and Juliette (Rogers) K.;m. Donna Chapman, June 24, 1966 (div. Aug. 1984); m. Joy Stringfellow, Oct. 22, 1987; children: Kent, Kim, Ryan McIntire. BA, Washington and Lee U., 1965; MA, George Washington U., 1966. Tchr. Pembroke Country Day Sch., Kansas City, Mo., 1966-67; salesman B. C. Christopher & Co., Kansas City, 1967-70; v.p. Faulkner, Dawking & Sullivan, N.Y.C., 1970-72, Donaldson, Lufkin Jenrett, N.Y.C., 1972-75; sr. v.p. White Weld, N.Y.C., 1975-76; v.p. Goldman Sachs, N.Y.C., 1976-80; gen. ptnr. Dakota Ptnrs., Ketchum, Idaho, 1980—. Trustee Sun Valley (Idaho) Sky Edn. Found., 1984-87, Ketchum Sun Valley Community Sch., 1986-89. Mem. Sun Valley Golf Club, Laker Club (Palm Desert, Calif.), Morris Country Golf Club (Morristown, N.J.). Republican. Episcopalian. Home: 81 Adams Gulch Rd Ketchum ID 83340 Office: Dakota Ptnrs 620 Sun Valley Rd Ketchum ID 83340

KREITZBERG, FRED CHARLES, engineering management company executive; b. Paterson, N.J., June 1, 1934; s. William and Ella (Bohen) K.; m. Barbara Braun, June 9, 1957; children: Kim, Caroline, Allison, Bruce, Catherine. BSCE, Norwich U., 1957. Registered profl. engr., Ala., Alaska, Ariz., Calif., Colo., Conn., D.C., Idaho, Ill., Ind., Md., Mass., Nev., N.J., N.Mex., N.Y., Ohio, Oreg., Pa., Va., Wash. Asst. supt. Turner Constrn. Co., N.Y.C., 1957; project mgr. Project Mercury RCA, N.J., 1958-62; schedule, cost mgr. Catalytic Constrn. Co., Pa., 1963-65, 65—; owner, pres., chief exec. officer O'Brien-Kreitzberg and Assocs. Inc., San Francisco, also bd. dirs.; lectr. Stanford (Calif.) U., U. Calif., Berkeley. Contbg. author Crit. Path Method Scheduling for Contractor's Mgmt. Handbook, 1971; tech. editor Constrn. Inspection Handbook, 1972; contbr. articles to profl. jours. bd. dirs. Partridge Soc. Norwich U. Served to 1st lt. C.E., U.S. Army, 1957-58. Recipient Disting. Alumnus award Norwich U., 1987; named Boss of Yr., Nat. Assn. Women in Construction, 1987; Kreitzberg Ampitheater named in his honor, 1987. Fellow ASCE (Constrn. Mgr. of Yr., 1982), Internat. Leaders in Achievement; mem. Am. Arbitration Assn., Constrn. Mgmt. Assn. Am. (founding, bd. dirs.), Soc. Am. Value Engrs., Community Field Assn. (Marin County bd. dirs.), Ross Hist. Soc., Construction Mgmt. Assn. Am. Clubs: Palm Springs (Calif.) Tennis; Marin Tennis, Tamalpa Runners. Home: 19 Spring Rd Box 1200 Ross CA 94957 Office: O'Brien-Kreitzberg & Assocs Inc 188 The Embarcadero San Francisco CA 94105

KREJCI, ROBERT HENRY, aerospace engineer; b. Shenandoah, Iowa, Nov. 15, 1943; s. Henry and Marie Josephine (Kubicek) K.; m. Carolyn R. Meyer, Aug. 21, 1967; children—Christopher S., Ryan D. B.S. with honors in Aerospace Engring., Iowa State U., Ames, 1967, M.Aerospace Engring., 1971. Commd. 2d lt. U.S. Air Force, 1968, advanced through grades to capt., 1978; served with systems command Space Launch Vehicles Systems Program Office, Advanced ICBM program officer; research asso. U.S. Dept. Energy Lawrence Livermore lab.; dept. mgr. advanced tech. programs Wasatch div. Thiokol Corp., 1978-84, mgr. space programs, 1984-85, mgr. Navy strategic programs, 1986—. Decorated A.F. commendation medal, Nat. Def. Service medal. Mem. AIAA. Home: 885 N 300 E Brigham City UT 84302 Office: Thiokol Corp PO Box 689 Brigham City UT 84302

KREMPEL, ROGER ERNEST, consultant; b. Waukesha, Wis., Oct. 8, 1926; s. Henry and Clara K.; m. Shirley Ann Gray, June 16, 1948; children—John, Sara, Peter. Student Ripon Coll., 1944, Stanford U., 1945; BCE, U. Wis.-Madison, 1950. Registered profl. engr., Wis., Colo.; registered land surveyor, Wis. Asst. city engr., Manitowoc, Wis., 1950-51; city engr. dir. pub. works, Janesville, Wis., 1951-75; dir. water utilities, pub. works Ft. Collins, Colo., 1975-84, dir. natural resources, streets and stormwater utilities, Ft. Collins, 1984-88; pub. works mgmt. cons., 1988-89; lectr. various univ., coll., nat. confs. and seminars. Contbr. articles to profl. pubs. Served with U.S. Army, 1944-46. Recipient numerous tech. and profl. awards. Fellow ASCE; mem. Water Pollution Control Fedn., Am. Water Works Assn., Am. Pub. Works Assn. (past pres. Colo. and Wis. chpts.), Pub. Works Hist. Soc. (bd. dirs., trustee), Research Found. of Am. Pub. Works Assn. Nat. Soc. Profl. Engrs., Wis. Soc. Profl. Engrs. (past pres.), Am. Acad. Environ. Engrs. (diplomate).

KREN, HAROLD EDWIN, business services company executive; b. San Francisco, Sept. 10, 1920; s. Hugo and Irene (Cohn) K.; m. Marilyn Newcomb, Apr. 2, 1971; children: Jennifer, Mary, Ellen, Alan, Michael, Valerie. BS, U. Calif, Berkeley, 1941; MBA, Calif. State U., San Jose, 1972. Personnel mgr. Ampex Corp., Redwood City, Calif., 1955-56; bus. mgr. Tech, Ops., Inc., Monterey, Calif., 1956-60; gen. mgr. LFE, Inc., Monterey, 1960-63; v.p. adminstrn. Data Dynamics, Inc., Monterey, 1963-64; v.p. fin., adminstrn. Tensor Corp., Monterey, 1964-70; prin. Harold E. Kren and Assocs., Monterey, 1970—; adj. prof. Golden Gate U., 1971-87; researcher in Econ. field. Pres. Council Monterey Bay, 1972-74; bd. dirs. Monterey County Indsl. Devel., 1964-70. Served with USAAF, 1943-46. Decorated D.F.C., Air Medal with four oak leaf clusters. Mem. Monterey C. of C. (dir. 1975-76, treas. 1976—), Pacheco Club, Rotary. Home and Office: 584 Houston St Monterey CA 93940

KRENGEL, PETER MARK, sales and marketing; b. Mpls., Mar. 11, 1956; s. Richard and Carol (Larson) K.; m. Barbara Ellen Malcolm, Mar. 24, 1979; 1 child, Stuart Lawrence. BA in English Lit., Seattle Pacific U., 1979; postgrad., Western Wash. U., 1980. English lit. and social justice instr. St. Mary's High Sch., Stockton, Calif., 1980-87; feed salesman and mktg. coord. Willowbrook Feeds, Inc., Petaluma, Calif., 1987—; instr. Mennonite Brethern Ch., Lodi, Calif., 1984-89. Vol. dir. CROP relief orgn., Stockton, Calif., 1984-87. Recipient Journalism edn. grant, Dow Jones News Fund, Stanford Univ., 1986. Mem. Calif. Feed and Grain Assn. Democrat. Mem. of Mennonite Brethern Ch. Home: 514 W Locust Lodi CA 95240 Office: Willowbrook Feeds Inc 40 Ely Rd Petaluma CA 94975-0818

KRENZKE, RAYMOND EUGENE, estate manager; b. Racine, Wis., Feb. 17, 1943; s. Edward Julius and Catherine Lavern (Undorf) K. BA, Dominican Coll., 1965; MA in Theatre, Saint Louis U., 1966; postgrad., Northwestern U., 1969. Cert. tchr. Tchr. Evanston (Ill.) Pub. Schs., 1969-71; tech. dir. of theatre Ashland (Ohio) Coll., 1971-73; costume designer Savoy Opera Co., Cleveland, 1973-74; chauffer Johnson Found., Racine, Wis., 1974-75; owner Bread Sales Bakery & Catering, Racine, Wis., 1975-77; gen. mgr. Racine Symphony Orchestra, Racine, Wis., 1977-80, Johnstown Symphony Orchestra, Johnstown, Pa., 1980-81; freelance theatre dir. Racine, Wis., 1981-83; mgr. private estate Pebble Beach, Calif., 1983—; pres. Region 8 Am. Theatre Conference, Ill. and Wis., 1970-71; parish council pres. Saint Marys Church, Racine, 1976-77. Author numerous plays. Roman Catholic. Home: 222 Cypress Ave Pacific Grove CA 93950

KREPAKEVICH, JERRY DAVID, film producer; b. Yorkton, Sask., Can., Nov. 20, 1946; s. Fred and Martha (Zederayko) K.; m. Barbara Jacqueline Mumns, June 29, 1967; children: Alanna, Robin, Shane. Student, U. Sask., 1965-68. Producer Sta. CJUS-FM, Saksatoon, Sask., 1966-68; prodn. asst., asst. editor, dir., writer Nat. Film Bd. of Can., Montreal, 1967-74; film editor, writer, dir., producer Nat. Film Bd. of Can., Winnepeg, Man., 1974-80, Edmonton, Alta., Can., 1980—. Mem. Syndicat Gen. du Cinema et TV (sec. office nat. du film, treas. 1972-73, synd. steward 1974-88). Office: Nat Film Bd Can, 120-9700 Jasper Ave, Edmonton, AB Canada T5J 4C3

KRESA, KENT, aerospace executive; b. N.Y.C., Mar. 24, 1938; s. Helmy and Marjorie (Boutelle) K.; m. Joyce Anne McBride, Nov. 4, 1961; 1 child, Kiren. B.S.A.A., MIT, 1959, M.S.A.A., 1961, E.A.A., 1966. Sr. scientist research and advanced devel. div. AVCO, Wilmington, Mass., 1959-61; staff mem. MIT Lincoln Lab., Lexington, Mass., 1961-68; dep. dir. strategic tech. office Def. Advanced Research Projects Agy., Washington, 1968-73; dir. tactical tech. office Def. Advanced Research Project Agy., Washington, 1973-75; v.p., mgr. Research & Tech. Ctr. Northrop Corp., Hawthorne, Calif., 1975-76; v.p., gen. mgr. Ventura div. Northrop Corp., Newbury Park, Calif., 1976-82; group v.p. Aircraft Group Northrop Corp., Los Angeles, 1982-86, sr. v.p. tech. devel. and planning, 1986-87, pres., chief operating officer, 1987—; bd. dirs. John Tracy Clinic.; mem. Chief of Naval Ops. exec. panel Washington, Def. Sci. Bd., Washington, DNA New Alternatives Working Group, Los Angeles, Dept. Aeronautics and Astronautics Corp. Vis. Com. MIT. Recipient Henry Webb Salsbury award MIT, 1959, Arthur D. Flemming award, 1975; Sec. of Def. Meritorious Civilian Service medal, 1975, USN Meritorious Pub. Service citation, 1975, Exceptional Civilian Service award USAF, 1987. Fellow AIAA; mem. Naval Aviation Mus. Found., Navy League U.S., Soc. Flight Test Engrs., Assn. of U.S. Army, Nat. Space Club, Am. Def. Preparedness Assn. Club: Mountaingate Country. Office: Northrop Corp 1840 Century Park E Los Angeles CA 90067

KREUTZER, MARY P., county official; b. Many, La., Feb. 26, 1937; d. Robert Burns and Mary Lee (Keith) J.; m. Neil R. Scott, Aug. 26, 1960 (div. Aug. 1972); 1 child, Bret Scott; m. Richard Miller Kreutzer, Dec. 27, 1976; 1 child, William Richard; stepchildren: Anne, Ellen, Ted. BA in History Edn., La. State U., 1959; MA in Polit. Sci., Duke U., 1966; credential in econ. devel, U. Okla.; spl. edn. credential, U. Calif. Tchr., adminstr. ednl. TV history program N.C. Sept. Pub. Instrn., 1961—; tchr. adminstr. spl. edn. programs Sequia Union High Sch. Dist., Menlo Park, Calif., 1961-71; dir. pub. rels. and devel. St. Mary's Acad., Englewood, Colo.; real estate salesman Bennett Perkins & Wafer, Englewood, 1972-76; dir. Industries for Jefferson County, Inc., Lakewood, Colo., 1976-79, Jefferson County Comprehensive Employment and Tng. Svcs., Lakewood, 1979—; bd. dirs. Jeffco Pvt. Industry Found., Inc., Lakewood, 1987—; speaker in field. Mem. adv. bd. Red Rocks Community Coll., 1979-85; mem. Colo. Job Tng. Coordinating Council, 1983-86; mem. adv. com. Colo. Dept. Commerce and Industry, 1977-83; mem. Colo. Export Council, 1978-82; past chmn. Dirs. Assn., Job Tng. Partnership Act in Colo.; speaker CETA Dirs. Conf.; mem. econ. devel. com. Colo. Gov.'s Front Range Blue Ribbon Project, 1980-82; mem. benefits council Denver Ballet Guild, 1986-87, v.p., 1988—; active local polit. campaigns; alumni officer Duke U., La. State U. Mem. Nat. Assn. Counties (speaker 1980-84, 87), Wheat Ridge C. of C. (bd. dirs. 1986—), Chi Omega, Lakewood Country. Democrat. Presbyterian. Home: 2518 Alkire St Golden CO 80401 Office: Jeffco Employment & Tng 8585 W 14th Ave Lakewood CO 80215

KREVANS, JULIUS RICHARD, university administrator, physician; b. N.Y.C., May 1, 1924; s. Sol and Anita (Makovetsky) K.; m. Patricia N. Abrams, May 28, 1950; children: Nita, Julius R., Rachel, Sarah, Nora Kate. B.S. Arts and Scis, N.Y. U., 1943, M.D., 1946. Diplomate: Am. Bd. Internal Med. Intern, then resident Johns Hopkins Med. Sch. Hosp., mem. faculty, until 1970, dean acad. affairs, 1969-70; physician in chief Balt. City Hosp., 1963-69; prof. medicine U. Calif. at San Francisco, 1970—, dean Sch. Medicine, 1971-82, chancellor. Contbr. articles on hematology, internal med. profl. jours. Served with M.C. AUS, 1948-50. Mem. A.C.P., Assn. Am. Physicians. Office: U Calif 3rd & Parnassus Aves San Francisco CA 94143 *

KRIEGER, DENNIS ABBA, homeopathic physician; b. Bklyn., Feb. 12, 1949; s. Seymour and Celia (Stupsky) K.; (div. 1987); 1 child, Leah. BS, Providence Coll., 1970; postgrad., Brandeis U., 1970-71, U. Grenoble (France) Med. Sch., 1972-73; D in Chiropractic, Western States Chiropractic Coll., Portland, Oreg., 1977. Diplomate Nat. Chiropractic Bd. of Examiners. Homeopathic physician Natural Healing Ctr., Carbondale, Colo., 1978—. Recipient Rsch. award Parker Chiropractic Rsch. Found., Acupuncture Soc. Am. Mem. Am. Assn. Nutritional Cons., Nat. Ctr. for Homeopathy, Internat. Found. of Homeopathy, Yoga Tchrs. Colo., Ctr. for Sci. in the Pub. Interest, Physicians for Social Responsibility, Sci. Against Nuclear Energy, Greenpeace, Valley Peace Alliance. Office: Natural Healing Ctr 734 Main St Carbondale CO 81623

KRIEGER, GARY ROBERT, environmental medical physician; b. Valdese, N.C., May 10, 1951; s. Marvin and Jean Sylvia (Elder) K.; m. Jeanne Faye Arrington, May. 6, 1978; children: Lauren, Taylor. AB, U. N.C., 1973, MD, 1978; MPH, Johns Hopkins, 1982. Diplomate Am. Bd. Internal Medicine, Am. Bd. Preventive Medicine. Resident in medicine Mayo Clinic,

Rochester, Minn., 1978-81; med. dir. Exxon Chem., Houston, 1982-83; dir. occupational, environ. medicine Boulder (Colo.) Med. Ctr., 1984-88; mgr. health effects group Dames & Moore, Golden, Colo., 1988—; cons. Circadian Physiology Lab. Harvard Med. Sch., Boston, 1983-84; research fellow French Red Cross, Paris, 1975-76; expert witness U.S. House Com. on Sci. Tech., Washington, 1983, Nuclear Regulatory Com. Task Force, Washington, 1984; med. dir. Ball Aerospace div., Boulder, 1985—; cons. in. field., Boulder, 1984—; adj. asst. prof. toxicology U. Colo., Boulder, 1986—. Advisor emergency preparedness Boulder Valley (Colo.) Sch. Dist., 1985. Mem. AAAS, ACP (assoc.), Rocky Mountain Acad. Occupational Medicine (bd. dirs. 1986—), N.Y. Acad. Scis., Am. Acad. Clin. Toxicology, Semi-Conductor Safety Assn., Am. Acad. Occupational Medicine, Phi Beta Kappa. Home: 7332 Island Circle Boulder CO 80301 Office: Dames & Moore 1626 Cole Blvd Golden CO 80401

KRIEGER, WILLIAM CARL, English educator; b. Seattle, Mar. 21, 1946; s. Robert Irving Krieger and Mary (McKibben) Durfee; m. Patricia Kathleen Callow, Aug. 20, 1966; children: Richard William, Robert Irving III, Kathleen Elizabeth. BA in English, Pacific Luth. U., 1968, MA in Humanities, 1973; PhD in Am. Studies, Wash. State U., 1986. Instr. Pierce Coll., Tacoma, 1969—; adj. prof. hist. and English Cen. Wash. State U., 1980; vis. prof. hist. and English So. Ill. U., Carbondale, 1981-84, Pacific Luth. U., Tacoma, 1981-84; Chmn. English dept. Pierce Coll., Tacoma, 1973-75, 76-79, 81-84, humanities div. chair, 1979-81; bd. dirs. Thoreau Cabin Project, Tacoma, 1979—; project dir. Campus Wash. Centennial Project, Tacoma, 1984—; spl. cons. Clover Park Sch. Dist., Tacoma, 1985. Apptd. Wash. St. Centennial Commn., Constitutions Com, Pierce County Centennial Com. Mem. Thoreau Soc. (life), Community Coll. Humanities Assn. (standing com. 1982-83), Am. Studies Assn., Wash. Community Coll. Humanities Assn. (bd. dirs. 1982-84, grantee, 1984), Western Wash. Ofcls. Assn. Home: 4415 68th St Ct NW Gig Harbor WA 98335 Office: Pierce Coll 9401 Farwest Dr SW Tacoma WA 98498

KRIENKE, CAROL BELLE MANIKOWSKE (MRS. OLIVER KENNETH KRIENKE), realtor, appraiser; b. Oakland, Calif., June 19, 1917; d. George and Ethel (Purdon) Manikowske; student U. Mo., 1937; BS, U. Minn., 1940; postgrad. UCLA, 1949; m. Oliver Kenneth Krienke, June 4, 1941 (dec. Dec. 1988); children: Diane (Mrs. Robert Denny), Judith (Mrs. Kenneth A. Giss), Debra Louise (Mrs. Ed Paul Davalos). Demonstrator, Gen. Foods Corp., Mpls., 1940; youth leadership State of Minn. Congl. Conf., U. Minn., Mpls. 1940-41; war prodn. worker Airesearch Mfg. Co., Los Angeles, 1944; tchr. L.A. City Schs., 1945-49; realtor DBA Ethel Purdon, Manhattan Beach, Calif., 1949; buyer Purdon Furniture & Appliances, Manhattan Beach, 1950-58; realtor O.K. Krienke Realty, Manhattan Beach, 1958—. Manhattan Beach bd. rep. Community Chest for Girl Scouts U.S., 1957; bd. dirs. South Bay council Girl Scouts U.S.A., 1957-62, mem. Manhattan Beach Coordinating Coun., 1956-68; mem. Long Beach Area Childrens Home Soc. (v.p., 1967-68, pres. 1979; charter mem. Beach Pixies, 1957—, pres. 1967; chmn. United Way, 1967); sponsor Beach Cities Symphony, 1953—. Mem. DAR (life, citizenship chmn. 1972-73, v.p. 1979, 83—), Colonial Dames XVII Century (charter mem. Jared Eliot chpt. 1977, v.p., pres. 1979-81, 83-84), Friends of Library, Torrance Lomita Bd. of Realtors, South Bay Bd. Realtors, Nat. Soc. New England Women (life, Calif. Poppy Colony), Internat. Platform Assn., Soc. Descs. of Founders of Hartford (life), Friends of Banning Mus., Manhattan Beach Hist. Soc., Manhattan Beach C. of C. (Rose and Scroll award 1985), U. Minn. Alumni (life). Republican. Mem. Community Ch. (pres. Women's Fellowship 1970-71). Home: 924 Highview St Manhattan Beach CA 90266 Office: OK Krienke Realty 1716 Manhattan Beach Blvd Manhattan Beach CA 90266

KRIESS, FRED LEWIS, JR., utility executive; b. Butler, Pa., Sept. 28, 1953; s. Fred Lewis and Edna Ruth (Kirker) K.; m. Sandra Kaye McPherson, Jan. 17, 1976; children: Jason, Matthew. BSc in Biology, Westminster Coll., 1975; MSc in Environ. Health, U. Pitts., 1977; postgrad., Ariz. State U., 1988—. Cert. environ. quality operator, Ariz. Sales cons. Fulton Piano and Organ Co., Pitts., 1976-77; operator Evans City (Pa.) Mcpl. Authority, 1977-78, ops. supr., 1979-83, asst. gen. mgr., 1983-88; mgr. Citizens Ulilities Co., Maricopa County, Ariz., 1989—; mem. adv. com. operator certification Ariz. Dept. Environ. Quality, 1988-89. Co-author: Environmental Protection Agency Technology Transfer, 1979. Minister music Hope Bapt. Ch., Phoenix, 1983-88, moderator, 1989—. Recipient Community Svc. award St. John's United Ch. of Christ, Evans City, 1978; named an Outstanding Young Man Am., 1988. Mem. Am. Water Works Assn., Northwest Valley C. of C. (asst. editor newsletter 1987—), Am. Bapt. Men (pres. Hope Bapt. chpt. 1985, sec. 1988), Lions. Republican. Home: 7109 W Carol Ave Peoria AZ 85345 Office: Citizens Utilities Co 15626 N Del Webb Blvd Sun City AZ 85351

KRILL, MARY ALICE, association executive; b. Longmont, Colo., Mar. 21, 1924; d. James Blaine and Agnes Elsie (Brown) Hitt; m. Arthur Melvin Krill, July 6, 1944; children: Susan Krill Smith, Juli Lapin, Arthur M. Jr. BA in Chemistry, U. Colo., 1941-44; MA, U. Denver, 1969-71, PhD, 1971-73. Asst. project dir. Ctr. for Research in Ambulatory Health Care Adminstrn., Denver, 1974-76, proj. dir., 1977-79, dir. research, 1979-85, adminstrv. dir., 1985—; assoc. dir. parent orgn. Med. Group Mgmt. Assn., Denver, 1986—; cons. Rand Corp., L.A., 1985—, Honolulu Med. Group Rsch. and Edn. Found. Honolulu, 1985—, Gov.'s Coun. on Phys. Fitness and Health, 1988—. Contbr. articles to profl. jours. Active Welcome Colo., Denver. Mem. Assn. Health Services Research, Nat. Ctr. Health Edn., Assn. Univ. Programs in Health Adminstrn., Sigma Xi, Phi Beta Kappa, Kappa Kappa Gamma. Republican. Episcopalian. Home: 450 Westwood Dr Denver CO 80206 Office: Ctr Rsch Ambulatory Health 1355 S Colorado Blvd Denver CO 80222

KRIM, ARTHUR B., motion picture company executive, lawyer; b. N.Y.C., Apr. 4, 1910; s. Morris and Rose (Ocko) K.; m. Mathilde Galland, Dec. 7, 1958; 1 child, Daphna. B.A., Columbia U., N.Y.C., 1930, J.D., 1932, LL.D. (hon.), 1982. Bar: N.Y. 1933. With Phillips, Nizer, Benjamin, Krim & Ballon, N.Y.C., 1932—, sr. ptnr., 1935-78, of counsel, 1978—; pres. Eagle Lion Films, N.Y.C., 1946-49; chmn. United Artists Corp., N.Y.C., 1951-78, Orion Pictures Corp., N.Y.C., 1978—; dir. Occidental Petroleum Corp., Los Angeles, Cities Service Corp., Tulsa, Iowa Beef Corp., Iowa City. Editor in chief Columbia Law Rev., 1931-32. Spl. cons. to Pres. U.S., 1968-69; mem. Pres.'s Gen. Adv. Com. Arms Control, 1977-80; chmn. Democratic Nat. Fin. Com., 1966-68, Dem. Adv. Council Elected Ofcls., 1973-76; bd. dirs. Weizmann Inst. Sci., 1948—, UN Assn., 1961—, Lyndon Baines Johnson Found., 1969—, John F. Kennedy Library Found., 1964—, Arms Control Assn., 1985—; chmn. bd. trustee Columbia U., 1977-82, chmn. emeritus, 1982—. Served to lt. col. U.S. Army, 1942-45. Decorated Cavaliere Ufficiale Della award Republic of Italy, Chevalier dans l'Ordre Nat. de la legion d'Honneur (France); recipient Jean Hersholt Humanitarian award Acad. Motion Picture Arts and Scis., 1975. also: Orion Pictures Corp 1888 Century Park E Los Angeles CA 90067 *

KRING, THOMAS CAROL, social services administrator; b. Kokomo, Ind., May 2, 1939; s. Carol Franklin and Mildred Bates (Smith) K.; m. Betsy Pauline Fredrickson, June 9, 1962; children: Cathy Ann Kring Hamilton, Bryan Thomas. BA, So. Meth. U., 1961, BD, MTh, 1965. Minister Vickery Meth. Ch., Dallas, 1963-65, Galt (Calif.) Community United Meth. Ch., 1965-69, 1st United Meth. Ch., Modesto, Calif., 1969-71; exec. dir. Planned Parenthood Assn., Sacramento, Calif., 1971-78, Los Angeles Regional Family Planning Council, 1978—, Calif. Family Planning Council, Los Angeles, 1983—; bd. dirs. Parinatal Adv. Com. Los Angeles. Cons., speaker in field. Recipient Vera Casey award Calif. Alliance Concerned with Sch. Aged Parents, 1985, Spl. Commendation award Planned Parenthhod Assn. Korea, 1988, Cheryl Kleinhammer award Outstanding and Enduring Contbr. to Family Planning in Calif., 1989. Mem. Am. Pub. Health Assn., Calif. Reproductive Health Assn. (founder, bd. dirs.), Population Assn. Am., Nat. Family Planning and Reproductive Health Assn. (bd. dirs., chmn. pub. affairs com. 1986-89, pres. bd. dirs. 1989), Large Councils Exec. Dirs. Assn. (founding chmn. 1981), Zero Population Growth (nat. bd. mem. 1989). Democrat. Home: 28819 Leah Circle Rancho Palos Verdes CA 90274 Office: LA Regional Family Planning Coun 3600 Wilshire Blvd #600 Los Angeles CA 90010

KRIPPNER, STANLEY CURTIS, psychologist; b. Edgerton, Wis., Oct. 4, 1932; s. Carroll Porter and Ruth Genevieve (Volenberg) K.; m. Lelie Anne Harris, June 25, 1966; stepchildren—Caron, Robert. BS, U. Wis., 1954; MA, Northwestern U., 1957, PhD, 1961; PhD (hon.), U. Humanistic Studies, San Diego, 1982. Speech therapist Warren Pub. Schs. (Ill.), 1954-55, Richmond Pub. Schs. (Va.), 1955-56; dir. Child Study Ctr. Kent State U. (Ohio), 1961-64; dir. dream lab. Maimonides Med. Ctr., Bklyn., 1964-73; prof. of psychology Saybrook Inst., San Francisco, 1973—; vis. prof. U. P.R., 1972, Sonoma State U., 1972-73, Univ. Life Scis., Bogotá, Colombia, 1974, Inst. for Psychodrama and Humanistic Psychology, Caracas, Venezuela, 1975, West Ga. Coll., 1976, John F. Kennedy U., 1980-82; lectr. Acad. Pedagogical Scis., Moscow, 1971, Acad. Scis., Beijing, China, 1981. Author: (with Montague Ullman) Dream Telepathy, 1973, rev. edit., 1989, Song of the Siren: A Parapsychological Odyssey, 1975; (with Alberto Villoldo) The Realms of Healing, 1976, Human Possibilities, 1980, (with Alberto Villoldo) Healing States, 1987; (with Jerry Solfvin) La Science et les Pouvoirs Psychiques de l'Homme, 1986, (with Joseph Dillard) Dreamworking, 1988, (with David Feinstein) Personal Mythology, 1988; editor: Advances in Parapsychological Research, Vol. 1, 1977, Vol. 2, 1978, Vol. 3, 1982, Vol. 4, 1984, Vol. 5, 1987, Psychoenergetic Systems, 1979; co-editor: Galaxies of Life, 1973, The Kirlian Aura, 1974, The Energies of Consciousness, 1975, Future Science, 1977; mem. editorial bd.: Gifted Child Quar., Internat. Jour. Paraphysics, Jour. Humanistic Psychology, Jour. Transpersonal Psychology, Revision Jour., Jour. Theoretical Parapsychology, Jour. Indian Psychology, Psi Research, Metanoia, Dream Network Bulletin, Humanistic Psychologist, Internat. Jour. Psychosomatics, Jour. Creative Children and Adults, InterAm. U. Press; contbr. 500 articles to profl. jours. Mem. adv. bd., bd. dirs. A.R.E. Clinic, Acad. Religion and Psychical Rsch., Survival Rsch. Found., Aesculapian Inst. for Healing Arts, Hartley Film Found., Inst. for Multilevel Learning, Internat. Horizon Ednl. Audio Recordings, John E. Fetzer Energy Medicine Rsch. Inst., Forest Inst. Profl. Psychology, Humanistic Psychology Ctr. N.Y., Ctr. Transcendence and Transintegration, Ky. Ctr. Psychosynthesis. Recipient Svc. to Youth award YMCA, 1959; recipient citation of merit Nat. Assn. Gifted Children, 1972, citation of merit Nat. Assn. Creative Children and Adults, 1975, cert of recognition Office of Gifted and Talented, U.S. Office Edn., 1976, Volker Medal South Africa Soc. Psychical Rsch., 1980. Fellow Am. Soc. Clin. Hypnosis, Am. Psychol. Assn., Am. Psychol. Soc., Soc. Sci. Study Sex; mem. Am. Soc. Psychical Rsch., N.Y. Soc. Clin. Psychologists (assoc.), Am. Acad. Social and Polit. Sci., AAAS, Am. Ednl. Rsch. Assn., Am. Assn. of Counseling and Devel., Internat. Council Psychologists, Assn. for Study of Dreams, Assn. Anthrop. Study of Consciousness, Assn. Transpersonal Anthropology Internat., Internat. Kirlian Rsch. Assn., Com. for Study Anomalistic Rsch., Inter-Am. Psychol. Assn., Assn. Humanistic Psychology (pres. 1974-75), Assn. Transpersonal Psychology, Internat. Psychomatics Inst., Internat. Soc. Hypnosis, Internat. Soc. for Study Multiple Personality and Dissociative States, Nat. Assn. for Gifted Children, Sleep Rsch. Soc., Soc. Sci. Exploration, Biofeedback Soc. Am., Coun. Exceptional Children, Soc. Accelerative Learning and Teaching, Soc. Gen. Systems Rsch., Swedish Soc. Clin. and Exptl. Hypnosis, Western Psychol. Assn., World Coun. for Gifted and Talented Children, Internat. Soc. Gen. Semantics, Menninger Found., Nat. Soc. Study of Edn., Parapsychol. Assn. (pres. 1983), Soc. Clin. and Exptl. Hypnosis, Soc. for Sci. Study of Religion, World Future Soc. Home: 79 Woodland Rd Fairfax CA 94930 Office: Saybrook Inst 1550 Sutter St San Francisco CA 94123

KRISTJANSON, LEO FRIMAN, college administrator; b. Gimli, Man., Can., Feb. 28, 1932; s. Hannes and Elin Thordis (Magnusdottir) K.; m. Jean Evelyn Cameron, June 29, 1957; children: Terri, Darryl, Brenda, Johanne. B.A., U. Man., 1954, M.A., 1959; Ph.D., U. Wis., 1963; LL.D., U. Winnipeg, 1980. Instr. history United Coll., Winnipeg, Man., 1956-57; research economist Centre for Community Studies, Saskatoon, Sask., Can., 1959-64; prof. econs., head dept. econs. U. Sask., Saskatoon, 1964-75, v.p., 1975-80, pres., 1980—; cons. agrl. marketing Govt. Sask., 1972—. Author 2 booklets in field. Mem. Am. Econ. Assn., Canadian Econ. Assn. (exec. mem.), Canadian Assn. U. Tchrs. (treas., exec. mem. 1970-72), Am. Farm Econs. Assn., Canadian Agrl. Econs. Soc. Office: U Sask, Office of Pres, Saskatoon, SK Canada S7N 0W0 *

KRITVITZKY, RICHARD ALAN, lawyer; b. Chgo., Oct. 1, 1952; s. Jacob and Pauline (Weisman) K. BA, Lake Forest Coll., 1973; JD, Wash. U., 1977. Assoc. counsel N. Central Life Ins. Co., St. Paul, 1980-82; asst. gen. counsel Inter-Am. Ins. Cos., Chgo., 1983-87; asst. v.p., asst. gen. counsel First Capital Life Ins.Co., San Diego, 1987—. Group leader, Weight Watchers of San Diego, 1976—. Mem. Life and Health Complinance Assn. (mem. com. 1988—), Internat. Claim Assn. (life ins. com. 1989). Democrat. Jewish. Office: First Capital Life 10241 Wateridge Circle San Diego CA 92021

KRITZMAN, JERRY JAY, giftware designing, manufacturing and importing company executive; b. L.A., Aug. 20, 1950; s. Norman and Doris (Dworman) K.; m. Denise Lisa Scheer, Sept. 8, 1951; children: Melinda Anne, Micah Allan. AA, Valley Coll., Van Nuys, Calif., 1970; BA, Northridge Coll., 1972. Sales mgr. Star Mdse. Corp., North Hollywood, Calif., 1968-71; chief exec. officer Gift Creations, Inc., North Hollywood, 1971—, Pacific Master Ltd., Hong Kong, 1984—, Gift Creations Internat. Ltd., Taipei, Republic of China, 1997—; ptnr. Na Pua O'Hana, Maui, Hawaii, 1987—. Mem. Internat. Assn. Amusements and Attractions (Outstanding Svc. award 1986, 87), Calif. Giftware Assn., Travel Exporters Assn., Hong Kong Bus. Assn. Office: Gift Creations Inc 7624 Varna Ave North Hollywood CA 91805

KROGH, ROBERT B., small business owner; b. Honolulu, Jan. 22, 1942; s. Roy John Krogh and Betty Lou (Mickelberry) Lamberto; m. Gabrielle Krogh. BBA, Calif. Western U., 1966. Supr. auditor U.S. Gen. Acctg. Office, L.A., 1966-72; v.p. sales, mktg. PCS, Inc., Phoenix, 1972-78; pres., owner Robert Krough Assocs., Inc., Scottsdale, Ariz., 1978-87; gen. mgr. MMS/Robert Krough Assoc., Scottsdale, 1987—; owner R.K. Mktg. Cons. Inc., Scottsdale, 1987—. Author: (Report to Congress) Indian Education, 1972. Mem. NRA, (Washington chpt. 1966—), Ariz. Desert Bighorn Sheep Soc., Med. Mktg. Assn. (pres. 1986-87), Rotary (pres. 1986-87). Republican. Roman Catholic. Home: 6350 E Joan d'Arc Scottsdale AZ 85254 Office: MMS/Robert Krough Assocs 7819 E Greenway #4 Scottsdale AZ 85260

KROGIUS, TRISTAN ERNST GUNNAR, food products executive; b. Tammerfors, Finland, Apr. 13, 1933; came to U.S., 1939; s. Helge Lorenz and Valborg Isolde (Antell) K.; m. Barbara Jane Brophy, Aug. 29, 1952; children—Ferril Anne, Lars Anthony, Karin Therese, Eric Lorenz, Marian Elaine, Rebecca Kristina. B.A., U. N.Mex., 1954; M.A., Calif. State U.-Los Angeles, 1962; grad. Advanced Mgmt. Program, Harvard U., 1980. With Scott Paper Co., Phila., 1960-65, Hunt-Wesson Foods, Fullerton, Calif., 1965-75; pres. Hunt-Wesson Foods Can., Ltd., Toronto, Ont., 1969-71, pres. frozen and refrigerated foods div., 1971-75; pres., chief exec. officer Dalgety Foods, Salinas, Calif., 1975-78; v.p., gen. mgr. food div. Tenneco West, Inc., Bakersfield, Calif., 1978-80, pres., chief exec. officer, 1981-87; pres. Landmark Mgmt., Inc., 1987-88; ptnr. The Cons. Co., South Laguna, 1988—. Bd. dirs. South Coast Med. Ctr., Laguna Beach, Calif., 1969-74, pres., chief exec. officer, 1974; bd. dirs. South Sierra council Boy Scouts Am., 1981-87, Calif. State Coll. Found., Bakersfield, 1983-87, Found. for 21st Century, 1987—. Served to capt. USMC, 1954-60. Recipient World Food award Ariz. State U., Tempe, 1982. Republican. Episcopalian. Office: The Consulting Co 31706 Coast Hwy Ste 401 South Laguna CA 92677

KROHN, KENNETH ALBERT, radiology educator; b. Stevens Point, Wis., June 19, 1945; s. Albert William and Erma Belle (Cornwell) K.; m. Marijane Alberta Wideman, July 14, 1968; 1 child, Galen. BA in Chemistry, Andrews U., 1966; PhD in Chemistry, U. Calif., 1971. Acting assoc. prof. U. Wash., Seattle, 1981-84, assoc. prof. radiology, 1984-86, prof. radiology and radiation oncology, 1986—, adj. prof. chemistry, 1986—; guest scientist Donner Lab. Lawrence Berkeley (Calif.) Lab., 1980-81; radiochemist, VA Med. Ctr., Seattle, 1982—. Contbr. numerous articles to profl. jours.; patentee in field. NDEA fellow. Mem. AAAS, Am. Chem. Soc., Radiation Research Soc., Soc. Nuclear Medicine, Acad. Council, Sigma Xi. Home: 11322 23d Ave NE Seattle WA 98125 Office: U Wash Imaging Rsch Lab RC-05 Seattle WA 98195

KROKENBERGER, LINDA ROSE, chemist, environmental analyst; b. Ridley Park, Pa., July 17, 1954; d. Roy Frank and Rose Marie (Kraffert) K. BS in Chemistry, Syracuse U., 1976. Radiopharm. chemist Upstate Med. Ctr., SUNY, Syracuse, 1976-78; chemist IT Corp. (formerly West Coast Tech. Services), Cerritos, Calif., 1978-80, analytical chemist, 1980-81, sr. chemist, 1981-84, asst. mgr. lab., 1984-85, project mgr. environ. protection agency, 1985-86; mgr. data control Enseco-Cal Lab., West Sacramento, Calif., 1987; asst. mgr. lab. Sci. Applications Internat. Corp., San Diego, 1987—. Recipient Citizenship award DAR, 1972. Mem. Am. Chem. Soc., ASTM, Assn. Official Analytical Chemists, Soc. Environ. Toxicology and Chemistry. Republican. Methodist. Home: 12974 Cree Dr Poway CA 92064 Office: Sci Applications Internat Corp 4224 Campus Point Ct San Diego CA 92121

KRONENBERG, JEFFREY NEIL, landscaping contractor; b. Bklyn., Feb. 2, 1951; s. Phil and Anne (Sachowkitz) K.; m. Harriet Ellen Dinnerman, Oct. 31, 1976. BS in Econs., U. Akron, 1973, BA in Sociology, 1973. Sportswear buyer M. Oneil Co., Akron, Ohio, 1974-78; div. pres. Beeba's Creations Inc., San Diego, 1978-81; pres. Pashion Warehouse, Inc., San Diego, 1981-82; v.p. Greenbrier, Inc., Spring Valley, Calif., 1982-86; owner S. Coast L & T Expert, San Diego, 1986—; cons., San Diego, 1986—. Mem. Calif. Landscape Assn., Mission Bay Ski. Democrat. Jewish. Home: 2579 Grandview St San Diego CA 92110

KRONINGER, LUTHER HENDRICKS, JR., medical computerization executive; b. Allentown, Pa., May 13, 1930; s. Luther Hendricks and Bea (Brobst) K.; m. Mary Esther Kunkel, June 21, 1952; children: Luther III, Amy Louise, Catharine Rhoads. BS, Cornell U., 1951; postgrad., George Washington U., 1952-53. Product mgr. Mead Johnson & Co., Evansville, Ind., 1969-70; mktg. dir. Bristol Myers Inc., N.Y.C., 1970-72; exec. v.p. Biochem. Procedures Inc., North Hollywood, Calif., 1972-74; pres. MD Systems Inc., Encino, Calif., 1974-78, chmn., chief exec. officer, 1978—. Inventor animal shaped chewable vitamin tablets. Served to 1st lt. U.S. Army, 1952-55. Recipient Pres.'s award Mead Johnson Co., 1965. Mem. Am. Mgmt. Assn., Newport Fleet. Home: 5244 Armida Dr Woodland Hills CA 91364 Office: MD Systems Inc 15821 Ventura Blvd Encino CA 91436

KRONK, BERNARD J., marketing executive; b. Amsterdam, N.Y., June 14, 1933; m. Donna Campbell Dybas, Sept. 6, 1958; children: David, Kathleen. BA in Mktg., Syracuse U., 1960; BS in Wood Product Engring., N.Y. State Coll. Forestry, 1960. Sales rep. Midstate Wholesale Corp., Binghamton, N.Y., 1962-66; sales mgr. Midstate Wholesale Corp., Syracuse, N.Y., 1966-70; mgr. eastern region Triangle Pacific Corp., Dallas, 1970-72; mgr. western region &, &, 1972-74; pres., owner Mktg. Enterprises West, Inc., Thousand Oaks, Calif., 1974—. Served with U.S. Army, 1953-55. Club: Calif. Bass Fedn. (pres. 1987—). Office: Mktg Enterprises West Inc 954 Calle Angosta Thousand Oaks CA 91360

KRONSTAD, WARREN ERVIND, genetics educator, researcher; b. Bellingham, Wash., Mar. 3, 1932; s. Ervind Raymond and Valintine (Ayers) K.; m. Mary Kathleen Holt, Sept. 19, 1952; children: Robin Kathleen, James Warren, Brian David, Nancy Ann. BS, Wash. State U., 1957, MS, 1959; PhD, Oreg. State U., 1963. Research asst. Wash. State U., Pullman, 1957-59; instr. Oreg. State U., Corvallis, 1959-63, asst. prof., 1963-69, assoc. prof., 1969-72, prof. plant breeding and genetics, 1972—; cons. in field, 1967—. Served with USNR, 1952-54. Recipient Alexander Von Humboldt award, 1981; Nixon Disting. Prof., 1980, Disting. Svc. award USDA, 1988, Disting. Prof. award Oreg. State U., 1989. Fellow Am. Soc. Agronomy, Crop Sci. Soc. Am. (Crop Sci. award 1983); mem. Nat. Assn. Fgn. Student Affairs, Sigma Xi, Gamma Sigma Delta, Phi Kappa Phi, Phi Sigma. Office: Oreg State U Coll Agr Corvallis OR 97331

KRONZEK, LYNN CHANNAH, public affairs specialist; b. Pitts., Apr. 8, 1955; d. Abraham and Helena (Stern) K.; m. Richard A. Flom, Dec. 28, 1980. BA, U. Mich., 1977; MPA, George Washington U., 1981. Vol. VISTA, Pitts., 1978-79; program analyst EPA, Washington, 1980-81; ind. mgmt. and editorial cons. Arlington, Va., 1981-83; sr. editor Windsor Publs., Northridge, Calif., 1984-85; exec. dir. Hollywood-Wilshire Fair Housing Coun., L.A., 1985-87; div. dir., cons. Jewish Fedn. Greater Long Beach/West Orange County, Calif., 1987-88; cons. in field. Contbr. articles to various publs. Bd. dirs., treas., So. Calif. Women's Substance Abuse Task Force, 1984-88. Mem. Pi Alpha Alpha. Democrat. Jewish. Home and Office: 8025 Redlands St Playa Del Rey CA 90293

KROPOTOFF, GEORGE ALEX, civil engineer; b. Sofia, Bulgaria, Dec. 6, 1921; s. Alex S. and Anna A. (Kurat) K.; came to Brazil, 1948, to U.S., 1952, naturalized, 1958; BSCE, Inst. Tech., Sofia, 1941; postgrad. in computer sci. U. Calif., 1968; m. Helen P., July 23, 1972. Tech. asst. Standard Eletrica S.A., Rio de Janeiro, 1948-52; structural designer Pacific Car & Foundry Co., Seattle, 1952-64; structural draftsman T.G. Atkinson Assocs., Structural Engrs., San Diego, 1960-62; structural engr. Tucker, Sadler & Bennett A-E, San Diego, 1964-74; rsch. engr. Gen. Dynamics-Astronautics, San Diego, 1967-68; structural engr. Engring. Sci., Inc., Arcadia, Calif., 1975-76; cons. Incomtel, Rio de Janeiro, Brazil, 1976; assoc. Bennett Engrs., structural cons., San Diego, 1976-82; project structural engr. Hope Cons. Group, San Diego and Saudi Arabia, 1982-84; cons. structural engr. Registered profl. engr., Calif. Mem. ASCE, Structural Engrs. Assn. San Diego, Soc. Am. Mil. Engrs., Soc. Profl. Engrs. Brazil. Republican. Orthodox. Home: 742 Brockton St El Cajon CA 92020

KROTKI, KAROL JOZEF, sociology educator, demographer; b. Cieszyn, Poland, May 12, 1922; emigrated to Can., 1964; s. Karol Stanislaw and Anna Elzbieta (Skrzywanek) K.; m. Joanna Patkowski, July 12, 1947; children—Karol Peter, Jan Jozef, Filip Karol. B.A. (hons.), Cambridge (Eng.) U., 1948, M.A., 1952; M.A., Princeton U., 1959, Ph.D., 1960. Civil ser. Eng., 1948-49; dep. dir. stats. Sudan, 1949-58; vis. fellow Princeton U., 1958-60; research adviser Pakistan Inst. Devel. Econs., 1960-64; asst. dir. census research Dominion Bur. Stats., Can., 1964-68; prof. sociology U. Alta., 1968-83, Univ. Prof., 1983—; vis. prof. U. Calif., Berkeley, 1967, U. N.C., 1970-73, U. Mich., 1975; coordinator program socio-econ. research Province Alta., 1969-71; cons. in field. Author 10 books and monographs; contbr. numerous articles to profl. jours. Served with Polish, French and Brit. Armed Forces, 1939-46. Recipient Achievement award Province of Alta., 1970; grantee in field. Fellow Am. Statis. Assn., Royal Soc. Can. (v.p. 1986-88), Acad. Humanities and Social Scis. (v.p. 1984-86, pres. 1986-88); mem. Fedn. Can. Demographers (v.p. 1977-82, pres. 1982-84), Can. Population Soc., Association des Demographes du Quebec, Cen. and E. European Studies Soc. (pres. 1986-88), Population Assn. Am., Internat. Union Sci. Study Population, Internat Statis. Inst. Roman Catholic. Home: 10137 Clifton Pl, Edmonton, AB Canada T5N 3H9 Office: U Alta, Dept Sociology, Edmonton, AB Canada T6G 2H4

KRUCHEK, THOMAS FRANCIS, psychiatrist; b. Montgomery, Minn., Aug. 15, 1922; s. Joseph and Nettie (Washa) K.; B.S., Coll. St. Thomas, 1944; M.D., Creighton U., 1946; m. Esther Kelly, Feb. 17, 1950; 1 son, Joseph. Intern. St. Mary's Hosp., Mpls., 1946-49; resident VA Hosp., Ft. Lyon, Colo., 1948-49, Norristown (Pa.) State Hosp., 1949-50, U. Pitts., 1953-54; practice medicine specializing in psychiatry, Chgo., 1954-62, Phoenix, 1962—; mem. staff St. Joseph's Hosp., chmn. dept. psychiatry, 1973-76; mem. staff Camelback Hosp., chief staff 1965-66; mem. staff Good Samaritan, St. Luke's, Dr.'s hosps., Phoenix, Scottsdale (Ariz.) Community/Hosps.; clin. instr. psychiatry Stritch Sch. Medicine, Chgo., 1955-62; prof. psychology St. Procopius Coll., Lisle, Ill., 1954-62; pres. Thomas F. Kruchek, M.D., Ltd. Served to capt. M.C., AUS, 1951-53. Diplomate Am. Bd. Psychiatry and Neurology. Fellow Am. Psychiat. Assn. (life), Royal Soc. Health; mem. AMA, Am. Psychotherapy Assn., Maricopa County Med. Soc., Ariz. Psychiat. Soc. (treas. 1968-69, pres. 1970-71), Phoenix Psychiat. Council, Chgo. Neurol. Soc., Am. Group Psychotherapy Assn., Acad. Psychosomatic Medicine, Ariz. Med. Assn. Office: 5051 N 34th St Phoenix AZ 85018

KRUEGER, CARYL WALLER, author, lecturer; b. Chgo., Apr. 1, 1929; d. Thomas Floyd and Astrid Alvina (Johnson) W.; m. Cliff W. Krueger, Aug. 11, 1951; children: Chris, Carrie, Cameron. BS, Northwestern U., 1950; postgrad., U. Chgo., 1951, U. Calif., 1971-73. Account exec. Advt. Div., Inc., Chgo., 1952-60, W. S. Meyers Co., Honolulu, 1961-70, Caryl Krueger

Assocs., Honolulu, 1963-68; ind lectr. on parent-child relationships, time mgmt. 1969--. Author: Six Weeks to Better Parenting, 1981, 2d edit., 1985, 1001 Things To Do With Your Kids, 1988; contbr. articles to Parade, Sunset, Parents, L.A. Times, C.S. Monitor, other publs. Pres. Oahu League Republican Women, Honolulu, 1968-69, Community Concert Assn., Rancho Santa Fe, Calif., 1983. Named Writer of Yr., Chgo. Advt. Club, 1959, Woman of Yr., Panhellenic Hawaii, 1968; recipient service award Camp Fire Girl Council, Honolulu. Mem. Women in Communications (pres. Honolulu chpt. 1968), Pen Women, AAUW, Phi Beta, Alpha Omicron Pi (pres. Honolulu chpt. 1963). Christian Scientist. Home and Office: 28455 Meadow Mesa Ln Escondido CA 92026

KRUEGER, CHERYL A(NN), actuary; b. Fairbury, Nebr., Jan. 2, 1962; d. Hilmar F. and M. Lucille (Forney) K. BS in Econs., U. Nebr., 1984. Sr. actuarial analyst, product devel. Lincoln Benefit Life Ins. Co., Lincoln, Nebr., 1982-87; asst. actuary product devel. staff, actuarial dept. GNA, Seattle, 1987—. Vol., Big Bros./Big Sisters, Lincoln, 1984-87/. Mem. Am. Acad. Actuaries, NAFE, U. Nebr. Alumni Assn., Seattle Economists Culb, Toastmasters, PEO, Mensa. Democrat. Lutheran. Office: GNA Ste 3300 1 Union Sq Seattle WA 98101

KRUEGER, JAMES, lawyer; b. N.Y.C., Oct. 27, 1938; s. Carl and Ida (Levey) K.; m. Merry Michael Hill, July 5, 1967; children—Melissa Carlton, James Michael. BA, UCLA, 1960; LLB, Loyola U., L.A., 1965. Bar: Hawaii 1966, U.S. Dist. Ct. Hawaii 1966, U.S. Ct. Appeals (9th cir.) 1967, U.S. Tax Ct. 1974, U.S. Supreme Ct. 1982. Assoc. firm Padgett, Greeley, Marumoto & Akinaka, Honolulu, 1967-72; pres. James Krueger Law Corp., Wailuku, Maui, Hawaii, 1973—; speaker, lectr. profl. orgn. convs.; spl. counsel County of Maui, 1974; spl. agt. Internat. Police Congress, Washington. Contbr. articles to profl. jours. Co-founder Nat. Bd. of Trial Advocacy, Hawaii Acad. of Plantiffs Attys.; Gold Trustee Thomas F. Lambert Chair; mem. Commn. Hawaii Ct. Annexed Arbitration, Hawaii State Com. on Lawyer Professionalism, 1988—; del. Hawaii Judicial Conf., 1986-88. Fellow Internat. Soc. Barristers, Internat. Acad. Trial Lawyers; mem. ABA (trial techniques com. 1974-76, com. medicine and law, nat. vice-chmn. sect. on tort and ins. practice 1977-81), Assn. Trial Lawyers Am. (gov. 1976-82, state committeeman 1975-76, constl. revisions com. 1977-78, nat. exec. com. 1981-82, amicus curiae com. 1979-80, fed. liaison com. 1980-81, nat. vice chmn. profl. research and devel. com. 1980-81, nat. vice-chmn. publs. dept. 1982-83, nat. vice chmn. edn. policy bd. 1983-84, chmn. Nat. Midwinter Conv. 1988, chmn. Nat. Pub. Relations Com. 1986-88), Hawaii Bar Assn., Fed. Bar Assn., Maui County Bar Assn. (pres. 1975), Melvin M. Belli Soc., Hawaii Acad. Plaintiffs Attys., Am. Coll. Legal Medicine, Am. Soc. Hosp. Attys., Western Trial Lawyers Assn. (pres. 1978-79, v.p. 1977-78, bd. govs. 1982-88), Calif. Trial Lawyers Assn., N.Y. Trial Lawyers Assn., Pa. Trial Lawyers Assn., Tex. Trial Lawyers Assn., NITA Advocates Assn., Phi Alpha Delta. Democrat. Jewish. Clubs: Outrigger Canoe (Honolulu); Transpacific Yacht (Los Angeles); Maui Country. Office: 2065 Main St PO Box T Wailuku HI 96793

KRUEGER, JAMES WAYNE, radon company executive; b. Ames, Iowa, May 6, 1957; s. Robert Wayne and Marilyn Jane (Woodall) K.; m. Shannon Le Earnshaw, June 9, 1984; children: Robert James, Stefan Mitchell. Student, U. Northern Iowa, 1981-83, Ariz. State U., 1985. Accredited instr. Mng. assoc. Krueger Mech., Griswold, Iowa, 1977-81; field mgr. McGuckin Inc., Phoenix, 1985-86; founder, chief exec. officer Am. Radon Corp., Scottsdale, Ariz., 1986—; Legis. resource environ. com. Ariz. Ho. of Reps., Phoenix, 1988—. Contbr. articles to profl. jours. Explorer leader Boy Scouts Am., Tempe, Ariz., 1986-87. Mem. ASTM (mem. EO6 com. 1988—), Am. Assn. Radon Scientists and Technicians (dir. 1987—), Nat. Radon Assn., Ariz. Bar Assn. (assoc., instr. 1988), Ariz. Assn. Realtors (resource advisor 1988—). Republican. Mormon. Office: Am Radon Corp 8300 N Hayden Rd Ste 100 Scottsdale AZ 85258

KRUEGER, ROBERT BLAIR, lawyer; b. Minot, N.D., Dec. 9, 1928; s. Paul Otto and Lila (Morse) K.; m. Virginia Ruth Carmichael, June 3, 1956 (div. 1987); children: Lisa Carmichael, Paula Leah, Robert Blair. A.B., U. Kans., 1949; J.D., U. Mich., 1952; postgrad., U. So. Calif., 1960-65. Bar: Kans. 1952, Calif. 1955, D.C. 1978. Practiced in Los Angeles, 1955-87; assoc. O'Melveny & Myers, 1955-59; ptnr. Nossaman, Krueger & Marsh and predecessor firms, 1961-83, Finley, Kumble, Wagner, Heine, Underberg, Manley, Myerson & Casey, 1983-86; counsel Lewis, D'Amato, Brisbois & Bisgaard, San Diego, 1988—; adj. prof. natural resource law U. So. Calif. Law Ctr., 1973-83; mem. Gov.'s Adv. Commn. on Ocean Resources, 1966-68, Calif. Adv. Commn. on Marine and Coastal Resources, 1968-73, chmn., 1970-73; mem. adv. council Inst. on Marine Resources, U. Calif., 1966-74, Commn. of the Californias, 1977—; mem. Nat. Security Council Adv. Com. on Law of Sea, 1972-82, chmn. internat. law and relations subcom., 1972-82; U.S. del. to UN Seabeds Com., 1973, 3d UN Law of Sea Conf., 1974-82; cons. energy and natural resources policy to UN, fgn. govts. U.S. Centre on Transnat. Corps.; vice chmn. Calif. Senate Task Force Waste Mgmt., 1988—; mem. exec. bd. Law of Sea Inst., U. Hawaii, 1977-83; mem. Nat. Adv. Com. on Oceans and Atmosphere, 1986—; fellow U. So. Calif. Inst. on Marine and Coastal Studies., 1977—; mem. policy com. U.S. Dept. Interior Outer Continental Shelf Adv. Abd., 1987—. Author: Study of Outer Continental Shelf Lands of the United States, 1968, The United States and International Oil, 1975, World Petroleum Policies Report, 1981; also articles on energy and natural resources.; Asst. editor: Mich. Law Rev., 1951-52; editor: Los Angeles Bar Bull., 1961-63; bd. editors: Calif. Bar Jour., 1962-68. Mem. com. visitors U. Mich. Law Sch.; charter founder Los Angeles Mus. Contemporary Art. Served to 1st lt. USMCR, 1952-54. Fellow Am. Bar Found.; mem. ABA (chmn. spl. com. on energy law 1979-83, chmn. coordinating group on energy law 1983-86), Los Angeles County Bar Assn., Internat. Bar Assn., Am. Soc. Internat. Law., Fellows Contemporary Art, Barristers, Tau Kappa Epsilon, Phi Alpha Delta. Republican. Clubs: Calif., University, Chancery (Los Angeles); La Jolla (Calif.) Beach and Tennis; Metropolitan (Washington); Princeton (N.Y.C.). Home: 9828 La Jolla Farms Rd La Jolla CA 92037 Office: Lewis D'Amato Brisbois & Bisgaard 101 W Broadway Ste 800 San Diego CA 92101

KRUGER, ALBERT AARON, chemist; b. Bklyn., Oct. 3, 1952; s. Louis Max and Shirley Judith (Linn) K.; m. Liza Lilly, June 9, 1974; children: Evelyne, Nathaniel R. BS with honors, Bklyn. Coll., 1974; MS in Chemistry, Syracuse U., 1974-75. Sr. tech. assoc. Bell Telephone Labs., Murray Hill, N.J., 1976-78; team leader, sr. chemist 3M Cen. Rsch. Lab., St. Paul, 1978-82; rsch. engr., project chief Saint-Gobain Recherche, Aubervilliers, France, 1982-87; adj. lectr. CUNY, Bklyn., 1987-88; sr. rsch. scientist Battelle, Pacific Northwest Lab., Richland, Wash., 1988—; lectr. continuing edn., 3M, St. Paul, 1978-80; adviser, Oakdale (Minn.) City Coun., 1980-81. Patentee in field; contbg. author: Surface and Near Surface Chemistry of Oxide Materials, 1988, NATO-ASI Surface and Interfaces in Ceramic Materials, 1989. Merit badge adviser, Boy Scouts Am., Paris, 1982-87, asst. dist. commr., 1983-86. Fellow Am. Inst. Chemists; mem. Am. Chem. Soc., Materials Rsch. Soc., Optical Soc. Am., Internat. Union Pure and Applied Chemistry, Sigma Xi. Home: 336 Sierra St Richland WA 99352 Office: Battelle PNL Battelle Blvd Richland WA 99352

KRUGER, BONNY BEATRICE, federal agency administrator; b. Tokyo, Mar. 3, 1950; d. Howard Albert and Edna Florence (Headley) K.; m. Michael Dean Bussey, Sr., Dec. 18, 1975 (July, 1978); 1 child, Michael Dean, Jr. BA, U. Colo., 1972; MA, Adams State Coll., 1984. Service clk. Smith-Colona Marchant, Denver, 1972; receptionist Dixson, Inc., Grand Junction, Colo., 1972-73; counter rep. Budget Rent-A-Car, Grand Junction, 1979; vol. coord. Mesa County Pub. Library, Grand Junction, 1979-84; claims rep. Social Security Administrn., Grand Junction, 1984—; commdg. officer The Lexington Div., a U.S. Naval Sea Cadet Unit, Grand Junction, 1988—. Vol. Youth Who Care, Grand Junction, 1978—, Assn. for Retarded Citizens, Grand Junction, 1988—. Lt. USN, 1973-76. Mem. Naval Res. Assn., Am. Legion, Navy League. Republican. Home: 503 Rado Dr #8 Grand Junction CO 81503

KRUM, NELSON CHARLES, JR., dentist, optical executive; b. Morristown, N.J., Feb. 15, 1953; s. Nelson Charles Sr. and Dorothy (Caress) K.; m. Nancy Jo Clark, Dec. 28, 1974 (div. 1989); children: Shaun, Jarod. BA, Dartmouth Coll., 1975; DDS, U. Colo., 1979. Pvt. practice Littleton, Colo., 1979—; pres., chief exec. officer X-Ray Vision, Inc., Littleton, 1987—; v.p., bd. dirs. Colo. Found. Dentistry for Handicapped, Denver, 1982-85; pres., bd. dirs. Hillcroft Acad., Littleton, 1983-87; pres., chief exec. officer X-Ray Vision, Inc., Littleton, 1987—; pres. Nelson C. Krum Jr., DDS, Littleton, 1987—. Guest Today Show, Hour Mag., PM Mag. Donor svcs. Nat. Found. Dentistry for Handicapped, 1979—; recipient Nine Who Care award, 1983. Mem. ADA, Colo. Dental Assn., Met. Denver Dental Soc. Republican. Episcopalian. Office: 5301 S Federal Circle Littleton CO 80123

KRUMM, JOHN MCGILL, bishop; b. South Bend, Ind., Mar. 15, 1913; s. William F. and Harriett Vincent (McGill) K. A.A., Pasadena Jr. Coll., 1933; A.B., U. Calif., 1935; B.D., Va. Theol. Sem., 1938, D.D. (hon.), 1974; Ph.D., Yale U., 1948; S.T.D. (hon.), Kenyon Coll., Gambier, Ohio, 1962; D.D. (hon.), Berkeley Div. Sch., Gen. Theol. Sem., 1975; L.H.D. (hon.), Hebrew Union Coll., Cin. Ordained to ministry Episcopal Ch., 1938; vicar Episc. chs., Compton, Lynwood and Hawthorne, Calif., 1938-41; asst. rector St. Paul's Ch., New Haven, 1941-43; rector Ch. of St. Matthew, San Mateo, Calif., 1943-48; dean St. Paul's Cathedral, Los Angeles, 1948-52; chaplain Columbia U., 1952-65; rector Ch. of Ascension, N.Y.C., 1965-71; bishop of So. Ohio, Episc. Ch., 1971-80; suffragan bishop in Europe Paris, 1980-83; assisting bishop Los Angeles, 1983—, St. Paul's Ch., Tustin, Calif., 1983—; vis. lectr. N.T. Berkeley Div. Sch., New Haven, 1942-43; ch. history Va. Theol. Sem., Alexandria, 1942; instr. Prospect Hill Sch., New Haven, 1942-43; instr. religion U. So. Calif., 1950-52; chmn. clergy div. U. Religious Conf., Los Angeles; pres. San Mateo-Burlingame (Calif.) Council Chs., 1947-48, Ch. Fedn. Los Angeles, 1951-52; chmn. nat. council Panel of Ams., 1953-61. Author: (with J.A. Pike) Roadblocks to Faith, 1953, Modern Heresies, 1961, The Art of Being a Sinner, 1967, Why Choose the Episcopal Church, 1974, (with others) Denver Crossroads, 1979, Letters from Lambeth, 1988, Flowing Like A River, 1989. Trustee Mt. Holyoke Coll., 1962-72, Bexley Hall of Colgate-Rochester, Kenyon Coll., Children's Hosp., Cin., 1971-80; chmn. Canterbury Irvine Found., U. Calif.-Irvine. Mem. Ch. Soc. for Coll. Work (bd. dirs.). Democrat. Clubs: Century Assn. (N.Y.C.); University (Cin.). Office: St Paul's Ch 1221 Wass Ave Tustin CA 92680

KRUMM, VICTOR CARL, lawyer; b. St. Paul, Mar. 1, 1947; s. Carl J. and Evelyn M. Krumm; m. Jean M. Ellsberg, May 23, 1969; children: Alexander, Andrew, Marissa. BA, Macalester Coll., 1969; JD, U. Minn., 1974. Ptnr. Christianson & Krumm, Sitka, Alaska, 1974-76; dist. atty. State of Alaska, Bethel, 1976-79, Ketchikan, 1979-81; asst. atty. gen. State of Alaska, Juneau, 1981-82; dist. atty. State of Alaska, Anchorage, 1982-87; pvt. practice Anchorage, 1988—. Served with U.S. Army, 1970-72.

KRUPNICK, MICHAEL IRA, marketing consultant; b. Chgo., Oct. 20, 1947; s. Simon S. and Elaine Sidel (Broude) K. BS, Case Western U., 1969; MA, Roosevelt U., 1971. Prin. Krupnick Cons., Chgo., 1975-76; mktg. dir. Natlsco/Kemper, Long Grove, Ill., 1976-80; dir. community rels. Westlake Hosp., Melrose Park, Ill., 1980-84; mgr. TPI Internat., Taipei, Taiwan, 1984-86; prin. The K Group, Tucson, 1986—. Bd. dirs. The Ctr. for Devel. of Human Resources, Tucson; chmn. 90's com. So. Ariz. Jewish Fedn. Mem. Nat. Assn. Law Firm Marketers, Tucson C. of C. (World Trade Fair sub-com.), ABA (mem. Econs. of Law sect., mem. spl. cons. com.), The Entrepreneurs Forum (chmn. pub. rels.), Old Pueblo Bus. and Profl. Assn. Jewish. Home: 7887 N La Cholla Blvd #2154 Tucson AZ 85741 Office: The K Group 7315 N Oracle #105 Tucson AZ 85704

KRUPP, EDWIN CHARLES, astronomer; b. Chgo., Nov. 18, 1944; s. Edwin Frederick and Florence Ann (Olander) K.; m. Robin Suzanne Rector, Dec. 31, 1968; 1 son, Ethan Hembree. B.A., Pomona Coll., 1966; M.A., UCLA, 1968, Ph.D. (NDEA fellow, 1970-71), 1972. Astronomer Griffith Obs., Los Angeles Dept. Recreation and Parks, 1972—, dir., 1976—; mem. faculty El Camino Coll., U. So. Calif., extension divs. U. Calif.; cons. in ednl. TV Community Colls. Consortium; host teleseries Project: Universe. Author: The Comet and You, 1986 (Best Sci. Writing award Am. Inst. Physics 1986), Echoes of the Ancient Skies, The Big Dipper and You, 1989; editor/co-author: In Search of Ancient Astronomies, 1978 (Am. Inst. Physics-U.S. Steel Found. award for Best Sci. Writing 1978), Archaeoastronomy and the Roots of Science; Editor-in-chief: Griffith Obs., 1974—. Mem. Am. Astron. Soc. (past chmn. hist. astronomy div.), Astron. Soc. Pacific (past dir., recipient Klumpke-Roberts outstanding contributions to the public understanding and appreciation of astronomy award 1989), Explorers Club, Sigma Xi. Office: Griffith Obs 2800 E Observatory Rd Los Angeles CA 90027

KRUPP, MICHAEL R., investor; b. El Paso, Tex., May 26, 1946; s. Leon B. and Merrill (Goldberg) K.; m. Nancy A. Krupp, May 26, 1968; children: Keri Beth, Robert Jason. BSBA, Babson Coll., 1967; MBA, Syracuse U., 1968. Registered rep. Quinn & Co., El Paso, 1968-72; chmn. Equity Cons. Group, Golden, Colo., 1972—, Southwestern Gen. Corp., Golden, 1980—; bd. dirs. Bldg. Techs. Industries, Cin., 1986—. Office: Southwestern Gen Corp 602 Park Point Dr #103 Golden CO 80401

KRUSE, ANN ELIZABETH, lawyer; b. Davenport, Iowa, Mar. 4, 1949; d. Donald Harry and Frances mary (Sunderbruch) K.; m. Curtis Dale Mobley, May 27, 1979. Student, Rosary Coll., River Forest, Ill., 1967-69; BA, U. Iowa, 1971; postgrad., U. Ill., 1971-72; JD, Georgetown U., 1977. Bar: Wash. 1978, U.S. Dist. Ct. (we. dist.) Wash. 1978, U.S. Ct. Appeals (9th cir.) 1978. Law clk U.S. Ct. Appeals (8th cir.), Fargo, N.D., 1977-78; assoc. Bogle & Gates, Seattle, 1978-82; from assoc. to ptnr. Edwards & Barbieri, Seattle, 1982-85; prin. Ann E. Kruse & Assocs., Woodinville, Wash., 1985—. Bd. dirs. Totem Council Girl Scouts U.S.A., Seattle, 1985-87, Northshore Sr. Ctr., Bothell, Wash., 1986—. Mem. ABA, Wash. Bar Assn. (legis. com. 1985-87, chmn. jud. recommendation com. 1987-88), Seattle-King County Bar Assn. (chmn. young lawyers sect. 1983-84), Wash. Women Lawyers, Woodinville C. of C. (pres. 1986-87), AAUW, Am. Alpine Club, Rotary. Office: 17311 135th Ave NE Woodinville WA 98072

KRUSE, CLIFTON BRYAN, JR., lawyer, educator; b. Hutchinson, Kans., July 16, 1934; s. Clifton Bryan Sr. and Merle Ilene (Hefling) K.; m. Carolyn Young, June 17, 1956; children: Stephen Paul Young, Angela Michele. BA, Washburn U., 1956, JD, 1963; STB, Boston U., 1959. Bar: Kans. 1963, Colo. 1963, U.S. Ct. Appeals (10th cir.) 1963.,. Assoc. Tullis & Craig, Colorado Springs, Colo., 1963-64; ptnr. Tullis, Craig, Kruse, Stumbo and McGinley, Colorado Springs, 1964-66, Kruse & Lynch, P.C., Colorado Springs, 1978--; pvt. practice, Colorado Springs, 1966-78; instr. bus. law seminars. Assoc. editor Washburn Law Journ., 196-263; probate and trust columnist Colo. Lawyer, 1987-88; contbr. articles to profl. jours. Bd. dirs. Pikes Peak chpt. ARC, Colorado Springs, 1986--; hon. bd. dirs. Silver Key Sr. Svcs., Colorado Springs, 1988--. Fellow Am. Coll. Probate Counsel, Colo. Bar Found.; mem. ABA, Colo. Bar Assn. (chmn.-elect probate and trust coun. 1986), El Paso County Bar Assn. (pres. 1983-84), Colo. Probate Coun. (chmn.-elect 1989--), Estate Planning Coun. (pres. Pikes Peak chpt. 1978-79), Confrerie Chevaliers du Tastevin, Broadmoor Golf Club, Broadmoor Figure Skating, Broadmoor Cooking Club. Home: 4 Crossland Rd Colorado Springs CO 80906 Office: Kruse & Lynch PC 350 Holly Sugar Bldg Colorado Springs CO 80903

KRUSE, JEFFREY RICHARD, electronics executive, financial counselor; b. Whittier, Calif., Apr. 17, 1958; s. Richard George and Darleen Delores (Colwell) K.; m. Karen Grace Davis, Aug. 4, 1979; children: Jamie Heather, David Jeffrey, Jennifer Dawn, Kimberly Joy. BA, Whitworth Coll., 1980; MBA, U. Puget Sound, 1984. CPA, Wash. Accts. payable clk. Whitworth Coll., Spokane, Wash., 1977-80; acctg. trainee Pioneer Bank, Lynnwood, Wash., 1977-80; ops. acct. Ace Tank and Equipment, Seattle, 1980-83; cons. Family Fin. Planning, Everett, Wash., 1984-85; controller Intelligent Controls Inc., Mountlake Terr., Wash., 1985, v.p. fin., 1985-86; v.p. fin. and ops. Intelligent Controls Inc., Lynnwood, Wash., 1986—. Leader Jr. Achievement, Spokane, 1978-79; tchr. of basketball Everett Commmunity Schs., 1987-88; fin. counselor New Life Ctr. Ch., Everett, 1986—; mem. steering com. bus. dept. Whitworth Coll., 1987. Named Scholastic scholar Whitworth Coll., 1979; recipient Leadership award Jr. Achievement, 1979. Mem. Am. Electronics Assn. (mem. Mfg. Com. 1988—). Republican. Mem. Pentacostal Ch. Office: Intelligent Controls Inc 6825 216th St SW Lynnwood WA 98036

KRUTSINGER, ANSEL JEROME, insurance agt.; b. Chariton, Iowa, Mar. 7, 1943; s. Clyle Jerome and Gladys Elizabeth (Van Pelt) K.; m. Teresa Lee Gardner, June 25, 1976; 1 child, Christian Lee. BA, U. Oreg., 1967. CLU, Charted Fin. Cons. Journalist USNR, 1967-69; news rep. Pacific Power and Light, Portland, Oreg., 1969-70; staff writer Pacific U., Forest Grove, Oreg., 1970-71, dir. univ. relations, 1971-78; sales Sta. KICE, Bend, Oreg., 1978-79; ins. agt. Northwestern Mutal Life, John Day, Oreg., 1979—. Contbr. articles to profl. jours. Served with USNR, 1967-69. Mem. Nat. Assn. Life Underwriters, Oreg. Life Underwriters, Am. Soc. CLU's, Cen. Oreg. Life Underwriters, Nat. Rifle Assn. Lodge: Elks. Office: Northwestern Mut Life 147 N Canyon Blvd PO Box 579 John Day OR 97845

KRUTZ, WILLIAM KEITH, computer systems software engineer, educator; b. Akron, Ohio, July 18, 1945; s. John William and Barbara (Baughman) K.; m. Marjorie Ann Church, Dec. 28, 1968; children: Michael, Peter, Justin. BS in Math., U. Akron, 1967; MS in Computer Sci., Johns Hopkins U., 1976; M in Fin. Mgmt., Southeastern U., 1978. Cert. Data Processor. Sr. programmer, analyst Mgmt. Sci. Systems, Alexandria, Va., 1972-74; sr. assoc. CACI-Fed., Arlington, Va., 1974-77; computer scientist systems div. Computer Scis. Corp., Falls Church, Va., 1977-79, Vandenberg AFB, Calif., 1979-81; data specialist ITT/Fed. Electric, Vandenberg AFB, Calif., 1981-83; sr. scientist B-K Dynamics, San Diego, 1983; software design specialist data systems div. Gen. Dynamics, San Diego, 1983-86; sr. software engr. Amex System div. Bendix Aerospace, Chula Vista, Calif., 1986-87; prin. engr. Calspan Corp. div. Arvin, Huntington Beach, Calif., 1987—; adj. faculty mem. Allan Hancock Coll., Lompoc, Calif, 1980-82, Chapman Coll., Vandenberg AFB, 1981, 83, Nat. Univ., San Diego, Vista, Calif., 1983-86, Palomar Coll., San Marcos, Calif., 1986—; presenter seminars in field. Contbg. author to books, mags. Mem. subcom. Ramona (Calif.) Planning Group South, 1988. Mem. Data Processing Mgmt. Assn. Republican. Methodist. Office: Zychros Software Engring PO Box 331 Ramona CA 92065-4221

KRYNICKI, PAUL FRANCIS, physician; b. Detroit, June 26, 1940; s. Francis Xavier and Helena (Raczyniski) K.; m. Jean Seinsheimer, Dec. 18, 1969; children: Beth Ann, Lynn, Jill. BS, U. Mich., 1962, MD, 1966. Intern Virginia Mason Hosp., Seattle, 1966-67, med. resident, 1967-69; chief med. resident Mason Clinic, Seattle, 1969-70; pvt. practice Seattle, 1974-75; mem. med. staff Polyclinic, Seattle, 1975—; pres. Polyclinic, 1987-89; clin. asst. prof. medicine, U. Wash., Seattle, 1983—; chief of medicine, Cabrini Hosp., Seattle, 1977-78; bd. dirs. Providence Hosp. Found., Seattle, 1987—; mem. med. bd., Blue Cross HMO, Seattle. Bd. dirs., Discover Dance, Seattle, Seattle Supernumary. Maj. M.C., U.S. Army, 1970-74. Mem. AMA, Wash. State Med. Assn., King County Med. Soc. Home: 11215 NE 58th Pl Kirkland WA 98033 Office: Polyclinic 1200 Harvard St Seattle WA 98122

KUBICZ, LAWRENCE, computer scientist; b. Detroit, Aug. 7, 1947; s. Edmund Anthony and Martha (Skuban) K.; m. Paula Gomez, Oct. 28, 1978; 1 child, David Lawrence. BS, U.S. Air Force Acad., 1969; MS, Cen. Mich. U., 1987. Commd. 2d lt. USAF, 1969, advanced through grades to capt., 1972, retired, 1985; computer programmer Aangstrom Precision Corp., Mt. Pleasant, Mich., 1985-87; software devel. engr. Hewlett-Packard, Sunnyvale, Calif., 1987—; owner, mgr. Neighborhood Computer Store, Lakewood, Colo., 1979-80. Democrat. Unitarian. Home: 2452 Scanlan Pl Santa Clara CA 95050 Office: Hewlett Packard 1272 Kifer Rd Sunnyvale CA 94086

KUBIDA, WILLIAM JOSEPH, patent lawyer; b. Newark, Apr. 3, 1949; s. William and Catherine (Gilchrist) K.; m. Mary Jane Hamilton, Feb. 4, 1984. B.S.E.E., U.S. Air Force Acad., 1971; J.D., Wake Forest U., 1979. Bar: N.C. 1979, U.S. Patent Office 1979, Ind. 1980, U.S. Dist. Ct. (no. dist.) Ind. 1980, U.S. Dist. Ct. (so. dist.) Ind. 1980, U.S. Ct. Appeals (7th cir.) 1981, U.S. Dist. Ct. (Ariz.) 1982, U.S. Ct. Appeals (9th cirs. and fed.) 1982, Ariz. 1982. Patent and trademark lawyer Lundy and Assocs., Ft. Wayne, Ind., 1979-81; patent atty. Motorola, Inc., Phoenix, 1981-85; Intellectual Property Counsel Nippon Motorola, Ltd., Tokyo, 1985-87; ptnr. Lisa & Kubida, P.C., Phoenix, 1987-89; sr. atty. Digital Equipment Corp., Colorado Springs, Colo., 1989—. Served to 1st lt. USAF, 1971-76. Mem. ABA (patent/trademark/copyright sect., litigation sect.), Am. Intellectual Property Law Assn., Am. C. of C. (patents, trademarks and lic. sect., Japan), Maricopa County Bar Assn., Mensa. Republican. Presbyterian. Club: Tokyo Am. Home: 4165 Regency Dr Colorado Springs CO 80906

KUBISKE, DAVID ARTHUR, civil engineer; b. Hamtramck, Mich., Aug. 8, 1954; s. Edward P. and Patricia (Piontkowski) K.; m. Irma Marie Cantu, June 25, 1983; children: Michael, Maureen. BCE, Mich. Technol. U., 1977. Registered profl. civil engr., Calif. Asst. civil engr. City of Thousand Oaks (Calif.), 1977-78; project mgr. Merco, Inc., Santa Monica, Calif., 1978-80; estimator Allied Constrn., Ventura, Calif., 1980-82; prin. Kubiske Engring., Ojai, Calif., 1982-86; pres., chief exec. officer KEAC Inc., Ventura, 1986—. CPR instr. ARC, Ojai, 1987. Mem. Am. Petroleum Inst., Ventura County Contractors Assn., Ventura Trade Club, Nat. Ski Patrol.

KUBSCH, KIM KAREN, commercial real estate consultant; b. Milw., Dec. 24, 1956; d. David Eugene and Jo Ann Myrtle (Fischer) K. BS in Home Econs., Silver Lake coll., 1979; postgrad., U. Wis., Stevens Point, 1980. Mall mgr., property mgr. Weingarten Realty, Inc., Houston, 1981-83; sr. property mgr. Stanley J. Williams Interests, Houston, 1983-84; regional property mgr. Patrician Group, Inc., N.Y.C., 1984-85; dir. property mgmt. Lincor Properties Ariz., Phoenix, 1985-87, Carmel-Givol Mgmt. Group, Hollywood, Calif., 1987-88; prin. cons. KK Consulting, L.A., 1988—; founder, pres. Networking for Phoenix Female Property Mgrs., 1986-87. Bd. dirs. Planned Parenthood, Wisconsin Rapids, Wis., 1979-80; Am. mktg. Assn., Houston, 1981-84. Mem. Inst. Real Estate Mgr. (cert. property mgr. candidate), Bldg. Owners Mgrs. Assn. (bd. dirs.), Nat. Assn. Women in Comml. Real Estate (hospitality chairwoman Houston chpt. 1981-84). Republican. Roman Catholic. Home: 340 S Cloverdale #106 Los Angeles CA 90036 Office: 3921 Wilshire Ste 505 Los Angeles CA 90010

KUCIJ, TIMOTHY MICHAEL, engineer, musician, theologian; b. Whittier, Calif., Sept. 2, 1954; m. Paulina V. Jimenez. BA in Music, Calif. Poly. U., Pomona, 1978; ThM cum laude, Christian Bible Coll., 1983; studies with Frank Sanucci, Edward D. Berryman, Thurla Wallis, Kathreen Prout, Eddy L. Manson, Henry Charles Smith, 1965-78; student, Sherwood Music Sch. of Chgo., 1965-68. Tech. writer Honeywell Inc., 1979-84; hydromech. reliability engr. Advanced Systems div. Northrop Corp., Pico Rivera, Calif., 1984-86; sr. engr. quality and reliability Swedlow, Inc., Garden Grove, Calif., 1986-88, mgr., quality assurance, composites div., 1988—. Performer Wiltern Theater, L.A., 1966-68, Busch-Reisinger Mus., Harvard U., Cambridge, Mass., 1972, 73, 74; composer over 40 piano compositions; contbr. numerous articles to newspapers and jours. Asst. to pastors local Bapt. Chs. in Tex., Ga., Wis., Minn. and Calif.; pastor Victory Bapt. Ch., Pine City, Minn., 1982-83; minister music, bible tchr. Calvary Bapt. Ch., La Verne, Calif., 1988—; musical compositions include Frolic, The Happy Whistler, The Little Toy March, Hope, Teardrops, Reminisce, Windchimes, A Place Somewhere, Rainbows, The Bicentennial Rag, The Pulsar Rag, Dazzling Fingers, The Butterfly Rag. Named one of Outstanding Young Men in Am., U.S. Jaycees, 1980; recipient First prize So. Calif. Organ Competition, 1966, Performer's certificate, 1967. Mem. Soc. Logistics Engring., Minn. Composer's Forum, Am. Symphony Orch. League, Fundamental Bapt. Fellowship Am., Dean Burgon Soc., Bible-Sci. Assn., Creation Rsch. Soc., Mensa. Republican. Home: 529 S Calvados Ave Covina CA 91723-2911 Office: Swedlow Inc 12122 Western Ave Garden Grove CA 92641

KUCKLINCA, STEPHEN JOHN, strategic planning consultant, lawyer; b. N.Y.C., May 9, 1943; s. Stephen and Helen (Fesko) K.; m. Jane E. Hepp, July 17, 1965; children: Janet H., Stephen H. BE, Cooper Union, 1965; MBA, Fairleigh Dickinson U., 1968; JD, Fordham U., 1972. Ter. mgr. Esso-Humble Oil Co., N.Y.C., 1965-67; N.Y. sales mgr. Honeywell Microswitch, N.Y.C., 1967-69; asst. v.p. Engrs., Inc., Newark, 1969-71; div. mgr. Raychem Corp., Menlo Park, Calif., 1971-81; pres. Sierracin Corp., Sylmar, Calif., 1981-82, SST Software Systems, Sunnyvale, Calif., 1982-83, LS Industries, Sunnyvale, Calif., 1985—; exec. v.p. Utilitech Corp., San Ramon, Calif., 1983-85; strategic planning cons. Crystalvision, Santa Clara, Calif., 1982, Zuckerboards, Inc., Sunnyvale, 1986, Gen. Tech. Co., Fremont, Calif., 1988—, Azuray Co., Scotts Valley, Calif., 1988—. Contbr. articles to profl. publs. Mem. ASME (sr.), IEEE. Home: 1633 Swift Ct Sunnyvale CA 94087 Office: LS Industries Inc 1556 Halford Ave Ste 263 Santa Clara CA 95051

KUCZEK, RICHARD EDWARD, economist; b. Waukegan, Ill., July 21, 1945; s. Edward Clarence and Helen Fay (Branson) K.; m. Melinda Ann Kuykendall, June 21, 1971 (separated Aug. 1977); children: Becky Lynn Dalton, Lee Kyle, Rex Thomas. Student, U. Oreg., 1963-66, 69-70; BS in Math., Polit. Sci., Portland (Oreg.) State U., 1973, MS in Polit. Sci., 1975; postgrad., W.Va. U., 1975-78. Teaching fellow W.Va. U., Morgantown, 1975-78; specialist human relations Met. Human Relations Commn., City of Portland, 1978-81; research dir. Urban League Portland, 1981-85; regional economist employment div. State of Oreg., Pendleton, 1986—. Editor Mid-Columbia Labor Trends, East Cen. Oreg. Labor Trends, Bus. and Employment Outlooks; contbr. articles to various newspapers; producer (TV program) Job Scene, 1983-85. Vice chmn. housing alternatives com. Met. Service Dist., Portland, 1979-81; mem. adv. com. on condominium conversions Portland Planning Commn., 1980; chmn. bd. dirs. Community Housing Resources, 1980-81; bd. dirs. N.W. Dist. Assn., 1980-82; treas. bd. dirs. Portland Cable Access Corp., 1983-85; mem. adv. com. on emergency services United Way of the Columbia/Willamette, 1984; chmn. housing subcom. cen. city plan City of Portland, 1985. Mem. Internat. Assn. Personnel in Employment Security. Democrat. Taoist. Home: 4794 Sunnyside Rd SE Salem OR 97302 Office: Oreg State Employment Div 875 Union St NE Salem OR 97311

KUDO, EMIKO IWASHITA, former state official; b. Kona, Hawaii, June 5, 1923; s. Tetsuzo and Kuma (Koga) Iwashita; B.S., U. Hawaii, 1944; M.S. in Vocational Edn., Pa. State U., 1950; postgrad. U. Hawaii, U. Ore., others; m. Thomas Mitsugi Kudo, Aug. 21, 1951; children: Guy J.T., Scott K., Candace F. Tchr. jr. and sr. high sch., Hawaii, 1945-51; instr. home econs. edn. U. Hawaii Tchrs. Coll., Honolulu, 1948-51, Pa. State U., State College, 1949-50; with Hawaii Dept. Edn., Honolulu, 1951-82, supr. sch. lunch service, 1951-64, home econ. edn., 1951-64, dir. home econ. edn., 1964-68, adminstr. vocat.-tech. edn., 1968-76, asst. supt. instructional services, 1976-78, dep. supt. State Dept. Edn., 1978-82; cons. Am. Samoa vocat. edn. state plan devel., 1970-71, vocat. edn. U. Hawaii, 1986, internat. secondary program devel. Ashiya Ednl. System, Japan, 1986-89; state coordinator industry-labor-edn., 1972-76; mem. nat. task force edn. and tng. for minority bus. enterprise, 1972-73; steering com. Career Info. Ctr. Project, 1973-78; co-dir. Hawaii Career Devel. Continuum project, 1971-74; mem. Nat Accreditation and Instl. Eligibility Adv. Council, 1974-77, cons., 1977-78; mem. panel Internat. Conf. Vocat. Guidance, 1978, 80, 82, 86, 88; state commr. edn. commn. of the states, 1986—; mem. Hawaii edn. coun., 1986—; dir. Dept. Parks and Recreation, City and County of Honolulu, 1982-84. Exec. bd. Aloha council Boy Scouts Am., 1978-88. Japan Found. Cultural grantee, 1977; Pa. State U. Alumni fellow, 1982; bd. trustees St. Louis High Sch., 1988-89. Mem. Pa. State U. Disting. Alumni, Western Assn. Schs. and Colls. (accreditation team mem. Ch. Coll. of Hawaii 1972-73), Am. Vocat. Assn., Hawaii Practical Arts and Vocat. Assn., NEA, Hawaii Edn. Assn., Hawaii State Ednl. Officers Assn., Am., Hawaii home econ. assn., Nat., Hawaii assns. for supervision and curriculum devel., Am. Tech. Edn. Assn., Omicron Nu, Pi Lambda Theta, Phi Delta Kappa, Delta Kappa Gamma. Author handbooks and pamphlets in field. Home and Office: 217 Nenue St Honolulu HI 96821

KUDRNA, KENNETH LYLE, aerospace company official; b. Clarkson, Nebr., Feb. 18, 1932; s. Adolph C. and Blanche (Mestl) K.; m. Betty Lu Stoklasa, June 29, 1954; children: Keith (dec.), Kevin, Kurt, Kendall, Kristen. AEE, Valparaiso Tech. Inst., 1956; BSEE, U. Colo., 1963. Staff asst. Sandia Corp., Albuquerque, 1956-58; engr. Gulton industries, Albuquerque, 1958-60, Ball Corp., Boulder, Colo., 1960-65; sect. engr. Ball Corp., 1965-69, communications mgr., 1969-79, program mgr., 1979-83, dept. mgr., 1983—, program devel. mgr., 1986—. Contbr. articles to profl. publs. Served with USAF, 1949-52. Mem. Am. Forces Communications and Electronics Assn. (bd. dirs. 1986, v.p. 1987), Optimist (pres. Boulder, dist. lt. gov.). Republican. Roman Catholic. Home: 4435 Burr Pl Boulder CO 80303 Office: Ball Corp 10 Longs Peak Dr Broomfield CO 80020

KUEHN, KLAUS KARL ALBERT, ophthalmologist; b. Breslau, Germany, Apr. 1, 1938; came to U.S., 1956, naturalized, 1971; s. Max and Anneliese (Hecht) K.; m. Eileen L. Nordgaard, June 22, 1961 (div. 1972); children—Stephan Eric, Kristina Annette; m. Lynda O. Hubbs, Oct. 2, 1974. Student, St. Olaf Coll., 1956-57; B.A., B.S., U. Minn., 1961; M.D., 1963. Diplomate Am. Bd. Ophthalmology. Resident in ophthalmology UCLA Affiliated Hosps., 1968-71; practice medicine specializing in ophthalmology, San Bernardino, Calif., 1971—; chief ophthalmology dept. San Bernardino County Med. Ctr., 1979-80; assoc. clin. prof. ophthalmology Jules Stein Eye Inst. and UCLA Med. Ctr., 1978-81. Served to capt. U.S. Army, 1963-64. Fellow Am. Acad. Ophthalmology; mem. AMA, Calif. Med. Assn., Calif. Assn. Ophthalmology (bd. dirs.). Office: 1920 N Waterman Ave San Bernardino CA 92404

KUHLKE, KIM LEE, prosthodontist; b. Denver, Feb. 8, 1946; s. Dale Leslie and Evelyn Lenore (Gurley) K.; m. Dana Boyd, Nov. 6, 1966 (div. 1969); m. Amy Inge, Nov. 3, 1973; children: Scott, Stephen, Mary. Student, U. Colo., 1969-71; DDS, Northwestern U., Chgo., 1975; MS in Prosthodontics, U. Iowa, 1977. Asst. prof. U. Md., Balt., 1977-78; pvt. practice dentistry specialty in prosthodontics Lakewood, Colo., 1978—. Contbr. articles to profl. jours. Mem. Am. Dental Assn., Am. Coll. Prosthodontists, Colo. Dental Assn., Black Forest Soaring Soc. Republican. Office: 7620 W 26th Ave Lakewood CO 80215

KUHN, IRVIN NELSON, hematologist, oncologist; b. Winnipeg, Man., Can., Aug. 18, 1928; s. Gottfried and Wanda Lena Kuhn; m. Doreen Mary L. Elvedahl, July 3, 1956; children: Jill A., Erin R., Jay N. BA in Chemistry, Loma Linda U., 1950; MD, Loma Linda (Calif.) U., 1955. Diplomate Nat. Bd. Med. Examiners, Am. Bd. Internat. Medicine; cert Thai Med. Bd., Clin. Hematology, Med. Oncology; lic. physician, Calif. Rotating intern then resident gen. internal medicine White Meml. Med. Ctr., L.A., 1955-59; resident gen. pathology U. B.C. at Vancouver Gen. Hosp., Can., 1961-63; instr. med. Loma Linda (Calif.) U., 1961-65, asst. prof., 1965-72, assoc. prof., 1972-78, prof., 1978—, cons. in clin. hematology and oncology, 1966—; dir. Adult Hemophilia Treatment Ctr., 1974-85; chief med. svc. Jerry L. Pettis Meml. VA Hosp., Loma Linda, 1977-80, assoc. chief staff edn., 1980—, active staff, 1977—; ind. investigator Nat. Cancer Inst. Leukemia and Chemotherapy, 1970-85; assoc. investigator Western Cancer Study Group, subcom. Lymphoma and Leukemia, 1972-76; mem. Loma Linda Med. Oncology rsch. team Coop. Group Outreach program/Puget Sound Oncology Consortium S.W. Oncology Group, 1985-88; com. grad. med. edn. Loma Linda U. Sch. Medicine, 1980—, health adv. com. 1980-83, chmn. rsch. funding adv. com. 1982-86, acad. com. 1977—, resident tng. com. 1979—, adv. com. Med. Record adminstrn. 1976-78, quality assurance com. 1972-76, transfusion com. 1972-80, risk mgmt. com. 1973-75; mem. clin. exec. coun. Jerry L. Pettis Meml. VA Hosp., 1979—, radiosotope and nuclear medicine com. 1977-89, clin. exec. bd. 1977—, pharmacy adn therapeutics com. 1977-80, rsch. devel. com. 1977-84, dean's com. 1980—, shmn. hosp. edn. com. 1980—, chmn. travel and tuition funds cons. 1980-84, joint conf. coun., 1982-85, chmn. Case Mix Mgmt. steering com. 1984-88; presenter numerous symposia, seminars and confs. to various agys., schs. and health orgns., 1970—; cons. in field. Contbr. articles to profl. jours. Blood Coagulation Rsch. Lab. fellow Churchill Hosp., 1964, Laboratoire d' Hemostase fellow St. Louis Hosp., 1964, clin. and rsch. fellow U. Wash., 1965-66. Fellow ACP (gov.'s adv. com. 1980-88), Royal Coll. Physicians and Surgeons of Can.; mem. AAAS, Walter E. MacPherson Soc. (charter), AMA, CAlif. Med. Assn. (legis. com. 1987, dist. II del. 1983-87, alt. del. 1974-83, comprehensive health plannig commn. 1974-76), San Bernardino County Med. Assn., Loma Linda U. Sch. Medicine Alumni Assn. (life, med. evangelism coun. 1975-76, conv. governing bd. dirs. 1983—, pres. elect., pres. 1988—), Am. Soc. Internal Medicine, Calif. Soc. Internal Medicine, Inland Soc. Internal Medicine, Am. Soc. Hematology, N.Y. Acad. Scis., Am. Soc. Clin. Oncology, L.A. Acad. Medicine, Nat. Assn. VA Physicians, Am. Coll. Physic Exec. San Bernardino County Med. Soc. (numerous offices and com. mems. found. med. care 1970—), Loma Linda Physicians Med. Group, Inc. (bd. dirs. 1969-73), Sigma Xi (life), Alpha Omega Alpha. Office: Loma Linda U Med Ctr Rm 1531 Loma Linda CA 92354 also: Jerry L Pettis Meml VA Hosp Office Assoc Chief Staff Edn 11201 Benton St Loma Linda CA 92357

KUHN, JOSEPH ANTHONY, areospace company executive; b. Roxborough, Pa., July 15, 1923; s. Joseph John and Gertrude (Haas) K.; m. Nancy Coleman, 1951; children: Kevin J., David A., Kathleen M., Carolyn A., Brian A., Christopher M., Dennis M. Student, U. Md., Wiesbaden, Germany, 1950-53, U. Md., Tackikawa, Japan, 1960-63. Commd. 2d lt. USAF, 1943, advanced through grades to col., 1969; stationed at USAF, Warner Robbins AFB, Ga., 1968-69, Saigon, Vietnam, 1969-70, Oklahoma City, 1970-74; retired USAF, 1974; exec. dir. Northrop-Iran Aircraft Industries, Tehran, Iran, 1974-77; supr. contracts Lockheed Aero. Systems Co., Burbank, Calif., 1977--. Mem. P-38 Nat. Assn. (pres. 1987--, editor newsletter 1988), Air Rescue Assn., Retired Officers Assn., Order Daedalians. Republican. Roman Catholic. Home: 25511 La Gosta Pl Valencia CA 91355

KUHNAU, WOLFRAM WILHELM, cell biologist; b. Breslau, Germany, July 23, 1910; s. Wilhelm and Susanna Berta Narie (Opitz) K. Student, Univs. Breslau, Munich, Vienna, 1928-33; MD, U. Vienna, 1934. Intern Univ. Hosps., Breslau, Berlin, Freiburg; staff physician dept. dermatology Doctors Univ. Hosp., 1934-39, Breslau Univ. Hosp., Bonn, 1934-39; staff physician dept. biochemistry U. Leipzig, 1935-37; pvt. practice Bingen, Fed. Republic of Germany, 1945-60, Egypt, Lybia, 1959-60, Wiesbaden, Egypt, Lybia, 1961-80; mem. staff cancer research hosp. Montego Bay, Jamaica, summer 1980, Santa Maria Hosp., Ensenada, Mex., 1980-81; live cell therapy specialist Am. Biologics Research Hosp., Tijuana, Mexico, 1981—; lectr. on live cell biology, Spain, France, Egypt, Iraq, India, Peru, Mex., USSR, Czechoslovakia, Romania, U.S., Belgium. Author: Live Cell Therapy: My Life with a Medical Breakthrough, 1983; contbr. numerous articles on anatomy, vitamins, hormones and sulfonamides to sci. jours.; exhibited paintings in France, Italy, Austria, U.S., Mex., Fed. Republic Germany, also others. With M.C. German Army, World War II. Home: PO Box 2014 San Ysidro CA 92073 Office: Am Biologics Mex SA 1180 Walnut Ave Chula Vista CA 92011

KUIPER, ERIKA LURA SCHMIDT, tax consultant; b. Ottawa, Ill., June 21, 1946; d. Erich Friedrich and Lura Florence (Strawn) Schmidt; children: Julie Anne Lura Kuiper. Student, U. Calif., Santa Barbara, 1965-66, 80, U. So. Calif., L.A., 1982-84. Cert. fin. planner. Office/adminstrv. acct. Faletti Knapp & Jarabin, Santa Barbara, Calif., 1968-73; sr. acct. MacFarlane Kueny & Lishman CPA's, Santa Barbara, 1977-85; pvt. practice tax cons. Santa Barbara, 1985—. Bd. dirs. Am. Heart Assn., Santa Barbara, 1988—, planned giving com. mem., 1986—, endowment bd. 1987—; treas. women's bd. Community Arts Music Assn., 1989—. Mem. Internat. Assn. Fin. Planners (treas. 1984-86), Calif. Soc. Enrolled Agts., Nat. Soc. Enrolled Agts., Am. Soc. Women Accts. Santa Barbara, The Little Town Club, La Cumbre Golf and Country Club, Gals Rep. Club, Channel City Club. Republican.

KUKLIN, JEFFREY PETER, lawyer, talent agency executive; b. N.Y.C., Dec. 13, 1935; s. Norman Bennett and Deane (Cable) K.; m. Jensina Olson, Nov. 18, 1960; 1 son, Andrew Bennett; m. 2d, Ronia Levene, June 22, 1969; children—Adam Blake, Jensena Lynne, Jeremy Brett. A.B., Columbia U., 1957, J.D., 1960. Bar: N.Y. 1962, U.S. Supreme Ct. 1965, Calif. 1973. Atty., TV sales adminstrn. NBC-TV, N.Y.C., 1966-67; asst. to dir. bus. affairs CBS News, N.Y.C., 1967-69; atty., assoc. dir. contracts ABC-TV, N.Y.C. and Los Angeles, 1969-73; v.p. bus. affairs and law Tomorrow Entertainment, Inc., Los Angeles, 1973-75; v.p. legal and bus. affairs Billy Jack Enterprises, Inc., Los Angeles, 1975-76; atty., bus. affairs exec. William Morris Agy., Inc., Beverly Hills, Calif., 1976-79, head TV bus. affairs, 1979-81, v.p., head TV bus. affairs, 1981—. Mem. ABA, Acad. TV Arts and Scis., Los Angeles Copyright Soc. Address: 151 El Camino Dr Beverly Hills CA 90212

KULACKI, FRANCIS ALFRED, engineer, educator; b. Balt., May 21, 1942; s. Frank Alfred and Ida (Jarowski) K.; m. Jane H. Davidson, Nov. 29, 1985; children: Sarah, Nancy. BSME, Ill. Inst. Tech., 1963, MS in Gas Engring., 1966; PhD, U. Minn., 1971. From asst. prof. to assoc. prof. mech. engring. Ohio State U., Columbus, 1971-79; prof., chmn. dept. mech. and aerospace engring. U. Del., Newark, 1980-85; dean engring. Colo. State U., Ft. Collins, 1986—; cons. in field. Contbr. numerous articles to profl. jours. V.p. Columbus Tech. Council, 1979; pres. Arbour Park Civic Assn., Newark, 1985. Fellow ASME (chmn. heat transfer div. 1987-88, pres. Columbus sect. 1978), AAAS, Am. Soc. Engring. Edn., Internat. Assn. Advancement Hydrogen Energy, NSPE: mem. Sigma Xi, Phi Kappa Sigma, Tau Beta Pi, Pi Tau Sigma. Home: 1612 Linden Lake Rd Fort Collins CO 80524 Office: Colo State U Coll Engring Fort Collins CO 80523

KULIKOV, HANYA JEAN, automotive executive; b. Fresno, Calif., Aug. 2, 1956; d. Roy Joe and Mary (Babeshoff) K. BA in Psychology/Russian, Calif. State U., Fresno, 1978. Adminstrv. asst. Berven Carpets, Fresno, 1980-82, Frontier Chevrolet, Fresno, 1983-88; fleet mgr. Michael Automotive Ctr., Fresno, 1988; fin. and ins. mgr. Giant Automotive Ctr., Visalia, Calif., 1988—. Home: 2167 Mayfair Dr West Fresno CA 93703 Office: Giant Automotive Ctr 615 E Main St Visalia CA 93291

KULKARNI, KARMEEN D., dietitian; b. Karachi, Pakistan, Dec. 22, 1953; came to U.S., 1973; d. Ardeshir S. and Mani (Irani) Devitre; m. Rajiv K. Kulkarni, Sept. 15, 1978; 1 child, Anjali. BS, Women's Christian Coll., Madras, India, 1973; MS, Eastern Mich. U., 1974. Registered dietitian; certified diabetes educator. Nutritionist Nebr. Diabetes Project, Lincoln, Nebr., 1978-81; clin. dietitian Kaiser Permanente, Fontana, Calif., 1981, Dept. of Endocrinology, City of Hope Nat. Med. Ctr., Duarte, Calif., 1982-83; nutrition cons. Metabolic Clinic, Utah Dept. of Health, Salt Lake City, 1983-84; dietitian Diabetes Control Program, Utah Dept. of Health, Salt Lake City, 1984-85; clin. dietitian Diabetes Treatment Ctr., Salt Lake City, 1985—; Editorial bd. mem. Diabetes Forecast, mag. of the Am. Diabetes Assn.; state media rep. Utah Dietetic Assn., 1985—. Author: (chpt. in text) Handbook of Diabetes/Nutrition Management, 1987; editor Nutrition Update, (column) The Diabetes Educator, 1982—. Mem. Diabetes Care and Edn. Practice Group of the Am. Dietetic Assn. (chmn. 1988-89; editor of newsletter, 1983-87). Home: 3920 Nora Circle Salt Lake City UT 84124 Office: Diabetes Treatment Ctr 1260 E 3900 S Salt Lake City UT 84124

KULKOSKY, PAUL JOSEPH, psychology educator; b. Newark, N.J., Mar. 3, 1949; s. Peter Francis and Rose Mary (Leonetti) K.; m. Tanya Marie Weightman, Sept. 16, 1978. BA, Columbia U., N.Y.C., 1971, MA, 1972; PhC, U. Wash., 1974, PhD, 1975. Research assoc. Cornell U., White Plains, N.Y., 1980-81, instr. psychiatry, 1981-82; asst. prof. psychology U. So. Colo., Pueblo, 1982-86, assoc. prof., 1986-89, chmn. dept. psychology, 1988—, prof., 1989—; bd. advisors Pueblo Zool. Soc., 1984-85, 1988—, bd. dirs. 1985-88. Ad hoc reviewer NIMH, 1989—; contbr. chpts. to books, articles to profl. jours.; referee psychol. jours. Named Hon. Affiliate Prof. Am. U., Washington, 1977-80; research grantee NIH, 1984—; staff fellow Nat. Inst. Alcohol Abuse and Alcoholism, 1976-80. Mem. N.Y. Acad. Scis., Internat. Brain Rsch. Orgn., Soc. Neurosc., Internat. Soc. Biomed. Rsch. on Alcoholism (charter), Psychonomic Soc., Soc. Study Ingestive Behavior (charter), U. So. Colo. Club Sigma Xi (treas. 1986—, Outstanding Faculty Rsch. award 1985-89), Colo.-Wyo. Acad. Sci. Home: 417 Tyler St Pueblo CO 81004 Office: U So Colo 2200 N Bonforte Blvd Pueblo CO 81001-4901

KULL, DOVE MONTGOMERY, former social welfare administrator; b. Perry, Okla.; d. Andrew J. and Polly Ann (McCurry) Montgomery; m. Alexander E. Kull, June 26, 1929; 1 son, John E. BA, U. Okla., 1922, MSW, 1940; MA, Columbia U., 1927; HHD (hon.), U. Alaska, 1988. Social worker United Providence Assn., Oklahoma City, 1921; head English dept. Fairfax (Okla.) High Sch., 1923-26; English instr. ext. div. U. Okla., Norman, 1927-33; prof. Oklahoma City U., 1933-35; social work intake dir. Fed. Emergency Relief Adminstrn., Okla., 1934-35; asst. state dir. intake and cert., asst. dir. employment div. Works Project Adminstrn., Okla., 1935-41, prin. social worker, 1941; head social svc. Campbell-Galbraith Clinic and Coyne Campbell Sanatorium, Okla., 1941; child welfare worker, asst. state supr., state cons. on foster care and adoption Okla. State Dept. Pub. Welfare, 1941-53; sec. community council Okla. Child and Family Welfare Div., 1953-54; welfare dir. Salvation Army, Okla., 1954-58; child welfare worker Anchorage, 1959-61; state child welfare supr. Juneau, Alaska, 1961-67; clin. social worker USPHS Hosp., Kotzebue, Alaska, 1967-69; exec. di. Episc. Ch. Holy Trinity, 1st United Meth. Ch., Juneau, 1969-76. Active sr. housing com. Commr. Community and Regional Affairs, Juneau, 1976; chmn. Sr. Citizens Adv. Bd., Juneau, 1977; del. Internat. Conf. ERA, Houston, 1977; commr. Older Alaska Commn., 1981—. Named Woman of Yr. Soroptimist Club, 1981, Bus. and Profl. Women's Club, 1981, Sr. Intern Congressman Don Young, 1988; recipient Disting. Svc. award Pioneer and Capital U.S. Jaycees, 1973, Commendation for Svcs. to Elderly Pres. Ronald Reagan, 1982, Citation for Outstanding Contrbns. to Humanity Alaska State Legis., 1987, Andres award Am. Assn. Retired Persons, 1988; Shelter for Victims of Violence named in her honor Aiding Women from Abuse and Rape Emergencies, 1986, Alaskan Sch. Social Work Scholarship (named in her honor) U. Alaska, Anchorage, 1987. Mem. Nat. Assn. Social Workers, Knife and Fork Dinner Club, Blue Pencil, Chi Omega, Theta Sigma Phi, Delta Psi Kappa. Congregationalist. Home: 4675 Glacier Hwy Juneau AK 99801

KULL, WILLIAM FRANKLIN, civil engineer, land surveyor; b. Houston, Nov. 21, 1956; s. William Fredrick and Rita Francis (Natiello) K. BSCE, U. Santa Clara, 1979. Registered civil engr., land surveyor, Calif. Jr. engr. Nowack & Assocs., San Jose, Calif., 1978-82; sr. engr. Sandis & Assocs., Mountain View, Calif., 1982-87; prin. engr. Civil Cons. Group, Cupertino, Calif., 1987-88; founder, prin. Giuliani & Kull Inc., Cupertino, 1988—. Bd. dirs. Community Services Agy., Mountain View, 1986—. Mem. ASCE. (assoc. 1978—). Republican. Episcopalian. Lodge: Kiwanis. Home: 505 Cypress Pt Dr #37 Mountain View CA 94043 Office: Giuliani & Kull Inc 20431 Stevens Creek Blvd #230 Cupertino CA 95014

KULLAS, DANIEL ALBERT, information systems consultant; b. Balt., Aug. 15, 1946; s. Albert John and Joyce May (Gladue) K.; m. Jean Stuart Hench, June 24, 1978; children: Heather Jean, Stephen Albert. BS in Applied Math., U. Colo., 1969; MBA, U. Denver, 1983. Cert. in data processing. Engr. Martin Marietta Aerospace, Denver, 1969-74; sr. systems analyst Sci. Applications, Inc., Englewood, Colo., 1974-80; data processing mgr. Exeter Drilling Co., Denver, 1980-86; ind. info. systems cons. Englewood, 1986--, pvt. practice, 1986--. Author computer software, including Service Control System, 1986. Active Perry Pines Homeowners Assn., Sedalia, Colo., 1975--, Cherry Creek Vista South Homeowners Assn., 1978--; mem. at large adminstrv. bd. Hope United Meth. Ch., Englewood, 1985--, long range planning com., 1987--. Recipient Letter of Commendation NASA, 1978. Mem. Nat. Prime Users Group, Digital Equipment Computer Users Soc., PC Users Group Colo., Data Based Forum, Colo. Prime Users Group (treas. 1985-87), Phi Kappa Psi, Beta Gamma Sigma.

KULSTAD, GUY CHARLES, public works official; b. Bend, Oreg., Feb. 28, 1930; s. John Marlyn and Annie Mildred (Boyd) Kulstad Ibison; B.S. in Civil Engring., U. Calif.-Berkeley, 1958; Registered profl. engr., Calif., Oreg., Wash.; registered traffic engr., Calif.; registered land surveyor, Oreg.; cert. community coll. instr., Calif. m. Bonnie Jane Sherman, Aug. 28, 1955; children—Anne Marie Kulstad Hurst, Mark, Alice Kulstad Krause. Engring. aide county rd. dept., Los Angeles, 1951, asst. civil engr., 1953-58; dir. pub. works, Benicia, Calif., 1958-59; dep. dir. pub. works, Solano County, Calif., 1959-65; dir. pub. works, Humboldt County, Calif., 1965—; gen. mgr. gen. Humboldt Bay Wastewater Authority 1975, 82-89. Mem. joint liaison com. Mcpl. Pub. Works Officers and Calif. County Civil Engrs. and Land Surveyors. Served with AUS, 1951-53. Recipient Outstanding Service award North Bay chpt. Calif. Soc. Profl. Engrs., 1964, Boss of the Year award Arcata Jaycees, Recognition award Humboldt Toastmasters. Fellow ASCE; mem. Nat. Soc. County Engrs. Calif. County Engrs., Nat. Soc. Profl. Engrs., Am. Congress Surveying and Mapping, Nat. Acad. Forensic Engrs., Calif. Land Surveyors Assn. (surveyor award Humbolt chpt.), Calif. County Engrs. Assn. Clubs: Commonwealth of Calif., Sons of Norway. Author profl. dissertations. Office: 1106 2d St Eureka CA 95501

KUM, JIMMY LEE, real estate corporation chief executive; b. San Francisco, Aug. 24, 1923; s. Koon Ting and Sue (Shew) K.; m. May Oy Wong, Mar. 29, 1964; children: Robert J., Lawrence J., David J. AA, City Coll. San Francisco, 1949; BS, U. Calif., Berkeley, 1951; MBA, Columbia Pacific U., 1980; JD, Southland U., 1983. Registered estate planner and mortgage agt., Calif. Head acct. City and County San Francisco, 1951-80; sole proprietor Kum Svcs. Co., San Francisco, 1980-86; chmn. bd., chief exec. officer J.L. Kum Inc., San Francisco, 1986—. Author: Tax Aspect of Real Estate, 1985. Cpl. U.S. Army, 1942-46. Mem. Nat. Soc. Pub. Accts., Internat. Org. Real Estate Appraisers, Nat. Assn. Real Estate Appraisers, Nat. Real Estate Assn. Inc., San Francisco Bd. Realtors, Chinese Am. Citizen Alliance. Democrat. Baptist. Home and Office: 3814 Moraga St San Francisco CA 94122

KUMAGAI, HIROYUKI, aerospace engineer; b. Sendai, Miyagi, Japan, Dec. 21, 1954; s. Ichiro and Shimeko (Nakazawa) K. BE in Astronautics and Astronautics, Tokai U., Hiratsuka, Japan, 1977; MS in Aerospace Engring., U. Kans., 1982, D of Engring., 1984. Post-doctoral research fellow U. Kans. Ctr. for Research Inc., Lawrence, 1984-85; research engr. U. Kans. Ctr. for Research Inc., 1985-87; project engr. Advanced Rotorcraft Tech. Inc., Mountain View, Calif., 1987-89; pres. Aerospace Computing, Inc., Boulder Creek, Calif., 1989—. Mem. AIAA, Am. Helicopter Soc., Sigma Gamma Tau. Office: NASA Ames Rsch Ctr Mail Stop 221-6 Moffett Field CA 94035

KUMAR, RAJENDRA, electrical engineering educator; b. Amroha, India, Aug. 22, 1948; came to U.S., 1980; s. Satya Pal Agarwal and Kailash Vati Agarwal; m. Pushpa Agarwal, Feb. 16, 1971; children: Anshu, Shipra. BS in Math. and Sci., Meerut Coll., 1964; BEE, Indian Inst. Tech., Kanpur, 1969, MEE, 1977; PhD in Electrical Engring., U. New Castle, NSW, Australia, 1980. Mem. tech. staff Electronis and Radar Devel., Bangalore, India, 1969-72; rsch. engr. Indian Inst. Tech., Kanpur, 1972-77; asst. prof. Calif. State U., Fullerton, 1981-83, Brown U., Providence, 1980-81; prof. Calif. State U., Long Beach, 1983—; cons. Jet Propulsion Lab., Pasadena, Calif., 1984—. Contbr. numerous articles to profl. jours. Recipient Best Paper award Internat. Telemetering Conf., Las Vegas, 1986, 4 New Technology awards NASA, Washington, 1987-88. Mem. IEEE (sr.), NEA, Am. Assn. Univ. Profs., Calif. Faculty Assn., Auto Club So. Calif. (Cerritos), Eta Kappa Nu. Home: 13910 Rose St Cerritos CA 90701 Office: Calif State U 1250 Bellflower Blvd Long Beach CA 90701

KUMAR, RAJESH NARAYAN, pediatrician; b. Dehra Dun, India, Feb. 2, 1950; came to U.S.; 1975; s. Brijlal and Subhadra (Gurwara) K.; m. Vinita Nath, June 24, 1979; children: Aditya, Abhishek. MBBS, Armed Forces Med. Coll., Poona, India, 1973. Diplomate Am. Bd. Pediatrics. Intern No. Railway Cen. Hosp., New Delhi, India, 1974, Ellis Hosp., Schenectady, N.Y., 1975-76; resident in pediatrics Luth. Gen. Hosp., Park Ridge, Ill., 1976-78; attending physician Guadalupe Med. Ctr., Carlsbad, N.Mex., 1978—; pres. Carlsbad Children's Med. Ctr., 1978—. Fellow Am. Acad. Pediatrics. Republican. Hindu. Home: 1607 Live Oak Pl Carlsbad NM 88220 Office: 2402 W Pierce #6G Carlsbad NM 88220

KUMLER, ROSE MARIE, career counselor; b. Detroit, Dec. 22, 1935; d. Charles and Aida (Oliveri) Fiorini; m. Frank Wozniak, May 17, 1958 (div. 1975); children: Corrine, Paul; m. John H. Kumler, Apr. 15, 1978 (div. 1988). BBA, Western Internat. U., 1982; MA, U. Phoenix, 1985. Lic. career counselor, Ariz. Sales rep. Vestal Labs., Phoenix, 1978-79; personnel cons. Ford Personnel Cons. Inc., Phoenix, 1979-81; owner, career counselor Specialized Employment Evaluation Devel., Phoenix, 1980—; dist. supr. Grand Canyon Color Lab., Phoenix, 1981-83; acad. dean Lamson Colls., Glendale, Ariz., 1983-86, instr. Phoenix Coll., Ottawa U., Phoenix, 1986—; speaker in field, 1987—. Chair subcom. of task force Ariz. Gov.'s Offices Women's Svcs. Mem. Fellow Impact (mem. strategic planning com. 1988, edn. com. 1988), The Network, Ariz. Career Devel. Assn., Am. Bus. Women's Assn. (sec. 1975), Soroptimist (judge 1988). Roman Catholic. Home and Office: 13630 N 34th Pl Phoenix AZ 85032

KUMMER, GLENN F., mobile home company executive; b. Park City, Utah, 1933; married. B.S., U. Utah, 1961. Sr. acct. Ernst & Ernst, 1961-65; trainee Fleetwood Enterprises Inc., Riverside, Calif., 1965-67, purchasing mgr., 1967-68, plant mgr., 1968-70, gen. mgr. recreational vehicle div., 1970-71, asst. v.p. ops. to v.p. ops., 1971-72, sr. v.p. ops., 1972-77, exec. v.p. ops., 1977-82, pres., 1982—, dir. Office: Fleetwood Enterprises Inc 3125 Myers St Box 7638 Riverside CA 92523 also: Fleetwood Motor Homes of Calif 5300 Via Ricardo Riverside CA 92502 *

KUNDINGER, MATHEW H., author, publisher; b. Wuerzburg, W.Ger., Aug. 7, 1955; s. Joseph and Erika (Endres) K. Diplom. Ingenieur, Fachhochschule, 1982. Sales rep. Michelin Tire Corp., Karlsruhe, W.Ger., 1977; trainee Mercedes-Benz, Wuerzburg, 1983; sales/project engr. Gerhard Schubert Machinery, Crailsheim, W.Ger., 1983-84; tech. support mgr. F&E Hedman-LA, Inc., L.A., 1985-87; gen. mgr. Diamond Copy Products, Gardena, Calif., 1987; pres. 140 Plus Mgmt. Cons., Inc., L.A., 1985--. Author: California Here I Come, 1987. Home: PO Box 34793 Los Angeles CA 90034

KUNIN, JAY S., data processing executive; b. Cleve., Nov. 27, 1949; s. K.C. and Roberta (Shine) K.; m. Gabrielle Pascu, June 5, 1983; 1 child, Lauren Michelle. BS, MIT, 1971, MS, 1972, PhD, 1982. Rsch. engr. West Indies Lab., Christiansted, V.I., 1972-75; software cons. Cambridge, Mass., 1978-81; sr. cons. Hammer & Co., Inc., Cambridge, 1981-83; v.p. Securities Ind. Software Corp., Evergreen, Colo., 1983-87; pres. Lasermax Corp., Golden, Colo., 1987--; chmn. bd. dirs. Legalsoft Corp., Lakewood, Colo., 1986--; mem. exec. com. MIT Ent. Forum Colo., Denver, 1984--; adj. prof. U. Denver, 1987--. Contbr. articles to profl. jours. Mem. IEEE, ACM, Sigma Xi. Office: Lasermax Corp 603 Park Point Dr Ste 220 Golden CO 80401

KUNKEE, RALPH EDWARD, viticulture and enology educator; b. San Fernando, Calif., July 30, 1927; s. Azor Frederick and Edith Electa (Engle) K. AB, U. Calif., Berkeley, 1950, PhD, 1955. Research biochemist E.I. Du Pont De Nemours, Wilmington, Del., 1955-60; prof. enology U. Calif., Davis, 1963—; cons. UNFAO, Bangalore, India, 1986. Co-author: Technology of Winemaking, 1971. Fulbright fellow, Mainz, Fed. Republic Germany, 1970-71, France fellow, Montpellier, France, 1977-78. Mem. Am. Chem. Soc., Am. Soc. Microbiology, Am. Soc. Enology and Viticulture (sec./treas. 1983-85). Home: 820 Radcliffe Dr Davis CA 95616 Office: U Calif Dept Viticulture and Enology Davis CA 95616

KUNKLE, STEVEN KENT, insurance agency executive; b. Ft. Worth, Nov. 11, 1953; s. Richard Patrick and Cherry Ann (Farmer) K.; m. Melissa Ann Boucher, May 29, 1976; children: Matthew, Rachel, Nathan, Hannah. BS, U. Okla., 1976. Area rep. Fellowship Christian Athletes, Okla., 1976-79; assoc. pastor Hoffmantown Bapt. Ch., Albuquerque, 1979-84; owner, mgr. State Farm Ins. Agy., Albuquerque, 1984—. Mem. adv. bd. Albuquerque Pregnancy Ctr., 1986—; vol. coord. Bernalillo County Corky Morris for U.S. Senate Campaign, 1988. Mem. Fellowship Christian Athletes (bd. dirs. N.Mex. 1988). Home: 9609 Camino del Sol NE Albuquerque NM 87111 Office: 1336 Wyoming NE Albuquerque NM 87112

KUNSMAN, DAVID MARVIN, nuclear engineer; b. Quakertown, Pa., Apr. 18, 1949; s. Marvin S. and Wanda S. (Zaleski) K. BS in Nuclear Engring., U. Va., 1971; MS in Nuclear Engring., U. N.Mex., 1972. Nuclear engr. Air Force Weapons Lab., Albuquerque, 1973-75; sect. supr. Falcon R & D Co., Albuquerque, 1976-80; dep. div. mgr. Sci. Applications Internat. Corp., Albuquerque, 1980-83; risk analyst Sandia Nat. Labs., Albuquerque, 1983—; instr. nuclear reactor safety U.S. Nuclear Regulatory Commn., Rockville, Md., 1982-84, IAEA, Chgo., 1987. Contbr. articles to profl. jours. Mem. Soc. for Risk Analysis, N.Y. Acad. Scis., Raven Soc., Tau Beta Pi, Omicron Delta Kappa. Republican. Lutheran. Home: 2904 Candelita Ct NE Albuquerque NM 87112

KUNTZ, NOELLA MAE, pharmacist; b. Harvey, N.D., Dec. 20, 1950; d. John Martin and Kathleen Otillia (Senger) K. BS, N.D. State U., 1974. Registered pharmacist, Wis., Ill., Colo., Ariz. Pharmacist intern Severson Drugs, Pelican Rapids, Minn., 1974-75, Walgreen Drugs, Milw., 1975-76; staff pharmacist Walgreen Drugs, Chgo., 1977-79; chief pharmacist Walgreen Drugs, Naperville, Ill., 1979-82; chief pharmacist Walgreen Drugs, Chgo., 1982-84, dist. pharm supr., 1984-87; pharmacy mgr. Walgreen Drugs, Sun City West, Ariz., 1987-89; supr. cen. dist. pharm. Walgreen Drugs, Phoenix, 1989—. Contbr. articles to profl. jours. Group speaker Walgreens, Chgo., 1979-87; bd. dirs. St. Luke's Cath. Ch., Phoenix, 1988. Mem. Am. Pharmacist Assn., Ill. Pharmacist Assn. (v.p. 1984-85), Ariz. Pharmacist Assn., Walgreen's Ambassador Club, Kappa Epsilon (v.p.). Home: 1010 E Rosemonte Dr Phoenix AZ 85024 Office: Walgreen Drug Co 4545 N 27th Ave Phoenix AZ 85017

KUNTZ, RICHARD PETER, investor; b. Flushing, N.Y., Feb. 21, 1957; s. Richard and Cosette Elaine (George) K. SB, MIT, 1979, SM, 1980; MM, Northwestern U., Evanston, Ill., 1983. Registered rep. Ops. analyst Tex. Internat. Air, Houston, 1980-81; v.p., corp. fin. Prudential Capital Corp., Los Angeles, 1983-89; v.p. 3i Capital Corp., Newport Beach, Calif., 1989—. Lutheran. Office: 3i Capital Corp 450 Newport Ctr Dr Ste 250 Newport Beach CA 92660

KUNZ, DANIEL JAMES, mining company executive; b. Butte, Mont., May 31, 1952; s. Harry Valentine and Mary Louise (McGrath) K.; m. Carol Ann Castiglioni, Aug. 10, 1974; children: Ashley Claire, Alexander Gregory, Andrea Halley. Student, St. Cloud Bus. Coll., 1972-73; BS in Engring. Sci., Mont. Tech. U., 1977; MBA, Boise State U., 1985. Mgr. spl. projects Fingerhut Mfg. Co., St. Cloud, Minn., 1972-73; assoc. engr. Anaconda Minerals Co., Butte, Mont., 1973-77; mining engr. Peter Kiewit Sons Co., Omaha, 1977-79; sr. mining engr. Morrison-Knudsen Co., Boise, Idaho, 1979-82; mgr. project engring., mining group Morrison-Knudsen Co., 1982-87, mgr. contracts, mining group, 1987—; officer, Wildhorse Industries, Sun Valley, Idaho, 1986-87; cons., Tech. Svcs. Contractors, Inc., Boise, 1987-88. Active, Nat. Rep. Congl. Com., Boise, 1984, Internat. Hunger Relief Group, Boise, 1985; fundraiser, Mont. Tech. Found., Butte, 1988. Mem. Northwest Mining Assn., Rocky Mountain Coal Mining Inst., The Planetary Soc., Nev. Mining Assn., Rocky Mountain Mineral Law Found., Mars Watch. Roman Catholic. Home: 1995 Roanoke Dr Boise ID 83712 Office: Morrison Knudsen Co Inc 740 Park Blvd Boise ID 83729

KUO, PING-CHIA, historian, educator; b. Yangshe, Kiangsu, China, Nov. 27, 1908; s. Chu-sen and Hsiao-kuan (Hsu) K.; m. Anita H. Bradley, Aug. 8, 1946. A.M., Harvard U., 1930, Ph.D., 1933. Prof. modern history and Far Eastern internat. relations Nat. Wuhan U., Wuchang, China, 1933-38; editor China Forum, Hankow and Chungking, 1938-40; counsellor Nat. Mil. Council, Chungking, China, 1940-46, Ministry Fgn. Affairs, 1943-46; participated in Cairo Conf. as spl. polit. asst. to Generalissimo Chiang Kai-shek 1943; during war yrs. in Chungking, also served Chinese Govt. concurrently in following capacities: mem. fgn. affairs com. Nat. Supreme Def. Council, 1939-46; chief, editorial and pubs. dept. Ministry Information, 1940-42, mem. central planning bd., 1941-45; tech. expert to Chinese delegation San Francisco Conf., 1945; chief trusteeship sect. secretariat UN, London; (exec. com. prep. commn. and gen. assembly), 1945-46; top-ranking dir. Dept. Security Council Affairs, UN, 1946-48; vis. prof. Chinese history San Francisco State Coll., summers 1954, 58; assoc. prof. history So. Ill. U., 1959-63, prof. history, 1963-72, chmn. dept. history, 1967-71, prof. emeritus, 1972—; sr. fellow Nat. Endowment for Humanities, 1973-74; Pres. Midwest Conf. Asian Studies, 1964. Author: A Critical Study of the First Anglo-Chinese War, with Documents, 1935, Modern Far Eastern Diplomatic History (in Chinese), 1937, China: New Age and New Outlook, 1960, China, in the Modern World Series, 1970; Contbr. to Am. hist. pubs. and various mags. in China and Ency. Brit. Decorated Kwang Hua medal A-1 grade Nat. Mil. Council, Chungking, 1941; Auspicious Star medal Nat. Govt., Chungking, 1944; Victory medal, 1945. Mem. Am. Hist. Assn., Assn. Asian Studies. Club: Commonwealth (San Francisco). Home: 8661 Don Carol Dr El Cerrito CA 94530

KUPERUS, JOHN HENRY, radiopharmicist; b. Meppel, The Netherlands, Mar. 3, 1949; came to U.S., 1956; s. Alric and Winnie K.; m. Robin Lorraine Usrey, Aug. 10, 1973; children: Jonathan, Lauren. BS in Pharmacy, U. of the Pacific, 1973; MS in Radiopharmacy, U. So. Calif., Los Angeles, 1975. Diplomte Am. Bd. Nuclear Pharmacists. Clin. pharmacist Orange County Med. Ctr., Orange, Calif., 1973-74; radiopharmacist VA Hosp., Long Beach, Calif., 1975-82; plant mgr., nuclear pharmacist Medi Nuclear, Baldwin Park, Calif., 1982-83; radiopharmacist Harbor LAC/UCLA Med. Ctr., Torrance, Calif., 1983—; radiopharmacist, research pharmacist, Research and Edn. Inst., Torrance, Calif., 1983—; cons. Med. Ancillary Svcs., Inc., Ft. Worth, 1987-88. Mem. Soc. Nuclear Medicine, Radiopharm. Sci. Council, Am.Soc. of Hosp. Pharmacists, Am. Pharm. Assn. Club: Seal Beach (Calif.) Yacht.

KUPFERMAN, BRUCE, financial company executive; b. San Francisco, May 14, 1947; s. Carl and Mildred Kupferman; m. Carol L. Deweert, Dec. 18, 1982; children: Michael, Brian. AA, Coll. San Mateo, 1971. Loan officer Calif. Tchrs. Union, Burlingame, 1969-73; ops. mgr. Safeway Credit Union Burlingame, 1973-76; collection mgr. Matthews TV, Daly City, Calif., 1976-79; agy. auditor Citicorp Credit Svcs., San Mateo, Calif., 1979-81; collection mgr. SCA Credit, Bellevue, Wash., 1981-84; gen. mgr. Bus. & Profl. Collection Services, Reno, 1984-85; pres., mgr. Credit Bur. Tahoe (Calif.), 1985—. Mem. Internat. Credit Assn. (cert. assoc. credit exec., collection agy. exec.), Sierra Nev. Credit Assn. (pres. 1985-87), Nev. Check Investigators, Calif. Check Investigators. Republican. Home: PO Box 892 Tahoe City CA 95730 Office: Credit Bur Tahoe PO Box 7467 Tahoe City CA 95730

KUPPERBERG, CLIFFORD IVAN, accountant; b. San Francisco, Oct. 2, 1941; s. Abraham and Sylvia (Beinacher) K.; m. Penny May Lewis, Apr. 7, 1961; children: Kenneth Charles, Peter Lewis. BS, San Francisco State U., 1967. CPA, Calif. Asst. gen. acct. Corn Products Corp., San Francisco, 1963-67, staff acct., 1967-69; mng. ptnr. John R. McKean Accts., San Francisco, 1969-85; pvt. practice San Francisco, 1985-87; pres. Kupperberg, Damasco & Assocs., San Francisco, 1987—; bd. dirs. The Lefcourt Group, Palo Alto, Calif., others; cons. in field. Cubmaster Boy Scouts Am., San Francisco, 1971-73, scoutmaster, San Mateo, 1976-77; mem. Riles Com. Edn., San Francisco, 1974. With USCG, 1960. Mem. Am. Inst. CPAs, Calif. Soc. CPAs, Olympic Club (San Francisco). Democrat. Jewish. Office: Kupperberg Damasco & Assocs 1 Market Pla Spear St Tower Ste 1501 San Francisco CA 94105

KURAISHI, AQDAS SARFARAZ, physician. came to U.S., 1979; divorced; children: Alia, Nadia. MD, U. Toronto, 1974. Diplomate Am. Bd. Family Practice. Intern. McMaster U., 1974-75, resident, 1975-76; with various hosps., 1976-79; pvt. practice Oreg., 1979-87; asst. prof. U. Calif., Irvine, 1987—; asst. prof. U. Calif., Irvine, 1988—. Author: When Someone is Dying, 1987. Chmn. PAC, Roseburg, Oreg., 1985; prs. Am. Diabetes Assn., Umpqua chpt., 1984; v.p. Umpqua Valley Horse Assn., Roseburg, 1980. Office: San Bernardino County Med 780 E Gilbert St San Bernardino CA 92409

KURODA, YASUMASA, political science educator, researcher; b. Tokyo, Apr. 28, 1951; came to U.S., 1951; s. Shohei and Take (Ishii) K.; m. Alice Kassis, Mar. 21, 1961; children: Kamilla, Kamil. Student, Waseda U., 1951; BA, U. Oreg., 1956, MA, 1958, PhD, 1960. From instr. to asst. prof. polit. sci. Mont. State U., Bozeman, 1960-64; asst. prof. polit. sci. U. So. Calif., L.A., 1964-66; from assoc. to prof. polit. sci. U. Hawaii-Manoa, Honolulu, 1966—; assoc. program officer advanced projects East-West Ctr., Honolulu, 1967-69; lectr. Japan-Am. Inst. Mgmt. Sci., Honolulu, 1973—; v.p. Minerva Rsch., Inc., Honolulu, 1981—. Author: Reed Town, Japan, 1974, Chiho Toshi no Kenryokukozo, 1976, (with others) Palestinians Without Palestine, 1978; co-editor: Studies in Political Socialization in the Arab States, 1987. Mem. bd. of govs. Japanese Cultural Ctr. Hawaii, Honolulu, 1988—, mem. program com., 1988—. Rockefeller Found. grantee, 1963-64, Social Sci. Rsch. Coun. grantee, 1966-67, Toyota Found. grantee, 1984-87, 87—. Mem. Am. Polit. Sci. Assn., Internat. Polit. Sci. Assn., Internat. Assn. Middle Ea. States (coll. of fellows 1986—). Democrat. Office: U Hawaii Dept Polit Sci Honolulu HI 96822

KUROKAWA, AKEMI, construction executive; b. Tokyo, Feb. 9, 1943; came to U.S., 1974; s. Akira and Aiko (Yokomakura) K.; m. Misako Fujikawa, June 30, 1971; children: Miki, Akito, Akihiro. Student, Calif. State Polytechnic U., 1962-64; BArch, U. So. Calif., 1968. Draftsman Skidmore, Owings & Merrill, Chgo., 1968, San Francisco, 1968-69; planner Mitsui Constrn. Co., Tokyo, 1970-71, Seibu Real Estate Co., Tokyo, 1972-80; project mgr. Seibu Constrn. Co., Tokyo, 1980-83; project mgr. Seibu Hawaii Inc, Maui, 1983-86, dir., 1986—. Mem. Japanese-American Soc. of Honolulu. Mem. United Ch. of Christ. Home: 3675 Woodlawn Terr Pl Honolulu HI 96822 Office: Seibu Hawaii Inc 2237 Kuhio Ave #303 Honolulu HI 96815

KURSEWICZ, LEE Z., marketing consultant; b. Chgo., Oct. 26, 1916; s. Antoni and Henryka (Sulkowska) K.; ed. Chgo. and Bata ind. schs.; m. Ruth Elizabeth Venzke, Jan. 31, 1940; 1 son, Dennis. With Bata Shoe Co., Inc., 1936-78, plant mgr., Salem, Ind., 1963-65, v.p., mng. dir., Batawa, Ont., Can., 1965-71; v.p., dir. Bata Industries, Batawa, 1965-71, plant mgr., Salem, 1971-76; pres. Bata Shoe Co., Inc., Belcamp, Md., 1976-77, sr. v.p., dir., 1977-79; gen. mgr. Harford Insulated Panel Systems div. Hazleton Industries, 1981-82. City mgr. City of Batawa, 1965-71; vice chmn. Trenton (Ont.) Meml. Hosp., 1970-71; pres. Priestford Hills Community Assn., 1979-80; chmn. adv. bd. Phoenix Festival Theatre, Hartford County Community Coll., 81; vice chmn. Harford County chpt. ARC, 1980-81, chmn., 1982-83; chmn. Harford County Econ. Devel. Adv. Bd., 1983-85; mem. Susquehanna Region Pvt. Industry Council, 1983-85. Mem. Am. Mgmt. Assn. Clubs: Rotary, Bush River Yacht (commodore 1956), Bush River Power Squadron (comdr. 1957), Western Hills Country of Salem (pres. 1975), Trenton Country (pres. 1968-69), Md. Country. Home and Office: 29707A Niguel Rd Laguna Niguel CA 92677

KURTH, JAMES EDWIN, aerospace program planning executive; b. Spokane, Wash., July 1, 1926; s. Edwin George and Mary Magadalene (Clancy) K.; m. Dorothy Ione Froland, Sept. 11, 1948 (dec. Mar. 1960); 1 child, James G.; m. Carol Joan Stidham, Jan. 23, 1965; children: Gretchen A., Gregory E., Garrison P., Eileen M., Carolyn J. BS in Physics, U. Portland, 1950. Methods engr. Boeing Co., Renton, Wash., 1950-53; schedule planner Boeing Co., Seattle, 1953-58, program planning mgr., 1958-69, sales coord., 1969-71, equipment mgr., 1971-81, program planning mgr., 1981-86, program requirements mgr., 1986-88, ret., 1988. With USN, 1944-46, PTO. Mem. Boeing Mgmt. Assn. Republican. Roman Catholic. Home: 15675 19th Ave SW Seattle WA 98166

KURTZ, EDMUND STEVEN, small business owner; b. N.Y.C.; s. Theodore G. and Bernice A. (Seioe) K; m. Bernadette Anne Schrader. BBA, Ohio U., 1974. Sales profl. Westlam Foods, Chino, Calif., 1974-78; v.p. sales Westlam Foods, Chino, 1978-84; v.p. Caplin Food Brokers, Beverly Hills, Calif., 1984-87; pres. Caplin Food Brokers, Reseda, Calif., 1987—, Promotional Concepts, Reseda, 1985--. Team mgr. Pony Baseball, Agouna, 1984-88; chmn. Pony Express Days. Mem. U.S. C. of C. (v.p. 1988). Office: Promotional Concepts 6925 Canby Ave # 106 Reseda CA 91335

KURTZIG, SANDRA L., software company executive; b. Chgo., Oct. 21, 1946; d. Barney and Marian (Boruck) Brody; children: Andrew Paul, Kenneth Alan; B.S. in Math., UCLA, 1967; M.S.in aeronaut. engring., Stanford U., 1968. Math analyst TRW Systems, 1967-68; mktg. rep., Gen. Electric Co., 1969-72; chmn. bd., chief exec. officer, pres. ASK Computer Systems, Mountain View, Calif., 1972-85, chmn. bd., 1986-89. Cited one of 50 most influential bus. people in Am., Bus. Week, 1985. Office: ASK Computer Systems Inc 2440 W El Camino Real Mountain View CA 94039-7640

KUSLER, DUANE ALLAN, nurse; b. Denver, Feb. 28, 1963; s. Clifford Edward and Caroline Ann (Lowell) K. AA in Nursing with honors, Highline Community Coll., 1984; BS in Nursing with honors, Pacific Luth. U., 1987. RN, Wash. Nurse emergency room St. Joseph Hosp. and Trauma Ctr., Tacoma, 1984-88, Scripps Meml. Hosp., La Jolla, Calif., 1988—; pub. edn. specialist Tacoma Fire Dept., 1987-88, cons. 1988—; lectr. in field. Contbr. articles to profl. jours. mem. com. Pierce County Emergency Med. Services, Tacoma, 1987-88; chmn. community project CPR Marathon, 1988. Mem. Emergency Nurses Assn. (Spl. Bd. Recognition award, 1988), Nat. Trauma Nurse Network, Wash. Nurses Assn., Am. Nurses Assn., Internat. Honor Soc. Nursing. Roman Catholic. Home: 6502 7th St E Tacoma WA 98424

KUSTAS, FRANK MARK, metallurgical engineer; b. New Haven, Oct. 6, 1953; s. Frank Anthony and Helen Mary (Waznis) K.; m. Gretchen Garnet Gruebele, Oct. 13, 1984. BS in Mech. Engring., U. Colo., 1976; MS in Metallurgical Engring., Colo. Sch. Mines, 1978, postgrad. Tchr. asst., research assoc. Dept. Metallurgical Engring. Colo. Sch. Mines, Golden, 1976-78; engr. research Battelle NW Labs., Richard, Wash., 1978-80; staff engr. Research and Tech. Dept. Martin Marietta Space Systems Co., Denver, 1981—. Contbr. articles to profl. jours. Recipient New Tech. award NASA, 1984. Mem. Am. Soc. Metals. Home: 8026 S Harrison Way Littleton CO 80122 Office: Martin Marietta Astronautics Group 12250 S Hwy 75 Waterton CO 80122

KUSTER, ROBERT KENNETH, scientist; b. Los Angeles, July 11, 1932; s. Arthur Rollo Kuster and Ermine Rosebud (Prittchett) Woodward. AS, Gavilan Coll., 1974, AA in Humanities, 1981; student, San Jose State U., 1955, 1974-76, UCLA, 1977. Installer Western Electric Co., Inc., Corpus Christi, Tex., 1951-52, 1955, San Jose, Calif., 1957-58, 1960-83; ptnr., scientist, cons. WE-Woodward's Enterprises, Morgan Hill, Calif., 1975—; technician AT&T Tech., Inc., San Jose, 1983-85; scientist pvt. pr ce, Gilroy, 1978—. Served to sgt. U.S. Army Corps Engrs., 1952-54. Mem. AAAS, Astron. Soc. Pacific, Calif. Acad. Scis., N.Y. Acad. Scis., Am. Legion, VFW. Baptist. Lodge: Elks. Home: 420 W 9th St PO Box 1113 Gilroy CA 95021 Office: Woodward's Enterprises 179 Bender Dr Morgan Hill CA 95037

KUTSKO, JACQUELYN PATTI, teacher, writer, speaker; b. Akron, Ohio, Mar. 27, 1945; d. Pete and Carolyn (Naglic) Patti; BA, U. Akron, 1967; MEd., Colo. State U., 1983; m. James Andrew Kutsko, June 10, 1967; 1 son, James Andrew. Tchr. bus. N.E. High Sch., Pasadena, Md., 1967, Athens-Draughon Bus. Coll., Athens, Ga., 1967, McAuley High Sch., Cin., 1971-72; tchr. bus., coord. Scarlet Oaks Joint Vocat. Sch., Cin., 1972-73; instr. bus. Barnes Bus. Coll., Denver, 1974-76; pres., owner Finishing Touches, Englewood, Colo., 1976-78; bus. and med. office cons., 1976-78; tchr. bus. Smoky Hill High Sch., Aurora, Colo., 1976—; lectr. profl. groups. Mem. Med. Office Asst.'s Adv. Bd., Community Coll. Denver, 1976; pres. bus. adv. com. Cherry Creek Schs., 1983-84; mem. Superintendent's Com. in Excellence, 1983-84; mem. Subcom. to Study the Content of the Curricular Program, 1983-84; mem. Secondary Computer Edn. Coun., 1983-84; co-chmn. Smoky Hill Computer Edn. Com., 1983-84; mem. com. to Plan Needs/Design of District's Fourth High Sch., 1983-84; chmn. Life Skills/Concepts task force, mem. staff devel. com., mem. composer Curriculum com., 1988—. Mem. NEA, Nat. Bus. Edn. Assn., Mountain Plains Bus. Edn. Assn., Colo. Vocat. Assn., Colo. Educators For and About Bus., Nat. Speaker's Assn., Colo. Speaker's Assn., Cherry Creek Tchrs. Assn., Am. Vocat. Assn., U.S. Figure Skating Assn., Delta Pi Epsilon, Phi Delta Kappa. Club: Denver Figure Skating. Author: Broncos: From Striped Socks to Super Bowl and Beyond, 1980; Houghton-Mifflin Typewriting-Keyboard Mastery and Applications, 1st and 2d yr. texts, 1984, Houghton Mifflin Keyboarding, 1987, Houghton-Mifflin Info. Processing, 1st and 2d yr. texts, 1989; contbr. articles in field; presenter rsch. studies to profl. assns. Home: 8378 E Jamison Circle S Englewood CO 80112 Office: Smoky Hill High Sch 16100 E Smoky Hill Rd Aurora CO 80015

KUTZSCHER, BERND MICHAEL, ophthalmologist; b. Oxnard, Calif., Apr. 12, 1950; s. Edgar Walter and Edith Hildegard (Wagner) K.; m. Marilyn Marchese, Oct. 16, 1982; children: Lauren, Elizabeth. AB in History, Stanford (Calif.) U., 1971, MD, 1981. Intern Georgetown U., Washington, 1981-82; resident Pacific Presbyn. Med. Ctr., San Francisco, 1982-85; mem. med. staff King Khaled Eye Specialist Hosp., Riyadh, Saudi Arabia, 1986-88; mem. clin. faculty Pacific Presbyn. Med. Ctr., San Francisco, 1988—, Stanford U. Med. Ctr., 1989; pvt. practice Daly City, Calif., 1988—. Home: 72 22nd Ave San Francisco CA 94121 Office: 1850 Sullivan Ave #540 Daly City CA 94015

KUVSHINOFF, BERTHA HORNE, painter, sculptor; b. Dungeness, Wash., Aug. 29, 1915; d. Mellon Tobias and Mariamagdalena (Volnagel) Horne; m. Nicolai V. Kuvshinoff. Represented in numerous mus., pvt. and pub. collections, including Evansville (Ind.) Art Mus., Miami (Fla.) Mus. Modern Art, Seattle Art Mus., World's Fair, Seattle, 1962-63. Recipient Diploma of Merit of Univ. of Arts, Univ. Delle Arti, Rome, Italy. Studio: 121 1/2 Yale Ave N Seattle WA 98109

KUVSHINOFF, NICOLAI VASILY, painter, sculptor. m. Bertha Horne. Exhibited in group shows at Cimaise de Paris Galerie, 1956, 57, La Galerie Norval, Paris, 1957, Smith Tower Gallery, Seattle, 1960, World's Fair, Seattle, 1962, 63, Wash. Capitol Mus., Olympia, 1965, Cath. Ctr. Art Gallery, Balt., 1967, Kupsick Art Gallery, 1969 and numerous others; represented in permanent collections Seattle Art Mus., Phoenix Art Mus., Santa Fe Art Mus., Tacoma Art Mus., Miami (Fla.) Art Mus. and many others; represented in numerous pub. and pvt. collections in France, Brazil, India, Can., Alaska, Japan, Tangier and U.S.; author: (books) Art Book, 1959, Drawings, 1966. Studio: 121 1/2 Yale Ave N Seattle WA 98109

KUWABARA, DENNIS MATSUICHI, optometrist; b. Honolulu, July 20, 1945; s. Robert Tokuichi and Toshiko (Nakashima) K.; m. Judith Naomi Tokumaru, June 28, 1970; children: Jennifer Tomiko, Susan Kazuko. BS, So. Calif. Coll. Optometry, 1968, OD cum laude, 1970. Pvt. practice optometry Waipahu, Honolulu, Hawaii, 1972—; Pres. 1st Study Club for Optometrists, Honolulu, 1982-83; chmn. bd. examiners in Optometry, Honolulu, 1982—; state dir. Optometric Extension Found., Honolulu, 1980—. Served to lt. Med. Service Corps, USN, 1970-72. Named Outstanding Young Person of Hawaii, Hawaii State Jaycees, 1979. Fellow Am. Acad. Optometry; mem. Hawaii Optometric Assn. (pres. 1979-80, Man of Yr. award 1976, Optometrist of Yr. 1983), Am. Optometric Assn., Armed Forces Optometric Soc. Home: 94-447 Holaniku St Mililani Town HI 96789 Office: 94-748 Hikimoe St Waipahu HI 96797 also: 1441 Kapiolani Blvd Ste 710 Honolulu HI 96814

KUZNIK, ROBERT WILLIAM, manufacturing company executive; b. Springfield, Ill., Sept. 5, 1947; s. Robert William and Margaret F. (Schuerman) K.; m. Carolyn Sue Winnett, Feb. 1, 1969; children: Brian, Cindy. BS, Calif. State U., Sacramento, 1969. Prodn. mgr. FMC Corp., L.A., 1969-71; asst. dir. pub. works City of Palm Springs, 1971-77; pres. Jaycox Disposal Co., Anaheim, Calif., 1977-88, Delaney Sash & Door Co., Los Alamitos, Calif., 1988—. Contbr. articles to profl. pubs. Council mem., mayor City of Placentia, Calif., 1982-85; dir. Anaheim Meml. Hosp. Med. Ctr., 1986—. Named Citizen of Yr., Cypress Coll., Calif., 1988, Mgr. of Yr. award, Soc. for Advancement of Mgmt., Orange Coast chpt., 1985. Mem. Pvt. Industry Coun., Anaheim C. of C. (pres. 1987-88). Republican. Home: 487 Kiolstad Placentia CA 92670 Office: Delaney Sash & Door Co 10850 Portal Dr Los Alamitos CA 90720

KWAN, CHO YIU, developer and entrepreneur; b. Hong Kong, Kowloon, U.K., Dec. 22, 1962; s. Shiu Lit Kwan and Wai KAm Tang. BArch, U. So. Calif., 1987. Registered architect, Calif. V.p. Canton Food Co., L.A., 1978; draftsman Choy & Assocs., Los Angeles, 1983—; designer Duplanty Architects, Los Angeles, 1984—, PBWS Architects, Los Angeles, 1986—; constrn. mgr. Hannon Devel., Los Angeles, 1986—; pres. K.S. Ventures, Inc., Los Angeles, 1988—, Kwan Devel. Corp., Los Angeles, 1988—; archtl. designer Kwan Devel., Los Angeles, 1988. Mem. AIA, Archtl. Guild, Sigma Alpha Mu. Office: Kwan Devel 1100 E 5th St Los Angeles CA 90013

KWOK, SAMUEL K., transportation executive; b. Hong Kong, Nov. 8, 1955; s. Po-Sin and Yuk Hing (Leung) K.; m. Ellen Y. Poon-Kwok, Sept. 5, 1986. BBA, Chaminade U., 1979. Mgr. C.L. Thomson Express Internat. Corp., San Francisco, 1984—. Recipient Tsuru award Japan Airlines, Honolulu, 1987, Grand Tsuru award, 1988, 89. Mem. Fgn. Travel Club. Home: 1571 Piikoi St 1101 Honolulu HI 96822 Office: CL Thomson Express Internat Corp 1585 Kapiolani Blvd 1838 Honolulu HI 96814

KWONG, LEONARD LON, dentist; b. Sacramento, Calif., Apr. 22, 1923; s. King Lamb and Kwan Ming (Lee) K.; m. Ellen Lun Luk, Nov. 25, 1956; children: Arden Lon, Lenelle Lon, Glenn Lon. BS, DDS, Coll. Physicians and Surgeons, San Francisco, 1947. Gen. practice dentistry Glendale, Calif., 1947-50, Sacramento, 1950-51, 52—. Deacon, elder Chinese Community Ch. Served to capt. U.S. Army, 1950-53, Korea. Decorated Korean Svc. medal with 2 battle stars, UN medal, Combat Med. badge. Mem. ADA (life), Calif. Dental Assn. (life), Sacramento Dist. Dental Soc. (life), Coll. Physicians and Surgeons Alumni Assn., Sacramento Chinese Bowling Assn., VFW (life). Office: 2430 L St Sacramento CA 95816

KYD, CHARLES WILLIAM, writer, consultant; b. Columbia, Mo., June 11, 1948; s. Charles Ream and Beverly (Steele) K.; m. Marilyn Joyce Gratton. BJ, U. Mo., 1970; MBA, U. Wash., 1979. Controller Summit-Dana Indsl. Corp., Bozeman, Mont., 1972-76; acctg. mgr. Hewlett-Packard, Corvallis, Oreg., 1979-81; v.p. fin. Gradco Systems, Inc., Santa Ana, Calif., 1981-82; v.p. Albert Computers, Thousand Oaks, Calif., 1982-83; v.p. fin. Jungle Growth Garden Product, Inc., Thousand Oaks, 1984-85; mgmt. cons. Arthur Young & Co., Seattle, 1986-87; pres. Cash Master Bus. Systems, Seattle, 1987—. Author: Financial Modeling Using Lotus 1-2-3, 1986, Microsoft Excel Business Sourcebook, 1988; columnist Inc. mag., 1986—, Lotus mag., 1985—, PC World, 1988. Lt. U.S. Navy, 1970-72. Mem. MENSA, Nat. Assn. Accts. Republican. Presbyterian. Office: Cash Master Bus Systems 12345 Lake City Way NE Ste 220 Seattle WA 98125

KYD, MARILYN GRATTON, writer, editor; b. Wichita, Kans., Jan. 26, 1948; d. Robert and Celia (Goldman) Gratton; m. Charles W. Kyd, Mar. 25, 1984. AA, Pasadena City Coll., 1967; BA in English and History, UCLA, 1969. Cert. secondary tchr., Calif. Tchr. English Glendora (Calif.) High Sch., 1970-72; tchr. English and creative writing Hueneme High Sch., Oxnard, Calif., 1972-76; employment counselor Snelling & Snelling, Oxnard, 1976-77; ptnr., mgr. MG Pers. Agy., Santa Monica, Calif., 1977-78; tech. writer, editor Stanwick Corp., Ventura, Calif., 1978-80; engring. writer Northrop Corp., Oxnard, 1980; logistics analyst Automation Industries, Vitro Labs., Oxnard, 1980-81; mgr. documentation Computer Data Corp., Westlake Village, Calif., 1981-82; dir. mktg. Kiely Profl. Svcs., Westlake Village, 1983-84; pres., owner CashMaster Bus. Systems, Inc., Seattle, 1984—; owner, operator profl. resume preparation bus.; free-lance tech. writer and editor. Author: It's A Good Thing I'm Not Married, 1975, The Question Caper: A Nosmo King Mystery; contbr. articles to profl. jours. Named Young Careerist Bus. Profl. Women, 1975; recipient 3rd pl. Nat. Writers Club articles contest, 1976, 2nd pl. for photography Port Hueneme Harbor Days, 1976, Honorable mention Writer's Digest Articles Contest, 1987. Mem. NAFE, Nat. Writers Club, Soc. Tech. Communication, UCLA Alumni Assn., Mensa (columnist 1978, proctor Channel Islands area). Office: Cashmaster Bus Systems Inc 12345 Lake City Way NE Ste 220 Seattle WA 98125

KYL, JON LLEWELLYN, congressman; b. Oakland, Nebr., Apr. 25, 1942; s. John and Arlene (Griffith) K.; m. Caryll Louise Collins, June 5, 1964; children: Kristine Elizabeth, John Jeffry. BA, U. Ariz., 1964, LLB, 1966. Atty. Jennings, Strouss & Salmon, Phoenix, 1966-86; mem. 100th, 101st Congresses from 4th Ariz. dist., 1987—. Founding dir. Crime Victim Found., Phoenix Econ. Growth Corp.; former bd. mem. Ariz. Acad., vice chmn. bd. litigation Mountain States Legal Found.; past chmn. Outstanidng Young Rep., 1969-70; gen. counsel Ariz. Young Rep. League; adv. dir. State Grand Old Party, 1971-75; precinct committeeman Ariz. Rep. Caucus. Mem. Ariz. State Bar Assn., Maricopa County Bar Assn., Phoenix Met. C. of C. (past chmn.). Office: US Ho of Reps 313 Cannon Bldg Washington DC 20515

KYLE, HENRY CHARLES, III, trade association executive; b. Washington, Jan. 19, 1951; s. Henry Charles and Lois Marion (Suter) K.; m. Glenise Madoline Kyle, June 24, 1973 (div. 1981); m. Susan Jean Thede, June 26, 1982; children: Brandon Charles, Cody Mathew. BA in Polit. Sci., Ottawa U., 1973; MPA, U. N.Mex., 1975. Supt. Heritage Bldrs., Gaithersburg, Md., 1973-74; personnel intern City of Albuquerque, 1974-75; asst. to exec. v.p. Albuquerque Bd. Realtors, 1976-77, dir. adminstrn., 1977-80; exec. dir. Ind. Ins. Agts. Colo., Inc., Denver, 1981-82; exec. v.p. Ind. Ins. Agts. Colo., Inc., 1982, Edn. Found., 1988—; exec. v.p. Ind. Ins. Agts. Svcs. Corp., Denver, 1988—; bd. dirs. Colo. Ins. Edn. Found., Denver, 1984—; pres. Computer Purchasing Group, Denver, 1986—. Editor Colo. Ins. News, 1981—. Mem. Am. Soc. Assn. Execs. (cert.), Colo. Soc. Assn. Execs. (bd. dirs. 1989—). Republican. Episcopalian. Home: 8064 Owens Way Arvada CO 80005 Office: Ind Ins Agts Colo Inc 1127 E 16th Ave Denver CO 80218

KYTE, LYDIANE, botanist; b. L.A., Jan. 6, 1919; d. Aurele and Helen Scott (Douglas) Vermeulen; m. Robert McClung Kyte, June 2, 1939; children: Katherine, Bobbin, William Robert. BS, U. Wash., 1964. Supt. Weyerhaeuser Co., Rochester, Wash., 1972-77; lab mgr. Briggs Nursery, Olympia, Wash., 1977-80; owner Cedar Valley Nursery, Centralia, Wash., 1980—; cons. Internat. Exec. Service Corps, Stamford, Conn., 1987. Author: Plants From Test Tubes: An Introduction to Micropropagation, 1983. Mem. Internat. Plant Propagators' Soc., Tissue Culture Assn., Internat. Assn. Plant Tissue Culture, Am. Assn. for Hort. Sci., Am. Assn. Univ. Women (treas. 1979). Home and Office: Cedar Valley Nursery 3833 McElfresh Rd Sw Centralia WA 98531

KYZER, HERBERT HAYNES, civil engineer; b. Conway, S.C., Apr. 20, 1934; s. Herbert Haynes and Elizabeth (Jones) K.; m. Sally Wetherby Stickney, June 28, 1954; children: Valery G., Herbert L., Christel L. AA, Mira Costa Coll., 1982. Rodman, transit man S.C. Highway Dept., 1947-54; party chief Middlesex (N.J.) Township Engring. Dept., 1960-64; prin. engring. tech. County Sanitation Dists. Orange County, Fountain Valley, Calif., 1964-76; sr. engring. tech. City of Carlsbad (Calif.) Water Dept., 1977-83; sr. civil engr. Ultra Systems, Inc., Irvine, Calif., 1982-89; asst. civil engr. J.F. Davidson Assocs., Inc., Rancho, Calif., 1989—; Served to 1st class surveyor USN, 1954-60. Mem. Am. Soc. Plumbing Engrs. Home: 24403 Trails End Dr Murrieta CA 92362 Office: JF Davidson Assocs Inc 27349 Jefferson Ave Rancho CA

LAACK, HELEN STIRMEL, underwriting and marketing consultant; b. Elkhorn, Wis., Nov. 5, 1945; d. George Benjamin and Virginia May (Brereton) Stirmel; m. James Emil Laack, July 4, 1964; children: Lance Erik, Darcie Meredith, Torrey Alan. Cert. in teaching, Sheboygan County Tchrs. Coll., 1967; BA, Ariz. State U., 1979. CPCU. Elem. sch. tchr. Riverview Mid. Sch./Plymouth (Wis.) Pub. Schs., 1968-69; market & opinion rsch. interviewer Roper, Sheboygan County, 1969-74; nutritional/mgmt. cons. Bell County Opportunity Workshop, Middlesboro, Ky., 1976; mgmt. intern, ops. supr. Prudential Property and Casualty Ins., Scottsdale, Ariz., 1979-82, underwriting/mktg. cons., 1983—. Founding bd. dirs., sec. Western Lee County Health Clinic, Ewing, Va., 1974-76; mem. exec. bd. Calvary Found., Calvary Rehab. Ctr., Phoenix, 1989—, 2d vice chmn. So. Scottsdale Community Council, 1988—; disaster preparedness vol. Christian Reformed World Relief Com., Middlesbrook (Ariz.), Phoenix, 1974-76, 82—. Mem. Mensa. Republican. Home: 8113 E Weldon Scottsdale AZ 85251 Office: Prudential Property & Casualty 7337 E Doubletree Ranch Rd Scottsdale AZ 85258

LAALY, HESHMAT OLLAH, research chemist, roofing consultant; b. Kermanshah, Iran, June 23, 1927; came to Germany, 1951, Can., 1967, U.S., 1984; s. Jacob and Saltanat (Afshani) L.; m. Parvaneh Modarai, Oct. 7, 1963; (div. 1971); children: Ramesh, Edmond S.; m. Parivash M. Farahmand, Feb. 7, 1982. BS in Chemistry, U. Stuttgart, Republic of Germany, 1955, MS in Chemistry, 1958, PhD in Chemistry, 1962. Chief chemist Kress Sohne, Krefeld, Republic of Germany, 1963-67; analytical chemist Gulf Oil Research Ctr., Montreal, Que., Can., 1967-70; material scientist Bell-Northern Research, Ottawa, Ont., Can., 1970-71; research officer NRC of Can., Ottawa, 1972-84; pres. Roofing Materials Sci. and Tech., Los Angeles, 1984—; scientist, bd. dirs. Non Smokers Assn. Ottawa, 1982; lectr. profl. assns., U.N. Devel. Programs worldwide. Mem. Inst. Roofing and Waterproofing Cons., Single-Ply Roofing Inst., Assn. Profl. Engrs. Ontario, AAAS (Can.), Am. Chem. Soc., ASTM, Internat. Union of Testing and Research Labs. for Material and Structures (tech. com. 1975), UN Indsl. Devels. Orgns., Internat. Conf. Bldg. Ofcls., Can. Standard Assn., Can. Gen. Standards Bd. Home and Office: 9037 Monte Mar Dr Los Angeles CA 90035

LABADIE, BRUCE ALAN, public relations executive; b. San Francisco, Sept. 4, 1950; s. Emile Lucian Jr. and Evelyn (Clow) L.; m. Geraldine Josephine Puth, Dec. 10, 1976; 1 child, Brian. BS, Santa Clara (Calif.) U., 1972; postgrad., San Jose (Calif.) State U., 1974. Owner Plantation Plant Stores, San Jose and Palo Alto, Calif., Calif., 1972-76; dir. pub. relations San Pedro Square Mchts. Assn., San Jose, 1976-78; owner Downtown Prods., San Jose, 1978-79; mgr. publicity Paul Masson Vineyards, Saratoga, Calif., 1979-84; dir. pub. relations Seagram Wine Co., Saratoga, Calif., 1984-87, Vitners Internat., Saratoga, Calif., 1987—; dir. Paul Masson Summer Series, Saratoga, 1979—. Bd. dirs. Woman's Alliance Shelter, 1980-86, Bus. Vols. for Arts, 1987—; active United Way (dir. special events com. 1983—); mem. San Jose Jazz Soc. (v.p. 1987—). Named Vol. of Yr. United Way, 1986. Mem. Santa Clara Winegrowers (bd. dirs. 1979-88, v.p. 1980-82), Monterey Winegrowers Council (bd. dirs. 1985-88), Market Devel. Wine Inst. Democrat. Roman Catholic. Office: Paul Masson Vineyards 14831 Pierce Rd Saratoga CA 95070

LABONTE, JOVITE, insurance company executive; b. Providence, R.I., Jan. 16, 1933; s. Jovite and Madeleine (Blake) LaB.; m. Jane Ann Lipscomb, Nov. 1, 1958; children: Joanne, David, Tracy. A.B. with honors, Brown U., 1956. Agt. N.Y. Life Ins. Co., Arlington, Va., 1960-62, asst. mgr., 1962-64; regional dir. Alexander Hamilton Life Ins. Co., Grosse Pointe, Mich., 1964-65; v.p. Alexander Hamilton Life Ins. Co., Farmington, Mich., 1965-71; exec. v.p. Gt. Am. Life Ins. Co., Los Angeles, 1971-72, pres., 1972—, chief exec. officer, 1972. Served to 1st lt. USMC, 1956-60. Mem Am. Council Life Ins. (chmn. exec. round table com. 1983-86, bd. dirs. 1984-88); mem. Assn. Calif. Life Ins. Cos. (dir. 1982—), Nat. Assn. Life Underwriters. Home: 807 Napoli Pacific Palisades CA 90272 Office: Great Am Life Ins Co 6330 San Vicente Blvd Los Angeles CA 90048

LA BOUNTY, HUGH ORVICE, university administrator; b. Chgo., Sept. 22, 1927; s. Hugh Orvice and Dorothy (Cooper) La B.; m. Judith Lane Hess, June 20, 1987. B.A., U. Redlands, 1950, M.A., 1951; Ed.D., UCLA, 1961. Mem. faculty Citrus Coll., Azusa, Calif., 1950-53; mem. faculty dept. social scis. and history Calif. State Poly. U., Pomona, 1953—; v.p. acad. affairs Calif. State Poly. U., 1967-77, pres., 1977—; cons., Tanzania, Greece, PRC, United Arab Emirates. Author: Government of California, 1957. Mem., trustee Pomona Econ. Devel. Corp. U. Redland Bd. Served with USNR, 1945-46. Mem. Pomona C. of C. (dir.). Office: Calif State Poly U Office of Pres 3801 W Temple Ave Pomona CA 91768-2290

LABOVITZ, LAURENCE BRIAN, lawyer; b. New Haven, Aug. 19, 1946; s. Abraham Isadore and Edith (DiVerniero) L.; m. Geraldine Fernandez, Aug. 12, 1985. BA, Calif. State U.-Northridge, 1970; JD, Southwestern U., 1975. Bar: Calif. 1976; cert. tchr., Calif. Tchr. L.A. Unified Sch. Dist., 1073-75; sole practice, L.A., 1976-81, 83—; exec. v.p., gen. counsel Mgmt. Three, Beverly Hills, Calif., 1981-82; spl. liaison Rep. Nat. Com., Washington, 1977-81. Office: 3055 Wilshire Blvd Ste 900 Los Angeles CA 90010

LACELL, JAMES LEROY, naval electronics technician; b. Rome, N.Y., Aug. 1, 1953; s. Glenn Leroy and Phoebe Ernestine (Pritchard) L.; m. Tania Marie Johnson, Sept. 25, 1976 (div. Mar. 1980); m. Gwendalyn Fern Russell, Oct. 18, 1980; children: Leah Anne, James Glenn, Rebekah Lyn. AS, SUNY, Morrisville, 1974. Enlisted USN, 1975; reactor operator USS Richard B. Russel USN, Groton, Conn., 1977-79, reactor ops. supr. USS Boston, 1979-82; reactor plant supr. USS Alabama USN, Bangor, Wash., 1983-86, personnel mgr. naval subase, 1987-89, reactor plant supr. USS Alaska, 1989—. Trustee, mem. choir Tracyton (Wash.) United Meth. Ch., 1987—. Republican. Office: USS Alaska SSBN 732 BLUE FPO Seattle WA 98799-2111

LACHAPELLE, FRANK J(OSEPH), data processing executive; b. San Francisco, May 31, 1940; m. Ann Lindstrom Scott, Jan. 19, 1962 (div. Mar. 1972); m. Carole Key Crane, Oct. 11, 1975; stepchildren: Steven Scott Crane, Shawn Marie Crane. BS in Math., U. Wash., 1961. Assoc engr. Boeing Aircraft Co., Seattle, 1962; programmer, analyst System Devel. Corp., Santa Monica, Calif., 1962-66; sr. programmer Bunker-Ramo, Heidelberg, Germany, 1966-69; group head System Devel. Corp., Santa Monica, 1969-71; designer, developer, researcher, Abacus Programming Corp., Santa Monica, 1971-73; v.p. Interscience Systems, Inc., Canoga Park, Calif., 1973-83; pres., owner Interscience Computer Corp., Agoura Hills, Calif., 1983—. Mem. IEEE, Nat. Computer Svc. Network, Computer Dealers & Lessors Assn., Assn. Computing Machinery, Las Virgenes C. of C., Malibu C. of C., Chief Exec. Officers Club, North Ranch Country Club (Westlake Village, Calif.). Republican. Office: Intersci Computer Corp 5171 Clareton Dr Agoura Hills CA 91301

LACK, LARRY HENRY, professional inventor; b. Richland, Wash., Aug. 27, 1952; s. Eugene Herman and Myrtle (Wellman) L.; m. Patricia Ann Henry, Aug. 19, 1978; children: Vicki Marie, Rachel Ann. Enlisted USAF, 1970; aircraft mechanic Ill., S.C., Okla. AFBs., 1970-78; inventor, prin. Lack Industries, Inc., Shreveport, La., 1979-85, Phoenix, 1985—; cons. U.S. Air Force, Altus AFB, 1978-80, Cates & Phillips Patent Attys., Phoenix, 1985—; pres. La. Innovators Tech., Shreveport, 1981-82; lectr. Glendale Community Coll. 1987-88. Republican. Home: 3010 W Colter Unit 6 Phoenix AZ 85017 Office: The Lack Group 4621 N 16th St Ste F-608 Phoenix AZ 85016

LACOMBE, RITA JEANNE, computer sales executive; b. Panama City, Fla., Sept. 28, 1947; d. Robert Rosairio and Virginia May (Mauldin) L. AA, Los Angeles Pierce Coll., 1967; BSBA, Calif. State U., Northridge, 1969; postgrad., Stanford U., 1986. Br. mgr. Security Pacific Nat. Bank, San Fernando Valley, Calif., 1970-78; bankcard compliance officer, asst. v.p. Security Pacific Nat. Bank, Woodland Hills, Calif., 1978-82; sect. mgr., v.p. Security Pacific Nat. Bank, Los Angeles, 1982-87; sr. sales rep. corp. microcomputer sales ComputerLand, L.A., 1987-88; corp. sales rep. microcomputer sales ComputerLand, Northridge, Calif., 1988—. Membership chair Sierra Club, Los Angeles, 1982. Mem. Nat. Assn. Female Execs. Democrat. Roman Catholic.

LACY, KENNETH E., customs broker; b. San Francisco, Apr. 22, 1956; s. Albert W. Sr. and Gladys M. Lacy. Grad. high sch., San Bruno, Calif. Lic. U.S. customhouse broker. Asst. sec. Internat. Activities Corp., Burlingame, Calif., 1973-80; owner KEL Internat., Burlingame, 1980—. pres., Carlmont Townehome House Owners Assn., Belmont, Calif., 1989, pres., 1988. Office: KEL Internat 1838 El Camino Real #111 Burlingame CA 94010

LACY, LEE MARVA LOU, educator; b. Longview, Tex., Dec. 28, 1942; d. Louis and Grace Tecumseh (Davis) Armstrong; BS in Math., Prairie View (Tex.) A&M U., 1965; MA in Secondary Math. Edn. (grantee Roosevelt Sch. Dist. 1977-78), Ariz. State U., 1978; m. Troy Lee Lacy, June 20, 1965; children: Corwyn Enrico, Aimee Siubhan, Gardenia Catriona. Tchr. math. schs. in Tex., Nebr., Md. and Ariz., 1965-68, 69-77; sr. gen. edn. instr., counselor Washington Jobs Corps, 1968; tchr. math., spl. tchr. for gifted C.O. Greenfield Jr. High Sch., Phoenix, 1978-82; math and gifted resource tchr. T.B. Barr Sch., Phoenix, 1982-85; instr. math. South Mountain Community Coll. at Ariz. State U., Tempe, 1985-87, Glendale Community coll. MCCCD, 1987—; faculty assoc. Prairie View A&M U., 1981-83; vis. math. tchr. South Mountain Community Coll., Phoenix, 1982-85; workshop leader, cons. in field. Vol., Arthritis Found., Leukemia Soc.; v.p., trustee sanctuary choir First Instl. Bapt. Ch., Phoenix. Mem. Nat. Council Tchrs. Math., NEA, Assn. Supervision and Curriculum Devel., Ariz. Edn. Assn., Ariz. Assn. Tchrs. Math., Roosevelt Classroom Tchrs. Assn., Ariz. State U. Alumni Assn., Am. Math. Assn. 2-Yr. Colls., Delta Sigma Theta Alumnae. Baptist. Home: 9404 S Kenneth Pl Tempe AZ 85284 Office: Glendale Community Coll 02-122 GCC Glendale AZ 85302

LACY, PAMELA KAY, nurse; b. Midland, Tex., Feb. 6, 1962; d. Ferrell Dean and Melba Darlene (Clark) Waddle. AS in Nursing, N.Mex. State U., 1982. RN, N.Mex. Charge nurse Lakeview Christian Home, Carlsbad, N.Mex., 1982-86, Guadalupe Med. Ctr., Carlsbad, 1986—. Named Outstanding Young Woman Am., 1987. Democrat. Home: 922 Valverde St Carlsbad NM 88220 Office: Guadalupe Med Ctr 2430 W Pierce Carlsbad NM 88220

LACY, SUZANNE L., marketing professional; b. Fond du Lac, Wis., Feb. 10, 1947; d. Roy Raymond and Mildred Marie (Buck) Ludvigsen; m. James David Lacy, Dec. 17, 1967; children: Merissa Anne, James Kenneth. Student, Hardbarger Bus. Coll., 1965-66. Office mgr. Indsl. Siding Co., Salt Lake City, 1979-81; adminstrv. asst. to dir. MIDECO, Salt Lake City, 1981-82; customer svc. mgr. MIDECO/Utah Biomed. Test Lab., Salt Lake City, 1982-85; sr. mktg. specialist, mgr. adminstrv. svcs. Utah Biomed. Test Lab., Salt Lake City, 1985—; pres., owner Metal Concepts Co., Salt Lake City, 1987—. Republican. Pentecostal. Office: Utah Biomed Test Lab 520 Wakara Way Salt Lake City UT 84108

LADD, ALAN WALBRIDGE, JR., motion picture company executive; b. Los Angeles, Oct. 22, 1937; s. Alan Walbridge and Marjorie Jane (Harrold) L.; m. Patricia Ann Beazley, Aug. 30, 1959 (div. 1983); children: Kelliann, Tracy Elizabeth, Amanda Sue; m. Cindra Kay, July 13, 1985. Motion picture agt. Creative Mgmt., Los Angeles, 1963-69; v.p. prodn. 20th Century-Fox Film Corp., Los Angeles, 1973-74; sr. v.p. 20th Century-Fox Film Corp. (Worldwide Prodns. div.), Beverly Hills, Calif., 1974-76; pres. 20th Century-Fox Pictures, 1976-79, Ladd Co., Burbank, Calif., 1979-83; pres., chief operating officer MGM/UA Entertainment Co., 1983-86; chief exec. officer MGM/UA Entertainment Co, from 1986, also chmn. bd. dirs.; chmn., chief exec. officer Metro-Goldwyn-Mayer Pictures, Inc., Culver City, Calif., until 1988; pres. Am. Pathe Entertainment, Los Angeles, 1989—. Producer: (films) Walking Stick, 1969, A Severed Head, 1969, TamLin, 1970, Villian Zee and Co, 1971, Fear is the Key, 1973; exec. producer: (films) Nightcomers, 1971, Vice Versa, 1988. Served with USAF, 1961-63. Office: Am Pathe Entertainment 640 S San Vicente Blvd Los Angeles CA 90048

LADD, DONALD MCKINLEY, JR., retired lawyer; b. Huntington Park, Calif., Oct. 24, 1923; s. Donald McKinley and Rose (Roberts) L.; B.A., Denison U., 1945; J.D., Stanford U., 1950; m. Eleanor June Martin, June 29, 1951; children—Donald, Richard, Cameron. Admitted to Calif. bar, 1950; asso. firm Anderson McPharlin & Conners, Los Angeles, 1951; legal staff Union Pacific RR, Los Angeles, 1953-56; sr. dep. prosecutor City of Pasadena (Calif.), 1956-58; with Office of Dist. Atty., Santa Clara County, Calif., 1958-88, asst. dist. atty., 1971-88. Served to capt. USMCR, 1943-46, 51-52. Certified criminal law specialist Calif. Mem. Bay Area Prosecutors Assn., Calif. State Bar, Calif. Dist. Attys Assn., Stanford Law Alumni Assn., Blue Key, Omicron Delta Kappa, Phi Alpha Delta. Clubs: Marines Meml., Am. Commons, English-Speaking Union, Brit. Am. Home: 1034 Golden Way Los Altos CA 94022 Office: Office of Dist Atty Santa Clara County 70 W Hedding St San Jose CA 95110

LADEHOFF, ROBERT LOUIS, bishop; b. Mar. 19, 1932; m. Jean Arthur Burcham; 1 child, Robert Louis Jr. Grad., Duke U., 1954, Gen. Theol. Sem., 1957, Va. Theol. Sem., 1980. Ordained deacon, priest The Episcopal Ch., 1957;. Priest in charge N.C. parishes, 1957-60; rector St. Christopher's Ch., Charlotte, N.C., 1960-74, St. John's Ch., Fayetteville, 1974-85; bishop, co-adjutor of Oreg. 1985, bishop, 1986—. Office: Diocese of Oreg PO Box 467 Lake Oswego OR 97034 *

LADEN, CYNTHIA See NEWMAN, CYNTHIA

LADION, GERTRUDES JUMAWAN, law librarian; b. San Antonio, Siquijor, Philippines, Nov. 15, 1937; came to U.S., 1974; d. Felix Samson and Felisa (Rubio) Jumawan; m. Caesar B. Ladion Sr., Oct. 5, 1963; children: Georgina, Caesar Jr., Pierre. BL, Silliman U., Dumaguete City, Philippines, 1960. Courts law librarian Dumaguete City, 1962-68, courts research atty., 1969-71, br. clk. cts., 1971-74; law librarian San Joaquin County, Stockton, Calif., 1975—; librarian pvt. law and acctg. libraries, Stockton; part-time mgr. retirement facility; cosmetics salesperson. Pres. Siquijor Protective Assn., Stockton, 1987—. Mem. Integrated Bar of the Philippines, Council of County Law Librarians of Calif., No. Calif. Assn. of Law Libraries. Republican. Roman Catholic. Home: 2210 N Orange Stockton CA 95204 Office: San Joaquin County Law Library 300 Courthouse Stockton CA 95202

LADMAN, JERRY R., economist, educator; b. Sioux City, Iowa, Dec. 30, 1935; s. Harry L. and Amy I. (Swearingen) L.; m. Mary E. Ladman, June 4, 1960; children—Jeffrey, James, Michael. B.S., Iowa State U., 1958, Ph.D., 1968. Placement officer Coll. Agr., Iowa State U., Ames, 1963-65, research asst., 1965-67; asst. prof. Ariz. State U., 1967-72, assoc. prof., 1972-78, prof. econs., 1979—, dir. Ctr. for Latin Am. Studies, 1976—; program asst. Ford Found., Mexico City, 1971-72; vis. prof. Nat. Sch. Agr., Chapingo, Mex., 1965-67, 71-72, Ohio State U., 1979; vis. scholar Stanford U., 1975; hon. prof. Cath. U. Bolivia, 1986; participant U.S.-U.S.S.R. Cultural Exchange, 1986. Author: The Development of Mexicali Regional Economy, 1975, United States-Mexican Energy Relationships: Realities and Prospects, 1981, Modern Day Bolivia: The Legacy of the Revolution and Prospects for the Future, 1982, Mexico: A Country in Crisis, 1987; contbr. articles to profl. jours., chpts. to books. Chmn. troop com. Boy Scouts Am., Tempe, Ariz., 1976-84; bd. dirs. Friends of Mexican Art, 1977-86. Served to capt. USAR, 1958-65. Fulbright lectr., Ecuador, 1974. Mem. Am. Econ. Assn., Am. Agrl. Econ. Assn., Latin Am. Studies Assn., Pacific Coast Council Latin Am. Studies (treas. 1977-86, v.p. 1986, pres. 1987), Rocky Mountain Council Latin Am. Studies (bd. dirs. 1976—), Phoenix Com. Fgn. Relations, Ariz.-Mex. Commn. (bd. dirs. 1982—), Assn. Borderlands Scholars (pres. 1983-85), PROFMEX (bd. dirs. 1983—). Home: 1201 E Loyola Dr Tempe AZ 85282 Office: Ariz State U Ctr Latin Am Studies Tempe AZ 85287

LAFARO, ANGELO JOHN, infosystems specialist; b. Poteau, Okla., June 2, 1949; s. Angelo John Sr. and Nettie Marie (Stephens) LaF.; m. Lydia Elizabeth Camozzo, June 9, 1979. BA, Northeastern Okla. State U., 1978; postgrad., Okla. State U., 1980-85. Cert. Data Processor. Successively applications programmer, systems analyst, project leader, EDP strategic planner Phillips Petroleum Co., Bartlesville, Okla., 1978-86, mgr., 1982-86; dir. Data Resources div. Maricopa County Govt., Phoenix, 1986-89; mgr. govt. accts. Computerland Major Accts., Phoenix, 1989—. Creator, marketer copyrighted Boone Busters T-Shirt, 1985. V.p. Green County March of Dimes, Bartlesville, 1982-84. Served with USAF, 1969-72. Fellow NSF, Boulder, Colo., 1977, Rotary Found., Taiwan, 1983. Mem. Rotary (treas. Phoenix Sunrise club 1988-89). Republican. Roman Catholic. Home: 1131 E Stephens Dr Tempe AZ 85283 Office: Computerland Major Accts 15002 N 25th Dr Ste 2 Phoenix AZ 85023

LAFAYETTE, MICHAEL EUGENE, nurse practitioner; b. Maquoketa, Iowa, July 8, 1949; s. Gerald George and Margaret Catherine (Jenkinson) L.; m. Nancy Joan Kampling, Aug. 8, 1980; children: Joan, Laura. BS, Iowa State U., 1972; BS in Nursing, U. Iowa, 1981; MS in Nursing, U. Colo., 1983; postgrad., U. Nebr., 1984-85. Lic. family nurse practitioner. Staff nurse St. Anthony's Hosp., Denver, 1981-82; instr. U. Nebr., Lincoln, 1983-85; nurse practitioner St. Francis Meml. Hosp., West Point, Nebr., 1986, Carrizozo (N.Mex.) Health Ctr., 1986-87, Lovelace Med. Ctr., Albuquerque, 1988—; cons. Lincoln Med. Edn. Found., 1984-85. Sgt. USAF, 1974-78. Mem. N.Mex. Nurses Assn., N.Mex. Nurse Practitioner Coun., Coun. Primary Health Care Nurse Practitioners, Sigma Theta Tau. Home: 6540 Esther NE Albuquerque NM 87109 Office: Lovelace Med Ctr 5400 Gibson Blvd SE Albuquerque NM 87108

LAFFEY, JAMES KEVIN, public safety communications management consultant; b. Seattle, June 2, 1952; s. Cyril Joseph and Mary Ann (Heinrich) L.; m. Maureen Patrice Alleman, Apr. 23, 1983. BA, St. Vincent Coll., 1975; MA, Ind. U., Pa., 1982. Emergency med. tech. and fire sci. coord. Westmoreland County Community Coll., Youngwood, Pa., 1974-78; exec. dir. Westmoreland County Emergency Mgmt., Greensburg, Pa., 1978-85; dir. communications City of Gainesville (Fla.) and Alachua County, 1985-88; sr. cons. The Warner Group, Woodland Hills, Calif., 1988—; instr. Am. Red Cross and Heart Assn., Greensburg, 1970-85; emergency mgmt. cons. Fed. Emergency Mgmt. Agy., Emmitsburg, Md., 1982; adv. bd. mem. Emergency Communications Profl. Assn., Gainesville, 1988—. Contbr. articles to profl. jours.; guest lectr. Coll. of Law U. Fla., 1986, 87, 88. Vol. firefighter Greensburg Vol. Fire Dept., 1968-85; emergency med. tech. Mutual Aid Ambulance Svc. Inc., Greensburg, 1968-85. Recipient award of excellence Nat. Assn. Counties, Washington, 1980, achievementaward, 1985. Mem. Am. Soc. Indsl. Security, Radio Club Am., Associated Pub. Safety Communications Officers (voice and data network com. 1987-88), Elks. Office: The Warner Group 5950 Canoga Ave Ste 600 Woodland Hills CA 91367

LAFLER, KIRK PAUL, computer information scientist; b. Penn Yan, N.Y., Feb. 27, 1956; s. Paul Alton and Eleanor Theresa (Gombar) L.; m. Darlynn Joan Lasky, July 7, 1984. BS, U. Miami, 1978, MS, 1982. Pvt. practice computer cons. Miami, Fla., 1976-78; jr. programmer analyst Rydacom Inc., Miami, 1978-79; systems engr. Electronic Data Systems Corp., Washington, 1979-81; programmer analyst Great Am. Fed., San Diego, 1981-82; systems analyst San Diego Gas and Electric Co., 1982-83; pres., chief exec. officer Software Intelligence Corp., San Diego, 1984—; instr. info ctr. So. Calif. Edison Co., Rosemead, 1983-85; computer seminar speaker, San Diego, 1983—. Contbr. articles to profl. jours. Sponsor and contbr. Children Inc., Richmond, Va., 1980—, Muscular Dystrophy Assn., N.Y.C., 1985—, Am. Heart Assn., San Diego, 1987—. Mem. Am. Assn. for Artificial Intelligence. Republican. Roman Catholic. Office: Software Intelligence Corp PO Box 1390 Spring Valley CA 92077-0220

LAFLER-BOTELHO, KENDRA LOIS, business owner; b. El Paso, Tex., Mar. 19, 1961; d. Kenneth Albert and Cynthia Anne (Witherspoon) Lafler; m. Paul Christopher Botelho, Jan. 16, 1982 (div. May 1983). Clk. Bank of the West, Santa Clara, Calif., 1978-81; customer svc. clk. Bankmatic Systems, Beaverton, Oreg., 1982-83; cons. Denver, 1983-86; sales rep. Dictaphone Corp., Portland, Oreg., 1985-87; owner, mgr. Lafler Svcs., Portland, 1986-88; pres. Premier Techs., Inc., 1988—. Recipient Good Citizenship award DAR, 1978. Mem. SW Profl. Assn., NAFE, Oreg. Cons. Assn. Democrat. Presbyterian. Office: Lafler Svcs Inc 1075 NW Murray Rd Ste 174 Portland OR 97229

LAFLEUR, LAWRENCE EUGENE, research chemist; b. Everett, Wash., Sept. 18, 1951; s. Eugene Harvey and Marie Margarett (Longberg) LaF. BS summa cum laude, U. Puget Sound, 1975; MS, U. Oreg., 1977. Cert. profl. chemist. Lab. technician U.S. Oil & Refining Co., Tacoma, 1972-75; research asst. U. Oreg., Eugene, 1975-77; research chemist Nat. Council Paper Industry for Air and Stream Improvement, Corvallis, Oreg., 1977-83, organic analytical program mgr., 1983—; environ. cons. forest products industry, 1979—. Recipient Student Affiliate award Am. Chem. Soc., 1975; La Pore award U. Puget Sound, 1974. Fellow Am. Inst. Chemistry; mem. Am. Chem. Soc., Am. Soc. Mass Spectrometry, Am. Pub. Health Assn. (standard methods com.). Assn. Ofcl. Analytical Chemists. Home: 27060 Forest Springs Ln Corvallis OR 97330 Office: NCASI 720 SW 4th St PO Box 458 Corvallis OR 97339

LAFONT, ROBERT JAMES, infosystems specialist; b. Long Beach, Calif., Nov. 21, 1952; s. Robert Lou LaFont and Evelyn Jean (Ovrid) Armijo. Grad. high sch., Long Beach, Calif. Software designer GTE, Long Beach, 1975—. Mensa. Republican. Roman Catholic. Home: 2052 Pine Ave Long Beach CA 90806 Office: GTE 200 W Ocean Blvd Long Beach CA 90802

LA FORGE, RALPH LEROY, JR., health care center executive, educator; b. Nashville, Dec. 10, 1946; s. Ralph Leroy and Dorthy (Flowers) La F.; 1 child: Frank. BS in Zoology, U. Tex., 1974; MS in Physiology, U. Wis., La Crosse, 1975. Dir. preventive medicine Sharp Healthcare, San Diego, 1978—; instr. health U. Calif., San Diego, 1981—; cons. Dept. Energy, Albuquerque, 1976-82, Nat. Ctr. for Health Promotion, Ann Arbor, Mich., 1985; instr. Nat. U., San Diego, 1980—, Rancho La Puerta, Tecate, Mex.; speaker in field. Contbr. articles to profl. publs. Bd. dirs., San Diego Heart Assn., 1985-. With USAF (Vietnam), 1965-69. Named Vol. of Yr., N. Mex. Heart Assn. 1977; recipient Pub. Edn. award San Diego Heart Assn., 1980. Mem. Am. Coll. Sports Medicine, Aerospace Med. Assn. Democrat. Home: 5390 Rimview Way San Diego CA 92124

LAGASSE, BRUCE KENNETH, structural engineer; b. Bklyn., Feb. 1, 1940; s. Joseph F. Lagasse and Dora S. Gould. BSME, U. Calif., Berkeley, 1964. Structures engr. Rockwell Internat., Canoga Park, Calif., 1964-69; mem. tech. staff Hughes Aircraft Co., Los Angeles, 1969-70; scientist/engr. Hughes Aircraft Co., El Segundo, Calif., 1972—; sr. engr. Litton Ship Systems, Los Angeles, 1971-72; lectr. Hughes Aircraft Co., El Segundo, 1980—; cons. in field, Van Nuys, Calif., 1979—. Libertarian state chmn., Los Angeles, 1977-79, nat. committeeman, Washington, 1979-81. Mem. ASME. Home: PO Box 5235 Sherman Oaks CA 91403

LAGESCHULTE, ROGER EARL, lawyer; b. Waverly, Iowa, June 16, 1936; s. Fred A. and Alice L. (Koenig) L.; m. Lee Olson, June 7, 1958; 1 child, Lisa Lynn. BA in Bus. cum laude, Wartburg Coll., 1960; LLB, U. Ill., 1963. Bar: Wash.1964. Assoc. Clodfelter et al, Seattle, 1964-67, ptnr., 1967-69; ptnr. Krutch, Lindell et al, Seattle, 1969-77, Blackburn, Moren & Lageschulte, Seattle, 1977-81, Moren, Lageschulte & Cornell, Seattle, 1981-88; pvt. practice Seattle, 1988—. Bd. dirs. Burden Bearers, Seattle, 1977-88, Underground Ministries, Bothell, Wash., 1985-88. Mem. ABA, Wash. State Bar Assn., Seattle-King Bar Assn. (chmn. tax sect. 1974-75), Alpha Chi. Republican. Home: 17030 14th St NW Seattle WA 98177 Office: 1155 N 130th St Ste 310 Seattle WA 98133

LAGINESS, DUANE AUGUST, furniture manager; b. Rockwood, Mich., Feb. 25, 1934; s. Legrand Jerome and Lucile Marie (Goniea) L. Grad. high sch., Trenton, Mich. Mgr., designer Design Imports, Pasadena, Calif., 1964-72, Mel Brown Furniture, Los Angeles, 1972—. Mem. Rep. Task Force. Roman Catholic. Home: 4621 Allott Ave Sherman Oaks CA 91423

LAGOMARSINO, ROBERT JOHN, congressman; b. Ventura, Calif., Sept. 4, 1926; s. Emilio J. and Marjorie (Gates) L.; m. Norma Jean Mabrey, Nov. 10, 1960; children: Dexter, Karen, Dana. B.A., U. Calif., Santa Barbara, 1950; J.D., U. Santa Clara, Calif., 1954. Bar: Calif. 1954. Individual practice law Ventura, 1954; mem. Ojai (Calif.) City Council, 1958-61, mayor, 1958-61; mem. Calif. Senate, 1961-74, 93d-101st Congresses from 19th Calif. Dist., 1974—; mem. fgn. affairs com., house interior and insular affairs com.; sec. Rep. Conf. Served with USNR, 1944-46. Recipient Pearl Chase Conservation Edn. award, 1970; recipient Legislator Conservationist of Year award Calif. Wildlife Fedn., 1965, Honor award Calif. Conservation Council, 1967, Peace Officers Research Assn. award, 1966. Mem. Calif. Bar Assn., Ventura County Bar Assn., D.C. Bar Assn. Republican. Roman Catholic. Clubs: Elks, Moose, Eagles, Rotary. Office: 2332 Rayburn House Office Bldg Washington DC 20515 *

LAGOPOULOS, BASIL SIMON, architect; b. Jerusalem, July 1, 1933; came to U.S., 1954; s. Simon K. Lagopoulos and Katherine Christedes; married; children: Cynthia, Ann. Student, Marquette U., 1956-58; AA, Milw. Inst. Tech., 1963; student, Heald Sch. of Architecture, San Francisco, 1963-64. Registered architect, Wis., Ariz., N. Mex. Designer, architect various archtl. firms, Milw., 1962-73; chief architect Donohue & Assocs., Sheboygan, Wis., 1973-77; project architect Lendrum Group, Sullivan, Masson and Fonce Architects, Phoenix, 1978-83; cons. architect B.S.L. Assocs., Phoenix, 1983—. Plan rev. bd. City of Glendale, Wis., 1970-73. Mem. AIA, Nat. Council Archtl. Registration, Scottsdale, Ariz. C. of C. (local affairs 1987-88, govtl. affairs rev. bd. 1988—). Lodge: Elks. Office: BSL Assocs 3883 E Thomas Phoenix AZ 85018

LAGUE, RICHARD P., publisher; b. Apr. 26, 1944; married; four children. BA, Coll. of the Holy Cross, 1966; postgrad., Purdue U., 1971; student bus. adminstr., U. Calif., Berkeley, 1971-72, UCLA, 1978-79. Product mgr. Yankee Motor Co., Schenectady, N.Y., 1972-73; dir. mktg. Can.-Am. Motorcycles, 1973-76; pub. Motorcyclist Mag. Petersen Pub., L.A., 1976-82, motorcycle div. Petersen Pub. Co., L.A., 1982—. Capt. USAF, 1967-70. Mem. Motorcycle Industry Coun. (bd. dirs. 1975-76, 1987—, public relations com. 1977-82, land use com. 1982-87, aftermarket com. 1987—), Am. Coalition of Recreational Pubs. (bd. dirs.). Home: 18434 Bermuda St Northridge CA 91326 Office: Petersen Pub Co 8490 W Sunset Blvd Los Angeles CA 90069

LAHL, LYNDA LEA, nurse; b. Decatur, Ill., Oct. 21, 1961; d. Paul Eddie and Linda Lee (Lynch) Hartig; m. Michael Gene Yonker, Sept. 23, 1978 (div. 1980); m. Dennis Anthony Lahl, July 19, 1986; children: Angela Sue, Mary Elizabeth. AA in Nursing, Lincolnland Community Coll., 1983. RN Calif., Ill. Nurse St. John's Hosp., Springfield, Ill., 1983-85, Alavarado Hosp. Med. Ctr., San Diego, 1985-89, Straub Clinic & Hosp., Honolulu, 1989—. Leader, San Diego coun. Girl Scouts Am., 1987-89. Mem. Nat. Assn. Orthopedic Nursing, Ill. Heart Assn. (co-chmn, 1980-81). Democrat. Lutheran. Office: Straub Clinic & Hosp 888 S King St Honolulu HI 96813

LAHO, RALPH, automation project engineer; b. Melrose Park, Ill., Feb. 22, 1942; s. Rudolph and Margaret (Greenway) L.; m. Nancy Elizabeth Madden, Sept. 28, 1985. BA in Engring. Sci., St. Procopius Coll., 1964; BSEE, U. Notre Dame, 1965. Weapons systems engr. Grumman Aerospace Corp., Bethpage, N.Y., 1965-73; product engr. Kulicke & Soffa, Santa Clara, Calif., 1973-74; equipment engr. Nat. Semiconductor Co., Santa Clara, 1974-80; maintenance mgr. Philips Corp., Eindhoven, Netherlands, 1985-87; maintenance mgr. Signetics Corp., Albuquerque, 1980-85, automation project engr., 1987—. Author: RIB Navigation System, 1972. Mem. Am. Vacuum Soc., Soc. Mfg. Engrs. Republican. Home: PO Box 541 Placitas NM 87043 Office: Signetics Corp 9201 Pan American Frwy NE Albuquerque NM 87184

LAI, SHIH-TSE JASON, chemistry researcher, educator; b. Chia-yi, Republic of China, Oct. 29, 1951; came to U.S., 1977, naturalized, 1985; s. Chi-Kuei and Yu-Lien (Kao) L.; m. Wei Bamboo Lee, June 25, 1980; 1 child, Jeffrey. BS, Nat. Chung-Hsing U., Taichung, Republic of China, 1974; PhD, CUNY, 1983; postgrad., West Coast U. Adminstrn. asst. Tunghai U., Taichung, 1976-77; adjunct lectr. CUNY, Bklyn., 1977-78; research fellow CUNY, Flushing, 1978-83; sr. chemist semicondtr. products div. Rockwell Internat., Newport Beach, Calif., 1983-85; head mass spectrometry lab., sr. staff scientist, project scientist Tech. & Ventures div. Baxter Healthcare Corp., Irvine, Calif., 1985-89, head gas, liquid chromatography, mass spectrometry lab., 1989—; vis. assoc. prof. Ta-Hwa Inst. Tech., Hsinchu, Republic of China, 1986, 87; instr. tech. workshops Analytical Svc. Ctr. Tech. & Ventures div. Baxter Healthcare Corp., Irvine, 1985—; seminar speaker Union Chem. Labs., Cen. Police Acad., Nat. Sun Yat-Sen U., Nat. Chung-Hsing U., Republic of China, 1987, mem. planning com., Pacific Conf. on Chemistry & Spectroscopy, 1989. Contbr. numerous articles to profl. jours. Coach Tunghai U. Rugby Team, 1976-77; patron Laguna Moulton Playhouse, Laguna Beach, Calif., 1986-87; mem. Orange County Sheriff's Adv. Bd. University fellow, CUNY, 1977; recipient Fellow A scholarship CUNY, 1978-83. Fellow Am. Inst. Chemists; mem. AAAS, N.Y. Acad. Scis., Am. Chem. Soc. (mem. program com. Orange County chpt. 1985-87), Chinese Culture Assn. (pres. CUNY chpt. 1978-80), Friends Orange County Performing Art Ctr., Nat. Chung-Hsing U. Alumni Assn. (v.p. So. Calif. chpt. 1986-88, pres. 1989—), Taiwan Benevolent Assn. (nat. advisor 1985—, adv. So. Calif. chpt. 1986—, v.p., dir. 1984-86), Asian Am. Alliance Calif. (co-founder, co-chmn.), Am. Soc. Mass Spectrometry, So. Calif. Mass Spectrometry (chmn. program com. 1988—), Fedn. Chinese Student Assn. in USA (bd. dirs. 1978-80), Joint Chinese U. Alumni Assn. So. Calif. (bd. dirs. 1988—), Sigma Xi.

LAI, WAIHANG, educator; b. Hong Kong, Jan. 7, 1939; s. Sing and Yuching (Wong) L.; came to U.S., 1964; BA, Chinese U. Hong Kong, 1964; MA, Claremont Grad. Sch., 1967; m. Celia Cheung, Aug. 13, 1966. Asst. prof. art Maunaolu Coll., Maui, Hawaii, 1968-70; instr. art Kauai (Hawaii) Community Coll., 1970—. Vis. prof. art Ariz. State U., Tempe, summer 1967. Mem. Am., Kauai (pres. 1974—) watercolor socs., Phila. Watercolor Club, Kauai Oriental Art Soc. (pres. 1981—). Author: The Chinese Landscape Paintings of Waihang Lai, 1966, The Watercolors of Waihang Lai, 1967. Home: PO Box 363 Lihue HI 96766 Office: Kauai Community Coll Lihue HI 96766

LAIDLAW, HARRY HYDE, JR., entomology educator; b. Houston, Apr. 12, 1907; s. Harry Hyde and Elizabeth Louisa (Quinn) L.; BS, La. State U., 1933, MS, 1934; Ph.D. (Univ. fellow, Genetics fellow, Wis. Dormitory fellow, Wis. Alumni Research Found. fellow), U. Wis., 1939; m. Ruth Grant Collins, Oct. 26, 1946; 1 dau., Barbara Scott Laidlaw Murphy. Teaching asst. La. State U., 1933-34, research asst., 1934-35; prof. biol. sci. Oakland City (Ind.) Coll., 1939-41; state apiarist Ala. Dept. Agr. and Industries, Montgomery, 1941-42; entomologist First Army, N.Y.C., 1946-47; asst. prof. entomology, asst. apiculturist U. Calif.-Davis, 1947-53, asso. prof. entomology, assoc. apiculturist, 1953-59, prof. entomology, apiculturist, 1959-74, asso. dean Coll. Agr., 1960-64, prof. entomology emeritus, apiculturist emeritus, 1974—; coord. U. Calif.-Egypt Agrl. Devel. Program, AID, 1979-83. Rockefeller Found. grantee, Brazil, 1954-55, Sudan, 1967. Trustee, Yolo County (Calif.) Med. Soc. Scholarship Com., 1965-83. Served to capt. AUS, 1942-46. Recipient Cert. of Merit, Am. Bee Jour., 1957; Spl. Merit award U. Calif.-Davis, 1959; Merit award, Calif. Central Valley Bee Club, 1974; Merit award Western Apicultural Soc., 1980, Gold Merit award Internat. Fedn. Beekeepers' Assns., 1986; recipient Disting. Svc. award Ariz. Beekeepers Assn., 1988. Cert. of Appreciation Calif. State Beekeepers' Assn., 1987: NIH grantee, 1963-66; NSF grantee, 1966-74. Fellow AAAS; mem. Am. Genetics Assn., Am. Inst. Biol. Scis., Am. Soc. Naturalists, Am. Soc. Zoologists, Entomol. Soc. Am. (C.W. Woodworth award Pacific br. 1981), Genetics Soc. Am., Internat. Bee Research Assn., Nat. Assn. Uniformed Services, Ret. Officers Assn. (2d v.p. Sacramento chpt. 1984-86), Scabbard and Blade, Sigma Xi (treas. Davis chpt. 1959-60, v.p. chpt. 1966-67), Alpha Gamma Rho (pres. La. chpt. 1933-34, counsellor Western Province 1960-66). Democrat. Presbyterian. Author books, the most recent being: Instrumental Insemination of Honey Bee Queens, 1977; Contemporary Queen Rearing, 1979; author slide set: Instrumental Insemination of Queen Honey Bees, 1976. Home: 761 Sycamore Ln Davis CA 95616 Office: U Calif Dept Entomology Davis CA 95616

LAINE, MAURICE DEE, JR., dentist; b. Highland Park, Mich., May 28, 1924; s. Maurice Dee Sr. and Helen Elizabeth (Coons) L.; m. Carol Ann Holzberger, Sept. 13, 1947 (div. Mar. 1973); children: Theodore Bruce, John Thomas, Donald Warren; m. Helen Marie Faulkner. DDS, Northwestern U., 1947. Gen. practice dentistry Missoula, Mont. Chmn. Missoula County Water Pollution Control, 1970-72, U. Mont. Excellence Fund, Missoula, 1988. Served to lt. USNR, 1950-52. Fellow Am. Coll. Dentists, Internat. Coll. Dentists, Acad. Gen. Dentistry; mem. ADA, Mont. Dental Assn. (pres. 1969-70, Disting. Service award 1978), West Mont. Fish and Game Assn., Phi Delta Theta, Omicron Kappa Upsilon. Republican. Lodge: Rotary (pres. Missoula chpt. 1970-71). Office: 1547 S Higgins Missoula MT 59801

LAIRD, JERE DON, news reporter; b. Topeka, Aug. 8, 1933; s. Gerald Howard and Vivian Gertrude (Webb) L.; m. Alexandra Berezowsky, Aug. 4, 1957; children: Lee, Jennifer, Christopher. BA in Journalism, U. Nev., 1960. Disc jockey Sta. KHBC Radio, Hilo, Hawaii, 1949-50; announcer, chief engr. Sta. KOLO Radio, Reno, Nev., 1951-58; program dir. Sta. KOLO-TV, Reno, 1958-60; news reporter Sta. KCRA Radio and TV, Sacramento, Calif., 1960-61, Sta. KRLA Radio, L.A., 1962-63; news reporter, editor Sta. KNXT-TV, L.A., 1964-68; news reporter, fin. editor Sta. KNX-CBS Radio, L.A., 1968—; lectr. U. So. Calif., L.A., 1984-85; instr. Calif. State U., Northridge, 1978-79. Cpl. U.S. Army, 1953-55. Recipient Emmy award, L.A., 1964, Peabody award, U. Ga., 1984, Best Bus. News award, L.A. Press Club, 1986, 87, 88, Martin K. Gainsburgh award, Fiscal Policy Coun., Fla., 1978. Mem. Radio TV News Assn. (bd. dirs. 1966-68, Golden Mike award 1984), Sigma Delta Chi. Home: 222 Monterey Rd #1105 Glendale CA 91206 Office: Sta KNX-CBS 6121 Sunset Blvd Los Angeles CA 90028

LAIRD, MARY See WOOD, LARRY

LAIRD, PAMELA SUE, marketing executive; b. Conneaut, Ohio, Aug. 6, 1955; d. Howard Duane and Joan Elaine (Walrath) L.; m. Paul Lyman Bixby, June 14, 1979 (div. June 1983); m. Mark Peter Jacobsen, May 30, 1987. BSJ, Northwestern U., 1978, M in Mgmt., 1979. Asst. brand mgr. Procter & Gamble, Cin., 1979-81; brand mgr. Clorox Co., Oakland, Calif., 1981-84; mgr. new bus. DHL Worldwide Express, Redwood City, Calif., 1984-86; ind. mktg. cons. San Francisco, 1986-88; pres., owner PSL Mktg. Resources, San Francisco, 1988—; cons. Leadership San Francisco, Jr. League of San Francisco. Bd. dirs. Advs. for Women, San Francisco, 1983-86. Office: 10 Lombard St #400 San Francisco CA 94111

LAIUPPA, MARK ANTHONY, military officer; b. Hartford, Conn., Oct. 22, 1957; s. Anthony Salvatore and Justina (Weiss) L.; m. Suzanne Meade Peters, May 16, 1981 (div. 1987). BS in Astronautical Engring., USAF Acad., 1980. Commd. 2nd lt. USAF, 1980, advanced through grades to capt., 1986; pilot 773 Tactical Airlift Squadron USAF, Dyess AFB, Tex., 1981-86; air ops. officer 463 Tactical Airlift Support Group, tactical airlift liaison officer 611 Mil. Airlift Support Group USAF, Osan, Korea, 1986-87; C12 pilot 1403 Mil. Airlift Squadron USAF, Osan, 1986-87; tactical airlift liaison officer 1702 Mobility Support Squadron USAF, Ft. Ord, Calif., 1987—; sr. pilot USAF, Ft. Ord, 1988—. Columnist: "773 TAS News" Peacemaker (newspaper), 1984-86. Judge Abiline (Tex.) Sci. Competition, 1982-86. Mem. Assn. Grads. USAF Acad., Air Force Assn., Assn. U.S. Army, Abiline Sailing Assn. (sec. 1985-86), Privat Hire Coun. (Camp Red Cloud). Lutheran. Home: 806 Estrada Ct Salinas CA 93907 Office: USAF Detachment 5 602 TAIRCW Fort Ord CA 93941

LAKE, CANDACE LOOMIS, literary agent; b. N.Y.C., Sept. 26, 1946; d. Alfred Lee Jr. and Virginia Nancy (Davis) Loomis; m. Peter A. Lake, Sept. 14, 1968 (div. 1979); m. Richard DiLello, Aug. 28, 1982; 1 child, Francesca Stimson. BA, Wellesley Coll., 1968; postgrad., UCLA, 1969-72. V.p. literary dept. Zeigler, Diskant & Roth, Los Angeles, 1974-78; motion picture literary agent Internat. Creative Mgmt., Los Angeles, 1978-79; pres. The Candace Lake Office, Los Angeles, 1979-85; chief exec. officer Lake & Douroux, Inc., Beverly Hills, Calif., 1985—. Mem. Acad. TV Arts and Scis. Republican. Episcopalian. Office: Lake & Douroux Inc 445 S Beverly Dr Beverly Hills CA 90212

LAKE, KELLY ORLAN, school system administrator; b. Ft. Wayne, Ind., Aug. 28, 1952; d. Francis Orlando and Christie Delight (Allen) L. BA in Sociology, Ind. U., 1976; MA in Counseling Psychology, Ball State U., 1978. Cert. Montessori presch. tchr., Ill. Clin. therapist, child and adolescent program Porter-Starke Svcs., Valparaiso, Ind., 1981-83; pvt. therapist, Valparaiso, 1983-84; exec. dir. Y Kids Koffeehaus, Valparaiso, 1983-84; Montessori dir. Chesterton Montessori, Ind., 1983-84, Montessori Community Sch., Durham, N.C., 1984-86, tutor, caregiver, 1986-87; mental health coord. Fresno County EOC, 1987-88; mental health, spl. needs coord. Tri-County Migrant Head Start, Fresno, Calif., 1988—. Membership chmn. Christian Community Action, Valparaiso, 1982, bd. dirs., 1983. Mem. Am. Montessori Soc., Am. Assn. for Counseling and Devel., Am. Mental Health Counselors Assn., Nat. Assn. for Edn. Young Child. Avocations: recreational sports, the arts, outdoors, spending time with friends. Home: 1257 N Van Ness Apt 1 Fresno CA 93728

LAKE, KEVIN BRUCE, medical association administrator; b. Seattle, Jan. 25, 1937; s. Winston Richard and Vera Emma (Davis) L.; B.S., Portland State U., 1960; M.D., U. Oreg., 1964; m. Suzanne Roto, Oct. 25, 1986; children from previous marriage: Laura, Kendrick, Wesley. Intern, Marion County Gen. Hosp. and Ind. Med. Center, Indpls., 1964-65; resident U. Oreg. Hosps. and Clinics, 1968-70; fellow in infectious and pulmonary diseases, 1970-71; fellow in pulmonary diseases U. So. Calif., 1971-72, instr. medicine, 1972-75, asst. clin. prof., 1975-79, assoc. clin. prof., 1979-84, clin. prof., 1986—; dir. med. edn. and research La Vina Hosp., 1972-75; dir. respiratory therapy Methodist Hosp., Arcadia, Calif., 1975—; mem. staff Los Angeles County/U. So. Calif. Med. Center, Santa Teresita Hosp., Duarte, Calif., Huntington Meml. Hosp., Pasadena, Calif.; attending physician, mem. med. adv. bd. Foothill Free Clinic, Pasadena. Mem. exec. com. Profl. Staff Assn. U. So. Calif. Sch. Medicine; 2d v.p. bd. mgmt. Palm St. br. YMCA, Pasadena, 1974, 1st v.p., 1975, chmn., 1976-78, met. bd. dirs., 1976-84; bd. dirs. Mendenhall Ministries, La Vie Holistic Ministries, Hospice of Pasadena, Hastings Found. co-pres. PTA, Allendale Grade Sch., Pasadena, 1975-76; deacon Pasadena Covenant Ch., 1976-79. Served to lt. U.S. Navy, 1965-68. NIH grantee, 1971-72. Fellow A.C.P., Am. Coll. Chest Physicians; mem. Am. Thoracic Soc., Calif. Thoracic Soc., Oreg. Thoracic Soc., Trudeau Soc., Am. Soc. Microbiology, N.Y. Acad. Scis., Calif. Med. Assn., Los Angeles County Med. Assn. Democrat. Contbr. articles to profl. jours. Home: 875 S Madison St Pasadena CA 91106 Office: 50 Alessandro Ste 330 Pasadena CA 91105

LAKE, STANLEY JAMES, security consulting company executive, motel chain executive, locksmith; b. Oklahoma City, June 3, 1926; s. Clyde Edward Lake and Helene Frances (Herndon) Hunnicut; m. Lila Marguarite Mosley, Mar 29, 1947 (div. Aug. 1952); children: Katherine, Marilyn, Stanley James II; Norma Jean Phelps, Jan. 18, 1961. Student, Mont. State U., 1946-48. Owner, mgr. Lake Oil Co., Glendive, Mont., 1949-53, Lake Mining Co., Salt Lake City, 1954-57, Lake Realty Co., Denver, 1958-63, Stanlake Corp., Denver, 1964—, Stanlake Luxury Budget Motels, Denver, 1979—, Lake's Security and Lock Svc., Englewood, Colo., 1979—; co-owner, instr. Colo. Karate Assn., Denver, 1965-73. Originator modular budget motel concept, 1963. Chmn. bd. for karate Rocky Mountain region AAU, 1972-73. With USAAC, 1945-46. Recipient Presdl. award for teaching karate to disadvantaged and civic orgns., 1972, numerous others. Mem. Assn. Locksmiths Am. (cert. profl. locksmith), Nat. Fire and Burglar Alarm Assn. (cert. alarm installer), Rocky Mountain Locksmiths Assn., Colo. Burglary and Fire Assn. (organizer), Japan Karate Assn. Rocky Mountain Area (chmn. bd. 1970-73), Masons, Shriners. Republican. Methodist. Home: 6026 S Elizabeth Way Littleton CO 80121 Office: Lake's Security & Lock Svc 6200 S Syracuse Way Ste 125 Englewood CO 80111

LAL, DEVENDRA, nuclear geophysics educator; b. Varanasi, India, Feb. 14, 1929; s. Radhe Krishna and Sita Devi (Gupta) L.; m. Aruna Damany, May 17, 1955. BS, Banaras Hindu U., Varanasi, 1947, MS, 1949, DSc, 1984; PhD, Bombay U., 1958. Research student Tata Inst. of Fundamental Research, Bombay, 1949-50, research fellow, fellow, assoc. prof., 1950-63, prof., 1963-70, sr. prof., 1970-72; dir. Phys. Research Lab., Ahmedabad, India, 1972-83; sr. prof. Phys. Research Lab., Ahmedabad, 1983-89; vis. prof. UCLA, 1965-66, 83-84; prof. Scripps Instn. Oceanography, La Jolla, Calif., 1967—. Editor: Early Solar System Processes and the Present Solar System, 1980. Recipient K.S. Krishnan Gold Medal Indian Geophys. Union, 1965, S.S. Bhatnagar award for Physics Govt. India, 1967, Padma Shri award Govt. India, 1971, award for Excellence in Sci. and Tech. Fedn. of Indian Chamber Com., 1974, Pandit Jawaharlal Nehru award for Scis., 1986. Fellow Royal Soc., Indian Nat. Sci Acad., Indian Acad. Scis.; mem. Nat. Acad. Scis. (fgn. assoc.), Third World Acad. Scis. (founding mem.), Royal Astron. Soc. (assoc.) Internat. Acad. Aeronautics, Internat. Union of Geodesy and Geophysics (pres. 1984-87), Internat. Assn. Phys. Scis. of the Ocean (pres. 1980-84). Hindu. Office: Scripps Inst Oceanography GRD A-020 La Jolla CA 92093

LAM, QUI, jewelry company executive; b. PhanRang, Vietnam, June 30, 1954; came to U.S., 1978; s. Chan and Loan Lam. Student, Vanhanh U., 1972-75, Kapidami Community Coll., 1980-82. Mgr. Gold Classics, Inc., Honolulu, 1982-85, Gold & Gems Collection, Inc., Honolulu, 1985—. Home: 1255 Nuuanu Ave #1315 Honolulu HI 96817 Office: Gold & Gems Collections Inc 334 Seaside Ave #707 Honolulu HI 96815

LAM, STEPHEN TANG-FEI, mechanical engineer; b. Hong Kong, China, Nov. 20, 1953; came to U.S., 1973; s. Wei-Chong and Giok-Yen (Wong) L.; m. Pauline NG, Feb. 13, 1980. BS in Civil Engring., U. Houston, 1977; MS in Mech. Engring., U. Calif., Berkeley, 1979, ME in Mech. Engring., 1980; postgrad., Stanford U., 1981—. Cons. engr. Cons. Computation Bur., Oakland, Calif., 1978-79; engr. GE Nuclear Energy, San Jose, Calif., 1980—; rsch. asst. Stanford U. Geothermal Program, Calif., 1981-86; cons. Varian Assocs. Inc., Santa Clara, 1988. contbr. articles to profl. jours. Recipient Earle C. Anthony scholarship U. Calif. Berkeley, 1977. Mem. ASME, Chi Epsilon, Phi Kappa Phi, Tau Beta Pi. Home: 1305 Garthwick Dr Los Altos CA 94022 Office: GE Co NF & ES /MS 769 175 Curtner Ave San Jose CA 95125

LAM, TONY CHIU-LEUNG, physician; b. Canton, People's Repubic of China, Jan. 12, 1958; came to U.S., 1968; s. Yui Wan and Pui Ching (Lee) L. BS, MIT, 1979; MD, Albert Einstein Coll. Medicine, 1983. Resident Temple U. Hosp., Phila., 1983-85, Loma Linda (Calif.) U. Med. Ctr., 1987-. Mem. AMA. Office: Loma Linda U Med Ctr Anderson and Campus Sts Loma Linda CA 92354

LAMASTER, TIMOTHY SHAWN, computer specialist; b. New Albany, Ind., Jan. 25, 1959; s. Dale Eugene and Beverly Jean (Risner) L.; m. Valerie Joan Mayer, June 25, 1983; 1 child, Ryan Shane. BA in Econs., U. Ariz., 1985. Acad. profl., mgr. econ. sci. systems devel. Econ. Sci. Lab. U. Ariz., Tucson, 1985—; prin. Computer Research and Cons., Tucson, 1984—. Pres. Tucson Kaypro Users Group, 1987-88. Home: 932 E King St Tucson AZ 85719 Office: U Ariz Econ Sci Lab Bldg #23 Tucson AZ 87521

LAMB, DAVID LAYTON, travel service executive; b. Bremerton, Wash., Nov. 8, 1960; s. Keith Hillary and Leana Dominga (Munguia) L. AA in Transp. Bus., Highline Community Coll., Midway, Wash., 1981. Outside sales rep. Am. Tours and Travel, Seattle, 1978-82; mgr. ops. Plus Travel

Prodns., Seattle, 1982-83; travel cons. Cosmos Travel, Tacoma, Wash., 1983-84; mgr. Cosmos Travel, Seattle, 1984-87, Klineburger Travel, Seattle, 1985; lead internat. agt. Doug Fox Travel/Travel Makers, Redmond, Wash., 1987-88, mgr. internat. ops., 1988—; instr. Highline Community Coll., 1981-83, Nat. Sch. Travel, Bellevue, Wash., 1985. Republican. Roman Catholic. Office: Doug Fox Travel 2053 152d Ave NE Redmond WA 98052

LAMB, JAMES ALLEN, health care facility executive; b. Memphis, Apr. 18, 1941; s. John Leonard and Victoria (Pyles) L.; m. Elsie Jane Adams, June 5, 1964; children: Jane Allison, Jennifer Ashley, Julie Ann. BS in Psychology, Memphis State U., 1964; MA in Hosp. Adminstrn., Duke U., 1966. Adminstrv. assoc. Bapt. Meml. Hosp., Memphis, 1966-69; asst. adminstr. Erlanger Med. Ctr., Chattanooga, 1969-73, pres., chief exec. officer, 1973-83; pres., chief exec. officer Washoe Med. Ctr., Reno, 1983—; chmn. bd. dirs. Washoe Health System, Reno. Bd. dirs. 1989 Internat. Winter Spl. Olympic Games, Reno-Tahoe, Nev., 1987—. Mem. Am. Coll. Health Care Execs., Nev. Hosp. Assn. (chmn. bd. trustees 1986-87), Reno-Sparks C. of C. (bd. dirs. 1986—, v.p. community affairs 1987-88). Presbyterian. Lodge: Rotary. Home: 2550 Lakeridge Shores W Reno NV 89509 Office: Washoe Med Ctr Office of Pres 77 Pringle Way Reno NV 89520

LAMB, JANE ADAMS, educator; b. Memphis, June 30, 1943; d. Roy Oliver and Hazel Jane (Mayhall) Adams; m. James Allen Lamb, June 5, 1964; children: Jane Allison, Jennifer Ashley, Julie Ann. BA, Rhodes Coll., 1964; MSW, U. N.C., 1966; EdD, U. Tenn., 1986. Cert. social worker. Med. social worker City of Memphis Hosps., 1966-67; instr. U. Tenn. Med. Sch., Memphis, 1966-67; cons. Vis. Nurses Assn., Memphis, 1968-69; clin. social worker Family & Children's Services, Chattanooga, 1970-75; asst. prof. U. Tenn., Chattanooga, 1977-83; assoc. prof. U. Nev., Reno, 1985—; pres. Nev. Bd. Examiners Social Workers, 1987—; bd. dirs. Suicide Prevention and Crisis Call, Reno, 1986—; cons. Nev. State Legis. Interim Study Com., Carson City, 1986. Contbr. articles to profl. jours. Bd. dirs. Young Audiences No. Nev., 1984-85; pres. Children's Internat. Summer Village Program, Chattanooga, 1979-80; active United Way, Reno, 1987—; State Task Force Drug Free Schs., Carson City, 1987-88; Nev. Juvenile Justice Project, 1987. Recipient Chancellor's citation U. Tenn., 1986. Mem. Nat. Assn. Social Workers (pres. 1980-82), Council on Social Work Edn. (del. 1983-84). Presbyterian. Home: 2550 Lakeridge Shores West Reno NV 89509 Office: U Nev-Reno Bus Bldg 525 Reno NV 89557

LAMB, VALERIE ANN, medical librarian; b. Lusk, Wyo., Nov. 23, 1960; d. Jerry Jay and Judith Valerie (Jassmann) L. Accredited record technician. With Community Hosp., Torrington, Wyo., 1981—; asst. supr. med. record dept., med. libr. Community Hosp., Torrington, 1981—; cons. in field. Mem. Am. Med. Record Assn., Wyo. Med. Record Assn., Southeast Wyo. Health Scis. Library Consortium (pres. 1983-84). Republican. Home: 3702 Johnson St Torrington WY 82240 Office: Community Hosp 2000 Campbell Dr Torrington WY 82240

LAMB, WILLIS EUGENE, JR., physicist, educator; b. Los Angeles, July 12, 1913; s. Willis Eugene and Marie Helen (Metcalf) L.; m. Ursula Schaefer, June 5, 1939. B.S., U. Calif., 1934, Ph.D., 1938; D.Sc., U. Pa., 1953, Gustavus Adolphus Coll., 1975; M.A., Oxford (Eng.) U., 1956, Yale, 1961; L.H.D., Yeshiva U., 1965. Mem. faculty Columbia, 1938-52, prof. physics, 1948-52; prof. physics Stanford, 1951-56; Wykeham prof. physics and fellow New Coll., Oxford U., 1956-62; Henry Ford 2d prof. physics Yale, 1962-72, J. Willard Gibbs prof. physics, 1972-74; prof. physics and optical scis. U. Ariz., Tucson, 1974—; Morris Loeb lectr. Harvard, 1953-54; cons. Philips Labs., Bell Telephone Labs., Perkin-Elmer, NASA.; Vis. com. Brookhaven Nat. Lab. Recipient (with Dr. Polykarp Kusch) Nobel prize in physics, 1955; Rumford premium Am. Acad. Arts and Scis., 1953; Research Corp. award, 1955; Guggenheim fellow, 1960-61; recipient Yeshiva award, 1962. Fellow Am. Phys. Soc., N.Y. Acad. Scis.; hon. fellow Inst. Physics and Phys. Soc. (Guthrie lectr. 1958), Royal Soc. Edinburgh (fgn. mem.); mem. Nat. Acad. Scis., Phi Beta Kappa, Sigma Xi. Office: U Ariz Dept Physics Tucson AZ 85721

LAMB-BRASSINGTON, KATHRYN EVELYN, writer, genealogist; b. Yakima, Wash., Apr. 3, 1935; d. Victor Earl and Anna (Kauzlarich) Lamb; m. Donald Morley Brassington, Dec. 27, 1956 (div. 1968); children: Andrew Stuart, Perry Sanford, Van Victor, Keith Bennett. Student, Wash. State U., 1954-55, U. Wash., 1955-56. Author: A Leg of Lamb, 1985; assoc. editor quar. newsletter Lamb's Pastures, 1985-88. Mem. New Eng. Historic Geneal. Soc., Geneal. Soc. Vt., Seattle Geneal. Soc., Towne Family Assn., DAR, Colonial Dames 17th Century, Chi Omega. Republican. Presbyterian. Home: 4509 Somerset Pl SE Bellevue WA 98006

LAMBERT, BERTUS LOREN, exporter, negotiant; b. Marshall, Okla., Mar. 1, 1937; s. Merle Loren and Martha Mae (Patterson) L.; m. Margaret Ann French, Nov. 9, 1963 (dec. Sept. 1982); children: Margan Rebekah, Jessica Irene. BS, Okla. State U., 1960; BA, Calif. State U., L.A., 1981. Sr. svc. engr. Lockheed Aircraft Corp., Burbank, Calif., 1960-68; pres. Enviro Logics Co., Pasadena, Calif., 1968-77; project mgr. Wittler-Young Co., L.A., 1977-84; ptnr. Pacific Agrl. Commodities Co., L.A., 1984—. Bd. dirs. Little Tokyo Svc. Ctr., L.A., 1986—. Mem. Japanese Am. Contractors Assn. (pres. 1981—). Republican.

LAMBERT, DENNIS ALVIN, radio news director; b. Allegan, Mich., Sept. 14, 1947; s. Alvin Millard and Myrta Gertrude (Ellinger) L.; m. Pamela Sue Hoeksema, Dec. 20, 1969; children: Matthew Dennis, Nicole Leigh. BA, Mich. State U., 1971. Disc jockey Sta. WAOP, Osego, Mich., 1969; asst. news dir. Sta. WJIM, Lansing, Mich., 1969-75; news reporter Sta. WVIC, East Lansing, 1975-76; news and sports anchor Sta. WCAR, Detroit, 1976; news reporter, editor Sta. WXYZ, Detroit, 1976-84; mng. editor Sta. KTAR, Phoenix, 1984-85, news dir., 1985—. Recipient various news related awards Ariz. AP, 1984, 86, 87. Mem. Ariz. Press Club, Radio, TV and News Dirs. Assn. Office: Sta KTAR Radio 301 W Osborn Phoenix AZ 85013

LAMBERT, KENNETH NELSON, data processing executive; b. Los Angeles, June 26, 1942; s. Charles F. Sr. and Lenora P. (Vezna) L.; m. Jane Ann Pinney (div. Nov. 1987); m. Cathy A. Little, Feb. 14, 1988; children: Kendell Ray, Katrina Marie. BS in Math., Calif. State Poly. U., 1965. Systems engr. IBM, Sacramento, 1966-71; dir. data processing Comdr. Industries, Red Bluff, Calif., 1971-74; mgr. data processing La. Pacific Corp., Red Bluff, 1974-75; v.p. ops. NW Farm Fur. Ins. Co., Salem, Oreg., 1975-85; dir. gen. service Polk County, Dallas, Oreg., 1985-86; mgr. info. systems United Telephone of NW, Hood River, Oreg., 1986—; cons. Salem, 1977-86; instr. Shasta Community Coll., 1971-75, Salem Community Coll., 1975-85, Western Oreg. State Coll., 1981-85, Treaty Oaks Community Coll., 1986—6. Fellow Data Processing Mgmt. Assn. Republican. Lutheran. Club: Tall Ships (Hood River). Lodges: Lions, Elks. Home: PO Box 588 Gas Locks OR 97014 Office: United Telephone of NW 601 State St #11 Hood River OR 97031

LAMBERT, LISA GAYE, sales representative; b. Roseville, Calif., Apr. 25, 1955; d. Lloyd Douglas and Dona (Holt) L. BS, Chico (Calif.) State U., 1977; MS, U. Conn., 1979. Clin. dietitian L.I. Coll. Hosp., Bklyn., 1980-81; chemist Novo Labs., Wilton, Conn., 1981-83; applications chemist Varian Assocs., Houston, 1984-85; sales rep. Varian Assocs., Austin, Tex., 1985-86; sales rep., magnetics rsch. Varian Assocs., Palo Alto, 1987—; sales rep. Spectra Physics, San Jose, 1986-87. Mem. Am. Chem. Soc., Am. Oil Chemist (pres., chmn. S. Cen. sect. 1985), Bay Area NMR Group. Republican. Mormon. Office: Varian Assocs 611 Hansen Way Palo Alto CA 94303

LAMBERT, NADINE MURPHY, psychologist, educator; b. Ephraim, Utah; m. Robert E. Lambert, 1956; children—Laura Allan, Jeffrey. Ph.D. in Psychology, U. So. Calif., 1965. Sch. psychologist Los Nietos Sch. Dist., Whittier, Calif., 1952-53, Bellflower (Calif.) Unified Sch. Dist., 1953-58; research cons. Calif. Dept. Edn., Los Angeles, 1958-64; dir. sch. psychology tng. program U. Calif., Berkeley, 1964—; asst. prof. edn. U. Calif., 1964-70, asso. prof., 1970-76, prof., 1976—; mem. Joint Com. Mental Health of Children, 1967-68; cons. state depts. edn., Calif., Ga., Fla.; cons. Calif. Dept. Justice; mem. panel on testing handicapped people Nat. Acad. Scis., 1978-81. Author: (with Windmiller and Cole) School Version of the AAMD Adaptive Behavior Scale, 2d edit, 1981; (with Wilcox and Gleason) Educationally retarded child: Comprehensive assessment and planning for the EMR and slow-learning child, 1974; (with Hartsough and Bower) Process for Assessment of Effective Functioning, 1981; (with Windmiller and Turiel) Moral Development and Socialization—Three Perspectives, 1979; assoc. editor Am. Jour. Orthopsychiatry, 1975-81, Am. Jour. Mental Deficiency, 1977-80; cons. editor to jours. NIMH grantee, 1965-87; Calif. State Dept. Edn. grantee, 1971-72, 76-78. Fellow Am. Psychol. Assn. (council reps. div. sch. psychologists, bd. dirs. 1983-86, bd. profl. affairs 1981-83, Disting. Service award 1980, award for Disting. Profl. Contributions 1986), Am. Orthopsychiat. Assn.; mem. Calif. Assn. Sch. Psychologists and Psychometrists (pres. 1962-63, Sandra Goff award 1985), Am. Ednl. Research Assn., NEA, Am. Bd. Profl. Psychology (diplomate in sch. psychology). Office: U Calif Dept Edn Berkeley CA 94720

LAMBETH, DEBORAH HAYES, interior designer; b. Thomasville, N.C., July 14, 1956; d. Wilburn Roy and Doris (Welborn) Hayes. AA, Davidson County Community Coll., 1976; BS in Econs. and Bus. Adminstrn., U. N.C., Greensboro, 1977. Adminstrv. design asst. Lambeth Ltd., Thomasville, 1979-80, cons., 1978-87; interior designer Furniture Galleries Inc., Denver, 1983-84; interior design adminstr. Aircoa, Denver, 1984-85, dir. design, 1985—; cons. L.J. Best Inc., Thomasville, 1986—; mem. nat. adv. coun. Allied Fibers. Active Jr. Symphony Guild, Denver, 1980-82, Denver Alliance, 1985—. Mem. Am. Soc. Interior Designers, Inst. Bus. Designers. Republican. Baptist. Club: Lone Tree Country (Littleton). Office: AIRCOA 4600 S Ulster St Ste 1200 Denver CO 80237

LAMEIRO, GERARD FRANCIS, computer network consultant, columnist; b. Paterson, N.J., Oct. 3, 1949; s. Frank Raymond and Beatrice Cecilia (Donley) L.; BS, Colo. State U., 1971, MS, 1973, PhD, 1977. Sr. scientist Solar Energy Research Inst., Golden, Colo., 1977-78; asst. prof. mgmt. sci. and info. systems Colo. State U., Fort Collins, 1978-82, lectr. dept. computer sci., 1983, lectr. dept. mgmt., 1983; pres. Successful Automated Office Systems, Inc., Fort Collins, 1982-84; product mgr. Hewlett Packard, 1984-88; computer networking cons., 1988—, Ft. Collins.; columnist The HP Chronicle, 1988—. Mem. Presdl. Electoral Coll., 1980. Recipient nat. disting. Service award Assn. Energy Engrs., 1981. Colo. Energy Research Inst. fellow 1976; NSF fellow 1978. Mem. Assn. for Computing Machinery. Roman Catholic. Contbr. articles in mgmt. and tech. areas to profl. jours. Home: PO Box 9580 Fort Collins CO 80525 Address: 3313 Downing St Fort Collins CO 80526 Office: Hewlett Packard Co 3313 Downing Ct Fort Collins CO 80526

LAMERE, DENIS CLIFFORD, real estate executive; b. Claremont, N.H., May 20, 1949; s. Clifford Alfred and Hazel Lillian (Martin) L.; m. Barbara Jean, Sept. 26, 1970; children: Kimberely Susanne, Kevin Michael. AAS, Grahm Coll., Boston, 1970; BS, U. N.H., Durham, 1976; MBA, N.H. Coll., 1982. V.p. Eagle Mgmt., Inc., Holiston, Mass., 1973-82; dir. real estate ops. Picerne Devel. Corp., Phoenix, 1982-83; property mgr. Fox and Carskadon, Scottsdale, Ariz., 1983-85; v.p. Balcor Property Mgmt., Tempe, Ariz., 1985—. Polit. action com., Ariz. Multihousing Assn., Phoenix, 1988, community service chmn., 1988, profl. devel. chmn., 1989, pres. Valley chpt. 1989; active Child Protective Svcs., Phoenix, fund raiser 1988, Area Food Bank/St. Vincent De Paul, Phoenix, fund raiser, 1988—. With U.S. Army, 1970-72, Vietnam. Decorated Bronze Star. Mem. Nat. Apt. Assn. (Cert. apt. property supr. 1988), Inst. Real Estate Mgmt. (Cert. property mgr. 1982). Republican. Roman Catholic. Office: Balcor Property Mgmt 5038 S Hardy Dr Tempe AZ 85282

LAMERS, ELIZABETH PYLE, bereavement consultant; b. Bryn Mawr, Pa., Mar. 18, 1939; d. William Clarkson and Elizabeth Scarlett (Phelps) Pyle; m. Rodney Fiske Du Bois, Dec. 4, 1958 (div. Apr. 1967); children: Sabrina Michelle Du Bois De Filippis, Monique Elizabeth; m. William Matthias Lamers, Jr., Dec. 31, 1982. BS cum laude, SUNY, New Paltz, 1972; MA, Sonoma State U., 1982. Cancer researcher, lab. technician dept. pathology Harvard U., Boston, 1959-60; cancer researcher, lab. technician Children's Cancer Rsch. Found.-Children's Hosp. Med. Ctr., Boston, 1959-60; asst. to guidance counselor Friends Sem., N.Y.C., 1969-70; tchr. sci. Da Nahazli Sch., Taos, N.Mex., 1972-73; tchr., reading specialist Bolinas (Calif.)-Stinson Union Sch. Dist., 1973-82; death-grief-bereavement of children-AIDS-neonatal loss cons. Malibu, Calif., 1982—; cons. Caring Beyond, neonatal loss, Calgary, Alta., Can., 1983-85. Contbr. chpts. to books. Mem. community health adv. com. Santa Monica-Malibu Unified Sch. Dist., 1987—; mem. com. on bioethics Los Angeles County Bar Assn., 1988—; mem. AIDS edn. task force Santa Monica chpt. ARC, 1988—; mem. profl. adv. bd. Chris Brownlie Hospice, L.A., 1988—. Mem. Internat. Reading Assn., Internat. Workgroup on Death, Dying and Bereavement, Nat. Speakers Assn., Kappa Delta Pi. Mem. Soc. of Friends. Home and Office: 9510 Yerba Buena Rd Malibu CA 90265-9705

LAMIT, LOUIS GARY, engineer, educator; b. Newberry, Mich., Feb. 3, 1949; s. Louis Joseph and Frances (Merlo) L.; m. Margaret Fennimore, Apr. 16, 1976 (div. Sept. 1984); children: Angela, Corina, James. BS, Western Mich. U., 1970; postgrad., Mich. State U., 1971-72, U. Calif., Berkeley, 1980. Engr. Boeing Aircraft, Phila., 1969-70; programmer Kolmorgan Optics, Northampton, Mass., 1970-71; tchr. Melby Jr. High, Warren, Mich., 1971-72; instr. Carroll Tech. Vocat. Sch., Carrollton, Ga., 1974-76, Heald Engring. Coll., San Francisco, 1976-80, No. Ky. U., Highland Heights, Ky., 1980-81, Mission Coll., Santa Clara, Calif., 1981-82, Santa Rosa (Calif.) Jr. Coll., 1982-83, Cogswell Polytech. Coll., Cupertino, Calif., 1984-86; dept. head De Anza Coll., Cupertino, 1984—. Author: Piping Drafting & Design, 1981, Industrial Model Building, 1981, Descriptive Geometry, 1983, Piping & Pipefitting Hand Book, 1984, Drafting For Electronics, 1986, CADD, 1987, Technical Drawing and Design, 1989; contbr. articles to profl. jours. Republican. Buddhist. Home: 1258 S Stelling Cupertino CA 95014 Office: Deanza Coll 21250 Stevens Creek Cupertino CA 95014

LAMM, RICHARD DOUGLAS, former governor of Colorado; b. Madison, Wis., Aug. 3, 1935; s. Arnold E. and Mary (Townsend) L.; m. Dorothy Vennard, May 11, 1963; children: Scott Hunter, Heather Susan. BBA, U. Wis., 1957; LLB, U. Calif., Berkeley, 1961. Bar: Colo. 1962; C.P.A., Colo. Accountant Salt Lake City, 1958, Ernst & Ernst, Denver, 1961-62; atty. Colo. Anti-Discrimination Commn., Denver, 1962-63, Jones, Meiklejohn, Kilroy, Kehl & Lyons, Denver, 1963-65; sole practice 1965-74; mem. Colo. Ho. of Reps., 1966-74, asst. minority leader, 1971-74; gov. Colo., 1975-87; asso. prof. law U. Denver, from 1969; chmn. natural resource and environ. mgmt. com. Nat. Gov.'s Assn., 1978-79, mem., from 1979, also mem. exec. com. and environment com., and chmn. task force on synthetic fuels. mem. Conservation Found., Denver Center Performing Arts Center for Growth Alternatives, Central City Opera House Assn. Served as 1st lt. U.S. Army, 1957-58. *

LAMME, DENNIS WAYNE, advertising executive; b. Trenton, Mo., Mar. 19, 1955; s. John Robert and Earlene Marie (Trump) L.; m. Cindy Kay Wright, July 30, 1977; children: Kelly Marie, Jacob Fremont, Kristen Kay, Kaylie Elizabeth. B.S., Northwest Mo. State U., 1976. Account exec. Sta. KKJO, St. Joseph, Mo., 1976-77; gen. mgr. Sta. KVMT-FM, Vail, Colo., 1977-78; sta. mgr. Sta. KYEZ-FM, Salina, Kans., 1978; account exec. Sta. WRMN, Elgin, Ill., 1978-79; v.p., corp. sales Brewer Broadcasting Co. (Stas. KUAD, KSGR, KKBG) Windsor, Colo. and Hilo, Hawaii, 1979-84; advt. exec. Jefferson-Pilot Communications, Stas. KIMN and KYGO, Denver, 1984-86; gen. mgr., v.p. Surrey Broadcasting, Stas. KATR and KYOU, Greely/ Denver, KDZA, Pueblo, Colo., KATM, Colorado Springs, 1986-89; gen. sales mgr. Sta. KDHT-AM, Denver, 1989—; mem. research bd. advisors Am. Biographical Inst. Inc. Chmn. bd. dirs. Thompson Valley Preschool, 1982-84. Mem.Nat. Assn. of Broadcasters, Colo. Broadcasters Assn., Mktg. Advt. and Communications Assn. (v.p.), Am. Advt. Fedn., Denver Advt. Fedn., Am. Mgmt. Assn., Am. Film Inst., Pikes Peak Advt. Fedn., Alpha Epsilon Rho. Republican. Presbyterian. Home: 545 Thames Dr Colorado Springs CO 80906 Office: 9351 Grant St Ste 600 Thornton CO 80229

LAMONICA, JOHN, food executive; b. Bklyn., Apr. 26, 1954; s. Lou and Alda (Merola) L.; m. Nancy Lamonica. BS in Acctg., Bklyn. Coll., 1977. With N.S.L. Enterprises, 1982—; with Aniellos Pizza, 1979—, Lamonicas N.Y. Pizza, 1980—; restaurant cons. Developer of new pizzas in field. Republican. Mem. Beverly Hills Gun Club, Shelby Am. Club. Office: 518 W 6th St Los Angeles CA 90014

LAMONT, DONALD MELVILLE, computer company executive, restaurateur; b. Seattle, Nov. 19, 1953; s. Joseph and Mildred Elizabeth (Robb) L.; m. Karen Sue Shrader, May 7, 1976; children: Joshua Ryan, Megan Elizabeth, Kelsey Lynn. BA in Sociology and Organizational Behavior, Geneva Coll., 1976. Programmer, analyst Boeing Computer Svcs., Seattle, 1978-87, mgr., 1987—; ptnr., cons. Associated Computer Svcs., Seattle, 1983-88. Recipient Spl. Achievement award Boeing Computer Svcs., 1986, 87. Presbyterian. Home: 5636 NE 200th Pl Seattle WA 98155

LA MONTAGNE, EDWARD WEIR, investment company executive; b. Mexico City, Jan. 11, 1939; s. Robert Weir and Mary Elizabeth (Ring) La M.; m. Kirsten Krueger, Feb. 11, 1967; children: Kendall, Evan Blake. BA in Econs., U. Tex., 1962. Stockbroker Rotan Mosle Inc., Houston, 1965-68; lending officer United Bank Denver, 1968-72; with corp. devel. dept. United Banks Colo., Denver, 1972-75; pres. Bear Creek Investment Co., Evergreen, Colo., 1975—; bd. dirs. Colo. Nat. Bank Evergreen, Mt. States Hardware and Implement Dealers, 1985—. Bd. dirs. Evergreen Scholarship Assn., 1980-82; pres. Nat. Repertory Orch., Evergreen, 1982-83, Bootstraps, Inc., Evergreen, 1984; trustee Colo. Acad., Denver, 1986—. Lt. USNR, 1963-65, Vietnam. Mem. Evergreen C. of C. (bd. dirs. 1984-87), Hiwan Golf (Evergreen), Sigma Alpha Epsilon. Republican. Home: 124 Antler Way Evergreen CO 80439 Office: Bear Creek Investment Co PO Box 1613 Evergreen CO 80439

LAMOREAUX, PHILLIP ADDISON, investment management company executive; b. Vallejo, Calif., May 8, 1941; s. Page Halleck and Marjorie Ruth (Nelson) L.; m. Sonia Ann Zeltin, Aug. 13, 1965 (div. 1988); children: Anne Elizabeth, Brian Brook. BA, Stanford U., 1963; MBA, Harvard U., 1967. Analyst Dean Witter & Co., San Francisco, 1963-65; portfolio mgr. Am. Express Investment Mgmt. Co., San Francisco, 1967-74; gen. ptnr. Lamoreaux, Glynn & Assocs., San Francisco, 1974-83, Lamoreaux Ptnrs., San Francisco, 1983—, Lamoreaux Ventures, San Francisco, 1983—. Pres. Interfaith Housing Found., Mill Valley, Calif., 1970-76; bd. dirs. Marin Theatre Co., Mill Valley, 1985–; bd. dirs., treas. Hospice Marin, San Rafael, Calif., 1978-84. Mem. Western Venture Capital Assn., Security Analysts San Francisco, Olympic Club, Family Club (San Francisco). Republican. Home: 1001 Bridgeway Blvd Box 205 Sausalito CA 94965 Office: Lamoreaux Ptnrs 600 Montgomery St 41st Fl San Francisco CA 94111

LAMOUREUX, GLORIA KATHLEEN, nurse, military officer; b. Billings, Mont., Nov. 2, 1947; d. Laurits Bungaard and Florence Esther (Nielsen) Nielsen; m. Kenneth Earl Lamoureux, Aug. 31, 1973 (div. Feb. 1979). BS, U. Wyo., 1970; MS, U. Md., 1984. Staff nurse, ob-gyn. DePaul Hosp., Cheyenne, Wyo., 1970; enrolled USAF, 1970, advanced through grades to lt. col.; staff nurse ob-gyn dept. 57th Tactical Hosp., Nellis AFB, Nev., 1970-71, USAF Hosp., Clark AB, Republic Phillipines, 1971-73; charge nurse ob-gyn dept. USAF Regional Hosp., Sheppard AFB, Tex., 1973-75; staff nurse ob-gyn dept. USAF Regional Hosp., MacDill AFB, Fla., 1976-79; charge nurse ob-gyn dept. USAF Med. Ctr., Andrews AFB, Md., 1979-80, MCH coordinator, 1980-82; chief nurse USAF Clinic, Eielson AFB, Alaska, 1984-86, Air Force Systems Command Hosp., Edwards AFB, Calif., 1986—. Named one of Outstanding Women Am., 1983. Mem. Nurses Assn. of Am. Coll. Obstetricians and Gynecologists (sec.-treas. armed forces dist. 1986-88, vice-chmn. armed forces dist. 1989—), Air Force Assn., Assn. Mil. Surgeons U.S., Bus. and Profl. Women's Assn. (pub. relations chair Prince George's County chpt. 1981-82), Sigma Theta Tau. Republican. Lutheran. Office: AFSC Hosp Edwards Edwards AFB CA 93523-5300

LAMPART, HANS HELMUT, real estate developer; b. Manheim, Fed. Republic of Germany, Nov. 29, 1957; came to U.S., 1960; s. Karl and Maria (Massinger) L.; m. Victoria Lampart. Student, UCLA, 1979-81. Lic. gen. contractor, Calif. Supt. Wittenberg Corp., Newport Beach, Calif., 1976-77; project coordinator Rebecca Builders, Van Nuys, Calif., 1977-78; project mgr. Womack Co., Diamond Bar, Calif., 1978-80; v.p. Tourtelot Devel., L.A., 1980-84; pres. Alamo Homes, Simi Valley, Calif., 1984—; bd. dirs. Presdl. Purchasing Council, L.A. Mem. Bldg. Industry Assn., Internat. Council Shopping Ctrs., Calif. Yacht Club. Republican. Office: Alamo Homes PO Box 7015-116 Canoga Park CA 91304

LAMPERT, ELEANOR VERNA, employment development specialist; b. Porterville, Calif., Mar. 23; d. Ernest Samuel and Violet Edna (Watkins) Wilson; student in bus., fin. Porterville Jr. Coll., 1977-78; grad. Anthony Real Estate Sch., 1971; student Laguna Sch. of Art, 1972, U. Calif.-Santa Cruz, 1981; m. Robert Mathew Lampert, Aug. 21, 1935; children—Sally Lu Winton, Lary Lampert, Carol R. John. Bookkeeper, Porterville (Calif.) Hosp., 1956-71; real estate sales staff Ray Realty, Porterville, 1973; sec. Employment Devel. Dept., State of Calif., Porterville, 1973-83, orientation and tng. specialist CETA employees, 1976-80. Author: Black Bloomers and Han-Ga-Ber, 1986. Sec., Employer Adv. Group, 1973-80, 81—; mem. U.S. Senatorial Bus. Adv. Bd., 1981-84; charter mem. Presdl. Republican Task Force, 1981—; mem. Rep. Nat. Congl. Com., 1982-88; pres. Sierra View Hosp. Vol. League, 1988-89 ; vol. Calif. Hosp. Assn., 1983-86, Calif. Spl. Olympics Spirit Team. Recipient Merit Cert., Gov. Pat Brown, State of Calif., 1968. Mem. Lindsay Olive Growers, Sunkist Orange Growers, Am. Kennel Club, Internat. Assn. Personnel in Employment Security, Calif. State Employees Assn. (emeritus Nat. Wildlife Fedn., NRA, Friends of Porterville Library, Heritage Found., DAR (Kaweah chpt. rec. sec. 1988—), Internat. Platform Assn., Dist. Fedn. Women's Clubs (recording sec. Calif. chpt. 1988—), Ky. Hist. Soc., Porterville Women's Club (pres. 1988—, dist. rec. sec. 1988—), Internat. Sporting and Leisure Club.

LAMPHER, JACQUELINE DIANE, teacher; b. Fullerton, Calif., June 16, 1938; d. Frederick H. and Eugenie O. (Rivers) Lampher; children: Babette, Brigitte Dennis (twins). AA, Fullerton Coll., 1958; BA, U. Calif., Fullerton, 1962, MA, 1982. Tchr. Anaheim (Calif.) City Sch. Dist., 1962—. Historian PTa, 1988—. Mem. Anaheim Elem. Educators Assn. (pres. 1982-83, 87—, chmn. polit. action com. 1984), Tchrs. United (sec. 1988—). Democrat. Roman Catholic. Home: 419 Wooden Dr Placentia CA 92670

LAMPLEY, NORMA MOSLEY, nurse; b. Homestead, Pa.; d. Mervin McKinley and Vashti (Taylor) Mosley; m. Edward C. Lampley, Sept. 11, 1959; children: E. Charles Jr., Margeaux, Karl. Diploma in Nursing, Howard U., 1958; BBA, Calif. State U., Hayward, 1970; BS in Nursing, Calif. State U., Sacramento, 1978; MS in Nursing, U. Calif., 1980; PhD, Columbia Pacific U., San Rafael, 1985. RN, Washington. Staff nurse Freedman's Hosp., Washington, 1959; head nurse in ophthalmology U. Chgo., 1961-63; emergency room nurse Detroit Receiving Hosp., 1960-61; head nurse in ob-gyn Sydenham Hosp., N.Y.C., 1963-64; pub. health nurse N.Y.C. Health Dept., 1964; clinician Planned Parenthood, Oakland, Calif., 1968-66; coordinator perinatal project Meml. Hosp., San Leandro, Calif., 1978-80; program dir. family communication project Family Service Agy., Oakland, Calif., 1983-84; pvt. practice adolescent and women's health East Oakland Ob-Gyn Med. Group, Oakland, 1980—; founder, mgr. CMK Mgmt. Co., Oakland, 1983—; lectr. Black Nurses State Bd. Rev., 1986-88, various community groups, 1980—; family planning nurse practitioner West Oakland Health Ctr., 1988. Editor: Newsletter Jack/Jill Am., Inc., Parenting, 1984; columnist Samoan News, 1985. Asst. chmn. adminstrv. council Down's Meml. United Meth. Ch., Oakland, 1988; bd. dirs. Family Service Agy., 1985—, East Oakland Girl's Assn., 1984—. Recipient Youth forum Plaque award Nat. Med. assn., Washington, 1982, Easter Seal Plaque Easter Found., Oakland, 1985. Mem. NAACP (life), Coalition Calif. Nurse Practitioners, Am. Coll. Obstetricians Gynecologists, Nat. Assn. Obstetricians Gynecologists, Aux. Nat. Med. Assn. (pres. 1973-74, treas., editor), Sinkler Miller Assn. (sec. 1982), Delta Sigma Theta, Sigma Theta Tau. Democrat. Clubs: Jack & Jill of Am. (Oakland) (treas., editor). Office: E Oakland Ob-Gyn Med Group 9925 E 14 St Oakland CA 94603

LAMY, JEFFREY L., winery, vineyard executive; b. Evanston, Ill., Apr. 23, 1938; s. Joseph Curwin and Eleanor Patricia (Headen) L.; m. Judith Irene Begley, Nov. 25, 1961; children: Christopher John, Ann Katherine, Michelle Irene. BS in Indsl. Adminstrn., Yale U., 1960; postgrad., U. R.I., 1961-62,

Syracuse U., 1964-65; MS in Bus. and Corp. Fin., U. Idaho, 1971. Plant location cons. Tec-Search, Inc., Evanston, 1960-61; systems mgr., sr. project engr., dist. mgr. Sealol, Inc. subs. EG&G, Inc., Providence, 1961-65, 66-67; exec. v.p. Hydro-Components Research and Devel., Inc., Chgo., 1965-66; gen. mgr. Moscow (Idaho) C. of C. 1967-71; dir. econ. devel. Eugene (Oreg.) Area C. of C., 1971-73; sr. v.p. Jack Jarvis & Co., Inc., Portland, Oreg., 1973-75; spl. asst. to fed. co-chmn. Pacific Northwest Regional Commn., Vancouver and Washington, 1975-77; pres., cons. Bus. Econs., Inc., Portland, 1977—; pres., gen. mgr., winemaker Montinore Vineyards, Ltd., Forest Grove, Oreg., 1983—; instr. in viticulture, enology and mgmt. Portland Community Coll., Rock Creek, 1983-87; instr. in urban land econs. Portland State U., 1979-80. Contbr. articles to profl. pubs. Active Oreg. Rep. Party, 1979—. Mem. Oreg. Winegrowers Assn. (bd. dirs. 1984-87, mem. legis. com. 1985-87). Roman Catholic. Lodge: Knights of Vine. Club: Multnmah Athletic (Portland). Home: 3410 SW Vista Dr Portland OR 97225 Office: Montinore Vineyards Ltd Rte 3 Box 193W Forest Grove OR 97116

LANCASTER, ELAINE, teacher; b. Washington, July 28, 1945; d. Edgar Willis and Marion Ruth (Hutchinson) L.; m. John Joseph Judge, Aug. 7, 1987. BS in Early Childhood Edn., U. Md., 1967. Tchr. Montgomery County Sch. Dist., Rockville, Md., 1967-69, Albermarle County Sch. Dist., Charlottesville, Va., 1969-70, Washoe County Sch. Dist., Reno, Nev., 1970—; No. Nev. Polit. Specialist Nev. State Edn. Assn., Carson City. 1985, polit. specialist, lobbyist, 1986-87. Mem. Washoe County Dem. Cen. Com., Reno, 1984—. Mem. AAUW (past pres.) NEA (bd. dirs. 1987—), Nev. State Tchrs. Assn. (bd. dirs. 1987—, govtl. relations and polit. leadership award 1988), Washoe County Tchrs. Assn. (bd. dirs. 1975-84, pres. award 1977, assn. leadership award), Delta Kappa Gamma. Home: 570 Greenstone Dr Reno NV 89512 Office: Pleasant Valley Elem Sch 405 Surrey Dr Reno NV 89511

LANCASTER, ROBERT BRICK, public health administrator, educator; b. Detroit, July 20, 1949; s. Jack Robert and Ruth Lucille (Hood) L.; m. Mary Sue Fisher, Aug. 12, 1972; children: Marc Owen, Amy Lynn. BS cum laude, Cen. Mich. U., 1971, MA, 1972. Dir. health edn. Cen. Mich. Dist. Health Dept., Mt. Pleasant, 1972-79; dep. chief office health edn. Mich. Dept. Pub. Health, Lansing, 1979-82, chief community health edn., 1982-83; chief mgmt. svcs. Kent County Health Dept., Grand Rapids, Mich., 1983-86; chief office health promotion and edn. Ariz. Dept. Health Svcs., Phoenix, 1986—; adj. prof., Cen. Mich. U., Mt. Pleasant, 1974-86, instr., 1983-86; nat. rev. panel mem. Edn. Devel. Ctr., Newton, Mass., 1988; cons. Alcohol Alley multimedia kit, Nat. PTA, Chgo., 1977. Co-author textbook: Community Health Education: Settings, Roles and Skills, 1985, 2d edit., 1989. Chmn., Mt. Pleasant Community Coun. on Drug Misuse, 1972-76; pres. Northwestern region, Mich. Lung Assn., Traverse City, 1977-78; group leader state govt. sect., Lansing United Way, 1980-83; mem. adv. com., Gov.'s Cup Walk, Phoenix, 1987. Fellow Soc. Pub. Health Edn. (v.p. 1982); mem. Am. Pub. Health Assn., Internat. Union Health Edn., Ariz. Pub. Health Assn. (sect. v.p. 1987), Assn. State and Territorial Dirs. Pub. Health Edn. (creativity award 1988, Hod Ogden award 1989). Methodist. Home: 1568 W Irisado Circle Mesa AZ 85202 Office: Ariz Dept Health Svcs 3008 N 3d St Phoenix AZ 85012

LAND, JUDY M., land developer and appraiser; b. Phoenix, Oct. 6, 1945; d. Sanford Karl Land and D. Latanne (Hilburn) Land Krauss; divorced; children: Neal McNeil III, Latanne Tahnee. Student, Geneva Sch., 1965; AA in Econs., Merritt Coll., 1967; MBA, Brklyn Bus. Sch., 1984. Cert. real estate developer, broker and appraiser. Gen. mgr. ACE Rent-A-Car, San Francisco, 1967-71; with real estate sales dept. Odmark/Welch Co/Mesa Realty, San Diego, 1971-76; v.p. Brehm Communities, San Diego, 1977; mgr. investment div. Ayers Realty, Encinitas, Calif., 1978-79; asst. v.p. Harry L. Summers Inc., La Jolla, Calif., 1982-85; pres. Land Co., Carlsbad, Calif., 1979-88; v.p. sales and mktg. Guttman Constrn., Inc., 1988—; bd.dirs. sale and mktg. coun. BIA. Fundraiser Hunger Project, 1979-86, Youth at Risk, 1984-86, Multiple Sclerosis Soc., 1984; mem. exec. com. U.S. Olympics, 1984; bd. dirs. Polit. Policies Com., San Diego, 1986. Mem. Nat. Assn. Real Estate Appraisers, Nat. Assn. Women Execs., Nat. Assn. Home builders, Home Builders Council (pres. 1985), Building Industry Assn. San Diego (bd. dirs. 1985), Econ. Devel. Corp. San Diego (membership com. 1984), Women Comml. Real Estate, Life Spike Club. Office: 409 Camino Del Rio S Ste 101 San Diego CA 92108

LAND, KENNETH DEAN, test and balance agency executive, energy and environmental consultant; b. Central City, Nebr., Oct. 5, 1931; s. Andrew Kenneth Land and Marie Eveline (Weaver) Gehrke; m. Christa Cawthern. AAME, El Camino Coll., 1957; student, Long Beach City Coll., 1958, Calif. State Coll., 1959. Cert. test and balance engr. Gen. mgr. Air Heat Engrs., Inc., Santa Fe Springs, Calif., 1956-61; sales and estimating engr. Thermodyne Corp., Los Alamitos, Calif., 1962-64; pres., founder Air Check Co., Inc., Santa Ana, Calif., 1964-69; engring. technician Nat. Air Balance Co., Los Angeles, 1969-73; gen. mgr. B&M Air Balance Co., South El Monte, Calif., 1973-78; chief exec. officer, founder Land Air Balance Tech. (LABTECH), Las Vegas, Nev., 1978—; bd. dirs. Energy Resources and Mgmt., Inc., 1980—, San-I-Pac, Internat., Inc., 1980—, Energy Equities Corp., 1980—. Mem. Las Vegas Founders Club/Las Vegas Internat. PGA Pro-Am Tournament, 1983—; trustee Associated Air Balance Council/Sheet Metal Workers Internat. Apprenticeship Tng. Fund. Mem. ASHRAE (pres. so. Nev. chpt. 1983-84, editor chpt. bull. 1979—), CSI (co-founder Las Vegas chpt., pres. 1989—, editor, founder chpt. bull., 1988—) Assn. Energy Engrs., Am. Soc. Profl. Cons., Associated Air Balance Council (cert. test and balance engr. 1965—, pres. 1988—, bd. mem. 1982—, mem. many coms.), Sheet Metal Workers Internat. Tng. Fund, Internat. Conf. Bldg. Officials Assn., Constrn. Specifications Inst. (Las Vegas chpt., pres., v.p., co-founder 1987—), Nat. Fedn. Ind. Businessmen, Rotary (editor So. Elmonte, Calif. chpt. Bulletin 1977-78, Las Vegas SW club 1979—, bd. dirs. 1984-85, photographer 1987—), Rotary Internat. (4 Paul Harris fellows), Citizens for Pvt. Enterprise, Nev. TaxpayersAssn., Univ. Nev. Las Vegas Golf Found., Desert Inn Country Club. Office: Land Air Balance Tech Inc PO Box 26389 Las Vegas NV 89126-0389

LANDA, BARRY MORRIS, sales executive; b. Saskatoon, Sask., Can., Apr. 2, 1936; s. Eastwood and Helen Dalores (Von Crum) L.; m. Stasia Bernice Poweska, Apr. 2, 1963; children: Tamara, Shana, John. BS, U. B.C., 1956. With Playtex div. Internat. Latex Corp., 1962-66; sales mgr. Grayson Broadcasting, Inc., 1966-68; environ. and tech. svcs. supr. Calif. div. Del Monte Corp., 1968-79; food div. mgr. Diversey Chems., 1979-80; cons. The Barange Co., Stockton, Calif.; ptnr. Gooding Assocs., Lodi, Calif., 1980-83; western regional sales mgr. Franrica & Prodo-Pak Corp., 1983-85, mgr. product sales and mktg. svcs., 1985-88; v.p. sales Precision Drying Systems, Inc., Stockton, Calif., 1988; v.p., gen. mgr. VID-Alert, Inc., Stockton, 1988—; mem. faculty Delta Coll., Stockton, 1973-86, U. Calif., Davis, 1973-79; lectr. in field. Mem. Canners League, Nat. Assn. Corrosion Engrs., Inst. Food Technologists, Calif. Food Processors Inst., Inst. for Thermal Processing Specialists, Am. Soc. Enologists. Home: 3079 Beaufort Ave Stockton CA 95209

LANDEL, ROBERT FRANKLIN, physical chemist, rheologist; b. Pendleton, N.Y., Oct. 10, 1925; s. Carlisle Oscar and Grace Elisabeth (McEachren) L.; m. Aurora Mamauag, Aug. 1, 1953; children: Carlisle P., Grace P., Hans F., Robert F. Jr., Kevin L., Matthew N. BA, U. Buffalo, 1949, MA, 1950; PhD, U. Wis., 1954. Rsch. assoc. U. Wis., Madison, 1954-55; sr. rsch. engr. Jet Propulsion Lab., Pasadena, Calif., 1955-59; sect. mgr. Jet Propulsion Lab., Pasadena, 1959-85, sr. rsch. scientist, 1984—; vis. prof. Ecole Poly. Fed., Lausanne, Switzerland, 1984; cons. Sandia Nat. Labs, Albuquerque, 1983; cons. in field; mem. U.S./U.K. Working Group on Antimisting Aircraft Fuels, 1978-82. Mem. editorial bd. various polymers jours.; contbr. over 90 articles to profl. jours.; patentee in field. Mem., officer YMCA Indian Guides, Altadena, Calif., 1960-74. With U.S. Army, 1943-46, ETO. French Govt. fellow Strasbourg, 1972, Sr. Fulbright fellow U. Naples, Italy, 1971-72; recipient Exceptional Sci. Achievement award NASA, 1976, Exceptional Svc. medal, 1989. Fellow Am. Phys. Soc. (exec. com. high polymer physics div.); mem. Soc. Rheology (v.p. 1983-1985, pres. 1985-87), Am. Chem. Soc., Council Sci. Soc. Pres's., Mgmt. Club, Sigma Xi (sec.-treas. Caltech chpt. 1974-75, v.p. 1975-76, pres. 1976-77). Office: Jet Propulsion Lab Calif Inst Tech 4800 Oak Grove Dr Pasadena CA 91109

LANDERS, ANNA, massage therapist; b. Bowdon, Ga., Nov. 1, 1953; d. Wilburn Fred and Mordie (Kitchens) L.; m. Stephen Foster, May 1971 (div.); 1 child, Stephen Adrian. Student, Inst. Psychol. Structural Balancing, San Diego, 1985, Orange Coast Coll., 1988. Lic. health therapist, Calif. Floral designer Anderson's Florist, Carrollton, Ga., 1972-76, Plants & Flowers, Houston, 1977-79; clk.-typist Fluor Corp., Irvine, Calif., 1979-81; personnel asst. Hughes Aircraft Co., Newport Beach, Calif., 1981-85; pvt. practice massage therapy Costa Mesa, Calif., 1985--. Home and Office: 249-A Ogle St Costa Mesa CA 92627

LANDERS, MILTON HAROLD, anesthesiologist; b. San Jose, Calif., Sept. 30, 1950; s. Allen B. and Laura (Handler) L.; m. Helena Kathleen Florence, Aug. 13, 1972; children: Samara P., David M., Daniel L., Rachel S. BS, U. Oreg., 1971, 72, MS, 1974; Phd., U. Vt., 1980; D.O., U. Health Sciences, Kansas City, Mo., 1984. Diplomate Am. Acad. Osteopathic Anesthesiologists. Research asst. U. Oreg., Eugene, 1973-74; research asst. Colo. State U., Ft. Collins, 1974-75; instr. Colo. State U., 1976, teaching asst., 1976-78; teaching fellow U. Vt., Burlington, 1978-80; chief resident anesthesia Doctors Hosp., Columbus, Ohio, 1986-87; staff anesthesiologist USAF Regional Hosp., Elmendorf Air Force Base, Ark., 1987-88; chief anesthesia svcs. USAF Regional Hosp., Elmendorf Air Force Base, 1988—. Contbr. articles to Insect Physiology, Anesthesiology. Gordon Lacy scholar Colo. State U., 1975, Health Professions scholar USAF. Mem. Alaska Anesthesia Soc., Am. Anesthesia Assn., Am. Osteo. Assn., Am. Assn. Osteo. Specialists (diplomat), Alaska Osteo. Med. Assn. (bd. dirs.), Am. Soc. Regional Anesthesia. Jewish. Office: USAF Regional Hosp SGHSA Elmendorf AFB AK 99506-5300

LANDERS, VERNETTE TROSPER, educator, author; b. Lawton, Okla., May 3, 1912; d. Fred Gilbert and LaVerne Hamilton (Stevens) Trosper; A.B. with honors, U. Calif. at Los Angeles, 1933, M.A., 1935, Ed.D., 1953; Cultural doctorate (hon.), Lit. World U., Tucson, 1985; m. Paul Albert Lum, Aug. 29, 1952 (dec. May 1955); 1 child, William Tappan; m. 2d, Newlin Landers, May 2, 1959; children: Lawrence, Marlin. Tchr. secondary schs., Montebello, Calif., 1935-45, 48-50, 51-59; prof. Long Beach City Coll., 1946-47; asst. prof. Los Angeles State Coll., 1950; dean girls Twenty Nine Palms (Calif.) High Sch., 1960-65; dist. counselor Morongo (Calif.) Unified Sch. Dist., 1965-72, coordinator adult edn., 1965-67, guidance project dir., 1967; clk.-in-charge Landers (Calif.) Post Office, 1962-82; ret., 1982. V.p., sec. Landers Assn., 1965—; sec. Landers Vol. Fire Dept., 1972—; life mem. Hi-Desert Playhouse Guild, Hi-Desert Meml. Hosp. Guild. Bd. dirs., sec. Desert Emergency Radio Service. Recipient internat. diploma of honor for community service, 1973; Creativity award Internat. Personnel Research Assn., 1972, award Goat Mt. Grange No. 818, 1987; cert. of merit for disting. service to edn., 1973; Order of Rose, Order of Pearl, 1989, Alpha Xi Delta, 1978; poet laureate Center of Internat. Studies and Exchanges, 1981; diploma of merit in letters U. Arts, Parma, Italy, 1982; Golden Yr. Bruin UCLA, 1983; World Culture prize Nat. Ctr. for Studies and Research, Italian Acad., 1984; Golden Palm Diploma of Honor in poetry Leonardo Da Vinci Acad., 1984; Diploma of Merit and titular mem. internat. com. Internat. Ctr. Studies and Exchanges, Rome, 1984; Recognition award San Gorgonio council Girl Scouts U.S., 1984, 85; Cert. of appreciation Morongo Unified Sch. Dist., 1984; plaque for contribution to postal service and community U.S. Postal Service, 1984; Biographee of Yr. award for outstanding achievement in the field of edn. and service to community Hist. Preservations of Am.; named Princess of Poetry of Internat. Ctr. Cultural Studies and Exchange, Italy, 1985; community dinner held in her honor for achievement and service to Community, 1984; Star of Contemporary Poetry Masters of Contemporary Poetry, Internat. Ctr. Cultural Studies and Exchanges, Italy, 1984; named to honor list of leaders of contemporary art and lit. and apptd. titular mem. of Internat. High Com. for World Culture & Arts Leonardo Da Vinci Acad., 1987; ABI medal of honor 1987; other awards and certs. Life fellow Internat. Acad. Poets, World Lit. Acad.; mem. Am. Personnel and Guidance Assn., Internat. Platform Assn., Nat. Ret. Tchrs. Assn., Calif. Assn. for Counseling and Devel., Am. Biog. Research Assn. (life dep. gov.), Nat. Assn. Women Deans and Adminstrs., Montebello Bus. and Profl. Women's Club (pres.), Nat. League Am. Pen Women (sec. 1985-86), Leonardo Da Vinci Acad. Internat. Winged Glory diploma of honor in letters 1982), Landers Area C. of C. (sec. 1985-86, Presdl. award for outstanding service), Desert Nature Mus., Phi Beta Kappa. Clubs: Whitter Toastmistress (Calif.) (pres. 1957); Homestead Valley Women's (Landers). Lodge: Soroptimists (sec. 29 Palms chpt. 1962, life mem., Soroptimist of Yr. local chpt. 19, Woman of Distinction local chpt. 1987-88); Whittier (Calif.) Toastmistress (pres. 1957); Homestead Valley Women's (Landers). Author: Impy, 1974, Talkie, 1975, Impy's Children, 1975; Nineteen O Four, 1976, Little Brown Bat, 1976; Slo-Go, 1977; Owls Who and Who Who, 1978; Sandy, The Coydog, 1979; The Kit Fox and the Walking Stick, 1980; contbr. articles to profl. jours., poems to anthologies. Home: 632 Landers Ln PO Box 3839 Landers CA 92285

LANDERSMAN, STUART DAVID, engineer; b. Bklyn., May 26, 1930; s. Joseph David and Thelma (Domes) L.; m. Martha Britt Morehead, Sept. 2, 1955; children: David Wesley, Mark Stuart. BA, Dakota Wesleyan U., Mitchell, S.D., 1953; MS, George Washington U., 1967. Commd. ens. USN, 1953, advanced through grades to capt., 1974, retired, 1982; engr. Applied Physics Lab., Johns Hopkins U., Laurel, Md., 1982—; convoy commodore USN, Royal Navy, Can. Armed Forces, 1984—. Contbr. articles to mags. Decorated Bronze Star, (3) Legion of Merit. Home: 13220 Cooperage Ct Poway CA 92064 Office: JHU/APL Rep COMNAVSURFPAC NAB Coronado San Diego CA 92155-5035

LANDES, ROBERT ALTON, pharmacist, management consultant; b. Inglewood, Calif., Aug. 31, 1942; s. Glen Alton and Edith Irene (Demmon) L.; m. Cara Lou Hutchinson, Aug. 13, 1966 (div. July 1978). AA, Compton Coll., 1962; PharmD, U. So. Calif., 1966, postgrad., 1974-75, 81-83; MBA, Calif. State U., 1989. Registered pharmacist Calif., Nev. Staff Pharmacist Titus Pharmacy, Santa Ana, CAlif., 1966-69; clin. pharmacist St. Francis Med. Ctr., Lynwood, Calif., 1968-88, Torrance Meml. Hosp. Med. Ctr., Lynwood, 1988—; owner, pres. Robert's Reports, Torrance, Calif., 1983—; ptnr., cons. Grier, Landes and Assocs, Marina Del Rey, Calif., 1987—. Contbr. articles to profl. jours. Tchr. Sunday Sch. Grace Missionary Bapt. Ch., Redondo Beach, Calif., 1983-84. Mem. Orange County Soc. Hosp. Pharmacists (chmn. clin. services com. 1979-80), Am. Mgmt. Assn., Soc. Advancement Mgmt. (pres. 1984, editor newsletter 1985), AAAS, Am. Soc. Hosp. Pharmacists, Los Angeles C. of C. (chmn.), Phi Delta Chi, Rho Chi. Clubs: Bikecentennial (Missoula, Mont.), SportsConnection (Torrance). Home: 21321 Marjorie Ave Torrance CA 90503-5443 Office: Grier Landes & Assocs 2554 Lincoln Blvd #141 Marina Del Rey CA 90291

LANDHOLM, WALLACE MARVEN, ophthalmologist; b. N. Platte, Nebr., Sept. 8, 1933; s. Marven K. and Alma L. (Phillips) L.; BA, U. Nebr., 1956, MD, 1959; m. Marcia Greenlee, 1955; children: James, Cheryl. Intern San Bernardino (Calif.) County Hosp., 1959-60; resident in ophthalmology State U. Iowa Hosp., 1963-65; pvt. practice, Newport Beach, Calif., 1967—; mem. staff Hoag Meml. Hosp.; asst. clin. prof. U. Calif. Med. Sch., Irvine; fellow intraocular lens implants Pacific Hosp., Long Beach, Calif., 1976. Served to capt. M.C., USAF, 1960-63. Decorated Air medal; diplomate Am. Bd. Ophthalmology. Mem. AMA, Soc. Eye Surgeons, Am. Acad. Ophthalmology, Am. Intraocular Implant Soc., Newport Beach C. of C., Balboa Bay Club, Alpha Omega Alpha. Lutheran. Office: 320 Superior Ave Ste 350 Newport Beach CA 92663

LANDIS, ROBERT BRUCE, real estate appraiser; b. Ashtabula, Ohio, July 3, 1951; m. Cindy Louise Fee, Sept. 26, 1987; 1 child, Ethan Owen. BS in Music, SUNY, Brockport, 1976. Prin. Landis Appraisal Service, Los Angeles, 1984—; cons. in field, Los Angeles, 1981—. Named Designated Rev. Appraiser, Boston Safe Deposit & Trust Co., 1987. Office: Landis Appraisal Svc 1522 Euclid St #16 Santa Monica CA 90404

LANDON, JACK NICHOLAS, III, railway official, security consultant; b. Wiesbaden, Fed. Republic Germany, Oct. 17, 1951; (parents Am. citizens); s. Jack Nicholas and Geneva (Oswalt) L.; m. Nancy Dunson, Dec. 1976 (div. 1979); m. Janis Kay Hendrickson, Dec. 29, 1979; children: Heather, Megan. BBA, Eastern N.Mex. U., 1974. Br. mgr. Clovis Nat. Bank, N.Mex., 1972-78; police officer City of Clovis, 1978-83; spl. agt. Santa Fe Rwy. Police, Albuquerque, 1983—; active operation lifesaver Santa Fe Rwy. Police, 1983—; instr. grade crossing accident investigation, r.r. safety N.Mex. State Police Acad., Albuquerque Police Acad. Mem. N.Mex. Sheriff's and Police Assn., FOP. Home: 3800 Oakmount Dr SE Rio Rancho NM 87124 Office: Santa Fe Ry Police 214 1st St SW Albuquerque NM 87102

LANDOVSKY, JOHN, artistic director; b. Riger, Latvia, Jan. 2, 1935; came to U.S., 1950; s. Jains and Olga (Kalnins) L. Dancer Weirtterberg Stadiis Opera House, Stuttgart, Fed. Republic Germany, 1965, Internat. Ballet Co., Chgo., 1960-70, Lyric Opera of Chgo., 1960-70; asst. prof. U. Ill., Urbana, 1976-80; director Duluth (Minn.) Ballet Co., 1980-82, Ballet Hawaii, Honolulu, 1982, Hawaii State Ballet, Honolulu, 1982—. Office: Hawaii State Ballet 1418 Kapiolani Blvd Honolulu HI 96814

LANDRE, DEBRA ANN, college mathematics instructor; b. Quantico, Va., Sept. 15, 1955; d. Thomas F. and Joy L. (Carstens) L. BA in French and Math., Bradley U., 1976, MS in Edn., 1977; MS in Math., Ill. State U., 1979. Math. instr. Bradley U., Peoria, Ill., 1977-79, Ill. Valley Community Coll., Peru, 1980, Ill. Wesleyan U., Bloomington, 1981; computer sci. instr. Lincoln Coll., Bloomington, 1981-85; math. instr. Ill. State U., Normal, 1979-85; pres. Quality Input Inc., Normal, 1983-85; dir. acad. computing San Joaquin Delta Coll., Stockton, Calif., 1985-88; math. instr. San Joaquin Delta Coll., Stockton, 1988—. Co-author: Mathematics: Theory into Practice, 1980, Microprocessor-Based Operations: Systems Software, 1985, Microprocessor-Based Operations, 1985, Data Acquisition, 1985; contbr. articles to profl. jours. Mem. Calif. Assn. Dirs. Acad. Computing (pres. 1988—), Calif. Ednl. Computer Consortium (bd. dirs. 1987—, editor 1988—), No. Calif. Community Coll. Computer Consortium (sec./editor 1986—), Phi Delta Kappa. Office: San Joaquin Delta Coll 5151 Pacific Ave Stockton CA 95207

LANDRUM, LARRY JAMES, computer engineer; b. Santa Rita, N.Mex., May 29, 1943; s. Floyd Joseph and Jewel Helen (Andreska) L.; m. Ann Marie Hartman, Aug. 25, 1963 (div.); children—Larry James, David Wayne, Andrei Mikhail, Donal Wymore; m. 2d, Mary Kathleen Turner, July 27, 1980. Student N.Mex. Inst. Mining and Tech., 1961-62, N. Mex. State U., 1963-65; A.A. in Data Processing, Eastern Ariz. Coll., 1971; B.A. in Computer Sci., U. Tex., 1978. Tech. svc. rep. Nat. Cash Register, 1966-73; with ASC super-computer project Tex. Instruments, Austin, 1973-80, computer technician, 1973-75, tech. instr., 1975-76, product engr., 1976-78, operating system programmer, 1978-80; computer engr. Ariz. Pub. Svc., Phoenix, 1980-84, sr. computer engr., 1984-87, lead computer engr., 1987-88, sr. computer engr., 1988—; instr. computer fundamentals Eastern Ariz. Coll., 1972-73, Rio Salado Community Coll., Phoenix, 1985-86; chmn. bd. trustees, 1988, chmn. bd. dirs. Epworth United Meth. Ch., 1989; community devel. adv. com. City of Glendale (Ariz.), 1988-90; local arrangements chmn. Conf. on Software Maintenance, 1988. Mem. Assn. Computing Machinery, Mensa, Phi Kappa Phi. Methodist. Home: 6025 W Medlock Dr Glendale AZ 85301 Office: Ariz Nuclear Power Project PO Box 52034 Phoenix AZ 85072-2034

LANDRY, CALISTE JOHN, JR., engineer, educator; b. Glendale, Calif., Aug. 28, 1941; s. Caliste John and Evangeline Priscilla (Wright) L.; m. Cathy Marie Peterson, May 5, 1983. BS, U. Calif., Santa Barbara, 1966, PhD, 1972. Lectr. U. Calif., Santa Barbara, 1972-76, head mechano-optics research Ctr. Robotic Systems, 1985—; engr. Gen. Research Corp., Santa Barbara, 1976-80; research specialist Lockheed Research, Palo Alto, Calif., 1980-82; project engr. Santa Barbara Research Ctr., 1982-84; pres. Electro-Optics Cons., Santa Barbara, 1983—; mem. faculty Brooks Inst. Photography, Santa Barbara, 1978—; co-founder and exec. dir. Sci. Discovery Ctr., Santa Barbara, 1984—. Contbr. numerous tech. publs.; patentee in field. Bd. dirs. Santa Barbara Sci. Fair Council, 1975—; mem. Sci. and Engring. Council., Santa Barbara, 1983—. Mem. AAAS, IEEE (Outstanding Tech. Paper, 1966), Seismol. Soc. Am., Optical Soc. Am., Aircraft Owner's and Pilots Assn., Santa Barbara C. of C., Santa Barbara Flying Club (bd. dirs. 1985), Sigma Xi. Democrat. Lutheran. Home: 663 Wakefield Rd Goleta CA 93117 Office: U Calif Ctr for Robotic Systems 6740 Cortona Dr Goleta CA 93106

LANDRY, LARRY DAVID, management and government relations consultant; b. May 8, 1948; s. Ernest and Charmain Landry; m. Luz Sarmina, 1971 (div. 1983); children: Lisa, David; m. Nancy Timmerman, May 22, 1988. BA in Govt., U. Notre Dame, 1970; MS in Urban Affairs, U. Wis., Milw., 1972. Dir. research South Bend (Ind.) C. of C., 1969-72; mgmt. asst. Phoenix City Council, 1973-74, exec. asst., 1974-78; asst. to gov. Ariz. State Govt. Office, Phoenix, 1978-79, exec. asst. to gov., 1979-83; dir. Office of Econ. Planning, Phoenix, 1979-83; pres. Landry and Assocs. Cons., Phoenix, 1983—; adj. faculty Ariz. State U. Ctr. for Pub. Affairs, Tempe, Ariz., 1976-80. Author: City Council Members: Issues in Policy Effectiveness; contbr. articles to profl. jours. Bd. dirs. OK Community adv. bd., 1986—, Arizonans for Cult. Devel., 1983—, Ariz. Park Lands Found., 1983-87; mem. Dean's adv. council Ariz. State U. Engring. Sch., U. Ariz. Engring. Sch. Recipient Gov.'s Citation, 1983, Very Outstanding Phoenician award, 1978, TOYM award Phoenix Jaycees, 1979. Fellow Council of State Planning Agys.; mem. Phoenix City Club (pres. 1986). Democrat. Roman Catholic. Office: Landry & Assocs 2 N Central #1950 Phoenix AZ 85004

LANDSBOROUGH, RON JAMES, healthcare executive; b. Jerome, Idaho, Oct. 9, 1955; s. James Ron and Lola Cora (Kinsey) L. BS in Engring., Ariz. State U., 1981, M in Health Service Adminstrn., 1985. Registered profl. engr., Ariz. Indsl. mfg. engr. Gen. Instrument Corp., Chandler, Ariz., 1981; systems engr. Samaritan health Service, Phoenix, 1982-85; healthcare systems cons. Shared Med. Systems, Phoenix, 1985—; cons. Ariz. Dept. Transp., Phoenix, 1980; bd. dirs. Tee-Vision Inc., Phoenix. Mem. Am. Coll. Healthcare Execs., Healthcare Fin. Mgmt. Assn., Health Adminstrs. Forum, Active 20/30 Internat., Soc. for Arts Phoenix, Toastmasters. Republican. Methodist. Office: SMS 2720 E Thomas Rd Bldg A Phoenix AZ 85016

LANE, DAVID CHRISTOPHER, humanities educator, author, researcher; b. Burbank, Calif., Apr. 29, 1956; s. Warren Joseph and Louise Lane; m. Jaquelyn Ann Godfrey, Dec. 16, 1978. BA in Religion, Calif. State U., Northridge, 1978; MA in Religious Studies, Grad. Theol. Union, Berkeley, Calif., 1983; MA in Sociology, U. Calif., San Diego, 1988, postgrad., 1988—. Tchr. Moreau High Sch., Hayward, Calif., 1979-81, Chaminade Prep., Canoga Park, Calif., 1981-82, San Diego U., H.S., 1982-84, U. Calif., San Diego, 1984—; adj. prof. Calif. Sch. Profl. Psychology, San Diego, 1987—; prof. U. for Humanistic Studies, Del Mar, Calif., 1988—; Fate Mag. book reviewer, Hyacinth, Ill., 1983—; cult analyst for various orgns., 1978—; Inst. for the Study of Am. Religion researcher, Santa Barbara, Calif.; faculty-student chmn. Moreau High Sch., 1980-81. Author: The Making of a Spiritual Movement, 1983; editor Understanding Cults Research Series, 1984—; contbg. author to profl. jours. and encycs. of religion. Coach St. Charles, 1978, N. Hollywood, Chaminade Coll. Prep., 1981-82. Regents fellow U. Calif., San Diego, 1984-85, also scholar, 1986-87; recipient U. Calif., San Diego travel grant, 1987. Mem. Am. Acad. Religion, Assn. for Sociology of Religion, Assn. for Transpersonal Psychology. Republican. Roman Catholic. Clubs: U. San Diego High Sch., Surf (San Diego) (pres. 1982-84), Del Mar Surf. Home: 615 Stratford Ct #5 Del Mar CA 92014 Office: U Calif San Diego Warren Coll Writing Program La Jolla CA 92093

LANE, GLORIA JULIAN, foundation administrator; b. Chgo., Oct. 6, 1932; d. Coy Berry and Katherine (McDowell) Julian; m. William Gordon Lane (div. Oct. 1958); 1 child, Julie Kay Rosewood. BS in Edn., Cen. Mo. State U., 1958; MA, Bowling Green State U., 1959; PhD, No. Ill. U., 1972. Cert. tchr. Assoc. prof. William Jewell Coll., Liberty, Mo., 1959-60; chair forensic div. Coral Gables (Fla.) High Sch., 1960-64; assoc. prof. No. Ill. U., DeKalb, 1964-70; prof. Elgin (Ill.) Community Coll., 1970-72; owner, pub. Lane and Assocs, Inc., San Diego, 1972-78; prof. Nat. U., San Diego, 1978—; pres., chief exec. officer Women's Internat. Ctr., San Diego, 1982—; founder, dir. Living Legacy Awards, San Diego, 1984—. Author: Project Text for Effective Communications, 1972, Project Text for Executive Communication, 1980, Positive Concepts for Success, 1983; editor Who's Who Among San Diego Women, 1984, 85, 86, Systems and Structure, 1984. Named Woman of Accomplishment Soroptimist Internat., 1985, Pres.'s Council San Diego, 1986, Ctr. City Assn., 1986, Woman of Yr. Girl's Clubs of San Diego, 1986; recipient Independence award Ctr. for Disabled, 1986. Home and Office: 6202 Friars Rd 311 San Diego CA 92108

LANE, JAMES F., software engineer; b. Jersey City, Nov. 6, 1953; s. Francis Robert and Margaret Ellen Lane. BS in Computer Sci., Worcester Poly. Inst., 1971-75; postgrad., U. Colo., 1978. Software engr. LFE Corp., Waltham, Mass., 1975-76, Martin Maretta, Waterton, Colo., 1976-77; sr. software engr. Digital Group, Denver, 1977; systems analyst Johns-Manville, Littleton, Colo., 1977-78; systems software designer, project leader Microsoft, Redmond, Wash., 1978-85; pres. Elvyn Software, Inc., Redmond, Wash., 1985-87; PDL group mgr. Hanzon Data Inc., Bothell, Wash., 1985—; owner Novelty Hill Software, Redmond, 1987—. Editor (newsletter) Madrone Leaf, 1983-84. Active Maple Valley Renaissance Faire, Maple Valley, Wash., 1979; vol. Sensible Growth Alliance, King County, Wash., 1988—, Seattle Folklife Fest., 1988-89. Mem. IEEE, Assn. Computing Machinery, Soc. Creative Anachronism, Seattle Dulcimer Soc. Home: 22006 NE 114th Redmond WA 98053 Office: Hanzon Data Inc 22032 23d Dr SE Bothell WA 98021

LANE, JOHN GARY, Canadian provincial official; b. Saskatoon, Sask., Can., May 2, 1942; s. Richard Louis and Kathleen May (Flanagan) L.; m. Liz McLaughlin, July 21, 1979; children: Caitlin, Glennie Ann, William. BA, U. Sask., Saskatoon, 1963, LLB, 1966. Bar: Can. 1966. Articled Dept. Justice Sask., Regina, Can., 1966-71; exec. asst. Office Atty. Gen. Sask., Regina, 1971; mem. Nicol Keith, Regina, 1971-76; sr. ptnr. Lane & Whitmore, Regina, 1976-82; minister of justice, atty. gen. Govt. Sask., Regina, 1982-85, minister fin., 1985—, minster revenue and fin. services, 1985-87; minister Sask. Computer Utility Corp., 1982-88, Employment Devel. Agy., 1983-85, Regina, 1983—, Potash Corp. Sask., 1986—. Mem. Sask. Legis. Assembly, Can., 1971—; pres. Progressive Conservative Party Sask., Can., 1979-81. Mem. Canadian Bar Assn., Regina Bar Assn., Law Soc. Sask. Office: Ministry of Fin, Legislative Bldg Rm 312, Regina, SK Canada S4S 0B3

LANE, LARRY SCOTT, producer, writer; b. N.Y.C.; s. Claude Benjamin and Betty Jo (Hostetler) L. BA, U. Tex., 1970; MFA, UCLA, 1972. Mng. artistic dir. City of L.A. Cultural Affairs Dept., L.A., 1975-79; pres. West Coast East Television, West Hollywood and N.Y.C., 1982—; bd. dirs. L.A. Opera Soc. Composer, lyricist: (musical) "1933", 1989; screenwriter: "Rebel Yell", 1987. Vol. L.A. Ctr. for Living, 1982—, G.M.H.C., N.Y.C., 1983—, AIDS Project L.A., 1986—, Nat. Gay and Lesbian Task Force, N.Y.C., 1982—. Recipient Dramalogue award, L.A. Press, 1976, Citipride award, Citicorp, N.Y.C., 1985. Mem. Hollywood Arts Council, Calif. Arts Council, Calif. Confedn. of the Arts. Democrat. Office: West Coast East TV 1217 N Formasa 5 West Hollywood CA 90046

LANE, TIMOTHY DOUGLAS, real estate associate; b. Northridge, Calif., Nov. 9, 1960; s. Fredric Varlic and Pamela Mary (Ames) L. Student, Pierce Jr. Coll., Woodland Hills, Calif., 1979-81, Theater Arts Acad., 1982-83. Host T.G.I. Fridays, Woodland Hills, 1979-83; spokesperson M&M Mars, Inc., Chgo., 1983-86; sales rep. World Title Co., Burbank, Calif., 1987—. Mem. Bd. of Realtors, San Fernando Valley Bd. Realtors, Reseda (bd. dirs. 1987—). Republican. Home: 18530 Hatteras St Ste 212 Tarzana CA 91356 Office: World Title Co 7530 N Glen Oaks Blvd Burbank CA 91504

LANEY, VERN RICHARD, marketing professional; b. Hanford, Calif., June 5, 1942; s. Vern W. and Berniece B. (Hawkins) L.; m. Catherine Marie Downs, July 15, 1961; children: Sherri, Sandi, David. Student, Coll. of Sequoia, 1960-61, Santa Ana Coll., 1970-71; cert., Am. Inst. Banking, Santa Ana, Calif., 1971. Br. mgr. Household Fin. Corp., L.A., 1964-69; consumer loan mgr. First Western Bank, Santa Ana, 1969-71; v.p. State Mutual Savs. & Loan, Newport Beach, Calif., 1971-74; v.p., mgr. Wells Fargo Bank, Fresno, Calif., 1974-79; pres. Union Fin. of Calif., Visalia, 1979--; sec.-treas. Quality Machinery Ctr., Tulare, Calif., 1983--; sec. Union Fin. of Calif., 1986--; bd. dirs. Delta Telephone, Quality Machinery Ctr. Bd. dirs. Mastern Coll. Mem. Western Assn. Equipment Lessors, Fresno C. of C., Visalia C. of C., Rotary. Republican. Baptist. Home: 122 W Victor Ct Visalia CA 93277 Office: Union Fin of Calif 1606 W Mineral King Suite A Visalia CA 93291

LANG, GEORGE F., insurance executive, consultant, lawyer; b. Orange, N.J., Aug. 21, 1937; s. Frank W. and Hilda I. (Pierson) L.; m. Grace B. Preisler, Jan. 30, 1960; children: Christine, Gregg, Cynthia; m. Valerie J. Hanson, Nov. 24, 1978. BS, Ill. Wesleyan U., 1960; JD, Ill. Inst. Tech., 1968. Account exec. Scarborough & Co., Chgo., 1960-67; dir. fin. inst. George F. Brown & Sons, Chgo., 1967-69; v.p., dir. Fin. Ins. Svc., Schaumburg, Ill., 1969-79; pres. City Ins. Svc., Elizabeth, N.J., 1980-84; mng. dir. Res. Fin. Mgmt., Miami, Fla., 1984-85; v.p. Beneficial Ins. Group, Newport Beach, Calif., 1985-86; v.p. Ask Ins. Svc., Irvine, Calif., 1986-89, product ctr. sales, 1989—; cons. in field. Bd. dirs. Woodview Civic Assn., Mt. Prospect, Ill., 1964-70, pres., bd. dirs., 1969; bd. dirs. Chippendale Assn., Barrington, Ill., 1972-76, v.p., bd. dirs., 1976. Home: 111 E Avenida Junipero San Clemente CA 92672 Office: Ask Ins Svc Inc 18581 Teller Ave Irvine CA 92715

LANG, MARGARET ROCHELLE, protective services official; b. Los Angeles, Aug. 29, 1947; d. Charles and Irene Eleanor (Kelley) Eaton; m. James Vincent Lang, Jan. 24, 1970; children: Michelle Lavon, James Patrick-Emil. AA, Cerritos Coll., Norwalk, Calif., 1967. Sec. Bechtel Co., Commerce, Calif., 1967, SWECO, Commerce, 1967-69, Union Oil of Calif., La Mirada, 1969, Assoc. Piping, Compton, Calif., 1969-70, County of San Bernardino, Calif., 1986; supr. San Bernardino Police Dept., 1986—. Active Norwalk counsel Boy Scouts Am., 1981-85, Camp Fire Girls, 1976-83. Recipient Woman of Yr. award Boy Scouts Am., 1983. Democrat. Roman Catholic. Home: 1077 Christobal Ln Colton CA 92324

LANG, MARGO TERZIAN, artist; b. Fresno, Calif.; d. Nishan and Araxie (Kazarosian) Terzian; m. Nov. 29, 1942; children: Sandra J. (Mrs. Ronald L. Carr), Roger Mark, Timothy Scott. Student, Fresno State U., 1939-42, Stanford U., 1948-50, Prado Mus., Madrid, 1957-59, Ariz. State U., 1960-61; workshops with, Dong Kingman, Ed Whitney, Rex Brandt, Millard Sheets, George Post. Maj. exhbns. include, Guadalajara, Mex., Brussels, N.Y.C., San Francisco, Chgo., Phoenix, Corcoran Gallery Art, Washington, internat. watercolor exhbn., Los Angeles, Bicentennial shows, Hammer Galleries, N.Y.C., spl. exhbn. aboard, S.S. France, others, over 50 paintings in various Am. embassies throughout world; represented in permanent collections, Nat. Collection Fine Arts Mus., Smithsonian Instn.; lectr., juror art shows; condr. workshops.; interviews and broadcasts on Radio Liberty, Voice of Am. Bd. dirs. Phoenix Symphony Assn., 1965-69, Phoenix Musical Theater, 1965-69. Recipient award for spl. achievements Symphony Assn., 1966, 67, 68, 72, spl. awards State of Ariz., silver medal of excellence Internat. Platform Assn., 1971. Mem. Internat. Platform Assn., Ariz. Watercolor Assn., Nat. Soc. Arts and Letters (nat. dir. 1971-72, nat. art chmn. 1974-76), Nat. Soc. Lit. and Arts, Phoenix Art Mus., Friends of Mexican Art, Am. Artists Profl. League, English-Speaking Union, Musical Theater Guild, Ariz. Costume Inst., Phoenix Art Mus., Scottsdale Art Center. Home: 6127 Calle del Paisano Scottsdale AZ 85251

LANG, NEVALON B., business college administrator; b. Seattle, Nov. 29, 1933; d. Arthur Roy and Beaulah Etta (Dasher) Thompson; m. Alfred Wayne Lang, Feb. 19, 1965; children: Linda Kay Boyle, Janice Rae Blaine. BS, Lewis Clark State Coll., Lewiston, Idaho, 1970; postgrad. Ariz. State U., Calif. State U., Los Angeles. Cert. vocat. edn., Calif. Bookkeeper, Idaho 1st Nat. Bank, Lewiston, 1952-53; sec. Boeing Aircraft, Seattle, 1953-56, State of Alaska, Soldatna, 1960-62; note teller Rainier Bank, Clarkston, Wash., 1962-65; dir., owner Valley Bus. Coll., Lewiston, 1970—; owner, tour guide Vacations Unltd., Lewiston; owner, mgr. several apts., Lewiston. Mem. Pacific N.W. Bus. Schs. Assn. (sec.-treas.), Wash. Bus. Edn. Assn., Western Bus. Edn. Assn., Nat. Bus. Edn. Assn., Idaho Bus. Edn. Assn., Am. Bus. Edn. Assn., Wash. Vocat. Assn., Am. Vocat. Assn., Lewiston C. of C. (past pres.). Methodist. Club: Jet Set Travel (Seattle). Office: Valley Bus Coll 508 Thain Lewiston ID 85301

LANG, THOMPSON HUGHES, publishing company executive; b. Albuquerque, Dec. 12, 1946; s. Cornelius Thompson and Margaret Miller (Hughes) L.; m. Kimberley M., Mar. 1980. Student, U. N.Mex., 1965-68, U. Americas, Mexico City, 1968-69. Advt. salesman Albuquerque Pub. Co., 1969-70, pres., treas., gen. mgr., dir., 1971—; pub., pres., treas., dir. Jour. Pub. Co., 1971—; pres., dir. Masthead, Internat., 1971—; pres. Magnum Systems, Inc., 1973—; pres., treas., dir. Jour. Ctr. Corp., 1979—; chmn. bd., dir. Starline Printing, Inc., 1985—; v.p., dir. Rio Tech, 1985—; dir. Sun West Bank of Albuquerque; chmn. bd. dirs. Corp. Security and Investigation, Inc., 1986—; pres., bd. dirs. Eagle Systems, Inc., 1986—. Mem. HOW Orgn., Sigma Delta Chi. Home: 8643 Rio Grande Blvd NW Albuquerque NM 87114 Office: 7777 Jefferson NE Albuquerque NM 87109

LANGAN, ROBERT THOMAS, research geophysicist; b. St. Louis, Nov. 14, 1948; s. Thomas Montgomery and Margaret Olive (Huf) L.; m. Susan Lynn Griesbach, Apr. 11, 1981. BSEE, Northwestern U., 1971, MS in Geol. Scis., 1974, MSCE, 1980, PhD in Geol. Scis., 1981. Registered profl. engr., Ill. Postdoctoral fellow Northwestern U., Evanston, Ill., 1980-81; rsch. geophysicist Gulf R & D Co., Harmarville, Pa., 1981-83, Houston, 1983-85; rsch. geophysicist Chevron Oil Field Rsch. Co., La Habra, Calif., 1985—. Contbr. numerous articles to profl. jours. Mem. Am. Geophys. Union, Soc. Exploration Geophysicists, Triathlon Fedn. (mem. rulse and safety com.). Office: Chevron Oil Field Rsch Co PO Box 446 La Habra CA 90631

LANGDON, B.J., nursing educator; b. Haxtum, Colo., July 24, 1937; d. Ivan L. and Mary Elizabeth (Ruch) Knode; m. Donald D. Langdon, Sept. 18, 1960; children: Brent Donald, Cherri Jo, Darla Dawn. Diploma, Swedish Covenant Hosp., 1960; BE, Colo. State U., 1977; postgrad., U. No. Colo. RN, Colo. Staff nurse Logan County Hosp., Sterling, Colo., 1960-63, 74-76, 87—; instr. nursing Northeastern Jr. Coll., Sterling, 1963—; staff nurse E. Colo. Health Dept., Sterling, 1966-67, Med-Care Home Health, Sterling, 1985-86. Singer in Ch. choir. Named Outstanding Young Woman Am., Federated Clubs Am., 1966. Mem. Colo. Edn. Assn. (pres. local chpt. 1984-85), 20th Century Club, Circle 8 Sq. Dance Club. Republican. Methodist. Office: Northeastern Jr Coll 100 College Dr Sterling CO 80751

LANGDON, VERNE LORING, composer; b. Oakland, Calif., Sept. 15, 1941; s. Vernon H. and Dorothy E. (Nichols) L.; m. Karen Dawn Carlson, Jan. 25, 1963 (div.). Student, San Jose (Calif.) State U., 1963. Disc jockey Sta. KLOK, San Jose, 1959-63; v.p. Don Post Studios, Hollywood, Calif., 1963-68; writer, producer Freberg, Ltd., Hollywood, 1969-73; creative cons. major studios and pvt. projects Hollywood, 1973-80; composer, lyricist 1973—. Albums include: An Evening with Boris Karloff & His Friends, Jaye P. Morgan-Lately!, April Stevens-A Very Special Time; mus. compositions include Carousel Dreams, Once Upon a Very Special Time, I Remember, Please Be Gentle, Lovers and Other Strangers, Children of the Night, Just a Memory, Giner Snaps, Circus Clown Calliope Ste., Bork Shuffle, Horror of Erik, The Devil's Love, Echoes of the Organ, Carnival of Souls, Flight of the Vampire, Waltz of the Ghouls, Dream Within a Dream. Mem. ASCAP. Office: Brookledge Music Co 8912 Appian Way Hollywood CA 90046

LANGE, ARTHUR LESLIE, geophysicist; b. Plainfield, N.J., Mar. 25, 1926; s. Moritz and Margaret (Schutte) L.; m. Judith Marian Hayford, Mar. 19, 1966; children: Vreli Rebecca, Gerda Lorena. BS, Stanford U., 1950. Registered geophysicist, Calif. Data analyst Office Naval Rsch., Stanford, Calif., 1949-51; speleologist Western Speleogical Survey, Santa Barbara, Calif., 1951-55; geophys. engr. Newmont Exploration Ltd., Danbury, Conn., 1956-58; geophysicist SRI Internat., Menlo Park, Calif., 1959-71; chief geophysicist AMAX Geothermal, Denver, 1971-81; geophysicist, v.p. Mincomp Corp., Denver, 1981-82; gen. ptnr. Albireo Ltd., Denver, 1983-85, owner, mgr., 1985—; mgr. ops. The Geophysics Group, Denver, 1986—. Editor Jour. Caves & Karst, 1960-72; contbr. articles to profl. jours. With USNR, 1944-46. Mem. Soc. Exploration Geophysicists, European Assn. Exploration Geophysicists, Geothermal Resources Coun., Am. Geophys. Union, Am. Cave Conservation Assn. Lutheran. Home: 257 Alpine Ave Golden CO 80401 Office: The Geophysics Group 3798 Marshall St Wheat Ridge CO 80033

LANGE, GILLIAN NORTHWAY, realtor, foundation executive; b. Hamilton, Ont., June 22, 1936; d. John Hayward and Vivian Lewis Northway; m. David Lange, Jan. 29, 1966 (div. Jan. 1976). Student, Havergal Coll., Toronto, 1953. Realtor Jon Douglas Co., Beverly Hills, Calif., 1975—. Founder, pres. The Amanda Found., Los Angeles, 1976—. Recipient St. Francis of Assisi award City of Los Angeles, 1980. Office: Jon Douglas Co 370 N Canon Dr Beverly Hills CA 90210

LANGE, JANE LOUISE, state agency administrator; b. Platteville, Wis., Sept. 16, 1947; d. Ervin W. and Marian B. (Salzmann) L. BS in Nursing, Viterbo Coll., LaCrosse, Wis., 1971; MPH, U. N.C., 1978. RN, Ariz. Nurse various hosps., Wis., 1971-75; nurse Dept. Pub. Health County of Dane, Madison, Wis., 1975-77; instr. community health nursing Ariz. State U. Coll. Nursing, Tempe, 1978-81; pub. health cons. Dept. Health Scis. State of Ariz., Phoenix, 1981-84, dir. patient care svcs. Hosps. Home Health Agy., 1984-85, mgr. med. rev. program Div. Motor Vehicles Dept. Transp., 1985—; mem. Profl. Adv. Bd. Am. Nursing Resources, Inc., Phoenix, 1987—, Task Force Adolescent Injury Prevention Dept. Health Svcs. State of Ariz., Phoenix, 1987—, MEDPACT Steering Com. Dept. Transp. State of Wis., Madison, 1988—. Creator self-instructional learning modules, 1980. Mem. Am. Pub. Health Assn., Ariz. Pub. Health Assn. (chmn. nursing sect. 1979-81), Assn. Advancement Automotive Medicine, Am. Nurses' Assn., Ariz. Nurses' Assn., Sigma Theta Tau. Office: Ariz Dept Transp 1801 W Jefferson St 512M Phoenix AZ 85007

LANGE, LOUISE MARIA, real estate executive; b. Sedalia, Mo., Apr. 6, 1945; d. Paul Gerhardt and Frances Louise (Donaldson) L.; m. Richard Glen Moore, May 3, 1976. Student, U. Mo., 1963-66. Owner Design World, San Francisco, 1966-73, London, 1973-77; owner Algarve (Portugal) Property Mgmt., 1977-82; real estate salesperson Santa Barbara, Calif., 1982-87; realtor assoc. Steve Schmidt & Co., Santa Barbara, 1987—; cons. Wonder Workshop, London, 1973-77. Mem. Nat. Assn. Realtors, Calif. Assn. Realtors, Santa Barbara Bd. Realtors. Office: Steve Schmidt & Co 1515 Chapala Santa Barbara CA 93103

LANGENDOEN, DONALD TERENCE, linguistics educator; b. Paterson, N.J., June 7, 1939; s. Garret and Wilhelmina (Van Dyk) L.; m. Sally Wicklund, Aug. 16, 1964, (div. Mar. 1982); 1 child, David; m. Nancy Susan Kelly, July 28, 1984. Grad., MIT, 1961, PhD, 1964. Asst. prof. Ohio State U., Columbus, 1964-68; vis. accos. prof. Rockefeller U., N.Y.C., 1968-69; prof. Bklyn. C. and Grad. Ctr., CUNY, N.Y.C., 1969-88, U. Ariz., Tucson, 1988—; exec. officer grad. linguistics program, CUNY, N.Y.C., 1971-78; head dept. linguistics, U. Ariz., Tucson, 1988—; vis. scientist IBM T.J. Watson Research Ctr., Yorktown Heights, N.Y., 1986-87; sr. lectr. Fulbright, Utrecht, Holland, 1977. Co-author: The Vastness of Natural Languages, 1984; author: The London School of Linguistics, 1968. Fellow N.Y. Acad. of Scis., N.Y.C., 1977; named Ptnr. in Edn., Bd. of Edn., N.Y.C., 1982. Mem. Linguistic Soc. of Am. (sec., treas. 1984-88), Assn. for Computational Linguistics, Assn. for Linguistic and Literary Computing. Office: Dept Linguistics U Ariz Douglass Bldg Rm 200E Tucson AZ 85721

LANGENHEIM, JEAN HARMON, biology educator; b. Homer, La., Sept. 5, 1925; d. Vergil Wilson and Jeanette (Smith) H.; m. Ralph Louis Langenheim, Dec. 1946 (div. Mar. 1961). BS, U. Tulsa, 1946; MS, U. Minn., 1949, PhD, 1953. Rsch. assoc. botany U. Calif., Berkeley, 1954-59, U. Ill., Urbana, 1959-61; rsch. fellow biology Harvard U., Cambridge, Mass., 1962-66; asst. prof. biology U. Calif., Santa Cruz, 1966-68, assoc. prof. biology, 1968-73, prof. biology, 1973—; academic v.p. Orgn. Tropical Studies, San Jose, Costa Rica, 1975-78; mem. sci.adv. bd. EPA, Washington, 1977-81; chmn. com. on humid tropics U.S. Nat. Acad. Nat. Research Council, 1975-77; mem. com. floral inventory Amazon NSF, Washington, 1975-87. Contbr. articles to profl. jours. Grantee NSF, 1966-88; recipient Disting. Alumni award U. Tulsa, 1979. Fellow AAUW, Bunting Inst., Calif. Acad. Scis.; mem. Botanical Soc. Am., Internat. Soc. Chem. Ecology (pres. 1986-87), Ecol. Soc. Am. (pres. 1986-87), Assn. Tropical Biology (pres. 1985-86). Home: 191 Palo Verde Terr Santa Cruz CA 95060 Office: U Calif Thimann Labs Santa Cruz CA 95064

LANGER, EVA MARIE, marketing executive; b. Oceanside, Calif., Sept. 23, 1958; d. William Frank and Clotilde (Gonzalo) L. B.S., San Diego State U., 1980. Audio engr. Peters Prodns., San Diego, 1980-83; news writer Sta. KSDO, San Diego, 1981-82; audio prodn. engr. Tuesday Prodns., San Diego, 1983-85; video technician Voice & Video, San Diego, 1983-84, ednl. sales staff, 1984-85, govt. and ednl. mktg. saleswoman, 1985-86,retail sales mgr., corp. and comml. mktg. saleswoman, 1986-88, med. sales specialist, 1988—; ind. radio producer, San Diego, 1984—, ind. music searcher, 1984-85. Producer Persons with AIDS Project, 1987, (documentary) Joyu, A Zen Priest, 1987. Camera operator Mothers Embracing Nuclear Disarmament, San Diego, 1985, Reiki Therapist, 1988. Mem. Am. Women in Radio and TV (dir.-at-large 1985, 1st v.p. 1986, editor newsletter 1985-86), Nat. Assn. Female Execs. Democrat. Home: 5046 Rockford Dr San Diego CA 92115 Office: Voice & Video Inc 5038 Ruffner St San Diego CA 92111

LANGER, JAMES STEPHEN, physicist, educator; b. Pitts., Sept. 21, 1934; s. Bernard F. and Liviette (Roth) L.; m. Elinor Goldmark Aaron, Dec. 21, 1958; children: Ruth, Stephen, David. B.S., Carnegie Inst. Tech., 1955; Ph.D., U. Birmingham, Eng., 1958. Prof. physics Carnegie-Mellon U., Pitts., 1958-82, assoc. dean, 1971-74; prof. physics U. Calif-Santa Barbara, 1982—; mem. solid state scis. com. NRC. Contbr. articles to profl. jours. Vice pres. physics Com. Concerned Scientists, 1979—. Guggenheim fellow, 1974-75; Marshall scholar, 1955-57. Fellow AAAS, Am. Phys. Soc.; mem. Nat. Acad. Scis., N.Y. Acad. Scis. Democrat. Jewish. Home: 1130 Las Canoas Ln Santa Barbara CA 93105 Office: U Calif Inst Theoretical Physics Santa Barbara CA 93106

LANGER, PAMELA JOYCE, molecular biologist; b. Phila., May 5, 1951; d. Albert George and Helen Dorothea (Mulranen) L. BS, Ind. U., 1973; PhD, MIT, 1980. IIT internat. fellow U. Nairobi, Kenya, 1980-81; research scientist Wellcome trust Kenya Med. Research Inst., 1981-82; postdoctoral research fellow Harvard U. Med. Sch., Boston, 1982-85; asst. prof. in molecular biology U. Wyoming, Laramie, 1986—. Contbr. articles to profl. jours. Recipient Postdoctoral award Inst. Internat. Edn., 1980-81, Med. Found., 1983; Nat. Sci. Found., 1986—, NIH grantee, 1987—. Office: U Wyo Dept Molecular Biology Box 3944 Univ Sta Laramie WY 82071

LANGEREIS-BACA, MARIA, speech-language pathologist; b. Hoorn, Netherlands, Dec. 16, 1930; came to U.S., 1956; d. Jan and Ditje (Schollée) Langereis; m. Stanley H. Skigen (dec.); 1 child, Michelle Arlene; m. Wilhelm Voebel (div.); children: George L., Helene Patimah; m. Gregorio Baca. BS, N.Mex. State U., 1982, MS in Speech, MS in Ednl. Mgmt. Devel., 1985, EdD in Ednl. Mgmt. Devel., 1989. Cert. elem. tchr., ednl. adminstr., speech-lang. pathologist. Asst. personnel mgr. D.M. Read Inc., Bridgeport, Conn., 1960-62; order librarian U. Bridgeport (Conn.), 1962-65; dir. community house Nichols Improvement Assn., Trumbull, Conn., 1960-65; speech-lang. pathologist Las Cruces (N.Mex.) Pub. Schs., 1984—, Hatch (N.Mex.) Pub. Schs., 1985-89; cons. Hospice Inc., Las Cruces, 1985—, Associated Health Service, Las Cruces, 1986—; ednl. cons., 1988—. Leader Girl Scouts Am., Las Cruces, 1976-77; leader 4H Club, Las Cruces, 1978-80; vol. Las Cruces Pub. Schs., 1978-79. Mem. Am. Speech Hearing and Lang. Assn., N.Mex. Speech Hearing and Lang. Assn., Assn. Supervision and Curriculum Devel., Phi Kappa Phi, Phi Delta Kappa. Republican. Roman Catholic. Club: Singles Scene (bd. dirs. 1985—). Home: 465 Milton Ave Las Cruces NM 88005

LANGFELD, MARILYN IRENE, creative art company director; b. St. Louis, Apr. 28, 1951; d. Norman Max and Celeste (Brown) L. Student, Vanderbilt U., 1966-70; B.A. cum laude, Sonoma State U., 1978-80. Printer, Sojourner Truth Press, Altanta, 1971-73; carpenter apprentice Housebuilders Union, Atlanta, 1973-74; self employed housebuilder, Perry, Me., 1974-75; graphic artist Cuthberts Printing, San Rafael, Calif., 1976-77; graphic Designer Community Type & Design, Fairfax, Calif., 1977-80; owner, creative dir. Langfeld Assocs., San Francisco, 1980—. Recipient Am. Corp. Identity award, 1986, Type Dirs. Club award, 1987, Desi award, 1987, Simpson Paper Co. award, 1987, Printing Industries of Am. award, 1987. Mem. People Speaking Adv. Bd., 1979-84. Sonoma State scholar, Bank of Sonoma County, 1979-80; Vanderbilt U. scholar, 1968-69, 69-70; bd. dirs. Horizons Found. Mem. San Francisco C. of C., Am. Inst. Graphic Artists, San Francisco Art Dirs. Club, Western Art Dirs. Club. Art Dirs. and Artists of Sacramento, San Francisco Better Bus. Bur. Clubs: San Francisco Ad, City, Advertising (San Francisco). Democrat. Jewish. Office: 381 Clementina St San Francisco CA 94103

LANGHORST, GARY ARLEN, army reserve officer, communications security consultant; b. Portland, Oreg., June 30, 1928; s. Walter C. and Elsie Lillian (Miles) Langhorst Norris; m. Helen Ruth Costner, Nov. 22, 1952 (dec. Feb. 1988); 1 child, Richard Arlen. BA in History, Wake Forest Coll., 1957. Pvt. investigator Ins. Co., Inc., San Francisco, 1958-63; claims agt. Pacific Intermountain Express, Oakland, Calif., 1963-64; staff adminstrv. specialist 361st Rgt. 91st Div. USAR, San Pablo, Calif., 1964-67; staff adminstrv. asst. 221st Mil. Police Brigade, USAR, San Pablo, 1967-73; tng. specialist 351st Civil Affairs Command, USAR, Mountain View, 1973-88; cons. communication security 351st Civil Affairs Command, USAR, 1975-88; exec. sec. Lamptey Sports Found., Santa Clara, Calif., 1988--. Asst. music dir. Bapt. Temple San Jose, 1967--, Sunday Sch. Tchr., 1967-88; bd. dirs. Am. Christians TV Network, 1987-88; advisor Correctional Instn. Chaplains, San Jose, Calif., 1980--. Mem. Kiwanis (sec. Milpitas, Calif. 1976-78, lt. gov. div. 12 1984-85, pres. San Jose chpt. 1987-88, editor Spirit of Kiwanis 1986-88, Disting. Pres. award 1980, Kiwanian of Yr. award 1983, Layman of Yr. award San Jose chpt. 1987). Republican. Home: 1580 Fallen Leaf Dr Milpitas CA 95035

LANGLEY, WILLIAM RAYMOND, electronics company executive; b. Milw., Sept. 26, 1961; s. William Wiley Langley and Linda Dianne (Mein) Seitz. Design dept. mgr. Hyteck Microsystems Inc., Los Gatos, Calif., 1981-87; sr. designer Intech Microsystems, Inc., Santa Clara, Calif., 1987-88; owner Pages, Los Gatos, Calif., 1988--; contract designer, Sequence, Inc., San Jose, Calif., 1986, Intech Microsystems, Inc., Santa Clara, Calif., 1986, Intech, Inc., Santa Clara, 1987. Home: 15900 Escobar Ave Los Gatos CA 95032 Office: Pages 15466 Los Gatos Blvd Ste 109 052 Los Gatos CA 95032

LANGONI, RICHARD ALLEN, civil engineer; b. Trinidad, Colo., Aug. 7, 1945; s. Domenic and Josephine (Maria) L.; A of Applied Sci., Trinidad State Jr. Coll., 1966; BSCE Colo. State U., 1968; MA, U. No. Colo., 1978; m. Pamela Jill Stansberry, Aug. 19, 1972; children: Kristi, Kerri. Civil engr. Dow Chem. Co., Golden, Colo., 1968-71; city engr., dir. public works City of Trinidad, 1971-74; civil engr. Clement Bros. Constrn. Co., 1974-75; instr. Trinidad State Jr. Coll., 1975-78; city engr., dir. public works City of Durango (Colo.), 1978-82; project engr. Colo. Dept. Hwys., Durango, 1982—. Recipient Meritorious Service award City of Durango; registered profl. engr. Colo., N.Mex. Mem. Nat. Soc. Profl. Engrs., ASCE, Am. Public Works Assn., Water Pollution Control Fedn., Profl. Engrs. Colo., Durango C. of C., Nat. Ski Patrol, Purgatory, Wolf Creek, Hesperus, Phi Theta Kappa, Chi Epsilon. Home: 30 Moenkopi Dr Durango CO 81301

LANGSTON, DEWEY FRANCIS, retired physical education educator; b. Palestine, Tex., July 17, 1920; m. Dessie Langston; children: Jackie Frances, Judy Kaye. BA in Edn. and Math., Eastern N.Mex. U., 1943; MEd, Springfield (Mass.) Coll., 1948; postgrad., Ind. U., 1950, PhD in Phys. Edn., 1952; postgrad., Stanford U., 1956. Grad. fellow, asst. prof. phys. edn. U. Ark., 1950-51; asst. prof. phys. edn. Eastern N.Mex. U., Portales, 1951-53, assoc. prof., 1953-57, prof. health and phys. edn., 1957—, prof. emeritus, 1986—; mem. grad. student com., faculty devel. com., program rev. com. ROTC Scholarship Selection Bd.; mem. grad. council, grad. recruitment com., com. to evaluate adminstrn. Coll. Edn. and Tech.; grad. coord. Sch. of Health, Phys. Edn. and Recreation; faculty advisor Phi Delta Kappa; several positions in intercollegiate athletics, adminstrv. athletics and phys. edn. Contbr. articles to profl. jours. Past bd. dirs. Portales Campfire Girls, Red Rose of N.Mex., Roosevelt County United Fund, Portales Explorer Soc., El Llano Grande Dist. Boy Scouts Am.; past chmn. Roosevelt County ARC, Roosevelt County Oral Vaccine Drive; active Mil. Acad. Rev. Bd., Portales Armory Bd., N.Mex. Nat. Guard; mem. phys. edn. adv. com. State of N.Mex., 1982-85, N.Mex. Devel. Disabilities Planning Council; bd. dirs. Southeastern N.Mex. Sr. Coalition, 1989. 2nd lt. USMC, 1943-46; capt. USMCR, 1946-62; lt. col. USAR, 1962-71. Decorated Purple Heart; Nat. Collegiate Athletic Assn. grantee 1976-78, 83, 85. Fellow N.Mex. Assn. Health, Phys. Edn., Recreation and Dance (pres. 1968, hon. award 1965); mem. NEA, Am. Sch. and Community Safety Assn. (bd. dirs. 1968-74, 77-80, v.p. 1977-78, Profl. Svc. award 1980), Am. Alliance Health, Phys. Edn.

and Recreation (sch. grad. coord., bd. govs. 1978-79, rep. to southwest dist. assembly N.Mex. chpt., v.p. 1965-67, pres. 1967-68, others), Sports Philatelist Internat., Nat. Rifle Assn., Am. Acad. Sports Medicine, Am. Coll. Sports Medicine, Roosevelt County C. of C., Antique Autos of Am., Masons, Shriners, (select master), Rotary (pres. 1958-59, Paul Harris fellow), Am. Legion, Alpha Phi Omega (Svc. Key 1958), Phi Delta Kappa (area copr. 1968-75, 77-78, chmn. adv. panel 1976-80, Disting. Svc. award 1974, 78, Svc. Key 1964, 84), Phi Epsilon Kappa (Hon. Key 1958), Phi Kappa Phi, Sigma Delt Psi. Baptist. Home: 1500 W 17th Ln Portales NM 88130

LANGSTON, TIMOTHY MICHAEL, sales executive; b. Vallejo, Calif., Feb. 16, 1953; s. Shelby T. and Laura (Sanchez) L.; m. Kathleen Louise Eddy, Dec. 26, 1986; children: Heather Christine, Jacqueline Marie. AA, Solano Coll., Vallejo, Calif., 1972. Sales mgr. Flintstone Motor Cars, Redding, Calif., 1976-79, Auburn (Calif.) Datsun, 1979-82, Gusruds Nissan, Mt. Vernon, Wash., 1982-86, Cosol Inc., Roseville, Calif., 1987-88; v.p. sales Watkins Marine Ctrs., Las Vegas, Nev., 1989; owner Marine Wholesale Distbn., Roseville, 1989—; fund-raiser, cons. Four Seasons Fund Raising, Auburn, Calif. 1979-82; dist. mgr. West coast Chris Craft Boats, Bradenton, Fla., 1986-88. Recipient Award of Merit, President's Council Physical Fitness, 1973. Mem. Kangaroo Kourts. Office: Marine Wholesale Distbn 639 Lyndhurst Ave Roseville CA 95678

LANIER, SIDNEY ARTHUR, business owner; b. Austin, Tex., Mar. 21, 1945; s. Sidney Alexandrea and Ruth D'Dee (Ruppenthal) L.; m. Marla Sue Davidson, Apr. 10, 1971; children: Heidi Rene, Bryanna, Katherine, Caleb. BS, Sam Houston U., 1967, postgrad., 1968. From sales rep. to dist. rep. Crown Zellerbach Corp., Lubbock, Tex., 1969-71; from asst. mgr. to mgr. Wilbur Ellis Co., Lubbock and Clovis, N.Mex., 1971-77; owner Lanier Commodities, Clovis, 1977—; pres. U.S. Mktg., Inc., Clovis, 1984—; cons. United Salvage Assocs., Dallas, 1978—. Bd. dirs. Mission to Am., Humble, Tex., 1986—, Believers Faith Ministries, Cloud, 1983—; ambassador People to People, China, 1989. Mem. Tex. Grain and Feed Assn., Tex. Cattle Feeders (assoc.), Com. of Fifty, Full Gospel Businessmen. Republican. Office: US Mktg Inc 200 Main St PO Box 69 Clovis NM 88101

LANKFORD, JEFFERSON LEWIS, lawyer, judge; b. Louisville, Oct. 5, 1951; s. Charles William and Anne Lewis (Scales) L.; m. Mildred Yates, Aug. 19, 1978; children: Katherine, John. BA, U. Ky., 1973; JD, U. Va., 1978. Bar: Ariz. 1978, U.S. Dist. Ct. Ariz. 1979, U.S. Ct. Appeals (6th cir.) 1979, U.S. Supreme Ct. 1982, U.S. Ct. Appeals (9th cir.) 1982, U.S. Ct. Appeals (10th cir. 1983), U.S. Ct. Appeals (D.C. cir.) 1988, U.S. Ct. Appeals (fed. dir.) 1988. Staff asst. U.S. Ho. of Reps., Washington, 1973-75; law clk. U.S. Ct. of Appeals, Cin., 1978-79; ptnr. Jennings, Strouss & Salmon, Phoenix, 1979—; judge pro tempore Maricopa County Superior Ct., Phoenix, 1986—; mem. appellate adv. com. Ariz. Ct. of Appeals, Phoenix, 1987—. Contbr. chpt. to book Arizona Civil Practice Manual, 1984, also articles to profl. jours.; editor Ariz. Litigations Guide, 1989. V.p., bd. dirs. Deer Valley Edn. Found., Phoenix, 1986—. Mem. Phoenix Assn. of Def. Counsel, ABA, Ariz. Bar Assn., Am. Judicature Soc., Fed. Bar Assn., Def. Rsch. Inst., Maricopa County Bar Assn. (chmn. continuing legal edn. com. 1988-89), Am. Arbitration Assn. Democrat. Office: Jennings Strouss & Salmon 2 N Central Ave Phoenix AZ 85004

LANKFORD, LINDA MARIE, construction executive; b. Lubbock, Tex., Aug. 24, 1947; d. Jimmie and Maryann Florence (Jones) Smyth; m. Bobby Ray Lankford, July 31, 1964 (div. 1974); children: Jimmie, Bobby, Michael. Grad. high sch.; student, Antelope Valley Coll., Lancaster, Calif. Cert. pvt. pilot. Haistylist 1963-75; adminstrv. asst., controller Pagosabode, Inc., Pagosa Springs, Colo., 1975-80; office mgr. Aspen Homes, Pagosa Springs, 1978-80; adminstrv. asst. Teroco Constrn., Pagosa Springs, 1980-85; site supt. Teroco Constrn., Lake Arrowhead, Calif., 1985-86; mgr. Mission Bell Inc., Ventura, Calif., 1986-87; quality control inspector Quality Cons., Inc., Federal Way, Wash., 1987-88; quality control supt. Kaufman and Broad Inc., Los Angeles, 1988—. Pres. PTO, Pagosa Springs, 1983; sec.-treas. Aspen Springs Owners Assn., 1979; founder Ennis Youth Soccer Assn., Ennis and Archuleta County Soccer Assn. Mem. Nat. Assn. Female Execs., Archuleta County Builders Assn. Republican. Baptist. Office: Kaufman and Broad 11601 Wilshire Los Angeles CA 90025-1748

LANKTREE, CHERYL BLANCHE, clinical psychologist, clinical director; b. Cambridge, Can., Jan. 4, 1953; came to U.S., 1985; d. Roy Henry Nelson and Beryl Olive (Black) L.; m. John Neale Briere, July 5, 1980. BA in Psychology with hons., U. Western Ont., 1975; MA in Devel. Psychology, U. Guelph, 1977; PhD in Clin. Psychology, U. Manitoba, 1984. Predoctoral intern dept. psychiatry Yale U., New Haven, Conn., 1982-83; lecturer U. Manitoba, Winnipeg, Man., Can., 1983-84, asst. prof. of psychology, 1984-85; post-doctoral fellow Harbor-UCLA Med. Ctr., Torrance, Calif., 1985-86; asst. prof. of counseling Calif. State U., Fullerton, 1986-87; asst. prof. clin. psychiatry U.S.C., Los Angeles, 1987-88; clin. psychologist LAC-USC Med. Ctr., Los Angeles, 1987-88; asst. clin. prof. U. Calif., Los Angeles, 1988—; clin. dir. Stuart House Rape Treatment Ctr., Santa Monica, Calif., 1988—; clin. cons. Children's Home, Winnipeg, Man., Can., 1985. Clin. cons. Man. Com. on Wife Abuse, Winnipeg, 1984-85. Man. Mental Health Found. research grantee, 1983-84. Mem. Am. Psychological Assn. Office: Stuart House Santa Monica Hosp 1336 16th St Santa Monica CA 90404

LANNI, JOSEPH TERRENCE, hotel corporation executive; b. Los Angeles, Mar. 14, 1943; s. Anthony Warren and Mary Lucille (Leahy) L. B.S., U. So. Calif., 1965, M.B.A., 1967. Vice pres. Intervest, Inc., Los Angeles, 1967-69; treas. Republic Corp., Los Angeles, 1969-76; chief fin. officer C.W.I., Inc., Los Angeles, from 1977; now pres., chief operating officer Caesars N.J., Inc. subs. Caesars World, Inc., Atlantic City; pres., chief operating officer Caesars World, Inc., Los Angeles, 1981—; dir. OnLine Distributed Processing Co. Author: Anthology of Poetry, 1965. Bd. dirs. Holy Family Services Counseling and Adoption Agy.; bd. regents Loyola Marymount U.; active So. Calif. Civic Light Opera Assocs. Mem. Los Angeles Jr. C. of C. (dir. Century City region), Am. Mgmt. Assn., Commerce Assocs. Clubs: Bachelors; Crockfords (London), Beach (London). Office: Caesars World Inc 1801 Century Pk E Ste 2600 Los Angeles CA 90067

LANS, CARL GUSTAV, architect, economist; b. Gothenburg, Sweden, Oct. 19, 1907; came to U.S., 1916; s. Carl and Ida Carolina (Schon) L.; m. Gwynne Iris Meyer, Dec. 21, 1935; children: Douglas C., C. Randolph. Student, CCNY, 1925-26, Sch. Architecture, Columbia U., 1926-30. Registered architect, Calif. Architect with Harry T. Lindeberg N.Y.C., 1930-32; architect Borgia Bros. Ecclesiastical Marble, N.Y.C., 1932-34; with architects Paist & Stewart, Miami, Fla., 1934-35; chief engr. insp. Dept. Agr., 1936-38; asst. tech. dir. FHA, 1938-48; tech. dir. Nat. Assn. Home Builders, Washington, 1948-52; with Earl W. Smith Orgn., Berkeley, Calif., 1952-56; architect, economist Huntington Beach, Calif., 1956—; ptnr. John Hans Graham & Assocs. Architects, Washington, 1947-55; spl. adviser Pres. Rhee, Republic of Korea, 1955-56; guest lectr. various univs., 1949-52. Author: Earthquake Construction, 1954. Chmn. bd. edn. adv. com., Arlington, Va., 1948. Recipient Outstanding and Meritorious Svcs. citation Republic of Korea, 1956. Mem. AIA (citation), Nat. Acad. Scis. (bldg. rsch. adv. bd. dirs.), S.W. Rsch. Inst., Seismol. Soc. Am., Prestressed Concrete Inst., Urban Land Inst., Nat. Press Club. Home and Office: 21821 Fairlane Circle Huntington Beach CA 92646

LANSDOWNE, KAREN MYRTLE, retired English language and literature educator; b. Twin Falls, Idaho, Aug. 11, 1926; d. George and Effie Myrtle (Ayotte) Martin; B.A. in English with honors, U. Oreg., 1948, M.Ed., 1958, M.A. with honors, 1960; m. Paul L. Lansdowne, Sept. 12, 1948; chilren—Michele Lynn, Larry Alan. Tchr., Newfield (N.Y.) High Sch., 1948-50, S. Eugene (Oreg.) High Sch., 1952; mem. faculty U. Oreg., Eugene, 1958-65; asst. prof. English, Lane Community Coll., Eugene, 1965-82, ret., 1982; cons. Oreg. Curriculum Study Center. Rep., Cal Young Neighborhood Assn., 1978—; mem. scholarship com. First Congl. Ch., 1950-70. Mem. MLA, Pacific N.W. Regional Conf. Community Colls., Nat. Council Tchrs. English, U. Oreg. Women, AAUW (sec.), Jaycettes, Pi Lambda Theta (pres.), Phi Beta Patronesses (pres.), Delta Kappa Gamma. Co-author: The Oregon Curriculum: Language/Rhetoric, I, II, III and IV, 1970. Home: 15757 Rim Rd La Pine OR 97739

LANSER, HERBERT RAYMOND, financial planner; b. Hollywood, Calif., Dec. 10, 1932; s. Hugo and Anna (Strandlund) L.; m. Evana E. Conway, Apr. 1, 1980 (div.); children: Lynn (dec.), Deborah, Cynthia, Karen, Rick; m. Judy Kay Skousen; children: Zachary, Joshua, Ezekiel. Cert. fin. planner. With Herb Lanser Fin. Svc's., San Mateo, Calif., 1956-62, financial planner, 1962-83, cons., 1971-83; fin. planner Herb Lanser Fin. Svc's., Morro Bay, Calif., 1986—; cons., fin. planner Lanser Vermiculture Svc's., Herb Lanser Fin. Svc's., Nurnberg, Fed. Republic Germany, 1983-85; cons. various orgns., 1975—. Author: Profit From Earthworms, 1976; contbr. articles to profl. jours. Sgt. U.S. Army, 1953-55. Named Nat. Sales Leader Prudential Ins. Co., Europe, 1985, 1987. Republican. Office: Herb Lanser & Assocs 895 Napa Ste B5 & B6 PO Box 834 Morro Bay CA 93442

LANTER, SEAN KEITH, mechanial engineer; b. Los Alamos, N.Mex., May 8, 1953; s. Robert Jackson and Norma Esther (Jonas) L.; m. Lauri Jane Willand, July 16, 1977; 1 child, Tully Erik. BA in Physics, U. Utah, 1974, MS in Mech. Engring., 1977. Registered profl. engr. Wash. Sr. engr. Boeing Comml. Airplane Co., Seattle, 1977-82; systems analyst Internat. Submarine Tech. Ltd., Redmond, Wash., 1982-83; engr. software Advanced Tech. Labs., Bellevue, Wash., 1983-84; engr. contract Rho Co., Redmond, 1984-85; sr. mem. tech. staff Cedar Software Inc., Redmond, 1985-87; pres. Connexions Engring. and Software, Woodinville, Wash., 1987-88; pres., chief engr. Connexions Engring., Inc., Woodinville, 1988—. Contbr. articles to profl. jours. Mem. Assn. Computing Machinery, NSPE. Lutheran. Office: Connexions Engring Inc PO Box 2449 Woodinville WA 98072

LANTERMAN, DOUGLAS V., electronics engineer; b. L.A., Feb. 22, 1939; m. Linda Coupe, July 26, 1964; children: John, Jeff. BSEE, Stanford U., 1961; MBA, Santa Clara U., 1969. Engr. Hewlett Packard Co., Palo Alto, Calif., 1965-72; chief engr. Litton Applied Tech., San Jose, 1972—. Contbr. articles to profl. jours. Lt. USN, 1962-64. Mem. IEEE (vice Chmn. 1987). Home: 1913 Deodora Dr Los Altos CA 94022 Office: Litton Applied Tech 4747 Hellyer Ave San Jose CA 94150-7101

LANTOS, THOMAS PETER, congressman; b. Budapest, Hungary, Feb. 1, 1928; m. Annette Tillemann; children: Annette, Katrina. B.A., U. Washington, 1949, M.A., 1950; Ph.D., U. Calif.-Berkeley, 1953. Mem. faculty U. Wash., San Francisco State U., 1950-83; TV news analyst, commentato, sr. econ. and fgn. policy adviser to several U.S. senators; mem. Presdl. Task Force on Def. and Fgn. Policy, 97th-101st Congresses from 11th Dist. Calif. (ranking mem. Mid. East subcom. of fgn. affairs com., chmn. employment and housing subcom. govt. ops. com.); founder study abroad program Calif. State U. and Coll. System. Mem. Millbrae Bd. Edn., 1950-66. Democrat. Office: US Ho of Reps 1526 Longworth House Office Bldg Washington DC 20515

LANTZ, PATRICK EUGENE, pathologist, educator; b. Bklyn., May 16, 1952; s. Robert Eugene and Patricia Ann (Hamilton) L.; m. Shelley Rae Kreiter, Feb. 10, 1987; 1 stepchild, Andrew. BS, U. Ill., 1978; MD, Southern Ill. U., 1983. Diplomate Am. Bd. Pathology. Resident in pathology U. N.Mex. Sch. Medicine, Albuquerque, 1983-86, 87-88, fellow in forensic pathology, Office Med. Investigators, 1986-87, instr. in pathology, 1988—; med. investigator Office Med. Investigator, 1988—. Co-author: Atlas and Text of Gastroentestinal Pathology, 1989. Mem. AMA, Am. Soc. Clinical Pathologists (hon. mention award 1987), U.S.-Can. Acad. Pathologists. Office: Office of Med Investigator 7000 Camino de Salud NE Albuquerque NM 87131

LANTZ, STEPHEN HAMILTON, public affairs executive; b. Pasadena, Calif., May 13, 1950; s. Glenn Burnell II and Joanne Ruth (Hamilton) L.; m. Terri Suzanne Skidmore, Dec. 27, 1975; 1 child, Patrick Brendon Skidmore. AA, Pasadena City Coll., 1970; BA, U. So. Calif., 1972. Exec. dir. Century City C. of C., L.A., 1972-80; editor, gen. mgr. Prime Communications Century City News, L.A., 1980-83; community rels. mgr. transp. commn. L.A. County, L.A., 1983—. Co-author: On the Road to the Year 2000, 1988. Republican. Office: LA County Transp Commn 403 W 8th St # 500 Los Angeles CA 90014

LANYI, JANOS KAROLY, biochemist, educator; b. Budapest, Hungary, June 5, 1937; came to U.S., 1957, naturalized, 1962; s. Istvan and Klara (Rosthy) L.; m. Carol Ann Giblin, Sept. 15, 1962 (div. Dec. , 1984); children: Clara Aileen, Sean Renton, Gabriella; m. Brigitte Schobert, Mar. 27, 1988. Student, Eotvos Lorand U. Scis., Budapest, 1955-56; B.S., Stanford U., 1959; M.A., Harvard U., 1961, Ph.D., 1963. Postdoctoral fellow Stanford U. Sch. Medicine, 1963-65; Nat. Acad. Scis. resident assoc. NASA-Ames Research Ctr., 1965-66; sr. scientist NASA-Ames Research Ctr., Moffett Field, Calif., 1966-80; prof. physiology and biophysics U. Calif.-Irvine, 1980—; vis. fellow Cornell U., 1976. Recipient NASA medal for exceptional sci. achievement, 1977; recipient H. Julian Allen award for best sci. paper Ames Research Ctr., 1978, Alexander von Humboldt award for sr. U.S. Scientists W.Ger., 1979-80. Mem. Am. Soc. Biol. Chemists, Biophys. Soc., Am. Soc. Microbiology, Phi Beta Kappa, Sigma Xi. Office: U Calif Dept Physiology & Biophysics Irvine CA 92717

LAOS, JEFFERY BAFFERT, health services specialist; b. Tucson, Oct. 11, 1954; s. Roy Elias and Annie (Baffert) L.; m. Carren Lee Wood, Jan. 7, 1984; children: Jeffrey Wood Jr., Jarred Wood. BS in Health Svcs., U. Ariz., 1983, postgrad., 1985—; cert. mgmt., Western Internat. U., Phoenix, 1985. Emergency med. technician II A&A Ambulance, Tucson, 1973-77; dialysis technician Dialysis Found. So. Ariz., Tucson, 1977-81, projects mgr., 1981-83; dept. mgr. renal service St. Joseph's Med. Ctr., Phoenix, 1983-85; adminstr., chief executive officer Desert Dialysis Ctr., Tucson, 1985-86; cons. Dialysis Cons., Inc., Littleton, Colo., 1987—; pres., cons. Jeffrey B. Laos & Assocs., Tucson, 1987—; instr. U. Ariz., Tucson, 1975-77, Pima Community Coll., Tucson, 1976-79. Contbr. articles to profl. jours. Bd. mem. Nat. Kidney Found. Ariz., Tucson, 1985, Catholic Community Svcs. Ariz., Tucson, 1985; mem. Republican. Com., Pima County, Tucson, 1977. Recipient Outstanding Citizen of Tucson award, Mayor of Tucson, 1972, 88; speakers award, Lions Internat. Tucson, 1987. Mem. Nat. Renal Adminstrs. Assn., U. Ariz. Alumni Assn., We. Internat. U. Mgmt. Soc. Republican. Roman Catholic. Office: Jeffrey B Laos & Assocs 9300 N Eagle Dancer Dr Tucson AZ 87541

LA PLANTE, DONALD EUGENE, printing company executive, academic administrator; b. Los Angeles, Jan. 27, 1955; s. Victor Donald and Elrose Muriel (Schwartz) LaP. BA, U. So. Calif., Los Angeles, 1976; postgrad., U. Nev., 1976-78. Mgr. graphic services dept. U. So. Calif., Los Angeles, 1978-85, Olympic Graphic systems, Los Angeles, 1985—. Mem. bd. edn. Downey (Calif.) Unified Sch. Dist., 1979, 83, 87; pres., del. Calif. Sch. Bd. Assn., 1983—. Mem. Skull and Dagger Soc. (pres. 1985-87), Delta Chi (chmn. constn. and by laws com., nat. parliamentarian). Democrat. Home: 11908 Susan St Downey CA 90242 Office: Olympic Graphic Systems 3516 E Olympic Blvd Los Angeles CA 90023

LA POLL, FRANCIS ALBERT, lawyer; b. West Hartford, Conn., Dec. 20, 1958; s. Albert Francis and Wilhemina Elvadora (Garrison) L.P. BA, U. Va., 1981; JD, Stanford U., 1984. Bar: Calif. 1984, U.S. Dist. Ct. (no. dist.) Calif. 1984, U.S. Tax Ct. 1986, U.S. Ct. Appeals (9th cir.) 1985. Law clk. U.S. Ct. Appeals 9th Cir., 1984-85; assoc. Fenwick, Davis and West, Palo Alto, Calif., 1985—. Editor-in-chief Stanford Jour. Internat. Law, 1983-84. Mem. bd. mgrs. Mid-Peninsula YMCA, 1988—. Mem. Raven Soc., Jefferson Soc. (sec. 1980, treas. 1980-81). Office: Fenwick Davis & West 2 Palo Alto Sq Ste 800 Palo Alto CA 94306

LAPPERT, MICHAEL ANDREW, ice cream manufacturing company executive; b. Caracas, Venezuela, Mar. 30, 1942; (parents Am. citizens); s. Walter Alexander and Eileen Mary (Molloy) L.; m. Jessica Dee King, May 14, 1985; 1 child, Andrew. Sous chef Hilton Internat., Caracas, 1967-68, chief steward, 1968-69; v.p. Lappert Enterprises, Sausalito, Calif., 1972-; pres. Lapperts Ice Cream Co., Novato, Calif., 1975-. Served with USN, 1969-72. Office: Lapperts Ice Cream Co 32 Levoroni Ct Ste 107 Novato CA 94947

LARAWAY, CHRISTIN SHEEHY, land planning and real estate development consultant; b. Methuen, Mass., Oct. 6, 1955; d. Joseph James and Christine Veronica (Shea) Sheehy; m. Daniel James Laraway, May 6, 1979. B of Landscape Architecture, Mich. State U., 1978. Engring. asst. Beery & Assocs., Okemos, Mich., 1978-79; land planner HLH Architecture Planning, Scottsdale, Ariz., 1979-81; real estate sales agt. Corp. Fin. Assocs., Phoenix, 1981-82; planner Ariz. Gov's. Office of Econ. Planning and Devel., Phoenix, 1982-83; dir. urban planning Ariz. State Land Dept., Phoenix, 1983-86; prin. Laraway & Assocs., Phoenix, 1986—; bd. dirs. Valley Partnership, 1988—. Planning commr. City of Scottsdale, 1988—. Named Adminstr. of Yr. Ariz. Adminstrs. Assn., 1986. Mem. Ariz. Planning Assn., Urban Land Inst. Republican. Office: Laraway & Assocs 2828 N Central Ave Phoenix AZ 85004

LARDY, BARBARA DAWE, foundation executive; b. Elkhorn, Wis., July 30, 1946; d. Lawrence William and Jean (Lucas) Dawe; m. Nicholas Richard Lardy, Aug. 29, 1970; children: Elizabeth Brooke, Lillian Henry. BA, U. Wis., 1968; M in Pub. Health, U. Mich., 1974. Dir. devel. Planned Parenthood of Conn., New Haven, 1975-83; dir. ann. giving U. Wash., Seattle, 1983-85; pres., chief exec. officer Found. of Group Health Coop., Seattle, 1985—. Mem. Nat. Assn. for Hosp. Devel., Nat. Soc. for Fund-Raising Execs., Northwest Devel. Officers Assn. (bd. dirs.). Club: Wash. Athletic (Seattle). Home: 3802 110th Pl NE Bellevue WA 98004 Office: Group Health Found 521 Wall St Seattle WA 98121

LARGENT, STEVE, professional football player; b. Tulsa, Sept. 28, 1954; m. Terry Largent; children: Kyle, Kelly, Kramer, Casie. BS in biology, U. Tulsa, 1976. Wide receiver Seattle Seahawks, NFL, Kirkland, Wash., 1976—; player Pro Bowl, 1979, 80, 82, 85-88. Holder NFL record for passes caught in consecutive games, also for career receiving yardage. Office: Seattle Seahawks 11220 NE 53d St Kirkland WA 98033 *

LARICK, KEITH TOLBERT, JR., educational administrator, educator; b. Pomona, Calif., Feb. 5, 1940; s. Keith Tolbert and Marian (De Vore) L.; m. Sharon Lucille Cooper, June 17, 1961; children—Lisa Raelene, Keli Beth. A.A., Chaffey Coll., 1959; B.A., La Verne Coll., 1961; M.A., Calif. State U.-Los Angeles, 1965; Ed.D., U. La Verne, 1979. Cert. tchr., adminstr., Calif. Tchr., Upland Sch. Dist., Calif., 1961-65, prin., 1965-73; dir. spl. projects Oceanside Unified Sch. Dist., Calif., 1973-74, dir. instrn., 1974-76; asst. supt. Placentia Unified Sch. Dist., Calif., 1976-78, dep. supt., 1978-79, supt., 1979-86; supt. Sacramento City Unified Sch. Dist., 1986—; faculty U. La Verne, Calif., 1980—; mem. Calif. State Tech. Commn. 1984—; chmn. Ctr. for Ednl. Adminstrv. Devel., Orange County, Calif., 1983-84; bd. dirs. Orange County Tech. Bd., 1982-84; cons., lectr. state, nat., local confs., 1973—. Author: Doing Something About Educational Failure, 1977; Strategic Planning—The Future, 1983, Classrooms of the Future, The Futurist, 1986, School Report Cards and Accountability Thrust May/June, 1988. Contbr. articles to profl. jours. Bd. dirs. YMCA—Camping, Ontario, Calif., 1965-73, Boys Club, Upland, 1965-73, So. Calif. Environ. and Leadership Found., 1982-84, Master Symphony Orch. Assn., Orange County, 1984. Recipient Century Club award YMCA, 1979; Mentor award So. Calif. Women in Ednl. Mgmt., 1984. Mem. U. La Vern Doctoral Assn. (pres. 1982-85), Assn. Calif. Sch. Adminstrs. (Exemplary Service award 1983), Am. Assn. sch. Adminstrs., Assn. Large Suburban Sch. Dists. (bd. dirs.), Assn. Supervision and Curriculum Devel. Mem. Christian Ch. (Disciples of Christ). Office: Sacramento City Sch Dist Office of Supt PO Box 2271 Sacramento CA 95810

LARISH, KENNETH, optical company executive; b. Vancouver, B.C., Can., Sept. 6, 1957; s. Fred and Herta (Vielweber) L. M.Ophthalmic Optics, ABO, Fairfax, Va. Optician Pieper Optic, Wiesbaden, W. Ger., 1977-78; owner Deutsche Luftwaffe, Hamburg, W. Ger., 1978-81; optician Brillen Bouffier, Wiesbaden, 1981-82; product mgr. Siegel Optic, Frankfurt, W. Ger., 1982-83; store mgr. Brillen Kessler, Wiesbaden, 1983-84, I-Care Optical, L.A., 1984-87; ops. mgr. Rodenstock, L.A., 1987-88; product mgr. Rodenstock, Chatsworth, Calif., 1988—. Patentee in field; contbr. articles to profl. jours. With German Air Force, 1978-81. Mem. Nat. Acad. Opticians, Opticians Assn. Am., Am. Mktg. Assn. Home: 4211 Arch Dr Studio City CA 91604 Office: Rodenstock 9722 Topanga Cyn Chatsworth CA 91311

LARIZADEH, M(OHAMMED) R(EZA), business educator; b. Tehran, Iran, Apr. 14, 1947; came to U.S., 1966; s. Hassan and Nosrat (Saremi) L.; m. Dianne Ellen Pincus, Mar. 25, 1973; children: Dariush, Darya Anna. BA in Econs., Bus., UCLA, 1972, cert. in acctg., 1974. Cert. colls. teaching credential, Calif. (life); lic. real estate agent, Calif. Auditor Peat, Marwick & Mitchell, Los Angeles, 1972-74; controller Petromain Constrn. Co., Tehran, 1975-77; v.p. fin. Pilary Marine Shipping Co., Tehran, 1977-79; prof. Iranian Inst. Banking, Tehran, 1975-78; pres. Audicount Acctg. and Auditing Group, Los Angeles, 1984—; prof. bus. and acctg. East Los Angeles Coll., 1980-87, vice-chmn. dept. bus. and acctg., 1987—, chmn. dept. bus. adminstrn., 1988—; prof. acctg. Santa Monica (Calif.) Coll., 1987—; mgmt. cons. L.P. Assocs. Mfg. Co., Los Angeles, 1981—; mng. dir. Barrington Enterprises, Los Angeles; prof. Santa Monica (Calif.) Coll., 1987. Author/translator: Accounting/Auditing, 1975. Mem. Am. Mgmt. Assn., Am. Acctg. Assn., Faculty Assn. Calif. Community Colls., NEA, Am. Fedn. Tchrs., Calif. Tchrs. Assn., Am. Entrepreneur Assn., Nat. Assn. Realtors, Calif. Assn. Realtors, Iranian Student Assn. (pres. UCLA chpt. 1969-70), Iranian Student Assn. (pres. UCLA chpt. 1969-70), Nat. Trust for Hist. Preservation, Smithsonian Assn., Alpha Kappa Psi.

LARK, NEIL L., physics, astronomy educator; b. Baker, Oreg., Sept. 10, 1934; s. David Vernon and Lenore K. (Null) L.; m. Elizabeth L. Knox, Oct. 4, 1958; children: Kenneth, David. AB, Calif. State U., Chico, 1955; PhD, Cornell U., 1960. Vis. scientist Inst. for Nuclear Research, Amsterdam, 1961-62; prof. physics U. of the Pacific, Stockton, Calif., 1962—; chemist Lawrence Radiation Lab., Berkeley, Calif., 1963, 66, Livermore, Calif., 1964, 65; Ford Found. fellow Niels Bohr Inst., Copenhagen, 1967-68; vis. mem. staff Los Alamos (N.Mex.) Sci. Lab., 1969; research collaborator, vis. physicist Brookhaven Nat. Lab., Upton, N.Y., 1971, 75; vis. fellow Australian Nat. U., Canberra, 1976; vis. colleague U. Hawaii Inst. for Astronomy, Honolulu, 1986, 87; vice-chmn. planetarium council San Joaquin Delta Coll., Stockton, 1986—. Contbr. numerous articles to profl. jours. Mem. Am. Phys. Soc., Am. Astron. Soc., Am. Assn. Physics Tchrs., AAUP, Astron. Soc. of the Pacific, Sigma Xi. Office: U of Pacific Dept Physics Stockton CA 95211

LARK, RAYMOND, artist, art scholar; b. Phila., June 16, 1939; s. Thomas and Bertha (Lark) Crawford. Student, Phila. Mus. Sch. Art, 1948-51, Los Angeles Trade Tech. Coll., 1961-62; B.S., Temple U., 1961; L.H.D., U. Colo., 1985. Ednl. dir. Victor Bus. Sch., Los Angeles, 1969-71; public relations exec. Western States Service Co., Los Angeles, 1968-70; owner, mgr. Raymond Lark's House of Fine Foods, Los Angeles, 1962-67; exec. sec. to v.p. Physicians Drug and Supply Co., Phila., 1957-61; lectr. Los Angeles Trade Tech. Coll., 1973, Compton (Calif.) Coll., 1972, Nat. Secs. Assn., Hollywood, Calif., UCLA, numerous others. One-man shows include, Dalzell Hatfield Galleries, Los Angeles, 1970-80, Arthur's Gallery Masterpieces and Jewels, Beverly Hills, Calif., 1971, Dorothy Chandler Pavillion Music Center, Los Angeles, 1974, Honolulu Acad. Arts, 1975, UCLA, 1983, U. Colo. Mus., 1984; group exhbns. include, Smithsonian Instn., 1971, N.J. State Mus., Trenton, 1971, Guggenheim Mus., N.Y.C., 1975, Met. Mus. Art, 1976, La Galerie Mauffe, Paris, 1977, Portsmouth (Va.) Mus., 1979, Ava Dorog Galleries, Munich, W. Ger., 1979, Accademia Italia, Parma, 1980, Ames Art Galleries and Auctioneers, Beverly Hills, 1980, Le Salon des Nations at Centre International d'Art Contemporain, Paris, 1983; represented in permanent collections, Library of Congress, Ont. Coll. Art, Toronto, Mus. African and African Am. Art and Antiquities, Buffalo, Carnegie Inst., numerous others; art commns. for tv. and film studios include, All in the Family, Carol burnett Show, Maude, The Young and the Restless, Universal City Studios, Palace of the Living Arts, Movie Land Wax Mus.; author works in field; author and contbr. more than 50 scholarly treatises on art, edn. and the hist. devel. of Black Ams., chpts. to encyclopedias and textbooks, articles to jours., introductions to mus. exhbn. catalogues. Recipient Gold medal Accademia Italia, 1980, also numerous other gold medals and best of show awards, and 3 presdl. proclamations; Nat. Endowment Arts grantee; ARCO Found. grantee; Colo. Humanities Program grantee; Adolph Coors Beer Found. grantee. Mem. Art West Assn. (pres. 1968-70). Address: PO Box 8990 Los Angeles CA 90008

LARKIN, NELLE JEAN, computer programmer, analyst; b. Ralston, Okla., July 4, 1925; d. Charles Eugene and Jennivea Pearl (Lane) Reed; m. Burr Oakley Larkin, Dec. 28, 1948 (div. Aug. 1969); children: John Timothy, Kenneth James, Donald Jerome, Valerie Jean Larkin Rouse. Student, UCLA, 1944, El Camino Jr. Coll., 1946-49, San Jose (Calif.) City Coll., 1961-62. Sr. programmer, analyst III Santa Clara County, San Jose, Calif., 1963-69; sr. analyst, programmer Blue Cross of No. Calif., Oakland, 1971-73; sr. programmer, analyst Optimum Systems, Inc., Santa Clara, Calif., 1973-75, Crocker Bank, San Francisco, 1975-77, Greyhound Fin. Service, San Francisco, 1977-78, TRW Vidar, Mt. View, Calif., 1978-79; sr. program analyst Memorex, Santa Clara, 1979-80; staff mgmt. cons. Am. Mgmt. System, Foster City, Calif., 1980-82; sr. programmer, analyst, project leader Tymeshare, Cupertino, Calif., 1982-83; sr. programmer, analyst Beckman Instruments, Palo Alto, Calif., 1983—. Mem. Calif. Scholarship Fedn. (lifemem. 1943), Alpha Sigma Gamma. Home: 3493 Londonderry Dr Santa Clara CA 95050 Office: Beckman Instruments 1050 Page Mill Rd Palo Alto CA 94304

LARKIN, WENDY DAVIS, advertising consultant; b. Mpls., May 6, 1944; d. Arthur Edward Jr. and Margaret Scott (Davis) L. BS in Am. Lit., Stanford U., 1966; MBA, Pepperdine U., 1977; MA in Clin. Psychology, John F. Kennedy U., 1985. Lic. counselor, Calif. Various positions Clinton E. Frank Advt., San Francisco, 1968-75, acct. exec., 1975-77; freelance broadcast producer Wendy Larkin Communications, San Francisco, 1977-79; acct. exec. Lynch & Rockey Advt., Inc., San Francisco, 1979-84; advt. cons. for therapists Wendy Larkin Communications, Terra Linda and Oakland, Calif., 1985—; pvt. practice counseling, Terra Linda and Oakland, 1987—; cons., bd. dirs. The Therapy Network, Oakland, 1988—; cons. Bioenergetic Soc. of North Calif., 1986-87; assoc. dir. Inst. for Jungian & Reichian Studies, Berkeley, Calif., 1983—; teaching asst. John F. Kennedy U., Orinda, Calif., 1983—, lectr. in psychology, 1988—. Editor: Jung and Reich: The Body as the Shadow, 1988. Commr. San Francisco Advt. Softball League, 1975. Mem. Assn. for Transpersonal Psychology, Calif. Assn. for Marriage and Family Therapists. Office: Wendy Larkin Communications 704 Las Colindas Rd Terra Linda CA 94903

LARKS, LEONARD, optical engineer; b. Chgo., Apr. 29, 1937; s. Saul David and Golda (Gezuk) L.; BA, UCLA, 1957; OD, L.A. Coll. Optometry, 1961; m. Eleanor Judith Glukes, June 14, 1959; children: Caryn, Deena. Practice optometry Glendale, Calif., 1961-64, L.A., 1962-64; bio./med., optical engr./scientist Hycon Mfg. Co. Monrovia, Calif., 1964-69; optical-lens designer engr. design, devel. interplanetary telescopes Jet Propulsion Lab., Calif. Inst. Tech. at Pasadena, 1969-78; cons. in optical design, interplanetary optical design, 1978—; optometrist So. Calif. Permanente Med. Group, West Covina, 1978—. Chief data processing observer L.A. County Dem. Party, 1967-75, mem. County Dem. Central Com., 1968-72, committeeman, chmn. 49th assembly dist. Delegation, 1968-70. Recipient Younger Lens award L.A. Coll. Optometry, 1961, NASA Group Achievement award for Mariner Venus/Mercury 1973 project TV Subsystem Devel. Team, 1974, for Viking Mars 1976 project Orbiter Design and Devel. Team, 1977, for Voyager Sci. Instrument Devel., Imaging Instrument 1981. Mem. Am. Inst. Physics, Optical Soc. Am., Optical Soc. So. Calif. Contbr. articles profl. jours. Patentee in field. Home: 1028 Blue Dr West Covina CA 91790 Office: So Calif Permanente Med Group 1249 Sunset West Covina CA 91720

LARMAN, SHYLA JUNE, real estate broker; b. Rochester, Minn., July 8, 1945; d. Clifford O. and Rita Elaine (Cramer) Clement; m. David Lee Larman, Mar. 28, 1984; children: Christine Beth Anderson, Wade Weston Zellmer. Student, Westmar Coll., LeMars, Iowa, 1963-64. Sales mgr. Realty World-Krueger Realty, Fairmont, Minn., 1976-84; comml. broker The Hanford Co., Tempe, Ariz., 1985-86, Remax, Mesa, Ariz., 1986-87; sr. investment analyst Elcor Fin. Corp., Phoenix, 1987—. Fundraiser Phoenix Symphony, 1988. Mem. Cert. Comml. Investment Assn., Realtors Nat. Mktg. Assn., Cen. Ariz. CCIM Chpt. (chmn. mktg., 1987-88, bd. dirs. 1987-88), Valley of Sun Real Estate Exchangors, Women in Comml. Real Estate. Republican. Roman Catholic. Office: Elcor Fin Corp 4742 N 24th St Ct 1 Ste 300 Phoenix AZ 85016

LAROCK, TERRANCE EDMOND, business executive; b. Detroit, Aug. 29, 1952; s. Wendell and Donna Jean (Elliott) LaR.; m. Bonnie Jo Campbell, July 21, 1979. A.A., Ohlone Jr. Coll., 1972; postgrad. Calif. State U.-Hawyard, 1976, U. N.Y., 1984; B. Polit. Sci., San Jose State U., 1974. Project planner Gould Inc., Santa Clara, Calif., 1977-79; materials mgr. Stanford Assocs., Menlo Park, Calif., 1979, Delta Assocs., Milpitas, Calif., 1979-81, Masstor Systems, Sunnyvale, Calif., 1981-84; purchasing/planning mgr. Fairchild ATS, San Jose, Calif., 1984—; v.p. USA ops. Prodstar America, 1986—; v.p. ops. REDIFAB, San Jose, 1984-86; mgr. Tandy Corp., San Jose, 1976-78; city mgr. Thrifty Rent-A-Car, San Francisco, 1975-76. Author: Manufacturing Terms and Definition, 1978. Recipient Region 7 & 10 Excellent award, Am. Prodn. & Inventory Control, 1983, Edn. award, 1980, Membership award, 1979. Mem. Am. Prodn. and Inventory Control Soc. (region 10 edn., pres. 1980-81, v.p. bd. dirs. 1986-88), Purchasing Mgmt. Assn. Republican. Lutheran.

LA ROCQUE, MARILYN ROSS ONDERDONK, communications executive; b. Weehawken, N.J., Oct. 14, 1934; d. Chester Douglas and Marion (Ross) Onderdonk; B.A. cum laude, Mt. Holyoke Coll., 1956; postgrad. N.Y. U., 1956-57; M. Journalism, U. Calif. at Berkeley, 1965; m. Bernard Dean Benz, Oct. 5, 1957 (div. Sept. 1971); children: Mark Douglas, Dean Griffith; m. 2d, Rodney C. LaRocque, Feb. 10, 1973. Jr. exec. Bonwit Teller, N.Y.C., 1956; personnel asst. Warner-Lambert Pharm. Co., Morris Plains, N.J., 1957; editorial asst. Silver Burdett Co., Morristown, 1958; self-employed as pub. relations cons., Moraga, Calif., 1963-71, 73-77; pub. relations mgr. Shaklee Corp., Hayward, 1971-73; pub. relations dir. Fidelity Savs., 1977-78; exec. dir. No. Calif. chpt. Nat. Multiple Sclerosis Soc., 1978-80; v.p. public relations Cambridge Plan Internat., Monterey, Calif., 1980-81; sr. account exec. Hoefer-Amidei Assocs., San Francisco, 1981-82; dir. corp. communications, dir. spl. projects, asst. to chmn. Cambridge Plan Internat., Monterey, Calif., 1982-84; dir. communications Buena Vista Winery, Sonoma, Calif., 1984-86, asst. v.p. communications and market support, 1986-87; dir. communications Rutherford Hill Winery, St. Helena, Calif., 1987-88; pres. LaRocque/Hannaford Pub. Rels. and Pub. Affairs, Napa, Calif., 1988—; instr. pub. relations U. Calif. Extension, San Francisco, 1977-79. Mem. exec. bd., rep-at-large Oakland (Calif.) Symphony Guild, 1968-69; co-chmn. pub. relations com. Oakland Museum Assn., 1974-75; cabinet mem. Lincoln Child Center, Oakland, 1967-71, pres. membership cabinet, 1970-71, 2d v.p. bd. dirs., 1970-71. Bd. dirs. Calif. Spring Garden and Home Show, 1971-77, Dunsmuir House and Gardens, 1976-77, San Francisco Symphony Assn., 1984—; mem. Calif. State Republican Central Com., 1964-66; v.p. Piedmont council Boy Scouts Am., 1977. Mem. DAR (chpt. regent 1960-61, 66-68), U. Calif. Alumni Assn., Public Relations Soc. Am. (chpt. dir. 1980-82; accredited), Sonoma Valley Vintners Assn. (dir. 1984-87), Napa Valley Wine Auction (pub. relations com.), Internat. Wine and Food Soc. (Marin chpt.), Calif. Hist. Soc., San Francisco Mus. Soc., Nat. Trust for Historic Preservation, Smithsonian Assocs., Sonoma Valley C. of C. (bd. dirs. 1984-87), Am. Inst. Wine and Food, W.I.N.O. (San Francisco chpt.), Knights of the Vine (master lady 1985—). Clubs: Commonwealth of Calif.; Mount Holyoke Coll. Alumnae. Author: Maestro Baton and His Musical Friends, 1968; Happiness is Breathing Better, 1976. Office: LaRocque/Hannaford Pub Rels 1804 Soscol Ave Ste 200 Napa CA 94559

LARRICK, PHYLLIS DALE, teacher; b. Stockton, Calif., May 31, 1930; d. Allen Dale and Lucile Genevieve (Copeland) Perry; m. James Milton Larrick, May 3, 1953; children: Michele Dale Pinkston, Marcia Louise Boer, James Matthew. AS, Modesto Jr. Coll., 1949; BS, U. Calif., Davis, 1951; postgrad., Calif. State U., Turlock, 1985-88. Seed analyst Calif. Crop Improvement Assn., Davis, 1951-53; comml. egg producer Waterford, Calif., 1957-85; horsemanship instr. Waterford, 1976—; sec. horse dept. 38th Dist. Agrl. Assn., Turlock, Calif., 1976-82, supt., 1983—; tchr. Hickman Elem.Sch., Hickman, Calif., 1984—. Adv. com. Oakdale High Sch. Agrl. Dept., 1986—; 4-H and resource leader, U. Calif. Extension Service, 1965—, 1975—; mem. Stanislaus County Form Bur. Agrl. Edn. Com. Recipient outstanding service award Flying W Riding Club, 1980, service to youth award Waterford Pomona Grange, 1981, Vol Service to Community and Youth award, Soroptomists Internat. of Waterford, 1986, Youth award Waterford Dist. C. of C., 1970. Mem. Calif. Women for Agr. (Stanislaus County Chpt.), Nat. Sci. Tchrs. Assn., Washington. Republican. Home: 14849 Yosemite Blve Waterford CA 95386

LARSEN, DEAN LE ROY, church official; b. May 24, 1927; B.A. in English, Utah State U., 1950. Pres. 1st Quorum of the 70, Mormon Ch., Salt Lake City, 1980—. Office: LDS Church 1st Quorum of the 70 50 E N Temple St Salt Lake City UT 84150 *

LARSEN, DONN EDWARD, electronics engineer; b. Aurora, Ill., Sept. 25, 1929; s. Albion Oliver Larsen and Anna (Augusta) Olson; m. Barbara Jean Simonson, Dec. 13, 1948 (div. 1976); children: Arne, Craig, Neil, Donna, Eric. BA in Physics and Math, Western Wash. U., 1951. Lab technician Superior Portland Cement, Concrete, Wash., 1951-54; electronics technician, systems analyst B-52 project Boeing, Seattle, 1954-57, quality control engr., 1954-57, elec. engr., designer Dynasoar project, 1957-61, logistics engr., 1961-62, elec. engr., designer Aerospace div., 1962-66, elec. engr., designer lunar orbiter project, 1966, elec. engr., designer black box project, 1967-72, elec. engr., designer Airborne Warning and Control System project, 1972-76, elec. engr., designer on-board test systems project, 1977-82, elec. engr., configurations and systems designer, 1982—. Patentee in field. Active SPHRT Ski Patrol Rescue Team, 1953—, Nat. Ski Patrol, Snoqualmie Pass, 1965—, Mountain Rescue Council, Seattle, 1975—. Mem. Seattle Profl. Engrs. Republican. Lutheran. Lodge: Elks. Address: 1966 Westlake Ave N Seattle WA 98109

LARSEN, RONALD JUSTIN, principal; b. L.A., Feb. 16, 1941; s. Justin Joshua Larsen and Willa Mae (Arnold) Larsen Salazar; children: Shelley Elizabeth Larsen Brunsvik, Heather Brooke; m. Kathleen Anne Hesse, Oct. 27,. 1979; 1 child, Emily Rose. BA cum laude, San Francisco State Coll., 1968; MA, U. San Francisco, 1985. Cert. tchr., ednl. adminstr., Calif. Tchr. Novato (Calif.) High Sch., 1970-85; asst. prin. Sinaloa Middle Sch., Novato, 1985-88; prin. Twin Hills Sch., Sebastopol, Calif., 1988—. Author: The United States and Canada, 1970. Cpl. USMC, 1958-62, Okinawa. Mem. Twin Hills Ednl. Found., Heritage Homes Petaluma, Assn. Suprs. and Curriculum Devel., Calif. Sch. Leadership Acad. (assoc.), Assn. Calif. Sch. Adminstrs., Sonoma County Assn. Sch. Adminstrs., Commonwealth Club, Phi Delta Kappa, Gamma Theta Upsilono. Democrat. Office: Twin Hills Sch 1685 Water Trough Rd Sebastopol CA 95472

LARSEN, SHERRYL ARLENE, executive secretary; b. Scotts Bluffs, Nebr., July 4, 1945; d. Donald La Verne and Leota Mildred (Rowley) Farmer; m. James M. Houston, Feb. 16, 1964 (div. Feb. 1973); m. Michael L. Larsen, Jan. 21, 1978; children: Brian J., Darcee A., Sumerlin C., Anna Serena. Student, Boise Jr. Coll., 1963-64. Profl. model free lance, 1967-79; adminstrv. clk. Benton County Dist. Ct., Kennewick, Wash., 1971-78; legal sec. Larsen/Cleavenger Law Firm, Kennewick, 1980; rep. collections Mid Columbia Mental Health Ctr. and Psychiat. Hosp., Richland, Wash., 1983-87; exec. sec. Doug Gross Cons., Richland, 1987—. Mem. Zonta (pres. 1986—, numerous other offices). Office: Doug Gross Cons PO Box 187 Richland WA 99352

LARSEN, TIMOTHY GORDON, health care executive; b. Susquehanna, Pa., Aug. 20, 1944; s. Norman James and Margarete Anne (Wunsch) L.; children: Erik Cristopher, Heather Louise. BA summa cum laude, Fla. Atlantic U., 1965; MA (NDEA fellow), Vanderbilt U., 1968; MBA, Pepperdine U., 1978, Dr. honoris causa, 1981; cert. hosp. adminstrn. U. So. Calif., 1980; PhD, Bedford U., 1981. Commd. 2d lt. USAF, 1968, advanced through grades to capt., 1971; aircraft comdr. March AFB, Calif., 1972-75; assoc. prof. aerospace studies Loyola Marymount U., L.A., 1975-76, U. So. Calif., L.A., 1976-78; admissions counselor Air Force Acad., USAF Res., 1978-82 ; asst. mgr. Lincoln Pacific Mktg. Corp., Long Beach, Calif., 1978-79; dep. dir. Social Rehab. Agy., L.A., 1979-81; adminstr. Colima Internal Medicine, Whittier, Calif., 1981-82; exec. dir. Diamond Bar (Calif.) Med. Center, 1982-84; asst. clin. prof. health svc. adminstrn. U. So. Calif., 1981-84; exec. v.p., prin. D'Argent Investment Network, Inc., 1984-85; exec. dir. COMPNET, Coll. of Osteopathic Medicine of the Pacific, 1985-87, The Petrofsky Inst., 1988—; pres. Diamond Bar Improvement Assn., 1984-86; v.p. Diamond Bar C. of C., 1984; bd. dirs. YMCA Diamond Bar, 1982-83. Maj. USAF Res. Decorated D.F.C., Air medal (3); Commendation medal (2), Republic Vietnam Campaign medal, Republic Vietnam Cross of Gallantry with palm. Mem. Am. Acad. Polit. and Social Sci., Med. Group Mgmt. Assn., Hosp. Fin. Mgmt. Assn., Assn. Western Hosps., Internat. Police Assn., Assn. Mental Health Adminstrs., Am. Mgmt. Assn., Diamond Bar Improvement Assn. (pres. 1984-86), Diamond Bar C. of C. (v.p. 1984), Air Force Assn., Soaring Soc. Am., Calif. Wildlife Fedn. Home: 2834 Hamner Ave #131 Norco CA 91760-1929

LARSON, BRENT T., broadcasting executive; b. Ogden, Utah, Sept. 23, 1942; s. George Theodore and Doris (Peterson) L.; m. Tracy Ann Taylor; children: Michelle, Brent Todd. Student, pub. schs., Los Angeles; diploma in radio operational engrng., Burbank, Calif., 1962. Owner, mgr. Sta. KAIN, Boise, Idaho, 1969-77; owner, operator Sta. KXA Radio, Seattle, 1975-83, Sta. KYYX Radio, Seattle, 1980-83, Sta. KCKO Radio, Spokane, Wash., 1978-84, Sta. KUUZ Radio, Boise, 1976-82, Sta. KOOS Radio, North Bend, Oreg., 1980-81, Sta. KODL Radio, The Dalles, Oreg., 1974-80, Sta. KKWZ Radio, Richfield, Utah, 1980—, Sta. KSVC Radio, Richfield, 1980—, Sta. KSOS-FM, Sta. KNKK-Am, Salt Lake City, 1984—; v.p. Casey Larson Fast Food Co., Oreg. and Idaho, 1976—, Imperial Broadcasting Corp., Idaho, 1970—, Sta. KSOS-FM and KNKK-AM, 1983—; pres. First Nat. Broadcasting Corp., 1970—; v.p. Larson-Wynn Corp., 1974—, Brentwood Properties, Ogden, 1977—; pres. Sta. KSIT Broadcasting, Rock Springs, Wyo., 1980—, Gold Coast Communications Corp., Oreg., 1980-81, Sevier Valley Broadcasting Co., Inc., Utah, 1980—, Brent Larson Group Stas., Western U.S., 1969—; v.p. mktg. Internat. Foods Corp., Boise, 1983—; ptnr. Larson Tours and Travel, Burley, Idaho, 1977-87; dir. Casey-Larson Foods Co., La Grande, Oreg. Bd. dirs. Met. Sch., 1981—. Served with U.S. Army, 1961-63. Mem. Am. Advt. Fedn., Nat. Assn. Broadcasters, Nat. Radio Broadcasters Assn., Wash. Broadcasters Assn., Oreg. Broadcasters Assn., Idaho Broadcasters Assn., Utah Broadcasters Assn., Citizens for Responsible Broadcasting (bd. dirs.). Republican. Mormon. Home: 4014 Beus Dr Ogden UT 84403 Office: First Nat Broadcasting Corp PO Box 2129 Salt Lake City UT 84110-2129

LARSON, CHARLES LESTER, television writer, producer, author; b. Portland, Oreg., Oct. 23, 1922; s. Charles Oscar and Ina May (Couture) L.; m. Alice Mae Dovey, Aug. 25, 1966; 1 stepson, Wyn Donavan Malotte. Student, U. Oreg., 1940. Contract writer MGM Studios, Culver City, Calif., 1943-46; freelance mag. writer 1941-51. Assoc. producer: TV program Twelve O'Clock High, 1964; producer: TV program The FBI, 1965-68, The Interns, 1970-71, Cades County, 1971-72; exec. producer: TV program Nakia, 1974; producer: TV movie Crime Club, 1973; co-creator: TV series Hagen, 1979-80; author: The Chinese Game, 1969, Someone's Death, 1973, Matthew's Hand, 1974, Muir's Blood, 1976, The Portland Murders, 1983. Mem. Writers Guild Am. West, Producers Guild, Mystery Writers Am. (spl. award 1974), Authors League Am. Democrat. Home: 2422 SW Broadway Dr Portland OR 97201

LARSON, DAYL ANDREW, architect; b. Denver, Aug. 13, 1930; s. Andrew and Esther (Freiberg) L.; m. Kay W. Larson; children: Linda, Lesli, Lucy. BS in Architecture, BSBA, U. Colo., 1953. Pres. Haller & Larson Architects, Denver, 1962—. Served to capt. C.E., U.S. Army, 1953-55. Mem. AIA (pres. Denver chpt. 1978, pres.-elect state sect. 1986-87, pres. Colo. sect. 1987—). Home: 2153 S Beeler Way Denver CO 80231 Office: Haller & Larson 1725 S Blake St Denver CO 80202 *

LARSON, DELWYN ERNEST, wholesale company executive; b. Storm Lake, Iowa, Nov. 21, 1940; s. Ernest Lloyd and Lea Amanda (Gerke) L.; m. Dolores Teresa Schuh, Aug. 12, 1972. Grad. high sch., Havelock, Iowa. Territory mgr. Cargill Inc., Mnpls., 1962-69; pres. Del-Rich Corp., Linden, Iowa, 1969-71; sales rep. Graybar Electric, Phoenix, 1971-75; pres. N.A.C. Agencies, Phoenix, 1975-79; mgr. Graybar Electric, Mesa, Ariz., 1979—. Mem. Mesa C. of C., Lions, Masons. Republican. Lutheran. Home: 5831 W Pierson Phoenix AZ 85031 Office: Graybar Electric Co Inc 1866 S Fraser Mesa AZ 85204

LARSON, KEITH DOUGLAS, cartoonist; b. Carmel, Calif., Mar. 29, 1957; s. Edwin Carl and Margaret Isabel (Cox) L.; m. Karen Jane Lindvall; 1 child, Wesley Alan. Student, Monterey Peninsula Coll., 1975; student, Calif. Coll. Arts & Crafts, Oakland, 1981-82. Custodian Pacific Grove Sch. Dist., 1976-79; gardener Carmel, Monterey, Calif., 1982-85; cartoonist free-lance Carlsbad, Calif., 1985—; guest cartoonist Art's Prog. Soledad (Calif.) State Prison, 1980. Cartoons pub. in Lear's, Cosmopolitan, others; cartoonist "Slice of Wry". Vol. Pacific S.W. Rwy. Mus. Assn., San Diego, 1987--. Mem. So. Calif. Cartoonists Assn., No. Calif. Cartoonists Assn., Greenpeace. Home: 2607-204 Pirineos Way Carlsbad CA 92009

LARSON, KEITH ROBERT, venture capital fund executive; b. L.A., Mar. 20, 1958; s. Jack Robert and Annie Magdelene (Endres) L.; m. Cynthia Ann Barnett, Sept. 17, 1982. BBA, U. So. Calif., 1080. CPA, Calif., Oreg. Sr. acct. Peat, Marwisk, Main & Co., L.A., 1980-83; asst. sec., chief fin. officer 1st Interstate Capital, Inc. & 1st Interstate Equities Corp., L.A., 1983-85; sec., chief fin. officer Interven Ptnrs.,Inc., Portland, Oreg., 1985--; gen. ptnr. InterVen II, L.P., Portland, Oreg., 1985--; bd. dirs. Northwest Pipe and Casing Co., Portland, Protocol Systems, Inc., Beaverton, Oreg. Mem. U. So. Calif. Acctg. Circle (assoc. dir. 1984-85), City Club. Office: InterVen Ptnrs Inc 227 SW Pine Ste 200 Portland OR 97204

LARSON, MAUREEN INEZ, rehabilitation company executive; b. Madison, Minn., Mar. 10, 1955; d. Alvin John and Leona B. (Bornhorst) L.; m. Michael Earl Klemetsrud, July 7, 1979 (div. Sept. 1988). BA in Psychology, BFA, U. Minn., 1977; MA in Counseling, U. N.D., 1978. Cert. rehab. counselor, ins. rehab. specialist. Employment counselor II, coordinator spl. programs Employment Security div. State of Wyo., Rawlins, 1978-80; employment interviewer Employment Security div. State of Wash., Tacoma, 1980; lead counselor Comprehensive Rehab. Counseling, Tacoma, 1980-81; dir. counseling Cascade Rehab. Counseling, Tacoma, 1981-87, dist. mgr., 1987—; state capt. legis. div. Provisions Project Am. Personnel and Guidance Assn., 1980. Advocate Grand Forks (N.D.) Rape Crisis Ctr., 1977-78. State of Minn. scholar, 1973-77; recipient Alice Tweed Tuohy award U. Minn., 1977, Nat. Disting. Services Registry award Library of Congress, 1987. Mem. Nat. Fedn. of Bus. and Profl. Women (rec. sec. 1978-80), Nat. Rehab. Counseling (bd. dirs. Olympic chpt. 1988—), Nat. Rehab. Assn. (pres. elect 1989—), Pvt. Rehab. Orgn. Wash., N.W. Regional Mgmt. Assn., Nat. Assn. of Rehab. Profls. of Pvt. Sector, Pierce County YMCA, Pi Gamma Mu. Home: 4014 Commencement Bay Dr N Tacoma WA 98407 Office: Cascade Rehab Counseling 917 Pacific Ave Ste 605 Tacoma WA 98402

LARSON, NANCY S., accountant; b. La Jolla, Calif., Aug. 28, 1954; d. Erwin L. and Mildred (Sasse) L. BS in Acctg., San Diego State U., 1977; MS in Taxation, Calif. State U., Fullerton, 1981. CPA, Calif. Tax mgr. Deloitte, Haskins & Sells, Costa Mesa, Calif., 1978-84, Coopers & Lybrand, Newport Beach, Calif., 1984-87; dir. tax Winchells Donut Houses, La Mirada, Calif., 1987—. Mem. AICPA (tax div.), Calif. State CPAs. Office: Winchell's Donut Houses 16424 Valley View Ave La Mirada CA 96037

LARSON, ROBERT WAYNE, communications executive; b. Myrtle Creek, Oreg., Sept. 17, 1957; s. Frank A. and Dorothy I. (Martin) L. Grad. high sch., Myrtle Creek. 3d class permit, FCC. Asst. mgr., projectionist Tri-City (Oreg.) Drive In, 1972-79, Starlite Theater Inc., Roseburg, 1972-79, Pine Drive In Inc., Roseburg, Oreg., 1975-79; announcer Sta. KRNR-Douglas Broadcasters Inc., Roseburg, 1977-83; asst. mgr. Tom Moyer Theaters, Roseburg, 1979-84; pres., bd. dirs. Cascade Pacific TV Assn. Inc., Myrtle Creek, 1979-84; pres., chief exec. officer Cascade Pacific Communications, Myrtle Creek, 1983—, Sta. KRGL-Gee Jay Broadcasting, Myrtle Creek, 1985—, Cinema West, Myrtle Creek, 1986—; mgr., projectionist Garden Valley Cinema, Roseburg, 1972-79; chief engr. Sta. KYES, Roseburg, 1972-79, Beterview Cable TV, Myrtle Creek, 1975-78; projectionist Rio Theatre, Myrtle Creek, 1972-75; owner Sta. KLRQ-FM, Tri City, Oreg., 1988—. Sponsor, TV studio time Jerry Lewis Telethon, Roseburg, 1983. Served with USAF, 1985—. Mem. Air Force Assn. Democrat. Club: Aereo. Home: 916 Douglas St Myrtle Creek OR 97457 Office: Gee Jay Broadcasting Inc PO Box 1555 Myrtle Creek OR 97457

LARUSSA, ANTHONY, JR., professional baseball manager; b. Tampa, Fla., Oct. 4, 1944; m. Elaine Coker, Dec. 31, 1973; 2 daus.: Bianca, Devon. Student, U. Tampa; B.A., U. So. Fla., 1969; LL.B., Fla. State U., 1978. Player numerous major league and minor league baseball team; mgr. Knoxville, So. League, 1978, Iowa, Am. Assn., 1979, Chgo. White Sox (Am. League), 1979-86, Oakland A's (Am. League), Oakland, Calif., 1986—; mgr. Am. League championship team, 1988, Am. League All-Star team, 1989. Named American League mgr. of the year, 1988. Office: Oakland A's Oakland-Alameda County Coliseum Oakland CA 94621 *

LASAK, LUBOMIR STEPHEN, metallurgist; b. Bratislava, Czechoslovakia, July 15, 1943; came to U.S., 1967; s. Ladislav Gabriel and Elena Lasak; m. Danuta Kurek, Dec. 12, 1970; children: Andrew, Ingrid, Rebecca, Monica. MetE, Coll. Tech., Kosice, Czechoslovakia, 1965; M Material Sci., Rensselaer Poly. Inst., 1976. Metallurgist GE, Schenectady, 1967-79; sr. materials engr. Garrett Corp., Phoenix, 1979-86; sr. engrng. specialist Fluid Systems div. Allied Signal Aerospace, Tempe, Ariz., 1986--. 1st lt. Czechoslovak Air Force, 1965-66. Mem. Am. Soc. for Metals. Republican. Roman Catholic. Office: Allied Signal Aerospace Co 1300 W Warner Rd Box 22200 Tempe AZ 85282

LASAROW, WILLIAM JULIUS, chief bankruptcy judge; b. Jacksonville, Fla., June 30, 1922; s. David Herman and Mary (Hollins) L.; m. Marilyn Doris Powell, Feb. 4, 1951; children: Richard M., Elisabeth H. B.A., U. Fla., 1943; J.D., Stanford U., 1950. Bar: Calif. 1951. Counsel judiciary com. Calif. Assembly, Sacramento, 1951-52; dep. dist. atty. Stanislaus County, Modesto, Calif., 1952-53; pvt. practice Los Angeles, 1953-73; bankruptcy judge U.S. Cts., Los Angeles, 1973—; chief judge U.S. Bankruptcy Ct., Central dist., Calif., 1978—; judge Bankruptcy Appellate Panel 9th Fed. Cir., 1980-82; faculty Fed. Jud. Ctr. Bankruptcy Seminars, Washington, 1977-82. Contbg. author, editor legal publs.; staff: Stanford U. Law Review, 1949. Mem. ABA, Los Angeles County Bar Assn., Wilshire Bar Assn., Blue Key, Phi Beta Kappa, Phi Kappa Phi. Democrat. Jewish. Lodge: Masons. Home: 11623 Canton Place Studio City CA 91604 Office: US Bankruptcy Ct 930 US Courthouse 312 N Spring St Los Angeles CA 90012

LASATER, GENE MARTIN, neurologist; b. Paris, Tenn., Apr. 8, 1924; s. John Porter and Frances Laurine (Martin) L.; m. Naomi Ruth Krahn, Oct. 8, 1951; children: Eric, Rand, Gene Jr., Scott. BA, Vanderbilt U., 1945, MD, 1948. Diplomate Am. Bd. Psychology and Neurology. Instr. U. Minn., Mpls., 1953-55; asst. prof. neurology U. Tenn., Memphis, 1955-58; practice medicine specializing in neurology Denver, 1958—; chief of staff Presbyn. Hosp., Denver, 1973-74. Contbr. articles to profl. jours. Served to 1st lt. U.S. Army, 1951-53. Fellow Am. Acad. Neurology. Club: Denver Country. Office: Western Neurol Group 2005 Franklin St Denver CO 80205

LASHER, SUE, councilwoman, investor; b. Split, Yugoslavia; came to U.S., 1932; d. Peter and Ida (Purisic) Sorich; 1 child, Eric Lasher. Councilwoman City of Santa Clara, Calif., 1983—; chmn. Modesto-Santa Clara-Redding (Calif.) Joint Power Agy., 1985—; mem. Santa Clara County Transp. commn., 1987—. Mem. League of Calif. Cities, 1984—. Mem. Santa Clara Women's League (pres. 1984-86). Lodge: Soroptomists. Office: City of Santa Clara 1500 Warburton Ave Santa Clara CA 95050

LASHLEY, VIRGINIA STEPHENSON HUGHES, computer science educator; b. Wichita, Kans., Nov. 12, 1924; d. Herman H. and Edith M. (Wayland) Stephenson; m. Kenneth W. Hughes, June 4, 1946 (dec.); children: Kenneth W. Jr., Linda Hughes Tindall; m. Richard H. Lashley, Aug. 19, 1954; children: Robert H., Lisa Lashley Van Amberg, Diane Lashley Tan. BA, U. Kans., 1945; MA, Occidental Coll., 1966; PhD, U. So. Calif., 1983. Cert. info. processor, tchr. secondary and community coll., Calif. Tchr. math. La Canada (Calif.) High Sch., 1966-69; from instr. to prof. Glendale (Calif.) Coll., 1970—, chmn. bus. div., 1977-81, coord. instructional computing, 1974-84; 88—; sec., treas., dir. Victory Montessori Schs., Inc., Pasadena, Calif., 1980—; pres. The Computer Sch., Pasadena, 1983—; pres. San Gabriel Valley Data Processing Mgmt. Assn., 1977-79, San Gabriel

Valley Assn. for Systems Mgmt., 1979-80; chmn. Western Ednl. Computing Conf., 1980, 84. Editor Jour. Calif. Ednl. Computing, 1980. NSF grantee, 1967-69, EDUCARE scholar U. So. Calif., 1980-82; John Randolph and Dora Haynes fellow, Occidental Coll., 1964-66. Mem. AAUP, Data Processing Mgmt. Assn., Calif. Ednl. Computing Consortium (bd. dir. 1979—, v.p. 1983—, pres. 1985-87), Orgn. Am. Historians, Phi Beta Kappa, Pi Mu Epsilon, Phi Alpha Theta, Phi Delta Kappa, Delta Phi Upsilon, Gamma Phi Beta. Republican. Congregationalist. Home: 1240 San Marino Ave San Marino CA 91108 Office: Glendale Coll 1500 N Verdugo Rd Glendale CA 91208

LASITER, JACK BRINKLEY, utility holding company executive; b. Ft. Smith, Ark., July 20, 1930; s. Brinkley Cyrus and Ruth Leona (Wear) L.; B.S., Pepperdine U., Los Angeles, 1954, M.B.A., 1975; m. Julia Clara Simmons, June 16, 1957; 1 son, Paul Brinkley. With Aerophysics Devel. Corp., Santa Barbara, Calif., 1956-57, Kibbee, Peterson & Co., C.P.A.'s, Hollywood, Calif., 1957-58; with So. Calif. Gas Co., Los Angeles, 1958—, audit coordinator, 1978—; audit support supr. Pacific Lighting Corp. (name now Pacific Enterprises), Los Angeles, 1980—. Served with U.S. Army, 1954-56. Cert. internal auditor. Mem. Inst. Internal Auditor (chmn. scholarship com. Los Angeles chpt. 1980-81), Town Hall Calif. Republican. Mem. Ch. of Christ. Home: 1330 N Valley Home Ave La Habra CA 90631 Office: Pacific Enterprises 801 S Grand Ave Los Angeles CA 90017

LASKO, ALLEN HOWARD, entrepreneur; b. Chgo., Oct. 27, 1941; s. Sidney P. and Sara (Hoffman) L.; B.S. (James scholar), U. Ill., 1964; m. Janice Marilynn Chess, Dec. 24, 1968; children—Stephanie Paige, Michael Benjamin. Staff pharmacist Michael Reese Hosp. and Med. Center, Chgo., 1964-68; clin. pharmacist City of Hope Med. Center, Duarte, Calif., 1968-73; chief pharmacist Monrovia (Calif.) Community Hosp., 1973-74, Santa Fe Meml. Hosp., Los Angeles, 1974-77; pvt. investor, 1977—. Recipient Roche Hosp. Pharmacy Research award, 1972-73. Mem. Magic Castle, Flying Samaritans, Mensa, Rho Pi Phi. Jewish. Author books: Diabetes Study Guide, 1972; A Clinical Approach to Lipid Abnormalities Study Guide, 1973; Jet Injection Tested As An Aid in Physiologic Delivery of Insulin, 1973. Home: 376 N Hill St Monrovia CA 91016

LASORDA, TOM CHARLES, professional baseball team manager; b. Norristown, Pa., Sept. 22, 1927; s. Sam and Carmella (Covatto) L.; m. Joan Miller, Apr. 14, 1950; children—Laura, Tom Charles. Student pub. schs., Norristown. Pitcher with Bklyn. Dodgers, 1954-55, Kansas City A's, 1956; with Los Angeles Dodger Orgn., 1956—; mgr. minor league clubs Pocatello (Idaho), Ogden (Utah), Spokane, Albuquerque, 1965-73; coach Los Angeles Dodgers, 1973-76, mgr., 1976—. Author: (with David Fisher) autobiography The Artful Dodger, 1985. Served with U.S. Army, 1945-47. Los Angeles Dodgers winner Nat. League pennant, 1977, 78, 81, winner World Championship, 1981; 2d Nat. League mgr. to win pennant first two yrs. as mgr.; named Mgr. of Yr. 1988. Mem. Profl. Baseball Players Am. Roman Catholic. Club: Variety of Calif. (v.p.). Office: care Los Angeles Dodgers 1000 Elysian Park Ave Los Angeles CA 90012 *

LASSELL, MICHAEL JOHN, writer, editor; b. N.Y.C., July 15, 1947; s. Michael Joseph and Catherine Elizabeth (Harneit) L. BA, Colgate U., 1969; MFA, Calif. Inst. Arts, 1973, Yale U., 1976. Assoc. editor L.A. Weekly, Los Angeles, 1983-85; theater critic Los Angeles Herald-Examiner, Los Angeles, 1985-87; mng. editor L.A. Style Mag., Los Angeles, 1985—. Author: Poems For Lost and Unlost Boys, 1986 (Amelia award 1986); contbr. poems and articles to various jours. Democrat. Office: LA Style 6834 Hollywood Blvd Los Angeles CA 90028

LASSWELL, JOHN EARL, corporate professional; b. Caddo, Okla., Sept. 17, 1930; s. Albert and Henrietta (Walla) L.; m. Sandra Simonick, Sept. 3, 1960; children: Marla Ann, Monica Lynn, Margo Leah. AA in Engring., El Camino Coll., 1955; BS in Fin., Calif. State U., Long Beach, 1961; MBA, U. So. Calif., 1963; postgrad., UCLA, 1964-65. Officer Crocker Citizens Nat. Bank, Los Angeles, 1961-63; dir. corp. investment TRW Inc., Redondo Beach, Calif., 1963-74; mgr. corp. investment Tektronix Inc., Beaverton, Oreg., 1974-85; controller, treas. Anthro Corp., Portland, Oreg., 1985-86; v.p. fin. United Epitaxial Tech., Beaverton, 1986-87; pres., chief exec. officer, chmn. EPI Corp., Portland, 1987—, also bd. dirs.; bd. dirs. Synertech Corp., Portland. Bd. dirs. West Union (Oreg.) Grade Sch., 1982-83; fin. advisor West Union Sch. Bd., 1984. Served as sgt. USMC, 1948-52. Mem. U. So. Calif. Assocs., Alpha Kappa Psi (life, pres. 1960). Republican. Home: Rte #2 Box 428A Portland OR 97231 Office: EPI Corp 13563 NW Cornell #124 Portland OR 97229

LAST, DIANNA LINN SCHNEIDER, data processing company executive; b. Canton, Ohio, Dec. 29, 1944; d. Ld Mervyn and Veronica Lee Schneider; m. David D. Last, Nov. 29, 1969; 1 child, Jason Holden. BA in German, Ohio State U., 1966. Rsch. asst., programmer trainee high-energy physics dept. Ohio State U., Columbus, 1964-66; mfg. programmer RANCO, Inc., Columbus, 1966-68; sr. edn. rep. Honeywell Info. Systems, Cleve., 1968-72; dist. mgr. Honeywell Info. Systems, Orlando, Fla., 1972-78, telecommunications cons., 1978-79; mgr. networking edn. Honeywell Info. Systems, Phoenix, 1979-81, mgr. distributed systems, 1981-84; account and tech. mgr. Honeywell Info. Systems, Beijing, People's Republic of China, 1985; resident dir., chief rep. Honeywell Bull (formerly Honeywell Info. Systems), Beijing, People's Republic of China, 1985-87; dir. Integrated Info. Architecture Honeywell Bull, Phoenix, 1987-88; dir. info. mgmt. U.S. mktg. Bull (formerly Honeywell Bull), Phoenix, 1988—; bd. advisor Internat. Bus. Orgn., Am. Grad. Sch. Internat. Mgmt., 1981-84; cons., speaker in field. Chalice bearer, lay reader, St. John Baptist Episc. Ch., Phoenix, 1983—, mem. bishop's com., 1980-83; mem. adv. bd. Ariz. Assn. Children and Adults with Learning Disabilities, 1983-84; mem. design task force Maricopa Community Colls., 1984; bd. dirs. Ctr. for New Dirs., 1987—, exec. com. employment adv. com., ctr. for continuing edn., 1972-79. Mem. IEEE (past vice chmn. programs). Home: 1274 E Marconi Ave Phoenix AZ 85022

LATHAN, REGINALD WILMONT, transportation executive; b. Harrisburg, Pa., Nov. 3, 1952; s. Reginald L. and Willetta Thazell (Bolen) L.; m. Nancy Jane Albin, May 18, 1981; children: Radford Carolyn, Reid Alexander. BS, U. So. Calif., 1976; MBA, U. Va., 1987. Personnel mgr. Bethlehem (Pa.) Steel Corp., 1975-82; adminstrn. mgr. A.H. Al Zamil Group, Al Khobar, Saudi Arabia, 1982-85; assoc. investment mgr. Prudential Capital Corp., Newark, N.J., 1987; chief exec. officer Chemical Transp., Long Beach, Calif., 1987—. Office: Chemical Transp 21119 Wilmington Ave Long Beach CA 90810

LATHEN, ROBERT LEE, accountant; b. Clarkston, Wash., Aug. 20, 1956; s. Wesley W. and Mary Lorita (York) L.; m. Rebecca A. Howard, Apr. 21, 1979; children: Scott, Jenny, Sarah. BA in Acctg., M in Taxation, Brigham Young U., 1981. CPA, Oreg. Tax acct. Arthur Andersen & Co., Portland, Oreg., 1981-84; tax mgr. Ch2m Hill, Corvallis, Oreg., 1984—. Contbr. articles to profl. jours. and mags. Varsity coach Boy Scouts Am., Corvallis, 1985-86; youth leader Ch. of Jesus Christ of Latter Day Saints, Corvallis, 1986—. Fellow Am. Inst. CPAs, Oreg. Inst. CPAs. Republican. Mormon. Office: CH2M HILL 2300 NW Walnut Blvd Corvallis OR 97339

LATHI, BHAGAWANDAS PANNALAL, electrical engineering educator; b. Bhokar, Maharashtr, India, Dec. 3, 1933; came to U.S., 1956; s. Pannalal Rupchand and Tapi Pannalal (Indani) L.; m. Rajani Damodardas Mundada, July 27, 1962; children: Anjali, Shishir. BEEE, Poona U., 1955; MSEE, U. Ill., 1957; PhD in Elec. Engring., Stanford U., 1961. Research asst. U. Ill., Urbana, 1956-57, Stanford (Calif.) U., 1957-60; research engr. Gen. Electric Co., Syracuse, N.Y., 1960-61; cons. to semicondr. industry India, 1961-62; assoc. prof. elec. engring. Bradley U., Peoria, Ill., 1962-69, U.S. Naval Acad., Annapolis, Md., 1969-72; prof. elec. engring. Campinas (Brazil) State U., 1972-78, Calif. State U., Sacramento, 1979—; vis. prof. U. Iowa, Iowa City, 1979. Author: Signals, Systems and Communication, 1965, Communication Systems, 1968 (transl. into Japanese 1977), Random Signals and Communication Theory, 1968, Teor ia Signalow I Ukladow Telekomunikacyjnych, 1970, Sistemy Telekomunikacyjne, 1972, Signals, Systems and Controls, 1974, Sistemas de Comunicacion, 1974, 86, Sistemas de Comunicacao, 1978, Modern Digital and Analog Communication Systems, 1983, 89 (transl. into Japanese 1986), Signals and Systems, 1987; contbr. articles to profl. jours. Mem. (sr.) IEEE. Office: Calif State U Elec Engring Dept Sacramento CA 94819

LATHOM, PATRICIA G., advertising and marketing systems executive; b. San Francisco, Oct. 30, 1925; d. A.S. and Ethelyn (Ross) Green; m. J.W. Lathom, Sept. 15, 1945 (div. Nov. 1965); children: Jan W., Christina R. Student, Scripps Coll., 1943-44; BA, Calif. State U., Los Angeles, 1969, postgrad., 1969-71; adult ednl. credential, UCLA, 1972; postgrad., San Francisco Theol. Sem., 1981—. Cert. in consumer sci., home econs., sociology, adult edn., social sci., systems research. Customer service rep. Western Lithograph Co., Los Angeles, 1956-57; west coast office mgr. Revere Corp. Am., Los Angeles, 1957-60; tchr. Glendora (Calif.) Adult Sch., 1973-75; moderator Smokenders, Los Angeles, 1976-80; regional mgr. World Wide Services, San Marino, Calif., 1981-84; franchise owner Successful Living, Inc. div. David C. Cook Pub. Co., Mpls., 1980—; owner, mgr. Lathom Assocs., San Marino, 1967—. Chmn. Community Chest, Monterey Park, Calif., 1953-54; pres. Repetto PTA, Monterey Park, 1955-56; charter mem. Reagan Presdl. Task Force, 1982-88, trustee, 1986-88; sponsor The Ronald Reagan Presdl. Found., 1987-88. Recipient Key Woman award, Inglewood Jr. Chamber Aux, 1953, Monterey Park Jr. Chamber Aux, 1955, Community Chest div. chmn. awards, 1953, 54, fellowship Internat. Biog. Assn., London, Eng., 1975. Mem. Nat. Assn. Female Execs., Mus. Contemporary Arts, Found. for Community Artists, Am. Soc. Profl. and Exec. Women, Soc. for Advancement Mgmt. (v.p. 1964-65, exec. cons. 1965-66ü, Phi Upsilon Omicron, Alpha Kappa Delta. Presbyterian. Home: 1925 Kerns Ave San Marino CA 91108 Office: Lathom Assocs 1613 Chelsea Rd Ste 123 San Marino CA 91108

LATHROP, DAVID DEAN, insurance executive; b. Denver, Apr. 30, 1961; s. Dean Allen and Shirley Anne (Gruis) L. Student, Ariz. State U., 1979-80. Svc. rep. Londen Ins. Group, Phoenix, 1978-81; acct. HBA/Legacy Life Ins. Co., Phoenix, 1981-84; sr. examiner Ariz. Dept. Ins., Phoenix, 1984—, profl. edn. coord., 1987-88; pres. Dave Lathrop Enterprises, Inc., Phoenix, 1985—; Dir., pres., treas. Manhattan Resources, Inc., Phoenix, 1989—. Mem. Soc. Fin. Examiners. Republican. Roman Catholic. Home: 20608 N 5th Ave Phoenix AZ 85027 Office: Dave Lathrop Enterprises 20608 N 5th Ave Phoenix AZ 85027

LATHROP, JAMES CAMERON, general contractor; b. Summit, N.J., Mar. 31, 1946; s. Palmer Jadwin and Caroline Marsh (Kinsey) L.; m. Kathy Jean Goodnite, July 17, 1984; children: Linsay, David. BA, U. Ariz., 1969; MBA, Thunderbird Grad. Sch., Glendale, Ariz., 1971. Pres. Cameo Mgmt. Inc., Steamboat, Colo., 1975-77; owner J.L. Construction, Steamboat, 1977-85; pres. Structural Contracting, Inc., Kona, Hawaii, 1987—. Mem. Keauhou Kona C. of C. Republican. Episcopalian. Office: Structural Construction Inc Box AS Kailua-kona HI 96745

LATHROP, KAYE DON, nuclear scientist, educator; b. Bryan, Ohio, Oct. 8, 1932; s. Arthur Quay and Helen Venita (Hoos) L.; m. Judith Marie Green, June 11, 1957; children: Braxton Landess, Scottfield Michael. B.S., U.S. Mil. Acad., 1955; M.S., Calif. Inst. Tech., 1959, Ph.D., 1962. Staff mem. Los Alamos Sci. Lab., 1962-67; group leader methods devel. Gen. Atomic Co., San Diego, 1967-68; with Los Alamos Sci. Lab., 1968-84, asso. div. leader reactor safeguards and reactor safety and tech. div., 1975-77, alt. div. leader energy div., 1977-78, div. leader computer sci. and services div., 1978-79, asso. dir. for engring. scis., 1979-84; assoc. lab dir., prof. applied research Stanford Linear Accelerator Ctr. Stanford U., Calif., 1984—; vis. prof. U. N.Mex., 1964-65, adj. prof., 1966-67; guest lectr. IAEA, 1969; mem. adv. com. reactor physics ERDA, 1973-77; mem. reactor physics vis. com. Argonne Nat. Lab., 1978-83; mem. mgmt. adv. com. y-12 div. Union Carbide Corp., 1979-82; mem. engring. nat. adv. com. U. Mich., 1983—; mem. steering com. Joint MIT-Idaho Nat. Engring. Lab. Research Program, 1985—; cons. in field. Author reports, papers, chpts. to books; mem. editorial adv. bd. Progress in Nuclear Energy, 1983-85. Served to 1st lt. C.E. U.S. Army, 1955-58. Spl. fellow AEC, 1958-61; R.C. Baker Found. fellow, 1961-62; recipient E.O. Lawrence Meml. award ERDA, 1976; Disting. Service award Los Alamos Nat. Lab., 1984. Fellow Am. Nuclear Soc. (chmn. math. and computation div. 1970-71, nat. dir. 1973-76, 79-82, treas. 1977-79, Outstanding Performance award 1980); mem. Am. Phys. Soc., Nat. Acad. Engring. Republican. Episcopalian. Home: 672 Junipero Serra Blvd Stanford CA 94305

LATHROP, LAWRENCE ERWIN, JR., state agency administrator; b. L.A., Dec. 4, 1942; s. Lawrence Erwin and Anna Maxine (Cypert) L.; m. Elaine Dorothy Baudin, May 16, 1964; 1 child, Lawrence Erwin III. AA in Forestry, Lassen Coll., Susanville, Calif., 1968; BA in Pub. Adminstrn., U. San Francisco, 1976. Cert. fire investigator, coll. instr. Forest firefighter Calif. Dept. Forestry and Fire Protection, Santa Clara, 1961; fire apparatus engr. Calif. Dept. Forestry and Fire Protection, Belmont and Yreka, 1962-64; fire capt. Calif. Dept. Forestry and Fire Protection, Riverside County, 1964-67, 68-73; fire prevention officer Calif. Dept. Forestry and Fire Protection, Clearlake, 1973; state forest ranger I Calif. Dept. Forestry and Fire Protection, Ione, 1973-82; state forest ranger II Calif. Dept. Forestry and Fire Protection, Susanville, 1982—; fire investigation and tng. cons. Nev. Dept. Forestry, Carson City, 1985—, U.S. Bur. Land Mgmt., Elko and Winnemuca, Nev., 1985—. Author, editor: Tailgate Safety Bulletin, 1984—; author of numerous in-service tng. programs, including Helicopter Safety, Air Attack, Powerline Inspections, 1978-82. Advisor Demolay, Amador County, Calif., 1976-78; active PTA, Amador County, 1975-82, Lassen County Arson Task Force, 1985—, State Arson Unit, 1974—. Mem. Am. Mensa Ltd., Masons (master 1977). Republican. Presbyterian. Home: 460-525 Janesville Grade Rd Janesville CA 96114-0717 Office: Dept Forestry 711-045 Center Rd Susanville CA 96130

LATHROP, MITCHELL LEE, lawyer; b. Los Angeles, Dec. 15, 1937; s. Alfred Lee and Barbara (Mitchell) L.; m. Denice Annette Davis, Dec. 1988; children: Christin Lorraine Newlon, Alexander Mitchell, Timothy Trewin Mitchell. B.Sc., U.S. Naval Acad., 1959; J.D., U. So. Calif., 1966. Bar: D.C., Calif. 1966, U.S. Supreme Ct. 1969, N.Y. 1981. Dep. counsel Los Angeles County, Calif., 1966-68; with firm Brill, Hunt, DeBuys and Burby, Los Angeles, 1968-71; ptnr. firm Macdonald, Halsted & Laybourne, Los Angeles and San Diego, 1971-80; sr. ptnr. Rogers & Wells, N.Y.C., San Diego, 1980-86, Adams, Duque & Hazeltine, Los Angeles, N.Y.C. and San Diego, 1986—; presiding referee Calif. Bar Ct., 1984-86, mem. exec. com., 1981-88; lectr. law Advanced Mgmt. Research Inc., Practicing Law Inst. N.Y., Continuing Edn. of Bar, State Bar Calif., ABA. Western Regional chmn. Met. Opera Nat. Council, 1971-81, v.p. and mem. exec. com., 1971—, now chmn.; trustee Honnold Library at Claremont Colls., 1972-80; bd. dirs. Music Ctr. Opera Assn., Los Angeles, sec., 1974-80; bd. dirs. San Diego Opera Assn., 1980-89, v.p., 1985-89; bd. dirs. Met. Opera Assn., N.Y.C. Served to capt. JAGC, USNR. Mem. ABA, N.Y. Bar Assn., Fed. Bar Assn., Fed. Bar Council, Calif. Bar Assn., D.C. Bar Assn., San Diego County Bar Assn. (chmn. ethics com. 1980-81, bd. dirs. 1982-85, v.p. 1985), Assn. Bus. Trial Lawyers, Assn. So. Calif. Def. Counsel, Los Angeles Opera Assos. (pres. 1970-72), Soc. Colonial Wars in Calif. (gov. 1970-72), Order St. Lazarus of Jerusalem, Friends of Claremont Coll. (dir. 1975-81, pres. 1978-79), Friends of Huntington Library, Am. Bd. Trial Advocates, Judge Advocates Assn. (dir. Los Angeles chpt. 1974-80, pres. So. Calif. chpt. 1977-78), Internat. Assn. Def. Counsel, Brit. United Services Club (dir. Los Angeles 1973-75), Mensa Internat., Calif. Soc., S.R. (pres. 1977-79), Phi Delta Phi. Republican. Clubs: California (Los Angeles); Valley Hunt (Pasadena, Calif.); Metropolitan (N.Y.C.). Home: 706 Stafford Pl San Diego CA 92107 Office: 401 West A St 23d Fl San Diego CA 92101 also: 551 Madison Ave 8th Fl New York NY 10022

LATNO, ARTHUR CLEMENT, JR., telephone company executive; b. Ross, Calif., May 14, 1929; s. Arthur Clement and Marie (Carlin) L.; m. Dorothy Sheldon Guess, June 27, 1953; children—Jeannine Marie, Michele Claire, Arthur Clement III, Mary Suzanne, Patrice Anne. B.S., Santa Clara U., 1951. With Pacific Tel. & Tel. Co., San Francisco, 1952—; v.p. Pacific Tel. & Tel. Co., 1972-78, exec. v.p., 1978—; also dir. PacTel Corp.; dir. Nev. Bell, Marin Health System; WestAm. Bank, WestAm. Bancorp. v.p., dir. Pacific Coast Elec. Assocs., Inc. Bd. dirs. San Francisco Fine Arts Mus., Alemany Scholarship Fund.; chmn. San Francisco Econ. Devel. Corp.; chmn. adv. bd. Berkeley Program in Bus. and Social Policy, U. Calif.; mem. exec. com. San Francisco Host Com.; bd. dirs. Fromm Inst. Lifelong Learning; chmn. bd. trustees St. Mary's Coll. Calif.; trustee Marin Gen. Hosp. Found.; former U.S. Ambassador, chmn. U.S. Delegation, WATTC 1988 Treaty Conf. Mem. Knights of Malta (vice chancellor, bd. dirs.), San Francisco C. of C. (chmn. port com.), Alpha Sigma Nu. Club: Meadow. Home: 67 Convent Ct San Rafael CA 94901 Office: Pacific Telesis Group 130 Kearny St San Francisco CA 94108

LATTANZIO, STEPHEN PAUL, astronomy educator; b. Yonkers, N.Y., June 29, 1949; s. Anthony Raymond and Anella Lattanzio; m. Barbara Regina Knisely, Aug. 14, 1976; 1 child, Gregory Paul. BA in Astronomy, U. Calif., Berkeley, 1971; MA in Astronomy, UCLA, 1973, postgrad., 1973-75. Planetarium lectr. Griffith Obs., Los Angeles, 1973-75; instr. astronomy El Camino Coll., Torrance, Calif., 1974-75; planetarium lectr. Valley Coll., Los Angeles, 1975; prof. astronomy Orange Coast Coll., Costa Mesa, Calif., 1975—, planetarium dir., 1975—; mem. adv. commn. Natural History Found. Orange County, Calif., 1988—. Co-author: Study Guide for Project: Universe, 1978, 2d rev. edition 1981; textbook reviewer, 1978—; co-screenwriter Project: Universe instructional TV series episode, 1979; contbr. articles to profl. jours. Mem. Astron. Soc. Pacific, Nat. Space Soc., The Planetary Soc., Space Studies Inst. Sigma Xi (assoc.), Phi Beta Kappa. Office: Orange Coast Coll 2701 Fairview Rd Costa Mesa CA 92628

LATTIMORE, LOUISE JOAN, elementary teacher; b. Wattis, Utah, July 3, 1934; d. John T. and Ruth A. (Craven) Maulsby; m. Roy Jay Lattimore, Jan. 29, 1955; children: Karen Lattimore Ervin, Katherine, John. BA in Edn. with honors, Fresno State U., 1956; MA in Adminstrv. Services with honors, Sonoma State U., 1985. Cert. lifetime elem. tchr. and administr., Calif. Tchr. Panama Sch. Dist., Bakersfield, Calif., 1956-57, Fresno (Calif.)-Scandinavian Sch. Dist., 1957-58, Petaluma (Calif.) City Schs., 1966-68; tchr.-in-charge Liberty Sch. Dist., Petaluma, 1969—; condr. workshops No. Calif. Kindergarten Conf., San Francisco, 1987, 89, Sonoma County Consortium, Santa Rosa, Calif., 1987, Petaluma City Schs., 1988. Margaret Thomas scholar Delta Zeta, 1956. Mem. Calif. Tchrs. Assn. (dist. negotiator 1985—), Delta Kappa Gamma. Methodist. Office: Liberty Sch Dist 170 Liberty Rd Petaluma CA 94952

LAU, DOUGLAS KAM, advertising company executive; b. Honolulu, June 18, 1947; s. Albert Y.S. and Anna N.W. Lau; m. Patricia A. Chown, Sept. 13, 1969; children: Michael K., Megan N. BA in English, U. San Francisco, 1969. Builders hardware estimator AmFac, Inc., Honolulu, 1969-70; pub. relations writer ROCOR Internat., Palo Alto, Calif., 1972-74; mktg. services mgr. Napko Corp., Fremont, Calif., 1974-79; advt. dir. Manteca (Calif.) News, 1979-81; sr. acct. exec. Michael-Stewart Advt., Stockton and San Mateo, Calif., 1981-82; v.p. client services Lighthouse Advt., Modesto, Calif., 1982-84; pres. Advt. Communications, Modesto, Calif., 1984—. Served with USNR, 1970-72. Mem. Modesto Ad. Club, Stockton Advt., Mktg. and Media Club (Sammy award 1987), Sacramento Art Dirs. Club. Democrat. Lutheran. Office: Advt Communications 808 14th St Modesto CA 95354

LAU, LAWRENCE JUEN-YEE, economics educator, consultant; b. Guizhou, China, Dec. 12, 1944; came to U.S., 1961, naturalized, 1974; s. Shai-Tat and Chi-Hing (Yu) Liu; m. Tamara K. Jablonski, June 23, 1984. B.S. with gt. distinction, Stanford U., 1964; M.A., U. Calif.-Berkeley, 1966, Ph.D., 1969. Acting asst. prof. econs. Stanford U., Calif., 1966-67, asst. prof., 1967-73, assoc. prof., 1973-76, prof., 1976—; cons. The World Bank, Washington, 1976—; vice chmn. Bank of Canton of Calif. Bldg. Corp. 1981-85; dir. Bank of Canton of Calif., San Francisco, 1979-85; dir. Property Resources Equity Trust, Los Gatos, 1987-88; vice-chmn. Complete Computer Co. Far East Ltd., Hong Kong, 1981—. Author: (with D.T. Jamison) Farmer Education and Farm Efficiency, 1982, Models of Development: A Comparative Study of Economic Growth in South Korea and Taiwan, 1986; contbr. articles in field to profl. jours. Mem. adv. bd. Self-Help for the Elderly, San Francisco, 1982. John Simon Guggenheim Meml. fellow, 1973; fellow Ctr. for Advanced Study in Behavioral Scis., 1982; Overseas fellow Churchill Coll., Cambridge U., Eng., 1984. Fellow Econometric Soc.; mem. Academia Sinica, Conf. Research in Income and Wealth. Republican. Episcopalian. Office: Stanford U Dept Econs Stanford CA 94305

LAUB, WILLIAM MURRAY, utility executive; b. Ft. Mills, Corregidor, Philippines, July 20, 1924; s. Harold Goodspeed and Marjorie M. (Murray) L.; m. Mary McDonald, July 26, 1947; children: William, Andrew, Mary, David, John. B.S. in Bus. Adminstrn, U. Calif. at Berkeley, 1947, LL.B., 1950. Bar: Calif. 1951. Practice law Los Angeles, 1951-55; with Southwest Gas Corp., Las Vegas, Nev., 1948—; v.p., gen. counsel Southwest Gas Corp., 1958-60, exec. v.p., 1960-64, pres., chief exec. officer, 1964-82, chmn., chief exec. officer, 1982-88, pres., 1984-87, also dir. Pres. Boulder Dam Area council Boy Scouts Am., 1967-69, So. Nev. Indsl. Found., 1967-68, So. Nev. Meth. Found., 1967-74; chmn. Nev. Equal Rights Commn., 1966-68; Chmn. Clark County Republican Central Com., 1964-66; nat. committeeman Nev. Rep. Com., 1968-80; trustee Sch. Theology at Claremont, Calif., 1977—; trustee Inst. Gas Tech., 1983; nat. bd. advisors, coll. bus. and pub. adminstrn. The U. Ariz., 1985—; bd. dirs. Alliance for Acid Rain Control, 1985—. Served to lt. (j.g.) USNR, 1941-45. Mem. ABA, Am. Gas Assn. (bd. dirs., chmn. 1986-87), Pacific Coast Gas Assn. (chmn. 1983,), Calif. Bar Assn., Nat. Coal Council. Methodist (trustee). Clubs: Jonathan (Los Angeles); Pauma Valley (Calif.) Country; Spanish Trail Golf & Country (Nev.), Las Vegas Country. Office: SW Gas Corp 5241 Spring Mountain Rd Las Vegas NV 89102

LAUBE, ROGER GUSTAV, financial consultant; b. Chgo., Aug. 11, 1921; s. William C. and Elsie (Drews) L.; m. Irene Mary Chadbourne, Mar. 30, 1946; children: David Roger, Philip Russell, Steven Richard. BA, Roosevelt U., 1942; postgrad., John Marshall Law Sch., 1942, 48-50; LLB, Northwestern U., 1960; postgrad., U. Wash., 1962-64. Cert. fin. cons. With Chgo. Title & Trust Co., Chgo., 1938-42, 48-50, Nat. Bank Alaska, Anchorage, 1950-72; mgr. mortgage dept. Nat. Bank Alaska, 1950-56, v.p., trust officer, mgr. trust dept., 1956-72; v.p., trust officer, mktg. dir., mgr. estate and fin. planning div. Bishop Trust Co., Ltd., Honolulu, 1972-82; instr. estate planning U. Hawaii, Honolulu, 1978-82; exec. v.p. Design Capital Planning Group, Inc., Tucson, 1982-83; pres., sr. trust officer, registered investment adviser Advanced Capital Advisory, Inc. of Ariz., Tucson, 1983—; registered rep., pres. Advanced Capital Investments, Inc. of Ariz., Prescott, 1983—; pres., chief exec. officer Advanced Capital Devel., Inc. of Ariz., Prescott, 1983—; mng. exec. Integrated Resources Equity Corp., Prescott, 1983—; pres. Anchorage Estate Planning Coun., 1960-62, Charter mem., 1960-72; Charter mem. Hawaii Estate Planning Coun., 1972-82, v.p., 1979, pres., 1980, bd. dirs., 1981-82; charter mem. Prescott Estate Planning Coun., 1986—, pres. 1988. Charter mem. Anchorage Community Chorus, pres., 1950-53, bd. dirs., 1953-72; mem. Anchorage camp Gideons Internat., 1946-72, Honolulu camp, 1972-82, mem. Cen.camp, Tucson, 1982-85, Prescott, 1985—; mem. adv. bd. Faith Hosp., Glennallen, Alaska, 1960—, Cen. Alaska Mission of Far Ea. Gospel Crusade, 1960—; sec.-treas. Alaska Bapt. Found., 1955-72; bd. dirs. Bapt. Found. of Ariz., 1985—, mem. investment com.; mem. mainland adv. coun. Hawaii Bapt. Acad., Honolulu, 1982—; pres. Sabinovista Townhouse Assn., 1983-85; bd. advisers Salvation Army, Alaska, 1961-72, chmn., Anchorage, 1969-72, bd. advisers, Honolulu, 1972-82, chmn. bd. advisers, 1976-78; asst. staff judge adv. Alaskan Command, 1946-48; exec. com. Alaska Conv., 1959-61, dir. music Chgo., 1938-42, 48-50, Alaska, 1950-72, Hawaii, 1972-82, Tucson, 1982-85, 1st So. Bapt. Ch., Prescott Valley, 1985—; chmn. bd. trustees Hawaii, 1972-81, Prescott Valley, 1986—; worship leader Waikiki Ch., 1979-82. 1st lt., JAGD U.S. Army, 1942-48. Recipient Others award Salvation Army, 1972. Mem. Am. Inst. Banking (instr. trust div. 1961-72), Am. Bankers Assn. (legis. com., trust div. 1960-72), Nat. Assn. Life Underwriters (nat com. for No. Ariz.), Yavapai County-Prescott Life Underwriters Assn. (charter), Anchorage C. of C. (mem. awards com. 1969-71), Internat. Assn. Fin. Planners, Anchorage chpt. 1969-72, treas., exec. com. Honolulu chpt. 1972-82, Ariz. chpt. 1982—, Del. to World Congress Australia and New Zealand 1987, Am. Assn. Handbell Ringers. Baptist. Home: 649 Filaree Dr Prescott AZ 86301 Office: Sun Pine Exec Ctr 915 E Gurley Ste 303 Prescott AZ 86301

LAUBER, MIGNON DIANE, food processing company executive; b. Detroit, Dec. 21; d. Charles Edmond and Maud Lillian (Foster) Donaker; student Kelsey Jenny U., 1958, Brigham Young U., 1959; m. Richard Brian Lauber, Sept. 13, 1963; 1 dau., Leslie Viane (dec.). Owner, operator Alaska World Travel, Ketchikan, 1964-67; founder, owner, pres. Oosick Soup Co.,

Juneau, Alaska, 1969—. Treas., Pioneer Alaska Lobbyists Soc., Juneau, 1977—. Mem. Bus. and Profl. Women, Alaska C. of C. Libertarian. Club: Washington Athletic. Author: Down at the Water Works with Jesus, 1982; Failure Through Prayer, 1983. Home: 321 Highland Dr Juneau AK 99801 Office: PO Box 1625 Juneau AK 99802

LAUCHENGCO, JOSE YUJUICO, JR., lawyer; b. Manila, Philippines, Dec. 6, 1936; came to U.S., 1962; s. José Celis Sr. Lauchengco and Angeles (Yujuico) Sapota; m. Elisabeth Schindler, Feb. 22, 1968; children: Birthe, Martina, Duane, Lance. AB, U. Philippines, Quezon City, 1959; MBA, U. So. Calif., 1964; JD, Loyola U., Los Angeles, 1971. Bar: Calif. 1972, U.S. Dist. Ct. (cen. dist.) Calif. 1972, U.S. Ct. Appeals (9th cir.) 1972, U.S. Supreme Ct. 1975. Banker First Western Bank/United Calif. Bank, Los Angeles, 1964-71; assoc. Demler, Perona, Langer & Bergkvist, Long Beach, Calif., 1972-73; ptnr. Demler, Perona, Langer, Bergkvist, Lauchengco & Manzella, Long Beach, 1973-77; sole practice Long Beach and Los Angeles, 1977-83; ptnr. Lauchengco & Mendoza, Los Angeles, 1983—; mem. commn. on jud. procedures County of Los Angeles, 1979; tchr. Confraternity of Christian Doctrine, 1972-79; counsel Philippine Presdl. Commn. on Good Govt., Los Angeles, 1986. Mem. So. Calif. Asian Dem. Caucus, Los Angeles, 1977; chmn. Filipino-Am. Bi-Partisan Polit. Action Group, Los Angeles, 1978. Recipient Degree of Distinction, Nat. Forensic League, 1955. Mem. Criminal Cts. Bar Assn., Calif. Attys. Criminal Justice, Los Angeles County Bar Assn., Assn. Trial Lawyers Am., Calif. Trial Lawyers Assn., Los Angeles County Trial Lawyers Assn., U. Philippines Vanguard Assn. (life), Beta Sigma. Roman Catholic. Lodge: K.C. Office: Lauchengco & Mendoza 2503 W Beverly Blvd Ste 4 Los Angeles CA 90057

LAUER, GEORGE, environmental consultant; b. Vienna, Austria, Feb. 18, 1936; came to U.S., 1943; s. Otto and Alice (Denton) L.; m. Sandra Joy Comp, Oct. 1, 1983; children by previous marriage: Julie Anne, Robert L. BS, UCLA, 1961; PhD, Calif. Inst. Tech., 1967. Mem. tech. staff N.Am. Aviation, Canoga Park, Calif., 1966-69; mgr. Rockwell Internat., Thousand Oaks, Calif., 1969-75; div. mgr. ERT, Inc., Westlake Village, Calif., 1975-78; dir. Rockwell Internat., Newbury Park, Calif., 1978-85; dir. Tetra-Tech Inc., Pasadena, Calif., 1985-86; pres. Environ. Monitoring and Services, Inc., 1986-88; sr. cons. Atlantic Richfield, Inc., Los Angeles, 1988—. Contbr. articles to profl. jours.; patentee in field. Served with U.S. Army, 1957-59. Fellow Assn. for Computing Machinery; mem. Am. Chem. Soc., Air Pollution Control Assn. Republican. Jewish. Home: 6009 Maury Ave Woodland Hills CA 91367 Office: Atlantic Richfield Inc 515 S Flower Los Angeles CA 90071

LAUFER, JOEL E., lawyer; b. Marshalltown, Iowa, Jan. 20, 1951; s. Warden Benjamin and Dorothy May (Serfoss) L. BA, Simpson Coll., 1973; JD, U. Iowa, 1976. Assoc. Clarke & Waggener, P.C., Denver, 1979-82; pvt. practice Englewood, Colo., 1982—; continuing legal edn. speaker, various seminars, Denver, 1984-89. Mem. Colo. Bar Assn., Arapahoe County Bar Assn. Home: 8550 E Temple Dr Denver CO 80237 Office: 5290 DTC Pkwy Ste 150 Englewood CO 80111

LAUGHLIN, LOUIS GENE, economic analyst, consultant; b. Santa Barbara, Calif., Sept. 20, 1937; s. Eston A. and Cornelia Helen (Snively) L.; student Pomona Coll., 1955-58; BA, U. Calif.-Santa Barbara, 1960; postgrad. Claremont Grad. Sch., 1966-70, 85-86, Sch. Bank Mktg., U. Colo., 1974-75, Grad. Sch. Mgmt., U. Calif.-Irvine, 1983. Mgr., Wheeldex-L.A. Co., 1961-62; v.p. Warner/Walker Assos., Inc., L.A., 1962; cons. Spectra-Sound Corp., L.A., 1964-65; rep. A.C. Nielsen Co., Chgo., 1962-64; rsch. analyst Security Pacific Nat. Bank, L.A., 1964-67, asst. rsch. mgr., 1967-68, asst. v.p., 1968-72, v.p., mgr. market info. and research div., 1972-76, v.p. rsch. adminstrn., pub. affairs/rsch. dept., 1976-82, v.p. govt. rels. dept., 1982-85; dir. rsch. and devel. Applied Mgmt. Systems, South Pasadena, Calif., 1986; pres. L.G. Laughlin & Assoc., Houston, 1987—; prin. Courtyard Holdings, Houston, 1988—; pres. chief exec. officer, Mastodon Capital Corp., Houston, 1988—; mem. Nat. Conf. on Fin. Svcs., 1982-84, mem. policy coun., 1983-84; mem. policy coun. Nat. Conf. on Competition in Banking, 1978-79, 81. Sec. econs. Town Hall of Calif., 1966. Mem. Am. Econs. Assn., Western Econ. Assn., Nat. Assn. Bus. Economists, L.A. C. of C. (food and agr. adv. com. 1981). Office: 7035 Highway 6 South Ste 336 Houston TX 77083

LAUNER, ROBERT DAVID, data processing executive; b. N.Y.C., May 10, 1951; s. Arthur and Eileen Ilona (Steingeisser) L.; m. Kris Vilma Launer, Sept. 27, 1985. BSEE., UCLA, 1973. Computer lab. instr. U. So. Calif., 1969-70; computer programmer I, Sch. Engring., UCLA, 1972-75; computer systems engr. Electronic Data Systems Corp., San Francisco, 1975-80; dir. data processing Summit Workshops, Inc., Redwood City, Calif., 1980-85; Dir. DP/MIS, Emeryville, Calif., 1983-87; computer bus. cons. RDL Enterprises, 1988—; sr. systems engr. ACP Corp., 1988—. L.A. Coun. of Engrs. and Scientists scholar, 1970-71, 71-72; recipient Men of Achievement award, Cambridge, Eng., 1982, 87. Inst. for Advancement of Engring. scholar, 1970-71. Mem. IEEE, Am. Soc. Engrs. and Architects, Am. Assn. for Artificial Intelligence, Engring. Soc. of UCLA, Data Processing Mgrs. Assn., Boston Computer Soc. Contbr. articles to profl. jours. Office: RDL Enterprises 160 Monterey Blvd Ste 19 San Francisco CA 94131

LAURE, PHILLIP JOHN, industrial engineer; b. Ann Arbor, Mich., May 9, 1949; s. Daniel Pierre and Elizabeth Ann (Arigan) L.; m. Nelda Jane Griffing, June 8, 1973; children: Michael James Witham, Steven Duane Witham, Charles Allen Witham, Deanna Jane Witham. BA, Calif. State U., San Bernardino, 1978. Sr. engring. technician County of San Bernardino, San Bernardino, 1974-80; prodn. planning supr. Lily-Tulip, Inc., Riverside, Calif., 1980-85; mfg. cons. Laure & Assocs., Riverside, 1985-86; indsl. engr. Northrop Corp., Hawthorne, Calif., 1986-88; sr. indsl. engr. Rohr Industries, Riverside, 1988—. Sponsor, Kids Against Durgs, Moreno Valley, Calif., 1988. Mem. Inst. Indsl. Engrs. (bull. editor 1988), Riverside C. of C., Elks. Democrat. Roman Catholic.

LAURSEN, WILLIAM KENNETH, art educator; b. Standardville, Utah, Feb. 26, 1948; s. Edward Chipman and Vivian Burdette (Babcock) L. BFA, Utah State U., 1972. Dept. chmn. Cottonwood High Sch., Salt Lake City, Utah, 1976—; set designer, Cottonwood High Sch., 1972-88; illustrator, Granite Sch. Dist., 1988—; tour dir., Ednl. Tours, 1978-88; instr. community edn. Recipient People Make a Difference award, Sta. KSL Radio, 1987, Best of Show award 1st Ann. Golden Spike Art Exhibit, 1973, Purchase award Brigham City Mus.-Gallery, 1973, Painting award Park City Arts Festival, 1974; named Tchr. of the Year, Granite Sch. Dist., 1987. Mem. NEA, Internat. Thespian Soc. (hon. mem.).

LAUTENBACH, DENNIS KENT, dairyman, real estate investor; b. Bellingham, Wash., Feb. 27, 1967; s. Sybren and Henrietta Rose (Van Weerdhuizen) L. Grad. high sch., Lynden, Wash. Herdsman De Haan Dairies, Inc., Lynden, Wash., 1984-87; prodn. mgr. Vanderhage Dairies, Inc., Everson, Wash., 1987--. Pres. Silver Bullet Com., Nooksack, Wash., 1988. Recipient Am. Farmer award Future Farmers Am., 1988. Mem. An. Agr. Appraisers, Holstein Freisian Assn. Am.

LAUTENSLAGER, BEN FRANKLIN, III, educator, consultant; b. Evanston, Ill., Mar. 13, 1949; s. Benjamin Franklin and Rosemary (Barrentine) L.; m. Sandra Kay Campa, June 12, 1968; children: Benjamin, Joshua, Amy. BA, U. La Verne, 1971, MA, 1979; postgrad., U. San Diego, 1984. Cert. gen. adminstr., tchr., Calif. Tchr. Ontario (Calif.)-Montclair Sch. Dist., 1971—, mentor, 1985-87, asst. prin., 1988—; soccer coach Chaffey High Sch., Ontario, 1983-85. State of Calif. computer grantee, 1986. Mem. Assn. Calif. Sch. Adminstrs., Assn. West End Sch. Adminstrs. Republican. Roman Catholic. Home: 8991 Whirlaway Ct Alta Loma CA 91701 Office: Edison Sch 515 E 6th St Ontario CA 91701

LAUTH, ROBERT EDWARD, geologist; b. St. Paul, Feb. 6, 1927; s. Joseph Louis and Gertrude (Stapleton) L.; student St. Thomas Coll., 1944; BA in Geology, U. Minn., 1952; m. Suzanne Janice Holmes, Apr. 21, 1947; children—Barbara Jo, Robert Edward II, Elizabeth Suzanne, Leslie Marie. Wellsite geologist Columbia Carbon Co., Houston, 1951-52; dist. geologist Witco Oil & Gas Corp., Amarillo, Tex., 1952-55; field geologist Reynolds Mining Co., Houston, 1955; cons. geologist, Durango, Colo., 1955—. Appraiser helium res. Lindley area Orange Free State, Republic of South Africa, 1988, remaining helium res. Odolanow Plant area Polish Lowlands, Poland, 1988. With USNR, 1944-45. Mem. N.Mex., Four Corners (treas., v.p., pres., symposium com.) geol. socs., Rocky Mountain Assn. Geologists, Am. Inst. Profl. Geologists, Am. Inst. Mining, Metall. and Petroleum Engrs., Am. Assn. Petroleum Geologists, Helium Soc., N.Y. Acad. Sci. Am. Assn. Petroleum Landman, Soc. Econ. Paleontologists and Mineralogists, The Explorers Club. Republican. Roman Catholic. K.C. Clubs: Durango Petroleum (dir.), Denver Petroleum, Elks. Author: Desert Creek Field, 1958; (with Silas C. Brown) Oil and Gas Potentialities of Northern Arizona, 1958, Northern Arizona Has Good Oil, Gas Prospects, 1960, Northeastern Arizona; Its Oil, Gas and Helium Prospects, 1961; contbr. papers on oil and gas fields to profl. symposia. Home: 2020 Crestview Dr PO Box 776 Durango CO 81302 Office: 555 S Camino Del Rio Durango CO 81301

LAVAL, CLAUDE CONSTANT, III, manufacturing executive; b. Fresno, Calif., May 9, 1935; s. Claude Constant Jr. and Marian B. (Kahn) L.; m. Betty Lou Scarbrough, Feb. 1, 1958; children: Melinda, Luann Laval Williams. BA, Stanford U., 1957. Sales mgr. Suppliers, Inc., Fresno, 1957-60; pres. A-V Electronics, Inc., Fresno, 1960-71, Claude Laval Corp., Fresno, 1971—; dir. bus. adv. council Calif. State U., 1984--. Chmn. Parking Authority Fresno, 1964-68. Mem. Irrigation Assn. (pres. 1983-84), Downtown Assn. Fresno (pres. 1966-68), No. Calif. Dist. Export Coun., Water Resource Export Coun., Young Pres.' Orgn. (chmn. 1983-84), World Bus. Forum (sec.-treas. 1985—), Am. Water Found. (exec. com. 1986—), Rotary, Sunnyside Country Club, Fig Garden Swim and Racquet Club, Beta Gamma Sigma. Office: Claude Laval Corp 1911 N Helm St Fresno CA 93727

LAVE, CHARLES ARTHUR, economics educator; b. Phila., May 18, 1938; s. Israel and Esther (Axlerod) L.; 1 child, Rebecca. BA, Reed Coll., 1960; PhD, Stanford U., 1968. Mem. faculty U. Calif., Irvine, 1966—, prof. econs., chmn. dept. econs., 1978-85; vis. prof., vis. scholar Hampshire Coll., 1972, Stanford U., 1974, MIT, 1982, Harvard U., 1982, U. Calif., Berkeley, 1988. Author: (with James March) An Introduction to Models in the Social Sciences, 1975, Education and Cognitive Development, 1979, Energy and Auto Type Choice, 1981, Urban Transit, 1985, others. Trustee Reed Coll., Portland, Oreg., 1978-82; chmn. bd. Irvine Campus Housing Authority, Inc., 1982—. Served with USAF, 1957. Dept. Energy grantee, 1975-83; Dept. Transp. grantee, 1977-89. Fellow Soc. Applied Anthropology; mem. Am. Econ. Assn., AAAS, Transp. Research Bd. Office: U Calif Dept Econs Irvine CA 92717

LAVELL, ALAN JOSEPH, informations systems executive; b. London, Nov. 14, 1946; came to U.S., 1987; s. George Charles and Marie Louise (Volpe) L.; m. Pamela Christina Bossy, June 30, 1984. BSc, U. W.I., Kingston, Jamaica, 1971. Cert. mgmt. cons. Mgr. computer ops. Honeywell Inc., Toronto, Ont., Can., 1972-74; mgr. systems engring. NCR Can., Halifax, N.S., 1974-81; mgr. profl. resources/mgmt. cons. Systemhouse Ltd., Halifax, 1981-86; mgr. info. systems Systemhouse Inc., Ottawa, Ont., Can., 1986-87; mgr. bus. ctr. Systemhouse Inc., Cerritos, Calif., 1987—. Mem. Inst. Cert. Mgmt. Cons. of Ont., Brit. Computer Soc., Toastmasters (pres. 1988). Home: 311 Vista Del Canon Anaheim Hills CA 92807 Office: Systemhouse Inc 18000 Studebaker Rd 4th Fl Cerritos CA 90701

LAVENTHOL, DAVID ABRAM, newspaper editor; b. Phila., July 15, 1933; s. Jesse and Clare (Horwald) L.; m. Esther Coons, Mar. 8, 1958; children: Peter, Sarah. A.B., Yale U., 1957; M.A., U. Minn., 1960; Litt.D., Dowling Coll., 1979; LLD, Hofstra U., 1986. Reporter, news editor St. Petersburg (Fla.) Times, 1957-62; asst. editor, city editor N.Y. Herald-Tribune, 1963-66; asst. mng. editor Washington Post, 1966-69; assoc. editor Newsday, L.I., N.Y., 1969, exec. editor, 1970, v.p., 1971-74, editor, 1970-78, pub., chief exec. officer, 1978-85, chmn., 1986—; group v.p. newspapers Times Mirror Co., 1981-85, sr. v.p., 1986-87, pres., 1987—; chmn., bd. dirs. Pulitzer Prize. Trustee Hartford-Courant Found., 1982—; bd. dirs. N.Y. Partnership, 1985-87, United Negro Coll. Fund, 1988, L.A. Times Post News Svc., Washington, 1988, Times Mirror Found., 1987; sec. Am. Com. Internat. Press Inst.; vice chmn. Internat. Press Inst. With Signal Corps AUS, 1953-55. Mem. Am. Soc. Newspaper Editors (treas. ASNE Found. 1980—, chmn. writing awards bd. 1980-83), Council Fgn. Relations. Club: Century. Home: 800 W First St Apt 3202 Los Angeles CA 90012 Office: The Times Mirror Co Times Mirror Sq Los Angeles CA 90053

LAVIER, ANNABELLE THERESA, computer science educator; b. Hillsboro, Oreg., Aug. 6, 1947; d. Emil William and Ellen Florence (Englund) Egger; m. Bruce Edward Lavier, Dec. 16, 1969; children: Kristen, Jack. Student, Schiller Coll., Kleiningsheim, Germany, 1967-68; BA in German and History, Linfield Coll., McMinnville, Oreg., 1969; MEd in Reading, Oreg. State U., 1972. Tchr., lang. coordinator Castle Rock (Wash.) Upper Elem., 1970-71; acad. advisor Treaty Oak Community Coll., The Dalles, Oreg., 1979-83; coordinator Adult Basic Skills TEch. Project, The Dalles, 1984—; instr. computer sci. Treaty Oak Community Coll., The Dalles, 1979—; cons. Apple Computer, Inc., N.W. Regional Labs., Cupertino, Calif., 1987—; editor software guides Dept. Edn., Olympia, Wash., 1985—; ESL coordinator USN-Navy Relief, San Diego, 1972-74. Editor: Recreational Guide to Software, 1987, 88. Bd. chmn. Wasco County Sch. Bd., The Dalles, 1987—; mem. bd. East Cascade Nat. Pub. Radio, Wenetchee, Wash., 1987—, Mid Columbia Hops., The Dalles, 1986, Congl. Ch., The Dalles, 1988—; mem. steering com. Wasco County Dem. Party, The Dalles, 1986. Recipient Disting. Svc. award Treaty Oak Community Coll., The Dalles, 1984, Appreciation award Calif. Lit. Assn., Sacramento, 1987, award Oreg. Lit., Portland, 1987. Mem. WABE, Am. Assn. Adult and Continuing Edn., Oreg. Devel. Edn., Oreg. Reading and Learning Assn., N.W. Coun. Computer Edn. (bd. 1987—), AAUW (pres. 1984-86), PEO. Office: Treaty Oak Community Coll 300 E 4th St The Dalles OR 97058

LAVIERI, ANNAMARIE, librarian; b. Hartford, Conn., Nov. 7, 1945; d. Sebastian and Mary (Minnelli) L.; m. Albert C. Gunther Jr., Oct. 7, 1977. AA, Hartford Coll. for Women, 1965; BS, Boston U., 1967; MS, Seattle U., 1980. Standard teaching cert., Wash. Tchr. Moore (Okla.) Pub. Schs., 1968-69; tchr., librarian Omaha (Nebr.) Pub. Schs., 1969-72, Seattle (Wash.) Pub. Schs., 1972-88; librarian Bainbridge Island (Wash.) Pub. Schs., 1988—. del. Wash. State Dem. Conv., Olympia, 1988. Mem. Wash. Library Assn., NEA (vol. reader 1983-84), LWV, AAUW, Wash. Library Media Assn., Phi Delta Kappa. Office: Ordway Sch 8555 Madison Ave NE Bainbridge Island WA 98110

LAVIGNE, LOUIS JAMES, JR., biotechnology company executive; b. Cheboygan, Mich., Apr. 24, 1948; s. Louis James and Shirley (Lahaie) L.; m. Rachel Joy Winikur, June 21, 1969; children: Stephanie Lynn, Gordon Scott. BSBA, Babson Coll., 1969; MBA, Temple U., 1976. Mgr. sales acctg. Pennwalt Corp., Phila., 1971-73, mgr. acctg. systems, 1973-74, mgr. acctg. info., 1974-79, asst. contr., 1979-82; asst. contr. Genentech Inc., South San Francisco, 1982-83, contr., 1983-84, contr., officer, 1984-86, v.p., contr., 1986-87, v.p., chief fin. officer, 1988—. Mem. Fin. Exec. Inst., Nat. Assn. Accts. Office: Genentech Inc 460 Point San Bruno Blvd South San Francisco CA 94080

LAVRAKAS, JOHN WILLIAM, software engineer; b. San Diego, Jan. 27, 1952; s. Lefteris and Billye C. L.; m. Melody Shipherd, May 12, 1979; children: Miranda, James, Robert. BS in Math., Harvey Mudd Coll., 1974; MA in Math., Claremont U., 1975. Tchr. Ind. Vocat. Tech. Coll., South Bend, 1975-78; mem. tech. staff Logicon Inc., San Pedro, Calif., 1978-88; dir. software engring. NAVSYS Corp., Monument, Colo., 1988—. Mem. Inst. of Navigation, Internat. Test and Evaluation Assn. Mem. Christian Sci. Ch. Office: Nausys Corp 18725 Monument Hill Rd Monument CO 80132

LAW, JOHN HAROLD, biochemistry educator; b. Cleve., Feb. 27, 1931; s. John and Katherine (Frampton) L.; m. Nancy Jean Floyd, June 8, 1956. BS, Case Inst. Tech., Cleve., 1953; PhD, U. Ill., 1957. Postdoctoral fellow Harvard U., Cambridge, Mass., 1958-59, from instr. to asst. prof. biochemistry, 1960-65; instr. Northwestern U., Evanston, Ill., 1959-60; prof. U. Chgo., 1965-81; prof. U. Ariz., Tucson, 1981—, chmn. dept. biochemistry, 1981-86, dir. biotech. program, 1986—, assoc. dean coll. agr., 1988—; mem. gov. bd. Internat. Ctr. Insects, Nairobi, Kenya, 1980-87. Fellow AAAS; mem. Am. Soc. Biochem. Molecular Biology. Home: 2540 E 7th St Tucson AZ 85716 Office: U Ariz Dept Bioscis West 364 Tucson AZ 85721

LAWLER, JUDY ANN, data processing executive; b. West Bend, Wis., Aug. 4, 1944; d. Alexander John and Elsie Frieda (Zumach) Boettcher; m. Michael Francis Lawler, Jan. 28, 1968 (div.); children: Timothy Shane, Alisandra Michelle. BS, U. Ariz., 1966, MEd, 1967. Systems engr. IBM Corp., Phoenix, 1967-71; systems mgr. Kaibab Industries, Phoenix, 1972-78; pres. System/3 Assocs. S.W. Inc., Scottsdale, Ariz., 1975-79; mgr. data processing Marathon Steel Co., Phoenix, 1978-82; dir. mgmt. info. systems Ariz. Mail Order, Inc., Tucson, 1982—; instr. N.Am. Coll. of Data Processing, Phoenix, 1980-81. Contbg. editor: Small Systems World, 1979-81. Sec. bd. dirs. COMMON (Nat. IBM Midrange Systems Users Group), Border Ariz. System 38 User's Group (chmn. and founder). Lutheran. Office: Ariz Mail Order Inc 3740 E 34th St Tucson AZ 85713

LAWLER, KATHY PRICE, small business owner; b. Rock Island, Ill., Feb. 26, 1958; d. Neal Wesley Price and Harriett Melisa (Garriet) Fudge; m. Michael Leo Lawler, Oct. 30, 1982. AA, Glendale (Ariz.) Community Coll., 1979; BBA in Mktg., U. Phoenix, 1981; MBA in Mgmt., Western Internat. U., 1983; cert. nanny, Glendale (Ariz.) Community Coll. Assoc. acct. Honeywell PMSD, Phoenix, 1981-83; profl. med. rep. Abbott Labs., Colorado Springs, Colo., 1984-86; med. sales mgr. Parke-Davis, Colorado Springs, 1986-87; dir., owner Attention Unltd., Colorado Springs, 1987—. Mem. Better Bus. Bur. Mem. Internat. Nanny Assn., Nat. Assn. for Edn. of Young Children, Valley of Sun for Edn. of Young Children, Nanny Network. Office: Attention Unltd Nanny Placement 3310 W Bell Rd Ste 19 Phoenix AZ 85023

LAWLESS, SARAH MADISON, theatrical executive; b. Milw., Feb. 1, 1934; d. Frederick William and Geraldine (Conover) Madison; m. Donald Buzard (div.); m. James J. Lawless, May 7, 1971; children: Julia, Mary, David Buzard. BS, Northwestern U., 1953. Assoc. mng. dir. Guthrie Theatre, Mpls., 1969-71; dir. communications Dayton Hudson Corp., Mpls., 1971-79; v.p. Padilla & Speer, Mpls., 1979-81; exec. dir. The Children's Theatre, Mpls., 1981-84, Denver Ctr. Theatre Co., 1984--. Bd. dirs. Children's Chorale, Denver, 1987—, TCG, N.Y.C., 1988—, LORT, N.Y.C., 1986-88, ASSITEJ/USA, Washington, 1987—. Office: Denver Ctr Theatre Co 1245 Champa St Denver CO 80204

LAWLOR, JAMES JOHN, JR., marine corps officer; b. San Diego, July 10, 1963; s. James John and Mary Catherine (Young) L.; m. Linda S. Alm, June 6, 1986 (div. May 1989). BA in History, Marquette U., 1985. Designated naval aviator, 1987. Commd. 2d lt. USMC, 1985, advanced through grades to 1st lt., 1987; squadron pilot, schedules officer USMC, Camp Pendleton, Calif., 1988—. Republican. Roman Catholic. Home: 3939Mesa Dr Apt 106 Oceanside CA 92056 Office: VMO-2 Marine Corps Air Sta Camp Pendleton CA 92055-6093

LAWRENCE, ANDREA MEAD, county official, recreational land use consultant; b. Rutland, Vt., Apr. 19, 1932; d. Bradford Belcher and Janet Brocket (Ross) Mead; m. David Lawrence, Mar. 31, 1951 (div. 1969); children: Cortlandt Bradford, Matthew David, Deirdre Bario, Leslie Peace, Quentin Andrea. Student pub. schs., Rutland. Competitive skier 1942-56; mem. U.S. Olympic Alpine Team, 1948, 52, 56; winner gold medals for slalom and giant slalom Internat. Olympics, 1952; 1st in downhill, slalom and giant slalom N.Am. Championships, 1953; winner downhill, slalom and giant slalom Am. Internat. Races, Stowe, Vt., 1952, 53, 54; Nat. Alpine champion in downhill, slalom and combined events 1949, 52, 55, Nat. Alpine giant slalom chamption, 1953, 55; mem. Mono County Bd. Suprs., Mammoth Lake, Calif., 1982—, vice chmn., 1983, 85, chmn., 1986; mem. Gt. Basin Unified Air Pollution Control Dist., Local Agy. Formation Commn., Mono County Hist. Records Commn., Ea. Sierra Com., Econ. Devel. Steering Com., Interagy. Com. on Owens Valley and Wildlife, Inyo-Mono Fish and Game Adv. Commn., Mono County Mental Health Adv. Bd., Long Valley Volcanic Hazards Adv. Coun., Mono County Housing Authority; spl. cons., ski resort cons. Allan O'Connor & Assocs., 1974-77, Wallace, McHarg, Roberts, Todd & Assocs., 1974-77, June Mountain Devel. Corp., 1974. Author: (with Sara Burnaby) A Practice of Mountains, 1980. Mem. Aspen (Colo.) Bd. Adjustment and Planning Commn., 1963-64; founder Friends of Mammoth, 1971-75; a founder Mammoth Adv. Coun., 1972-76; mem. Mono County Grand Jury, 1973; mem. citizens working group for long range plans for allocation winter sports resources in Inyo Nat. Forest, U.S. Forest Svc.; mem. Citizen's Com. To Rev. U.S. Forest Svc. Practices in Calif., 1979. Named to New Eng. Hall of Fame, 1952, Helms Hall of Fame, 1953, Ski Hall of Fame, 1958; recipient Athlete of Yr. award Helms Found. and Sportfolio mag., 1947, Am. Ski Trophy, 1950; inducted into Women's Sports Found. Hall of Fame, 1983; on cover Time mag., Jan. 21, 1952. Mem. Nat. Assn. Counties (pub. lands steering com.), County Suprs. Assn. Calif. (housing, land use and transp. com., transp. task force subcom.), So. Calif. Regional Assn. County Suprs., Mountain Counties Water Resources Assn., Sacramento-Mother Lode Regional Assn. County Suprs. Democrat. Home: PO Box 43 Mammoth Lakes CA 93546 Office: Mono County Bd Suprs HCR 79 Box 221 Mammoth Lakes CA 93546

LAWRENCE, BRENT CHRYST, software company executive; b. Portland, Oreg., Aug. 11, 1958; s. Mark Edward Lawrence and Hazel Marylee (Chryst) Leitch. BA, Oreg. State U., 1980; M Internat. Mgmt., 1983. Sales rep. Verbatim Corp., Sunnyvale, Calif., 1984-85; v.p. Machinery Market, Inc., Portland, Oreg., 1985-87; market analyst MicroDisk Svcs., Inc., Redmond, Wash., 1987-88; prodn. mgr. Taito Software, Inc., Bothell, Wash., 1988—; cons. to software industry, Redmond, 1988—. Mem. Seattle World Affairs Coun. Republican. Methodist. Home: 9411 NE 32nd Bellevue WA 98004

LAWRENCE, DANIEL JOSEPH, electrical engineer; b. Tacoma, July 26, 1953; s. Joseph Alvin Jr. and Angelina Mary (Campos) L.; m. Carolee Myers, June 15, 1974; children: Matthew Garrett, Cheri Renee. AA, San Joaquin Delta Coll., Stockton, Calif., 1980; BS, U. Pacific, 1986. Registered profl. engr., Calif. Electrician, journeyman Lawrence & Sons Electric Co., Tracy, Calif., 1971-78, Tracy, 1978-81; elec. engr. Lawrence Livermore (Calif.) Nat. Lab., 1981—; cons., designer Crawford Engring., Stockton, 1986—; tutor Tracy Area Schs., 1972—; instr. Calif. Dept. Fish and Game. 2d lt. Calif. Air N.G., 1986—. Lawrence Livermore Nat. Lab. scholar, 1984-86. Mem. IEEE (vice chmn. 1987—), Soc. Am. Mil. Engrs., NRA, Tau Beta Pi, Phi Kappa Phi, Eta Kappa Nu. Republican. Baptist. Office: Lawrence Livermore Nat Lab PO Box 808 L-654 Livermore CA 94550

LAWRENCE, DEAN GRAYSON, retired lawyer; b. Oakland, Calif.; d. Henry C. and Myrtle (Grayson) Schmidt; A.B., U. Calif.-Berkeley, 1934, J.D., 1939. Admitted to Calif. bar, 1943, U.S. Dist. Ct., 1944, U.S. Ct. Appeals, 1944, Tax Ct. U.S., 1945, U.S. Treasury Dept., 1945, U.S. Supreme Ct., 1967; asso. Pillsbury, Madison & Sutro, San Francisco, 1944, 45; gen. practice Oakland, 1946-50, San Jose, 1952-60, Grass Valley, 1960-63, 66—; county counsel Nevada County, 1964-65. Nevada County Bd. Suprs., 1969-73, chmn., 1971. Sec. Nev. County Humane Animal Shelter Bd., 1966-86; state humane officer, 1966-82; pres. Nev. County Humane Soc., 1974-86, mem. Humane Soc. U.S., Fund for Animals; bd. dirs. Nevada County Health Planning Council, Golden Empire Areawide Health Planning Council, 1974, 75. Mem. Bus. and Profl. Women's Club, AAUW, Animal Protection Inst. Am. (Humanitarian of Yr. 1986), Animal Legal Defense Fund, Golden Empire Human Soc. Phi Beta Kappa, Sigma Xi, Kappa Beta Pi, Pi Mu Epsilon, Pi Lambda Theta. Episcopalian. Office: PO Box 66 Grass Valley CA 95945

LAWRENCE, FRANCES ELIZABETH, teacher; b. Glendale, Calif., Feb. 26, 1925; d. Felix William and Bessie Marie Powers; m. Vester Blount Lawrence, Apr. 2, 1955; children: Elizabeth Gail, Mark William, Cynthia Sue Cherry. AA, Pasadena Jr. Coll., 1945; BA, Whittier Coll., 1949. Tchr. Victor Sch. Dist., Victorville, Calif., 1949-56, Adelanto (Calif.) Sch. Dist., 1965—; mem. planning bd. San Bernardino County Spelling Connection Com., 1985, Adelanto Dist. Curriculum Com., 1985-86. Served with USNR, 1945-49. Mem. Nat. Assn. for Edn. Young Children, Calif. Assn. for Edn. Young Children, Early Childhood Caucus Calif. Tchrs. Assn., Adelanto Dist. Tchrs. Assn. (rep.). Democrat. Lodges: Job's Daus. (majority mem.), Order Eastern Star. Home: 18258 Symeron Rd Apple Valley CA 92307

LAWRENCE, GARY DEAN, art gallery director; b. El Reno, Okla., Jan. 15, 1940; m. Mary Carole Pitts., June 13, 1971; children: Brad, Brent, Angela. Student, Humboldt State Coll., Arcata, Calif., 1958-60. Territorial mgr., then west coast mgr. Sherwin-Williams Co., various locations, 1962-69;

automotive tchr. Benson High Sch., Portland, Oreg., 1969-70; owner, mgr. Lawrence Gallery, Sheridan, Oreg., 1977—; pres. Lawrence/Lawrence, Inc. Sheridan, Oreg., 1980—; v.p. Lawrence/Maveety, Inc., Salishan, Oreg., 1979-85; pres. Art Focus Enterprises, Inc., Portland, 1982-84. Mem. Yamhill County (Oreg.) Parkway Com., 1988-89. Republican. Episcopalian. Home: 9920 Gilbert Creek Rd Willamina OR 97396 Office: Lawrence Gallery 19706 SW Hwy 18 McMinnville OR 97128

LAWRENCE, JACOB, painter, educator; b. Atlantic City, Sept. 7, 1917; s. Jacob and Rosealee (Armstead) L.; m. Gwendolyn Knight, July 24, 1941. Student, Harlem Art Workshop, N.Y.C., 1932-39; scholar, Am. Artists Sch., N.Y.C., 1938-39; AFD, Denison U., 1970; DFA (hon.), Pratt Inst., 1970, Colby Coll., 1976, Md. Inst. Coll. Art, 1979, Carnegie-Mellon U., 1981, Rutgers U., 1988, Parsons Sch. Design, N.Y.C., 1988; L.H.D. (hon.), Howard U., 1985, Tulane U., 1989; DFA (hon.), Yale U., 1986, Yale U., 1986, Spelman Coll., 1987. Artist Yaddo Found., Saratoga, 1954-55; instr. Pratt Inst. Art Sch., N.Y.C., 1958-65, Art Students League, N.Y.C., 1967-69, New Sch. Social Research, N.Y.C., 1966-71; artist in residence Brandeis U., 1965—; coordinator of the arts Pratt Inst., 1970—, prof. art, 1970; prof. art U. Wash., Seattle, 1970-83, prof. emeritus, 1983—; Disting. Faculty lectr. U. Wash., 1978; mem. Nat. Council Arts, 1979—. Exhibits include John Brown Series, under auspices Am. Fedn. Art, 1947, 30 paintings on history U.S., Alan Gallery, 1957, mural GSA, Jamaica, N.Y.; one-man shows include Migration Series, Mus. Modern Art, 1944, Downtown Gallery, N.Y.C., 1941, 43, 45, 47, 50, 53, M'Bari Artists and Writers Club, Nigeria, 1962, Terry Dintenfass Gallery, N.Y.C., 1963, Francine Seders Gallery, Seattle, 1985; works included Johnson Wax Co. World tour group exhbn., 1963, U.S. State Dept. group exhbn. in, Pakistan, 1963, retrospective exhbn., Whitney Mus. Am. Art, 1974, traveling retrospective Exhbn., Seattle Art Mus., 1986-87; commd. for graphic impressions 1977 Inauguration, Washington, mural commd., Kingdome Stadium, Seattle, 1979, Mural Howard U., 1980, 85, U. Wash., 1985, others; represented in, Met. Mus. Art, Mus. Modern Art, Whitney Mus., Phillips Meml. Gallery, Wash., Portland (Oreg.) Mus., Worcester (Mass.) Mus., Balt. Mus. Art, Wichita Art Mus., Albright Art Gallery, Buffalo, AAAL, N.Y.C., Mus. Modern Art, Sao Paulo, Brazil, R.I. Sch. Design, Va. Mus. Fine Arts, Bklyn. Mus., IBM Corp., Container Corp. Am., various univs.; Author: Harriet and the Promised Land, 1968; illustrator: Aesop's Fables, 1970; (book catalogue for retrospective exhbn.: Jacob Lawrence-American Painter, 1986; executed mural Theatre, 1985; executed, instatted mural Orlando Fla. Internat. Airport, 1988. Bd. govs. Skowhegan Sch. Painting and Sculpture; mem. Fulbright Art Com., 1966-67, Wash. State Arts Commn., 1976—; elector Hall of Fame for Gt. Americans, 1976—; mem. Nat. Endowment for Arts, 1978—. Rosenwald fellow, 1940, 41, 42; recipient purchase prize Artists for Victory, 1942, purchase prize Atlanta U., 1948; Guggenheim fellow, 1945; Opportunity mag. award, 1948; Norman Wait Harris medal Art Inst. Chgo., 1948; Acad. Arts and Letters grantee, 1953; Chapelbrook Found. grantee, 1955; 1st prize in mural competition for UN Bldg. Nat. Council U.S. Art, Inc., 1955; recipient Retrospective Exhbn. with Definitive Catalogue Ford Found., 1960, Retrospective Exhbn. with Definitive Catalogue Whitney Mus. Modern Art, 1974; works selected as part of exchange exhibit with Soviet Union, 1959; Spingarn medal N.A.A.C.P., 1970; ann. citation Nat. Assn. Schs. Art, 1973. Mem. Artist Equity Assn. (past sec., pres. N.Y. chpt. 1957), Nat. Inst. Arts and Letters. Address: 4316 37th Ave NE Seattle WA 98105

LAWRENCE, JAMES LESTER, college dean and official; b. N.Y.C., Oct. 22, 1941; s. Ernice B. and Telete Zorayda (Lester) L.; BA, Tex. Christian U., 1963, MA, 1965; PhD, U. Maine, 1968. Asst. prof. biology Hartwick Coll., Oneonta, N.Y., 1968-70, asst. dean faculty, 1970-71, asst. v.p., assoc. dean of coll., 1971-74, v.p. ednl. affairs, dean coll., 1974-75; dean of coll. Huron Coll., S.D., 1979-81; sr. v.p., dean of coll. Marycrest Coll., Davenport, Iowa, 1981-88; v.p. acad. and student affairs Coll. of Santa Fe, 1988—; mem. student life council Colls. Mid-Am., Sioux Falls, S.D., 1979-81, mem. deans' council, Sioux Falls, 1979-81, chmn., 1981; mem. adv. bd. Huron Coll./Huron Regional Med. Ctr. Sch. Nursing, 1979-81, mem. com. accreditation, 1980-81; mem. Council Ind. Colls. Nat. Cons. Network, Washington, 1980—, dir. New Deans' Mentor Program, 1987—; mem. program rev. panel Quad-Cities Grad. Study Ctr., Rock Island, Ill., 1981-87, bd. govs., 1987-88, mem. Council of Mem. Insts., 1987-88; mem. Edn. Task Force Quad-Cities Visions for Future, 1987-88; presenter workshops and seminars. Contbr. articles and poetry to profl. pubs. Fulbright fellow, 1972-73; Helene Wurlitzer Found. grantee, 1975. Bd. dirs. Community Chorale, Oneonta, N.Y., 1974-78, Huron Symphony, 1979-81, Community Theatre, Huron, 1980-81, Glimmerglass Opera Theatre, Cooperstown, N.Y., 1976-78, Davenport Med. Ctr., Iowa, 1985-87, Santa Fe Community Orch.; vestryman Grace Ch., Huron, 1980-81, chmn. religious edn. com., 1980-81. Mem. Davenport C. of C. (edn. com. 1981-83, small bus. council 1986-88, steering com.), Huron C. of C. (edn. com. 1980-81), Santa Fe C. of C. (edn. coun. 1988—), Am. Assn. Higher Edn., Am. Assn. Acad. Deans, Council Adult Exptl. Learning, N.Y. Acad. Scis. Democrat. Episcopalian. Avocations: writing, cooking, singing. Home: 835 Colonitas Campestres Santa Fe NM 87501 Office: Coll of Santa Fe St Michael's Dr Santa Fe NM 87501

LAWRENCE, JEROME, playwright, director, educator; b. Cleve., July 14, 1915; s. Samuel and Sarah (Rogen) L. BA, Ohio State U., 1937, LHD (hon.), 1963; DLitt, Fairleigh Dickinson U., 1968; DFA (hon.), Villanova U., 1969; LittD, Coll. Wooster, 1983. Dir. various summer theaters Pa. and Mass., 1934-37; reporter, telegraph editor Wilmington (Ohio) News Jour., 1937; editor Lexington Daily News, Ohio, 1937; continuity editor radio Sta. KMPC, Beverly Hills, Calif., 1937-39; sr. staff writer CBS, Hollywood, Calif. and N.Y.C., 1939-42; pres., writer, dir. Lawrence & Lee, Hollywood, N.Y.C. and London, 1945—; vis. prof. Ohio State U., 1969, Salzburg Seminarin Am. Studies, 1972, Baylor U., 1978; prof. playwriting U. So. Calif. Grad. Sch., 1984—; co-founder, judge Margo Jones Award, N.Y.C., 1958—; co-founder, pres. Am. Playwrights Theater, Columbus, Ohio, 1970-85; bd. dirs. Am. Conservatory Theater, San Francisco, 1970-80, Stella Adler Theater, Los Angeles, 1987—. Scenario writer Paramount Studios, 1941; master playwright NYU Inst. Performing Arts, 1967-69; author-dir. for: radio and television UN Broadcasts; Army-Navy programs D-Day, VE-Day, VJ-Day; author: Railroad Hour, Hallmark Playhouse, Columbia Workshop; author: Off Mike, 1944, (biography, later made into PBS-TV spl.) Actor: Life and Times of Paul Muni, 1978 (libretto and lyrics by Lawrence and Lee, music by Billy Goldenberg); co-author, dir.: (album) One God; playwright: Live Spelled Backwards, 1969, Off Mike, (mus. with Robert E. Lee) Look, Ma, I'm Dancin', 1948 (music by Hugh Martin), Shangri-La, 1956 (music by Harry Warren, lyrics by James Hilton, Lawrence and Lee), Mame, 1966 (score by Jerry Herman), Dear World, 1969 (score by Jerry Herman), (non-mus.) Inherit the Wind (translated and performed in 33 langs., named best fgn. play of year London Critics Poll 1960), Auntie Mame, 1956, The Gang's All Here, 1959, Only in America, 1959, A Call on Kuprin (now called Checkmate), 1961, Diamond Orchid (revised as Sparks Fly Upward, 1966), 1965, The Incomparable Max, 1969, The Crocodile Smile, 1970, The Night Thoreau Spent in Jail, 1970, (play and screenplay) First Monday in October, 1978, (play and screenplay) The Night Thoreau Spent in Jail, 1971, (written for opening of Thurber Theatre, Columbus) Jabberwock, 1974, (with Norman Cousins and Robert E. Lee) Whisper in the Mind, 1989; Decca Dramatic Albums, Musi-Plays.; contbg. editor Dramatics mag.; Lawrence and Lee collections at Library and Mus. of the Performing Arts, Lincoln Ctr., N.Y., Harvard's Widener Library, Cambridge, Mass., Jerome Lawrence & Robert E. Lee Theatre Research Inst. at Ohio State U., Columbus, est. 1986. A founder, overseas corr. Armed Forces Radio Service; mem. Am. Theatre Planning Bd.; bd. dirs. Nat. Repertory Theatre, Plumstead Playhouse; mem. adv. bd. USDAN Center for Creative and Performing Arts, East-West Players, Performing Arts Theatre of Handicapped., Inst. Outdoor Drama; mem. State Dept. Cultural Exchange Drama Panel, 1961-69; del. Chinese-Am. Writers Conf., 1982, 86, Soviet-Am. Writers Conf., 1984, 85; Am. Writers rep. to Hiroshima 40th Anniversary Commemorative, Japan, 1985; mem. U.S. Cultural Exchange visit to theatre communities of Beijing and Shanghai, 1985. Recipient N.Y. Press Club award, 1942, CCNY award, 1948, Radio-TV Life award, 1948, Mirror awards, 1952, 53, Peabody award, 1949, 52, Variety Showmanship award 1954, Variety Critics poll 1955, Outer-Circle Critics award 1955, Donaldson award, 1955, Ohioana award, 1955, Ohio Press Club award, 1959, Brit. Drama Critics award, 1960, Moss Hart Meml. award, 1967, State Dept. medal, 1968, Pegasus award, 1970, Lifetime Achievement award Am. Theatre Assn., 1979, Nat. Thespian Soc. award, 1980, Pioneer Broadcasters award, 1981, Ohioana Library career medal, Master of Arts award Rocky Mountain Writers Guild, 1982, Centennial Award medal Ohio State U., 1970, William Inge award and lectureship Independence Community Coll., 1983, 86, 87, 88, 89; named Playwright of Yr. win-Wallace Coll., 1960. Mem. Acad. Motion Picture Arts and Scis., Acad. TV Arts and Scis. (2 Emmy awards 1988), Authors League (council), ANTA (dir., v.p.), Ohio State U. Assn. (dir.), Radio Writers' Guild (a founder, pres.), Writers Guild Am. (dir., founding mem. Valentine Davies award), Dramatists Guild (council), ASCAP, Phi Beta Kappa, Sigma Delta Chi, Zeta Beta Tau.

LAWRENCE, JULIE ANNE, insurance agency executive; b. Cin., Nov. 17, 1963; d. James Orlando and Louise Anne (Davis) L. BSBA, No. Ariz. U., 1985. CLU; registered Nat. Assn. Securities Dealers. Sales mgr. Desert House Inc., Tucson, 1981-85, now bd. dirs.; ins. adviser Northwestern Mut. Life Ins. Co., 1985—; investment officer Robert W. Baird Inc., 1988—. Fund raiser YMCA, Tucson, 1986-89, Brester Ctr., Tucson, 1988-89, Cedric Dempsey Cancer Run, Tucson, 1988; vol. Spl. Olympics, Flagstaff, Ariz., 1982-85. Mem. Greater Tucson Assn. Life Underwriters (bd. dir. 1988-89, awards chmn., chmn. pub. rels. 1988-89, Rookie of Yr. award 1986), Tucson C. of C., Resources for Women, No. Ariz. U. Alumni Assn., Physicians Nationwide, Desert Dwellers Ski Club. Republican. Home: 4601 N Via Entrada Apt 1003 Tucson AZ 85718 Office: 310 S Wilmot Ste 100 Tucson AZ 85711

LAWRENCE, PAULA DENISE, physical therapist; b. Ft. Worth, May 21, 1959; d. Roddy Paul and Kay Frances (Spivey) Gillis; m. Mark Jayson Lawrence, Apr. 20, 1985. BS, Tex. Women's U., 1982. Lic. phys. therapist, Tex., Calif. Sales mgr. R. and K Camping Ctr., Garland, Tex., 1977-82; staff physical therapist Longview (Tex.) Regional Hosp., 1982-83, dir. phys. therapy, 1983-87, dir. rehab. svcs., 1987-88; staff phys. therapist MPH Home Health, Longview, Tex., 1983-84; pres. DRCA Phys. Therapy Corp., Hemet, Calif., 1988—; mem. adv. com. div. health occupations Kilgore (Tex.) Coll., 1985-88; mem. profl. adv. bd. Hospice Longview, 1985-88. Mem. Am. Phys. Therapy Assn., Tex. Phys. Therapy Assn., Nat. Assn. Female Execs., Am. Bus. Women;'s Assn. (v.p. 1987, Woman of Yr. award 1988), Calif. Physical Therapy Assn., Psi Chi, Omega Rho Alpha. Home: 899 Kristin Ln Hemet CA 92343 ffice: DRCA Physical Therapy Clinic Physical Rehab Ctrs Calif 850 E Latham Ste G Hemet CA 92343

LAWRENCE, RICK L(EE), architect; b. Loveland, Colo., Jan. 15, 1954; s. Virgil Walter and Twila Lea (Brown) L.; m. Terri Ann Clayton, Oct. 26, 1955 (div. Dec. 1987); children: Shandra Denise, Adam Clayton. BArch, U. Idaho, 1977. Registered architect, Colo., N.Mex., Utah, Wyo. Surveyors aide engring. dept. City of Loveland, 1972-77; draftsman The Neenan Co., Ft. Collins, Colo., 1977-78; job capt. Victor Huff & Assocs., Inc., Aurora, Colo., 1978-81; project architect Bourn & Dulaney Architects, AIA, Englewood, Colo., 1981-82, Urban Design Group, Denver, 1982-84; project mgr. Blizzard/Lehman Partnership, Denver, 1984-85; owner, architect Rick L. Lawrence Architect Cons., Littleton, 1985-87; project architect Kenmar Assocs., Inc., Englewood, 1987-88; architect VHA, Inc., Aurora, 1988--. Mem. Nat. Trust for Hist. Preservation, Nat. Bldg. Mus., Internat. Conf. Bldg. Ofcls. Home: 7580 E Harvard Ave 108 Denver CO 80231 Office: VHA Inc 2675 S Abilene St 200 Aurora CO 80014

LAWRENCE, SANFORD HULL, physician; b. Kokomo, Ind., July 10, 1919; s. Walter Scott and Florence Elizabeth (Hull) L. AB, Ind. U., 1941, MD, 1944. Intern Rochester (N.Y.) Gen. Hosp., 1944-45; resident Halloran Hosp., Staten Island, N.Y., 1946-49; dir. biochemistry research Lab. San Fernando (Calif.) VA Hosp.; asst. prof. UCLA, 1950—; cons. U.S. Govt., Los Angeles County; lectr. Faculte de Medicine, Paris, various colls. Eng., France, Belgium, Sweden, USSR, India, Japan. Author: Zymogram in Clinical Medicine, 1965; contbr. articles to sic. jours. Mem. Whitley Heights Civic Assn., 1952—; pres. Halloran Hosp. Employees Assn., 1947-48. Served to maj. U.S. Army, 1945-46. Recipient Research award TB and Health Assn., 1955-58, Los Angeles County Heart Assn., 1957-59, Pres.' award, Queen's Blue Bookaward, Am. Men of Sci. award; named one of 2000 Men of Achievement, Leaders of Am. Sci., Ky. Col., named Hon. Mayor of West Point, Ky. Mem. AAAS, AMA, N.Y. Acad. Scis., Am. Fedn. Clin. Research, Am. Assn. Clin. Investigation, Am. Assn. Clin. Pathology, Am. Assn. Clin. Chemistry, Los Angeles County Med. Assn. Republican. Methodist. Home: 2014 Whitley Ave Hollywood CA 90068 Home: 160 rue St Martin, Paris 75003, France

LAWRENCE, STEPHEN, small business owner; b. San Francisco, Mar. 10, 1954; s. Leonard George and Vera (Lissina) L.; m. Effie Pappas, Nov. 22, 1987. BS, San Francisco Sch. Bus., 1983. V.p. Nat. Bus. Factors, San Francisco, 1980-83, Nat. Credit Svc., Foster City, Calif., 1983-86; pres. TCAA Inc/TCA Collections, San Leandro, Calif., 1986—. Author: Last Right, 1979. Active various charitable orgns. With USN, 1971-76. Mem. Am. Collection Assn., Profl. Photographers Assn., Nikon Profl. Assn., Calif. Collectors Assn. Home: 2101 9th Ave San Francisco CA 94116 Office: TCA Collections 14425 Catalina St San Leandro CA 94577

LAWRENCE, WILLIAM GERALD, electronic design company executive, engineering consultant; b. Oakland, Calif., Aug. 4, 1927; s. William John and Hazel Marie (Heathcote) L.; m. Darcy Joan Thomas, Aug. 18, 1951; children: Kristen, Susan, David, Carolyn. BS in Mech. Engring., U. Wash., 1949, BS in Indsl. Engring., 1949, postgrad., 1953-56; postgrad. U. Pa., 1966. Supr. engring. Boeing Aircraft, Seattle, 1953-60, Douglas Aircraft, Santa Monica, Calif., 1960-62; project engr. Gen. Electric Co., Phila., 1962-69, engring. mgr., Tokyo, 1970-74; pres. AAVCOM, Phoenix, 1974—, Aavsystems, Phoenix, 1981—, AAVCOM World Trade Svcs., Ltd., Phoenix, 1987—. Advanced Precision Tool Co. Ltd., Phoenix, 1984-85. Office: AAVCOM World Trade Svcs 3035 W Thomas Rd Phoenix AZ 85017

LAWRENCE, ZAN, computer consultant; b. Cedar Rapids, Iowa, Jan. 19, 1945; s. Stanley Alexander and Doris (Cornelius) L. Student, Calif. State-Fullerton, 1973-75. Sales cons. Computerland, Newport Beach, Calif., 1979-80, 85-86; regional sales mgr. Microbyte Electronic, Newport Beach, 1981-85; sr. sales rep. Pac Tel Infosystems, Irvine, Calif., 1986-87; owner Western Computer Systems, Laguna Beach, Calif., 1987—. Author: (tng. manual) Effective Sales of AT&T, 1985. Sponsor Children's Hosp., Orange, Calif., 1988; quartermaster Orange County Marine Inst., Dana Pt., Calif., 1988. Served with USMC, 1963-66. Republican. Office: Western Computer Systems 490 Third St Unit I Laguna Beach CA 92651

LAWSHE, CHARLES DAVID, real estate executive; b. Greenwood, Miss., Feb. 19, 1955; s. William Harvey and Louise (Worrell) L. BS, U. So. Miss., 1979. Cert. property mgr. Dir. mgmt. services Elkington & Keltnor Group, Memphis, 1983-85; dist. mgr. Southmark Comml. Mgmt., Memphis, 1985-86; regional mgr. Southmark Comml. Mgmt., Dallas, 1986-87; v.p. Benequity Properties, Los Angeles, 1987—. Mem. Mastership, Inst. Real Estate Mgmt. (exec. dir. 1985-86), Internat. Council Shopping Ctrs., Nat. Assn. Realtors. Republican. Methodist. Office: Benequity Properties 3700 Wilshire 10th Fl Los Angeles CA 90010

LAWSON, BERT ALLEN, communication executive; b. Lexington, Ky., Jan. 8, 1947; s. Delbert Henry and Mary Jane (Sams) L.; m. Carol Brewer, June 25, 1982; 1 child, Carrie E. BSEE, U. Ky., 1970; MBA, U. Mo., Kansas City, 1979. Registered profl. engrs., Kans. Account exec. IBM, Louisville, 1973-75, Kansas City, Mo., 1975-78; v.p. SUNCOM, Inc., Kansas City, 1978-81; regional mgr. Honeywell, Inc., Mpls., 1981-83; v.p. Internat. Office System, Mpls., 1983-85; pres. Executone Northwest Inc., Billings, Mont., 1985—; prof. aviation studies Rocky Mountain Coll, Billings, 1988—. mem. City Council, City of Lenexa, Kans., 1975-78. Major Air Nat. Guard, 1968-88. Republican. Office: Executone NW Inc 2110 Overland Ave Ste 115 Billings MT 59102

LAWSON, CAROLYN RUTH, educator, consultant; b. Orlando, Fla., June 11, 1948; d. Robert Earl and Emma Cleo (Hockaday); m. John Calvin Lawson. BA, Scripps Coll., 1977; MA in Edn., Wash. State U., 1984. Adminstrv. asst. Gen. Telephone, Kennewick, Wash., 1978-81; computer systems analyst State of Wash., Olympia, 1981-83, computer cons., 1983-84, HRD specialist, 1984-87; curriculum specialist Western Wash. Univ., Olympia, 1987—; cons., owner Abacus Edn. & Consulting, Olympia, 1986—. Chmn. Career Planning Resource Council, Scripps Coll., 1975-77. Mem. Wash. State Univ. Alumni Assn., Am. Assn. Univ. Women (editor 1979-80), Interagency Trainers Assn. (chmn. 1986-87), Capital Area Info. Processors, Toastmasters (pres. 1986-87). Home: PO Box 1373 Olympia WA 98507

LAWSON, JAMES LEE, health care consultant; b. Alhambra, Calif., Jan. 7, 1949; Charles French and Helen Marie (Gregory) L.; m. Ilene Eleanor Sweeney, Apr. 8, 1973 (div. 1983); children: Charles J., Sara C.; m. Marguerite Adams King, Feb. 25, 1984; 1 child, Zachary David. AA in Polit. Sci., Cypress (Calif.) Coll., 1970; AS in Nursing, Victor Valley Coll., Victorville, Calif., 1980; BBA, Calif. We. U., 1976, MBA, 1978; postgrad., We. State U., 1970-71. Cert. instr., Calif.; RN, Calif., Fla., Ky., Idaho, Ill., Ind., Tex., Wis.; cert. emergency nurse practioner, Calif. Head nurse, charge nurse La Palma (Calif.) Intercommunity Hosp. and Pioneer Hosp., 1974-76; from adminstrv. asst. to staff analyst San Bernadino (Calif.) County Med. Ctr., 1976-79; dir. nursing services Barstow (Calif.) Community Hosp., 1979-80; adminstr. Disabled and Vietnam Vets. Outreach Program Vets House, Inc., Madison, 1981; exec. dir. So. Wis. Emergency Med. Services Council, Inc., Madison, 1981-83; charge nurse, acting head nurse West Side Dist. Hosp., Simi Valley (Calif.) Adventist Hosp., 1983-84; dir. ops. Pasadena Children's Tng. Soc., Altadena, Calif., 1984-86; staff asst. Kapner, Wolfberg & Assocs., Inc., Van Nuys, Calif., 1987-88; v.p. Kapner, Wolfberg & Assocs., Inc., Van Nuys, 1988—. Contbr. articles to profl. jours. Loaned exec., Arrowhead United Way, San Bernadino, 1979; mem. Calif. State Bd. of Edn. Child Advisory Nutrition Council, 1986—, Selective Service Bd. Local 14, Wis., 1981-83, ARC, Am. Heart Assn.; vol. campaign worker for Repub. Party. Served with USN, 1966-74. Mem. Am. Mgmt. Assn., Am. Hosp. Assn., Nat. League for Nursing, Am. Nurses Assn., Am. Public Health Assn., Am. Soc. Nursing Svc. Admistrs., Am. Trauma Soc., Calif. Soc. Nursing Svc. Administrs., Hosp. Mgmt. Systems Soc. of So. Calif. (charter), Hosp. Internal Auditors, Med. Auditors Assn. Calif., Nat. Emergency Nurses Assn. (charter), Nat. Assn. for Emergency Paramedics (charter), Pasadena (Calif.) C. of C., Hosp. Fin. Mgmt. Assn. Republican. Home: 20224 Sherman Way #13 Canoga Park CA 91306 Office: Kapner Wolfberg & Assocs Inc 7120 Hayvenhurst Ste 204 Van Nuys CA 91406

LAWSON, MARGUERITE PAYNE, small business owner; b. Detroit, Apr. 30, 1935; d. LeRoy and Marguerite Lenore (Archambeau) Payne; m. William Allen Stanke, Sept. 4, 1954 (div. Sept. 1962); children: Elizabeth Susan Hankey, Elaine Kathryn Dinwiddie; m. Vernon Arthur Lawson, Aug. 15, 1975. BA in Social Sci., Mich. State U., E. Lansing, 1957. Tchr. El Segundo Unified Sch. Dist., Calif., 1957-58, Las Virgenes Unified Sch. Dist., Calif., 1962-66, Timber Unified Sch. Dist., Thousand Oaks, Calif., 1966-72, Muroc Unified Sch. dist., Edwards, Calif., 1972-78; store owner Margie Lawson's Gourmet Ctr., Lancaster, Calif., 1978—; speaker various local clubs, television station, Lancaster, Palmdale, Calif., 1977—. Contbr. newspaper articles to Antelope Valley Press, 1975—; photojournalist Antelope Valley Press. Candidate Lancaster City Council, Calif., 1977. Mem. Mensa, Intertel, Asst. League Antelope Valley, Am. Assn. U. Women, Desert Amigas-Domestic Violence (affiliate), Alpha Charter Guild. Republican. Home: 2849 W Ave J-4 Lancaster CA 93536 Office: Margie Lawson's Gourmet Ctr 906 W Lancaster Blvd Lancaster CA 93534

LAWSON, ROSANNE TAUBER, psychotherapist; b. Allentown, Pa., Dec. 19, 1946; d. Herbert J. and Sylvia (Annoni) Tauber; m. Alphonzo S. Lawson, Jan. 15, 1971 (div. 1979); 1 child, Gregory Michael. BA, Notre Dame Coll., Cleve., 1968; MSW, Rutgers U., 1971. Psychotherapist Bonnie Brae Residential Treatment Ctr., N.J., 1971-73, Somerset County (N.J.) Family Counseling Service, Bound Brook, 1973-76; social worker Walnut Creek (Calif.) Hosp., 1980-81; pvt. practice psychotherapy Flanders, N.J., 1976-80, San Francisco, 1980—. Editor book revs. Women and Therapy, N.Y.C., 1983-86. Mem. Internat. Transactional Analysis Assn. (trustee 1982-85, program chmn. 1981-84). Democrat. Office: 2247 Union St San Francisco CA 94123

LAWSON, THOMAS CHENEY, security, information and credit bureau company executive; b. Pasadena, Calif., Sept. 21, 1955; s. William McDonald and Joan Bell (Jaffee) L.; m. Cathy Lee Taylor. Student Calif. State U., Sacramento, 1973-77. Pres., Tomatron Co., Pasadena, 1970-88, Tom's Tune Up & Detail, Pasadena, 1971-88, Tom's Pool Service, Sacramento, 1975-78, Tom Supply Co., 1975—; mgmt. trainee Permoid Process Co., Los Angeles, 1970-75; regional sales cons. Hoover Co., Burlingame, 1974-76; mktg. exec. River City Prodns., Sacramento, 1977-78; prof. automechanics Calif. State U., Sacramento, 1973-75; territorial rep. Globe div. Burlington House Furniture Co., 1978; So. Calif. territorial rep. Marge Carson Furniture, Inc., 1978-80; pres. Ted L. Gunderson & Assos., Inc., Westwood, Calif., 1980-81; pres., chief exec. officer Apscreen, Newport Beach, Calif., 1981—; chmn. bd. dirs. Creditbase Co., Newport Beach, Worldata Corp., Newport Beach. Calif. Rehab. scholar, 1974-77. Mem. Christian Businessmen's Com. Internat., Council Internat. Investigators, Am. Soc. Indsl. Security (cert., vice-chmn. Orange County chpt. 1989), Nat. Pub. Records Research Assn., Personnel and Indsl. Relations Assn. Office: 2043 Westcliff Dr Ste 300 Newport Beach CA 92660

LAWTON, ERIC, lawyer, photographer, visual artist; b. N.Y.C., Apr. 9, 1947; s. Leo and Vira (Michaels) L. AB, UCLA, 1969, photographic studies, 1980-81; JD, Loyola U., Los Angeles, 1972. Bar: Calif. 1972, U.S. Dist. Ct. (cen. dist.) Calif. 1974, U.S. Ct. Appeals (9th cir.) 1973, U.S. Supreme Ct. 1976. Assoc. West & Girardi, Los Angeles, 1972-76; sole practice Los Angeles, 1976—; guest lectr. UCLA Law Sch., 1986. one-man shows include Los Angeles Children's Mus., 1980-81, Am. Film Inst., 1981, Marc Richards Gallery, Los Angeles, 1986, U. Art Gallery Calif. State U. Northridge, 1987, John Nichols Gallery, Santa Paula, Calif., 1988; exhibited in group shows at Stockholm Art Fair, Sweden, 1986, Francine Ellman Gallery, 1986-87, Artists' Soc. Internat. Gallery, San Francisco, 1986-87, Fla. State U. Fine Arts Gallery and Mus., Tallahassee, 1988, Silvermine Gallery, Stamford, Conn., 1988, City Hall of West Hollywood, 1988, others; spl. film photographer in The Last Day, 1979, Chiva, Getting on in Style, 1980, Child's Play, 1981, others; multi-media prodns. include The Power, 1979, The Tie That Binds, 1981, Large-Screen Photographic Slide Montage with performance of Los Angeles Philharm. Orch. at Hollywood Bowl, 1986, Floating Stone performance, Japan Am. Theater, Los Angeles, 1987, others; represented in permanent collections including Bibliotheque Nationale, Paris, Los Angeles Children's Mus., Westwood Nat. Bank, Gibralter Savs., L.A., Mobius Soc., Los Angeles, Western Bank, Internat. Photography Mus., Oklahoma City, others; spl. assignment White House photographer, 1983; record album covers include Gyuto Monks, Tibetan Tantric Choir, Jungle Suite; poster Japanese Boats; contbr. photographs to newspapers and mags. including, N.Y. Times Mag., Fortune Mag., Traveler Mag., Chgo. Tribune, Variety, Gente (Italy), Dukas Femina (Switzerland), The World of Photography (China), Popular Photography, others. Active organizing com., citizens adv. and cultural and fine arts adv. commns. XXIII Olympic Games, Los Angeles, 1983-84; mem Cultural and Fine Arts Adv. Commn, 1983-84. Recipient award Fla. Nat. '88, Artquest awards 1987, 88. Mem. ABA, Los Angeles Trial Lawyers Assn., Los Angeles County Bar Assn., Santa Monica Bar Assn. Office: 2001 Wilshire Blvd 600 Santa Monica CA 90403

LAWTON, GREGORY MOSS, financial analyst; b. Youngstown, Ohio, Jan. 10, 1958; s. Edward Rigby Lawton and Peggy Lou (Egan) Albert. BS, Ft. Lewis Coll., 1981; postgrad., Fordham U., 1984-85. Pres. San Juan Mountaineering Inc., Telluride, Colo., 1978-82; sales mgr. W.S.V. Inc., N.Y.C., 1982-83; nat. sales mgr. CitiCorp Devel. Div., N.Y.C., 1983-85; exec. v.p. A.E. Stephenson & Co., Inc., Denver, 1985—; bd. dirs. Charter Bank and Trust, Denver, Larson Heavy Industries, Denver. Chmn. Denver Art Mus. Exhibits Com., Denver, 1987—. Mem. Telluride C. of C. (dir. festival transp. 1980, 81). Office: Stephenson & Co 100 Garfield St Denver CO 80206

LAWTON, MICHAEL JAMES, entomologist, pest management specialist; b. Balt., Aug. 6, 1953; s. James William and Mary Eileen (O'Connor) L.; m. Barbara Ann Byron, Dec. 19, 1983. BS, U. Md., 1975. Registered profl. entomologist. Technician, tech. dir. Atlas Exterminating Co., Towson, Md., 1975-78; asst. tech. dir. Western Exterminator Co., Irvine, Calif., 1978-83, tng. and tech. dir., 1984—. Republican. Office: Western Exterminator Co 1732 Kaiser Ave Irvine CA 92714

LAWYER, THOMAS CARLTON, mechanical service company executive; b. Huntington, Mass., Aug. 18, 1940; s. Denzil T. and Charlotte (Wills) L.; m. Bonnie Clappier, June 10, 1965; children—Anne, Sara, B.S.M.E., Purdue U., 1962; M.B.A., U. Nev., 1971. Registered profl. engr., Nev., Tenn. Sales engr. The Trane Co., Memphis, 1962-69, dist. mgr., Las Vegas, 1969—; sec., treas. Nevada Supply, Inc., Las Vegas, 1976—; pres. Lawyer Mech. Service, Las Vegas, 1969—; lectr. econs. dept. U. Nev., Las Vegas, 1979—, instr. continuing edn., 1980—. Mem. steering com. Nev. State Energy Forum, Reno, 1982-84; mem. Com. to Write Nev. Energy Standards for New Constrn., 1982; v.p. Nat. Kidney Found. Nev., Las Vegas, 1984. Recipient Nev. Energy award, Gov. State of Nev., 1982. Mem. ASHRAE (pres. 1976-77). Republican. Methodist. Club: Executive Association (pres. 1978-79) (Las Vegas). Office: The Trane Co 3040 S Valley View Blvd Las Vegas NV 89102

LAXALT, JOHN PAUL, political fund raiser; b. San Francisco, Aug. 8, 1952; s. Paul Dominique and Jackalyn (Ross) L.; m. Cynthia Rae Glauner, June 10, 1978; children: Jackalyn, David, Kevin. BS in Hotel Adminstrn., U. Nev., Las Vegas, 1974. Mgmt. trainee Marriott Hotel Corp., Arlington, Va., 1976; framing carpenter Carson City, Nev., 1977-79; youth coord. Laxalt for U.S. Senate Com., Reno, 1980; mktg. rep. Lincoln Properties Co., Reno, 1980-81; western regional rep. Rep. Nat. Fin. Com., Carson City, 1981—; rsch. cons. E.I.C. Group, Carson City, 1988—. Mem. Carson City Rep. Cen. Com., 1986. Mem. Lions. Roman Catholic. Office: Rep Nat Fin Com 1100 E Williams St Ste 100 Carson City NV 89701

LAXALT, PAUL, former senator; b. Reno, Aug. 2, 1922; s. Dominique and Theresa (Alpetche) L.; m. Jackalyn Ross, June 23, 1946 (div.); children: Gail, Sheila, John, Michelle, Kevin, Kathleen; m. Carol Wilson, Jan. 2, 1976; 1 child, Denise. Student, Santa Clara U., 1940-43; B.S., LL.B., Denver U., 1949. Bar: Nev. 1949. Practice in Carson City; partner firm Laxalt, Ross & Laxalt, 1954-62; dist. atty. Ormsby County, 1951-54; city atty. Carson City, 1954-55; lt. gov. Nev., 1962-66, gov., 1966-70; sr. partner Laxalt, Berry & Allison, Carson City, 1970-74; U.S. senator 1974-86; assoc. Finley, Kumble, Wagner, Heine, Underberg, Manley, Myerson & Casey, Washington, 1987-88, Laxalt, Washington, Perits and Dubuc, Washington, 1988—; pres., gen. mgr. Ormsby House Hotel and Casino, Carson City, 1972-75. Gen. chmn. Nat. Rep. Party, 1983—; chmn. Ronald Reagan Pres., 1976, 80, 84; co-chmn. George Bush Pres., 1988. Mem. Am. Bar Assn., Am. Legion, VFW. Club: Eagles. Office: Laxalt Washington Perito & Dubuc/Ste 975 1455 Pennsylvania Ave NW Washington DC 20004

LAY, KENNETH LEE, diversified energy company executive; b. Tyrone, Mo., Apr. 15, 1942; s. Omer and Ruth E. (Reese) L.; m. Linda Ann Phillips, July 10, 1982; children: Robyn Anne, Mark Kenneth, Todd David, Elizabeth Ayers, Robert Ray. BA, U. Mo., 1964, MA, 1965; PhD, U. Houston, 1970. Corp. economist Exxon Corp., Houston, 1965-68; assoc. prof. and lectr. in econs. George Washington U., 1969-73; tech. asst. to commr. FPC, 1971-72; dep. undersec. for energy Dept. Interior, 1972-74; v.p. Fla. Gas Co. (now Continental Resources Co.), Winter Park, Fla., 1974-76, pres., 1976-79; exec. v.p. The Continental Resources Co. subs. The Continental Group, Winter Park, 1979-81; pres., chief operating officer, dir. Transco Energy Co., Houston, 1981-84; chmn., pres., chief exec officer Houston Natural Gas Corp., 1984-85; pres., chief exec. officer, chief operating officer, dir. HNG/InterNorth (now Enron Corp.), Omaha, 1985—; also chmn. bd. dirs. HNG/InterNorth (now Enron Corp.), Houston; now also chief exec. officer, dir. Enron Corp. (formerly Internorth), Houston; bd. dirs. Baker Hughes, Inc., Compaq Computer Corp., Tex. Commerce Banchares, Inc., Houston Met. YMCA. Chmn. bd. regents U. Houston. Served with USN, 1968-71. Decorated Navy Commendation award; N.A.M. fellow; State Farm fellow; Guggenheim fellow. Mem. Interstate Natural Gas Assn. Am. (dir.), River Oaks Country Club. Office: Enron Corp PO Box 1188 Houston TX 77251

LAY, KERRY LYNN, county government official; b. Baker, Oreg., Feb. 2, 1938; s. Deshler Coleman and Myrtle Yvonne (Inman) L.; m. Janice Irene Ervin, Sept. 30, 1958; children: Geoffrey Lynn, Bradley Kevin, Christopher Ervin. Student, Oreg. State U., 1956-57; BS in Sociology, U. Oreg., 1961. Resident planner Bur. Govtl. Rsch. and Svc., U. Oreg., Pendleton, 1964-66, Tillamook, 1966-68; county planner County of Tillamook, Tillamook, 1968-69; asst. planning dir. Jackson County Planning Dept., Medford, Oreg., 1969-76; dir. Jackson County Dept. Planning and Devel., Medford, 1976—. With AUS, 1961-64. Mem. Redcoats of Oreg. Shakespearean Festival Assn. Mem. Baha'i faith. Home: 965 Graden Way Ashland OR 97520 Office: Jackson County Courthouse Medford OR 97501

LAYCRAFT, JAMES HERBERT, judge; b. Veteran, Alta., Can., Jan. 5, 1924; s. George Edward and Hattie (Cogswell) L.; m. Helen Elizabeth Bradley, May 1, 1948; children: James B., Anne L. BA, U. Alta., Edmonton, 1950; LLB, U. Alta., 1951; LLD (hon.), U. Calgary, Alta., 1986. Bars: Alta. Barrister Nolan Chambers & Co., Calgary, 1952-75; justice trial div. Supreme Ct. of Alta., Calgary, 1975-79; justice Ct. of Appeal of Alta., Calgary, 1979-85; chief justice of Alta. Calgary, 1985—. Contbr. articles to law jours. Served to lt. Royal Can. Arty., 1941-46, PTO. Mem. United Ch. of Can. Office: Alta Ct of Appeal, 530 7th Ave SW, Calgary, AB Canada T2P 0Y3

LAYDEN, FRANCIS PATRICK, professional basketball team executive, former coach; b. Bklyn., Jan. 5, 1932; m. Barbara Layden; children: Scott, Michael, Katie. Student, Niagara U. High sch. basketball coach L.I., N.Y.; head coach, athletic dir. Adelphi-Suffolk Coll. (now Dowling Coll.); head basketball coach, athletic dir. Niagara U., Niagara Falls, N.Y., 1968-76; asst. coach Atlanta Hawks, 1976-79; gen. mgr. Utah Jazz, Salt Lake City, 1979-88, head coach, 1981-88, v.p. basketball ops., until 1988, pres., 1989—. Bd. dirs. Utah Soc. Prevention Blindness; bd. dirs. Utah chpt. Multiple Sclerosis Soc., Utah Spl. Olympics. Served to 1st lt. Signal Corps, AUS. Office: Utah Jazz 5 Triad Ctr Ste 500 Salt Lake City UT 84180 *

LAYHON, CHRISTINE MARIE, nurse, educator; b. Everett, Wash., Nov. 14, 1955; m. Patrick Layhon, Aug. 10, 1985. BS in Nursing, Wash. State U., 1978; MS in Nursing, U. Wash., 1987. Cert. critical care RN. Staff nurse Caldwell Health Ctr., Seattle, 1978-82, West Seattle Community Hosp., Seattle, 1982-83, Riverton Hosp., Seattle, 1983-88, Va. Mason Hosp., Seattle, 1987—; instr. nursing Highline Community Coll., Seattle, 1984-86, 87—. Mem. Am. Heart Assn. (council on cardiovascular nursing), Am. Assn. Critical Care Nurses, Am. Nurses' Assn.

LAYTON, HARRY CHRISTOPHER, artist, lecturer; b. Safford, Ariz., Nov. 17, 1938; s. Christopher E. and Eurilda (Welker) L.; LHD, Sussex Coll., Eng., 1969; DFA (hon.), London Inst. Applied Research, 1972, DSc (hon), 1972; DD (hon.), St. Matthew U., Ohio, 1970, PhD (hon.), 1970; m. Karol Barbara Kendall, July 11, 1964 (div. Jan. 1989); children: Deborah, Christopher, Joseph, Elisabeth, Faith, Aaron, Gretchen, Benjamin, Justin, Matthew, Peter. Cert. clin. hypnotherapist. Lectr. ancient art Serra Cath. High Sch., 1963-64, Los Angeles Dept. Parks and Recreation, summer 1962, 63, 64; interior decorator Cities of Hawthorne, Lawndale, Compton, Gardena and Torrance (Calif.), 1960-68; one-man shows paintings; Nahas Dept. Stores, 1962, 64; group shows include: Gt. Western Savs. & Loan, Lawndale, Calif., 1962, Gardena (Calif.) Adult Sch., 1965, Serra Cath. High Sch., Gardena, 1963, Salon de Nations Paris, 1983; represented in permanent collections: Sussex Coll., Eng., Gardena Masonic Lodge, Culver City-Foshey Masonic Lodge, Gt. Western Savs. & Loan; paintings include: The Fairy Princess, 1975, Nocturnal Covenant, 1963, Blindas Name, 1962, Creation, 1962. Elder Ch. of Jesus Christ of Latter-day Saints, Santa Monica, Calif., 1963—. Recipient Golden Poet award, World of Poetry, 1986, 88. Mem. Am. Hypnotherapy Assn., Gardena Valley Art Assn., Centinella Valley Art Assn., Internat. Soc. Artists, Internat. Platform Assn., Am. Security Council, Soc. for Early Historic Archaeology, Am. Councilor's Soc. of Psychol. Counselors, Le Salon Des Nation Paris Geneva, Ctr. Internat. d'Art Contemporain, Am. Legion, Alpha Psi Omega. Republican. Clubs: Masons (32 deg.), Shriners, K.T. Home: 3658 Centinela Ave Ste 6 Los Angeles CA 90066 Office: Layton Studios Graphic Design PO Box 66849 Los Angeles CA 90066

LAYTON, KAREN ELAINE, mechanical design engineer; b. Tulsa, Oct. 21, 1960; d. James Edward and Judith Ann (Hughes) H.; m. George Allen Layton, June 6, 1981. AS in Mech. Design Technology, Okla. State U., 1980, B Mech. Design Technology, 1988. Design draftsman George Moody, Inc., Broken Arrow, Okla., 1981-83, Safety Tng. Systems, Tulsa, 1983-84; sr. mech. designer Flight Safety Internat., Tulsa, 1984-86; mech. design engr. LaHatt Engring., Bellingham, Wash., 1988—. Mem. Northwest Engrs. Club, Soc. Mfg. Engrs., Tau Alpha Pi. Mem. Assembly of God Ch. Home: 2701 Lakeridge Ln Bellingham WA 98226

LAZAR, EUGENE JAMES, V, consultant; b. Riverside, Calif., Aug. 3, 1952; s. Donna Faye (Folkers) L.; m. Nancy Mae Ricker, Nov. 5, 1971. Grad., Calif. Bapt. Coll., 1989, postgrad., 1989--. Police officer Riverside (Calif.) Police Dept., 1971-77; technician Sears Roebuck & Co., Riverside, Calif., 1977-79; police officer Stockton (Calif.) Police Dept., 1979-86; edn. cons. Calif. Bapt. Coll., Riverside, 1986--. Mem. Masons. Republican. Home: 11868 Venetian Moreno Valley CA 92387

LAZARA, VINCENT ANTHONY, brokerage house executive; b. Bklyn., Oct. 2, 1946; s. Vincent S. and Rosalind (Donadio) L.; m. Nancy E. Ash, Mar. 24, 1984. BA, NYU, 1968; MA, U. Ariz., 1971, PhD, 1973. Account exec. Blythe Eastman Dillon, Tucson, 1979, Paine Webber, Tucson, 1979-82; v.p. investments Prudential Bache Securities, Tucson, 1982—; adj. instr. Coll. Fin. Planning, 1980-85; cons. Nat. Ctr. Fin. Edn., 1984—, Dima Coll. Fin. Edn., 1987-88. Treas. Humane Soc. Tucson, 1982. Mem. Inst. Cert. Fin. Planners (pres. Tucson chpt.), Southwestern League Fine Arts (v.p. 1987-88, pres. 1988—). Office: Prudential Bache Securities 5255 E Williams Circle 205 Tucson AZ 85711

LAZAROF, HENRI, composer; b. Sofia, Bulgaria, Apr. 12, 1932. Private study with Paul Ben Haim, Israel; student, New Conservatory of Music, Jerusalem, Santa Cecilia Musical Acad., Rome, 1955-57; MFA, Brandeis U., 1959. Teacher French lang., lit. UCLA, 1959-62, instr. dept. music, from 1962, prof. then prof. emeritus; artist-in-residence Berlin, Fed. Republic of Germany, 1970-71; Organizer, Festival of Comtemporary Music, 1963; artistic dir., Contemporary Music Festival, UCLA, 1973-75; conductor various orchs. Composer concerti, other works for orch., chamber ensembles, piano, organ, chorus; recipient first Internat. Prize of Milan for Structures Sonores, 1966; compositions include Cadence I-Cadence VI, Volo, Canti, ballet work Mirrors, Mirrors, Intonazione et Variazioni. Office: UCLA Dept Music Los Angeles CA 90024 *

LAZARSKI, MARGARET ANN, small business owner; b. Chgo., Apr. 13, 1950; d. Walter Michael and Antoinette Helen (Makowski) L. BS in Home Econs., Bradley U., Peoria, Ill., 1972. With Fashion Bar Store, Denver, 1972-73; lease analyst Ralston Oil & Gas Co., Denver, 1973-74, Kissinger Petroleum Corp., Denver, 1974-76; landman Marmik Oil Co., Denver, 1976-77; landman, coord. Amoco Prodn. Co., Denver, 1977-80; sr. landman Home Petroleum Corp., Denver, 1980-86; owner, gen. mgr., inventor PAL Products, Denver, 1987—. Inventor KOOL KOVERS. Mem. Denver Assn. Petroleum Landmen (bd. dirs. 1984-85). Office: PAL Products PO Box 6594 Denver CO 80206

LAZERSON, JACK, pediatrician, educator; b. Bronx, Jan. 9, 1936; s. Mayer and Jennie (Gerson) L.; (div.); children: David, Deborah, Darlene, Donna; (div.); 1 child, Samuel. AB, NYU, 1957; MD, U. Chgo., 1961. Diplomate Am. Bd. Pediatrics. Rotating internship L.A. County Gen. Hosp., 1961-62; resident in pediatrics Stanford-Palo Alto (Calif.) Hosp., 1962-64; chief resident in pediatrics, instr. U. Wash. Hosp., Seattle, 1966-67; asst. prof. dept. pediatrics Sch. of Medicine Stanford U., 1969-72; from asst. to assoc. prof. dept. pediatrics U. So. Calif., L.A., 1972-76; assoc. prof. dept. pediatrics U. Wis., Milw., 1976-79; prof. dept. pediatrics Sch. of Medicine U. Calif., Davis, 1979-86, prof. dept. pathology, 1980-86; prof., chmn. dept. pediatrics Sch. of Medicine U. Nev., Las Vegas, 1986—; chief hemophilia svc. Children's Hosp. Stanford U. Sch. of Medicine, 1969-72; assoc. hematologist div. hematology and oncology Children's Hosp. L.A., 1972-76. Contbr. numerous articles to profl. jours. Bd. dirs. hemostasis program Milw. Children's Hosp., 1976-79; med. dir. Great Lakes Hemophilia Found., 1976-79. Armour and Hyland Labs. grantee, 1969-72, 72-76, Med. Coll. of Wis. grantee, 1976-79, HEW grantee, 1976-79, Cutter Labs. grantee, 1981-82, 82-83; recipient Rsch. Funds award U. Calif.-Davis, 1981-82, Outstanding Alumnus award U. Chgo., 1981. Fellow Am. Acad. Pediatrics; mem. Am. Fedn. for Clin. Rsch., N.Y. Acad. Scis., Nat. Hemophilia Found., Am. Chem. Soc. (biochemistry sect., med. chemistry sect.), Hemostasis Assn. of Calif., Internat. Soc. Thrombosis and Hemostasis, Am. Heart Assn. Coun. on Thrombosis Basic Sci. Coun., Am. Soc. Hematology, Am. Soc. for Exptl. Pathology, World Fedn. Hemophilia, Am. Assn. Blood Banks, Am. Soc. Pediatric (hematology and oncology credentials and by-laws com., membership com.), Alpha Omega Alpha. Office: U Nev Sch Medicine 2040 W Charleston Blvd #503 Las Vegas NV 89102

LAZZ, MARYJANE VERNON, city official; b. Wenatchee, Wash., Apr. 29, 1948; d. Thomas E. and Jane Irene (Beckman) Vernon; m. Keith Douglas Lazz, Feb. 3, 1968. BA in Anthropology, Wash. State U., 1972; M in Pub. Adminstrn., U. Laverne, 1979. Asst. to city mgr. City of Oxnard, Calif., 1973-80; asst. city mgr. City of Thousand Oaks, Calif., 1980—; instr. U. Laverne, Oxnard, Calif. Luth. U., Thousand Oaks. Bd. dirs. Conejo Valley Days Assn., Thousand Oaks, 1982—, Child Care Task Force, Thousand Oaks, 1987—. Named Outstanding Citizen Conejo Valley C. of C., 1987. Mem. AAUW, Internat. City Mgmt. Assn., League Calif. Cities (chair com. women and minorities 1988, Outstanding Asst. 1986). Office: City of Thousand Oaks 2150 W Hillcrest Thousand Oaks CA 91360

LAZZARO, ANTHONY DEREK, university official; b. Utica, N.Y., Jan. 31, 1921; s. Angelo Michael and Philomena (Vanilla) L.; m. Shirley Margaret Jones, Dec. 20, 1941; 1 child, Nancy. B.S. in Indsl. Engring, U. So. Calif., 1948; LL.D., Pepperdine U., 1974. Registered profl. engr., Calif. Asst. bus. mgr. U. So. Calif., L.A., 1948-60, asst. bus. mgr., dir. campus devel., 1960-65, asso. bus. mgr., dir. campus devel., 1965-71, asso. v.p. bus. affairs, 1971-72, v.p. bus. affairs, 1972-86, sr. v.p. bus. affairs, 1986-88, univ. v.p., 1988—; bd. dirs. RFS Devel. Corp., RFS Mortgage Corp.; cons. HEW. Editorial cons. College and University Business, 1955-58. Mem. nat. adv. coun. United Student Aid Funds, N.Y.C., 1973-78, chmn., 1976-77; dir. Rep. Fed. Savs. & Loan Assn. and subs. corps., L.A.; spl. studies cons. div. higher edn. Office Edn. HEW, 1956-59; mem. citizens com. Palos Verdes Bd. Edn., 1955-57; mem. Hoover urban renewal adv. com. Community Redevel. Agy. City of L.A., 1960-88. Lt. USNR, 1941-46. Mem. Nat. Assn. Coll. and Univ. Bus. Officers (pres. 1979, dir. 1972-80, chmn. goals and programs com. 1978, chmn. large inst. com. 1986, Disting. Bus. Officer award 1986), Western Assn. Coll. and Univ. Bus. Officers (pres. 1972), Soc. Coll. and Univ. Planning, Blue Key, Phi Kappa Phi, Tau Beta Pi. Club: Jonathan (Los Angeles). Home: 4012 Via Largavista Palos Verdes Estates CA 90274 Office: University Park OWH 100 Los Angeles CA 90089

LE, QUANG DINH, architect; b. Hai Phong, Vietnam, Mar. 11, 1950; came to U.S., 1975; s. Teo Le and Thi (Ty) Huynh; m. Myle Le; children: Dao, Diem, Uyen, Vy. AA, U. Toledo, 1979. Architect, project mgr., designer William M. Simpson and Assocs., Newport Beach, Calif., 1980—. Home: 16060 Mt Lister Ct Fountain Valley CA 92708 Office: William M Simpson & Assocs 2222 Newport Blvd Newport Beach CA 92663

LE, TRUC HUY, quality assurance executive; b. Socialist Republic of Vietnam, Apr. 10, 1952; s. Chinh Le., 1977;. BSME, Kanto Gakuin, Yokohama, Japan, 1975; MBA, U. Redlands, 1982. Gen. mgr. Cal-Best Inc., Los Alamitos, Calif., 1975-78; sr. quality engr. Pioneer Electronic Tech, Los Alamitos, Calif., 1978-79; quality assurance and test mgr. Gen Dynamic, Upland, Calif., 1979-82; quality assurance and regulatory affair mgr. Johnson and Johnson, Surgikos, Claremont, Calif., 1982—. Mem. Am. Soc. Quality Control, Am. Mgmt. Assn., Soc. Mfg. Engrs., Soc. Plastic Engrs. Office: Johnson & Johnson Surgikos 26001 Pala Dr Mission Viejo CA 92688

LEA, LILLIAN RICHARDS, accountant; b. New Brunswick, NJ, June 10, 1941; d. Royce Joseph Lea and Lillian Baird (Boudinot) Doran; m. Manuel Mendoza Cruz, Sept. 5, 1987. BA, Duke U., 1963. Enrolled agt. Ind. acct. Oakland, Calif., 1974—. Editor (newsletter) Networker, 1986—; contbr. articles to jours. Mem. Nat. Assn. Enrolled Agts., Nat. Soc. Pub. Accts., Calif. Assn. Ind. Accts. (bd. dirs. 1986-88), East Bay Assn. of Enrolled Agts. (bd. dirs. 1986-89). Democrat. Office: 478 W MacArthur Blvd Oakland CA 94609

LEACH, JEFFREY KENT, accountant, consultant; b. Monte Vista, Colo., Jan. 27, 1959; s. Darrell Willis and Marian (Hesler) L. BS, U. Colo., 1981; M of Profl. Acctg., U. Tex., 1985. CPA, Calif. Head clk. King Soopers, Inc., Boulder, Colo., 1977-84; cons. Shibui Systems Ltd., Austin, Tex., 1984-85; sr. cons. Deloitte, Haskins & Sells, Costa Mesa, Calif., 1986—. Author: Management Information System for a Home Health Care Company, 1985, EBS Computer Resource Guide, 1988. Vol. Orange County Performing Arts, Costa Mesa, 1987-88. Named one of Outstanding Young Men of Am. State of Ala., 1987. Mem. Grad. Bus. Coun. (rep. 1985). Republican. Home: PO Box 10306 Newport Beach CA 92658 Office: Deloitte Haskins & Sells 695 Town Center Dr Costa Mesa CA 92626

LEACH, LARRY ALLEN, county public health official; b. Ft. Leonard Wood, Mo., Mar. 8, 1955; s. Robert Allen and Rose Claire (Williams) L.; m. Doncella Hamby, Sept. 13, 1975; 1 child, James A. BA, Western Ky. U., 1977, MPS, 1978; postgrad. bus. adminstrn., Nova U., 1988—. Registered sanitarian, Ariz. Dir. pub. health Yuma County Dept. Pub. Health, Yuma, Ariz., 1983—. Capt. U.S. Army, 1978-82. Recipient Dist. Merit award Boy Scouts Am., Stuttgart, Fed. Republic Germany, 1982, Woodbadge, Tucson, 1982. Mem. Am. Pub. Health Assn., U.S. Conf. Local Health Officers, Nat. Assn. County Health Ofcls., Nat. Environ. Health Assn., Ariz. County Health Officers Assn. (pres. 1988-89), Ariz. Pub. Health Assn. (v.p. 1987-88), Ariz. Environ. Health Assn. (bd. dirs. 1987-88). Home: 3416 Cuadrillia Ln Yuma AZ 85365 Office: Yuma County Dept Pub Health 201 S 2d Ave Yuma AZ 85364

LEACH, LOIS ELLEN, public relations executive; b. Kingston, Pa., Jan. 12, 1943; d. Fabian and Edna A. (Spray) Bogdan; m. Willis Roy Leach Jr., Nov. 21, 1969; children: Bradley Thomas, Ryan Roy. Student, Long Beach (Calif.) City Coll., 1967-68. Pub. relations rep. Long Beach Promotions, 1965-67; adminstrv. asst. United Foam Corp., Compton, Calif., 1967-69; outside sales rep. Control Data Corp., La Mirada, Calif., 1969-72; sales mgr. Embassy Suites Hotel, Downey, Calif., 1985; pres., owner L.E. Leach Pub. Relations, Downey, 1984—. Mem. task force and mktg. com. Downey Family YMCA, 1985, chmn.'s roundtable, 1986; exec. com. Downey Community Hosp., 1985-86, bd. trustees, 1985-86, steering com. charter ball, 1985-86, 12:15 club, 1985—, Million Dollar club, 1985, 86, 87; active Assistance League of Downey; pub. relations rep. Downey Rose Float Assn., 1984-85. Mem. Downey C. of C. (bd. dirs. 1985-87, Appreciation of Service award 1985), WomanCare, (adv. bd. 1986—), Am. Bus. Women's Assn. (chmn. publicity, fashion show1987), Profl. Secs. Internat. (program chmn. 1980-82), Pub. Relations Soc. Am., Publicity Club of Los Angeles, Greater Los Angeles Press Club, Lions (3rd v.p. Downey chpt. 1988-89). Republican. Baptist. Lodge: P.E.O. Sisterhood (program chmn. 1985-86). Home: 7823 4th Pl Downey CA 90241 Office: 11002 Downey Ave Downey CA 90241

LEACH, NORMAN EDWARD, minister; b. Farmingdale, N.Y., May 17, 1940; s. George Alexander and Irene Alice (Bowen) L. AB, U. Mo., 1962; postgrad., Mo. U. Sch. Social Work, 1962-63; MDiv, San Francisco Theol. Sem., 1970, D in Ministry, 1973. Ordained to ministry Presbyn. Ch., 1971. Mgr. Third Rail Coffee House First Presbyn Ch., San Anselmo, Calif., 1968-70; adj. staff cons. Golden Gate Mission Area Ch. and World Com. United Presbyn. Ch. USA, San Francisco, 1970-72; dir. San Francisco Bay Area Healing Community Program, 1975—; program adminstr. San Fransicso Council Chs., 1976-82, interim acting exec. dir., 1982-84, acting exec. dir., 1984; exec. dir. San Fransicso Coun. Chs., 1984-89; chmn. Presbytery Program Coordinating Council; mem. Presbytery Gen. Council, Presbytery Long-Range Planning Com., Presbytery Nominations Com., Presbytery Permanent Jud. Commn., Interfaith BiCentennial Com., San Francisco, 1975-76, No. Calif. Ecumenical Council, 1975-78, World Council Chs., Vancouver, B.C., Can., 1983; founding mem., pres. Presbyn. Disabilities Concerns Caucus 1981; bd. dirs. World Conf. on Religion and Peace West, 1975-77; founding mem., task force on disabilities Archdiocese of San Francisco, 1975-80. Editor, pub.: Heritage and Hope, 1978, (newspaper) To Free Mankind; mem. editorial bd. Caring Congregation Mag.; contbr. columns to mags., chpts. to books. Mem. Congress on Racial Equality, U. Mo., Columbia, 1958-63, Coalition on Nat. Priorities and Mil. Policy, Washington, 1967-71; bd. dirs. Cambodian-Am. Benevolent Assn., 1975-78, Ind. Living Expn., San Francisco, 1983-87, Am.-Israel Friendship League 1984-89, assoc. United Way Execs., San Francisco, 1982-89; founding mem. San Francisco Intergroup Clearinghouse, 1982-89; founder, pres. emeritus San Francisco Mayor's Council on Disabilities Concerns, 1982—. Recipient God and Country award Boy Scouts Am., 1955, Vigil Honor award, 1974, CORLE/Nat. Council Chs. award, 1977, cert. of merit Mayor Dianne Feinstein, 1985, Freedom award No. Calif. Bd. Rabbis, 1987; named to Gov.'s Hall of Fame for Persons with Disabilities, 1988. Mem. Am. Acad. Polit. and Social Scis., Alpha Sigma Phi, Alpha Phi Omega, Pi Omicron Sigma. Home: 1459 46th Ave San Francisco CA 94122 Office: San Francisco Coun of Chs 942 Market St Ste 402 San Francisco CA 94102

LEACH, RICHARD MAXWELL, JR. (MAX LEACH), corporate professional; b. Chillicothe, Tex., June 14, 1934; s. Richard Maxwell and Lelia Booth (Page) L.; m. Wanda Gail Groves, Feb. 4, 1956; children: Richard Clifton, John Christopher, Sandra Gail, Kathy Lynn. BS in Acctg. magna cum laude, Abilene Christian U., 1955. Registered Fin. Planner., CLU. Asst. dir. agys. Am. Founders Ins. Co., Austin, Tex., 1960-62; owner A.F. Ins. Planning Assocs., Temple, Tex., 1962-65; v.p. sales Christian Fidelity Life Ins. Co., Waxahachie, Tex., 1966-67; exec. v.p. Acad. Computer Tech., Inc., Dallas, 1968-69; pres., chief exec. officer Inta-Search Internat., Inc., Dallas, 1969-71; prin., chief exec. officer, fin. cons. Leach and Assocs., Albuquerque, 1971—; chmn. bd. United Quest Inc., Albuquerque, Hosanna Inc., Albuquerque; real estate broker; commodity futures broker; exec. dir., bd. dirs. New Heart, Inc., Albuquerque, 1975-85; owner Insta-Copy, Albuquerque, 1973-76, Radio Sta. KYLE-FM, Temple, 1963-64. Editor, author Hosanna newspaper, 1973-74. Gen. dir. Here's Life, New Mexico, Albuquerque, 1976; exec. dir. Christians for Cambodia, Albuquerque, 1979-80. Served with U.S. Army, 1955-57. Home: 3308 June NE Albuquerque NM 87111 Office: 7200 Montgomery Blvd NE Albuquerque NM 87109

LEACH, STEVEN CONRAD, electrochemical and software engineer, consultant; b. Berkeley, Calif., May 30, 1955; s. Barbara Jean (Miller) L. BS, U. Calif., Davis, 1977; MS, Stanford U., 1986, Kensington U., Glendale, Calif., 1988. Electrochemist SRI Internat., Menlo Park, Calif., 1977-86, electrochem. engr., 1987-88; software engr. Spectra Physics, San Jose, Calif., 1986-87, Finnigan MAT, San Jose, 1988—; pres., owner Micro Faces Unltd., San Jose, 1986—. Contbr. articles to profl. jours.; inventor methane from CO2 and silicon prodn. Mem. Electrochem. Soc. (sec. San Jose 1985—), Assn. Apple 32 Users (v.p. 1985—). Republican. Home: 2568 Pebble Beach Dr San Jose CA 45051 Office: Xinix Corp 3500 Thomas Rd Bldg A Santa Clara CA 95054

LEACH, SUZANNE CARPENTER, nurse administrator; b. Phoenix, Aug. 22, 1956; d. Jimmie Juan and Marylou (Arnold) Carpenter; m. Stephen Gordon Leach, Dec. 21, 1976; children: Nicole Catherine, Brandon Matthew. BS in Nursing, Ariz. State U., 1979, postgrad., 1988—. RN, Ariz. Staff nurse St. Joseph's Hosp., Phoenix, 1978-84, Good Samaritan Hosp., Phoenix, 1983-84; supr. home care Am. Nursing Resources, Phoenix, 1984-85, exec. dir., 1988%; dir. Am. Nursing Pediatric Care, Phoenix, 1985—; clin. instr. Gateway Community Coll., Phoenix, 1985-86; bd. dirs., sec. SKIP Nat. N.Y.C., 1985—; bd. dirs., v.p. Ariz. Consortium Children with Chronic Illness, Phoenix, 1988—. Chmn. Maricopa Adv. Coun. for Devel. Disabilities, Phoenix, 1985-87. Mem. Nat. Assn. Home Care, Ariz. Assn. Home Care, Assn. Care Childrens Health, Nat. Assn. Nurses in Bus., Ariz. Assn. Health Care Agys. (bd. dirs. v.p. 1988—). Office: Am Nursing Resources Inc 2001 W Camelback Rd Ste 360 Phoenix AZ 85015

LEACH, TERRY LYNN, architect; b. Tucumcari, N.Mex., Apr. 25, 1948; s. Wallace Ancel and Lula M. (Gates) L.; m. Onorina M. Wilson, Apr. 8, 1972; children: Jessica, Tisha, Ashley. BA in Architecture, U. N.Mex., 1983, M in Architecture, 1986. Pres. GPOS, Inc., Gallup, N.Mex., 1971-81; project architect Richard Elliott, Architects, Albuquerque, 1981-84; project mgr. Holmes & Narver, Inc., Albuquerque, 1984—. Editor: Mass Mag., 1981-82, 82-83. Bd. dirs. Heights YMCA, Albuquerque, 1981-82; dir. McKinley Area Svcs. for the Handicapped, 1979-80. Recipient Scholarhsip, Painting and Decorting Contractors Am., 1982, 83; named Outstanding Young Man Am.,

1978. Mem. AIA, Gallup C. of C. (dir. YEIS 1976-81), Order Demolay (master counciler, 1966, life). Republican. Roman Catholic. Office: Holmes & Narver 6501 Americas Pkwy Albuquerque NM 87110

LEACH, WILLIAM HENRY, JR., oil company executive; b. Pitts., Jan. 31, 1931; s. William Henry and Harriet (Leahy) L.; BS in Petroleum Engring., U. Pitts., 1953; postgrad. U. Tulsa, 1958; m. Janet L. Evans, July 9, 1954; 1 child, Christine April. Petroleum engr. Magnolia Petroleum Co., Electra, Tex., 1953-59; petroleum engr., v.p. LeClair Operating Co., Inc., Abilene, Tex., 1959-73; pres. LeClair-Westwood, Inc., Denver, 1973-85, Miles Petroleum, Inc., N.Y.C., 1982-83, Antares Oil Corp., 1983-86, Am. Petresearch Inc., Denver, 1986-87, cons. petroleum engr. Denver, 1987; pres. OilSearch Corp., Albuquerque, 1987-88, TriSearch, Inc., Albuquerque, 1988—; sec. Andover Internat., Inc., Denver; v.p. Am. Petresearch Inc., Denver, 1982-88; past dir. Tomahawk Oil and Minerals Inc.; contbg. editor Western Oil Reporter, Denver, 1970-75; past dir. McRae Oil Co., Houston; v.p. explorations Brent, Inc., Denver, 1973-74. Explorer scout adviser Boy Scouts Am., Electra, Tex., 1954-55. Chmn. petroleum engring. U. Pitts. Alumni Fund, 1965. Recipient Betty McWhorter award Denver Desk and Derrick Club, 1982. Mem. Jr. C. of C. (pres. 1955), Soc. Petroleum Engrs., Soc. Petroleum Evaluation Engrs., Ind. Producers Assn. Am., Ind. Producers Assn. Mountain States (pres. 1981-84), Tanoan Country Club, Denver Petroleum Club, Sigma Pi. Presbyterian (deacon, elder). Contbr. articles to profl. jours. Home: 820 E Maplewood Ave Littleton CO 80121 Office: Tri-Search Inc 7801 Academy Blvd NE Albuquerque NM 87109

LEAHEY, PATRICK LEONARD, mechanical engineer; b. Greensburg, Pa., Oct. 20, 1961; s. Robert Michael and Anne Ethel (Latterner) L. BSME, Pa. State U., 1984. System test engr. Lockheed Missile & Space Co., Sunnyvale, Calif., 1984-85; jr. design engr. Lockheed Missile & Space Co., Sunnyvale, 1985-87, sr. design engr., 1987—. Mem. ASME, Pa. State U. Alumni Assn. (treas. 1986-88), Sigma Pi. Republican. Roman Catholic. Home: 2250 Monroe St #161 Santa Clara CA 95050 Office: Lockheed Missile & Space Co PO Box 3504 Sunnyvale CA 94089-3504

LEAKE, DONALD LEWIS, oral and maxillofacial surgeon, oboist; b. Cleveland, Okla., Nov. 6, 1931; s. Walter Wilson and Martha Lee (Crowe) L.; m. Rosemary Dobson, Aug. 20, 1964; children: John Andrew Dobson, Elizabeth, Catherine. AB, U. So. Calif., 1953, MA, 1957; DMD, Harvard U., 1962; MD, Stanford U., 1969. Diplomate Am. Bd. Oral and Maxillofacial Surgery. Intern Mass. Gen. Hosp., Boston, 1962-63; resident Mass. Gen. Hosp., 1963-64; postdoctoral fellow Harvard U., 1964-66; practice medicine specializing in oral and maxillofacial surgery; asso. prof. oral and maxillofacial surgery Harbor-UCLA Med. Center, Torrance, 1970-74; dental dir., chief oral and maxillofacial surgery Harbor-UCLA Med. Center, 1970—, prof., 1974—; asso. dir. UCLA Dental Research Inst., 1979-82, dir., 1982-86; cons. to hosps.; dental dir. coastal health services region, Los Angeles County, 1974-81; oboist Robert Shaw Chorale, 1954-55; solo oboist San Diego Symphony, 1954-59. Contbr. articles to med. jours.; rec. artist: (albums on Columbia label) The Music of Heinrich Schütz, Stockhausen, Zeitmasse for 5 Winds, Schönberg, Orchestra Variations-Opus 31; freelance musician various film studio orchs., Carmel Bach Festival, 1949, 52-53, 67-81, numerous concerts with Coleman Chamber Music, The Cantata Singers, Boston, Baroque Consortium, Los Angeles, others. Recipient 1st prize with greatest distinction for oboe and chamber music Brussels Royal Conservatory Music Belgium, 1956. Fellow ACS; mem. Internat. Assn. Dental Research, So. Calif. Soc. Oral and Maxillofacial Surgeons, Internat. Assn. Oral Surgeons, AAAS, Soc. for Biomaterials, Biomedical Engring. Soc. (sr. mem.), Los Angeles County Med. Assn., N.Y. Acad. Sci., Los Angeles Acad. Medicine, ASTM, European Assn. Maxillofacial Surgeons, Brit. Assn. Oral and Maxillofacial Surgeons, Internationale Gesellschaft fur Kiefer-Gesichts-Chirurgie, Phi Beta Kappa, Phi Kappa Phi. Clubs: Harvard (Boston and N.Y.C.); Beefeater (N.Y.C.). Home: 2 Crest Rd W Rolling Hills CA 90274 Office: Harbor-UCLA Med Ctr 1000 W Carson St Torrance CA 90509 also: 701 E 28th St Ste 415 Long Beach CA 90806

LEALE, OLIVIA MASON, import marketing company executive; b. Boston, May 5, 1944; d. William Mason and Jane Chapiin (Prouty) Smith; m. Euan Harvie-Watt, Mar. ll, 1967 (div. Aug. 1979); children: Katrina, Jennifer; m. Douglas Marshall Leale, Aug. 29, 1980. BA, Vassar Coll., 1966. Sec. to dir. Met. Opera Guild, N.Y.C., 1966; sec. to pres. Friesons Printers, London, 1974-75; guide, trainer Autoguide, London, 1977-79; ptnr. Inmark Internat. Mktg. Inc., Seattle, 1980—. Social case worker Inner London Ednl. Authority, 1975-76. Democrat. Presbyterian. Home and Office: 5427 NE Penrith Rd Seattle WA 98105

LEAMING, MARJ P(ATRICIA), strategic management and marketing consultant, researcher; b. Denver; d. Taylor J. Sr. and Augie R. Leaming. BA, U. Colo., 1969, MBA, 1970; PhD, Colo. State U., 1979. Cert. cons., trainer. Asst. supr. State Approving Agy. Vets. Edn., Denver, 1973-82; asst. assoc. dir. State Bd. Community Colls. and Occupational Edn., Denver, 1982-85; mgmt. cons. div. mgmt. services Denver Dept. Adminstrn., 1985-86; pres. Edventure Systems, Lakewood, Colo., 1986—; bd. dirs. Colo. Retail Coun., Denver, 1982-85; dir. mgmt. devel. Mng. for Success, Denver, 1985-86; asst. grad. prof. MBA program Regis Coll., Denver, 1982; vis. asst. prof. Bus. Leadership Inst. U. Alaska, Fairbanks, 1986; pres. Nat. Entrepreneurship Consortium, 1984-85; commr. Colo. Productivity-Study Team, 1988-89. Author: (coll. textbook) Administrative Office Management, 1970, (coll. casebook) Administrative Management Cases, 1970, (handbook) Entrepreneurship, 1988; author, editor: Entrepreneurship Models, 1985, Economic Value of Entrepreneurship, 1985; contbr. articles to nat. jours. Active fin. devel. ARC, Jefferson County, 1988, Mile High, 1988; mem. Denver Art Mus., 1983-88; mem. adv. com. Red Rocks Community Coll., 1986, Jefferson County Pub. Schs., 1986-88, Jefferson County Small Bus. Ctr.; mem. Gov. apptd. commn. on privatization, 1988—. NSF grantee, Denver, 1972. Mem. SBA (bd. dirs. region VIII, 1987-88) Women Bus. Owners Assn., Exec. Women Internat. (nat. del., 1986), U.S. Assn. for Small Bus., Am. Entrepreneurs Assn., LWV, Am. Golf Club, Phi Kappa Phi. Office: Edventure Systems PO Box 15767 Lakewood CO 80215

LEAR, NORMAN MILTON, writer, producer, director; b. New Haven, July 27, 1922; s. Herman and Jeanette (Seicol) L.; children: Ellen Lear Reiss, Kate B. Lear LaPook, Maggie B.; m. Lyn Davis; 1 child, Benjamin Davis. Student, Emerson Coll., 1940-42, HHD, 1968. Engaged in pub. relations 1945-49. Comedy writer for TV, 1950-54; writer, dir. for TV and films, 1954-59; writer, producer: films Come Blow Your Horn, 1963, Divorce American Style, 1967, The Night They Raided Minsky's, 1968; writer, producer, dir.: film Cold Turkey, 1971; creator, producer: TV shows TV Guide Awards Show, 1962, Henry Fonda and the Family, 1963, Andy Williams Spl., also, Andy Williams Series, 1965, Robert Young and the Family, 1970; developer: TV shows All in the Family, 1971 (4 Emmy awards 1970-73, Peabody award 1977); creator: TV show Maude, 1972; co-developer: TV show Sanford and Son, 1972; developer: TV show Good Times, 1974, The Jeffersons, 1975, Hot L Baltimore, 1975, Mary Hartman, Mary Hartman, 1976, One Day At a Time, 1975, All's Fair, 1976, A Year at the Top, 1977; co-creator: TV show All That Glitters, 1977; creator: TV show Fernwood 2 Night, 1977; developer: TV show The Baxters, 1979, Palmerstown, 1980; creator, developer TV spl. I Love Liberty, 1982; creator a.k.a. Pablo, 1984; exec. producer Heartsounds, 1984, The Princess Bride, 1987. Pres. Am. Civil Liberties Found. So. Calif., 1973—; trustee Mus. Broadcasting; bd. dirs. People for the American Way. Served with USAAF, 1942-45. Decorated Air medal with 4 oak leaf clusters; named One of Top Ten Motion Picture Producers, Motion Picture Exhibitors, 1963, 67, 68, Showman of Yr., Publicists Guild, 1971-77, Assn. Bus. Mgrs., 1972, Broadcaster of Yr., Internat. Radio and TV Soc., 1973; Man of Yr. Hollywood chpt. Nat. Acad. Television Arts and Scis., 1973; recipient Humanitarian award NCCJ, 1976, Mark Twain award Internat. Platform Assn., 1977, William O. Douglas award Pub. Counsel, 1981, 1st Amendment Lectr. Ford Hall Forum, 1981, Gold medal Internat. Radio and TV Soc., 1981. Disting. Am. award, 1984, Mass Media award Am. Jewish Com. Inst. of Human Relations, 1986, Internat. award of Yr., Nat. Assn. TV Program Execs., 1987; inducted into TV Acad. Hall of Fame, 1984. Mem. Writers Guild Am. (Valentine Davies award 1977), Dirs. Guild Am., AFTRA, Caucus Producers, Writers, and Dirs. Office: Act III Communications 1800 Century Park E Los Angeles CA 90067 *

LEASE, JANE ETTA, librarian; b. Kansas City, Kans., Apr. 10, 1924; d. Joy Alva and Emma (Jaggard) Omer; B.S. in Home Econs., U. Ariz., 1957; M.S. in Edn., Ind. U., 1962; M.S. in L.S., U. Denver, 1967; m. Richard J. Lease, Jan. 16, 1960; children—Janet (Mrs. Jacky B. Radifera), Joyce (Mrs. Robert J. Carson), Julia (Mrs. Earle D. Marvin), Cathy (Mrs. Edward F. Warren); stepchildren—Richard Jay II, William Harley. Newspaper reporter Ariz. Daily Star, Tucson, 1937-39; asst. home agt. Dept. Agr., 1957; homemaking tchr., Ft. Huachuca, Ariz., 1957-60; head tchr. Stonebelt Council Retarded Children, Bloomington, Ind., 1960-61; reference clk. Ariz. State U. Library, 1964-66; edn. and psychology librarian N.Mex. State U., 1967-71; Amway distbr., 1973—; cons. solid wastes, distressed land problems reference remedies, 1967; ecology lit. research and cons., 1966—. Ind. observer 1st World Conf. Human Environment, 1972; mem. Las Cruces Community Devel. Priorities Adv. Bd. Mem. ALA, Regional Environ. Edn. Research Info. Orgn., Nat. Assn. Female Execs., P.E.O., D.A.R., Internat. Platform Assn., Las Cruces Antique Car Club, Las Cruces Story League, N.Mex. Library Assn. Methodist (lay leader). Address: 2145 Boise Dr Las Cruces NM 88001

LEASE, RICHARD JAY, former police officer, educator, consultant; b. Cherokee, Ohio, Dec. 10, 1914; s. Harold and Mabelle (Fullerton) L.; m. Marjorie Faye Stoughton, Sept. 2, 1939 (div. Apr. 1957); children: Richard Jay II, William Harley; m. Jane Etta Omer, Jan. 16, 1960; stepchildren: Janet Radifera, Joyce Garson, Julia Marvin, Catherine Warren. Student, Wittenberg U., 1932-33; BA, U. Ariz., 1937, MA, 1961; postgrad., Ind. U., 1950, 60, Ariz. State U., 1956, 63-65, 67—; grad., U. Louisville So. Police Inst., 1955. Grad. asst . U. Ariz., Tucson, 1937-38; with Tucson Police Dept., from 1938; advanced from patrolman to sgt., also served as safety officer Pima County Sheriff's Dept., Tucson, 1953, patrol supr., 1953-55, investigator, 1955-56; tchr. sci. pub. schs. Tucson, 1957-59; lectr. dept. police adminstrn. Ind. U., Bloomington, 1960-65; asst. prof. dept. police sci. N.Mex. State U., Las Cruces, 1965—; cons. law enforcement problems HEW, 1960, Indpls. Police Dept., 1962, Harrisburg Community Coll. Police Sci. Dept., 1967, Phoenix Police Dept., 1968—; advisor police tng. programs several small city police depts., Ind., 1960-63, Indpls., 1962; mem. oral bd. for selection chief in Bateville, Ind., 1962, oral bd. for selection sgts. and lts., Las Cruces Police Dept., 1966—. Author: (with Robert F. Borkenstein) Alcohol and Road Traffic: Problems of Enforcement and Prosecution, 1963; cons. editor Police, various research publs. on chem. intoxication tests, psychol. errors of witnesses, reading disabilities, delinquency. Participant numerous FBI seminars; active youth work, philanthropy, among Am. Indians in Southwest; founder awards outstanding ROTC cadets N.Mex. State U., 1967—; founder Wiltberger ann. awards Nat. Police Combat Pistol Matches; scoutmaster Yucca council Boy Scouts Am., 1966—. Served to 1st lt. USMCR, 1942-45, PTO. Fellow Am. Acad. Forensic Scis. (sec. gen. sect.); mem. Internat. Assn. Chiefs of Police, Internat. Assn. Police Profs., Brit. Acad. Forensic Scis., Can. Soc. Forensic Sci., Am. Soc. Criminology, Ret. Officers Assn., Assn. U.S. Army (2d v.p. 1969—), NEA, N.Mex. Edn. Assn., N.Mex. Police and Sheriffs Assn., Internat. Crossroads, NRA (benefactor mem.), Marine Corps League (life), Sigma Chi. Lodges: Masons, Elks. Home and Office: 2145 Boise Dr Las Cruces NM 88001

LEASON, JODY JACOBS, newspaper columnist; b. Margarita, Venezuela, June 8, 1926; came to U.S., 1928; d. Jose Cruz Caceres and Graciela Rodriguez; m. Russell L. Jacobs (div.); 1 child, Jessica Jacobs Vitti; m. Barney Leason, Dec. 29, 1976. BA, Hunter Coll., 1940's. Assoc. fashion editor Women's Wear Daily, N.Y.C., 1975-72; West Coast fashion editor Los Angeles, 1957-72; society editor Los Angeles Times, 1972-86; columnist Post Newspaper Corp., Los Angeles, 1986—. Author: (novel) The Right Circles, 1988. Office: PO Box 17 The Sea Ranch CA 95457

LEATHERBY, JOANN, lawyer; b. L.A., May 13, 1955; d. Ralph William and Eleanor Augustine (Samson) L.; M. Emroy L. Watson, Oct. 1, 1983 (div. 1988). BA in English, Iowa Wesleyan Coll., 1977; JD, UCLA, 1980. Bar: Calif., 1980. Exec. dir. Women's Legal Clinic, L.A., 1978-81; v.p. adminstrn. UniCare Ins., Irvine, Calif., 1981-82; pvt. practice Newport Beach, Calif., 1982-84; gen. counsel Ricoh Electronics, Inc., Tustin, Calif., 1984-88; dir. adminstrn. and legal dept. Ricoh Electronics, Inc., Tustin, 1988—; bd. dirs. UniCare Fin. Corp., Irvine. Mem. Calif. Women Lawyers Assn., Am. Corp. Counsel Assn., Orange County Bar Assn. Democrat. Office: Ricoh Electronics Inc 1100 Valencia Ave Tustin CA 92680

LEAVEY, TERRANCE CHARLES, systems programmer, consultant; b. Sacramento, Feb. 11, 1947; s. Henry Harold and Harriet T. (Ferguson) L.; m. Frances Elaine Morrone, Nov. 3, 1973; stepchildren: Brena Elaine Richmond, David Benton Richmond. Student, Calif. Inst. of the Arts, 1965-66, Merced (Calif.) Coll., 1974-76; cert. bus. practices, Rio Salado Coll., 1985. Pvt. practice band leader, musician Calif., 1964-69; computer programmer Williams Turkey Breeding Farms, Oakdale, Calif., 1969-70; computer tech. asst. Computer Scis. Corp., L.A., 1970; system programmer Computer Scis. Corp., Sacramento, 1978-81; computer cons. Am. Info. Devel., San Francisco, 1970-71; cattle man Favier Cattle Co., Merced, 1971-72; computer programmer Merced County, 1973-76; owner Cody Enterprises, Merced, 1976-78; systems programmer Ariz. Pub. Svc., Phoenix, 1981—; bd. dirs. Leavey Found. for Hist. Preservation, Inc., Phoenix. Editor, pub. newsletter AZRA News, 1988—. Chmn. bd. Leavey Found. for Hist. Preservation, Inc., 1988—. Recipient Jefferson Davis medal United Daughters of the Confederacy, 1988, Svc. award City of Phoenix, 1988. Mem. Ariz. Civil War Coun., Inc. (pres. 1984-88, bd. dirs. 1986-88), 602 Ariz., Metro Phoenix Film Bd., Ariz. Reenactors Assn. (pres. 1988—), Electric Horsemen (startup chmn. Phoenix chpt. 1988), SAG, YWCA Camera Club (pres. Phoenix chpt. 1982-84). Republican. Roman Catholic. Office: Leavey Found 10000 N 31st Ave Ste A107 Phoenix AZ 85051-9568

LEAVITT, LOIS HUTCHEON, consumer and homemaker educator; b. Whiterocks, Utah, Nov. 6, 1920; d. Arthur James and Ada E. (Peterson) Hutcheon; m. Jack William Leavitt, June 19, 1943; children—VaLoy, Joyce, LaJean. B.S., Brigham Young U., 1943, postgrad. 1955-83. Cert. vocat. home econs., secondary edn. tchr. Utah. Tchr. consumer and homemaking edn. Spanish Fork (Utah) High Sch., 1943-45, Roosevelt (Utah) High Sch., 1945-47, Union High Sch., Roosevelt, 1954-83; chpt. advisor Future Homemakers Am. Named Outstanding Utah Home Econs. Tchr., Utah Cowbells of Utah Cattlemen's Assn.; Adviser of Yr., Utah chpt. Future Homemakers Am. 1983. Mem. Am. Home Econs. Assn., Utah Home Econs. Assn. (Home Econs. Tchr. of Yr. 1982), Nat. Assn. Vocat. Home Econs. Tchrs. Vocat. Assn., Utah Assn. Vocat. Home Econs. Tchrs. Vocat. Assn., Am. Vocat. Assn., Utah Vocat. Assn., Bus. and Profl. Women (pres., sec.). Mormon. Home: Box 235 Neola UT 84053 Office: Union High Sch PO Box 400 Roosevelt UT 84066

LEAVITT, RICHARD FORD, mechanical engineer; b. Salt Lake City, Dec. 8, 1957; s. Richard Shaw and Norma (Ford) L.; m. Jolene Williams, Oct. 10, 1980; children: David Richard, Trevor James. BSME, Utah State U., 1986. Cert. engr. in training. Elec. mech. designer Key Engring., Salt Lake City, 1979-81; student engr. U.S. Dept. Air Force, Ogden, Utah, summers 1982-84; CAD/CAM teaching asst. dept. mech. engring. Utah State U., Logan, Utah, 1985-86; devel. engr. IOMEGA Corp., Roy, Utah, 1986; advanced mfg. engr. IOMEGA Corp., 1986-87, sr. mfg. engr., 1987—. Coach AYSO Soccer Orgn., Layton, Utah, 1988—. Mem. Soc. Mfg. Engrs. (chpt. pres. 1985-86), ASME (assoc.). Republican. Mormon. Home: 3479 N 2400 East Layton UT 84040-8468 Office: IOMEGA Corp 1821 W 4000 South Roy UT 84067

LEAVITT, TODD PAGE, entertainment executive; b. Detroit, Mar. 27, 1951; s. Gerald Matthew and Ann (Ruttenberg) L.; m. Lauren Iris Luchnick, Jan. 6, 1979; children: Julia Paige, Chloe Gabrielle, Eliza Layne Gambier. AB, Kenyon Coll., Gambles, Ohio, 1973; JD, NYU, 1977. Bar: N.Y. 1978. Counsel Viacom Internat., Inc., N.Y.C., 1977-79; assoc. Franklim, Weinrib, Rudell & Vassallo, N.Y.C., 1979-81; dir. bus. affairs Rainbow Programming, Woodbury, N.Y., 1981-82; sr. v.p. programming CBS/Fox Video, N.Y.C., 1982-86; chief operating officer D.L. Taffner Ltd., N.Y.C., 1986-87; exec. v.p. Reeves Entertainment Group, Burbank, Calif., 1987—. Recipient 1st prize Nathan Burkan Copyright Competition, ASCAP, 1977. Mem. ABA, Hollywood Radio and TV Soc., Phi Beta Kappa. Jewish. Office: Reeves Entertainment 3500 W Olive Ave Burbank CA 91505

LEAVY, BRIAN DAVID, geologist; b. Bklyn., Nov. 5, 1951; s. David M. and Mildred (Richters) L.; m. Helen Pendleton. BS in Geology, U. R.I., 1974, MS in Geology, 1979; PhD in Geology N.Mex. Inst. Mining and Tech., 1987. Geologist U.S. EPA, Narragansett, R.I., 1975-78, U.S. Geol. Survey, Reston, Va., 1979—; staff rsch. asst. Earth and Space Scis. div. Los Alamos (N.Mex.) Nat. Lab., 1986-87. Sigma Xi rsch. grantee, 1977, 85; N.Mex. Geol. Soc. rsch. grantee, 1982; Am. Fedn. Mineral. Socs. grad. scholar, 1982-83; Associated Western Univs. grad. rsch. fellow, 1983-85, fellow N.Mex. Inst. Mining and Tech., 1982. Mem. Geol. Soc. Am. (Outstanding Mention grantee 1985, rsch. grantee 1985), Geochem. Soc., Am. Assn. Petroleum Geologists, Mineral. Soc. Am., Am. Geophys. Union, N.Mex. Geol. Soc., Geol. Soc. Washington, Sigma Gamma Epsilon, Phi Kappa Psi.

LEBARON, RUTHANN HAYES, biology educator, management consultant; b. Denver, Nov. 8, 1925; d. John Edward and Anna Elizabeth (Hansen) Hayes; m. Marshall John LeBaron, Sept. 7, 1948 (div. Feb. 1980); children: Anne, Michael Roy. BA cum laude, U. Colo., 1946; MA in Zoology, Mt. Holyoke Coll., 1948; postgrad., U. Idaho, 1948-70. Instr. histology U. Idaho, Moscow, 1948-49; from asst. prof. to assoc. prof. biology Coll. So. Idaho, Twin Falls, 1965-70, prof., 1970-76, chmn. dept. sci., 1965-73; prof. biology Linfield Coll., McMinnville, Oreg., 1983—, Linn Benton Community Coll., Newport, Oreg., 1986-88, Oreg. Coast Community Coll., Newport, 1988—; bd. dirs. Regional Studies Ctr., Caldwell, Idaho, 1972-77. Author: Hormones: A Delicate Balance, 1972; contbr. articles to profl. jours. Pres. Idaho Fedn. Music Clubs, Twin Falls, 1963-65. Recipient award of recognition Oreg. and Wash. Community Coll. Couns., 1988; NSF grantee, 1966, 67, 73. Mem. Am. Inst. Biol. Sci., AAAS, Idaho Acad. Sci. (pres. 1972-73), Phi Beta Kappa, Sigma Xi. Republican. Episcopalian. Home: 1713 Sandpiper Dr PO Box 886 Waldport OR 97394 Office: care SM Paulsen 2831 NW Westover Rd Portland OR 87210

LEBEDEFF, NICHOLAS BORIS, consulting executive; b. Hollywood, Calif., Apr. 16, 1944; s. Boris Paul and Alexandra Esidorovna (Koshell) L.; m. Judith Leah Moffett, Nov. 22, 1969 (div. Aug. 1985); children: Christina, Christopher. BBA, Loyola U., Los Angeles, 1967; MBA, U. So. Calif., 1970. Budget and adminstrv. analyst City of Los Angeles, 1967-73; mgr. budget and fiscal ops. Van de Kamp's Holland Dutch Bakers div. Gen. Host Corp., Los Angeles, 1973-74; mgr. fin. planning and analysis dept. U.S. Borax and Chem. Co., Los Angeles, 1974-75; pres. NBL Assocs., Los Angeles, 1976-85, Micro-Software, Inc., Los Angeles, 1977—, Planning Systems Group, Los Angeles, 1982-85, Forecasting and Fin. Planning Group, 1982—. Bd. dirs. Am. Med. and Ednl. Services in Africa. Mem. U. So. Calif. Alumni Assn., Commerce Assocs. Republican. Mem. Orthodox Ch. Am. Home: 17400 Flanders St Granada Hills CA 91344

LEBIEDZ, JAMES FRANCIS, naval officer; b. Newport, R.I., Nov. 28, 1957; s. Edward Francis and Anna Dorthea (Conner) L.; m. Jamie Angela Hoppus, May 3, 1986. BCE, Villanova U., 1980; MSCE, U. Calif., Berkeley, 1988. Registered profl. engr., Calif. Commd. ensign USN, 1980; engring. officer Naval Support Force Antarctica, Port Hueneme, Calif., 1980-82; staff civil engr. Naval Sta. Treasure Island, San Francisco, 1982-83; asst. to prodn. officer Navy Pub. Works Ctr., San Francisco Bay, 1983-85; facility planning officer Phila. Naval Shipyard, 1985-87; resident officer in-charge USN, Amchitka, Alaska, 1988—. Mem. ASCE. Home: 6710 Reynard Dr Springfield VA 22152

LEBLANC, LEONARD JOSEPH, electronics company executive; b. Amherst, N.S., Can., Feb. 4, 1941; came to U.S., 1952 naturalized 1959; s. Edgar Marcel and Mary Catherine (Bourgeois) LeB.; m. Janice May Dittrich, Sept. 11, 1965; children: Bryan, Jeffrey, Steven. B.S., Coll. of Holy Cross, 1962, M.S., 1963; M.S., George Washington U., 1966. Fin. analyst to mgr. Philco-Ford Corp., Blue Bell, Pa., 1966-72; asst. corp. controller Centainteed Corp., Valley Forge, Pa., 1972-73; sr. v.p. fin. Data Tech. Corp., Costa Mesa, Calif., 1973-76; v.p., controller Memorex Corp., Santa Clara, Calif., 1976-82; v.p. fin., treas. Saga Corp., Menlo Park, Calif., 1982-87, Cadence Design Systems Inc., San Jose, Calif., 1987—. Mem. Monte Sereno Archtl. Com., Calif., 1981—; bd. dirs. Eastfield Children's Ctr., Campbell, Calif., 1984-87. Served to lt.(j.g.) USN, 1963-66. Recipient commendation U.S. Navy Med. Sch., Bethesda, Md., 1966; fellow Coll. of Holy Cross, 1962. Mem. Fin. Execs. Inst., Nat. Assn. Corp. Treas., Assn. Corp. Growth. Office: Cadence Design 555 River Oaks Pkwy San Jose CA 95134

LE BLANC, SISTER SHIRLEY MAURIE, social worker; b. Port Sulphur, La., Sept. 18, 1939; d. Elton Gustave and ira Mae (Ayers) Le Blanc. BA in Psychology, Coll. Santa Fe, 1988. Bus. svcs. coord., asst. bus. office mgr. St. Joseph Hosp., Albuquerque, 1975-81; exec. treas. Villa Therese Clinic, Santa Fe, 1981-86; founder, exec. dir. St. Elizabeth Shelter, Santa Fe, 1986—. Mem. Sisters of Charity Cin., 1981—. With USAF, 1961-65. Roman Catholic. Home and Office: 804 Alarid St Santa Fe NM 87501

LEBLANG, STEVEN CRAIG, television executive; b. N.Y.C., Aug. 13, 1959; s. Allan and Barbara Joan (Chapin) L. BA, SUNY, Oswego, 1981. Media buyer Grey Advt., N.Y.C., 1981-83; program analyst MMT Sales, Inc., N.Y.C., 1983-85; dir. domestic research Metromedia Producers Corp., Hollywood, Calif., 1985-86; dir. research 20th Century Fox TV, Beverly Hills, Calif., 1986, v.p. TV research, 1987-88; v.p. programming Fox Televison Stations, Inc., Beverly Hills, Calif., 1988—. Home: 1144 10th St Santa Monica CA 90403 Office: 20th Century Fox TV 10201 W Pico Blvd Beverly Hills CA 90215

LEBOFSKY, LARRY ALLEN, astronomer, consultant; b. Bklyn., Aug. 31, 1947; s. Harry and Clara (Goodman) L.; m. Marcia Jean Keyes; m. Nancy Ruth Moore, May 9, 1980; 1 child, Miranda Blythe. BS, Calif. Tech. Coll., 1969; Phd, MIT, 1974. With Dept. Earth and Planetary Scis., MIT, Cambridge, Mass., 1969-70, teaching asst., 1971-72, rsch. assoc., 1974; cons. Jet Propulsion Lab., Pasadena, Calif., 1975-78, mem. nat. rsch. coun., rsch. assoc., 1975-77; rsch. assoc. lunar and planetary lab. U. Ariz., Tucson, 1977-82, assoc. rsch. scientist, 1982-89, sr. rsch. scientist, 1989—; cons. Jet Propulsion Lab., Pasadena, 1981—. Contbr. numerous articles to profl. jours. Mem. twp. 2000 Tucson Unified Sch. Dist., 1988—. Mem. Internat. Astrom. Union, Am. Astrom. Soc. Scis. (div. planetary sec., treas. 1988—), Meteoritional Soc., AM. Geophys. Soc., Astrom. Soc. of the Pacific. Democrat. Jewish. Home: 2333 E 7th St Tucson AZ 85719 Office: U Ariz Lunar and Planetary Lab Tucson AZ 85721

LEBOWITZ, MICHAEL DAVID, epidemiologist; b. Bklyn., Dec. 21, 1939; s. Harry and Rachel (Dick) L.; m. Joyce Marian Schmidt, Sept. 9, 1960; children: Jon A., Kirk L., Debra M. AB, U. Calif., 1961, MA, 1965; PhC, U. Wash., 1969, PhD, 1971. Resch. assoc. preventive medicine U. Wash., Seattle, 1967-70, rsch. assoc. environ. health, 1970-71; asst. prof. internal medicine U. Ariz., Tucson, 1971-75, assoc. prof. internal medicine, 1975-80, prof. internal medicine, 1980—; vis. fellow Postgrad. Cardiothoracic Inst. U. London, 1978-89; cons. US NIH, Bethesda, Md., 1975—, US EPA, Washington, 1969—, WHO, Geneva, 1979—, Italian Nat. Rsch. Council, Rome and Pisa, 1979—, Ednl. Guidelines for Studies in Environ. Epidemics, 1983, Polish Nat. Inst. Hygiene and Acad. Scis., 1981—, Pan Am. Health Orgn., 1985—, numerous others; co-chmn. indoor air pollutents commn. Nat. Acad. Sci./NRC, Washington, 1979-81. Contbr. articles to profl. jours.; mem. editorial bd.: J. Behai Med., 1977—. Chmn. Pima County Air Quality Adv. Commn., Tucson, 1975-78; cons. Ariz. State Dept. Health Svcs., Phoenix, 1972—, Ariz. Lung Assn., Phoenix, 1971—, State Dept. Environ. Quality, Phoenix, 1987—, Gov. of Ariz., 1987—; senator U. Ariz. Faculty Senate, Tucson, 1976-78. Recipient Ariz. Clean Air award Ariz. Lung Assn., 1987; numerous epidemiology/disease grants and contracts, NIH, EPA, FDA, EPRI and others, 1964—. Fellow Am. Coll. Chest Physicians; mem. Am. Epidemiological Soc., Am. Thoracic Soc., Internat. Epidemilogical Assn., European Soc. Clin. Respiratory Physiology, Biometrics Soc., Ariz. Thoracic Soc. (chmn. council 1973-77, 83—), Soc. Epidermal Resources, AAAS, Internat. Soc. Environ. Epidemiology, Am. Pub. Health Assn., Hungar Soc., Am. Stats. Assn. Office: U Ariz Coll Medicine Div Respiratory Scis 1501 N Campbell Ave Tucson AZ 85724

LE CLAIR, DOUGLAS MARVIN, lawyer; b. Montreal, Nov. 13, 1955; s. Lawrence M. and Joan B. Le Clair; m. Debra L. Garland, Oct. 12, 1985. BA, Loyola U., 1977; JD, Southwestern U., 1980; peace officer cert.,

Mesa Community Coll. Law Enforcement Acad., 1985. Bar: Ariz. 1982, U.S. Dist. Ct. Ariz. 1983, U.S. Ct. Appeals (9th cir.) 1983, U.S. Tax. Ct. 1987, U.S. Claims Ct. 1987, U.S. Supreme Ct. 1987. Corp. counsel Great Western Trading Co., Los Angeles, 1982-83; pvt. practice Mesa, Ariz., 1983—; chief exec. officer, gen. counsel DL Industries, Inc., Mesa, 1983—; corp. counsel various corps., Ariz. Author: Le Clair/Morgan Income Tax Organizer, 1982-83; prodn. editor Computer Law Jour., 1979-80; producer TV Advt., 1983; co-founder, editor Arizona Domestic Relations Reporter, 1988. Res. officer Mesa Police Dept., 1984—. Named One of Outstanding Young Men Of Am., 1979. Mem. ABA (taxation sect.), Ariz. Bar Assn., Maricopa County Bar Assn., Internat. Platform Assn., Southwestern Student Bar Assn. (exec. bd. 1978-79), Southwestern U. Tax Law Soc., Mesa C. of C., Delta Theta Phi, Phi Alpha Theta. Home: PO Box 223 Mesa AZ 85211-0223 Office: 805 First Interstate Bank Bldg 20 E Main St Mesa AZ 85201

LECLERC, STEPHEN ALLYN, mechanical engineer; b. Salem, Mass., Apr. 22, 1942; s. Charles Joseph Leclerc and Elizabeth (Carolyn) Grieco; m. Pamela Jean Salvati, Aug. 14, 1965; children: Christopher Mark, Carolyn Nicole. BS in Mech. Engring., U. Mass., 1964; MS in Engring. Mgmt., Northeastern U., 1970; postgrad., MIT, 1974. Registered profl. engr., Mass., La. Field/constrn. engr. Stone & Webster Engring. Corp., Boston, 1964-68, engr., lead mechanic, asst. project engr., 1969-75; project engr. Stone & Webster Engring. Corp., Denver, 1975-82, mgr. mech. engring., 1983-85, project mgr., 1983-89; project mgr. Pyropower Corp., San Diego, 1989—; pres. bd. dirs. Beaver Run Resort and Conf. Ctr., Breckenridge, Colo. Contbr. articles to profl. publs. Precinct chmn. Rep. com. Arapahoe County, Colo., 1976-82; treas. Cherry Creek Vista Homeowner Assn., Arapahoe County, 1976-78; coach various sports teams, Arapahoe County, 1976-82. Mem. United Ch. of Christ. Home: 582 Shadywood Dr Escondido CA 92026 Office: PyroPower Corp 5120 Shoreham Pl San Diego CA 92122

LECRON, MARY FRAZER See **FOSTER, MARY FRAZER**

LECZINSKI, DENNIS WALTER, interior designer, architectural consultant; b. Yonkers, N.Y., Feb. 14, 1942; s. Walter John and Mary Agnes (Seman) L. AS in Constrn. Tech., Westchester Community Coll., 1961; BS in Archtl. Design, Mont. State U., 1964, BA in Interior Design, 1965, MA in Interior Design, 1966. Designer Richard Himmel, ASID, Chgo., 1966-71, Robert Caudle, ASID, Denver, 1971-72; v.p. Claus Heppner & Assocs., Denver, 1972-85; owner, mgr., designer Leczinski Design Assocs., Denver, 1985—; prin., designer Design Collaborative, Denver; instr. art history Northwestern U., Evanston, Ill., 1969-71; lectr. Colo. State U., U. Colo., Interior Design Internship, Colo. Inst. Art; designer Saturday Night Alive Gala, Denver Performing Arts Ctr.; mem. adv. bd. Colo. Design Profls.; career day lectr. to high schs., Denver. Work featured in numerous mags. Vol. Christmas Tree Design Gala, Denver Art Mus.; vol. Am. Cancer Soc., Make A Wish Found., March of Dimes Telethon. Recipient 1st place award Hospitality mag., 1969, W.O.O.D. Inc., 1988. Mem. Am. Soc. Interior Designers (profl., pres. Colo. chpt. 1984-85, nat. bd. dirs. 1986-87, industry found. com. 1988-89, nat. chmn. fask force on homeless 1989, ways and means com. 1989, 1st place award Colo. chpt. 1978, Rocky Mountain region 1978, nat. competition award 1982, merit award 1984, Lowell Batchelder Meml. award Colo. chpt. 1987), Colo. Coalition for Interior Design (founding), Historic Denver, Denver Zoo Found. Republican. Office: 1000 S Monaco Pkwy Ste 56 Denver CO 80222

LEDBETTER, CARL SCOTIUS, counselor, educator; b. Pyatt, Ark., Aug. 19, 1910; s. James Oliver and Lillie Belle (Wall) L.; student Phillips U., Enid, Okla., 1930-32; A.B., Ky. Christian Coll., 1937; A.B., Butler U., 1939, M.A., 1940; M.A., U. Redlands, 1967; postgrad. Claremont Grad. Sch., 1961-64, Mankato (Minn.) State Coll., 1970-73, Calif. State Coll., 1974-76; m. Ruth Slocum Weymouth, June 20, 1948; children—Carla Sue Ledbetter Holte, Carl Scotius, Charles Stephen, Craig Slocum, Candace Sybil Ledbetter Heidelberger, Christa Sharyn Ledbetter Sanders. Ordained to ministry Christian Ch., 1933; student pastor, Huntington, W.Va., 1935-36, Russell, Ky., 1936-39, Atlanta, Ind., 1939-40; mem. editorial staff Standard Pub. Co., Cin., 1940-41; commd. 1st lt. U.S. Army, 1941; advanced through grades to col., 1961; command chaplain Augsburg (W. Ger.) area, 1950-53; div. chaplain 3d Inf. Div., 1953-55; dep. army chaplain 6th U.S. Army, 1955-58; command chaplain 5th Region Army Air Def. Command, 1959-61; ret., 1961; dean men U. Redlands, 1961-69; dir. counseling, v.p. acad. affairs Lea (Minn.) Coll., 1969-74; rehab. counselor J.O.B. Work Activities Ctr., Hesperia, Calif., 1976-80, dir., 1980-85, dir. emeritus, 1985—; adj. prof. psychology and religion Chapman Coll., 1976-85. Recipient award of merit Boy Scouts Am., 1967, Silver Beaver award, 1969. Mem. Am. Personnel and Guidance Assn., Nat. Vocat. Guidance Assn., Am. Rehab. Counselors Assn., Alpha Phi Gamma, Phi Delta Kappa, Pi Ch, Pi Gamma Mu, Alpha Phi Omega. Democrat. Club: Masons. Home: 611 Juniper Ct Redlands CA 92374

LEDERER, JEROME, aerospace safety consultant, engineer; b. N.Y.C., Sept. 26, 1902; m. Sarah Bojarsky, Nov. 1, 1935; children—Nancy, Susan. B.Sc. in Mech. Engring., NYU, 1924, M.Engring., 1925. Registered profl. engr., N.Y. Engr. Aero Ins. Underwriters, N.Y.C., 1929-40; dir. safety bur. CAB, Washington, 1940-42; pres. Flight Safety Found., N.Y.C., 1947-67; dir. Office Manned Space Flight Safety, NASA, Washington, 1967-70, dir. safety, 1970-72; ret., 1972; bd. govs. Flight Safety Found., Arlington, Va., 1947—; mem. adv. council Inst. Nuclear Power Ops., Atlanta, 1980-85; cons., Laguna Hills, Calif., 1974—. Author books and articles on aviation and space safety. Recipient NASA Exceptional Service medal, Daniel Guggenheim medal, Wright Bros. award, Amelia Earhart medal, Ziolkowski Medal Soviet Fedn. Cosmonauts, many others. Fellow AIAA (hon.), Am. Astronautics Assn., Royal Aero. Soc., Royal Soc. Arts, Human Factors Soc.; mem. Mil. Order Daedalions (hon.), Nat. Acad. Engring. Club: Wings (N.Y.). Home: 468-D Calle Cadiz Laguna Hills CA 92653

LEDERER, JOHN MARTIN, aeronautical engineer; b. Solomon, Kans., May 12, 1930; s. George Martin and Angie Belle (Faubion) L.; m. Joan Elizabeth Patrick, June 15, 1963; children: Jeffrey Mark, Carol Elizabeth. BS in Aero. Engring., Kans. State U., 1953; MSEE, Air Force Inst. Tech., 1955; postgrad., U. N.Mex., 1962-63. Registered profl. aero. engr., Ohio. Project engr. Air Force Spl. Weapons Ctr., Albuquerque, 1955-63, chief project engring. div., 1963-67, chief electromagnetics div., 1967-70; tech. adviser Air Force Weapons Lab., Albuquerque, 1970-73, 76-87, chief nuclear systems surety div., 1988—; tech. dir. 4900th test group, Albuquerque, 1973-76; chmn. Dept. of Def. Design Rev. and Acceptance Group, Albuquerque, 1979—. Co-inventor digital distance measuring instrument. Founder One of Ten Young Am. Football League, Albuquerque, 1964. Served to 1st lt. USAFR, 1953-58. Recipient Outstanding Performance award Dept. Air Force, Albuquerque, 1965, 66, 68, 73, 74, 79, Sustained Superior Performance award Dept. Air Force, Albuquerque, 1961, 81, 83, 84, 85, 86, 88. Mem. NSPE, Inst. Aerospace Scis. Republican. Episcopalian. Home: 3012 El Marta Ct NE Albuquerque NM 87111-5618 Office: Air Force Weapons Lab NTS Kirtland AFB NM 87117-6008

LEDERER, MARIÒN IRVINE, cultural administrator; b. Brampton, Ont., Can., Feb. 10, 1920; d. Oliver Bateman and Eva Jane (MacMurdo) L.; m. Francis Lederer, July 10, 1941. Student, U. Toronto, 1938, UCLA, 1942-45. Owner Canoga Mission Gallery, Canoga Park, Calif., 1967—; cultural heritage monument Canoga Mission Gallery, 1974—; Vice pres. Screen Smart Set women's aux. Motion Picture and TV Fund, 1973—; founder sister city program Canoga Park-Taxco, Mexico, 1963; Mem. mayor's cultural task force San Fernando Valley, 1973—; mem. Los Angeles Cultural Affairs Commn., 1980-85; bd. dirs. Muses (Mus. Sci. and Industry Los Angeles). Mem. Los Angeles Cultural Affairs Commn., 1980-85. Recipient numerous pub. service awards from mayor, city council, C. of C. Mem. Canoga Park C. of C. (cultural chmn. 1973-75, dir. 1973-75). Presbyn. Home: PO Box 32 Canoga Park CA 91305 Office: Canoga Mission Gallery 23130 Sherman Way Canoga Park CA 91307

LEDFORD, BRENT RALEIGH, lawyer; b. Monterey Park, Calif., Dec. 13, 1950; s. Wilson Marion and Helen Elizabeth (Johnson) L.; m. Cathleen Doherty, May 14, 1978. BS in Criminal Justice, Calif. State U., Long Beach, 1981; JD, Southwestern U., L.A., 1988. Bar: Calif. 1988. Dep. marshal L.A. County Marshal's Dept., Long Beach, Calif., 1974-82; Bonus I dep., supr. dep. L.A. County Marshal's Dept., Long Beach, 1982-89; assoc. Morgan, Wenzel & McNicholas, L.A., 1989—. Ssgt., USAF, 1969-73, Italy. Recipient Letter of Commendation., L.A. County Marshal Dept., 1979. Mem. L.A. County Bar Assn.

LEDFORD, DAVID FULLER, electronic technician; b. Bremerton, Wash., Nov. 12, 1964; s. Dennis Andrew and Patricia Ann (Murray) L. Electronic technician diploma, DeVry Inst. Tech., Phoenix, 1985, AS in Electronics, 1987. Electronic test technician Hughes Aircraft Co., Tucson, 1985--. Home: 2410 S Mission Rd #1192 Tucson AZ 85713

LEDFORD, GERALD EDWARD, JR., psychologist; b. Huntsville, Ala., Apr. 21, 1951; s. Gerald Edward and Lois Aileen (Falk) L.; m. Heather Ann Wictum, Nov. 8, 1986. BA in Psychology, George Washington U., 1973; MA in Psychology, U. Mich., 1979, PhD, 1984. User svcs. specialist Gen. Electric Co., Gaithersburg, Md., 1973-74; writer, researcher Bicentennial Youth Debates, Washington, 1974-75; research assoc. Inst. Social Research, U. Mich., Ann Arbor, 1976-82; research scientist Ctr. for Effective Orgns., U. So. Calif., L.A., 1982-88; sr. research scientist Ctr. for Effective Orgns., U. So. Calif., 1988--; mgmt. cons. in field. Editor: (with others) Research That is Useful for Theory and Practice, 1985, Large Scale Organizational Change, 1989; author: (with others) Employee Involvement in America: A Study of Contemporary Practice, 1989; contbr. articles to profl. jours. Mem. Am. Psychol. Assn., Acad. Mgmt., Phi Beta Kappa. Democrat. Office: U So Calif HOH501L Los Angeles CA 90089

LEDGERWOOD, HELEN DIANE, accountant; b. Chattanooga, Sept. 24, 1946; d. Howard Brown and Helen Irene (Boettcher) Blakely; m. Larry Ledgerwood, Aug. 12, 1967; children: Jennifer, Cheryl. BS in Acctg., Calif. State U., Long Beach, 1976. Asst. contr. Don Roberto Jewelers, El Toro, Calif., 1979-80; staff acct. Nicholas Terpstra, CPA, Santa Ana, Calif., 1980-81; sr. acct. Rusty Pelican Restaurants, Irvine, Calif., 1981-83; acctg. mgr. Adams Fin. Group, Costa Mesa, Calif., 1983-85, cons., 1985—; acct. The Lusk Co., Irvine, 1985-88, sr. acct., 1988—. Republican.

LEE, ALDORA G., social psychologist; b. Schenectady, N.Y.; d. Alois W. and M. Dorothy (Swigert) Graf. AB, Ind. U.; MA, Stanford U.; PhD, U. Colo. Dir. women studies Wash. State U., Pullman, 1976-78, dir. unit on aging, 1976-81; cons. in market research Syva, Palo Alto, Calif., 1982; market research analyst Allstate Research and Planning Ctr., Menlo Park, Calif., 1983—; rep. Wash. Assn. Gerontol. Edn., N.W. region rep. Nat. Women's Studies Assn., 1978-81. Contbr. articles to profl. jours. Mem. Menlo Park Libr. Commn., chmn. 1985-87; instr. Resource Ctr. for Women, Palo Alto, 1984-87. Mem. Am. Mktg. Assn., Am. Psychol. Soc., Am. Sociol. Assn., Western Psychol. Assn., Phi Beta Kappa, Sigma Xi.

LEE, ALFRED THEODORE, research psychologist; b. Port Washington, Wis., June 25, 1946; s. Alfred and Gladys (Loomis) L. BA cum laude Psychology, San Jose State U., 1972, MA in Exptl. Psychology, 1974; PhD in Exptl. Psychology, U. Calif.-Riverside, 1979. Lic. pvt. pilot. Rsch. scientist U. Dayton (Ohio), 1979-82, NASA-Ames Rsch. Ctr., Moffett Field, Calif., 1983--; lectr. U. Calif., 1978, teaching asst., 1974-78; rsch. cons. U.S. Dept.Justice, 1978-79, VA, 1978; rsch. asst. San Jose State U., 1972-74. Contbr. articles to profl. jours. Sgt. USAF, 1964-68. Regents fellow U. Calif., 1979. Mem. Human Factors Soc., Soc. Automotive Engrs., IEEE, Assn. Aviation Psychologists. Office: NASA Ames Rsch Ctr MS239-21 Moffett Field CA 94035

LEE, BERNARD TUNGHAO, import-export company executive; b. Shantung, Republic of China, Feb. 20, 1944; came to U.S., 1969; s. Tze-Ching and Sheng-Fei (Wang) Li; m. Cathy Maywen Wang, July 21, 1988. BS, Tamkang U., Taipei, Republic of China, 1968; MS, U. Tex., El Paso, 1971; PhD, Va. Poly. U., 1975. Applications chemist Hewlett-Packard Co., Avondale, Pa., 1975-76; tech. dir. SGL-Homalite Co. Inc., Wilmington, Del., 1976-78; mktg. mgr. Cosmopolitan Internat. Co., Inc., Martinsville, Va., 1978-79; owner, gen. mgr. Berwen Internat. Co., Yorba Linda, Calif., 1979—. Mem. Rep. Presdl. Task Force, Nat. Rep. Senatorial Com., Washington, 1982—. 2d lt. Chinese Army, 1968-69.

LEE, BERTRAM, financier, professional basketball team owner. Grad.in political sci., N. Central Coll., Naperville, Ill. Chmn. The Boston (Mass.) Bank of Commerce; pres. BML Assocs. Inc., Boston; formerly pres. WNEV-TV, Boston; co-owner Denver Nuggets, NBA, Denver, Colo., 1989—. Address: care Denver Nuggets McNichols Sports Arena PO Box 4658 Denver CO 80204 *

LEE, BRIAN DALVIN, pediatric dentist; b. Berkeley, Calif., Dec. 23, 1942; s. David Alan and May (Hum) L.; m. Dorlene Sandria Yee, Aug. 13, 1966; children: Lisa Ann, Jonathon Everett. Student, U. Calif., Berkeley, 1960-62; DDS, U. Calif., San Francisco, 1966; MSD, Ind. U., 1970. Diplomate Am. Bd. Pedodontics. Practice pediatric dentistry Foster City, Calif., 1972—; guest lectr. U. Calif. Sch. Dentistry; clin. instr. Ind. U. Sch. Dentistry; dental examiner Calif. Bd. Dental Examiners. Contbr. articles to profl. jours. Served as capt. Dental Corps, U.S. Army, 1966-68. Decorated Army Commendation medal with oak leaf cluster; Crippled Children's fellow, 1968-70. Fellow Am. Acad. Pedodontics, Am. Coll. Dentists; mem. Am. Bd. Pedodontics (examiner), Am. Soc. Dentistry for Children, Calif. Soc. Dentistry for Children, Calif. Soc. Pediatric Dentists, ADA, Calif. Dental Assn., Golden Gate Pedodontic Study Club, Am. Bd. Pediatric Dentistry (chmn. 1986—), Foster City C. of C. Lodge: Lions. Home: 198 Flying Mist Isle Foster City CA 94404 Office: 1289 Hillsdale Blvd Foster City CA 94404

LEE, CANDIE CHING WAH, retail executive; b. Hong Kong, British Crown Colony, June 17, 1950; came to U.S., 1973:; d. Willard W. and Yuk Ching (Yau) L. Student, Hong Kong Tech. Coll., Kowloon, 1968-70. Office mgr. Crown Enterprises, Ltd., Hong Kong, 1970-73; buyer, mgr. Hawaii Resort Industries, Inc., Honolulu, 1973-76, v.p., 1976-82; pres. Hawaii Resort Shops, Inc., Honolulu, 1983—. Mem. Am. Mgmt. Assn. Republican. Office: Hawaii Resort Shops Inc 2270 Kalakaua Ave Ste 1000 Honolulu HI 96815

LEE, CURTIS HOWARD, mechanical engineer, consultant; b. San Francisco, June 7, 1928; s. Lum Quong and Kum Ho (Lee) L.; B.S. with honor, Calif. State Poly. Coll., 1952; postgrad. McGeorge Coll. Law, 1964-67; m. Mildred Lee; children—Melinda, Roberta, Lorie, Sabrina, Kristina. Mech. engr. Buonaccorsi & Assos., cons. engrs., San Francisco, 1953-57, Eagleson Engrs., cons. engrs., San Francisco, 1957-59; 60-63; chief engr. C.S. Hardeman, San Francisco, 1959-60; spl. project engr. A.E. D'Ambly, cons. engrs., Phila., 1963-64; self-employed as cons. engr., Sacramento, 1964-67; chief engr. George W. Dunn & Assos., cons. engrs. San Diego, 1967-69; prin. Dunn-Lee-Smith-Klein & Assocs., San Diego, 1969-87, Curtis H. Lee Cons. Group, Chula Vista, 1987—. Mem. Accrediting Commn. of Assn. of Ind. Colls. and Schs., 1970-76; mem. adv. panel Calif. State Bldg. Standards Commn., 1971-76; mem. San Diego City Bd. Bldg. Appeals, 1974-79; mem. Chula Vista City Bd. Appeals, 1980-88—. Served with AUS, 1947-48. Registered profl. engr., Ariz., Calif., Colo., Fla., Ga., Wash., Nev., N.Mex., Ohio, Oreg., Pa., Tex. Fellow ASHRAE; mem. Am. Arbitration Assn. (mem. nat. panel 1969—, regional adv. bd. 1977—), Am. Acad. Forensic Scis., Nat. Soc. Profl. Engrs. (pres. San Diego chpt. 1972-73, state dir. 1973-74, nat. dir. 1974-76), ASME, Am. Soc. Plumbing Engrs. (charter pres. San Diego chpt. 1970, nat. 3d v.p. 1970-72), Constrn. Specifications Inst. (dir. San Diego chpt. 1974-75, pres. 1976-77, Inst. com. 1978—, named fellow 1983), Am. Soc. Profl. Estimators, Am. Soc. Quality Control, Instrument Soc. Am., Am. Soc. Testing and Materials, Internat. Assn. Plumbing and Mech. Ofcls., Nat. Fire Protection Assn. Office: 492 3d Ave #101 Chula Vista CA 92010-4614

LEE, DANIEL DAVID (LE-DINH-PHUOC), clinical psychologist; b. Danang, Vietnam, Dec. 14, 1941; married; 2 children. BA in Sociology and Psychology, Trinity Coll., Deerfield, Ill., 1970; MSW in Psychiatric Social Work, U. Ill.-Chgo., 1972, postgrad., 1972-73; PhD in Clin. Psychology, U.S. Internat. U., 1979. Lic. clin. psychologist; Diplomate Am. Bd. Med. Psychotherapy. Clin. intern U. Ill. Hosp. Med. Sch., Chgo., 1970-71, Luth. Gen. Hosp., Park Ridge, Ill., 1971-72; psychiatric social worker Salvation Army Family Svcs., Chgo., 1972-73; predoctoral intership in community and clin. psychology County of Orange (Calif.) Dept. of Mental Health, 1978-79; postdoctoral intern County of L.A. Dept. of Mental Health, 1980-81; pvt. practice Garden Grove, Calif., 1981—; mem. panel of psychologists State of Calif. Dept. Social Svcs., 1981—, Superior Ct. Calif., 1986—; clin. psychologist Indochinese Mental Health Clinic, Asian/Pacific Counseling and Treatment Ctr., County of L.A. Dept. Mental Health, 1980-83; mental health svcs. cons. State of Ariz., 1985—, State of Calif. , 1976-81; contract cons. State of Calif. Dept. Edn., 1978, Indochinese Community Health and Edn. Project HEW Social Security Adminstrn., 1978-79; ednl. svcs. cons. for Southeast Asians, World Vision Internat. Inc., Monrovia, Calif., 1974-75; asst. clin. prof. psychiatry and behavioral scis. U. So. Calif. Sch. Medicine, 1980-84; field instr. UCLA Grad. Sch. Social Welfare, 1980-81; prof. sociology and social welfare Dalat (Vietnam) U. Sch. Govt. and Bus., 1974-75, Van Hanh U. Faculty Social Scis., Saigon, Vietnam, 1973-75; cons. child welfare and family svcs. Ministry of Social Welfare, Vietnam, 1973-75; project dir. Southeast Asian Family Counseling Program and Southeast Asian Refugee Resettlement Project Internat. Inst. of L.A., 1975-77. Contbr. articles to profl. jours. Chairperson health and mental health com. Refugee Forum of L.A., 1983-84; cons. and trainer cultural awareness program Dept. Pub. Social Svcs. County of L.A., 1975-77, cons. Asian Community Svcs. Ctr. Dept. Community Svcs., 1975-77; mem. Asian-Am. Mental Health Task Force, L.A., 1975-77. Fellow Am. Coll. Forensic Psychology; mem. Am. Psychol. Assn. , World Fedn. Mental Health, Acad. Psychologists in Marital, Sec, and Family Therapy, Forensic Mental Health Assn. Calif., Calif. Neuropsychology Soc., Calif. State Psychol. Assn., Orange County Psychol. Assn. Office: 9872 Chapman Ave Ste 204 Garden Grove CA 92641

LEE, DEBRA ANN, marketing executive; b. Salt Lake City, Sept. 10, 1953; d. Glenn Alfred and Evelyn Mary (Bridges) Gale L. Student, Glendale Community Coll., 1971, Santa Ana Community Coll., 1974. Cert. paralegal in family and bus. law. Legal sec. various orgns., Phoenix, Santa Ana, Orange, Ariz., Calif., 1972-77; with sales, training dept. Lifespring, Inc., Orange, Calif., 1977-79; west coast dir., trainer Lifespring, Inc., 1979-80; v.p. Lee Enterprises, Ltd., San Diego, 1980-81; asst. developer Denro Interests, Ltd., Phoenix, 1981-82; acct. exec. Baker Pub., Inc., 1983-85; owner Competitive Concepts, Phoenix, 1985-87, Irvine, Calif., 1987—; mktg. cons. The Estes Co., Phoenix, 1988, Orange Coast Equities, Fountain Valley, Calif., 1987-88; advt. agy. Bellamah Community Devel., Phoenix, 1985-88. Com. mem. Gov. Apptd. Land-Use Com, Phoenix, 1985-86. Mem. Homebuilders Assn. of Cen. Ariz., Sales and Mktg. Coun., Bldg. Industry Assn., Calif. Bldg. Industry Assn., Sales and Mktg. Coun., Homebuilders Coun., Nat. Assn. of Homebuilders, Orange County Ad Club, Phoenix Ad Club. Republican.

LEE, DONNA LYNN, auditor, accountant; b. San Francisco, Dec. 1, 1956; d. Arthur J. and Myrtle Joan (Haynes) L. BS in Acctg., U. San Francisco, 1983. Acctg. clk. 3/33 Ins. Co., San Francisco, 1979-80; advt. acct. San Francisco Newspaper Agy., 1980-83; sales supr. Macy's Calif., 1974-84; supr. sr. auditor Arthur Young and Co., 1984-87; internal auditor Hewlett-Packard Co., Palo Alto, Calif., 1987—. Mem. Nat. Assn. Black Accts. Democrat. Roman Catholic. Office: Hewlett-Packard Co 3000 Hanover St Palo Alto CA 94304

LEE, EDGAR KWAN MING, structural engineer; b. Honolulu, Nov. 16, 1934; s. Edgar Kon Yan and Margaret Kui Lan (Ching) L.; m. Amy F.M. Lau, June 22, 1957; children: Kenton, Randall, Lorina, Andrew. BS with honors, U. Calif., Berkeley, 1957, MS, 1958. Registered profl. engr., Calif., Hawaii. Project engr. Chin & Hensolt, San Francisco, 1958-67, Alf A. Yee & Assocs., Honolulu, 1967-69, SSFM Co., 1969-72; pres. Engring. Design Group, Inc., 1972—. Mem. ASCE, Structural Engrs. Assn. Hawaii (treas. 1980, sec. 1984), Prestressed Concrete Inst., Am. Concrete Inst., Tau Beta Pi, Chi Epsilon. Home: 3143 Alani Dr Honolulu HI 96822 Office: Engring Design Group Inc 1525 Young St Honolulu HI 96826

LEE, ELEANOR M., state legislator; b. Elgin, Ill., July 17, 1931; d. Earl H. and Catherine (Goldback) S.; m. David H. Lee, 1951; children: Virginia Boylan, Phyllis Kenworthy, Marcia. BA, Evergreen State Coll., 1973. Bus. mgr. Fairman B. Lee Co., Inc., Burien, Wash., 1969—; state senator State of Wash., Olympia, 1977—; mem. State Land Planning Commn., Wash., 1971-73; chair Jt. Adminstrv. Rules Com., 1982, Econ. Devel. and Labor Com., 1989; co-chair SeaTac Task Force, Visitors and Conv. Com.; founder, past chair Puget Sound Air Quality Coalition. Past chair Fire Dist. Civil Service Bd. Mem. Bus. and Profl. Women (Woman of Yr. 1986), LWV (former pres.), Burien C. of C., Soroptimists (Women Helping Women award 1982, 86), Seattle Mountaineers, Des Moines Yacht Club. Republican. Office: Wash State Senate 102 Institutions Bldg Olympia WA 98504

LEE, FAITH HOPE, electronics engineer; b. Steubenville, Ohio, Dec. 2, 1925; d. Raymond Abraham and Marie Belle (Kellar) Miller; m. Raymond M. Lee, Jr., Sept. 8, 1947 (div. 1977); children: Sharon Melanie Lee Gamble, Cynthia Laura, Raymond Marvin III. AA, Orlando Coll., 1958; BEE, Ariz. State U., 1963, MEE, 1969. Staff engr. research and devel. Motorola Semiconductor Products Div., Phoenix, 1963-69; cons. engr. digital circuits Societa Generale Semiconduttori Co., Milan, Italy, 1969-70; project engr. research and devel. labs RCA, Somerville, N.J., 1970-79; mgr. custom facility microwave devel./research Motorola Solid State Div., Phoenix, 1979—. Contbr. articles to profl. jours. Officer, Lulac, Tempe, Ariz., 1968, PTA, various locations, 1960-69. Mem. IEEE (svc. award 1977), Soc. Women Engrs. (Engr. of Year 1976), ASME, Nat. Soc. Profl. Engrs., Electro Chemical Soc. (officer 1970), Ariz. Council Scientists and Engrs. (pres. elect 1969), Mensa, Orlando Astronomy Club, N.J. Table Tennis, Ariz. Table Tennis, New Orleans Astronomy, Eta Kappa Nu. Republican. Home: 1057 E Butler Dr 1C Phoenix AZ 85020 Office: Motorola SSD Price & Elliott Rds Tempe AZ 85283

LEE, GLEN K., dentist; b. Honolulu, Nov. 10, 1950; s. Kenneth Kam Chun Lee and Audrey (Mew Wun) Chun; m. Barbara Lynn Dunnett, Feb. 14, 1981; children: Jayna Christine, Jeffrey Ryan, David Michael. BS, Loyola U., L.A., 1972; DDS, Creighton U., 1976. Pvt. practice Santa Barbara, Calif., 1976--; mem. med. staff St. Francis Hosp., Santa Barbara, 1976--, Santa Barbara Cottage Hosp., 1976--, Goleta Valley Hosp., Goleta, Calif., 1976--. Mem. ADA, Am. Acad. Implant Dentistry, Am. Acad. Cosmetic Dentistry, Calif. Dental Assn., Santa Barbara-Ventura County Dental Soc., Old Towne Mchts. Assn. Democrat. Roman Catholic. Home: 3641 Tierra Bella Santa Barbara CA 93105 Office: 1919 State St Ste 201 Santa Barbara CA 93101

LEE, GRACE TZE, controller; b. Taipei, Republic of China, Aug. 11, 1953; came to U.S., 1974; d. Tang Chi and Ming (Shu) L. BA, Nat. Taipei U., 1974; BS, U. Nev., 1977; postgrad., UCLA, 1988. Fgn. currency specialist Deak-Perera Co., L.A., 1977-80; asst. mgr. Universal Supply Co., L.A., 1980; controller AJR Electronics Inc., L.A., 1981-84; western zone asst. mgr. Samsung Electronics Co., L.A., 1984; controller Gideon Nol Inc., L.A., 1985-87, James G. Wiley Co., L.A., 1987—; pres. G.L. Fin. Svc., 1988—, Real Estate Investment Svc., 1988—. Home: 23442 Batey Ave Harbor City CA 90710

LEE, HU, realtor, mechanical engineer; b. Saigon, Socialist Republic of Vietnam, July 8, 1959; came to U.S., 1978; parents Yen and Si (Chen) L. BSME, U. Miss., 1984; grad., Real Estate Trainers Sch., 1988. Lic. real estate broker. Engr. assoc. U-V-P, Inc., San Gabriel, Calif., 1985-86; realtor Coldwell Banker, Arcadia, Calif., 1986-87, Amb. Real Estate, Temple City, Calif., 1987—. Mem. Am. Soc. Mech. Engrs., Calif. Assn. Realtors. Democrat. Home: 215 S McPherrin Ave #D Monterey Park CA 91754 Office: Amb Real Estate PO Box 1402 Temple City CA 91780

LEE, IVY, JR., public relations consultant; b. N.Y.C., July 31, 1909; s. Ivy and Cornelia (Bigelow) L.; m. Marie F. Devin, Oct. 14, 1988; children: Peter Ivy III (dec.), Jean Downey. BA, Princeton U., 1931; MBA, Harvard U., 1933. Ptnr. Ivy Lee & T.J. Ross, N.Y.C., 1933-45; with Pan Am. World Airways, Miami, Fla. and San Francisco, 1942-45; adminstrv. asst. S.D. Bechtel, Bechtel Cos., San Francisco, 1950-54; pres. Ivy Lee Jr. & Assocs., San Francisco, 1945-55; pres., cons. Ivy Lee Jr. & Assocs., Inc., San Francisco, 1955—. Trustee Princeton (N.J.) U., 1965-69; bd. dirs. San Francisco TB Assn., Bay Area Red Cross, San Francisco, Edgewood Childrens Ctr. Mem. Pub. Relations Soc. Am., Internat. Pub. Relations Assn. (pres. 1976-77). Republican. Presbyterian. Clubs: Bohemian, Pacific Union.

Home: 1940 Broadway San Francisco CA 94109 Office: 210 Post St San Francisco CA 94108

LEE, JAMES FORREST, manufacturing executive; b. Bromerton, Wash., Feb. 17, 1951; s. Joe and Dorothy Grace (Lewis) L.; m. Debra Sue Neeley, June 20, 1987; children: Jason Farish, Crystal Joe, James Justin. AA, Olympic Community Coll., Bremerton, Wash., 1973; BSBA, City U., 1982; BA im mfg. tech., Nat. U., 1985, MBA, 1987. Cert. mfg. engr. Numerical control programmer Boeing Aircraft Co., Seattle, 1973-76, 1977; numerical control contractor Rockwell Internat., Columbus, Ohio, 1976-78; numerical control cons. Lockheed Space/Missle Co., Sunnyvale, Calif., 1978-79; numerical control programmer Tacoma (Wash.) Boat Co., 1977-78; numerical control cons. Chrysler Tank Plant, Lima, Ohio, 1979-80, Northrup Aircraft Co., Hawthorne, Calif., 1980-82; numerical control programmer Smiley Industries Co., Lakeside, Calif., 1982-83; numerical control mgr. Ametek, El Cajon, Calif., 1983--. Mem. Soc. Mfg. Engrs., Nat. Alumni Assn., Employee Assn. Club (El Cajon, pres.). Home: 220 Holly Oak Dr El Cajon CA 92020 Office: Ametek PO Box 666 El Cajon CA 92022

LEE, JAMES MAHNGILL, financial executive; b. Seoul, Republic of Korea, Feb. 22, 1942; s. Young Keun and Sung Duck (Hwang) L.; m. Atsuko Sasaki, Mar. 15, 1987; 1 child, Geoffrey. BA, Yonsei U., 1966; MBA, U. Calif., Berkeley, 1970. CPA, Calif. Jr. acct. Litton Industries, Inc., Beverly Hills, Calif., 1971-72; acct. J.H. Snyder Co., L.A., 1972-74; agt. Equitable Fin. Cos., L.A., 1975-78, dist. mgr., 1978-87, agy. mgr., 1988—. Buddhist. Club: NSA (L.A.). Home: 7917 Kentwood Ave Los Angeles CA 90045 Office: Equitable Fin Cos 11440 San Vicente Blvd Los Angeles CA 90049

LEE, JETSON SCOTT, orthodontist; b. San Francisco, Oct. 16, 1959; s. Sunny Fook and Bicky (Chan) L.; m. Lisa Marie Wayne, May 14, 1988. AB, U. Calif.-Berkeley, 1981; DDS, U. Pacific, 1984, MSD, 1986. Pvt. practice San Francisco, 1986--; asst. prof. Sch. Dentistry, U. Pacific, San Francisco, 1986--. Contbr. numerous articles to profl. publs. Mem. ADA, Calif. Dental Assn., San Francisco Dental Soc., Am. Assn. Orthodontists, Calif. State Soc. Orthodontists, Pacific Coast Soc. Orthodontists, Lowell High Sch. Alumni Assn. (bd. dirs. 1985--), Omicron Kappa Upsilon, Tau Kappa Omega, Delta Sigma Delta. Republican. Office: 4141 Geary Blvd Ste 209 San Francisco CA 94118

LEE, JOEL MARVIN, marketing executive; b. San Antonio, Aug. 13, 1949; s. Lewis C. and Charlotte (Lippman) L. AB in English, Oberlin Coll., 1971; MA, U. Chgo., 1972. Asst. librarian Lake Forest (Ill.) Coll., 1972-77; hdqrs. librarian ALA, Chgo., 1977-86, sr. mgr. info. tech. publ., 1986-88; mgr. mktg. Auto-Graphics, Inc., Pomona, Calif., 1988—. Assoc. editor ALA World Encyclopedia, 1980, 86; editor-in-chief Who's Who in Library and Information Services, 1982; co-editor As Much To Learn As To Teach, 1979; mem. edit. bd. Library Software Rev., 1988; contbr. articles to various pubs. Mng. trustee 860 Lake Shore Dr. Trust, Chgo., 1984-86. Mem. ALA, Spl. Libraries Assn., Am. Soc. for Info. Sci. Jewish.

LEE, JOHN JIN, lawyer; b. Chgo., Oct. 20, 1948; s. Jim Soon and Fay Yown (Young) L.; m. Jamie Pearl Eng, Apr. 30, 1983. BA magna cum laude, Rice U., 1971; JD, Stanford U., 1975; MBA, 1975. Bar: Calif. 1976. Assoc. atty. Manatt Phelps & Rothenberg, L.A., 1976-77; asst. counsel Wells Fargo Bank N.A., San Francisco, 1977-79, counsel, 1979-80, v.p., sr. counsel, 1980, v.p., mng. sr. counsel, 1981—. Bd. dirs. Asian Bus. League of San Francisco, 1981—, gen. counsel, 1981. Mem. ABA (chmn. subcom. on housing fin., com. on consumer fin. svcs., bus. law sect. 1983—), Consumer Bankers Assn. (lawyers com.), Asian Am. Bar Assn. of Greater Bay Area, Soc. Physics Students. Democrat. Baptist. Office: Wells Fargo Bank NA Legal Dept 111 Sutter St San Francisco CA 94163

LEE, JONG HYUK, accountant; b. Seoul, Korea, May 6, 1941; came to U.S., 1969, naturalized, 1975; s. Jung Bo and Wol Sun Lee; B.A., Sonoma State U., Rohnert Park, Calif., 1971; M.B.A. in Taxation, Golden Gate U., San Francisco, 1976; m. Esther Kim, Jan. 24, 1970. Cost acct., internal auditor Foremost-McKesson Co., San Francisco, 1971-74; sr. acct. Clark, Wong, Foulkes & Barbieri, C.P.A.s, Oakland, Calif., 1974-77; pres. J.H. Lee Accountancy Corp., Oakland, 1977—; instr. Armstrong Coll., Berkeley, Calif., 1977-78. Bd. dirs. Korean Residents Assn., 1974, Multi-service Center for Koreans, 1979, Better Bus. Bur., 1984-87; chmn. caucus Calif.-Nev. ann. conf. United Methodist Ch., 1977; commr. Calif. State Office Econ. Opportunity, 1982-86; pres. Korean-Am. Democratic Network; mem. Dem. Nat. Fin. Council; regional chmn. Adv. Council on Peaceful Unification Policy, Republic of Korea; commr. Asian Art Mus. San Francisco, 1988—. Served with Korean Marine Corps, 1961-64; 1st lt. Calif. State Mil. Res. C.P.A., Calif. Mem. Am. Inst. C.P.A.s, Nat. Assn. Asian Am. C.P.A.s (dir.), Am. Acctg. Assn., Nat. Assn. Accountants, Internat. Found. Employee Benefit Plans, Calif. Soc. C.P.A.s, Oakland C. of C., Korean Am. C. of C. (pres. Pacific North Coast, Democrat. Club: Rotary. Author tax and bus. column Korea Times, 1980. Home: 180 Firestone Dr Walnut Creek CA 94598 Office: 369 13th St Oakland CA 94612

LEE, KAREN ROSAMOND, lawyer; b. Washington, July 30, 1950; d. Charles Benjamin Pegs and Hazel Marie (Drew) Payne; m. Sidney Edward Lee, Aug. 10, 1970 (div. Feb. 1976); 1 child, Desiree Yvette. AA, Long Beach City Coll., 1973; BA, U. Calif., Berkeley, 1976, JD, 1980. Bar: Calif. 1980. Law clk. U.S. Dist. Ct., New Orleans, 1980-81; assoc. Orrick Herrington and Sutcliffe, San Francisco, 1981-82; paralegal Safeway Stores Inc., Oakland, Calif., 1987—. Ford Found. scholar 1973, James Wheeler scholar 1975; recipient I Dare You award DAR, 1962. Mem. Calif. Bar Assn., Delta Sigma Theta. Democrat.

LEE, LAURENCE KENNETH, utility company executive; b. Jesup, Ga., Apr. 16, 1937; s. Lewis Kimbrough and Adele Lucille (Tomberlin) L.; m. June Adele Foerstner, Nov. 22, 1956; children: Laurence Kenneth Jr., Lorena Adele Lee Williams, Lewis Carl. Student, Ariz. State Coll., 1956-59, Calif. Western U., 1959. Powerhouse operator Power Authority State of N.Y., various cities, 1959-63; journeyman operator Grant County Pub. Utility Dist., Wanapum Dam, Wash., 1963-67; asst. power dispatcher Grant County Pub. Utility Dist., Ephrata, Wash., 1967-74; sr. power system dispatcher Grant County Pub. Utility Dist., Ephrata, 1974—. Councilman, City of Soap Lake, Wash., 1970—; sr. warden, St. John's Episc. Ch., Ephrata, 1970-72; asst. scoutmaster, Soap Lake area Boy Scouts Am., 1970-72; Mayor pro-tem, City of Soap Lake, 1986-88. Mem. Am. Power Dispatchers Assn. (nat. pres. 1981-85), Northwest Power Pool, IBEW, Elks, Masons (past master). Republican. Home: 127 Fir St N Soap Lake WA 98851 Office: Grant County Power Utility 30 C St SW Ephrata WA 98823

LEE, LOU S., printing company executive, developer; b. Liuzhou, Guangsi, Peoples Republic of China, Nov. 5, 1943; came to U.S., 1959; s. So Sat and Yuen Ching (Leung) L.; m. Irene Woo Lee, Apr. 21. 1971; children: Derrick Chin-Chang, Aaron Cin-Hung. AA, Los Angeles City Coll., 1965; BA, San Jose (Calif.) State U., 1968; MBA, Golden Gate U., 1971. Cert. coll. instr., Calif. Mktg. rep. IBM, San Francisco, 1973-75; chief exec. officer VIP Litho, San Francisco, 1976—; assoc. producer Gold Mountain Prodns., San Francisco, 1986. Active Cathedral Sch. for Boys Christmas Boutique, San Francisco, 1981-82, Merola Opera program, San Francisco, 1983-84, Katherine Delmar Burke Sch. Festival, San Francisco, 1985; v.p. and bd. dirs. Marin Chinese Cultural Group, Calif., 1985; mem. fin. com. Kentfield Sch. Found., Calif., 1986-88; dir. Kentfield Sch. Found., 1987-88; hon. com. mem. San Francisco Boys Chorus Bracebridge Feast, 1986, San Francisco Opera Ctr. Shanghai Fund, 1987—; adv. bd. Asian Performing Arts, San Francisco, 1988; mem. Calif. Spl. Olympic spirt Team, San Francisco, 1988. Named Man of the Yr., Univ. High Sch., San Francisco, 1987. Mem. Asian Bus. Assn., Sierra Club Found., Calif. Club. Club: City (San Francisco). Office: VIP Litho 363 6th St San Francisco CA 94104

LEE, MARGARET ANNE, psychotherapist; b. Scribner, Nebr., Nov. 23, 1930; d. William Christian and Caroline Bertha (Benner) Joens; m. Robert Kelly Lee, May 21, 1950 (div. 1971); children: Lawrence Robert, James Kelly, Daniel Richard. AA, Napa Coll., 1949; student, U. Calif., Berkeley, 1949-50; BA, Calif. State Coll., Sonoma, 1975; MSW, Calif. State U., Sacramento, 1977. Lic. clin. social worker, marriage and family counselor, Calif.; tchr. Columnist/stringer Napa (Calif.) Register, 1946-50; eligibility worker, supr. Napa County Dept. Social Services, 1968-75; instr. Napa Valley Community Coll., 1978-83; practice psychotherapy Napa, 1977—; bd. dirs. Project Access, 1978-79. Trustee Napa Valley Community Coll., 1983—, v.p. bd. trustees, 1984-85, pres. bd. trustees, 1986, clk., 1988-89; bd. dirs. Napa County Council Econ. Opportunity, 1984-85, Napa Chpt. March of Dimes, 1957-71, Mental Health Assn. of Napa County, 1983-87, mem. 1983—; vice chmn. edn. com. Calif. Community Coll. Trustees, 1987-88, chmn. edn. com., 1988-89, also legis. com. 1985-87, bd. dirs., 1989—. Recipient Fresh Start award Self mag., Mental Health Assn. Napa County, 1983-87, award Congl. Caucuson Women's Issues, 1984. Mem. Nat. Assn. Social Workers, Mental Health Assn. Napa County, Calif. Assn. Physically and Handicapped, Women's Polit. Caucus, Calif. Elected Women's Assn. Edn. and Rsch., Am. Assn. Women in Community and Jr. Colls. Democrat. Lutheran. Home: 15 Camilla Dr Napa CA 94558 Office: 1100 Trancas PO Box 2099 Napa CA 94558

LEE, MICHAEL CHARLES, landscape architect; b. Renton, Wash., July 27, 1948; s. Charles Edmund and Doris Darlene (Litch) L. BA, U. Wash., 1974. Landscape designer Robert W. Chittock, Seattle, 1973, Jongejan-Gerrard-McNeal Assocs., Bellevue, Wash., 1973-79; owner, mgr. Michael Lee Landscape Architect, Seattle, 1979—; instr. horticulture U. Wash. Exptl. Coll., Seattle, 1974-86. Author: Trees of Western Washington, 1975; garden columnist Highline Times, Burein, Wash., 1977-78; contbr. articles to profl. jours. Mem. Arboretum Found. Office: 1931 2d Ave Ste 215 Seattle WA 98101

LEE, MURLIN E., software engineer; b. Crescent, Calif., Jan. 4, 1957; s. George Lee and Ida Burl (Wilson) M.; m. Jeanine Marie Metcalfe, Apr. 13, 1985; children:, Kimberly, Kristen. BS in Bus. Adminstrn., Calif. Poly. U., Pomona, 1981; MS in Software Engring., Nat. U., San Jose, Calif., 1988. Mgr. George M. Lee Enterprises Inc., Crescent City, Calif., 1979-80, Wells Aviation, Ontario, Calif., 1980-81, Bard Software, San Jose, Calif., 1982-84; software engr. Applied Technologies, San Jose, 1984—. Republican. Home: 4081 Will Rogers Dr San Jose CA 95117 Office: Litton Applied Tech 4747 Hellyer Ave San Jose CA 95150-7012

LEE, PALI JAE (POLLY JAE STEAD LEE), librarian, writer; b. Nov. 26, 1929; d. Jonathan Everett Wheeler and Ona Katherine (Grunder) Stead; m. Richard H.W. Lee, Apr. 7, 1945 (div. 1978); children: Lani Kay Lee, Karin Lee Robinson, Ona Lee Yee, Laurie Lee Lam, Robin Louise Lee Halbert; m. John K. Willis, 1979; stepchildren: Stacie K., Paia Erin K., Johnna A. Willis Thomas. Student, U. Hawaii, 1944-46, Mich. State, 1961-64. Cataloguer and processor U.S. Army Air Force, 1945-46; with U.S. Weather Bur. Film Library, New Orleans, 1948-50, FBI, Wright-Patterson AFB, Dayton, Ohio, 1952, Ohio Wholesale Winedealers, Columbus, Ohio, 1956-58, Coll. Engring., Ohio State U., Columbus, 1959; writer tech. manual Annie Whittenmeyer Home, Davenport, Iowa, 1960; with Grand Rapids (Mich.) Pub. Library, 1961-62; dir. Waterford (Mich.) Twp. Libraries, 1962-64; acquisition librarian Pontiac (Mich.) Pub. Libraries, 1965-71, dir. East Side br., 1971-73; librarian Bishop Mus., Honolulu, 1975-83. Author: Mary Dyer, Child of Light, 1973; Giant: Pictorial History of the Human Colossus, 1973; History of the Kaneohe Bay Area, 1976; Na Po Makole--Tales of the Night Rainbow, 1981, rev. edit., 88, Mo'olelo O Na Pohu Kaina, 1983; contbr. articles to Aloha and Honolulu mags., other pubs. Chmn. Oakland County br. Multiple Sclerosis Soc., 1972-73, co-chmn. Pontiac com. of Mich. area bd., 1972-73; sec. Ohana o Kokua, 1979-83, Paia-Willis Ohana, 1982—, Ohana Kame'ekua, 1988—; bd. dirs. Detroit Mulitple Sclerosis Soc., 1971; mem. Mich. area bd. Am. Friends Service com., 1961-69. Recipient Mother of Yr. award Quad City Bus. Men, Davenport, Iowa, and Moline, Ill., 1960. Mem. Internat. Platform Assn., Soc. Friends. Office: Night Rainbow Pub PO Box 10706 Honolulu HI 96816

LEE, PAMELA ANNE, accountant; b. San Francisco, May 30, 1960; d. Larry D. and Alice Mary (Reece) L. BS in Bus., San Francisco State U., 1981. CPA, Calif. Typist, bookkeeper, tax acct. James G. Woo, CPA, San Francisco, 1979-85; tutor bus. math. and statistics San Francisco State U., 1979-80; teller to ops. officer Gibraltar Savs. and Loan, San Francisco, 1978-81; sr. acct. Price Waterhouse, San Francisco, 1981-86; corp. acctg. mgr. First Nationwide Bank, Daly City, Calif., 1986-89, v.p., 1989—; acctg. cons. New Performance Gallery, San Francisco, 1985, San Francisco Chamber Orch., 1986. Founding mem., chair bd. trustees Asian Acctg. Students Career Day, 1988—. Mem. Am. Inst. CPA's, Calif. Soc. CPA's, Nat. Assn. Female Execs., Nat. Assn. Asian-Am. CPA's (bd. dirs. 1986, news editor 1987, pres. 1988). Republican. Avocations: reading, music, travel, personal computing. Office: First Nationwide Bank 455 Hickey Blvd Daly City CA 94015

LEE, QWIHEE PARK, plant physiologist; b. Republic of Korea, Mar. 1, 1941; d. Yong-sik and Soon-duk (Paik) Park; m. Ick-whan Lee, May 20, 1965; children: Tina, Amy, Benjamin. MS, Seoul Nat. U., Republic of Korea, 1965; PhD, U. Minn., 1973. Head dept. plant physiology Korea Ginseng and Tobacco Inst., Seoul, 1980-82; instr. Sogang U., Seoul, 1981, Seoul Women's U., 1981; research assoc. U. Wash., Seattle, 1975-79, 86—. Exec. dir. Korean Community Couseling Ctr., Seattle, 1983-86. Named one of 20 Prominent Asian Women in Wash. State, Chinese Post Seattle, 1986. Mem. AAAS. Buddhist. Home: 13025 42d Ave NE Seattle WA 98125 Office: U Wash Dept Pharm SJ-30 1959 NE Pacific Seattle WA 98195

LEE, REX E., university president, lawyer; b. Los Angeles, Feb. 27, 1935; s. Rex E. and Mabel (Whiting) L.; m. Janet Griffin, July 7, 1959; children: Diana, Thomas Rex, Wendy, Michael, Stephanie, Melissa, Christie. B.A., Brigham Young U., 1960; J.D., U. Chgo., 1963. Bar: Ariz., D.C., Utah. Law clk. Justice Byron R. White, U.S. Supreme Ct., 1963-64; atty. Jennings, Strouss & Salmon, 1964-72, ptnr., 1967-72; founding dean J. Reuben Clark Law Sch., Brigham Young U., Provo, Utah, 1972-81; solicitor gen. U.S.A., Washington, 1981-85; ptnr. Sidley & Austin, Washington, from 1985; pres. Brigham Young U., Provo, Utah, 1989—; asst. U.S. atty-gen. in charge civil div. Justice Dept., Washington.; lectr. Am. Inst. Fgn. Trade, 1966-68, U. Ariz. Sch. Law, 1968-72; George Sutherland prof. law Brigham Young U., 1985—. Mem. gen. bd. Young Men's Mut. Improvement Assn., Ch. of Jesus Christ of Latter-day Saints, 1958-60; bd. dirs. Theodore Roosevelt council Boy Scouts Am., 1967-72. Mem. Am. Law Inst. Republican. Home: 2840 Iroquois Dr Provo UT 84604 Office: Sidley & Austin 1722 Eye St NW Washington DC 20006 also: Brigham Young U Office of the Pres Provo UT 84602 *

LEE, RICHARD CAVETT, innkeeper, transport and real estate executive; b. Oklahoma City, Mar. 13, 1951; s. M. Stanley and Geraldine (Cavett) L.; m. Melinda Kathryn Botkin, Dec. 30, 1971; children: Elijah, Annabelle, Tobias, Nelson. BA in Polit. Sci., U. Okla., 1974; MPA, Am. U., 1976. Budget analyst Alaska Dept. Health and Social Svcs., Juneau, 1978-81; spl. asst. to commr. Alaska Dept. Fish and Game, Juneau, 1981-84; co-owner, mgr. Silverbow Inn, Juneau, 1984—; pres. Merrilees, Oklahoma City, 1984—; ptnr. Ptarmigon Ptransport & Ptours, Juneau, 1987--. Mem. Downtown Bus. Assn., Juneau Conv. and Visitors Bur. Office: Silverbow Inn 120 2d St Juneau AK 99801

LEE, ROBERT ANDREW, librarian; b. Washington, Dec. 7, 1923; s. Frederic Edward and Edna (Stewart) L. BA in English, Oberlin Coll., 1947; MLS, U. So. Calif., 1966. Jr. cataloger Columbia U. Law Library, 1950-51; reference librarian N.Y. Daily Mirror, 1952-54; researcher for Dore Schary MGM, Culver City, Calif., 1955; with Universal City Studios, Calif., 1955—, research librarian, 1960-69, head research dept., 1969-89. Contbr. articles to profl. jours. Served with AUS, 1943-46. Decorated Bronze Star with oak leaf cluster. Mem. Acad. Motion Picture Arts and Scis. (gov. 1973-75), Acad. TV Arts and Scis., Am. Film Inst., Los Angeles Internat. Film Exposition, Spl. Libraries Assn. Home: 2212 Cahuenga Blvd Apt 104 Los Angeles CA 90068 Office: Universal City Studios 100 Universal City Pla Universal City CA 91608

LEE, ROBERT DEEMER, political science educator; b. Estherville, Ia., June 4, 1941; s. Deemer and Everyld (Anderson) L; m. Susan A. Ashley, Sept. 9, 1967; children: William, Matthew. BA, Carleton Coll., 1963; MS, Columbia U., 1965, MA, 1968, PhD, 1972. Reporter Mpls. Tribune, 1963-65; free-lance journalist Africa, 1965-66; asst. prof. polit. sci. Colo. Coll., Colorado Springs, 1971-79, assoc. prof., 1979-89, prof., 1989—. Pulitzer Traveling fellow Columbia Sch. Journalism, 1965; William P. Gray fellow Fgn. Correspondence Overseas Press Club N.Y., 1965-66. Mem. Am. Polit. Sci. Assn., Middle East Studies Assn., Middle East Inst., Phi Beta Kappa. Democrat. Home: 1425 N Tejon St Colorado Springs CO 80907 Office: Colo Coll Dept Polit Sci Colorado Springs CO 80903

LEE, ROGER BING, oncologist; b. Oakland, Calif., Mar. 10, 1941; s. Robert F. and Jean (Chin) L.; m. Sylvia Kwong, June 26, 1966. BA, Stanford U., 1962; MD, Hahnemann U., 1968. Diplomate Am. Bd. Ob-Gyn. Commd. 2d lt. U.S. Army, 1968, advanced through grades to col., 1982; asst. chief dept. ob-gyn. Silas B. Hays Army Hosp., Ft. Ord, Calif., 1972-77; chief ob-gyn clinic Walter Reed Army Med. Ctr., Washington, 1977-80; chief gynecologic oncology Madigan Army Med. Ctr., Tacoma, 1980-88; ret. 1988; dir. div. gynecologic oncology Tacoma Gen. Hosp., 1988—; asst. prof. U. Wash., Tacoma, 1988—. Author: Cervical Carcinoma in Pregnancy, 1981, Bladder Dysfunction Following Radical Hysterectomy, 1981, Malignant Melanoma in the Vagina, 1984. Cons. Tacoma Opera Guild, 1980-88; mem. Spl. Olympics, 1984-85. Decorated Legion of Merit. Fellow Am. Coll. Ob-Gyn (best sci. exhibit award 1985); mem. Am. Uro-Gynecology Soc. (bd. dirs. 1978-81), Tacoma Ob-Gyn Soc. (sec.-treas. 1986, pres. 1987), Tacoma Med. Computer Users Group (pres. 1983-85), Puget Sound Oncology Consortium, Masons, Rotary. Republican. Roman Catholic. Home: 10827 Evergreen Terr SW Tacoma WA 98498 Office: Tacoma Gen Hosp 315 South K St Tacoma WA 98405

LEE, SAMMY, I, physician, surgeon; b. Fresno, Calif., Aug. 1, 1920; s. Soonkee Rhee and Eunkee Chun; m. Rosalind M.K. Wong, Oct. 1, 1950; children: Pamela Alicia, Sammy Lee II. BA, Occidental Coll., 1943; MD, U. So. Calif., 1947, DSc (hon.), 1984. Diplomate Am. Bd. Otorhinolaryngology. Pvt. practice limited to otology Orange, Calif.; intern Orange County Hosp., Calif., 1946-47; resident in otolaryngology Letterman Army Hosp., 1949-53; presdl. rep. Melbourne Olympics, 1956, Munich Games, 1972, Seoul Olympics, 1988;coach diving U.S. Olympics, Rome, 1960, Bob Webster, Rome Olympics, 1960, Tokyo Olympics, 1964, Greg Louganis, Montreal Olympics, 1976; cons. Mission Viejo Nadadores Diving Team, Mission Viejo, Calif.; mem. President's Coun. on Phys. Fitness and Sports, 1971-80; adv. U.S. Internat. Olympic Diving Com. Author: (with other) DIVING, 1983, Not Without Honor, 1987; editor: The New Book of Knowledge, Diving, 1986. Commr. Pres. Commn. on White House Fellows, 1981-88; hon. chmn. Korean Am. Coalition, L.A., 1986-88, Korean Am. Rep., Orange County, Calif., 1986-88. Maj. U.S. Army, 1943-55, Korea; olympic flag bearer, torch runner, 1984. Named Outstanding Am. Korean Ancestry, Am. Korean Soc., 1967, Outstanding Am. Korean Ancestry, League of Korean Ams., 1986; recipient Gold and Bronze medal 3 meter springboard diving London Olympics, 1948, Gold medal Helsinki Olympics, 1952, James E. Sullivan award; named Outstanding Amateur Athlete in U.S.A. 1953. Republican. Home: 16537 Harbour Ln Huntington Beach CA 92649 Office: Sammy Lee MD Inc 1310 W Stewart Dr Ste 210 Orange CA 92668

LEE, STANLEY TAK, dentist; b. Chungshan, Canton, China, Mar. 1, 1946; s. Man Hoy and Bo Yuk (Lau) L.; m. Rita Sook Chin, July 3, 1976; children—Winnie Sita, Jennie Wanda. A.S., City Coll. San Francisco, 1971; B.S., U. Calif.-Berkeley, 1973; D.D.S., Loma Linda U., 1977. Gen. practice dentistry, San Jose, Calif., 1978—. Mem. ADA, Calif. Dental Assn., Santa Clara County Dental Soc. (dental care com. 1983-84), Am. Endodontic Soc., Chungshan Benevolence Assn., Chinese Cultural Assn., Alpha Gamma Sigma, Beta Gamma Sigma. Office: Lee Dental Ctr 1832 Tully San Jose CA 95136 also: 1095 Branham Ln San Jose CA 95122

LEE, TIMOTHY GUY, physician educator; b. Taipei, Formosa, June 16, 1939; came to U.S., 1957; s. Donald K.Y. and Launa (Wan) L.; m. Suellen Ross; children: Elsa J., Timothy R. BA, Monmouth Coll., 1961; MD, U. Ill., Chgo., 1965. Intern Ill. Masonic Hosp., Chgo., 1965-66; resident in radiology West Suburban Hosp., Oak Park, Ill., 1966-69, Wesley Meml. Hosp., Chgo., 1968, Children's Meml. Hosp., Chgo., 1969; staff radiologist 121 Evacuation Hosp., Korea, 1969-70, Madigan Gen. Hosp., Tacoma, 1970-71, West Suburban Hosp., Oak Park, 1972; from fellowship in radiology to assoc. prof. radiology U. Oreg. Med. Sch., Portland, 1972-77; assoc. prof. U. of Utah Med. Sch., Salt Lake City, 1978-81; prof. radiology, ob-gyn. U. Utah Med. Sch., Salt Lake City, 1981-85, clin. prof. radiology og-gyn, 1985—; dir. ultrasound Latter-day Saints Hosp., Salt Lake City, 1985—; cons. Nat. Insts. of Health, Bethesda, Md., 1971—. Reviewer American Journal Roentgenology, 1977—; advisor editorial bd. Journal of Clinical Ultrasound, 1978-81, Journal of Ultrasound in Medicine, 1981—; contbr. scientific papers and articles to profl. jours. Maj. U.S. Army, 1969-71, Korea. Fellow Am. Coll. Radiology; mem. AMA, Am. Inst. Ultrasound in Medicine, Am. Roentgen Ray Soc., Radiological Soc. of North Am., Utah State Med. Soc., Salt Lake County Med. Soc. Office: Univ Utah Med Ctr Salt Lake City UT 84132

LEE, TONY CHUNG, publishing company executive, management consultant; b. Taipei, Republic of China, Nov. 14, 1963; came to U.S., 1973; s. Pao-Yu (Li) Lee. AA in Childhood Edn., Bellevue Coll., 1986; BA in Communications, U. Wash., 1986; MA in Communications, Miami U., 1989. Asst. buyer Sumner's Inc., N.Y.C., 1981; restaurant mgr. Majestic Chef Inc., Jackson, Miss., 1982; acad. dir. Far Eastern Lang. Inst., Taipei, 1983; asst. mgr. Videospace Inc., Bellevue, Wash., 1984; instr. Tam-Kang U., Tamsui, Republic of China, 1986-87; v.p. mktg. Ruth Pub. Inc., Seattle, 1986—; co-exec. producer China TV Enterprises, Taipei, 1986; mgmt. cons. Crane Day Care and Kindergartens, Taipei, 1986-87; orgnl. cons. VCCP Corp., Taipei, 1986-87; bd. dirs. Thunderbird Pub. Co., Taipei. Co-author: High School Composition, 1980, Children's Talk, 1983, Daily American English, 1986. Mem. Chinese-Am. Assn. for Profls., Seattle Chinese C. of C. Office: Box 712 Mercer Island WA 98040

LEE, VIN JANG THOMAS, financial company executive, physicist; b. Honan Province, China, Feb. 14, 1937; came to U.S., 1958; s. Tsin-Yin and Hwa-Neu (Mar) L.; m. Y.T. Margaret Nee, Dec. 29, 1963; 1 child, Maxwell. Diploma in ChemE, Ordnance Engring. Coll., Taipei, Taiwan, 1958; MSChemE, U. Notre Dame, 1959; PhD, U. Mich., 1963. Assoc. prof. chem. engring. U. Mo., Columbia, 1965-74; pres. Econo Trading Co., Santa Monica, Calif., 1975-80, Cyberdyne Inc., Santa Monica, 1980—; vis. prof. catalysis and physical chemistry UCLA, 1972-73. Contbr. numerous articles to sci. jours. Mem. Sigma Xi. Lodge: Masons. Office: Cyberdyne Inc 1045 Ocean Ave Ste 2 Santa Monica CA 90403

LEE, WILLIAM MORRIS, JR., interior designer; b. Waco, Tex., Nov. 30, 1943; s. William Morris Lee and Lady Ann (Mayfield) Thomason; m. Susan Carroll, Jan. 25, 1964 (div. 1980); children: William III, Robert, Peter; m. Dorothy Lou Ziemke, Feb. 27, 1981; children: Eric, John. BS, Okla. City U., 1967. Interior designer Nelson's Bartlesville (Okla.) Furniture, 1968-70, Lee & Statham Co., Bartlesville, 1970-72, Kashian Bros. Interiors, Wilmette, Ill., 1972-74, Phyllis Morris Originals, Chgo., 1974-75; & E.W. Rost & Son, Janesville, Wis., 1975-80, owner, interior designer, 1980-85; owner, interior designer Collectibles Outlet, San Jose, Calif., 1986—; mem. Edn. Adv. Bd. U. Wis., Madison, 1982-85. Pres. Blackhawk Epilepsy Ctr., Janesville, 1978-85. Recognized for Haye residence, House Beautiful Bldg. Guide, 1980, Dunn Residence, Edgerton Chronicle, 1981, Kochell residence, Janesville Gazette, 1984. Mem. Janesville C. of C. (bd. dirs. 1980-83, treas. 1981, v.p. 1982), Am. Soc. Interior Design (bd. dirs. 1976-85, treas. 1978-79, admissions chmn. 1979-81). Lodge: Masons. Office: Collectibles Outlet 1899 W San Carlos San Jose CA 95128

LEE, YONG TSUN, lawyer; b. Shanghai, China, June 12, 1952; s. Kwong Cheong and Ching So (Lee) L.; came to U.S., 1970, naturalized, 1973; student Orange Coast Coll., 1971-72, So. Calif. Coll., 1970-71; J.D. and B.S. in Law, Am. Coll. Law, 1978; m. Josephine Suen; children—Mia, Erin, Jennifer, Christin, Candice, Robin. Lab. instr. math. Orange Coast Coll., Costa Mesa, Calif., 1971; mgr. Shanghai Pine Garden, Balboa Island, 1973-78; admitted to Calif. bar, 1978; practice law, Costa Mesa, 1979—. Mem. Am. Bar Assn., Orange County Bar Assn. Democrat. Roman Catholic. Office: 628 W 19 St Costa Mesa CA 92627

LEE, YUAN T(SEH), chemistry educator; b. Hsinchu, Taiwan, China, Nov. 29, 1936; came to U.S., 1962, naturalized, 1974; s. Tsefan and Pei (Tasi) L.;

m. Bernice Wu, June 28, 1963; children: Ted, Sidney, Charlotte. BS, Nat. Taiwan U., 1959; MS, Nat. Tsinghua U., Taiwan, 1961; PhD, U. Calif., Berkeley, 1965. From asst. prof. to prof. chemistry U. Chgo., 1968-74; prof. U. Calif., Berkeley, 1974—, also prin. investigator Lawrence Berkeley Lab. Contbr. numerous articles on chem. physics to profl. jours. Recipient Nobel Prize in Chemistry, 1986, Ernest O. Lawrence award Dept. Energy, 1981, Nat. Medal of Sci., 1986, Peter Debye award for Phys. Chemistry, 1986; fellow Alfred P. Sloan, 1969-71, John Simon Guggenheim, 1976-77; Camille and Henry Dreyfus Found. Tchr. scholar, 1971-74. Fellow Am. Phys. Soc.; mem. Am. Acad. Arts and Scis., Am. Chem. Soc., AAAS, Nat. Acad. Scis. Office: U Calif Dept Chemistry Berkeley CA 94720

LEEB, CHARLES SAMUEL, clinical psychologist; b. San Francisco, July 18, 1945; s. Sidney Herbert and Dorothy Barbara (Fishstrom) L.; m. Storme Lynn Gilkey, Apr. 28, 1984; 1 child, Morgan Evan. BA in Psychology, U. Calif.-Davis, 1967; M.S. in Counseling and Guidance, San Diego State U., 1970; Ph.D. in Edn. and Psychology, Claremont Grad. Sch., 1973. Counselor Mayor's Com. on Unemployment, San Diego, 1969-70, VA, San Diego State Coll., 1969-70, Claremont Coll. Counseling Ctr., 1971-72; assoc. So. Regional Dir. Mental Retardation Ctr., Las Vegas, Nev., 1976-79; pvt. practice, Las Vegas, 1978-79; dir. biofeedback and athletics Menninger Found., Topeka, 1979-82, dir. children's div. biofeedback and psychophysiology ctr. The Menninger Found., 1979-82; dir. of psychol. services Horizon Hosp., 1986-88; chief psychologist Raleigh Hills Hosp., San Gabriel, Calif., 1982-83; pvt. practice, Claremont, Calif., 1982—; lectr. in field. Contbr. articles to profl. jours. Mem. Biofeedback Soc. Am., Nev. Psychol. Assn. Office: 232 Harrison PO Box 1084 Claremont CA 91711

LEECH, JOHN WILLIAM, data processing executive; b. Tacoma, Dec. 16, 1957; s. Jack Warren and Doris Donna (Ristuct) L.; m. Brenda K. Grosser. BS magna cum laude, U.S. Air Force Acad., 1980; MS summa cum laude, U. So. Calif., 1983, U. Wash., 1986. Commd. 2d lt. USAF, 1980, advanced through grades to capt., 1984, systems analyst space div., 1980-83; infosystems mgr. fgn. tech. div. Wright-Patterson AFB USAF, Dayton, Ohio, 1985-87; acctg. and fin. officer McChord AFB USAF, Tacoma, 1987-88; comptroller, comdr. McChord AFB USAF, 1988-89; dir. info. systems Xytec Inc, Tacoma, 1989—; computer cons. Mem. Omega Row Ops, Inst. Mgmt. Sci., Assn. Mil. Comptrollers. Home: 1213 Starling St Steilacoom WA 98388 Office: Xytec Inc 9350 47th St SW Tacoma WA 98499

LEECING, WALDEN ALBERT, educator; b. Glendale, Calif., Sept. 6, 1932; s. Horace Walden and Leona Belle (Dudek) L.; m. Elizabeth Joan Miller, Aug. 16, 1958; children: Jeffrey Scott, Brian Walden. BA, U. Redlands, 1954; MA, Stanford U., 1956, postgrad., 1973—. Tchr. El Rancho High Sch., Whittier, Calif., 1957-59, Santa Ana (Calif.) High Sch., 1959-66; from instr. to assoc. prof. lang. arts Chabot Coll., Hayward, Calif., 1967-86, prof., 1986—; chmn. speech dept. Author: The Santa Ana Community Players: 1920-27, 1956, (with James Armstrong) The Curious Eye, 1970, Viva la Causa! A Historiographic Survey of Chicano Studies Programs at Five Bay Area Colleges and Universities. V.p. Santa Ana Community Players, 1964-66; asst. organist Danville Congl. Ch., 1968—. Mem. Nat. Council English Tchrs., AAUP, No. Calif. Forensics Assn., Am. Guild Organists, Stanford Alumni Assn. (life). KRON-NBC Viewer Adv. Council. Republican. Congregationalist. Home: 697 Paradise Valley Ct S Crow Canyon Country Club Danville CA 94526 Office: Chabot Coll 25555 Hesperian Blvd Hayward CA 94545

LEEDS, SANFORD EDGAR, surgeon; b. San Francisco, Nov. 14, 1909; s. Louis and Amelia (Snoek) Levy; m. Syra Florence Nahman, Apr. 9, 1941. AB, U. Calif., Berkeley, 1931; MD, U. Calif., San Francisco, 1936. Rsch. assoc. Vanderbilt Med. Sch., Nashville, 1936-38; resident surgeon U. Calif. Med. Sch., San Francisco, 1938-41; pvt. practice San Francisco, 1946-80; dir. exptl. surgery lab. Mt. Zion Hosp., San Francisco, 1950—. Contbr. articles to profl. jours. Col. M.C., U.S. Army, 1936-39. NIH rsch. grantee, 1936-38. Fellow ACS; mem. Am. Thoracic Surg. Assn., Pacific Coast Surg. Assn., San Francisco Med. Soc., San Francisco Surg. Soc. (v.p. 1960), Bay Area History of Medicine Club (pres. 1968), Internat. Soc. Lymphology (coun. 1985), Lake Merced Golf and Country Club, Civil War Roundtable. Home: 3440 Washington St San Francisco CA 94118

LEEDS-HORWITZ, SUSAN BETH, speech-language pathology educator; b. Los Angeles, Mar. 14, 1950; d. Henry Herbert and Lee (Weiss) Leeds; m. Stanley Martin Horwitz, Nov. 28, 1975; 1 child, Brian David. BA, Calif. State U., Northridge, 1971; MEd, U. S.C., 1973; adminstrv. credential, U. LaVerne, 1984. Itinerant speech pathologist Los Angeles City Schs., 1973-74; severe lang. disorders tchr. Los Angeles County Bd. Edn., Downey, Calif., 1974-88; tchr. on spl. assignment Santa Clarita Valley Spl. Edn. Local Plan Area, Newhall, Calif., 1986-88; coord. spl. projects and migrant edn. Castaic (Calif.) Union Sch. Dist., 1988—. Active Santa Clarita Valley Spl. Edn. PTA, Newhall, 1984—. Mem. Am. Speech-Lang.-Hearing Assn. (cert.), Down Syndrome Congress, Assn. Calif. Sch. Adminstrs., San Fernando Valley Panhellenic Assn. (rep. 1976—), Delta Kappa Gamma, Alpha Xi Delta (Edna Epperson Brinkman award 1985), Phi Delta Kappa. Office: Castaic Union Sch Dist 31616 N Ridge Rt Rd Castaic CA 91384

LEE-GULLEY, PATRICIA AMY, production and inventory control executive; b. Pasadena, Calif., Jan. 25, 1953; d. Seward and Simone (Yoh) Lee; m. Kyle Walter Gulley, Dec. 2, 1985; 1 child, Kyle William. BA in Communications and Social Sci. magna cum laude, U. So. Calif., 1974; MBA, East Carolina U., 1981; JD, Western State U., Fullerton, Calif., 1988. Cert. in prodn. and inventory mgmt. With publs. dept. Airstream, Cerritos, Calif., 1975-80; reporter Jacksonville (N.C.) Daily News, 1980; supr. prodn. inventory control Digitran, Pasadena, 1981-83; sr. planner Endevco, San Juan Capistrano, Calif., 1983-84; prodn. and inventory control mgr. Distributed Logic, Anaheim, Calif., 1984—; teaching asst. legal analysis Western State U., Fullerton, 1987-88, acad. support Western State U., Fullerton, 1988—. Contbr. articles to profl. jours. and newspapers. Recipient J. Brower Achievement award Western State U., 1988, Am. Jurisprudence award Western State U. and Lawyers Co-operation, 1986-87. Mem. Am. Production and Inventory Control Soc. (seminar chmn. 1985, denl. curriculum chmn., com. mem. 1988, Cert. of Appreciaton 1985-88), Asian Am. Law Students Assn. (pres. 1987-88), Beta Gamma Sigma. Republican. Roman Catholic.

LEEMING, FRANK, JR., newspaper editor, publisher; b. Oklahoma City, Aug. 10, 1938; s. Frank and Louise (Lindner) L.; m. Sally Schuske, 1960 (div. 1968); children: Patricia, Frank III; m. Joyce Barnett, Sept. 20, 1973; children: Dusty, Scott, Lewis. B in Bus. and Pub. Adminstrn., U. Mo., 1960. Reporter St. Louis Dispatch, 1960-69; corr. Life Mag., St. Louis, 1967-69; editor Lindsay-Schaub Newspapers, Decatur, Ill., 1969-70; bus. editor The Phila. Inquirer, 1970-71, city editor, 1972, asst. to exec. editor, 1973-75, circulation sales and mktg. mgr., 1976-78; circulation sales and mktg. mgr. Daily News, Phila., 1976-78; pub. Kinsport (Tenn.) Times-News, 1978-83; editor, pub. Jour. of San Juan Islands, Friday Harbor, Wash., 1983—. Contbr. editorials, news series and columns. Bd. dirs. Econ. Devel. Coun. San Juan County, Wash., 1986-89. Mem. Lions. Presbyterian. Home: 3031 Hasley Rd Friday Harbor WA 98250 Office: Leeming Communications Co PO Box 519 301 Tucker Ave Friday Harbor WA 98250

LEEPER, RAMON JOE, physicist; b. Princeton, Mo., Apr. 1, 1948; s. Joe Edd and Jeanne (Gaul) L.; m. Sumiko Yasuda, Dec. 21, 1976; 1 son, Joe Eric. BS, MIT, 1970; PhD, Iowa State U., 1975. Research assoc. Ames Lab., U.S. Dept. Energy, Iowa, 1975-76; mem. tech. staff Sandia Nat. Labs., Albuquerque, 1976-86, supr. diagnostics div., 1986—; guest scientist Argonne Nat. Lab., Ill., 1971-76; invited lectr. NATO Advanced Study Inst., Italy, summer 1983. Contbr. articles to profl. jours., patentee in field. Recipient Outstanding Teaching award Iowa State U., 1973; NDEA fellow, 1971-73. Mem. Am. Phys. Soc., IEEE (session chmn. 1984), Sigma Xi. Republican. Home: 6905 Rosewood Rd NE Albuquerque NM 87111 Office: Sandia Nat Labs Diagnostics Div 1234 Albuquerque NM 87185

LEETH, DAN STEVEN, banker, educator; b. Waverly, Iowa, Jan. 11, 1949; s. Daryl Eugene and Betty Louise (Stevenson) L.; m. Beverly Dianne Wilson, Apr. 21, 1968 (div. 1972); 1 child, Steven Spencer; m. Dianne Ruth Giles, Aug. 28, 1981. BS, U. Ariz., 1971; basic cert., Am. Inst. Banking, Washington, 1973. Credit supr. Montgomery Ward Co., Tucson, 1969-72; ops. officer 1st Nat. Bank Ariz., Tucson, 1972-75; asst. v.p. Nev. Nat. Bank, Reno, 1975-83; v.p., cashier Am. Nat. Bank Aurora (Colo.), 1983-85, Republic Nat. Bank Englewood (Colo.), 1985—; instr. Am. Inst. Banking, Reno, 1976-83, Denver, 1985—. Contbr. articles to outdoor mags. Named Mem. of Yr., Ad Lib Toastmasters, Reno, 1981. Mem. Am. Inst. Banking (bd. govs. 1981-83 Reno chpt., chmn. high attitude mountaineering sect.), Colo. Mountain Club (leader 1985—, Chmn.'s Spl. award 1988), Sierra Club (San Francisco (outdoor guide 1987—). Home: PO Box 440289 Aurora CO 80044 Office: Republic Nat Bank Englewood PO Box 1418 Englewood CO 80150

LEEWARD, LINDA, dentist; b. Salt Lake City, June 24, 1946; d. Harold Baxter and Yvonne (Allen) Williams; adopted d. George Ferwerda; m. Stephen Lory, Dec. 3, 1983. BS, U. Calif., Davis, 1968, MA, 1969; DMD, Tufts U., 1983. Tchr. pub. schs. Sacramento, 1969; rsch. assoc. U. Calif., Davis, 1969-79; pvt. practice Boston, 1983--; dental cons. Lake Wash. Vo-Tech. Inst., Kirkland, 1986-88. NDEA scholar, 1966-68. Mem. Wash. Assn. Women (sec. 1986-88), Totem Lake Study (pres. 1988-). Democrat.

LEFEBVRE, JAMES KENNETH, professional baseball manager; b. Inglewood, Calif., Jan. 7, 1943. Player minor league baseball teams, Reno, 1962, Salem, 1963, Spokane, 196, with Los Angeles Dodgers, Nat. League, 1965-72, player with Lotte Orions, Japanese Baseball League, 1973-76, coach, 1977, coach, Los Angeles Dodgers, 1978-79, coach, San Francisco Giants, 1980, 82, dir. player devel., 1983, 84, mgr., Phoenix minor league team, 1985, 86, coach, Oakland Athletics, Am. League, 1987, 88, mgr., Seattle Mariners, Am. League, 1988—; played in World Series, 1965, 66, All-Star Game, 1966. Named Nat. League Rookie of the Yr., Baseball Writers' Assn. Am., 1965, Pacific Coast League Mgr. of the Yr., 1985, 86. Office: care Seattle Mariners PO Box 4100 Seattle WA 98104 *

LEFEVRE, GREG (LOUIS), news correspondent; b. Los Angeles, Jan. 28, 1947; s. Robert Bazille and Anna Marie (Violé) L.; m. Mary Deborah Bottoms, July 10, 1971. AA, Valley Coll., 1970; BS, San Diego State U., 1972, postgrad. Asst. news dir. Sta. KDEO, San Diego, 1971-73; reporter Sta. KFMB-TV, San Diego, 1973-76; sr. reporter Sta. KDFW-TV, Dallas, 1976-81; news dir. Sta. KSEE-TV, Fresno, Calif., 1981-83; corr. Cable News Network, San Francisco, 1983—. Mem. AP Broadcasters (bd. dirs. 1981—), Soc. Profl. Journalists (pres. 1979-81), Radio and TV News Dirs. Assn. (bd. dirs. 1988—). Club: Dallas Press (v.p. 1978-81). Office: Cable News Network 50 California St Ste 835 San Francisco CA 94111

LEFEVRE, SUSAN MARGARET, architect; b. Rochester, N.Y., Sept. 27, 1956; d. Eugene DeDaugherty and Barbara Joan (Calkins) LeF. BS in Architecture, Calif. Poly. State U., 1979. Registered architect, Calif. Designer Marshall-McDaniel, Los Altos, Calif., 1979-81; designer, job capt. Griffin-Joyce Assocs., San Jose, Calif., 1981-83; mgr. project Design & Engring. Systems, Fremont, Calif., 1983-85; architect Ehrlich-Rominger Inc., Los Altos, 1985—. Mem. Nat. Soc. Hist. Preservation, Sierra Club (Loma Prieta chpt.). Democrat. Methodist. Office: Ehrlich Rominger 4800 El Camino Real Los Altos CA 94022

LEFFEL, KAY JEANNE, legal administrator; b. Spokane, Wash., Oct. 15, 1943; d. Arnold Maynard and Mary Ellen (Mansfield) Pearson; m. Harold Patrick Leffel, Mar. 20, 1961; children: Christopher A., Jon Patrick, Scott M. BA, Evergreen State Coll., 1985. Service rep. Pacific Northwest Bell, Spokane, 1963-66; instrl. asst. Vancouver (Wash.) Sch. Dist., 1974-76; legal adminstr. Landerholm, Memovich, Lansverk & Whitesides, Vancouver, 1977-86, Underwood, Campbell, Brock & Cerutti, Spokane, 1986—. Author newletter for Wash. State Community Colleges Assn. Paralegal Rev., 1987. Sec., treas. local Boy Scouts Am., Spokane, 1968-71; bd. dirs. 4th of July celebration, VAncouver, 1981-83; mem. adv. bd. Western Bus. Colls., Portland, Oreg., 1979-80, Clark Community Coll., Vancouver, 1983-86. Named Woman of Yr. Am. Bus. Women's Assn., Vancouver, 1981. Mem. ABA, Assn. Legal Adminstrs. (edn. chmn. Oreg. Legal Mgrs. chpt., 1981, publicity chmn. Oreg. Legal Mgrs. chpt. 1983-84, v.p. 1987, pres. 1988— Inland Empire chpt.). Presbyterian. Home: 1245 E Crystal Bay Rd Post Falls ID 83854 Office: Underwood Campbell Brock & Cerutti 1100 Seafirst Financial Ctr Spokane WA 99201

LEFOND, ANNE MAY, real estate broker; b. Ashland, Wis., Apr. 26, 1917; d. Charles and Anna (Erickson) Newman; BA cum laude, Northland Coll., Ashland, 1939; MLS, U. Wis., 1940; m. Stanley J. Lefond, Dec. 26, 1946 (dec. Nov. 1985); children: Dennis C., Robert E.; m. George V. VonVihl, 1986. Reference librarian Colgate U., Hamilton, N.Y., 1945-46, U. Mich., Ann Arbor, 1949-52; librarian Euclid (Ohio) Public Schs., 1953-66; sales assoc. Lloyd C. Helgager Co., Woodland Hills, Calif., 1967-70; broker New Eng. Realty Co., Westport, Conn., 1970-72; broker-mgr. Crown Realty Co., Evergreen, Colo., 1972-75; broker-assoc. Junction Realty Co., Evergreen, 1976-84, Remax-Evergreen, 1984—; v.p. Indsl. Minerals, Inc., Evergreen, 1976-85. Mem. Evergreen Bd. Realtors (dir.), Colo. Assn. Realtors, Nat. Assn. Real Estate Brokers, Nat. Inst. Real Estate Brokers. C. of C., Hiwan Country Club, Swedish Club of Denver. Lutheran. Home: 29983 Canterbury Circle Evergreen CO 80439

LEFOR, NICOLETTE ANN, nurse; b. Dickinson, N.D., Mar. 16, 1954; d. Nick and Elizabeth (Willer) Biel; m. Randall Lefor, Apr. 21, 1973 (div. 1978); children: Wade, Danielle. AA in Nursing, Dickinson State Coll., 1976; BS, Ariz. State U., 1985, postgrad., 1985--. RN, Ariz., Calif. Staff RN Rapid City (S.D.) Regional Hosp., 1976-77; clin. II RN Desert Samaritan Hosp., Mesa, Ariz., 1977--; substitute instr. clin. nursing Mesa Community Coll., 1985--; RN Norrell Home Health Care, Tempe, 1985--; cons. health Health Advancement Service, Tempe, 1987; lectr. health promotion various seminars and orgns., Ariz., 1987--. Mem. Ariz. Pub. Health Assn., Ariz. Assn. Occupational Health Nurses, Ariz. Nurses' Assn. (bd. dirs. local dist. 1986--, chairperson legis. com. 1986--, nursing scholarships 1985, 88), Sigma Theta Tau, Profl. Bus. Women's Orgn. Home: 2426 W Knowles Mesa AZ 85202

LEGARE, HENRI FRANCIS, archbishop; b. Willow-Bunch, Sask., Can., Feb. 20, 1918; s. Phillippe and Amanda (Douville) L. B.A., U. Ottawa, 1940; theol. student, Lebret, Sask., 1940-44; M.A., Laval U., 1946; Dr. Social Sci., Cath. U. Lille, France, 1950; LL.D. (hon.), Carleton U., Ottawa, 1959, Windsor (Ont.) U., 1960, Queens U., Kingston, Ont., 1961, U. Sask., 1963, Waterloo (Ont.) Luth. U., 1965, U. Ottawa, Can., 1984; Doctor of Univ., U. of Ottawa. Ordained priest Roman Cath. Ch., 1943; prof. sociology Laval U., 1947, U. Ottawa, 1951; exec. dir. Cath. Hosp. Assn. Can., 1952-57; dean faculty social scis. U. Ottawa, 1954-58, pres., 1958-64; provincial Oblate Fathers, Winnipeg, Man., 1966-67; bishop of Labrador, 1967-72; archbishop Grouard-McLennan, Alta., 1972—. Contbr. articles to profl. jours. Chmn. Canadian Univs. Found., 1960- 62. Decorated grand cross merit Order Malta, 1964; order merit French Lang. Assn. Ont., 1965. Mem. Assn. Canadian Univs. (pres. 1960-62), Can. Conf. Cath. Bishops (pres. 1981-83), Internat. Assn. Polit. Sci. Address: Archbishop's House, CP 388, McLennan, AB Canada T0H 2L0

LEGGE, CHARLES ALEXANDER, judge; b. San Francisco, Aug. 24, 1930; s. Roy Alexander and Wilda (Rampton) L.; m. Janice Meredith Sleeper, June 27, 1952; children: Jeffrey, Nancy, Laura. AB with distinction, Stanford U., 1952, JD, 1954. Bar: Calif. 1955. Assoc. Bronson, Bronson & McKinnin, San Francisco, 1956-64, ptnr., 1964-84, chmn., 1978-84; judge U.S. Dist. Ct. (no. dist.) Calif., San Francisco, 1984—. Served with U.S. Army, 1954-56. Fellow Am. Coll. Trial Lawyers; mem. Calif. Bar Assn. (past chmn. adminstrn. justice com.). Republican. Clubs: Bohemian, World Trade (San Francisco); Orinda (Calif.) Country. Office: US Dist Ct 450 Golden Gate Ave PO Box 36060 San Francisco CA 94102

LEGRAND, SHAWN PIERRE, computer systems programmer; b. San Diego, Nov. 27, 1960; s. Roger and Violet Louise (Howe) L. Grad. high sch., El Cajon, Calif. Cert. computer programmer. Computer operator Grossmont CCD, El Cajon, 1978-79; computer systems programmer ICW, San Diego, 1979—. Recipient Math. Achievement award Bank of Am., 1978. Mem. IEEE, Assn. Computing Machinery. Republican. Office: ICW 10140 Campus Point Dr San Diego CA 92121

LEGRANT, RANDY LEO, institute executive; b. Enid, Okla., Aug. 12, 1949; s. Arlie Leo and Norma Jean (McKee) LeG.; m. Deborah Ann Smith, May 29, 1975; children: Christopher James, Alexandra Elizabeth. B.S., Phillips U., 1971. Chmn. lang. arts dept. Ottawa Pub. Schs., Kans., 1976-79; mgr. sales devel. Am. Inst. Fgn. Study, Greenwich, Conn., 1979-80, v.p., dir. admissions, 1980-85, v.p., dir. program devel., 1985—, liaison officer, London, 1985; dean summer sch. Richmond Coll., Eng., 1982-85; prin. Desert Bloom Publs., Woodland Park, Colo.; founder Traveler's Info. Service. editor electronic newsletter Ednl. Travel Connection, 1985; asst. editor InstiToots, 1980. Contbr. articles to profl. jours. Chief negotiator Ottawa Ednl. Assn., Kans., 1979; head swim program Ottawa Recreational Commn., 1977-79; chmn. polit. action com. Goodland Ednl. Assn., Kans., 1976. Named Dir. of Admissions of Yr., Ambassador Mag., 1982; recipient Silver Cup, Am. Inst. Fgn. Study, 1984. Mem. Nat. Assn. Fgn. Student Advisors. Republican. Roman Catholic. Avocations: computers; boating; photography. Home: 2756 Woody Creek Ct PO Box 6309 Woodland Park CO 80866

LEHMAN, RICHARD HENRY, congressman; b. Sanger, Calif., July 20, 1948; m. Patricia Ann Kandarian, Aug. 9, 1971. AA, Fresno City Coll., 1968; BA, U. Calif., Santa Cruz, 1971. Adminstrv. aide to Calif. State Assemblyman George N. Zenovich, Sacramento, 1969-76; mem. 98th-101st Congresses from 18th Dist. Calif., 1983—; regional whip 99th and 100th Congresses; mem. Calif. State Assembly, 1976-82, asst. majority leader, 1980-82. With Calif. NG, 1970-76. Democrat. Office: US Ho of Reps 1319 Longworth House Office Bldg Washington DC 20515

LEHMAN, SCOTT NELSON, sales company executive; b. Ripon, Wis., Apr. 12, 1961; s. Arland Nelson and Mabel Irene (Sell) L. BS in Mktg., U. Wis., La Crosse, 1984. Office mgr. Am. Millionaires, San Diego, 1984-85; salesman Internat. Male, San Diego, 1985-87; sales rep. Gordon & Smith, San Diego, 1987-88; v.p. West Coast Sales Orgn., San Diego, 1988—. Mem. Action Sports Retailers Assn. Home: 12946 Carmel Creek Rd #99 San Diego CA 92130 Office: 7950 Silverton Ave Ste 211 San Diego CA 92126

LEHMANN, HELMUTH AUGUST, human resource manager, consultant; b. Teaneck, N.J., Aug. 14, 1956; s. Horst August and Lore (Luikart) L.; m. Gretchen Elizabeth Lehmann; 1 child, Erin Margaret. BA in Govt., U. Tex., 1983, MA in Pub. Adminstrn., 1985. Mgr. office svcs. Farmers Ins. Group, Austin, Tex., 1983-86; tng. specialist Safeco Corp., Seattle, 1986-87; human resource specialist Dept. Labor and Industry State of Wash., Olympia, 1987, computer cons. Dept. Info. Svcs.; human resource specialist Dept. Social and Health Svcs. State of Wash., Tacoma; pres. Newtechs Cons. Co., 1988—; tng. cons. State Bd. Community Colls., Olympia, Puget Sound Devel Coun., Seattle, 1988—. Vol. Disabled Student Svcs. U. Tex., Austin, 1983-84, counselor Juvenile Ct. Conf. com. King County Superior Ct., 1986—; bd. dirs. Capital Metro Transp., Austin, 1984-86. Mem. Am. Soc. Tng. and Devel., Orgn. Devel. Network. Office: Newtechs Tng Co 30839 49th Ct S Auburn WA 98001

LEHR, JAMES JEROME, bank executive, university public board member; b. Witcha, Kans., Apr. 1, 1931; s. Anton and Vertress (Tucker) L.; m. Rose Marie Shenuk, Aug. 22, 1954; children: Kim Marie, Kathleen Ann, Kevin Anthony, Karen Sue. AA, U. Calif. at Los Angeles, 1955, AB, 1956, MS, 1957. Prodn. news rep. NBC, Burbank, Calif., 1958-61; asst. cashier Union Bank, Los Angeles, Pasadena, Calif., 1962-68; v.p. Bank Calif., Beverly Hills, Calif., 1968-76; pres. Pacific Funding Group, Beverly Hills, 1976-84; v.p. Guardian Bank, Los Angeles, 1984—. Contbr. various articles to Los Angeles Times, 1956, Los Angeles Herald-Examiner, 1957; writer, editor: NBC polit. news., 1960. Mem. San Gabriel Rep. Club, Calif., 1986—. Served to 1st Lt. U.S. Army, 1951-54, Korea. Decorate Bronze Star; recipient cert. commendation Occidential Coll., Los Angeles, 1987; named Calif. State U. Grad. Research Competition juror San Jose State U., 1988. Mem. Am. Bankers Assn., Independent Bankers Assn., Calif. State U. (Univ. Devel. Bd., 1987—), Calif. State U. (The Inter-Colligiate Athletic Bd., 1987—). Republican. Roman Catholic. Club: Los Angeles Stock Exchange. Lodge: Lions. Office: Guardian Bank 800 S Figueroe Los Angeles CA 90017

LEHRHOFF, IRWIN, psychologist; b. Newark, June 4, 1929; s. Carl and Esther (Israelow) L.; m. Barbara Laufer, June 6, 1952 (div. July 1988); children: Terri, Debra, Howard, Steven. MA in Psychology, U. So. Calif., PhD, 1954. Cert. marriage, family and child counselor, Calif., psychologist, speech pathologist. Dir. Dept. Communicative Disorders Childrens Hosp., Los Angeles, 1950-55, Dept. Communicative Disorders Harbor Gen. Hosp., Torrance, Calif., 1955-58; pvt. practice psychology and speech and lang. pathology Irwin Lehrhoff and Assocs., Inc., 1954-86. Contbr. articles to profl. jours. Advisory bd. Am. Acad. Child Psychiatry; community advisory com. Internat. Health Resources; exec. vice chmn. Thailians Community Mental Health Ctr. Mem. Am. Psychol. Assn., Calif. Psychol. Assn., Los Angeles County Psychol. Assn., Internat. Soc. Mental Health, Am. Assn. Marriage and Family Counselors, Am. Orthopsychiatric Assn., Assn. for Advancement Science, N.Y. Acad. Science, Am. Speech-Lang.-Hearing Assn., Calif. Speech and Hearing Assn., Calif. Speech Pathologists and Audiologists in Pvt. Practice (dir. and pres. 1973-77), Am. Acad. Pvt. Practice in Speech Pathology and Audiology (dir. and nat. pres. 1974-78). Office: Irwin Lehroff & Assocs 11755 Wilshire Blvd #1830 Los Angeles CA 90025

LEIBERT, RICHARD WILLIAM, producer of public spectacles; b. N.Y.C., Nov. 11, 1948; s. Richard William and Rosemarie Martha (Bruns) L. BS, Boston U., 1966-70; student, Northwestern U., 1971. Producer Sta. WBZ AM/FM, Boston, 1968-70; prodn. dir. Sta. WMMR-FM, Phila., 1970; exec. producer Sta. WIND-AM, Chgo., 1970-72; program dir. Sta. KGB AM-FM, San Diego, 1972-80; pres. Events Mktg., Inc., L.A., 1980—88, 1988—; dir. Nat. Fireworks Ensemble, Los Angeles, Calif., 1985—. Creator (mascot, publicity stunts) Sta. KGB Chicken, 1974; creator, producer (radio fireworks show) Sta. KGB Sky Show, 1976; writer, producer (network radio show) New Music News, 1983; creator, dir. (touring co.) Nat. Fireworks Ensemble, 1985. Recipient Emmy award, 1978; named Program Dir. of Yr. Billboard Mag., 1976, Radio Program of Yr. Billboard Mag., 1976. Office: Events Mktg Inc PO Box 65694 Los Angeles CA 90065

LEIBSON, NORMAN HOWARD, information technology executive; b. Pitts., Mar. 20, 1945; s. Philip Adam and Freda (Bronstein) L.; m. Jeri Elyse Amber, Dec. 24, 1969; children: Daniel, Katherine. BS, Calif. State U., Northridge, 1968, MS, 1969. 1st v.p. Security Pacific Nat. Bank, Los Angeles, 1969-83; v.p. Carter Hawley Hale Stores, Inc., Los Angeles, 1983—; bd. dirs. Assn. for Retail Mgmt. Info. Systems, Los Angeles, 1985—; mem. adv. com. Golden Gate U., San Francisco, 1982—. Mem. Mktg. Com. The Orange County United Way. Served with USAR, 1969. Republican. Jewish. Home: 22302 Pine Glen Mission Viejo CA 92692 Office: Carter Hawley Hale Stores Inc 1600 N Kraemer Anaheim CA 92806

LEIFER, LARRY JOHN, mechanical engineering design educator, health science facility administrator; b. Ely, Nev., July 2, 1940; s. Lewis Carl and Nelle Nadine (Evasovic) L.; m. Aimee Dorr, Sept. 20, 1963 (div. Oct. 1973); 1 child, Simeon Kel; m. Ines Jenal, Aug. 26, 1976; children: Tjarko Zuri, Sascha Bjorn, Kalani Kai. BS, Stanford U., 1962, MS, 1963, PhD, 1969. Staff scientist, human machine integration NASA Ames Research Ctr., Calif., 1969-73; scientist, man-vehicle lab MIT, Cambridge, 1972-73; asst. prof. Inst. Biomed. Systems Analysis Swiss Fed. Inst. Tech., Zurich, Switzerland, 1973-76, prof., 1976—; assoc. prof. mech. engring. Stanford (Calif.) U., 1978—; dir. rehab. research and devel. ctr. VA Med. Ctr., Palo Alto, Calif., 1978—; dir. Smart Product Design Lab., Stanford U., 1977—, Ctr. for Design Research, Stanford U., 1984—; prof. mech. engring. Stanford (Calif.) U., 1988—. Editor: Distribute Nerve Conduction Velocity, 1981; contbr. articles to profl. jours. NASA, VA, NSF, IBM grantee. Mem. AAAS, ASME, IEEE, Biomed. Engring. Soc., Assn. Computer Machinery, Artificial Intelligence Soc., Rehab. Engring. Soc. N.Am. Office: Stanford U Dept Mech Engring Stanford CA 94305

LEIGHNINGER, DAVID SCOTT, cardiovascular surgeon; b. Youngstown, Ohio, Jan. 16, 1920; s. Jesse Harrison and Marjorie (Lightner) L.; m. Margaret Jane Malony, May 24, 1942; children: David Allan, Jenny. BA, Oberlin Coll., 1942; MD, Case Western Res. U., 1945. Intern Univ. Hosps. of Cleve., 1945-46, resident, 1949-51, asst. surgeon, 1951-68; rsch. fellow in cardiovascular surgery rsch. lab. Case Western Res. U. Sch. Medicine, Cleve., 1948-49, 51-55, 57-67, instr. surgery, 1951-55, sr. instr., 1957-64, asst. prof., 1964-68, asst. clin. prof., 1968-70; resident Cin. Gen. Hosp., 1955-57; practice medicine specializing in cardiovascular surgery, Cleve., 1957-70; pvt. practice medicine specializing in cardiovascular and gen. surgery Edgewater Hosp., Chgo., 1970-82, staff surgeon, also dir. emergency surg. services, 1970-82; staff surgeon, also dir. emergency surg. svcs. Mazel Med. Ctr., Chgo., 1970-82; emergency physician Miner's Hosp., Raton, N.Mex., 1982-83, 84-85, No. Colfax County Hosp., Raton, 1983-84, Mt. San Rafael Hosp., Trinidad, Colo., 1984-85; assoc., courtesy, or cons. staff Marymount Hosp., Cleve., Mt. Sinai Hosp., Cleve., Geauga Community Hosp., Chardon, Ohio, Bedford Community Hosp (Ohio), 1957-70. Tchr. tng. courses in CPR for med. personnel, police, fire and vol. rescue workers, numerous cities, 1950-70. Served to capt., M.C., AUS, 1946-48. Recipient Chris award Columbus Internat. Film Festival, 1964, numerous other award for sci. exhibits from various nat. and state med. socs., 1953-70; USPHS grantee, 1949-68. Fellow Am. Coll. Cardiology, Am. Coll. Chest Physicians; mem. AMA, N.Mex. Med. Assn., Colfax County Med. Assn., Ill. Med. Assn., Chgo. Med. Assn., U. Cin. Grad. Sch. Surg. Soc. Contbr. numerous articles to med. jours., chpts. to med. texts; spl. pioneer research (with Claude S. Beck) in physiopathology of coronary artery disease and CPR; developed surg. treatment of coronary artery disease; achieved 1st successful defibrillation of human heart, 1st successful reversal of fatal heart attack; provided 1st intensive care of coronary patients. Home: HCR 68 BX77 Fort Garland CO 81133

LEIGHT, BETSY LEVY, data processing executive, consultant; b. N.Y.C., July 22, 1946; d. Maurice and Elaine (Lind) Levy; m. Gary Allan Leight, Aug. 17, 1975; children: Debbie, David. BS, Carnegie Inst. Tech., 1966. Programmer, instr. IBM Can., Toronto, Ont., 1966-72; systems engr. World Trade Corp div IBM, Poughkeepsie, N.Y., 1972-73, HP Palo Alto, Palo Alto, 1973-76; exec. v.p., owner Ops. Control Systems, Palo Alto, 1976—, also bd. dirs. Leader local troop Girl Scouts U.S., Los Altos, 1984—. Named one of 1985 Women of Achievement in Bus., Santa Clara County (Calif.) Commn. on Status of Women, 1986. Mem. Am. Assn. Artificial Intelligence, EDP Auditors Assn., AAUW, Data Processing Mgmt. Assn. Jewish. Home: 14200 Sholes Ct Los Altos Hills CA 94022 Office: Ops Control Systems 560 San Antonio Rd Palo Alto CA 94022

LEIGHTON, HENRY ALEXANDER, physician; b. Manila, Philippines, Nov. 12, 1929; (parents U.S. citizens).; s. Raymond Harry and Theola Marie (Alexander) L.; m. Helga Maria Hell, Jan. 17, 1970; children: Alan Raymond, Henry Alexander, Michael Ballinger, John, Marni, Tammy Ballinger. BA in History, U. Calif., Berkeley, 1952, MPH, 1971; MD, U. Calif., San Francisco, 1956. Diplomate Am. Bd. Preventive Medicine. Intern So. Pacific Gen. Hosp., San Francisco, 1956-57; resident in surgery Brooke Gen. Hosp., Ft. Sam Houston, Tex., 1960-62; commd. 2d. lt. U.S. Army, 1957, advanced through grades to col., 1971; div. surgeon 8th Inf. div. U.S. Army, Germany, 1964-66; comdr. 15th Med. Bn. U.S. Army, Vietnam, 1966-67; instr.Med. Field Service Sch. U.S. Army, San Antonio, 1968-70; resident preventive medicine U.S. Army, Ft. Ord, Calif., 1971-72, chief preventive medicine, 1973-76; chief preventive medicine U.S. Army-Europe, 1976-79, ret., 1979; chief occupational health MEDDAC U.S. Army, Ft. Ord, 1981—. Neighborhood commr. Boy Scouts Am., 1964-66; bd. dirs. Am. Lung Assn. of Calif., 1982-84, and of affiliate, 1980-86; pres. The Bluffs Homeowners Assn., 1986. Decorated Air medal with oak leaf cluster, Bronze Star, Legion of Merit, Meritorious Service medal. Fellow Am. Coll. Preventive Medicine; mem. Am. Pub. Health Assn., Am. Occupational Med. Assn., Assn. Mil. Surgeons, Ret. Officers Assn., Assn. U.S. Army, Theta Xi. Lodges: Masons, Shriners. Office: US MEDDAC Occupational Health Fort Ord CA 93941

LEIGHTON, ROBERT B(ENJAMIN), physicist; b. Detroit, Sept. 10, 1919; s. George Benjamin and Olga Ottilie (Homrig) L.; m. Alice M. Winger, July 31, 1943 (div. 1973); children: Ralph Edward, Alan Paul; m. Margaret Laura Lauritsen, Jan. 7, 1977; step-children: Eric, Margaret Ann. AA, Los Angeles City Coll., 1938; BSEE, Calif. Inst. Tech., 1941, MS in Physics, 1944, PhD in Physics, 1947. Resident fellow Calif. Inst. Tech., Pasadena, 1947-49, asst. prof., 1949-53, assoc. prof., 1953-59, prof., 1953-85, William R. Valentine prof. physics, 1984-85, prof. emeritus, 1985—, chmn. div. physics, math, and astronomy, prin. investigator, 1971-75. Author: Principals of Modern Physics, 1960; editor: Feynman Lectures on Physics, Vol. I, 1963; designer/inventor in field. Fellow Am. Physics Soc.; mem. Nat. Acad. Sci. (James Craig Watson medal 1988), AAAS (Rumford prize 1986), Am. Astron. Soc. Democrat. Office: Calif Inst Tech Dept Physics Pasadena CA 91125

LEINBERGER, CHRISTOPHER BROWN, urban development consultant, writer; b. Charleston, W.Va., Jan. 2, 1951; s. Fredrick Arthur and Helen (Brown) L.; m. Madeleine LeMoyne McDougal, Aug. 25, 1973; children: Christopher Jr., Rebecca. BA in Urban Sociology, Swarthmore Coll., 1972; MBA, Harvard U., 1976. Asst. to pres. ARA Food Services, Inc., Phila., 1973-74, 76-77; dir. concept devel. Saga Corp., Menlo Park, Calif., 1977-79; exec. v.p. Robert Charles Lesser & Co., Beverly Hills, Calif., 1979-82, mng. ptnr., co-owner, 1982—; mng. ptnr. Met. Futures Group, 1989—. Contbr. articles to profl. jours. and nat. print media including The Wall Street Jour., Los Angeles Times and The Atlantic Monthly. Vice chmn. Swarthmore Coll. Capital Funds Dr., Los Angeles, 1986. Fellow NSF, 1971, NCAA, 1972, Coro Found., 1972-73. Mem. Urban Land Inst. (council mem. 1984—). Democrat. Clubs: Zamarono (Los Angeles); Juan Tomas (Santa Fe, N.Mex.). Home: Las Milpas PO Box 489 Tesuque NM 87574 Office: Robert Charles Lesser & Co 1323 Paseo de Peralta Santa Fe NM 87501

LEINER, ROSEANN HARTKE, plant pathologist; b. Little Rock, Apr. 8, 1960; d. Richard H. and Rosalie Ann (Stradnicky) Hartke; m. John Leiner, June 12, 1982; children: Jonathan Carl, Rosalie Catherine. BS, Cornell U., 1981. Pest scout Coop. Extension Svc., Palmer, Alaska, 1982; lab. technician U. Alaska, Palmer, 1982—. Contbr. articles to profl. jours. Mem. Nature Conservancy. Republican. Roman Catholic. Home: PO Box 2053 Palmer AK 99645 Office: U Alaska Agrl and Forest Expt Sta 533 E Fireweed Palmer AK 99645

LEINO, DEANNA ROSE, educator; b. Leadville, Colo., Dec. 15, 1937; d. Arvo Ensio Leino and Edith Mary (Bonan) Leino Malenck; adopted child, Michael Charles Bonan. B.S. in Bus. Adminstrn., U. Denver, 1959, M.S. in Bus. Adminstrn., 1967; postgrad. Community Coll. Denver, U. No. Colo., Colo. State U., U. Colo., Met. State Coll. Cert. tchr., vocat. tchr., Colo. Tchr. Jefferson County Adult Edn., Lakewood, Colo., 1963-67; tchr. bus., coordinator coop. office edn., Jefferson High Sch., Edgewater, Colo., 1959—; instr. Community Coll. Denver, Red Rocks, 1967-81, U. Colo. Denver, 1976-79, Parks Coll. Bus. (name now Parks Jr. Coll.), 1983—; dist. adviser Future Bus. Leaders Am. Active City of Edgewater Sister City Project Student Exchange Com.; pres. Career Women's Symphony Guild; treas. Phantoms of Opera, 1982—; active Opera Colo. Assocs. & Guild, I Pagliacci; ex-officio trustee Denver Symphony Assn., 1980-82. Recipient disting. service award Jefferson County Sch. Bd. 1980; Jefferson High Sch. Wall of Fame 1981. Mem. NEA (life), Colo. Edn. Assn., Jefferson County Edn. Assn., Colo. Vocat. Assn., Am. Vocat. Assn., Colo. Educators for and about Bus., Profl. Secs. Internat., Career Women's Symphony Guild, Profl. Panhellenic Assn., Colo. Congress Fgn. Lang. Tchrs., Wheat Ridge C. of C. (edn. and scholarship com.), Delta Pi Epsilon, Phi Chi Theta, Beta Gamma Sigma, Alpha Lambda Delta. Republican. Roman Catholic. Club: Tyrolean Soc. Denver. Avocations: decorating wedding cakes, crocheting, sewing, music, world travel Home: 3712 Allison St Wheat Ridge CO 80033

LEISEY, DONALD EUGENE, learning systems company executive; b. Pa., Sept. 23, 1937; s. Alvin L. and E. Marie L.; BS in Edn., West Chester (Pa.) State U., 1959; MA in Adminstrn., Villanova (Pa.) U., 1962; EdD in Adminstrn., U. So. Calif., 1973; m. Patricia M. Leisey; children: Kristen, Kendra. Tchr., Coatesville, Pa., 1959-62; prin., Downingtown, Pa., 1962-64; prin. Dept. Def. Dependent Schs., Tachikawa, Japan, 1964-67; asst. supt. Lennox Schs., Inglewood, Calif., 1967-71; dir. adminstrv. services San Rafael (Calif.) City Sch. Dist., 1971-73, supt. schs., 1973-79; v.p., regional mgr. Am. Learning Corp., Huntington Beach, Calif., 1979-80; v.p., treas. Kittredge Sch. Corp., San Francisco, 1980-83; pres., chmn. bd. Merryhill Schs. Inc., Sacramento, 1980—; gen. ptnr. L&L Investments Ltd., 1980—. Appointed to Gov.'s Child Care Task Force, Calif., 1984, Gov.'s Child Devel. Programs Adv. Com., Calif., 1985—. Recipient Disting. Alumnus award West Chester State U., 1983, Disting. Service award Los Angeles County Sheriff, 1969, Hon. Service award PTA, 1970. Mem. Nat. Assn. Child Care Mgmt., Nat. Ind. Pvt. Schs. Assn. (bd. dirs.), Nat. Assn. Edn. Young Children, Am. Assn. Sch. Adminstrs., Assn. Calif. Sch. Adminstrs., Delta Epsilon, Phi Delta Kappa. Certifications: gen. adminstrv., gen. secondary, gen. elementary, Calif. Home: 10 Oak Mountain Ct San Rafael CA 94903 Office: Merryhill Schs Inc 2730 Eastern Ave Sacramento CA 95821

LEITCH, CLARENCE MERVIN, barrister; b. Creelman, Sask., Can., Jan. 13, 1926; s. Peter Harold and Martha Ann (Walker) L.; m. Ardine Catherine Brissette, Feb. 23, 1980; children: Margaret Jan, Catherine Anne, James Harold. BA, U. Alta., 1951, LLB, 1952. Called to Alta. bar, 1953, created queen's counsel, 1968; Mem. firm Macleod Dixon, Calgary, Alta., Can., 1952-71, 1983—; atty. gen. Province of Alta., 1971-75, provincial treas., 1975-79, min. energy and natural resources, 1979-82; dir. Can. Pacific Ltd., Alta. Energy Co. Ltd., Alta. Govt. Tels. Commn., Bank Montreal, Can. Utilities Ltd., Chieftain Internat., Inc. With Royal Can. Navy, 1943-45. Conservative. Clubs: Calgary Golf and Country, Mission Hills Country. Office: Macleod Dixon, 3700 Canterra Tower, 400 Third Ave SW, Calgary, AB Canada T2P 4H2

LEKSTRUM, JOHN MARVIN, telecommunications/computer company executive; b. Hollywood, Calif., Sept. 24, 1932; s. Conrad Fritjoff Lekstrum and Mildred Mary Frank; m. Margaret Rose Moulder, Aug. 29, 1958; children: Valarie Ann, Tamara Lynn. BS in Physics, Va. Mil. Inst., 1955. Research & devel. engr. Hughes Aircraft Co., Culver City, Calif., 1958-59; project leader Rockwell Collins, Newport Beach, Calif., 1959-60; project mgmt. engr. Jet Propulsion Lab., Pasadena, Calif., 1960-62; staff engr. Astrodata, Anaheim, Calif., 1962-71; pres. Plantronics Internat. Corp., Frederick, Md., 1971-81; group v.p. Computer Sciences Corp., Falls Church, Va., 1981-82; v.p. internat. ops. ISC Systems Corp., Spokane, Wash., 1982-87; pres., chief exec. officer Multipoint Networks, San Carlos, Calif., 1987—. Pres. Inland NW World Trade Coun., Spokane, 1985-86; vice chmn. Export Assistance Coun. Wash., Seattle, 1984-87. Capt. USAF, 1955-57. Republican. Home: S 5805 Campbell Rd Greenacres WA 99016 Office: Multipoint Networks 953 Washington St San Carlos CA 94070

LEM, RICHARD DOUGLAS, painter; b. Los Angeles, Nov. 24, 1933; s. Walter Wing and Betty (Wong) L.; B.A., UCLA, 1958; M.A., Calif. State U.-Los Angeles, 1963; m. Patricia Ann Soohoo, May 10, 1958; 1 son, Stephen Vincent. Exhibited in one-man shows at Gallery 818, Los Angeles, 1965; group shows at Lynn Kottler Galleries, N.Y.C., 1973, Palos Verdes Art Gallery, 1968, Galerie Mouffe, Paris, France, 1976, Le Salon des Nations, Paris, 1984, numerous others; represented in permanent collections; writer, illustrator; Mile's Journey, 1983. Served with AUS, 1958-60. Mem. UCLA Alumni Assn. Address: 1861 Webster Ave Los Angeles CA 90026

LEMAY, JAMES EDWARD, educational materials marketing manager; b. St. Paul, Dec. 26, 1925; s. Eugene Noel Phillip and Ruberta (Pieper) L.; m. Mary Rose Dicks, Aug. 5, 1950; children: Steven, Susan, Jean, Robert, Peter, Phillip, Judith. BA, Coll. St. Thomas, 1950; MS, Ind. U., 1951. Edn. instr. Coll. St. Thomas, St. Paul, 1951-54; edn. specialist USAF U., Maxwell AFB, Ala., 1954-57; regional mgr. Ozalid div. GAF Corp., Bloomington, Minn., 1957-59; product mgr. Ozalid div. GAF Corp., Johnson City, N.Y., 1959-61; sales mgr. Coronet Films, Chgo., 1961-70, v.p. mktg., 1970-77, gen. mgr., 1977-81; exec. v.p. The Media Guild, San Diego, 1981-85; telecourse mktg. mgr. Coastline Community Coll., Fountain Valley, Calif., 1985—; cons. Medcom Corp., Garden Grove, Calif., 1985. Co-author: They See What You Mean, 1959. Alderman Park Ridge (Ill.) City Council, 1977-81. Served with U.S. Army, 1946-48. Recipient Dean Larsen Alumni award Ind. U. Audiovisual Ctr., 1980. Mem. Community Coll. Assn. for Instructional Tech. Roman Catholic. Home: 9 Madrona Irvine CA 92715 Office: Coastline Community Coll 11460 Warner Ave Fountain Valley CA 92708

LEMBERG, MILTON BREWSTER, real estate broker; b. N.Y.C., Nov. 19, 1941; s. Jack and Rose (Zuckerman) L.; m. Barbara Elaine Cahn, July 1, 1963; children: Jason Michael, Ira Bruce, Howard Jay, Adina Beth. BSME, Ariz. State U., 1963. Registered profl. mech. engr., Ariz.; lic. real estate broker, Ariz. Design engr. Rocketdyne, Canoga Park, Calif., 1963-64; pres., chief exec. officer Sun Valley Industries, Phoenix, 1964-81; ops. mgr. and tech. dir. membrane switch facility EECO, Phoenix, 1981-82; prin. Fin. Evaluation Services, Phoenix, 1983-85; real estate agt. ERA Rainbow Realty, Phoenix, 1983-86; real estate broker Execunet Realty, Scottsdale, Ariz., 1986-88; stockbroker Blinder Robinson & Co. Inc., Scottsdale, 1988-89, Rocky Mountain Securities & Investments Inc., Scottsdale, 1989—; real estate broker Milton Lemberg Investment Co., Phoenix, 1988—; cons. and expert witness Creare, Inc., Phoenix, 1982—. Mem. Ariz. Watercolor Assn. (juried, treas. 1982-86). Republican. Jewish. Home: 14249 N Piping Rock Ct Phoenix AZ 85023 Office: Milton Lemberg Investment Co 14249 N Piping Rock Ct Phoenix AZ 85023

LEMIEUX, LINDA DAILEY, museum director; b. Cleve., Sept. 6, 1953; d. Leslie Leo LeMieux Jr. and Mildred Edna (Dailey) Tutt. BA, Beloit Coll., 1975; MA, U. Mich., 1979; assoc. cert., Mus. Mgmt. Program, Boulder, Colo., 1987. Asst. curator Old Salem, Inc., Winston-Salem, N.C., 1979-82; curator Clarke House, Chgo., 1982-84; curator Western Mus. Mining and Industry, Colorado Springs, Colo., 1985-86, dir., 1987—. Author: Prairie Avenue Guidebook, 1985; editor: The Golden Years--Mines in the Cripple Creek District, 1987; contbr. articles to mags. and newspapers. Fellow Historic Deerfield, Mass., 1974—; active Colorado Springs Jr. League. Research grantee Early Am. Industries Assn., 1978. Mem. Am. Assn. Mus., Am. Assn. State and Local History, Colo.-Wyo. Mus. Assn., Colo. Mining Assn., Mountain Plains Assn. Mus., Women in Mining. Republican. Presbyterian. Home: 1337 Hermosa Way Colorado Springs CO 80906 Office: Western Mus of Mining & Industry 1025 N Gate Rd Colorado Springs CO 80921

LEMIEUX, MARJORIE DIX, educator; b. Laurel, Mont., Nov. 11, 1921; d. Dale C. and Cora jerome (Bradley) Dix.; m. Andrew Wear Elting, 1940 (div. 1962); children: Clayton Ross, Paula Jan; m. Archie L. Lemieux. Student, Wash. State Coll., Pullman, 1940-42, Fullerton Jr. Coll., 1945-46, Colo. State Coll., Ft. Collins, 1955-60. Lease clk. Carter Oil Co., Miles City, Mont., 1956; ins. agt. Western Life, Miles City, 1956-60; copy writer Women's News div. Sta. KGO, Missoula, Mont., 1961-63; sales woman Sta. KMSO-TV, Missoula, 1963-64; sec. Hilton Inn, San Francisco, 1964-66; exec. housekeeper trainee Hilton Hotels, 1966-67; exec. housekeeper Huntington Hotel, San Francisco, 1967-74, Oakland (Calif.) Hosp., 1974-83; asst. dir. house-keeping and laundry Peralta Hosp., Oakland, 1983-85; tchr. UAW-Learning Edn. Tng. Corp., San Francisco, 1988—. Vassar Summer Inst. scholar, 1954. Mem. Nat. Exec. Housekeepers Assn. (pres., sec.), Internat. Tng. in Communication (life, past pres.). Republican. Office: Hospitality Industry Tng 1255 Post St Ste 510 San Francisco CA 94109

LEMIRE, DAVID STEPHEN, teacher; b. Roswell, N.Mex., May 23, 1949; s. Joseph Armon and Jeanne (Longwill) L.; BA, Linfield Coll., 1972, MEd, 1974; EdS, Idaho State U., 1978; postgrad. U. Wyo.; Ed. S.in Ednl. Adminstrn. and Instructional Leadership, U. Wyo., 1988; postgrad. U. Wyo. Cert. sch. counselor, student personnel worker, psychology instr., Calif. Sch. counselor, psychol. technician and tchr. Goshen County Sch. Dist. 1, Torrington, Wyo., counselor Aspen High Sch., Aspen, Colo.; sch. counselor Unita County Sch. Dist., Evanston, Wyo., coord. rsch. and devel. Lifelong Learning Ctr. 1986-87; dir. spl. svcs. and sch. psychologist Bighorn County Sch. Dist. #4, Basin, Wyo., 1989—; pres. David Lemire Software Enterprises, Evanston; dir. Inst. for Advanced Study of Thinkology. Mem. Nat. Assn. Sch. Psychologists (cert.), Am. Psychol. Assn., Am. Assn. for Counseling and Devel. Editor WACD Jour.; mng. editor Jour. Humanistic Edn.; contbr. articles to profl. jours. Address: PO Box 1325 Laramie WY 82070-1325 Office: U Wyo Box 4285 Laramie WY 82071 also: Creative Self Inst Adminstrv Offices 2390 Riviera St Reno NV 89509

LEMME, CHARLES DANIEL, engineer; b. Los Angeles, Feb. 26, 1944; s. Daniel Christian Lemme and Ruth Irene (Cyriacks) Davenport; m. Alice Ella Jones, Oct. 6, 1965 (div. Apr. 1985); children: Chris, Eric; m. Linda Mae Mahler, June 14, 1987. BS in Engring., Harvey Mudd Coll., 1966; MS in Mech. Engring., Ill. Inst. Tech., 1971. Registered profl. engr., Ariz., Ill. Engr. Maremont Corp., Chgo., 1969-74; dir. engring. Pathfinder Corp., Chgo., 1974-75; sr. engr. Triodyne Corp., Chgo., 1975-77; founder, gen. Centerline Cons., Chgo. and Tucson, 1977—; founder, pres. Copernicus Corp., Tucson, 1985—; bd. dirs. Blazer Internat. Corp., Chgo., 1977—. Patentee in field; contbr. articles to profl. jours. Recipient Excellence in Design award Design News mag., 1985. Mem. ASME, AAAS, Soc. Automotive Engrs.

LEMON, OLA TESS GOODRICH, nurse; b. Tridell, Utah, May 9, 1932; d. Forrest Odra and Ethel (McConkie) Goodrich; m. Boyd R. Lemon, June 20, 1951; children: John, Edna, James, Charles, Ethel, Kathie, Susan, Rick. Student in nursing, U. Utah, 1949-51, 67-68, U. Philippines, Manila, 1965-66, U. Nebr., 1969-71; AS in Nursing, Weber State Coll., 1973, student. R.N., Utah. Dir. nursing Snyders Convalescence Villa, Roosevelt, Utah, 1973-76; night supr. Duchesne County Hosp., Roosevelt, 1976-80, 85—, supr. labor/delivery, 1982-85; dir. nursing Stewart's Nursing Home, Roosevelt, 1981-82. Mem. PTA, March of Dimes, Cancer Drive, Blood Drive. Recipient Appreciation award ARC, 1964-71. Mem. Utah Nursing Assn., Am. Nursing Assn., No. Utah Basin Dist. Nursing Assn. Republican. Mormon.

LEMONS, CHARLES THURMAN, sales executive; b. Nashville, June 8, 1949; s. Charles Griffin and Nellie Gray (Bandy) L.; m. Sandra Kay Puckett, Feb. 24, 1973; children: Tullie Jean, Rachael Claire, Kellee Renae. Inventory clk. Winn-Dixie Stores, Inc., Huntsville, Ala., 1970-72; asst. sales mgr. Inst. Wholesale Co., Cookeville, Tenn., 1972-75; account specialist Shamrock Foods Co., Phoenix, 1975-79; mgr. dist. sales SYSCO/Continental-Phoenix, 1979—; cons., v.p. Sahuaro Equipment Dist., Inc. Tucson, 1982-83; master's circle CFS Continental, Phoenix, 1981-88. Sgt. USMC, 1966-70. Mem. Am. Mgmt. Assn., Disabled Am. Vets. Office: SYSCO/Continental-Phoenix 4545 N 43d Ave Phoenix AZ 85705

LEMUS, GEORGE, Latin American studies educator; b. Del Rio, Tex., Apr. 14, 1928; s. Leopoldo and Ines (Suarez) L.; student U. Nacional Autónoma de México, 1946-48; B.A., U. Tex., 1952, M.A., 1956, Ph.D., 1963; m. Carmen Garcia, Aug. 6, 1957; children—Agnes Marie, Sarita Ann, Henry Edward, Robert Leopold, William Anthony. Tchr. pub. high sch., Aberdeen, Idaho, 1953-54; teaching fellow U. Tex., Austin, 1955-57; instr. USAF Lang. Sch., Lackland AFB, Tex., 1957-58, Loyola U., Los Angeles, 1958-60; asst. prof. Spanish, San Diego State U., 1960-64, assoc. prof., 1965-68, prof., 1968—, dir. summer program, 1964, 65, chmn. Latin Am. Studies Com., 1963-66, grad. adv. Latin Am. Studies Program, 1966-70; vis. prof. U. Colo., summer 1968. Sec.-treas. Pacific Coast Council Latin Am. Studies, 1964, mem. governing bd., 1967-69. Direccion General de Relaciones Culturales fellow, Madrid, 1957; Del Amo Found. fellow, 1970. Mem. Am. Assn. Tchrs. Spanish and Portuguese, Assn. Latin Am. Studies, Real Sociedad Bascongada de los Amigos del Pais, Sigma Delta Pi, Alpha Mu Gamma. Democrat. Roman Catholic. Author: Francisco Bulnes: su vida y sus obras, 1965. Contbr. articles to profl. jours. Home: 5730 Lance St San Diego CA 92120

LENHARD, ROBERT EARL, JR., mergers and acquisitions consultant; b. Quakertown, Pa., July 31, 1941; s. Robert E. and Ruth Lloys (Hoffman) L.; m. Linda Stitzer Lenhard, Aug. 29, 1964; children: Robert E. III, Courtney L. BA, U. Ariz., 1964. Mgr. Wells Fargo Bank, San Francisco, L.A. and San Diego, 1965-76; v.p., mgr. United Bank Ariz., Tucson, 1976-82; ptnr. VR Bus. Brokers, Tucson, 1983-88; pres. Hallmark Bus. Cons., Tucson, 1988—. Dir. Southern Ariz. Multiple Sclerosis Soc., Tucson, 1978-80; loaned exec. United Way, Tucson, 1979. With U.S. Army, 1964-65. Ford found. scholar U. Ariz., 1963-64. Mem. Ariz. Assn. Bus. Brokers (sec. Tucson 1986-89). Republican. Episcopalian. Home and Office: Hallmark Bus Cons Inc 6820 N Columbus Blvd Tucson AZ 85718

LENHOFF, HOWARD MAER, political and biological sciences educator, academic administrator; b. North Adams, Mass., Jan. 27, 1929; s. Charles and Goldy Sarah (Rubin) L.; m. Sylvia Grossman, June 20, 1954; children: Gloria, Bernard. B.A., Coe Coll., 1950, D.Sc. (hon.), 1976; Ph.D., Johns Hopkins U., 1955. USPHS fellow Loomis Lab., Greenwich, Conn., 1954-56; vis. lectr. Howard U., Washington, 1957-58; postdoctoral fellow Carnegie Instn., Washington, 1958; investigator Howard Hughes Med. Inst., Miami, 1958-63; prof. biology, dir. Lab. for Quantitative Biology U. Miami, Coral Gables, 1963-69; prof. biol. scis. U. Calif., Irvine, 1969—, prof. polit. sci., 1986—, dir. marine biology program, 1969-73, assoc. dean biol. scis., 1969-71, dean grad. div., 1971-73, asst. to vice chancellor of student affairs for grant devel. and faculty rels., 1986-88, chair faculty senate, 1988—; vis. scientist, Louis Lipsky fellow Weizmann Inst. Sci., Rehovot, Israel, 1968-69; vis. prof. chem. engring., Rothschild fellow Israel Inst. Tech., 1973-74; vis. prof. Hebrew U., Jerusalem, spring 1970, fall 1971, 77-78; Hubert Humphrey Inst. fellow Ben Gurion U., Beersheva, Israel, 1981; dir. Nelson Rsch. & Devel. Co., Irvine, 1971-73; bd. dirs. BioProbe Internat., Inc., Tustin, Calif., 1983-89, chmn. bd., 1983-86; chmn. bd. and pres. Bravo Enterprise, Inc., 1988—. Editor: Biology of Hydra, 1961, Hydra, 1969, Experimental Coelenterate Biology, 1972, Coelenterate Biology—Review and Perspectives, 1974, Hydra: Research Methods, 1983, Enzyme Immunoassay, 1985, From Trembley's Polyps to New Directions in Research on Hydra, 1985, Hydra and the Birth of Experimental Biology, 1986, Biology of Nematocysts, 1988; mem. editorial bd.: Jour. Solid Phase Biochemistry, 1976-80. Vice chmn. So. Calif. div. Am. Assn. Profs. for Peace in Middle East, 1972-80; bd. dirs. Am. Assn. for Ethiopian Jews, 1973—, pres., 1978-82; bd. govs. Israel Bonds Orange County, Calif., 1974-80, Dade County Heart Assn., Miami, 1958-61, So. Calif. Technion Soc.,1976; pres. Hillel Coun. of Orange County, 1976-78; nat. chmn. faculty div. State of Israel Bonds, 1976; mem. sci. adv. bd. Am. Friends of Weizmann Inst. Sci., 1980-84; bd. dirs. Hi Hopes Identity Discovery Found., Anaheim, Calif., 1982-87, pres. bd. govs., 1983-85. 1st lt. USAF, 1956-58. Recipient Career Development award USPHS, 1965-69; Louis Lipsky fellow, 1968-69; Disting. fellow Iowa Acad. Sci., 1986. Fellow AAAS, Iowa Acad. Sci.; mem. Am. Chem. Soc., Am. Biophys. Soc., History of Sci. Soc., Am. Soc. Cell Biologists, Am. Soc. Biol. Chemists, Biophysics Soc., Soc. Gen. Physiologists, Soc. Growth and Devel., Phi Beta Kappa, Sigma Xi, Phi Kappa Phi. Home: 304 Robin Hood Ln Costa Mesa CA 92627 Office: U Calif Sch Biol Scis Irvine CA 92717

LENNOX, SHIRLEY ANN, artist, educator, consultant; b. San Francisco, Nov. 8, 1931; d. James Joseph and Mildred Mae (Hall) Amos; m. Arthur James Lennox, Jan. 6, 1951; children: Sharron Kay, Kathleen Melanie, Bonnie Marie, Colleen Leta. Student pub. schs., South Glens Falls, N.Y. Window display artist Fowlers' Inc., Glens Falls, 1948-51; owner, operator Discovery House Gallery, Palo Alto, Calif., 1969-71; owner, operator, tchr. porcelain painting Lennox Art Sutdio, Santa Maria, Calif., 1972—; cons. art, Santa Maria, 1985—; owner, operator Gallerie 272, Morton, N.Y., 1979-81; resident artist, gallery mgr. Options Gallery, Shell Beach, Calif., 1985. Exhibited paintings in one-woman shows: Village Gallery, Hilton, N.Y., Lake George Inst. History and Art, N.Y., 1974, Swan Gallery, Albion, N.Y., 1979, Options Gallery, Shell Beach, Calif., 1984, Morro Bay Mus. Natural History, 1985; group shows include: The Calif. Scene (with Ansel Adams and others), Foothill Coll., Los Altos, Calif., 1970, Suburban Rochester Art Group shows, N.Y., 1976-80, Santa Ynez Art Shows, Calif., 1983-84, Los Padres Artists Guild Shows, 1983-86, Faulkner Gallery, 1985, Gallery 113, Santa Barbara, 1987, Sheldon Swope Art Gallery, Terre Haute, Ind., 1987, Internat. Soc. Marine Painters Exhibit, San Luis Obispo (Calif.) Art Ctr Gallery; represented in permanent collections: Old Courthouse Mus., Lake George, N.Y., Shelter Cove Lodge, Pismo Beach, Calif; represented by Gallery 912 1/2, Santa Maria, Calif., The Sandpiper Art Gallery, Pismo Beach, Calif., Visions Fine Art Gallery, Morro Bay, Calif. Active Santa Maria Arts Council, 1988—. Mem. Internat. Porcelain Arts Tchrs., Internat. Soc. Marine Painters Inc. (juried profl. mem., west coast rep.), Nat. Soc. Painters in Casein and Acrylic (assoc.), Santa Maria Women's Network, Santa Barbara Art Assn. (juried), Cen. Coast Watercolor Soc., San Luis Obispo Art Assn., Artists Guild of Santa Ynez Valley, Porcelain Portrait Soc., Nat. Mus. Women in the Arts (charter mem.), Nat. Assn. Female Execs. Republican. Mem. Unity Ch. Avocations: photography, camping. Address: Lennox Art Studio 4123 Mayfield St Santa Maria CA 93455

LENT, BERKELEY, retired judge; b. L.A., Sept. 22, 1921; s. Oscar Paul and Patricia Lucile (Berkeley) L.; m. Joan Kay Burnett, Dec. 27, 1968; children: Patricia Brandt, Deirdre, Eric, Terry Ling. Student, Reed Coll., 1941, 46-47, Occidental Coll., 1944-45; J.D., Willamette U., 1950. Bar: Oreg. 1950. Assoc. editor Bancroft-Whitney Law Pub. Co., San Francisco, 1950; with office of gen. counsel Bonneville Power Adminstrn., Portland,

Oreg., 1950-51, 52-53; pvt. practice law Coos Bay, Oreg., 1951-52; assoc. Peterson & Pozzi, Portland, 1952-53; ptnr. Lent, York, Paulson & Bullock (and predecessor firms), Portland, 1953-70; pvt. practice law Portland, 1970-71; judge Cir. Ct., Multnomah County, 1971-77; assoc. Oreg. Supreme Ct., Salem, 1977-82, 83-88, chief justice, 1982-83. Mem. Oreg. Ho. of Reps., 1957-65, minority whip, 1965; mem. Oreg. Senate, 1967-71, majority leader, 1971. With USNR, 1942-45. Mem. VFW, Am. Legion, Elks. Democrat. Office: 530 Center St NE Ste 425 Salem OR 97301

LENTES, DAVID EUGENE, corporate executive; b. Spokane, Wash., Dec. 14, 1951; s. William Eugene and Ellen Elsie L.; m. Debra Kay White, May 19, 1973 (div. 1984); children: Janette Adele, Damon Arthur. AA, Spokane Falls Community Coll., 1972; BBA, Gonzaga U., 1975. V.p. Dellen Wood Products, Inc., Spokane, 1972—, also bd. dirs.; v.p. Custom Computer Services, Inc., Spokane, 1980-87, also bd. dirs.; mng. ptnr. Com-Lease, 1980-87, Len-Lease, 1980—; v.p., bd. dirs. DWP Trucking, Inc., 1982-85, Sentel Corp., 1983-88, BDR Investment Corp., 1983—; pres., bd. dirs. ASA Mgmt. Corp., 1984—, also Link Internat., Inc., 1985. Treas. Dishman Hills Natural Area Assn., 1970—; elder Bethany Presbyn. Ch., 1980-83; active Spokane Econ. Devel. Council. Mem. Assn. Wash. Bus., Nat. Fedn. Ind. Businessmen, Am. Fedn. Bus., Better Bus. Bur. (Spokane chpt.), U.S. C. of C., Spokane C. of C., Timber Products Mfrs., Hoo-Hoo Internat. Republican. Office: N 3014 Flora Rd Spokane WA 99216

LENZ, PHILIP JOSEPH, municipal administrator; b. Monterey Park, Calif., Sept. 15, 1940; s. Philip George and Irene Mary (Bowers) L.; m. Mary Lou Antista, July 16, 1966; children: Brian Joseph, Jonathan Thomas. BA, Calif. State U., L.A., 1966; MS, Pepperdine U., 1974. Dir. West Valley div. San Bernardino County (Calif.) Probation Dept., 1977-79, dir. juvenile div., 1979-82, dir. adminstrv. services, 1982-88, dir. dist. services, 1988—; instr. dept. social rels. Loma Linda U., 1988. Sec. bd. trustees Upland (Calif.) Sch. Dist., 1985—, pres. sch. bd., 1989; mgr., coach Upland Am. Little League, 1981—, bd. dirs. 1982—; pres. Fontana (Calif.) Family Service Agy., 1972-74; mem. adv. com. corrections Chaffey Coll., Alta Loma, Calif., 1977—; mem. City of Upland Parks and Recreation com., 1986—, chmn., 1989-90; mem., bd. dirs. Highlander Ednl. Found.; mem. Calif. youth authority CADRE of Cons. Recipient Tim Fitzharris award Chief Probation Officers of Calif., 1987. Mem. Calif. Probation, Parole and Correctional Assn. (regional v.p. 1981-83, 2d v.p. 1985-86, 1st v.p. 1986—, pres. 1987—), Probation Bus. Mgr.'s Assn. (regional chmn. 1984-86, v.p. 1987), Western Correctional Assn., Calif. Probation Parole and Correctional Assn. (liaison). Democrat. Roman Catholic. Home: 1375 N Stanford Ave Upland CA 91786 Office: San Bernardino County Dept Probation 175 W 5th St San Bernardino CA 92415

LEO, MARGARET ELENA, vice principal, teacher; b. Nyack, N.Y., Apr. 12, 1940; d. Salvatore and Elena Marie (Prattico) Ingafu; m. Robert Joseph Leo, Aug. 5, 1962; children: Christopher Matthew, Nicholas Andrew. BS in Edn., SUNY, Oneonta, 1962; postgrad., Calif. State U., Northridge, 1983-. Cert. tchr., N.Y. Tchr. 5th grade Garfield Elem. Sch., Long Branch, N.J., 1962-64; tchr. 5th grade Emerson Elem. Sch., Everett, Wis., 1964-65, tchr. 6th grade, 1965-66; tchr. 5th grade, music coord. St. Euphrasia Sch., Granada Hills, Calif., 1977-82; vice prin., tchr. 4th grade Our Lady of Peace Sch., Sepulveda, Calif., 1984-89; vice prin., tchr. 3d grade L.A. Unified Sch. Dist., 1989—; mem. ind. TV Archdiocese Telecommunications Svcs., L.A., 1988--. Div. rep. AVSO Soccer Bd., 1985-86; mem. Oak Cliff Soc. Fine Arts, Dallas, 1983-84. Mem. Nat. Cath. Ednl. Assn., L.A. Jr. C. of C. (pro-am com. open golf tournament 1983--), Northridge C. of C., United Tchrs. L.A. Home: 12055 Woodley Ave Granada Hills CA 91344

LEO, MARY GAYE, school administrator; b. Colorado Springs, Colo., Oct. 19, 1951; d. Bernard Johnston and Mary Ellen (Hardy) Lamar; m. Dominick Louis Leo; 1 child, Dominick Christopher. BA, U. Colo., 1973, MA, 1978; PhD in Ednl. Adminstrn. Denver U., 1985. Communications, group dynamics instr., Denver area, 1972-73; with Denver Public Sch. System, 1973—, arts mgmt./theater dir., 1973-87; asst. prin. Lake Middle Sch., 1987-89, Martin Luther King Middle Sch., Denver Pub. Schs., 1989—. Vol., Colo. Arts and Humanities Council as lectr., workshop coordinator, 1974-75. Cert. bicultural/bilingual instr. Mem. Am. Theatre Assn., Women in Theatre, Nat. Council Tchrs. English, Nat. Assn. Female Execs., Colo. Assn. Sch. Execs., ASCD, Colo. Partnership. Author: Celebration (rock musical), 1979; Bob, The Magical Unicorn (children's fantasy), 1981; The Raven and I-E Locus of Control as Measures of High Ability; dir., designer, producer profl. and ednl. theatrical prodns. including Godspell, 1974, Guys and Dolls, 1975, My Fair Lady, 1976, Carousel, 1977, Music Man, 1978, Celebration!, 1979, Annie Get Your Gun, 1980, Jesus Christ Superstar, 1982, Grease, 1982, Camelot, 1983, Guys and Dolls, 1987, Authentic School Project for Drop Out Prevention. Home: 11224 E Harvard Dr Aurora CO 80014 Office: 1620 Lowell Blvd Denver CO 80204

LEO, ROBERT JOSEPH, association executive, consultant; b. Paterson, N.J., Nov. 24, 1939; s. Dewey J. and Jean (Bianco) L.; m. Margaret Elena Ingafu, Aug. 5, 1962; children—Christopher, Nicholas. B.A. in Speech, Temple U., 1960, M.A., 1962; Ph.D., U. Wash., 1968. Instr. Monmouth Coll., West Long Branch, N.J., 1962-64; spl. asst. to chancellor Dallas County (Tex.) Community Coll. Dist., 1968-71, dir. spl. services and gov. relations, 1971-76; assoc. exec. dir. League for Innovation in the Community Coll., Los Angeles, 1976-80, exec. dir., Dallas, 1980-82; exec. dir. Los Angeles Jr. C. of C., 1982—; founding pres. Nat. Council Resource Devel., adj. assoc. prof. East Tex. State U., 1975-76; chmn. Tex. Health Planning Council. Recipient Disting. Service award Oak Cliff Jaycees, 1973; Spl. Recognition award Nat. Council Resource Devel., 1981; named Significant Contbr. to Fair Housing, Greater Dallas Housing Opportunity Ctr., 1973. Mem. Am. Soc. Tng. and Devel., Am. Soc. Assn. Execs., Nat. Council Resource Devel., Am. Youth Soccer Orgn. Roman Catholic. Clubs: Rotary, Los Angeles Athletic, Univ. Author articles in field. Home: 12055 Woodley Ave Granada Hills CA 91344 Office: LA Jaycees 404 S Bixel St Los Angeles CA 90017

LEON, HAYDEN LOUIS, small business consultant, tax practitioner; b. Balt., Nov. 4, 1911; s. Harry Louis and Irene (Fiske) L.; m. Virginia Wallis, June 4, 1935; children: Hayden Louis Jr., Ann, Peter, Gordon. BS, U.S. Naval Acad., 1933; MA in Aero. Engring., MIT, 1942; postgrad. in mgmt., Harvard U., 1952. Registered profl. engr., Calif. Commd. ensign USN, 1933, advanced through grades to capt., 1957; ret. 1963; mgr. McDonnell Douglas Coorp., Long Beach, Calif., 1964-76; owner, mgr. Gen. Bus. Svcs., Palos Verdes, Calif., 1982—; mem. Svc. Corps Ret. Execs., L.A., 1976—, now chmn. Fellow AIAA, King Harbor Yacht Club (Redondo Beach, Calif., port chpt., fleet capt.). Republican. Episcopalian. Home and Office: 30413 Via Cambron Rancho Palos Verdes CA 90274

LEONARD, DAVID LEE, electronics engineer; b. Dayton, Ohio, Sept. 9, 1934; s. Lee Homer and Beulah Gerald (McLaughlin) L.; m. Helen M. Powell, Feb. 9, 1957; children: Victoria Dee, David Scott. AA, Centralia Jr. Coll., Wash., 1954; BS, U. Wash., 1957; MS, U. So. Calif., 1970. Lab. worker various cos., 1955-56; engr. trainee Shell Chem., Ventura, Calif., 1959-61, technologist, 1961-64; with Rocketdyne div. Rockwell Internat., Canoga Park, Calif., 1964—, project engr., 1982-87, project mgr., 1987—. Patentee non-circular expulsion process. Vol. County Detention Camp Outreach, Newhall and Los Angeles, 1981-83, YMCA, Woodland Hills, 1967-73. Served with U.S. Army, 1957-59. Mem. AIAA, Odd Fellows. Republican. Mem. Internat. Ch. of Four Square Gospel.

LEONARD, LARRY GIVENS, plastic surgeon; b. Greenville, S.C., Feb. 23, 1946; m. Claire Offutt, Dec. 23, 1968; children: Christopher, Kathleen. BA, Johns Hopkins U., 1968, MD, 1971. Diplomate Am. Bd. Surgery, Am. Bd. Plastic Surgery; lic. MD in Md., Colo., Calif., Utah. Intern in surgery U. Colo., Boulder, 1971-72, residency in surgery, 1971-75; residency in plastic surgery Johns Hopkins U., Balt., 1975-79; fellow in maxillo-facial trauma Md. Inst. Emergency Medicine, Balt., 1979; fellow in hand surgery Raymond M. Curtis, M.D., Hand Ctr. Union Meml. Hosp., Balt., 1980; asst. prof. Johns Hopkins U., Balt., 1979-81; asst. prof. U. Utah, Salt Lake City, 1981-83, assoc. prof., vice chair plastic surgery, 1985, clin. assoc. prof. plastic surgery, 1988—; staff U. Utah Med. Ctr., Salt Lake City, VA Med. Ctr., Salt Lake City, Latter Day Saints Hosp., Salt Lake City, Primary Childrens Hosp., Salt Lake City, Holy Cross Hosp., Salt Lake City, St. Mark's Hosp., Salt Lake City. Contbr. articles to profl. jours. Maj. USAF, 1975-77. Fellow Am. Soc. Surgery Hand; mem. Am. Soc. Plastic and Reconstructive Surgery, Am. Assn. Hand Surgeons, Plastic Surgery Rsch. Council, AMA, Utah State Med. Assn., Utah State Plastic Surgery Soc. (pres. 1984-86), Rocky Mt. Assn. Plastic and Reconstrucitve Surgeons, John Staige Davis Soc. Md., Salt Lake City Surg. Soc., Salt Lake Surg. Soc., Interplast (founder, sec./treas. 1987). Home: 1445 Wilton Way Salt Lake City UT 84108 Office: Hand Care Ctr 702 E South Temple Salt Lake City UT 84102

LEONARD, MARY MCCREA, substance abuse counselor; b. Kansas City, Mo., Oct. 4, 1952; d. Robert McCrea Leonard and Constance Lee (Carter) Bergendoff. BA in Social Work, Washburn U., 1976; M in Adminstrn. Justice, Wichita State U., 1983. Cert. substance abuse counselor, Nev. Prevention specialist Nat. Council on Alcoholism, Topeka, 1977-85; alcoholism counselor Salvation Army Treatment Facility, Honolulu, 1985-86; pvt. practice substance abuse counseling Honolulu, 1986-87; prevention-intervention coordinator Positive Lifestyles, Inc., Las Vegas, Nev., 1987—. Pres. Topeka Battered Women Task Force, 1983-85. Mem. Phi Kappa Phi. Episcopalian. Home: 3540 W Sahara St Las Vegas NV 89102 Office: Positive Lifestyles Inc 1934 E Charleston St Las Vegas NV 89104

LEONARD, MAURICE F(RANKLIN), air conditioning technician, real estate developer; b. Alexander City, Ala., Feb. 11, 1935; s. M.E. and Odessa L. (Thomas) L.; m. Mary Joyce Hill, Oct. 5, 1959 (div. Oct. 1977). AS, L.A. Trade Tech. Coll., 1969. Air conditioning mechanic Montgomery Ward, L.A., 1965; air conditioning fabricator Supreme Air Mfg. Co., Inc., L.A., 1966-67; air conditioning mechanic Systems Devel. Corp., Santa Monica, Calif., 1967-68; air conditioning start-up man United Air Conditioning Corp., Monterey Park, Calif., 1968; svc. engr. Air Conditioning Co., Inc., Glendale, Calif., 1969; bldg. engr. Engring. Supervision Co., L.A., 1970-71, Confinental Hyatt House, Hollywood, 1971-73; instr. air conditioning Nat. Sch., L.A., 1975; air conditioning mechanic Hughes Aircraft Co., El Segundo, Calif., 1975—. With USN, 1959-63, U.S. Army, 1954-57. Tuskegee Inst. scholar, 1953. Mem. Refrigeration Svc. Engrs. Soc., Holiday Club Internat. Republican. Home: Playa del Rey CA 90293 Office: PO Box 4044 Culver City CA 90231

LEONARDO, SUSAN ANN, protective services offical; b. Sharon, Conn., July 23, 1953; d. Joseph Lewis and Madalaine Christine (Duffy) Aluffo; m. Michael, Feb. 5, 1983; 1 child, Laura Marie. AS, Allan Hancock Jr. Coll., 1973; BS, Calif. State U., Fresno, 1976, MS, 1981. Cert. tchr., Calif. Correctional officer I Fresno County Sheriff's Dept., 1976-77, correctioanl officer II, 1977-80, correctioal sgt., 1980--; tchr., trainer Fresno City Coll., 1981--, correctional coordinator, 1987--; instr. Coll. of Sequioas, Visilia, Calif., 1982-84; lectr. Calif. State U., Fresno, 1982-83. Mem. Criminal Justice Alternatives (sec. 1982-85, v.p. 1986--), Am. Correctional Assn., Am. Jail Assn., Cen. Calif. Trainers Assn. (v.p. 1984-85). Democrat. Roman Catholic. Office: Fresno County Sheriff's Dept 2200 Fresno St Fresno CA 93721

LEONG, ALLEN MERRITT, musician; b. Glendora, Calif., Nov. 9, 1958; s. Donald Francis and Marian (Wong) L. Student, U. Ha., 1976-79. Keyboardist/vocalist Livewire, Honolulu, 1976-78, Nueva Vida, Honolulu, 1981—; Contbr. Brouhaha mag., 1986—. Contbr. articles to various publs. Mem. Mus. Assn. of Ha. (local 677).

LEONG, CAROL JEAN, electrologist; b. Sacramento, Jan. 9, 1942; d. Walter Richard and Edith (Bond) Bloss; m. Oliver Arthur Fisk III, Apr. 12, 1964 (div. 1973); 1 child, Victoria Kay. BA in Sociology, San Jose (Calif.) State Coll., 1963; degree, Western Bus. Coll., 1964; cert. in electrolysis, Bay Area Coll. Electrolysis, 1978. Registered and cert. clin. profl. electrologist, Calif. Model various orgns., Calif., 1951-64; employment counselor Businessmen's Clearinghouse, Cin., 1966-67; dir. personnel Kroger Food Corp., Cin., 1967-68; prin. Carol Leong Electrolysis, San Mateo, Calif., 1978—; prin. Designs by Carol, San Mateo, 1987—; mem. Profl. Women's Forum, 1988—. Contbr. articles to profl. publs. Recipient Cert. of Appreciation San Francisco Lighthouse for the Blind, 1981-82, 83. Mem. Internat. Guild Profl. Electrologists (mem. continuing edn. com.), NAFE, Profl. Women's Forum, Peninsula Humane Soc., San Francisco Zool. Soc., Friends of Filoli, Am. Electrologists Assn., Electrologists Assn. Calif., Chi Omega. Republican. Methodist. Home: 3339 Glendora Dr San Mateo CA 94403 Office: Carol Leong Electrolysis 36 S El Camino Real Ste 205 San Mateo CA 94401

LEON-GUERRERO, DAVID MESA, communications executive; b. Honolulu, Apr. 29, 1955; s. Mariano Cepeda and Josefina (Cruz) L-G.; m. Alicia Laurentina Ceja, Nov. 18, 1984; children: Jessica Alicia, Jake David. AS, San Diego City Coll., 1979; BBA cum laude, Nat. U., 1980. Sales assoc. Pacific Telephone, San Diego, 1979-81; sales assoc. AT&T, San Diego, 1981-85, account exec., 1985-87, tech. cons., 1987-88, tech. cons. II, 1988—; guest speaker Nat. Univ., San Diego, 1986—. Bd. mem. Econ. Devel. Com. Chula Vista C. of C., 1986, Windsor Heights Homeowners Assn., Chula Vista, Calif., 1985, Foreign Language & Global Studies Magnet Program, Chula Vista, 1989; adv. mem. Congressman Duncan Hunter Veterans Affairs Council, San Diego, 1979. Sgt. U.S. Army, 1973-77. Mem. Am. Telephone & Telegraph. Republican. Roman Catholic. Office: AT&T 750 B St 16th Fl San Diego CA 92101

LEONHARD, WILLIAM EDWARD, engineering and construction company executive; b. Middletown, Pa., Dec. 9, 1914; s. Charles Frank and Ruth Eva (Wagner) L.; m. Wyllis Mary Rocker, Feb. 8, 1940; children: William Edward, Richard W., D. Jeanne. BEE, Pa. State U., 1936; MSEE, Mass. Inst. Tech., 1940; LLD, Pepperdine U., 1987. Commd. 2d lt. U.S. Army, 1936; Commd. lt. col. USAF, 1950, advanced through grades to brig. gen., 1960; ret. 1964; with Ralph M. Parsons Co., Pasadena, Calif., 1966—; pres. Ralph M. Parsons Co., 1974—, gen. mgr., 1974-75, chief exec. officer, 1975—, also dir, chmn. bd.; pres., chmn., chief exec. officer The Parsons Corp., 1978—. Bd. visitors, bd. overseers UCLA; assoc. Calif. Inst. Tech.; mem. corp. vis. com. dept. civil engring. MIT; trustee Harvey Mudd Coll., 1986—. Decorated Bronze Star, Legion of Merit (3); recipient Corp. Leadership award M.I.T., 1977; named Chief Exec. of Yr. Fin. World, 1982, 83, 84, 85, Outstanding CEO Wall Street Transcript, 1981, 83; recipient Disting. Alumnus award Pa. State U., 1982, Golden Beaver award in mgmt., 1984. Mem. ASME (Newman award 1961), Nat. Acad. Engring., Council on Fgn. Relations, Los Angeles World Affairs Council. Clubs: California (Los Angeles); Marrakesh Country (Palm Desert, Calif.); Annandale Golf (Pasadena), Pasadena Breakfast, Forum (Pasadena), Twilight (Pasadena).

LEONHARDT, KENT ALBIN, military officer; b. Buffalo, N.Y., Apr. 2, 1954; s. Herbert Albin and Arlene (Bassler) L.; m. Linda Lee Jagels, June 21, 1973 (div. 1981); 1 child, Kyle Robert; m. Shirley Aleta Lawrence, Aug. 4, 1984. BS in Wildlife Mgmt., U. Mo., 1976; MA in Mgmt. and Supervision, Cen. Mich. U., 1982; postgrad., Def. Intelligence Coll., 1985-86. Commd. 2d lt. USMC, 1976, advanced through grades to major, with, 1977-83; comdg. officer Co. A Marine Support Battalion, Ft. Meade, Md., 1983-84; officer Nat. Security Agy., Ft. Meade, 1984-85, 7th Marine Air Base, Twentynine Palms, Calif., 1986—. Mem. NRA, Nat. Assn. Realtors, Ruffed Grouse Soc. Republican. Home: 8403 WB and A Rd Severn MD 21144

LEOPOLD, IRVING HENRY, physician, medical educator; b. Phila., Apr. 19, 1915; s. Abraham and Dora (Schlow) L.; m. Eunice Robinson, June 24, 1937; children—Ellen Robinson, John. BS, Pa. State U., 1934; MD, U. Pa., 1938, DSc, 1943. Diplomate Am. Bd. Ophthalmology (chmn. bd. 1971-72, examiner 1974-81, subcom. impaired vision and blindness 1967-69, task force on ocular pharmacology, 1967-69, cons. 1975-79, assoc. examiner 1974-81). Intern U. Pa. Hosp., 1938-40; fellow, instr. ophthalmology U. Pa. Hosp., U. Pa. Med. Sch., 1940-45; assoc. Hosp. U. Pa., also U. Pa. Med. Sch., 1945-54; research investigator chem. warfare OSRD, 1941-45; mem. faculty U. Pa. Grad. Sch. Medicine, 1946-64, successively assoc., asst. prof., assoc. prof., 1946-55, prof., head dept. ophthalmology, 1955-64; chief dept. ophthalmology Grad. Hosp., 1955-64; dir. research Wills Eye Hosp., 1949-64, attending surgeon, 1952-64, med. dir., 1961-64, cons. surgeon, 1965-73; chmn. sci. adv. com. Allergan, Inc., 1974, Sr. v.p., 1975; prof., chmn. dept. ophthalmology Mt. Sinai Sch. Medicine, 1965-75; dir. dept. ophthalmology Mt. Sinai Hosp., N.Y.C., 1964-75; prof., chmn. dept. ophthalmology U. Calif. at Irvine, 1975-85, prof. pharmacology, 1982—, prof. emeritus ophthalmology, 1985—; clin. prof. ophthalmology Coll. Physicians and Surgeons, Columbia, 1964-67; cons. ophthalmologist St. Joseph's Hosp., 1959-64, Albert Einstein Med. Center, 1959-64; Proctor lectr. U. Calif., 1962; Gifford Meml. lectr., Chgo., 1967; Edwin B. Dunphy lectr. Harvard, 1968; Walter Wright lectr. U. Toronto, 1969; Richardson Cross lectr. Royal Soc. Medicine, 1970; Doyne Meml. lectr. Ophthal. Soc. U.K., 1971; DeSchweinitz Meml. lectr., Phila., 1972; Jules Stein lectr. UCLA, 1974; Bedell lectr., Phila., 1975; Edwin B. Dunphy lectr. Harvard, 1975; Francis H. Adler lectr., Phila., 1980, Dwight Towne lectr., Ky., 1979, C.S. O'Brien lectr., New Orleans, 1979; Disting. vis. lectr. Jefferson Med. Coll., 1980, Moorfields Hosp., Eng., 1980, U. Helsinki, Finland, 1980, Third Francis Heed Adler lectr., 1980, 2d ann. Tullos O. Coston lectr., 1981, Sir Stewart Duke-Elder lectr., 1982, Everett R. Viers lectr., Scott and White Clinic and Tex. A&M U. Coll. Medicine, Temple, Tex., 1982, U. Phillipines 1st lectr, 1st Irving H. Leopold lectr. Wills Eye Hosp, 1987—. Eye Resident Soc., Eye Referral Ctr., 1982, Royal Soc. Medicine lectr., London, 1985; lectr. Internat. Congress Ophthalmology, Japan, 1978, Phillipine Bd. Opthalmology; cons. Chem. Warfare Service, U.S. Army, 1948-52, 81; surgeon gen. USPHS, 1952-58, FDA, HEW, 1963; mem. med. adv. com. Orange County chpt. Multiple Sclerosis Soc., 1979-81; chmn. ophthalmology panel U.S. Pharmacopeia, 1960-70, mem. revision panel, 1970—; chmn. panel drug efficacy in ophthalmology Nat. Acad. Scis.-NRC, 1966-67, 80—; mem. tng. grants com. USPHS, 1952-58, mem. spl. sensory study sect. research neurol. diseases and blindness, 1954-58; mem. field investigating com. Nat. Inst. Neurol. Diseases and Blindness, 1959-61, mem. neurol. project com., 1961-63, chmn. vision research tng. com., 1967-68; mem. adv. bd. Am. Behcet's Found., Inc., 1980, 81; Expert Agree to Ministry of Health, France, 1981-87; curator ophthalmic pharmaceuticals Found. Am. Acad. Ophthalmology, 1983-89; mem. nat. adv. eye council panel on cataract sect. Nat. Eye Inst. and HEW, 1981-85; mem. med. research and devel. command-chemical welfare U.S. Army, 1981-85. Editor-in-chief: Survey of Ophthalmology, 1958-62; cons. editor, 1962—; editorial bd.: Am. Jour. Diabetes, 1956-73, Investigative Ophthalmology, 1961-74; assoc. editor: Am. Jour. Ophthalmology, 1974-88, now mem. editorial bd.; assoc. editor Archives of Ophthalmology, 1974-81; cons. Jour. AMA, 1974-81; editorial cons. Jour. Ocular Pharmacology, 1985—; editor: Ocular Inflammation and Therapeutics, 1981. Trustee Seeing Eye Guide. Recipient Zentmayer award, 1945, 49; honor award Am. Acad. Ophthalmology, 1955, Sr. Hon. award, 1984; Edward Lorenzo Holmes citation and award, 195iedenwald medal Assn. Research Ophthalmology, 1960; Disting. Research award U. Calif., Irvine, Calif., 1980; Disting. Research award U. Calif. Alumni Assn., 1980, Disting. Service to Opthalmology, 1988; Physician's award Pa. Acad. Ophthalmology and Otolaryngology, 1981; Sir Steward Duke-Elder award, Lederle Medal and Prize for Research in Glaucoma Internat. Glaucoma Congress VI and Am. Soc. Contemporary Ophthalmology, Orlando, Fla., 1982. Mem. N.Y. Acad. Medicine, Am. Ophthal. Soc. (Verhoeff Meml. lectr. 1973, Lucien Howe medal 1974), Am. Acad. Ophthalmology and Otolaryngology (chmn. drug com. ophthalmology 1963-74, Edward Jackson Meml. lectr. 1965, honor guest 1971, 75, Philip M. Corboy Perpetual Excellence award 1988, Disting. Service to Ophthalmology award 1988), Am. Soc. Contemporary Ophthalmology (chief cons. editorial bd. 1981), Assn. Research Ophthalmology (trustee, chmn.), Nat. Soc. Prevention Blindness (dir. 1974-81, v.p., exec. com., hon. bd. dirs.), A.C.S., AAAS, Art Alliance Phila., John Morgan Soc., Coll. Physicians Phila., Am. Diabetes Assn., AMA (chmn. residency rev. com. ophthalmology 1970-72, Physician's Recognition award 1980-87), N.Y. Acad. Sci., Pan Am. Assn. Ophthalmology, Pan Pacific Surg. Assn., Royal Soc. Medicine (London), N.Y. State, N.Y. County, Philadelphia County med. socs., Calif., Orange County med. assns., Orange County Soc. Ophthalmology, Am. Med. Student Assn., Nat. Soc. to Prevent Blindness (hon. bd. dirs. 1986—), Med. Biochemist Club, Vesper Club, Newport Beach Tennis Club, Sigma Xi, Alpha Omega Alpha. Clubs: Medical Biochemist, Vesper (Phila.); Big Canyon Country, Balboa Bay (Newport Beach, Calif.); Century Country, Purchase (N.Y.C.). Home: 1484 Galaxy Dr Newport Beach CA 92660 Office: Allergan Inc 2525 DuPont Dr Irvine CA 92715

LEPAPE, HARRY LEONARD, energy company executive; b. Sonora, Calif., Nov. 26, 1930; s. Harry Lepape and Ruth (Freitas) Lepape Woodhams; B.S., Stanford U., 1952, J.D., 1956; m. Marilyn J. Earley, Mar. 21, 1955; children—Linda Gay, Jeanne Carolyn. Admitted to Calif. bar, 1956; atty. Honolulu Oil Corp., San Francisco, 1956-61; v.p. U.S. Natural Gas Corp., Beverly Hills, Calif., 1962-64; with Pacific Enterprises, L.A., 1964—, v.p., from 1981; chmn., chief exec. officer Pacific Interstate Co., 1973—, Pacific Enterprises Oil Co., 1983—; dir. Foothills Pipelines Ltd. Mem. Pacific Coast Gas Assn., Interstate Natural Gas Assn. Am. (bd. dirs.), Am. Gas Assn., Am. Petroleum Inst., Am. Bar Assn., Los Angeles County Bar Assn. Club: Los Angeles Athletic. Office: Pacific Enterprises Oil & Gas Co 801 S Grand Ave Ste 1200 Los Angeles CA 90060

LEPERA, LEONARD J., real estate executive; b. Gilroy, Calif., Feb. 16, 1941; s. Louis and Louisa (Carpignano) L.; B.S., U. Calif., Berkeley, 1966, M.B.A. (fellow), 1967; m. Meriel Mura, Feb. 3, 1973; 1 child, Alexander. Rep. Pacific Mut. Life Ins. Co., Los Angeles, 1969-70, supr., 1970-71, mgr., 1971-73, dir., 1973-74, asst. v.p., 1974-76, 2d. v.p., 1976-77, v.p., 1977-80; partner Property Corrs., Irvine, Calif., 1980—. Mem. Urban Land Inst., Alpha Kappa Psi (life). Home: 3592 South Mall Irvine CA 92714

LEPORIERE, RALPH DENNIS, quality engineer; b. Elizabeth, N.J., Nov. 8, 1932; s. Maximo and Christian (Lello) L.; m. Judith Louise Crowhurst, Nov. 19, 1960; children: Bonnie Ann, David Anthony. BS in Chemistry, Rutgers U., 1954. Registered profl. engr., Calif. Chemist N.Y. Quinine & Chemical Works, Newark, 1954-55; asst. to chief quality control C.D. Smith Pharmacal Co., New Brunswick, N.J., 1955-56; asst. supr. quality control White Labs., Kenilworth, N.J., 1958-60; statistician Calif. and Hawaiian Sugar Co., Crockett, Calif., 1960—; instr., chmn. of quality control dept. Laney Community Coll., Oakland, Calif., 1986-87, asst. prof., chmn. quality control dept. John F. Kennedy U., Martinez, Calif., 1967-72; instr., mem. adv. com. annual statis. short course U. Calif., Davis, Calif., 1969—. Pres. PTA Napa Junction Elem. Sch., Napa County, Calif., 1971-73; mem. early childhood com., program adv. com. Napa Valley Unified Sch. Dist., Napa County, 1972-76; v.p. Am. Canyon County Water Dist., American County, Calif., 1971-73, pres., 1973-83, gen. mgr., 1981. Recipient Hon. Service award Calif. State PTA, 1973. Fellow Am. Soc. Quality Control (cert., chmn. San Francisco sect., founder East Bay Subsect. 1970-71); mem. Soc. Mfg. Engrs. (sr.), Am. Statis. Soc., Am. Chem. Soc. Republican. Roman Catholic. Home: 618 Kilpatrick St Vallejo CA 94589 Office: Calif & Hawaiian Sugar Co 830 Loring Ave Crockett CA 94525

LEPS, ANTS ARVO, mass communication educator, consultant; b. Pärnu, Estonia, Jan. 26, 1936; came to U.S., 1949; parents Erich and Pauline (Elfriede) L.; m. Virve Põld, Sept. 1963. Student, Wesleyan U., Middletown, Conn., 1954-57; BA, U. Ill., 1961, MA, 1965; PhD, UCLA, 1979. Asst. physicist Nuclear Chgo. Corp., Des Plaines, Ill., 1959-60; engring. writer Gen. Dynamics Corp., Pomona, Calif., 1962-65; tech. publs. analyst System Devel. Corp., Santa Monica, Calif., 1965-70; instr. Santa Monica Coll., 1968-70; research assoc. Inst. for Ednl. Devel., El Segundo, Calif., 1970-71; cons. instructional design Northridge, Calif., 1972—; prof. dept. Radio-TV-Film Calif. State U., Northridge, 1979—, coord. MA program in mass communication, 1981—, prof., 1988—. Author, editor: (with others) Art of Multi-Image, 1978; author: (with others) Mass Media and the Individual, 1983; presenter various media confs., 1980-89; contbr. articles to profl. jours. Bd. dirs. Build Rehab. Industries, North Hollywood, Calif., 1980-87. Instructional Improvement grantee Northridge Found., 1985. Mem. Acad. TV Arts and Scis., Soc. Motion Picture and TV Engrs., Internat. TV Assn., Assn. For Multi-Image (publs. bd, devel. bd., coord., chmn. bd. dirs.), Am. Psychol. Assn., Internat. Interactive Communications Soc., Broadcast Edn. Assn., UCLA Alumni Assn., Grad. Sch. Edn. Assn. (v.p. 1988-89, bd. dirs.), Textbook Authors Assn., Assn. Visual Communicators (exec. com. 1988—, bd. dirs., pres. L.A. chpt. 1989—), Assoc. for Ednl. Communications and Tech., Am. Ednl. Rsch. Assn., Internat. Visual Literacy Assn., Am. Ednl. Rsch. Assn., Spl. Interest Group-Computer Graphics (L.A. chpt.), L.A. Nat. Soc. for Performance and Instrn., Soc. for Performance and Instrn., Los Angeles County Mus. Art, Am. Film Inst., Sierra Club, Calif. Faculty Assn., AAUP. Office: Calif State U Dept Radio-TV-Film Northridge CA 91330

LERAAEN, ALLEN KEITH, arbitrageur, trader; b. Mason City, Iowa, Dec. 4, 1951; s. Myron O. and Clarice A. (Handeland) L.; m. Mary Elena Partheymuller, Apr. 14, 1978. BBA in Data Processing and Acctg., No. Ariz. U., 1975. Chartered fin. analyst. Data processing supr. Stephenson & Co., Denver, 1978-81, contr., 1981-85, arbitrageur, trader, 1985—, v.p.,

1986—; asst. sec. Satellink Corp., Denver, 1984-89; v.p. Isis Entertainment Inc., Denver, 1985—; v.p., sec., bd. dirs. Circle Corp., Denver, 1985—, Level I CFA Candidate. Home: 5692 S Robb St Littleton CO 80127 Office: Stephenson & Co 100 Garfield St 4th Fl Denver CO 80206

LERCH, STANFORD EARL, lawyer; b. Newberrytown, Pa., Aug. 24, 1933; s. Mizpah Earl and Julia Elizabeth (Smith) L.; m. Isabella Middleton Barnwell, June 2, 1959; children: Susan, Bradley, Michael. J.D., U. Ariz., 1961. Bar: Ariz. 1961, U.S. Supreme Ct. 1967. Ptnr. Jones Hunter & Lerch (P.A.), Phoenix, 1961-79, pres., 1974-79; ptnr. Harrison & Lerch, P.C., 1979-88, Kennedy, Wilson & Lerch, 1988—; Evaluator legal services program OEO, 1967-68. Bd. editors Fair Share Mag., 1982—. Maricopa County chmn. Young Citizens for Johnson-Humphrey, 1964; mem. Planning Task Force for Democratic Party Reorgn. in Maricopa County, 1965-66, Dem. state committeeman, 1962-64, mem. Dem. Fin. Council, 1983-84, mem. Dem. Bus. Council, 1984—; bd. dirs. Maricopa County Legal Aid Soc., 1964-70, Maricopa County Cancer Soc., 1967-68; bd. visitors Ariz. State U. Law Sch., 1974-77; mem. youth and govt. com. Ariz. YMCA, 1966-78; mem. jud. selection com. City of Phoenix, 1974-78; mem. Ariz.-Mex. Commn., 1978—. Recipient A. Louis Slonaker award as outstanding alumnus U. Ariz., 1970. Fellow Am. Bar Found., Ariz. Bar Found. (founding), Young Lawyers Assn.; mem. ABA (ho. of dels. 1969-87), state del. 1984-87, chmn. retirement com. 1974-75, mem. resolutions com. 1979-84, chmn. family law sect. 1981-82, mem. scope and correlation com. 1981-86, chmn. 1983-85, vice chmn. ad hoc com. on assembly 1981-82 mem. hearings com. 1984-86, com. on constn. and by laws 1985—), State Bar Ariz. (chmn. young lawyers sect. 1965-66, chmn. bankruptcy sect. 1968-72, treas., v.p., gov. 1973-77, del. White House Conf. on Families 1980), Fed. Bar Assn. (nat. council 1974-79), Nat. Conf. Lawyers and Social Workers, U. Ariz. Alumni Assn. (dir. 1971-77), U. Ariz. Pres.'s Club, 20-30 Internat. (internat. pres. 1970-71), Phi Delta Theta, Delta Sigma Rho, Phi Alpha Delta, Blue Key. Episcopalian. Clubs: Phoenix Country, University. Home: 2102 Encanto Dr SW Phoenix AZ 85007 Office: Harrison & Lerch PC 1001 N Central Ste 900 Phoenix AZ 85004

LERMAN, EILEEN R., lawyer; b. N.Y.C., May 6, 1947; d. Alex and Beatrice (Kline) L. BA, Syracuse U., 1969; JD, Rutgers U., 1972; MBA, U. Denver, 1983. Bar: N.Y. 1973, Colo. 1976. atty. FTC, N.Y.C., 1972-74; corp. atty. RCA, N.Y.C., 1974-76; corp. atty. Samsonite Corp. and consumer products div. Beatrice Foods Co., Denver, 1976-78, assoc. gen. counsel, 1978—, asst. sec., 1979-85; ptnr. Davis, Lerman, & Weinstein, Denver, 1985—; bd. dir. Legal Aid Soc. of Met. Denver, 1979-80. Bd. dirs., vice chmn. Colo. Postsecondary Ednl. Facilities Authority, 1981-89; bd. dirs., treas. Am. Jewish Com., also v.p.; mem. Leadership Denver, 1983. Mem. ABA, Colo. Women's Bar Assn. (bd. dir. 1980-81), Colo. Bar Assn. (bd. govs.), Denver Bar Assn. (bd. trustee), N.Y. State Bar Assn. (bd. trustees), Rutgers U. Alumni Assn. Lodge: Soroptimists. Home: 1018 Fillmore St Denver CO 80206 Office: Davis Lerman & Weinstein 50 S Steele St Ste 420 Denver CO 80209

LERNER, SHELDON, plastic surgeon; b. N.Y.C., Mar. 3, 1939; s. Louis and Lillian L.; AB with honors, Drew U., Madison, N.J., 1961; MD, U. Louisville, 1965. Intern, resident Albert Einstein Coll. Medicine, Bronx-Mcpl. Hosp. Center, 1965-73; practice medicine, specializing in plastic surgery Plastic Cosmetic and Reconstructive Surgery Center, San Diego, 1973—. Served with USPHS, 1968-70. Mem. AMA, Am. Soc. Plastic and Reconstructive Surgeons, Calif. Med. Soc., San Diego County Med. Soc., San Diego Internat. Plastic Surgery Assn. Clubs: Masons, Shriners. Office: 3399 First Ave San Diego CA 92103

LE ROUX, JEAN-LOUIS, orchestra conductor; b. Le Mans, France, Apr. 15, 1927; came to U.S., 1959; s. Joseph M. and Lucienne (Papin) L.; m. Marie-Louise Malnou, 1952 (div. 1956); children: Olivier, Hervé; m. Marta Bracchi, Dec. 13, 1957; 1 child, Cécile. Diploma, Ecole Superieur de Commerce, Paris, 1945, Conservatoire Superieur de Musique, Paris, 1949. Musical dir. "Guanabara" Chamber Orch., Belo Horizonte, Brazil, 1951-54, Euterpe Chamber Orch., Montevideo, Uruguay, 1955-60; conducting instr. San Francisco Conservatory of Music, 1964-68; musical dir. San Francisco Contemporary Music Players, 1975-88; conductor San Francisco Ballet, 1975—; music dir. Chamber Symphony of San Francisco, 1982—. Prin. oboe Belo Horizonte Symphony, 1950-54, SODRE Network (Servicio Oficial para Difusion Radio Electrica y Espectaculos), Uruguay, 1954-60, San Francisco Symphony, 1960-80; featured on several recs. including ballet The Tempest, 1983. Decorated Chevalier de l'Ordre des Arts et Lettres, Govt. France, 1981. Democrat. Roman Catholic. Home: 2874 Washington St San Francisco CA 94115 Office: Chamber Orch San Francisco 710 Van Ness Ave San Francisco CA 94102

LEROY, DAVID HENRY, lawyer, state official; b. Seattle, Aug. 16, 1947; s. Harold David and Lela Fay (Palmer) L.; m. Helen LaVonne Transue, Aug. 5, 1972; 2 children. B.S., U. Idaho, 1969, J.D., 1971; LL.M., NYU, 1972. Bar: Idaho 1971, N.Y. State 1973, U.S. Supreme Ct. 1976. Law clk. Idaho 4th Dist. Ct., Boise, 1969; legal asst. Boise Cascade Corp., 1970; asso. firm Rothblatt, Rothblatt, Seijas & Peskin, N.Y.C., 1971-73; dep. prosecutor Ada County Prosecutor's Office, Boise, 1973-74; pros. atty. Ada County Prosecutor's Office, 1974-78; atty. gen. State of Idaho, Boise, 1978-82, lt. gov., 1983-87; ptnr. Runft, Leroy Coffin & Matthews, 1983-88, Leroy Law Offices, 1988—; candidate for Gov. of Idaho, 1986; motivation speaker, writer Leading Edge, Boise. Mem. State Task Force on Child Abuse, 1975; mem. Ada County Council on Alcoholism, 1976; del. Republican Nat. Conv., 1976, 80; chmn. Nat. Rep. Lt. Gov.'s Caucus, from 1983; bd. dirs. United Fund, 1975-81; del. Am. Council Young Polit. Leaders, USSR, 1979, Am. Council for Free Asia, Taiwan, 1980, U.S./Taiwan Investment Forum, 1983; del. leader Friendship Force Tour USSR, 1984; legal counsel Young Republicans, 1974-81. Mem. Nat. Dist. Attys. Assn., Idaho Prosecutors Assn., Am. Trial Lawyers Assn., Idaho Trial Lawyers Assn., Nat. Assn. Attys. Gen. (chmn. energy subcom., exec. com., del to China 1981), Western Attys. Gen. Assn. (vice chmn. 1980-83, chmn. 1981), Nat. Lt. Govs. Assn. (exec. bd. 1983), Idaho Bar Assn., Sigma Alpha Epsilon. Presbyterian. Office: The Leroy Offices PO Box 193 Boise ID 83701

LERUDE, WARREN LESLIE, journalism educator; b. Reno, Oct. 29, 1937; s. Leslie Raymond and Ione (Lundy) L.; m. Janet Lagomarsino, Aug. 24, 1961; children: Eric Warren, Christopher Mario Leslie, Leslie Ann. BA in Journalism, U. Nev., 1961. Reporter, editor, correspondent The AP, Las Vegas, Reno, Nev., 1960-63; reporter, editor, pub., pres. Reno Evening Gazette, Nev. State Jour., 1963-81; prof. journalism U. Nev., Reno, 1981—; bd. dirs. Oakland (Calif.) Tribune; lectr. Am. Press Inst.; cons. ABA, Nat. Broadcasting Co., Nat. Jud. Coll. Co-author: American Commander in Spain, Robert Hale Merriman and the Abraham Lincoln Brigade, 1986; mem. editorial bd. USA Today, 1982—. Trustee U. Nev.-Reno Found.; trustee, mem. community adv. bd. Sta. KNPB-TV, Reno; mem. legis. com. Greater Reno C. of C.; mem. exec. bd. Biggest Little City Com., Reno, 1988—. Served with USNR, 1957-59. Co-recipient Pulitzer prize, 1977. Mem. Nev. State Press Assn. (past pres.), Calif.-Nev. News Execs. Council of the AP, Calif. Newspaper Pub. Assn. (editors conf.), Sigma Delta Chi. Club: Rotary. Home: 3825 N Folsom Dr Reno NV 89509 Office: U Nev Reynolds Sch Journalism Reno NV 89557

LERVICK, ROGER O., frozen foods company executive. Office: Twin City Foods Inc 10120 269th Pl NW Stanwood WA 98292

LESATZ, STEPHEN, JR., lawyer; b. Greeley, Colo., Aug. 5, 1937; s. Stephen J. and Rose (Scholz) LeS.; m. LaDonna M. Distel, June 10, 1961; 1 son, Eric S. B.S. in Bus. Adminstrn., U. Denver, 1959, LL.B., 1961. Bar: Colo. 1962, Minn. 1968, Mich. 1969. Assoc. Haskell, Helmick, Carpenter & Evans, Denver, 1962-68, Arthur E. Anderson, LeSueur, Minn., 1968-69; atty. Whirlpool Corp., Benton Harbor, Mich., 1969-74; assoc. gen. counsel Rocky Mountain Energy Co., Denver, 1974-87, Union Pacific Corp., 1987-89; assoc. gen. counsel USPCI, Inc., Oklahoma City, Okla., 1989—; prin. Vista Properties, Denver, 1983—. Mem. Denver Art Mus., Denver Mus. Natural History, U. Denver Chancellor's Soc. Mem. ABA, Colo. Bar Assn., Denver Bar Assn. Republican. Congregationalist. Office: 1919 14th St Boulder CO 80302

LESCHINE, THOMAS MICHAEL, marine studies educator; b. Sewickley, Pa., July 12, 1945; s. Michael and Julia Louise (Ponticello) L.; m. Susan Jean Bingman, Apr. 28, 1968 (div. 1979); m. Kathleen O'Neill, Dec. 19, 1981. BS, U. Pitts., 1967, MA, 1970, PhD, 1975. Assoc. prof. math. U. Pitts., Greensburg, 1970-76; rsch. fellow Woods Hole (Mass.) Oceanographic Inst., 1976-78, policy assoc., 1978-83; rsch. assoc. prof. Inst. Marine Studies, U. Wash., Seattle, 1983-88, assoc. prof., 1988—; vis. scientist Nat. Ctr. Atmospheric Rsch., Boulder, Colo., 1983, Battelle Meml. Inst., Seattle, 1988—; cons. in field. Contbr. articles to profl. publs. Tech. advisor U.S. EPA, Seattle, 1985-86, Puget Sound Water Quality Authority, Seattle, 1987—. Grantee Woods Hole Oceanographic Inst., 1976, NSF, 1978-88, numerous other fed. and state agys. Mem. Inst. Mgmt. Sci., AAAS, Ops. Rsch. Soc. Am., Soc. Judgement and Decision Making. Democrat. Office: Inst Marine Studies U Wash 3707 Brooklyn Ave NE Seattle WA 98195

LESH, PAUL LESTER, mechanical engineer, educator; b. Arkansas City, Kans., Oct. 30, 1935; s. Paul Earl and Clara (League) L.; m. Ruth Aline Webb, July 21, 1956; children: David Paul, Stephanie Elaine. AA, U. Cin., 1973, BS, 1974; MBA, U. Phoenix, 1986. Registered profl. engr. Ohio, Ariz., Tex.; cert. community coll. tchr. Drafting apprentice Gen. Electric Co., Evendale, Ohio, 1954-58, designer, 1962=63; draftsman Aerojet-Gen. Corp., Sacramento, 1958-62; machine designer Cin. Minlacron, Inc., 1963-74; mech. designer Flanco Svcs., Inc., Phoenix, 1974-76; machine design engr. S.I.I. Drillco Indsl., Midland, Tex., 1976-77; mech. engr. supr. CIBA-GEIGY Corp., Burkburnett, Tex., 1977-79; sr. devel. engr. Loral Corp., Def. Systems Group, Litchfield Park, Ariz., 1979--; instr. Miami Valley Inst. Tech., Hamilton, Ohio, 1970, Acad. Drafting, Tempe, Ariz., 1974-76, Glendale (Ariz.) Community Coll., 1980-82, Phoenix Coll., 1983-84. Pvt. 1st class U.S. Army, 1958-60. Mem. Am. Mgmt. Assn. Republican. Office: Loral Def Systems Group Ariz 100 S Litchfield Rd Litchfield Park AZ 85340

LESHER, MARGARET LISCO, newspaper publishing executive, songwriter; b. San Antonio, Tex., May 4, 1932; d. Lloyd Elmo Lisco and Dovie Deona (Maynard) Lisco Welch; m. William Jarvis Ryan (dec.); children: Patricia D., Wendi L. Ryan Alves, Jill A. Ryan Heidt; m. Dean Stanley Lesher, Sr., Apr. 4, 1972; children: Dean S. II, Melinda K., Cynthia A. Student Coalinga (Calif.) Jr. Coll., 1957-59. Dir. sales Chatmar, Inc., Concord, Calif., 1970-73; dir. community services Contra Costa Times Newspaper, Walnut Creek, Calif., 1973—; 1st v.p. corp. bus. Lesher Communications, Inc., Walnut Creek, 1974—, Calif. Delta Newspapers, Inc., Antioch, 1975—, No. Calif. Newspapers, Inc. Composer, lyricist gospel song Margaret Lesher Album, 1976 (So. Calif. Motion Picture Council Bronze Halo award 1982); author 14 published poems. Regent Holy Names Coll., Oakland, Calif., 1979-86; chief of protocol Contra Costa County, 1980—; dir. Bay Area Sports Hall of Fame, San Francisco, 1982—; bd. overseers U. Calif., San Francisco, 1983—; mem. San Francisco Host Com., 1983—, Internat. Visitors Ctr., San Francisco, 1983-85, Internat. Host Com. of Calif., 1983-86, Nat. Reading Initiative Coordinating Com., 1988—; developed Citizen Recognition Awards Program with County Police Chiefs Assn.; founded Contra Costa Literacy Alliance; commr. Port of Richmond, Calif., 1983-86; chmn. adv. bd. Crisis Nursery of Bay Area, Concord, 1983-86; adv. bd. Oakland A's Baseball Team, 1984-85, Battered Women, 1983—; pres. bd. dirs. Mt. Diablo Hosp. Found., 1980-81; bd. dirs. Contra Costa Council, 1984—; mem. adv. bd. Las Trampas Sch. Mentally Retarded, chmn., 1984—; trustee Oakland Symphony Orch., 1985-86; host Informed Viewer pub. svc. program Sta. KFCB-TV. Recipient Spl. Merit award State of Calif., 1982. Mem. Am. Newspaper Pub. Assn. (ednl. svcs. com. 1988—), Gospel Music Assn., ASCAP, Nat. TV Acad. Arts & Scis. Republican. Christian. Clubs: Blackhawk Country. Office: care Contra Costa Times Lesher Communications Inc 2640 Shadelands Dr Walnut Creek CA 94598

LESHY, JOHN DAVID, lawyer, educator; b. Winchester, Ohio, Oct. 7, 1944; s. John and Dolores (King) L.; m. Helen M. Sandalls, Dec. 15, 1973; 1 child, Alec. AB, Harvard U., 1966, JD, 1969. Bar: Ohio 1969, Calif. 1972, D.C. 1977. Atty. U.S. Dept. Justice, Washington, 1969-72; regional counsel Nat. Resourses Def. Coun., Palo Alto, Calif., 1972-77; assoc. solicitor energy and resources U.S. Dept. Interior, Washington, 1977-80; prof. law Ariz. State U., Tempe, 1980—; bd. dirs. Ariz. Raft Adventures, Flagstaff, Grand Canyon Trust, Washington. Author: The Mining Law: A Study in Perpetual Motion, 1987. Rsch. grantee Ford Found., 1981; Robinson Cox fellow, 1985. Mem. ABA. Democrat. Office: Ariz State U Coll Law Tempe AZ 85287-0604

LESLIE, DONALD MICHAEL, software engineer; b. Chgo., June 5, 1943; s. Howard and Estelle (Mansowitz) L.; m. Patricia A. Stauffer, May 30, 1969; 1 child, Elizabeth. BS in Math., N.Mex. State U., 1967, MS in Computer Sci., 1972. Programmer RCA, Riverton, N.J., 1969-71, Siemens Co., Munich, 1972-73, Travelers Ins. Co., Hartford, Conn., 1973-74; sr. software engr. Raytheon Co., Bedford, Mass., 1975-78, White Sands, N.Mex., 1982—; cons. Danet Co., Munich, 1979-82; conf. presenter. Mem. Southwestern Assn. for Artificial Intelligence (v.p. 1987-88), HP-1000 Users Group (pres. 1984-88). Home: 1121 N Reymond St Las Cruces NM 88005 Office: Raytheon Co PO Box B White Sands Missile Range NM 88002

LESLIE, REO NAPOLEON, JR., clergyman, naval officer; b. Chgo., May 8, 1953; s. Reo Napoleon and Ernestine (Brown) L.; m. Elanda Lee Larsen, Feb. 19, 1980; children: Pammie, Ronald, Erica, Hatshepsut. MDiv, Garrett Theol. Sem., 1977; DMin, Chgo. Theol. Sem., 1979; MS in Theology, McCormick Sem., 1982; MA in Internat. Rels., U.S. Internat. U., 1989. Ordained to ministry United Ch. of Christ 1977. Chaplain Way Out Drug Abuse Ctr., Evanston, Ill., 1975-76, Evanston Twp. High Sch., 1976, Met. Ctr. for Corrections, Chgo., 1976-77; student liason person Univ. Ch., United Ch. of Christ, Chgo., 1977-78; protestant chaplain Westside VA Hosp., Chgo., 1978; chaplaincy dir. Community Hosp., Evanston, 1978-79; chaplain, spiritual dir. Boysville of Mich., Detroit, 1980-81; assoc. pastor Shrine of Black Madonna United Ch. of Christ, Detroit, 1972-81; commd. officer USN, 1981; advanced through grades to lt. comdr. Chaplain Corps, San Diego, 1981--; bd. dirs., Ctr. for Studies of Person, LaJolla, Calif., 1988--; appointed asst. work ctr. coordinator, Svc. Sch. Command Chaplain Div., Naval Tng. Cr., 1988--. Author: Sermons for Stormy Seas, 1984, Peace in Troubled Waters, 1987. Bd. dirs. San Diego County Ecumenical Conf., 1981-83, Jackie Robinson YMCA, San Diego, 1987-88. Recipient cert. of appreciation Bethel Bapt. Ch., San Diego, 1988, Navy Achievement Medal, USS Ranger, 1986. Mem. Southeast Ministerial Alliance (sec. San Diego), Point Loma Ministerial Assn., Nat. Naval Officers Assn. Office: US Naval Tng Sta Chaplain Dept San Diego CA 92133-1000

LESLIE, ROBERT LORNE, lawyer; b. Adak, Alaska, Feb. 24, 1947; s. J. Lornie and L. Jean (Conelly) L.; children—Lorna Jean, Elizabeth Allen. B.S., U.S. Mil. Acad., 1969; J.D., Hastings Coll. Law, U. Calif.-San Francisco, 1974. Bar: Calif. 1974, D.C. 1979, U.S. Dist. Ct. (no. dist.) Calif. 1974, U.S. Ct. Claims 1975, U.S. Tax Ct. 1975, U.S. Ct. Appeals (9th and D.C. cirs.), U.S. Ct. Mil. Appeals 1980, U.S. Supreme Ct. 1980. Commd. 2d lt. U.S. Army, 1969, advanced through grades to maj., 1980; govt. trial atty. West Coast Field Office, Contract Appeals, Litigation Div. and Regulatory Law Div., Office JAG, Dept. Army, San Francisco, 1974-77; sr. trial atty. and team chief Office of Chief Trial Atty., Dept. Army, Washington, 1977-80; ret., 1980; ptnr. McInerney & Dillon, Oakland, Calif., 1980—; lectr. on govt. contracts CSC, Continuing Legal Edn. Program; lectr. in govt. procurement U.S. Army Materiel Command. Decorated Silver Star, Purple Heart, Meritorious Service medal. Mem. ABA, Fed. Bar Assn. Club: Commonwealth (San Francisco). Home: 4144 Greenwood Ave Oakland CA 94602 Office: Ordway Bldg 18th Fl Oakland CA 94612

LESNICK, MICHAEL THOMAS, foundation administrator; b. Bridgeport, Conn., July 27, 1952; s. Thomas Richard and Joann Clara (Miccio) L.; m. Martha Agnes McCann, July 17, 1976; children: Eric McCann, Kaitlan McCann. BA, Fairfield U., Conn., 1974; MS in N.R. Policy, U. Mich., 1981, PhD (postdoctoral fellow), 1986. Asst. dir. Drug Edn. Ctr. City of Bridgeport, 1971-72, Youth Employment Prog., 1973; dir. Youth Drop-In Ctr. Stratford (Conn.) YMCA, 1973-75, Youth in Crisis Project, Coun. of Chs., Bridgeport, 1975-78; rsch. assoc. Sch. Natural Resource, U. Mich., Ann Arbor, 1978-83, Resource & Devel. Cons. Internat., Inc., Ann Arbor, 1980; assoc. dir. Environ. Conflict Project, U. Mich., 1983-86; v.p. The Keystone Ctr., Colo., 1986—; bd. dirs. Colo. Aquatic Inst., Frisco, 1988—; cons. Sec. of Interior, Nat. Adv. Com. on Strategic Matl. & Minerals, 1987, USAID/U.S. Forest Svc., Internat. Forestry Seminar, 1985-86. Contbr. articles to profl. jours. Mem. Summit County Sch. Dist. accountability com., Colo., 1986-87; chmn. Parent/Tchr./Student Assn. fin. com. for sch. play, Summit County, 1988—; coach Summit County Little League, 1986—. Recipient Ayers Brinser award, Sch. Natural Resources, U. Mich., 1983; U. Mich. Horace H. Rackham dissertation grantee, 1984. Democrat. Roman Catholic. Home: PO Box 554 Frisco CO 80443 Office: The Keystone Center Box 606 Keystone CO 80435

LESTER, JOHN CLAYTON, life insurance company executive; b. Cheyenne, Wyo., Sept. 26, 1940; s. Arthur C. and Harleen E. (Gorman) L.; m. Ruth A. Whatley, Nov. 21, 1959; children: John Clayton, Connie Sue. BBA, Wichita State U., 1965. CLU. Office supr. State Farm Fire & Casualty Co., Greeley, Colo., 1965-69; agt. Equitable Life Assurance Soc., Greeley, 1969-70, from dist. mgr. to agy. mgr., Denver, 1970-78, regional agy. v.p., 1978-84, agy. mgr., Woodland Hills, Calif., 1984—. Served with USN, 1958-61. Mem. Am. Soc. CLU's, San Fernando Valley Life Underwriters, Gen. Agts. and Mgrs. Assn. (past pres. San Fernando Valley chpt.). Republican. Home: 29372 Castlehill Dr Agoura Hills CA 91301 Office: Equitable Life Assurance Soc 21041 Burbank Blvd Ste 200 Woodland Hills CA 91365

LESTER, JOHN JAMES NATHANIEL, II, engineer, environmental analyst; b. Houston, May 7, 1952; s. John James Nathaniel Lester and Margaret Louise (Tisdale) Sharp; m. Leslie Ann Yarab, Oct. 5, 1980. Student, U. Tex., 1970, Lee Coll., 1971; AS, Grossmont Coll., 1979; BA in Behavioral Sci., Nat. U., 1987, postgrad., 1987—. Registered profl. stationary engr.; ordained to ministry Am. Fellowship Ch. Nuclear power specialist USN, various, 1971-77; microbiology lab. technician VA, San Diego, 1978; prin. engring. asst. San Diego Gas & Electric, 1979-85, engring. environ. analyst, 1985-88; owner Calif. Triad Gem & Mineral Co. Logistics dir. and regional bd. mem. Gary Hart Presdl. Campaign, San Diego, 1984; founding mem. Inlet drug crisis ctr., Houston, 1970; vol. Dir. Aid for Guatemalan Refugees and Orphans, Guatemala, 1988. Served with USN, 1971-77. Mem. ASME, IEEE (interim pres. and founding mem. San Diego region Ocean Engring. Soc. 1984-85), Mensa, Assn. Humanistic Psychology, Amnesty Internat., Hunger Project, Earth Stewards, Human Rights Watch, Sierra Club. Democrat. Home and Office: 2588-D El Camino Real Suite 193 Carlsbad CA 92008

LESTER, TERRY LEROY, actor; b. Indpls., Apr. 13, 1950; s. Ernest LeRoy and Carol Ann (Gipson) L. BA, DePauw U., 1975. Actor "The Young and the Restless" Sta. CBS-TV, L.A., 1980—. With U.S. Army, 1971-74. Mem. Acad. TV Arts and Scis. (daytime Emmy awards com. 1988—, nominated for Best Actor Emmy awards 1983-86). Office: 413 Prodns Inc 1925 Century Park E Ste 920 Los Angeles CA 90067

LESTER, THOMAS FRANCIS JOSEPH, mathematics and computer consultant; b. Butte, Mont., Aug. 23, 1940; s. Joseph abd Margaret Esther (Torpy) L.; m. Mary Lynn Maloney; children: Christopher Joseph, Cara Nicole. BS, Iona Coll., 1962; MA, Manhattan Coll., 1966. Dir. project SEED, Detroit, Sacramento and Bay Area, Calif.; instr. Calif. State U., Sacramento, 1973—; resource tchr. math. and computer San Juan Unified Sch. Dist., Carmichael, Calif., 1974-84, math./computer program specialist, 1984-88; dir. live-in program U. Calif., Davis, summer 1970; vice prin. North Ave. Sch., Del Paso Heights, Calif., 1969-70; co-dir. discovery program Calif. State U., Sacramento, summers 1978-81, acad. partnership project grant Calif. State U. and U. Calif., 1984-87; dir. math. Talent Search, Sacramento, summers 1982—; mem. Math. Com. for Assessment Program, State of Calif., 1978-88, math. diagnostic testing project Calif. State U. and U. Calif., 1983—, testing adv. com. Ednl. Testing Svc., Princeton, 1986—; maths. cons. Calif. State Dept. of Edn., 1988—. Co-author Plexers and More Plexers, 1983, Trigonometry, 1983-84, Calculus, 1983-84; editor edn., contbg. author Sacramento Valley Computer News, 1984-85; mem. working symposium booklet Teaching: Making It An Effective and Attractive Profession, 1984-86. Coach Pony Baseball League, Citrus Heights, Calif., 1980-83, San Soccer League, Citrus Heights, 1980-85; co-dirs. NSF, Calif. Acad. Partnership Program. Mem. Nat. Coun. Tchrs. of Math., Calif. Math. Coun., San Juan Adminstrs. Assn. Democrat. Roman Catholic. Club: Gold River Racquet (Rancho Cordova, Calif.). Home: 8419 Kroeger Ct Fair Oaks CA 95628 Office: San Juan Unified Sch Dist 3938 Walnut Ave Carmichael CA 95609

LESTER, WILLIAM ALEXANDER, JR., chemist, educator; b. Chgo., Apr. 24, 1937; s. William Alexander and Elizabeth Frances (Clark) L.; m. Rochelle Diane Reed, Dec. 27, 1959; children: William Alexander III, Allison Kimberleigh. B.S., U. Chgo., 1958, M.S., 1959; postgrad., Washington U., St. Louis, 1959-60; Ph.D., Cath. U. Am., 1964. Phys. chemist Nat. Bur. Standards, Washington, 1961-64; asst. dir. Theoretical Chemistry Inst. of U. Wis.-Madison, 1965-68; research staff mem. IBM Research Lab., San Jose, Calif., 1968-75; mgr. 1976-78; mem. tech. planning staff IBM T.J. Watson Research Center, Yorktown Heights, N.Y., 1975-76; dir. Nat. Resource for Computation in Chemistry, Lawrence Berkeley (Calif.) Lab., 1978-81, also assoc. dir., staff sr. scientist, 1978-81, faculty sr. scientist, 1981—; prof. chemistry U. Calif.-Berkeley, 1981—; lectr. chemistry U. Wis., 1966-68; cons. NSF, 1976-77, mem. chem. div. adv. panel, 1980-83, adv. com. Office Advanced Sci. Computing program, 1985-87, chmn., 1987; mem. U.S. nat. com. Internat. Union Pure and Applied Chemistry, 1976-79; mem. com. on recommendations for U.S. Army Basic Sci. Research NRC, 1984-87, mem. steering com., 1987-88; chemistry research evaluation panel AF Office Sci. Research, 1974-78; chmn. Gordon Conf. Atomic and Molecular Interactions, 1978; mem. NRC panel on chem. physics Nat. Bur. Standards, 1980-83; mem. com. to survey chem. scis. NRC, 1982-84. Editor: Procs. of Conf. on Potential Energy Surfaces in Chemistry, 1971; mem. editorial bd. Jour. Phys. Chemistry, 1979-81, Internat. Jour. Quantum Chemistry, 1979-87, Jour. Computational Chemistry, 1980-87, Computer Physics Communications, 1981-86. Recipient Alumni award in sci. Cath. U. Am., 1983. Fellow Am. Phys. Soc. (chmn. div. chem. physics 1986); mem. Am. Chem. Soc. (sec.-treas. Wis. sect. 1967-68, chmn. div. phys. chemistry 1979, treas. div. computers in chemistry 1974-77), Nat. Orgn. Black Chemists and Chem. Engrs. (Percy L. Julian award 1979, Outstanding Tchr. award 1986, exec. bd. 1984-87), AAAS (com. on nominations 1988—). Home: 4433 Briar Cliff Rd Oakland CA 94605 Office: U Calif Dept Chemistry Berkeley CA 94720

LESTER, WILLIAM WALTER, real estate executive, orchardist; b. Santa Clara, Calif., July 17, 1916; s. William Walter and Ethel Viola (Gerrans) L.; student San Jose (Calif.) State U., 1935-38, U. Calif., Davis, 1938-40, U. Santa Clara, 1941, Columbia U., 1942; m. Hazel Marie Barnes, Mar. 6, 1944; children: Stanley, Marie, William, III, George, Russell. Sr. v.p., treas., gen. ptnr. Vallco Park, Ltd., 1964—; owner Lester & Lester, orchard, Cupertino and Sacramento Valley, Calif., 1940—; dir. Orchard Supply Bldg. Corp., 1960-77. Mem. Santa Clara County Planning Commn., 1956-64, Rt. 280 Penninsula Hwy. Design Commn., Cupertino Public Safety Commn., 1971-75; bd. dirs. Santa Clara County Water Dist., 1965-66; pres. Calif. History Ctr. Found., 1979-83. Served to lt. USNR, World War II. Named Man of Year, Cupertino C. of C., 1981. Mem. Internat. Council Shopping Centers, Am. Inst. Plant Engrs., Western Water Assn., Calif. Water Resources Assn., Farm Bur. Fedn., Council Calif. Growers, U.S. C. of C., Calif. C. of C., Cupertino C. of C., U. Calif. Davis Chancellors Club (funded 1st chair for pemological rsch., Disting. Jerry Fielder award 1986), Commonwealth Club of Calif., Masons. Home: 10650 Linnet Ln Cupertino CA 95014 Office: 10050 N Wolfe Rd Ste SW 2-106 Cupertino CA 95014

LETTICH, SHELDON BERNARD, screenwriter; b. N.Y.C., Jan. 14, 1951; s. Max and Sonja (Shapell) L.; m. Toni Dorothea Williams, Mar. 5, 1954; children: Micheline, Jessica, Angelique. Student, Brooks Inst., Santa Barbara, Calif., 1974; AA, Santa Monica Coll., 1974-76; student, Am. Film Inst., Beverly Hills, 1977-78. Author: (with others) play Tracers, 1980 (Los Angeles Drama Critics award, 1981), film Russkies, 1987, Rambo III, 1988; author: film Bloodsport, 1988. Served to cpl. U.S.M.C., 1969-72, Vietnam. Mem. Writers Guild Am. Office: Hard Corps Prodns Inc 5225 Wilshire Blvd 1103 Los Angeles CA 90036

LETTINI, MICHAEL JOHN, aviation company executive; b. Rahway, N.J., Oct. 7, 1942; s. Anthony and Antoinetta (Anginoli) L.; m. Ingeborg K. V. Betzler, July 1, 1972; children: Kim, Kara. BS in Physics, Stevens Inst. Tech., 1964. Engr. Boeing, Seattle, 1964-71, 72-74, lead engr., 1974-84, supr., 1984-87, mgr. elec. processes, engring. standards, 1987—; chief engr.

King Elec. Mfg., Seattle, 1971-72; cons., Mercer Island, Wash., 1981—. Inventor, patentee Electrical Terminal, 1975. Mem. Planetary Soc. Roman Catholic. Home: 9728 SE 41st St Mercer Island WA 98040

LEUENBERGER, MARTIN JAKOB, lawyer; b. Zurich, Switzerland, May 3, 1949; came to U.S., 1951; s. Hans and Marie (Weilenmann) L.; m. Gayle Raye Downing, Feb. 23, 1979; 1 child, Edward Santiago. BS, Oreg. State U., 1971; JD, U. Oreg., 1975. Bar: Oreg. 1975, U.S. Dist. Ct. Oreg. 1976. Pvt. practice Baker, Oreg., 1975-76, 81-82; ptnr. Leuenberger & Hadley, Baker, Oreg., 1977-80, Coughlin, Leuenberger & Moon, Baker, Oreg., 1983—; bd. dirs. Anthony Lakes Ski Corp., La Grande, Oreg. Bd. dirs. Baker County Coun. on Alcohol, 1976-78, Baker Family YMCA, 1979-82; chmn. Baker County campaign United Way, 1978-79; mem. Baker County Planning Com. to Draft Recreational Use Ordinance, 1987. Mem. Oreg. Bar Assn. (exec. com. debtor/creditor sect. 1985-87), Baker County Bar Assn., Elks (justice Baker 1979-83). Republican. Home: 1 Western Heights Baker OR 97814 Office: Coughlin Leuenberger & Moon 1650 Dewey Ave Baker OR 97814

LEUNG, DAVID KAM-FAI, restaurateur; b. Guangzhou, China, June 19, 1950; came to U.S., 1978; s. Yue Wing and Mui Yung (Cherng) L.; m. Audrey K. So, Jan. 29, 1986. Diploma in mech. engring., Hong Kong Tech. Coll., 1974-76. Design engr. Vector Electronic Co., Sylmar Valley, Calif., 1979-81; mgr., ptnr. Panda Inn, Santa Monica, Calif., 1981-88; mgr., owner Cathay Palisades, Pacific Palisades, 1988—. Home: 16521 Wain Pl Hacienda Heights CA 91745 Office: Cathay Palisades 15315 Antioch St Pacific Palisades CA 90272

LEUNG, FREDERICK CHI-CHING, endocrinologist; b. Hong Kong, Dec. 1, 1952; came to U.S., 1970; Hung-Sum and Lai-Ching L.; m. Judy A. Charles, Feb. 3, 1978; children: Brandon, Amber, Trevor. BA in Physiology and Anatomy, U. Calif., 1974, PhD in Endocrinology, 1978. Asst. prof. endocrinology Calif. State U., Hayward, 1978; postdoctoral fellow Mich. State U., East Lansing, 1978-80; sr. rsch. biochemist Merck & Co., Rahway, NJ, 1980-84; rsch. fellow Merck & Co., Rahway, 1984-85; sr. rsch. scientist Battelle NW Labs., Richland, Wash., 1985—; adj. asst. prof. Rutgers U., 1982-85; adj. assoc. prof., Wash. State U., 1985—; researcher in field. Contbr. chpts. to med. texts and jours.; patentee in field. Travel grantee Internat. Congress Endocrinology; recipient Nat. Rsch. Svc. award NIH, 1978. Mem. AAAS, Am. Soc. Zoologists, Endocrine Soc., Am. Physiol. Soc., N.Y. Acad. Sci. Home: 714 Redwood Ln Richland WA 99352 Office: Battelle Pacific NW Labs PO Box 999 Richland WA 99352

LEUSCHEN, DONALD M., energy company executive. BSEE, Mont. St. U., 1950. With Mont. Power Co. 1950—, groundman, Lewistown, 1950-51, jr. elec. engr., 1951-54, asst. elec. engr., Missoula, 1954-57, Butte, 1957-58, asst. div. supt., Bozeman, 1958-60, Glasgow, 1958-63, dist. mgr., Glasgow, 1963-65, div. supt. Great Falls, 1965-66, div. mgr., Billings, 1966-74, Missoula, 1974-82, v.p. adminstrn., 1982-84, pres., 1984—, also dir. Served with USN, 1943-46. Office: Mont Power Co 40 E Broadway Butte MT 59701 *

LEUS MCFARLEN, PATRICIA CHERYL, water chemist; b. San Antonio, Mar. 12, 1954; d. Norman W. and Jacqueline S. (Deason) Leus; m. Randy N. McFarlen, June 28, 1986; 1 child, Kevin Bryant. AA, Highline Community Coll., 1974; BS in Chemistry, Eastern Wash. U., 1980. Lab. technician, oil analyst D.A. Lubricant, Vancouver, Wash., 1982-83; plant chemist Navajo Generating Sta., Page, Ariz., 1983—. Sci. judge Page Schs. Sci. Project Fair, 1985; chemist Navajo Generating Sta./Page Sch. Career Day, 1986, 89; life mem. Girl Scouts Am. Mem. Am. Chem. Soc., Sigma Kappa (treas. 1976-78, life). Methodist. Office: Navajo Generating Sta Dept Chem PO Box W Page AZ 86040

LEVADA, WILLIAM JOSEPH, archbishop; b. Long Beach, Calif., June 15, 1936; s. Joseph and Lorraine (Nunez) L. B.A., St. John's Coll., Camarillo, Calif., 1958; S.T.L., Gregorian U., Rome, 1962, S.T.D., 1971. Ordained priest Roman Catholic Ch., 1961, consecrated bishop, 1983. Assoc. pastor Archdiocese of L.A., 1962-67, aux. bishop, vicar for Santa Barbara County, 1983-86; prof. theology St. John's Sem., Camarillo, Calif., 1970-76; ofcl. Doctrinal Congregation, Vatican City, Italy, 1976-82; exec. dir. Calif. Cath. Conf., Sacramento, 1982-84; archbishop Archdiocese of Portland, Oreg., 1986—. Mem. Nat. Conf. Cath. Bishops (com. on doctrine, com. for pro-life activities, com. for pastoral letter on women in ch. and soc.), U.S. Cath. Conf., Cath. Theol. Soc. Am., Canon Law Soc. Am. Office: Archdiocese 2838 E Burnside St Portland OR 97214

LEVENSON, ROBERT MONTIE, physician; b. Yakima, Wash., Jan. 10, 1921; s. Montie T. and Ellen (Sharkey) L.; m. Marie E. Hofmeister, Sept. 21, 1947; children: Robert Jr., Albert D., David A., Nancy, Linda, Mary. MD, U. Louisville, 1946. Diplomate Am. Bd. Internal Medicine, 1955. Intern King County Hosp., Seattle, 1946-47; pvt. practice in internal medicine Seattle, 1954-88; resident Providence Hosp., Seattle, 1949-51, U. Calif. Hosp., San Francisco, 1951-52; clin. prof. U. Wash. Med. Sch., Seattle, 1974—. Trustee Swedish Hosp. Med. Ctr., Seattle, 1985-88, King County Med. Blue Shield, Seattle, 1985—, J.L. Locke Trust, Seattle, 1974—. Fellow Am. Coll. Cardiology, Am. Coll. Physicians, Council Clin. Cardiology; mem. Am. Heart Assn. (award of merit 1982). Home: 3406 72nd Pl SE Mercer Island WA 98040 Office: 801 Broadway Seattle WA 98122

LEVENSTEIN, ROSLYN M., advertising consultant, writer; b. N.Y.C., Mar. 26, 1920; d. Leo Rapoport and Stella Schimmel Rosenberg; m. Justin Seides, June 7, 1943 (div. 1948); 1 child, Leland Seides.; m. Lawrence Levenstein, June 25, 1961. BA in Advt., NYU, 1940. Sr. v.p., assoc. creative dir. Young and Rubicam, Inc., N.Y.C., 1962-79; cons. Young and Rubicam, Inc., Los Angeles and San Diego, 1979-83; advt. cons., writer mag. articles La Jolla, Calif., 1979—. Creator: Excedrin Headache commls. (Andy awards 1967, 68, 69), I'm Only Here for the Beer (Cannes award 1970, Clio Jury award 1970). Recipient: Silver Lion award Cannes Film Festival, 1968, multiple advt. awards U.S. and Eng.; named one of YWCA Women of Yr., 1978. Mem. Charter 100, Women's Com. Brandeis U., Nat. Pen Women. Home: 5802 Corral Way La Jolla CA 92037

LE VEQUE, MATTHEW KURT, state legislative consultant, marketing professional; b. Los Angeles, May 24, 1958; s. Edward Albert and Vera Eleanora (Behne) LeV. BA in Polit. Sci., UCLA, 1981. Reapportionment cons. Calif. State Legislature, Sacramento, 1981; cons. Berman and D'Agostino Campaigns, Inc., Los Angeles, 1982—; coordinator Los Angeles Olympic com., 1984; spl. asst. Congressmen H. Waxman and H. Berman, Calif., 1982-85; cons. Spallino Internat., Newport Beach, Calif., 1984-86; sr. cons. Calif. State Senate, Los Angeles and Sacramento, 1985—. Active numerous local and nat. Dem. polit. campaigns. Office: Calif State Senate 1950 Sawtelle Blvd #210 Los Angeles CA 90025

LEVER, JANET RAE, sociology educator, television talk show host; b. St. Louis, Dec. 5, 1946; d. Harry H. and Sophia (Goldberg) L. BA summa cum laude, Wash. U., St. Louis, 1968; M in Philosophy, Yale U., 1971, PhD, 1974. Instr. Yale U., New Haven, 1974; asst. prof. sociology Northwestern U., Evanston, Ill., 1974-82; vis. asst. prof. U. Calif. San Diego, La Jolla, 1983-85; vis. lectr. UCLA, 1985-87; cons. The RAND Corp., Santa Monica, Calif., 1987—; vis. lectr. U. So. Calif., 1989; sr. analyst readers' sex survey Playboy Mag., Chgo., 1981-83; cons. Playboy Cable Channel, Los Angeles, 1983—, talk show host, 1983—; numerous TV appearances as expert on health aspects of sexuality. Author: Soccer Madness, 1983; co-author: Women at Yale, 1971; contbr. articles to mags. and profl. jours. Pew Health Policy Career fellow, 1987-88; grantee Am. Found. AIDS Rsch., 1988-89. Mem. Am. Sociol. Assn., Nat. Women's Studies Assn., Internat. Com. Sociology of Sport, Phi Beta Kappa. Office: RAND Corp BSD/3A 1700 Main St Santa Monica CA 90406

LEVERT, JOSEPH ALBERT, mechanical engineer; b. New Orleans, Oct. 25, 1959; s. Joseph Richard and Virginia (Leicht) L. BS in Engring., Tulane U., 1981; postgrad., Ariz. State U., 1985—. Registered profl. engr., Calif. Engr. Chevron USA, El Segundo, Calif., 1981-85, Allied Signal Aerospace Co., Tempe, Ariz., 1985—. Mem. ASME (assoc.). Office: Allied Signal Aerospace Co Fluid Systems Div 1300 W Warner Rd Tempe AZ 85282

LEVESQUE, JOSEPH D., personnel consultant; b. Seattle, May 9, 1944; s. Joseph and Ellen Ruth (Garner) L.; children: Larry, DeeAnn, Corrine. BA, Calif. State U., Hayward, 1971; MA, Calif. State U., Northridge, 1974; MPA, John F. Kennedy U., 1980. Sr. pers. analyst City of Fremont, Calif., 1972-80; pers. dir. City of Roseville (Calif.), 1980-83; pers. cons. Pers. Systems Cons., Citrus Heights, Calif., 1983—; vis. lectr. in field. Author: Manual of Personnel Policies, Procedures and Operations, 1986, People in Organizations: A Guide to Solving Critical Human Resource Problems, 1989. With U.S. Army, 1967-69, Korea. Recipient Disting. Writers award Small Bus. Illustrated, 1986. Mem. Am. Soc. Pers. Adminstrs. (dist. dir.), Pers. Assn. Sacramento (v.p. 1987), Am. Soc. Tng. and Devel., Internat. Pers. Mgmt. Assn. Republican. Office: Pers Systems Cons 5530 Birdcage St Ste 110 Citrus Heights CA 95610

LEVIN, ALVIN IRVING, educator, composer; b. N.Y.C., Dec. 22, 1921; s. David and Frances (Schloss) L.; B.M. in Edn., U. Miami (Fla.), 1941; M.A., Calif. State U., Los Angeles, 1955; Ed.D. with honors, UCLA, 1968; m. Beatrice Van Loon, June 5, 1976 (div. 1981). Composer, arranger for movies, TV, theater Allied Artists, Eagle-Lion Studios, Los Angeles, 1945-65; tng. and supervising tchr. Los Angeles City Schs., 1957-65, adult edn. instr., 1962-63; research specialist Los Angeles Office Supt. Edn., 1965-67; asst. prof. ednl. research Calif. State U., Los Angeles, 1968; asst. prof. elem. edn. Calif. State U., Northridge, 1969-73; self-employed, Northridge, 1973—; founder, pres. Alvin Irving Levin Philanthropic Found., 1973—; ordained to ministry Ch. of Mind Sci., 1975; founder, pres. Divine Love Ch.-An Internat. Metaphys. Ch., 1977—, Meet Your New Personality, A Mind Expansion Program, 1975-77. Bd. overseers Calif. Sch. Profl. Psychology, 1974—; gen. chmn., producer Fiftieth Anniversary Pageant of North Hollywood Park, 1977. Composer: Symphony for Strings, 1984, Tone Poem for Male Chorus and Brass, 1984. Recipient plaque State of Calif., 1977, Golden Merit medal Rep. Presdl. Task Force, 1985. Named to Rep. Task Force Presdl. Commn., 1986. Mem. Nat. Soc. for Study Edn., AAUP, Am. Statis. Assn., Internat. Council Edn. for Teaching, Los Angeles World Affairs Council, Internat. Platform Assn., North Hollywood C. of C. (dir. 1976—), Phi Delta Kappa. Author: My Ivory Tower, 1950; (music-drama) Happy Land, 1971; Symposium: Values in Kaleidoscope, 1973; America, America! (TV series), 1978-79; (docu-drama) One World, 1980; Symphony for Strings, 1984; Tone Poem for Male Chorus and Brass, 1984; (mus. play) A Tale of Two Planets, 1988; compiler and contbr. U.S. Dept. Edn. reports; Adult Counseling and Guidance, 1967, Parent Child Presch. Program, 1967, English Classes for Foreign Speaking Adult Profls., 1967. Home and Office: 9850 Reseda Blvd #314 Northridge CA 91324

LEVIN, EMIL, physician; b. Lvov, Ukraine, USSR, Jan. 13, 1946; came to U.S., 1974; s. Afroim and Sarah (Buchman) L.; m. Maria Levin, Oct. 13, 1978. MD, Dushanbe (USSR) State Med. Inst., 1969. Resident Tb Hosp., Doushanbe, 1969-72, Polyclinic #11, Lvov, 1972-74; fellow Goldwater Meml. Hosp., N.Y.C., 1978; intern Cath. Med. Ctr., N.Y.C., 1978-79, resident, 1979-81; practice medicine specializing in homeopathy, geriatrics and allergy Holistic Med. Ctr., Beverly Hills, Calif., 1981—. Fellow Am. Coll. Advancement Sci.; mem. Nat. Health Fedn. Jewish. Office: Holistic Med Ctr 450 S Beverly Dr Beverly Hills CA 90212

LEVIN, MARIO, computer consultant; b. Mexico City, July 30, 1953; came to U.S., 1978; s. Sommer and Clara (Desatnik) L.; m. Deborah Feiner, Jan. 16, 1982; 1 child, Jonathan. BEE, U. Mex., 1976; MS in Engring., Princeton U., 1980. System programmer Nat. Semiconductor Co., Santa Clara, Calif., 1980-81; computer cons. Mexico City, 1981-83; software engr. Norton & Co., Westport, Conn., 1983-84, Cipherlink Corp., L.A., 1984-87; ind. computer cons. L.A., 1987--. Jewish. Home and Office: 3631 Gleneagles Dr Tarzana CA 91356

LEVIN, MARK JAY, television lighting director; b. Mpls., July 30, 1957; s. Myron Yale and Phyllis (Goodman) L. BA, U. Wis., 1979. Lighting dir., cameraman Sta. WHA-TV, Madison, Wis., 1978-79, NBC, 1980, ABC, Hollywood, 1982—; lighting dir. Columbia Pictures TV, 1985-88, ABC-TV, comedy prodn., dramatic prodn., music and variety prodn., news and talk format prodn., 1984—, Bob Booker/Universal TV, 1984, Platypus Prodn., 1983-85, Dick Clark Prodn., 1982-83, Sta. KABC-TV, 1984-86; dir. photography Amos Prodn., 1982. Lighting dir. numerous TV series including The New Love American Style, 1985, Charmed Lives, 1986, Sweet Surrender, 1986, The Charmings, 1986-87, Facts of Life, 1987, Women in Prison, 1987-88, Who's the Boss, 1985-89 (Emmy award nomination 1986, 87, 88), General Hospital, 1984—, Faerie Tale Theater, 1983-85 (Ace award 1983), American Bandstand, 1983-86, The Love Boat Spl., 1984, Home Movies, 1982, The Love Connection, 1984-85, ABC's World News Tonight, 1984-86, Married With Children, Nat. Cerebral Palsey Telethon, 1985, 87, 89, One at the Boys, 1989, numerous local prodns.; contbg. editor Lighting Dimensions mag., 1980-85. Active Big Bros. of Greater L.A., 1984—. Recipient Patriotic Svc. award U.S. Dept. of the Treasury, 1984, Outstanding Excellence award Am. Soc. Lighting Designers, 1988. Mem. Am. Soc. of Lighting Dirs., Internat. Assn. Theatrical Stage Employees, World Underwater Fedn., Nat. Assn. Broadcast Employees and Technicians, Soc. Operating Cameramen, Profl. Assn. Diving Instrs. (divemaster), Underwater Photographic Soc. Home: 9318 Via Ferrara Burbank CA 91504 Office: Capitol Cities/ABC-TV 4151 Prospect Ave Hollywood CA 90027

LEVIN, MARTIN HOWARD, computer consultant, retired air force officer; b. Hazleton, Pa., Feb. 9, 1941; s. Benjamin and Selma Louise (Rosen) L.; B.S. in Bus. Adminstrn., Pa. State U., 1962; M.S. in Retailing, N.Y. U., 1963; m. Rosa Bernardina Fernandez Rosado, Aug. 15, 1965; children—Maya Ann, Richard Benjamin. Commd. 2d lt. U.S. Air Force, 1963, advanced through grades to maj., 1973; comdr. 825th Services Squadron, Little Rock AFB, Ark., 1968-69; commissary officer Anderson AFB, Guam, 1969-72; comdr. 635th Services Squadron, U-Tapao, Thailand, 1972-73; services staff officer Hdqrs. 15th Air Force, SAC, 1973-75; camp comdr. Anderson AFB Indochina Refugee Camp, 1975; dep. comdr. Korea Regional Exchange, Seoul, 1975-78; chief USAF Acad. Cadet Dining Hall, 1978-79; dir. housing and services Aerospace Def. Command, Colorado Springs, Colo., 1979-80; services requirements mgr. SAC, 1980-83; ret., 1983; course dir., instr. Am. Inst. Profl. Edn., Madison, N.J., 1982-84; pres. Levin and Assocs., Inc., Colorado Springs, 1984— ; sr. v.p. Tech. Internat. Corp., 1986—; cons. microcomputer applications and edn., 1982—; instr. Pikes Peak Community Coll., Colorado Springs, 1980-82. Decorated Air Force Commendation medal with 3 oak leaf clusters, Meritorious Service medal, Joint Service Commendation medal. Jewish. Home: 5850 Escapardo Way Colorado Springs CO 80917 Office: Levin & Assocs 2120 Academy Circle Executive Park Ste E Colorado Springs CO 80917

LEVIN, MICHAEL MOSHE, electronics company executive; b. Tel Aviv, Mar. 26, 1955; came to U.S., 1958; s. Harry P. and Zipora (Ban Jacob) L.; m. Beth Ard, Oct. 21, 1972; children: Joyce, Laura, Brian. Student, UCLA, 1972, Calif. Luth. Coll., 1987, Stanford U., 1988. Engr. Astro-Metrix Corp., Burbank, Calif., 1975-76, Teledyne Controls, El Segundo, Calif., 1976-77; product engr. Nucleonic Products, Canoga Park, Calif., 1977-79; founder, exec. v.p., bd. dirs., dir. electronics rsch. and devel. Silent Radio-Cybernetic Data Products Co., Chatsworth, Calif., 1979—; bd. dirs. Electro Energy Corp., Burbank. Patentee in field. Office: Cybernetic Data Products Co 20732 Lassen St Chatsworth CA 91311

LEVIN, PAMELA JEAN, counselor; b. Rockford, Ill., Oct. 26, 1942; d. Clifton Elgin and Zola Brenice (Griffith) Backus; children: Eric Daniel, Jennifer Jean Levin-Landheer. BS, U. Ill., 1964. RN. Staff nurse, med. nursing Boston VA Hosp., 1964-65; chief nursing dept. Washingtonian Hosp., Boston, 1965-66; staff nurse Highland, Cowell and Alta Bates Hosps., Oakland and Berkeley, Calif., 1967-70; asst. dir. Day Treatment Ctr. Gladman Hosp., Oakland, 1970; pvt. practice transactional analysis San Francisco Bay Area and No. Calif., 1971—; internat. lectr. transactional analysis and devel.; co-pres., v.p. Eric Berne Seminars of San Fransisco, 1977-78; co-founder Group House Inc., Berkeley, 1971; coodinator N.W. Fla. Alcoholic Rehab. Clinic, 1966; co-founder Orr's Hot Springs Healing Retreat Community, Ukiah, Calif., 1974-79. Author: Becoming The Way We Are, An Introduction to Personal Development in Recovery and In Life, 1988, Cycles of Power, A Users Guide To The Seven Seasons of Life, 1988, French transl., 1986, How to Develop Your Personal Powers, A Workbook for your Life's Time, 1982, (children's book) The Fuzzy Frequency, 1978; author, founder Experiencing Enough, human potential tng. course, 1984; founding mem., editorial bd. quar. jour. Women & Therapy, 1982-86; contbr. numerous articles to profl. jours.; developer instructional aids including blocks, cymbals, devel. cycle and deviations chart, growth and devel. chart, series of comparative charts of psychol. theory; featured commentator/ analyst in film Hello Up There, Eric!, Rogers Prodns., Inc., 1979. Recipient Eric Berne Sci. award for article The Cycle of Development, 1984. Mem. Internat. Transactional Analysis Assn. (cert. Level I and II, 1st woman teaching and clin. mem., co-founder women's caucus 1970, bd. trustees 1973, 74, 75, chair pub. info. and profl. relations com. 1987—, press screeing com. 1976-78, women's editorial bd. jour. 1977, editor Script, internat. newsletter 1983-85, co-editor 1986), Can. Assn. for Transactional Analysis, Am. Assn. Counselling & Devel., Inst. Devel. Edn. and Psychotherapy, Nat. Assn. Female Execs., AAUW, New Directions in Edn. & Psychotherapy, Internat. Soc. for Study of Innovative Psychotherapies, Media Alliance, Feminist Writer's Guild, Author's Guild, Author's League. Home and Office: Box 1429 Ukiah CA 95482

LEVIN, THOMAS AUGUSTUS, health science association executive; b. Montgomery, Ala., Dec. 8, 1946; m. Carolyn Dahlgren; children: Daniel, Carey. BA, U. Ala., 1968; JD, U. N.C., 1971. Bar: N.C. 1971, D.C. 1972, N.Mex. 1974. Staff counsel N.Mex. Blue Cross & Blue Shield, Albuquerque, 1974-76, v.p. legal affairs, 1976-81, pres., chief exec. officer, 1981-86; chief exec. officer Rocky Mountain Health Care Corp., 1986—, Blue Cross and Blue Shield plans Colo., N.Mex., Nev.; bd. dirs. First Interstate Bank; bd. dirs., exec. com. Blue Cross and Blue Shield Assn.; chmn. bd. Health Plan Capital Svcs. Corp., Firstsource, HMO Colo., Inc., Rio Grande HMO, Rocky Mountain Life Ins. Co. Mem. policy rev. bd. U. Colo., Denver, The Pub. Edn. Coalition Steering Com. Served with U.S. Army, 1972-74. Mem. N.Mex. Bar Assn., Nat. Health Lawyers Assn., The Econ. Club Colo., Colo. Forum. Office: Rocky Mountain Health Care Corp 700 Broadway Denver CO 80273

LEVIN, WILLIAM MICHAEL, insurance company executive; b. Westwood, Calif., Apr. 3, 1949; s. Herman G. and Ruth Mae (MacArthur) L.; m. Ann Christine Lickel, Sept. 18, 1981; children: Richard Christo, Alexandre Michael. BS, U. Oreg., 1971. Field underwriter N.Y. Life Ins. Co., Portland, Oreg., 1982-83; mktg. dir. Security First Group, Los Angeles, 1983-85; dir. ins. Baraban Securities, Inc., Los Angeles, 1985-88, Drake Capital Securities, Santa Monica, Calif., 1988—. Served to lt. (j.g.) USN, 1971-77. Mem. Nat. Assn. Securities Dealers, Life Underwriters, Delta Chi. Republican. Jewish. Club: Exchange (Culver City, Calif.). Office: Drake Capital Securities Inc 520 Broadway Santa Monica CA 90901

LEVINE, ALAN NEAL, air force officer; b. Manhasset, N.Y., Jan. 26, 1960; s. Frederick Irwin and Betty Ann (Simson) L. BS in Indsl. Engring., Purdue U., 1982. Commd. 2d lt. USAF, 1982, advanced through grades to capt., 1986; instr. pilot USAF, Vance AFB, Okla., 1984-87; aircraft comdr. USAF, McChord AFB, Wash., 1987—. Mem. Order of Daedalians. Democrat. Jewish. Home: 5509 77th St Ct NW Gig Harbor WA 98335 Office: USAF 4 MAS/DOP McChord AFB WA 98438

LEVINE, MELDON EDISES, congressman, lawyer; b. Los Angeles, June 7, 1943; s. Sid B. and Shirley B. (Blum) L.; m. Jan Greenberg; children: Adam Paul, Jacob Caplan, Cara Emily. AB, U. Calif., Berkeley, 1964; MPA, Princeton U., 1966; JD, Harvard U., 1969. Bar: Calif. 1970, D.C. 1972. Assoc. Wyman, Bautzer, Rothman & Kuchel, 1969-71; legis. asst. U.S. Senate, Washington, 1971-73; ptnr. Levine Krom & Unger, Beverly Hills, Calif., 1973-77; mem. Calif. Assembly, Sacramento, 1977-82, 98th-101st Congresses from 27th Calif. dist., Washington, 1983—. Author: The Private Sector and the Common Market, 1968; contbr. articles to various publs. Mem. governing bd. So. Calif. chpt. Anti-Defamation League, So. Calif. chpt. Am. Jewish Com., So. Calif. chpt. Am. Jewish Congress, So. Calif. chpt. NAACP Legal Def. Fund, U. Judaism, City of Hope, U. Calif. Alumni Council. Mem. Calif. Bar Assn., Los Angeles Bar Assn. Office: Ho of Reps care The Postmaster Washington DC 20515

LEVINE, MICHAEL, public relations executive, author; b. N.Y.C., Apr. 17, 1954; s. Arthur and Virgiaia (Gaylor) L. Student, Rutgers U., 1972-77. Owner, operator TV News Mag., Los Angeles, 1977-83; pres., owner Michael Levine Pub. Relations, Los Angeles, 1982—; mem. Gov.'s adv. bd. State Calif., Sacramento, 1980-82; pres., owner Aurora Pub., Los Angeles, 1986—. Author: The Address Book: How to Reach Anyone Who's Anyone, 1984, The New Address Book, 1986, The Corporate Address Book, 1987, The Music Address Book, 1989. Mem. Ronald Reagan Pres.'s Libr., Rosey Grier's Are You Committed, L.A., 1986—, Neil Bogart Labs. of Cancer Rsch., 1986—; founder The Acton's Conf. Mem. TV Acad. Arts and Scis., Entertainment Industries Council, West Hollywood C. of C. (bd. dirs. 1980-82). Republican. Jewish. Office: 8730 Sunset Blvd 6th Fl Los Angeles CA 90069

LEVINE, MICHAEL JOSEPH, insurance company executive; b. Boston, Mar. 23, 1945; s. Sam and Helen Alice (Michelman) L.; m. Margaret Mary Gutierrez, Aug. 6, 1983; 1 child, Samuel Jacob Gutierrez. BA, Boston U., 1967. Supr. underwriting Comml. Union. Ins., Boston, 1969-73; mgr. Harris-Murtagh Ins., Boston, 1973-75, Cohen-Goldenberg Ins. Agy., Boston, 1975-77; v.p. Southwest Underwriters Ins., Deming, N.Mex., 1977-83, pres., 1983-86; pres. Consol. Ins. Cons., Deming, N.Mex., 1985—. V.p. Border Area Mental Health Svcs., So. N.Mex., 1978—; pres. Deming Arts Council, 1979-81; treas. Luna County (N.Mex.) Crimestoppers, Inc., 1979—. Mem. Mensa, Soc. CPCU's (cert.), Soc. Cert. Ins. Counselors (cert.), Ins. Mktg. Assocs., Luna County C. of C. (v.p. 1981-84), Ind. Ins. Agts. N.Mex. (state dir. 1985—), Southwest N.Mex. Ind. Ins. Agts. (treas. 1981-83, pres. 1983-85), B;Nai Brith Lodge, Moose. Democrat. Jewish. Home: 1920 S Silver St Deming NM 88030 Office: Consol Ins Cons Inc 318 S Columbus Rd Deming NM 88031

LEVINE, STEPHEN, safety engineer; b. N.Y.C., Aug. 9, 1935; s. Al and Sophie (Gritzer) L.; m. Brenda M. Reid, Mar. 16, 1964 (div. Mar. 1985); children: David, Paul, Deborah, Aaron. BS in Adminstrn., U. N.H., 1974; MS in Areo., Emery Riddle Aero. U., 1980. Commd. 2d lt. USAF, 1954, advanced through grades to lt. col., 1975, ret., 1980; loss control mgr. Nat. Farmers Union Ins., Denver, 1980-81; loss control cons. pvt. practice Denver, 1982-84; sr. safety cons. Home Ins., Englewood, Colo., 1985-88; risk mgr., safety dir. U.S. Recycling Industries, Denver, 1988—. Author: Telecom Industry Safety, 1980. Decorated D.F.C., Air medal (13), Meritorious Service medal. Mem. Soc. Safety Engrs., Risk and Ins. Mgmt. Soc. Clubs: D.T.C. Sporting, Colo. Mountain. Home: 9347 E Chenango Ave Englewood CO 80111 Office: US Recycling Industries 2441 Broadway Denver CO 80205

LEVINSON, KENNETH LEE, lawyer; b. Denver, Jan. 18, 1953; s. Julian Charles and Dorothy (Milzer) L.; m. Shauna Titus, Dec. 21, 1986. BA with distinction, U. Colo.-Boulder, 1974; JD, U. Denver, 1978. Bar: Colo. 1978, U.S. Ct. Appeals (10th cir.) 1978. Assoc. atty. Balaban & Lutz, Denver, 1979-83; shareholder Balaban & Levinson, P.C., 1984—. Contbr. articles to profl. jours. Pres., Dahlia House Condominium Assn., 1983-85; intern Reporters Com. For Freedom of the Press, Washington, 1977. Recipient Am. Jurisprudence award Lawyers Co-op., 1977. Mem. ABA, Denver Bar Assn., Colo. Bar Assn., Am. Arbitration Assn. (arbitrator), Internat. Platform Assn. Clubs: Denver Law, Denver Athletic.

LEVISEUR, CARL RICHARD, physician; b. Youngstown, Ohio, Sept. 29, 1939; s. Carl Joseph and Rosalind Jeannette (Vose) LeV.; m. Ethel Ann Claar, July 16, 1961; children: Theresa, Albert, Charles. BAAS, Southwest Tex. State U., 1979; MD, Tex. Tech. U., 1983. Diplomate Am. Bd. Family Practice. Commd. 2d lt. USAF, 1958, advanced through grades to lt. col., 1975; navigator, pilot various locations, 1958-79; ret.; resident in family practice Tex. Tech U., Lubbock, 1983-86; pvt. practice family medicine Pahrump, Nev., 1986—. Mem. AMA, Am. Acad. Family Practice, Nev. Assn. Family Practice. Republican. Home: PO Box 2360 Pahrump NV 89041 Office: Pahrump Community Med Ctr Calvada Blvd Pahrump NV 89041

LEVITAN, ROGER STANLEY, lawyer; b. Washington, Jan. 31, 1933; s. Simon Wolfe and Bessie (Abramson) L.; m. Maria Anneli Stennius, May 27, 1975 (div. 1980); 1 child, Mark Howard; m. Laurel Lynn Allen, July 9, 1982; 1 child, Brandon Wolfe. BS in Econs., U. Pa., 1954; JD, Columbia U., 1957. Bar: D.C. 1957, U.S. Ct. Appeals (D.C. cir.) 1957, Ariz. 1976. Tax specialist, reorgn. br. IRS, Washington, 1957-62; atty. McClure & Trotter, Washington, 1962-65; assoc. ptnr. Main Lafrentz, Washington and N.Y.C., 1970-72; dir. taxes U.S. Industries, Inc., N.Y.C., 1972-73; asst. tax counsel Am. Home Products Co., N.Y.C., 1973-75; atty., stockholder Bilby & Shoenhair, P.C., Tucson, 1976-89; ptnr. Snell & Wilmer, Tucson, 1989—; lectr. Am. Law Inst., State Bar Ariz. Trustee, Tucson Community Found., 1981—. Mem. ABA (chmn. ann. report com. 1965-67, continuing legal edn. com. 1969-70), Ariz. Bar Found., State Bar Ariz. (chmn. sect. taxation 1987-88), D.C. Bar Assn. Contbr. articles to profl. jours. Office: PO Box 871 Tucson AZ 85702

LEVITON, ALAN EDWARD, museum curator; b. N.Y.C., Jan. 11, 1930; s. David and Charlotte (Weber) L.; m. Gladys Ann Robertson, June 30, 1952; children: David A., Charlotte A. A.B., Stanford U., 1949, M.A., 1953, Ph.D., 1960; student, Columbia U., summers 1947, 48, 53, N.Y. U., 1948, U. Nebr., 1954. Asst. curator herpetology Calif. Acad. Scis., San Francisco, 1957-60, assoc. curator, 1960-61, chmn., curator, 1962-82, 89—, curator, 1983-88; chmn. computer services Calif. Acad. Scis., 1983—; assoc. curator zool. collections Stanford, 1962-63; lectr. biol. sci. 1963-70; professorial lectr. Golden Gate U., 1953-63; adj. prof. biol. sci. San Francisco State U., 1967—. Author: North American Amphibians and Reptiles, 1972; contbr. numerous articles to sci., profl. jours. Am. Philos. Soc. grantee, 1960; NSF grantee, 1960-61, 77-79, 80, 83-86, 86-89, Belvedere Sci. Fund grantee, 1958-59, 1962. Fellow Calif. Acad. Scis., AAAS (council 1976—, com. council affairs 1983-85, sec.-treas. Pacific div. 1975-79, exec. dir. 1980—), Explorers Club; mem. Am. Soc. Ichthyologists and Herpetologists (bd. govs. 1960-84), Soc. Systematic Zoology (sec.-treas. Pacific sect. 1970-72), Forum Historians of Sci. in Am. (coordinating com. 1986-88, sec.-treas. 1988-91), Herpetologists League (pres. 1961-62), Soc. Vertebrate Paleontologists, History of Sci. Soc., Geol. Soc. Am. (vice-chmn. history of geology div. 1989—), Sigma Xi. Home: 571 Kingsley Ave Palo Alto CA 94301 Office: Calif Acad Scis Golden Gate Pk San Francisco CA 94118

LEVITON, FRED J., health foundation administrator; b. Chgo., Feb. 10, 1953; s. Lawrence and Roselle D. (Lisdovsky) L.; m. Ann G. Poter, Dec. 28, 1974; children: Brandon, Tory. BS, U. Ill., 1973; MS in Health Adminstrn., U. Colo., Denver and Boulder, 1976. Adminstrv. asst. Westside Neighborhood Health Program, Denver, 1974-76; asst. exec. dir. Nat. Found. Dentistry for Handicapped, Denver, 1976—; exec. dir. Acad. Dentistry for Handicapped, Denver, 1978-83; course presenter Tech. Assistance Ctr., Denver, 1981—. Bd. dirs. Rsch. Found. for Crohn's Disease, Denver, 1986—. Recipient Vol. of Yr. award Tech. Assistance Ctr., 1985. Mem. U. Colo. Health Adminstn. Alumni Assn., Gun Club Green HOA (bd. dirs. 1988—), Optimists. Office: Nat Found Dentistry 1600 Stout St Ste 1420 Denver CO 80202

LEVITT, LAWRENCE DAVID, insurance agent; b. Los Angeles, Apr. 18, 1944; s. Albert Herbert and Reva (Narvey) L.; m. Cinda Sue Coffee, Apr. 8, 1967; 1 child, Rachel Diane. AA, Solano Community Coll., 1970; B, U. San Francisco, 1976. Officer, detective Fairfield (Calif.) Police Dept., 1968-78; officer, supr. Douglas (Wyo.) Police Dept., 1978-79; comdr. Rock Springs (Wyo.) Police Dept., 1979-83, chief of police, 1983-86; owner CoServe, Rock Springs, 1986—; instr. Solano Community Coll., Fairfield, 1972-78, Western Wyo. Coll., Rock Springs, 1979—; mem. curriculum com. Wyo. Law Enforcement Acad., Douglas, 1985—. Mem. adv. bd. Youth Home, Inc., Rock Springs, 1980, S.W. Wyo. Alcohol Rehab. Assn., Rock Springs, 1984-86; mem. Upper Solano County Assn. For Retarded Children, Fairfield, 1974-78. Recipient Red Cross Life Saving award ARC, 1970; named Police Officer of Yr., Fairfield-Suisun Exchange Club, 1973. Mem. Internat. Assn. Chiefs of Police, Wyo. Assn. Chief's Police (v.p. 1985-86, chmn. edn. com. 1985—), Wyo. Peace Officers Assn., Rock Springs C. of C., Am. Assn. Life Underwriters, Wyo. Assn. Life Underwriters. Democrat. Jewish. Club: Wyo. Paint Horse (Douglas). Lodges: Lions, Shriners, Masons, Elks. Home: 248 Cherokee Dr Rock Springs WY 82901 Office: Allstate Ins 175 Riverview Ste F Green River WY 82935

LEVITT, MICHAEL KENT, psychiatrist; b. Detroit, May 6, 1941; s. Samuel and Molly (Strossky) L.; m. Mary Ritchie, Oct. 25, 1974; children—Hollis, Jonathan. B.A. in Zoology, U. Mich., 1962, M.D., 1966. Sr. med. student extern in child psychiatry Hawthorn Ctr., Northville, Mich., 1965; intern Sinai Hosp., Detroit, Wayne State U. Sch. Medicine, 1966-67; resident in psychiatry Albert Einstein Coll. Medicine, Mcpl. Hosp. Center, Bronx, N.Y., 1967-71; practice medicine specializing in psychotherapy, Ann Arbor, Mich., 1973-74; practice medicine specializing in psychiatry Tri-County Mental Health Assn., Southfield, Mich., 1974-81, Hickory (N.C.) Meml. Hosp. 1981-84; assoc. dir. pain ctr. Frye Hosp., Hickory, 1981-84, med. dir. Meadow View Hosp., Lake Charles, La., 1984-86, CPC Meadow Wood Hosp., Baton Rouge, 1986-88, pres. med. staff E. Valley St. Luke's Hosp., Chandler, Ariz., 1987—. Served to maj. USAF, 1971. Mem. Am. Psychiat. Assn., Am. Acad. Childhood and Adolescent Psychiatry, Am. Soc. Adolescent Psychiatry, AMA. Avocations: photography, hiking, music. Home: 850 S Longmore #203 Mesa AZ 85202

LEVITZ, JOEL JACOB, community developer; b. Phila., Jan. 4, 1935; s. Milton and Sophia (Kurtz) L.; B.S., CCNY, 1958; M.A., Sacramento State Coll., 1964; postgrad CCNY, 1959-60, Columbia U., 1960-61, U. Denver, 1961-62; Ed.D., Temple U., 1973; m. Karen R. Bell, Sept. 17, 1977; children—Michael Seth, John, Susan, Robin, Michael Kimball. Tchr. emotionally disturbed children Hawthorne (N.Y.) Cedar Knolls, 1958-60; tng. supr., tech. rep. Am. Machine & Foundry, Stamford, Conn., 1960-62; engring. psychologist Aerojet Gen. Corp., Sacramento, 1962-64, Philco Ford, Willow Grove, Pa., 1964-66; program mgr. ednl. systems Burroughs Corp., Ardmore, Pa., 1966-70; dir. spl. support serviced Federal City Coll., Washington, 1970-71; v.p. mktg., Ill. and Ariz. ops. Environ. Devels., Inc., 1971-78; pres. Executive Homes Inc., Denver, 1977—, Calvan Properties Inc., 1978—, Paragon Realty (USA) Ltd., 1979—; pres. The Levitz Group, 1982—; mem. U.S. Senatorial Bus. Adv. Com. Mem. Human Factors Soc. (exec. council at large 1966-67), Am. Psychol. Assn., (asso.), Nat. Assn. Homebuilders, Nat. Assn. Realtors, Psi Chi, Phi Delta Kappa, Phi Theta Tau. Home: 6859 N 79th Pl Scottsdale AZ 85253 Office: 7527 E 1st St Scottsdale AZ 85251

LEVY, ALAN DAVID, real estate executive; b. St. Louis, July 19, 1938; s. I. Jack and Natalie (Yawitz) L.; grad. Sch. Real Estate, Washington U., 1960; m. Abby Jane Markowitz, May 12, 1968; children—Jennifer Lynn, Jacqueline Claire. Property mgr. Solon Gershman Inc., Realtors, Clayton, Mo., 1958-61; gen. mgr. Kodner Constrn. Co., St. Louis, 1961-63; regional mgr. Tishman Realty & Constrn. Co., Inc., N.Y.C., 1963-69, v.p., Los Angeles, 1969-77; exec. v.p., dir. Tishman West Mgmt. Corp., 1977-88; pres. Tishman West Cos., 1988—; guest lectr. on real estate mgmt. to various forums. Mem. Los Angeles County Mus. Art; trustee Archives Am. Art; chmn. bd. trustees Westlake Sch. Mem. bldg. owners and mgrs. assns. Los Angeles (dir.), N.J. (co-founder, hon. dir.), Inst. Real Estate Mgmt. (cert. property mgr.), Urban Land Inst., Internat. Council Shopping Centers. Contbr. articles on property mgmt. to trade jours. Office: 10960 Wilshire Blvd Los Angeles CA 90024

LEVY, BARBARA RIFKIN, theater company and fund raising executive, consultant; b. Schenectady, Apr. 25, 1941; d. Sam and Jane (Goodman) Rifkin; m. Martin Ray Levy, July 21, 1963; children: Douglas Marc, Mitchell Brent. BS, U. Vt., 1962; postgrad., Ithaca Coll. Music, 1962, Ohio U., 1964-65, U. Ariz., 1973-75. Tchr. music Vernon Pub. Schs., Rockville, Conn., 1962-63, Northwood Pub. Schs., Toledo, 1963-64; supr. music therapy Athens (Ohio) State Hosp., 1964-66; dir. devel. Ariz. Opera Co., Tucson, 1974-78, Ariz. Theatre Co., Tucson, 1978-89; devel. officer U. Ariz. Mus. Art, Tucson, 1989—; cons. Ariz. Commn. on Arts, 1984—, Found. for Extension and Devel. Am. Profl. Theatre, 1985—; mem. pvt. sector adv. com. NAAG Model Law, 1986-87; mem. ad hoc com. to devel. state legis. Phoenix Solicitation Bd., 1988—. Mem. Nat. Soc. Fund Raising Execs. (cert., mem. exec. com. nat. bd. dirs., vice chmn. 1987-88, Outstanding Fund Raising Exec. award 1988), Nat. Assn. Attys. Gen. Office: Univ Ariz Found 1111 N Cherry Ave Tucson AZ 85721

LEVY, DAVID, lawyer, insurance company executive; b. Bridgeport, Conn., Aug. 3, 1932; s. Aaron and Rachel (Goldman) L. BS in Econs., U. Pa., 1954; JD, Yale U., 1957. Bar: Conn. 1958, U.S. Supreme Ct. 1963, D.C. 1964, Mass. 1965, N.Y. 1971, Pa. 1972; CPA, Conn. Acct. Arthur Andersen & Co., N.Y.C., 1957-59; sole practice Bridgeport, 1959-60; specialist tax law IRS, Washington, 1960-64; counsel State Mut. Life Ins. Co., Worcester, Mass., 1964-70; assoc. gen. counsel taxation Penn Mut. Life Ins. Co., Phila., 1971-81; sole practice Washington, 1982-87; v.p., tax counsel Pacific Mut. Life Ins. Co., Newport Beach, Calif., 1987—. Author: (with others) Life Insurance Company Tax Series, Bureau National Affairs Tax Management Income Tax, 1970-71. Mem. adv. bd. tax conf. Wharton Sch. Bus. U. Pa., 1977-84, Tax Mgmt., Washington, 1975—; bd. dirs. Citizens Plan E Orgn., Worcester, 1966-70. With U.S. Army, 1957. Mem. ABA (vice-chmn. employee benefits com., 1980-86, ins. cos. com. 1984-86, torts and ins. practice sect.), Assn. Life Ins. Counsel, Am. Inst. CPA's, Phila. C. of C. (chmn. state tax com. 1972-80), Beta Alpha Psi. Jewish.

LEVY, DAVID STEVEN, college administrator; b. Los Angeles, Mar. 9, 1955; s. Henry and Gloria Grace (Barouh) L.; m. Stephanie Brashears. B.A., Occidental Coll., 1977; M.A., 1979. Asst. dir. fin. aid Calif. State Coll., San Bernardino, 1978-79; fin. aid counselor Calif. State U.-Northridge, 1979-80; assoc. dir. student fin. aid Calif. State U.-Dominguez Hills, 1980-82; dir. fin. aid Occidental Coll., Los Angeles, 1982-88; dir. fin. aid Calif. Inst. Tech., Pasadena, Calif., 1988—; mem. Title IA Adv. Com. Calif., 1977—. Mem. life-long learning com. Calif. Postsecondary Edn. Commn., 1980—, mem. student fin. aid issues com., 1984—. Recipient NASFAA Meritorious Achievement award, 1988; Richter fellow Princeton U., 1976; Calif. State U. adminstrv. fellow, 1981—. Mem. Mortar Board Alumni Assn. (pres. 1977—), Calif. Assn. Student Fin. Aid Adminstrs. (ind. segmental rep. 1984, sec. 1985, treas. 1986-88), Western Assn. Student Fin. Aid Adminstrs., Nat. Assn. Student Fin. Aid Adminstrs., Phi Beta Kappa, Delta Phi Epsilon, Psi Chi, Phi Alpha Theta, Sigma Alpha Epsilon. Jewish. Co-editor Calif. Student Aid Commn. Student Aid Workbook, 1977—. Home: 41 Northwoods Ln La Crescenta CA 91214 Office: CalTech 515 S Wilson Pasadena CA 91125

LEVY, EUGENE HOWARD, planetary sciences educator, researcher; b. N.Y.C., May 6, 1944; s. Isaac Philip and Anita Harriet (Guttman) L.; m. Margaret Lyle Rader, Oct. 13, 1967; children: Roger P., Jonathan S., Benjamin H. AB in Physics with high honors, Rutgers U., 1966; PhD in Physics, U. Chgo., 1971. Teaching asst. dept. physics U. Chgo., 1966-69, rsch. asst. Enrico Fermi Inst., 1969-71; postdoctoral fellow dept. physics and astronomy U. Md., 1971-73; asst. prof. physics and astrophysics Bartol Rsch. Found., Franklin Inst., Swarthmore, Pa., 1973-75; asst., then assoc. prof. U. Ariz., Tucson, 1975-83, prof. planetary scis., 1983—, mem. faculty applied math. program, 1981—, head dept. planetary scis., dir. lunar and planetary lab., 1983—, mem. theoretical astrophysics program, 1985—; mem. com. on planetary and lunar exploration of space sci. bd., Nat. Acad. Scis., 1976-79, chmn., 1979-82, co-chair Space Sci. Bd. Study on Exploration Primitive Solar-System Bodies, 1978, mem. Space Sci. Bd., 1979-82, head U.S. del., co-chair Nat. Acad. Scis.-European Sci. Found. Joint Working Group on Cooperation in Planetary Exploration, 1982-84, mem. steering group com. on major directions for space sci. 1995-2015, 1984-86, chair adv. com. on internat. cooperation for Mars sample return, 1986-88; mem. Comet Halley Sci. Working Group, NASA, 1977, mem. spacelab phys. sci. rev. panel space sci. steering com., 1979, mem. rev. panel on origin plasmas in Earth's neighborhood, 1980, mem. solar system exploration com. of Adv. Coun., 1980-83, mem. Ames Rsch. Ctr. Planetary Detection Study, 1983, Solar System Exploration Mgmt. Coun., 1983-87, mem. com. on future space-sta. sci. projects, 1985, mem. Space Sta. Sci. Users' Working Group, 1985-86, Space and Earth Sci. Adv. Com., 1985-88, chair Comet Rendevous and Asteroid Flyby Rev. Panel, 1986, mem. Mars Exploration Strategy Adv. Group, 1986, Mars Rover Sample Return Sci. Working Group, 1987—; sci. cons. Rockwell Internat. Corp., 1980; mem. COSPAR Internat. Tech. Panel on Comets, 1980-82; U.S.-NASA del. to discussions on internat. cooperation investigations of Comet Halley, Padua, Italy, 1981, to U.S.-USSR Joint Working Group on Near-Earth Space, the Moon and Planets, 1981; mem. program adv. bd. Internat. Conf. on Cometary Exploration, Budapest, Hungary, 1982; mem. exec. com. univs.' space sci. working group Assn. Am. Univs., 1982-86; study panel U.S.-Soviet cooperation in space sci. U.S. Cong. Office of Tech. Assessment, 1984; chair planetary exploration panel Pacific Rim Nations Internat. Space Yr. Conf., Kona, Hawaii, 1987; cons. and lectr. in field. Contbr. numerous articles to profl. jours.; author articles for gen. pub., adv. reports for Congl. Record, abstracts, book reviews, others. Recipient Disting. Pub. Svc. medal NASA, 1983; Disting. vis. scientist Jet Propulsion Lab., Calif. Inst. Tech., 1985-89; NASA predoctoral fellow U. Chgo., 1966-69, fellow Ctr. for Theoretical Physics, U. Md., 1971-73; rsch. grantee NASA, NSF. Mem. AAAS, Am. Astron. Soc., Am. Geophys. Union, Am. Phys. Soc., Internat. Astron. Union, Phi Beta Kappa, Sigma Xi. Home: 5442 E Burns St Tucson AZ 85711 Office: U Ariz Lunar and Planetary Lab Tucson AZ 85721

LEVY, HAROLD P., public relations cons.; b. Trinidad, Colo., Mar. 8, 1907; s. Phan and Fannie (Akerman) L.; AB, U. Wash., 1929; m. Alice Klund, Sept. 9, 1938. Reporter, Seattle Union Record and Seattle Post-Intelligencer, 1926-29; reporter, editor Seattle Times, 1929-34; resident writer Henry St. Settlement, N.Y.C., 1934-35; dir. publicity Nat. Conf. Social Work, Columbus, Ohio, 1935-39; rsch. assoc. Russell Sage Found., N.Y.C., 1939-45; nat. dir. pub. relations Commn. Community Interrelations, N.Y.C., 1945-47; founder, pres. Harold P. Levy Pub. Rels., L.A., 1947-87; faculty U. Calif. Extension, 1947-49. Bd. dirs. Tb and Health Assn. L.A. County, 1958-64, pres., 1962-63; bd. dirs. Calif. Orgn. Pub. Health Nursing, 1949-52, Pasadena Symphony Orch., 1981-84. Mem. Pub. Rels. Soc. Am. (charter; nat. dir. 1954, chpt. dir. 1950-54), Sigma Delta Chi. Clubs: Assocs. of Calif. Inst. Tech., Athenaeum. Author: There Were Days Like That, 1985, Public Relations for Social Agencies, 1956; Building a Popular Movement, 1944; A Study in Public Relations, 1943; contbr. articles to profl. jours. Address: 2980 Edgewick Rd Glendale CA 91206

LEVY, JONATHAN MICHAEL, radiologist; b. N.Y.C., Jan. 25, 1946; s. Herbert Spencer and Freida (Pollack) L.; m. Sue Garber, Aug. 30, 1970; children: Ariel Rebecca, David Spencer. BA in Math., Boston U., 1965; MD, U. Louisville, 1969. Intern Cook County Hosp., Chgo., 1969-70; fellow in radiology Mayo Clinic, Rochester, Minn., 1970-71, 1973-75; radiologist Scottsdale (Ariz.) Meml. Hosp., 1975—, chief radiologist, 1980—; adj. asst. prof. U. Ariz. Med. Sci. Ctr., Tucson, 1983—; v.p. Race West, Inc., Phoenix, sec. Hosp. Radiologist, Ltd., Scottsdale, Scottsdale Med. Imaging. Author: contbr. several articles to profl. radiology jours. Maj., U.S. Army, 1971-73. Mem. Ariz. Radiological Soc. (pres. 1987), Ariz. Med. Assn. (del. alt. 1982-85), AMA, Soc. for Magnetic Resonance Imaging, Inst. for Ultrasound in Medicine, Soc. for Cardiovascular and Interventional Radiology, Am. Roentgen Ray Soc.; fellow, Am. Coll. of Radiology, Alpha Omega Alpha, Plaza Club (Phoenix). Jewish. Home: 5822 Via Los Caballos Paradise Valley AZ 85253 Office: Scottsdale Med Imaging Ltd 3604 Wells Fargo #C Scottsdale AZ 85251

LEVY, MARK ALLAN, musician, educational association administrator; b. Trenton, N.J., Oct. 21, 1950; s. Gilbert Levy and Bernice Etzcovitz; m. Helene Elisabeth Oppenheimer, Oct. 24, 1982. BA in Sociology, Pa. State U., 1972, BA in Philosophy, 1972. Founder, coord. Santa Cruz (Calif.) Acoustic Music Soc., 1977-78; founder, pres. New Clear Records, Felton, Calif., 1979—; co-founder Peace Edn. Project, Felton, Calif., 1981—, Freedom Song Network, San Francisco, 1982—; advisor Escuela Pacifica (Peace Sch.), Santa Cruz, 1985—; bd. dirs. Western Workers Labor Heritage Festival, Santa Cruz, 1987—; co-owner, mgr. Wintercreek Enterprises, Boulder Creek, Calif., 1985—. Writer, performer (recs.) Leviathan, 1980, Risin' Wind, 1981, Live and Nuclear Free, 1986, Take Off Your Clothes, 1987, You and I, 1989. Mem. San Francisco Folk Music Club, Am. Fedn. Musicians, ASCAP. Democrat. Jewish. Office: New Clear Records PO Box 559 Felton CA 95018

LEVY, PHILIP LAZARUS, ophthalmologist; b. N.Y.C., Mar. 9, 1931; s. David Emanuel and Anna F. (Berstein) L. m. Roslyn Finkelstein, Dec. 19, 1954 (div. 1979); children: Leonard Robert, Amy Rachel; m. Lynn Marie Jenkins, June 12, 1983. BA in Biology, NYU, 1952; MD, N.Y. Med. Coll., 1956. Diplomate Am. Bd. Ophthalmology. Intern Michael Reese Hosp., Chgo., 1956-57; resident U. Pa., Phila., 1957-58, Wills Eye Hosp., Phila., 1960-62; practice medicine and surgery specializing in ophthalmology Sacramento, 1962—; clin. prof. ophthalmology Sch. Medicine U. Calif., Davis, 1979-85, clin. prof., 1985—; cons. USAF, 1962—, State of Calif., 1967—, U.S. HHS, 1968—; lectr. in field. Contbr. articles to profl. jours. Bd. dirs. Jewish Fedn., Sacramento, 1966-69, 72-78. Served to capt. MC., USAF, 1958-60. Recipient Cor et Manus Honor award N.Y. Med. Coll., 1956; Bausch & Lomb Co. grantee, 1978. Fellow ACS, Am. Acad. Ophthalmology, Kerato-Refractive Soc., Am. Intraocular Implant Soc. (founder), Am. Soc. Cataract and Refractive Surgery (founder), Conrerie de la Chaine des Rotisseurs (pres. greater Sacramento chpt. 1988—), Calif. Assn. Ophthalmology (v.p. 1986—). Jewish. Office: Med Corp 77 Scripps Dr Ste 202 Sacramento CA 95825

LEVY, ROBERT NATHAN, unit supervisor; b. Saint Louis, Aug. 7, 1950; s. Dave and Esther Mollie (Brick) L.; m. Cynthia Leslie Rosenberg, July 12, 1981. Student, Forest Park Community Coll., 1968-69; BA, U. Mo., 1972; MA, Webster U., 1978. Juvenile corrections officer Mo. State Bd. Tng. Sch., Saint Louis, 1972-73; juvenile counselor University Ctr., Ann Arbor, Mich., 1973-74; pre-trial counselor, investigator Mo. State Probation & Parole, Saint Louis, 1975-76; probation and parole officer Mo. State Probation and Parole, Saint Louis, 1976-84; probation officer Pima County Adult Probation, Tucson, 1984-85, sr. probation officer, 1988—; co-founder, sr. probation officer Intensive Probation Supervision, Pima County, 1985-87, unit supr., 1988—; cons. APC Skills Co., W. Palm Beach, Fla., 1979-80. Contbr. articles to profl. jours. Mem. Universal Great Brotherhood (v.p. 1980-82, pres. 1982-84) Saint Louis; marshal Pima County Election Bd., 1988—; treas., pubs. dir., Cosmobiology Dept. dir. Mem. Am. Correctional Assn., Ariz. Probation, Parole & Corrections Assn., Am. Probation and Parole Assn. Republican. Jewish. Office: Pima County Adult Probation 1951 W Grant Ste 180 Tucson AZ 85745

LEVY, SALOMON, mechanical engineer; b. Jerusalem, Apr. 4, 1926; came to U.S., 1945; s. Abraham Isaac and Sultana Claire (Elyachar) L.; m. Eileen Dolores Jaques, Oct. 14, 1951; children: Marshall Douglas, Linda C. BSME, U. Calif., Berkeley, 1949, MME, 1951, PhD in Mech. Engring., 1953. Engr. Gen. Electric Co., Schenectady, N.Y. and San Jose, Calif., 1953-59; mgr. heat transfer Gen. Electric Co., San Jose, 1959-66, mgr. systems engring., 1966-68, mgr. design engring., 1968-71, gen. mgr., 1971-75, gen. mgr. boiling water reactor ops., 1975-77; pres. S. Levy Inc., Campbell, Calif., 1977—; adj. prof. UCLA, 1986-87; Springer prof. U. Calif., Berkeley, 1979-80; bd. dirs. Iowa Electric Utilities, Cedar Rapids. Patentee in field. Fellow Am. Soc. Mech. Engrs. (chmn. heat transfer div. 1964-65, heat transfer meml. award 1966, heat transfer conf. award 1963, 50th Ann. Heat Transfer Div. award 1988), Nat. Acad. Engring; mem. Am. Nuclear Soc. (chmn. thermal hydraulics div. 1985-86, Thermal Hydraulics Div. Achievement award 1987, Power Div. Walter H. Zinn award, 1989). Democrat. Mem. Unitarian Ch. Home: 1829 Dry Creek Rd San Jose CA 95124 Office: S Levy Inc 3425 S Bascom Ave Campbell CA 95008

LEW, RONALD S. W., federal judge; b. L.A., 1941; s. Chowlan and Suey Woon L.; m. Mamie Wong, 1970; children: Leslie, Leila, Lorelei, David. BA in Polit. Sci., Loyola U., L.A., 1964; JD, Southwestern U., 1971. Dep. city atty. L.A. City Atty's. Office, 1972-74; ptnr. Avans & Lew, L.A., 1974-82; commr. fire and police pension City of L.A., 1976-82; mcpl. ct. judge County of L.A., 1982-84, superior ct. judge, 1984-87; judge U.S. Dist. Ct. (cen. dist.) Calif., L.A., 1987—; Bar: Calif. 1971. Mem. World Affairs Council of L.A., 1976—, Christian Businessmen's Com. of L.A., 1982—. 1st It. U.S. Army, 1967-69. Recipient Vol. award United Way of L.A., 1979, cert. of merit L.A. Human Relations Commn., 1977, 82. Mem. Am. Judicature Soc., Calif. Assn. of Judges, So. Calif. Chinese Lawyer's Assn. (charter mem. 1976, pres. 1979), Chinese Am. Citizens Alliance, San Fernando Valley Chinese Cultural Assn., Delta Theta Phi. Office: US Dist Ct 312 N Spring St Los Angeles CA 90012

LEWAN, PAUL CHARLES, psychology and sociology educator; b. Detroit, May 19, 1929; s. Samuel John and Jennie Josephine (Mattson) L.; m. Carolyn May Sherry, Mar.23, 1957; children: Kathryn Grace, Paul Charles Jr. BS in Psychology, U. Wash., 1954, MS in Psychology, 1959. Personnel rep., tooling insp., facilities coordinator Boeing Aircraft Co., Seattle, 1954-59; instr. psychology Wenatchee (Wash.) Valley Coll., 1959-60; tchr., counselor Sylvester Jr. High Sch., Burien, Wash., 1960-65; instr. psychology and sociology Green River Community Coll., Auburn, Wash., 1965--; pres. council, 1974-75; bd. dirs, Presbyn. Counseling Service, Seattle, 1978-81. Mem. Burien Workshop Theater, Lake Burien Players, 1960-82; committeeman, conv. del. Seattle Democratic Com., 1962--; bd, dirs. Highline Symphony, Burien, 1984-85, Federal Way (Wash.) Symphony, 1984-87. Served with U.S. Army, 1951-53, capt. USAR ret. Mem. Am. Psychol. Assn., Wash. State Psychol. Assn., Green River Coll. Fedn. Tchrs. (sec., v.p., pres. 1980--), Phi Delta Kappa., Masons (32 degree)), Shriners. Presbyterian. Home: 27020 8th Ave S Kent WA 98032 Office: Green River Community Coll 12401 SE 320th St Auburn WA 98002

LEWANDOWSKI, STANLEY RICHARD, JR., utility company executive; b. Hammond, Ind., Sept. 1, 1937; s. Stanley Richard Sr. and Helen (Owczarak) L.; m. Gayle Marcia Anderson, Dec. 2, 1967; children: Paula, Ann-Marie, John. AA, San Diego City Coll., 1960; BS, San Diego State U., 1962. Ops. analyst Rural Electric Adminstrn., Washington, 1962-66; regional rep. Rural Electric Adminstrn., Denver, 1966-71; exec. v.p. San Isabel Electric Co., Pueblo, Colo., 1971-72; gen. mgr. Intermountain Rural Electric Assn., Sedalia, Colo., 1972—; bd. dirs. Affiliated Littleton (Colo.) Nat. Bank. Served with USN, 1954-58. Mem. Am. Mgmt. Assn., Castle Rock C. of C., Parker C. of C., Douglas County Econ. Devel. Council, Teller County Econ. Devel. Council. Republican. Roman Catholic. Lodges: Rotary, Elks. Home: 2426 S Zephyr Way Lakewood CO 80227 Office: Intermountain Rural Electric Assn 5496 N US Hwy 85 Sedalia CO 80135

LEWIN, FRANK EDMUND, data processing executive; b. L.A., Nov. 30, 1953; s. Arthur Wolfe and Deborah Kathryn (Pincus) L. BS in Math. and Computer Sci., UCLA, 1974. Data processing mgr. NHM Corp., North Hollywood, Calif., 1979—. Mem. Boston Computer Soc. (assoc.). Office: NHM Corp PO Box 3923 North Hollywood CA 91609

LEWIN, IAN, lighting sciences company executive, engineer; b. Newcastle, Eng., Dec. 10, 1942; came to U.S. 1967; s. Albert and Jennie (Reilly) L.; m. Enid Howes, Aug. 12, 1967; children: Jennifer Lesley, Sarah Kay. BS, U. Newcastle, 1964, PhD, 1967. Rsch. mgr. Holophane div. Manville Corp., Newark, Ohio, 1967-73; dir. Environ. Rsch. Labs., Scottsdale, Ariz., 1973-79; pres. Lighting Scis., Inc., Scottsdale, 1979—; bd. dirs. Lighting Scis. Can. Ltd., Waterloo, Ont. Patentee in field of illumination, 1973-87; contbr. articles to profl. jours. Sml. Bus. Innovation Research grantee, U.S. Army, 1987, Fed. Hwy. Adminstrn., 1987. Fellow Illuminating Engring. Soc. (bd. dirs. 1986); mem. Am. Phys. Soc., Optical Soc. Am., Rotary (chpt. pres. 1979-80). Republican. Home: 11408 Saint Andrews Hwy Scottsdale AZ 85254 Office: Lighting Scis Inc 7830 E Evans Rd Scottsdale AZ 85260

LEWINTER, ANTHONY ALAN, lawyer; b. L.A., Mar. 9, 1952; s. Richard Zachary and Marion Mildred (Zuckerman) LeW.; m. Julia Edith Merkin, June 4, 1978; children: Vanessa, Garrick. Student, U. Calif., Irvine, 1969-71; BA, UCLA, 1973; JD, Harvard U., 1976. Bar: Calif., U.S. Tax Ct. Assoc. DeCastro, West and Chodorow, L.A., 1976-79, Armstrong and Hendler, L.A., 1979-83; ptnr. Armstrong and Hirsch, L.A., 1983-86; pvt. practice Encino, Calif., 1986—. Mem. Calif. State Bar Assn., L.A. County Bar Assn., Century City Bar Assn., Encino C. of C. Democrat. Jewish. Office: 16530 Ventura Blvd #208 Encino CA 91436

LEWIS, BARBARA CLINE, city clerk, personnel executive; b. Sapulpa, Okla., Sept. 7, 1948; d. Frank Edwin and Dorothy Jean (Morris) C.; children from previous marriage: Lisa Kay, Michelle Ann., Jenny Rebecca Williams; m. David Leroy Lewis, July 7, 1984. Student, Glendale Community Coll., 1980-85; diploma Mcpl. Clks.' Inst., Ariz. State U., 1987. Cert. mcpl. clk. Clk. typist Arlington County (Va.) Govt., 1968-70, USMC, Cherry Point, N.C., 1970-71; sec. Hunt County Govt., Greenville, Tex., 1972-73; exec. sec. Wolfe City (Tex.) Ind. Sch. Dist., 1975-79; personnel adminstrv. asst. Del Webb Devel. Co., Sun City, Ariz., 1979-82; exec. sec. City of Tolleson (Ariz.), 1983-84, city clk., 1984—. Dep. registrar Maricopa County Rep. Orgn., 1984. Mem. Internat. Inst. Mcpl. Clks., Ariz. Mcpl. Clks. Assn.,

Internat. Records Mgmt. Assn., Internat. Personnel Mgrs. Assn., Ariz. Personnel Mgrs. Assn. Roman Catholic. Office: City of Tolleson 9555 W Van Buren Tolleson AZ 85353

LEWIS, BRENT RENAULT, computer company executive; b. Mpls., May 23, 1958; s. Willard Russell and Reatha (Landon) Kay L. Student, Brown Inst., 1978. Computer operator Northwestern Hosp., Mpls., 1977-78; programmer, supr. Dakota County, Mendota Heights, Minn., 1979-81; pres. Renault Sound Video, Mpls., 1981-85; system analyst Compucare, Inc., Mpls., 1981-84; mgr. data processing Golden Valley (Minn.) Health Ctr., 1985-86; prin. mng. ptnr. Logic 1 Computers, Scottsdale, Ariz., 1986—; dir. Data Map Internat., Scottsdale, 1986—. Mem. Ariz. Council Black Engrs., Ind. Computer Cons. Assn., Data Processing Mgmt. Assn., Assn. Vertical Market Computing, Microcomputer Industry Assn., Scottsdale C. of C. Home: 4940 E Columbine Dr Scottsdale AZ 85254 Office: Logic 1 Computers 7317 E 6th Ave Scottsdale AZ 85251

LEWIS, CHADWICK TERRY, business educator; b. Seattle, July 7, 1951; s. William Howard and Eva Lombard (Colkett) L.; m. Patricia Ann Gordon, Feb. 14, 1978; children: David, Kevin. AAS, Edmonds Community Coll., 1971; BA, Evergreen State Coll., 1973; MEd, Western Wash. U., 1974; MBA, U. Puget Sound, 1980. Fin. aid officer Ft. Steilacoom Community Coll., Tacoma, 1974-78; planning analyst Seattle Cen. Community Coll., Seattle, 1979; instr. bus. Everett (Wash.) Community Coll., 1979--. Author: (with Phil Lewis) The Donut Franchise: A Microcomputer Simulation, 1984; (with Lewis and Conrad Boyle) Marketing Peanut Butter: A Microcomputer Simulation, 1985; (with Fred Fiedler and Joe Garcia), People, Management, and Productivity, 1986; contbr. articles to profl. jours. Co-founder Nippon Bus. Inst., Everett and Bellingham, Wash., 1986. Recipient recognition for outstanding contbns. Everett Community Coll. Assn. Students, 1983, gold award mktg. competition Admissions Mktg. Report, 1987, 88; named Faculty of Yr., Everett Community Coll. Assn. Students, 1988. Mem. Educators for Social Responsibility, Japan-Am. Soc. Office: Everett Community Coll 801 Wetmore St Everett WA 98201

LEWIS, CHARLES D., insurance executive, rancher; b. Denver, June 22, 1936; s. Harry Thompson and Margretta (Borrmann) L.; m. Penelope Hall, June 18, 1956; children: C. Randel, Christina, Vanda H. Student, Dartmouth Coll., 1954-55; BSBA, U. Denver, 1959, MBA, 1961. Tax mgr. Arthur Andersen & Co., Denver, 1959-64; exec. v.p., treas. Vail (Colo.) Assocs., Inc., 1964-67, Writer Constrn. Corp., Denver, 1967-69; pres., chief exec. officer, founder Copper Mountain (Colo.), Inc., 1969-82; gen. ptnr. Williams Fork Ranches, Parshall, Colo., 1979—; gen. ptnr., dir. Boettcher & Co., Denver, 1982-85; pres. L.W.P. Svcs., Inc., Golden, Colo., 1985—; bd. dirs. Aircoa, Denver. Chmn. Copper Mountain Water & Sanitation Dist., 1972-82, Copper Mountain Met. Dist., 1972-82. With U.S. Army, 1955-57. Recipient Industry and Environ. award Rocky Mountain Ctr. on Environment, 1974; named Outstanding Design, Ski Mag., 1975, Colo. Ski Hall of Fame, 1989. Mem. Colo. Soc. CPAs, AICPAs, Nat. Ski Areas Assn. (chmn. 1981-83), Colo. Ski Country USA (chmn. 1978-79), Am. Ski Fedn. (vice chmn. 1980-82), Am. Arbitration Assn., Denver Club. Republican. Episcopalian. Home: 1421 Grand City 34 Parshall CO 80468 Office: LWP Svcs Inc 350 Indiana Golden CO 80401

LEWIS, CRISMON SMITH, newspaper editor; b. Ajo, Ariz., Dec. 30, 1948; s. Malin W. and Myreel Lewis; m. Vivienne Smith, Jan. 16, 1975; children: Ondalynn, Seth Corwin, Alice-Anne, Vivienne, Dallin, Meredith, Crimson Jr. BA in Communications, Brigham Young U., 1972. Photo editor Assoc. Press, Chgo., 1971; fed. ct. reporter Las Vegas (Nev.) Review Jour., 1974-75; editor The Tampa (Fla.) Neighbor, 1975-78; pres., editor The Latter-Day Sentinel Newspapers, Phoenix, 1979—. Contbr. articles to various publs. in Peru, 1969-70. Second counselor Phoenix Stake of Mormon Ch. With U.S. Army, 1972-74. Office: Latter Day Sentinel PO Box 2440 Phoenix AZ 85002

LEWIS, DAVID FRANKLIN, land investor, broker; b. Kingman, Ariz., Feb. 17, 1948; s. Dean W. and Ethel (Tolle) L.; m. Judy Anne Paine, Dec. 4, 1976; children: Luke D., Mark D. BS, No. Ariz. U., 1971. Licensed Real Estate Broker, Ariz. V.p. Double L-W Ranches, Phoenix, 1971-73; v.p. Luke Land, Inc., Phoenix, 1973-74, pres., 1975—; pres. Luke Land Realty & Investment, Phoenix, 1987—. Mem. Area D Adv. Com., Phoenix, 1985-87. Mem. Exec. Internat. Republican. Office: Luke Land Inc 7801 N Black Canyon Hwy Phoenix AZ 85021

LEWIS, DEREK LAMONT, advertising sales executive; b. Los Angeles, May 28, 1956; s. Arthur Alexander Lewis and Maxine Kennedy; m. Elizabeth Aileene Campfield, July 11, 1981; children: Jonathan, Paul. BA in English, UCLA, 1981. With sales dept. Cal Stereo, West Los Angeles, Calif., 1978-79; pub. relations rep. CBS Television, Los Angeles, 1979-80; sales rep. Lewis Vending Co., Los Angeles, 1973-81; acct. exec. Sta. KACE, Los Angeles, 1981-88; adv. exec., ptnr. Biko Mktg. Group, Los Angeles, 1988—; co-ptnr. Creative Images and Designs Co., 1988—. Mem. Nat. Assn. Broadcasters, So. Calif. Broadcasting Assn., So. Calif. Media Network, UCLA Alumni Assn. Democrat. Office: Biko Mktg Group 200 W Chestnut Ave Ste 202 Glendale CA 91204

LEWIS, EDWARD, producer, writer; b. Camden, N.J., Dec. 16, 1919; s. Max and Florence (Kline) L.; m. Mildred Gerchik, Sept. 6, 1946; children: Joan, Susan. BS, Bucknell U., 1940. Producer Edward Lewis Prodns., L.A., 1953—. Author screenplays Careless Years, Brothers, 1953; author: The Good Life, 1988, Zone D, 1989; producer feature films including Spartacus, The Fixer, Seven Days in May, Grand Prix, Seconds, Executive Action, Missing, The River, Lonely are the Brave. Capt. MAC, U.S. Army, 1945-48. Recipient Acad. Award nominations, 1956, 87, Golden Globe awards, 1956, 87. Mem. Producers' Guild (Best Producer 1960), Screen Writers' Guild. Democrat.

LEWIS, EDWARD B., biology educator; b. Wilkes-Barre, Pa., May 20, 1918; s. Edward B. and Laura (Histed) L.; m. Pamela Harrah, Sept. 26, 1946; children—Hugh, Glenn (dec.), Keith. B.A., U. Minn., 1939; Ph.D., Calif. Inst. Tech., 1942; Phil.D., U. Umea, Sweden, 1982. Instr. biology Calif. Inst. Tech., Pasadena, 1946-48; asst. prof. Calif. Inst. Tech., 1949-56, prof., 1956-66, Thomas Hunt Morgan prof., 1966—; Rockefeller Found. fellow Sch. Botany, Cambridge U., Eng., 1948-49; mem. Nat. Adv. Com. Radiation, 1958-61; vis. prof. U. Copenhagen, 1975-76, 82; researcher in developmental genetics, somatic effects of radiation. Editor: Genetics and Evolution, 1961. Served to capt. USAAF, 1942-46. Fellow AAAS; mem. Genetics Soc. Am. (sec. 1962-64, pres. 1967-69), Nat. Acad. Scis., Am. Acad. Arts and Scis. Home: 805 Winthrop Rd San Marino CA 91108 Office: Calif Inst Tech Div Biology Pasadena CA 91125

LEWIS, EDWIN REYNOLDS, biomedical engineering educator; b. Los Angeles, July 14, 1934; s. Edwin McMurtry and Sally Newman (Reynolds) L.; m. Elizabeth Louise McLean, June 11, 1960; children: Edwin McLean, Sarah Elizabeth. AB in Biol. Sci., Stanford U., 1956, MSEE, 1957, Engr., 1959, PhD in Elec. Engring., 1962. With research staff Librascope div. Gen. Precision Inc., Glendale, Calif., 1961-67; mem. faculty dept. elec. engring. and computer sci. U. Calif., Berkeley, 1967—, dir. bioengring. tng. program, 1969-77, prof. elec. engring. and computer sci., 1971—, assoc. dean grad. div., 1977-82, assoc. dean interdisciplinary studies coll. engring., 1988—; chair joint program bioengring. U. Calif. Berkeley and U. Calif. San Francisco, 1988—. Author: Network Models in Population Biology, 1977, (with others) Neural Modeling, 1977, The Vertebrate Inner Ear, 1985, also numerous articles. NSF, Nat. Aero. and Space Adminstrn. grantee, 1984, 87; Neurosci. Research Program fellow, 1966, 69; recipient Disting. Teaching Citation U. Calif., 1972; named Jacob Javits Neurosci. Investigator, NIH, 1984—. Fellow IEEE; mem. AAAS, Assn. Research in Otolaryngology, Acoustical Soc. Am., Soc. Neurosci., Sigma Xi. Club: Toastmasters (area lt. gov. 1966-67). Office: U Calif Dept Elec Engring & Computer Scis Berkeley CA 94720

LEWIS, FREDERICK THOMAS, insurance company executive; b. Tacoma, Apr. 1, 1941; s. Arthur Thomas and June Louise (Levenhagen) L.; m. Sarah Carolyn Boyette, Apr. 18, 1971; adopted children: Johanna, Elizabeth, Sarah, Jonathan, Matthew. Student, Concordia Coll., Portland, Oreg., 1959-61, Dominican Coll., San Rafael, Calif., 1967-71. Registered health underwriter. Enroute coord. Trans World Airlines, N.Y.C., 1961-62, 64-66; customer svc. rep. Trans World Airlines, Oakland, Calif., 1966-75; dist. rep. Aid Assn. for Luths., Twin Falls, Idaho, 1975-84, dist. mgr., 1984—. Vocalist Oakland Symphony Chorus, 1972-75; soloist Magic Valley Chorale, Twin Falls, 1979-83. Cantor Immanuel Luth. Ch., Twin Falls, 1984—; organizer Theos of Magic Valley, Filer, Idaho, 1984. Served with U.S. Army, 1962-64. Mem. Nat. Assn. Life Underwriters (tng. coun. fellow 1984, nat. quality award, nat. sales achievement award, health ins. quality award, 1978-85), , So. Idaho Life Underwriters (pres. 1980-81, edn. chmn. 1984-86, nat. local com. mem. 1986-89), So. Idaho Health Underwriters (bd. dirs. 1986-88), Idaho State Assn. Life Underwriters (area v.p. 1988-89, sec. 1989—), Idaho Fraternal Congress (ins. counselor 1976, bd. dirs. 1976-85, pres. 1981-82). Republican. Lodges: Lions (local v.p. 1979-81, pres. 1982-83, organizer Women's aux. 1983, sec. 1986-87). Home: RR 2 Box 5902 Twin Falls ID 83301 Office: Aid Assn for Luths 1210 Addison Ave E Twin Falls ID 83301

LEWIS, GEORGE RAYMOND, social work administrator; b. Bridgeton, N.J., July 7, 1944; s. Raymond and Evelyn Rhoda (Mitchell) L.; m. Tenelia Kay Boykin, Sept. 3, 1966. BA, U. N.Mex., 1966; MSW, Our Lady of the Lake Coll., 1971. Cert. social worker. With N.Mex. Health and Social Services Dept., 1971—; dist. tng. officer N.Mex. Health and Social Services Dept., Roswell, 1972-73, field office mgr., 1973-75, social worker cons., 1975-84, dist. ops. mgr., 1984—; behavioral sci. specialist Community Guidance Ctr., San Antonio, 1971; adj. instr. N.Mex. State U., Las Cruces, 1971, 83, 85, Eastern N.Mex. U., Roswell, 1973-76; clin. dir. Chaves County 1st Offender Program, Roswell, 1974-77; field instr. Tex. Tech U., Lubbock, 1981; bd. dirs. Assurance Home Inc., Roswell. Bd. dirs. Chaves County Home Health Agy. Inc., Roswell, 1973-76, Parents Anonymous of N.Mex. Inc., 1978-79. Named an Outstanding Young Man of Am., U.S. Jaycees, 1978, 81. Mem. Nat. Assn. Social Workers, Acad. Cert. Social Workers, Order of the Arrow, Blue Key. Democrat. Baptist. Home: 1018 N Plains Park Roswell NM 88201 Office: NMex Dept Human Svcs Social Svcs Div 1101 S Main St Roswell NM 88201

LEWIS, GERALD JORGENSEN, judge; b. Perth Amboy, N.J., Sept. 9, 1933; s. Norman Francis and Blanche M. (Jorgensen) L.; m. Laura Susan McDonald, Dec. 15, 1973; children by previous marriage: Michael, Marc. AB magna cum laude, Tufts Coll., 1954; JD, Harvard U., 1957. Bar: D.C. 1957, N.J. 1961, Calif. 1962, U.S. Supreme Ct. 1968. Atty. Gen. Atomic, LaJolla, Calif., 1961-63; ptnr. Haskins, Lewis, Nugent & Newnham, San Diego, 1963-77; judge Mcpl. Ct., El Cajon, Calif., 1977-79; judge Superior Ct., San Diego, 1979-84; assoc. justice, Calif. Ct. of Appeal, San Diego, 1984-87; dir. Fisher Scientific Group, Inc., 1987—; of counsel Latham & Watkins, 1987—; dir. Wheelabrator Techs., Inc., 1987—, Henley Mfg., Inc., 1987—; adj. prof. evidence Western State U. Sch. Law, San Diego, 1977—, exec. bd., 1977—; faculty San Diego Inn of Ct., 1979—, Am. Inn of Ct., 1984—. Cons. editor: California Civil Jury Instructions, 1984. City atty. Del Mar, Calif., 1963-74, Coronado, Calif., 1972-77; counsel Comprehensive Planning Orgn., San Diego, 1972-73; trustee San Diego Mus. Art., 1986—; bd. dirs. Air Pollution Control Dist., San Diego County, 1972-76; trustee San Diego Mus. Art, 1986—. Served to lt. comdr. USNR, 1957-61. Named Trial Judge of Yr., San Diego Trial Lawyers Assn., 1984. Mem. Am. Judicature Soc., Soc. Inns of Ct. in Calif., Confrerie des Chevaliers du Tastevin, Friendly Sons of St. Patrick. Republican. Episcopalian. Clubs: Bohemian; LaJolla Country (dir. 1980-83); Honkers Hunting (Niland, Calif.); Prophets. Home: 6505 Caminito Blythfield La Jolla CA 92037 Office: Latham & Watkins 701 B St Ste 2100 San Diego CA 92101

LEWIS, HARDIE DOSSIE, architectural drafting company owner; b. Duncan, Okla., Aug. 24, 1939; s. Dossie Humbred and Veda Ruth (Rowe) L.; m. Linda Faye Cantwell, June 4, 1960 (div. Feb. 1979); children: Tami Lynn, Kristi Leigh; m. Barbara Francis Clevenger, Dec. 27, 1984. Student, Chaffey Coll., 1957-59. Draftsman Harnish Morgan Causey, Ontario, Calif., 1959-62, Criley McDowell, Claremont, Calif., 1962-64; sr. draftsman Everet Tozier, Pomona, Calif., 1964-66; project coord. Cooke Frost Greer Schmandt, Santa Barbara, Calif., 1966-67, Arendt Mosher Grant, Santa Barbara, Calif., 1967-68, Ruhnau Evans Steinman, Riverside, Calif., 1968-70; office mgr. Robert miller, Riverside, Calif., 1970-72; v.p. Shaker and Robinson Constrn. Co., Riverside, Calif., 1972-77; owner H.D. Lewis Designs, Riverside, 1977—. Chmn. N.A.B. Job Fair, Riverside, 1970, Riverside 500 Parade, 1971, A. Childs Estate Chils's Zoo, Santa Barbara, 1967. Mem. Am. Inst. Bldg. Design, Jaycees (pres. Riverside 1972-73, bd. dirs. Santa Barbara 1967). Republican. Baptist. Home: 2223 Black Oak Pl Riverside CA 92506

LEWIS, JAMES B., state government official; b. Roswell, N.Mex., Nov. 30, 1947; m. Armandie Johnson; children: Terri, James Jr., Shedra, LaRon. BS in Edn., Bishop Coll., 1970; MA in Pub. Adminstrn., U. N.Mex., 1977, BS in Bus. Adminstrn., 1981. Coord., counselor pub. svcs. careers program N.Mex. State Personnel Office, Albuquerque; adminstr. consumer affairs div., investigator white collar crime sect., then dir. purchasing div. Bernalillo County Dist. Atty.'s Office; adminstr., educator U. Albuquerque; county treas. Bernalillo County, 1982-85; state treas. State of N.Mex., 1985—. Mem. adv. bd. Victims of Domestic Violence; past chmn. Dem. precincts and ward, Albuquerque; mem. N.Mex. State Bd. of Fin., Edn. Found. Bd., State Investment Coun., Oil and Gas Ad-Hoc Com., NAACP. With U.S. Army, 1970-72. Mem. Nat. State Treas.'s Assn., Pub. Employees Retirement Assn., Edn. Retirement Assn., Mortgage Fin. Authority, N.Mex. Assn. of Counties (past pres. treas.'s affiliate), Nat. Assn. County Treas. and Fin. Officers (chmn. membership com., bd. dirs.), Am. Soc. for Pub. Adminstrn. (past treas. N.Mex. chpt.), Am. GI Forum, Am. Legion, Internat. Alumni Assn. Bishop Coll., Am. Soc. for Pub. Adminstrn. (pres. elect 1989), Taylor Ranch Neighborhood Assn., Western State Treas.'s Assn. (v.p.), Omega Psi Phi (life), Alpha Beta Psi CPA Soc. Lodges: Kiwanis, Masons. Office: Office State Treas Villa Rivera Bldg PO Box 608 Santa Fe NM 87504

LEWIS, JAMES LUTHER, savings and loan executive; b. Bridgeport, Ohio, Sept. 29, 1912; s. William Luther and Gwen (Evans) L.; grad. Mercersburg Acad., 1931; B.A., Yale U., 1935; m. Mary Anne Glen, Oct. 26, 1943; children—William Luther II, Gwendolyn. Salesman, asst. sales dist. mgr. Chgo. Pneumatic Tool Co., 1935-43, asst. to pres., 1946-55; v.p., adminstrn. and sales, dir. Van Norman Industries, Inc., 1956; pres. Insuline Corp., 1956-58; v.p. corp. devel. Norris Thermador Corp., Los Angeles, 1959-65; chmn. bd., dir. Am. Savs. & Loan Assn., Reno, 1965—, Sierra Fin. Corp., 1968—; dir. Firth Sterling Steel Corp., 1956-58. Served to lt. USNR, 1943-46. Decorated Purple Heart, Presdl. Unit citation. Presbyterian. Home: 7755 Lakeside Dr Reno NV 89511 Office: 67 W Liberty St Reno NV 89501

LEWIS, JAMES WILLIAM, sales executive; b. L.A., Jan. 27, 1937; s. Kenneth Edward Lewis and Martha Magdalen (Butler) McNally; m. Máire Agnes O'Connor, Sept. 23, 1961; children: Kenneth Robert, Maureen Therese, Irene Bernadette, Erin Patricia. AA, L.A. City Coll., 1961; cert., UCLA, 1964, Loyola U., Westchester, Calif., 1971-72. Grocery mgr. King Cole Markets Inc., L.A., 1954-61; liquor mgr. Hughes Markets Inc., L.A., 1961-69; rep. spl. accounts Paul Masson Vineyards, L.A., 1969; supr. sales Almaden Vineyards, L.A., 1969-72; dist. mgr. Almaden Vineyards, Scottsdale, Ariz., 1972-77; western regional mgr. Almaden Vineyards, L.A., 1977-78, mgr. nat. accounts, 1978-84; southwestern regional mgr. Charles Lefranc Cellars, L.A., 1984-87; mgr. so. div. Parrott & Co., Irvine, Calif., 1987—; cons. Wine Club of Month, Palos Verdes, Calif., 1984—. Author, sports editor: Liberty Lantern, 1954; contbg. corr. Burbank Rev., 1952-54. Tchr. Confraternity Christian Doctrine, Canoga Park, Calif., 1971; booster Scottsdale Little League, 1974; booster Westlake High Sch. Track, 1984-85. With USNR, 1954-62. Named Man of Rhone Chapoutier & Cie France, L.A., 1986; recipient Cert. Merit German Wine Acad. Wine, 1983, Cert. Achievement Wine Inst. Calif., 1961. Mem. North Coast Prestige Wine Soc., Wine Investigative Oenophile Orgn., Les Amis du Vin, Kappa Phi Delta (treas. 1954-55). Democrat. Roman Catholic. Clubs: Los Santos (Burbank); Order of Palate (pres. 1967-68). Lodge: K.C. Home: 8 Cabrini Irvine CA 92714 Office: Parrott & Co 18004 Sky Park Blvd #155 Irvine CA 92714

LEWIS, JASON ALVERT, JR., communications executive; b. Clarksville, Tex., Aug. 17, 1941; s. Jason Allen and Mary (Dinwiddie) L. Student, Stockton Coll., 1959-60, San Jose Jr. Coll., 1962-63. Field engr. telephone tech. Pacific Bell, San Francisco, 1983-84; systems technician AT&T, San Francisco, 1984—. Patentee in field. With U.S. Army, 1964-66. Mem. Cousteau Soc., Astron. Soc. Pacific, San Francisco Zool. Soc. Democrat. Home: 139 Pecks Ln S South San Francisco CA 94080

LEWIS, JAY H., sociologist, educator; b. Mt. Pleasant, Ark., July 24, 1940; s. Osmer Homer and Artie Mae (Weatherford) L.; m. Karen Mary Ericson, Aug. 15, 1965; children: Jason Eric, Jonathon William, Julie Ann. BS in Sociology, Union Coll., Lincoln, Nebr., 1967; MA in Psychology, U. Nebr., 1971; MSW, U. Nebr., Omaha, 1976. Counselor Nebr. Penal Complex, Lincoln, 1967-69, rehab. adminstr., 1969-73; rehab. adminstr. Nebr. Ctr. Women, York, 1973-74; alcohol & drug adminstr. Dept. Edn., Lincoln, 1974-77; asst. prof. Union Coll., Lincoln, 1977-81, Atlantic Union Coll., South Lancaster, Mass., 1981-86; assoc. prof. social work, dir. undergrad. tng. Pacific Union Coll., Angwin, Calif., 1986-89, bd. chmn. Prep Sch. dept., 1989—. Mem. Nat. Assn. Social Workers, Coun. Social Work Edn. (ho. del. 1986—), Nebr. Rehab. Assn. (state pres. 1977-78). Mem. Seventh Day Adventist. Office: Pacific Union Coll Angwin CA 94508

LEWIS, JAYNE, park development official; b. East Orange, N.J., Mar. 2, 1956. BS in Civil Engring., Wash. U., 1978; postgrad., Ariz. State U., 1983-84. Lic. civil engr. Colo. Design engr. Brown & Root, Houston, 1978-79; structural engr. Stearns Roger, Denver, 1979-82; structural engr. Salt River Project, Phoenix, 1984-85, project mgr., 1985-87, asst. devel. mgr., 1987—. Tutor Boys Club Scottsdale, Ariz., 1989. Mem. Coun. Urban Econ. Devel., Project Mgmt. Inst. Office: Salt River Project PO Box 52025 Phoenix AZ 85072

LEWIS, JERRY, congressman; b. Oct. 21, 1934. BA, UCLA, 1956. Former underwriter life ins. underwrite; field rep. for former U.S. Rep. Jerry Pettis; mem. Calif. State Assembly, 1968-78; vice chmn. rules com., chmn. subcom. on air qualit; mem. 96th-101st Congresses from 35th Calif. dist., 1979—; mem. appropriation com., ranking minority mem. legis. br. subcom., mem. fgn. ops. subcom., ind. agys. subcoms. HUD. Presbyterian. Office: 2312 Rayburn House Office Bldg Washington DC 20515 *

LEWIS, JOHN CLARK, JR., manufacturing company executive; b. Livingston, Mont., Oct. 15, 1935; s. John Clark and Louise A. (Anderson) L.; m. Carolyn Jean Keesling, Sept. 4, 1960; children: Robert, Anne, James. BS, Fresno (Calif.) State U., 1957. With Service Bur. Corp., El Segundo, Calif., 1960-70, Computer Scis. Corp., 1970; with Xerox Corp., El Segundo, 1970-77, pres. bus. systems div., 1977; pres. Amdahl Corp., Sunnyvale, Calif., 1983-87, chief exec. officer, 1983—, chmn., 1987—. Served with USNR, 1957-60. Roman Catholic. Office: Amdahl Corp 1250 E Arques Ave Sunnyvale CA 94088 *

LEWIS, JOHN THOMSON CONDELL, aerospace company executive; b. Castro Valley, Calif., Nov. 18, 1955; s. Ernest Edward John and Catherine Evangeline (Thomson) L. BA, U. Calif., Santa Barbara, 1977; MBA, Santa Clara U., 1980. Systems analyst Gen. Electric Co., Sunnyvale, Calif., 1978-82; mem. tech. staff Applied Research, Inc., Santa Clara, Calif., 1982-83; co-founder, mng. ptnr. The Delphi Group, Fremont, Calif., 1982-83; aerospace planner Ford Aerospace Corp., Sunnyvale, Calif., 1983—. Republican. Episcopalian. Clubs: Commonwealth of Calif. (San Francisco); Kenna(U. Santa Clara). Home: 7835 Crossridge Rd Dublin CA 94568 Office: Ford Aerospace Corp 1260 Crossman Ave Sunnyvale CA 94089

LEWIS, JOHN WILSON, political scientist; b. King County, Wash., Nov. 16, 1930; s. Albert Lloyd and Clara (Lewis) Seeman; m. Jacquelyn Clark, June 19, 1954; children: Cynthia, Stephen, Amy. Student, Deep Springs Coll., 1947-49; A.B. with highest honors, UCLA, 1953, M.A., 1958, Ph.D., 1962; hon. degree, Morningside Coll., 1969, Lawrence U., 1986. Asst. prof. govt. Cornell U., 1961-64, assoc. prof., 1964-68; prof. polit. sci. Stanford U., 1968—, William Haas prof. Chinese politics, 1972—, co-dir. NE Asia U.S. Forum on Internat. Policy, co-dir. arms control and disarmament program, 1971-83, co-dir. Ctr. for Internat. Security and Arms Control; chmn. Internat. Strategic Inst. 2; chmn. joint com. on contemporary China Social Sci. Research Council-Am. Council Learned Socs., 1976-79; former vice chmn. and bd. dirs. Nat. Com. on U.S.-China Relations; cons. Senate Select Com. on Intelligence, 1977-81, Lawrence Livermore Nat. Lab., Los Alamos Nat. Lab.; chmn. com. advanced study in China Com. Scholarly Communication with People's Republic of China, 1979-82; mem. com. on internat. security and arms control Nat. Acad. Scis., 1980-83; organizer first univ. discussion arms control and internat. security matters Chinese People's Inst. Fgn. Affairs, 1978, first academic exchange agreement Dem. People's Rep. of Korea, 1988; negotiator first univ. tng. and exchange agreement People's Rep. of China, 1978. Author: Leadership in Communist China, 1963, Major Doctrines of Communist China, 1964, Policy Networks and the Chinese Policy Process, 1986; co-author: The United States in Vietnam, 1967, Modernization by Design, 1969, China Builds the Bomb, 1988; editor: The City in Communist China, 1971, Party Leadership and Revolutionary Power in China, 1970, Peasant Rebellion and Communist Revolution in Asia, 1974; contbr.: Congress and Arms Control, 1978, China's Quest for Independence, 1979, others.; mem. editorial bd.: Chinese Law and Govt, China Quar., Survey, The Pacific Rev. Served with USN, 1954-57. Mem. Assn. Asian Studies, Am. Polit. Sci. Assn., Council Fgn. Relations, Phi Beta Kappa. Home: 541 San Juan St Stanford CA 94305 Office: Stanford U 320 Galvez St Stanford CA 94305

LEWIS, KENNETH, shipping executive; b. N.Y.C., Aug. 23, 1934; b. Nathaniel and Hana Evelyn (Kotler) L.; A.B., Princeton U., 1955; J.D., Harvard U., 1958; m. Carol Ann Schnitzer, Aug. 3, 1958 (div. 1982); children—Scott, Laurence, Kathleen; m. 2d, Colleen Anne Wesche, Nov. 27, 1983. Admitted to N.Y., Oreg. bars, 1959; law clk. to judge U.S. Dist. Ct., N.Y.C., 1958-59; asso. King, Miller, Anderson, Nash & Yerke, Portland, Oreg., 1959-61; gen. counsel Indsl. Air Products Co., Portland, 1961-63; v.p. to exec. v.p. Lasco Shipping Co., Portland, 1963-79, pres., 1979—; bd. dirs. Britannia Steam Ship Ins. Assn., Ltd., London, 1986—, The Swedish Club, Gothenburg, 1987—, dep. chmn., 1988—. Mem. Port of Portland Commn., 1974-81, treas., 1977, v.p., 1978, pres., 1979; trustee Lewis and Clark Coll., 1974-83; bd. dirs. Columbia River Maritime Mus., 1987—, Oreg. Community Found., 1982—, treas., 1986—; mem. Portland Met. Area Boundary Commn., 1974-74, Portland Met. Mass Transit Dist. Bd., 1973-74; pres. Portland Zool. Soc., 1970, World Affairs Council of Oreg., 1969. Mem. Am., Oreg. Bar Assns., Soc. Maritime Arbitrators, Inc. Democrat. Jewish. Clubs: Multnomah Athletic, Arlington, University, Masons, City (Portland). Office: 3200 NW Yeon Ave Portland OR 97210

LEWIS, MARY ETTA, special education teacher; b. Ontario, Calif., Oct. 23, 1928; d. Franklin Carr and Marguerite Mae (Wood) McMakin; m. Charles Jesse Lewis, Dec. 15, 1946; children: Kenneth Arnold, Linda Marie. AA, Chaffey Coll., Alta Loma, Calif., 1963; BA, LaVerne Coll., 1965; MA, Calif. State U., Los Angeles, 1979. Cert. elem. tchr., learning handicapped specialist. Tchr. Chino (Calif.) Unified Sch. Dist., 1965-67; tchr. Ontario-Montclair Sch. Dist., 1967-79, spl. edn. tchr., 1979-80, resource specialist, 1980-88; resource specialist Morongo Unified Sch. Dist., Yucca VAlley, Calif., 1988—. Tchr. Presby. Ch., Upland, CAlif., 1956-78, deacon 1976-79, Alta Loma, Calif., 1980-83. Recipient Delta Kappa GAmma award Teaching Colleagues, 1982-88. Mem. AAUW (sec. 1967-69), Pilot's Internat. Assn., NEA, Calif. Tchrs. Assn., orton Dyslexia Soc., Council for Exceptional Children, ZONTA, Calif. Assn. Resource Specialists, 99er's Club, Assistance League Club. Republican. Home: PO Box 2349 Yucca Valley CA 92286 Office: Mels Learning Sta 56020 Santa Fe Tr Ste Q Yucca Valley CA 92284

LEWIS, MICHAEL, playwright, columnist; b. Washington, May 4, 1950; s. Melvin Earl and Beatrice (Fleischman) L.; m. Divona Fae Tyrrell, July 2, 1978; children: Anna-Lisa, Jonathan, Eric. BA, Brandeis U., 1972. Freelance playwright 1972—; resident playwright Street 70 Theatre Co., Washington, 1972-73, performer, tchr., 1972-73; cons. in field., L.A., 1978—; writer, script analyst Celebrity Ctr. Theatre, L.A., 1985—; script analyst, cons. Orbit Entertainment div. Paramount Studios, 1987—; sec., co-founder My Dad's Gotta Barn Prodns., Inc. Author: (plays) Sunrise on the Earth, 1983, The Pot of Gold, 1987, Girls in Warm Snow, 1986, Alive and Kicking, 1988, The Heart Beats in Waltz Time, 1989; (TV script) Facts of Life, 1987; columnist Needs and Wants, 1986—. Recipient Montgomery County award

Montgomery County TB & Respiratory Disease Found., 1968, Franklin Giddon Playwriting award Brandeis U., 1971, 72, Dramalogue award Dramalogue (publ.) 1986. Mem. Dramatist's Guild Am. (assoc.), Author's League Am. (assoc.). Scientologist.

LEWIS, MICHAEL EARLE, financial executive; b. Portland, Oreg.; s. Michael Dale and Gail Carole Lewis. B in Bus., Portland State U., 1989, postgrad., 1989—. Govtl. intern Oreg. State Senate, Salem, 1985-86; placement advisor Portland State U., 1986-87; asst. adminstr. Bernard Haldane Assoc., Portland, 1988—. Fin. Analyst scholar Portland Soc., 1989. Mem. Assn. Students Internat. Commerce & Econs., Oreg. Internat. Coun., Fin. Mgmt. Assn., Kiwanis (chartered), Builder's Club. Republican. Home: 4517 SW Fairvale Ct Portland OR 97221

LEWIS, NANCY PATRICIA, speech-language pathologist; b. Miami, Fla., Sept. 23, 1956; d. James and Sara (Gilman) L. BS, U. Fla., 1978; MS, U. Ariz., 1980. Postgrad. fellow U. Tex. Med. Br., Galveston, 1979-80, speech lang. pathologist, 1980-81; speech lang. pathologist Albuquerque Pub. Schs., 1982-84; child devel. specialist Albuquerque Spl. Presch., 1984—; pvt. practice speech pathology Albuquerque, 1985—; coordinator Project Ta-kos, 1987—; speaker in field. Author (dianostic procedure) Khan-Lewis Phonological Analysis, 1986; (therapeutic materials) Familiar Objects and Actions, 1985. Labor coord. Lama Found., 1988; bd. dirs. Vols. for the Outdoors, Albuquerque, 1984—. Fellow U. Tex. Med. Br., Galveston, 1981. Mem. Am. Speech Lang. and Hearing Assn., N.Mex. Speech Lang. and Hearing Assn. Democrat. Office: PO Box 240 San Cristobal NM 87564

LEWIS, NORMAN, English language educator, writer; b. N.Y.C., Dec. 30, 1912; s. Herman and Deborah (Nevins) L.; m. Mary Goldstein, July 28, 1934; children—Margery, Debra. B.A., CUNY, 1939; M.A., Columbia U., 1941. Instr., lectr CUNY, N.Y.C., 1943-52; assoc. prof. English NYU, N.Y.C., 1955-64; instr. Compton Coll., Calif., summers 1962-64, UCLA, 1962-69; prof. English Rio Hondo Coll., Whittier, Calif., 1964—, chmn. communications dept., 1964-75. Author: (with Wilfred Funk) Thirty Days to a More Powerful Vocabulary, 1942, rev. edit., 1970, Power with Words, 1943, How to Read Better and Faster, 1944, rev. edit., 1978, The Lewis English Refresher and Vocabulary Builder, 1945, Better English, 1948, Word Power Made Easy, 1949, rev. edit., 1978, The Rapid Vocabulary Builder, 1951, rev. edit., 1980, 3d edit., 1988, How to Get More Out of Your Reading, 1951, Twenty Days to Better Spelling, 1953, The New Roget's Thesaurus in Dictionary Form, 1961, rev. edit., 1978, Dictionary of Correct Spelling, 1962, Correct Spelling Made Easy, 1963, rev. edit. 1987, Dictionary of Modern Pronunciation, 1963, New Guide to Word Power, 1963, The New Power with Words, 1964, Thirty Days to Better English, 1964, The Modern Thesaurus of Synonyms, 1965, RSVP-Reading, Spelling, Vocabulary, Pronunciation, elem. texts, I-III, 1966, coll. edit., 1977, See, Say, and Write!, books I and II, 1973, Instant Spelling Power, 1976, R.S.V.P. for College English Power, book II, 1978, book III, 1979, R.S.V.P. with Etymology, book I, 1980, book II, 1981, book III, 1982, R.S.V.P. books I-III, rev. edits., 1982-83, books A-B, 1985-86, Instant Word Power, 1981, Dictionary of Good English, 1987; also numerous articles in nat. mags.

LEWIS, ORME, JR., real estate company executive, natural resources company executive; b. Phoenix, Apr. 26, 1935; s. Orme and Barbara (Smith) L.; m. Elizabeth Bruening, Oct. 17, 1964; children: Orme Joseph, Elizabeth Blaise. BS, U. Ariz., 1958. Assoc. Coldwell Banker, Phoenix, 1959-64; v.p. Braggiotti Constrn., Phoenix, 1964-65; pvt. practice investment brokerage Phoenix, 1966-69; dep. asst. sec. Dept. Interior, Washington, 1969-73; dir. Devel. Ariz. Biltmore Estates, 1973-76; v.p. World Resources Co., Phoenix and McLean, Va., 1978—; pres. Applewhite, Laflin and Lewis, Phoenix, 1979—; gen. ptnr. Equity Interests, Phoenix, 1982—; co-chmn. U.S. Adv. Com. Mining and Mineral Rsch., Washington, 1982—; mem. U.S. Emergency Minerals Adminstrn., 1986—; mem. State Plant Site Transmission Line Com., Phoenix, 1974-85. Mem. Ariz. State Senate, 1966-69; bd. dirs. Phoenix Children's Hosp., 1981—, Polycystic Kidney Rsch. Found., Kansas City, Mo., 1983—, Ariz. Community Found., 1986—, Ariz. Parks and Conservation Coun., 1985—, Ariz. State U. Found., Tempe, 1981—, Ariz. Hist. Found., 1984—; Desert Bot. Garden, 1987-89. Republican. Clubs: Metropolitan (Washington); Ariz. Valley Field Riding and Polo (Phoenix); Paradise Valley Country (Scottsdale, Ariz.). Home: 4325 E Palo Verde Dr Phoenix AZ 85018 Office: Applewhite Laflin & Lewis 4250 E Camelback Rd 175-K Phoenix AZ 85018-2784

LEWIS, PATRIC ROBERT, meat packing and food distribution executive; b. Kanab, Utah, Aug. 4, 1947; s. Harold Bernell and Elva L.; m. Carla Inglish, June 3, 1970; children: Lindsey, Ryan, Sydney, Courtney, Tyler. BS, Brigham Young U., 1970. Cert. secondary tchr., Utah. Exec. Lewis Meats, Inc., St. George, Utah, 1970-81, sec.-treas., 1977-89, pres., 1989—; exec. Anthony Motors, Inc., St. George, 1981-84; sec., treas. Lewis Meats, Inc., St. George, 1977—; cons. Dixie Jr. Coll. Vocational Edn., St. George, 1979-82. Bd. dirs. Alcohol and Drug Abuse St. George Area, 1979-81, Wash. County Sch. Dist. Found., St. George, 1985-89; campaign chmn. County Sheriff race, St. George, 1986, State Sen. race, Dist. 19, Utah, 1988. With U.S. Army, 1970. Mem. Western States Meat Assn., Jaycees (bd. dirs. 1972), St. George Area C. of C. (bd. dirs. 1984-88, pres. 1987), Exchange Club. Republican. Mormon. Home: 521 Churchill Dr St George UT 84770 Office: Lewis Meats Inc 1845 Sunset Blvd St George UT 84770

LEWIS, RALPH JAY, III, management and human resources educator; b. Balt., Sept. 25, 1942; s. Ralph Jay and Ruth Elizabeth (Schmeltz) L. BS in Engring., Northwestern U., 1966; MS in Adminstrn., U. Calif., Irvine, 1968; PhD in Mgmt., UCLA, 1974. Research analyst Chgo. Area Expressway Surveillance Project, 1963-64, Gen. Am. Transp. Co., Chgo., 1965-66; assoc. prof. mgmt. and human resources mgmt. Calif. State U., Long Beach, 1972—; cons. Rand Corp., Santa Monica, Calif., 1966-74, Air Can., Montreal, Que., 1972-73, Los Angeles Times, 1973;. Co-author: Studies in the Quality of LIfe, 1972; author instructional programs, monographs; co-designer freeway traffic control system. Bd. dirs. Project Quest, Los Angeles, 1969-71. Mem. AAAS, Am. Psychol. Assn., Assn. for Humanistic Psychology, The World Future Soc., Soc. of Mayflower Desc., SAR (Ill. soc.), Internat. Arabian Horse Assn., Sierra Club, Beta Gamma Sigma. Democrat. Office: Calif State U Dept Human Resources Mgmt Long Beach CA 90840

LEWIS, RALPH MILTON, real estate developer; b. Johnstown, Pa., Nov. 9, 1919; s. Morris and Sarah (Galfond) L.; m. Goldy Sarah Kimmel, June 12, 1941; children: Richard Alan, Robert Edward, Roger Gordon, Randall Wayne. AA, Los Angeles City Coll., 1939; BS, UCLA, 1941; postgrad., U. So. Calif., 1945-48. Bar: Calif. 1952. Pvt. practice acctg. Los Angeles, 1945-55; practice law Los Angeles, 1953-55; founder Lewis Homes, 1957; chmn. bd. Lewis Construction Co., Upland, Calif., 1959—, Lewis Bldg. Co., Las Vegas, 1960—; Republic Sales Co., Inc. Lewis Bldg. Co., Upland, 1956—; dir., v.p. Kimmel Enterprises, Inc., 1959—; mng. partner Lewis Homes of Calif., 1973—, Lewis Homes of Nev., 1972—, Western Properties, Upland, 1972—, Foothill Investment Co., Las Vegas, 1971—, Republic Mgmt. Co., Upland, 1978-86; dir. Gen. Telephone Co. Calif., 1981-86; mem. adv. bd. Inland div. Security Pacific Nat. Bank; instr. U. So. Calif., UCLA, Los Angeles City Coll., 1948-54, Dooley Law Rev. Course, 1953-54; guest lectr. numerous colls., univs. Contbr. articles to mags., jours. Mem., com. chmn. Calif. Commn. of Housing and Community Devel., 1965-67; mem. Calif. Gov.'s Task Force on the Home Bldg. and Construction Industry, 1967; pres. Bd. of Edn. Citrus Community Coll. Dist., Azusa, Calif., 1969, 73, mem., 1967-73; mem. Citizens Planning Council, Los Angeles County Regional Planning Commn., 1972-73, UCLA Found., Chancellor's Assoc.; mem. dean's council UCLA Grad. Sch. Architecture and Urban Planning.; bd. dirs. Regional Research Inst. So. Calif., 1983-84; chmn. land use and planning com. Citizens' Adv. Council, Calif. Senate Housing Com., 1983-84; founding mem. Rancho Cucamonga Community Found., 1987-88. Recipient Humanitarian award NCCJ, 1979; Builder of Year award Bldg. Industry Assn. So. Calif., 1970; named as U. So. Calif.'s 1st Developer in Residence, 1988 at Lusk Ctr. for Real Estate Devel.; recipient Good Scout award Old Baldy council Boy Scouts Am., 1984; recipient (with wife) Builder of Yr. award Profl. Builder mag., 1987; inducted Nat. Housing Ctr.'s Hall of Fame, Washington, 1988. Mem. Am. Bar Assn., Calif. Soc. C.P.A.'s, Nat. Assn. Home Builders (dir.), Calif. Bldg. Industry Assn. (dir., chmn. affordable housing task force 1978-80, named to Hall of Fame 1987), Bldg. Industry Assn. So. Calif. (past treas., pres., dir., Bldg. Industry Medal of Honor, 1986). Office: Lewis Homes 1156 N Mountain Ave Upland CA 91786

LEWIS, RICHARD NEWBURN, environmental technician; b. Jacksonville, Tex., Oct. 25, 1951; s. Henry Richard Lewis and Mary Joyce (Newburn) Gandy; m. Charlyn Gail, Dec. 26, 1985; 1 child, Christopher. BS, Stephen F. Austin State U., 1975, postgrad., 1976. Asst. dir. quality control Temple-Eastex Corp., Diboll, Tex., 1977-79; environmental quality technician Basin Electric Power Coop., Wheatland, Wyo., 1979&. Mem. pub. relations com. Wyo. AFL-CIO, 1980-83; vice-chmn. Platte County (Wyo.) Dems., 1980—; vol. Mike Sullivan for Gov., Platte County, 1987. Mem. Internat. Brotherhood Elec. Workers, Wyo. Wildlife Fedn., Ducks Unlimited, Arbor Day Found. Democrat. Baptist. Lodges: Shriners (sec., trustee 1981—), Masons (Master 1987-88, trustee), Moose. Home: 518 N Wheatland Hwy Wheatland WY 82201 Office: Basin Electric Power Coop Laramie River Sta Wheatland WY 82201

LEWIS, ROBERT LEE, III, health facility executive; b. San Francisco, Sept. 20, 1949; s. Robert Lee Jr. and Dolores Patricia (Brady) L.; m. Kari B. Hanson, May 1989. BS, Calif. State U., Fresno, 1971, MBA, 1978; cert. advanced mgmt., Stanford U., 1983. Ops. officer, adminstrv. asst. to v.p. Security Pacific Nat. Bank, Fresno, 1971-74; service chief County Health Dept., Fresno, 1974-79; adminstrv. dir. clin. labs. Stanford (Calif.) U. Hosp., 1979-84; pres. Western Div. Internat. Clin. Labs., Dublin, Calif., 1984-86; v.p. Performance Health Care, Inc., Danville, Calif., 1986—; adminstr. Good Samaritan Med. Group, San Jose, Calif., 1987—; mem. hiring bds. Calif., Fresno County, 1978-79; cons. Performance Health Care, 1986—, Abbott Diagnostics, 1984-86, Nichols Inst. 1984, Syva Co. 1983-84, 86, hosp. mgmt. 1982—; adj. faculty Coll. Profl. Studies U. San Francisco, 1988—. Author: Optimizing Productivity: Capital Equipment Acquisition, 1985; mem. editorial bd. Syva Monitor, 1984. Officer Fresno County Council for Developmentally Disabled, 1975-79; mem. Mayor's Com. on Hiring Handicapped, 1976-79; mem. adv. bd. Goodwill Industries, 1977-78. Served with USNG, 1971-76. Mem. Calif. Clin. Lab. Assn. (bd. dirs. 1984-86), Clin. Lab. Mgmt. Assn. (founder No. Calif. chpt.), Calif. Assn. Rehab. Facilities, Fresno Assn. for Retarded (bd. dirs. (1975-78). Home: 108 Durham St Menlo Park CA 94025 Office: Good Samaritan Med Group 2585 Samaritan Dr San Jose CA 95124

LEWIS, ROBERT TURNER, psychologist; b. Taft, Calif., June 17, 1923; s. D. Arthur and Amy Belle (Turner) L.; m. Jane Badham, Mar. 23, 1946; children—Jane, William, Richard. B.A., U. So. Calif., 1947, M.A., 1950; Ph.D., U. Denver, 1952. Lic. psychologist, Calif. Chief psychologist Hollywood Presbyn. Hosp., Los Angeles, 1953-58; dir. psychol. services Salvation Army, Pasadena, Calif., 1958-68; dir. Pasadena Psychol. Ctr., 1964-74; successively asst. prof., assoc. prof. and prof., Calif. State U.-Los Angeles, 1952-83, prof. emeritus, 1984—; assoc. dir Cortical Function Lab., Los Angeles, 1972-84; clin. dir. Diagnostic Clinic, West Covina, Calif., 1983-85; dir.·Job Stress Clinic, Santa Ana, Calif., 1985—. Author: Taking Chances, 1979; co-author: Money Madness, 1978; Human Behavior, 1974; The Psychology of Abnormal Behavior, 1961. Served to lt. (j.g.) USNR, 1943-46, PTO. Mem. Am. Psychol. Assn., Calif. State Psychol. Assn., Los Angeles County Psychol. Assn., Nat. Acad. Neuropsychology. Republican. Office: Job Stress Clinic 1200 N Main St #525 Santa Ana CA 92701

LEWIS, ROSEMARY ADELE, accountant, insurance agent; b. St. Louis, Jan. 2, 1937; d. Stephen F. and Eileen (Leahy) Harke; m. Robert D. Lewis, II, Oct. 9, 1954. Student, St. Louis U., 1954-55. Lic. ins. agt., Calif. Bookkeeper Brady-Drake Photocopy Co., St. Louis, 1954-55; bookkeeper, office mgr. ABC Constrn. Co., Norwalk, cALIF., 1956-61, Bission Ins. Agy., Garden Grove, Calif., 1967-73; acctg. mgr. Ky. Fried Chicken, Long Beach, Calif., 1961-66; acctg. exec. Mahar Ins. Svc. Inc., Garden Grove, Calif., 1973--. Mem. Ind. Ins. Agts. Assn., Am. Agts. Alliance Co. Democrat. Roman Catholic. Home: 11162 Yana Dr Garden Grove CA 92641

LEWIS, RUTH ADAMS, writer; b. Hartford, Conn., Feb. 26, 1943; d. Christopher A. and Ruth Clark (Horan) Adams; m. John Simpson Lewis, Aug. 1, 1964; children: J. Vandenbergh, Margaret L. Martell, Christopher, Katherine, Elizabeth, Peter. AB, Smith Coll., 1965. Fgn. manuscript editor Jour. Phys. Chemistry, La Jolla, Calif., 1967-68; translator French MIT Press, Cambridge, Mass., 1982-83; translator French and German HP Books, Tucson, Ariz., 1983-84, editor, 1984-86; free lance writer Tucson, 1984—; tchr. sci. Carden Sch. Tucson, Inc., 1984-89; pres. ASPERA, Inc. Editor: Symptoms, 1985, Sports Medicine, 1986; translator numerous books including Atoms of Silence, 1982-86; co-author: Space Resources: Breaking the Bonds of Earth, 1987; contbr. articles to profl. jours. Mem. The Authors' Resource Ctr., Tucson Space Soc. Republican. Mormon. Home: 5010 W Sweetwater Dr Tucson AZ 85745 Office: 1745 N Campbell Ave Tucson AZ 85719

LEWIS, SAMELLA SANDERS, artist, educator; b. New Orleans, Feb. 27, 1924; d. Samuel and Rachel (Taylor) Sanders; m. Paul Gad Lewis, Dec. 22, 1948; children—Alan Stephen, Claude Anthony. Student, Dillard U., 1941-43; B.S., Hampton Inst., 1945; M.A., Ohio State U., 1947, Ph.D., 1951; postgrad., U. So. Calif., 1964-66; L.H.D. (hon.), Chapman Coll., 1976. Asst. prof. Hampton (Va.) Inst., 1945-47; asso. prof. art Morgan State Coll., 1950-52; chmn. dept. art, prof. Fla. A&M U., 1953-58; prof. SUNY, Plattsburgh, 1958-67; coordinator edn. Los Angeles County Mus. Art, 1968-69; prof. Asian, African, Afro-Am. Art History Scripps Coll., Claremont, Calif., 1970-84; prof. emerita Scripps Coll., 1984—; artistic cons.; curator Richard Hunt: Sculptures and Drawings (8 countries in Africa), USIA, Arts Am., 1986-87, Jacob Lawrence: Paintings and Drawings for Africa and the Caribbean, USIA, Arts Am., 1988-89. Author: Art, African American Textbook, 1978, The Art of Elizabeth Catlett, 1984; producer five films on Black Am. artists; founder Mus. African Am. Art, Los Angeles, 1976; founder, dir., The Gallery, Los Angeles, 1969-79, Asanti Gallery, Pomona, Calif., 1980; Art editor Internat. Rev. African Am. Art, 1976—; One woman shows, Clark Mus., Claremont, Calif., 1979, Univ. Union Gallery, 1980, group shows include, Huntsville (Ala.) Mus., 1979, Smithsonion Instn. travelling exhbn., 1980-81, Vorpal Gallery, San Francisco, 1989; curator Masters Exhbn., Salvador, Bahia, Brazil, 1988; represented in permanent collections, Balt. Mus. Art, Oakland Mus. Art, High Mus., Atlanta, Palm Springs Mus., Va. Mus. Art. Recipient Faculty Recognition award Scripps Coll., 1984, Honor award for outstanding achievement in visual arts Women's Caucus for Art, 1989; Fulbright fellow, 1962, NDEA post doctoral fellow, 1964-66; Ford Found. grantee, 1965, 81. Mem. Assn. Asian Studies, Nat. Conf. Artists, So. Calif. Art History Assn., Coll. Art Assn. Am. Home: 1237 S Masselin Ave Los Angeles CA 90019

LEWIS, SHIRLEY JEANE, instructor; b. Phoenix, Aug. 23, 1937; d. Herman and Leavy (Hutchinson) Smith; AA, Phoenix Community Coll., 1957; BA, Ariz. State U., 1960; MS, San Diego State U., 1975, MA, 1986; MA, Azusa Pacific U., 1982; PhD, U. So. Calif., 1983. Cert. Tchr., Calif.; m. Edgar Anthony Lewis, June 25, 1966 (div. May 1980); children—Edgar Anthony, Roshaun, Lucy Ann, Jonathan. Recreation leader Phoenix Parks and Recreation Dept., 1957-62; columnist Ariz. Tribune, Phoenix, 1958-59; tchr. phys. edn. San Diego Unified Schs., 1962—; adult educator San Diego Community Colls., 1973—, instr. psychology, health, Black studies, 1977—, counselor, 1981—; community counselor S.E. Counseling and Cons. Svcs. and Narcotics Prevention and Edn. Systems, Inc., San Diego, 1973-77; counselor educator, counselor edn. dept. San Diego State U., 1974-77; marriage, family, child counselor Counseling and Cons. Ctr., San Diego, 1977—; inservice educator San Diego Unified and San Diego County Sch. Dists., 1973-77; lectr. in field. Girl Scout phys. fitness cons., Phoenix, 1960-62; vol. community tutor for high sch. students, San Diego, 1963; sponsor Tennis Club for Youth, San Diego, 1964-65; troop leader Girl Scouts U.S., Lemon Grove, Calif., 1972-74; vol. counselor USN Alcohol Rehab. Center, San Diego, 1978. Named Woman of Year, Phoenix, 1957, One of Outstanding Women of San Diego, 1980; recipient Phys. Fitness Sch. award and Demonstration Sch. award Pres.'s Coun. on Phys. Fitness, Taft Jr. High Sch., 1975; Delta Sigma Theta scholar, 1957-60; Alan Korrick scholar, 1956. Mem. NEA, Calif. Tchrs. Assn., San Diego Tchrs. Assn., Assn. Marriage and Family Counselors, Am. Personnel and Guidance Assn., Calif. Assn. Health, Phys. Edn. and Recreation, Am. Alliance of Health, Phys. Edn. and Recreation, Delta Sigma Theta. Democrat. Baptist. Contbr. articles to profl. jours. Home: 1226 Armacost Rd San Diego CA 92114 Office: 2630 B St San Diego CA 92102

LEWIS, TED HOWARD, electrical engineer; b. Chgo., Apr. 4, 1942; s. Howard Estes and Vivian Irene (Lay) L.; m. Susan Lynn Schuffler, May 9, 1971 (div. Feb. 1979); m. Judith Ann Hindes, June 2, 1984. BSEE, Ill. Inst. Tech., 1968, MSEE, 1969. Registered profl. engr.; lic. real estate broker. Project engr. Motorola Communications and Electronics, Ft. Lauderdale, Fla., 1970-72; account exec. Motorola Communications and Electronics, Los Angeles, 1972-74; electrical engr. County of Los Angeles, 1974-78, communications engr. Sheriff's Dept., 1978-84; sales engr. Great Am. Rep. Co., Encino, Calif., 1984-87; sr. engr. So. Calif. Rapid Transit Dist., Los Angeles, 1987—. NASA Trainee fellow, Ill. Inst. Tech. Mem. Inst. Elec. and Electronic Engrs., Mensa, Tau Beta Pi, Eta Kappa Nu. Home: 4057 Warner Ave Huntington Beach CA 92649 Office: So Calif Rapid Transit Dist 425 S Main St Los Angeles CA 90013

LEWIS, TERRENCE ANN, teacher; b. San Jose, Calif., Oct. 28, 1952; d. John Howard and Carol Ann (Sullivan) O'Brien; m. Randall Keith Lewis, . BA in English, San Francisco State U., 1974; secondary teaching creden, Calif. Poly. Inst., 1981. Cert. tchr., Calif. Tchr. English King City (Calif.) Elem. Sch. Dist., 1981--. Vol. King City Library, 1986-87, Grace Luth. Ch., 1988; So. Monterey County. Mem. King City Elem. Tchrs. Assn., Calif. Tchrs. Assn. (negotiator 1987-88), Orton Dyslevia Soc. (bd. dirs. South county contact cen. coast chpt.). Democrat. Office: San Lorenzo Sch 415 Pearl St King City CA 93930

LEWIS, THOMASINE ELIZABETH, magazine editor-in-chief; b. Manila, Phillipines, Sept. 20, 1958; d. Thomas Donald and Elizabeth Jane (Munson) L. Student, Broward Community Coll., 1977, Universidad de las Americas, Mexico City, 1977, U. Fla., L.A. Valley Coll., 1979, UCLA, 1984. Copy editor, reporter Mexico City News, 1979-80; mng. editor LF Pub., L.A., 1980-82; editor Eton Pub., Hollywood, Calif., 1982-83; editor in chief Playgirl Mag., Santa Monica, Calif., 1983-86; exec. editor mag. devel. Petersen Pub., Hollywood, Calif., 1986-87; exec. editor Japan Jour. Mag., Marina del Rey, Calif., 1987-88; assoc. pub., dir. Radio Guide Mag., L.A., 1988—. Bd. dirs. Santa Monica Red Cross; mem. League of Women Voters, NOW, People for the Am. Way.

LEWIS, VERIN G., data processing executive; b. Sept. 9, 1952. Chief exec. officer VGL & Assocs., Ashland, Oreg., 1983—. Editor: (newsletter) Microcomputer Resources, 1986—. Recipient Hon. Speaker award PNNA, 1986. Office: VGL & Assocs 43 Emerick St Ashland OR 97520

LEWIS, VICKIE L., photojournalist; b. Hillsboro, Oreg., Feb. 24, 1959; d. Melvin Gene and Elizabeth Ann (VanDyke) L. BA, Oreg. State U., 1981; postgrad., Ohio U., 1981-83. Photographer Albuquerque Tribune, 1985—. Author-photographer spl. sect. The Story of Sage, 1987 (Roy Howard award for pub. service 1987), illustration Hats, 1987 (Poy award for best fashion photo 1987). Mem. Nat. Press Photographers Assn. Democrat.

LEWITT, MILES MARTIN, computer engineering company executive; b. N.Y.C., July 14, 1952; s. George Herman and Barbara (Lin) L.; m. Susan Beth Orenstein, June 24, 1973; children: Melissa, Hannah. BS summa cum laude, CCNY Engring., 1973; MS, Ariz. State U., 1976. Software engr. Honeywell, Phoenix, 1973-78; software engr., architect iRMX line ops. systems Intel Corp., Santa Clara, Calif., 1978; engring. mgr. Intel, Hillsboro, Oreg., 1978-80, 1981-89, corp. strategic staff, 1981-82; engring. mgr. Intel, Israel, 1980-81; v.p. engring. Cadre Techs., Inc., Beaverton, Oreg., 1989—; instr. Maricopa Tech. Coll., Phoenix, 1974-75. Contbr. articles to profl. jours. Recipient Engring. Alumni award CCNY, 1973, Eliza Ford Prize CCNY, 1973, Advanced Engring. Program award, Honeywell, 1976, Product of Yr. award Electronic Products Mag., 1980. Mem. IEEE Computer Soc. (voting mem.), IEEE (voting mem.), Assn. Computing Machinery (voting mem.). Democrat. Office: Cadre Techs Inc 19545 NW Von Newmann Dr Beaverton OR 97006

LEWITZKY, BELLA, choreographer; b. Los Angeles, Jan. 13, 1916; d. Joseph and Nina (Ossman) L.; m. Newell Taylor Reynolds, June 22, 1940; 1 dau., Nora Elizabeth. Student, San Bernardino Valley (Calif.) Jr. Coll., 1933-34; hon. doctorate, Calif. Inst. Arts, 1981; PhD (hon.), Occidental Coll., 1984, Otis Parsons, 1989. Chmn. contemporary dance dept. U. So. Calif., Idyllwild, 1956-72; adv. panel U. So. Calif., 1972—; founder Sch. Dance, Calif. Inst. Arts, 1969, dean, 1969-72; vice chmn. dance adv. panel Nat. Endowment Arts, 1974-77, mem. artists-in-schs. adv. panel, 1974-75; mem. Nat. Adv. Bd. Young Audiences, 1974—, Joint Commn. Dance and Theater Accreditation, 1979—; com. mem. Am. chpt. Internat. Dance Council of UNESCO, 1974—; bd. dirs. Am. Arts Alliance, 1977-82, Arts, Edn. and Americans, 1978—; trustee Nat. Found. Advancement Arts, 1982—, Lake Placid Ctr. for Arts, 1982-84, Calif. Arts Council, 1983-86, Calif. Assn. Dance Cos., 1976-81, Nat. Found. Advancement in Arts; trustee Idyllwild Sch. Music and the Arts, 1986—. Co-founder, co-dir., Dance Theatre, Los Angeles, 1946-50: founder, dir., Dance Assocs., Los Angeles, 1951-55; founder 1966, since artistic dir., Lewitzky Dance Co., Los Angeles; choreographer, 1948—; founder, artistic dir. The Dance Gallery, Los Angeles; contbr. articles in field. Mem. adv. com. Actors' Fund of Am., 1986—, Women's Bldg. Adv. Council. 1985—, Calif. Arts Council, 1983-86, City of Los Angeles Task Force on the Arts, 1986. Recipient ann. award Dance mag., 1978; Dir.'s award Calif. Dance Educators Assn., 1978; Women of Achievement award, 1988; Disting. Svc. award, Western Alliance Arts Adminstrs., 1987, Achievement award YWCA, 1982; Mellon Found. grantee, 1975, 81, 86; Guggenheim Found. grantee, 1977-78; Nat. Endowments for Arts grantee, 1969-86. Mem. Am. Arts Alliance (bd. dirs. 1977), Internat. Dance Alliance (adv. council 1984—), Dance/USA (bd. dirs. 1988).

LEYDET, FRANÇOIS GUILLAUME, author; b. Neuilly-sur-Seine, France, Aug. 26, 1927; s. Bruno and Dorothy (Lindsey) L.; AB, Harvard, 1947, postgrad. Bus. Sch., 1952; postgrad. Johns Hopkins Sch. Advanced Internat. Studies, 1952-53; Bachelier-es-lettres-philosophie, U. Paris (France), 1945; m. Patience Abbe, June 17, 1955 (div.); step children: Catherine Abbe Geissler, Lisa Amanda O'Mahony; m. 2d, Roslyn Carney, June 14, 1970; step-children: Walter E. Robb IV, Rachel R. Avery, Holly H. Prunty, Mary-Peck Harris. Came to U.S., 1940, naturalized, 1956. Bd. advisers Research Ranch, Elgin, Ariz., Am. Wilderness Alliance; past dir. Marin County Planned Parenthood Assn., Planned Parenthood Center Tucson. Served to 1st lt. French Army, 1947-48. Mem. Nat. Parks Assn., Wilderness Soc., Sierra Club, Nat. Audubon Soc., World Wildlife Fund, Am. Mus. Natural History, Union Concerned Scientists, Environ. Def. Fund, Friends of the Earth, Ariz.-Sonora Desert Mus., Am. Internat., Ariz. Hist. Soc., Common Cause, World Affairs Council No. Calif., Western Writers Assn. Clubs: Commonwealth, Harvard (San Francisco). Author: The Last Redwoods, 1963; Time and the River Flowing: Grand Canyon, 1964; The Coyote: Defiant Songdog of the West, 1977. Editor: Tomorrow's Wilderness, 1963; contbr. to Nat. Geog. mag. Address: 183 Oak Ave San Anselmo CA 94960 also: 948 E Camino Diestro Tucson AZ 85704

LEYLEGIAN, JACK H., II, investment management company executive; b. Providence, Oct. 26, 1935; m. Dorothy Patricia Aprahamian, July 21, 1957; children: George A., Debra A. BSBA, Boston U., 1957; MBA, U. So. Calif., 1960. Vice pres. No. Trust Co., Chgo., 1966-71; pres. Dreyfus Mgmt. Inc., N.Y.C., 1971-77, Bank Am. Investment Mgmt. Co., San Francisco, 1977-81, Leylegian Investment Mgmt. Inc., Menlo Park, Calif., 1981--; bd. dirs. Imperial Bank, Los Angeles. Trustee, Claremont (Calif.) Econ. Inst., 1985--; bd. dirs. Med. Research Inst., San Francisco, 1986--. Mem. Chartered Fin. Analysts Soc., San Francisco Security Analysts Soc. Office: Leylegian Investment Mgmt 855 Oak Grove Ave Ste 200 Menlo Park CA 94025

LIANG, JASON CHIA, research chemist; b. Beijing, Peoples Republic China, Feb. 24, 1935; came to U.S., 1978, naturalized 1984; s. Tsang Truan and Shulin (Tang) L.; m. Joan Chorng Chen, June 11, 1960; children: Cheryl, Chuck. BS in Pharm. Chemistry, U. Beijing, 1957; postgrad., Pharm. Research Instn., Beijing, 1961; MS in Organic Chemistry, U. Oreg., 1980. Chemist Beijing Chem. Factory, 1961-71; research chemist Beijing Pharm. Factory, 1971-78; research chemist Tektronix Inc., Beaverton, Oreg., 1980-85, sr. reasearch chemist, 1985-88; research chemist Kalama (Wash.)

Chemical Inc., 1988—; presenter Internat. Pitts. Conf. on Analytical Chemistry and Applied Spectroscopy, 1988. Contbr. articles to profl. jours.; patentee in field. Fellow Am. Inst. Chemists; mem. Am. Chem Soc. (organic chemistry div., paper presenter 1984-88), Internat. Union Pure and Applied Chemistry (affiliate). Office: Kalama Chem Inc 1296 NW 3d St Kalama WA 98625

LIANG, JEFFREY DER-SHING, retired electrical engineer, civil worker; b. Chungking, People's Republic China, Oct. 25, 1915; came to U.S., 1944, naturalized, 1971; s. Tze-hsiang and Sou-yi (Wang) L.; m. Eva Yin Hwa Tang, Jan. 2, 1940; 1 child, Shouyu. BA, Nat. Chengchih U., Chungking, 1940; BAS, U. B.C., Vancouver, 1960. Office asst. Ministry of Fgn. Affairs, Chungking, 1940-43; vice consul Chinese consulate Ministry of Fgn. Affairs, Seattle, 1944-50; consulate-gen. Ministry of Fgn. Affairs, San Francisco, 1950-53; consul Chinese consulate-gen. Ministry of Fgn. Affairs, Vancouver, 1953-56; engr.-in-tng. Can. Broadcasting Corp., Vancouver, 1960-65; assoc. engr. Boeing Co., Seattle, 1965-67, rsch. engr., 1967-70, engr., 1970-73, sr. engr., 1973-75, specialist engr., 1975-78; cons. Seattle, 1979-81. Mem. chancelor's cir. Wesbrook Soc., U. B.C., Vancouver, 1986—, Seattle-King County Adv. Council on Aging, 1984-88, Gov.'s State Council on Aging, Olympia, 1987-88. Mem. IEEE (life), Hwa Sheng Chinese Music Club (v.p. 1978-79, chmn. nomination com. 1981-88), Eastside Athletic Club. Republican. Mem. Christian Ch.

LIAO, ERIC NAN-KANG, structural and mechanical engineer; b. Wu-Feng, Taiwan, China, Nov. 29, 1938; came to U.S., 1964; s. Swei-Mu and Ging-Kwan (Chen) L.; m. Fanny Ho-mei Yen, Feb. 10, 1968; children: Willy, Royce. BS, Cheng-Kung U., Taiwan, 1961; MS, Okla. State U., 1966; PhD, U. Wis., 1970. Registered profl. engr., Wis., Pa.; lic. real estate agt. N.J., Calif. Sr. engr. Westinghouse Electric Corp., Pitts., 1970-71; mem. research faculty U. Wis., Madison, 1971-72; research engr. United Engrs. & Constructors Inc., Phila., 1972-74; prin. engr. Stone & Webster Engrng. Corp., Cherry Hill, N.J., 1974-80; mem. tech. staff TRW Def. & Space Systems, Redondo Beach, Calif., 1980-81; staff engr. Aerospace Corp., El Segundo, Calif., 1981—; cons. engrng., Cherry Hill, 1973-80. Contbr. articles to profl. jours. Fundraiser Park Jr. High, Fullerton, Calif., 1981-82. Served to lt. Taiwan Air Force, 1961-62. NSF scholar, 1966-68; Wis. Alumni Rsch. fellow U. Wis., 1968-70. Mem. ASME (com. applied mechanics Phila. sect. 1975-78), Sigma Xi, Pi Mu Epsilon, Chi Epsilon. Republican. Buddhist. Club: Realty Investment (Orange County, Calif.). Home: 1912 Avenida Del Ossa Fullerton CA 92633

LIBERMAN, ROBERT PAUL, psychiatry educator, researcher, writer; b. Newark, Aug. 16, 1937; s. Harry and Gertrude (Galowitz) L.; m. Janet Marilyn Brown, Feb. 16, 1973; children—Peter, Sarah, Danica, Nathaniel, Annalisa. A.B. summa cum laude, Dartmouth Coll., 1959, diploma in medicine with honors, 1960; M.S. in Pharmacology, U. Calif.-San Francisco, 1961; M.D., Johns Hopkins U., 1963. Diplomate Nat. Bd. Med. Examiners, Am. Bd. Psychiatry and Neurology; cert. community coll. instr., Calif. Intern Bronx (N.Y.) Mcpl. Hosp.-Einstein Coll. Medicine, 1963-64; resident in psychiatry Mass. Mental Health Ctr., Boston, 1964-68; postdoctoral fellow in social psychiatry Harvard U., 1966-68, teaching fellow in psychiatry, 1964-68; mem. faculty group psychotherapy tng. program Washington Sch. Psychiatry, 1968-70; with Nat. Ctr. Mental Health Service, Tng. and Research, St. Elizabeths Hosp., also mem. NIMH Clin. and Research Assocs. Tng. Program, Washington, 1968-70; asst. clin. prof. psychiatry UCLA, 1970-72, assoc. clin. prof., 1972-73, assoc. research psychiatrist, 1973-76, research psychiatrist, 1976-77, prof. psychiatry in residence, 1977—; adj. faculty mem. Antioch Coll. West/U. Without Walls, 1971-73; lectr. Calif. Luth. Coll., 1973-74; cons. div. mental health and behavioral scis. edn. Sepulveda (Calif.) VA Hosp., 1975-80; cons. in psychiatry to hosps.; practice medicine specializing in psychiatry, Reston, Va., 1968-70, Thousand Oaks, Calif., 1977—; staff psychiatrist Fairfax Hosp., Falls Church, Va., 1968-70, Ventura County Mental Health Dept., 1970-75; staff psychiatrist Ventura County Gen. Hosp.; mem. med. staff UCLA Neuropsychiatric Inst. and Hosp., Ventura Gen. Hosp., Camarillo State Hosp., West Los Angeles VA Med. Ctr.; dir., prin. investigator Mental Health Clin. Research Ctr. for Schizophrenia and Psychiat. Rehabilitation, NIMH, 1977—; chief rehab. medicine service Brentwood div. west Los Angeles VA Med. Ctr., 1980—; dir. clin. research unit Camarillo State Hosp., 1970—; dir. Rehab. Research and Tng. Ctr. Mental Illness, 1980-85. Bd. dirs. Lake Sherwood Community Assn., 1978—, pres., 1979-81; mem. Conejo Valley Citizens Adv. Bd., 1979-81. Served as surgeon USPHS, 1964-68. Research grantee. Mem. Assn. Advancement Behavior Therapy (exec. com. 1970-72, dir. 1972-79), Am. Psychiat. Assn., Assn. Clin. Psychosocial Research (exec. com. 1985—), Phi Beta Kappa. Author: (with King, DeRisi and McCann) Personal Effectiveness: Guiding People to Assert Their Feelings and Improve Their Social Skills, 1975; A Guide to Behavioral Analysis and Therapy, 1972; (with Wheeler, DeVisser, Kuehnel and Kuehnel) Handbook of Marital Therapy: An Educational Approach to Treating Troubled Relationships, 1980, Psychiatric Rehabilitation of Chronic Mental Patients, 1987, Social Skills Training for Psychiatric Patients, 1989, Rehabilitation of the Psychiatrically Disabled, 1989; mem. editorial bd. Jour. Applied Behavior Analysis, 1972-78, Jour. Marriage and Family Counseling, 1974-78, Jour. Behavior Therapy and Exptl. Psychiatry, 1975—, Behavior Therapy, 1979-84, Assessment and Invervention in Devel. Disabilities, 1980-85; assoc. editor Jour. Applied Behavior Analysis, 1976-78, Schizophrenia Bull., 1981-87; internat. reviewer Jour. Psychiatry, 1988—; contbr. over 200 articles to profl. jours., chpts. to books. Home: 528 E Potrero Rd Thousand Oaks CA 91361 Office: 11301 Wilshire Blvd B117 Los Angeles CA 90073

LIBKE, ALBERT WALTER, physician; b. Seattle, Apr. 3, 1944. BA in Econs., U. Wash., 1967, MD, 1971. Diplomate Nat. Bd. Med. Examiners. Intern in surgery Stanford (Calif.) U. Med. Ctr., 1971-72; resident in cardiac surgery Santa Clara (Calif.) Valley Med. Ctr., 1972; acting emergency room dir. San Mateo (Calif.) County Hosp., 1973-74; with Jalbert Prodns., N.Y.C., 1975-77; assoc. in cardiovascular surgery Encino (Calif.) Hosp., 1978-79; emergency dept. physician Calif. Hosp., L.A., 1980-81; cons. physician Dhahran Armed Forces Hosp., Saudi Arabia, 1981-83; pres. Doctors Group, 1984-85; founder, pres., chief exec. officer, chmn. Bioanalogics, Inc., L.A., 1985—; cons. Pritikin Longevity Ctr., Santa Monica, Calif., 1981; researcher in field. Contbr. articles to profl. publs. Mem. Nutritional Medicine Found., Alpha Omega Alpha, Phi Delta Theta (chmn.). Office: Bioanalogics Inc 11726 San Vilente Blvd #500 Los Angeles CA 90049

LIBMAN, ALAN DAVID, investment executive, lawyer, financial consultant; b. Toronto, Ont., Can., Aug. 3, 1943; came to U.S., 1977; s. Louis and Ruth (Organ) L.; m. Donna McLellan O'Shea, Oct. 13, 1986; children: Bryn-Erin, Warren, Kelly, Danny. LLB, Osgoode Hall Law Sch., 1967. Bar: Ont. 1969. Sole practice law, Toronto, 1969-77; TV producer T.M.I., Los Angeles, 1977-83; fin. cons. Los Angeles, 1977—; guest speaker Toronto High Schs., 1969-75; tchr., lectr. adult edn. and law, Toronto, 1969-75; exec. various cos., Los Angeles, 1982-86; pres. Sunset West Internat., Los Angeles, 1986—. Author: The Law and You, 1968. Mem. Acad. TV., Arts and Scis. Jewish. Office: Sunset West Internat 9000 Sunset Blvd Ste 1100 Los Angeles CA 90069

LICHTENBERG, LARRY RAY, chemist, consultant, researcher; b. Marceline, Mo., July 25, 1938; s. Kenneth Ray and Evelyn (Lauck) L.; m. Clarice Elaine Dameron, Dec. 23, 1961; children: Julia-Isabel Dameron. BS in Chemistry, Northeast Mo. State U., 1962. Chemist Bell & Howell, Chgo., 1962-62; jr. chem. engr. Magnavox Corp., Urbana, Ill., 1963-64; process engr. Gen. Electric Co., Bloomington, Ill., 1964-70; mfg. engr. Burr-Brown, Tucson, 1970-72; sr. staff engr. Motorola, Scottsdale, Ariz., 1972—; mem. corp. tech. council Motorola, Scottsdale, 1982—. Contbr. articles to profl. jours. Mem. Am. Chem. Soc., Internat. Soc. Hybrid Microelectronics (pres. Phoenix chpt. 1981-82). Republican. Baptist. Home: 13018 N 32 Ave Phoenix AZ 85029 Office: Motorola GEG 8220 E Roosevelt Rd Scottsdale AZ 85252

LIDICKER, WILLIAM ZANDER, JR., zoologist; b. Evanston, Ill., Aug. 19, 1932; s. William Zander and Frida (Schroeter) L.; m. Naomi Ishino, Aug. 18, 1956 (div. Oct., 1982); children: Jeffrey Roger, Kenneth Paul. B.S., Cornell U., 1953; M.S., U. Ill., 1954, Ph.D., 1957. Instr. zoology, asst. curator mammals U. Calif., Berkeley, 1957-59; asst. prof., asst. curator U. Calif., 1959-65, assoc. prof., assoc. curator, 1965-69; assoc. dir. Mus. Vertebrate Zoology, 1968-81, acting dir., 1974-75, prof. zoology, curator mammals, 1969—. Contbr. articles to profl. jours. Bd. dirs. No. Calif. Com. for Environ. Info., 1971-77; bd. trustees BIOSIS, 1987—; N. Am. rep. steering com., sect. Mammalogy IUBS, UNESCO, 1978—; chmn. rodent specialist group Species Survival Commn., IUCN, 1980—; mem. sci. adv. bd. Marine World Found. at Marine World Africa USA, 1987—. Fellow AAAS, Calif. Acad. Scis.; mem. Am. Soc. Mammalogists (dir., 2d v.p. 1974-76, pres. 1976-78, C.H. Merriam award 1986), Am. Soc. Naturalists, others. Club: Berkeley Folk Dancers (pres. 1969). Office: U Calif Mus Vertebrate Zoology Berkeley CA 94720

LIEBAU, FREDERIC JACK, JR., securities analyst; b. Palo Alto, Calif., Sept. 30, 1963; s. Frederic Jack and Charlene (Conrad) L. BA, Stanford U., 1985. Press aide Office of V.P., Washington, 1982; intern L.A. Times, 1983; analyst Capital Rsch. Co., L.A., 1984-86; assoc. Primecap Mgmt. Co., Pasadena, Calif., 1986—. Office: Primecap Mgmt Co 225 S Lake Ave Pasadena CA 91101

LIEBENSON-REX, NANCY JOY, artist; b. N.Y.C., Jan. 7, 1957; d. Herman and Bessie Liebenson; m. Robert Erle Rex, May 12, 1984. BA, Scripps Coll., 1978; MFA, Claremont (Calif.) U., 1982. Exhibiting artist, 1974—; tchr. Fresno (Calif.) Arts Ctr. Mus., 1979-80. Millard Sheets fellow Scripps Fine Arts Found., 1981.

LIEBERMAN, GERALD J., statistics educator; b. N.Y.C., Dec. 31, 1925; s. Joseph and Ida (Margolis) L.; m. Helen Herbert, Oct. 27, 1950; children—Janet, Joanne, Michael, Diana. B.S. in Mech. Engrng., Cooper Union, 1948; A.M. in Math. Stats., Columbia U., 1949; Ph.D., Stanford U., 1953. Math. statistician Nat. Bur. Standards, 1949-50; mem. faculty Stanford U., 1953—, prof. statistics and indsl. engrng., 1959-67, prof. statistics and operations research, 1967—, chmn. dept. operations research, 1967-75, assoc. dean Sch. Humanities and Scis., 1975-77, acting v.p. and provost, 1979, vice provost, 1977-85, dean research, 1977-80, dean grad. studies and research, 1980-85; cons. to govt. and industry, 1953—. Author: (with A. H. Bowker) Engineering Statistics, 1959, 2d edit., 1972, (with F.S. Hillier) Introduction to Operations Research, 1967, 4th edit., 1986. Ctr. Advanced Studies in Behavioral Scis. fellow, 1985-86. Fellow Am. Statis. Assn., Inst. Math. Statistics, Am. Soc. Quality Control (Shewhart medal 1972), AAAS; mem. Nat. Acad. Engrng., Inst. Mgmt. Sci. (pres. 1980-81), Ops. Research Soc. Am., Nat. Acad. Engrng. (elected), Sigma Xi, Pi Tau Sigma. Home: 811 San Francisco Terr Stanford CA 94305

LIEBERSON, STANLEY, sociologist, educator; b. Montreal, Que., Can., Apr. 20, 1933; s. Jack and Ida (Cohen) L.; m. Patricia Ellen Beard, 1960; children—Rebecca, David, Miriam, Rachel. Student, Bklyn. Coll., 1950-52; M.A., U. Chgo., 1958, Ph.D., 1960. Asso. dir. Iowa Urban Community Research Center, U. Iowa, 1959-61, instr., asst. prof. sociology, 1959-61; asst. prof. sociology U. Wis., 1961-63, asso. prof., 1963-66, prof., 1966-67; prof. sociology U. Wash., 1967-71, dir. Center Studies Demography and Ecology, 1968-71; prof. sociology U. Chgo., 1971-74, assoc. dir. Population Research Center, 1971-74; prof. sociology U. Ariz., Tucson, 1974-83; head dept. U. Ariz., 1976-79; prof. sociology U. Calif.-Berkeley, 1988—; vis. prof. Stanford U., summer 1970; Claude Bissell disting. vis. prof. U. Toronto, 1979-80; mem. com. on sociolinguistics Social Sci. Research Council, 1964-70; mem. sociology panel NSF, 1978-81. Author: (with others) Metropolis and Region, 1960, Ethnic Patterns in American Cities, 1963; Editor: Explorations in Sociolinguistics, 1967, (with Beverly Duncan) Metropolis and Region in Transition, 1970, Language and Ethnic Relations in Canada, 1970, A Piece of the Pie, 1980, Language Diversity and Language Contact, 1981, Making It Count, 1985, (with Mary C. Waters) From Many Strands, 1988; assoc. editor: Social Problems, 1965-67, Sociol. Methods and Research, 1971—; editorial cons. Sociol. Inquiry, 1965-67; adv. editor: Am. Jour. Sociology, 1969-74; editorial bd. Lang. in Society, 1972-74, Internat. Jour. Sociology of Lang, 1974—, Canadian Jour. Sociology, 1975—, Social Forces, 1980-83; adv. council Sociol. Abstracts, 1972-73, Language Problems and Language Planning, 1984-87. Recipient Colver Rosenberger Ednl. prize, 1960; Guggenheim fellow, 1972-73. Fellow Am. Acad. Arts and Scis.; mem. Am. Sociol. Assn. (disting. contbn. to scholarship award 1982, council 1985-87), Population Assn. Am. (dir. 1969-72), Internat. Population Union, Pacific Sociol. Assn. (v.p. 1984-85, pres. 1986-87), Sociol. Research Assn. (exec. com. 1976-81, pres. 1981), Oakland Sch. Sociology. Home: 560 Valle Vista Ave Oakland CA 94610 Office: Harvard U Dept Sociology William James Hall Cambridge MA 02138

LIEBHAUSER, WILLIAM JOSEPH, federal agency administrator; b. Oroville, Calif., Aug. 22, 1953; s. Harry Joseph and Mary Alice (Megerle) L.; m. Ellen Ruth Shuffield, Oct. 16, 1976 (div. 1984); m. Janis Lyn Lewis, Sept. 26, 1987. AA, Yuba Community Coll., 1973; BA in Polit. Sci., Calif. State U., 1976. Realty specialist U.S. Bur. Land Mgmt., Las Vegas, Nev., 1978-82; sr. realty specialist U.S. Bur. Land Mgmt., Tok, Alaska, 1982-83; area realty specialist U.S. Bur. Land Mgmt., Tonopah, Nev., 1983-85, Ridgecrest, Calif., 1988—; sr. land use specialist, Sierra Pacific Power Co., Reno, 1985-88; project mgr., corridor study com., Western Utility Group, Reno, 1985-88. Contbr. articles to profl. publs. Post leader, adviser Explorer Scouts, Las Vegas, 1980-82. Capt. USAR, 1976-84. Mem. Am. Planning Assn., Internat.Right of Way Assn. (chpt. sec. 1986-87), The Packard Club, W.P. Chrysler Club. Republican. Presbyterian. Office: Bur Land Mgmt 112 E Dolphin Ave Ridgecrest CA 93555

LIEBSON, DONALD CHARLES, oil and gas executive; b. N.Y.C., Dec. 27, 1952; s. Milton Joseph and Lila (Jacobs) L. BA, Syracuse U., 1974, MBA, 1976; MA, Claremont (Calif.) Grad. Sch., 1984, MBA, 1986, post-grad., 1986—. Fin. analyst Ford Motor Co., Dearborn, Mich., 1976-79; evaluation cons., mgr. planning and evaluation Atlantic Richfield Co., L.A. and Phila., 1979-86; dir. bus. devel. GATX Terminals Corp., Chgo., 1986-88; pres. Oil Pipeline Research Inst., Torrance, Calif., 1988—; also bd. dirs. Oil Pipeline Research Inst., Torrance; bd. dirs. DL Investments, Inc., Torrance; sec. GATX Pipe Line Co., Chgo., 1987-88; rep. Assn. Oil Pipe Lines, Washington, 1988. Author: United States Oil Pipelines, 1988, United States Gas Pipelines, 1988. Mem. L.A. Energy Analysts' Group, Am. Petroleum Inst., Nat. Petroleum Refiners' Assn.

LIEBSON, EDWARD, insurance company executive; b. Detroit, Dec. 12, 1928; s. Fred and Mollie (Pliskow) L.; m. Clara Klein, Dec. 24, 1950 (div. June 15, 1962); children: Andrea Ellen, Sherry Esther, Karen Ruth; m. Rosara Wine, Feb. 12, 1970; children: Carrie Ann, Susan B., Joanne C. BA, Wayne State U., 1950, MEd, 1952, EdD, 1961. Various ednl. positions Mich., 1952-64; adv. specialist Wayne City Int. Schs., Detroit, 1965-67; dir. inst. rsch. Macomb County Community Coll., Warren, Mich., 1968-69; exec. dir. NARCO, Detroit, 1969-71; mental health cood. Wayne City Mental Health Bd., Detroit, 1971-73; dir. Wayne County Dept. Substance Abuse, Detroit, 1973-77; exec. dir. Alameda Contra Costa Health System Agy., Oakland, Calif., 1977-82; medi-cal negotiator State of Calif. Gov.'s Office, Sacramento, Calif., 1982-83; dir., provider contracting Blue Cross Calif., Oakland, 1983—; cons. in field; lectr. in field. Mem. Alcohol Credentialling Task Force, Sacramento, Calif., 1986, Ambulatory Surgery Task Force, 1988, San Francisco Opera Soc., San Francisco Museum Soc., 1977-89. Sgt. U.S. Army, 1950-52. Mem. Am. Pub. Health Assn., Am. Health Planning Assn. Democrat. Jewish. Home: 642 Buzzie Ct Lafayette CA 94549

LIEDTKE, ARMIN ADOLF, data processing executive; b. Koenigsberg, Fed. Republic Germany, Jan. 9, 1941; came to U.S., 1963; s. Adolf and Margaret (Kretschman) L.; m. Susan Beth Day, Nov. 24, 1968; children: Armin Gregory, John Charles. Grad., State Bus. Sch., Hamburg, Fed. Republic Germany. Sales mgr. Memorex Corp., Seattle and Denver, 1968-74; regional mgr. Wabash Magnetics Corp., Denver and San Francisco, 1974-76; pres., owner Data Northwest Inc., Seattle, 1976—. With German mil., 1960-62. Recipient Life Saving medal City of Hamburg, 1961. Mem. Software Assn. Lutheran. Home: 13032 7th St NW Seattle WA 98133 Office: Data NW Inc 3831 Stone Way N Seattle WA 98103

LIEM, SCOTT ROBBINS, real estate broker; b. Phoenix, Jan. 14, 1955; s. Donald Robbins and Barbara Kay (Nasser) L.; m. Christy Rojas, July 25, 1980; children: Lindsey, Laura, Joanna, Jessica. BSBA, No. Ariz. U., 1981. Sales assoc. Knoell Homes, Phoenix, 1979-85; v.p. sales and mktg. Global Village Corp., Phoenix, 1985-86; broker Scott Jackson Brokerage, Tempe, Ariz., 1986-88, Iliff, Thorn & Co., Phoenix, 1988—. Bd. dirs., v.p. Tempe (Ariz.) Leadership, 1986—; bd. dirs. Tempe Diablos, 1983—; com. mem. Fiesta Bowl, 1988—. Recipient Disting. Alumni Leadership award Nat. Assn. of Community Leadership Orgs. 1988. Mem. Home Builders Assn. of Central Ariz., Valley Partnership. Republican. Presbyterian. Home: 1535 E McNair Dr Tempe AZ 85283 Office: Iliff Thorn & Co 3636 N Central Ave #600 Phoenix AZ 85012

LIENAU, BONNIE L(OUISE) ROSZAK, nurse adminstrator; b. Langley, Va., Aug. 9, 1944; d. Cleo Mitchell and Annie Christine (Brown) Groves; m. Rudy Roszak, July 1, 1966 (div.); 1 son, Christopher Thomas; m. Richard M. Lienau, Jan. 1, 1987. Diploma Gen. Hosp. Sch. Nursing, Nashville, 1965; BS, Belmont Coll., 1969; postgrad. U. Colo., 1978, Calif. Coast U. Cert. ARC nurse. Staff nurse Vanderbilt U. Hosp., Nashville, 1966; head nurse Bapt. Hosp., Nashville, 1966-72; physician asst. Anesthesiology Assocs., Nashville, 1972-73, Middle Tenn. Anesthesiology, P.C., Nashville, 1973-75; head nurse Rose Med. Ctr., Denver, 1975-76, asst. dir. surgery, 1976-77, dir. surgery, 1977-78; dir. surgeries Good Samaritan Hosp., Corvallis, Oreg., 1978-80; dir. surg. services Santa Monica (Calif.) Hosp. Med. Ctr., 1980-87; assoc. dir. nursing Panorama Community Hosp., Panorama City, Calif., 1988-89; assoc. dir. surg. svcs. Brotman Med. Ctr., Culver City, Calif., 1989—; operating room cons. Pacific Health Resources, Los Angeles. Mem. Assn. of Oper. Room Nurses (L.A. chpt.), Calif. Soc. Nursing Svc. Adminstrs., Internat. Assn. Quality Cirs. Office: Brotman Med Ctr 3828 Delmas Terr Culver City CA 90231

LIENAU, RICHARD MICHAEL, electronics manufacturing engineering advisor; b. Los Angeles, Apr. 26, 1933; s. Peter Cecil and Jean Rose (Knoeller) L.; m. Caroline Ray Acosta, Oct. 7, 1972 (div. Apr. 1982); m. Bonnie Louise Groves, Jan. 1, 1987; children: Steven, Leslie Lienau Gibbs, Christopher. Student, U. Denver, 1951-52, U. N.Mex., 1955-56, 68-71. Customer engr. IBM, various, 1956-63; ptnr., supr. San Ysidro Constrn. Co., Albuquerque, 1963-65; sr. field engr. Benson-Lehner Corp., Albuquerque, 1963-65; contract field engr. Ampex Corp., Albuquerque, 1966-71; sr. field engr. Harris Corp., Albuquerque, 1972-74, Data 100 Corp., Albuquerque, 1974-79; dir., mgr. Varex Corp., Los Angeles, 1979-80; sr. instr. computers Pertec Corp., Los Angeles, 1980-81; pres. Pesonal Electronics Consulting Firm, Los Angeles, 1981-82; mfg. support engr. advisor Teradata, Los Angeles, 1982—. Author: The Hawk Leaves No Shadow, 1974, The Truchas Light, 1985; patentee in field. Sgt. USAF, 1951-55. Mem. Soc. Mfg. Engrs. Democrat. Home: 1236 Wellesley Ave #1 Los Angeles CA 90025-1139 Office: Teradata 12945 Jefferson Blvd Los Angeles CA 90066

LIES, BERT A., JR., orthopedic surgeon; b. Buffalo, Apr. 22, 1939; children: Elizabeth, Rebecca. MD, SUNY, Buffalo, 1964. Diplomate Nat. Bd. Med. Examiners, Am. Bd. Orthopedic Surgery. Intern in gen. surgery Edward J. Meyer Meml. Hosp., Buffalo, 1964-65; resident in orthopedic surgery Edward J. Meyer Meml. Hosp., Buffalo Children's Hosp., Buffalo Gen. Hosp., 1965-69; asst. attending orthopedic surgery. pediatrics Buffalo Children's Hosp., 1969-83; asst. attending orthopedic surgery Buffalo Gen. Hosp., 1969-83; staff PHS Indian Hosp., St. Vincent Hosp., Santa Fe, 1983—; sect. chief St. Vincent Hosp., Santa Fe, 1988-89; pediatric orthopedic cons. to numerous schs., hosps.; asst. clin. prof. orthopedic surgery SUNY, Buffalo, 1979-83. Contbr. articles to profl. jours. Pres., bd. trustees Wheelright Mus. of the Am. Indian, Santa Fe, 1987-90, found. bd. dirs., 1985-86; mem. Parents Reach Out Program of N.Mex. Recipient award for achievement in clin. surgery Buffalo Surg. Soc., 1964, Research award Bacelli Club, 1964. Fellow Am. Acad. Orthopedic Surgeons, Am. Acad. Pediatrics; mem. Am. Acad. Cerebral Palsy, Pediatric Orthopedic Soc. of N.Am., AMA, Am. Coll. Sports Medicine, Am. Trauma Soc., Nat. Rehab. Assn., Assn. of Children's Prosthetic and Orthotic Clinics, Ea. Orthopedic Assn., N.Mex. Med. Soc., Santa Fe County Med. Soc., N.Mex. Pediatric Soc., Nat. Assn. Disability Evaluating Physicians, Wilderness Med. Soc., Western Orthopedic Assn., U.S. Ski Assn., Am. Med. Tennis Assn., Far Western Ski Assn., Delta Kappa Epsilon, Alpha Omega Alpha. Office: 539 Harkle Rd Ste D Santa Fe NM 87501 also: Wheelwright Mus Am Indian PO Box 5153 Santa Fe NM 87502

LIGHTER, ERIC AARON, real estate developer, consultant; b. Chico, Calif., Aug. 6, 1950; s. Bruce Clyde and Katherine Bernice (Stutsman) L.; m. Gitte Gadix, Dec. 18, 1976 (div. Feb. 1978); m. 2d, Janet Shellen Wong, Apr. 20, 1982 (div. July 1985). Grad. Grad. Realtors Inst., 1973; student U. Hawaii. Salesman Fin. Security Life, Honolulu, 1970; founder, treas. 3d Eye Prodns., Honolulu, 1974-76; pres. Home Rent Hawaii, Honolulu, 1976; pres. A. Lighter Cons., Graphic and Media, 1977—; pres. Lighter Properties Corp., Developers, Honolulu, 1978—; founder Quality Income Systems, Honolulu, 1983; mem. Honolulu Realtor Pub. Relation Com., 1983-84. Editor: Ke Alaka'i, 1984. Bd. dirs. Hawaii Alliance for Arts in Edn., 1984, Inst. Human Services, Honolulu, 1984; Hawaii Statue of Liberty Program Mgr., 1986; founder Diamond Cross Ministries, 1985, performing Gospel guitarist, 1985. Mem. Hawaii Assn. Realtors, Bldg. Industry Assn. Hawaii (Parade of Homes Award of Excellence 1983), Hawaii Jaycees (project initiator Silver Jubilee Project 1983, mgr. Outstanding Hawaii Jaycees program mgr., founding pres. Capital Dist. 1982, chaplin Honolulu Chinese 1982-84, King of King award 1982, 83), Nat. Assn. Bed and Breakfast. Republican. Episcopalian. Club: Scandinavian of Hawaii. Lodge: Lions (Honolulu) (var. offices, including treas.). Avocation: playing Gospel guitar. Home: Honolulu Inn 1045 Spencer St Honolulu HI 96813

LIGHTFOOT, LOUIS NORMAN, urban planner; b. Pitts., July 25, 1948; s. Louis Norman and Sylvia (Kaniecki) L.; m. Lynne Adrienne Kirwin, Jan. 11, 1973; children: Adrienne, Jenna. Cert. planner. Planner City Oceanside, Calif., 1973-75; planning dir. City Oceanside, Calif., 1975-78; pres., owner The Lightfoot Planning Group, 1978—. Chmn. Oceanside Econ. Devel. Council, 1988. Served to USNR, 1970-73. Mem. AICP, Am. Planning Assn., Urban Land Inst. (assoc.), Bldg. Industry Assn. Republican. Office: The Lightfoot Planning Group 702 4th St Oceanside CA 92054

LIGHTWOOD, CAROL WILSON, writer; b. Tacoma, Wash., Oct. 2, 1941; d. Harry Edward and Cora H. Wilson; m. Keith G. Lightwood (div. Dec. 1968; children: Miles Francis, Clive Harry. BA, Smith Coll., 1963. Writer various advt. agencies, 1968-82; v.p. Wakeman & DeForrest, Newport Beach, Calif., 1985-86; owner Lightwood & Ptnrs., Long Beach, Calif., 1986—. Author: Malibu, 1984; contbr. articles to profl. jours. Chair mus. coun. Long Beach Mus. Art. Mem. Sierra Club. Episcopalian.

LIJPHART, AREND, political scientist; b. Apeldoorn, Netherlands, Aug. 17, 1936; came to U.S., 1955; s. Anthonius and Mathilde Theodora (d'Angermond) L.; m. Eva Tamm Lijphart, Aug. 10, 1959 (div. Mar. 1980); children: Antony Sune, Anna Margaretha; m. Gisela Meyers Lijphart, June 24, 1988. BA, Principia Coll., Elsah, Ill., 1958; MA, Yale U., 1959, PhD, 1963. Instr. polit. sci. Elmira (Ill.) Coll., 1961-63; asst. prof. polit. sci. U. Calif., Berkeley, 1963-68, assoc. prof. polit. sci., 1968-69; prof. internat. relations U. Leiden, Netherlands, 1968-78; vis. prof. govt. Harvard U., Cambridge, Mass., 1970; vis. research fellow Inst. of Advanced Studies, Australian Nat. U., Canberra, 1971-72; fellow Netherlands Inst. for Advanced Study, Wassenaar, 1974-75; prof. polit. sci. U. Calif., San Diego, 1978—. Author: (books) The Trauma of Decolonization: The Dutch and West New Guinea, 1966, The Politics of Accommodation: Pluralism and Democracy in the Netherlands, 1968, Democracy in Plural Societies: A Comparative Exploration, 1977, Democracies: Patters of Majoritarian and Consensus Government in 21 Countries, 1984, Power-Sharing in South Africa, 1985; editor: World Politics: The Writings of Theorists and Practitioners, Classical and Modern, 1966, Politics in Europe: Comparisons and Interpretations, 1969, (with Bernard Grofman, Robert McKay, and Howard Scarrow), Representation and Redistricting Issues, 1982, (with Bernard Grofman) Choosing an Electoral System: Issues and Alternatives, 1984, Electoral Laws and their Political Consequences, 1986; contbr. articles to profl. jours. Sec. Am. Polit. Sci. Assn., 1983-84, v.p. 1987-88; exec. com. mem. Am. Polit. Sci. Assn. Sect. on Representative and Electoral Systems, 1985-87; mem. Am. Polit. Sci. Assn Sect. Polit. Orgns. and Coms., Am. Sect. Legis. Studies, Western Polit. Sci. Assn., Midwest Polit. Sci. Assn., So. Polit. Sci. Assn., Ctr. for Study of Dem. Insts. Fulbright grantee, 1955-58; Helen Dwight Reid Ednl. Found. fellow, 1958-59, Cowles fellow, Yale U., 1958-59, Hosford-U. fellow, Yale U., 1959-60, Univ. fellow, 1960-61, vis. research fellow, Inst. of Advanced Studies, Australian Nat. U., 1971-72, fellow Netherlands Inst. for Advanced Study, Wassenaar, 1974-75, fellow German Marshall Fund of the U.S., 1983-84, Guggenheim fellow, 1984-95; recipient Ralph J. Bunche award Am. Polit. Sci. Assn., 1979, Excellence in Teaching award Revelle Coll., U. Calif. San Diego, 1982. Mem. Am. Assn. Netherlandic Studies, Internat. Polit. Sci. Assn., (v.p. 1976-77) Can. Polit. Sci. Assn., Am. Assn. for Netherlandic Studies, European Consortium Polit. Research (exec. com. 1976-78), Nederlands Genootschap voor Internat. Zaken, Nederlandse Kring voor Wetenschap der Polit. (exec. com., 1977-78), Council for European Studies (steering com. 1982-85, exec. com. 1983-85). Home: 4276 Caminito Terviso San Diego CA 92122 Office: U Calif San Diego Dept Polit Sci La Jolla CA 92093-0060

LIKENS, SUZANNE ALICIA, physiologist, researcher; b. Chgo., Nov. 12, 1945; d. Harry Ross and Sibyle Lovelett (Butler) L. BS in Biology, U. N.Mex., 1969, MS in Physiology, 1982. Research asst. biology dept. U. N.Mex, Albuquerque, 1969; sr. research technologist Inhalation Toxicology Research Inst., Albuquerque, 1974—. Contbr. sci. papers and articles to profl. jours. Mem. Costeau Soc., N.Mex. Zool. Soc., Humane Soc. of U.S., N.Mex. Herpetological Soc. (charter), Women in Sci. and Engring., AAAS, Ctr. Envrion. Edn. Whale Protection Fund, Magic Park Dressage Sch., U.S. Dressage Fedn., N.Mex. Dressage and Combined Tng. Assn., Inc., Internat. Platform Assn., S.W. Dressage Assn. (bd. dirs. 1989), N.Y. Acad. Scis., Sigma Xi. Republican. Presbyterian. Home: 1311 Dartmouth NE Albuquerque NM 87106 Office: Inhalation Toxicology Research Inst PO Box 5890 Albuquerque NM 87185

LILJEQUIST, RAGNAR STAPLES, small business owner; b. Chgo., May 8, 1933; s. Leon Rogner and Muriel Alice (Staples) L.; m. Donna Kay Ray, May, 1969 (div. 1979); children: Bradley, Garth, Dag. BA, North Cen. Coll., Naperville, Ill., 1959. Cert. comml. investment mem. Copywriter Continental Assurance Co., Chgo., 1960-63; mgr. sales promotion Instns. Mag., Chgo., 1964; dir. advtg. Container Corp. of Am., Chgo., 1965; v.p. Robert Vogele, Inc., Chgo., 1966-68; mgr. acct. D'Arcy MacManus-Internat., Chgo., 1969-71; dir. advtg. Woodmoor Corp., Monument, Colo., 1972-73; mgr. research and planning Pacific NW Bell, Seattle, 1974-79; salesman Kushner, Stringer & Hill, Winslow, Wash., 1980-85; pres., chief exec. officer Dansk Co., Inc., Bainbridge Island, Wash., 1986—. Lodge: Rotary.

LILLARD, LOUISE DAVIS, lawyer; b. St. Louis, Mar. 4, 1919; d. Louis Ensenore and Maude Adele (Clamorgan) D.; m. Laurence E. Dunn, Dec. 25, 1941 (div. 1948); m. Richard G. Lillard, Aug. 27, 1949; 1 child, Monique. AB, UCLA, 1940, MA, 1941, JD, 1985. Bar: Calif. 1985; cert. tchr., Calif. Tchr. French Beverly Hills (Calif.) High Sch., 1941-76; supr. student tchrs. in fgn. langs. Calif. State U., Northridge, 1969-82; assoc. Law Offices Christopher Dieterich, Santa Monica, Calif., 1985—; freelance writer, editor L.A., 1976—. Co-author French textbook: L'Hexagone, c'est la France, 1983; contbr. articles to various publs. Mem. ABA, Calif. Bar Assn., Am. Assn. Tchrs. of French, Phi Beta Kappa. Democrat.

LILLBERG, JOHN WAYNE, electrical engineer; b. Butte, Mont., Apr. 17, 1936; s. John Eino and Ellen (Pohia) L.; m. Margaret Anne Babich, Mar. 17, 1955; children: Eric, Vanessa. BSEE, Mont. State U., 1962; MSCSEE, U. N.Mex., 1975. Elec. engr. Control Data Corp., Mpls., 1962-63, U. Chgo., 1963-68, Los Alamos Nat. Lab., 1968—. Contbr. articles to profl. jours.; patentee apparatus and method for reading two-dimensional electrophorotograms. With U.S. Army, 1955-58. Mem. IEEE (sr.). Home: 2349-A 33d St Los Alamos NM 87544 Office: Los Alamos Nat Lab PO Box 1663 Los Alamos NM 87545

LILLEJORD, LORI JOAN, editor, computer programmer, word processor; b. Kirkland, Wash., July 3, 1963. ATA in Computer Sci., City U., Bellevue, 1984, BS in Computer Sci., 1986; cert. in tech. writing/editing, U. Wash., 1989. Lead word processor Envirosphere Co., Bellevue, Wash., 1981-85, programmer, analyst, 1985-86, tech. editor, 1986--. Altrusa Club. vocat. scholar, 1981. Mem. Wash. Public Interest Research Group. Democrat. Lutheran. Home: 13344 NE 80th St Redmond WA 98052 Office: Envirosphere Co 10900 NE 8th St Bellevue WA 98004

LILLIE, ELEANOR HELDSTAB, educator; b. McCloud, Calif., Mar. 26, 1929; d. Reinhard and Ada Mae (Godfrey) Heldstab; m. John Allen Lillie, June 19, 1948 (dec. 1989); children: John Alan, James Reinhard, Michelle Mariann. AA, U. Calif., Berkeley, 1947; BA, Calif. State U., Stanislaus, 1972; MA, U. San Francisco, 1978. Cert. elem. and secondary tchr., sch. adminstr., Calif. Tchr. Columbia (Calif.) Union Elem. Sch., 1974—, mentor tchr., 1988—; edn. advisor Tuolumne County Jail Com., Sonora, Calif., 1987—. Editor, advisor (short stories) From Thought to Print, 1986-87; (poetry) Words, Words, Words, 1987. Mem. NEA, Calif. Tchrs. Assn., Columbia Tchrs. Assn. (pres. 1987—), Calif. Tchrs. English, Tuolumne Council on Reading, Columbia Coll. Found., Global Edn. Republican. Presbyterian. Home: PO Box 4001 Sonora CA 95370 Office: Columbia Elem Sch 22540 Parrotts Ferry Rd Columbia CA 95310

LILLIE, JOHN MITCHELL, retail executive; b. Chgo., Feb. 2, 1937; s. Walter Theodore and Mary Ann (Hatch) L.; m. Daryl Lee Harvey, Aug. 23, 1987; children: Alissa Ann, Theodore Perry. B.S., Stanford U., 1959, M.S., M.B.A., 1962-64. Various positions including dir. systems devel., also asst. to pres. Boise Cascade Corp., 1964-68; v.p., chief financial officer Arcata Nat. Corp., Menlo Park, Calif., 1968-70; exec. v.p., chief operating officer Arcata Nat. Corp., 1970-72; pres., chief exec. officer Leslie Salt Co., Newark, Calif., 1972-79; exec. v.p. Lucky Stores Inc., Dublin, Calif., 1979-81, pres., 1981-86, chmn., chief exec. officer, 1986—, also dir. Trustee Stanford (Calif.) U., 1988. Mem. Beta Theta Pi, Tau Beta Pi. Office: Lucky Stores Inc 6300 Clark Ave Dublin CA 94568

LILLO, LAWRENCE EDWARD, theater director; b. Kinuso, Alta., Can., Sept. 20, 1946; s. Marvin Victor and Ruth Lenore (Hingly) L. BA with honors, St. Francis Xavier U., Antigonish, N.S., 1967. Actor Vancouver, B.C., 1968-70; dir., founder Tamahnous Theatre, Vancouver, 1970-81; freelance theatre dir. Can. and U.S., 1981-86; dir. Grand Theatre, London, Ont., Can., from 1986; artistic dir. Vancouver Playhouse, Vancouver, B.C., 1988—; mem. arts adv. panel Can. Council, 1984—. Dir. plays including Pal Joey, Top Girls (Jessie Richardson award 1983), Streetcar Named Desire, Blood Relations (Jessie Richardson award 1984). Recipient Arts award Can. Council, 1982. Mem. Can. Actors Equity Assn., Profl. Assn. Can. Theatres, Assn. Cultural Execs. Office: Vancouver Playhouse, 543 W 7th Ave, Vancouver, BC Canada V5Z 1B4 *

LILLY, LUELLA JEAN, university administrator; b. Newberg, Oreg., Aug. 23, 1937; d. David Hardy and Edith (Coleman) L. BS, Lewis and Clark Coll., 1959; postgrad., Portland State U., 1959-61; MS, U. Oreg., 1961; PhD, Tex. Woman's U., 1971; postgrad., various univs., 1959-72. Tchr. phys. edn. and health, dean girls Cen. Linn Jr.-Sr. High Sch., Halsey, Oreg., 1959-60; tchr. phys. edn. and health, swimming, tennis, golf coach Lake Oswego (Oreg.) High Sch., 1960-63; instr., intramural coach Oreg. State U., Corvallis, 1963-64; instr., intercollegiate coach Am. River Coll., Sacramento, 1964-69; dir. women's phys. edn., athletics U. Nev., Reno, 1969-73, dir. women's athletics, 1973-75, assoc. dir. athletics, 1975-76, assoc. prof. phys. edn., 1971-76; dir. women's intercollegiate athletics U. Calif., Berkeley, 1976—; organizer, coach Lue's Aquatic Club, 1962-64. Author: An Overview of Body Mechanics, 1966, 3d rev. edit., 1969. Vol. instr. ARC, 1951; vol. Heart Fund and Easter Seal, 1974-76; ofcl. Spl. Olympics, 1975; mem. Los Angeles Citizens Olympic Com., 1984. Inducted Lewis and Clark Coll. Athletic Hall of Fame, 1988. Mem. AAHPER (life), AAUW, Nat. Soc. Profs., Women's Athletic Caucus, Council Collegiate Women Athletics Adminstrs., Western Soc. Phys. Edn. Coll. Women (membership com. 1971-74, program adv. com. 1972, exec. bd. 1972-75), Western Assn. Intercollegiate Athletics for Women (exec. bd. dirs. 1973-75, 79-82), Oreg. Girls' Swimming Coaches Assn. (pres. 1960, 63), Cen. Calif. Bd. Women Ofcls. (basketball chmn. 1968-69), Calif. Assn. Health, Phys. Edn. and Recreation (chmn.-elect jur. coll. sect. 1970), Nev. Bd. Women Ofcls. (chmn. bd., chmn. volleyball sect., chmn. basketball sect. 1969), No. Calif. Women's Intercollegiate Conf. (sec. 1970-71, basketball coordinator 1970-71), No. Calif. Intercollegiate Athletic Conf. (volleyball coordinator 1971-72), Nev. Assn. Health, Phys. Edn. and Recreation (state chmn. 1974—), No. Calif. Athletic Conf. (pres. 1979-82), Phi Kappa Phi, Theta Kappa. Mem. Soc. Friends. Lodge: Soroptimists (bd. dirs. 1988—). Home: 60 Margrave Ct Walnut Creek CA 94596 Office: U Calif 177 Hearst Gym Berkeley CA 94720

LILLY, MICHAEL ALEXANDER, lawyer; b. Honolulu, May 21, 1946; s. Percy Anthony, Jr. and Virginia Craig Lilly; children from previous marriage: Cary J., Laura B., Claire F., Winston W. AA, Menlo Coll., Menlo Park, Calif., 1966; BA, U. Calif., Santa Cruz, 1968; JD with honors, U. of Pacific, 1974. Bar: Calif. 1974, U.S. Dist. Ct. (no., so. and ea. dists.) Calif. 1974, U.S. Ct. Appeals (9th cir.) 1974, Hawaii 1975, U.S. Dist. Ct. Hawaii 1975, U.S. Ct. Appeals (D.C. cir.) 1975, U.S. Supreme Ct. 1978, U.S. Ct. Appeals (7th cir.) 1979. Atty. Pacific Legal Found., Sacramento, 1974-75; dep. atty. gen. State of Hawaii, Honolulu, 1975-79, 1st dep. atty. gen., 1981-84, atty. gen., 1984-85; ptnr. Feeley & Lilly, San Jose, Calif., 1979-81, Green, Ning, Lilly & Jones, Honolulu, 1985—; faculty Hastings Litigation Trial Advocacy Sch., San Francisco, 1984. Alumni rep. U. Calif., Santa Cruz, 1982—, Menlo Coll.; leader sustaining membership drive YMCA, Honolulu, 1984—; chmn. 17th senatorial dist. Rep. Party Hawaii. Served to lt. USN, 1968-71, Vietnam; capt. USNR. Named Hon. Ky. Col.; recipient Navy Commendation medal, 1988. Mem. Nat. Assn. Attys. Gen., Hawaii Law Enforcement Ofcls. Assn., Naval Res. Assn. (pres. 14th dist.), Navy League (contbg. editor Fore 'N Aft mag., dep. judge adv. to bd. Honolulu coun.), MADD, U. Pacific Alumnae Assn. Hawaii (pres.). Club: Outrigger Canoe. Home: 2769 Laniloa Rd Honolulu HI 96813 Office: Green Ning Lilly & Jones 707 Richards St Ste 700 Honolulu HI 96813

LILLYMAN, WILLIAM JOHN, German language educator; b. Sydney, Australia, Apr. 17, 1937; came to U.S., 1963, naturalized, 1974; s. John and Christina Mary (Munro) L.; m. Ingeborg Wolz, Sept. 14, 1962; children: Gregory, Christina. AB, U. Sydney, 1959; PhD, Stanford U., 1964. Asst. prof. Stanford (Calif.) U., 1964-67; assoc. prof. U. Calif., Santa Cruz, 1967-72; prof. German U. Calif., Irvine, 1972—, dean humanities, 1973-81, vice chancellor acad. affairs, 1981-82, exec. vice chancellor, 1982-88. Author: Otto Ludwig's Zwischen Himmel und Erde, 1967, Otto Ludwig: Romane und Romanstudien, 1977, Reality's Dark Dream The Narrative Fiction of Ludwig Tieck, 1979, Goethe's Narrative Fiction, 1983. Mem. MLA, Am. Assn. Tchrs. German. Office: U Calif Dept German Irvine CA 92717

LIM, LARRY KAY, university official; b. Santa Maria, Calif., July 4, 1948; s. Koonwah and Nancy (Yao) L.; m. Louise A. Simon, Aug. 15, 1988. BA, UCLA, 1970, teaching cert., 1971. Asst. engr. Force Ltd., L.A., 1969; teaching asst. UCLA, 1970-71; tchr. L.A. Sch. Dist., 1971-82; dir. minority programs, adminstr. Sch. Engring., U. So. Calif., L.A., 1979—; presenter minority math.-based intervention symposium U. D.C., Washington, 1988. Newsletter editor, 1981—. Bd. dirs. Developing Ednl. Studies for Hispanics, L.A., 1983—. Named Dir. of Yr., Math. Engring. Sci. Achievement Ctr. Adv. Bd., 1986. Mem. Nat. Assn. Pre-Coll. Dirs., Lotus/West Club (pres. 1977-83). Home: 3050 Veteran Ave Los Angeles CA 90034 Office: U So Calif Sch Engring OHE 104 Los Angeles CA 90089-1455

LIMA, DONALD ALLAN, oil company executive; b. Pasadena, Calif., Nov. 21, 1953; s. John Kenneth and Fay Gwynneth (Strangman) L.; m. Tina Marie Clark, Nov. 23, 1979 (div. May 9, 1984); m. Joyce Close Cirre, Jan. 17, 1985 (div. Oct. 15, 1987). BS, Calif. State U., Long Beach, Calif., 1982. Research technician Union Oil Co. Calif., Brea, Calif., 1979-84; chief chemist Pennzoil Products Co., Vernon, Calif., 1984-86; tech. service engring. ICI Tribol, Woodland Hills, Calif., 1986-88; Asian Pacific engring. mgr. ICI Tribol, Woodland Hills, 1988—. Mem. Am. Soc. Lubrication Engrs. (publicity chmn. 1986-87), Soc. Automotive Engrs. Office: ICI Tribol 21031 Ventura Blvd Woodland Hills CA 91364-2297

LIMON, LILIA LUZ, teacher; b. El Paso, Tex., Oct. 1, 1961; d. Enrique B. and Irma Soccoro (Valles) L. BS in Edn., No. Ariz. U., 1985. Cert. elem. bilingual tchr., Ariz., Calif. Tchr. Murphy Elem. Sch. Dist., Phoenix, 1985-87; bilingual tchr. Fontana (Calif.) Unified Sch. Dist., 1987—; sch. site dir. Rio Salado Family Math. Workshop, Phoenix, 1987; liaison South Phoenix Mental Health Ctr., 1986-87. Author: Mosaic Mathematics, 1985. Campaign worker Carolyn Warner for Gov. Ariz., 1986-87; mem. com. Reinstate Martin Luther King Day Commn., 1987. Recipient outstanding Ednl. Service award Murphy Sch. Dist., 1987, cert. of merit Elks Lodge, Phoenix, 1987. Mem. Nat. Tchrs. Assn., Calif. Tchrs. Assn., Fontana Tchrs. Assn. Democrat. Home: 922 East J St Ontario CA 91764 Office: Fontana Unified Sch Dist 9680 Citrus Ave Fontana CA 92335

LIN, HUN-CHI, molecular biologist; b. Yun-Lin, Taiwan, Republic of China, Nov. 8, 1953; came to U.S., 1980; s. Shun-Tsu and Yu-Hwa (Tsai) L.; m. Shau-Ping Lei, July 6, 1980; 1 child, Victoria Lei. BS, Nat. Taiwan U., Taipei, 1976, MS, 1978; PhD, UCLA, 1984. Teaching asst. UCLA, 1983; rsch. scientist Ingene, Santa Monica, Calif., 1984-85, project dir., 1985-87, prin. investigator, 1985-87; rsch. dir. Sinogen, L.A., 1987; pres., dir. rsch. Trigen Inc., Santa Monica, 1987—. Contbr. articles to profl. jours. Lt. Chinese Army, 1978-80. Mem. AAAS, Am. Soc. Microbiology. Office: Trigen Inc 2211 Michigan Ave Santa Monica CA 90404

LIN, KAREN SHAO-CHI, reseach biologist; b. Amoy, Fukien, China, July 4, 1947; came to U.S., 1969.; d. Lieh and Shih-Chu (Yin) Lin; m. Peter Yung Tai Lin, May 26, 1979; 1 child, Y i Ning. BA in Zoology, Nat. Taiwan U., 1969; MA in Biology, Wake Forest U., 1971; postgrad., San Francisco State U. Rsch. scientist Michael Reese and St. Luke Hosps., Chgo., 1971-85, Xoma Corp., Berkeley, Calif., 1985--. Fellow Am. Soc. Clin. Pathologists. Democrat. Presbyterian. Office: Xoma Corp 2910 7th St Berkeley CA 94710

LIN, LAWRENCE SHUH LIANG, accountant; b. China, July 5, 1938; s. Wan Chow and Inn Chi Lin; came to U.S., 1967, naturalized, 1979; LLB, Soochow U., 1963; MBA, Pepperdine U., 1970; m. Grace Yu, July 31, 1966; children: Ray, Lester. Spl. project acctg. supr. Motown Records, Hollywood, Calif., 1975; chief acct. Elektra/Asylum/Nonesuch Records, Beverly Hills, Calif., 1976-77, United Artists Music Pub. Group, Hollywood, 1977-80; controller-adminstr. Pasadena (Calif.) Guidance Clinics, 1980-86; v.p. Stew Kettle Corp., L.A., 1986-87; pres. LKL Corp., L.A., 1987—. Mem. Nat. Assn. Accts. Baptist. Office: LKL Corp 10926 W Pico Blvd Los Angeles CA 90064

LIN, TAO, electronics engineer; b. Shanghai, People's Republic of China, Aug. 6, 1958; came to U.S., 1986; s. Zeng-hui Lin and Wei-jing (Wu) Wu. BS, East China Normal U., Shanghai, 1982; MS, Tohoku U., Sendai, Japan, 1985; postgrad., Tohoku U., 1985-86. Technician Dongtong Electronics Inc., Shanghai, 1977-78; rsch. asst. Electronics Rsch. Lab U. Calif., Berkeley, 1986-87, postgrad. researcher, 1987-88; application engr. Integrated Device Technology Inc., Santa Clara, Calif., 1988—. Contbr. articles to profl. jours. Mem. IEEE (student). Home: 3552 Rockett Dr Fremont CA 94538 Office: Integrated Device Tech Inc 3001 Stender Way Santa Clara CA 95051

LIN, WEN H., aeronautical engineer; b. Huh-Wei, Taiwan, Jan. 3, 1948; s. Muh-Shuh and Ya (Liu) L.; m. Lih-Yuh Wang, July 23, 1973; children: Clark, Jolie. EdB, Nat. Taiwan U., 1971; EdM, Princeton U., 1974, MA, 1975, PhD, 1977. Mech. engr. Argonne (Ill.) Nat. Lab., 1977-85; MTS AT&T Bell Labs., Naperville, Ill., 1985-87; sr. engr. Rocketdyne div. Rockwell Internat., Canoga Park, Calif., 1987—. Tech. reviewer Applied Mechanic Revs., N.Y.C. , 1981—. Mem. ASME, Acoustical Soc. Am. (tech. reviewer 1983—), Am. Acad. Mechanics, Sigma Xi. Home: 11934 Maplecrest St Moorpark CA 93021 Office: Rockwell Internat Rocketdyne div Canoga Ave Canoga Park CA 91306

LIN, YI-CHING, electrical engineer, educator; b. Tounan, Taiwan, Republic of China, Sept. 8, 1949; came to U.S., 1974; s. Wun-Chang and Su-Jen (Sen) L.; m. Shiou-Ling Lieu, Aug. 24, 1977; children: Teresa Cynthia, Karen Alice. BSEE, Nat. Taiwan U., Taipei, 1972; MSEE, U. Houston, 1976; PhD, U. Calif., Berkeley, 1981. Testing engr. Acurex, Inc., Mt. View, Calif., 1976-77; research asst. U. Calif., Berkeley, 1977-81; mem. tech. staff Tex. Instruments, Dallas, 1981-84; sr. engring. specialist Monolithic Memories, Santa Clara, Calif., 1984-87; staff engr. Intel Corp., Santa Clara, 1987—; mem. faculty/lectr. San Jose (Calif.) State U., 1986—. Contbr. articles to profl. jours.; patentee in field. Served to 2d lt. Army Republic of China, 1972-74. Recipient Incentive award Tex. Instruments, Dallas, 1984. Mem. IEEE. Buddhist.

LINCICUM, MICHAEL SCOTT, state agency administrator; b. Portland, Oreg., Feb. 11, 1946; s. Milo Scott and Shirley Eileen (Jones) L.; m. Bernice Louise Balcomb, June 14, 1969; children: Shirley Joanne, Jon Michael. BA, Willamette U., 1968; MA, U. Wis., 1969; postgrad., U. Oreg., 1969-70. Planning specialist Oreg. Ednl. Coordinating Council, Salem, 1970-74; sr. budget analyst Oreg. Exec. Dept., Salem, 1974-80, budget supr., 1980-84; asst. adminstr. Oreg. Children's Services Div., Salem, 1984-85; asst. adminstr. Oreg. Mental Health Div., Salem, 1985-87, acting adminstr., 1987-88, dep. adminstr., 1988—; Mem. Oreg. Commn. on Futures Research, Salem, 1983-87, Oreg. Criminal Justice Council, Salem, 1987-88. Chmn. Highland Neighborhood Adv. Commn., Salem, 1973-74; chmn. local parent com. Boy Scouts Am., Salem, 1987-88; bd. dirs. Salem Youth Symphony, 1987-89. Club: Salem Golf. Office: Oreg Mental Health Div 2575 Bittern St NE Salem OR 97310

LINCOLN, ALEXANDER, III, financier, lawyer; b. Boston, Dec. 1, 1943; s. Alexander Jr. and Elizabeth (Kitchel) L.; m. Isabel Fawcett Ross, Dec. 27, 1969. BA, Denver U., 1967; JD, Boston U., 1971. Bar: Colo. 1972, U.S. Ct. Appeals (10th cir.) 1972, U.S. Supreme Ct. 1979. Atty. Dist. Ct. Denver, 1973-78, Colo. Ct. Appeals, Denver, 1978-80; mng. ptnr. Alexander Lincoln & co., Denver, 1980—. Mem. Colo. Bar Assn. (fin. com. 1975-76), Colo. Soc. Mayflower Descendants (life, bd. dirs. 1975—), Order of Founders and Patriots (life). Republican. Home: 121 S Dexter St Denver CO 80222 Office: 121 S Dexter St Denver CO 80222

LINCOLN, MARY KATHLEEN, bakery owner, operater; b. Buffalo, N.Y., Nov. 22, 1949; d. Samuel Edward and Gertrude Mary (Brennan) Shea; m. Timothy Craig Lincoln, May 16, 1976; children: Anna Rosemarie, Guy Bross, Curtiss Hart, Samuel Kingman, Matthew Shea. Student, Marygrove Coll., 1967-69, Loyola Inst. for Ministry, 1986—. Owner, operator Slice-O-Life Bakery, Palisade, Colo., 1980—; tchr. Culinary Corner, 1987-88; speaker in field. Bd. dirs. Child and Migrant Svcs., Palisade, 1988—; bd. dirs., booth chmn., Palisade Peach Festival, 1986-88; mem. Sta. KPRN-FM Pub. Radio, Community Forum Mesa County Commns., Grand Junction, Colo., 1988; precint chmn. Paliside Dem. Party, 1988; cake decorating tchr., Paliside 4-H, 1980; lay min. Roman Cath. Ch. Mem. Paliside C. of C. (bd. dirs., sec./treas. 1986-88, pres. 1989-90), Culinary Arts Guild, Women's Book Club, St. Anne's Lectors (acting head). Office: Slice-O-Life Bakery 105 W 3d St PO Box 299 Palisade CO 81526

LINCOLN, SANDRA ELEANOR, chemistry educator; b. Holyoke, Mass., Mar. 11, 1939; d. Edwin Stanley and Evelyn Ida (Mackie) L. BA magna cum laude, Smith Coll., 1960; MSChem, Marquette U., 1970; PhD in Inorganic Chemistry, SUNY, Stony Brook, 1982. Tchr., prin. Oak Knoll Sch., Summit, N.J., 1964-74; tchr. Holy Child High Sch., Waukegan, Ill., 1974-76; lectr. chemistry, dir. fin. aid Rosemont (Pa.) Coll., 1976-78; teaching asst. SUNY, Stony Brook, 1978-82; assoc. prof. chemistry U. Portland, Oreg., 1982—; researcher Oreg. Grad. Ctr., Beaverton, 1982—; bd. dirs. Portland Chemists for Pauling Symposium. Contbr. articles to profl. jours. Cath. sister Soc. Holy Child Jesus, 1963—. Recipient Pres.'s award for Teaching, SUNY, Stony Brook, 1981; Burlington No. Outstanding scholar, 1987. Mem. Am. Chem. Soc., Phi Beta Kappa, Sigma Xi. Democrat. Home: 5431 N Strong St Portland OR 97203 Office: U Portland 5000 Willamette Blvd Portland OR 97203

LIND, BRUCE ELVIN, land developer; b. Twin Falls, Idaho, June 25, 1941; s. Wyland Herman and Helen Eileen (Bailey) L.; B.S., Utah State U., 1967, B.S. in Bus. Edn., 1968, M.S. in Mktg., 1969; m. Patricia Zohner; children—Billie Jean, Bonita, Ben, Katy, Tyler, Tara, Corbin, Jess. Product mgr., wholesaler Boise Cascade Corp. (Idaho), 1968-70; asst. to nat. sales mgr. Trus-Joist Corp., Boise, 1970-71; founder, pres. A.M.R. Corp., Idaho Falls, Idaho, 1971—, chmn. bd., 1972—. Mem. Delta Phi Kappa. Club: Lions. Office: A M R Corp 244 Broadway Idaho Falls ID 83402

LIND, GREGORY ALAN, nurse; b. Mpls., July 15, 1953; s. Raymond Pernal and Barbara (Haddad) L.; m. Diane Nancy Erpenbach, Dec. 28, 1974; children: Brienne Jo, Kacie Barbara. BS in Nursing, Viterbo Coll., 1976; MS in Nursing, U. Mo., 1980; PhD in Nursing, U. Kans., 1988. Staff nurse Truman Vet.'s Hosp., Columbia, Mo., 1976-78; family nurse practitioner Callaway Family Clinic, Fulton, Mo., 1979-83; prin. Family Nurse Practitioner Care, Unlimited, Columbia, 1983-87; asst. prof. Sch. Nursing U. Mo., Columbia, 1986-87; assoc., advanced nurse practitioner Primary Health Care Assocs., Seattle, 1988—; asst. prof. dept. community health care, primary health care pathway, Sch. Nursing, U. Wash., Seattle, 1988—. Contbr. to profl. publs.; health columnist, local newspaper, 1982-87. Sec.-treas., Cedar Lake homeowners Assn., Columbia, 1982-86; mem. Corrections Health Task Force, Jefferson City, Mo., 1986; mem. Columbia City/County Bd. Health, 1986. Mem. Am. Nurses Assn. (exec. mem. cabinet 1988—, mem. exec. coun. 1986-88), Wash. State Nurses Assn., King County Nurses Assn., Sigma Theta Tau. Roman Catholic. Home: 2310 233d Ave NE Redmond WA 98053 Office: U Wash CHCS SM-24 T502A Seattle WA 98195

LIND, KENDRA JOHNSON, materials manager; b. Whitefish, Mont., Nov. 3, 1947; d. Harold Norman and Laura Beryl (Schooley) Johnson; m. L. Harold Lind, July 3, 1976; 1 child, Toni Lynn. BS, No. Mont. Coll., 1972; postgrad., Flathead Valley Community Coll., 1984—. Instr. sci. Powell County High Sch., Deer Lodge, Mont., 1972-74; with ins. sales N.Am. Life & Casualty, Billings, Mont., 1975; dir. pub. rels. Mid Yellowstone Areawide Planning Orgn., Billings, Mont., 1976; mill maintenance clk. W.R. Grace & Co., Libby, Mont., 1976-80, warehouse clk., 1981, warehouse supr., 1982—; mem. adv. com. Kellogg Found.for Lincoln County Intermountain Communication, Learning & Info. System, 1988—; bd. dirs. Zonolite Emplyees Credit Union, sec. 1978—. Editor-producer: MYAPO Newsletter, 1976, Grace Safety Newsletter, 1977-81; author-illustrator: Field Guide to Alpine & Sub-alpine Flora of the Deer Lodge Valley, 1973; author: Coloring Book Guide to Endangered Species, 1973. Campaign coord. L.H. Lind for Nat. Jr. Commdr. in chief VFW, 1985-88. Mem. VFW Aux. (#7311 dist. 3 chmn. bicentennial celebration1975-76, convention credentials com. 1976, encampment planning com. 1988), DAV Aux. (#21 life, adj.-treas. 1984—), Mont. Mining Assn. (sec., treas. Lincoln County chpt. 1983-85), Sigma Tau Sigma, Order Ea. Star (worthy matron Libby chpt. 1986-87, treas. 1988—, unit 1 chmn. ESTARL 1987-88, grand teller 1988-89), Women of the Moose (Libby chpt.). Republican. Home: PO Box 467 Libby MT 59923 Office: WR Grace & Co PO Box 609 Libby MT 59923

LIND, MAURICE DAVID, research physicist; b. Jamestown, N.Y., July 25, 1934; s. Paul William Frederic and Florence Rosemond (Hedstrom) L.; m. Carol Norma Dickson, Apr. 21, 1962; 1 child, Diana Nadine. BS, Otterbein Coll., 1957; PhD, Cornell U., 1962. Postdoctoral fellow Cornell U., Ithaca, N.Y., 1962-63; research scientist Union Oil Co., Brea, Calif., 1963-66, Rockwell Internat., Thousand Oaks, Calif., 1966—; vis. prof. applied physics Tech. U. Denmark, Lyngby, 1985. Contbr. articles to profl. jours. Recipient Pub. Service award NASA, 1976. Mem. Am. Phys. Soc., Am. Crystallographic Assn., Am. Assn. Crystal Growth, Sigma Xi. Home: 1690 Stoddard Ave Thousand Oaks CA 91360 Office: Rockwell Internat 1049 Camino Dos Rios Thousand Oaks CA 91360

LIND, TERRIE LEE, program administrator, speech pathologist; b. Spokane, Wash., June 5, 1948; d. Clifford and Edna Mae (Allenbach) Presnell; m. Stephen George Lind, Aug. 29, 1970 (div. Mar. 1981); children: Erica Rachel, Reid Christopher. BA cum laude, Wash. State U., 1970, MA, 1971. Cert. tchr., Wash., Ariz.; cert. in Porch Index Communicative Ability. Specialist communication disorders U. Tex., Houston, 1971-73; clin. supr. The Battin Clinic, Houston, 1973-76; specialist communication disorders Spokane Guilds Sch., 1980-82; program coordinator, adminstr. Fresno (Calif.) Community Hosp., 1982-87; program adminstr. Advantage 65* sr. access program Health Dimensions, Inc., San Jose, Calif., 1987—; cons. Adolescent Chem. Dependency Unit, Fresno, 1984-87. Mem. Am. Speech and Hearing Assn. (cert., Continuing Edn. award 1985-86), Wash. Speech and Hearing Assn. (co-chmn. state conv. program com. 1981-82), AAUW (officer 1976-82), Wash. State U. Alumni Assn. Home: 866-D Apricot Ave

Campbell CA 95008 Office: Health Dimensions Inc Advantage 65 SM 1275 S Winchester Blvd #D San Jose CA 95128

LINDAHL, ROGER MATHEWS, executive editor; b. Orange, N.J., July 22, 1955; s. Melvin August and Barbara (Davenport) L.; m. Po-Yee Au, June 12, 1979; one child, Patricia Si-Ling. BA, Franklin and Marshall Coll., 1977; MBA, U. Mich., 1982. Research assoc. Bus. Internat. Asia/Pacific, Hong Kong, 1982-83; editor Daily Comml. News, San Francisco, 1984-86; exec. editor Diagnostic Imaging Scan newsletter, San Francisco, 1986—. Bd. dirs. Night Ministry, San Francisco. Mem. Phi Beta Kappa. Democrat. Office: Miller Freeman Pubs 500 Howard St San Francisco CA 94105

LINDAUER, THEODORE, psychiatrist; b. N.Y.C., July 17, 1935; s. Harry and Anne (Kurtz) L. AB, Columbia Coll., 1956; MD, U. Pitts., 1960; cert. in adult psychiatry, U. Ill., 1963; cert. in child psychiatry, Harvard U., 1965. Intern Michael Reese Hosp., Chgo.; resident adult psychiatry U. Ill., Chgo.; resident child psychiatry Harvard U., Boston; dir. mental health svcs. L.A. Unified Sch. Dist., 1971-73; asst. clin. profl. UCLA, 1973-75, 79-81; dir. adolescent svcs. Kellogg Psychiat. Hosp., Corona, Calif., 1977-79; med. dir. Hathaway Home for Children, L.A., 1980-82; cons. psychiatrist Chaparral Treatment Ctr., San Bernadino, Calif., 1987-89; cons. mental health AIDS L.A. Project, Long Beach, Calif., 1987-89; cons. psychiatrist Med. Sq. Counseling Ctr., Garden Grove, Calif., 1987—. Mem., speaker Common Cause, L.A., 1971—; mem., writer Amnesty Internat., L.A., 1971—. Recipient N.Y. State Regents scholar, 1952-56. Mem. Am. Psychiat. Assn., Am. Assn. Child and Adolescent Psychiatry, So. Calif. Psychiat. Soc. Home: 2811 Tucker Ln Los Angeles CA 90720

LINDBERG, DAVID NILS, geologist; b. Pitts., Feb. 19, 1954; s. Olof Herman and Teresa Francis (Milewski) L.; m. Sylvia Lynn Bagley, Apr. 4, 1975. BA in Geology, Humboldt State U., 1981, MS in Geology, 1989. Trail crew foreman U.S. Forest Service, Somes-Bar, Calif., 1978-79; wilderness ranger U.S. Forest Service, Covelo, Calif., 1980; wellsite geologist Analex, Inc., Denver, 1981, Exploration Logging, Inc., Sacramento, Calif., 1981-86; field geologist Humboldt State U. Found., Arcata, Calif., 1986; tchrs. asst. geology dept. Humboldt State U., Arcata, 1987; field geologist Woodward-Clyde Cons., Oakland, Calif., 1987; instr. geology dept. Humboldt State U., 1988—. Mem. Northwest Scientific Assn. (grantee 1988), Geologic Soc. Am. (grantee 1988), AAAS, Humboldt State U. Geology Club. Democrat. Office: Humboldt State U Geology Dept Arcata CA 95521

LINDBLAD, JOHN PAUL, architect; b. Seattle, Sept. 4, 1952; s. Elwood Glen and Janet May (Jones) L. AA, Seattle Community Coll., 1973; BA in Environ. Design, U. Wash., 1975; MArch, Tex. A&M U., 1980. Registered architect, Calif. Designer, Blunk Assoc., Architects, Burlingame, Calif., 1977-78; project mgr. James D. Fessenden, Architect, Portola Valley, Calif., 1978-79, Woodford & Bernard Architects, L.A., 1981; project mgr. Hunter & Appel Architects, 1981-82; pres., chief exec. officer Lindblad Architecture, Sherman Oaks, Calif., 1982—; cons. VA, Sepulveda, Calif., 1980; instr. Woodbury U., 1984—; spkr. Pacific Design Ctr. symposium, 1987; exhibitor Tex. A&M U. Architecture Hall., 1980, Ambulatory Care Outpatient Bldg., Aspen Med. Ctr., Simi Valley, Calif., Anaheim Conv. Ctr., Sepulveda, Assn. Western Hosps., 1986. Contbr. articles to profl. jours. Researcher Stop the 3d Lake Washington Bridge, Seattle, 1967; coordinator Save Seattle's Pub. Market, 1967. U. Wash. innovative rsch. grantee, 1975; active Save the Sepulveda Basin, 1988—. Mem. L.A. Mcpl. Art Gallery, Am. Inst. Planners, AIA (health com.), Nat. Trust Historic Preservation, Van Nuys C. of C., Assn. Gen. Contractors, Nautilus Plus Club. Roman Catholic. Office: Lindblad Architecture 13437 Ventura Blvd Ste 228 Sherman Oaks CA 91423

LINDBLAD, WILLIAM JOHN, utility executive; b. Oakland, Calif., May 22, 1929; s. William N. and Johnina B. (Moore) L.; B.S. in Elec. Engring., U. Calif., Berkeley, 1951; m. Rosella J. Allender, July 4, 1953; children—Catherine, Nancy, Thomas, Christopher, Margaret, Michael, Therese, Paul. Various engring. and mgmt. positions Pacific Gas & Electric Co., San Francisco, 1954-77; v.p. engring. and constrn. Portland (Oreg.) Gen. Electric Co., 1977-80, pres., dir., 1980—; bd. dirs. Portland Gen. Corp., 1986—. . Mem. adv. bd. Providence Med. Center, 1981—; bd. dirs. Portland State U. Found., 1981—; trustee St. Mary's Acad., Served 1982-83. with USN, 1951-54. Registered profl. engr., Calif. Mem. ASME, Am. Soc. Naval Engrs., IEEE. Republican. Roman Catholic. Club: Univ. Office: Portland GE Co 121 SW Salmon St Portland OR 97204 *

LINDE, HANS ARTHUR, state supreme court justice; b. Berlin, Germany, Apr. 15, 1924; came to U.S., 1939, naturalized, 1943; s. Bruno C. and Luise (Rosenhain) L.; m. Helen Tucker, Aug. 13, 1945; children: Lisa, David Tucker. B.A., Reed Coll., 1947; J.D., U. Calif., Berkeley, 1950. Bar: Oreg. 1951. Law clk. U.S. Supreme Ct. Justice William O. Douglas, 1950-51; atty. Office of Legal Adviser, Dept. State, 1951-53; individual practice law Portland, Oreg., 1953-54; legis. asst. U.S. Sen. Richard L. Neuberger, 1955-58; asso. prof., prof. U. Oreg. Law Sch., 1959-76; justice Oreg. Supreme Ct., Salem, 1977—; Fulbright lectr. Freiburg U., 1967-68, Hamburg U., 1975-76; cons. U.S. ACDA, Dept. Def., 1962-76; mem. Adminstrv. Conf. U.S., 1978-82. Author: (with George Bunn) Legislative and Administrative Processes, 1976. Mem. Oreg. Constl. Revision Commn., 1961-62. Served with U.S. Army, 1943-46. Fellow Am. Acad. Arts and Scis.; mem. Am. Law Inst. (council), Order of Coif, Phi Beta Kappa. Office: Oreg Supreme Ct Supreme Ct Bldg Salem OR 97310

LINDEMULDER, CAROL ANN, interior designer, artist; b. San Diego, May 2, 1936; d. Franklin Geert and Leone Augusta (Oltman) L. BA in Decorative Arts, U. Calif., Berkeley, 1959; postgrad. in fine arts, San Diego State U., 1965-67. Tchr. interior design and fine arts adult edn. div. San Diego City Schs., 1960-67; with Milo of Calif., Inc. subs. Milo Electronics Corp., 1968-73, corp. staff asst., 1972, asst. to dir. mktg., 1972-73; with Frazee Industries 1975-77; owner, designer-artist Call Carol, San Diego, 1976-; former instr. U. Calif. Extension, San Diego. One-woman show Point Loma Art Assn., 1967, Scandia Interiors, 1977, Cen. Fed. Savs. & Loan, 1978, John Duncan Interiors, 1979, Villa Montezuma Mus., 1981; exhibited in group shows Calif. Western U., 1963, Jewish Community Ctr., 1963-64, So. Calif. Expn., 1964, San Diego Mus. Art, 1966, 71, 75, San Diego State U., 1974, Spectrum Gallery, 1985, A.R.T. Beasley Gallery, 1985. Coord. Christmas program San Diego Community Vol. Bur., 1961; a founder, treas., bd. dirs. Save Our Heritage Orgn., 1969-71, pres., 1974-75, 79-81; mem. San Diego Hist. Sites Bd., 1985—, vice chmn., 1987—; founder, pres. Save the Coaster Com., 1981-83. Named Vol. of Month, San Diego Community Vol. Bur., 1961; recipient President's commendation Save Our Heritage Orgn., 1984. Mem. Jr. League San Diego. Republican. Office: PO Box 81718 San Diego CA 92103

LINDEN, CRAIG LEIGH, energy company executive; b. Upland, Calif., Oct. 21, 1947; s. Bernard Harry Jr. and Barbara Jean (Newnon) L.; m. Lindsey Sue Elkins, Aug. 24, 1968; children: Mitri Leigh, Merritt Leigh. BS, San Diego State U., 1970. Tech. writer, editor Glenn Mitchell Manuals, San Diego, 1970-71; owner, pres. Design Systems Research and Devel., Inc., Alpine, Calif., 1976—; v.p. research and devel. Micro Cogen Systems Inc., Irvine, Calif., 1985—. Patentee cogeneration energy systems. Served to capt. USCG, 1971-75. Mem. Assn. Energy Engrs. Home and Office: 1335 Midway Dr Alpine CA 92001

LINDENBERG, KATJA, chemistry educator; b. Quito, Ecuador, Nov. 2, 1941; came to U.S., 1957; d. Manea Sifnaghel and Gerda (Gumpel) Anders; m. Andras Lakatos, Aug. 26, 1961 (div. 1969); m. Semmy Lindenberg, July 1, 1970 (dec. 1988); children: Misha, Dania. BA, Alfred U., 1962; PhD, Cornell U., 1967. Lectr. chemistry U. Rochester (N.Y.), 1967-69; prof. U. Calif. at San Diego, La Jolla, 1969-; cons. Oak Ridge (Tenn.) Nat. Lab., 1973-76; assoc. La Jolla Inst., 1982-. Research grantee Nat. Sci. Found., 1969-, Dept. Energy, 1986-. Mem. AAUP, Am. Phys. Soc., Am. Chem. Soc., Am. Geophys. Union, Am. Women in Sci. Office: U Calif B-040 La Jolla CA 92093-0340

LINDER, MARK RICHARD, public relations executive; b. Bucyrus, Ohio, July 27, 1946; s. Carl Edward Linder Jr. and Juanita Mae Richard; m. Mary Susan Dean. BA, Macalester Coll., St. Paul, 1969. Coord. Community Improvement Program, St. Paul, 1969-71; assoc. Canterfes Urban Encounter, Mpls., 1971-72; staff dir. Orgn. for a Better St. Paul, 1972-73, Community Focus, York, Pa., 1974-75, Lincoln (Nebr.) Alliance, 1975-77, Valley Coalition, San Jose, Calif., 1977-78; assoc. Dale Watson & Assoc., Inc., San Jose, Calif., 1978-80; v.p. adminstr. Allstane Investment Corp., San Jose, Calif., 1980-82; with Santa Cruz (Calif.) Met. Transit Dist., 1982—; assoc. Dalewatson & Assoc., Inc., San Jose. Pres. Christ Good Shepherd Luth. Ch., San Jose, 1983, Terrace Hills Townhome Assn., 1983; vista vol. Angel Job Corps. Ctr. Mem. Am. Pub. Transit Assn., Calif. Transit Assn. Democrat. Office: Santa Cruz Met Transit Dist 230 Walnut Ave Santa Cruz CA 95060

LINDGREN, ROBERT KEMPER, securities trader, insurance company executive; b. LaPorte, Ind., Sept. 25, 1939; s. Ralph Arthur and Georgia Lillian (Kemper) L.; m. Charmaine Katherine Freeman, Feb. 2, 1963; children: Scott Edward, Amber Louise, Vincent Kemper. BS, Western Mich. U., 1963. Comml. printing mgr. Livingston Enterprise Comml. Printing, Livingston, Mont., 1968-70; prodn. mgr. Mont. Graphic Arts Ctr., div. of Lee Enterprises, Helena, Mont., 1970-71; ptnr., sales mgr. Ashton Printing Co., Butte, Mont., 1971-72; ptnr., sales mgr., corp. sec. Thurber Printing Co./Office Supplies, Helena, 1972-86; securities and investments trader Helena, 1968—; ins. agt. Am. Bankers Life Ins. Co. and Continental Gen. Ins. Co., Helena, 1988—; instr. Officer Candidate Sch., Mont. Mil. Acad., Mont. Army NG, Helena, 1974-75; adv. staff Civil Def. of the Mont. NG, Helena, 1975-76; chmn. Helena Demolition Derby of the annual Rodeo and Stampede, Helena, 1982-87. Scout leader, Webelo Cub Scouts, Boy Scouts Am., Helena, 1973-76; bd. mem. Lewis & Clark County Planning Bd., Helena, 1977-79, Sch. Dist. No. 4 Bd. Trustees, Canyon Creek, Mont., 1981—, bd. chmn., 1984—; mem. Lewis & Clark Sheriff's Res., Helena, 1988—. Capt. (Signal Corps) U.S. Army, 1963-68. Recipient Certs. of Achievement, Boy Scouts Am., Helena, 1975, 85; Certs. of Service, County Commrs., Helena, 1977, 79. Mem. Toastmasters Internat., Lions. Republican. Home and Office: Am Bankers Life Ins Co 4930 Birdseye Rd Helena MT 59601

LINDH, PATRICIA SULLIVAN, banker, former government official; b. Toledo, Oct. 2, 1928; d. Lawrence Walsh and Lillian Winifred (Devlin) Sullivan; m. H. Robert Lindh, Jr., Nov. 12, 1955; children: Sheila, Deborah, Robert. B.A., Trinity Coll., Washington, 1950, LL.D., 1975; LL.D., Walsh Coll., Canton, Ohio, 1975, U. Jacksonville, 1975. Adoption case worker Cath. Charities, Chgo., 1954-55; editor Singapore Am. Newspaper, 1957-62; spl. asst. to counsellor to Pres. 1974, spl. asst. to Pres., 1975-76; dep. asst. sec. state for ednl. and cultural affairs Dept. State, 1976-77; v.p., dir. corp. communications Bank Am., Los Angeles, 1978-84, World Banking P.R. Bank Am., San Francisco, 1985—. Trustee La. Arts and Sci. Center, 1970-73, Calif. Hosp. Med. Ctr., 1979-84; bd. dirs. Jr. League of Baton Rouge, 1969, Children's Bur. Los Angeles, 1979, 84, USO Northern Calif.; Rep. state vice chairwoman La., 1970-74; Rep. nat. committeewoman, La., 1974; mem. pub. affairs com. San Francisco World Affairs Coun., 1985; adv. bd. Jr. League Los Angeles, 1980-84; bd. visitors Southwestern U. Sch. Law. Roman Catholic. Home: 850 Powell St San Francisco CA 94108

LINDHEIM, ELAINE LAVIS, educational evaluation consultant; b. L.A., Sept. 25, 1942; d. Salvo and Stella (Amado) Lavis; m. Richard David Lindheim, Dec. 22, 1963; children: Susan, David. BA with honors in English, Stanford U., 1963; MEd, UCLA, 1977, EdD, 1983. Tchr., program adminstr., counselor L.A. City Schs., 1964-75; dir. test devel. IOX Assessment Assocs., L.A., 1975-83; ednl. evaluation cons. Beverly Hills, Calif., 1983—. Co-author: Teaching and Measuring the Skills of Composition, 1980, How to Measure Performance, 1988. Mem. Nat. Soc. for Performance and Instrn. (v.p., pres. L.A. chpt. 1986—), Am. Ednl. Research Assn., Nat. Council on Measurement in Edn., Am. Occupational Therapy Assn. (pub. mem.), Phi Beta Kappa. Jewish.

LINDHOLM, RICHARD THEODORE, university professor; b. Eugene, Oreg., Oct. 5, 1960; s. Richard Wadsworth and Mary Marjorie (Trunko) L. m. Valaya Nivasananda, May 8, 1987. BA, U. Chgo., 1982, MA, 1983. Adj. asst. prof. U. Oreg., Eugene, 1988—; pres. Rubicon Inst., Eugene, 1988—; ptnr. Lindholm and Osanka, Eugene, 1986—. Co-campaign chmn. Lane Community Coll. Advocates, Eugene, 1988; coord., planner numerous state rep. campaigns, Oreg., 1988; precinct committeeperson Oreg. Rep. Party, 1988; bd. dirs. Rubicon Soc., Eugene, 1987. Republican. Lutheran. Home: 2710 Garfield St Eugene OR 97405

LINDHOLM, STEVEN MORGAN, engineer; b. Santa Ana, Calif., Aug. 16, 1960; s. Richard Vinton and Nancy Jean (Morgan) L.; m. Marianne Ruth Nenzell, July 11, 1987. BS in Engring., U. Calif., Berkeley, 1983. Registered profl. engr., Calif. Jr. engr. Ocean Design Engring. Corp., Irvine, Calif., 1980-81; jr. marine engr. Todd Pacific Shipyards Corp., San Pedro, Calif., 1982-84; naval architect IMODCO, L.A., 1984-85; systems engr. Ametek Offshore Rsch., Santa Barbara, Calif., 1985-87; materials engr. USN, CBC Port Hueneme, Port Hueneme, Calif., 1987—; dir. Advanced Concepts Rsch., Santa Barbara, 1989—. Mem. Am. Soc. Testing Materials, Soc. Naval Architects and Marine Engrs., U. Calif. Alumni Assn., Sigma Alpha Mu (sec. 1982). Office: USN Civil Engring Support CBC Port Hueneme Code 1564L Port Hueneme CA 93043

LINDLEY, NORMAN DALE, physician; b. Henrietta, Tex., July 18, 1937; s. Hardie Lindley and Hope (Clement) Mourant; m. Luise Ann Moser, May 29, 1964; children: Norman Dale Jr., Roger Paul. BS, N.M. Highlands U., 1960; MD, U. Colo., 1964. Diplomate Am. Bd. Ob-Gyn. Rotating intern Kans. City (Mo.) Gen. Hosp., 1964-65; resident in ob-gyn. St. Joseph Hosp., Denver, 1965-68; med. officer USAF, Cheyenne, Wyo., 1968-70; pvt. practice physician Alamogordo, N.M., 1970—; dir. N.M. Found. for Med. Care, Albuquerque, 1985-88, N.M. Med. Review Assn., Albuquerque, 1985-88; physician liaison Am. Assn. Med. Assts., Chgo., 1987—; physician adv. N.M. Soc. Med. Assts., 1984—. Dir. Otero County Boys' and Girls' Club, Alamogordo, 1977—, Otero County Assn. for Retarded Citizens, Alamogordo, 1985—, Am. Cancer Soc., Otero County, Alamogordo, 1970-72. Capt. USAF, 1968-70. Recipient Research grant Nat. Sci. Found., U. Utah., 1959, Nat. Sci. Found., N.M. Highlands U., 1960, Service Above Self award Rotary Club of Alamogordo, 1979, Paul Harris Fellowship, Rotary Internat., 1987. Fellow Am. Coll. Ob-Gyn.; mem. Am. Fertility Soc., AMA, N.M. Med. Soc. (councilor 1985-88), Otero County Med. Soc. (pres. 1972-73, 83-84), Rotary Club of Alamogordo (pres. 1981-82, dir. 1988—). Home: 2323 Union Ave Alamogordo NM 88310 Office: Thunderbird Ob-Gyn 1212 Ninth St Alamogordo NM 88310

LINDLEY, TODD JAMES, financial analyst; b. Aberdeen, Wash., Mar. 23, 1960; s. James Earl and Luella May (Trautman) L.; m. Gerrilyn Marie Pyle. BA, West Wash. U., Bellingham, 1983. Shop floor planner Western Farmers, Bellingham, Wash., 1980-83; choker setter Weyerhaeser Co., Cosmopolis, Wash., 1980-83; mgmt. trainee K. Mart Corp., Beaverton, Ore., 1983; fin. planner Lindley Fin. Svcs., Montesano, Wash., 1984—. Bd. dirs. Montesano Community Schs., Wash., 1985; chmn., co-chmn. Doug Sayan 35th Dist. State Rep., Grays Harbor, 1986-88; Sunday Sch. Tchr. Presbyn. Ch., 1984—. Recipient New Orgn. Leader award Lincoln Nat. Life 1984--, Nat. Sales. Mem. Nat. Assn. Life Underwriters (program chmn. 1986-88, v.p., treas., sec. 1986—), Pres. Club. (Agt. of Yr. 1987-88, Nat. Career winner1985). Democrat. Office: Lindley Fin Svcs 107 E Broadway PO Box 607 Montesano WA 98563

LINDNER, ALAN WALTER, electrical engineer; b. Las Vegas, Nev., June 7, 1960; s. John Herman and Miriam Charlotte (Zucker) L. BSEE, Ariz. State U., 1982; postgrad., U. N.Mex., 1983-84, San Diego State U., 1987—. Engring. intern Physics Internat., San Leandro, Calif., 1980, INESCO, La Jolla, Calif., 1981; elect. engr. BDM Corp., Albuquerque, 1983-84, IRT Corp., San Diego, 1984-86, Teledyne Ryan Electronics, San Diego, 1986—. Recipient So. Nev. Home Builders award So. Nev. Home Builders Assn., 1987. Mem. IEEE. Republican. Jewish. Home: 5226 Cobb Pl San Diego CA 92117 Office: Teledyne Ryan Electronics 8650 Balboa Ave San Diego CA 92123

LINDNER, KENNETH ROBERT, JR., manufacturing executive, composer, musician; b. Bethlehem, Pa., Apr. 27, 1949; s. Kenneth Robert and Betty Irene (Gillespie) L.; m. Leslie A. Watson, Apr. 3, 1971 (div. Apr. 1987); 1 child, Robert Alan. B Music Edn., Oberlin Conservatory Music, 1971. Tchr. Hamilton (N.Y.) Cen. Sch., 1971-74; electronics technician Digital Equipment Corp., Maynard, Mass., 1974-75, chief technician, work coord., 1975-76; test supr. Digital Equipment Corp., Phoenix, 1976-78; quality engr. ITT Courier Terminal Systems, Tempe, Ariz., 1978-79; quality engr. Intel Corp., Phoenix, 1979-81, staff reliability engr., 1981-85; quality engring. mgr. ADR Ultrasound, Tempe, 1985-86; dir. quality Hamilton Co., Reno, 1986—. Composer various works. Mem. IEEE (referee 1984—), Am. Fedn. Musicians. Democrat. Unitarian. Home: 135 Regier Springs Dr Sparks NV 89436 Office: Hamilton Co 4960 Energy Way Reno NV 89520

LINDQUIST, JOHN A., utility company executive; b. Ogden, Utah, 1919. Grad., Weber State Coll., 1939. Chmn. Utah Power and Light Co., Salt Lake City; chmn. Lindquist and Sons, Ct. Western Ins. Co. Office: Utah Power & Light Co 1407 W N Temple St Salt Lake City UT 84116 *

LINDSAY, CRAIG CURTIS, automobile company executive; b. Elyria, Ohio, Feb. 13, 1952; s. Walter Lowry and Wilma Evelyn (Harnack) L.; m. Cindy Lee Ritchie, Nov. 7, 1983; 1 child, David Christopher. BS, Ariz. State U., 1977, MBA, 1984. CPA, Ariz. Staff acct. Coopers and Lybrand, Phoenix, 1977-79; tax supr. J. McDonald and Co., Phoenix, 1979-84; tax mgr. Peat Marwick Mitchell, Phoenix, 1984-85; fin. cons. Phoenix, 1986-87; chief fin. officer The Ryerson Co., Phoenix, 1987-88, Scottsdale (Ariz.) Automotive Group, 1988—; Founder Mountaineers Inc., Phoenix. Contbr. articles to profl. jours. Vice-chmn. Citizen's Adv. Com. South Mountain Master Plan, Phoenix, 1987-88. Recipient Environ. Action award Valley Forward, Phoenix, 1987. Mem. AICPA, Ariz. Soc. CPAs. Republican. Office: Scottsdale Automotive Group 6825 E McDowell Scottsdale AZ 85257

LINDSAY, DONALD GENE, dermatologist, educator; b. Kokomo, Ind., Mar. 27, 1922; s. Clifford George and Velma Lindsay; m. Catharine Smith, June 20, 1945 (div. 1972); children: Jan Corwin, Diane Kay, James Christopher; m. Donann Sisler, July 10, 1986. BS, U. Ill., 1945; MD, U. Ill., Chgo., 1947; postgrad in Medicine, UCLA, 1971-72. Diplomate Am. Bd. Dermatology, Am. Bd. Dermatopathology. Intern Calif. Hosp., Los Angeles, 1947-48; resident in gen. practice San Luis Obispo County Hosp., San Luis Obispo, Calif., 1948-49; pvt. practice medicine Dinuba, Calif., 1949-51; tng. in psychiatry U.S. Army Hosp., Ft. Sam Houston, Tex., 1951-52; resident in internal medicine Good Samaritan Hosp., Los Angeles, 1954-55; resident in dermatology Long Beach (Calif.) VA Hosp., 1955-58; pvt. practice dermatology Ventura, Calif., 1958-71, 74--; fellow in endocrinology and endocrine research Harbor Hosp., UCLA, Torrance, Calif., 1972-74; assoc. clin. prof. medicine U. So Calif. Med. Sch., Los Angeles, 1961--; pres. Found. for Research in Aging, Ventura, Calif., 1965--; research cons. Pickard, Lowe & Garrick Inc., Newport Beach, Calif., Washington, 1987-88. Author 12 video tapes on skin surgery; co-author artificial intelligence software. Capt. M.C., U.S. Army, 1951-53. Mem. AMA, Am. Acad. Dermatology, Pacific Dermatol. Soc., Am. Gerontol. Soc., Calif. Med. Assn., Ventura County Med. Soc., Alpha Omega Alpha. Home: 5300 Cliffside Circle Ventura CA 93003

LINDSAY, RICHARD PAUL, artist, jewelry designer; b. Aurora, Colo., Nov. 21, 1945; s. Paul Francis and Geraldine Evelyn (Goulet) L.; m. Susan Lynn Greenwood, Dec. 28, 1982; 1 child, Jared Nicholas. BA in Polit. Sci., Colo. State U., 1967. Profl. ski patrol Santa Fe (N.M.) Ski Basin, 1974-80; prin. Richard Lindsay Designs, Santa Fe, 1973—. Copyrighted designs include Walking Trout (R), Happy Critters (R), Roadkill Rabbit (R), Kachina Klan (R); exhibited in numerous galleries, N.Y.C., Colo., N.M., Tex., France, also others. Served to lt. U.S. Army, 1968-71, Vietnam. Recipient Design award Silversmith Santa Fe Film Festival, 1983, Best Ad Yr., Colo. Press Assn., 1972; decorated bronze star, Army Commendation medal. Mem. Jewelers Bd. of Trade. Office: Richard Lindsay Designs 1404 Luisa St Ste 4 Santa Fe NM 87501

LINDSAY, SHANNON DAVID, architect; b. Nassau, New Providence, Bahamas, Dec. 21, 1962; s. Miltol and Hazel (Thompson) L. Student, Howard U., 1981-86, U. London, 1977-79; BArch, 1986. Draftsman Leroy Brown Assoc., Washington, 1984-85, Austin Spriggs Assoc., Washington, 1985-86; designer Interior Architect Inc., San Francisco, 1986-87; cons., architect Design Staff Inc., Oakland, Calif., 1987-88; mgr. project Kardan Constrn. Inc., Oakland, 1988—; project designer, CADD technician Designers Collective, Oakland, 1988—. Home: 1134 Chatham Rd09 Oakland CA 94610 Office: Designers Collective 1201 Park Ave Ste 204 Oakland CA 94608

LINDSAY, WILLARD LYMAN, soil science researcher, educator; b. Dingle, Idaho, Apr. 7, 1926; s. William Henry and Phoebe May (Humpherys) L.; m. Lorna Lance, Nov. 19, 1951; children: Diane, Janice, Cheryl, Calvin Willard. BS, Utah State U., 1952, MS, 1953; PhD, Cornell U., 1956. Grad. research asst. Utah State U., Logan, 1952-53; grad. research and teaching asst. Cornell U., Ithaca, N.Y., 1953-56; research soil chemist TVA, Muscle Shoals, Ala., 1956-60; from asst. prof. to prof. soil scientist Colo. State U., Ft. Collins, 1960-70, Centennial prof. agronomy, 1970—; cons. in field, 1966—. Author: Chemical Equilibria in Soils, 1979; contbr. articles to profl. jours.; author scientific papers. Served with USN, 1945-46. Fellow Geigy Travel, Scotland, 1966, Geigy Travel, Australia, 1968; recipient Andrew G. Clark award Colo. State U., 1970, Shepardson Outstanding Teaching award, 1983, Burlington Northern Faculty Achievement award 1985; nominee USDA Superior Service award 1987. Fellow Am. Soc. Agronomy, Soil Sci. Soc. Am. (co-author: Micronutrients in Agriculture, 1972); mem. Internat. Soil Sci. Soc., Western Soil Sci. Soc., Soc. Environ. Geochem. and Health, Sigma Xi, Phi Kappa Phi, Gamma Sigma Delta, Delta Phi Kappa. Mormon. Home: 208 Tulane Dr Fort Collins CO 80525 Office: Colo State U Dept Agronomy Fort Collins CO 80523

LINDSAY, WILLIAM EDWARD, manufacturing engineer; b. Newhall, Calif., May 16, 1948; s. Newton Edward and Bertie Cathilene (Throgmorton) L.; m. Donna Estells, Apr. 3, 1978 (div. May 1979); 1 child, William E. II; m. Laurie Annette Felton, May 19, 1979; 1 child, Jeffrey. AA, Ventura Coll., 1968. Indsl. engr. Fansteel Reflective Laminates, Newbury Park, Calif., 1966-76; owner The We-Do-It Shop, Lone Pine, Calif., 1976-79; mechanic Cyprus Bagdad, Bagdad, Ariz., 1980-83; indsl. engr. McDonnell-Douglas Helicopter Mfg. Co., Mesa, Ariz., 1984—. Home: 6545 E Rustic Dr Mesa AZ 85205 Office: McDonnell-Douglas Helicopter Mfg Co 5000 E McDowell Rd Mesa AZ 85205

LINDSAY, WILLIAM NEISH, III, insurance company executive; b. Hartford, Conn., Aug. 24, 1947; s. William N. Jr. and Margaret A. (Fraser) L.; m. Pamela J. Laine (div.); children: William N., Elizabeth Ruth; m. Camilla M. Falotico, Dec. 16, 1978; children: Katherine Anne, Sarah Fraser. BA, Gettysburg Coll., 1969. CLU. Asst. regional dir. Aetna Life & Casualty, Hartford, Conn., 1972-74; tng. specialist Aetna Life & Casualty, Hartford, 1974-75; dir., sales edn. Aetna Life & Casualty, 1975-78; brokerage gen. agt. Aetna Life & Casualty, Denver, 1978-81, gen. mgr., Rocky Mt. branch, 1981-84; pres. Benefit Mgmt. & Design, Inc., Denver, 1984—; gen. mgr. Aetna Life & Casualty, Hartford, 1983-84; adv. coun. Personal Fin. Security Div.; cons. Robert Wood Johnson Found., Denver, 1985-89. Capt. USMC, 1969-72, Vietnam. Mem. Nat. Assn. Life Underwriters, CLU Assn., Greater Denver C. of C. (bd. mem. 1989—), Jr. Achievement of Colo. (bd. mem. 1982-86), Phi Gamma Delta (pres. 1981-84, Denver Grad. Chpt.). Republican. Roman Catholic. Home: 8247 S Jasmine Ct Englewood CO 80112 Office: Benefit Mgmt & Design Inc 6025 S Quebec Ste 220 Englewood CO 80111

LINDSEY, GARY PHILIP, legal investigator, photographer; b. Washington, Mar. 14, 1947; s. Frank Charles Sr. and Audrey Elizabeth (Miller) L.; m. Natalie Suzanne Colley, Aug. 31, 1968; Gary Philip Jr., Nathan Miller. Cert., New Thing Art & Archl. Ctr., 1973; BA in Communications, D.C. U., 1972; MA in Communications, Howard U., 1983; MA in Criminal Justice, Calif. State U., Sacramento, 1988. Profl. photographer Neighborhood Consumer Info. Ctr., Washington, 1965-73; sports, news reporter Washington Afro-Am. Newspaper, Washington, 1966-70; sports reporter Washington Evening Star Newspaper, 1970-74; legal investigator Colley Lindsey Colley Law Office, Sacramento, 1974—; instr. self def. for women, photographer Glamour World, 1983—. Author: Something Else

About Photography, 1984; columnist: The Lockerroom. Mem. Am. Taekwondo Assn. (instr. 1986—, author press releases for schs. 1977-79, 83—, recipient numerous awards, honors), Omega Psi Phi (pub. rels. writer 1976-88). Democrat. Congregationalist. Home: 5613 Delcliff Circle Sacramento CA 95822 Office: Glamour World Prodns 2743 Franklin Blvd Sacramento CA 95817

LINDSEY, JOHN HALL, JR., software company executive; b. Malvern, Ark., July 29, 1938; s. John Hall and Jeannette Francis (Stuart) L.; m. Renetta Louise Harms, July 14, 1962; children: Sabra, Lemecia, Lance. Student, Ark. Poly. U., 1956-58, Okla. State U., 1958-60; BS in Bus., U. Utah, 1964; MBA, U. So. Calif., 1968. Data base mgr. NCR corp., Rancho Bernardo, Calif., 1966-75; data base adminstr. Kal Kan Foods, Vernon, Calif., 1975-77; data base supr. Kaiser Steel, Fontana, Calif., 1977-79; mgr. data base and tech. support Western Gear, Lynwood, Calif., 1979-84; mgr., sr. cons. data base Citicorp/TTI, Santa Monica, Calif., 1984-86; prin. Lindsey & Assocs., Eureka, Calif., 1986-88; ptnr. Lindsey/Milligan Cos., Houston; mem. computer adv. com. Ontario/Montclaire Schs., Calif., 1980-82; mem. industry advisor Cullinet Corp., Westwood, Mass., 1986—; bd. dirs. IDMS User Assn., Westminster, chmn. large users adv. com., 1985-88; bd. dirs. S.W. User Assn., Los Angeles; guest lectr. U. So. Calif., 1975-76. Author: IDMS DB Design Review, 1982. Elder local Presbyn. Ch., 1980-82; vol. Culver City (Calif.) YMCA, 1986, Santa Monica (Calif.) Real Soccer Club, 1985-86; pres. Mt. Baldy Swim Team, Upland, Calif., 1975-80; bd. dirs. Ontario Community Credit Union, 1979-80. Served with USNG, 1956-64. Mem. IDMS User Assn., S.W. Area IDMS User Assn. (chmn. 1982-84), Assn. System Mgmt. (v.p. 1966-68), Soc. for Mgmt. Info. (co-founder 1979), Eureka C. of C. (Humboldt pvt. industry coun.). Home and Office: 10 W Seventh St Ste 202 Eureka CA 95501

LINDSTRAND, DOUGLAS WILLARD, artist; b. Winthrop, Minn., July 5, 1943; s. August Joel and Blandina H. (Draeger) L.; m. Patti Faye Herron, Nov. 15, 1982. BFA, Mankato U., 1968. Artist Dart Corp., Mpls., 1968-70; artist and owner Sourdough Studio, Anchorage, 1970—. Author and artist: Alaskan Sketchbook # 1, 1981, Alaskan Sketchbook # 2, 1984, Alaskan ABC-Numbers Book, 1985, Sourdough Snow and the Magic Valley, 1985. Sgt. Paratroopers, U.S. Army, 1965-68, Vietnam. Republican. Lutheran. Office: Sourdough Studio 2000 E Dowling Rd # 5 Anchorage AK 99507

LINDSTROM, NINA LUCILLE, school administrator, director; b. Cleveland, Tenn., Dec. 9, 1940; d. Noah Haskins Jones and Grace (Mae) Burke; m. Larry Lance Lindstrom, June 26, 1966; children: Anton Lee, Kristina Mae. BS in Edn., Biology, U. Tenn., 1963; MS in Edn., Portland (Oreg.) State U., 1970. Cert. tchr., Oreg., Calif. Tchr. sci. Hudson Sch. Dist., LaPuente, Calif., 1963-64, Baldwin (Calif.) Park Dist., 1964-67; tchr. biology Beaverton Sch. Dist. 48, Portland, 1968-70; student tchr. supr. Portland State U., 1971; tchr. Portland Community Coll., 1971-72; prin., dir., founder Belmont Sch., Portland, 1973—; co-owner Riverview Properties, Portland, 1973—; v.p. Mt. Park Vet. Clinic, Lake Oswego, 1978—. Chmn. Sunnyside Neighborhood, Portland, 1987; childcare advisor Portland Pub. Schs., 1976-87. Mem. Portland C. of C. (distinguished service award 1985), Belmont Bus. Assn. (treas. 1985-86, sec. 1986-87, pres. 1989—), Oreg. Fedn. Pvt. Schs. (pre-sch. com. 1986-87, treas. 1988-89, sec. 1989—). Republican. Baptist. Office: Belmont Sch 3841 SE Belmont Portland OR 97219

LINDZEY, GARDNER, psychologist, educator; b. Wilmington, Del., Nov. 27, 1920; s. James and Marguerite (Shotwell) L.; m. Andrea Lewis, Nov. 28, 1944; children: Jeffrey, Leslie, Gardner, David, Jonathan. AB, Pa. State U., 1943, MS, 1945; PhD, Harvard U., 1949. Research analyst OSRD, 1944-45; instr. psychology Pa. State U., 1945-46; teaching fellow Harvard U., Cambridge, Mass., 1946-47, research fellow, 1947-49, research assoc., asst. prof., 1949-53, lectr., chmn. psychol. clinic staff, 1953-56, prof., chmn. dept., 1972-73; prof. psychology Syracuse (N.Y.) U., 1956-57, U. Minn., 1957-64; prof. psychology U. Tex., 1964-72, chmn., 1964-68, v.p. acad. affairs, 1968-70, v.p. ad interim, 1971, v.p., dean Grad. Studies, prof. psychology, 1973-75; dir. Ctr. for Advanced Study in Behavioral Scis., Stanford (Calif.) U., 1975—; mem. psychopharmacology study sect. NIMH, 1958-62, mem. program-project com., 1963-67, mem. adv. com. on extramural research, 1968-71; mem. com. faculty research fellowships Social Sci. Research Council, 1960-63, bd. dirs., 1962-76, mem. com. problems and policy, 1963-70, 72-76, chmn., 1965-70, mem. exec. com., 1970-75, chmn., 1971-75, mem. com. genetics and behavior, 1961-67, chmn., 1961-65; mem. com. biol. bases social behavior, 1967—; mem. com. work and personality in middle years, 1972-77; mem. sociology and social psychology panel NSF, 1965-68, mem. spl. commn. social scis., 1968-69, mem. adv. com. research, 1974—, mem. Waterman award com., 1976—; mem. exec. com., assembly behavioral and social sci. Nat. Acad. Sci.-NRC, 1970—, mem. com. life sci. and pub. policy, 1968-74, mem. panel nat. needs for biomed. and behavioral research personnel, 1974—, mem. com. social sci. in NSF, 1975—, mem. Inst. Medicine, 1975—; mem. com. on drug abuse Office Sci. and Tech., 1962-63; mem. Presdl. Com. Nat. Medal Sci., 1966-69; bd. dirs. Found.'s Fund Research in Psychiatry, 1967-70; bd. dirs. Am. Psychol. Found., 1968-76, v.p., 1971-73, pres., 1974-76. Author: (with Hall) Theories of Personality, 1957, 70, 78; (with Allport and Vernon) Study of Values, 1951, 60; Projective Techniques and Cross-Cultural Research, 1961; (with J.C. Loehlin and J.N. Spuhler) Race Differences in Intelligence, 1975; (with C.S. Hall and R.F. Thompson) Psychology, 1975; also articles; editor: Handbook of Social Psychology, Vols. 1 and 2, 1954, Vols. 1-5, 1969, Assessment of Human Motives, 1958, Contemporary Psychology, 1967-73, History of Psychology in Autobiography, Vol. 6, 1974; assoc. editor Psychol. Abstracts, 1960-62, Ency. Social Scis., 1962-67; co-editor Century Psychology Series, 1960-74, Theories of Personality: Primary Sources and Research, 1965, History of Psychology in Autobiography, Vol. V, 1968, Behavioral Genetics: Methods and Research, 1969, Contributions to Behavior-Genetic Analysis, 1970. Fellow Ctr. Advanced Study Behavioral Scis., Stanford, 1955-56, 63-64, 71-72, Inst. Medicine, 1975—. Fellow Am. Psychol. Assn. (bd. dirs. 1962-68, 70-74, mem. publs. bd., 1956-59, 70-73, chmn. 1958-59, mem. council of reps. 1959-67, 68-74, pres. div. social and personality psychology 1963-64, mem. policy and planning 1975, 78, pres. assn. 1966-67, mem. council of editors 1968-73, chmn. com. sci. award 1968-69, pres. div. gen. psychology 1970-71), Am. Acad. Arts and Scis., Am. Philos. Soc., AAAS, Am. Sociol. Assn.; mem. Am. Eugenics Soc. (bd. dirs. 1962-70), Soc. Social Biology (bd. dirs. 1972—, pres. 1978—), Am. Psychol. Assn. (dir. ins. trust 1973—), Univs. Research Assn. (bd. dirs. 1973-75). Club: Cosmos. Home: 890 Robb Rd Palo Alto CA 94306

LINFORD, LAURANCE DEE, cultural organization administrator; b. Cheyenne, Wyo., Mar. 2, 1951; s. Dee Verl and Helen Grace (Bagley) L.; m. Karen Page Stephens, Nov. 23, 1971; children: Justin D., Micah Robert. BA, U. N.Mex., 1973; MA, U. Ariz., 1978. Archaeologist Sch. Am. Research, Santa Fe, 1967-75, Ariz. State Mus., Tucson, 1975-77, Nat. Park Service, Tucson, 1977-78, Navajo Nation, Window Rock, Ariz., 1978-82; exec. dir. Inter-Tribal Indian Ceremonial Assn., Gallup, N.Mex., 1982—; bd. dirs. St. Michaels (Ariz.) Hist. Mus., 1979-86. Author, editor; The Pinon Project, 1982. Pres. Indian Country Tourism Coun., 1982-86; mem. tourism com. Gallup McKinley County Chamber, 1985-86; bd. dirs. Gallup Conv. and Visitors Bur., 1987—. Mem. N.Mex. Assn. Execs. Democrat. Office: Inter-Tribal Indian Ceremonial Assn PO Box 1 Church Rock NM 87311

LING, SHUI-CHEUNG CHARLES, microelectronic engineer; b. Shanghai, Republic of China, May 15, 1952; came to U.S., 1971; BS in Physics, U. Hawaii, 1975, MS in Info. & Computer Sci., 1978. CAD engr., Microelectronic Components Div. Burroughs Corp., Rancho Bernardo, Calif., 1979-81; design automation engr., LSI products div. TRW Corp., La Jolla, Calif., 1981-85; CAD/CAE mgr. Brooktree Corp., San Diego, 1985—. Mem. IEEE. Office: Brooktree Corp 9950 Barnes Canyon Rd San Diego CA 92121

LING, THEODORE JAMES, civil engineer; b. Inglewood, Calif., Apr. 18, 1941; s. Myron T. and Isabell Alberta (Deming) L.; m. Patricia Ann Williams, Aug. 21, 1965 (div. 1984); children: Morgan Williams, Jason Theodore. BCE, Calif. State U.-Long Beach, 1965, MCE, 1968. Engr., Bur. Engring. City of Los Angeles, 1965-67; plant engr. Ford Motor Co., Pico Rivera, Calif., 1968-81; project engr. Varco, Orange, Calif., 1981-82, Hydril, San Francisco Springs, Calif., 1982-83; facility engr. Toyota Motors, Long Beach, Calif., 1983—; cons. facility engr. Garrett Air Research, Torrance, Calif., 1987-88. Editor mag. Computers in Drafting, 1988. Mem. Sigma Nu. Republican. Home: 1645 Clark Ave #218 Long Beach CA 90815 Office: Toyota Auto Body Inc Calif 6375 Paramount Blvd Long Beach CA 90801

LINN, BRIAN JAMES, lawyer; b. Seattle, July 8, 1947; s. Bruce Hugh and Jeanne De V. (Weidman) L.; m. Renee Dianne Mousley; children—Kelly, Kareem, Kari. B.A. in Econs., U. Wash., 1972; J.D., Gonzaga Sch. Law, 1975. Bar: Wash. 1975. Mng. atty. Legal Services for Northwestern Pa., Franklin, 1975-76; staff atty. The Nat. Ctr. for Law and the Handicapped, 1976-78, U. Notre Dame Law Sch., South Bend, Ind., 1976-78; pvt. practice, Seattle, 1978—; lectr. Seattle U., 1980-85. Chmn. civil and legal rights subcom. Gov.'s Com. on Employment of the Handicapped, 1981-87; mem. Wash. State Devel. Disabilities Planning Council, 1980-83; trustee Community Service Ctr. for the Deaf and Hard of Hearing, Seattle, 1982-84; chmn. legal rights task force Epilepsy Found. Am., 1979-81. Editor Gonzaga Law Rev., 1973-75. Served with U.S. Army, 1967-69; Vietnam. Mem. Wash. State Bar Assn. (exec. com. world peace through law sect.), Washington State Trial Lawyers Assn., Omicron Delta Epsilon. Democrat. Methodist. Hon. editor DePaul Law Rev., 1978; contbr. articles to profl. jours. Home: 21211 21st Ave S Seattle WA 98188 Office: 245 SW 152d St Seattle WA 98166

LINN, CAROLE ANNE, dietitian; b. Portland, Oreg., Mar. 3, 1945; d. James Leslie and Alice Mae (Thorburn) L. Intern, U. Minn., 1967-68; BS, Oreg. State U., 1963-67. Nutrition cons. licensing and cert. sect. Oreg. State Bd. Health, Portland, 1968-70; chief clin. dietitian Rogue Valley Med. Ctr., Medford, Oreg., 1970—; cons. Hillhaven Health Care Ctr., Medford, 1971-83; lectr. Local Speakers Bur., Medford. Mem. Am. Dietetic Assn., Am. Diabetic Assn., Oreg. Dietetic Assn. (sec. 1973-75, nominating com. 1974-75, young dietitian of yr. 1976), Oreg. diabetic Assn., Alpha Lambda Delta, Omicron Nu. Democrat. Mem. Christ Unity Ch. Office: Rogue Valley Med Ctr 2825 Barnett Rd Medford OR 97504

LINN, GEORGE BYRON, academic administrator, writer; b. Hillmont, Wyo., Aug. 19, 1913; s. George Toney and Laura Adelaide (Osborn) L.; m. Ruby Fonda, Aug. 6, 1938 (dec. Mar. 1973); 1 child, Kent Landen; m. Reta Nayoma Faler, June 28, 1977. BA, U. Wyo., 1936, MA, 1941; postgrad., U. Wash., 1955; EdD, U. So. Calif., 1965. Speech instr. U. Wyo., Laramie, 1937-38; tchr. various schs., Wyo., 1938-42; supt. various schs., Oreg. and Ak., 1942-1954; instr. U. Ariz., Tucson, 1946-47; speech clinician Santa Paula (Calif.) Sch. Dist., 1955-59; adminstr. Cerebral Palsy Sch., Santa Paula (Calif.) Sch. Dist., 1960-62; coordinator of spl. edn. South Bay Area Sch. Dists., Redondo Beach, Calif., 1962-66; dir. of spl. edn. Ventura County (Calif.) Supt. of Schs. Office, 1966-78; lectr. Calif. Luth. Coll., Thousand Oaks, 1975; ret. 1978. Author: Broadax Artists, 1984; contbr. articles to profl. jours. Recipient cert. of appreciation Ventura County Assn. for the Retarded, 1967, hon. membership Ventura County Council for Neurological Handicapped Children, 1968, award for service to exceptional Children Ventura County Council For Exceptional Children, 1977, Outstanding Service award Calif. State Dept. of Edn., 1978. Mem. NEA, Calif. Tchrs. Assn., AAAS, Am. Speech-Lang.-Hearing Assn., Calif. Speech and Hearing Assn., Delta Sigma Rho, Delta Epsilon. Democrat. Presbyterian. Lodges: Kiwanis (pres. East Ventura, Calif. Club 1974-75; lt. gov. 1977-78), Masons. Home: 1229 Woodland Dr Santa Paula CA 93060

LINN, STUART MICHAEL, biochemist, educator; b. Chgo., Dec. 16, 1940; s. Maurice S. and Pauline L.; m. Priscilla K. Cooper; children: Matthew S., Allison D., Meagan S. B.S. with honors in Chemistry, Calif. Inst. Tech., 1962; Ph.D. in Biochemistry, Stanford U., 1967. Asst. prof. biochemistry U. Calif., Berkeley, 1968-72, assoc. prof., 1972-75, prof., 1975-87, head div. Biochemistry and Molecular Biology, 1987—. Mem. editorial bd.: Nucleic Acids Research, 1974—, Molecular and Cellular Biology, 1987—; mem. editorial bd.: Jour. Biol. Chemistry, 1975-80; contbr. articles to profl. jours., chpts. to books. Helen Hay Whitney fellow, 1966-68; John Simon Guggenheim fellow, 1974-75; recipient USPHS Merit Grant award, 1988—. Mem. Am. Soc. Biol. Chemists, Am. Soc. Microbiologists, AAAS. Office: U Calif Dept Biochemistry Berkeley CA 94720

LINSSEN, ROBERT JOSEPH, finance company executive; b. Green Bay, Wis., Mar. 23, 1940; s. Robert Philip and Cecelia Ann (Allen) L.; m. Arlene Ann Vanden Heuvel, Aug. 18, 1962; children: Sheryl, Victoria, Jeffrey, Renee, Craig. BEE, Marquette U., 1965; MBA, Mich. Tech. U., 1976. Registered profl. engr., Wis.; registered investment advisor. Staff engr. Wis. Elec. Power Co., Milw., 1962-66; sr. engr. Wis. Elec. Power Co., Appleton, Wis., 1966-69; engring. supr. Wis. Elec. Power Co., Iron Mountain, Mich., 1969-78; engring. supr. Ariz. Pub. Service Co., Phoenix, 1978-81, engring. mgr., 1981-86; v.p. Corp. Assistance Inc., Scottsdale, Ariz., 1986—; bd. dirs. Ariz. Blue Stake, Inc., Phoenix, 1981-84, Am. Pub. Works Assn., Phoenix, 1980-83. Mem. Inst. Cert. Fin. Planners, IEEE, Elks, K.C., Greater Paradise Valley C. of C. (pres. 1988, bd. dirs. 1982—), Rotary (pres. Paradise Valley chpt. 1987, bd. dirs. 1984-88). Republican. Roman Catholic. Home: 2735 E Ironwood Dr Phoenix AZ 85028 Office: Corp Assistance Inc 8070 E Morgan Trail #120 Scottsdale AZ 85258

LINSTONE, CLARK RAYMOND, banker; b. L.A., Feb. 9, 1958; s. Harold Adrian and Hedy (Schubach) L. BA, Claremont (Calif.) U., 1979; MBA, U. So. Calif., L.A., 1985. With Union Bank, L.A., 1979—, v.p. asset based fin. div., 1985-88, v.p. loan adminstrn., 1988—. Mem. Claremont McKenna Coll. Alumni Assn. (bd. dirs. 1979—), Robert Morris Assocs., Beta Gamma Delta. Office: Union Bank 445 S Figueroa St Los Angeles CA 90051

LINTHICUM, GARY REX, construction company executive; b. Tulsa, Mar. 3, 1940; s. Rex R. and Theo Murtle (Mace) L.; m. Dianne Davis, May 28, 1960; children: David, Dana, Eric. BS in Engring. and Constrn., Ariz. State U., 1964; postgrad., U. Ariz., 1974, Stanford U., 1980. Field engr. Craig & Keithline Emgrs., Tulsa, 1960-61; project engr. Kitchell Contractors, Phoenix, 1964, estimator, project mgr., ops. mgr., exec. v.p., pres., 1980-84; pres. Linthicum Constructors Inc., Scottsdale, Ariz., 1984—. Named Mgr. of Yr. City of Scottsdale, 1986. Mem. Associated Gen. Contractors (special contracting methods com. 1980-82, bd. dirs. 1982-83, collective bargaining com. 1983, contract documents coordinating com. 1983, spl. contracting methods com. 1983, chmn. edn. com. Ariz. chpt. 1980-82, bd. dirs. 1982-83, chmn. collective bargaining com. 1982-83, 2d v.p. 1987, 1st v.p. 1988, pres. Ariz. chpt. 1989), Ariz. State Alumni Assn. (bd. dirs. 1983-85). Republican. Methodist. Office: Linthicum Constructors Inc 9322 N 94th Way Suite 102 Scottsdale AZ 85258

LINTON, ARLENE MAE, trade association executive; b. Lynwood, Calif., July 13, 1949; d. Virginia Mae Cassel; children from previous marriage: Brian Scott, Dustin Gabriel. Grad. high sch., Colorado Springs, Colo., 1967. Lic. nursing home adminstr. Adminstrv. asst. Four Seasons Nursing Home, Colorado Springs, 1972-74; adminstr. Springs Valley Recovery Ctrs., Colorado Springs, 1974-83; exec. dir. Colo. Health Care Assn., Denver, 1983—. Apptd. Colo. Legis. Long Term Care Task Force 1988-89, chmn. spl. pop. needs subcom.; mem. Colo. Case Mix Reimbursement Study Com. 1987-89, Fiscal Agt. Evaluation Com., 1988, Alternative Care Devel. Com., 1984-85; mem. long term care adv. com. Dept. Social Svcs., 1984, 85, 86, 87, 88, 89, Colo. Dept. Health, 1986, 87, 88, 89; mem. long term care adv. com. to Rep. Dan Schaeffer. Recipient Disting. Svc. award Long Term Care Industry, 1986. Mem. Am. Soc. Health Care Assn. Execs., Am. Health Care Assn. (nat. payment for svcs. com. 1986, 87. Republican. Lutheran. Office: Colo Health Care Assn 1600 Sherman St #1000 Denver CO 80203

LINTON, STEVEN JAY, public safety diving educator; b. Dalton, Nebr., June 11, 1949; s. Elwin W. and Barbara J. (Cruise) L.; m. Donna Jeanne McLaughlin, June 2, 1984. Student, Colo. State U., 1967-70. Gen. mgr. Midwest Divers Inc., Ft. Collins, Colo., 1971-74; investigator Larimer County Sheriff, Ft. Collins, 1974-77; pres. Dive Rescue Inc. Internat., Ft. Collins, 1977--. Author: Ice Rescue, 1985, Dive Rescue Specialist Training Manual, 1986; contbr. articles to profl. jours. Recipient Leadership Ft. Collins award Ft. Collins C. of C., 1986. Mem. Internat. Assn. Dive Rescue Specialists (bd. dirs. 1980--), Nat. Assn. Search and Rescue (bd. dirs. 1988), Am. Soc. Assn. Execs., Larimer County Dive Rescue Team (pres. 1972--), Sertoma. Republican. Office: Dive Rescue Inc Internat 2619 Canton Ct Fort Collins CO 80525

LINXWILER, LOUIS MAJOR, JR., finance company executive; b. Blackwell, Okla., Mar. 7, 1931; s. Louis Major and Flora Mae (Horton) L.; m. Susan Buchanan, July 27, 1963; children: Louis Major III, Robert William. BS, Okla. State U., 1954. Mgr. credit dept. Valley Nat. Bank, Phoenix, 1957-60; sales rep. Vega Industries, Syracuse, N.Y., 1960-62; program dir. Am. Cancer Soc., Phoenix, 1962-67; v.p., mgr. credit dept. United Bank Ariz., Phoenix, 1967-76; dean edn. Am. Inst. Banking, Phoenix, 1976-80; cons. Phoenix, 1980-81, United Student Aid Funds Inc., Phoenix, 1981-82; pres., chief exec. officer Ariz. Student Loan Fin. Corp., Phoenix, 1982—, also bd. dirs.; chmn., chief exec. officer Western Loan Mktg. Assn., Phoenix, 1984—, also bd. dirs. Editor: Money and Banking, 1978. Pres. City Commn. Sister Cities, Phoenix, 1986-87, Am. Inst. Banking, Phoenix, 1973-74, Phoenix YMCA Bd. Dirs., 1974-75; v.p. North Mountain Behavioral Inst., Phoenix, 1975-77. Served to 1st lt. U.S. Army, 1954-56. Mem. Nat. Council Higher Edn. Loan Programs, Newcomen Soc. Republican. Presbyterian. Club: Arizona (Phoenix). Lodge: Rotary (bd. dirs. 1982-83), Shriners. Office: Western Loan Mktg Assn 6991 E Camelback Ste A200 Scottsdale AZ 85251

LIONAKIS, GEORGE, architect; b. West Hiawatha, Utah, Sept. 5, 1924; s. Pete and Andriani (Protopapadakis) L.; student Carbon Jr. Coll., 1942-43, 46-47; B. Arch., U. Oreg., 1951; m. Iva Oree Braddock, Dec. 30, 1951; 1 dau., Deborah Jo. With Corps Engrs., Walla Walla, Wash., 1951-54; architect Liske, Lionakis, Beaumont & Engberg, Sacramento, 1954—. Mem. Sacramento County Bd. Appeals, 1967—, chmn., 1969, 75, 76; pres. Sacramento Builders Exchange, 1976. Served with USAAF, 1943-46. Mem. AIA (pres. Central Valley chpt., 1972—), Constrn. Specifications Inst. (pres. Sacramento chpt., 1962; nat. awards, 1962, 63, 65), Sacramento C. of C. (code com., 1970—). Club: North Ridge Country (pres. 1987). Lodge: Rotarian (pres. East Sacramento 1978-79). Prin. works include Stockton (Calif.) Telephone Bldg., 1968, Chico (Calif.) Main Telephone Bldg., 1970, Mather AFB Exchange Complex Sacramento, 1970, Base Chapel Mather AFB, Sacramento, 1970, Woodridge Elementary Sch., Sacramento, 1970, Pacific Telephone Co. Operating Center Modesto, Calif., 1968, Sacramento, 1969, Marysville, Calif., 1970, Red Bluff, Calif., 1971, Wells Fargo Banks, Sacramento, 1968, Corning, Calif., 1969, Anderson, 1970, Beale AFB Exchange Complex, Marysville, 1971, Cosumnes River Coll., Sacramento, 1971, base exchanges at Bergstrom AFB, Austin, Tex., Sheppard AFB, Wichita Falls, Tex., Chanute AFB, Rantoul, Ill., McChord AFB, Tacoma, Wash., health center Chico State U., Sacramento County Adminstrn. Center, Sacramento Bee Newspaper Plant. Home: 160 Breckenwood Way Sacramento CA 95825 Office: Lionakis Beaumont Design Group 401 Watt Ave Sacramento CA 95864

LIPKIN, MARY CASTLEMAN DAVIS (MRS. ARTHUR BENNETT LIPKIN), retired psychiatric social worker; b. Germantown, Pa., Mar. 4, 1907; d. Henry L. and Willie (Webb) Davis; student grad. sch. social work U. Wash., 1946-48; m. William F. Cavenaugh, Nov. 8, 1930 (div.); children—Molly C. (Mrs. Gary Oberbillig), William A.; m. 2d, Arthur Bennett Lipkin, Sept. 15, 1961 (dec. June 1974). Nursery sch. tchr. Miquon (Pa.) Sch., 1940-45; caseworker Family Soc. Seattle, 1948-49, Jewish Family and Child Service, Seattle, 1951-56; psychiat. social worker Stockton (Calif.) State Hosp., 1957-58; supr. social service Mental Health Research Inst., Fort Steilacoom, Wash., 1958-59; engaged in pvt. practice, Bellevue, Wash., 1959-61. Former mem. Phila. Com. on City Policy. Former diplomate and bd. mem. Conf. Advancement of Pvt. Practice in Social Work. Mem. Acad. Cert. Social Workers, Nat. Assn. Social Workers, Linus Paul Inst. Sci. and Medicine, Menninger Found., Union Concerned Scientists, Physicians for Social Responsibility, Center for Sci. in Pub. Interest, Jr. League, Seattle Art Mus., Asian Art Council, Wing Luke Mus., Bellevue Art Mus., Pacific Sci. Center, Western Wash. Solar Energy Assn., Nature Conservancy, Wilderness Soc., Sierra Club, Common Cause, ACLU, Pa. Acad. Fine Arts. Clubs: Cosmopolitan, Cricket (Phila.); Women's University (Seattle); Nassau (Princeton, N.J.), Friday Harbor Yacht (Washington). Home: 10022 Meydenbauer Way SE #202 Bellevue WA 98004

LIPMAN-BLUMEN, JEAN CAROL, sociologist, educator; b. Brookline, Mass., Apr. 28, 1933; d. Myer Edward and Ann Ruth (Perlman) L.; m. Louis J. Blumen, Oct. 11, 1953 (div. May 1974); children: Lorna, Lesley, Peter; m. Harold Jack Leavitt, Mar. 19, 1987. AB in English Lit., Wellesley Coll., 1954, AM in Sociology, 1958; Phd in Sociology and Edn., Harvard U., 1970; postgrad. in math. stats., Carnegie-Mellon U., 1971, Stanford U., 1972. Tutor social relations dept. Harvard U., Cambridge, Mass., 1961-63; research asst. social sci. unit Harvard Sch. Pub. Health, Cambridge, 1962-65; research assoc., dir. life plans of married women project Radcliffe Inst., Cambridge, Mass., 1966-72; sr. med. sociologist urban and social systems div. med. ser. Stanford Research Inst., Menlo Park, Calif., 1972-73; asst. dir. Nat. Inst. Edn., dir. women's research program HEW, Washington, 1973-78; spl. advisor domestic policy staff White House, Washington, 1978; fellow in residence Ctr. for Advanced Study in Behavioral Scis., Palo Alto, Calif., 1978-79; sr. assoc. Ctr. for Women Policy Studies, Washington, 1979-82; pres. LBS Internat., Ltd., 1979—; Thornton F. Bradshaw prof. pub. policy and profl. orgnl. Peter F. Drucker Grad. Mgmt. Ctr., Claremont (Calif.) Grad. Sch., 1983—; disting. guest lectr. U. Bergen (Norway), 1976, U. Oslo, 1976; vis. prof. sociology U. Conn., Storrs, 1980; vis. prof. orgnl. behavior and sociology, acting dir. women's studies program U. Md., College Park, Md., 1980-82; vis. research scholar Stanford U. Grad. Sch. Bus., 1987; cons., lectr. presenter in field; guest numerous TV programs, 1970—. Author: Gender Roles and Power, 1984; editor: (with J. Bernard) Sex Roles and Social Policy, 1979; assoc. editor Ednl. Researcher, 1978—; cons. assoc. editor Psychology Women Quar., 1978—; contbr. numerous articles to profl. jours., chpts. to books. Recipient numerous fellowships. Fellow AAAS; mem. Am. Inst. Energy Economists, AAUP, AAUW, Am. Psychol. Assn., Am. Sociol. Assn., Am. Women in Sci., Internat. Inst. Sociology, Internat. Sociol. Assn., NOW, Nat. Women's Polit. Caucus, Sociologists for Women in Soc., Women's Equity Action League. Democrat. Jewish. Office: Claremont Grad Sch Peter F Drucker Grad Mgmt Ctr Jagels Bldg Rm 205 Claremont CA 91711

LIPOMI, MICHAEL JOSEPH, health facility administrator; b. Buffalo, Mar. 9, 1953; s. Dominic Joseph and Betty (Angelo) L.; m. Brenda H. Lipomi, Dec. 23, 1977; children: Jennifer, Barrett. BA, U. Ottawa, 1976. Mktg. dir. Am. Med. Internat. El Cajon Valley Hosp., Calif., 1980-83; dir. corp. devel. Med. Surg. Ctrs. Am., Calif., 1983-85; exec. dir. Stanislaus Surgery Ctr., Modesto, Calif., 1985—. Author: Complete Anatomy of Health Care Marketing, 1988; co-host med. TV talk show Health Talk Modesto. Bd. dirs. Am. Heart Assn., Modesto, 1988—; pres. Modesto Community Hospice, 1987—; active local govt.; sec.-treas. Modesto Industry and Edn. Council. Mem. No. Calif. Assn. Surgery Ctrs. (pres. 1986-88), Federated Ambulatory Surgery Assn. (govt. rels. com. 1988). Lodge: Rotary. Office: Stanislaus Surgery Ctr 1421 Oakdale Rd Modesto CA 95355

LIPPE, PHILIPP MARIA, neurosurgeon, educator; b. Vienna, Austria, May 17, 1929; s. Philipp and Maria (Goth) L.; came to U.S., 1938, naturalized, 1945; m. Virginia M. Wiltgen, 1953 (div. 1977); children: Patricia Ann Marie, Philip Eric Andrew, Laura Lynne Elizabeth, Kenneth Anthony Ernst; m. Gail B. Busch, Nov. 26, 1977. Student Loyola U., Chgo., 1947-50; BS in Medicine, U. Ill. Coll. Medicine, 1952, MD with high honors, 1954. Rotating intern St. Francis Hosp., Evanston, Ill., 1954-55; asst. resident gen. surgery VA Hosp., Hines, Ill., 1955, 58-59; asst. resident neurology and neurol. surgery Neuropsychiat. Inst., U. Ill. Research and Ednl. Hosps., Chgo., 1959-60, chief resident, 1962-63, resident neuropathology, 1962, postgrad. trainee in electroencephalography, 1963; resident neurology and neurol. surgery Presbyn.-St. Luke's Hosp., Chgo., 1960-61; practice medicine, specializing in neurol. surgery, San Jose, Calif., 1963—; instr. neurology and neurol. surgery U. Ill., 1962-63; clin. instr. surgery and neurosurgery Stanford U., 1965-69, clin. asst. prof., 1969-74, clin. assoc. prof., 1974—; staff cons. in neurosurgery O'Connor Hosp., Santa Clara Valley Med. Center, San Jose Hosp., Los Gatos Community Hosp., El Camino Hosp. (all San Jose area); chmn. div. neurosurgery Good Samaritan Hosp, 1989—; founder, exec. dir. Bay Area Pain Rehab. Center, San Jose, 1979—; clin. adviser to Joint Commn. on Accreditation of Hosps.; mem. dist. med. quality rev. com. Calif. Bd. Med. Quality Assurance, 1976-87, chmn., 1976-77. Served to capt. USAF, 1956-58. Diplomate Am. Bd. Neurol. Surgery, Nat. Bd. Med. Examiners. Fellow ACS; mem. AMA (Ho. of Dels. 1981—), Calif. Med. Assn. (Ho. of Dels. 1976-80, sci. bd., council 1979-87, sec. 1981-87), Santa Clara County Med. Soc. (council 1974-81, pres. 1978-79), Chgo. Med.

Soc., Congress Neurol. Surgeons, Calif. Assn. Neurol. Surgeons (dir. 1974-82, v.p. 1975-76, pres. 1977-79), San Jose Surg. Soc., Am. Assn. Neurol. Surgeons (dir. 1983-86, 87—), Western Neurol. Soc., San Francisco Neurol. Soc., Santa Clara Valley Profl. Standards Rev. Orgn. (dir., v.p., dir. quality assurance 1975-83), Fedn. Western Socs. Neurol. Sci., Internat. Assn. for Study Pain, Am. Pain Soc. (founding mem.), Am. Acad. Pain Medicine (sec. 1983-86, pres. 1987-88), Alpha Omega Alpha, Phi Kappa Phi. Contbr. articles to profl. jours. Pioneered med. application centrifugal force using flight simulator. Office: 2100 Forest Ave Ste 106 San Jose CA 95128

LIPPITT, ELIZABETH CHARLOTTE, writer; b. San Francisco; d. Sidney Grant and Stella Lippitt; student Mills Coll., U. Calif.-Berkeley. Writer, performer own satirical monologues; contbr. articles to 85 newspapers including N.Y. Post, Los Angeles Examiner, Orlando Sentinel, Phoenix Republic, also advt. Recipient Congress of Freedom award, 1959, 71-73, 77, 78; writer on nat. and polit. affairs for 85 newspapers including Muncie Star, St. Louis Globe-Democrat, Washington Times, Utah Ind., Jackson News. Mem. Commn. for Free China, Conservative Caucus. Mem. Nat. Assn. R.R. Passengers, Nat. Trust for Hist. Preservation, Am. Security Council, Internat. Platform Assn., Am. Conservative Union, Nat. Antivivisection Soc., High Frontier, For Our Children, Childhelp U.S.A., Free Afghanistan Com., Humane Soc. U.S., Young Ams. for Freedom, 8 antivivisection orgns. Clubs: Metropolitan, Olympic, Commonwealth. Pop singer, recorder song album Songs From the Heart. Home: 2414 Pacific Ave San Francisco CA 94115

LIPPMAN, JOHN AARON, television station executive; b. Chgo., Sept. 12, 1949; s. Jordan Howard and Kaleen Wool L.; m. Barbara Gay Heinen, Aug. 24, 1977 (div. 1980); 1 dau., Sarah Rosanne; m. Julie Jueling Neff, June 15, 1984; stepchildren: Britt Jueling, John David. A.B., Dartmouth Coll., 1971; pastgrad. Am. Mgmt. Assn., 1982-83; Notre Dame, 1985. Intern Sta. WBZ-TV, Boston, 1970; news reporter, anchorman Sta. KING-TV, Seattle, 1971-76; news and pub. affairs dir. Sta. KSTW-TV, Tacoma, Wash., 1976-79; v.p., TV news dir. Sta. KIRO-TV, Seattle, 1979-86, exec. v.p. news, 1986—. Active Leadership Tomorrow, Seattle, 1983-84, Alumni Bd. of Leadership Tomorrow, 1988; bd. dirs. Wash. Research Council, 1985—, Seattle Urban League, 1988—. Recipient Best Newscast in U.S.A. award, UPI, 1984, Better Understanding award Wash. Edn. Assn., 1978; Wash. Internat. fellow, 1986-87. Mem. Radio TV News Dirs. Assn., World Affairs Coun. Washington, Nat. Broadcast Editorial Assn., Nat. Acad. TV Arts and Scis. (Emmy for news 1983, 84, 85), Wash. AP Broadcasters Assn. (pres. Seattle 1982-85, bd. dirs.), Wash. Club, Broadmoor Golf Club. Athletic. Office: Sta KIRO-TV 2807 3d Ave Seattle WA 98111

LIPPOLD, ROLAND WILL, surgeon; b. Staunton, Ill., May 1, 1916; s. Frank Carl and Ella (Immenroth) L.; m. Margaret Cookson, June 1, 1947; children: Mary Ellen Lippold Elvick, Catherine Anne Lippold Rolf, Carol Sue Lippold Webber. Diplomate Am. Bd. Surgery. Intern Grant Hosp., Chgo., 1941-42, resident in surgery, 1942-43, 47-48; resident in surgery St. Francis Hosp., Evanston, Ill., 1946-47; fellow in pathology Cook County Hosp., Chgo., 1947-48, resident in surgery, 1949-50; practice medicine specializing in surgery Chgo., 1950-53; also asst. in anatomy U. Ill., Chgo., 1950-53; practice medicine specializing in surgery Sacramento, 1953-68; chief med. officer No. Reception Ctr.-Clinic, Calif. Youth Authority, Sacramento, 1954-68, chief med. services, 1968-79; cons. in med. care in correctional instns.; cons. Calif. State Personnel Bd. Contbr. articles to med. publs. Chmn. Calif. Expn. Hall of Health, 1971-72. Comdr. M.C., USNR, 1943-73, PTO. Mem. Sacramento Surg. Soc., Sacramento County Med. Soc., Calif. Med. Assn., AMA, Assn. Mil. Surgeons U.S., Sacramento Hist. Soc. (life). Republican. Lutheran. Home: 1811 Eastern Ave Sacramento CA 95864

LIPSCOMB, ANNA ROSE FEENY, hotel executive; b. Greensboro, N.C., Oct. 29, 1945; d. Nathan and Matilda (Carotenuto) L. B.A. in English and French summa cum laude, Queens Coll., 1977. Reservations agt. Am. Airlines, St. Louis, 1968-69, ticket agt., 1969-71; coll. rep. CBS, Holt Rinehart Winston, Providence, 1977-79, sr. acquisitions editor Dryden Press, Chgo., 1979-81; owner, mgr. Taos Inn, N.Mex., 1981—; bd. dirs. N.Mex. Hotel and Motel Assn., 1986—; sem. leader Taos Women Together, 1989. Editor: Intermediate Accounting, 1980; Business Law, 1981. Contbr. articles to profl. jours. Bd. dirs., 1st v.p. Taos Arts Assn., 1982-85; founder, bd. dirs. Taos Spring Arts Celebration, 1983—; founder, dir. Meet-the-Artist Series, 1983—; bd. dirs. and co-founder Spring Arts N.Mex., 1986; founder Yuletide in Taos, 1988, A Taste of Taos, 1988; bd. dirs. Music from Angel Fire, 1988—; founding mem. Assn. Hist. Hotels, Boulder, 1983—; organizer Internat. Symposium on Arts, 1985; bd. dirs. Arts in Taos, 1983, Taoschool, Inc., 1985—. Recipient Outstanding English Student of Yr. award Queens Coll., 1977; named Single Outstanding Contributor to the Arts in Taos, 1986. Mem. Millicent Rogers Mus. Assn., Taos Lodgers Assn. (mktg. task force 1989), Taos Restaurant Assn., Taos County C. of C. (1st v.p. 1988-89, bd. dirs. 1987—, advt. com. 1987-90, chmn. nominating com. 1989), Internat. Platform Assn., Phi Beta Kappa. Democrat. Home: Talpa Rte Taos NM 87571 Office: Taos Inn PO Drawer N Taos NM 87571

LIPSKY, IAN DAVID, contracting executive; b. Bklyn., May 26, 1957; s. Eugene Herman and Janet Dorothy (Heller) L. BS in Marine Engring., Maine Maritime Acad., 1979. Commd. 2nd lt. USNR, 1979; third asst. engr. Interlake Steamship Co., Cleve., 1979-81; port engr. Exxon Internat. Co., Florham Park, N.J., 1981-84; prodn. supr. Alfred Conhagen Inc. Calif., Hercules, 1984-87, gen. mgr., 1987-89, v.p., 1989—. Mem. Soc. Naval Architects & Marine Engrs., Marine Port Engrs. N.Y., Inst. Marine Engrs., Port Engrs. San Francisco. Democrat. Jewish. Home: 153 Koch Rd Corte Madera CA 94925 Office: Alfred Conhagen Inc Calif 444 Railroad Ave Hercules CA 94529

LIPSON, MELVIN ALAN, chemical company executive; b. Providence, R.I., June 1, 1936; s. Nathan and Esta (Blumenthal) L.; m. Jacqueline Ann Barclay, July 2, 1961; children: Donna, Robert, Michelle, Judith. BS, U. R.I., 1957; PhD, Syracuse U., 1963. Chemist ICI Organics, Providence, 1963, Philip A. Hunt Chem. Co., Lincoln, R.I., 1964-67; rsch. mgr. Philip A. Hunt Chem. Co., Lincoln, 1967-69; tech. dir. Dynachem div. Morton Thiokol Inc., Tustin, Calif., 1969-72; v.p. Morton Thiokol Inc., Tustin, 1979-82, sr. v.p., 1972-82, 1982-85, exec. v.p., 1985-86, pres., 1986-89; v.p. technology devel. Specialty Chemicals Group Morton Internat. Inc., Tustin, 1989—. Home: 1715 Plaza del Sur Newport Beach CA 92661 Office: Morton Thiokol Inc Specialty Chemicals Group 2631 Michelle Dr Tustin CA 92680

LIPSTONE, HOWARD HAROLD, television production executive; b. Chgo., Apr. 28, 1928; s. Lewis R. and Ruth B. (Fischer) L.; m. Jane A. Nudelman, Apr. 7, 1957; children—Lewis, Gregory. BS in Cinema, U. So. Calif., 1950. Asst. to gen. mgr. Sta. KTLA, Los Angeles, 1950-54, program dir. Sta. KNBC-TV, Los Angeles, 1955-61; film and program dir. Sta. KABC-TV, Los Angeles, 1954-63, exec. asst. to pres., exec. producer Selmur Prodns., Inc. subs. ABC-TV, Los Angeles, 1963-69, exec. v.p. Ivan Tors Films and Studios, Inc., 1969-70, pres. Alan Landsburg Prodns., Inc., Los Angeles, 1970-85, pres. The Landsburg Co., Los Angeles, 1985—. Mem. Soc. Motion Picture and TV Engrs., ATAS, Motion Picture Acad. Arts and Scis. Club: Radio of Am. Office: The Landsburg Co 11811 W Olympic Blvd Los Angeles CA 90064

LIQUIDO, NICANOR JAVIER, entomology educator; b. Calamba, Philippines, Jan. 10, 1953; s. Francisco Lajara Liquido and Isidra (Mailom) Javier; m. Susan Heftel, Apr. 14, 1984. BS in Applied Zoology, Entomology and Microbiology, U. Philippines, 1975, MS in Entomology and Genetics, 1978; PhD in Entomology and Biometry, U. Hawaii, 1982. Instr. in biology and Entomology U. Philippines, Los Baños, 1976-77; sr. rsch. asst. The Internat. Rice Rsch. Inst., Los Baños, 1978-79; mem. rsch. faculty U. Ill., Champaign, 1983-85; mem. grad. faculty U. Hawaii-Manoa, Honolulu, 1985—; rsch. entomologist Agrl. Rsch. Svc. USDA, Hilo, Hawaii, 1985—; lectr. Internat. Atomic Energy Agy. Guatemala; cons. Food and Agr. Orgn. U.N., Mex., Venezuela, 1987-89. Editor The Exuviae Quar. newsletter, 1978; corr. The Weekly Notes newsletter U. Philippines, 1977-78; contbr. articles to profl. jours. Fellow Ill. Natural Hist. Survey, Champaign, 1983-85; East-West Ctr. scholar, Honolulu, 1979-82; grantee Kasetsart U., Thailand, U. Hawaii, East-West Ctr., 1981. Mem. AAAS, Entomol. Soc. Am. (chair subsect. Ecology, Bionomics and Behavior), Entomol. Soc. Can., Ecol. Soc. Am., Hawaiian Entomol. Soc. (sec.), Am. Inst. Biol. Scis., Assn. Philippine Entomologists, Pest Control Council of Philippines, Hawaii Acad. Sci., N.Y. Acad. Scis., Sigma Xi (pres. Hilo chpt.), Gamma Sigma Delta, Phi Sigma. Roman Catholic. Club: Yacht (Hilo). Home: 2296 Kalanianaole Ave Hilo HI 96720 Office: USDA Agrl Rsch Svc PO Box 4459 Hilo HI 96720

LIRA, SUZANNE MARIE, accountant; b. Pueblo, Colo., Apr. 15, 1963; d. John Francis and Gloria Mary (Weinman) Crist. BSBA in Acctg., U. So. Colo., 1985. Acct. ABLE Internat., Pueblo, 1985-86, Energy Fuels Coal, Inc., Florence, Colo., 1987—. Mem. Nat. Assn. Accts., Golden Z Club, Omicron Delta Epsilon, Alpha Chi. Republican. Roman Catholic. Home: 125 Abarr Dr Pueblo CO 81007

LIRELY, SAMUEL CHRISTOPHER, corporate professional; b. Cape Girardeau, Mo., Nov. 24, 1941; s. Samuel Albert and Dorothy Berniece (Hinck) L. BA, U. Tulsa, 1964; MBA, UCLA, 1966; cert. in profl. devel., Harvard U., 1988. Rsch. dir. Saul Bass & Assocs., L.A., 1966-68; dir. mktg. Dreyer's Ice Cream, Oakland, Calif., 1968-80; pres. Holsinger, Inc., Burlingame, Calif., 1981—. Bd. dirs. San Francisco Opera Ctr., 1986-88; chmn. Menola Opera Advanced Tng. Program, San Francisco, 1986-88. Mem. Am. Soc. Interior Designers (bd. dirs. 1986-87), Inst. Bus. Designers (bd. dirs. 1988), AIA, City Club (San Francisco). Republican. Presbyterian. Home: 11 San Andreas Way San Francisco CA 94127 Office: Holsinger Inc 577 Airport 260 Burlingame CA 94010

LISTER, HUGH LAWRENCE, social work educator; b. Portland, Oreg., July 14, 1935; s. Hugh Lawrence and Honor Farrell (Youngson) L.; m. Constance Louise Clark, June 21, 1958; children: Jennifer Louise, Cheryl Ann. BA, Willamette U., 1957; MSW, U. Wash., 1959; DSW, Columbia U., 1970. Social worker Family Counseling Service, Portland, 1959-66; research assoc. psychiat. epidemiology research unit N.Y. State Psychiat. Inst., N.Y.C., 1966, 68-70; assoc. prof. U. Hawaii Sch. of Social Work, Honolulu, 1970-86, prof., 1986—; cons., Hawaii, 1970—; lectr., U.S. and Hawaii, 1970—. Editor: (with others) Human Sexuality in Medical Social Work, 1984, Human Sexuality, ETHNOCULTURE, and Social Work, 1986. Pres. The House, Inc., Honolulu, 1985—; active Am. Cancer Soc. Career teaching fellow Columbia U., 1968. Mem. AAUP, NEA, Nat. Assn. Social Workers. Democrat. Home: 648 Paopua Loop Kailua HI 96734 Office: U Hawaii Sch Social Work 2500 Campus Rd Honolulu HI 96822

LISTERUD, MARK BOYD, surgeon; b. Wolf Point, Mont., Nov. 19, 1924; s. Morris B. and Grace (Montgomery) L.; m. Sarah C. Mooney, May 26, 1954; children: John, Mathew, Ann, Mark, Sarah, Richard. BA magna cum laude, U. Minn., 1949, BS, 1950, MB, 1952, MD, 1953. Diplomate Am. Bd. Surgery. Intern King County Hosp., Seattle, 1952-53; resident in surgery U. Wash., Seattle, 1953-57; practice medicine specializing in surgery Wolf Point, 1958—; mem. admission com. U. Wash. Med. Sch., Seattle, 1983—. Contbr. articles to med. jours. Mem. Mont. State Health Coordinating Council, 1983, chmn. 1986—; bd. dirs. Blue Shield, Mont., 1985—. Served with USN, 1943-46. Fellow Am. Coll. Surgeons; mem. N.E. Mont. Med. Soc. (pres.), Mont. Med. Assn. (pres. 1968-69), AMA (alt. del., del. 1970-84). Club: Montana. Lodge: Elks. Home: Rodeo Rd Wolf Point MT 59201 Office: 100 Main Wolf Point MT 59201

LISTON, ALBERT MORRIS, administrator, educator, investor; b. Carlinville, Ill., Aug. 6, 1940; s. Joseph Bostick and Hazel Marie (Smalley) L.; AB in Econs., U. Calif., Davis, 1963; MA in Govt., Calif. State U., Sacramento, 1970; m. Phyllis Clayton, Feb. 27, 1967 (div. July 1970). Rsch. analyst Ombudsman Activities Project polit. sci. dept. U. Calif., Santa Barbara, 1970-72; asst. prof. polit. sci. dept. Calif. State U., Fullerton, 1973-79; investor, 1980—. Lt. Supply Corps, USNR, 1963-66. Mem. Am. Polit. Sci. Assn., Am. Soc. for Pub. Adminstrn., Town Hall of Calif., Commonwealth Club Calif., Kappa Sigma, Phi Kappa Phi. Democrat. Office: PO Box 96 Tiburon CA 94920

LISTROM, DANIEL ERIC, real estate executive; b. St. Louis, May 1, 1954; s. Donald Leo and Joanne (Patrick) L.; m. Margaret Louise Barron Listrom, June 3, 1978; children: Daniel, Michael. BA, U. Va., Charlotesville, 1976; postgrad., U. Richmond, 1976; MBA, Coll. William and Mary, Williamsburg, Va., 1978. Grad. student asst. Grants Fiscal Office-Coll. William and Mary, 1977-78; sales rep. Met. Ins. Cos., Charlottesville, Va., 1978-80; trust banker Albuquerque, 1980-83; v.p., dir. CenterWest Properties, Inc., Albuquerque, 1984-86; v.p., mgr. Comml. Brokers, Inc. & Land Am., Tucson, 1986-88; prin. The Parliament Group of Cos., Albuquerque, 1988—; mem. mktg. faculty MBA and BBA programs U. Phoenix; instr. Life Underwriters Tng. Coun., 1979-80; Mktging. Chmn. Am. Inst. Banking. Author: Officer's Trust Guide, 1982; contbr. various articles to profl. jours. Mem. Albemarle Chorus, Charlottesville, 1979-80; vol. Nat. Election Campaigns, 1980, 82, 84, 86; New Mex. Symphony Chorus, Albuquerque, 1981-82; bd. dirs, panel mem. Nat. Christian Conciliation Svc., Albuquerque, 1982-83; bd. dirs. Christian Broadcasting Acad., Albuquerque, 1983-86; active in local ch. Recipient Nat. Sales and Nat. Quality awards Nat. Assn. Life Underwriters, 1980;named outstanding 1st yr. jaycee U.S. Jaycees, Charlottesville, 1980, out standing young man Am. Outstanding Young Men Am., 1982, outstanding chmn. dir. Am. Inst. Banking, Albuqurque, 1982. Mem. Cert. Comml. Investment (candidate, 1988), Tucson Bd. Realtors (ins. com. 1987—), Nat. Assn. Realtors, U.S. Jaycees. Republican.

LITES, LARRY TOMMIE, religious organization human resources manager; b. Lake City, Fla., Mar. 5, 1947; s. Tommie Jordan and hennie Mae (Smith) L.; m. Buris Joan Adkinson, June 14, 1968; children: David hamilton, Jonathan Andrew, Jason Alexander. AS in Turf Mgmt., Lake City Jr. Coll., 1968; Bible Tng. Cert., Internat. Sch. Theology, San Bernardino, Calif., 1972; BSBA, U. Phoenix So. Calif., Costa Mesa, Calif., 1985. Golf course mgr. The Deerwood Club, Jacksonville, Fla., 1969-72; conf. svcs. adminstr. Campus Crusade for Christ, San Bernardino, 1972-76; prayer/care counseling adminstr. Campus Crusade for Christ, 1976-80, human resources adminstr., 1980-84, human resources and staff benefits fund mgr., 1985—; recruitor Campus Crusade for Christ, San Bernardino, 1980—, seminar tchr., 1974—. Vol. chaplain Loma Linda (Calif.) Vets. Hosp., 1980-86; soccer coach Am. Youth Soccer Assn., San Bernardino, 1980-88, baseball coach Little League Baseball, San Bernardino, 1980-89; mission bd. chmn. Immanuel Baptist Ch., San Bernardino, 1978-85. Sgt. USNG, 1968-74. Mem. Christian Ministries Mgmt. Assn., Christian Businessmen's Com. Republican. Baptist. Home: 5654 Wadsworth Ave Highland CA 92346

LITTELL, JEFFREY D., real estate executive; b. Lansing, Mich., June 23, 1954; s. Edward G. and Alice (W.) L. BS, U. So. Calif., 1976. Property mgr. Norris, Beggs & Simpson, Los Angeles, 1976-79, Westfield Devel., Irvine, Calif., 1979-82; real estate broker, advisor Irvine, 1982—. Roman Catholic. Club: Newport Harbor Yacht (Newport Beach, Calif.). Office: 18662 MacArthur #200 Irvine CA 92715

LITTLE, JOHN RUSSELL, JR., lawyer; b. Monte Vista, Colo., June 30, 1932; s. John Russel and Lois Alberta (Powell) L.; m. Joanne Jean Bartelma, Sept. 2, 1955; children: David Russell, Mark Douglas, Robert Michael. BA, U. Colo., 1955, LLB, 1956. Bar: Colo. 1956, U.S. Dist. Ct. Colo. 1956, U.S. Supreme Ct. 1961, U.S. Ct. Appeals (10th cir.) 1978. Atty. advisor U.S. Dept. Interior, Denver, 1956-69, asst. regional solicitor, 1969-73, regional solicitor, 1974-83; assoc. solicitor energy and resources U.S. Dept. Interior, Washington, 1980; assoc. Duncan, Weinberg, Miller & Pembroke, Denver, 1983—; instr. Rocky Mtn. Mineral Law Found. 1983-87. Contbr. articles to profl. jours. Cited for Meritorious Services U.S. Dept. of Interior, Denver, 1980. Mem. ABA, Colo. Bar Assn., Am. Judicature Soc. Democrat. Presbyterian. Office: Duncan Weinberg Miller & Pembroke 717 17th St #1670 Denver CO 80202

LITTLE, JULIA ELIZABETH, medical technologist, educator; b. Canton, Ohio, Aug. 23, 1932; d. Nicholas Charles and Julie Ella (Boldizsar) Psenka; children: Linda Marie, Lori Elizabeth. BS, Mt. Union Coll., 1954. Registered med. technologist Am. Soc. Clin. Pathologists, Calif. Med. technologist Aultman Hosp., Canton, 1955-56; supr. chemistry Barberton (Ohio) Citizens Hosp., 1956-57; supr. bacteriology Massillon (Ohio) City Hosp., 1957-63; chief technologist Lynwood (Calif.) Clin. Lab., 1964-65; med. technologist Los Altos Hosp., Long Beach, Calif., 1966-70, Newhall (Calif.) Community Hosp., 1973-79; med. technologist, hemotology educator Eisenhower Med. Ctr., Rancho Mirage, Calif., 1980—. Mem. Am. Soc. Clin. Pathology, Calif. Assn. Med. Lab. Technologists (pres. Palms to Pines chpt. 1988-89, treas. 1986-87, 87-88). Republican. Home: 34161 Linda Way Cathedral City CA 92234 Office: Eisenhower Med Ctr 39000 Bob Hope Dr Rancho Mirage CA 92270

LITTLE, WILLIAM HENRY, oceanographer; b. Balt., May 23, 1948; s. Robert Henry and Ruth Alice (Brehm) L.; m. Sally Jeanne Schoppert, June 13, 1971; children: Rachel, Jessica. BS in Geology and Geol. Oceanography, U. Wash., 1971; MS in Air-Ocean Sci., Naval Postgrad. Sch., Monterey, Calif., 1980. Anti-submarine warfare officer USS Horne, San Diego, 1971-74; ops. officer Naval Facility, Coos Head, Oreg., 1975-78; oceanographer Naval Oceanography Ctr., Guam, 1980-82; oceanographer, instr. Anti-Submarine Warfare Sch., San Diego, 1982-84; oceanographer USS Constellation, San Diego, 1984-86; ops. officer Naval Western Oceanography Ctr., Pearl Harbor, Hawaii, 1986-89; oceanographer Comthirdflt, Pearl Harbor, 1989—. Mem. Hawaii Ballroom Dance Assn. (v.p. Miliani chpt. 1988-89). Lutheran. Office: Comthirdflt FPO San Francisco HI 96601-6001

LITTLEJOHN, BRUCE EVERY, film and television producer; b. Washington, Mar. 28, 1951; s. William F. and Barbara B. (Bairnsfather) L. BA in History, U. Va., 1973. Film distbr. United Artists Corp., Boston, 1975-78; media coord. Clements for Gov. campaign, Austin, Tex., 1978; exec. producer Klein & Co., L.A., 1979—. Assoc. producer (albums) Tom Scott Streamlines, 1987 (Grammy nomination), Flashpoint, 1988; exec. producer (TV series) Against the Odds, 1982. Recipient Album Art Direction award Art Dirs. Club N.Y., 1988, Clio award for TV music, 1985, Best of Broadcasting award New England Broadcasting Assn., 1985, Cine Golden Eagle award Coun. on Internat. Nontheatrical Events, 1982. Home: 2279 Parnell Ave Los Angeles CA 90064 Office: Klein & Co 1111 S Robertson Blvd Los Angeles CA 90035

LITTMAN, JONATHAN RUSSELL, writer; b. San Francisco, Apr. 10, 1958; s. Allan Norman and Caroline (Russell) L. BA in Rhetoric, U. Calif., Berkeley, 1982. Contbg. editor PC World Mag., San Francisco, 1983-84; staff reporter PC Week, Belmont, Calif., 1984-86; contbg. editor Mac Week, San Francisco, 1987—; speaker various univs. and nat. TV, 1985—. Author: Once Upon a Time in Computerland, 1987; also articles to Forbes, Los Angeles Times.

LITTRELL, DAVID LEE, promotion company executive; b. Roanoke, Va., Apr. 29, 1949; s. Wilbur L. and Geraldine (Gedling) L.; m. Melinda Ann Miles; 1 stepchild, Heather. Student U. Louisville. Div. mgr. Golden Star Prodns., Santa Rosa, Calif., 1969-71; account exec. Sta. WDRB-TV, Louisville, 1971-76; gen. sales mgr. Sta. WLRS-FM, Louisville, 1977-79; cons. Sta. KBDF, Sta. KZEL, Eugene, Oreg., 1980; v.p., gen. mgr. Sta. KEZX-AM-FM, Seattle, 1981-88; v.p. concert/entertainment promotion co. Media One, Seattle, 1988—; Western region mgr. Park Broadcasting, 1981-88; dir. ABC Entertainment Radio Network, N.Y.C. Eurotrade Internat., Seattle. Bd. dirs. Seafair, Seattle, 1982-87, King County Boys and Girls Clubs; mem. Middletown City Council, Ky., 1979-80; commr. Seattle Zoo, 1984-86. Recipient Seattle First Citizen arad, 1986. Mem. Puget Sound Radio Broadcasters, Wash. State Assn. Broadcasters, Woodland Park Zool. Soc., (bd. dirs. 1986—). Democrat. Presbyterian. Lodge: Rotary. Home: 6839 31st Ave NE Seattle WA 98115 Office: Media One 6300 Southcenter Blvd Seattle WA 98188

LITTY, CAROLYN LOUISE ELMER, counseling educator; b. Susanville, Calif., Jan. 7, 1941; d. Edward Elden Elmer and Hazel Pauline (Morgan) Elmer Haws; m. Paul Francis Litty, Oct. 6, 1961 (div. 1976); children: Paul Francis II, Jon Joseph. BSN with honors, U. Calif., San Francisco, 1966, MSN, 1968; MS, U. Oreg., 1982, PhD, 1988. RN, Calif.; cert. psychiat. nurse, counseling psychologist. Resident nurse St. Elizabeth's Home, San Francisco, 1967-68; nurse San Mateo Pub. Health Dept., S. San Francisco, 1968-71; co-owner, funeral dir. Litty Funeral Dirs., Inc., Brookings, Oreg., 1971-76; nurse counselor, cons. Weight Loss Clinics Am., Tukwila, Wash., 1976-78; dir. clinic Weight Loss Clinics Am., Eugene, Oreg., 1978-81; instr. counseling Lane Community Coll./U. Oreg., Eugene, 1981—; mem. Speaker's Bur., 1981—; assoc. counselor St. Jude Ch., Eugene, 1978—; assoc. coord. Community Ctr. for Family Counseling, Eugene, 1981—. Editor various manuals. Mem. steering com. Eugene-Springfield Met. Vicariate Marriage Prep. Program, 1981—. Mem. Am. Inst. Adlerian Studies (assoc.; cert.), N.Am. Soc. Adlerian Psychology, Oreg. Soc. Individual Psychology, Oreg. Counselors Assn., Sigma Theta Tau. Home: 4330 Willamette St Eugene OR 97405

LIU, GERALD HANMIN, organization administrator, educator; b. San Francisco, Aug. 24, 1944; s. Howard Y. and Patricia Marian (Lee) Low; m. Jennifer Mei, Sept. 6, 1969. BA, U. Pacific, 1966; DDS, NYU, 1970; PhD, Union for Experimenting Colls. and Univ.'s, 1978. Lectr. U. Calif., San Francisco, 1974-75; exec. dir. Min An Health Ctr., San Francisco, 1979-82, also bd. dirs.; founder, pres. U.S.-China Ednl. Inst., San Francisco, 1978—, also bd. dirs.; bd. dirs. San Francisco-Shanghai Friendship City Com., 1983—, Min An Health Ctr., 1987-89; cons. W.K. Kellogg Found., Battle Creek, Mich., 1984-87, 89—, MacArthur Found., Chgo., 1986—, William T. Grant Found., N.Y.C., 1988—, Kellogg Internat. Fellowship Program in Health, Mich. State U., East Lansing; project dir. Workshops on Edn. and Culture, 1984—; mem. steering com. Kellogg Internat. Fellowship program Mich. State U., East Lansing, 1985—; hon. advisor Shanghai Mental Health Ctr., People's Rep. China, 1987, Shanghai 1st People's Hosp., Beijing Med. U., 1985; cons. Apple Computer, Inc., 1989—. Project dir. (textbook) Essential Book of Traditional Chinese Medicine, Vols. I and II, 1986. Coord. Cultural Tng. Program Peace Corps, 1989—. Served to capt. U.S. Army, 1971-73. Grantee Ednl. Found. Am., 1981-85, Ettinger Found., 1980, 86, 87, 89, Ednl. Comm. Fgn. Med. Grads., 1982, L.J. and M.C. Skaggs Found., 1985, W.K. Kellogg Found., 1986. Mem. AAAS, Omicron Kappa Upsilon. Office: US China Ednl Inst 1144 Pacific Ave San Francisco CA 94133-4212

LIU, KATHERINE CHANG, artist, art educator; b. Kiang-si, Peoples Republic of China; came to U.S., 1963; d. Ming-fan and Ying (Yuan) Chang; m. Yet-zen Liu; children: Alan S., Laura Y. MS, U. Calif., Berkeley, 1965. lectr. N.J. Watercolor Soc., Pitts. Watercolor Soc., Oreg. Watercolor Soc., Tex. Watercolor Soc., Ohio Watercolor Soc., Ariz. Watercolor Assn., Rocky Mountain Watercolor Workshop, U. Va. extension, Longwood. Coll., Va. One-man shows include Harrison Mus., Utah State U., Riverside (Calif.) Art Mus., Ventura (Calif.) Coll., Roanoke (Va.) Mus. Fine Arts, Fla. A&M U., Louis Newman Galleries, L.A., Lung-Men Gallery, Taipei, Republic of China, L.A. Artcore, 1989; sole juror Watercolor State Open Competitions, N.J., Oreg., Pa. 1988; Western Fedn. Exhibition, Houston, 1986, San Diego Internat. Watercolor Exhbn., 1986, Ohio Watercolor Soc., 1986, Watercolor State Open Competitions, Fla., S.C., 1989. Recipient Rex Brandt award San Diego Watercolor Internat., 1985, Purchase Selection award Watercolor USA and Springfield (Mo.) Art Mus., 1981, Gold Medal, 1986, Mary Lou Fitzgerald Meml. award Allied Arts Am. Nat. Arts Club, N.Y.C., 1987; NEA grantee, 1979-80. Mem. Nat. Watercolor Soc. (life, chmn. jury 1985, pres. 1983, Top award 1984, cash awards 1979, 87.), Watercolor USA Honor Soc., Nat. Soc. Painters in Casein and Acrylic (2d award 1985), Rocky Mountain Nat. Watermedia Soc. (juror 1984, awardee 1978, 80, 86), West Coast Watercolor Soc.

LIU, SANDRA SHOU-MING, pharmacologist; b. Taipei, Taiwan, Sept. 5, 1954; came to U.S. 1978; d. Shaw Gi and Chun-Ying (Chen) L. BS in Pharmacy, Taipei Med. Coll., 1977; MS in Preventive Med., Ohio State U., 1980, MS in Pharmacology, 1983; MBA, Pepperdine U., 1988. Sales trainer Bristol-Myers (Taiwan) Pharm. Co., Taipei, 1977-78; tchr. assoc. to research assoc. Ohio State U., Columbus, 1979-83; mem. profl. staff Allergany, Inc., Irvine, Calif., 1983-86; clin. research assoc. Allergany, Inc., Irvine, 1986-88, sr. clin. research assoc., 1988-89; product mgr. E. Asia Allergany, Inc., Irvine, 1989—; program coordinator Ohio Dept. Health, Columbus, 1979; intern pharmacist Thrifty Pharmacy, Costa Mesa, Calif., 1987-88. Contbr. articles to profl. jours. Mem. Am. Pharm. Assn., Assn., Clin. Pharmacology, L.A. Asian Bus. League (activity coordinator 1986-87). Baptist. Office: Allergan Inc 2525 Dupont Dr Irvine CA 92715

LIU, SHIN-TSE, chemical consultant; b. Taipei, Republic of China, Sept. 27, 1932; s. Teng-mien and Alee (Chen) L. BSChemE, Taiwan Nat. U., Taipei, 1956; Diplom-Chemiker, Technische-Hochschule, Aachen, Fed. Republic Germany, 1962, Dr. rer. nat., 1966. Research chemist ITT Rayonier, Whippany, N.J., 1967-70, UCLA, 1970-72; research engr. Jet Propulsion Lab., Pasadena, Calif., 1972-73; pres. S.T. Liu & Co., Los Angeles, 1974—. Mem. Am. Chem Soc. Office: PO Box 17457 Los Angeles CA 90017

LIVELY, BRIGITTE, cartographer, executive; b. Stuttgart, Fed. Republic Germany; came to U.S., naturalized, 1963; d. Eugen K.E. and Hermine J. (Geiger) Ebert; m. Lewis E. Lively; children: Ursa, Karma, Dara. Ed., Stuttgart. Exploration clk. Conoco, Inc., Anchorage, 1960-62, Mobil Oil Co., Anchorage, 1962-63; sr. geol. cartographer Phillips Petroleum Co., Anchorage, 1963-65; founder, mgr. The Mapmakers, Palmer, Alaska, 1969—; sec., treas. Planning, Inc., Palmer, 1972; founder, mgr. DataBank Mat-Su, Palmer, 1988. Author: Agriculture-Matanuska-Susitna Bourough, 1983, A Balance-Matanuska-Susitna Borough, 1985, 50 Years Matanuska Colony, 1985; editor: Minerals, Matanuska-Susitna Borough, 1983, Tourism-Matanuska-Susitna Borough, 1984; author maps of gas and oil leases in Alaskan and Arctic region. Mem. Palmer C. of C. (pres. 1985-86, 88-89), Alaska State C. of C. (bd. dirs. 1986—). Office: The Mapmakers 259 S Alaska St Palmer AK 99645

LIVERMORE, DONALD RAYMOND, elementary teacher; b. Stockton, Calif., May 14, 1947; s. Harry Guy and Cora Edith (Ambrose) L. AA, Delta Jr. Coll., Stockton, Calif., 1967; BS, BA, Chico State U., 1971. Cert. elem., sec. tchr., Calif. Salesman/mgr. Magor's Mens Wear, Tracy, Calif., 1961-75; tchr., K-6 Monterey (Calif.) Peninsula Unified Sch. dist., 1971-89; tchr. Chapman Coll., Monterey, 1982—; mentor tchr., cons. Monterey Unified Sch. Dist., 1984-89; aquarium guide, Monterey Bay Aquarium, 1985-89, mentor guide, trainer, 1986-89; program quality reviewer, State of Calif., Monterey County Office of Edn., Salinas, 1982-89. Collaborator (with Randy Reinstedt): More Than Memories, 1985. Pres. bd. Parent Tchr. Assn., Olson, 1976-78, Hayes, 1986-88. Recipient award, Kern County Hist., Social Sci. Consortium, Fresno, Calif., 1985; named Tchr. in Marine Research, Monterey County Office of Edn., Salinas, 1988. Mem. Monterey Bay Tchrs. Assn. (faculty rep. 1975-77). Democrat. Lutheran. Office: Hayes Elem Sch MPUSD PO Box 1031 Monterey CA 93940

LIVERMORE, ROBERT NEAL, construction project manager; b. Taunton, Mass., Apr. 11, 1953; s. Lawrence William and Dorothy Jane (Mason) L.; m. Debra Ann Vieira, June 16, 1973. AS, Wentworth Inst., Boston, 1973; BSBA, Northestern U., Boston, 1978. Estimator Varasso Bros. Inc., Braintree, Mass., 1973-74; draftsman Space Bldg. Corp., East Taunton, Mass., 1974-75, Bayside Assocs., Boston, 1975-76; hdqrs. cost engr. Stone & Webster Engring. Corp., Boston, 1976-80; field cost engr. Bechtel Cnstrn. Co. Inc., Palo Verde, Ariz., 1980-86; project mgr. Bapt. Hosps., Phoenix, 1986—; cnstrn. specialist Joseph M. Davis & Assocs., Tempe, Ariz., 1984. Mem. Am. Assn. cost Engrs. (Ariz. chpt. pres. 1981), Project Mgmt. Inst. Episcopalian. Club: Cen. Ariz. Hiking (Phoenix). Home: 1 E Surrey Ave Phoenix AZ 85022

LIVESAY, THOMAS ANDREW, museum administrator; b. Dallas, Feb. 1, 1945; s. Melvin Ewing Clay and Madge Almeda (Hall) L.; m. Jennifer Clark, 1985; children: Heather Marie, Russell Lee. B.F.A., U. Tex., Austin, 1968, M.F.A., 1972; postgrad., Harvard U. Inst. Arts Adminstrn., 1978. Curator Elisabet Ney Mus., Austin, 1971-73; dir. Longview (Tex.) Mus. and Arts Center, 1973-75; curator of art Amarillo (Tex.) Art Center, 1975-77, dir. center, 1977-80; asst. dir. for adminstrn. Dallas Mus. Fine Arts, 1980-85; dir. Mus. of N.Mex., Santa Fe, 1985—; mem. touring panel Tex. Commn. Arts; mem. panel Nat. Endowment Arts, Inst. Mus. Services. Author: Young Texas Artists Series, 1978, Made in Texas, 1979; editor: video tape American Images, 1979, Ruth Abrams, Paintings, 1940-85, NYU Press. Served with U.S. Army, 1969-71. Mem. Am. Assn. Museums (council 1986—), Tex. Assn. Museums (v.p. 1981, pres. 1983), N.Mex. State Records and Archives Commn. (chmn. 1986—). Office: Mus NMex PO Box 2087 Santa Fe NM 87503

LIVINGSTON, KAY ANN, personnel executive; b. Ft. Collins, Colo., Nov. 6, 1955; d. Clark and Ann (Garney) L. BSBA, Colo. State U., 1978. With Am. Hosp. Supply Corp., Denver, 1978-81; office mgr. Manpower, Inc., Boulder, Colo., 1981-82; office mgr. Manpower, Inc., Denver, 1982-84, br. mgr., 1984-87, area mgr., 1987—. Mem. Denver Women in Bus., Denver C. of C., Bus. and Profl. Women's Clubs. Home: 3515 28th St 101 Boulder CO 80301 Office: Manpower Inc 1401 17th St #560 Denver CO 80202

LIVINGSTON, MARLENE JOHNSON, investor; b. Clarkston, Wash., Dec. 29, 1947; d. Carroll Richard and Verta Rose (Rogers) Johnson; m. Gordon Wesley Livingston, June 12, 1967 (dec. Aug. 1985); children: Joel W., Mark W., Lynee M. BS in Health Edn., U. Nev., 1984. Coord. hospitality convs. svcs. Reno (Nev.) Conv. Authority, 1979-82; instr. Truckee Meadows Community Coll., 1982-83; exec. dir. Nev. Pharmacists Assn., 1985-86; pvt. practice Spokane, 1985—. Recipient Bob Davis scholarship U. Nev., 1982-84. Mem. AAUW, Spokane Coll. Women's Assn. Republican.

LIVINGSTON, MYRA COHN, poet, writer, educator; b. Omaha, Nebr., Aug. 17, 1926; d. Mayer L. and Gertrude (Marks) Cohn; m. Richard Roland Livingston, Apr. 14, 1952; children: Joshua, Jonas Cohn, Jennie Marks. B.A., Sarah Lawrence Coll., 1948. Profl. horn player 1941-48; book reviewer Los Angeles Daily News, 1948-49, Los Angeles Mirror, 1949-50; asst. editor Campus Mag., 1949-50; various public relations positions and pvt. sec. to Hollywood (Calif.) personalities 1950-52; tchr. creative writing Dallas (Tex.) public library and schs., 1958-63; poet-in-residence Beverly Hills (Calif.) Unified Sch. Dist., 1966-84; sr. instr. UCLA Extension, 1973—; cons. to various sch. dists., 1966-84, cons. poetry to publishers children's lit., 1975—. Author: Whispers and Other Poems, 1958, Wide Awake and Other Poems, 1959, I'm Hiding, 1961, See What I Found, 1962, I Talk to Elephants, 1962, I'm Not Me, 1963, Happy Birthday, 1964, The Moon and a Star and Other Poems, 1965, I'm Waiting, 1966, Old Mrs. Twindlytart and Other Rhymes, 1967, A Crazy Flight and Other Poems, 1968, The Malibu and Other Poems, 1972, When You Are Alone/It Keeps You Capone: An Approach to Creative Writing with Children, 1973, Come Away, 1974, The Way Things Are and Other Poems, 1974, 4-Way Stop and Other Poems, 1976, A Lollygag of Limericks, 1978, O Sliver of Liver and Other Poems, 1979, No Way of Knowing: Dallas Poems, 1980, A Circle of Seasons, 1982, How Pleasant to Know Mr. Lear!, 1982, Sky Songs, 1984, A Song I Sang to You, 1984, Monkey Puzzle, 1984, The Child as Poet: Myth or Reality?, 1984, Celebrations, 1985, Worlds I Know and Other Poems, 1985, Sea Songs, 1986, Earth Songs, 1986, 1987, Higgledy-Piggledy, 1986, Space Songs, 1988, There Was a Place and Other Poems, 1988, others; co-editor: The Scott-Foresman Anthology, 1984; Author: The Writing of Poetry; film strips; editor 23 anthologies of poetry; contbr. articles on children's lit. to ednl. publs., contbr., essays on lit. and reading in edn. to various books; mem. editorial adv. bd. The New Advocate. Officer Beverly Hills PTA Council, 1966-75; pres. Friends of Beverly Hills Public Library, 1979-81; bd. dirs. Poetry Therapy Inst., 1975—, Reading is Fundamental of So. Calif., 1981—. Recipient Honor award N.Y. Herald Tribune Spring Book Festival, 1958, Excellence in Poetry award Nat. Council Tchrs. of English, 1980, Commonwealth Club award, 1984, Nat. Jewish Book award, 1987. Mem. Authors Guild, Internat. Reading Assn., Soc. Children's Book Writers (honor award 1975), Tex. Inst. Letters (awards 1961, 80), So. Calif. Council on Lit. for Children and Young People (Comprehensive Contribution award 1968, Notable Book award 1972), PEN. Address: 9308 Readcrest Dr Beverly Hills CA 90210

LIVINGSTON, PATRICIA ANN, marine biologist, researcher; b. Detroit, Dec. 10, 1954. BS, Mich. State U., 1976; MS, U. Wash., 1980, M in Pub. Adminstrn., 1987. Ecosystem modeller Nat. Marine Fish Service, Seattle, 1977-82, trophic interactions program leader, 1983—; mem. sci. and tech. bd. The Sea Use Council, Seattle, 1986—. Contbr. articles on ecosystem modelling and marine fish trophic interactions to profl. jours. Mem. Am. Fisheries Soc. (officer and regional fish corr. Marine Fish sect., 1982-84), Am. Soc. Pub. Adminstrn., AAAS. Office: NW and Alaska Fisheries Ctr 7600 Sand Point Way NE Bldg 4 Bin C15700 Seattle WA 98115

LIVINGSTON, ROBERT BURR, neuroscientist, educator; b. Boston, Oct. 9, 1918; s. William Kenneth and Ruth Forbes (Brown) L.; m. Mandana Beckner, Dec. 21, 1954 (div. 1977); children: Louise, Dana, Justyn. AB, Stanford U., 1940, MD, 1944. Intern, asst. resident internal medicine Stanford Hosp., Palo Alto, Calif., 1943-44; instr. physiology Yale U., New Haven, Conn., 1946-48; asst. prof. Yale U., New Haven, 1950-52; rsch. asst. psychiatry Harvard U., Cambridge, Mass., 1947-48; NRC sr. fellow neurology Inst. Physiology, Geneva, Switzerland, 1948-49; Wilhelm Gruber fellow neurophysiology Switzerland, France, Eng., 1949-50; exec. asst. to pres. NAS—NRC, 1951-52; assoc. prof. physiology and anatomy UCLA, 1952-56, prof., 1956-57; dir. basic rsch. NIMH and Nat. Inst. Neurol. Diseases and Blindness, 1956-61; chief neurobiology lab. NIMH, 1960-65; prof. dept. neuroscis. U. Calif., San Diego, 1965—, chmn. dept. neuroscis., 1965-70; Gast prof. U. Zurich, Switzerland, 1971-72; Ernest Sachs lectr. Dartmouth Med. Sch., 1981; cons. NRC, VA, NASA, HEW, NSF, Dept. Def.; assoc. neuroscis. rsch. program MIT, 1963-76, hon. assoc., 1976—; emissary to 6 Arab nations for Internat. Physicians for the Prevention of Nuclear War, Sept., 1986; del. Internat. Conflict Resolution in Cen. Am., Rust, Austria, Internat. Conf. The Cen. Am. Challenge, Costa Rica, 1988; neuroscis. tutor to Dalai Lama, Dharamsala, India, Oct., 1987. Adv. editorial bd.: Jour. Neurophysiology, 1959-65; editorial bd.: Internat. Jour. Psychobiology, 1970-80, Neurol. Rsch., 1979—; cons. editor: Jour. Neurosci. Rsch., 1975-85. Bd. dirs. Foundations' Fund for Rsch. in Psychiatry, 1954-57; bd. incorporators Jour. History of Medicine and Allied Scis.; incorporator Inst. Policy Studies, 1963, Elmwood Inst., 1984. Lt. (j.g.) M.C. USNR, 1944-46. Decorated Bronze Star; recipient Award for Excellence Matrix: Midland Festival, 1981. Fellow AAAS (chmn. commn. sci. edn. 1968-71), Am. Acad. Arts and Scis.; mem. Am. Physiol. Soc., Am. Assn. Anatomists, Am. Neurol. Assn., Am. Acad. Neurology, Assn. for Rsch. in Nervous and Mental Diseases, Am. Assn. Neurol. Surgeons, Soc. for Neurosci.

LIVINGSTON, THOMAS MATHIAS, advertising agency executive, writer; b. White Plains, N.Y., July 18, 1935; s. Warren Putnam Livingston and Emily Celeste (Mathias) Beard; m. Christine Turpin, Feb. 21, 1964; children: Tracy Emilie, Terence Howard. AB, Stanford U., 1959. Freelance writer Europe, 1959-66; lectr. Rutgers U., New Brunswick, N.J., 1966-68, San Jose (Calif.) State U., 1969-73; v.p. Regis McKenna Advt., Palo Alto, Calif., 1973-76, exec. v.p., 1979-80, creative dir., 1973-76, 79-80; v.p. mktg. Saga Corp., Menlo Park, Calif., 1976-79; pres., chief exec. officer Livingston-Sirutis Advt., San Francisco, 1980--. Author: (novel) Paper Walls of Innocence, 1964, The Tower Is Down, 1966; contbr. short stories to mags. Michael Karolyi Found. fellow, Vence, France, 1964; Music Corp. Am. fellow, 1966. Office: Livingston-Sirutis Advt 2 Embarcadero Ctr San Francisco CA 94111

LIVSEY, DEANNA LYNN, dance, aerobic instructor; b. Reno, June 14, 1960; d. Herbert Frederic and Geraldine Sally (Grieve) L. BA, U. Oreg., 1983; MA, UCLA, 1988. Tchr., choreographer Hamilton H.S., Los Angeles, 1983-84; dresser, stitcher Theatrical Wardrobe, 768, Los Angeles, 1984—, sec., 1986—; stitcher Ctr. Theatre Group, Los Angeles, 1986—; adminstrv. asst. LTD Unlimited, Los Angeles, 1985—; substitute dance tchr. Cypress (Calif.) Jr. Coll., 1983—; dance tchr. Orange Coast Coll., Costa Mesa, Calif., 1986—; pvt. coach Aerobics West, Arcadia, Calif., 1987—; tchr. UCLA, 1985. Mem. Theatrical Wardrobe, Local 768. Republican. Home: 3735 Kelton Ave Los Angeles CA 90034 Office: Orange Coast Coll 2701 Fairview Rd Costa Mesa CA 92628

LIVZIEY, JAMES GERALD, secondary school teacher; b. Buffalo, July 30, 1927; s. James Ephlyn and Helena Charlote (Kiener) L.; m. June Ellen Andersen, July 25, 1955; children: Naomi Lynn, Patricia Ellen. AA, Southwestern Jr. Coll., 1970; BA, San Diego State U., 1972. Enlisted U.S. Navy, 1945, advanced through grades to lt. comdr., ret., 1969; high sch. instr. SWHS Dist., Chula Vista, Calif., 1972—. Fellow Taft Inst, 1977, Pacific Acad. Advanced Studies, 1978. Fellow Alpha Gamma Sigma; mem. Naval Inst. USN, Masons (tiler 1985-88). Home: 675 Mariposa Cir Chula Vista CA 92011

LIZARDY, ANDONI, consulting company executive; b. Akron, Ohio, June 9, 1947; s. Themistocles Anthony and Katherine (Chembithes) L.; m. Peggy Wicks, Aug. 31, 1967 (div. 1974); 1 child, Michael. Student, Kent State U., 1965-67. Asst. sales mgr. Kelly & Cohen, Warren, Ohio, 1967-71; self-employed in real estate 1971-75; pres. Lizardy Assocs., San Diego, 1975—; cons. USAir, Pitts., 1979-81, Maersk Lines/Moller U.S., N.Y.C., Copenhagen, 1979-86, Hilton Internat., London, 1987; lectr. in field. Author 12 books on selling and psychology, audio cassette series, From the First Impression to Your Presentation, 1988, Closing Games, 1988. Served with U.S. Army, 1968-71, Vietnam. Office: Lizardy Assocs PO Box 270468 San Diego CA 92128

LIZARRAGA, MARI EUDORA, marketing company executive; b. Pomona, Calif., July 27, 1964; d. Garry Lad and Patricia Jean (Maddox) Usnick; m. Frank J. Lizarraga, May 21, 1983 (div. Dec. 1987); m. Michael Altenhofen, Aug. 6, 1988. Grad. high sch., Pomona. Saleswoman Gallenkamp Shoes, Montclair, Calif., 1980-81, asst. mgr., 1981-82; mgr. Gallenkamp Shoes, Glendale, Calif., 1982-83; computer mktg. rep. Radio Shack Computer Ctr., Tandy Corp., Montclair, 1983-84; West Coast sales mgr. Hopes Industries, Montclair, 1984-85; owner, founder, mgr. Marisco Mktg. Co., Rancho Cucamonga, Calif., 1985—. Republican. Lutheran. Office: Marisco Mktg Co 9045 Haven St Ste 109-B Rancho Cucamonga CA 91730

LIZZUL, LEE ANN, clinical audiologist; b. Teaneck, N.J., June 12, 1960; d. Aldo Matthew and Georgia Lee (Rossillon) L. Student bus., Drake U., 1978-79; BS, Colo. State U., 1982, MS, 1984. Audiology intern N.Y. League for Hard of Hearing, N.Y.C., 1984-85, audiology cons., 1985; clin. audiologist Ctr. for Hearing, Speech and Lang., Colorado Springs, Colo., 1985--. Mem. Am. Speech-Lang.-Hearing Assn. (cert. clin. competence in audiology), Colo. Speech-Lang.-Hearing Assn., Assn. Colorado Springs Audiologists, Self Help for Hard of Hearing People in Pikes Peak Region, Phi Beta Kappa. Office: Ctr for Hearing 1785 N Academy Blvd Ste 405 Colorado Springs CO 80909

LJUBICIC DROZDOWSKI, MILADIN PETER, consulting engineer; b. Zajecar, Yugoslavia, Sept. 28, 1921; came to U.S., 1959; s. Peter Miladin and Martha Jovan (Viktorovic) Ljubicic; m. Dusica Cile Pavic, Sept. 9, 1948. Diploma in engring., U. Belgrade, Yugoslavia, 1951, 52; cert., Nat. Higher Sch. Armanents, Paris, 1956; MSME, UCLA, 1964, PhD in Mec. Engring., 1971. Design and test engr. Fed. Mogul Bower, El Monte, Calif., 1959-62; chief advanced armament analytical support Hughes Helicopters, Culver City, Calif., 1962-78; engring. supr. Bechtel Power Corp., Norwalk, Calif., 1978-80; engring. adviser Bechtel Espana, Madrid, 1980-87; v.p. Koach Engring., Sun Valley, Calif., 1987; ind. cons. Mission Viejo, Calif., 1987—; asst. to chmn. continuum mechanics, Belgrade, 1955-56; guest lectr. Sch. Engring. and Applied Sci., UCLA, 1971; prof., Loyola Marymount U., L.A., 1978-80. Contbr. to profl. publs. Mem. Am. Soc. Mech. Engrs., Am. Def. Preparedness Assn., Spanish Nuclear Soc. Democrat. Eastern Orthodox. Home and Office: 26426 Lope de Vega Mission Viejo CA 92691

LLEWELLYN, FREDERICK EATON, mortuary executive; b. Mexico, Mo., Mar. 28, 1917; s. Frederick William and Mabel (Eaton) L.; BS, Calif. Inst. Tech., 1938; MBA (Baker scholar), Harvard, 1942; LLD, Pepperdine U., 1976; m. Jane Althouse, Aug. 15, 1940; children: Richard, John, Ann Marie. Asst. gen. mgr., dir. Forest Lawn Life Ins. Co., Glendale, Calif., 1940-41, pres., 1959-61; asst. to gen. mgr. Forest Lawn Meml. Park, Glendale, 1941-42, exec. v.p., 1946-66, gen. mgr., 1966—; pres. Forest Lawn Found., 1961—, Forest Lawn Co., 1967-88; chmn. bd. Am. Security & Fidelity Corp., Forest Lawn Co., 1988—, Founders Fin. Corp., Glendale, 1971—, Upstairs Galleries Inc., 1974—, Met. Computer Center, 1973-81, Calif. Citrus Corp., 1971-80, Forest Lawn Mortgage Corp., 1974-81; dir. Calif. Fed. Savs. & Loan, IT Corp. Recon Optical; chmn. Trust Services Am., Inc., 1983—. Mem. Found. for the 21st Century, 1986—, Orthopaedic Hosp., 1976—, chmn., 1980; chmn. Glendale Meml. Hosp., 1980, trustee, 1982-85; pres. So. Calif. Visitors Council, 1976-77; chmn. Council of Regents, Meml. Ct. of Honor. Mem. Mayor's Ad Hoc Energy Com., Los Angeles, 1973-74, Los Angeles County Reorgn. Commn., 1978; bd. dirs. Los Angeles County Heart Assn., 1957; trustee U. Redlands, 1966-77, chmn. bd., 1969-72; mem. Univ. Bd., Pepperdine Coll., 1966—, chmn. bd. regents, mem. exec. bd., 1977-86 ; bd. dirs. Pasadena Found. Med. Research, 1967-72, So. Calif. Bldg. Funds, 1975—, Met. YMCA Los Angeles, 1975—; trustee San Gabriel Valley council Boy Scouts Am., 1968-74; trustee Calif. Mus. Sci. and Industry, 1977—, pres., 1983-85, chmn., 1985-86; bd. govs. Dept. Mus. Natural History, Los Angeles County, 1968-72; mem. Los Angeles County Energy Commn., 1974-80; chmn. Mayor's Ad Hoc Water Crisis Commn., 1977—. Served with USNR, 1942-45. Decorated knight Order of Merit (Italy). Mem. Nat. Assn. Cemeteries (pres. 1956-57), Los Angeles Area C. of C. (dir. 1969-78, bd. chmn. 1974, pres. 1973), Calif. C. of C. (dir. 1977—), Newcomen Soc., Tau Beta Pi. Clubs: California, San Marino, Lincoln, One Hundred, Twilight, Walnut Elephant. Lodge: Order of St. Hubertus. Contbr. articles to profl. jours. Home: 1521 Virginia Rd San Marino CA 91108 Office: 1712 S Glendale Ave Glendale CA 91205

LLEWELLYN, JOHN FREDERICK, cemetery executive; b. L.A., Nov. 16, 1947; s. Frederick Eaton and Jane Elizabeth Llewellyn; m. Linda Garrison, Apr. 15, 1989. BA, U. Redlands, 1970; MBA, U. So. Calif., 1972. Foreman Pacific T&T, Orange, Calif., 1970; underwriter Allstate Ins. Co., Santa Ana, Calif., 1971-72; asst. to controller Forest Lawn Co., Glendale, Calif., 1972-73, v.p., 1973-75, exec. v.p., 1976-88, treas., chief fin. officer, 1978-83, sec., bd. dirs., 1983—, pres., 1988—; various offices, bds. dirs. divs. Forest Lawn Co., Glendale, Calif., 1974—; exec. v.p. Founders Fin. Corp., Glendale, 1974-75, pres. 1975-82, also bd. dirs.; chief exec. officer Met. Computer Ctr., Glendale, 1974-81, Upstairs Gallery Inc., Glendale, 1974—, also vice chmn. bd. dirs.; bd. dirs. Beneficial Standard Life Ins. Co., L.A., Braille Inst., L.A.; trustee Glendale Meml. Hosp. Bd. dirs., pres. Greater Los Angeles Visitors and Convention Bur., 1988-89; bd. dirs. Glendale Devel. Council, Los Angeles area Council Boy Scouts Am., vice chmn., 1987. Mem. Am. Cemetery Assn. (bd. dirs. 1977-81, 83-86, 88—, v.p. 1985-86, pres.-elect 1986-87, pres. 1987-88), Internment Assn. Calif. (bd. dirs 1984—, state v.p. 1987-88, pres. 1988-89), Calif. Mortuary Alliance (bd. dirs.), Western Cemetery Alliance (bd. dirs., v.p. 1987—), Econ. Round Table (sec.-treas. 1983-85), Newcomer Soc. N.Am., Claif. Club, Lincoln Club. Home: 1130 Oakwood Pl Sierra Madre CA 91204 Office: Forest Lawn Meml-Parks & Mortuaries 1712 S Glendale Ave Glendale CA 91205

LLOYD, ARTHUR LEONARD, railroad official; b. San Francisco, May 21, 1925; s. Arthur Leonard and Ella Caroline (Rosburg) L.; m. Eleanor Graham Hutson, Apr. 20, 1946; children: Lynne, Lawrence, Liane. BS, U. Calif., Berkeley, 1948. Yard clk. San Francisco & Napa Valley R.R., Napa, Calif., 1942-43; ptnr. Eastshore Lines Bus Co., Berkeley, 1946-49; asst. dir. pub. rels. Western Pacific R.R., San Francisco, 1949-6l; owner, mgr. Clift Travel Svc., San Francisco, 196l-7l; mgr. travel agy. sales Amtrak, Washington, 1971-74; regional sales mgr. Amtrak, L.A., 1974-75; dir. pub. and govt. affairs Amtrak, San Francisco, 1975—; mem. faculty Echols Travel Coll., San Francisco, 1977—; bd. dirs. San Mateo County Transp. Authority, Burlingame, Calif., 1988—. Mem. Calif. Transp. Deptl. Adv. Com., Sacramento, 1977—, chmn. Calif. Train Citizens Adv. Com., San Francisco, 1989. With AUS, 1943-45. Mem. R.R. Pub. Rels. Assn., Ry. and Locomotive Hist. Soc. (exec. v.p. 1988—, chmn. 1989). Republican. Episcopalian. Home: 20 Arapahoe Ct Portola Valley CA 94025 Office: Amtrak One California St Ste 1250 San Francisco CA 94111

LLOYD, BRUCE GREGORY, chef; b. Artesia, Calif., Mar. 16, 1950; s. Steven James and Frances Anne (Milovich) L. AA, Long Beach (Calif.) City Coll., 1972. Jr. draftsman Arthur G. McKee, San Mateo, Calif., 1974-77; sr. draftsman Brown and Root, San Francisco, 1977-79; from sr. draftsman to piping designer Bechtel Power Corp., San Francisco, 1979-84; from pantry chef to pastry chef Rings Restaurant, San Francisco, 1986-88; luncheon chef Alta Plaza Restaurant, San Francisco, 1988—. Contbr. recipes to B & B Salutes the Great Chefs of America, 1988. With USN, 1969-73. Democrat. Home: 505 Connecticut St San Francisco CA 94107 Office: Alta Plaza Restaurant 2301 Fillmore St San Francisco CA 94115

LLOYD, ELLEN HOLOHAN, marketing executive; b. Phoenix, Jan. 27, 1957; d. William Andrew and Kathryn Irene (Dewey) H.; m. Russell L. Lloyd Jr., Sept. 17, 1983; l child, Mallory Lloyd. BA, U. Ariz., 1978. Asst. promotions coordinator 1st Interstate Bank Ariz., Phoenix, 1979-82; acct. exec. John A. Pratt & Assocs., Denver, 1982-83; product mgr. 1st Interstate Bank Denver, 1983-86; div. mktg. dir. TCI Central, Inc., Denver, 1986—. Mem. Cable TV Adminstrn. and Mktg. Soc. (Rocky Mountain chpt.), Ad 2 Phoenix (bd. dirs. 1980-82). Republican. Office: TCI Central Inc 355 Union Blvd Ste 200 Lakewood CO 80228

LLOYD, LLYN ALLAN, association executive; b. Evergreen Park, Ill., Jan. 14, 1938; s. Russell Donald and Gladys Marie (Bladholm) L.; m. Helen Elizabeth Main, Mar. 22, 1959; children: Leanne, Douglas, Bradley. BS in Pharmacy, Ohio No. U., 1960; MA in Pub. Adminstrn., Boise State U., 1980. Lic. pharmacist, Ohio, Idaho, Ariz. With various pharmacies, Ohio and Idaho, 1960-63; pharmacist, owner Arco (Idaho) Drug, 1963-76; pharmacist city of Boise, Idaho, 1976-82; exec. dir. Idaho Bd. Pharmacy, Boise, 1982-86, Ariz. State Bd. Pharmacy, Phoenix, 1986—. Chmn. Butte County unit ARC, Arco, Idaho, 1968-74; mem. forest adv. com. Challis (Idaho) Nat. Forest, 1969-72. Recipient A.H. Robbins Bowl of Hygiene award Challis Nat. Forest, 1973. Mem. Nat. Assn. Bds. Pharmacy (exec. com. 1986—), Ariz. Pharmacy Assn., Ariz. Soc. Hosp. Pharmacists (Svc. to Pharmacy award 1988), Rotary, Lions, Masons. Home: 3044 W Myrtle St Phoenix AZ 85051 Office: Ariz State Bd Pharmacy 5060 N 19th Ave Phoenix AZ 85015

LLOYD, R(USSELL) DUANE, federal agency official; b. Soda Springs, Idaho, Feb. 11, 1930; s. Russell Carl and Annetta (Norstrom) L.; m. Joyce E. Bush, Sept. 8, 1952; children: Karen, Kathryn, Leslie, Michael, David, Annette, Mary, Susannah, Spencer, Rebecca, Rachel. BS in Forestry, U. Idaho, 1952; PhD, Utah State U., 1959. Rsch. economist econ. rsch. svc. USDA, Reno, Nev., 1957-61; staff economist Bur. Land Mgmt. U.S. Dept. Interior, Washington, 1961-65; asst. sta. dir. Forest Svc. Rsch., Ft. Collins, Colo., 1965-70; spl. staff asst. Forest Svc. Rsch., Washington, 1970-71, rsch. program leader, 1971-74; dep. sta. dir. Forest Svc. Rsch., Broomall, Pa., 1974-80; asst. sta. dir. Forest Svc. Rsch., Ogden, Utah, 1980-88; dep. sta. dir. Forest Svc. Rsch., Ogden, 1988—. With U.S. Army, 1952-54. Recipient creative scholarship U. Idaho, 1952, Pub. Svc. award The Nature Conservancy, 1985. Mem. Soc. for Range Mgmt. Mormon. Office: Intermountain Rsch Station 324 25th St Ogden UT 84401

LO, WAITUCK, artist; b. Honolulu, June 9, 1919; s. Wai Tong and Kam T. Lo; m. Agnes Lo Ching; Jan. 4, 1958; children: Edwina, Felix, Lisa Ann. BS, Utopia U., Shanghai, China, 1942; postgrad., Yen Yu Inst. Fine Art, Shanghai, Ind. U. Exhibited in group shows at Assn. Honolulu Artists Jury Art Show, 1956, 57 (Most Decorative award 1956, 57), Assn. Honolulu Artists non-jury show, 1957 (Popular award 1957), Narcissus Festival Art Exhibition, 1960 (Kaiser award 1960, Most Popular award 1960), Maui County Fair Art Exhibition, 1963 (2d prize 1963). Recipient 1st Place Water Color award Assn. Honolulu Artists, 1965, 68, Hayward award Assn. Honolulu Artists, 1968, 1st Place Water Color award Home Builders Assn. Art Show, 1966; Honorable Mention in Oil and Water Color, Assn. Honolulu Artists, 1966, Internat. Assn. Artists, 1979. Club: Toastmasters (Honolulu) (pres. 1986). Home: 6080 Keoki Pl Honolulu HI 96821

LOBELL, WILLIAM JOSEPH, retail executive; b. Washington, May 10, 1947; s. Henry and Mary Catherine (Paul) L.; m. Beverly Ann Barker, Feb. 19, 1966; children: April Ann, Angie Ann, Aaron William Lobel. Student, San Diego City Coll., 1966-68. Pvt. practice as music tchr., dance band mgr., guitarist San Diego, 1959-64; retail drug clk. Sav-On Drug Inc. (div. Am. Drug Stores), San Diego, 1964-66, receiving dept. mgr., 1966-67, svc. mgr., 1967-68, mdse. mgr., 1969-70, asst. mgr., 1970-72, asst. gen. mgr., 1972-74; gen. store mgr. Sav-On Drug Inc. (div. Am. Drug Stores), Solana Beach, Calif., 1974-82; dist. mgr. Sav-On Drug Inc. (div. Am. Drug Stores), Anaheim, Calif., 1982—. Founding mem. Community Ch. Delmar (Calif.), 1978, program dir., 1979. Republican. Home: 552 S Willowspring Dr Encinitas CA 92024 Office: Sav-On Drugs Inc 1500 S Anaheim Blvd Anaheim CA 92805

LOBNER, KNEELAND HARKNESS, lawyer; b. Sacramento, Calif., Feb. 2, 1919; s. Leo Kneeland and Laura (Roberts) L.; m. Adele Frances Ohe,

Dec. 20, 1941 (dec. Sept. 1987); children: Breton K., Robert K., Susan. A. Lobner Schroeder; m. Marilyn Mahaffey Dowden, Dec. 30, 1988. A.A., Sacramento City Coll., 1939; J.D., Hastings Coll. Law, 1944. Bar: Calif. 1946, U.S. Supreme Ct. 1960. Atty. City of Auburn, Calif., 1946-47; asso. firm K.D. Robinson, Auburn, 1946-47; dep. dist. atty. Sacramento County, 1947-49; atty. Calif. Automobile Assn., Sacramento, 1949-52; ptnr. Lobner and Bull, Sacramento, 1958—; advocate Am. Bd. Trial Advocates, 1972, pres. Sacramento chpt., 1985; bd. dirs. Hastings Coll. Law, 1986. Councilman, City of Sacramento, 1957-62, vice mayor, 1962; mem. Sacramento Met. Adv. Com., 1957-59; mem. Sacramento Redevel. Agy., 1964-73, chmn., 1970-72; mem. Sacramento Estate Planning Council, 1960—, Sacramento County Republican Central Com., 1955-57, Calif. Rep. Central Com., 1962-68; bd. dirs. Am. Cancer Soc., Sacramento, 1956-64, pres., 1963-64; bd. dirs. Calif. Mus. Assn., 1968-73, pres., 1969-71; bd. dirs. Am. Heart Assn., Sacramento, 1958-68; bd. govs. Hastings Law Coll., 1960—, pres., 1966, bd. dirs. 1986—; pres. Hastings 1066 Found., 1976; bd. dirs. Sacramento Symphony Found.; bd. dirs., pres. Crystal Shores West Assn. Nev. Served with AUS, 1944-46. Recipient Outstanding Alumnus award Hastings Coll. Law, 1976. Fellow Am. Coll. Probate Counsel; mem. Internat. Assn. Def. Counsel, Am. Bd. Trial Advocates (advocate), Def. Rsch. Inst., ABA, Sacramento County Bar Assn. (pres. 1973), State Bar Calif., Am. Judicature Soc., Better Bus. Bur. Sacramento (pres. 1967), Sacramento Zool. Soc. (pres. 1965), Am. Legion, Sacramento County Bar Coun. Clubs: Del Paso Country, Elks, Grandfathers Club Am. (Sacramento chpt.). Office: 717 20th St Sacramento CA 95814

LOCATELLI, PAUL LEO, university administrator, educator; b. Santa Cruz, Calif., Sept. 16, 1938; s. Vincent Dino and Marie Josephine (Piccone) L. B.S., Santa Clara U., 1961; M. Div., Jesuit Sch. Theology, 1974; D.B.A., U. So. Calif., 1971. C.P.A., Calif. Ordained priest Roman Catholic Ch., 1974. Acct., Kasch, Lautze & Lautze, San Jose, Calif., 1960-61, Wolf & Co., San Francisco, 1973-74; prof. acctg. Santa Clara U., Calif., 1974-86, assoc. dean Sch. Bus., 1975-78, acad. v.p., 1978-86, pres., 1988—; sr. commr. Western Assn. Schs. and Colls., from 1982; rector, prof. acctg. Loyola Marymount U., Los Angeles, 1986-88. Trustee, Bellarmine Coll. Prep., San Jose, 1975—, U. San Francisco, 1979-86, Seattle U., 1983—. Named Outstanding Tchr. of Yr., Santa Clara U., 1978. Mem. Calif. Soc. CPAs, Am. Inst. CPAs, Am. Acctg. Assn. Democrat. Club: Commonwealth (San Francisco). Office: Santa Clara U Office of Pres Santa Clara CA 95053 *

LOCH, PATRICIA ANN, software company executive, consultant; b. Omaha, May 2, 1944; d. Frank and Elizabeth (Duffield) Barrick; m. Charles Joseph Loch, Nov. 25, 1967; children: Michelle Kathleen, Justin Randall. BS in Math., Wake Forest U., 1966. Programmer IBM, Raleigh, N.C., 1966-68, Almay Cosmetics, Raleigh, N.C., 1968; contract programmer Kelly Assocs., Mpls., 1969-70, Bre-Mar Systems, N.Y.C., 1971; systems analyst Met. Life Ins. Co., N.Y.C., 1970-71; cons. Bd. Coop. Edn. Svcs., Yorktown, N.Y., 1972-75; pres., cons. P. Loch Assocs., Danville, Calif., 1975—; cons. Target Pub., Pleasanton, Calif., 1976-88. Mem. Assn. Small System Users (dir. membership 1981-82, dir. facilities 1985-87), NAFE, AAUW, Round Hill Country (Alamo, Calif.), Amador Athletic Club (Pleasanton). Home and Office: 181 Emmons Canyon Ln Ste 200 Danville CA 94526

LOCHMILLER, KURTIS L., real estate entrepreneur; b. Sacramento, Dec. 30, 1952; s. Rodney Glen and Mary Margaret (Frauen) L.; m. Mariye Susan Mizuki, Nov. 9, 1951; children: Margaux Sian, Chase Jordan. BA in Econs. and Fin., U. Denver, 1975. Dist. sales mgr. Hertz Truck Div., Denver, 1975-76; drilling foreman Shell Oil, Alaska, Mont., Colo., 1976-79; pres., owner Kurtex Mortgage & Devel. Co., Denver, 1979—, Kurtex Properties Inc., Denver, 1980-86; pres., chief exec. officer Kurtex Inc., Denver, 1981—, Bankers Pacific Mortgage, Denver, 1980—, Bankers Fin. Escrow Corp., Denver, 1984—, Northwest Title & Escrow, Denver, 1984—; pres., chief. exec. officer Steamboat Title, Steamboat Springs, Colo., 1985—, First Escrow, Denver, 1986—, Fidelity-Commonwealth-Continental Escrow, Denver, 1984—; pres. Colonnade Ltd., Denver, 1981-88. V.p., founder Colfax on the Hill, Denver, 1984; mediator, arbitrator Arbitrator/Mediation Assn., Denver, 1986; mem. Police Athletic League, Denver, 1988. Recipient Pres. Spl. Achievement/Founder award Colfax on the Hill, Denver, 1984, Spl. Mayor's award, City & County of Denver, 1985. Mem. Nat. Assn.of Real Estate Appraisers, Internat. Brotherhood of Teamsters, Colo. Mortgage Bankers Assn., Mortgage Banking Assn., Denver C. of C., Phi Beta Kappa, Omicron Delta Epsilon. Clubs: U.S. Karate Assn. (Phoenix) (3d degree Black Belt), Ferrari (Portland). Lodge: Internat. Supreme Council Order of Demolay. Home: 1 Carriage Ln Littleton CO 80121 Office: Bankers Fin Escrow Corp 360 Garfield Ste 630 Denver CO 80209

LOCK, ALEXANDER, accountant. BA, Calif. State U., Stanislaus. Ops. mgr. Western U. Mfg. Co., San Francisco, 1968-74; chief exec. officer A. Lock & Assocs., Sunnyvale, Calif., 1972—; sr. acct. Oroweat Foods Co., South San Francisco, 1976-80; acctg. mgr. FMC Corp., San Jose, Calif., 1980-81; fin. acct. Magic Pan Internat., San Francisco, 1981-86; pres., chief exec. officer The Alock Corp., San Francisco, 1982-85; with San Mateo County (Calif.) Transit Dist., Burlingame, 1988—. Bd. mgrs. YMCA of San Francisco, 1975-79, 1987—, dir. Endowment Devel. Com., 1986—, gen. chmn. Sustaining Membership Com., 1988, charter mem. Heritage Club, 1981— (membership achievement award 1988, named Benefactor of Youth, 1980); Big Bro., Big Bros./Big Sisters of Santa Clara County, San Jose, 1985—; mem. Chinese for Affirmative Action, Asian Bus. League, 1981—, West Coast Motor Coach Mus., 1980—. Mem. Nat. Assn. Accts., Am. Assn. of Individual Investors, The Press Club of San Francisco, Internat. Bus Collectors (Jackie Wilson award 1986), Commonwealth Club of Calif., Motor Bus Soc., Vizsla Club of Am., Chinese Hist. Soc., San Francisco Hist. Soc., Bay Area Electrical Railway Assn., Electrical Railway Hist. Assn. of Southern Calif., Western Transit Soc. Office: A Lock & Assocs PO Box 2562 Sunnyvale CA 94087

LOCKARD, THOMAS SWIFT, JR., communications executive; b. Columbia, Pa., Aug. 12, 1924; s. Thomas Swift and Bertha Mary (Jewell) L.; m. Blanche Galbraith Miller, June 12, 1955; children: Christianne Jewel, Rebecca Galbraith, Katherine Rossiter. BA in Econs., Franklin and Marshall Coll., 1950. Assoc. sales dir. N.Y. Mag., 1967-72; v.p. mktg. Mag. Pubs. Assn., N.Y.C., 1972-74; v.p., assoc. pub. Saturday Review, N.Y.C., 1974-76; dir. mktg. Petersen Pub., N.Y.C., 1976-77; v.p., assoc. pub. New West Mag., Beverly Hills, Calif., 1978-80; dir. spl. mag. projects Knapp Communications Corp.; nat. sales mgr. UPI; lectr. pub. procedures Radcliffe Coll.; lectr. U. So. Calif. Mem. Montclair (N.J.) Bd. Edn., 1969-71. Lt. comdr. USNR, 1943-46, 50-53. Mem. Advt. Club Los Angeles, Mag. Pubs. Assn., Western Pub. Assn. (dir.), Los Angeles Club, Ironwood Country Club (Palm Desert, Calif.). Republican.

LOCKART, BARBETTA, counselor, jeweler, artwear designer; b. Sacramento, Calif., Feb. 28, 1947; d. Bernard Elwood and Naomi Joyce (Wilson) L.; m. Michael Stanley Ray, Dec. 29, 1982 (div.). AA in English, Southwestern Coll., Chula Vista, Calif., 1974; BA, San Diego State U., 1975; MA in Edn. Adminstrn., N.Mex. State U., Las Cruces, 1979, MA in Counseling and Guidance, 1981. Sec., interim coord., tchr. Indian Edn. Project, Palm Springs (Calif.) Unified Sch. Dist., 1976-79; outreach counselor Tecumseh House/Boston Indian Coun., 1980-81, asst. dir., 1981; acad. counselor, coord. native Am. affairs Ea. N.Mex. U., Portales, 1981-82; ind. researcher in field of counseling, Albuquerque, 1982—; counseling family therapy, Albuquerque, 1988—; owner Dearwater Designs, Albuquerque, 1985—; speaker in field of community edn., alcoholism, urban native Am. women. Rockefeller Found. fellow, 1978-79; Nat. Inst. Edn. fellow, 1979-80. Author: Resolving Discipline Problems for Indian Students: A Preventative Approach, 1981, Auctions and Auction-Going: Make Them Pay Off for You; contbr. articles to profl. jours.

LOCKE, JAMES DONALD, mechanical engineer; b. Bolivar, Mo., Oct. 12, 1924; s. James William and Bernice Melissa (Shuck); m. Grace Frances Cassidy, Dec. 26, 1952. AA, SW Bapt. Coll., 1944; ME, U. Mo., 1948. Registered profl. engr., Ariz. Engr. U.S Bur. Reclamations, Phoenix, 1948-51; engr. various positions Goodyear Aerospace Corp., Litchfield Park, Ariz., 1951-87; pvt. practice Phoenix, 1987—; cons. in field. Mem. Am. Soc. Mech. Engrs., Soc. Plastics Engrs. (treas. 1976-82), Am. Soc. Testing Materials (good service award 1987), Nat. Soc. Profl. Engrs., Am. Inst. Aero. and Astronautics. Republican. Baptist. Home and Office: 1731 W Highland Ave Phoenix AZ 85015

LOCKE, RANDY LEE, property management executive; b. Athens, Ohio, July 16, 1944; s. Bernard Leroy Porter and Wyona Gail (Stauffer) Chapon; m. Eve Gayle Resnik, Aug. 31, 1975 (div. Jan. 1984); children: Dahvia Yvette, Kiptyn Randahl. BA, Stanford U., 1972. Mktg. mgr. Kampgrounds of Am., Inc., Billings, Mont., 1973-75; wholesaler Crestwood Lumber, Inc., South San Francisco, 1975-80; pres. Earthsong Homes, Inc., Pacifica, Calif., 1980-84; mng. assoc. H.E.B. Properties, Mountain View, Calif., 1984—. Author: Resident Manager's Handbook, 1987, Mission to South Vietnam, 1968. Pres. Pacificans for Individual and Economic Rights (PIER), Pacifica, Calif., 1980-81. With USAF, 1962-66. Mem. Inst. Real Estate Mgmt., SPAUG. Republican. Methodist. Home: 322 Bryant St Palo Alto CA 94301 Office: HEB Properties 2330 California St Ste 17 Mountain View CA 94040

LOCKE, RICHARD COUTANT, telecommunications executive; b. Charlottesville, Va., Mar. 5, 1948; s. William Webber and Doreen Louise (Thomas) L.; m. Tracey Barker, Oct. 10; 1 child, Andrew. BS in Urban Planning, U. Wash., 1970. Dir. planning Skid Row Community Council, Seattle, 1972-75; housing dir. Pike Place Market Preservation and Devel. Authority, Seattle, 1976-79; chief exec. Locke Systems Inc., Seattle, 1980—; v.p. govt. info. svcs. pub. works div. GTE. Pres. Plymouth Housing Group, Seattle, 1975.

LOCKE, WILLIAM LOUIS, pharmacist; b. Reno, May 20, 1946; s. John William and Janice Elizabeth (Leavy) L.; m. Sarah Elizabeth Witherell, June 19, 1978 (div. Apr. 1983); children: Kate MacKenzie, Nicholas Kristopher; m. Katherine Ann Beach, Sept. 26, 1987. BS in Pharmacy, U. Pacific, 1969. Registered pharmacist. Treas. Nev. Pharmacists Assn., Reno, 1982-84, bd. dirs., 1984-87, pres., 1987—. With US Air N.G., 1969-75. Republican. Home: 4310 Elmwood Ln Reno NV 89509 Office: Hales Drug Inc 975 Ryland Reno NV 89520

LOCKHART, JAMES BICKNELL, JR., manufacturing company executive; b. Taunton, Mass., Mar. 27, 1918; s. James Bicknell and Charlotte Bradford (Babbitt) L.; m. Mary Ann Reigel, Oct. 2, 1943; children: Joan Riegel, James B. II, Ann Murchie, Brenda Margaret. BS, Yale U., 1940; MBA, Northwestern U., 1941; MS, USN Acad., 1945. Cost acct. GE, Lynn, Mass., 1941-42; mgmt. cons. MacDonald Bros., Boston, 1945-48; chief indsl. engr. Riegel Paper Corp., N.Y.C., 1948, purchasing agt., 1948-50, asst. to v.p. prod., 1950-51, mill mgr., 1951-54, N.Y. mgr. indsl. and mcht. sales, 1954-57, corp. sec., 1955-63, dir., 1957-67, v.p., 1957-63, corp. controller, 1958-63; dir., pres., chief exec. officer Conwed Corp., St. Paul, 1963-71, Lockhart & Conwed, Orange, Calif., 1971-74, Monier Co., 1974-78; pres., chief exec. officer Isolite Corp., Hawthorne, Calif., 1978-85, Locknell Corp., Orange, 1985—. Authro: SMG: The Stock Market Game, 1987. Pres., dir. Riegelsville (Pa.) Cemetery; v.p., dir. Minn. Sci. Mus. (permanent exhibit named in honor 1974), Big Bros. of Am. (recipient Svc. award 1975, 77); mem. com. Nat. UN Day, 1978; founder, dir., Old Town Restorations, 1970. Lt. USNR, 1942-46, PTO. Recipient Honor award Wisdom Soc., 1975, Key to City San Bernadino (Calif.), 1977. Mem. Specialty Paper and Bd. Assn. (exec. com. N.Y. sect.), Acoustical Insulating Materials Assn. (pres., dir.), Mayflower Soc., Travelers Century Club, Circumnavigators Club. Republican. Episcopalian. Home: 635 E Palmdale Ave Orangedale CA 92665 Office: Locknell Corp 1400 E Katella Ave Ste 224 Orange CA 92667

LOCKHART, KENNETH BURTON, architectural company executive; b. Charles City, Iowa, Oct. 2, 1916; s. Louis James and Dorothy Hildred (Hurst) L.; m. Mary Francis Coan, July 10, 1945 (div.): children: Brian, Leslie; m. Susan Jacobs, Sept. 27, 1964. Project adminstr. Fla. So. Coll., Lakeland, 1946-50; farm mgr. Frank Lloyd Wright Found., Spring Green, Wis., 1951-52, mem. staff, 1952-62; dir. quality assurance Taliesin Assoc. Architects, Spring Green and Scottsdale, Ariz., 1963—. Mem. Constrn. Specifications Inst. (cert. constrn. specifier, chmn. reg. tech. 1983—, spectext com. 1986-88, bd. dirs. Phoenix chpt. 1985-86, sec. Phoenix chpt. 1986-88, recipient Hon. Mention 1982, 83, 86, 87, 89, Honor award 1984, S.W. region Dir.'s Citation 1986, Outstanding Profl. award 1986, chpt. pres.'s cert. 1987-88). Home and Office: Frank Lloyd Wright Found 13201 N 108th St Scottsdale AZ 85261-4430

LOCKHART, PATRICK GALE, real estate corporation officer; b. Portland, Oreg., Aug. 20, 1947; s. Gale Anthony and June Alice (Mathews) L.; m. Janelle Lockhart, Aug. 10, 1968 (div. 1978); 1 child, Sona; m. Rosemary Thorp, Mar. 25, 1977; children: Anne Marie, Patricia. BS in Mktg. and Econ., Portland State U., 1972. Lic. real estate broker, Oreg., Wash. Sec., treas. Execulodge Corp., Portland, 1978—; pres. Exec. Properties, Portland, 1981—, Exec. Mortgage and Investment Co., Portland, 1986—, Exec. Appraisal, Portland, 1985—; v.p. Exec. Group, Portland, 1986—; pres. Key Property Mgmt., Portland, 1986-88, Nendels Corp., Portland, 1987-88. Mem. Internat. Soc. Financiers, Nat. Assn. Realtors, Oreg. Assn. Realtors., Washington County Bd. Realtors, Hotel/Motel Brokers Am., Portland C. of C., Portland State U. Alumni (bd. dirs. 1987), Multnomah Athletic Club, Rotary. Republican. Roman Catholic. Office: Exec Properties 12725 SE 66th Ave Ste 102 Portland OR 97223

LOCKWOOD, IONA LOUISE, tax consultant; b. Bremerton, Wash., Oct. 21, 1942; d. Owen Orville and Frances Maude (Fisher) Majorowicz; m. Merwyn Robert Jens Lockwood, Sept. 17, 1966. BS, Oreg. State U., 1965. Rsch. asst. oceanography Oreg. State U., Corvallis, 1966-69; tax cons. H&R Block, Portland, Oreg., 1969-75, Scheer & Stewart, Milwaukie, Oreg., 1976-77; prin. Iona Lockwood Tax Svc., Milwaukie, 1978—; owner, mgr. Clackamas Book Exchange, Milwaukie, 1981—. Mem. Oreg. Assn. Tax Cons., Romance Writers Am. (local chpt. treas. 1983-88, pres. 1988—). Republican. Baptist. Home: 11635 SE Home Ave Milwaukie OR 97222 Office: Iona Lockwood Tax Svc 7000 SE Thiessen Rd Milwaukie OR 97267

LOCKWOOD, MICHAEL JAMES, management executive; b. Casa Grande, Ariz., May 12, 1948; s. Donald L. and Helen M. (Robins) L. BS, U. Nebr., 1977; postgrad., Troy State U. Sales rep. The Upjohn Co., Bakersfield, Calif., 1980-81; administrv. resident Luth. Hosp. and Home Soc., Fargo, N.D., 1981; adminstr. Luth. Hosp. and Home Soc., Soldotna, Alaska, 1981-88; sr. adminstr. LHS Mgmt. Co., Soldotna, 1988—; chmn. Lutheran Hosp. and Home Soc. SP Network, Anchorage, 1988—. Pub. rels. chmn., Dem. Dist. 5, Soldotna, 1988; instr. Jr. Achievement, Soldotna, 1988; treas. Women's Resource and Crises Ctr., Soldotna, 1982-84; bd. dirs. Community Care Ctr., Soldotna, 1986-88; chmn. Polit. Action Com., 1988-89; chmn. United Way Allocations Com., 1988-89, bd. dirs., 1989—. Mem. Am. Coll. Health Care, Health Assn. of Alaska (chmn. 1986-87, legis. chmn., 1987-88, allocation com. chmn. 1988—), Rotary, Elks. Democrat. Office: Cen Peninsula Gen Hosp 250 Hospital Pl Soldotna AK 99669

LODICO, ANTHONY THOMAS, medical diagnostic products executive; b. Chgo., Aug. 4, 1929; s. Leonard L. and Antoinette (Loguidice) L.; m. Gloria Erikson, Aug. 1, 1982 (div. 1987); 1 child, Mark Alan. LLB, U. Chgo., 1947; M of Internat. Mgmt., Am. Grad. Sch. of Internat. Mgmt., Phoenix, 1949; MA in Bus. Mgmt., Claremont (Calif.) Grad. Sch., 1980, PhD in Exec. Mgmt., 1982. Br. mgr. mktg., ethical drugs Sterling Drug Co., Lima, Peru, 1952-58; regional dir. Home Products Internat., Inc., N.Y.C., 1958-66; gen. mgr. Incolgrasos, S.A., Medellin, Colombia, 1966-70; mng. dir. Avionics Del Mar Biomedical, Inc., L.A., 1970-72; pres. Cardio Dynamics Internat., Inc., L.A., 1972-80, Biognostic Internat. Inc., San Diego, 1981—; internat. cons. Eisai Co., Ltd., Tokyo, 1987—, Barnes Hind Japan, Tokyo, 1987—, Mizuko Medy Co., Ltd., Saga, Japan, 1987—. 1st lt. U.S. Army, 1950-51, Korea. Democrat. Office: Biognostic Internat Inc 1201 Camino Del Mar Del Mar CA 92014

LODMELL, JOHN STEPHEN, chemist, aerial photographer; b. Washington, June 28, 1962; s. John Gary Lodmell and Susan (Maxwell) Law. BS, U. Mont., 1985, postgrad., 1988—. Chemist, aerial fire photographer U.S. Forest Service, Missoula, Mont., 1984-88. Watkins research scholar U. Mont., 1984. Home: Box 9064 Missoula MT 59807

LODMER, EMILY LEVIN, English language educator; b. Denver, Mar. 1, 1948; d. Nathaniel Ira and Selma Carolyn (Weintraub) Levin; m. Sheldon Ira Lodmer, Nov. 28, 1970; children: Abby Rebecca, Zachary Harris. Student, Universidad Nacional Autonoma de Mex., Mexico City, 1967; BA in Spanish and French, UCLA, 1969, MA in Applied Linguistics, 1979. Cert. secondary, community coll. tchr., Calif. Tchr. Los Angeles Children's Ctrs., 1969-70; tchr. Spanish, ESL Anaheim (Calif.) Union High Sch. Dist., 1970-75; tchr. Spanish, French Santa Monica (Calif.) Unified Sch. Dist., 1975-76; prof. ESL Santa Monica Coll., 1977—; mem. Santa Monica Coll. ESL Adv. Council, 1983—; presenter Jerusalem Conf. ESL, Eng. as a Fgn. Lang., Hebrew U., 1985, Catesol State Conf., 1986, 88, Santa Monica Coll. ESL Consortium, 1986; bd. dirs. Latin Am. Bookfair, Los Angeles, 1988. Sch. Bd. pres. Malibu (Calif.) Jewish Ctr. and Synagogue, 1980-81. Mem. Calif. Tchrs. ESL (presenter conf. Oakland 1986, San Francisco, 1988), acting coordinator Santa Monica Coll. 1988, Alpha Mu Gamma. Office: Santa Monica Coll Dept English 1900 Pico Blvd Santa Monica CA 90405-1628

LOEB, JOYCE LICHTGARN, interior designer, civic worker; b. Portland, Oreg., May 20, 1936; d. Elias Lichtgarn and Sylvia Amy (Margulies) Freedman; m. Stanley Robinson Loeb, Aug. 14, 1960; children: Carl Eli, Eric Adam. Student U. Calif.-Berkeley, 1954-56; B.S., Lewis and Clark Coll., 1958; postgrad. art and architecture, Portland State U., 1976. Tchr. art David Douglas Sch. Dist., Portland, 1958-59, 61-64; tchr., chmn. art dept. Grant Union High Sch. Dist., Sacramento, 1959-60; designer, pres. Joyce Loeb Interior Design, Inc., Portland, 1976—; cons. designer to various developers of health care facilities. Chairperson fundraisers for civic orgns. and Jewish orgns.; mem. women's com. Reed Coll.; bd. dirs. Met. Family Services, Portland, 1968-71, Young Audiences, Inc., Portland, 1970-76, 78-80, Portland Opera Assn., 1978-84, Arts Celebration, Inc., Portland, 1984—, Congregation Beth Israel, 1986—; chmn. Artquake Festival, 1985, Operaball, 1987; v.p. Beth Israel Sisterhood, 1981-83; trustee Congregation Beth Israel, 1986—, chmn. art interior design com. Mem. Soc. Interior Designers, Nat. Council Jewish Women. Democrat. Club: Multnomah Athletic. Home: 1546 SW Upland Dr Portland OR 97221

LOEBNER, EGON EZRIEL, physicist; b. Plzen, Czechoslovakia, Feb. 24, 1924; s. Emil and Josephine (Koeser) L.; came to U.S., 1947, naturalized, 1952; BA in Physics, U. Buffalo, 1950, PhD in Physics, 1955; m. Sonya S. Sajovics, June 18, 1950; children: Gary Emil, Benny Joseph, Mindy Sue. Draftsman, Danek & Co., Bolevec, Czechoslavakia, 1941-42, asst. to chief engr. Terezin Waterworks, 1942-44; sr. engr. Sylvania Electric Products, Inc., Buffalo and Boston, 1952-55; mem. tech. staff RCA Labs., Princeton, N.J., 1955-61; mgr., rsch. specialist H.P. Assos., Palo Alto, Calif., 1961-65; dept. head, rsch. adviser Hewlett-Packard Labs., 1965-74, lab. assoc., 1976-77, mgr. data base mgmt. systems dept., 1977-80, mgr. cognitive interface dept., 1980-85, counselor sci. and tech. 1985—; counselor sci. and technol. affairs U.S. embassy, Moscow, 1974-76; lectr. Stanford U., part-time 1968-74; lectr. U. Calif. at Santa Cruz, 1972-74. Mem. N.J. Commn. on Radiation Protection, 1960-62; mem. lay adv. com. on math. Unified Palo Alto Sch. Dist., 1964-66. Bd. dirs. Jewish Center, Princeton, 1957-59. Fellow IEEE; mem. Am. Phys. Soc., Semiotics Soc. Am., Am. Assn. Artificial Intelligence, Am. Optical Soc., AAAS, Sigma Xi, Assn. for Computing Machinery, Cognitive Sci. Soc., N.Y. Acad. Scis., Calif. Acad. Scis., Soc. Hist. Tech., Hist. Sci. Soc., Sigma Alpha Mu. Democrat. Jewish. Club: Palo Alto Hills Golf and Country, Commonwealth. Research in physics, chemistry, electronics, metalurgy, psychology, biophysics, cybernetics, math., sci. policy, linguistics, neural networks, data processing, constitutional law, hist. tech. and hist. sci. Patentee in optoelectronics. Home: 2934 Alexis Dr Palo Alto CA 94304 Office: Hewlett Packard Labs 1501 Page Mill Rd Palo Alto CA 94304

LOEN, RAYMOND ORDELL, management consultant; b. Howard, S.D., July 15, 1924; s. Lauris and Selina Edith (Langorgen) L.; m. Omeline Janelle, June 17, 1950; children: Kurtis, Jon, Philip, Pamela, Brock. BS, Columbia U., 1948, MS, 1949. Salesman, sales trainer, city sales mgr. Uarco, Inc., N.Y.C. and Phila., 1949-53; staff cons., sr. cons. H.B. Maynard & Co., Inc., Pitts., 1953-59; sales tng. mgr., dir. mgmt. services Fibreboard Corp., San Francisco, 1959-63; prin. R.O. Loen Co., San Anselmo, Calif. and Lake Oswego, Oreg., 1963—; founder, dir. Loen, Brandt Inc., Palo Alto, Calif. 1965-70; bd. dirs., founder Swift Energy Co., Houston. Author: Manage More by Doing Less, 1971; contbr. articles to profl. jours. Served to lt. (j.g.) USNR, 1943-46, PTO. Mem. Salmon & Steelhead Anglers of Oreg., Sons of Norway, Mountain Park Racquet Club, Columbia Univ. Sch. Bus. Alumni Assn., Oreg. Trout, Alpha Kappa Psi. Republican.

LOESER, JOHN DAVID, neurosurgeon, educator; b. Newark, Dec. 14, 1935; s. Lewis Henry and Rhoda Sophie (Levy) L.; m. Susan Winifred Becker, June 11, 1961 (div. 1974); children: Sally Ann, Thomas Eric, Derek William; m. Karen Winslow, Dec. 29, 1977; 1 child, David Winslow. BA, Harvard U., 1957; MD, NYU, 1961. Diplomate Am. Bd. Neurol. Surgery; cert. Nat. Bd. Med. Examiners.; lic. neurosurgeon, Wash. Intern dept. surgery U. Calif., San Francisco, 1961-62; resident neurol. surgery U. Wash., Seattle, 1962-67; asst. prof. neurosurgery U. Calif., Irvine, 1967-68; asst. prof. neurol. surgery U. Wash., Seattle, 1969-75, assoc. prof., 1975-80, prof., 1980—, dir. Multidisciplinary Pain Clinic, 1983—; chief div. of neurosurgery Children's Hosp. & Med. Ctr. Contbr. articles to profl. jours. Served as maj. U.S. Army, 1968-70. Mem. Internat. Assn. Study of Pain (sec. 1985—), Am. Pain Soc. (treas. 1980-85, pres. 1986-87), Am. Assn Neurol. Surgeons, AAAS, Am. Soc. Functional and Stereotactic Neurosurgery, N. Pacific Soc. of Neurology and Psychiatry, Wash. Assn. Neurosurgery, Western Neurosurg. Soc., Am. Assn. Pain Medicine, King County Med. Soc., Cong. Neurol. Surgeons, Phi Beta Kappa, Alpha Omega Alpha. Home: 1142 38th Ave Seattle WA 98122 Office: U Wash Dept Neurol Surgery RI-20 Seattle WA 98195

LOEW, DAVID N., insurance company executive; b. Santa Monica, Calif., May 20, 1949; s. Marcus and Ethel L.; m. Fran, Aug. 29, 1970; children: Jeremy, Kevin, Sarah, Matthew. BS in Mkgt., San Jose State Coll.; MBA, Calif. State U., San Jose. CLU, Chartered Fin. Cons. Pres. Loew & Assocs., L.A., 1974—; spkr. in field; tchr. mktg. Calif. State U., San Jose. Past pres., bd. mem. Bay Cities Jewish Community Ctr.; bd. dirs. Jewish Community Ctrs. Assn.; personnel grievance com., Jewish Fedn., Council of Greater L.A.; vol. Jewish Big Brothers, 1976-81; pres. advisory council, Jewish Community Found.; cons. Jewish Fedn. Council Personnel benefits subcom., pension adminstrn. subcom., cafeteria benefits com.; bd. dirs. Southern Calif. Golf Assn. Recipient Rabbi Edgar F. Magnin Svc. award, 1988, Outstanding Achievement award, Jewish Big Bros., 1981. Mem. (life) Million Dollar Round Table. Office: 12121 Wilshire Blvd Los Angeles CA 90025

LOEWENSTEIN, WALTER BERNARD, nuclear power technologist; b. Gensungen, Hesse, Germany, Dec. 23, 1926; came to U.S., 1938; s. Louis and Johanna ((Katz) L.; m. Lenore C. Pearlman, June 21, 1959; children: Mark Victor, Marcia Beth. BS cum laude, U. Puget Sound, 1949; postgrad., U. Wash., 1949-50; PhD, Ohio State U., 1954. Registered profl. engr., Calif. Rsch. asst., fellow Ohio State U., Columbus, 1951-54; rsch. asst. Los Alamos Nat. Lab., 1952-54; sr. physicist, div. dir. Argonne (Ill.) Nat. Lab., 1954-73; dept. dir., dep. div. dir. Electric Power Rsch. Inst., Palo Alto, Calif., 1973—, mem. Large Aerosol Containment Experiment project br., 1983—; mem. Marviksen project bd. Studsvik Rsch. Ctr., Stockholm, 1978-85; mem. LOFT project bd. Nuclear Energy Agy., Paris, 1982—. With USNR, 1945-46. Fellow Am. Phys. Soc., Am. Nuclear Soc. (v.p., pres. 1989—). Jewish. Home: 515 Jefferson Dr Palo Alto CA 94303 Office: Electric Power Rsch Inst 3412 Hillview Palo Alto CA 94303

LOFF, BETTY GARLAND, religious educator; b. L.A., Aug. 18, 1932; d. Lewis Michael and Bernice (Siberz) Hohenthaner; m. Daniel David Loff, May 1, 1951; children: Dana Elizabeth, Tamra Marie. Grad., Lamson Dental Coll., L.A., 1950-51; M in Cathechist, Diocese Phoenix, 1975; postgrad., U. San Francisco, 1986—. Dental asst.various offices L.A., 1952-53; office mgr. Supply Co, Phoenix, 1968-71; adminstrv. asst. Diocese Phoenix Religious Edn., 1971-75; adminstrv. aast., intern religious edn. St. Theresa Ch., Phoenix, 1975-79; dir. religious edn. St. Paul Ch., Phoenix, 1979—; chmn. Catechetical Congress Diocese, 1971—, Diocesan Religious Edn. Adv. Bd., Phoenix, 1983-86; mem. steering & formation com., co-chmn., spirituality com. CADRE-Profl. Orgn. for Dirs. & Coords. Religious Edn., Phoenix, 1986—. Author-editor Catechetical Congress Job Description booklet, 1974; contbr. articles to profl. jours. Mem. Religious Edn. Assn.

Phoenix (sec. 1972-83). Home: 3801 E Laurel Ln Phoenix AZ 85028 Office: St Paul Cath Ch 330 W Coral Gables Dr Phoenix AZ 85023

LOFFICIER, RANDY JOANNE, writer; b. Phila., Feb. 3, 1953; d. Max Apfelbaum and Irene Marcia (Rosenberg) Gerken; m. Jean-Marc Lofficier, May 5, 1979. Grad. high sch., Rosemont, Pa. Cert. x-ray technologist. Free-lance writer 1979—; v.p. prodn. Starwatcher Graphics, Encino, Calif., 1985—. Author: The Best Video Films, 1984, Your Movie Guide to Musicals on Videotape, 1985, Basil, The Great Mouse Detective, 1986, (with Jean-Marc Lofficier) Doctor Who Programme Guide 1 and 2, 1981, Les Maitres de L'Insolite, 1985; (comic books) Fury of Firestorm #32, 1984, Arak #45-50, 1985, Action #579, 1986, Teen Titans #44 (screenplays) Mayday, 1982, Royal Flush, 1984, Terminus Four, 1985, The Airtight Garage, 1988; (tv screenplays) Science-Fiction Plus!, 1983, The Real Ghostbusters, 1986, Duck Tales, 1986, Bionic Six, 1987, others; contbg. and cons. editor L'Anee du Cinema Fantastique, 1983, The Official Explorers Moviebook, 1985, others; contbr. to Am. Cinematographer, Starlog, Heavy Metal, Twilight Zone mag., Weekley Reader, numerous others in U.S., France and Eng.; translator: Moebius, 1987, The Incal, 1988, French Ice, 1987-88, 1989. Mem. Animation Writers Am., Women in Film. Home: 6539 Jamieson Ave Reseda CA 91335 Office: Starwatcher Graphics Inc PO Box 17270 Encino CA 91416

LOFGREN, WILLIAM ARTHUR, small business owner; b. Denver; s. Roy Fredrick L. and Anita Nellie (Bach) Raia; m. Barbara Ann Basse, June 15, 1948 (div. July 1950); m. Mary Joan Bates, July 14, 1956; children: Chernelyn, Michelle, Michael, Madeline. Student, Colo. Sch. of Mines, Golden, 1947-49. Cert. mech. engr. Line driver Ringsby Trucking, Denver, 1950-52; foreman Manly Heating and Sheet Metal, Arvada, Colo., 1953-57; owner Bills Sheet Metal, Westminster, Colo., 1957—. With USN, 1952-53. Democrat. Roman Catholic. Home and Office: 3744 W 85th Ave Westminster CO 80030

LOFGREN, ZOE, county government official; b. San Mateo, Calif., Dec. 21, 1947; d. Milton R. and Mary Violet L.; m. John Marshall Collins, Oct. 22, 1978; children: Sheila Zoe Lofgren Collins, John Charles Lofgren Collins. BA in Polit. Sci., Stanford U., 1970; JD cum laude, U. Santa Clara, 1975. Bar: Calif., 1975. D.C. Adminstrv. asst. to Congressman Don Edwards, San Jose, Calif., 1970-79; ptnr. Webber and Lofgren, San Jose, 1979-81; mem. Santa Clara County Bd. Suprs., 1980—; part-time prof. Law, U. Santa Clara, 1978-80. Exec. dir. Community Housing Developers, Inc., 1979-80; trustee San Jose Community Coll. Dist., 1979-81; bd. dirs. Community Legal Svcs., 1978-81, San Jose Housing Svc. Ctr., 1978-79; pres. Calif. Voter Group, Inc., 1977, mem. adv. bd. 1978—; mem. steering com. sr. citizens housing referendum, 1978; del. Calif. State Bar Conv., 1979-82, Dem. Nat. Conv., 1976; active Assn. Immigration and Nationality Lawyers, 1976-82, Calif. State Dem. Cen. Com., 1975—, Santa Clara County Dem. Cen. Com., 1974-78, Notre Dame High Sch. Blue Ribbon Com., 1981—, Victim-Witness Adv. Bd., 1980—. Recipient Bancroft-Whitney award for Excellence in Criminal Procedure, 1973. Mem. Santa Clara County Bar Assn. (trustee 1979—), Santa Clara County Women Lawyers Com. (exec. bd. 1979-80), Santa Clara Law Sch. Alumni Assn. (v.p. 1977, pres. 1978), Nat. Women's Polit. Caucus, Assn. of Bay Area Govts. (exec. bd. 1981—). Office: Bd Suprs 70 W Hedding St San Jose CA 95110

LOFTHOUSE, RUSS WILBERT, school administrator; b. Chgo., Jan. 21, 1945; s. Russell Wilber and Anne Marie (Daker) L.; m. Pamlin I. Axelson, Aug. 7, 1976; one child, James. BA in Elem. Edn., U. Denver, 1971; MA in Elem. Edn., U. Colo., Denver, 1978. Cert. elem tchr., Colo., elem. prin., Colo. Tchr. Cherry Creek Schs., Englewood, Colo., 1971-86, prin., 1986—; mem. adv. bd. Teaching and Computers, N.Y.C., 1986—. Recipient Disting. Tchr. award Cherry Creek Schs., 1985; named Colo. Tchr. of Yr., Colo. Dept. Edn., 1986; runner-up Nat. Tchr. of Yr., 1986. Mem. Assn. Supervision and Curriculum Devel., Am. Acad. and Inst. Human Reason (dir. community leaders and succesful schs.), Fulbrite Tchrs. Alumni Assn., NEA, Nat. State Tchs. of Yr., Phi Delta Kappa. Home: 8505 E Temple Dr #502 Denver CO 80237 Office: Cherry Creek Sch Dist 4700 S Yosemite Englewood CO 80111

LOFTUS, THOMAS DANIEL, lawyer; b. Seattle, Nov. 8, 1930; s. Glendon Francis and Martha Helen (Wall) L. BA, U. Wash., 1952, JD, 1957. Bar: Wash. 1958, U.S. Ct. Appeals (9th cir.) 1958, U.S. Dist. Ct. Wash. 1958, U.S. Ct. Mil. Appeals, U.S. Supreme Ct. Trial atty. Northwestern Mut. Ins. Co., Seattle, 1958-62; sr. trial atty. Unigard Security Ins. Co., Seattle, 1962-68, asst. gen. counsel, 1969-83, govt. rels. counsel, 1983—; mem. Wash. Commn. on Jud. Conduct (formerly Jud. Qualifications Commn.), 1982-88, vice-chmn., 1987-88; judge pro tem Seattle Mcpl. Ct., 1973-81. Sec., treas. Seattle Opera Assn., 1980—; pres., bd. dirs. Vis. Nurse Svcs., 1979-88; pres., v.p. Salvation Army Adult Rehab. Ctr., 1979-86; vice chmn. Young Rep. Nat. Fedn., 1963-65; pres. Young Reps. King County, 1962-63; bd. dirs. Seattle Seafair, Inc., 1975; bd. dirs., gen. counsel Wash. Ins. Coun., 1984-86, sec., 1986-88, v.p., 1988—; bd. dirs. Arson Alarm Found. 1st lt. U.S. Army, 1952-54, col. Res., 1954-85. Fellow Am. Bar Found.; mem. Am. Arbitration Assn. (nat. panel arbitrators 1965—), Wash. Bar Assn. (gov. 1981-84), Seattle King County Bar Assn. (sec., trustee 1977-82), ABA (ho. of dels. 1984—), Internat. Assn. Ins. Counsel, Def. Rsch. Inst., Washington Def. Trial Lawyers Assn., Am. Judicature Soc., Res. Officers Assn., Judge Advocate General's Assn., U. Wash. Alumni Assn., Pi Sigma Alpha, Delta Sigma Rho, Phi Delta Phi, Theta Delta Chi. Republican. Presbyterian. Clubs: Coll. of Seattle, Wash. Athletic. Lodges: Masons, Shriners. Home: 3515 Magnolia Blvd West Seattle WA 98199 Office: 1215 4th Ave 18th Fl Seattle WA 98161

LOGAN, DAVID WALKER, graphic designer, art director; b. Boston, Apr. 15, 1948; s. Alexander Miller and Margaret (Wilson) L. AA, Pasadena City Coll., 1968; BA, U. Calif., Berkeley, 1970, Art Ctr. Coll. of Design, L.A., 1975. Asst. curator Pasadena City Coll., 1971-73; asst. art dir. John Coy Design, L.A., 1975-78; art dept. dir. Bryan Hardwick & Assoc., Palos Verdes, Calif., 1978-82, Engle Advt., L.A., 1982-85; pres. David Logan Design, L.A., 1985—. Mem. Art Dirs. Club of L.A. Democrat. Episcopalian. Office: David Logan Design 1942 Chariton St Los Angeles CA 90034

LOGAN, JAMES DAVID, electrical engineer; b. Ontario, Oreg., Oct. 10, 1940; s. Harry C. and Nellie O. (Kenward) L.; m. Linda C. McSweeney, Nov. 11, 1967 (div. 1988); children: Jeffrey D., Scott A., Yolanda Andersen. BS in Elec. Engring., U. Idaho, 1963, MS in Elec. Engring., 1965. Registered profl. engr., Wash., Oreg., Idaho. With staff U. Idaho, Moscow, 1961-63; with faculty dept. elec. engring. Wash. State U., Pullman, 1963-75, instr., 1963-69, asst. prof. elec. engring., 1969-75; v.p. Metriguard, Inc., Pullman, 1973-82, pres., chmn., 1982—; cons. Morrison-Knudsen Co., Boise, Idaho, 1983—, Greater Pullman Econ. Devel. Corp., 1985—. Patentee in field; inventor ultrasonic sheet material testing apparatus. Mem. ASTM, IEEE, Forest Products Rsch. Soc. Republican. Methodist. Home: NW 340 Janet Pullman WA 99163 Office: Metriguard Inc PO Box 399 Pullman WA 99163

LOGAN, LEE ROBERT, orthodontist; b. Los Angeles, June 24, 1923; s. Melvin Duncan and Margaret (Seltzer) L.; m. Maxine Nadler, June 20, 1975; children: Fritz, Dean, Scott, Gigi, Chad, Casey. BS, UCLA, 1952; DDS, Northwestern U., 1956, MS, 1961. Gen. practice dentistry, Reseda, Calif., 1958-59; practice dentistry specializing in orthodontics, Northridge, Calif., 1961—; pres. Lee R. Logan DDS Profl. Corp.; mem. staff Northridge Hosp., Tarzana Hosp.; owner Maxine's Talent Agy Inc.; guest lectr. UCLA, U. So. Calif. Served to lt. USNR, 1956-58. Diplomate Am. Bd. Orthodontics. Named (with wife) Couple of Yr. Austic Children Assn., 1986; recipient Nat. Philanthropy award, 1987. Fellow Internat. Acad. Nutrition; mem. Am., San Fernando Valley dental assns., Am. Assn. Orthodontists, Pacific Coast Soc. Orthodontists (dir., pres. so. sect. 1974-75, chmn. membership 1981-83), Found. Orthodontic Research (charter mem.), Calif. Soc. Orthodontists (chmn. peer rev. 1982-89), G.U. Black Soc. (charter mem.), Angle Soc. Orthodontists (pres. 1986-87, bd. dirs. 1982-89, nat. pres. 1985-87), Xi Psi Phi. Club: U.S.C. Century. Contbr. articles to profl. jours. Home: 4830 Encino Ave Encino CA 91316 Office: 18250 Roscoe Blvd Northridge CA 91324

LOGAN, NANCY JANE, broadcast sales and marketing executive; b. Buffalo, Oct. 29, 1957; d. Harry Lee and MaryJane (Redinger) Logan. AA, Erie Community Coll., Buffalo, 1977; BS, SUNY, Brockport, 1979. Account exec. Sta. WBUF Radio, Buffalo, 1979-80; account exec. Sta. WBEN Radio, Buffalo, 1980-82; regional mgr. Westwood One Radio Networks, L.A., 1983-84; mktg. rep. TV Guide Mag., L.A., 1984-88, broadcast mktg. supr., 1988-89, western mgr. tune-in advt., 1989—. Mem. NATAS, Am. Women in Radio & TV (pres. so. Calif. chpt. 1988-89), Publicity Club L.A. Democrat. Presbyterian. Home: 2627 5th St Santa Monica CA 90405 Office: TV Guide 9000 Sunset Blvd Ste 300 Los Angeles CA 90069

LOGAN, STEVE J., infosystems specialist; b. Smithcenter, Kans., Sept. 12, 1952; s. James Author and Virgie (Ray) L.; m. Christie Dee Dellos, July 21, 1973; children: Stephanie Dawn, Clayton James, Cole Adam. AAS, Northwest Community Coll., Powell, Wyo., 1973. Prodn., salesperson Fremont Beverages, Inc., Worland, Wyo., 1970-74, programmer analyst, 1974-76, dir. data processing, 1976-86, mgr. systems analysis, 1986—. Mem. NSDA Fin. Mgmt. Com., Washington, 1987—. Republican. Baptist. Lodges: Masons (Master 1981-82), Shriners. Home: 111 Country Dr Worland WY 82401 Office: Fremont Beverages Inc PO Box 58 Worland WY 82401

LOGAN, WILLIAM ALFRED, law enforcement agent; b. Spokane, Wash., Nov. 26, 1933; s. James William and Mary Ada (Farmer) L.; m. Anna Virginia Loomis, 1956 (div. 1976); children: Laura Louise, Karla Christine, Doris Elaine, Elmer Palo; m. Marilyn Kay Nay, Feb. 11, 1978; 1 child, Denise Ann Nay. ATA LE, Centralia Coll., 1974; postgrad., N.W. Law Enforcement Exec. Command Coll., 1987, FBI Nat. Acad., 1988. Jailor, dispatcher Lewis County Sheriff's Office, Chehalis, Wash., 1963-65, records and identification officer, 1965-69, patrol dep., 1969-71, patrol sgt., 1971-78, patrol lt., 1978-86, sheriff, 1987—. Bd. dirs. Sch. Dist. 300, Onalaska, Wash., 1967, 69. Served to sgt. U.S. Army, 1953-61, Korea, Vietnam. Recipient Disting. Service award US Jaycees, Chehalis, 1968. Democrat. Lodge: Eagles. Home: 285 SW 2d St Chehalis WA 98532 Office: Lewis County Sheriff's Office 345 Main St Chehalis WA 98532

LOGGINS, DAVID HAROLD, business broker; b. Fulton, N.Y., Aug. 8, 1957; s. Harold Joseph Loggins and Agnes Elizabeth Izzo; m. Marie Vinci, Jan. 17, 1986. AS in Culinary Arts, Culinary Inst. Am., Hyde Park, N.Y., 1978; BSBA, Regis Coll., Denver, 1988. Chef, mgr. White Mountain Convention Ctr., Waterville Valley, N.H., 1978-79; owner, mgr. Toucan Builders, Denver, 1980-84; broker assoc. Corp. Investment Bus. Brokers, Denver, 1984-86, Bus. Acquisitions Ltd., Denver, 1986—; broker Colo. Real Estate Commn., Denver, 1985—. Mem. Water Quality Assn., Naperville, Ill., 1988. Mem. Am. Assn. Individual Investors, Profl. Ski Instrs. Am. (cert. coach, cert. Nordic Alpine). Home and Office: 8164 S Kearney Ct Englewood CO 80112

LOGIE, DENNIS WAYNE, clergyman; b. Longmont, Colo., Mar. 18, 1940; s. Wayne Edward and Fern Maxine (Jacobson) L.; m. Burgl Dagmar Kaiser, Jan. 15, 1961; children: Hans Dennis, Heidi Elisabeth. Student, Stanford U., 1958-60, Fuller Sem., 1978--. Ordained to ministry Christian Ch., 1977. Systems officer Crocker Nat. Bank, San Francisco, 1964-76, dir. data processing edn., 1976-78; minister 1st Christian Ch., Redwood City, Calif., 1978--, sr. minister, 1981--; del. Heavenly Hills Christian Camp, Twain-Harte, Calif., 1978--; founder, bd. dirs. No. Calif. Ministers Retreat, San Rafael, Calif., 1983--. Contbr. articles and essays to various publs. Mem. parents adv. group Selby Lane Sch., Atherton, Calif., 1974-76; treas. Band-Aids, Woodside (Calif.) High Sch., 1976-79; co-founder, bd. dirs. Lay Inst. for Tng., Redwood City, 1976-81; bd. dirs. San Jose (Calif.) Bible Coll., 1976-82, 88--. Mem. No. Calif. Evangelistic Assn. (bd. dirs. 1987--), Redwood City Clergy Assn. (pres. 1979-85, 88--), Calif. PTA (life). Republican. Home: 164 Oakfield Ave Redwood City CA 94061 Office: 1st Christian Ch 233 Topaz St Redwood City CA 94062

LOH, PHILIP CHOO-SENG, virology educator; b. Singapore, Singapore, Sept. 14, 1925; came to U.S., 1947; s. Poon Lip and Soh Choo (Teo) L.; m. Susie Sook Han Lau, Feb. 5, 1955; children: Valerie Kia Hee, Rhonda Kia Hiong. BS, Morningside Coll., 1950; MS, State U. Iowa, 1953; MPH, U. Mich., 1954, PhD, 1958. Rsch. assoc. U. Mich., Ann Arbor, 1959-61, asst. prof., 1961; assoc. prof. virology U. Hawaii, Honolulu, 1961-65, prof., 1965—, chmn. dept., 1985—. Contbr. over 125 articles to profl. jours. Recipient Regent's award U. Hawaii, 1965; Horace Rackham fellow, 1959, USPHS fellow, 1967-68, Am. Cancer Soc. Eleanor Roosevelt fellow, 1975. Fellow AAAS, Am. Acad. Microbiology (diplomate); mem. Am. Soc. Virology, Am. Soc. for Microbiology, Soc. for Exptl. Biology and Medicine, Tissue Culture Assn., Am. Water Works Assn., Sigma Xi. Office: U Hawaii 2538 The Mall Honolulu HI 96822

LOHAFER, DOUGLAS ALLEN, chemical engineer; b. Holstein, Iowa, June 7, 1949; s. Walter Jessen and Dorothy Ann (Thies) L. AA in Liberal Arts magna cum laude, Waldorf Coll., 1975; student, Mayo Sch. Health-Related Scis., Iowa State U., 1976; BA in Biology, Chemistry, Luther Coll., 1977, St. Olaf Coll., 1977; postgrad., San Jose State U. Sr. satellite ops. engr. Lockheed Missiles & Space Co., Inc., Sunnyvale, Calif., 1978-87, Lockheed Tech. Ops. Co., Inc., Sunnyvale, Calif., 1987—. Active Gideons Internat. Mem. Calif. Acad. Scis., Nat. Eagle Scout Assn., Am. Chem. Soc. (assoc. Santa Clara Valley sect. 1979, div. biol. chemistry 1979, div. nuclear chemistry and tech. 1986), Health Physics Soc. (assoc. No. Calif. chpt.), Ctr. for Theology and Natural Scis., Internat. Platform Assn., N.Y. C.S. Lewis Soc., U.S.A. Søren Kierkegaard Soc., Phi Theta Kappa. Democrat. Lutheran. Home: 403 Los Encinos Ave San Jose CA 95134

LOHMAN, LORETTA CECELLIA, social scientist, consultant; b. Joliet, Ill., Sept. 25, 1944; d. John Thomas and Marjorie Mary (Brennan) L. BA in Polit Sci., U. Denver, 1966, postgrad., 1985—; MA in Social Sci., U. No. Colo., 1975. Lectr. Ariz. State U., Tempe, 1966-67; survery researcher Merrill-Werthlin Co., Tempe, 1967-68; edn. asst. Am. Humane Assn., Denver, 1969-70; econ. cons. Lohman & Assocs., Littleton, Colo., 1971-75; rsch. assoc. Denver Rsch. Inst., 1976-85; rsch. scientist Milliken Chapman Rsch. Group, Littleton, 1986—; cons. Constrn. Engring. Rsch. Lab., 1984—; peer reviewer NSF, 1985-86; manuscript referee Social Studies Jour. Contbr. articles to profl. jours. Researcher legis. campaigns Arapahoe County, Colo., 1988; vol. Metro Water Conservation projects, 1986—. Recipient Huffsmith award Def. Rsch. Inst., 1983; Nat. Ctr. for Edn. in Politics grantee, 1964-65. Mem. ASCE (social and environ. objectives com.), Am. Water Works Assn., Am. Water Resources Assn., Water Pollution Control Fed., Am. History Assn., Freshwater Found., Colo. Water Congress, Sigma Xi, Pi Gamma Mu, Phi Alpha Theta. Democrat. Home: 3375 W Aqueduct Ave Littleton CO 80123 Office: Chapman Rsch Group 6631 S University Blvd Littleton CO 80121

LOHMAN, MARION BETH SIMPSON BECKER, retired educational administrator; b. Sheridan, Mont., Nov. 30, 1918; d. Thomas Alexander and Maude Murilla (Bullerdick) Simpson; m. Peter Wilson Becker, June 28, 1941 (dec.); children—Laura Lynn, Karen Lee, Joyce Lenore; m. 2d, Michael S. Lohman, July 12, 1976 (dec.). Teaching degree Mont. State Normal Coll., 1939; B.S., Gonzaga U., 1956, M.S., 1964. Cert. librarian, Calif. Tchr., Mont. State Orphans Home, Twin Bridges, 1939-41, Post Falls, Idaho, 1952-54; librarian Greenacres Jr. High Sch., Spokane, Wash., 1956-63; media coordinator Edison High Sch., Huntington Beach, Calif., 1963-87; exec. rep. Crescent Cement Co., Costa Mesa, Calif., 1977-83. Sponsor Chess Club (nat. championship 1975), other sch. clubs. Served to chief yeoman USCG, 1942-45. Mem. Calif. Tchrs. Assn., Nat. Curriculum, Assn. Supervision and Curriculum Devel., Am. Bus. Profl. Women. Republican. Lodge: Order Eastern Star (life). Home: 3244 New York Ave Costa Mesa CA 92626 Office: Edison High Sch 21400 Magnolia St Huntington Beach CA 92646

LOHR, GEORGE E., state supreme court justice; b. 1931. B.S., S.D. State U.; J.D., U. Mich. Bar: Colo. 1958, Calif. 1969. Former judge Colo. 9th Dist. Ct., Aspen; assoc. justice Colo. Supreme Ct., Denver, 1979—. Office: Colo Supreme Ct State Judicial Bldg 2 E 14th Ave Denver CO 80203

LOKEN, SARAH FREDRIKA (SALLY LOKEN), library administrator; b. Seattle, Nov. 12, 1938; m. Thomas Wesley Settle, Dec. 19, 1959 (div. 1976); children: James Gilbert, Gregory Thomas, Vernon Wesley, Neil Douglas. BA, U. Wash., 1971, M of Librianship, 1974; M of Pub. Adminstrn., The Evergreen State Coll., Olympia, Wash., 1982. Cert. librarian, Wash. Head outreach services Kitsap Regional Library, Bremerton, Wash., 1971-73, adult services librarian, 1974, head extension services, 1974-76; supr. cen. services Timberland Regional Library, Olympia, 1976-78, asst. dir. cen. services, 1978—; mem. council Wash. Library Network, 1980-82, Western Library Network Computer Services Council, Olympia, 1986—, vice-chmn., 1988—. Jail Ministry St. John's Episcopal Ch., Olympia, 1986—. Mem. ALA (councillor 1979-83, booklist editorial adv. bd. 1982-84), Wash. Library Assn. (conf. co-chmn. 1987), Phi Beta Kappa, Mortar Board. Democrat. Episcopalian. Office: Timberland Regional Libr 415 Airdustrial Way SW Olympia WA 98501

LOMBARDI, PATRICK ARNOLD, insurance agent; b. Boulder, Colo., Oct. 4, 1950; s. Clement Anthony and Beatrice Louise (Rosser) L.; m. Deborah Ann DeSantis, July 1, 1972; children: Jennifer Michelle, Julianne Marie. Student, Metro State Coll., Denver, 1968-71, U. Colo., Boulder, 1971-72. Agt. Farmers Ins. Group, Colorado Springs, Colo., 1973—. Mem. Elks. Office: Farmers Ins Group Ste 121 400 S McCaslin Blvd Louisville CO 80027

LOMELI, JESSE, teacher, realtor; b. Aguascalientes, Mexico, Nov. 16, 1943; came to U.S., 1954; s. Jesus and Guadalupe (Ascencio) L.; m. Teresa Lomeli, Aug. 16, 1969; 1 child, Veronica Cynthia. AA, Palomar Jr. Coll., 1965; BA, San Diego State U., 1967, MA, 1976. Tchr. Vista (Calif.) Unified Sch. Dist., 1967—; realtor Century 21 Amigos Realty, Vista, 1984-85, James D. Downs, Broker, Oceanside, Calif., 1985—; panelist, bilingual assessment panel Dept. Edn. San Diego County, 1978-86. Rep. Dem. State Conv., Vista, 1986. Fellow Am. Assn. Tchrs. Spanish and Portuguese (chmn. nat. exams 1974, 88). Home: 1315 Vista Colina Dr San Marcos CA 92069

LOMELÍ, REFUGIO (JESSE LOMELÍ), athletics educator; b. Aguascalientes, Mex., July 23, 1941; came to U.S., 1954, naturalized, 1965; s. J. Jesus and Maria Guadalupe (Ascencio) L.; m. Barbara L. McMinn, Aug. 24, 1968; children: Lorena, Maya, Marc. Assoc., Palomar Coll., 1962; B, U. of the Americas, Mexico City, 1965; M, San Diego State U., 1972; postgrad., U. Pitts., 1972-74. Firefighter U.S. Forest Service, So. Calif. region, 1962-66; tchr. Santana H.S., Santee, Calif., 1967-73; counselor, tchr., soccer coach Mira Costa Coll., Oceanside, Calif., 1973—. Named Community Coll. Soccer Coach of Yr., Pacific Coast Conf., 1985. Mem. Nat. Assn. Fgn. Student Advisors, Am. G.I. Forum. Lodge: KC. Home: 1250 Vista Colina Dr San Marcos CA 92069 Office: Mira Costa Coll 1 Barnard Dr Oceanside CA 92056

LOND, HARLEY WELDON, editor, publisher; b. Chgo., Feb. 5, 1946; s. Henry Sidney and Dorothy (Shaps) L.; m. Marilyn Moss, Aug. 20, 1981. BA in Journalism, Calif. State U., L.A., 1972. Adminstrv. dir. Century City Ednl. Arts Project, L.A., 1972-76, hon. dir., 1982—; founder, editor Intermedia mag., L.A., 1974-80; prodn. mgr. FilmRow Publs., L.A., 1981; assoc. editor Boxoffice mag., Hollywood, Calif., 1981-84; editor, assoc. pub. Boxoffice mag., Hollywood, 1984—; syndicated columnist McNaught Syndicate, Greenwich, Conn., 1986—; hon. dir. Monterey (Calif.) Film Festival, 1987; mem. media adv. bd. Cinetex Internat. Film Festival, 1988; cons. Take 3 Info. Svc.; editor Entertainment Media Electronic Info. Svc. contbr. articles to profl. publs. Calif. Arts Council grantee, 1975, Nat. Endowment for Arts grantee, 1976-77. Mem. Soc. Profl. Journalists, MLA, Assn. for Edn. in Journalism and Mass Communication. Office: Boxoffice Mag 1800 N Highland Ave Ste 710 Hollywood CA 90028

LONDON, RAY WILLIAM, clinical psychologist; b. Burley, Idaho, May 29, 1943; s. Loo Richard and Maycelle Jerry (Moore) L. AS, Weber State Coll., 1965, BS, 1967; MSW, U. So. Calif., 1973, PhD, 1976, Exec. MBA, 1987-89. Diplomate: Am. Bd. Psychol. Hypnosis (dir. 1984—, pres. 1989—), Am. Acad. Behavioral Medicine, Am. Bd. Psychotherapy, Am. Bd. Med. Psychotherapy, Internat. Acad. Medicine and Psychology, Am. Bd. Profl. Neuropsychology, Am. Bd. Adminstrv. Psychology, Am. Bd. Examiners Clin. Soc. Work; cert. Am. Assn. Sex Therapists, Soc. Med. Hypnosis. Congl. asst. U.S. Ho. of Reps., 1964-65; research assoc. Bus. Advs., Inc., Ogden, Utah, 1965-67; dir. counseling and consultation services Meaning Found., Riverside, Calif., 1966-69; mental health and mental retardation liaison San Bernardino County (Calif.) Social Services, 1968-72; clin. trainee VA Outpatient Clinic, Los Angeles, 1971-72, Children's Hosp., 1972-73, clin. fellow, 1973-74; clin. trainee Reiss Davis Child Study Ctr., Los Angeles, 1973-74, Los Angeles County-U. So. Calif. Med. Center, 1973; psychotherapist Benjamin Rush Neuropsychiat. Ctr., Orange, Calif., 1973-75; clin. psychology postdoctoral intern Orange County (Calif.) Mental Health, 1976-77; postdoctoral fellow U. Caif.-Irvine-Calif. Coll. Medicine, 1978; clin. psychologist Orange Police Dept., 1974-80; pvt. practice consultation and assessment, Santa Ana, Calif., 1974—; cons. to public schs., agys., hosps., bus., nationally and internationally, 1973—; pres. bd. govs. Human Factor Programs, Ltd., 1976—; pres. Internat. Bd. Medicine and Psychology, 1980—; chief exec. officer Human Studies Ctr., 1987—, London Assocs. Internat., Organizational Behavior-Crisis-Devel. Cons., 1987—; research affil. Ctr. for Crisis Mgmt. U. So. Calif. Grad. Sch. Bus. Adminstrn., 1988—; mem. faculty UCLA, U. So. Calif., Calif. State U., U. Calif., Irvine, Calif. Coll. Medicine, Internat. Cong. of Hypnosis and Psychosomatic Medicine, Soc. Clin. and Exptl. Hypnosis, Internat. Coll.; research assoc. Nat. Commn. for Protection of Human Subjects of Biomed. and Behavioral Research, 1976; fellow Inst. for Social Scientists on Neurobiology and Mental Illness, 1978. Editor: Internat. Bull. Medicine and Psychology, 1980, A.B.C.D. Report, 1988 behavioral medicine Australian Jour., 1980, adv. editor Internat. Jour. Clin. and Exptl. Hypnosis, 1981; cons. editor Internat. Jour. Psychosomatics, 1984; Experimentelle und Klinische Hypnose, 1987, cons. Am. Jour. Forensic Psychology, 1986; pub.: London Behavioral Medicine Assessment, 1982; producer: TV series Being Human, 1980; contbg. author World Book Ency. and books; contbr. articles to profl. jours. Recipient Congl. recognition U.S. Ho. of Reps., 1978; named scholar laureate Erickson Advanced Inst., 1980. Fellow Internat. Acad. Medicine and Psychology (dir. 1981—), Soc. Clin. Social Work (dir. 1979-80), Royal Soc. Health, Am. Coll. Forensic Psychology, Soc. Clin and Experimental Hypnosis (bd. dirs. 1985—, treas. 1987—); mem. Acad. Mgmt., Acad. Psychosomatic Medicine, Am. Psychol. Assn., Am. Group Psychotherapy Assn., Am. Orthopsychiat. Assn., Assn. Profl. Cons., Internat. Soc. Hypnosis, N.Y. Acad. Sci., Soc. Behavioral Medicine, Internat. Psychosomatic Inst., Australian Coll. Pvt. Clin. Psychologists, Australian Psychol. Soc., Toastmasters Club, Elks, Phi Delta Kappa, Delta Sigma Rho, Tau Kappa Alpha, Pi Rho Phi, Lambda Iota Tau. Office: 1125 E 17th St Ste E-209 Santa Ana CA 92701

LONDRIE, BARBARA SISSON, company executive; b. St. Louis, Nov. 29, 1963; d. Richard Leslie and Annetta Maria (Murray) Sisson; m. David Alan Londrie, Sept. 12, 1982. Cert. fashion merchandise, Patricia Stevens, St. Louis, 1982. Telephone sales rm. mgr. Olan Mills, Phoenix, 1982-83; receptionist Health Industries, Phoenix, 1983; office adminstr. CRW Engring. Group, Anchorage, 1984-85; facilities coordinator Micro-Rel, Tempe, Ariz., 1986-88, tng. adminstr., coordinator, 1988—. Democrat. Baptist. Home: 9539 E Dallas St Mesa AZ 85207 Office: Micro-Rel 2343 W 10th Pl Tempe AZ 85281

LONERGAN, MARY CAROLYN, interior designer; b. Ottumwa, Iowa, Dec. 7, 1952; d. Robert Joseph and Verna Mae (Hamman) Sprengelmeyer; m. Richard Louis Lonergan, June 30, 1979. AA, Napa Valley Coll., 1976. Interior designer Allen and Benedict Furniture Co., Napa, Calif., 1976—; career day and salesmanship speaker area high schs., 1986-88. Co-designer showcase house, 1986. Vol. Cancer Soc., Napa, 1982—, pastoral council mem. St. John the Bapt. Cath. Ch., Napa, 1986—. Mem. Soroptimist Internat. of Napa (jr. dir. 1981-82, sr. dir. 1982-83, corr. sec. 1983-84, rec. sec. 1984-85, conf. del. 1988—), Rotary Internat. (career speaker, vol. 1985—). Republican. Roman Catholic. Club: Napa Council of Navy League (historian 1985-86, 1989-90). Lodge: Moose. Home: 2546 Patricia Dr Napa CA 94558 Office: Allen & Benedict Furniture 815 Freeway Dr Napa CA 94558

LONERGAN, S. J., III, small business owner; b. Albion, Mich., Dec. 29, 1950; s. Simon Joseph Jr. and Beverlye (Wogan) L.; m. Suzanne Marie Richter, Apr. 17, 1976; children: Kelly Anne, Nicole. BSBA, Menlo Coll., 1973. Sales rep. Equitable Life Assurance, San Diego, 1973-74; mgmt.

trainee Union Oil Co., San Diego, 1974-75, area rep., 1975-76; mgr. ops. Pacific Freeport Warehouse Co., Reno, Nev., 1976-78; owner Reno Indsl. Products, Reno, 1978—, Discount Desks Etc., Sparks, Nev., 1986—; ptnr. Reno Indsl. Exposition, Reno, 1981—, Singularity Inc., Reno, 1987—. Bd. dirs. Nev. Waterfowl Assn., 1988—. Mem. Ducks Unltd. Republican. Roman Catholic. Office: Discount Desks Etc 100 E Glendale Ave Sparks NV 89431

LONERGAN, THOMAS FRANCIS, III, criminal justice consultant; b. Bklyn., July 28, 1941; s. Thomas Francis and Katherine Josephine (Roth) L.; BA, Calif. State U., Long Beach, 1966, MA, 1973; MPA, Pepperdine U., 1976; postgrad. U. So. Calif.; m. Irene L. Kaucher, Dec. 14, 1963; 1 son, Thomas F. Dep. sheriff Los Angeles County Sheriff's Dept., 1963-70; U.S. Govt. program analyst, 1968—; fgn. service officer USIA, Lima, Peru, 1970-71; dep. sheriff to lt. Los Angeles Sheriff's Office, 1971-76, aide lt. to div. chief, 1976-79; dir. Criminal Justice Cons., Downey, Calif., 1977—; cons. Public Adminstrv. Service, Chgo., 1972-75, Nat. Sheriff's Assn., 1978, 79; cons. Nat. Inst. Corrections, Washington, 1977—, coordinator jail ctr., 1981-82 ; tchr. N. Calif. Regional Criminal Justice Acad., 1977-79; lectr. Nat. Corrections Acad., 1983—; monitor Chancery Ct. Davidson County, Tenn.; spl. master Chancery Ct. Davidson County, Tenn., 1980-82, U.S. Dist. Ct. (no. dist.) Ohio, 1984-85, Santa Clara Superior Ct. (Calif.), 1983-89, U.S. Dist. Ct. Ga., Atlanta, 1986-87, U. S. Dist. Ct. (no. dist.) Calif., 1984—, U.S. Dist. Ct. (no. dist.) Idaho, 1986—, U.S. Dist. Ct. Oreg. 1986, U.S. Dist. Ct. Portland 1987, U.S. Dist. (no. dist.) Calif. 1984—; also ct. expert. Mem. Am. Correctional Assn., U.S. Strategic Inst., Nat. Sheriff's Assn., Zeta Beta Tau. Roman Catholic. Author: California-Past, Present & Future, 1968; Training-A Corrections Perspective, 1979; AIMS-Correctional Officer; Liability-A Correctional Perspective; Liability Law for Probation Administrators; Liability Reporter; Probation Liability Reporter; Study Guides by Guides.

LONERGAN, WALLACE GUNN, college dean, management consultant; b. Potlatch, Idaho, Mar. 18, 1928; s. Willis Gerald and Lois (Gunn) L.; m. Joan Laurie Penoyer, June 1, 1952; children: Steven Mark, Kevin James. BA, Coll. Idaho, 1950; MBA, U. Chgo., 1955, PhD, 1960. Asst. dir., asst. prof. bus. Indsl. Relations Ctr. U. Chgo., 1960-70, assoc. dir., assoc. prof., 1970-74, dir., prof., 1974-84; vis. prof. Rikkyo U., Tokyo, 1985; vis. fellow Merton Coll. Oxford (Eng.) U., 1986; dean, prof. J.A. Albertson Sch. Bus. Coll. Idaho, Caldwell, 1987—; v.p. Human Resources Research Cons., Chgo., 1980-87. Author: Leadership and Morale, 1960, Group Leadership, 1974, Performance Appriasal, 1978, Leadership and Management, 1979. Chmn. Episcopal Commn. on Higher Edn., Chgo., 1970-80, mgmt. com. United Way Chgo., 1982-85. 1st lt. U.S. Army, 1950-53, Korea. Named Disting. Alumni Coll. Idaho, 1962; vis. scholar Internat. Anglican Exchange, N.Y.C., 1976, Tokyo, 1986. Mem. Internat. House Japan, Internat. Indsl. Relations Research Assn., Acad. Mgmt., Rotary. Home: 812 E Linden Caldwell ID 83605 Office: Coll Idaho Sch Bus 2112 Cleveland Blvd Caldwell ID 83605

LONETREE, GEORGIA L., rehabilitation counselor; b. Portage, Wis., Sept. 22, 1946; d. Edward and Minnie I. (Decorah) L.; children—Lucinda J., Aaron E. Yazzie. B.S. in Vocat. Rehab., U. Wis.-Stout, 1976, postgrad., 1976-77; M.S. in Vocat. Rehab. Counseling, U. Wis., 1981, postgrad., 1981-82. Team tchr. U. Wis.-Stout, 1976, Native Am. coordinator ednl. and cultural enrichment program, 1977-78; statewide specialist Indian edn. and community programs U. Wis. Extension, 1978-79; sec. to tribal atty. Wis. Winnebago Bus. Com., Madison, 1980; rehab. counselor intern Waisman Ctr. Mental Retardation and Human Devel., U. Wis., 1981, project evaluator Madison Indian parent com., 1981-82; vocat. evaluator, edn. coordinator Project Hogan Naa Nish, Navajo Vocat. Rehab. Program, Tuba City, Ariz., 1982-83; instr. rehab. edn. Navajo Community Coll., Tsaile, Ariz., 1983; homeliving specialist guidance dept. Shonto (Ariz.) Boarding Sch., 1984—. Vocat. adv. com. Tuba City High Sch., 1982; treas. Wisconsin Dells chpt. Native Am. Ch., 1979-80; sec.-treas. Ho-Chunk Housing Authority, Wis. Winnebago Bus. Com., Nekoosa, 1979-80; past officer, mem. Native Am. Awareness Club, U. Wis.-Stout, 1972-76. Continuing edn. scholar Dells Indian Club, Inc., 1982; Am. Indians into Grad. Edn. fellow, 1981-82; Advanced Opportunity fellow, 1980-81; recipient Am. Indian Scholarship award, 1976, Chancellor's award for high acad. achievement, 1975; Outstanding Alumni award U. Wis.-Stout, 1986. Mem. Am. Rehab. Counseling Assn., Am. Personnel and Guidance Assn. Home: 752 Spruce St PO Box 364 Shonto AZ 86054

LONG, HOWARD MARTIN, dentist; b. Denver, Apr. 3, 1930; s. Howard Everit and Mable Doris (Cameron) L.; m. Doris Rae Blew, July 26, 1953; children: Howard W., Marcus D., Berry W. DDS, Emory U., 1961. Intern U. Chgo., 1961-62; trainee in human genetics Tokyo Med. and Dental U., 1962-63; pvt. practice gen. dentistry Commerce City, Colo., 1963-67, Wheat Ridge, Colo., 1967-81, Coal Creek Canyon, Colo., 1981—. Bd. dirs. Coal Creek Improvement Assn., 1967-68; fireman Coal Creek Vol. Fire Dept., 1964-84, bd. dirs., 1983-84; scoutmaster Coal Creek Canyon area Boy Scouts Am., 1969-79. With USN, 1951-55. NIH grantee, 1962-63. Mem. ADA, Colo. Dental Assn., Denver Dental Study Club. Republican. Mem. Evangelical Free Church. Home: 11132 Circle Dr Golden CO 80403

LONG, JOHN HOLMES, manufacturing company executive; b. Chgo., June 4, 1947; s. Richard Alan Grest and Audrey (Holmes) Rhodes; m. Lynn M. Cancellieri, Sept. 18, 1976. BA in Chemistry, Ill. Wesleyan U., 1970; MBA in Mgmt., Pepperdine U., 1982. Factory mgr. Chemold Corp., Maspeth, N.Y., 1972-76; chief process engr. AMF Voit, Santa Ana, Calif., 1976-81, factory mgr., 1982-85; mng. coordinator South Coast Carriers, Vernon, Calif., 1985, pres., 1987—. Bd. dirs., pres. Harbor View Knoll Community Assn., Newport Beach, Calif., 1977-88. Mem. Am. Chem. Soc., Los Angeles Rubber Group Inst. Republican. Home: 2745 Hillview Dr Newport Beach CA 92660 Office: South Coast Carriers 4376 Soto St Vernon CA 90058

LONG, MARJORIE JEAN, lawyer; b. Elmhurst, Ill., June 15, 1950; d. Kenneth A. and June M. (Dudgeon) L.; m. Walter J. Downing, Aug. 6, 1983; children: Leigh Anne, Kellan. BA, U. Colo., Boulder, 1972, JD, 1982. Bar: Colo. 1983. Editorial asst. Sphere Mag., Chgo., 1972; asst. registrar U. Colo., Boulder, 1975-79; sr. editor Shepard's/McGraw-Hill Inc., Colorado Springs, 1982-84; staff atty. Children's Legal Clinic, Denver, 1984-85; adj. prof. Regis Coll., Colorado Springs, Colo., 1982—; sr. atty The Legal Ctr., Denver, 1985—; guardian ad Litem Juvenile Ct., Denver, 1985—; faculty Continuing Legal Edn., Denver, 1988; cons. Colo. Dept. Edn., Denver, 1988. Author: Rights to Special Education in Colorado, 1988. Vol. Aurora (Colo.) Assn. for Retarded Citizens, 1987—. Recipient Best Performance in Legal Aid Clinic award U. Colo. Law Sch., Boulder, 1982. Mem. ABA, Colo. Bar Assn. Democrat. Clubs: Bernese Mountain Dog Club of Am. (OFA chmn. 1977-80), Alaskan Malamute Club of Am. Home: 455 Sherman St Denver CO 80203 Office: The Legal Ctr 455 Sherman St Denver CO 80203

LONG, RICHARD ALLAN, ranch manager; b. Dayton, Ohio, Apr. 16, 1940; s. James Otto and Dorothy (Derr) L.; m. Jane Leigh Feuz, Feb. 7, 1974 (div. June 1987); children: Luke Richard, Peter James. BA in Philosophy, San Jose State U., 1966. Tchr. pub. schs. Happy Camp, Calif., 1968-71, Yreka, Calif., 1978-71; owner, mgr. Big Foot Beef, organic cattle, Happy Camp, 1967-72; range boss Jackson Hole (Wyo.) Cattlemen Assn., 1972-78; ranch mgr. for Laurance S. Rockefeller, JY Ranch, Moose, Wyo., 1978—; math. cons., Yreka, 1968-71; rodeo cowboy, Jackson Hole, 1976—. Appeared in ednl. film A Day in Life of a Rancher, 1975, also actor in TV commls. Named Outstanding Young Rancher, Jackson Hole Jaycees, 1979; recipient citation Nat. Park Svc., 1986, 88. Mem. Profl. Rodeo Cowboys Assn. Republican. Home and Office: JY Ranch Moose WY 83012

LONG, ROBERT MERRILL, retail drug company executive; b. Oakland, Calif., May 19, 1938; s. Joseph Milton and Vera Mai (Skaggs) L.; m. Eliane Quilloux, Dec. 13, 1969. Student, Brown U., 1956-58; B.A., Claremont Men's Coll., 1960. With Longs Drug Stores Inc., Walnut Creek, Calif., 1960—, dir., 1968—, pres., 1975-77, pres., chief exec. officer, 1977—. Mem. Nat. Assn. Chain Drug Stores (dir.). Office: Longs Drug Stores Corp 141 N Civic Dr Walnut Creek CA 94596

LONG, ROGER VALE, environmental engineer; b. Honolulu, May 7, 1934; s. Leon A. and Judith (Williams) Burt; m. Carol Ann Lamb, May 7, 1955; children: Dulcie Ann, Robert Vale, James La Mont. BS in Chemistry, No. Ill. U., 1962. Registered profl. engr., Ill., Colo., Alaska. Chemist Valspar Paint Co., Rockford, Ill., 1958-66; chief chemist Testor Corp., Rockford, 1965-68; process engr. Ill. Water Treatment Co., Rockford, 1968-73; water treatment engr. Stearns Roger Inc., Denver, 1973-80; environ. engr. Stone & Webster Engring. Inc., Denver, 1980—. Contbr. articles to profl. publs. With U.S. Army, 1955-58. Mem. Am. Inst. Chem. Engrs., ASME (indsl. subcom. research com. on water in thermal power systems). Office: Stone & Webster Engring Inc PO Box 5406 Denver CO 80217

LONG, ROSALEE MADELINE, law librarian; b. Concordia, Kans., Aug. 27, 1931; d. James Albert and Mary Clara (McConnell) Vincent; m. Robert Long, Mar. 5, 1954. AB in Library Sci., Kans. State U., 1953; JD, U. Santa Clara, 1973. Bar: Calif. 1976, U.S. Dist. Ct. (no. dist.) Calif. 1976. Cataloger San Jose (Calif.) State U., 1954-56, head cataloging dept., 1956-58; cataloger Law Library Stanford (Calif.) U., 1958-60, spl. project librarian, 1974-75, assoc. law librarian, 1975—; faculty mem. Am. Assn. Law Libraries Ins., Mpls., 1974; cons. Nat. U. Singapore Law Library, 1983. Author: Author Notation, 1966, Stanford Library Classification, 1968. Mem. Am. Assn. Law Libraries (western Pacific chpt.), No. Calif. Assn. Law Libraries. Office: Stanford U Law Library Stanford CA 94305

LONG, SARAH ANN, librarian; b. Atlanta, May 20, 1943; d. Jones Lloyd and Lelia Maria (Mitchell) Sanders; m. James Allen Long, 1961 (div. 1985); children: Andrew C., James Allen IV; m. Donald J. Sager, May 23, 1987. BA, Oglethorpe U., 1966; M in Librarianship, Emory U., 1967. Asst. librarian Coll. of St. Matthias, Bristol, Eng., 1970-74; cons. State Library of Ohio, Columbus, 1975-77; coordinator Franklin County Pub. Library, Columbus, 1977-79, dir. Fairfield County Dist. Library, Lancaster, Ohio, 1979-82, Dauphin County Library System, Harrisburg, Pa., 1982-85, Multnomah County Library, Portland, Oreg., 1985—; chmn. Portland State U. Library Adv. Council. Contbr. articles to profl. jours. Bd. dirs. Dauphin County Hist. Soc., Harrisburg, 1983-85, ARC, Harrisburg, 1984-85; pres. Lancaster-Fairfield County YWCA, Lancaster, 1981-82; vice-chmn. govt. and edn. div. Lancaster-Fairfield County United Way, Lancaster, 1981-82; sec. Fairfield County Arts Council, 1981-82; adv. bd. Portland State U.. Recipient Dir.'s award Ohio Program in Humanities, Columbus, 1982; Sarah Long Day Fairfield County, Lancaster, Bd. Commrs., 1982. Mem. Oreg. Library Assn. (chmn. legis. com. 1987-89), Pacific N.W. Library Assn., Pub. Library Assn. (v.p., pres.-elect.), ALA, Western Library Network (network services council). Club: City (Portland). Office: Libr Assn/Portland Multnomah County Libr 205 NE Rusell St Portland OR 97212-3708

LONG, WILLIAM JUSTUS, pharmacist; b. St. Louis, July 30, 1940; s. Vincent Charles and Marie Margaret (Fehr) L.; m. Linda Marie Simpson, June 22, 1969; children: Christopher Charles, Timothy Shane, Molly Anne. BS in Pharmacy, St. Louis Coll. Pharmacy, 1963; postgrad., N.Mex. State U., 1964-65. Pharmacist Glaser Drug, St. Louis, 1963-64, Days Pharmacy, Las Cruces, N.Mex., 1964-65, 68-72; owner, pharmacist Medi-Kare Pharmacy, Las Cruces, 1972-83; dairyman Longs Dairy, Las Cruces, 1981-84; pharmacist, mgr. Revco, Ruidoso, N.Mex., 1984—. Lt. U.S. Army, 1965-68, Vietnam. Mem. N.Mex. Pharm. Assn., Sales and Leads Assn., Odd Fellows. Republican. Methodist. Home: Box 2095 Ruidoso NM 88345

LONGBRAKE, WILLIAM ARTHUR, banker; b. Hershey, Pa., Mar. 15, 1943; s. William Van Fleet and Margaret Jane (Barr) L.; m. Martha Ann Curtis, Aug. 23, 1970; children—Derek Curtis, Mark William, David Robert, Dorothy Eleanor Lois. BA, Coll. of Wooster, 1965; MA, U. Wis., 1968, MBA, 1969; DBA, U. Md., 1976. Jr. asst. planner Northeastern Ill. Planning Commn., Chgo., 1966; instr. Coll. Bus. and Mgmt., U. Md., 1969-71, lectr., 1976, 79-81; fin. economist FDIC, Washington, 1971-75, sr. planning specialist Office Corp. Planning, 1975-76, spl. asst. to chmn., acting contr., 1977-78; assoc. dir. div. banking rsch. Office Compt. of Currency, Treasury Dept., Washington, 1976, dep. dir. econ. rsch. and analysis div., 1976-77; dep. compt. for rsch. and econ. programs, 1978-81, acting sr. dep. compt. for policy, 1981-82, sr. dep. compt. for resource mgmt., 1982; exec. v.p., chief fin. officer Wash. Mut. Savs. Bank, Seattle, 1982-85; exec. v.p. finance and ops., 1985-86, sr. exec. v.p., 1986-88, sr. exec. v.p., chief fin. officer, 1988—; small bus. cons. Mem. College Park (Md.) Citizen's Adv. Com. on Code Enforcement, 1973-74, cons., 1975; lectr. Albers Sch. Bus. Seattle U., 1985. bd. dirs. Puget Sound Coun. Fin. Insts., Seattle, v.p., 1988, pres., 1989—. Mem. Seattle Mcpl. League, 1986—, King County Housing Partnership, Seattle, 1988—, exec. com., 1989—; mem. adv. com. Ctr. for the Study of Banking and Fin. Markets U. Wash., Seattle, 1983—, chmn., 1986-89; mem. of initiative support corp. Seattle/Tacoma Adv. Bd.; bd. dirs. Diabetes Rsch. Coun., Seattle, 1984—, v.p., 1987-88; bd. dirs. N.W. Symphony Orch., Seattle, 1987—. Recipient Kenneth E. Trefftz prize Western Fin. Assn., 1971, cert. of recognition William A. Jump Meml. Found., 1978. Mem. Am. Econs. Assn., Am. Fin. Assn., Fin. Mgmt. Assn. (dir. 1978-80), Fin. Execs. Inst. (bd. dirs. 1988—, chmn. acad. rels. com. 1988—), Coll. of Wooster Alumni Assn. (pres. Washington chpt. 1976, pres. Seattle chpt. 1983—, trustee 1988—, alumni bd. 1988—), Columbia Tower Club. Presbyn. (trustee 1973-75, chmn. 1975, elder, 1979-82, clk. 1980-81, deacon 1985-88). Assoc. editor Fin. Mgmt., 1974-78; mem. editorial adv. bd. Issues in Bank Regulation, 1977-84, Jour. Econs. and Bus., 1980-83; contbr. articles to profl. jours. Avocations: jogging, painting, singing, playing piano. Home: 939 18th Ave E Seattle WA 19812 Office: 1101 2nd Ave Seattle WA 98101

LONGFELLOW, LAYNE ALLEN, psychologist; b. Jackson, Ohio, Oct. 23, 1937; s. Hershel Herman and Opal Edna (Pursley) L. BA in Psychology magna cum laude with honors, Ohio U., 1959; MA, U. Mich., 1961, PhD, 1967; postgrad. (NIMH fellow), Ctr. for Studies of the Person, 1968-70. Asst. prof. psychology Reed Coll., Portland, Oreg., 1967-68; asst. prof. psychology Prescott (Ariz.) Coll., 1970-71, chmn. dept., 1971-72, acad. v.p., 1972-74; dir. exec. seminars Menninger Found., Topeka, 1975-78; co-dir. Ctr. for Mgmt. of Stress, L.A. and Santa Barbara, Calif., 1978-80; dir. wilderness exec. seminars Banff Ctr., Alta., Can., 1978—; sr. assoc. Health Edn. Inst. Phoenix Bapt. Hosp., 1980-81; pres. Lecture Theater, Inc., Prescott, Ariz., 1981—; internat. lectr., cons. 1978—; adj. faculty Union Grad. Sch. and Humanistic Psychology Inst., 1974—. Composer: Ten Songs, 1969, Uncommon Festival of Christmas, 1974; author, creator Body Talk, 1970, The Feel Wheel, 1972, Stress, The American Addiction. 1982, From Adolescence to Middlescence, 1983, Leadership, Power and Productivity in the 80's, 1983; TV documentary The Mountain Waits, 1983. Bd. dirs. Prescott Ctr. Coll., 1976-81, Am. Inst. Productivity and Creativity, 1981-82. Mem. Am. Psychol. Assn., Nat. Speakers Assn., Assn. for Humanistic Psychology, ACLU, Phi Beta Kappa, Beta Theta Pi. Home: 1860 Idylwild Dr Prescott AZ 86301 Office: Lecture Theatre Inc 1490 W Gurley Prescott AZ 86301

LONGHI, ROBERT J., restaurant executive; b. Torrington, Conn., Mar. 19, 1933; s. Paul Joseph and Eleanor (Barrette) L.; children: Gabrielle, Carol, Peter, Charles; m. Gail Gordon, Jan. 19, 1985; children: Ian Wetzel, Genafer. BA, Cornell U., 1956. Sales rep. Proctor & Gamble, 1956; sales mgr. Mass. Mutual Life Ins., 1956-64; v.p. sales Valic, 1964-76; prin. Longhi's, Lahaina, Hawaii, 1976—. With U.S. Army, 1956-58. Office: Longhi's 888 Front St Lahaina HI 96761

LONGO, LAWRENCE DANIEL, physiologist, gynecologist; b. Los Angeles, Oct. 11, 1926; s. Frank Albert and Florine Azelia (Hall) L.; m. Betty Jeanne Mundall, Sept. 9, 1948; children: April Celeste, Lawrence Anthony, Elizabeth Lynn, Camilla Giselle. B.A., Pacific Union Coll., 1949; M.D., Coll. Med. Evangelists, Loma Linda, Calif., 1954. Diplomate: Am. Bd. Ob-Gyn. Intern Los Angeles County Gen. Hosp., 1954-55, resident, 1955-58; asst. prof. ob-gyn UCLA, 1962-64; asst. prof. physiology and ob-gyn U. Pa., 1964-68; prof. physiology and ob-gyn Loma Linda U., 1968—; head div. perinatal biology Loma Linda U. (Sch. Medicine), 1974—; mem. perinatal biology com. Nat. Inst. Child Health, NIH, 1973-77; chmn. reprodn. scientist tng. program NIH; NATO prof. Consiglio Nat. delle Richerche, Italian Govt. Contbr. numerous articles to profl. jours.; editor: Respiratory Gas Exchange and Blood Flow in the Placenta, 1972, Fetal and Newborn Cardiovascular Physiology, 1978, Charles White and A Treatise on the Management of Pregnant and Lying-in Women, 1987; editor classic pages in ob-gyn: Am. Jour. Ob-Gyn, 1970—; editorial bd., 1970—; co-editor: Landmarks in Perinatology, 1976—. Served with AUS, 1945-47. Recipient Research Career Devel. award NIH, 1967; NIH grantee, 1966—. Mem. Am. Assn. History Medicine, Am. Coll. Obstetricians and Gynecologists, Am. Osler Soc. (bd. govs., sec.-treas.), Am. Physiol. Soc., Assn. Profs. Ob-Gyn, Perinatal Research Soc., Soc. Gynecologic Investigation (past pres.). Adventist. Office: Div Perinatal Biology Sch of Medicine Loma Linda Univ Loma Linda CA 92350

LONG-RUSSELL, SHARON LEE, data processing educator; b. Baldwin, Wis., Apr. 13, 1947; d. Alden Edward and Catherine (McDonough) Helgeson; m. Richard Lee Russell; children: Mary-Catherine, Christopher Lee. BS in Bus., Chapman U., 1987; postgrad., U. Phoenix. Lic. real estate broker, Wyo. Instr. Laramie County Community Coll., Cheyenne, Wyo., 1977-83; instr. data processing Info. Ctr., State of Wyo., Cheyenne, 1983—; presenter seminars, cons., speaker in field. Author workbooks; contbr. articles to profl. publs. Mem. Solid State Data Processing Mgmt. Assn. (chmn. scholarship com. 1988, chmn. fundraising com. 1986; Performance award 1986, 87), Am. Soc. Tng. and Devel. (steering com. 1988), Info. Systems Network, Am. Soc. Pub. Adminstrn., Women's Christian Group, Am. Soc. Info. and Devel. (bd. dirs. No. Rockies chpt.). Home: 5317 Greybull St Cheyenne WY 82009

LONGSWORTH, EILEEN CATHERINE, library director; b. N.Y.C., Feb. 7, 1950; d. Francis L. and Maurine E. (Romkey) Brannigan; m. Laurence S. Woodworth, June 16, 1970 (div. 1982); 1 child, David; m. Bruce Todd Longsworth, May 28, 1983. Student, Dunbarton Coll., 1966-68; BA, U. Md., 1970; MS in Libr. Sci., Cath. U., Washington, 1973. Dept. head Anne Arundel County Pub. Libr., Annapolis, Md., 1974-75, br. librarian, 1975-79; adult services specialist Enoch Pratt Free Libr., Balt., 1979-84; asst. dir. Salt Lake City Pub. Libr., 1984-87; dir. Salt Lake County Libr. System, 1987—. Mem. ALA (chmn. tech. com. 1985-87), Utah Libr. Assn. (chmn. legis com. 1987—). Democrat. Home: 860 N Terrace Hills Salt Lake City UT 84103 Office: Salt Lake County Libr System Whitmore Libr 2197 E 7000 S Salt Lake City UT 84121

LONGVAL, MARK J., legal researcher; b. Boston, Mar. 26, 1957; s. Leo H. and Mary T. (Gallegher) L. BS in Biology, U. Miami, 1981; JD, Nat. U., San Diego, 1987. Ct. clk. Dade County, Miami, Fla., 1981; law clk. U.S. Small Bus. Adminstrn., Los Angeles, 1982; ptnr. Longval and Sells, San Diego, 1986-87; pvt. practice San Diego, 1987—. Mem. Nat. U. Alumni Assn. Office: 4807 Wightman St San Diego CA 92105

LONIE, CLAYTON CARLYLE, aerospace executive; b. Mishawaka, Ind., Aug. 28, 1940; s. Louis Carlyle and Carol Lucille (Peik) L.; m. Julie Anne Asher, June 30, 1962 (div. Nov. 1980); children: Clayton Carlyle Jr., Richard Andrew, John Asher; m. Judith Ann Agee, Jan. 17, 1981. BS in Econs., Purdue U.; MA in Mgmt., U. Nebr.; postgrad., Claremont Grad. Sch. Commd. 2d lt. USAF, 1962, advanced through grades to lt. col.; minuteman launch officer SAC, Great Falls, Mont., 1962-68; minuteman missile officer SAC, Omaha, 1968-80; plant rep. USAF-United Techs., Sunnyvale, Calif., 1980-81; dir. European ops. ctr. USAF, Stuttgart, Fed. Republic of Germany, 1981-82; ret. USAF, 1982; mgr. mfg. McDonnell Douglas Helicopter, Mesa, Ariz., 1982—; instr. mgmt. Chapman Coll., Orange, Calif., 1975-78, Bellevue (Nebr.) Coll., 1973-74. Mem. Am. Philatelic Soc., Pi Kappa Alpha. Republican. Home: 2192 E Chesapeake Dr Gilbert AZ 85234 Office: McDonnell Douglas Helicopter Co 5000 E McDowell Mesa AZ 85202

LONNER, THOMAS DUNSTAN, museum director; b. San Francisco, May 27, 1942; s. Ernest B. and Lisa K. Lonner; m. Elizabeth Ward. BA, San Francisco State U., 1966, MA, 1970; PhD, U. Calif., San Francisco, 1976. Projects coordinator Peat, Marwick, Mitchell & Co, Anchorage, 1976-79; dir. subsistence div. Alaska Fish and Game, Juneau, 1979-81; dir. Ctr. for Alcohol Studies, Anchorage, 1981-85, Alaska State Museums, Juneau, 1986—. Contbr. articles to profl. jours. Home: PO Box 22238 Juneau AK 99802 Office: Alaska State Mus 395 Whittier Juneau AK 99801

LOO, YEN-HOONG, research biochemist; b. Honolulu, Dec. 19, 1914; s. Goon and Sun (Luke) L. BA, Barnard Coll., N.Y.C., 1937; MS, U. Mich., 1938, PhD, 1943. Postdoctoral fellow U. Tex., Austin, 1943-44; rsch. asst. U. Ill., Urbana, 1944-51, Eli Lilly and co., Indpls., 1952-68; assoc. rsch. scientist N.Y. State Inst., S.I., 1968-85. Contbr. articles to jours., chpts. to books. Barbour scholar, 1943-44; NIH fellow, 1966-67, grantee, 1970-71, 76-85. Fellow AAAS; mem. Am. Soc. Biol. Chemists, Am. Soc. Neurochemistry. Home: 1212 Punahou St #1906 Honolulu HI 96826

LOOK, VIVIAN ANN, management analyst, consultant; b. San Francisco; d. Hing Mon and Dor Fook Look; m. Scott Stephen Krieger, Mar. 25, 1988. BS with honors, U. Calif., Berkeley, 1972; MPH, U. Mich., 1980; MPA, Ariz. State U., Tempe, 1984. Trainer, nutritionist Community Nutrition Inst., Washington, 1973-74; tchr. spl. vocat. edn. Springfield (Oreg.) Pub. Schs., 1974-75; asst. prof. Lane Community Coll., Eugene, Oreg., 1974-75; nutritionist Lane County Dept. Health and Social Svcs., Eugene, 1975-79; project cons. Ariz. Dept. Health Svcs., Tempe, 1980-83; rsch. asst. Ariz. State U., Tempe, 1983-84; performance auditor State of Ariz., Phoenix, 1984-87; mgmt. analyst Maricopa County Mgmt., Phoenix, 1987-88; adminstrv. asst. to dep. city mgr. City of Barstow, Calif., 1988—; mem. task force Western Oreg. Health Systems Agy., Eugene, 1978-79; program chairperson Lane Nutrition Coun., Eugene, 1978-79. Mem. Am. Soc. for Pub. Adminstrn., Calif. Mgmt. Assts. Assn., Cen. Ariz. Dist. Dietetic Assn. (mem. exec. bd. 1982-83, mem. community nutrition sect. chairperson 1981-82, Phi Kappa Phi. Democrat. Presbyterian. Office: 220 E Mountain View Barstow CA 92311

LOOMIS, CHRISTOPHER KNAPP, metallurgical engineer; b. San Francisco, May 6, 1947; s. Richard and Evaline Elsie (Crandal) L.; m. Merril Ellen Purdy, Dec. 8, 1968; 1 child, Nicole Lee. Profl. Engring., Colo. Sch. Mines, 1969. Process engr. Alcan Aluminum Corp., Riverside, Calif., 1969-73, prodn. supt., 1973-76; process engr. Alcan Aluminum Corp., Oswego, N.Y., 1976-78, maintenance engr., 1978-80; metall. engr. Hazelett Strip-Casting Corp., Colchester, Vt., 1980-81; chief engr. ARCO Metals Co., Chgo., 1981-84; maintenance supt. Cerro Metal Products, Paramount, Calif., 1984-85, mgr. engring. and maintenance, 1985-86; supt. tech. svcs. Golden Aluminum Co., Ft. Lupton, Colo., 1987-88; process devel. engr. Golden Aluminum Co., Lakewood, Colo., 1988—. Mem. Am. Soc. for Metals, Metall. Soc., Colo. Sch. Mines Alumni Assn., Fedn. Fly Fishers (life), Trout Unltd. (life). Episcopalian. Home: 11928 Clay Ct Westminster CO 80234 Office: Golden Aluminum Co 3000 Youngfield Ste 230 Lakewood CO 80215

LOOMIS, DAVID NICHOLAS, aerospace company official; b. Kansas City, Mo., Oct. 4, 1945; s. William Virgil and Frances Lenore (Thomas) L.; m. Marcia Holder, Mar. 31, 1968; children: Christopher Scott, Eric Nicholas. BA in Physics, William Jewell Coll., 1967; postgrad., U. Ark., 1968; MSSM, U. So. Calif., 1989. Engr. U.S. Naval Ship Weapon Systems Engring. Sta., Port Hueneme, Calif., 1968-75, head Test and Evaluation br., 1975-77, head weapons div., 1977-79; owner, mgr. Sun Country Solar Co., Klamath Falls, Oreg., 1979-81; engr. Peacekeeper test Martin Marietta Co., Denver, 1981-84, supr. Peacekeeper test requirements, 1984-85, mgr. Space Based Laser test, 1985-86, mgr. assembly, test and launch ops., 1986—. Mem. Soc. Photo Instrumentation Engrs. Republican. Methodist. Home: 7834 Native Dancer Trail Evergreen CO 80439 Office: Martin Marietta Co PO Box 179 Denver CO 80201

LOOMIS, MARY JEANETTE, editor-in-chief; b. Houston, July 21; d. Richard William and Mary Evelyn (Richards) Roby; m. Robert Lindsey Loomis, Feb. 10, 1965; children: Robert Duncan, Richard Roby. BA in Fine Art, Scripps Coll., 1966. Pres., editor-in-chief L.A. West Media mag., Santa Monica, 1985—. Editor, designer (datebooks) Datebook for Westsiders, 1982, Yesterday Tripping, 1984; contbr. articles to profl. jours.; fiber artist banners Corpus Christi Ch., Pacific Palisades, 1980; speaker in field. Mem. Civic Action Com., Pacific Palisades, Calif., 1983-85. Mem. Soc. Profl. Journalists, Mag. Pubs. Assn., Western Pubs. Assn., Prodn. Club. Los Angeles. Republican. Roman Catholic. Office: Santa Monica Bay Printing & Pub 919 Santa Monica Blvd #245 Santa Monica CA 90272

LOONEY, CARL GRANT, computer science and electrical engineering educator; b. Christoval, Tex., May 23, 1935; s. Claude Emil and Inez (Wamble) L.; m. Laurette Chamson, Nov. 25, 1967; children: Erin Claude, Adrianne May. BS, U. Nev., 1965, MS, 1968; PhD, U. Iowa, 1972. Assoc.

prof. U. Toledo, 1974-78; sr. engr. Veda, Inc., Dayton, Ohio, 1978-80; sr. data analyst Kentron Internat., Hill AFB, Utah, 1980-81; systems engr. Hughes Ground Systems, Fullerton, Calif., 1981-83; analyst Logicon, Inc., Vanderburg, Calif., 1983-84; cons. Hughes, Fullerton, Calif., 1984; assoc. prof. U. Nev., Reno, 1984—; computer cons. Looney Assocs., Sparks, Nev., 1986—. Contbr. articles to profl. jours. Served with U.S. Army, 1956-58, PTO. Mem. IEEE, Assn. for Computing Machinery, Am. Assn. for Artificial Intelligence, Internat. Soc. for Mini and Microcomputers. Republican. Home: 1462 Winterwood Ave Sparks NV 89431 Office: U Nev Dept Elect Engring Computer Sci Reno NV 89557

LOONEY, CLAUDIA ARLENE, health facility executive; b. Fullerton, Calif., June 13, 1946; d. Donald F. and Mildred B. (Gage) Schneider; m. James K. Looney, Oct. 8, 1967; 1 child, Christopher K. BA, Calif. State U., 1969. Dir. youth YWCA No. Orange County, Fullerton, Calif., 1967-70; dir. dist. Camp Fire Girls, San Francisco, 1971-73; asst. exec. dir. Camp Fire Girls, Los Angeles, 1973-77; asst. dir. community resources Childrens Hosp., Los Angeles, 1977-80; dir. community devel. Orthopaedic Hosp., Los Angeles, 1980-82; sr. v.p. Saddleback Health Found. and Hosp. & Health Ctr., Laguna Hills, Calif., 1982—. Mem. steering com. United Way, Los Angeles, 1984-86. Fellow Nat. Assn. Hosp. Devel. (chmn. program Nat. Edn. Conf. 1986); mem. Nat. Soc. Fund Raising Execs. Found. (vice- chmn. 1985—), Nat. Assn. Hosp. Devel. (regional dir. 1985—), So. Calif. Assn. Hosp. Devel. (past pres., bd. dirs.), Profl. Ptnrs. (chmn. 1986), Philanthropic Ednl. Orgn. (past pres. 1968, 70, 72). Office: Saddleback Health Found 24451 Health Ctr Dr Laguna Hills CA 92653

LOONEY, RALPH EDWIN, newspaper editor; b. Lexington, Ky., June 22, 1924; s. Arville Zone and Connie Elizabeth (Boyd) L.; m. Clarabel Richards, Dec. 7, 1944. B.A., U. Ky., 1948. Successively proof reader, photographer, chief photographer, sports writer, reporter Lexington Leader, 1943-52; reporter Albuquerque Tribune, 1953-54; reporter, copy editor, chief copy editor St. Louis Globe-Democrat, 1955-56; city editor Albuquerque Tribune, 1956-68, asst. mng. editor, 1968-73, editor, 1973-80; editor Rocky Mountain News, Denver, 1980—. Author: Haunted Highways, the Ghost Towns of New Mexico, 1969; contbr.: articles to mags. including Nat. Observer; others, photographs to mags. Founder, mem. N.Mex. Motion Picture Commn., 1967-76; v.p., dir. Albuquerque C. of C., 1971-75; bd. dirs. Albuquerque Indsl. Devel. Service, 1971-80; bd. advisors Lovelace Med. Center, Albuquerque, 1976-80; bd. advs. UPI, 1983-86; bd. dirs. Newspaper Features Council, 1984—; mem. exec. council St. Joseph Hosp., 1986—. Recipient N.Mex. medal of Merit, 1968, Robert F. Kennedy Journalism award, 1970, George Washington Honor Medal Freedoms Found., 1969, 19 E.H. Shaffer awards for editorial writing, reporting and photography N.Mex. Press Assn., 1965-80. Mem. N.Mex. Press Assn. (state pres. 1976), Colo. Press Assn. (bd. dirs. 1982-85), Sigma Delta Chi (N. Mex. pres. 1960). Methodist. Office: Rocky Mountain News 400 W Colfax St Denver CO 80204

LOPATA, MARTIN BARRY, service executive; b. Bronx, N.Y., Apr. 6, 1939; s. Julius A. and Rose (Silverman) L.; m. Sarah G. Lopata, July 4, 1965 (div. 1978); children: Warren A., Lawrence M. Grad., High Sch. of Art and Design, N.Y.C.; attended N.Y.C. Community Coll., Bklyn. Sales mgr. H. Natoway Co., Los Angeles, 1961-62; contract mgr. A.S. Aloe Co., Los Angeles, 1962-64; merchandise mgr. S.E. Rykoff Co., Los Angeles, 1964-70; v.p. Kirby Sales, Los Angeles, 1970-71; pres. MBL Industries Inc., Santa Ana, Calif., 1971-87, Unicorn Seminars Inc., Huntington Beach, Calif., 1987—, Unicorn Internat., Huntington Beach, 1988—; bd. dirs. Internat. Sanitary Supply Assn., 1979-81; vice chmn. Soviet Am. Internat. Co., 1988—. Patron Am. Mus. Nat. History, N.Y.C., 1984—; bus. chmn. Ctr. for Soviet-Am. Dialogue, Washington, 1987—; chmn. Com. on Bus.-A New Way of Thinking in a New Age, Moscow, 1987; bd. dirs. Three Mountain Found., Lone Pine, Calif., 1987-88, Inside Edge, Irvine, Calif., 1987—; vice chmn. United Ch. Religious Science, Los Angeles, 1986-87, pres. Huntington Beach Ch. Religious Sci., 1985. Lodges: (Masons 32d degree), Shriners. Home: 16391 Wimbledon Huntington Beach CA 92649 Office: 16902 Bulsa Chica Rd #203 Huntington Beach CA 92649

LOPER, D. ROGER, retired oil company executive; b. Mpls., Dec. 14, 1920; s. Donald Rust and Agnes (Yerxa) L.; m. Sylvia Lee Brainard, Aug. 16, 1946 (dec. Apr. 1973); children: Ann Kathleen, Michael Brainard, Joyce Elizabeth, Nancy Jean Loper Woods; m. Genevieve Jean Kusles, May 4, 1974. BSMetE, Carnegie Tech. Inst., 1947. Registered chem. engr., Calif. Div. supr. Standard Oil of Calif., San Francisco, 1958-64, asst. chief engr., 1964-74; gen. mgr. Chevron Petroleum, London, 1974-80; pres. Chevron Shale Oil Co., Denver, 1980-82; v.p. Chevron Overseas Petroleum, San Francisco, 1982-85; cons. Loper Assocs., Redwood City, Calif., 1985—. Inventor hydrocracking reactor, remote inspection device. Pres. Our Saviour Luth. Ch., Lafayette, Calif., 1971-72. Maj. U.S. Army, 1942-46. Republican. Home and Office: 2804 Pradera Rd Carmel CA 93923

LOPER, DAVID EUGENE, nurse anesthesiologist; b. Ogden, Utah, Apr. 9, 1950; s. Ira Don and Donna Jane (Vance) L.; m. Sally Ann Long, June 1, 1973; children: David Ryan, Cassandra Dawn, Ann Marie, Grant Eugene, Blake Sterling. AS in Nursing, So. Oreg. State Coll., 1976, BS, 1978. Cert. registered nurse anesthetist. Missionary Mormons, Dallas, 1969-71; cement found. laborer Medford, Oreg., 1972-73; dept. mgr. K-Mart Stores, Medford, 1974; nurses aid Rogue Valley Meml. Hosp., Medford, 1974-75; intensive care, coronary cared RN Grande Rhonde Hosp., La Grande, Oreg., 1976-78; anesthetist Grace Harper Sch. of Anesthesia, Detroit, 1978-80; freelance anesthetist, exec. dir. Columbia Basin Anesthesia Assocs., Hermiston, Oreg., 1980—; owner Del n' Sal's Sports Hause Farm, Hermiston, 1984—; trauma team anesthetist, Good Shepherd Community Hosp., Hermiston, 1987—, anesthesia cons., 1980—, surgery com., 1982—, quality assurance com., 1988—; speaker, Community Hosp. Ob. classes, Hermiston, 1985—. Mem. Am. Soc. Regional Anesthesia, Am. Assn. Nurse Anesthetists, Jackson County Nurse Assn. (scholarship 1975), Oreg. Assn. Nurse Anesthetists (bd. dirs. 1982-85), Hermiston C. of C., Latter-day Saint Student Assn. (pres. 1971-72), Latter-day Saint Elders Quorum (pres. 1988—). Republican. Mormon. Office: Columbia Basin Anesthesia Rt 2 Box 2282 Hermiston OR 97838

LOPER, JAMES LEADERS, broadcasting executive; b. Phoenix, Sept. 4, 1931; s. John D. and Ellen Helen (Leaders) L.; m. Mary Louise Brion, Sept. 1, 1955; children: Elizabeth Margaret, James Leaders. BA, Ariz. State U., 1953; MA, U. Denver, 1957; PhD, U. So. Calif., 1967; DHL (hon.), Columbia Coll., 1973; LLD (hon.), Pepperdine U., 1978. Asst. dir. bur. broadcasting Ariz. State U., Tempe, 1953-59; news editor, announcer Sta. KTAR, Phoenix, 1955-56; dir. ednl. TV, Calif. State U., Los Angeles, 1960-64; v.p. Community TV So. Calif., Los Angeles, 1962-63; asst. to pres. Sta. KCET-Pub. TV, Los Angeles, 1963-65, sec., 1965-66, dir. ednl. services, 1964-65, asst. gen. mgr., 1965-66, v.p., gen. mgr., 1966-69, exec. v.p., gen. mgr., 1969-71, pres., gen. mgr., 1971-76, pres., chief exec. officer, 1976-82; exec. dir. Acad. TV Arts and Scis., 1983—; chmn. bd. Pub. Broadcasting Service, Washington, 1969-72; adj. prof. Sch. Cinema and TV U. So. Calif., 1984—; sr. lectr. U. So. Calif., Los Angeles, 1969-70; pres. Western Ednl. Network, 1968-70; mem. Gov.'s Ednl. TV and Radio Adv. Com., Calif., 1968-74; U.S. rep. CENTO Conf. Radio and TV, Turkey, 1978, trustee Internat. Council Nat. Acad. TV Arts and Scis., 1988—. Contbr. articles to profl. jours; contbr. to ETV: The Farther Vision, 1967, Broadcasting and Bargaining: Labor Relations in Radio and Television, 1970. Mem. adv. bd. Jr. League of Los Angeles, 1970-76, Jr. League of Pasadena, 1972-75, Los Angeles Jr. Arts Ctr., 1968-72; exec. v.p. Assocs. of Otis Art Inst., 1971-77, pres., 1975-77; chmn., dir. The Performing Tree, Los Angeles; bd. dirs. Los Angeles Civic Light Opera Co., 1974—, v.p., 1975—; bd. dirs. Sears-Roebuck Found., 1976-79; chmn. bd. visitors Annenberg Sch. Communications, U. So. Calif., 1975-80; trustee Poly. Sch., Pasadena. Recipient Disting. Alumnus award Ariz. State U., 1972; Alumni award of Merit, U. So. Calif., 1975; Gov's. award Hollywood chpt. Nat. Acad. TV Arts and Scis., 1975; Alumni Achievement award Phi Sigma Kappa, 1975; named Centennial Alumnus Nat. Assn. of State Univs. and Land Grant Colls., 1988. Mem. Acad. TV Arts and Scis. (past gov., v.p. Hollywood chpt., trustee nat. acad.), TV Acad. Found., Hollywood Radio and TV Soc. (treas., dir.), Western Ednl. Soc. Telecommunications (past pres.), Assn. Calif. Pub. TV Stas. (past pres.), Young Pres.'s Orgn., Phi Sigma Kappa, Pi Delta Epsilon, Alpha Delta Sigma, Sigma Delta Chi. Presbyterian (chmn. Mass Media Task Force So. Calif. synod 1969-75). Clubs: Valley Hunt (Pasadena), Bel-Air Bay, California, Los Angeles, 100 of Los Angeles, Valley of San Marino, Sunset, Calif. (Los Angeles). Office: Acad TV Arts and Scis 3500 W Olive Rd Burbank CA 91505

LOPER, KEITH ALLEN, physician, anesthesiologist; b. Inglewood, Calif., Sept. 23, 1958. AB with honors, U. Calif., Berkeley, 1980; MD, Wash. U., St. Louis, 1984. Intern and resident U. Calif., Davis, 1984-87; fellow U. Wash. Sch. of Medicine, Seattle, 1987-88; anesthesiologist U. Hosp., U. Wash., Seattle, 1987—; physician Multidisciplinary Pain Ctr. U. Wash., Seattle, 1988—, Acute Pain Svc. U. Hosp., Seattle, 1988—. Contbr. articles to profl. jours. and publs.; presenter in field. Recipient Young Investigator award Am. Heart Assn., 1978, Chancellor's Research award, 1979, 80, Sigma Xi Merit award for Research, 1980. Mem. Am. Soc. of Anesthesiology, Wash. State Soc. of Anesthesiology, Canadian Soc. of Anesthesiology, Internat. Anesthesiology Research Soc., Am. Soc. for Regional Anesthesia, Internat. Assn. for the Study of Pain, Am. Pain Soc., Western Pain Soc. Office: Univ Wash Clinical Pain Ctr RC-76 Seattle WA 98195

LOPER, WARREN EDWARD, computer scientist; b. Dallas, Aug. 2, 1929; s. Leon Edward and Belva (Fannin) L.; BS in Physics, U. Tex. at Austin, 1953, BA in Math. with honors, 1953; m. Ruth M. Wetzler, June 17, 1967; 1 child, Mary Katherine. Commd. ensign U.S. Navy, 1953, advanced through grades to lt., 1957; physicist U.S. Naval Ordnance Test Sta., China Lake, Calif., 1956-61; operational programmer U.S. Navy Electronics Lab., San Diego, 1962-64; project leader, systems programming br., digital computer staff U.S. Fleet Missile Systems Analysis and Evaluation Group, Corona, 1964-65, sr. systems analyst digital computer staff U.S. Naval Ordnance Lab., Corona, 1965-69; head systems programming br. Naval Weapons Center, Corona Labs, 1969; computer specialist compiler and operating systems devel., Naval Electronics Lab. Center, San Diego, 1969-76; project leader langs., operating systems and graphics Naval Ocean Systems Ctr., San Diego, 1977—; Navy rep. on tech. subgroup Dept. Def. High Order Lang. Working Group, 1975-80. Recipient Disting. Svc. award Dept. Def., 1983. Mem. IEEE, Assn. Computer Machinery. Democrat. Roman Catholic. Home: 6542 Alcala Knolls Dr San Diego CA 92111 Office: Naval Ocean Systems Ctr/Code 412 271 Catalina Blvd San Diego CA 92152

LOPES, BARBARA KETCHAM, foundation administrator; b. Mineola, N.Y., June 17, 1945; d. Jame Rowland and Katherine (Baker) Ketcham; m. Daniel Antone Lopes, June 18, 1977. BA, William Smith, 1967. Lic. real estate sales, N.C. Spl. edn. tchr. Lochland Sch., Geneva, N.Y., 1967-68; field exec. Conn. Valley Girl Scout Coun., Hartford, Conn., 1968-70; adminstrv. tng. specialist Traveler's Ins. Co., Hartford, 1970-72; asst. to program coordinator Hartford (Conn.) Easter Seal Rehab. Ctr., 1972-78; dir. pub. info. Currituck County (N.C.) Pub. Schs., 1978-79; membership specialist Colonial Coast Girl Scout Coun., Norfolk, Va., 1979-80; dir. devel. County of Currituck, N.C., 1980-83; field exec. Greater Long Beach Girl Scout Coun., Calif., 1984—. Republican. Episcopalian. Office: Greater Long Beach Coun Girl Scouts Am PO Box 8215 Long Beach CA 90808

LOPES, RAFAEL, banker; b. San Diego, Sept. 24, 1966; s. Joseph Lopes and Rosa (Moreno) Iniguez. BS, Calif. State U., L.A., 1989. Prodn. asst. L.A. Arts Ctr., 1983-84; sales assoc. J. W. Robinsons, L.A., 1984-85; teller Security Pacific Nat. Bank, Beverly Hills, Calif., 1985, new accounts rep., 1985-86; banking supr. City Nat. Bank, Beverly Hills, Calif., 1986-. Fellow Toastmasters Internat. (ednl. v.p. 1988). Democrat. Roman Catholic. Home: 4401 Griffin Ave Los Angeles CA 90031 Office: City Nat Bank 400 N Roxbury Dr Beverly Hills CA 90210

LOPEZ, ARTHUR CESAR, microcomputer systems engineer; b. Los Angeles, Apr. 2, 1954; s. Arthur Sanabria and Eleanor (Montero) L.; m. Joann-Chicako-Haak, Sept. 15, 1984; 1 child, Arthur Cesar Jr. BA, Calif. State U., 1979. From digital tech. C to digital tech. A ITT-Fed. Electric Corp., Pasadena, CA, 1981-88; systems engr. Orbiting Astron. Obs. Corp., Pasadena, 1988—; pres. ACL Enterprises, Sylmar, Calif., 1988, ACL Computer Service, Sylmar, 1988, ACL Video Prodns., Sylmar, 1988, Art Lopez Publs., Sylmar, 1988. Author, editor How to Build XT Micros, 1988, Amazing Road to Riches, 1988. Pres. Olivemountain View Townhouse Assn., Sylmar, 1987. Mem. Soc. Profl. Hispanic Engrs. Home and Office: 13540 Hubbard St Suite 12 Sylmar CA 91342

LOPEZ, BARRY HOLSTUN, writer; b. Port Chester, N.Y., Jan. 6, 1945; s. Adrian Bernard and Mary Frances (Holstun) L.; m. Sandra Jean Landers, June 10, 1967. BA, U. Notre Dame, 1966, MA in Teaching, 1968; postgrad., U. Oreg., 1968-69; LHD (hon.), Whittier Coll., 1988. Free-lance writer 1970—, free-lance photographer, 1970-81; assoc. Gannett Ctr. for Media Studies, N.Y.C., 1985—. Author: Desert Notes, 1976, Giving Birth to Thunder, 1978, Of Wolves and Men, 1978 (John Burroughs Soc. medal 1979, Christophers of N.Y. medal 1979, Pacific Northwest Booksellers award in nonfiction 1979), River Notes, 1979, Winter Count, 1981 (Disting. Recognition award Friends Am. Writers in Chgo. 1982), Arctic Dreams, 1986 (Am. Book award in nonfiction 1986, Christopher medal 1987, Pacific Northwest Booksellers award 1987, Frances Fuller Victor award in nonfiction Oreg. Inst. Literary Arts 1987), Crossing Open Ground, 1988; author various essays and stories; contbg. editor Harper's mag., 1981-82, 84—, N.Am. Rev., 1977—; contbr. articles to profl. jours.; works translated into Japanese, Swedish, German, Dutch, Italian, French, Norwegian, Chinese, Finnish, and Spanish. Recipient Award in Lit., Am. Acad. and Inst. Arts and Letters, 1986; John Simon Guggenheim Found. fellow, 1987. Mem. PEN Am. Ctr., Authors Guild, Poets and Writers.

LOPEZ, CHARLES TYRONE, retail executive; b. Charleston, Miss., June 2, 1959; s. Manual G. and Ada Belle (Campbell) L.; m. Shirley Ann Pucket, June 1, 1983 (div. 1986). Student, Boise State U., 1981--. Mgr. Briscoe Builders, Inc., Meridian, Idaho, 1984-86; territorial sales rep. R & S Beauty Supply, Inc., Boise, Idaho, 1986-87; bus. mgr. Wolfe Automotive Group, Inc., Caldwell, Idaho, 1987--; pres. Jones Wood Stores Distbn., Meridian, 1987--; chmn. bd. dirs. Double L Enterprises, Inc., Garden City, Idaho. Contbr. articles to trade publs. Founder, guest speaker The Outspoken Against Drugs, 1982—; pres. Boise Big Bros. Club, 1982-83. Sgt., U.S. Army, 1977-80. Mem. Assoc. League Mex.-Ams. (pres. Boise chpt. 1981-82), Idaho State Jaycees (Chmn. of Yr. award local chpt. 1983), Civitan. Republican. Mormon. Home: 3403 Meadow Dr Boise ID 83706

LOPEZ, DAVID JOSEPH, military officer; b. Syracuse, N.Y., Oct. 20, 1961; d. Joseph Frank and Lucille Jane (Conmme) L. BS in Phys. Sci., U. Ct., 1983. Commd. ensign USN, Miramar, Calif., 1985, advanced through grades to lt., 1987. Contbr. articles to profl. jours. Mem. Tailhook Assn., NRA, Audubon Soc., N.Am. Hunting Club, Miramar Gun Club. Republican. Roman Catholic. Office: Fighter Squadron 213 NAS Miramar San Diego CA 92145

LOPEZ, DIANE DORAN, elementary teacher, principal; b. L.A., Feb. 24, 1931; d. Clifford Wilmoth Doran and Rowena Louise (Buell) Little; m. M.T. Lopez, June 5, 1954 (dec. May 1966); children: M. James, Rowena R. Yates, Clifford O. BA, Biola U., 1956; MA, Tex. Women's U., 1979. Cert. tchr., Calif., Tex. Tchr. rural sch., Plattsmouth, Nebr., 1950-51; elem. tchr. San Gabriel (Calif.) Christian Sch., 1956-58, pvt. sch., Northridge, Calif., 1960-61; founder sch., missionary, tchr. CAM Internat., Puelba, Mex., 1962-69; tchr. Dallas Christian Acad., 1970-74; tchr. and prin. Trinity Christian Acad., Dallas, 1975-83; dir. pilot program and curriculum writer L'Abri Fellowship Personnel, Greatham, Eng. and Dallas, 1983-85; prin. Benthany Christian Sch., Sierra Madre, Calif., 1985-88; coordinator various workshop, Dallas and Calif., 1975—; pvt. practice cons., Arcadia, Calif., 1985-88; pvt. practice curriculum con. Author: Teaching Children, 1988. Mem. Internat. Reading Assn., Assn. for Supervision and Curriculum Devel. Republican. Interdenominational. Home: 508 S 3 Ave Arcadia CA 91006

LOPEZ, LARRY S., technical writer; b. Delta, Colo., Apr. 1, 1932; s. Dionicio Arcenio and Abelina (Gonzalez) L.; m. Liesel Lampert, Dec. 5, 1955; children: David Alexandre, Charles Eugene. BA in History, U. N. Mex., 1974, MA in History, 1976. Tech. writer Sandia Nat. Labs., Albuquerque, 1977-86, specs. engr., 1986--. Contbr. articles to profl. jours.; author: Taos Valley, 1975. Coordinator Mardi Gras Festivals and Parades German Am. Club, Albuquerque, 1982-87. With USN, 1951-70. Mem. Edelweiss German Am. Club (v.p. 1980), Outdoors Club (pres. 1988). Home: 508 Jefferson St Albuquerque NM 87108

LOPEZ, THOMAS MARSH, entrepreneur; b. Wilmington, Del., Apr. 2, 1943; s. S. Henry and Kate Wedston (Hawley) L.; m. Su-Allan Latchum, Aug. 28, 1968 (div. 1972); m. Margaret Judd Jacoby, Aug. 20, 1983. BS in Mktg., U. Del., 1967. Recruiter RCA Corp., Camden, N.J., 1970-72; exec. dir. Am. Heart Assn., N.Y.C., 1972-77, Juvenile Diabetes Found., N.Y.C., 1977-79; v.p. ComputerMaster, Inc., Ft. Lee, N.J., 1979-80; account supr. J. Walter Thompson Co., San Francisco, 1980-81; sr. v.p. Activision, Inc., Mt. View, Calif., 1981-84; pres. Cytation Inc., San Francisco, 1984-86; v.p. Microsoft Inc., Redmond, Wash., 1986-88; chmn. bd. Mammoth MicroProdns., Seattle, 1988—; cons. Interactive Communications Corp., San Jose, 1984. Inventor CD-ROM software, 1985. Lt. (j.g.) USCG, 1968-70. Mem. St. Bart's Club. Republican. Episcopalian.

LOPEZ-POWELL, JOYCE ANN, corporate cash manager; b. Phoenix, Feb. 23, 1954; d. Rosario Felix and Alice Nancy (Hunt) Lopez; m. Stratton Rhonnelle Powell, Mar. 4, 1973; children: Christopher, Angela Rollings, Tiffany Megan. AA, Phoenix Community Coll., 1974; BA in Mgmt., U. Phoenix, 1986, MBA, 1988. With pub. relations State of Ariz., Phoenix, 1977; with cash mgmt. The Tanner Cos., Phoenix, 1977—. Dir.: (plays) Sleeping Beauty, Wizard of Oz, Heidi at Phoenix Children's Theater, 1968—. Mem. Valley Leadership, Phoenix, 1986—, mem. task force on edn., 1988; bd. dirs. Phoenix Children's Theater, 1970—, Maricopa County Vol. Bur., Phoenix, 1988. Mem. Ariz. Cash Mgmt. Assn. Democrat. Unitarian. Club: Phoenix City. Home: 707 E Whitton Ave Phoenix AZ 85014

LORANCE, ELMER DONALD, organic chemistry educator; b. Tupelo, Okla., Jan. 18, 1940; s. Elmer Dewey and Imogene (Triplett) L.; m. Phyllis Ilene Miller, Aug. 31, 1969; children: Edward Donald, Jonathan Andrew. BA, Okla. State U., 1962; MS, Kansas State U., 1967; PhD, U. Okla., 1977. NIH research trainee Okla. U., Norman, 1966-70; asst. prof. organic chemistry So. Calif. Coll., Costa Mesa, 1970-73, assoc. prof., 1973-80, prof., 1980—, chmn. div. natural scis. and math., 1985—. Contbr. articles to profl. jours. Cons. Harbor Christian Sch., Costa Mesa, 1974. Mem. AAAS, Am. Chem. Soc., Internat. Union Pure and Applied Chemistry (assoc.), Am. Inst. Chemists, Am. Sci. Affiliation, Phi Lambda Upsilon. Republican. Mem. Ch. Assembly of God. Office: So Calif Coll 55 Fair Dr Costa Mesa CA 92626

LORCH, WILLIAM CHARLES, transportation executive; b. Peoria, Ill., Nov. 17, 1945; s. Carl and Marie (Huffman) L.; m. Mary Kay Hull, Aug. 20, 1983; 1 child, William Eric. BS, U.S. Mcht. Marine Acad., Kings Point, N.Y., 1967; postgrad., U. Wash., 1968-70, Alaska Pacific U., 1988—. Ops. mgr. Cascade Shipping Co., Seattle, 1970-77; port mgr. Alaska Maritime Agys., Valdez, 1977-86; gen. mgr. Alaska Maritime Agys., Anchorage, 1986—; mgr. mktg. Cen. Steamship Internat., 1989—; info. rep. U.S. Mcht. Marine Acad., 1984—. Commr. Alaska Bd. Marine Pilots, 1988—; chmn. Transp. Commn., Valdez, 1982-86; mem. Soviet-Am. com. Alaska Hist. Soc. Mem. U.S. Naval Inst., Propeller Club U.S. Clubs: Am. Alpine, Valdez Alpine (v.p. 1978-84), Valdez Yacht (pres. 1980-82). Office: Alaska Maritime Agys 2000 W Internat Airport Rd Anchorage AK 99519

LORD, ARTHUR ABRAM, television producer; b. N.Y.C., Mar. 3, 1942; s. Benjamin and Kathryn (Zucker) L.; m. Susan E. Tallman, Aug. 28, 1965; children: Michael, Sharon. Student, Ohio Wesleyan U., 1961; BS in Journalism, U. Fla., 1963. Newswriter NBC, N.Y.C., 1967-71; war corr. NBC, Saigon, Vietnam, 1971-73; S.W. bur. dir. NBC, Houston, 1973-79; network news dir. NBC, Burbank, Calif., 1979-82, producer, 1982—; cons. (TV movie) Special Bulletin, 1983. Producer news feature Heart Transplant, 1980 (Emmy award 1981): Writer news spl. Apollo to the Moon, 1970 (Emmy award 1970); contbr. articles to TV Guide. Served to capt. USAF, 1963-67. Recipient Nat. Merit award Houston Urban League, 1975, Peabody award, 1985. Mem. TV News Dirs. Assn. Jewish. Club: Mid Valley Athletic. Office: NBC News 3000 W Alameda Burbank CA 91523 *

LORD, HAROLD WILBUR, electrical engineer and electronics consultant; b. Eureka, Calif., Aug. 20, 1905; s. Charles Wilbur and Rossina Camilla (Hansen) L.; B.S., Calif. Inst. Tech., 1926; m. Doris Shirley Huff, July 25, 1928; children—Joann Shirley (Mrs. Carl Cook Disbrow), Alan Wilbur, Nancy Louise (Mrs. Leslie Crandall), Harold Wayne. With Gen. Electric Co., Schenectady, 1926-66, electronics engr., 1960-66; pvt. cons. engr., Mill Valley, Calif., 1966—. Coffin Found. award Gen. Electric Co., 1933. Fellow IEEE (life, tech. v.p. 1962, Centennial medal 1984, IEEE Magnetics Soc. 1984 Achievement award). Contbr. articles to profl. jours. Patentee in field. Home and Office: 336 Corte Madera Ave Mill Valley CA 94941

LORD, JACK, actor, director, producer; b. N.Y.C., Dec. 30, 1930; s. William Lawrence and Ellen Josephine (O'Brien) Ryan; m. Marie de Narde, Apr. 1, 1952. BS in Fine Arts, NYU, 1954. pres. Lord and Lady Enterprises, Inc., 1968—. Works exhibited in galleries, museums including Corcoran Gallery, Nat. Acad. Design, Whitney Mus., Bklyn. Mus., Met. Mus. Art, N.Y.C., Library of Congress, Brit. Mus., London, Bibliotheque Nationale, Paris, Mus. Modern Art, N.Y.C., Met. Mus. Art, Brit. Mus., Bklyn. Mus., Bibliotheque Nationale, Paris, Fogg Mus., Harvard U., Santa Barbara (Calif.) Mus. Art, John and Mable Ringling Mus. Art, Sarasota, Fla., Grunwald Graphic Arts Found., UCLA, Brooks Meml. Art Gallery, Memphis, Cin. Art Mus., Atkins Mus. Art, Kansas City, Mo., Fine Arts Gallery, San Diego, Colby Coll. Art Mus., Waterville, Maine, Ga. Mus. Art, U. Ga., Atlanta, DePauw U. Art Mus., Greencastle, Ind., Chouinard Art Inst., Los Angeles, Free Library Phila., Columbia U., N.Y.C., Lycoming Coll., Williamsport, Pa., Rutgers U., New Brunswick, N.J., U. Maine, Orono; represented in permanent collections, Dartmouth Coll., Hanover, N.H., Colgate U. Library, Hamilton, N.Y., Simmons Coll., Boston, Kalamazoo Inst. Arts, U. N.C., Chapel Hill, Evansville (Ind.) Mus. Arts, Massillon (Ohio) Mus., Hebrew Union Coll., Cin., N.Y.C., Los Angeles, Jerusalem, Flint (Mich.) Inst. Arts, Lehigh U. Coll. Arts, Bethlehem, Pa., Birmingham (Ala.) Mus. Art, Case Western Res. U., Cleve., Coll. of Wooster (Ohio), Calif. Inst. Arts; Broadway appearances include Traveling Lady, Cat on a Hot Tin Roof, Flame-Out, The Illegitimist, (TV shows) Stoney Burke (star); producer, star of 280 hours in 12 yrs. of series Hawaii Five-O; creator (TV series) The Hunter; creator, dir., producer: (TV film) M Station: Hawaii, 1980; writer (original screenplay) Melissa, 1968; dir. episodes Hawaii Five-O; appeared in feature films The Court Marshall of Billy Mitchell, Williamsburg, The Story of a Patriot, Tip on a Dead Jockey, God's Little Acre, Man of the West, The Hangman, Walk Like a Dragon, Dr. No, Ride to Hangman's Tree, Doomsday Flight; leading TV roles include Omnibus, Playhouse 90, Goodyear Playhouse, Studio One, U.S. Steel Hour, Have Gun Will Travel, Untouchables, Naked City, Rawhide, Bonanza, Americans, Route 66, Gunsmoke, Stagecoach West, Dr. Kildare, Greatest Show on Earth, Combat, Chrysler Theater, 12 O'Clock High, Loner, Laredo, FBI, Invaders, Fugitive, Virginian, The Man from UNCLE, High Chaparral, Ironside, Alcoa Theatre, Loretta Young Show, The Millionaire, Checkmate, Climax, Kraft, Philco, Danger, Suspense, The Web, You Are There, Lineup, Grand Hotel, Kraft Suspense Theatre. Served as 2d officer U.S. Merchant Marines. Recipient St. Gauden's Artist award, 1948, Fame award, 1963, Spl. Law Enforcement award, Am. Legion, 1973, Adminstr.'s award VA, 1980, Legend in His Own Time award State of Hawaii, 1980; named to Cowboy Hall of Fame, 1963. Mem. Dirs. Guild Am., Screen Actors Guild. *

LORD, JACKLYNN JEAN, student services representative; b. Sacramento, Feb. 2, 1940; d. Jasper Jackson and Celia (Moreno) Opdyke; m. Brent Andrew Nielsen, Aug. 6, 1966 (dec. Sept. 1974); 1 child, Taumie Celia; m. Mark William Lord, Mar. 5, 1983; 1 child, Jacklynn Michelle. Student, Sacramento State U., 1958-60, Cabrillo Coll., 1962-66, Sacred Coll. of Jamilian Theology and Div. Sch., Reno, 1976—. Communications cons. Pacific Telephone Co., San Jose, Calif., 1966-74, Nev. Bell Co., Reno, 1974-76; student services rep. for extension program Jamilian U. of Ordained, Reno, 1976—; asst. music dir. Internat. Community Christ, Reno, 1980—; choral instr. Jamilian Parochial Sch., Reno, 1976—; sexton Jamilian Handbell Choir, Reno, 1981—; organist Symphonietta, Reno, 1983—. Mem. Nat. League Concerned Clergywomen. Republican. Mem. Ch. Internat. Community Christ (ordained to ministry). Home: 1990 Humboldt Reno NV 89509 Office: Internat Community Christ 643 Ralston St Reno NV 89503

LORD, SUZANNE MARY, university official; b. Redbank, N.J., Feb. 16, 1962; d. William Francis Lord and Jacqueline Maria (Lester) Pisarro. BA in Polit. Sci., Pa. State U., 1984; postgrad. in polit. sci., San Diego State U., 1984--. Conf. desk asst. San Diego State U., 1985, computer operator, 1985-86, night security supr., 1985-86, clerical asst., office mgr., 1987--. Mem. Centre Region Code Enforcement Bd. Appeals, State College, Pa., 1983-84. Mem. Pa. State U. Alumni Assn., Skull and Bones. Democrat. Home: 3639 Caminito Carmel Landing San Diego CA 92130 Office: San Diego State U Housing and Residential Life Office San Diego CA 92182-0568

LORDS, KEVIN JAMES, dentist; b. Salt Lake City, May 9, 1957; s. James Lafayette and Katherine R. (Reeves) L.; m. Janet Eileen Elifritz, June 20, 1987. BS, U. Utah, 1981; DMD, Wash. U., St. Louis, 1985. Pvt. practice Salt Lake City, 1988--. Lt. USN, 1985-88. Mem. ADA, Ariz. Dental Assn., Utah Dental Assn., Kappa Sigma. Roman Catholic. Office: 4885 S 900 E Ste 106 Salt Lake City UT 84117

LORENTS, ALDEN CONRAD, data processing educator; b. Bagley, Minn., Apr. 29, 1937; s. Joseph Conrad and Elsa (Anderson) L.; m. Olivia Leigh Gordon, June 18, 1960; children: Heidi, Troy. BS, Concordia Coll., 1960; MBA, U. Minn., 1963, PhD, 1971. Programmer, analyst Honeywell, Mpls., 1960-66; dir. computer ctr. Bemidji (Minn.) State U., 1966-69; assoc. dir. Project PRIME, State of Minn., Mpls., 1970-71; prof. mgmt. info. systems No. Ariz. U., Flagstaff, 1971—; intern Lawrence Livermore (Calif.) Labs., 1981, Sandia Nat. Labs., Albuquerque, 1983, Ariz. Pub. Svc., 1987-88; cons. U. Kuwait, 1983, No. Ariz. Guidance Ctrs., Flagstaff, 1974, 80. Contbr. articles to profl. jours. Named Outstanding Educator of Am., 1972. Mem. Soc. Info. Mgmt., Data Processing Mgmt. Assn., Soc. Data Educators, Info. Resources Mgmt. Assn., Decision Scis. Inst. Democrat. Lutheran. Home: Rte 4 Box 737 Flagstaff AZ 86001 Office: No Ariz U 15066 Coll Bus Flagstaff AZ 86001

LORENTSON, HOLLY JEAN, health facility executive; b. Mpls., Nov. 27, 1956; d. Leslie Arnold and Mary Ann Jean (Anderson) L. BA in Nursing, Coll. St. Catherine, St. Paul, 1978; MPH, U. Minn., 1986. RN, Minn.; registered pub. health nurse. Nurse Abbott/Northwestern Hosp., Mpls., 1978-79; acting dir. community nursing services Ebenezer Soc., Mpls., 1979-81, pub. health nurse supr., 1981-82; charge nurse Ebenezer Hall nursing Home, Mpls., 1982-84; patient services coordinator San Diego Hospice Corp., 1984-85, exec. dir., 1985-88, pres., 1988—; mem. fiscal intermediary provider task force Region X Health Care Financing Adminstrn., 1984-88. Mem. Nat. Hospice Orgn., Internat. Soc. Pres. Non-Profit Orgns., Calif. State Hospice Assn. (v.p. 1985-88), Calif. Assn. Health Services at Home (com. mem.), Sierra Club, Soroptimists. Office: San Diego Hospice Corp 9797 Aero Dr Ste B San Diego CA 92123

LORENZ, JACQUELINE GABRIAL, sales and marketing executive; b. Seattle, Feb. 8, 1948; d. Melvin John McAbee and Theresa (Haman) Bickford; m. George A. Lorenz, Jan. 19, 1985. BA, U. Wash., Seattle, 1971; MBA, UCLA, 1979. Supr. Seattle 1st Nat. Bank, 1973-75; sales mgr. Bristol Myers Products, N.Y.C., 1975-79; sales trainer Johnson & Johnson, New Brunswick, N.J., 1979-80; sales mgr. Borg Warner, St. Louis, 1980-84; v.p. sales and mktg. div. Key Trust Co., Seattle, 1984—. Co-author: Bank Telemarketing, 1986. Bd. dirs. Seattle Mental Health Inst. Mem. Bank Mktg. Assn. (bd. dirs. Chgo. chpt. 1988—), Seattle C. of C., Bellevue (Wash.) C. of C., Anchorage C. of C., World Affairs Coun., Alpha Xi Delta (alumni pres. 1980, membership advisor 1978). Roman Catholic. Office: Key Trust Co 1000 2d Ave Fl 11 Seattle WA 98104

LORENZ, TIMOTHY CARL, real estate agent; b. Glendale, Calif., June 9, 1947; s. Raymond Jerome and Majorie Nadine (Bevis) L.; m. Jeanann Carrington, Apr. 16, 1966 (div. 1982); children: Julianne, Todd; m. Nadyne Claire Buck, Sept. 11, 1982; stepchildren: Ron, Eve, SeAnn, Dray. BA in Psychology, Calif. State U., Los Angeles, 1969, MA in Psychology, 1972. Lic. real estate agt., Calif. Chief investigator L.A. County Dept. Consumer Affairs, 1976-81; co-owner Newport Holistic Health Clinic, Newport Beach, Calif., 1981-83; chief investigator Orange County Office Consumer Affairs, Santa Ana, Calif., 1983-86; agt. Century 21 Niguel, Laguna Niguel, Calif., 1986—; instr. psychology Mt. San Antonio, Walnut, Calif., 1976-83; chmn. bd. dirs. Real Reasons, Laguna Niguel; distbr. Amway, Dana Point, Calif., 1983—. Co-author Renter Rights and Responsibilities, 1978; producer T.V. talk show Coping in Today's World, 1982 (Best of Pub. Access award 1982). Pres. Bur. Electronic and Appliance Repair Bd., Sacramento, Calif., 1980, 86, legis. com., 1979; founding mem. Nat. Automobile Dealers Consumer Action Panel, L.A., 1978-81. Recipient Letter Commendation Atty. Gen., L.A., 1980. Mem. Nat. Assn. Realtors, Assn. Foster Parents North Cen. South Orange County (pres. 1986-88), State Calif. Foster Parent Assn. (pres. 1985—), Dana Point C. of C., Newport Beach C. of C. Republican. Home: PO Box 7676 Laguna Niguel CA 92677 Office: Century 21 Niguel Realty 30232 Crown Valley Pkwy Laguna Niguel CA 92677

LORENZEN, ROBERT FREDERICK, ophthalmologist; b. Toledo, Ohio, Mar. 20, 1924; s. Martin Robert and Pearl Adeline (Bush) L.; B.S., Duke, 1948, M.D., 1948; M.S., Tulane U., 1953; m. Lucy Logsdon, Feb. 14, 1970; children—Roberta Jo, Richard Martin, Elizabeth Anne. Intern, Presbyn. Hosp., Chgo., 1948-49; resident Duke Med. Center, 1949-51, Tulane U. Grad. Sch., 1951-53; practice medicine specializing in ophthalmology, Phoenix, 1953—; mem. staff St. Joseph's Hosp., St. Luke's Hosp., Good Samaritan Hosp., Maricopa County Hosp. Pres. Ophthalmic Scis. Found., 1970-73; chmn. bd. trustees Rockefeller and Abbe Prentice Eye Inst. of St. Luke's Hosp., 1975—. Recipient Gold Headed Cane award, 1974; named to Honorable Order of Ky. Colonels. Fellow Internat. Coll. Surgeons, A.C.S., Am. Acad. Ophthalmology and Otolaryngology, Soc. Eye Surgeons; mem. Am. Assn. Ophthalmology (sec. of ho. of dels. 1972-73, trustee 1973-76), Ariz. Ophthal. Soc., Royal Soc. Medicine. Republican. Lodge: Rotary (pres. Phoenix 1984-85). Editor-in-chief Ariz. Medicine, 1963-66, 69-70. Home: 2921 W Manor Dr Phoenix AZ 85014 Office: 367 E Virginia Ave Phoenix AZ 85004

LORENZETTI, REGINA ANNE, apartment management company executive; b. Los Banos, Calif., Aug. 15, 1948; d. Donald Grey and Patricia Ann (Farley) Estep; m. Frederick Mario Lorenzetti, Dec. 16, 1966; children: Stephanie, Freddie. Student, Merced Coll., U. Berkeley. Head clk. San Joaquin Cotton Oil Co., Ora Loma, Calif., 1968-69; salesman Les Abbott Realty, Dos Palos, Calif.; owner, mgr. Le Boutique, Firebaugh, Calif., 1978-81; owner, mgr. apts. Merced, Calif., 1971—. Home: 1037 Dos Palos Ave Dos Palos CA 93620

LORHAN, GEORGE JOSEPH, manufacturing engineer; b. Kansas City, Kans., Jan. 3, 1949; s. Paul Herman and Grace Evelyn (Hemphill) L.; m. Connie Linn Johnson, June 22, 1985 (div. June 1989). BS in ChemE, Carnegie-Mellon U., 1971; M in Engring., Calif. Poly. U., 1978. Material engr. Fluor Corp., Irvine, Calif., 1974-85; sr. mfg. engr., composites Northrop Aircraft Corp., Pico Rivera, Calif., 1985—. Club: Toastmasters (Pico Rivera) (sec., treas. 1987). Home: 913 Via Mirola Palos Verdes Estates CA 90274

LORINSKY, LARRY, international trade executive, consultant; b. New Britain, Conn., July 31, 1944; s. Jacob and Bernice Edythe (Horn) L.; BA, U. Conn., 1966, MA, 1968; m. Laurie Clark Griffin, June 9, 1968; children: Michael Bliss, Jennifer Bartlett, Jessica Clark. Ops. mgr., then trading mgr. Norwich Iron & Metal Co. (Conn.), 1965-75; ferrous export mgr. Comml. Metals Co., Dallas, 1975-77, br. mgr., San Francisco, 1977-81 , West Coast area mgr., 1980-81; exec. v.p. Technalloy Inc., San Jose, Calif., 1981-83; dir. nonferrous alloys David Joseph Co., 1983-84; pres., chief exec. officer Lornat Metals Trading, Inc., 1984-87; project mgr. Mindseed Corp., 1987-89; gen. mgr. Custom Alloy, 1989—; ltd. dir., rep. METALSASIA Internat., 1983—. Mem. Nat. Inst. Scrap Iron and Steel (nat. export council), Seaguard Svcs. Inc. (dir.), Locell Assocs. Ltd., Nat. Assn. Recycling Industry (nat. traffic com.), Brisbane (Calif.) C. of C. (dir. 1977-81). Democrat. Jewish. Club: Masons.

LORMAN, WILLIAM RUDOLPH, civil engineer, retired naval officer; b. Cleve., Sept. 26, 1910; s. Rudolph Calman and Theresa Mary (Pollock) L.; m. Hulda Wanita Babel, May 2, 1936 (dec. May 1980); children: Jonathan, Timothy. BS, Case Western Res. U., 1933; MS, U. Colo., 1939, profl. degree CE, 1956. Asst. dep. engr. Cuyahoga County Engrs., Cleve., 1935-36; asst. engr. U.S. Bur. Reclamation, Denver and Redding, Calif., 1936-42; commd. lt. (j.g.) USN, 1942, advanced through grades to lt. comdr., 1948, ret., 1970; spl. projects officer USN, Vanuatu, 1943-44; helium officer USN, Moffett Field Air Station, Calif., 1944; flag staff officer USN fleet aircraft command, Alameda, Calif., 1945-46; civil engr. USN, San Francisco, 1946-48; materials research engr. USN, Solomons, Md., Port Hueneme, Calif., 1948-82; cons. USN liason DuBridge Oil Lease Panel, Los Angeles, 1969, Com. Status of Cement and Concrete Research in U.S., Washington, 1979-81. Contbr. over 80 articles to profl. jours. Fellow ASCE (life), Am. Concrete Inst.; mem. ASTM, The Ret. Officers Assn. (life, sec. Ventura County, Calif. chpt. 1983-87), Nat. Assn. Retired Fed. Employees (life), Sigma Xi (emeritus). Republican. Home: 510 Ivywood Dr Oxnard CA 93030

LORTI, DANIEL CAESAR, engineer; b. Dec. 13, 1936; s. Dante Antonio, Marie Therese (Butrago) L.; m. Jane Susann Perkins, Aug. 15, 1959 (div. Feb. 1979); children: Daniel C., Dean J., Susan D., David S.; m. Gloria Jean Hooper, May 3, 1980. BSEE summa cum laude, Ariz. State U., 1966, MS in Engring., 1967; postgrad., U. Calif., Irvine, 1968-69. Registered profl. engr., Ariz. Mem. radar systems analysis staff Ford Aeronutronic, Newport Beach, Calif., 1966-68; mem. tech. staff Gen. Rsch. Corp., Santa Barbara, Calif., 1968-71, Spectra Rsch. Systems, Newport Beach, 1971-74, 75-76; pres. Data Tec, Irvine, 1974-81; v.p. Corp. Benefit Cons., Tustin, Calif., 1974-75; sr. scientist Xonics, Inc., L.A., 1976-78; v.p. Xonics, Inc., Van Nuys, Calif., 1979-80; v.p., prin. XonTech, Inc., Van Nuys, 1980-85; chief radar engr. Advanced Concepts Northrop Electronics Systems Div., Hawthorne, 1985—. Contbr. articles to profl. jours.; patentee precision ignition adjustment device. With USAF, 1955-59. Mem. IEEE, Phi Kappa Phi, Tau Beta Pi, Eta Kappa Nu. Home: 425 Vista Parada Newport Beach CA 92660 Office: 2301 W 120th St Hawthorne CA 90250

LOSCH, JOSEPH GEORGE, development engineer; b. El Monte, Calif., Jan. 29, 1964; s. Franz and Maria (Oppermann) L. AS, Don Bosco Tech. Inst., 1983; BSME summa cum laude, Calif. Polytech. State U., San Luis Obispo, 1987. Tool and die design draftsman Precision Pattern and Tooling, Alhambra, Calif., 1982-83; engring. summer hire Radar Systems Group Hughes Aircraft Co., El Segundo, Calif., 1984-86; devel. engr. Allied Signal Aerospace Co. Airesearch, Torrance, Calif., 1987—. Mem. ASME, AIAA, Tau Beta Pi, Phi Kappa Phi. Democrat. Roman Catholic. Home: 8627 E Scott St Rosemead CA 91770 Office: Allied Signal Aerospace Co Airsearch 2525 W 190th St Torrance CA 90504

LOSS, ROBERT FREDERICK, III, aerospace company executive; b. Allen, Md., June 14, 1940; s. Robert F. Jr. and Olive May (Butler) L.; m. Eleanor Catherine Quirin, Sept. 8, 1962; children: Cathi, Robin, Rick. BEE, U. Del., 1962; postgrad. in modern bus., Alexander Hamilton Inst., 1972. Mgr. computer applications Frederic R. Harris, Inc., cons. engrs., N.Y.C., 1967-70; account rep. McDonnell Douglas Co., N.Y.C., 1971-73, mgr. tech. sales support area, br. sales mgr., 1973-82; mgr. European tech. sales support McDonnell Douglas Co., Woking, Eng., 1982-83; mgr. bus. unit McDonnell Douglas Co., St. Louis, 1983-84; dir. product mgmt., bus. mgmt. and mktg. McDonnell Douglas Co., Cypress, Calif., 1984-88; v.p. devel. and ops. McDonnell Douglas Mfg. & Engring. Systems Co., Cypress, 1988—. Capt. U.S. Army, 1963-67. Republican. Methodist. Home: 9561 Henderson Way Villa Park CA 92667 Office: McDonnell Douglas M&E Sys 5701 Katella Ave Cypress CA 90630

LOTT, DAVIS NEWTON, advertising agency executive, publisher; b. San Antonio, May 8, 1913; s. James and Sissilla (Davis) L.; m. Arlene Marion Peterson, Nov. 1, 1942; children: Vicki Arlene, Christy Sue, Laurie Ann. B.S., Northwestern U., 1935; post-grad. UCLA. With Better Homes and Gardens and Successful Farming, Des Moines, Iowa, 1935-36; with Abbott, Labs., North Chicago, Ill., 1936-37; copywriter J. Walter Thompson, Chgo., 1938-39; owner and pres. Lott Advt. Agy., L.A., 1939-41, 46—; pres. USA Corp., Marina Del Rey, Calif.; pres. Lott Publs., Santa Monica, Calif.; pub. Am. Carwash Rev., Am. Personal Protection Rev., Candy World, Tobacco, Sundries and Fancifoods World, Chocolate and Nut World, Gourmet and Giftpack World, Sugarless World, Cheese and Crackers World, Organic World, Teen Scene, Tennis Illustrated, Surfing Illustrated, Sweater's Digest, Books and Authors World, New Products and Mail Order World and many others; dir. spl. projects Microlert Systems Internat. Past bd. dirs. Los Angeles Library Assn. Comdr. USNR, 1941-46, 1951-52, World War II, Korea. Named Assoc. Dean of Candy Industry, Nat. Candy Wholesalers Assn., 1974. Author: Rules of the Road, 1942, Handbook of the Nautical Road; Emergency Shiphandling Manual, 1943; Collision Prevention, 1947; Treasure Trail, 1944; Star Spangled Broadcast, 1950; Mystery of Midnight Springs, 1954; Dodge City Justice, 1957; The Inaugural Addresses of the American Presidents, 1964; The Presidents Speak, 1965; See How They Ran 1972; The Presidents Illustrated, 1976; Jimmy Carter-And How He Won, 1976; co-author: (with Bruce Greenland) musical comedy The Music Room, 1982. Home: 13222 B Admiral Ave Marina Del Rey CA 90292 Office: PO Lockbox 9669 Marina Del Rey CA 90291

LOTT, JULIA DAWN, insurance company executive; b. Mesa, Ariz., Feb. 13, 1951; d. Connley J. and Clara Mae (Cluff) Tyron; m. Clyde Edwin Lott, July 9, 1971; children: Stuart Allen, Dallan Richard, Susan Ranae, Stephanie Dawn, Janeil Lynn, Nathan Warren. Ins. and securities saleswoman Ariz.; regional mgr. A.L. Williams Co., Phoenix, 1985—. Home: Rte 1 Box 95 Buckeye AZ 85235

LOUBET, LOUIS BERNARD, vacuum and cryogenic specialist; b. Pomona, Calif., Feb. 16, 1933; s. John Louis and Florence (Strona) L.; m. Barbara Mae Viverto, July 22, 1961; children: Maria A. Rode, Gregory L. Loubet. BSME, Calif. Polytechnic U., 1960; BSBA, Redlands U., 1979. Engr. Aerojet Gen. Corp., Sacramento and Azusa, Calif., 1959-62; tech. staff Space Gen. Corp., El Monte, Calif., 1962-64; applied rsch. engr. N.Am. Aviation, Inc., Downey, Calif., 1964-67; tech. staff specialist Aerojet Electro Systems, Azusa, Calif., 1967-82, engring. supr., 1982--; cons. Joel-Loubet, La Verne, Calif., 1980--. Author of numerous articles in field. Served in U.S. Army, 1957-59, Germany. Mem. AIAA, Am. Vacuum Soc. Roman Catholic. Home: 1948 Clear Falls Ave La Verne CA 91750 Office: Aerojet Electrosystems 1100 W Hollyvale Ave Azusa CA 91702

LOUCHE, KEVIN ANDREW, management consultant; b. N.Y.C., Sept. 11, 1951; s. Andrew Wagner and Trina (Cusiamano) L.; m. Dawn Alice, Aug. 11, 1973; children: Erica, Lisa, Jessica. B Engring., Stevens Inst., Hoboken, N.J., 1973. Registered profl. engr., Oreg. Engr. Jersey Cen. Power and Light, Morristown, N.J., 1973-77; sr. engr. NUS Corp., Rockville, Md., 1977-80; sr. cons. SCI Software, Crystal River, Fla., 1980-87; cons. Mgmt. Analysis Corp., San Diego, 1987-88; pres. Champion Cons., Orangevale, Calif., 1988—. Mem. Am. Nuclear Soc. Republican. Roman Catholic. Home: 100 Judah Ct Folsom CA 95630 Office: Champion Cons PO Box 1976 Orangevale CA 95662

LOUCKY-RAMSEY, JOANNA RUTH, clergyperson; b. Syracuse, N.Y., Oct. 13, 1954; d. Lubomir George and Mildred Mary (Droppa) Loucky; m. William John Ramsey, Aug. 9, 1980. BA in English, Stephens Coll., 1976, BFA in Creative Writing, 1976; MA in Religious Studies, N.Am. Bapt. Sem., 1983; cert. in urban ministry, Sem. Consortium Urban Pastoral Edn., 1982; MDiv., N.Am. Bapt. Sem., 1981. Ordained to ministry Am. Bapt. Ch., 1985. Minister music and youth Emerson Ave. Bapt. Ch., Indpls., 1983-87; chaplain Marion County Children's Guardian Home, Indpls., 1983-86; assoc. pastor First Bapt. Ch., Portland, Oreg., 1987—. Mem. Fellowship Am. Bapt. Musicians, Am. Guild English Handbell Ringers, Am. Choral Dirs. Assn., Am. Bapt. Ch.'s (ministers coun.), Downtown Ministries Cluster, Portland Worship Network. Office: First Bapt Ch 909 SW 11th Ave Portland OR 97205

LOUDERBACK, TRUMAN EUGENE, environmental management consultant; b. Sterling, Colo., Jan. 17, 1946; s. George DeWayne and Lillian Louise (Harrach) L.; m. Dena Marie Chambers, June 1, 1985; children: Nicole Marie, Kyle Eugene, Matthew Joseph. BS, Colo. State U., 1968; postgrad., U. Colo., 1974-75. Project investigator and biologist, research inst. Colo. Sch. Mines, Golden, 1972-78; adminstr. quality assurance Cleveland-Cliffs Iron Co., Casper, Wyo., 1979, dir. environ. affairs, 1980-83; dir. environ. affairs Cleveland-Cliffs Iron Co., Rifle, Colo., 1984-88, Cliffs Engring., Inc., Rifle, Colo., 1984-88; pvt. practice cons. Lakewood, Colo., 1978-79, Rifle, 1988—; chmn. environ. com. Pacific Shale Project, Rifle, 1983-87, also mgr. environ. impact statement, 1983-84. Contbr. articles to profl. jours. Industry rep. Colo. Joint Rev. Process Team, Colo. Dept. Nat. Resources, 1983. Mem. Nat. Assn. Environmental Profls., Rocky Mountain Assn. Environmental Profls. Republican. Methodist. Lodge: Rotary (bd. dirs. Rifle chpt. 1984), Masons. Home and Office: 1544 S Flower Ct Lakewood CO 80226

LOUGHEED, PETER, lawyer, politician; b. Calgary, Alta., Can., July 26, 1928; s. Edgar Donald and Edna (Bauld) L.; m. Jeanne Estelle Rogers, June 21, 1952; children—Stephen, Andrea, Pamela, Joseph. B.A., U. Alta., 1950, LL.B., 1952; M.B.A., Harvard U., 1954. Bar: Alta 1955. With firm Fenerty, Fenerty, McGillivray & Robertson, Calgary, 1955-56; sec. Mannix Co., Ltd., 1956-58, gen. counsel, 1958-62, v.p., 1959-62, dir., 1960-62; individual practice law from 1962; formerly mem. Alta. Legislature for Calgary West; formerly leader Progressive Conservative Party of Alta., 1965-85; premier Alta., 1971-85; sr. ptnr. Bennett Jones, Calgary, 1985—. Office: Bennett Jones, 3200 Shell Ctr, 400 4th Ave, Calgary, AB Canada T2P 0X9 *

LOUGHLIN, RICHARD J., real estate company executive; b. 1932. Gen. mgr. no. Calif. ops. Century 21 Real Estate Corp., 1974-81, pres., chief exec. officer, 1981—; also bd. dirs. Office: Century 21 Real Estate Corp PO Box 19564 Irvine CA 92714 *

LOUGHRAN, JAMES NEWMAN, university president, philosophy educator; b. Bklyn., Mar. 22, 1940; s. John Farley and Ethel Margaret (Newman) L. A.B., Fordham U., 1964, M.A., 1965, Ph.D. in Philosophy, 1975; Ph.D. (hon.), Loyola Coll., Balt., 1985. Joined S.J., 1958; ordained priest Roman Catholic Ch., 1970. Instr. philosophy St. Peter's Coll., Jersey City, 1965-67; asst. dean Fordham U., Bronx, N.Y., 1970-73; tchr. philosophy Fordham U., Bronx, 1974-79, 82-84, dean, 1979-82; pres. Loyola Marymount U., Los Angeles, 1984—. Contbr. numerous articles and revs. to popular and scholarly jours. Trustee St. Peter's Coll., Jersey City, 1972-78, Xavier U., Cin., 1981-84. Mem. Am. Philos. Assn. Home and Office: Loyola Marymount U Loyola Blvd at W 80th St Los Angeles CA 90045

LOUIS, WILLIAM CHARLES, III, physicist; b. Chgo., July 24, 1951; s. William Charles Jr. and Clementina Scott (Ransom) L.; m. Catherine Ann Gribler, July 4, 1980. BS, Ga. Inst. Tech., Atlanta, 1973; PhD, U. Mich., 1978. Lic. physicist. Rsch. assoc. Rutherford Lab., Chilton, U.K., 1978-81; asst. prof. Princeton (N.J.) U., 1981-87; mem. staff Los Alamos (N.Mex.) Lab., 1987--. Contbr. numerous articles to profl. jours. Named Jr. Investigator, U.S. Dept. Energy, 1984-87. Mem. N.Y. Acad. Scis., Am. Pys. Soc. Office: Los Alamos Nat Lab MS H846 Los Alamos NM 87544

LOUSBERG-HOAL, LUCINDA, college administrator; b. Sterling, Colo., Nov. 9, 1962; d. Dean K. and E. Vay (Archbold) Lousberg; m. Charles Alan Hoal. BA in Speech, U. No. Colo., 1985, MA in Speech, 1987. Dir. student activities Morgan Community Coll., Ft. Morgan, Colo., 1988—; trainer Excel, Ft. Morgan, 1988. Fellow Colo. Speech Communications Assn., Speech Communication Assn., AAUW. Republican. Roman Catholic. Office: Morgan Community Coll 17800 County Rd 20 Fort Morgan CO 80701

LOUVAU, GORDON ERNEST, management consultant, educator; b. Oakland, Calif., May 29, 1928; s. Ernest and Ella Meta (Meins) L.; student U. Calif., 1946-49; postgrad. Calif. State U., Hayward, 1975-77; M.B.A., John F. Kennedy U., 1980; m. Lois Louvau Peterson, June 9, 1984; children—John Pierre, Tanya Lissette, Charles Frederic. Accountant, Oakland, 1950-59; asst. controller U.S. Leasing, Inc., San Francisco, 1960-61; pres. Louvau Systems Co., Oakland, 1962-66; v.p., gen. mgr. Prescolite div. U.S. Industries Co., San Leandro, Calif., 1966-68; cons. acctg. systems, 1969—; vis. prof. acctg. U. S.Africa, 1970-71; dir. Inst. Research and Bus. Devel., asst. prof. acctg. Calif. State U. at Hayward, 1972-80; asst. dean., asso. prof. mgmt., dir. acctg. programs J.F. Kennedy U., 1979-85. Cert. mgmt. acct., 1975. Mem. Nat. Assn. Acct. (dir. 1972-74), Am. Acctg. Assn. Republican. Author: Financial Management of the Clinical Laboratory, 1974; Management and Cost Control Techniques for the Clinical Laboratory, 1977; Computers in Accountant's Offices, 1981. Office: PO Box 5808 Carmel CA 93921

LOVATT, ARTHUR KINGSBURY, JR., manufacturing company executive; b. Ventura, Calif., Mar. 12, 1920; s. Arthur Kingsbury and Flora (Mercedes) L.; B.S., U. So. Calif., 1941; M.B.A., Queens U., 1943; m. Juanita Gray, Feb. 1, 1946; children—Sherry Lynn, Tim Arthur. Leaseman, Shell Oil Co., Los Angeles, 1946-51; dir. indsl. relations Willys-Overland Motors, Inc., Los Angeles, 1952-55; asst. to pres. and gen. mgr. Pastushin Aviation Corp., Los Angeles, 1955-57; pres. Lovatt Assos., Los Angeles, 1957-66; chemn. bd., pres., gen. mgr. Lovatt Tech. Corp., Santa Fe Springs, Calif., 1966—, also dir.; chmn. bd. Lovatt Sci. Corp., Santa Fe Springs, Metal Ore Processes, Inc., Santa Fe Springs; dir. Lovatt Industries, Inc., others. Mem. Calif. Republican State Central Com., 1964—; state adviser U.S. Congl. Adv. Bd.; chartered mem. Republican Pres. Task Force. Served with U.S. Army, 1943-45. Mem. Am. Legion (post comdr. 1946), AAAS, Nat. Space Inst., Am. Soc. Metals, Los Angeles C. of C., U. So. Calif. Alumni Assn. (life), Nat. Hist. Soc. (founding assoc.), N.Y. Acad. Scis., Internat. Oceanographic Found., Smithsonian Assos., Am. Ordnance Assn., Disabled Am. Vets., U.S. Senatorial Club, Nat. Rifle Assn. Club: Masons (past master, Shriner). Inventor, developer tech. processes. Office: Lovatt Tech Corp 10106 Romandel Ave Santa Fe Springs CA 90670

LOVE, COLLEEN CARNEY, health science facility administrator; b. Feb. 27, 1956; d. John Patrick and Mary Louise (Hoffmann) Carney; m. James Warren Love, June 14, 1980; children: James Wesley, Christopher Carney. AAS, Adirondack Community Coll., Glens Falls, N.Y., 1976; BSN magna cum laude, SUNY, Utica, 1978; MA in Nursing, U. Iowa, 1986; postgrad., U. Calif., San Francisco, 1986--. RN, Calif., Iowa. Nurse clinician med.-psychiat. unit Mercy Hosp., Cedar Rapids, Iowa, 1982-86; dir. Cen. Coast Psychiat. Ctr., San Luis Obispo, Calif., 1986--; pres. Anorexia Nervosa and Related Eating Disorders, Inc., San Luis Obispo, 1986--; lectr. Nursing div. Cuesta Coll., San Luis Obispo, 1986--; research asst. U. Calif., San Francisco. Author (with others) Psychiatric Nursing, 1986, (with others) Nursing Interventions for the Institutionalized Elderly. Chmn. San Luis Obispo Psychiat.-Mental Health Clin. Specialist Council, 1986--; fellow mem. San Luis Obispo Mental Health Adv. Bd., 1986--. Nursing scholar N.Y. State Bd. Regents, 1974. Mem. Am. Nurses Assn. (cert. psychiat.-mental health nurse), Calif. Nurses Assn., U. Iowa Alumni Assn., Sigma Theta Tau. Office: Cen Coast Psychiat Ctr 1911 Johnson San Luis Obispo CA 93403-8127

LOVE, JAMES EDWARD, clinical chemist, army officer; b. Phila., Apr. 30, 1948; s. James Edward and Helen Josephine (Turner) L.; m. Sondra Eleanor Walker, June 7, 1969; children: Jaime Eleanor, Jonathan Edward. BS, Temple U., 1969; MS, Wayne State U., 1976; MBA, Austin Peay State U., 1981; PhD, Ohio State U., 1985. Commd. 2d lt. U.S. Army, 1969, advanced through grades to lt. col., 1987; exec. officer drug testing lab. U.S. Army, Long Binh, Vietnam, 1971-72; chief lab. svs., Rader Army Health Clinic U.S. Army, Ft. Meyer, Va., 1972-74; chief clin. lab., Blanchfield Army Hosp. U.S. Army, Ft. Campbell, Ky., 1976-81; chief of chemistry, Letterman Army Med. Ctr. U.S. Army, San Francisco, 1981—; accreditation inspector, Coll. Am. Pathologists, San Francisco, 1986—. Assoc. editor, Am. Jour. Med. Tech., Houston, 1980-83; contbr. articles, abstracts to sci. publs. Bd. dirs., Christian County Sickle Cell Found., Hopkinsville, Ky., 1979-81. Decorated Bronze Star medal. Mem. Am. Assn. Clin. Chemists, Soc. Armed Forces Med. Lab. Scientists, Officers' Club. Mem. Assemblies of God Ch. Home: 1235 C Ramsel Ct San Francisco CA 94129 Office: Letterman Army Med Ctr Bldg 1100 Rm 202 San Francisco CA 94129

LOVE, MILDRED LOIS (JAN LOVE), public relations executive; b. Iowa City, July 9, 1928; d. Joseph R. and Gladys M. (Parsons) Casey; BS in Bus. Adminstrn., U. Iowa, 1951; m. Gerald Dean Love, Apr. 4, 1952; children: Laura Anne Love Parris, Cynthia Love-Hazel, Gregory Alan, Linda Love Mesler, Geoffrey Dare. Vocal soloist Sta. KXEL, Waterloo, Iowa, 1944-46; sec. to lawyer, La Porte City, Iowa, 1944-46; administrv. aide Office of Supt., La Porte City High Sch., 1947-48; office mgr. Minn. Valley Canning Co.,

Iowa div. offices, LaPorte City, 1947-48; sec. dept. mktg. U. Iowa, 1948-51; asst. dept. pub. rels. Chgo. Bd. Trade, 1949-51; exec. sec. patent dept. Collins Radio Co., Cedar Rapids, 1951-52; vol. VA Hosp., Albany, N.Y., 1965-73; adminstrv. dir. Tri-Village Nursery Sch., Delmar, N.Y., 1960-61; participant Internat. Lang. Teaching Exch., Cambodia, 1961; vol. hosps. in Concord, N.H., 1963-64; vol. Chgo. Maternity Center, 1973-74; mgr. Wolf Trap Assocs. Gift Shop, Vienna, Va., 1975-80; gen. mgr. Travelhost of Washington, 1980-81; cons. mgmt., 1980—; chmn. Nat. Cherry Blossom Festival, Washington. Participant community pageants on local and dist. levels, Iowa, 1950-51; Sunday sch. tchr. Meth. Ch., 1941-61; mem. Flossmoor (Ill.) Planning and Zoning Commn., 1973-74, McLean (Va.) Planning and Zoning Commn., 1975—; precinct worker in Iowa, 1946-52, N.Y., 1956-61, N.H., 1963-64, Va., 1979—; pres. I.O.W.A. Inc., Washington, 1980-81; active various community fund raising drives; mem. LWV, Ladies Aux., McCosh Infirmary, Princeton, N.J. Mem. AAUW, Am. Mkgt. Assn., NAFE, Nat. Conf. State Socs. (pres. 1983), Ariz. Opera League, Princeton Club, Can. Club, Normanside Country Club, Olympia Fields Winter Club, Kenilworth Club, Delta Zeta. Republican. Home: 1167 Blanc Ct The Vintage Hills Pleasanton CA 94566

LOVE, SANDRA RAE, information specialist; b. San Francisco, Feb. 20, 1947; d. Benjamin Raymond and Charlotte C. Martin; B.A. in English, Calif. State U., Hayward, 1968; M.S. in L.S., U. So. Calif., 1969; m. Michael D. Love, Feb. 14, 1971. Tech. info. specialist Lawrence Livermore (Calif.) Nat. Lab., 1969—. Mem. Spl. Libraries Assn. (sec. nuclear sci. div. 1980-82, chmn. 1983-84, bull. editor 1987-89), Beta Sigma Phi. Democrat. Episcopalian. Office: Lawrence Livermore Nat Lab PO Box 808 L-389 Livermore CA 94550

LOVEGROVE, ROBERT EMERSON, mayor, realtor; b. Bridgeport, Conn., June 30, 1943; s. Robert Emerson and Sylvia (Tyack) L.; m. Martha Robertson, July 25, 1964; children: Lisa Lynn, Brian Scott, Joseph Lee, Carmen Marie. Student, U. N.Mex., 1962; BS in Forestry, U. Mont., 1966; MS in Forestry, Harvard U., 1967; PhD in Econs., Colo. State U., 1971. Asst. prof. Adams State Coll., Alamosa, Colo., 1970-72; research assoc. U. Mont., Missoula, 1972-74; regional economist U.S. Forest Service, Missoula, 1974-78; realtor Lambros Realty, Missoula, 1978-84; real estate broker Lovegrove Ltd., Missoula, 1984-85; mayor City of Missoula, 1986—; econs. cons. various corps., 1978—. Contbr. articles to profl. jours. Active Boy Scouts Am.; deacon Ch. of Christ. Mem. Nat. League Cities (small cities council, steering com.), Mont. League Cities and Towns, Western Mont. Fish and Game Assn. (treas.). Republican. Home: 825 Parkview Way Missoula MT 59803 Office: City of Missoula 201 W Spruce Missoula MT 59802

LOVELACE, JON B., investment management company executive; b. Detroit, Feb. 6, 1927; s. Jonathan Bell and Marie (Andersen) L.; m. Lillian Pierson, Dec. 29, 1950; children: Carey, James, Jeffrey, Robert. A.B. cum laude, Princeton U., 1950. Personnel asst. Pacific Finance Co., 1950-51; with Capital Research & Mgmt. Co., L.A., 1951—, treas., 1955-62, v.p., 1957-62, exec. v.p., 1962-64, pres., 1964-75, 82-83, chmn. bd., 1975-82, 83—, also dir.; chmn. bd. Investment Co. Am., 1982—, Capital Income Builder, 1987—, Am. Mut. Fund Inc., 1971—; bd. dirs. Capital Research Co., 1967—, Am. Pub. Radio; pres., dir. New Perspective Fund; vice chmn. Capital Group, Inc. Trustee Claremont McKenna Coll.; mem. bd. fellows Claremont U. Ctr.; mem. adv. bd. Stanford U. N.E. Asia/U.S. Forum on Internat. Policy; mem. adv. council Stanford U. Grad. Sch. Bus.; trustee Calif. Inst. Arts, chmn., 1983-88; trustee Santa Barbara Med. Found. Clinic, J. Paul Getty Mus., chmn. 1988—. Mem. Council on Fgn. Relations, Sierra Club. Clubs: Princeton (N.Y.C.), University (N.Y.C.); Calif. (Los Angeles). Home: 800 W 1st St Los Angeles CA 90012 also: 780 El Bosque Rd Santa Barbara CA 93108 Office: Capital Rsch & Mgmt Co 333 S Hope St Los Angeles CA 90071

LOVELAND, RICHARD KENNETH, headmaster; b. Scranton, Pa., Jan. 10, 1930; s. Ernest Kenneth and Ethel Mae (Cobley) L.; m. Margot Gilbert, June 14, 1952; 1 child, Richard Wardell. AB cum laude, Princeton (N.J.) U., 1951; MA, Trinity Coll., 1957; PhD, U. Conn., 1963; postgrad., U. Buffalo, 1962-63. Asst. dean, head history dept. Avon Old Farms Sch., Conn., 1953-60; asst. headmaster Buffalo Seminary, N.Y., 1960-63; acad. dean Sidwell Friends Sch., Washington, 1963-65; headmaster Kimberley Sch., Montclair, N.J., 1965-73, Crystal Springs Uplands Sch., Hillsborough, Calif., 1973—. Contbr. articles to profl. jours. Trustee Montclair Hist. Soc., 1969-73, Phillips Brooks Sch., 1976-81, Cen. Presbyn. Ch., 1968-73; bd. dirs. Montclair Fine Arts Festival, 1968-69. 1st lt. U.S. Army Artillery, 1951-53, Korea. Walks Found. grantee, 1958. Mem. Calif. Assn. Ind. Schs. (v.p. 1983-86), N.J. Assn. Ind. Schs. (v.p., treas. 1968-72), Montclair C. of C., Nat. Assn. Prins. Schs. for Girls (v.p. 1987—, pres. San Francisco Bay area coun. 1988-89), Princeton, Montclair Country, Nassau, Peninsula Country, Univ. San Francisco, Phi Kappa Phi. Republican. Office: Crystal Springs Upland Sch 400 Uplands Dr Hillsborough CA 94010

LOVELAND, WALTER DAVID, chemist, chemistry educator; b. Chgo., Dec. 23, 1939; s. Walter Hubert and Anna Emelia (Reese) L.; m. Patricia Marie Rice, Sept. 7, 1962. SB, MIT, 1961; PhD, U. Wash., Seattle, 1965. Postdoctoral fellow Argonne (Ill.) Nat. Lab., 1966-67; rsch. asst. prof. Oreg. State U., Corvallis, 1967-68, from asst. to prof., 1968—; vis. scientist Argonne (Ill.) Nat. Lab., 1968, 76, Lawrence Berkeley (Calif.) Lab., 1976-77, 83-84. Author: Radiotracer Methods, 1975, Nuclear Chemistry, 1982; contbr. numerous articles to profl. jours. NSF fellow, 1962, Tartar fellow Oreg. State U., 1977. Mem. Am. Chem. Soc., Am. Phys. Soc., AAAS, MIT Alumni Assn., Sigma Xi. Democrat. Office: Oreg State U Radiation Ctr Corvallis OR 97331

LOVELASS, NANCY JEAN, insurance agency manager; b. Biloxi, Miss., May 16, 1948; d.William Dysart and Marguerite Louise (Hershey) Berryhill; m. William Coy Cox Jr., Dec. 18, 1967 (div. 1979); 1 child, Kristen Louise; m. Larry DeanLovelass, Apr. 8, 1982. Student, U. Ariz., 1966-69. Advt. placer Tucson Newspapers, Inc., 1968-69; real estate specialist D-M Realty and Trust Co., Tucson, 1969-74; owner, designer N. Cox Originals, Tucson, 1974-77; regional mgr. Blue Cross/Blue Shield Wyo., Cheyenne, 1977-79; comml. ins. specialist Wallick and Volk, Inc., Cheyenne, 1979-83; real estate specialist Century-21 Bell Real Estate, Cheyenne, 1983—; agy. mgr. Key Ins. Svcs., Cheyenne, 1984—; instr., Profl. Ins. Agts. Wyo., Cheyenne, 1988-89, Laramie (Wyo.) Ins. Co. Agts. Tng. Sch., 1989. Bd. dirs., past pres., Mountain Meadows Homeowners Assn., Cheyenne, 1980-89; mem. City of Cheyenne Green Ribbon Task Force. Mem. Profl. Ins. Agts. Wyo, Ind. Ins. Agts. Am., Soc. Cert. Ins. Counselors, Acad. Producer Ins. Studies, Cheyenne Bd. Realtors, Cheyenne C. of C., Classical Glass Corvette Club, Profl. Ins. Agts. Wyo. (bd. dirs.), Southeast Wyo. Ins. Assn.. Republican. Roman Catholic. Office: Key Ins Svcs 2200 E Lincolnway Cheyenne WY 82001

LOVELL, CHARLES C., federal judge; b. 1929; m. Ariliah Carter. BS, U. Mont., 1952, JD, 1959. Assoc. Church, Harris, Johnson & Williams, Helena, Mont., 1959-85; judge U.S. Dist. Ct. Mont., Great Falls, 1985—; chief counsel Mont. Atty Gen.'s Office, Helena, 1969-72. Served to capt. USAF, 1952-54. Mem. ABA, Am. Judicature Soc., Assn. Trial Lawyers Am. Office: US Dist Ct 301 S Park PO Drawer 10112 Helena MT 59626

LOVELL, EMILY KALLED, journalist; b. Grand Rapids, Mich., Feb. 25, 1920; d. Abdo Rham and Louise (Claussen) Kalled; student Grand Rapids Jr. Coll., 1937-39; B.A., Mich. State U., 1944; M.A., U. Ariz., 1971; m. Robert Edmund Lovell, July 4, 1947. Copywriter, asst. traffic mgr. Sta. WOOD, Grand Rapids, 1944-46; traffic mgr. KOPO, Tucson, 1946-47; reporter, city editor Alamogordo (N.Mex.) News, 1948-51; Alamogordo corr., feature writer Internat. News Service, Denver, 1950-54; Alamogordo corr., feature writer El Paso Herald-Post, 1954-65; Alamogordo news dir., feature writer Tularosa (N.Mex.) Basin Times, 1957-59; co-founder, editor, pub. Otero County Star, Alamogordo, 1961-65; newscaster KALG, Alamogordo, 1964-65; free lance feature writer Denver Post, N.Mex. Mag., 1949-69; corr. Electronics News, N.Y.C., 1959-63, 65-69; Sierra Vista (Ariz.) corr. Ariz. Republic, 1966; free lance editor N.Mex. Pioneer Interviews, 1967-69; asst. dir. English skills program Ariz. State U., 1976; free-lance editor, writer, 1977—; part-time tchr., lectr. U. Pacific, 1981-86; part-time interpreter Calif., 1983—, Interpreters Unlimited, Oakland, 1985—; sec., dir. Star Pub. Co., Inc., 1961-64, pres., 1964-65. 3d v.p., publicity chmn. Otero County Community Concert Assn., 1950-65; mem. Alamogordo Zoning Commn., 1955-57; mem. founding com. Alamogordo Central Youth Activities Com., 1957; vice chmn. Otero County chpt. Nat. Found. Infantile Paralysis, 1958-61; charter mem. N.M. Citzens Council for Traffic Safety, 1959-61; pres. Sierra Vista Hosp. Aux., 1966; pub. relations chmn. Ft. Huachuca chpt. ARC, 1966. Mem. nat. bd. Hospitalized Vets. Writing Project, 1972—. Recipient 1st Pl. awards N.Mex. Press Assn., 1961, 62. Pub. Interest award Nat. Safety Council, 1962. 1st Pl. award Nat. Fedn. Press Women, 1960, 62; named Woman of Year Alamogordo, 1960. Editor of Week Pubs. Aux., 1962, adm. N.Mex. Navy, 1962, col. a.d.c. Staff Gov. N.Mex., 1963, Woman of Yr., Ariz. Press Women, 1973. Mem. N.Mex. (past sec.), Ariz. (past pres.) press women, N.Mex. Fedn. Womens Clubs (past dist. pub. relations chmn.), N.Mex. Hist. Soc. (life), N.Mex. Fedn. Bus. and Profl. Womens Clubs (past pres.), Pan Am. Round Table Alamogordo, Theta Sigma Phi (past nat. 3d v.p.), Phi Kappa Phi. Democrat. Moslem. Author: A Personalized History of Otero County, New Mexico, 1963; Weekend Away, 1964; Lebanese Cooking, Streamlined, 1972; A Reference Handbook for Arabic Grammar, 1974, 77; contbg. author: The Muslim Community in North America, 1983. Home: PO Box 7152 Stockton CA 95207

LOVEN, CHARLES JOHN, advertising executive; b. N.Y.C., Feb. 17, 1937; s. John and June Emma (Custer) Azzaro. BA, Occidental Coll., 1962; MA, Calif. State U., L.A., 1967. Group scheduler Douglas Space Systems, Huntington Beach, Calif., 1963-65; personnel rep. Shell Oil Co., L.A., 1965-71; dir. indsl. rels. Calif. Computer Products, Anaheim, 1971-80; sr. v.p., dir. personnel dept. Thompson Recruitment Advt., L.A., 1980—. With USCG, 1954-58. Mem. Employment Mgrs. Assn., Personnel and Indsl. Rels. Assn., Am. Soc. Personnel Adminstrs., Exec. Human Resources Round Table. Office: Thompson Recruitment Advt 4201 Wilshire Blvd #600 Los Angeles CA 90010

LOVENTHAL, MILTON, librarian, writer, playwright, lyricist; b. Jan. 19, 1923; s. Harry and Clara (Feldman) L.; m. Jennifer McDowell, July 2, 1973. BA, U. Calif., Berkeley, 1950, MLS, 1958; MA in Sociology, San Jose State U., 1969. Researcher Hoover Instn., Stanford, Calif., 1952-53; librarian San Diego Pub. Library, 1957-59; librarian, bibliographer San Jose (Calif.) State U., 1959—; tchr. writing workshops, poetry readings, 1969-73; coproducer lit. and culture radio show Sta. KALX, Berkeley, 1971-72; editor, pub. Merlin Press, San Jose, 1973—. Author: Books on the USSR 1917-57, 1957, Black Politics, 1971, A Bibliography of Material Relating to the Chicano, 1971, Autobiographies of Women 1946-70, 1972, Blacks in America, 1972, The Survivors, 1972, Contemporary Women Poets an Anthology, 1977, Ronnie Goose Rhymes for Grown-Ups, 1984; co-author: (Off-Off-Broadway plays) The Estrogen Party To End War, 1986, Mack the Knife: Your Friendly Dentist, 1986, Betsy & Phyllis, 1986, The Oatmeal Party Comes to Order, 1986; co-writer: (musical comedy) Russia's Secret Plot to Take Back Alaska, 1987. Recipient Bill Casey award in Letters, 1980; grantee San Jose State U., 1962-63, 84. Mem. ALA, Assn. Calif. State Profs., Calif. Alumni Assn., Calif. Assn. Research Librarians, Calif. Theatre Council. Office: PO Box 5602 San Jose CA 95150

LOVETT, CRISTINE LOUISE, electronics manufacturing company executive; b. Las Animas, Colo., Aug. 8, 1951; d. Ivan Eugene and Rosalee (Pemberton) Brenton; m. Daryle A. Lovett, May 19, 1972. BS in Journalism, U. Colo., 1972; MBA in Fin., U. Colo.-Denver, 1980. Office mgr. B.C. Christopher & Co., Englewood, Colo., 1973-74; office mgr. OWL Tech. Assocs. Inc., Louisville, Colo., 1974-75, mktg. mgr., 1975-80; v.p. mktg. OWL Tech. Assocs. Inc., Longmont, Colo., 1980-82, v.p., gen. mgr., 1982--. Contbr. articles to various publs. Founder Exec. and Profl. Women's Council, Denver, 1978; mem. exec. com. Women and Bus. Conf., Denver, 1981-86. Mem. Assn. Info. and Image Mgmt. (treas. 1988--), Instrument Soc. Am., Denver C. of C. (corp.), Longmont Mfrs. Council. Office: OWL Tech Assocs Inc 1111 Delaware Ave Longmont CO 80501

LOVGREN, BETTE JEAN, interior designer; b. Tacoma, Aug. 27, 1941; d. John R. Torgerson and Dorothy May (Wheeler) Lloyd; m. Leonard Duane Lovgren, Sept. 9, 1960; children: Joyce Elaine Lovgren Pederson, Janice Lynn. Student art edn., Cen. Wash. U., 1959-60. Lic. Nat. Council Interior Designer. With Puget Sound Office Interiors, Tacoma, 1970-78, A.T. Noman Interiors, Tacoma, 1978-81, Design Concepts, Inc., Tacoma, 1981-84; owner, mgr. Lovgren Design Assocs., Inc., Gig Harbor, Wash., 1984—; cons. in color/design U.S. Gypsum Co., Chgo., Reliance Universal, Salem, Oreg., Charleston Carpet Mfrs. Contbr. articles to profl. publs. Mem. Am. Soc. Interior Designers (profl., v.p., Inst. Bus. Designers (profl.), Color Mktg. Group (profl. bd. dirs.), Constrn. Specifications Inst. (profl. bd. dirs.). Office: 19 Point Fosdick Dr Gig Harbor WA 98335

LOVING, JEAN FRANKLIN, retired elementary school administrator, consultant; b. Kansas City, Kans., Sept. 28, 1925; d. James Wesley and Nine Jane (McMullen) L.; m. Betty Lou Pearsall, May 30, 1947; children: Janet Kay, Donald Franklin. BS in Edn., Ariz. State Coll., 1950, MA in Sch. Adminstrn., 1958; EdS in Sch. Adminstrn., No. Ariz. U., 1966. Cert. elem. tchr., Ariz. Tchr. Prescott (Ariz.) Pub. Schs., 1950-65; asst. supt. bus. Prescott Pub. Schs., 1972-74, elem. prin., 1974-85; adminstrv. asst. No. Ariz. U., 1965-66; asst. prin. Prescott Jr. High, 1966-72; cons. reading programs, Prescott, 1983; speaker Nat. Elem. Sch. Prins. Conv., Denver, 1985; creator edn. computer program, 1984; creator reading program Million Minutes of Reading, 1983. Scoutmaster Boy Scouts of Am., Prescott, 1950-60; active fund drives Big Brothers Big Sisters, Prescott, 1982-84; elder Church of Christ, Prescott, 1985. Served to staff sgt. U.S. Army Air Force 1943-45. No. Ariz. U. fellow, 1965-66. Mem. Ariz. Sch. Admins. (prof. growth com. 1985-86, speaker workshops, Ariz Disting. Elem. Prin. 1985), Nat. Elem. Sch. Adminstrs. (Nat. Disting. Elem. Prin. 1985). Republican. Church of Christ. Clubs: Smoki, Am. Bowling Congress (Prescott). Address: 519 Highland Ave Prescott AZ 86301

LOVINS, AMORY BLOCH, energy consultant; b. Washington, Nov. 13, 1947; s. Gerald Hershel and Miriam (Bloch) L.; m. L. Hunter Sheldon, Sept. 6, 1979. Student, Harvard U., 1964-65, 66-67, Magdalen Coll., Oxford, Eng., 1967-69; MA, Merton Coll., Oxford, 1969-71; DSc (hon.), Bates Coll., 1979, Williams Coll., 1981, Kalamazoo Coll., 1983, U. Maine, 1985; LLD (hon.), Ball State U., 1983. Jr. research fellow Merton Coll., 1969-71; Brit. rep., policy advisor Friends of the Earth, San Francisco, 1971-84; regent's lectr. U. Calif., Berkeley and Riverside, 1978, 81; v.p., dir. research Rocky Mountain Inst., Old Snowmass, Colo., 1982—; cons. physicist, 1963-68; govt. energy cons., 1971—; vis. prof. Dartmouth Coll., 1982; distg. vis. prof. U. Colo., 1982. Author: (also layout artist and co-photographer) Eryri, The Mountains of Longing, 1971, The Stockholm Conference: Only One Earth, 1972, Openpit Mining, 1973, World Energy Strategies: Facts, Issues, and Options, 1975, Soft Energy Paths: Toward a Durable Peace, 1977; co-author: (with J. Price) Non-Nuclear Futures: The Case for an Ethical Energy Strategy, 1975, (with L.H. Lovins) Energy/War: Breaking the Nuclear Link, 1980, Brittle Power: Energy Strategy for National Security, 1982, (with L.H. Lovins, F. Krause, and W. Bach) Least-Cost Energy: Solving the CO2 Problem, 1982, 89, (with P. O'Heffernan, sr. author, and L.H. Lovins) The First Nuclear World War, 1983, (with L.H. Lovins, sr. author, and S. Zuckerman) Energy Unbound: A Fable for America's Future; co-photographer (book) At Home in the Wild: New England's White Mountains, 1978; author numerous poems; contbr. articles to profl. jours., reports to tech. jours.; patentee in field. Recipient Right Livelihood award Right Livelihood Found., 1983, Sprout award Internat. Studies Assn., 1977, Pub. Edn. award Nat. Energy Resources Orgn., 1978, Pub. Service award Nat. Assn. Environ. Edn., 1980, Mitchell prize Mitchell Energy Found., 1982, Delphi Prize Onassis Found., 1989. Fellow AAAS, World Acad. Art and Sci., Lindisfarne Assn.; mem. Fedn. Am. Scientists. Home and Office: 1739 Snowmass Creek Rd Old Snowmass CO 81654-9199

LOVOI, PAUL ANTHONY, physicist; b. Palo Alto, Calif., Apr. 10, 1947; s. Anthony Henry and Clarice (Colmar) L.; m. Janice Marie Craig, Oct. 23, 1976; children: Coleen Marie, Schuyler, Trevor. BS in Math. and Physics, Pacific U., 1969; MS in Physics, U. N.Mex., 1973, PhD in Physics, 1975. Dir. R&D ILC Tech., Sunnyvale, Calif., 1975-80; exec. v.p., founder Internat. Tech. Assocs., Santa Clara, Calif., 1980—. Contbr. articles to profl. jours.; patentee in field. Mem. IEEE, AAAS, No. Calif. Optical Soc. (pres. 1983), Soc. Mfg. Engrs., Optical Soc. Am., APS. Democrat. Episcopalian. Home: 19152 Dehavilland Dr Saratoga CA 95070 Office: Internat Tech Assocs 2281 Calle de Luna Santa Clara CA 95054-1002

LOVROVICH, SHERI L., commercial fisherman; b. Lewistown, Mont., Nov. 13, 1961; d. Robert Lee and Barbara Joann (Sherk) Grant; m. Gregg George Lovrovich, May 20, 1983. Student, Pierce Coll., Lakewood, Wash., 1981. With Dick's Camera & Sound, Inc., Burian, Wash., 1980, Kit's Cameras, Federal Way, Wash., 1981, Safeway Stores, Inc., Wash., 1981-85; comml. fisherman F/V Sentinel, Gig Harbor, Wash., 1985--; asst. horse trainer Gig Harbor, 1987--. Mem. Wash. State Horsemen, People for Ethical Treatment of Animals, Gig Harbor Horsemen. Address: 8101 Bayridge Ave Gig Harbor WA 98335

LOVVIK, DARYL VAUGHN, consulting geologist; b. Eau Claire, Wis., July 26, 1941; s. Oscar W. and Pearl B. (Johnson) L.; m. Perla Ivonne Vargas; children: Alexander Wilhelm, Rodolfo, Sheila Najivi. B.S. in Geology, W. Tex. State U., 1975. Cert. profl. geologist; registered profl. geologist, Alaska, Ariz. Cons. geologist, Golden, Colo., 1975-77; exploration geologist Cotter Corp., Moab, Utah, 1977-79; pres. Southwestern Geol. Survey, Mesa, Ariz., 1979-86; water resource dir. Tohono O'Odham Nation, Sells, Ariz., 1986-89, pres. Southwestern Geol., Tempe, Ariz. Author articles. Served with USAF, 1960-64; Far East. Mem. Am. Inst. Profl. Geologists, Geol. Soc. Am., Am. Assn. Petroleum Geologists, Soc. Mining Engrs. Republican. Episcopalian. Home: 410 E Beatryce St Tempe AZ 85281

LOWBER, STEPHEN SCOTT, manufacturing executive; b. Gainesville, Fla., Apr. 17, 1951; s. Leslie Vernon and Grace Irene (Townsend) L.; m. Susan Irene LeClair, Aug. 28, 1976; children: Jessica Renee, Allison Susanne. BA in Acctg., Western Wash. U., 1975; MBA, Seattle U., 1978. CPA, Wash. Sr. audit mgr. Ernst & Whinney, Seattle, 1978-84; v.p., chief fin. officer Xytec, Inc., Tacoma, 1984—. Served with U.S. Army, 1969-71, Socialist Republic Vietnam. Mem. Am. Inst. CPA's, Wash. Soc. CPA's, Nat. Assn. Accts. (bd. dirs. 1983). Republican. Mem. Assembly of God. Club: Pacific West. Home: 4629 Kent Ct Kent WA 98032 Office: Xytec Inc 9350 47th Ave SW Tacoma WA 99057

LOWE, DORIS JEAN, social worker; b. Pompano, Fla., July 9, 1943; d. Richard Carl and Dorothy May (Malson) Ladeburg; m. Alfred Lewis Lowe, Aug. 29, 1964; children: Lorrie, Wayne. AA, Casper Coll., 1963; BSW, U. Wyo., 1979, MS in Counselor Edn., 1986. Sch. social worker Natrona Schs., Casper, Wyo., 1979—; mem. State Task Force on roles of counselors and social workers in schs., 1984, Forms Com. for Spl. Edn. in Natrona County Schs., 1983-86, Dist. Parent Ctr. Adv. Council, 1983—; liaison Natrona County Sch. Social Workers to Adminstrv. Com., 1983-85. Bd. dirs. Windy Cities Corp. for rehab. of the Developmentally Disabled, Natrona County, 1983—; bd. dirs. Overcomers Corp., 1974—; chairperson Natrona County Child Protection Team, 1986-88, coordinator of first state wide meeting, 1985; mem. God's Fenced Flock prison ministry, 1985-86. Mem. Nat. Assn. Social Workers (1st v.p. and pres. Wyo. chpt., regional rep. 1988), NEA, AAUW (pres. 1984-85, 1st v.p. 1982-83, state bull. editor 1987-89), Natrona County Edn. Assn. (mem. negotiations com. 1985—, mem. grievance com. 1985—), Kappa Kappa Iota (pres. elect 1985-86, pres. 1986-87). Democrat. Mem. Assemblies of God Ch. Home: 2919 Belmont Casper WY 82604 Office: Natrona County Sch Dist #1 970 Glenn Rd Casper WY 82601

LOWE, MARGARET MARY (PEGGY LOWE), financial consultant; b. Los Angeles, June 12, 1951; d. J.F. and Ann (Reitinger) Klecker; m. Barry E. Lowe, Aug. 3, 1974; 1 child, Jennifer Julianna. BA, U. Colo., 1973. Credit and collection mgr. Boulder (Colo.) Med. Ctr., 1978-82; br. mgr. Credit Fax, Inc., Denver, 1982-83; program mgr. Strategic Direct Mktg., Inc., Agoura, Calif., 1984-86; asst. planner Fin. Perspectives, Inc., Clinton, N.J., 1987; fin. cons. Century Fin. Services of Colo., Boulder, 1988. Contbr. articles to profl. jours. Mem. Metro Denver Consumer Credit Assn. (bd. dirs. 1983). Roman Catholic. Office: Century Fin Svcs 1800 30th St #308 Boulder CO 80301

LOWE, OARIONA, dentist; b. San Francisco, June 17, 1948; d. Van Lowe and Jenny (Go) Lowe-Silva; m. Evangelos Rossopoulos, Dec. 18, 1985; 1 child, Thanos G. BS, U. Nev., Las Vegas, 1971; MA, George Washington U., 1977; DDS, Howard U., 1981; pediatric dental cert., UCLA, 1984. Instr. Coll. Allied Health Scis. Howard U., Washington, 1974-76, asst. prof., 1976-77; research asst. Howard U. Dental Sch., Washington, 1977-81; resident gen. practice Eastman Dental Ctr., Rochester, N.Y., 1981-82; dir. dental services City of Hope Med. Ctr., Duarte, Calif., 1984-86; vis. lectr. pediatric dentistry UCLA; mem. oral cancer task force Am. Cancer Soc., Pasadena, Calif., 1985—. Contbr. articles to profl. jours. Del. People to People Internat. Mem. ADA, Nat. Soc. Autistic Children, Calif. Dental Assn., Am. Acad. Pedeatric Dentistry, Am. Soc. Dentistry for Children (v.p.), Sigma Xi, Alpha Omega. Republican. Presybterian. Office: 11822 E Floral Dr Ste D Whittier CA 90601

LOWE, RICHARD GERALD, JR., computer programmer manager; b. Travis AFB, Calif., Nov. 8, 1960; s. Richard Gerald and Valerie Jean (Hoefer) L. Student, San Bernardino Valley Coll., 1978-80. Tech. specialist Software Techniques Inc., Los Alamitos, Calif., 1980-82, sr. tech. specialist, 1982-84, mgr. tech. services, 1984-85; mgr. cons. services Software Techniques Inc., Cypress, Calif., 1985-86; sr. programmer BIF Accutel, Camarillo, Calif., 1986-87; systems analyst BIF Accutel, Camarillo, 1987-88; mgr. project Beck Computer Systems, Long Beach, Calif., 1986—. Contbr. articles to profl. jours. Mem. Assn. Computing Machinery, Digital Equipment Corp. Users Group. Office: Beck Computer Systems 5372 Long Beach Blvd Long Beach CA 90805

LOWER, ROBERT D., marketing professional; b. Long Beach, Calif., Jan. 21, 1936; s. Jack Creech and Helen Louise Lower; m. Judy Lynn Bisgaard, June 27, 1959 (div. 1980); children: Robin Elise Baum, Kristen Kim Ronchetto, Robert Brian, Allison Jane. AA, Coll. of San Mateo, 1956; BA, San Francisco State U., 1959; MBA, Pepperdine U., 1976. Sales corr. Du Pont Co., Inc., Burlingame, Calif., 1962-65; slaes rep. Du Pont Co., Inc., Houston, 1965-66; div. sales mgr. PPG Industries, Inc., Torrance, Calif., 1966-71; pres. Anico Industries, Inc., Cerritos, Calif., 1971-75; regional sales mgr. Farboil Co., Inc., Balt., 1975-77, Matcote Co., Houston, 1977-85; regional mgr., dir. Far East ops. Internat. Paint Co., 1985-87; v.p. A.L. Kilgo Co., Inc., Honolulu, 1987—. With U.S. Army. Home: 400 Hobron Ln #3001 Honolulu HI 96815

LOWERY, E(MERSON) FRED(ERICK), civil engineer; b. Macom, Mo., Feb. 2, 1942; s. Emerson Frederick and Annabelle (Moehle) L.; m. Sept. 5, 1965 (div. 1986); children: Michael, Michelle, Shawn, Todd, Sondra. BCE, U. Mo., 1965; MCE, U. So. Calif., 1968; postgrad., U. Ariz., 1970. Registered civil engr. Ariz., Calif. Civil engr. U.S. BLM, Reno, Nev., 1962-64, L.A. Dept. Water and Power, 1965-69; prin. civil engr. Cella Barr Assocs., Tucson, 1970-80, WLB Group, Tucson, 1981—. Mem. Ariz. Soc. Civil Engrs., Tucson C. of C., U. So. Calif. Alumni Club (pres., v.p. 1978-87), So. Ariz. Homebuilders Assn. Republican. Episcopalian. Home: 5670 N Via Umbrosa Tucson AZ 85715 Office: WLB Group 4444 E Broadway Tucson AZ 85711

LOWERY, JACQUE CHARLENE, realtor, escrow manager; b. Williams, Ariz., Aug. 16, 1950; d. Halsey Peter and Sue Ann (Locke) Holloway; m. Ernest Dale Lowery, Aug. 27, 1969; children: Nathan K., Marsha K. BEd with honors, U. Nev., 1972; AA, Reno Bus. Coll., 1988. Sec. N.Y. Life Ins., Reno, Nev., 1972-74; sec., life ins. agt. Peek Ins., Reno, 1974-76; office mgr. Lemmon Valley Land Co., Reno, 1976-79; real estate sales rep. Peek-Flowers Realty, Reno, 1979-85; mgr. Flowers Escrow Co. Inc., Sparks, Nev., 1979—; real estate sales rep. Ona Flowers Realty, Sparks, 1985—. Active Com. Aid Abused Women, 1985. Mem. Reno Bd. Realtors (chmn. grievance com. 1985-87). Republican.

LOWERY, WILLIAM DAVID, congressman; b. San Diego, May 2, 1947; s. Thomas Henry and Eve (Howard) L.; m. Kathleen Ellen Brown, Sept. 7, 1968; children: Ashley Colleen, Alison Elizabeth, Thomas Harrington. Student, San Diego State Coll., 1965-69, Calif. Western Sch. Law, 1970. Self-employed 1973-77; with Calif. Group, 1977-79; councilman City of San Diego, 1977-80, dep. mayor, 1980; mem. 97th-101st Congresses from

41st Calif. dist., 1981—; mem. Congl. adv. bd. Future Bus. Leaders Am., Grace Caucus. Art Caucus, Congl. Coalition for Soviet Jewry, Caucus for Ethiopian Jews, Environ. and Energy Study Conf., Travel and Tourism Caucus, Congl. Hispanic Caucus (hon.). Bd. dirs. Calif. Water Found., 1978-79; council liaison Unified Port Commn.; mem. Commn. Californias; founder, chmn. Calif. Concord Group; mem. San Diego Sch. Fin. Task Force; chmn. Calif. League Cities; dir. Aseltine sch. San Diego council Boy Scouts Am.; chmn. San Diego March of Dimes, 1981; active Republican orgns. Recipient YMCA Red Triangle award; Amigo de Distinction Mex. and Am. Found. Mem. Urban League San Diego, Navy League. Roman Catholic. Office: 2433 Rayburn House Office Bldg Washington DC 20515 *

LOWI, ALVIN, JR., mechanical engineer, consultant; b. Gadsden, Ala., July 21, 1929; s. Alvin R. and Janice (Haas) L.; m. Guillermina Gerardo Alverez, May 9, 1953; children: David Arthur, Rosamina, Edna Vivian, Alvin III. BME, Ga. Inst. Tech., 1951, MSME, 1955; postgrad., UCLA, 1956-61. Registered prof. engr., Calif. Design engr. Garrett Corp., Los Angeles, 1956-58; mem. tech. staff TRW, El Segundo, Calif., 1958-60, Aerospace Corp., El Segundo, 1960-66; prin. Alvin Lowi and Assocs., San Pedro, 1966—; pres. Terraqua Inc., San Pedro, Calif., 1968-76; v.p. Daeco Fuels and Engring. Co., Wilmington, Calif., 1978—; also bd. dirs. Daeco Fuels and Engring. Co.; vis. research prof. U. Pa., Phila, 1972-74; sr. lectr. Free Enterprise Inst., Monterey Park, Calif., 1961-71; bd. dirs. So. Calif. Tissue Bank; research assoc. Heather Found., San Pedro, 1966—. Contbr. articles to profl. jours.; patentee in field. Served to lt. USN, 1951-54, Korea. Fellow Inst. Humane Studies; mem. ASME, NSPE, Soc. Automotive Engrs., Soc. Am. Inventors, So. Bay Chamber Music Soc., Scabbard and Blade, Pi Tau Sigma. Jewish. Home and Office: 2146 Toscanini Dr San Pedro CA 90732

LOWNDES, DAVID ALAN, systems analyst; b. Schenectady, N.Y., Oct. 28, 1947; s. John and Iris Anne (Hepburn) L.; m. Peggy Welco, May 3, 1970; children: Diana Justine, Julie Suzanne. AB, U. Calif., Berkeley, 1969, postgrad., 1972-73. Acct., credit mgr. The Daily Californian, Berkeley, 1973-75; bus. mgr. The Daily Californian, 1975-76; acct. Pacific Union Assurance Co., San Francisco, 1976-77, acctg. mgr., 1977-78; sr. acct. U. Calif., San Francisco, 1978-88, sr. systems analyst, 1988—. Bd. dirs., auditor, Thornhill Sch. Parent-Faculty Club, Oakland, Calif., 1988—. Home: 1829 Gaspar Dr Oakland CA 94611 Office: U Calif 145 CED 1855 Folsom St San Francisco CA 94143

LOWREY, CHARLES FREDERICK, securities company executive; b. San Francisco, Oct. 27, 1927; s. Alan Jewett and Mary Louise (Black) L.; m. Mary Coolidge Rentschler, June 7, 1952; children: Mary Lowrey Gregory, Charles Frederick Jr. BA, Yale U., 1950. With Chem. Bank, N.Y.C., 1951-55; asst. cashier Wells Fargo Bank, San Francisco, 1956-61; ptnr. Schwabacher & Co., San Francisco, 1961-70; v.p. Blair & Co., San Francisco, 1970; sr. v.p. Davis Skaggs & Co., Inc., San Francisco, 1971-83, Sutro & Co., Inc., San Francisco, 1983-84, Morgan Olmstead Kennedy & Gardner, San Francisco, 1984-87, Hutchinson Securities, San Francisco, 1987—. Treas., fin. v.p. Citizens for Better Govt., San Francisco, 1958-62. With USAAF, 1946-47. Mem. Securities Industry Inst. (trustee, chmn. 1978-79), Bond Club San Francisco (pres. 1978-79), Bohemian Club, Pacific Union Club, St. Francis Yacht Club. Republican. Episcopalian. Office: Hutchinson Securities 160 Sansome St San Francisco CA 94104

LOWRY, CANDACE E., human resource administrator, consultant; b. Miles City, Mont., Sept. 27, 1950; d. James A. and Nathlee (Azar) Zadick; m. Michael Roy Lowry, June 7, 1980; 1 child, Natalie. BSW with high honors, U. Mont., 1971; MSW with high honors, U. Iowa, 1975; DSW, U. Utah, 1984. Clin. social worker, Utah; cert. marriage and family therapist and supr.; diplomate clin. social work, 1987—. Inpatient social worker II U. Iowa Psychiat. Hosps., Iowa City, 1975-76, inpatient social worker III, 1976-79, coordinator, Iowa Autism Program, 1979-80; coordinator, social work specialist U. Utah Counseling Ctr., Salt Lake City, 1980-86, assoc. dir., 1986; program dir. adult unit Wasatch Canyons Hosp., Salt Lake City, 1986—; clin. instr. U. Utah, Salt Lake City, 1981—. Co-author: Meeting the Needs of Autistic Children, 1980; contbr. articles to profl. jours. Grantee NIMH, 1986—. Mem. Nat. Assn. Social Workers, Acad. Cert. Social Workers (cert.), Nat. Register Clin. Social Workers, Am. Group Psychotherapy Assn., Salt Lake City C. of C. Home: 2384 S Summit Circle Salt Lake City UT 84108 Office: Wasatch Canyons Hosp 5770 S 1500 W Salt Lake City UT 84123

LOWRY, LARRY LORN, management consulting company executive; b. Lima, Ohio, Apr. 12, 1947; s. Frank William and Viola Marie L.; m. Jean Carroll Greenbaum, June 23, 1973; 1 child, Alexandra Kristin. BSEE, MIT, 1969, MSEE, 1970; MBA, Harvard U., 1972. Mgr. Boston Consulting Group, Menlo Park, Calif., 1972-80; sr. v.p. Booz, Allen & Hamilton Inc, San Francisco, 1980—; pres. Booz,Allen Capital Inc., San Francisco, 1987—. Western Electric fellow, 1969, NASA fellow, 1970. Mem. Sigma Xi, Tau Beta Pi, Eta Kappa Nu. Presbyterian. Home: 137 Stockbridge Ave Atherton CA 94025

LOWRY, MIKE, former congressman; b. St. John, Wash., Mar. 8, 1939; s. Robert M. and Helen (White) L.; m. Mary Carlson, Apr. 6, 1968; 1 child, Diane. B.A., Wash. State U., Pullman, 1962. Chief fiscal analyst, staff dir. ways and means com. Wash. State Senate, 1969-73; govtl. affairs dir. Group Health Coop. Puget Sound, 1974-75; mem. council King County Govt., 1975-78, chmn., 1977; mem. 96th-100th congresses from 7th dist. Wash., 1979-1989. Chmn. King County Housing and Community Devel. Block Grant Program, 1977; pres. Wash. Assn. Counties, 1978. Democrat. Address: PO Box 4246 Seattle WA 98104 *

LOZANO, IGNACIO EUGENIO, JR., newspaper editor; b. San Antonio, Jan. 15, 1927; s. Ignacio E. and Alicia E. de Lozano; m. Marta Navarro, Feb. 24, 1951; children: Leticia Eugenia, José Ignacio, Monica Cecilia, Francisco Antonio. A.B. in Journalism, U. Notre Dame, 1947. Asst. pub. La Opinion, Los Angeles, 1947-53, pub., editor, 1953-76, 77-83, 84-86; pub. La Opinion, 1983-84, editor-in-chief, 1986—; ambassador El Salvador, 1976-77; Am. ambassador to El Salvador 1976-77; bd. dirs. BankAmerica Corp., Bank of Am. NT & SA, Pacific Enterprises., The Walt Disney Co., Calif. Econ. Devel. Corp. Bd. dirs. Nat. Pub. Radio, Los Angeles World Affairs Council, Santa Anita Found., Youth Opportunity Found., Orange County Performing Arts Ctr.; mem. Council on Fgn. Relations, Council of Am. Ambassadors; trustee U. Notre Dame, Occidental Coll., South Coast Repertory Company; overseer The Rand Corp. Inst. for Civil Justice; bd. govs. Calif. Community Found. Mem. Calif. Newspaper Pubs. Assn. (bd. dirs.), Calif. Press Assn., Cath. Prss Council of So. Calif., Greater Los Angeles Press Club, Inter Am. Press Assn. (pres.), Sigma Delta Chi. Office: La Opinion 1436 S Main St Los Angeles CA 90015 *

LOZZI, EDWARD RHODES, III, public relations consultant, television producer; b. Hawthorne, N.J., Mar. 8, 1952; s. Virgil Paul Lozzi and Elizabeth Ann (Rhodes) Nead; m. Oct. 22, 1968 (div.); 1 child, Brandon V. Lozzi Bonser. Student, U. Tenn., 1968-69; BBA, NYU, 1972; postgrad Bus. Sch., Harvard U., 1972. Lic. ins. broker, N.J.; lic. realtor, Calif., N.J. Aviation ins. underwriter Hartford Ins. Co., N.Y.C., 1971-73; v.p. mktg. Raymond Rhodes Agy. Inc., Hawthorne, 1973-77; chief exec. officer Am. Cookie Co. Inc., N.Y.C., 1977-78; editor Dow Jones-Irwin Pubs., L.A., Chgo., 1979; publicist Paramount Pictures Corp., N.Y.C., 1979; publicist, officer mgr. Pub. Info. Network, Studio City, Calif., 1979-80; pres. Edward Lozzi & Assocs. Pub. Relations and Mgmt., Beverly Hills, Calif., 1980--, N.Y.C., 1980--, London, 1980--; v.p. Brandon Prodns. Ltd., L.A., N.Y.C., London, 1980--; mem. adv. bd. dirs. Alexander Hamilton Savs. & Loan, Hawthorne; fin. news columnist Century City News, 1981; guest commentator CNN Cable News Network, L.A. and Atlanta, 1986--; dir. pub. relations Assoc. Visual Talent Internat., L.A., 1987--. Author: The Garbo Interviews, 1986; co-editor Cover Girl mag., 1985--. Mem. Nat. Med. Publicists Assn., N.Y. Soc. Ins., Publicity Club L.A. (com. 1987-88), Rotary (entertainment and publicity com. Hawthorne and L.A. 1973--). Mem. Ch. of England. Office: 9348 Civic Ctr Dr Ste 101 Beverly Hills CA 90210

LUBARY, JORGE, photography laboratory owner; b. Argentina, Feb. 18, 1943; came to U.S., 1968; s. Jorge Mario and Leonor (Garcia-Uriburu) L.; m. Mary Margaret Ross, Aug. 3, 1966; children: Jorge Maria, James. BS, Colegio Champagnat, Buenos Aires, 1961. Flight attendant Pan-Am. Grace Airways Flight Svc., Lima, Peru, 1964-68; owner, exporter Occidental Trading Corp., Miami, Fla., 1968-72; properties adminstr. Standard Investment Co., Los Angeles, 1972-79; owner, operator Tahoe Photo Labs. Inc., Incline Village, Nev., 1979—; exporting cons. various Argentinian importers, 1979—. Lt. Argentine Air Force, 1962-63. Mem. Jockey Club de Buenos Aires. Republican. Roman Catholic. Home: PO Box 7538 Thousand Oaks CA 91359 Office: Tahoe Photo Labs Inc PO Box 8181 Incline Village NV 89450

LUBATTI, HENRY JOSEPH, physicist, educator; b. Oakland, Calif., Mar. 16, 1937; s. John and Pauline (Massimino) L.; m. Catherine Jeanne Berthe Ledoux, June 29, 1968; children: Karen E., Henry J., Stephen J.C. A.A., U. Calif.-Berkeley, 1957, A.B., 1960, Ph.D., 1966; M.S., U. Ill., 1963. Research assoc. Faculty Scis. U. Paris, Orsay, France, 1966-68; asst. prof. physics MIT, 1968-69; assoc. prof., sci. dir. visual techniques lab. U. Wash., 1969-74, prof., sci. dir. visual Techniques lab., 1974—; vis. lectr. Internat. Sch. Physics, Erice, Sicily, 1968, Herceg-Novi, Yugoslavia Internat. Sch., 1969, XII Cracow Sch. Theorectical Physics, Zapokane, Poland, 1972; vis. scientist CERN, Geneva, 1980-81; vis. staff Los Alamos Nat. Lab., 1983-86; mem. physics editorial adv. com. World Sci. Pub. Co. Ltd., 1982—. Contbr. numerous articles on high energy physics to profl. jours. Alfred P. Sloan research fellow, 1971-75. Fellow Am. Phys. Soc.; mem. Sigma Xi; mem Tau Beta Pi. Office: U Wash Visual Techniques Lab Physics FM 15 Seattle WA 98195

LUBECK, MARVIN JAY, ophthalmologist; b. Cleve., Mar. 20, 1929; s. Charles D. and Lillian (Jay) L.; A.B., U. Mich., 1951, M.D., 1955, M.S., 1959; m. Arlene Sue Bitman, Dec. 28, 1955; children—David Mark, Daniel Jay, Robert Charles. Intern, U. Mich. Med. Center, 1955-56, resident ophthalmology, 1956-58, jr. clin. instr. ophthalmology, 1958-59; practice medicine, specializing in ophthalmology, Denver, 1961—; mem. staff Rose, Children's, Mercy, St. Luke's hosps.; asso. clin. prof. U. Colo. Med. Center; cons. ophthalmologist State of Colo. Served with U.S. Army, 1959-61. Diplomate Am. Bd. Opthalmology. Fellow ACS; mem. Am. Acad. Ophthalmology, Denver Med. Soc., Colo. Ophthalmol. Soc., Am. Intraocular Lens Implant Soc. Home: 590 S Harrison Ln Denver CO 80209 Office: 3865 Cherry Creek N Dr Denver CO 80209

LUBER, JAY ROSS, sales executive, consultant; b. Bklyn., Feb. 6, 1946; s. Morris and Ruth (Whitehorn) L.; m. Sheila Ross, May 17, 1981; 1 child, Alexandra Ross. BA, U. Md., 1972. V.p., co-founder R.J. Learning Ctrs., Washington, 1974-76; mktg. v.p. RWZ Devel., N.Y.C., 1976-81; sales mgr. Control Data Corp., Boston, 1981-85; exec. v.p. Pet Express, Scottsdale, Ariz., 1985—; cons. in field. Republican. Jewish. Home: 8545 N 49th St Paradise Valley AZ 85253

LUBNAU, KATHRYN LEE, speech and language pathologist; b. Gillette, Wyo., Apr. 9, 1961; d. Thomas Edwin and Cynthia L'Vere (Kirkland) L. BS, U. Wyo., 1983, MS, 1985. Speech and lang. pathologist Campbell County Sch. Dist., Gillette, 1985—; rep. Com. for Revision Wyo. Rules and Regulations for Handicapped Children, 1985-86. Asst. youth group leader Episcopal Ch., 1988-89, Sunday Sch. tchr., 1987--. Mem. Am. Speech-Lang.-Hearing Assn., Wyo. Speech-Lang.-Hearing Assn. (sec. 1987), Zeta Phi Eta, Chi Omega, Gilette Jaycees (Outstanding Young Women of Am. 1983, 85, 86, 88). Office: Rozet Sch PO Box 200 Rozet WY 82727

LUBOCKI, DAVID JOSEPH, medical electronics company executive; b. L.A., Aug. 2, 1949; s. Meilach and Malka (Rabinov) L.; m. Sydelle M. Feinstein Haas, May 18, 1969 (div. Oct. 1987); children: Marlene, Brian; m. Jackie S. Calderon, Nov. 28, 1987; stepchildren: Anne Marie, Brett, Jack. BS, Calif. State U., Northridge, 1971, MS, 1975; JD, Southwestern U., L.A., 1979. Med. sales and tng. Electro Med. Engring. Co., Burbank, Calif., 1969-71; med. sales and mktg. Med. Measurements Corp., West Los Angeles, Calif., 1971-74; with med. sales and mktg. Cardio Monitoring, Inc., Marina Del Ray, Calif., 1974-77; med. sales engr. A.O. med. div. Warner Lambert, Newport Beach, Calif., 1977-79; S.W. sales mgr. Litton Med. Electronics, Elk Grove, Ill., 1980-82; western div. sales mgr. Biochem. Internat., Milw., 1982-84; mktg. mgr. Spacelabs, Inc., Squibb, Chatsworth, Calif. and Redmond, Wash., 1984-86; ECG sales and mktg. mgr. Del Mar Avionics, Irvine, Calif., 1986-88; ECG product mgr. Quinton, A. H. Robins, Seattle, 1988—; med. practice mgmt. specialist Wright Line Corp., Sherman Oaks, Calif., 1979; fin. mgmt. cons. U.S. Fin. Corp., Valencia, Calif., 1981; market rsch. cons. Market Rsch. Corp., Van Nuys, Calif., 1975. Contbr. articles to profl. jours. Expert witness computerized monitoring State of Hawaii, Hilo, 1986. With Calif. Nat. Guard, 1969-75. Mem. B'nai B'rith, New Connections, Hillel (L.A.). Republican. Jewish. Home: 12121 SE 15th St Bellevue WA 98005 Office: Quinton Instrument Co 2121 Terry Ave Seattle WA 98121

LUBRAN, ALBERT SAUL, supervisory contract administrator; b. Pitts., Nov. 13, 1942; s. Walter Heinz and Pearl Amstey L. BS in Physics, Bethany Coll., 1965. Quality assurance specialist Def. Contract Adminstrn. Svc. Mgmt. Area, Denver, 1972-77; procurement agt. Duluth (Minn.) AFB, 1977-78, supr. procurement agt., 1978-80; supr. procurement agt. Fitzsimons Army Med. Ctr., Aurora, Colo., 1980-82; contract adminstr. Office Civilian Health and Med. Program of Uniformed Svcs., Aurora, 1982-87; supr. contract adminstr. Directorate of Contracting, Ft. Carson, Colo., 1987—. Capt. USAF, 1967-71. Mem. Nat. Contract Mgmt. Assn. (cert. assoc. contracts mgr., 1981, v.p. logistics, 1986-87, treas., 1987-88, 2nd v.p. Colo. Springs 1988-89), Nat. Ski Patrol (scheduling chmn. 1983-89), Sno Jets Ski Club (v.p. 1974-75, pres., 1975-76). Democrat. Jewish. Home: 950 Pulpit Rock Ct Colorado Springs CO 80918 Office: Directorate of Contracting Fort Carson CO 80913

LUCAS, DONALD LEO, entrepreneur; b. Upland, Calif., Mar. 18, 1930; s. Leo J. and Mary G. (Schwamm) L.; BA, Stanford U., 1951, MBA, 1953; m. Lygia de Soto Harrison, July 15, 1961; children: Nancy Maria, Alexandra Maria, Donald Alexander. Assoc. corp. fin. dept. Smith, Barney & Co., N.Y.C., 1956-59; gen., ltd. partner Draper, Gaither & Anderson, Palo Alto, Calif., 1959-66; pvt. investor, Menlo Park, Calif., 1966—; chmn. bd. Oracle Corp., Inc., Belmont, Calif., Tri-Data Corp.; bd. dirs. HBO & Co., Atlanta, ICOT Corp., Mountain View, Liconix, Mountain View, Robinton Products, Inc., Sunnyvale, Calif., Kahler Corp., Cadence Design Systems, Santa Clara, Calif., Cadence, Inc. Mem. bd. regents Bellarmine Coll. Prep., 1977—; regent emeritus U. Santa Clara, 1980—. 1st lt. AUS, 1953-55. Mem. Am. Council for Capital Formation, Stanford U. Alumni Assn., Stanford Grad. Sch. Bus. Alumni Assn., Commonwealth Club (San Francisco), Stanford Buck Club, Vintage Club (Indian Wells, Calif.), Menlo Country Club (Woodside, Calif.), Menlo Circus Club (Atherton, Calif.), Jackson Hole Golf and Tennis Club, Teton Pines Club, Zeta Psi. Home: 224 Park Ln Atherton CA 94025 Office: 3000 Sand Hill Rd #3 Menlo Park CA 94025

LUCAS, DONNA JEAN S., vocational rehabilitation consultant; b. Portland, Oreg., Apr. 7, 1944; d. Howard Joseph and Lorraine L. (Anderson) Schaefer; m. Roy Lucas, Oct. 2, 1966 (div. Dec., 1971); 1 child, Michael Aaron. BS, Portland State U., Oreg., 1971. Manpower specialist III State of Oregon Vocat. Rehab., Portland, 1974-79; area supr. State of Oregon Workers' Compensation Dept., Portland, 1979-82; vocat. rehab. counselor Helen Accra Rehab., Beaverton, 1982, Cascade Rehab. Counseling, Portland, 1982-83; pres., owner Crossroads Consulting Inc., Portland, 1983—. Mem. Nat. Assn. Rehab. Profls. (cert. vocat. rehab. counselor), Workers Compensation Claims Assn., Nat. Assn. Female Execs. Democrat. Office: Crossroads Consulting Inc 3150 SE Belmont Portland OR 97214

LUCAS, GEORGE W., JR., film director, producer, screenwriter; b. Modesto, Calif., May 14, 1944. Student, Modesto Jr. Coll.; BA, U. So. Calif., 1966. Chmn. Lucasfilm, Ltd., San Rafael, Calif. Creator short film THX-1138 (Grand prize Nat. Student Film Festival, 1967); asst. to Francis Ford Coppola on The Rain People; dir. Filmmaker (documentary on making of The Rain People); dir., co-writer THX-1138, 1970, American Graffiti, 1973; dir., author screenplay Star Wars, 1977; exec. producer More American Graffiti, 1979, The Empire Strikes Back, 1980, Raiders of the Lost Ark, 1981, Indiana Jones and the Temple of Doom, 1984, Labyrinth, 1986, Howard the Duck, 1986, Willow, 1988, Tucker, 1988; exec. producer, co-author screenplay Return of the Jedi, 1983; co-exec. producer Mishima, 1985; co-author, co-exec. producer: Indiana Jones and the Last Crusade, 1989. Office: Lucasfilm Ltd PO Box 2009 San Rafael CA 94912

LUCAS, MALCOLM MILLAR, state chief justice; b. Berkeley, Calif., Apr. 19, 1927; s. Robert and Georgina (Campbell) L.; m. Joan Fisher, June 23, 1956; children: Gregory, Lisa Georgina. B.A., U. So. Calif., 1950, LL.B., 1953. Bar: Calif. 1954. Partner firm Lucas, Deukmejian and Lucas, Long Beach, Calif., 1955-67; judge Superior Ct., Los Angeles, 1967-71, U.S. Dist. Ct., Central Dist., Calif., 1971-84; assoc. justice Calif. Supreme Ct., 1984-87, chief justice, 1987—. Office: Calif Supreme Ct 455 Golden Gate Ave #4250 San Francisco CA 94102 *

LUCAS, SUZANNE, statistician; b. Baxter Springs, Kans., Jan. 16, 1939; d. Ralph Beaver and Marguerite (Sansocie) L.; B.A. in Math., Calif. State U., Fresno, 1967, M.A. in Ednl. Theory, 1969; M.S. in Stats., U. So. Calif., 1979; children—Patricia Sue Jennings, Neil Patric Jennings. Asst. to dir. NSF Inst., Calif. State U., Fresno, 1968; Tchr. secondary math. Fresno city schs., 1968-78; statistician corp. indsl. relations Hughes Aircraft Co., Los Angeles, 1979-80; personnel adminstr. Hughes Aircraft Co. Space and Communications Group, Los Angeles, 1981-82, mem. tech. staff in math., 1982-85, staff engr., 1986-87; mem. tech. staff cost analysis The Aerospace Corp., 1987—; lectr. in biostats. U. So. Calif., 1979. Kiwanis scholar, 1958. Mem. Internat. Assn. Parametric Analysts, Inst. Cost Analysis, Air Force Assn., Armed Forces Communications and Electronics Assn., U. So. Calif. Alumni Assn. (life), Kappa Mu Epsilon. Home: 13430 Isis Ave Hawthorne CA 90250 Office: The Aerospace Corp 2350 E El Segundo Blvd M1-021 El Segundo CA 90245

LUCAS-WARREN, CLAIRE MARION, gerontologist; b. Auckland, New Zealand, Apr. 16, 1961; d. Ronald James and Marion Lily Lucas; m. Peter James Warren, July 9, 1988. BA Psychology with honors, San Jose State U., 1984; MS in gerontology, U. So. Calif., 1986. Care mgr. Ind. Aging, San Jose, Calif., 1982-84; counseling intern Andrus Older Adult Ctr., L.A., 1984-86; rsch. asst. Andrus Gerontology Ctr.-U. So. Calif., L.A., 1985-86; social worker LaPaz Geropsychiat. Ctr., Norwalk, Calif., 1986-87; clin. coord. U. So. Calif.-Alzheimer's Disease Rsch. Ctr., L.A., 1987-89; cons. spl. programs Hillhaven Corp., Aurora, Colo., 1989—. Author gerontol. resource materials. Mem. Am. Soc. on Aging, Geriatric Soc. Am., Alzheimers Disease and Related Disorder Assn. Democrat. Episcopalian. Office: Hillhaven Corp 3000 Jamaica Ct Ste 390 Aurora CO 80014

LUCCHESI, MARIANNE VEGLIA, writer; b. Sacramento, Nov. 23, 1952; d. Eugene Francis and Ramona Alice (Reeves) Veglia; m. John Joseph Figueira, Oct. 14, 1972 (dec. Apr. 1976); m. Jeffrey Foster Lucchesi, Apr. 22, 1979. Student, St. Mary's Coll., Moraga, Calif., 1970-72. Asst. employment and claims dept. employment devel. State of Calif., Sacramento, 1974-78; coordinator dist. safety dept. motor vehicles State of Calif., Santa Ana, 1978-81; mgr. prodn. Regis McKenna Pub. Relations, Palo Alto, Calif., 1981-82; account exec., copywriter The Agy., 1982; asst. dir. San Jose (Calif.) Film and Video Commn., 1982-84; dir. advt. and pub. relations Positive Video, Orinda, Calif., 1984-85; pres., owner PR*SCRIPT*ions, Belmont, Calif., 1985—. Editor Cue mag., 1988—; columnist No. Calif. Film and Video Prodn., 1982—; producer Emmy Awards, No. Calif. and Hawaii, 1987—; contbg. editor various newspapers and mags., 1982—; contbr. articles to profl. jours. Producer fundraiser United Cerebral Palsy, San Carlos, Calif., 1985; team capt. Jr. Achievement, San Jose, 1987. Mem. Nat. Acad. TV Arts and Scis. (voting mem., bd. dirs., editor newsletter 1986—, publicist 1986—), Assn. Ind. Comml. Producers San Francisco (publicist 1986-88), Assn. Film Commrs. (assoc., program editor, advt. coordinator), Am. Film Inst., Profl. Media Network (voting mem., v.p., sec. 1983-86, Joey awards, Awards of Merit 1985-88), San Jose Film Festival (coordinator event, publicity com.), Am. Film Inst., Writer's Connection, Internat. Olympic Hospitality Com. Republican. Roman Catholic. Club: Alpine Hills Swim and Tennis (Portola Valley, Calif.). Home and Office: 2308 Casa Bona Ave Belmont CA 94002

LUCENTE, ROSEMARY DOLORES, educational administrator; b. Renton, Wash., Jan. 11, 1935; d. Joseph Anthony and Erminia Antoinette (Argano) Lucente; B.A., Mt. St. Mary's Coll., 1956, M.S., 1963. Tchr. pub. schs., Los Angeles, 1956-65, supr. tchr., 1958-65, asst. prin., 1965-69, prin. elem. sch., 1969-85, 86—, dir. instrn., 1985-86; nat. cons., lectr. Dr. William Glasser's Educator Tng. Ctr., 1968—; nat. workshop leader Nat. Acad. for Sch. Execs.-Am. Assn. Sch. Adminstrs., 1980; Los Angeles Unified Sch. Dist. rep. for nat. pilot of Getty Inst. for Visual Arts, 1983-85, site coordinator, 1983-86. Recipient Golden Apple award Stanford Ave. Sch. PTA, Faculty and Community Adv. Council, 1976, resolution for outstanding service South Gate City Council, 1976. Mem. Nat. Assn. Elem. Sch. Prins., Los Angeles Elem. Prins. Orgn. (v.p. 1979-80), Assn. Calif. Sch. Adminstrs. (charter mem.), Assn. Elem. Sch. Adminstrs. (vice-chmn. chpt. 1972-75, city-wide exec. bd., steering com. 1972-75, 79-80), Asso. Adminstrs. Los Angeles (charter), Pi Theta Mu, Kappa Delta Pi (v.p. 1982-84), Delta Kappa Gamma. Democrat. Roman Catholic. Home: 6501 Lindenhurst Ave Los Angeles CA 90048 Office: Roscomare Rd Sch 2425 Roscomare Rd Los Angeles CA 90077

LUCERO, ORLANDO JUAN, dentist; b. La Jara, Colo., Dec. 20, 1943; s. Steve and Vincentita (Gallegos) L.; children: Patricia, Teri, Toni, Tracey. BS, Adams State Coll., Alamosa, Colo., 1965; DDS, St. Louis U., 1969. Gen. practice dentistry Colorado Springs, 1971—; pres. Colo. State Bd. Dental Examiners, Denver, 1980-81. Lt. USN, 1969-71. Home: 1121 Terrace Rd Colorado Springs CO 80904 Office: 1855 Austin Bluffs Pkwy Colorado Springs CO 80918

LUCHT, MARIA CECILE, teacher; b. L.A., June 18, 1955; d. Kenneth Warren and Genevieve Rose (Blechel) L. BS, U. Nev., 1977; postgrad., Liberal Studies, Calif. State U., 1986; postgrad., Nat. U., 1986. Cert. multisubject (1-6), learning handicapped (K-12) tchr. Tchr. Humboldt Sch. Dist., Winnemucca, Nev., 1977-79; instructional asst. Methods Edu-Care, Sacramento, 1979-80; substitute instructional asst. San Juan Unified Sch. Dist., Carmichael, Calif., 1980-83, instructional asst., 1983-87, substitute tchr., 1987—. Vol. Sta. KVIE-TV. Mem. Am. Diabetes Assn., Zool. Soc., Smithsonian Assocs., Beta Sigma Phi. Republican. Roman Catholic.

LUCHTERHAND, RALPH EDWARD, financial planner; b. Portland, Oreg., Feb. 9, 1952; s. Otto Charles II and Evelyn Alice (Isaac) L.; m. JoAnn Denise Adams, Aug. 13, 1983; children: Anne Michelle, Eric Alexander. B.S., Portland State U., 1974, MBA, 1986. Registered profl. engr., Oreg., Wash.; gen. securities broker NYSE/NASD. Mech. engr. Hyster Co., Portland, 1971-75, service engr., 1975-76; project engr. Lumber Systems Inc., Portland, 1976-79; prin. engr. Moore Internat., Portland, 1979-81, chief product engr., 1981-83; project engr. Irvington-Moore, Portland, 1983, chief engr., 1983-86; ind. cons. engr., 1986; engring. program mgr. Precision Castparts Corp., Portland, 1986-87; reg. rep./personal fin. planner IDS Fin. Services, Clackamas, Oreg., 1987—. Treas. Village Bapt. Ch., Beaverton, Oreg., 1988—. Mem. ASME (pres. student chpt. 1973-74). Republican. Home: 3000 NW 178th Ave Portland OR 97229 Office: IDS Fin Svcs Inc 8800 SE Sunnyside Rd Ste 300 Clackamas OR 97015

LUCKETT, BYRON EDWARD, JR., air force chaplain; b. Mineral Wells, Tex., Feb. 2, 1951; s. Byron Edward and Helen Alma (Hart) L.; m. Kathryn Louise Lambertson, Dec. 30, 1979; children: Florence Louise, Byron Edward III, Barbara Elizabeth, Stephanie Hart. BS, U.S. Mil. Acad., West Point, 1973; M of Divinity, Princeton Theol. Sem., 1982; MA, The Claremont (Calif.) Grad. Sch., 1987. Platoon leader Company B, 2nd Engr. Bn., Camp Edwards (East), Korea, 1974-75; bn. supply officer 563rd Engr. Bn., Kornwestheim, Germany, 1975-76; platoon leader, exec. officer 275th Engr. Co., Ludwigsburg, Germany, 1976-77; boy scout project officer Hdqrs., VII Corps, Stuttgart, Germany, 1977-78; student intern Moshannon Valley Larger Parish, Winburne, Penn., 1980-81; protestant chaplain Philmont Scout Ranch, Cimarron, N.Mex., 1982; asst. pastor Immanuel Presbyn. Ch., Albuquerque, 1982-83, assoc. pastor, 1983-84; tchr. Claremont High Sch., 1985-86; protestant chaplain 92nd Combat Support Group, Fairchild AFB, Wash., 1986—; mem. Intern Program Council, Claremont Grad. Sch. Contbr. articles to profl. jours. Bd. dirs. Parentcraft, Inc., Albuquerque, 1984, United Campus Ministries, Albuquerque, 1984, Proclaim Liberty, Inc., Spokane, 1987—, Nat. Assn. Presbyn. Scouters (western region sec. Irving,

Tx., 1986—); mem. Old Baldy Council, BSA, Claremont, Calif. 1986; chmn. Fairchild Parent Co-Op, Fairchild AFB, 1986-87; pres. Co. Grade Officers Council, Fairchild AFB, 1987-88. Recipient Dist. award of Merit (Germany) 1977, Aubrey Douglas award Claremont Grad. Sch. 1986; named Outstanding Young Man of Am. U.S. Jr. C. of C., Albuquerque, 1983. Mem. Mil. Chaplains Assn. Presbyn. Club: Soc. of the Cincinnati of Maryland. Home: 8191 Palm Fairchild AFB WA 99011 Office: 92 CSG/HC Fairchild AFB WA 99011

LUCKETT, RICHARD (LUCKY LUCKETT), architect; b. Tucson, Sept. 14, 1943; s. Harry Nolen and Lois Alene (Wachter) L.; m. Lauren Freedman, Dec. 27, 1974 (div. Nov. 1981); children: Katherine, Meghan. BA in Architecture, U. Ariz., 1981. Lic. profl. architect. Intern CNWC Architects, Tucson, 1979; designer Anderson DeBartolo Pan, Tucson, 1979-81; sr. designer Architecture One, Ltd., Tucson, 1982-83; project mgr. Pflueger Architects, San Francisco, 1983-86; sr. designer Architecture One, Ltd., Tucson, 1986-87; dir. bus. devel. Blanton & Co., Tucson, 1987—; ptnr. The Design Alliance, Inc., Tucson, 1989—; chmn. Landuse Regulatory Task Force, 1988--; mem. Landuse Com., Tucson, 1988--; Eastside Bus. Com., Tucson, 1988--; vis. design reviewer Coll. Architecture U. Ariz., Tucson, 1987--. Bd. dirs. Big Brothers-Big Sisters of Tucson, 1988; mem. Leadership Tucson 1988; bd. dirs. Alumni Coun. Coll. of Architecture U. Ariz., 1988—; adv. coun. Salvation Army Hospitality House, Tucson, 1989. Mem. AIA, So. Ariz. Chpt. AIA, The Soc. for Mktg. Profl. Svcs., Ariz. Soc. Am. Inst. Architects, Tucson Met. C. of C., Kiwanis (Palo Verde chpt.). Democrat. Baptist. Home: 5820 E 7th St Tucson AZ 85711 Office: Blanton & Co 300 W Paseo Redondo Tucson AZ 85714

LUDEMAN, KATE, human resources executive; b. San Antonio, Aug. 14, 1946; d. Ben and Annette (Martin) L.; 1 child from previous marriage, Catherine. BS in Engring., Tex. Tech U., 1967, MA in Psychology, 1972; postgrad., U. Tex., 1974-76; PhD in Psychology, Saybrook Inst., 1979. Project leader Control Data, Saigon, Socialist Republic of Vietnam, 1970-71; cons. Dallas, 1972-79; interviewer morning news ABC Sta. WFAA-TV, Dallas, 1976-77; mgr. tng. and devel. Shaklee Corp., San Francisco, 1979-81; mgr. human resources Impell Corp., San Francisco, 1981-83; corp. v.p. human resources KLA Instruments, Santa Clara, Calif., 1984-88; pres. Worth Ethic Tng. Co., 1988—; developer profl. stress mgmt. conf. for use in Dallas, Albuquerque, and Atlanta. Author: Worth Ethic: How to Profit from changing Values of the New Work Force, 1989; contbr. articles to profl. jours. Chemstrand & Am. Dyers scholar Tex. Tech U., 1965-67. Mem. Am. Soc. Personnel Adminstrs., Am. Soc. Tng. and Devel., Tau Beta Phi. Home: 19644 Montevina Rd Los Gatos CA 95032 Office: Worth Ethic Tng Co 24863 Olive Tree Ln Los Altos Hills CA 94022

LUDWIG, DORENE MARIE, arts executive, entertainer, playwrite; b. Washington, July 29, 1949; d. Donald Jemison and Margaret Aurore (Grenon) L. BA with honors, U. South Fla., 1972; MFA with honors, UCLA, 1974. Cer. community coll. tchr. lifetime, Calif. Pres, artistic dir. Am. Living History Theater, Hollywood, Calif., 1976—; speaker, seminar leader, corp. trainee, cons. in field; instr., UCLA, U. So. Calif., L.A., Calif. Poly., various community colls. Author: 12 plays, 1978-89; co-author: 6 plays, 1975-83; actress over 40 prodns.; dir. over 25 plays. Steering com. Project image, Los Angeles, 1986—; pres., founder Interguild Women's Caucus, Los Angeles, 1980-85. Mem. AFTRA (bd. dirs. L.A. chpt. 1975-76), Screen Actors Guild (mem. nat. bd. 1978-80), Black Women in Theater (bd. dirs. 1986—), Am. Assn. Univ. Profs., Dramatists Guild, Phi Kappa Phi, Zeta Phi Eta. Office: Am Living History Theater PO Box 2677 Hollywood CA 90078

LUDWIG, MARK ALLEN, small business owner; b. Cin., Aug. 5, 1958; s. Jerome Howard and Genevieve Carolyn (Edwards) L.; m. Patricia Gaye Smithson, June 30, 1984. MS in Physics, Caltech, 1980. Product engr. Tusonix, Inc., Tucson, 1982-83; research physicist U. Ariz., Tucson, 1984-85, Ariz. Carbon Foil Co., Inc., Tucson, 1985-86; bus. owner Am. Eagle Publs., Inc., Tucson, 1987—. Editor The Captive, 1988; inventor in field. Precinct committeeman Rep. Party, Tucson, 1987—. Mem. Am. Sci. Affiliation, ANA. Republican. Office: Am Eagle Publications Box 41401 Tucson AZ 85717

LUDWIG, R. MARTHA, architect; b. Great Falls, Mont., Dec. 7, 1924; d. Henry William and Ruth M. Ludwig. BS, U. Wash., 1948, Mont. State U., 1952; MS, Mont. State U., 1961. Registered architect, Calif., Mont. With various archtl. firms Mont., Cal, 1952-69; pvt. practice architecture Sacramento, 1969—. With USNR, 1945-46. Mem. Model A Ford Club of Am. Address: 108 S Fork Way Folsom CA 95630

LUDWIG, ROLF MARTIN, internist; b. Bautzen, Germany, June 3, 1924; came to U.S., 1953; s. Martin Max and Doris (Metz) L.; m. Shirley Jean Ray, Oct. 26, 1956 (div. June 1983); 1 child, Mark Stephen. M.D., Eberhard Karls U. Tuebingen, Germany, 1953. Intern, Mary's Help Hosp., San Francisco, 1953-54, then resident in internal medicine; resident in internal medicine Franklin Hosp., San Francisco, Huntington Meml. Hosp., Pasadena, Calif., Wadsworth VA Gen. Hosp., Los Angeles, 1959-60. Internist, Kaiser/Permanente, Fontana, Calif., 1960-63, 73-87; practice medicine specializing in internal medicine, Yucaipa, Calif., 1963-72; retired, 1987. Served to capt. M.C., U.S. Army, 1956-59. Mem. Am. Soc. Internal Medicine, Calif. Soc. Internal Medicine, Inland Soc. Internal Medicine. Republican. Lutheran. Home: 11711 Holmes St Yucaipa CA 92399

LUENBERGER, DAVID GILBERT, electrical engineer, educator; b. Los Angeles, Sept. 16, 1937; s. Frederick Otto and Marion (Crumly) L.; m. Nancy Ann Iversen, Jan. 7, 1962; children: Susan Ann, Robert Alden, Jill Alison, Jenna Emmy. B.S.E.E., Calif. Inst. Tech., 1959; M.S.E.E., Stanford U., 1961, Ph.D. in Elec. Engring., 1963. Asst. prof. elec. engring. Stanford (Calif.) U., 1963-67, assoc. prof. engring.-econ. systems, 1967-71, prof., 1971—, dept. chmn., 1980—; tech. asst. dir. U.S. Office Sci. and Tech., Exec. Office of Pres., Washington, 1971-72; vis. prof. MIT, Cambridge, 1976; bd. dir. Optimization Tech., Inc., Auburn, Ala.; guest prof. Tech. U. of Denmark, Lyngby, 1986. Author: Optimization by Vector Space Methods, 1969, Linear and Nonlinear Programming, 1973, 2d edit., 1984, Introduction to Dynamic Systems, 1979; contbr. articles to tech. jours. Fellow IEEE; mem. AAUP, Am. Fin. Assn., Econometric Soc., Soc. for Promotion Econ. Theory, Inst. Mgmt. Sci., Soc. Econ. Dynamics and Control (pres. 1987-88), Math Programming Soc., Palo Alto Camera Club, Sigma Xi, Tau Beta Pi. Lutheran. Office: Stanford U Dept Engring-Econ Systems Terman Ctr 306 Stanford CA 94305-4025

LUEVANO, FRED, JR., computer systems executive; b. Alamogordo, N.Mex., June 21, 1943; s. Fred Macias and Margaret (Baca) L.; m. Lupe Olmos, July 11, 1964; children: Michael, James Paul. AA in bus., Fullerton Coll., 1975; BA in Mgmt., U. Redlands, 1979, MA in Mgmt., 1985. Cert. data processing mgr. Mgr. computer ops. Hoffman Electronics, El Monte, Calif., 1971-76; mgr. computer ops. and tech. services City of Anaheim, Calif., 1976-79; mgr. data processing Wyle Data Services, Huntington Beach, Calif., 1979-83; mgr. corp. computer ops. Northrop Corp., Hawthorne, Calif., 1983, mgr. corp. computing, 1985—, dir. disaster revovery program, 1983—; cons. info. systems, La Habra, Calif., 1971—. Cub master Boy Scouts Am., La Habra, 1979-84, chmn. com. 1975-79; councilman candidate City of La Habra Heights, Calif., 1982; pres. Red Coach Club, 1979-80, 86-88; pres. La Habra Parents for Swimming Inc., 1986-88. Served with USN, 1961-65. Mem. Am. Mgmt. Assn., Telecommunications Assn., Assn. Computer Ops. Mgrs. (speaker 1983-86), Northrop Mgmt. Club. Republican. Roman Catholic. Office: Northrop Corp 1 Northrop Ave Hawthorne CA 90250

LUFF, CARL R., mutual fund executive; b. Doylestown, Pa., Apr. 30, 1954; s. J. Hibbs and Dolores (Bloom) L.; m. Gloria LaNoce, Apr. 21, 1978; children: Gloria Sofia, Cara, Virginia. BS, Drexel U., Phila., 1977. CPA, N.M. Exec. v.p. Venture Advisers, L.P., Santa Fe, N. Mex., 1977—. Mem. Am. Inst. CPA's, N.M. Soc. CPA's. Office: Venture Advisers LP 124 E Marcy St Santa Fe NM 87501

LUFKIN, JAIME PATRICIA, illustrator; b. Seattle, Apr. 17, 1921; d. Bradley Woodruff and Jaime Marie (Singletary) Young; widowed; children: Patrick Brian and Shannon Jerome. Student, U. Wash., 1941, Coll. of Sequoias, Visalia, Calif., 1952, Inst. Art Edn., Berkeley, Calif., 1958, Peralta Community Coll., Oakland, Calif., 1980-86. Freelance artist, illustrator, portrait painter Wash. and Calif., 1950-64. Illustrator: work appeared in U. Calif. pubs., Sci. Am., Ariz. Highways; also on Dinosaur T shirts issued by U. Calif. Paleontology Mus.; exhibition in Lawrence Hall of Sci., Berkeley, Calif., 1985, video film Showcase of the Ages, 1988. Mem. U. Calif. Art Mus., Mendocino Art Ctr. Home: 2151 1/2 Russell St Berkeley CA 94705 Office: U Calif Paleontology Mus Berkeley CA 94720

LUFT, HAROLD S., health economist; b. Newark, N.J., Jan. 6, 1947; s. George and Kay (Grossman) L.; m. Lorraine Ellin Levinson, May 24, 1970; children: Shira Levinson, Jana Levinson. A.B., Harvard U., 1968, AM, 1970, Ph.D., 1973. Systems analyst, research asst. Harvard Transport Research, Cambridge, Mass., 1965-68; systems analyst Harvard Econ. Research Project, Cambridge, Mass., 1968-72; instr. econs. Tufts U., Medford, Mass., 1972-73; postdoctoral fellow Harvard Ctr. Community Health, Boston, 1972-73; asst. prof. health econs. Stanford U., Calif., 1973-78; prof. health econs. Inst. Health Policy Studies, U. Calif., San Francisco, 1978—; cons. Applied Mgmt. Scis., Silver Spring, Md., 1979—, Robert Wood Johnson Found., Princeton, N.J., 1982—; study sect. Nat. Ctr. Health Services, Rockville, Md., 1981-83. Author: Poverty and Health, 1978; Health Maintenance Organizations, 1981, 88 (2d edit.). Contbr. chpts. to books, articles to profl. jours. Advisor, fin. planning com. Mid-Peninsula Health Service, Palo Alto, Calif., 1984—. NSF fellow, Carnegie Found. fellow, Grad. Prize fellow Harvard U., 1968-72, fellow Ctr. for Advanced Study in Bahavioral Scis., 1988-89. Mem. Am. Pub. Health Assn., Am. Econ. Assn., Inst. Medicine (mem. coun.), Western Econ. Assn. Home: 1020 Ramona St Palo Alto CA 94301 Office: U Calif Inst Health Policy Studies 1326 3d Ave San Francisco CA 94143

LUFT, RENE WILFRED, civil engineer; b. Santiago, Chile, Sept. 21, 1943; came to U.S., 1968; s. David and Malwina (Kelmy) L.; m. Monica Acevedo, Aug. 24, 1970; children: Deborah Elaine, Daniel Eduardo. CE, U. Chile, 1967; MS, MIT, 1969, DSc, 1971. Registered profl. engr., Alaska, Calif., Mass., N.H., R.I., Republic of Chile; registered structural engr., Vt. Asst. prof. civil engring. U. Chile, 1967-68; research asst. MIT, Cambridge, Mass., 1969-71, vis. lectr., 1983-84; staff engr. Simpson, Gumpertz & Heger Inc., Arlington, Mass., 1971-74, sr. staff engr., 1975-78, assoc., 1978-83, sr. assoc., 1984-86; sr. assoc., asst. branch mgr. Simpson, Gumpertz & Heger Inc., San Francisco, 1986—; sec. seismic adv. com. Mass. Bldg. Code Commn., 1978-80, chmn., 1981-82; mem. Boston seismic instrumentation com. U.S. Geol. Survey. Contbr. articles to profl. jours. Mem. design overview com., bldg. seismic safety council, Earthquake Hazards Reduction Program, also chmn. research com. 1987-88. Mem. ASCE, Boston Soc. Civil Engrs. (chmn. seismic design adv. com. 1981-86, Clemens Herschel award for tech. paper 1980, pres.'s award for leadership in earthquake engring. 1984), Am. Concrete Inst., Earthquake Engring. Research Inst., Structural Engrs. Assn. Calif., NSPE (Young Engr. of Yr., 1979), Sigma Xi, Chi Epsilon. Home: 109 Ardith Dr Orinda CA 94563 Office: 221 Main St Suite 1500 San Francisco CA 94105

LUGO, ANDRE M., horticulturist; b. Prescott, Ariz., Oct. 3, 1949; s. John R. and Joyce (Bowen) L.; m. Claudia Lugo, May 31, 1975; children: Justin r., Elyce T. BS in Horticulture, Ariz. State U., 1972. Owner, operator Wind Bell Farms, Paradise Valley, Ariz., 1970-83; pres. The Green Goddess, Paradise Valley, Ariz., 1983—. Mem. Scottsdale C. of C., Phoenix Convention Bur. Office: The Green Goddess 8626 N Morning Glory Rd Paradise Valley AZ 85253

LUI, JAMES HAROLD, manufacturing executive; b. Chgo., June 20, 1965; s. Pac Chong and Ann aiko (Kamikawa) L.; m. Patricia Kimberly Yarbrough, June 20, 1987. BS in Bus. Mgmt., Calif. State Poly. U., 1986, MBA in Fin., 1988. Contract adminstr. Jacobs Engring. Group, Pasadena, Calif., 1986-87; purchasing agt. Gen. Dynamics, Pomona, Calif., 1987-88; v.p. mktg. and ops. Scantech Inc., Irwindale, Calif., 1988-89; contracts mgr. Ralph M. Parsons Co., Pasadena, Calif., 1989—; lectr. Calif. State Poly U., Ponoma, 1985-87, asst. prof., 1987—. Contbr. articles to profl. jours. Mem. NSF, Nat. Contract Mgmt. Assn., Mensa, Phi Kappa Phi, Delta Mu Delta. Home: 1151 W Arrow Hwy #A7 Azusa CA 91702 Office: Ralph M Parsons Co 100 W Walnut St Pasadena CA 91124

LUJAN, MARIO GUILLERMO, personnel director; b. Raton, N. Mex., Mar. 3, 1953; s. William Bronson and Otilia (Guaderrama) L. AA, N. Mex. State U., 1984. Adminstrv. asst. Dean of Grad. Sch. N. Mex. State U., Las Cruces, 1979-84; dir. purchasing and personnel Digital Cartographic Systems, Englewood, Colo., 1984—. Republican. Roman Catholic. Home: 5100 McIntyre St Golden CO 80403 Office: Digital Cartographic 9 Inverness Dr Englewood CO 80112

LUKASIK, STEPHEN JOSEPH, aerospace company executive; b. S.I., N.Y., Mar. 19, 1931; s. Stephen Joseph and Mildred Florence (Tynan) L.; m. Marilyn Bertha Trappiel, Jan. 31, 1953 (div. 1982); children: Carol J., Gregory C., Elizabeth A., Jeffrey P.; m. Virginia Dogan Armstrong, Feb. 11, 1983; stepchildren: Elizabeth L., Alan D. B.S., Rensselaer Poly. Inst., 1951; M.S., MIT, 1953, Ph.D., 1956. Dir. Advanced Research Project Agy., Washington, 1966-74; v.p. Xerox Corp., Rochester, N.Y., 1974-76; chief scientist and sr. v.p. Rand Corp., Santa Monica, Calif., 1977-79; chief scientist FCC, Washington, 1979-82; v.p. and mgr. Northrop Research and Tech. Ctr., Palos Verdes, Calif., 1982—; cons. numerous gov. orgns. Assoc. editor: The Info. Soc. Trustee Stevens Inst. Tech., Hoboken, N.J.; mem. computer sci. adv. com. Stanford U. Served to capt. USAR. Recipient Sec. Def. Disting. Civilian Service medal, 1973, 74. Mem. Am. Phys. Soc., AAAS. Club: Cosmos. Home: 1714 Stone Canyon Rd Los Angeles CA 90077 Office: Northrop Corp 1840 Century Pk E Los Angeles CA 90067

LUKE, ERIC NEVILLE, screenwriter; b. Palo Alto, Calif., Dec. 17, 1956; s. Richard Carlen and Johanna Theodora (Loerwald) L.; m. Jane Elizabeth van Tamelen, Sept. 11, 1982; children: Kristin Johanna, Alexandra Carlen. BA, UCLA, 1978. Editor Pvt. Stock Effects, Hollywood, Calif., 1981-82; screenwriter Paramount Studios, Los Angeles, 1982-86, Walt Disney Studios, Burbank, Calif., 1986—. Dir.: (films) Train Station, 1976 (De Anza award 1976), The Farmer and the Wise Man, 1977 (Morrison award 1977, Diablo award 1980), Dark Ages, 1978 (Diablo award 1980); screenwriter (film) Explorers, 1985. Presdl. grantee motion picture div., UCLA, 1978. Mem. Writers Guild Am. West, Screen Actors Guild. Democrat.

LUKENBILL, GREGG, real estate developer, professional basketball team executive. Mng. gen. ptnr. Sacramento Kings, NBA, 1984—. Office: care Sacramento Kings 1 Sports Pkwy Sacramento CA 95834 *

LUKENS, LAURA GREEVER, marketing consultant; b. Hutchinson, Kans., Apr. 10, 1959; d. David and Olive Zahn (Belcher) L. BA in French, Kans. State U., 1981; Master's, Am. Grad. Sch. Internat. Mgmt., Glendale, Ariz., 1983. Owner LGL Quarter Horses, Hutchinson, 1971-81; intern internat. dept. Mellon Bank, Pitts., 1982; asst. v.p., mktg. mgr. Securoty Pacific Nat. Bank, L.A., 1983-86; v.p. mktg. Cross Assocs., L.A., 1987; pvt. practice in cons., Beverly Hills, Calif., 1988—; mgr. corp. communications Security Pacific State Trust Co., L.A., 1988—; ednl. counselor Am. Grad. Sch. Internat. Mgmt., Glendale, L.A., 1984—. Mem. L.A. Jr. C. of C. (project leader 1987-88), Phi Beta Kappa, Phi Kappa Phi. Presbyterian.

LUKER, PAUL ADRIAN, computer scientist, educator; b. Dartford, Kent, Eng., Jan. 6, 1947; came to U.S., 1985; s. Alfred Reginald Thomas and Dora Arabella (Chidgey) L.; m. Christine Taylor, Dec. 22, 1970; children: Ellen Catherine, Beth Harriet, Anna Victoria. BSEE, U. London, 1968; MS in Computer Sci., City U., London, 1972; PhD in Computer Sci., U. Bradford, Eng., 1982. Systems engr. Elliott Flight Automation, Rochester, Eng., 1968-71; lectr. computer sci. Hatfield (Eng.) Poly. U., 1971-74, U. Bradford, 1974-85; prof. computer sci. Calif. State U., Chico, 1985—; cons. Lockheed Artificial Intelligence Ctr., Menlo Park, Calif., 1987—. Author: Good Programming Practice in ADA, 1987; assoc. tech. editor Simulation, 1987—; joint editor Advances in Simulation, 1986—; contbr. articles to profl. jours. Mem. Soc. Computer Simulation (dir. at large 1981—, conf. organizer 1985—), Assn. for Computing Machinery. Office: Calif State U 1st and Normal Sts Chico CA 95929-0410

LUKOSKIE, WILLIAM MATTHEW, JR. (W. M. LUKE LUKOSKIE), food industry executive; b. Duluth, Minn., Nov. 24, 1946; s. William Matthew and Janeatte (Josephine) L.; m. Soon Kim, May, 7, 1978; children: Suluh Kim, Dmitria Kim. BA, Carroll Coll., 1968; MBA, PhD, U. Wash., 1971. Cert. Montessori tchr. Ptnr. I.S. Constrn., Bothell, Wash., 1971-76; chief exec. officer Island Spring Inc., Vashon, Wash., 1976—; founding ptnr. Am. Sea Vegetable Co., Vashon, 1985. Mem. NRA, Wash. Kite-Flyers Assn., Vashon Golf and Country Club, Wash. Athletic Club. Republican. Roman Catholic. Home: Rte 1 Box 1054 Vashon WA 98070 Office: Island Spring Inc PO Box 747 Vashon WA 98070

LUM, BARBARA LOUISE, nurse; b. Cottage Grove, Oreg., Feb. 5, 1944; d. Robert John Jones and Wilberta O. (Wilson) Price; m. Prasanna K. Pati, Aug. 15, 1966 (div. 1970); children: Jeffrey A., Michael M.; m. Henry T. Lum, Jr., May15, 1981. Diploma, Sacred Heart Sch. Nursing, Eugene, Oreg., 1965; BA in Psychology, Willamette U., 1970; MBA, U. Portland, 1980. RN, Oreg., Wash. Clin. nurse Willamette U., Salem, Oreg., 1965-66; staff nurse Salem Meml. Hosp., 1966; instr. nursing Oreg. State Hosp., Salem, 1970; dir. nursing Columbia View Hosp., Vancouver, Wash., 1971-76; nursing cons. Brim & Assocs., Portland, Oreg., 1976-80, dir. profl. services, 1980-88; cons. Virginia Mason Health Services Consortium, Seattle, 1988; pres. B. L. Cons., Vancouver, 1988—. Contbr. articles to nursing publs. Mem. Nat. League Nursing, Sports Car Club Am. (sec. bd. dirs. Oreg. region) 1987--). Republican. Roman Catholic. Office: BL Cons 1110 NE 125th Ave Vancouver WA 98684

LUM, HERMAN TSUI FAI, chief justice Hawaii Supreme Court; b. Honolulu, Nov. 5, 1926; s. K.P. and Helen (Tom) L.; m. Almira Ahn, June 17, 1949; children: Forrest K.K., Jonathan K.K. Student, U. Hawaii, 1945-46; LL.B., U. Mo., 1950. Bar: Hawaii 1950. Asst. public prosecutor City and County Honolulu, 1950-52; chief atty. Hawaii Ho. of Reps., 1955, chief clk., 1956-61; partner Suyenaga, Sakamoto & Lum, Honolulu, from 1956; U.S. atty. Dist. Hawaii, 1961-67; judge Circuit Ct. Honolulu, 1967-76, sr. judge Family Ct., 1977-80; assoc. justice Supreme Ct. Hawaii, 1980-83, chief justice, 1983—; Pres. Jr. Bar Assn. Hawaii, 1957. Mem. ABA, Bar Assn. Hawaii, Fed. Bar Assn. Hawaii (pres. 1963), Phi Delta Phi, Lambda Chi Alpha. Home: 2508 Makiki Heights Dr Honolulu HI 96822 Office: Hawaii Supreme Ct PO Box 2560 Honolulu HI 96804 also: Hawaii Supreme Ct Honolulu HI 96813 *

LUM, JEAN LOUI JIN, nurse educator; b. Honolulu, Sept. 5, 1938; d. Yee Nung and Pui Ki (Young) L. BS, U. Hawaii, Manoa, 1960; MS in Nursing, U. Calif., San Francisco, 1961; MA, U. Wash., 1969, PhD in Sociology, 1972. Registered nurse, Hawaii. From instr. to prof. Sch. Nursing U. Hawaii-Manoa, Honolulu, 1961—, acting dean, 1982, dean, 1982—; project coordinator Analysis and Planning Personnel Services, Western Interstate Commn. Higher Edn., 1977; extramural assoc. div. Research Grants NIH, 1978-79; mem. mgmt. adv. com. Honolulu County Hosp., 1982—; mem. exec. bd. Pacific Health Research Inst., 1980-88; mem. health planning com. East Honolulu, 1978-81. Contbr. articles to profl. jours. Recipient Nurse of Yr. award Hawaii Nurses Assn., 1982; USPHS grantee, 1967-72. Fellow Am. Acad. Nursing; mem. Am. Nurses Assn., Am. Pacific Nursing Leaders Conf. (pres. 1983-87), Council Nurse Researchers, Nat. League for Nursing (bd. rev. 1981-87), Western Council Higher Edn. for Nurses (chmn. 1984-85), Western Soc. for Research in Nursing, Am. Sociol. Assn., Pacific Sociol. Assn., Assn. for Women in Sci., Hawaii Pub. Health Assn., Hawaii Med. Services Assn. (bd. dirs. 1985—), Mortar Bd., Phi Kappa Phi, Sigma Theta Tau, Alpha Kappa Delta, Delta Kappa Gamma. Episcopalian. Office: U Hawaii-Manoa Sch Nursing Webster 416 2528 The Mall Honolulu HI 96822

LUNA, DENNIS R., lawyer; b. L.A., Aug. 21, 1946; BS in Petroleum Engring., U. So. Calif., 1968, MS in Petroleum Engring., 1969, MBA, 1971; JD, Harvard U., 1974. Bar: Calif. 1974; Assoc. firm McCutchen, Black, Verleger & Shea, L.A., 1974-81, ptnr., 1981—. Commr. Bd. Recreation and Parks, City of Los Angeles, 1984—; alt. commr., L.A. Meml. Coliseum Commn., 1987—; bd. dirs. Econ. Devel. Corp. of L.A. County, 1988—. Commr. Community Redevel. Agy., City of L.A., 1989—. Contbr. articles to legal jours. Registered profl. petroleum engr., Calif. Mem. ABA (sect. of corp., banking and bus. law, sect. natural resources law), Calif. State Bar Assn., Soc. Petroleum Engrs. Office: 600 Wilshire Blvd Los Angeles CA 90017

LUNAS, JOHN PAUL, physician; b. Glen Ridge, N.J., Mar. 11, 1936; s. Lawrence John and Pauline Howell (MacGahan) L.; children: William Alan, Terese Barrett, Lisa Kirsten, Fredric Warren; m. Sharron Leverne Sumrall, Oct. 18, 1984; children: William Louis, Colin Watson, Philip Leighton. BA, Johns Hopkins U., 1958; MD, Duke U., 1962. Cert. Am. Bd. Internal Medicine. Intern U. Pitts. Health Ctr. Hosps., 1963; resident in internal medicine U. Oreg., Portland, 1970; commd. surgeon USPHS, 1963, advanced through grades to lt. col., 1970; med. officer USPHS, various cities, Alaska, 1963-67; chief medicine USPHS, Mt. Edgecumbe, Alaska, 1970-71; practice medicine specializing in internal medicine Sitka, Alaska, 1971—; affiliate faculty mem. Advanced Cardiac Life Support, Alaska Heart Assn., 1979—; pres. Sitka Community Hosp. Med. staff, 1976-77. Pres. Alaska Heart Assn., 1979—; actor Baranof Little Theater, Sitka, 1976-83; singer Sitka Community Chorus. Named winner Islands Community Coll. Debating Pub. Forum, Sitka, 1983; poetry contest winner Southeast Alaska State Fair, 1983. Mem. ACP, AMA, Alaska Med. Assn., Sitka-Mt. Edgecumbe Med. Assn., Internat. Soc. for Philosophical Enquiry, Triple Nine Soc. Republican. Roman Catholic. Lodges: Moose, Elks. Home: 311 Erler St Sitka AK 99835 Office: Box 58 Sitka AK 99835

LUNCH, WILLIAM M., political science educator, broadcast political analyst; b. Detroit, Feb. 16, 1947; m. Caroline, Apr. 10, 1971; children: Benjamin, Claire. BA, U. Calif., Riverside, 1965-69; MA, U. Calif., Berkeley, 1969-70, PhD, 1970-76. Asst. prof. Oregon State U., 1984—; polit. analyst Oreg. Pub. Broadcasting, Portland and Corvallis, 1988—; research asst. and prin. investigator Ctr. for Study of Social and Polit. Change, Smith Coll., Northhampton, Mass., 1985—. Author: The Nationalization of American Politics, 1987. Recipient Chancellor's award U. Calif. Riverside, 1969, Prof. of Year award Oreg. State U. Interfrat. and Panhellenic Council, 1986-87. Mem. Am. Polit. Sci. Assn., Phi Beta Kapp. Office: Oreg State U Dept Polit Sci Corvallis OR 97331

LUND, ARTHUR KERMIT, lawyer; b. Chinook, Wash., May 2, 1933; s. Arthur K. and Lillian (Lee) L.; children: Michael Lee, Karen Elizabeth Near, Nancy Marie; m. Agnieszka Winkler. AB in Bus. Adminstrn., San Jose State U., 1955; JD, U. Calif., Berkeley, 1961. Bar: Calif. 1962 U.S. Dist. Ct. (no. dist.), Calif., U.S. Ct. Appeals (9th cir.), U.S. Dist. Ct. (no. dist.) Calif., U.S. Supreme Ct.1971. Ptnr. Rankin, Oneal, Center, Luckhardt & Lund, San Jose, Calif.; chmn. bd. San Jose Nat. Bank; bd. dirs. Coast Counties Truck & Equipment Co., Semi Con Systems, Inc., Winkler McManus; pres. O'Connor Profl. Bldg., Inc.; adv. bd. San Jose State U.; past lectr. law sch. Lincoln U., San Jose. Chmn. bd. O'Connor Found.; bd. trustees Presentation High Sch.; bd. dirs. San Jose Conv. and Visitors Bur.; past pres., bd. dirs. Spartan Found. San Jose State U.; past pres. Health Facilities Planning Council Santa Clara County. 2d lt. USMC, 1955, capt. USMCR. Mem. ABA, Am. Acad. Hosp. Attys., State Bar Calif., Santa Clara County Bar Assn., San Jose C. of C. (chmn. aviation com.), Aircraft Owners and Pilots Assn., Navy League, San Jose State U. Alumni Assn. (life, past pres.). Clubs: St. Claire. Lodge: Rotary (past pres.). Home: 52 Isabella Ave Atherton CA 94025 Office: 152 N 3d St Ste 400 San Jose CA 95115

LUND, LYDIA MARIE, retired teacher; b. Centerdale, Iowa, Nov. 17, 1907; d. Nels Peter and Julie Anne (Andersen) Olsen; m. John Jorgensen Lund, June 27, 1934; children: John William, Carol Jane. Student, Dana Coll., 1925-27; BEd magna cum laude, Chico State U., 1959; postgrad., U. Calif.-Berkeley, 1961, 66, 67, Dominican Coll., San Rafael, Calif., 1963-71. Cert. tchr., Iowa, Calif. Tchr. elem. schs. Ringsted, Iowa, 1927-30, Elkhorn, Iowa, 1930-32, Walnut, Iowa, 1932-34, Susanville, Calif., 1959-63; tchr., asst. prin. Janesville (Calif.) Sch., 1956-59; elem. tchr. San Rafael (Calif.) City Sch., 1963-72, master tchr., 1968-72; ret. 1972. Mem. Rogue Valley Handweavers Guild (sec., treas. 1977, 83), Sat. Weavers Guild (pres. 1978), AAUW, Delta Kappa Gamma, Order Eastern Star (organist 12978-86). Democrat.

LUND, MORRIS DUANE, educator, consultant; b. Effie, Minn., Aug. 1, 1930; s. Jesse Ira and Ruth Ellen (Randall) L.; m. Jacqueline Mae Johnston, Apr. 24, 1954; children: Jenelle, Joelle, Jay, Jon. BS, Bemidji State U., 1958; MA, Denver U., 1971; EdS, U. Idaho, 1981, PhD, 1987. English tchr. Henning (Minn.) Pub. Schs., 1958-66; counselor Jefferson County Schs. R-1, Lakewood, Colo., 1966-86; student, instr. U. Idaho, Moscow, 1986-87; counselor, cons. Jeffco Schs. R-1, Golden, Colo., 1987—; cons. Colo. Dept. Edn., Denver, 1970-85; bd. dirs. Jeffco Schs. Credit Union, Lakewood, Colo., 1985—; staff devel. acad., instr./cons., Jeffco, Golden, 1970—; pres., chief exec. officer, New Horizons Human Relations, Golden, 1982—. Vol. Hospice of St. John, Lakewood, 1981-85, Dem. Party Elections, Colo., 1980-88; instr. Am. Cancer Research Hosp., Lakewood, 1986-87. Named High Sch. Counselor of the Yr., Jeffco Sch. Counselor Assn., Lakewood, 1988, Clifford Houston award, Colo. Assn. Counselors and Devel., 1988. Mem. Colo. Sch. Counselors Assn. (pres. 1981-82), Am. Assn. Counseling Devel., Jefferson County Counselors Assn. (pres. 1978), Jefferson County Edn. Assn., Colo. Nat. Edn. Assn., Colo. Assn. Counseling and Devel. (chmn. human rights com. 1987-89), VFW, Elks.

LUNDAHL, E. CORDELL, small business owner; b. Logan, Utah, Jan. 23, 1923; s. Ezra Christen and Leatha (Marler) L.; m. Shirleen Laura Bramwell, Apr. 14, 1950; children: Chris, Mark, Jeff, Leanna, Dewey, Allison, Todd. Student, Utah State U. Asst. to pres. Hesston Corp., Hesston, Kans., 1966-71; dir. sales Hall Way Mfg., 1971-73; advanced concept research cons. John Deere & Co., Moline, Ill., 1974-82; pres. Ezra C. Lundahl, Inc., Logan, Utah, 1982—; cons. John Deere & Co., Logan, 1982—. Patentee in field, over 100 patents. Advisor to Ctr. Excellence for State of Utah, Salt Lake City; mem. fin. com. U.S. House of Reps., Salt Lake City; worker for U.S. senator, Salt Lake City; worker for Gov. of Utah, Salt Lake City; del. White House Conf. Small Bus., 1989; adv. coun. intermountain region SBA. With USN, 1943-46. Recipient Small Bus. award SBA, 1987; named for Outstanding Innovation in Product System Tech., Agrl. Engrs. Soc., 1986-87. Mem. Interant. Fed. Inventors (exec. bd.), Cache County Econ. Com., Utah State Ctr. Excellence (advisor), Nat. Congress Inventors Orgn. (v.p.), Lions (pres. Lodgan chpt. 1986, Outstanding Citizen award). Republican. Mormon. Office: Ezra C Lundahl Inc 710 N 600 W Logan UT 84321

LUNDE, DONALD THEODORE, physician; b. Milw., Mar. 2, 1937; m. Marilynn Krick; children: Montgomery, Christopher, Glenn, Evan, Bret. BA with distinction, Stanford U., 1958, MA in Psychology, 1964, MD, 1966. Diplomate Nat. Bd. Med. Examiners. Ward psychologist Palo Alto (Calif.) VA Hosp., 1965-66, chief resident in psychiatry, 1969-70, assoc. chief tng. and research sect., 1970-72, acting chief tng. and research sect., 1971-72; intern in internal medicine Palo Alto/Stanford Hosp., 1966-67; resident in psychiatry Stanford (Calif.) U. Sch. Medicine, 1967-69, instr. psychiatry, 1969-70, asst. prof. psychiatry, 1970-75, dir. med. sch. edn. in psychiatry, 1971-74, clin. assoc. prof. psychiatry, 1978—; staff physician Atascadero (Calif.) State Hosp., 1968. Author books and articles in field. Served with USN, 1958-61. Fellow Am. Psychiat. Assn.; mem. Am. Coll. Forensic Psychiatry, Am. Psychiat. Assn., No. Calif. Psychiat. Soc., Phi Beta Kappa, Alpha Omega Alpha. Office: Stanford U 900 Welch Rd #400 Palo Alto CA 94304

LUNDEEN, ROBERT WEST, electronics company executive; b. Astoria, Oreg., June 25, 1921; s. Arthur Robert and Margaret Florence (West) L.; m. Betty Charles Anderson, Dec. 26, 1942; children: John Walter, Peter Bruce, Nancy Patricia. B.S., Oreg. State U., 1942; postgrad., Inst. Meteorology, U. Chgo., 1942-43. With Dow Chem. Co., 1946-87; dir. bus. devel. Dow Chem. Internat., Midland, Mich., 1963-66; pres. Dow Chem. Pacific, Hong Kong, 1966-77, Dow Chem. Latin Am., from 1978; exec. v.p. Dow Chem. Co., 1978-82, chmn. bd., 1982-87, dir., 1973-87; chmn. Tektronix Inc., Beaverton, Oreg., 1987—. Chmn. City Planning Commn., Concord, Calif., 1960-61; trustee Kettering Found., Dayton, Ohio, Monterey Inst. Internat. Studies, Calif., Oreg. State U. Found., Corvallis, Orcas Island Library Dist., 1987—. Served with U.S. Army, 1942-46. Decorated Bronze Star. Mem. AICE, Am. Chem. Soc. Republican. Clubs: Hong Kong, Royal Hong Kong Yacht; Orcas Tennis, Orcas Island Yacht, Beach and Tennis Club (Pebble Beach, Calif.). Office: Tektronix Inc PO Box 500 Beaverton OR 97077

LUNDELL, BARBARA MILDRED, car wash owner; b. Mpls., Feb. 15, 1934; d. Arthur Edwin and Mildred Cordella (Dammen) Swenson; m. Erling Alvin Lundell, Mar. 27, 1954; children: Cynthia Mae, Julie Ann Lundell Chandler. Student, St. Olaf Coll., Northfield, Minn., 1952-53. Dental asst. Dr. C.L. Rowley, P.C., Longmont, Colo., 1967-74; owner, mgr. U-Neda Car Wash, Inc., Longmont, 1980--. Mem. Longmont United Hosp. Aux., pres., 1970, 71, 76, trustee, 1980—; chmn. spl. events Am. Cancer Soc., Boulder county, 1974-81, chmn. locating drivers for cancer patients, med. supplies; co-leader Am. Cancer Golf Tournament, 1974-87. Mem. Am. Legion Aux. (pres. 1971), Colo. Hosp. Assn. Aux. (dist. counselor 1977, pres. 1981, 82, trustee rep., 1983, 84), Soroptimist, Boulder County Dental Soc. (pres. 1970-72), Eastern Star. Republican. Lutheran. Home: 7232 Rozena Dr Longmont CO 80501 Office: U-Neda Car Wash Inc PO Box 1474 Longmont CA 80502

LUNDERVILLE, GERALD PAUL, English language educator; b. Springfield, Mass., Feb. 22, 1941; s. Leon Albert and Florence Marion (Jolivette) L.; m. Martha Ann Sumner, Mar. 26, 1966 (div. Aug. 1971); m. Bony Lek, June 30, 1984. BA cum laude, U. N.H., 1963; MA, Middlebury Coll., 1969, U. Rochester, 1973; postgrad., Calif. State U., Long Beach, 1981-84, 86—. Instr. Spanish Berwick Acad., South Berwick, Maine, 1963-64; tchr. French, Spanish Barnstable High Sch., Hyannis, Mass., 1967-68; instr. Spanish Cape Cod Community Coll., West Barnstable, Mass., 1968-71; tchr. French, Spanish Stevens High Sch. Annex, Claremont, N.H., 1973-74; tchr. English Centro de Estudios Norteamericanos, Valencia, Spain, 1974-75; dept. head fgn. langs. Merrimack (N.H.) High Sch., 1975-80; tchr. Spanish El Camino Coll., Torrance, Calif., 1980-85; tchr. ESL Wilson High Sch., Long Beach, Calif., 1980-87, dept. head ESL, 1987—. Contbr. articles to Am. Atheist Mag. Active Long Beach Area Citizens Peace, 1982—, Animal Protection Inst. Am., Sacramento., 1983—. Served with U.S. Army, 1964-67, Vietnam. Mem. ACLU, Nat. Assn. Tchrs. Spanish and Portuguese, NEA, Modern and Classical Lang. Assn. of So. Calif., Tchrs. of English as a Second Lang., Merrimack Tchrs. Assn. (sec. 1977-80), Lambda Pi. Home: 1740 Washington St Long Beach CA 90805

LUNDGREN, DAVID ALBERT, product design engineer; b. Englewood, N.J., Nov. 22, 1959; s. Daniel Paul and Janet Norma (Nutt) L. BE, Stevens Inst. Tech., 1981; BSME, MIT, 1985. Design engr. Hewlett-Packard, Greeley, Colo., 1981-86; devel. engr. Pixar Co., San Rafael, Calif., 1986—. Mem. The Solstice Soc., Sigma Xi, Tau Beta Pi. Democrat. Home: 305 Wickham Dr Mill Valley CA 94941 Office: Pixar Co 3240 Kerner Blvd San Rafael CA 94901

LUNDGREN, SUSAN ELAINE, college program director; b. Martinez, Calif., May 31, 1949; d. Elmer Alfred and Shirley (Bright) L.; 1 child, Alicia Hadiya. AA, Diablo Valley Coll., 1969; BA in English, San Francisco State U., 1971, MA in Counseling, 1975; EdD, U. San Francisco, 1983; cert. in gen. mgmt., John F. Kennedy U., 1988. Instr., counselor Diablo Valley Coll., Pleasant Hill, Calif., 1976—, coordinator, 1986—, dir. faculty women's ctr., 1983-85; lectr. dept. grad. career devel. John F. Kennedy U., Orinda, Calif., 1982—. Sec., bd. dirs. Rape Crisis Ctr., Concord, Calif., 1985. Named participant in leadership devel. inst. AAUW and Nat. Assn. Community Colls., 1985. Mem. NOW (pres. East Bay chpt. 1982-84, bd. dirs. Calif. chpt.), Am. Assn. Women Community Jr. Colls., Nat. Mus. Women in Arts, Calif. Advs. for Re-entry Edn., I-Pride, Eureka Consortium (conf. speaker 1984, 86). Home: 2015 Cedar Berkeley CA 94709 Office: Diablo Valley Coll 321 Golf Club Rd Pleasant Hill CA 94523

LUNDIN, ANN FRANCES, chemist, medical technologist; b. Dallas, Pa., Sept. 22, 1941; d. Walter Stanley and Frances Evelyn (Sholes) Black; m. Lars Norman Lundin, June 10, 1967; children: Lori, Terri, Wendy. BS in Chemistry, Coll. Misericordia, 1963; MS in Chemistry, Villanova U., 1967. Chem. asst. Worcester Found. for Exptl. Biology, Shrewsbury, Mass., 1963-67; research chemist Dow Chem. Co., Wayland, Mass., 1967-71; chem. technologist Children's Hosp., Boston, 1975-80, VA Med. Ctr., San Francisco, 1980-83; quality control chemist Nobel Sci., Alexandria, Va., 1983-84; chemist Nat. Health Labs., Englewood, Colo., 1984—; cons. sci. projects Randolph Mass., 1975-80.. Sec. Jr. League of Swedish Charitable Soc., Boston, 1970-72. Grantee NSF, 1959. Mem. Am. Chem. Soc. Democrat. Roman Catholic. Club: Gen. Fedn. Womens. Lodge: Order of Eastern Star, Ind. Order Vikings. Home: 11442 E Adriatic Pl Aurora CO 80014 Office: Nat Health Labs S Alton Way Englewood CO 80111

LUNDQUIST, VIOLET ELVIRA, state agency administrator; b. Bristol, Conn., Jan. 28, 1912; d. Otto Nimrod and Mabel Elvira (Lindeen) Ebb; diploma music Augustana Coll., Rock Island, Ill., 1932; postgrad. mgmt. systems U. Mo., 1969; m. Vernon Arthur Lundquist, May 14, 1935; children—Karen Ebb, Jane Christine. Tchr. music, public schs., Olds, Iowa, 1932-35; editor Warsaw (Mo.) Times, 1935-45, Anthon (Iowa) Herald, 1945-57; field dir. Iowa Heart Assn., Des Moines, 1957-66; exec. dir. S.E. Iowa Community Action Program, Burlington, 1966-74; adminstrn. dir. S.E. Ariz. Govts. Orgn. Community Services, Bisbee, Ariz., 1975-77; statewide advocate developmentally disabled adults, 1977—; adminstr. Arizona City Med. Ctr., part-time, 1979-80; adminstr. Dist. V Council on Devel. Disabilities, 1980-87. Bd. dirs. Cen. Ariz. Health Systems Agy., 1979—, chmn., 1986—; chmn. Arizona City Home and Property Owners Assn., 1979-82; bd. dirs. Ariz. State Health Planning Council, 1986—; mem. Ariz. Statewide Health Coordinating Council, 1986—, Ariz. Dist. V Human Rights Com., 1986—; pres. Pinal County Assn. for Retarded Citizens, 1987—, v.p., vice chmn. state assn. Recipient Carol Lane award Nat. Safety Council, 1956, 1st place award Nat. Fedn. Press Women, 1952, 53, 55, 57; USPHS scholar, Columbia U., summers 1963, 64; cert. vocat. rehab. adminstr. Mem. Nat. Soc. Community Action Program Dirs. (dir. 1966-75), Ariz. Fedn. Press Women. Lutheran. Clubs: Zonta (area dir. 1984-86), Women of Moose. Home and Office: 15686 S Reef PO Box 2265 Arizona City AZ 85223

LUNDQUIST, WEYMAN IVAN, lawyer; b. Worcester, Mass., July 27, 1930; s. Hilding Ivan and Florence Cecilia (Westerholm) L.; m. Joan Durrell, Sept. 15, 1956 (div. July 1977); children—Weyman, Erica, Jettora, Kirk; m. Kathryn E. Taylor, Dec. 28, 1978; 1 child, Derek. BA magna cum laude, Dartmouth Coll., 1952; LLB, Harvard U., 1955. Bar: Mass. 1955, Alaska 1961, Calif. 1963. Assoc. Bowditch & Dewey, Worcester, 1957-60; atty. U.S. Attys. Office, Mass. and Alaska, 1960-62; assoc. Heller, Ehrman, White & McAuliffe, San Francisco, 1963-65, ptnr., 1967—; counsel, v.p. State Mut. Life Ins. Co., Worcester, 1965-67; vis. prof. environ. studies Dartmouth Coll., Hanover, N.H., 1980, 84. Author: (fiction) The Promised Land, 1987; contbr. articles to profl. jours. Trustee, Natural Resources Def. Council, Hastings Coll. Advocacy. Recipient CPR Significant Achievement award, 1987. Fellow ABA (chmn. Soviet Bar Assn. liaison com. 1986, chmn. litigation sect. 1978-79, co-chmn. spl. com. for study discovery abuse 1976-83, spl. com. on tort liability system 1981-84, superfund 301e study group advisor to U.S. Congress, 1983); mem. Am. Coll. Trial Lawyers, Lawyers Alliance for Nuclear Arms Control (co-founder), Am. Antiquarian Soc., Fgn. Relations Council, Am. Coll. Trial Lawyers, Assn. Life Ins. Council, U.S. Supreme Ct. Hist. Soc., No. Dist. Hist. Soc., Sierra Club, Friends of the Earth, Sequoia, Dartmouth Lawyers Assn., Swedish Am. C. of C. (pres., bd. dirs. western area U.S. 1982-85). Clubs: Bohemian, Olympic (San Francisco). Home: 3725 Broderick San Francisco CA 94123 Office: Heller Ehrman White & McAuliffe 333 Bush Ste 3320 San Francisco CA 94104

LUNDRY, JERRY LEE, aeronautical engineer; b. Canton, Ill., Jan. 18, 1937; s. Lester Berlyn and Leta Dell (Keefauver) L.; m. Coral Margaret Moser, Feb. 2, 1968 (div. 1988); children: Christopher, David. BS in Aero. Engring., U. Ill., 1958, MS in Aero. Engring., 1959. Aero. engr. Douglas Aircraft Co., Long Beach, Calif., 1959-70; aerodynamicist Boeing Comml. Airplanes Co., Seattle, 1970-77, mgr. aero. engring., 1977--, tech. staff mgr. airborn optical adj., 1984-87. Contbr. articles to profl. jours.; inventor aerodynamic wing fins. Fellow Am. Inst. Aero. Scis. (assoc., sec. NW region 1979-80). Home: 1000 Sunset Way Bellevue WA 96004 Office: Boeing Comml Airplanes Mail Stop 6N-98 PO Box 3707 Seattle WA 98124

LUNDY, VERLAND L., graphic arts specialist; b. Clearbrook, Minn., June 26, 1942; s. Curtis Olander and Lois Geniveve (Hetland) L.; m. Linda Lou Marshall, Apr. 12, 1968 (div. 1980); 1 child, Eric Todd; m. Diann Louise Hastings, Feb. 7, 1981; children: Mary West Norris, Edward West, J. Randy Young. AA, Scottsdale (Ariz.) Community Coll., 1979; BA in Mgmt., U. Phoenix, 1986. Mech. draftsman Motorola Inc., Phoenix, 1965-67; elec. draftsman Motorola Inc., Scottsdale, 1967-69, tech. illustrator, 1969-76, sr. tech. illustrator, 1976-78, dept. Q.A., 1978-81, art dir., 1981-85, forms adminstr., 1985-88; forms and procedures analyst III Ariz. Dept. Econ. Security, Phoenix, 1988—. Mem. Scottsdale Artist League, 1976-80; res. dep. sheriff Maricopa County, 1967-72. Served with U.S. Army, 1962-65, 68, Vietnam. Recipient awards in comml. art, fine art, sculpture, 1978-81. Mem. Bus. Forms Mgmt. Assn., Am. Mgmt. Assn., U. Phoenix Alumni Assn. (organizer 1986-87), Ariz. Philatelic Assn. (resident artist 1969—). Republican. Lutheran. Home: PO Box 3097 Scottsdale AZ 85271-3097 Office: Ariz Dept Econ Security 1300 W Washington Phoenix AZ 85007

LUNGREN, DANIEL EDWARD, lawyer; b. Long Beach, Calif., Sept. 22, 1946; s. John Charles and Lorain Kathleen (Youngberg) L.; m. Barbara Kolls, Aug. 2, 1969; children: Jeffrey Edward, Kelly Christine, Kathleen Marie. A.B. cum laude, Notre Dame U., 1968; postgrad., U. So. Calif. Law Sch., 1968-69; J.D., Georgetown U., 1971. Bar: Calif. 1972. Staff asst. Sen. George Murphy, Sen. William Brock, 1969-71; spl. asst. to co-chmn. Rep. Nat. Com., dir. spl. programs, 1971-72; assoc. Ball, Hunt, Hart, Brown & Baerwitz, Long Beach, 1971-78, ptnr., 1978; mem. 96th-97th Congresses from 34th, 98th-100th Congresses from 42d Calif. Dist., 1979-1989, Rep. State Cen. Com. Calif., 1974-89; ptnr. Diepenbrock, Wulff, Plant & Hannegan, Sacramento, 1989—. Committeeman Rep. Nat. Com., Calif., 1989; bd. dirs. Long Beach chpt. ARC, Boy's Club. Recipient Good Samaritan award Los Angeles Council Mormon Chs., 1976. Republican. Roman Catholic. Office: Diepenbrock Wulff Plant & Hannegan 300 Capitol Mall 17th Fl Sacramento CA 95812

LUNINE, JONATHAN IRVING, planetary scientist, educator; b. N.Y.C., June 26, 1959. BS magna cum laude, U. Rochester, 1980; MS, Calif. Inst. Tech., 1983, PhD, 1985. Research assoc. U. Ariz., Tucson, 1984-86, asst. prof., 1986—; vis. asst. prof. U. Calif., Los Angeles, 1986; lectr. Flandrau Planetarium, Tucson, 1987, Sierra Vista (Ariz.) Astronomy Club, 1985; mem. com. planetary and lunar exploration space sci. bd. Nat. Acad. Scis. Contbr. articles to profl. jours. Mem. solar system exploration mgmt. counc. NASA. Mem. Am. Astronomical Soc. (Harold C. Urey prize 1988), Am. Geophys. Union, Sigma Xi. Office: U Ariz Lunar and Planetary Lab Tucson AZ 85721

LUNINGHAM, ROBERT DONALD, radio marketing consultant; b. Russellville, Ark., June 14, 1955; s. Carrel A. and Clara J. (Chenowith) L.; m. Barbara Potts, July 4, 1955; children: Terri Luningham Zolyniak, Randall, Martin. Student, Ark Sch. Broadcasting, 1957; cert. radio mktg. cons., Radio Advt. Bur., 1988. Announcer Sta. KWAK, Stuttgart, Ark., 1957-59, Sta. KYVA, Gallup, N.Mex., 1959-61; program dir. Sta. KRZE, Farmington, N.Mex., 1961-63; sales mgr. Sta. KRZE, Farmington, 1963-65, sta. mgr., 1965-67; gen. mgr. Sta. KRSY, Roswell, N.Mex., 1967-72; account exec. Sta. KCUB-KIIM, Tucson, 1972--, radio mktg. cons., 1988--. Bd. govs. West Tex. Beautify Council, El Paso, 1980-81. With USN, 1953-57. Named Mr. DJ USA, Sta WSM, Nashville, 1960. Mem. Tucson Advt. Club (chmn. media auction 1987, Advt. Person of Yr. award 1984), Optimists (pres. Roswell 1970-71, Tucson 1974-75, lt. gov. West Tex. 1971-72, Outstanding Ariz. Pres. award 1975). Libertarian. Home: 5531 Arroyo Grande Tucson AZ 85718

LUNN, BRUCE KEVIN, respiratory therapist; b. St. Louis, Dec. 23, 1950; s. Clarence Alfred and Bonnie Sue (Slack) L.; m. Carol Elizabeth Rhodes, 1972 (div. 1977); m. Patricia Ann Lyons, July 29, 1978; children: Meghan, Heather. Student, Glendale (Ariz.) Community Coll., 1969-70, Maricopa Community Coll., Phoenix, 1970-71, Maricopa Community Coll., Phoenix, 1975-77, Biosystems Inst., Phoenix, 1975. Cert. respiratory therapy technician; registered respiratory therapist. Staff respiratory technician Maricopa County Gen. Hosp., Phoenix, 1971-72, Phoenix Bapt. Hosp., 1972-75; supr. respiratory therapy Phoenix Bapt. Hosp. and Med. Ctr., 1975-77, dir. respiratory care, 1977—; bd. dirs. Biosystems Inst., Inc., Phoenix, 1977-85, Long Med. Inst., Phoenix, 1979—; tech. site inspector Nat. Assn. Trade and Tech. Schs., Phoenix, 1984. Mem. Ariz. Soc. Respiratory Therapy, Am. Assn. Respiratory Care. Office: Phoenix Bapt Hosp and Med Ctr 6025 N 20th Ave Phoenix AZ 85015

LUNSFORD, REBECCA LYNN, service representative; b. LaMesa, Calif., Feb. 10, 1956; d. Cletis Melvin Jr. and Janice Marie (Brandell) Williams; m. Charles Alton Lunsford, July 1, 1978; children: Charles Daniel, Stephanie Christine. AA, Grossmont Coll., 1980. Svc. rep. Automobile Club of So. Calif., LaMesa, 1987-88, supr., 1988—; owner Hats by Rebecca, LaMesa, 1987. Sec., treas. Lindo Lake Townhomes Bd. dirs., Lakeside, Calif., 1982-87; vol. Lindo Pk. Sch., Lakeside, 1987—, Rep. Party, Santee, Calif., 1988; mem. sch. site counsel. Mem. Automobile Club So. Calif. Home: PO Box 1244 La Mesa CA 92041

LUNT, ANITA, video production company executive; b. Mpls., July 19, 1960; d. Richard Arnold and Dorie Anita (Merrill) Erickson; m. Dennis Allen Lunt, Feb. 14, 1986; 1 child, Crystal Robin. BS in Info. Systems, U. Colo., 1981. Coop. programmer prodn. applications Rockwell Internat., Golden, Colo., 1981-82; programmer/analyst Rockwell Internat., 1982-84, computer security engr. computer and telecommunications, 1984-89; systems integration engr. Nat. Jewish Ctr., Denver, 1989—; owner, mgr., Erickson Enterprises, Boulder, Colo., 1982-85; pres. Pinewood Images, Inc., Lyons, Colo. 1987—. Author: Toothpick Building Illustrated, 1978. Am. Sch. Chgo. scholar, 1977. Mem. Am. Entrepreneurs Assn., Nat. Assn. Female Execs., Toastmaster (Rockwell-Golden) (treas. 1982). Republican. Home: 3293 Pinewood Springs Lyons CO 80540 Office: Pinewood Images Inc PO Box 18028 Boulder CO 80308 also: Nat Jewish Ctr 1400 Jackson St Denver CO 80206

LUNT, OWEN RAYNAL, biologist, educator; b. El Paso, Tex., Apr. 8, 1921; s. Owen and Velma (Jackson) L.; m. Helen Hickman, Aug. 8, 1953; children: David, Carol, Janet. BA in Chemistry, 1947, PhD in Agronomy, 1951. Mem. faculty UCLA, 1951—, prof. plant nutrition, 1964-72, prof. biology, 1972—, acting chmn. dept. biophysics, 1965-70; dir. Lab. Biomed. and Environ. Scis., 1968—; researcher in soil chemistry, fertility, plant physiology. Served with USN, 1944-46. Fellow Am. Soc. Agronomy, Soil Sci. Soc. Am.; Internat. Soc. Soil Sci., AAAS, Am. Nuclear Soc. (L.A. chpt.), Sigma Xi. Home: 1200 Roberto Ln Los Angeles CA 90077 Office: UCLA 900 Veteran Ave Los Angeles CA 90024

LUPINI, DANTE, school superintendent; b. Montreal, Que., Aug. 14, 1933; s. Pietro and Maria Lupini Massanti; m. Louise Mary Talevi, June 30, 1956; children—Lora, Linda, Peter, Andrea. B.A., Thomas More Inst., 1959; B.Ed., U. Montreal, 1960, M.Ed., 1962; Ph.D., U. Alta., Can., 1965. Tchr., Montreal Sch. Bd., 1953-62, prin., 1962-68, asst. supt., 1968-73; supt. Vancouver Sch. Bd., B.C., 1973—. Office: Vancouver Sch Bd, 1595 W 10th Ave, Vancouver, BC Canada V6J 1Z8 *

LURIE, ROBERT A. (BOB LURIE), professional sports team executive, businessman. Owner San Francisco Giants (Nat. League) baseball team, 1976—, now chmn. Office: San Francisco Giants Candlestick Pk San Francisco CA 94124 *

LURIE, RON, mayor. Former city councilman Las Vegas, Nev.; mayor 1987—. Office: Office of Mayor 400 E Stewart Ave Las Vegas NV 89101 *

LUST, PETER, JR., microwave engineer; b. Montreal, Que., Can., Apr. 21, 1960; came to U.S., 1975, naturalized, 1987; s. Peter Clark and Evelyn (Heymanson) L.; m. Gloria Ruth Bingle, Apr. 5, 1985; 1 child, Peter Alexander III. Student, Lowry Tech. Tng. Ctr., Community Coll. A.F., Albuquerque, USAF Acad. Enlisted USAF, 1979, resigned, 1982; computer meterologist Electro Rent, Burbank, Calif., 1982-84; microwave engr., program mgr. satellite and space shuttle communications systems Transco Products, Camarillo, Calif., 1984—; prin. Electronic Note Enterprises, Port Hueneme, Calif., 1984—; cons. in field, Port Hueneme, 1984—. Recipient Technol. award USAF, 1980, Discovery award NASA, 1987, Internat. Leaders in Achievement award, Cambridge. Mem. Assn. Old Crows, Channel Islands Health Club. Republican. Office: Electronic Note Enterprises PO Box 460 Ste 16 Port Hueneme CA 93041

LUSTECK, CLAUDIA ANN DUFEK, principal; b. Phoenix, Sept. 2, 1948; d. John Allen and Teresa Magdolin (Lazok) D.; 1 son, Ryan Alexander. BS, U. Ariz., 1971; MEd, 1974. High sch. tchr. Tucson Unified Sch. Dist., 1971-85; curriculum specialist Pueblo High Sch., Tucson, 1985-89; asst. prin. Tucson (Ariz.) Magnet High Sch., 1989—; tchr. adult edn. program Pima (Ariz.) Community Coll., 1974-75; workshop facilitator; lectr. in field. Author: Activity Guide for Guide to Good Food, 1982, Activity Guide for Housing Decisions, 1983. Mem. exec. bd. Tucson Boy's Chorus Parent's Assn., 1985-87. Named Ariz. Tchr. of Yr., Ariz. Home Econs. Assn., 1981. Mem. Assn. for Supervision and Curriculum Devel., Phi Delta Kappa, Pi Lambda Theta. Office: Tucson Magnet High Sch 400 N 2nd Ave Tucson AZ 85705

LUSTGARTEN, SONDRA ANN, lawyer; b. Pampa, Tex., Sept. 12, 1939; d. Claude L. and Katherine J. (Mosely) Sullins; m. Maurice V. Lustgarten, Aug. 11, 1964; children: Kevin M., Lisa Katherine. BS, West Tex. State U., 1961; MA, Calif. State U., Northridge, 1965; JD, U. Puget Sound, 1986. Bar: Wash. 1987. Dist. dir. Girl Scouts of Am., Amarillo, Tex., 1961-62; communications therapist Children's Speech and Hearing Ctr., Van Nuys, Calif., 1967-69; gen. ptnr. Racquette Pointe, Palos Verdes, Calif., 1972-75; communications disorders specialist Bellevue (Wash) Sch. Dist., 1980-83; legal intern Attorney Gen., Olympia, Wash., 1985-86; sole practice Bellevue, 1987—. Mem. canidate evaluation com. Municipal League, Seattle, 1987—. Recipient Outstanding Achievement award Bellevue Parents Tchrs. Students Assn., 1983. Mem. ABA, Seattle-King County Bar Assn. (vol. Neighborhood Legal Clinic 1987—, vol. mentor Family Law Mentor Program 1988—), E. King County Bar Assn., Wash. State Bar Assn., Wash. State Trial Lawyers Assn., Assn. Trial Lawyers Am., Seattle Forensic Inst, Phi Delta Phi. Office: 1299 156th Ave NE Bellevue WA 98007

LUSTIG, JUDITH JOY, real estate executive; b. L.A., June 7, 1943; d. Harry and Beatrice (Labovitz) Moret; m. Floyd Sheldon Lustig, Aug. 22, 1980; 1 child, Helene Stacy Lessner. Controller, gen. mgr. Calif. Connection, Inc., L.A., 1975-83; real estate sales assoc. Coldwell Banker, Sherman Oaks, Calif., 1986-89, Fred Sands Realtors, Studio City, Calif., 1989—. Mem. Calif. Assn. Realtors, San Fernando Valley Bd. Realtors. Republican. Jewish. Home: 5450 Nagle Ave Van Nuys CA 91401 Office: Fred Sands Realtors 12345 Ventura Blvd Studio City CA 91604

LUTALI, A. P., governor; b. Aunu'u, American Samoa, Dec. 24, 1919; married. Governor AS, 1985—. Office: State Capitol Office of Gov Pago Pago AS 96799 *

LUTER, JOHN, newsman, educator; b. Knoxville, Tenn., Jan. 17, 1919; s. John Thomas and Bertha Mae (Carver) L.; m. Mary Hickey, 1948 (dec.); 1 child, Linda; m. Yvonne Spiegelberg, 1966 (div. 1971); m. Nan Hoyt Lawrence, 1974. BA, St. Mary's U., Tex., 1939, postgrad., 1939-42; fellow Time Inc., Sch. Advanced Internat. Studies, Washington, 1945. Reporter San Antonio Light, 1939-42, Washington Star, 1942-44; corr. Time mag., 1944-45; war corr. Time mag., Pacific, 1945; fgn. corr. Time and Life mags., Southeast Asia, 1945-46, Japan, 1946-47, Israel, 1948-49, Italy, 1949-54; asst. editor internat. edit. Life mag., 1954-56; reporter, writer CBS News, 1957-58; asso. editor Newsweek mag., 1958-61; radio news commentator stas. Stas. WQXR and QXR-FM Network, 1960-61; coord. advanced internat. reporting program Columbia Grad. Sch. Journalism, 1961-72; dir. Maria Moors Cabot Prize Program, 1961-74; mem. profl. staff Bank St. Coll. Edn., 1973-74; prof., dir. journalism U. Hawaii, Honolulu, from 1974, now prof. and chmn. journalism dept. Adv. editor: Columbia Journalism Rev., 1961-72. Chmn. internat. rels. com. N.Y.C. Protestant Coun., 1968-71; chmn. adv. screening com. communications Sr. Fulbright Program, 1970-73; trustee Overseas Press Club Found., 1962-72, chmn., 1964-65; bd. dirs. UN Assn. N.Y., 1973-74; chmn. Honolulu Community Media Coun., 1982-84. Mem. Assn. Edn. Journalism and Mass Communications, Assn. Schs. Journalism and Mass Communications, Honolulu Com. Fgn. Relations, Pacific and Asian Affairs Coun., Soc. Profl. Journalists (mem. chpt. exec. coun. 1966-69,

89—), Japan Am. Soc. Clubs: Overseas Press (pres. N.Y.C. 1960-62), Honolulu Press, Outrigger Canoe. Home: 1451 Kalanikai Pl Honolulu HI 96821 Office: U Hawaii 208 Crawford Hall 2550 Campus Rd Honolulu HI 96822

LUTH, WILLIAM CLAIR, research management; b. Winterset, IA, June 28, 1934; s. William Henry Luth and Ora Anna (Klingaman) Sorenson; m. Betty L. Heubrock, Aug. 23, 1953; children: Linda Diane, Robert William, Sharon Jean. BA in Geology, U. of Iowa, 1958, MS in Geology, 1960; PhD in Geochemistry, Penn State U., 1963. Research assoc. in geochemistry Pa. State U., University Park, Pa., 1963-65; asst. prof. geochemistry MIT, Cambridge, Mass., 1965-68; assoc. prof. geology Stanford U., 1968-77, prof. of geology, 1977-79; supr. geophysics div. Sandia Nat. Labs, Albuquerque, N. Mex., 1979-82; mgr. geosciences dept. Sandia Nat. Labs, Albuquerque, 1982—; geoscientist US ERDA/DOE Washington, 1976-78; faculty sabbatical Sandia Laboratories, Albuquerque, N. Mex., 1975, visiting staff mem. Los Alamos Nat. Lab, 1978. Contbr. articles to profl. jours. Served with U.S. Army, 1953-56. Grantee NSF, 1964-78. Home: 1600 LaCabra Dr SE Albuquerque NM 87123 Office: Sandia Nat Labs Geosciences Dept 6230 Albuquerque NM 87185

LUTIN, DAVID LOUIS, real estate development and finance consultant; b. East Hartford, Conn., Apr. 18, 1919; s. Solomon and Esther (Newman) L.; A.B., Ohio No. U., 1946; M.B.A., Syracuse U., 1949; m. Dorothy Marmor, Dec. 3, 1944; children—Gary, Marnie (Mrs. George Wittig). Housing economist and field rep. HHFA, Washington, 1950-57; dir. urban renewal City of Brookline, Mass., 1957-58; cons. on urban renewal and housing Com. for Econ. Devel., N.Y.C., 1958-59; propr. David L. Lutin Assocs., real estate devel. and fin. cons., Rye, N.Y., 1959-73, Phoenix, 75—; v.p. real estate and mortgages Am. Bank and Trust Co., N.Y.C., 1973-75. Research assoc. Albert Farwell Bemis Found., M.I.T., 1951-52. Served to capt. AUS, 1942-46. Decorated Purple Heart. Mem. Am. Econ. Assn., Nat. Planning Assn., Mortgage Bankers Assn., Urban Land Inst., Am. Planning Assn., Am. Statis. Assn., Nat. Assn. Home Builders. Contbr. articles and reports on econs., housing and urban devel. to profl. jours. Home and Office: 11419 N Century Ln Scottsdale AZ 85254

LUTSKY, SHELDON JAY, financial and marketing consultant, writer; b. New Kensington, Pa., Jan. 13, 1943; s. Hyman I. and Rose S. (Schwartz) L.; B.S., Kent State U., 1967; postgrad. U. Colo., 1969-70. Chemist B.F. Goodrich, Akron, Ohio, 1966; with United Bank of Denver, 1968-75; founder Mountain States Ski Assn., pub. Mountain States Recreation, Denver, 1976-81; pres. Dolphin Assocs., Denver, 1981—; instr. penny stocks Denver U. Bd. mem. Colo. 4-H Adv. Council. Recipient Burr Photog. Achievement award Kent State U., 1965. Mem. Denver C. of C., Denver Conv. Bur., Nat. Ski Writers Assn., Rocky Mountain Ski Writers Assn., Rocky Mountain Fin. Writers Assn. (pres. 1982-84). Developer Slope Scope, ski slope evaluation system. Home: 4807 S Zang Way Morrison CO 80465 Office: Lutsky & Assocs 2124 S Dayton St Denver CO 80231

LUTZ, ARNOLD, teacher; b. Detroit, July 26, 1949; s. Walter and Tessie Lutz; m. Charlene Howells, Jan. 3, 1980 (div. 1987); children: Stara Lynn, Mista Lea. BE, Cen. Mich. U., 1971, MEd, 1975; cert., West L.A. Law Sch., 1985. Cert. tchr., Calif. Tchr. Inkster Pub. Schs., Mich., 1972-73, Beaverton Rural Schs., 1975-76, Garden City Pub. Schs., 1976-80, L.A. Unified Schs., 1980-84, Lynwood Unified Schs., Calif., 1984—; adminstr. City of Inkster, 1973-74. Administr. City of Inkster, 1973-74. Mem. NEA, Calif. Tchrs. Assn., Lynwood Tchrs. Assn. Home and Office: 18202 Saint Andrews Pl Torrance CA 90504

LUTZ, JOHN SHAFROTH, lawyer; b. San Francisco, Sept. 10, 1943; s. Frederick Henry and Helena Morrison (Shafroth) L.; m. Elizabeth Boschen, Dec. 14, 1968; children: John Shafroth, Victoria. BA, Brown U., 1965; JD, U. Denver, 1971. Bar: Colo. 1971, U.S. Dist. Ct. Colo. 1971, U.S. Ct. Appeals (2d cir.) 1975, D.C. 1976, U.S. Supreme Ct. 1976, U.S. Dist. Ct. (so. dist.) N.Y. 1977, U.S. Tax Ct. 1977, U.S. Ct. Appeals (10th cir.) 1979, N.Y. 1984. Trial atty. Denver regional office U.S. SEC, 1971-74; spl. atty. organized crime, racketeering sect. U.S. Dept. Justice, So. Dist. N.Y., 1974-77; atty. Kelly, Stansfield and O'Donnell, Denver, 1977-78; gen. counsel and gen. ptnr. Boettcher & Co., Denver, 1978-87, Kelly, Stansfield and O'Donnel, Denver, 1987; spl. counsel, 1987-88, ptnr., 1988—. allied mem. N.Y. Stock Exch., 1978-87; speaker on broker, dealer, securities law and arbitration issues to various profl. orgns. Contbr. articles to profl. jours. Bd. dirs. Cherry Creek Improvement Assn., 1980-84, Spalding Rehab. Hosp., 1986—. Lt. (j.g.), USNR, 1965-67. Mem. ABA, Colo. Bar Assn., Denver Bar Assn., Am. Law Inst., Securities Industry Assn. (state regulations com. 1982-86), Nat. Assn. Securities Dealers, Inc. (nat. arbitration com. 1987—), St. Nicholas Soc. N.Y.C., Denver Law Club, Denver Country Club, Denver Tennis Club, Denver Athletic Club, Rocky Mountain Brown Club (founder, past pres.), Racquet and Tennis Club. Republican. Episcopalian. Home: 144 Race St Denver CO 80206 Office: Kelly Stansfield & O'Donnell 550 15th St Denver CO 80202

LYBARGER, MARJORIE KATHRYN, nurse; b. Holland, Mich., Apr. 23, 1956; d. Richard Simon and Mary Kathryn (Homan) Denuyl; m. John Steven Lybarger Aug. 22, 1981; 1 child, Ashley Ann. BA in Psychology, Biola U., Calif., 1979, BS in Nursing, 1984. RN, Calif. Staff nurse Presbyn. Intercommunity Hosp., Whittier, Calif, 1985-86, Healthcare Med. Ctr., Tustin, Calif., 1986-88; staff nurse med.-telemetry unit Friendly Hills Regional Med. Ctr., La Habra, Calif., 1988—. Mem. Calif. Nurses Assn., Gammma Phi Beta. Republican. Home: 530 Stone Harbor Circle La Habra CA 90631

LYDICK, LAWRENCE TUPPER, judge; b. San Diego, June 22, 1916; s. Roy Telling and Geneva (Lydick) L.; m. Gretta Grant, Aug. 7, 1938; children: Gretta Grant, Lawrence Tupper; m. Martha Martinez, Oct. 1969; 1 son, Chip. A.B., Stanford U., 1938, LL.B. (Crothers law scholar), 1942; Sigma Nu exchange scholar, U. Freiburg, Germany, 1938-39; postgrad., Harvard U., 1943, Mass. Inst. Tech., 1943-44. Bar: Calif. 1946. Since practiced in Los Angeles; dir. disputes div. 10th region Nat. War Labor Bd., San Francisco, 1942-43; asst. to pres., gen. counsel U.S. Grant Export-Import, Ltd., Los Angeles, 1946-48; assoc. Adams, Duque & Hazeltine, Los Angeles, 1948-53; partner Adams, Duque & Hazeltine, 1953-71; U.S. dist. ct. judge Central Dist. Calif. 1971—. Bd. vis. Stanford Law Sch. Lt. USNR, 1943-46. Mem. Am. Law Inst., Sigma Nu. Republican. Congregationalist. Office: US Dist Ct 312 N Spring St Los Angeles CA 90012

LYE, WILLIAM FRANK, university administrator; b. Kimberley, B.C., Can., Feb. 19, 1930; came to U.S., 1955, naturalized, 1981; s. Arthur Percy and Jessie Loretta (Prince) L.; m. Velda Campbell, Oct. 16, 1953; children: William Mark, Matthew Campbell, David Arthur, Victoria, Regina. Student Ricks Coll., 1953-55, Duke U., 1963; BS, Utah State U., 1959; MA, U. Calif.-Berkeley, 1959; PhD, UCLA, 1969. Instr. polit. sci. Ricks Coll., Rexburg, Idaho, 1959-63, 67-68, head dept. polit. sci., 1959-63; teaching asst. dept. history UCLA, 1964-65; asst. prof. Utah State U., Logan, 1968-69, acting head dept. history and geography, 1969-70, assoc. prof., head dept. history and geography, 1970-73, prof., head dept. history and geography, 1973-76, dean Coll. Humanities, Arts and Social Scis., 1976-83, v.p. for univ. relations, prof. dept. history and geography, 1983—; vis. lectr. dept. history Brigham Young U., Provo, Utah, 1970; temporary lectr. dept. history U. Cape Town, Republic of South Africa, 1974; social cons. for project design teams in land conservation, U.S. Agy. for Internat. Devel. Khartoum, Sudan, 1978, Maseru, Lesotho, 1979; mem. higher edn. taskforce on telecommunications, Utah, 1977-82; chmn. State of Utah Telecommunications Coop., 1987, Regents' Com. on Credit by Exam., Utah, 1976; mem. adv. com. Sta. KULC-TV, State Ednl. Telecommunications Operating Ctr., 1986—; bd. dirs., exec. com. Children's Aid Soc. Utah, 1985-88; pres.-elect Utah Alliance for Arts Edn. Author: (with Colin Murray) Transformations on the Highveld: The Tswana and Southern Sotho, 1980, paperback edit., 1985; editor: Andrew Smith's Journal of His Expedition into the Interior of South Africa, 1834-36, 1975. Producer (TV series) Out of Africa, 1977, The God Seekers, 1978; contbr. articles and book revs. to profl. publs. Chmn. State Day celebration, Logan, Utah, 1973, univ. drive for new Logan Regional Hosp. Recipient Leadership award Standard of Calif., 1957, Idea of Yr. award Utah State U., 1971, Faculty Service award Associated Students, Utah State U., 1977-78; Woodrow Wilson Nat. fellow 1958, Foreign Area fellow Social Sci. Research Council, Republic of South Africa, England, 1966-67, 67-68; faculty devel. grantee Utah State U., 1972, Human Sci. Research Council of South Africa publ. grantee, 1975, Mauerberger Trust grantee, 1976, 79. Mem. African Studies Assn., Royal African Soc., Western Assn. Africanists (program chmn. 1972-74, pres. 1974-76), Am. Soc. Landscape Architects (accreditation bd. 1967—), Council for Advancement and Support Edn., Phi Kappa Phi, Phi Alpha Theta. Mormon. Lodge: Rotary. Home: 696 E 400 N Logan UT 84321 Office: Utah State U Dept History & Geography Logan UT 84322-1440

LYKINS, JAY ARNOLD, economic development director; b. Shattuck, Okla., Feb. 13, 1947; s. George Eldridge and Lucy Lee (Croom) L.; m. (Mary) Lynn Turner, Jan. 3, 1970; children: Mary Lee and Amy Lynn (twins), Jason. BA, Covenant Coll., 1973; MBA in 3rd World Econ. Devel., Kennedy-Western U., 1987, PhD in Internat. Bus., 1988. Credit specialist Gen. Electric Supply Co., Nashville, 1974-75; owner, mgr. Environment Control Co., Nashville, 1975-78; bus. adminstr. Youth for Christ, Atlanta, 1978-81; controller Young Life, Colorado Springs, Colo., 1981-82, internat. adminstr., 1982-86; exec. dir. Global Reach, Milpitas, Calif., 1982—; cons. Royal Donuts, Lima, Peru, Barnabas Group, Vancouver. B.C, Manna Corp., Bulawayo, Zimbabwe, Denver Bridge Corp. Author: Values in the Marketplace, 1985, Development and Technology: Economics for the Third World, 1987, Islamic Business: Philosophy and Methods, 1988. Served with USN, 1966-68. Mem. Internat. Council for Small Bus., Am. Cons. League, Assn. MBA Execs., Ctr. Enterpreneurial Mgmt. Club: Nob Hill Country (Snellville, Ga.) (pres. 1980). Office: Global Reach 25 Corning Ave Milpitas CA 95035

LYNCH, ALLAN WILLIAM, law enforcement official; b. Weehawken, N.J., Dec. 12, 1942; s. Joseph Andrew and Theresa Josephine (Bracco) L.; m. Rose Mary Perez, Sept. 7, 1968; 1 child, Joseph Henry. AA, Fullerton Coll., 1963; BS, Calif. State U., Long Beach, 1967; cert., FBI Nat. Acad., Quantico, Va., 1985. Supervisory and mgmt. certs. Calif. Commn. on Peace Officer Standards and Tng. Officer La Palma (Calif.) Police Dept., 1965-70; dep. probation officer Riverside County, Riverside, Calif., 1970-73, investigator, 1973-76, sr. investigator, 1976-80; sr. supervisory investigator Office Riverside County Dist. Atty., Riverside, 1980-85, asst. chief investigator, 1985—; mgr. security wrestling venue L.A. Olympic Organizing Com. XX111rd Olympiad, Anaheim, Calif., 1984. Vol. 1st lt. Calif. State Mil. Res., 1983—. Recipient resolution Calif. Assembly, 1983, cert. of achievement U. Va., 1985. Mem. Calif. Peace Officers Assn. (life, legis com. 1965—, Outsdanding Svc. award 1985), Calif. Dist. Atty. Investigators Assn. (pres. 1982-83, citation 1988), FBI Nat. Acad. Assocs., Fraternal Order Police, Elks. Republican. Roman Catholic. Office: Riverside County Dist Atty's Office 4080 Lemon St 2d Fl Riverside CA 92501

LYNCH, ÁRTHUR JOSEPH, teacher, retired; b. Chgo., Sept. 2, 1936; s. James Franklin and Mabel Ursula (Woods) L.; m. Rene Dudney, June 25, 1960; children: Frank Woods, James Arthur, George Fairbanks. BA in Soc. Studies, San Francisco State U., 1958; MA in History, San Jose State U., 1969. Calif. Gen. Teaching Credential. Tchr. Drew Sch., San Francisco, 1957-59, Ravenswood Sch. Dist., East Palo Alto, Calif., 1960-67, Cupertino (Calif.) Union Sch. Dist., 1967-81; instr. Stanford (Calif.) U., 1987. Mem. US/USSR Initiatives, San Francisco, 1987-89; host Soviets Meet Middle Am., Los Altos, Calif., 1988; mem. Calif. Dem. State Exec. Com., 1988—, Santa Clara County Cen. Com., 1987—; pres. Pen. Dem. Coalition Los Altos, 1987-88; mem. Los Altos Children's Theater Support, 1978-80; bd. dirs. Palo Alto Area Indian Guides, 1974; mem. Los Altos Gen. Plan Com., 1968. Rsch. fellow San Jose State U., 1968. Mem. Pen. Dem. Coalition (pres. 1987-88). Home: 520 Benvenue Ave Los Altos CA 94022

LYNCH, AUBREY JAMES, aerospace company executive; b. Memphis, Nov. 23, 1938; s. John Gibson and Ruth (Patton) L.; m. Paulette Parker, Sept. 14, 1964 (div. 1975); children: Aubrey, Collin, Eric. BS, U. Detroit, 1962; MA, U. Mich., 1972, PhD, 1975. Projects mgr. GM Inst., Flint, Mich., 1969-74, prof. psychology, 1974-76; pers. dir. City of Flint, 1976-77; sr. assoc. Rensis Likert Assocs., Ann Arbor, Mich., 1976-77; mgmt. cons. Mobil Oil Corp., N.Y.C., 1977-80; pvt. practice mgmt. cons. Oakland, N.J., 1980-86; assoc. prof. psychology William Paterson Coll., Wayne, N.J., 1984-86; mgr. human resources devel. McDonnell Douglas Astronautics Co., Huntington Beach, Calif., 1986-88, McDonnell Douglas Aircraft Co., Torrance, Calif., 1988—. Pres. Millstream Homeowners Assn., Huntington Beach, 1989. Capt. USAF, 1962-68. Mem. Am. Psychol. Assn. Office: McDonnell Douglas Aircraft 19503 S Normandie Ave Torrance CA 90502

LYNCH, CHARLES ALLEN, home furnishings executive; b. Denver, Sept. 7, 1927; s. Laurence J. and Louanna (Robertson) L.; m. Linda Bennet, June 14, 1952; children: Charles A., Tara O'Hara, Casey Alexander. B.S., Yale U., 1950. With E.I. duPont de Nemours & Co., Inc., Wilmington, Del., 1950-69, dir. mktg., 1965-69; corp. v.p. SCOA Industries, Columbus, Ohio, 1969-72; corp. exec. v.p., also mem. rotating bd. W.R. Grace & Co., N.Y.C., 1972-78; chmn. bd., chief exec. officer Saga Corp., Menlo Park, Calif., 1978-86, also dir.; chmn., chief exec. officer DHL Airways, Inc., Redwood City, Calif., 1986-88; pres., chief exec. officer Levolor Corp., 1988—; bd. dirs. Pacific Mut. Life Ins. Co., Nordstrom, Inc., SRI Internat., Palo Alto Med. Found., Syntex Corp.; trustee Conf. Bd. Bd. dirs. San Francisco YMCA; vice chmn. Bay Area Council; former chmn. Calif. Bus. Roundtable; trustee Occidental Coll., 1987; adv. bd. U. Calif., Berkeley Bus. Sch., Governance Bd., Coll. of Notre Dame, Belmont, Calif.; chmn. 1987 Bay area campaign United Way. Served with USNR, 1945. Republican. Clubs: Yale (N.Y.C.); Internat. Lawn Tennis; Menlo Country (Calif.), Menlo Circus (Calif.); Pacific Union (San Francisco); Ponte Vedra (Fla.); Beach and Tennis; Coral Beach and Tennis (Bermuda); Vintage (Indian Wells, Calif.). Office: Levolor Corp 1 Upper Pond Rd Parsippany NJ 07054

LYNCH, CHARLES THOMAS, radio, television and film educator; b. Waterbury, Conn., Oct. 10, 1918; s. Charles Thomas and Sara (Carroll) L.; m. Helen Victoria Kaliss, Aug. 4, 1941; children: Charles Thomas III, Jean, Christopher. Student, U. Ala., 1935-37, Mich. State U., 1960; B.A., Western Mich. U., 1963, M.A., 1966; Ph.D., So. Ill. U., 1972. Announcer, producer, writer various radio stas. Conn., Pa., Fla. and Mich., 1938-49; program dir., exec. producer Fetzer Broadcasting Co., Kalamazoo, 1949-67; asst. prof. radio-TV, sta. mgr. Sta. WSIU, So. Ill. U., 1967-74, assoc. prof., chmn. dept. radio-TV, 1974-79; chmn. dept. radio-TV-film Calif. State U., Northridge, 1979-87, prof., 1979—. Author various documentaries, spl. broadcast programs; contbr. articles profl. jours. Pres. Kalamazoo Area PTA Council, 1960-61, Kalamazoo Civic Players, 1962-64, Community Theatre Assn. Mich., 1963-65, Am. Cancer Soc., Kalamazoo, 1965-67. Recipient Broadcast Preceptor award Broadcast Industry Conf., 1976. Mem. Hollywood Chpt. Acad. TV Arts and Scis., St. Louis Chpt. Nat. Acad. TV Arts and Scis., Am. Film Inst., Broadcast Edn. Assn., Soc. Profl. Journalists, Ill. News Broadcasters Assn., Hollywood Radio and TV Soc., Am. Women in Radio and TV (bd. dirs. So. Calif. chpt. 1985—), Broadcast Pioneers, Pacific Pioneer Broadcasters (bd. dirs. 1983-86), Sierra Club, Alpha Epsilon Rho, Phi Kappa Phi. Office: Calif State U Dept Radio-TV-Film Northridge CA 91330

LYNCH, DAVID DILLON, transportation executive, educator; b. Richmond Heights, Mo., July 24, 1940; s. David Dillon and Alice Ann (Eubank) L.; m. Judy Anton, Aug. 13, 1960; children: Gwynn, Christine, Jennifer. BSEE, Washington U., Clayton, Mo., 1962, MSEE, 1965; postgrad., Bklyn. Poly. Inst., 1966, UCLA, 1974, 84. Project engring. asst. Union Electric Co., St. Louis, 1961; project engr. Mo. Research Lab., St. Louis, 1962-64; mem. tech. staff Bell Labs., Murray Hill, N.J., 1964-65; group supr. Emerson Electric Co., St. Louis, 1966-70; group v.p., mgr. engring. div. Hughes Aircraft Co., L.A., 1970—; bd. dirs. Hughes S.C. Inc.; instr. UCLA, 1971-76, U. So. Calif., L.A., 1973-76; asst. prof. U. Mo., Rolla, 1964-67; cons. Evolving Technology, San Diego, 1973—. Co-author books on radar and signal processing; contbr. articles to profl. jours.; patentee in field. Recipient Hyland Patent award Hughes Aircraft Co., 1978. Sr. mem. IEEE, AIAA; mem. Computer Soc. of IEEE (pres. and v.p. chpt.), Am. Soc. Metals, Hughes Mgmt. Club, Sigma Xi, Phi Delta Theta. Episcopalian. Home: 18651 Gledhill St Northridge CA 91324 Office: Hughes Aircraft Co Radar Systems Group PO Box 92426 Los Angeles CA 90009

LYNCH, DELL MARIE RYAN, civic worker, writer, artist; b. Scranton, Pa.; d. Cornelius James and Alice Wall (Burke) Ryan; BA, Manhattanville Coll., 1922; m. James Merriman Lynch, Apr. 6, 1926 (dec. Feb. 1982); 1 child, Nathaniel Merriman. Exhibited in group shows Pala Art Show, Showcase of Arts, Bank Am. Exhibit, Fireside Restaurant Exhibit, Country Squire Exhibit; one-woman show Woman's Club, 1979; publicity chmn. Santa Barbara County Med. Aux., 1947-48; co-chmn. Garden sect. Palomar Meml. Hosp. Aux., 1958-61; bd. mem. Friends of Leonell Strong Cancer Found., 1969-70; v.p. Yole Dames, 1928-29, Friends of Pala Indian Mission Sch., 1967-72, Friends of Escondido Library, 1972-73; chmn. Showcase of Arts Gallery, 1967-68; project chmn. Exceptional Girl Scouts U.S.A., 1957-58. Recipient award for over 20 yrs. vol. service Palomar Meml. Hosp., 1981; hon. mention state poetry award Women's Club, 1980. Mem. Felicita Found. (life), Escondido Hist. Soc. (life), Palomar Meml. Hosp. Aux. (life), Friends of Escondido Library (life), Escondido Art Assn. (life), Chaparral Poets, AAUW (life; area rep. for cultural interests 1964-65, courtesy chmn. 1968-77, cultural interests chmn. 1977-78, creative writing chmn. 1978-81, cert. of appreciation 1977-78). Clubs: Woman's (chmn. creative writing 1977-81, creative writing chmn. 1977-81, , cert. of appreciation 1977-78, 1st place poetry, writing contest 1978, 1st, 2d, 3d places poetry, 1979, 3 1st place awards for poetry, 2d place for prose 1980, 1st place and 2d place for poetry 1981), Escondido Garden (therapy co-chmn., Cert. Appreciation, 1986). Author (poetry) Bright Orbits, 1974, Have A Nice Day, 1980, Challenge, 1984; contbr. poems to poetry anthologies and jours. AAUW Ednl. Found. grad. student fellowship named in her honor, 1977. Home: 810 Omar Dr Escondido CA 92025

LYNCH, DONALD FRANCIS, geography educator; b. Seattle, Wash., June 1, 1931; s. Roger Edward and Florence Leone (Casey) L.; m. Elizabeth Dunne, July 3, 1954 (div. 1971); children: Sean R.T.L., Lesley B.E.A., Niall C.D.C. BA, Yale U., 1952, PhD, 1965. Geography prof. U. Alaska, Fairbanks, 1970—. Mem. Assn. Am. Geographers, APCG, Rotary (pres. 1988-89), Elks (loyal knight 1989—), Phia Kappa Phi, Sigma Xi, Gamma Theta Upsilon. Home: 1151 Kennicott Ave Fairbanks AK 99701 Office: U Alaska-Fairbanks Dept Geography Fairbanks AK 99775-0780

LYNCH, FRANK WILLIAM, aerospace company executive; b. San Francisco, Nov. 26, 1921; s. James Garfield and Med (Kelly) L.; m. Marilyn Leona Hopwood, June 24, 1950; children: Kathyn Leona, Molly Louise. A.B., Stanford U., 1943, postgrad., 1946-48. Research engr. Boeing Airplane Co., Seattle, 1948-50; with Northrop Corp., Hawthorn, Calif., 1950-57, Los Angeles, 1959—; sr. v.p. ops. corp. hdqrs. Northrop Corp., 1974-78, sr. v.p. and group exec. Tactical and Electronic Systems Group, 1978-82, pres., chief operating officer, 1982-87, vice chmn. of bd., 1987—; div. v.p. engring. Lear-Siegler Corp., Anaheim, Calif., 1957-59. Vice-chmn. Found. for Joffery Ballet; trustee Calif. State U. Found., L.A.; bd. govs. L.A. Music Ctr. Served with USAAF, 1942-46. Mem. IEEE (sr. mem.), AIAA (sr. mem.), Assn. U.S. Army, Am. Def. Preparedness Assn., Air Force Assn., Navy League, Balboa Yacht Club, City Club, Ctr. Club. Home: 1933 Altura Dr Corona Del Mar CA 92625 Office: Northrop Corp 1840 Century Pk E Los Angeles CA 90067

LYNCH, JAMES EDWARD, architect; b. Pendleton, Oreg., Apr. 20, 1946; s. Edward John and Barbara Jean (Moore) L.; m. Judy Lee Tyack, Dec. 29, 1968; 1 child, David James (dec.). BArch, U. Oreg., 1970. Lic. profl. architect, Colo., Oreg. Designer, draftsman Balzhiser, Rhodes, Smith & Morgan, Eugene, Oreg., 1970-71; architect, planner Woodmoor Corp., Monument, Colo., 1971-74; designer, architect Architectonics, Inc., Colorado Springs, Colo., 1974-75; constrn. supr. Hartman Constrn. Co., Colorado Springs, 1975; prin. Enviro-Synthesis Assocs., Eugene, 1976-77, AJS/Lynch Architects & Planners, Pendleton, 1977-81, James Lynch & Assocs., Pendleton, 1981-85, Lynch Fitzgerald & Assocs., Pendleton, 1985—; officer, dir. Contemp. Methods, Pendleton, 1982—; dir. Round-Up City Devel. Corp., Pendleton, 1985—. Editor bus. newsletter Update, 1986—; author and presenter seminars; inventor constrn. systems. Bd. dirs. E. Oreg. Regional Arts Coun., LaGrande, 1985-88; officio dir. Pendleton Arts Coun., 1986-88; commr. Capital Improvements Commn., Pendleton, 1982-85; mem. various adv. coms. in E. Oreg., 1979—. Recipient Award of Excellence Hist. Preservation League Oreg., 1985. Mem. AIA (cor), Nat. Trust for Hist. Preservation. Democrat. Roman Catholic. Office: Lynch Fitzgerald & Assocs 215 SW 1st St Pendleton OR 97801

LYNCH, ROBERT BERGER, lawyer; b. LaCrosse, Wis., June 10, 1931; s. Jan P. and Eve (Berger) L.; B.S., U.S. Merchant Marine Acad., 1955; J.D., U. of the Pacific, 1967; m. Ann Godfrey, May 30, 1980; 1 son, Jan Fredrick. Sr. engr. Aerojet Gen. Corp., Sacramento, Calif., 1955-61, proposal mgr., 1961-63, asst. contract adminstrn. mgr., 1963-66, contract adminstrn. mgr., 1967-70; admitted to Calif. bar, 1969, U.S. Supreme Ct. bar, 1972; individual practice law. Rancho Cordova, Calif., 1969—; instr. bus. law Solano Community Coll., 1977-79, San Joaquin Delta Coll., 1978-79. Monthly columnist Mil. History Rev. Active various charity fund-raising campaigns in Sacramento Calif., 1966-68; mem. mission com. St. Clements Episcopal Ch., Rancho Cordova, Calif., 1967-68; trustee Los Rios Community Coll. Dist., Calif., 1971-79. Served with USCG, 1949-51. Fellow Brit. Interplanetary Soc.; mem. Am. Bar Assn., Assn. of Trial Lawyers of Am., Calif. Trial Lawyers Assn., IEEE, Calif. Wildlife Fedn., Internat. Turtle Club, Marines Meml. Assn., Am. Legion, Mensa. Home and Office: 10615 Coloma Rd Rancho Cordova CA 95670

LYNDE, EDWARD JAMES, financial executive; b. Boston, Feb. 23, 1938; s. Kenneth R. and Mildred T. (Cassidy) L.; m. Kristina Kratzer, Aug., 1974 (dec. Aug. 1986); m. Anne Gibson Beeler, May 1, 1987. AB in Philosophy, Brown U., 1959. Group sales rep. Union Mut. Life Ins., Boston and Portland, Maine, 1962-66; pvt. practice broker N.Y.C., 1966-67; asst. regional mgr. Prin. Fin. Group (formerly Bankers Life), N.Y.C., 1967-73; regional mgr. Prin. Fin. Group (formerly Bankers Life), Seattle, 1973—. With U.S. Army Inf., 1959-62. Mem. Western Pension Conf., Brown U. Alumni Assn. Roman Catholic. Home: 1100 E Harrison #401 Seattle WA 98102 Office: Prin Fin Group 1111-3d Ave Ste 620 Seattle WA 98101

LYNGBAEK, PETER, computer scientist; b. Nakskov, Denmark, Mar. 9, 1955; came to U.S., 1979; s. Viggo and Helen Beate (Skotte) L.; m. Manon Janssen, Aug. 3, 1985. MSEE, Tech. U. Denmark, 1979; PhD in Computer Sci., U. So. Calif., 1984. Rsch. asst. computer sci. dept. U. So. Calif., L.A., 1981-83, rsch. fellow, 1983-84; mem. tech. staff Hewlett Packard Labs., Palo Alto, Calif., 1984-88; project mgr. Hewlett Packard Labs., Palo Alto, 1988—; mem. rsch. staff IBM Rsch. Lab., San Jose, Calif., 1982; speaker in field. Contbr. articles to profl. jours. Rotary Found. grad. fellow, 1979-80, IBM fellow, 1983-84; Otto Monsted found. scholar, Copenhagen, 1980-82, Egmont H. Petersens Found. scholar, 1980-82, Danish Employers' Assn. Jubilee Found. scholar, 1980; danish Natural Sci. Rsch. Coun. grantee, Copenhagen, 1983-84. Mem. Assn. for Computing Machinery, Sigma Xi (assoc.). Home: 385 Foxborough Dr Mountain View CA 94041 Office: Hewlett Packard Labs 1501 Page Mill Rd Palo Alto CA 94304

LYNN, CHARLES RANDAL, engineering executive; b. Dumas, Tex., July 18, 1954; s. Orden Jr. and Mildred Ruth (Johnson) L.; m. Susan Marie Barber, May 28, 1977; children: Patrick Randal, Christopher Charles. BSEE, Tex. Tech. U., 1977, MS in Indsl. Engring., 1979. Process engr. Phillips Petroleum Co., Borger, Tex., 1975-79; assoc. engr. IBM Corp., Tucson, 1979, mfg. mgr., 1980, quality assurance mgr., 1981, current products project mgr., 1983, adv. engr., mgr., 1985-86, mgr. devel. engring., 1986-87, mgr. printed circuit bd. process/assembly engring., 1987—. Deacon Palo Verde Ch. of Christ, 1986. Mem. IEEE (jr., v.p. 1976-77), AIEE (v.p. 1977-79), Alpha Pi Mu (sec. Lubbock, Tex. chpt. 1978-79), Tau Beta Pi (sec. Lubbock chpt. 1979). Home: 1401 N Arbor Circle Tucson AZ 85715

LYNN, KATHERINE LYN, materials engineer, chemist; b. Nagoya, Japan, June 25, 1954; (parents Am. citizens); d. Jimmie Frank and Barbara Sue (Whiteside) Sutton; m. Richard Shelly Lynn, Feb. 28, 1981. BS in Chemistry cum laude, Calif. State U., Fullerton, 1979. Technician U.S. Borax Corp., Anaheim, Calif., 1974-79; chemist Armstrong World Industries, Southgate, Calif., 1979-82; project engr. Hydril Co., Whittier, Calif., 1982-84; materials engr. So. Calif. Gas Co., Los Angeles, 1984—. Patentee fluorspar flotation. Bd. dirs. East Side Christian Ch., 1987-89. Mem. So. Calif. Thermal Analysis Group (chair 1988, sec. 1985-87), Soc. Plastic Engrs., N. Am. Thermal Analysis Soc., Am. Chem. Soc., Sierra Club. Mem.

Christian Ch. Home: 5120 Faust St Lakewood CA 90713 Office: So Calif Gas Co Box 3249 Terminal Annex ML730B Los Angeles CA 90051

LYNN, MICHAEL KENTON, graphic design and advertising company executive; b. Las Vegas, Nev., June 17, 1953; s. Russell Kenton and Hazel Alene (DeLong) L.; m. Sandra Diane Reed, June 3, 1978 (div. 1988); children: Daniel Kenton, Trevor Reed. BS in Journalism, U. Kans., 1976. Bus. mgr. Colo. Country Life mag., Denver, 1976-79; founder, owner, mgr. PrePress Advt., Denver, 1979-85; pres. Kenton & Assocs. Inc., Denver, 1985—. Mem. Nat. Agri-Mktg. Assn. (bd. dirs. Rocky Mountain chpt. 1988—, chmn. awards 1987—, Best of Region award 1987), BMW Car Club Am. Republican. Home: 4433 S Zenobia St Denver CO 80236 Office: Kenton & Assocs Inc 10200 E Girard St Ste 306A Denver CO 80231

LYON, KEITH DAVID, mortgage company executive, finance executive; b. Geneva, N.Y, Jan. 1, 1956; s. Scott Robert and Arlene Ann (Picarello) L.; m. Janis Barton, Oct. 12, 1981 (div. Oct. 1981); m. Lezlie Lyon, Dec. 27, 1986, 1 child, Jesse Lyon. BBA, Utah State U., 1979. Asst. mgr. Taurus Corp. Restaurants, Cedar City, Utah, 1975-79; engr. drilling fluids Baroid Corp., Houston, 1981-88; owner, pres. Lyon Mortgage Co., Las Vegas, Nev., 1981-85; owner, pres. Western Acceptance Corp., Las Vegas, 1985—, also bd. dirs.; bd. dirs. Profl. Ins. Agts., Las Vegas. Navy Wives Assn. scholarship, 1974. So. Utah State Coll., scholarship, 1977. Mem. PGA Las Vegas (founder 1984), Jaycees.

LYON, MARK ANDREW, dentist; b. Bethesda, Md., Apr. 8, 1953; s. Harvey William and Margaret (Siggelkow) L.; m. Patti Lynn Wagner, Aug. 8, 1988; 1 child, Gunnar Andrew. BS in Chemistry, Colo. State U., 1975; DDS, Northwestern U., 1979. Chemistry research asst. Colo. State U., Ft. Collins, 1974-75; dental research asst. ADA, Chgo., 1975-79; pvt. practice Santa Fe, N.Mex., 1979--. Commodore Santa Fe Sailboard Fleet, 1987. Recipient Cert. of Exemplary Performance, State N.Mex. Corrections Dept., Santa Fe, 1987. Mem. ADA, Santa Fe Dental Soc. (pres. 1987-88), Santa Fe Rugby Club. Republican. Lutheran. Home: 2876 Vereda de Pueblo Santa Fe NM 87505 Office: 1418 Luisa St Ste 5A Santa Fe NM 87501

LYONS, JAMES ELLIOTT, lawyer; b. Lexington, Mo., Mar. 10, 1951; s. james Elliott and Elouise (Blackman) L.; m. Mary Jane McCarthy, June 30, 1979; children: Sean Austin, Caitlan Maureen. BA with honors, U. Mo., 1973; JD, NYU, 1976. Bar: Mo. 1976, N.Y. 1977, Calif. 1984. Assoc. Stinson Mag Thompson McEvers & Fizzell, Kansas City, Mo., 1976-77; assoc. Skadden, Arps, Slate et al., N.Y.C., L.A., 1977-84; law clk. U.S. Dept. Justice, N.Y.C., 1978; ptnr. Skadden, Arps, Slate et al., L.A., 1984—. Mem. ABA (chmn. securities trials & takeover litigation subcom. 1986—), Mo. Bar Assn., City Club (L.A.), Wilshire Country Club. Democrat. Home: 332 S Arden Blvd Los Angeles CA 90020 Office: Skadden Arps Slate et al 300 S Grand Ave 3400 Los Angeles CA 90071

LYONS, JAMES MICHAEL, chemical engineer; b. Long Beach, Calif., Apr. 30, 1961; s. Herbert Brian and Rosalie Jean (Bultena) L.; m. Irma Ruth Hernandez, Mar. 20, 1982. BS in Chemistry cum laude, U. Calif., Irvine, 1983; MS in Engring., UCLA, 1985. Air resources engr. assoc. Calif. Air Resources Bd., El Monte, 1985—. Mem. Am. Chem Soc., Phi Beta Kappa, Phi Lambda Upsilon. Democrat. Lutheran. Office: Calif Air Resources Bd 9528 Telstar St El Monte CA 91731

LYONS, MARTIN JESSE, protective services official; b. Walla Walla, Wash., July 22, 1952; s. Joseph Denzel and Maxine Della (Stephens) L.; m. Mary Ellen Joy, June 12, 1971; children: Lisa, Dawn, Andrea. AA, Walla Walla Community Coll., 1982; BA, Cen. Wash. U., 1984. Correctional officer Washington State Penitentiary, Walla Walla, 1978-81, correctional sgt., 1981-83, adminstrv. asst., 1984-86, correctional unit supr., 1986--; correctional counselor Cedar Creek Correctional Ctr., Littlerock, Wash., 1983-84; research advisor Whitman Coll., Walla Walla, 1984--; speaker Wash. State Penitentiary, 1984--. Mem. law enforcement torch run com. Spl. Olympocs, Wash., 1987—; bd. dirs. Walla Walla Camp Fire Council, 1989—. Served with USAF, 1971-75. Recipient Appreciation award Spl. Olympics, 1988. Mem. Wash. Correctional Assn. (co-chair 1986--), Exchange, Elks. Mem. Assembly of God. Home: 1520 Truman Walla Walla WA 99362 Office: Wash Dept Corrections PO Box 520 Walla Walla WA 99362

LYONS, (MARY) RUTH, retail automotive company executive; b. Milw., May 18, 1949; d. Thomas Desmond and Mary Ruth (Keogh) L. BA, St. Mary's Coll., Notre Dame, Ind., 1971. Bus. mgr. Sunnyvale (Calif.) Ford, 1978-80; bus. mgr. Victory Toyota, Seaside, Calif., 1982-86, gen. mgr., 1987--. Bd. dirs. Vols. in Action, Monterey, Calif., 1986--, United Way, Monterey, 1987, 88; sec. Leadership Monterey Peninsula, 1985-86. Mem. Monterey Peninsula Bus. Mgrs. Assn. (pres. 1986—), Monterey Peninsula Alumni Assn. (sec. leadership). Republican. Office: Victory Toyota 5 Heitzinger Pla Seaside CA 93955

LYSAK, WILLIAM, psychologist; b. Newark, Jan. 14, 1926; s. Alexander and Anna (Borsuk) L.; m. Louise Alma Hayes, 1948 (div. 1962); children: William Hayes, Thomas Pennington, John Foard; m. Jo Ann Matthes, July 7, 1964. BA, U. Mich., 1948; MA, U. Wis.-Madison, 1951, PhD, 1953. Commd. 2d lt. U.S. Army, 1949, advanced through grades to lt. col., 1967; asst. chief psychology service Letterman Army Med. Ctr., San Francisco, 1959-62; chief psychology service 97th Gen. Hosp., Frankfurt, Fed. Republic Germany, 1962-66, Madigan Army Med. Ctr., Tacoma, 1966-69; ret. 1969; psychology cons. Rohrer, Hibler & Replogle, Seattle, 1969-70, Wash. Correctional Ctr., Shelton, 1966-69; cons. div. vocat. rehab. Wash. Dept. Social and Health Svcs., Olympia, 1970--; cons. NIMH, San Francisco, 1960; instr. psychology European div. U. Md., Frankfurt, 1962-66. Contbr. articles to psychol. jours. Decorated Bronze Star. Mem. Ranier Psychol. Assn. (pres. 1968-69), Am. Psychol. Assn., Wash. State Psycol. Assn., Sigma Xi. Home: 9342 Lohrer Ln NE Olympia WA 98506 Office: Dept Social and Health Svcs Vocat Rehab Div PO Box 2487 Olympia WA 98507

LYTLE, MARALYN CELESTE, banker; b. Lewistown, Mont., Feb. 1, 1952; d. John P. and Caroline B. (Koch) Strunk; m. Laurence A. Lytle, Aug. 12, 1972; children: Lyla C., Kari D. BA in Elem. Edn., Carroll Coll., 1974. Cert. tchr., Mont. Teller Western Fed. Savs., Helena, Mont., 1983-84, head teller, savs. cashier, 1984-86, br. mgr., 1986—. Mem. Am. Bus. Women, Helena Kennel. Lutheran. Office: Western Fed Savs 601 N Montana Ave Helena MT 59601

MA, FAI, mechanical engineering educator; b. Canton, People's Republic of China, Aug. 6, 1954; came to U.S., 1977, naturalized, 1988; s. Rui-Qi and Shao-Fen (Luo) M. BS, U. Hong Kong, 1977; MS, PhD, Calif. Inst. Tech., 1981. Sr. rsch. engr. Weidlinger Assocs., Menlo Park, Calif., 1981-82; rsch. fellow IBM, Yorktown Heights, N.Y., 1982-83; sr. engr. Standard Oil Co., Cleve., 1983-86; asst. prof. mech. engring. U. Calif., Berkeley, 1986—. Co-author: Probabilistic Analysis, 1983; contbr. articles to profl. jours. Recipient Presdl. Young Investigator award NSF, grantee, 1987; IBM rsch. grantee, 1987, Digital Equipment Corp. rsch. grantee, 1987, GE grantee, 1987. Fellow Instn. Diagnostic Engrs.; mem. ASME. Office: U Calif Dept Mech Engring Berkeley CA 94720

MAACK, DEBRA KEOSA, retail executive; b. Hardin, Mont., Apr. 13, 1955; d. Ernest Fredrick Herman and Helene Keosa (Olind) M. BA in Polit. Sci., U. Mont., 1977, postgrad., 1980-81. Microfilm tech. Dept. Pub. Safety, Juneau, Alaska, 1973; caretaker Yellowtail Dam Bur. of Reclamation, Ft. Smith, Mont., 1974-76; intern State Commn. on Local Govt., Helena, Mont., 1975; parts salesman John Deere Distbr., Missoula, 1977-78, 80-81; legis. liaison Dept. Community Affairs, Helena, 1978; owner, mgr. Mac-A-Tack Horse Racing Supplies, Yakima, Wash., 1982—; cons. race horse sales D&D Tack, Seguin, Tex, 1984. Author: Consolidation of Rural Police and Fire Departments, 1975, How to Write a Grant Proposal, 1980. Recipient DAR Good Citizen award, 1973. Mem. Horse Benevolent Protection Assn., Alpha Phi (pledge trainer Missoula chpt. 1974-77). Lutheran. Home and Office: 311 Hazen Rd Yakima WA 98903

MAARTMANN-MOE, PETER SIGVAL, electrical engineer; b. Concord, Mass., Aug. 22, 1955; s. Ragnvald and Constance (Platine) Maartman-M.; m. Lorraine Gail Jackie, Oct. 8, 1988; 1 child, Amanda Marie. BSEE, U. Mass., 1983. Mgr. Amherst (Mass.) Audio, 1980-81; tech. sales support Computer Automation, Irvine, Calif., 1983-84, Genrad, Inc., Irvine, Calif., 1984-87; mgr. test engring. Harman Electronics, Northridge, Calif., 1987—; pres. P & G Resume Svc., Northridge, Calif., 1987—. Chmn. Bounce for Beats, Amherst, 1982. Mem. IEEE, Sigma Alpha Mu (chpt. pres. 1976), Sons Norway. Home: 8502 Grove Ave Northridge CA 91325 Office: Harman Electronics 8500 Balboa Blvd Northridge CA 91329

MAAS, SALLY ANN, magazine editor; b. Portage, Wis., Apr. 10, 1947; d. Franklin Arthur and Mabel Gladys (Engen) Maas; m. Robert A. Marshall, Aug. 3, 1973. BJ, U. Wis., 1969. Reporter, The Paper, Oshkosh, Wis., 1969-70; feature writer The Press, Binghamton, N.Y., 1970-71; feature writer The Press-Enterprise, Riverside, Calif., 1971-76, lifestyle editor, 1976-83, feature editor, 1983-85, asst. mng. editor features and art, 1985—. Recipient Outstanding Woman of Achievement award Bus. and Profl. Women's Club, 1981. Mem. Soc. Newspaper Design, Women in Communications, LWV, Sigma Delta Chi. Club: Twin Cities Press (past pres.). Home: 30001 Live Oak Cyn Rd Redlands CA 92373 Office: The Press-Enterprise Co 3512 14th St Riverside CA 92502

MAAS, TERRY LEO, investment banker; b. St. Louis, Dec. 6, 1946; s. Clifford Joseph and Dorothy Marie (Mayernick) M.; m. Sharon Eileen Schick, Aug. 26, 1972; children: Brett Charles, Bryan Clifford. BS with honors, UCLA, 1968; MBA, Calif. State U., Dominguez Hills, 1975, M of Pub. Adminstrn., 1978. Adminstrv. mgr. KMS Tech. Ctr., Los Angeles, 1972-75; investment broker Merrill-Lynch, Los Angeles, 1975-78; mgr. West Coast Rauscher Pierce Refsnes, Inc., Los Angeles, 1978-81; asst. regional mgr. Rauscher Pierce Refsnes, Inc., Phoenix, 1981-86; SW regional mgr. Security Pacific Mcht. Bank, Phoenix, 1986-88; sr. v.p. Citibank, Phoenix, 1988—; faculty Nat. Real Estate Devel. Conf., San Francisco, 1984-85; group leader Valley Leadership Conf., Phoenix, 1985; speaker forum in pub. fin. UCLA, 1984. Bd. dirs. East Scottsdale Little League, 1982-88. Served to 1st lt. USAF, 1969-72. Mem. UCLA Alumni Assn., Lambda Chi Alpha. Republican. Lutheran. Club: Phoenix Stock and Bond. Home: 9300 N 58th St Paradise Valley AZ 85253 Office: Citibank 3300 N Central Ave Phoenix AZ 85012

MAASS, ANDREW WARREN, management information systems manager; b. Madison, Wis., Mar. 24, 1949; s. Alfred Ronald and Eleanor Grace (Anderson) M.; m. Linda Marie Summy, Oct. 6, 1984 (div. Mar. 1983); children: Adam, Eleanor, Meredith, April. BA, U. Pa., 1971. Mgr. Hitachi Am. Ltd., San Bruno, Calif., 1983—. Office: Hitachi Am Ltd 2000 Sierra Point Pkwy Brisbane CA 94005

MAASS, JANET EMILY, health facility executive; b. Green Bay, Wis.; d. Norman H. and Verla Esther Maass. BS, U. Wis., Green Bay, 1976; MEd in edn. for profl. devel., U. Wis., Eau Claire, 1980. Cert. histotechnologist, cytotechnologist. Sec. Seymour (Wis.) Press, 1965-66; med. stenographer St. Vincent Hosp., Green Bay, 1966-68; histology technician Deaconess Hosp., Milw., 1969-70, St. Mary's Hosp., Green Bay, 1970-74; teaching asst. U. Wis., Green Bay, 1972-74, 76; histology supr., edn. coordinator Marshfield (Wis.) Clinic, 1976-80; mgr. histology, cytology U. Colo. Health Scis. Ctr., Denver, 1980-81; lab. mgr. Westpath Labs., Fort Collins, Colo., 1981-83; owner, pres. Colo. Histo-Prep, Inc., Fort Collins, 1983—; cons. Colo. Histo-Prep, Inc., 1983—. Editor Technology Sample, 1980. Mem. Nat. Soc. for Histotechnology (sec. 1978-82, v.p. 1984-88), Colo. Soc. Histotechnology (pres. 1981-83), Am. Soc. Cytology, Am. Soc. Clin. Pathologists. Office: Colo Histo-Prep Inc PO Box 8644 Fort Collins CO 80524

MABEY, EDWARD MILO, insurance agency executive; b. Bountiful, Utah, Feb. 26, 1919; s. Charles Rendell and Afton (Rampton) M.; student U. Utah, 1936-38, 40, San Francisco Trade Sch., 1941-42, U. Tenn., 1944; m. Edrice Louise Haslam, July 23, 1940 (div.); children: James Edward, Afton Louise Mabey Wettstein, Charlynn Edrice Mabey Clark; m. Gun Sundberg, Aug. 27, 1979; 1 child, Amanda Gun. Book salesman, mgr. Edward Brown & Sons Gen. Ins. Co., Oakland, Calif., 1940-41; pres., dir. Western Gen. Agy., Inc., Salt Lake City, 1947-81; pres. Brother Christopher Inc. Western Underwriters, Inc.; chmn. bd., dir. Investment Mgmt. Corp.; pres., chmn. bd. Western Indsl. Shares, Inc.; chmn. bd. Bountiful State Bank, 1965-68; pres., dir. Western Holding Corp., 1973-76; mng. dir. Internat. Guaranteed Fund, Ltd.; dir., owner-developer Oakridge Improvement Co., Farmington, Utah; mng. dir. Bahamian Investment Mgmt. Ltd.; dir. Natural Resources, Inc., New Hemisphere Life Ins. Co., Victoria Falls Enterprises, Inc., Bayview Park Devel. Co., Woods Cross, Utah, Zions First Nat. Bank, Bountiful, Foursquare Fund, Boston. Exec. dir. Utah Opera Co., 1979, pres., 1980-82, chmn. bd., 1982-85. With USNR, World War II. Mem. Intercollegiate Knights, Ambassador Club, Oakridge Country Club, Beta Theta Pi. Republican. LDS. Address: 780 E South Temple Salt Lake City UT 84102

MABIE, RUTH MARIE, realtor; b. Pueblo, Colo., Feb. 7; d. Newton Everett and Florence Ellen Allen; M.B.A., La Jolla U., 1980, Ph.D., 1981; m. Richard O. Mabie, Nov. 29, 1946; 1 son, Ward A. Mgr., LaMont Modeling Sch., San Diego, 1962; tchr. Am. Bus. Coll., San Diego, 1964-66; fashion modeling, 1960-72; owner, broker Ruth Mabile Realty, San Diego, 1972—; asst. v.p. Skil-Bilt, Inc., 1976—; dir. Mabie & Mintz, Inc. Bd. dirs. Multiple Sclerosis Dr., 1971—. Mem. San Diego Bd. Realtors, Nat. Assn. Female Execs. Republican. Office: 2231 Camino del Rio So #302 San Diego CA 92108-3605

MABUS, CYNTHIA ANNE, architect; b. Johnstown, Pa., Mar. 28, 1958; d. Roy John and Anne Cynthia (Sova) M. BArch, Calif. Poly. State U., 1980. Registered architect, Calif. Architect Pulliam-Matthews & Assocs., L.A., 1981-83, Prochnow-Frew Architects, Santa Monica, Calif., 1983-84, Scott Adams Assocs., San Francisco, 1984, Kaplan-McLaughlin Diaz, San Francisco, L.A., 1984-88, Bobrow Thomas & Assocs., L.A., 1988--. Lutheran. Home: 10731 Northgate St Culver City CA 90230 Office: Bobrow Thomas & Assocs 1001 Westwood Blvd Los Angeles CA 90024

MACALISTER, ROBERT STUART, oil company executive; b. L.A., May 22, 1924; s. Robert Stuart and Iris Grace (Doman) MacA.; m. Catherine Vera Willby, Nov. 15, 1947; children: Rodney James, Sara Marjorie Pfirrmann. Student, Brighton Coll., Sussex, Eng., 1945; BSME, Calif. Inst. Tech., 1947. Registered profl. engr., Tex. Petroleum engr. Shell Oil Co., 1947-56; mgmt. trainee Royal Dutch Shell, The Hague, Netherlands, 1956-57; with exec. staff, mgr. Shell Oil Co., Netherlands, 1957-68; v.p., ops. mgr. Occidental Petroleum Corp., Tripoli, Libya, 1968-71; mng. dir.various subs. London, 1971-76; mng. dir., pres. Occidental Internat. Oil, Inc., London, 1976-78; pres., chmn. bd. Can. Occidental Petroleum Ltd., Calgary and Alberta, 1978-81; mng. dir. Australian Occidental Petroleum Ltd., Sydney, 1982-83, Hamilton Bros. Oil & Gas Ltd., London, 1983-86; petroleum cons. Hamilton Bros. Oil & Gas Ltd., Camarillo, Calif., 1986—; mem. adv. bd. Vista Pacific Resources, Oxnard, Calif., 1988—, exec. U.K. Offshore Operators, London, 1972-78, 83-86. Cubmaster Boy Scouts Am., Larchmont, N.Y., 1964-65, scoutmaster, Houston, 1965-68. Sgt. U.S. Army, 1944-45, ETO. Mem. Am. Assn. Petroleum Geologists, Soc. Petroleum Engrs.,Las Posas Country Club, Gold Coast Srs. Republican. Episcopalian. Home and Office: 78 Lopaco Ct Camarillo CA 93010

MACALLISTER, JACK ALFRED, telephone company executive; b. Humeston, Iowa, July 12, 1927; s. Maxwell A. and Opal E. (Caldwell) MacA.; m. Marilyn Anderson, June 12, 1950; children: Steven, James, Sue. B.Commerce, Iowa State U., 1950; student, Iowa State Tchrs. Coll., Cedar Rapids, 1947-48. With Northwestern Bell Telephone Co., 1950-65, 67-83; v.p. ops. Northwestern Bell Telephone Co., Omaha, 1974-75, pres., 1965-82, chmn., 1982-83; pres., chief exec. officer U.S. West, Inc., Englewood, Colo., 1984-86, chmn. bd. dirs., chief exec. officer, 1986—; mem. staff AT&T, N.Y.C., 1965-67; bd. dirs. 1st Interstate Bank of Los Angeles, The St. Paul Cos., Western Strategy Ctr. for Regional Devel.; mem. adv. bd. U. Pa. Wharton Sch. Fishman-Davidson Ctr. for study of service sector; mem. nat. adv. bd. U. Ariz.; mem. internat. adv. bd. Stanford Research; mem. Bus. Higher Edn. Forum. Mem. Found. Bd. Denver Art Mus.; mem. exec. bd. Denver Area council Boy Scouts Am.; bd. dirs. U. Iowa Found.; co-chair Ednl. Commn. of the States. Office: US West Inc 7800 E Orchard Rd Englewood CO 80111

MACASKILL, RODERICK BURNS, engineer; b. Boston, May 31, 1933; s. Daniel and Margaret H. (Burns) M.; m. Margaret Elizabeth Tait; children: Susan, Malcolm. BS in Engring., Letourneau Coll., 1960. Registered profl. engr., Calif. Engr. Stanley Aviation Corp., Denver, 1960-62, Emerson Elect. Co., Colorado Springs, Colo., 1962-66, Coors Porcelain Co., Golden, Colo., 1966-71, Storage Technology Corp, Louisville, Colo., 1971-84, McData Corp., Broomfield, Colo., 1985—. Cpl. U.S. Army, 1953-55, Germany. Mem. Internat. Facilities Mgmt. Assn., Toastmasters, Denver (area gov. 1982-84).

MACBRIDE, THOMAS JAMISON, federal judge; b. Sacramento, Mar. 25, 1914; s. Frank and Lotta Kirtley (Little) MacB.; m. Martha Harrold, Nov. 7, 1947; children—Peter, Thomas Jamison, David, Laurie. A.B., U. Calif. at Berkeley, 1936, J.D., 1940. Bar: Calif. 1940. Dep. atty. gen. Calif., 1941-42; pvt. practice Sacramento, 1946-61; U.S. dist. judge Eastern Dist. Calif., Sacramento, 1961-67; chief judge Eastern Dist. Calif., 1967-79, sr. judge, 1979—; mem. U.S. Temporary Emergency Ct. Appeals, 1982-87; mem. Criminal Justice Act Com., U.S. Jud. Conf., 1969-88; mem. U.S. Jud. Conf., 1975-78; chmn. Criminal Justice Act Com. of U.S. Jud. Conf., 1979-88; mem. U.S. Fgn. Intelligence Surveillance Ct., 1979-80. Pres. Town Hall, Sacramento, 1952, N.E. area YMCA, 1960; mem. Calif. Legislature from Sacramento County, 1955-60 mem. Nat. Commn. on Reform Fed. Criminal Laws, 1967-71; bd. dirs. Sacramento YMCA; trustee U. Calif., San Francisco Found., 1982—; bd. dirs. Sacramento Regional Found., 1988—; founding dir. League to Save Lake Tahoe, 1965. Lt. USNR, 1942-46. Mem. Am. Bar Assn., U. Calif. Alumni Assn. (v.p. 1955, 60), Kappa Sigma, Phi Delta Phi. Democrat. Clubs: Mason (33 deg., Shriner, Jester), Rotarian (pres. 1966-67), Sutter, University (pres. 1953), Comstock (pres. 1975-76), Senator Outing (sec.-treas.). Home: 1800 Rockwood Dr Sacramento CA 95864 Office: US Ct of Appeals 2014 US Courthouse 650 Capitol Mall Sacramento CA 95814

MACCALLUM, (EDYTHE) LORENE, pharmacist; b. Monte Vista, Colo., Nov. 29, 1928; d. Francis Whittier and Berniece Viola (Martin) Scott; m. David Robertson MacCallum, June 12, 1952; children: Suzanne Rae MacCallum Homiak and Roxanne Kay MacCallum Batezel (twins), Tracy Scott, Tamara Lee MacCallum Johnson, Shauna Marie MacCallum Bost. BS in Pharmacy U. Colo., 1950. Registered pharmacist, Colo. Pharmacist Presbyn. Hosp., Denver, 1950, Corner Pharmacy, Lamar, Colo., 1950-53; research pharmacist Nat. Chlorophyll Co., Lamar, 1953; relief pharmacist, various stores, Delta, Colo., 1957-59, Farmington, N.Mex., 1960-62, 71-79, Aztec, N.Mex., 1971-79; mgr. Med. Arts Pharmacy, Farmington, 1966-67; cons. pharmacist Navajo Hosp., Brethren in Christ Mission, Farmington, 1967-77; sales agt. Norris Realty, Farmington, 1977-78; pharmacist, owner, mgr. Lorene's Pharmacy, Farmington, 1979-88; tax cons. H&R Block, Farmington, 1968; cons. Pub. Service Co., N.Mex. Intermediate Clinic, Planned Parenthood, Farmington. Advisor Order Rainbow for Girls, Farmington, 1975-78. Mem. Nat. Assn. Bds. Pharmacy (com. on internship tng., com. edn., sec., treas. dist. 8, mem. impaired pharmacists adv. com., chmn. impaired pharmacists program N.Mex., 1987—, mem. enforcement legis. com.), N.Mex. Bd. Pharmacy (first woman pres. 1987-88), Nat. Assn. Retail Druggists, N.Mex. Pharm. Assn. (mem. exec. council 1977-81). Methodist. Lodge: Order Eastern Star (Farmington). Home: 1301 Camino Sol Farmington NM 87401 Office: 901 W Apache Farmington NM 87401

MACCAULEY, HUGH BOURNONVILLE, banker; b. Mt. Vernon, N.Y., Mar. 12, 1922; s. Morris Baker and Alma (Gardiner) MacC.; m. Rachael Gleaton, Aug. 30, 1943 (div. May 1980); m. Felice Cooper, Dec. 2, 1980. Student, Rutgers U., 1939-41, Tex. Christian U., 1948-50, U. Omaha, 1957-59. Commd. 2d lt. U.S. Army, 1943; advanced through grades to col. U.S. Army, USAF, Washington, 1943-73; v.p. Great Am. Securities, San Bernardino, Calif., 1979—; chmn. bd. Desert Community Bank, Victorville, Calif., 1980—. bd. dirs. Air Force Village West, 1986-88; chmn. bd. Gen. and Mrs. Curtis E. Lemay Found., 1987—. Decorated Air medal, Legion of Merit. Mem. Dadaelian Soc., Rotary. Republican. Presbyterian. Home: 1630 Monroe St Riverside CA 92504 Office: Great Am Securities Inc 334 W 3d Ste 201 San Bernardino CA 92401

MACCRACKEN, PETER JAMES, marketing executive; b. Trieste, Italy, Dec. 27, 1952; came to U.S., 1956; s. James and Kirsten (Koch) MacC. BA summa cum laude, Albion Coll., 1975; MA, U. Calif., Santa Barbara, 1978. Asst. mgr. GranTree Furniture Rental, San Leandro, Calif., 1979-81; freelance writer San Diego, 1981-82; corp. editor Scripps Meml. Hosps., La Jolla, Calif., 1982-84; sr. v.p. Berkman & Daniels Mktg., San Diego, 1984-89; v.p. Stoorza, Zeigaus & Metzger, Inc., San Diego, 1989—. Contbr. over 400 articles, photographs to numerous publs. Com. chmn., San Diego sect. Am. Cancer Soc., 1986-87, vice-chmn. mktg. communications com., 1988-89. Recipient 23 bus. communications awards. Mem. Pub. Rels. Soc. Am., Med. Mktg. Assn., Internat. Assn. Bus. Communicators (pres. San Diego chpt. 1985), Phi Beta Kappa. Democrat. Office: Stoorza Ziegaus & Metzger Ste 1600 225 Broadway San Diego CA 92101

MAC CREADY, PAUL BEATTIE, aeronautical engineer; b. New Haven, Sept. 29, 1925. BS in Physics, Yale U., 1947; MS, Calif. Inst. Tech., 1948, PhD in Aeros. cum laude, 1952. Founder, pres. Meteorology Research Inc., 1951-70, Atmospheric Research Group, 1958-70; founder, 1971, since pres., now also chmn. AeroVironment Inc., Pasadena, Calif.; leader team that developed Gossamer Condor, 1976-77, Gossamer Albatross for human-powered flight across English Channel, 1979, Solar Challenger, ultralight aircraft powered by solar cells, 1981, Gossamer Penguin; cons. in field, 1951—; mem. numerous govt. tech. adv. coms. Author research papers in field. Recipient Collier trophy Nat. Aero. Assn., 1979, Edward Longsreth medal Franklin Inst., 1979, Gold Air medal Fedn. Aero. Internat., 1981; Inventor of Yr. award Assn. Advancement Innovation and Invention, 1981; named Engr. of Century ASME, 1980. Mem. Nat. Acad. Engring., Am. Acad. Arts and Scis., Am. Meteorol. Soc. (chmn. com. atmospheric measurements 1968-69, councillor 1971-74), AIAA (Reed Aero. award 1979). Office: Aerovironment Inc 825 Myrtle Ave Monrovia CA 91106-3424

MACDONALD, NORVAL WOODROW, retired safety engineer; b. Medford, Oreg., Dec. 8, 1913; s. Orion and Edith (Anderson) MacD.; m. Elizabeth Ann Clifford, Dec. 8, 1937; children: Linda (Mrs. Bob Comings), Peggy (Mrs. Don Lake), Kathleen. Student, U. So. Calif., 1932-34. Registered profl. safety engr., Calif. Safety engr. Todd Shipyards, San Pedro, Calif., 1942-44, Pacific Indemnity Ins. Co., San Francisco, 1944-50; area safety engring. mgr. Indsl. Ind., San Francisco, 1950-76; v.p. loss control Beaver Ins. Co., 1976-78; tchr. adult evening classes U. San Francisco, 1960-63, Golden Gate U., 1969—. Contbr. articles to profl. jours. Mem. Am. ASME, Soc. Safety Engrs. (pres. 1958-59). Methodist. Club: Las Posas Country (Camarillo, Calif.). Lodge: Masons. Home: 1710 E Shoreline Camarillo CA 93010 Office: Beaver Loss Control 100 California St San Francisco CA 94111

MACDONALD, PETER, SR., tribal official, electrical engineer; b. Teec-NosPos, Ariz., Dec. 16, 1928; s. Dyahthini and Lucy (Ute) Begay; m. Wanda L. LeClere, June 1973; children: Hope Marie, Faith Ann, Charity Lynn; children by previous marriage: Linda, Peter. AA, Bacone Coll., 1952; BSEE, U. Okla., 1957; postgrad., UCLA. Project engr., mem. tech. staff Hughes Aircraft Co., El Segundo, Calif., 1957-63; dir. mgmt. and procedures Navajo Tribe, Window Rock, Ariz., 1963-65; exec. dir. Office of Navajo Econ. Opportunity, Ft. Defiance, Ariz., 1965-70; chmn. Navajo Tribal Council, 1970-82, from 1986. Mem. N.Mex. Gov.'s Econ. Devel. Adv. Group, 1963-67, N.Mex. State Planning Com., 1963-67; mem. nat. task force for mgmt. and career devel. OEO, 1968-69; mem., v.p. Leadership Inst. for Community Devel., 1968; mem. Four Corners Regional N.Mex. tech. action panels, 1968; del. Rep. Nat. Conv., 1972. Served as cpl. USMC, 1944-46, PTO. Republican. Baptist. Office: Navajo Tribal Coun PO Box 308 Window Rock AZ 86515

MACDONALD, VIRGINIA BROOKS, architect; b. Denver, July 17, 1918; d. Emmet Earl and Lulu (Gatchel) Stoffel; widowed; m. Russell A. Apple, Oct. 18, 1981; children: Philip Brooks, Anne Brooks Hormann, Bill Brooks, Mike Brooks. BArch, Case Western Res. U., 1946. Registered architect, Hawaii. Dir. Timberline Camp., Honolulu, 1962-67; planner State of Hawaii, Honolulu, 1967-77; pvt. practice architecture Volcano, Hawaii, 1977—. Author: West Hawaii, 1972; (book/report) Na Ala Hele, 1973. Active Volcano Community Assn., 1980—. Recipient Innovative Energy award U.S. Dept. Energy, 1984, Energy Saving award State of Hawaii, 1984. Mem. AIA (pres. elect. local sect. 1988), Sierra Club (past state bd. dirs), Hawaii Conservation Council (past state pres.).

MACDONOUGH, ROBERT HOWARD, consulting engineer; b. Chgo., Jan. 24, 1941; s. John Haaf and Helen Margaret (McWilliams) MacD.; m. Joan Carol Rosecrants, Dec. 28, 1963 (div. Nov. 1975); children: John Haaf, Thomas William, Mark Peter. BS in Engring. Ops., Iowa State U., 1962; MA in Econ., Drake U., 1966. Registered profl. engr., Iowa. Assoc. Mgmt. Sci. Am., Palo Alto, Calif., 1969; mng. assoc. Theo. Barry & Assoc., Los Angeles, 1970-72; mgr. indsl. engring. Advanced Memory Systems, Sunnyvale, Calif., 1972-73; mgr. planning and engring. Signetics, Sunnyvale, 1973-75; pres. Facilities Cons., Mountain View, Calif., 1976—. Mem. Inst. Indsl. Engrs. (sr.), Am. Inst. Plant Engrs., Am. Contract Bridge League, Phi Gamma Delta. Republican.

MACDOUGALL, WILLIAM RODERICK, lawyer, county official; b. Nevada City, Calif., May 14, 1914; s. William Stewart and Ethel Martha (Hutchison) McDougall; m. Carol Bernie Keane, May 1, 1937; children: Marcia MacDougall Williams, James Stewart. AA, Sacramento City Coll., 1930-32; student U. Calif.-Berkeley, 1933-34; JD, U. of Pacific, 1941. Bar: Calif. 1941, U.S. Dist. Ct. (no. dist.) Calif. 1941, U.S. Supreme Ct. 1950. Library page Calif. State Library, Sacramento, 1932-33; sr. auditor Office of Controller, State of Calif., Sacramento, 1934-37; chief bur. of collections Calif. Social Welfare Dept., Sacramento, 1937-42; gen. counsel County Suprs. Assn. Calif., Sacramento, 1946-70; exec. dir. U.S. Intergovt. Relations Commn., Washington, 1970-75; planning commr. County of Orange, Santa Ana, Calif., 1976-84; chief counsel Calif. Alcoholic Beverage Control Appeals Bd., 1984—; exec. dir. Calif. County Govt. Edn. Found., 1965-69; chmn. home rule com. Nat. Assn. Counties, 1963-67. Mem. Fed. Public Assistance Adv. Council, 1959-60, Gov.'s Commn. on Met. Problems, Calif., 1960; pres. Laguna Beach Sch. of Art (Calif.), 1983-84. Mem. Am. Planning Assn., Nat. Assn. County and Pros. Attys. (hon.), Calif. County Planning Commrs. Assn. (dir. 1981-84). Republican. Presbyterian. Office: 1001 Sixth St #401 Sacramento CA 95814-3324

MACDOWELL, PAUL WILLIAM, JR., finance executive; b. Denver, Colo., Apr. 14, 1925; s. Paul William and Jessica (Sechler) MacD.; m. Cynthia L. Tupper, May 1950 (div. May 1971); children: Barrie Rouse, Paul W. III, Tupper G., Peter C.; m. Genevieve Courtney, June 21, 1975. BSBA, U. Denver, 1949. Acct. Beatrice Foods Co., Denver, 1946-52; controller Mid-Continent Wholesale Co., Inc., Denver, 1952-69, v.p., 1970-84; treas. Colo. Corp., Denver, 1969-70; chief fin. officer Core Mark Mid-Continent, Inc., Denver, 1984-87, Bershof and Assoc., Inc., Denver, 1987—. Served to chief sgt. USAAC, 1943-45, PTO. Decorated with Air medal with two oak leaf clusters and one bronze star, Philippine Liberation medal. Republican. Episcopalian. Club: The Valley Country (Denver). Home: 7009 E Girard Ave Denver CO 80224 Office: Bershof & Assoc Inc 9745 E Hampden Ave Denver CO 80231

MACEK, ANNA MICHAELLA, cosmetics executive; b. Lancashire, Eng., Aug. 10, 1950; came to U.S., 1974; d. Wasyl and Maria (Litynska) Flaszczak; m. Frank Macek, Aug. 18, 1977. MA, U. Manchester, Eng., 1973; grad., Ecole des Estheticiennes Inst. de Beaute, Geneva, 1974. Asst. to pres., chief exec. officer Reed-Ingram Corp., N.Y.C., 1974-77; coordinator corp. pub. relations Northrop Corp., Los Angeles, 1978-82; pres. Annastasia Cosmetics, Gardena, Calif., 1983—. Contbr. articles to profl. jours. Mem. Beauty and Barber Supply Inst.

MACEK, CARL FRANK, JR., television and motion picture writer-producer, author; b. Pitts., Sept. 21, 1951; s. Carl F. and Leona (Felicione) M.; m. Joan Leasman (div.); m. Svea Stauch, Aug. 22, 1981. BA, Calif. State U., Fullerton, 1974, postgrad. in Am. studies, 1976. Producer, creative dir. Harmony Gold U.S.A., L.A., 1984-86; developer, story editor DIC Enterprises, Burbank, Calif., 1987-88; prin., founder Streamline Picutres, West Hollywood, Calif., 1989—; toy design cons. Palmtree Prodns., Santa Monica, Calif., 1987-88. Author: Heavy Metal Animation for the '80's, 1981, The Making of the Sentinels, 1988; co-editor: Film Noir, 1979, McGill's Survey of Cinema, 1980; producer TV series Robotech, 1985; writer, dir. motion picture Robotech, 1986. Recipient Inkpot award San Diego Comic Conv., 1980. Mem. Animation Writers Am. (founding), Am. Philatelic Soc. Republican. Home: PO Box 691418 West Hollywood CA 90069

MACELWEE, HELENE C., civic worker, club woman, business executive; b. Stevens Point, Wis.; d. Joseph Victor and Jeannette M. (Gasche) Collins; B.E., U. Wis., Stevens Point; postgrad. Carroll Coll.; B.Lit. Sci., U. Wis., Madison, 1918; m. Irvin Reed MacElwee, Dec. 29, 1927; children—Marilyn Jean Macelwee Throckmorton, Donald Beall. Dir. Fibremold, Inc., Woburn, Mass. Apptd. to 1960 Assay Commn. Mem. bd. Phila. Cancer Dr., 1954-64; hon. pres. St. Christopher's Hosp. Auxiliary, 1957-61. Mem. advisory com. Phila. Com. on Alcoholism. Pres. Pa. Council Republican Women, 1960-62; pres. Rep. Women Pa., 1954-60; mem. bd. Nat. Fedn. Rep. Women, 1960-64, mem. exec. bd., 1962-64; alternate del. Rep. Nat. Conv., 1972, 76. Bd. dirs. Soc. Retarded Children, March of Dimes, Phila., Women's Soc. Prevention Cruelty to Animals; active Tucson Symphony, 1978-82, Ariz. Theater Co. Recipient Plaque for citizenship work in Swarthmore, Lions Club, 1966; Alumni Achievement award, U. Wis., 1969. Mem. D.A.R. (Phila. chpt. regent 1956-59, state program chmn. 1957-67), Am. Acad. Polit. and Social Scis., Los Angeles Mus. Art, Daus. 17th Century, Colonial Dames Am., Needlework Guild Am. (dir. Swarthmore br. 1935-79), Woman's Med. Coll. Aux., Sons and Daus. Pilgrims, Soc. Preservation Old Landmarks, AAUW, Am. Contract Bridge Assn., Nat. Geog. Soc., U. Wis. Phila. Alumni Assn. (v.p. 1958-61, 64-69), Internat. Platform Assn., Smithsonian Assocs., Strawberry Mansion and Com. of 1926, Delta Zeta (dir. eastern region 1926-34). Presbyterian. Clubs: Nat. Travel; Union League; Springhaven Golf (Wallingford, Pa.); Capitol Hill (Washington). Home: care Murray 115 W Esperanza Blvd #1 Green Valley AZ 85614-2626

MACER, GEORGE ARMEN, JR., orthopedic hand surgeon; b. Pasadena, Calif., Oct. 17, 1948; s. George A. and Nevart Akullian M.; m. Celeste Angelle Lyons, Mar. 26, 1983; children: Christiana Marilu, Marina Lynn. BA, U. So. Calif., 1971, MD, 1976. Diplomate Am. Bd. Med. Examiners, Am. Bd. Orthopaedic Surgery. Intern Meml. Hosp. Med. Ctr., Long Beach, Calif., 1976; resident Orthopaedic Hosp. at U. S. Calif., 1977-81; pvt. practice hand surgery, Long Beach, 1981—; cons. Harbor UCLA Med. Ctr., Torrance, 1983—; asst. clin. prof. orthopaedics UCLA, 1983—. Joseph Boyes Hand fellow, 1982; mem. AMA, Calif. Med. Assn., L.A. County Med. Assn., Western Orthopaedic Assn., Am. Soc. for Surgery of Hand. Republican. Office: 701 E 28th St Ste 418 Long Beach CA 90806

MACEY, LAWRENCE HENRY, electrical engineering executive; b. Chgo., Feb. 26, 1948; s. Henry Hillary and Evelyn (Babincsak) M. BSEE, Purdue U., 1971. Engr. Northern Ind. Public Service Co., Hammond, Ind., 1971-74; sr. Southern Edison Co., Rosemead, Calif., 1974-78; sales Bussman Fuse, San Francisco, 1978-79; western sales mgr. HTC Corp., Los Angeles, 1979-81; nat. sales mgr. Consolidated Am. System, Los Angeles, 1981-85; chief exec. officer, design, mktg. L4 Technologies Ltd., Los Angeles, 1985—; cons. Hai Tek, Inc., Diamond Bar, Calif., 1986--, 21 Century Systems, Palm Springs, Calif., 1985--. Patentee in field. Mem. IEEE, Am. Vacuum Soc. Democrat. Roman Catholic. Home: 9111 Amethyst St Rancho Cucamonga CA 91730 Office: L4 Technologies 9111 Amethyst St Rancho Cucamonga CA 91730

MACFARLANE, GORDON FREDERICK, telephone company executive; b. Victoria, B.C., Can., Sept. 21, 1925; s. Frederick Randolph and Nora Margaret (La Fortune) MacF.; m. Hazel Louise Major, June 1946; children: Michael Gordon, Ann L. MacFarlane Patterson, Katherine M. MacFarlane Bernard. B.S.E.E., U. B.C. Chief engr., dir. plant services B.C. Telephone Co., Vancouver, 1966-67, v.p. ops., 1967-70, v.p. corp. devel., 1970-76, v.p. adminstr., 1976; chmn., chief exec. officer B.C. Telephone Co., Burnaby, 1977—; pres., chief exec. officer GTE Automatic Elec., Brockville, Ont., Can., 1976-77; chmn. Microtel Pacific Research Ltd.; chmn. Microtel Ltd.; chmn., pres., chief exec. officer North-West Telephone Co., dir. Air Can., Fletcher Challenge Canada Ltd., Telecom Leasing Can. Ltd., Can. Telephones and Supplies Ltd., BC Gas Inc.; bd. trustees Advanced Systems Found., Advanced Systems Inst. Mem. bd. govs. Vancouver Pub. Aquarium Assn. Recipient First Communications Can. award, 1988. Mem. IEEE, Assn. Profl. Engrs. B.C., Telephone Pioneers Am., Premier Econ. Adv. Council. Office: BC Telephone Co, 21-3777 Kingsway, Burnaby, BC Canada V5H 3Z7

MACGREGOR, DONALD LANE, JR., banker; b. Duluth, Minn., June 21, 1930; s. Donald Lane and Julia (Waldo) MacG.; m. Mary Jo Rouse, Sept. 27, 1959; children—Jeffrey Lane, Steven Scott, John Rouse. Student, Carleton Coll., 1948-51; B.A. in Econs., Macalester Coll., 1956. Asst. cashier 1st Nat. Bank of Mpls., 1956-61; v.p. United Calif. Bank, San Francisco, 1961-69; pres. Ormand Industries, Dallas, 1969-70; v.p. United Calif. Bank, Los Angeles, 1970-71; pres., chief operating officer Am. Security Bank (name now Interstate Bank of Hawaii), Honolulu, 1972-83, pres., chief exec. officer, 1983—. Hon. trustee Hawaii Army Mus. Soc., Honolulu, 1978—; bd. regents Chaminade U., Honolulu; trustee Hawaii Conf. Found., 1985—. Served to capt. USAF, 1951-55. Mem. Am. Bankers Assn. (leadership del. 1984—), Hawaii Bankers Assn., Hawaii C. of C. (bd. dirs. 1985—). Republican. Clubs: Outrigger Canoe, Pacific, Waialae Country (Honolulu). Office: First Interstate Bank Hawaii 1314 S King St Honolulu HI 96814

MACGREGOR, STEVEN DOUGLAS KRUCH, telecommunications official; b. Cleve., Nov. 14, 1957; s. Douglas Alfred and Claire (Snider) MacG.; m. Jane Elizabeth Kruchten, Sept. 6, 1986. BS in Bus., U. Colo., 1980. Lic. broker SEC. Keypunch supr. NCNB Nat. Bank, Raleigh, N.C., 1980-81, proof supr., 1981-83; mgr. verfications Oppenheimer Shareholder Svcs., Denver, 1983-84, mgr. quality assurance, 1984-86, mgr. telephone svcs., 1986-88, mgr. voice communication, 1988—. Mem. Tele-Communications Assn., Assn. Colo. Telecommunications Profls., Teknekron-Infoswitch Users Group. Office: Oppenheimer Shareholder Svc 3410 S Galena St Denver CO 80231

MACH, FRANKLIN CHRIST, aerospace manufacturing company executive; b. Wessington, S.D., Jan. 26, 1933; s. Anton Joseph and Hermina (Wormsbecker) M.; m. Linda Cargen, May 14,1983. BS, U. So. Miss., 1965; MS, Air Force Inst. Tech., 1968. Commd. 2d lt. USAF, 1954, advanced through grades to lt. col., 1972; ops. mgr. mil. assistance command USAF, Saigon, Vietnam, 1968-69; sr. cons. Am. mission USAF, Tehran, Iran, 1973-75; mgr. electronic warfare ops. USAF, Charleston, S.C., 1975-80; dep. dir., then exec. dir. def. contract mgmt. USAF, N.Y.C., 1980-84; ret. USAF, 1984; test dir. Rockwell Internat., Palmdale, Calif., 1985-88; mgr. quality assurance engring. Crane Co. Hydro-Aire div., Burbank, Calif., 1988—; cons. in computer-aided performance evaluation, Raleigh, N.C., 1984-85. Mem. Air Force Assn., Assn. Old Crows. Republican. Baptist. Home: 306 Susan Ct Palmdale CA 93551 Office: Crane Co Hydro-Aire Div 3000 Winona Ave Burbank CA 91510

MACHANIC, BENNETT IRVINE, neurologist; b. Burlington, Vt., June 3, 1943; s. Allen and Goldye Pearl (Seltzer) M.; m. Paula L. Nasbarg (div. 1985); 1 child, Adam Paul. BA, U. Vt., 1965; MD, Johns Hopkins U., 1969. Diplomate Am. Bd. Psychiatry and Neurology. Intern Georgetown U., Washington, 1969-70; neurology resident U. Calif., Los Angeles, 1972-76; fellow in neurology NIH, Los Angeles, 1975; asst. clin. prof. of neurology U. Colo., Denver, 1976—; neurologist Neurol. Cons., Denver, 1976—; chmn. neurology com., Rose Med. Ctr., Denver, 1978-82. Mem. Am. Acad. Neurology, Am. Assn. Electromyography and Electrophysiology, AMA, Colo. Soc. Clin. Neurologists (treas. 1978-80). Jewish. Office: Neurol Cons PC 4545 E 9th Ave #650 Denver CO 80220 also: Denver Injury Evaluation Treatment Ctr 1777 S Hanson Denver CO 80210

MACHON, RICHARD DANIEL, infosystems specialist; b. Boston, July 19, 1946; s. Charles Melville and Jesse Marie (Lebrocqvy) M.; m. Barbara Ann Saba, Dec. 10, 1967; children: Danielle, Emilie. BSME, Northeastern U., 1970. Registered profl. engr., Mass., N.Y. Test engr. Gen Dynamics, Groton, Conn., 1968-74; system engr. Yankee Atomic Electric Co., Westboro, Mass., 1974-77; plant mgr. Boston Editon, 1977-83; div. mgr. Impell Corp., Melville, N.Y., 1983-85; pres., gen. mgr. Impell Corp., Portland, Oreg., 1985—; bd. dirs. AppCo, Vancouver, Wash. Coach, Plymouth (Mass.) Youth Soccer, 1981-83, YMCA Soccer, L.I., N.Y., 1984-85, Columbia Youth Soccer, Vancouver, 1987—; chmn. Long Pond Assn., Plymouth, 1981-83. Roman Catholic. Home: 2801 SE Bella Vista Rd Vancouver WA 98684 Office: Impell Pacific 825 NE Mahnomah St Ste 1375 Portland OR 97232

MACIAS, DEAN RICHARD, interior designer; b. Keosauqua, Iowa, Mar. 28, 1958; s. Richard Jr. and Gertrude Mary (Stevenson) M. BS in Interior Design, San Jose State U., 1982. Designer Kyn/Hill Assocs., San Francisco, 1979-80; free-lance designer 1980-81, 85-86; designer Ruth and Going Inc., San Jose, Calif., 1981-82, Rick Guidice Design, Los Gatos, Calif., 1982-84; facilities designer, mgr. project Raychem Corp., Menlo Park, Calif., 1986—. Inventor portfolio case, 1988. Republican. Methodist. Home and Office: 1518 Lexington Dr San Jose CA 95117

MACIAS, JULIE ANN, interior designer; b. Long Beach, Calif., Apr. 1, 1967; d. Joel Joseph and Daniella (Misczcak) M. AA magna cum laude, The Fashion Inst. of Design & Merchandising, 1987. With sales dept. Handmade Sandals, Orange, Calif., 1983-84, Mayco Sales Assocs., Orange, 1984-86; interior designer, cons. Creative Design Cons., Costa Mesa, Calif., 1986—. Vocat. scholar Bank of Am., Orange, 1987; Crocsill scholar The Broadway, Los Angeles, 1987. Mem. Fashion Inst. Design and Merchandising Associated Student Body.

MACINTOSH, MICHAEL KIRK, minister; b. Portland, Oreg., Mar. 26, 1944; s. Wilbur MacIntosh and Ruth (Lane) Osborn; m. Sandra Crill Riddet, Apr. 3, 1971 (div. 1968), remarried Apr. 1971; children: Melinda, David, Megan, Jonathan, Phillip. M of Ministry, Azusa Pacific U., Calif., 1988, MDiv, 1989. Ordained to ministry Calvary Chapel, 1972. Asst. pastor Calvary Chapel, Santa Ana, Calif., 1971-72; dir. Maranatha Music, Santa Ana, Calif., 1972-74; pastor Horizon Christian Fellowship, San Diego, 1975—; pres. Youth Devel. Inc., San Diego, 1988—, Horizon Internat. Ministries, San Diego, 1980—; guest speaker Billy Graham Evang. Crusade, Anaheim, Calif., 1985. Author: Attributes of a Christian Woman, 1979, Finding God, 1989; creator, host TV program Wake Up America, 1977 (Emmy award); speaker various radio programs. Police chaplain San Diego Police Dept., 1988—, reserve officer, 1983-89; commr. San Diego Crime Commn., 1988-89; assisted in release of 7 Siberians from U.S. Embassy in Moscow, 1982. With USNG, 1962-65. Mem. San Diego Evang. Assn., Internat. Assn. Police Chaplains. Office: Horizon Internat 4575 Ruffner St San Diego CA 92111

MACK, BRENDA LEE, sociologist, public relations consulting company executive; b. Peoria, Ill., Mar. 24; d. William James and Virginia Julia (Pickett) Palmer; A.A., Los Angeles City Coll.; B.A. in Sociology, Calif. State U., Los Angeles, 1980; m. Rozene Mack, Jan. 13 (div.); 1 child, Kevin Anthony. Ct. clk. City of Blythe, Calif.; partner Mack Trucking Co., Blythe; ombudsman, sec. bus facilities So. Calif. Rapid Transit Dist., Los Angeles, 1974-81; owner Brenda Mack Enterprises, Los Angeles, 1981—; lectr., writer, radio and TV personality; co-originator advt. concept View/Door Project; pub. News from the United States newsletter through U.S. and Europe. Past bd. dirs. Narcotic Symposium, Los Angeles. Served with U.S. WAC. Mem. Women For, Calif. State U. Los Angeles Alumni, German-Am. C. of C. Home: 8749 Cattaraugus Ave Los Angeles CA 90034 Office: Brenda Mack Enterprises PO Box 5942 Los Angeles CA 90055

MACK, CHARLES DANIEL, III, labor union executive; b. Oakland, Calif., Apr. 16, 1942; s. Charles Daniel and Bernadine Zoe (Ferguson) M.; m. Marlene Helen Fagundes, Oct. 15, 1960; children—Tammy, Kelly, Kerry, Shannon. B.A., San Francisco State Coll., 1964. Truck driver Garrett Freight Lines, Emeryville, Calif., 1962-66; bus. agt. Teamsters Local No. 70, Oakland, 1966-70, sec.-treas., 1972—; legis. rep. Calif. Teamsters Pub. Affairs Council, Sacramento, 1970-71; trustee Western Conf. Teamsters Pension Trust Fund, 1980—, mem. policy com., 1980-82, pres. Teamsters' Joint Council 7, San Francisco, 1982—; rep. Internat. Botherhood Teamsters, Chauffeurs, Warehousemen & Helpers of Am., 1984—. Bd. dirs. Econ. Devel. Corp. of Oakland, 1980—, Pvt. Industry Council, Oakland, 1983-84, Children's Hosp. of East Bay, 1981-83, Calif. Compensation Ins. Fund, San Francisco, 1980-86, Alameda County Easter Seals, 1983-85, United Way, 1978-82. Democrat. Roman Catholic. Office: Teamsters' Joint Counc 7 Executive Pk Blvd Ste 2900 San Francisco CA 94134

MACK, JOANNE MARYLYNNE, anthropology educator, archaelogy researcher, consultant; b. San Francisco, July 16, 1943; d. Charles Fredrick and Eunice Helena (Humphreys) M.; m. James Joseph McKenna, Sept. 9, 1973; 1 child, Jeffrey William. AA, Coll. Marin, 1962; BA cum laude, San Francisco State Coll., 1964; MA, U. Wyo., 1971; PhD, U. Oreg., 1979. jr. coll. tchr., Calif. Instr. dept. anthropology U. Oreg., Eugene, 1972-74, research supr. aracheol. survey, 1975; researcher Galleries of Claremont Colls., Calif., 1979; asst. regional officer San Bernardino County Site Files Redlands, Calif., 1980; dean of freshmen Pomona Coll., Claremont, Calif., 1981-82, dir. freshman program, 1984, asst. prof. research assoc., 1988; instr. Mt. San Antonio Coll., Walnut, Calif., 1983-84, Riverside Community Coll., Calif., 1984-88; vis. researcher Lowie Mus. Anthropology, Berkeley, Calif., 1975-77; archaeol. supr. Mud Springs Lab., Redlands, 1979-88; archaeol. cons., Claremont, 1980—; ceramic cons. Infotec Rsch., Sonora, Calif., 1986—. Contbr. papers to profl. publs.; co-author: Native American Art from the Permanent Collection, 1979. Mem. Am. Anthropology Assn., Soc. Am. Archaeology, Am. Soc. Conservation Archaeology, AAAS, AAUP, Phi Kappa Phi. Office: Pomona Coll Dept Sociology and Anthropology Claremont CA 91711

MACK, SUSAN CATHERINE, advertising agency executive; b. Kansas City, Mo., Oct. 25, 1952; d. James Owen and Betty (Frey) M. BS in Journalism, W.Va. U., 1974. Copywriter Paris Dept. Store, Salt Lake City, 1974-75; advt. saleswoman Newspaper Agy. Corp., Salt Lake City, 1975-79; br. mgr. Thompson Recruitment Advt., Salt Lake City, 1979-83; pres. Mack Advt., Salt Lake City, 1983—. publicity chmn. Utah Heritage Found., Salt Lake City, 1986; vol. women's aux. U. Utah Hosp., Arboretum Guild. Mem. Utah Assn. Women Bus. Owners, Salt Lake Area C. of C. Democrat. Presbyterian. Office: Mack Advt 342 West 200 S Ste 125 Salt Lake City UT 84101

MACKAY, ALEXANDER RUSSELL, surgeon; b. Bottineau, N.D., Oct. 8, 1911; s. Alexander Russell and Eleanor (Watson) M.; BS, Northwestern U., 1932, MD, 1936; MS in Surgery, U. Minn., 1940; m. Marjorie Andres, July 16, 1941; children: Andrea, Alexander Russell. Intern, Med. Center, Jersey City, 1935-37; fellow in surgery Mayo Clinic, Rochester, Minn. 1937-41; practiced medicine specializing in gen. surgery, Spokane, Wash., 1941-82, now ret.; former staff Deaconess, Sacred Heart hosps., Spokane. Capt., M.C., AUS, 1942-45. Diplomate Am. Bd. Surgery. Fellow ACS; mem. Spokane Surg. Soc., North Pacific Surg. Assn., Alpha Omega Alpha, Phi Delta Theta, Nu Sigma Nu, Phi Beta Kappa. Home: E 540 Rockwood Blvd Spokane WA 99202

MACKAY, PATRICK MICHAEL, child care center executive; b. Duluth, Minn., Apr. 21, 1959; m. Tracey Martin, Mar. 3, 1979; children: Alisa Marie, April Michelle. Founder, dir. Agape Child Care Ctr., Seattle, 1982--; dir. children's ministry Calvary Fellowship Ch., Seattle, 1985-86; cons., 1980--. Mem. Nat. Assn. for Edn. Young Children, Child Care Dirs. Assn. Greater Seattle, Greater Seattle C. of C. Office: Agape Child Care Ctr 4400 Interlake Ave N Seattle WA 98103

MACKENROTH, JOYCE ELLEN, teacher; b. Portland, Oreg., June 22, 1946; d. Ferrel Adelbert and Ellen Ellenora (Setala) McKinney; m. Glen MacKenroth, Sept. 21, 1968; 1 child, Tonia Lynn. BS, Western Oreg. State Coll., 1968; postgrad. U. Oreg., 1980, 81, 83, 85, Portland State U., 1984. Cert. elem. tchr., Oreg. Salesperson Avon, Tucson, Toledo, 1969-70, 73-77; tchr. Lincoln County Sch. Dist., Newport, Oreg., 1970—; bd. dirs. Curriculum Coordinating Council, Newport; computer instr. and coordinator Lincoln County Sch. Dist., 1984-87; mem. various lang. arts and writing coms., 1981—. Sec. State Assn. Pagent Bds., Seaside, Oreg., 1984-85; active Miss Lincoln County Scholarship Pagent, Toledo, Oreg., 1979-87; founder, pres. Youth Activities Council, 1988. Mem. Internat. Reading Assn., Oreg. Reading Assn., Seacoast Reading Assn., Oreg. Edn. Assn. (uniserv treas. 1979-81, bd. dirs. 1981-82), Lincoln County Edn. Assn. (sec. 1974, v.p. 1975, pres. 1976, 81), NEA, Bus. and Profl. Women, Beta Sigma Phi (sec. 1983-84, v.p. 1985-86, pres. 1986—). Democrat. Home: 264 NE 1st Toledo OR 97391 Office: Toledo Mid Sch 600 SE Sturdevant Rd Toledo OR 97391

MACKENZIE, MARY THERESA, director of human resources; b. Quincy, Mass., May 18, 1952; d. Paul James and Teresa Ann (Mullen) MacK. Student, Champlain Coll., 1970-71, Northeastern U., 1973. Dir. food services Ventura TowneHouse, Ventura, Calif., 1980-82; personnel Channel Island Community Hosp., Oxard, Calif., 1982-86; human resources AMI-Rancho Encino Hosp., Encino, Calif., 1986--; advisory bd. mem. West Valley Occupational Ctr., Woodland Hills, Calif., 1987-88. Com. chairperson, Encino Health Faire, 1987; United Way, 1985-87; mem. United Way Allocation Com., Ventura, Calif., 1985. Mem. Healthcare Human Resources Mgmt. Assn., Women in Healthcare Adnimstrn., Bus. and Profl. Women (sec. 1985, treas. 1986). Republican. Roman Catholic.

MACKENZIE, STUART IAN GUSTAV, lawyer; b. Toronto, Dec. 24, 1952; came to U.S., 1954; s. Ian and Inger Maria (Delbanco) MacK. Student, U. Calif., Santa Barbara, 1971-73; BA in Rhetoric, U. Calif., Berkeley, 1976; JD, Golden State U., San Francisco, 1979, LLM in Taxation, 1986. Bar: Calif. 1980. Sole practice Oakland, Calif., 1980—. Mem. MENSA. Home: 9057 Skyline Blvd Oakland CA 94611 Office: 5920 Thornton Ave Ste D Newark CA 94560

MACKIE, WILLIAM BRUCE, comptroller; b. New Rochelle, N.Y., Nov. 7, 1942; s. Joseph Fleming Mackie and Gladys Leslie (Craigans) Kemp; m. Margaret Ann Davis, June 5, 1965; children: Mary Louise, Diana Leigh. BS in Health Svcs. Adminstrn., George Washington U., 1980, MBA, 1982. Enlisted USN, 1960, advanced through grades to lt. comdr., Med. Svc. Corps, 1986, hosp. corpsman, 1960-76; systems analyst med. command Naval Aerospace Med. Inst. USN, Washington, 1981-83, program analyst chief naval ops., 1983-84; head hosp. fiscal dept. U.S. Naval Hosp., Guantanamo Bay, Cuba, 1976-79; compt. U.S. Naval Hosp., Portsmouth, Va., 1984-88; dir. adminstrn. U.S. Naval Hosp., Twentynine Palms, Calif., 1988—. Mem. Am. Soc. Mil. Comptrollers, Am. Assn. Individual Investors (life), VFW. Presbyterian. Office: Naval Hosp MCAGCC Twentynine Palms CA 92278

MACKINTOSH, FREDERICK ROY, oncologist; b. Miami, Fla., Oct. 4, 1943; s. John Harris and Mary Carlotta (King) MacK.; m. Judith Jane Parnell, Oct. 2, 1961 (div. Aug. 1977); children: Lisa Lynn, Wendy Sue; m. Claudia Lizanne Flournoy, Jan. 7, 1984. BS, MIT, 1964, PhD, 1968; MD, U. Miami, 1976. Intern then resident in gen. medicine Stanford (Calif.) U., 1976-78, fellow in oncology, 1978-81; asst. prof. med. U. Nev., Reno, 1981-85, assoc. prof., 1985—. Contbr. articles to profl. jours. Fellow ACP; mem. Am. Soc. Clin. Oncology, Am. Cancer Soc. (pres. Nev. div. 1985, pres. 1987—), No. Nev. Cancer Council (bd. dirs. 1981—, pres.-elect 1985-87, pres. 1987-89), No. Calif. Cancer Program (bd. dirs. alt. 1983-87, bd. dirs. 1987—). Office: Nev Med Group 781 Mill St Reno NV 89502

MACKLER, SCOTT EDWARD, sales executive; b. Springfield, Mass., Feb. 25, 1954; s. Leslie George and Ruth (Goldman) M.; m. Deborah I. Friedman, May 24, 1987. BSME, Rensselaer Poly. Inst., 1976; MBA, U. Houston, 1987. Eng. Union Carbide, Linde div., Tonawanda, N.Y., 1976-78; asst. staff engr. Union Carbide, Linde div., 1978-79; staff engr. Union Carbide, EP&P, Tarrytown, N.Y., 1979-81; project engr. Union Carbide, EP&P, 1981-82; account rep. Union Carbide, EP&P, Houston, 1982-84; sr. account rep. Union Carbide, EP&P, 1984-85, tech. licensing mgr., 1985-87; mgr. tech. sales UOP Inc., Garden Grove, Calif., 1987—. Contbr. articles to profl. jours. Mem. L.A. World Affairs Council. Mem. Assn. MBA Execs., Pacific Energy Assn., Am. Inst. Chem. Engrs., Am. PetroleumInst., Licensing Execs. Soc., Nat. Petroleum Refining Assn., U. Houston Alumni Assn. Office: UOP Inc 12399 Lewis St #201 Garden Grove CA 90803

MACKNIGHT, MILDRED HOOVER, nurse; b. Ord, Nebr., Apr. 3, 1914; d. Joseph Edward and Hazel Vivian (Cummings) Hoover; m. Walter K. MacKnight, Dec. 20, 1942 (dec. 1944); 1 child, Jerri Kaye. Diploma, Mont. Deaconess Hosp. Sch. Nursing, 1935. RN Mont., Ill. Head nurse surg.

Mont. Deaconess Hosp., Great Falls, 1935-37; nurse VA, Dwight, Ill., 1937-41, Bronx, N.Y., 1941-43; nurse Great Falls Clinic, 1944-48; dep. chief nurse ARC Blood Program, Great Falls and Chgo., 1948-52; nurse Dr. Andrew J. McGee Office, Dwight, 1952-60; nurse student health U. Mont., Missoula, 1960-64; nurse occupational health Chgo. Title and Trust Co., 1968-76, CNA, Chgo., 1976—. Contbr. articles to newspapers. Democrat. Roman Catholic.

MACLAREN, WALTER ROGERS, allergist, educator; b. Yokohama, Japan, Dec. 7, 1910; s. Walter Wallace and Zaidee (Rogers) McL.; m. Dorothy Agnes Goodwin, June 1942 (div. 1970); children: Walter Jr., Jean, Anne, Elizabeth, Catherine; m. Dorothy Hamblen, July 7, 1971. BA, Queens U., 1933; MD, Harvard U., 1938. Diplomate Am. Bd. Allergy and Immunology (bd. dirs., sec. 1978-83). Practice medicine specializing in asthma, allergy and immunology Pasadena, Calif., 1947—; clin. prof. medicine U. So. Calif. Sch. Med., Los Angeles, 1948—; dir. Allergy and Immunology Cons. Labs., Inc., Pasadena, 1978—. Contbr. 32 articles to profl. jours. Bd. dirs. Pasadena Symphony Orch., 1976-82, Pasadena Chamber Orch., 1984-86. Fellow Am. Acad. Allergy and Immunology, Am. Coll. Allergists, Assn. Clin. Immunology and Allergy (pres.), Sigma Xi. Republican. Club: Valley Hunt (Pasadena). Office: 94 N Madison Ave Pasadena CA 91101

MACLAUCHLIN, ROBERT KERWIN, communications artist, educator; b. Framingham, Mass., Oct. 8, 1931; s. Charles Lewis and Elinor Frances (Kerwin) MacL.; m. Elizabeth D'Ann Willson, June 13, 1964. BA in Sociology, U. Mass., Amherst, 1954; MEd, Bridgewater State Coll., 1958; MS in Radio and TV, Syracuse U., 1959; PhD in Speech, Radio, TV, Mich. State U., 1969. Personnel trainee Nat. Security Agy., Washington, 1954-55; elem. sch. tchr. Mattapoisett (Mass.) Pub. Schs., 1957-58; asst. prof., dir. programming Maine Ednl. TV Network, Orono, 1959-66; assoc. prof. speech communications, dir. TV-Radio instrn. Colo. State U., Ft. Collins, 1969-76, prof., dir. TV-Radio instrn., 1976—; cons. U. Maine, Orono, 1968, Ft. Collins Presbyn. Ch., 1976-78, Sta. KCOL-AM-FM, Ft. Collins, 1978, Pub. Health Assn., Ft. Collins, 1985; archives program guest Maine Pub. Broadcast, Orono, 1983. Served with inf. U.S. Army, 1955-57. Recipient Excellence in Teaching award Mich. State U., 1969, Friend of Broadcasting award Colo. Broadcasters Assn., 1985; named Disting. Vis. Prof. U. Vt., Burlington, 1983, A Teacher Who Makes A Difference Denver's Rocky Mountain News, KCNC-TV, 1987. Mem. NATAS (panelist Colo. chpt. 1989—), Broadcast Edn. Assn. (panelist 1989—), Colo. Broadcasters Assn. (edn. com. 1972—, Hall of Fame com. 1980—, Friend of Broadcast award 1985), Western Speech Communications Assn., Speech Communications Assn., Broadcast Edn. Assn. Industry State (chmn. 1981-86), State Assn. Communications (chmn. 1981-86). Republican. Lodge: Kiwanis (Ft. Collins chpt. Disting. Past Pres. 1979-80). Home: 1407 Country Club Rd Fort Collins CO 80524 Office: Colo State U Dept Speech Communication Fort Collins CO 80523

MACLEOD, JACK (J. M. MACLEOD), oil company executive; b. Beddeck, N.S., Can., 1931; m. Beverley Ann Thurston; children: Heather, Carol, Sandra. Alan. B in Engring., Tech. U. N.S., Halifax, 1954, D in Engring. (hon.), 1982, DCL (hon.), 1987. Petroleum engr. Shell Can. Ltd., Calgary, Alta., 1954-69, mgr. dept. prodn., 1969-71, gen. mgr. frontier div., exploration and prodn., 1971-72; gen. mgr. prodn. Shell Can. Ltd., Calgary, 1972-73; gen. mgr. supply & logistics Shell Can. Ltd., Toronto, Ont., 1973-75; v.p. corp. planning and pub. affairs Shell Can. Ltd., Calgary, 1975-77, v.p. exploration and prodn., sr. v.p. resources, 1977-82, exec. v.p., 1982-83, pres., chief exec. officer, 1985—, also bd. dirs.; coord. natural gas Shell Internat. Petroleum Co., London, 1983-85; chmn. C.D. Howe Inst. Bd. dirs. The Coun. for Can. Unity, The Coun. for Bus. and the Arts in Can. Mem. Assn. Profl. Engrs. Geologists and Geophysicists Alta., Can. Inst. Mining and Metallurgy, Bus. Coun. on Nat. Issues, Calgary Petroleum Club, Calgary Golf and Country Club, Mississauga Golf and Country Club. Office: Shell Can Ltd, 400 4th Ave SW, Calgary, AB Canada T2P 0J4

MACLEOD, NORMAN CLOUD, electronics company executive; b. Bristol, Pa., Feb. 16, 1931; s. William Cloud and Viola (Kath) MacL.; m. Ruth Lillian Helm, Dec. 15, 1951; children: Ronald, Alan, Brian. Student, Menlo Coll., 1949-50, Naval Electronics Inst., 1950-51, Philco Inst., 1956-57. Project mgr. Astro Tech. Corp., Mountain View, Calif., 1963-67; program mgr. Ford Aerospace, Palo alto, Calif., 1967-69; program mgr. Dalmo Victor div. Textron Ford Aerospace, Belmont, Calif., 1969-71; program mgr. RAndtron Systems Loral, Menlo Park, Calif., 1979-80; v.p. rsch. Intersci. systems, San Jose, Calif., 1971-72, Farallon Industries, Belmont, 1972-77; dir. Tech. Devel. Corp., Sunnyvale, Calif., 1977-78; chmn. MacLeod Labs., Inc., San Jose, 1981-86; pres. Metrotech Corp., Mountain View, 1986—; bd. dirs. Macrowave Tech. Corp., Sunnyvale. Patentee in field. Pres. Sunnyvale PTA, 1969. With USN, 1950-55. Mem. IEEE, soc. Petroleum Engrs., Am. Mgt. Assn., Masons. Home: 1142 Revere Dr Sunnyvale CA 94087 Office: Metrotech Corp 331 Fairchild Dr Mountain View CA 94043

MACMILLAN, DANIEL JAMES, petroleum engineer, researcher; b. Denver, June 9, 1953; s. Joseph Ellsworth and Virginia Marie (Massard) M.; m. Lois Betty Doolittle, May 31, 1986; 1 child, Michelle Renae. BS in Chem. Engring., U. Colo., 1976; MS in Math., Colo. Sch. of Mines, Golden, 1985. Registered profl. engr., Colo. Advanced engr. Marathon Oil Co., Littleton, Colo., 1976--. Author: The Gambler's Palm Revisted, 1977; contbr. articles to profl. jours. Mem. Am. Inst. Mech. Engrs., Soc. Petroleum Engrs. of Am. Inst. Mech. Engrs., Mile High Magicians Soc. (v.p. 1977-78), Soc. for Indsl. and Applied Maths. Republican. Home: 1290 E Jamison Ave Littleton CO 80122 Office: Marathon Oil Co 7400 S Broadway Littleton CO 80122

MACMILLAN, ROBERT SMITH, electronics engineer; b. L.A., Aug. 28, 1924; s. Andrew James and Moneta (Smith) M.; BS in Physics, Calif. Inst. Tech., 1948, MS in Elec. Engring., 1949, PhD in Elec. Engring. and Physics cum laude, 1954; m. Barbara Macmillan, Aug. 18, 1962; 1 son, Robert G. Rsch. engr. Jet Propulsion lab. Calif. Inst. Tech., Pasadena, 1951-55, asst. prof. elec. engring., 1955-58; assoc. prof. elec. engring. U. So. Calif., L.A., 1958-70; mem. sr. tech. staff Litton Systems, Inc., Van Nuys, Calif., 1969-79; dir. systems engring. Litton Data Command Systems, Agoura Hills, Calif., 1979—; treas., v.p. Video Color Corp., Inglewood, 1965-66. Cons. fgn. tech. div. USAF, Wright-Patterson AFB, Ohio, 1957-74, Space Tech. Labs., Inglewood, Calif., 1956-60, Space Gen. Corp., El Monte, Calif., 1960-63. With USAAF, 1943-46. Mem. IEEE, Am. Inst. Physics, Am. Phys. Soc., Sigma Xi, Tau Beta Pi, Eta Kappa Nu. Research in ionospheric, radio-wave, propagation; very low frequency radio-transmitting antennas; optical coherence and statist. optics. Home: 350 Starlight Crest Dr La Canada CA 91011 Office: Litton Data Command Systems 29851 Agoura Rd Agoura Hills CA 91301

MACMULLEN, DOUGLAS BURGOYNE, writer, editor, retired army officer, publisher; b. Berkeley, Calif., Dec. 26, 1919; s. T. Douglas and Florence (Burgoyne) MacM.; ed. San Francisco State U., 1937-41, Stanford U., U. Calif., Fgn. Service Inst., Air War Coll., Army Mgmt. Sch.; m. Sherry Bernice Auerbach, Mar. 11, 1942; 1 son, Douglas Burgoyne. Commd. 2d lt. F.A. Res. U.S. Army, 1941; advanced through grades to col. M.I., 1967; Army gen. staff Psychol. Ops. Fgn. Svc., PTO; ret., 1972; exec. editor Am. Research Assoc., Sherman Oaks, Calif.; cons. in communication; accredited corr. Def. Dept. Bd. govs. Monte Vista Grove Homes, Pasadena, Calif., Shriners Hosps. for Crippled Children, L.A.; pres. Clan MacMillan Soc. N.Am., 1973-77, trustee, 1975—; mem. L.A. Olympics Citizens Adv. Commn., 1982-84; mem. L.A. Philanthropic Found.; bd. dirs. Masonic Press Club, Los Angeles, 1975, 84-88; mem. steering com. Mayor Los Angeles Council Internat. Visitors and Sister Cities, 1969; chmn. Los Angeles-Glasgow Sister Cities Ad Hoc Com.; former mem. San Francisco Mayor's Mil. and Naval Affairs Com.; mem. wills and gifts com. Shriners Hosp. Crippled Children, Al Malaikah Temple, Los Angeles, 1974-80; cons. com. on pub. info. Masons Grand Lodge of Calif., 1985-86. Decorated Legion of Merit, Army Commendation medal (U.S.), Red Cross of Constantine; Knight Royal Order Scotland. Mem. Internat. Inst. Strategic Studies, Nat. Mil. Intelligence Assn., Assn. Former Intelligence Officers (pres. chpt.), U.S. Naval Inst., Assn. U.S. Army, Company Mil. Historians, Am. Def. Preparedness Assn., St. Andrew's Soc. Los Angeles (past pres., trustee), Air Force Assn., Stanford U. Alumni Assn., Calif. Newspaper Pubs. Assn., Nat. Def. Exec. Res., Sigma Delta Chi. Republican. Presbyterian. Clubs: Press, Caledonian (London); San Francisco Press. Lodges: Masons (32 deg.), K.T., Shriners (editor, pub. The Al Malaikahan, imperial news editor Shrine of N.Am.), Quatuor Coronati C.C. Co-author: Psychological Profile of Cambodia, 1971; author-editor: A Sentimental Journey--The History of the First Hundred Years, 1988; numerous other publs. and articles; radio commentator and newspaper columnist on mil., polit. and internat. affairs. Address: PO Box 5201 Sherman Oaks CA 91413

MACNAMARA, ROBERT A., real estate executive; b. San Francisco, June 7, 1947; s. Arthur George and Jean Catherine (Hird) M.; m. Susan Spurgin (div. 1984); 1 child, Kelly. BA, Occidental Coll., 1969. Tchr., adminstr. Brentwood Sch., L.A., 1973-76; account exec. Merrill Lynch, Beverly Hills, Calif., 1976-78; real estate exec. Daley Corp., San Diego, 1978--; bd. dirs. Comml. Indsl. Council San Diego, 1988--. Trustee, San Diego Repertory Theater. Mem. Bldg. Industry Assn., Golden Eagle Club San Diego. Republican. Home: 13258 Ocean Vista Rd San Diego CA 92130 Office: Daley Corp PO Box 20188 San Diego CA 92120

MACNAUGHTON, ANGUS ATHOLE, finance company executive; b. Montreal, Que., Can., July 15, 1931; s. Athole Austin and Emily Kidder (MacLean) MacN.; children—Gillian Heather, Angus Andrew. Student, Lakefield Coll. Sch., 1941-47, McGill U., 1949-54. Auditor Coopers & Lybrand, Montreal, 1949-55; acct. Genstar Ltd., Montreal, 1955; asst. treas. Genstar Ltd., 1956-61, treas., 1961-64, v.p., 1964-70, exec. v.p., 1970-73, pres., 1973-76, vice chmn., chief exec. officer, 1976-81, chmn. or pres., chief exec. officer, 1981-86; pres. Genstar Investment Corp., 1987—; bd. dirs. Can. Pacific Ltd., Sun Life Assurance Co. Can. Ltd., Am. Barrick Resources Corp., Stelco Inc., Varian Assocs. Inc.; past pres. Montreal chpt. Tax Exec. Inst. Bd. govs. Lakefield Coll. Sch.; sr. mem. Conf. Bd. N.Y.; bd. dirs. San Francisco Bay Area Council, Boy Scouts Am. Mem. Pacific Union, World Trade Club (San Francisco), Mount Royal (Montreal), Toronto Club. Office: Genstar Investment Corp 801 Montgomery St Ste 500 San Francisco CA 94133 also: Am Barrick Resources Corp, 24 Hazelton Ave, Toronto, ON Canada M5R 2E2

MAC NEIL, JOSEPH NEIL, archbishop; b. Sydney, N.S., Can., Apr. 15, 1924; s. John Martin and Kate (Mac Lean) Mac N. BA, St. Francis Xavier U., Antigonish, N.S., 1944; postgrad., Holy Heart Sem., Halifax, N.S., 1944-48, U. Perugia, 1956, U. Chgo., 1964; JCD, U. St. Thomas, Rome, 1958. Ordained priest Roman Cath. Ch., 1948. Pastor parishes in N.S., 1948-55; officialis Chancery Office, Antigonish, 1958-59; adminstr. Diocese of Antigonish, 1959-60; rector Cathedral Antigonish, 1961; dir. extension dept. St. Francis Xavier U., Antigonish, 1961-69, v.p., 1962-69; bishop St. John, N.B., Can., 1969-73; archbishop of Edmonton, Alta., 1973—; chancellor U. St. Thomas, Fredericton, N.B., 1969-73. Vice chmn. N.S. Voluntary Econ. Planning Bd., 1965-69; exec. Atlantic Provinces Econ. Council, 1968-73, Can. Council Rural Devel., 1965-75; bd. dirs. Program and Planning Agy. N.S. Govt., 1969, Futures Secretariat, 1981, Ctr. for Human Devel., Toronto, Ont., Can., 1985—. Mem. Canadian Assn. Adult Edn. (past pres. N.S.), Canadian Assn. Dirs. Univ. Extension and Summer Schs. (past pres.), Inst. Research on Public Policy (founding mem.), Can. Conf. Cath. Bishops (pres. 1979-81, mem. comm. on ecumenism 1985—). Address: Archbishop of Edmonton, 10044 113th S., Edmonton, AB Canada T5K 1N8

MACQUEEN, ROBERT MOFFAT, solar physicist; b. Memphis, Mar. 28, 1938; s. Marion Leigh and Grace (Gilfillan) MacQ.; m. Caroline Gibbs, June 25, 1960; children: Andrew, Marjorie. BS, Rhodes Coll., 1960; PhD, Johns Hopkins U., 1968. Asst. prof. physics Rhodes Coll., 1961-63; instr. physics and astronomy Goucher Coll., Towson, Md., 1964-66; sr. research scientist Nat. Ctr. for Atmospheric Research, Boulder, Colo., 1967—, dir. High Altitude Obs., 1979-86, asst. dir., 1986-87, assoc. dir., 1987-89; prin. investigator NASA Apollo program, 1971-75, NASA Skylab program, 1970-76, NASA Solar Maximum Mission, 1976-79, NASA/ESA Internat. Solar Polar Mission, 1978-83; lectr. U. Colo., 1968-79, adj. prof., 1979—; mem. com. on space astronomy Nat. Acad. Scis., 1973-76, mem. com. on space physics, 1977-79; mem. Space Sci. Bd., 1983-86. Recipient Exceptional Sci. Achievement medal NASA, 1974. Fellow Optical Soc. Am.; mem. Am. Astron. Soc. (chmn. solar physics div. 1976-78), Assn. Univ. Research Astronomy (dir.-at-large 1984—, chmn. bd. 1989—), Am. Assn. Physics Tchrs., Sigma Xi. Home: 1366 Northridge Ct Boulder CO 80304 Office: Nat Ctr Atmospheric Rsch 1850 Table Mesa Dr PO Box 3000 Boulder CO 80307

MACY, GARY ALLAN, history educator; b. Milw., Mar. 24, 1950; s. Leland Francis and Joan Marie (LaValle) M.; m. Saralynn T. Ferrara, June 20, 1987. BA, Marquette U., 1971, MA, 1973; PhD, U. Cambridge (Eng.), 1978. Prof. history U. San Diego. Author: Theologies of the Eucharist, 1984. Founding mem. Peace Through Law Inst., San Diego, 1987. Recipient Best Fictional Honor award Assoc. Ch. Press, 1984. Mem. Ecclesiastical History Soc. Eng., Coll. Theology Soc., Medieval Acad. Am., Am. Cath. Hist. Soc. Office: U San Diego Alcala Park San Diego CA 92110

MADANI, SAM MOHAMMAD, electrical engineer, researcher; b. Teheran, Iran, Mar. 21, 1953; came to U.S., 1979; s. Mir Ahmad and Mansour (Khanome) S-M. BS, Teheran U., 1975; BSEE, U. Colo., Denver, 1985; MSEE, U. Colo., Boulder, 1988. Project mgr. A.S. Co. Ltd., Altricham, Cheshire, Eng., 1978-79; rsch. asst. U. Colo., Boulder, 1983-87; data analyst NOAA, Boulder, 1988-89; corp. tech. specialist Hwelett-Packard, Palo Alto, Calif., 1989—. Mem. Am. Phys. Soc., Optical Soc. Am., SPIE, Eta Kappa Nu, Tau Beta Pi. Home: 20875 Valley Green Dr #102 Cupertino CA 95014 Office: Hewlett-Packard MS 20CX 3000 Hanover St Palo Alto CA 94304

MADDEN, NENA, therapist, director; b. Big Rapids, Mich., Dec. 26, 1948; d. Dean Sherman and Mary Louise (Brack) Arnold; m. John Anthony Scuderi Jr.; children: Keesha Lisbeth, Peter Michael. Cert. therapy, Massage Inst. Am., 1985. Bookkeeper various orgns., Van Nuys, Calif., 1971—; pvt. practice Van Nuys, 1981—; v.p., mgr. Mad-Den, Inc., Van Nuys, 1982—; co-owner, trainer Anthony Brito Seminars, Sherman Oaks, Calif., 1987—; founder, dir. Pinnacle-Wellness, Caring & Sharing Ctr., Sherman Oaks, 1988—; co-owner, co-writer Creative Empathics, Sherman Oaks, 1989—. Editor, graphic artist: Things You Never Learned in School or at Home, 1988; screenwriter: Cause and Effect. Office: Creative Empathics 13601 Ventura Blvd Ste 193 Sherman Oaks CA 91423

MADDEN, PAUL R., lawyer; b. St. Paul, Nov. 13, 1926; s. Ray Joseph and Margaret (Meyer) M.; student St. Thomas Coll., 1944; AB, U. Minn., 1948; JD, Georgetown U., 1951; m. Rosemary R. Sorel, Aug. 7, 1974; children—Margaret Jane, William, James Patrick, Derek R. Sorel, Lisa T. Sorel. Admitted to Ariz., Minn., D.C. bars; asso. firm Hamilton & Hamilton, Washington, 1951-55; legal asst. to commr. S.C., Washington, 1955-56; asso. Lewis and Roca, Phoenix, 1957-59, partner, 1959—; counsel to The Indsl Devel. Authority of City of Phoenix; asso. gen. counsel Blood Systems, Inc., Scottsdale, Ariz. Sec. Minn. Fedn. Coll. Rep. Clubs, 1947-48; chmn. 4th dist. Minn. Young Rep. Club, 1948; nat. co-chmn. Youth for Eisenhower, 1951-52; mem. Ariz. Rep. Com., 1960-62; bd. dirs., past. pres. Ariz. Club, Phoenix, Mesa Airlines, Farmington, N.Mex., East Valley Cultrual Alliance, Mesa, Mesa Symphony Orch.; bd. dirs., past chmn. Found. for Sr. Living, Phoenix; bd. dirs., vice chmn., Cen. Ariz. chpt. ARC; past bd. dirs., past pres. Jr. Achievement Cen. Ariz., Inc.; bd. dirs. Camelback Hosps., Inc., Scottsdale. With USNR, 1946-48. Mem. Am., Ariz., Maricopa County, Fed. Bar Assns., Internat. Assn. Ins. Counsel, Fedn. Ins. Counsel, Nat. Health Lawyers Assn., Am. Soc. Hosp. Attys., Nat. Assn. Bond Lawyers, Ariz. Assn. for Indsl. Devel., East Valley Partnership, Phi Delta Phi. Clubs: The Barristers (Washington), Arizona. Home: 3732 E Pierson St Phoenix AZ 85018 Office: 100 W Washington Phoenix AZ 85003

MADDEN, RICHARD BLAINE, forest products executive, educator; b. Short Hills, N.J., Apr. 27, 1929; s. James L. and Irma (Twining) M.; m. Joan Fairbairn, May 24, 1958; children: John Richard, Lynn Marie, Kathryn Ann, Andrew Twining. B.S., Princeton U., 1951; J.D., U. Mich., 1956; M.B.A., NYU, 1959. Bar: Mich. 1956, N.Y. 1958. Gen. asst. treas.'s dept. Socony Mobil Oil Corp., N.Y.C., 1956-57; spl. asst. Socony Mobil Oil Corp., 1958-59, fin. rep., 1960; asst. to pres. Mobil Chem. Co.; also dir. Mobil Chems. Ltd. of Eng., 1960-63; exec. v.p., gen. mgr. Kordite Corp.; also v.p. Mobil Plastics, 1963-66; v.p. Mobil Chem. Co., N.Y.C., 1966-68; group v.p. Mobil Chem. Co., 1968-70; asst. treas. Mobil Oil Corp., 1970-71; chmn. Mobil Oil Estates Ltd., 1970-71; pres., chief exec. to chmn., chief exec. officer Potlatch Corp., San Francisco, 1971—; bd. dirs. Pacific Gas and Electric Co.; from lectr. to adj. assoc. prof. fin. NYU, 1960-63. Bd. dirs. Am. Paper Inst., Nat. Park Found.; trustee, exec. com. Am. Enterprise Inst.; bd. govs. San Francisco Symphony; bd. dirs. San Francisco Opera Assn. Lt. (j.g.) USNR, 1951-54. Mem. N.Y., Mich. bar assns. Roman Catholic. Clubs: University (N.Y.C.); Pacific Union (San Francisco), Bohemian (San Francisco); Lagunitas (Ross, Calif.); Metropolitan (Washington).

MADDEN, TIMOTHY JOHN, writer, editor; b. American Fork, Utah, Oct. 13, 1943; s. John Edward and Hazel (Monson) M.; m. Kristin Alice Moren; children: Kirin Leslie, Jonathan Tyler. BA, U. Utah, 1980; cert., Def. Lang. Inst. Writer AP, Buffalo; broadcast exec. AP, Salt Lake City, 1972-78; pub. rels. specialist Primary Children's Hosp., Salt Lake City, 1980-84; sr. editor, writer Latter Day Saints Hosp., Salt Lake City, 1984—. Writer, editor med. manuals. Purchasing agt., St. Paul's Episcopal Ch., Salt Lake City, 1983—; del., Utah State Dem. party, Salt Lake City, 1985; bd. dirs., Nat. Kidney Found. Utah, 1987—. With U.S. Army, 1963-66, USNR, 1980—. Mem. Internat. Assn. Bus. Communicators (bd. dirs. Utah chpt. 1983-87), Utah Soc. Hosp. Mktg. and Pub. Rels., Kappa Tau Alpha. Democrat. Home: 2175 S 19th E Salt Lake City UT 84106 Office: LDS Hosp 8th Ave at C St Salt Lake City UT 84106

MADDOCK, ROSEMARY SCHROER, library administrator; b. Coldwater, Ohio, Dec. 19, 1919; d. Henry Herman and Rose Elizabeth (Schlagheck) Schroer; m. Ernest A. Maddock, May 28, 1942 (div. 1951); children: Ernest H., Barbara A., Rosemary E. BE, Bowling Green State U., 1941; MS in Adminstrn., Cen. Mich. State U., 1976; postgrad., U. Ariz. Tchr. math. and sci. Ohio Pub. Schs., Spencerville, Grafton, and Coldwater, 1941-45; radio-chemistry rsch. asst. U. Mich., Ann Arbor, 1952-63; technical info. specialist Analytical Chemistry div. Nat. Bur. Standards, Washington, 1975-79, writer-editor tech. pubs. Nat. Measurement Lab., 1979-81; asst. to curator of collections Ariz. State Mus. U. Ariz., Tucson, 1982-86, film library admistr./researcher, 1986-88; with NSF-Ariz. Accelerator Mass Spectrometry Facility NSF, Tucson, 1988—. Author, editor: Radiochemistry Monographs, 1959-62; asst. editor: ULTRASONIC IMAGING, 1979-81; contbr. articles to profl. jours. Vol. Archeology dept. Ariz. State Mus., 1982-87; program coord. Nuclear Chemistry Monographs, 1963-65. Recipient Bronze award U.S. Dept. Commerce, 1973; Spl. Act award Nat. Bur. Standards, 1980. Mem. Soc. for Tech. Communications (Spl. Merit award 1980), Soc. for Scholary Pub., Juror, CINE Film Festival (mem. Coun. on Internat. Nontheatrical Events-Secondary Edn.), Golden Key Nat. Honor Soc. Democrat. Office: NSF Physics and Atmospheric Scis Bldg Tucson AZ 95721

MADDOCK, THOMAS MICHAEL, lawyer, reserve officer; b. San Francisco, July 3, 1946; s. James Michael and Josephine Mary (Genco) M.; m. Janet Marie Wilson, July 14, 1984; children: Thomas James, Patrick Michael. BA, U. Calif., Davis, 1968; JD, U. Calif., San Francisco, 1977. Bar: Calif. 1977, U.S. Dist. Ct. (no. dist.) Calif. 1977, U.S. Ct. Appeals (9th cir.) 1983. Author: Practice Guide for Siting Processes, 1989. Mem. Am. Legion. Lafayette and Placerville, Calif., 1982; treas. ARC Mt. Diablo chpt., Concord, Calif., 1983. Comdr. USCGR, 1969-89. Mem. El Dorado County Bar Assn., Contra Costa County Barristers Assn. (bd. dirs. 1978-80), Res. Officer Assn. (chpt. pres. 1980-81). Republican. Roman Catholic. Home: PO Box 251 Placerville CA 95667 Office: Calif Energy Commn MS-12 1516 9th St Sacramento CA 95628

MADER, KELLY FORBES, real estate company executive, senator; b. Sheridan, Wyo., Jan. 21, 1952; s. Richard August and Ena Cora (Forbes) M.; m. Nancy Gay Murray, Nov. 16, 1975; children: Amy, Angie, Ian. Student, Bob Jones U., 1970-71, Grace Coll., 1971-72, Tex. A&M U. Owner, pres. Kelly F. Mader & Assocs., Gillette, Wyo., 1973—; rep. Wyo. State Legis., Cheyenne, 1982-84, senator, 1984—. Officer Campbell County Sheriffs Res., Gillette, 1981—, Campbell County Search and Rescue Team, Gillette 1981—. Named one of Outstanding Young Men of Am., 1982, 85. Mem. Am. Legis. Exchange Council (state chmn. 1984—), Nat. Rifle Assn. Republican.

MADERA, JOSEPH J., bishop; b. San Francisco, Nov. 27, 1927. Ed., Domus Studiorum of the Missionaries of the Holy Spirit, Coyoacan, D.F., Mexico. Ordained priest Roman Cath. Ch., 1957; ordained coadjutor bishop of Fresno, Calif., 1980; bishop of Fresno, 1980—. Office: PO Box 1668 Fresno CA 93717

MADIA, ASHWIN M., microbiologist; b. Lathi, Gujarat, India, Dec. 5, 1946; s. Mohanlal D. and Jakunvar (Bhayani) M.; m. Nirupama A. Shah, Feb. 20, 1973; children: Jigar, Surbhi, Virat. BS in Microbiology, U. Bombay, 1969; MS in Microbiology with honors, U. Baroda, 1971, PhD in Microbiology, 1976. Rsch. assoc. dept. biochemistry Sch. Medicine, Boston U., 1977-78, dept. nutrition and food sci. MIT, Cambridge, 1978-79; microbiologist A.E. Staley Mfg. Co., Decatur, Ill., 1979-81, sr. rsch. microbiologist, 1981-83, sr. scientist, 1983-84; sr. scientist Genencor, Inc., South San Francisco, 1985—. Contbg. author articles to publs. India, U.S., Europe. Patentee hydrolysis of cellulose. Mem. Am. Soc. Microbiology, Soc. Indsl. Microbiology, Am. Chem. Soc. (div. microbial and biochem. tech.), Mycol. Soc. Am., Assn. Microbiologists of India. Home: 842 Morningside Dr Millbrae CA 94030 Office: Genencor Inc 180 Kimball Way South San Francisco CA 94080

MADILL, EDWIN JOSEPH, consultant, former foreign service officer; b. Charlevoix, Mich., Feb. 19, 1911; s. Robert G. and Elaine J. (Orlowski) M.; m. Margaret A. Shea, May 9, 1934; children: Margaret Ann Madill Baptie, Mary Paula Madill Jarrett, Edwin Joseph, Michael Shea. Student, Georgetown U., 1929-32, Columbus U., 1936-37, 41-42; grad., U.S. Army War Coll., 1957, Breveted Brig. Gen., 1972. Tax analyst Mich. Tax Commn., 1933-34; asst. supt. HOLC, 1934-36; successively acct., tech. adviser, classification agt., personnel dir. Office of Treas. U.S. Treasury Dept., 1936-45; asst. dir. Office Contract Selttlement Exec. Office of Pres., 1945-46, spl. adminstrv. cons., 1946; mgmt. analyst U.S. Dept. State, 1946-48; mem. civil service com. expert examiners 1948, spl. liaison officer to Brit. and Can. govts. on emergency planning problems, 1947-56; spl. rep. to Paris U.S. Dept. State, 1948, 50, spl. rep. to Rome and London, 1949, spl. rep. to Philippines, Thailand and India, 1949, spl. rep. to Rome and Geneva, 1950, spl. rep. to Panama, France, Germany, Austria, Italy, 1952, spl. rep. to France, Italy, Saudi Arabia, East Africa, 1953, spl. rep. to Italy, 1954, spl. rep. to Italy, Austria, France, Eng., Germany, Spain, Greece, Turkey, Lebanon, 1955, spl. asst. to adminstr. Bur. Security and Consular Affairs, 1955-56, spl. coordinator to Italy, Lebanon, Syria, Jordan, Israel, Cyprus, Egypt, Iraq, 1956-57; U.S. Consul Calgary, Alta., Can., 1957-63; dean Calgary Consular Corps, U.S. Consul Auckland, N.Z., 1963-64; ret. 1964; cons. pub. relations adminstrn. and mgmt. engring. Author: Position Classification in the Federal Service, 2d edit., 1945, Manual on Emergency Procedures and Practices, 1950, edits. 1952-56, History of Emergency Planning, 1957, Genealogy of Five Families, 1977, The Madill Chronicles, 5 vols., 1983, Verse & Worse, 6 vols., Madill's 20th Century, 7 vols., Why Travel, 10chpts. Mem. Canukeena Club (hon.), Lord Strathcona's Horse, The Queen's Own Rifles, King's Own Armored Regt., H.M.C.S. Tecumseh, Sarcee Tribe (hon. chief). Clubs: Ranchmen's (Calgary), Royal N.Z. Yacht Squadron, Auckland, Northern. Lodges: KC. Home: 5630 E Calle Del Paisano Phoenix AZ 85018

MADISON, PALMER BROOKS, small business owner; b. Ottawa, Kans., Aug. 17, 1941; s. Palmer B. and Gertrude Lilly (Todd) M.; m. Johanne Towers Kuntz, July 10, 1965 (div. Nov. 1982); children: Paul, Christian. BBA, San Diego State U., 1964. From mgmt. trainee to dist. merchandiser Montgomery Ward Co., varous, 1964-80; store mgr. Montgomery Ward Co., Gt. Falls, Mont., 1980-85; stockbroker Dain Bosworth, Gt. Falls, 1985-87; prin. Kidstuff, Gt. Falls, 1987—. Exec. bd. Mil. Affairs Com., 1980—. Mem. Lewis & Clark Found. Republican. Methodist. Home: 8 17th Ave S Great Falls MT 59405 Office: Kidstuff Holiday Village Mall Great Falls MT 59405

MADNI, ASAD MOHAMED, engineering executive; b. Bombay, India, Sept. 8, 1947; came to U.S., 1966; s. Mohamed Taher and Sara Taher (Wadiwalla) M.; Gowhartaj Shahnawaz, Nov. 11, 1976; 1 child, Jamal

Asad. Gen. cert. edn., U. Cambridge, Bombay, 1964; AAS in Electronics, RCA Insts., Inc., 1968; BS in Engring., UCLA, 1969, MS in Engring., 1972; postgrad. exec. inst., Stanford U., 1984; cert. in engring. mgmt., Calif. Inst. Tech., 1987; PhD in Engring., Calif. Coast U., 1987. Sr. instr. Pacific States U., Los Angeles, 1969-71; electronics auditor Pertec Corp., Chatsworth, Calif., 1973-75; project engr., sr. engr., program mgr., dir. advanced programs Microwave div. Systron Donner, Van Nuys, Calif., 1975-82, dir. engring., 1982—, gen. mgr., 1985—; tech. advisor Test and Measurement World, Boston, 19806. Mem. editorial rev. bd., West coast chmn. Microwave Systems News and Communications Tech., 1982—; contbr. more than 50 articles to numerous tech. publs.; patentee in field. Mem. IEEE (sr.), Assn. Old Crows, Nat. Rifle Assn. (life), Calif. Rifle and Pistol Assn. (life). Home: 3582 Greenfield Ave Los Angeles CA 90034 Office: Systron Donner Corp Microwave Div 14844 Oxnard St Van Nuys CA 91409

MADRID, DONNA KAY, personnel executive; b. Mt. Ayr, Iowa, May 29, 1937; d. Clete Hewitt and Murice Marjorie (Cornwall) Madison; married; children: Murice Elaina Scanlon, Cathy Lynne Carlson. AA, Interior Designers Guild, Sherman Oaks, Calif., 1987. Owner Home Cleaning Service, Canoga Park, Calif., 1970-79; designer Beam Interiors, Northridge, Calif., 1979-80; owner, mgr. Innovative Interiors, Chatsworth, Calif., 1980-81; office mgr. Jardine Emett & Chandler, Los Angeles, 1981—, asst. v.p., 1988—. Mem. Personnel and Indsl. Rels. Assn., NAFE, Women Referral Svc. Office: Jardine Emett & Chandler LA Ins Brokers 11835 W Olympic Blvd Los Angeles CA 90021

MADSEN, DAVID ANDRE, director, programs or activities, architectural designer; b. Mason City, Iowa, July 23, 1947; s. George John and Jeanne (Morasaglou) M.; m. Judith R. Dial, Oct. 16, 1976; children: Michael D. Taylor, Britt A., David P. BS, Oreg. State U., 1970, MEd, 1976. Tchr. Centennial High Sch., Gresham, Oreg., 1970-72; mem. faculty Clackamas Community Coll., Oregon City, Oreg., 19726; dept. chmn. Clackamas Community Coll., 1976-82, 86—; ind. archtl. designer, 1972--; bldg. contractor, 1978-87. Author: Geometric Dim and Tol, 4th edit. 1976, Civil Drafting Tech, 1978, Architectural Drafting, 1986, Mechanical Drafting, 1986, Autocad and its Applications, 1988, Architectural Autocad, 1989, Engineering Drafting, 1989. Mem. Am. Inst. Design/Draft, Epsilon Pi Tau. Home: 3440 Riverknoll Way West Linn OR 97068 Office: Clackamas Community Coll 19600 S Molalla Ave Oregon City OR 97045

MADSEN, DAVID MARTIN, computer systems executive; b. Salt Lake, Dec. 29, 1955; s. Carlos A. and Margaret Lee (Young) M.; m. Heidi Lassig, Sept. 14, 1979; children: Melissa, Camille, Erika. Sales rep. Code 3 Corp., Salt Lake City, 1979-83; sales mgr. 3M Health Info. Systems, St. Paul, 1983-85; nat. sales tng. mgr. 3M Health Info. Systems, Salt Lake City, 1985-86, area sale mgr., 1986—. Editor: Diagnostic Selling, 1989. Mem. Boy Scouts Am. 386, 1985--. Fellow Prime Resource Inst.; mem. Health Com. Fin. Mgmt. Republican. Office: 3M Health Info Systems 575 W Murray Blvd Murray UT 84157

MADSEN, ELIZABETH KARLENE, librarian; b. Swarthmore, Pa., Aug. 16, 1944; d. Roy Harding and Katharine (Walters) M. BA, Western Wash. State U., 1966; MLS, U. Hawaii, 1972, postgrad.; MA, Stanford U., 1985. Editor Kodiak (Alaska) Daily Mirror 1967-68; outreach librarian Fairbanks (Alaska) North Star Borough Library, 1972; asst. librarian A. Holmes Johnson Library, Kodiak, 1973-74, Bothell Library King County (Alaska), 1974-76; coll. librarian Matanuska-Susitna Coll. U. Alaska, Palmer, 1976—; del. Alaska Gov.'s Conf. on Libraries, 1979. Contbr. articles to profl. jours. Chmn. steering com. Alaska Collection Devel., 1982—; bd. dirs. Alaska Pub. TV, Anchorage, 1978-80. Mem. ALA, Pacific N.W. Library Assn., Alaska State Library Assn. (chmn. Mat-Su chpt. 1976, state treas. 1979-80), Internat. Platform Assn., Mensa, Stanford U. Alumni Assn. Republican. Home: PO Box 499 Palmer AK 99645 Office: U Alaska Matanuska-Susitna Coll Mile 2 Trunk Rd Palmer AK 99645

MADSEN, ELMA MERRILL, real estate associate; b. Salt Lake City, Nov. 11, 1929; d. Thais Abia and Alice (Sessions) Merrill; m. Von Peter Madsen, July 21, 1953; 1 child, Shirley Yvonne Madsen Dodson. BS with distinction, Wash. State U., 1950; cert., Utah State U., 1952, Calif. Sch. of Real Estate, 1987. Med. technologist Nat. Registry, 1952-63; prodn. mgr. Ch. of Jesus Christ Latter-day Saints Temple, Oakland, Calif., 1965-85; adminstrv. asst. John Grobe Comml. Real Estate, Walnut Creek, Calif., 1985-86; real estate assoc. Mason-McDuffie, Pleasanton, Calif., 1986-88; real estate assoc., notary pub. Homeowners Real Estate, San Ramon, Calif., 1988, John M. Grubb Real Estate, San Ramon, 1988—. Mem. Nat. Women's Coun. Realtors (network mem. Chgo. chpt. 1987—), Contra Costa Women's Coun. Realtors, So. Alameda County Women's Coun. Realtors, NAFE, Bus. Women's Network (fundraising com. Pleasanton chpt. 1988—), Commonwealth Club of Calif. Republican. Home: 3085-4 Lakemount Dr San Ramon CA 94583 Office: John M Grubb Real Estate 2432 San Ramon Valley Blvd San Ramon CA 94583

MADSEN, KENNETH ANDREW, JR., dentist; b. Kalispell, Mont., Aug. 21, 1953; s. Kenneth Andrew Sr. and Bernice Margarite (Carr) M.; m. Rita Lynn Root; children: Jacob, Alex. DDS, U. Minn., 1982. Sole practice dentistry Kalispell, Mont., 1982—; cons. dentist Flathead Co. Nursing Home, Kalispell, 1986—. Chmn. bd. Flathead Valley Community Coll. Trustees, Kalispell, 1988; state chmn. Assn. Community Coll. Trustees, Washington, 1987, 88. Served with USAF, 1972-76. Mem. Elks. Office: 673 1st Ave WN Kalispell MT 59901

MADSEN, KENNETH RUSSELL, lawyer; b. Provo, Utah, July 24, 1925; s. Parley Wm. and Christina (Nuttall) M.; m. Sandra Snow, July 15, 1953; children: Mark R., Dale R., Laural, Christine, Garth. BS, Brigham Young U., 1948; JD, U. Utah, 1951. Bar: Utah 1951. Atty. AT&T, N.Y.C., 1953-58; mem. regional coun. AT&T, Kansas City, Mo., 1958-67, San Francisco, 1967-75; gen. atty. Mt. States Tel. & Tel. Co., Salt Lake City, 1975-87; pvt. practice Washington, 1951-53, Salt Lake City, 1987—; chmn. corp. counsel Utah Bar, Salt Lake City. Founder, trustee Utah Assn. Alternative Dispute Resolution Providers, Salt Lake City, 1988—; mem. govs. com. law and edn. With U.S. Army, 1943-45, ETO. Decorated Bronze Star, Purple Heart. Mormon. Home: 4171 Cecil Dr Salt Lake City UT 84124

MAEDA, J. A., data processing executive; b. Mansfield, Ohio, Aug. 24, 1940; d. James Shunso and Doris Lucille (Moore) M.; m. Robert Lee Hayes (div. May 1970); 1 child, Brian Sentaro Hayes. BS in Math., Purdue U., 1962, postgrad., 1962-63; postgrad., Calif. State U., Northridge, 1968-75; cert. profl. designation in tech. of computer operating systems and tech. of info. processing, UCLA, 1971. Cons., rsch. asst. computer ctr. Purdue U., West Lafayette, Ind., 1962-63; computer operator, sr. tab operator, mem. faculty Calif. State U., Northridge, 1969, programmer cons., tech. asst. II, 1969-70, supr. acad. applicatons, EDP supr. II, 1970-72, project tech. support coord. programmer II, office of the chancellor, 1972-73, tech. support coord. statewide timesharing tech. support, programmer II, 1973-74, acad. coord., tech. support coord. instrn., computer cons. III, 1974-83; coord. user svcs. info. ctr., mem. tech. staff IV CADAM INC subs. Lockheed Corp., Burbank, Calif., 1983-86, coord. end user svcs., tech. specialist computing dept., 1986-87; v.p., bd. dirs. Rainbow Computing, Inc., Northridge, 1976-85; pres. Akiko Maeda Tech./Design Cons., Northridge, 1980—; mktg. mgr. thaumaturge Taro Quipu Tech./Design Cons., Northridge, 1987—; tech. cons. Digital Computer Cons., Chatsworth Calif., 1988; cons. computer tech., fin. and bus. mgmt., systems integration, 1988—. Author 100 user publs., 1969-83, 98 computer user publs., 1983-87, basic computer programming language; contbr. articles and papers and photos to profl. jours. Mem. IEEE, SHARE, Digital Equipment Computer Users Soc. (author papers and presentations 1977-81, ednl. spl. interest group 1977-83, steering com. Resource Sharing Timesharing System/Extended (RSTS/E), 1979-82). Home: 18257 Shepley Pl Northridge CA 91326

MAEHL, WILLIAM HARVEY, historian, educator; b. Bklyn., May 28, 1915; s. William Henry and Antoinette Rose (Salamone) M.; m. Josephine Scholl McAllister, Dec. 29, 1941; children: Madeleine, Kathleen. BSc, Northwestern U., 1937, MA, 1939; PhD, U. Chgo., 1946. Asst. prof. history St. Louis U., 1941-42, Tex. A&M U., College Sta., 1943, De Paul U., Chgo., 1944-49; historian Dept. of Def., Karlsruhe, Stuttgart, Fed. Rep. Germany, 1950-52; chief briefing office U.S. hdqrs. EUCOM, Frankfurt, Fed. Rep. Germany, 1952-53; chief historian Artillery Sch. Ft. Sill, Okla., 1954, war plans office Hdqrs. NAMAE, USAF, Burtonwood, Eng., 1954-55; assoc. prof. European history Nebr. Wesleyan U., Lincoln, 1955-57, prof., 1958-62, 65-68; prof. German history Auburn (Ala.) U., 1968-81, prof. emeritus, 1981—; vis. prof. U. Nebr., 1962, U. Auckland, New Zealand, 1963-64, Midwestern U., Wichita Falls, Tex., 1965. Author: German Militarism and Socialism, 1968, History of Germany in Western Civilization, 1979, A World History Syllabus, 3 vols., 1980, August Bebel, Shadow Emperor of the German Workers, 1980, The German Socialist Party: Champion of the First Republic, 1918-33, 1986; monographs, chpts. to books; contbr. articles to profl. jours. Grantee Nebr. Wesleyan U., 1959, Auburn U., 1969-73, 79-80, Am. Philosophical Soc., 1973-74, Deutscher Akademischer Austauschdienst, 1978. Mem. Am. Hist. Assn., Phi Kappa Phi, Phi Alpha Theta.

MAEHL, WILLIAM HENRY, historian, university administrator; b. Chicago Heights, Ill., June 13, 1930; s. William Henry and Marvel Lillian (Carlson) M.; m. Audrey Mae Ellsworth, Aug. 25, 1965; 1 child, Christine Amanda. B.A., U. Minn., 1950, M.A., 1951; postgrad (Fulbright fellow), King's Coll., U. Durham, Eng., 1955-56; Ph.D., U. Chgo., 1957. Asst. prof. Montclair (N.J.) State Coll., 1957-58; asst. prof. Washington Coll., Chestertown, Md., 1958-59, U. Okla., Norman, 1959-64; asso. prof. U. Okla., 1964-70, prof. English history, 1970-86; dean Coll. Liberal Studies, 1976-86, vice provost for continuing edn. and public service, 1979-86; pres. The Fielding Inst., Santa Barbara, Calif., 1987—; vis prof. U. Nebr., summer, 1965; vis. fellow Wolfson Coll. Oxford (Eng.) U., spring, 1975; fellow Salzburg Seminar in Am. Studies, 1976. Author: The Reform Bill of 1832, 1967; editor: R.G. Gammage, Chartist Reminiscences, 1981, Continuum: Jour. of the Nat. Continuing Edn. Assn., 1980-83, also articles. Served with AUS, 1953-55. Leverhulme Research fellow, 1961-62; grantee Am. Philos. Soc., 1961-62, 67-68, 71, 76. Fellow Royal Hist. Soc., Assn. of Grad. Liberal Studies Programs; mem. Am. Hist. Assn., Conf. on Brit. Studies, Soc. for Study Labour History. Office: 2112 Santa Barbara St Santa Barbara CA 93105

MAGALONG, ROMEO, civil engineer; b. Bayambang, Philippines, June 27, 1948; came to U.S., 1961; s. Felix Buyao and Sandra (Gloria) M.; m. Constance May Ebia, Nov. 15, 1970. BSCE, U. Hawaii, 1970. Registered profl. engr., Colo., Pa. Hwy. engr. trainee Fed. Hwy. Adminstrn., Denver, 1971-73; asst. area engr. Fed. Hwy. Adminstrn., Harrisburg, Pa., 1973-75; area engr. Fed. Hwy. Adminstrn., Harrisburg, 1975-77, program coord., 1977-78ngr.; civil engr. Nat. Park Svc., Denver, 1978—; hwy. engr., Wendleton Consulting, Inc., Nederland, Colo., 1982-84; owner, mgr. Asian Pacific Imports, Lakewood, Colo., 1984—. Mem. Asian Edn. Adv. Com., Denver, 1987—. Mem. Am. Soc. Civil Engrs., Nat. Filipino Am. Coun. (regional dir. 1986—), Philippine Am. Soc. Colo. (chmn., dir. 1986—), Asian. Am. Found. Colo. (steering com. 1988—)., Lions. Republican. Roman Catholic. Home: 1314 S Kendall St Lakewood CO 80226 Office: Nat Park Svc 12795 W Alameda Pkwy Lakewood CO 80228

MAGARAM, PHILIP SIDNEY, lawyer; b. N.Y.C., July 29, 1937; s. Bernard and Ida (Weiss) M.; widowed; children: Justin B., Jodi C. BS, UCLA, 1958, LLB, 1961. Bar: Calif. 1963. Ptnr. Magaram, Riskin, Wayne & Minikes, L.A., 1963-83, Irell & Manella, L.A., 1983-84, Valensi, Rose & Magaram, PLC, L.A., 1984--. Contbr. articles to legal publs. Mem. bd. govs. So. Calif. chpt. Arthritis Found., 1980--; bd. dirs. Joseph Drown Found., L.A., 1982--, Nat. Found. for Ileitis and Colitis, L.A., 1987--; trustee UCLA Found., 1984--. Mem. Regency Club. Democrat. Jewish. Office: Valensi Rose & Magaram PLC 1800 Ave of the Stars Ste 1000 Los Angeles CA 90067

MAGARET, PATRICIA MAIXNER, artist; b. Lincoln, Nebr., Jan. 8, 1944; d. Frank William and Elizabeth (Barrows) Maixner; m. David Ernest. BS in Med. Technol., U. Nebr., 1966. Med. technol. U. Nebr. Coll. Medicine, Omaha, 1966-69, Northgate Hosp., Seattle, 1970-71; quilt artist Pullman, Wash., 1986—. Inventee in field 1987-88. Recipient Best Fiber Arts award Palouse Visual Arts Juried Show 1987, 1st Place Miniature Quilt award Edmonds Quilt Show 1988. Mem. Am. Quilt Soc., NQA, Wash. State Quilters, Palouse Patchers (treas.). Home: SE 800 Derby St Pullman WA 99163

MAGEE, SUSAN CAROL, corporate administrator; b. Santa Monica, Calif., Dec. 18, 1959; d. Richard Myhr and Ruth Marie (Prentice) M. BA in Theatre, Calif. State U., Long Beach, 1986. Prodn. asst. Long Beach City Coll., 1985-86; adminstrv. asst. Matlack, Inc., Long Beach, 1986-89, Southland Industries, Long Beach, 1989—. Mem. Orange County Horse Show Assn. Republican.

MAGER, ARTUR, retired aerospace company executive, consultant; b. Nieglowice, Poland, Sept. 21, 1919; came to U.S., 1939, naturalized, 1944; s. Herman and Ella (Kornbluh) M.; m. Phyllis R. Weisman, Aug. 19, 1942; 1 child, Ilana Gail. B.S., U. Mich., 1943; M.S., Case Inst. Tech., 1951; Ph.D. in Aeros., Calif. Inst. Tech., 1953. Registered profl. engr., Ohio. Aero. research scientist NASA Lewis Labs., Cleve., 1946-51; research scientist Marquardt Corp., Van Nuys, Calif., 1954-60; dir. Nat. Engring. Sci. Co., Pasadena, Calif., 1960-61; dir. spacecraft scis. Aerospace Corp., El Segundo, Calif., 1961-64, gen. mgr. applied mechanics div., 1964-68, v.p., gen. mgr. engring. sci. ops., 1968-78, v.p. engring. group, 1978-82, cons., 1982—; mem. BSD Re-entry Panel, 1961-63, NASA com. missile and space vehicle aerodynamics, 1963-65; mem. adv. com. AFML, 1971-72; mem. NASA Adv. Council, 1982-86 ; chmn. NASA Space Applications Adv. Com., 1982-86 ; mem. Aeros. and Space Engring. Bd., NRC, 1982-87; mem. Space Sta. Task Force, NRC, 1983-87, Shuttle Criticality and Hazard Analysis Rev. Bd., 1986-88, DSB NASP Task Force, 1987-88, AFSB Hypersonic Task Force, 1987-88. Contbr. articles to profl. jours. Mem. alumni fund council Calif. Inst. Tech., 1972-74; trustee West Coast U.; bd. councilors U. So. Calif. Sch. Engring., 1976-86; mem. devel. disabilities bd. Area X, 1976-80, chmn., 1976-78; 1st v.p. Calif. Assn. Retarded, 1983-85 ; pres. Exceptional Children's Found., 1970-72. Recipient Disting. Alumni award U. Mich., 1969, Golden Rule award Calif. Assn. Retarded, 1977. Fellow Inst. Advanced Engring., AIAA (chmn. Los Angeles sect. 1967-68, bd. dirs. 1975-77, pres. 1980-81), AAAS; mem. Technion Soc., Nat. Acad. Engring., Sigma Xi. Home and Office: 1353 Woodruff Ave Los Angeles CA 90024 *

MAGGIO, KAREN KAY, training manager; b. Topeka, Feb. 21, 1954; d. Ray Albert and Dorothy Rachel (Bell) McMillen; m. Guy Phillip Maggio, Oct. 13, 1972. BBA, U. Phoenix, 1988. Presch. tchr. La Petite Acad., Kansas City, Mo., 1972-75; ctr. dir. La Petite Acad., Kansas City, 1975-80, asst. dir. ops., 1980-83; ctr. dir. Children's World, Golden, Colo., 1983-86; sales tng. dir. Children's World, Golden, 1986-87, tng. mgr., 1987—; speaker Colo. Assn. Edn. Young Children, Ft. Collins, 1987, Va. Assn. Early Childhood Edn., Washington, 1987. Mem. ASTD, Nat. Assn. Edn. Young Children. Office: Childrens World Learning Ctrs 573 Park Point Dr Golden CO 80401

MAGID, GAIL AVRUM, neurosurgery educator; b. Chgo., Oct. 15, 1934; s. Harry M. and Henrietta (Busch) M.; m. Janet Louise Reinhardt, June 15, 1962 (div.); children: Allison Drew, Jonathan Alward; m. Roseanne Cipra Muirhead, Sept. 4, 1982; children: Heather Marie, John Scott IV, Mark Andrew. BSc, U. Ill., 1954; MD, Chgo. Med. Sch., 1958. Diplomate Am. Bd. Neurol. Surgery. Intern Cook County Hosp., Chgo., 1958-59; resident, then fellow neurol. surgery Mayo Clinic, Rochester, Minn., 1959-61, 63-65; clin. instr. neurosurgery U. Calif., San Francisco, 1965-70, asst. clin. prof., 1970-79, assoc. prof., 1979—; chmn. Dominican Neurol. Inst., Santa Cruz, Calif., 1975—, bd. dirs. Dominican Found.; sr. v.p. Frank Magid Assocs., Cedar Rapids, Iowa; cons. neurosurgeon U.S. Army; cons. neurosurgeon San Francisco Gen. Hosp. Assoc. editor: Clinical Neurosurgery, 1974. Bd. dirs. Santa Cruz Symphony Assn., 1983-85, U. Calif. Friends of Arts, Santa Cruz, 1985-86. Served to lt. comdr. USN, 1961-63. Fellow ACS, Internat. Coll. Surgeons; mem. AMA, Calif. Med. Assn., Internat. Soc. Pediatric Neurosurgeons, Am. Assn. Neurol. Surgeons, Western Neurosurg. Soc., Cong. Neurol. Surgeons, San Francisco Neurol. Soc. (v.p. 1988—). Republican. Club: St. Francis Yacht (San Francisco). Home: 241 4th Ave Santa Cruz CA 95062 Office: 1661 Soquel Dr Santa Cruz CA 95065

MAGINNITY, GERALD FRANCIS, librarian; b. Boston, Nov. 11, 1950; s. Paul Morris and Mary Ann (Roberts) M.; m. Evelyn Elaine Espinosa, Aug. 16, 1986; 1 child, Paul Edward. BS, Ohio State U., 1972; MLS, U. Western Ont., London, Can., 1974. Advisor Inst. Tech., Monterrey, Mex., 1974-76; asst. county librarian Lassen County Library, Susanville, Calif., 1977-78; reference coordinator Imperial Valley Serra Coop. Library System, San Diego, 1978-80; Vallejo region librarian Solano County Library, Fairfield, Calif., 1980-82; assoc. county librarian Fresno (Calif.) County Library, 1982—. Mem. El Concilio de Fresno, 1988. Mem. ALA, Calif. Library Assn., Bibliotecas Para La Gente. Democrat. Roman Catholic. Office: Fresno County Libr 2420 Mariposa Fresno CA 93721

MAGLIARO, LORNA BETH, health services facility executive; b. Chgo., Sept. 4, 1953; d. Anthony P. Magliaro and Laurel (Moulton) Lundh. Student, U. Nev., Las Vegas, 1971-73. Social worker Clark County Social Services, Las Vegas, 1974-79; word processing specialist Data Processors Nev., Las Vegas, 1983-84; mgr. user support Sierra Health Services, Las Vegas, 1984-88; supr. customer svcs. Family Health Plan, Costa Mesa, Calif., 1988—. Democrat. Home: 1933 Whittier Ave Costa Mesa CA 92627 Office: Family Health Plan MIS Dept 1620 Sunflower Ave Bldg A Costa Mesa CA 92626

MAGNANO, JOSEPH ANTONIO, food importer; b. Seattle, Apr. 1, 1945; s. Angelo Cooper and Mary Dealtry (Sanderson) M.; m. Mary Margaret Beuerle. BBA, U. Notre Dame, 1967. V.p., co-owner The Napoleon Co., Seattle, 1978—. Active Naval War Coll., Newport, R.I., 1985; mem. century club Bellevue (Wash.) Boys and Girls Club. Mem. Nat. Food Brokers Assn., Seattle Food Brokers Club, Bellevue Athletic Club, Notre Dame Alumni Club. (past. pres.), Overlake Golf Club. Roman Catholic. Home: 9057 NE 26th Bellevue WA 98004 Office: The Napoleon Co 355 118 Ave SE PO Box 1457 Bellevue WA 98009

MAGNESS, BOB JOHN, telecommunications executive; b. Clinton, Okla., 1924; married. Attended, South Western State Coll. Chmn. Tele-Communications, Inc., Denver. Office: Tele-Communications Inc 4643 S Ulster St #360 Denver CO 80237-2863 *

MAGNESS, RHONDA ANN, microbiologist; b. Stockton, Calif., Jan. 30, 1946; d. John Pershing and Dorothy Waneta (Kelley) Wetter; m. Barney LeRoy Bender, Aug. 26, 1965 (div. 1977); m. Gary D. Magness, Mar. 5, 1977; children: Jay D., Troy D. BS, Calif. State U., 1977. Lic. clin. lab. technologist, Calif., med. technologist; cert. clin. lab. scientist. Med. asst. C. Fred Wilcox, MD, Stockton, 1965-66; clk. typist Dept. of U.S. Army, Ft. Eustis, Va., 1967, Def. Supply Agy., New Orleans, 1967-68; med. asst. James G. Cross, MD, Lodi, Calif., 1969, Arthur A. Kemalyan, MD, Lodi, 1969-71, 72-77; med. sec. Lodi Meml. Hosp., 1972; lab. aide Calif. State U., Sacramento, 1977; phlebotomist St. Joseph's Hosp., Stockton, 1978-79; microbiologist supr. Dameron Hosp. Assn., Stockton, 1980—. Active Concerned Women Am., Washington, 1987-88. Mem. AAUW, Calif. Assn. Clin. Lab. Technologists, San Joaquin County Med. Assts. Assn., Nat. Geog. Soc., Nat. Audubon Soc. Baptist. Lodge: Jobs Daus. (chaplain 1962-63). Home: 9627 Knight Ln Stockton CA 95209 Office: Dameron Hosp Lab 525 W Acacia St Stockton CA 95203

MAGNUS, DEBORAH, educational administrator; b. N.Y.C., Feb. 2, 1939; d. Jerome J. and Helen (Kleppel) Stone; divorced; children: David Christopher, Victoria Robin. Cert., Cooper Union Coll., N.Y.C., 1959; BA, U. Calif., Riverside, 1971, MA, 1975. Cert. regular and spl. edn. tchr., Calif. Tchr. kindergarten Riverside (Calif.) Unified Sch. Dist., 1972-73, tchr. learning handicapped, 1973-75, tchr. severely handicapped, 1975-79; prin.-coordinator Riverside County Office of Edn., 1979—; lectr. U. Calif., Riverside, 1979-84. Co-author: tng. manual Responsible Communication, 1982. Advisor spl. edn. dept. U. Calif., Riverside, 1979-85, United Cerebral Palsy, Riverside, 1982-84. Mem. Council for Exceptional Children, Assn. Calif. Sch. Adminstrs., Phi Delta Kappa, Phi Beta Kappa. Home: 401 Massachusetts Riverside CA 92507 Office: Riverside County Office Edn 3939 13th St Riverside CA 92502

MAGNUSON, ALAN DOUGLAS, banking executive; b. Valparaiso, Ind., Jan. 22, 1942; s. Douglas Harold and Alice Elizabeth (Burch) M.; m. Rose Becerra, Apr. 25, 1971; children: Lori, Kathi, Juli. Diploma, South Bend Coll. Commerce, 1962. Officer trainee Crocker-Citizens Bank, Los Angeles, 1967-70, ops. officer, 1967-70; ops. officer So. Calif. 1st Nat. Bank, San Diego, 1970-73; loan officer 1st Nat. Bank Nev., Las Vegas, 1973-80; br. mgr. 1st Interstate Nev., Las Vegas, 1980-82, v.p., 1984—; instr. Clark County Community Coll., Las Vegas; speaker SBA, Las Vegas.; mem. speakers bur. First Interstate Bank Nev., Las Vegas. Active First Interstate Bank, Nev. Speakers Bur. Served as sgt. U.S. Army, 1960-63. Mem. Am. Inst. Banking (gov. So. Nev. chpt. 1971-77, plaque 1977), Bank Adminstrn. Inst. (pres. So. Nev. chpt. 1982-83, plaque 1983), Henderson C. of C., Boulder City C. of C. (v.p. 1980-81), North Las Vegas C. of C. (comml. com., chmn. audit com., chmn. fairshow, chmn. funds appropriation subcom., import-export com., chmn. fin. subcom., pub. relations com.). Republican. Lodge: Lions (chmn. Nev. zone 1982-83, sec. Nev. cabinet 1983-84, gov. Nev. dist. 1985-86, chmn. council govs. Calif./Nev. 1985-86). Office: 1st Interstate Nev PO Box 98588 Las Vegas NV 89193-8588

MAGNUSON, DONALD RICHARD, insurance executive, consultant; b. Chgo., Apr. 23, 1951; s. Donald Orville and Olive June (O'Keefe) M.; m. Debra Michelle Ruzek, June 9, 1973; children: Jennifer Jean, Erick Richard. Diploma, No. Ill. U., summer 1968; student, Coll. of Du Page, 1971. Tchr. pro-tennis Westside Racquet Club, Oakbrook Terr., Ill., 1971-73; broker Teichen Ins. Agy., Villa Park, Ill., 1973-74; underwriter Hanover Ins. Co., Chgo., 1974-76; spl. risk underwriter Am. Ins. Group, Chgo., 1976-78; with mgmt. Sayre & Toso, Inc., Chgo., 1978-82, L.A., 1986-87; sr. underwriter Mead Reinsurance Corp., Dayton, Ohio, 1982-86, Sayre & Toso, Inc., L.A., 1986-88, Montgomery & Collins, Inc., L.A., 1988—; pres., founder Magnuson & Assocs., Yorba Linda, Calif., 1987—. Mem. Porsche Club Am. Roman Catholic. Office: 19866 Ridge Manor Way Yorba Linda CA 92686

MAGOWAN, PETER ALDEN, grocery chain executive; b. N.Y.C., Apr. 5, 1942; s. Robert Anderson and Doris (Merrill) M.; m. Jill Tarlau (div. July 1982; children—Kimberley, Margot, Hilary; m. Deborah Johnston, Aug. 14, 1982. B.A., Stanford U.; M.A., Oxford U., Eng.; postgrad., Johns Hopkins U. Store mgr. Safeway Stores Inc., Washington, 1968-70; dist. mgr. Safeway Stores Inc., Houston, 1970-71; retail ops. mgr. Safeway Stores Inc., Phoenix, 1971-72; div. mgr. Safeway Stores Inc., Tulsa, 1973-76; mgr. internat. div. Safeway Stores Inc., Toronto, Ont., Can., 1976-78; mgr. western region Safeway Stores Inc., San Francisco, 1978-79; chmn. bd., chief exec. officer Safeway Stores Inc., Oakland, Calif., 1980—; also pres. Safeway Stores Inc., Oakland, 1988—; bd. dirs. Pacific Gas and Electric, Chrysler Corp., Vons Cos. Inc. Mem. U.S. C. of C., Food Mktg. Inst. (bd. dirs.), Bus. Roundtable. Office: Safeway Stores Inc 201 4th St Oakland CA 94660

MAGUIRE, ALEXANDER, publishing company executive; b. Glasgow, Scotland, Apr. 26, 1934; came to U.S., 1963; s. Patrick Joseph and Marion Hunter Coulter (McConnell) M.; m. Margaret Hay, Mar. 1, 1957; children: Steven, Mark, Karen Lesley. Master printer, U. Strathclyde, Glasgow, Scotland. Apprentice Gilmour & Dean, Glasgow, 1949-56; sect. leader Rolls-Royce, Glasgow, Blantyre, Scotland, 1956-63; asst., plant mgr. Haddon Craftsmen, Scranton, Pa., 1963-73; ops. mgr. Banta West, Sparks, Nev., 1973-76; plant mgr. Waller Press, San Francisco, 1976-79; v.p. ops. Mariposa Press, Benicia, Calif., 1979-85; plant mgr. Recorder-Sunset Press, San Francisco, 1985-87, Consolidated Printers, Berkeley, Calif., 1987—; instr. vocat. edn. Washoe County, Reno, 1973-74. Adv. bd. middle sch., Bloomsburg, Pa., 1965-67; bd. dirs. Jaycees, Bloomsburg, 1964-67, Post 273 Am. Legion, Bloomsburg, 1967-70. With Royal Engrs., British Army, 1952-54. Mem. Amateur Boxing Fedn. (referee, judge), Masons (Master Mason Clarkston, Scotland). Home: 877 Rose Dr Benicia CA 94510

MAGUIRE, JOHN DAVID, university president, educator; b. Montgomery, Ala., Aug. 7, 1932; s. John Henry and Clyde (Merrill) M.; m. Lillian Louise Parrish, Aug. 29, 1953; children—Catherine Merrill, Mary Elizabeth, Anne King. A.B. magna cum laude, Washington and Lee U., 1953, Litt.D. (hon.), 1979; Fulbright scholar, Edinburgh (Scotland) U., 1953-54; B.D. summa cum laude, Yale, 1956, Ph.D., 1960; postdoctoral research,

Yale U. and U. Tübingen, Germany, 1964-65, Univ. of Calif.-Berkeley, 1968-69, Silliman U., Philippines, 1976-77. Acting chaplain Washington and Lee Univ., 1952-53; acting dir. Internat. Student Ctr., New Haven, 1956-58; asst. in instrn. systematic theology Yale U. Div. Sch., 1958-59; mem. faculty Wesleyan U., Middletown, Conn., 1960-70; asso. provost Wesleyan U., 1967-68; vis. lectr. Pacific Sch. Religion and Grad. Theol. Union, Berkeley, 1968-69; pres. SUNY Coll. at Old Westbury, 1970-81, Claremont (Calif.) U. Ctr. and Grad. Sch., 1981—. Author: The Dance of the Pilgrim: A Christian Style of Life for Today, 1967; also numerous articles. Mem. Conn. adv. com. U.S. Commn. Civil Rights, 1961-70; participant White House Conf. on Civil Rights, 1966; advisor, permanent trustee and 1st chmn. bd. dirs. Martin Luther King Ctr. for Social Change, Atlanta, 1968—; bd. dirs. Nassau County Health and Welfare Coun., 1971-81, pres., 1974-76; trustee United Bd. Christian Higher Edn. in Asia, 1975-81, Inst. Internat. Edn., 1980-86, The Tomás Rivera Ctr., Claremont, Calif., 1984—, Assn. Ind. Calif. Colls. and Univers., 1985—, The Calif. Achievement Coun., 1985—, Transylvania U. Faculty Enhancement Fund, 1987—, Lincoln Found., Lincoln Inst. of Land Policy, Inc.; bd. dirs. Assn. Am. Colls., 1981-86, chmn., 1984-85; bd. dirs. west coast div. NAACP Legal Def. and Edn. Fund, 1981—, Thacher Sch., Ojai, Calif., 1982—, vice chmn., 1986—; mem. Am. Com. East-West Accord, 1981—, Blue Ribbon Calif. Commn. on Teaching Profession, 1984-86; mem. governing coun. Aspen Inst. Wye Faculty Seminar, 1984—, mem. Coun. on Fgn. Rels., 1983—, L.A. Humanitas Coun., 1986—; sr. fellow Inst. Trustee Leadership, Assn. Governing Bds., 1985—; mem. Pres.'s Adv. Coun. to Commn. on Calif. Master Plan for Higher Edn., 1986-87. Recipient Julia A. Archibald High Scholarship award Yale Div. Sch., 1956; Day fellow Yale Grad. Sch., 1956-57; Kent fellow, 1957-60; Howard Found. postdoctoral fellow Brown U. Grad. Sch., 1964-65; Fenn lectr., 7 Asian countries, 1976-77; recipient Conn. Prince Hall Masons' award outstanding contbns. human rights in Conn., 1965; E. Harris Harbison Gt. Tchr. prize Danforth Found., 1968. Fellow Soc. Values Higher Edn. (pres. 1974-81, bd. dirs. 1972-88); mem. Phi Beta Kappa, Omicron Delta Kappa. Democrat. Office: Claremont U Ctr & Grad Sch Office of Pres 160 E 10th St Claremont CA 91711-6165

MAHAFFAY, WILLIAM EDWARD, mechanical engineer. s. James W. and Ida (Hyink) M.; m. Carolyn Dahlquist, Oct. 15, 1935; 1 son, John W. B.S., Northwestern U., 1933. Registered engr., Ind. Various positions Internat. Harvester Co., 1935-42; plant engr. Internat. Harvester Co. (Refrigeration div.), 1942-45, chief engr. advanced engring sect., 1945-51; exec. engr. Whirlpool Corp., St. Joseph, Mich., 1951-53; dir. engring. and rsch. Whirlpool Corp., 1953-56, v.p. engring. and rsch., 1956-65, group v.p., 1965-70; dir. Robbins Myers, Dayton, Ohio, 1970-87, Ranco Inc., Columbus, Ohio, 1970-87; engring. cons.; adj. prof. U. Mich., 1970; vis. prof. Purdue., 1970; Life regent Northwestern U.; tech. adv. com. Purdue U. Mem. ASHRAE, ASME, Acacia, Northwestern U. Alumni Assn., Instrument Soc. Am., Union League Club (Chgo.), Paradise Valley Country Club, Lomas Santa Fe Country Club, (Solana Beach, Calif.), Sigma Xi, Tau Beta Pi, Pi Tau Sigma. Home: 86 Colonia Miramonte Scottsdale AZ 85253

MAHAFFEY, MARCIA JEANNE HIXSON, school administrator; b. Scoby, Mont., Oct. 21, 1927; d. Edward Goodell and Olga Marie (Frederickson) Hixson; m. Donald Harry Mahaffey (div. Aug. 1976); 1 child, Marcia Anne. BA in English, U. Wash.; MA in Secondary Edn., U. Hawaii, 1967. Cert. secondary and elem. tchr. and adminstr. Tchr. San Lorenzo (Calif.) Sch. Dist., 1958-59; tchr. Castro Valley (Calif.) Sch. Dist., 1959-63, vice prin., 1963-67; vice prin. Sequoia Union High Sch. Dist., Redwood City, Calif., 1967-77, asst. prin., 1977—; tchr. trainer Project Impact Sequoia Union Sch. Dist., Redwood City, 1986—, mem. supr.'s task force for dropout prevention, 1987—, mentor tchr. selection com., 1987—; mem. Stanford Program Devel. Ctr. Com., 1987—; chairperson gifted and talented Castro Valley Sch. Dist.; mem. family services bd., San Leandro, Calif. Vol. Am. Cancer Soc., San Mateo, Calif., 1967, Castro Valley, 1965; Sunday sch. tchr. Hope Luth. Ch., San Mateo, 1970-76; chair Carlmont High Sch. Site Council, Belmont, Calif., 1977—. Recipient Life Mem. award Parent, Tchr., Student Assn., Belmont, 1984; named Woman of the Week, Castro Valley, 1967. Mem. Assn. Calif. Sch. Adminstrs. (Project Leadership plaque 1985), Sequoia Dist. Mgmt. Assn. (pres. 1975, treas. 1984, 85), Sequoia Dist. Goals Commn. (chair subcom. staff devel. 1988), Met. Mus. Art, Smithsonian Inst., AAUW, DAR, Animal Welfare Advocacy, Delta Kappa Gamma, Alpha Xi Delta. Club: Carlmont Social.

MAHAFFEY, MARTHA BERNAL, psychologist; b. San Francisco, June 17, 1959; d. Octavio Segundo and Aurora Nellie (Cirio) Bernal; m. Michael Lambert Mahaffey, Aug. 8, 1981; children: Christopher Michael, Steven Anthony. BS in Psychology magna cum laude, Santa Clara (Calif.) U., 1980; PhD in Clin. Psychology, U. Nev., 1986. Cert. psychologist. Psychologist Nev. Mental Health Inst., Reno, 1987; pvt. practice Reno, 1987—; clin. psychologist VA Med. Ctr., Reno, 1988—; adj. prof. Truckee Meadows Community Coll., Reno, 1987, asst. prof. U. Nev., Reno, 1988—. Mem. Am. Psychol. Assn., Nev. Psychol. Assn., No. Nev. Assn. Cert. Psychologists, Western Psychol. Assn., Bicultural Assn. Spanish Speaking Therapists and Advocates, Rocky Mtn. Psychol. Assn., Psi Chi, Phi Beta Kappa, Sigma Xi. Home: 6066 White Water Way Reno NV 89523 Office: VA Med Ctr 1000 Locust St 116B Reno NV 89520

MAHAY, STEPHEN THOMAS, river guide, emergency medical technician; b. Saratoga Spring, N.Y., May 6, 1947; s. Joseph J. and Shirly J. (Thomas) M.; m. Kristine D. Drumm, Apr. 29, 1970; children: Israel, Judah, Noah. Grad. high sch., Schuylerville, N.Y. Cert. emergency med. technician, Alaska. Pres. Mahay's Riverboat Service, Inc., Talkeetna, Alaska, 1977—; chief Talkeetna Ambulance Dept., 1987—. adv. bd. mem. Mat-Suе Visitor Bur., Wasilla, Alaska, 1986-87; dir. Trout Unlimited, Anchorage, 1987; emergency mgmt. coord. Fed. Emergency Mgmt. Agy., 1984-89; warrant officer, Alaska State Def. Force, 1987-89; instr., trainer CPA, Am. Heart Assn., 1985-89; first aid instr. State of Alaska Dept. Labor., 1988-89. Mem. Alaska Sports Fishing Assn., Alaska Fly Fishing Assn. Republican. Home: Box 133 Talkeetna AK 99676 Office: Mahays Riverboat Service Box 705 Talkeetna AK 99676

MAHER, DENNIS PATRICK, manufacturing executive; b. Chgo., Feb. 17, 1938; s. James Paul and Eleanor Margret (Heniken) M.; m. Sarah Francis Clark, Dec. 30, 1973 (div. Oct. 1978); children: Dennis Patrick, Cari Louise. Ba in Econs., Drake U., 1961. Salary adminstrn. mgr. Philco-Ford Corp., Phila., 1969-70; personnel mgr. Philco-Ford Corp., Newport Beach, Calif., 1970-73; indsl. rels. dir. Philco-Ford, Sao Paulo, Brazil, 1973-76; employee rels. dir. Ford Aerospace Corp., Sunnyvale, Calif., 1976—. Mem. U.S. English, Washington, 1988—; donor Good Samaritan Hosp. Soc., San Jose, Calif., 1988—. Mem. Am. Compensation Assn., Am. Electronic Assn., Calif. Mfg. Assn. (steering com. 1988—). Republican. Roman Catholic. Home: 226 Bachman Ave Los Gatos CA 95030 Office: Ford Aerospace Corp 1260Crossman Ave Sunnyvale CA 94089

MAHER, JOHN FRANCIS, financial executive; b. Berkeley, Calif., Apr. 25, 1943; s. Edward John and Emilia A. (Radovan) M.; m. Ann Elizabeth Breeden (div. 1975); children: Edward John II, Elizabeth Ann; m. Helen Lee Stillman, Mar. 20, 1976; children: Michael Stillman, Helen Cathline. BS, Menlo Coll., 1965; MBA, U. Pa., 1967. Gen. ptnr. Eastman Dillon, N.Y., 1971; 1st v.p. Blyth Eastman Dillon, N.Y., 1972; exec. v.p. Blyth Eastman Dillon, Los Angeles, 1976-79; exec. v.p., chief fin. officer Gt. Western Fin., Beverly Hills, Calif., 1973-76, also bd. dirs.; mng. dir. Shearson Lehman Bros., Los Angeles, 1979-86; pres., chief operating officer Great Western Fin. Corp., Beverly Hills, 1986—; bd. dirs. Gt. Western Fin. Corp., Beverly Hills, Baker Hughes Internat., Gt. Western Bank. Bd. dirs. Los Angeles Big Bros., Inc., Baker Hughes, Inc. Joseph Wharton fellow U. Pa., 1965-67. Office: Gt Western Fin Corp 8484 Wilshire Blvd 10th Fl Beverly Hills CA 90211-3212

MAHER, LEO THOMAS, bishop; b. Mt. Union, Iowa, July 1, 1915; s. Thomas and Mary (Teberg) M. Ed., St. Joseph's Coll., Mountain View, Calif., St. Patrick's Sem., Menlo Park, Calif.; LHD, U. San Diego, 1986. Ordained priest Roman Catholic Ch.; asst. pastor in San Francisco, 1944-47, sec. archbishop of, 1947-61; chancellor Archdiocese San Francisco, 1956-62, dir. vocations, 1957-62, archdiocesan consultor, 1959-62; apptd. domestic prelate 1954; bishop Santa Rosa, Calif., 1962-69; 3d bishop of San Diego, 1969—; prior Western Lieutenancy of Knights and Ladies of Holy Sepulchre. Bd. dirs. Soc. Propagation of Faith, Youth's Director, Cath. Youth Orgn.; chmn. bd. trustees U. San Diego.; Del. Ecumenical Council, Rome, Italy, 1962, 63, 64, 65. Home: 2031 Sunset Blvd San Diego CA 92103 Office: Diocesan Office Alcala Pk San Diego CA 92110

MAHLER, DANIEL ARTHUR, social worker; b. Salt Lake City, Apr. 20, 1950; s. Anton and Elfriede (Butchereit) M.; m. Lisa R. Goodroad, Mar. 7, 1981; children: P. Simon, Sarah. BS in Sociology, Social Welfare, U. Utah, 1973, MSW, 1975. Group counselor, supr. Neighborhood House, Salt Lake City, 1970-73; social service worker Bur. Indian Affairs, Fairbanks, Alaska, 1974; unit dir. N. Idaho Children's Home, Lewiston, 1975-78, dir. residential services, 1978-85; exec. dir. Christie Sch., Marylhurst, Oreg., 1985—; lit. reviewer Child Welfare Resource Exchange, Washington, 1978-80; foster parent trainer Boise (Idaho) State U., 1978-80; instr. Lewis Clark State Coll., Lewiston, 1980-85. Named Disting. Employee N. Idaho Children's Home, 1980, 81. Mem. Nat. Assn. Social Workers (pres. Idaho chpt. 1982-85, Social Worker Yr., 1982), Am. Assn Children's Residential Ctrs. Home: 16890 SW Cortez Ct Lake Oswego OR 97035 Office: Christie Sch Marylhurst OR 97036

MAHLER, DAVID, chemical company executive; b. San Francisco; s. John and Jennie (Morgan) M.; PhC, U. So. Calif., 1932; children: Darrell, Glenn. Pres., United Drug Co., Glendale, Calif., 1934-37, Blue Cross Labs., Inc., Saugus, Calif., 1937—. Active Fund for Animals, Friends of Animals, Com. for Humane Legislations; patron Huntington Hartford Theatre, Hollywood, Calif. Mem. Packaging and Rsch. Devel. Inst. (hon.), Anti-Defamation League, Skull and Daggar, Rho Pi Phi. Office: 26411 N Golden Valley Rd Saugus CA 91350

MAHLKE, AMY GERILYN, pre-school teacher; b. Winona, Minn., Jan. 21, 1959; d. Alan Eugene and Barbara Ann (Lelwica) Smith; m. David Allen Mahlke II; children: Katherine, David III. Student, Coll. St. Teresa, Winona, 1977-78; BS in Elem. Edn., Winona State U., 1982. Cert. tchr., Minn. Interim tchr. Jefferson Elem. Sch., Winona, 1985; tchr. learning disabled students Goodview Elem. Sch., Winona, 1985-86; tchr. of mildly handicapped Burlington Elem. Sch., Billings, Mont., 1986-88; tchr. Kid Kollege Preschool, Billings, 1988—. Mem. Mont. Edn. Assn. Republican. Roman Catholic. Home: 157 Erickson Ct Billings MT 59105 Office: Kid Kollege Preschool 375 Westchester Sq N Billings MT 59105

MAHLUM, DALE DUANE, small business owner, horseman; b. Bowman, N.D., June 12, 1930; s. Lloyd S. and Ragna (Paulson) M.; m. Sandra Sue Little, Dec. 21, 1956; children: Douglas, Connie, Thomas, Dee Ann, Michele. BS, U. Mont, 1956. Mgr. Super Foods, Kalispell, Mont., 1954-58; store owner Coast to Coast, Missoula, Mont., 1959—, thoroughbred farm owner, breeder, 1981—; chmn. Mont. Bank Bd., Missoula, 1974—; bd. dirs. Mont. Hardware Implement, Helena, Community Hosp., Missoula; chmn. adv. bd. sch. bus U. Mont., Missoula, 1985-88. Mem. Western Mont. Fair Commn., Missoula, 1974—. With USN, 1950-54. Mem. Mont. Thoroughbreds Breeders Assn. (pres.). Republican. Lutheran. Home: 10955 Hwy 93 N Missoula MT 59802 Office: Coast to Coast Store 2301 Brooks Missoula MT 59801

MAHONEY, JAMES P., bishop; b. Saskatoon, Sask., Can., Dec. 7, 1927. Ordained priest Roman Cath. Ch., 1952; bishop Saskatoon, 1967—. also: Chancery Office, 106 5th Ave N, Saskatoon, SK Canada S7K 2N7 *

MAHONEY, LEE CLYDE, engineer, consultant; b. Phoenix, Apr. 10, 1938; s. Selden C. and Ardith (Brown) M.; m. Nancy Markley, Feb. 14, 1959 (div. 1965); children: Timothy Michael, Shelley Anne. Tool engr. Zephyr Mfg., Inglewood, Calif., 1965-66; diamond, carbide tool engr. Craig Tools, Inc., El Segundo, Calif., 1967-70; bus. developer, cons. Princeton, Oreg., 1970—; pres. B&D Distbrs., Inc., Englewood, 1973-79, Mission Bell Ranch, Inc., Rogue River, Oreg., 1976-80, Rocking L. Ranch, Inc., Princeton, Oreg., 1980—. Designer, builder racing aircraft, automotive prodn. machinery. Winner Cleve. Nat. Air Races, 1967. Home and Office: HC-72 Box 180 Princeton OR 97721

MAHONY, ROGER MICHAEL, archbishop; b. Hollywood, Calif., Feb. 27, 1936; s. Victory James and Loretta Marie (Baron) M. A.A., Our Lady of Queen of Angles Sem., 1956, B.A., St. John's Sem. Coll., 1958, B.S.T., 1962; M.S.W., Catholic U. Am., 1964. Ordained priest Roman Cath. Ch., 1962, ordained bishop, 1975. Asst. pastor St. John's Cathedral, Fresno, Calif., 1962, 68-73, rector, 1973—; residence St. Genevieve's Parish, Fresno, Calif., 1964—, adminstr., 1964-67, pastor, 1967-68; titular bishop of Tamascani, aux. bishop of Fresno 1975-80; chancellor Diocese of Fresno, 1970, vicar gen., 1975-80; bishop Diocese of Stockton (Calif.), 1980-85; archbishop Diocese of Los Angeles, 1985—; diocesan dir. Cath. Charities and Social Service Fresno, 1964-70, exec. dir. Cath. Welfare Bur., 1964-70; exec. dir. Cath. Welfare Bur. Infant of Prague Adoption Service, 1964-70; chaplain St. Vincent de Paul Soc., Fresno, 1964-70; named chaplain to Pope Paul VI, 1967; mem. faculty extension div. Fresno State U., 1965-67; sec. U.S. Cath. bishops ad hoc com. on farm labor Nat. Conf. Bishops, 1970-75; chmn. com. on pub. welfare and income maintenance Nat. Conf. Cath. Charities, 1969-70; bd. dirs. West Coast Regional Office Bishops Com. for Spanish-Speaking, 1967-70; chmn. Calif. Assn. Cath. Charities Dirs., 1965-69; trustee St. Patrick's Sem., Archdiocese of San Francisco, 1974-75. Mem. Urban Coalition of Fresno, 1968-72; mem. Fresno County Econ. Opportunities Commn., 1964-65, Fresno County Alcoholic Rehab. Com., 1966-67, Fresno City Charter Rev. Com., 1968-70, Mexican-Am. Council for Better Housing, 1968-72, Fresno Redevel. Agy., 1970-75; bd. dirs. Fresno Community Workshop, 1965-67; trustee St. Agnes Hosp., Fresno. Named Young Man of Yr. Fresno Jr. C. of C., 1967. Mem. Canon Law Soc. Am., Nat. Assn. Social Workers. Home: 114 E 2nd St Los Angeles CA 90012 Office: Archdiocese of Los Angeles 1531 N 9th St Los Angeles CA 90012 *

MAI, HAROLD LEVERNE, federal judge; b. Casper, Wyo., Apr. 5, 1928. B.A., U. Wyo., 1950, J.D., 1952. Bar: Wyo. 1952, U.S. Supreme Ct. 1963. Sole practice, Cheyenne, Wyo., 1953-62, 67-71; judge Juvenile Ct., Cheyenne, 1962-67; U.S. bankruptcy judge, Cheyenne, 1971—. Mem. adv. bd. Salvation Army. Wyo. Mem. ABA, Wyo. Bar Assn., Laramie County Bar Assn., Nat. Conf. Bankruptcy Judges. Home: 5428 Walker Rd Cheyenne WY 82009 Office: US Dist Ct PO Box 763 Cheyenne WY 82003

MAIER, CORNELL C., aluminum and chemical company executive; b. Herreid, S.D., Jan. 12, 1925; s. Phillip and Ann (Riedlinger) M. B.S. in Engring, U. Calif. at Berkeley, 1949. With Kaiser Aluminum & Chem. Corp., Oakland, Calif., 1949-87; v.p., mgr. European region Kaiser Aluminum Internat., 1963-68; v.p., gen. mgr. European region Kaiser Aluminum Internat. (Mill Products div. parent co.), 1969; v.p., gen. mgr. European region Kaiser Aluminum Internat. (N.Am. aluminum ops.), 1969-70, exec. v.p., 1970-72; corp. gen. mgr. Kaiser Aluminum and Chem. Corp., Oakland, Calif., 1971-72, pres., 1972-82, chief exec. officer, 1972-87, chmn., 1978-87, mem. exec. com., also bd. dirs.; vice chmn., pres. KaiserTech Ltd., Oakland, 1987, now bd. dirs.; mem. Bus. Roundtable; bd. dirs. Anglesey Aluminum Metal Ltd., London, Bank of Am. N.T. and S.A., Volta Aluminum Co. Ltd., BankAm. Corp. Co-chmn. Calif. Commn. on Campaign Financing; mem. adv. bd. U. Calif. Sch. Bus., Berkeley; bd. dirs., bd. dirs., mem. exec. com. Bay Area Council Inc.; bd. dirs. Calif. Econ. Devel. Corp. Served with USAAF, 1943-45. Named Mfr. of Yr., Calif. Mfrs. Assn., 1983. Mem. Calif. C. of C. (dir.), Aluminum Assn. (chmn. adv. council). Clubs: Round Hill Country, Alamo, Silverado Country, Pacific Union. Office: Kaiser Aluminum & Chem Corp Kaiser Ctr 300 Lakeside Dr Oakland CA 94643 *

MAILHOT, JAMES, cardiologist; b. Providence, June 6, 1938; s. Frederick Ludger and Gracia Prue M.; m. Elisabeth Ann Hozen, July 27, 1968; children: Mark, James Christine, Thomas, Andrew, Peter. AB in Biology, Providence Coll., 1960; MD, Georgetown U., 1964. Diplomate Am. Bd. Internal Medicine. Intern Univ. Hosp. Boston, 1964-65; resident in internal medicine Boston City Hosp., 1967-69; fellow in cardiology Mt. Zion Hosp., San Francisco, 1969-71, assoc. dir. cardiology, 1971-78, dir. cardiology, 1978—; fellow cardiology Stanford U., 1970-71; med. advisor Blue Shield M.O., San Francisco, 1979-88. Contbr. articles to profl. jours. Adult leader Boy Scouts Am., Millbrae, Calif., 1978-88. Lt. USMC, 1965-67. Fellow Am. Coll. Cardiology, Am. Heart Assn. (clin. coun.); mem. Am. Fed. Clin. Rsch., Am. Soc. Clin. Rsch. Roman Catholic. Home: 60 Manzanita Ct Millbrae CA 94030 Office: Cardiology Med Group San Francisco 2299 Post St San Francisco CA 94115

MAIN, ALICE LEE, municipal administrator; b. St. Louis, Mar. 11, 1941; d. George and Lillie (Poleos) M.; m. Waldemar Schimming, June 1, 1974 (div. 1988); 1 child, Nicole Maria. BA, Webster U., 1963, U. Mo., 1967; MA, U. No. Colo., 1981; arts mgmt. cert., N.C. State U., 1981. Asst. rsch. librarian Fed. Res. Bank, St. Louis, 1964-66; tchr. drama and English Riverview Gardens Sch. Dist., St. Louis, 1966-69; div. fashion specialist Helene Curtis, Inc., Chgo., 1969-70; asst. buyer Fashion Bar, Denver, 1970-72; credit mgr. Montgomery Wards, Aurora, Colo., 1973; cultural arts adminstr. City of Aurora, 1973—. Founder, treas., v.p. Aurora Arts and Humanities Council, 1978—; theater cons. renovation bd., Fox Arts Ctr., Aurora, 1982-85; cons. Colo. Council Arts and Humanities, Denver, 1979-84; speech judge Voice of Dem., VFW, Colo., 1980-81; coach Aurora Girls' Softball Assn., 1987—; chmn. com. Colo. Parks and Recreation Assn., 1979-82; bd. dirs. Colo. Dance Alliance, 1985-89; mem. Denver Ballet Guild, 1988-89. Named Woman of Yr. Aurora Bus. and Profl. Women, 1984; recipient Svc. award Aurora Dance Arts, 1987. Mem. Aurora C. of C. (chmn. arts com. 1988—), Assn. Coll. U. and Community Arts Adminstrs, Zonta Internat. (treas. 1989). Democrat. Roman Catholic. Home: 11661 E Colorado Dr Aurora CO 80012 Office: City of Aurora Bicentenn Art Ctr 13655 E Alameda Ave Aurora CO 80012

MAIN, CHARLES VERNON, speech and writing educator; b. Eureka, Calif., Aug. 3, 1952; s. Justin Vernon and Aimee Mae (Nowlin) M. AA in English, Coll. of Redwoods, 1972; BA in Speech, Humboldt State U., 1974, MA in Speech, 1979. Cert. community coll. instr., lang. arts and lit. tchr., Calif. Account exec. Sta. KXGO-FM, Arcata, Calif., 1976-78; account exec., mktg. cons. Sta. KQDQ, Eugene, Oreg., 1981-82; mktg. cons., freelance writer Eugene and Eureka, 1982—; advt. mgr. Coll. of Redwoods, Eureka, 1971-72, instr. speech and writing, 1985—, pub. info. cons., 1987—. Contbr. over 100 articles to various publs. Mem. Gideons Internat. Democrat. Mem. Assemblies of God Ch. Office: Coll of Redwoods 7351 Tompkins Hill Rd Eureka CA 95501

MAIN, ROBERT GAIL, communications and training consultant, television and film producer, educator, former army officer; b. Bucklin, Mo., Sept. 30, 1932; s. Raymond M. and Inez L. (Olinger) M.; m. Anita Sue Thoroughman, Jan. 31, 1955; children: Robert Bruce, David Keith, Leslie Lorraine. BS magna cum laude, U. Mo., 1954; grad. with honors, Army Command and Gen. Staff Coll., 1967; MA magna cum laude in Communications, Stanford U., 1968; PhD, U. Md., 1978. Commd. 2d lt. U.S. Army, 1954, advanced through grades to lt. col., 1968; various command and staff assignments field arty., 1954-64; sr. instr. and div. chief Pershing missile div. U.S. Army Arty. and Missile Sch., Ft. Sill, Okla., 1964-66; mem. faculty U.S. Army Command and Gen. Staff Coll., 1968-70; chief speechwriting and info. materials div. U.S. Army Info. Office, 1971, chief broadcast and film div., 1972-73; dir. def. audiovisual activities Office of Info. for Armed Forces, 1973-76, ret., 1976; prof., grad. adv. Coll. Communications, Calif. State U., Chico, 1976-87; pres. Grant & Main, Inc., corp. communications and tng. cons. Author: Rogues, Saints and Ordinary People, 1988; contbr. articles on audiovisual communications to profl. publs.; producer: Walking Wounded, TV documentary, 1983; producer army info. films, army radio series, 1972-73; creating family heritage videos. Decorated Legion of Merit, Meritorious Service medal, Commendation medal with oak leaf cluster, combat Inf. Badge; Vietnamese Cross of Gallantry; recipient Freedom Found. awards, 1972, 73, 74; Bronze medal Atlanta Film Festival, 1972; Best of Show award Balt. Film Festival, 1973; Creativity award Chgo. Indsl. Film Festival, 1973; Cine gold award Internat. Film Producers Assn., 1974; named an Outstanding Prof. Calif State U., 1987-88. Mem. Assn. for Ednl. Communications Tech., Am. Soc. of Curriculum Developers, Nat. Assn. Ednl. Broadcasters, Phi Eta Sigma, Alpha Zeta, Phi Delta Gamma, Omicron Delta Kappa, Alpha Gamma Rho. Mem. Christian Ch.

MAINES, CLIFFORD BRUCE, insurance company executive; b. Tacoma, Wash., Aug. 14, 1926; s. Clifford McLean and Ida Vera (Wardall) M.; m. Mary Jean Marshall, Sept. 4, 1948; children—Molly, Janet Lynn. Student, Central Coll., Fayette, Mo., 1944-45, U. Mich., 1945-46; B.S., U. Wash., 1948, LL.B., 1949, J.D., 1949. Bar: Wash. bar 1950. Mem. legal staff Safeco Corp., Seattle, 1950-62, asso. gen. counsel, 1962-66, gen. counsel, 1966-68, v.p., gen. counsel, 1968-74, sr. v.p., 1974-81, pres., 1981—, pres., chief exec. officer, 1986-89, dir., 1977—, chmn., chief exec. officer, 1989—; exec. v.p., chief operating officer, dir. Gen. Ins. Co. Am., 1974-77, pres., 1977-81; now dir.; exec. v.p. 1st Nat. Ins. Co. Am., 1974-77, pres., 1977-81; now dir.; exec. v.p. Safeco Ins. Co., 1974-77, pres., 1977-81, now dir.; dir. Safeco Life Ins. Co.; exec. v.p. GSL. Served with USNR, 1944-46. Mem. ABA, Wash. Bar Assn., Seattle-King County Bar Assn. (past trustee), Wash. Ins. Council (past pres.), Pacific Ins. and Surety Conf., Washington Athletic Club, Broadmoor Golf Club, Seattle Golf Club, Columbia Tower Club, Beta Theta Pi. Methodist. Office: Safeco Corp Safeco Pla Seattle WA 98185

MAING, I. YOUNG, food company executive; b. Seoul, Republic of Korea, July 9, 1942; came to U.S., 1968, naturalized, 1968; s. Kwang Ho Maing and In Sun Lee; m. Jeanne Lee, Aug. 12, 1968; children: Michelle, John-Michael. BS, Seoul Nat. U., 1967; MS, U. Ga., 1970; PhD, U. Wis., 1972. Sr. food technologist Armour Foods, Oak Brook, Ill., 1974-75; project leader Gen. Foods, Tarrytown, N.Y., 1975-77, group leader, 1977-79, sr. research specialist, 1980-82; exec. mgr. Gen. Foods Internat., Honolulu, 1982—; also bd. dirs. Gen. Foods Internat., Seoul; dir. USDA, Washington, 1980-82; exec. dir. Korea Indsl. Research Inst., Seoul, 1982—, strategy and policy com. Gen. Foods, Korea, 1985—; invited scientist German Research Inst., Kulmbech, 1972-74. Inventor in field. Mem. Rep. Presdl. Task Force, Washington, 1984, Statue of Liberty Ellis Island Found., N.Y.C., 1984. Grantee Internat. Child Health Found., N.Y.C., 1969; FDA fellow U. Ga., Athens, 1967. Mem. Am. Cereal Chemists Soc., Inst. Food Technologists (counselor 1984—), Am. Chem. Soc., Korean-Am. Food Scientists Assn. (chmn. 1978). Home: 722 Post Rd Darien CT 06820 Office: Gen Foods Worldwide 250 North St White Plains NY 10625

MAIROSE, PAUL TIMOTHY, mechanical engineer, consultant; b. Mitchell, S.D., Aug. 4, 1956; s. Joseph E. and Phyllis R. (Glissendorf) M. BSME, S.D. Sch. Mines and Tech., 1978; postgrad., Tulane U., 1986. Registered profl. engr., Wash. Mech. engr. UNC Nuclear Industries, Richland, Wash., 1979-80, Wash. Pub. Power Supply System, Richland, 1980-85; cons. La. Power & Light Co., New Orleans, 1985-86, Erin Engring. & Rsch. Inc., Walnut Creek, Calif., 1986-87, Sacramento Mcpl. Utility Dist., 1987—, Wash. Pub. Power Supply System, Richland, 1989—. Mem. polit. action com. Sacramento Mcpl. Utility Dist., 1988. Mem. ASME (assoc.), ASHRAE (assoc.), Aircraft Owners and Pilots Assn., Sierra Club, Bards of Bohemia. Republican. Roman Catholic. Home: 205 Casey Ave Richland WA 99352 Office: Wash Pub Power System 300 George Washington Way WNP-2 Richland WA 99352

MAIRS, NANCY PEDRICK, poet; b. Long Beach, Calif., July 23, 1943; d. John Eldredge Smith Jr. and Anne (Pedrick) Cutler; m. George Anthony Mairs, May 18, 1963; children: Anne Eldredge, Matthew Anthony. AB, Wheaton Coll., Norton, Mass., 1964; MFA, U. Ariz., 1975, PhD, 1984. Jr. editor Smithsonian Astrophys. Observatory, Cambridge, Mass., 1966-69; editorial asst. Internat. Tax Program Harvard U. Sch. Law, Cambridge, 1970-72; tchr. Salpointe Cath. High Sch., Tucson, 1973-77; project dir. S.W. Inst. for Rsch. on Women, Tucson, 1983-85; lectr. in writing UCLA, 1986-87; freelance writer Tucson, 1987—. Author: Instead It Is Winter, 1977, In All The Rooms of the Yellow House, 1984 (Western States Book Award 1984), (essays) Plaintext, 1986, Remembering the Bone House: An Erotics of Place and Space, 1989. Time Inc. scholar Bread Loaf Writers Conf., Middlebury, Vt., 1982; William P. Sloane fellow Bread Loaf Writers Conf., 1984. Mem. Catholics for Peace and Justice, Nat. Women's Studies Assn., Poets and Writers Inc. Democrat. Roman Catholic. Home: 1527 E Mabel St Tucson AZ 85719

MAISEL, ANDREW CODDON, computer company executive; b. Mpls., Oct. 8, 1956; s. Melvin and Renée (Levin) M.; m. Vicki L. Weir, Aug. 5, 1983. AB, BS, Stanford U., 1979; MBA, Harvard U., 1983. Economist Dames & Moore, San Francisco, 1979-81; fin. analyst GE, San Francisco,

1982; cons. The Boston Cons. Group, San Francisco, 1983-86; product mgr. Sun Microsystems, Mountain View, Calif., 1986-87; mgr. strategic planning Sun Microsystems, Mountain View, 1987-88, mgr. mkt. devel. group, 1988—. Swim coach, Stanford U., Palo Alto, Calif., 1979—; mgr. govt. rels. X/Open, 1989—. Mem. Am. Inst. Mining Engrs., U.S. Synchronized Swimming, Inc. (dir., bd. govs. 1985-89), Coll. Coaches Assn. (pres. 1984-89). Office: Sun Microsystems Inc 2550 Garcia Ave Mountain View CA 94043

MAISEL, TERRI LYNN, organization administrator; b. Tucson, Dec. 28, 1951; d. John Louis and Irene (Ellis) Gunby. Student, U. N.Mex., 1975-80; cert., Inst. Orgn. Mgmt., 1985. Cert. chamber exec. New accounts rep. SunWest Bank, Albuquerque, 1971-74, employment adminstr., 1974-76, communications dir., 1976-78; pub. info. dir. Albuquerque C. of C., 1978-81, gen. mgr., 1981-83, pres., 1983—; pres. N.Mex. C. of C. Execs. Assn., 1986-87, bd. dirs., 1980—; bd. regents Inst. for Orgn. Mgmt.; bd. dirs. Hosp. Home Health, Inc. Recipient Bus. Devel. award Expn. Mgmt. Inc., 1985, Women on Move award YWCA, 1986; named one of Outstanding Women of Am., 1984. Mem. Am. Chamber Execs. (bd. dirs. 1986—), U.S. C. of C. (bd. dirs., mem. populous regional com.). Republican. Office: Greater Albuquerque C of C PO Box 25100 Albuquerque NM 87125

MAITLAND, JAMES DEAN, sales executive; b. Redondo Beach, Calif., Aug. 19, 1960; s. James Preston and C. Dean (Adams) M. BA in Psychology, Calif. State U., Sacramento, 1985, postgrad., 1988—. Asst. instr. San Juan Unified Sch. Dist., Carmichael, Calif., 1985-87. Active Civil Air Patrol, North Highlands, 1983. Democrat. Home: 6242 Pine Creek Way Citrus Heights CA 95621

MAITZEN, DOLORES ANN, educator; b. Chgo., Nov. 2, 1952; d. Joseph Thomas and Angeline G. (Butz) Svacik; m. Robert H. Maitzen Jr., Apr. 15, 1978. BS, Ill. State U., 1973; student, John Robert Powers Modeling Sch., 1975-76; MS, Chgo. State U., 1976. Tchr., Josephinum High Sch., Chgo., 1973-75, Queen of Peace High Sch., Burbank, Ill., 1976-79; coordinator home econs. related occupations and tchr. home econs. North High Sch., Phoenix Union Dist., 1979-81; asst. prof. Ariz. State U., 1981-86; tchr. fashion merchandising Paradise Valley High Sch., 1988—. Mem. Ariz. Assn. Vocat. Home Econs. Educators (state membership chmn. 1981-83, state pres. 1986), Am. Vocat. Assn. (del. nat. conf.), Ariz. Vocat. Assn. (sec. 1983-84, bd. dirs., exec. bd.), Am. Home Econs. Assn., Ariz. Home Econs. Assn. (profl. awards chmn. 1983-86, profl. recognition award 1982, Elem.-Secondary Adult Edn. award 1982, state del. to conv. 1989, Ariz. Home Econs. Tchr. of Yr. 1989), Ill. State U. Alumni Assn., Ariz. State U. Women's Faculty Assn., Ariz. State Home Econs. Adv. Coun., Nat. Restaurant Assn., Assn. Supervision and Curriculum Devel., Chgo. State U. Alumni Assn., NEA, Ariz. Edn. Assn., Young Ladies of St. Joseph Ch. Club, Alpha Gamma Delta. Home: 3702 E Dahlia Dr Phoenix AZ 85032 Office: Ariz State U Dept Home Econs Tempe AZ 85287

MAJER, CHRISTOPHER DEAN, company executive; b. Spokane, Wash., Feb. 9, 1951; s. Norman Archibald and Virginia Leigh (Holmes) M.; m. Carla Lee Sawyer, Mar. 21, 1983 (div. 1984); m. Cheri Rose Michel, Sept. 5, 1987. BA, U. Wash., 1973, MPA, 1976. Asst. to county exec. King County, Seattle, 1974-76; dir. village mgmt. program Sheldon Jackson Coll., Sitka, Ark., 1976-78; ptnr. Modern Product Mktg., Seattle, 1978-80; founder, pres. Sportsmind Inc., Seattle, 1980—. Contbr. articles in field to profl. jours. Bd. trustees Univ. Bookstore, Seattle, 1971-75, chmn., 1974-75. Mem. Old Puget Sound Club (Seattle, pres. 1981-83), Beach Rugby Football Club.

MAJOR, MARGUERITE LOUISE, magazine editor; b. Kansas City, Mo., Jan. 26, 1929; d. Ray Clark and Celia Marguerite (Fowler) M. AB in Journalism, San Jose State U., 1950. Reporter, editor Sunnyvale (Calif.) Standard, 1951-52; alumni dir. San Jose State U., 1953-57; pubs. dir. Santa Clara (Calif.) U., 1957-60, news dir., 1960-78, pub. affairs dir., 1978-83; editor Santa Clara Today, Santa Clara U., 1983-86, Santa Clara mag., Santa Clara U., 1986—. Mem. Am. Coll. Pub. Rels. (regional dir. 1974-75), Pub. Rels. Soc. Am. (accredited), Coun. Advancement & Support Edn. (trustee 1975-77). Republican. Episcopalian. Home: 7135 Via Solano San Jose CA 95135 Office: Santa Clara U Santa Clara CA 95053

MAKANSI, TAREK, electrical engineer; b. Wilmington, Del., Oct. 21, 1957. BSEE, Cornell U., 1980; MSEE, U. Calif., Berkeley, 1982, PhD in Elec. Engring., 1985. Coop. engr. Gen. Elec., Schenectady, N.Y., 1978-80; teaching asst. U. Calif., Berkeley, 1980-82, research asst., 1982-84; engr. Ampex Corp., Redwood City, Calif., summers 1981, 82; staff engr. IBM, San Jose, Calif., 1985-86, mgr., 1986—; cons. SRI Internat., Menlo Park, Calif., 1984; cons., chmn. bd. dirs. Digital Kinetics Corp., Pleasanton, Calif. Scholar McMullen Dean Cornell U., 1976, Earl C. Anthony, U. Calif., Berkeley, 1980. Mem. IEEE, Communications Soc. IEEE, Control Sytems Soc. IEEE, Magnetic Soc. IEEE, Tau Beta Pi, Eta Kappa Nu. Office: IBM Corp 5600 Cottle Rd San Jose CA 95193

MAKEBAKKEN, MARK PETER, small business owner; b. Akron, Ohio, May 7, 1963; s. Bjarne and Elin Makebakken; m. Cathy Makebakken, Sept. 7, 1984 (div. Jan. 1988). Student, Mesa Coll., 1983. Pres. Moremakr Painters Inc., San Diego, 1982—. Mem. adv. bd. Youth for Christ, Calif., 1987-88; trustee local Lukemia Soc. Mem. San Diego C. of C., Assn. Bldg. Contractors, Rotary. Republican. Home: 2510 Clairemont Dr San Diego CA 92117 Office: Moremakr Painters Inc 7915 Silverton Ave #305 San Diego CA 92109

MAKEPEACE, DARRYL LEE, manufacturing company executive; b. Pitts., Oct. 24, 1941; s. Thomas Henry Makepeace and Nevada Ruth (Wagner) Desin; m. Maryanne Stright, Aug. 16, 1977; children: Krisanne, Erin. BS in Indsl. Engring., Pa. State U., 1969; MBA, Pepperdine U., 1982. Dept. mgr. Procter & Gamble, Cin., 1969-72; plant mgr. CBS Mus. Instruments, Fullerton, Calif., 1972-76; dir. mfg. Frigid Coil/Wolf Range, Whittier, Calif., 1977-79; mgr. materials mgmt. Nat. Supply, Los Nietos, Calif., 1979-85, mgr. mfg., 1985-86; program mgr. Armco Cumberland Group, Middletown, Ohio, 1986; ptnr., cons. Armco Cumberland Group, Mason, Ohio, 1986-87, ptnr., prin., 1988—; assoc. prof. mgmt. Wright State U., Dayton, Ohio, 1987-88, Miami U., Oxford, Ohio., 1988—. Contbr. articles to profl. jours. Served with U.S. Army, 1960-61. Named to Honorable Order of Ky. Cols. Mem. Am. Prodn. and Inventory Control Soc., Inst. Indsl. Engrs., Alpha Pi Mu, Tau Beta Pi, Sigma Tau.

MAKI, KAZUMI, physicist, educator; b. Takamatsu, Japan, Jan. 27, 1936; s. Toshio and Hideko M.; m. Masako Tanaka, Sept. 21, 1969. B.S., Kyoto U., 1959, Ph.D., 1964. Research asso. Inst. for Math. Scis., Kyoto U., 1964; research asso. Fermi Inst., U. Chgo., 1964-65; asst. prof. physics U. Calif., San Diego, 1965-67; prof. Tohoku U., Sendai, Japan, 1967-74; vis. prof. Universite Paris-Sud, Orsay, France, 1969-70; prof. physics U. So. Calif., Los Angeles, 1974—; vis. prof. Inst. Laue-Langevin, U. Paris-Sud, France, 1979-80, Max-Planck Inst. für Festkörper Forschung, Stuttgart, Fed. Republic of Germany, 1986-87. Assoc. editor Jour. Low Temperature Physics, 1969—; contbr. articles to profl. jours. Recipient Nishina prize, 1972, Alexander von Humboldt award, 1986-87; Fulbright scholar, 1964-65; Guggenheim fellow, 1979-80. Fellow Am. Phys. Soc.; Mem. Phys. Soc. Japan, AAAS. Office: U So Calif Dept Physics Los Angeles CA 90089-0484

MAKINSON, DWIGHT LELAND, land surveyor, consultant; b. Baker, Oreg., Apr. 16, 1946; s. Ralph Leland and Ruth Irene (Bisbee) M.; m. Doris Berquist, Aug. 1, 1965 (div. 1978); m. Denise Mary Kneifl; 1 child, Cassie Corene. BS, Oreg. State U., 1969; postgrad., Nat. Advanced Resource Tech., 1982. Lic. profl. land surveyor, Wash. Asst. forest land surveyor USDA Forest Svc., Corvallis, Oreg., 1973-76; cadastral surveyor USDA Forest Svc., Coeur d'Alene, Idaho, 1976-81, supervisory forest land surveyor, 1981—; prin. Makinson & Assocs., Coeur d'Alene, 1982—; co-owner Property Info. Systems, Inc., Coeur d'Alene, 1988—. Author: Mineral Surveys in the Coeur d'Alene Jour., 1981; co-editor: Gem State Surveyor Jour., 1981. Mem. Idaho Assn. Land Surveyors (bd. dirs. No. chpt. 1986-87, chmn. 1987), N. Idaho Enological Soc. (sec. Coeur d'Alene chpt. 1986), Rocky Mountain Elk Found. Democrat. Office: Idaho Panhandle Nat Forests 1201 Ironwood Dr Coeur d'Alene ID 83814

MAKOWSKI, CAROL JEAN, interior designer; b. Phoenix; d. Elwood C. and Letha J. Evans; m. Michael G. Makowski, Dec. 23, 1979. BS in Interior Design, No. Ariz. U., 1987. Interior designer Cunninghams Interiors, Flagstaff, Ariz., 1987—. Author: Reality, 1979. Recipient Outstanding Student Book award Inst. B Bus. Designers, 1987; Industry Found. scholar, 1986. Mem. Am. Soc. Interior Designers (assoc., alumni corr. No. Ariz. U. chpt. 1985-87). Office: Cunningham's Interiors 2221 E 7th Ave Flagstaff AZ 86004

MAKOWSKI, EDGAR LEONARD, obstetrician and gynecologist; b. Milw., Oct. 27, 1927; s. Adam and Ernestine (Horn) M.; m. Patricia M. Nock, Nov. 1, 1952; children: Peter, James, Ann, Mary, Thomas, Paul. B.S., Marquette U., 1951, M.D., 1954. Intern Deaconess Hosp., Milw., 1954-55; resident in Ob/Gyn U. Minn., Mpls., 1955-59; asst. prof. U. Minn., 1959-66, asso. prof., 1966; asso. prof. Ob/Gyn U. Colo., Denver, 1966-69; prof. U. Colo., 1969—, chmn. dept., 1976-88. Contbr. articles to sci. jours., chpts. to books. Served with AUS, 1946-47. NIH spl. fellow in physiology Yale U., 1963. Mem. Am. Gynecol. and Obstet. Soc. (pres.), Am. Coll. Obstetricians and Gynecologists, Soc. Gynecol. Investigators, Central Assn. Obstetricians and Gynecologists, Colo. Soc. Ob/Gyn., Perinatal Research Soc. (pres.). Roman Catholic. Office: U Colo Sch Medicine 4200 E 9th Ave Denver CO 80262

MALA, THEODORE ANTHONY, physician, university institute director; b. Santa Monica, Calif., Feb. 3, 1946; s. Ray and Galina (Liss) M.; m. Emma Sahagun, Dec. 25, 1975 (div. 1980); children: Theodore S., Galina T. BA in Philosophy, DePaul U., 1972; MD, Autonomous U., Guadalajara, Mex., 1976; MPH, Harvard U., 1980. Spl. asst. for health affairs Alaska Fedn. Natives, Anchorage, 1977-78; chief health svcs. Alaska State Div. of Corrections, Anchorage, 1978-79; founder, dir. Internat. Inst. for Circumpolar Health U. Alaska, Anchorage, 1982—; founder Siberian med. rsch. program U. Alaska, 1982, Magadan (USSR) med. rsch. program, 1988; Alaska rsch. and publs. com. mem. USPHS Indian Health Svs., 1987—; advisor WHO Nordic Council Meeting, Greenland, 1985. Contbr. articles to profl. jours. Trustee United Way Anchorage, 1978-79. Recipient Gov.'s award, 1988, Nat. Indian fellowship U.S. Dept. Edn., 1979, Outstanding Service award Alaska Commr. Health, 1979. Mem. Assn. Am. Indian Physicians, Am. Assn. University Profs., N.Y. Acad. Scis., Internat. Physicians for Prevention of Nuclear War, Native Am. Sci. Edn. Assn., Internat. Union for Circumpolar Health (permanent sec.-gen. 1987—, mem. organizing com. 8th Internat. Congress on Circumpolar Health 1987—), Am. Pub. Health Assn., Alaska Pub. Health Assn., Harvard Club of Boston, Am. Orthopsychiatric Assn. Home: PO Box 23-2228 Anchorage AK 99523 Office: U Alaska Inst Circumpolar Health Studies 3211 Providence Dr Anchorage AK 99508

MALAKOFF, JAMES LEONARD, data processing executive; b. Phila., June 20, 1933; s. John and Ida Vera (Partman) M.; m. Anne Bronstein Frisch, June 26, 1955; children: Randi Ellen, John Seymour. B in Aerospace Engring., Rensselaer Poly. Inst., 1954, MS, 1955. Structural methods specialist Grumman Aircraft, Bethpage, N.Y., 1955-62; mem. tech. staff Northrop Corp., Hawthorne, Calif., 1962-65; chief, math. analyst Beckman Instruments, Inc., Fullerton, Calif., 1965-68; dir. data processing Beckman Instruments, Inc., Fullerton, 1968-82, v.p. data processing, 1982-85, v.p., mgmt. info., 1985—; bd. dirs. San Pedro (Calif.) Peninsula Hosp.; vis. prof. Calif. State U., Fullerton. Fellow AIAA (assoc.); mem. IEEE (computer group), U.S. Council Internat. Bus. (bus. and industry adv. com., West Coast com. Internat. Info. and Telecommunications Policy), Assn. Computing Machinery, Data Processing Mgmt. Assn. Office: Beckman Instruments Inc 2500 Harbor Blvd Fullerton CA 92634

MALBOUVIER, KATHRYN ANNE VERONICA, microwave electrical engineer; b. N.Y.C., Apr. 18, 1954; d. William Henry and Patricia Anne (Lynch) Irwin; m. Alain Daniel Malbouvier, July 8, 1976. B.S., U. Calif.-Davis, Engr. Avantek, Folsom, Calif., 1985-87 . Served to capt. USAF, 1974-80, Air NG, 1980—. U. Calif.-Davis Ann. Fund scholar, 1984; Nat. Guard Assn. Calif. scholar, 1983; Elliott Adkisson Meml. scholar Am. River Coll., 1981; Tenco Tractor Engring. scholar, 1983; Women's Social and Cultural League scholar, 1982; Soroptimist scholar, 1981. Mem. IEEE, Soc. Women Engrs. Republican. Roman Catholic. Avocations: architectural design; art; aerobics; weight training. Office: HP Roseville MS R5th 8020 Foothills Blvd Roseville CA 95678

MALCOLM, GERALD LINDBURG, electric company executive; b. Genola, Utah, Dec. 18, 1927; s. John Leo and Rhoda (Steele) M.; m. Edith Jackson, Oct. 4, 1952; children: Guy David, Roger Allan, JoAnn, Tracy Dale, Gerald Leo, Edith Christine. Student, U. Utah, Salt Lake City, 1957-59. Master electrician, Utah; lic. elec. contractor. Electrician, Excel Neon Sign Co., Salt Lake City, 1946-48; owner, operator Malcolm Electric Co., Santaquin, Utah, 1948-52; journeyman electrician Dept. Army, Dugway Proving Grounds, Utah, 1952-60; sr. constrn. foreman A. Thiokol Chem. Corp., Tremonton, Utah, 1960-62; electrician leader VA Med. Ctr., Salt Lake City, 1962-73, constrn. mgr., 1973-81; owner, operator Malcolm Electric Co., Salt Lake City, 1965—; instr. Utah Tech. Coll., Salt Lake City, 1974-76; lectr. in field. Active Soil Conservation, Utah County, U.S. Dept. Agr., 1950-51. Mem. Ch. Jesus Christ Latter-Day Saints. Home: 1549 S 1300 W Salt Lake City UT 84104 Office: Malcolm Electric Co 1549 S 1300 W Salt Lake City UT 84104

MALCOR, MICHAEL JOSEPH, newspaper official; b. L.A., July 12, 1963; s. Joseph Vern and Joan Lois (Cooley) M.; m. Sherri Esther Stickles, June 1, 1985. Grad. high sch., Alhambra, Calif. Computer operator Architects & Engrs. Supply Co., Monrovia, Calif., 1977-85; sr. systems coord. L.A. Times, 1985-89. Democrat. Mem. Christian Ch. (Disciples of Christ).

MALDONADO, ELIZABETH G., fundraiser; b. Los Angeles, June 24, 1954; d. Fernando M. and Ursula (Gruenwald) M. BA, UCLA, 1977. Mgr. Acapulco y Los Arcos Restaurant, Pasadena, Calif., 1979-81; asst. dir. UCLA Alumni Assn., Los Angeles, 1981-86; asst. dir., ann. fund UCLA Pub. Affairs, Los Angeles, 1986—. Democrat. Mormon. Office: UCLA Ann Fund 405 Hilgard Ave Los Angeles CA 90024-1359

MALDONADO, FRANK PARKER, orthopaedic surgeon, investor; b. Buenos Aires, Argentina, Feb. 28, 1938; came to U.S., 1939; s. Frank Medina and Maria Ortiz (Toro) M.; m. Kathleen Ann Fox, May 18, 1963; children: Craig, Eileen, Parker, Frank J., Erin. BS, U. Calif., Berkeley, 1960; MD, N.Y. Med. Coll., 1964. Diplomate Am. Bd. Orthopaedic Surgery. Intern Akron (Ohio) City Hosp., 1964-65; resident in orthopaedic surgery U. Okla., Oklahoma City, 1965-69; orthopaedic surgeon Lovelace Clinic, Albuquerque, 1971-73, Norte Vista Med. Ctr. Ltd., Hobbs, N.Mex., 1973-87, Hobbs Orthopaedic Surgery Assocs., Hobbs, 1989—; asst. prof. Sch. Medicine U. N.Mex., 1971—; bd. dirs. Sunwest Bank, Hobbs, 1978—, Lea Regional Hosp., Hobbs, 1980-87. Exec. bd. Conquistador coun. Boy Scouts Am., 1980-87; bd. dirs. N.Mex. Physician Mutual Co., Albuquerque, 1983-87. Lt. comdr. USN, 1969-71. Fellow Am. Acad. Orthopaedic Surgeons; mem. N.Mex. Orthopaedic Assn. (pres. 1986, exec. bd. dirs. 1984—). Republican. Roman Catholic. Home: 1933 N Vega Hobbs NM 88240 Office: Hobbs Orthopaedic Surgery Assocs 5419 Lovington Hwy Ste 18 Hobbs NM 88240

MALDONADO-CALZADA, LYDIA, educational director; b. L.A., Jan. 3, 1945; d. Ramona Calzada; 1 child, Amelia Garcia. BA, BFA, Mt. St. Mary's Coll., 1977; MA in Adminstrn., U. San Francisco, 1986. Cert. tchr., Calif. Tchr. Roman Cath. Archdiocese of L.A., 1969-85, prin., 1985-87; on-site-coord. Soledad Enrichment Actions Schs., Pomona, Calif., 1987—; dir. Hispanic affairs Edward's Photography, El Toro, Calif.; guest speaker Hermenet, Inc., Logonet, Inc. Mem. Am. Assn. Sch. Adminstrs., Assn. Calif. Sch. Adminstrs., Assn. for Supervision and Curriculum, Nat. Cath. Ednl. Assn., Western Cath. Edn. Assn. (evaluator), Inst. for Cath. Ednl. Leadership. Democrat. Home: 1133 Cardiff Ct Pomona CA 91767 Office: SEA Sch 655 W 3d St Pomona CA 91766

MALECHA, MARVIN JOHN, architect, academic administrator; b. Lonsdale, Minn., June 26, 1949; s. George and Barbara Malecha; m. Cynthia Marie Miller, Aug. 8, 1970; children: Peter, Michelle. Student, St. Thomas Coll.; BArch, U. Minn.; M in Design, Harvard U. Registered architect, Calif. Designer Wallace and Mundt Architects, Edina, Minn., 1969-73, Hugh Stubbins and Assocs., Cambridge, Mass., 1973-76; instr. Cambridge Urban Awareness Program, 1973-76, Boston Archtl. Ctr., 1974-76; asst. chmn., asst. prof. dept. architecture Sch. Environ. Design, Calif. State Poly. U., Pomona, 1976-77, chmn., assoc. prof., 1979-82, prof., dean Coll. Environ. Design, 1982—; chmn. Assn. Collegiate Sch. Architecture Adminstrs Conf., Washington, Dec. 1985, Univ. Fall Conf. com. Calif. State Poly. U., 1984; mem. steering com. Architects for Social Responsibility; mem. bd. advisors Tchrs. cert. program City Bldg. Edn. Program, planning com. So. Calif. Assn. Govts.; vis. critic UCLA, 1985, U., Minn., 1981-83, 87, U. So. Calif., 1980-87, Calif. Poly. State U., San Luis Obispo, 1979-87, Clemson U., 1988; lectr. to schs. and archtl. assns.; cons. in architecture and research, Claremont, Calif., 1976—; master juror Nat. Council Archtl. Registration Bds.; mem. edn. equity com. Calif. State U. System, 1985-86; pres. Calif. Coun. Archtl. Edn., 1986-88, Assn. Collegiate Schs. Architecture, 1988-89; mem. accreditation vis. team for collegiate programs in landscape architecture, 1988—, Nat. Archtl. Accreditation Bd., 1988—. Contbr. aticles to profl. jours. Mem. Art and Liturgy com. Our Lady Assumption Ch., Claremont, Calif. Recipient Ellerbe Archtl. award, 1972, Hon. Mention Mass. Housing Dept., 1976; Rotch scholar, 1980. Mem. AIA (bd. dirs. Los Angeles chpt. 1982-83, chmn. state and nat. awards coms. 1983-85, chmn. Monterey design conf. com., Henry Adams award 1973, presl. citation Los Angeles chpt. 1987), Soc. Am. Registered Architects, Calif. Council of Archtl. Edn. (pres.), Assn. Collegiate Schs. Architecture (v.p. 1989—). Home: 4143 Las Casas Claremont CA 91711 Office: Calif State Poly U Coll Environ Design 3801 W Temple Ave Pomona CA 91768

MALES, WILLIAM JAMES, film producer, make-up artist; b. Mesa, Ariz.; s. James W. and Oveta (Bradshaw) M. Student, Pepperdine U., 1982-86; studies with Vincent J. R. Kehoe, 1980-82, studies with Dick Smith, 1981-83. Make-up artist William J. Males and Assocs., Hollywood, Calif., 1976—; line producer Azrak Films, Inc., Hollywood, 1986—. Studio make-up artist for numerous projects including (films) Aftershock, Family Reunion, Winds of War, Necromancer, Conan the Barbarian, Return of the Living Dead, Cat People, Scanners, Ragedy Anne, (TV shows) The Blue and the Gray, Crisis at Central High, Skyward, Printer to the Territory, Golden Girls, Hollywood Squares, 21 Jump Street, 9 to 5, (theatrical prodns.) Man of La Mancha, The Gospel Truth, Camelot, Chorus Line (nat. tour), Grease, Godspell, Crucible; line producer (films) Aftershock, Necromancer, Ms. Frankenstein, Family Reunion, Rocky I; assoc. producer (films) Castle of Revenge, Alien Warrior, Californio, (TV commls.) Coppertone, Pepsi, Beechcraft, Levi Strauss, Chanel. Mem. Nat. Acad. TV Arts and Scis., Acad. TV Arts and Scis. (Emmy nomination 1982), Brit. Acad. Film and TV Arts, Soc. Motion Picture and TV Engrs., Assn. Film Craftsmen (local 531), Nat. Assn. Broadcast Employees and Technicians, Producers Guild Am., Alpha Psi Omega (faculty dir. local chpt. 1986—). Republican. Office: 7095 Hollywood Blvd Ste 703 Hollywood CA 90028

MALHAM, CHRISTIAN VICTOR, landscape development company executive; b. Gary, Ind., Feb. 28, 1960; s. Howell Joseph and Martha (Karas) M.; m. Tracy Leigh Samaha, June 4, 1988. BS, Ariz. State U., 1983. Lic. landscape and irrigation contractor, Ariz. Account exec. Cityscape, Inc., Austin, Tex., 1983-86; pres., mng. ptnr. Cityscape-Phoenix, Inc., 1986—. Assoc. Valley Partnership, Phoenix; sponsor Valley Big Bros. Club. Mem. Ariz. Landscape Contractors Assn., Ariz. Nursery Man Assn., Nat. Assn. Indsl. Office Parks (assoc.), Assn. Gen. Contractors (affiliate). Republic. Roman Catholic. Office: Cityscape-Phoenix Inc 2737 W Baseline Rd Ste 21 Tempe AZ 85283

MALIAN, IDA MARGUERITE, professor; b. Detroit, Mar. 25, 1950; d. Artin Ghevont and Agavnie Agnes (Eknayan) M. BA, Oakland U., 1970; MA, U. Mich., 1971, PhD, 1977. Dir. ednl. tng. Children's Psychiat. Hosp., Ann Arbor, Mich., 1974-75; instr. U. Mich., Ann Arbor, 1974-75; behavior mgmt. cons. Med. Ctr. U. Nebr., Omaha, 1975-78, asst. prof., 1975-78; assoc. prof. Sch. Tchr. Edn. San Diego State U., 1978—, dir. field experiences, 1987—; state hearing officer Legal Officer State Dept., Sacramento, 1979-83; state mediator State Legal Office, 1980-83; cons. San Diego City Schs., 1979-81. Author: (with C.M. Charles) Special Student: Practical Help for the Classroom Teacher, 1980; contbr. articles to profl. jours. Bur. Edn. Handicapped grantee, 1975, fellow, 1973. Mem. Council for Exceptional Children, Council for Behavior Disorders (regional dir. 1980-82), Ctr. for Study of Sensory Integrative Dysfunction (dir. 1982-83). Democrat. Eastern Orthodox. Home: 5405 Baltimore Dr #78 La Mesa CA 92042 Office: San Diego State U Sch Tchr Edn San Diego CA 92182

MALIN, EVANGELINE MAY, social services case worker, retired; b. L.A., Dec. 19, 1928; d. Ray and Mary Alice (Yandell) Wheeler; m. Robert E. Zipperer, Feb. 6, 1953 (div. 1973); 1 child, Robert Eugene.; m. Sigmund John Malin, Sept. 9, 1976. AA, Pasadena City Coll., 1950; BA, Pasadena Coll., 1952; cert. in social svcs., U. Calif., Berkeley, 1969; 2 certs. in social work, Ethel Percy Andrus Gerontology Ctr. U. So. CAlif., 1971, 72. Social worker San Bernardino (Calif.) Co. Social Svcs., 1953-56; social worker Santa ClaraDept. Social Svcs., San Jose, Calif., 1966-81, ret., 1981. Mem. Pasadena & Point Loma Alumni Assn., Santa Clara Co. Employees Assn., Castle Med. Ctr. Aux., Mid-Pacific Country Club. Republican. Methodist. Home: 998 Iopono Loop Kailua HI 96734 also: 2308 Back Nine Oceanside CA 92056

MALIN, MICHAEL CHARLES, geology educator; b. Burbank, Calif., May 10, 1950; s. Jack and Beatryce (Solomon) M. AB, U. Calif., Berkeley, 1971; PhD, Calif. Inst. Tech., 1976. Sr. scientist Jet Propulsion Lab., Pasadena, Calif., 1975-78, mem. tech. staff, 1978-79; asst. prof. geology Ariz. State U., Tempe, 1979-82, assoc. prof., 1982-87, prof., 1987—. Co-author: Earthlike Planets, 1981; contbr. articles to profl. jours. MacArthur fellow, 1987—. Mem. Am. Geophys. Union, Am. Astron. Soc. (div. Planetary Scis.). Office: Ariz State U Dept Geology Tempe AZ 85287-1404

MALINA, ROGER F., astronomer; b. Paris, July 6, 1950; married; 1 child, Xavier. BS in Physics, MIT, 1972; PhD in Astronomy, U. Calif., Berkeley, 1979. Rsch. aide MIT Ctr. for Space Rsch., Cambridge, 1969-72; summer rsch. aide Cambridge (Mass.) Electron Accelerator, 1971; teaching asst. U. Calif., Berkeley, 1972-73, rsch. asst. space scis. lab., 1973-79, assoc. rsch. astronomer space scis. lab., 1980—; project mgr. for NASA sounding rockets, 1974; organizer Sierra Astrophysics Conf., 1974-76; project scientist for NASA sounding rockets, 1976-78, Berkeley-London-Utrecht extreme ultraviolet spectrometer, 1979-82, FAUST Spacelab 1 Instrument, 1977-84, Extreme Ultraviolet Explorer, 1978-86; co-investigator IUE observations of HZ43, 1981, NGC4242, 1983; co-dir. grant from the Nat. Endowment for the Arts to the Jour. Leonardo, 1984; dir. grant from the Nat. Endowment for the Arts to the Jour. Leonardo, 1985-87; prin. investigator Extreme Ultraviolet Explorer Sci. Instruments, 1985—. Exec. editor Jour. Leonardo, 1982—; co-author and contbr. various articles to profl. jours., 1974—; author numerous papers delivered to sci. meetings, 1974—; speaker on profl. confs., 1977—. Bd. dirs. Bay Area Energy Action, San Francisco, 1977-80, Sun Found. Fellow Brit. Interplanetary Soc. (assoc. 1976), Royal Astron. Soc.; mem. Am. Astron. Soc., Optical Soc. of Am., Internat. Soc. for the Arts, Scis. and Tech. (chmn. bd.), Internat. Acad. of Astronautics (corr. mem. 1987), Sigma-Xi. Office: U Calif Space Scis Lab Grizzly Peak Blvd Berkeley CA 94720

MALLARD, THOMAS IRVIN, retail company executive; b. L.A., July 12, 1946; s. Thomas Gibson and Bernice Pearl (Tubbs) M.; m. JoAnne Morning, 1971 (div. 1976). AA, Seattle Cen. Community Coll., 1974; student, U. Wash., 1972—. Night mgr.computer prodn. REI Co-op, Seattle, 1974-76; owner The Works Co., Seattle, 1976; gen. ptnr. Suspended Elevations, Seattle, 1982-88; owner Proton Mfg. Products, Seattle, 1987—. With U.S. Army, 1969-72. Mem. Nat. Audobon Soc., Cascade Bicycle Club, Am. Canoe Assn., U.S. Cycling Fedn. Presbyterian. Home: 15201 16th Pl NE #8-12 Bellevue WA 98007 Office: Proton Mfg Products Kitesport 15600 NE 8th St #SL-2 Bellevue WA 98008

MALLENDER, WILLIAM HARRY, lawyer; b. Detroit, May 21, 1935; s. Milton F. and Eleanor M. (Rainey) M.; m. Carole Miller, Aug. 8, 1964; children: W. Drew, Gregory. B.A., Yale U., 1957; L.L.B., U. Mich., 1960. Bar: Mich. 1960, N.Y. 1962, Fla. 1970. Assoc. Donovan Leisure, Newton, Irvine, N.Y.C., 1960-69; atty. Ritter & Co., Gibraltar Mgmt. Co., GAC

Corp., Fort Lauderdale, Fla., 1969-71; v.p., gen. counsel Talley Industries, Inc., Mesa, Ariz., 1971-78, exec. v.p., gen. counsel, sec., 1978-81, dir., 1975—; pres., chief exec. officer Talley Industries, Inc., Phoenix, 1981-83, chmn. bd., chief exec. officer, 1983—. Chmn. Phoenix Econ. Growth Corp.; pres. Combined Phoenix Arts & Scis.; bd. regents Brophy Coll. Preparatory; sec. Internat. Heart Found., Phoenix, 1983. Mem. ABA, Mich. State Bar, Fla. State Bar, N.Y. State Bar. Office: Talley Industries Inc 2800 N 44th St Phoenix AZ 85008 *

MALLETTE, LEO ALBERT, aerospace company executive; b. Detroit, May 26, 1953; s. Albert Gedeon and Dolores Marguerite (Carriere) M.; m. Kathryn Joan Abrahamzon, Aug. 10, 1985; 1 child, Andrea. BEE, U. Cen. Fla., 1975, MEE, 1977; MBA, Pepperdine U., 1985. Instr. U. Cen. Fla., Orlando, 1977-78; cons. Martin Marietta, Orlando, 1977, USN, Orlando, 1978; with Hughes Aircraft Co., Los Angeles, 1978—; bd. dirs. Aerospace Applications Conf., MTS Assocs. Contbr. articles to profl. jours. Mem. IEEE (sr., many coms.). Republican. Roman Catholic. Home: 2309 S Santa Anita Ave Arcadia CA 91006 Office: Hughes Aircraft Co PO Box 92919 S41-B322 Los Angeles CA 90009

MALLON, JOSEPH ROBERT, JR., engineer executive; b. Phila., July 10, 1945; s. Joseph Robert and Elizabeth Rose (Novack) M.; 1 child, Joseph Michael. BS in Physics, Farleigh Dicksinson U., 1978. V.p. engr. Kulite Semiconductor Products Inc., Teaneck, N.J., 1965-85; co-pres NovaSensor, Fremont, Calif., 1985—; editorial bd. Sensors & Actuators, Switzerland, 1985—; editorial bd. and dir. IECI Transactions, N.Y.C., 1972-78. Patentee in field; contbr. numerous profl. papers to jours. Mem. IEEE, Electrochem. Soc., ISA. Home: 43517 Ocaso Ct Fremont CA 94539 Office: NovaSensor 1055 Mission Ct Fremont CA 94539

MALLORY, C. SHANNON, bishop; b. Dallas, Sept. 9, 1936; s. William Lee and Hazelle (Wisdom) M.; children: Karin, Teresa, James, Mary, Patrick. BA, UCLA, 1958; MDiv, Gen. Sem., N.Y.C., 1961; MA, Rhodes U., Republic South Africa, 1970; ordained to ministry. Rector Parish Districts of Namibia, Africa, 1961-62; mission dir. Diocese of Damaraland, Africa, 1962-69, archdeacon, 1964-69; coll. chaplain U. Rhodes, 1970-71; lectr. Makerere (Uganda) U., 1971-72; diocesan bishop Diocese of Botswana, 1972-78; asst. bishop Diocese of L.I., N.Y., 1978-80; diocesan bishop Diocese of El Camino (Calif.) Real, 1980—. Office: Diocese El Camino Real PO Box 1903 Monterey CA 93942

MALLOTT, BYRON IVAR, holding corporation executive; b. Yakutat, Alaska, Apr. 6, 1943; s. Jay B. and Emma M. (Brown) M.; m. Evelyn Anderson Converse, 1964 (div. 1971); children: Byron, Meredith; m. Antoinette Mary Evans, May 7, 1972; children: Anthony, Joseph. Student, Eastern Wash. State Coll., 1961-62, Western Wash. State Coll., 1962-64. Spl. asst. U.S. Senator Mike Gravel, 1969; exec. dir. Rural Alaska Action Program, Anchorage, 1970; dir. State of Alaska Local Affairs Agy., Juneau, 1971, commr. State Dept. Community and Regional Affairs, 1972-74; chmn. SeaLaska Corp., Juneau, from 1976, chief exec. officer, 1982—; co-owner Alaska Native Mgmt., Yakutat, 1974-80; dir. B.M. Behrends Bank, Juneau, 1978—, Alaska Airlines Inc., Seattle, 1982—, Alaska Permanent Fund, Juneau, 1982—, Fed. Res. Bank, Seattle, 1983—. Mayor City of Yakutat, 1965; mem. Alaska Reapportionment Bd., Juneau, 1980—, chmn., 1980; mem. U. Alaska Found., Fairbanks, 1981—. Recipient Gov.'s award Alaskan of Year Com., 1982. Mem. Alaska Fedn. Natives (Citizen of Year 1982). Democrat. Roman Catholic. Club: Alaska Native Brotherhood (v.p. 1968-69). Office: SeaLaska Corp 1 SeaLaska Plaza Juneau AK 99801 *

MALLOY, JOHN THORNTON, general engineering contractor; b. L.A., Aug. 15, 1943; s. Emmett James and Louise (Thornton) M.; m. Elizabeth Ann Miller, Aug. 21, 1965; children: Justin, Hilary, Emmett, Brendan, Coley. BA in Polit. Sci., U. San Francisco, 1965. Foreman Malloy Equip Co., L.A., 1965-70; supt. M&M Pipeline Co., L.A., 1970-74; pres. John T. Malloy Inc., L.A., 1974—. V.p. Calif. Pediatric Ctr., L.A., 1988-89; bd. dirs. Cath. Big Bros., L.A., 1983—. Mem. Engring. Contractors Assn. (v.p. 1988-89), Jonathan Club, Wilshire Country Club. Democrat. Roman Catholic. Office: 606 N Larchmont Blvd Los Angeles CA 90004

MALMBERG, JOHN HOLMES, physics educator; b. Gettysburg, Pa., July 5, 1927; s. Constantine F. and Margaret Eloise (Dysinger) M.; m. Vilma Ruth Martinus, June 21, 1952; children: David Gabriel, Lori Ann. BE, Ill. State U., 1949; MS in Physics, U. Ill., 1951, PhD in Physics, 1957. Research, teaching asst. U. Ill., Champaign, 1949-57; staff mem. Gulf Gen. Atomic, San Diego, 1957-69; prof. physics U. Calif., San Diego, 1967—. Contbr. numerous sci. articles to jours.; patentee in field. Served with U.S. Army, 1946. Recipient Tech. Innovation award NASA. Fellow Am. Phys. Soc. (Maxwell prize in plasma physics 1985). Home: 445 Van Dyke Del Mar CA 92014 Office: U Calif San Diego Dept Physics B 019 La Jolla CA 92093

MALMGREN, RENÉ LOUISE, academic arts administrator; b. Mpls., Nov. 14, 1938; d. Albert William and Hildegarde Ann (Topel) Erickson; m. Donald Elwin Malmgren, Dec. 27, 1958; D. Gustaf, Ericka Susan, Tavus Val, Beret Kristina. BA in Theatre, Speech and English, Colo. Women's Coll., 1966; MA in Ednl. Adminstrn and Curriculum Devel., U. Colo., 1981. Cert. supt., Ariz.; cert. type D adminstr., Colo. Cons. creative drama Cultural Arts Program Denver Pub. Schs., 1970-72; tchr. APS Crawford Elem. Sch., Aurora, Colo., 1972-78; instr. Colo. Women's Coll., Denver, 1974-75; tchr. English Hinkley High Sch., Aurora; ednl. dir. Colo. Children's Theatre Co., Denver, 1977-86; adminstrv. intern Aurora Pub. Schs., 1981-82, coordinator curriculum, 1982-85; asst. dir. instrn. fine arts Tucson Unified Sch. Dist., 1985—; external auditor lang. arts Jefferson County Pub. Schs., Littleton, Colo., 1984; curriculum evaluator North Cen. Assn., Grand Junction, Colo., 1985; editor performing arts curriculum Ariz. Dept. Edn., Phoenix, 1989, mem. visual art textbook selection com., 1988, performing arts essential skills com., 1989; rev. panelist Ariz. Commn. on Arts, Phoenix, 1986-87. Co-author satellite TV curriculum, 1987; appeared in premier of play The Only Woman Awake, 1984. Del. Colo. Dem. Conv., Denver, 1980; peacekeeper Take Back the Night March-Rape Assistance and Awareness Program, Denver, 1982-84; mem. policy com. Tucson Cable Arts Channel, 1986-87; mem. edn. com. Tucson Symphony Orch., 1988—; mem. So. Ariz. Opera Guild, 1988—; mem. corp. bd. Ariz. Arts Alliance 1988—; bd. dirs. Arts Genesis, 1988—. Colo. Council on Arts and Humanities grantee, 1978. Mem. Nat. Art Edn. Assn., Assn. for Supervision and Curriculum Devel., Arts in Edn. Council, Nat. Adminstrv. Women in Edn., Ariz. Arts Supervisory Coalition (bd. dirs. 1985—), Ariz. Theatre Educators Assn. (bd. dirs. 1985-89, pres. 1988-89), Phi Delta Kappa. Home: 2612 E La Cienega Dr Tucson AZ 85716 Office: Tucson Unified Sch Dist 2025 E Winsett St Tucson AZ 85719

MALMROS, MELINDA SUE, accountant; b. Sayre, Pa., Dec. 5, 1945; d. Jack Robert and Mary Elizabeth (Eike) Armstrong; m. Richard Alf Malmros, Dec. 14, 1968. BS in Bus. Edn., Bloomsburg U., 1967; postgrad., U. Calif., Berkeley, 1978. CPA, Colo. Sr. acct. IBM Corp., Westlake, Calif. and Owego, N.Y., 1967-69, Litton Industries, Woodland Hills, Calif., 1969-70; acct. various orgns., Colo., 1970-78; staff acct. Monahan and Morton, P.C., Glenwood Springs, Colo., 1978-79; controller TMD Corp., Rife, Colo., 1979-80; mgr. Irvine and Patterson, P.C., Denver, 1980-85; sole practice Golden, Colo., 1985—; instr. acctg. U. Denver, 1983-84, Arapahoe Community Coll., Englewood, Colo., 1984-85. Chmn. fin. Holiday Project, Denver, 1980; treas. Community Living Alternatives, Denver, 1985-87, sec., 1988—. Mem. Am. Inst. CPA's, Colo. Soc. CPA's (chmn. career edn. com. 1984-85, co-chnm. acctg. edn. com. 1987-88, chmn. acctg. edn. com. 1989—). Republican. Episcopalian. Club: Denver Fin. Partnership. Office: 1746 Cole Blvd Ste 225 Golden CO 80401

MALNAR, JAMES PAUL, financial executive; b. Aurora, Ill., May 2, 1948; s. Rudolph and Alice Viola (Johnson) M.; m. Carol Anne Baker, Oct. 24, 1975; children: Douglas, Lori. BA, Augustana Coll., Rock Island, Ill., 1970. Auditor Deere & Co., Moline, Ill., 1970-72, mgr., acctg., 1976-79; acctg. supr. John Deere Co., Portland, Oreg., 1972-75; supr. acctg. parts div. John Deere Co., East Moline, Ill., 1975-76; controller John Deere Co., Portland, 1980-87; v.p. fin. Evergreen Internat. Airlines, McMinnville, Oreg., 1987—. Accounts mgr. United Way, Portland, 1983-85. Mem. Nat. Assn. Accts. (dir. 1988), Toastmasters (v.p. 1983). Democrat. Club: Portland Kennel (treas. 1985-87). Home: 16050 NE Stanton Portland OR 97230

MALOHN, DONALD A., manufacturing executive; b. South Bend, Ind., Mar. 26, 1928; s. Harry A. and Opal (Baker) M.; m Myla Claire Lockwood, Feb. 9, 1948; 1 child, Chris. BSEE, Tri-State U., Angola, Ind., 1952. Engr. jet engine div. Studebaker Corp., South Bend, Ind., 1952-54; prodn. rsch. engr. Ford Motor Co., Dearborn, Mich., 1954-61; sr. analytical engr. Solar, San Diego, 1961-62; dept. mgr. Sundstrand Aviation, Denver, 1962-66; asst. dir. engring. Ai Rsch. Mfg. Co., Phoenix, 1966-78; exec. v.p. Tiernay Turbines, Phoenix, 1978—. Inventor: Vaporizing Igniter, 1963; contbr. tech. jours. Mem. ASME., Am. Soc. Metals, Soc. Automotive Engrs. Republican. Home: 7848 E Sage Dr Scottsdale AZ 85253 Office: Tiernay Turbines Inc 1301 E Jackson St Phoenix AZ 85034

MALONE, ALAN LEE, engineer; b. Lincoln, Nebr., Mar. 8, 1953; s. William Franklin and Iona Belle (Norwood) M.; m. Elaine Rose Walters, July 24, 1957; children: Andrew Nathan, Sean William. BS in Arch., U. Nebr., 1977, postgrad., 1979. Electrician Malone Electric, Waverly, Nebr., 1971-77; solar engr. Solar, Inc., Mead, Nebr., 1977; commd. 2nd lt. USAF/Air Nat. Guard, 1974, advanced through grades to capt., 1987; weapon systems operator Nebr. Air Nat. Guard, Lincoln, 1974-77, pilot, 1977-84; architect Cons. Engring. Group, Omaha, 1980-81, Hoskins-Western-Sondregger, Lincoln, 1981-82; environ. and design engr. Nebr. Air Nat. Guard, Lincoln, 1982-84; base civil engr. Oreg. Air Nat. Guard, Portland, 1984—. Referee Orchards Soccer Club, Vancouver, Wash., 1987-88. Mem. Soc. Mil. Engrs., Air Nat. Guard Civil Engr. Assn., Internat. Coun. Bldg. Ofcls. Home: 2107 NE 124th Ave Vancouver WA 98684 Office: Oreg Air Nat Guard 6801 Cornfoot Dr Portland OR 97218

MALONE, MIKE, state senator, police officer; b. Saginaw, Mich., Jan. 13, 1932; s. Archie Ralph and Helen Mary (Johnson) M.; m. Theresa Nancy Tankavich, Jan. 1, 1982. Grad., Las Vegas (Nev.) Metro. Police Acad. With USN, 1948-68, ret., 1968; police officer Las Vegas Metro. Police Dept., 1968—. Mem. Nebraska Legis., 1978—; counsellor, Boulder Dam Area Boy Scouts Am., 1983-88. Mem. Sons of Erin. Republican. Home: 3660 Thom Blvd Las Vegas NV 89130-3015 Office: Office of State Senate State Capitol Carson City NV 89710

MALONE, MINDY SARA, radiation health physicist; b. Cleve., Jan. 12, 1952; d. Irving Bernard Bookatz and Thelma (Glassman) Brooks; m. Jesse Edwin Malone Jr., June 26, 1977; 1 child, Laura Ilene. Student, San Diego State U., 1969-71. Cert. radiologic tech., Calif. Radiologic technologist San Mateo (Calif.) County Chope Hosp., 1973-79; radiation protection specialist, health physicist Radiologic Health br. Calif. Dept. Health Svcs., Berkeley, 1979—. Mem. Am. Assn. Physicists in Medicine, No. Calif. Soc. Health Physicists. Democrat. Jewish. Office: Calif Dept Health Svcs 2151 Berkeley Way Berkeley CA 94704

MALONE, ROBERT GEORGE, investment banker; b. Wadena, Minn., Sept. 18, 1940; s. Robert Joseph and Elizabeth R. (Spahn) M.; children: Patty, Molly, Shelly, Betsy, Michael. BS in Bus., U. Minn., 1961, postgrad., 1963-65. Registered rep. B.C. Christopher Corp., Denver, 1970-74, Barton and Co., Denver, 1974; exec. v.p., registered rep. E.J. Pittock and Co., Inc., Denver, 1974-82; pres., prin. Malone and Assocs., Inc., Denver, 1982—. Pub. newsletter Malone's Letter, 1976—. Mem. Regis Coll. Pres.'s Club, Denver, U. Colo. Pres.'s Club, Boulder. Mem. Denver Stock Traders Assn. (mem. arbitration panel 1986—, mem. chief exec. officer roundtable 1986—), Securities Industry Assn., Nat. Assn. Securities Dealers. Republican. Roman Catholic. Office: Malone & Assocs Inc 1401 17th St Ste 1550 Denver CO 80202

MALONE, THOMAS WILLIAM, lawyer; b. Seattle, Sept. 16, 1946; s. James Edward and Marie Cecilia (Anderson) M.; m. Drexel Cox, June 19, 1978; children: Jason, Cary. BA, U. Wash., 1968, JD, 1972; MBA, Golden Gate U., 1982. Bar: Wash. 1972, U.S. Ct. Appeals (9th cir.) 1972, U.S. Tax Ct. 1980, U.S. Ct. Claims 1981, U.S. Supreme Ct. 1980. Prin. Treece, Richdale, Malone & Corning, Inc., P.S., Seattle, 1973—. Pres., Seattle Marine Bus. Coalition, 1983-86; bd. dirs. Ballard Community Hosp., 1982—, North Seattle Community Coll. Found., 1989—; chmn. bd. dirs. Ballard Community Hosp., 1986-88. Mem. ABA, Wash. Bar Assn., Seattle-King County Bar Assn., Ballard C. of C. (pres. 1981-84). Home: 2116 NW 93d St Seattle WA 98117

MALOOF, GILES WILSON, mathematics educator; b. San Bernardino, Calif., Jan. 4, 1932; s. Joseph Peters and Georgia (Wilson) M.; m. Mary Anne Ziniker, Sept. 5, 1958 (dec. Oct. 1976); children—Mary Jane, Margery Jo. B.A., U. Calif. at Berkeley, 1953; M.A., U. Oreg., 1958; Ph.D., Oreg. State U., 1962. Petroleum reservoir engr. Creole Petroleum Corp., Venezuela, 1953-54; mathematician electronics div. research dept. U.S. Naval Ordnance Research Lab., Corona, Calif., 1958-59; asst. prof. math. Oreg. State U., Corvallis, 1962-68, research assoc. dept. oceanography, 1963-68, vis. prof. math., 1977-78; prof. math. Boise (Idaho) State U., 1968—, head dept., 1968-75, dean grad. sch., 1970-75; project dir. Dept. Energy Citizens' Workshop Energy Environment Simulator for Eastern Oreg., No. Nev. and Idaho, 1976—. Served with Ordnance Corps, AUS, 1950, 54-56. Recipient Carter award, 1963, Mosser prize, 1966, Oreg. State U. Mem. Math. Assn. Am., Am. Math. Soc., Soc. Indsl. and Applied Math., Northwest Coll. and Univ. Assn. for Sci. (dir. 1973—), Northwest Sci. Assn. (trustee 1977-80), Sigma Xi, Pi Mu Epsilon, Phi Kappa Phi. Editor Ida. Council of Tchrs. of Math. Newspaper, 1971-73. Home: 1400 Longmont Ave Boise ID 83706

MALORRUS, FARLEY MARTIN, astrologer; b. St. Louis, Aug. 11, 1948; s. Fred Max and Beatrice (Cuttler) M. B.A. in Speech, Drama and English, Central Meth. Coll., Fayette, Mo., 1970; postgrad. in English, UCLA, 1974, in Astrology, 1974-76. Pvt. practice astrology, Culver City, Calif., 1975—; ship's astrologer, lectr. Sun Princess, Queen Elizabeth 2, Sitmar, Cunard, Princess and Carnival Cruise Lines, 1980—; columnist Redondo Beach (Calif.) Community Network News, 1982—; astrologer Sta. KROQ-FM, 1983—; ships astrologer Holland Am. Cruise lines, 1985—; dir., host astrology series for cable TV, 1983; astrologer various TV shows, 1983-86; host Astrology Hour, Sta. KFOX-FM, 1983—, Astrology and You, Sta. KIEV-AM, 1983—; ship astrologer S.S. Rotterdam, 1985, Nieu Amsterdam, 1986; sports astrologer Los Angeles Times, 1985, with TV show The Late Show, 1987; with L.A. Times, 1988; guest lectr. United Astrology Congress, 1986. Address: PO Box 2988 Culver City CA 90230

MALOTT, DWIGHT RALPH, accountant; b. Medford, Oreg., Mar. 24, 1947; s. Ralph Joseph and Eugenia (Romanchuk) M.; m. Janet Gail Born, June 28, 1975; children: Jennifer, Paul, Michelle. A.Tech. Arts, Everett Jr. Coll., 1967; BBA, U. Wash., 1969. CPA, Wash. Acct. Main Hurdman, Everett, Wash., 1973-81; controller Shaffer Crane, Inc., Everett, 1981-83; prin. acct. Dwight Malott & Co., P.S., Arlington, Wash., 1983-88; ptnr. Wintch Tobiason & Co. PS CPA, Everett, Wash., 1988— . Loaned exec. United Way of Snohomish County, Everett, 1977, mem. allocations panel, 1980, 81, 82; bd. dirs. Lions Sight and Hearing Found. of Snohomish County, Everett, 1979—; mem. acctg. adv. com. Everett Community Coll., 1979—. Served with USAF, 1969-73. Mem. Wash. Soc. CPAs, AICPA, Smokey Point C. of C., U. Wash. Alumni Assn. (life), Lions (local pres. 1981-82), Beta Alpha Psi. Democrat. Office: Wintch Tobiason & Co PS CPA 3326 Smokey Point Dr Ste 103 Arlington WA 98223

MALPHURS, ROGER EDWARD, insurance company executive; b. Lake Worth, Fla., Dec. 15, 1933; s. Cecil Edward and Muriel Thelma (Ward) M.; m. Carolyn Sue Calapp, Feb. 2, 1963; children: Steven, Brian, Darren, Regina, Victoria. BS, U. Utah, 1961. Cert. med. technologist. Supr. spl. chemistry Cen. Pathology Lab., Santa Rosa, Calif., 1968-73; mgr. lab. Community Hosp., Santa Rosa, 1973-76; supr. chem., staff asst. Meml. Hosp., Santa Rosa, 1976-85; pres., chief exec. officer R.E. Malphurs Co., Sunnyvale, Calif., 1972—; owner, developer REMCO Mktg. Assocs., Santa Rosa, 1970-72, Better Bus. Forms and Typeset, Santa Rosa, 1977-81. Author: A New, Simple Way to Win at Blackjack, 1972. Served as squadron commdr. CAP USAF Aux., 1982-84. Mem. Am. Chiropractic Assn., Calif. Chiropractic Assn., Optimists Internat. (youth awards chmn. 1969-74), Am. Pub. Health Assn., Toastmasters (sec./treas. 1988-89). Republican.

MALSON, REX RICHARD, drug and health care corporation executive; b. Stanberry, Mo., Nov. 26, 1931; s. Albert J. Curtis and Nellie E. Coburn (Bussey) M.; m. Jimmie S., May 25, 1956 (dec. 1980); children: Richard Gary, Gregory Neil; m. Vicki L., Feb. 10, 1983 (div. Aug. 1984). B.B.A., Ga. State U., 1961; postgrad. exec. program hon., Stanford U., 1983. Gen. transp. mgr. John Sexton & Co., Chgo., 1964-68; dir. distbn. system Keebler Co., Chgo., 1968-73; with drug and health care group McKesson Corp., San Francisco, 1973—, vice pres., 1984-86, exec. v.p. ops., 1986—, also bd. dirs.; bd. dirs. Sunbelt Beverage Co., Balt., Stationers Distbg. Co., Ft. Worth. Served with U.S. Navy, 1951-55, Korea. Mem. Am. Soc. Traffic and Transp. Republican. Office: McKesson Corp One Post St San Francisco CA 94104

MALTIN, FREDA, university administrator; b. Calgary, Alta., Can., June 4, 1923; d. Meyers Wolfe and Ida (Kohn) Rosen; m. Manny Nayton Maltin, Aug. 25, 1950; 1 child, Richard Allan. came to U.S., 1958; diploma Garbutt's Bus. Coll., Calgary, 1942. Various secretarial and bookkeeping positions, 1951-61; mem. adminstrv. staff U. So. Calif., 1961—, asst. to exec. dir. Davidson Conf. Ctr., 1987, Grad. Sch. Bus. Adminstrn., 1981—. Mem. Exec. Women Internat. Club: U. So. Calif. Staff (charter). Office: U So Calif DCC 111 401 University Park Los Angeles CA 90089-0871

MALVICK, ANN CARLA, medical foundation administrator; b. Independence, Iowa, Feb. 9, 1945; d. Walter Theodore and Dell Rose (Willenborg) Mangerich; children: Anne Sara, Katherine Rose. BA, Clarke Coll., 1967. Sales acct. The Paper, Prescott, Ariz., 1970-73; account exec. Payne-Prescott Broadcasting, Prescott, 1982-84; gen. sales mgr. LaPaz Pub. Co., Prescott, 1984-85; devel. officer Prescott Coll., 1985-87, Kingman (Ariz.) Regional Med. Ctr. Found., 1988—. Bd. dirs. Yavapai Big Bros./Big Sisters, Prescott, 1987, Prescott Forward, 1985. Mem. Nat. Soc. Fund Raising Execs., Ariz. Hosp. Assn., Kingman Area C. of C. (bd. dirs.) Rotary Internat. Republican. Roman Catholic. Office: Kingman Regional Med Ctr Found 3269 Stockton Hill Rd Kingman AZ 86401

MAMULA, RICHARD ALLEN, behavior management specialist; b. East Chicago, Ind., July 4, 1943; s. Michael and Irene (Macak) M. BS cum laude, Ind. State U., Terre Haute, 1965; MSW, Fla. State U., 1967; PhD, St. Stephens Coll., 1978; DD, St. Stephens Theol. Sem., 1978. Psychiat. social worker Calif. Bur. Social Work, Vallejo, Calif., 1967-69; dist. office adminstr. Calif. Community Svcs. Div., Fresno, Calif., 1969-72; acting dir., chief counseling svcs. Kern Regional Ctr. for Retarded, Bakersfield, Calif., 1972-74; exec. dir. Future of Youth, Inc., Santa Barbara, Calif., 1974-77; sr. counselor Regional Ctr. Orange County, Orange, Calif., 1977-81; pvt. practice psychotherapist L.A., 1981-86; dir. program svcs. CEDCO-DIAZ Corp., Pomona, Calif., 1984-86, Habilitation, Inc., Bakersfield and Fresno, 1986—; chmn. Fresno County Coord. Coun. for Svcs. to Retarded, 1969-72; v.p., El Granito Found., Porterville, Calif., 1978—; pres., Separate Realities, Inc., Santa Barbara, 1988—. Author: Community Placement Programs for the Retarded, 1973. Mem. adv. bd., Citizen's Mental Health Assn., Fresno, 1971-72; bd. dirs. Help and Health Found., Santa Barbara, 1976-78, Found. for Autistic Svcs., Orange, 1978-84, Grace Community Chapel, Bakersfield, 1987—. Fellow Am. Assn. Mental Deficiency (nat. steering com. 1968-72), Am. Orthopsychiat. Assn.; mem. Nat. Assn. Social Workers, Am. Psychol. Assn. Democrat. Methodist. Home: 409 Sperry St Bakersfield CA 93307 Office: Habilitation Inc Ste 102 2519 W Shaw St Fresno CA 93711

MAN, GUY KEE, aerospace and mechanical engineer; b. Kowloon, Hong Kong, May 27, 1951; came to U.S., 1970, naturalized, 1985; s. Hon Kwong and Sau Ching (Luk) M.; BS, U. Redlands, 1974; MS, Stanford U., 1975, ME, PhD, 1979; m. Debra Y. K. Ching, Dec. 15, 1979. Sr. engr. guidance and control sect. Jet Propulsion Lab., Calif. Inst. Tech., Pasadena, Calif., 1979-82, tech. group leader, 1982-83, tech. group, supr. guidance and control analysis group, 1982-86, tech. group supt. system design and integration guidance and control sect., 1986—; cons. in dynamics, kinematics, controls, automation, seismic analysis and software devel., 1982-84. Registered profl. engr., Calif. Mem. AIAA, ASME, Calif. Soc. Profl. Engrs., Nat. Soc. Profl. Engrs., Sigma Xi. Contbr. tech. articles to various publs. Home: 2158 Valentine Pl San Marino CA 91108

MANARY, RICHARD DEANE, manufacturing executive; b. Des Moines, Nov. 11, 1944; s. Robert Claude and Veronica (Cornwell) M.; m. Eileen Cecile, Aug. 16, 1986; children: (Erica (dec.), Matthew, Stephen, Lauren. AA in Indsl. Engring., Southwestern Coll., 1976; BA in History, Calif. State U., San Diego, 1967, BS in Edn., 1973. Registered profl. engr., Calif. Mfg. engr. Rohr Industries, San Diego, 1967-78; chief research and devel. div. Rohr Industries, Riverside, Calif., 1978-80, project mfg. mgr., 1980-84; dep. program mgr. Rohr Industries, Wichita, Kans., 1984-87; mgr. Titan 3d, Titan IV missile programs Rohr Industries, Riverside, 1987—. Contbr. articles to profl. jours. Chmn. Rohr Industries Co. Employee and Community Assistance Program, Riverside, 1981-85; adv. Jr. Achievement, Riverside chpt., 1978-79. Mem. Soc. Mfg. Engrs (sr., assoc., chmn. 1978-79), Soc. Automotive Engrs., Soc. Material and Process Engrs., Am. Soc. Metals, Nat. Mgmt. Assn. (chmn. 1980-81), Air Force Assn. Democrat. Roman Catholic. Home: 6523 West View Dr Riverside CA 92506 Office: Rohr Industries 8200 Arlington Blvd Riverside CA 92503

MANATOS, JOSEPH W., land surveyor; b. Rock Springs, Wyo., Mar. 10, 1950; s. William T. and Elsie (Sergakis) M. AA, Western Wyo. Coll., 1971. Registered land surveyor, Wyo. Surveyor Johnson-Fermelia & Crank, Inc., Rock Springs, 1971-75, profl. land surveyor, 1975-79, surveying supr., 1979-84; prin., dir. surveying Johnson-Fermelia Co., Inc., Rock Springs, 1984—. Editorial bd.: Standards of Practice-Wyo. Fellow Am. Congress on Surveying and Mapping; mem. Profl. Land Surveyors Colo., Profl. Land Surveyors Wyo. (pres. 1985), Wyo. Assn. Cons. Engrs. and Surveyors (sec.-treas.), Elks. Democrat. Greek Orthodox. Home: 520 Wasatch Cir Rock Springs WY 82901 Office: Johnson Fermalia Co Inc 1515 9th St Rock Springs WY 82901

MANAUT, FRANK J., banker; b. Alhambra, Calif., Feb. 16, 1924; married. B.S., UCLA, 1947. With Standard Oil Co., 1947-50; with Bank of Hawaii, Honolulu, 1950—, chmn. bd., chief exec. officer, dir.; chmn. bd., chief exec. officer Bancorp Hawaii, Honolulu, 1980—. Office: Bancorp Hawaii Inc 111 S King St Box 2900 Fin Pla of the Pacific Honolulu HI 96846 *

MANCINI, JOHN E., small business owner; b. Trenton, N.J., Feb. 26, 1945; s. John and Antoinette (Cichetti) M.; m. Sandra, Feb. 7, 1967 (div. 1975). Credit mgr. Gaudin Ford, Las Vegas, Calif., 1977-80; pres. John Mancini Inc., Long Beach, Calif., 1980—; cons. Whittlesey Motors, Torrance, Calif., Whittlesey Jaguar, Torrance Suzuki. Chmn. Heart Assn., Long Beach, 1982. With USMC, 1963-67, Vietnam. Mem. KC. Republican. Roman Catholic. Home: 3400 Ave of the Arts #A401 Costa Mesa CA 92626

MANCINI, LOUIS JOSEPH, airline executive; b. Chgo., May 6, 1950; s. Edward August and Adeline Josephine (Renella) M.; m. Christine Ann Fourness, Aug. 13, 1976; children: Edward John, Louis Charles. BS in Gen. Engring., U. Ill., 1972; MS in Ops. Rsch., Stanford U., 1975, PhD in Ops. Rsch., 1975. Rsch. engr. Shell Devel. Co., Houston, 1975-78; ops. rsch. supr. Chevron Corp., San Francisco, 1978-80; staff planner strategic planning Chervon USA, San Francisco, 1980-82, staff planner bus. evaluation, 1982-84; ventures mgr. Chevron Pipe Line Co., San Francisco, 1984-85; dir. maintenance analysis and rsch. United Airlines, San Francisco, 1985-87, dir. maintenance automation, 1987—; cons. Chase Manhattan Bank, N.Y.C., 1978-80; guest speaker ops. rsch. dept. Grad. Sch. Bus., Stanford (Calif.) U. Contbr. articles to profl. jours. Stanford U. fellow, 1972, NSF fellow, 1973-75. Mem. Prodn. and Inventory Control Soc., Elks. Presbyterian. Office: United Airlines SFORX San Francisco Internat Airport San Francisco CA 94128-3800

MANCINI, WILLIAM F., public relations executive; b. Downey, Calif., Jan. 16, 1959. BA in Polit. Sci., Calif. State U., 1980. Parts lister and scheduling analyst Rockwell Internat. Corp., Downey, Calif., 1976-78; prodn. asst. Winner/Wagner and Assocs., Los Angeles, 1978-83; protocol officer U.S. Dept. of State, Washington, 1983-84; advance rep. for the Pres. The White House, Washington, 1984-85; asst. to the chmn. Com. for the 50th Am. Presdl. Inaugural, Washington, 1984-85; confidential asst. to the dir. Pub. Affairs Agy. U.S. Dept. of Commerce, Washington, 1985-86; pres.

Mancini Communications, Newport Beach, Calif., 1986—; cons. Embassy of Oman, Susan Davis Cos., Washington, Niles Internat., Burbank, Calif., Vincent T. Lombari Found., Washington, The Greater Alarm Co., Inc., Huntington Beach, Calif., 1986-87, The Challenger Ctr. for Space Sci. Edn., Washington, 1986, Realty Bus. Group, Newport Beach, 1986. Patentee in field. Mem. The Big Bros. of Greater Los Angeles and Washington. Mem. Profl. Ski Instrs. Am., Aircraft Owners and Pilots Assn. Office: Mancini Communications PO Box 7652 Newport Beach CA 92658

MANDARICH, DAVID D., real estate corporation executive; b. 1948. With Majestic Savs. and Loan, 1966-67; formerly chief operating officer, exec. v.p. MDC Holdings Inc.; pres., co-chief operating officer MDC Holdings Inc., Denver, from 1986, now pres., chief operating officer. Office: MDC Holdings Inc 3600 S Yosemite St Denver CO 80237 *

MANDATO, JOSEPH MICHAEL, medical products company executive; b. Everett, Mass., May 17, 1944; s. Vito and Marianne (Nanfria) M.; m. Elizabeth Rea, May 25, 1974; children: Lucy, Sarah. BS, Nasson Coll., 1967; MA, L.I. U., 1971. Dir. internat. mktg. Gulf & Western Industries, N.Y.C., 1977-81; pres. Altman Internat., N.Y.C., 1981-82; v.p. mkgt. and sales Sonometrics Systems, Inc., N.Y.C., 1982-83; mng. dir. Cilco AG, Zug, Switzerland, 1983-86; pres. Ioptex Research, Inc., Azusa, Calif., 1986—. Served to capt. U.S. Army, 1968-72. Mem. N.Y. Athletic Club. Republican. Roman Catholic. Office: Ioptex Rsch Inc 1301 Optical Dr Azusa CA 91702-1375

MANDEL, ALFRED JAY, communications executive; b. L.A., Feb. 25, 1952; s. Alexander and Marilyn R. (Newman) M. BA in Environ. Studies cum laude, U. Calif., Santa Barbara, 1974; M in Environ. Design cum laude, U. Oreg., 1976. Owner A & M Enterprises, Downey, Calif., 1968-70, Solar Rsch., Palo Alto, Calif., 1976-77; v.p. sales Electrolabs, Palo Alto, 1977-79; owner Photon Electronic Sales, Palo Alto, 1979-82; mktg. mgr. Apple Computer Inc., Cupertino, Calif., 1982-86; ptnr., exec. v.p. Redgate Communications Corp., San Francisco, Vero Beach, Fla.; speaker, panelist computer trade shows various univ. MBA programs. Contbr. articles to profl. jours. Co-chmn. Western Ballet Theatre, Palo Alto. Calif. State scholar U. Calif. Santa Barbara, 1970-74, U. Calif. Regents scholar, 1970-74, Calif. Sci. Found. scholar, 1970-74; recipient Addy awards 1986-88. Mem. Bus. Profl. Advt. Assn.

MANDEL, JEFF, writer, director, composer; b. L.A., May 27, 1952; s. Sheldon Charles and Renee Babette (Donatt) M. BA, U. Calif., L.A., 1973. V.p. Warren Lockhart Productions, L.A., 1980-82; exec. script cons. Ohara/Warner Bros. TV, L.A., 1987-88; advisor Slavko Vorkapich, L.A., 1974-76. Writer and co-writer for TV and cable; writer, co-writer, producer, directed various films; composed musical material for film and TV, 1975—; contbr. articles to profl. jours. Mem. Libertarian Cen. Com., L.A., 1982, 83; patron Museum of Neon Arts, L.A., 1983—. Mem. Writers Guild Am., Am Soc. Composers, Authors and Pubs.

MANDERS, BONNIE JASMINE, cosmetics executive; b. Rockville Centre, N.Y., Feb. 11, 1950; d. Lawrence Albert and Eileen Jeanette (Hewitt) Zonker. Grad, high sch., Jacksonville, Fla. With traffic dept. Sta. WEAR-TV, Pensacola, Fla., 1971-73; media buyer William Cook Advt., Jacksonville, 1974-76, Photo Corp. Am., Charlotte, N.C., 1976; local account rep. Sta. WXIA-TV, Atlanta, 1977-78; nat. account exec. Katz Communications, Chgo., 1979-83, San Francisco, 1983, L.A., 1983-86; nat. account exec. TeleRep Inc., L.A., 1986; pvt. practice makeup and hair artist L.A., 1987—.

MANDLER, GEORGE, psychologist; b. Vienna, Austria, June 11, 1924; came to U.S., 1940, naturalized, 1943; s. Richard and Hede (Goldschmied) M.; m. Jean Matter, Jan. 19, 1957; children: Peter Clark, Michael Allen. B.A., NYU, 1949; M.S., Yale U., 1950, Ph.D., 1953; postgrad., U. Basel, Switzerland, 1947-48. Asst. prof. Harvard U., 1953-57, lectr., 1957-60; prof. U. Toronto, Ont., Can., 1960-65; prof. psychology, dir. Ctr. Human Info. Processing U. Calif.-San Diego, 1965—, chmn. dept. psychology, 1965-70; hon. research fellow Univ. Coll. London. Author: books the most recent being Mind and Emotion, 1975, (German edit.), 1980, Mind and Body, 1984, (Japanese edit.), 1987, Cognitive Psychology, 1985; contbr. articles and revs. to profl. jours.; editor: Psychol. Rev., 1970-76. Served with U.S. Army, 1943-46. Fellow Ctr. for Advanced Study in Behavioral Scis., 1959-60; vis. fellow Oxford U., Eng., 1971-72, 78; Guggenheim fellow, 1971-72; hon. research fellow Univ. Coll., London U., 1977-78, 82—. Fellow AAAS; mem. AAUP, Am. Assn. Advancement Psychology (1974-82); Psychonomic Soc. (governing bd., chmn. 1983), Am. Psychol. Soc., Am. Psychol. Assn. (pres. div. exptl. psychology 1978-79, pres. div. gen psychology 1982-83, mem. council reps. 1978-82, William James prize 1986), Internat. Union Psychol. Scis. (U.S. com. 1985—), Soc. Exptl. Psychologists, Fedn. Behavioral Psychol. and Cognitive Scis. (pres. 1981). Home: 1406 La Jolla Knoll La Jolla CA 92037 Office: U Calif San Diego Dept Psychology La Jolla CA 92093 also: 3 Perrins Ln, London NW3 1QY, England

MANDLER, JEAN MATTER, psychologist, educator; b. Oak Park, Ill., Nov. 6, 1929; d. Joseph Allen and May Roberts (Finch) Matter; m. George Mandler, Jan. 19, 1957; children: Peter Clark, Michael Allen. Student, Carleton Coll., 1947-49; B.A. with highest honors, Swarthmore Coll., 1951; Ph.D., Harvard U., 1956. Research asso. lab. social relations Harvard U., 1957-60; research asso. dept. psychology U. Toronto, Ont., Can., 1961-65; asso. research psychologist, lectr. U. Calif. at San Diego, La Jolla, 1965-73, asso. prof., 1973-77, prof. psychology, 1977-88, prof. cognitive sci., 1988—; mem. adv. com. on memory and cognitive processes NSF, 1978-81. Author: (with G. Mandler) Thinking: From Association to Gestalt, 1964; Stories, Scripts, and Scenes, 1984; asso. editor Psychol. Rev., 1970-76; mem. editorial bd. Child Devel., 1976—, Discourse Processes, 1977—, Jour. Exptl. Psychology, 1977-85, Text, 1979—, Jour. Verbal Learning and Verbal Behavior, 1980-88, Lang. and Cognitive Processes, 1985—; contbr. articles to profl. jours. Pres. San Diego Assn. Gifted Children, 1968-71; v.p. Calif. Parents for Gifted, 1970-71; mem. alumni council Swarthmore Coll., 1975-78. NIMH research grantee, 1968-81; NSF research grantee, 1981—. Fellow Am. Psychol. Assn. (exec. com. div. 3 1983-85); mem. Psychonomic Soc. (governing bd. 1982-87, chmn. 1985-86), Soc. Research in Child Devel., Cognitive Sci. Soc., Soc. Exptl. Psychologists, Phi Beta Kappa. Office: U Calif San Diego Dept Cognitive Sci D-015 La Jolla CA 92093

MANDRA, YORK T., geology educator; b. N.Y.C., Nov. 24, 1922; s. Raymond and Irene (Farruggio) M.; m. Highoohi Kechijian, Jan. 26, 1946. BA, U. Calif., Berkeley, 1947, MA in Paleontology, 1949; PhD in Geology, Stanford U., 1958. From instr. to assoc. prof. geology San Francisco State U., 1950-63, prof., 1964—, head geology sect., chmn. dept., 1960-67; vis. prof. U. Aix-Marseille, France, 1959, Syracuse U., summer 1963, U. Maine, summer 1969, U. Calif., Santa Barbara, summers 1972—; research assoc. U. Glasgow, 1959, Calif. Acad. Scis., 1966-88; vis. scientist New Zealand Geol. Survey, fall 1970. Contbr. numerous articles to profl. jours. Pres. David S. Sohigian Found., 1975—. Served with USAAF, 1942-46. Teaching fellow Danforth Found., 1958, NSF, 1959; research grantee NSF, 1967-77; recipient Neil Miner Disting. Coll. Teaching award, 1984. Fellow Calif. Acad. Scis., Geol. Soc. Am., AAAS; mem. Nat. Assn. Geology Tchrs. (pres. Far Western sect. 1953-54, 73-74, Robert Wallace Webb award 1977), Paleontol. Soc., Soc. Econ. Mineralogists and Paleontologists, Soc. for Environ. Geochemistry and Health. Office: San Francisco State U Dept Geoscis 1600 Holloway Ave San Francisco CA 94132

MANDRICK, NICHOLAS TIMOTHY, telecommunications company executive; b. Detroit, Aug. 20, 1956; s. Donald Joseph and Edna (Mikula) M. BS, BA, Wayne State U., 1980. Ops. mgr., service coordinator Rikal W., Inc., Santa Ana and Burlingame, Calif., 1984-85; regional ops. mgr. Datatec Industries, Hayward, Calif., 1984-85; owner, mgr. Diversified Data Network Systems, Castro Valley, Calif., 1985--. Patentee baseball tng. device. Mem. Communications Workers Am. (local organizer 1986--), Phi Gamma Chi Alumni Assn. Home and Office: 20353 Park Way Ste 28 Castro Valley CA 94546

MANDRY, ROY HUNTER, JR., marketing executive; b. Burbank, Calif., May 10, 1949; s. Roy Hunter Sr. and Helen Elizabeth (Goldner) M.; m. Andrea Lynn Grant, Mar. 7, 1970; children: Michael David, Nicholas John. Student, Pierce Coll., 1968, Valley Coll., 1969. Sr. computer operator Litton D.S.D., Van Nuys, Calif., 1967-74; sales mgr. Finco Industries, Van Nuys, Calif., 1974-75, Triple A, Gardena, Calif., 1976-77; ptnr., pres. Merlan Co. dba Alamo Constrn. Co., Westminster, Calif., 1977-82; ptnr., co-owner Triad Constrn. Co., North Hollywood, Calif., 1983; v.p. sales and mktg. Ben-Wal Printing, Glendora, Calif., 1983—. Mem. Direct Mktg. Club Orange County. Republican. Home: 8356 Lakeside Dr Riverside CA 92509 Office: Ben-Wal Printing 2011 E Financial Way Glendora CA 91740

MANDT, DAVID WILLIAM, insurance claim analyst; b. E. Cleveland, Ohio, Jan. 30, 1945; s. Robert D. Mandt and Ruth Virginia (Varnes) Knauss; m. Susan Jane Wakefield, Aug. 2, 1969; children: Diana, Steven. BA, Coll. of Wooster, 1967; postgrad., U. Denver, 1967-68. Chartered property-casualty underwriter. Claims rep. Safeco Corp., Denver, 1973-75, claim supr., 1975-78; area mgr. Safeco Corp., Albuquerque, 1978-82; claim analyst Safeco Corp., Denver, 1982-88; environ./hazardous waste claim adminstr. Safeco Corp., Seattle, 1988—; cons. to ins. defense bar, Denver, 1986-87. Active Better Bus. Bur., Denver, 1986-87; ruling elder Covenant Presbyn. Ch., Albuquerque, 1980-82; stated clk. Genesis Presbyn. Ch., Littleton, Colo., 1987-88. Staff sgt. USAF, 1969-73. Mem. Colo. Claims Assn., Soc. Chartered Property Casualty Underwriters. Office: Safeco Corp Safeco Plaza T 18 Seattle WA 98185

MANEA-MANOLIU, MARIA ION, linguistics educator; b. Galatz, Romania, Mar. 12, 1934; came to U.S., 1978; d. Ion T. and Ana S. (Codescu) Manoliu; m. Ion S. Manea, Nov. 26, 1968. BA, French Coll., Galatz, 1951; MA, U. Bucharest, Romania, 1955, PhD, 1966. Asst. prof. linguistics U. Bucharest, 1957-61, assoc. prof., 1961-68; prof. U. Calif., Davis, 1978—; vis. prof. U. Chgo., 1972-74; cons. NEH, 1980—; mem. adv. bd. Romance Philology, Berkeley, Calif., 1984—. Author: Sistematica Substitutelor, 1968 (Ministry of Edn. award 1968), Gramatica Comparată a limbilor romanice, 1971, El Estructuralismo Lingüistico, 1979, Tipologia e Historia, 1985; editor-in chief Bull. de la S.R.L.R., Bucharest, 1975-78; corresponding editor Revue Romane, Copenhagen, 1972—; contbr. articles to profl. jours. Grantee Internat. Com. Linguists, 1972, Fulbright, 1972-74, U. Calif., 1979—. Mem. Am. Romanian Acad. (pres. 1982—), Soc. de Linguistique Romane, Soc. Roumaine de Linguistique Romane (v.p. 1974-78), Internat. Assn. Hist. Linguistics, MLA, Linguistics Soc. Am. Office: U Calif Dept French and Italian 506 Sproul Hall Davis CA 95616

MANEATIS, GEORGE A., utility company executive; b. 1926. BS in Elec. Engring., Stanford U., 1949, MS in Elec. Engring., 1950. With Gen. Elec. Co., 1950-53; with Pacific Gas & Elec. Co., San Francisco, 1953—, v.p., 1979-81, sr. v.p., 1981-82, exec. v.p., 1982-86, pres., 1986—, also dir. Office: Pacific Gas & Electric Co 77 Beale St San Francisco CA 94106

MANEN, CAROL-ANN, toxicologist, marine environmentalist; b. Newark, Feb. 4, 1943; d. Edward Adolph and Dorothy Helen (Wolfe) M. BA, Gettysburg Coll., 1964; MS, U. Ill., 1966; PhD, U. Maine, 1973. Postdoctoral fellow U. Ariz. Med. Sch., Tucson, 1973-77; rsch. assoc. Roche Inst. Molecular Biology, Nutley, N.J., 1977-78; asst. prof. biology U. Ala., Tuscaloosa, 1978-82; toxicologist Nat. Oceanic Atmospheric Adminstrn., Anchorage, 1984—; "Fate and Effects" coordinator for Alaska Outer Continental Shelf Environ. Assessment Program, quality assurance officer for NOAA's Nat. Status and Trends Program. Contbr. articles to sci. publs., chpts. to books. NSF fellow, 1964-66, NDEA fellow, 1970, Univ. fellow, 1971-73, NIH postdoctoral fellow, 1975-77. Mem. Am. Chem. Soc., Soc. for Devel. Biology. Home: 7337 Foxridge Circle Apt 1 Anchorage AK 99518 Office: NOAA NOS OMA OAD 701 C St Box 56 Anchorage AK 99513

MANETH, ALVIN LEE, real estate company executive; b. Great Bend, Kans., June 12, 1934; s. Henry J. and Lena (Hlavaty) M.; m. Jolene Clara Schremmer, June 9, 1959; children: Darrin, Tamee, Danielle. BS, Fort Hays State U., 1960. Indsl. engr. Boeing Corp., Wichita, Kans., 1962-63; owner Maneth Constrn., Wichita, 1962-72, 1972—; owner A&J Co., Phoenix, 1972—, Direct Fin., Scottsdale, Ariz., 1983—; bus. specialist Realty Internat., Scottsdale, 1988—. Author: How to Sell U.S. Real Estate to Hong Kong Investors, 1986, Sell It and Get the Cash, 1987. With U.S. Army, 1954-57. Mem. Scottsdale Bd. Realtors, Optimists (Wichita) (pres. 1970, lt. gov. 1971). Republican. Roman Catholic. Office: Direct Financial 6925 5th Ave #E184W Scottsdale AZ 85251

MANFREDI, EUGENE TRENT, microbiologist; b. Long Beach, Calif., Nov. 6, 1944; m. Anne Reid Horne, Sept. 26, 1964. AS, Long Beach City Coll., 1971; BS, Calif. State Univ., 1973, MS, 1975; PhD, Univ. Wash., 1986. Computer operator/programmer McDonnell-Douglas Aerospace Ctr., Huntington Beach, Calif., 1968-71; teaching asst. Calif. State Univ., Long Beach, 1971-75; research assoc. Univ. Wash., 1975-80; microbiologist Washinton State Fisheries Cooperative, Seattle, 1980-81; research microbiologist Nat. Fisheries Research Ctr., 1981-83; dir. research Bio-Techniques Labs, Inc., Redmond, Wash., 1983-87, The Bonaparte Co., Bellevue, 1987-88; cons. Bio-Techniques Labs, Inc., 1987-88. Patentee, Application 915, 279 Lactobacillus acidophilus strain dietary supplement, 1987; contbr. articles to profl. jours. With USMC, 1964-67, Vietnam. Named Wilbert McLeod Chapman scholar, W. F. Thompson scholar. Mem. Am. Soc. for Microbiology, Am. Assn. for Lab Animal Sci., Am. Chem. Soc., Soc. of Animal Sci., Soc. of Indsl. Microbiology, N.Y. Acad. of Sci. Roman Catholic.

MANGEL, LEROY DWIGHT, information systems professional; b. Westby, Mont., Oct. 18, 1945; s. Ervin LeRoy and Phyllis Delphine (Hereim) M.; m. Jane Irene Wisness, Dec. 27, 1969; children: Lisa Jane, Lori Jo. AS in Data Processing, N.D. State Sch. of Sci., 1969; BS in Computer Mgmt. Sci., Met. State Coll., Denver, 1985; postgrad., U. Denver. Cert. systems profl., data processor. Programmer Blue Cross/Blue Shield, Fargo, N.D., 1969-72; programmer analyst Northwestern Nat. Ins. Corp., Milw., 1972-74; systems analyst Green Giant Co., Le Sueur, Minn., 1974-79; systems and programming mgr. Homestake Mining Co., Golden, Colo., 1979-81, system planning and support mgr., 1982-85, computer systems mgr., 1985—. Served with USAF, 1963-67. Mem. Data Processing Mgmt. Assn., Golden Key Nat. Hon. Soc. (life). Lutheran. Office: Homestake Mining Co 1726 Cole Blvd Golden CO 80401

MANGELS, JOHN DONALD, banker; b. Victoria, B.C., Can., Apr. 14, 1926; s. August and Marguerite E. M.; m. Mary Ann Hahn, Nov. 25, 1954; children: Susan, Meg, John Donald. BA in Bus. and Econs., U. Wash., 1950. With Security Pacific Bank Wash., Seattle, 1950—, pres., 1984-87, chmn., chief exec. officer, 1987—, pres., 1976-86, chmn. bd. dirs., 1986-87, chmn., chief exec. officer, 1987—; vice-chmn. Security Pacific Bancorp. N.W., Seattle, 1975-84; bd. dirs. PEFCO, ISC Systems, Inc. Trustee Downtown Seattle Assn., Corp. Council for Arts, 5th Ave. Theatre Assn., Seattle-King County Econ. Devel. Council, U. Wash. Devel. Bd., Wash. Roundtable, Children's Hosp. Found. Served with USNR, 1944-46. Mem. Wash. Inst. C.P.A.s, Assn. Res. City Bankers, Robert Morris Assocs. Presbyterian. Clubs: Rainier, Broadmoor Golf, Seattle Tennis.

MANGIAFICO, EDGAR, department store executive. Chmn. May Co., North Hollywood, Calif. Office: May Co Calif 6160 Laurel Canyon Blvd North Hollywood CA 91606 *

MANGIARELLI, RICHARD DONALD, energy company executive; b. Providence, Apr. 23, 1940; s. Santo and Jennie (Granieri) M.; divorced; children: Richard Donald Jr., Lisa Ann, Maria Lucia, Gina Sue. BA, U. Conn., 1963; MBA, Pepperdine U., 1975. CLU. Profl. football player Ottowa (Ont., Can.) Rough Riders, 1963-65; pres. Profl. Athletes Mgmt. Co., San Diego, 1969-76, Socalso Inc., San Diego, 1978-85; pres. U.S.A. Energy Corp., Solana Beach, Calif., 1985—, also bd. dirs. Author: Predicting Success of N.F.L. Draft Choices, 1975. Mem. Presdl. Task Force, Washington, 1980-88. Served to col. USMC, 1965-68, Vietnam, Res. Mem. Bldg. Contractors Assn., Marine Corps Res. Officers Assn. (v.p. 1987-88, bd. dirs. 1985-87). Republican. Roman Catholic. Club: Fairbanks Ranch (Calif.) Country. Home: Box 250 Rancho Santa Fe CA 92067

MANGLONA, BENJAMIN T., commonwealth senator; b. Rota, Mariana Islands; s. Prudencio M. and Maria T. M.; m. Magdalena Manglona Manglona, 1959; children: Lillian Manglona Matsumoto, Rebecca Manglona Taisague, Theodore, Marie Manglona Apatong, Joann Manglona San Nicolas, Benjamin M., Jr., Harold M., Debra M., Selina M. Grad., Surveyor's Sch., Palua, 1957; student Internat. Correspondence Sch., Scranton, Pa., 1964-65, Honolulu Community Coll., 1966-67; AS Civil Engring. Tech., U. Guam, 1973. Registered profl. land surveyor. Jr. engring. aide Rota Dist. Adminstrn., 1957, sr. engring. aide, 1958, supr. engring., 1958-59, asst. surveyor and cartographic engr., 1959-68, asst. clk. ct., Rota, part-time 1962-66, sta. mgr. Continental/Air Micronesia, Rota, 1968-69; pub. works office, Rota, 1970-75; pres. Rota Petroleum Co., B & M Constrn. Co., Rota Community Project Assn.; mem. Mariana Islands Dist. Legislature, 1963-65; mem. Ho. of Reps. Congress of Micronesia, 1965-70, resigned; chmn. Ho. resources and devel. com. 1969-70; appointed Mariana Islands Dist. Legislature, 1975; mem. No. Marianas Legislature, 1976-78; mem. No. Mariana Islands Commonwealth Legislature (Senate), 1978—, pres. Senate, floor leader, Republican mem. Cen. Com., chmn. appointments and govt. investigation com., 1978-80, 80-82, v.p., chmn. senate fiscal affairs com., 1982-84, v.p., legis. sec., chmn., 1984-85, chmn., 1986-87; elected Senate pres., 1988—; Trust Terr. rep. S. Pacific Commn. Conf., New Caledonia, 1968; mem. Congress of Micronesia Joint Commn. on Polit. Status, Washington, 1969-70; No. Marianas rep. to numerous USA, UN confs.; 1st v.p. No. Mariana Constl. Conv., 1976; numerous other govtl. appointments and coms.; mem. Trust Terr. Bd. of Land Surveying Examiners, 1972-75; mem. Rota Mcpl. Scholarship Bd., 1969-75. Mem. Am. Soc. Bldg. and Constrn. Inspectors. Roman Catholic. Home: Songsong Village Rota MP 96951 Office: No Mariana Commonwealth Legislature The Senate PO Box 129 Saipan MP 96950

MANGOTICH-GRIER, MARY ELIZABETH, lawyer; b. Chgo., July 31, 1953; d. Edward and Elizabeth (Hanlon) M.; m. Michael Anthony Grier, Aug. 14, 1982; children: Matthew, Megan. BA in Communications, Calif. State U., Northridge, 1974; JD, U. Ariz., 1977. Bar: Ariz. 1977, U.S. Dist. Ct. Ariz., U.S. Ct. Appeals (9th cir.). Assoc. Bilby & Shoenhair, P.C., Tucson, Ariz., 1977-82; mem. Bilby & Shoenhair, P.C., Tucson, 1982-89. Bd. dir. Agnese Nelms Lindley Found., Tucson, 1985-88; active City Coun. Campaign Com., Tucson, 1987, magistrate selection com. City of Tucson, 1987-88. Fellow Ariz. Bar Found. (v.p., bd. dirs. 1984-89, pres.-elect 1989); mem. ABA, Pima County Bar Assn., Am. Bankruptcy Inst., Ariz. Women Lawyers' Assn. (pres. so. Ariz. chpt. 1983-84), Order of Coif. Republican.

MANGUM, JAMES KENNETH, lawyer; b. Pasadena, Calif., Feb. 24, 1945; s. Eugene Kenneth and Marzelle (Jesperson) M.; m. Cherie Boothe, June 20, 1975; children: Christopher Kenneth (dec.), Ryan Todd. Student, U. Ariz., 1963-64; BA in Polysci. magna cum laude, Brigham Young U., 1969; JD, U. Chgo., 1972; postgrad., George Washington U., 1973-74. Bar: Ariz. 1972. Clk. Lewis and Roca, Phoenix, 1972, Sherman, Dunn, Cohen and Leifer, Washington, 1976; assoc. Robbins and Green, Phoenix, 1976—. Chmn. career awareness Theodore Roosevelt Council Boy Scouts Am., Phoenix, 1985—, also scoutmaster and various positions, Chgo. and Phoenix, 1970—. Lt. U.S. Navy, 1972-76. Mem. Maricopa County Bar Assn. (young lawyer's div. bd. dirs. 1979-81, sec. 1981-82, practice manual com. 1980-84), Ariz. Bar Assn., Phoenix Assn. Defense Counsel, Nat. Ctr. Decency (bd. dirs. 1982—), Phi Eta Sigma, Phi Kappa Phi, Phi Delta Phi. Republican. Mormon. Club: U. Chgo. (v.p. Phoenix 1978—). Lodge: Rotary (sec. 1986-87, pres. 1988-89). Home: 1729 E Rose Ln Phoenix AZ 85016-1820 Office: Robbins & Green 3300 N Central Ave #1800 Phoenix AZ 85012

MANGUM, MARK ALAN, publishing executive; b. Flagstaff, Ariz., Dec. 28, 1962; s. Richard Karl Mangum and Joyce Orms-Stowers. BS, Ariz. State U., 1984. Researcher Goodson & Allen, Phoenix, 1981-84; salesman LawForms, Inc., Phoenix, 1984-85, sales mgr., 1985-86, v.p., chief exec. officer, 1986—. Asst. Scottsdale Symphony Orch.; mem. Amnesty Internat. Mem. Phoenix C. of C., Rotary Internat. Home: 7050 E Belleview Scottsdale AZ 85257 Office: LawForms Inc 101 S Central Phoenix AZ 85003

MANIERI, MICHAEL JOSEPH, JR., industrial hygienist, safety engineer; b. Jersey City, Dec. 16, 1951; s. Michael Joseph and Lucille (De Luca) M.; m. Lori Frances Thresher, Oct. 6, 1984. BS, N.Y. Inst. Tech., 1973; MS in Indsl. Hygiene, Wayne State U. Sch. Medicine, 1976. Indsl. hygienist, rsch. analyst SRI Internat. (formerly Stanford Rsch. Inst.), Menlo Park, Calif., 1976-77; corp. indsl. hygienist Employees Benefits Ins. Cos., San Jose, Calif., 1977-80; assoc. indsl. hygienist Calif. Dept. Occupational Safety and Health, San Jose, 1980-81; corp. mgr. indsl. hygiene safety AVANTEK, Inc., Santa Clara, Calif., 1981-83; corp. indsl. hygienist, occupational safety specialist Applied Materials, Inc., Santa Clara, 1983-84; program mgr. occupaational and environ. health svcs., Safety Specialists, Inc., Sacramento, 1984-85; assoc. safety engr., Calif. Occupational Safety and Health Standards Bd., Sacramento, 1985—. Commr. City of Sacramento Toxic Substances Commn., 1985—. Mem. Am. Electronics Assn., Am. Indsl. Hygiene Assn. (symposium com. No. Calif. sect. 1983, contbr. Hygienic Guide Series 1976-78), Am. Soc. Safety Engrs., Peninsula Indsl. Bus. Assn., Bay Area Electronics Safety Group, Soc. Bio-Med. Scis., Nat. Off-Rd. Bicycle Assn., Sacramento Sports Assn., Sacramento Bike Hikers, Sierra Club, U.S. Far West Ski Assn., Tau Epsilon Phi. Roman Catholic. Contbr. articles to profl. jours. Home: 7042 Charolais Way Citrus Heights CA 95610 Office: State Calif Occupational Safety and Health Standards Bd 1006 4th St 3d Fl Sacramento CA 95834

MANION, RICHARD MICHAEL, architectural designer; b. Torrington, Conn., Dec. 26, 1961; s. Thomas Richard Manion and Carol Ann (Audia) Ramonas. BA, Columbia U., 1984. Draftsman Torrington Co., Torrington, Conn., 1979-81, Venturi, Rauch and Scott Brown, N.Y.C., 1983-84; project architect asst. Robert Stern Architects, N.Y.C., 1984-86; project architect Lee Manners and Assocs., N.Y.C., 1986-87; prin. Richard Manion and Assocs., Santa Monica, Calif., 1987—; cons. in field. Astor Found. Scholar, Columbia U., 1980-84. Mem. AIA, Nat. Trust for Hist. Preservation, Santa Monica C. of C. Home: 1714 Wellesley Dr Santa Monica CA 90405 Office: Richard Manion & Assocs 1714 Wellesley Dr Santa Monica CA 90405

MANKOFF, ALBERT WILLIAM, cultural organization administrator, consultant; b. Newark, Aug. 24, 1926; s. Albert and Dorothy (Kline) M.; m. Milicent Jessie Morgan, Apr. 4, 1953 (div.); m. Audrey Emery, Mar. 18, 1972; 1 child, Robert Morgan. BLS, U. Okla., 1967. With Am. Airlines, Inc., 1947-69, regional mgr. mgmt.tng. and devel., 1957-67; mgr. orgn. devel. Am. Airlines, Inc., Tulsa, 1968-69; dir. personnel Peat, Marwick, Mitchell & Co., Chgo., 1969-72; ptnr. Lexicon, Inc. Cons., Raleigh, N.C., 1972-77; Pacific area mgr. safety and tng. dept. Trailways, Inc., L.A., 1978-80; tng. cons. State of Calif., Sacramento, 1980—; pres. Inst. Am. Hist. Tech., Sacramento, 1987—. Author: Trolley Treasures, 4 vols., 1986-87, The Golden Decade, 1989, Cat Nooze Of The Werld, 1989; contbr. articles to profl. jours. Bd. dirs., v.p. OASIS: Midwest Centre for Human Potential, Chgo., 1970-72, Tulsa Urban League, 1962-69. Cpl. A.C., U.S. Army, 1945-46, PTO. Recipient Commendation Letter, Pres. Lyndon B. Johnson, 1968. Home and Office: 2237-3 Woodside Ln Sacramento CA 95825-7456

MANLEY, CHARLES DENNIS, economic developer; b. Galena Park, Tex., Feb. 8, 1952; s. Charles Norman and Ida E. (McLemore) M. AA, Ariz. Western U., 1973; BSBA, U. Ariz., 1979; Cert. in Basic Industrial Devel., Tex. A&M U., 1981; Cert. in Econ. Devel. Inst., U. Okla., 1987. Indsl. developer So. Pacific Indsl. Devel. Co., Houston, 1979-83, Kans. Dept. Commerce, Topeka, 1983-88; exec. dir. Oceanside (Calif.) Econ. Devel. Coun., 1988—. With U.S. Army, 1973-76. Mem. Am. Econ. Devel. Coun., So. Indsl. Devel. Coun., Calif. Assn. Local Econ. Devel., Urban Land Inst. Republican. Baptist. Office: Oceanside Econ Devel Coun 510 4th St Oceanside CA 92054

MANLEY, WILL, library director. Former dir. Tempe (Ariz.) Pub. Library, now asst. community svcs. dir.; columnist Wilson Library Bull. Office: Tempe Pub Library 3500 S Rural Rd Tempe AZ 85282 *

MANN, DONALD ROBERT See VALA, ROBERT DONALD

MANN, GENIE GRANT, hospital administrator; b. Mount Carmel, Ill., July 24, 1951; d. Stewart Eugene and R. Joann (Mobley) Grant; m. Stephen I. Mann, July 21, 1988. BA, Western Ill. U., 1980; Masters in Health and Hosp. Adminstrn., Xavier U., 1981. Fellow Gov.'s Office, State of Ill.,

Springfield, 1980-82; adminstrv. asst. St. Elizabeth's Hosp., Boston, 1982; dir. planning Health Northeast, Manchester, N.H., 1983-86; dir. strategy support Sutter/Health, Sacramento, Calif., 1986—; cons. in field. Local coordinator campaign John Glenn for Pres., Derry, N.H., 1984; active Camellia Festival, Sacramento, Community Svcs. Planning Coun., 1988—; bd. dirs. Jr. Achievement, Sacramento Child Abuse Coun., 1988—, Community Svcs. Planning Coun., 1988—; active Sacramento County Health Coun. Named Outstanding Young Woman Am., 1984. Mem. Soc. Hosp. Planning and Mktg., Am. Hosp. Assn., Women Healthcare Execs. No. Calif., Sacramento C. of C. (Leadership award 1987-88). Democrat. Clubs: Harry S. Truman, Ambassador (Sacramento). Office: Sutter Health 1111 Howe Ave Ste 600 Sacramento CA 95864

MANN, GORDON LEE, JR., insurance broker; b. Taylor, Tex., May 5, 1921; s. Gordon L. and Ruth (Kirkpatrick) M.; student, UCLA, 1939, Loyola U., L.A., 1961. Claims mgr. Traders and Gen. Ins. Co., L.A., 1948-52, Fireman's Fund Am. Ins. Cos., 1952-70; account exec., claims cons. Behrendt-Levy Ins. Agy., 1970-72; asst. div. mgr. Argonaut Ins. Co., L.A., 1972-78; v.p. Frank B. Hall & Co., L.A., 1978—. Lt. USNR, 1946. Recipient Meritorious Pub. Svc. citation Dept. Navy, 1965; Nat. Scroll of Honor, Navy League, 1968. CPCU. Mem. Am. Soc. CPCUs (pres. L.A. chpt. 1972, gen. chmn. nat. conv. 1970), Navy League U.S. (nat. dir. 1963-75, v.p. for adminstrn. 11th region 1974-75, pres. L.A. council 1962, state pres. 1965), Am. Legion (past comdr.) Nat. Soc. Colonial Wars (gov. Calif. soc. 1967, nat. dep. gov. gen. 1969), Children Am. Revolution (past nat. com. chmn.), S.R., Mil. Order World Wars, Men of All Saints' Soc. (past pres.), Naval Order U.S. Rep., Masons, L.A. Club, American Club. Episcopalian. Speaker and writer on ins. and patriotic subjects. Home: 435 S Curson Ave Los Angeles CA 90036 Office: 3200 Wilshire Blvd Los Angeles CA 90010

MANN, MICHAEL MARTIN, electronics company executive; b. N.Y.C., Nov. 28, 1939; s. Herbert and Rosalind (Kaplan) M.; m. Mariel Joy Steinberg, Apr. 25, 1965. BSEE, Calif. Inst. Tech., 1960, MSEE, 1961; PhD in Elec. Engring. and Physics, U. So. Calif., 1969; MBA, UCLA, 1984. Mgr. high power laser programs office Northrop Corp., Hawthorne, Calif., 1969-76; mgr. high energy laser systems lab. Hughes Aircraft Co., El Segundo, Calif., 1976-78; mgr. E-0 control systems labs. Hughes Aircraft Co., El Segundo, 1978-83, asst. to v.p., space & strategic, 1983-84; exec. v.p. Helionetics Inc., Irvine, Calif., 1984-85, pres., chief exec. officer, 1985-86, also bd. dirs.; ptnr. Mann Kavanaugh Chernove, 1986—; sr. cons. Arthur D. Little, Inc., 1987—; chmn. bd., pres., chief exec. officer Blue Marble Devel. Group, Inc., 1988—; mem. Army Sci. Bd., Dept. Army, Washington, 1986—; chmn. Ballistic Missile Def. Panel, Directed Energy Weapon Panel, Rsch. and New Initiatives Panel; cons. Office of Sec. of Army, Washington, 1986—, Inst. of Def. Analysis, Washington, 1978—, Dept. Energy, 1988—; bd. dirs. Datum, Inc., 1989—, Safeguard Health Enterprises, Inc., Am. Video Communications, Inc., Meck Industries, Inc., 1987-88, Datum Inc. 1988—; bd. dirs., mem. adv. bd. Micro-Frame, Inc., 1988—; chmn. bd. HLX Laser, Inc., 1984-86; rsch. assoc., mem. extension teaching staff U. So. Calif., L.A., 1964-70; chmn. Ballistic Missile Def. Subgroup, 1989—, Tactical Directed Energy Weapons Subgroup, 1988—. Contbg. editor, mem. adv. bd. Calif. High-Tech Funding Jour., 1989—; contbr. over 50 tech. articles to profl. jours.; Patentee in field. Adv. com. to Engring Sch., Calif. State U., Long Beach, 1985—; chmn. polit. affairs Am. Electronics Assn., Orange County Council, 1986—, mem. exec. com. , 1986—; adv. com. several Calif. congressmen, 1985—; mem. dean's council UCLA Grad. Sch. Mgmt., 1984-85; bd. dirs. Archimedes Circle U. So. Calif., 1983-85, Ctr. for Innovation and Entrepreneurship, 1986—, Caltech/MIT Venture Forum, 1987—. Hicks fellow in Indsl. Rels. Calif. Inst. Tech., 1961, Hewlett Packard fellow. Mem. So. Calif. Tech. Execs. Network, IEEE (sr.), Orange County CEO's Roundtable, Aerospace/Def. CEO's Roundtable, Am. Defense Preparedness Assn., Security Affairs Support Assn., Internat. Platform Assn., King Harbor Yacht Club. Republican. Office: 4248 Via Alondra Palos Verdes Estates CA 90274

MANN, RICHARD GERRIT, computer company executive; b. Buffalo, July 15, 1945; s. Bernard Watson and Alice Viola (Walberg) M.; m. Ellen Louise Grauer, July 24, 1971; children: Barbara Alice, Sylvia Louise. AA in English, West Valley Coll., San Jose, Calif., 1966; BA in English Lit., San Francisco State Coll., 1968; BA in Math., U. Calif., Berkeley, 1972. Programmer/analyst Nat. Cash Register Corp., L.A., 1968-69; asst. systems analyst U.S. Army, Anchorage, 1969-70; data analyst Bell Telephone Labs., Oakland, Calif., 1971-72; programmer/analyst Boeing Computer Svcs., Kent, Wash., 1973-74, Evans Products, Inc., Portland, Oreg., 1974-76; owner, mgr. Stone Art, Beaverton, Oreg., 1976-79, Handyman Computing, Beaverton, 1979-84; mgr. svc., info. systems Tektronix, Inc., Beaverton, 1984-88; pres. Mindnet, Inc., Beaverton, 1988—. Pres., Prepared Childbirth Assoc., Portland, 1977. Office: Mindnet Inc Ste 200 1865 NW 169th Pl Beaverton OR 97006-4873

MANN, RICHARD O'BRIAN, accountant; b. Murray, Utah, Nov. 10, 1946; s. Edward O'Brian and Elaine (Peterson) M.; m. Ramona Rollins, Nov. 26, 1975; children: Mary Elizabeth, Edward O'Brian. BS, Brigham Young U., 1972. CPA, Colo., Utah. Staff auditor Arthur Young & Co., Denver, 1973-77; sr. auditor Arthur Young & Co., Salt Lake City, 1977-79; contr. Bennett Enterprises, Salt Lake City, 1979-84; audit supr. LDS Ch., Salt Lake City, 1984-85, 87—; v.p., chief fin. officer Kenman Corp., Salt Lake City, 1985-87; pvt. practice, Salt Lake City, 1979—. Contbr. articles to profl. jours. Fin. clk, auditor, lay priesthood leader LDS Ch., Salt Lake City, 1977—. Sgt. USAF, 1966-70. Mem. AICPA, Colo. Soc. CPA's, Utah Assn. CPA's, Inst. Internal Auditors, Computer Press Assn. Republican. Home: 5998 S 3100 W Roy UT 84067 Office: LDS Ch Auditing Dept 50 E N Temple 16th Fl Salt Lake City UT 84150

MANN, ROBERT SAMUEL, video producer; b. Pitts., Feb. 5, 1936; s. Albert Samuel and Hilda Clara (Kalson) M.; children: Curtis, Kelly, Gary. Student, U. Fla., 1973-78. Pvt. practice as real estate developer Daytona Beach, Fla., 1962-68; golf. profl., mfr. Bomman Golf, Daytona Beach, 1968-73; pvt. practice as golf profl. Daytona Beach, 1979-82; pvt. practice as video producer and author Santa Monica, Calif., 1982—. Author: Automatic Golf, 1986; produced and performed in numerous videos including Fitness Testing, 1987, Automatic Golf, 1982-83, Instant Karate, 1986, Isometric Stretch, 1986, Weight Training, 1987. Served with U.S. Army, 1961. Office: 28955 Pacific Coast Hwy Malibu CA 90265

MANNING, DARRELL V., state adjutant-general; b. Preston, Idaho, July 17, 1932; s. Virgil and Olive Ann (Jenks) M.; m. Rochelle Manning, June 4, 1954; children: David Scott, Michael Alan. BS, Utah State U., 1955; postgrad., Idaho State U., 1969. Enlisted USAF, 1955, pilot, 1955-60, advanced through grades to maj. gen.; v.p. Manning Inc., Pocatello, Idaho, 1960-71; dir. Idaho Dept. Aeronautics, Boise, 1971-74, Idaho Dept. Transp., Boise, 1974-85; adjutant-gen., chief Idaho N.G., Boise, 1985—; chmn. Trans Research Bd. Nat. Acad. Scis., 1982. State rep., Boise, 1960-63; Idaho sen., 1970-71. Mem. Am. Assn. State Hwy. and Transp. Officials (nat. pres. 1978, Disting. Service award 1985, MacDonald Meml. award 1985), Western Assn. State Hwy. and Transp. Officials, Adjutant-Gens. Assn. U.S., N.G. Assn. U.S., Air Force Assn., Assn. U.S. Army, VFW, Rotary. Home: 8260 Golse Circle Boise ID 83704 Office: Idaho Mil Div Gowen Field PO Box 45 Boise ID 83707

MANNING, DONALD O., protective services official. Fire chief L.A. Office: Los Angeles Fire Dept Office of the Fire Chief 200 N Main Los Angeles CA 90012 *

MANNING, MARLOU, psychotherapist; b. Tucson, June 2, 1956; d. William Herman and Carole Eleanor (Musgrove) McBratney. BA U. Ariz., 1981; MA Calif. Grad. Inst., 1983, PhD, 1987. Lic. marriage, family and child counselor. Asst. to pres. Western Psychol. Svcs., L.A., 1978-81; crisis counselor Cedars-Sinai Med. Ctr., L.A., 1980-84; counselor South Bay Therapeutic Clinic, Hawthorne, Calif., 1982-84; psychotherapist PMC Treatment Systems, L.A., 1984-85, Beverly Hills Counseling Ctr., 1984-85, Comprehensive Care Corp., L.A., 1985-86; pvt. practice, L.A., 1986—; counselor Brotman Med. Ctr., L.A., 1982-83, Julia Ann Singer Ctr., Los Angeles, 1984. Mem. AAUW, NAFE, Internat. Assn. Eating Disorders Profls, Nat. Assn. Women Bus. Owners, Women in Health, Women's Referral Svc., Am. Anorexia-Bulimia Assn., Calif. State Psychol. Assn., Calif. Assn. Marriage & Family Therapists. Democrat. Office: 9911 W Pico Blvd Ste 670 Los Angeles CA 90035

MANNING, MARY (WHITAKER), journalist, photographer; b. Marlboro, Mass., Apr. 2, 1947; d. John Francis and Mary Virginia (Bordeleau) Manning; m. Frank D. Whitaker, July 15, 1975 (div. May 1980); 1 child, Michelle. BA in English, U. Nev., 1970. Copy girl Las Vegas Sun, Nev., 1965, corr. for nature, 1966-71, Sunday editor, 1976-78, journalist, 1978—; info. officer Clark County Health Dist., Las Vegas, 1971-73; reporter AP Stanford, San Francisco, 1973-76. Mem. State and Las Vegas Pen Women (recording sec.), Sigma Delta Chi (bd. dirs. 1986-88). Democrat. Unitarian. Office: Las Vegas Sun 121 S Martin L King Blvd Las Vegas NV 89127

MANNING, MICHAEL MARCUS, accountant; b. L.A., Nov. 23, 1939; s. Earl Francis and Isabel mary (Hanley) M.; m. Phyllis M.H. Underwood, May 11, 1963; children: Phyllis E., Helen, Patrick and Michael G. (twins). BS, Golden Gate U., 1964. CPA, Calif. Pub. acct., staff acct. San Francisco, 1960-64; resident auditor in charge States S.S. Co., Maritime Adminstrn., Dept. Commerce, San Francisco, 1965-70; prin. Michael M. Manning, CPA, San Francisco, 1971-80; ptnr. Manning & Carroll CPA's, Mill Valley, Calif., 1980—; bd. dirs. Nat. Real Estate Fund.. Mem. AICPA, Calif. Soc. CPA's, Fed. Govt. Accts. Assn., Soc. Calif. Accts. (pres. North Bay 1976-77), Marin Estate Planning Council (bd. dirs. 1987-88), Native Sons Golden West, Rotary (pres. Mill Valley 1985-86), Elks. Republican. Roman Catholic. Office: Manning & Carroll CPA's 169 Miller Ave Mill Valley CA 94941

MANNING, PATRICIA KAMARAS, biochemist, consultant; b. Harlingen, Tex., May 26, 1953; d. Henry Julius and Audrey Marie (Klimas) Kamaras; m. Steven Allan Manning, Feb. 26, 1983. BS, U. Ariz., 1975, MS, 1978. Grad. rsch. asst. U. Ariz., Tucson, 1976-78, sponsor grad.rsch., 1986-88; rsch. scientist Armour Dial, Inc., Scottsdale, Ariz., 1978-79; sr. chemist Armour Rsch. Ctr., Armour Food Co., Scottsdale, Ariz., 1979-86; exec. v.p., tech. dir. Manning, Batson & Assocs., Inc., Seattle, 1986—; owner, mgr., cons. Phoenix Rsch. & Devel. Ctr., Gilbert, Ariz., 1987—. Inventor in field. Vol. Humane Soc Ariz., 1986—, Humane Soc. Am., 1987—. Mem. Inst. Food Technologists (profl.), Nat. Fisheries Inst. (tech. subcom. 1988—, govt. rels. com. 1988—), Assn. Ofcl. Analytical Chemists, Am. Oil Chemists Soc., Alaska Fisheries Devel. Found. (voting cons. 1986—, rsch & devel. grantee 1986—), N.Y. Acad. Scis., So. Ariz. Runners Club. Roman Catholic. Home and Office: 1341 W Windrift Way Gilbert AZ 85234

MANNING, RICHARD DALE, newspaper reporter and columnist; b. Flint, Mich., Feb. 7, 1951; s. Harold J. Manning and Juanita Mayo; m. Margaret B. Saretsky, June 5, 1971 (div.); 1 child, Joshua. AB in Polit. Sci., U. Mich., 1973. News dir. Sta. WATZ, Alpena, Mich., 1975-79; reporter Alpena News, 1977-79; city editor Post-Register, Idaho Falls, Idaho, 1979-81; editor, columnist Wood River Jour., Hailey, Idaho, 1981-82; city editor, columnist Times-News, Twin Falls, Idaho, 1982-85; reporter, columnist Missoulian, Missoula, Mont., 1985—. Recipient Blethen award for investigative reporting Allied Newspapers, 1986-87. Mem. Nat. Assn. Newspaper Columnists (award 1985), Soc. Profl. Journalists (award for column 1986), Missoula Press Club (pres.). Office: Missoulian PO Box 8029 Missoula MT 59807

MANNINI, RICHARD JOSEPH, university football coach; b. San Francisco, May 17, 1933; s. Joseph and Dina (Pacchelli) M.; m. Sandra Rae White, Feb. 15, 1958; children: Denise Marie, Janice Lynn, Lisa Anne. BS, Calif. Poly. State U., 1958, MA, 1960. Tchr., asst. coach Chowchilla (Calif.) High Sch., 1959-60; instr., asst. coach Hancock Coll., Santa Maria, Calif., 1960-62, Rio Hondo Coll., Whittier, Calif., 1965-73; tchr., head football coach Santa Maria High Sch., 1963-65; asst. coach San Jose (Calif.) State U., 1974-76; head football coach St. Mary's Coll., Moraga, Calif., 1977-83; asst. football coach Stanford (Calif.) U., 1984—. Contbr. articles to profl. jours. Sgt. USMC, 1951-54, Korea. Mem. Assn. Am. Football Coaches. Home: 460 Ives Terr Sunnyvale CA 94087 Office: Stanford U Dept Athletics 1 galvez Stanford CA 94305

MANNINO, J. DAVIS, psychotherapist; b. Patchoque, N.Y., Sept. 27, 1949; s. Joseph I. and Adrienne Adele (Davis) M. BA magna cum laude, SUNY, Stony Brook, 1971; MSW summa cum laude, San Francisco State U., 1974; EdD in Counseling and Ednl. Psychology, U. San Francisco, 1989. Lic. psychotherapist, Calif.; lic. clin. social worker, Calif., marriage, family and child counselor. Instr. U. Malaysia, 1974-76; dir. refugee programs City San Francisco, 1979-82; instr. U. San Francisco, 1979-85; pvt. practice specializing in psychology San Francisco, 1979—; cons. foster care Calif. State Legis., 1980, community rels., San Francisco Police Dept., 1982-87; forensic task force on A.I.D.S., San Francisco Pub. Health Dept., 1984-85; child abuse investigation supr. City of San Francisco, 1985-88; supr. Reasonable Efforts to Families Unit, 1988—; project coord. Edna McConnell Clark Found. Family Mediation Demonstration Grant. Contbr. articles to profl. jours.; local psychology columnist, 1986—. Mem. Am. Psychol. Assn., Nat. Assn. Social Workers (diplomate clin. social work), Orthopsychiat. Assn., Am. Assn. Counseling and Devel., Calif. Assn. Marriage Family and Child Therapists, Golden Gate Bus. Assn. (ethics com. 1986, Disting. Svc. award, 1985), Am. Assn. Marriage and Family Therapists, Nat. Register Clin. Social Workers, Lions (Helen Keller Humanitarian award, bd. dirs. San Francisco chpt. 1986). Address: PO Box 14031 San Francisco CA 94114-0031

MANOLAS, ELLI LIZA, janitorial supplies company executive; b. Chgo., Nov. 30, 1962; d. E. Van and Olga (Tsarouhi) Vlahakis; m. John A. Manolas, Jan. 19, 1985; children: Nicole, Stacy. Grad., Elmhurst Coll., 1985. Salesperson Venus Labs., Inc., Wood Dale, Ill., 1980-85; office mgr. Venus Labs., Inc., Huntington Beach, Calif., 1985-87; sec. bd. Venus Labs., Inc., Huntington Beach, 1987—; pres. bd. Barco Chem., Inc., Opa Locka, Fla., 1987—. Democrat. Greek Orthodox. Office: Venus Labs Inc 855 Lively Blvd Wood Dale IL 60191

MANON, EDUARDO, finance company executive; b. Mexico City, Dec. 4, 1943; came to U.S., 1963; s. Adrian and Carlota (Tavarez) M.; m. Dora Pasquel, June 29, 1966; children: Eduardo, Robert, Arthur, Adrian. Student, Calif. Computer Sch., Upland, 1987-88. Mgr. ops. Etan Products, Culver City, Calif., 1964-65; plant mgr. Direct Mail Co. of Am., L.A., 1966-67, Calif. Mktg. Corp., L.A., 1968-70; plant mgr. Fin. Communications Clearing House, L.A., 1970-75, v.p., 1976-84, pres., dir., 1985—. Pres. Universal Soccer League, L.A., 1975-78, Pasadena Soccer League, 1978-81; equipment mgr. Little League Football, Culver City, 1972-73. Mem. Western Fulfillment. Roman Catholic. Home: 663 Bowcreek Dr Diamond Bar CA 91765 Office: Fin Communications Clearing House 3691 Bandini Blvd Los Angeles CA 90002-0003

MANRING, DOROTHY FRANCES, exporter; b. Tientsin, Republic of China, Nov. 23, 1926; came to U.S., 1941; d. Jess T. and Mara Naomi (Wilson) Peyton; m. Alvin Benjamin Manring, Dec. 26, 1946; children: Rebecca, Nicholas, Keith. BA in French, Old Dominion U., Norfolk, Va., 1970; postgrad., Creighton U., Omaha, 1942, Whitman Coll., Walla Walla, Wash., 1943-46. Tchr. Fallbrook (Calif.) High Sch., 1970-71; ptnr. Mancor, Bellevue, Wash., 1971--. Mem. adv. bd. Econ. Devel. State of Wash.; active various charitable orgns. Mem. AAUW, World Trade, Interservice Club, China of Seattle (pres. 1984-87).

MANROSS, MARY ANN, human resource consultant; b. Titusville, Pa., Oct. 15, 1949; d. Harold Eugene and Louise Miriam (Reid) Williams; m. George Gary Manross, June 1, 1969 (div. 1978); 1 child, Shanna Ann. BA in Sociology, Calif. State U., Fullerton, 1978; postgrad., Calif. State U., L.A. Rsch. specialist Ducommun Metals, L.A., 1973-78; v.p. rsch. Multi-facet Communications, Inc., Irvine, Calif., 1978-82; mgr. human resources Coastcom, Concord, Calif., 1982-87; ind. human resource and survey rsch. cons. Martinez, Calif., 1988—. Mem. NAFE, Pvt. Industry Coun. Contra Costa County. Republican Roman Catholic. Office: 521 Frumenti Ct Martinez CA 94553 Mailing Address: PO Box 1654 Lafayette CA 94549

MANS, WALTER A., space planner; b. Inglewood, Calif., July 11, 1942; s. Walter Adolf and Grace (Louis) M.; m. Martha Laverne Voiner, Aug. 10, 1968; children: Wade Walter, Shane Michael. BS, Mont. State U., 1964; MS, U. So. Calif., 1971. Enlisted USAF, 1964, advanced through grades to maj.; mathematician Nat. Security Agy., Ft. Meade, Md., 1964-68; project officer U.S. Dept. Def., El Segundo, Calif., 1968-72; asst. prof. ROTC USAF, Waterville, Maine, 1972-74; chief engr. USAF, El Segundo, 1974-76; regional area comdr. CAP, Great Falls, Mont., 1976-80; chief planner USAF, Sunnyvale, Calif., 1981-85, Albuquerque, N.Mex., 1985—; sr. project engr. Hughes Aircraft Co.; registered rep. Dain, Kalman, Boswell, Great Falls, 1976-80. Author: NASA/Department of Defense: Ten Years of the Future, 1971, Economic Balance 1983, 1983; contbr. articles to profl. jours. Pres. La Palma (Calif.) Homeowners Assn., 1979-81. Mem. IEEE, IAAA. Methodist. Lodges: Optimists (v.p. Great Falls club 1978-80), Rotary. Office: USAF Kirtland AFB NM 87117-6008

MANSEL, WENDELL BRIAN, quality assurance engineer; b. Lake Charles, La., Apr. 4, 1958; s. Hisbray George and Willie Dean (Guillory) M.; m. Karen Dell Taff, June 23, 1979; children: Brian Keith, Ethan James. Student, U. Houston, 1978-80, Houston Bapt. U., 1978; BME, Kensington U., Glendale, Calif., 1982, M Petroleum Engring., 1986. Lab. chemist Fertilizer Co. of Tex. Inc., Pasadena, 1977; engr. Hughes Drilling Fluids, Inc., Houston, 1979-81; ops. mgr. P.D.F. Chems., Inc., Houston, 1982; engr. Fenix & Scisson, Inc., Las Vegas, Nev., 1983-87, U.S. Dept. Energy, Las Vegas, 1987—. Mem. ASME, Soc. Petroleum Engrs., Am. Petroleum Inst., Am. Soc. Quality Control, Kiwanis. Republican. Baptist. Home: 6116 Rymer Ct Las Vegas NV 89130 Office: US Dept Energy 101 Convention Ctr Dr Phase II Ste 200 Las Vegas NV 89109

MANSFIELD, ROGER LEO, aerospace publisher; b. Boston, Feb. 18, 1944; s. Roy D. Sr. and Nellie E. (Venzlowski) M.; m. Alice Lee Waring, Nov. 1, 1969 (div. Mar. 1983); 1 child, Jason Benjamin; m. Karen June Sprout, June 27, 1987. BS in Chemistry with high honors., U. Cin., 1965; MA in Math., U. Nebr., 1972. Chemist Lockheed Missiles & Space Co., Palo Alto, Calif., 1967; orbital analyst USAF, Offutt AFB, Nebr., 1967-73; instr. Dept. of Math. USAF Acad., Colorado Springs, Colo., 1973-74; aerospace engr. Philco-Ford Crp, Palo Alto, 1974-75, Data Dynamics Inc., Mountain View, Calif., 1975-76; aerospace engr. Ford Aerospace & Communications Corp., Colorado Springs, 1976-78, team leader, 1978-84, prin. engr., 1984-86; supr. Ford Aerospace Corp., Colorado Springs, 1986—; owner Astron. Data Svc. Pub. Skywatcher's Almanac, Local Planet Visibility Report, Photographer's Almanac, Comparative Ephemeris, Space Birds; contbr. articles to profl. jours. Mem. Am. Astron. Soc., Math. Assn. of Am., Internat. Planetarium Soc., Rocky Mountain Planetarium Assn., Nat. Space Soc., Phi Beta Kappa, Phi Eta Sigma. Home: 3922 Leisure Ln Colorado Springs CO 80917-3502

MANSON, DAVID JOSEPH, producer; b. N.Y.C., Jan. 6, 1952; s. Eddy Lawrence and Margery May (Abramson) M.; m. Arla Mae Nudelman, Apr. 4, 1982; 1 stepchild, Elena Jo Sorkin. BA magna cum laude, U. Calif., Irvine, 1974. Dir. devel. Stonehenge Prodns., Los Angeles, 1975-76, v.p. creative affairs, 1977-80; chmn. Sarabande Prodns., Los Angeles, 1980—. Producer: (feature films) including Bring on the Night, 1985 (Grammy award 1986), Birdy, 1985 (Cannes Spl. Jury prize 1985), (TV films) including Eye on the Sparrow, 1987 (Christopher award 1988), Sessions, 1983, (TV miniseries) A Rumor of War, 1980 (Writers Guild award 1980). Mem. devel. com. Children Now, Los Angeles, 1988. Office: Sarabande Prodns 10000 W Washington Blvd Culver City CA 90232

MANSON, MICHAEL IRVING, accountant; b. Glendale, Calif., Aug. 25, 1951; s. Arnold James and Jennie (McGowan) M.; m. Simcha Nahari, Dec. 17, 1972; children: Ahmi, Elon, Leor. BS, Calif. State U., Long Beach, 1974; MBA, U. So. Calif., 1975. CPA, Calif. Fin. analyst Relta Steamship Co., Long Beach, 1975-76; auditor CCH Computax, El Segundo, Calif., 1976; sr. acct. L.M. Wurth & Co., Anaheim, Calif., 1976-77; tax mgr. Ernst & Whinney, Irvine, Calif., 1977-82; pres. Michael Manson, Inc., Laguna Hills, Calif., 1982—. Mem. Calif. Soc. CPA's. Republican. Home: 25251 Derby Hill Laguna Hills CA 92653 Office: Michael Manson Inc 23231 S Pointe Dr #101 Laguna Hills CA 92653

MANSOOR, JOHN JIRIUS, sports management executive; b. New Ulm, Minn., July 13, 1955; s. Khalil Audi Mansoor and Audre Helen (Woebke) McGranahan. AA, Am. River Jr. Coll., Sacramento, 1975; BA, Ohio State U., 1978; MA, U. Calif., Davis, 1979. Coach U. Calif., Davis, 1979-81; exec. dir. Sacramento Long Distance Running Assn., 1984—; chmn. Pacific Assn./The Athletics Congress, Sacramento, 1980—. Bd. dirs. Am. River Parkway Commn., Sacramento, 1984-85, Save the Am. River Assn., 1986-88. Home: 800 Bonita Dr El Dorado Hills CA 95630

MANSOUR, TAG ELDIN, pharmacologist; b. Belkas, Arab Republic of Egypt, Nov. 6, 1924; came to U.S., 1951, naturalized, 1956; s. Elsayed and Rokaya (Elzayat) M.; m. Joan Adela MacKinnon, Aug. 6, 1955; children—Suzanne, Jeanne, Dean. BSc, Cairo U., 1946; PhD, U. Birmingham, Eng., 1949, DSc, 1974. Lectr. U. Cairo, 1950-51; Fulbright instr. physiology Howard U., Washington, 1951-52; sr. instr. pharmacology Western Res. U., 1952-54; asst. prof., assoc. prof. pharmacology La. State U. Med. Sch., New Orleans, 1954-61; assoc. prof., prof. pharmacology Stanford U. Sch. Medicine, 1961—, Donald E. Baxter prof., chmn. dept. pharmacology, 1977—; cons. USPHS, WHO, Nat. Acad. Scis.; Mem. adv. bd. Med. Sch., Kuwait U.; Heath Clarke lectr. London Sch. Hygiene and Tropical Medicine, 1981. Contrbr. sci. articles to profl. jours. Commonwealth Fund fellow, 1965; Macy Found. scholar NIMR, 1982. Fellow AAAS; mem. Am. Soc. Pharmacology and Exptl. Therapeutics, Am. Soc Biol. Chemists, Am. Heart Assn., Sierra Club. Club: Stanford Faculty. Office: 300 Pasteur Dr Stanford CA 94305

MANSOURI, LOTFOLLAH, opera stage director; b. Tehran, June 15, 1929; s. Hassan and Mehri (Jalili) M.; m. Marjorie Anne Thompson, Sept. 18, 1954; 1 child, Shireen Melinda. AB, UCLA, 1953. Asst. prof. UCLA, 1957-60; resident stage dir. Zurich Opera, 1960-65; chief stage dir. Geneva Opera, 1965-75; gen. dir. Can. Opera Co., Toronto, Ont., from 1976, San Francisco Opera, 1988—; dramatic coach Music Acad. West, Santa Barbara, Calif., 1959; dir. dramatics Zurich Internat. Opera Studio, 1961-65, Centre Lyrique, Geneva, 1967-72; artistic adviser Tehran Opera, 1973-75; opera adviser Nat. Arts Centre, Ottawa, Ont., 1977; v.p. Opera America, 1979—; operatic cons. dir. Yes, Giorgio, MGM, 1981; dir. opera sequence for film Moonstruck (Norman Jewison), 1987. Guest dir. opera cos. including Met. Opera, San Francisco Opera, N.Y.C. Opera, Lyric Opera of Chgo., Houston Grand Opera, La Scala, Covent Garden, Australian Opera, Vienna Staatsoper, Vienna Volksoper, Salzburg Festival, Amsterdam Opera, Holland Festival, Nice (France) Opera, Festival D'Orange, France; co-author: An Operatic Life, 1982 (initiated above-stage projection of Surtitles (a simultaneous transl. of opera) 1983). Mem. Am. Guild Mus. Artists, Can. Actors Equity Assn. Office: San Francisco Opera War Meml Opera House San Francisco CA 94102 *

MANTLEY, JOHN, producer, director; b. Toronto, Ont., Can., Apr. 25, 1920; s. Cecil Clayton Van Manzer (Mantley) and Violet Patillo; m. Angela Maria Gabriella De Dino Carabello; children: Clay, John, Maria. BA, U. Toronto, 1942; M in Theatrical Arts magna cum laude, Pasadena Playhouse, 1947. Director (in Can.) The Little Foxes, Candida, What Every Woman Knows, A Murder Has Been Arranged; choreographer fencing sequences Elizabeth the Queen, Hamlet; appeared playhouses nationally; star, dir., producer numerous live TV dramas; writer Kraft Theatre, Desilu Playhouse, Outer Limits, The Untouchables, Gunsmoke, Great Adventure, Rawhide, others; exec. producer Gunsmoke, The Wild, Wild West, How The West Was Won, Dirty Sally, Buck Rogers, McGyver, (TV movies) Cutter's Trail, The Macahans, Gunsmoke/Return to Dodge; co-producer Firecreek; writer My Blood Runs Cold; author: The 27th Day (English, Am. and Doubleday Sci. Fiction Book-of-the-Month Club Selection), The Snow Birch (English, Am. Book-of-the-Month Selection). With Royal Can. Air Force, 1943-45, ETO, India. Recipient Mass Media Brotherhood award Nat. Conf. Christians and Jews, 1971, Cert. of Extraordinary Merit for Compassionate and Understanding Treatment of the Mentally Retarded Pres.'s Council on Mental Retardation, 1976, 1979, Charles Russell "Wrangler" award Western Heritage Ctr., 1969, 70, 71, 72, 73, 74, 75, 76, 77, 78, 79, Outstanding Overall Contribution to the Western Heritage, 1980, Fame award Best Western Series T.V. Today, 1969-73, William F. Cody award Old West Trail Found.,

1977; spl. salutes from Am. Film Inst., Acad. TV Arts and Scis. Mem. SAG, Actors' Equity, Writers' Guild Am., Producers' Guild Am. (bd. dirs.), Caucus Producers, Writers & Dirs. (founding mem., chmn., co-chmn., life mem. steering com. and exec. com.), Am. Film Inst. (bd. dirs.).

MANTON, LINDA MARIE, academic administrator, home economist; b. Hanford, Calif., Nov. 17, 1949; d. John Batista and Evelina Garcia (Miranda) Nunes; m. Frank P. Manton, Apr. 14, 1971. AA, Coll. of Sequoias, Visalia, Calif., 1970; BS, Calif. State U., Fresno, 1972; BA, U. Ill., 1983. Cert. home economist. County extension advisor U. Ill. Cooperative Extension, Urbana, 1973-85; county dir. U. Calif. Cooperative Extension, Oakland, 1985. Author: Factors Contributing to Job Turnover, 1982; contbr. articles to profl. jours. Bd. dirs. health com. County Head Start, Merced County, Calif., 1986-88. Named one of Outstanding Young Women of Am., 1981. Mem. Calif. Assn. of Extension Home Economists, Nat. Assn. Extension Home Economists, Am. Home Economists Assn., Nat. Assn. Extension 4-H Agents (bd. dirs. 1984, Disting. Svc. award 1982), Ill. Assn. Youth Advisors (pres. 1980, Disting. Svc. award 1982), Calif. Assn. for the Edn. of Young Children, AAAW, Calif. Women for Agr. (v.p.), Toastmasters (v.p.), Epsilon Sigma Phi, Phi Kappa Phi. Democrat. Roman Catholic. Office: U Calif Coop Extension 2145 W Wardrobe Ave Merced CA 95340

MANTOS, LINDA JACOBS, small business owner; b. Miami, July 10, 1955; d. Martin Jacque and Doris Harriet (Stucker) Jacobs; m. JohnJoseph Mantos, Jan. 1, 1984 (dec. 1988). Student, U. South Fla., 1977. Mgr., cons. Werner Erhard & Assocs., San Francisco, 1978-82, program leader, 1979—; asst. exec. dir. The Breakthrough Found., San Francisco, 1982-88; owner MantagarisGalleries, San Francisco, 1988—. Vol. The Hunger Project, Fla., 1977-78. Democrat. Jewish. Homw: 75 Milland Dr Mill Valley CA 94941 Office: Mantagaris Galleries 77 Geary San Francisco CA 94108

MANZANO, EUGENE GERARD, food products executive; b. Hilo, Hawaii, Oct. 30, 1954; s. Teofilo and Nicanora (Beguio) M. Student, Hawaii Community Coll., 1974; Cert., Okla State U. Sch. of Tech. Tng., 1976. Pastry chef Sheraton Waiakea Village, Hilo, 1977-83; mgr. KTA Superstores, Hilo, 1983—; guest instr. Waiakea High Sch., Hilo, 1984-88, Hawaii Community Coll., Hilo, 1987-88, instr. Liberty House Dept. Store, Hilo, 1987—. Food Svc. Scholar Hawaii Hotel Assn., Hilo, 1974. Mem. Am. Culinary Fedn., Big Island Culinary Assn., (sec. 1980, pres. 1984, treas. 1989—). Home: PO Box 223 Keaau HI 96749 Office: KTA Superstores 50-E Puainako St Hilo HI 96720

MANZO, ANTHONY JOSEPH, painter; b. Saddle Brook, N.J., Apr. 25, 1928; s. Michael and Jennie (Spinneli) M.; m. Ruth Hendricks, Jan. 27, 1956; children—Kathleen, Joanne. Student NAD, N.Y.C., 1946-49, Phoenix Sch. Design, N.Y.C., 1955-58; studied privately with Salvatore Lascari N.A., 1945-65. Freelance comml. illustrator, 1956-59; painter and sculptor, 1958—; instr. pvt. art classes Renaissance Sch. Art, N.J. Served with U.S. Army, 1950-52. Recipient Ray A. Jones award N.J. Painters and Sculptors Soc., 1976. Mem. The Artists Fellowship, Salmagundi Club. Roman Catholic. Address: Box 2708 Taos NM 87571

MAOLI, GIUSEPPE, real estate executive; b. Cittaducale, Italy, May 17, 1923; came to U.S., 1982; s. Ferninando and Anita (Bonafaccia) M.; m. Vittoria Sabatini, Apr. 29, 1950; children: Eligio, Anna B., Rosella, Alessandra. BS, PhD in Agr., U. Di Perugia, Italy, 1946; PhD in Zoology, U. Rome, 1956. Exec. mgr. real estate holdings Italy, 1947-76; prof. zool. dept., mem. faculty of biol. scis. U. Rome, 1964-76; chief exec. officer State Inst. Zootech of Rome, 1962-68, State Inst. Olive Culture of Pescara, Italy, 1968-70; asst. tchr. Experimental Inst., San Rafael, Calif., 1975-78; chief exec. officer Arbiter of Calif., 1975-78; owner Maoli Consolidated Enterprises, 1978—. Author (zoology text book): Zootecina Speciale; contbr. entry to ency. Served with Italian Army, 1943-45, Palatine Guard State of Vatican. Decorated Cross of Merit Rep. of Italy; recipient civic awards for outstanding achievements in agr., Donato Militare ordine di Malta, commendatore della rep. Italiana by order Pres. of Italy., 1965. Mem. Higher Council, Medallian Soc., Assn. Calif. Inst., Marin County Club, Rotary. Republican. Roman Catholic. Office: Maoli Consol Enterprises 68 Mitchell Blvd Ste 200 San Rafael CA 94903

MAPELLI, ROLAND LAWRENCE, food company executive; b. Denver, June 10, 1922; s. Herman M. and Della (Borelli); m. Neoma Robinson, Apr. 1942; children—Terralyn Mapelli DeMoney, Geraldine Mapelli Gustafson. Student, Regis Coll., 1959-61. Pres. Mapelli Bros. Distbg. Co. div. Monfort of Colo., Greeley, 1969—; chmn. bd., sr. v.p. Monfort of Colo., Inc., Greeley, 1971—; owner, operator Mapelli Farms, Eaton, Colo., 1974—; chmn. bd. Denver Union Stock Yards Co., 1969-70; dir. United Banks Colo., United Bank of Greeley; mem. Colo. Bd. Agr.'s Frozen Food Provisioners Bd., 1967-71; mem. Colo. Agrl. Adv. Com., 1966-73. Chmn. Denver Off-Street Parking Commn., 1960-72; mem. Denver City Coun., 1955-59, Colo. Ho. of Reps., 1961-62, Colo. State Senate, 1962-66; mem. adv. bd. Ft. Logan Mental Health Ctr., 1961-64, St. Anthony's Hosp., 1960-65; bd. dirs. N. Denver Civic Assn., 1955-65, Better Bus. Bur., 1966-69; mem. bd. Ambassadors Loretto Heights Coll., 1960-65; bd. dirs., exec. com. Nat. Western Stock Show, 1966—; dir. Colo. State U. Land Coun., 1984—. 2d lt. USAF, 1942-46, ETO. Recipient Knute Rockne award, 1961; Water for Colo. Conservation award, 1985; named one of 12 Outstanding Transp./ Logistics Profs. in U.S. and Can. Internat. Intermodal Exbn., 1989. Mem. Mountain/Plains Meat Assn. (pres. 1968-69), Colo. Cattlemen's Assn., Colo. Cattlefeeders Assn., Colo.-Wyo. Restaurant Assn., Nat. Assn. Meat Purveyors. Roman Catholic. Home: 18979 Weld County Rd 78 Eaton CO 80615 Office: PO Box G Greeley CO 80632

MAPLES, ROBERT LEE, school system administrator; b. Phila., July 26, 1933; s. Amos Leonard Maples and Helen May (Dolan) Saunders; m. Marjorie June Brockwehl, Mar. 18, 1956; children: Christopher Lee, Jeffrey Lee, Jennifer Lee. BS in Pub. Adminstrn., U. So. Calif., L.A., 1958; MA in Geography, Calif. State U., Northridge, 1965. Personnel dir. City of Santa Monica, Calif., 1957-70; instr. Calif. State U., Northridge, 1965-69; dir. employee rels. Washoe County Sch. Dist., Reno, Nev., 1970-84, assoc. supt. personnel dept., 1984—; cons. in field. Lt. (j.g.) USNR, 1958-64. Mem. Internat. Personnel Mgmt. Assn., Assn. Ednl. Negotiators, Am. Assn. Sch. Adminstrs., Western Govtl. Rsch. Assn., Nat. Pub. Employer Labor Rels. Assn. Republican. Home: 3165 Wedgewood Ct Reno NV 89509 Office: Washoe County Sch Dist 425 E 9th St Reno NV 89520

MAPLES-PACHECO, ELIZABETH MAE, psychotherapist, counselor psychology; b. St. Petersburg, Fla., July 22, 1941; d. Samuel Ernest Jr. and Mamie Belle (France) Maples; m. Henry Kenneth Camacho, June 27, 1959 (div. 1963); children: Michael D., Deborah C., Linda Louise; m. Joseph Felimon Pacheco, July 8, 1972; children: Joseph L., Alicia Maria. Student, U. Albuquerque, 1981-84, Sierra U., 1987-88; human devel. tng., Hypnotherapy Albuquerque, 1988. Field dir. Girl Scouts U.S., Albuquerque, 1984-86; counselor, therapist Westside Counseling Assocs., Albuquerque, 1987—, Counseling & Psychotherapy Inst., Inc., Albuquerque, 1987—; cons. N.Mex. Health & Social Svcs., Albuquerque, Bernalillo and Rio Rancho, 1988—. Pres. AAU N.Mex., 1975-84, chmn. Women's Basketball, 1980-84, nat. men's bd. dirs. AAU, 1981-83. Mem. Am. Assn. Counseling & Devel., Am. Assn. Family Counselors & Mediators, Am. Coun. Hypnotists, SW Hypnotherapists Examining Bd. Democrat. Home: 10308 Timan Pl NW Albuquerqe NM 87114 Office: Westside Counseling Assocs PO Box 1222 Corrales Albuquerque NM 87048

MAPP, JERRY WALTER, medical foundation executive; b. Columbia, Miss., Sept. 1, 1945; s. Jerry M. and Louise E. (Foreman) M.; divorced; 1 child, Michael A.; m. Regina Falsetto. BA in Religion, Abilene Christian U., 1968; postgrad. in religion, Earlham Coll., 1968-69. Minister Tex. Ch. of Christ, 1968; residential treatment social worker Good Samaritan Ctr., adminstrv. asst. in charge devel. and pub. rels.; assoc. for devel. Daniel Freeman Med. Ctr., 1974-76; with spl. edn. dept. Santa Monica (Calif.) United Sch. Dist., 1976-77; assoc. dir. devel. Anaheim (Calif.) Meml. Hosp. Devel. Found., 1977-78; dir. devel. and community rels. York Sch., Calif., 1978-83; cons. not-for profit orgns. Calif., 1983-84; exec. dir. Pacific Presbyn. Med. Found., San Francisco, 1984--; v.p. for devel. Pacific Presbyn. Med. Ctr., San Francisco, 1984--; dir. workshops on planned giving, grantsmanship and trusteeship; former instr. devel. and community rels. for non-profits Hartnell Coll., Monterey Peninsula Coll.; speaker regional confs. Calif. Assn. Ind. Schs., Coun. for Advancement and Support Edn., Nat. Assn. Hosp. Devel., Nat. Soc. Fund Raising Execs.; cons. to numerous orgns. including Festival Theater Calif., Monterey Peninsula Found., Family Svc. Agy., Ctr. for Attitudinal Healing, Eskaton Monterey Hosp., West Coast U., Notre Dame Sch.; campaign cons. Merritt Peralta Med. Ctr. Former mem. tech. adv. bd. L.A. Mental Health Planning and Devel. Commn.; past mem. svc. com. Am. Cancer Soc.; cons. not for profit orgns. With Chaplain Corps, U.S. Army, 1969-7l, Vietnam. Decorated Bronze Star. Mem. Nat. Assn. for Hosp. Devel., Nat. Soc. Fund Raising Execs., Commonwealth Club, Rotary. Office: Pacific Presbyn Med Found 2340 Clay St Ste 425 San Francisco CA 94115

MAR, STEVE, data processing executive; b. Seattle, Nov. 30, 1948; s. Albert and Pamalai (Tze) M.; m. Betty Lam, Sept. 9, 1972; 1 child, Andrew. BA in Bus., U. Wash., 1971; MBA, Seattle U., 1977. Auditor, br. ops. First Interstate Bank, Portland, Oreg., 1971-74; EDP auditor SeaFirst Bank, Seattle, 1974-79, tech. audit svc. mgr., 1979-83, corp. data security mgr., 1983-85; mgmt. reports mgr. control svcs. dept. Bank of Am., San Francisco, 1985-86; EDP audit mgr. Continental Ill. Nat. Bank, Chgo., 1986-88; EDP audit mgr., mgr. info. tech. Peat Marwick Main, San Francisco, 1989—; chmn. Data Security Com. Bank Adminstrn. Inst., Rolling Meadows, Ill., 1984-88; v.p. Edn. EDP Auditors Found., Carol Stream Ill., 1986-87. Chmn. Citizen Transit Authority, Metro Transit, 1980-86, Affirmative Action Com., Bellevue Sch. Dist., 1973-79. Mem. EDP Auditors Assn. (sec. 1987—, Puget Sound chpt. 1982-85, Chgo. chpt. 1986-88, San Francisco chpt. 1989—), Info. Systems Security Assn. Home: Two Fallon Pl Ste 50 San Francisco CA 94111 Office: Peat Marwick Main Three Embarcadero F-17 San Francisco CA 94111

MARABLE, DON SCOTT, food products executive; b. Tyler, Tex., June 10, 1959; s. Don Hartwell and Dana Gene (Scott) M. BS in Bldg. Constrn., Tex. A&M U., 1982. Lectr. Tex. A&M U., 1982-83; young adult mktging. coord. Adolph Coors Co., Houston, 1983-84; asst. area sales mgr. Adolph Coors Co., Arlington, Tex., 1984; area sales mgr. Adolph Coors Co., Lubbock, Tex., 1984-86; field svc. project mgr. Adolph Coors Co., Golden, Colo., 1986-87, dist. devel. project mgr., 1987, asst. brand devel. mgr., 1987—; lectr. mktging. seminars various colls., 1985—. Fund-raiser Am. Cancer So., 1987—. Mem. Century Club, 'Aggie' Club. Republican. Methodist. Home: 12584 W 1st Pl Lakewood CO 80228 Office: Adolph Coors Co 311 10th St #NH440 Golden CO 80401

MARAFINO, VINCENT NORMAN, aerospace company executive; b. Boston, June 8, 1930; m. Doris Marilyn Vernall, June 15, 1958; children: Marli Ann, Sheri Louise, Wendi Joan. A.B. in Acctg. and Econs., San Jose State Coll., 1951; M.B.A., Santa Clara U., 1964. Chief acct. Am. Standard Advance Tech. Lab., Mountain View, Calif., 1956-59; with Lockheed Missiles & Space Co., Sunnyvale, Calif., 1959-70; chief acct. Lockheed Missiles & Space Co., 1967-68, dir. fin. mgmt. and controls, R & D div., also asst. dir. fin. ops., 1968-70; asst. controller Lockheed Corp., Burbank, Calif., 1970-71, v.p., controller, 1971-77, sr. v.p. fin., 1977-83, exec. v.p., chief fin. and adminstrv. officer, 1983-88, vice chmn. bd., chief fin. and adminstrv. officer, 1988—, also dir.; bd. dirs. Lockheed Missiles & Space Co., Inc., Dataproducts Corp., Woodland Hills, Calif., Newport Corp., Fountain Valley, Calif.; chmn. bd. dirs. Lockheed Fin. Corp. Chmn. bd. trustees Holy Cross Med. Ctr., Mission Hills, Calif. Served with USAF, 1953-56. Mem. Fin. Execs. Inst., Am. Inst. CPAs, Jonathan Club, North Ranch Country Club. Office: Lockheed Corp 4500 Park Granada Blvd Calabasas CA 91399

MARAMAG, AURORA VALLE, educational administrator; b. Manila, Nov. 26, 1947; came to U.S., 1958; d. Russell Maramag and Fidela (Valle) Alavazo. BA, San Francisco State Coll., 1970; teaching credentials, Calif. State U., San Francisco, 1972; MA in Ednl. Adminstrn., Calif. State U., 1974; MA Bilingual Edn., U. San Francisco, 1977. Cert. gen. supr., Calif. Tchr. Burnett Sch., San Francisco, 1974-77, Filipino Edn. Ctr., San Francisco, 1978-79; bilingual resource tchr. San Francisco Unified Sch., 1977-78; tchr., ESL Newcomer High Sch., San Francisco, 1979-82; tchr./ advisor Ctr. for Ind. Study, San Francisco, 1982-83; reading resource tchr. Roosevelt Middle Sch., San Francisco, 1983-85; dean students Balboa High Sch., San Francisco, 1985-86; asst. prin. Commodore Stockton Sch., San Francisco, 1986—. Office: Commodore Stockton Sch 950 Clay St San Francisco CA 94106

MARANTO, MATTHEW PHILIP, engineer; b. Durango, Colo., Apr. 24, 1963; s. Philip Caroll and Loretta Margret (Brock) M. BS, Embry-Riddle Aero. U., 1985; MA, Webster U., 1987. Engr. Martin Marietta Astronautics Group, Denver, 1986-88, quality engr., 1988—. Squadron comdr. Civil Air Patrol, Pinellas County, Fla., 1982. Named Wing Cadet of the Yr., Civil Air Patrol, 1981, Group Cadet of the Yr., Civil Air Patrol, 1980. Mem. Am. Inst. Aero. and Astronautics, Soc. Logistics Engrs., Lambda Chi Alpha, 1988. Republican. Roman Catholic. Home: 9178 S Bitterweed Ct Highlands Ranch CO 80126 Office: Martin Marietta Astronautics PO Box 179 M/S DC 1826 Denver CO 80201

MARAVICH, MARY LOUISE, realtor; b. Fort Knox, Ky., Jan. 4, 1951; d. John and Bonnie (Balandzic) M. AA in Office Adminstrn., U. Nev., Las Vegas, 1970; BA in Sociology and Psychology, U. So. Calif., 1972; grad. Realtors Inst. Cert. residential specialist. Adminstrv. asst. dept. history U. So. Calif., L.A., 1972-73; asst. personnel supr. Corral Coin Co., Las Vegas, 1973-80; Realtor, Americana Group div. Better Homes and Gardens, Las Vegas, 1980-85, Jack Matthews and Co., 1985—. Mem. Nev. Assn. Realtors (cert. realtors inst.), Las Vegas Bd. Realtors, Nat. Assn. Realtors, Women's Council of Realtors, Am. Bus. Women's Assn., NAFE, Million Dollar Club, Pres.'s Club. Office: Jack Matthews & Co 3100 S Valley View Blvd Las Vegas NV 89102

MARBUT, GARY S., public policy consultant; b. Denver, Sept. 24, 1946; s. Gary R. Marbut; m. Ellen Senechal O'Farrel; children: Scott Carleton, Tyrel Matthew. Student polit. sci., U. Mont., 1964-66. Propr., mgr. B.I.T. Enterprises, Missoula, Mont., 1978—, Pub. Policy Rsch. and Analysis, Missoula, 1985—; cons. on emergency med. delivery systems, residential energy conservation; ski instr; instr. fire sci. and emergency medicine U. Alaska, Tanana Valley Community Coll. Founder, pres., chmn. bd. dirs. Mont. Coun. Orgns.; founder, chmn. bd. dirs., pres. Mont. Legal Found., Inc.; Mont. coordinator Conservative Caucus, Inc.; founder, bd. dirs. Mont. Edn. Excellence Assn.; Rep. candidate for Missoula County commr., for Mont. Ho. of Reps.; founding mem. Mont. Liability Coalition; mem. comprehensive plan steering com. Energy Task Force and Rural Task Force, Ad Hoc Task Force on Local Govt. Affairs; active in other civic orgns. Served with U.S. Army, 1966-69. Recipient numerous awards for community activities. Mem. Missoula Area C. of C. (govtl. affairs com.), NRA, Mont. Rifle and Pistol Assn. (pres., bd. dirs., chmn. pub. rels. com., mem. legis. com.), Western Mont. Fish and Game Assn. (sec., bd. dirs., chmn. legis. com.), Mont. Action Shooting Coun. (chmn. adv. coun., pub. policy and issues com.), Big Sky Practical Shooting Club (bd. dirs, membership chmn., chmn. pub. policy and issues com.). Office: PO Box 4924 Missoula MT 59806

MARCA, JERRY, financial analyst; b. Agrigento, Sicily, Italy, Dec. 8, 1951; came to the U.S., 1955; s. Emanuele and Maria (Digiovanni) M.; m. Chiara Stella Acacia, April 27. Student, Rio Salado Community Coll., 1982. Operation mgr. Heath, Schlumberger Products Corp., North White Plaines, N.Y., 1972-79; gen. agent Marca Ins, Phoenix, 1979-81; sr. analyst, coord. Am. Express Co., Phoenix, 1981—; editor, publisher numerous short stories, 1970-73. Office: Am Express Co PO Box 31744 Phoenix AZ 85046

MARCELYNAS, RICHARD CHADWICK, manufacturing company manager; b. New London, Conn., Aug. 21, 1937; s. Anthony F. and Elizabeth A. (Chadwick) M.; m. Betty A. Forray, July 1, 1961; children: Michael R., Thomas R. B.A. in Bus. Adminstrn., U. Wash., 1961; postgrad. Seattle U., 1971-72. Mgmt. trainee, installation foreman Pacific Bell, Fullerton, Calif., 1964-65; cost acct. Scott Paper Co., Everett, Wash., 1965-68; asst. v.p. personnel and adminstrn. Nat. Pub. Service Ins. Co., Seattle, 1968-77; mgr. indsl. relations Heath Tecna Precision Structures Inc., Kent, Wash., 1978-85; mgmt. con. Pilon Mgmt. Co., Seattle, 1985— ; cons., lectr. Served to maj. USMCR, 1961-77. Decorated commendations for bravery and tech. expertise, 1962, 63, 64; recipient Seattle Pacific N.W. Personnel Mgrs. Assn. Bd. Dirs. award, 1975. Mem. Am. Soc. Personnel Adminstrs., Pacific N.W. Personnel Mgrs. Assn. (past pres. Tacoma chpt.), Am. Soc. Safety Engrs. Republican. Roman Catholic. Office: Tower Bldg Seattle WA 98101

MARCHAND, RUSSELL DAVID, II, fire captain; b. Lafayette, Ind., May 14, 1950; s. Russell David and Mable May (Gean) M.; m. Sandra Green, June 12, 1951 (div. Nov. 1986); 1 child, Russell David III; m. Carol Bella Flashenburg, May 31, 1987. AA in Fire Sci., Clark County Community Coll., Las Vegas, Nev., 1979. Cert. fire service instr., supr. instr. Firefighter N. Las Vegas Fire Dept., 1973-78, engr., 1978-82, capt., 1982—; pres. Local 1607 Internat. Assn. Fire Fighters, Las Vegas, 1980— (v.p. 1976-80); instr. N. Las Vegas Fire Dept., 1986. Chmn. N. Las Vegas Firefighters Polit. Action Com., 1980—, Muscular Dystrophy Assn., 1980-83, 85; served to sgt. U.S.M.C. 1968-72, S. Vietnam. Named fireman of the year Optimist Club, 1981; received citation of merit Muscular Dystrophy Assn., 1982, commendation City of N. Las Vegas, 1980, 83, 85. Mem. Fed. Firefighters Nev. (received commendation 1982). Club: Nat. Assn. Miniature Enthusiasts. Office: 2626 E Carey Las Vegas NV 89030

MARCHESE, LAMAR VINCENT, broadcasting executive; b. Tampa, Fla., Dec. 11, 1943; s. Thomas and Catherine (Palmer) M.; m. Patricia Davis, June 23, 1966; children: Peter, Julia. BA, U. So. Fla., 1964; MA, U. Fla., 1972. Media specialist Morehead (Ky). State U., 1969-72; program coordinator Clark County Library Dist., Las Vegas, Nev., 1972-78; gen. mgr. Sta. KNPR-FM, Las Vegas, 1979—; mem. adv. com. Legis. Subcom. on Pub. Broadcasting, Carson City, Nev., 1983-85; bd. dirs. Sta. KUNV, Las Vegas; chmn. Nev. Pub. Broadcasting Assn., 1986—; pres. Rocky Mountain Pub. Radio, 1988—. Pres. Nev. Alliance for the Arts, Las Vegas, 1983-86; chmn. Citizens Against 12, Las Vegas, 1984; mem. steering com. Library Bond Election, Las Vegas, 1985. Recipient Gov.'s Arts award Nev. State Council on Arts, 1985; named Outstanding Fundraising Exec., Nat. Soc. Fund Raising Execs., Las Vegas, 1985. Mem. Clark County Cable Communications Adv. Bd. (vice chmn. adv. bd. 1988—), Las Vegas C. of C., Las Vegas Blues Soc. (pres./founder 1988—), Rocky Mountain Pub. Radio (pres. 1988—). Democrat. Office: Sta KNPR-FM 5151 Boulder Hwy Las Vegas NV 89122

MARCHI, JON, cattle rancher, exporter, former investment brokerage executive; b. Ann Arbor, Mich., Aug. 6, 1946; s. John Robert and Joan Trimble (Toole) M.; m. Mary Stewart Sale, Aug. 12, 1972; children: Aphia Jessica, Jon Jacob. Student Claremont Men's Coll., 1964-65; BS, U. Mont., 1968, MS, 1972. Sec., treas. Marchi, Marchi & Marchi, Inc., Morris, Ill., 1968-69; account exec. D. A. Davidson & Co., Billings, Mont., 1972-75, asst. v.p., office mgr., 1976-77, v.p. mktg. and adminstrn., Great Falls, Mont., 1977—; sec., dir., v.p. fin. services and exec. devel., D. A. Davidson Realty Corp., Great Falls, 1978-85, chmn. research com., 1980; cattle rancher, Polson, Mont., 1985—; bd. dirs. Big Sky Airlines, Billings, Mont., Energy Overthrust Found., Mansfield Found., Mont. Beverages, Mont. Venture Capital Network. Chmn. Mont. Gov.'s Subcom. for Venture Capital Devel.; chmn. investment com., State of Mont. Sci. and Tech. Alliance, 1985—; chmn. seed capital com. State of Mont., bd. dirs. job svc. com.; mem. Mont. Peoples Action; sec.-treas. Valley View Assn., 1987—. With U.S. Army, 1969-71. Mem. Nat. Cattlemen's Assn. (fgn. trade com.), Polson C. of C. (bd. dirs.), Valley View Assn. (bd. dirs.), Mont. Cattle Feeders Assn., Montana Angus Assn., Am. Angus Assn., Western Mont. Stock Growers Assn., Am. Angus Assn., Western Mont. Stockgrowers Assn., Securities Industry Assn., Mont. Stock Growers Assn., Polson C. of C. (dir.), Leadership Great Falls Club, Ski Club, Mont. Club, Helena Wilderness Riders Club, Rotary. Episcopalian. Home: 7783 Valley View Rd Polson MT 59860 Office: Marchi Angus Ranches 7783 Valley View Rd Polson MT 59860

MARCHOL, PAUL JEROME, senior engineering specialist; b. Chester, Pa., Apr. 30, 1948; s. James and Anna Elizabeth (Paluobyte) M.; m. Katherine Dianne Bloedorn, Dec. 23, 1972; children: Nikolas Paul, Max Adam. BS in PHysics, Drexel U., Phila., 1971; MS in Physics, U. Wis., 1975. Rsch. engr. Gen. Dynamics Corp., Pamona, Calif., 1973-74; mem. tech. staff Gen. Rsch. Corp., Santa Barbara, Calif., 1976-79; staff scientist Fiber Materials, Inc., Biddeford, Maine, 1979-82; sr. engring. specialist Aerojet Strategic Propulsion Co., Sacramento, Calif., 1982-87, Aerojet Tech. Systems Co., Sacramento, Calif., 1987—. Contbr. articles to profl. books. Mem. Soc. Am. Materials and Process Engrs, Am. Ceramics Soc. Home: 8224 Warhorse Ct Orangevale CA 95662 Office: Aerojet Tech Systems Co PO Box 13222 Sacramento CA 95813

MARCIANO, RICHARD ALFRED, research institute executive; b. Providence, Apr. 9, 1934; s. Eugene and Venera (Stramondo) M.; m. Norma Ann Mulford, June 20, 1964; children: Melissa, Cristina. Student Brown U., 1951-52; BA, Syracuse U., 1970. Computer programmer RAND Corp., Santa Monica, Calif., 1956-58; computer scientist, mgr. System Devel. Corp., Santa Monica, 1958-65; sr. staff SRI Internat., Menlo Park, Calif., 1965-76, dir. edn. research, 1976-81, asst. to pres., 1981—, v.p. technology commercialization, 1983-87, v.p. commercialization and ventures, 1987—; dir. SRI Devel. Co., Menlo Park; mem., chmn. bd. dirs., Confirma Technology Corp., Menlo Park. Mem. Assn. Computing Machinery, Ops. Research Soc. Am., Inst. Mgmt. Scis. Office: SRI 333 Ravenswood Ave Menlo Park CA 94025

MARCIL, GERALD JOFFRE, real estate developer; b. Inglewood, Calif., Jan. 14, 1953; s. Joffre and Bertha (Boehm) M.; m. Carol Lee Paterson, Aug. 13, 1988; 1 child, Adriana. AA with honors, El Camino Coll., 1974; BS with honors, U. So. Calif., L.A., 1976. Real estate broker Dale Marks Realtors, Torrance, Calif., 1973—; pres. Property Dynamics, Inc., Torrance, 1980—, Palos Verdes (Calif.) Developers, 1983—. Charter mem. Issues Mobilization Fund, Washington, 1984—; mem. Nat. Tax Limitation Com., Washington, 1985—, U.S. Senatorial Soc., Washington, 1986—, Torrance YMCA Chmn.'s Round Table, 1988—; v.p. Malage Cove Homeowners Assn., Palos Verdes Estates, Calif., 1986-88. U. So. Calif. scholar, 1975; recipient Beautification award City of Torrance, 1981. Mem. Nat. Assn. Real Estate Brokers, Calif. Assn. Realtors, Torrance and Lomita Bd. Realtors, Nat. Fedn. Ind. Bus., Calif. Assn. Apt. and Motel Owners and Mgrs., U. So. Calif. Alumni Assn., U. So. Calif. Assocs., Torrance C. of C., Rancho Verdes Racquet Club. Republican. Home: 544 Paseo Del Mar Palos Verdes Estates CA 90274 Office: Property Dynamics Inc 43-D Malaga Cove Pla Palos Verdes Estates CA 90274

MARCILLAC, SHARON LEE, financial company executive, nurse; b. Exeter, Calif., July 27, 1947; d. Senette Grant Keck and Hazel Ruth (Hausner) Laiosa; m. George E. Marcillac, Feb. 15, 1969 (div. Aug. 1984); children: Monique Marie, Nichole Marie. Diploma, St. Luke's Hosp., San Francisco, 1968. RN, Calif. Critical care nurse St. Luke's Hosp., San Francisco, 1968-69, Seaton Med. Ctr., Daly City, Calif., 1969-76, Santa Rosa (Calif.) Meml. Hosp., 1976-79; ins. broker Marcillac Ins. Agy., Santa Rosa, 1979-84; asst. mng. dir. Double Eagle Fin. Corp., Santa Rosa, 1984—; owner, mgr. Fin. Data Svcs. Bus. Cons., Santa Rosa, 1986—. Bd. dirs. Redwood Empire Ballet, Santa Rosa, 1982-83. Republican. Office: Double Eagle Fin Corp PO Box 6265 Santa Rosa CA 95406

MARCKWARDT, HAROLD THOMAS, assn. exec.; b. Chgo., May 4, 1920; s. Herman and Carrie (Polachek) M.; AB, U. So. Calif., 1949, AM, 1953; MS, U. Calif., 1970, postgrad., 1970—; m. Patricia Ann Hoffman, Apr. 7, 1945; children: Craig, Diana, Brad, Glenn. Tool and machinery designer Douglas Aircraft, Santa Monica, Cal., 1939-43; playground leader County Los Angeles, 1946-47; community program dir. Hollywood (Calif.) YMCA, 1947-51, dir. community program and bldg., 1952-55; exec. dir. Westchester YMCA, Los Angeles, 1955-63; area dir. Nat. Council YMCA, 1963-66, pres. Western Center Assocs., Los Angeles, 1966—; internat. mgmt. cons., Indonesia, 1985-86, Sri Lanka, 1989; field assoc. Internat. Exec. Service Corps, 1987. Exec. dir. Calif. Youth and Govt. Statewide Com., 1965, del. seminar UN, 1959. Colliver lectr. U. Pacific, 1965. Trainer, Leadership Devel. Camp, Los Angeles, 1959; mem. Mayor's Steering Com., 1973-75, chmn. Mayor's Facilitators com. Conf. Children, Youth and Sr. Citizens, 1974; mem. employment and tng. subcom. Los Angeles County Task Force, 1977; mem. Task Force on Equity for Women in Employment, 1976-77. Served to 1st lt., USAAF, 1943-46, USAF, 1950-52. Recipient One of Hollywood's Top Ten Young Men award, 1954. Mem. Am. Soc. Tool Engrs.

(charter mem.), Pacific S.W. Area YMCA Assn. Profl. Dirs. (pres. 1963-66), Orgn. Devel. Network, Airplane Owner's and Pilots Assn., Am. Soc. Tng. and Devel. (v.p. 1979, pres. 1980), Internat. Fedn. Tng. and Devel. Orgns., Pacific Area Travel Assn, Indonesian Bus. Soc., Am. Soc. Travel Agts., Indonesian Trade Mission. Democrat. Author: The Leader Makes The Difference, 1968; Leading Discussion Groups, 1972; How to Make Executive Decisions About Training, 1976; 16 Steps to the Job You Want, 1979; The Quality Circles Kit, 1982. Home: 4216 Colbath Sherman Oaks CA 91423 Office: 15910 Ventura Blvd Ste A-3 Encino CA 91436

MARCO, DAVID DUANE, biomedical engineer; b. Apollo, Pa., Feb. 3, 1951; s. Peter M. and Jean M. (Merlo) M.; m. Nancy Elizabeth Bierman, Nov. 16, 1985. BS in Biomed. Engring., Rensselaer Polytechnic Inst., 1973. Operating engr. Shock & Trauma Unit Albany (N.Y.) Med. Ctr., 1973-75; research technician Abcor Inc., Boston, 1975-76; clin. engr. Boston U. Med. Ctr. Hosp., 1975-77; field clin. engr. Arco/Med. Products, San Francisco, 1977-81; sales rep. Siemens-Elema, Oakland, Calif., 1981-85; field clin. engr. Siemens-Pacesetter, Oakland, 1985—. Contbr. articles to profl. jours. Vol. Shiloh Christian Fellowship, Oakland, 1983—; lay counselor Shiloh Counseling Ctr., Oakland, 1983—. Mem. N.Am. Soc. Pacing & Electrophysiology, Full Gospel Businessmen Fellowship. Republican. Office: Pacesetter Systems 333 Hegenberger Rd #208 Oakland CA 94621

MARCOE, GEORGE ISADORE, social service administrator; b. Tacoma, Wash., Oct. 13, 1946; s. George Isadore Marcoe and Clara Belle (Emerson) McFarland; m. Carol Marie Pierce, Jan. 3, 1970 (div. 1980); m. Terese Ann Aston, July 13, 1986. BA, Cen. Wash. State U., 1970; Cert. Rehab. Adminstr., U. San Francisco, 1976; Cert. Prosthetics & Orthotics, UCLA, 1980. Fundraising mgr. United Cerebral Palsy Wash., Spokane, 1970-71; workshop dir. United Cerebral Palsy Benton/Franklin County, Kenniwick, Wash., 1973-74, exec. dir., 1973-74; assoc. dir. United Cerebral Palsy King/Snohomish County, Seattle, 1974-76, cons., 1985; vocat. rehab. supr. Dept. Labor & Industry, Seattle, 1976-79; pvt. practice prothetics and orthotics Mt. Vernon, Wash., 1980-85; field service dir. Found. for Handicapped, Seattle, 1985-87, exec. dir., 1987—; cons. Resource Ctr. for Handicapped, Seattle, 1985. Mem. The Assembly (bd. dirs.), Exec. Dirs. Coalition. Office: Found for Handicapped 1550 W Armory Way Ste 205 Seattle WA 98119

MARCUS, ALLAN JEFFERY, nurse; b. Long Beach, Calif., Sept. 15, 1953; s. Max and Gertrude Mariam (Abrams) M.; m. Deborah Michelle Glasser; children: Tivon Benjamin, Oren Gabriel. Student, Yeshiva Aish Hatorah, Los Angeles and Jerusalem, 1976-78; semitics student, U. South Africa, Pretoria, 1984-85; student, Berkeley Sch. Nursing, Santa Monica, Calif., 1979-80. Ironworker Fed. Steel Corp., Long Beach, 1971-79; emergency med. technician-1 Goodhew Ambulance, L.A., 1979; emergency med. technician VA Med. Ctr. - Wadsworth, L.A., 1979-80; emergency room nurse L.A. County Olive View, Van Nuys, Calif., 1980-81, Beit Holim Yosef Tal, Nahariah, Israel, 1981; ICU nurse Beit Holim Belenson, Petah Tikua, Israel, 1982; emergency room and triage nurse El Cajon (Calif.) Hosp., 1985; psychiat. nurse, spl. treatment and rehab. unit team leader Dept. Health Svcs., San Diego County, Santee, Calif., 1985-88; with OSS, San Diego, 1989—. Mem. Chabad Club. Jewish.

MARCUS, BURTON H., marketing executive; b. Jamaica, N.Y., May 27, 1934; s. Julius W. and Gertrude (Konigsberg) M.; m. Frances Mary Kolacz, Nov. 10, 1968; children: Julie Anne, Keith Alan. BA in Psychology, Queens Coll., N.Y.C., 1956; MA in Indsl. Psychology, Syracuse U., 1957; PhD in Bus. Adminstrn., Northwestern U., Evanston, Ill., 1965. With Gen. Elec. Radio & TV Receiver div., Syracuse, N.Y., 1956-57, U.S. Rubber, Gen. Products div., Mishawaka, Ind., 1961-62; asst. prof. IIT, Chgo., 1962-66; assoc. prof. U. So. Calif., L.A., 1966-86; mktg. rsch. dir. BL&D Advt. Agy., L.A., 1969-70; pres. Nat. Rsch. Ctr., L.A., 1972-73; exec. v.p., dir. Higgins, Marcus & Lovett, Inc., L.A., 1981—; cons. in field; dir. Anabolic Labs, Irvine, Calif. Contbr. articles to profl. jours.; co-author: Modern Marketing, 1975, Marketing Analysis and Decision Making, 1979, Modern Marketing Management, 1980. Northwestern U. fellow, 1957-62. Mem. Am. Mktg. Assn., Am. Soc. Appraisers. Office: Higgins Marcus & Lovett 800 S Figueroa St Ste 710 Los Angeles CA 90017

MARCUS, JEFFREY HOWARD, security company executive; b. Albany, N.Y., June 4, 1950; s. Paul and Phyllis (Zippert) M.; m. Claudia Kramlich, Aug. 22, 1981. BS in Elec. Engring. and Computer Sci., U. Colo., Denver, 1977; MBA, U. Phoenix, Denver, 1985. Specialist counter intelligence U.S. Army, Washington, 1971-73; v.p. engring. Securus, Inc. (formerly Photo-Scan of Colo.), Denver, 1977-81, pres., 1981—; also bd. dirs. Securus (formerly Photo-Scan of Colo.), Denver; Bd. dirs. PSA Fin. Services, Inc., Westminster; vice chmn. bd., tech. com. chmn. PSA Security Network, Westminster. Democrat. Office: Securus Inc 12411 E 37th Ave Denver CO 80239

MARCUS, ROBERT, aluminum company executive; b. Arlington, Mass., Feb. 24, 1925; s. Hymen David and Etta (Arbetter) M.; m. Emily Patricia Ulrich, 1988; children: Lawrence Brian, Janie Sue, Clifford Scott, Emily. AB, Harvard U., 1947; MBA, U. Mich., 1949; MEd, Tufts U., 1950. Market analyst Govt. Commodity Exch., N.Y.C., 1952-54; market rsch. analyst Gen. Electric Co., 1954-55; corp. market analyst Amax Inc., N.Y.C., 1955-62, staff market mgr. aluminum group, 1962-65, pres. internat. aluminum div., 1965-70, v.p., 1970-71; exec. v.p. Amax Pacific Corp., San Mateo, Calif., 1971-72; exec. v.p., dir. Alumax Inc., San Mateo, 1973-82, pres., chief exec. officer, dir., 1982-86; ptnr. Am. Indsl. Ptnrs., San Francisco, 1987—; bd. dirs. Domtar, Inc., Montreal. Trustee World Affairs Coun., 1974—; bd. dirs. With USN, 1943-46. Mem. Japan Soc. (bd. dirs.). Clubs: Harvard (N.Y.C.); University, Commonwealth, (San Francisco). Home: 2700 Scott St San Francisco CA 94123 Office: Am Indsl Ptnrs 1 Maritime Pla 23rd Fl San Francisco CA 94111

MARCUS, RUDOLPH ARTHUR, chemist; b. Montreal, Que., Can., July 21, 1923; came to U.S., 1949, naturalized, 1958; s. Myer and Esther (Cohen) M.; m. Laura Hearne, Aug. 27, 1949; children: Alan Rudolph, Kenneth Hearne, Raymond Arthur. BS, McGill U., 1943, PhD, 1946, DSc (hon.), 1988; DSc (hon.), U. Chgo., 1983, Poly. U., 1986, U. Göteborg, Sweden, 1987. Postdoctoral research assoc. NRC of Can., Ottawa, Ont., 1946-49, U. N.C., 1949-51; asst. prof. Poly. Inst. Bklyn., 1951-54, assoc. prof., 1954-58, prof., 1958-64; prof. U. Ill., Urbana, 1964-78; Arthur Amos Noyes prof. chemistry Calif. Inst. Tech., Pasadena, 1978—; temp. mem. Courant Inst. Math. Scis., N.Y. U., 1960-61; trustee Gordon Research Confs., 1966-69, chmn. bd., 1968-69, mem. council, 1965-68; mem. rev. panel Argonne Nat. Lab., 1966-72, chmn., 1967-68; mem. rev. panel Brookhaven Nat. Lab., 1971-74; mem. rev. com. Radiation Lab., U. Notre Dame, 1975-80; mem. panel on atmospheric chemistry climatic impact com. Nat. Acad. Scis.-NRC, 1975-78, mem. com. kinetics of chem. reactions, 1973-77, chmn., 1975-77, mem. com. chem. scis., 1977-79, mem. com. to survey opportunities in chem. scis., 1982-86; adv. council in chemistry Princeton U., 1972-78; vis. com. div. chemistry and chem. engring. Calif. Inst. Tech., 1977-78; adv. council chemistry Poly. Inst. N.Y., 1977-80; adv. com. for chemistry NSF, 1977-80; vis. prof. theoretical chemistry U. Oxford, Eng., 1975-76; also professorial fellow Univ. Coll. Mem. editorial bd. Jour. Chem. Physics, 1964-66, Ann. Rev. Phys. Chemistry, 1964-69, Jour. Phys. Chemistry, 1968-72, 80-84, Accounts of Chem. Research, 1968-73, Internat. Jour. Chem. Kinetics, 1976-80, Molecular Physics, 1977-80, Chem. Physics Letters, 1980—, Laser Chemistry, 1982—; Advances in Chem. Physics, 1984—, Theoretica Chimica Acta, 1985—, World Sci. Pub., 1987—, Internat. Revs. in Phys. Chemistry, 1988—, International Reviews in Physical Chemistry, 1988; contbr. articles to profl. jours. Recipient Anne Molson prize in chemistry McGill U., 1943, Alexander von Humboldt Found. Sr. U.S. Scientist award, 1976, Robinson medal Faraday div. Royal Soc. Chemistry, 1982, Centenary medal Faraday div. Royal Soc. Chemistry, 1988, Chandler medal Columbia U., 1983, Wolf prize in chemistry, 1985; Alfred P. Sloan fellow, 1960-63; NSF sr. postdoctoral fellow, 1960-61; sr. Fulbright-Hays scholar, 1972. Fellow Am. Acad. Arts and Scis. (exec. com. Western sect., co-chmn. 1981-84, rsch. and planning com. 1989—); mem. Nat. Acad. Scis., Am. Chem. Soc. (past div. chmn., mem. exec. com., mem. adv. bd. petroleum research fund, Irving Langmuir award Chem. Physics 1978, Peter Debye award Phys. Chemistry 1988, Willard Gibbs medal Chgo. sect., 1988), Royal Soc. London (fgn. mem.), Internat. Acad. Quantum Molecular Sci., Am. Phys. Soc. (exec. com. div. chem. physics), AAUP, Alpha Chi Sigma. Home: 331 S Hill Ave Pasadena CA 91106

MARCUS, STEPHEN GARRETT, physician, biotechnology executive, researcher; b. Bklyn., Sept. 5, 1953; s. Seymour and Miriam Marcus. BS, Bklyn. Coll., 1973; MD, N.Y. Med. Coll., 1976. Diplomate Am. Bd. Internal Medicine. Intern, then resident Lenox Hill Hosp., N.Y.C., 1976-79; fellow cancer rsch. inst. U. Calif., San Francisco, 1979-81; emergency physician Children's Hosp., San Francisco, 1981-84; assoc. dir. clin. rsch. Triton Bioscis. div. Shell Oil Co., Alameda, Calif., 1985-86, dir. clin. rsch., 1986-88, sr. dir. med. affairs, 1988—. Aem. AMA (Recognition award 1981), Internat. Soc. Inteferon Rsch., Am. Acad. Med. Dirs., Soc. for Biolog. Therapy, Internat. AIDS Soc., Calif. Med. Assn., Internat. Soc. for Antiviral Rsch. Home: 9 Captain's Dr Alameda CA 94501 Office: Triton Bioscis 1501 Harbor Bay Pkwy Alameda CA 94501

MARDINLY, A. JOHN, scientist, metallurgical engineer; b. Phila., Apr. 15, 1949; s. Ashe J. and Jane E. (Fish) M. BS in Engring. Physics, U. Mich., 1972, MS in Engring. Metallurgy, 1974, PhD in Metallurgy, 1982. Registered profl. engr., Mich. Materials specialist Northrop Corp., L.A., 1982-83; materials specialist Lockheed Missiles & Space Co., Sunnyvale, Calif., 1983-85, lead engr. for failure analysis, 1985—; mem. faculty part-time San Jose (Calif.) State U., 1988. Mem. Electron Microscopy Soc. Am. (Predls. scholar 1979), Micro Beam Analysis Soc., West Coast chpt. Micro Beam Analysis Soc. (program chair 1985-86, pres. 1986-87), Am. Soc. for Metals, Am. Inst. Metall. Engrs. Home: 655 S Fair Oaks #F 105 Sunnyvale CA 94086

MAREI, IBRAHIM, medical technologist; b. Marowe, Sudan, Dec. 6, 1939; s. Hassan and Shafika (Mohamed) M. BS in Chemistry, U. Cairo, 1966; MS in Med. Tech., Calif. State U., 1980. Lic. clinical chemist tech., Calif., clinical lab. tech., Calif. Clinical chemist Biosci. Lab., Van Nuys, Calif., 1969-71; supr. ctr. critically ill lab. Hollywood Presbyn. Med. Ctr., L.A., 1971-75; sr. toxicologist, clin. chemist spl. chemistry dept., instr. on the job tng. and edn. new students, tech. staff Reference Labs., Newbury Park, Calif., 1975-88; clin. chemist endochronology dept., med. technologist Smith Kline Biosci. Labs., Van Nuys, Calif., 1988—. Mem. Am. Soc. Clinical Pathologists (cert.), Am. Chem. Soc., Am. Assn. Clinical Chemists (cert.), Am. Pub. Health Assn. Calif. Assn. for Med. Lab. Tech. Home: 7441 Hazeltine Ave Apt 107 Van Nuys CA 91405 Office: Smith Kline Biosci Labs 7600 Tyrone Ave Van Nuys CA 91405

MARES, GRACIELA EUGENIA, service company executive; b. Chihuahua, Mex., Jan. 14, 1950; came to U.S., 1965; d. Ruben P. and Graciela (Gonzalez) M.; m. Philip Arroyo, June 2, 1975 (div. Nov. 1979). Legal asst. cert., U. West Los Angeles, 1975; BA in Comparative Lit., Calif. State U., Long Beach, 1981. Cert. legal asst., Calif. Legal asst. Ira Eugene Bank Law Offices, L.A., 1982-88; pres. Santa Fe Paralegal Svcs. Inc., Brea, Calif., 1989—. Translator (play and art book) Mexican Masks, 1980; contbr. articles to newspaper. Mem. Nat. Notary Assn., Brea C. of C., Am. Bus. Women Assn., Latin Bus. Assn., Network Cerretos Chpt., Phi Kappa Phi. Democrat. Office: Santa Fe Paralegal Svcs Inc 521 Tomarack Ave Brea CA 92621

MARES, JESUS MARIA, electrical engineer; b. Durango, Mex., Mar. 4, 1963; came to U.S., 1969; s. Jose Cruz and Manuela (Rodriguez) Marez; 1 child, Jennifer A. BS in Elec. Engring., Calif. State U., L.A., 1988. Registered profl. elec. engr., Calif. Prodn. asst. Thrifty Ice Cream Plant, El Monte, Calif., 1982-86; elec. engr. asst. U.S. Army Corps of Engrs., L.A., 1986—; traffic engr. Calif. State Dept. of Transp., L.A., 1987-88; elec. engr. asst. L.A. Dept. of Water and Power, 1988—. Nat. Action Coun. Minorities in Engring. scholar, 1981-85, TRW Inc. scholar, 1981-82. Mem. IEEE, Soc. Hispanic Engring. and Sci. Students (Calif. State U. student chpt. pres. 1986-87), Soc. Hispanic Profl. Engrs., Mex. Am. Legal Def. and Edn. Fund,. Lodge: Kiwanis. Home: 2110 Almadale St Los Angeles CA 90032

MARGALITH, ELI, laser scientist; b. Lodz, Poland, Aug. 16, 1945; came to U.S., 1987; s. Abraham and Miriam (Schwadron) M.; m. Michal Kochva, Aug. 9, 1973; children: Tal, Ayal. BSc in Aeros., Technion, Haifa, Israel, 1970, MSc, 1973; PhD in Aero. and Astronautics, U. Wash., Seattle, 1978. Research asst. U. Wash., Seattle, 1973-78; laser scientist Govt. of Israel, Beer Sheva, 1978-84; sr. scientist laser div. Helionetics, San Diego, 1978-85; sr. scientist, mgr. comml. lasers HLX Laser Inc., San Diego, 1985-87; tech. dir. Gen. Dynamics Laser Systems Lab., San Diego, 1987—; presenter in field. Contbr. articles to profl. publs. With Israel Def. Forces, 1964-66. Office: Gen Dynamics Laser Systems Lab 5452 Oberlin Dr San Diego CA 92121

MARGARITA, PETER A., personnel company executive; b. N.Y.C., Jan. 27, 1947; s. Albert J. and Rose (Sonessa) M.; m. Wendy Newell, Apr. 5, 1970; children: Brian, Allison. BS, Drexel U., 1969; MBA, Monmouth (N.J.) Coll., 1975. Duplicator capital specialist Xerox Corp., Princeton, N.J., 1970-75; br. mgr. A.B. Dick Co., Chgo., 1975-81; sr. v.p. Olsten Corp., Westbury, N.Y., 1981—. Mem. Calif. Assn. Temporaries (v.p. 1988), Irvine Racquet Club. Republican. Lutheran. Office: Olsten Corp 7777 Center Ave Huntington Beach CA 92647

MARGERUM, J(OHN) DAVID, chemist; b. St. Louis, Oct. 20, 1929; s. Donald Cameron and Ida Lee (Nunley) M.; m. Virginia Bolen, June 5, 1954; children: John Steven, Kris Alan, Julie Ellen. A.B., S.E. Mo. State Coll., 1950; Ph.D., Northwestern U., 1956. Rsch. chemist Shell Oil Co., Wood River, Ill., 1954-55; chief spectoscopy sect. U.S. Army QMR&E Center, Natick, Mass., 1957-59; research specialist Sundstrand Corp., Pacoima, Calif., 1959-62; with Hughes Research Labs., Malibu, Calif., 1962—, sr. scientist, head chemistry sect., 1967—, head material scis. sect., 1988—. Contbr. articles to profl. jours.; patentee in field. Served with U.S. Army, 1955-57. Recipient Holley medal ASME, 1977. Fellow AAAS; mem. Am. Chem. Soc., Electrochem. Soc., Soc. Info. Display, Inter-Am. Photochem. Soc., Sigma Xi. Democrat. Unitarian. Home: 5433 Rozie Ave Woodland Hills CA 91367 Office: 3011 Malibu Canyon Rd Malibu CA 90265

MARGOLF, CHARLES WEAVER, coal mining executive; b. State College, Pa., Sept. 7, 1926; s. Paul Henry and Anne Elizabeth (Weaver) M.; m. Barbara Anne Keefer, Sept. 1, 1951; children: Kristin, Kimberly, Hunter Keefer. BS in Indsl. Engring., Pa. State U., 1950; JD, U. Pitts, 1953. Bar: Va. 1954, Wyo. 1971. Atty. Reynolds Metals Co., Richmond, Va., 1953-65; div. mgr. Wyo. Reynolds Mining Corp., Buffalo, Wyo., 1965-72; v.p. coal, water, environ. affairs Cameron Engrs. Inc., Denver, 1972-73; dir. western coal ops. W.R. Grace & Co., Denver, 1974-81; v.p. western coal devel. Natural Resources Group div. W.R. Grace & Co., Denver, 1981-87; v.p. coal devel. Colowyo Coal Co., Denver, 1988—; vice chmn. Supply Tech. Adv. Task Force Fed. Power Commn., Washington, 1973-75; mem. royalty mgmt. adv. com. Dept. Interior, Denver, 1985-87. Author: (book) Federal Coal Lease Readjustments - Will Reason Prevail?, 1988. With USN, 1944-46. Mem. Soc. Mining Engrs. Am., Inst. Mining Metallurgy & Petroleum Engrs., Rocky Mountain Coal Mining Inst. (pres. 1985-86), Colo. Mining Assn., Va. Bar Assn., Wyo. Bar Assn, Denver Coal Club (chmn. bd.). Home: 2140 9th St Boulder CO 80302 Office: Colowyo Coal Co 14062 Denver West Pkwy Bldg 52 Ste 250 Denver CO 80401

MARGOLIN, PHILLIP MICHAEL, lawyer; b. N.Y.C., Apr. 20, 1944; s. Joseph Harold and Eleonore (Leftcourt) M.; m. Doreen Stamm, Dec. 22, 1968; children: Daniel Scott, Amy Elaine. BA, Am. U., Washington, 1965; JD, NYU, 1970. Bar: Oreg. 1972, U.S. Dist. Ct. Oreg. 1973, U.S. Ct. Appeals (9th cir.) 1974, U.S. Supreme Ct. 1977. Tchr. N.Y.C. Pub. Schs., 1968-70; law clk to presiding judge Oreg. Ct. Appeals, Salem, 1970-71; dep. dist. atty., spl. agt. Multnomah County, Portland, Oreg., 1971-72; pvt. practice Portland, 1973, 80-86; ptnr. Nash & Margolin, Portland, 1974-80, Margolin & Margolin, Portland, 1986—; lectr. in field. Author: Heartstone, 1978, The Last Innocent Man, 1981, numerous short stories; contbr. articles to profl. jours. Vol. Peace Corps., Liberia, 1965-67; coach Hayhurst Elem. Chess Team, Portland, 1981—. Mem. Oreg. Criminal Def. Lawyers Assn., Oreg. State Bar Assn. Democrat. Jewish. Office: Margolin & Margolin 1020 SW Taylor Ste 330 Portland OR 97205

MARGOLIS, BERNARD ALLEN, library administrator, antique book merchant and appraiser; b. Greenwich, Conn., Oct. 2, 1948; s. Sidney S. and Rose (Birkenfeld) M.; m. Amanda Batey, Nov. 2, 1973. BA in Polit. Sci., U. Denver, 1970, MLS, 1973. Cert. librarian, Mich. Library asst. Denver Pub. Library, 1970-72; br. head Virginia Village Library, Denver Pub. Library, 1972-73; dep. dir. Monroe County Library System, Mich., 1973-75; dir. Raisin Valley Library System, Monroe, 1976-78, S.E. Mich. Regional Film Library, Monroe, 1976-88 , Monroe County Library System, 1976-88, Pikes Peak Library Dist., Colorado Springs, Colo., 1988—; cons. in library pub. relations, 1976—; lectr. Western Mich. U., Kalamazoo, 1978-81; appraiser rare books, Monroe, 1970—. Contbr. articles to profl. jours; assoc. editor Bottom Line Mag. Fin. Mgmt. for Libraries, 1986—. Bd. dirs. Monroe Sen. Citizens Ctr., 1976-80, Monroe Fine Arts Council, 1978-81; chmn. Blue Cross-Blue Shield Consumer Council, Detroit, 1984-88 ; mem. adv. bd. Mercy Meml. Hosp., Monroe, 1984-86; Dem. candidate for Mich. Senate, 1986. Recipient Mayoral Cert. Commendation award Denver, 1972, 73. Mem. ALA (governing council 1986—, cons. annual swap and shop 1979-84; John Cotton Dana award 1977, Library Awareness Idea Search award Washington 1982), Library Adminstrv. Mgmt. Assn., Pub. Library Assn., Library Pub. Relations Council. Democrat. Jewish. Home: 10640 Hungate Rd Colorado Springs CO 80908 Office: Pikes Peak Libr Dist Penrose Pub Libr 20 N Cascade PO Box 1579 Colorado Springs CO 80901

MARGOLIS, LORRAINE ELIZABETH, small business owner; b. London, July 4, 1945; came to U.S., 1976; d. James Cornelius and Daisy Doris (Hartwell) Goss; m. Stanley Margolis, May 8, 1963 (div. 1978); children: Alex Campbell, Rachel Sarah. GCE, Oxford U., 1962. Clk. Barclays Bank, Reading, Eng., 1962-64; acct. Contra Costa Times, Walnut Creek, Calif., 1978-84; bookkeeper Atty.'s Office, Merced, Calif., 1984-85; restaurant owner, mgr. Limey's Lunchbox, Merced, 1985—. Mem. Women's Royal Vol. Svc., London, 1972-76. Mem. Merced C. of C., Merced County C. of C., Merced Downtown Assn., Am. MENSA. Home: 3066 Meridian Way Atwater CA 95301 Office: Limeys Lunchbox 709 W Main St Merced CA 95340

MARGOLIS, ROBERT SI, nuclear engineer; b. La Mesa, Calif., May 13, 1965; s. Leo and Eva (Schaeffer) M. BS in Nuclear Engring., U. Calif., Santa Barbara, 1987. Cert. engr. in tng. Nuclear engring. trainee So. Calif. Edison Co., San Onofre, 1985-88; nuclear engr. MDM Engring. Corp., San Clemente, Calif., 1988—. Reuben H. Fleet Found. grantee, 1983. Mem. Am. Nuclear Assn. (judge sci. fair San Diego 1988), Fusion Power Assocs., San Diego Aerospace Mus. (life), U. Calif. Santa Barbara Alumni Assn. Republican. Home: 4329 Alamo Dr San Diego CA 92115

MARIETTA, MARY BLACKFORD, clinical social worker; b. Gallup, N.Mex., Mar. 17, 1929; d. Clyde Walter and Edna (Elder) Blackford; m. Wallace Cameron Sweat, Aug. 31, 1951 (div. Mar. 1958); children: Eric Kevin (dec.), Cynthia Eileen Moriarty; m. George Albert Marietta, June 18, 1967. BS, Ariz. State U., 1951; MSW, UCLA, 1967. Lic. clin. social worker, Calif. Social worker Los Angeles County Dept. Welfare, 1953-57; probation officer Los Angeles Dept. Probation, 1957-70, clin. social worker, 1967-70; social services dir. Epworth Village, York, Nebr., 1970-71; clin. social worker Mental Health Ctr., Lincoln, Nebr., 1971-77; child protective services social worker San Diego County Dept. Social Services, Oceanside, Calif., 1977-87, supr., 1988—; pvt. practice clin. social worker Oceanside, 1977—; cons. Group Home for Girls, Lincoln, 1972-77; field instr. U. Nebr., Lincoln, 1970-77. Mem. Nat. Assn. Social Workers, Nat. Assn. Social Workers Clin. Registry, N. County Child Abuse Coalition (treas. 1986), Sierra Club. Baha'i. Home: 851 Loma Alta Terr Vista CA 92054 Office: San Diego County Dept Social Svcs 318 N Hocne St Oceanside CA 92054

MARIGOLD, LAWRENCE LEE, management consultant; b. Tehachapi, Calif., Oct. 14, 1940; s. George Austin and Pauline Marie (Vukich) M.; m. Julie Ann Chohon, Sept. 9, 1978; children: Eric, Michelle. AA, Contra Costa Coll., 1960; BS, U. San Francisco, 1964; MBA, Golden Gate U., 1967. Exchange analyst, Standard Oil (Calif.), San Francisco, 1960-64; v.p. Unigas Inc. subs. Unical Oil Co., Denver, 1964-69, corp. mgr. residual products Union Oil Calif., Chgo., 1969-74; corp. mgr. energy planning and devel. Anheuser-Busch Inc., St. Louis, 1974-82; dir., corp. rep. Anheuser-Busch, Sacramento, 1982-84; mgr. aviation and alternate fuels Wickland Oil Co., Sacramento, 1984-85; internat. mgmt. cons. State of Calif. Energy Commn. and the Oil and Chemical Industry, 1985—; energy cons. food industry; mem. Coal Industry Adv. Com. to U.S. Dept. Energy, 1978—. Mem. Soc. Automotive Engrs., Assn. Energy Engrs., Porsche Club Am. Republican. Roman Catholic. Lodge: Elks (Carmichael, Calif.). Home and Office: 4925 St Thomas Dr Fair Oaks CA 95628

MARIK, MARGARET JANE, college official; b. Phila., Apr. 28, 1943; d. Robert J. and Eleanor Jane (Simon) Knox; m. Charles Weldon Marik, Sept. 7, 1963 (dec. June 1966); 1 child, Steven Scott. BA in History, Old Dominion U., 1969; MLS in Info. Sci., San Jose State U., 1977. Med. librarian Elmbrook Meml. Hosp., Brookfield, Wis., 1973-77; dir. midwest regional found. collection Marquette U., Milw., 1977-79; program coord. U. Wis. Extension, Madison, 1980, assoc. dir. spl. programs, 1980-83; exec. dir. coll. rels. Western Oreg. State Coll., Monmouth, 1983--, exec. dir. found., 1983--. Editor, author: Foundations in Wisconsin, 1978. Bd. dirs. Valley Community Hosp., Dallas, Oreg., 1988--; exec. treas. Wolfpack Athletic Assn., Monmouth, 1985--. sem. Am. Assn. Univ. Adminstrs. (bd. dirs. 1986--), Nat. Assn. Women Deans, Adminstrs. and Counselors (moderator 1985), Nat. Soc. Fund Raising Execs. (bd. dirs. Oreg. chpt. 1987--), Am. Assn. Higher Edn., Am. Assn. State Colls. and Univs. (fed. liaison person 1983-86), Salem C. of C., Monmouth-Independence C. of C. (com. mem. 1984--), AAUW (corp. rep. Polk County chpt. 1985--), Polk County Bus. and Profl. Women's Club (founding pres. 1984-85). Office: Western Oreg State Coll Office Coll Rels Monmouth OR 97361

MARINER, JOHN MARTIN, marketing executive; b. N.Y.C., July 16, 1953; s. Louis Anthony and Caroline Elizabeth (Brugman) M.; m. Marguerite Nichols, May 4, 1971; children: Christopher R., Jason L., Elibzaeth Marguerite. BS in Bus. Mgmt., Brigham Young U., 1979. Nat. mktg. mgr. Continental Candle Co., Carson, Calif., 1982-83; corp. mktg. dir. Lincoln Health Resources, Phoenix, 1983-85; v.p. mktg. Southside Hosp., Bay Shore, N.Y., 1985-87; pres. Mariner Mktg., Phoenix, 1987—; cons. to numerous health care and non-health care orgns. Explorer post leader Boy Scouts Am., Phoenix, 1987—. Sgt. USAF, 1971-76. Named Hon. Citizen of Tucson C. of C., 1972. Mem. Am. Mktg. Assn., Healthcare Mktg. Soc. Republican. Mormon. Home: 7745 W Cholla St Peoria AZ 85345

MARINER, WILLIAM MARTIN, chiropractor; b. Balt., Jan. 2, 1949; s. William Joseph and Ellen (Dexter) M. AA, Phoenix Coll., 1976; BS in chiropractic, L.A. Coll. of Chiropractic, 1980, D of chiropractic (hons.), 1980; DD, Universal Life Ch., Modesto, Calif., 1986. Health food restaurant mgr. Golden Temple of Conscious Cookery, Tempe, Ariz., 1974-75; health food store mgr. Guru's Grainery, Phoenix, 1975; physical therapist A.R.E. Clinic, Phoenix, 1975-76; research dir., founder G.R.D. Healing Arts Ctr., Phoenix, 1974-77; aminstrv. asst., acad. dean L.A. Coll. Chiropractic, Glendale, Calif., 1977-80; faculty Calif. Acupuncture Coll., L.A., 1978-80; ednl. cons. Amici Tng. and Information Seminars, San Francisco, 1985—; found, dir., head clinician Pacific Healing Arts Ctr., Del Mar, Calif., 1980—. Patentee in field. Co-dir. "We Care We Share" Charitable Orgn., San Diego, 1985-86. Named Outstanding Sr., L.A. Coll. Chiropractic, 1980. Mem. San Diego Chiropractic Soc., Calif. Chiropractic Assn., Am. Chiropractic Assn., Internat. Coll. Applied Icnesiology, Holistic Dental Assn., British Homopathic Assn., Rotary, Del Mar C. of C. Office: Pacific Healing Arts Ctr PO Box 5000 Del Mar CA 92014

MARINOFF, RONALD H., manufacturing executive; b. Chgo., Feb. 27, 1934; s. Hyman and Rose (Goldstein) M.; m. Margaret Virginia Norman, July 25, 1960; children: Alan J., David H. AA, Los Angeles Community Coll., 1953; BA, UCLA, 1955. Mfg. rep. Selig Mfg. Co., Leominster, Mass., 1958-62, Sherman Bertram Co., L.A., 1963-68, Bassett (Va.) Furniture Industries, 1969—. Mem. Jewish Community Relations Council, San Francisco, 1978-79; treas. Marin Jewish Community Ctr., San Rafael, Calif., 1972-73; pres. Lucas Valley Homeowners Assn., San Rafael, 1980; chmn. zoning and planning com. Community Homeowners Assn., San Rafael, 1981—; vol. fire fighter, Marinwood Fire Dept., 1967-80, battalion chief, fire commr. County Svc. Area #13, 1981—; chmn. Marinwood Fire Commn., 1984—. Served with U.S. Army, 1956-58. Named Man of Mark, Internat.

Home Furniture Reps., 1981, Citizen of Yr., Marinwood Community Svc. Dist., 1981. Mem. Home Furniture Reps. Assn. (pres. 1977, bd. trustees 1978—). Home: 66 Mount Rainier Dr San Rafael CA 94903 Office: Weil/ Marinoff Assocs 1355 Market St San Francisco CA 94103

MARIONI, JOHN DONALD, systems engineering consultant; b. Cin., Feb. 26, 1933; s. John Dominic and Jennie Rita (Geiss) M.; m. Gail Virginia Dickson, July 26, 1969; children: Lisa, Laura, John, Mark. BS, U. Cin., 1956; MS, Stanford U., 1958; postgrad., UCLA, 1963. Analyst, supr. Lockheed Missiles & Space Co., Sunnyvale, Calif., 1956-62, staff engr., 1974-79; br. mgr. SDC, Santa Monica, Calif., 1962-72; v.p. Med. Bus. Systems, Campbell, Calif., 1972-74; systems engring. mgr. Argosystems, Sunnyvale, 1979-86; pvt. practice systems engring. cons., Port Townsend, Wash., 1986—. Pres., v.p., sec. Los Gatos (Calif.) Jaycees, 1964-67; chmn. Los Gatos Drug Abuse Edn. Commn., 1968-69; active Los Gatos Youth Activities Commn., 1970, Am. Youth Soccer Orgn., San Jose, Calif., 1974-76. Fellow AIAA (assoc., tech. com. 1970-72); mem. IEEE, Tau Beta Pi. Republican. Roman Catholic. Home and Office: 301 Windship Dr Port Townsend WA 98368

MARK, ADOLF DEROY, architect; b. Phila., July 6, 1931; s. Josef deRoy Mark and Claire (Broome-Newman) Mark Ingraham; m. Fay Sheldon, June 22, 1955 (dec.); children: Calleen St. Claire, Courtney deRoy, Carrie Hale (dec.). BA, Pa. State U., 1951; MArch, U. Pa., Phila., 1955. Registered architect, Pa., Ariz., N.J., Va., Calif., N.C. With USAF, 1951-81, advanced through grades to lt. col.; pvt. practices, Calif. and Ariz. Prin. works includes Cottonwoods of Tempe, Phoenix, Rancho Villas, Phoenix, Papago Place, Scottsdale; publs. in Life, 1970, Salvaged Treasures, 1983, Town and Country, 1988, Metro Home Mag., 1988-89, and many more. Mem. improvement dist. Upgrade of Old Scottsdale. Lt. col. USAF, 1951-81. Recipient Nat. Urban Design award, 1977, Pacific Coast Builders Conf., 1983, Metro. Home of Yr., 1984, City of Tempe Beautification, 1984, 85, City of Phoenix Visual Improvement, 1986, Phoenix Home and Garden Homes of Yr., 1987, Phoenix Family Housing, 1989, and many more. Episcopalian. Home: PO Box 1052 Carefree AZ 85377 Office: 10229 No Scottsdale Rd Scottsdale AZ 85253

MARK, ARTHUR, information systems specialist; b. San Francisco, Aug. 1, 1948; s. Bo You and Chew Lin (Oyoung) M.; m. Alice Look, Sept. 1, 1975 (div. Oct. 1987); children: Jennifer, Brandon. BS, Calif. State U., 1971, MS, 1977. Cert. data processor, systems profl., Calif. Lectr. bus. Calif. State U., Sacramento, 1978—; internal auditor State of Calif., Sacramento, 1977-85, 88—. Chmn. EEO, Kansas City, Mo., 1986-87; mem. Internat. Relations Coun., Kansas City, 1987. Major USMC, 1985-88. Mem. Mensa, EDP Auditors. Republican. Home: 3216 Normington Dr Sacramento CA 95833

MARK, DAVID FU-CHI, molecular biologist; b. Hong Kong, Dec. 10, 1950; came to U.S., 1970; s. Hua Cheuk and Patricia Li M.; m. Joyce Lai-Jean Yee, July 1, 1973; children: Jonathan, Jennifer, Andrew. BA summa cum laude, U. Mass., 1973; PhD, Harvard U., 1977. Postdoctoral fellow Stanford (Calif.) Med. Sch., 1977-79; scientist Cetus Corp., Emeryville, Calif., 1979-83, project mgr., 1981—; dir. molecular biology Cetus Corp., 1982—, sr. scientist, 1983—; sci. advisor China Nat. Ctr. for Biotech. Devel., Beijing, 1984. Contbr. articles to profl. jours.; patentee in field. Named Outstanding Young Scientist, Sci. Digest mag., N.Y.C., 1984, Inventor of Yr. Intellectual Property Owners, Washington, 1986; Commonwealth of Mass. scholar U. of Mass., 1971-73. Mem. AAAS, Am. Soc. for Microbiology, Am. Assn. Immunologists. Republican. Baptist. Office: Cetus Corp 1400 53d Emeryville CA 94608

MARK, EVAN, pattern technician; b. San Francisco, Apr. 18, 1964. AA, City Coll. San Francisco, 1984; diploma, Fashion Inst. Design, L.A., 1985. Asst. mgr. Bing and Lai Co., San Francisco, 1979-84; first and prodn. pattern maker Eber Internat., San Francisco, 1985-86; first and prodn. pattern technician Jessica McClintock, Inc., San Francisco, 1986—; pattern technician Bugi Bugi, San Francisco 1988. Mem. Honor Soc.

MARK, LAURENCE MAURICE, film producer; b. N.Y.C., Nov. 22, 1949; s. James Mark and Marion Lorraine (Huebner) Green. BA, Wesleyan U., 1971; MA, NYU, 1973. Exec. dir., publicity Paramount Pictures, N.Y.C., 1978-80; v.p., West Coast mktg. Paramount Pictures, L.A., 1980-82, v.p., prodn., 1982-84; exec. v.p., prodn. Twentieth Century Fox, L.A., 1984-86; pres. Laurence Mark Prodns., L.A., 1986—. Exec. producer Black Widow, 1987, My Stepmother is an Alien, 1988, Working Girl, 1988; producer Cookie, 1989. Mem. Acad. Motion Pictures Arts and Scis. Home: 7888 Woodrow Wilson Dr Los Angeles CA 90046 Office: Twentieth Century Fox 10201 W Pico Blvd Los Angeles CA 90214

MARKEN, WILLIAM RILEY, magazine editor; b. San Jose, Calif., Sept. 2, 1942; s. Harry L. and Emma Catherine (Kraus) M.; m. Marilyn Tonascia, Aug. 30, 1964; children—Catherine, Elizabeth, Michael, Paul. Student, Occidental Coll., 1960-62; B.A., U. Calif.-Berkeley, 1964. Writer, mng. editor, now editor-in-chief and v.p. Sunset Mag., Menlo Park, Calif., 1964—. Bd. dirs. Calif. Tomorrow, 1979-83. Democrat. Office: Sunset Mag Lane Pub Co 80 Willow Rd Menlo Park CA 94025

MARKER, MARC LINTHACUM, lawyer, leasing company executive; b. Los Angeles, July 19, 1941; s. Clifford Harry and Voris (Linthacum) M.; m. Sandra Yocom, Aug. 29, 1965; children—Victor, Gwendolyn. B.A. in Econs. and Geography, U. Calif.-Riverside, 1964; J.D., U. So. Calif., 1967. Asst. v.p., asst. sec. Security Pacific Nat. Bank, Los Angeles, 1970-73; sr. v.p., chief counsel, sec. Security Pacific Leasing Corp., San Francisco, 1973—; pres. Security Pacific Leasing Services Corp., San Francisco, 1977-85, dir., 1977—; bd. dirs., sec. Voris, Inc., 1973-86; bd. dirs. Refiners Petroleum Corp., 1977-81, Security Pacific Leasing Singapore Ptc Ltd., 1983-85; lectr. in field. Served to comdr. USCGR. Mem. ABA, Calif. Bar Assn., D.C. Bar Assn., San Francisco Bar Assn., Am. Assn. Equipment Lessors. Republican. Lutheran. Club: University (Los Angeles). Office: Security Pacific Leasing Corp 4 Embarcadero Ctr #1200 San Francisco CA 94111

MARKHAM, J. DAVID, state official; b. Austin, Tex., Dec. 26, 1945; s. James Walter and Myrtle (Sturges) M.; m. Barbara Ann Munson, May 14, 1983. BS, U. Iowa, 1971; MA, U. No. Iowa, 1972; postgrad., So. Ill. U., 1972-74, U. Wis., 1981-82. Instr. sociology U. Wis., Fond du Lac/Stevens Point, 1974-76; dir. Vietnam edn. grants Wis. Dept. Vet. Affairs, Madison, 1979-83; coordinator internat. edn. AFSCME, Phoenix, 1983-84; vets. svc. officer Ariz. Vets. Service Commn., Phoenix, 1984-86; asst. to dir. Commn. on Ariz. Environ., Phoenix, 1986-88; div. supr. Ariz. Dept. Liquor Lics. and Control, Phoenix, 1988—; instr. sociology and polit. sci., Maricopa Community Coll. Dist., Phoenix, 1985—. Mem. Ariz. Right to Choose, 1985—; bd. dirs. World Affairs Council Ariz., 1987—. With U.S. Army, 1968-69, Vietnam. Decorated Bronze Star. Mem. Am. Sociol. Assn., Am. Soc. Sex Educators, Counselors and Therapists, Sierra Club, Nature Conservancy, Zero Population Growth, Am. Polit. Items Collectors, Napoleonic Soc. Am., Ariz. Polit. Collectors (pres. 1984-86), Alpha Kappa Delta. Democrat. Home: 13008 N 24th St Phoenix AZ 85032

MARKMAN, STEVEN JULES, retail executive; b. Bklyn., Apr. 14, 1947; s. Murray and Esther (Modell) M.; m. Harriet White, June 10, 1973; 1 child, Joseph. BA in English with honors, Calif. State U., 1972. Asst. buyer Broadway Dept. Stores, L.A., 1972-76; store mgr. Hickory Farms of Ohio, Glendale, Calif., 1976-77; owner, mgr. 7-Eleven Food Store, Alhambra, Calif., 1977—; Bd. dirs. so. Calif. chpt. 7-Eleven Franchise Owners Assn. Contbr. articles to profl. jours. Served with USN, 1964-68. Republican. Jewish. Home: 2229 Woodlyn Rd Pasadena CA 91104-3330 Office: 7-Eleven Store 1723 W Main St Alhambra CA 91801

MARKOE, M. ALLEN, leasing company executive; b. St. Paul, Feb. 23, 1927; s. Julius and Bernice (Jacobson) M.; student Drake, 1947-48; BS U. Wis., 1950; m. Joan B. Lewensohn, Aug. 7, 1949; children: Guy Leigh, Sara Lynne, Robin Dawn. Owner, Diversified Bus., Milw., 1950-54; dir. mgmt. adv. services Profit Counselors, Inc., Chgo., N.Y.C., 1954-60; pres. Pacific Am. Leasing Corp., Phoenix, 1961-80; ret., 1980; founder, pres. Markoe Fin. Group, Markoe Leasing; pres. AM Leasing Ltd., Phoenix; chmn., chief operating officer Shillelagh Ventures, Chartered Pub. Co., Phoenix; bd. dirs. Sunsounds, Rio Salade Community Coll. System. Served with AUS, 1945-46. Mem. Am. Indsl. Devel. Council, Ariz. Assn. Mfrs., Am. Mgmt. Assn., Soc. for Advancement Mgmt., N.Am. Soc. Sci. Mgmt., Assn. Equipment Lessors, Western Assn. Lessors, Phoenix C. of C., Am. Legion, Frat. Order Police (assoc.). Republican. Jewish. Clubs: Ariz. Aikido Kai, Lions. Home: 7050 N Wilder Rd Phoenix AZ 85021 Office: 5815 N Black Canyon Hwy Phoenix AZ 85015

MARKOVICH-TREECE, PATRICIA HELEN, economist; b. Oakland, Calif.; s. Patrick Joseph and Helen Emily (Prydz) Markovich; BA in Econs.; MS in Econs., U. Calif.-Berkeley, postgrad. (Lilly Found. grantee) Stanford U., (NSF grantee) Oreg. Grad. Rsch. Ctr., DD World Christian Ministries; children: Michael Sean, Bryan Jeffry, Tiffany Helene. With pub. rels. dept. Pettler Advt., Inc.; pvt. practice polit. and econs. cons.; aide to majority whip Oreg. Ho. of Reps.; lectr., instr., various Calif. instns., Chemeketa (Oreg.) Coll., Portland (Oreg.) State U. Commr., City of Oakland (Calif.), 1970-74; coord. City of Piedmont, Calif. Gen. Planning Commn.; mem. Piedmont Civic Assn., San Francisco Community Archives Calif. Art, Oakland Mus., Berkeley Art Ctr. Mem. Mensa, Bay Area Artists Assn. (coord., founding mem.), CFRTP (bd. dirs.), BACA, San Francisco Arts Commn. File, Index for Contemporary Arts, Pro Arts.

MARKOWITZ, RHEA-BETH, research scientist; b. Meriden, Conn., Feb. 10, 1949; d. Herman and Frances Shirley (Naviasky) M.; m. William Shelley Dynan, May 1, 1988. BA, Boston U., 1971; MS, Albert Einstein Coll. Medicine, Bronx, N.Y., 1979, PhD, 1984. Tchr. J.D. Sanderson High Sch., Raleigh, N.C., 1971-73; asst. for rsch. Rockefeller U., N.Y.C., 1973-77; postdoctoral fellow Columbia U., N.Y.C., 1984-85; asst. prof. N.Y. Med. Coll., Valhalla, 1985-87; sr. research assoc. Dept. Chemistry and Biochemistry, U. Colo., Boulder, 1987—. Contbr. articles to profl. jours. U.S. Pub. Health Service grant, 1987. Mem. Am. Soc. Microbiology, Am. Soc. Cell Biology, Assn. Women Sci., AAAS. Office: U Colo Dept Chemistry and Biochemistry Campus Box 215 Boulder CO 80309

MARKOWSKI, GREGORY RAY, consulting aerosol scientist; b. Milw., June 23, 1947; s. Casimir Ray and Blanche Dorothy (Dzik) M. BS with honors, Calif. Inst. Tech., 1969; MS, U. Calif., Berkeley, 1972. Sr. scientist Meteorology Research Inc., Altadena, Calif., 1973-84; cons. aerosol scientist Altadena, 1984--. Contbr. articles to profl. jours. Mem. AAAS, Am. Assn. for Aerosol Research, Air Pollution Control Assn., So. Calif. Soaring Assn. (treas. 1981-88). Democrat. Home and Office: 2009 N Madison Ave Altadena CA 91001

MARKS, DOROTHY LIND, mathematics tutor; b. N.Y.C., Apr. 30, 1900; d. Alfred Daniel and Martha (Herzog) Lind; m. Norman Lincoln Marks, May 29, 1923 (dec. 1959); 1 son, Alfred Lind (dec. 1980). B.A., Barnard Coll., 1921. Substitute tchr. N.Y. high schs., 1921-28; math tutor The Brearley Sch., N.Y.C., 1953-62, The Marlborough Sch., Los Angeles, 1973—, pvt. and pub. secondary schs., Los Angeles, 1973—, NYU, 1965-72; chmn. math dept. The Lenox Sch., N.Y.C., 1960-70. Bd. dirs. women's orgn. Temple Rodeph Sholem, N.Y.C., 1925-50, fin. sec., 1925-47. Mem. Phi Beta Kappa (recipient Kohn Math. Prize 1921, sec.-treas. Barnard chpt. 1925-50, chartermem. alumnae in N.Y.). Republican. Jewish. Avocations: reading, music, theatre, concerts, ballet.

MARKS, GORDON HOWARD, commercial real estate developer; b. Bremerton, Wash., Sept. 16, 1947; s. Howard Keylor and Mary Eleanor (Thompson) M.; m. Linda Lee Lockhart, Aug. 8, 1981; children: Darcy, Gerby, Meagan. BA, Harvard U., 1969; MBA, Stanford U., 1971. Asst. to pres. Westgate Corp., McLean, Va., 1971-78; chief exec. officer Alexandria Mgmt. Corp., McLean, 1978-79; gen. ptnr. Nat. Inns Co., McLean, Va., 1979—; ops. v.p. West Group Hotel div., Scottsdale, Ariz., 1980-82; gen. ptnr. Pima Grande Devel., Scottsdale, Ariz., 1981—; gen. ptnrs. TN Properties, Scottsdale, 1983—, THM Properties, Scottsdale, 1986—, TH Properties, Scottsdale, 1985—; pres. SW RealCorp, Scottsdale, 1986—; co-developer of largest shopping ctr. ever built on Am. Indian land; cons. in field; dir. E. Phoenix Redevel. Group, 1985-87. Author: She's Gone, 1987. Coach Arcadia Soccer Club, Scottsdale, 1983. Mem. Internat. Assn. Shopping Ctrs., Urban Land Inst., Harvard Club (pres 1989—). Office: SW RealCorp 6040 N Scottsdale Rd Scottsdale AZ 85253

MARKS, IRA ALAN, executive search company executive; b. Bklyn., Apr. 11, 1942; s. Samuel Alex and Sylvia Ruth (Schiller) M.; m. Jo-Ann Marks, July 11, 1968; children: Meredith, Marissa. BA, Pace Coll., 1965. Tchr. N.Y.C. Sch. System, Bklyn., 1965-71; N.Y. sales mgr. Harper & Row Pub., N.Y.C., 1971-77; pres. J.M. Meredith & Assoc. Inc., Phoenix and Santa Cruz, Calif., 1977—; v.p. Nova Strategies, Santa Cruz, 1987—; founder Ariz. Search Assn., 1981. Bd. dirs. Paradise Valley Soccer Club, Phoenix, 1979-84. Mem. Ariz. Assn. Personnel Cons. (v.p. 1979-80). Republican. Jewish. Home: 2240 N Rodeo Gulch Rd Soquel CA 95073

MARKS, MILTON, state senator; b. San Francisco, July 22, 1920; s. Milton and Olita M. (Meyer) M.; B.A., Stanford U., 1940; LL.B., San Francisco Law Sch., 1949; m. Carolene Wachenheimer, Aug. 14, 1955; children—Carol, Milton, Edward David. Mem. Calif. Assembly, from 1959; judge mcpl. ct., San Francisco, 1966-67; mem. Calif. Senate, 1967—, chmn. election coms., select com. on maritime industry, com. on disabled. Bd. dirs. Nat. Council on Alcoholism, Calif. League for Handicapped, St. Anthony's Dining Room, Mex. Am. Polit. Assn., Chinese-Am. Citizens Alliance. Served with U.S. Army, World War II. Recipient numerous awards including: Bronze Key award Nat. Council on Alcoholism; Man of Yr. award Council for Civic Unity of San Francisco Bay Area, 1973; Legislator of Yr. award Calif. Assn. Physically Handicapped, 1973; Consumer Legislator of Yr. award, 1981; Calif. Preservation award, 1982; Legislator of Yr. award Students of Calif. State Univ. System; Legislator of Yr. award Planning and Conservation League Calif., 1984. Mem. Am. Legion, VFW. Democrat. Jewish. Club: Press Club (San Francisco). Lodge: Lions. Office: Office of State Senate State Capitol Sacramento CA 95814

MARKS, PETER AMASA, technical company administrator; b. Passaic, N.J., Dec. 5, 1948; s. Amasa A. and Eunice L. (Irwin) M.; B.S. in Design Engring., U. Cin., 1972, M.A. in Media Communications, 1973, postgrad. in human factors engring. Research asst. dept. mech. engring. U. Cin., 1972; sr. engr. Ford Motor Co., Sharonville, Ohio, 1972-75; prin. Design Insight Cin., 1976—; mng. dir. SDRC TEC Services, Milford, Ohio, 1978-84, dir. product planning and devel., SDRC, Inc., Milford, 1981-84; sr. v.p. ops. Automation Tech., Campbell, Calif., 1985-88; lectr., cons. on product design tech. implementation, U.S., Asia, Europe, also for Am. Mgmt. Assns. Grad. fellow; Gen. Motors grantee in design, 1970; winner nat., internat. competitions for tech. programs. Mem. ASME, Soc. Mfg. Engrs. (bd. dirs.), Soc. for Tech. Communication, Computer and Automated Systems Assn. (bd. dirs.), Mensa. Author books, articles and films in field. Office: Design Insight PO Box 37 Los Gatos CA 95031

MARKS, SHARON LEA, nurse; b. Arroyo Grande, Calif., June 12, 1942; d. Donald Elmore and Gertrude (Grieb) Shaffer; m. George Conrad Schmidt, June 23, 1963 (div. 1975); children: Kerrilynn, Robert, Marianne; m. Keith Dalton Marks, June 4, 1978; children: Joseph, Erik, Alice. Diploma, Sch. Nursing Samuel Merritt Hosp., 1963; BS in Nursing, Lewis and Clark State Coll., 1984, BS in Mgmt., 1986. RN, Calif., Wash., Idaho. Staff nurse Vesper Meml. Hosp., San Leandro, Calif., 1968-74; night nurse supr. Tuolumne Gen. Hosp., Sonora, Calif., 1975; nurse Orleans (Calif.) Search and Rescue Team, 1975-78; instr. nursing Pasadena (Calif.) City Coll., 1978-79; resource coord. learning ctr. div. health sci. Spokane (Wash.) Community Coll., 1979-84; staff nurse Kootenai Med. Ctr., 1979-85; instr. North Idaho Coll., Coeur d'Alene, 1984-85; staff nurse North Idaho Home Health, Coeur d'Alene, 1985-86; coord. br. office Family Home Care, Spokane, 1986-87; devel., dir. Good Samaritan Home Health Plummer, Idaho and Fairfield, Washington, 1987-88; mgr. patient svcs. VNS Seattle-King County, Tukwila, Wash., 1988—; emergency med. technician instr. Orleans campus Coll. Redwoods, Eureka, Calif., 1977-78; book reviewer Brady Co.; film reviewer Olympia Media Info. Mem. Rural Nurses Orgn (v.p.), Nat. Head Injury Found., Wash. State Head Injury Found., South County Human Svcs. King County, Eastside Aging Providers. Home: 17410 Maple Valley Hwy Renton WA 98058 Office: VNS Seattle-King County 6510 Southcenter Blvd Tukwila WA 98188

MARKSHEFFEL, EDWARD EVERETT, merchant marine officer; b. Omaha, July 4, 1949; s. Charles Claude and Betty Jane (Detweiler) M.; m. Penny Marie Riddle, Aug. 18, 1972; 1 child, Amy Ruth. Parts mgr. Volkswagen of Am., Ketchikan, Alaska, 1964-67; various positions to sr. asst. purser Alaska Marine Highway System, Juneau, Alaska, 1969-78; chief purser Motor Vessel TAKU, Juneau, 1978—; trustee, Unlicensed Vessel Annuity Retirement Plan, 1987—. Mem. Inlandboatman's Union of the Pacific (exec. bd. 1978-81, del. to conv. in San Francisco, 1980). Democrat. Home: PO Box 962 Ward Cove AK 99928 Office: Alaska Marine Hwy System TAKU PO Box R Juneau AK 99811

MARLANE, JUDITH SCHLEIN, television producer, author, educator; b. N.Y.C., May 26, 1937; d. Samuel R. and Rose (Friedman) Schlein; student Cornell U., 1954-56; B.F.A. cum laude, Columbia U., 1958, M.A., 1962, Ed.D., 1974; m. Stanley Gelfman, July 14, 1957 (div. Jan. 1985); chilren—Debra Dawn, Sari Susanne. Producer, broadcaster Channel 13, WNET, 1962-66; freelance television writer, cons., 1966-71; pres. JSG Prodns., N.Y.C., 1974; producer writer TV series Out of Work, Feeling Female; producer Hispanic Horizons, Meet the Mayors, Point of View, Sta. WOR-TV, N.Y.C., 1982-87; pres. Videocom Internat., Inc.; instr. Tchrs. Coll., Columbia; adj. prof. communication Hunter Coll., N.Y.C.; prof., chair dept. radio, TV and film Calif. State U., Northridge, 1987—; dir. Ctr. for Communications Studies; guest Internat. Shanghai TV Festival, People's Republic of China; interview on radio Beijing, People's Republic of China. Recipient Broadcast Preceptor award Women in TV News, 1977, Silver medal Internat. Film and TV Festival, 1983, Silver Angel Religion in Media award, 1984, 85, 86, 87. Mem. Actors Equity Assn., Screen Actors Guild, AFTRA, Nat. Acad. TV Arts and Scis., Internat. Radio and TV Soc., Hollywood Radio-TV Soc., Broadcast Edn. Assn., Pi Lambda Theta, Kappa Delta Pi, Phi Kappa Phi. Author: Women in Television News, 1976; A Woman's Place. Home: 4267 Marina City Dr Marina del Rey CA 90292 Office: Calif State U Dept Radio TV Film Northridge CA 91330

MARLENEE, RONALD CHARLES, congressman; b. Scobey, Mont., Aug. 8, 1935; m. Cynthia Tiemann; children—Sheila, Casey, Allison. Student, Mont. State U., U. Mont., Reisch Sch. Auctioneering. Farmer, rancher; mem. 95th-101st Congresses from 2d Mont. Dist., 1977—; congressional committeeman 2d Congressional dist. Mont., 1975-76. Mem. Mont. Stockgrowers Assn., Daniels County Farm Bur., Daniels Fair Assn., Mont. Beef Performance Assn., Mont. Grain Growers Assn. Republican. Lutheran. Clubs: Safari Internat., Masons, Lions. Office: 2465 Rayburn House Office Bldg Washington DC 20515

MARLER, STEVE JOHN, protective services official; b. Mission City, B.C., Can., July 11, 1959; s. Edward William and Edna Eleanor (Kilback) M.; m. Karen Theodora Carson, Mar. 20, 1982; children: Stephanie Virginia, Jonathan David William. Student, Columbia Coll., 1977-79, Modesto Jr. Coll., 1979-83, Santa Rosa Jr. Coll., 1983—. Firefighter Tuolumne County Fire Dept., Moccasin, Calif., 1977-79, City of Ceres Fire Dept., Calif., 1979-83; capt. City of Sonoma Fire Dept., Calif., 1983—. Co-chmn. Norcal com. Calif. Code Regulations. Mem. Sonoma County Fire Prevention Officers, Norcal Fire Prevention Officers Assn. Republican. Roman Catholic. Office: City of Sonoma Fire Dept 32 Patten St Sonoma CA 95476

MARLOW, ROBERT ALLEN, family physician; b. Brighton, Colo., Mar. 13, 1948; s. Herbert Allen and Ima Jean (Campbell) M.; m. Iva Loraine Warren, Aug. 14, 1971; children: Courtney, Kimberly. BA cum laude, U. Colo., 1970, MD magna cum laude, 1974. Diplomate Am. Bd. Family Practice, Nat. Bd. Med. Examiners. Resident in family practice U. Colo. Med. Ctr., Denver, 1974-77, asst. prof., 1977-78; pvt. practice Sterling, Colo., 1978-84; asst. prof. family practice U. Wyo., Cheyenne, 1984-88; asst. dir. family practice residency program Scottsdale (Ariz.) Meml. Hosp., 1988—; med. officer Wyo. Wing, CAP, 1986-88. Contbr. articles to med. jours. Chmn. Coalition for Tobacco-Free Wyo., 1986-88; pres.-elect. Am. Heart Assn. Wyo., 1987-88. Recipient Outstanding Program Leadership award Am. Heart Assn. Wyo., 1987, 88; Boettcher Found. scholar, 1966-70. Fellow Am. Acad. Family Physicians; mem. Soc. Tchrs. Family Medicine, Ariz. Med. Assn., Maricopa County Med. Soc., Ariz. Acad. Family Physicians, Alpha Omega Alpha. Republican. Baptist. Office: Scottsdale Meml FP Ctr 7301 E 4th St Ste 22 Scottsdale AZ 85251

MARMADUKE, ARTHUR SANDFORD, educational administrator; b. Long Beach, Calif., May 29, 1926; s. William Sandford and Nina Belle (Romberger) M.; m. Carolyn Ann Tilden, Aug. 21, 1949; children: Jennifer, Stephen, Scott. AB, Occidental Coll., 1950; MPA, U. Mich., 1952; DPA (hon.), U. Pacific, 1970. Adminstrv. analyst Office Legis. Analyst Calif. State Legis., Sacramento, 1951-55; dir. admissions Occidental Coll., L.A., 1955-60; dir. Calif. Student Aid Commn., L.A., 1960-85; exec. dir. Eureka Project, Sacramento, 1986—; cons. Weingart Found., 1987, Bush Found., 1985; vice chmn. nat. task force on student aid programs Keppel Com., 1974-75; chmn. Coll. Scholarship Svc., Coll. Entrance Examination Bd., 1967-69. Contbr. author several student aid books. Recipient Disting. Service award Calif. Student Fin. Aid Adminstrs., 1982, Raol Wallenberg New Traditional High Sch., San Francisco, 1985, Coll. Bd. Scholarship Service, N.Y.C., 1985. Home: 1516 Del Dayo Dr Charmichael CA 95608 Office: Eureka Project 428 J St #400 Sacramento CA 95814

MARMOR, JUDD, psychiatrist, educator; b. London, May 1, 1910; came to U.S., 1911, naturalized, 1916; s. Clement K. and Sarah (Levene) M.; m. Katherine Stern, May 1, 1938; 1 son, Michael Franklin. AB, Columbia U., 1930, MD, 1933; DHL, Hebrew Union Coll., 1972. Diplomate: Am. Bd. Psychiatry and Neurology, Nat. Bd. Med. Examiners. Intern St. Elizabeth Hosp., Washington, 1933-35; resident neurologist Montefiore Hosp., N.Y.C., 1935-37; psychiatrist Bklyn. State Hosp., 1937; psychoanalytic tng. N.Y. Psychoanalytic Inst., N.Y.C., 1937-41; pvt. practice psychiatry, psychoanalysis and neurology N.Y.C., 1937-46, L.A., 1946—; instr. assoc. in neurology Columbia Coll. Physicians and Surgeons, 1938-40; adj. neurologist, neurologist-in-charge clinic Mt. Sinai Hosp., N.Y.C., 1939-46; lectr. New Sch. Social Rsch., N.Y.C., 1942-43; instr. Am. Inst. Psychoanalysis, N.Y.C., 1943; lectr. psychiatry N.Y. Med. Coll., 1944-46; lectr. social welfare UCLA, 1948-49, vis. prof. social welfare, 1949-64, clin. prof. psychiatry sch. medicine, 1953-80, adj. prof. psychiatry, 1980—; vis. prof. psychology U. So. Calif., 1946-49; tng. analyst, also pres. So. Calif. Psychoanalytic Inst., 1955-57; sr. attending psychiatrist L.A. County Gen. Hosp., 1954—; dir. divs. psychiatry Cedars-Sinai Med. Ctr., L.A., 1965-72; Franz Alexander prof. psychiatry U. So. Calif. Sch. Medicine, 1972-80, emeritus, 1980—; sr. cons. regional office social svc. VA, L.A., 1946-50; cons. psychiatry Brentwood VA Hosp., Calif., 1955-65; mem. Coun. Mental Health of Western Interstate Commn. Higher Edn., 1966-72. Editor: Sexual Inversion-The Multiple Roots of Homosexuality, Modern Psychoanalysis: New Directions and Perspectives, Psychiatry in Transition: Selected Papers of Judd Marmor, Homosexual Behavior: A Modern Reappraisal, (with S. Woods) The Interface Between the Psychodynamic and Behavioral Therapies; editorial bd.: Jour. Sex and Marital Therapy, Am. Jour. Psychoanalysis, Contemporary Psychoanalysis, Psychiatry Digest, Archives Sexual Behavior, Am. Jour. Community Psychology; contbr. articles in field to profl. jours. Served as sr. attending surgeon USPHS USNR, 1944-45. Fellow Am. Psychiat. Assn. (life mem., pres. 1975-76), N.Y. Acad. Medicine (life mem.), Am. Acad. Psychoanalysis (pres. 1965-66), Am. Orthopsychiat. Assn. (dir. 1968-71), AAAS, Am. Coll. Psychiatrists; mem. AMA, Calif. Med. Assn., Group for Advancement Psychiatry (dir. 1968-70, pres. 1973-75), Am. Fund for Psychiatry (dir. 1955-57), So. Calif. Psychiat. Soc., So. Calif. Psychoanalytic Soc. (pres. 1960-61), Am. Psychoanalytic Assn., Los Angeles County Med. Soc., Phi Beta Kappa, Alpha Omega Alpha. Home: 655 Sarbonne Rd Los Angeles CA 90077 Office: 1100 Glendon Ave Ste 921 Los Angeles CA 90024

MARMOR, RACHELLE ADINA, entertainment company official; b. N.Y.C., May 5, 1959; d. Seymour and Micheline (Kaplan) M. BA, Ariz. State U., 1982. Mgr. aerobics div. Fitness West Inc., Mesa, Ariz., 1980-82; office mgr. Health Force, Flushing, N.Y., 1983-84; sales and ter. mgr. SmithKline Bio-Sci. Labs., Lake Success, N.Y., 1984-87; mgr. bus. Morning Star, Tempe, Ariz., 1987—. Office: Morning Star 517-I E Huntington Dr Tempe AZ 85282

MARNELL, ANTHONY AUSTIN, II, architect; b. Riverside, Calif., Mar. 30, 1949; s. Anthony Austin and Ida Marie (Comforti) M.; m. Sandra Jean

Graf, June 24, 1972; children: Anthony, Alisa. BArch, U. So. Calif., 1972. Architect, draftsman firms in Calif. and Nev. 1969-72; project coordinator Zuni Constrn. Co., Las Vegas, Nev., 1973-74; office mgr., architect Corrao Constrn. Co., Inc., Las Vegas, Nev., 1973-74, 1974-82; chmn. bd. Marnell Corrao Assocs., Las Vegas, Nev., 1976—; pres. Marinelli Internat., Inc., Las Vegas, Nev., 1978—, A.A. Marnell II, Architect, Las Vegas, Nev., 1978—, 1980—; pres. Air Continental Jet Charter, Inc., Las Vegas, Nev., 1980—; mem. ethics com. Nev. Bd. Architects, 1974. prin. works include Maxim Hotel, Sundance Hotel, Sam's Town, Golden Nugget Strip Hotel, Excalibur, Rio, additions to Caesar's Palace, Desert Inn, Sands, Stardust, California, Frontier, and Dunes hotels (all Las Vegas), Caesar's Atlantic City, others. Mem. Nat. Council Archtl. Registration Bds., Post Tensioning Inst. Roman Catholic. Office: Marnell Corrao Assoc Inc 4495 S Polaris Ave Las Vegas NV 89103

MAROIS, HARRIET SUKONECK, computer scientist; b. Newark, Jan. 30, 1945; d. Edward and Mae S.; m. George Marois, Oct. 18, 1986. B.A., Rutgers U., 1966; M.A., U. So. Calif., 1968, Ph.D. (NIMH fellow), 1971. NIMH clin. postdoctoral fellow, div. psychiatry Children's Hosp. of Los Angeles, 1971-73; lectr. Calif. State U., Los Angeles, 1971-76; core faculty research series Calif. Sch. Profl. Psychology, Los Angeles, 1973-78, clin. psychologist in pvt. practice, Santa Monica, Calif., 1973-78; vis. asst. prof. Loyola Marymount U., Los Angeles, 1976-78; research assoc. Neuropsychiat. Inst., UCLA, 1978-79, adminstrv. analyst office of vice chancellor UCLA, 1979; sr. mem. tech. staff, project leader Computer Scis. Corp., El Segundo, Calif., 1979-81; systems cons./project adminstr. First Interstate Services Co., El Segundo, Calif., 1981-83; dir. research and product planning Data Line Service Co., 1983-84; project mgr. Xerox Corp., El Segundo, 1984—; founder, bd. dirs. Brainstorms, Los Angeles, 1985—.Lic. psychologist, Calif. Mem. Assn. Computing Machinery, Am. Psychol. Assn., AAAS. Contbr. articles to profl. jours. Editor et al, social sci. jour., 1971-76. Bd. dirs. So. Calif. Hot Jazz Soc. Los Angeles, 1988.

MARONDE, ROBERT FRANCIS, internist, clinical pharmacologist, educator; b. Monterey Park, Calif., Jan. 13, 1920; s. John August and Emma Florence (Palmer) M.; m. Yolanda Cerda, Apr. 15, 1970; children—Robert George, Donna F. Maronde Varnau, James Augustus, Craig DeWald. B.A., U. So. Calif., 1941, M.D., 1944. Diplomate: Am. Bd. Internal Medicine. Intern Los Angeles County-U. So. Calif. Med. Center, 1943-44, resident, 1944-45, 47-48; asst. prof. physiology U. So. Calif., Los Angeles, 1948-49; asst. clin. prof. medicine U. So. Calif., 1949-60, asso. clin. prof. medicine, 1960-65, asso. prof. medicine and pharmacology, 1965-67, prof., 1968—; cons. FDA, 1973. Served to lt. (j.g.) USNR, 1945-47. Fellow ACP; mem. Am. Soc. Clin. Pharmacology and Therapeutics, Alpha Omega Alpha. Home: 785 Ridgecrest St Monterey Park CA 91754 Office: U So Calif 2025 Zonal Ave Los Angeles CA 90033

MARQUARDT, EDWARD RALPH, management consultant; b. Chgo., Mar. 2, 1943; s. Edward Ralph Marquardt Sr. and Elizabeth Ann (Stickney) Shelton; m. L. Sue Rath, Sept. 25, 1977; children: Fred, Elizabeth Clark, Edward Ralph. AA, Pensacola Jr. Coll., 1972; BS, Daniel Webster Coll., 1985. Sect. mgr. Dynamics Rsch. Corp., Wilmington, Mass., 1980-84; engring. dept. mgr. GTE, Billerica, Mass., 1984-86; group v.p. Hay Systems Inc., Phoenix, 1986-88; mng. ptnr. Systems Specialists Inc., Phoenix, 1988—. With USN, 1961-80. Mem. Soc. Logistic Engrs., Am. Soc. Naval Engrs. Republican. Home: 11011 N 66th St Scottsdale AZ 85254

MARQUARDT, JAMES LEONARD, producer; b. Phoenix, Oct. 30, 1957; s. James Delmore and Helen Irene Marquardt. BS in Telecommunications Mgmt., No. Ariz. U., 1981. Dir. NBC-TV, Flagstaff, Ariz., 1979-81, ABC-TV, Phoenix, 1981-82; producer Garrett, L.A., 1982-86; ind. producer Laguna, Calif., 1986—; judge student films Acad. Motion Picture Arts and Scis., Los Angeles, 1982—. Vol. Stop AIDS edn. program, Orange County, Calif., 1986—, Laguna (Calif.) Shanti. Recipient Award of Excellence U.S. Indsl. Film Festival, 1985. Mem. Internat. TV Assn. (Gold Angel award 1985), Am. Film Inst., Soc. Motion Picture and TV Engrs., Assn. of Cinematograph TV and Allied Techs.

MARQUESS, LAWRENCE WADE, lawyer; b. Bloomington, Ind., Mar. 2, 1950; s. Earl Lawrence and Mary Louise (Coberly) M.; m. Barbara Ann Bailey, June 17, 1978; children: Alexander Lawrence, Michael Wade. BS in Elec. Engring., Purdue U., 1973; JD, W.Va. U., 1977. Bar: W.Va. 1977, Tex. 1977, U.S. Dist. Ct. (so. dist.) W.Va. 1977, U.S. Dist. Ct. (no. dist.) Tex. 1977, Colo. 1980, U.S. Dist. Ct. Colo. 1980, U.S. Ct. Appeals (10th cir.) 1980, U.S. Supreme Ct. 1984, U.S. Dist. Ct. (no. dist.) Ohio 1988. Assoc. Johnson, Bromberg, Leeds & Riggs, Dallas, 1977-79, Bradley, Campbell & Carney, Golden, Colo., 1979-82, ptnr., 1983-84; assoc. Stettner, Miller & Cohn P.C., Denver, 1984-85, ptnr., 1985-87; of counsel Nelson & Harding, Denver, 1987-88; ptnr. Heron, Burchette, Ruckert & Rothwell, 1989—. Mem. faculty Am. Law Inst.-ABA Advanced Labor and Employment Law Course, 1986, 87. Mem. ABA (labor and litigation sects.), Colo. Bar Assn. (program com., labor law com.), Denver Bar Assn. (program com., labor law com.), 1st Jud. Dist. Bar Assn., Sierra Club, Nat. Ry. Hist. Soc., ACLU. Democrat. Methodist. Home: 2293 Yellowstone St Golden CO 80401 Office: Heron Burchette Ruckert & Rothwell 717 17th St Ste 2600 Denver CO 80202-3357

MARQUEZ, ALFREDO C., federal judge; b. 1922; m. Linda Nowobilsky. B.S., U. Ariz., 1948, J.D., 1950. Bar: Ariz. Practice law Mesch Marquez & Rothschild, 1957-80; asst. atty. gen. State of Ariz., 1951-52; asst. county atty. Pima County, Ariz., 1953-54; adminstrv. asst. to Congressman Stewart Udall 1955; judge U.S. Dist. Ct. Ariz., Tucson, 1980—. Served with USN, 1942-45. Office: US Dist Ct US Courthouse Rm 327 55 E Broadway Tucson AZ 85701

MARQUEZ, ANTHONY PHILIP, deputy legislative counsel, lawyer; b. L.A., Oct. 10, 1950; s. Tony Marquez and Helen (Ruiz) Frescas; m. June Aurora Jaramillo, June 7, 1975 (div. Jan. 1977); m. Kimberly Lou Hill, Feb. 9, 1986. BA, Columbia U., 1972; JD, Harvard U., 1975. Bar: N.Mex. 1976, Calif. 1978, Tex. 1986. Mng. atty. Legal Aid Soc., Albuquerque, 1975-77; legal counsel Legis. Counsel, Sacramento, Calif., 1977-78; asst. atty gen. Atty. Gen. Office, Santa Fe, N.Mex., 1978-82; chief counsel Transp. Dept., Santa Fe, 1982-83, deputy sec., 1983-84; adminstrv. asst. N.Mex. Supreme Ct., Santa Fe, 1984-86; ptnr. Diamond & Marquez, El Paso, Tex., 1986-88; deputy legis. counsel Legis. Counsel, Sacramento, 1988—; mem. contracts com. Nat. Transp. Bd., Washington, 1979-84; supreme ct. liaison, N.Mex. Compilation Commn., Santa Fe, 1984-86; judge pro tem Superior Ct., 1989. Editor Harvard Civil Rights-Civil Liberties Law Rev., 1974; staff mem. Harvard Civil Liberties Law Rev., 1974. Del. State Dem. Party, Albuquerque, 1984; mem. arts coun., Santa Fe, 1983-86; pres. Film Adv. Bd., Santa Fe, 1983-84; v.p. Ctr. for Contemporary Arts of Santa Fe, 1983-86; mem. adv. bd. Hidden Gallery, 1989. Recipient Outstanding Service award, N.Mex. Supreme Ct., Santa Fe, 1985, Outstanding Young Man award, Jaycees, 1978, Outstanding Service award, Legal Assts. of N.Mex., Albuquerque, 1986. Mem. ABA (task force on undocumented workers 1978-81), Capitol Latino Staff Assn., La Raza Lawyers Assn., Deputy Legis. Counsel Assn., Ferrari Club Am., Sports Car Club Am. Democrat. Roman Catholic. Office: Legis Counsel 3021 State Capitol Sacramento CA 95814

MARQUEZ, CARLOS LUIS, electronics company official; b. Albuquerque, Dec. 18, 1957; s. Peter J. and Evangeline (Castillo) m.; m. Carol Marie House, June 20, 1981; children: Mario Luis, Analisa Marie. BS in Biomed. Engring., U. N. Mex., 1981. Research asst. U. N. Mex., Albuquerque, 1980-81; product engr. Motorola Semicondr. Inc., Austin, Tex., 1981-82; sales engr. Alliance Electronics, Albuquerque, 1982-84; field sales engr. Hewlett-Packard Co., Albuquerque, 1984—. Home: 2515 E 7th St Tucson AZ 85716 Office: Hewlett-Packard Co 3400 E Britannia Bldg C Ste 124 Tucson AZ 85706

MARQUEZ, MARTINA ZENAIDA, reading teacher; b. Santa Rosa, N.Mex., Nov. 5, 1935; d. Jose Zenon and Adelina (Romero) Sanchez; m. George J. Marquez, June 17, 1972. Student, Mt. St. Scholastica Coll., 1954-56, Regis Coll., 1956-59; BA, Coll. Santa Fe, 1963; MA, U. N.Mex., 1968. Cert. tchr., N.Mex. Elem. tchr. St. Rose Lima Sch., Santa Rosa, 1959-67, Cristo Rey Sch., Santa Fe, 1967-68, Los Lunas (N,Mex.) Consol. Schs., 1975-78, head tchr. adults operation; SER Manpower Devel. Tng. Act, Albuquerque, 1968-71, 73-75; tchr., cons. Regional Resource Ctr., N.Mex. State U., Las Cruces, 1971-72; counselor, coord. Taos (N.Mex.) Career Edn. Program, 1972-73; chpt. I reading tchr. Grants (N.Mex.) & Cibola County Schs., 1978—; chmn. ethics com. Profl. Standards Commn., N.Mex. Dept. Edn., 1986-88. Dir. choir St. Vivian's Ch., Milan, N.Mex., 1978—; del. Dem. Women's Club, Grants, N.Mex., 1981—. Mem. Internat. Reading Assn. (1st v.p. Malpais coun.1988-89. pres. 1989-90, Local Literacy award 1986, State Literacy award 1987), AAUW (bylaws chmn. 1984—, Grants Woman of Yr award 1988), Delta Kappa Gamma (pres. Psi chpt. 1986-88). Democrat. Roman Catholic. Home: PO Box 11 Bluewater Village NM 87005 Office: Grants-Cibola County Schs Jemez and Del Norte Sts Grants NM 87020

MARQUIS, JAMES FREDERICK, petroleum company executive; b. Kingsport, Tenn., July 17, 1953; s. James F. Jr. and Emma Lou (Shipley) M. BA in Lit., BS in Psychology, U. of the South, 1975; MBA, Tulane U., 1978. Land mgr. Amoco Prodn. Co., New Orleans, 1978-79; land man Meany & Johnson Energy Corp., Denver, 1979-82; mgr. exploration Tango Petroleum Co., Denver, 1983-86; land mgr. Trans-Western Petroleum, Inc., Golden, Colo., 1986—; bd. dirs. B-W Resources, Inc., Breckenridge Resources, Inc., Denver. Mem. Denver Assn. Petroleum Landmen, Mid-Continent Exploration Assn., Ind. Petroleum Assn. Am. Republican. Episcopalian. Office: Trans-Western Petroleum PO Box 276 Golden CO 80402

MARR, JEROME SOO WHAN, zoo director; b. Honolulu, Nov. 30, 1939; s. Jacob P. and Edna Esh (Han) M.; m. Eloise H. Tateishi, Aug. 15, 1970; children—Jonathan K., Michelle M. B.A., U. Hawaii, 1963. Sci. illustrator Bishop Mus., 1963; biologist Nat. Marine Fisheries, Hawaii, 1964-68; curator Honolulu Zoo, 1968-79, dir., 1979—. Bd. dirs. Eye Dog of the Pacific, 1971. Served with USAR, 1962-68. Fellow Am. Assn. Zool. Parks and Aquarium. Office: Honolulu Zoo 151 Kapahulu Ave Queen Kapiolani Park Honolulu HI 96815

MARRA, P(ETER) GERALD, manufacturers representative distributor firm executive; b. Cranbrook, B.C., Can., June 29, 1940; came to U.S., 1964, naturalized, 1973; s. John and Angela Rose Marra; B.Sc., U. B.C., 1963, postgrad., 1963-64; divorced; children: Amber Eileen, Anne-Marie Geraldine. Computer engr. Canadair Ltd., Montreal, Que., 1962-63; research engr. Boeing Corp., Seattle, 1964-68; hardware specialist Computer Sci. Corp., Toronto, Ont., Can., 1969; pres., gen. mgr. D.I.S.C., Seattle, 1970-74; sales mgr. Hayes Tech. Co., Seattle, 1975; owner, pres. Marra & Assocs., Bellevue, Wash., 1976—; cons. small bus., 1970—. Republican party platform chmn. King County, 1976-78, legis. dist. chmn., 1978; pres., dir. fundraising for U. B.C., Friends of U. B.C., 1975—; asst. chmn. archery com. Wash. State Sportsmen's Council, 1980, chmn., 1981-83, chmn. big game com. 1981-83; mem. Mt. Rainier Wildlife Com., 1981—. IBM scholar, 1964. Mem. Can. Soc. of Northwest (exec. com. 1985-88), U. B.C. Alumni (pres. Seattle, Pacific N.W. chpt. 1974—). Clubs: Cedar River, Bowman Archery, Bellevue Athletic. Home: 1739 172d Pl NE Bellevue WA 98008

MARRACCI, THOMAS KENNETH, computer company executive, consultant; b. Oakland, Calif., Apr. 29, 1965; s. Louis Thomas and Susan Joan (Stormont) M. Student, Grinnell (Iowa) Coll., 1983-84; BA in Math., UCLA, 1989. Programmer Synergy, Inc., Torrance, Calif., 1984-85, chief programmer, 1985-86, v.p., 1986; v.p. Computers for Industry & Fin., Inc., Torrance, 1986-88, pres., 1988—; v.p. Internat. Software Techs., Inc., Glendale, Calif., 1987-88; cons. Continental Airlines, Houston, 1985—, Banco Do Brasil, Internat., L.A., 1987—; bd. dirs. C.I.F., Inc., Torrance. Developer L.C. software, banking and trucking software. Grinnell Coll. athletic scholar, 1983. Mem. UCLA Bus. Soc., So. Calif. Assn. Pick Profls., Am. Trucking Assn. Republican. Roman Catholic. Office: Computers Industry & Fin 22700 S Crenshaw Ste 117 Torrance CA 90505

MARRACK, ALEXANDER CASE, lawyer; b. Honolulu, May 12, 1933. BA cum laude, Amherst Coll., 1955; LLB cum laude, Harvard U., 1958. Bar: Hawaii 1958. Ptnr., Reinwald, O'Connor and Marrack, Honolulu. Mem. Hawaii State Bar Assn., ABA. Home: 512 Portlock Rd Honolulu HI 96825 Office: Reinwald O'Connor Marrack Hoskins & Playdon 733 Bishop St Honolulu HI 96813

MARRONE, JOSEPH FRANCIS, sales executive; b. N.Y.C., May 31, 1943; s. Joseph Francis and Ethel (Szabo) M.; m. Linda Joyce Redling, June 3, 1978; 1 child, Jarrett Thomas. Grad. high sch., Queens, N.Y. Sales rep. PRAM Labs., N.Y.C., 1965; sales rep. Addressograph Multigraph Corp., N.Y.C., 1966-72, Honolulu, 1972-74; sales Best Copy Products, San Diego, Calif., 1975, San Diego Office Supply, 1976-78; sales rep. Johnson Staley, San Diego, 1978-80, Dennison Mfg., San Diego, 1980-87; pres. Jarrett Thomas Marrone Inc., La Jolla, Calif., 1985—. Mem. La Jolla Hist. Soc., San Diego, 1988-89, San Diego Hist. Soc., 1988-89; mem. La Jolla Town Coun., 1989—. With NG. Mem. Price Club (San Diego). Roman Catholic. Home and Office: 7150 Monte Vista Ave La Jolla CA 92037

MARRONE, KRISTAN JO, real estate executive; b. Olean, N.Y., June 5, 1952; d. Hermans Charles and Josephine (Kelsey) M. BS, Edinboro (Pa.) U., 1973. Tchr. elem. Otto Eldred Sch. Dist., Duke Center, Pa., 1974-86; asst. mgr. Johnstown Am., Colorado Springs, Colo., 1986; exec. v.p. Colo. Apt. Assn. Colo. Springs, 1986—. Bd. dirs. Colo. Apt. Assn., Denver, 1987, 88. Mem. Nat. Apt. Assn. (sec. exec. coun. 1989—), NAFEE. Home: 2585 E Pikes Peak T-206 Colorado Springs CO 80909 Office: Colo Apt Assn 2812 E Bijou #102 Colorado Springs CO 80909

MARROW, MARVA JAN, photographer, author; b. Denver, Apr. 22, 1948; d. Sydney and Helen Berniece (Garber) M. Student, Carnegie-Mellon U., 1965-67. Singer, songwriter RCA Records, Italy, 1972-77; pvt. practice photography Italy and U.S., 1976—; represented by Shooting Star Photo Agy., USA, Agenzia Marka, Italy; correspondent, photographer Italian TV Guide, Milan, 1979—; collaborator, photographer for other U.S. and European publs. Author numerous songs for Italian pop artists, including: Lucio Battisti, Battiato, Premiata Forneria Marconi (PFM), Patty Pravo, 1972—; author: (photobook) Inside the L.A. Artist, 1988; contbr. photographs for covers and articles to nat. and internat. mags. Mem. Motion Picture Assn. of Am., Fgn. Press Assn. Democrat. Home and Studio: 2080 N Garfield Ave Altadena CA 91001 Office: Shooting Star Agy PO Box 93368 Los Angeles CA 90093

MARRS, JAMES STUART, II, military officer; b. Rantoul, Ill., July 31, 1955; s. James Stuart I and Helen Louise (Stiles Groskopf) D.; children: James Stuart III, Amanda Grace. BS in Aero Engring., Ariz. State U., 1977; MS in Systems Mgmt., U. So. Calif., 1988. Cert. FAA Pilot. Commd. officer U.S. Army, 1977, advanced through grades to maj., 1989; armor platoon leader 2d infantry div. U.S. Army, Republic Korea, 1977-78; attack helicopter platoon commdr. 6th calvary brigade U.S. Army, Ft. Hood, Tex., 1979-82; flight simulator systems mgr. U.S. Army, Ft. Rucker, Ala., 1983-86; space ops., tactical support officer U.S. Army Space Command, Peterson AFB, Colo., 1986—; chmn. civic service com. U.S. Army, Peterson AFB, Colo., 1988—. Republican. Lutheran. Office: US Army Space Command Peterson AFB CO 80914-5000

MARRS, LEO RICHARD, JR., materials manager, educator; b. Birmingham, Ala., June 29, 1949; s. Leo Richard Sr. and Oma Lee (Stone) M.; m. Penny Ann Boals, Dec. 26, 1971; children: Hilary Anne, Thomas Richard. BA, U. So. Ala., 1974; MBA, U. Phoenix, 1985. Lab. asst. U. So. Ala., Mobile, 1973-75; rep. Marrs Electric Co., Tarrant, Ala., 1975-79; buyer Magma Copper Co., San Manuel, Ariz., 1979-81; sr. buyer Magma Copper Co., San Manuel, 1981-85, materials control supr., 1985-86, chief warehouse supr., 1986, warehousing mgr., 1986—; mem. faculty U. Phoenix, 1987—. Mem. Nat. Assn. Purchasing Mgmt., Purchasing Mgmt. Assn. So. Ariz., Am. Prodn. and Inventory Control Soc. Methodist. Home: 7911 N Hopdown Ave Tucson AZ 85741 Office: Magma Copper Co PO Box M State Hwy 77 San Manuel AZ 85631

MARRS, LOIS MARIE, former educator; b. Grand Island, Nebr., Feb. 21, 1919; d. John Wesley and Mildred Rena (Hiller) Burnett; m. Roy Merton Marrs, Oct. 27, 1940 (dec.); children: John, Richard, Valerie. BA, U. Omaha, 1940; postgrad., UCLA, U. Calif., Santa Barbara. Life kindergarten, elem. credentials, Calif. Tchr. Ocean View Sch. Dist., Oxnard, Calif., 1950-51, Mound Sch. Dist., Ventura, Calif., 1952-61; substitute tchr. Mound Sch. Dist., Ventura, 1957-61; kindergarten tchr. Mount and Ventura Unified Sch. Dist., 1962-76. Sunday sch. tchr. Community Presbyn. Ch., Ventura, 1946-89, pres. voyagers club, 1981, deacon, 1985-87; pres. kindergarten tchrs. group Ventura County. Mem. AAUW (travel sec., curator Ventura 1980-89), Juanamaria PTA (life), Quill and Scroll, Panhellenic, San Buenaventura Women's Club (Ventura, ways and means chmn. 1979-88, bus. mgr. 1985), Order Eastern Star (organist 1988-89, treas. Ladies Oriental Shrine 1984, organist 1985, 87-88), Daughters of Nile, Job's Daus. (past honored queen 1938), Delta Kappa Gamma (rec. sec. 1961-62), Kappa Delta Phi (pres. 1936), Chi Omega (pres. 1980). Republican. Home: 322 Palomares Ave Ventura CA 93030

MARRS, RICHARD PRESTON, gynecologist/obstetrician; b. Paducah, Tex., Dec. 6, 1947; s. Benjamin Verne and Mary Angela (Mattei) M.; m. Joyce Marie Vargyas, Nov. 1, 1980; children: Ashley Marie, Austen Michael. AA, Schreiner Inst., Kerrville, Tex., 1968; BA, U. Tex., Austin, 1970; MD, U. Tex., Galveston, 1974. Lic. MD Tex, 1974, Calif., 1977; diplomate Am. Bd. Ob-Gyn, Am. Bd. Reproductive Endocrinology. Resident in Ob-Gyn U. Tex. Med. Br., Galveston, 1974-77, asst. prof., 1979-82; fellow in reproductive endocrinology U. So. Calif. Sch. Medicine, L.A., 1977-79, clin. instr. dept Ob-Gyn, 1977-79, from asst. to assoc. prof. dept. Ob-Gyn, 1979-86; dir. div. reproductive endocrinology and infertility Cedars-Sinai Med. Ctr., L.A., 1986-88; prof. dept. Ob-Gyn UCLA Sch. Medicine, 1986-88; dir. inst. for reproductive rsch. Hosp. Good Samaritan, L.A., 1988—; Mem. Outpatient Surgery com., Hosp. Good Samaritan, L.A., 1986-88; pres. Marrs/Vargyas Corp., 1983. Mem. editorial bd. Jour. In Vitro Fertilization and Embryo Transfer, Jour. Clin. Endocrinology and Metabolism; contbr. over 75 articles to med. jours.; contbr. chpts. to books. Recipient Squibb prize Pacific Coast Fertility Soc., 1979, Sci. Exhibit award Am. Coll. Ob-Gyn, 1980, Mem. Found. award 49th Ann. Mtg. Pacific Coast Ob-Gyn Coc., 1982, sr. residents award for excellence in teaching, 1980. Fellow Am. Coll. Obstetrics and Gynecology, Jeanne Kemper Found.; mem. In Vitro Fertilization Spl. Interest Group (chmn. 1986-88, pres. 1987-88), Los Angeles Obstetrics and Gynecology Soc., Salerni Collegium, AMA, Soc. for Gynecol. Investigation, Endocrine Soc., Soc. for Study of Reproduction, Am. Inst. Ultrasound In Medicine. Office: Marrs/Vargyas Corp 1425 Wilshire Blvd Ste 905 Los Angeles CA 90017

MARS, ROBERT, lawyer, real estate associate, financial planner; b. Willimantic, Conn., May 11, 1955; s. David and Marien (Weisser) M. BS, U. So. Calif., L.A., 1977, MPA, JD, 1980. Bar: Calif. 1980, U.S. Dist. Ct. (cen. dist.) Calif. 1984, U.S. Ct. Appeals (9th cir.) 1984, U.S. Supreme Ct. 1989. Pvt. practice Torrance, Calif., 1980—. Author: Foreclosures!, 1988, Guide to Living Trusts, 1988. Named Lawyer of Yr., So. Calif. Assn. Fin. Planners, 1987. Mem. Calif. Trial Lawyers Assn., L.A. Trial Lawyers Assn. Home and Office: 3838 Carson St Torrance CA 90503

MARSDEN, GILLIAN, health insurance executive; b. Chester, England, Feb. 25, 1943; came to U.S., 1966; d. Philip and Muriel (Teasdill) M.; m. Arthur C. Haug, Sept. 28, 1974; children: Nicola, Deryn. BA with honors, U. Southampton, Eng., 1964; MS in Pub. Health, U. Wash., 1975. Head econs. dept. Woking (Eng.) County Grammar Sch., 1964-66; account exec. Cons. Services Corp., Seattle, 1966-70; asst. dir. Wash./Alaska Regional Med. Program, Seattle, 1970-71, Seattle Indian Health Bd., 1971-75; research assoc. Soc. Pub. Health U. Wash., Seattle, 1975-76; adminstv. asst. Dept. Pub. Health Seattle King County, 1976; mgr. emergency med. services King County Health Dept., Seattle, 1976-78; dir. staff services Seattle/King County Dept. Pub. Health, Seattle, 1978-80; dir. Seattle div. Seattle/King County Dept. Pub. Health, 1980-85, dep. dir., 1985-86; v.p. Network Health Plan Inc., Mercer Island, Wash., 1986—, Network Mgmt., Inc., Mercer Island, Wash., 1986—; cons. Native Am. Health Orgns. U.S. Congress, 1973-77. Contbr. articles to profl. jours. Mem. Affordable Health Com., Seattle, 1983—, Joint Adv. Com. Edn., Seattle, 1988. Named Mgr. Yr. Seattle Mgmt. Assn., 1985. Mem. Seattle Women Govt. (v.p. 1984-86). Office: Network Health Plan PO Box 9005 Mercer Island WA 98040-9005

MARSH, HELENA ROSA, financial consultant; b. Pitts., Oct. 9, 1947; d. Serafino and Maria Petronella (Van den Bussche) Murano; m. Keith Walter Marsh, Sept. 17, 1983; children: David Christopher Tinsley, Dana Renee Tinsley. Student, U. Hawaii, 1968. V.p., mgr. Great Western Bank, Corte Madera, Calif., 1975-86; securities rep. Great Western Fin. Securities, San Rafael, Calif., 1986-87; exec. v.p., proprietor Western Capital Planning Corp., San Rafael, 1987—, Marsh & Assocs. Real Estate Appraisers and Cons., San Rafael, 1988—. Mem. Inst. Fin. Edn. (bd. dirs. 1978-80, instr. 1977-80), Corte Madera C. of C. (bd. dirs. 1982—). Roman Catholic. Office: 834 Mission Ave San Rafael CA 94901

MARSH, PAUL, public relations executive; b. Lorain, Ohio, Oct. 19, 1910; s. George Thomas and Marie Agnes (Buckleigh) M.; m. Ruth Dannenbaum, Nov. 5, 1950; children: Rolf Maxwell, Alan Jonathan, Melinda Jane. BA, Miami U., Oxford, Ohio, 1932; MA, Western Res. U., 1945. Tchr. Lorain (Ohio) High Sch., 1935-45; prin. Paul Marsh & Assocs., 1950—. Served with USN, 1942-45. Mem. Delta Upsilon. Republican. Roman Catholic. Club: Los Angeles Press. Home: PO Box 2119 Toluca Lake CA 91602

MARSH, SAM BENJAMIN, educator; b. Long Beach, Calif., June 25, 1927; s. Grant Mordestus and Ella Lelia (Koch) M.; m. Barbara Ann Hatchett,. BA, U. Colo., 1954; MA, San Fernando Valley State U., 1961. Operator Schauer Printing, Santa Barbara, Calif., 1953-54; tchr. Ventura (Calif.) United Schs., 1954—; dept. head Driver Instr., Ventura, 1963-70, div. head Applied Arts. Contbr. articles to profl. jours. Sgt. U.S. Army, 1950-51. Mem. NEA, Ventura United Edn. Assn., Calif. Tchrs. Assn. Home: 3706 Maple Ventura CA 93003 Office: Ventura United Schs 2155 E Main Ventura CA 93001

MARSH, STEPHEN MACFARLANE, entrepreneur; b. Mukwonago, Wis., Jan. 29, 1941; s. Ralph Independence and E. Elisabeth (McFarlane) M.; m. Pamela Ann Thatcher, Jan. 14, 1967; children: Sean MacFarlane, Christophe Thatcher. Student, U. Wis., 1959-61; DDS, Northwestern U., 1965, postgrad., 1967-68. Diplomate Am. Bd. Oral and Maxillofacial Surgery. Pvt. practice Mukwonago, 1965-66; resident in oral and maxillofacial surgery Cook County (Ill.) Hosp., 1968-71; pvt. practice Colorado Springs, Colo., 1971-83, Assocs. Oral and Maxillofacial Surgery, P.C., Colorado Springs, 1984-87; inventor Colorado Springs, 1987—; bd. dirs. Elsinore Cattle Co., Colorado Springs. Capt. U.S. Army, 1966-68. Fellow Am. Soc. Oral and Maxillofacial Surgeons; mem. Colo. Soc. Oral and Maxillofacial Surgeons, Rocky Mountain Soc. Oral and Maxillofacial Surgeons. Republican. Episcopalian.

MARSHAL, KIT, restaurateur; b. L.A., Dec. 2, 1939; s. Alan Marshal and Mary (Grace) Borel. Pres. Au Petit Cafe, Hollywood, Calif., 1963-82; pres., dir. Au Petit Cafe, Honolulu, 1988—; chmn. bd. Cruvinet, L.A., 1980-85; sec., dir. Langan's Brasserie, L.A., 1986-88; ptnr., mgr., distbr. Cruvinet Wine Preserving and Dispensing System, 1981, pres., chmn., 1982-86; wine cons. to numerous restaurants. Publ., wine critic: Goodlife Newsletter, 1982-84.

MARSHALL, ANNE BRADLEY, lawyer; b. Hartford, Conn., May 29, 1952; d. George A. and Anne Elizabeth (Bradley) M.; m. Bruce Rea Elworthy, Aug. 25, 1979. BA, Wellesley Coll., 1974; JD, Yale U., 1977. Bar: Calif., Tex.; cert. tax specialist. Assoc. Bracewell and Patterson, Houston, 1977-79; assoc. Pettit and Martin, San Francisco, 1981-82, Bronson, Bronson & McKinnon, San Francisco, 1982-83; ptnr. Elworthy and Marshall Profl. Corp., Tahoe City, Calif., 1983—; lectr. World Trade Inst., N.Y.C., 1978-80, Am. Mgmt. Assn., 1979, Calif. Continuing Edn. of Bar, Berkeley, 1982. Durant scholar, Wellesley Coll., 1974, Trustee scholar, 1974. Mem. ABA, Bar Assn. San Francisco, Monterey County Bar Assn., State Bar Calif. (estate planning sect.), Placer County Bar Assn., Greater Carmel Valley C. of C. (past bd. dirs.), Phi Beta Kappa. Clubs: Elizabethan (New Haven); Monterey Peninsula Country; Yale of Monterey (past bd. dirs.); Yale (Sacramento); Monterey Bay Wellesley. Office: Elworthy and Marshall Profl Corp 740 N Lake Blvd P O Box 7044 Tahoe City CA 95730-7044

MARSHALL, ARTHUR K., lawyer, judge, arbitrator, educator, writer; b. N.Y.C., Oct. 7, 1911. B.S., CCNY, 1933; LL.B., St. John's U., N.Y.C., 1936; LL.M., U. So. Calif., 1952. Bar: N.Y. State 1937, Calif. 1947. Practice law N.Y.C., 1937-43, Los Angeles, 1947-50; atty. VA, Los Angeles, 1947-50; tax counsel Calif. Bd. Equalization, Sacramento, 1950-51; inheritance tax atty. State Controller, Los Angeles, 1951-53; commr. Superior Ct. Los Angeles County, 1953-62; judge Municipal Ct., Los Angeles jud. dist., 1962-63, Superior Ct., Los Angeles, 1963-81,; supervising judge probate dept. Superior Ct., 1968-69, appellate dept., 1973-77; presiding judge Appellate Dept., 1976-77; pvt. practice 1981—, arbitrator, referee, judge protem, 1981—; acting asst. prof. law UCLA, 1954-59; mem. grad. faculty U. So. Calif., 1955-75; lectr. Continuing Edn. of Bar; vice chmn. Calif. Law Revision Commn., 1984-86, chmn. 1986—; past chmn. com. on efficient economy Conf. Calif. Judges, past chmn. spl. action com. on ct. improvement; past chmn. probate law cons. group Calif. Bd. Legal Specialization. Author: Joint Tenancy Taxwise & Otherwise, 1953, Branch Courts, 1959, California State and Local Taxation, Text, 2 vols, 1962, rev. edit., 1969, supplement, 1979, 2d edit., 1981, California State and Local Taxation Forms, 2 vols, 1961-75, rev. edit., 1979, California Probate Procedure, 1961, 10th rev. edit., 1989, Guide to Procedure Before Trial, 1975. Served with AUS, 1943-46; lt. col. Res. ret. Named Judge of Yr. Lawyers Club of Los Angeles County, 1975; first recipient Arthur K. Marshall Award established by estate planning, trust and probate sect. Los Angeles Bar Assn., 1981; Disting. Jud. Career award Los Angeles Lawyers Club. Fellow Am. Bar Found.; mem. Internat. Acad. Estate and Trust Law (academician, founder, 1st pres., now chancellor), ABA (probate litigation com. real property, probate and trust sect.), Calif. State Bar (adv. to exec. com. estate planning, probate and trust sect. 1970-83), Santa Monica Bar Assn. (pres. 1960), Westwood Bar Assn. (pres. 1959, bd. dirs. 1987—), Los Angeles Bar Assn., Lawyers Club, Am. Judicature Soc., Am. Legion (comdr. 1971-72), U. So. Calif. Law Alumni Assn. (pres. 1969-70), Phi Alpha Delta (1st justice alumni chpt. 1976-77, arbitrator, judge pro tempore). Office: 300 S Grand Ave 28th Fl Los Angeles CA 90071

MARSHALL, FRED CHARLES III, electronics executive; b. Portland, Oreg., June 10, 1939; s. Fred Charles Jr. and Anne (Ferrando) M.; m. Julie Ellen Branford, Sept. 14, 1985; children: Fred Charles IV, Gina Marie, Robert John Aragon. Bachelor Engring. Sci., U. Portland, 1962; MS in Engring., UCLA, 1967, PhD in Engring., 1970. Engr. Naval Oceans System Ctr., Pasadena, Calif., 1962-73; program mgr. Naval Oceans System Ctr., San Diego, 1973-78; dir. submarine and antisubmarine warfare programs Office of Asst. Sec. of Navy Research, Engr. and Systems, Washington, 1978-83; tech. dir. Antisubmarine Warfare Systems Project Office, Washington, 1983-84; chief engr. Honeywell Marine Systems, Seattle, 1984-86; bus. area mgr. Honeywell Marine Systems, Everett, Wash., 1986-88; dir. bus. devel. Honeywell Marine Systems, Everett, 1988--. Contbr. papers to profl. pubs. Mem. IEEE (sr.), Assn. Computing Machinery. Office: Honeywell Marine Systems 6500 Harbour Heights Pkwy Everett WA 98204

MARSHALL, JAMES KENNETH, academic administrator; b. Providence, Dec. 25, 1952; s. James William and Eileen Frances (O'Connell) M.; m. Mary H. Jackson, Mar. 17, 1987. BA in Chemistry, SUNY, Plattsburgh, 1974; MBA in Fin., U. R.I., 1977; postgrad., U. Wash., 1978-79. Fin. instr. U. R.I., Kingston, 1978; teaching assoc. U. Wash., Seattle, 1978-79; asst. dir. facilities mgmt. U. Colo., Boulder, 1979-86, dir. buying and contracting, 1986—; honorarium instr. U. Colo., Denver, 1981—; bd. dirs. Minority Enterprises, Inc. Mem. Colo. Gov.'s Procurement Adv. Council. Recipient Job Well Done award U. Colo. Boulder Dept. Facilities Mgmt., 1983. Mem. Rocky Mountain Assn. Phys. Plant Adminstrs., Assn. Phys. Plant Adminstrs., Nat. Assn. Ednl. Buyers, Nat. Inst. Govtl. Purchasing, Beta Gamma Sigma, Phi Kappa Phi. Office: U Colo Campus Box 380 Dept Buying and Contracting Boulder CO 80309

MARSHALL, JAMES THOMAS, composer, educator; b. Seattle, Oct. 12, 1941; m. Karen Ruth (Pape); children. Sara, Erica. BA, Whitman Coll., 1963; MA, U. Wash., 1966; DMA, U. Cin., 1977. Instr. Drake U., Des Moines, Iowa, 1966-68, Montclair State Coll., Upper Montclair, N.J., 1968-71; asst. prof. Cleve. State U., 1974-81; asst. prof. Whitman Coll., Walla Walla, Wash., 1981-85, assoc. prof., 1986—. Composer: Later, Perhaps, 1970, Multisone, 1973, Rondellus, 1973, Elevation of Imagery, 1973, Consone, 1980, Symphony Number 1, 1977, Convergence, 1985, Patterns for Solo Trumpet, 1984, Duo for Oboe and Bassoon, 1987, Contraharmonia, 1989. Recipient Consortium Commn. Nat. Endowment for the Arts, 1983. Mem. Soc. Composers, Coll. Music Soc., Am. Fed. Musicians, Nat. Assn. Coll. Wind and Percussion Instrs., Nat. Assn. Composers. Home: 21 Stone St Walla Walla WA 99362

MARSHALL, JOANNE MARIE, retail excutive; b. Chgo., Oct. 14, 1934; d. Joseph and Kathryn Agnes (Conley) Pupello; m. Frank William Marshall, Jan. 25, 1957 (div. Jan. 1965). Grad. high school, Newton Mass. Travel agt. Garber's Travel Inc., Boston, 1956-63; asst. buyer Jordan Marsh Inc., Boston, 1963-65; cons. retail services Revlon Inc., Boston, 1965-66; supr. cons. Revlon Inc., Chgo., 1966-67; dir. retail services Revlon Inc., N.Y.C., 1967-72; v.p. sales and mktg. Hawaiian Fragrances Inc., Honolulu, 1972-74; cosmetic buyer I. Magnin, Los Angeles, 1975-77; cosmetic buyer May Co., Los Angeles, 1977-80, divisional v.p., 1980—. Recipient Spirit of Life award Cosmetic Industry of the City of Hope, 1987. Mem. Calif. Cosmetic Assn. (pres. 1988—), Fragrance Found., Fashions Group. Republican. Roman Catholic. Home: 651 N Wilcox #3A Los Angeles CA 90004 Office: May Co 6160 Laurel Canyon Blvd North Hollywood CA 91606

MARSHALL, JOHN PAUL, broadcast engineer; b. Hadjeb El-Aioun Gare, Tunisia, Dec. 21, 1941; came to U.S., 1967; Degree, de l'Academie de Grenoble (France), 1963, U. Munich, 1965; student, San Francisco State, 1969-71. Filmmaker Cinemalab, San Francisco, 1970; engr. film and TV Able Studios, San Francisco, 1971-73; radio and TV engr. Sta. KALW-FM-TV (Nat. Pub. Radio), San Francisco, 1973-74; broadcast engr. Sta. KRON-TV (NBC), San Francisco, 1974—; freelance audio visual tech. advisor, San Francisco area, 1975—, lectr. radio, TV, motion pictures, 1975—, cons. customized electronic effects. Translator tech. pubs. and manuals, 1975—. Mus. dir., participant in theater prodns., 1950-59; active Boy Scouts Am. Club: Rolls Royce Owners. Home: Cathedral Hill Pla 1333 Gough St #4G San Francisco CA 94109

MARSHALL, LESTER BELL, medical technologist; b. Chgo., Feb. 10; s. Gillman and Ethel (Robinson) M.; student, San Francisco State U., 1950; AA, City Coll. San Francisco, 1957; BS, U. Puget Sound, 1961; DSc, London Inst., Eng., 1972; m. Esther Wood, Sept. 28, 1961; 1 child, Lelani. Pres., Med. Offices Health Services Group Inc., San Francisco, 1964—. Mem. NAACP. With U.S. Army, 1947-53. Decorated Bronze Star, Med. Combat Badge; recipient Cert. Appreciation Pres. Nixon, 1973, Urban League, 1973, Calif. Dept. Human Resources, 1973. Mem. Am. Calif. Assns. Med. Technologists, Calif. State Sheriff's Assn. (assoc.), Black Am. Polit. Assn. Calif., Oyster Point Yacht Club, Press Club, Commonwealth Club (San Francisco). Home: 765 San Pedro II Rd San Rafael CA 94901

MARSHALL, LYNNOR BEVERLEY, biotechnology company executive; b. Melbourne, Victoria, Australia, Mar. 11, 1943; came to U.S., 1971; d. John A. and Evelyn M. (Post) Gilmore; m. Noel Marshall, 1965 (div. 1977); children: Neil D., David. K. BS with honors, U. Melbourne, Australia, 1963; BEd, U. Melbourne, 1967; PhD, Monash U., Melbourne, 1971. Sr. biochemist, mgr. product, mktg. Beckman Instruments, Palo Alto, Calif., 1972-79; pres. Calif. Medicinal Chemistry Corp., South San Francisco, 1979-83; v.p. corp. devel. Creative Biomolecules, South San Francisco, 1983; v.p. rsch. Advanced Polymer Systems, Redwood City, Calif., 1984-85; exec. v.p. Agen USA Inc., Mt. View, Calif., 1985-86; chmn. Alta Biomed., Los Altos, Calif., 1987—; pres. Paravax Inc., Palo Alto, Calif., 1988—; bd. dirs. Chromatochem, Missoula, Mont., Yellowstone Diagnostics, Palo Alto. Mem. Am. Chem. Soc., AAAS.

MARSHALL, MARILYNN JOYCE, social services administrator; b. Cleve., Sept. 3, 1952; d. William Edward Marshall and Anne Loretta (Macon) Johnson. BA in Psychology, Chgo. State U., 1975. Adminstrv. asst. Chgo. State U., 1975-76; social worker Manteno (Ill.) Mental Health Ctr., 1976-78, Dept. of Children's Services, Los Angeles, 1978—. Democrat. Office: Aenon Guest Homes Inc 2077 Lime Ave Long Beach CA 90805

MARSHALL, MAUREEN GRETA, management company executive; b. Yorkshire, Eng., Aug. 14, 1921; d. George Cyril and Greta Beatrice (Hall) Stevenson; came to U.S., 1952; B.A. with distinction, U. Calif. at Berkeley, 1969, M.A., 1970; m. Sherwood Barnett Marshall, Nov. 1, 1952; 1 dau., Virginia Maureen Marshall Lang. Vice pres. Alameda (Calif.) Convalescent Hosp., 1968-70, Sonoma (Calif.) Convalescent Hosp., 1970-74; gen. ptnr. Valley View Lodge, Walnut Creek, Calif., 1974-82; exec. v.p. SAV Service Corp., Walnut Creek, 1975—; pres. Tri-County Supply Inc., Walnut Creek, 1978—; v.p. Kristina Odysseys, Ltd., Del., 1979; co-gen. ptnr. Messenger Ariz. I, 1989—. Served with Canadian Women's Army Corps, World War II. Mem. San Francisco Women's Artists (pres. 1977-79), Phi Beta Kappa. Episcopalian. Paintings exhibited at Calif. Inst. Art, Mus. Modern Art, San Francisco, Worth Ryder Gallery, San Francisco, U. Calif. at Berkeley, San Francisco Art Commn. Gallery, St. Mary's Coll., Moraga, Calif., Internat. Ctr. for Contemporary Art, Paris, 1983, Percy Basse Gallery, London, 1985, also at juried shows. Office: Messenger Ariz I 4808 N 22d St Phoenix AZ 85016

MARSHALL, PAUL MACKLIN, oil company executive; b. Toronto, Ont., Can., Sept. 21, 1923; s. Griffith Macklin and Josephine Angela (Hodgson) M.; m. Carol Ann Dickie; children: Blake, Gregory, Jonathan, Kirk. B.C.L., McGill U., Montreal, Que., Can., 1949. Bar: called to bar Que. 1949. Legal asst. Sun Life Assurance Co., Montreal, 1949-52; exec. asst. to Canadian minister nat. def., Ottawa, Ont., 1952-54; with Canadian Chem. & Cellulose Co. Ltd., Montreal, 1955-69; v.p. Canadian Chem. & Cellulose Co. Ltd., 1958-59; v.p., sec.-treas. Chemcell Ltd., 1959-67, chmn. bd., 1967-69; v.p., treas. Columbia Cellulose Co. Ltd., 1959-62, pres., chief exec. officer, 1962-66; v.p., treas. Can. Chem. Co. Ltd., Celgar Ltd., 1959-62; v.p. Hamilton Bros. Petroleum Corp., 1969-72; pres. Hamilton Bros. Exploration Co., Denver, 1972; exec. v.p. Hamilton Bros. Oil Co., 1972; pres. Canadian Hydrocarbons Ltd., Calgary, Alta., 1972-77, Westmin Resources, Ltd., 1978—; vice chmn. Brascan Ltd., 1987—; pres., dir. Brascade Resources, Inc., Brascade Holdings, Inc.; dir. Brascan Ltd., Noranda Mines Inc.; chmn. Norcen Energy Resources Ltd., North Can. Oils Ltd.; bd. dirs. Westinghouse Can. Inc., Journey's End Corp. Bankeno Resources, Ltd. Lt. Royal Can. Army, 1943-45. Club: Toronto; Petroleum (Calgary). Office: Commerce Ct, Postal Sta Box 48, Toronto, ON Canada M5L 1B7

MARSHALL, SCOTT, advertising agency executive. V.p. Ogilvy & Mather, N.Y.C., sr. v.p., 1986-88; pres. Cole & Weber, Inc., Seattle, 1988—. Office: Cole & Weber Inc 308 Occidental Ave S Seattle WA 98104 *

MARSHALL, WOLF, music educator; b. N.Y.C., Dec. 19, 1949; m. Magee Smith, Feb. 14, 1989. BA, UCLA, 1977. Performer, musical dir. Starlicks Instrnl. Tapes, L.A., 1981-87; music dir., cons. Noma Video, L.A., 1985-87; contbg. editor Guitar mag., Port Chester, N.Y., 1985—; music cons., product devel. specialist Cherry Lane Music Co., Port Chester, 1988—. Author: Original Randy Rhoads, 1985, Original Gary Moore, 1987; author, performer songbooks, instrnl. audios, 1981—. Mem. Malibu C. of C., Rolls Royce Owners Club So. Calif. Republican. Office: Marshall Arts 22653 Pacific Coast Hwy Ste 300 Malibu CA 90265

MARSHALL-WALKER, ROBERT WILLIAM, financial consultant, economist, tax lawyer; b. San Marcos, Tex., July 4, 1945; s. Robert William and Martha Ann (Westenbarger) W. BA, Calif. State U., 1969; postgrad., U. Calif.-Davis, 1969-72, Calif. State U., San Francisco; JD, New Coll. Sch. Law, 1984. Bar: Calif. 1985; U.S. Dist. Ct. (9th cir.), U.S. Dist. Ct. Appeals (9th cir.), U.S. Tax Ct.; lic. real estate broker, Calif. With African Tradeways, Inc., San Francisco, 1973-86 , pres., 1976-86 ; mng. ptnr. Marshall-Walker Assocs., San Francisco, 1977—; chief exec. officer Diversified Real Estate Investments Am., San Francisco, Fresno, Calif. and Tokyo, 1980—; prin. Grannis-Cox-Walker Assocs., Fresno and Patterson, Calif., 1980—; trainer Motivation Services, San Francisco, 1975-79; cons. Govt. Mali, Agrl. Trade Devel., 1979-81; cons. Somiex, Mali, 1980-82; v.p., trustee Pets Unltd. Richard M. Weaver fellow, 1969; Arthur Mellinger Found. Fellow, 1969. Mem. Am. Philatelic Soc., Bar Assn. San Francisco, The Barristers Club, Fresno County Bar Assn., Bay Area Lawyers for Individual Freedom, Calif. Lawyers for the Arts, King Hall Counselors, Am. Numismatic Soc., ABA (com. taxation, com. real property, com. probate and trust law). Office: PO Box 352 San Francisco CA 94101

MARSLAND, DIANE MARY, research engineer; b. Milw., Jan. 28, 1963; d. Jerome Joseph and Irene Helen (Zirbel) M.; m. Robert Alvin Marsland, Jr., Aug. 16, 1986. BSEE, U. Wis., 1985; MS, Ariz. State U., 1986. Engring. asst., engr. Lawrence Livermore Nat. Lab., Livermore, Calif., summers 1984-85; research engr. SRI Internat., Menlo Park, Calif., 1987—. Contbr. articles profl. jours. Mem. Nat. Right to life Com., Washington, 1986—. Recipient dept. scholarship, Elect. Engring. dept. U. Wis., 1984-85, dean's grad. scholarship Ariz. State U., 1985-86. Mem. IEEE (antennas and propagation soc.). Republican. Roman Catholic.

MARSTON, GARY LEE, medical instrumentation manufacturing company; b. Phoenix, May 1, 1951; s. Carroll Jack and Martha Edna (Ward) M.; m. Martha Jane Curtin, Aug. 15, 1975; children: Brooke Curtin, Allison Jeanne. BS, U. Redlands, 1973, MS, 1975. Speech therapist Behavioral Sci. Inst., Carmel, Calif., 1975-77; supr. Community Speech Ctr., Encino, Calif., 1977-80; owner, mgr. Community Speech Ctr., Tempe, Ariz., 1980-82; account exec. IVAC, Albuquerque, 1982—. Home: 6109 Caminito Ct NE Albuquerque NM 87111

MARSTON, MICHAEL, urban economics, real estate asset manager; b. Oakland, Calif., Dec. 4, 1936; s. Lester Woodbury and Josephine (Janovic) M.; m. Alexandra Lynn Geyer, Apr. 30, 1966; children: John, Elizabeth. BA, U. Calif., Berkeley, 1959; postgrad. London Sch. Econs., 1961-63. V.p. Larry Smith & Co., San Francisco, 1969-72, exec. v.p. urban econ. div., 1969-72; chmn. bd. Keyser Marston Assocs., Inc., San Francisco, 1973-87; gen. partner The Sequoia Partnership, 1979—; pres. Marston Vineyards and Winery, 1982—, Marston Assocs., Inc., 1982—. Cert. rev. appraiser Nat. Assn. Rev. Appraisers and Mortgage Underwriters, 1984—. Chmn., San Francisco Waterfront Com., 1969-86; chmn. fin. com., bd. dirs., mem. exec. com., treas. San Francisco Planning and Urban Research Assn., 1976-87, Napa Valley Vintners, 1986—; trustee Cathedral Sch. for Boys, 1981-82, Marin Country Day Sch., 1984—; v.p. St. Luke's Sch., 1986—; pres. Presidio Heights Assn. of Neighbors, 1983-84; v.p., bd. dirs., mem. exec. com. People for Open Space, 1972-87, chmn. adv. com., 1988—; mem. Gov.'s Issue Analysis Com. and Speakers Bur., 1966; mem. speakers bur. Am. embassy, London, 1961-63; v.p., bd. dirs. Democratic Forum, 1968-72; v.p., trustee Youth for Service. Served to lt. USNR. Contbr. articles to profl. jours. Mem. Nat. Assn. Rev. Appraisers and Mortgage Underwriters (cert. 1984—), Napa Valley Vintners, Urban Land Inst., World Congress Land Policy (paper in field), Order of Golden Bear, Commanderie de Bordeaux, Bohemian Club, Pacific Union Club, Lambda Alpha. Contbr. articles to profl. articles. Home: 3375 Jackson St San Francisco CA 94118

MARSTON, RICHARD ALAN, geography educator, consultant; b. Bethesda, Md., Apr. 6, 1952; s. Alan Douglas and Nancy (Burdick) M.; m. Linda Mary Crowe, July 16, 1977. BA, UCLA, 1974; MS, Oreg. State U., 1976, PhD, 1980. Environ. sci. V.T.N.-Colo., Denver, 1974-76, EPA, Corvallis, Oreg., 1976-77; hydrologist U.S. Forest Service, Waldport, Oreg., 1978-79; asst. prof. geography U. Tex., El Paso, 1980-86; asst. prof. geography U. Wyo., Laramie, 1986-88, assoc. prof., 1988—; cons. environ. geoscis., El Paso, 1980—. Contbr. articles to profl. jours. Grantee Assn. Western Univs., 1984, Horizon Communities Improvement Assn., 1983, Ft. Bliss Mil. Reservation, 1981, U.S. Forest Service 1979. Mem. Assn. Am. Geographers (Warren Nystrom award 1981), Am. Geomorphological Field Group, Am. Soc. Photogrammetry, Am. Water Resources Assn. Geol. Soc. Am. Home: 144 New Orleans Dr El Paso TX 79912 Office: U Tex at El Paso Dept Geol Scis El Paso TX 79968

MARTCH, THEODORE, teacher; b. Pitts., Mar. 24, 1949; s. Nicholas Martch and Helen (Belajac) Humes; m. Darlene Frances Carlin, June 18, 1983; children: Nathan, Benjamin. AA in Fine Arts, Community Coll. Allegheny County, 1973; BE, Calif. (Pa.) State Coll., 1975; MEd, U. Pitts., 1979. Counselor ARC Camp Mentally Retarded, Legioner, Pa., 1975; head tchr. Pa. Assn. Retard Citizens, Pitts., 1975-79; tchr. Allegheny Community Coll., Pitts., 1975-76, Ednl. Service Dist. Douglas County, Roseburg, Oreg., 1979—; com. mem. Transition Team Douglas County, 1985—. Vol. Douglas County Spl. Olympics, Roseburg, 1979—, presenter Spl. Olympics Internat., Washington, 1987—, bd. dirs. Oreg. Spl. Olympics, Portland; bd. dirs. Douglas County Respite Care, 1980—; mem. adv. counsel Agrl. Vocat. Adv. Council, Winston, Oreg., 1986—; mem. Portland region Spl. Olympics Ednl. Com., 1987—; organized first time entry spl. olympians in Boston marathon, 1988. Recipient hon. degree Future Farmers Am., 1988; named Vol. of Yr. Assn. for Retarded Citizens, 1983, Tchr. of Yr. Assn. for Retarded Citizens, 1985. Mem. VFW, Assn. for Severely Handicapped, U. Pitts. Alumni. Democrat. Serbian Orthodox. Clubs: Roseburg Track, Ediweiss Ski. Home: 734 NE Knoll Roseburg OR 97470 Office: Douglas County Spl Olympics PO Box 1368 Roseburg OR 97470

MARTENS, DAVID BAKER, publishing executive; b. St. Paul, June 3, 1942; s. Henry C. and Harriette C. (Baker) M.; m. Mary Jo Noack, Aug. 22, 1969; children: Jennifer Jo, Patrick Henry. BA, Mich. State U., 1965. Regional mgr. Times Mirror Cable, San Clemente, Calif., 1971-72; pub. The Advertiser-Tribune, Tiffin, Ohio, 1973-78; pub. York (Pa.) Daily Record, 1978-83, pres., 1983—; v.p. Buckner News Alliance, Seattle, Wash., 1983—; also bd. dirs. Buckner News Alliance, Bellingham, Wash.; mem. adv. bd. Am. Press Inst., Reston, Va., 1985—. Presbyterian. Office: Buckner News Alliance 221 1st Ave W Ste 315 Seattle WA 98119

MARTENS, HERMAN HELLMUTH, retired analytical chemist; b. Hamburg, Federal Republic of Germany, Mar. 23, 1923; came to U.S., 1936; s. Hellmuth Heinrich and Ottilie (Hirschfeld) M.; m. Agnes Rose Galligan, Apr. 25, 1942; children: Margaret R., Carol A., Janice M., Linda K. BS in Chemistry, St. Mary's U., San Antonio, 1952. Analytical chemist S.W. Research Inst., San Antonio, 1952-56; scientist III Biochem. Inst. U. Tex., Austin, 1956-57; research chemist Am. Potash and Chem. Co., Los Angeles, 1957-59; supr. quality control lab. Lockheed Propulsion Co., Redlands, Calif., 1959-61; research chemist Aerojet Gen. Corp., Azusa, Calif., 1961-66; project mgr. USAF/AFSC-AFRPL, Edwards AFB, Calif., 1966-83; cons. in field, Sparks, Nev., 1983—. Contbr. articles to profl. jours.; inventor dogbone in liquid tester. Served as cpl. USAAF, 1943-45, ETO. Mem. AAAS, Am. Chem. Soc. (sec.-treas. Sierra Nev. sect. 1986), Nat. Assn. Ret. Fed. Employees (2d v.p., program chmn. 1986), Sigma Xi. Republican. Home: 863 E Greenbrae Dr Sparks NV 89434

MARTILLA, JOHN ALAN, sanitary supply company executive; b. Tacoma, Wash., Aug. 21, 1941; s. Arne William and Esther Lempi (Anderson) M.; m. Frieda Beth Grimsrud, June 23, 1967; children: Kathy Lynn, Julie Marie. BBA summa cum laude, Pacific Luth. U., 1963; MBA with honors, U. Oreg., 1966, PhD, 1969. Prof. bus. adminstrn. Pacific Luth. U., Tacoma, 1969-77; v.p. mktg. Western Mgmt. Corp., Portland, Oreg., 1974-75; v.p. Paulsen and Roles Labs., Portland, Oreg., 1977—; mktg. cons. Weyerhaeuser Co., Tacoma, 1968, Mead Corp., Dayton, Ohio, 1969, Olympia (Wash.) Brewing Co., 1976. Contbr. articles to profl. publs. Raoynier Found. scholar, 1959-63; NDEA fellow, 1964-67. Mem. Am. Mktg. Assn. (v.p. local chpt. 1972-73, bd. dirs. 1974-76), Sales and Mktg. Execs., Beta Gamma Sigma, Alpha Kappa Psi (faculty adviser 1963-64). Home: 11675 SW Ridgecrest Dr Beaverton OR 97005 Office: Paulsen & Roles Labs 1836 NE 7th Ave Portland OR 97212

MARTIN, ANA M., business owner; b. Habana, Cuba, May 8, 1948; d. Reinaldo Martin-Jimenez and Maria J. (Marco) M.; m. Charles M. Lakamp, June 17, 1972 (div. Mar. 1980). BA, U. of the Pacific, 1969; cert. data processing, Acad. Computer Tech., 1969; M in Bus. Mgmt., Calif. State U., San Francisco, 1981. From jr. programmer to mgr. systems analysis Levi Strauss & Co., San Francisco, 1969-80; mgr. systems analysis Wells Fargo Bank, San Francisco, 1980-82, v.p., mgr. data processing dept., 1982-83; divemaster, underwater photographer Hydronaut Charters, Lahaina, Hawaii, 1983-84, 85-86; capt., owner, operator Sundance Scuba Charters, Lahaina, 1986—; cons. data processing Wells Fargo Bank, 1984. Capt. USCG, 1986—. Mem. Nat. Assn. Underwater Instrs. Profl. Assn. Diving Instrs. Republican. Roman Catholic. Home and Office: Sundance Scuba Charters PO box 12491 Lahaina HI 96761

MARTIN, BERNARD LEE, college dean; b. Dayton, Ohio, May 29, 1923; s. Harley L. and Clare (Murphy) M.; m. Mary Patricia McDonald, Nov. 23, 1950; children: Joseph, Mary, David, Patrick, Paul, Timothy, Michael, Christopher. B.A., Athenaeum of Ohio, 1941-45; M.A. in History, Xavier U., 1950, M.B.A., 1955; Ph.D. in Econs, U. Cin., 1963; Ph.D. honoris causa, Canisius Coll., 1978. Mem. faculty Xavier U., Cin., 1948-65; asst. prof. bus. adminstrn. Xavier U., 1955-62, assoc. prof. mktg., 1962-65, chmn. mktg. dept., 1961; chmn., prof. mktg. Eastern Mich. U., Ypsilanti, 1965-66; dean Sch. Bus. Adminstrn. Canisius Coll., Buffalo, 1966-71, 1973-78, acting acad. v.p. of coll., 1971-73; dean McLaren Coll. Bus. Adminstrn., U. San Francisco, 1978-86, prof. mktg., 1986—; bd. dirs. Empire of Am.-Calif. Fed. Savs. Bank. Author: (with others) Contemporary Economic Problems and Issues, 3d edit, 1973. Ford Found. grantee Harvard, 1964. Mem. Am. Mktg. Assn., Am. Econ. Assn. Club: Rotary Internat. Home: 224 Greenview Dr Daly City CA 94014 Office: 2130 Fulton St San Francisco CA 94117

MARTIN, BOYD ARCHER, emeritus political science educator; b. Cottonwood, Idaho, Mar. 3, 1911; s. Archer Olmstead and Norah Claudine (Imbler) M.; m. Grace Charlotte Swingler, Dec. 29, 1933; children: Michael Archer, William Archer. Student, U. Idaho, 1929-30, 35-36, B.S., 1936; student, Pasadena Jr. Coll., 1931-32, U. Calif. at Los Angeles, summer 1934; A.M., Stanford, 1937, Ph.D., 1943. Research asst. Stanford U., 1936-37, teaching asst., 1937-38; instr. polit. sci. U. Idaho, 1938-39; acting instr. polit. sci. Stanford U., 1939-40; John M. Switzer fellow, summer 1939-40; chief personnel officer Walter Butler Constrn. Co., Farragut Naval Tng. Center, summer 1942; instr. polit. sci. U. Idaho, 1940-43, asst. prof. polit. sci., 1943-44, asso. prof. polit. sci., 1944-47; prof., head dept. social sci., asst. dean U. Idaho (Coll. Letters and Sci.), 1947-55, dean, 1955-70, Borah Distinguished prof. polit. sci., 1970-73, prof., dean emeritus, 1973—; Vis. prof. Stanford U., summer 1946, spring 1952, U. Calif., 1962-63; affiliate Center for Study Higher Edn., Berkeley, 1962-63; mem. steering com. N.W. Conf. on Higher Edn., 1960-67, pres. conf., 1966-67; mem. bd. Am. Assn. of Partners of Alliance for Progress; chmn. Idaho Adv. Council on Higher Edn.; del. Gt. Plains UNESCO Conf., Denver, 1947; chmn. bd. William E. Borah Found. on Causes of War and Conditions of Peace, 1947-55; mem. Commn. to Study Orgn. Peace; dir. Bur. Pub. Affair Research, 1959-73, dir. emeritus, 1973—; dir. Inst. Human Behavior, 1970—. Author: The Direct Primary in Idaho, 1947, (with others) Introduction to Political Science, 1950, (with other) Western Politics, 1968, Politics in the American West, 1969, (with Sydney Duncombe) Recent Elections in Idaho (1964-70), 1972, Idaho Voting Trends: Party Realignment and Percentage of Voters for Candidates, Parties and Elections, 1890-1974, 1975, In Search of Peace: Starting From October 19, 1980, 1980, Why the Democrats Lost in 1980, 1980, On Understanding the Soviet Union, 1987; editor: The Responsibilities of Colleges and Universities, 1967; contbr. to: Ency. Britannica, 1974; also articles. Mem. Am. Polit. Sci. Assn. (exec. council 1952-53), Nat. Municipal League, Am. Soc. Pub. Adminstrn., Fgn. Policy Assn., UN Assn., AAUP, Western Polit. Sci. Assn. (pres. 1950), Phi Beta Kappa, Pi Gamma Mu, Kappa Delta Pi, Pi Sigma Alpha. Home: 516 Eisenhower Moscow ID 83843

MARTIN, CHRISTOPHER BRUCE, military officer; b. Staten Island, N.Y., Feb. 14, 1948; s. Sydney Burkhardt and Helen (Smith) M.; m. Barbara Partridge Buzbee, Feb. 10, 1973; children: Warren, James, Christine. BA in Spanish, U. S.C., 1970; MPA in Urban, State, Fed. Govt., Golden Gate U., 1980. Commd. USN, 1974, advance through grades to commdr., 1989; grad. asst. U. S.C., Columbia, 1970-71; intelligence analyst Supreme Allied Commdr.Atlantic, Norfolk, Va., 1971-74; main propulsion asst. USS MIssiissinewa, Norfolk, Va., 1974-75, USS Ichon, Norfolk, Va., 1975-77; aide-de-camp Armed Forces Staff Coll., Norfolk, Va., 1977-80; weapons officer USS Blandy, Norfolk, Va., 1980-83; 1st lt. USS Iowa, Norfolk, Va., 1983-86; exec. officer USS Wabash, Long Beach, Calif., 1986-88; asst. ops. officer Fleet Tng. Group, San Diego, 1988—; cons. City Norfolk Devel. Review, 1979; mem. planning Bicentennial Mil. Parade & Review, Yorktown, Va., 1983. Coord. Humanitarian Devel. USN USS Iowa, 1984-86; bd. dirs. DOD Bicentennial Constn. Unit, Long Beach, 1986-88, Adopt A Sch., Long Beach, 1986-88; active PTA White's PT Sch., San Pedro, Calif., 1986-88, Palmquist Elem. Sch., 1988—, Lincoln Jr. High Sch., 1988—. Mem. USS Iowa VA, So. Calif.

Golf Assn., U. S.C. Alumni Assn., Sigma Delta Pi, Omicron Delta Kappa, Sigma Phi Epsilon, Alpha Phi Omega. Republican. Roman Catholic. Home: 3421 Summerset Way Oceanside CA 92056 Office: Fleet Tng Group Nimitz Rd and Harbor Blvd San Diego CA 92109

MARTIN, CLYDE VERNE, psychiatrist; b. Coffeyville, Kans., Apr. 7, 1933; s. Howard Verne and Elfrieda Louise (Moehn) M.; m. Barbara Jean McNeilly, June 24, 1956; children—Kent Clyde, Kristin Claire, Kerry Constance, Kyle Curtis. Student Coffeyville Coll., 1951-52; A.B., U. Kans., 1955; M.D., 1958; M.A., Webster Coll., St. Louis, 1977; J.D., Thomas Jefferson Coll. Law, Los Angeles, 1985. Diplomate Am. Bd. Psychiatry and Neurology. Intern, Lewis Gale Hosp., Roanoke, Va., 1958-59; resident in psychiatry U. Kans. Med. Ctr., Kansas City, 1959-62, Fresno br. U. Calif.-San Francisco, 1978; staff psychiatrist Neurol. Hosp., Kansas City, 1962; practice medicine specializing in psychiatry, Kansas City, Mo., 1964-84; founder, med. dir., pres. bd. dirs. Mid-Continent Psychiat. Hosp., Olathe, Kans., 1972-84; adj. prof. psychology Baker U., Baldwin City, Kans., 1969-84; staff psychiatrist Atascadero State Hosp., Calif., 1984-85; clin. prof. psychiatry U. Calif., San Francisco, 1985—; chief psychiatrist Calif. Med. Facility, Vacaville, 1985-87; pres., editor Corrective and Social Psychiatry, Olathe, 1970-84, Atascadero, 1984-85, Fairfield, 1985—. Contbr. articles to profl. jours. Bd. dirs. Meth. Youthville, Newton, Kans. 1965-75, Spofford Home, Kansas City, 1974-78. Served to capt. USAF, 1962-64, col. USAFR. Fellow Royal Soc. Health, Am. Assn. Mental Health Profls. in Corrections, World Assn. Social Psychiatry, Am. Orthopsychiat. Assn., Am. Psychiat. Assn.; mem. AMA, Assn. for Advancement Psychotherapy, Am. Assn. Sex Educators, Counselors and Therapists (cert.), Assn. Mental Health Adminstrs. (cert.), N.Y. Acad. Sci., Phi Beta Pi, Pi Kappa Alpha. Methodist (del. Kans. East Conf. 1972-80, bd. global ministries 1974-80). Clubs: Carriage; Kansas City. Lodge: Mason. Office: PO Box 3365 Fairfield CA 94533

MARTIN, DAVID LOUIS, financial systems analyst; b. Oak Park, Ill., Dec. 20, 1950; s. Donald Maxwell and Marian Sylvia (Goers) M.; m. Norma Kay Allen, June 7, 1975. BA, Calif. State U., Fullerton, 1972. Mgr. programming Mortgage Systems, Anaheim, Calif., 1974-79; sr. programmer McDonnell Douglas, Huntington Beach, Calif., 1979-80; systems analyst Downey Savs., Costa Mesa, Calif., 1980-83; sr. project mgr. Columbia Savs., Irvine, Calif., 1983-89; free lance data processing cons. 1989—; cons., Santa Ana, Calif., 1973—. Lutheran. Home: 2041 N Ross Santa Ana CA 92706 Office: Columbia Savs & Loan 17911 Von Karman Ave Irvine CA 92714

MARTIN, DAVID WILLIAM, psychology educator; b. Indpls., June 28, 1943; s. Daniel William and Martha (Parker) M. BA, Hanover Coll., 1965; MA, Ohio State U., 1966, PhD, 1969. Asst. prof. N.Mex. State U., Las Cruces, 1969-75, assoc. prof., 1975-83, head dept. psychology, 1981—, prof. psychology, 1983—, chmn. faculty senate, 1980-81. Author: Doing Psychology Experiments, 2d rev. edit., 1985; contbr. articles to profl. jours. Mem. Rocky Mountian Psychol. Assn. (pres. 1984-85), Am. Psychol. Assn., Rio Grande Human Factors Soc. (pres. 1986), Human Factors Soc., Psychonomic Soc., Sertoma Club, Las Cruces Club (pres. 1977-78, dist. gov. So. N.Mex. chpt., West Tex. chpt. 1986-88). Home: 3251 Solar Ridge Las Cruces NM 88001 Office: NMex State U Dept Psychology Las Cruces NM 88003

MARTIN, DAVID WILLIAM, JR., biomedical research company executive, educator; b. West Palm Beach, Fla., Jan. 15, 1941; s. David W. Sr. and Joanna (Law) M.; m. Kathleen McKinnon, Aug. 22, 1964; children: David McKinnon, Gillian Hope. Student, MIT, 1958-60; MD, Duke U., 1964. Intern in internal medicine Duke U. Med. Ctr., Durham, N.C., 1964-65; asst. resident dept. medicine Duke U. Med. Ctr., Durham, 1965-66; research assoc. lab. molecular biology, Nat. Inst. Arthritis and Metabolic Diseases Nat. Insts. Health, Bethesda, Md., 1966-69; instr. dept. medicine, dept. biochemistry and biophysics U. Calif., San Francisco, 1969-70, asst. prof. medicine, chief med. genetics service, lectr. dept. biochemistry and biophysics, 1970-75, assoc. prof. medicine in residence and biochemistry in residence, chief med. genetics service, 1975-79, prof. medicine in residence and biochemistry in residence, chief med. genetics service, 1979-82; v.p. research Genentech, Inc., South San Francisco, Calif., 1983—; adj. prof. medicine and biochemistry U. Calif., San Francisco, 1983—, investigator Howard Hughes Med. Inst., 1974-82, dir. Med. Scientist Tng. Program, 1978-82; mem. adv. bd. Forum on Drug Devel. and Regulation, 1987—, Recombinant DNA Adv. Com., NIH, 1981-85, adv. com. U. Calif. Biotech. Research and Edn. Program, 1986—; bd. dirs. UCLA Symposia, 1986—. Mem. editorial bd. Harper's Rev. Biochemistry, 18th and 19th edits., 1980-85, Sci. Yr., World Book Ency., 1981-86, Jour. Biol. Chemistry, 1983-87; contbr. numerous articles to profl. jours. Mem. adv. council Research and Devel. Council Cystic Fibrosis Found., 1983—; bd. overseers Duke U. Comprehensive Cancer Ctr., 1985-88. Served to Sr. Surgeon, USPHS. Named Disting. Alumnus of Duke U. Sch. Medicine, 1985. Mem. Am. Fedn. Clin. Research, Am. Soc. Biol. Chemists, Am. Soc. Clin. Investigation, Assn. Am. Physicians, Western Assn. Physicians, Alpha Omega Alpha. Office: Genentech Inc 460 Point San Bruno Blvd South San Francisco CA 94080

MARTIN, DONALD WALTER, author, publisher; b. Grants Pass, Oreg., Apr. 22, 1934; s. George E. and Irma Ann (Dallas) M.; m. Kathleen Elizabeth Murphy, July, 1970 (div. May 1979); children: Daniel Clayton, Kimberly Ann; m. Betty Woo, Mar. 18, 1985. Enlisted USMC, 1952; advanced through grades to staff sgt. USMC, Japan, Republic of Korea, Republic of China, 1956-61; reporter Blade-Tribune, Oceanside, Calif., 1961-65; entertainment editor Press-Courier, Oxnard, Calif., 1965-69; mng. editor Argus-Courier, Petaluma, Calif., 1969-70; assoc. editor Motorland mag., San Francisco, 1970-88; founder, prin. Pine Cone Press, Columbia, Calif., 1988—. Author: Best of San Francisco, 1986, Best of the Gold Country, 1987, San Francisco's Ultimate Dining Guide, 1988; contbr. articles on travel to various publs. Recipient Diane Seely award Ventura County Theatre Council, 1968. Republican. Home and Office: 11362 Jackson St Box 1494 Columbia CA 95310

MARTIN, EDWARD HENRY, aerospace engineer; b. Lakewood, Ohio, July 15, 1933; s. Paul Joseph and Susan Rose (Kudravy) M.; m. Janice Joy Morgan, June l, 1957; children: Kim Luise, Michael Edward. Student, Fenn Coll., 1951-53; BS in Elec. Engring., Ohio State U., 1957, MS in Elec. Engring., 1964. Registered profl. engr., Calif. Mem. tech. staff Hughes Aircraft Co., Culver City, Calif., 1957-59; aerospace specialist U.S. Air Force Systems Command, Dayton, Ohio, 1962-64; sr. research engr. N.Am. Aviation, Anaheim, Calif., 1964-67; analysis supr. N.Am. Rockwell, Anaheim, Calif., 1967-72; mgr. advanced systems Magnavox Govt. Indsl. & Elec. Co., Torrance, /5, 1972-78; tech. dir. Rockwell-Collins Co.; mgr. global positioning system program devel. Rockwell Internat. Corp., 1981—; lectr. Tech. Mktg. Soc. Am., 1978-82. Patentee synthetic aperture aiding. Capt. USAF, 1959-62. Mem. IEEE, Inst. Navigation (organizer, chmn. satellite navigation session 1980), Air Force Assn., Corona Del Mar Club, Beta Theta Pi. Republican.. Home: 5221 Nantucket Ln Anaheim CA 92807 Office: Rockwell Internat Corp S&SED PO Box 3644 2600 Westminster Blvd Seal Beach CA 90740-7644

MARTIN, FRED KENNETH, JR., solar energy and real estate executive; b. Fresno, Calif., Nov. 21, 1942; s. Fred K. and Emma B. (Balmer) M.; m. Maria Armanno, June 5, 1976; children: Kenneth, Mario. AA, Fresno City Coll., 1964; Sec. of the Navy nomination to US Naval Acad., 1965; student, U. Santa Clara, 1986. With Travelers Corp., San Jose Calif. and Hartford, Conn., 1967-72, regional sales dir. L.H. & F.S., prodn. mgr., 1972-75; with Fafco Inc., Menlo Park, Calif., 1976—, nat. comml. sales mgr., 1971-78, gen. mgr., Bay Area Distbn. Co., 1978; pres., Fafco Solar Systems, 1979-83; dir., v.p. Solar Energy Sales, Inc.; pres., chmn. bd. Martin & Mickle Ins. and Fin. Corp., 1983-85; mgmt. cons., 1985-86; exec. v.p. Century 21 Bonus Realty, 1986—, also bd. dirs.; pub. Bonus News Inc., 1986—; mem. Century 21 Brokers Council and Advt. Com.; solar energy advisor Pacific Gas & Utility Co., U.S. Congressman Pete McCloskey, Calif. Solar Energy Commn., 1983-84. Bd. dirs. The Ark; chmn. BSA Camp Stewart Summer Camp. Contbg. author articles to profl. jours. Served with USMCR, 1960-68. Mem. Calif. Solar Energy Soc. (state bd. dirs.), Calif. Solar Energy Industries Assn., Calif. Insulation Contractors Assn. (dir., chmn. govtl. affairs, chmn. polit. action com.), Internat. Solar Energy Soc., UNICO (bd. dirs., sec. San Jose chpt. 1988—), Nat. Assn. Realtors, Calif. Assn. Realtors, San Jose Real Estate Bd., Los Gatos-Saratoga Real Estate Bd. Republican. Lutheran.

MARTIN, GEORGE, psychologist, educator; b. L.A., May 8, 1940; s. George Leonard and Margaret (Padigamus) M.; m. Penny Harrell, July 18, 1963 (div. 1984); children: Jeni, Kimberle; m. Judy Ann Peralta, June 22, 1985. BA, UCLA, 1965; MA, Calif. State U., L.A., 1967; MS, Calif. State U., Fullerton, 1988. Systems analyst L.A. Dept. Water & Power, 1965-67; project coord. L.A. Police Dept., 1967-70, edn. cons., 1980-83; alcohol researcher Pomona (Calif.) Coll., 1970-73; tng. systems researcher Lanterman State Hosp., Pomona, 1973-77; prof. psychology Mt. San Antonio Coll., Walnut, Calif., 1970—, dir. rsch., 1986—. Contbr. articles to profl. jours. Rsch. dir. Orange County Dem. Party, 1985-86. With U.S. Army, 1959-61. Grantee Nat. Inst. Law Enforcement, 1967-70, Nat. Inst. Alcohol, 1970-74. Mem. Am. Psychol. Assn., Nat. Sci. Assn., Lions. Home: 1313 N Grand Ave Ste 326 Walnut CA 91789 Office: Mt San Antonio Coll 1100 N Grand Ave Walnut CA 91789

MARTIN, GEORGE MAYBEE, lawyer; b. Mohler, Idaho, June 18, 1906; s. George Sylester and Janet Dove (Maybee) M.; m. Elizabeth Harrington Stafford, June 14, 1930; children: Elizabeth Jean, Dorothy Jane, George Stafford, Jonathon Harrington. BSEE, U. Wash., 1928, JD, 1940. Bar: Wash. 1940; registered profl. engr., 1928. Pvt. practice electrical contractor Seattle and Harrah, Wash., 1929-37; gen. merchant Martin & Martin, Harrah, 1930-37; pvt. practice law Yakima, Wash., 1940—; dep. prosecuting atty. Yakima County, Yakima, 1941-43; ptnr. Martin & Marquis, Yakima, 1975—. Author (book): Yakima, 1960, Yakima Centennial, 1985; editor: U.S. Post Card Catalog, 1955-60; philatelic columnist. Pres. Maybee Soc.; trustee Yakima Valley Meml. Hosp., Yakima Valley Regional Library, 1944-46, Yakima Valley Mus., 1946—. Named Distingished Citizen, Am. Legion, 1969; recipient Others award, Salvation Army, 1976, Silver Beaver, Silver Antelope award Boy Scout Am. Mem. ABA, Yakima County Bar Assn. (past pres.), Wash. State Bar Assn., Rotary, Mason, Am. Philatelic Soc. (Luff award 1974). Republican. Presbyterian. Home: 216 S 28th Ave Yakima WA 98902

MARTIN, GERRY RICHARD, construction executive; b. Washington, July 30, 1958; s. Richard Dudley and Frances May (Gordon) M.; m. Joy Ann Mueller, July 30, 1983; children: Amanda Renee, Andrea Marie. BS in Acctg., No. Ariz. U., 1980. Asst. mgr. Sherwin-Williams Co., Flagstaff, Ariz., 1978-80; mgr. ops. Credit Bur. Phoenix, 1980-84; asst. credit mgr. Tanner Cos., Phoenix, 1984-86; regional credit mgr. The Ceco Corp., Phoenix, 1986—. Active Worldwide Marriage Encounter, Phoenix, 1986—. Mem. Nat. Assn. Credit Mgrs., Nat. Inst. Credit. Republican. Roman Catholic. Home: 8042 N 32d Dr Phoenix AZ 85051 Office: The Ceco Corp 4500 S Lakeshore Dr #450 Tempe AZ 85282

MARTIN, HARRY (JOE), JR., advertising executive; b. Detroit, July 19, 1931; s. Harry M. and Irene Louis (McClung) M.; m. Linda Garn, Feb. 15, 1976; children—Monique, Michael, Jeffrey. BA, Mich. State U., 1957. Advt. mgr. Gate City Sash & Door Co., Ft. Lauderdale, Fla., 1955-56; advt. brand mgr. Coca Cola Co., 1958-59; founder, pres. Martin Advt., Inc., Tustin, Calif., 1960—. Served with USCGR, 1953-55. Mem. Pub. Relations Soc. Am., Western States Advt. Assn. Am. (bd. dirs.), Nat. Assn. Home Builders, Sales and Mktg. Council, The Constrn. Industries Alliance for City of Hope (v.p. Orange County chpt.), Bldg. Industries Am. Clubs: Lincoln, Pacific, Center, Balboa Bay, Shark Island Yacht, Irvine Racquet. Republican. Avocations: sailing, photography. Office: 18141 Irvine Blvd Tustin CA 92680

MARTIN, JAMES PATRICK, florist; b. Seattle, May 25, 1946; s. John Dennis and Catherine (Kirley) M.; m. Denise Marie Widen, Apr. 24, 1982; children: Michele, David, Nicholas, Patrick, Christopher. BA in Humanities, Gonzaga U., 1968, BS in Philosophy, 1968; MBA in Bus., U. Seoul, Seoul, Korea, 1969. Capt. U.S. Army 7th Infantry Div., Korea, 1968-70; retail sales mgr. Pacific Coast Comml., Los Angeles, 1970-71; v.p. Ballard Blossom Inc., Seattle, 1971—; fin. com. mem. Florists Transworld Delivery, Southfield, Mich., 1983-86. V.p. Seattle Allied Florists, Seattle, 1974-78; asst. soccer coach Seattle Pacific U., 1980—. Named Bus. Person of the Year Seattle C. of C.; recipient Small Bus. award Washington Gov., 1985, Florists Transwordl Delivery Top 100 award, 1977—. Mem. FTD, Am. ACad. Floraculture, Seattle Allied Florists (v.p. 1974-78). Republican. Roman Catholic. Home: 11931 Stendall Dr N Seattle WA 98133 Office: Ballard Blossom Inc 1766 NW Market St Seattle WA 98107

MARTIN, JANE D., interior designer; b. Bloomington, Ind., Sept. 9, 1943; d. Charles Henry and Dorothy D. (Robison) Dunn; m. Don Russell Martin, June 27, 1965; children: Don R., Robert Dunn. Student, Stephens Coll., 1963; BS, Ind. U., 1965; AA, Nashville Sch. Design, 1987. Ptnr. First Choice Designs, San Francisco, 1976-8l; owner, mgr. First Choice Designs, Nashville, 198l-87, Boulder, Colo., 1987-88; ptnr. Martin Lodge Design Assn., Boulder, 1988%. Mem. Am. Soc. Interior Design (allied). Democrat. Home and Office: 2230 Knollwood Dr Boulder CO 80302

MARTIN, JOSEPH, JR., lawyer, diplomat; b. San Francisco, May 21, 1915; m. Ellen Chamberlain Martin, July 5, 1946; children: Luther Greene, Ellen Myers. AB, Yale U., 1936, LLB, 1939. Assoc. Cadwalader, Wickersham & Taft, N.Y.C., 1939-41; ptnr. Wallace, Garrison, Norton & Ray, San Francisco, 1946-55, Pettit & Martin, San Francisco, 1955-70, 73—; gen. counsel FTC, Washington, 1970-71; ambassador, U.S. rep. Disarmament Conf., Geneva, 1971-76; mem. Pres.'s Adv. Com. for Arms Control and Disarmament, 1974-78; bd. dirs. Arcata Corp., Allstar Inns, Astec Industries, Inc., Opco Holding, Inc. Pres. Pub. Utilities Commn., San Francisco, 1956-60; Rep. nat. committeeman for Calif., 1960-64; treas. Rep. Party Calif., 1956-58; bd. dirs. Patrons of Art and Music, Calif. Palace of Legion of Honor, 1958-70, pres., 1963-68; bd. dirs. Arms Control Assn., 1977-84; pres. Friends of Legal Assistance to Elderly, 1983-87. Lt. comdr. USNR, 1941-46. Recipient Ofcl. commendation for Outstanding Service as Gen. Counsel FTC, 1973, Distinguished Honor award U.S. ACDA, 1973, Lifetime Achievement award Legal Assistance to the Elderly, 1981. Fellow Am. Bar Found. Clubs: Burlingame Country, Pacific Union. Home: 2580 Broadway San Francisco CA 94115 Office: Pettit & Martin 101 California St 35th Fl San Francisco CA 94111

MARTIN, JULIE ELAINE, retail store executive; b. Ft. Bragg, Calif., Sept. 7, 1949; d. Elmer O. and Hazel Elaine (Johnson) Harju; m. Robert E. Coltrane, Jan. 2, 1975 (dec. Feb. 1978); children: Julie, Sara, Joanna, Faith; m. Jim Lee Martin, Jan. 25, 1986. Student, Casper Coll., 1974-75, Coll. of Redwoods, 1983-85. Exec. sec. Job Svc. Wyo., Casper, 1974-78; mgr. Sprouse-Reitz, Santa Rosa, Calif., 1981-83; office mgr. Safeway Stores, Inc., Ft. Bragg, Calif., 1983-85; mgr. trainee Payless Store, Ft. Bragg, 1985-86; mgr. Beno's Clothing Store, Sonora, Calif., 1986-88; innkeeper/mgr. Barretta Gardens Inn, Sonora, Calif., 1988—; relief mgr. Walnut Apts., Ft. Bragg, Calif., 1989—. Author: Literary Pathways, World of Poetry (Golden Poet award 1989). Mem. NAFE, Motherlode Artists Guild, Art Ctr. Tuolumne County. Democrat. Home: 190 S Cory #4 PO Box 2194 Fort Bragg CA 95437 Office: Walnut Apts 311 Walnut Ave Fort Bragg CA 95437

MARTIN, JUNE JOHNSON CALDWELL, journalist; b. Toledo, Oct. 6; d. John Franklin and Eunice Imogene (Fish) Johnson; A.A., Phoenix Jr. Coll., 1939-41; B.A., U. Ariz., 1941-43, 53-59; student Ariz. State U., 1939, 40; m. Erskine Caldwell, Dec. 21, 1942 (div. Dec. 1955); 1 son, Jay Erskine; m. 2d, Keith Martin, May 5, 1966. Free-lance writer, 1944—; columnist Ariz. Daily Star, 1956-59; editor Ariz. Alumnus mag., Tucson, 1959-70; book editor, gen. feature writer Ariz. Daily Star, Tucson, 1970—; panelist, co-producer TV news show Tucson Press Club, 1954-55, pres., 1958; mem. editorial bd. Clarion, women's issues newspaper. Contbg. author: Rocky Mountain Cities, 1949; contbr. articles to World Book Ency., and various mags. Mem. Tucson CD Com., 1961; vol. campaigns of Samuel Goddard, U.S. Rep. Morris Udall, U.S. ambassador and Ariz. gov. Raul Castro. Recipient award Nat. Headliners Club, 1959, Ariz. Press Club award, 1957-59, Am. Alumni Council, 1966, 70. Mem. Nat. Book Critics Circle, Jr. League of Tucson, Tucson Urban League, Pi Beta Phi. Democrat. Methodist. Club: Tucson Press. Home: PO Box 2631 Tucson AZ 85702 Office: PO Box 26807 Tucson AZ 85726

MARTIN, LAURA ANNE, banker; b. Pasadena, Calif., Dec. 11, 1958; d. Warren Leicester and Laura Paez (Reed) M.; m. Daniel Andrew Medina, July 16, 1983. Student Wellesley Coll., 1976-78; BA, Stanford U., 1980; MBA, Harvard U., 1983. Fin. analyst AG Becker, Los Angeles, 1980-81; assoc. Drexel Burnham Lambert, Los Angeles, 1983-86, v.p., 1986-88, 1st v.p. 1988—. Office: Drexel Burnham Lambert 131 S Rodeo Dr Ste 300 Los Angeles CA 90212

MARTIN, LUCY Z., public relations executive; b. Alton, Ill., July 8, 1941; d. Fred M. and Lucille J. Kirk; m. Jerry Martin, 1967 (div. 1979). BA, Northwestern U., 1963. Adminstrv. asst., copywriter Batz-Hodgson-Neuwoehner, Inc., St. Louis, 1963-64; news reporter, Midwest fashion editor Fairchild Publs., St. Louis, 1964-66; account exec. Milici Advt. Agy., Honolulu, 1967; publs. dir. Barnes Med. Ctr., St. Louis, 1968-69; communications cons. Fleishman-Hillard, St. Louis, 1970-74, Fleishman-Hillard (now Lucy Z. Martin & Assocs.), Portland, Oreg., 1974-86; pres., chief exec. officer Lucy Z. Martin & Assocs., Inc., Portland, 1987—. Chmn. women's adv. com. Reed Coll., Portland, 1977-79; mem. Oreg. Commn. for Women, 1984-87; bd. dirs. Ronald McDonald House Oreg., 1986, Oreg. Sch. Arts & Crafts, 1988-90. Recipient MacEachern Citation Acad. Hosp. Pub. Relations, 1978, Rosey awards Portland Advt. Fedn., 1979, Achievement award Soc. Tech. Communications, 1982, Disting. Tech. Communication award, 1982, Exceptional Achievement award Council for Advancement and Support Edn., 1983, Monsoon award Internat. Graphics, Inc., 1984; named Woman of Achievement Daily Jour. Commerce, 1980. Mem. Pub. Relations Soc. Am. (pres. Columbia River chpt. 1984, chmn. bd. 1980-84, Oreg. del. 1984-86, judicial panel N. Pacific dist 1985-86, exec. bd. health care sect. 1986-87, mem. Counselors Acad., Spotlight awards 1985, 86, 87), Portland Pub. Relations Roundtable (chmn. 1985, bd. dirs. 1983-85), Assn. Western Hosps. (editorial adv. bd. 1984-85), Best of West awards 1978, 80, 83, 87), Oreg. Hosp. Pub. Relations Orgn. (pres. 1981, chmn. bd. 1982), Acad. Health Service Mktg., Am. Hosp. Assn., Am. Mktg. Assn., Am. Soc. Hosp. Mktg. & Pub. Relations, Healthcare Communicators Oreg., Internat. Assn. Bus. Communicators (18 awards 1981-87), Oreg. Assn. Hosps. Oreg. Press Women, Nat. and Oreg. Soc. Healthcare Planning & Mktg., Women in Communications (Matrix award 1977). Office: 4380 SW Macadam Ave Ste 285 River Forum Bldg Portland OR 97201-6408

MARTIN, MARI LACRESSA, clinical social worker; b. Glendale, Calif., Apr. 4, 1962; d. Leroy Martin and Cecil Dell (Flemmings) M. BA in Social Work and Psychology, Azusa Pacific U., 1984; MSW, U. Houston, 1985. Lic. clin. social worker. Counselor Youth for Christ, Covina, Calif., 1982-83; social work intern St. Joseph Hosp., Houston, 1984; psychotherapist Tex. Rsch. Inst. Mental Scic., Houston, 1984-85; social worker Angelic Christian Daycare, Pasadena, Calif., 1985-86; clin. social worker Pacific Clinics Child Adolescent Programs, Pasadena, Calif., 1986—; dir. community and outreach svcs. Salvation Army Booth Meml Ctr. for Pregnant Adolescents, L.A., 1988—. Mem. Nat. Assn. Social Workers.

MARTIN, MARSHALL GEORGE, lawyer; b. Carlsbad, N.Mex., Sept. 11, 1938; s. William Leslie and Marie (Johnson) M. ; m. Sallie Sue Schirmer, Nov. 24, 1962 (div. Dec. 1982); children: Jessica Blair, Benjamin Johnson; m. Mary Margaret Parkin, Jan. 13, 1964. BA, So. Meth. U., 1960, JD, 1963. Bar: N.Mex. 1963. Assoc. Trower, Still & Keeling, London, 1963-64, Iden & Johnson, Albuquerque, 1964-70; ptnr. Poole, Tinnin & Martin, Albuquerque, 1970--; mem. N.Mex. Bd. Bar Examiners, 1977-82. Organizer, officer Alternatives to Trial, Inc., Albuquerque, 1987--. Fellow N. Mex. Bar Found.; mem. ABA, N.Mex. State Bar Assn. (chmn. alternative dispute resolution com. 1986-87, comml. litigation and antitrust sect. 1986-87, Disting. Service award 1984), N.Mex. Jud. Council (chmn. 1963-64), Albuquerque Country Club. Democrat. Office: Poole Tinnin & Martin 219 Central St NW Ste 700 Albuquerque NM 87103

MARTIN, MICHAEL LAWTON, real estate broker, developer; b. Berkeley, Calif., May 31, 1948; s. Edward Lawton and Jeanne-Marie (Willi) M.; m. Christine Veronique, Feb. 15, 1975; children: Matthew Michael, Julie Willi. BBA in Fin., U. Denver, 1972. Asst. ops. mgr. United Calif. Bank, San Francisco, 1972-74, IDS/Equico Lessors, San Francisco, 1975-76; sales mgr. Gelco Equpment Leasing, San Francisco, 1976-77; dist. sales mgr. Pinnacle Leasing, Berkeley, 1977-78; pres. Bailey & Martin Fin. Services, Bellevue, Wash., 1979-84; dir. sales Ocean Colony Realty, Half Moon Bay, Calif., 1984—. Mem. transp. com. San Mateo County Econ. Devel. Assn., 1986-87. Mem. Rotary Club. Republican. Episcopalian. Office: Ocean Colony Realty 2000 Fairway Dr Half Moon Bay CA 94019

MARTIN, MICHAEL LEE, orthotist; b. Long Beach, Calif., May 30, 1947; s. Troy Lee and Ruth Elizabeth (Hummer) M.; m. Sharon Lee Johnson, Aug. 23, 1969; 1 child, Tanya Lee. Student, Northwestern U., 1973; AA, Cerritos (Calif.) Coll., 1976; student, UCLA, 1976. Diplomate Am. Bd. Orthotists and Prosthetist. Cable splicer Gen. Telephone, Dairy Valley, Calif., 1965-66; orthotic technician Johnson's Orthopedic, Santa Ana, Calif., 1969-73, orthotist, 1974—; pres. Johnson's Orthopedic, Orange, Calif., 1989—; rsch. orthotist Rancho Los Amigos Hosp., Downey, 1973. With U.S. Army, 1966-68, Vietnam. Mem. Am. Acad. Orthotists and Prosthetists (sec., pres. So. Calif. chpt. 1976-79, sec., pres. Region IX 1979-87), Orthotic and Prosthetic Provider Network (pres. Calif. chpt. 1988—). Democrat. Home: 1179 Hillcrest Corona CA 91720 Office: Johnson's Orthopedic 1920 E Katella Ste G Orange CA 92667

MARTIN, NANCY L., communications exective; b. Phoenix, Dec. 6, 1931; d. Donald Mackenzie and Mary (Wilson) M. BA, U. Calif., 1954. Reporter Phoenix Gazette, 1951-52; creative dir. Modern Advtg., Santa Monica, Calif., 1954-60; publicist Los Angeles, 1960-63; exec. v.p. Ad Mktg., Beverly Hills, Calif., 1963-68; pres. Martin Ptnrs., Inc., Beverly Hills, 1968-75, Los Angeles, 1986—; supr. Sitmar Cruises, Los Angeles, 1975-86, cons., 1986—. Recipient Design Excellence award Type Dirs. Club, 1963. Mem. Am. Soc. Tng. & Devel., Internat. Soc. Gen. Semantics, Nat. Soc. Performance and Instr. Democrat. Roman Catholic. Home: 1820 Midvale Ave Los Angeles CA 90025

MARTIN, PAUL EGLEY, investment banker; b. St. Louis, Mar. 25, 1958; s. Frederick William and Dorothy Jean (Egley) M.; m. Georgia Remington, July 31, 1982; 1 child, Katherine Remington. AB in Econs., Princeton U., 1980; MBA in Fin., U. Chgo., 1984. Fin. analyst Blyth Eastman Paine Webber, N.Y.C., 1980-82; asst. to chmn. Farley Inds., Chgo., 1983-84; assoc. Paine Webber, N.Y. & San Francisco, 1984-85, Smith Barney Harris Upham, San Francisco, 1986; v.p. Smith, Barney, Harris, Upham, San Francisco, 1987—. Bd. dirs. ARC Golden Gate Chpt., San Francisco, 1988. Princeton Club of No. Calif. (pres. 1989). Republican. Home: 201 Magellan Ave San Francisco CA 94116 Office: Smith Barney et al 350 California St San Francisco CA 94104

MARTIN, PRESTON, savings and loan executive; b. L.A., Dec. 5, 1923; s. Oscar and Gaynell (Horne) M.; 1 child, Pier Preston. BS in Fin., U. So. Calif., 1947, MBA, 1948; PhD in Monetary Econs., U. Ind., 1952. Rsch. fellow U. Ind., Bloomington, 1948-49; prin. in housebldg. firm 1952-56; with mortgage fin. and consumer fin. instns., 1954-57; prop. econ. rsch. group specializing in savs. and loan banks, 1956-66; developer, adminstr. Pakistan Project for Grad. Bus. Edn., L.A., 1960-63; developer, dir. Programs for Bus. and Govt. Execs. U. So. Calif., L.A., 1959-63; commr. savs. and loan State of Calif., 1967-69; chmn. Fed. Home Loan Bank Bd., Washington, 1969-72; chmn., chief exec. officer PMI Mortgage Ins. Co., 1972-80; chmn., chief exec. officer Seraco Group subs. Sears, Roebuck & Co., 1980-81, also bd. dirs. parent co.; chmn., chief exec. officer H.F. Holdings, Inc., San Francisco, 1988—; chmn. bd. Fed. Home Loan Bank Bd., 1969-72; vice chmn. Fed. Res. Bd., Washington, 1982-86; bd. dirs. Honolulu Fed. Savs. Bank, Fed. Home Loan Mortgage Corp. Adv. Com.; Policy Adv. Bd. Ctr. for Real Estate and Urban Econs. U. Calif.; chmn., chief exec. officer SoCal Holdings, Inc., San Francisco, 1987—, WestFed Holdings, Inc., San Francisco, 1988—, Wespar Fin. Svcs., Inc., San Francisco, 1987—. Author: Principles and Practices of Real Estate, 1959; contbr. articles to profl. jours. Mem. Joint Ctr. Urban Studies MIT; sr. advisor Reagan Adminstrn. Commn. on Housing, 1980-81. With AUS, 1943-46. Recipient House and Home award, 1969, award Engring. News Record, 1971, NAHB Turntable award, 1973. Mem. Am. Econs. Assn., Am. Fin. Assn., Lambda Chi Alpha. Presbyterian.

MARTIN, ROBERT BURTON, consultant; b. Takoma Park, Md., Mar. 17, 1935; s. Herbert Lester and Lenora Marie (Sponseller) M.; m. Mary Lou Rushworth, Sept. 7, 1959 (div. Dec. 1982); children: Laurajean, Kenneth, Donna Beth. BEE, Cornell U., 1958; MS, Northwestern U., 1966, PhD, 1967. Dir. mgmt. systems Denver and Rio Grande Western R.R., 1967-71; v.p. Mgmt. Design Assoc., Denver, 1971-79; owner Martin & Assoc., Denver, 1979—; treas. Rocky Mountain Chpt., Inst. of Mgmt. Sci., Denver, 1968-70; opening speaker Am. Inst. CPA's, Las Vegas, Nev., 1988. Author and Pub. Martin Reports, newsletter, 1981—. Served to lt. USN, 1958-63. Mem. Inst. of Mgmt. Cons., Alpha Pi Mu, Sigma Xi. Home and Office: 180 Cook St Ste 110 Denver CO 80206

MARTIN, ROBERT EDWARD, JR., forestry educator, scientist, researcher; b. Flint, Mich., Jan. 9, 1931; s. Robert Edward and Sarah Catherine (Royal) M.; m. Patricia Ann Meyer, Nov. 7, 1953; children—Steven Francis, Michael Philip, Kathleen Marie. B.S. in Physics, Marquette U., 1953; B.S. in Forestry, U. Mich., 1958, M. in Forestry, 1959, Ph.D., 1963. Researcher forester Forest Service, U.S. Dept. Agr., Macon, Ga., 1960-63; from asst. prof. to prof. Va. Poly. Inst., Blacksburg, Va., 1963-71; prof., research physicist Forest Service, U.S. Dept. Agr. and U. Wash., Seattle, 1971-75; research forester Forest Service, U.S. Dept. Agr., Bend, Oreg., 1975-82; prof. forestry U. Calif.-Berkeley, 1982—; forestry cons. REMAR, Oakland, Calif., 1984—. Served to lt. USN, 1953-56. Mem. Soc. Am. Foresters, AAAS, Soc. Range Mgmt., Sigma Xi, Phi Kappa Phi, Xi Sigma Pi. Club: Toastmasters (Berkeley). Home: 75 Chadbourne Way Oakland CA 94619 Office: U Calif Berkeley Dept Forestry and Rsch Mgmt 145 Mulford Hall Berkeley CA 94720

MARTIN, ROBERT GREGORY, chemist; b. Denver, Apr. 24, 1959; s. Harold Gregory and Margaret C. (Mayer) M. BS, U. Denver, 1982. Computer distbr. Tronics Sales Corp., Ft. Worth, 1983; lab. technician Hager Labs., Denver, 1983-84, chem. analyst I, 1984-85, chem. analyst II, 1985-86, chem. analyst III, 1986-87, operator GC/MS, 1987-88; chemist IV, operator GC/MS Rocky Mountain Analyical Labs, Environ. Svc. Co., Arvada, Colo., 1988—. Recipient Hornbeck award U. Denver, 1982; scholar U. Denver, 1982. Mem. AAAS, Am. Chem. Soc., N.Y. Acad. Sci., Am. Inst. Chemists, The Planetary Soc., Gold Key, Alpha Lambda Delta, Alpha Epsilon Delta. Roman Catholic. Home: 1370 Oneida St Denver CO 80220 Office: Rocky Mountain Analytical Labs ENSECO 4955 Yarrow St Arvada CO 80002

MARTIN, ROBERT LORNE, city manager; b. Yreka, Calif., Aug. 28, 1954; s. Lorne Irwin and Mary (Grove) M.; m. Frieda Ruff, June 18, 1977. BSBA, No. Ariz. U., 1977. Acct. Mt. States Engrs., Tucson, 1977-78; adminstrv. asst. II Tucson Parks & Recreation Dept., 1978-80, adminstrv. asst. III, 1980-83, adminstrv. asst IV, 1983-87, asst. dir., 1987—, state conf. chmn., 1986. Mem. Nat. Recreation & Parks Assn., Ariz. Parks & Recreation Assn. (state treas. 1987, Profl. Svc. award 1986), Delta Sigma Pi. Home: 4634 N Melpomene Way Tucson AZ 85749-9023

MARTIN, STANLEY LAWRENCE, hotel/restaurant company executive; b. Pitts., Mar. 17, 1938; s. Leonard and Nancy Lee (Broder) M.; m. Elinor Scher, Aug. 1, 1964; children: Deborah Joyce, Miriam Denise. Student, San Antonio Jr. Coll., 1958-59, Ariz. State U., 1959, 60, 61. Cert. hotel adminstr. Div. mgr. Performance Systems, Inc., Nashville, 1969-72; ptnr., gen. mgr. Stamar Ent., Inc., Phoenix, 1972-75; mgr. Little Am., Flagstaff, Ariz., 1975-78; sr. v.p. Fin. Devel. Svcs., Inc., Phoenix, 1978-83; ptnr. Pasatiempo Inn, Santa Cruz, Calif., 1983-85; pres. PMG Ltd., Flagstaff, 1983—; ptnr., gen. mgr. Poco Diablo Resort, Sedona, Ariz., 1985—. Reviewer text books, 1975-78; contbr. articles to profl. jours. Bd. dirs. Navajo Nations adv. Council, Window Rock, Ariz., 1988—, Sedona Villa Adv. Council, 1988—. Mem. Ariz. Restaurant Assn. (bd. dirs. 1987—), Sedona C. of C. (pres. 1988), Am. Motel/Hotel Assn., Nat. Restaurant Assn., Calif. Restaurant Assn., Sedona Film Commn., Sedona Innkeepers Assn. Republican. Jewish. Home: 301 William Rd Flagstaff AZ 86001

MARTIN, W. MIKE, educator; b. Las Vegas, Feb. 21, 1943; s. Bill Earl Martin and Marie M. Murray; m. Patricia K. Mowbray, Dec. 28, 1965; children: Brandi Leigh, Calleen Mallinda. BArch, U. Colo., 1969; MArch, U. Wash., 1971; PhD in Architecture, U. Calif., Berkeley, 1983. Cert. architect, Calif. Assoc. prof., head pre-design professions Kans. State U., Manhattan, 1971-76, assoc. prof. dept. architecture, 1979-80; tchng. assoc. dept. architecture U. Calif., Berkeley, 1976-78; dean, assoc. prof. coll. environ. design U. Colo., Boulder, 1980-85; head, prof. dept. architecture Calif. Polytech. State U., San Luis Obispo, 1985—; prin. Ctr. for Environ. Design and Architecture, San Luis Obispo, 1985—, Flatiron Shelter Co., Boulder, 1980-85. Contbr. articles to profl. jours. Bd. dirs. Boulder Energy Commn., 1982-85. Tasheira fellow U. Calif., 1976. Mem. AIA (vice chmn. AIE com. 1988), Calif. Council Archl. Edn. (pres. 1989—). Office: Calif Polytech State U Dept Architecture San Luis Obispo CA 93407

MARTIN, WILLIAM FRANKLIN, JR., rancher; b. Dallas, May 21, 1919; s. William Franklin and Willie Ida (McCreary) M.; m. Wanda Walker, Jan. 11, 1950. Student, McMurray Coll., Abilene, Tex., 1937-38; LLB, U. Tex., 1941. Bar: Tex. 1941. Ptnr. Turner & Martin Atty's at Law, Hamlin, Tex., 1946-48, Ritchie & Martin, Mineral Wells, Tex., 1948-50; rancher Stonewall & Fisher Counties, Mineral Wells, Tex., 1945-57, Colfax County, N.Mex., 1957-81, Gladstone, N.Mex., 1981—; spl. county judge Stonewall County, Aspermont, Tex., 1953. Pres. N.Mex. U. Found., Las Cruces, 1981; mem. adv. bd. Clayton Rsch. Ctr., 1976—. Recipient Father of Yr. award N.Mex. Cowbelle Assn., 1984. Mem. Nat. Cutting Horse Assn., Am. Quarter Horse Assn., N.Mex. Cattlemens Assn. (pres. 1987-88), Nat. Cattlemens Assn. (v.p. region IV 1982-84, Commendation award 1985). Republican. Methodist. Home: PO Box 6124 Santa Fe NM 87502 Office: Carrizo Ranch PO Box 518 Gladstone NM 88422

MARTINDALE, LOREN DAVID, personnel director; b. Wichita, Kans., Sept. 5, 1939; s. Herbert Willard and Maude Merle (Mills) M.; m. Sandra Ann Hahn, July 3, 1965; children: Bradley Kane, Stanley David, Geoffrey Kent. BA, Wichita State U., 1967. Position classifier U.S. Army, Sukiran CPO, Okinawa, 1968-69; personnel officer U.S. Air Force, Tainan Air Base, Taiwan, 1969-70; chief classifier Rocky Mt. Arsenal, Denver, 1970-72; dir. personnel Savanna (Ill.) Army Depot, 1973-75; chief classifier Corps of Engrs., Jacksonville, Fla., 1975-80; dir. personnel U.S. Army Yuma (Ariz.) Proving Ground, 1980—; owner Martindale Software, Yuma, Ariz., 1988—. Inventor: (software program) Exit Q 1988; contbr. articles profl. jours. With USAF, 1957-61. Recipient Nick Hoge award Dept. U.S. Army, Washington, 1985. Mem. Am. Assn. for Artificial Intelligence, Assn. U.S. Army (sec. golf chpt. 1988—), Mexican Am. Golf Assn. (sec. 1982-84). Republican. Home: 1746 W 25th Ln Yuma AZ 85364 Office: US Army Yuma Proving Ground Yuma AZ 85365

MARTINETTI, RONALD ANTHONY, lawyer; b. N.Y.C., Aug. 13, 1945; s. Alfred Joseph and Frances Ann (Battipaglia) M. Student, U. Chgo., 1981-82; JD, U. So. Calif., 1982. Bar: Calif. 1982, U.S. Dist. Ct. (cen. and no. dists.) Calif. 1982, U.S. Ct. Appeals (9th cir.) 1982. Ptnr. Kazanjian & Martinetti, Glendale, Calif., 1984—. Author: James Dean Story, 1975; contbr. articles to profl. jours. Mem. Calif. Bar Assn., L.A. Bar Assn., Samuel Williston Soc. Found. (chmn. 1981—). Roman Catholic. Home: 3700 Los Feliz Blvd Los Angeles CA 90027 Office: Kazanjian & Martinetti 520 E Wilson Ave Los Angeles CA 91206

MARTINEZ, BRIAN MICHAEL, flight test and aircraft guidance and control engr; b. Shreveport, La., May 9, 1957; s. Clyde Emmanuel and Christine (Lemon) M.; m. Arlene Joyce Dunster, Jan. 19, 1988; 1 child, Sten Michael. Student, U.S. Mil. Acad., 1975-76; BS in Aerospace Engring., Calif. State Poly. U., 1980. Enging. aide Aerojet Liquid Rocket Co., Sacramento, 1977; tech. aide Jet Propulsion Lab., Pasadena, Calif., 1978; engr. Rockwell Internat., Downey, Calif., 1980-83, Northrop, Pico Rivera, Calif., 1983--. Dep. sheriff Orange County Sheriff Search and Rescue Res., 1983-85. Lt. USNR, 1986--. Mem. AIAA, Exptl. Aircraft Assn. Republican. Home: 41746 Crispi Ln Quartz Hill CA 93536 Office: Northrop AB-2 Div 8900 E Washington Pico Rivera CA 93536

MARTINEZ, CAMILLA MARIA, lawyer; b. Santa Fe, Feb. 26, 1954; d. Eloy A. and Frances (Roybal) M. BS, U. N.Mex., 1975, MA with honors, 1978; JD, U. Denver, 1985. Classroom tchr. Albuquerque Pub. Schs., 1975-82; with staff Martinez Bail Bond Co., Santa Fe, 1975-82; with legal staff Willis A. Belford, Jr. Law Offices, Colorado Springs, Colo., 1985—. Reader Mother of God Catholic Ch., Denver, 1983—, eucharistic minister, 1985—. Named one of Outstanding Young Women Am., 1985. Mem. Am. Trial Lawyers Assn., Colo. Trial Lawyers Assn., Student Am. Bar Assn., Mexican-Am. Law Students Assn., Phi Alpha Delta. Democrat. Home: 412 Alta Vista Santa Fe NM 87501

MARTINEZ, DAVID JOSEPH, municipal official, energy consultant; b. Loma Linda, Calif., May 1, 1950; s. Joseph S. and Annie (Trevino) M.; m. Nadine G. Luine, Spt. 27, 1971; children: Robbie A., Ryan J. AA, San Bernardino Valley Coll., 1982; cert., Riverside City Coll., 1984. Bldg. advisor City of Redlands, Calif., 1972-76, chief bldg. ofcl., 1987—; bldg. inspector II Riverside (Calif.) County, 1976-79, plans examiner, 1979-84; prin. D.J.'s Energy Cons., Redlands, 1979—; sr. plans examiner Riverside (Calif.) County, 1984-85; bldg. inspector Willdan & Assoc., San Bernardino, 1985-86; bldg. official City of Claremont, Calif., 1986—; chief bldg. ofcl. City of Redlands, Calif., 1987—. Served with USMC, 1969-71, Vietnam. Named Citizen of Yr., Nat. Rifle Assn., 1984. Mem. Internat. Conf. Bldg. Officials (Riverside chpt. parliamentarian 1986, Foothill chpt. sec.-treas. 1987, pres. 1987-88). Democrat. Presbyterian. Office: City of Redlands 30 Cajon St Redlands CA 92373

MARTINEZ, HENRY R., manufacturing company executive, researcher; b. Torrance, Calif., Dec. 8, 1955; s. Henry L. and Maria Luisa (Ramirez) M.; m. Sylvia, Aug. 27, 1978; children: Leon, Vivian, Yvonne. BEE, UCLA, 1977. Devel. engr. Garrett Airesearch Mfg. Co., Torrance, 1977-80; R&D unit mgr. Northrop Electronics Corp., Hawthorne, Calif., 1980-83; chief engr. Powerline Industries, Inc., Torrance, 1983-84; dir. rsch. Leviton Mfg. Co., Inc., Gardena, Calif., 1984—; cons. Elco Engring., L.A., 1978—. Contbr. articles to profl. jours. Lectr. Youth Motivation Task Force, Los Angeles, 1982-84. Mem. IEEE, Nat. Elec. Mfrs. Assn., Washington (com. mem. 1987—). Unitarian. Home: 21825 Barbara St Torrance CA 90503-6204 Office: Leviton Mfg Co Inc 747 W Redondo Beach Blvd Gardena CA 90247

MARTINEZ, JILL MARIE, community relations director, minister; b. Hayward, Calif., July 29, 1950; d. Reuben Alva and Willie Mae (Montgomery) M.; (div. Feb. 1978); 1 child, Marie. BA in Sociology, U. Hawaii, 1972; MDiv, San Francisco Theol. Sem., 1983, postgrad., 1989—. Tchr. Lucia Mar Unified Sch. Dist., 1973-74, 77-78, Madison Sch. Dist., 1974-77; tchr. Presbyn. Ch., Stockton, Calif., 1984-85, Morro Bay, Calif., 1982-83; cons., ethnic rsch. and devel. Presbyn. Ch. (Calif.) Synod of the Pacific, 1983-84; probe dir., ethnic rsch. and devel. Presbyn. Ch. (U.S.A.) Stockton Presbytery, Sacramento, Calif., 1985-85; supr., instruction support svcs., dir. community relations Calif. State U., Stanislaus, 1985—; cons. Hispanic Ministries, Presbyn Ch. (USA) Stockton, 1984—, Palm Springs, Calif., 1987; bd. dirs. Coun. for the Spanish Speaking; rsch. assoc. Louisville Presbyn. Theol. Sem. Del. State Dem. Cen. Com. Assembly, Dist. 26, 1989—; corr. sec. Comite Patriotico, 1987-88; city civil service commr., City Coun,; v.p. Stockton Hispanic Regional Found.; chaplain, Stockton Police Dept.; chair, Edni. Equity Adv. Coun., Calif. State U., Stanislaus, 1986-88; bd. dirs United Way, San Josquin, Calif. Mem. Nat. Coun. Churches (governing bd. 1986-88). Democrat. Presbyterian. Office: Calif State U/ Stanislaus 5151 Pacific Ave Locke 119 Stockton CA 95209

MARTINEZ, JOHN STANLEY, aerospace engineer; b. Phila., Apr. 14, 1930; s. Joseph Vincent and Helen Leeds (Simpson) M.; m. Britta K. Ponder, Dec. 29, 1987; children: John Jr., Joseph G., Mary Lynn. BChemE, Rensselaer Poly. Inst., 1951; diploma, Oak Ridge Sch.Tech., 1957; PhD, U. Calif., Berkeley, 1962. Rsch. engr. N.Am. Aviation Co., Santa Suzanna, Calif., 1954-55, Jet Propulsion Lab., Calif. Inst. Tech., Pasadena, Calif., 1955-61; rsch. asst. Livermore (Calif.) Nat. Lab., 1959-61; with TRW Systems Group, Redondo Beach, Calif., 1961-76, mgr. high energy laser bus. area, 1970-76; pres. Physics Internat. Co., San Leandro, Calif., 1976-84, Jamar Enterprises, Moraga, Calif., 1970—, HLX Laser Inc., San Diego, 1986-87, Jamar Tech. Co., San Diego, 1987—, Air-Sea Communications Corp., San Diego, 1988—; supervisory dir. Pisces Internat., Netherlands, 1982-84; pres., chmn. Hermosa Entertainment Corp., Hermosa Beach, Calif., 1969-72. Contbr. articles to profl. publs.; patentee in field. Chmn. Hermosz Beach City Improvement Commn., 1968-70. Capt. USMC, 1951-54, Korea. AEC fellow, 1958, Ford Found. fellow, 1960. Mem. IEEE, Sigma Xi, Tau Beta Pi. Home: PO Box 1030 Del Mar CA 92014 Office: 3956 Sorrento Valley Blvd San Diego CA 92014

MARTINEZ, LARRY FRANK, educator; b. Covina, Calif., July 16, 1953; s. Frank Robert and Lois Margaret (Weber) M.; m. Catherine Mary Boggs, July 9, 1988. AA in Liberal Arts, Cuesta Coll., San Luis Obispo, Calif., 1973; BA in Polit. Sci., U. Calif., Santa Barbara, 1975, MA in Polit. Sci., 1978, PhD in Polit. Sci., 1984. Assoc. lectr. dept. polit. sci. U. Calif., Santa Barbara, 1981-83; vis. lectr. dept. polit. sci. Calif. State U., Fullerton, 1984-85; vis. asst. prof. dept. polit. sci. Calif. State U., Long Beach, 1988—; adj. lectr. SUNY, Albany, 1986, George Washington U., Washington, 1986-87; internat. policy analyst nat. telecommunications adminstrn. U.S. Dept. Commerce, Washington, 1985-87; internat. policy analyst office comml. space transp. U.S. Dept. Transp., Washington, 1987-88; space industry specialist U.S. Dept. Commerce, Washington, 1989; cons. to space and telecommunications firms, 1988—. Author: Communications Satellites: Power Politics in Space, 1985; contbr. articles to profl. jours. German Academic Exch. grantee, 1982, Grad. Inst. of Internat. Studies fellow, 1978-79. Mem. Assn. of U.S. Members of Internat. Inst. of Space Law (sec. 1988—), Am. Polit. Sci. Assn., Internat. Studies Assn. Democrat. Office: Calif State U Dept Polit Sci 1250 Bellflower Blvd Long Beach CA 90840

MARTINEZ, MATTHEW GILBERT, congressman; b. Walsenburg, Colo., Feb. 14, 1929; children: Matthew, Diane, Susan, Michael, Carol Ann. Cert of competence, Los Angeles Trade Tech. Sch., 1959. Small businessman and bldg. contracto; mem. 97th-101st Congresses from 30th Calif. dist., 1980—. Mem. Monterey Park Planning Commn., 1971-74; mayor City of Monterey park, 1974-75; mem. Monterey Park City Council, 1974-80, Calif. State Assembly, 1980-82; bd. dirs. San Gabriel Valley YMCA. Served with USMC, 1947-50. Mem. Congl. Hispanic Caucus, Hispanic Am. Democrats, Nat. Assn. Latino Elected and Apptd. Ofcls., Communications Workers Am., VFW, Am. Legion, Latin Bus. Assn., Monterey Park C. of C., Navy League (dir.). Democrat. Lodge: Rotary. Office: 240 Cannon House Office Bldg Washington DC 20515 *

MARTINEZ, ROBERT ASA, construction executive; b. Raton, N.Mex., July 7, 1943; s. George Robert and Helen Marie (West) M.; m. Sharon Ann Morrison, Feb. 4, 1974; children: Courtney, Robert Travis, Alyson, Jessica. BBA, N.Mex. State U., 1965, MBA, 1967. V.p. Nat. Econ. Devel. Assn., Los Angeles, 1971-75; program mgr. SBA, Washington, 1975-76; asst. regional dir. SBA, Denver, 1976-77; pres. Martinez-Alvarado Constrn., Denver, 1977-79, Great Southwestern Constrn. Inc., Castle Rock, Colo., 1980—; sec. Colo. Power Council, Denver, 1987-88; mem. Tech. Hazard Liquid Pipeline Com., Washington, 1987-88; v.p. CBM Inc., Denver, 1987—. Active U.S. Senate Task Force on Hispanic Affairs, 1988; chmn. Douglas County Rep. Com., 1983-84; state chmn. Rep. Nat. Hispanic Assembly, Denver, 1979-85, exec. com., Washington, 1987; guardian Nat. Fedn. Ind. Bus., Denver, 1987; exec. com. Ind. Inst., Golden, Colo., 1987. Served to capt. U.S. Army, 1967-70, Vietnam. Decorated Bronze Star, Honor medal Republic of South Vietnam, 1970, Vietnam Service and Campaign medal, U.S. Army, 1970. Mem. Power & Communications Contractors Assn., Colo. Assn. Commerce & Industry (50 for Colo. award 1987), Southwest Bus. Network (chmn. 1987, annual award 1987), VFW, KC. Roman Catholic. Home: 29 Oakridge Dr Castle Rock CO 80104 Office: Gt Southwestern Constrn Inc 511 S Gilbert St Castle Rock CO 80104

MARTINEZ, RUBEN MARTIN, senior logistics engineer; b. L.A., Mar. 12, 1948; s. Elias and Emma Louise (Jurado) M.; m. Deanna Jean Rein, May 1969 (div. 1976); children: Ruben Jr., Victor; m. Linn Ann Hampton, Apr. 5, 1980; children: Michael, Martin, Linnita, Loretta. AA in Bus., Rio Hondo Coll., 1973; AA in Logistics, BA in Computer System, Nat. U. Registered engr., Calif. Sr. data analyst Continental Data Graphics, Culver City, Calif., 1972-79; provisioning engr. Hughes Aircraft, Ground Systems, Fullerton, Calif., 1979-83; sr. logistics engr. Rockwell Internat., Anaheim, Calif., 1983-87; sr. tech. writer B-2 div. Northrop Corp., Pico-Rivera, Calif., 1987—. Officer Civil Air Patrol, Compton, Calif., 1984. Mem. Soc. Logistics Engr., Am. Defense Preparedness Assn., Nat. Mgmt. Assn., KC. Republican. Roman Catholic. Home: 9605 Armley Ave Whittier CA 90604

MARTINEZ Y FERRER, MARCELINO CODILLA, JR., hospital official; b. San Francisco, Sept. 28, 1947; s. Jacinta (Codilla) M. y F. BA, Calif. State U., Sacramento, 1972; BS, U. Md., 1986; postgrad. pub. adminstrn., Calif. State U., 1986—. Adminstrv. asst. Sacramento County, Sacramento, 1970-72; elections supr. Yolo County (Calif.), 1972-73; supr. mil. personnel Naval Hosp., Camp Pendleton, Calif., 1974-76; supr. psychiat. unit. Naval Hosp., Subic Bay, The Philippines, 1976-78, Oakland, Calif., 1978-84, Okinawa, Japan, 1984-86; asst. coord. med. credentials Naval Hosp., Oakland, 1986—; cons. joint legis. com. on aging Calif. Assembly, 1970-74, adminstrv. asst. to speaker, 1973-74; bd. dirs., cons. Toyo Corp., Tokyo and Manila, 1974—. Sustaining mem. Rep. Nat. Com., 1980—; mem. Rep. Presdl. Task Force, 1980—, Calif Rep. League, 1986—, Rep. Congl. Leadership Coun., 1989—. Recipient Order of Merit, Pres. U.S., 198l, Medal of Merit U.S. Pres. George Bush, 1989. Mem. Am. Acad. Polit. Sci., Am. Acad. Social and Polit. Sci., Wilson Ctr., Am. Legion, Asian/Pacific Students Union (treas. 1978-80, Calif. State Filipino coordinating com. 1970-73), Commonwealth Club, Phi Kappa Phi, Pi Sigma Alpha, Psi Chi, Sigma Phi Epsilon, Phi Alpha Theta. Republican. Roman Catholic. Office: Naval Hosp Credentials 8750 Mountain Blvd Oakland CA 94627-5000

MARTIN-HALL, PATRICIA JEAN, educator; b. San Francisco, Sept. 30, 1949; d. William Edward and Rosemary Patricia (Casey) M. RDA, Northwest Coll., W. Covina, Calif., 1968. Cert. community coll. tchr., Colo. Dental asst. Ronald Schrader DDS, Riverside, Calif., 1969-71; instr. Colo. Coll. of Med. and Dental Asst., Denver, 1971-73; office mgr. RDA Robert M. Bley, DDS, San Diego, 1973-80; instr. Pacific Coll. of Med. and Dental Careers, San Diego, 1980-82, mem. adv. bd., 1986-88; co-owner PFI Personnel Svc., San Diego, 1982-87; nat. sales mgr. The James Wittmack Collections, LaJolla, Calif., 1987-88; instr., acting dir. Apollo Coll. Med. and Dental Careers, San Diego, 1988—; edn. dir. Calif. Acad. of Registered Dental Assts., San Diego, 1977-79; sec. Nat. Assn. of Women Bus. Owners, San Diego, 1985-87; adv. bd. Cabrillo Sch. of Nursing, San Diego, 1986. Republican. Roman Catholic. Home: 15246 Avenida Rorras San Diego CA 92128

MARTINI, ARTHUR PETE, manufacturing company executive; b. El Paso, Sept. 19, 1943; s. Arthur Peter and Beatrice (Kleinman) M.; m. Linda Louise Fowler, July 11, 1968 (div. 1983); children: Russell Robert, James Dale, Bradwell Peter. BS in Anthropology, U. Oreg., 1972, postgrad., 1975-76. With Harold Club, Reno, 1966-68; salesman Cougill & Hansen Realtors, Eugene, Oreg., 1972-76; v.p. Duco-Lam, Inc., Drain, Oreg., 1976-77, pres., chief exec. officer, 1977-81; pres., chief exec. officer Am. Laminators, Inc., Eugene, 1982—. Mem. exec. bd. Boy Scouts Am., Eugene, 1980—, coun. City of Yoncalla, Oreg., 1980-81; active Rep. Party, Portland, Oreg. With U.S. Army, 1962-65. Mem. Am. Inst. Timber Constrn. (bd. dirs. 1979-86, pres. 1984-85), Pres's. Assn. N.Y., Eugene Athletic Club, Rotary (community svc. chmn. 1984—), Elks. Home: 403 Alder St PO Box 336 Yoncalla OR 97499 Office: Am Laminators Inc 1839 Garden Ave Eugene OR 97403

MARTINI, EMIL P., JR., wholesale pharmaceutical distribution company executive; b. Teaneck, N.J., 1928. Grad., Purdue U., 1950. With Bergen Brunswig Corp., Los Angeles, 1952—, now chmn., chief exec. officer; pres., mgr. Bergen Drug Co. div., Los Angeles, 1956-69, corp. pres., chief exec. officer, from 1969, also dir.; dir. Bro-Dart Industries. Office: Commtron Corp 1501 50th St West Des Moines IA 50265 also: Bergen Brunswig Corp 4000 Metropolitan Dr Orange CA 92668 *

MARTINI, ROBERT E., wholesale pharmaceutical and electronic products company executive; b. Hackensack, N.J., 1932. B.S., Ohio State U., 1954. With Bergen Brunswig Corp., Orange, Calif., 1956—, v.p., 1962-69, exec. v.p., 1969-81, pres., chief operating officer, dir., 1981—, now chmn. exec. com., pres., dir.; also chmn., dir. Bergen Brunswig Drug Co., Orange, Calif. Served to capt. USAF, 1954. Office: Bergen Brunswig Corp 4000 Metropolitan Dr Orange CA 92668

MARTINO, FRANK, physicist, university provost; b. Boston, Apr. 10, 1937; s. Giuseppe and Anna (Oster) M.; married; 1 child, Carlo Bartolomeo. AB, Harvard U., Cambridge, 1959; MS, U. Ill., 1961; PhD, MIT, 1966. Rsch. assoc. MIT, Cambridge, 1966-67, Uppsala U., Sweden, 1967-68; prof. physics CCNY, 1968-87, dean sci., 1981-87; prof. physics, provost Portland State U., Oreg., 1987—. Contbr. numerous articles to profl. jours. Mem. Am. Phys. Soc. (chmn. com. internat. sci. affairs 1988—), Am. Assn. Univ. Adminstrs. (bd. dirs.). Office: Portland State U Office of Provost PO Box 751 Portland OR 97207

MARTINS, DONALD HENRY, astrophysics educator, researcher; b. Poplar Bluff, Mo., July 31, 1945; s. Otto Henry and Winnifred Fanny (Bellamy) M.; m. Joyce Ann Stoecklein, Aug. 1, 1969; 1 child, Winifred M. BS, U. Mo., 1967; MS, U. Md., 1969; PhD, U. Fla., 1974. Rsch. assoc. NASA and NRC, Houston, 1974-76; instr. U. St. Thomas, Houston, 1976-77; asst. prof. U. Ga., Athens, 1977-82; asst. prof. astrophysics U. Alaska, Anchorage, 1982-83, assoc. prof., 1983—. Contbr. articles to profl. jours. With U.S. Army, 1968-69. MMem. Am. Phys. Soc., Am. Astron. Soc., Internat. Astron. Union, Astron. Soc. Pacific, Am. Orchid Soc., Phi Kappa Phi. Home: 6020 Craig Dr Anchorage AK 99504 Office: U Alasks Physics-Astronomy 32ll Providence Dr Anchorage AK 99508

MARTINS, EVELYN MAE, theatre owner; b. Salinas, Calif., June 12, 1929; d. Earl Baldwin and Esther Martine (Harding) Andersen; m. Nolan Anthony Martins, Aug. 20, 1946 (dec. June 1982); children: Dennis, Noelyn, Antonette, Darrin. Owner Skyview Drive-In Theatres, Salinas, 1948—. Mem. Nat. Assn. Theatre Owners, Showest (Calif. Woman Exhibitor of Yr. 1976), Variety Club, Jr. Women's Club (publicity dir. 1965-67), Optimist Youth Found. (treas. 1966-68). Republican. Roman Catholic. Home and Office: Skyview Drive-In Theatres 201 Harrison Rd Salinas CA 93907-1612

MARTINSON, CONSTANCE FRYE, television program hostess, producer; b. Boston, Apr. 11, 1932; d. Edward and Rosalind Helen (Sperber) Frye; m. Leslie Herbert Martinson, Sept. 24, 1955; 1 child, Julianna Martinson Carner. BA in English Lit., Wellesley Coll., 1953. Dir. pub. relations Coro Found., Los Angeles, 1974-79; producer/host KHJ Dimensions, Los Angeles, 1979-81, Connie Martinson Talks Books, Los Angeles, 1981—; instr. dept. humanities UCLA, 1981—; celebrity advisor Book Fair-Music Ctr., Los Angeles, 1986. Author Dramatization of Wellesley After Images, 1974; book editor, columnist Calif. Press Bur. Syndicate, 1986—. Pres. Mayor's adv. council on volunteerism, Los Angeles, 1981-82; chmn. community affairs dept. Town Hall of Calif., Los Angeles, 1981-85; bd. dirs. legal def. fund NAACP, Los Angeles, 1981-84. Mem. Women in Cable, Am. Film Inst., Jewish TV Network (bd. dirs. 1985-87). Democrat. Jewish. Clubs: Wellesley Coll. (pres. 1979-81), Mulholland Tennis. Home and Office: 2288 Coldwater Canyon Blvd Beverly Hills CA 90210

MARTINSON, JOHN ROBERT, oil company executive; b. Chgo., Sept. 9, 1935; s. Warren Charles Martinson and Jane (Martin) Finlayson; m. Kathryn Hellyer, June 14, 1958 (div. Dec. 1970); children: Kate, Robert, Johanna; m. Patricia Richardson, Nov. 17, 1973 (div. Sept. 1981); children: Erik, Torgen; m. Jaclyn Norwood, Aug. 30, 1986; 1 stepson, Jack Thomas. BSE, Princeton U., 1957; MBA, Northwestern U., Chgo., 1959. Planning assoc. Mobil Oil Corp., N.Y.C., 1959-62, 65-66, London, 1967-69; stockbroker Kidder Peabody & Co., N.Y.C., 1962-65, Oppenheimer & Co., N.Y.C., 1969-73; owner Hawthorne Exploration Co., N.Y.C., 1973—; owner MVP, Ketchum, Idaho, 1984—, also bd. dirs.; owner, mng. dir. Wood Roberts & Co., Ketchum, 1988—; v.p. Parker Technology, Houston, 1988—, also bd. dirs.; owner Hawthorne Exploration Co., Ketchum, 1988—. Inventor radio controlled electric load mgmt. Bd. dirs. Boise (Idaho) Philharmonic Assn., 1988—. Mem. Vikings of Scandia. Republican.

Presbyterian. Home: 161 Laurel Ln Ketchum ID 83340 Office: Wood Roberts & Co 620 Sun Valley Rd Box 1017 Ketchum ID 83340

MARTINSON, JOHN SIROTA, tea company executive; b. N.Y.C., Jan. 27, 1954; s. Paul and Frances Sirota (Steyer) M. Grad. high sch., Avon, Conn. Pres. Martinson Dist. Co., Inc., Scottsdale, Ariz., 1979-82, Restaurant Tea Svc., Inc., Scottsdale, 1982—, China Mist Tea Co. Inc., Scottsdale, 1982—. Mem. Gov.'s Task Force on State Parks and Recreation, Phoenix, 1980-81. Mem. Phoenix City Club (bd. dirs. 1986-87). Democrat.

MARTINSON, JULIA ELLENOR, health science administrator; b. Paso Robles, Calif., May 1, 1951; d. John Elwyn and Betty Jeanne (Fruehling) M. BA in Journalism, U. Nev., 1973, BA in Phys. Edn., 1976. Store mgr. S. S. White, Reno, 1979, Kelly Dental Supply Co., Reno, 1979-81; office mgr. Fine Arts Dental Studio, Reno, 1981-88; sec., treas. Superior Dental Lab. Inc., Reno, 1988—. treas. Campus Christian Assn., 1987-88; mgr. Reno Royals, 1979-88. Mem. Women's Softball Alumni Assn. (treas. 1983— U. Nev. Reno chpt.), U. Nev. BoostHers (v.p. 1986—), Campus Christian Assn. (treas. 1986—), U. Nev. Boosters (treas. 1987-88). Democrat. Episcopalian. Home: 1600 Idlewild #5 Dr Reno NV 89509 Office: Superior Dental Lab Inc 190 Mill St Ste 5 Reno NV 89501

MARTYN, LINDA LABONTE, human resources executive; b. Salem, Mass., Apr. 5, 1961; d. C.Joseph and Donna Marie (Chiaradonna) LaBonte; m. Patrick A. Martyn, May 21, 1983 (div. 1989); 1 child, Jennifer Nicole. Student, El Camino Coll., L.A., 1983-85, Antioch U., L.A., 1988—. Pers. asst. 20th Century-Fox Film Corp., L.A., 1982-83; adminstrv. mgr. McCormack & Dodge Corp., L.A., 1983-85; event planner Le Bon Event!, L.A., 1984—; human resources specialist Imperial Corp. Am., L.A., 1988—; coord. bridal show So. Calif. Wedding Assn., L.A., 1985-87; mem. bus. devel. com. Wedding and Spl. Event Assn., L.A., 1987-88. Guest, TV program, 1988. Republican. Roman Catholic. Home: 7515 Winnetka Ave #106 Canoga Park CA 91306 Office: Le Bon Event 800 S Pacific Coast Hwy 8-213 Redondo Beach CA 90277-4778

MARTYN, ROBERT GORDON, human resource management consultant; b. Weiser, Idaho, Aug. 15, 1930; s. Bernard S. and Florence E. (Turner) M.; m. Dolores A. Sorenson, Nov. 24, 1950 (div. 1974); children: Linda, Kathryn, Tamara; m. Donna M. Harwood, Dec. 9, 1980. BA in Sociology and Math., Linfield Coll., 1952, MEd, 1959. Profl. baseball player N.Y. Yankees and Kansas City Athletics, 1952-60; employment specialist Tektronix, Inc., Beaverton, Oreg., 1961-62, mgr. salary adminstrn., 1963-68, mgr. employment, 1969-71; mgr. personnel ops. Tektronix, Inc., Beaverton, 1972-73, personnel dir., 1973-76, mgr. indsl. rels., 1977-83; pres., sr. cons. Sloan Silver Floren Martyn, Inc., Portland, 1983—; mem. human resource mgmt. adv. bd. Commerce Clearing House, Inc., Chgo., 1982—. Com. resource person Oreg. Ho. of Reps., Salem, 1977-83. With U.S. Army, 1952-54. Mem. Am. Soc. for Personnel Adminstrn. (accredited exec. in personnel, com. chmn. 1980-83), Assoc. Oreg. Industries (com. chmn. 1986—). Republican. Baptist. Office: 13535 NW Science Park Dr Portland OR 97229

MARTZ, CARL SCOTT, aerospace engineer; b. Grand Rapids, Mich., June 18, 1958; s. Kenneth Wayne and Edwina Pauline (Goodheart) M. BS in Biol. Sci., U. Calif., Irvine, 1981; cert. in artificial intelligence, UCLA, 1987. Mem. tech. staff Rockwell Internat., Downey, Calif., 1981—. judge Los Angeles Sci. Fair, 1984, 85. Mem. Nat. Space Soc., Smithsonian Inst., U. Calif. Irvine Century Club. Democrat. Home: 21513 Juan Ave #2 Haw Gardens CA 90716 Office: Rockwell Internat 12214 Lakewood Blvd MLS FA19 Downey CA 90241

MARVIT, ROBERT CHARLES, psychiatrist; b. Lynn, Mass., Jan. 23, 1938. BS summa cum laude, Mass. Coll. Pharmacy, 1960; MD, Tufts U., 1964; M.Sc., Harvard U., 1970. Intern New Eng. Med. Ctr., Pratt Diag. Hosp., 1964-65; resident in psychiatry, neuropsychol. medicine Mass. Gen. Hosp., Boston, 1967-70; pvt. practice medicine, specializing psychiatry Honolulu, 1970—; prof. pub. health U. Hawaii, Honolulu, 1974-78, adj. prof. Sch. Pub. Health, 1978—; forensic advisor Hawaii Mental Health Div., 1977—; dir. Health Info. Sys. Office, Dept. Health, 1976-80; cons. in field; lectr. in field. Contbr. articles to profl. jours. Served with USPHS, 1965-67 to lt. comdr. Recipient Alpha Omega Alpha Research award Tufts U., 1963. Fellow Am. Coll. Preventive Medicine, Internat. Soc. Social Psychiatry of Am. Pub. Health Assn., Am. Psychiat. Soc.; mem. Am. Acad. Psychiatry and the Law, Hawaii Psychiat. Soc., AAAS, Harvard Med. Soc., Boston Soc. Neurology and Psychiatry, Hawaii Neurol. Soc.,. Internat. Soc. Neurosci., Am. Acad. Forensic Psychiatry, Alpha Omega Alpha. Home: 929 Pueo St Honolulu HI 96816 Office: 1314 S King St Ste 1463 Honolulu HI 96814

MARX, NICKI D., sculptor; b. L.A., Oct. 3, 1943; d. Donald F. and Ruth H. (Ungar) M.; m. Jonathan H. Rice, Sept. 3, 1983. BA in Philosophy, U. Calif., Riverside, 1965; postgrad., U. Calif., Santa Cruz, 1973. One-woman shows include Rocklands Gallery, Monterey, Calif., 1983, Kirk De Gooyer Gallery, L.A., 1982, Weston Gallery, Carmel, Calif., 1981, Phoenix Art Mus., 1975, Julie Artisans Gallery, N.Y.C., 1975, Palm Springs Desert Mus., 1977, others; group exhbns. include Jordan Gallery, Taos, N.Mex., 1988, Stables Art Gallery, Taos, 1988, Fetish Gallery, Taos, 1988, Albuquerque State Fair Grounds, 1986, San Francisco Mus. Modern Art, 1977, 78, The Elements Gallery, Greenwich, Conn., 1977, Pacific Design Ctr., L.A., 1976, Lester Gallery, Inverness, Calif., 1976, numerous others; work included in sixteen invitational shows; represented in pvt. collections IBM, Milford, Conn., N.Y.C., San Jose, Calif., Bank of Am., San Francisco, The Continental Group, Inc., Stamford, Conn., Cedars-Sinai Hosp., L.A., Farm Bur. Fedn., Sacramento, Calif., Sherman Fairchild Sci. Ctr., Stanford, Calif., Palm Springs (Calif.) Desert Mus., Univ. Mus., Ariz. State U. at Tempe, Mills Coll. Art Gallery, Berkeley, Calif.; exhibited in pvt. collections of Eugene Klein, Estate of Louise Nevelson, Estate of Georgia O'Keeffe, Fritz Scholder, Ray Graham, Bunny Horowitz, Sue and Otto Meyer, Burt Sugarman, Craig Moody, Paul Pletka, others; subject of numerous articles in jours. and mags. MacDowell Colony fellow, 1975. Home: PO Box 1135 Ranchos de Taos NM 87557

MARXMILLER, HUGH O'NEIL, food products executive; b. Danville, Ill., Jan. 13, 1930; s. Homer and Ora Lee (Spears) M.; m. Linda Nehls, Sept. 14, 1962, (div. Dec. 1976); m. Patricia Ann Bean, Nov. 15, 1986; children: Laurie Lynn, Lisa Ann, Jason O'Neil, Douglas Phillips, Kimberly Phillips. BA in Bus., L.A. State U., 1965; data system specialist, Nortronics, Van Nuys, Calif., 1970. Ops. control chief Calif. Inst. Tech.-JPL, Pasadena, 1954-72; data systems mgr. Ralph M. Parsons Co., Pasadena, 1974-86; pres., owner South Fork BBQ Catering Co., Newhall, Calif., 1986—; surveyor spacecraft ops. control team, NASA, Jet Propulsion Lab, 1965, mariner spacecraft ops. control team, NASA, Jet Propulsion Lab, 1966. Inventor heart rate pulse counter, 1958; special BBQ sauce, (1st place award 1988). Cpl. USMC, 1952-54, Korea. Republican. Home: 24658 Sagecrest Cir Newhall CA 91321

MARYLANDER, STUART JEROME, hospital administrator; b. Oakland, Calif., Nov. 13, 1931; s. Philip and Lilyan (Wolf) M.; m. Judith Rosenblatt, June 3, 1956; children: Steven Mark, Grant. M.P.H. in Hosp. Adminstrn, U. Calif.-Berkeley, 1956. Research asst. med. care adminstrn. Sch. Pub. Health, U. Calif.-Berkeley, 1955-56; adminstrv. resident Mt. Zion Hosp., San Francisco, 1956-57; asst. adminstr. Cedars of Lebanon Hosp., Los Angeles, 1957-62; adminstr. Mt. Sinai Hosp. div. Cedars-Sinai Med. Center, Los Angeles, 1963-64; adminstrv. dir. center Mt. Sinai Hosp. div. Cedars-Sinai Med. Center, 1964-66, asso. exec. dir. and adminstrv. dir., 1967-71, exec. dir., 1971-74, exec. v.p., 1974-78, pres., 1979-88; vice chmn. of Bd., Hosp. Ops. Nu-Med. Inc., Encino, Calif., 1989—; instr. U. So. Calif. Sch. Pub. Adminstrn., 1965-70. Bd. dirs. Commn. Adminstrv. Services to Hosps., 1967-76; bd. dirs. Hosp. Council So. Calif., 1968-76, pres., 1975-76; chmn. Council Teaching Hosps., 1980-81, mem. adminstrv. bd., 1977-82. Served with AUS, 1953-55. Fellow Am. Pub. Health Assn., Royal Soc. of Health (Eng.), Am. Coll. Hosp. Adminstrs.; mem. Am. Hosp. Assn. (, bd. trustees 1987—, rep. to ho. of dels. 1983-88), Calif. Hosp. Assn. (dir. 1974-80, chmn. 1979), Assn. Am. Med. Colls. (mem. assembly 1977-82, exec. council 1979-82), Nat. Assn. Biomed. Research (bd. dirs. 1986—), Internat. Hosp. Fedn., Blue Cross of Calif. (bd. dirs. 1987—), Sigma Alpha Mu.

MARZANO, MARYANN ROSE, lawyer; b. N.Y.C., Dec. 2, 1955; d. Anthony Michael and Ann Rose (Florio) M. BA, Rutgers U., 1977; JD, Pepperdine U., 1980. Bar: Calif. 1980, U.S. Dist. Ct. (cen. dist.) Calif. 1981, U.S. Ct. Appeals (9th cir.) 1982. Assoc. Miller & Nolan, Inc., Beverly Hills, Calif., 1980-83, Haight, Dickson, Brown & Bonesteel, Santa Monica, Calif., 1983-85; from assoc. to ptnr. Finley, Kumble, Wanger, Heine, Underberg, Manley et al., Beverly Hills, 1985-87; ptnr. Charlston, Revich & Williams, L.A., 1988—; bd. dirs. Woodcraft Rangers, L.A. Vol. Calif. Legal Aid Soc., L.A., 1984-85, 87. Mem. ABA, L.A. County Bar Assn. (vol. Domestic Violence Project 1987), Woman Lawyer's Assn. Am. Office: Charlston Revich & Williams 2049 Century Park E 42nd Fl Los Angeles CA 90067

MASCARENAS, ALBERTO LUCERO, junior high school educator; b. Salinas, Calif., Aug. 14, 1952; s. Juan Indalecio and Marie Rita (Lucero) M.; m. Etta Delgado, Oct. 22, 1977; children: Xavier, Alberto, Ana, Sofia, Jennifer. Student, Monterey Pen. Coll., 1970-71, U. Md., 1974-76, San Jose State U., 1976-80; BS in Liberal Arts, SUNY, Albany, 1987. Secondary teaching credential. Organizer United Farmworkers AFL-CIO, Chgo., 1971-73; race relations instr. U.S. Army, West Germany, 1973-76; child care ctr. dir. Mexican Am. Community Svcs. Agy., San Jose, Calif., 1977; counselor Am. G.I. Forum, San Jose, 1978; driver Greyhound Lines, San Francisco, 1980-81; support counselor Ctr. for Employment Tng., San Jose, 1983; mgr. Phoenix Books & Espresso Cafe, San Jose, Calif., 1983-85; tchr. Migrant Edn. Pajaro Valley Unified Sch. Dist., Watsonville, Calif., 1987-88, S. Valley Jr. High SCh. Gilroy Unified Sch. Dist., Gilroy, Calif., 1988—. Editor Mestizo Forum. Mem. NEA, Nat. Council for Self-Esteem, Assn. Mexican Am. Educators, Mensa. Home: 104 Montebello Dr Watsonville CA 95076 Office: South Valley Jr High Sch 7663 Church St Gilroy CA 95020

MASCHA, ALFRED RICHARD, marketing executive; b. N.Y.C., Sept. 10, 1931; s. Alfred and Viola M.; m. Olive E. Moore, June 21, 1969. BBA, Toledo U., 1975; MBA, Cen. Mich. U., 1984. Mgr. field engring. parts and supplies Burroughs Corp., Detroit, 1975-77, mgr. field engring. ops. planning, 1977-80, dir. advanced svc. devel., 1983-84; mgr. western region, field engring. Burroughs Corp., Newport Beach, Calif., 1980-81; mgr. western region, customer svc. and support Burroughs Corp., Irvine, Calif., 1981-83; v.p. Nat. Advanced Systems, Santa Clara, Calif., 1984—. Mem. Assn. Field Svc. Mgrs. Internat. (pres. 1983-84, bd. dirs. 1985-88). Republican. Lutheran. Home: 5982 Via Del Cielo Pleasanton CA 94566 Office: Nat Advanced Systems 750 Central Expwy Santa Clara CA 95052

MASDEN, FRANK DOLAN, JR., accountant; b. Kansas City, Mo., Aug. 3, 1931; s. Frank Dolan and Allee (Young) M.; m. Barbara Jeanette Schall, Oct. 13, 1962; children: John Andrew, Jeanette Allee, James Elmer, Jayne Evaline. ABA, Kansas City Jr. Coll., 1950; BS, Cen. Meth. Coll., 1952; MA in Acctg., U. Mo., Columbia, 1955. CPA, Mo., Ariz. Staff acct. Touche, Ross & Co., CPAs, Kansas City, 1952-55, 1959; sr. acct. Touche, Ross & Co., CPAs, Denver, 1959-60; asst. to credit mgr. to mgr. spl. accounts The Vendo Co., Kansas City, 1961-67; mgr. gen. acctg., cost acctg. Misco Div. Howard Corp., Muskegon, Mich., 1967-71; founder, pres. Masden and Green, P.C., Lake Havasu City, Ariz., 1972—; mem. faculty Mohave Community Coll., Lake Havasu City, 1975-88; mem. adv. bd. Mera Bank, Lake Havasu City, 1982—; bd. dirs. Community Coll. Campus Found., Lake Havasu City. Chmn. Bond Election of Sch. Consolidation City Coun., Lake Havasu City, 1978-79; v.p. So. dist. Boulder Dam Area Coun. Boy Scouts Am., Las Vegas, Nev., 1986— (Silver Beaver award, 1984); elected Rep. Precinct Com., Mohave County, Lake Havasu City, 1988. Cpl. U.S. Army, 1952-54. Mem. AICPA, Am. Assn. Accts., Rotary. Republican. Presbyterian. Home: 2725 Empress Ct Lake Havasu City AZ 86403 Office: Masden and Green PC 2240 McCulloch Blvd Lake Havasu City AZ 86403

MASILAMONEY, SAM, not-for-profit foundation administrator, minister; b. Palayamkottai, Madras, India, May 17, 1944; came to U.S., 1977; s. Thachanamoorthi and Nancy (Arumainayagam) Thangiah; m. Leona Pushpa Prasangi, Dec. 29, 1970; children: Bonnie Josephine, Daniel Paul. BS, U. Madras, 1965; ThD, Calcutta Bible Coll., India, 1970; BTh, Allahabad Bible Sem., India, 1975; DD, Am. Bible Sem., 1979; PhD, Western Evang. Sch. Theology, 1985. Area dir. Collegiate Ambassadors, Calcutta, 1970-75; missions dir. N.Am. Evangelistic Assn., Everett, Wash., 1976-79; founder, dir. Op. India Internat., Watsonville, Calif., 1979—; asst. supt. N.Am. Evangelistic Assn., 1979—; prof. San Jose Bible Coll., Calif., 1986. Author: Christ Changed My Karma, 1971; editor Action mag., 1972. Pastor home mission dept. East Indian Bapt. Mission So. Bapt. Conv.; bd. dirs. Multi-cultural Mission of San Jose Bible Coll. Mem. Evang. for Social Action, Am. Coun. of Counselors and Educators. Lodge: Rotary (editor newsletter Asanol, India chpt. 1977, chmn. 3H program Kailua-Kona, Hawaii chpt. 1978). Home: 18C Bent Tree Ct Watsonville CA 95076 Office: Op India Internat Inc PO Box 7521 San Jose CA 95150

MASINI, JERRY DAVID, real estate developer; b. Cin., July 18, 1954; s. Anthony Frances and Eura Nunley (Gay) M. BA in History, U. Nev., 1976. Grad. Realtors Inst. Realtor Sahara Realtors, Las Vegas, 1978-82; realtor Award Realty, Las Vegas, 1982-89, prodn. leader, 1989—; prodn. leader Sahara Realtors. Recipient Most Listings award Las Vegas Bd. Realtors, 1987. Mem. Nat. Assn. Real Estate Brokers, Nat. Bd. Realtors (mem. audit com., grievance com.), Nat. Assn. Realtors (cert., chmn. membership com. Las Vegas chpt.). Home: 7333 Mission Hills Las Vegas NV 89113 Office: Award Realty 801 S Rancho B2 Las Vegas NV 89106

MASKALL, MARTHA JOSEPHINE, executive recruiter; b. Kearny, N.J., Mar. 30, 1945; d. Charles Edgar and Mathilda (Comba) M. BA in Biology, Stanford U., 1966; MA, Duke U., 1969. Cert. data processor, 1979. Data base adminstr. Armco Steel, Ashland, Ky., 1972-74; project mgr. Rand Info. Systems, San Francisco, 1974-78; mgr. systems devel. Itel Corp., San Francisco, 1978-79; sales rep. Datacom ADR, San Francisco, 1980-81; systems engr. Four-Phase Systems, Sacramento, Calif., 1981-83; data processing recruiter Mgmt. Recruiters, Sacramento, 1983-86; executive recruiter Telos, Sacramento, 1986—; coord. data base series info sci. seminars Golden Gate U., 1979-80. NDEA fellow, 1966-68. Mem. Data Processing Mgmt. Assn. (program dir. 1980, 82, sec. 1983), NOW, Sierra Club, Toastmaster (v.p. 1985, pres. 1986, div. gov. 1987, speakers bur. 1988, Silver award 1987). Democrat. Home: 8456 Hidden Valley Circle Fair Oaks CA 95628 Office: Telos 106 K St Ste 310 Sacramento CA 95814

MASLIN, HARRY, music business executive; b. Phila., Apr. 4, 1948; s. Philip and Sarah (Jacobs) M.; m. Ada Allister, Mar. 4, 1985. Rec. engr. Regent Sound, N.Y.C., 1969-71; chief engr. Hit Factory Studios, N.Y.C., 1971-73, 74-75; rec. engr. Record Plant Studios, N.Y.C., 1973-74; record producer HRM Prodns., Hollywood, Calif., 1975—; co-owner, pres. Image Rec. Studios, Hollywood, 1983—. Recipient 20 gold and platinum records Rec. Industry Assn. of Am. Mem. Nat. Acad. Rec. Arts and Scis., ASCAP, Audio Engring. Soc. Office: Image Rec Studios 1020 N Sycamore Ave Hollywood CA 90038

MASOERO, ARTHUR ROGER, retired military officer; b. Seattle, Nov. 25, 1935; s. Arthur Joseph and Margaret M.; m. Celeste Suzann Moore, Aug. 24, 1957; children: Arthur R. Jr., Christina A., Anthony J. Student, U. Wash., 1953-58; diploma, U.S. Army War Coll., 1981. Commd. 2d lt. U.S. Army, 1958, advance through grades to col., Sept. 1980; instr. 6236th Res. Sch., Tacoma, 1970-74, sec., 1972-74, dept. commdt., 1974-77; dep. chief staff ops., intelligence 124th Res. Command, Ft. Lawton, Wash., 1977-80; sr. res. advisor Armor Ctr. & Sch., Ft. Knox, Ky., 1980-82, Tng. & Doctrine Command, Ft. Monroe, Va., 1982-85; sr. res. advisor Western Command, Ft. Shafter, Hawaii, 1985-88, ret., 1988. Patentee in field. Mem. Assn. U.S. Army, Res. Officers Assn. (Ft. Monroe chpt.), U.S. Army Armor Assn., Sr. Army Res. Comdrs. Assn., Phi Gamma Delta. Roman Catholic. Home: 240 C Dockside Dr Hampton VA 23669

MASON, ANTHONY HALSTEAD, real estate corporation officer, lawyer; b. N.Y.C., Dec. 23, 1938; s. Anthony Taylor and Margaret Adams (Halstead) M.; m. Brenda Lee Reingold, Sept. 3, 1962; children: Linda Gaye, David Anthony. BA, U. Denver, 1961, JD, 1965. Bar: Colo. 1965, Ariz. 1966. Atty. Ariz. Atty. Gen.'s Office, Phoenix, 1966-67, Maricopa County Atty.'s Office, Phoenix, 1967-69; ptnr. McCall & Mason, Phoenix, 1969-71, Mason, McCall & Ross, Phoenix, 1971-74, Mason & Ross, Phoenix, 1974-77, Carmichael, McClue, Stephens, Mason & Toles, Phoenix, 1977-78, Levy, Mason, Spector & Sherwood, Phoenix, 1978-84, Deltacor, Phoenix, 1984—; guest lectr., moot ct. judge Ariz. State U., Tempe; lectr. continuing legal edn. State Bar Ariz., 1978, Crittenden Real Estate Conf., 1984—. Chmn. City of Phoenix Planning Commn., 1974-76, Mayor's Task Force on Drug Abuse, Phoenix, 1987-88; pres. bd. dirs. Phoenix Symphony Assn., 1981-84; mem. steering com. Phoenix 40, 1988, 89; candidate for Gov. Ariz., 1986. Named Best Land Use Planner in U.S. Am. Soc. Planning Ofcls., 1975. Mem. Ariz. Bar Assn., Maricopa County Bar Assn. (pres. 1975-76), Plaza Club, University Club, Ariz. Club, Mansion Club. Democrat. Office: Deltacor 3300 N Central Ave Ste 2100 Phoenix AZ 85012

MASON, BENJAMIN JORDAN, soil scientist; b. Camden, Ark., May 5, 1935; s. Roy Markham Mason and Addie Olivia (Gardner) Stinnett; m. Virginia Marie Field, June 7, 1957 (div. Dec. 1969); children: Virginia, Fredrick; m. Rosemary Ann Miller, Apr. 6, 1974; children: Kathryn, Deborah, Todd. BS, U. Wash., 1957; MS, Oreg. State U., 1962, PhD, 1967. Cert. soil scientist, agronomist. Asst. in soils Oreg. State U., Corvallis, 1962-66; sect. chief USPHS, Las Vegas, 1966-69; cons. Batelle Meml. Inst., Las Vegas, 1969-71; div. dir. U.S. EPA, Research Triangle, N.C., 1971-72; mgr. Logos Corp., Moapa, Nev., 1974-76; prin. scientist Geomet Techs. Inc., Germantown, Md., 1977-81; owner ETHURA, Rockville (Md.) and Grants Pass (Oreg.), 1981—. Contbr. articles to profl. jours. Mem. Md. State Adv. Com. on Environ. Protection Plan, Balt., 1984-86; elder Ch. of Living Word, Grants Pass and Washington, 1979—. Capt. USMC, 1957-60; comdr. USPHS, 1966-69. Mem. Soil Sci. Soc. Am., Argonomy Soc. Am., Soc. Am. Foresters, Hazardous Materials Rsch. Inst. Republican. Home: 13785 N Applegate Rd Grants Pass OR 97527

MASON, BERT E., podiatrist; b. Ryderwood, Wash., Mar. 17, 1944; s. Jean Grenette and Bette Evelyn (Phillips) M.; m. Susan Renee Swenson, Dec. 28, 1977. BA with honors, U. Calif., San Diego, 1971; B in Basic Med. Sci., Calif. Coll. Podiatric Medicine, 1975; D Podiatric Medicine, Calif. Coll. Podiatric Med., 1977. Diplomate Am. Bd. Podiatric Surgery, Am. Bd. Podiatric Orthopedics. Pvt. practice Fairfield, Calif., 1977-79; chied podiatry sect., dir. podiatric residency VA Med. Ctr., Huntington, W.Va., 1983-87; pvt. practice San Diego, 1987—; asst. prof. podiatric surgery Ohio Coll. Podiatric Medicine, Cleve., 1984-87; asst. prof. dept. surgery and community medicine Marshall U. Sch. Medicine, Huntington, 1985-87; v.p. Smithsonian Med. Group. Alumni mem. scholarship com. U. Calif., San Diego, 1988—. Maj. U.S. Army, 1979-83. Luth. Hosp. Soc. scholar, 1968. Fellow Am. Coll. Foot Surgeons, Am. Coll. Foot Orthopedics, Am. Assn. Hosp. Podiatrists; mem. Am. Podiatric Med. Assn., AAAS, U. Calif. San Diego Alumni Assn. (bd. dirs.). Democrat. Home: 31249 Hiawatha Ct Temecula CA 92390 Office: Smith Hanna Med Group 3939 Iowa St San Diego CA 92104

MASON, CHARLES EDMOND (BUD MASON), property manager; b. Kamiah, Idaho, Dec. 11, 1938; s. Byron E. and Orla (Lucas) M.; m. Kathleen Burke, Feb. 21, 1976; children: Michael, Maureen. BSBA, U. Nev., 1962. Mgr. dept. store Diamonds div. Dayton Hudson, 1968-79; mgr. Broadway S.W. div. Carter Hawley, Phoenix, 1980-83; shopping ctr. mgr. Westcor, Phoenix, 1983—. Mem. Pilot Parents Assn. (bd. dirs.). Home: 46 W Verde Ln Tempe AZ 85284 Office: Paradise Valley Mall 4568 E Cactus Rd Phoenix AZ 85032

MASON, DAVID LAUN, gas company executive; b. Salt Lake City, July 21, 1943; s. Laun H. and Betty Jane (Ross) M.; m. Connie Criddle, Dec. 28, 1967; children: Anthony, Elizabeth, Katherine, Jonathan, Megan. BBA, U. Utah; postgrad., Brigham Young U. Ordained bishop Mormon Ch., 1988. Staff auditor Utah Power and Light Co., Salt Lake City, 1970-73; supr. staff auditor Mountain Fuel Supply co., Salt Lake City, 1973-76, dir. purchasing, warehousing, 1976-78, dir. materials, equipment and office services, 1978-80, mgmt. cons. in material mgmt., 1978-80; mgr. adminstrv. services Mountain Fuel Resources Inc., Salt Lake City, 1980—; mng. rep. Hometown Am. project, Am. Express; assoc. instr. U. Utah, Salt Lake City, 1975-78. Contbr. articles to profl. jours. Chmn. Rep. Voting Dist., Salt Lake City, 1988; councilman Holladay (Utah) Community, 1985, chmn. Holladay Boy's Baseball Assn., 1982-83; scoutmaster Boy Scouts Am., Holladay, 1984—; chmn. planning United Way, Greater Salt Lake, chmn. allocation coms. 1982—, chmn. mgmt. assistance programs, 1987—; mem. nat. bd. to determine local agy. for privatization of juvenile ct, 1987. Served as sgt. USNG, 1960-67. Recipient Community Avc. award, 1987; nominated Young Man of Yr., Jaycees, Salt Lake City, 1972. Mem. Pacific Coast Gas Assn. (chmn. materials mgmt. 1979-80), Am. Gas Assn. (chmn. materials mgmt. 1984-85), Salt Lake City Area C. of C. (edn. com. 1985-86, pres's. club 1982-86, pres. plaque 1983).,. Mormon. Office: Questar Pipeline Co 79 S State Salt Lake City UT 84147

MASON, DEAN TOWLE, cardiologist; b. Berkeley, Calif., Sept. 20, 1932; s. Ira Jenckes and Florence Mabel (Towle) M.; m. Maureen O'Brien, June 22, 1957; children: Kathleen, Alison. B.A. in Chemistry, Duke U., 1954, M.D., 1958. Diplomate: Nat. Bd. Med. Examiners, Am. Bd. Internal Medicine (cardiovascular diseases). Intern, then resident in medicine Johns Hopkins Hosp., 1958-61; clin. asso. cardiology br., sr. asst. surgeon USPHS, Nat. Heart Inst., NIH, 1961-63, asst. sect. dir. cardiovascular diagnosis, attending physician, sr. investigator cardiology br., 1963-68; prof. medicine, prof. physiology, chief cardiovascular medicine U. Calif. Med. Sch., Davis-Sacramento Med. Center, 1968-82; dir. cardiac ctr. Cedars Med. Ctr., Miami, Fla., 1982-83; physician-in chief Western Heart Inst., San Francisco, 1983—; chmn. dept. cardiovascular medicine St. Mary's Med. Ctr., San Francisco, 1986—; co-chmn. cardiovascular-renal drugs U.S. Pharmacopeia Com. Revision, 1970-75; mem. life scis. com. NASA; med. research rev. bd. VA, NIH; vis. prof. numerous univs., cons. in field; mem. Am. Cardiovascular Splty. Certification Bd., 1972-78. Author: Cardiovascular Management, 1974, Congestive Heart Failure, 1976, Advances in Heart Disease, Vol. 1, 1977, Vol. 2, 1978, Vol. 3, 1980, Cardiovascular Emergencies, 1978, Principles of Noninvasive Cardiac Imaging, 1980, Myocardial Revascularization, 1981, Cardiology, 1981, 82, 83, 84, 85, 86, 87, 88, Clinical Nuclear Cardiology, 1981, Love Your Heart, 1982; also numerous articles.; assoc. editor: Clin. Cardiol. Jour; editor-in-chief: Am. Heart Jour; mem. editorial bds. sci. jours. Recipient Research award Am. Therapeutic Soc., 1965; Theodore and Susan B. Cummings Humanitarian award State Dept.-Am. Coll. Cardiology, 1972, 73, 75, 78; Skylab Achievement award NASA, 1974; U. Calif. Faculty Research award, 1978; named Outstanding Prof. U. Calif. Med. Sch., Davis, 1972. Fellow Am. Coll. Cardiology (pres. 1977-78), A.C.P., Am. Heart Assn., Am. Coll. Chest Physicians, Royal Soc. Medicine; mem. Am. Soc. Clin. Investigation, Am. Physiol. Soc., Am. Soc. Pharmacology and Exptl. Therapeutics (Exptl. Therapeutics award 1973), Am. Fedn. Clin. Research, N.Y. Acad. Scis., Am. Assn. U. Cardiologists, Am. Soc. Clin. Pharmacology and Therapeutics, Western Assn. Physicians, AAUP, Western Soc. Clin. Research (past pres.), Phi Beta Kappa, Alpha Omega Alpha. Republican. Methodist. Club: El Marcero Country. Home: 3015 Country Club Dr El Macero CA 95618 Office: Western Heart Inst St Mary's Med Ctr 450 Stanyan St San Francisco CA 94117

MASON, JAMES ALBERT, university dean; b. Eureka, Utah, 1929; married, 1956; 3 children. BA, Brigham Young U., 1955, MA, 1957; EdD, Ariz. State U., 1970. Cons., clinician in fine arts, 1955—; former chmn. dept. music Brigham Young U., Provo, now dean Coll. Fine Arts and Communications; vis. prof., lectr. Ind. U., Northwestern U., Cin. Coll.-Conservatory, U. Tex., Central Conservatory, Beijing, Internat. Soc. Music Edn., Warsaw; chmn. nat. symposium Applications of Psychology to the Teaching and Learning of Music; co-founder, 1st pres. Utah Valley Symphony Orch.; past condr. Utah Valley Youth Orch. Editor: The Instrumentalist, Orch. News, Utah Music Educator, Research News column, Jour. Research in Music Edn. Bd. dirs. Presser Found. Mem. Music Educators Nat. Conf. (past nat. pres., council), Nat. Music Council (past bd. dirs.), Am. Music Conf. (past bd. dirs.). Office: Brigham Young U/Coll Fine Arts & Communications A-410 Harris Fine Arts Ctr Provo UT 84602

MASON, JEFFREY LYNN, lawyer; b. Phila., Nov. 1, 1944; s. Herbert Lester and Phyllis Louise (Reader) M.; m. Michele Meyer, Aug. 12, 1967 (div. 1989); children: Jeffrey, Meredith. BA in Polit. Sci., Stanford U., 1966, JD, 1969. Bar: Calif. 1970, U.S. Dist. Ct. (no. dist.) Calif. 1970, U.S. Mil. Appeals 1970, U.S. Ct. Appeals (9th cir.) 1970, U.S. Supreme Ct. 1973, U.S. Dist. Ct. (so. dist.) Calif. 1974. Assoc. staff legal counsel Stanford (Calif.) U., 1969-70; assoc. Seltzer Caplan Wilkins & McMahon, San Diego, 1974-77, ptnr., 1977—; adj. prof. U. San Diego, 1979-81. Bd. dirs. Francis W. Parker Sch., San Diego, 1978-87, pres. 1982-85. Capt. JAGC, U.S. Army, 1970-74. Decorated Bronze Star. Mem. ABA, San Diego County Bar Assn., Calif. Trial Lawyers Assn., San Diego Trial Lawyers Assn., Sigma Alpha Epsilon. Office: Seltzer Caplan Wilkins & McMahon 3003-43 4th Ave San Diego CA 92103

MASON, RAYMOND DAE, software engineer; b. Monterey, Calif., Nov. 6, 1959; s. Raymond Lewis and Linda (Chin) M. BSBA, San Diego State U., 1984. Vax cluster mgr. San Francisco French Bread Co., Oakland Calif., 1984-85; systems mgr.and programmer Digital Research Inc., Monterey, 1986; applications programmer Poolman, Shil & Platton, San Francisco, 1986-87; mgr. Basic Measuring Instruments, Foster City, Calif., 1988—; software cons. Sports Car Racing Assn. Monterey Peninsula, Monterey, 1988—. Mem. Upsilon pi epsilon. Home: 405 Sycamore Ave #4 Hayward CA 94544 Office: Basic Measuring Instruments 335 Lakeside Dr Foster City CA 94404

MASON, WILLIAM A(LVIN), psychologist, educator, researcher; b. Mountain View, Calif., Mar. 28, 1926; s. Alvin Frank and Ruth Sabina (Erwin) M.; m. Virginia Joan Carmichael, June 27, 1948; children—Todd, Paula, Nicole, Hunter. B.A., Stanford U., 1950, M.S., 1952, Ph.D., 1954. Asst. prof. U. Wis.-Madison, 1954-59; research assoc. Yerkes Labs. Primate Biology, Orange Park, Fla., 1959-63; head dept. behavioral sci. Delta Primate Research Ctr., Tulane U., Covington, La., 1963-71; prof. psychology, research psychologist U. Calif.-Davis, 1971—; cons. USPHS, 1968-75; leader behavioral biology unit Calif. Primate Research Ctr., Davis, 1972-85; bd. dirs. Jane Goodall Inst., 1979—, Karisoke Research Ctr., 1980-86. Contbr. numerous chpts., articles to profl. publs.; editorial bd. Animal Learning and Behavior, 1973-76, Internat. Jour. Devel. Psychobiology, 1968—, Internat. Jour. Primatology, 1980—. Served with USMC, 1944-46. USPHS spl. fellow, 1963-64. Fellow Am. Psychol. Assn. (pres. Div. 6 1982), AAAS, Animal Behavior Soc.; mem. Internat. Primatological Soc. (pres. 1976-80, 81-84), Am. Soc. Primatologists (pres. 1988—), Internat. Soc. Devel. Psychobiology (pres. 1971-72, Best Paper of Yr. award 1976), Sigma Xi. Home: 2809 Anza Ave Davis CA 95616 Office: U Calif Dept Psychology Davis CA 95616

MASSA, EDWARD CLEMENT, realtor, civic leader; b. Hayward, Calif., May 7, 1907; s. Manual Maria and Camilla (Cotta) M.; m. Grace Francis Tomley, Sept. 28, 1935 (dec. June 1980); children: Michael, Valerie; m. Alice Burgren, Sept. 12, 1987. AB, St. Mary's Coll. Calif., 1929; JD, U. Notre Dame, 1933; postgrad., Stanford U. Mgr. war fin. commn. U.S. Treasury, San Francisco, 1942-44; mem. Nat. Adv. Council and San Francisco Adv. Council of SBA. Chmn. San Francisco Adv. Council and Nat. Bd. U.S. Bus. Adminstrn., San Francisco, 1975-79; trustee Mid-Pacific region Nat. Italian Am. Found., San Francisco, 1984—; chmn. bd. trustees City of Hope, San Francisco, No. Calif., Washington, No. Nev., Idaho, Mont., Wyoming, Utah, 1988— (recipient Spirit Life award 1975); past pres. Portuguese Union Calif. and Nev., 1958; active numerous civic and charity orgns. Mem. Calif. Assn. Realtors (hon. life), So. Alameda County Bd. Realtors, Hayward Merchants Assn. (past pres., hon. life), Nat. Alumni Assn. (pres. 1957-58), U. Notre Dame Alumni No. Calif., Infantile Paralysis Com., Monogram Club. Republican. Roman Catholic. Office: 3401 Investment Block Ste 204 Hayward CA 94545 Office: City of Hope 31 Geary St 3d Fl San Francisco CA 94103

MASSE, WILLIAM ERIC, bank executive; b. Bklyn., Dec. 19, 1951; s. Harry and Lillian (Kass) M.; m. Kathy Freitas, May 21, 1988. BA in History cum laude, SUNY, Albany, 1973. Programmer U.S. Geodetic Survey/NOAA, Bethesda, Md., 1976-77, Hwy. Loss Data Inst., Washington, 1977-78; programmer/analyst C.A.C.I., Rosslyn, Va., 1978-82; programmer/analyst Wells Fargo Bank, San Francisco, 1982-85, systems mgr., 1986-88, v.p., 1988—. Crisis line vol., San Francisco Suicide Prevention Agy., 1986. Democrat. Jewish. Home: 40 Black Log Rd Kentfield CA 94904

MASSELL, THEODORE BENEDICT, vascular surgeon; b. Boston, May 26, 1907; s. James Hirsch and Regina Goldie (Chaloff) M.; m. Helen C. Weinberg, Dec. 5, 1930 (dec. 1971); m. Margaret A. Hansen, Mar. 17, 1973; 1 child, Diane Massell Edmisten. AB, Harvard U., 1926, MD, 1931, AM, 1934. Practice medicine specializing in surgery Worcester, Mass., 1937-41; chief vascular surgery Birmingham VA Hosp., Van Nuys, Calif., 1946-49; practice medicine specializing in vascular surgery Los Angeles, 1950—; cons. Calif. Dept. Health, 1973-78; chief vascular surgery Cedars-Sinai Med. Ctr., 1955-71; asst. prof. surgery Coll. Med. Evangelists, 1947-57; ind. med. examiner Workmen's Appeal Bd., 1975—; med. cons. Calif. Dept. Rehab., 1978—. Assoc. editor Angiology, 1967-70; contbr. 42 articles to med. jours. Served to maj. AUS, 1942-46. Mem. Soc. for Cardiovascular Surgery, Am. Coll. Angiology (past pres.), Internat. Coll. Angiology (past v.p.), Phi Beta Kappa, Alpha Omega Alpha. Home: 2175 S Beverly Glen Los Angeles CA 90025

MASSIE, ERIN LYNN, accountant; b. Quantico, Va., Sept. 12, 1963; d. Thornton and Patricia Adele (Padgett) Boyd; m. Timothy Wayne Massie, Nov. 6, 1982; children: Laila Jasmyn, Alexander Jordan. AS in Bus., Coll. of Alameda, Calif., 1989; student, Tidewater Community Coll., Virginia Beach, Va., 1984, Am. Inst. Banking, Washington, 1981-83. Asst. bookkeeper C.D.P.C. Constrn. Co., Washington, 1978-81; asst. head teller Nat. Savs. & Trust Bank, Washington, 1981-83; controller Va. Beach Air Conditioning Corp., Virginia Beach, 1983-86, Terra Nova Industries, Walnut Creek, Calif., 1986-89; acct. Lawrie Devel. Corp., Danville, Calif., 1989—; owner, acct. Erin Boyd Massie Co., Alameda, Calif., 1989—; notary pub., Va., Calif. Bd. dirs. Community Media Svcs., Inc., Washington, 1981-85; founding mem. Dunwood Civic Assn., Virginia Beach, 1985. Mem. Nat. Notary Assn., U.S. Navy E.O.D. Wives Club, Women Constrn. Owners & Execs. Office: Laurie Devel Corp 521 Sycamore Valley Rd W Danville CA 94526 also: Erin Boyd Massie Co Alameda CA 94501

MAST, JAMES LEE, dentist; b. Dover, Ohio, Apr. 1, 1948; s. Leland Henry and Hazel Myra (Dienst) M.; m. Kathryn Marie Contini, June 17, 1972; children: Michael James, Marie Lynn, Joseph Lee. DDS, Ohio State U., 1972. Staff dentist USPHS Indian Hosp., Winslow, Ariz., 1972-73, chief dentist, 1973-75; gen. practice dentistry Flagstaff, Ariz., 1975—; tchr. gardening Flagstaff Community Schs., 1985-87. Gardening leader 4-H, Flagstaff, 1982—; v.p. Coconino County 4-H Leaders Council, 1985-87 (leader of yr. 1986). Mem. ADA, Ariz. State Dental Assn., No. Ariz. Dental Soc. Democrat. Office: 3011 N West St Flagstaff AZ 86004

MASTALER, RICHARD MICHAEL, healthcare executive; b. Miami, Fla., Jan. 31, 1946; s. Michael George and Margaret (Jeren) M.; m. Sherilyn Eileen Sullestad, Oct. 4, 1972; children: Jason R., Brett R.. BS, Fla. State U., 1968; MA, George Washington U., 1972. Adminstrn. resident Samaritan Health Services, Inc., Phoenix, 1971-72; asst. adminstr. U. N.Mex. Hosp., Albuquerque, 1972-75; adminstr. Beverly Glen Hosp., Los Angeles, 1975-76; exec. dir. Humana Hosp.-West Hills, Canoga Park, Calif., 1976-79, Humana Hosp., Phoenix, 1979-83; v.p. mktg. and sales Humana-Group Health div., Louisville, Ky., 1983-87; pres., chief exec. officer Preferred Health Network, Los Angeles, 1987—. Served to 1st lt. U.S. Army, 1968-70. Mem. Am. Coll. Health Care Execs., Am. Assn. Preferred Provider Orgns. Republican. Mem. Ch. of Christ. Club: Hunting Cree Country (Louisville, Ky.). Office: Preferred Health Network 4700 Ramona Blvd Monterey Park CA 91754

MASTELLER, ROBERT MICHAEL, chiropractor; b. Cedar Rapids, Iowa, Sept. 21, 1950; s. Margaret Frances (Michalek) M.; m. Cindy Sue Hamilton, June 24, 1982; 1 child, Marissa Leigh, Catlin Rose. AS, Kirkwood Community Coll., Cedar Rapids, Iowa, 1972; D Chiropractor, Palmer Coll., Davenport, Iowa, 1978. With Mountain Vista Chiropractic, Longmont, Colo., 1978—. Mem. Colo. Chiropractic Assn. (bd. dirs. 1986—, 2d v.p. 1988-89, Chiropractor of Yr. 1988). Roman Catholic. Lodge: Moose. Office: Mountain Vista Chiropractic 1750 Mountain View Ave Longmont CO 80501

MASTERS, LOWELL FORREST, human resources administrator; b. LaGrande, Oreg., Sept. 16, 1946; s. Forrest Edmond and Alice (Hughes) M.; m. Susan Ann Fish; children: Jessica Anne, Jamie Sue. AAS, Clark Coll., Vancouver, Wash., 1966; BS, Eastern Oreg. Coll., LaGrande, 1971; MS, Ind. State U., 1972; DEd, U. Northern Colo., 1976. Cert. tchr. Tchr. Samuel Kirk Developmental Ctr., Palatine, Ill., 1972-73, Battle Creek (Mich.) Central High Sch., 1973-74, Golden (Colo.) Sr. High Sch., 1975-76; asst. prof. U. Nev., Las Vegas, 1976-78, U. Ark., Fayetteville, 1978-79; psychologist So. Nev. Mental Retardation Svcs., Las Vegas, 1979-80; cons. Nev. Dept. Edn., Las Vegas, 1980-83; adminstr. Clark County Sch. Dist., Las Vegas, 1983-86; adminstr., psychologist So. Nev. Mental Retardation Svcs, Las Vegas, 1986-88, regional dir., 1988—; adj. faculty U. Nev., Las Vegas, 1985—; self-employed magician, Las Vegas, 1977—. Co-author: Teaching the Severely Mentally Retarded, 1980, Physical Education and Recreation for the Handicapped, 1983, Teaching Secondary Students with Mild Learning and Behavior Problems, 1986; editor Jour. Career Edn., 1988—. Mem. Nev. Coun. Occupational Edn., 1985-88; mem. First Presbyn. Presch. Bd., Las Vegas, 1983-85; mem. Nat. Adv. Bd. on Metric Edn. for Mentally Retarded Kennedy Found., Washingotn, 1980-82. U.S. Office Edn. tng. grantee, 1980-83. Mem. Am. Assn. Mental Retardation, Darwin Soc. Republican. Presbyterian. Home: 3236 Surfline Dr Las Vegas NV 89117 Office: So Nev Mental Retardation 1300 S Jones Blvd Las Vegas NV 89158

MASTERS, WALLACE ELLSWORTH, manufacturing executive; b. Cottage Grove, Oreg., June 4, 1937; s. Roy Franklin and Sonia (Hackstead) M.; m. Shirley Ileen Murrey, June 27, 1959; children: Gregory, Nancy. BS in Engring., Oreg. State U., 1959. Indsl. engr. Boeing co., Seattle, 1959-63; prodn. mgr. Tektronix, Inc., Beaverton, Oreg., 1963-78; producibility engring. mgr. Electro Sci. Industries, Portland, Oreg., 1978-80, mfg. mgr., 1980-82, v.p. mfg., 1982-87; pres. Spectronics, Inc., Portland, 1987—. Republican. Presbyterian. Office: Spectronics Inc 11230 NW Reeves Portland OR 97229

MASTERSON, MARGARET MARY, lawyer, banker; b. N.Y.C., Sept. 24, 1955; d. Edward and Margaret (Gallogly) M. BS cum laude, U. Pitts., 1976; JD, No. Ill. U., 1981. Asst. to staff atty. Village of Downers Grove, Ill., 1978-80; legal asst. Walters & Ward, San Diego, 1981-82, Ellsworth & Tibbitts, Laguna Hills, Calif., 1982-83; sales exec. Sand Dollar Devel. Co., Orange, Calif., 1983-85; v.p., mgr. Newport Beach (Calif.) trust and investment office Wells Fargo Bank, L.A., 1986—. Mem. Orange County Estate Planning Coun. Mem. Orange County Trust Officer's Assn. Republican. Roman Catholic. Office: Wells Fargo Bank 660 Newport Center Dr Newport Beach CA 92660

MASTERSON, WILLIAM A., state judge; b. N.Y.C., June 25, 1931; s. John Patrick and Helen Audrey (O'Hara) M.; m. Julie Dohrmann Cosgrove; children: Mark, Mary, Timothy, Barbara. BA, UCLA, 1953, JD, 1958. Bar: Calif., U.S. Supreme Ct. Assoc. Sheppard, Mullin, Richter & Hampton, L.A., 1958-62; ptnr., 1962-79; ptnr. Rogers & Wells, 1979-83, Skadden, Arps, Slate, Meagher & Flom, 1983-87; judge L.A. Superior Ct., 1987—. Author, editor: Civil Trial Practice: Strategies and Techniques, 1986. With inf. U.S. Army, 1953-55. Fellow Am. Coll. Trial Lawyers; mem. Order of Coif. Office: Los Angeles Superior Ct 111 N Hill St Los Angeles CA 90012

MASTRIANNI, RONALD RAYMOND, marketing company executive; b. Detroit, Dec. 22, 1947; s. Joseph Paul and Virginia Alice (Wise) Master; m. Alyce Kay Sherock, July 5, 1975; children: Michael Shawn, Alice Meredith. BS, Calif. State U., Northridge, 1972, MS, 1976. Dir. Children's Neurological Clinic, Newport Beach, Calif., 1973-74; owner Ron Master Gen. Contractor, Westminster, Calif., 1974-83; facilities mgr. Harte Hanks Calif. Direct Mktg. Inc., Brea, Calif., 1983-84, mailroom mgr., 1984-85, dir. mailing ops., 1985-86; plant mgr. Harte Hanks Calif. Direct Mktg. Inc., Mira Loma, Calif., 1986—. Bd. dirs. Inland Empire Postal Customer Coun., San Bernardino, Calif., 1986—. Mem. Am. Heart Assn. (steering com. 1985—), Sierra Club (chmn. rock climbing sect. 1981-83). Office: Harte Hanks Calif CDM Inc 3885 Wabash Dr Mira Loma CA 91752

MASTRINI, JANE REED, social worker, consultant; b. Lincoln, Nebr., July 23, 1948; d. William Scott and Ellen (Daly) Cromwell; m. Charles James Mastrini, July 19, 1969. BA, Western State Coll., Gunnison, Colo., 1970; MSW, U. Denver, 1980. Cert. alcoholism counselor; lic. social worker. Tchr. Flandreau (S.D.) Indian Sch., 1970; social worker S.D. Dept. Welfare, Pierre, 1970-75; child care worker Sacred Heart Home, Pueblo, Colo., 1975-76; counselor Fisher Peak Alcohol Treatment Ctr., Trinidad, Colo., 1976-77; family therapist West Nebr. Gen. Hosp., Scottsbluff, 1980-81; adolescent coordinator St. Luke's Hosp., Denver, 1981-86; exec. dir. New Beginnings At Denver, Lakewood, Colo., 1986—; cons. Colo. Counseling Consortium, Denver, 1984—; field work supr. U. Denver, 1983—. Lectr., group leader Colo. Teen Inst., Denver, 1984-85. Mem. Nat. Assn. Social Workers (cert.), Mile High Council on Alcoholism, P.E.O. (pres. 1984-87), Am. Coll. Alcohol Treatment Adminstrs. Democrat. Episcopalian. Home: 3231 Alkire Ct Golden CO 80401 Office: New Beginnings at Denver 1325 Everett Ct Lakewood CO 80215

MASTRODONATO, GEORGE CARL, lawyer; b. Rochester, N.Y., Aug. 7, 1950; s. George Carl and Jennie (Scognetti) M; m. Rosalyn Eppley, June 23, 1978; children: Anne Lesley, Michael Jay. AS, Monroe Community Coll., Rochester, 1970; BA, Syracuse U., 1972; JD, Gonzaga U., 1976. Bar: Wash. 1977. Tax examiner State of Wash., Olympia, 1976-77, adminstrv. law judge Dept. Revenue, 1977-84, legal affairs officer Dept. Revenue, 1984-85, chief taxpayer info. Dept. Revenue, 1985-87; pvt. practice Olympia, 1987—. Contbr. articles to profl. jours.; speaker continuing legal edn., 1984—. Mem. Thurston County Econ. Devel. Coun., Olympia, 1987-88. Mem. Nat. Assn. Tax Adminstrs.-Fedn. Tax Adminstrs. (sect. chair 1985-87), Wash. State Bar Assn. (chair taxation sect. subcom. 1987—), Thurston County Bar Assn. Roman Catholic. Home: 4940 Orvas Ct SE Olympia WA 98501 Office: 1702 E 4th Ave Olympia WA 98506

MASURSKY, HAROLD, geologist; b. Fort Wayne, Ind., Dec. 23, 1923; s. Louis and Celia (Ochstein) M.; 4 children. B.S. in Geology, Yale U., 1943, M.S., 1951; D.Sc. (hon.), No. Ariz. U., 1981. With U.S. Geol. Survey, 1951—, chief astrogeologic studies br., 1967-71; chief scientist U.S. Geol. Survey (Center Astrogeology), Flagstaff, Ariz., 1971-75; sr. scientist U.S. Geol. Survey (Center Astrogeology), 1975—; lunar orbiter Surveyor Missions, 1965-67; team leader, prin. investigator TV experiment (Mariner Mars), 1971; co-investigator Apollo field geol. team Apollo 16 and 17, also mem. Apollo orbital sci. photog. team, Apollo site selection group; leader Viking Mars Missions Site Selection and cert. team, 1975; mem. imaging teams Voyager (Jupiter, Saturn, Uranus, Neptune), 1977; chmn. mission ops. group Venus Pioneer Mission 1978, co-chmn. mission operational group Galileo Mission, 1981, mission ops. leader, radar team Magellan mission Magellan Mission, 1981—; mem. camera team Mars observer, 1986; mem. Space Sci. Adv. Com., 1978-81, solar system exploration com., 1980-86; mem. Space Sci. Bd., 1982-85; pres. intedisc com. B, COSPAR; sec. Coordinating Com. of Moon and Planets. Assoc. editor: Icarus, Geophys. Rev. Letters, Geodynamics. Served with AUS, 1943-46. Fellow Geol. Soc. Am. (assoc. editor bull., pres. planetary geol. div.), AAAS, Am. Geophys. Union (pres. nomenclature workgroup), Internat. Astron. Union (exec. com. compar planet interan. Union Geol. Sci.), Am. Astron. Assn. (dir. planet studies, mem. exec. com. 1987). Office: US Geol Survey 2255 N Gemini St Flagstaff AZ 86001

MATAN, LILLIAN KATHLEEN, designer, home economics educator, academic administrator; b. Boston, Aug. 18, 1937; d. George Frances and Lillian May (Herbert) Archambault; m. M. Joseph Anthony Matan, Aug. 6, 1960; children—Maria, Meg, Tony, Liz, Joan. B.S. in Home Econs., Seton Hill Coll., postgrad. Tex. A&I, 1971, U. Tex., 1972, Towson State U., 1973; Rudolph Schaeffer Sch. Design, 1977-80; M.A. in Home Econs., San Francisco State U., 1985. Cert. tchr., Md. Tchr. home econs. Surrattsville High Sch., Md., 1960-61; edn. cons. Head Start, Frederick, Md., 1971-72; head home econ. dept. Brunswick High Sch., Md., 1972-73, tchr. adult edn., 1973-74; designer Dudley Kelly & Assocs., San Francisco, 1977-82; designer, prin. Kay Matan Antiques & Interiors, Ross, Calif., 1983-87; dean of students St. Rose Acad., San Francisco, 1988—. Bd. dirs. Cath. Social Services, Marin County, Calif., 1984—, Parnow Friendship House, Marin County, 1984—, Cath. Charities, Archdiocese San Francisco, 1987—, McGucken House, 1987—; del. Joint Community County Wide Plan, Marin County, 1984—; active in Marin Ecumenical Assn. Housing, 1981-83, Ross Valley Ecumenical Housing, Marin County, 1981-83. Mem. Women in Design, Home Economists Bus., Am. Assn. Home Economists, Am. Assn. Housing Educators, Calif. Assn. Home Economists, Environ. Forum of Marin, Marin Conservation League.

MATAS, MYRA DOROTHEA, interior designer, consultant; b. San Francisco, Mar. 21, 1938; d. Arthur Joseph and Marjorie Dorothy (Johnson) Anderson; m. Michael Richard Matas Jr., Mar. 15, 1958; children: Michael Richard III, Kenneth Scott. Cert. interior design, Canada Coll.; cert. interior design, Calif. Owner, operator Miquel's Antiques Co., Millbrae, Calif., 1969-70, Miguel's Antiques & Interiors Co., Burlingame, Calif., 1970-79, Country Elegance Antiques & Interiors Co., Menlo Park, Calif., 1979-84, La France Boutique Co., 1979-84, Myra D. Matas Interior Design, Burlingame, 1984—; mgr. La France Imports, Inc., 1982—; pres. Artisans 3 Inc., Burlingame, 1988—; instr. interior design dept. Canada Coll. Mem. Nat. Home Fashion League, Am. Soc. Interior Designers (asso.), Menlo Park C. of C. Contbr. articles in field to profl. jours. Office: 200 Kansas St San Francisco CA 94103 Office: 1209 Bellevue Ave #S Burlingame CA 94010

MATHAUDHU, SUKHDEV SINGH, mechanical engineer; b. Dhamtan Sahib, Haryana, India, Sept. 11, 1946; came to U.S., 1965; s. Kesho Ram and Channo Devi (Dhiman) M.; m. Veena Chand, Aug. 20, 1972; children: Suveen Nigel, Suneel Adrian. BSME, Walla Walla (Wash.) Coll., 1970. Registered profl. engr., Calif., Pa. Mech. engr. McGinnis Engring., Inc., Portland, Oreg., 1970-71, Can. Union Coll., LaCombe, Alta., Can., 1971-72, H.D. Nottingham & Assocs., McLean, Va., 1972; project engr. Shefferman & Bigelson Co., Silver Spring, Md., 1973-77; mech. engr. Buchart Assocs., York, Pa., 1977-78; sr. mech. engr. Gannett Fleming, Harrisburg, Pa., 1978-80; chief mech. engr. Popov Engrs., Newport Beach, Calif., 1981-83; pres. Mathaudhu Engring., Inc., Riverside, Calif., 1983—. Vice chmn. LaSierra Acad. of Seventh Day Adventists, Riverside, 1978-88; mem. lay adv. counselor SE Conf. Seventh Day Adventists, 1987—. Mem. ASHRAE (chpt. pres. 1988—), Calif. Soc. Profl. Engrs. (pres. 1985-86 ,state dir. 1986-87), NSPE, Am. Soc. Plumbing Engrs., Soc. Am. Mil. Engrs., Am. Cons. Engrs. Council, Cons. Engrs. Assn. Calif. Republican. Seventh-Day Adventist. Home: 5394 College Ave Riverside CA 92505 Office: 3903 Brockton Ave Ste 5 Riverside CA 92501

MATHENY, RICHARD EDWIN, educational administrator, consultant; b. Spokane, Wash., June 22, 1940; s. Fredrick Elwin and Ethel Christine (Hanson) M.; m. Phyllis Ann Cheever, June 10, 1961; children—Richelle Ann, Dwight, Richard. B.A., Wash. State U., 1962; M.P.A., U. So. Calif.-L.A., 1973; postgrad. Harvard U., summer 1982; Ed.D., Gonzaga U., 1985. Sr. real estate agt. County of Orange, Santa Ana, Calif., 1962-73; exec. v.p. Internat. Right of Way Assn., L.A., 1973-77, Whitworth Found., Spokane, Wash., 1977-81, v.p., 1981-84; assoc. vice chancellor U. Calif.-Irvine, now chancellor; ednl. cons. Lilly Endowment, Indpls., Northwest Area Found., St. Paul, Z. Smith Reynolds Found., N.C., 1980—. Author: Creating Charitable Trusts with Real Estate, 1982; contbr. articles on mgmt. to profl. jours. Bd. dirs. Presbyn. Ministries Inc., Seattle; bd. govs. Holy Family Hosp., Spokane. Recipient Journalism award Am. Soc. Assn. Execs., 1977. Mem. Council Advancement and Support of Edn. Office: U Calif Office of Vice Chancellor Davis CA 92717

MATHER, JOSEPH RAY, manufacturers representative; b. Los Angeles, Apr. 16, 1934; s. Lawrence Cooper and Gertrude Helen (McElhose) M.; m. Mary Janis MacMillan, Aug. 15, 1965; children—Mark Joseph, Seth Allen, David Billings Larson. Student Los Angeles City Coll., 1952, El Camino Coll., Torrance, Calif., 1957-63. Telemetry technician TRW Systems Co., Redondo Beach, Calif., 1956-58; sales engr. H. Joe Meyer Co., Hollywood, Calif., 1958-60; salesman La Grange Inc., Hollywood, 1960-62; v.p., gen. mgr. Meyer Assocs., Inc., Hollywood, 1962-68; sales mgr. La Grange Inc., 1968-73; dir. mktg. Norman Enterprises, Inc., Burbank, Calif., 1973-75; owner Mather & Assocs., Napa, Calif., 1975—; pres. J.M. Internat. Inc., Napa, 1987—; cons. lighting with electronic flash. Mem. Dep. Sheriff Res., Los Angeles County, 1963-74; commr. Los Angeles Area council Boy Scouts Am., 1966-69; treas. Granada Hills Homeowners Assn., 1975-78. Served with USNR, 1952-56. Mem. Profl. Photographers Am., Profl. Photographers Calif., Nat. Assn. Mfrs. Reps., West Profl. Photographers Assn., Ariz. Profl. Photographers Assn., Nat. Assn. Ind. Photog. Mfrs. Reps., Peace Officers Assn. So. Calif., So. Calif. Photog. Golf Assn., VFW. Republican. Club: Napa Valley Country. Lodge: Masons. Address: 106 Kerns Court Napa CA 94558-4122

MATHEW, VINCENT BOSE MANNOORAMPARAPMIL, service executive; b. Piravom, Kerala, India, Apr. 5, 1961; came to U.S., 1984; m. Rosemole K. Abraham, Jan. 18, 1987. Teller Bayview Check Cashing, Inc. and Western Union, San Francisco, 1984-85, head teller, 1985-86, mgr. office, 1986-87, gen. mgr., 1987—; gen. mgr. San Francisco Check Cashing Co. and Western Union, 1989—. Office: Bayview Check Cashing Inc 4901-32d St San Francisco CA 94124

MATHEWS, CHARLES ANDERSON, electronics company executive; b. Cardiff, Wales, Feb. 23, 1938; came to U.S., 1969, naturalized 1984; s. Mervyn Charles and Bertha Annie (Farrow) M.; m. Stephanie Rose, Aug. 30, 1980; children: Charles, Clare, Vicki. BS, Imperial Coll. Sci., London, 1960. Project dir. ITT, London, 1965-69; asst. controller ITT Gilfillan, Van Nuys, Calif., 1969-71; dir. ops. ITT Cannon Electric, Santa Ana, Calif., 1971-73; dir. tech. services Plessey Co., Ltd., London, 1973-76; v.p. Plessey, Inc., Plessey Trading Corp., Plessey Materials; pres. Plessey Peripheral Systems Inc., 1976-84; pres., chief operating officer, bd. dirs. Cipher Data Products, Inc., San Diego, 1984-85; pres., bd. dirs. Sci. Micro Systems Inc., Mountain View, Calif., 1985-88; pres. CharterMast, Ltd., San Marcos, Calif., 1988—; bd. dirs. Bluebird Systems, Internat. Mktg. Channels, Ltd. Home: 1759 La Plaza Dr Lake San Marcos CA 92069 Office: CharterMast Ltd PO Box 846 San Marcos CA 92069

MATHEWS, JAMES MELTON, air weapons director; b. Ft. Dix, N.J., Mar. 20, 1950; s. Charles Jerome and Katie May (McCraw) M.; m. Barbara Clair Hensel, Aug. 6, 1969; children: James Mark, Paula, Jill. BS, Livington U., 1977; MPA, Golden Gate U., San Francisco, 1982. Commd. 2d lt. USAF, 1979, advanced through grades to capt., 1983; instr. 3625 TCTS USAF, Tyndall AFB, Fla., 1979-82; chief standardization and evaluation 631 TCF USAF, Wurzburg, Fed. Republic Germany, 1982-85; air force advisor 107 tactical control squad AZANG USAF, Phoenix, 1986-88; subject matter expert USAF, Luke AFB, Ariz., 1988—. Scoutmaster, mem. dist. com. Boy Scouts Am., Mesa, Ariz., 1982—. Mem. Air Force Assn. Republican. Methodist. Home: 5053 E Evergreen Mesa AZ 85205 Office: USAF Det 2 602 TAIRCW Luke AFB AZ 85309-5260

MATHEWS, JEROME RODNEY, orthodontist; b. Ione, Wash., Sept. 3, 1911; s. Jerome Salisbury and Valesta Lilly (Hlava) M.; m. Marylin Claire Mino, Dec. 19, 1949; children: Robert George, Nancy Mathews Hanson, Thomas William. BA in Bacteriology, UCLA, 1934; MA in Bacteriology, U. Calif.-Berkeley, 1936; DDS, U. Calif.-San Francisco, 1949. Diplomate Am. Bd. Orthodontics. Bacteriologist City Health Dept., Oceanside, Calif., 1936-40; part-time prof. U. Calif.-San Francisco, 1949-79; pvt. practice Berkeley, 1949-87; assoc. prof. U. Calif.-San Francisco, 1980-83, prof. emeritus, 1984-87; lectr. in field. Contbr. articles to profl. jours. Orthodontist, Berkeley Clinics Aux., Calif., 1980-87. Lt. comdr. USN, 1940-46, USNR, 1946-71. Mem. Edward H. Angle Soc. Orthodontists (chpt. pres. 1969), Pacific Coast Soc. Orthodontists (Profile of a Profl. award 1983), Am. Assn. Orthodintics, Berkeley Dental Soc., Am. Dental Soc., 49er's Investment Club, Polygon Study Club, Sigma Xi, Omicron Kappa Upsilon. Republican. *Died, 1987.*

MATHEWS, LINDA MCVEIGH, journalist; b. Redlands, Calif., Mar. 14, 1946; d. Glenard Ralph and Edith Lorene (Humphrey) McVeigh; m. Thomas Jay Mathews, June 15, 1967; children—Joseph, Peter, Katherine. B.A., Radcliffe Coll., 1967; J.D., Harvard U., 1972. Gen. assignment reporter Los Angeles Times, 1967-69, Supreme Ct. corr., 1972-76, corr., Hong Kong, 1977-79, China corr., Peking, 1979-80, op-ed page editor, 1980-81, dep. nat. editor, 1981-84, dep. fgn. editor, 1985-88, editorial writer, 1988—; corr. Wall St. Jour., Hong Kong, 1976-77; lectr.; freelance writer; books include: (with others) Journey Into China, 1982; One Billion: A China Chronicle, 1983. Mem. Women's Legal Def. Fund, 1972-76; co-founder, pres. Hong Kong Montessori Sch., 1977-79; docent Pasadena Heritage, 1982—. Mem. Fgn. Corrs. Club Hong Kong, Am. Soc. Newspaper Editors. Office: Los Angeles Times Times Mirror Sq Los Angeles CA 90053

MATHEWS, LYNDA JENNINGS, social services administrator; b. Salt Lake City, June 5, 1951; d. Willaim M. and Myrtle H. (Jensen) J.; m. Dennis R. Amerson, Apr. 9, 1978 (div. Dec. 1983); m. Mark Phillip Mathews, Mar. 27, 1987; children: Ian S. Calegory, Cameron T. Caputo, Tracy M. Amerson. BS, U. Utah, 1973. Technician Denver Social Services, 1975-76; asst. supr. Boulder (Colo.) Social Services, 1976-80; reviewer State of Colo., Denver, 1980-82; lead reviewer, office mgr. State of Colo., Grand Junction, 1982—. Mem. Social Services Tech. and Bus. Soc. Republican. Office: State of Colo 222 S 6th Rm 215 Grand Junction CO 81501

MATHEWS, RAYMOND IRVIN, obstetrician, gynecologist; b. Chanute, Kans., Feb. 11, 1927; s. William Raymond and Ethel Elizabeth (Ogborn) M.; m. Mildred Amelia Yost, Aug. 28, 1947; children: Launa Rae, Michael Larry, Marla Kae, LaRelle. BA in Biology, Walla Walla Coll., 1949; D in Medicine, Loma Linda U., 1954. Diplomate Am. Bd. Ob-gyn. Intern Deaconess Hosp., Spokane, Wash., 1954-55; resident ob-gyn White Meml. Hosp., 1958-61; clin. instr. L.A. County Gen. Hosp., 1961-65; assoc. clin. prof. ob-gyn U. Calif., Irvine, 1983—; mem. adv. coun. Dist. IX ACP, 1982-88, chmn. sect. 4, 1986-88. Capt. USAF, 1955-57. Mem. Long Beach Ob-Gyn. Soc. (pres. 1971). Republican. Office: 2865 Atlantic Ave Ste 101 Long Beach CA 90806

MATHIAS, BETTY JANE, communications and community affairs consultant, writer, editor, lecturer; b. East Ely, Nev., Oct. 22, 1923; d. Royal F. and Dollie B. (Bowman) M.; student Merritt Bus. Sch., 1941, 42, San Francisco State U., 1941-42; 1 dau., Dona Bett. Asst. publicity dir. Oakland (Calif.) Area War Chest and Community Chest, 1943-46; pub. relations Am. Legion, Oakland, 1946-47; asst. to pub. relations dir. Cen. Bank of Oakland, 1947-49; pub. relations dir. East Bay chpt. of Nat. Safety Council, 1949-51; propr., mgr. Mathias Public Relations Agy., Oakland, 1951-60; gen. assignment reporter and teen news editor Daily Rev., Hayward, Calif., 1960-62; freelance pub. relations and writing, Oakland, 1962-66, 67-69; dir. corp. communications Systech Fin. Corp., Walnut Creek, Calif., 1969-71; v.p. corp. communications Consol. Capital companies, Oakland, 1972-79, v.p. community affairs, Emeryville, Calif., 1981-84, v.p. spl. projects, 1984-85; v.p., dir. Consol. Capital Realty Services, Inc., Oakland, 1973-77; v.p., dir. Centennial Adv. Corp., Oakland, 1976-77; communications cons., 1979—; cons. Mountainair Realty, Cameron Park, Calif., 1986-87; lectr. in field; bd. dirs. Oakland YWCA, 1944-45, ARC, Oakland, So. Alameda County chpt., 1967-69, Family Ctr., Children's Hosp. Med. Ctr. No. Calif., 1982-85, March of Dimes, 1983-85, Equestrian Ctr. of Walnut Creek, Calif., 1983-84, also sec.; adult and publs. adv. Internat. Order of the Rainbow for Girls, 1953-78; communications arts adv. com. Ohlone (Calif.) Coll., 1979-85, chmn., 1982-84; mem. adv. bd. dept. mass communications Calif. State U.-Hayward, 1985; pres. San Francisco Bay Area chpt. Nat. Reyes Syndrome Found., 1981-86; vol. staff Columbia Actors' Repertory, Columbia, Calif., 1986-87, 89; mem. exec. bd., editor newsletter Tuolumne County Dem. Club, 1987; publicity chmn. 4th of July celebration Tuolumne County C. of C., 1988. Recipient Grand Cross of Color award Internat. Order of Rainbow for Girls, 1955. Order Eastern Star (publicity chmn. Calif. state 1955). Editor East Bay Mag., 1966-67, TIA Traveler, 1969, Concepts, 1979-83. Home: 20575 Gopher Dr Sonora CA 95370

MATHIAS, CORINNE FLORENCE, consultant company executive; b. Buffalo, June 10, 1926; d. Sidney and Florence (Vincent) O'Neill; m. Richard Charles Mathias, Sept. 6, 1947 (dec. Apr. 20, 1972); children—Richard Charles, Micheal William, Corinne Mary, Marc Francis. A.A., Citrus Coll., 1979. Dir. Universal Product Code and Direct Store Set-UP, Vons Grocery Co., El Monte, Calif., 1958-78; pres., owner Direct Delivery Data, Glendora, Calif., 1978—. Author receiving clerk's manual, 1966. Fellow mem. Los Angeles Art Mus., 1984—, Com. Against Govt. Waste, Washington, 1984—, Redlands Community Music Assn., Calif., 1984—. Women in Mgmt. scholar, 1979. Fellow So. Calif. Grocers Assn., Bus. and Profl. Women. Democrat. Roman Catholic. Avocations: bridge; golf; tennis; travel; photography.

MATHIAS, HARRY MICHAEL, cinematographer, consultant, author; b. London, Aug. 15, 1945; came to U.S., 1949.; s. Eric Manfred and Elsa (Herbst) M.; m. Ann C. Johnston, Oct. 4, 1987. AA, San Francisco City Coll., 1965; BA, Calif. State U., 1968, MA, 1974. Dir. photography numerous motion pictures, 1969-88; sr. cons. Panavision Inc., Tarzana, Calif., 1981—; cons. Eastman Kodak Co., Rochester, N.Y., 1982-84; pres. Image Tech. Inc., Santa Monica, Calif., 1986—; mem. faculty UCLA, 1984—; lectr. Swedish Film Inst., Am. Film Inst., Stanford U. Author: Electronic Cinematography, 1985; author (with others) Image Quality, 1984, The American Cinematographers Handbook, 1986; contbr. articles to profl. jours; dir. photography Solly's Dinner, 1980 (Oscar nomination). Mem. Mus. Contemporary Art, Los Angeles, 1988, Los Angeles County Mus. Art, 1987, 88. Mem. Soc. Motion Picture and T.V. Engrs., Working Group on High Definition Electronic Prodn. Standards (chmn. film splty. com.). Democrat. Clubs: Pacific Mariners (Marina Del Rey), Yacht. Home: PO Box 11083 Marina Del Rey CA 90295

MATHIAS, ROBERT BRUCE, marketing executive; b. Tulare, Calif., Nov. 17, 1930; s. Charlie Milford and Lillian (Harris) M.; m. Melba Wiser, 1953 (div. 1976); children: Romel, Megan, Marissa; m. Gwen Haven, Dec. 31, 1977. BA in Edn., Stanford U., 1953. Actor Mathlon Prodns., Los Angeles, 1953-54, Batjac Prodns., Los Angeles, 1956-58; pres. Bob Mathias Sierra Boys Camp, Fresno, Calif., 1962-78; dir. Olympic Tng. Ctr., Colorado Springs, Colo., 1977-83; exec. dir. Nat. Fitness Found., Los Angeles, 1983-86; pres. Am. Kids Sports Assn., Fresno, Calif., 1984—; bd. dirs. HDL, Costa Mesa, Calif., Sigma Group Mut. Funds, Wilmington, Del. Rep. U.S. Congress, 1967-75. Capt. USMC, 1954-56. Nominated U.S. Track and Field Hall of Fame, Indpls., U.S. Olympic Com. Hall of Fame, Colorado Springs, 1983; named one of 10 Outstanding Young Men Am., U.S. Jaycees, 1949. Mem. U.S. Decathlon Assn. (dir. 1986—). Republican. Methodist.

MATHIS, RONALD FLOYD, physicist; b. L.A., July 26, 1942; s. Darrell Floyd and Gladys Mae (Buckles) M.; m. Charlotte Anne Gibson, June 5, 1964; children: Melanie Kay, Stephen Ronald, David Darrell, Michael Lee. BA, Fullerton (Calif.) State U., 1966; MS, U. Mo., Rolla, 1971, PhD, 1973. Sr. physicist IRT Corp., San Diego, 1973-75; sr. engr. Cubic Corp., San Diego, 1975-78; sr. engring. specialist electronics div. Gen. Dynamics, San Diego, 1978—. Contbr. articles to profl. publs.; patentee in field. Mem. Am. Phys. Soc., Optical Soc. Am., IEEE, Soc. Photooptical Instrumentation Engrs., Creation Rsch. Soc. Republican. Office: Gen Dynamics Electronics div PO Box 85310 MZ7207-H San Diego CA 92138

MATHISON-BOWIE, STEPHEN LOCH, minister; b. Leonia, N.J., Dec. 31, 1955; s. Glenn Edward and Doreen Maye (Lindo) B.; m. Tiare Louise Mathison, Sept. 11, 1982. BA, U. Wash., 1977; MDiv, Fuller Theol. Sem., 1987. Ordained Presbyterian Minister. Program officer Flintridge Found., Pasadena, Calif., 1985—; assoc. pastor Cen. Presbyn. Ch., Eugene, Oreg., 1988-89. Mem. Cascades Presbytery, U.S.G.A., Eugene Ministerial Alliance. Democrat. Presbyterian. Home: 2885 Harlow Rd Eugene OR 97401 Office: Cen Presbyn Church 1475 Ferry St Eugene OR 97401

MATHISON-BOWIE, TIARE LOUISE, minister; b. Seattle, Apr. 17, 1953; d. Maynard John and Elain Marie (Anderson) M.; m. Stephen Loch Bowie, Sept. 11, 1982. BA, Evergreen St. Coll.; MDiv, Fuller Theol. Sem., Pasadena, Calif., 1987. Ordained Presbyterian Minister. Program officer Flintridge Found., Pasadena, Calif., 1984-87; devel. dir. Connelly Sch. for Girls, Anahiem, Calif., 1987-88; assoc. pastor Cen. Presbyn. Ch., Eugene, Oreg., 1988—. Mem. Am. Acad. of Religion, Evang. Women's Caucus, Cascades Presbytery, Eugene Ministerial Alliance. Democrat. Presbyterian. Home: 2885 Harlow Rd Eugene OR 97401 Office: Cen Presbyn Church 1475 Ferry St Eugene OR 97401

MATHUR, ASHOK, telecommunications engineer, educator, researcher; b. Gorakhpur, Uttar Pradesh, India; came to U.S., 1979; s. Raj Swarup and Savitri Mathur; m. Jayanti Srivastava, May 31, 1978; children: Menka, Puja. BS, U. Agra, India, 1963, MS, 1965; PhD, U. Southampton, Hampshire, Eng., 1974. Cert. telecommunications engr., Calif.; teaching credential, Calif. Lectr. upper atmospheric physics Kanpur, India, 1965-68; doctoral researcher U. Southampton, 1968-73; postdoctoral research fellow U. Poitiers, Vienne, France, 1973-74; assoc. prof., research supr U. Kanpur, 1974-79; mem. tech. staff telecommunications sci. and engring. div. Jet Propulsion Lab. Calif. Inst. Tech., Pasadena, 1979—. Contbr. numerous publs. to profl. jours.; mem. editorial bd. Acta Ciencia Indica Jour., 1975-78. Recipient 5-Year Service award Jet Propulsion Lab. Calif. Inst. Tech., 1984, Overseas Students award Brit. Council, London, 1968, Délégation Générale a la Recherche Scientifique et Technique award, Paris, 1973. Mem. IEEE, AIAA (vice chmn. pub. policy San Gabriel Valley, sec. Los Angeles 1987—), The European Phys. Soc., Calif. Inst. Tech. Mgmt. Club., Armed Forces Communications and Electronics Assn., Am. Biog. Inst. (rsch. bd. advisors 1988—). Republican. Hindu. Home: 1923-B Huntington Dr Duarte CA 91010 Office: Calif Inst Tech Jet Propulsion Lab 4800 Oak Grove Dr MS T-1202 Pasadena CA 91109

MATIN, ABDUL, microbiology educator, consultant; b. Delhi, India, May 8, 1941; came to U.S., 1964, naturalized, 1983; s. Mohammed and Zohra (Begum) Said; m. Mimi Keyhan, June 21, 1968. BS, U. Karachi, Pakistan, 1960, MS, 1962; PhD, UCLA, 1969. Lectr. St. Joseph's Coll., Karachi, 1962-64; research assoc. UCLA, 1964-71; sci. officer U. Groningen, Kerklaan, The Netherlands, 1971-75; from asst. to assoc. prof. microbiology Stanford U., Calif., 1975—; cons. Engenics, 1982-84, Monsanto, 1984—; chmn. Stanford Recombinant DNA panel; convener of microbiological workshop and confs. Mem. editorial bd. Jour. of Bacteriology; guest mem. editorial bd. Ann. Rev. Microbiol., Rev. of NSF and other Grants; contbr. numerous publs. to sci. jours. Fellow Fulbright Found., 1964, NSF, 1981—, Ctr. for Biotech. Research, 1981-85, EPA, 1981-84, NIH, Coll. Biotech., U.N. Tokten, 1987. Mem. AAAS, AAUP, Am. Soc. Microbiology, Soc. Gen. Microbiology, Soc. Indsl. Microbiology, No. Soc. Indsl. Microbiology (bd. dirs.), Biophys. Soc. Home: 690 Coronado Ave Stanford CA 94305 Office: Stanford U/Dept of Microbiology & Immunology Fairchild Sci Bldg Stanford CA 94305

MATINKI, RAILA ELISABETH, real estate company official, interior designer; b. Helsinki, Apr. 21, 1963; came to U.S., 1968; d. Raimo Kalevi Matinki and Eila Elisabeth (Pennanen) Lindgren. Student, U. Helsinki, 1981-83; BFA, Acad. Art, San Francisco, 1986; student, Chamberlin Real Estate Sch., Campbell, Calif., 1987. Lic. realtor, Calif. Travel specialist Finland Tourist Bur., Helsinki, 1980-83; sales coord. Finnair Airlines, San Francisco, 1984; freelance interior designer 1984-86; realtor assoc. Grubb & Ellis, Greenbrae, Calif., 1987--. Com. mem. San Rafael (Calif.) Consumer Protection Bd., 1988-89. English Sch. Helsinki scholar, 1978, State of Calif. scholar, 1985-86. Mem. Nat. Assn. Realtors, Calif. Assn. Realtors, Marin County Bd. Realtors. Republican. Lutheran. Home: 204 Cutlass Dr Novato CA 94947 Office: Grubb & Ellis 350 Bon Air Ctr Greenbrae CA 94904

MATIS, KATINA, management consultant; b. Westchester Ct., N.Y., Feb. 10, 1946; d. Stephen and Barbara Matis. AA, Foothill Coll., 1975; BA, U. Calif.-Berkeley, 1977. With IBM Corp., 1965-71; legal adminstr. Wilson, Sonsini & Goodrich, Palo Alto, Calif., 1974-75; mgmt. cons. McKinsey & Co., Inc., San Francisco, 1974-75; legal adminstr. Pillsbury, Madison & Sutro, San Francisco, 1976-78; mktg. rep. Burroughs Corp., San Francisco, 1979-80; pres. Tina Matis Cons. Svcs., Inc., Palm Desert, Calif., 1980-88; mktg. cons. Bird Products Corp., Palm Springs, Calif., 1988--; dir. St. Mary's Tennis Masters, Moraga, Calif., 1980-86; systems devel. cons. San Francisco State U., 1980; orgn. devel. cons. Crown Zellerbach, San Francisco, 1980-81; lectr. St. Mary's Coll., Moraga, 1982-83; orgn. devel. cons. Varian Assocs., Inc., Palo Alto, Calif., 1984-85; lectr. bus. mgmt. Chapman Coll., Orange, Calif., 1986-87; mktg. mgmt. cons. Desert Personnel Svcs., Palm Desert, Calif., 1986; bus. devel. mgr. County of Riverside (Calif.), 1987; lectr. Calif. State U.-San Bernardino. Mem. Am. Prodn. and Inventory Control Assn., U.S. Tennis Assn. (developer jr. tennis Coachella Valley, Calif. 1985), Intercollegiate Tennis Coaches Assn., Soroptomist (treas. La Quinta chpt. 1987).

MATISOFF, BERNARD SYDNEY, electronic packaging engineer, consultant; b. L.A., Apr. 4, 1930; s. Sam and Reva (Sorrich) M.; m. Louise Ann Breskin, June 20, 1953; children: Martin, Glen. BSE, West Coast U., 1957. Registered profl. engr., Calif. Mgr. mech. engring. and engring. svcs. Computer Control Co. Inc., L.A., 1960-66; mech. projecy engr. Librascope Corp., Glendale, Calif., 1966-70; mgr. mech. engring. Data Recall Corp., El Segundo, Calif., 1970-75; engr. guidance control & systems div. Litton, Woodland Hills, Calif., 1975-76; mgr. mech. engring. Teledyne Systems Co., Northridge, Calif., 1976-77, Vector Gen. Inc., Woodland Hills, 1977-79; product engr. EMM Sesco, Chatsworth, Calif., 1979-81; leader physical design group Textron Inc., Valencia, Calif., 1981-84; mgr. mfg. engring. optical techs. div. Sundstrand, Newbury Park, Calif., 1984-85; editor-in-chief Inst. Packaging and Mfg. Electronics, Anaheim Hills, Calif., 1986—; cons. on mfg. analysis BMA Engring. Co., Anaheim Hills, 1966—; instr. L.A. Pierce Coll., 1988, UCLA. Author: Handbook of Electronic Manufacturing Engineering, 1978, Handbook of Electronic Packaging Design and Engineering, 1980, Handbook of Electrostatic Controls, 1986, Handbook of Design and Manufacturing with Surface Mount Technology, 1988, Handbook of Wiring and Cable Design, 1988. Scoutmaster Boy Scouts Am., Woodland Hills, 1971-79. With USN, 1948-52, Korea. Mem. Soc. Mfg. Engrs. (sr., cert., v.p. 1988—). Republican. Jewish. Home and Office: 5584 Vista Del Estes Anaheim CA 92807

MATO, WILLIAM MICHAEL, systems analyst; b. Phila., Apr. 5, 1942; s. Michael Paul and Mary Bertha (Telichan) M.; m. Michelle Brymer, Oct. 18, 1987. BS, LaSalle Coll., 1968; MBA, Widener U., 1972. Electronic technician G.E. Missile and Space Vehicle, Phila., 1961; electronic environ. technician Controls Co. Am., Folcroft, Pa., 1962-63; programmer/analyst Boeing Vertol Co., Morton, Pa., 1963-66; rep. computer mktg. RCA Computer Systems, Phila., 1966-71, RCA Industry Systems, Burlington, Mass., 1972-73; sr. system analyst/project mgr. Boeing Computer Svcs., Phila., 1976-87; adminstr. systems integration Allied-Signal Garrett Group, Torrance, Calif., 1987--; cons. including Erie and Lackawanna R.R., Cin., 1974-75. Served to 2nd petty officer USNR, 1961-67. Mem. IEEE (sec. 1966-67). Republican. Roman Catholic. Home: 4451 Pacific Coast Hwy #H-103 Torrance CA 90505

MATOVICH, MITCHEL JOSEPH, JR., motion picture producer, executive; b. Watsonville, Calif., Dec. 16, 1927; s. Mitchel Joseph and Mildred Florence (Ingrom) M; widowed, 1968; divorced, 1983; children: Wayne, Mark, Laura. Student, San Jose State U., 1946-49. Mechanical designer Stanford Rsch. Inst., Menlo Park, Calif., 1955-59; rsch. specialist Lockheed Missiles & Space Co., Sunnyvale, Calif., 1959-70; mgr. NASA and Dept. of Def. bus. sect. Engineered Systems Div. FMC Corp., San Jose, Calif., 1970-77; pres. and chief exec. officer Morton Co. Div. of Haycor Corp., Hayward, Calif., 1977-82; pres. Concept Devel. Co., Newark, Calif., 1982-87, Matovich Productions, Hollywood, Calif., 1987—, Stereotronics Inc., Beverly Hills, Calif., 1988—. Author: The Image Machine; author feature length screenplays, stories for screenplays, short stories; patentee in field. With USN, 1945-46, 51-52, Korea. Mem. MENSA, Intertel. Home: 10660 Wilshire Blvd # 1104 Los Angeles CA 90024 Office: Matovich Prodns Inc 6253 Hollywood Blvd Ste 714 Hollywood CA 90028

MATSEN, JEFFREY ROBERT, lawyer; b. Salt Lake City, Nov. 24, 1939; s. John Martin and Bessie (Jackson) M.; B.A. cum laude, Brigham Young U., Provo, Utah, 1964; J.D. with honors, UCLA, 1967; m. Susan Davis, July 27, 1973; children—Gregory David, Melinda Kaye, Brian Robert, Jeffrey Lamont, Kristin Sue, Nicole, Brett Richard. Admitted to Calif. bar, 1968, also U.S. Supreme Ct., U.S. Tax Ct., D.C. Ct. Appeals bars; practice in Los Angeles, 1968, Newport Beach, 1971—; mng. ptnr. firm Jeffrey R. Matsen & Assocs., 1978—; prof. law Western State U. Coll. Law, Fullerton, Calif., 1969—; instr. Golden Gate U. Grad. Taxation Program, 1978—. Served as capt. USMCR, 1968-71. Decorated Navy Commendation medal. Mem. Am. Bar Assn., State Bar Calif. (certified taxation specialist), Order of Coif. Mormon. Author: Business Planning for California Closely-Held Enterprises. Contbr. articles to legal jours. Office: 4000 MacArthur Blvd Ste 600 Newport Beach CA 92660

MATSON, MERWYN DEAN, educational consultant; b. Forest City, Iowa, Aug. 6, 1937; s. Archie Alvin and Henrietta (Wittgreve) M.; m. Audrey Christine Gaydos, Apr. 9, 1988; children: Candace, Kevin, Shaunna, Dan, Cathy, Matthew, Mindy. AB, Northwest Nazarene Coll., 1959; MEd, Oreg. State U., 1962; EdM, U. Oreg., 1962. Cert. tchr., sch. counselor, sch. psychologist, Iowa. Elem. sch. guidance coord. Pottawattami County Schs., Council Bluffs, Iowa, 1969-70; sch. psychologist Hancock County Schs., Garner, Iowa, 1970-71; dir. career edn. Mason City (Iowa) Pub. Schs., 1971-73; regional dir. Am. Coll. Testing Program, Springfield, Mo., 1973-84; Midwest regional dir. career planning svcs. Am. Coll. Testing Program, Lincolnshire, Ill., 1984-86; Mountains/Plains regional dir. career planning svcs. Am. Coll. Testing Program, Aurora, Colo., 1986—. Mem. Am. Assn. Counseling and Devel., Rotary (Denver). Lutheran. Home: 8121 S Marion Ct Littleton CO 80122 Office: Am Coll Testing Program 3131 S Vaughn Way Ste 218 Aurora CO 80014

MATSON, SANDRA LOU, small business owner; b. Seattle, Dec. 14, 1953; d. Donald Ivar and Donna Jean (LaNore) M.; m. Robert Allen Petek, Dec. 11, 1981 (div. Sept. 1984); children: Christopher Donald. AAS, No. Seattle Community Coll., 1978. Cert. profl. estimator. Estimator, office mgr. Estimates, Inc., Seattle, 1978-82; estimator Eastside Constrn., Bellevue, Wash., 1982-84; cost engr. The NBBJ Group, Seattle, 1984-88; cost engr., owner Matson/Carlson/Whitacre, Seattle, 1988—; instr. No. Seattle Community Coll., 1983-84. Author: Lab Designing, 1988. Mem. Am. Soc. Profl. Estimators (v.p. 1983-84), Soc. Am. Value Engrs. Office: Matson/Carlson/Whitacre 209 1/2 1st Ave S Seattle WA 98104

MATSUDA, FUJIO, research administrator; b. Honolulu, Oct. 18, 1924; s. Yoshio and Shimo (Iwasaki) M.; m. Amy M. Saiki, June 11, 1949; children: Bailey Koki, Thomas Junji, Sherry Noriko, Joan Yuuko, Ann Mitsuyo, Richard Hideo. B.S. in Civil Engring., Rose Poly. Inst., 1949; D.Sc., Mass. Inst. Tech., 1952; D. Engring. (hon.), Rose Hulman Inst. Tech., 1975. Research engr. Mass. Inst. Tech., 1952-54; research asst. prof. engring. U. Ill., Urbana, 1954-55; asst. prof. engring. U. Hawaii, Honolulu, 1955-57; assoc. prof. U. Hawaii, 1957-62, chmn. dept. civil engring., 1960-63, prof., 1962-65, 74-84, dir. engring. expt. sta., 1962-63, v.p. bus. affairs, 1973-74, pres., 1974-84; exec. dir. Research Corp. U. Hawaii, 1984—; dir. Hawaii Dept. Transp., Honolulu, 1963-73; v.p. Park & Yee, Ltd., Honolulu, 1956-58; pres. SMS & Assos., Inc., 1960-63; pvt. practice as structural engr., 1958-60; dir. C. Brewer & Co., Ltd., UAL Corp., First Hawaiian Bank, First Hawaiian Inc., Pacific Internat. Ctr. for High Tech. Research, Kuakini Health System and Kuakini Med. Ctr.; adv. bd. Duty Free Shoppers Ltd.; mem. Bd. Water Supply, Honolulu, 1963-73; mem. Airport Ops. Council Internat., 1968-73; pres. Pacific Coast Assn. Port Authorities, 1969; mem. sci. bd. Dept. Army, 1978-80; mem. U.S. Army Civilian Adv. Group, 1978—; bd. dirs. Hawaii Inst. Electronic Research; mem. exec. com. transp. research bd. NRC, 1982-86. Bd. dirs. Aloha United Way, 1973-76; trustee Kuakini Health Systems, 1984-86; trustee Nature Conservancy. Served with AUS, 1943-45. Recipient Honor Alumnus award Rose Poly. Inst., 1971; recipient Disting. Service award Airport Ops. Council Internat., 1973, Disting. Alumnus award U. Hawaii, 1974, 87; named Hawaii Engr. of Yr., 1972. Mem. ASCE (Parcel-Sverdrup Engring. Mgmt. award 1986), Nat. Acad. Engring., Nat. Soc. Profl. Engrs., Social Sci. Assn., Western Coll. Assn. (exec. com. 1977-84, pres. 1980-82), Japanese-Am. Soc. Honolulu (trustee 1976-84, adv. council 1984—), Beta Gamma Sigma, Sigma Xi, Tau Beta Pi. Office: U Hawaii Rsch Corp 1110 University Ave Rm 408 Honolulu HI 96826

MATSUHASHI, YUKO, pediatrician; b. Iwate, Japan, Dec. 8, 1946; came to U.S., 1986; d. Makitaro and Keiko (Yoshida) Watanabe; m. Masakazu Matsuhashi, July 22, 1972. MD, physician lic., Keio U., Tokyo, 1973, PhD in Med. Sci., 1981. Resident in pediatrics Keio U., Tokyo, 1973-79, fellow in pediatrics, 1979-81, instr. in pedicatrics, 1982-86; dep. dir. maternal and child health Ministry of Health and Welfare, Tokyo, 1981-82; research fellow adolescent medicine U. Calif. Med. Ctr., San Diego, 1987, clin. instr. pediatrics, 1988—. Mem. Soc. for Adolescent Med., Soc. Behavioral Pediatrics, University City Racket Club. Office: U Calif San Diego Med Ctr 225 Dickinson St San Diego CA 92103

MATSUI, ROBERT TAKEO, congressman; b. Sacramento, Sept. 17, 1941; s. Yasuji and Alice (Nagata) M.; m. Doris Kazue Okada, Sept. 17, 1966; 1 child, Brian Robert. A.B. in Polit. Sci, U. Calif.-Berkeley, 1963; J.D., Hastings Coll. Law, U. Calif., San Francisco, 1966. Bar: Calif. 1967. Practiced law Sacramento, 1967-78; mem. Sacramento City Council, 1971-78, vice mayor, 1977; mem. 96th-101st Congresses from 3d Calif. dist., 1979—, mem. ways and means com.; chmn. profl. bus. forum Dem. Congl. Campaign Com.; congl. liaison nat. fin. council Dem. Nat. Com.; mem. adv. council on fiscal policy Am. Enterprise Inst. chmn. Profl. Bus. Forum of the Dem. Congl. Co. and Com.; congl. liaison Nat. Fin. Council, Dem. Nat. Com.; mem. Am. Enterprise Inst. Adv. Council on Fiscal Policy. Named Young Man of Yr. Jr. C. of C., 1973; recipient Disting. Service award, 1973. Mem. Sacramento Japanese Am. Citizens League (pres. 1969), Sacramento Met. C. of C. (dir. 1976). Democrat. Clubs: 20-30 (Sacramento) (pres. 1972), Rotary (Sacramento). Office: 2419 Rayburn House Office Bldg Washington DC 20515 *

MATSUMURA, KAZUYOSHI, materials engineer; b. Yokohama, Japan, Dec. 28, 1947; s. Akio and Hisuko (Mori) M.; m. Mikiko Tamura, May 5, 1982; 1 child, Sayako. BEngring., Tohoku U., Sendai, Japan, 1970. Asst. mgr. Kawasaki Steel Corp., Tokyo, 1978-85; mgr. Kawasaki Steel Am. Inc., Los Angeles, 1986—; sr. tech. officer Iron and Steel Inst., Tokyo, 1979-82. Mem. Iron and Steel Inst. Japan, Materials Properties Council. Office: Kawasaki Steel Am Inc 444 S Flower St Ste 1590 Los Angeles CA 90071

MATSUNAGA, SPARK MASAYUKI, senator; b. Kauai, Hawaii, Oct. 8, 1916; s. Kingoro and Chiyono (Fukushima) M.; m. Helene Hatsumi Tokunaga, Aug. 6, 1948; children: Karen (Mrs. Hardman), Keene, Diane, Merle, Matthew. Ed.B. with honors, U. Hawaii, 1941; J.D., Harvard U., 1951; LL.D. (hon.), Soochow U., 1973, St. John's U., 1977, Eastern Ill. U., 1978, U. Md., 1979; H.L.D., Lincoln U., 1979. Bar: Hawaii 1952. Vets. counsellor U.S. Dept. Interior, 1945-47; chief priority claimants div. War Assets Adminstrn., 1947-48; asst. pub. pros. City and County of Honolulu, 1952-54; practice of law Honolulu, 1954-62; mem. Hawaii Ho. of Reps., 1954-59, majority leader, 1959; mem. U.S. Ho. Reps. 88th-94th Congresses; mem. Rules, Aging, Steering and Policy coms., dep. majority whip; U.S. senator from Hawaii, 1976—; mem. Fin., Energy and Natural Resources, Vets.' Affairs coms., chief dep. whip.; Mem. Hawaii statehood delegations to Congress, 1950, 54, Pacific War Meml. Commn., 1959-62; adv. com. Honolulu Redevel. Agy., 1953-54. Author: Rulemakers of The House, 1976. Chmn. bd. Kaimuki YMCA; pres. Naturalization Encouragement Assn. Honolulu.; Bd. dirs. World Brotherhood. Soc. Crippled Children and Adults, Honolulu Council Social Agys. Served from 2d lt. to capt., inf. AUS, 1941-45; ret. lt. col. JAGC 1969. Decorated Bronze Star with valor clasp, Purple Heart with oak leaf cluster. Mem. ABA, Hawaii Bar Assn., DAV, VFW, Japan-Am. Soc., U. Hawaii Alumni Assn. Democrat. Episcopalian. Clubs: Lions (Honolulu), 100 (Honolulu). Office: US Senate 109 Hart Senate Office Bldg Washington DC 20510 *

MATSUO, GEORGE, management and marketing executive; b. Tokyo. BA, Ea. Wash. U., 1980, MBA, 1982. Pres. Network Services, Inc., Honolulu, 1986—; bd. dirs. Royal Coast Realty Corp., Honolulu, Fujio Enterprises Ltd., Honolulu, CK Investment Co., Honolulu, N&N Enterprises, Honolulu, Taketsu Internat. Hawaii, Inc., Honolulu, Network Investment Co., Honolulu. Office: Pacific Network Svcs Inc 1600 Kapiolani Blvd #717 Honolulu HI 96814

MATSUYAMA, JAMES DAVID, director of environemtal health; b. Cheyenne, Wyo., Aug. 10, 1948; s. William M. and Mary Y. (Arima) M.; m. Melody Ann Meade, Aug. 21, 1971; children: Karen Lynn, Lisa Kay, Jessica Ann. BS in Prevention Med., U. Wash., 1970. Co. commdr. 551 Med. Co. Ambulance, Ft. Lewis, Wash., 1971-73; environ. health specialist Stevens County Health Dept., Colville, Wash., 1973-75, dir., environ. health, 1975-77; dir., environ, health Northeast Tri-County Health Dist., Colville, Wash., 1977—. Mem. Colville City Bd. of Adjustment, 1986—. Cpt. U.S. Army, 1971-73. Mem. Wash. State Environ. Health Assn., Nat. Environ. Health Assn., Wash. State Registered Sanitarians (chmn. 1988). Independent. Home: 567 E 3rd Colville WA 99114 Office: NE TriCounty Health Dist PO Box 270 Colville WA 99114

MATTA, JUDITH KAIN, customs broker, manager; b. L.A., July 12, 1941; d. Herbert Eugene and Patsy Fern (Kain) Haymaker; m. Ronald J. Matta,

Oct. 31, 1960 (wid. 1976); children: Daniel J., Kenneth J.; m. I. David Hoops, Sept. 15, 1984. Student, Pasadena Community Coll., 1960-61, Glendale Community Coll., 1988. Lic. customs broker, U.S. Dept. Treasury. Prin., v.p. Div. M., Inc., Schiller Park, Ill., 1973-77; zone mgr. William F. Joffroy, Inc., Phoenix, 1983-86; proprietor Matta Cons. Svcs., Glendale, Ariz., 1986-88; gen. mgr. William F. Joffroy, Inc., Phoenix, 1988—. Author personalized import manuals. Mem. Chgo. Customhouse Brokers Assn. (v.p. 1977), Phoenix Customs Brokers Assn. (1st pres. 1989), Phoenix Traffic Club, Internat. Traffic Mgmt. Assn. (bd. dirs. 1989). Republican. Office: 2627 S 21st St Phoenix AZ 85034

MATTEUCCI, DOMINICK VINCENT, real estate developer; b. Trenton, N.J., Oct. 19, 1924; s. Vincent Joseph and Anna Marie (Zoda) M.; BS, Coll. of William and Mary, 1948; BS, Mass. Inst. Tech., 1950; m. Emma Irene DeGuia, Mar. 2, 1968; children: Felisa Anna, Vincent Eriberto. Owner, Matteucci Devel. Co., Newport Beach, Calif.; pres. Nat. Investment Brokerage Co., Newport Beach. With USAAC, 1943-46. Recipient NASA achievement award, 1974; registered profl. engr., Calif.; lic. gen. bldg. contractor, real estate broker. Home: 2104 Felipe Newport Beach CA 92660 Office: PO Box 8328 Newport Beach CA 92660

MATTHEW, LYN, art marketing consultant, educator; b. Long Beach, Calif., Dec. 15, 1936; d. Harold G. and Beatrice (Hunt) M.; m. Wayne Thomas Castleberry, Aug. 12, 1961 (div. Jan. 1976); children—Melanie, Cheryl, Nicole, Matthew. BS, U. Calif.-Davis, 1958; MA, Ariz. State U., 1979. Pres., Davlyn Cons. Found., Scottsdale, Ariz., 1979-82; cons., vis. prof. The Art Bus., Scottsdale, 1982—; vis. prof. Maricopa Community Coll., Phoenix, 1979—, Ariz. State U., Tempe, 1980-83; cons. Women's Caucus for Art, Phoenix, 1983-88. Bd. dirs. Rossom House and Heritage Square Found., Phoenix, 1987-88. Author: The Business Aspects of Art, Book I, 1979, Book II, 1979; Marketing Strategies for the Creative Artist, 1985. Mem. Women Image Now (Achievement and Contbn. in Visual Arts award 1983), Women in Higher Edn., Nat. Women's Caucus for Art (v.p. 1981-83), Ariz. Women's Caucus for Art (pres. 1980-82, hon. advisor 1986-87), Vocat. Edn. Assn. (sec. 1978-80), Ariz. Visionary Artists (treas. 1987—), Ariz. Acad. Performing Arts (v.p. bd. dirs. 1987—, pres. 1988—).

MATTHEWS, BARBARA LEE, teacher, consultant; b. Columbus, Colo., Oct. 28, 1940; d. Walden M. and Ruth May (Williams) W.; m. Ron D. Gary, June 18, 1966 (div. Dec. 1977); 1 child, Dean; m. Cecil A. Matthews, July 2, 1981; stepchildren: David, Bruce. BS in Edn., Ohio State U., 1962; MA in Reading, U. Northern Colo., 1969. Cert. tchr., Colo. Tchr. English and Bus. Olentangy High Sch., Delaware, Ohio, 1962-64, Aurora (Colo.) Cen. High Sch., 1964-66; tchr. English Adams City High Sch., Commerce City, Colo., 1966-68; tchr. Reading Isaac Newton Jr. High Sch., Littleton, Colo., 1968-69; tchr. Reading Campus Mid. Unit Cherry Creek Schs., Englewood, Colo., 1972-75, reading specialist Laredo Mid. Sch., 1975—; instr. U. No. Colo., Greeley; conductor workshops bus. and reading edn., U. No. Colo., Aurora Pub. Schs., presentations Cherry Creek Council on Learning Disabilities. Mem. north central evaluation team Colo. mid. sch. programs. Recipient various teaching grants, awards, 1975—. Mem. Colo. Coun. Internat. Reading Assn. (regional conf. com., 1976, Outstanding Secondary Reading Tchr. Continuing Edn. award, 1976, holder numerous offices, editor newsletter), Nat. Mid. Sch. Assn. (planning com mem., registration chairperson), Colo. Assn. Mid. Level Edn. (session presentor, nominations chairperson), Nat. Assn. Student Councils (nat. conv. planning com. 1980, registration chairperson), Arapahoe County Coun. Internat. Reading Assn., Phi Delta Kappa. Democrat. Presbyterian. Office: Laredo Mid Sch 5000 S Laredo St Aurora CO 80015

MATTHEWS, CHRIS LONG, real estate executive; b. Washington, Nov. 9, 1954; s. Homer Burtis and Patricia Marian (Milner) M.; m. Liz Burton, July 14, 1976; children: Sara, Rachel, Jacob, Ruth, Mary. BS, U. Utah, 1979, MBA, 1981. Cert. property mgr. Real estate salesman Ler Burton Co., Salt Lake City, 1977-79; property mgr. Woodbury Corp., Salt Lake City, 1979-81, Equitable Life, Denver, 1981-84; regional leasing mgr. Equitable Real Estate, Denver, 1984-86, v.p., 1986—; faculty mem. Inst. Real Estate Mgmt., Chgo., 1987—. Mem. Bldg. Owner's and Mgr.'s Assn. (chmn. bd. 1988—, real property adminstnr.), Inst. Real Estate Mgmt. (cert. shopping ctr. mgr.), Internat. Coun. Shopping Ctrs., Beta Gamma Sigma, Honor Soc. Office: Equitable Real Estate 1225 17th St #2525 Denver CO 80202

MATTHEWS, JACK EDWARD, real estate executive; b. El Paso, Oct. 29, 1928; s. Jack C. and Helen (Guidry) M.; A.A., Los Angeles City Coll., 1951, U. So. Calif., 1953; m. Willa Blaine Davis, May 29, 1948; children—Jon E., Vikki. Gen. sales mgr. Volk-McLain Co., San Diego, 1956-60; co-owner Brent-Matthews & Co., San Diego, 1960-62; v.p. Am. Savs. & Loan, No. Calif., 1962-67; sr. v.p. 1st Western Savs. & Loan, Las Vegas, Nev., 1967-69; pres. Jack Matthews & Co., Realtors, Las Vegas, 1969-80, Merrill Lynch Realty/Jack Matthews, 1981-84; prin. Jack Matthews Co., Las Vegas, 1984—; chmn. bd. Continental Nat. Bank, Las Vegas, from 1983; now bd. dirs. Pres. Lions Club, 1975-76, named Lion of Year, 1976; state baseball chmn. Am. Legion. Served with USNR, 1946-48; PTO. Mem. Nat. Homebuilders Assn. (Sales Mgr. of Year 1959), Realtors Inst. (cert. residential specialist, designation), Nat. Assn. Realtors (cert. residential broker, bd. dirs. 1978-85, nat. regional v.p. 1985, Realtor of Yr. 1984, State Realtor or Yr. 1985), Nev. Assn. Realtors (pres. 1982), Las Vegas Bd. Realtors (pres. 1976), Reno Bd. Realtors, Bay Area Sales Mgrs. Club (charter), Las Vegas Execs. Club. Democrat. Club: Las Vegas Country. Office: 3100 S Valley View St Las Vegas NV 89102 *

MATTHEWS, JANA B., management consultant; b. Chgo., Oct. 23, 1940; d. L. Emmet and Helen J. (Severson) Beauchamp; m. Samuel R. Matthews, June 1, 1963 (div. 1971); 1 child, Carolyn E.; m. Charles C. Halbower, May 13, 1975. BA, Earlham Coll., 1962; MA, U. R.I., 1970; EdD, Harvard U., 1979. Tchr. Portsmouth (N.H.) and Coventry (R.I.) Pub. Schs., 1963-68; asst. provost Mass. State Coll. System, Boston, 1970-73; sr. staff Arthur D. Little, Inc., Cambridge, Mass., 1973-76; div. dir. NCHEMS, Boulder, Colo., 1980-83; pres. NCHEMS Mgmt. Svcs., Inc., Boulder, Colo., 1983-85, M & H Group, Inc., Boulder and Herndon, Va., 1985—; appointed commr. Colo Advanced Tech.Inst., 1988—. Co-authors: Managing the Partnership Between Higher Edn. and Industry, 1984, Effective Use of Management Consultants in H.E., 1983; contbr. articles to profl. jours. Commr. Colo. Advanced Tech. Inst., 1988—. Mem. Assn. Univ. Related Rsch. Parks (dir. 1987—), Soc. Coll. & Univ. Planning (v.p. 1973-75), Assn. Instl. Researchers, Harvard Club. Home: 49 Alder Ln Boulder CO 80302 Office: M&H Group Inc PO Box 1888 Boulder CO 80306

MATTHEWS, JOHN LOUIS, military officer, educator; b. Copperton, Utah, June 27, 1932; m. Darlene Davis, 1956; 3 children. BS in Geology, Brigham Young U., 1955, MEd in Edml. Adminstrn., 1967; Air War Coll. Grad., 1976. Commd. 2d lt. USAF, 1954; advanced through grades to instr. pilot, Laredo, Tex., 1955-58; mem. Utah Air N.G., 1959—, Colo. Air N.G., 1961-62, commdr. 151st Air Refueling Group, asst. adj. gen. for Air, 1981-82, chief of staff, 1982, adj. gen. State of Utah, 1982—; tchr. math. and sci. Dixon Jr. High Sch., Provo, Utah, 1962-67, prin., 1967-73; prin. Timpview High Sch., Provo, 1976-79. Decorated Legion of Merit, Vietnam Svc. medal, Nat. Def. Svc. medal, others. Mem. N.G. Assn. Utah, N.G. Assn. of U.S., Adjs. Gen. Assn. of U.S., Air Force Assn., Assn. U.S. Army, Rotary.

MATTHEWS, NORMAN SHERWOOD, JR., insurance company executive; b. San Antonio, Tex., Apr. 23, 1944; s. Norman Sherwood and Alice Ann (Hathaway) M.; student Middle Tenn. State U., 1962-64, Ventura Coll., 1965, Calif. State U., 1965-66, U. Md., 1968-70; BBA, U. Tex., 1972; postgrad. U. Hawaii, 1977-79; m. Masayo Nakamura, Sept. 1, 1970; children: Debbie Ann, Scott Tsuyoshi. Research asst. State Farm Ins. Co., Murfreesboro, Tenn., 1963-64; inventory control analyst Minn. Mining & Mfg. Co., Camarillo, Calif., 1964-65; sr. acct. Peat, Marwick, Mitchell & Co., Honolulu, 1973-75; dir. mgmt. analysis Hawaii Med. Service Assn., Honolulu, 1975-89; asst. v.p. mgmt. analysis and security Hawaii Med. Svc. Assn., 1989—. With USAF, 1966-70. Decorated Air medal with 8 oak leaf clusters. CPA, Hawaii; cert. internal auditor. Mem. AICPA, Hawaii Soc. CPAs, Nat. Assn. Accts., Am. Acctg. Assn., Inst. Internal Auditors, EDP Auditors Assn., Am. Mgmt. Assn. Home: 2724 Kahoaloha Ln Apt 1903 Honolulu HI 96826 Office: Hawaii Med Service Assn 818 Keeaumoku St Honolulu HI 96814

MATTHEWS, PHILIP RICHARD, lawyer; b. San Francisco, Aug. 27, 1952; s. Richard Thomas and Marjorie Hilda (Dean) M.; m. Dana Lynn Meier, Aug. 8, 1981; children: Lauren Alison, Lyndsey Ann. BA in Polit. Sci., George Washington U., 1974; JD, U. Calif.-San Francisco, 1977. Bar: Calif. 1978, U.S. Ct. Appeals (9th cir.) 1978, U.S. Dist. Ct. (no., and so.dists.) Calif. 1978, U.S. Dist. Ct. (ea. dist.) Calif. 1980. Assoc. Dinkelspiel, Pelavin, San Francisco, 1978-80; assoc. Hancock, Rothert & Bunshoft, San Francisco, 1980-85, ptnr., 1985—. Mem. ABA, State Bar Assn. of Calif., Bar Assn. of San Francisco, Commonwealth Club. Democrat. Episcopalian. Office: Hancock Rothert & Bunshoft 4 Embarcadero Ctr Ste 1000 San Francisco CA 94111

MATTHEWS, ROBERT LLOYD, banker; b. Omaha, Sept. 23, 1937; s. Lloyd Dale and Henrietta Anna (Voss) M.; m. Elizabeth Ann Martell, Feb. 17, 1962; children: Charles Robert, John Lloyd. B.A., U. Nebr.-Omaha, 1959; grad., Am. Inst. Banking, 1968, Pacific Coast Banking Sch., 1970. With Ariz. Bank, Phoenix, 1959—, beginning as mgmt. trainee, successively loan officer, br. mgr., loan supr., asst. to pres., exec. v.p. charge loan div., 1959-75, exec. v.p. charge earning assets div., 1975-77, pres., 1978-85, pres., chief operating officer, 1985-87, pres., chief exec. officer, 1987-88, chmn. bd. dirs., chief exec. officer, 1988—; bd. dirs., past chmn. Pacific Coast Banking Sch.; bd. dirs. Babbitt Bros. Trading Co., U.S. West Communications; bd. dirs., pres., mem. exec. com. COMPAS; mem. Ariz. state exec. bd. Life mem. Phoenix Thunderbirds, Fiesta Bowl Adv. Bd.; mem. bd. regents, Brophy Prep. Coll.; adv. bd. Sun Angel Found.; bd. dirs. Phoenix Community Alliance, Heard Mus., Herberger Theater Ctr., Phoenix Civic Ctr., Phoenix Together, Valley Big Bros., adv. dir., former pres.; chmn. bd. dirs. United for Ariz.; trustee emeritus, hon. bd. dirs. St. Luke's Health System; mem. adv. coun. Engring. Sch., Ariz. State U.; mem. bd. advisors U. Ariz. Bus. Sch. With Air N.G., 1959-65. Mem. Robert Morris Assos. (past pres.), Ariz. Bankers Assn. (dir., past pres.), Am. Bankers Assn. (past council), Phoenix Met. C. of C. (dir., past chmn.), Phoenix 40. Republican. Roman Catholic. Office: Security Pacific Bank Ariz 101 N 1st Ave Phoenix AZ 85003 also: Security Pacific Nat Bank PO Box 2097 Terminal Annex Los Angeles CA 90051

MATTHEWS, STEVEN RICHARD, culinary instructor, chef, consultant; b. Lowell, Mass., Mar. 31, 1962; s. Edward Joseph and Elizabeth Anne (Howcroft) M.; m. Carmen DeJesus Orellana, June 28, 1985; children: Christine, Adrian, Tania. Student, U. Lowell, 1981, Santa Monica (Calif.) Coll., 1982-83. Banquet sous chef Windsor, Dracut, Mass., 1976-80; head chef Charmer's Market, Santa Monica, 1981-83; exec. chef Rose Cafe, Venice, Calif., 1984—; instr. culinary arts U. Calif.-L.A., Westwood, Calif., 1987—; cons. co-owner So. Calif. Chef, L.A., 1986; cons. Chatter's Restaurant, Sherman Oaks, Calif., 1988. Mem. Am. Culinary Fedn., Chef's De Cuisine Assn. Calif., The Wine Soc. of Am. Roman Catholic. Office: Rose Chef 220 Rose Ave Venice CA 90291

MATTHEWS, WARREN WAYNE, state supreme court justice; b. Santa Cruz, Calif., Apr. 5, 1939; s. Warren Wayne and Ruth Ann (Maginnis) M.; m. Donna Stearns, Aug. 17, 1963; children: Holly Maginnis, Meredith Sample. A.B., Stanford U., 1961; LL.B., Harvard U., 1964. Bar: Alaska 1965. Assoc. firm Burr, Boney & Pease, Anchorage, 1964-69, Matthews & Dunn, Matthews, Dunn and Baily, Anchorage, 1969-77; justice Alaska Supreme Ct., Anchorage, 1977-87, chief justice, 1987—. Bd. dirs. Alaska Legal Services Corp., 1969-70. Mem. Alaska Bar Assn. (bd. govs. 1974-77), ABA, Anchorage Bar Assn.

MATTHEWS, WILLIAM JOHN, small business owner; b. Croswell, Mich., Jan. 1, 1919; s. Silas Oliphant and Lois O. (Arnot) M.; divorced; children: Lois, Carol, James, John, Robert. B of Music, U. Calif., Santa Barbara, 1941; student, Florence Conservatory, Italy, 1945. Owner, operator Wm. J. Matthews Piano Studio, Long Beach, Calif., 1946—. Author: Matthews Modern Music Methods for Piano and Organ (6 vol.), 1965—. Served to sgt. Signal Corps, U.S. Army, 1942-46. Republican.

MATTHIAS, JUDSON STILLMAN, civil engineering educator, consultant; b. Scofield Barracks, Hawaii, Oct. 6, 1931; s. Norman Arthur and Charlotte Aleta (Stillman) M.; m. Georgia Stewart, June 9, 1956; children: Mary, Elizabeth, Judson Jr., Anne. BS, grad. U.S. Mil. Acad., 1954; MSCE, Oreg. State U., 1963; PhD, Purdue U., 1967. Commd. 2d lt. U.S. Army, 1954, resigned, 1961; instr. Oreg. State U., Corvallis, 1962-64, Purdue U., West Lafayette, Ind., 1964-67; prof. civil engring. Ariz. State U., Tempe, 1967—. Contbr. articles to profl. jours. Mem. Traffic Accident Reduction Program, Phoenix, 1982-85, Valley Forward, Phoenix, 1972-84. Grantee Fed. Hwy. Adminstrn., Evanston, Ill., 1980, Washington, D.C., 1982; elected Outstanding Engr. of Yr., Ariz. Soc. Profl. Engrs., 1986. Fellow Inst. Transp. Engrs.; mem. ASCE (hwy. and traffic safety), Am. Rd. and Transp. Builders Assn. (pres. edml. div. 1984-185, bd. dirs. 1984-85), Transp. Research Bd. of Nat. Acad. of Scis. (univ. rep. 1971—). Home: 2032 E Laguna Dr Tempe AZ 85282 Office: Ariz State U Dept Civil Engring Tempe AZ 85287

MATTISON, CHARLES ALBERT, minister; b. Anderson, S.C., Dec. 30, 1939; s. Charles Henry and Alma (Watkins) M.; m. Patricia Ann Rich, Nov. 11, 1980; children: Robyn, Charles, Chad, Cayce. BS, Johnson C. Smith U., 1962; DDS, Meharry Med. Coll., Nashville, 1968; MA, Fuller Theol. Sem., Pasadena, Calif., 1984; D of Ministry, Calif. Grad. Sch. Theology, Glendale, 1987. Pvt. practice dentistry L.A., 1970-83; assoc. pastor Pilgrim Congl. Ch., L.A., 1985-88; pastor Lincoln Meml. Congl. Ch., L.A., 1988—. With USN, 1968-70. Home and Office: 4573 Don Milagro Dr Los Angeles CA 90008

MATTISON, ELISA SHERI, industrial psychologist; b. Grand Rapids, Mich., Apr. 24, 1952; d. Andrew and Loraine R. Wierenga; m. John H. Mattison, Sept. 29, 1978. BS cum laude, Western Mich. U., 1974, MA, 1979. Trainer No. Inst., Anchorage, 1980; mgmt. cons.,trainer Alaska Assocs. Human Devel. Inc., Anchorage, 1980-82; job devel. specialist Collins, Weed and Assocs., Anchorage, 1982-83; owner Mattison & Assocs., Anchorage; mem. adj. faculty Anchorage Community Coll., 1981-82; work environment and design coord. ARCO Alaska Inc., 1983-86; cons. Employee Assts. Cons. Alaska, Anchorage, 1982; v.p. Human Resource Mgmt. and Mktg. Alaskan Fed. Credit Union, 1986—. Mem. Am. Soc. Tng. and Devel., Am. Soc. Personnel Adminstrs., Credit Union Execs. Soc. Contbr. articles to profl. publs. Office: 3400 La Touche St Anchorage AK 99508

MATTISON, LEE JESSE, small business owner; b. Fairmont, Minn., Nov. 7, 1949; s. Glenn B. and Mildred Opel (Thouson) M.; m. Janice Erwin Walla, Aug. 29, 1971; 1 child, Krista. BS in Dairy Mgmt., Loma Linda U., 1972. Asst. mgr. Loma Linda U., 1967-72; farmer Loma Linda, 1972-74; owner Lee's Hay Loading & Unloading, Chino, Calif., 1974—. Republican. Seventh-Day Adventist. Office: Lees Hay Loading 12168 Mount Vernon #18 Grand Terrace CA 92324

MATTSON, DAVID ROALD, real estate developer; b. Grand Forks, N.D., Feb. 21, 1947; s. Alf S. and Sharlot (Hanson) M.; m. Carol Jean Haupt, Mar. 8, 1969; children: David R. Jr., Kirstin M., Suzanne A., Michael S. BS, N.D. State U., 1969. Project supt. Baukol Constrn. Inc., Scottsdale, Ariz., 1974-75; project mgr. Mattson Constrn. Inc., Phoenix, 1975-76, C.W. Jackson Constrn. Co., Tempe, Ariz., 1976-78; constrn. mgr. Anmar Constrn., Chandler, Ariz., 1978-79; pres., chief exec. officer J.B. Contractors, Inc., Phoenix, 1979-85; sr. v.p., chief operating officer Double AA Constructors, Inc., Phoenix, 1985-86; v.p., dir. devel. The Pensus Group, Phoenix, 1986--; lectr. Ariz. State U., 1978--. Bd. dirs. Hacienda de Los Angeles, Phoenix, 1988--. Capt. USMC, 1970-74. Mem. Am. Inst. Constructors (pres. Ariz. chpt. 1982-84), Project Mgmt. Inst. (pres. Phoenix chpt. 1988--), Assoc. Gen. Contractors (bd. dirs. Ariz. chpt. 1982-86), Sons of Norway. Republican. Roman Catholic. Home: 2046 E Manhatton Dr Tempe AZ 85282 Office: The Pensus Group 2201 E Camelback Rd Ste 226B Phoenix AZ 85016

MATTSON, HARRY AUWAE, business and risk management services company executive; b. Honolulu, Mar. 9, 1951; s. James Auwae and Marguerite Kauilani (Boyd) M.; m. JoAnn Namie Gondo, Aug. 9, 1975. BA in Polit. Sci., BBA, U. Hawaii, 1973. Mgr. Kam's Ltd. (Vintage Wine Cellar and Village Market), Honolulu, 1973-75; orgnl. analyst Office of Gov., State of Hawaii, Honolulu, 1975-77; ptnr. Mattson & Co., Honolulu, 1977—; exec. v.p. Risk Mgmt. Group, Inc., Honolulu, 1985-87. Past commr. Scandinavian Centennial Commn., Hawaii Found. on Culture and Arts; mem Hawaii Dem. Com., 1970—, mem. Oahu County com., 1974, 76; del. Hawaii Dem. Conv., 1970—. Home: 2299-B Round Top Dr Honolulu HI 96822 Office: 1188 Bishop St Ste 3109 Honolulu HI 96813

MATTSON, JAMES ALLEN, clinical psychologist; b. Seattle, July 4, 1949; s. Glenn Arthur and Lillian B. (Schnaidt) M.; m. Charyl B. Thurber, July 22, 1972; children: Robert Charles, David James. BS in Psychology, U. Wash., 1971; PhD in Clin. Psychology, U. Tex., Austin, 1975. Lic. psychologist, Wash. Assoc. dir. planning and evaluation N. Cen. Community Mental Health Ctr., Columbus, 1975-78; exec. dir. Drug Abuse Council, Everett, Wash., 1978—; co-founder Substance Abuse Treatment Assn.; mgr. Creative Investments. Treas. Wash. Assn. TASC programs. Mem. Am. Psychol. Assn. Unitarian. Office: Pacific Treatment Svcs 2720 Rucker Everett WA 98201

MATTSON, ROY HENRY, engineering educator; b. Chisholm, Minn., Dec. 26, 1927; s. Gust and Hilma (Appel) M.; m. June Eileen Lindstrom, June 14, 1948; children—Kristi Lynn, Lisa Kay, Greta Lee, Linnea Jean, Marla Jo, Brent Anders, Brian Alan. B.Elec. Engring., U. Minn., 1951, M.S. in Elec. Engring, 1952; Ph.D., Iowa State U., 1959. Registered profl. engr. Mem. tech. staff Bell Telephone Labs., Inc., 1952-56; asst. prof., then asso. prof. Iowa State U., 1956-61; asso. prof. U. Minn., 1961-66; prof. elec. engring., head dept. U. Ariz., 1966-86, prof. elect, comp. engring,, 1986-88; acad. v.p. Nat. Technol. U., Ft. Collins, Colo., 1988—; Del. to A.S. Popov Congress, Moscow, USSR, 1972; non-govt. observer to UN Conf. on Human Environment, Stockholm, 1972; chmn. grad. faculty, acad. exec. com. Nat. Tech. U., 1986-88. Author: Basic Junction Devices and Circuits, 1963, Electronics, 1966, also articles; patentee in field. Mem. Amphitheater Bd. Sch. Trustees, 1971-76, pres., 1976. Served with USNR, 1946-47. Fellow IEEE (editor Transactions on Edn. 1970-73, chmn. validation of ednl. achievement program 1976-82), AAAS; mem. Am. Soc. Engring. Edn., Sigma Xi, Theta Tau, Eta Kappa Nu, Tau Beta Pi. Home: PO Box 97 Bellvue CO 80512 Office: Nat Technol U PO Box 700 Fort Collins CO 80522

MATULL, JOHN FRANKLIN, industrial relations specialist; b. Arno, Va., Sept. 11, 1938; s. John Dominicus and Lena Della (Gabera) M.; m. Lorene Blocker, Feb. 16, 1960; children: Michael, Carolyn, Tonya. BA, U. Beverly Hills (Calif.), 1982. Mill worker U.S. Borax and Chem. Corp., Boron, Calif., 1960-64; local v.p. Internat. Chem. Workers Union, Boron, 1962-64; internat. rep. Internat. Longshoremens Union, Los Angeles, 1964-70; union negotiator Teamsters Union, Los Angeles, 1970-78; cons., arbitrator Matull and Assocs., Inc., San Pedro, Calif., 1978—; bd. dirs. Marathon Office Supply, Los Angeles, 1986—. Mem. Harbor Area Ethnic Polit. Group, San Pedro, 1975; coach Miraleste High Sch. Girls Softball, Rancho Palos Verde, Calif., 1978, Am. Fast Pitch Assn., San Pedro, 1980. Served with USN, 1957-59. Named Coach of Yr. Calif. Interscholastic Fedn., 1986. Mem. UCLA-IRIA (v.p.), Soc. Prof. In Dispute Resolution. Democrat. Roman Catholic. Office: Matull & Assocs Inc Ports-O-Call Village San Pedro CA 90731

MATYAS, JANET, consultant; b. Garden Grove, Calif., Oct. 6, 1962; d. George Edwin Hood and Joan Elaine (McFarland) Thorn; m. Nicholas J. Matyas, Oct. 30, 1987; 1 daughter, Ashley Anne. AA, Auraria Community Coll., Denver, 1984; Secretarial Cert., Barns Bus. Coll., Denver, 1984. Sec. to pres. TSP Colorado, Denver, 1982-83; accounting staff Dirt Magnet, Denver, 1983-85; accounting supr. All State Distributing, Denver, 1984-85; account rep. AT&T Communications, Van Nuys, Calif., 1985-87; adminstrv. supr. Liberty Woods Internat., Huntington Beach, Calif., 1987-88; v.p. Matyas & Assoc. Inc., Phoenix, 1988—. Mem. Mt. Park Ranch Adv. Com., Phoenix, 1988. Mem. Xerox Ventura Pub. Users Group. Office: Matyas & Assoc Inc PO Box 51180 Phoenix AZ 85076

MAUGHAN, JOYCE BOWEN, psychologist, educator, writer, sculptor; b. Rupert, Idaho, June 26, 1928; d. John Henry and Sara (Stewart) Bowen; m. Dean L. Maughan, Nov. 4, 1949 (div.); children: JoDean Dunn, LaRee Olson, Randon B., Teresa Abney, Melanie Brimley, Kristine Nance. BS, U. Idaho, 1958; MA, MC in Counseling, Ariz. State U., 1974. Tchr. elem. schs. Spokane, Wash., 1958-64; instr. Mesa (Ariz.) Community Coll., 1973-76; coord., psychologist Kyrene Dist. Program for Gifted & Talented Children, Tempe, Ariz., 1975-81; pvt. practice in psychology Mesa, 1981—. Author: Talks for Tots, vol. I, 1964, vol. II, 1967, Talk Themes for Sub-Teens, 1964, Stories You'll Want to Remember, 1969, Stories That Never Grow Old, 1965, Unicornucopia, 1977; columnist Thoughts in Passing, Sun Valley newspaper, 1968-69; sculptor portrait busts, 1969—. Mem. Am. Assn. Counseling, Ariz. Personnel & Guidance Assn., Am. Personnel & Guidance Assn., Nat. League Am., Pen Women (pres. 1975-76), Coun. Exceptional Children, Calif. Assn. Gifted, Ariz. Assn. Gifted, Internat. Platform Assn., NOW. Mormon. Home and Office: 735 E 3rd Mesa AZ 85203

MAUK, THOMAS GREGORY, city manager; b. Oakland, Calif., Oct. 21, 1943; s. James R. and Constance Ivy (Jensen) Nourse; m. Rebecca V. Mauk, Mar. 18, 1968; children—Donald, Katherine, Laura, Danielle. B.B.A., Calif. State U.-Pomona, 1966; M.P.A., U. So. Calif., 1972. Adminstrv. analyst City of Los Angeles, 1967-70; asst. city adminstr. City of Montclair (Calif.), 1970-76; city mgr. City of Norco (Calif.), 1976-80, City of Whittier (Calif.), 1980—; pub. speaker; tchr. Named Man of Yr., Norco C. of C., 1977. Mem. Internat. City Mgrs. Assn., Los Angeles World Affairs Council, Town Hall of Calif. Club: Lions. Home: 10015 Santa Gertrudes St Whittier CA 90603 Office: City of Whittier 13230 Penn St Whittier CA 90601

MAUL, TERRY LEE, psychologist, educator; b. San Francisco, May 6, 1946; s. Chester Lloyd and Clella Lucille (Hobbs) M.; AB, U. Calif., Berkeley, 1967, MA, 1968, PhD, 1970; student Coll. San Mateo, 1964-65; m. Gail Ann Retallick, June 27, 1970 (div. Dec. 1986); 1 son, Andrew Eliot. Assoc. prof. psychology San Bernardino Valley Coll., San Bernardino, Calif., 1970—, chmn. dept., 1979-82; researcher self-actualization. Mem. Am. Psychol. Assn., AAUP (chpt. pres. 1971-73), Audubon Soc., Mensa, Nature Conservancy, Rachel Carson Council, Wilderness Soc., Sierra Club. Democrat. Author: (with Eva Conrad) Introduction to Experimental Psychology, 1981; (with Gail Maul) Beyond Limit: Ways to Growth and Freedom, 1983; contbg. author other psychol. texts. Home: 6155 Bluffwood Dr Riverside CA 92506 Office: San Bernardino Valley Coll 701 S Mount Vernon Ave San Bernardino CA 92410

MAULIK, JERRI EILEEN, teacher's aide; b. Newcastle, Wyo., Mar. 5, 1957; d. Jerry Arnold and Dorcas Ann (McKean) Pridgeon; m. Douglas Alec Maulik, Aug. 5, 1978; children: Jillian Anne, David Alec. Grad. high sch., Sundance, Wyo.; student, Casper (Wyo.) Coll. Cert. substitute tchr., Wyo. Dispatcher, sec. Campbell County Sheriff's Office, Gillette, Wyo., 1975-76; dormitory proctor Casper Coll., 1977-78; clk., buyer, then dept. head Bi-Rite Payless Drug Store, Riverton, Wyo., 1978-85; tchr.'s aide, substitute tchr. Riverton High Sch., 1985—. Vol., Riverton Friends of Library, 1983—, Riverton area Girl Scouts U.S., 1988—. Mem. Wyo. Star Quilters Guild (co-founder, 1987). Republican. Roman Catholic. Home: 1003 E Adams St Riverton WY 82501 Office: Riverton Sr High Sch Sunset Ave Riverton WY 82501

MAULIN, JACK DOOLIN, construction company executive; b. Buffalo, Mo., Nov. 7, 1934; s. George Washington and Gussie Dean (Doolin)M.; m. Jane Lois Eason, Sept. 1, 1957 (div. 1979); children: Debra, John, Robert; m. Stpehanie Anne Liesk, Oct. 25, 1980. BS, U. Mo., 1957. Asst. project engr. Morrison-Knudsen, Calif., Mo. and Wyo., 1959-63; project engr./project mgr. multiple constrn. projects Morrison-Knudsen, Wyo., N.D. and Calif., 1963-66; ea. regional engr. Morrison-Knudsen, N.Y., 1966-71; project mgr. multiple constrn. projects Morrison-Knudsen, N.D. and Calif., 1970-73; v.p. corp. mktg. and planning Morrison-Knudsen, Boise, Idaho, 1973-83, sr. v.p. corp. mktg. and planning, 1983-87, sr. v.p. constrn., 1987—. 1st lt. U.S. Army, 1957-59. Republican. Home: 1727 Trout Rd Eagle ID 83616 Office: Morrison-Knudsen M-K Plaza Boise ID 83729

MAUPIN, ERNEST JUSTIN, lawyer; b. Reno, Nev., Sept. 10, 1946; s. Ernest Justin and Hazel Helen (Prudler) M.; m. Catherine Ann Kelly, June

19, 1971; children: Darren J., Ryan D., Jason E., Ann M. BS in Acctg., U. Nev., 1968; JD, U. Calif., Berkeley, 1971. Bar: Nev. 1971, U.S. Dist. Ct. Nev. 1971, U.S. Dist. Ct. Calif. 1971, Calif. 1972, U.S. Tax Ct. 1973, U.S. Claims Ct. 1976, U.S. Ct. Appeals (9th cir.) 1977; CPA, Nev. Acct. Semenza, Kottinger & McMullen (now Grant Thornton), Reno, 1971-73; ptnr. Walther, Key, Maupin, Oats, Cox, Lee & Klaich, Reno, 1973—. Bd. dirs. Sierra Arts Found., Reno, 1984-86. Mem. ABA, State Bar Nev., State Bar Calif., Am. Inst. CPAs, Nev. Soc. CPAs, Estate Planning Coun. Reno (pres. 1977-78), Nev. Tax Found. (dir. 1981—), Hidden Valley Country Club (pres. 1985), U.S. Golf Assn. (sectional affairs com. 1982—), Nev. State Golf Assn. (pres. 1988), No. Nev. Golf Assn. (pres. 1983-85). Republican. Methodist. Home: 2551 Lakeridge Shores Circle Reno NV 89509 Office: Walther Key Maupin Oats Cox Lee & Kaaich 3500 Lakeside Ct Ste 200 PO Box 30000 Reno NV 89520

MAURICE, LOIS JANE, electronics technologist; b. Trona, Calif., Apr. 6, 1953; d. George Owen and Wilma Jane (Simmons) Williams; m. Francis Jerome Maurice, Dec. 21, 1979. Assoc., Cerro Coso Coll., 1979; student, La. State U., 1974-75. Cert. electronics tech. Meteorology instruction asst. target acquisition dept. Army Field Artillery Sch., Ft. Sill., Okla., 1972-73; copy editor asst. Bradenton Herald Newspaper, Bradenton, Fla., 1973-74; electronics tech. Naval Weapons Ctr. Spl. Projects, China Lake, Calif., 1975-78, Naval Weapons Ctr. Parachute/Aerosystems, China Lake, 1978-80, Naval Weapons Ctr. Super Sonic Naval Ordnance Research Track, China Lake, 1980-83, Naval Weapons Ctr. Computer Aided Engring., China Lake, 1983-87, Naval Weapons Ctr. Electromagnetics Compatibility, China Lake, 1987—; ATE & RF measurements Naval Weapons Ctr. Spl. Projects, China Lake, 1976-78; test & instrumentation Naval Weapons Ctr. Parachute/Aerosystems, China Lake, 1978-80, Naval Weapons Ctr. Super Sonic Naval Ordnance Research Track, China Lake, 1980-83; CAM (photoplotting) Naval Weapons Ctr. Computer Aided Engring., China Lake, 1983-87, test mgr. EMC Sect., 1987—. Career day presenter Sierra Sands Sch. Dist., Ridgecrest, Calif., 1984. Mem. Elks (press/recording sec. 1982-84, pub. relations, newsletter writer 1980-85 Ridgecrest chpt.). Republican. Home: 231 S Sunland Dr Ridgecrest CA 93555 Office: Naval Weapons Ctr Mail Code 36254 China Lake CA 93555

MAURO, JOHN ROCCO, JR., building and development executive; b. Orange, Calif., Nov. 17, 1945; s. John Michael and Elizabeth (Watkins) M.; m. C. Karen, Feb. 17, 1967 (div. Sept. 1969); 1 child, Stacey Michelle; m. Detra Kay, Mar. 31, 1984; 1 child, Ryan Joseph. AA in Psychology, Fullerton Coll., 1968; BA in Psychology, Calif. State U., Long Beach, 1974; MA in Behavioral Sci., Calif. State U. Dominquez Hills, Carson, 1975. Camp dir. Orange YMCA, Orange, Calif., 1963-66; cen. office equipment mgr. Pacific Bell, Santa Ana, Calif., 1966-74; assoc. Dr. Lee Cordrey & Assocs., Psychologists, Orange, 1974-80; exec. dir. Jewish Family Svc. Orange County, Garden Grove, Calif., 1974-80; project mgr. Century Am. Corp., Orange, 1980-84; v.p., gen. mgr. Marinita Devel. Co., Newport Beach, Calif., 1984-86; project mgr. Century Am. Corp., Orange, 1986-88; v.p., div. mgr. Glenfed Devel. Corp., Encino, Calif., 1988—. Exec. v.p. bd. dirs. Orange YMCA, 1976-80, Chapman Coll. Athletic Found., Orange, 1988—; committeeperson Gaddi Vasques Campaign Com., Orange, 1987. mem. Building Industry Assn. So. Calif. (com. chairperson 1986-88), Home Builders Coun. Orange County. Republican. Roman Catholic. Office: Glenfed Devel Corp 16601 Ventura Blvd Encino CA 91463

MAURO, RICHARD FRANK, lawyer, educator, businessman; b. Hawthorne, Nev., July 21, 1945; s. Frank Joseph and Dolores D. (Kreimeyer) M.; m. LaVonne M. Madden, Aug. 28, 1965; 1 child, Lindsay Anne. AB, Brown U., 1967; JD summa cum laude, U. Denver, 1970. Bar: Colo. 1970. Assoc. Dawson, Nagel, Sherman & Howard, Denver, 1970-72; assoc. Van Cise, Freeman, Tooley & McClearn, Denver, 1972-73, ptnr., 1973-74; ptnr. Hall & Evans, Denver, 1974-81, Morrison & Forester, Denver, 1981-84, Parcel, Mauro, Hultin & Spaanstra, Denver, 1984—; pres. Sundance Oil Exploration Co., 1985-88; adj. prof. U. Denver Coll. Law, 1981-84. Symposium editor: Denver Law Jour., 1969-70; editor: Colorado Corporation Manual; contbr. articles to legal jours. Pres. Colo. Open Space Coun., 1974; mem. law alumni coun. U. Denver Coll. Law. Francis Wayland scholar, 1967; recipient various Am. jurisprudence awards. Mem. ABA, Colo. Bar Assn., Denver Bar Assn., Colo. Assn. Corp. Counsel. (pres. 1974-75), Am. Arbitration Assn. (comml. arbitrator), Order St. Ives. Club: Denver Athletic (bd. dirs. 1986-89). Home: 3264 Taft Ct Wheat Ridge CO 80033 Office: 1801 California St Ste 3600 Denver CO 80202

MAUS, JOHN ANDREW, computer systems engineer; b. Whittier, Calif., July 13, 1945; s. Kenneth Waring and Bertha Estella (Eckman) M.; M. Diana Barba, April 16, 1977 (div. May 1, 1983); m. Colette An Moschelle, Nov. 23, 1985; stepchildren: BreAnn, Adam; children: Steven Andrew, Terra An. BA in Physics, U. Calif., Riverside, 1963-67; MS in Physics, San Diego State U., 1967-70. Cert. data processor, 1983. Programmer, analyst San Diego State Found., 1970-72; instr. bus. San Diego State U., 1971-73; systems programmer San Diego State U., San Diego, 1971-74; data processing mgr. M.H. Golden Co., San Diego, 1974-79; computer systems engr. Hewlett-Packard Co., Spokane, Wash., 1979-84, sr. systems engr., 1984-86, network systems engr., 1986—; physics lab. asst. USDA Salinity Lab., Riverside, Calif., 1965-67; underwater acoustics programmer Naval Undersea Ctr., San Diego, 1967-70; programmer San Diego Inst. Pathology, 1972-76. Co-author: Chemical Physics Letters, 1971, Electronic and Atomic Collisions, 1971. Merit badge counselor Spokane chpt. Boy Scouts Am., 1983—. Mem. Assn. Computing Machinery (founder Spokane chpt., chpt. chmn. 1980-82, service award 1981). Home: W 12417 Sunridge Dr Nine Mile Falls WA 99026 Office: Hewlett-Packard Co N 1225 Argonne Rd Spokane WA 99212-2657

MAUSER, KEVIN EDWARD, finance executive; b. Plattsburgh, N.Y., Nov. 22, 1959; s. Edward Anton and Josie Agnes (Collins) M. BS, Sacramento State U., 1981. Loan processor Am. Savs., Sacramento, 1983-84; underwriter United Guaranty Ins., San Ramon, Calif., 1984-85, Ticor Investment Securities, L.A., 1985; asst. v.p. Portfolio Svcs., Inc., L.A., 1986—; cons. in field. Mem. Nat. Assn. Rev. Appraisers (sr.), Mortgage Underwriters. Roman Catholic. Office: Portfolio Svcs Inc 6300 Wilshire Blvd #1400 Los Angeles CA 90048

MAUTER, WARREN EUGENE, chemist, business development manager; b. Denver, Aug. 27, 1951; s. Jacob Martin and Harriette June (Kaiser) M.; m. Deborah Lee Long, Jan. 22, 1983 (div. 1987). BS in Chemistry, Met. State Coll., 1976; MBA, U. Colo., 1986. Rech. chemist Manville Corp., Denver, 1973-80, group leader, 1980-83; applications mgr. Cardinal Chem., Columbia, S.C., 1983-84; prin. Alpine Cons., Denver, 1984-88; corp. mgr. COBE Labs., Inc., Lakewood, Colo., 1988—; instr. econs. and fin. U. Colo. Coll. Engring, 1987-89; mem. bd. advs. Shock Found., 1986-88. Bd. reviewers Jour. Vinyl Tech., 1981-83; contbr. articles to profl. jours. Sci. and Tech. Colo. scholar Met. State Coll., 1972-75. Mem. ASTM, Soc. Plastics Engrs. (bd. dirs. vinyl div. 1982-86), Nat. Sanitation Found. (industry adv. bd. 1980-84), Am. Chem. Soc., Am. Mgmt. Assn., Colo. Mountain Club, U. Colo. Execs. Club (Denver, v.p. 1987, pres. 1988). Republican. Home: 1649 S Marion St Denver CO 80210 Office: COBE Labs Inc 1185 Oak St Lakewood CO 80215

MAW, SAM H., restaurant chain executive; b. Easley, SC, 1933. Grad., Wofford Coll., Spartanburg, S.C., 1956. Formerly v.p. for r & d Spartan Food Systems Inc., Spartanburg, S.C.; pres., chief exec. officer Denny's Inc., La Mirada, Calif., 1988—. Office: Denny's Inc 16700 Valley View La Mirada CA 90637 *

MAXEY, KEREN LOUISE, nurse; b. Scottsbluff, Nebr., Sept. 5, 1953; d. I. Parker and Edith Louise (Morehouse) M. Diploma, Luth. Hosp. Sch. for Nurses, 1973; postgrad., Graceland Coll., 1988—. RN, Ill., Calif. Staff nurse Franciscan Hosp., Rock Island, Ill., 1973-75, Ill. Migrant Head Start, Edgington, Ill., 1984; night supr. Luth. Hosp., Moline, 1976-77, head nurse oncology, 1985-87; adminstr. maternal/pediatric clinic Evangelistic Faith Missions, Inc., Honduras, 1977-83; chemotherapy nurse Med. Arts Assocs., Moline, 1983; charge nurse obstetrics Dominican Santa Cruz (Calif.) Hosp., 1987-88, utilization rev. nurse, 1988—; lectr. God's Bible Sch., Cin., 1985; pub. speaker Evangelistic Faith Missions, Inc., 1980-81. Contbr. articles on med. work in Cen. Am. profl. jours., 1977-83. Republican. Home: 4414 10th Ave Rock Island IL 61201

MAXEY, VALERIE KRIZ, writer, communications consultant; b. Berkeley, Calif., Oct. 16, 1954; d. Leland and Rita Rose (Webber) Kriz; m. Lyle D. Maxey, June 2, 1979. BA in Communications, Stanford U., 1976. Analyst Ford Motor Co., Pico Rivera, Calif., 1977-79; account supr. Bozell & Jacobs, Inc., Newport Beach, Calif., 1979-82; corp. communications mgr. Smith Internat. Inc., Newport Beach, 1982-85; freelance writer, communications cons. Newport Beach, 1985—. Mem. Women in Communications (Orange County chpt. pres. 1985-86), Pub. Relations Soc. Am.

MAXON, JAMES CLARK, archaeologist, environmental education specialist; b. Alamosa, Colo., Dec. 19, 1935; s. Leo Gilbert and Mary Edith (Taylor) M.; student U.S. Mil. Acad., 1954; B.A. in Anthropology, U. Denver, 1958; M.A. in Archaeology, U. Wis., 1969; m. Sharon Kay Sullivan, Aug. 16, 1958; children—Kevin Joseph, Clark Christopher, Dianne Marie; m. 2d, Kristin Jane Lenning, Jan. 3, 1982. Archaeologist, Aztec Ruins Nat. Monument, 1958-61, Bandelier Nat. Monument, 1961-67; environ. edn. specialist Lake Mead Nat. Recreation Area, 1967-74; instr. continuing edn. U. Nev., Las Vegas, 1972—; with U.S. Bur. Reclamation, Lower Colo. River region, Boulder City, Nev., 1975-85, regional archaeologist, 1976-85, chief archaeologist, Denver, 1986—. Pres. Nev. Environ. Edn. Council 1974—. Mem. Soc. Am. Archeology, Am. Soc. Conservation Archeology, Nev. Hist. Soc., Boulder City First Nighters. Author: Indians of the Lake Mead Country, 1971; Boating Guide to Lake Mohave, 1971; Lake Mead: The Story Behind the Scenery, 1980. Office: US Bur Reclamation Engring and Rsch Ctr DFC PO Box 25007 Denver CO 80225

MAXSON, ROBERT C., university president. Former sr. v.p. acad. affairs U. Houston Systems, Houston; pres. U. Nev., Las Vegas, 1984—. Office: U of Nev-Las Vegas Office of Pres 4505 S Maryland Pkwy Las Vegas NV 89154 *

MAXWELL, COLIN, Canadian provincial cabinet minister; b. Tillicoultry, Scotland, Dec. 16, 1943; arrived in Can., 1966; s. Colin and Molly (Drummond) M.; m. Cherry Harvey, July 6, 1966; children: Ashley, Kirstin, Brigham. Grad. Jordanhill Coll., 1965, Grad. diploma in Edn., 1966; BEdn, U. Regina, 1975. Cert. tchr., Scotland, Sask. Tchr., Sturgis Sch. Dist., Preeceville, Sask., 1966-67; prin. Nipawin Sch. Dist., Smeaton, Sask., 1968; phys. edn. tchr. Melville, Sask., 1968-74; univ. lectr. U. Regina, 1974-76; prin. Spiritwood High Sch., Sask., 1976-82; head coach Legion Track and Field Camp., Sask., 1974-75. Mayor Spiritwood Town Council, 1978-82; mem. legis. assembly Prog. Conservative Govt. Sask. Legislation, Regina, 1982—; re-elected mem. Turtleford Constituency, 1986; cabinet minister of advanced edn. and manpower, 1983, cabinet minister of parks and renewable resources, Regina, 1985. Pres. Melville local Sask. Tchrs. Fedn., 1970-72, councillor, 1970-74, Mem. Commonwealth Parliamentary Assn. Lutheran. Lodges: Lions, Masons. Office: Sask Legis Assembly, Legislative Bldg Rm 340, Regina, SK Canada S4S 0B3

MAXWELL, DONALD STANLEY, publishing executive; b. Los Angeles, May 30, 1930; s. Harold Stanley and Margaret (Trenam) M.; m. Martha Helen Winn, Dec. 5, 1952; children: Sylvia Louise, Cynthia Lynn, Bruce Stanley, Bradley Erl, Walter James, Wesley Richard, Amy Bernice. Student, Long Beach City Coll., 1948-50; B.B.A., Woodbury Coll., 1956. C.P.A. Ptnr. Robert McDavid & Co. (C.P.A.'s), Los Angeles, 1955-61; controller Petersen Pub. Co., Los Angeles, 1961-68; v.p. fin. Petersen Pub. Co., 1969; controller Los Angeles Times, 1969-79, v.p., 1977-79, v.p. fin., 1979-81; asst. treas. Times Mirror Co., 1971-82, v.p., controller, 1982-87, v.p., chief acctg. officer, 1987—. Trustee Woodbury U., 1981—, chmn. bd. trustees, 1984-87. Served with AUS, 1950-52. Mem. Fin. Execs. Inst. (dir. 1979-82, pres. Los Angeles chpt. 1973-74), Internat. Newspaper Fin. Execs. (dir. 1978-82, pres. 1980-81), Am. Inst. CPAs, Calif. Soc. CPAs, Am. Horse Council, Internat. Arabian Horse Assn., Arabian Horse Assn. So. Calif., Friendly Hills Country Club. Republican. Baptist. Home: 2160 LeFlore Dr La Habra Heights CA 90631 Office: Times Mirror Co Times Mirror Sq Los Angeles CA 90053

MAXWELL, JEROME EUGENE, electronics company executive; b. Princeton, Ill., June 2, 1944; s. Emmett Eugene and June (Erickson) M.; BSEE, So. Meth. U., 1967, MSEE, 1971; m. Cynthia Jane O'Connell, July 30, 1977; children: Eric Vaughn, Christina Dawn, Jeremy Emmett, Jason Daniel, Nicholas Mark. Maintainability engr. product support div. Collins Radio Co., Richardson, Tex., 1965-67; jr. engr. computer systems div., 1967-70; sr. engr. TRW Electronic Products, Inc., Colorado Springs, 1970-73, mgr. engring., 1973-79, mgr. program mgmt. office, 1979-81, gen. mgr. space electronics mfg. div., 1981-86; pres., chief exec. officer G&S Systems, Inc., Bedford, Mass., 1986-87; pres., chief exec. officer Atec, Inc., Houston, 1987—. Mem. adv. council U. Colo., Colorado Springs, 1973-86, U. So. Colo., Pueblo, 1974-78; Weblo leader, asst. pack leader Boy Scouts Am., 1976-77; fin. chmn. Ascension Luth. Ch., 1981-86; cons. to community edn. coordinator for computer systems and equipment, 1980-86. Republican. Patentee in field.

MAXWELL, LEROY MAHLON, construction company executive, consultant; b. Sheridan, Wyo., May 23, 1935; s. James Alfred and Blanche Edith (Stallings) M.; divorced; children: Sheree Maxwell Bench, Daniel, David, Kerri Maxwell Bradford, Jonathon. C.E., Colo. State U., 1959. Constrn. mgr. Lloyd M. Hill, Inc., Salem, Oreg., 1968-71, Cabax Mills, Eugene, Oreg., 1971-78; owner, mgr. Maxwell Cons., Eugene, 1978-80; v.p., mgr. Gen. Constrn. Co. of Hawaii, Honolulu, 1980-82; v.p., ops. mgr. Arctic Slope/Wright Schuchart Constrn. Co., Anchorage, 1982—; v.p. Keystone Devels., Inc., Anchorage, 1985-87, Frontier Equipment Co., Anchorage, 1985-87; owner, mgr. Image Seminars, Anchorage; owner C&M Enterprises, Anchorage; cons. U.S. Forest Service. Mem. Pres.'s Republican Task Force (charter), U.S. Senatorial Club. Mem. Am. Mgmt. Assn. Republican. Club: Plaza (Honolulu); Elks (Eugene). Office: 3942 Lunar Dr Anchorage AK 99504

MAXWELL, NEAL A., church official. m. Colleen Hinckley; four children. B in Polit. Sci., M in Polit. Sci., U. Utah, LLD (hon.); LLD (hon.), Brigham Young U.; LittD (hon.), Westminster Coll.; HHD (hon.), Utah State U. Legis. asst. U.S. sen. Wallace F. Bennett, Utah; various adminstrv. and teaching positions U. Utah, Salt Lake City; various secular positions including bishop Salt Lake City's Univ. Sixth Ward, mem. gen. bd. youth orgn., adult correlation com. and one of first Regional Reps. of the Twelve; elder Ch. Jesus Christ Latter Day Sts., Asst. to the Council of Twelve, 1974-76, mem. of Presidency of First Quorum of the Seventy, 1976-81, mem. of Council of Twelve Apostles, 1981—; bd. dirs. Quester Corp., Deseret News Pub. Co., Zions First Nat. Bank. Mem. Quorum of the Twelve Ch. of Jesus Christ of Latter-Day Saints, Salt Lake City. Recipient Liberty Bell award Utah State Bar, 1967; named Pub. Adminstr. of Yr. Inst. Govt. Service Brigham Young U., 1973. Office: LDS Ch Quorum of the Twelve 50 E N Temple St Salt Lake City UT 84150

MAXWELL, SCOTT KEVIN, software engineer, computer consultant; b. Glasgow AFB, Mont., Mar. 27, 1966; s. Charles Lee and Patricia Lynn (Clark) M. Grad. high sch., Camarillo, Calif. Salesman Computer Horizons, Camarillo, 1982-83, Quality Computer, Ventura, Calif., 1983-84; with quality control dept., programmer Qubie, Camarillo, 1984; sr. software engr. Inkwell Systems, San Diego, 1984-85, Progressive Peripherals & Software, Denver, 1985-87; software engr. Starpoint Software, Gazelle, Calif., 1985; v.p. R & D, Pacific Datawork Internat., Agoura, Calif., 1987-88; head software devel. Capcom U.S.A., Santa Clara, Calif., 1988-89; software engr., cons. Am. Design Capcom Co., Ltd., Osaka, Japan, 1989—; computer cons. various customers, 1981—. Author video game Side Arms, computer programs Flexidraw and Flexifont. Mem. Fantasy Game Club (pres. 1982-83), Petigrees Club (librarian 1982-84). Republican. Roman Catholic. Office: Capcom USA 3303 Scott Blvd Santa Clara CA 95054

MAXWELL-BROGDON, FLORENCE MORENCY, school administrator; b. Spring Park, Minn., Nov. 11, 1929; d. William Frederick and Florence Ruth (LaBrie) Maxwell; m. John Carl Brogdon, Mar. 13, 1957; children: Carole Alexandra, Cecily Ann, Daphne Diana. B.A., Calif. State U., L.A., 1955; MS, U. So. Calif., 1957; postgrad. Columbia Pacific U., San Rafael, Calif., 1982-86. Cert. tchr., Calif. Dir. Rodeo Sch., L.A., 1961-64; lectr. Media Features, Culver City, Calif., 1964—; dir. La Playa Sch., Culver City, 1968-75; founding dir. Venture Sch., Culver City, 1974—, also chmn. bd.; bd. dirs., v.p. Parent Coop. Preschools, Baie d'Urfe Quebec, Calif., 1964—. Author: Let Me Tell You, 1973; Wet 'n Squishy; 1973; Balancing Act, 1977; (as Morency Maxwell) Framed in Silver, 1985; (column) What Parents Want to Know, 1961—; editor: Calif. Preschooler, 1961-74; contbr. articles to profl. jours. Treas. Democrat Congl. Primary, Culver City, 1972. Mem. Calif. Council Parent Schs. (bd. dirs. 1961-74), Parent Coop. Preschools Internat. (advisor 1975—), Pen Ctr. USA West, Mystery Writers of Am. (affiliate), Internat. Platform Assn. Libertarian. Home: 10814 Molony Rd Culver City CA 90230 Office: Venture Sch 5333 S Sepulveda Blvd Culver City CA 90230

MAY, CHARLES EDWARD, educator; b. Paintsville, Ky., Feb. 18, 1941; s. Howard Edward and Kathleen (Newsom) M.; m. Joan C. Trivett, Dec. 1, 1961 (div. 1978); children: Hillary Ellen, Hayden Alexander; m. Patricia Ruth Treadway, Mar. 29, 1980; 1 child, Jordan Elizabeth. BA, Morehead State U., 1963; MA, Ohio Univ., 1964, PhD, 1966. Asst. prof. Ohio Univ., Athens, 1966-67; asst. prof. advanced to prof. Calif. State U., Long Beach, 1967—. Editor: Short Story Theories, 1977, numerous articles in profl. jours. Awarded generous grant, Calif. Dept. Edn., 1986. Democrat. Presbyterian. Office: Calif State U 1250 Bellflower Blvd Long Beach CA 90840

MAY, DIANE ELIZABETH, designer in leather; b. Oakland, Calif., Sept. 30, 1947; d. Clayton Adam and Lorraine Marie (Chapman) M.; m. Horace B. Washington, Oct. 22, 1976 (div. Feb. 1988). BFA, San Francisco Art Inst., 1971. Section head East West Leather, San Francisco, 1972-76; owner Designs by D, San Francisco, 1976—; design cons. Banana Republic, San Francisco, 1987-88. Democrat. Buddhist. Home and Office: 350 Francisco St 1 San Francisco CA 94133

MAY, GERALD WILLIAM, university administrator, civil engineering consultant; b. Kenya, Jan. 2, 1941; s. William and Ruth (Koch) M.; m. Mary Joyce Pool, July 27, 1963; children: Erica Ruth, Christian William, Heidi Clara. B.S., Bradley U., 1962; M.S., U. Colo., 1964, Ph.D., 1967. Registered profl. engr., N.Mex. Civil engr. Ill. Hwy. Dept., Peoria, summer 1959-63; instr. U. Colo., Boulder, 1964-67; asst. prof. to prof. engring. U. N.Mex., Albuquerque, 1967-77; dean Coll. Engring., U. N.Mex., Albuquerque, 1980-86; pres. U. N.Mex., Albuquerque, 1986—; dir. accident study program, Albuquerque, 1970-75, cons. to corps., govtl. agys. Contbr. articles to profl. jours., chpts. to books. Recipient Borden Freshman award Bradley U., 1958. Mem. ASCE (pres. N.Mex. sect. 1982-83), Am. Soc. Engring. Edn. (Outstanding Young Faculty award 1973), Nat. Soc. Profl. Engrs., Sigma Xi, Chi Epsilon, Tau Beta Pi, Phi Eta Sigma. Office: U NMex Office of Pres Albuquerque NM 87131

MAY, JERRY RUSSELL, psychologist; b. Seattle, Apr. 24, 1942; s. Harold Russell May and Anne Margret (Jones) DeGolier; m. Carolyn Marlene May; children: Darin, Christopher, Laurel. Student, Sorbonne U., Paris, 1961-62; BA, Western Wash. U., 1966; PhD, Bowling Green State U., 1974. Prof. psychiatry sch. medicine U. Nev., Reno, 1974—, dean admissions sch. medicine, 1977—; cons. VA Med. Ctr., Reno, 1974—, U.S. Olympic Sports Medicine Program, Colorado Springs, Colo., 1977—; pvt. practice clin. psychology, Reno, 1977—; team psychologist U.S. Ski Team, Park City, Utah, 1977—; chmn. U.S. Olympic Psychology Com., Colorado Springs, 1985—; mem. U.S. Olympic Sports Medicine Council, Colorado Springs, 1985—. Author/editor: Sports Psychology: The Psychological Health of the Athlete, 1987; contbr. articles to profl. jours., chpts. to books. Pres. West Coast Group on Student Affairs, 1981-82. Served to lt. USN, 1968-71. Mem. No. Nev. Assn. Cert. Psychologists (pres. 1979-82), Am. Psychol. Assn., Western Psychol. Assn., Am. Assn. Med. Colls., Nev. Psychol. Assn. Home: PO Box 2661 Truckee CA 95734 Office: U Nev Sch Medicine Reno NV 89557

MAY, KEITH TERRILL, art director; b. Atlanta, Nov. 1, 1966; s. Billy Garfield and Mary Ann (King) M. Grad. high sch., Douglasville, Ga. Paste-up artist Sweetwater News Enterprise, Austell, Ga., 1983-84; prodn. asst. Cycle News East, Atlanta, 1984-86; assoc. art dir. Katherine Phelps Advt., Atlanta, 1986-88, Autobuff mag., Sports Car Illustrated, Newport Beach, Calif., 1986-88; art dir. Sports Car International, Newport Beach, 1988—. Democrat. Baptist. Home: 323 N Euclid #36 Santa Ana CA 12703 Office: Sports Car International 3901 Westerly Pl #120 Newport Beach CA 92660

MAY, MICHAEL WAYNE, broadcast school executive; b. Springhill, La., Mar. 31, 1949; s. Willie Wilmer and Ethel Florene (Sigler) M.; student So. Ark. U., 1968-70, La. Tech. U., 1970-71. Prodn. dir. Sta. KKAM, Pueblo, Colo., 1973-75; quality control dir. Sta. KBOZ, Bozeman, Mont., 1975-78; music dir., dir. research, disk jockey Sta. KOOK, Billings, Mont., 1978-80; founder, operator May Sch. Broadcasting and Bus., Billings, 1980—. Mem. Nat. Assn. Trade and Tech. Schs. (Key mem. for Mont.). Author: Building with the Basics: Radio Personality Development, 1979. Home: 80 Skyline Dr Billings MT 59105 Office: PO Box 127 Billings MT 59103

MAY, RONALD VARNELLE, county official, historic archaeologist; b. Salt Lake City, Oct., 26, 1946; s. Russell Varnelle and Dorothy (Jensen) M.; m. Dale Ellen Ballou, May 8, 1983. AA, Mesa Coll., 1967; BA, San Diego State U., 1970; grad. cert. Pub. History, 1988. Dist. liaison archaeologist Calif. Div. Hwys. San Diego County, 1970-73; supervisory archaeologist San Diego State U. Found., San Diego County, 1971, 73; archeol. cons. pvt. contractor, Calif., 1971—; sr. archaeologist David D. Smith & Assocs., So. Calif., 1972-74; anthropology instr. Mesa Coll., San Diego, 1976-77; environ. mgmt. specialist II County San Diego, 1974—; judge Tijuana-San Diego In ernat. History Fair, 1986-88. Contbr. articles on Spanish fortifications, shorewhaling and Calif. Indian pottery to acad. and history jours.; editor Fort Guijarros Quar.; chmn. bd. dirs. Fort Guijarros Mus. Found., San Diego, 1981—; mem. staff County Hist. Site Bd., 1986—; mem. Calif. Com. for Promotion of History, 1987—. Recipient Award of Merit Inst. History, 1982; San Diego Community Found. conservation grant, 1983, Cabrillo award for Maritime History Inst. of History, 1985, Community Svc. award Peninsula C. of C., 1987, Mark Raymond Harrington award for Conservation Archaeology, 1987; decorated knight's officer Cross of Civil Mert, Spain, 1989. Mem. E Clampus Vitus (Clamper of Yr. 1985), Soc. Am. Archaeology, Soc. Profl. Archaeologists, Assn. Conservation Archaeology (regional coord. 1988), Soc. Hist. Archaeology, San Diego County Archeol. Soc. (pres. 1980-82), Soc. Calif. Archaeology (v.p., ethics chmn., editor 1977-82, assoc. editor 1988, Spl. Achievement award 1983), Archeol. Resource Mgmt. Soc. (treas., fund raising chmn. 1980-82), Nature Conservancy, Greenpeace, San Diego Maritime Soc., Soc. Calif. Archivists, Sigma Xi. Republican. Clubs: San Diego State U. Anthro. Soc. (pres. 1969, 72), Coun. on Am. Mil. Past. Office: San Diego County Planning Dept 5201 Ruffin Rd Ste 5B San Diego CA 92123

MAYBERRY, GLEN ERIC, educator, tennis professional; b. Portland, Maine, Sept. 7, 1953; s. Gerald Ellis and Jeanne Estelle (McKenney) M.; m. Sheila Ann Howe, Apr. 16, 1983. BA, U. So. Maine, 1975, cert. spl. edn., 1976. Tchr. Portland Sch. Systems, 1976-83; tennis profl. Tennis of Maine, Falmouth, 1976-83; tchr. Dept. Def. Dependents Schs., Hanau, Fed. Republic of Germany, 1983-87, Okinawa, Japan, 1987—. Organizer Spl. Olympics, Frankfurt, Fed. Republic of Germany, 1984-87. Mem. Maine Tennis Assn. (sec. 1976-82, Player of Yr. 1980), Am. Educators Assn. (v.p. Okinawa chpt. 1986—), Okinawa Tennis Assn. (v.p. 1986—), Dependents Coun. on Edn. (bd. dirs. Okinawa chpt. 1988—). Home: PO Box 507 Camp Foster Seattle FPO WA 98774 Office: Dodds Kubasaki High Sch Camp Butler Seattle FPO WA 98773

MAYBERRY-STEWART, MELODIE IRENE, information systems executive; b. Cleve., Sept. 4, 1948; 1 child, George Julian. BS, Union Coll., Lincoln, Nebr., 1970; MA, U. Nebr., 1972; MBA, Pepperdine U., 1983; MA, Claremont Grad. Sch., 1988. Project evaluator Nat. Hwy. Traffic Safety Adminstrn., Lincoln, 1972-76; with IBM Corp., 1976-88; systems support mgr. IBM Corp., L.A., 1986-87, telecommunications mgr., 1987-88; v.p. infosystems, chief info. officer Community Health Corp., Riverside, Calif.,

1988—. Author: Telecommunications Networks, 1982 (Edn. Excellence aware 1982), Managing Networks, 1983 (Edn. Excellence award 1983). Vol. United Negro Coll. Fund, L.A., 1984—. Recipient Disting. Alumni award Pine Forge Acad., 1978, Cert. Appreciation, United Negro Coll. Fund, 1985, Women of Achievement award Voice News, 1988, Black Women Achievement award NAACP Legal Def. Fund, 1989. Mem. NAACP, Nat. Assn. Female Execs., Nat. Black MBA Assn., Nat. Assn. Bus. Women, Nat. Assn. Healthcare Execs., Info. Sytems Soc. AMA. Riverside C. of C. (ethic com. 1988—). Democrat. Seventh Day Adventist. Office: Community Health Corp 4445 Magnolia Ave Riverside CA 92501

MAYDEW, RANDALL CLINTON, engineer; b. Lebanon, Kans., Jan. 29, 1924; s. Kermit and Lelia M.; m. Maxine Norvell, Sept. 2, 1944 (dec.); m. Susanna Jean Glaze, Dec. 1, 1971; children: Jenan Louise, Randall Paul, Barbara Ann. BS, U. Colo., 1948, MS in Engring., 1949. Rsch. scientist NASA Ames Lab., Moffett Field, Calif., 1949-52; staff mem. aerodynamics dept. Sandia Nat. Labs, Albuquerque, 1952-57, supr. exptl. aerodynamics div., 1957-65, mgr. aerodynamics dept., 1965-88, mem. mgmt. staff, 1988—. Contbr. numerous articles to profl. jours.; patentee in field. 1st lt. USAAF, 1943-45. Decorated Dist. Flying Cross with 3 oak leaf clusters. Fellow AIAA (assoc.); mem. Supersonic Tunnel Assn. (pres. 1969-70), Sigma Xi, Pi Tau Sigma. Republican. Methodist. Home: 5305 Queens Ct NE Albuquerque NM 87109 Office: Sandia Nat Labs Org 400 Albuquerque NM 87185

MAYER, ADOLPH, university official; b. Denver, Feb. 16, 1919; s. Adolph and Aimee (Levy) M.; m. Eileen Mayer, Sept. 14, 1943; children: Reed F., Meredith A. BA in Journalism, U. Colo., 1941. Account exec. Max Goldberg Advt. Agy., Denver, 1941-42; reporter Rocky Mountain News, Denver, 1942-44; news editor NBC, San Francisco, 1944-47; news dir. Sta. KFBK, Sacramento, 1947-49; dir. pub. rels. U. Denver, 1949-86, spl. asst. to chancellor, 1986—; cons. in field. Mem. editorial rev. bd. Pub. Rels. Quar., 1966—. Bd. dirs. Auraria Community Ctr., Denver, 1954-56, Colo. TB Assn., 1956-58, Found. for Pub. Rels. Edn., 1968-74; v.p. Mile Hi ARC, 1968-72, bd. dirs. 1964-72; mem. Denver Community Coun., 1963-71. Mem. Pub. Rels. Soc. Am. (assembly del. 1968-71, mem. grievance bd. 1969-72, chmn. Rocky Mountain dist. 1968., pres. Colo. chpt. 1963), Am. Coll. Pub. Rels. Assn. (mem. nat. bd. 1966-72, dist. dir. 1958, 65, chmn. nat. honors competition 1972, nominated to Hall of Fame 1968), Denver C. of C., Colo. Assn. Commerce and Industry, Cen. City Opera Assn., Sigma Delta Chi. Jewish. Club: Denver Press. Home: 3665 S Jersey St Denver CO 80237 Office: U Denver University Park Denver CO 80208

MAYER, CHARLES ANTHONY, dentist; b. Mayville, Wis., Oct. 10, 1930; s. Victor Charles and Phyllis Cecile (Bachhuber) M.; m. Mary Alice Linsmeier, Jan. 29, 1955; children: Kathleen, Julie, Jean, Elizabeth, Mary Nell. DDS, Marquette U., 1955. Pvt. practice Albuquerque, 1957—. Cochmn. Bernalilio County Rep. Com., Albuquerque, 1988—. Capt. USAF, 1955-57. Fellow Internat. Coll. Dentists, Acad. Gen. Dentistry; mem. N.Mex. Dental Assn. (pres. 1977-78), N.Mex. Acad. Gen. Dentistry (pres. 1980-81), Greater Albuquerque C. of C., N.Mex. Marquette Alumni Assn. (bd. dirs. 1988—), Delta Sigma Delta. Republican. Roman Catholic. Home and Office: 7304 Aztec NE Albquerque NM 87110

MAYER, HENRY, filmmaker, doctor; b. N.Y.C., June 13, 1914; s. Henry and Adele (Lederman) M.; m. Olive G. Hendricks, Dec. 31, 1941; children: Robert Bruce, Judith Mayer O'Brien. BA, Princeton, 1935; MD, Columbia U., 1939. Diplomate Am. Bd. Internal Medicine. Clinical prof. of medicine Stanford U., Palo Alto, Calif., 1975—. Producer: (documentaries) The Survivors (Chris award 1968), Tomorrow's Children (Golden Eagle award, 1970), A Baby is Born (1st Prize Nat. Ednl. Film Festival 1975), Are You Ready for Sex? (Top 20 award Cleve. Instructional Film Festival 1978), Solar Promise (Chris Plaque, Columbus Film Festival 1979), Kilowatts from Cowpies (1st prize, EKO Film Festival). Bd. dirs. Planned Parenthood, San Mateo, Calif., 1978—, Californians for Population Stabilization, Sacramento, Calif., 1978—. Served to lt. comdr. USN, 1942-46. Fellow Am. Coll. of Physicians; mem Phi Beta Kappa. Democrat. Jewish. Home: 245 Josselyn Ln Woodside CA 94062 Office: 945 Middlefield Rd Redwood City CA 94063

MAYER, HERBERT CARLETON, JR., management information systems educator; b. Newton, Mass., Aug. 2, 1922; s. Herbert Carleton and Elsie Marie (Hauser) M.; m. Maryetta Brodkord, Aug. 21, 1948; children: Judith Marie, Christine Louise. BS, Parsons Coll., 1943; MS, U. Iowa, 1947; PhD, U. So. Calif., 1975. Instr. math. U. Idaho, Moscow, 1947-48, U. Utah, Salt Lake City, 1949-51; edn. adminstr. Gen. Electric co., Richland, Wash., 1951-59; systems engr., univ. industry specialist IBM, Chgo., 1959-81; adj. assoc. prof. mgmt. info. systems Wash. State U., Pullman, 1980-82; assoc. prof. U. Wis.-Parkside, Kenosha, 1982-85, Eastern Wash. U., Cheney, 1985—; adj. prof. mgmt. U. Tex., El Paso, 1976-78. Pres. Tri-City Heights Assn., Kennewick, Wash., 1956-58, PTA, Kennewick, 1957-58; v.p. Kennewick Sch. Bd., 1958, pres., 1959. Mem. Math. Assn. Am., Internat. Assn. of Computing in Edn., Am. Soc. Engring. Edn., Data Processing Mgmt. Assn. (bd. dirs., sec. Spokane chpt. 1988, v.p. edn. Spokane chpt. 1989), Phi Delta Kappa. Home: S 3334 Bernard Spokane WA 99203 Office: Ea Wash U 316 Kingston Hall Cheney WA 99004

MAYER, JAMES HOCK, lawyer; b. Neptune City, N.J., Nov. 1, 1935; s. J. Kenneth and Marie Ruth (Hock) M.; m. Carol I. Keating, Sept. 20, 1958 (div. Feb. 1981); children: Craig, Jeffrey; m. Patrisha Renk, Mar. 28, 1981. AB with distinction, Dartmouth Coll., 1957; JD, Harvard U., 1964. Bar: Calif. 1965, U.S. Dist. Ct (no. dist., so. dist.) Calif. 1965, U.S. Ct. Appeals (9th cir.) 1965, U.S. Supreme Ct. 1974. Assoc. Pillsbury, Madison & Sutro, San Francisco, 1964-72, ptnr., 1973—. Rear adm. USNR, 1957—. Rufus Choate scholar Dartmouth Coll., 1956-57. Mem. Newcomen Soc., Navy League, Naval Order of U.S., Harvard Club (San Francisco). Office: Pillsbury Madison & Sutro 4250 Executive Sq Suite 800 La Jolla CA 92037

MAYER, PAMELA JEAN, computer company executive; b. Mitchel, S.D., May 31, 1958; d. Richard R. and Beverly J. (Kayser) M. BS in Accting., U. Minn., 1980; MBA in Mktg., St. Thomas Coll., St. Paul, 1985. Jr. auditor Touche Ross & Co., Mpls., 1980-82, sr. auditor, 1982-83; gen. acct. Edge Computer Corp., Mpls., 1983-85, sr. systems analyst, 1985-88; mgr. mktg. communications Edge Computer Corp., Scottsdale, Ariz., 1988, dir mktg., corp. communications, 1988—. Sec., bd. dirs. Big Bros./Big Sisters Assn., Mpls., 1983-85; mem. Mpls. Citizen's League, 1983-85. Mem. Enterprise Network (mktg. com. 1988—). Republican. Roman Catholic. Office: Edge Computer Corp 7320 E Butherus Dr Scottsdale AZ 85260

MAYER, PATRICIA JAYNE, fraternal organization executive; b. Chgo., Apr. 27, 1950; d. Arthur and Ruth (Greenberger) Hersh; m. William A. Mayer Jr., Apr. 30, 1971. AA, Diablo Valley Coll., 1970; BSBA, Calif. State U., Hayward, 1975. Staff acct., auditor Elmer Fox Westheimer and Co., Oakland, Calif., 1976; supervising auditor Auditor's Office County of Alameda, Oakland, 1976-78; asst. acctg. mgr. CBS Retail Stores doing bus. as Pacific Stereo, Emeryville, Calif., 1978-79; contr. Oakland Unified Sch. Dist., 1979-84; v.p. fin. YMCA of San Francisco, 1984—; instr. acctg. to staff YMCA, San Francisco, 1984—, CBS Retail Stores, 1978-79. Draft counselor Mt. Diablo Peace Ctr., Walnut Creek, Calif., 1970-72; dep. registrar of voters Contra Costa County Registrar's Office, Martinez, Calif., 1972-77. Mem. Nat. Assn. Accts., Dalmatian Club No. Calif., Dalmatian Club Am. Democrat. Jewish. Home: 2395 Lake Meadow Circle Martinez CA 94553 Office: YMCA 220 Golden Gate Ave 3d Fl San Francisco CA 94102

MAYER, VIRGINIA ANNE, dietitian; b. Cortez, Colo., June 14, 1929; d. James Edward and Anna May (Coleman) Casey; m. Frederick Henry Mayer, Feb. 7, 1954; children: Jennifer, Valorie, Helen, Lydia. AS, Cottey Coll. for Women, Nevada, Mo., 1949; BS, U. Colo., 1951. Dietitian Columbia Presbyn. Med. Ctr., N.Y.C., 1952-55; food service dir. Luth. Sanitarium, Wheatridge, Colo., 1955-57; adminstrv. dietitian VA Hosp., Grand Junction, Colo., 1961-65; nutritionist Maricopa County Health Dept., Phoenix, 1965-68; food service dir. ARA Services, Phila., 1968-72, supr. dietitian, 1972-75, area exec. dietitian, 1975-76, dist. mgr., 1976-81; pres., chief exec. officer SunWest Services, Inc., Tempe, Ariz., 1981--. Alt. del. White House Conf. on Small Bus., Ariz., 1986. Named Pacesetter, Roundtable for Women in Food Service, Chgo., 1988. Mem. Am. Dietetic Assn., Ariz. Dietetic Assn. (bd. dirs., chmn. 1987-88), Nat. Assn. Women Bus. Owners (pres. 1988-89), The Exec. Com. (Phoenix), PEO Sisterhood (pres. Tempe, Ariz. chpt. 1970-72). Office: SunWest Svcs Inc 420 E Southern Ave Tempe AZ 85282-5203

MAYERS, LESLIE LEE, marketing executive; b. Los Angeles, Jan. 30, 1945; s. Louis Spencer and Helen Septima (Grossman) M.; m. Kathy Ann Kent, July 3, 1977; 1 child, Samantha Lee. BS, U. So. Calif., 1967. Acct. exec. trainee Doyle, Dane, Bernbach, Los Angeles, 1967-68; nat. sales mgr. Monogram Industries, Inc., Los Angeles, 1968-73; Western sales mgr. Meyers Mfg. Co., N.Y.C., 1976-81; pres. Les Mayers & Co., Los Angeles, 1975—; pres., chief exec. officer Gen. Merchandising Corp., Los Angeles, 1985-87; nat. mktg. dir. Broco, Inc., Rialto, Calif., 1988—. Jewish. Home: 14423 Dickens St #8 Sherman Oaks CA 91423

MAYERS, MARVIN KEENE, college dean, educator; b. Canton, Ohio, Oct. 25, 1927; s. Homer Douglas and Irma Hope (Kean) M.; m. Marilyn Ann Piepgrass, May 24, 1952; children: Margaret, Donna. BA, Wheaton Coll., 1949; MDiv, Fuller Sem., 1952; MA, U. Chgo., 1958, PhD, 1960. Translator Wycliffe Bible Translators, Huntington Beach, Calif., 1952—; dean Wycliffe Bible Translators, Huntington Beach, 1989—; prof. Wheaton (Ill.) Coll., 1965-74; adj. prof. U. Tex., Arlington, 1974-82; dean, prof. Biola U., La Mirada, Calif., 1982-89. Author: Christianity Confronts Culture, 1972, rev. 1987, A Look at Latin American Lifestyle, 1976, rev. 1987, A Look at Filipino Lifestyle, 1980; co-author: Cultural Anthropology, 1978, rev. 1988, Ministering Crossculturally, 1986; editor: Languages of Guatemala, 1965. Fellow Am. Anthrop. Assn. Republican. Presbyterian. Office: Biola U Sch Intercultural Studies La Mirada CA 90639

MAYFIELD, DAVID MERKLEY, library administrator; b. Salt Lake City, Nov. 29, 1942; s. Orson Smith and Isabell (Merkley) M.; m. Judy Rae White, Dec. 17, 1965; children: Celeste, Melody, Michael, Paul, Nathan, Heather, Christopher, Benjamin. BA in German, U. Utah, 1967, MA in German, 1969; MLS, UCLA, 1971. Instr. Brigham Young U., Provo, Utah, 1971-72; mgr., dir. hist. dept., mem. and stats. records dept., info. systems dept. Ch. of Jesus Christ of Latter-day Saints, Salt Lake City, 1972-80; dir. family history library of Ch. of Jesus Christ of Latter-day Saints, Salt Lake City, 1980—; v.p. Geneal. Soc. Utah, 1988—. Contbr. articles to profl. jours. Fellow NDEA, 1967, HEW Title II, 1970. Mem. Internat. Fedn. Library Assns. and Insts. (voting del.), Nat. Geneal. Soc. (chmn. inst. services com. 1983-85), ALA, Nat. Soc. Sons of Utah Pioneers (v.p. 1982-83), Phi Beta Kappa. Republican. Mormon. Office: Family History Libr 50 E N Temple Salt Lake City UT 84150

MAYFIELD, ROBERT GIL, real estate developer; b. Salina, Kans., June 16, 1946; s. Bobby M. and Mary Ann (Lee) M.; m. Ronalee A. Bray, Feb., 1972 (div.); m. Mary E. Oliver, Oct. 8, 1978; children: Robert Oliver, Catherine Lee. BA, U. Colo., 1969. Salesman Regiment, Ltd., Boulder, Colo., 1965-69, Bray Realty, Loveland, Colo., 1970-71; v.p. Bellamah Corp., Albuquerque, 1972-78; exec. v.p. Bellamah Devel. Co., Phoenix, 1979-81; exec. v.p., bd. dirs. Western Devcor, Inc., Phoenix, 1982--; bd. dirs. R.L. Kotrozo Option Fund, Scottsdale, Ariz. Mem. Men's Art Coun., Phoenix, 1984--; active Charros, Scottsdale, 1988--. Mem. Internat. Coun. Shopping Ctrs. (cert.), White Mountain Country. Republican. Office: Western Devcor Inc 4141 N Scottsdale Rd Ste 300 Scottsdale AZ 85251

MAYHEW, LAWRENCE LEE, electronics company executive; b. Santa Paula, Calif., Mar. 17, 1933; s. Paul Donald and Lucille Frances (Winkler) M.; m. Kathleen Joan McCown, Feb. 6, 1955; children: Taryn Lee, Jeffrey Park, Kimberly Anne. BS, Calif. State Poly. U., 1961. Design engr. Tektronix Inc., Beaverton, Oreg., 1961-65; ops. mgr. Tektronix Inc., Netherlands, 1965-69; div. gen. mgr. Tektronix Inc., Beaverton, 1969-73; div. v.p. Tektronix Inc., 1973-78, group v.p., 1978-82; pres., chief exec. officer Data I/O Corp., Redmond, Wash., 1982—. Lt. USN, 1953-58. Mem. IEEE (sr.). Republican. Office: Data I/O Corp 10525 Willows Rd NE Redmond WA 98052

MAYNARD, HAL BRUCE, management consultant; b. Dandridge, Tenn., June 1, 1926; s. Robert Bruce and Carrie Lee (Irwin) M.; m. Mary LaVerne Wolfe, Feb. 17, 1946; children: Diana, Laura, Karen. Student, Carson-Newman Coll., 1958-59; AA, U. Tenn., 1960; student, Troy State U., 1973-74. Office mgr. Appalachian Electric Co., Jefferson City, Tenn., 1950-66; asst. mgr. Co-Mo Electric Co., Tipton, Mo., 1967-70; office mgr. Cen. Ala. Electric Co., Prattville, 1970-80; mgr. office and staff Orcas Power and Light Co., Eastsound, Wash., 1980-88; cons. Mgmt. Info. Systems, Eastsound, 1988—; lectr. Digital Systems, Inc., Columbia, S.C., 1984, N.W. Pub. Power, Vancouver, Wash., 1985, Nat. Rural Electric Co., Washington, 1986. Author: (pamphlets) Info. Handbooks, 1962, 85. Mem. Inst. Indsl. Engrs. (sr. pres. 1966-67, 73-74, Award of Excellence 1967, 74, Outstanding Service award 1974), Soc. Advancement Mgmt. (v.p. Montgomery, Ala. chpt. 1976-79, historian Knoxville, Tenn. chpt., 1962), Jaycees (pres. Jefferson City chpt., 1959). Republican. Lutheran. Lodges: Lions (Lion Tamer Eastsound club 1985-86), Masons (sec. 1950-54). Home and Office: Rte 1 Box 299 Calvert City KY 42029

MAYNARD, JOHN LELAND, software publishing executive; b. Arco, Idaho, Dec. 16, 1927; s. Henry Harrison and Lydia Lornell (Toombs) M. ABA, Golden Gate Coll., 1953, BBA, 1954; MA in Econs., UCLA, 1955. Cert. computer profl. Data processing system analyst Security Pacific Bank, Los Angeles, 1956-60, Price Watehouse Mgmt. Advisory, Los Angeles, 1960; computer system analyst Bendix Computer Div., Los Angeles, 1960-62; programmer, writer Packard Bell Corp., Los Angeles, 1962-64, Control Data Corp., Los Angeles, Sunnyvale, Calif., 1964-68; software documentation mgr. Xerox Data Systems, El Segundo, Calif., 1969-76; mgr. large-scale computer documentation Honeywell Large Scale Computer Div., Phoenix, 1976-86; pres. Maynard Desktop Pubs., Phoenix, 1986—, Maynard Publs. Cons., Inc., Phoenix, 1986—. With U.S. Navy, 1945-48, 50-51. Mem. IEEE. Mormon.

MAYNARD, KENNETH DOUGLAS, architect; b. Hackensack, N.J., Aug. 16, 1931; s. Douglas Harry and Eva (Whiting) M.; m. Myrna Myrtle James, Feb. 4, 1956; children: Colin, Vivien Regan. Cert. in Architecture, U. Natal, Durban, Republic of South Africa, 1958. Registered architect Alaska. Draftsman Morross & Graff, Johannesburg, Republic of South Africa, 1950-51, Anglo-Am. Corp., Johannesburg, Republic of South Africa, 1951-54, Moir & Llewellyn, Empangeni, Zululand, Republic of South Africa, 1955-57; architect Pearse Aneck-Hahn & Bristol, Johannesburg, 1957-60, Manley & Mayer, Anchorage, 1960-61, FAA, Anchorage, 1961-62, Crittenden Cassetta Wirum & Jacobs, Anchorage, 1962-65; prin. Schultz & Maynard, Anchorage, 1965-68, Kenneth Maynard Assocs., Anchorage, 1968-78; pres. Maynard & Partch, Anchorage, 1978—. Active We. Alaska Council Boy Scouts Am., Anchorage, 1965-84; bd. dirs. Salvation Army Adv. Bd., Anchorage, 1981-87, Anchorage Mus. Assn., 1969-86, Anchorage Opera Co., 1983—. Fellow AIA (pres. Alaska chpt. 1969, Northwest regional rep. for nat. com. on design 1976—); mem. Constrn. Specification Inst., Soc. Am. Mil. Engrs. Republican. Lodge: Rotary. Home: 2237 Forest Park Dr Anchorage AK 99517-1324 Office: Maynard & Partch 800 F St Anchorage AK 99501-3595

MAYNARD, LIBBY, artist, arts administrator; b. Washington, Sept. 21, 1948; d. Paul John and Antoinette (Lebris) M. BA in Art, Humboldt State U., 1970, MA, 1982. Bus. office supr. St. Joseph's Hosp., Eureka, Calif., 1972-78; instr. art Humboldt State U., Arcata, Calif., 1982-84; arts coordinator Assn. Humboldt Artists, Eureka, 1984-87; exec. dir. Humboldt Arts Council, Eureka, 1987—; pres. Rural Arts Services, Mendocino, Calif., 1984—; founder, dir. The Ink People, Eureka, 1979—. Artist etching The Vision, Calif. Arts Council commn., 1987; several one-person shows. Mem. Nat. Assembly Local Arts Agys. (chair rural interest sect. 1986-88), Calif. Assembly Local Arts Agys. (founder, pres. 1987-88), Calif. Confedn. of the Arts, Redwood Art Assn., Nat. Assn. Female Execs. Taoist. Lodge: Soroptimists. Home: 2318 Harris Eureka CA 95501 Office: Humboldt Arts Coun 422 1st St Eureka CA 95501

MAYNARD, STEVEN HARRY, writer; b. San Diego, July 4, 1954; s. Harry Clark and Ruby Kristina (Odna). BA in Communications, U. Wash., 1976; MA in Theology, Fuller Theol. Seminary, 1979. Religion writer, gen. news reporter Walla Walla (Wash.) Union-Bulletin, 1979-84; religion writer Houston Chronicle, 1984-87; religion, higher edn. reporter Morning News Tribune, Tacoma, Wash., 1987—. Recipient Mng. Editors award Tex. Associated Press, 1984, Wilbur award Religious Pub. Relations Council, 1981. Mem. Religion Newswriters Assn., Soc. Profl. Journalists. Office: 1950 S State St Tacoma WA 98411

MAYO, DONALD GLENN, management executive; b. San Francisco, July 20, 1946; s. Donald Gurden and Evelynn Jennie (Herron) M.; m. Linda Kaye Aud, Oct. 10, 1970; children: Ann Katherine, Laura Michele, Erin Elizabeth. Student, Ill. Inst. Tech., 1964-66, UCLA, summer 1965, Fresno City Coll., 1966-67. Engr. in tng. Oil Ins. Assocs., Chgo., 1964-66; sr. field supr. Pacific Fire Rating Bur., San Francisco, 1969-72; tech. svcs. rep. Fred S. James & Co., San Francisco, 1972-76; sales engr. Pacific Fire Extinguisher Co., San Francisco, 1976, Automatic Sprinkler Corp. Am., San Francisco, 1976-77; staff cons. Kemper Ins. Cos., San Francisco, 1977-78; v.p. Frank B. Hall & Co., San Francisco, 1978-87; pres., chmn. bd. Donald Mayo Fire Protection Cons., Pleasant Hill, Calif., 1987—. With USNR, 1966-72, Vietnam. Recipient Exceptional Performance award Nordstrom, Inc., 1985. Mem. Soc. Fire Protection Engrs. (assoc.), Nat. Fire Protection Assn., Am. Water Works Assn. Democrat. Home and Office: 150 Grove Cir Pleasant Hill CA 94523

MAYO, FRANK JOSEPH, charitable organization administrator; b. Tacoma, Wash., Dec. 26, 1925; s. Willis and Arvilla Marchetta (Anderson) M.; diploma Simpson Coll., 1949; postgrad. UCLA, 1965, Kennedy Sinclaire Estate Planning Sch., 1966, 72, 78; m. Ruth Rustad, July 18, 1947 (div. Sept. 1983); children—Karen Ruth, Sharon Darlene, Rebekah Kay, Deborah Jean; m. 2d Virginia Faith Cole Bubna, Jan. 13, 1984; stepchildren—Kurt, Kevin, Kraig, Kimberly. Ordained to ministry Christian and Missionary Alliance, 1951; pastor chs., Wolf Creek, Oreg., Boise, Idaho, Ellensberg, Wash., Dallas, Oreg., Sherman Oaks, Calif.; field rep. planned gifts Christian and Missionary Alliance, Western U.S. area, 1966-72; v.p. planned giving Le Tourneau Coll. Fund, Longview, Tex., 1972-76; planned gifts cons. Western ter. Salvation Army, Rancho Palos Verdes, Calif., 1976-84; v.p. St. Joseph Med. Center Found., Burbank, Calif., 1984-88; pres. Frank Mayo and Co., planned giving consultants, 1980—; planned giving officer St. Vincent Med. Found., Portland, Oreg., 1988—; bd. commrs. North Hollywood Rotary Found., 1984—; pres. So. Calif. Planned Giving Roundtable, 1984-87. Bd. dirs. Simpson Coll. Found., 1974-79; trustee Simpson Coll., San Francisco, 1963-79. Served with USAF, 1944-46. Mem. Nat. Assn. for Hosp. Devel., Rotary (North Hollywood, Calif. chpt.). Home: 4361 Browns Creek Rd The Dalles OR 97058 Office: Buena Vista and Alameda Sts Burbank CA 91505

MAYO, PHYLLIS JEAN, teacher, rancher; b. Buffalo, Wyo., May 5, 1950; d. Allen Gene and Rosa Bell (Key) Wagoner; m. William H. Mayo, Apr. 26, 1981; children: Misti, Matthew. AS, Sheridan (Wyo.) Coll., 1970; BA, U. Wyo., 1972. Sec. United Presbyn. Ch., Laramie, Wyo., 1972-73; bus. tchr. Uinta County Sch. Dist., Evanston, Wyo., 1973-77, Sweetwater County Sch. Dist. #1, Rock Springs, Wyo., 1977—; Advisor Future Bus. Leaders of Am., Farson, Wyo., 1981—, Farson Sch. Yearbook, 1981—, Farson Sch. Newspaper, 1981—; class sponsor. Mem. Sweetwater Edn. Assn., Wyo. Edn. Assn., NEA, Farm Bur., Wyo. Bus. Edn. Assn., Nat. Bus. Edn. Assn. Home: Star Rte Boulder WY 82923

MAYOL, RICHARD THOMAS, advertising executive, political consultant; b. Springfield, Ill., Oct. 30, 1949; s. Richard McFaren and Marjorie (Maddox) M. AA, Springfield Coll., 1969; BS, U. Tulsa, 1972. Co-owner First Tuesday Inc., Phoenix, 1976-85; pres. Mayol and Assocs., Phoenix, 1985—; cons. Dem. candidates, Western U.S., 1976—, Mo Udall for Congress, Tucson, 1982—, Mayor Terry Goddard, Phoenix, Senator John Melcher, Mont. Mem. Phoenix Film Commn., 1985—. Mem. Am. Assn. Polit. Cons., Phoenix Grand Prix Commn. Home and Office: Mayol and Assocs 2329 N 57th Pl Scottsdale AZ 85257-1907

MAZA, AGGIE LAM, medical laboratory administrator; b. Hong Kong, Mar. 14, 1940; came to U.S., 1959; d. John Yuk Hon and Anna Nap (Chan) Lam; m. Raymond Maza, June 12, 1965; children: John, Paul, Matthew. BS, Seattle U., 1962; MBA, City U., Seatte, 1981. Med. technologist Stanford U. Hosp., Palo Alto, Calif., 1963-68; sr. med. technologist O'Connor Hosp., San Jose, Calif., 1968-71, Evergreen Hosp., Kirkland, Wash., 1971-72, Valley Med. Ctr., Renton, Wash., 1972-73; rsch. devel. technician VA Hosp., Seattle, 1974; chief technologist Eastside Med. Lab., Inc., Redmond, Wash., 1974-76, lab. ops. mgr., 1976-84, gen. mgr., 1984-87, chief exec. officer, 1988--; mem. adv. bd. Cascade Nursing Home, Redmond, 1985--. Mem. Lab. Assembly Scientists Assn. (treas. 1985-88), Clin. Lab. Mgmt. Assn. (pres. Western Wash. chpt. 1987-88). Office: Eastside Med Lab Inc 2205 152d Ave NE Redmond WA 98052

MAZA, VIC FRANCISCO, radiologist; b. Sibalom, Philippines, May 5, 1937; came to U.S., 1962; s. Ramon and Rita (Mostacho) M.; m. Vicky Tan, Sept. 6, 1976. MD, U. Philippines, 1962. Diplomate Am. Bd. Radiology. Intern St. Francis Gen. Hosp., Pitts., 1962-63; intern internal medicine Newark (N.J.) City Hosp., 1963-64; resident radiology N.Y. Med. Coll. Met. Med. Ctr., N.Y.C., 1964-68, clin. fellow in radiology, 1968-69; attending radiologist Catholic Med. Ctr., Queens, N.Y., 1972-76; pvt. practice Borger, Tex., 1976-81; chief radiology dept. VA Med. Ctr., Salem, Va., 1983-86; radiologist Med. Imaging of Carlbad, Carlsbad, N.Mex., 1986—, Guadalupe Med. Ctr., Carlsbad, 1986—; asst. prof. clin. radiology U. Va.-Charlottesville, Roanoke, 1983-86. Mem. Radiol. Soc. N. Am., Assn. Univ. Radiologists, Southwest Va. Assn. Philippine Physicians (pres. 1984—). Episcopalian. Office: Sullesta & Maza 411 N Canyon St Carlsbad NM 88220

MAZELIS, MENDEL, plant biochemist, educator, researcher; b. Chgo., Aug. 31, 1922; s. Jacob and Anna (Brvarnick) M.; m. Noreen Beimer, Mar. 24, 1969; 1 son, Jacob Russell. B.S., U. Calif.-Berkeley, 1943, Ph.D., 1954. Jr. research biochemist U. Calif.-Berkeley, 1954-55; research assoc., instr. U. Chgo., 1955-57; assoc. chemist Western Regional Research Lab., Albany, Calif., 1957-61; asst. prof. U. Calif.-Davis, 1961-64, assoc. prof., 1964-73, prof., 1973—. Served to lt. (j.g.) USN, 1943-46. Mem. Am. Soc. Plant Physiologists, Am. Soc. Biochemists and Molecular Biologists, Biochem. Soc. London, Phytochem. Soc. N.Am., Phytochem. Soc. Europe, Inst. Food Technologists. Office: U Calif Dept Food Sci/Tech 1480 Chemistry Annex Davis CA 95616

MAZENKO, DONALD MICHAEL, aerospace engineering consultant, educator; b. Benld, Ill., July 11, 1925; s. Mike George and Anna Agnes (Kozak) M.; m. Joyce Christine Patrick, Apr. 22, 1950; children: Donna Nijmeh, Joyce Ann, Martha Jane Nishimura. Student, Mont. Sch. Mineral Sci. and Tech., 1944, U. Wash., 1945-46; BSME, U. Ill., 1949; MBA, U. Santa Clara, 1965. Tech. supt. Reynolds Metals Co., Listerhill, Ala., 1949-62; sr. staff engr. Lockheed Missiles and Space Co., Sunnyvale, Calif., 1962-89; cons. Saratoga, Calif., 1976—; instr. De Anza Community Coll., Cupertino, Calif. 1973—. Contbr. articles to profl. jours. Lt. USNR, 1947-67, PTO. Fellow Soc. Adv. Material and Process Engring. (various offices); mem. Soc. Automotive Engrs., Aero. Material Specifications, Ascension Men's Club, KC (dep. grand knight 1958-62), Delta Upsilon. Republican. Roman Catholic. Home: 19361 Bellwood Dr Saratoga CA 95070

MAZUR, MARGIE ELLA HANDLEY MEREDITH, reading educator; b. Tulsa, Mar. 27, 1941; d. Joyce Samuel and MaryPaul (Ellsworth) Handley; m. Don Leroy Mazur, Aug. 31, 1962 (div. Nov. 1974); children: Susan Diane, Michael. BA in Art, U. Tulsa, 1962, M of Teaching Arts in Spl. Edn., 1967; postgrad., Calif. State U., L.A., UCLA, Purdue U., Calumet, Ind., San Jose State U. Accredited tchr., reading specialist, adminstr., Calif. Classroom tchr. Tulsa Pub. Schs., 1963-65; fellow, clinician, diagnostician, instr. Mabee Reading Clinic, U. Tulsa, 1965-67; instr. So. Meth. U. Reading Clinic, Dallas, fall 1969; classroom tchr. L.A. Unified Sch. Dist., 1975-76; reading specialist Sierramont Middle Sch., Berryessa Union Sch. Dist., San Jose, Calif., 1976—; pvt. tutor, San Jose, 1976—; owner, operator Eastside Learning Ctr. and Reading Clinic, San Jose, 1978-82. Cons., activist in women's and children's rights in child-support enforcement; chmn. child-support enforcement task force San Jose-South Bay chpt. NOW, 1984-85; mem. child support div. rev. ad-hoc. com. Santa Clara County Bd. Suprs. Entrance Exam. scholar U. Tulsa, 1959; John Mabee grad. fellow, 1966; recipient 1st place Bronze award Am. Waltz, Palo Alto, Ca., 1987, 1st Place Silver award Am. Fox Trot, 1989. Mem. Calif. Reading Assn., Mortar Bd.,

Alpha Delta Kappa, Kappa Alpha Theta (chpt. pres. 1961-62). Mem. Baháí Faith Ch. Avocations: ballroom dancing, skiing, sailing, reading, sewing. Home: PO Box 32744 San Jose CA 95152 Office: Sierramont Mid Sch 3155 Kimlee Dr San Jose CA 95132

MAZZA, DENNIS FITZGERALD, accountant; b. Milw., Feb. 6, 1946; s. Charles John and Elsie (Sorgi) M.; m. Carol M. Mazza, June 27, 1970; children: Brett, Jackie. BSBA, Marquette U., 1969. CPA, Wis., Ariz. Acct. 1972—. Mem. AICPA, Wis. Inst. CPA's, Ariz. Inst. CPA's. Office: Mazza Spero & Hougham 4203 E Indian School Rd Phoenix AZ 85018

MCADAM, JOANNE FARRIS, retail store executive; b. Orange, N.J., July 3, 1924; d. William Clayton and Alice (Carr) Farris; children: David Coursen, Richard Coursen, Sarah Coursen, Jennifer Coursen. AB, Vassar Coll., 1944; MA, U. Oreg., 1964. Columnist McNaught Syndicate, N.Y.C., 1974-78; owner, mgr. Made in Oreg., Eugene, 1980—; small bus. cons. Small Bus. Devel. Ctr., Eugene, 1986—. Mem. Oreg. Racing Commn., 1985—, vice chmn., 1988—; trustee Oreg. Health Scis. U. Found., Portland, 1987—; mem. Eugene Small Bus. Adv. Bd., 1987—, Consumer Credit Counseling Svc. Bd., Eugene, 1988—. Mem. Assn. Racing Commrs. Internat., Profl. Women's Network Oreg. (bd. dirs. 1983-85), Sigma Delta Chi. Office: Made in Oregon 295 E 5th Ave Eugene OR 97401

MCADAM, THOMAS HUGH, investment banker; b. Urbana, Ill., July 4, 1955; s. Robert Everett and Grace Lucille (Ford) McA.; children: Nicholas Landon, Jeffrey Bradford. Bachelor's, U. Ill., 1977. CPA, Ind., Ariz., Colo. Acct. Ernst & Whinney, Indpls., 1977-80, Miller Wagner & Co., Phoenix, 1980-82, Schulman Klock & Co., Phoenix, 1982-84; investment banker J.W. Gant & Assocs., Englewood, Colo., 1984—. Recipient 1st pl. award U.S. Options Trading Championship, 1988. Mem. Am. Inst. CPAs, Colo. Soc. CPAs. Office: JW Gant & Assocs 7600 E Orchard Rd #160 Englewood CO 80111

MCALEAR, PETER JAMES PATRICK, accounting and business management consultant; b. Boston, Oct. 8, 1949; s. Thomas Joseph and Europa Ann (Angelucci) McA. BA in Music Edn., Northwestern U., 1971. Tax auditor Franchise Tax Bd., Los Angeles, 1975-78; co-owner Best Sellers Cafe, Los Angeles, 1976-78; pres., chief. exec. officer McAlear Martines, Los Angeles, 1978—; bd. dirs. Cal Neva Corp., Los Angeles, 1984—, Jacques Allen, Inc., Los Angeles, 1986—, Dynamic Enterprise Internat., Ltd., Parker, Colo., 1976—; bd. dirs., sec. San Marcos Leather, Inc., Los Angeles, 1987—. Planning commr. W. Hollywood, Calif., 1986-87; chmn. Employee Benefits Com., W. Hollywood, 1986; mem. Mcpl. Elections Com. L.A., W. Hollywood, 1980—. Recipient Citizen of Future award, Boston, 1967. Mem. Los Angeles Bus. and Profl. Assn., W. Holly C. of C. Democrat. Roman Catholic. Office: McAlear Martines 8455 Beverly Blvd 601 Los Angeles CA 90048

MCALLISTER, BYRON LEON, mathematics educator; b. Midvale, Utah, Apr. 29, 1929; s. Donald Leon and Julia Vilate (Roundy) McA.; m. Kay Marie Keithley, Nov. 29, 1957; children: Marie Elizabeth, Galen Arthur, Tamara Ann. BA, U. Utah, 1951, MA, 1955; PhD, U. Wis., 1966. Asst. prof. to assoc. prof. S.D. Sch. of Mines and Tech., Rapid City, 1958-67; assoc. prof. to prof. Mont. State U., Bozeman, 1967—; instr. U. Wis., Menasha, 1961-62. Contbr. articles to profl. jours. With U.S. Army, 1952-54. Mem. Am. Math. Soc., Math. Assn. of Am., Assn. for Computing Machinery, History of Sci. Soc., Assn. for Women in Math. Office: Mont State U Dept Math Scis Bozeman MT 59717

MCALLISTER, DARRELL DEAN, banker; b. Russell, Kans., July 3, 1948; s. Everett and Anna Marie (Bean) McA.; m. Connee Daughe, Apr. 23, 1988. BBA, U. Colo., 1972. CPA, Colo. Asst. nat. bank examiner Office of Comptroller of Currency, Ft. Collins, Colo., 1976-79; asst. v.p. United Bank, Ft. Collins, 1979-81, 1st Interstate Bank, Ft. Collins, 1981-82; v.p. Greeley (Colo.) Nat. Bank, 1982-83; pres., chmn. Cache Nat. Bank, Greeley, 1983—. Active United Way, Greeley, 1985-87; bd. dirs. Partners, Greeley, 1986-87. Served to 1st lt. U.S. Army, 1972-76. Club: Toastmasters. Lodges: Lions, Sertoma. Office: Cache Nat Bank 2600 11th Ave Greeley CO 80631

MCALLISTER, JAMES CHARLES, real estate consultant; b. Tuscaloosa, Ala., Nov. 16, 1954; s. Roy L. and Zedell (Ward) McA. BSBA and Commerce, U. Ala., 1977. Lic. real estate salesman, Calif. Fund raiser U. Ala., Tuscaloosa, 1975-77, lectr. Coll. Commerce and Bus., 1977; dir. alumni affairs U. South Ala., Mobile, 1978-80; v.p., sales cons. Morehead & Co., L.A., 1980-84; loan agt. lst Fed. Savs. Bank Calif., Santa Monica, Calif., 1984-86; sr. loan cons. Brookside Savs. & Loan, L.A., 1986-88; real estate fin. cons. Santa Monica, 1988—. Editor Looking South, 1978-80. Mem. Ala. Election Law Commn., 1980-81. Mem. U. Ala. Nat. Alumni Assn. (regional v.p. L.A. 1984). Democrat. Home: llll S Crescent Heights Los Angeles CA 90035 Office: 2730 Wilshire Blvd Ste 500 Santa Monica CA 90403

MCALPINE, STEPHEN A., state official, lawyer; b. Yakima, Wash., May 23, 1949; s. Robert Eugene and Myrtle B. (Loomis) McA.; m. Dana Sue Hill, Jan. 15, 1982; 1 child, Sean Michael. B.A., U. Wash., 1972; J.D., U. Puget Sound, 1976. Bar: Alaska. With Alaska Dept. Health and Social Svcs., Valdez, 1972-73; contracts adminstr. Fluor Alaska, Valdez, 1974-75; assoc. Law Offices James Ginotti, Valdez, 1977-80; pres. Ginotti & McAlpine, Valdez, 1980-82; lt. gov. State of Alaska, Juneau, 1982—; mem. Alaska Resource Devel. Council, 1978—, exec. com. Council of State Govts., Nat. Conf. Lt. Govs.,chmn., 1988. Mem. Valdez City Council, 1979-82; mayor City of Valdez, 1980-82; bd. dirs. Alaska Mcpl. League, 1979-82; chmn. Nat. Conf. lt. govs., 1988; del. Alaska Dem. Party Nat. Conv., 1988. With USAR, 1968-71. Named Young Alaskan of Yr., Anchorage Jaycees, 1982; Toll fellow Council of State Govts., Lexington, 1988. Mem. Alaska Bar Assn., ABA, Assn. Trial Lawyers Am., Valdez Fisheries Devel. Assn., Nat. Assn. Secs. of States, Alaska Native Brotherhood, Am. Legion, Elks, Moose. Democrat. Roman Catholic. Office: Office of Lt Gov PO Box AA Juneau AK 99811

MCANANEY, PATRICK, counseling educator; b. Salinas, Calif., Oct. 19, 1954; s. Donald Jack and Margaret Mary (Miller) McA.; m. Kate Peggy Divine, Feb. 23, 1985; children: Mahlon Andersen, Michael Robert. Grad. high sch., Salinas; hon. degree, Berkeley Psychich Inst., 1974. Pres., chmn. McDragon Enterprises, Carmel Valley, Calif., 1976—, Human Factor Consulting Svcs., Carmel Valley, 1980—, People-Reading Inc., Carmel Valley, 1980—. Contbr. articles self-help pubs.; producer: The Human Potential Hour (radio), Pacific Grove, Calif., 1981-88; producer, writer: Exploring the Psychic World (radio), Pacific Grove, 1982-88; host: The Love Show (radio), Monterey, Calif., 1987-88; lectr. tours on the inspiration circuit, 1984—. Regional chairperson, United Cerebral Palsy Telethon, Monterey County, 1987. Mem. Psikikos (Monterey) (sec. 1987-88). Democrat. Unitarian. Office: Human Factor Consulting Box 745 Carmel Valley CA 93924

MCANUFF, DES, artistic director; b. Princeton, Ill., June 19, 1952; s. John Nelson and Ellen Boyd; m. Susan Berman, Jan. 1, 1984. founding mem. Dodger Prodsn.; former faculty Julliard Sch.; now adj. prof. theatre U. Calif. San Diego. Dir.: (Broadway prodns.) Big River (Tony award 1985), A Walk in the Woods (San Diego Critics Circle award); (off-Broadway prodns.) Gimme Shelter (Soho Arts award 1979), The Crazy Locomotive, Chelsea Theatre Ctr., Mary Stuart, How It All Began, Henry IV Part One, The Death of Von Richthofen as Witnessed from Earth (Villager award 1982), N.Y. Shakespeare Festival; A Mad World My Masters, Romeo & Juliet, As You Like It (San Diego Critics Circle award), The Sea Gull, Shout Up A Morning, Gillette, The Matchmaker, Two Rooms, 80 Days, La Jolla Playhouse; Macbeth, Stratford Festival Can.; A Walk in the Woods, Yale Repertory Theatre, others; playwright Leave it to Beaver is Dead (Soho Arts award), The Death of Von Richthofen as Witnessed from Earth (Villager and Bay Area Circle Critics awards), Troll, A Lime in the Morning, Silent Edward; contbg. editor Am. Theatre Mag. Can. Council grantee, Rockefeller grantee. Mem. Theatre Communications Group (past bd. dirs.). Office: La Jolla Playhouse PO Box 12039 La Jolla CA 92037

MCARTHUR, SUSANNE MEYER, controller; b. Portland, Oreg., Mar. 11, 1953; d. Edward T. and Frances B. (Benner) Meyer; m. Stephen Walker McArthur, Aug. 12, 1985. BBA, Portland State U., 1983. CPA, Oreg. Tech. specialist acctg. N.W. Regional Ednl. Lab., Portland, 1971—; ptnr. Hare Doktor Volkswagen Svc., Portland, 1980-83; acct. Clean Copy, Portland, 1982-88; sr. acct. audit dept. Coopers & Lybrand, Portland, 1983-85; contr. Oil Can Henry's Corp., Portland, 1985-88, Willamett Cable TV, Beaverton, Oreg., 1988.

MCAULEY, BRUCE JEFFREY, cardiologist; b. Pasadena, Calif., Aug. 28, 1950; s. Clyde Burton and Ruth Ann (Tease) McA.; m. Susan Gail Kritzik, June 9, 1984; 1 child, Kyle Lawrence. BA, U. Calif., Berkeley, 1972; postgrad., Oxford U., 1975-76; MD, Harvard U., 1977. Intern U. Calif., San Francisco, 1977-78, resident, 1978-80; fellow Stanford U. Hosp., 1981-83; clin. instr. Stanford (Calif.) U., 1983—; attending cardiologist Sequoia Hosp., Redwood, Calif., 1983—; mem. adv. bd. Advanced Cardiovascular Systems, Mountain View, Calif., 1985—. Mem. Am. Heart Assn. Knox fellow Harvard U., 1975-76. Fellow Am. Coll. Cardiology. Office: Cardiovascular Medicine 770 Welch Rd #100 Palo Alto CA 94304

MCBEATH, GERALD ALAN, political science educator, researcher; b. Mpls., Sept. 13, 1942; s. Gordon Stanley and Astrid Elvira (Hjelmeir) McB.; m. Jenifer Huang, June 7, 1970; children—Bowen, Rowena. B.A., U. Chgo., 1963, M.A., 1964; Ph.D., U. Calif.-Berkeley, 1970. Vis. asst. prof. polit. sci. Rutgers Coll., New Brunswick, N.J., 1970-72; asst. prof. John Jay Coll., CUNY, N.Y.C., 1972-74, 75-76; assoc. prof. Nat. Chengchi U., Mucha, Taipei, Taiwan, 1974-75; prof. U. Alaska, Fairbanks, 1976—; cons. Inst. Social and Econ. Research, Anchorage, 1976-77; contract researcher Alaska Dept. Natural Resources, Alaska Dept. Edn., Nat. Inst. Edn., others; staff dir. task force on internat. trade policy Rep. Conf., U.S. Senate. Sr. author: Dynamics of Alaska Native Self-Government, 1980; author monograph: North Slope Borough Government and Policymaking, 1981; jr. author: Alaska's Urban and Rural Governments, 1984; sr. editor Alaska State Government and Politics, 1987; editor: Alaska's Rural Development, 1982. Mem. bd. edn. Fairbanks North Star Borough, 1986—. Named Outstanding Faculty Mem., Assn. Students U. Alaska, Fairbanks, 1979, Alumni Assn. U. Alaska, Fairbanks, 1981; grantee Nat. Inst. Edn., 1980-83, Alaska Council on Sci. and Tech., 1982-84, Spencer Found., 1987-88. Mem. Asian Studies on Pacific Coast (program chmn. 1983, bd. dirs. 1982-83), Assn. Asian Studies, Western Polit. Sci. Assn., Am. Polit. Sci. Assn., Am. Soc. Pub. Adminstrn., Fairbanks N. Star Borough Bd. Edn. Democrat. Home: 1777 Red Fox Dr Fairbanks AK 99709 Office: U Alaska Dept Polit Sci Fairbanks AK 99775

MCBETH, RUBEN JOSE, JR., criminal justice administrator; b. St. Louis, May 2, 1945; s. Ruben Andrew McBeth and Doris Augusta (Bell) Sweet; m. Pauline Marie Martinez, Dec. 26, 1970; 1 child, Lisa Christine. BS in Criminal Justice, Pacific Western U., Los Angeles, 1980; grad., Nat. Inst. Corrections, FBI Tng. Acad.; postgrad., U. Colo., Denver, 1987—. Cert. instr. self-defense, tactical instr. With Sheriff's Dept. City of Denver, 1970—, cpl., 1974-75, sgt., 1975-78, lt., 1978-79, capt., 1978—, tng. capt., 1987—; instr. jail ops. Nat. Sheriffs Assn., Alexandria, Va., 1980—. Served as sgt. USAF, 1965-68; Vietnam. Mem. Am. Correctional Assn. (auditor accreditation com. 1986—, mem. affirmative action com. 1978-80), Am. Jail Assn., Nat. Assn. Blacks in Criminal Justice, Nat. Sheriffs Assn., Nat. Assn. Criminal Justice, Colo Assn. Blacks in Law Enforcement, Am. Legion. Home: 6365 S Florence Way Englewood CO 80111 Office: Denver Sheriff Dept PO Box 1108 Denver CO 80201-1108

MC BRIDE, GUY THORNTON, JR., college president emeritus; b. Austin, Tex., Dec. 12, 1919; s. Guy Thornton and Imogene (Thrasher) McB.; m. Rebekah Jane Bush, Sept. 2, 1942; children: Rebekah Ann, William Howard, Ellen McBride McCarty. B.S. in Chem. Engring., U. Tex., 1940; Sc.D., MIT, 1948; D.P.S. (hon.), Regis Coll., 1979; D.Engring. (hon.), Colo. Sch. Mines, 1984. Registered profl. engr., Tex. La., N.Y., Colo. Instr. chem. engring. Mass. Inst. Tech., 1942-44, research assoc., 1946-48; job engr. Standard Oil Co. Calif., 1944-46; asst. prof. chem. engring Rice Inst., 1948-55, assoc. dean students, 1950-57, dean, 1957-58, assoc. prof., 1955-58; cons. Tex. Gulf Sulphur Co., 1950-58, asst. mgr. research dept., 1958-59, mgr., 1959-60, v.p., mgr. research, 1960-63; v.p. Tex. Gulf Sulphur Co. (Phosphate div.), 1963-70, gen. mgr., 1966-70; pres. Colo. Sch. Mines, Golden, 1970-84; dir. Halliburton Co., Kerr-McGee Corp., Hercules, Inc.; hon. dir. Texasgulf Inc. Mem. Am. Chem. Soc., Am. Inst. Chem. Engrs., Nat. Soc. Profl. Engrs., Sigma Xi, Phi Lambda Upsilon, Tau Beta Pi. Club: Mile High (Denver). Home: 2615 Oak Dr #13 Lakewood CO 80215

MCBRIDE, SHERRY LOUEEN (SHARON MCBRIDE), magazine editor; b. Eureka, Kans., Aug. 1, 1937; d. Marvin Chester and Vera Minnie Shaw; m. William Thomas McBride Jr., Sept. 12, 1959 (div. Apr. 1972); children: Erin, Sean. BA, UCLA, 1964. Mng. editor Hi-Way Herald Trailer Life Enterprises Inc., Agoura, Calif., 1979-81, editor Hi-Way Herald, 1981-83, mng. editor MotorHome mag., 1983-84, sr. editor MotorHome and Trailer Life mags., 1984—; sr. editor Trailers Life's Campground & RV Svcs. Directory, 1989—. Mem. Western Publs. Assn. Democrat.

MC BRIDE, THOMAS FREDERICK, university dean, former government official; b. Elgin, Ill., Feb. 8, 1929; s. Thomas Wallace and Sarah Rosalie (Pierce) McB.; m. Catherine Higgs Milton, Aug. 23, 1975; children: Matthew (dec.), Elizabeth, John, Raphael, Luke. B.A., NYU, 1952; LL.B., Columbia U., 1956. Bar: N.Y. 1956, D.C. 1966, U.S. Supreme Ct. 1963. Asst. dist. atty. N.Y. County, 1956-59; trial atty. organized crime sect. Dept. Justice, 1961-65; adviser to Home Ministry, Govt. India, 1964; ofcl. Peace Corps, 1965-68; dep. chief counsel select com. on crime Ho. of Reps., 1969-70; assoc. dir., staff dir. Police Found., 1970-73; assoc. spl. prosecutor Watergate, 1973-75; dir. bur. enforcement CAB, 1975-77; insp. gen. U.S. Dept. Agr., Washington, 1977-81, U.S. Dept. Labor, Washington, 1981-82; assoc. dean Stanford Law Sch. (Calif.), 1982—; mem. Pres.'s Commn. Organized Crime, 1983-86, Calif. Council on Mental Health, 1986—. Co-author: Team Policing, 1973. Served with AUS, 1946-47. Mem. D.C. Bar Assn. Home: 837 Cedro Way Stanford CA 94305 Office: Stanford U Sch Law Stanford CA 94305

MCBRIDE, WILLIAM, legal consultant, transportation company executive; b. Pitts., June 21, 1928; s. Albert Sr. and Mabelle (Danhart) McB.; m. Jennie Francis Pelloni, Sept. 30, 1960; children: Blair A. Weaver, Dale W. Weaver, Scott R. Weaver, Lorraine D. BA, U. Pitts., 1953; JD, Dickinson Sch. Law, 1956. Safety inspector U.S. Steel Corp., Ellwood City, Pa., 1957-60; tng. rep. N. Am. Aviation, Anaheim, Calif., 1960-65; mgr. personnel services Food Giant Markets, Santa Fe Springs, Calif., 1965-66; adminstr. employee relations Auto Club So. Calif., Los Angeles, 1967-71, asst. mgr. safety and security, 1971-83, adminstr. safety, 1983-88, staff cons., mem. legal svcs., 1988—; instr. N. Orange County Jr. Coll. Dist., Anaheim, Calif., 1965-70, Cerritos Coll., Norwalk, Calif., 1968. Dist. chmn. Boy Scouts Am., Ellwood City, 1957-59; petitioner Various Civic Causes, Los Angeles, 1975—; communicator State and Fed. Reps., Sacramento and Washington, 1975—; mem. bus. adv. com. Rep. Assemblyman Frank Hill, 1986—; donor Heritage Found., Washington, 1983—, Rep. Presdl. Task Force, Washington, 1980—. Served to sgt. USAF, 1946-53, PTO. Mem. Am. Soc. Safety Engrs. Lodges: Masons, Shriners (life). Office: Auto Club So Calif 2601 S Figueroa St Los Angeles CA 90007

MCBRYDE, KIMBERLY ELIZABETH, dental hygienist; b. Chgo., Apr. 16, 1956; d. Salvatore John and Ruth Eileen (Polson) Gallo; m. Larry Alan McBryde, July 18, 1955. AAS, Clark County Community Coll., 1981. Registered dental hygienist. With ARC, Las Vegas, Nev., 1972-77; head lifeguard Caesars Palace Hotel, Las Vegas, 1972-78; swimming instr. 1974-77; sec. St. Viator Cath. Ch., Las Vegas, 1972-78; dental asst. Dr. John Hirsh, DDS, Las Vegas, 1975-76; med. asst. Dr. Earl Jacobson, MD, Las Vegas, 1979-80; dental hygienist Dr. James A. Callaway, DDS, Las Vegas, 1981—. Contbr. articles to profl. jours. CPR instr., ARC, 1975-77, water safety instr. 1972-77; dental health educator Clark County Pub. Schs., 1986—, dental hygiene adv. bd. and technical occupational skills com.; mem. adv. bd. Clark Community Coll., 1988-89. Recipient Clin. Dental Hygiene Excellence award Clark County Community Coll. Mem. Am. Dental Hygiene Assn., Nev. Dental Hygiene Assn. Republican. Roman Catholic. Office: Dr James A Callaway 3100 W Sahara #217 Las Vegas NV 89102

MCCABE, DONALD LEE, physician; b. Phila., Nov. 5, 1925; s. Joseph Grant and Agnes Muriel (Lee) McC.; student Ursinus Coll., 1944-45, Haverford Coll., 1946; D.O., Phila. Coll. Osteo. Medicine, 1950; D. Social Sci., World U., 1983; m. Jean Smallwood, June 25, 1977; children—Geoffrey, Timothy, Karen, Ellie, Derek, Traill. Intern, Phila. Osteo. Hosp., 1950-51; resident in psychiatry Del. Valley Mental Health Found., 1973-74; individual practice medicine, specializing in gen. practice, Towanda, Pa., 1951-68, specializing in psychoanalysis, gen. medicine, Harrisburg, Pa., 1968-71; psychiatrist Harrisburg State Hosp., also Delaware Valley Mental Health Found., 1970-73; individual practice medicine specializing in gen. practice and psychiatry, 1974—; faculty Phila. Coll. Osteo. Medicine, 1971; preceptor Mich. State Osteo. Med. Coll., 1978; founder Coll. Osteo. Medicine of Pacific, 1979; cons. in field. Original clin. research and publs. on kryptopyrroles. Lic. physician Calif. Fellow Am. Public Health Assn., Acad. Psychosomatic Medicine, Am. Coll. Gen. Practitioners in Osteo. Medicine and Surgery (pres. Pa. 1968-71, nat. dir. 1970-71, pres. Calif. Soc., 1977); mem. Osteo. Physicians and Surgeons Calif. (pres. 1979) editor jour. 1975-79), Calif. Soc. Orthomolecular Medicine (founding), Am. Osteo. Assn. (Calif. del. 1978-79), Am. Coll. Neuropsychiatry, AAAS, Academie Internationale de Lausanne, other orgns. Club: Vallejo Yacht (Calif.). Author, illustrator: Diary from the Orient, Eat and Reduce Diet; children's bokks illustrator. Office: Freeland Med Ctr 1689 E Main St Ste 1 Freeland WA 98249

MCCABE, KEVIN MICHAEL, real estate development executive; b. Evanston, Ill., May 1, 1961; s. Charles McCabe and Maryanne (Massmann) Anderson. BS in Architecture with high honors, U. Notre Dame, 1984; MBA in Real Estate Fin., U. So. Calif., 1986. Architect Skidmore, Owings & Merrill, Chgo., 1985; rsch. asst. fin. dept. U. So. Calif., L.A., 1985-86; fin. analyst Century West Devel. Co., Santa Monica, Calif., 1986—. Recipient scholarship Am. Soc. Real Estate Counselors, 1986. Mem. Notre Dame Alumni Club of L.A., U. So. Calif. Alumni Club, Tau Sigma Delta, Tau Beta Pi. Republican. Roman Catholic. Home: 11940 Goshen Ave Brentwood CA 90049 Office: Century West Devel Inc 1401 Ocean Ave #300 Santa Monica CA 90401

MCCABE, ROBERT R., architect, city planner. BArch, U. Calif., Berkeley, 1965; postgrad., Mich. State U., 1967-68; M in Community Planning, U. Cin., 1971. Vol. Peace Corps, Columbia; city planner 5, chief planner model cities physical planning program Cin. City Planning Commn.; prin. Flatow, Moore, Bryan, Shaffer, McCabe, Inc., Albuquerque, 1984—; instr. U. N.Mex. 1976-79, Grad. Dept. Community Planning, Cin., 1972, Urban Conservation Project, Cin., 1968, Mich. State U., 1968; assoc. prof. community planning Sch. Art, Architecture and Design, U. Cin., 1972. Prin. works include Albuquerque Acad. Mid. Sch., St. Joseph Rehab. Hosp., Westside Auto Ctr., others. Mem. Cen. Ave. Corridor Corp. Com., Downtown Action Planning Com., Comprehensive Plan Oversight Com.; bd. dirs. Greater Albuquerque C. of C., v.p. met. affairs, v.p. govtl. affairs, Albuquerque Mus. Found., mem. exec. com.; mem. bus. adv. council Gov. Garry Carruthers, chmn. long-range planning tasl force. Mem. AIA (nat. planning and urban design com.), Am. Planning. Assn., Nat. Council Archtl. Registration Bds. Office: Flatow Moore Bryan Shaffer McCabe Inc PO Box 8266 Albuquerque NM 87198

MCCAFFERTY, SANDRA LEE, real estate broker; b. Cleve., June 12, 1940; d. Michael and Julie (Verdi) Malinas; children: Elizabeth, Matthew, Ryan. EdB, Kent (Ohio) State U., 1963. Instr. Jefferson Community Coll., Watertown, N.Y., 1970-71; sales person C-21 Greathouse, Missoula, Mont., 1981-83; mgr. residential sales, broker Security Agy., Missoula, 1983-85; prin. Properties 2000, Missoula, 1985—; instr. U. Mont., Missoula, 1987-88, Missoula Vo-Tech., Missoula, 1984-88. Recipient Linus award for advtg., 1985, 86, 87, 88. Mem. Mont. Assn. Realtors (state media chairperson; state instr., 1984-87), Missoula County Bd. Realtors (bd. dirs. 1982-87, pres. 1986-87, Salesperson of Yr. 1986). Office: Properties 2000 2806 Garfield Missoula MT 59801

MCCAIN, JOHN SIDNEY, III, senator; b. Panama Canal Zone, Aug. 29, 1936; s. John Sidney and Roberta (Wright) McC.; m. Cindy Hensley, May 17. 1980; children: Douglas, Andrew, Sidney, Meghan, Jack. Grad. U.S. Naval Acad., 1958; grad., Nat. War Coll., 1973. Commd. ensign U.S. Navy, 1958, capt., 1977; prisoner of war Vietnam, 1967-73; dir. Navy Senate Liaison Office, Washington, 1977-81; mem. 98th-99th Congress from 1st Ariz. Dist.; U.S. senator from Ariz. 1987—. Bd. dirs. Community Assistance League, Phoenix, 1981-82. Decorated Legion of Merit; decorated Silver Star, Bronze Star, Purple Heart, D.F.C., Vietnamese Legion of Honor. Mem. Soc. of the Cin., Am. Legion, VFW. Republican. Episcopalian. Office: US Senate 111 Russell Senate Office Bldg Washington DC 20510

MCCAIN, WARREN EARL, supermarket company executive; b. Logan, Kans., Dec. 17, 1925. A.A., Oreg. State U., 1948; postgrad., U. Ill. Supr. sales Mountain States Wholesale Co., 1951-59; with Albertson's Inc., Boise, Idaho, owner, operator supermarkets, 1959—, became mgr. non-foods, 1959, mgr. store, 1962-65, supr. merchandise, 1965-67, dir. intermountain region, 1967-68, v.p. ops., 1968-72, exec. v.p., 1972-74, pres., 1974-84, chmn. bd., chief exec. officer, 1976—, also dir.; dir. Idaho 1st Nat. Bank. Office: Albertson's Inc 250 Parkcenter Blvd Boise ID 83726 *

MCCALL, JAMES ANDREW, data processing executive; b. Paterson, N.J., Apr. 1, 1947; s. James Andrew and Grace Marie (Schultheis) McC.; m. Carol Cox, July 25, 1981; children: Andy, Julianne, Christopher. BS in Engring., U.S. Mil. Acad., 1969; MS in Ops. Research, MS in Engring.-Econs., Stanford U., 1971. Commd. U.S Army, 1969, advanced through grades to capt., 1971; co. comdr. U.S Army, Vietnam, 1971-72; ADP officer U.S Army, Ft. Belvoir, Va., 1972-75; resigned U.S Army, 1975; infosystems analyst Gen. Electric Space div., Sunnyvale, Calif., 1975-79; mgr. techn. programs Gen. Electric Space div., Sunnyvale, 1979-82; mgr. software sect. SAIC, La Jolla, Calif., 1982-84, v.p., 1985—. Co-Author: Software Quality Management, 1979; contbr. articles to profl. jours. Mem. IEEE, Assn. Computing Machinery. Home: 1751 Via Allondra San Marcos CA 92069 Office: SAIC 10260 Campus Point Dr La Jolla CA 92121

MCCALL, KATHRYN LOUISE, advertising agency executive; b. Newport Beach, Calif., Apr. 20, 1964; d. James Lyons and Sylvia Louise (Langston) McC. BSBA, U. So. Calif., 1987. Product support specialist Trax Softwords, Inc., Los Angeles, 1987-88; asst. acct. exec. Lintas: CECO Communications, L.A., 1988—. Mem. U. So. Calif. Alumni Assn., Beta Gamma Sigma, Alpha Delta Pi. Republican. Methodist. Office: CECO Communications 10920 Wilshire Blvd Los Angeles CA 90024

MCCALL, ROBERT THE, artist; b. Columbus, Ohio, Dec. 23, 1919; s. Harry and Lena (Storch) M. Student, Columbus (Ohio) Fine Art Sch., 1938-39. Freelance artist, Chgo., 1939-42, 45-49, N.Y.C., 1949-71, Paradise Valley, Ariz., 1971—. Co-author: Our World in Space, 1973, Vision of the Future, 1983. With USAF, 1942-45. Mem. Rotary. Republican. Presbyterian. Home and Office: 4816 Moonlight Way Paradise Valley AZ 85253

MCCALL, WILLIAM CALDER, oil and chemical company executive; b. Hoquiam, Wash., Feb. 1, 1906; s. Dougall Hugh and Hughena (Calder) McC.; m. Marian Hall, Mar. 22, 1946; children—Ernest, Robert. Student U. Oreg., 1924-28. Asst. sales mgr. Anaconda Sales Co., Chgo., 1932-39; chmn. McCall Oil & Chem. Corp., Portland, Oreg., 1939—, Gt. Western Chem. Co., Portland, 1955—, Chemax, Inc., Portland, 1975—; dir. Oreg. Bank, Portland, King Broadcasting Co., Seattle. Pres. Oreg. Art Mus., Portland; trustee Lewis and Clark Coll., Portland; exec. v.p. Oreg. Symphony Soc.; dir. Med. Research Found., Good Samaritan Hosp. Found., Portland. Republican. Episcopalian. Clubs: Eldorado Country (Indian Wells, Calif.) (pres. 1978-79); Arlington (Portland); Pacific-Union (San Francisco); Los Angeles Country, Vintage (Palm Desert, Calif.), Waverley Country, Rainier (Seattle). Office: McCall Family Corp 808 SW 15th Ave Portland OR 97205

MCCALLA, DOUGLAS BRUCE, revenue analyst; b. Oakland, Calif., July 29, 1949; s. Howard Lewis and Faye Louise (Teas) McC.; m. Judy Rae Mullison, Aug. 15, 1981 (div. 1984); children: Kristin Anne, Heather Lynn. BA, San Diego State U., 1972. Data analyst Navy Personnel Rsch. and Devel. Ctr., San Diego, 1975-77; recreation ctr. dir. City of San Diego, 1977-82, risk mgmt. analyst, 1982-87, revenue analyst, 1987—; cons. fin. and taxation, San Diego, 1979—. Co-author Management Information Systems and Organizaitonal Behavior, 1985. Vol., fundraiser Am. Cancer Soc., San

Diego, 1986-88, Nat. Multiple Sclerosis Soc., San Diego, 1987-88; bd. dirs. City of San Diego Retirement Bd., 1987—. Mem. Nat. Mgmt. Assn. (chpt. bd. dirs. 1986-88), Internat. Found. Employee Benefit Plans. Home: 5430 Baltimore Dr #8 La Mesa CA 92042 Office: City of San Diego 202 C St MS 8A San Diego CA 92101

MCCALLISTER, ROSS ANDREW, JR., real estate development company executive; b. Albuquerque, Jan. 27, 1953; s. Ross Andrew and Nancy (McCulloch) M.; m. Patty F. Bentley, June 5, 1974; children: Amanda, Ann. BBA, N.Mex. State U., 1975. Regional v.p. Sandia Fed. Savs. & Loan, Albuquerque, 1976-83; pres. E.C. Garcia & Co., Tucson, 1983-85, The McCallister Co., Tucson, 1985—. Pres. Gallup Country Club, 1980-83; fund devel. com. Girl Scouts, Tucson, 1988; bd. dirs. United Way, Gallup, N.Mex., 1978. Democrat. Roman Catholic. Home: 8172 E Galinda Tucson AZ 85715 Office: The McCallister Co 5546 E 4th St Tucson AZ 85711

MCCALLON, LARRY KEITH, aerospace company executive; b. Mayfield, Ky., Oct. 21, 1939; s. Clyde Dawson and Annie Dee (Burnett) McC.; m. Su-Chun Lee, Apr. 10, 1981; children: James, Bryan, David, Monica. BS in Engring. Math. and Aero. Engring., U. Mich., 1962; MSin Aero. Engring., Air Force Inst. Tech., 1963. Commd. 2d lt. USAF, 1962, advanced through grades to maj., 1972; research assoc. Lawrence Radiation Lab., Livermore, Calif., 1966-69; br. chief USAF Weapons Lab., Albuquerque, 1969-71; chief research and devel. div. U.S. Mil. Assistance Group, Seoul, Republic of Korea, 1975-81; br. chief program office USAF Space Div., Los Angeles, 1981-83; ret. USAF, 1983; mgr. strategic missile program office, electronics div. Northrop Corp., Hawthorne, Calif., 1983—; pres., chief exec. officer McFam Corp., Huntington Beach, Calif., 1984—. Decorated Bronze Star. Mem. Air Force Assn., Am. Def. Preparedness Assn., Tau Beta Pi. Republican.

MCCAMMON, BOB, professional hockey coach. Formerly hockey player Port Huron Flags, Internat. League; formerly coach Philadelphia Flyers (Nat. Hockey League); coach Vancouver Canucks, 1987—. Office: care Vancouver Canucks, 100 N Renfrew St, Pacific Coliseum, Vancouver, BC Canada V5K 3N7 *

MC CANDLESS, ALFRED A., congressman; b. Brawley, Calif., July 23, 1927; s. Max T. and Fleta (Beaty) Mc C.; m. Gail W. Glass, Nov. 26, 1982; children: Cristina, Alfred A., Craig, Blaine, Ward. B.A. in Polit. Sci. and Pub. Adminstrn., UCLA, 1951. Mem. Riverside County Bd. Suprs., Calif., 1971-82, chmn. bd., 1971-72, 80-81; founder McCandless Motors, Indio, Calif., 1953-75; mem. 98th-101st Congresses from 37th dist. Calif. Founding mem. South Coast Air Quality Mgmt. Dist.; mem. Riverside County Housing Authority; founding mem. Sunline Transit Agy.; founder Coachella Valley Assn. Govts.; exec. com., dir. County Suprs. Assn. Calif. Served to capt. USMC, 1945-46, 50-52. Mem. Indio Co. of C. (hon. life), Greater Riverside C. of C. Lodge: Indio Rotary (past pres.). Office: US Ho Reps 435 Cannon House Office Bldg Washington DC 20515

MCCANN, CECIL VINCENT, III, electronics engineer; b. Kissimmee, Fla., Oct. 31, 1962; s. Cecil Vincent McCann Jr. and Marian Fern (Wagner) Paulding; m. Cynthia Sue Hillenburg, Nov. 23, 1984; children: Matthew Thomas, Christopher Ryan. BS in Computer Sci., U. Cen. Fla., 1985. Simulation analyst Ednl. Computer Corp., Orlando, Fla., 1985-86; project software engr. Honeywell, Sperry Comml. Flight Systems, Phoenix, 1986-89; sr. electronics engr. McDonnell Aircraft Co., Mesa, Ariz., 1989—. Rep. Go Club, Honeywell Corp., 1988. Republican. Lutheran. Office: McDonnell Aircraft Corp 5000 E McDowell Rd Mesa AZ 85205

MCCANN, JACK ARLAND, former construction and mining equipment company executive, consultant; b. Chestnut, Ill., Apr. 16, 1926; s. Keith Ogden and Miriam Imogene McC.; m. Marian Adele Gordon, Mar. 31, 1956; 1 son, Christopher John. A.B., Bradley U., 1950. Mgr. Washington Office, R.G. LeTourneau Inc., 1950-53; mgr. def. and spl. products Westinghouse Air Brake Co., 1958-64, mgr. nat. accounts, 1964-67, mng. dir. Belgian plant and European mktg., 1967-70; gen. sales mgr. WABCO div. Am. Standard Inc., Peoria, Ill., 1970-73, v.p. mktg., 1973-80, v.p. staff, 1980-82; ret., 1982; now cons. Bd. dirs. Green Valley Community Fund. With USNR, 1944-46. Decorated chevalier Ordre de la Couronne (Belgium). Mem. Nat. Def. Transp. Assn. (life), U.S. C. of C., Green Valley Bd. Realtors (bd. dirs.), Am. Legion, Bradley Chiefs Club, Old Pueblo Club, Country Club Green Valley, Green Valley Rep. Club (bd. dirs.), Shriners, Masons.

MCCANN, ROBERT RAY, health service administrator; b. Paintsville, Ky., July 29, 1940; s. Charles Huey and Pearl (Cassidy) McC.; m. Kyoko Kamamuta, Feb. 19, 1962; children: Jim, Fred. BS with distinction in Bus. Adminstrn., Colo. State U., 1966; MA in Pub. Adminstrn., U. No. Colo., 1977. Enlisted USAF, 1958, advanced through grades to capt., 1969; mgmt. analyst USAF Systems Command, Dayton, Ohio, 1966-70; with med. service corps USAF Med. Service, 1970-78; ret. USAF, 1978; adminstr. Cigna Health Plan of Ariz., Phoenix, 1978-83; owner, pres. Med.-Solo, Inc., Phoenix, 1983-88; mktg. exec. Rainsoft, Phoenix, 1988—. Editor: Drawing for Life, 1985. Rep. precinct committeeman, Glendale, 1987. Decorated Air medal. Mem. Ret. Officers' Assn. (pres. Ariz. council 1984-85). Home: 20401 N 6th Ave #6 Phoenix AZ 85027

MCCANSE, A. ROSS, film director, consultant; b. Madison, Wis., Dec. 1, 1938; s. Ralph Alan and Jessie Methven (Hill) McC.; (div. Dec. 1979). BS, U. Wis., 1960; MA, UCLA, 1963. Producer J. Walter Thompson Co., N.Y.C., 1963-69; producer, dir. Sachs, Finley & Kaye, L.A., 1969-72; owner, exec. producer Ross McCanse & Assoc., L.A., 1972-75; pres., dir. Ross McCanse & Assoc., Inc., L.A., 1975-83; dir. The Film Tree, L.A., 1983-87; freelance dir., cons. Studio City, Calif., 1987—; cons. Ednl. Film Ctr., Annandale, Va., 1975—. Cons. film TV series Footsteps, 1974-75; cons., dir. film TV series Powerhouse, 1979, 80; dir. videotape program It Does a Body Good, 1988, I Can, 1989. Film producer, dir. TV commls. several polit. candidates, 1974-84. Recipient Clio award TV Commls. Festival, 1979. Mem. Dirs. Guild Am., Assn. Ind. Comml. Producers (bd. dirs. 1981-84). Democrat. Presbyterian. Home and Office: 3315 Oakdell Rd Studio City CA 91604

MC CARDLE, RANDALL RAYMOND, real estate developer; b. Phila., Sept. 2, 1931; s. Russell Henry and Ruth Hertha (Snyder) McC.; m. Yong Suk; 1 child, Mark. A.A., Orange Coast Coll., 1956; B.A., Chapman Coll., 1958, M.A., 1966; Ph.D., Western Colo. U., 1974; Real estate broker, Newport Beach, Calif., 1953-61; founder, pres. The Real Estaters, Orange County, Calif., 1961—, Treeco Escrow Co., Inc., Costa Mesa, Calif., 1971-—; founder Bank of Costa Mesa, 1972, dir. bus. devel., 1973—; also newspaper columnist, lectr., investment counselor. Fund-raising chmn. Boys' Club of Am., Harbor area, 1979-80; bd. dirs. Boys Club Harbor Area; mem. adv. com. Orange Coast Coll., 1964—, Golden West Coll., 1969—. With USNR, 1950-53. Recipient Appreciation award Bd. Realtors, 1967, 68, 70, 76, 80; inducted into Orange Coast Coll. Hall of Fame, 1983. Mem. Calif. Assn. Realtors (state dir. 1963-67), Calif. Assn. Real Estate Tchrs. (state dir. 1966-80), Orange County Coast Assn. (dir. 1974—), C. of C., Nat. Assn. Real Estate Appraisers, Bd. Realtors (pres. 1966-67 long-range planning com. 1981), U. So. Calif. Faculty Assn., Red Baron Flying Club, Mason (Shriner). Contbr. articles to profl. jours. Home: 12 Geneve Newport Beach CA 92660 Office: 1000 Quail St Ste 260 Newport Beach CA 92660

MCCARTER, NEELY D., seminary president. s. Robert William and Nell (Dixon) McC.; m. Jean Maxwell, May 28, 1954; children: Robert Sidney, Robin, Jeanette, Shirley, Jean. AB, Presbyn. Coll., 1950; BD, Columbia Theol. Sem., 1953, postgrad., 1968; ThM, Union Theol. Sem., 1958; MA, Yale U., 1959, PhD, 1961. Ordained to ministry Presbyn. Ch. U.S., 1953. Pastor U. Fla., Gainesville, 1953-58; prof. Christian edn. Columbia Theol. Sem., Decatur, Ga., 1961-66; Robert and Lucy Reynolds Critz prof. Christian edn. Union Theol. Sem., Va., 1966, deacon, 1973; now pres. Pacific Sch. Religion, Berkeley, Calif. Author: Hear the Word of the Lord, 1964; co-author: The Gospel on Campus, 1959, Help Me Understand, Lord, 1978. Office: Pacific Sch of Religion 1798 Scenic Ave Berkeley CA 94709 *

MCCARTHY, BRIAN NELSON, retail and real estate company executive; b. Detroit, May 24, 1945; s. Andrew Nelson and Ruth Elizabeth (Hill) McC.; m. Linda Lang, Aug. 10, 1974; children: Amanda Lang, Kelly Elizabeth, Meghan Virginia. BS in Engring. Sci., Oakland U., Rochester, Mich., 1966; MBA, Harvard U., 1972. Engr. Gen. Motors Corp., Pontiac, Mich., 1965-67; co-owner Sound Wave Systems, Costa Mesa, Calif., 1971-78; chief fin. officer, controller A&W Gershenson Co., Farmington, Mich., 1972-75; chief op. officer Devel. Group, Southfield, Mich., 1975-81; chief exec. officer Brichard & Co., San Francisco, 1982-87; pres., chief exec. officer Watermark Corp., Sausalito, Calif., 1987—. Lt. USNR, 1967-70, capt. S.C. USNR. Recipient Navy Commendation medal with gold star. Mem. Internat. Council Shopping Ctrs., Nat. Assn. Realtors, Real Estate Securities and Syndications Inst., Nat. Assn. Security Dealers, Navy Supply Corps Assn. (bd. dirs. 1987—), Harvard Bus. No. Calif. Club, Commonwealth Club. Republican. Office: Watermark Corp 1505 Bridgeway Blvd Sausalito CA 94965

MCCARTHY, JAMES PATRICK, financial planner; b. Milw., Aug. 19, 1930; s. Emmet and Lucille (Doonan) McC.; m. Terri Schiller, June 10, 1955; children: Terrence, Mary, Anne, Matt, Michael, Paul. BS with distinction, Ind. U., 1961; MBA, Wayne State U., 1967. Commd. 2d lt. USAF, 1951, advanced through grades to col., 1951-73, ret., 1973; fin. planner McCarthy & Assocs., Phoenix, 1973—; faculty assoc. Scottsdale (Ariz.) Community Coll., 1976-79, Ariz. State U., Tempe, 1979-86; bd. dirs. Rea Graham Fund, L.A. Author: A,B,C,D,D's of Mutual Fund Investing, 1989; contbr. numerous articles to nat. mags. Decorated D.F.C., Bronze Star, 12 Air medals, USAF Commendation medal. Mem. Aircraft Owners and Pilots Assn. Republican. Roman Catholic. Home: 10014 N 61st Pl Scottsdale AZ 85253

MCCARTHY, JOANNE ELIZABETH, teacher, consultant; b. Allentown, Pa., May 6, 1943; d. Robert Franklin and Sarah Elizabeth (Knauss) Schall; m. William James McCarthy, June 21, 1969. B.A., UCLA, 1968; M.Ed., U. Rochester, 1974; M.S., U. LaVerne, 1981; M.A., Mills Coll., 1983. Elem. tchr. Centralia Sch. Dist., Buena Park, Calif., 1968-70; reading specialist elem. sch. Spencerport (N.Y.) Sch. Dist., 1973-74, Wayne Central Sch. Dist., Ontario, N.Y., 1974-75; tchr. State Demonstration Project, Pittsburg (Calif.) Unified Sch. Dist., 1977-78; English and reading tchr. Vallejo (Calif.) City Unified Sch. Dist., 1978—; staff devel. cons. Profl. Devel. Ctr. Mem. NEA, Assn. Supervision and Curriculum Devel., Calif. Assn. Tchrs. English, Nat. Council Tchrs. English, Phi Delta Kappa, Pi Lambda Theta; Nat. Audubon Soc. Author publ. in field. Home: 105 Poshard St Pleasant Hill CA 94523 Office: Vallejo City Unified Sch Dist 840 Nebraska St Vallejo CA 94591

MCCARTHY, JOHN FRANCIS, aerospace engineer; b. Trenton, N.J., Sept. 2, 1951; s. John F. and Margaret T. (Horton) McC.; m. Sarah Anne Sheard, July 6, 1985; 1 child, Kathleen. BA, U. Pa., 1973; MS, Cornell U., 1976, PhD, 1979. Research asst. astronomy dept. Cornell U., Ithaca, N.Y., 1976-79; system analyst Hughes Aircraft Corp., El Segundo, Calif., 1979-82, propulsion system engr. intelsat VI program, 1982-85, system engring. mgr. Magellan program, 1987-. Contbr. articles to profl. jours. Mem. Phi Beta Kappa. Democrat. Roman Catholic. Home: 1723 Clark Ln Redondo Beach CA 90278

MCCARTHY, LEO TARCISIUS, state lieutenant governor; b. Auckland, N.Z., Aug. 15, 1930; came to U.S., 1934, naturalized, 1942; s. Daniel and Nora Teresa (Roche) McC.; m. Jacqueline Lee Burke, Dec. 17, 1955; children: Sharon, Conna, Adam, Niall. BS, U. San Francisco, 1955; JD, San Francisco Law Sch., 1961. Bar: Calif. 1963. Supr. Bd. of Supr., San Francisco, 1964-68; assemblyman Calif. State Legislature, Sacramento, 1969-82, assembly speaker, 1974-80; lt. gov. State of Calif., Sacramento, 1983—; Democratic nominee U.S. Senate, 1988. Chmn. Econ. Devel. Commn. of Calif., 1983—; regent U. Calif., 1983—; trustee State Coll. and Univ. System Calif., 1983—; chmn. Task Force on Nursing Home Care, Calif., 1982—; mem. Democratic State Central Com., 1969—. Served with USAF, 1951-52. Named Outstanding Legislator Planning and Conservation League of Calif., 1971; named Outstanding Legislator in U.S. Nat. Council Sr. Citizens, 1972; recipient Torch of Liberty award B'nai B'rith, 1976. Roman Catholic. Office: Office of Lt Gov State Capitol Rm 1114 Sacramento CA 95814

MCCARTHY, MARY ANN BARTLEY, electrical engineer; b. Drummond, Okla., Nov. 27, 1923; d. William Clifford and Estella Florence (Williams) Bartley; m. Joseph Manderfield McCarthy, Aug. 23, 1946 (dec. 1983); 1 child, Mary Ann McCarthy Morales. BEE, B of Material Sci., U. Calif., Berkeley, 1976. Aircraft radio technician U.S. Civil Svc., San Antonio and Honolulu, 1942-45; salesperson Sears Roebuck & Co., Enid, Okla., 1947-53; specialist reliability engring. Lockheed, Sunnyvale, Calif., 1977-82, engr. program components, 1986—; rsch. engr. Lockheed, Austin, Tex., 1982-86. Mem. Soc. Women Engrs. (pres. S.W. Tex. chpt. 1984, counsel reps. sec. 1985, pres. Santa Clara Valley chpt. 1986-87, nat. v.p. 1987-88, chmn. nat. career guidance 1988-89), AAUW (com. chmn. 1984, co-chmn. literacy com. 1984), Toastmasters. Republican. Roman Catholic. Home: 6103 Edenhall Dr San Jose CA 95129

MCCARTHY, ROGER LEE, mechanical engineer. AB in Philosophy with high distinction, U. Mich., 1972, BSME summa cum laude, 1972; MS in Mech. Engring., MIT, 1973, MechE, 1975, PhD in Mech. Engring., 1977. Registered profl. engr., Calif., Ariz. Project engr. machine design and devel. engring. div. Proctor & Gamble, Inc., Cin., 1973-74; program mgr. Spl. Machinery Group Foster-Miller Assocs., Inc., Waltham, Mass., 1976-78; prin. design engr. Failure Analysis Assocs., Palo Alto, Calif., 1978—; pres., 2d chmn. Failure Analysis Assocs., Palo Alto, 1982—. Co-contbr. numerous articles to profl. jours. NSF fellow, 1972-75. Mem. Am. Soc. Metals, ASME, Soc. Automotive Engrs., Am. Welding Soc., Am. Soc. for Testing and Materials, Human Factors Soc., Nat. Soc. Profl. Engrs., ASHRAE, Nat. Fire Protection Assn., Phi Beta Kappa, Sigma Xi (James B. Angell scholar). Office: Failure Analysis Assocs 149 Commonwealth Dr PO Box 51470 Menlo Park CA 94025

MCCARTHY, RORY (JOSEPH RORICK MCCARTHY), designer; b. N.Y.C., Nov. 2, 1948; s. Joseph Allen McCarthy and Katharine Page; m. Leslie Whitelaw, Oct. 11, 1980; children: Quinn, Oona. Student, U. Ariz, Tucson, 1966-70. Owner, prin. Design & Fabrication Studio, Tucson, 1972—. Active Downtown Adv. Com., Tucson, 1987&, Arts Dist. Implementation Com., 1987—, Pimo County Arts Council, Tucson, 1987—, Transit Ctr. Adv. Com., Tucson, 1987—. Recipient Young Am. award, Am. Crafts Council, N.Y.C., 1977, Design Rev. award for excellence, Indsl. Design Mag., N.Y.C., 1984, Post Modern Color award, Victoria & Albert Mus., London, 1984, Internat. Furniture Composition award, Progressive Architecture mag., 1985. Office: Rory McCarthy Design 8 E Toole Tucson AZ 85701

MCCARTNEY, PATRICK KEVIN, newspaper reporter, political consultant; b. L.A., Sept. 9, 1948; s. Warren Phil and Mildred Pauline (Weiler) McC. BA, U. San Diego, 1970; MA, U. So. Calif., 1983. Statis. analyst L.A. County Probation Dept., Downey, Calif., 1973-79; writer Free Venice (Calif.) Beachhead, 1984-88; editor, reporter Westchester (Calif.) Jour., 1987-88; reporter Citizen Newspaper, Solana Beach, Calif., 1988—; press relations cons. to Daniel Tabor, Inglewood, Calif., 1988. Contbr. articles to newspapers. Pres. Venice Town Council, 1984-86, Coalition Concerned Communities, L.A., 1986-87; bd. dirs. Not Yet N.Y., L.A., 1986-87; v.p. Marina-Mar Vista-Venice Democratic Club, 1987-88; candidate for L.A. City Council, 1987. Mem. San Diego Press Assn., Venice Hist. Soc. (co-founder, bd. dirs. 1986-88), Heal the Bay. Home: 117 Rosebay Dr Apt 32 Encinitas CA 92024

MCCARTY, ELIZABETH ANN, realty company executive; b. Phoenix, Jan. 30, 1954; d. James Douglas McCarty and Doris Jean (Kay) Witt; m. John Arley Vallery, June 1, 1974 (div. Mar. 31, 1982); m. Howard Alton Jones, Sept. 15, 1984; 1 child, Tempest Rochelle Jones. Student, Phoenix Coll., 1972; student, Ariz. State U., 1973-74. Salesperson Aztec Investment & Realty, Show Low, Ariz., 1978-82; broker, owner McCarty Realty & Devel., Show Low, 1983—. Bd. dirs. Foster Care Rev. Bd., Holbrook, Ariz., 1981-83; mem. Show Low Airport Commn., 1984-86. Mem. Nat. Assn. Realtors, Real Estate Brokerage Coun. Democrat. Home: PO Box 2155 Show Low AZ 85901 Office: Coldwell Banker Realty 3191 S Wt Mountain Rd Show Low AZ 85901

MCCASLIN, PHILLIP RAY, engineering modeler; b. Altus, Okla., Mar. 10, 1950; s. Harold Hugh and Wadie V. (Branscum) McC.; m. Betty Sue Marcella Maynard, Aug. 19, 1969; children: Karen Sue, Sandra Lee, Cherri Lynn, Steven Phillip, Stacy Susanne. BS, Fla. State U., 1971. Tech. supr. Scottsdale (Ariz.) Police Dept., 1974-81; dir. graphic div. Attention Getters Inc., Phoenix, 1981-85; v.p. Ariz. Archtl. Models, Tempe, 1985-88; dir. project devel. Ariz. Western, Tempe, 1988—; archtl. cons. Mobie Land Devel. Corp., Dallas, 1985-86. Orgn. mem. Ariz. March of Dimes, 1988. Recipient mktg. achievement award Bus. Owners and Mgrs. Assn., 1984, McSamm mktg. award Tex. Home Builders Assn., 1985, mktg. excellence award Ariz. Home Builders Assn., 1986. Mem. Am. Engring. Model Soc. (bd. dirs. 1989—). Republican. Mem. Ch. of Christ. Office: Ariz Western 6102 S Maple Ave Ste 2 Tempe AZ 85283

MCCAW, JOHN WHEELER, casino owner; b. New Brighton, Pa., Mar. 17, 1956; s. John B. and Margaret (Wheeler) McC.; m. Debra Patricia Brooks, Aug. 2, 1986; children: Jesse M., John D. Student, Pa. State U., 1974-76. Assoc. v.p. Dean Witter Reynolds, Las Vegas, Nev., 1981-83; acct. exec. Prudential-Bache, Las Vegas, 1983-86; pres. Larine, Inc., Las Vegas, 1983—. Mem. Masons, Moose. Republican. Episcopalian. Office: 5480 W Spring Mtn Rd Las Vegas NV 89102

MCCLAIN, PAMELA KAY, periodontist; b. Monterey, Calif., Mar. 8, 1958; d. Robert George and JoAnn Kay (Rohrbach) Schallhorn; m. Michael John McClain, June 14, 1980; children: Michael James, Brian Robert. BS in Dental Hygiene, U. Colo., 1980, DDS cum laude, 1985. Dental hygienist Dr. Robert Schallhorn, Denver, 1980-85; practice dentistry specializing in periodontics Aurora, Colo., 1987—; clin. instr. U. Colo., 1988. Contbr. research articles to profl. jours. Bd. mem. youth ministry Mt. Olive Luth. Ch., Aurora, 1988—. Mem. ADA, Colo. Dental Assn., Am. Acad. of Periodontology, Western Soc. of Periodontology, Rocky Mountain Soc. of Periodontists, Met. Denver Dental Soc., Columbine Periodontal Study Club, Omicron Kappa Upsilon. Lutheran. Office: 11200 E Mississippi Ave Aurora CO 80012

MCCLAIN, RICHARD STAN, cinematographer; b. Los Angeles, Oct. 7, 1951; m. Kim Girard, Nov. 7, 1987. Astrovision technician Continental Camera Systems, Van Nuys, Calif., 1974-82; aerial cameraman TV shows Magnum P.I., Airwolf, Murder She Wrote, Simon & Simon, Universal City, Calif., 1981—, Super Carrier, Captain Power; aerial cameraman feature films The Right Stuff, The Iceman, Rambo, Innerspace, Buster, U2 Rattle and Hum; aerial cameraman music videos Stevie Wonder, Journey, U2; pres. Pasadena Camera Systems, Inc.; distbr. WESCAM gyro-stabilized helicopter mounts,. Mem. Internat. Photographers, Screen Actors Guild, Guild of Am. (bd. dirs.). Office: Pasadena Camera Systems Inc 47 E Walnut St Pasadena CA 91003

MC CLANAHAN, MOLLY, mayor; b. San Jose, Calif., 1937; children: Patricia, David, Cynthia. Student, U. Redlands, 1955-57; AA in Bus. Mgmt., Fullerton Coll., 1982. Farmer San Luis Obispo County, Calif.; dir. YWCA Youth Employment Svc., Anaheim, Calif., 1982—; mem. Fullerton (Calif.) City Coun., 1982—; mayor City of Fullerton, 1988—. Pres. Fullerton Beautiful; trustee Fullerton Coll. Found.; Fullerton City Coun. rep., pact chmn. Tri-City Park Authority; past chmn. Fullerton Human Rels. Commn., Orange County Housing Authority Adv. Com., Arbor Day Com.; mem. Sr. Citizens Task Force, Fullerton Arboretum Commn., Fullerton Hist. Bldg. Survey, Fullerton Sch. Dist. Master Plan Task Force, Wilshire Jr. High Sch. Bd., Fullrton-Morelea sister City Assn., Fullerton Mus. Ctr., Muckenthaler Cultural Ctr., Friends of the Library, Friends of the Arboretum, Fullerton Friends of Music, Calif. State U.-Fullerton Art Alliance, CSUF Music Assocs. Named Fullerton Coll. Woman of Distinction, 1982, YWCA Vol. of Yr., 1981. Mem. LWV, Anaheim C. of C. (women's div., Woman of Yr. 1977). Office: City Hall 303 W Commonwealth Ave Fullerton CA 92632

MCCLATCHY, JAMES B., editor, publisher; b. Sacramento; s. Carlos K. and Phebe (Briggs) McC.; m. Susan Brewster; children: Carlos F., William B. B.A., Stanford U.; M.S., Columbia U. Reporter, editor Sacramento Bee; reporter, editor Fresno Bee, Calif.; pub. McClatchy Newspapers, Sacramento. Pres. French Am. Bilingual Sch., 1974-76. Served with USAF, 50-52. Mem. InterAm. Press Assn. (bd. dirs.), Calif. Nature Conservancy (bd. dirs.). Office: McClatchy Newspapers 21st & Q Sts Sacramento CA 95813

MCCLAVE, DONALD SILSBEE, assocation executive; b. Cleve., May 7, 1941; s. Charles Green and Anne Elizabeth (Oakley) McC.; m. Christine Mary Tomkins, Feb. 19, 1966; 1 child, Andrew Green. BA, Denison U., 1963. Mktg. research officer Bank of Calif., San Francisco, 1968-70; v.p. Cen. Nat. Bank, Chgo., 1970-75; v.p. First Interstate Bank, Portland, Oreg., 1975-77, sr. v.p., 1977-79, exec. v.p., 1979-86; pres., chief exec. officer Portland Met. C. of C., 1987—; bd. dirs. Bank Mktg. Assn., Chgo., 1976-79, Consumer Bankers Assn., Washington, 1980-82; instr. Grad. Sch. Mktg. and Strategic Planning, Athens, 1982-84, Pacific Coast Sch. Banking, Seattle, 1976-78. Pres. Oreg. Episcopal Sch. Bd., Portland, 1983-84; pres. Assn. Oreg. Industries Found., Salem, Oreg., 1984-85; co-chmn. Japan-Am. Conf. of Mayors and C. of C., Portland, 1985—. Office: Portland C of C 221 NW 2nd Ave Portland OR 97209

MCCLELLAN, CRAIG RENE, lawyer; b. Portland, Oreg., June 28, 1947; s. Charles Russell and Annette Irene (Benedict) McC.; m. Susan Armistead Nash, June 7, 1975; children: Ryan Alexander, Shannon Lea. BS in Econs., U. Oreg., 1969; JD magna cum laude, Calif. We. U., 1976. Bar: Calif. 1976, U.S. Dist. Ct. (so. dist.) Calif. 1976. Compliance specialist Cost of Living Coun. and Price Commn., Washington, 1972-73, dir. Oil Policy subcom., 1973; ptnr. Luce, Forward, Hamilton & Scripps, San Diego, 1976-87; owner McClellan & Assocs., San Diego, 1987—. Chairperson Sta. KPBS Annual Fundraising Auction, 1984. With USMC, 1969-72. Mem. Assn. Trial Lawyers Am., Calif. State Bar Assn., San Diego County Bar Assn., Calif. Trial Lawyers Assn. (bd. govs. 1985-87), San Diego Trial Lawyers Assn. (bd. dirs. 1983—), Nat. Forensics League, Phi Gamma Dela, Phi Alpha Delta. Republican. Presbyterian. Office: McClellan & Assocs 1144 State St San Diego CA 92101

MCCLELLAN, JANE LEE, legal assistant; b. Phoenix, Oct. 27, 1962; d. Hugh Mac and Mildred (Mount) McC.; m. Earl Wesley Beatty, Oct. 31, 1985. BA magna cum laude, Ariz. State U., 1984; cert. legal asst., U. San Diego, 1984. Legal asst. Fennemore, Craig, von Ammon, Udall & Powers, Scottsdale, Ariz., 1984-85, Quarles & Brady & Fannin (and predecessor firm), Phoenix, 1985—. Mem. (assoc.) ABA, Ariz. Paralegal Assn. (voting), Gamma Phi Beta (ritual chmn. 1982-83). Democrat. Home: 7333 W Turney Ave Phoenix AZ 85033 Office: Quarles & Brady & Fannin 1 E Camelback Ste 470 Phoenix AZ 85012

MCCLELLAN, ROGER ORVILLE, toxicologist; b. Tracy, Minn., Jan. 5, 1937; s. Orville and Gladys (Paulson) McC.; m. Kathleen Mary Dunagan, June 23, 1962; children—Eric John, Elizabeth Christine, Katherine Ruth. D.V.M. with highest honors, Wash. State U., 1960; M.Mgmt., U. N.Mex., 1980. diplomate Am. Bd. Vet. Toxicology, cert. Am. Bd. Toxicology. From biol. scientist to sr. scientist Gen. Electric Co., Richland, Wash., 1957-64; sr. scientist biology dept. Pacific N.W. Labs., Richland, Wash., 1965; scientist med. research br. div. biology and medicine AEC, Washington, 1965-66; asst. dir. research, dir. fission product inhalation program Lovelace Found. Med. Edn. and Research, Albuquerque, 1966-73; v.p., dir. research adminstrn., dir. Lovelace Inhalation Toxicology Research Inst., Albuquerque, 1973-76, pres., dir., 1976-88; chmn. bd. dirs. Lovelace Biomedical and Environ. Research Inst., Albuquerque, 1988—; pres. Chem. Industry Inst. Toxicology Research, Triangle Park, N.C., 1988—; mem. research com. Health Effects Inst., 1981—; bd. dirs. Toxicology Lab. Accreditation Bd., 1982—, treas., 1984—; adj. prof. Wash. State U., 1980—, U. Ark., 1970—; clin. assoc. U. N.Mex., 1971—, adj. prof. toxicology, 1985—; adj. prof. toxicology Duke U., 1988—. mem. dose assessment adv. group U.S. Dept. Energy, 1980-87, mem. health and environ. research adv. com., 1984-85; mem. exec. com. sci. adv. bd. EPA, 1974—, mem. environ. health com., 1980-83, chmn., 1982-83, chmn. radionuclide emissions rev. com., 1984-85, chmn. Clean Air Sci. Adv. Com., 1987—; mem. com. on toxicology Nat. Acad. Sci.-NRC, 1979-87, chmn., 1980-87, ad hoc mem. bd. environ. studies and toxicology, 1980-87; mem. Dept. Labor adv. com. , 1988; bd.

dirs. Lovelance Anderson Endowment Found.; pres. Am. Bd. Vet. Toxicology, 1970-73; mem. adv. council Ctr. for Risk Mgmt., Resources for the Future, 1977—; council mem. Nat. Council for Radiation Protection, 1970—. Contbr. articles to profl. jours. Editorial bd. Jour. Toxicology and Environ. Health, 1980—, assoc. editor, 1982—; editorial bd. Fundamental and Applied Toxicology, 1984—, assoc. editor, 1987—; editorial bd. Toxicology and Indsl. Health, 1984—; editor CRC Critical Revs. in Toxicology, 1987—; assoc. editor Inhalation Toxicology Jour., 1987—. Recipient Herbert E. Stokinger award Am. Conf. Govtl. Indsl. Hygienists, 1985, Alumni Achievement award Wash. State U., 1987, Disting. Assoc. award Dept. Energy, 1987. Fellow AAAS, Am. Acad. Vet. and Comparative Toxicology; mem. Radiation Research Soc. (sec.-treas. 1982-84, chmn. fin. com. 1979-82), Health Physics Soc. (chmn. program com. 1972, Elda E. Anderson award 1974), Soc. Toxicology (v.p.-elect to pres. 1987-90; inhalation specialty sect. v.p. to pres. 1983-86; bd. publs. 1983-86, chmn. 1983-85), Am. Assn. Aerosol Research (bd. dirs. 1982—, treas. 1986—), Soc. Risk Analysis, Am. Vet. Med. Assn., Gesellschaft fur Aerosolforschung, Sigma Xi, Phi Kappa Phi, Phi Zeta. Republican. Lutheran. Home: 1111 Cuatro Cerros SE Albuquerque NM 87123 Office: Lovelace Biomed and Environ Rsch Inst PO Box 5890 Albuquerque NM 87185 also: Chem Industry Inst Toxicology PO Box 12137 Triangle Park NC 27709

MCCLELLAND, JOHN MORRIS, retired publishing executive; b. Rogers, Ark., May 31, 1915; s. John Morgan and Adlyn (Morris) McC.; m. Burdette Craig, June 24, 1939; children: John M. III, Genevieve Sue. BA, Stanford U., 1937. Editor, pub. Daily News, Longview, Wash., 1950-77; founder, editor, pub. Jour.-Am., Bellevue, Wash., 1976-86; pres. Evergreen Pub. Co., Seattle, 1984-86. Author: R.A. Long's Planned City-Longview, 1971, Cowlitz Corridor, 1964, Wobbly War, The Centralia Story, 1987. Chmn. State Parks and Recreation Commn., Washington, 1952-56; mem. Wash. Bd. Geographic Names, 1978—; bd. dirs. Health and Hosp. Services, Bellevue, 1977—, N.W. Kidney Ctr., Seattle, 1979—, Annie Wright Sch., Tacoma, 1986—. Served to lt. USNR, 1942-45. Named Internat. Boss of Yr., Nat. Secs. Assn., 1968; named to Wash. Newspaper Hall of Honor, Wash. State U., 1984. Fellow Soc. Profl. Journalists; mem. Am. Soc. Newspaper Editors, Am. Antiquarian Soc., Wash. State Hist. Soc. (pres. 1982-88), AP (bd. dirs. 1968-71, 72-81), Am. Legion, Golf Collectors Soc., Sigma Delta Chi, Kappa Sigma. Clubs: Royal and Ancient Golf of St. Andrews (Scotland); Broadmoor Golf, Seattle Golf. Lodge: Elks. Office: 777 108th 650 Security Pacific Bank Pla Bellevue WA 98004

MC CLELLAND, JOHN PETER, winery executive; b. N.Y.C., Aug. 17, 1933; s. Harold Stanley and Helen Lucille (Gardner) McC.; m. Ann Carolyn Campbell, Aug. 27, 1954; children: John, Kristen. Student, UCLA, 1951-53. With Almadén Vineyards, Inc., San Jose, Calif., 1958-83; v.p. sales, then v.p. mktg. Almadén Vineyards, Inc., 1970-76, pres., 1976-83; chmn. bd., chief exec. officer Geyser Peak Winery, 1983—. Served with AUS, 1954-56. Mem. Wine Inst. (chmn. public relations com. 1977—, exec. com. 1979—, chmn. 1986-87), Sonoma County Wine Bd., Internat. Wine and Food Soc., Supreme Knight of the Vine, Chaine Des Rotisseurs. Republican. Presbyterian. Office: Geyser Peak Winery PO Box 25 Geyserville CA 95441

MCCLELLAND, NANNETTE EVETTE, furniture installation company official; b. Detroit, Oct. 20, 1956; d. Samuel August Jr. Darbous and Helen Margaret (Williams) Schmidt; m. Jeffrey D. McClelland, Mar. 10, 1989. AA, Everett Community Coll., 1980. Ops. mgr. Oasis, Inc., Seattle, 1986—. Author poems. With U.S. Army, 1974-75. Mem. NAFE. Office: Oasis Inc 3415 Stone Way N Seattle WA 98103

MCCLENDON, IRVIN LEE, SR., data processing executive; b. Waco, Tex., June 12, 1945; s. Irvin Nicholas and Evelyn Lucile (Maycumber) McC.; m. Mary Helen Burrell Swanson, June 26, 1982; 1 son, Richard Lester children by previous marriage: Michael Boyd, Irvin Lee Jr., Laura Ann, Paul Nicholas; stepchildren: Brenda Irene, Kevin Ray, Perry Lee. Student El Camino Coll., 1961-63, U. So. Calif., 1962-66; BA in Math., Calif. State U.-Fullerton, 1970, postgrad. in bus. adminstrn., 1971-76; cert. nat. security mgmt. Indsl. Coll. Armed Forces, 1974; postgrad. in religion Summit Sch. Theology, 1982-84. Engring. lab. asst. Rockwell Internat. Corp., Anaheim, Calif., 1967-68, test data analyst, 1968, assoc. computer programmer, 1968-70, mem. tech. staff, 1970-82; systems programmer A-Auto-trol Tech. Corp., Denver, 1982-84, sr. tech. writer, 1984-86; sr. tech. writer, editor Colo. Data Systems, Inc., Englewood, Colo., 1986-87; engring. writer III CalComp subs. Lockheed Co., Hudson, N.H., 1987; sr. tech. writer CDI Corp., Arvada, Colo., 1987-88; office automation cons. Volt temporary Svcs., 1989, word processing cons., Aurora, Colo., 1989—; staff cons. CAP GEMINI AM., 1989—. Sec. of governing bd. Yorba Linda Libr. Dist., 1972-77; trustee Ch. of God Seventh Day Advent, Bloomington, Calif., 1979-81, treas., 1980-81, mem. Calif. State U. and Coll. Statewide Alumni Coun., 1976-77; 2d v.p. Orange County chpt. Calif. Spl. Dists. Assn., 1976, pres., 1977; mem. Adams County Rep. Cen. Com., 1984—, vice-chmn. 32d House Dist. Vacancy com., 1984-86, chmn., 1986—; dist. capt., mem. exec. com. , 1988—; mem. Luth. Chorale, 1982-85, Colo. Choir, 1988—, Northland Chorale, 1988—. With USAFR, 1967-71. USAF Nat. Merit scholar, 1963-67. Mem. Calif. Assn. Libr. Trustees and Commrs. (exec. bd., So. Calif. rep. 1976-77), Assn. Computing Machinery, Air Force Assn., Nat. Eagle Scout Assn., Calif. State U.-Fullerton Alumni Assn. (dir. 1975-77). Home: 9835 Pennsylvania Dr Thornton CO 80229-2117 Office: Southgate II D200 6892 S Yosemite Ct Englewood CO 80112

MCCLENDON, ROBERT FRANK, architect; b. Seattle, Feb. 26, 1946; s. Don and Gracey (Carmicle) Whittemore; m. Meredith R. McClendon, Mar. 26, 1970; children: Anna Michel, Ian Robert. BArch, Wash. state U., 1970; MEd magna cum laude, Yale U., 1972; Assoc. MBA, Harvard U., 1972. Assoc. Ibsen Nelsen, Seattle, 1972-76; lead designer TRA, Seattle, 1976-78; dir. design and planning Media 5, Honolulu, 1978-80; dir. office CDA, Seattle, 1980-82; v.p. and gen. mgr. mgmt. services CADI, Seattle, 1982-89; pres. MSG Devel. Mgmt. Co., Bellevue, Wash., 1989—. Contbr. articles to profl. jours. Recipient Platz BoBo Peace award, France, 1972; Progressive Architecture Design award, 1978, 80, Progressive Architecture South Lake Union Master Plan award, Plastics Inst. award, Italy, 1973, Golden Nugget award, Kako Master Plan for Honolulu award, Bagdad Internat. Design award; named to U.S. Olympic Swim Team, 1964, All-Am. Swimmer, 1966, 67. Mem. AIA, AICP. Clubs: Tower, Coll., Washington Athletic (Seattle). Office: MSG Devel Mgmt Co 10800 Northeast St Bellevue WA 98112

MCCLENNEN, MIRIAM J., former state official; b. Seattle, Sept. 16, 1923; d. Phillip and Frieda (Golub) Jacobs; m. Louis McClennen, Apr. 25, 1969; stepchildren: Peter Adams, James C.A., Helen, Persis, Crane, Emery. BA, U. Wash., 1945; MBA, Northwestern U., 1947. Exec. trainee Marshall Field & Co., Chgo., 1945-47; asst. buyer Frederick & Nelson (subs. of Marshall Field), Seattle, 1947-49; buyer Frederick & Nelson (subs. of Marshall Field), 1949-57; fashion coordinator, buyer Levy Bros., Burlingame/San Mateo, Calif., 1957-63; buyer Goldwaters, Phoenix, 1963-67; adminstrv. asst. to pres. Ariz. State Senate, Phoenix, 1973-76; dir. publs. Office of Sec. of State, Phoenix, 1976-87; chairwoman legis. subcom. adminstrv. procedure Ariz. State Legislature, Phoenix, 1984-85. Compiler, editor publ. Ariz. Adminstrv. Code, 1973-87, Ariz. Adminstrv. Digest, 1976-87. Bd. dirs., mem. exec. com. Phoenix Art Mus. League, 1972—, Phoenix Symphony Guild, 1970-88; bd. dirs., sec. Combined Metro. Phoenix Arts & Scis., 1974—; bd. dirs. Phoenix Arts Coun., Master Apprentice Programs, 1980-83; bd. dirs., mem. exec. com. Heard Mus., 1982-88, chmn. publs. com., 1982-88; mem. Ariz. State Hist. Records and Archives Bd., 1987—. Recipient Disting. Svc. award Atty. Gen. Ariz., 1987, Outstanding Svc. to People, Ariz. State Senate, 1987, Nat. Assn. Secs. of State award, 1987. Mem. English Speaking Union, Nat. Soc. Arts and Letters, Charter 100 (bd. dirs. 1981-85), Phoenix County Club, Ariz. Club. Home: 5311 LaPlaza Cir Phoenix AZ 85012

MCCLINTICK, ROBERT ROY, insurance company executive; b. Walnut, Kans., Nov. 19, 1924; s. A.W. and Louella (Burnett) McC.; m. Hazel Jean Wathen, Aug. 12, 1950; children—Suzanne McClintick Dinsmore, Stephanie Owens. B.S., U. Kans., 1949; postgrad. U. Kansas City, 1950-52. CPCU; CLU. With Farmers Ins. Group, Kansas City, 1949-51, Austin, Tex., 1952-55, underwriting mgr., Merced, Calif., 1956-58, gen. underwriting mgr., Los Angeles, 1959-62, dir. underwriting adminstrn. and personal lines, 1963-68, regional mgr. Pacific Northwest, 1969-74, v.p., mgr. Great Lakes region, 1975-76, v.p. claims, Los Angeles, 1977-78, v.p. field ops., 1979-84, sr. v.p. property and casualty ops., 1985—; pres. Fire Underwriters Assn., Los Angeles, 1982—, also dir.; dir. Farmers Underwriters Assn., Truck Underwriters Assn., Mid-Century Ins. Co., A.I.F. Holding Co.; mem. Farmers Ins. Group Safety Found. Investment Com.; v.p., gen. mgr. Farmers Ins. Co. of Wash., 1969-74; pres. Farmers Ins. Co. Oreg., 1969-74, Ill. Farmers Ins. Co., 1974-76; chmn. Oreg. steering com. Western Ins. Info. Service, 1973-74; dir. Oreg. Ins. Guaranty Assn., Assn. Oreg. Industries, Ill. Ins. Info. Service. Mem. U.S. C. of C., C.P.C.U. (Los Angeles chpt.), C.L.U. Office: Farmers Group Inc 4680 Wilshire Blvd Los Angeles CA 90010 also: Fire Ins Exch PO Box 2478 Terminal Annex Los Angeles CA 90051

MCCLURE, ALLAN HOWARD, space contamination specialist, space materials consultant; b. Phila., Mar. 29, 1925; s. C. Howard and Edda Cherry (Speirs) McC.; m. Jean Florence Hall, May 31, 1947; children: Joyce Ann, Allan Hall. BS, Widener U., 1949; postgrad., Command & Gen. Staff Coll., 1972. Chemist Am. Cyanamid, Pitts., 1950-52; materials engr. Piasecki/Vertol Helicopter Co., Morton, Pa., 1952-59; lead engr. Boeing Aerospace Co., Seattle, 1959-71; sr. specialist engr. Boeing Aerospace Co., Kent, Wash., 1974-85; tech. cons. Adhesive Engring. Co., San Carlos, Calif., 1971-74. Author, investigator spacecraft contamination control documents and govt. reports. Pres. Seattle Crime Prevention League, 1974-84. Served to maj. U.S. Army, 1943-46, ETO, PTO; sec. Boeing Employees Amateur Radio Soc., 1984; membership chmn. Amateur Radio Emergency Services, 1984-85. Recipient Silver Beaver award and William H. Spurgeon III award Boy Scouts Am., Seattle, 1964. Mem. Am. Chem. Soc., Soc. for Advancement of Material and Process Engring. (nat. dir., pres. Seattle chpt.), Rainier C. of C., Res. Officers Assn. (life). Republican. Home: 12026 SE 216th St Kent WA 98031

MCCLURE, FRANK EDWARD, structural engineer; b. San Francisco, June 3, 1924; s. Denny Hanks and Irma (Vose) McC.; m. Augusta Tolles, Apr. 12, 1946; children: Edward Denny, Anne Elizabeth, Robert Coke Hill, Julia Margaret. BS, U. Calif., Berkeley, 1944. Field engr. Peter Kiewit Sons Co., Friant Kern Canal, Calif., 1946; chief engr. Thomas F. Chace Cons., San Francisco, 1947-52; ptnr. Jennings & McClure Cons. Engrs., Berkeley, 1952-54; sr. structural engr. Oakland Pub. Schs., 1954-55; cons. engr. Frank McClure, Cons. Engr., Oakland, Calif., 1955-62; ptnr. McClure & Messinger, Cons. Engrs., Oakland, 1962-75; univ. engr. U. Calif., Berkeley, 1976-77; sr. structural engr. Lawrence Berkeley Lab., Berkeley, 1978—; Mem. Com. on Earthquake Engring., Nat. Research Council, Washington, 1983-85, Seismology Code Devel. Com., Internat. Conf. of Bldg. Officials, Whittier Calif., 1980-85; made field reports and investigations on earthquake damage in U.S. and abroad, 1952-85. Served to lt. j.g. CEC, USNR, 1943-46, Okinawa. Mem. ASCE, Structural Engrs. Assn., Calif., Seismol. Soc. Am., Internat. Conf. Bldg. Ofcls. (Seismology Code Devel. Com., 1980-85), Earthquake Engring. Research Inst. (pres. 1987-89), Order of Golden Bear, Tau Beta Pi, Chi Epsilon. Democrat. Presbyterian. Home: 54 Sleepy Hollow Ln Orinda CA 94563 Office: Lawrence Berkeley Lab 1 Cyclotron Rd Berkeley CA 94720

MCCLURE, JAMES A., senator; b. Payette, Idaho, Dec. 27, 1924; s. W. R. and Marie McC.; m. Louise Miller; children: Marilyn, Kenneth, David. J.D., U. Idaho, 1950; J.D. hon. doctorate, 1981; DL (hon.), Coll. Idaho, 1986. Mem. Idaho State Senate, 1961-66; asst. majority leader 1965-66; city atty. City of Payette (Idaho); pros. atty. Payette County; Mem. 90th-92d Congresses from 1st Idaho Dist., 1967-73; U.S. Senator from Idaho 1973—; Energy and Natural Resources Com.; mem. Com. on Rules and Adminstrn., Com. on Appropriations; subcom. on Interior and related agys.; mem. subcoms. on agrl., def., energy/water devel. Trustee Kennedy Center; bd. govs. Council for Nat. Policy; mem. subcoms. Labor HHS. Mem. Phi Alpha Delta. Methodist (trustee). Clubs: Elks, Masons, Kiwanis. Office: US Senate 309 Hart Senate Bldg Washington DC 20510

MCCOLLUM, LISA COLLEEN, business official, educator; b. Ajo, Ariz., Apr. 25, 1955; d. Ralph C. and Frances (Downey) McC. AS, Olympic Community Coll., 1984; BS in Health Care Adminstrn., City U., Bellevue, Wash., 1989. Teaching aide No. Kitsap Marine Environ. Ctr., Poulsbo, Wash., 1971; staff mem. Seabeck (Wash.) Conf. Grounds, Wash., 1972-75; med. asst. Robert B. Bright, M.D., Bremerton, Wash., 1975--, office mgr., 1980--; instr. med. asst. program Olympic Community Coll., Bremerton, 1986-89, mem. adv. bd. med. asst. program, 1980—. Mem. Am. Assn. Med. Assts. (cert. med. asst., adminstrv. cert., clin. cert., curriculum rev. bd. 1985-, Profl. Achievement award 1983), Wash. State Soc. Med. Assts. (co-editor Statline 1981-82, pres. 1986-87, pres. Kitsap chpt. 1979-80, editor Monitor 1983-84). Home: PO Box 2237 Bremerton WA 98310 Office: 245 4th St Bldg 405 Bremerton WA 98310

MCCOLLUM, SUDI BEL, artist, designer, printmaker; b. Berkeley, Calif., Dec. 17, 1950; d. Alfred James II and Helen Charlotte (Grimsley) McC. BFA with distinction, Calif. Coll. Arts and Crafts, 1973. Art dir. Boysen Paint Co., Oakland, Calif., 1974-76; v.p., art dir. Faron, Melrose and McCollum, Palo Alto, Calif., 1976-85; pres., ptnr. McCollum & Pitcher Pub., Palo Alto, 1981-87; pres., owner Sudi McCollum Design, Glendale, Calif., 1984—. Fine art posters and serigraphs commd. by GTE Spirit, Nat. Coun. Jewish Women, Am. Heart and Lung Assn., numerous others. Mem. Western Art Dirs. Club, L.A. Art Dirs. Club. Office: McCollum Design 3244 Cornwall Dr Glendale CA 91206

MCCOMB, DAVID GLENDINNING, history educator; b. Kokomo, Ind., Oct. 26, 1934; s. John Floyd and Jennie (Glendinning) McC.; m. Mary Alice Collier, Sept. 6, 1957; children: Katherine, Susan, Joseph. BA, So. Meth. U., 1956; MBA, Stanford U., 1958; MA, Rice U., 1962; PhD, U. Tex., 1968. Purchasing agt. McRan Co., Houston, 1958-60; instr. South Tex. Jr. Coll., Houston, 1962, U. Houston, 1966-68; asst. prof. San Antonio Coll., 1962-66; rsch. assoc. U. Tex., Austin, 1968-69; asst. prof. history Colo. State U., Ft. Collins, 1969-72, assoc. prof., 1972-77, prof., 1977—; interviewer, dir. Oral History of Colo. Project, 1973-77, Big Thompson Disaster Oral History, 1976-78, Olympic Tng. Ctr. Oral History, 1983-87. Author: Houston, a History, 1969 (Tullis award 1969), Galveston, a History, 1986 (Tex. History award 1987), also others; editor: World History Ann. Edits., 1987; contbr. articles to hist. jours. Recipient award of merit Am. Assn. for State and Local History, 1980, Disting. Svc. award Colo. State U., 1986; Danforth Found. grantee, 1978, also others, 1966-85. Fellow Tex. Hist. Assn.; mem. Oral History Assn. (program chmn. 1980), N.Am. Assn. for Sports History, World History Assn., Western History Assn. (program chmn. 1979), Rocky Mountain World History Assn. (chmn. 1988—). Democrat. Unitarian. Office: Colo State U Dept History Fort Collins CO 80523

MC COMIC, ROBERT BARRY, real estate development company executive; b. Selmer, Tenn., Nov. 6, 1939; s. Richard Donald and Ila Marie (Prather) McC.; m. Judith Joseph; children by previous marriage: Thomas Christopher, Robert Geoffrey. B.S., Union U., 1961; LL.B. (Thomas Dewey Nelson award), Tulane U., 1964; postgrad. in law (Ford Found. grantee, Fredrich Ebert Found. fellow), U. Freiburg, W. Ger., 1964-65, Hague (Netherlands) Internat. Acad. Law, 1965. Bar: Tenn. 1964, N.Y. 1966, Calif. 1971. Assoc. firm Donovan Leisure Newton & Irvine, N.Y.C., 1965-68; assoc. gen. counsel Avco Corp., Greenwich, Conn., 1968-70; v.p., sec., gen. counsel Avco Community Developers, Inc., San Diego, 1970-73; exec. v.p. Avco Community Developers, Inc., 1973-75, pres., 1975-82, chief exec. officer, 1977-82; chmn., chief exec. officer R.B. McComic, Inc., 1982—; dir., sec. Avco Savs. and Loan Assn., Los Angeles, 1969-73. Chmn. San Diego campaign coms., United Negro Coll. Fund, 1976-80, S.D. Inst. Arts Edn.; bd. dirs. San Diego Econ. Devel. Corp., Western Behavioral Sci. Inst., La Jolla, 1981-86, San Diego Opera Assn., 1985—, U. Calif.-San Diego Found., 1985, Child Abuse Prevention Fedn.; trustee U.S. Naval Acad. Found., 1982-86. Honoree Human Relations Inst.; Honoree Am. Jewish Com., 1981. Mem. Am., Calif., N.Y., Tenn., San Diego County bar assns., Assn. Bar City N.Y., San Diego Bldg. Contractors Assn. (dir., treas. 1974-75), Order of Coif, Omicron Delta Kappa, Sigma Alpha Epsilon. Clubs: San Diego Yacht, City of San Diego, City of Los Angeles (chmn.). Home: 2032 Via Casa Alta La Jolla CA 92037 Office: RB McComic Inc 6920 Miramar Rd Ste 104 San Diego CA 92121

MCCONNEL, JAMES HOWARD, entrepreneur, consultant; b. Durango, Colo., Oct. 11, 1950; s. John Howard and Ellen Gertrude (Carbis) M.; m. Janice Rea Hill, Aug. 28, 1987. Student, Ft. Lewis Coll., 1975. Vice-comdr. DAV, Grand Juction, Colo., 1984-85; v.p. Citizens Against Legal Injustice, Durango, 1986—. Mem. Rodeo Com., Durango, 1985—. With USN, 1969-73, Vietnam. Mem. Entrepenuers Am., VFW, DAV. Office: Circle J Enterprises 1111 Camino Del Rio Durango CO 81301

MCCONNEL, RICHARD APPLETON, aerospace company official; b. Rochester, Pa., May 29, 1933; s. Richard Appleton Sr. and Dorothy (Merriman) McC.; m. Mary Francis McInnis, 1964 (div. 1984); children: Amy Ellen, Sarah Catherine. BS in Naval Engring., U.S. Naval Acad., 1957; MS in Aerospace Engring., USN Postgrad. Sch., 1966. Commd. ensign USN, 1959, advanced through grades to comdr., 1971, ret., 1982; program mgr. Electromagnetic Systems div. Raytheon Co., Goleta, Calif., 1982-87, SRS Techs., Inc., Camarillo, Calif., 1987--. With USN, 1957. Mem. Internat. Test and Evaluation Assn., Assn. Old Crows. Republican. Home: 1665 Pierside Ln Camarillo CA 93010 Office: SRS Techs Inc 1317 Del Norte Rd Ste 100 Camarillo CA 93010

MCCONNELL, CALVIN DALE, clergyman; b. Monte Vista, Colo., Dec. 3, 1928; s. Roy and Leota Fern (Taylor) McC.; m. Mary Caroline Bamberg, Sept. 2, 1952 (dec. Apr. 1986); children: David William, Mark Andrew; m. Velma Duell, Dec. 17, 1988. B.A., U. Denver, 1951; M.Div., Iliff Sch. Theology, 1954; S.T.M., Andover Newton Theol. Sem. Ordained to ministry United Meth. Ch.; pastor Meth. Ch., Williams, Calif., 1955-58, 1st United Meth. Ch., Palo Alto, Calif. and Stanford U. Wesley Found., 1958-61; chaplain and asst. prof. religion Willamette U., Salem, Oreg., 1961-67; pastor Christ United Meth. Ch., Denver, 1968-72; pastor 1st United Meth. Ch., Boulder, Colo., 1972-79, Colorado Springs, Colo., 1979-80; bishop of United Meth. Ch., Portland Area, 1980-88, Seattle Area, 1988—. Trustee U. Puget Sound, Iliff Sch. Theology. Club: Rotary. Office: 2112 3d Ave Ste 301 Seattle WA 98121

MCCONNELL, DAVID SCOTT, sales and marketing executive; b. Lafayette, Ind., Feb. 3, 1949; s. David Lee and Caroline (Snyder) McC.; m. Marilyn Anne Schumaker, Aug. 26, 1972; 1 child, Kelly Anne. Student, Purdue U., 1971. Sales engr. Ross Gear div. TRW, Lafayette, 1971-73; sales mgr. Ross Gear div. TRW, Detroit, 1973-76; salesman Vecco Instruments, Richmond, Va., 1976-78, Gen. Electric Med. Group, N.Y.C., 1978-82; nat. accounts mgr. Gen. Electric Med. Group, L.A., 1982-86, Surgidev Corp., Santa Barbara, Calif., 1986-88; mgr. sales and mktg. Transmatic, Inc., Santa Barbara, 1988—. Chmn. Santa Barbara New Comers, 1987. Mem. Nat. Account Mgr. Assn., Sigma Chi Alumni. Democrat. Presbyterian. Home: 3615 Capri Dr Santa Barbara CA 93105 Office: Transmatic Inc 6145 Delfield Indsl Waterford MI 48095

MCCONNELL, HARDEN MARSDEN, biophysical chemistry researcher, chemistry educator; b. Richmond, Va., July 18, 1927; s. Harry Raymond and Frances (Coffee) McC.; m. Sophia Milo Glogovac, Oct. 6, 1956; children: Hunter, Trevor, Jane. B.S., George Washington U., 1947; Ph.D., Calif. Inst. Tech., 1951. NRC fellow dept. physics U. Chgo., 1950-52; research chemist Shell Devel. Co., Emeryville, Calif., 1952-56; asst. prof. chemistry Calif. Inst. Tech., 1956-58, prof. chemistry and physics, 1963-64; prof. chemistry Stanford U., Calif., 1964-79, Robert Eckles prof. chemistry, 1979—; founder Molecular Devices Corp., 1983—; cons. in field. Contbr. numerous articles to profl. publs.; patentee (in field). Recipient Calif. sect. award Am. Chem. Soc., 1961; recipient award in pure chemistry Am. Chem. Soc., 1962, Irving Langmuir award in chem. physics Am. Chem. Soc., 1971, Dickinson prize for sci. Carnegie-Mellon U., 1982, Wolf prize in chemistry, 1984, ISCO award, 1984, Pauling medal Puget Sound and Oreg. sects. Am. Chem. Soc., 1987, Wheland medal U. Chgo., 1988. Fellow AAAS, Am. Phys. Soc.; mem. Nat. Acad. Scis. (award in chem. scis. 1988), Am. Acad. Arts and Scis., Am. Soc. Biol. Chemists. Office: Stanford U Dept Chemistry Stanford CA 94305

MCCONNELL, ROBERT ANDREW, lawyer; b. Seattle, May 31, 1949; s. Neil Lathrop and Suzanne Katherine (Schaefer) M.; m. Joanne Christine McConnell, Aug. 17, 1974. BA, Cen. Washington U., 1971; JD, Golden Gate U., 1974. Bar: Wash. Prin. East, Lagerquist, McConnell & McDonough, Inc. predecessors, Seattle, 1975—; prof. paralegal program, real estate law Edmonds Community Coll., Edmonds, Wash., 1981-82; bd. dirs., mem. exec. com. Shoreline Savs. Bank, Seattle, 1984-88. Bd. dirs. Firland Correctional Adv. Com., 1976-77, Seattle Youth and Community Svcs., 1986— (pres. 1988—); judge moot ct. U. Wash. Law Sch., 1985—. Mem. Wash. State Bar, Wash. State Trial Lawyers Assn., Wash. Savings League (attys. com.), Tower Club. Republican. Office: East Lagerquist McConnell & McDonaugh Inc 9725 3d Ave NE #600 Seattle WA 98115

MCCONVILLE, JOHN FRANK, cosmetics executive, consultant, chemist; b. Flushing, N.Y., May 21, 1936; s. Frank and Josephine (Carpenter) McC.; m. Anna Marie Potter, Dec. 15, 1974; children: Dina, Daniel. BS in Biology, U. Miami, Fla., 1963, BS in Chemistry, 1964; postgrad., Fla. State U., 1965-66; MBA in Mgmt., Pepperdine U., 1978. Sr. rsch. scientist U. Miami, 1963-65; supr. ensymology dept. Dade Regents, Coral Gables, Fla., 1967-68; sales engr. Coutler Electronics, Miami, 1968-69; quality control microbiologist Max Factor & Co., Hollywood, Calif., 1969-71, assoc. mgr. R & D, 1971-78, mgr. R &D, 1979-81; dir. microbiology dept. Vidal Sassoon, Chatsworth, Calif., 1978-79; tech. dir. Cosmetic Labs. of Am., Chatsworth, 1981—; pvt. practice cons., Valencia, Calif., 1985—. Contbr. articles to profl. jours. With USAF, 1955-59, CBI. Mem. Soc. Cosmetic Chemists (Paul W. Jewel award 1983), Am. Soc. for Microbiology, Cosmetic, Toiletries and Fragrances Assn. (microbiology com.). Republican. Roman Catholic. Home: 25874 Anzio Way Valencia CA 91355 Office: Cosmetic Labs of Am 20245 Sunburst St Chatsworth CA 91311

MCCOPPIN, PETER, symphony orchestra conductor; b. Toronto; m. Roswitha McCoppin. BMus in Performance Art, U. Toronto; studied conducting with, Erich Leinsdorf. Former head orch. dept. Cleve. Inst. Music; resident conductor Edmonton (Alta.) Symphony; prin. conductor Alta. Ballet Co., 1981-84; former guest conductor, prin. guest conductor Vancouver (B.C.) Symphony Orch., 1988—; music dir. Victoria (B.C.) Symphony Orch., 1989—; prin. guest conductor Thunder Bay (Ont.) Symphony Orch., 1989—. Office: Vancouver Symphony Orch, 601 Smithe St, Vancouver, BC Canada V6B 5G1 *

MCCORD, THOMAS B., geophysicist, educator; b. Elverson, Pa., Jan. 18, 1939; s. Thomas M. and Hazel Violet (Bard) M.; m. Carol S. Bansner, Dec. 20, 1962. BS, Pa. State U., 1962; MS, Calif. Inst. Tech., 1964, PhD, 1968. From asst. to assoc. prof. (tenured) MIT, Boston, 1969-77; sr. research scientist Ctr. for Space Research, MIT, Boston, 1977-86; prof. planetary scis., depts. geology and geophysics, and physics and astronomy U. Hawaii, Honolulu, 1986—; vis. assoc. Planetary Sci., Calif. Inst. Tech., 1969-72; dir. George R. Wallace Jr. Astrophys. Obs., MIT, Boston, 1970-77; asst. dir. Inst. for Astronomy, U. Hawaii, Honolulu, 1976-79; chmn. div. planetary sci. Hawaii Inst. Geophysics U. Hawaii, 1979—, SETS Inc., Honolulu, 1978—; mem. NASA teams on 6 past and current missions , positions included team leader Comet Rendezvous Asteroid Flyby Project and chmn. Asteroid and Comet Data Processing Sci. Adv. Com. Pres. Pacific Space Ctr. Served with USAF 1958-62. Named Research Fellow in Planetary Sci., Calif. Inst. Tech., 1968; recipient numerous research grants from various govt. and private agencies including NASA, Jet Propulsion Lab., Nat. Oceans and Atmospheres Adminstrn., and NSF, 1980-87, W.M. Keck Found. grant, 1986, Honolulu City and County award; asteroid discovered in 1985 named for him. Fellow Am. Geophys. Union (pres. 1986—), AAAS; mem. Am. Astron. Soc., Am. Astronautical Soc., Internat. Astron. Union, Explorers Club; active on many coms. in profl. sci. orgs. Office: U Hawaii Planetary Geosciences Div Hawaii Inst Geophysics Honolulu HI 96822 also: SETS Inc Mililani Technology Park Honolulu HI 96789

MCCORD, VINCENT ABBOTT, JR., data processing company executive; b. Nashville, July 24, 1946; s. Vincent Abbott and Mary Helen (Kropf) McC.; m. Nancy Elizabeth Stark, Nov. 17, 1973; children: Hunter Stark, Haven Elizabeth. BS in Math., Ga. Inst. Tech., 1969; MBA, Harvard U., 1974. Mktg. rep. IBM, L.A., 1974-78; fin. exec. IBM, White Plains, N.Y., 1978-82, San Jose, Calif., 1982-88; fin. exec. Conner Peripherals, Inc., San Jose, 1988—. Bd. dirs. City Lights Theatre Co., San Jose, 1987-89. Capt. USAF, 1969-72. Republican. Episcopalian. Home: 965 Foxswallow Ct San Jose CA 95120

MCCORKINDALE, LAURA ANN, feature film and theater producer; b. Teaneck, N.J., Mar. 19, 1966; d. Douglas Hamilton and Gloria Ann Gallo. BA with honors, San Diego State U., 1988. Adv. asst. The Rochester (N.Y.) Democrat & Chronicle, 1981; reporter The Rochester Times Union, 1982; wire corr. Pacific News Service, Marin County, Calif., 1982-84; city reporter The Ind. Jour., Marin County, 1982-84, columnist, 1984-86; actress various films and TV, L.A.; 2nd asst. dir., asst. producer New Horizons, L.A., 1988—; producer The Attic Theatre, L.A., 1989. Named #1 U.S. Journalist of Yr. Journalism Edn. Assn., 1984, Calif. Journalist of Yr., 1984; recipient Marin County Outstanding Achievement award Buck Found., Nat. Investigative Reporting award Quill and Scroll. Mem. Sigma Delta Chi, Delta Gamma.

MCCORKLE, CHESTER OLIVER, JR., agricultural and environmental sciences educator; b. Gilroy, Calif., Jan. 18, 1925; s. Chester Oliver and Avis Jacqueline (Kickham) McC.; m. Nina Grace Mathews, June 11, 1945; children: Sandra Lee, Kenneth Carl, Timothy Kevin. Student, Calif. Poly. State U., San Luis Obispo, 1941-43, U. Redlands, 1943-44; BS, U. Calif., Berkeley, 1947, MS, 1948, PhD, 1952. Research asst. U. Calif., Berkeley, 1947-48, asst. specialist, 1949-51; agrl. analyst Bank of Am., San Francisco, 1948-49; from research asst. to dean Coll. Agrl. and Environ. Scis. U. Calif., Davis, 1952-70, prof. agrl. econs., 1978—; v.p. Universitywide Office, Berkeley, 1970-78; research economist Ctr. for Econ. Research, Athens, Greece, 1961-62; econ. cons. Ministry Coordination, Kingdom of Greece, 1965; chmn. agr. and renewable resources bd. NRC-Nat. Acad. Scis., 1977-80, mem. commn. on natural resources, 1976-81. Served with USMCR, 1943-46, 51-52. Mem. AAAS, AAUP, Am. Western Agrl. Econ. Assn. (past pres.). Club: Bohemian (San Francisco). Home: 637 Eisenhower St Davis CA 95616 Office: U Calif Voorhies Hall Rm 210 Davis CA 95616

MCCORKLE, SHERMAN, banker; b. Elida, N.Mex.; m. Cathy Weaver; children: Ashley Danielle, Shelby Arrielle. Student, U. N.Mex., 1966-68; degree, U. Colo., 1984. With Southwest Investment Co, Albuquerque; 1973-76 Sunwest Bank of Albuquerque, 1976—, asst. cashier, 1977, asst. mgr. Master Charge dept., 1978, asst. v.p., 1979, v.p., mgr. Mesa Grande Bank Cards, 1980-85, sr. v.p., dir. electronic banking svcs. div., 1985-87, exec. officer, 1987; pres., chief exec. officer Sunwest Credit Svcs. Corp., 1988—; mem. faculty U. Okla. Bd. dirs. Albuquerque Civic Light Opera Assn., N.Mex. Mus. Natural History Found., Landsun Home, Greater Albuquerque C. of C., chmn. 1988-89. Mem. Am. Bankers Assn. (mem. numerous coms.), N.Mex. Bankers Assn. (bd. dirs.), Plus System, Inc. (exec. com. bd., 1981—). Home: 1125 Turner NE Albuquerque NM 87123 Office: Sunwest Credit Svcs Corp PO Box 3257 Albuquerque NM 87190-3257

MCCORMAC, VIRGINIA HICKS, social services administrator; b. San Antonio, Apr. 8, 1935; d. Frank M. and Virginia M. (Obergfell) Hicks; m. John S. McCormac, June 26, 1954; children: Anne C., Karen D. BA cum laude, Trinity U., 1954. Pub. rels. dir. 1982-83, pres., exec. dir., 1983--. Chmn. Ada County Community Action Com., Boise, 1966-67; pres. Boise Jr. League, 1972-73; pub. rels. chmn. Silver Sage Girl Scout Coun., Boise, 1973-75; bd. dirs. Puget Sound Big Sisters, Seattle, 1978-81. Named Outstanding Young Woman in Am., 1967, Outstanding Civic Leader, 1968; recipient Disting. Citizen award Idaho Daily Statesman, 1974. Mem. Rotary of Seattle, Met. Soroptimist. Republican. Presbyterian. Office: Seattle Goodwill 1400 S Lane St Seattle WA 98144

MC CORMAC, WESTON ARTHUR, retired educator and army officer; b. Tacoma, Mar. 5, 1911; s. Jesse Carney and Jessie (Myron) McC.; B.A., Golden Gate U., M.B.A., 1968; diploma Nat. War Coll., 1956; M.P.A., U. So. Calif., 1972; M.A., Calif. Poly. State U., 1975. m. Mary Jeanne Rapp, Sept. 5, 1940. Account exec. Merrill, Lynch, Pierce, Fenner & Beane, Tacoma, Seattle, 1929-40; commd. lt. U.S. Army, 1940, advanced through grades to col., 1946; asst. chief of staff 7th Army G 1, 1952-54; comdg. officer 35th F.A. Group, Germany, 1956-58; dep. chief of staff V Corps, 1958-60, asst. chief of staff G 1, Pacific, 1962-65; ret., 1966; prof. bus., dept. chmn. Calif. Poly. State U., San Luis Obispo, 1968-80, ret., 1980. Decorated Legion of Merit with 2 oak leaf clusters, Silver Star, Bronze Star medal, Commendation medal with oak leaf cluster. Fellow Fin. Analysts Fedn.; mem. Los Angeles Soc. Fin. Analysts. Club: San Luis Obispo Golf and Country. Home: 176 Country Club San Luis Obispo CA 93401

MCCORMACK, DENNIS K., clinical psychologist. m. Nancy K. McCormack; children: Kelly, Karen. BA in Math., Calif. Western U., 1969; MA, U.S. Internat. U., 1971, PhD in Leadership and Human Behavior, PhD in Psychology, 1974, 78. Diplomate Internat. Council Profl. Counseling and Psychotherapy, Am. Inst. Counseling and Psychotherapy, Internat. Acad. Health Care Profls. Pvt. practice family therapist Coronado, Calif.; guest speaker at numerous clubs, lodges and local orgns. Contbr. articles to profl. jours. Mem. Sr. Citizen Adv. Com., 1982—, Land Use Adv. Com., Coronado, 1979-80; chmn. Coronado Planning Commn., 1978-83, St. Paul's United Meth. Ch., 1978-81, personnel com., 1978-81, mem. adminstrv. bd., 1983—; pres. Coronado Coordinating Council, 1983—; mem. adv. bd. Mil. Affairs Com., 1984—; bd. dirs. Vietnam Vets. Leadership Program, 1984—, Coronado Hosp. Found., 1988—; mem. Southbay Chember Exec. Com., 1986—, Coronado Visitor Promotion Bd., 1986—. Fellow Internat. Council of Sex Edn. and Parenthood of Am. U., Am. Bd. Med. Psychotherapists (clin. assoc.), S.D. Acad. Psychologists (chmn. membership com. 1988—), Coronado C. of C. (pres. 1986—). Office: 1017 Isabella Ave PO Box 583 Coronado CA 92118

MCCORMACK, JOSEPH ANDREW, executive research consultant; b. N.Y.C., Dec. 15, 1944; s. Joseph Patrick McCormack and Cecelia (Posch) Swisher; m. Patty Hall Neff, Sept. 12, 1981; children: Annette Gano, Caroline Cecelia. Student, U. Santa Clara, 1962-64; BA in English Lit., U. Calif., Berkeley, 1967. Pub. rels. exec. Rockefeller Ctr., Inc., N.Y.C., 1972-74; program dir. Young Pres.'s Orgn., N.Y.C., 1974-77; mgr. Arthur Young & Co., N.Y.C., 1977-79; v.p. Billington, Fox & Ellis, N.Y.C., 1979-82, Paul R. Ray & Co., Inc., L.A., 1982-83; ptnr., founder McCormack & Farrow, Costa Mesa, Calif., 1984-88; ptnr. Ward Howell Internat., L.A., 1988—; cons. L.A. Music Ctr. Opera Assn., 1988—; bd. dirs. Epilogics, Los Gatos, Calif., 1988—. Active Town Hall of Calif., L.A., 1982—. Lt. (s.g.) USNR, 1968-71. Mem. Japan-Am. Soc., Australian-Am. C. of C., Univ. Club (N.Y.C.), L.A. Athletic Club. Republican. Episcopalian. Office: Ward Howell Internat 800 W 6th St #400 Los Angeles CA 90017

MCCORMACK, MIKE, professional football team executive. Pres., gen. mgr. Seattle Seahawks, NFL. Office: Seattle Seahawks 11220 NE 53rd St Kirkland WA 98033 *

MCCORMICK, ADELE VON RÜST, psychotherapist; b. San Francisco, Dec. 11, 1929; d. George Washington and Adele E. von Rüst; clin. cert. Moreno Inst., SUNY, 1968; Ph.D. in Psychology, Columbia Pacific U., 1980; m. Thomas E. McCormick, Dec. 11, 1971; 1 child, Deborah. Profl. actress with Warner Bros., 1950-62; appeared in films including My Enemy The Sea, 1961, Days of Wine and Roses, 1962; co-founder Charila Found., San Francisco, 1968; instr. psychiat. residents Agnews (Calif.) State Hosp., 1966-72; cons. in psychotherapy Belmont Psychiat. Ctr., 1972-75; founder, dir. Psychotherapy Inst., San Francisco, 1970, dir., 1970-81; exec. dir. Clin. Psychotherapy Inst., 1983—; condr. clin. workshops in group dynamics and psychodrama in Switzerland, Eng., Spain, U.S., 1971-78; hon. prof. U. Madrid, 1977; founder, exec. dir. adult and adolescent treatment units McCormick Found., Inc., 1979—; founder Equine Therapy for the Psychosis, 1985—. Sponsor Wine Country Film Festival. Recipient Medal of Honor U. Madrid, 1977. Mem. Am. Assn. of Owners and Breeders of Peruvian Paso Horses (sec. bd. dirs. 1989—), Soc. Analytic Psychotherapy, Internat. Assn. Group Psychotherapy, Orthopsychiat. Soc., Friends of the Psychoanalytic Soc. Republican. Episcopalian. Contbr. articles on group psychotherapy to profl. publs. Home: 9000 Franz Valley Rd Calistoga CA 94515 Office: 227 Indian Creek Santa Rosa CA 94963

MCCORMICK, DONALD WILLIAM, educator; b. L.A., Aug. 5, 1954; s. James Lincoln and Esther Veronica (Mayo) McC. AB in Psychology with honors, U. Calif., Santa Cruz, 1977; PhD in Orgnl. Behavior, Case Western Res. U., 1985. Adj. faculty Calif. Sch. Profl. Psychology, L.A., 1985-87, U. So. Calif. Sch. Bus., L.A., 1986-87; mem. faculty Antioch U., L.A., 1987—; cons., assoc. The Orgn. Devel. Ctr., L.A., 1986—; mem. faculty Nat. U., L.A., 1985-87; orgn. devel. intern The White House, Washington, 1980. Editor book Business Communications, 1988. Recipient Spl. Citation U.S. Office of Personnel Mgmt., 1980. Mem. Acad. of Mgmt., Orgn. Devel. Network, NTL Inst. Democrat. Buddhist. Home: 1535 Veteran Ave Los Angeles CA 90024 Office: Antioch U 4800 Lincoln Blvd Los Angeles CA 90292

MCCORMICK, FLOYD GUY, JR., agricultural educator; b. Center, Colo., July 3, 1927; s. Floyd Guy and Gladys (Weir) McC.; m. Constance P. Slane, Sept. 18, 1965; children: Angela Lynn, Craig Alan, Kim Ann, Robert Guy. BS, Colo. State U., 1950, MEd, 1959; PhD, Ohio State U., 1964. Tchr. vocat. agr. State Colo., 1956-62; asst. prof. agrl. edn. Ohio State U., 1964-67; mem. com. agr. edn. Commn. Edn. in Agr. and Natural Resources, Nat. Acad. Sci., 1967-69; prof. agrl. edn., head dept. U. Ariz., 1967—; cons. in-svc. edn., div. vocat. edn. Ohio Dept. Edn., 1963-64; vis. prof. Colo. State U., 1973; external examiner U. Sierra Leone, 1984, 85, 87; adv. trustee Am. Inst. Cooperatives, Washington, 1985-88; mem. Nat. Council Vocat. and Tech. Edn. in Agriculture, Washington, 1985-88. Co-author Teacher Education in Agriculture, 1982, Supervised Occupational Experience Handbook, 1982; Author instructional units, tech. bulls., articles in profl. jours.; Spl. editor: Agrl. Edn. mag, 1970-74. Trustee Nat. FFA Found. Served with USNR, 1945-46. Named hon. state farmer Colo., 1958, hon. state farmer Ariz., 1968; Hon. Am. Farmer, 1972; Outstanding Educator in Am., 1972; Tchr. fellow Nat. Assn. Coll. Tchrs. Agr., 1988; recipient Centennial award Ohio State U., 1970; E.B. Knight award NACTA Jour., 1980. Mem. Am. Vocat. Assn. (mem. policy com. agrl. edn. div. 1976-79, v.p. div. 1985-88, chmn. membership com. 1980-83, sec. agrl. edn. div. 1983-86, pres. 1985-88), Nat. Vocat. Agr. Tchrs. Assn. (life, Outstanding Svc. award Region I 1974, 83), Am. Assn. Tchr. Educators in Agr. (disting. lectr. 1984, editor newsletter 1975-76, pres. 1976-77, Disting. Svc. award 1978, 88, Rsch. award western region rsch. 1988), Alpha Zeta, Alpha Tau Alpha (hon.), Gamma Sigma Delta, Phi Delta Kappa, Epsilon Pi Tau. Home: 6933 Paseo San Andres Tucson AZ 85710

MCCORMICK, RICHARD DAVID, telecommunications company executive; b. Fort Dodge, Iowa, July 4, 1940; s. Elmo Eugene and Virgilla (Lawler) McC.; m. Mary Patricia Smola, June 29, 1963; children: John Richard, Matthew David, Megan Ann, Katherine Maura. B.S. in Elec. Engring., Iowa State U., 1961. With Bell Telephone Co., 1961-85; v.p., chief exec. officer for N.D. Northwestern Bell Telephone Co., Omaha, 1974-77; asst. v.p. human resources AT&T, Basking Ridge, N.J., 1977-78; sr. v.p. Northwestern Bell, Omaha, 1978-82, pres., chief exec. officer, 1982-85; exec. v.p. U.S. West Inc., Englewood, Colo., 1985-86, pres., chief operating officer, 1986—; dir. Super Valu Stores, Norwest Corp., Prin. Fin. Group. Bd. dirs. Regis Coll. Mem. Phi Gamma Delta. Office: US West Inc 7800 E Orchard Rd Englewood CO 80111 *

MCCORMICK, WILLIAM MALLORY, financial services company executive; b. Hartford, Conn., Aug. 21, 1940; s. Ernest W. and Esther M. McCormick; B.S., Yale U., 1962; M.S., George Washington U., 1967; children—James and Skye (twins). Mgmt. cons. McKinsey & Co., N.Y.C., 1967-72; investment banker Donaldson, Lufkin & Jenrette, N.Y.C., 1972-75; with Am. Express Internat. Banking Corp., 1975-78, sr. v.p. fin., systems and ops., 1977-78; sr. v.p. fin. and planning card div. Am. Express Co., 1978-79, pres. travel div., 1979-80, pres. card div., 1980-81, pres. consumer fin. services group, 1981-82, pres. travel related services, 1982-83; chmn., chief exec. officer Fireman's Fund Ins. Co., 1984—; bd. dirs. Bay Area Council, Ctr. for Excellence in Edn.; mem. adv. council SRI. Served to lt. USNR, 1962-67. Mem. Commonwealth Club of Calif., Calif. Bus. Roundtable. Office: Fireman's Fund Ins Co 777 San Marin Dr Novato CA 94998 also: Fireman's Fund Corp 646 Steamboat Rd Greenwich CT 06830 *

MCCOY, EUGENE LYNN, civil engineer; b. Ridgefield, Wash., Apr. 9, 1926; s. Eugene Victor McCoy and Thelma Lucinda (Ayres) Martin; m. Marcia Helen Schear, Sept. 14, 1955 (div. 1974); children: Thomas Edwin, Susan Lynn, Molly Kay (dec.). AS, Lower Columbia Coll., 1948; BS, Wash. State U., 1950; MS, U. Wash., 1955. Registered profl. engr., Wash. Successively civil engr. soils, chief engr. soils sect., chief geotechnical br. Portland dist., chief North Pacific div. U.S. Army Corps. Engrs., Portland, Oreg., 1955-85; staff cons. Shannon and Wilson, Portland, 1985-88, Cornforth Cons. Inc., Tigard, Oreg., 1988—; tech. specialist delegation for design of Longtan Dam, U.S. Army Corps. Engrs., Beijing, 1981, People to People's delegation Dams and Tunnels, 1987. Contbr. articles to profl jours. Active camp com. Campfire Girls, 4-H Clubs, Oregon City. Cpl. U.S. Army, 1950-52. Mem. ASCE, U.S. Com. Large Dams, Oreg. Master Gardeners Club. Democrat. Unitarian. Home: 20551 S Fischers Mill Rd Oregon City OR 97045 Office: Cornforth Cons Inc 7440 SW Hunziker Rd Tigard OR 97223

MCCOY, KATHLEEN ANNE, telemarketing representative; b. Detroit, June 28, 1950; d. George Malcolm and Florence Mae (Caddy) Sutton; m. Donald James Gregory, Aug.30, 1974 (div.1980); m. John Franklin McCoy, Jr., Feb. 28, 1981. BA, Spring Arbor Coll., 1972. Substitute tchr. Warren (Mich.) Woods Schs., Mich., 1972-74, Warren Consolidated Schs., Mich., 1972-74; telemkting. rep. Amtech. Corp., Irvine, Calif., 1975-78, Prudential Sys., Parmount, Calif., 1978—. Republican. Methodist. Home: 14459 Fairbury St Hacienda Heights CA 91745 Office: Prudential Systems Inc 7330 Adams St Paramount CA 91745

MC COY, LOIS CLARK, county official, magazine editor; b. New Haven, Oct. 1, 1920; d. William Patrick and Lois Rosilla (Dailey) Clark; m. Herbert Irving McCoy, Oct. 17, 1943; children: Whitney, Kevin, Marianne, Tori, Debra, Sally, Daniel. BS, Skidmore Coll., 1942; student Nat. Search and Rescue Sch., 1974. Asst. buyer R.H. Macy & Co., N.Y.C., 1942-44, assoc. buyer, 1944-48; instr. Mountain Medicine & Survival, U. Calif. at San Diego, 1973-74; cons. editor Search & Rescue Mag., 1975, Rescue mag., 1988—; coordinator San Diego Mountain Rescue Team, La Jolla, Calif., 1973-75; exec. sec. Nat. Assn. for Search and Rescue, Inc., Nashville and La Jolla, 1975-80, comptroller, 1980-82; disaster officer San Diego County, 1980-86, Santa Barbara County, 1986—; contbr. editor Rescue Mag., 1989—, editor-in-chief Response! mag., 1982-86; cons. law enforcement div.; Calif. Office Emergency Services, 1976-77; pres. San Diego Com. for Los Angeles Philharmonic Orch., 1957-58. Bd. dirs. Search and Rescue of the Californias, 1976-77, Nat. Assn. for Search and Rescue, Inc., 1980-87, pres., 1985-87, bd. trustees, 1987—; mem. Gov.'s Task Force on Earthquakes, 1981-82; chmn. Earthquake Preparedness Task Force, Seismic Safety Commn., 1982-85. Recipient Hal Foss award for outstanding service to search and rescue, 1982, Nasar Service award, 1985. Mem. Am. Astronautical Soc., AIAA, IEEE, Am. Soc. Indsl. Security, Nat. Assn. for Search and Rescue (Service award 1985), Council for Survival Edn., Mountain Rescue Assn., Nat. Jeep Search and Rescue Assn., San Diego Mountain Rescue Team, San Diego Amateur Radio Club, Sierra Club. Episcopalian. Author: Search and Rescue Glossary, 1974; contbr. to profl. jours. Office: PO Box 91648 Santa Barbara CA 93190

MCCRACKEN, JOHN HARVEY, artist, sculptor; b. Berkeley, Calif., Dec. 9, 1934; s. John H. and Marjorie (Strain) McC.; children: David Gordon, Patrick Daniel. BFA, Calif. Coll. Arts & Crafts, 1962, postgrad., 1962-65. tchr., U. Calif., Irvine, 1965-66, L.A., 1966-68, Santa Barbara, 1974-85, Sch. Visual Arts, N.Y.C., 1968-69, Hunter Coll., N.Y.C., 1970-71, U. Nev., Reno, 1971-72, Las Vegas, 1972-75. One man shows include: Robert Elkon Gallery, N.Y.C., 1966, 67, 68, 72, 73, Galerie Ileana Sonnabend, Paris, 1969, Sonnabend Gallery, N.Y.C., 1970, Ace Gallery, L.A., 1985, HoffmanBorman Gallery, Santa Monica, Calif., 1988; group exhbns. include: Solomon R. Guggenheim Mus., N.Y.C., 1967, Saatchi Gallery, London, 1985, Venice (Italy) Biennale, 1986, Centro de Arte Reina Sofia, Madrid, 1987, Musee St. Pierre Art Contemporain, Lyon, France, 1988; represented in mus. collections including: Art Inst. Chgo., Solomon r. Guggenheim Mus., N.Y.C., Mus. Modern Art, N.Y.C., San Francisco Mus. Art, Whitney Mus. Modern Art, N.Y.C., Mus. Contemporary Art, L.A. Grantee, NEA, 1968.

MCCRACKEN, SARAH ELIZABETH, lawyer; b. Cambridge, Mass., May 24, 1950; d. Frank Smith and Jane (Spencer) Fussner; m. Kenneth R. McCracken, Mar. 21, 1981 (div. Sept. 1988); 1 child, J. Russell. BA, Harvard/Radcliffe, 1972; JD, U. Oreg., 1975. Bar: Alaska 1976, U.S. Dist. Ct. Alaska 1976, U.S. Ct. Appeals (9th cir.) 1976, U.S. Supreme Ct. 1980. Assoc. Ely, Guess & Rudd, Anchorage, 1975-77; asst. atty. gen. State of Alaska, Anchorage, 1977—; workshop leader U. Oreg. Law Sch., Eugene, 1989. Mng. bd. editor U. Oreg. Law Rev., Eugene, 1975. Mem. Citizens' Adv. Bd., Land Conservation & Devel. Bd., Salem, Oreg., 1975. Mem. Alaska Bar Assn. Law Examiners, Phi Delta Phi.

MCCRADY, HOWARD C., bank holding company executive; b. 1931; married. B.S., U. So. Calif., 1953. Fin. analyst U.S. Steel Corp., 1956-61; fin. cons. Robert Heller & Assocs., 1961-64; mgr. EDP cost planning Mohasco Industries, 1964-67; sr. v.p. ops. and control 1st Western Bank & Trust, 1967-74; sr. v.p., chief fin. officer Valley Nat. Bank Ariz., Phoenix, 1974-78, exec. v.p. mktg., chief fin. officer, 1978-82, vice chmn., 1982-83, chmn. bd., chief exec. officer, 1983—; exec. v.p. Valley Nat. Corp., Phoenix, 1981-82, pres., 1982-83, chmn. bd., chief exec. officer, 1983—. Served with U.S. Army, 1954-55. Office: Valley Nat Corp PO Box 71 Phoenix AZ 85001 *

MC CRAKEN, ROBERT STANTON, newspaper and broadcasting executive; b. Washington, June 1, 1924; s. Tracy Stephenson and Lillian G. (Davis) McC.; m. A. Anne Wright, May 6, 1960; children—Michael, Cindy. Student, Washington and Lee U., 1945, U. Denver, 1946; B.A., U. Wyo., 1948. Reporter Rawlins (Wyo.) Daily Times, 1948-50; promotion mgr. Cheyenne (Wyo.) Newspapers, Inc.; pubs. Wyo. Eagle, Wyo. State Tribune, Wyo. Tribune Eagle, 1950-54, asso. pub., 1955-58, pres., pub., 1958—; chmn. bd. Laramie Newspapers, Inc., Rawlins Newspapers, Inc., Rock Springs Newspapers, Inc., Big Horn Basin Newspapers, Inc.; dir. Wyo. Broadcasting Co., Cheyenne Nat. Bank. Trustee U. Wyo., 1961-67. Served with AUS, World War II. Mem. Cheyenne C. of C., Kappa Sigma, Kiwanis. Presbyterian. Office: Wyo Eagle 702 W Lincolnway Cheyenne WY 82001

MCCRAVEN, CARL CLARKE, health services administrator; b. Des Moines, May 27, 1926; s. Marcus Henry and Buena Vista (Rollins) McC.; BS in Elec. Engring., Howard U., 1950; MS in Health Services Adminstrn., Calif. State U.-Northridge, 1976; m. Eva Louise Stewart, Mar. 18, 1978; 1 son, Carl B. Radiation physicist Nat. Bur. Standards, 1951-55; research engr. Lockheed Calif. Co., 1955-63; mem. tech. staff TRW Systems, 1963-72; assoc. adminstr. Pacoima Meml. Hosp., Lake View Terrace, Calif., 1972-74; founder, chief exec. officer Hillview Mental Health Ctr., Inc., Lake View Terrace, 1974—; asst. prof. Calif. State U., Northridge, 1976-78. Regent Casa Loma Coll.; bd. dirs. San Fernando Valley Girl Scout Council, Pledgerville Sr. Citizens Villa, ARC; treas. San Fernando Valley Mental Health Assn. Recipient citation Calif. Senate, 1971, 88, Calif. Assembly, 1971, 88, City of Los Angeles, 1971, 78, 88, County of Los Angeles, 1988. Fellow Assn. Mental Health Adminstrs.; mem. Am. Public Health Assn., Am. Mgmt. Assn., Nat. Assn. Health Services Execs., NAACP (pres. so. area Calif. conf. 1967-71, nat. dir. 1970-76), Sigma Pi Phi. Lodge: North San Fernando Valley Rotary (pres.). Home: 17233 Chatsworth St Granada Hills CA 91344

MCCRAVEN, EVA STEWART MAPES, health services administrator; b. Los Angeles, Sept. 26, 1936; d. Paul Melvin and Wilma Zech (Ziegler) Stewart; B.S. magna cum laude, Calif. State U., Northridge, 1974, M.S., Cambridge Grad. Sch. Psychology, 1987; postgrad.; m. Carl Clarke McCraven, Mar. 18, 1978; children—David Anthony, Lawrence James, Maria Lynn Mapes. Dir. spl. projects Pacoima Meml. Hosp., 1969-71, dir. health edn., 1971-74; asst. exec. dir. Hillview Community Mental Health Center, Lakeview Terrace, Calif., 1974—; past dir. dept. consultation and edn. Hillview Ctr., developer, mgr. long-term residential program, 1986—; program mgr. Crisis Residential Program. Former pres. San Fernando Valley Coordinating Council Area Assn., Sunland-Tujunga Coordinating Council; bd. dirs. N.E. Valley Health Corp., 1970-73, Golden State Community Mental Health Ctr., 1970-73. Fellow Assn. Mental Health Adminstrs.; mem. Am. Pub. Health Assn., Women in Health Adminstrn., Health Services Adminstrn. Alumni Assn. (former v.p.), Bus. and Profl. Women (v.p.), LWV. Office: Hillview Community Mental Health Ctr 11500 Eldridge Ave Lake View Terrace CA 91342

MCCRAW, LESLIE GLADSTONE, construction and design engineering executive; b. Sandy Springs, S.C., Nov. 3, 1934; s. Leslie Gladstone and Cornelia (Milam) McC.; m. Mary Earle Brown; children: Leslie Gladstone III, James C., John. BSCE, Clemson U., 1956. Registerd profl. engr., Del. Design engr. Gulf Oil Corp., Phila., 1956-57; various engring. and constrn. positions E.I. duPont Co., Wilmington, Del., 1960-75; v.p., mgr. div. Daniel Constrn. Co., Greenville, S.C., 1975-82, pres., 1982-84; pres., chief exec. officer Daniel Internat., Greenville, 1984-86, Fluor Daniel, Greenville and Irvine, Calif., 1986-88; pres. Fluor Daniel, Irvine, 1988—; bd. dirs. Fluor Corp., Irvine, Palmetto Bank, Greenville. Trustee Columbia Coll., S.C., Hampden sydney Coll.; mem. engring. adv. council Clemson U., chmn. pres.' adv. council; bd. dirs. Greenville Tech. Coll. Found. Served to capt. USAF, 1957-60. Mem. Bus. Roundtable (constrn. com., adv. com., contractor), S.C. State C. of C. (bd. dirs.). Republican. Presbyterian. Club: Greenville Country, Commerce (bd. govs.); Vintage Country (Indian Wells, Calif.); Center (Cosa Mesa, Calif.); Pacific (Newport Beach, Calif.). Home: 57 Hillside Dr Newport Beach CA 92660 Office: Fluor Daniel 3333 Michelson Dr Irvine CA 92730 *

MCCREADY, KENNETH F., electric utility executive; b. Edmonton, Alta., Can., Oct. 9, 1939; s. Ralpha and Lillian McCready; m. Margaret E. Randall, Sept. 2, 1961; children: Joh, Brian, Janet. BSc, U. Alta., 1963. Supr. data processing and systems Calgary (Alta.) Power Ltd., 1965-67, supr. rates and contracts, 1967-68, adminstrv. asst. to exec. v.p., 1968-72, v.p. adminstrn., 1976-80; asst. mgr. mgmt. cons. div. Montreal Engring. Co., Calgary, 1972-75, mgr. mgmt. systems dept., 1975-76; sr. v.p. ops. TransAlta Utilities, Calgary, 1980-85, pres., chief operating officer, 1985—, also bd. dirs., 1988—; gen. mgr. Monenco Computing Svcs. Ltd.; bd. dirs. Keyword Office Techs. Ltd., Maloney Steel Ltd., Selkirk Communications ltd., University Techs. Internat. Inc. Past dep. chmn. bd. govs. So. Alta. Inst. of Tech. Mem. Assn. Profl. Engrs., Geologists and Geophysicists of Alta., Can. Elec. Assn. (dir.), Constrn. Owners' Assn. Atla. (past pres.), Northwest Electric Light and Power Assn. (dir.), Calgary C. of C., Men's Can. Club of Calgary (past pres.), Ranchmen's Club, Winter Club. Office: TransAlta Utilities Corp, 110 12th Ave SW, Calgary, AB Canada T2R 0G7

MCCROBIE, DANIEL EDMOND, human factors engineer; b. Buffalo, Mar. 29, 1957; s. George Louis and Dorothy Ann (Cammeleri) McC.; m. Chantal Isabelle Rolland, July 9, 1977; children: Aja Rae, Ryan Daniel. BA, U. Calif., San Diego, 1979; PhD, Claremont Grad. Sch., 1985. Research asst. U. Calif., San Diego, 1977-79; instr. Chaffey Community Coll., Alta Loma, Calif., 1979-84; evaluation specialist Coll. Osteo. Med., Ponoma, Calif., 1982-84; research assoc. Essex Corp., Westlake Village, Calif., 1984; sr. research engr. Gen. Dynamics Valley Systems, Cucamonga, Calif., 1984--; cons. in field. Patentee in field. Mem. Human Factors Soc., Soc. Info. Display. Office: Gen Dynamics Valley Systems PO Box 50-800 MZ 601-21 Ontario CA 91761

MCCUBBIN, SUSAN BRUBECK, real estate executive; b. Decatur, Ill., Mar. 16, 1948; d. Rodney Earl Brubeck and Marilyn Jean (McMahon) Hopkins; m. Martin Charles Resnik, May 18, 1967 (div. 1974); 1 child, Martin Charles Jr.; m. William James McCubbin, May 30, 1987. LLB, Western State U., Fullerton, Calif., 1977. Bar: Calif. 1989; lic. real estate broker, Calif. Ptnr. Blue Chip Constrn. Co., Santa Ana, Calif., 1969-73; pres. Brubeck Co., San Francisco and Newport Beach, Calif., 1973-78; sole practice San Francisco, 1978-79; sr. mktg. cons., broker Grubb & Ellis Co., San Francisco, 1979-87; pres. Greenwich Corp., San Rafael, Calif., 1987—. Columnist Automotive Age Mag., 1974-75. Chmn. U.S. Senate Primary Campaign, Orange County, Calif., 1976. Republican.

MCCULLEN, DOUGLAS LEE, data processing executive; b. Waseca, Minn., May 18, 1957; s. John M. and Shirley S. (Stageberg) McC.; m. Lauri Schauer, Aug. 11, 1979; 1 child, Caitlin. Student, Boise State U., 1975-78; BA, Evergreen State Coll., 1987. Data technician Boise (Idaho) Cascade Corp., 1978-81; programmer/analyst Crown Zellerbach Corp., Portland, Oreg., 1981-83; sr. systems analyst Tektronix, Inc., Beaverton, Oreg., 1983-85; info. systems mgr. Tektronix, Inc., Vancouver, Wash., 1986—; instr. Evergreen State Coll., Vancouver, Wash., 1987. Vol.-in-parks Ft. Vancouver Nat. Hist. Site, 1983—; membership activities vol. Portland Art Assn., 1984-86. Mem. Soc. Info. Mgmt., Colonial Williamsburg Found. Avocations: tennis, running, basketball, hist. preservation.

MCCULLOCH, FRANK WALTER, JR., editor; b. Fernley, Nev., Jan. 26, 1920; s. Frank Walter and Frieda (Sieke) McC.; m. Jakie Caldwell, Mar. 1, 1942; children—Michaele Lee McCulloch Parman, Candace Sue, David Caldwell. B.A. in Journalism, U. Nev., 1941. With UP, San Francisco, 1941-42; with San Francisco Chronicle, 1945-46; gen. assignment reporter, legis. reporter, sports editor Reno Evening Gazette, 1946-53, Time Inc., 1953-60, 63-72; bur. chief Time Life News Service, Dallas, 1954-56, Los Angeles, 1957-60; mng. editor Los Angeles Times, 1960-64; bur. chief Time Life, Hong Kong and Saigon, 1964-68, Life, Washington, 1968-69, Time-Life, N.Y.C., 1969-72; v.p., editor Learning Mag., Palo Alto, Calif., 1972-75; mng. editor Sacramento Bee, 1975-80; dir. McClatchy Newspapers, Sacramento, 1978-85, exec. editor, 1980-85; mng. editor San Francisco Examiner, 1985—. Served with USMCR, 1942-45. Mem. Sigma Delta Chi, Phi Kappa Phi, Kappa Tau Alpha, Sigma Nu. Office: San Francisco Examiner 110 5th St PO Box 7260 San Francisco CA 94120

MCCULLOCH, MICHAEL REED, architect; b. Milw., July 29, 1949; s. Gerald Edward and Elizabeth (Reed) M.; m. Patricia Louise Clement, June 4, 1972; children: Katherine, Andrew. BArch, Cornell U., 1972. Registered architect, Ill., Oreg. Architect Harry Weese and Assocs., Chgo., 1972-76, Michael R. McCulloch, Architect, Eugene, Orteg., 1976-78; design architect W.E. Group Architects, Eugene, 1978-79, Driscoll & Hess Architects, Eugene, 1979-81, ZGF Architects, Portland, Oreg., 1981-84; sr. assoc. SRG Partnership, P.C., Architects, Portland, 1984--; adj. prof. architecture, U. Oreg., 1979-81; lectr. Oreg. Sch. Design, Portland, 1986--; founder Archtl. Discussion Group, Portland, 1986--. Author: (with others) Style & Vernacular, 1981; art work commd. by Am. Craft Mus., N.Y.C., 1988. Organizer N.E. 26th Neighbors, Alameda, Oreg. and Portland, 1985; land-use chmn. Santa Clara Community Orgn., Eugene, 1980-81; chmn. River Rd./Santa Clara Task Force, 1980-81; mem. Willamette Greenway Com., Eugene, 1978-79. Mem. AIA (bd. dirs. Portland chpt. 1987-89). Office: SRG Partnership PC 520 SW Yamhill St Portland OR 97204

MCCUNE, ELLIS E., university president; b. Houston, July 17, 1921; s. Ellis E. and Ruth (Mason) McC.; m. Hilda May Whiteman, Feb. 8, 1946; 1 son, James Donald. Student, Sam Houston State U., 1940-42; B.A., UCLA, 1948, Ph.D., 1957. Teaching asst. UCLA, 1949-51; instr. polit. sci. Occidental Coll., Los Angeles, 1951-56; chmn. applied politics and econs. curriculum Occidental Coll., 1956-59; asst. prof. Calif. State U., Northridge, 1959-61; assoc. prof., chmn. dept. polit. sci. Calif. State U., 1961-63, prof., 1963, dean letters and sci., 1963; dean acad. planning Calif. State Univs. and Colls., 1963-67; pres. Calif. State U., Hayward, 1967—; cons. govtl. units and agys.; lectr., panelist; mem. Calif. State Scholarship and Loan Commn., 1964-68, chmn., 1967-68; pres. Govtl. Adminstrn. Group Los Angeles, 1959. Chmn. univs. and colls. div. United Bay Area Crusade, 1969-70, 73-74; bd. dirs. Oakland (Calif.) Museum Assn., 1974-77, 86—, mem. arts adv. council, 1986—, devel. com., 1988—, Bay Area Urban League, bd. trust Calif. Coun. Econ. Edn. No. sect., Emergency Shelter Program Adv. Coun., Hayward Area Hist. Assn., NAACP Oakland Chpt.; trustee Calif. Council Econ. Edn.; sec. bd. dirs. Eden Community Found., 1978-79; rsch. fellow Haynes Found, 1957. Served with USAAF, 1942-46. Mem. Am. Coun. Edn. (adv. com. 1970-72, inst. coll. & univ. adminstrs. 1973-74, bd. dirs. 1985-86), Western Assn. Schs. & Colls. (accrediting commn. sr. colls. & univs. 1974-78, chmn., 1978-82, pres. 1979-81), N.W. Assn. Schs. & Colls. (commn. colls. 1974-80), Assn. Am. Colls. (bd. dirs. 1972-75, vice chmn. 1975-76), Assn. Western Univs. (bd. dirs.), Coun. Postsecondary Accreditation (bd. dirs. 1977—, exec. com. 1979—, chmn. 1985-87, chmn. com. recognition 1982-84), Am. Assn. State Colls. & Univs. (chmn. accreditation com. 1983-86, com. acad. personnel & acad. freedom 1987—), Calif. Coun. Edn. (trustee), Western Polit. Sci. Assn. (exec. coun. 1958-61), Hayward C. of C. (dir. 1968-71, 73-76, 77-80, 82-85, 86—), Regional Assn. East Bay Colls. & Univs. (exec. com. 1974—, sec. 1975-76, 87—, vice chmn. 1976-77, 84-85, chmn. 1977-79, 85-86), Rotary, Phi Beta Kappa, Pi Gamma Mu, Pi Sigma Alpha. Clubs: Bohemian, Commonwealth (San Francisco). Lodge: Rotary. Office: Calif State U Office of Pres Hayward CA 94542-3001

MCCUNE, WILLIAM MINTON, construction company executive; b. L.A., Oct. 13, 1922; s. William Wade and Lola Jewel (Minton) McC.; m. Lorraine R. Juelson, Dec. 4, 1943; children: Carol McCune Mann, Scott M. Chief estimator Diversified Builders, Paramount, Calif., 1948-56; v.p. Diversified Builders, Paramount, 1956-63, pres., 1963-69; exec. v.p. Zapata Constructors, Paramount, 1969-71, pres., 1971-78; exec. v.p. Zapata Corp., Houston, 1978-81; pres., chief exec. officer Macco Constructors, Inc., Paramount, 1981—. With U.S. Army, 1942-46. Mem. L.A. World Affairs Coun., Nat. Assn. Corp. Dirs., Huntington Harbour Anglers, Huntington Harbour Yacht Club, Jonathan Club. Republican. Home: 3822 Seascape Dr Huntington Harbour CA 92649 Office: Macco Constructors Inc 14409 Paramount Blvd Paramount CA 90723

MCCURDY, JOHN ANDREW, JR., plastic surgeon; b. Kingsville, Tex., July 17, 1945; s. John Andrew and Elizabeth (Smith) McC.; AB in Chemistry, Duke U., 1967; MD, Wake Forest U., Winston-Salem, N.C., 1971; divorced; children: John Andrew, Elizabeth Anne. Intern, Letterman Gen. Hosp., San Francisco, 1971-72; resident Madigan Army Med. Ctr., Tacoma, 1972-76; practice medicine specializing in cosmetic surgery, Wailuku, Hawaii, 1979—; mem. staff Tripler Army Med. Ctr., Maui Meml. Hosp., Castle Meml. Hosp.; asst. clin. prof. surgery U. Hawaii Med. Sch. Lt. col. M.C., USAR, 1971-79. Decorated Army Commendation medal; diplomate Am. Bd. Otolaryngology, Am. Bd. Cosmetic Surgery. Fellow ACS, Am. Acad. Facial Plastic and Reconstructive Surgery, Am. Acad. Head and Neck Surgery. Author: The Complete Guide to Cosmetic Facial Surgery, 1981, Beautiful Eyes, 1984, Sculpturing Your Body: Diet, Exercise and Lipo Suction, 1987. Home: 3126 Mapu Kihei HI 96753 Office: 1063 E Main St Ste 225 Wailuku HI 96793 also: 1188 Bishop St Ste 2402 Honolulu HI 96813

MCCUTCHEN, EDNA ELIZABETH, counselor; b. Washington, Iowa, Sept. 6, 1914; d. Charles Sanford and Gertrude Josephine (Swift) Ragan; m. Carl Richard McC., July 3, 1938; children: Evelyn Hitchcock, Carl Richard III, Charles. BA cum laude, Calif. State U., Long Beach, 1971. Researcher State Univ. System, Iowa, 1953-62, Gallup Poll, Palos Verdes (Calif.) Estates, and Iowa, 1954-68, Palos Verdes Estates, 1960-69; counselor for family service Long Beach, 1971-73; social worker L.A. County, 1973-83; pvt. practice in counseling Long Beach, 1983—; vol. Gov.'s Study of Aged State of Iowa, 1960-69; lectr., substitute tchr. for Confraternity of Christian Doctrine at St. Bartholomew's. Insp. election bds., Los Angeles County, Long Beach, 1964—; crew leader U.S. Census, Washington County, Iowa, 1950; Christian minister St. Bartholomews, Long Beach, 1987-88. Recipient Commendation Community Service award Family Service, Long Beach, 1972. Mem. Nat. Social Workers, Consumer's Union-Consumer's Research, DAR (sec. 1948-49), Dau. Am. Colonists, Friends of Library, League of Women Voters, AAUW, Phi Kappa Phi. Home: 3435 E First St Long Beach CA 90803

MCCUTCHEON, MICHAEL ANTHONY, real estate executive; b. Oakland, Calif., Jan. 5, 1939; s. James George and Barbara (Sweet) McC. BS, Calif. Maritime Acad., 1962. Lic. real estate broker. Ptnr. C.C. Richardson Devel., San Diego, 1968—; regional mgr. Prometheus Devel., Cupertino, Calif., 1984-87; cons. Casitas Homeowners Assn., Alameda, Calif., 1985-87; co-founder Okla City Apt. Owners Assn., 1974-75. Bd. dirs. Alameda (Calif.) Boys Club, 1968-73, Citizens for Good Housing, Ann Arbor, Mich., 1973-74. Served with USNR, 1962-64. Mem. Inst. Real Estate Mgmt., Building Owners and Mgrs. Assn. Republican. Episcopalian. Clubs: Corinthian Yacht (San Francisco), Treasure Island Yacht.

MCDAID, JANET LITWINOWICH, educational administrator; b. Kittery, Me.; d. Zenon John and Ada Margaret (Pacelt) Litwinowich; m. Edward Patrick McDaid, Aug. 28, 1969; children: Michael Fitzpatrick, Ashley Margaret. BS, Gorham State Coll., 1965; MEd, U. Wash., 1970; PhD, Claremont Grad. Sch., 1986. Cert. state adminstr., pupil personnel svcs., Calif.; lic. ednl. psychologist, Calif. Tchr. Waterville (Me.) Sch. Dist., 1967-68, Bellevue (Wash.) Sch. Dist., 1968-69; psychologist Newport New (Va.) Pub. Schs., 1970-72, Edmonds (Wash.) Sch. Dist., 1972-73; rsch. assoc. U. Wash., Seattle, 1974-76; early childhood assessment coord. Seattle Sch. Dist., 1977-81; sp. edn. program psychologist San Diego City Schs., 1981-85, program evaluator, 1986—; lectr. Hampton (Va.) Inst., 1972; cons. USIA, Washington, 1988; mem. evaluation working com. Calif. State Dept. Edn., Sacramento,1987-89; program effectiveness Task Force, 1987-88; evaluation cons. Calif. State Dept. Justice and Edn., Sacramento, 1986—. Author: Special Education in United States, 1988. Vol. U.S. Peace Corp, Kabul, Afghanistan, 1965-67; troop leader San Diego-Imperial Council Girl Scouts U.S.A., San Diego, 1984—. Grantee, Wash. State Dept. Edn., Olympia, 1979-81, Calif. State Dept. Edn., Sacramento, 1983-84. Mem. Assn. Calif. Sch. Adminstrs., Council Exceptional Children, Council Adminstrs. Spl. Edn., Am. Ednl. Rsch. Assn., Calif. Ednl. Rsch. Assn. Democrat. Roman Catholic. Office: San Diego City Schs Planning Rsch and Evaluation 4100 Normal St San Diego CA 92103

MCDANIEL, JOSEPH CHANDLER, lawyer; b. Covington, Va., Mar. 24, 1950; s. Everts Hardin and Betty (Chandler) McD.; m. Sandra Lee Bonds, Dec. 27, 1976; children: Sean Kenneth, Caitlin Bonds. BA in Philosophy, Ariz. State U., 1974, JD, 1980. Bar: Ariz. 1980, U.S. Dist. Ct. Ariz. 1981. Law clk. U.S. Bankruptcy Ct., Phoenix, 1980-82; pvt. practice Phoenix, 1982-84; ptnr. McDaniel and Jaburg, P.C., Phoenix, 1984-89, McDaniel and Lee, Phoenix, 1989—; mem. Scriveners Com. Local Rules of Ct. for Dist. of Ariz. Bankruptcy Cts., Phoenix, 1980. Author: A Guide to Researching Bankruptcy Law, 1980; editor: (with others) Arizona Civil Remedies, 1982. Bd. dirs. St. Patrick's Day Parade, 1988-89, Irish Cultural Assn. Phoenix, 1988-89. Mem. ABA (gen. practice sect. bankruptcy com., newsletter editor), Ariz. Bar Assn. (lectr., co-chmn. continuing legal edn. com., bankruptcy sect. 1987-88, chmn. bankruptcy sect. 1988-89), Maricopa County Bankruptcy Practitioners (chmn.), Ariz. Bankruptcy Coalition (bd. dirs. 1986—), Maricopa County Bar Assn., Am. Bankruptcy Inst. Democrat. Roman Catholic. Office: McDaniel & Lee 3636 N Central Ave Ste 1150 Phoenix AZ 85012

MCDERMOTT, CHERYL LYNN, entertainment company executive; b. Glendale, Calif., Dec. 28, 1953; d. Henry Lawrence McDermott and Phyllis (Markel) Grisso. Student, U. Colo., 1977-78; BA, Immaculate Heart Coll., L.A., 1980; JD, Loyola U., L.A., 1983. Legal researcher MGM/UA Entertainment Co., Culver City, Calif., 1983-85, sr. contract adminstr., 1985-86; dir. internat. TV distbn. Turner Entertainment Co., Culver City, 1986—; panelist, judge Emmy awards, 1987-88. Participant Names Project, L.A., 1988. Mem. Acad. TV Arts and Scis. (blue ribbon panel for Emmy awards 1987-88), Lawyers for Human Rights. Office: Turner Entertainment Co 10100 Venice Blvd Culver City CA 90232

MCDERMOTT, JAMES A., congressman, psychiatrist; b. Chgo., Dec. 28, 1936. BS, Wheaton Coll.; MD, U. Ill. Mem. Wash. Ho. of Reps., 1970-73, Wash. Senate, 1974-87; regional med. officer U.S. Fgn. Svc., 1987-88; mem. 101st Congress from 7th Wash. Dist., 1989—. With Med. Corps USN. Democrat. Office: US Ho of Reps Office of the Mems Washington DC 20510 *

MCDONALD, ALAN ANGUS, judge; b. Harrah, Wash., Dec. 13, 1927; s. Angus and Nell (Britt) Mc/d.; m. Ruby K., Aug. 22, 1949; children: Janelle Jo, Saralee Sue, Stacy. BS, U. Wash., 1950, JD, 1952. Dep. pros. atty. Yakima County, Wash., 1952-54; assoc. Halverson & Applegate, Yakima, 1954-56; ptnr. Halverson, Applegate & McDonald, Yakima, 1956-85; judge U.S. Dist. Ct. (ea. dist.) Wash., Spokane, 1985—. Fellow Am. Coll. Trial Lawyers; Yakima C. of C. (bd. dirs.). Clubs: Yakima Country, Royal Duck (Yakima). Office: US Dist Ct PO Box 2186 Spokane WA 99210

MCDONALD, ALLAN JAMES, aerospace engineering administrator; b. Cody, Wyo., July 9, 1937; s. John William and Eva Marie (Gingras) M.; m. Linda Rae Zuchetto, Apr. 20, 1963; children—Gregory Allan, Lisa Marie, Lora Lynn, Meghan Rae. B.S. in Chem. Engring, Mont. State U., 1959, D. in Engring. (hon.), 1986; M.S. in Engring. Adminstrn., U. Utah, 1967. Engr. Wasatch div. Morton Thiokol Inc., Brigham City, Utah, 1959-67, project engr. solid rocket motor programs, 1967-74, mgr. devel. project dept., 1974-76, mgr. propellant devel. dept. 1976-79, mgr. project engring. div., 1979-84, dir. space shuttle solid rocket motor project, 1984-86, dir. space shuttle solid rocket motor verification task force, 1986-87, v.p., space engr., 1987—; mem. Air Force/AIAA Space Tech. Propulsion Panel, 1982—. Judge sci. fair com. Weber State Coll., 1978-84; bd. dirs. St. Joseph High Sch., 1976-85, trustee, 1981-85, pres. 1976-79; coach Little League Football, 1972-75; coach Little League Baseball, 1971-72, pres., 1972-74; pres. CCD program St. James Catholic Ch., 1976-79. Named Outstanding Engr. of Utah, AIAA, 1971, 86; recipient Cert. of Recognition AIAA Propulsion Community, 1986, NASA Manned Flight Awareness, 1986; named Engr. of Yr. Utah Engring. Coun., 1987; recipient Presdl. award Nat. Space Soc., 1987, Disting. Centennial Alumni award Montana State U., 1987, Achievement award Design News, 1988, Astronaut's Silver Snoopy award, 1988; Eastern Mont. Coll. scholar, 1955-57; Mont. State U. scholar, 1958-59. Fellow AIAA (assoc., past chmn. Utah sect., mem. solid rocket tech. com. 1979-83, chmn., 1984-86, space task force, 1986—, Shuttle Flag award 1984); mem. Air Force Assn., Internat. Platform Assn., Tau Beta Pi, Phi Kappa Phi, Sigma Chi. Republican. Clubs: K.C., Elks, Ogden Athletic. Patentee solid rocket, pyrotechnic systems; contbr. articles to profl. jours., publs. Home: 4050 N 900 W Pleasant View UT 84414 Office: Morton Thiokol Wasatch Div PO Box 524 m/s EOO Brigham City UT 84302 also: Space Ops PO Box 707 m/s L00 Brigham City UT 84302-0707

MCDONALD, CAPERS WALTER, mechanical engineer; b. Georgetown, S.C., Nov. 29, 1951; s. Wabern and Cecilia (Lockwood) McD.; m. Marion E. Kiper, Aug. 23, 1975; 1 child, Adam Capers. BS in Engring., Duke U., 1974; MS in Mech. Engring., MIT, 1976; MBA, Harvard U., 1983. Registered profl. engr., N.C. Dir. mktg. dept. Becton Dickinson Co., Sunnyvale, Calif., 1978-81; cons. Booz, Allen & Hamilton, San Francisco, 1982-84; v.p. Siegen Corp., Mountain View, Calif., 1984, HP Genenchem, S. San Francisco, Calif., 1985-87; bio-analytic systems mgr. Hewlett-Packard Corp., Palo Alto, Calif., 1987; v.p. Orion Instruments, Inc., Redwood City, Calif., 1987-89, Spectroscopy Imaging Systems, Fremont, Calif., 1989—; guest lectr. Wwizmann Inst., Rehovot, Israel, 1977, All-Union Cardiology Ctr., Moscow, 1978, Christ Church (New Zealand) Clin. Sch., 1980, U. Edinburgh, Scotland, 1981. Author: chpt. Flow Cytometry and Sorting, 1979; patentee flow microfluorometer; contbr. articles to profl. jours. Asst. scout master Boy Scouts Am., Georgetown, 1965-66. Duke U. scholar, 1970-74, MIT scholar, 1974-76; NSF fellow, 1974. Mem. N.C. Acad. Scis., Harvard U. Alumni Assn., Duke U. Alumni Assn., Rotary, Sigma Xi, Tau Beta Pi. Republican. Methodist. Home: 628 Twelve Acres Dr Los Altos CA 94022

MCDONALD, DANIEL ROBERT, senator; b. Seattle, Feb. 4, 1944; s. Robert William and Josephine Dorothy (Quigley) McD.; m. Norah Jane Cornwall, Dec. 28, 1966; children: Tod Robert, Evan Daniel. BSME, U. Wash., 1965, MA in Econs., 1975. Registered profl. engr., Calif., Wash. Mem. Wash. Ho. of Reps., Olympia, 1979-83, floor leader, 1983; mem. Wash. Senate, Olympia, 1983—, floor leader, 1985-86, chmn. Ways and Means Com., 1987—; mem. revenue forecast council, Olympia, 1984—, chmn. 1984-85; mem. legis. evaluation and accountability program, Olympia, 1983—; commr. exec. bd. Western Interstate Com. on Higher Edn., 1983-87; mem. State Investment Bd. Mem. Seattle/King County Drug Commn., 1978-79, Mcpl. League, Seattle, 1979—. Served to lt. (j.g.) USN, 1966-69, Vietnam. Mem. Am. Pub. Works Assn., Am. Waterworks Assn., Bellevue (Wash.) C. of C. Republican. Presbyterian. Lodge: Rotary. Home: 4650 92nd NE Bellevue WA 98004 Office: Wash State Senate 105 JAC Bldg Olympia WA 98504

MCDONALD, DONALD MICHAEL, minister, consultant; b. Birmingham, Ala., Oct. 4, 1947; s. John Wesley and Lulu (Teague) M.; m. Judith Brown, Aug. 23, 1969; children: Barbara Ann, Amy Lynn, Carol Elizabeth. BA in Indsl. Design, Auburn U., 1971; MBA in Mgmt., Calif. State U., San Bernadino, 1985; MA in Biblical Studies, Internat. Sch. Theology, 1985; postgrad., Tex. A&M U., 1989—. Ordained to Bapt. ministry, 1976. Staff to dir. internat. summer projects Campus Crusade for Christ, San Bernardino, 1972-79; founder, dir. mgmt. discipling Crusade for Christ, San Bernardino, 1980—. Author: (with others) Magnetic Fellowship, 1988; contbr. articles to profl. jours. Mem. Am. Soc. for Tng. and Devel., Acad. of Mgmt., Am. Mgmt. Assn. Office: Campus Crusade for Christ 2700 Little Mountain Dr San Bernardino CA 92414

MC DONALD, MRS. JOHN B. See GRAY, JEANNE

MCDONALD, MARIANNE, classicist; b. Chgo., Jan. 2, 1937; d. Eugene Francis and Inez (Riddle) McD.; children: Eugene, Conrad, Bryan, Bridget, Kirstie, Hiroshi. BA magna cum laude, Bryn Mawr Coll., 1958; M.A., U. Chgo., 1960; Ph.D., U. Calif., Irvine, 1975, doctorate (hon.) Am. Coll. Greece, 1988. Teaching asst. classics U. Calif., Irvine, 1972-74, instr. Greek, Latin and English, mythology, modern cinema, 1975-79, researcher Thesaurus Linguae Graecae Project, 1979—; dir. Centrum. Bd. dirs. Am. Coll. of Greece, 1981—, Scripps Hosp., 1981; Am. Sch. Classical Studies, 1986—; ; mem. bd. overseers U. Calif. San Diego, 1985—; nat. bd. advisors Am. Biog. Inst., 1982—. Recipient Ellen Browning Scripps Humanitarian award, 1975; Disting. Service award U. Calif.-Irvine, 1982, Irvine Medal, 1987, 3rd Prize Midwest Poetry Ctr. Contest, 1987; named Philanthropist of Yr. Honorary Nat. Conf. Christians and Jews, 1986, Woman of Yr. AHEPA, 1988. Mem. Am. Philol. Assn., Am. Classical League, Philol. Assn. Pacific Coast, MLA, Am. Comparative Lit. Assn., Modern and Classical Lang. Assn. So. Calif., AAUP, Hellenic Soc., Calif. Fgn. Lang. Tchrs. Assn., Internat. Platform Assn. Republican. Greek Orthodox. Clubs: KPBS Producers, Hellenic Univ. (dir.). Author: Terms for Happiness in Euripides, 1978; Semilemmatized Concordances to Euripides' Alcestis, 1977; Cyclops, Andromache, Medea, 1978; Heraclidae, Hippolytus, 1979; Hecuba, 1982; Hercules Furens, 1984; Electra, 1985; Ion, 1985; Trojan Women, 1988; Iphigenia in Taurus, 1988; Euripides in Cinema: The Heart Made Visible, 1983; Hercules Furens, 1984, Electra, 1985, Ion, 1985; translator: The Cost of Kindness and Other Fabulous Tales (Shinichi Hoshi), 1986; contbr. numerous articles to profl. jours. Home: Box 929 Rancho Santa Fe CA 92067 Office: U Calif Thesaurus Linguae Gracae Project Irvine CA 92717

MCDONALD, MICHAEL DENNIS, health products executive; b. New Haven, Dec. 22, 1955; s. Vincent Paul and Zaida (McKenzie) McD.; m. Barbara Story, July 4, 1986; 1 child, Mikayla Zaida. BA, U. Calif., San Diego, 1981; MPH, U. Calif., Berkeley, 1983. Bus. mgr. Softshell Surfboards, San Diego, 1977-80; exec. producer Video Echo, Berkeley, 1982-84; pres., producer, developer, designer, researcher Windom Health Enterprises, Berkeley, 1982—; bd. dirs. Communications and Computer Applications in Pub. Health, Berkeley, 1984—, Environ. Scis. and Policy Inst.; cons. in field, 1985—. Patentee in plastics and hydrodynamics. Primary health care worker Berkeley Community Health Project, 1982-87. Grantee U. Calif. Grad. Assembly, 1982, Pacific Bell, 1988. Mem. Am. Assn. for Med. Systems and Informatics, Am. Pub. health Assn., Calif. Pub. Health Assn. (bd. dirs. 1983-84), Soc. for Prospective Medicine, Videotex Industry Assn., U. Calif. Alumni Assn. Office: Windom Health Enterprises 2600 10th St Ste 407 Berkeley CA 94710

MCDONALD, ROBERT, art museum curator, director; b. Phila., Jan. 13, 1933; s. William Anthony and Dorothy Elizabeth (Herwick) McD. BA, U. Calif., Berkeley, 1954, MA, 1959. Cert. Mus. Mgmt. Inst., 1983. Dir. Daniel Weinberg Gallery, San Francisco, 1974-76; adminstrv. asst. to dir. U. Calif. Art Mus., Berkeley, 1977-79; chief curator La Jolla (Calif.) Mus. Contemporary Art, 1979-82; dir. The Art Mus. of Santa Cruz County, Calif., 1982-84; chief curator Laguna Beach (Calif.) Art Mus., 1984-85; art critic L.A Times San Diego Edit., 1985-87; syndicated columnist Copley News Svc., San Diego, Calif., 1985-86; lectr. U. San Diego, 1986-87; dir. de Saisset Mus. Santa Clara (Calif.) U., 1987—. Author (exhibition catalog): Craig Kauffman, 1981, Terry Allen, 1983, D.J. Hall, 1986; contbr. articles to profl. publs.; contbg. editor: Artweek, 1973-88, Zyzzyva, 1987—. Visual arts panelist, Calif. Arts Council, Sacramento, 1981-83; bd.dirs. New Langton Arts, San Francisco, 1977-79; mem. Pub. Arts Policy Adv. Commn., Laguna Beach, 1985-86; mem. San Diego Community Concourse Art Selection com., 1985-86. With U.S. Army. 1954-56. Recipient scholarship U. Calif., 1953, J. Paul Getty Trust, 1983. Mem. Calif. Confedn. of the Arts., Coll. Art Assn., Am. Assn. Mus., Internat. Assn. Art Critics, U. Calif. Alumni Assn., Phi Beta Kappa. Democrat. Roman Catholic. Office: de Saisset Mus Santa Clara U Santa Clara CA 95053

MCDONALD, STANLEY BYRON, finance company executive; b. Alberta, Can., Oct. 13, 1920; came to U.S., 1923; s. David Elwood and Ethel Ann (Anderson) McD.; m. Barbara Jane Balkema, Apr. 2, 1944; children: Kirby B., Laurie McDonald-Jonsson. BBA, U. Wash., 1943. Pres., founder Air-Mac, Inc., Seattle, 1946-69, Princess Cruises, Seattle, L.A., 1965-80, Sundance Cruises, Seattle, 1983-88; gen. ptnr. McDonald Enterprises, Seattle, 1975—; chmn. bd. McDonald Industries, Seattle, Stellar Internat., Seattle. Active Nat. Rep. Party, Washington, 1970, Wash., 1960. With USN, 1943-45. Mem. World Bus. Counsel (founder, pres. 1972-73), Chief Execs. Orgn., Young Pres. Orgn., Rainer Club, Seattle Yacht Club, Wash. Athletic Club, Columbia Tower Club, Overlake Golf Club. Presbyterian. Office: Stellar Internat 520 Pke St Ste 2200 Seattle WA 98101

MCDONALD, STEPHEN EUGENE, forest services administrator; b. Orofino, Idaho, Apr. 25, 1940; s. Eugene Maurice and Sundy Carolyn (Crum) McD.; m. Janet (Jill) Ilene Lawrence; children: Kenneth Frederick, Robert Norman. BS in Forestry, U. Idaho, 1962, MF, 1975; PhD in Forestry, Colo. State U., 1981. Forester U.S. Forest Svc. Clearwater Nat. Forest, Orofino, 1962-65; supr. forester U.S. Forest Svc. Coeur D'Alene (Idaho) Nat. Forest, 1965-75; western nursery specialist U.S. Forest Svc. Region 2, Denver, 1975-80; nursery, tree improvement staff U.S. Forest Svc. Chief's Office, Washington, 1980-83; dir. U.S. Forest Svc., Broomall, Pa., 1983-84; rsch. biologist U.S. Forest Svc. Timber Mgmt., Washington, 1984-87; supr. rsch. biologist, asst. dir. U.S. Forest Svc. Rocky Mountain Sta., Ft. Collins, Colo., 1987—. Mem. Soc. Am. Foresters, Xi Sigma Pi, Sigma X, Phi Kappa Phi. Office: Rocky Mountain Forest and Range Expt Sta 240 W Prospect Fort Collins CO 80524

MCDONALD, THOMAS EDWIN, JR., electrical engineer; b. Wapanucka, Okla., June 19, 1939; s. Thomas Edwin and Rosamond Bell (Enoch) McD.; m. Myrna Kay Booth, Sept. 10, 1961; children: Stephen Thomas, Jennifer Kay, Sarah Lynn. BSEE, U. Okla., 1962, MSEE, 1963; PhDEE, U. Colo., 1969. Asst. prof. elec. engring. U. Okla., Norman, 1969-70; planning engr. Okla. Gas and Electric Co., Oklahoma City, 1970-72; staff mem. Los Alamos (N.Mex.) Nat. Lab., 1972-82, group leader, 1974-80, program mgr., 1980-86; program mgr. Centurion Program, Los Alamos, 1986—; adj. prof. elec. engring. U. Okla., 1970-72; cons. Los Alamos Tech. Assocs., 1980—. Researcher: Inertial Confinement Fusion; Contbr. articles to profl. jours. Bd. dirs., mem. United Ch. Los Alamos, 1987—. Served to capt. U.S. Army, 1963-67. Mem. IEEE, AAAS, Los Alamos Gynmastics Club (treas., bd. dirs. 1984—), Sigma Xi, Eta Kappa Nu. Republican. Home: 4200 Ridgeway Dr Los Alamos NM 87544 Office: Los Alamos Nat Lab PO Box 1663 Los Alamos NM 87544

MCDONALD-JONSSON, LAURIE JEAN, small business owner; b. Seattle, Apr. 14, 1949; d. Stanley B. and Barbara J. (Balkema) McD.; m. Lars H. Jonsson, Apr. 27, 1986; 1 child, Jonas. Student, Sophia U., Tokyo, 1969; BA, U. Wash., 1971; MSW, U. Mich., 1974; postgrad., U. Wash., 1983, Stanford U., 1986. Dir. adminstrn. U. YWCA, Seattle, 1976-77; owner McDonald Real Estate, Seattle, 1978-80; co-owner Sundance Tours Inc., Seattle, 1984-86, bd. dirs.; co-owner, sr. v.p. Sundance Cruises Inc., Seattle, 1984-87, bd. dirs.; co-owner Royal Hwy. Tours, Seattle, 1984-87, bd. dirs.; co-owner Admiral Cruises Inc., Miami, Fla., 1988—; bd. dirs. Admiral Cruises Inc., Miami; co-owner McDonald Enterprises, Seattle, 1980—; pres., chief exec. officer, co-owner Stellar Internat./Stellar Travel, Seattle, 1987—, Stellar Connections, Seattle, 1988—; Bd. dirs. Commerce Bank Wash., Seattle. Invitation for Women Entrepreneurs Pres. Ronald Reagan, Washington, 1986; treas., founding mem., bd. dirs. Rainier Found. Recipient Earthquake Relief award/Mex. Salvation Army, 1985. Mem. Leadership Am. Found., Com. of 200 (regional vice chair 1986—), Internat. Women's Forum, Wash. State Women's Forum (founding mem.), Seattle Women's Network. Lodge: Rotary. Clubs: Columbia Tower (Seattle), Wash. Athletic (Seattle), Bellevue Athletic. Office: Stellar Internat Inc 520 Pike St Ste 2200 Seattle WA 98101

MCDONNELL, PATRICK HOY, insurance industry executive; b. Mpls., July 18, 1934; s. Lawrence Patrick and Anastasia Cecelia (Hoy) McD.; m. Jane Blanche Ott, July 23, 1966 (div. Nov. 1984). BA, St. Thomas, 1958. CLU, chartered fin. cons.; registered health underwriter. With CNA Ins. Co., Chgo., 1958-78; v.p. mktg. Cen. United Life, Sioux City, Iowa, 1978-81, First Penn Pacific, Oak Brook, Ill., 1981-86; pres., owner McDonnell and

Assocs., El Cajon, Calif., 1986—. Author numerous articles ins. field. Sgt. USMC, 1952-55. Mem. Internat. Assn. Fin. Planners and Life Underwriters. Roman Catholic. Office: McDonnell & Assocs 3755 Avocado Ave Ste 506 La Mesa CA 92020

MCDONOUGH, ROBERT DAVID, JR., drilling fluids engineer; b. Denver, Nov. 25, 1946; s. Robert David and Edith Irene (Rogers) McD.; m. Willa Bell, Sept. 11, 1970 (div. May 1971); m. Janice LaVonne Fuglevand, Oct. 6, 1979; children: Padraic Thomas, Caitlin Kristen. BA, Carroll Coll., 1968; postgrad., Idaho State U., 1968-70. Chief chemist D.L. King div. FarBest Corp., Berkeley, Calif., 1977-78; plant mgr. D.L. King div. FarBest Corp., Berkeley, 1978-80; drilling fluids engr. Magcobar Group, Riverton, Wyo., 1980-83; v.p. research and devel. Overthrust Drilling Specialists, Worland, Wyo., 1983; drilling fluids engr. Hughes Drilling Fluids, Casper, Wyo., 1983—. Precinct worker Ind. Dems., Chgo., 1972-77; ward committeeman Dem. Party, Worland, 1984—. Roman Catholic. Home: PO Box 1516 Worland WY 82401

MCDONOUGH, THOMAS REDMOND, astrophysicist; b. Boston, Apr. 10, 1945; s. Redmond Augustus and Sophie Theresa (Stankewich) McD. SB in Physics, MIT, 1966; PhD in Astrophysics, Cornell U., 1973, postdoctoral study, 1973-75. Resident research assoc. Jet Propulsion Lab., Pasadena, Calif., 1976-77; astrophysical cons. Jet Propulsion Lab., 1978-81; lectr. in engring. Calif. Inst. Tech., Pasadena, 1979—; SETI coord. The Planetary Soc., Pasadena, 1981—. Author: The Search for Extraterrestrial Intelligence, 1987, Space: The Next 25 Years, 1987, 2nd edit., 1989, (novels) The Architects of Hyperspace, 1987, The Missing Matter, 1989. Repicient Spl. Citation for Pioneer/Saturn Mission, NASA, 1979. Fellow British Interplanetary Soc.; mem. Internat. Astron. Union (SETI comm. mem.), Am. Aston. Soc., Am. Physical Soc., Sci. Fiction Writers Am. Office: 138 78 Calif Inst Tech Pasadena CA 91101

MCDOUGALL, GEORGE DOUGLAS, engineering consultant; b. Indpls., July 20, 1930; s. Shirley Alton and Deborah Cleveland (Hall) McD.; student Asbury Coll., 1949-51, Mt. San Antonio Coll., 1960-61, Milw. Sch. Engring., 1977, Calif. State Poly. U., 1978; m. Maria Celia Velasquez, Aug. 4, 1956. Surveyor, Tidelands Exploration Co., Houston, 1954; with Vard, Inc., Pasadena, Calif., 1954-60, Gen. Dynamics, Pomona, Calif., 1960-62; researcher Aerojet Gen. Corp., Azusa, Calif., 1962-68; engr. Davidson Optonics, West Covina, Calif., 1968-69; mfg. mgr. Angeles Metal Systems, L.A., 1969-79; cons. Fremont Gen. Corp., L.A., 1979—; mem. automation rsch. project Inst. Indsl. Relations, U. So. Calif., 1966-68; mem. rsch. team U.S. Govt./U. So. Calif., 1979-81. Adv. bd. Automobile Club So. Calif., 1966-71; bd. dirs. St. Martha's Episcopal Sch., West Covina, 1978-81; lic. lay reader Episcopal Diocese of L.A.; vestryman St. Martha's Episc. Ch., West Covina, 1969-70, 77-79, 81-83; mem. U.S. Congl. Adv. Bd., 1982—; gen. conv. del. Episc. Diocese of L.A., 1970-78; instnl. rep. Boy Scouts Am., 1978-79, coord. San Gabriel Valley council, 1978-79. With JAGC, AUS, 1951-53, Korea. Cert. in mfg. engring., Canadian Council Profl. Cert., 1977; registered profl. engr., Calif. Fellow Internat. Biog. Assn.; mem. Soc. Engrs. (exec. council, sec. 1982; cert.), Computer and Automated Systems Assn. (charter), Nat. Soc. Profl. Engrs., Am. Soc. Safety Engrs., Calif. Soc. Profl. Engrs. (v.p.), Clan MacDougall Soc. U.S. and Can. (life), Highlands Clans and Family Soc. (exec. council 1982), St. Andrews Soc. L.A. (life), 101st Airborne Div. Assn. (life), Am. Legion, SAR, Town Hall of Califf. Club, Masons (life), Shriners. Republican. Home: PO Box 848 Azusa CA 91702 Office: Fremont Gen Corp 9 W 8th St Los Angeles CA 90017

MCDOUGALL, ISAAC EDWIN, lawyer; b. Pocatello, Idaho, Aug. 18, 1929; s. Isaac Edwin and Grace (Zudreele) McD.; m. Ann Reading, Apr. 27, 1957; children: Allison, Isaac, John. BA, U. Idaho, 1949; LLB, Cornell U., 1953—. Bar: N.Y., Idaho, U.S. Ct. Mil. Appeals, U.S. Ct. Appeals (9th cir.), U.S. Supreme Ct. Ptnr. McDougall & Murray, Pocatello, 1953—. Served to capt. USAF, 1952-53. Mem. ABA, Assn. Trial Lawyers Am., Idaho Trial Lawyers Assn.

MCDOWELL, JENNIFER, sociologist, playwright, publisher; b. Albuquerque, May 19, 1936; d. Willard A. and Margaret Frances (Garrison) McD.; m. Milton Loventhal, July 2, 1973. BA, U. Calif., 1957, MLS, 1963; MA, San Diego State U., 1958; PhD, U. Oreg., 1973. Tchr. English Abraham Lincoln High Sch., San Jose, Calif., 1960-61; freelance editor Soviet field, Berkeley, Calif., 1961-63; research asst. sociology U. Oreg., Eugene, 1964-66; editor, pub. Merlin Papers, San Jose, 1969—, Merlin Press, San Jose, 1973—; research cons. sociology San Jose, 1973—; music pub. Lipstick and Toy Balloons Pub. Co., San Jose, 1978—; composer Paramount Pictures, 1982-88; tchr. writing workshops; poetry readings, 1969-73; co-producer radio show lit. and culture Sta. KALX, Berkeley, 1971-72. Author: Black Politics: A Study and Annotated Bibliography of the Mississippi Freedom Democratic Party, 1971, Contemporary Women Poets: An Anthology of California Poets, 1977, Ronnie Goose Rhymes for Grown-ups, 1984; co-author (plays off-off Broadway) Betsy and Phyllis, 1986, Mack The Knife Your Friendly Dentist, 1986, The Estrogen Party To End War, 1986, The Oatmeal Party Comes to Order, 1986; contbr. poems, plays, essays, short stories, book revs. to lit. mags. and anthologies; researcher women's autobiog. writings, contemporary writings in poetry, Soviet studies, civil rights movement and George Orwell, 1962—; writer: (songs) Money Makes A Woman Free, 1976, 3 songs featured in Parade of Am. Music; co-creator: musical comedy Russia's Secret Plot to Take Back Alaska, 1988. Recipient 8 awards Am. Song Festival, 1976-79, Bill Casey award in Letters, 1980; AAUW doctoral fellow, 1971-73; grantee Calif. Arts Council, 1976-77. Mem. Am. Sociol. Assn., Soc. Sci. Study of Religion, Soc. Study of Religion under Communism, Poetry Orgn. for Women, Dramatists Guild, Phi Beta Kappa, Sigma Alpha Iota, Beta Phi Mu, Kappa Kappa Gamma. Democrat. Office: care Merlin Press PO Box 5602 San Jose CA 95150

MCDOWELL, JOHN RAY, microfiltration company executive; b. Duluth, Minn., Aug. 2, 1941; s. Oliver George and Dora Louise (Mayville) McD.; m. Sally Kay Brokaw, May 29, 1967; children: Rebbeca, Amy, Carrie. BS, U. Minn., 1964. Tchr. Superior (Wis.) schs., 1964-67; prodn. trainee Green Giant Corp., Beaver Dam, Wis., 1967-69; plant supt. Green Giant Corp., Rosendale, Wis., 1969-74; plant mgr. Pillsbury Corp., Lafayette, Ind., 1978-85; dir. operation Seneca Foods, Marian, N.Y., 1985-87; gen. mgr. Rocky Mountain Canning Co., Brighton, Colo., 1987-88; western regional mgr. Atam, Inc., Denver, 1988--. Pres. adv. bd. Jr. Achievement, Lafayette, 1983; chmn. indsl. div. United Way, Lafayette, 1984-85. Recipient Nat. Bronze Leaders award Nat. Jr. Achievement, 1983. Home: 1096 Purdue Dr Longmont CO 80010 Office: Atam Inc 3250 Oakland St Aurora CO 80010

MCDOWELL, LEAH PALKI, labor management specialist in telecommuniations; b. Cottage Grove, Oreg., Jan. 3, 1952; d. Arvid Henry and Dora Berniece (Mericle) P.; m. James Russell Hardisty, Apr. 8, 1972 (div. 1980); children: Russell Alan, Sarah Desiree Elaine; m. S. Bruce McDowell, Feb. 25, 1989. Grad. high sch. With U.S. West Communications, Eugene, Oreg., 1971--, sales rep., 1978-86, facilitator, trainer, part-time 1981-, organizational devel. cons., 1986—, seminar designer, 1986—, labor rels. trainer communications workers, 1985—, conf. planner, 1987—. Editor, writer newsletter Livewire, 1982-83, 84. Vol., organizer Spl. Olympics, 1981--. Mem. Communications Workers Am. (edn. chmn. Local 7906, 1984-88), Assn. for Quality & Participation, Assn. for Creative Change. Democrat. Mem. Christian Ch. Home: 198 Blackfoot Ave Eugene OR 97404

MCDOWELL, ROBIN SCOTT, physical chemist; b. Greenwich, Conn., Nov. 14, 1934; s. James Duffil and Aimee Marguerite (Lavers) McD.; m. Arlene R. Egertsen, Nov. 23, 1963; children: Jennifer Ellen, Allison Elizabeth. BA, Haverford Coll., 1956; PhD, MIT, 1960. Mem. staff Los Alamos (N.Mex.) Nat. Lab., 1960-81, asst. group leader, 1981-82, fellow, 1983—. Contbr. articles to profl. jours. Chmn. Los Alamos County Library Bd., 1981-82. Mem. AAAS, N.Mex. Acad. Sci., Optical Soc. Am., Coblentz Soc., Inc. (pres. 1987—), Soc. Applied Spectroscopy, Sigma Xi. Home: 885 Camino Encantado Los Alamos NM 87544 Office: Los Alamos Nat Lab Los Alamos NM 87545

MCELHANEY, RONALD M., software development consultant; b. Superior, Ariz., Jan. 15, 1943; s. William Monroe and Leta Mae (Lasater) McE.; m. Therese Lam Fan Chen, July 15, 1970; children: Kevin, Christine. BS, San Jose State U., 1968; MS, U. Hawaii, 1970, PhD, 1973. Postdoctoral assoc. U. Wis., Madison, 1973-75; mgr. software devel. Gen. Automation, Inc., Anaheim, Calif., 1975-77; cons. MCS, Inc., Costa Mesa, Calif., 1977-79, Auto-Trol Technology, Denver, 1979-80; pres., founder Graftek, Inc., Boulder, Colo., 1980-83, Unicad, Inc., Boulder, 1983-87; cons. The Jonathan Corp., Norfolk, Va., 1987-88; dir. software devel. Autodesk, Inc., Sausalito, Calif., 1988; v.p. software devel. Autodoski, Inc., Sausalito, Calif., 1989—; cons., Renault Co., Paris, 1982-83, EDS, Detroit, 1985, Framatome, Paris, 1986. Contbr. articles to various publs. With U.S. Armfy, 1962-65. Mem. IEEE.

MCELROY, EDDIE KEITH, accountant; b. Libby, Mont., Oct. 1, 1945; s. Tracy E. and Lillian M. (Tucker) McE.; m. Karen Richardson, June 10, 1967; children: Jeff, Laurie, Julie, Mark. BS in Commerce and Bus. Adminstrn. Acctg., Mont. State U., 1969. CPA Mont. Acct. Gallatin Nat. Life Co., Boxeman, Mont., 1964-69; treas. Continental Investors Life Co., Denver, 1969-72; pres. McElroy and Assocs., P.C., Missoula, Mont., 1972—; advisor Maria Mgmt., Missoula, 1972—, Bob Ward & Sons, Inc., Missoula, 1981—; bd. dirs. Mont. Bank Mineral County, Superior, Mustard Seed Inc., Missoula. Treas. YMCA, Missoula, 1979-87, Mont. Eye Bank, Missoula, 1984—. Fellow Life Office Mgmt. Assn.; mem. Am. Inst. CPA's (Outstanding Cons. Team Capt. award 1981), Mont. Soc. CPA's, Kiwanis. Office: 1800 Russell St Missoula MT 59801

MCELROY, FRED DEE, small business owner; b. Seattle, Oct. 3, 1934; s. Ted Adolph and Faye Eunice (Fraser) McE.; m. Marilyn Rae Stubbs, May 4, 1955; children: Julie Rae, Jeffrey Dean, James Neal. BS in Agriculture, Wash. State U., 1960; PhD in Plant Pathology, U. Calif., Riverside, 1967. Research tech. Wash. State U., Prosser, 1960-63; research scientist Canada Agriculture, Vancouver, B.C., 1967-77, Scottish Crops Research Inst., Dundee, Scotland, 1974-75; owner Strawberry Lane Nursery, Kingston, Wash., 1977-85; owner Peninsu-Lab, Kingston, 1977—, also bd. dirs.; lectr. (hon.) U. B.C., Vancouver, 1967-77. Author: Nematodes as Vectors of Plant Viruses: A Current Review, 1977, (with others) Economic Nematology, 1972, Nematode Vectors of Plant Viruses, 1975, Disease and Insect Pests and Their Management in PNW Bare Root Forest Nurseries, 1989. With U.S. Army, 1954-57. Hort. Research Inst. grantee, 1987, NSF grantee 1989. Mem. Am. Soc. Agrl. Cons., Soc. Nematologists (chmn. several coms. 1965—), Am. Phytopath. Soc., Eur. Soc. Nematologists, Wash. State Nurserymen Assn. (chpt. pres. 1979-80, research and scholarship bd. 1980-86, bd. dirs. 1979-80). Mem. Christian Ch. Office: Peninsu-Lab Box 3000 23976 Newellhurst Ct Kingston WA 98346

MCELROY, LEO FRANCIS, communications consultant, journalist; b. Los Angeles, Oct. 12, 1932; s. Leo Francis and Helen Evelyn (Silliman) McE.; m. Dorothy Frances Montgomery, Nov. 3, 1956 (div. 1981); children—James, Maureen, Michael, Kathleen. BS in English, Loyola U., L.A. 1953. News dir. KFI, KRLA, KABC Radio, L.A., 1964-72; pub. affairs host Sta. KCET, Pub. TV, L.A., 1967-74; v.p. Sta. KROQ AM/FM, L.A., 1972-74; polit. editor Sta. KABC-TV, L.A., 1974-81; pres. McElroy Communications, L.A. and Sacramento, 1981—; pres. sec. Lt. Gov.'s Office, Sacramento, 1983-84; chmn. Calif. AP Broadcasters, 1972-74; cons. State Office Migrant Edn., Sacramento, 1974, Californians for Water, L.A. , 1982, Calif. Water Protection Coun., Sacramento, 1982, Planning and Conservation League, Sacramento, 1984—, Common Cause, Sacramento, 1988—. Author: Uneasy Partners, 1984; author plays: Mermaid Tavern, 1956, To Bury Caesar (Christopher award 1952), 1952. State del. Western Am. Assembly on Prison Reform, Berkeley, Calif., 1973; chmn. State Disaster Info. Task Force; Calif., 1973-74; campaign media cons. statewide issues, various candidates, Sacramento, L.A., 1981-88; bd. dirs. Vols. in Victim Assistance, Sacramento, 1984, Rescue Alliance, Sacramento, 1987-88, Mental Health Assn., Sacramento, 1985—. Recipient Gabriel award Cath. Archdiocese, L.A., 1972, Golden Mike award Radio-TV News Assn., L.A., 1973; Hon. Resolution, Calif. State Assembly, Sacramento, 1981. Mem. ASCAP, AFTRA, Screen Actors Guild, Am. Assn. Polit. Cons. Republican. Roman Catholic. Office: McElroy Communications 2410 K St Ste C Sacramento CA 95816 also: 3111 S Valley View Ste A-112 Las Vegas NV 89102

MC ELWAIN, JOSEPH ARTHUR, retired power company executive; b. Deer Lodge, Mont., Nov. 13, 1919; s. Lee Chaffee and Johanna (Petersen) McE.; m. Mary Cleaver Witt, Mar. 8, 1945; children—Lee William and Lori Louise (twins). B.A., U. Mont., 1943, LL.B., 1947. Bar: Mont. 1947. Individual practice law Deer Lodge, 1947-63; Washington legis. counsel Mont. Power Co., Butte, 1954-63, counsel, 1963-65, asst. to pres., 1965-67, v.p., 1967-70, exec. v.p., dir., 1970, then chmn., chief exec. officer, now ret.; dir. Mont. Power Co., First Bank System 1975-84, Devel. Credit Corp. Mont.; MHD Devel. Corp. 1986—; mem. U.S. nat. com. World Energy Conf.; Mont. dir. for U.S. Savs. Bonds, 1980-81; cons. in field. Mem. Mont. Pub. Land Law Rev. Adv. Com. City atty. Deer Lodge, 1950-57, 60-63; mem. Mont. Ho. of Reps., 1949-55, majority floor leader, 1951; mem. Mont. State Senate, 1962-64; state chmn. Republican Central Com., Mont., 1952-54; mem. adv. com. Edison Electric Inst., U. Mont. Found., Missoula, Rocky Mountain Coll., Billings; bd. dirs. Mont. Internat. Trade Commn. Served with AUS, World War II and Korea. Recipient Judstin Miller award, 1947. Mem. Mont., Am. bar assns. Episcopalian. Clubs: Masons, Shriners, Kiwanis. Home: 40 E Broadway Butte MT 59701

MCELYEA, ULYSSES, JR., veterinarian; b. Ft. Collins, Colo., Oct. 29, 1941; s. Ulysses and Hazel (Hall) McE.; m. Rexanna Bell, Dec. 29, 1975 (div. 1980). BS in Pharmacy, U. N.Mex., 1963; DVM, Colorado State U., 1967, MS, 1968. Diplomate Am. Bd. Vet. Practicioners; cert. in companion animals. Owner Alta Vista Animal Clinic, Las Cruces, N.Mex., 1970—; dir. N.Mex. Acad. Vet. Practice, Albuquerque, 1976-82; bd. dirs. state of N.Mex. Bd. Vet. Examiners, 1987—, v.p., 1989—. Pres. Las Cruces Community Theater, 1974; founder, bd. dirs. Dona Ann Arts Coun., Las Cruces, 1976-80. Capt. U.S. Army, 1968-70. Mem. AVMA, Am. Pharm. Assn., Am. Assn. Feline Practitioners, Am. Soc. Vet. Ophthalmologists, N.Mex. Vet. Med. Assn. (bd. dirs. 1976-82), So. N.Mex. Vet. Assn. (pres. 1974, 84), N.Mex. State U. Athletic Assn. (bd. dirs. 1976—), N.Mex. State U. Pres.'s Assn. (bd. dirs. 1988—), U. N.Mex. Alumni Assn. (bd. dirs. 1976-80). Republican. Home: 2635 Fairway Dr Las Cruces NM 88001 Office: Alta Vista Animal Clinic 725 S Solano Las Cruces NM 88001

MCENERY, THOMAS, mayor; b. San Jose, Calif., Sept. 23, 1945; s. John Patrick and Margaret (Sellers) McE.; m. Jill Rodrick, Sept. 21, 1971; children: Sarah, Erin, Molly. B.A. in Sci. and Commerce, U. Santa Clara, 1967, M.A. in History, 1969. Tchr. St. Joseph's Middle Sch., San Jose, 1970-71; pres. Farmers Union Corp., San Jose, 1974-82; mayor City of San Jose, San Jose, 1983—. Author: California Cavalier-The Journal of Captain Thomas Fallon, 1978. Mem. of hist. renovation and downtown planning coms., San Jose. Fellow U. Santa Clara Bd. of Fellows; mem. U.S. Conf. of Mayors. Democrat. Roman Catholic. Office: San Jose Mayor's Office 801 N First St San Jose CA 95110 *

MCEUEN, JAMES ANDREW, manufacturing engineer; b. Thatcher, Ariz., Aug. 2, 1936; s. Vernon Perry and Beatrice (Woods) M.; m. Audrey Droney (div.); 1 child, Cynthia Ann; m. Janet Sorensen (div.); children: Thomas Ralph, Dana K. Grad. high sch., Norwalk, Calif. Registered profl. engr., Calif. Planning engr. Hughes Aircraft, El Segundo, Calif., 1959-60; wire harness designer Hughes Aircraft, Fullerton, Calif., 1960-62, Nortronics, Hawthorne, Calif., 1962-63; planning engr. Hughes Aircraft, El Segundo, Calif., 1963-67, sr. devel. engr., supr. and head of planning, 1967-73, head of microelectronics and material control, 1973-85, head mfg. planning, 1985-89; head mfg. engring. Hughes Aircraft, El Segundo, 1989—. Served with USAF, 1955-59. Mem. Soc. Mfg. Engrs., Hughes Mgmt. Club, Moose. Republican. Mormon. Home: 1115 D Catlin St Simi Valley CA 93065 Office: Hughes Aircraft 8433 Fallbrook Ave Canoga Park CA 91304

MCEWEN, WILLIAM JAMES, advertising executive; b. Montclair, N.J., Aug. 14, 1943; s. Lester Vincent McEwen and Harriet Eleanor (Toner) Mitchell; m. Florence Marie Witkop, Aug. 21, 1965; children: James Garrett, Megan Alicia. BA, St. Anselm Coll., 1965; MA, Mich. State U., 1967, PhD, 1969. Research analyst Leo Burnett Co., Chgo., 1969-70; assoc. prof. U. Conn., Storrs, 1970-76; supr. research Needham Harper & Steers, Chgo., 1975-76; v.p., dir. rsch. and mktg. D'Arcy-MacManus & Masius, San Francisco, 1976-81, pres., 1981-82; dir. product devel. Calif. Milk Adv. Bd., Modesto, 1982-83; sr. v.p., dir. research Foote, Cone & Belding, Chgo., 1983-84; sr. v.p., dir. stategic planning McCann-Erickson, Inc., San Francisco, 1984—; adj. prof. communications Annenberg Sch. Communications U. So. Calif., Los Angeles, 1980-81; cons. Dunlap and Assocs., Darien, Conn., 1973-77, Ctr. for Environment and Man, Hartford, Conn., 1974-77. Author: Communication and Behavior, 1977; contbr. articles to profl. jours. Mem. Coventry (Conn.) Town Council, 1975-76, Dem. Town Com., Coventry, 1975-76; scoutmaster Boy Scouts Am., Barrington , Ill. 1983-84. Mem. Am. Mktg. Assn. (local v.p. programs 1980-81, pres. 1985-87, exec. fellow in residence 1986, Keynoter 1986—). Republican. Roman Catholic. Home: 238 Reed Blvd Mill Valley CA 94941 Office: McCann-Erickson 201 California San Francisco CA 94111

MCFADDEN, LEON LAMBERT, artist, inventor; b. St. Paul, Apr. 19, 1925; s. Frank Grover and Irene Manilla Lambert (Deane) McF.; m. Karyn Flannery, Nov. 6, 1986. Student, several colls., univs., art insts. Prin. McFadden Commercial Studios, 1946-50; with McFadden-Kaump Art Service, 1952-54; pres. McFadden Advt. (merger with Sundial Services, Inc.), 1954-70; mktg. dir. Kinelogic Corp., Mountain View, Calif., 1965-70; held position in research and devel. proprietary patents Sundial Systems div. Sundial Services, Inc., 1968-70; art instr. various Calif. community colls., 1972-74; minority bus. cons. VISTA/ACTION, 1974-75; pres., chief exec. officer Libr. Painting Corp., Yreka, Calif., 1975—. Inventor, patentee seventeen mechanical tools and devices. Prin. artistic works include large assemblage painting of Statue of Liberty, found image works (represented in White House spl. collection). Served with USN, 1942-46, PTO. Mem. IEEE, AIAA, AAAS, N.Mex. Solar Energy Assn., Mensa, Artists Equity Assn. Inc., Artists Equity Assn. of N.Y., Siskiyou Artists Assn., , Sierra Club (life). Home: 418 3d St Yreka CA 96097-2436 Studio: Liberty Painting Corp 6725 Old Hwy 99 Yreka CA 96097-9725

MCFADDEN, LUCY-ANN ADAMS, planetary scientist; b. N.Y.C., May 23, 1952; d. Louis Ettlinger and Ruth Enright Neilson; m. Gregory Smith McFadden, Dec. 15, 1982; children: Whitney Carroll, Katherine Smith. BA, Hampshire Coll., 1974; MS, MIT, 1977; PhD, U. Hawaii, 1983. Research asst. dept. geography U. Md./NASA Goddard Space Flight Ctr., Greenbelt, 1983-84; research assoc. astronomy prog. U. Md., College Park, 1984-86; asst. research scientist U. Md., 1986-87, Calif. Space Inst., UCSD, LaJolla, 1987—. Contbr. articles to profl. jours. Mem. AAAS, Am. Astron. Soc. (nominating com. 1986-88), Am. Geophys. Union, Meteoritical Soc. Office: U Calif San Diego Calif Space Inst A016 2274 Sverdrup Hall La Jolla CA 92093-0216

MCFADDEN, RICHARD, civil service administrator, auditor; b. Pitts.; s. Guy E. and Monika M. (Wipplinger) McF. BS in Math., Pacific Luth. U., 1973. Budget analyst intern Comptroller Office, Ft. Lewis, Wash., 1976-77, quality edit reviewer, auditor, 1977-83, quality rev. analyst, 1983—. Office: Hdqrs I Corps 9th FSU Attn: AfZH-RMH-RMF-Q Fort Lewis WA 98433-5000

MC FADDEN, WILMOT CURNOW HAMM, retired librarian; b. Lead, S.D., Oct. 30, 1919; d. William and Ingeborg (Christianson) Curnow; student S.D. State Coll., 1938-41; m. Kenneth G. Hamm, Jan. 8, 1944 (div. 1963); 1 dau., Wilmot Christine (Mrs. Charles Bice); m. John Stinson McFadden, Mar. 1965. Asst. librarian Rock Springs (Wyo.) Pub. Library, 1947-48, head librarian, 1953-86; appointed to mayoral adminstrv. bd. Rock Springs, 1987—. State committeewoman Dem. Party, 1952-74, also state vice chmn., del. Dem. State Conv., 1970, 72; del. Dem. Nat. Conv., 1956, 64; adv. bd. Fed. Commn. Civil Rights, 1963—; treas. Sch. Bd. Dist. 4, 1966-69, clk. dist. 1, 1969-77; bd. dirs. State Library, Archives, Hist. Bd.; adv. bd. Western Wyo. Community Coll.; mem. Wyo. Citizens for Arts, 1977—, ctr. adv. counc. Wyo. Community Coll. Commn., 1983-85, Literacy Com., 1986, Western Wyo. Coll. Learning Ctr., Community Fine Arts Bd.; mem. Wes. Recipient Nat. Grolier award Nat. Library Week, 1969, Librarian Service award Eagles Aux., 1982, cert. of commendation Western Wyo. Community Coll., 1985. Mem. Federated Woman's Club, Am. Legion Aux., Mountain Plains (exec. bd. 1967—, pres. 1972-73), ALA, Wyo. Library Assn. (chmn. conf. 1966, 70, pres. 1958-59, 72-73; Librarian of Yr. 1977, Georgia Shovlain Spl. Projects award 1980, Wyo.'s Outstanding Librarian 1985), Zonta (charter), Am. Library Trustees Assn., Wyo. Sch. Bds. Assn. (life; commendation 1979), Alpha Delta Kappa. Author: Handbook Wyoming Library Trustees. Home: 28 Cedar St Rock Springs WY 82901 Office: 400 C St Rock Springs WY 82901

MCFARLAND, KEVIN JOHN, foundation administrator; b. Mt. Clement, Mich., Mar. 18, 1958; s. Chuck Paul and Myrna (Bell) McF.; m. Betty Ann Bolton, Nov. 26, 1976; children: Michelle, Michael, Melinda. BS in Biblical Studies, Abilene Christian U., Tex., 1980; postgrad., Tex. Tech. U., 1980-81, Stanford U., 1982-83. Resident asst. Abilene (Tex.) State Sch., 1976-78; pvt. landscaping bus. Abilene, 1978-80; research assoc., home and family life dept. Tex. Tech. U., Lubbock, 1980-81; youth and family minister Redwood City (Calif.) Ch. of Christ, 1981-84; pres. Manna Internat. Relief and Devel. Corp., Redwood City, 1984—. Mem. Alpha Chi. Democrat. Home: 837 Madison Ave Redwood City CA 94061 Office: Manna Internat PO Box 3507 Redwood City CA 94064

MC FARLAND, NORMAN FRANCIS, bishop; b. Martinez, Calif., Feb. 21, 1922; student St. Patrick's Sem., Menlo Park, Calif.; J.C.D., Cath. U. Am. Ordained priest Roman Catholic Ch., 1946, consecrated bishop, 1970; titular bishop of Bida and aux. bishop of San Francisco, 1970-74; apostolic adminstr. Diocese of Reno; 1974-76; bishop Diocese of Reno-Las Vegas, 1976-87, Diocese of Orange, Calif., 1987—. Office: Marywood Ctr 2811 E Villa Real Dr Orange CA 92667

MCFARLAND, STEPHEN PAUL, engineer; b. Springfield, Ill., Feb. 23, 1956; s. James Ernest and Virginia Lee (Carley) McF.; m. Connie Louise Shepperd, Apr. 15, 1978; children: Rebecca Lynn, Carrie Elaine, Jonathan David. AS, Okla. State U., 1980. Fitter welder CMI Corp., Oklahoma City, Okla., 1977-78; tech. assoc. Sandia Nat. Labs, Albuquerque, N.Mex., 1980—. Co-inventor: Via Coater, 1981. Founder and chief exec. officer N.Mex. SAR Support Team, Albuquerque, 1987—; mem. Amateur Radio Emergency Svcs., Albuquerque, 1981—, Civil Air Patrol, Albuquerque, 1983—, Nat. ELT Location Team, N.Mex., 1982—. Sgt. U.S. Army, 1974-77. Mem. Amateur Radio Caravan, Upper Rio FM Soc. Republican. Christian Reformed. Home: 12321 Summer Ave NE Albuquerque NM 87112 Office: Sandia Nat Labs PO Box 5800 Albuquerque NM 87185

MCFARLAND, WILLARD YALE, engineer; b. Palmerton, Pa., Oct. 8, 1935; s. Willard Clayton and Valera Marion (Ritter) McF.; m. Carol Virginia Crowe, May 1, 1971; children: Kelly Lynn, Laurie Ann. Student, Pa. State U., 1953-54, 58-60; BSEE, Lafayette Coll., 1969. Draftsman Western Electric Co., Allentown, Pa., 1960-62, assoc. engr., 1962-70, product engr., 1970-78; product engr. Western Electric Co., Denver, 1978-84; product engr. info. systems AT&T, Denver, 1984-85, sr. engr. info. systems, 1985—; mem. adv. bd. Mountain States Electronics Expo, Denver, 1987-88; chmn. ESD com. Denver Works AT&T, 1982-88, AT&T Corp. ESD com., Berkley Heights, N.J., 1982-88; speaker tech. seminar on ESD program, 1981, 87, 88. Served as cpl. U.S. Army, 1954-57. Mem. EOS/ESD Assn. Republican. Presbyterian.

MCFARLIN-KOSIEC, BARBARA ANN, teacher, small business owner; b. Lamesa, Tex., Oct. 4, 1937; d. Roy W. and Laura Corine (Daniel) McFarlin; m. Leonard E. Kosiec; 1 child, James Daniel. BA in Spanish, Tex. Christian U., 1960, MA in Spanish, 1964; EdD, Gonzaga U., 1985. Tchr. Mercedes (Tex.) Pub. Schs., 1962, Dayton (Wash.) High Sch., 1962-65; tchr. Spanish and Latin Am. history Peninsula Community Coll., Port Angeles, Wash., 1965-68; tchr. Columbia High Sch., Burbank, Wash., 1968-73, Pasco (Wash.) Pub. Schs., 1973-82, Lutacaga Elem. Sch., Othello, Wash., 1985-86; pres. McFarlin-Kosiec Enterprises, Fernie, B.C., Can., 1986—; instr. ESL Inst. Tech. y de Estudios Superios de Monterrey, Mex., 1962, East Kootenay Community Coll., Fernie, 1983-84, Big Bend Community Coll., Moses Lake, Wash., 1986-87, Seattle Pacific U., 1986, Columbia Basin Community Coll. Pasuo, Wash., 1973-80, 87-79; cons. in field. Bd. dirs. Mid Columbia Regional Ballet Co., Richland, Wash.; active various Rep. convs.; deaconess Disciples of Christ Ch., Richland. Mem. AAUW (scholarship, legis. coms., rep. to legis. conf. 1977), NEA, Wash. Edn. Assn., Pasco Edn. Assn. (grievance rep. 1975-77, bldg. rep. 1980), Columbia Edn. Assn. (legis. com.

1968-73), Peninsula Community Coll. Edn. Assn. (profl. rights and negotiations com. 1966-68), Can. Fedn. Univ. Women, Internat. Platform Assn. Home: 635 N Fisher Kennewick WA 99336 Office: PO Box 1275, Fernie, BC Canada V0B 1M0

MCFARREN, SANDRA KOCH, gynecologist/obstetrician; b. Boston, May 3, 1955; d. James and Harriet (Foss) Koch; m. Timothy Charles McFarren, May 7, 1988. BA, Middlebury Coll., 1977; MD, Tufts U., 1983. Intern U. Colo., Denver, 1983-84, resident in ob-gyn., 1984-86, chief resident in ob-gyn., 1986-87; pvt. practice Visalia, Calif., 1987—. Fellow Am. Coll. Ob-Gyn.; mem. AMA, Calif. Med. Assn. Office: Sierra Med Group 1700 S Court Box 469 Visalia CA 93277

MCFEELEY, MARK B., federal judge; b. Orlando, Fla., May 5, 1944; s. William Joseph and Belle (Levy) M.; m. Patricia Anne Josephson, June 10, 1972; children—Matthew Randolph, Morgan Diana. B.S., U.S. Mcht. Marine Acad., 1966; J.D. cum laude, U. N.Mex., 1972. Bar: N.Mex. 1972, U.S. Dist. Ct. N.Mex. 1972, U.S. Ct. Appeals (10th cir.) 1972. Law clk. presiding judge U.S. Ct. Appeals, 10th Cir., 1972-73; ptnr. Felker & McFeeley, 1974-77, officer, dir. Felker, McFeeley & Ish, 1977-83; judge U.S. Bankruptcy Ct. Dist. N.Mex., Albuquerque, 1981-83, 83—. Mem. editorial bd. N.Mex. Law Rev., 1971-72. Contbr. articles to profl. jours. Served with USNR, 1966-78. Mem. ABA, Nat. Conf. Bankruptcy Judges, Comml. Law League Am., N.Mex. Bar Assn., Albuquerque Bar Assn. Office: US Dist Ct PO Box 546 Albuquerque NM 87103

MCFEETERS, TOM LEE, chemist; b. San Antonio, Apr. 18, 1938; s. Marshall Melvin and Grace Pearl (Holloway) McF.; m. Doris Jean McKelvey, Sept. 5, 1970; children: Thomas, Robert. BS, Northwestern State Coll., 1959; MS, Okla. State U., 1963. Analytical chemist Rocky Flats Plant Dow, Golden, Colo., 1963-68; analytical specialist Rocky Flats Plant Dow, Golden, 1968-73, sr. analytical chemist, 1973-77; analytical specialist Rocky Flats Rockwell Internat., Golden, 1977-85, sr. analytical specialist, 1985—. Contbr. articles to profl. jours. Scoutmaster Boy Scouts Am., Erie, Colo., 1981-88; bd. dirs. Parkland Homeowners Assn., Erie, 1983-86; vacuum sci. and tech. del. to Australia, New Zealand; citizen ambassador People to People Program. Mem. Soc. Applied Spectroscopy, Am. Vacuum Soc., Nat. Mgmt. Assn., Phi Lambda Upsilon, Phi Kappa Tau (chaplain 1961-62). Baptist. Office: Rockwell Internat PO Box 464 Golden CO 80402

MCFERSON, THOMAS KIMBALL, accountant; b. L.A., Aug. 19, 1943; s. Morris H. and Eunice M. (Oaks) McF.; m. Judith E. Aldrich, Aug. 21, 1965; children: Tom, Ryan, Sean. BS, Calif. State U., Fresno, 1965. CPA, Calif. Acct., ptnr. Stoughton Davidson Accountancy Corp., Fresno, 1965—; part-time instr. Calif. State U., Fresno; mem. state bd. accountancy qualificatins com. Trustee Fresno Bulldog Found.; dir. Fresno Hall of Fame, 1987—; mem. Calif. State U. Bus. Adv. Coun., Fresno, 1986—, acctg. adv. com., 1986—. Mem. AIC, Calif. Soc. CPAs, Calif. State U. Bus. Alumni Assn. (officer), Delta Sigma Phi (alumni officer 1967-76), Fresno State U. Pres.'s. Office: Stoughton Davidson Accountancy Corp 3433 W Shaw Ste 100 Fresno CA 93711

MCFIE, MARSHALL N., aerospace executive; b. Anaheim, Calif., Mar. 7, 1944; s. Marshall N. and Ruth W. (Perry) McF.; m. Mary Louise Emmons, Aug. 20, 1984. BS in Chem., Calif. State U., Fullerton, 1967; MBA in Quantitative Methods, Calif. State U., 1971; MS in Computer Sci., UCLA, 1974, PhD Computer Sci. and Info. Sci., 1977. Cert. educator community colls., Calif. Assoc. prof. quantitative methods, dir. instructional computing Calif. State U., Fullerton, 1970-79; prof. bus. adminstrn. Pacific Christian Coll., Fullerton, 1978-80, Chapman Coll., Orange, Calif., 1979-81; program mgr. engring. productivity McDonnell Douglas Corp., Long Beach, Calif., 1980-83; mgr. quality productivity improvement McDonnell Douglas Corp., Long Beach, 1984—; computer cons. MIS and Assocs., Anaheim, 1977—; mgmt. practices cons. Quality Mgmt., Anaheim, 1982—. Author (book): Computer Glossary, 1977; contbr. articles to profl. jours. Mem. steering com. Am. Productivity Ctr., Houston, 1986— (Outstanding Leadership award 1986); mem. Boy Scouts Am., Anaheim. Mem. IEEE, Assn. Computing Machinery, Am. Legion, Beta Gamma Sigma, Upsilon Pi Epsilon. Home: 4140 Church Haven Way Anaheim CA 92807 Office: McDonnell Douglas Corp 3855 Lakewood Blvd Long Beach CA 98046

MCFLYNN, TIMOTHY, lawyer; b. Chgo., Oct. 14, 1942; s. John Joseph and Dorothy Susan (Brown) F.; m. Patricia Jo Shafer, 1963 (div. 1969); children: Jane, Timothy Jr.; m. Donna Marie McGuirk, Oct. 30, 1976; children: Travis, Abigael, Sara. BA with honors, Stanford U., 1964, JD, 1967. Bar: Calif., 1968, Colo., 1987, U.S. Supreme Ct., 1978. Assoc. Luce, Forward, Hamilton and Scripps, San Diego, 1967-69; spl. prosecutor Los Angeles County Dist. Atty., 1970-73; staff atty. Ctr. for Law in the Pub. Interest, Los Angeles, 1974-82; exec. dir. Pub. Justice Found., Santa Monica, Calif., 1982-87; sole practice Aspen, Colo., 1987—; asst. prof. law U. West Los Angeles, 1973-75; dir., counsel The Mallinson Sch. of Malibu (Calif.), 1982-86. Co-author: (screenplays) Conspiracy, 1973, The Mayflower Number, 1974, (law sch. casebook) Biography of Legal Dispute, 1969; coproducer teleplays. Dir., counsel Community Emergency Services, Inc., Malibu, 1983-86, Malibu Emergency Clinic, 1983-86; dir., treas. Weingart Rehab. Ctr., Los Angeles, 1983-87; dir. Aspen Ctr. for Environ. Studies, 1988—; mem. protocol com. Los Angeles Summer Olympics 1984. Served USAF, 1960. Named Civil Rights Lawyer of Yr., Mexican Am. Legal Def. and Edn. Fund, Los Angeles, 1979. Mem. ABA, Los Angeles County Bar Assn., Calif. State Bar Assn., Colo. Bar Assn., Pitkin County Bar Assn. Roman Catholic. Lodge: Kiwanis. Home: 0093 Horseshoe Dr Emma CO 81621 Office: Pub Justice Found 315 E Hyman Ave Ste 305 Aspen CO 81611

MCGAGH, WILLIAM GILBERT, financial consultant; b. Boston, May 29, 1929; s. Thomas A. and Mary M. (McDonough) McG.; m. Sarah Ann McQuigg, Sept. 23, 1961; children: Margaret Ellen, Sarah Elizabeth. BSBA, Boston Coll., 1950; MBA, Harvard U., 1952; MS, MIT, 1965. Fin. analyst Ford Motor Co., Dearborn, Mich., 1953-55; mem. staff treas. office Chrysler Corp., Detroit, 1955-64; compt., treas. Canadian div. Chrysler Corp., Windsor, 1965-67; staff exec.-fin. Latin Am. ops. Chrysler Corp., Detroit, 1967-68, asst. treas., 1968-75, treas., 1975-76, v.p., treas., 1976-80; sr. v.p. fin. Northrop Corp., Los Angeles, 1980-88; owner McGagh Assocs., Beverly Hills, Calif., 1988—; dir. Pacific Am. Income Shares, Inc. Bd. dirs. Greater Los Angeles Zoo Assn., Ind. Colls. of So. Calif., Sta. KCET-TV, John Tracy Clinic. Served with USAF, 1952-53. Sloan fellow MIT, 1965. Mem. Fin. Execs. Inst. (pres. Detroit chpt. 1979-80). Clubs: Orchard Lake Country; Harvard (N.Y.C. and Boston); Beach (Santa Monica, Calif.); Los Angeles Country, California (Los Angeles), Eastward Ho Country, (Chatham, Mass.). Home: 2189 Century Hill Los Angeles CA 90067 Office: McGagh Assocs 9601 Wilshire Blvd Ste 500A Beverly Hills CA 90210

MCGANN, JOHN MILTON, real estate executive; b. Omaha, Mar. 18, 1948; s. John Byron and Donna M. (Rehnquist) McG.; m. Barbara June Scott, June 2, 1978. BSBA, cert. real estate, U. Nebr., Omaha, 1971. Property mgr. Boetel & Co., Omaha, 1971-73; asst. office bldg. mgr. The Irvine Co., Newport Beach, Calif., 1973-74; property mgr. Harbor Investment Co., Corona Del Mar, Calif., 1974-76, Robert A. McNeil Corp., Santa Ana, Calif., 1976-78; gen. mgr. Daon Mgmt., Newport Beach, 1978-80; v.p. August Mgmt. Inc., Long Beach, Calif., 1980-82, Calif. Fed. Asst. Mgmt., Los Angeles, 1982-83; pres. Wespac Mgmt. Realty Corp., Newport Beach, 1983-87; v.p., dir. asset mgmt., pres. CalFed Asset Mgmt. Co., Los Angeles, 1987—. Mem. Inst. Real Estate Mgmt. (Orange County chpt.), Internat. Council Shopping Ctrs., Lambda Chi Alpha, Delta Sigma Pi, Rho Epsilon (pres.). Republican. Mem. Christian Sci. Ch. Home: 3151 Barkentine Rd Rancho Palos Verdes CA 90274 Office: Calif Fed Investment Mgmt Corp 5670 Wilshire Blvd Ste 940 Los Angeles CA 90036

MCGARRITY, JACK JOHNSTON, architect; b. Rocksprings, Wyo., Nov. 12, 1936; s. Carl A. Hawks and Dess (Johnston) Steuart. Registered architect, Hawaii, Calif., Ariz., Oreg., Tex., N.Mex., Colo., Wyo., Wash., Fla., Fiji. Architect, Jack J. McGarrity AIA, Honolulu, 1968—; interior designer Interspace Ltd., Honolulu, 1972—; resort developer Johnston Hawks Ltd., Honolulu, 1978—; architect, pres. Jack J. McGarrity AIA Assocs. Ltd., Honolulu, 1971-87; architect, ptnr. Architects Internat. Ltd., 1987— . Mem. Design Profl. Conciliation Panel, State of Hawaii, 1983—. Mem. AIA, Societas Damien (gov. gen. 1984—), Pacific Fleet Submarine Meml. Assn. (life, bd. dirs. 1984—), Rotary (sec. 1978, Paul Harris fellow 1979). Episcopalian. Home: PO Box 15697 Honolulu HI 96830-5697 Office: Architects Internat Ltd 539 Cooke St 201 Honolulu HI 96813

MC GAUGH, JAMES LAFAYETTE, psychobiologist; b. Long Beach, Calif., Dec. 17, 1931; s. William Rufus and Daphne (Hermes) McG.; m. Carol J. Becker, Mar. 15, 1952; children: Douglas, Janice, Linda. B.A., San Jose State U., 1953; Ph.D. (Abraham Rosenberg fellow), U. Calif. - Berkeley, 1959; sr. postdoctoral fellow, Nat. Acad. Scis.-NRC, Istituto Superiore di Sanita, Rome, 1961-62. Asst. prof., assoc. prof. psychology San Jose State U., 1957-61; assoc. prof. psychology U. Oreg., 1961-64; assoc. prof. U. Calif., Irvine, 1964-66, founding chmn. dept. psychobiology, 1964-67, 71-74, 86-89, prof., 1966—; dean Sch. Biol. Sci. U. Calif. at Irvine, 1967-70, vice chancellor acad. affairs, 1975-77, exec. vice chancellor, 1978-82, dir. Ctr. Neurobiology of Learning and Memory, 1983—; Mem. adv. coms. NIMH, 1965-78. Author: (with J.B. Cooper) Integrating Principles of Social Psychology, 1963, (with H.F. Harlow, R.F. Thompson) Psychology, 1971, (with M.J. Herz) Memory Consolidation, 1972, Learning and Memory: An Introduction, 1973, (with R.F. Thompson and T. Nelson) Psychology I, 1977, (with C. Cotman) Behavioral Neuroscience, 1980; editor: (with N.M. Weinberger, R.E. Whalen) Psychobiology, 1966, Psychobiology-Behavior from a Biological Perspective, 1971, The Chemistry of Mood, Motivation and Memory, 1972, (with M. Fink, S.S. Kety, T.A. Williams) Psychobiology of Convulsive Therapy, 1974, (with L.F. Petrinovich) Knowing, Thinking, and Believing, 1976, (with R.R. Drucker-Colin) Neurobiology of Sleep and Memory, 1977, (with S.B. Kiesler) Aging, Biology and Behavior, 1981, (with G. Lynch and N. M. Weinberger) Neurobiology of Learning and Memory, 1984, (with N.M. Weinberger and G. Lynch) Memory Systems of the Brain, 1985, Contemporary Psychology, 1985, (with C.D. Woody and D.L. Alkon) Cellular Mechanisms of Conditioning and Behavioral Plasticity, 1988, (with N.M. Weinbergen and G. Lynch) Brain Organization and Memory: Cells, Systems and Circuits, 1989; editor Behavioral Biology, 1972-78, Behavioral and Neural Biology, 1979—. Fellow Am. Psychol. Assn. (chief sci. advisor 1986-88, Disting. Sci. Contbn. award 1981), AAAS; mem. NAS, Am. Psychol. Soc. (pres. 1989—), Internat. Brain Rsch. Orgn., Soc. Neurosci., Am. Coll. Neuropsychopharmacology, Psychonomic Soc., Phi Beta Kappa, Sigma Xi. Office: U Calif Ctr Neurobiology of Learning and Memory Irvine CA 92717

MCGAUGHY, WILLIAM CHRIS, construction executive; b. Denver, Mar. 31, 1949; s. Bert and Mary (Barth) McG.; m. Donna Lee Whitman, Dec. 2, 1982 (div. Jan. 1989); 1 child, Lauren Rachel. AA, Paloma Coll., 1972; BA, Sanoma State Coll., 1974. Cert. gen. contractor, Calif. Owner City Limits, Camp Meeker, Calif., 1974-76, Custom Creations, L.A., 1979—. With USN, 1968-71, Vietnam. Mem. Glendale C. of C. Republican. Scientogolist.

MCGAW, SIDNEY EDWIN, educational consultant; b. Toronto, Ont., Can., Sept. 21, 1908; s. Sidney Anson and May (Bigelow) McG.; student Fresno State Coll., 1928-31; B.S., U. Calif. at Berkeley, 1944, M.A., 1948, Ed.D., 1952; m. Clara E. Eca da Silva, June 15, 1931; children—Bruce A., Laurie A., Kathleen C. (Mrs. Richard Chylinski). Instr., counselor pub. schs., Oakland, Calif., 1941-47; asst. supr. trade and tech. tchr. trng. Calif. State Dept. Edn., 1947-50, regional supr., 1950-65; dean instrn. San Jose City Coll., 1965-74; ednl. cons., 1974—; lectr. U. Calif. at Berkeley, summers 1948-66; workshop lectr. U. Nev., summers 1955-56. Pres., Calif. League for Nursing, 1967-69; chmn. edn. and tng. commn. Redwood Region Conservation Council, 1953-65. Mem. Nat. League for Nursing (bd. dirs. 1967-69), Rotary (Berkeley, bd. dirs. West San Jose chpt. 1969-70), Commonwealth Club of Calif. (San Francisco). Home: 1023 Ordway St Albany CA 94706

MCGEE, KEITH ISHAM, design administrator; b. Poplar Bluff, Mo., Jan. 28, 1950; s. George Wesley and Edna Juanita (Puckett) McG.; m. Mary Lynn Beasley, Oct. 18, 1975; 1 child, Kelly Ilene. AS in Indsl. Tech., Palm Beach Jr. Coll., Lake Worth, Fla., 1971; BFA, Fla. Atlantic U., 1973. Space planner Fla. Atlantic U., Boca Raton, 1971-76; sr. designer T.E. Beasley & Assocs., Boca Raton, 1976-78; owner Exterior Design Cons., Inc., Boca Raton, 1977-79; structural designer Midwest Tech., Inc., Kingsport, Tenn., 1979-80, Systems Design, Inc., Johnson City, Tenn., 1980-82; archtl. designer Interglobal, Inc., Tucson, 1982-83; design mgr. A.D.&D., Inc., Tucson, 1983-85; dist. mgr. CDI Corp.-West, Tucson, 1985—. Mem. CADAM Users Exch., NMRA, Toy Train Oper. Soc. Republican. Mormon. Office: CDI Corp-West 7820 E Broadway #110 Tucson AZ 85710

MCGEE, MICHAEL JAY, fire marshal, educator; b. Ft. Worth, June 9, 1952; s. Cecil Carl and Helen Ruth (Peeples) McG.; m. Carol Lee Garbarino, Sept. 18, 1982; children: Megan Rose, John Michael, Molly Caitlin. Student, U. Tex., 1970-73, Colo. Mountain Coll., 1977, Western Oreg. State U., 1983. Driver Massengale Co., Austin, Tex., 1970-73; gen. mgr. Sundae Palace, Austin, 1973-74; staff mem. Young Life, Colorado Springs, Colo., 1970-75; mgr. Broadmoor Mgmt. Co., Vail, Colo., 1974-76; technician Vail Cable Communications, 1976-77; fire marshal Vail Fire Dept., 1977—; instr. Colo. Mountain Coll., 1980—; dist. rep. Joint Coun. Fire Dist. Colo., 1983-85; co-chmn. Eagle County Hazardous Materials, 1984-85, mem. planning com., 1987—. ARC Eagle County chpt. chmn., 1980-83, disaster chmn., 1977-80; tng. officer Eagle Vol. Fire Dept., 1988—. Mem. Nat. Fire Protection Assn., Colo. State Fire Marshals Assn., Colo. State Fire Chiefs Assn., Internat. Platform Assn. Office: Vail Fire Dept 42 W Meadow Dr Vail CO 81657

MCGIBBON, WILLIAM ALEXANDER, rancher, photographer; b. Evanston, Ill.; s. Edmund L. and Catherine (Klink) M.; m. Nancy Hornaday, Aug. 27, 1966; children: Heather M., Andrew W. BA, U. Pa., 1966; postgrad., U. Ariz., 1970-71. Pres., chief exec. officer Santa Rita Ranch, Inc., Green Valley, Ariz., 1970--; adv. com. Coll. Agr., U. Ariz., Tucson. Photographer: photographs pub. in numerous agrl. and livestock publs., 1980--. Mem. Continental Sch. Bd. Green Valley, 1976-84, pres., 1978-84; mem. Ariz. Bd. Pesticide Control, Phoenix, 1983-86; bd. dirs. Green Valley Community Fund, 1988--. Mem. Ariz. Cattlemen's Assn. (bd. dirs.), Nat. Cattlemen's Assn., Green Valley Rotary Club (pres. 1986, v.p. Green Valley Rotary Club Found. 1988--), So. Ariz. Cattlemen's Assn. (pres.), Cattle Growers Assn. (v.p., pres.-elect), Freelance Photographers Orgn. Republican. Home and Office: Santa Rita Ranch Inc 8200 E Box Canyon Rd PO Box 647 Green Valley AZ 85622

MCGILL, DOROTHY JUNE, real estate professional; b. Altus, Okla., Jan. 16, 1930; d. V.N. Sr. and Pearl (Beecham) Compton; m. Henry L. McGill Jr., Sept. 5, 1954 (div. 1981); 1 child, Corey G. Cert., Calif. Sch. Real Estate, 1978. Sales assoc. Old Town Real Estate, Hesperia, Calif., 1978-80; sales mgr. Mira Vista Corp./Red Carpet Real Estate, Silver Lakes, Calif., 1981-86; sales assoc. Century 21 Jerl Realty, Silver Lakes, 1986—. Mem. Nat. Assn. Realtors, Calif. Assn. Realtors, Victor Valley Bd. Realtors, Silver Lakes Realtors Assn. (bd. dirs. 1987-88). Office: Century 21 Jerl Real Estate PO Box 204 Helendale CA 92342

MCGILL, LEIGH CRAIG, pediatric surgeon; b. Phoenix, Apr. 6, 1949; s. Richard Oliver and Jean Ellen (Niles) McG.; m. Mary Louise Cordell, June 4, 1983; children: Anna Elizabeth, Leigh Clinton. BA, U. Tex., Austin, 1971; MD, U. Colo., 1975. Am. Bds. of Surgery/Pediatric Surgery. Attending pediatric surgeon Phoenix Children's Hosp., 1983—. Mem. Am. Pediatric Surgery Assn., Am. Coll. Surgeons, Am. Acad. Pediatrics. Methodist. Home: 7102 N 1st St Phoenix AZ 85020 Office: 1301 E McDowell #100 Phoenix AZ 85006

MCGILVRAY, DENNIS BEATON, anthropology educator; b. Palo Alto, Calif., Aug. 16, 1943; s. Alexander Seawall and Susan (Hays) McG.; m. Beth Fippinger, June 21, 1973; children: Cameron Hays, Grant Righter, Miriam Beth. BA, Reed Coll., 1965; MA, U. Chgo., 1968, PhD, 1974; MA (hon.), Cambridge U., Eng., 1973. Asst. prof. U. Santa Clara, Calif., 1972-73; asst. lectr. Cambridge U., 1973-78; A.W. Mellon postdoctoral fellow Cornell U., Ithaca, N.Y., 1978-80; assoc. prof. anthropology U. Colo., Boulder, 1980—. Editor: Caste Ideology and Interaction, 1982; contbr. articles to profl. jours., chpts. to books. Grantee Am. Inst. Indian Studies, 1983, Social Sci. Research Council, 1984; recipient Stirling award for contributions to psychol. anthropology, 1987. Fellow Am. Anthropol. Assn., Royal Anthropol. Inst.; mem. Assn. Social Anthropologists, Am. Ethnol. Soc., Assn. Asian Studies, Phi Beta Kappa. Home: 1315 5th St Boulder CO 80302 Office: U Colo Dept Anthropology Boulder CO 80309-0233

MCGINN, CHARLES EVANS, architect; b. Ft. Polk, La., Mar. 3, 1953; s. Ferdinand Magnus and Mary Phallie (Evans) M.; m. Eileen Harper Lindsay, June 30, 1984; children: Forrest Fontenot Lindsay-McGinn, Claire Harper Lindsay-McGinn. Student, Rice U., 1971-73; BS in Art and Design, MIT, 1977, MS in Interdisciplinary Sci., 1977; PhD in Ecology, U. Calif., Davis, 1982. Registered architect, Calif.; cert. construction specifier. Research dir. CA Windbreaks Demonstration Project, Calif., 1982-83; assoc. engr. I.L. Welty and Assocs., Mendocino, Calif., 1983-85; assoc. architect Roger Scott Group, Architects, Sacramento, Calif., 1985-87; jr. civil engr. Calif. Dept. Transp., Sacramento, 1987; prin. Charles E. McGinn AIA, Sacramento, 1987--. Active Construction Codes Adv. and Appeals Bd., Sacramento, 1987--; trustee St. Marks United Meth. Ch., Sacramento, 1988--. With U.S. Merchant Marines. Mem. Construction Specifications Inst., AIA. Democrat. Home and Office: 2017 Mercury Way Sacramento CA 95864

MCGINNIS, MICHAEL PATRICK, psychotherapist; b. Madison, Wis., Oct. 4, 1950; s. James and Patricia Jane (Cole) McG.; m. Carol Ann Bailey, Aug. 8, 1982; children: Arielle Dominque, Chandra Eden. Student, U. Wis., 1968-69, U. Maine, 1971-73; BA, Sonoma State U., 1980, MA, 1984. Cert. marriage, family and child counselor, Calif. Offset printer Portland (Maine) Printing Co., 1970-71, Pronto Prints, Madison, 1972-74; mental health specialist Sheltered Workshop, Madison, 1975-77; mental health worker social svc. dept. Treatment Alternatives to Street Crimes, Santa Rosa, Calif., 1977-79; counselor Nat. Coun. on Alcoholism, Santa Rosa, 1978-79, exec. dir. Sonoma County, 1979-81; counselor, trainer Sonoma County Family Svc. Agy., Santa Rosa, 1981-86; pvt. practice, Healdsburg, Calif., 1985—; trainer, cons. domestic violence treatment Calif. Dept. Mental Health, 1979-84, YWCA Women's Emergency Shelter, Santa Rosa, 1980-86. Mem. Calif. Assn. Marriage and Family Therapists (clin.), Am. Profl. Soc. on Abuse on Children (clin.), Calif. Profl. Soc. on Abuse of Children (clin.). Democrat. Home and Office: 610 Alta Vista Dr Healdsburg CA 95448

MCGINNIS, ROBERT WILLIAM, electronics company executive; b. Modesto, Calif., Oct. 31, 1936; s. George Crawford and Lola May (Provis) McG.; B.S. in Elec. Engring. with highest honors, U. Calif., Berkeley, 1962; postgrad. N.Y. U., 1962-63; m. Sondra Elaine Hurley, Mar. 1, 1964; children—Michael Fredrick, Traci Anne, Patrick William. Mem. tech. staff Bell Telephone Labs, Murray Hill, N.J., 1961-63; devel. engr., engring. mgr., product mgr., ops. mgr. Motorola Semiconductor Group, Phoenix, 1963-73, ops. mgr. for hybrid circuits group, communications div., Fort Lauderdale, Fla., 1973-76, solar ops. mgr., 1976-79; v.p., gen. mgr. Photowatt Internat., Inc., Tempe, Ariz., 1979-83; gen. mgr. SAFT Electronic Systems Div., 1983-85, pres., Safe Power Systems, Inc., Tempe, 1985—. Mem. Ariz. Solar Energy Commn., 1977-83; chmn. photovoltaic subcom. Am. Nat. Standards Inst., 1978-83; mem. coordinating council Solar Energy Research Inst. Standards, 1977-82. Served with USNR, 1955-58. Mem. IEEE, Phi Beta Kappa, Tau Beta Pi, Eta Kappa Nu. Republican. Methodist. Contbr. articles in field to profl. jours. Home: 7887 Via Bonita Scottsdale AZ 85282 Office: Safe Power Systems Inc 528 W 21st Tempe AZ 85202

MCGINTY, ANNE, music publishing executive; b. Findlay, Ohio, June 29, 1945; d. John E. and Elisabeth J. (Harlow) Staley; m. Dennis D. McGinty, 1964 (div. 1969); m. John Baldwin Edmondson, Dec. 31, 1977. MusB summa cum laude, Duquesne U., 1973, MusM, 1975. Flutist various orchs., chamber groups, 1964-83; prin. flutist Tucson Symphony Orch., 1967-69; editor, arranger Hansen Publs., Miami Beach, Fla., 1976-77; co-owner, pub. Edmondson & McGinty, Inc. div. Queenwood Publs., Scottsdale, Ariz., 1986—; instr. flute, Duquesne U., Carroll Coll., Trinity Coll., others, 1974-79; composer, arranger for various music pubs., 1978-86; guest conductor, U.S. and Can., 1985—. Composer works for concert band, solo, duet and trio flute, solo flute and solo clarinet with band accompaniment. Mem. ASCAP (Composer award 1986, 87, 88), Nat. Flute Assn. (co-editor newsletter 1974-76), Women Band Dirs. Nat. Assn. (Golden Rose award 1988). Republican. Office: Queenwood Publs 11101 E Mercer Ln Scottsdale AZ 85259

MCGIRR, JACKELEN RICHARDSON, clothing designer; b. San Francisco, July 13, 1941; d. Jack Covell and Helen (York) Richardson; m. Douglas Jones, Dec. 22, 1969 (div. 1982); 1 child, Jackelen Anne; m. Wesley Neil McGirr, Feb. 7, 1987. BA, Calif. State U., Sacramento, 1963, gen. secondary credential, 1964; lic. in real estate, Fresno State Coll., 1965; MA in Clothing Design, Pacific Union Coll., 1968. Tchr. home econs. Kingsburg (Calif.) High Sch., 1963-65, Napa (Calif.) Valley Unified Sch. Dist., 1965-82; ptnr. Bottle Shop, St. Helena, Calif., 1965-71; clothing designer, Alturas, Calif., 1982-88; owner, mgr. Jackelen Custom Designed Garments, St. Helena, 1988—; cons. on cottage industry Coll. Siskeyou, Weed, Calif., 1983-85, Lassen Coll., Susanville, Calif., 1984. Exhibited designs Calif. State Fair, 1986—. Mem. Alturas Tourism Com., 1983—. Mem. AAUW, Order of Ea. Star. Republican. Presbyterian. Home and Office: 2080 Spring Mountain Rd Saint Helena CA 94574

MCGLOTHEN, SHEILA ELAINE, nurse; b. Jasper, Tex., Mar. 29, 1959; d. Calvin Coolidge and Barbara Bell (Smith) Barnett; m. Jody Ray McGlothen, June 5, 1982; children: Laura Anne, Leah Rhea. BS in Nursing, U. Tex., Arlington, 1984. R.N., Tex., Calif. Staff nurse Garland (Tex.) Community Hosp., 1985-86; home health nurse MPH Home Health Agy., Garland, 1986-87; staff nurse med./surg. Bakersfield Meml. Hosp., 1989—. Baptist.

MCGLYNN, BETTY HOAG, art historian; b. Deer Lodge, Mont., Apr. 28, 1914; d. Arthur James and Elizabeth Tangey (Davey) Lochrie; m. Paul Sterling Hoag, Dec. 28, 1936 (div. 1967); children: Peter Lochrie, Jane Hoag Brown, Robert Doane; m. Thomas Arnold McGlynn, July 28, 1973. BA, Stanford U., 1936; MA, U. So. Calif., 1967. Cert. secondary tchr., Calif. Rsch. dir. So. Calif. Archives of Am. Art, L.A., 1964-67; rsch. dir. Carmel (Calif.) Mus. Art, 1967-69, Triton Mus. Art, Santa Clara, Calif., 1970; archivist, librarian San Mateo County (Calif.) Hist. Soc. Mus., 1971-74; cons. Monterey Peninsula, Calif., 1964—; tchr. art extension Monterey Peninsula Coll., Calif., 1970, San Jose City Coll., 1971; lectr. in field. Author: The World of Mary DeNeale Morgan, 1970, Carmel Art Association: a History, 1987; contbg. author: Plein Air Painters of California The North, 1986; editor, author of jours.: La Peninsula, 1971-75, Noticias, 1983-88; author of booklets and mus. catalogs; contbr. articles to profl. jours. Appraiser art work City of Carmel, 1967, City of Monterey, 1981. Mem. Butte (Mont.) Arts Chateau, Carmel Art Assn. (hon.), Carmel Heritage Soc., Calif. Hist. Soc., Chinese Hist. Soc., Friends of Bancroft Libr., Monterey History and Art Assn. (art cons.), Monterey Peninsula Mus. Art (acquisitions bd.), Robinson Jeffers Tor House Found. (art cons.), Hawaiian Hist. Soc., Nat. Mus. of Women in the Arts, The Westerners, P.E.O. Republican. Home and Office: PO Box 5034 Carmel-by-the-Sea CA 93921

MCGOODWIN, JAMES RUSSELL, anthropology educator, writer; b. Houston, Dec. 26, 1941; s. James V. and Tina (Wait) McG. BBA, U. Tex., 1964, MBA, 1965, PhD, 1973. Assoc. prof. anthropology U. Colo., Boulder, 1973—; expert in fisheries and developing nations FAO, Rome, 1983—. Editor: The Colo. Bowhunter mag., 1986-87; contbr. articles to profl. jours. Served to 1st lt. U.S. Army, 1965-67, Vietnam. Decorated Bronze Star, Purple Heart; research fellow Woods Hole Oceanographic Instn., 1978-79. Mem. Rocky Mountain Elk Found. (chmn. coordinating com. Denver chpt. 1985-86), The Wildlife Soc., Soc. Applied Anthropology, Sigma Xi. Office: U Colo Dept Anthropology Campus Box 233 Boulder CO 80309

MCGOON, CLIFFORD DUANE, publisher; b. Bismarck, N.D., Dec. 18, 1939; s. Clifford D. and Norma S. McGoon; m. Nancy Schonfeld, May 31, 1986; 1 child from previous marriage, Amie. BS in Communication, U. Ill., 1963. Publs. mgr. Hercules Inc., Wilmington, Del., 1968-76; dir. Big Brothers/Big Sisters Lake County, Calif., 1976-78; v.p. communication Internat. Assn. Bus. Communicators, San Francisco, 1978—; editor, publisher Communication World Mag., San Francisco, 1978—. Served to capt. USAF, 1963-68. Recipient Maggie award Western Publs. Assn., Los Angeles, 1984, 86, 88. Mem. Am. Soc. Assn. Execs. (Gold Circle award 1983, 84, 85, 86), Pub. Relations Soc. Am. Office: Internat Assn Bus Communicators 1 Hallidie Pl San Francisco CA 94102

MCGOUGH, PETER MYLES, physician; b. Culver City, Calif., Mar. 27, 1952; s. Myles Douglas and Cecelia Marie (McVay) McG.; m. Colleen Ann Dolan, May 30, 1987. BA in Biology with hons., U. Calif.-San Diego, 1974; MD, U. So. Calif., 1979. Intern then resident Providence Med. Ctr., Seattle, 1979-82, practice medicine specializing in family practice, 1982—; rsch. assoc. S.M. Grundy VA Hosp., San Diego, 1973-75; asst. clin. prof. U. Wash., Seattle, 1987—. Contbr. articles to profl. jours. Pres. Physicians for Social Responsibility, Seattle, 1987--. George Gerber scholar, 1976-79; Calif. State scholar, 1971-74. Fellow Am. Acad. Family Physicians; mem. Wash. Med. Soc., Wash. Acad. Family Physicians (chmn. legis. com. 1986--). Democrat. Office: 3400 California Ave SW Seattle WA 98116

MCGOURTY, STEPHEN LAWRENCE, computer systems engineer; b. Ozark, Ala., Feb. 26, 1954; s. Wayne Edward and Ida Mae (Latchaw) McG.; m. Charmaine Louise Hencher, Apr. 3, 1976. AA, Pensacola Jr. Coll., 1982; BS, U. West Fla., 1985. Site rep., network analyst technology div. Everett (Wash.) Systems Design engr. Boeing Computer Services, 1985—, systems design engr. network mgmt. Everett site. Served with USN, 1976-82. Democrat. Club: United Mutations. Office: Boeing Computer Svcs M/S 07-21 PO Box 24346 Seattle WA 98124

MCGOVERN, MICHAEL PATRICK, computer systems consultant; b. Santa Monica, Calif., Nov. 17, 1951; s. Patrick Francis and Marilyn Lucille (Taylor) McG. BA in Econs., U. Calif., San Diego, 1973. Pres., owner Fern Forest Exports, Hilo, Hawaii, 1973-77; leasing adminstr., asst. controller Eurocars of Hawaii Ltd., Honolulu, 1976-80; computer systems mgr. Daiei (USA), Inc., Honolulu, 1980-85; systems coordinator Holmes & Narver, Inc., Honolulu, 1985-88; cons. Holmes & Narver, Inc., San Francisco, 1988—; cons. Internat. Trading Group, Ltd. Republican. Clubs: Windward Orchid Soc. (Honolulu); Chicken Alice Group. Home: 775 Post St #410 San Francisco CA 94109

MCGOVERN, RICKY JAMES, architect, educator; b. Tacoma, June 16, 1948; s. James Patrick and Betty Irene (Baxter) McG.; m. Kathleen Joy Kerrone, June 14, 1968; children—Jamie Francis, Brandon James. B.Arch., Wash. State U., 1973, B.S., 1973. Registered architect, Wash. Architect Burr Assocs., Tacoma, 1973-79, Erickson-Hogenson Architects, Tacoma, 1979-81; ptnr. Erickson-McGovern Architects, Tacoma, 1981—; instr. Tacoma Community Coll., 1979-85; vocat. advisor Bethel Sch. Dist., Spanaway, Wash., 1981—; sec. Avitar Inc., Tacoma, 1980—; bd. dirs. Sound Ventures, Inc., Plaza Hall. Co-chmn. Clearwood Community Assn., Pierce County, Wash., 1976-82; designer Bethel Community Daffodil Float, Spanaway, 1983-84. Recipient appreciation award Clearwood Community Assn., 1982; named Citizen of Yr., 1988. Mem. AIA, Council Ednl. Facilities Planning, Soc. Am. Value Engrs. (bd. dirs. 1982-83), Shelter Industry Coalition (vice chmn. 1983—), Parkland-Spanaway C. of C. (chmn. Community Days 1984, pres. 1987-88, citizen of yr. award 1985, 86), Winner's Circle (v.p. 1983—). Clubs: Plaza Hall (bd. dirs. 1985—) City. Lodge: Kiwanis (pres. 1984-85, Kiwanian of Yr. award 1982, 83, 84, Citizen of Yr. 1988). Office: Erickson-McGovern Architects 130 S 131st St Tacoma WA 98444

MC GOVERN, WALTER T., judge; b. Seattle, May 24, 1922; s. C. Arthur and Anne Marie (Thies) McG.; m. Rita Marie Olsen, June 29, 1946; children: Katrina M., Shawn E., A. Renee. B.A., U. Wash., 1949, LL.B., 1950. Bar: Wash. 1950. Practiced law in Seattle, 1950-59; mem. firm Kerr, McCord, Greenleaf & Moen; judge Municipal Ct., Seattle, 1959-65, Superior Ct., Wash., 1965-68, Wash. Supreme Ct., 1968-71, U.S. Dist. Ct. (we. dist.) Wash., 1971—; chief judge 1975-87; mem. subcom. on supporting personnel Jud. Conf. U.S., 1981-87, chmn. subcom., 1983, mem. adminstrn. com., 1983-87, chmn. jud. resources com., 1987—. Mem. Am. Judicature Soc., Wash. State Superior Ct. Judges Assn., Seattle King County Bar Assn. (treas.), Phi Delta Phi. Club: Seattle Tennis (pres. 1968). Office: US Dist Ct US Courthouse 5th Fl 1010 5th Ave Seattle WA 98104

MCGOWAN, JOSEPH ANTHONY, JR., news executive; b. Sheridan, Wyo., May 16, 1931; s. Joseph Anthony and Eda B. (Harris) McG.; m. Patricia Donnette Mitchell, June 7, 1958 (div. 1980); children—Joseph Howard, Colleen Diane; m. Catherine Doris Netick, June 12, 1982. B.S., U. Wyo. Newsman AP, Miami, Fla., 1960-64; bur. chief AP, New Delhi, India, 1965-68, Lima, Peru, 1968-70, Indpls., 1970-75, Boston, 1975-78, Denver, 1978—; lectr. U. Denver, 1978—, Colo. U., Boulder, 1978—, Northeastern U., Boston, 1975-78. Scoutmaster Boy Scouts Am., Sudbury, Mass., 1977-78. Served with USNR, 1953-55. Mem. Denver Press Club (bd. dirs.), Press Club Boston, Colo. Assn. Commerce and Industry (communications council), Sigma Delta Chi (Big Hat award 1983). Republican. Office: AP 1444 Wazee St Ste 130 Denver CO 80202

MCGRADY, JOHN FREDERICK, computer consultant, author; b. Munich, Federal Republic of Germany, Sept. 29, 1948; s. Gale Charles and Irene Matilda (Peelaerts) McG.; m. Linda Anne Curley, 1968 (div. 1974); 1 child, Rain Juli; m. Daven Temple, Sept. 5, 1985; children: Paul Temple Witherspoon, Caroline Witherspoon. BS in Zoology, U. Wash., 1970, DDS, 1974. Owner Burton Dental Clinic, Burton, Wash., 1974-83; cons. U.S. Peace Corps, Kingston, Jamaica, 1978; instr. dentistry U. Wash., Seattle, 1978-80; owner Sound Software Systems, Tacoma, 1980-82, Coconut Info., Honolulu, 1986—; developer, cons. Computerland, Apple Computer, Honolulu, 1986—; cons. Hawaii Dental Assoc., Honolulu, 1986; tchr. tng. Apple Computer/Computerland, Univ. Hawaii, Honolulu, 1987-89. Author: Journeying Teeth, 1980, Gone Forever, 1989; editor Lanikite Monthly Newsletter, Lanikai, Hawaii; author (software) cephalometric analysis, WetPaint, Overweight & Stackmoney. Mem. Manele Bay Yacht Club. Office: Coconut Info PO Box 75453 Honolulu HI 96836

MCGRANAHAN, SHELLEY ANNE, teacher; b. Rochester, N.Y., Mar. 16, 1950; d. Robert William and Beverly June (Ames) Carter; m. Patrick Brian McGranahan, Aug. 21, 1971; children: Matthew Shawn and Michael Ryan (twins), Mark Travis. B of Music Edn. with honors, Grove City Coll., 1972. Cert. music edn. tchr., Colo. Choir dir. 1st Bapt. Ch., Sidney, Ohio, 1974-77; youth dir. 1st United Presbyn. Ch., Sidney, 1977-80, 81; dealer Tupperware, Sidney, 1980, mgr., 1980-82; dir. Cambridge (Nebr.) Sr. Ctr., 1982-85; tchr. music. Montrose (Colo.) City Schs., 1985—; color guard advisor Montrose High Sch. Band, 1986-88. Mem. Home Extension Group, Cambridge, 1983-85; emergency med. technician Cambridge Rescue Squad, 1983-85, sec., 1985. Named one of Outstanding Vols., ARC, 1979, 80. Mem. NEA, Colo. Edn. Assn.

MCGRATH, FRANK EDWARD, insurance company executive; b. Port Chester, N.Y., May 23, 1946; s. Frank Edward Sr. and Eleanor Marie (Kelly) McG.; m. Marcia Brown, Mar. 18, 1981; children: Casey, Kelly, Frank, Kerry. BBA, St. Michael's Coll., 1968. Mgr. sales Allstate Ins., N.Y.C., 1968-77; mktg. dir./br. mgr. CNA Ins., Chgo., 1977-79; mgr. mktg. Carpezzi Agy., Nanuet, N.Y., 1979-80; asst. v.p. Home Ins., N.Y.C., 1982-87; v.p. Allianz Ins. Co., Los Angeles, 1987—. Mem. Soc. Chartered Property and Casualty Underwriters. Roman Catholic. Home: 29749 Kimberly Dr Agoura HIlls CA 91301 Office: Allianz Ins Co 6435 Wilshire Blvd Los Angeles CA 90048

MCGRATH, LARRY WILLIAM, automotive parts company executive; b. Lamar, Colo., Feb. 26, 1940; s. Guy Dean and Zoe C. (Bishop) McG.; m. Jane Lee Williams, Dec. 22, 1969. BA in Edn., Ariz. State U., 1962, MA in Edn., 1964, EdD, 1974. Tchr. Scottsdale (Ariz.) Pub. Schs., 1962-82; v.p., gen. mgr. Powerformance Internat. Corp., Phoenix, 1982—, also bd. dirs. Office: Powerformance Internat Corp 2225 W Mountain View Ste 6 Phoenix AZ 85021

MCGRATH, PHYLLIS NEYER, nurse; b. Lancaster, Pa.; d. Wellington Clair and Vera Rae (Drumm) Neyer; div.; children: Kristine, Kathryn. Student Sch. Nursing, Lancaster Gen. Hosp., 1961-63; AS in Nursing, U. Albuquerque, 1976; BS in Nursing, U. Calif.-San Francisco, 1984, MS in Nursing, 1986. RN, Calif. Nurse USAF Hosp., Yokota, Japan, 1976-79; surg. nurse VA Med. Ctr., Livermore, Calif., 1979-81; ICU cardiovascular nurse instr. VA Med. Ctr., Livermore, 1981-85; vascular clin. nurse specialist, cons., instr. VA Med. Ctr., Palo Alto, Calif., 1986--. Past sec. bd. dirs. Mainland Japan area Girl Scouts U.S.; mem. Flying Drs. flying med. vols. Mem. Am. Assn. Critical Care Nurses (cert.). Home: 51 Sea Crest Ct Half Moon Bay CA 94019 Office: VA Med Ctr Vascular Surg 3801 Miranda Ave Palo Alto CA 94304

MCGRATH, RICHARD WILLIAM, osteopathic physician; b. Hartford, Conn., Nov. 17, 1943; s. William Paul and Stephanie Gertrude (Romash) McG.; B.S., St. Ambrose Coll., 1965; D.Osteo. Medicine and Surgery, Coll. Osteo. Medicine and Surgery, Des Moines, 1971; m. Mariette VanLancker, June 24, 1967; children—Shaun, Megan, Kelley. Osteo. physician Weld County Gen. Hosp., Greeley, Colo., 1971-72, Granby (Colo.) Clinic, 1972-75, Timberline Med. Ctr., P.C., Granby, 1975—; pres. Timberline Med. Center, 1976—, Bighorn Properties Inc., 1978—, Thia of Am. Corp., 1980—; med. coordinator/dir. regional emergency systems Colo. State Health Dept., 1978-79; mem. Colo. Comprehensive Health Planning Agy., 1975-77; assoc. prof. clin. medicine Tex. Coll. Osteo. Medicine; med. advisor Grand County Ambulance System, 1977—; vice chief staff Kremmling Meml. Hosp.; bd. dirs. M&L Bus. Machine Co., Denver, Sun-Flo Internat., Inc., Silver Creek Devel. Co. and Ski Area. Mem. steering com. to develop Colo. Western Slope Health System Agy., 1975-76, bd. dirs., 1977—; bd. dirs. St. Anthony Hosp. Systems Emergency Rooms, 1984—; med. dir. Community Hosp. and Emergency Ctr., Granby; officer, police surgeon Grand Lake and Granby, 1977—; mem. parent adv. bd. Granby Sch. System, 1975-76; chmn. East Grand County Safety Council, 1974-76; dep. coroner Grand County, 1973-75; med. advisor Grand County Rescue Team, 1974-78. Recipient award Ohio State U. Coll. Medicine, 1977. Mem. AMA, ACS (com. on trauma), Am. Coll. Emergency Physicians, Western Slope Physicians Alliance Assn., Colo. State Emergency Med. Technicians (med. chmn. 1982-84), Colo. Union of Physicians (dir.), C. of C. of Granby, Grand Lake and Fraser Valley. Republican. Roman Catholic. Home: PO Box 706 Granby CO 80446 Office: PO Box 857 Granby CO 80446

MCGREGOR, JOHN H., deputy sheriff; b. Minot, N.D., July 8, 1929; s. William Elmer and Mildred Georgiana (Blessum) McG.; m. Norma Jean Kinshella, Oct. 6, 1951; children: Jaqueline, John H., Carolyn E. BS, U. Mont., 1957. Registered pharmacist, Mont., Wash.; teaching cert., Wash. Pharmacist, mgr. Kalispell (Mont.) Drug, 1957-59, Standard Drug Co., Spokane, Wash., 1959-62, Hart & Dilatush Pharmacy, Spokane, 1965-74; instr., law enforcement Spokane Community Coll., 1968-86; div. commdr. Spokane County Sheriff Dept., Spokane, 1962—; law enforcement adv. Spokane Community Coll., 1972—; expert witness Spokane County Cts., 1969—; cons. in field. Named Law Enforcement Officer of Year Exchange Club, 1986, Vets. of Foreign Wars, 1976. Mem. Wash. State Law Enforcement Assn. (pres. 1978-79), Reserve Officers Assn. Am., Air Force Assn., Am. Legion, Kappa Psi Pharmacy Honorary (regent 1955-56), Loyal Order of Moose, Eagles. Roman Catholic. Home: N 5726 C St Spokane WA 99205 Office: Spokane County Sheriff Dept County/City Pub Safety Bldg Spokane WA 99260

MCGREGOR, JOHN JOSEPH, lawyer; b. Fort Knox, Ky., Nov. 18, 1946; s. Arden Durham and Ruth Marguerite (Funkner) McG. AB, U. San Francisco, 1968; JD, U. Calif. Hastings Sch. Law, 1971; LLM, NYU, 1974. Cert. specialist in taxation law. Sports info. dir. U. San Francisco, 1966-68; staff atty. Community Legal Svcs., San Jose, Calif., 1972-73; cons. IRS Project, Washington, 1974-75; assoc. Thomas, Snell, Jamison, Russell, Williamson & Asperger, Fresno, Calif., 1975-78; shareholder Thomas, Snell, Jamison, Russell & Asperger, Fresno, 1978—; asst. sec., gen. counsel The Vendo Co., Fresno, 1985-88. Author: Taxation of Real Property Transfers, 1981. Bd. dirs. Fresno (Calif.) Storyland, 1976-81; mem. Fresno Ski Patrol, 1976—, Sierra Summit Ski Patrol, Lakeshore, Calif., 1985—, The Acad., Fresno, 1981—. Named Vol. Atty. of the Year Fresno County Bar Assn., 1983. Mem. Calif. State Bar, Fresno County Bar (dir. 1982-86), The Downtown Club, San Joaquin Country club. Roman Catholic. Home: 5049 N Van Ness Blvd Fresno CA 93711 Office: Thomas Snell Jamison et al 2445 Capitol St Fresno CA 93721

MCGREW, SANDRA MOODY, nurse; b. Boise, Idaho, Aug. 10, 1939; d. Ivan Vance and Marjorie Mae (Charlton) Moody; m. Donald C. Sperling, Aug. 11, 1956 (div. 1963) 1 child, Seana Lee; m. Herschel Dean McGrew, Jan. 18, 1964; children: Ronald, Lynn. BS in Nursing, Idaho State U., 1979. Lic. practical nurse; RN. Practical nurse St. Anthony Hosp., Pocatello, Idaho, 1970-79, nurse, 1979-80; nurse St. Alphonsus Regional Med. Ctr., Boise, 1980—; mem. adv. bd. Idaho State Bd. NUrsing, 1988—. Mem. NOW. Democrat. Mem. Seventh-Day Adventist. Home: 9620 Pattie Ct Boise ID 83704 Office: St Alphonsus Regional Med Ctr 1055 N Curtis Blvd Boise ID 83704

MCGUIGAN, SHERRYL ANN, educator; b. Oklahoma City, May 4, 1961; d. William Donald and Carolyn Frances (Svymbersky) McG. BS in Edn., Western Oreg. State Coll., 1985, MS in Edn., 1987. Cert. elem. tchr., reading specialist, handicapped learner, Oreg. Tchr. learning disabilities Dillard Elem. Sch., Dillard, Oreg., 1985-87, Fir Grove Elem. Sch., Roseburg, Oreg., 1987—; dir. handi-camp, trainer spl. sitters Willamtte Council Campfire, Salem, Oreg., 1985. Vol. Polk County Spl. Olympics, Dallas, Oreg., 1984-85. Mem. Council for Exceptional Children, Assn. for Retarded Citizens. Home: 366 W Laurelwood Ct Roseburg OR 97470 Office: Fir Grove Elem Sch 1360 W Harvard Blvd Roseburg OR 97470

MCGUIRE, JAMES CHARLES, aircraft company executive; b. St. Louis, Aug. 8, 1917; s. John Patrick and Anna Beulah (Erbar) McG.; A.B., Washington U., St. Louis, 1949, M.A. (Univ. fellow), 1953, Ph.D., 1954; m. Ingrid Elisabeth Getreu, Sept. 16, 1954. Research assoc. Ohio State U., 1953-56; research psychologist Aeromed. Lab., Wright-Patterson AFB, Ohio, 1956-59; group supr. Boeing Airplane Co., Seattle, 1959-61; dept. mgr. Internat. Electric Corp., Paramus, N.J., 1961-62; sr. human factors scientist System Devel. Corp., Santa Monica, Calif., 1962-67; v.p. Booz-Allen Applied Research, Saigon, Vietnam, 1967-72; v.p. Assoc. Cons. Internat., Saigon, 1972-75, Bethesda, Md., 1975-78; br. chief Human Factors, System Tech. Devel., 1978-82; prin. staff engr. tech. modernization methodology Douglas Aircraft Co., Long Beach, Calif., 1982-85; program mgr. cockpit automation tech. program, Northrop Aircraft div., Hawthorne, Calif., 1985-87; sect. mgr. aircraft programs dept. human factors engring. Douglas Aircraft Co., Long Beach, 1987—; lectr. Nat. Def. Coll., Vietnamese Armed Forces, Saigon, 1971. Served with AUS, 1940-46. Decorated Bronze Star medal with oak leaf cluster. Mem. Am. Psychol. Assn., IEEE, Computer Soc. of IEEE, Human Factors Soc., Am. Assn. Artificial Intelligence, Phi Beta Kappa, Sigma Xi. Republican. Home: 23201 Mindanao Circle Monarch Beach CA 92677 Office: Douglas Aircraft Co 78-73 3855 Lakewood Blvd Long Beach CA 90846

MCGUIRE, MICHAEL DENNIS, rhetoric educator; b. Oak Park, Ill., May 22, 1948; s. Wilbur Vernon McGuire and Helen Ruth Reeves; m. Patti A. Rompf, May 22, 1984; 1 child, Tahoe Lorraine. AB, U. Calif., Davis, 1970; MA, U. Iowa, 1972, PhD, 1975. Asst. prof. speech U. Ga., Athens, 1974-80, assoc. prof., 1982-88; vis. assoc. prof. U. Calif., Davis, 1980-82; prof. speech communication Calif. State U., Long Beach, 1988—; vis. lectr. U. Marburg (Fed. Republic Germany), 1978; exchange prof. U. Erlangen (Fed. Republic Germany)-Nuernberg, 1987; cons. Scott-Foresman, Houghton Mifflin; speech writer Communication Design, Sacramento, 1981; editorial advisor Rhetoric Soc. Quar., Quar. Jour. Speech, Communication Monographs, also others; presenter in field. Contbr. articles to profl. jours., chpts. to books. Named Outstanding Faculty Mem., U. Ga. Student Speech Assn., 1983. Mem. Speech Communication Assn. (div. chmn. 1981-82, Ralph Cooley rsch. award internat. and intercultural communication div. 1983, 88, best pub. rsch. article award 1987), Internat. Communication Assn., Western Speech Communication Assn., Golden Key (hon.). Office: Calif State U Dept Speech 1250 Bellflower Blvd Long Beach CA 90840-2407

MCGUIRE, MICHAEL FRANCIS, plastic/reconstructive surgeon; b. St. Louis, Oct. 4, 1946; s. Arthur Patrick and Virginia Claribel (Gannon) McG. BA, Columbia U., 1968, D of Medicine, 1972. Diplomate Am. Bd. Surgery, Am. Bd. Plastic Surgery. Intern UCLA, 1972-73, resident in gen. surgery, 1973-77, resident in plastic surgery, 1978-80; fellow in plastic surgery rsch. Stanford (Calif.) U., 1977-78; traveling fellow in plastic surgery Gt. Britain, 1980; chief plastic surgery L.A. County-Olive View Med. Ctr., Sylmar, Calif., 1980-85; pvt. practice Santa Monica, Calif., 1980—; pres. Pacific Coast Plastic Surgery Ctr., Inc., Santa Monica, 1987—, asst. clinical prof. of surgery U. Calif., Los Angeles, 1980—, vice chmn. plastic surgery St. John's Hosp., Santa Monica, 1987—, cleft palate team dir. Los Angeles County-Olive View Med. Ctr., 1986—. Charter patron Los Angeles Music Ctr. Opera, 1983, sponsoring patron Los Angeles County Art Mus., 1986, patron Colleague Helpers in Philanthropic Service, Bel Air, Calif., 1987. Fellow ACS, Royal Soc. Medicine (affiliate); mem. Am. Soc. Plastic and Reconstructive Surgeons, Inc., Los Angeles County Med. Assn., Calif. Soc. Plastic Surgery (exec. com., auditor 1988—), Alpha Omega Alpha. Democrat. Episcopalian. Office: 1301 20th St Ste 460 Santa Monica CA 90404

MC GUIRE, MICHAEL JOHN, environmental engr.; b. San Antonio, June 29, 1947; s. James Brendan and Opal Mary (Brady) McG.; BS in Civil Engring., U. Pa., 1969; MS in Environ Engring., Drexel U., 1972, PhD in Environ. Engring., 1977; diplomate Am. Acad. Environ. Engring.; m. Deborah Marrow, June 19, 1971; children: David, Anna. San. engr. Phila. Water Dept., 1969-73; rsch. assoc. Drexel U., Phila., 1976-77; prin. engr. Brown & Caldwell Cons. Engrs., Pasadena, Calif., 1977-79; water quality engr. Met. Water Dist. of So. Calif., L.A., 1979-84, water quality mgr., 1984-86, dir. water quality, 1986—; cons. environ. engr., 1979—; instr. Temple U., Phila., 1974; cons. to subcom. on absorbents, safe drinking water com. Nat. Acad. Scis., 1978-79. Registered profl. engr., Pa., N.J., Calif. Mem. Am. Water Works Assn. (Acad. Achievement award 1978, edn. div. chmn. 1982-83, chmn. Calif.-Nev. sect. water quality and resources div. 1982-83, governing bd. 1984-87, trustee Research Found. 1983-86), Am. Chem. Soc., ASCE, Water Pollution Control Fedn., Sigma Xi, Sigma Nu, Sigma Tau. Editor: (with I.H. Suffet) Activated Carbon Adsorption of Organics From the Aqueous Phase, 2 vols., 1980; Treatment of Water by Granular Activated Carbon, 1983; contbr. articles to profl. jours. Office: Met Water Dist So Calif PO Box 54153 Los Angeles CA 90054

MCGULPIN, ELIZABETH JANE, nurse; b. Toledo, Oct. 18, 1932; d. James Orville and Leah Fayne (Helton) Welden; m. Daivd Nelson Buster, Apr. 9, 1956 (div. Nov. 1960); children: David Hugh, James Ray, Mark Stephen; m. Fredrick Gordon McGulpin, Oct. 7, 1973. AA in Nursing, Pasadena City Coll., 1968. RN. Lic. nurse Las Encinas Hosp., Pasadena, Calif.; nurse Hopi Indian Reservation HEW, Keams Canyon, Ariz., 1969-70; nurse, enterostomal therapist Pasadena Vis. Nurse Assn., 1972-74; nurse Seattle King County Pub. Health, 1977-81; home care nurse Victorville, Calif., 1983-85; nurse Adult Family Home, Woodinville, Wash., 1986—; vol. nurse, counselor Child Protective Services, Victorville, 1984. Vol. nurse Am. Cancer Soc., Pasadena, 1973-75, United Ostomy Assn., Los Angeles, Victorville, 1973-84. Am. Cancer Soc. grantee. Mem. Vis. Nurse Assn. (Enterostomal Therpay grantee 1973). Home: 22366 Woodinville Duvall Rd Woodinville WA 98072

MCHARG, GERALD BARRON, real estate executive; b. Wichita, Kans., Feb. 1, 1932; s. Glen U. and Prudence Elizabeth (Skelton) McH.; m. Willo Lou Lovell, May 27, 1953 (div. Apr. 1978); children: Jeffrey Clay, Kevin Brent, Shannon Leigh; m. Rita S. Daniel, July 28, 1984. BA, Phillips U., 1953, MDiv, 1956. Ordained to ministry Christian Ch. (Disciples of Christ) 1956. Pastor 1st Christian Ch., Brawley, Calif., 1956-60, Kearny Mesa Christian Ch., San Diego, 1960-64; dist. pastor Christian Ch. (Disciples of Christ) of Pacific S.W., L.A., 1964-69, assoc. regional pastor, 1969-80; v.p. Real Estate Trainers, Inc., Santa Ana, Calif., 1980—; bd. dirs. Universal Tng. Corp., Santa Ana. Author: California Real Estate Agency, 1987. Home: 5514 Greenleaf Ave Whittier CA 90601 Office: Real Estate Trainers Inc 2428 N Grand Ave Santa Ana CA 92701

MCHENRY, ROBERT WILLIAM, landscape architect; b. Warren, Ohio, Apr. 3, 1953; s. William Sparks and Adelaide Mathilda (Kowaleski) McH.; m. Ruth Evelyn Berry, Sept. 20, 1987. B in Landscape Architecture, U. Ill., 1976. Lic. real estate salesperson, Colo.; lic. landscape architect, Kans., Calif. Landscape architect Copper Mountain (Colo.) Resort, 1977-79; resident mgr. Ten Mile Haus Condominiums, Copper Mountain, 1978-80; landscape architect Matthews & Assocs., Vail, Colo., 1979-83; resident mgr. Timber Creek Condominiums, Copper Mountain, 1980-86; front desk mgr. Resort Properties Mgmt., Copper Mountain, 1983-86; pvt. practice landscape architect Alpine Landscape Cons., Copper Mountain, 1984-86; pvt. practice Indian Hills, Colo., 1986-87; landscape architect, project mgr. The Pekarek Group, San Diego, 1987—. Named Best Landscape Project Eagle Valley Home Builders Assn., 1985, 86. Mem. Am. Soc. Landscape Architects, BMW Car Club Am.

MCHUGH, JOSEPHINE FLAHERTY, medical facility administrator; b. Pontiac, Mich., May 13, 1947; d. Joseph Francis and Mary Burns Flaherty; m. Richard Alan McHugh, Aug. 31, 1974; children: Sean Joseph, Bridget Kathleen. Grad. summa cum laude, Romana Sch., Rome, 1967; grad., Chandler Secretarial Sch., 1969. Sr. sec. Mass. Eye and Ear Infirmary, Boston, 1969-73; exec. sec. Dean's Office Preventative Medicine U. Colo. Health Scis. Ctr., Denver, 1973-80; clin. coordinator U. Hosp., Denver, 1980—; Mem. task force U. Hosp., 1986—, communications focus group leader, 1986—. Mem. Communications subcom. Douglas County (Colo.) Sch. Dist., 1987, 88, long-range planning commn., 1988. Mem. Am. Soc. Profl. and Exec. Women, NAFE, Parker Club, Breakfast Club (pres. 1987, 88), Kiwanis (sec. Parker chpt. 1988). Republican. Roman Catholic. Home: 11464 Bonanza Circle Franktown CO 80116 Office: U Hosp Denver CO 80262

MC HUGH, MARGARET ANN GLOE, psychologist; b. Salt Lake City, Nov. 8, 1920; d. Harold Henry and Olive (Warenski) Gloe; BA, U. Utah, 1942; MA in Counseling and Guidance, Idaho State U., 1964; PhD in Counseling Psychology, U. Oreg., 1970. Lic. psychologist; nat. cert. counselor; m. William T. McHugh, Oct. 1, 1943; children: Mary Margaret McHugh-Shuford, William Michael, Michelle. Tchr. kindergarten, Idaho Falls, Idaho, 1951-62, tchr. high sch. English, 1962-63; counselor Counseling Center, Idaho State U., Pocatello, 1964-67; instr. U. Oreg., Eugene, 1967-70; asst. prof. U. Victoria, B.C., Can., 1970-76; therapist Peninsula Counseling Center, Port Angeles and Sequim, Wash., 1976-81, McHugh & Assocs. Counseling Center, 1981—. Served with WAVES, 1943-44. Mem. Am. Psychol. Assn., Am. Assn. for Counseling and Devel., Am. Assn. Marriage and Family Therapy, Wash. Psychol. Assn. (rsch. women rels's., depression and women, sexual abuse). Home: 249 F Cameron Rd Sequim WA 98382

MCHUGH, MICHAEL LYN, military officer; b. Madison, Wis., Aug. 3, 1946; s. Raymond Joseph and Phoebe Rose (Sutmeyer) McH.; m. Margaret Suzanne Harvey, Dec. 28, 1968 (div. Apr. 1983); children: Rebecca Suzanne, Michael Aaron; m. Fay Margaret Maidment, Oct. 8, 1983. BS, U.S. Naval Acad., 1968; MS in Mech. Engring., U.S. Naval Postgrad. Sch., 1969. Commd. ensign USN, 1968—, advanced through grades to capt., 1989; div. officer USS Henry L. Stimson (SSBN 655), New London, Conn., 1970-74; engr. officer USS L.A. (SSN 688), Newport News, Va., 1974-78; insp. Nuclear Propulsion Examining Bd., Norfolk, Va., 1978-80; exec. officer USS Birmingham (SSN 695), Norfolk, 1980-83; commanding officer USS Haddock (SSN 621), San Diego, 1984-87, USS Sword Fish (SSN 579), Pearl Harbor, Hawaii, 1987—. Mem. U.S. Naval Acad. Alumni Assn., Naval Inst., U.S. Naval Submarine League. Republican. Roman Catholic. Home: 94-810 Leomana Way Waipahul HI 96797 Office: USS Sword Fish (SSN 579) FPO San Francisco CA 96678

MC ILHANY, STERLING FISHER, publishing company executive; b. San Gabriel, Calif., Apr. 12, 1930; s. William Wallace and Julia (Fisher) M. B.F.A. with high honors, U. Tex., 1953; postgrad. UCLA, 1953-54, 55-57, Universita per Stranieri, Perugia, Italy, 1957, Accademia delle Belle Arti, Rome, 1957-58. Teaching asst., lectr. in art history UCLA, 1953-54, 55-57; art supr. Kamehameha Prep. Sch., Honolulu, 1954-55; instr. Honolulu Acad. Arts, 1955; assoc. editor Am. Artist mag., N.Y.C., 1958-61, editor, 1969-70; host Books and the Artist network series Sta. WRVR, N.Y.C., 1961-62; sr. editor Reinhold Book Corp., N.Y.C., 1962-69; pres. IFOTA Inc., Los Angeles, 1981—; instr. Sch. Visual Arts, N.Y.C., 1961-69. Fellow Christ Coll., Cambridge. Author: Banners and Hangings, 1966; Art as Design—Design as Art, 1970; Wood Inlay, 1972; Simbari, 1975; also articles. Recipient First award tour European art ctrs. Students Internat. Travel Assn., 1952; Rotary fellow Accademia delle Belle Arti, 1957-58. Fellow Internat. Inst. Community Service London; mem. Nat. Soc. Lit. and Arts, Human Resource USA. Roman Catholic. Address: 6376 Yucca St Los Angeles CA 90028

MCILWRAITH, CYRIL WAYNE, veterinary surgery educator; b. Oamaru, New Zealand, Dec. 12, 1947; came to U.S., 1975; s. Cyril Alfred and Kathleen Avaca (O'Grady) McI.; m. Nancy Lynn Goodman, June 22, 1984. DVM, Massey U., Palmerston North, New Zealand, 1970; MS, Purdue U., 1977, PhD, 1979. Diplomate Am. Coll. Vet. Surgeons. Resident in vet. surgery Purdue U., West Lafayette, Ind., 1975-77, instr., 1977-79; asst. prof. equine surgery Colo. State U., Ft. Collins, 1979-81, assoc. prof., 1981-86, prof., 1986—; cons. surgeon. equine vet. practices, 1981—. Author: (textbook) Techniques in Large Animal Surgery ,1982, 2d edition, 1988; Diagnostic and Surgical Arthroscopy in the Horse, 1984, 2d edition 1989, Advanced Techniques in Equine Surgery, 1986; pioneered the technique of arthroscopic surgery in the horse. Recipient Colo. State U. Am. Assn. Equine Practitioners Faculty award for Teaching Equine Medicine and Surgery, 1982, Colo. State U. Alumni Outstanding Faculty award, 1983. Mem. AVMA, Royal Coll. Vet. Surgeons, Am. Assn. Vet. Surgeons, Colo. Vet. Med. Assn., Am. Assn. Equine Practitioners, Vet. Orthopedic Soc., Orthopedic Rsch. Soc. Home: 108 Blueridge Ct Fort Collins CO 80524 Office: Colo State U Vet Teaching Hosp 300 W Drake Fort Collins CO 80523

MCINTOSH, DAVID KLOSS, marketing executive; b. Arlington, Va., Mar. 27, 1954; s. Robert and Lillian (Kloss) McI.; m. Sandra Haber, July 20, 1986. BS in Communications, U. Colo., Boulder, 1980; MS in Telecommunications, U. Colo., 1984. Teleconferencing specialist Colo. Video, Boulder, 1984-88, dir. mktg., 1988—. Contbr. articles to profl. publs. Chmn. Boulder Community Broadcast Assn., 1981-82, 83-84; blockade vol. Shutdown/Rocky Mountain Peace Ctr., Rocky Flats Nuclear Weapons Plant, 1987. Mem. Internat. Teleconferencing Assn. Democrat. Home: PO Box 1405 Boulder CO 80306 Office: Colorado Video PO Box 928 Boulder CO 80306

MCINTOSH, PAUL EUGENE, county government official; b. Wabash, Ind., June 23, 1951; s. Jay Morton and Catherine Louise (Parsley) McI.; m. Susan Marie Hegedus, Sept. 5, 1981; children: Erin, Ian. B Pub. Affairs, Ind. U., 1978, MPA, 1980. Intern HEW, Washington, 1979; legis. analyst Ind. Legislature, Indpls., 1980-81; mgmt. cons. Hughes, Heiss and Assocs., San Mateo, Calif., 1981-82; adminstrv. analyst County of Solano, Fairfield, Calif., 1982-86; dep. county adminstr. County of Solano, 1986-88; chief adminstrv. officer County of El Dorado, Placerville, Calif., 1988—; project mgr., Solano County Justice Ctr., Fairfield, 1984-88. Withg USN, 1970-74, Vietnam. Mem. Am. Correctional Assn., Pi Alpha Alpha. Office: El Dorado County Adminstr 330 Fair Ln Placerville CA 95667

MCINTYRE, PATRICK LYNN, construction executive; b. Omaha, Mar. 10, 1955; s. Robert Lee and Marcia Lea (Michelsen) McI.; m. Nancy J. Brazda, May 22, 1975 (div. Sept. 1980); m. Marianne Ensworth, Aug. 30, 1986. Student, U. Nebr., Omaha, 1973-74. Journeyman electrician Omaha, 1976-83; elec. estimator Peter Kiewit Sons/So. Elec. Contractors, Omaha, 1983-84; project engr. Gilbert Indsl. Corp., Arlington, Tex., 1984-85; elec. mgr. Fluor Daniel, Sunnyvale, Calif., 1985-87; project mgr. Fluor Daniel, Santa Clara, Calif., 1987—. Asst. designer sub-micron computer chip prodn. facility. Office: Fluor Daniel PO Box 3770 Santa Clara CA 95955

MCINTYRE, ROBERT MALCOLM, utility company executive; b. Portland, Oreg., Dec. 18, 1923; s. Daniel A. and Bessie W. (Earsley) McI.; m. Marilyn Westcott, Aug. 27, 1949; 1 child, Julie. BA, UCLA, 1950; postgrad., UCLA, U. Soc. Calif., Columbia U. Gen. sales mgr. So. Calif. Gas Co. (subs. Pacific Enterprises), L.A., 1952-70, v.p., 1970-74, sr. v.p., 1974-80, pres., 1980-85, chmn., chief exec. officer, 1985-88, dir., 1988—; also bd. dirs. So. Calif. Gas Co. (subs. Pacific Enterprises). Mem. Korean Am. Centennial Commn., Huntington Libr. Soc. Fellows, L.A. Olympic Citizens Adv. Comm.; mem. bus. coun. Newport Harbor Art Mus.; mem. steering com. Orange County Bus. Com. for Arts; mem. ad hoc com. on city fin., L.A.; bd. dirs. NCCJ, Calif. Coun. Environ. and Econ. Balance, Calif. Found. Environment and Economy, L.A. United Way, Hoag Meml. Hosp.; trustee UCLA Found., L.A. Orthopaedic Hosp., mem. exec. com. Lt. USN, 1940-46. Decorated Order of the Rising Sun with Gold Rays and Ribbon (Japan); recipient Outstanding Svc. award Mex. Am. Legal Def. Fund, 1981, Humanitarian award NCCJ, Roy Wilkins award L.A. chpt. NAACP, others. Mem. Pacific Coast Gas Assn. (past dir., 49er Club award 1979), Am. Gas Assn., Inst. Gas Tech. (trustee), U.S.-Mex. C. of C., L.A. C. of C. (past chmn., Medici award), Calif. Club, L.A. Club, Phi Kappa Psi. Republican. Presbyterian. Office: So Calif Gas Co 810 S Flower St Los Angeles CA 90017

MCKAIN, MARY MARGARET, musician; b. Spokane, Wash., June 11, 1940; d. Neil Dunn and Elinore (Bien) McK. BA in Music and Police Sci., Calif. State U., L.A., 1968; studied trumpet with Rafael Mendez, Jane Sager, Sidney Lazar, and others. Trumpet player Peter Meremblum Jr. Symphony, 1954-59, Jack Benny at Greek Theater, 1963, Highland Park Symphony, L.A., 1955-66, Beverly Hills (Calif.) Symphony, 1960-66, South East Symphony, Downey, Calif., 1957-70, Santa Monica (Calif.) Elks Club, 1965-70, The Foresters, 1965-69, Latin Am. Symphony, L.A., 1961-63, L.A. Concert Band, Mexican Tipica Orch. Symphony, West Covina (Calif.) Symphony, 1976-79, Monterey Park (Calif.) Band, 1970-81, Calif. Concert Band, 1978-81, L.A. Police Dept. Concert Band, 1956-65, San Fernando Valley (Calif.) Opera, 1955-61, Iturbi on Tour, 1961; leader, trumpet player Pieces of 8 Polka Band, L.A., 1961—; 1st female dep. marshal, L.A., 1973. Trumpet player with Peter Meremblum Jr. Symphony, Jack Benny at Greek Theater, Highland Park Symphony, L.A., 1955-66, Beverly Hills (Calif.) Symphony, South East Symphony, Downey (Calif.) Symphony, Santa Monica (Calif.) Elks Club, The Foresters, Latin Am. Symphony, L.A., L.A. Concert Band, Mexican Tipica Orch., W. Covina (Calif.) Symphony, Calif. Concert Band, Monterey Park (Calif.) Band, L.A. Police Dept. Concert Band, San Fernando Valley (Calif.) Opera, 1955-61, Iturbi on tour, 1961; leader, trumpet player with Pieces of 8 Polka Band, L.A., 1961—. Mem. Musicians Local 47, Sons and Daughters Mont. Pioneers (life), Wild Life Fedn., U.S. Humane Soc., Marshals Assn. (sec., dir.), Internat. Police Assn. Home: 43212 45th St W Quartz Hill CA 93536

MC KAUGHAN, HOWARD PAUL, linguistics educator; b. Canoga Park, Calif., July 5, 1922; s. Paul and Edith (Barton) McK.; A.B., UCLA, 1945; M.Th., Dallas Theol. Sem., 1946; M.A., Cornell U., 1952, Ph.D., 1957; m. Barbara Jean Budroe, Dec. 25, 1943; children—Edith (Mrs. Daniel Skene Santoro), Charlotte (Mrs. Martin Douglas Barnhart), Patricia (Mrs. Stephen B. Pike), Barbara (Mrs. Ronald Chester Bell), Judith (Mrs. Frank L. Achilles III). Mem. linguistic research team Summer Inst. Linguistics, Mexico, 1946-52; asso. dir. Summer Inst. Linguistics, Philippines, also assoc. dir. summer sessions U. N.D., 1952-57, dir. Philippine br., 1957-61; research asst. prof. anthropology U. Wash., 1961-62; research assoc. prof., 1962-63; assoc. prof. linguistics U. Hawaii, 1963-64, prof. linguistics, 1964-88, prof. emeritus, 1988—, chmn. dept., 1963-66, dir. Pacific and Asian Linguistics Inst., 1964, 1966-69, assoc. dean grad. div., 1965-72, dean grad. div., dir. research, 1972-79, acting chancellor, 1979, interim vice chancellor acad. affairs, 1981-82, acting dir research, 1982-84, acting dean grad. div., 1982-83, dean, 1984-87, dir. research relations, 1987-88; lectr. linguistics U. Philippines, summers, 1954, 60; Fulbright vis. prof. Philippine Normal Coll.-Ateneo Consortium, Philippines, 1977; prin. Wycliffe Sch. Linguistics, summers 1953, 61; vis. prof. Australian Nat. U., Canberra, 1970; adj. prof. linguistics U. Okla., summers 1984, 85, 86; vis. prof. linguistics Payap U., Chiang Mai, Thailand, 1988—. Sr. scholar East-West Center, Honolulu, 1964; NDEA Maranao-Philippines research grantee, 1963-65; Office of Edn. Hawaii English grantee, 1965-66; NSF Jeh Language of South Vietnam grantee, 1969-70, Maranao Linguistic Studies, 1971-72, numerous other research grants. Mem. linguistic socs. Am., Philippines, Western Assn. Grad. Schs. (pres. 1978), Hawaii, Linguistic Circle N.Y., Philippine Assn. Lang. Tchrs., Hawaii Govt. Employees Assn., Phi Beta Kappa, Phi Kappa Phi. Author (with B. McKaughan): Chatino Dictionary, 1951; (with J. Forster) Ilocano: An Intensive Language Course, 1952; The Inflection and Syntax of Maranao Verbs, 1959; (with B. Macaraya): A Maranao Dictionary, 1967. Editor: Pali Language Texts: Philippines, 21 vols., 1971; The Languages of the Eastern Family of the East New Guinea Highlands Stock, 1973. Contbr. articles, chpts. to books, sci. jours. Home: 420 S Hill Rd McMinnville OR 97128

MCKAY, ALICE VITALICH, school system administrator; b. Seattle, Sept. 6, 1947; d. Jack S. and Phyllis (Bourne) Vitalich; m. Larry W. McKay, Aug. 14, 1973 (div. Jan. 1983). BA, Wash. State U., 1969; MEd, U. Nev., Las Vegas, 1975; EdD, U. Nev., Reno, 1986. High sch. tchr. Clark County Sch. Dist., Las Vegas, 1972-77, specialist women's sports, 1977-80, high sch. counselor, 1980-84, high sch. asst. prin., 1984—; pres. Lotus Profit, Inc., Las Vegas, 1985-86. Mem. Am. Assn. Counseling and Devel. (committee on women 1985—), Nev. State Counseling and Devel. (pres. 1985-86), Nat. Assn. Female Execs., AAUW, Phi Delta Kappa (exec. bd. 1980-82). Office: Clark County Sch Dist 2832 E Flamingo Rd Las Vegas NV 89121

MCKAY, D. BRIAN, lawyer, attorney general; b. Billings, Mont., Jan. 18, 1945. A.B., Colgate U., 1971; J.D., Albany Law Sch., 1974. Bar: Nev., U.S. Dist. Ct. Nev., N.Y., U.S. Dist. Ct. (no. dist.) N.Y., U.S. Ct. Appeals (9th cir.) 1978, U.S. Supreme Ct. Former mem. Sully, McKay & Lenhard, Las Vegas, Nev.; atty. gen. State of Nev., Carson City, 1983—; mem. adv. policy bd. Nat. Crime Info. Ctr., 1986—; chmn. Conf. of Western Attys.-Gen., 1987. Dir., chmn. fundraising Internat. Winter Spl. Olympics, 1989. Served with USAF, 1966-69. Mem. ABA, State Bar Nev., N.Y. State Bar Assn., Nat. Assn. Attys. Gen. Office: Office of Atty Gen Heroes Meml Bldg 198 S Carson St Capitol Complex Carson City NV 89710

MCKAY, THOMAS LEE, solar thermal electric power engineer; b. Tucson, Nov. 22, 1941; s. Thomas Hugh and Naidene Mable (Eisiminger) McK. Cert. solar thermal electric power engr. Chief exec. officer Cone Assymetrical Motor Power Systems, Inc., Seattle, 1976--, Solar Powered Pool Systems, Inc., Seattle, 1977--, Marcron Corp., Longmont, Colo., 1981-88; chief project engr. Andersen Mfg. Co., Idaho Falls, Idaho, 1988--; mktg. cons. Marcron Corp., Lake Havasu City, Ariz., 1986--. Designer Project Shenandoah Power Facility, Newnan, Ga.; patentee solar electronic and thermal devices. With USN, 1964-67. Republican. Home: 1641-25 McCulloch Blvd Apt 163 Lake Havasu City AZ 86403 Office: Marcron Corp 2800 McCulloch Blvd Ste 5A Lake Havasu City AZ 86403

MCKAY, TODD L., interior designer; b. Boulder, Colo., July 23, 1963; s. Lawrence Daniel McKay and Debra Louise (Anderson) Babcock. BA, New York U., 1985; AA, Internat. Fine Arts, Miami, 1986. Owner/designer Todd McKay Designer, San Francisco, 1985—, Phoenix, 1987; cons., Denver Design Dist., 1985-86. Designer, Best New Table Designer, Paisley, 1986, PWA, 1986, Car finishes first 1986, PWA, 1986, Best original interior, Working Environ., 1987 SFA, 1987. Organizer, John McCain for U.S. Senate, Phoenix, Ariz., 1986; Scheduler. Mem. Am. Soc. of Interior Designers, Internat. Bus. Designers. Republican Lutheran.

MCKEAN, THOMAS EDWARD, small business owner; b. Salt Lake City, Nov. 12, 1948; s. Thomas M. and Karyl Ann (Ikerd) McK.; m. Silvia Baste, Oct. 18, 1986. BA magna cum laude, U. Utah, 197l; MBA, Harvard U., 1975. Account exec. Leo Burnett, Chgo., 1975-78; account supr. Foote, Cone & Belding, San Francisco, 1978-82; dir. client svc. Foote, Cone & Belding, Barcelona, Spain, 1982-84; sr. v.p., dir. client svc. Latin Am. Foote, Cone & Belding, N.Y.C., 1984-86; v.p., dir. mktg. Freixenet USA, Sonoma, Calif., 1987-88; owner Create It! Copy It! Mail It!, Sonoma, Calif., 1989—; guest tchr. advt. high schs., San Francisco, 1980-82. Bd. dirs. Tudor City Coop., N.Y.C., 1986-87. lst lt. C.E., U.S. Army, 1971-73. Mem. Harvard Bus. Sch. Club (San Francisco, v.p. membership 1979-82), Phi Beta Kappa, Phi Kappa Phi. Home: 1479 Nut Tree Ln Sonoma CA 95476 Office: Create It Copy It Mail It 812 W Napa St Sonoma CA 95476

MCKECHNIE, DUSÉ E(ILEEN) (DAISY MCKECHNIE), substance abuse counselor; b. Wilsey, Kans., Aug. 1, 1928; d. Donald Monroe and Garnet Edna (Edwards) Love; m. Gordon F. McKechnie, May 2, 1952 (div. 1974); 1 child, Laurie Anne. AA, Clark Coll., 1974; BA, Marylhurst Coll., 1981. Cert. alcoholism and drug abuse counselor, CADC. Counselor, adminstrv. aide Alcoholism Counseling and Recovery Program, Portland, Oreg., 1974-76; counselor Alcoholic Rehab. Assocs., Portland, 1978, DePaul Alcohol Treatment Ctr., Portland, 1979; alcohol svcs. coordinator Multnomah County Alcoholism and Drug Office, Portland, 1979-81; dir. Metro Council on Alcoholism, Portland, 1981-82; counselor Project Stop, Portland, 1981-85; pvt. practice Portland, 1983—; mem. faculty Oreg. Inst. Alcohol Studies, Salem, 1982-83, Portland Community Coll., 1984; trainer State of Oreg., 1982--. Mem. Assn. of Alcoholism and Drug Abuse Counselors of Oreg. (charter, bd. dirs. 1978-82, Counselor of Yr. 1987), Nat. Assn. Alcoholism and Drug Abuse Counselors (bd. dirs. 1982). Home and Office: 2217 NE 20th St Portland OR 97212

MCKECHNIE, JAMES ARTHUR, municipal judge; b. Monticello, Ky., Dec. 12, 1923; s. James Craig and Elizabeth (Wray) M.; m. Faith Miller, 1952 (div. 1975); children: Lucy Elizabeth, Hugh Randolph, Donald Bryan, Anne Alexa. BS, U. Calif., Berkely, 1949; LLB, Hastings Coll. Law, 1952, Doctor of Jurisprudence, 1952. Dep. Div. Corps., L.A., Calif., 1953-54; pvt. practice, Whittier, Calif., 1954-78; judge Whittier Mcpl. Ct., Calif., 1978—; dir. So. Calif. BanCorp., Downey, 1981—, So. Calif. Bank, Downey, 1981—. Dir. Boys & Girls Club Whittier, 1974-75. Sgt. U.S. Army, 1943-46, ETO. Mem. Whittier Bar Assn. (pres. 1973-74). Democratic. Unitarian. Office: Mcpl Whittier Jud Dist 7339 S Painter Ave Whittier CA 90602

MC KEE, JOHN ANGUS, oil company executive; b. Toronto, Ont., Can., Aug. 31, 1935; s. John William and Margaret Enid (Phippen) McK.; m. Susan Elizabeth Harley, May 30, 1970; children: John Andrew, Mary Susan. Student, U. Toronto, 1954-58. With Dominion Securities Corp. Ltd., Toronto, 1958-61; v.p. Patino Mining Corp., Toronto and London, Eng., 1962-72; pres. J. Angus McKee & Assos. Ltd., 1973-83; pres., chief exec. officer Can. Occidental Petroleum Ltd., 1983—; dir. Teradyne Can. Ltd., Stone & Webster Can. Ltd., Cullman Ventures Inc., others.; Mng. dir. Consol. Tin Smelters Ltd., 1968-71. Bd. govs. Trinity Coll. Sch. Mem. Alpha Delta Phi. Clubs: Toronto, York, Badminton and Racquet; Knickerbocker (N.Y.C.). Office: Can Occidental Petroleum Ltd, 1500 635 8th Ave SW, Calgary, AB Canada T2P 3Z1 *

MCKEE, JOHN CAROTHERS, management consultant; b. San Diego, Apr. 25, 1912; s. John Joseph and Margaret (Giesman) McK.; BA, U. So. Calif., 1935, MA, 1937; PhD, Tulane U., 1947; m. Gladys Irene Michel, Jan. 10, 1941 (Dec. Feb. 1968); children—John Michael, Hillary Barbara; m. Sara Forman, June 25, 1968; 1 child, Evan. Gen. mgr. Hotel Royal, La Ceiba, Honduras, 1932-33; mgmt. cons. Douglas Aircraft Co., Long Beach, Calif., 1942-67, exec. adviser, dir. ops. control, 1967—, also pres. mgmt. assn. Douglas Space Systems Center; exec. adviser fin. mgmt. McDonnell Douglas Astronautics, v.p. Santa Monica Health Spot Shoe Corp., 1949—; pres. McKee Mgmt. Ctr., Volumetrics, Inc., Mentron Corp.; exec. v.p. Consearch Inc.; pres. McKee Mgmt. Ctr., Stanton, Calif., Quantek Internat. Inc.; ptnr. McKee & Wright and Assn., Stanton; v.p. Advion Corp.; lectr. Acad. of Justice, Riverside, Calif.; cons. Space Systems Ctr., Huntington Beach, Calif., 1964—; cons. Hanford, Orange, Cypress police depts. (all Calif.), Saanich Police Dept., Victoria, B.C., Can., 1988; mem. Fed. Res. Fin. Bd., Washington; bd. dir. Consultron, Inc. Author: Law Enforcement Manager's Handbook. Pres. sports coun. YMCA; bd. dirs. Long Beach YMCA. Assoc. dir. mgmt. ctr. Chapman Coll., bd. dirs. mgmt. ctr. McKee Wright La Verne Coll., Cavaliers Fencing Schs., 1935—, Law Enforcement Mgmt. Ctr., Calif.; mgr. Stanton Bd. Trade, 1978—; Olympic fencing coach, 1984; pres. Ctr. for Strategic Planning, Orange County, Calif.; mem. fed. res. adv. bd. Recipient Personagraph Speaker of Yr. award Indsl Mgmt. Assn, Outstanding Law Enforcement Work award Calif. Atty. Gen., 1984; named to Am. Police Hall of Fame, 1984; recipient Charles R. Able citation for co. mgmt., Cert. of Merit Amateur Fencers League Am., Citizen of Yr. award Calif. Office Atty. Gen., 1984; resolution of thanks for work with police City of Hartford; resolution of Excellence Hartford City Coun.; Calif. Gov.'s award for civilian svc. to law enforcement; named Cavalier Fencing Coach of Yr., 1982; named to Pub. Hall of Fame, 1985; Nat. Police Hall of Fame, 1985; cert. instr. Calif. Dept. Justice POST program. Mem. Internat. Platform Assn., Am. Statis. Assn. (past pres., mem. nat. coun.). Nat. Mgmt. Assn. (recipient Silver Knight of Mgmt., 1961, v.p. area coun.), Nat. Assn. Chiefs of Police, Internat. Assn. Chiefs Police, Calif. Assn. Police Tng. Officers, Fedn. Internationale D'Esgrime, (hon.) Can. Mounted Police, Amateur Fencers League Am., AAAS, C. of C. (mem. rsch. com. of L.A.), Inst. Mgmt. Scis., Am. Assn. Indsl. Editors, Internat. Coun. Indsl. Editors, So. Calif. Indsl. Editors Assn., Nat. Assn. Bus. Economists, Orange County Econ. Roundtable (Exec. of Yr. award, pres.), Am. Soc. Quality Control (chmn. criminal justice sect.), Calif. Adminstrn. Justice Educators, Calif. Assn. Peace Officers, Can. N.W. Mounted Police, Phi Beta Kappa. Author: Learning Curves, Quantity-Cost Curves, Estimating Engineering Costs, Systems Analysis, Cost and Budgeting Analysis and Statistics for Non-Mathematical Managers; Zero Base Budgeting, The Fencer's Work Book, Fiscal Management, The Police Chief's Financial Handbook. Home: 16509 Harbour Ln Huntington Beach CA 92649 Office: Law Enforcement Mgmt Ctr 10801 Dale St Ste J-1 Stanton CA 90680

MC KEE, RAYMOND WALTER, accountant; b. Joplin, Mo., Dec. 24, 1899; s. Charles Edward and Sarah Ellen (Epperson) McK.; student pub. schs., Joplin; m. Frances Ida Howe, Nov. 1, 1947; children—Michael, David, Roderick, Duncan, Malcolm, Brude. Acct., Price, Waterhouse & Co., 1923-25, Haskins & Sells, 1925-26; pvt. practice acctg., La Puente, Calif., 1964—; lectr. St. Louis U., 1923-24; v.p. Richfield Oil Corp., Pan Am. Petroleum Corp., 1928-30; sec. West Coast Air Transport, 1926-30; sec.-treas. West Coast div. Anchor Hocking Corp.; dir., v.p. Maywood Mut. Water Co.; pres. Cross Water Co. Co-founder Nat. Paraplegia Found. (name now Nat. Spinal Cord Found.), 1947. C.P.A., Calif. Mem. Petroleum Accts. Soc. (co-founder). Club: Lions. Author: Accounting for Petroleum Industry, 1925; Petroleum Accounting, 1938; Saludos California, 1947; Book of McKee, 1959. Home and Office: 738 S 3d Ave La Puente CA 91746

MCKEE, RAYMOND WILLIAM, lawyer; b. Phila., July 25, 1948; s. Charles William and Catherine Marie (Keelan) McK.; m. Sharyn Udell, Sept. 12, 1976; l child, Carly Jahye. BA, Trinity Coll., Hartford, Conn., 1970; JD, U. Pa., 1973; LLM in Taxation, Georgetown U., 1979. Bar: Pa. 1973, U.S. Tax Ct. 1977, Calif. 1984. Law clk. to presiding justice Superior Ct. Pa., Phila., 1973-75; atty. Pa. Dept. Justice, St. Davids, 1975-77, IRS, Washington, 1977-81; assoc. tax counsel Security Pacific Corp., L.A., 1981-84, v.p., 1982-88, tax counsel, 1984-88, 1st v.p., sr. tax counsel, 1988-89, sr. v.p., 1989—. Mem. ABA, L.A. County Bar Assn., Calif. Bar Assn. Home: 2330 Midvale Ave Los Angeles CA 90064 Office: Security Pacific Corp 333 S Beaudry Ave Los Angeles CA 90017

MCKEE, ROBERT BRUCE, JR., engineering professor; b. Kalispell, Mont., Jan. 15, 1924; s. Robert Bruce and Myrtle Izora (Flaten) McK.; m. Ann Jameson, June 22, 1949 (div. 1970); m. Kathryn Joyce Vinyard, Oct. 8, 1970; children: Janet, James, Jane. BSME, Mont. State U., 1948; MSME, U. Wash., 1952; PhD, UCLA, 1967. Registered profl. engr., Nev. Engr. Pratt Whitney Aircraft, Hartford, Conn., 1948-50, Dow Chem. Co., Midland, Mich., 1952-56; chief engr. Mastro Plastics, N.Y.C., 1956-57; asst. prof. U. Nev., Reno, Nev., 1957-65; dir. indsl. extension U. Nev., Reno, 1966-69, prof. mech. engring., 1969—; engring. cons. Naval Weapons Ctr., China Lake, La., 1958-67. Author: Descriptive Geometry, 1966, Machine Design, 1984. Served with USAF, 1943-46. Mem. ASHRAE (pres. No. Nev. 1977), ASME. Republican. Methodist. Home: 590 Greenstone Reno NV 89512 Office: U Nevada Dept Mech Engring Reno NV 89557

MCKEE, ROGER CURTIS, judge, instructor; b. Waterloo, Iowa, Feb. 11, 1931; s. James A. and Leonace (Burrell) McK.; m. Roberta Jeanne Orvis, Sept. 3, 1954; children: Andrea Jane, Brian Curtis, Paul Robert. BA, State Coll. of Iowa, 1955; MA, U. Ill., 1960; JD, U. San Diego, 1968. Telegrapher, agt. Ill. Cen. R.R., 1950-55; tng. asst. No. Ill. Gas Co., Aurora, 1959-60; with indsl. rels. dept. Convair div. Gen. Dynamics Corp., San Diego, 1960-68; contract adminstr. and supr. Datagraphix div. Gen. Dynamics Corp., San Diego, 1968-69, asst. counsel, 1969-70; ptnr. Powell & McKee, San Diego, 1970-75, Millsberg, Dickstein & McKee, San Diego, 1975-83; judge U.S. Dist. Ct. (so. dist.) Calif., San Diego, 1983—. Bd. trustees So. Calif. Presbyn. Homes, L.A., 1979-81; moderator Presbytery of San Diego, 1980. Capt. USNR, 1949-85. Mem. Calif. Bar Assn., Nat. Coun. U.S. Magistrates, Navy League U.S., Naval Res. Officers Assn., Res. Officers Assn., Dixieland Jazz Soc. (bd. dirs. San Diego chpt. 1984—). Republican. Office: US Cts Bldg 940 Front St San Diego CA 92111

MCKEEL, R. BRUCE, investment banker; b. Oregon City, Oreg., Apr. 13, 1942; s. Ralph Orman and Gladys Anna (Palmer) McK.; m. Lynn E. Mackey, Feb. 14, 1976; children: Amber Lynn, Elizabeth Ann, Janette Kathryn, Tiffany Lane. B.A., U. Oreg., 1964. Investment banker Davis Skaggs & Co., San Francisco, 1968-73; v.p. HBE Leasing Corp., San Francisco, 1973-75; v.p. leverage leasing Equilease Corp. subs. Eltra Corp., San Francisco, 1975-77; pres., founder, dir. Qartel Corp., San Francisco, 1977-79; v.p. leverage leasing, spl. fin. project Prescott Ball & Turben, San Francisco, 1979-80; founder, chmn. bd., pres. McKeel & Co. Inc. and subs., 1980—; chmn. Pacific Air Lease Ltd., 1989—; spl. project fin. cons. to various nat. cos., 1979—. Vice chmn. spl. gifts United Crusade, 1978. Recipient Cert. distinction N.Y. Inst. Fin., 1968. Mem. Western Assn. Equipment Lessors (past officer, dir.), Am. Assn. Equipment Lessors, Olympic of San Francisco Club, City Club of San Francisco, Hillsborough Racquet Club. Republican. Episcopalian. Home: 560 Hayne Rd Hillsborough CA 94010 Office: 155 Sansome St San Francisco CA 94104

MCKELLAR, DARLENE IRIS, restaurant owner; b. Waukegan, Ill., Dec. 30, 1945; d. Glen Wiley and Lillian Ann Root; divorced; children: Ken, John, Bruce. Grad. high sch., Tucson. Owner, operator McDonald's Restaurant, Santa Fe, N.Mex., 1977—. V.p. Cochise County Children's Ctr., 1984-85. Recipient Ken Ferguson award Sierra Vista C. of C., 1986, Outstanding Leadership award, 1989. Mem. Women Operators Network (founder, chmn. 1988--), So. Ariz. Operators Assn. (pres. 1986-88).

MCKELVEY, GEORGE IRWIN, III, college executive; b. Glen Ridge, N.J., May 5, 1925; s. George Irwin, Jr., and Florence (Samuel) McK.; m. Velma E. Vergara, June 28, 1959; 1 son, George Stuart. A.B. in History, U. Rochester, 1950, M.A. in Govt., 1958. Exec. sec. Alumni Assn. U. Rochester, N.Y., 1950-56, Alumni Fedn., U. Rochester, 1953-56, dir. alumni relations, 1955-56; assoc. dir. Am. Alumni Council, Washington, 1956-57; dir. devel. Harvey Mudd Coll., Claremont, Calif., 1957-68, v.p. devel. and planning, 1968-88, v.p., 1988—. Trustee Raymond M. Alf Mus., Claremont, 1982—; bd. dirs. Bates Found. for Aero. Edn., Claremont. Served with USN, 1943-46. Mem. Council for Advancement and Support of Edn., Psi Upsilon. Republican. Presbyterian. Club: University (Los Angeles). Office: Harvey Mudd Coll 12th St Claremont CA 91711

MCKENNA, JOHN DWAINE, financial company executive, stockbroker; b. Monticello, N.Y., Oct. 31, 1946; s. John Atkins and Catherine Francis (O'Toole) McK.; m. June Lynn, May 24, 1976. Student, U. Miami, 1964-65, Sullivan County Community Coll., South Fallsburg, N.Y., 1965-66, Borough Manhattan Community Coll., 1966-67, The Colo. Coll., 1968-69; cert. teaching, The Options Inst., 1985. Lic. resident agt., Colo. Stockbroker, sales mgr. Richey Frankel and Co., Colorado Springs, Colo., 1981-84; v.p., registered options prin. Malone and Assocs., Denver, 1984-85; v.p., br. mgr. Nat. Securities Network, Inc., Colorado Springs, 1985-88; v.p., syndications mgr. corp. office Nat. Securities Network, Inc., Englewood, Colo., 1988—. Contbr. articles to bus. mags. Arbitrator Better Bus. Bur., Colorado Springs, 1988; fundraiser Am. Cancer Soc., Colorado Springs, 1988; presenter Urban League, Colorado Springs, 1986-87. Mem. Bd. Arbitrators, Nat. Assn. Securities Dealers (arbitrator 1986—). Republican. Methodist. Home: 6570 Ashcroft Dr Colorado Springs CO 80918 Office: Nat Securities Network Inc 5500 S Greenwood Plaza Blvd Ste 240 Englewood CO 80111

MCKENNA, PATRICK JAMES, management consultant; b. Edson, Alta., Can., Oct. 31, 1951; s. James Edward and Madeline (Watson) McK.; C.I.M., Can. Inst. Mgmt., Toronto, Ont., 1979, P. Mgr., 1977, M.B.A., 1982, I.C.I.A., 1985. Asst. div. mgr. Hudsons Bay Co., Edmonton, Alta., 1973-75; gen. mgr. Alta. C. of C. Edmonton, 1975-78; mng. dir. QCTV Ltd., Edmonton, 1978-81; v.p. Achieve Enterprises Ltd., Edmonton, 1981-83; ptnr. The Edge Group, Edmonton, 1983—; dir. Nebula Holdings Ltd., Edmonton, 1980—, Can. Inst. Mgmt., 1981-85; chmn. bd. Saxby Payne & Cook Inc., Edmonton, 1988. Co-author: Creating the Marketing Mindset, 1989; editor: The Enterprizer Quar., 1976. Contbr. articles to profl. jours. Advisor on bus. administrn. Lakeland Coll., Lloydminister, Sask., 1984; bd. dirs. Jr. Achievement of Alta., 1984; dir. Edmonton Ctr. P.C. Party Assn., Alta., 1988. Mem. Can. Inst. Mgmt. (bd. dirs. 1981-84), Guild ICIA (chmn. 1986—), Cert. Gen. Accts. Assn. of Alta (mem. profl. conduct com. 1988—), Am. Mktg. Assn., Internat. Assn. Strategic Planning Cons. (founding mem.), Canadian Bar Assn., ABA, Alta. Entrepreneurs Assn. (founding mem.), Alta. Conf. Soc. (founding mem.), Inst. Outdoor Conservation (founding mem.). Conservative.). Home: 4242 111th Ave, Edmonton, AB Canada T5W 0K2

MCKENZIE, JACK VERNER, municipal official; b. Friday Harbor, Wash., June 6, 1934; s. William Bruce and Mary Emmaline (McCall) McK.; m. Mary Alice McMullen, Sept. 7, 1957; children: William Joseph, Elizabeth Ann. BBA, U. Wash., 1957. Cert. mcpl. fin. adminstr., profl. fin. officer, Wash. Sr. systems analyst GTE Northwest, Everett, Wash., 1965-69; revenue acctg. mgr. GTE Northwest, Everett, 1967-69, data processing mgr., 1969; fin. and budget dir. City of Everett, 1969-73; comptroller, treas. County of King, Seattle, 1973-74; pres. Precision Airmotive Corp., Everett, 1974-75; fin. advisor Harper, McLean & Co., Seattle, 1976-79; pres. McKenzie Moving and Storage, Inc., Seattle, 1979-82; asst. treas. City of Seattle, 1982--. Mem. Mcpl. Treas. Assn. of U.S. and Can., Wash. Fin. Officers Assn. (pres. 1973-74), Wash. Mcpl. Treas. Assn. (bd. dirs. 1989—). Office: City of Seattle 103 Municipal Bldg Seattle WA 98104

MCKENZIE, JAN ADELE, nurse, educator; b. Portland, Oreg., Aug. 19, 1953; d. Lyle Gordon and Dorothy May (Robinson) Nicholson. BS in Nursing with honors, Oreg. Health Scis. U., 1976; postgrad., Idaho State U., 1986—. Staff nurse Oreg. Health Scis. U., Portland, 1978-80; clinic nurse Sylvan Med. Clinic, Portland, 1981-82; staff nurse Magic Valley Regional Med. Ctr., Twin Falls, Idaho, 1983—; clin. instr. nursing students Coll. So. Idaho, —, 1988—. Mem. Am. Nurses Assn., Idaho Nurses Assn. (jr. dir. 1988—), Sigma Theta Tau. Office: Coll So Idaho Nursing Dept 315 Falls Ave Twin Falls ID 83301

MCKENZIE, LAURA ELIZABETH, travel critic, author; b. Kansas City, Mo., June 4, 1956; d. Leonard Ralph and Marcella (Neise) Yocum; m. David L. McKenzie, July 21, 1979. AA, Wash. U., St. Louis, 1976. Entertainer Serendipity Singers, internat. locations, 1975-80; news, weather reporter Sta. KMIR-TV, Calif., 1980-82; feature reporter Sta. LPN News Svc., L.A., 1982-87; TV travel reporter Travel Tips News Features, 1988—; host, producer Travel Tips Home Video Guides, L.A., 1988—; cons. Rep. Pictures, Los Angeles, 1986—. Author: London, 1988, San Francisco, 1988, Rome, 1988, Travel Tips Guidebooks, 1988—. Mem. NAFE, Screen Actors Guild, Writers Guild Am. Club: Magic Castle (Hollywood, Calif.). Office: Associated Entertainment Releasing PO Box 4180 Hollywood CA 90078

MCKENZIE, MERLE, aerospace engineer; b. Denver, Aug. 30, 1954; s. Keith Edward and Betsy Louise (Vogel) Gehrke. BS, Calif. Inst. Tech., 1977; postgrad., U. So. Calif., 1985-86. Engr. Jet Propulsion Lab., Pasadena, Calif., 1976-79, sr. engr., 1979-81, group leader, 1981-83, group supr., 1983-87, mgr. space sta. software issues, 1986-87, mgr. space sta. info. system analysis, 1987, tech. asst. to dirs. office, 1988—; cons. aerospace and telecommunications orgns., 1986—. Reviewer Engring. Mgmt. Internat. jour., 1984; contbr. articles to profl. jours. Scholar Calif. Inst. Tech., 1972-76, Boettcher, 1972, U. Colo., 1972. Mem. AIAA (chmn. econs. tech. com., publs. subcom. 1983-86, chmn. econs. standards com. 1986-87, nat. and L.A. sect. pub. policy com. 1983-85), Sigma Xi. Office: Jet Propulsion Lab MS 180-900 4800 Oak Grove Dr Pasadena CA 91109

MCKENZIE, TOM H., real property analyst; b. Spokane, Wash., Dec. 21, 1938; s. Walter A. and Myrtle A. (Hagaman) McK.; m. Beverly K. Good, July 19, 1969 (div.); 1 son, Brad; m. Betty J. Pearson, July 25, 1981. MA, Western States U., PhD. Lic. broker, Calif. Salesman, br. mgr. Hawaii The Pillsbury Co., 1964-67; sales mgr. So. Star Spice & Tea Co., L.A., 1967-68; dist. sales mgr. So. Claif., Ariz., Nev. Fairmont Foods Co., San Lorenzo, Calif., 1968-69; loan officer Calif. Mortgage Svc., Santa Ana, 1969-73; real property analyst/pres. AAA Appraisals Inc. and predecessor, Santa Ana, 1972—; expert witness superior and fed. cts.; instr. profl. courses Acad. of Real Estate Appraisal, NW Ctr. Profl. Edn., Soc. of Real Estate Appraisers, Calif. Sch. Real Estate Appraisal. With U.S. Army, 1961-63. Mem. Am. Soc. Appraisers, Am. Inst. Real Estate Appraisers (MAI designation), Soc. Real Estate Appraisers, Nat. Assn. Rev. Appraisers (sr.), Soc. Subdiv. Appraisers (sr.), Masons. Republican. Presbyterian. Home: 2351 Fig Tree Dr Tustin CA 92680 Office: AAA Appraisals Inc 415 N Sycamore St Ste 100 Santa Ana CA 92701

MCKEON, JOHN ALOYSIUS (JACK MCKEON), professional baseball team executive; b. South Amboy, N.J., Nov. 23, 1930; m. Carol McKeon; children: Kelly, Kasey, Kristi, Kori. BA in Phys. Edn. and Sci., Elon Coll. Baseball mgr. in 13 maj. and minor league citie; mgr. Kansas City Royals, Am. League, 1973-75, Oakland A's, 1977-78; v.p. baseball ops. San Diego Padres, Nat. League, 1980—, mgr., 1988—. bd. dirs. San Diego Make-a-Wish Found. Office: San Diego Padres PO Box 2000 San Diego CA 92120 *

MCKIM, HARRIET MEGCHELSEN, educator; b. Keokuk, Iowa, Oct. 17, 1919; d. Herbert John and Florence Josephine (Ottowa) Megchelsen; m. Lanier McClure, Nov. 1, 1944 (div. 1948); 1 child, Janet Gray; m. L.A. McKim, July 28, 1950 (div. 1968). BA, Sacramento State U., 1952; MA, U. So. Calif., 1963, EdD, 1979. Tchr., prin. Cumberland County Schs., Crossville, Tenn., 1939-42; sec. Tenn. Valley Authority, Oak Ridge Def. Plant, Mare Island Naval Shipyard and Cal-West Ins., 1942-52; tchr., vice-prin., reading specialist, dir. ESEA I various pub. schs., Oxnard, Orcutt, Sacramento, Edwards AFB, Calif. and Spokane, Wash., 1950-64; cons. Calif. Dept. Edn., Yuba County, 1964-83; coordinator Yuba County Schs., 1964-83; supr. student tchrs. Calif. State U., Sacramento, 1984; adj. prof. edn. Nat. U., Sacramento, 1986-88; part-time instr. Alan Hancock Community Coll., Santa Maria, Calif., Polytech. U., San Luis Obispo, Calif., U. Calif., Davis, Santa Barbara, 1960-70; supr. student tchrs. Calif. State U., Sacramento, 1984; adj. prof. edn. Nat. U., Sacramento, 1986-88. Vol. tchr. Am. Red Cross parenting classes, Sacramento, 1984-85; active Dukakis campaign, 1988; docent, speaker Crocker Art Mus.; vol. Loaves and Fishes; bd. dirs. Sacramento Internat. Students' Coun.; docent Sacramento History Ctr.; deacon Fremont Presbyn. Ch. Mem. AAUW, Nat. Assn. Edn. Young Children, Calif. Retired Tchrs., Am. Assn. Retired Persons Assn., Profs. of Early Childhood Edn., Sacramento Affiliates, Amnesty Internat., Delta Kappa Gamma, Sierra Club. Address: 5332 State Ave Sacramento CA 95819

MCKINLEY, JOSEPH WARNER, health science facility executive; b. Champaign, Ill., Jan. 9, 1943; s. Lyle Warner and Eloise M. (Coleman) McK. BS, Georgetown U., 1968; MBA, George Washington U., 1973. Asst. adminstr. Weiss Meml. Hosp., Chgo., 1973-75; assoc. v.p. Rockford (Ill.) Meml. Hosp., 1975-78; v.p. ops. Phoenix Meml. Hosp., 1978-84, exec. v.p., chief exec. officer, 1984-88; exec. v.p. St. Francis Med. Ctr., Lynwood, Calif., 1988—. Capt. U.S. Army, 1968-71, Vietnam. Mem. Am. Coll. of Healthcare Execs., Am. Hosp. Assn., Ariz. Club, Plaza Club. Republican. Episcopalian. Home: 5339 E Broadway Long Beach CA 90803 Office: St Francis Med Ctr 3630 E Imperial Hwy Lynwood CA 90262

MCKINLEY, MARK LEE, marketing professional; b. Pasadena, Calif., Jan. 30, 1953; s. William White and Ann Elise (Young) McK.; m. Teresa Marie Huberd, Nov. 15, 1985; 1 child, Michelle Marie. BA in Bus. and Lit., U. Redlands, 1975; MA in Econs., U. Oreg., 1977. Ptnr. Hansen & McKinley Cons., Ashland, Oreg., 1977-81; pres. Monarch Systems, Inc., Lake Oswego, Oreg., 1982—; instr. econs. So. Oreg. State Coll., Ashland, 1977-78, instr. stats., 1978-81. Chmn. Jackson County Econ. Devel. Commn., 1978. Office: Monarch Systems Inc 9 Monroe Pkwy Lake Oswego OR 97035-1425

MC KINLEY, ROYCE BALDWIN, business executive, lawyer; b. Ann Arbor, Mich., Feb. 20, 1921; s. Earle B. and Leola (Royce) McK.; m. Roberta Schreck, Apr. 15, 1943; 1 dau., Martha Lee; m. Anne de Beixedon, July 7, 1973. Student, Harvard U., 1938-40; A.B., U. Mich., 1942; J.D., Harvard U., 1948; LL.M., George Washington U., 1951. Bar: D.C. 1949, Mo. 1953, Ill. 1959. Practiced in Washington 1948-52; counsel Ralston Purina Co., St. Louis, 1952-55; assoc. McKinsey & Co., Inc., Chgo. and London, 1955-60; v.p., sec. Electro-Sci.-Investors, Inc., Dallas, 1960-63; v.p. finance and adminstrn. Space Gen. Corp., El Monte, Calif., 1963-66; asst. dir. mgmt. systems TRW, Inc., Redondo Beach, Calif., 1967-68; v.p. fin., sec.-treas. Santa Anita Consol., Inc., Los Angeles, 1968-73; exec. v.p., chief operating officer Santa Anita Consol., Inc., 1973-79; also dir.; pres., chief exec. officer Santa Anita Realty Enterprises, Inc., Los Angeles, 1980—, also dir.; dir. Santa Anita Operating Co., Arcadia, Calif., Los Angeles Turf Club, Arcadia, Minn. Racetrack Inc. Served to lt. (j.g.) USNR, 1943-46. Mem. Nat. Assn. Real Estate Investment Trusts (bd. govs. 1981—, pres. 1985-86). Club: California (Los Angeles). Home: 262 S Orange Dr Los Angeles CA 90036 Office: Santa Anita Realty Enteprises Inc 1 Wilshire Bldg Ste 1709 Los Angeles CA 90017

MCKINNEY, JAMES WARREN, regional sales manager; b. Poplar Bluff, Mo., Oct. 21, 1932; s. James Franklin and Helen Marie (Gatlin) McK.; m. Wanda Jean Wagner, Apr. 4, 1953 (div. 1959); m. Doris Maxine Bladwin, Feb. 22, 1963; children: Joan Marie McKinney McCune, Phyllis Ann Cate, Vanessa Lynn. BS in Cemistry, Kansas City U., Mo., 1957; PhD in Chemistry (hon.), Kansas City U., 1972. Ordained deacon, Bapt. Ch. Chemist Mo. Pacific R.R. Co., Kansas City, Mo., 1955-61; chief water chemist Mo. Pacific R.R. Co., Little Rock, 1961-67; rsch. chemist Midwest Rsch. Inst., Kansas City, 1959-60; territory mgr. Frank J. Brogan Co., Dallas, 1967-75; v.p. sales Frank J. Brogan Co., 1975-80; regional sales mgr. Felt Products Mfg., Inc., Skokie, Ill., 1980—. Bd. trustees Ednl. and Scholastic Found. A.B.C.I., Glenview, Ill., 1988—. Mem. N.Mex. Automotive Whoesaler Assn., Automotive Wholesaler Idaho (chmn. 1985—), rocky Mountain Wholesaler Assn., NRA (life), Nat. Geographi Soc., Automotive Booster Club (life, chmn., bd. dirs. 1988—, Man of Yr. award 1988). Republican. Home: 11894 So Aspen Ridge Rd Sandy UT 84094 Office: Felt Products Mfg Inc Box C 1103 Skokie IL 60076

MC KINNEY, MONTGOMERY NELSON, advertising executive; b. Chgo., June 20, 1910; s. William Ayer and Roberta (Montgomery) McK.; m. Virginia Dickey, Nov. 2, 1957; children by previous marriage: Jane McKinney McDonald, William; children: Beth McKinney Lavarn, Robert. BA, Oberlin Coll., 1934, HHD (hon.), 1989. Treas., with sales, advt. and sales promotion depts. Kitchen Art Foods, Inc., Chgo., 1934-40; v.p. Earle Ludgin & Co., Chgo., 1940-55; account supr. Leo Burnett Co., Inc., Chgo., 1956; v.p. Doyle Dane Bernbach, Inc., Los Angeles, 1957-69, sr. v.p. client services, 1969-75; exec. v.p., dir. client services Chiat/Day, Inc., Los Angeles, 1975-76, chmn. bd., 1976-83; chmn. Doyle Dane Bernbach/West, Los Angeles, 1983-86, DDB Needham West (merger Doyle Dane Bernbach and Needham, Harper and Steers), Los Angeles, 1986-87; vice chmn. Kresser, Craig/D.I.K., 1988—; mem. faculty Inst. Advanced Advt. Studies, 1964-68. Chmn. campaign Winnetka (Ill.) Community Chest, 1950, pres., 1952; trustee John Thomas Dye Sch., Bel Air, Calif., 1966-75, pres., 1973-75; trustee Oberlin Coll., 1971-85, emeritus trustee, 1986— ; trustee, chmn. fin. com. Winnetka Congregational Ch., 1950-56. Served to lt. USNR, 1944-46. Recipient silver medal Am. Advt. Fedn., 1983. Mem. Am. Assn. Advt. Agys. (gov. So. Calif. council 1972-76, sec.-treas. 1972, vice chmn. 1973, chmn. 1974-75, nat. dir. 1981-83), West States Assn. Advt. Agys. (dir. 1978-83, Advt. Leader of Yr. 1980), Los Angeles Advt. Club. Methodist (trustee 1970-74, vice chmn. 1973-74). Clubs: Riviera Country (Pacific Palisades, Calif.); Los Angeles Athletic. Home: 140 Ocean Park Blvd #625 Santa Monica CA 90405 Office: Kresser Craig/DIK 2029 Century Park E Ste 520 Los Angeles CA 90067

MCKINNEY, SALLY VITKUS, realty company executive, business owner; b. Muncie, Ind., Aug. 6, 1944; d. Robert Brookins and Mary (Mann) Gooden; m. Alan George Vitkus (div. Jan. 1979); m. James Larry McKinney, Feb. 1, 1986; children: Robert, James, Lee Alice. AA, William Woods Coll., 1964; BSBA, U. Ariz., 1966; postgrad., U. Nev., Las Vegas, 1966-68. Tchr. Las Vegas Day Sch., 1972-76; salesperson Globe Realty, Las Vegas, 1976-79; owner, pres. Realty West, Las Vegas, 1979—. Rec. sec. Clark County Rep. Cen. Com., Las Vegas, 1982, 1st vice chmn., 1985; vice chmn. Nev. Rep. com., 1986, chmn., 1987-88; mem. Assistance League Las Vegas. Recipient award Nat. Assn. Home Builders, 1981, 82, 83. Mem. Nat. Assn. Realtors, Las Vegas Bd. Realtors, Greater Las Vegas C. of C., Gen. Fedn. Womens Clubs (Outstanding Young Womam Am. 1979, exec. bd. 1980-82), Jr. League Las Vegas, Mesquite Club (chmn. pub. affairs com. 1986-87, past pres.). Presbyterian. Home: 3114 Pradera Circle Las Vegas NV 89121 Office: Realty West 3340 S Topaz St Ste 40B Las Vegas NV 89121

MCKINNIS, STEVEN RAY, electrical engineer; b. Lyons, Kans., Jan. 3, 1952; s. Richard I. and Marian J. (Link) McK.; m. Donna K. Copen, Nov. 19, 1989. BS in EE, Kans. State U., 1974; MS in EE, Minn. U., 1982. Registered profl. engr., Minn. Engr. govt. electronics div. Motorola, Scottsdale, Ariz., 1975-78, Honeywell Def. Systems, Hopkins, Minn., 1978-82; staff engr. Motorola Semiconductor Products, Phoenix, 1982. Inventor low side power switch. Mem. IEEE, Tau Beta Pi. Office: Motorola SLAICG 7402 S Price Rd Tempe AZ 85283

MC KINNON, CLINTON D., editor, former congressman; b. Dallas, Feb. 5, 1906; s. John C. and Tennie Clifdell (Hawkins) McK.; m. Lucille Virginia McVey, Oct. 15, 1932; children—Clinton Dan, Michael, Connie. A.B., U. Redlands, Calif., 1930, L.H.D. (hon.), 1967; postgrad., U. Geneva, Switzerland, 1930. Reporter, editor, advt. mgr. on various So. Calif. newspapers, 1931-35; pres., gen. mgr. Valley News Corp., North Hollywood, Calif., 1935-43; established San Fernando Valley Times, 1935, Los Angeles Aircraft Times, 1940, Long Beach Shipyard Times, 1941; established San Diego Daily Jour., 1944, editor, pub. and owner, 1944-48; co-owner Coronado Jour., 1953-72; owner Radio Sta. KSDJ (Columbia affiliate), San Diego, 1945-48; pres., editor and pub. Los Angeles Daily News, 1954; pres., gen. mgr. Alvarado Television Co., Inc., KVOA-TV, Tucson and KOAT-TV, Albuquerque, 1955-63; chmn. San Diego North Shores Pub. Co., San Diego, 1953-72, Sentinel Savs. and Loan Assn., 1963-69, San Diego Transit Co., 1966-71; sec. South Tex. Telecasting Co. Inc., 1963-79; Chmn. Indsl. Devel. Commn., San Diego, 1964-66, Econ. Devel. Corp., San Diego County, 1966-67, San Diego Urban Coalition, 1967-69; mem. Gov.'s Bus. Adv. Council, Calif. Bd. dirs. U. Calif., San Diego Sch. Medicine, 1979—; bd. dirs. Cancer Center Research Bd., U. Calif., San Diego, 1981—; Mem. 81st-82d Congresses from Calif.; vice chmn. Democratic State Central Com. of Calif., 1952-54. Recipient San Diego Golden Man and Boy award, 1968; San Diego Mayor's award of merit, 1971; named to San Diego Transit Hall Fame, 1987. Clubs: Rotarian, San Diego Yacht. Home: 1125 Pacific Beach Dr Apt 401 San Diego CA 92109 Office: 4425 Cass St San Diego CA 92109

MCKINNON, JAMES BUCKNER, real estate salesman, writer; b. Tacoma, Dec. 5, 1916; s. James Mitchell and Rochelle Lenore (Buckner) McK.; m. Marylyn Adelle Coote, Mar. 12, 1967 (div. May 1977); children: Michelyn, James H.C. McK.; m. Martha Sackmann, June 12, 1977. BA in Internat. Studies, U. Wash., 1983, H.M. Jackson Sch. Police detective Los Angeles Police Dept., 1946-50; bn. security officer 1st med. bn. 1st Marine div. Fleet Marine Force, 1950-53; owner, operator, mgr., dir. promotional sales The Saucy Dog Drive-In, Venice, Calif., 1953-63; salesman new car sales and leasing Burien Mercury, Seattle, 1963-66; real estate salesman and appraiser various firms Seattle, 1966—; instr., lectr. U.S. Naval Support Activity, Sandpoint, Wash., 1964-74; mem., lectr. NRC 11-8, Naval Postgrad. Sch., Monterey, Calif., 1975-76; Burien Mercury announcer KOMO TV. Published poetry in anthologies; contbr. articles to various newspapers and mil. jours. Served with USN, 1939-53, PTO, Korea. Recipient Wilmer Culver Meml. award Culver Alumni Fictioneers, Seattle, 1979; Occidental Coll. scholar, 1935, Silver Poet award, 1986, Golden Poet award, 1987, 88; named to Honorable Order Ken. Cols., 1976, One of Best New Poets, Am. Poetry Assn., 1988. Mem. Internat. Platform Assn., U.S. Naval Inst., N.W. Writers Conf., Ret. Officers Assn. (life), Mensa, KP, Masons. Republican. Home: 2312 41st Ave SW Seattle WA 98116

MCKNIGHT, EDWARD LAURENCE, psychologist; b. Portland, Oreg., July 30, 1927; s. Edward Prescott and Florence Margaret (Markmann) McK.; m. Eleanor May McGill, Aug. 22, 1955; children: Edward Laurence, John Prescott. BA in Music, U. Wash., 1957; MS in Psychology, Wash. State U., 1961. Cert. sch. psychologist, Wash.; lic. psychologist, Wash. Ednl. diagnostician, tchr. Wash. State Cerebral Palsy Ctr., Seattle, 1957-59, resident psychologist, sch. dist. cons., 1960-65, supt., 1973-79; sch. psychologist, coord. spl. edn. Highline Pub. Schs., Seattle, 1965-67; sch. psychologist Mercer Island (Wash.) Pub. Schs., 1967-73, 79-83, coord. spl. edn., 1967-73; pvt. practice Edmonds, Wash., 1983—; park ranger Olympic Nat. Park, Nat. Park Svc., Port Angeles, Wash., summers 1970-77; psychol. cons. Resource Child Ctr., Mountlake Terrace, Wash., 1982—; speaker in field. Contbr. articles to various publs. Scoutmaster Boy Scouts Am., Edmonds, 1968-71, trainer explorer search and rescue, Seattle, 1971-79, ops. leader, 1971—, chmn., 1987—. With U.S. Mcht. Marine, 1945-47, PTO, USAF, 1950-54. Recipient dist. award of merit Chief Seattle coun. Boy Scouts Am., 1987. Fellow Am. Assn. on Mental Retardation (ret.). Republican. Episcopalian. Home and Office: 8203 215th St SW Edmonds WA 98020

MCKNIGHT, LENORE RAVIN, child psychiatrist; b. Denver, May 15, 1943; d. Abe and Rose (Steed) Ravin; student Occidental Coll., 1961-63; B.A., U. Colo., 1965, postgrad. in medicine, 1965-67; M.D., U. Calif., San Francisco, 1969; m. Robert Lee McKnight, July 22, 1967; children—Richard Rex, Janet Rose. Cert. adult and child psychiatrist Am. Bd. Psychiatry. Intern pediatrics Children's Hosp., San Francisco, 1969-70; resident in gen. psychiatry Langley Porter Neuropsychiat. Inst., 1970-73, fellow child psychiatry, 1972-74; child psychiatrist Youth Guidance Center, San Francisco, 1974-74; pvt. practice medicine specializing in child psychiatry, Walnut Creek, Calif., 1974—; asst. clin. prof. Langley Porter Neuropsychiat. Inst., 1974—; asst. clin. prof. psychiatry U. Calif. San Francisco Med. Center. Diplomate Am. Bd. Psychiatry and Neurology. Internat. Insts. Edn. fellow U. Edinburgh, summer 1964; NIH grantee to study childhood nutrition, summer 1966. Mem. Am. Acad. Child Psychiatry, Am. Psychiat. Assn., Psychiat. Assn. No. Calif., Am. Med. Women's Assn., Internat., Diablo arabian horse assns. Breeder Arabian horses. Home: 3441 Echo Springs Rd Lafayette CA 94549 Office: 130 LaCasa Via Walnut Creek CA 94598

MC KOY, BASIL VINCENT CHARLES, theoretical chemist, educator; b. Trinidad, W.I., Mar. 25, 1938; came to U.S., 1960, naturalized, 1973; s. Allan Cecil and Doris Augusta McK.; m. Anne Ellen Shannon, Mar. 18, 1967; 1 son, Christopher Allan. B.Chem. Eng., N.S. Tech. U., 1960; Ph.D. in Chemistry (Univ. fellow), Yale U., 1964. Instr. chemistry Calif. Inst. Tech., 1964-66, asst. prof. chemistry, 1966-69, asso. prof., 1969-75, prof. theoretical chemistry, 1975—, chmn. of faculty, 1985-87; cons. Lawrence Livermore Lab., U. Calif., Livermore, 1974—, Inst. Def. Analysis, 1984—; vis. prof. Max Planck Inst., Munich, Ger., 1976—, U. Paris, 1968—, U. Campinas, Brazil, 1976—; lectr. Nobel Symposium, Goteborg, Sweden, 1979. Contbr. articles to Jour. Physics, London, Chem. Physics Letters, Phys. Rev., Jour. Chem. Physics.; bd. editors: Chem. Physics Jour., 1977-79; co-editor: Electron-Molecule and Photon-Molecule Collisions, 1979, 83, Swarm Studies and Inelastic Electron-Molecule Collisions, 1986; co-author: Electron-Molecule Collisions and Photoionization Processes, 1982. Recipient medal Gov.-Gen. Can., 1960; Alfred P. Sloan Found. fellow, 1969-73; Guggenheim fellow, 1973-74. Fellow Am. Phys. Soc. Home: 3855 Keswick Rd Flintridge CA 91011 Office: Calif Inst Tech Div Chemistry Pasadena CA 91125

MCLAIN, WILL KING, information systems executive; b. Pitts., Mar. 8, 1937; s. Benjamin McLain and Margaret Charlotte (Swinston) Kittle; m. Norma Lucille Butler, Feb. 6, 1964 (div. Mar. 1984); children: Matthew King, Erin Margaret, Michael John; m. Lois Evelyn Dodds, Oct. 12, 1984. BS in Mining Engring., U. Ariz., 1961. Field engr. various positions, Southeast Asia, 1964-67; dep. mng. dir. Techdata, Ltd., Bangkok, 1967-68; project mgr. Geotronics, Teledyne, L.A., 1968-69; pres. Resource Cons., Inc., Tucson and Phoenix, 1970-78; exec. v.p., pres., chief exec. officer Dyna Resources, Inc., Phoenix, 1979-85; pres., chief exec. officer Internat. Geographics Corp., Phoenix, 1986—, Cad-Tel Systems, Inc., Phoenix, 1987-89; pres., chief exec. officer Internat. GeoGraphics Corp., Phoenix, 1989—, also bd. dirs. Bd. dirs. Enterprise Network, Phoenix, 1989—. Maj. USMCR, 1955-77. Mem. Nat. Computer Graphics Assn., AM/FM Internat. Republican. Episcopalian. Office: Internat Geographics Corp 740 E Highland #107 Phoenix AZ 85014

MCLAIN, WILLIAM ALLEN, lawyer; b. Chgo., Oct. 19, 1942; s. William Rex and Wilma L. (Raschka) McL.; divorced; children: William A., David M., Heather A. BS, So. Ill. U., 1966; JD, Loyola U., Chgo., 1971. Bar: Ill. 1971, U.S. Dist. Ct. (no. dist.) Ill. 1971, U.S. Ct. Appeals (7th cir.) 1971, Colo. 1975, U.S. Dist. Ct. Colo. 1975, U.S. Ct. Appeals (10th cir.) 1975. Law clk. U.S. Dist. Ct. (no. dist.) Ill., Chgo., 1971-72; assoc. Sidley & Austin, Chgo., 1972-75; ptnr. Welborn, Dufford, Brown & Tooley, Denver, 1975-86; pres. William A. McLain PC, 1986—, Interact, Inc., 1986—. Mem. Dist. 10 Legis. Vacancy Commn., Denver, 1984-86. Served with U.S. Army, 1966-68. Recipient Leadership and Scholastic Achievement award Loyola U. Alumni Assn., 1971. Mem. ABA, Colo. Bar Assn. (lobbyist 1983-85), Denver Bar Assn., Assn. Trial Lawyers Am., Colo. Assn. Commerce and Industry (legis. policy coun. 1983-88), Colo. Mining Assn. (state and local affairs com. 1978—). Republican. Clubs: Denver Athletic, Roundup Riders of the Rockies. Lodges: Masons, Shriners, Scottish Rite, York Rite. Home and Office: 304 Lincoln St Denver CO 80203

MCLANE, SUSAN MARGARET, investment company executive; b. San Francisco, Feb. 4, 1956; d. Roy E. and Sally McLane; m. Robert N. Block, Mar. 8, 1980. BA in Communication Studies with honors, UCLA, 1979, MBA in Fin. with honors, 1987. Acct. Kendall & Warner, CPA's, Los Angeles, 1981; v.p., treas. Pacific Fin. Research, Beverly Hills, Calif., 1981—; treas. Clipper Fund, Inc., Beverly Hills, 1984—, also bd. dirs., 1984—. Edward M. Carter fellow UCLA, 1987. Mem. Phi Beta Kappa, Beta Gamma Sigma, Alpha Phi. Home: 2697 Deep Canyon Dr Beverly Hills CA 90210 Office: Pacific Fin Rsch 9601 Wilshire Blvd Ste 828 Beverly Hills CA 90210

MCLAREN, ARCHIE CAMPBELL, JR, marketing executive; b. Atlanta, Sept. 25, 1942; s. Archie Campbell and Virginia Lynn (Sides) McL.; m. Georgia Mae Blunt; 1969 (div. 1971); 1 child, Leslie Michelle. BA, Vanderbilt U., 1964; JD, Memphis State U., 1968. Clk. FBI, Memphis, 1965-66; tchr., tennis coach Memphis U. Sch., 1966-68; tchr. Hunt High Sch., Columbus, Miss., 1968-69; tennis coach Miss. State U., Starkville, Miss., 1968-69; concierge The Roosevelt Hotel, New Orleans, 1969-70; sales rep. West Pub. Co., St. Paul, 1970-84, adminstr. internat. mktg. The Orient, 1985—; freelance wine cons. 1985—; cons. Calif. Cen. Coast Wine Growers Assn., Santa Maria, 1987—; lectr. advanced wine appreciation Calif. Poly. U. Extended Edn., San Luis Obispo, 1986—; dir. KCBX Cen. Coast Wine Classic, San Luis Obispo, 1985—, KHPR, Wine Classic, Honolulu, 1987—, Winesong, Ft. Bragg, Calif., 1987—, WETA Washington Wine Classic, 1989—. Bd. dirs. San Luis Obispo Calif. Mozart Festival, 1988—. Mem. Calif. Cen. Coast Wine Soc. (pres. 1985), Am. Soc. Wine Educators, Bailli Cen. Coast Calif. Confrerie Chaine Rotisseurs, Calif. Wine Writers Forum, San Luis Bay Inn Wine Food Soc., German Wine Soc. Honolulu, Vintners Club San Francisco, Alaska Les Amis Vin (bd. dirs), Ferrari. Food, Wine & Travel Writers' Assn., Austrian Wine Brotherhood, Ferrari Owners Club, Honolulu Club. Office: 4100 Vachell Ln San Luis Obispo CA 93401

MCLAREN, MARY LEE, real estate professional; b. St. Louis, Apr. 7, 1919; d. William Adolphus and Beulah Kirk (Radford) Seeger; m. Joseph Shapiro, July 2, 1939 (div.); children: David A., Daniel L.; m. Ennis C. McLaren, Feb. 27, 1953; 1 child, D. Michael. Student, U. Mo., 1938-40. Broker McLaren Realtors, Honolulu. Home: 98-1548 Akaaka St Aiea HI 96701 Office: McLaren Realtors 100 N Beretania St Honolulu HI 96817

MCLARNAN, DONALD EDWARD, banker, corporation executive; b. Nashua, Iowa, Dec. 19, 1906; s. Samuel and Grace (Prudhon) McL.; m. Virginia Rickard, May 5, 1939; children: Marilyn, Marcia, Roxane. A.B., U. So. Calif., 1930; grad., Southwestern U. Law Sch., 1933; postgrad., Cambridge U. Trust appraiser, property mgr. Security-Pacific Nat. Bank, Los Angeles, 1935-54; regional dir. SBA for, So. Calif., Ariz., Nev., 1954-61; area adminstr. SBA for, Alaska, Western U.S., Hawaii, Guam, Samoa, U.S. Trust Terr., 1969-73; pres. Am. MARC, Inc. (offshore oil drillers and mfr. diesel engines), 1961-63, Terminal Drilling & Prodn. Co., Haney & Williams Drilling Co., Western Offshore, 1961-63; v.p., dir. Edgemar Dairy, Santa Monica Dairy Co., 1954-70; founder, pres., chmn. bd. Mission Nat. Bank, 1963-67; pres. Demco Trading Co., Mut. Trading Co.; dir. Coast Fed. Savs. & Loan; cons. numerous corps.; guest lectr. various univs. Contbr. articles on mgmt. and fin. to profl. jours. Chmn. fed. agys. div. Community Chest, 1956; nat. pres. Teachers Day, 1956; bd. councillors U. So. Calif.; founder, chmn., pres. Soc. Care and Protection Injured Innocent; adv. bd. Los Angeles City Coll.; bd. dirs. Calif. Easter Seal Soc.; nat. chmn. U. So. Calif. Drug Abuse Program. Recipient Los Angeles City and County Civic Leadership award, 1959. Mem. Nat. Assn. People with Disabilities (pres.); Mem. Skull and Dagger, Delta Chi. Clubs: Mason (Los Angeles) (K.T., Shriner), Los Angeles (Los Angeles), Jonathan (Los Angeles). Home: 135 S Norton Ave

Los Angeles CA 90004 Office: 1111 S Crenshaw Blvd Los Angeles CA 90019

MCLAUGHLIN, JAMES DANIEL, architect; b. Spokane, Wash., Oct. 2, 1947; s. Robert Francis and Patricia (O'Connel) McL.; B.Arch., U. Idaho, 1971; m. Willa Kay Pace, Aug. 19, 1972; children—Jamie Marie, Robert James. Project architect Neil M. Wright, Architect, AIA, Sun Valley, Idaho, 1971-74, McMillan & Hayes, Architects, Sun Valley, 1974-75; now pres., prin. McLaughlin Architects Chartered, Sun Valley. Prin. works include Oakridge Apts., Moscow, Idaho (Excellence in Design award AIA), Walnut Ave. Mall, Ketchum, Idaho (Excellence in Design award AIA, 1987), McMahan Residence, Sun Valley (Excellence in Design award AIA, 1987). Chmn., Ketchum Planning and Zoning Commn., Ketchum Planning Commn., Ketchum Zoning Commn.; vice chmn. Sun Valley Planning and Zoning Commn. Served to 1st lt. U.S. Army. Registered architect, 8 states including Idaho. Mem. AIA , Nat. Council Archtl. Registration Bds., Nat. Home Builders Assn., Ketchum-Sun Valley C. of C. (dir.). Roman Catholic. Club: Rotary. Prin. archtl. works include James West Residence, First Fed. Savs., Fox Bldg. Rehab., Walnut Ave. Mall, First St. Office Bldg. Home: Lot #5 Red Cliffs Subdiv Box 6 Ketchum ID 83340 Office: McLaughlin Architects Chartered PO Box 479 Sun Valley ID 83353

MCLAUGHLIN, MARGUERITE P., state senator, logging company executive; m. Bruce McLaughlin; 3 children. Owner, operator contract logging firm, Orofino, Idaho; former mem. Idaho Ho. of Reps.; now mem. Idaho Senate, 4th term. Trustee Joint Sch. Dist. 171; pres. Orofino Celebration, Inc. Democrat. Office: Idaho State Senate State Capitol Boise ID 83720

MCLAUGHLIN, VANESSA LEIGH, marketing executive; b. Eugene, Oreg., Aug. 27, 1956; d. Jerald P. and Gloria J. Totman; m. Todd S. McLaughlin, Mar. 27, 1982; children: Colin Bryce, Gavin Taggart. Student U. Ariz., 1975-77; BS in Real Estate Fin., U. Oreg., 1979. Account exec. Sta. KYES, Roseburg, Oreg., 1981; account exec. KRSB-FM, Roseburg, 1982; account exec. Sta. KPNW-AM-FM, 1982; owner AdSpectrum Mktg. Cons., Roseburg, 1982—; with WestCom Prodns., 1989—; mktg. advisor Phoenix Sch., Roseburg; dir. pub. rels., bd. dirs. Consumer Credit Counseling. Mem. brochure com. Visitors and Conv. Bur., Roseburg; bd. dirs. Umpqua Valley Arts Assn., 1984, Mercy Found.; chair Phoenix Sch. Endowment Found, 1988. Mem. Mid-Oreg. Advt. Club (Woody Award of Excellence, 1985), Roseburg C. of C. (pub. rels. com., 1986—, pioneer award com., greeter's com., 1981), Rotary. Republican. Presbyterian. Home: 338 W Riverside Dr Roseburg OR 97470 Office: PO Box 2098 Roseburg OR 97470

MC LAURIN, FRANCIS WALLIN (FRANK MC LAURIN), radio broadcasting executive; b. Sioux Falls, S.D., Sept. 24, 1923; s. Archibald A. and Clementine B. (Wallin) McL.; student Calif. Jr. Coll., 1941-42; m. Barbara Lee Jones, May 26, 1956; 1 dau., Barbara Lyn. Announcer sta. KGGM, Albuquerque, 1946; in prodn., sta. KFXM, San Bernardino, Calif., 1947-51; gen. mgr. sta. KWRN, Reno, 1951-52; account exec. KFMB TV, San Diego, 1953-54; gen. mgr. sta. KSRO, Santa Rosa, Calif., 1954—; dir., v.p. Finley Broadcasting Co. (now owns KSRO AM and KREO FM), Santa Rosa. Mem. broadcast adv. bd. UPI. Bd. dirs. Boy Scouts Am. Recipient Young Man of Yr. award, Santa Rosa Jr. C. of C., 1957; Calif. Broadcasters Disting. award, 1984. Mem. Calif. Broadcasters Assn. (dir., past chmn.), Nat. Assn. Broadcasters (dir.), Santa Rosa C. of C. (pres. 1960). Republican. Presbyterian. Rotarian (pres. 1966-67). Home: 1708 Pamela Dr Santa Rosa CA 95404 Office: Stas KSRO/KREO FM College Ave Santa Rosa CA 95403

MCLEAN, DAVID STUART, JR., navy officer; b. Valparaiso, Ind., July 30, 1960; m. Lis M. Riley, June 3, 1989. BA, U. Colo., 1982; MB, U. San Diego, 1988. Commd. lt. USN, 1982; helicopter pilot USN, SH-3H Seaking, USS Enterprise, 1983-86; student pilot USN, Sh60B Seahawk, San Diego, 1986-87, instr. pilot, 1987—. Mem. Navy Helicopter Assn., Grad. Bus. Assn., Phi Kappa Psi (v.p. 1980-81). Office: HSL-41 NASNI San Diego CA 92135

MCLEAN, HUGH ANGUS, management consultant; b. Salt Lake City, Feb. 19, 1925; s. George Mark and Rose (Powell) McL.; m. Martha Lane Green, Nov. 23, 1949; children: Michael Hugh, Merrie Smithson. Student, U. Kans., 1943-44; BSME, Iowa State U., 1946; postgrad., U. Utah, 1946, 61-66. Registered profl. engr., Utah. With Utah Oil Refining Co., Boise, Idaho, Twin Falls, Idaho and Salt Lake City, 1953-61, Am. Oil Co., Salt Lake City and 11 western states, 1961-66; cons. Standard Oil (Ind.), Chgo., 1966-69; v.p. Mahler Assocs., Midland Park, N.J., 1969-76; pres. McLean Mgmt. Systems, Wyckoff, N.J., 1976-84, Heber City, Utah, 1984—. Author: There Is a Better Way to Manage, 1982, Developmental Dialogues, 1972, Career Planning Program, 1975; creator, host (TV) live shows and commls., 1956-57; creator stewardship mgmt. system, 1987. Rep. election judge, Salt Lake City, 1964, Operation Eagle Eye, Chgo., 1968; pub. communications dir. Ch. Jesus Christ Latter-day Saints, N.Y. metro area, 1981-84; introduced SAFE HOMES in county and state, 1987. Served to lt. (j.g.) USNR, 1943-46. Recipient Silver award Am. Petroleum Inst., 1957. Mem. Am. Soc. Tng. Devel. (chmn. N.Y. metro chpt. field trips 1972-74). Home: 3384 S Mill Rd Heber City UT 84032 Office: McLean Mgmt Systems PO Box 251 Heber City UT 84032

MCLEAN, ROBIN JENNIFER, marketing professional; b. Denver, Dec. 15, 1960; d. Robert Earl and Marjorie Lee (Worland) McL. BA, U. Denver, 1983, postgrad., 1986—. Prodn. asst. Sta. KOA, Denver; advt. intern Colle & McVoy, Englewood, Colo.; advt. sales rep. Dow Jones & Co., Inc., Englewood, 1983-85; acct. exec. Univ. Graphics, Inc., Englewood, 1985-86; mktg. asst. MPS, Inc., Denver, 1986—; v.p. Columbine Mktg., Denver, 1986—; advisor U. Denver, 1985—. Mem. Internat. Assn. Bus. Communicators, Bus./Profl. Advt. Assn., Denver Art Mus., Nat. Hist. Preservation Soc. Republican. Roman Catholic. Home: 1601 Hudson St Denver CO 80220 Office: Columbine Mktg 255 Clayton St Denver CO 80206

MCLEAN, SEAN ALAN, radio announcer; b. Wichita, Kans., Oct. 4, 1967; s. Marc Alan and Joanne Arlene (Saur) McL. AA, Aims Community Coll., Greeley, Colo., 1987. Announcer, disk jockey Surrey Broadcasting Co., Greeley, 1983—; linesman Weld County Airport, Greeley, 1988—. Home: 2640 Sunset Ln Greeley CO 80631

MCLEOD, JAMES RICHARD, English educator; b. Spokane, Wash., Jan. 8, 1942; s. Richard Leland and Bernice Lola (Smith) McL.; m. Judith Ann Osterberg Sylte, June 10, 1982; children: Anne, Brock, Rory, John. BA in English, U. Wash., 1966; MA in English, Ea. Wash. U., 1969. Cert. tchr., Wash. Psychiat. group worker Ryther Child Ctr., Seattle, 1961-63; tchr. Cen. Valley Sch. Dist., Spokane, 1966-69; prof. English North Idaho Coll., Coeur d'Alene, 1970—, dir. Scottish studies program, 1982—; coord. two-yr. coll. programs, mem. exec. com. Associated Writing Programs, 1974-75. Author: Theodore Roethke: A Manuscript Checklist, 1971, Theodore Roethke: A Bibliography, 1973, Mysterious Lake Pen d'Oreille and its Monster, 1987; contbr. to scholarly publs. Bd. dirs., Kootenai County Coun. Alcoholism, Coeur d'Alene, 1977-80; mem.-at-large, United Ministries in Higher Edn., Seattle, 1979-85; cubmaster, Kootenai County coun. Boy Scouts Am., 1983-84; coord., Kootenai County Centennial Com., Ft. Sherman Day, Coeur d'Alene, 1988—. Named honored author, Wash. State Arts Commn., 1972, Idaho State Library, Boise, 1976. Mem.An Comunn Gaidhealach, Internat. Soc. Cryptozoology, Prince Edward Island Heritage Found., Community Coll. Humanities Assn., Nat. Trust Scotland, Clan MacLeod Soc. USA (nat. v.p. 1982-86), Wash. Poets Assn. (bd. dirs. 1973-76), Spokane Piobaireachd Soc. (treas. 1983—), North Idaho Coll. Rowing Club, North Idaho Coll. Cryptozoology Club. Democrat. Episcopalian. Home: 701 S 12th St Coeur d'Alene ID 83814 Office: North Idaho Coll 1000W Garden Ave Coeur d'Alene ID 83814

MCLEOD, JOHN HUGH, JR., mechanical and electrical engineer; b. Hattiesburg, Miss., Feb. 27, 1911; s. John Hugh and Martha (Caldwell) McL.; m. Suzette Boutell, June 23, 1951; children: John Hugh III, Robert Boutell. BS, Tulane U., 1933. Registered profl. engr., Calif. Engr. various firms, 1933-39; field engr. Taylor Instrument Co., Rochester, N.Y., 1940-42; rsch. and devel. engr. Leeds & Northrup Co., Phila., 1943-47; sect. head guidance systems and guided missiles U.S. Naval Air Missile Test Ctr., Point Mugu, Calif., 1947-56; design specialist Gen. Dynamics/Astronautics, San Diego, 1956-63, cons., 1963-64; pvt. practice mech. and elec. engring. cons., La Jolla, Calif., 1964—; disting. vis. prof. Calif. State U. Chico, 1975; mem. exec. com. Fall Joint Computer Conf. Am. Fedn. Info. Processing Socs., 1965. Co-founder San Diego Symposium for Biomed. Engring., 1961. Author: Simulation: The Dynamic Modeling of Ideas and Systems with Computers, 1968, Computer Modeling and Simulation: Principles of Good Practice, 1982; editor, pub.: Simulation Council Newsletter, 1952-55; editor: Simulation, 1963-74; assoc. editor Instruments & Control Systems, 1955-63, Behavioral Sci., 1973—; tech. editor Simulation in the Service of Soc., 1971—; co-author: Large-Scale Models for Policy Evaluation, 1977. With USN, 1942-43. Recipient Sr. Sci. Simulation award Electronic Assocs., Inc., 1965, TIMS award Inst. Mgmt. Scis., 1986; NEH, NSF grantee, 1983. Mem. IEEE, AAAS, Soc. Computer Simulation (publs. advisor, John McLeod award 1987). Home: 8484 La Jolla Shores Dr La Jolla CA 92037 Office: Soc Computer Simulation PO Box 17900 San Diego CA 92117

MCLEOD, ROBERT ALLYN, retired state agency administrator, consultant; b. San Francisco, Oct. 21, 1929; s. John Gustav McLeod and Henrietta Marie (Crane) Luther; m. Connie Frances Messina, Oct. 10, 1953; children: Michael Robert, Susan Joan, Kenneth Andrew, Patricia Marie, Robert Francis, Joan Grace. BS in History, U. San Francisco, 1951. With State Compensation Ins. Fund, San Francisco, 1953-69, claims mgr., 1963-67, rehab. supr., 1967-69; with Calif. State Div. Indsl. Accidents, San Francisco, 1969-89, chief rehab. bur., 1969-78, 86-89, chief info. and assistance bur., 1978-86; cons. in field. Mem. Gov.'s Com. for Employment of Handicapped, Sacramento, 1970-77; chmn. San Francisco Mayor's Com. for Employment of Handicapped, 1973-75. With USN, 1951-53. Mem. Calif. Assn. Rehab. Profls., Internat. Assn. Indsl. Accident Bds. and Commns., Our Lady of Mercy Men's Club, P.A.C.E. Republican. Roman Catholic. Home: 757 Wimbledon Rd Walnut Creek CA 94598

MCLESKEY, CHARLES HAMILTON, anesthesiology educator; b. Phila., Nov. 8, 1946; s. W. Hamilton and Marion A. (Butts) McL.; m. Nanci S. Simmons, June 3, 1972; children: Travis, Heather. BA, Susquehanna U., 1968; MD, Wake Forest U., 1972. Diplomate Am. Bd. Anesthesiology. Intern Maine Med. Ctr., Portland, 1972-73; resident in anesthesiology U. Wash. Sch. Medicine, Seattle, 1973-76, NIH rsch. trainee, 1974-75; clin. teaching assoc. dept. anesthesiology U. Calif., San Francisco, 1976-78; asst. prof. anesthesiology Wake Forest U. Bowman Gray Sch. Medicine, Winston-Salem, N.C., 1978-83, assoc. prof., 1983-84; assoc. prof. U. Tex. Med. Br., Galveston, 1985-87; assoc. prof. anesthesiology, dir. acad. affairs U. Colo. Health Sci. Ctr., Denver, 1987—; cons., lectr. Janssen Pharmaceutica, Piscataway, N.J., 1980—, Alza Corp., Palo Alto, Calif., 1986—; lectr. to over 150 nat. and state med. orgns., 1982—. Editor: Geriatric Anesthesiology, 1989; contbr. numerous articles to med. jours. Mem. choir Friendswood (Tex.) Meth. Ch., 1985-87; mem. Friendswood Fine Arts Commn., 1985-87. Lt. comdr. M.C., USN, 1976-78. Woodruff-Fisher scholar, 1964-68. Mem. Am. Soc. Anesthesiologists (del. 1983-85), Colo. Soc. Anesthesiologists, Soc. for Edn. in Anesthesia, Nat. Speakers Assn., Internat. Platform Assn., Evergreen Newcomers, Oenophile Soc., Alpha Omega Alpha. Republican. Presbyterian. Home: 30480 Monarch Ct Evergreen CO 80439 Office: U Colo Health Sci Ctr 4200 E 9th Ave Denver CO 80262

MCLIN, STEPHEN T., investment banker; b. St. Louis, Nov. 11, 1946; s. Leonard Dale and Hazel (Goodlett) McL.; m. Rebecca Missen, Dec. 26, 1965 (div. 1975); children: Cynthia Jeanne, Stephen Dale; m. Catherine Anne Crespi, Oct. 12, 1981; children: Scott Thomas, Stephanie Therese. B-SChemE, U. Ill.-Urbana, 1968; MSME, Stanford U., 1970, MBA, 1972. Rch. engr. Atlantic Richfield Corp., Anaheim, Calif., 1968-69; staff officer First Chgo. Corp., 1972-74; asst. v.p. Bank of Am., San Francisco, 1972-75, v.p., 1975-81, sr. v.p., 1979-86, exec. v.p., 1986-87; pres. Am. First Fin. Corp., San Francisco, 1987—; vice chmn., dir. Eureka Fed. Savs., San Francisco, 1988—; profl. lectr. Golden Gate U., San Francisco, 1976-82; bd. dirs. Charles Schwab & Co., San Francisco; vice-chmn. Eureka Fed. Savs., San Carlos, Calif. Bd. regents JFK U., Orinda, Calif., 1977-81. Recipient Disting. Svc. award Golden Gate U., 1982. Mem. Coun. Planning Execs., San Francisco Golf Club, Bankers Club, Conta Costa Country Club. Office: Am First Fin Corp 555 California St #4490 San Francisco CA 94104

MC LURE, CHARLES E., JR., economist; b. Sierra Blanca, Tex., Apr. 14, 1940; s. Charles E. and Dessie (Evans) McL.; m. Patsy Nell Carroll, Sept. 17, 1962. B.A., U. Kans., 1962; M.A., Princeton U., 1964, Ph.D., 1966. Asst. prof. econs. Rice U., Houston, 1965-69, assoc. prof., 1969-72, prof., 1972-79, Allyn R. and Gladys M. Cline prof. econs., 1973-79; exec. dir. for research Nat. Bur. Econ. Research, Cambridge, Mass., 1977-78, v.p., 1978-81; sr. fellow Hoover Instn., Stanford U., 1981—; dep. asst. sec. Dept. Treasury, 1983-85; sr. staff economist Council Econ. Advisers, Washington, 1969-70; vis. lectr. U. Wyo., 1972; vis. prof. Stanford U., 1973; cons. U.S. Treasury Dept., Labor Dept., World Bank, UN, Com. Econ. Devel., IMF, govts. Can., Colombia, Malaysia, Panama, Jamaica, Bolivia, Indonesia, Trinidad, Tobago, Venezuela, Guatemala. Author: Fiscal Failure: Lessons of the Sixties, 1972, (with N. Ture) Value Added Tax: Two Views, 1972, (with M. Gillis) La Reforma Tributaria Colombiana de 1974, 1977, Must Corporate Income Be Taxed Twice?, 1979, Economic Perperspectives on State Taxation of Multijurisdictional Corporations, 1986, The Value Added Tax: Key to Deficit Reduction, 1987; co-author: Taxation of Income from Business and Capital in Colombia, 1988; also numerous articles on econs. and public finance. Ford Found. faculty research fellow, 1967-68. Mem. Am. Econ. Assn., Nat. Tax Assn., Beta Theta Pi. Home: 250 Yerba Santa Ave Los Altos CA 94022 Office: Stanford U Hoover Instn Stanford CA 94305

MCLURKIN, THOMAS CORNELIUS, JR., lawyer; b. Los Angeles, July 28, 1954; s. Thomas Cornelius and Willie Mae (O'Connor) McL. BA, U. So. Calif., Los Angeles, 1976; MPA, U. So. Calif., 1980, postgrad., 1986—; JD, U. San Fernando Valley, 1982. Bar: Calif. 1984, U.S. Dist. Ct. (cen. dist.) Calif. 1984, U.S. Dist. Ct. Hawaii 1984, U.S. Ct. Appeals (9th cir.) 1984, U.S. Dist. Ct. (ea. dist) Calif. 1985, U.S. Dist. Ct. (so dist.) 1985, U.S. Dist. Ct. (no. dist.) Calif. 1985, U.S. Tax Ct. 1988, U.S. Mil. Ct. Appeals 1989. Law clk. Dept. Water and Power City of L.A., 1979-82; jud. clk. U.S. Dist. Ct. (cen. dist.) Calif., L.A., 1982-83; law clk. Office City Atty., Los Angeles, 1983-84, Dep. City Atty., 1984—. Author (with others): Facts in American History, 1968, 2nd edit. 1989. Bd. dirs. L.A. World Affairs Council, 1980—, Smithsonian Assocs., L.A. Area Council Boy Scouts Am.; mem. L. World Affairs Coun. Capt. USAR JAG, 1987—. Recipient Eagle Scout badge, 1971, Heroism award Boy Scouts Am., 1984; named Outstanding Young Man of Am. Jaycees, 1984. Mem. ABA, Los Angeles County Bar Assn., Assn. Trial Lawyers Am., Langston Law assn. of L.A., Am. Soc. of Pub. Adminstrs., U. So. Calif. Gen. Alumni Assn. (bd. govs., exec. bd. 1986—), U. So. Calif. Black Alumni Assn.-Ebonics (pres. 1988-89), U. So. Calif. Pres.'s Circle, Optimist, Phi Alpha Delta. Republican. Methodist. Office: LA City Atty Office Dept Water and Power PO Box 111 Beaudry 1848 Los Angeles CA 90051

MCMAHAN, DARRELL HUBERT, alloy company executive, consultant; b. Richmond, Va., Oct. 28, 1929; s. Clifford Lyman and Dora-Isabel (Wilson) McM.; m. Feb. 13, 1954; children: Denise, Michael, Kevin. BS, Cen. Mich. U., 1953. Owner D&M Heating Co., Midland, Mich., 1958-59; sr. field engr. Dow Chem. Co., Midland, 1967-70; zone mgr., specialist Murex Welding Products, Seattle, 1970-72; sr. field engr. Airco Welding Products, Union, N.J., 1975-77; sr. field engr. Stellite div. Cabot Corp., Kokomo, Ind., 1977-78, 80-82; zone mgr., specialist Metall. Industries, Tinton Falls, N.J., 1978-80; v.p. Specialty Products and Alloy, Vancouver, Wash., 1982—. With U.S. Army, 1953. Mem. Am. Soc. Metals. Republican. Home: 1112 NW 103d St Vancouver WA 98685

MCMAHON, GERALD LAWRENCE, lawyer; b. Youngston, Ohio, July 16, 1935; s. Lawrence J. and Lee Z. McM.; m. Donna Ghio, June 17, 1956; children: Maria, Michael, Mark, Matthew, Angela. BS cum laude, U. So. Calif., 1956; JD summa cum laude, U. San Diego, 1964. Bar: Calif. 1965, U.S. Ct. Claims 1966, U.S. Ct. Appeals (9th cir.) 1966. Chief contracts Centaur space vehicle program Gen. Dynamics/Astronautics, San Diego, 1960-64; from assoc. to sr. ptnr. Seltzer, Caplan, Wilkins & McMahon, San Diego, 1964—. Editor: San Diego Law Rev., 1963-64. Chmn. Bd. Vis., U. San Diego Law Sch., 1979-80. With USN, 1956-59. Fellow Am. Coll. Trial Lawyers; mem. ABA, San Diego Bar Assn., State Bar of Calif. (disciplinary referee pro tem 1977-79), Am. Judicature Soc., Calif. Trial Lawyers Assn., Am. Arbitation Assn., Am. Acad. Matrimonial Lawyers, San Diego Inn of Ct. (panelist 1975, dir. 1979), Phi Alpha Delta. Republican. Roman Catholic. Office: Seltzer Caplan Wilkins & McMahon 3003 4th Ave San Diego CA 92103

MCMAHON, GERALD THOMAS, obstetrician/gynecologist; b. Yonkers, N.Y., Feb. 5, 1932; s. Francis Joseph and Catherine (Connelly) McM.; m. Cay McMahon; children: Rob, Les, Lori, Melody, Cait, Margaret, Bryan, Darrin, Gerald T. Jr. BS, U. N.C., 1953, MD, 1957. Diplomate Am. Bd. Ob-Gyn. Intern Rex Hosp., Raleigh, N.C., 1957-58; residency in ob-gyn. Parkland Meml. Hosp., Southwestern Med. Sch., Dallas, 1961-64; pvt. practice Flagstaff, Ariz., 1964—; chmn. dept. ob-gyn. Flagstaff Hosp., 1965-71, 75-80, bd. dirs., chief of staff, 1972; chief of surgery Flagstaff Med. Ctr., 1981-83, chief of obstetrics, 1983-84, 86—. Med. chmn. Coconino County-Medicolegal Adv. Council, 1966-76; No. Ariz. coord. for Ariz. Perinatal Program, 1976-80, mem. exec. com. 1976-80; mem. adv. com. Ariz. Perinatal Trust, 1980—; pres. Flagstaff Amateur Hockey Assn., 1976—. Capt. USAF, 1958-61. Mem. Coconino County Med. Soc. (pres. 1969), Ariz. Med. Assn. (maternal and child health care com. 1974—), Am. Coll. Ob-Gyn. (rep. adv. council Ariz. perinatal program 1975-80), S.W. Ob/Gyn Soc., Flying Physicians Assn., Airplane Owners and Pilots Assn., Am. Assn. Gynecological Laparoscopists, Am. Assn. Colposcopy and Colpomicroscopy, Am. Fertility Soc., Mus. No. Ariz. Home: 1400 N Rockridge Rd Flagstaff AZ 86001

MCMAHON, KEVIN C., lawyer; b. Mpls., Sept. 4, 1944; s. Gerald J. and Jane M. (Williams) McM.; m. Pamela Phillips, June 8, 1968; children: Lisa, Brooks, Michael. AB maga cum laude, Harvard U., 1966, JD maga cum laude, 1969. Bar: N.Y. 1969, Wash. 1972. Law clk. to presiding justice U.S. Ct. Appeals (2nd cir.), N.Y.C., 1969-70; assoc. Debevoise and Plimpton, N.Y.C., 1970-71, Stoel, Rives, Boley, Jones and Grey, Seattle, 1971-75; ptnr. Stoel, Rives, Boley, Jones and Grey, 1975—. Contbr. chpts. to books. Mem. ABA (fed. regulation of securities com.), Wash. State Bar Assn. (mem. corp. act revision com., past chmn. corp., bus. and banking sect., securities com.), Phi Beta Kappa. Club: Rainier (Seattle). Office: Stoel Rives Boley Jones & Grey 1 Union Sq 36th Fl Seattle WA 98101

MCMAHON, MARGHE MAY, sculptor; b. Palo Alto, Calif., May 7, 1954; d. Merritt Norval and Ruth Evelyn McMahon. BA in Psychobiology, U. Calif., Santa Cruz, 1975, postgrad., 1977-78. Biologist, neuropharmacology Syntex Rsch., Palo Alto, 1975-76; freelance artist Santa Cruz, Calif., 1976-81; sculptor, modelmaker Lucas Film, San Rafael, Calif., 1981—, 20th Century Fox Orion, Chris Walas Inc., L.A., 1983-88; freelance sculptor San Francisco, 1981-88. Sculptor, modelmaker GJP Prodns., Gaffney, S.C., Westport, Wash., 1988, Premavision, Sausalito, Calif., 1987, 88; painter/model maker Colossal Pictures, San Francisco, 1986, USFX, San Francisco, 1985, Indsl. Light & Magic, San Rafael, Calif., 1985; painter Rob Bottin Prodns., L.A., Dallas, Pitts., 1986, Indsl. Light & Magic, San Rafael, 1984; sculptor Indsl. Light & Magic, San Rafael, 1985; others. Home: 2382 45th Ave San Francisco CA 94116

MCMAHON, MICHAEL EDWARD, retail chain executive; b. Castro Valley, Calif., Aug. 2, 1955; s. John Jostph and Diane Lucille (Marta) McM.; m. Susan Dodds, Apr. 25, 1981; c hildren: Christopher, Rebecca, Stephanie. BS, Calif. State U.-Hayward, 1977. Auditor Marvyn's, Hayward, Calif., 1979-83, asst. mgr., 1983-84, mgr. new accts., 1984-86, mgr. collections, 1986--. Pres. Mervyn's Credit Union; lst v.p. East Bay Credit Granters; bd. govs. So. Alameda chpt. Calif. Credit Union League. Mem. Calif. State U.-Hayward Alumni Assn. (past pres.). Republican. Home: 333 Haight Ave Alameda CA 94501 Office: Mervyn's 22301 Foothill Blvd Hayward CA 94541

MCMAHON, MICHAEL JAMES, aerospace engineer; b. Reno, Jan. 5, 1959; s. John Patrick and Gwen Louise (Guyan) McM.; m. Stephanie Frances Cimino, July 21, 1983. BSEE, Ariz. State U., 1989. Project engr. flight systems group Honeywell-Sperry Comml., Phoenix, 1981—; v.p. Career Connections Inc., Phoenix, 1986—. Vol., mem. Young Republicans, Phoenix, 1987—. Mem. IEEE, Smithsonian Assocs., Wilson Ctr. Assocs., Nat. Audubon Soc. Roman Catholic. Home: 15834 N 56th Way Scottsdale AZ 85254 Office: Honeywell Phoenix AZ 85036

MCMAHON, STEPHANIE FRANCES, placement company president/owner; b. Rochester, N.Y., Apr. 10, 1959; d. Richard Joseph and Santina Eleanor (Mangiavellano) Cimino; m. Michael James McMahon, July 21, 1983. AA, Glendale Community Coll., Glendale, Ariz., 1983. Mgr. Three Gold Boutiques, Phoenix, 1977-79; sales mgr. R&G Sales, Tempe, 1979-83; personnel cons. LJL Inc., Phoenix, 1983-86, Career Connections Inc., Phoenix, 1986—. Active in Young Republicans, Phoenix, 1980, 1987—. Republican. Roman Catholic. Home: 15834 N 56th Way Scotsdale AZ 85254 Office: Career Connections Inc 301 E Bethany Home Rd #C-284 Phoenix AZ 85012

MCMANUS, EDWIN CHARLES, JR., airline captain; b. Phila., Apr. 2, 1955; s. Edwin C. and Elinor Rita (Teschemacher) M. BS with honors, Embry Riddle U., 1977; MBA, U. Colo., 1987. Cert. airline transport pilot, flight instr. Flight capt. Continental Airlines, Denver, 1977—; rep. Continental Employee Action Group, Denver, 1984—; commr. Eagle County Airport. Mem. Vail Athletic Club, Vail Racquet Club, Vail Golf Club. Republican. Roman Catholic. Office: Stapleton Internat Airport PO Box 38291 Denver CO 80238

MCMANUS, PATRICK FRANCIS, educator, writer; b. Sandpoint, Idaho, Aug. 25, 1933; s. Francis Edward McManus and Mabel Delana (Klaus) DeMers; m. Darlene Madge Keough, Feb. 3, 1954; children: Kelly C., Shannon M., Peggy F., Erin B. BA in English, Wash. State U., 1956, MA in English, 1962, postgrad., 1965-67. News reporter Daily Olympian, Olympia, Wash., 1956; editor Wash. State U., Pullman, 1956-59; with Ea. Wash. U., Cheney, 1959—; news reporter Sta. KREM-TV, 1960-62; assoc. prof. Ea. Wash. U., Cheney, 1971-74, prof. emeritus, 1983—. Author: A Fine and Pleasant Misery, 1978, Kid Camping from Aaaiii! to Zip, 1979, They Shoot Canoes, Don't They?, 1981, Never Sniff a Gift Fish, 1983, The Grasshopper Trap, 1985, Rubber Legs & White Tail-Hairs, 1987, The Night The Bear Ate Goombaw, 1989; assoc. editor Field & Stream mag. Recipient Booksellers award P.N.W. Booksellers, 1983, Gov.'s award Wash. State Libr., 1985. Mem. Authors Guild, Outdoor Writers Am. (bd. dirs. 1981-84, Excellence award 1986). Roman Catholic. Office: PO Box 28216 Spokane WA 99228-8216

MCMANUS, RICHARD PHILIP, lawyer, financial executive; b. Keokuk, Iowa, Oct. 20, 1929; s. Edward William and Kathleen (O'Connor) M.; m. Marjorie Theresa Mullaney, Nov. 5, 1955; children: Michael L., Mark J., Matthew A. BA, St. Ambrose U., Davenport, Iowa, 1949; JD, U. Mich., 1952; MBA, Roosevelt U., Chgo., 1965. Bar: Calif. 1982, Ill. 1958, Iowa 1952. Ptnr. McManus & McManus, Keokuk, 1952-63; div. counsel USN Facility Engring. Command, Great Lakes, Ill., 1963-66; v.p., dir. law Household Fin. Corp., Chgo., 1966-81; exec. v.p., sec., gen. counsel Security Pacific Fin. Svcs., Inc., San Diego, 1981—; bd. dirs. Security Pacific Fin. Svcs. and subs., San Diego; chmn. Calif. Fin. Systems Assn. Law Com., Sacramento, 1981—; mem. gen. com. Conf. Consumer Fin. Law, Chgo., 1975—. Contbr. articles to profl. jours. Mem. ABA, Calif. Bar Assn., Ill. Bar Assn., San Diego Bar Assn., Stone Ridge Country Club. Democrat. Roman Catholic. Club: Univ., Stone Ridge Country. Lodges: Lions, Elks, KC. Home: 17305 Campillo Dr San Diego CA 92128

MCMASTER, BRIAN JOHN, artistic director; b. Hitchin, Eng., May 9, 1943; s. Brian John and Mary Leila (Hawkins) McM.; student Wellington Coll., 1955-60; LL.B., Bristol U., 1963. With internat. artists dept. EMI, 1968-73; controller opera planning English Nat. Opera, 1973-76; mng. dir. Welsh Nat. Opera, Cardiff, 1976—; artistic dir. Vancouver Opera (B.C., Can.), 1983-89. Office: Welsh Nat Opera, John St, Cardiff CF1 4SP, Wales

MCMASTER, MARY JANE, college educator; b. Nunda, N.Y., Feb. 15, 1943; d. Earl Lloyd and Marion Cecilia (Stewart) McM. BS, SUNY, 1965;

M in Sci., U. Oreg., 1970; PhD, U. Wis., 1975. Teaching asst. U. Wis., Madison, 1970-75; prof. math. U. Iowa, Cedar Falls, 1974-75; prof. Orange Coast Coll., Costa Mesa, Calif., 1977-79, Compton (Calif.) Coll., 1986—, W. Los Angeles Coll., Culver City, 1980—; book reviewer Brooks Publs., San Francisco, 1987-88. Mem. Los Angeles Math Council. Clubs: Sierra (Los Angeles), Canyon Explorers (Los Angeles) (leader 1980—). Office: West Los Angeles Coll Freshman Dr Culver City CA

MCMATH, CARROLL BARTON, JR., past college administrator, retired army officer; b. Godfrey, Wash., Sept. 18, 1910; s. Carroll Barton and Grace Jenness (Matthews) McM.; BS, Oreg. State U., 1932; MS (A. Olson Research scholar), N.Y. U., 1936; m. Betty Ruth Thompson, Nov. 26, 1937; children: Robert Thompson, Carol. With Sacramento Bee Newspaper, 1932-35; jr. exec. Lord & Taylor, N.Y.C., 1936-39; head dept. bus. Boise (Ida.) Jr. Coll., 1939-40; Res. officer on active duty U.S. Army, 1940-46, assigned gen. staff War Dept., 1943-45; commd. capt. regular U.S. Army 1947, advanced through grades to lt. col., assigned Joint Chiefs of Staff, 1951-53, Office Sec. of Army, 1953-55, ret., 1963; campaigns include Okinawa, Korea, Vietnam; mem. faculty U. Hawaii, Honolulu, 1964-77, asst. to dir. research, profl. adviser to faculty on rsch., 1964-77; faculty Indsl. Coll. of Armed Forces, Washington, 1945-46; asst. prof. retailing N.Y. U., N.Y.C., 1946-47. Mem. Assn. U.S. Army, AAAS, AAUP, Ret. Officers Assn., Honolulu Acad. Arts, Hawaiian Hist. Soc., Am. Theatre Organ Soc., Hawaii Found. History and Humanities, Scabbard and Blade, Alpha Delta Sigma, Alpha Kappa Psi, Eta Mu Pi, Elk, Koa Anuenue. Democrat. Home: 1624 Kanunu St PH-B Honolulu HI 96814

MCMICHAEL, J(ACK) RICHARD, real estate developer; b. Berkeley, Calif., Mar. 9, 1943; s. Jack R. and Dorothy (Dwyer) McM.; m. Karen Lois Moore, Nov. 15, 1964; children: J. Richard IV, Erik C. BA, U. Calif., Berkeley, 1964, JD, 1969. Bar: Calif.; lic. real estate broker, Calif. Assoc. Pettit and Martin, San Francisco, 1969-71; pres. Sutter Hill Ltd., Palo Alto, Calif., 1971-78; exec. v.p. Genstar Pacific Corp., San Francisco, 1978-79; gen. mgr. investment property div. Citation Builders, San Leandro, Calif., 1979-84; prin. JRM Properties, Palo Alto, 1984-88; pres. The Fairway Land Co., Laguna Niguel, Calif., 1988—; bd. dirs., Western Real Estate Fund, Inc., Menlo Park, Calif. Chmn., Scholar Opera, Palo Alto, 1982-85; bd. mgrs., Palo Alto YMCA, 1987—; chmn. troop com., Palo Alto area Boy Scouts Am., 1987-88. Comdr. USN, 1964-66, Vietnam. Mem. Internat. Coun. Shopping Ctrs. Democrat. Methodist. Office: Fairway Land Co Ste 130 33971 Selva Rd Laguna Niguel CA 92677

MCMILLAN, DON FRAIZER, audio-visual specialist; b. Denver, Apr. 11, 1958; s. James J. and Betty Sue (Neff) McM.; m. Janis Kay Longfield. AA, Yavapai Coll., 1979; BS, U. Ariz., 1981; MS, Idaho State U., 1984. Hearing aid sales No. Ariz. Hearing Aid Co., Presscott, 1984; audiologist, sales mgr. Benson Optical Co., Phoenix, 1984-86; audiologist Ariz. Dept. Health, Phoenix, 1986—. Advisor Community Hearing Aid. Mem. Am. Speech and Hearing Assn., Ariz. Speech and Hearing Assn. (chmn.). Lutheran.

MCMILLAN, EDWIN MATTISON, physicist, educator; b. Redondo Beach, Calif., Sept. 18, 1907; s. Edwin Harbaugh and Anna Marie (Mattison) McM.; m. Elsie Walford Blumer, June 7, 1941; children—Ann B., David M., Stephen W. B.S., Calif. Inst. Tech., 1928, M.S., 1929; Ph.D., Princeton U., 1932; D.Sc., Rensselaer Poly. Inst., 1961, Gustavus Adolphus Coll., 1963. Nat. research fellow U. Calif. at Berkeley, 1932-34, research asso., 1934-35, instr. in physics, 1935-36, asst. prof. physics, 1936-41, asso. prof., 1941-46, prof. physics, 1946-73, emeritus, 1973—; mem. staff Lawrence Radiation Lab., 1934—, asso. dir., 1954-58, dir., 1958-73; on leave for def. research at Mass. Inst. Tech. Radiation Lab., U.S. Navy Radio and Sound Lab., San Diego, and Los Alamos Sci. Lab., 1940-45; mem. gen. adv. com. AEC, 1954-58; mem. commn. high energy physics Internat. Union Pure and Applied Physics, 1960-67; mem. sci. policy com. Stanford Linear Accelerator Center, 1962-66; mem. physics adv. com. Nat. Accelerator Lab., 1967-69; chmn. 13th Internat. Conf. on High Energy Physics, 1966; guest prof. CERN, Geneva, 1974. Trustee Rand Corp., 1959-69; Bd. dirs. San Francisco Palace Arts and Scis. Found., 1968—; trustee Univs. Research Assn., 1969-74. Recipient Research Corp. Sci. award, 1951; (with Glenn T. Seaborg) Nobel prize in chemistry, 1951; (with Vladimir I. Veksler) Atoms for Peace award, 1963; Alumni Distinguished Service award Calif. Inst. Tech., 1966; Centennial citation U. Calif. at Berkeley, 1968; Faculty Research lectr. U. Calif. at Berkeley, 1955. Fellow Am. Acad. Arts and Scis., Am. Phys. Soc.; mem. Nat. Acad. Scis. (chmn. class I 1968-71), Am. Philos. Soc., Sigma Xi, Tau Beta Pi. Office: U Calif Lawrence Berkeley Lab Berkeley CA 94720

MCMILLAN, ROBERT SCOTT, astronomer; b. Pitts., Feb. 26, 1950; s. William Robert and Mary Eunice (Amos) McM.; m. Gloria Lee Ptacek, Dec. 22, 1980; 1 child, Christopher Norman. BS in Astronomy, Case Inst. Tech., 1972; MA in Astronomy, U. Tex., 1974, PhD in Astronomy, 1977. Research asst. Dept. Astronomy, U. Tex., Austin, 1972-75, teaching asst., 1975-77; Nat. Acad. Sci.-Nat. Rsch. Coun. research assoc. space sci. lab. Marshall Space Flight Ctr., NASA, Ala., 1977-79; research assoc. Lunar & Planetary Lab., U. Ariz., Tucson, 1979-81, sr. research assoc., 1981—; proposal reviewer NSF, Washington, 1981—. Grantee NSF, 1981—, NASA Ames Research Ctr., Moffett Field, Calif., 1981-87, NASA, Washington, 1987—. Mem. Am. Astron. Soc., Soc. Photo-Optical Instrumentation Engrs., Internat. Astron. Union. Office: U Ariz Lunar and Planetary Lab Space Scis Bldg Tucson AZ 85721

MCMORDIE, ROBERT KENNETH, thermal engineer; b. Austin, Tex., Dec. 30, 1932; s. Warren C. and Mamie A. (Jones) McM.; m. Elizabeth Jane Bodenhamer, June 5, 1957; children: Laurie, Cynthia, Robin, Michelle, Carol, Katie. BSME, U. Tex., 1955, MSME, 1959; PhD in ME, U. Wash., 1965. Jr. engr. Creole Petroleum Corp., Venezula, 1955-57; assoc. engr. Boeing Corp., Seattle, 1959-65; assoc. prof. U. Wyoming, Laramie, 1965-69; tech. mgr. Martin Marietta Corp., Denver, 1969--; pres. Energy Engring., Inc., Denver, 1980--. Contbr. articles to profl. publs. Named Outstanding Engring. Prof. Tau Beta Pi, U. Wyo., 1969. Mem. ASME, Sigma Xi. Republican. Office: Martin Marietta Corp MS D1140 PO Box 179 Denver CO 80201

MCMORROW, KATHRYN ANN, financial executive; b. Detroit, Aug. 16, 1962; d. James Richard and J. Aileen (Reid) McM. B in Pub. Adminstrn., U. San Francisco, 1986, postgrad. in Bus. Adminstrn. Adminstrv. asst. Ernest A. Bates MD Inc., Am. Shared Hosp. Services, San Francisco, 1983-87; chief fin. officer On/Off Site Med., Oakland, Calif., 1987—. Mem. Nat. Assn. Females Execs., NOW, Commonwealth Club. Home: 6071 Colton Blvd Oakland CA 94611 Office: On/Off Site Med 2976 Summit St Oakland CA 94609

MCMULLEN, JOHN WALTER, marketing executive; b. Des Moines, July 10, 1945; s. Donald Charles and Miriam Elaine (Arms) McM.; m. Rebecca Sue Sickler, June. BS, San Diego State U., 1970; MBA, Nat. U., 1982. Mgr. Oscar Padilla Ins., San Diego, 1970-72; communications cons. Arcata Communications, Phoenix, 1972; sales rep. Procter and Gamble Distbg. Co., Cin., 1972-76, unit mgr., 1976-83; regional mgr. Alberto Culver Co., Melrose Park, Ill., 1983-86; exec. v.p., dir. mktg. Property Tax Mgmt. Group, San Diego, 1986—; guest lectr. Nat. Univ. Grad. Sch. Bus. Served to E-4 USN, 1965-67. Mem. Calif. Bus. Properties Assn., Internat. Council Shopping Ctr., Inst. Property Taxation, Sigma Alpha Epsilon. Republican. Office: Property Tax Mgmt Group 4849 Ronson Ct Ste 105 San Diego CA 92111

MCMURDIE, JOHN ARTHUR, state agency executive; b. Ft. Smith, Ark., May 1, 1943; s. Chatley Neil and Shirley (McArthur) McM.; m. Sharron Gail Cartwright, Dec. 26, 1966; children: Kathryn Marie, Todd Kristjan, Aaron John, Celeste Michelle. BA, U. Utah, 1967; MEd, Ariz. State U., 1980. Cert. Spanish tchr., Ariz. Tchr. Spanish U. Tex., Austin, 1971-73, Tolleson (Ariz.) Union High Sch., 1973-81; adminstrn. svcs. officer Dept. Emergency and Mil. Affairs, Phoenix, 1981—; insp. gen. Ariz. Army N.G., Phoenix, 1974—; chmn. Pub. Safety Personnel Retirement System Pension Bd., Phoenix, 1986—. Sch. bd. clk. Tolleson Union High Sch. Dist. 214, 1983—; Bishop Estrella Ward Latter-day Saints Ch., Tolleson, 1983-88; dist. commr. White Tanks Dist. Boy Scouts Am., Phoenix, 1983. Capt. U.S. Army, 1967-71. Recipient Order of Merit Boy Scouts Am., 1983. Mem. Ariz. Soc. Cert. Pub. Mgrs. Republican. Home: 9513 W Fillmore Tolleson AZ 85353 Office: Dept Emergency Mil Affairs 5636 E McDowell Rd Phoenix AZ 85008

MCMURRY, L. L., horse breeding executive; b. Wamic, Oreg., May 1, 1927; s. John Carroll and Leona Grace (Willard) McM.; m. Vivian Harris, June 18, 1951 (div. 1968); children: Pamela McMurry Larson, Timothy J., Kathleen Susan (dec.); m. Julia Jean Elzeer, May 18, 1980; 1 child, Amy Racheal Haller. BA, Olympic Jr. Coll., 1947; BS, Wash. State U., 1949. Farm mgr. George C. Newell, Kingston, Wash., 1950-53, T90 Ranch, Tenino, Wash., 1953-66; field sec. Wash. Thoroughbred Breeders Assn., Renton, Wash., 1966-71; owner, pres. McMurry Bloodstock, Renton, 1971-74, McMurry Bloodstock & McMurry Thoroughbred Breeding Farm, Enumclaw, Wash., 1974—; chmn. horse mgmt. course adv. com. Green River Coll., Auburn, Wash., 1983-86. Contbr. articles to profl. jours. Served to cpl. U.S. Army, 1944-46. Mem. Washington Thoroughbred Breeders Assn. (bd. dirs., sales com. 1982—), Horsemans Benevolent Protective Assn. (bd. dirs. 1980—), Horseman's Short Course Com. Republican. Lodge: Elks. Office: McMurry Bloodstock Agy 45206 244th Ave SE Enumclaw WA 98022

MCMURTRY, BURTON JOHN, venture capital investor, electrical engineer; b. Houston, Mar. 26, 1935; s. James G. and Alberta Elizabeth (Matteson) McM.; m. Ann Kathryn Meck, June 9, 1956; children—Cathryn Ann, John Eric. BA, Rice U., 1956, BSEE, 1957; MSEE, Stanford U., 1959, Ph.D. in Elec. Engring. (Raytheon fellow), 1962. Engr. Microwave Tube div. Sylvania, Mountain View, Calif., 1957-62; rsch. asst. Stanford U., 1960-62; head lab. rsch. and devel. in electro-optics GTE, Sylvania, Mountain View, 1962-66; mgr. Equipment Engring. Labs., 1967-68; dir., gen. mgr. electro-optics orgn. Sylvania Electronic Systems, 1968-69; asso. Jack L. Melchor (personal venture capital investment bus.), Los Altos, Calif., 1969-70; pres. Palo Alto Investment Co., Calif., 1970-73; gen. partner Dennis, Jamieson & McMurtry, Menlo Park, Calif., 1973—, TVI Mgmt., TVI Mgmt.-2, TVI Mgmt.-3, Menlo Park, 1980—; bd. dirs. DAVID Systems, Veri-Fone, Nellcor, MCM Labs, VMX. Contbr. articles, chpts. to electronics publs., mainly on microwave tubes, lasers, optical detectors. Bd. dirs. El Camino Hosp. Found.; elder Menlo Park Presbyn. Ch.; mem. major gifts com. Stanford U.; trustee Rice U. Recipient Alfred Noble prize, 1964. Mem. Nat. Venture Capital Assn. (pres. 1986-87, chmn. 1987-88), Western Assn. Venture Capitalists (pres. 1972-73), Am. Phys. Soc., Optical Soc. Am., Sigma Xi (sr. award 1957), Sigma Tau, Tau Beta Pi. Home: 7 Coalmine View Portola Valley CA 94025 Office: Tech Venture Investors 3000 Sand Hill Rd Menlo Park CA 94025

MCNABB, ROBERT LESLIE, insurance company executive; b. Columbus, Ohio, July 17, 1927; s. Addison John and Thelma Audrey (Noble) McN.; m. Jane Elizabeth Kennedy,. BFA, Ohio State U., 1950. Claims supr. Nationwide Ins. Co., Columbus, 1951-57; spl. agt. Hartford Ins. Co., Columbus, 1957-59; br. mgr. Safeco Ins. Co., San Diego, 1959-74; mgr. comml. sales Allstate Ins. Co., San Diego, 1974-75; v.p. Bayly Martin & Fay Ins. Co., San Diego, 1975-87, Frank B. Hall Ins. Agy., San Diego, 1987-89, Pacific Ins. Agy., San Diego, 1989—; bd. dirs. Crime Victims Fund, Inc., San Diego, 1983-; chmn. bd. dirs. Vols. in Probation, Inc., San Diego, 1984-86. Bd. dirs. Crime Victims Fund, Inc., San Diego, 1983—; chmn. bd. dirs. Vols. in Probation, Inc., San Diego, 1984-86. Recipient Silver Bowl Vol. award Carnation Milk Co., San Diego, 1974; named Vol. of Yr. San Diego County Probation Dept., 1979, Hon. Probation Officer, 1986; S&H Found. grantee, 1979. Mem. University Club, San Diego, Kiwanis. Republican. Office: Pacific Ins Agy 3635 Ruffin Rd San Diego CA 92123

MCNABB, STEVEN DENNIS, career navy officer; b. San Bernardino, Calif., Aug. 13, 1949; s. Dennis G. and Amy Chloe (Haskins) M.; m. Cynthia Ann Skog, June 14, 1969. BA in Econs., Chapman Coll., 1981; MBA, Nat. U., San Diego, 1988. Commd. ensign USN, 1977, advance through grades to lt. commdr.; adminstrn. officer USS Samuel Gompers San Diego, 1977-80, asst. flag sec. Commdr. Naval Surface Force U.S. Pacific Fleet, 1981-83; exec. dept. head USS Enterprise Alameda, Calif., 1983-86; officer-in-charge Personnel Support Detachment Miramar, San Diego, 1986—; dir. Navy Relief-Miramar Auxilliary 1986-88; exec. officer pers. support activity San Francisco, 1989—. Mem. U.S. Naval Inst., Apple Corps of San Diego, Nat. Rifle Assn. Republican. Home: 8150 Cinnabar Dr La Mesa CA 92041 Office: Persuppact San Francisco CA 94130

MCNAIR, JOHN TIMOTHY, physician; b. Fargo, N.D., Feb. 1, 1949; s. John Hastings and Mary (Sevenants) M.; m. Francea Ann Levine, Oct. 10, 1976;children: Andrew William, Eric Michael. BS, N.D. State U., 1971; BS in Medicine, U. N.D., 1973; MD, So. Ill. U., 1975. Resident in emergency medicine Akron (Ohio) City Hosp., 1975-77, chief resident, 1977-78; co-residency dir. Madison Army Med. Ctr., 1978-80; dir. E.D. Humana Hosp., Tacoma, 1980—; interim dir. Pierce County Health Dept., 1986-87. Bd. dirs. Pantages Ctr., Tacoma, 1987-89. Capt. U.S. Army, 1978-80. Fellow Coll. Emergency Physicians, AMA, Wash. State Med. Soc., Pierce County Med. Soc. Office: Humana Hosp Tacoma 19th and Union Tacoma WA 98498

MCNALL, BRUCE, numismatist, professional sports executive. m. Jane Cody; children: Katie, Bruce. Student, UCLA, Oxford U. Founder, chmn. bd. Numismatic Fine Arts, Inc., L.A.; owner, chmn. bd. Summa Stable, Inc.; chmn. bd. Gladden Entertainment Corp.; former ptnr. Dallas Mavericks NBA; co-owner L.A. Kings, 1986-87, sole owner, 1988—; also gov., pres. Office: Los Angeles Kings 3900 W Manchester Blvd PO Box 17013 Inglewood CA 90306 *

MCNALLY, JAMES HENRY, physicist; b. Orange, N.J., Dec. 18, 1936; s. James Osborne and Edith Maude (Jones) McN.; B. in Engring. Physics, Cornell U., 1959; PhD, Calif. Inst. Tech., 1966; m. Nancy Lee Eudaley, July 4, 1976. staff mem. program mgr. Los Alamos (N.Mex.) Nat. Lab., 1965-74, asst. dir for laser and isotope separateion tech. AEC/ERDA, Washington, 1974-75; assoc. div. leader, dep. for inertial fusion, 1975-81, asst. for nat. sec. issues, 1981-86, dir. 1988—; dep. asst. dir. Arms Control and Disarmament Agy., Washington, 1986-88, with dirs. office Los Alamos Nat. Lab., 1988—; U.S. del. Geneva Conf. on Disarmament, 1969, 73, 74, Threshold Test Ban Treaty, Moscow, 1974, Nuclear Testing Talks, Geneva, 1986-88. Bd. dirs. Wilson Mesa Met. Water Dist., 1976-88 . Mem. Am. Phys. Soc., AAAS, Internat. Inst. Strategic Studies. Office: Los Alamos Nat Lab Los Alamos NM 87545

MCNAMARA, JESSICA CATHERINE, nurse; b. Cleve., Apr. 30, 1940; d. Joseph Andrew and Sylvia (Jankowski) Pluto; m. Gerald McNamara, May 13, 1961; children: Susan, Diane, Mary Lynne (dec.), Gerald. A.Nursing, Cuyahoga Commmunity Coll., Parma Hts., Ohio, 1970; BSN, Gwynedd-Mercy Coll., Pa., 1975; MS in Nursing, Loyola U., Chgo., 1978. RN, Calif. Staff nurse Kaiser Hosp., Cleve., 1970-72, Lakewood Hosp., Calif., 1972-73; clin. specialist VA Med. Ctr., Palo Alto, Calif., 1978-85, Peninsula Hosp., Burlingame, Calif., 1985-88, VA Med. Ctr., Menlo Park, 1988—; instr. Hosp. Consortium, Burlingame, 1985—, Evanston Hosp. Sch., Harper Coll., Schaumburg, Ill., 1978; lectr. in field. Mem. Calif. Nurses Assn. (cert.), Am. Assn. Critical Care Nurses (cert.). Democrat. Roman Catholic. Home: 724 Vespucci Ln Foster City CA 94404 Office: VA Med Ctr Willow Rd Menlo Park CA 94404

MCNAMARA, JOHN J., educator; b. Rochelle, Ill., Dec. 6, 1909; s. John and Grace (Campbell) McN.; B.E., No. Ill. U.; M.A., U. Iowa; Ph.D., Purdue U.; m. Hazel D. Dionne, Aug. 11, 1936; children—John, Denise, Carole, Michael, Terrence, Kevin. Tchr., St. Albans Acad., Sycamore, Ill., 1932-34; faculty St. Viator Coll., Kankakee, Ill., 1934-37; asso. prof. U. Detroit, 1937-43; head tng. div. Republic Aviation Corp., 1943-45; pres. M & M Candy, Hackettstown, N.J., 1945-59; dir. M & M Mars (now Mars Inc.), McLean, Va., 1952-62; chmn. bd. Uncle Ben's Rice, Houston, 1959-62; corp. mktg. adv. Warner Lambert Pharm. Co., Morris Plains, N.J., 1966-67; prof. No. Ill. U., DeKalb, 1970-78; prof. dept. mktg. Calif. State Coll., Bakersfield, 1978-80. Calcot-Kennedy disting. prof., 1980—. Recipient Chick Evans award and service award No. Ill. U., 1971; inducted into NIU Football Hall of Fame, 1984. Mem. Am. Assn. Advt. Agys. Sigma Xi, Phi Delta Kappa. Club: Stockdale Country. Contbr. articles to profl. publs. Home: 508 Malibu Ct Bakersfield CA 93309 Office: 9001 Stockdale Hwy Bakersfield CA 93309

MC NAMARA, JOSEPH DONALD, chief of police; b. N.Y.C., Dec. 16, 1934; s. Michael and Eleanor (Shepherd) McN.; m. Rochelle Wall, Jan. 25, 1964; children—Donald, Laura, Karen. B.S., John Jay Coll., 1968; fellow, Harvard Law Sch., 1970; D.P.A. (Littauer fellow), Harvard U., 1973. Served to dep. insp. Police Dept., N.Y.C., 1956-73; police chief Kansas City, Mo., 1973-76, San Jose, Calif., 1976—; adj. instr. Northeastern U., 1972, John Jay Coll., 1973, Rockhurst Coll., 1975-76, San Jose State U., 1980; cons. U.S. Civil Rights Commn., 1978; lectr., appearances on nat. TV; apptd. nat. adv. bd. U.S. Bur. Justice Stats., 1980. Author: (non-fiction) Safe and Sane Fawcett, 1984, (novel) The First Directive Crown, 1985, Fatal Command, 1987. Contbr. articles to profl. jours. Active NCCJ. Served with U.S. Army, 1958-60. Named one of 200 Young Am. Leaders Time mag., 1975; recipient disting. alumni award John Jay Coll., 1979, Western Soc. Criminology pres.'s award, 1979; Kansas City police named Best in Country by Nat. Newspaper Enterprises, 1974, San Jose Police Dept. named Nat. Model U.S. Civil Rights Commn., 1980. Mem. Internat. Assn. Chiefs of Police, Calif. Police Chiefs Assn., Calif. Peace Officers Assn., Major Cities Police Chiefs Assn., Police Exec. Research Forum (dir.). Office: 201 W Mission San Jose CA 95510

MCNAMEE, PETER CHARLES, management consultant; b. Bklyn., Oct. 19, 1937; s. Charles Reynolds and Agnes (Herman) McN.; m. Tereza Cristina Fite, Aug. 16, 1975; children: Patrick Francis, Christina Elizabeth, Andrew Charles. AB, Fordham U., 1962; MS, PhD, Stanford U., 1967; MDiv, Woodstock Coll., 1970. Lektor Universiteit Leuven, Louvain, Belgium, 1971-72; assoc. prof. Pontificia Universidade Catolica, Rio de Janeiro, 1972-74; vis. assoc. prof. U. Ariz., Tucson, 1974-76, U. Va., Charlottesville, 1976-77; cons. SRI Internat., Menlo Park, Calif., 1977-83; sr. assoc. Strategic Decisions Group, Menlo Park, 1983—. Author: Decision Analysis for the Professional, 1987; author computer software Supertree, 1985; contbr. articles to profl. jours. Woodrow Wilson fellow, 1962; predoctoral fellow Nat. Sci. Found., 1962. Mem. Am. Phys. Soc. Office: Strategic Decisions Group 2440 San Hill Rd Menlo Park CA 94025

MC NEAR, DENMAN KITTREDGE, transportation company executive; b. San Francisco, July 20, 1925; s. E. Denman and Mary H. (Kittredge) McN.; m. Susan L. Anderson, Jan. 27, 1962; children: Denman K., Stephen A., George D. BSCE, MIT, 1948; MBA, Stanford U., 1950. Registered profl. engr., Calif., Ariz., N.Mex., Tex. With So. Pacific Transp. Co., San Francisco, 1948—, asst. to pres., 1963-67, v.p., 1967-75, v.p. ops., 1975-76, pres., 1976—, chmn. bd., chief exec. officer, 1982—, also bd. dirs.; chmn., pres. St. Louis Southwestern Ry. Co., 1983. Mem. corp. MIT, Cambridge, 1977-88; bd. dirs. Jr. Achievement, Inc. Served with USN, 1944-46. Mem. Assn. Am. R.R.s (bd. dirs.), ASCE, Calif. Council Econ. Edn., Calif. C. of C. (bd. dirs.). Republican. Clubs: Bohemian, Pacific-Union, Stock Exchange. Office: So Pacific Transp Co So Pacific Bldg 1 Market Plaza San Francisco CA 94105 *

MCNEELY, ALMA GRETCHEN, nurse, educator; b. Detroit, Mar. 29, 1941; d. Carl Bertil and Katherine Rose (Brown) Orman; m. Joseph Francis Cavon, June 26, 1962 (div. 1981); children: Leslie Muriel Cavon Tatum, Joseph Anthony Cavon; m. Richard Irving McNeely, Dec. 18, 1981. Diploma, Harper Hosp. Sch. Nursing, 1962; BS in Nursing, Biola U., 1981; MS in Nursing, Loma Linda U., 1983; D Nursing Sci., U. San Diego, 1989. R.N., Mich., Mont., Calif. Staff nurse Harper Hosp., Detroit, 1962, Midway Hosp., St. Paul, 1963; pediatric charge nurse St. John Hosp., Detroit, 1963-64; staff nurse Mo. Bapt. Hosp., St. Louis, 1965-66; office nurse, mgr. pvt. practice plastic and reconstructive surgeon, Santa Ana, Calif., 1967-81; asst. prof. nursing Mont. State U., Missoula, 1983-86; doctoral fellow, rsch. asst. U. San Diego, 1986—. Contbg. author: Family Health Nursing, 1989, American Nursing: A Biographical Dictionary, 1988. Facilitator, Parents Anonymous, Missoula, 1984-86. Mem. Am. Nurses Assn., Mont. Nurses Assn., Am. Pub. Health Assn., Am. Assn. History of Nursing, Sigma Theta Tau. Republican. Presbyterian. Home: 2750 Terrace Dr Missoula MT 59803

MC NEELY, E. L., manufacturing company executive; b. Pattonsburg, Mo., Oct. 5, 1918; s. Ralph H. and Viola (Vogel) McN.; m. Alice Elaine Hall, Sept. 18, 1948; children: Sandra (Mrs. Ronald Gessl), Gregory, Mark, Kevin. Student, Central Bus. Coll., Kansas City, Mo., 1935-36, U. Mo., 1936-37; A.B., No. Mo. State U., Kirksville, 1940; student, Rockhurst Coll., Kansas City, Mo., 1942. With Montgomery Ward & Co., 1940-64, divisional mdse. mgr., 1961-64; dir. marketing Wickes Corp., Saginaw, Mich., 1964-65; sr. v.p. Wickes Corp., 1965-69, pres., 1969-74, chief exec. officer, chmn., 1974-80; chmn. bd., chief exec. officer Wickes Cos., Inc., 1980-82, also dir.; chmn., chief exec. officer Oak Industries Inc.; bd. dirs. Pacific Telesis Group, Transam. Corp. Served as officer USNR, 1942-46, PTO. Mem. Beta Gamma Sigma, Alpha Phi Omega. Republican. Presbyterian. Clubs: Union League, Metropolitan (Chgo.); La Jolla Country; Fairbanks Ranch Country, Cuyamaca (San Diego; San Francisco Golf; Deepdale Golf (N.Y.). Office: Oak Industries Inc 16510 Via Esprillo Rancho Bernardo CA 92127

MCNEELY, JIM MADISON, information services executive; b. Dos Palos, Calif., Feb. 14, 1956; s. James M. and Martha Ellen (Sarrels) McN.; m. Kristi Robin Borboa, Jan. 19, 1980. BS in Acctg., Calif. State U., Fresno, 1979. Cost acct. Manlift Inc., Fowler, Calif., 1977-78, programmer, 1978-79, mgr. data processing, 1979-82; cons. Expedata Inc., Fresno, 1982-85; dir. info. services Grundfos Pumps Corp., Clovis, Calif., 1985—. Mem. IEEE, Am. Mgmt. Assn., Assn. for Computing Machinery, Assn. for System Mgmt., Data Processing Mgmt. Assn. Office: Grundfos Pumps Corp 2555 Clovis Ave Clovis CA 93612

MCNEELY, RICHARD IRVING, minister, educator, retired military officer; b. Goodland, Kans., Nov. 24, 1928; s. Henry Irving and Emma Madeline (Dendurent) McN.; m. Jean Paton Graham, June 17, 1950 (div. Nov. 1981); children: Dennis Dean, Kathleen Jean McNeely Comer, Michael Craig; m. Alma Gretchen Orman, Dec. 18, 1981. BA, Westmont Coll., 1950; ThM, Dallas Theol. Sem., 1954, ThD, 1963; PhD, U. So. Calif., L.A., 1986. Ordained to ministry Presbyn. Ch. Dir. choral edn. Royal Ln. Bapt. Ch., Dallas, 1952-54; asst. pastor 1st Brethren Ch., Long Beach, Calif., 1954-58; min. of music Scofield Meml. Ch., Dallas, 1958-59; prof. Midwest Bible Coll., St. Louis, 1959-60, Biola Coll., La Mirada, Calif., 1960-66, 69-80; assoc. dean Biola Coll., La Mirada, 1980-81; chaplain USN Destron 21, San Diego, 1966-68; pastor 1st Presbyn. Ch., Libby, Mont., 1989—. Author: I II Kings, 1979; contbr. articles to profl. jours. Capt. USNR, 1962—. Mem. Evang. Theol. Soc. (chpt. pres. 1979), Am. Sci. Affiliates, Kiwanis (spiritual aims dir., bd. dirs. 1985—). Republican. Home: 2750 Terrace Dr Missoula MT 59803 Office: 1st Presbyn Ch PO Box 734 Libby MT 59923

MCNEESE, JACK MARVIN, communications executive; b. Seattle, Jan. 9, 1929; s. William Joseph and Mary Elizabeth (Fritz) McN.; m. Dolores May Winkler, Apr. 20, 1940 (div. 1953); 1 child John Martin; m. Natoma June Young. Grad. high sch., Seattle. Telephone installer Pacific N.W. Bell, Seattle, 1948-60; with telephone mktg. dept. Pacific N.W. Bell, Tacoma, 1960-67; communictions cons. Communication Mgmt. Concepts, Seattle, 1967-73; pres., founder, communications cons. Telcom Mgmt. Concepts, Federal Way, Wash., 1973—. With U.S. Army, 1955-59. Mem. Soc. Telecommunications Consultants, Twinlakes Golf and Country Club, Masons. Republican. Home: 2618 SW 323d Place Federal Way WA 98023 Office: Telcom Mgmt Concepts Inc 30915-18th Ave S Federal Way WA 98023

MCNEIL, HEIDI LORETTA, lawyer; b. Preston, Iowa, Apr. 7, 1959; d. Archie Hugo and Heidi (Waltert) McN. BA in Journalism and Broadcasting with distinction, U. Iowa, 1981, JD with distinction, 1985. Bar: Ariz. 1985, U.S. Dist. Ct. Ariz. 1985, U.S. Ct. Appeals (9th cir.) 1985. Sports journalist The Daily Iowan, Iowa City, 1977-81, Quad City Times, Davenport, Iowa, 1981-82; assoc. Snell & Wilmer, Phoenix, 1985—. Mem. ABA, Ariz. Bar Assn., Maricopa County Bar Assn. (bd. dirs. Young Lawyers Div. 1987-89), Ariz. Women Lawyers, Phoenix Assn. Def. Counsel, Phi Beta Kappa, Phi Eta Sigma. Lutheran.

MCNEIL, ROBERT DUELL, investment company executive; b. Chehalis, Wash., Sept. 16, 1935; s. Robert Maxwell Donahoe and Alice Julia (Duell) McN.; m. Lila G. Davis, Sept. 5, 1958 (div. 1961); children: Katrina, Kathleen; m. Virginia Allen, June 1964 (div. 1966); children: Mark, Marceline; m. Rita Camille Grove, June 29, 1972. Student, U. Oreg., 1953. Mgr. retail sales Standard Oil Calif., Santa Monica, 1956-63; dist. mgr. Questor Corp., 1963-65; regional sales mgr. Perfection Gear Co., L.A., 1965-66; gen. mgr. San Diego Tool Co., 1966-68; pres. F. Mohling Co., San Diego, 1968-70; with Midas Internat., Inc., L.A., Chgo., 1970-72; pres. Muffco, Inc., Lakewood, Colo., 1972-78; v.p. devel. Glassrock Med. Co., Atlanta, 1978-80; prin. R.D. McNeil & Assocs., Scottsdale, Ariz., 1981-86; gen. ptnr. Vaughn-McNeil & Assocs., Denver, 1986—; bd. dirs. Uniform & Equipment Co., Denver. With USMC, 1954-56. Mem. Met. Club. Roman Catholic. Home: 7040 W Fairview Dr Littleton CO 80123 Office: Vaughn McNeil & Assocs Ltd 5299 DTC Blvd Ste 500 Englewood CO 80111

MCNEILL, VICKI S., mayor. m. James P. McNeill; 2 children. BS, Simmons Coll., 1947. Appointed mem. Spokane (Wash.) City Council, 1982, elected mem., 1983-85; mayor City of Spokane, 1985—. Pres. Wash. State Pavilion Fund; trustee Spokane Symphony Soc., Spokane C. of C., Spokane Centennial Commn. Recipient Golden Deeds award Exchange Club, 1975, Distinction award Women in Communications, 1979, Outstanding Achievement Leadership award YWCA, 1983. Office: City of Spokane W 808 Spokane Falls Blvd Spokane WA 99201 *

MCNEILLIE, STANLEY RAY, automotive company executive; b. Santa Clara, Calif., Aug. 6, 1948; s. Reagon Harrison McNeillie and Betty Jean (Neeley) Gomez; m. Phyllis Lindsay Greig, Feb. 28, 1979; 1 child, Erica Lee. Student, Fresno City Coll., 1967-68, Fresno State U., 1969-70. Store mgr. Lee's Furniture, Fresno, Calif., 1971-73; sales rep. Breuners Furniture, Fresno, Calif., 1974-75, Levitz Furniture, Fresno, Calif., 1976-77; store mgr. Sherman Clay Music, Fresno, Calif., 1978-80; automobile sales rep. Toyota Motors Sales Co., Fresno, Calif., 1980--. Republican. Home: 6325 N Poplar Fresno CA 93704

MCNEW, JULIE ANN, real estate administrator; b. Pomona, Calif., Aug. 17, 1964; d. Robert L. and Edith A. (Head) Keller; m. Shawn T. Bridgett, Dec. 12, 1984 (div. Aug. 1986); m. John McNew, Nov. 11, 1988. Student, Cypress Coll., 1982-84. Ride operator Knott's Berry Farm, Buena Park, Calif., 1983-85; sec. Century 21 Beachside, Huntington Beach, Calif., 1985-87; office mgr. The Housing Market, Cypress, Calif., 1985—, exec. sec., 1987—; graphic cons. Buena Park Bd. Realtors, 1987—. Actress in numerous local theater prodns. Vol. Orange County Animal Shelter, 1988, MADD program, Orange, 1988—. Republican. Mem. Christian Ch. Home: 1132 S Citron Anaheim CA 92805 Office: The Housing Market 5241 Lincoln C-6 Cypress CA 90630

MCNEY, CRAIG STEWART, construction executive; b. Inglewood, Calif., Dec. 27, 1946; s. Stuart Lawrence and Ada Blanche (Honey) McN.; m. Sherry Lou Shipstead, June 14, 1969; children: Matthew, Joshua, Andrew, Jonathan. BA in Sociology, Calif. Luth. U., 1969, MBA, 1975. V.p. Norwal, Inc., Canoga Park, Calif., 1973-83, pres., 1984-85; pres., chief exec. officer Craig McNey, Inc. (doing bus. as Norwal II), Agoura Hills, Calif., 1986-88, Stewart Devel. Inc., Westlake Village, Calif., 1989—. Trustee Conejo Future Found., 1975-81, vice-chmn., 1981; founder Alliance for Arts, 1979; co-chmn. fund raising U.S. Olympic Com., Ventura County, 1982-84; bd. dirs. Am. Youth Soccer Orgn., 1977-78; bd. dirs. Big Bros. Greater L.A., 1979—, v.p. devel., 1983-84, exec. v.p., 1985-86, pres., 1986-88. Recipient Cert. of Appreciation City of Thousand Oaks (Calif.), 1980, Cert. of Appreciation Life Spike, 1988, Cert. of Appreciation Nat. Assn. Homebuilders, 1981, Cert. of Commendation L.A. County Bd. Suprs., 1987; named Outstanding Alumnus Calif. Luth. U., 1978, Caring Californian May Co. Dept. Stores, 1987. Mem. So. Calif. Drywall Contractors Assn. (bd. dirs. 1987—, sec. 1988), Bldg. Industry Assn. Greater Angeles (v.p. 1987—), L.A. County Painting and Decorating Contractors Assn., Bldg. Industry Assn. So. Calif. (bd. dirs. Greater L.A. chpt. 1976—, 2d v.p. 1979-80), North Ranch Club. Republican. Episcopalian. Home: 196 Dirt Rd Lake Sherwood CA 91360 Office: Stewart Devel Inc 5743 Corsa Ave Ste 217 Westlake Village CA 91362

MCNUTT, STEPHEN RUSSELL, volcanologist, geophysical scientist; b. Hartford, Conn., Dec. 21, 1954; s. Elmer Ellsworth and Leona (LaPointe) McN. BA, Wesleyan U., Middletown, Conn., 1977; MA, Columbia U., 1982, MPhil, 1984, PhD, 1985. Sr. seismologist Calif. Div. Mines and Geology, Sacramento, 1984-86, 1984—; cons. U. Costa Rica, San José, 1982-83. Contbr. articles to profl. jours. Mem. Seismol. Soc. Am., Am. Geophys. Union, Internat. Assn. Volcanology and Chemistry of Earth Interior. Democrat. Roman Catholic. Club: Buffalo Chips Running (Sacramento) (bd. dirs. 1986-88). Office: Calif Div Mines and Geology 630 Bercut Dr Sacramento CA 95814

MCOMBER, WARREN KINGSLEY, investment banker; b. Canton, Ohio, May 18, 1935; s. Monroe Frank and Carolyn (Palmer) McO.; m. Virginia Griffith, Oct. 9, 1965; 1 child, Elisabeth Mellen. BA, Williams Coll., Williamstown, Mass., 1957; MBA, Harvard U., 1959. V.p. The First Boston Corp., N.Y.C., 1961-71; sr. v.p. Shearson Hammill, N.Y.C., 1971-74, Shearson Hayden Stone Inc., N.Y.C., 1974-75, Eppler Guerin and Turner Inc., Dallas, 1975-81, Geo Kinetics Inc., Salt Lake City, 1981-85; chmn. bd. McOmber and Travis Inc., Salt Lake City, 1985-88; pres. McOmber and Assocs. Inc., Salt Lake City, 1988—; bd. dirs. geoKinetics Inc., E.I. Internat. Inc., Idaho Falls. Bd. dirs. Utah Symphony, Salt Lake City, 1986—, investment com., 1987—, pres. Maestro Club, 1986-87. Mem. The Alta Club. Republican. Episcopalian. Office: McOmber & Assocs Inc 380 N 200 West Bountiful UT 84010

MCPARTLAND, THOMAS JOSEPH, historian, educator; b. Oakland, Calif., July 30, 1945; s. Richard Joseph and Anne Josephine (Calmes) McP. BA, U. Santa Clara, 1967; MA, U. Wash., 1969, PhD, 1976. Acting asst. prof. U. Wash., Seattle, 1976-79; lectr. Pacific Luth. U., Tacoma, 1977, U. Wash., Seattle, 1985; instr. Bellevue (Wash.) Community Coll., 1981—; cons. to psychotherapists, Seattle, 1977—; instr. Telos, Clyde Hill, Wash., 1985-86, Issaquah, Wash., 1986—. Contbr. articles to profl. jours. Recipient scholarship Calif. State Scholarship Fedn., 1983-87; grantee for lecture Santa Clara U., 1985, Lonergan Workshop of Boston Coll., 1986. Mem. West Coast Methods Inst. Office: Bellevue Community Coll Dept Hist 3000 Landerholm Circle SE PO Box 92700 Bellevue WA 98009-2037

MCPHAIL, KARIN RUTH TAMMEUS, teacher, realtor, musician; b. Urbana, Ill., Nov. 23, 1938; d. Wilber Harold and Bertha Amanda Sofia (Helander) Tammeus; m. David Pendleton McPhail, Sept. 7, 1958 (div. 1972); children: Julia Elizabeth, Mark Andrew. BS, Juilliard Sch. Music, 1962; postgrad., Stanford U., 1983-84, L'Academia, Florence and Pistoia, Italy, 1984-85. Cert. tchr., Calif.; lic. real estate broker, Calif. Tchr. Woodstock Sch., Musoorie, India, 1957, Canadian, Tex., 1962-66; tchr. Head Royce Sch., Oakland, Calif., 1975-79, 87—, Sleepy Hollow Sch., Orinda, Calif., 1985—; realtor Freeholders, Berkeley, Calif., 1971-85, Northbrae Properties, Berkeley, 1985—; organist Kellogg Meml., Musoorie, 1956-57, Mills Coll. Chapel, Oakland, 1972—; cashier Trinity U., San Antonio, 1957-58; cen. records sec. Riverside Ch., N.Y.C., 1958-60; sec. Dr. Rollo May, N.Y.C., 1959-62, United Presbyn. Nat. Missions, N.Y.C., 1960, United Presbyn. Ecumenical Mission, N.Y.C., 1961, Nat. Coun. Chs., N.Y.C., 1962; choral dir. First Presbyn. Ch., Canadian, 1966; assoc. in music Montclair Presbyn. Ch., Oakland, 1972-88. Produced and performed maj. choral and orchestral works, 1972-88. Orinda Union Sch. Dist. grantee, 1988. Mem. Choral Condrs. Guild, Berkeley Bd. Realtors, East Bay Regional Multiple Listing Svc., Commonwealth Club (San Francisco). Democrat. Home: 7360 Claremont Ave Berkeley CA 94705 Office: Northbrae Properties 1600 Hopkins Berkeley CA 94707

MC PHAIL, WILLIAM K. V., construction executive, consultant; b. Tucson, Sept. 15, 1960; s. James Harry and Lydia Jo (Mechkoff) McP.; m. Stephanie Kay Langley, July 16, 1983. BS in Constrn. Engring., Mont. State U., 1983. Project leader, estimator Sletten Constrn. Co., Great Falls, Mont., 1983-87, cons., 1988—; v.p., owner Profl. Systems, Inc., Great Falls, 1987—; project mgr., owner Broadwater Mcpl. Devel. Group, Ltd., Great Falls, 1987—; pres., owner BMRJ Devels., Ltd., Great Falls, 1988—; cons. Morgen & Oswood Constrn. Co., Great Falls, 1987—, CD Contractors, Helena, Mont., 1988—; fellow IBM Mktg. Assistance Program. Contbr. articles to various publs. Chmn. United Way Cascade County, Great Falls, 1985—. Mem. Am. Correctional Assn., Great Falls Soc. Architects, Associated Gen. Contractors, Great Falls C. of C., Downtown Optomists Club, Universal Sports Club, Elks. Republican. Presbyterian. Home: 716 56th St S Great Falls MT 59405 Office: Profl Systems Inc 20 3d St N Ste 203 Great Falls MT 59401

MC PHERSON, ROLF KENNEDY, clergyman, church official; b. Providence, Mar. 23, 1913; s. Harold S. and Aimee Elizabeth (Semple) McP.; m. Lorna De Smith, July 21, 1931; children—Marlene (dec.), Kay. Grad., So. Cal. Radio Inst., 1933; D.D. (hon.), L.I.F.E. Bible Coll., 1944; LLD (hon.), L.I.F.E. Bible Coll., Los Angeles, 1988. Ordained to ministry Internat. Ch. Foursquare Gospel, 1949. Pres. emeritus Internat. Ch. Foursquare Gospel, L.A., 1988—. Mem. Echo Park Evangelistic Assn. (pres. 1944—). Office: 1910 W Sunset Blvd Ste 600 Los Angeles CA 90026

MCQUAID, SALLI LOU, writer, educator; b. Eugene, Oreg., May 17, 1943; d. William D. Randall and Mary Lou (Robertson) Duwell; m. Patrick C. Wiley, July 15, 1962 (div. Oct. 1972); children: James W., Colleen L., Darren P.; m. Michael James McQuaid, June 27, 1987. BA, San Jose State U., 1975; MA in Art, 1983; grad., Nikon Sch. Photography, 1978. Freelance writer numerous newspapers, San Francisco and others, 1975-78, Eugene and Springfield, Oreg., 1978-81; prof. San Jose State U., 1973-75, San Francisco State U., 1975; prof. of English Calif. State U., Hayward, 1987—; catalog essay writer, lectr. panelist Triton Mus. Art, Santa Clara, 1988. Author: (poetry) I Looked Into Narcissus and Discovered a Mirror, 1977, (novella) In Oregon the Rain Is Gray, 1987, (movie) Death Quest, 1988. Vol. Am. Cancer Soc., Pleasanton, Oreg., 1988. Named Foremost Art Critic, San Jose Art League, 1988. Mem. San Jose State U. Art Alumni Assn. (bd. dirs. 1984-86), Calif. Faculty Assn., World Kuk Sool Won Assn., Nat. Assn. Underwater Instrs. Democrat. Roman Catholic. Office: Calif State U Hayward CA 94542

MCQUAIN, DONNA MARIE, nurse; b. Omaha, July 14, 1953; d. Willis Walter and Doris May McQ. AA, Maricopa Community Coll., Phoenix, 1973; BS in Nursing, U. Phoenix, 1987. Cert. missionary, family nurse practitioner, nurse. Staff nurse Maynard McDougal Meml. Hosp., Nome, Alaska, 1973-74; family nurse practitioner Valley Wide Health Service, Alamosa, Colo., 1976-77, Apache Junction (Ariz.) Med. Ctr., 1977-78, Ariz. State U., Tempe, 1978-80; staff nurse Metrocenter Emergency, Phoenix, 1980-81; family nurse practitioner SIM Internat. Missions, Liberia, 1982, Dr. Norman, DO, Avondale, Ariz., 1983-85, Dr. R.W. Meyers, Willcox, Ariz., 1985-86, No. Cochise Community Hosp., Willcox, 1986-88, Harmon Clinic, Willcox, 1988—. Leader First Bapt. Youth Fellowship, Willcox, 1985—, First Bapt. Youth Choir, 1988. Mem. Am. Acad. Nurse Practitioners, Jr. Women Am. Republican. Office: Harmon Clinic 524 Maley Willcox AZ 85643

MCQUILLIN, MAHLON BRICE, II, television producer, director; b. Chgo., Apr. 3, 1950; s. Brice and Eleanor Valey (Lindskog) McQ. AA, Coll. San Mateo, 1970. Mem. advt .dept. San Mateo (Calif.) Times, 1970-71; audio systems mgr. Foremans Co., San Mateo, 1971-73; video systems mgr. Brooks Co., San Francisco, 1973-76; pres. gen. mgr. MicroVision Systems, San Mateo, 1976—; owner, cons. McQ Prodns.; producer, dir., editor TV programs for broadcast, corp. communications, syndication, commls.; dir. cable series Comedy Showcase; instr. Coll. San Mateo, 1981-84; faculty mem. N.Am. TV Inst.; bd. dirs. San Francisco Film/Tape Council, sec., 1986-87. Author: The Video Production Guide 1983, Computers in Video Production, 1986; (with others) The Handbook of Private Television, 1982; designer Edit Master videotape editing system; developer computer software; editor Internat. TV News, 1975-79; contbg. editor Video Systems mag., 1978-81; contbr. articles to industry publs. Active Poplar Ctr., San Mateo. Served with USAFR, 1970-73. Winner Silver and Bronze awards Internat. Film and TV Festival of N.Y., 1979, 81, 82, Gold award Internat. Film and TV Festival of N.Y., 1983. Mem. Internat. TV Assn. (Golden Reel of Excellence), Soc. Motion Picture and TV Engrs., Nat. Acad. TV Arts and Scis. Office: PO Box 1676 San Mateo CA 94401

MCQUOWN, THERESA ANN, computer company executive; b. Sisseton, S.D., Mar. 25, 1949; d. Stephen Nick and Clairce Telfreda (Skogen) Oswskey; m. Thomas Richard McQuown, Nov. ll, 1967 (div. July 1984); 1 child, Edward Spencer. Student, Mesa Community Coll., 1969-73, Phoenix Coll., 1983-84. Credit investigator Chilton Credit Bur., Mesa, Ariz.z, 1972-73; automobile leasing ops. mgr. Ariz. Bank, Phoenix, 1973-8l; br. mgr., cons. Computer Task Group, Inc., Phoenix, 198l—. Mem. Soc. for Tech. Communications, NAFE. Office: Computer Task Group Inc 7600 N l5th St Ste 250 Phoenix AZ 85020

MCRAE, HAMILTON EUGENE, III, lawyer; b. Midland, Tex., Oct. 29, 1937; s. Hamilton Eugene and Adrian (Hagaman) McR.; m. Betty Hawkins, Aug. 27, 1960; children: Elizabeth Ann, Stephanie Adrian, Scott Hawkins. BSEE, U. Ariz., 1961; student, USAF Electronics Sch., 1961-62; postgrad., U. Redlands, Calif., 1962-63; JD with honors and distinction, U. Ariz., 1967. Bar: Ariz. 1967, U.S. Supreme Ct. 1979. Elec. engr. Salt River Project, Phoenix, 1961; assoc. Jennings, Strouss & Salmon, Phoenix, 1967-71, ptnr., 1971-85, chmn. real estate dept., 1980-85, mem. policy com., 1982-85, mem. fin. com., 1981-85, chmn. bus. devel. com., 1982-85; ptnr. and co-founder Stuckey & McRae, Phoenix, 1985—; co-founder, chmn. bd. Republic Cos., Phoenix, 1985—; magistrate Paradise Valley, Ariz., 1983-85; juvenile referee Superior Ct., 1983-85; pres., dir. Phoenix Realty & Trust Co., 1970—; officer Indsl. Devel. Corp. Maricopa County, 1972-86; instr. and lectr. in real estate; officer, bd. dirs. other corps. Contbr. articles to profl. jours. Elder Valley Presbyn. Ch., Scottsdale, Ariz., 1973-75, 82-85, corp. pres., 1974-75, 84-85, trustee, 1973-75, 82-85, chmn. exec. com., 1984; trustee Upward Found., Phoenix, 1977-80, Valley Presbyn. Found., 1982-83, Ariz. Acad., 1971—; trustee, mem. exec. com. Phi Gamma Delta Ednl. Found., Washington, 1974-84; trustee Phi Gamma Delta Internat., 1984-86; bd. dirs. Archon, 1986-87; founder, trustee McRae Found.; bd. dirs. Food for Hungry (Internat. Relief), 1985—, exec. com., 1986—, chmn. bd. dirs., 1987—; trustee, mem. exec. com. Ariz. Mus. Sci. and Tech., 1984—, 1st v.p., 1985-86, pres., 1986-88, chmn. bd. dirs., 1988—; Lambda Alpha Internat. Hon. Land Econs. Soc, 1988—; sec.-treas. Ariz. State U. Council for Design Excellence, 1989—, bd. dirs. 1988—, sec.-treas. 1989—; bd. dirs. Crisis Nursery Office of the Chair, 1988—, Maricopa Community Colls. Found., 1988—, Phoenix Community Alliance, 1988—, Interchurch Ctr. Corp., 1987—, Western Art Assocs., 1989—, Phoenix Com. on Fgn. Rels., 1988—, U. Ariz. Pres.'s Club, 1984—, Econ. Club of Phoenix, 1987-88; vol. fund raiser YMCA, Salvation Army, others; mem. Taliesin Council, Frank Lloyd Wright Found., 1985—; mem. fin. com. Kyl for Congress, 1985—; mem. bond com. City of Phoenix, 1987-88; bd. dirs. Food for Hungry (Internat. Relief), 1985—, exec. com., 1986—, chmn. bd. dirs. 1987—; mem. Ariz. State U. Coun. of 100, 1985-89, investment com., 1985-89. With USAF, 1961-64. Recipient various mil. awards. Mem. ABA, Ariz. Bar Assn., Maricopa County Bar Assn., AIME, Ariz. Acad., U. Ariz. Alumni Assn., U. Ariz. Pres.'s Club (bd. dirs. 1984—), Econ. Club Phoenix (bd. dirs. 1987—), Clan McRae Soc. N.Am., Tau Beta Pi. Republican. Clubs: Phoenix Exec., Phoenix Country, Ariz., Continental Country, Jackson Hole Racquet (Wyo.). Home: 8101 N 47th St Paradise Valley AZ 85253 Office: Republic Cos 2425 E Camelback Rd Ste 900 Phoenix AZ 85016

MCREYNOLDS, R. BRUCE, interior designer; b. Taft, Calif., Dec. 30, 1940; s. Aylmer Guy and Marie Elizabeth (Miller) Swayze; m. Linda H. Rogovin, Dec. 26, 1964; 1 child, Stacey Alyn. BS, Calif. Poly. Inst., 1963. Adminstr. Computer Machine Corp., Los Angeles, 1970-73; dir. adminstrn. services WANGCO, Los Angeles, 1973-75; v.p. design REEL/Grobman & Assoc., Los Angeles, 1975-83; pres. RBM Design, Los Angeles, 1983—. Active Calif. Conf. on Interior Design. Mem. Am. Soc. Interior Designers, Inst. Bus. Designers, Internat. Facility Manage Assn. Office: RBM Design 1296 S La Cienega Blvd #210 Los Angeles CA 90035

MCSWEENY, JOHN EDWARD, defense industry executive; b. San Mateo, Calif., July 19, 1936; s. Edward Joseph and Alice (Barrett) McS.; m. Aug. 26, 1967; children: Sean Edward, Patrick Michael, Erin Marie, Kevin Joseph. BSEE, Loyola U., L.A., 1959; MSEE, U. Colo., 1961. Registered profl. engr., Calif. Electronics engr. Gen. Dynamics Pomona (Calif.) Div., 1961-66, design specialist, 1966-69, sect. head, 1969-70, sr. project engr., 1970-72, dir. phalanx program, 1972-76, v.p., program dir. Navy moderate range tactical weapons, 1976-80, v.p., dep. gen. mgr. programs, 1980-81, v.p., dep. gen mgr. fin. and adminstrn., 1981-82; v.p., gen. mgr. Gen. Dynamics Convair Div., San Diego, 1982—. Mem. Am. Def. Preparedness Assn., Navy League. Roman Catholic. Office: Gen Dynamics/Convair Div PO Box 85357 San Diego CA 92138 also: Gen Dynamics Corp Pierre Laclede Ctr Saint Louis MO 63105

MCTIERNAN, MIRIAM, government executive; b. Limerick, Ireland, May 2, 1952; arrived in Can., 1973; d. Michael and Marjorie (Woulfe) Lynch; m. Timothy Patrick McTiernan, Oct. 31, 1972; 1 child, Leah Rhiannon. BA with honors, Nat. U. Ireland, U. Coll. Dublin, 1972, diploma in archival studies, 1973; diploma in pub. sector mgmt. U. Victoria, 1985. Coll. archivist Douglas Coll., New Westminster, B.C., 1973-76; univ. archivist U. B.C., Vancouver, 1975; credit union archivist B.C. Cen. Credit Union, Vancouver, 1976-79; govt. records archivist Govt. of Yukon, Whitehorse, Yukon Ter., 1979-80, territorial archivist, 1980-84, dir. libraries and archives, 1984—. Contbr. articles to profl. jours. Mem. Assn. Can. Archivists (bus. archives com. 1976-79, treas. 1981-83, v.p. 1983-84, pres. 1984-85, chmn. nominations and elections com. 1985-87), Bur. Can. Archivists, Assn. B.C. Archivists (sec.-treas. 1976-78, pres. 1978-80), Can. Council of Archives (Yukon rep. 1985—, bd. dirs. 1987—, chair planning and priorities com. 1987—), Yukon Geog. Names Bd., Yukon Hist. and Mus. Assn. (treas. 1981), Soc. Am. Archivists, Assn. Records Mgr. and Adminstrs., Inst. Pub. Adminstrn. Can.

MCTIGHE, E. JAMES, freelance writer, researcher; b. Mitchell, S.D., Feb. 8, 1930; s. Gilbert Townsend and Gladys Irene (Cummings) McT.; m. Mary Lucile Dougherty, Aug. 23, 1952 (dec. Jan. 1988); children: James, Thomas, Michele, Christine, Margaret, Patrick, Martha, Catherine, Monica. BS in Journalism, Marquette U., 1952; MA in Polit. Sci., Georgetown U., 1958. Reporter Daily Republic, Mitchell, 1947-48, 52; intelligence analyst U.S. Govt., Washington, 1955-58; polit. officer Am. Embassy, The Hague, Netherlands, 1958-6l, Quito, Ecuador, 1970-73; polit. analyst Am. Embassy, Paris, 1963-67; polit. analyst Office Polit. Rsch. CIA, Washington, 1975-77; rsch. fellow Ctr. for Study Intelligence, Washington, 1977-78; freelance writer Boulder, Colo., 1978—. Author: Roadside History of Colorado, 1984, Survival Manual for Consumers, 1986; contbr. articles to Colo. Outdoors. Lay min. St. Martin's Cath. Ch., Boulder, 1978-79; vol. Boulder Dem. Com., 1980, Easter Seals, Boulder, 1986; bd. dirs. Mother House Women's Shelter, Boulder, 1984. With USAF, 1952-55.

MCUNE, ROGER WARREN, security consultant; b. Burns, Oreg., Oct. 30, 1932; s. George and Esther Ann (Eby) McU.; m. Mary Elizabeth Hostler, Aug. 27, 1963; children: Deborah Ann, Michael Andrew, Matthew Scott, Donna Michelle. Student, RCA Institutes, 1965-67. Electronics technician USCG, 1950-78; security systems analyst E G & G, Albuquerque, 1978-79; security devices engr. Shorrock/Greyhound, Albuquerque, 1980-81; security cons. McUne Security Consulting, Albuquerque, 1982-85, MSC Analytics, Albuquerque, 1986—. Cub master Cub Scouts Am., Albuquerque, 1978-81. Home and Office: 5 Del Fuego Circle NE Albuquerque NM 87113

MCVAY, JOHN EDWARD, professional football club executive; b. Bellaire, Ohio, Jan. 5, 1931; s. John A. and Helen (Andrews) McV.; m. Eva Lee; children: John R., James P., Timothy G. B.S. in Edn., Miami U., Oxford, Ohio, 1953; M.A. in Sch. Adminstrn., Kent (Ohio) State U., 1963. Asst. football coach, instr. phys. edn. Mich. State U., 1962-65; head coach, dir. athletics U. Dayton, Ohio, 1965-74; head coach, gen. mgr. Memphis in World Football League, 1974-76; head football coach New York Giants, Nat. Football League, 1976-78; dir. player personnel San Francisco 49ers, Nat. Football League, 1979-80, dir. football ops., 1980-81, v.p. adminstrn., 1981-83, gen. mgr., v.p., 1983—. Exec. dir. Catholic Youth Council, Canton, Ohio, 1959-62. Named to Miami U. Athletic Hall of Fame. Mem. Sigma Chi, Phi Epsilon Kappa, Phi Delta Kappa. Office: care San Francisco 49ers 4949 Centennial Blvd Santa Clara CA 95054

MCVEIGH-PETTIGREW, SHARON CHRISTINE, communications consultant; b. San Francisco, Feb. 6, 1949; d. Martin Allen and Frances (Roddy) McVeigh; m. John Wallace Pettigrew, Mar. 27, 1971; children: Benjamin Thomas, Margaret Mary. B.A. with honors, U. Calif.-Berkeley, 1971; diploma of edn. Monash U., Australia, 1975; M.B.A., Golden Gate U., 1985. Tchr., adminstr. Victorian Edn. Dept., Victoria, Australia, 1972-79; supr. Network Control Ctr., GTE Sprint Communications, Burlingame, Calif., 1979-81, mgr. customer assistance, 1981-84, mgr. state legis. ops., 1984-85, dir. revenue programs, 1986-97; communications cons. Flores, Pettigrew & Co., San Mateo, Calif., 1987—; telecommunications speaker Dept. Consumer Affairs, Sacramento, 1984. Panelist Wash. Gov.'s Citizens Council, 1984; founding mem. Maroondah Women's Shelter, Victoria, 1978; organizer nat. conf. Bus. Women and the Polit. Process, New Orleans, 1986; mem. sch. bd. Boronia Tech. Sch., Victoria, 1979. Recipient Tchr. Spl. Responsibilities award Victoria Edn. Dept., 1979. Mem. Women in Telecommunications (panel moderator San Francisco 1984), Am. Mgmt. Assn., Peninsula Profl. Women's Network, Women's Econ. Action League. Democrat. Roman Catholic. Office: Flores Pettigrew & Co 445 Georgetown Ave San Mateo CA 94402

MC VIE, CHRISTINE PERFECT, musician; b. Eng., July 12, 1943; m. John McVie (div.); m. Eddy Quintela. Student art sch., pvt. student sculpture. Singer, keyboardist, Fleetwood Mac, from 1970; albums with Fleetwood Mac include: Bare Trees, 1972, Penguin, Mystery To Me, Heroes Are Hard to Find, 1975, Fleetwood Mac, 1976, Rumours, 1977, Tusk, 1979, Mirage, 1982, Tango in the Night, 1987; solo albums include Christine Perfect, 1969, Christine McVie, 1984; composer: songs including Spare Me a Little of Your Love, Don't Stop, You Make Loving Fun, Over and Over, Hold Me, Songbird, Got a Hold on Me, Heroes Are Hard to Find. Office: care Warner Bros Records 3300 Warner Blvd Burbank CA 91510

MCWILLIAMS, GORDON MASLEN, architect; b. Keene, N.H., June 18, 1949; s. Norman Beattie and Micheline Yvone (Deane) McW.; m. Mary Oliver Davidson, Mar. 19, 1976; children: Angus Deane, Kathryn Taylor. AB, Dartmouth Coll., 1971; MArch, U. Pa., 1979. Registered architect, Oreg., Pa. Architect Stephen Mark Goldner Assoc., Phila., 1976-79, Carles Enric Vallhonrat, Phila., 1979-81, Vincent Kling Assoc., Phila., 1981-83; sr. assoc. architect SRG Partnership, P.C., Portland, Oreg., 1983--. Prin. works include Dupont Plant Sci Research Ctr., Wilmington, Del., Boise Cascade Research and Devel. Ctr., Swan Island, Portland, Oreg. Dales fellow, 1979. Mem. Am. Inst. Architects, Found. for Architecture, Multnomah Athletic Club, City Club of Portland (mem. research bd. 1988--). Democrat.

MC WILLIAMS, ROBERT HUGH, judge; b. Salina, Kans., Apr. 27, 1916; s. Robert Hugh and Laura (Nicholson) McW.; m. Catherine Ann Cooper, Nov. 4, 1942 (dec.); 1 son, Edward Cooper; m. Joan Harcourt, Mar. 8, 1986. A.B., U. Denver, 1938, LL.B., 1941. Bar: Colo. bar 1941. Colo. dist. judge Denver, 1952-60; justice Colo. Supreme Ct., 1961-68, chief justice, 1969-70; judge 10th Circuit Ct. Appeals 1970—. Served with AUS, World War II. Mem. Phi Beta Kappa, Omicron Delta Kappa, Phi Delta Phi, Kappa Sigma. Republican. Episcopalian. Home: 137 Jersey St Denver CO 80220 Office: US Ct Appeals C-402 US Courthouse 1929 Stout St Denver CO 80294

MEACHAM, CHARLES HARDING, government official; b. Newman, Calif., Sept. 21, 1925; s. Vernon A. and Sara (Paulsen) M.; m. June Lorraine Yunker, June 22, 1946; children—Charles Paulsen, Bruce Herbert. B.S., Utah State U., 1950. Biologist Calif. Dept. Fish and Game, 1950-56, Alaska Dept. Fisheries, 1956-59; regional supr. regions II and III Alaska Dept. Fish and Game, 1959-68; dir. internat. fisheries Office Gov. Alaska, 1968-69; commr. U.S. Fish and Wildlife Service, Dept. Interior, 1969-70; spl. asst. to area dir. U.S. Fish and Wildlife Service, Dept. Interior, Alaska, 1971-74; dir. internat. affairs Office of Gov., Juneau, Alaska, 1975-80; pres. Meacham & Assocs., Anchorage, 1980—; commr. U.S. North Pacific Fur Seal Commn.; mem. Pacific and North Pacific Fisheries Mgmt. Councils, 1976-81; chmn. nat. park system adv. bd. U.S. Dept. Interior. Served with USMCR, 1943-46. Mem. Am. Fisheries Soc., Wildlife Soc., Pacific Fisheries Biologists, Internat. Assn. Game, Fish and Conservation Commrs., Ducks Unlimited, Alaska Miners Assn., Am. Legion. Club: Elks. Office: 3438 Stanford Dr Anchorage AK 99504

MEACHAM, CRAIG LEI, police chief; b. Pasadena, Calif., Mar. 5, 1931; s. William Albert and Edna May (Hornbeck) M.; m. Carolyn June Stentz, Feb. 22, 1971; children—Alan, Pamela, Craig, Janelle, Cynthia. A.A., Rio Hondo Coll., 1964; B.A., Calif. Western U., 1976, M.A., 1976. With Whittier (Calif.) Police Dept., 1955-69, div. comdr., until 1969; cons. criminal justice Gov. Ronald Reagan, 1969-70; dep. chief West Covina Police Dept., 1970-78, chief of police, 1978—, pub. safety div. mgr., 1981—; instr. Rio Hondo Coll. With USAF, 1950-54. Mem. Los Angeles County Chiefs of Police Assn. (pres. 1982), San Gabriel Valley Police Chiefs Assn. (pres. 1982), Calif. Police Chiefs Assn. (pres. 1988), Peace Officers Assn. Los Angeles County (pres. 1986—), San Gabriel Valley Peace Officers Assn. (pres. 1983), West Covina C. of C. (legis. com.). Club: West Covina Lions. Office: 1444 W Garvey Ave West Covina CA 91790

MEADE, EDWARD PENNINGTON, II, computer cable industry executive; b. Rochester, N.Y., May 2, 1940; s. Edward Pennington Sr. and Elizabeth Jeannett (Fuller) M.; m. Sylvia Van Note, Aug. 17, 1963 (div. 1973); children: Edward P. III, Cara Gwen, Christopher Phillip; m. Carol Ann Cochran, Mar. 2, 1974; 1 child, Arianne Fuller. BA, San Diego State U. Quality control inspector Keafott Arionics, San Marcos, Calif., 1964-66; sales engr. Continental Device Corp., Hawthorne, Calif., 1966-69; sales mgr. Western Transistor Corp., El Monte, Calif., 1969-71; dist. sales mgr. Sprague Electric Co., Worcester, Mass., 1971-73; sales mgr. Sloan Micro Electronics, El Segundo, Calif., 1973; dist. sales mgr. Fairchild Semiconductor, Denver, 1973-76; gen. mgr. Ratel Electronics, Denver, 1976-79; founder, pres. Mountain Cable Industries, Inc., Golden, Colo., 1979—. Mem. Rep. Nat. Com., Washington, 1984. Mem. Colo. Electronics Assn. (bd. dirs. 1987—), Greater Denver C. of C., Bear Creek Country Club, Art Reach, Colo. Republicans., Jefferson County C. of C. Office: Mountain Cable Industries 16026 W 5th Ave Golden CO 80401

MEADE, JACK SOMMERS, sales executive, consultant; b. Poughkeepsie, N.Y., May 30, 1929; s. Harold David and Edythe Adele (Brown) M.; m. Patricia Ann Reinckens, Mar. 17, 1949; children; Gregory, Susan, Brad. BA in Air Transp. Engring, Purdue U., 1953. Ops. engr. Pan Am. World Airways, Miami, Fla., 1953-59; sales rep. Boeing Airplane Co., Renton, Wash., 1959-65; mgr. sales dept. Douglas Aircraft Co., Long Beach, Calif., 1965-66; dir. sales dept. Fairchild-Hiller Co., Hagerstown, Md., 1966-67; sr. dir. sales div. Lockheed Calif. Co., Burbank, 1967-84; v.p. mktg. dept. Tracor Aviation, Inc., Goleta, Calif., 1984—; bd. dirs. Contact Systems, N.Y.C. Mem. Sigma Alpha Tau. Republican. Presbyterian. Home: 1895 Ringstep Dr Solvang CA 93463 Office: Tracor Aviation Inc 495 S Fairview Ave Goleta CA 93117

MEADE, JAMES PENNY, JR., family therapist, counselor, public speaker; b. Forest Grove, Oreg., Jan. 19, 1947; s. James Penny Meade and Christine Jane (Williams) Boyed; m. Marie-Louise deBranac, July 30, 1978; children: James, Dava-Lee, Shawna, Christopher. AS, Mt. Hood Community Coll., 1970; BS, Portland State U., 1973; MA, Calif. State U., Fresno, 1981; PhD, Internat. Coll., Sacramento, 1984. Sales rep. Hunt-Wesson Foods, Inc., Salem, Oreg., 1974-83; vets. outreach specialist, psychologist VA, Fresno, 1984-86; family therapist, counselor Lt. David E. Meade Meml. Found., San Diego, 1986—; instr. San Diego Community Coll. Dist., 1989—; speaker in field. Author: Personal Asset Development Workbook, 1988, The Searching of Willie Gene Wright, 1984, Making Reality, 1981. Bd. dirs. San Diego Head Injury Found., 1988—; chmn. vets. com. San Diego County Task Force on Self-Esteem, 1988—; active Rep. Jim Bates Subcom. on Disability, San Diego, 1989—. With U.S. Army, 1965-68, Vietnam. Recipient Cert. for Outstanding Community Achievement of Vietnam Era Vet. Pres. Jimmy Carter, 1980, D.F.C., Bronze Star with Oak Leaf Cluster, Purple Heart, Air Medals with Silver Oak Leaf Clusters. Mem. Vietnam Vets. Am. (pres. San Diego chpt. 1989—), Calif. Assn. Marriage and Family Therapists, Nat. Speakers Assn. Democrat. Home and Office: 850 State St #108 San Diego CA 92101

MEADER, JONATHAN GRANT (KYTHE ASCIAN), artist; b. Orange, N.J., Aug. 29, 1943; s. William Granville and Audrey Meader. One-man shows Corcoran Dupont Center, 1969, Lunn Gallery, Washington, 1972, Pyramid Gallery, Washington, 1973, 74, Plum Gallery, Md., 1976, 78, 78, Klein-Vogel Gallery, Mich., 1976, Harlan Gallery, Tucson, 1977, Swearingen Gallery, Ky., 1977, Schoolhouse Gallery, Fla., 1978, 83, Ethel Putterman Gallery, Mass., 1978, Washington Project for Arts, 1981, Galerie Grüner Panther, Frankfurt, W. Ger., 1982, Illuminarium Gallery, Los Angeles, 1985, Illuminarium Gallery, Larkspur, Calif., 1985; Illuminarium, Mill Valley, Calif., 1982, 83, Gallery Show, Tokyo, 1985, Kraskin Gallery, Potomac, Md., 1986, Midtown Gallery, Washington, 1986, Kunst-Utmsyknig Gallery, Norway, 1987, House of Artists, Moscow, 1989; group shows include Corcoran Gallery Art, Washington, 1972, Balt. Mus. Traveling Show, 1972, Phillips Collection, Washington, 1972, Iowa U. Mus., 1975, Plum Gallery, 1975; represented in permanent collections, Whitney Mus. Am. Art, N.Y.C., Met. Mus. Art, N.Y.C., Nat. Gallery, Washington, Hirshhorn Mus., Washington, Zenith Gallery, Washington, 1987, Hall of Artists, Moscow, 1989. Wurlitzer Found. grantee, 1967; Stern Family grantee, 1970; Nat. Endowment Arts grantee, 1974. Address: 758 Marin Dr Mill Valley CA 94941

MEADERS, FRANK BARTLEY, JR., general manager; b. Abilene, Tex., Nov. 4, 1937; s. Frank Bartley and Julia Francis (McCary) M.; m. Roberta Baltosser, July 26, 1969; 1 child, Aprille Michelle. BBA, U. Okla., 1960, MBA, 1969, postgrad. Territory mgr. Walker Mfg. Co., Racine, Wis., 1960-67; system analyst U. Okla., Norman, Okla., 1968-71; dir. mgt. svcs. U. Okla., Norman, 1971-72, dir. auxiliary svcs., 1972-76; owner, operator Dunkin Donuts of Norman, 1976-79; pres. Med. Staffing Svcs., Okla. City, 1978-85; mgt. cons. George S. May Internat. Co., Redwood City, 1985-87; gen. mgr. Jason & Son Natural Foods, Rancho Cordova, Calif., 1987—. Mem. Delta Upsilon (Okla. chpt. Man of Yr. 1971). Republican. Episcopalian.

MEADES, KENNETH RICHARDSON, broadcasting and electronics consultant; b. Montreal, Que., Can., Mar. 2, 1943; came to U.S., 1963; s. Harold and Frances (Richardson) M. AA, Los Angeles City Coll.; student, Calif. State U., Los Angeles. Cons. in broadcasting, electronics and music Los Angeles. Mem. Soc. Broadcast Engrs. Democrat. Roman Catholic.

MEADOR, JAMES G., health care management consultant; b. Belton, Mo., Jan. 9, 1936; s. Chester Ray and Marie M. (Dodson) M.; m. Mary Lee Anderson, Apr. 7, 1957 (div. 1971); children: Amy Lynne, Janice Kay; m. Nancy Lee Pyles, Nov. 26, 1972. BA in Econs. with honors, U. Mo., 1957; postgrad., U. Kans. City, 1962. V.p. Citizens Bank, Belton, 1960-62; pvt. practice as health care mgmt. cons. Denver, Seattle, 1962—; v.p., bd. dirs. Practice Mgmt., Inc., St. Petersburg, Fla. Author: Why Physicians in Group Practice Earn Less Than Comparable Colleagues, 1977. Served as capt. USMC, 1957-60. Mem. Phi Eta Sigma, Phi Beta Kappa. Republican. Methodist. Home: 1540 Alki Ave SW Seattle WA 98116 Office: Regional Radiation Therapy Ctr 500 Keene St Columbia MO 65102

MEADOR, RICHARD ESTEN, furniture manufacturing executive; b. Balt., May 12, 1945; s. Francis Xavier and Doris Virginia (Hardy) M.; m. Patricia Burgess, Apr. 26, 1986. BS in Furniture Mfg. and Mgmt., N.C. State U.-Raleigh, 1968; MBA, U. N.C., 1970. With DMI Furniture, Inc., 1971—, v.p. mfg., 1978-80, exec. v.p. ops., 1980-83, pres., chief operating officer, 1983-85; gen. mgr. Brother Furniture Industries, Inc., 1985-87; pres. and chief operating officer San Diego Design, Inc., 1987-88, , also dir.; gen. mgr. Sheppard Office Systems, Seattle, 1988—. Pres., chmn. bd. Hardwood Rsch. Council, Asheville, N.C., 1983-85. Capt. Ind. Army N.G., 1968-76. Mem. Am. Furniture Mfrs. Assn. (dir. prodn. div. 1983-85), Young Pres.'s Orgn., Nat. Model RR Assn., Christmas Lake Golf and Tennis Club. Republican. Episcopalian. Editor: Production Woodworking Machinery, 1968; Furniture Construction, 1968. Office: Sheppard Office Systems 4975 3rd Ave S Seattle WA 98134

MEADOR, ROBERT LYMAN, dentist; b. Portland, Oreg., Jan. 20, 1934; m. Sharon Lynn Caillouet, Apr. 10, 1967 (div. June 1978); m. Charlotte Ann Dodson, Sept. 14, 1985. BS, U. Oreg., 1957; DMD, U. Oreg., Portland, 1959. Lic. dentist, Calif., N.Mex., Oreg. Chief, attending dental staff Orange (Calif.) County Med. Ctr., 1966-67, chief, restorative dental service, 1971-77; assoc. prof. dentistry Loma Linda (Calif.) U., 1969-70; clin. assoc. prof. diagnostic scis., oral diagnosis and emergency clinic. U. So. Calif., Los Angeles, 1981-83, clin. assoc. prof.; dir., gen. practice residency and clin. restorative service U. Calif., Irving, 1974-77; chief, attending dental staff Fullerton (Calif.) Community Hosp., 1982-83. Contbr. articles to profl. jours. Mem. Am. Heart Assn. (bd. dirs. Orange County chpts. 1981—, active dental CPR program 1975—, chmn. emergency services com. 1975—, co-chmn. hypertension control com. 1975-78); active Allied Health Profls., Yorba Linda City Planning Commn.; pres. Richard M. Nixon Birthplace Found., 1982-86. Served to Capt. USAF, 1959-62. Named one of Outstanding Young Men Am., 1966, Outstanding State Dir., Calif. Jaycees, 1965; Paul Harris fellow, Yorba Linda Rotary club, 1980. Mem. Acad. Gen. Dentistry (mastership 1984), Am. Assn. Hosp. Denstists (Calif. vice-chmn. 1974-80), Am. Dental Assn. and Local Components, Am. Dental Soc. of Anesthesiology, Am. Edodontic Soc., Calif. Soc. Anesthesiology (pres.-elect 1983-84, pres. 1984-85), Orange County Dental Soc. (chmn. continuing edn. com. 1973-74, chmn. children's dental clinic com 1970-71), Yorba Linda C. of C. (pres. 1971-72), North Orange County Jaycees (dist. gov. state of Calif., 1968-69, outstanding dist. chmn. 1966), Yorba Linda Jaycees (pres. 1966-67, disting. service award 1967, Kay Man award 1967).

MEADOWCROFT, HERBERT JAMES, federal agency administrator; b. Washington, Feb. 26, 1941; s. Allan James and Lousia Marian M.; m. Sheron E. Huntzinger, Apr. 12,1976 (div. 1987); 1 child, Jason T. BS, Stanford U., 1963. Pilot Northwest Airlines, Mpls., 1970; aviation safety inspector FAA, Oakland, Calif., 1976-80, Long Beach, Calif., 1981—. Active Cub Scouts, Boy Scouts Am., Fountain Valley, Calif., 1988—. Capt. USAF, 1964-69, major USAFR, 1971-76. Decorated Air Medal, DFC. Republican. Presbyterian. Office: Aircraft Evaluation FAA 3229 E Spring St Long Beach CA 90806-2425

MEAGHER, PAUL CHRISTOPHER, nuclear engineer; b. Albany, N.Y., Sept. 13, 1953; s. John Joseph and Caroline Hedwig (Glatz) M.; m. Kathleen Niebuhr, Jan. 23, 1982; 1 child, Eric James. BS in Nuclear Engring., Rensselaer Poly. Inst., 1975; MS in Nuclear Engring., MIT, 1977; MS in Engring. Econ. Syst, Stanford U., 1987, postgrad., 1987—. Engr.-economist SRI Internat. Energy Ctr., Menlo Park, Calif., 1976-80; energy legis. asst. to Sen Charles Percy U.S. Senate, Washington, 1980-81; supr. load mgmt. project devel. and coordination load mgmt. Pacific Gas & Electric Co., San Francisco, 1981-85; electronics engr. Systems Rsch. Group, Lawrence Livermore (Calif.) Nat. Lab., 1986-88; project mgr. Electric Power Rsch. Inst., Palo Alto, Calif., 1988—. Contbr. papers to profl. publs. Mem. IEEE, Sigma Xi, Tau Beta Pi. Roman Catholic. Home: 1001 E Evelyn Terr #181 Sunnyvale CA 94086 Office: Electric Power Rsch Inst 3412 Hillview Ave Palo Alto CA 94303

MEAGHER, THOMAS FRANCIS VINCENT, research and development company executive; b. Ellensburg, Wash., Aug. 9, 1935; s. Martin C. and Agnes C. (Heraty) M.; m. Alberta Frances Hatzenbeler, June 9, 1956; children: Michael, Brian, Kathy, Scott, Chris, Keri, Tim. BSEE, U. Wash., 1960; MS in Applied Sci., U. Calif., Davis, 1966. Staff mem. Sandia Nat. Labs., Livermore, Calif., 1960-67; program mgr. Kaman Scis. Corp., Colorado Springs, Colo., 1967-79; pvt. cons. practice, Colorado Springs, 1979-80; chmn., pres., chief exec. officer, founder Aptek, Inc., Colorado Springs, 1980—. With U.S. Army, 1953-56. Mem. AIAA, Am. Def. Preparedness Assn., U.S. Space Found., Colorado Springs C. of C. Republican. Roman Catholic. Office: Aptek Inc 1257 Lake Plaza Dr Colorado Springs CO 80906

MEANS, ROBERT B., management consultant; b. Kansas City, Mo., Dec. 6, 1940; s. Robert Ross and Beulah (Barrett) M.; m. Diane Wood (div.); children: Kathleen, Robert; m. Yvonne V. Hughes, Mar. 19, 1978; 1 child, Rebecca. BA, U. Mont., 1962; MS in Indsl. Psychology, Purdue U., 1964, MS in Indsl. Adminstrn., 1966; PhD, Purdue, 1966. Mgr. Pickands Mather & Co., Cleve., 1966-69; sr. assoc. McKinsey & Co., San Francisco, 1969-74; v.p. Crocker Bank, San Francisco, 1974-77; prin. Meredith Assocs., Walnut Creek, Calif., 1977-79; pres. OXICON, Lafayette, Calif., 1979—; bd. dirs. George Lithograph, San Francisco. Contbg. editor Today's Distbr., 1988—. Fellow Am. Psychol. Assn.; mem. Am. Soc. for Personnel Adminstrn., Employment Mgmt. Assn., Sigma Xi, Phi Kappa Phi. Office: OXICON 3732 Mt Diablo Blvd Ste 290 Lafayette CA 94549

MEARS, SUSAN JANE, optometrist, low vision consultant; b. Slayton, Minn., Mar. 28, 1961; d. Dorothy Anna (Auschinsky) M. Student, Concordia Coll., Moorhead, Minn., 1979-81, U. Minn., 1981-82; B Visual Sci., Ill. Coll. Optometry, 1985, OD, 1986. Teller Marquette Nat. Bank, Mpls., 1981-83; receptionist Ill. Coll. Optometry, Chgo., 1983-84, with Placement Office, 1983-86, tchr.'s asst., 1986; intern Mpls. Soc. for Blind, 1985-86; pvt. practice, Poulsbo, Wash., 1986-89, Silverdale, Wash., 1989—; assoc. Nat. Fedn. Blind, 1987—. Alliss Found. scholar, 1979, 80. Mem. Am. Optometric Soc., Wash. Optometric Soc., Kitsap Optometric Soc., Vol. Optometric Svcs. to Humanity. Lutheran. Office: Kitsap Mall #J1 PO Box 3337 10315 Silverdale Way NE Silverdale WA 98383

MEBANE, MARY VIRGINIA, accountant; b. Dallas, Feb. 24, 1959; d. David Mitchell and Helen Marie (Wallis) M. BA, U. Colo., 1981. Mgr. construction, property acctg. Chilis, Inc., Dallas, 1982-87; controller, acct. Internat. Eaterings, Santa Barbara, Calif., 1988; acct., asst. to chief fin. officer Day Dream Pub., Santa Barbara, 1988; cost acct. Tracor Aviation, Santa Barbara, 1988—; investment tax credit, Chilis, Inc., Dallas, 1983-85. Docent Dallas Museum of Art, 1986, 87; patron Santa Barbara Symphony League, 1988-89. Mem. Nat. Assn. Female Execs. Democrat. Episcopalian. Office: Tracor Aviation 495 S Fairview Goleta CA 93117

MEBLIN, SAMUEL DAVID, public relations executive; b. Grand Forks, N.D., June 25, 1928; s. Isidor and Sadie (Wolovitch) M.; m. Gail Messina, Oct. 29, 1958 (div. 1972); children: Matthew, Daniel, Margaret. BA, U. N.D., 1953. Account exec. Graham Kislingbury Pub. Rels., San Francisco, 1957-67; v.p. Arnold & Palmer & Noble Pub. Rels., San Francisco, 1967-82, Carl Byoir & Assocs., San Francisco, 1982-87, Hill and Knowlton, Inc., San Francisco, 1987—. Bd. dirs. Mgmt. Ctr., San Francisco, 1982—; mem. media adv. com. Bur. Jewish Edn., San Francisco, 1987. Mem. Pub. Rels. Round Table San Francisco, Bohemian Club. Democrat. Home: 1120 Grizzly Peak Blvd Berkeley CA 94708 Office: Hill and Knowlton Inc 177 Post St Ste 400 San Francisco CA 94108

MECHAM, EVAN, former governor of Arizona; b. Duchesne, Utah, May 12, 1924; m. Florence Lambert; seven children. Student, Utah State U., 1942-43, Ariz. State U., 1947-50. Owner Pontiac agy. franchise, Ajo, Ariz., 1950-54, Glendale, Ariz., 1954-88; sen. State of Ariz., 1961-62, gov., 1987-88; past pub. Am. Newspaper Group. Author: Come Back America, 1982. Active Ch. Jesus Christ of Latter-day Sts. Served with USAF, 1943-46, prisoner of war, Germany. Address: PO Box 970 Glendale AZ 85311

MECHAM, GLENN JEFFERSON, lawyer; b. Logan, Utah, Dec. 11, 1935; s. Everett H. and Lillie (Dunford) M.; BS, Utah State U., 1957; JD, U. Utah, 1961; m. Mae Parson, June 5, 1957; children: Jeff B., Scott R., Marcia, Suzanne. Admitted to Utah Bar, 1961, Supreme Ct. U.S., U.S. Ct. Appeals 10th Cir., U.S. Dist. Ct. Utah, U.S. Ct. Claims; engaged in gen. practice, Roy, Utah, 1961-65; Duchesne County atty., 1962, Duchesne City atty., 1962; city judge Roy City, 1963-66; judge City of Ogden, Utah, 1966-69; lectr.-in-law and govt. Stevens-Henager Coll., Ogden, 1963-75; asst. U.S. atty. Dist. Utah, 1969-72; ptnr. Mecham & Richards, Ogden, Utah, 1972-82; pres. Penn Mountain Mining Co., South Pacific Internat. Bank, Ltd.; mem. Bur. Justice Stats. Adv. Bd., U.S. Dept. Justice. Chmn. Ogden City Housing Authority; chmn. instl. coun. Utah State U.; trustee Space Dynamics Lab. Utah State U.; asst. mayor City of Ogden; pres. Utah League Cities and Towns, 1981-82. Col. USAF, 1957. Mem. Weber County (pres. 1966-68), ABA, Utah Bar Assns., Am. Judicature Soc., Weber County Bar Legal Svcs. (chmn. bd. trustees 1966-69), Utah Assn. Mcpl. Judges (sec.), Sigma Chi, Phi Alpha Delta. Home: 1748 Victoria Ct Ogden UT 84403

MECKLENBURG, DIANNE JORGI, speech pathologist, audiologist; b. Los Angeles, Feb. 22, 1945; d. Ralph Anthony Mecklenburg and Pauline Rae (Sherman) Sherman. BA, Calif. State U., Los Angeles, 1971, MA, 1972; PhD, Bowling Green State U., 1977. Trainee VA, Los Angeles, 1971; research asst. Wayne State Med. Hosp., Detroit, 1976-77; lectr. audiology U. Melbourne, Australia, 1978-80; owner, pres. Cavale Cons., Boulder, Colo., 1980—; clin. coordinator Cochlear Corp., Englewood, Colo., 1980-85, dir. clin. studies, children's program, 1985-87; pres. MindLight Inc., Boulder, 1987—; internat. cons. Locklear Implants, 1987—; lectr. continuing edn. Fla. Lang. Speech and Hearing Assn., Calif. Speech and Hearing Assn., 1985-86. Asst. editor Australian Jour. Speech and Hearing, 1979-80. Grad. assistantship Calif. State U., 1971; fellow Bowling Green (Ohio) State U., 1973-76. Mem. Am. Speech Lang. and Hearing Assn., Am. Auditory Soc., Rehab. Engring. Soc. N.Am., Alexander Graham Bell Soc., Assn. for Research in Otolaryngology. Office: Mindlight Inc 975 8th St Boulder CO 80302

MEDAVOY, MIKE, motion picture company executive; b. Shanghai, China, Jan. 21, 1941; came to U.S., 1957, naturalized, 1962; s. Michael and Dora M.; m. Patricia Duff; 1 child, Brian. B.A., UCLA, 1963. With Casting dept. Universal Studios, 1963; agt. Bill Robinson Assos., Los Angeles, 1963-64; v.p. motion picture dept. GAC/CMA Co., 1965-71, IFA Co., 1971-74; sr. v.p. United Artists Corp., 1974-78; exec. v.p. Orion Pictures Co., Burbank, Calif., 1978-82, Orion Pictures Corp. (formerly Orion Pictures Co.), Burbank, 1982—. Mem. vis. com. Boston Museum Fine Arts.; chmn. Ctr. Internat. Strategic Affairs , UCLA, Com. to Cure Cancer through Immunization UCLA; co-chmn. Olympic Sports Fedn. Com., Music Ctr. Unified Fund Campaign; bd. govs. Sundance Inst., 1980-86; bd. dirs. Calif. Mus. Sci. and Industry, 1984-87. Recipient Academy award for One Flew over the Cuckoo's Nest, Rocky, Annie Hall, Amadeus, Platoon. Mem. Acad. Motion Picture Arts and Scis. (gov. 1977-81), UCLA Found., UCLA Chancellors Assocs. Office: Orion Pictures Corp 1888 Century Pk E 7th Fl Los Angeles CA 90067 also: Orion Pictures Corp 711 Fifth Ave New York NY 10022

MEDAVOY, PATRICIA DUFF, film producer; b. L.A., Apr. 12, 1955; d. Robert Thomas and Mary Elizabeth (Bogle) Orr; m. M. Mike Medavoy, May 24, 1986. Student, Internat. Sch. Brussels, 1971; BS in Internat. Econs., Georgetown U., 1976. Spl. asst. to chief counsel U.S. Ho. of Reps., Washington, 1976-78; writer, researcher John McLaughlin-NBC, Washington, 1979; asst. rsch. dir. Dem. Nat. Com., Washington, 1980; v.p. Caddell Assocs., Washington, 1980-82; advt. cons. Communications Co., Washington, 1982-83; assoc. Show Coalition, L.A., 1984; contbg. editor west coast Vogue Mag.; ind. producer Columbia Pictures, Burbank, Calif., 1988—. Co-producer: (films) Limit Up, 1989, For Your Family's Sake, 1989. Celebrity coord. Mondale for Pres., L.A., 1984, Americans for Hart, L.A., 1984; founder, chair show coalition, 1988-89; founder, bd. dirs. Education 1st., Calif. 1988, Share Our Strength, 1986-89; bd. visitors Gerogetown U., 1988—. Democrat. Office: Columbia Pictures Hollywood Way Gate Producer 4 #27 Burbank CA 90210

MEDEIROS, DENIS MICHAEL, nutritionist, educator; b. Acushnet, Mass., June 12, 1952; s. Joseph Medeiros and Rita Irene (Brassard) Wilkie; m. Lydia Claire Wiggins, Dec. 28, 1981; 1 child, Kathryn Claire. BS, Cen. Conn. State U., 1974; MS, Ill. State U., 1976; PhD, Clemson U., 1981. Registered dietitian, Wyo. Asst. prof. Miss. State U., Starkville, 1981-84; assoc. prof. nutrition U. Wyo., Laramie, 1984—; chair U. Wyo. Faculty Senate, 1989—. Mem. editorial bd., Biol. Trace Element Rsch., 1984, Nutrition Rsch., 1988; contbr. articles to profl. publs. Grantee, NSF, 1986, NIH, 1988. Mem. Am. Inst. Nutrition, Am. Dietetic Assn., Inst. Food Technologists, Am. Pub. Health Assn., Sigma Xi, Gamma Sigma Delta. Democrat. Roman Catholic. Home: 508 S 11th St Laramie WY 82070 Office: Univ Wyo Box 3354 Union Station Laramie WY 82071

MEDEMA, RALPH GERHARD, mechanical engineer; b. Redlands, Calif., Dec. 24, 1959; s. Gerhard Fillipus and Joanne Hendrika (Tober) M.; m. Jan Weber, July 13, 1985. BSME, Calif. Poly. Inst., 1984. Design engr. Lockheed Calif. Co., Burbank, 1984-87; mech. engr. Holly Sugar Co., Santa Marie, Calif., 1987—. Republican. Mem. Christian Reformed Ch. Home: 385 Via Vicente Nipomo CA 93444 Office: Holly Sugar 2820 W Betteravia Rd Santa Maria CA 93455

MEDINA, THOMAS JULIAN, management consultant, educator; b. Denver, July 24, 1928; s. Frank John and Francis Josephine (Grasmuck) M.; m. Maryem McKell, Apr. 16, 1973; children: Kim Jordan, Vickie Jeanne, Michael McKell. AA, Mira Costa Coll., 1968; BA, San Diego State U., 1969; PhD, Pacific Western U., 1982. Lic. computer scientist, career counselor, Calif. Commd. 2d. lt. USMC, 1953, advanced through grades to maj., 1945-65, computer specialist, 1945-66, ret., 1966; owner, mgr. Medina Fish Finding Co., San Diego, 1970-82; instr. entrepreneurship San Diego County Schs., 1972-82, San Diego Unified Schs., 1984—; computer scientist Computer Scis. Corp., San Diego, 1982-83, Sci. Applications, Inc., San Diego, 1983-84; cons. entrepreneurship Calif. Dept. Edn., 1985—; owner The Entrepreneur, Solana Beach, Calif., 1988—; mem. adv. bd. Internat. U. Sch. Info. Mgmt., Santa Barbara, Calif., 1986—, mem. faculty, 1988—. Calif. Entrepreneur Ednl. grantee, 1986, 87. Mem. Am. Assn. Artificial Intelligence, U.S. Assn. for Small Bus. and Entrepreneurship, Calif. Bus. Edn. Assn., Am. Entrepreneur Assn. (dir. acad. rels. 1985-88), World Future Soc. (adv. coun. 1988—), Calif. Sheriffs Assn., Southwestern Yacht Club (port capt. 1985-86), Thalians. Republican. Mormon. Office: The Entrepreneur 505 N Granados Solana Beach CA 92075 Office: Calif State Bd Edn 721 Capital Mall Sacramento CA 95814-4785

MEDITCH, JAMES STEPHEN, electrical engineering educator; b. Indpls., July 30, 1934; s. Vladimir Stephen and Alexandra (Gogeff) M.; m. Theresa Claire Scott, Apr. 4, 1964; children: James Stephen Jr., Sandra Anne. B.S. in Elec. Engring, Purdue U., 1956, Ph.D., 1961; S.M., M.I.T., 1957. Staff engr. Aerospace Corp., Los Angeles, 1961-65; assoc. prof. elec. engring. Northwestern U., 1965-67; mem. tech. staff Boeing Sci. Research Labs., Seattle, 1967-70; prof. U. Calif., Irvine, 1970-77; prof. U. Wash., 1977—, chmn. dept. elec. engring., 1977-85, assoc. dean engring., 1987—. Author: Stochastic Optimal Linear Estimation and Control, 1969; co-editor: Computer Communications Networks, 1984. Fellow IEEE (disting. mem. control systems soc., 1983, editor proceedings 1983-85, Centennial medal 1984); mem. AAAS, Assn. for Computer Machinery. Office: U Wash Coll Engring FH-10 Seattle WA 98195

MEDLINSKY, ALBERT STANLEY, radio executive; b. Shaft, Pa., Mar. 30, 1932; s. Stanley Albert and Helen Ann (Stepulitis) M.; grad. high sch.; m. Fraun Yvonne Reeves, Nov. 15, 1958; 1 child, Stanley. Pres. Medlinsky Enterprises, Palmdale, Calif., 1963—, KOTE-FM, Lancaster, Calif., 1969-74, A.S.M.E. Corp., Palmdale, 1970—, North Antelope Valley Broadcasting, Inc., Lancaster, Calif., 1972-74; pres. Stan's Stuff, Reno, 1975—, Computer Systems West, 1977-86, Locator Mktg. Co. Inc., 1988—. Served with USAF, 1949-52. Mem. Nat. Assn. Broadcasters, Nat. Assn. F.M. Broadcasters. Home: 1325 Davidson Way Reno NV 89509 Office: 39 E Freeport Blvd Sparks NV 89431

MEDUSKI, JERZY WINCENTY, nutritionist, biochemist; b. Kalusz, Poland, Oct. 29, 1918; s. Dobieslaw Antoni and Katarzyna (Barbowska) M.; came to U.S., 1962, naturalized, 1969; M.D., Warsaw (Poland) Med. Sch., 1946; Ph.D. in Biochemistry, U. Lodz (Poland), 1951; 1 son, Jerzy Dobieslaw. Organizer, chief pharmacology labs. Polish Nat. Inst. Hygiene, Warsaw, 1945-52, organizer, head lab. of intermediary metabolism, 1952-59; asso. prof. biochemistry Warsaw Med. Sch., 1955-59; asst. prof. neurology U. So. Calif. Sch. Medicine, Los Angeles, 1973—; pres. Nutritional Cons. Group, Inc. Mem. Los Angeles County Bd. Suprs. Task Force on Nutrition. WHO fellow, Holland, Scotland, 1948-49; research grantee, USSR, 1956. Mem. Polish Acad. Sci. (sci. sec. biochem. com. 1952-59), Polish Med. Assn. (sci. sec. nat. bd. 1958-59), Polish Biochem. Soc. (founding mem.), Biochem. Soc. London, Royal Soc. Chem. London, Internat. Soc. on Toxinology, AMA, Am. Soc. Microbiology, Internat. Soc. on Oxygen Transport to Tissues, Sigma Xi. Author 3 books on biochemistry; contbr. more than 80 articles to internat. jours.; author textbook on nutritional biochemistry, 1977. Home: 1066 S Genesee Ave Los Angeles CA 90019 Office: U So Calif Sch Medicine 2025 Zonal Ave Los Angeles CA 90033

MEEHAN, PATRICK MICHAEL, dentist; b. Watertown, Wyo., Feb. 14, 1938; s. Augustine Edward and Lucille C. (Mondloch) M.; m. Maurita Anne Redle, June 15, 1963; children: Kathleen Anne, Maureen Anne, Michael Patrick, Michelle Lynn. DDS, Creighton U., 1962. Gen. pracctice dentistry

Sheridan, Wyo., 1964—; bd. dirs. First Wyo. Bank, Sheridan. Bd. dirs. Am. Legion Baseball, Sheridan, 1984—. Served as col. USNG, 1964. Recipient Medicine and Health award Sheridan Jaycees, 1986. Mem. ADA, Wyo. Dental Assn., NE Wyo. Dental Soc. (pres. 1967-68). Club: Sheridan Quarterback. Lodge: KC (grand knight), KP (grand knight 1980—). Home: 822 Victoria St Sheridan WY 82801 Office: 50 E Works St Sheridan WY 82801

MEEHAN, TIMOTHY MICHAEL, electronics company executive; b. Harrisburg, Ill., Dec. 13, 1944; s. John Edward Meehan and Georgia (Gram) Richards; m. Ronnie Lynn Klase, July 10, 1982; 1 child, Stephanie. Student, Rose Polytech. Inst., 1962-63; BS, U.S. Naval Acad., 1967; postgrad., John Hopkins U., 1971; MBA, Ind. U., 1973. Mgr. mktg. and sales Standard Oil Col, San. Francisco, 1974-78, Raychem Corp., Menlo Park, Calif., 1979-83, Chomerics Inc., Woburn, Mass., 1983-84; mng. dir. Dynametrics Electronics, San Francisco, 1985—; cons. Beta Phase Inc., Menlo Park, 1988—, Netherlands Fgn. Investment Agy., San Francisco and Amsterdam, 1988—, AKZO Co., Arnhem, Netherlands, 1986—, Impell Corp., Walnut Creek, Calif., 1988-89, Sharon (Pa.) Steel Corp., 1989—, Metcal Corp., Menlo Park, 1989—. Served as lt. U.S. Navy, 1967-71. Mem. Am. Soc. Naval Engrs., IEEE, Am. Electronics Assn., Soc. Advancement Material and Process Engring., Am. Inst. Avionics and Astronautics, Sigma Iota Epsilon, Beta Gamma Sigma. Home: 1554 Masonic Ave San Francisco CA 94117

MEEK, MARCELLUS ROBERT, lawyer, business consultant; b. N.Y.C., Nov. 20, 1929; s. Marcellus W. and Lillian D. (Hilward-Younes) M.; children: Susan J., Marcellus W. II, Mary F., Adam M. Student U. Ill., 1948-51; JD, DePaul U., 1954; LLM (James Nelson Raymond fellow), Northwestern U., 1955. Bar: Ill. 1955, U.S. Supreme Ct. 1971, U.S. Dist. Ct. (no. dist.) Ill. 1955, U.S. Ct. Appeals (7th cir.) 1955, U.S. Ct. Appeals (5th cir.) 1971. Ptnr. Baker & McKenzie, firm specializing in internat. law, Chgo., 1956-77; pvt. practice, Chgo., 1977—; cons. fed. tax, bus., related fields to former internat. law practice; lectr. internat. law Marquette U., Milw., 1959-65; instr., dir. internat. law dept. John Marshall Law Sch., Chgo., 1964-69. Founder, chmn. bd. dirs. Tucson Jazz Soc., 1979—; founder, pres. Found. For Imagery Guidance and Healing Therapies Against Cancer. Recipient citation for work with law rev. DePaul Law Sch., 1954; hon. justice Chgo. chpt. Moot Ct. competition, 1955; Nathan Burkan Meml. first award, ASCAP, 1954; Cert. contbg. author recognition DePaul Law Rev., 1966; Cert. distinction DePaul U., 1980. Mem. Ill. Bar Assn., ABA, Am. Judicature Soc., Am. Fgn. Law Assn., Celtic Legal Soc. Chgo., Am. Soc. Internat. Law, Chgo. Natural History Mus., Chgo. Hist. Soc., Art Inst. Chgo., Artists Guild Chgo., Mountain Oyster Club (bd. dirs.), Racquet Club, MG T Registry Club, Rod and Gun Club, Gun Le Group Club, Foothills Yacht Club, Jaguar of So. Ariz. Club (pres., bd. dirs.), Racquet Club (Chgo.), Pima County Polo Club. Author: Antiques, the Law and Taxes, 1964; Cases and Materials--International Commercial Transactions, 1964; (with H.J. Stitt) International Transactions, Commentaries and Forms, 1967; International Commercial Agreements, 1977; contbr. articles to profl. jours. Republican. Presbyterian. Home: 3020 E Weymouth St Tucson AZ 85716

MEEKER, ANTHONY, state treasurer; b. Amity, Oreg., Mar. 18, 1939; s. P.E. and Iona (Davis) M.; m. Carolyn Morton, Sept. 1, 1962; children: Tracy Michelle, Ryan Edwin. BA in Polit. Sci., Willamette U., 1961. Oregon state rep. Salem, 1968-72, Oregon sen., 1972-87, Senate Rep. leader, 1981-87, Oregon state treas., 1987—; bd. dirs. First Fed. Savs. and Loan Assn. McMinnville, Oreg. 1st lt. USAF, 1961-66, Vietnam. Named Disting. Alumni Willamette U., 1986. Mem. Nat. Assn. State Treas., Lions (pres. Amity club 1977). Republican. Methodist. Office: Treasury Dept 158 State Capitol Bldg Salem OR 97310

MEEKER, RICHARD HALLIDAY, publisher, lawyer; b. Washington, Jan. 20, 1949; s. Leonard Carpenter and Christine Rhoda (Halliday) M.; m. Ellen Frances Rosenblum, June 13, 1982; children: Catherine Lily Rosenblum, William Eyra Rosenblum. BA, Amherst Coll., 1970; JD, U. Oreg., 1974. Author Ticknor & Fields, N.Y.C., 1980-83; editor Willamette Week, Portland, Oreg., 1977-80, pub., 1983—. Author: Newspaperman, 1983. Mem. Assn. Alternative Newsweeklies (pres.), Inst. Alternative Journalism (bd. dirs.), Portland (Oreg.) Downtown Retail Coun. Democrat. Office: Willamette Week 2 NW Second Ave Portland OR 97209

MEEKER, WILLIAM MAURICE, manufacturing company executive; b. Cropsey, Ill., May 28, 1915; s. Maurice Siebert and Clara Louise (Hood) M.; m. Dorothy Corwina MacCauley, Sept. 5, 1945 (dec. Mar. 1965); 1 child, Nancy Lee Bordier; m. Arlene Dorothy Hallin, Aug. 19, 1966; 1 child, William Michael. Student, Whittier Coll., 1933-34, Lingnam U., Canton, People's Republic China, 1934-35, Sorbonne U., Paris, 1936; BBA, U. So. Calif., 1938. With engring. Lockheed Aircraft Corp., Burbank, Calif., 1938-45; gen. mgr. Am. Diecast Corp., San Gabriel, Calif., 1945-46; owner Mode Products Corp., Alhambra, Calif., 1946-49; gen. mgr., dir. Grover Mfg. Corp., San Gabriel, Calif., 1950-55; pres., bd. chmn. Grover Mfg. Corp., Montebello, Calif., 1950—, also bd. dirs. patentee in field. Reepublican. Congregationalist. Clubs: Friendly Hills Country, Newport Harbor Yacht. Office: Grover Mfg Corp Box 986 Montebello CA 90640

MEEKS, HENRY SPIENGLER, III, metallurgy company executive; b. Queens, N.Y., Feb. 6, 1949; s. Henry S. and Barbara (Wenzel) M.; m. Janet Anne Hirner, May 2, 1970; children: Jessica, Jonathan, Alison. AS in Design Engring., Acad. Aeronautics, 1970; BS in Engring. Materials, Calif. State U., Long Beach, 1974. Plant metallurgist Valeron Corp., Riverside, Calif., 1974-82; plant mgr., metallurgist GTE/Valeron Corp., Monument, Colo., 1982-86; dir. ops. and tech. Advanced Materials Group Nat. Forge Co., Colorado Springs, Colo., 1986—; v.p. mfg. and tech. Champion Horseshoe Co., Pound Ridge, N.Y., 1986—; v.p. Ti Industries, Inc., 1987; pres. Centrepointe Engring., Ltd., 1988—; cons. Surface Tech., Ft. Collins, Colo., 1983-86, MimTech., Denver, 1986—. Mem. Am. Soc. Metals, Am. Inst. Metall. Engrs., Soc. Carbide and Tool. Engrs., Metal Powder Industries Fedn.f. Mormon.

MEEKS, JAMES DONALD, librarian, educator; b. Kansas City, Mo., May 10, 1920; s. Walter James and Mary Elizabeth (Mershon) M.; B.A. in English Lit., U. Kansas City, 1941; B.S. in Library Sci., U. Denver, 1946; M.S., Columbia U., 1951; m. Patricia Ann Lowe, Feb. 27, 1953 (div.); children—Mary, Ann, Robert. Head reference dept., then asst. library dir. Yonkers Pub. Library (N.Y.), 1947-49; dir. library services USIS, Calcutta, India, 1949-50; br. asst. Bklyn. Pub. Library, 1950-51; dir. Enid Pub. Library (Okla.), 1951-53, St. Joseph Pub. Library (Mo.), 1953-55, Dallas Pub. Library, 1955-61; library coordinator Cherry Creek Sch. Dist., Englewood, Colo., 1962-69; instr. U. Denver, 1963-69; dir. Colo. State Library, 1969-74; mem. faculty U. Denver, 1974-75; city librarian, Eugene, Oreg., 1975—; mem. faculty U. Oreg. Sch. Librarianship; vis. prof. Grad. Sch. Library Studies, U. Hawaii, Manoa, fall 1982. Mem. Tex. Library Assn. (pres. 1960), Colo. Library Assn. (pres. 1970), Oreg. Library Assn. (pres. 1980), ALA. Served with AUS, 1942-45. Mem. Pacific N.W. Library Assn. Episcopalian. Home: 1162 Charnelton St Apt 5 Eugene OR 97401 Office: 100 W 13th Ave Eugene OR 97401

MEEKS, JOHN COXON, microbiology educator; b. Great Bend, Kans., June 4, 1941; s. Ira Elmer and Mary Bernadine (Coxon) M. BA, Cen. Wash. U., 1966, MS, 1967; PhD, U. Oreg., 1972. Leverhulme vis. fellow U. Dundee, Scotland, 1972-74; vis. asst. prof. U. So. Fla., Tampa, 1974-75; res. assoc. Mich. State U., E. Lansing, 1975-77; prof. U. Calif., Davis, 1977—; Mem. sci. bd. Cyanotech Corp., 1987—; mem. edn. bd. J. Gen. Microbiology, Reading, Eng., 1988—, A. Van Leeuwenhoek J. Microbiology, 1987—. Contbr. articles to profl. jours. Mem. Am. Soc. for Microbiology, Am. Soc. Plant Physiology, Phycological Soc. Am., Soc. Gen. Microbiology. Roman Catholic. Home: 902 Pennsylvania Pl Davis CA 95616 Office: U Calif Dept Microbiology Davis CA 95616

MEENAN, ALAN JOHN, clergyman, theological educator; b. Belfast, No. Ireland, Feb. 7, 1946; came to U.S., 1970; s. John and Elizabeth (Holland) M.; m. Vicky Lee Woodall, May 6, 1974; children: Kelly Elizabeth, Katie Michelle, Kimberly Brooke. BA, Queen's U., Belfast, 1970; MDiv, Asbury Theol. Sem., Wilmore, Ky., 1972, ThM, 1975; PhD, Edinburgh U., 1981. Ordained to ministry Presbyn. Ch., 1972. Pastor Wilmore Presbyn. Ch., 1972-74; asst. pastor St. Giles' Cathedral, Edinburgh, Scotland, 1974-77; head staff 3d Presbyn. Ch., Richmond, Va., 1977-84, Canoga Park (Calif.) Presbyn. Ch., 1984—; vis. lectr. Nairobi (Kenya) Grad. Sch. Theology, 1983, 89. Contbr. revs. to religious publs. Tchr. Chogoria High Sch., Meru, Keyna, 1965-66. Yale U. rsch. fellow, 1976-77. Mem. Tyndale Fellowship for Bibl. Rsch., Theta Phi. Office: Canoga Park Presbyn Ch 22103 Vanowen St Canoga Park CA 91303

MEENAN, PATRICK HENRY, state legislator; b. Casper, Wyo., Sept. 24, 1927; s. Hugh Martin and Margaret (Kelly) M.; B.S. cum laude, U. Notre Dame, 1949; m. Shirley Louise Byron, Dec. 30, 1950; children—Maurya Ann, Kevin Patrick, Michael James, Patricia Kelly. CPA Raab, Roush & Gaymon, Casper, 1949-53, partner 1960-68; asst. treas. Williston Oil & Gas Co., 1953-55; partner Meenan & Higgins, Casper, 1955-60; pres. KATI-AM & FM, Casper, 1963-81, KAWY Stero Radio, 1967-81; ptnr. Meenan, Miracle & Sherrill, C.P.A.'s, 1975-76; sec. dir. Bank of Casper, 1980-87; pres. PM Enterprises, Inc., 1981—; Erin Corp. Councilman City of Casper, 1956-65, v.p., 1961, mayor, 1962, 65; mem. Wyo. Ho. of Reps., 1969-88, majority floor leader, 1983-85, Speaker Pro Tem, 1985-87, Speaker of the House, 1987-88, chmn. house-rules com., chmn. mgmt. council, 1987-89; mem. exec. com. Western Legis. Conf. Council of State Govts., 1983-88; chmn. Nat. Conf. State Legis. Energy and Environ. Com., 1985. Named Young Man of Year, Jr. C. of C., Casper, 1962; Boss of Year, 1965; Distinguished Pub. Servant award City of Casper. Mem. AICPA, Casper Country Club, Notre Dame Alumni (nat. dir. 1972-75), Wyo. So. CPAs, Nat., Wyo. assns. broadcasters. Elk, K.C. Republican. Roman Catholic. Home: 3070 E 4th St Casper WY 82609 Office: PM Enterprises Inc 300 Country Club Rd Ste 211 Hilltop Nat Tower PO Box 9727 Casper WY 82609

MEERDINK, KENNETH JAMES, electrical engineer; b. Yakima, Wash., July 13, 1929; s. John Henry and Helen Lucille (Kinney) M.; m. Janet Evelyn Mack, Aug. 11, 1951; children: Douglas, Richard, Stephen, Eric. BSEE, Wash. State U., 1951. Engr. Gen. Electric Co., Ft. Wayne, Ind., 1951, Westinghouse Co., Balt., 1953-56; engr. Boeing Aerospace Co., Seattle, 1956-65, engring. mgr., 1965-84; engring. mgr. Boeing Advanced Systems Co., Seattle, 1984-. 1st lt. USAF, 1951-53. Mem. Phi Kappa Phi, Tau Beta Pi, Sigma Tau. Office:

MEESE, CELIA EDWARDS, pharmaceutical company executive; b. San Diego, May 10; d. Roy Clifford Edwards and Bessie Lucille (Lang) Hill; m. Jed D. Meese, July 6, 1963; 1 son, Scott Edwards. BA, U. Wis., 1964; BA (hon.), U. Taiwan, 1965. Office mgr. Pacific Telephone, San Jose, Calif., 1965-72; pres. Vitaline Corp., Ashland, Oreg., 1972—; v.p. RenalChem, Inc., San Jose, Calif., 1982—, Formulations Tech., Inc., Oakdale, Calif., 1982—; dir. Spectra Diagnostics, San Jose. Bd. dirs. So. Oreg. State Coll. Found.; vol. Tudor Guide. Mem. Pharm. Mfrs. Assn., Am. Soc. Bariatric Physicians, Mensa. Home: PO Box 162 Ashland OR 97520 Office: Vitaline Corp 722 Jefferson Ave Ashland OR 97520

MEESE, MARY BETH, publishing executive; b. Napoleon, Ohio, Sept. 9, 1945; d. Rudolph Frederich and Elda Anna (Maassel) Dehnbostel; m. Kenneth Newman Meese, Sept. 17, 1967; children: Kristian Leigh, Brooke Anne. Student, Riverside City Coll., Calif., 1972-74, Solano Community Coll., Fairfield, Calif., 1979-82, Windward Community Coll., Kaneohe, Hawaii, 1984-85. Linotype operator Glanz Lithograph Co., Wauseon, Ohio, 1963-67; linotype operator, printer Cummins Printing Co., Ft. Wayne, Ind., 1967-71, Burck's Advt. Co., San Bernadino, Calif., 1971-74; graphic artist Altus (Okla.) Times Democrat, 1974-77; account exec. Fairfield (Calif.) Daily Republic, 1977-84; advt. mgr. Off Duty Mag., Honolulu, 1985-87; account exec. Honolulu Mag., 1987—; cons. Hawaii Advt. Fedn., Honolulu, 1988. Asst. leader Girl Scouts U.S., Vacaville, Calif., 1982-83; pres. St. John Lutheran Ch. LCW; mem. task force revising constitution Women of Evang. Luth. Ch.; treas. S.W. King Intermediate Ohana, Kaneohe, Hawaii, 1985-87; vol. Am. Cancer Soc., Honolulu, 1987. Mem. Am. Logistics Assn. (bd. dirs. 1986-87), Hawaii Food Industry Assn., Bldg. Industry Assn., Internat. Mil. Club Exec. Assn., Sales and Mktg. Exec. Honolulu (Disting. Sales award 1988, 89). Republican. Club: Ahuimanu Ohana (Kaneohe), Castle High Sch. Band Boosters. Home: 47-748-3 Hui Kelu St Kaneohe HI 96744 Office: Honolulu Pub Co 36 Merchant St Honolulu HI 96813

MEGDAL, SHARON BERNSTEIN, economics educator, consultant; b. Newark, Apr. 4, 1952; d. William B. and Ann (Kopatonsky) Bernstein; m. Ronald G. Megdal, Aug. 18, 1974. AB in Econs., Rutgers U., 1974; MA in Econs., Princeton U., 1977, PhD in Econs., 1981. Asst. prof. econs. U. Ariz., Tucson, 1979-87, pres., owner MegEcon Cons. Group, 1987—; vis. assoc. prof. No. Ariz. U., 1987-88; commr. Ariz. Corp. Commn., 1985-87; speaker, panelist in field. Chairwoman Ariz. Joint Select Com. on State Revenues and Expenditures, 1989; bd. dirs. Tucson Issues Forum, Tucson Tomorrow, United Way, So. Ariz. Water Resources Assn.; mem. First Leadership Am. Class. Contbr. articles on econs. to profl. jours. Vol. United Way of Greater Tucson, 1982-85, 87-88. Richard D. Irwin fellow, 1977-78; fellow Princeton U., 1974-78, Sloan Found., 1976-78; U. Ariz. Rsch. grantee, 1982, 83, Figgle Corp. grantee, 1984. Mem. Am. Econs. Assn. (com. on status of women 1983—), Women Execs. in State Govt., Nat. Assn. Regulatory Utility Commrs. (com. on electricity), Phi Beta Kappa, Beta Gamma Sigma. Democrat.

MEHDIZADEH, PARVIZ, insurance company executive; b. Tehran, Iran, Sept. 15, 1934; came to U.S., 1981; s. Alexander and Sedigheh (Siavooshy) M.; m. Manijeh Sadri, Sept. 12, 1961; children: Sheida, Peyman, Pejman. BS, Forestry Sch., Tehran, 1958; MS, N.C. State U., 1963, PhD, 1966. Pres. Research Inst. Natural Resources, Tehran, 1968-73; assoc. prof. U. Tehran, 1973-74; prof. environ. sci. U. Tabriz, Iran, 1974-76; chmn. resolution com. FAO, Rome, 1976-77; chmn. natural resources Cen. Treaty Orgn., Ankars, Turkey, 1977-78; spl. adviser to sec. Ministry of Agr., Tehran, 1978-79; dist. mgr. Am. Family Life Assurance Co., Beverly Hills, Calif., 1981—; v.p. Point Internat. Corp. Inc., Los Angeles, 1986—; cons. Ministry of Sci., Tehran, 1972-75, UN U., Tokyo, 1975-76. Author: Flowering Plants of Semi-Arid Regions, 1976, Economizing of Water Use in Agriculture, 1977; editor Khandamhayeh Hafteh, 1979. Mem. U.S. Senatorial Club, Washington, 1984; charter mem. Rep. Presdl. Task Force, Washington, 1984. Mem. Life Underwriters Assn. (Los Angeles chpt., Health Ins. Quality award 1985, 88). Club: Friars (Los Angeles). Lodge: Rotary (pres., founder Los Angeles chpt. 1985-86.). Office: Am Family Life Assurance 9301 Wilshire Blvd #311 Beverly Hills CA 90210

MEHLMAN, LON DOUGLAS, data processing professional; b. Los Angeles, Apr. 29, 1959; s. Anton and Diane Mehlman. BA, UCLA, 1981; MBA, Pepperdine U., 1983. Systems programmer Ticom Systems Inc., Century City, Calif., 1978-81; systems analyst NCR Corp., Century City, 1981-83; sr. systems analyst Tandem Computers Inc., Los Angeles, 1983—. Mem. Sierra Club, Assn. MBA Execs., Am. Mgmt. Assn., Phi Delta Theta. Office: Tandem Computers Inc 444 S Flower St Los Angeles CA 90071

MEHLUM, JOHAN ARNT, banker; b. Trondheim, Norway, Nov. 11, 1928; came to U.S., 1950, naturalized, 1955; s. Hans Aage and Olga (Nygaard) M.; diploma Norwegian Bus. Coll., 1946, postgrad. Rutgers U., 1971; m. Ladona Marie Christensen, May 30, 1951 (dec. 1983); children—Ann Marie, Katherine, Susan Jane, Rolf Erik; m. Emel Hekimoglu, Sept. 27, 1986. Clk. Forretningsbanken, Trondheim, 1946-50, First Nat. Bank Oreg., Astoria and Corvallis, 1952-57; cashier, mgr. Bank of Shedd, Brownsville, Oreg., 1958-63; pres., chmn. Siuslaw Valley Bank, Florence, Oreg., 1963—; chmn. bd. Community Bank Creswell (Oreg.), 1970-79; founding dir., pres. Western Banker Svc. Corp., 1983-84; dir. Siuslaw Valley Plaza, Inc., 1966—. Mayor, Dunes City, Oreg., 1973-75. Trustee Lane Community Coll. Found., 1971-78; chmn. bd. dirs. NW Intermediate Banking Sch., Lewis and Clark Coll., Portland, Oreg., 1975-77; trustee, past chmn. Western Lane County Found., 1976-82. With Royal Norwegian Army, 1948-49. Named Jr. First Citizen, Astoria, 1955, First Citizen, Brownsville, 1962; recipient internat. rels. award U.S. Jr. C. of C., 1960; inducted Oreg. Bankers Hall of Fame, 1988. Mem. Western Ind. Bankers (mem. exec. coun. 1970-74), Am. Bankers Assn. (mem. exec. com. community bankers div. 1976-78, governing coun. 1982-84), Oreg. Bankers Assn. (exec. coun. 1977-83, pres. 1981-82), Western States Bankcard Assn. (bd. dir. 1987—), Florence Area C. of C. (pres. 1970), Banking Profession Polit. Action Com. (state chmn. 1973-76), Sons of Norway, Elks, Rotary (pres. 1967-68), Norsemen's League (pres. 1954). Home: PO Box 131 Florence OR 97439 Office: PO Box 280 Florence OR 97439

MEHREN, LAWRENCE LINDSAY, investment company executive; b. Phoenix, May 26, 1944; s. Lawrence and Mary Teresa (Stelzer) M.; B.A., U. Ariz., 1966; M.A., U. Ariz., 1968; m. Lynn Athon McEvers, June 5, 1965; children—Lawrence Lindsay, John Eskridge. Bus. mgr. Rancho Santa Maria, Peoria, Ariz., 1968-69; traffic mgr. Glen-Mar Mfg. Co., Phoenix, 1969-70; account exec. Merrill Lynch, Pierce, Fenner and Smith, Inc., Phoenix, 1970-77, sr. account exec., 1977-78, asst. v.p., 1978-80, v.p., 1980-82; v.p. Harbor Equity Funds, Inc., 1982-84; sr. v.p. Harbor Fin. Group, Inc., Phoenix, 1984-87; pres. Charles and Pierce Asst. Mgmt., Inc., 1987-89; pres. Lawrence Fine Art Inc., Phoenix, 1989—. Chmn. Madison Citizens Adv. Com., 1973-74; mem. Phoenix Art Mus., Phoenix Town Hall; bd. dirs. Planned Parenthood, 1972-75, Brophy Coll. Prep. Sch., 1981-87, Prescott Coll., 1984-85. Recipient award Ariz. Hist. Found., 1968. Mem. Phoenix Stock and Bond Club (bd. dirs. 1979-82), Ariz. Acad. Pub. Affairs, Internat. Wine and Food Soc., Beta Theta Pi. Club: Valley Field Riding and Polo. Home: 515 E Grant Rd #141-318 Tucson AZ 85705 Office: 5515 N 7th St #5107 Phoenix AZ 85016

MEHRING, CLINTON WARREN, engineering executive; b. New Haven, Ind., Feb. 14, 1924; s. Fred Emmett and Florence Edith (Hutson) M.; m. Carol Jane Adams, Mar. 9, 1946; children—James Warren, Charles David, John Steven (dec.), Martha Jane. B.S., Case Inst. Tech., 1950; M.S., U. Colo., 1956. Registered profl. engr., Wyo., Colo., Nev. Design engr. U. S. Bur Reclamation, Denver, 1950-56; design engr. Tipton & Kalmbach, Denver, 1956-58; asst. resident engr. Tipton & Kalmbach, Quito, Equador, 1959-61; asst. chief design engr. Tipton & Kalmbach, Lahore, Pakistan, 1962-65; v.p. Tipton & Kalmbach, Denver, 1966-73, exec. v.p., 1973-79, pres., 1979—, also bd. dirs. Served with AUS, 1943-45. Recipient Theta Tau award as outstanding grad. Case Inst. Tech., 1950. Fellow ASCE; mem. Am. Cons. Engrs. Council, Colo. Soc. Engrs., U.S. Com. on Large Dams, Am. Concrete Inst. (life), U.S. Com. Irrigation and Drainage, Sigma Xi, Tau Beta Pi, Theta Tau, Sigma Chi, Blue Key. Methodist. Club: Denver Athletic. Home: 1821 Mt Zion Dr Golden CO 80401 Office: 1331 17th St Denver CO 80202

MEHTA, PRAN NATH, service executive; b. Rajinder Nagar, New Delhi, India, Nov. 24, 1951; came to U.S., 1970; s. Ram Lal and Thakur Devi (Popli) M.; m. Neeru Mallik, Mar. 7, 1978; children: Shaan Pran, Prem Dev. Student, Indian Inst. of Tech., 1968-70, Chaffey Coll., 1970-73. Area mgr. Pacific Personnel Svc., Inc., Montclair, Calif., 1974-84; gen. mgr., v.p. Creative Personnel Svc., Inc., Rancho Cucamonga, Calif., 1984-86; pres. Temps R Us Personnel Svc., Inc., Rancho Cucamonga, 1986—. Mem. Calif. Assn. of Temporary Svcs., Rancho Cucamonga, Chino and Pomona C. of C. Republican. Hindu. Office: Temps R Us Personnel Svcs 9140 Haven Ave Rancho Cucamonga CA 91730

MEIER, HAROLD ELLSWITH, lawyer; b. Denver, Feb. 6, 1932; s. Henry A. and Ruth (Winsor) M.; m. Joan C. Preis, Sept. 1, 1958 (div. 1984); children: Scott W., Celia Ann, Douglas C.; m. Suzanne M. Faris, July 5, 1985. BS, U. Wyo., 1954, JD, 1959. Bar: Wyo. 1959, U.S. Dist. Ct. Wyo. 1959, U.S. Ct. Appeals (10th cir. ct.), U.S. Supreme Ct. 1974, U.S. Ct. of Claims 1979. Ptnr. Crofts, Mockler and Meier, Lander, Wyo., 1959-69, Meier, Gist and Moffat, Lander, Wyo., 1969-77; v.p., gen. counsel Teton Exploratin Drilling, Casper, Wyo., 1977-82; of counsel Schwartz, Bon, McCrary and Walker, Casper, Wyo., 1982-88; ptnr. Lonabaugh and Riggs, Sheridan, Wyo., 1988—; pres. Wester Energy, Sheridan. Mem. Wyo. House of Reps., Cheyenne, 1969-77. With U.S. Army, 1954-56. Mem. ABA, Assn. Trial Lawyers Am., Wyo. State Bar Assn., Wyo. Trial Lawyer's Assn., Rotary, Masons, Shriners, Elks. Republican. Home: PO Box 6128 Sheridan WY 82801 Office: Lonabaugh & Riggs 50 E Laucks PO Box 5059 Sheridan WY 82801

MEIKLEJOHN, ALVIN J., JR., state senator, lawyer, accountant.; b. Omaha, June 18, 1923; B.S., J.D., U. Denver, 1951; m. Lorraine J. Meiklejohn; children—Pamela Ann, Shelley Lou, Bruce Ian, Scott Alvin. Mem. Colo. Senate from 19th dist., 1976—, chmn. com.; edn.; mem. Edn. Commn. of States, 1981—. Mem. Jefferson Sch. Dist. No. R-1 Bd. Edn., 1971-77, pres., 1973-77; commr. Commn. on Uniform State Laws, 1988—. Served to capt. U.S. Army, 1940-46; to maj. USAF, 1947-51. Mem. Colo. Bar Assn. (bd. govs. 1989—), Denver Bar Assn., Colo. Soc. CPA's, Arvada C. of C. Republican. Clubs: Masons, Shriners. Home: 7540 Kline Dr Arvada CO 80005 Office: Jones Meiklejohn Kehl & Lyons 1600 Dome Tower Bldg 1625 Broadway St Denver CO 80202

MEIKLEJOHN, RAYMOND HARRY, government official; b. Quill Lake, Sask., Can., Nov. 7, 1935; s. Robert James and Ada Maria (Woodbury) M.; divorced; children: Laurel, Craig, Catherine. BE, U. Sask., 1965, postgrad. diploma, 1975. Profl. A teaching cert. Tchr. Wadena (Sask.) Sch. Unit, Can., 1955-69, asst. supt., 1969-74; program coordinator Govt. of Sask. Dept. Edn., Melfort, 1974-76, spl. edn. cons., 1977-79; asst. supt. Sask. East Sch. Div., 1979-86, supt., 1986; minister sci., tech. and consumer affairs Province of Sask., Regina, 1986. Northern v.p. Progressive Party of Sask., 1981-83; candidate Kelvington-Wadena Condstituency, 1978, Humbolt-Lake Ctr. Constituency, 1984; pres. Council for Exceptional Children, Sask. Fedn., 1980-81, Can. Council for Exceptional Children, 1984-85. Progressive Conservative. Home: 201-317 Cree Crescent, Saskatoon Can S7K 7Y3 Office: Cabinet of Sask, Legislative Bldg Rm 307, Regina, SK Canada S4S 0B3

MEINEKE, STEVEN ERIC, family therapist, clergyman; b. Cin., Sept. 26, 1949; s. Howard Albert and Lucille Marian (Droop) M.; m. Susan Trueblood, June 16, 1972; children: Summer Lynn, Ryan Cameron. BS, U. Cin., 1971; MA, U. Santa Clara, 1974; MDiv, Sem. of West, Berkeley, Calif., 1975. Lic. marriage, family and child counselor, Calif; ordained to ministry, United Ch. of Christ, 1976. Campus minister Colo. State U., Ft. Collins, 1976-78, We. Wash. U., Bellingham, 1978-84; pvt. practice marriage and family therapy Solana Beach, Calif., 1985—; v.p., Esperanza Consulting Found., San Diego, 1987—; lectr. in field. Columnist, San Diego Family Press, 1985—. Mem. Am. Assn. Marriage and Family Therapy, Am. Assn. Pastoral Counselors, Calif. Assn. Marriage and Family Therapists (bd. dirs. San Diego chpt. 1988). Democrat. Office: 141 N Acacia St Solana Beach CA 92075

MEININGER, SHERI LYNN, teacher; b. Las Vegas, Nev., Sept. 29, 1963; d. Edward Calvin and Marilyn June (Ray) M. BA in Bus. Edn., Utah State U., 1986, BA in English, 1986. Clk. typist Utah State U., Logan, 1984-86; tchr. Clark County Schs., Las Vegas, 1986—; exec. sec. Flamingo Hilton, Las Vegas, 1986—. Mem. Nat. Bus. Educators Assn., Nat. Council Tchrs. English. Republican. Mormon. Home: 6666 W Washington Las Vegas NV 89107 Office: Clark County Schs Frank F Garside Jr High 300 S Torrey Pines Las Vegas NV 89107

MEISSINGER, HANS F(RIEDRICH), areospace engineer; b. Villingen, Baden, Germany, Nov. 25, 1918; came to U.S., 1947; m. Karl August and Rosa (Oppenheimer) M.; m. Hannah Gerber, Nov. 23, 1949; 1 child, Joyce K. Arnon. Engring. Diploma, Tech. U., Berlin, 1942; MS in Math., NYU, 1949. Research engr. German Aero. Research Establishment, Berlin, 1942-45; asst. proj. mgr. Reeves Instrument Corp., N.Y.C., 1947-54; sr. staff engr. Hughes Aircraft Co., Culver City, Calif., 1955-62, TRW, Redondo Beach, Calif., 1962—; bd. dirs. Western Simulation Council, Calif., 1960-62, 83-85. Contbr. articles on aerospace tech. to profl. jours. Fellow AIAA (assoc., mem. tech. com.); mem. Soc. for Computer Simulation (sr., regional chmn. 1984-85). Home: 4157 Don Luis Dr Los Angeles CA 90008 Office: TRW Space & Tech Group 1 Space Park R11-2337 Redondo Beach CA 90278

MEISTER, FREDERICK WILLIAM, state official, lawyer; b. Waterbury, Conn., May 21, 1938; s. William Frederick and Marion Callender (Tracy) M.; m. Joanne Marie Babich, June 12, 1982. B.A., Swarthmore Coll., 1960; M.B.A., Harvard U., 1962; J.D., U. Pitts., 1975. Bar: Pa. 1975, D.C. 1980. Fin. analyst First Pa. Bank, Phila., 1966-67; asst. comptroller Am. Friends Service Com., Phila., 1967-72; program analyst HEW, Washington, 1976-77; project mgr., program analyst Health Care Financing Adminstrn., Balt., 1977-82; chief Bur. of Fiscal and Contract Mgmt., Ariz. Health Care Cost

Containment System, Phoenix, 1982-84, chief policy, planning and research, 1984-87; chief policy devel., 1987—; lectr. Sch. Pub. Affairs Ariz State U., 1988—. Founding chmn. troop com. Valley Forge council Boy Scouts Am., Media, Pa., 1966-68; bd. dirs., mem. bus. com. Fellowship House and Farm, Inc., Phila., 1968-72; county dir. U.S. Senate Primary Campaign for H. John Heinz, Montgomery County, Pa., 1976., mem. fin. com. Am. Friends Sevice Com., Balt., 1980-82; mem. contracts task force Ariz. Dept. Health Services, Phoenix, 1983-84. Served to lt. USNR, 1962-65. Recipient Bur. Dirs. citation Bur. Quality Control, Health Care Financing Adminstrn., 1982. Mem. ABA, Nat. Health Lawyers Assn., Fed. Bar Assn., Am. Soc. Pub. Adminstrn. Republican. Mem. Soc. Friends. Club: Harvard Bus. Sch., Harvard of Phoenix, Phoenix City. Home: 1722 W Earll Dr Phoenix AZ 85015 Office: Ariz Health Care Cost Containment System 801 E Jefferson St Phoenix AZ 85034

MEISTER, JOHN EDWARD, JR., infosystems specialist; b. Elgin, Ill., Nov. 17, 1956; s. John Edward and Marilyn Barbara (Futter) M.; m. Rebecca Marie Buehner, Nov. 15, 1975; children: Christine Marie, Mark Christopher. AA, Cen. Tex. Coll., 1979, U. Md., 1980; BS cum laude, U. Md., 1981; postgrad., Western Conservative Baptist Sem., 1982-83. Enlisted U.S. Army, 1974, advance through grades to staff sgt., 1980; electronics technician Frankfurt, Fed. Republic of Germany, 1974-77; maintenance supr. Darmstadt, Fed. Republic of Germany, 1978-81; transferred from 232d Signal Co. Telecommunications, 1981; sr. instr. U.S. Army Signal Sch., Ft. Gordon, Ga., 1981-82; resigned U.S. Army, 1982; sr. electronics instr. ITT Tech. Inst., Portland, Oreg., 1982-83; equipment engr., engrng. svcs. technician Intel Corp., Aloha, Oreg., 1983-85; electronic designer Boeing Electronics Co., Everett, Wash., 1985-89; systems analyst Boeing Commercial Airplanes, Everett, Wash., 1989—; electronics engr. Innovative Designs and Electronic Systems Techs., Portland, 1982-85. Bd. dirs. Machias Ridge East Homeowner's Assn.; fin. advisor Jr. Achievement, Everett High Sch., 1988-89. Mem. Apollo Domain User's Soc. Republican. Baptist. Home: 2111 159th Ave SE Snohomish WA 98290 Office: Boeing Comml Airplane Co M/S 01-90 PO Box 3707 Seattle WA 98124

MEISTER, VERLE MARTIN, management recruiter; b. Moville, Iowa, Mar. 16, 1937; s. Otto John Fred and Ruth Louise (Hughes) M.; m. Connie Margaret Sturm, May 11, 1968; 1 child, John Martin. BA in Bus. and Econs., Wartburg Coll., 1964. Employment interviewer J.I. Case Co., Bettendorf, Iowa, 1964-65; employment mgr. J.I. Case Co., Terre Haute, Ind., 1966-68, Am. Air Filter Co., Moline, Ill., 1965-66; adminstrv. asst. to pres. Vindale Corp., Dayton, Ohio, 1968-75; mgr. labor rels. Robbins & Myers, Springfield, Ohio, 1975-78; pres. Mgmt. Recruiters Cheyenne, Wyo., 1978—; del. White House Conf. on Small Bus., 1985. Chmn. spl. events Am. Cancer Soc., Cheyenne, 1979-80. With U.S. Army, 1960-63. Mem. Am. Soc. Pers. Adminstrs. (pres. 1986), Small Bus. Coun. (chmn. 1987-89), bd. dirs. 1989—), Cheyenne C. of C., Kiwanis. Home: 123 Longs Peak Dr Cheyenne WY 82009 Office: Mgmt Recruiters Cheyenne 1008 E 21st St Cheyenne WY 82001

MELANSON, EDWARD JOSEPH, electrical engineer; b. L.A., Apr. 21, 1961; s. Alfred R. and Anna Lee (Tidwell) M.; m. Nancy Darby, July 9, 1988. Student, Orange Coast Coll., Costa Mesa, Calif., 1980-82, Diablo Valley Coll., Pleasant Hill, Calif., 1982-84. Designer Infra-red Dynamics, Costa Mesa, 1979-80; design engr. Babcock Electro Mech., Costa Mesa, 1980-82; elec. engr. Trans-dyn Control Systems, Concord, Calif., 1982—. Mem. Ducks Unltd., Calif. Waterfowl Assn., NRA, Mu Alpha Theta. Republican. Office: Trans-dyn Control Systems 4040 Pike Ln Concord CA 94520

MELCHER, JOHN, former U.S. senator; b. Sioux City, Iowa, Sept. 6, 1924; m. Ruth Klein, Dec. 1, 1945; children: Terry, Joan, Mary, Robert, John. Student, U. Minn., 1942-43; D.V.M., Iowa State U., 1950. Ptnr. Yellowstone Valley Vet. Clinic, Forsyth, Mont., operator cattle feed lot, 1953-55; alderman City of Forsyth, 1953-55; mayor City of Foryth, 1955-61; mem. Mont. Ho. of Reps. from Rosebud County, 1961-62, 69, Mont. Senate, 1963-67, 91st-94th congresses from 2d Mont. Dist., 1969-77; U.S. senator from Mont. 1977-89; Former mem. Mont. Legis. Council. Democratic candidate for U.S. Ho. of Reps., 1966. Served with AUS, 1943-45, ETO. Decorated Purple Heart, Bronze Star, Combat Infantryman's Badge; recipient Disting. Service award Nat. Assn. Conservation Dists., 1985, Centennial medal U. Pa. Sch. Vet. Medicine, 1984. Democrat. *

MELDRUM, RONALD MURRAY, English professor; b. Penticton, Canada, Jan. 31, 1927; came to U.S., 1950; s. George and Jennie Josephine (Love) M.; m. Barbara Ruth Howard, Aug. 30, 1960; children: Deirdre Ruth, Cynthia Leigh. BA, U. British Columbia, Vancouver, 1949; MA, U. Wash., 1956; PhD, Ariz. State U., 1965. Teaching fellow U. Wash., Seattle, 1952-55; instr. U. Colo., Boulder, Colo., 1955-59, U. Redlands, Calif., 1960; assoc. prof. English U. Calif., Riverside, 1961-62; instr. Ariz. State U., Tempe, 1964-65; asst. prof. Washington State U., Pullman, 1965-72, assoc. prof., 1972-81, prof., 1981—; pres. Pacific N.W. Renaissance Conf., 1977-80, N.W. Conf. on British Studies, 1976-79; acting dir. Inst. Renaissance Studies, Ashland, Oreg., 1972. Contbr. various articles to profl. jours.; editor The Letters of King James I to King Christian IV, 1977. Recipient Canadian Studies Faculty & Research Grant, 1985-86; named Visiting Prof., U. Conn., 1985-86. Mem. Wranglers (chief 1971-72, scribbler 1972-73). Democrat. Episcopalian. Home: 420 N Polk St Moscow ID 83843 Office: Washington State U Dept English 202H Avery Hall Pullman WA 99164-5020

MELEIS, AFAF IBRAHIM, nursing educator; b. Alexandria, Egypt, Mar. 19, 1942; d. Abdel Baki Ibrahim and Soad Hussein Hassan; m. Mahmoud Meleis, Aug. 21, 1964; children: Waleed, Sherief. BS magna cum laude, U. Alexandria, 1961; MS, UCLA, 1964, MA, 1966, PhD, 1968; D of Pub. Svc. (hon.), 1989. Instr. U. Alexandria, 1961-62; acting instr. UCLA, 1966-68, asst. prof. nursing, 1968-71; assoc. prof., dean Health Inst., Kuwait, 1975-77; prof. nursing U. Calif., San Francisco, 1977—, also dir. Study Immigrant Health and Adjustment; vis. prof. colls. in Sweden, Brazil, Japan, Saudi Arabia, Kuwait, Egypt; cons., speaker in field. Author: Theoretical Nursing: Development & Progress, 1985 (Book of Yr., Am. Jour. Nursing 1985); contbr. articles to profl. jours. Recipient Helen Nahm award, 1981, Teaching awards, 1981, 85; Kellogg Internat. fellow, 1986-89. Fellow Am. Acad. Nursing; mem. Coun. Nurse Researchers, Western Soc. Research in Nursing, Am. Nurses Assn. Home: 39 Corte Ramon Greenbrae CA 94904 Office: U Calif San Francisco Sch Nursing N511Y San Francisco CA 94143-0608

MELENDEZ, RODRIGO CUAUHTEMOC, dentist; b. L.A., Oct. 23, 1943; s. Jose Chauhtemoc and Helen Antionette (Huhn) M.; m. Winifred Yoshiye. BS, U. So. Calif., 1966, DDS, 1968; MS, George Washington U., 1975; cert. prosthodontics Nat. Naval Dental Sch., 1976; lic. dentist, Calif. Commd. ensign USN Dental Corps, 1965, advanced through grades to capt., 1984; asst. dental officer NAS Alameda (Calif.), 1971-72, USS Sanctuary, Mayport, Fla., 1972-74; resident prosthodontics Nat. Naval Dental Ctr., Bethesda, Md., 1974-76; head prosthodontic dept. Naval Sta., Rota, Spain, 1974-80, Br. Dental Clin., NTC, San Diego, 1980-81, Br. Dental Clin., Miramar, San Diego, 1981-82, 82-84; head prosthodontic dept. Naval Dental Clin., Camp Pendleton, Calif., 1984-86, exec. officer, 1986-89; comdg. officer Naval Dental Clin., Yokosuka, Japan, 1989—; guest lectr., cons. Naval Dental Clinic, San Diego, 1980-88, Naval Hosp., Camp Pendleton, 1984-88. Mem. ADA, Assn. Mil Surgeons U.S., Am. Coll. Prosthodontics, Acad. Gen. Office: Naval Dental Clinic Yokosuka Japan FPO Seattle WA 98765-1690

MELLE, CHRIS F., software engineer; b. Bittburg, Ger., Mar. 2, 1956; s. Charles F. and G. Marge (Marcus) M.; m. Donna Weber, June 25, 1988. B.Computer Mgmt. Sci., Metro. State U., Denver, 1981. Grad. engr. Storage Tech. Inc., Louisville, Colo., 1981-83; software engr. Comtech Communications Corp., Boulder, Colo., 1983-85, Telwatch (formerly OneCom), Boulder, 1985-89; mem. tech. staff US West Adv. Tech., Denver, 1989—. Mem. Nat. Ski Patrol System, Aircraft Owners and Pilots Assn., U.S. Hang Gliding Assn. Democrat. Home: 2231 Grant St Longmont CO 80501

MELLISH, DONALD LEROY, banker; b. Fairbanks, Alaska, Nov. 1, 1927; s. William and Monica (Hugg) M.; m. Susan H. Schmelzer; children: Gabriele, John, Robert. Student U. B.C., Can.), Vancouver, 1946-47; grad., Pacific Coast Banking Sch., 1963. With Nat. Bank of Alaska, Anchorage, 1953—; exec. v.p. Nat. Bank of Alaska, 1962-65, pres., 1965-75, chmn. exec. com., 1975—; dir. Seattle br. Fed. Res. Bank San Francisco, 1978-82, Alascom Inc., MAPCO, Inc., Tulsa, Northwest Capital Corp.; mem. Nat. Export Expansion Council, Small Bus. Adv. Council, Regional Adv. Com. on Banking Policies and Practices, 1968-69. Chmn. Alaska Radio Free Europe, 1971-74. Mem. Am. Bankers Assn., Alaska Nippon Kai. Office: PO Box 600 Anchorage AK 99510

MELLO, DONALD R., state senator; b. Owensboro, Ky., June 22, 1934; s. Jack and Gladys (Jasper) M.; student U. Nev.; grad. B.F. Goodrich Co. Mgmt. Sch., Sacramento; m. Barbara Jane Woodhall; children—Donald, David. Condr., S.P. Transp. Co.; mem. Nev. Assembly from 30th Dist., 1963-82, chmn. Interim Finance com., 1975-77, chmn. Legis. Commn., 1973-74, chmn. Ways and Means com., 1973-80, sr. Democratic assemblyman, 1973-82, sr. assemblyman, 1977-82, Nev. state senator, 1983—; chmn. com. on transp., 1985, vice chmn. com. on fin., 1985. Mem. adv. com. Title III, Nev. Dept. Edn. Mem. Washoe County Democratic Central Com., 1968—; mem. Pres.'s Club, United Transp. Union, PTA (life). Served with USNR. Recipient Friend of Edn. award Washoe County Tchrs. Assn., 1974, Appreciation award Nev. N.G., 1973-75, Assembly Speaker's award, 1977, Appreciation award Ret. Public Employees Nev., 1979, award Clark County Classroom Tchrs., 1981, appreciation award United Transp. Union, 1981, Pres.' award Nev. State Edn. Assn., 1981, 85, Nev. AFL-CIO, 1981; commd. hon. Ky. col.; named One of 10 Outstanding Legislators in U.S., Assembly State Govtl. Employees, 1976; Don Mello Sports Complex named in his honor City of Sparks (Nev.). Democrat. Lodge: Masons. Office: 2590 Oppio St Sparks NV 89431

MELLON, WILLIAM DANIEL, communications executive; b. Darby, Pa., June 22, 1951; s. William and Eleanor M.; m. Nikki Dersin; 1 child, William D. III. BA, St. Louis U., 1972, MA, 1974. Dir. regional pub. rels. Boeing Co., Seattle, 1978-85; dir. corp. communications Beech Aircraft Corp., Wichita, Kans., 1985-87; dir. news and info. Rockwell Internat., El Segundo, Calif., 1987—. Capt. USAF, 1973-78. Mem. Pub. Rels. Soc. Am., L.A. Press Club, Assn. Aero. and Astronautics, Internat. Assn. Bus. Communicators, Am. Mktg. Assn., Coun. of Communications Mgmt., Nat. Investor Rels. Inst., Aviation and Space Writers Assn., N.Y. Aero Club. Office: Rockwell Internat Corp Hqrs 2230 E Imperial Hwy El Segundo CA 90245

MELLOR, NANCY AHLBERG, educator; b. Battle Creek, Mich., Oct. 1, 1937; d. Gilbert and Arlene K. Ahlberg; m. Reed T. Mellor, June 8, 1959; children: Reed Grant, Katherine A. BA, Mt. Holyoke Coll., 1959; MS, Johns Hopkins U., 1985. Teaching credential, Calif.; Cert. Advanced Profl. Tchr., Md. Tchr. Roanoke (Va.) City Schs., 1959-60, Nottoway County (Va.) Schs., 1977-78, Cecil County (Md.) Schs., 1978-84, Coalinga (Calif.) Jr. High Sch., 1984—; gifted program originator, dir. Coalinga-Huron Unified Sch. Dist., 1985—; founder, dir. Coalinga-Huron House, Berkeley, Calif., 1987—; instr. U. Calif-Berkeley Academic Talent Devel., 1988—. Designer curriculum for gifted, San Jose (Calif.) State U. (award 1987). Mem. AAUW (1st v.p. Coalinga chpt. 1986—), Calif. Assn. for Gifted (tchr.'s com. 1986—), Nat. Assn. for Gifted Children, Cen. Calif. Educators for Gifted and Talented Edn. (sec. 1988—). Mem. Society of Friends.

MELLOR, SANDY BALLENGER, association executive; b. Ft. Payne, Ala., Nov. 10, 1947; d. W.H. and Lillian (Brock) Ballenger; m. Tony Mellor, July 6, 1973 (div. 1984); 1 child, Gabriel; m. Dennis Taylor, Apr. 4, 1987. Student, Pima Community Coll., Tucson, 1979-81. Convention sales John Q. Hammons Hotels, Inc., Tucson, 1984-86; mgr. corporate sales Ariz. Cine Equipment, Inc., Tucson and Denver, 1986-88; exec. dir. Tucson Trade Bureau, 1975-81. Bd. dirs. Mental Health Assn. Greater Tucson, 1982-85, ARC, Tucson, 1982-85. Mem. Exec. Women's Council (charter). Club: El Centro Breakfast (Tucson) (program chair 1987-88). Home: 3243 E Waverly Tucson AZ 85716

MELMON, KENNETH LLOYD, physician, biologist, consultant; b. San Francisco, July 20, 1934; s. Abe Irving and Jean (Kahn) M.; m. Elyce Edelman, June 9, 1957; children: Bradley S., Debra W. AB in Biology with honors, Stanford U., 1956; MD, U. Calif. at San Francisco, 1959. Intern, then resident in internal medicine U. Calif. Med. Ctr., San Francisco, 1959-61; clin. assoc., surgeon USPHS, Nat. Heart, Lung and Kidney Inst., NIH, 1961-64; chief resident in medicine U. Wash. Med. Ctr., Seattle, 1964-65; chief div. clin. pharmacology U. Calif. Med. Ctr., 1965-78; chief dept. medicine Stanford U. Med. Ctr., 1978-84, Arthur Bloomfield prof. medicine, prof. pharmacology, 1978—; dir. office new clin. program devel. Stanford U. Hosp., 1986—; mem. sr. staff Cardiovascular Rsch. Inst.; chmn. joint commn. prescription drug use Senate Subcom. on Health, Inst. Medicine and HEW-Pharm. Mfrs. Assn.; mem. Nat. Bd. Med. Examiners, 1987—; pres. Bio 2000, Woodside, Calif., 1983—; founder, Immulogic, Boston, Palo Alto, Calif., 1988; sci. advisor Syntex, Hoffman LaRoche, Recordati, LTI, Cetus, other cons. FDA, 1965-82, Office Tech. Assessment, 1974-75, Senate Subcom. on Health, 1975—; bd. dirs. Pharmatrix, Techno-Gentics, N.Y.C.; cons. to govt. Author articles, chpts. in books, sects. encys.; Editor: Clinical Pharmacology: Basic Principles in Therapeutics, 2d edit, 1978, Cardiovascular Therapeutics, 1974; assoc. editor: The Pharmacological Basis of Therapeutics (Goodman and Gilman), 1984; mem. editorial bd. numerous profl. jours. Surgeon USPHS, 1961-64. Burroughs Wellcome clin. pharmacology scholar, 1966-71; John Simon Guggenheim fellow Weizman Instn., Israel, 1971; NIH fellow, Bethesda, 1972. Fellow AAAS (nat. coun. 1985—); mem. Am. Fedn. Clin. Rsch. (pres. 1973-74), Am. Soc. Clin. Investigation (past pres. 1978-79), Assn. Am. Physicians, Western Assn. Physicians (past pres. 1983-84), Am. Soc. Pharmacology and Exptl. Therapeutics, Inst. Medicine of Nat. Acad. Sci., Am. Physiol. Soc., Calif. Acad. Medicine, Med. Friends of Wine, Phi Beta Kappa. Democrat. Jewish. Home: 51 Cragmont Way Woodside CA 94062 Office: Stanford U Med Ctr Dept Medicine S025 Stanford CA 94305

MELOAN, TAYLOR WELLS, marketing educator; b. St. Louis, July 31, 1919; s. Taylor Wells and Edith (Graham) M.; m. Anna Geraldine Leukering, Dec. 17, 1944 (div. 1974); children: Michael David, Steven Lee; m. Jane Innes Bierlich, Jan. 30, 1975. B.S. cum laude, St. Louis U., 1949; M.B.A., Washington U., St. Louis, 1950; D of Bus. Admin., Ind. U., 1953. Advt. mgr. Herz Corp., St. Louis, 1941-42; sales promotion supr. Liggett & Myers Tobacco Co., St. Louis, 1942-43; asst. prof. mktg. U. Okla., Norman, 1953; asst., then assoc. prof. mktg. Ind. U., Bloomington, 1953-59; prof., chmn. dept. mktg. U. So. Calif., Los Angeles, 1959-69; dean Sch. Bus. Adminstrn. U. So. Calif., 1969-71, assoc. v.p. acad. adminstrn. and research, 1971-81, prof. mktg., 1959—; prof. bus. adminstrn. U. Karachi, Pakistan, 1962; vis. prof. mktg. Istituto Post U. Per Lo Studio Dell Organizzazione Aziendale, Turin, Italy, 1964; disting. vis. prof. U. Witwatersrand, Johannesburg, 1978; editorial adviser bus. adminstrn. Houghton Mifflin Co., Boston, 1959-73; cons. to industry and govt., 1953—; bd. dirs. Council Better Bus. Burs., Inc., 1978-84, Nat. Advt. Rev. Bd., 1985—. Author: New Career Opportunities, 1978, Innovation Strategy and Management, 1979, Direct Marketing: Vehicle for Department Store Expansion, 1984, Preparing the Exporting Entrepreneur, 1986, The New Competition: Dilemma of Department Stores in the 1980's, 1987, Franchise Marketing: A Retrospective and Prospective View of a Contractual Vertical Marketing System, 1988; co-author: Managerial Marketing, 1970, Internationalizing the Business Curriculum, 1968, Handbook of Modern Marketing, contbg. author, 1986; bd. editors: Jour. Mktg., 1965-72. Served with USNR, 1943-46. Mem. Newcomen Soc. N.Am., Am. Mktg. Assn. (pres. Los Angeles chpt. 1963-64), Order of Artus, Beta Gamma Sigma, Delta Pi Epsilon. Clubs: Calif. Yacht, University (Los Angeles). Lodge: Rotary. Home: 59 Lakefront Irvine CA 92714 Office: U So Calif Los Angeles CA 90089

MELTON, ROBERT BRUCE, publishing executive; b. Marion, N.C., Dec. 5, 1930; s. John Edwin and Paralie (McGuinn) M.; m. Rita Claudia Chudkowsky, May 2, 1964. BA in Journalism, U. N.C., 1952. Mng. editor Daily Tar Heel, Chapel Hill, N.C., 1951-52; copy editor UN, N.Y.C., 1956; reporter, news editor Fairchild Publs., N.Y.C., 1956-71; mng. editor Lebhar-Friedman, Inc., N.Y.C., 1971-72; editor Mags. for Industry, Inc., N.Y.C., 1974; mng. editor Dempa Publs., Inc., N.Y.C., 1975-76; editor BMT Publs., Inc., N.Y.C., 1977, Met. Restaurant News, N.Y.C., 1980-81; exec. editor, co-owner Restaurant Exch. News, Inc., N.Y.C., 1981-88, contbng. editor, co-owner, 1988—. Editor, pub.: USS Charles S. Sperry, 1953; contbng. editor: The Public Record, 1988—. Lt. (j.g.) USN, 1952-55. Named Person of Yr. L.I. Restaurant and Caterers Assn., 1983; recipient Citations Anti-Defamation League, 1967, 63, Internat. Food Service Execs. Assn., 1988. Mem. N.Y.C. Press Club (fin. sec. 1963-64), Desert Press Club, Roundtable for Women in Food Svc. (sec. 1984-85). Home and Office: 2266 Los Alamos Rd Palm Springs CA 92262

MELTON, RONALD BENJAMIN, electrical engineer; b. Los Alamos, N.Mex., Apr. 23, 1955; s. Benjamin Johnson and Marjorie Laurene (Dinsmore) M.; m. Carol Jean Geier, June 10, 1978; children: Christopher Geier, Andrew Geier, Timothy Geier. BSEE, U. Wash., 1977; MS in Engring. Sci., Calif. Inst. Tech., 1978, PhD in Engring Sci., 1981. Sr. research scientist Battelle Northwest, Richland, Wash., 1980-88; tech. group leader Battelle Northwest, Richland, 1987—, sect. mgr., 1988—. Contbr. articles, papers to profl. publs. Mem. IEEE, Am. Assn. Artificial Intelligence, Assn. Computing Machinery, AAAS. Office: Battelle NW Battelle Blvd Richland WA 99352

MELTON, TERRY RAYMOND, arts federation executive; b. Gooding, Idaho, Nov. 20, 1934; s. Omar D. and Loyce (Lue) M.; m. Glenda Smith, 1961 (div. Dec. 1974); children: Robert W., Susan N. BA, Idaho State U., 1959; MFA, U. Oreg., 1964. Dir. Yellowstone Art Ctr., Billings, Mont., 1964-67, C.M. Russell Mus., Gt. Falls, Mont., 1967-70; exec. dir. Oreg. Arts Commn., Salem, 1970-75; regional rep. Nat. Endowment for Arts, Seattle, 1975-84; exec. dir. Western States Art Fedn., Santa Fe., 1984--, chmn. artist com. Santa Fe Inst. Fine Arts, 1986. One-man shows and group exhbns., 1959-82; contbr. poetry to various publs. Chmn. Capitol Planning Commn., Salem, 1973-75; bd. overseers Lewis and Clark Coll., Portland, Oreg., 1975-80; mem. adv. com. Santa Fe Mus. Fine Arts, 1987-88; vice chmn. Santa Fe Arts Commn., 1988--. Recipient Luther A. Richman award Mont. Arts Council, 1970; Ina McLung scholar, 1963. Mem. Western Assn. Art Mus. (v.p. 1971-73, bd. dirs. 1971-78), Western States Arts Fedn. (bd. dirs. 1984--), Am. Assn. Mus. Home: 2491 Sawmill Rd Apt 201 Santa Fe NM 87505 Office: Western States Arts Fedn 207 Shelby St Ste 207 Santa Fe NM 87501

MELVIN, DANIEL SEAN, radio station executive; b. Richmond, Va., Oct. 6, 1961; s. Thomas J. and Jane Louise (Abernathy) M. Student, Ga. State U., 1982-84; BA, U. Ga., 1985. Account exec. Sta. KMTN-FM, Jackson, Wyo., 1985-87, sales mgr., 1987; account exec., asst. sales mgr. Sta. KIZN AM-FM, Boise, Idaho, 1987-88, sales mgr., 1988, gen. mgr., 1988—; gen. mgr. Sta. WUOG-FM (U. Ga.), Athens, Ga., 1984-85. Writer, producer interview with G. Gordon Liddy, 1983. Office: Sta KIZN AM/FM 1002 W Franklin Boise ID 83702

MELVIN, PEGGY LOUISE, court reporter; b. Tacoma, Wash., Mar. 26, 1950; d. John Douglas and Margaret (Fullinwider) M.; m. Ben Earl McCoy, June 10, 1979. Student, Tacoma Community Coll., 1968-69, Seattle Community Coll., 1969-71. Legal sec. Office of Pub. Defender, Okanogan, Wash., 1975-77, firm Mansfield & Thomas, Okanogan, Wash., 1977-80, firm Mansfield, Thomas & Reinbold, Okanogan, Wash., 1981-82; legal sec., office mgr. Office of Pub. Defender, Saipan, MP, 1980-81; adminstr., ct. reporter Okanogan County Superior Ct., 1982—. Mem. Wash. Assn. Superior Ct. Adminstrs., Nat. Assn. Ct. Adminstrn. Wash. Shorthand Reporters Assn., ABA, Judicial Assoc. Home: PO Box 20 Malott WA 98829 Office: Okanogan County Superior Ct PO Box 112 Okanogan WA 98840

MENARD, E. DEAN, manufacturing executive; b. Placentia, Calif., July 6, 1933; s. Ernest R. and Velma Winnie (Williams) M.; m. Marlene MacKenzie, June 28, 1958; 1 child, Lori Ann. BS in Bus., San Diego State U., 1957. Systems analyst Ryan Aero Co., San Diego, 1959-60, contract analyst, 1960-62, sr. contract adminstr., 1966-71, chief contracts, 1971-77, mgr. contracts, 1977-82; dir. contracts and pricing The Marquardt Co., Van Nuys, 1982-87, v.p. contracts, 1987—; corp. sec. The Marquardt Co., 1986—. Originator U. Cert. course in contract adminstrn., 1978. Pres. Ramona (Calif.) Outdoor Community Ctr., 1974. Served with U.S. Army, 1953-55. Scholarship awarded in his name San Diego State U., 1987. Mem. Nat. Contract Mgmt. Assn. (pres. 1979-80, edn. chmn. 1977-82, treas. 1975-77, award 1982), Valley Industry and Commerce Assn. (dir. 1988—). Republican. Club: Mgmt. Office: The Marquardt Co 16555 Saticoy St Van Nuys CA 91409

MENDEL, PETER PAUL, lawyer; b. Surabaya, Indonesia, Jan. 14, 1949; came to U.S., 1956; s. Henri Matthijs Caspar and Debora (Van Gelderen) M.; m. Lori Marie Wray, Oct. 10, 1975; children: Joshua, Kimberly, Heather, Alexandra, Matthew, Megan. BA, Brigham Young U., 1974; JD, Fordham U., 1981. Bar: N.Y. 1983, Calif. 1986. Legal asst. Lord, Day & Lord, N.Y.C., 1974-76, Walter Conston Schurtman & Gumpel, N.Y.C., 1976-77, Donovan Leisure Newton & Irvine, N.Y.C., 1977-83; assoc. Davidson & Matsen, Newport Beach, Calif., 1983-84; asst. v.p. Fin. Market Ins. Svcs., Orange, Calif., 1984-87; gen. counsel Hill Williams Devel. Corp., Anaheim, Calif., 1987—; pvt. practice Anaheim, 1987—. Mem. ABA, Calif. Bar Assn., N.Y. State Bar Assn., Am. Youth Soccer Assn. Club. Republican. Mormon. Home: 18172 Rainier Dr Santa Ana CA 92705 Office: Hill Williams Devel Corp 5500 E Santa Ana Canyon Rd Anaheim CA 92807

MENDENHALL, CARROL CLAY, physician; b. Missouri Valley, Iowa, July 26, 1916; s. Clay and Maude (Watts) M.; student U. So. Calif., 1942-44, Chapman Coll., 1946-47, Los Angeles City Coll., 1947-48; D.O., Coll. Osteo. Physicians and Surgeons, 1952; M.D., Calif. Coll. Medicine, 1962; m. Lucille Yvonne Bonvouloir, June 14, 1946 (div. July 1957); 1 son, Gregory Bruce; m. 2d, Barbara Marilyn Huggett-Davis, Sept. 28, 1974. Intern, Los Angeles County Osteo. Hosp., 1952-53; gen. practice medicine, 1953-82, specializing in weight control, Gardena, Calif., 1961-74, specializing in stress disorders and psychosomatic medicine, Ft. Worth, 1974-78, specializing in integral medicine and surgery, Santa Clara, Calif., 1978—; med. dir. Green's Pharms., Long Beach, Calif., 1956-64; v.p. Internat. Pharm. Mfg. Co., Inc., San Pedro, Calif., 1965-66; pres. Chemico of Gardena, Inc., 1964-69; staff Gardena Hosp.; active staff O'Connor Hosp., San Jose, Calif., 1979—; tchr., lectr. biofeedback, prevention and treatment of stress, creative thought; founder, dir. Eclectic Weight Control Workshop, 1971-74, Longevity Learning, Longevity Learning Seminars, 1980; past mem. adv. bd. dirs. Los Angeles Nat. Bank. Cadre med. dir. Gardena Civil Def., 1953-54, asst. to chief med. dir., 1954-60, chief med. and first aid services, 1960-64. Served as pharmacist's mate USNR, 1944-46. Fellow Royal Soc. Health, Am. Acad. Med. Preventics, Am. Acad. Homeopathic Medicine; mem. Calif. Med. Assn., Santa Clara County Med. Soc., Acupuncture Research Inst. (also alumni assn.), Los Aficionados de Los Angeles (pres. 1964-66), Am. Soc. Clin. Hypnosis. Flamenco Soc. No. Calif. (bd. dirs. 1986—). Republican. Address: 255 Crestview Dr Santa Clara CA 95050

MENDEZ, CELESTINO GALO, mathematics educator; b. Havana, Cuba, Oct. 16, 1944; s. Celestino Andres and Georgina (Fernandez) M.; came to U.S., 1962, naturalized, 1970; BA, Benedictine Coll., 1965; MA, U. Colo., 1968, PhD, 1974, MBA, 1979; m. Mary Ann Koplau, Aug. 21, 1971; children—Mark Michael, Matthew Maximilian. Asst. prof. maths. scis. Met. State Coll., Denver, 1971-77, assoc. prof., 1977-82, prof., 1982—, chmn. dept. math. scis., 1980-82. Mem. advt. rev. bd. Met. Denver, 1973-79; parish outreach rep. S.E. deanery, Denver Cath. Community Svcs., 1976-78; mem. social ministries com. St. Thomas More Cath. Ch., Denver, 1976-78, vice-chmn., 1977-78, mem. parish council, 1977-78; del. Adams County Rep. Conv., 1972, 74, Colo. 4th Congl. Dist. Conv., 1974, Colo. Rep. Conv., 1988; del. Douglas County Rep. Conv., 1980, 82, 84, 88; alt. del. Colo. Rep. Conv., 1984, 5th Congl. dist. conv., 1976; mem. rules com., 1978, 80, precinct committeeman Douglas County Rep. Com., 1976-78, mem. cen.

com., 1976-78; bd. dirs. Rocky Mountain Better Bus. Bur., 1975-79, Rowley Downs Homeowners Assn., 1976-78; mem. exec. bd., v.p. Assoc. Faculties of State Inst. Higher Edn. in Colo., 1971-73; trustee Hispanic U. Am., 1975-78; councilman Town of Parker (Colo.), 1981-84, chmn. budget and fin. com. 1981-84; chmn. joint budget com. Town of Parker-Parker Water and Sanitation Dist. Bds., 1982-84. Recipient U. Colo. Grad. Sch. excellence in teaching award, 1965-67; Benedictine Coll. grantee, 1964-65. Mem. Math. Assn. Am., Am. Math. Soc., Nat. Coun. Tchrs. of Math., Colo. Coun. Tchrs. of Maths., Colo. Internat. Edn. Assn., Asso. Faculties of State Insts. Higher Edn. in Colo. (v.p. 1971-73). Republican. Roman Catholic. Contbr. articles to profl. jours. and newspapers. Home: 11482 S Regency Pl Parker CO 80134 Office: 1006 11th St Denver CO 80204

MENDEZ, JANA LYNN, senator; b. Moscow, Idaho, Jan. 18, 1944; d. Earl Dean and Alverta (Dalberg) Hall; m. Richard Albert Mendez, Sept. 16, 1965; children: Amy, Jennifer, Christopher. BS in Journalism, U. Colo., 1981. Community and issue activist Boulder County Housing Authority and Citizens for the Right To Vote, Longmont, Colo., 1975-83; legis. asst. Senate Minority Leader, Denver, 1982-84; Colo. state senator, 1985—; asst. whip minority leader, 1986. Author: (with others) Chile From The Ground Up, 1982. Dem. precinct leader, area coordinator, senate dist. chmn. Boulder County, Colo., 1975-84; chair, commr. Boulder County Housing Authority, 1974-83. Regents scholar, 1963, Cervi scholar, 1980; U. Colo. Women's Ctr. grantee, 1980; named Outstanding Freshman Senator Colo. Social Legis. Com., 1985. Mem. Kappa Tau Alpha. Avocations: gardening, reading, photography, cooking. Office: State Capitol Rm 274 Denver CO 80203

MENDONCA, DAVID VINCENT, corporate executive; b. San Jose, Calif., May 18, 1948; s. Walter Vincent and LaVerne M. (Vieira) M.; m. Robin Rust, Nov. 21, 1976; children: Lianne, Jenna. BS, San Jose State U., 1972. Pres. T.M.A., Inc., Vacaville, Calif., 1974-77; gen. mgr. Yamanaka Trading Co., Sacramento, 1977-79; purchasing mgr. I.A.P., Inc., Sacramento, 1979-81; gen. mgr. F.P.D., Inc., Hialeah, Fla., 1981-83; pres. Direct Source Internat., Rancho Cordova, Calif., 1983—; cons. Grand Auto, Inc., Oakland, Calif., 1985—, I.T.M., Inc., Cerritos, Calif., 1987—. Republican. Roman Catholic. Office: Direct Source Internat 11315 K Sunrise Gold Circle Rancho Cordova CA 95742

MENDOZA, O. NICHOLAS, art director; b. Mexico City, Apr. 25, 1941; s. Nicolas and Guillermina (Oliveros) M.; m. Orlette Mendoza, July 1, 1989. BFA, Calif. Inst., 1965. Art dir. Carson Roberts Inc., Los Angeles, 1965-67, Chiat Day Inc., Los Angeles, 1966-67; art dir. Young & Rubicam Inc., N.Y.C., 1968-70, Venezuela, S.A., 1970-71; v.p., creative dir. Young & Rubicam Inc., Mexico City, 1971-79, Mendoza Dillon Inc., New Port Beach, Calif., 1980-84; pres. Nick Mendoza Prod., Hollywood, Calif., 1985--. Recipient Clio awards, Advt. Excellence, N.Y.C., 1987. Mem. Dirs. Guild Am. Republican. Home: 1000 Escondido Cyn Rd Agua Dulce CA 91350 Office: Nick Mendoza Prodn Inc 4411 W Magnolia Blvd Burbank CA 91505

MENEZES, STEPHEN, lawyer; b. Honolulu, Dec. 28, 1947; s. Clarence L. and Stella (Awana) M.; m. Janice M. Swearingen, Nov. 20, 1972 (dec. 1983). BBA, U. Hawaii, 1969; JD, Tex. Tech. U., 1976. Bar: Hawaii 1976. Dep. corp. counsel County of Hawaii, Hilo, 1977-80, corp. counsel, 1980-85; pvt. practice Hilo, 1985-87; ptnr. Menezes, Tsukazaki and Yeh, Hilo, 1987—. Mem. ABA, Hawaii State Bar Assn., Hawaii County Bar Assn. (pres. 1982), Hawaii Island Portuguese C. of C. (pres. 1988). Office: Menezes Tsukazaki & Yeh 100 Pauahi St Ste 204 Hilo HI 96720

MENGHINI, LENO H., highway engineer, state official; b. Superior, Wyo., Jan. 25, 1925; s. Egidio and Costantina (Prevedel) M.; m. Caroline Trontel, Oct. 21, 1950 (dec. 1969); children—Paul, Mark, Karen, Gary, John, Linda. B.C.E., U. Wyo., Laramie, 1950. Registered profl. engr., Wyo. With Wyo. Hwy. Dept., 1950—, stat constrn. engr., Cheyenne, 1967-72, dir. planning, 1972-76, supt., chief engr., 1976—. Bd. dirs. Seton Cath. High Sch., Cheyenne, 1980-84; v.p. bd. dirs. DePaul Hosp., Cheyenne, 1984-85. Served as sgt. U.S. Army, 1943-46. Mem. Wyo. Engring. Soc., Am. Assn. State Hwy Transp. Ofcls. (v.p. 1987, pres. 1988, chmn. maintenance com. 1980-84, mem. exec. com. 1978-81, hwy. com. 1982-84), Western Assn. State Hwy. Transp. Ofcls. (pres. 1980). Roman Catholic. Lodge: Cheyenne Rotary (dir. 1984-87). Home: 907 Shoshoni St Cheyenne WY 82009 Office: Wyo Hwy Dept PO Box 1708 Cheyenne WY 82001

MENKES, JOHN HANS, pediatric neurologist; b. Vienna, Austria, Dec. 20, 1928; came to U.S., 1940; s. Karl and Valerie (Tupler) M.; m. Miriam Trief, Apr. 14, 1957 (div. Feb. 1978); m. Joan Simon Feld, Sept. 28, 1980; children: Simon, Tamara, Rafael C. AB, U. So. Calif., 1947, MS, 1951; MD, Johns Hopkins U., 1952. Diplomate Am. Bd. Pediatrics, Am. Bd. Neurology. Intern, jr. asst. resident Children's Med. Ctr., Boston, 1952-54; asst. resident pediatrics Bellevue Hosp., N.Y.C., 1956-57; resident neurology, trainee pediatric neurology Columbia-Presbyn. Med. Ctr., Neurological Inst. N.Y., N.Y.C., 1957-60; asst. prof. pediatrics Johns Hopkins U., Balt., 1960-63, assoc. prof., 1963-66, asst. prof. neurology, 1964-66, chief pediatric neurology div., 1964-66; prof. pediatrics and neurology UCLA, 1966-74, chief pediatric neurology div., 1966-70, prof. psychiatry, 1970-74; chief Neurology-Neurochem. Lab. Brentwood (Calif.) VA Hosp., 1970-74; clin. prof. psychiatry, neurology and pediatrics UCLA, 1974-77, clin. prof. pediatrics and neurology, 1977-84, prof. pediatrics and neurology, 1985—; mem. metabolism study sect. NIH, 1966-70, project com. 1969-70; mem. adv. com. Nat. Inst. Child Health and Human Devel., 1985-87; mem. Dept. Health Services, Calif., 1980-87; mem. Council Child Neurology Soc., Dysautonomia Found; bd. trustees Dystonia Med. Research Found., Vancouver, Can., 1985—. Author: Textbook of Child Neurology, 3d edit., 1985; (play) The Last Inquisitor, 1985 (Drama Logue Critics award 1985), The Salvation of Miguel Toruna, 1987; (screen play) Miguel Open Ward, 1989; contbr. numerous articles to pediatric jours. Served with USAF, 1954-56. Mem. Am. Acad. Neurology, Am. Acad. Pediatrics, Am. Chem. Soc., Soc. for Pediatric Research, Sociedad Peruana de Neuro-Psychiatria (hon.), Am. Neurochem. Soc., Am. Neurol. Assn., Am. Pediatric Soc., Child Neurology Soc. (Hower award 1980), editorial bds. of related jours., Dramatist Guild. Jewish. Home: 1201 Park Way Beverly Hills CA 90210 Office: UCLA Reed Neurologic Rsch Ctr Los Angeles CA 90024

MENKES, LILIANE, educator; b. Paris, Apr. 9, 1952; came to U.S., 1960; d. Oscar and Aurelie (Goldstein) Grosz; m. Avi Menkes, June 30, 1974 (div. 1980). BA in French, UCLA, 1975; elem.-spl. edn. credential, Calif. State U., Northridge, 1977. Spl. edn. tchr., tutor L.A. Unified Sch. Dist., 1978—, mentor tchr., 1986—. Vol. L.I.F.E. (Love Is Feeding Everyone), L.A., 1986—. Democrat. Jewish. Office: LA Unified Sch Dist 600 S McCadden Pl Los Angeles CA 90005

MENKIN, CHRISTOPHER (KIT), leasing company executive; b. Manhattan, N.Y., Jan. 1, 1942; s. Lawrence and Columbia (Riland) M.; children: Dashiel, Tascha, Ashley. Student, Julliard Sch. of Music, 1960, Santa Monica Coll., 1959-61, UCLA, 1961-64. News editor, dir. Sta. KRFC Radio, San Francisco, 1964-67; adminstrv. asst. to assemblyman Leo J. Ryan South San Francisco, 1967-68; mng. editor Sta. KGO TV News, San Francisco, 1968-69; news producer west coast Sta. ABC TV, Los Angeles, 1969; city mgr. City of San Bruno (Calif.), 1970; owner Menkin & Assocs., Santa Clara, Calif., 1971—; sr. ptnr. Am. Leasing, Santa Clara, 1971—; ptnr. Medallon Leasing, Santa Clara, 1974-80; pres. Monte Sereno Wine Co., Santa Clara, 1978—; dir. Meridian Nat. Bank, 1982-84. Chmn. nominating com. San Jose (Calif.) Symphony, 1988—; sec. Salvation Army, Santa Clara, 1968—; bd. dirs. Community Against Substance Abuse, Los Gatos, Calif., 1988—, Valley Inst. of Theater Arts, Saratoga, Calif., 1987-88, San Jose Trolley, 1988—. Mem. Santa Clara Valley Wine Soc. (pres. 1988—), Assn. Credit Grantors (past pres.), Credit Women Internat. (first male pres.), Santa Clara C. of C. (past pres. 1973-76), Kiwanis (v.p. 1968), Optimists (v.p. 1970). Democrat. Office: Am Leasing 2175 De La Cruz Blvd Ste 11 Santa Clara CA 95050

MENNELLA, VINCENT ALFRED, automotive manufacturing and airplane company executive; b. Teaneck, N.J., Oct. 7, 1922; s. Francis Anthony and Henrietta Vernard (Dickson) M.; B.A. in Acctg., U. Wash., 1948; m. Madeleine Olson, Aug. 18, 1945; children—Bruce, Cynthia, Mark, Scott, Chris. Sales and bus. mgmt. positions Ford div. Ford Motor Co., 1949-55; founder, pres. Southgate Ford, Seattle, 1955-80; pres. Flightcraft, Inc., Seattle, 1973-86; chmn. bd. Stanley Garage Door Co., 1981-86. Former chmn. March of Dimes. Served to capt. USNR, 1942-45. Republican. Roman Catholic. Clubs: Rainier Golf, Seattle Tennis, Wash. Athletic, Rotary (past pres.). Home: 1400 SW 171st Pl Seattle WA 98166

MENSINGA, NANNY MAREINA, small business owner; b. Amsterdam, The Netherlands, June 4, 1939; came to U.S., 1961; d. Albert and Hendrika (VanGelder) M.; m. John Lee Colbert, Dec. 17, 1988. Student, Inst. Schoevers, Amsterdam, 1959. Adminstrv. asst. Dutch-French C. of C., Paris, 1959-61; editorial sec. David McKay Pubs., N.Y.C., 1962-65; editorial asst. Pocket Books, Inc., N.Y.C., 1965-67; asst. fashion editor Woman's Day mag., N.Y.C., 1967-72, tech. how-to writer, 1974-77; asst. knit/crochet editor McCall's Needlework & Crafts mag., N.Y.C., 1977-80; pres. Party Works, Inc., Visalia, Calif., 1985—. Author: (craft book) Beautiful Baby Clothes; editor: (craft book) The Best of Woman's Day Crochet, 1976. Vol. Shelter for Battered Women, Visalia, 1983, Visalia Community Ctr. Democrat. Jewish. Home: 617 Verde Vista Visalia CA 93277 Office: Party Works Inc Visalia CA 93277

MENSINGER, PEGGY BOOTHE, retired mayor; b. Modesto, Calif., Feb. 18, 1923; d. Dyas Power and Margaret (Stewart) Boothe; m. John Logan Mensinger, May 25, 1952; children: John B., Stewart I., Susan B. AB in Polit. Sci, Stanford U., 1944. Reporter San Francisco Red Cross Chpt. News Bur., 1944; acting mgr. Boothe Fruit Co., Modesto, Calif., 1945; asst. dir. Stanford (Calif.) Alumni Assn., 1947; exec. sec. pub. exercises com. Stanford U., 1949-51; mem. Modesto City Council, 1973-79, mayor, 1979-87; ret. 1987; Mem. adv. bd. Agrl. Issues Ctr. U. Calif., 1988—. Bd. dirs. Nat. council Girl Scouts U.S.A., 1978-87; chmn. Citizens Com. for Internat. Students, 1965-70; pres. Modesto PTA Council, 1967-69, Modesto chpt. Am. Field Svc., 1969-70, Stanislaus County Hist. Soc., 1970-71, state bd. Common Cause, 1973-75; chmn. Modesto City Cultural Commn., 1968-73; del. White House Conf. on Families, L.A., 1980; chmn. Stanislaus Area Assn. Govts., 1976-77; chmn. air quality subcom. U.S. Conf. Mayors, 1985-87. Recipient Woman of Year award VFW Aux., 1980, Man of Yr. award Am. Legion, 1987. Mem. Nat. League Am. Pen Women (asso.), AAUW (grant honoree Edn. Found. 1978), Stanford Assocs. (pres. 1985-87), Soroptimist (hon., Women Achievement award 1980), Local Govt. Commn., Phi Beta Kappa, Gamma Phi Beta. Unitarian. Home: 1320 Magnolia Ave Modesto CA 95350 Office: 801 11th St Modesto CA 95354

MENTOCK, RICHARD MICHEAL, mathematician; b. Sheridan, Wyo., Sept. 15, 1950; s. Raymond George and Alice Georgetaa (Demchock) M.; m. Sabrina Marie Greco, Dec. 10, 1978; children: Ryan Micheal, Shannon Marie. BS in Math, U. Wyo., 1976, MS in Math, 1981. Software engr. Lockheed Missiles and Space Corp., Aurora, Colo., 1981—. Author: Astrorhythms: A Scientific Approach to Astrology, 1988, Earth Throbs: A New View of Earth History, 1989. Mem. Math. Assn. of Am., Assn. for Computing machinery, Nat. Mgmt. Assn. Democrat. Roman Catholic. Home: PO Box 14023 Research Triangle Park NC 27709

MENZIES, JEAN STORKE, retired newspaperwoman; b. Santa Barbara, Calif., Dec. 30, 1904; d. Thomas More and Elsie (Smith) Storke; B.A., Vassar Coll., 1927; M.A. in Physics, Stanford, 1931; m. Ernest F. Menzies, Oct. 20, 1937; children—Jean Storke (Mrs. Dennis Wayne Vaughan), Thomas More. Teaching asst. dept. physics Stanford, 1927-29; instr. of physics Vassar Coll., 1929-30; tchr. math., chemistry, gen. sci. Sarah Dix Hamlin Sch., San Francisco, 1931-34; sec. to Dr. Samuel T. Orton, N.Y.C., 1935-36; press reporter, spl. writer Santa Barbara News-Press, 1954-63. Vol. rec. sec. nat. YWCA, India, Burma and Ceylon, 1941-42; rec. sec., Calcutta YWCA, 1942-47, v.p., 1949-51; sec. Tri-County adv. council Children's Home Soc., Santa Barbara, 1952-54; founding dir., sec. corp. Santa Barbara Film Soc., Inc., 1960-66. Bd. dirs. Santa Barbara County chpt. Am. Assn. UN, 1954-59, Friends U. Calif. at Santa Barbara Library, 1970-74, Small Wilderness Area Preservation, 1971-79; sec. bd. trustees Crane Country Day Sch., 1955-57; trustee Mental Hygiene Clinic of Santa Barbara, 1956-60, U. Calif. Santa Barbara Found., 1974-80, Santa Barbara Mus. Natural History, 1977-81; adv. council Santa Barbara Citizens Adult Edn., 1958-62, v.p., 1960-62; bd. dirs. Internat. Social Sci. Inst., sec., 1963-68, mem. adv. bd., 1969; bd. dirs. Planned Parenthood Santa Barbara County, Inc., 1964-65, adv. council, 1966-67; trustee Santa Barbara Botanic Garden, 1967-81, hon. trustee, 1981—; trustee. Santa Barbara Trust for Historic Preservation, 1967-68, 72-77; mem. affiliates bd. dirs. U. Calif. at Santa Barbara, 1960-61, 67-70, 72-77; sec. Santa Barbara Mission Archive-Library, 1967—; mem. Santa Barbara Found., 1977-81. Mem. Santa Barbara Hist. Soc. (dir. 1957-62, founding mem. women's projects com. 1959-63, sec. 1961-62), Channel City Women's Forum (v.p. 1969-73, bd. dirs. 1973-87), Phi Beta Kappa, Sigma Xi. Club: Vassar of Santa Barbara and the Tri-Counties (1st v.p., founding com. 1956-57, 2d v.p. 1959-61, chmn. publicity com. 1961-73). Home: 2298 Featherhill Rd Santa Barbara CA 93108

MENZIES, THOMAS NEAL, art consultant, art critic; b. Long Beach, Calif., Mar. 1, 1945; s. Thomas Warren and Frances (Starks) M. BA, U. Calif., Irvine, 1972; MA, U. So. Calif., 1978. Libr. dir. Parsons Sch. Design, L.A., 1980-82; art coord. Hirsch/Bedner & Assocs., Santa Monica, Calif., 1982-84; pres. Neal Menzies Contemporary Art Inc., L.A., 1984—. Contbg. editor ARTWEEK mag., Oakland, Calif., 1979-83. Chartered founder Mus. Contemporary Art, L.A.; docent Venice (Calif.) Art Walk. Mem. So. Calif. Art Writers Assn., L.A. Contemporary Exhbns. (friend), Pres.' Circle L.A. County Mus. of Art. Office: 170 S La Brea Ave Los Angeles CA 90036

MEOLA, FRANK ANTHONY, teacher; b. N.Y.C., Sept. 29, 1948; s. Daniel Benny and Camille Phyllis (Tocci) M.; m. Mary A. Agro, Sept. 12, 1970; children: Christopher, Robert, Marisa. BS, N.Y. Inst. Tech., 1980; MS, Iona Coll., 1983; postgrad., Nova U. Cert. tchr., adminstr., community coll. instr., Calif. Indsl. engr. U.S. Postal Svc., N.Y.C., 1973-80; tchr. math. John S. Burke Cath. High Sch., Goshen, N.Y., 1980-81; chmn. dept. math. Don Bosco Preparatory High Sch., Ramsey, N.J., 1981-84; tchr. math. North Rockland Cen. Sch. Dist., Stony Point, N.Y., 1984-87; instr. math. Dominican Coll. of Blauvelt, Orangeburg, N.Y., 1983-87; tchr. math. Rialto (Calif.) Unified Sch. Dist., 1987—; instr. math., Saddleback Community Coll. Dist., Irvine, Calif., Coast Community Coll. Dist., Costa Mesa,Calif., 1988—. Assoc. dir., St. Paul's Religious Edn. Program, Valley Cottage, N.Y., 1980-82; dir. publicity, Valley Cottage Indians Recreation Program, 1985-87, umpire-in-chief, 1985-86, v.p. fin., 1986-87. Mem. Nat. Coun. Tchrs. Math., Assn. Supervision and Curriculum Devel., Math. Assn. Am., Am. Soc. Mech. Engrs. Republican. Roman Catholic. Home: 5132 Yearling Irvine CA 92714 Office: Rialto Unified Sch Dist 182 E Walnut Ave Rialto CA 92376

MERCER, JANET CLARE, contracting company executive; b. Zumbrota, Minn., Mar. 25, 1955; d. Tracy M. and Helen Gene (Rockwood) M. Student, U. Mont., 1976, N. Bennett State Indsl. Sch., Boston, 1978. Owner, ptnr. Artisan Carpentry, Boston, 1978-81; owner, mgr. Inside Dimensions Gen. Contracting, Boston, 1981-87, Hale Ali: Builders, Haiku, Hawaii, 1987—. Mem. Women in Constrn. (pres. 1983-87), Maui Contractors Assn. Home and Office: 868 Kaupakalua Rd Haiku HI 96708

MERCER, JOSEPH HENRY, lawyer, former state senator; b. Peoria, Ill., Feb. 1, 1937; s. Maurice D. and Dorothy J. M.; children: Stephen, Jennifer, Matthew. BA, U. N. Mex., 1961; JD, Harvard U., 1964. Bar: N. Mex. 1966. With Hanna and Mercer, Mercer and Carpenter, Mercer and McCash, to 1980; ptnr. Mercer, Lock, and Keating, Albuquerque, 1980-86, Mercer Profl. Assn., Albuquerque, 1986—; mem. N.Mex. Ho. of Reps., 1975-76; mem. N. Mex. Senate, 1977-84, minority floor leader, 1980-84. Chmn. Albuquerque Com. on Fgn. Relations, 1975-76, mem., 1967—, jud. council, 1981-84; mem. Gov.'s Organized Crime Prevention Commn., chmn., 1988—, mem. oversight com., 1981-84. Served to 1st lt. arty U.S. Army, 1955-58. Mem. N. Mex. State Bar (Outstanding Service award 1974), Albuquerque Bar Assn. (dir. 1977-78). Republican. Presbyterian. Office: 4221 Silver SE Albuquerque NM 87108

MERCHANT, RHONDA RENE, accountant, consultant; b. Waco, Tex., June 8, 1962; d. Wilson Morgan and Maria Dolores (Carrasco) Camp. Student, Anchorage Community Coll., 1984-85, U. Alaska, 1985-89. Acct. Consol. Leather, Inc., N. Hollywood, Calif., 1980-83, Am. Restaurant Group, Anchorage, 1983-89; acctg. cons. Anchorage Econ. Devel. Corp., 1988—, Ernst & Whinney, CPA's., Anchorage, 1989—. Acctg. tutor Anchorage Community Coll., 1986—; vol. Vol. Income Tax Assistance Program, 1987-88. Mem. Nat. Assn. Accts. (bd. dirs. Anchorage chpt. 1988—). Home: PO Box 230424 Anchorage AK 99523-0424 Office: Stuart Anderson's Cattle Co 300 W Tudor Rd Anchorage AK 99503

MERCHANT, ROLAND SAMUEL, SR., hospital administrator, educator; b. N.Y.C., Apr. 18, 1929; s. Samuel and Eleta (McLymont) M.; m. Audrey Bartley, June 6, 1970; children—Orelia Eleta, Roland Samuel, Huey Bartley. B.A., N.Y.U., 1957, M.A., 1960; M.S., Columbia U., 1963, M.S.H.A., 1974. Asst. statistician N.Y.C. Dept. Health, 1957-60, statistician, 1960-63; statistician N.Y. TB and Health Assn., N.Y.C., 1963-65; biostatistician, adminstrv. coordinator Inst. Surg. Studies, Montefiore Hosp., Bronx, N.Y., 1965-72; resident in adminstrn. Roosevelt Hosp., N.Y.C., 1973-74; dir. health and hosp. mgmt. Dept. Health, City of N.Y., 1974-76; from asst. adminstr. to adminstr. West Adams Community Hosp., Los Angeles, 1976; spl. asst. to assoc. v.p. for med. affairs Stanford U. Hosp., Calif., 1977-82, dir. office mgmt. and strategic planning, 1982-85, dir. mgmt. planning, 1986—; clin. assoc. prof. dept. family, community and preventive medicine Stanford U., 1986-88, dept. health research and policy Stanford U. Med. Sch., 1988—. Served with U.S. Army. 1951-53. USPHS fellow. Fellow Am. Coll. Healthcare Execs., Am. Pub. Health Assn.; mem. Am. Hosp. Assn., Nat. Assn. Health Services Execs., N.Y. Acad. Scis. Home: 953 Cheswick Dr San Jose CA 95121 Office: Stanford U Hosp Stanford CA 94305

MERCHANT, RONALD, economist, educator; b. Joseph, Utah, Dec. 25, 1938; s. James Carl and Uella (Mills) M.; m. Glenda Marie Steenbergen, July 17, 1961; children: Michael James, Steven Charles, Paul Ronald, Rhonda Marie. BS in Econs., Utah State U., 1965; MBA, Gonzaga U., Spokane, Wash., 1969; postgrad., U. Tenn., 1983-84. Reliability coord. Am. Mach. & Fdy., Mt. Home, Ida., 1961-62; inspector Thiokol Chem. Corp., Tremonton, Utah, 1961-63; tchr. math/sci. Kuna (Ida.) Sch. Dist., 1963-64, McCall (Ida.) Sch. Dist., 1965-66; economist U.S. Dept. Interior, Spokane, 1966-69; tchr. bus. Spokane Falls Community Coll., 1969—; cons. and lectr. in field; coord. Coll. Needs Assessment, Spokane, 1978—. Author: Quotes for Teachers, 1986, Business Math with Elec. Accuracy, 1987, Calculator Proficiency, 1988, Business Math and Calculators, 4th edit. 1989. Active in Boy Scouts Am. Capt. USNR, 1968—. Wash. Internat. Trade Found. fellow, 1986; Found for Econ. Edn. fellow, 1986; NSF fellow 1973. Mem. Nat. Speakers Assn., Naval Res. Assn., Nat. Bus. Edn. Assn., Am. Voc. Assn., SPCC Assn. for Higher Edn., Toastmasters (pres. 1987-88). Home: E 24 Salmon Spokane WA 99218-1620

MERCURIO, EDWARD PETER, natural science educator; b. Orange, Calif., Dec. 28, 1944; s. Peter Amadeo and Jeanne (Monteleone) M.; m. Jeanne Roussel Gable, Oct. 18, 1980 (div. Dec. 1984); 1 child, Katherine Roussel; m. Patricia Ann Kahler, Apr. 12, 1987; 1 child, Peter Edward. BA, UCLA, 1967, MA, 1970, CPhil, 1978. Research asst. UCLA, 1971, teaching asst., 1968-71; instructional assoc. Golden West Coll., Huntington Beach, Calif., 1972-73; cons. Monterey County Planning Dept., Salinas, Calif., 1980; prof. Hartnell Coll., Salinas, Calif., 1973—; photographer in field, Calif., 1961—; lectr. in field, Calif., 1970—; cons. in field, 1980—. Fellow Woodrow Wilson Nat. Fellowship Found., 1967. Mem. AAAS, Sierra Club. Democrat. Home: 647 Wilson St Salinas CA 93901 Office: Hartnell Coll 156 Homestead Ave Salinas CA 93901

MEREDITH, LAURIE R., organizational business specialist; b. Ft. Collins, Colo., Jan. 2, 1960; d. D. Roscoe and Marlyn A. (Kirkpatrick) M. Student, Bethany Coll., 1978-79; BS in Bus. Mgmt., U. Denver, 1985. Office mgr. Thomas Leadabrand & Assocs., Lakewood, Colo., 1985-86; adminstrv. asst. Denver Tech. Coll., 1986-87; pres. Key Profl. Support, Inc., Denver, 1986-88; office mgr. strategic info. network USWest, Inc., Englewood, Colo., 1988—; cons. resumes, Denver, 1981—. Intern Gov.'s Citizen Adv. Office, Denver, 1978, 79; vol. Repub. Com. County of Adams, Westminster, Colo., 1980, election judge, 1980, 84. Named Outstanding Keyworker United Way, 1988. Mem. NAFE, Bus. and Profl. Women's Club (roster chmn. 1983-85, runner-up Young Career Woman 1984). Baptist. Home: 5310 S Broadway Circle #207 Englewood CO 80110 Office: 9785 Maroon Circle Ste 440 Englewood CO 80112

MERIAN, HAROLD ARTHUR, naval officer, nurse; b. Andrews AFB, Md., Nov. 18, 1959; s. Harold Holmes Merian and Peggy (Sutton) Dunn. Student, Linfield Coll., 1978-79; student, Wash. State U., 1979-80; BS in Nursing, U. State of N.Y., Albany, 1987. RN, Calif., Wash. Enlisted man USN, 1981-87, commd. ensign, 1987, lt. (j.g.), 1988; hosp. corpsman Charleston, S.C., 1981-82; lab. technician USS Constellation, 1982-83; histopathology technician Camp Pendleton, Calif., 1984-87; nurse Navy Hosp., Naval Air Sta. Whidbey, Oak Harbor, Wash., 1987—; advanced cardiac life support provider Am. Heart Assn., 1986-88, instr. basic cardiac life support, 1988—. Music and theatre scholar Linfield Coll., 1978-79; music scholar Eastern Wash. State U., 1978. Mem. Am. Assn. Critical Care Nurses. Democrat. Roman Catholic. Home: 8673 80th St NW Apt 21 Oak Harbor WA 98277 Office: Naval Air Sta Navy Hosp Whidbey Oak Harbor WA 98278

MERIGAN, THOMAS CHARLES, JR., physician, medical researcher, educator; b. San Francisco, Jan. 18, 1934; s. Thomas C. and Helen M. (Greeley) M.; m. Joan Mary Freeborn, Oct. 3, 1959; 1 son, Thomas Charles III. B.A. with honors, U. Calif., Berkeley, 1955; M.D., U. Calif., San Francisco, 1958. Diplomate: Am. Bd. Internal Medicine. Intern in medicine 2d and 4th Harvard med. services Boston City Hosp., 1958-59, asst. resident medicine, 1959-60; clin. assoc. Nat. Heart Inst., NIH, Bethesda, Md., 1960-62; asso. Lab. Molecular Biology, Nat. Inst. Arthritis and Metabolic Diseases, NIH, 1962-63; practice medicine specializing in internal medicine and infectious diseases Stanford, Calif., 1963—; asst. prof. medicine Stanford U. Sch. Medicine, 1963-67, assoc. prof. medicine, 1967-72, head div. infectious diseases, 1966—, prof. medicine, 1972—, George E. and Lucy Becker prof. medicine, 1980—; dir. Diagnostic Microbiology Lab., Univ. Hosp., 1966-72, Diagnostic Virology Lab., 1969—, Ctr. AIDS Rsch. Stanford U., 1988—; hosp. epidemiologist, 1966-88; mem. microbiology rsch. tng. grants com. NIH, 1969-73, virology study sect., 1974-78; cons. antiviral substances program Nat. Inst. Allergy and Infectious Diseases, 1970—, mem. AIDS clin. drug devel. commn., 1986—; mem. Virology Task Force, 1976-78, bd. sci. counselors, 1980-85; mem. U.S. Hepatitis panel U.S. and Japan Coop. Med. Sci. Program, 1979—, AIDS subcom. Nat. Adv. Allergy and Infectious Diseases Coun., 1988—; co-chmn. interferon evaluation Group Am. Cancer Soc., 1978-81; mem. vaccines and related biol. products adv. com. Ctr. for Drugs and Biols., FDA, 1984-88; mem. internat. adv. com. on biol. sci. Sci. Council, Singapore, 1985-88; mem. adv. com. J.A. Hartford Found., 1979-84; mem. Albert Lasker awards jury, 1981-84; mem. peer review panel U.S. Army Med. Rsch. and Devel. Com., 1986-88. Contbr. numerous articles on infectious diseases, virology and immunology to sci. jours.; editor: Antivirals with Clinical Potential, 1976, Antivirals and Virus Diseases of Man, 1979, 2d edit., 1984, 3d edit., 1989, Regulatory Functions of Interferon, 1980, Interferons, 1982, Interferons as Cell Growth Inhibitors, 1986; assoc. editor: Virology, 1975-78, Cancer Research, 1987—; co-editor: monograph series Current Topics in Infectious Diseases, 1975—; editorial bd.: Archives Internal Medicine, 1971-81, Jour. Gen. Virology, 1972-77, Infection and Immunity, 1973-81, Intervirology, 1973-85, Proc. Soc. Expt. Biology and Medicine, 1978-87, Reviews of Infectious Diseases, 1979—, Jour. Interferon Research, 1980—, Antiviral Research, 1980-86, Jour. Antimicrobial Chemotherapy, 1981—, Molecular and Cellular Biochemistry, 1982—, AIDS Research and Human Retroviruses, 1983—, Jour. Virology, 1984—, Biotechnology Therapeutics, 1988—, Jour. Infectious Diseases, 1989—, Drug Investigation, 1989—. Recipient Borden award for Outstanding Research Am. Assn. Med. Colls., 1973, Maxwell Finland award Infectious Diseases Soc. Am., 1988; Guggenheim Meml. fellow, 1972. Mem. Assn. Am. Physicians, Western Assn. Physicians, Am. Soc. Microbiology, Am. Soc. Clin. Investigation (coun. 1977-80), Am. Assn. Immunologists, Am. Fedn. Clin. Rsch., Western Soc. Clin. Rsch., Soc. Exptl. Biology and Medicine (publ. com. 1985-89), Infectious Diseases Soc. Am., Am. Soc. Virology, Inst. Medicine, Pan Am. Group for Rapid Viral Diagnosis, AMA, Internat. Soc. Interferon Rsch. (coun. 1983-89), Calif. Med. Assn., Santa Clara County Med. Soc., Calif. Acad. Medicine, Royal Soc. Medicine, AAAS, Alpha Omega Alpha. Home: 148 Goya Rd Portola Valley CA 94025 Office: Stanford U Sch Medicine Div Infectious Diseases Stanford CA 94305

MERILATT, RANDALL LEE, computer software developer; b. Kansas City, Mo., Oct. 23, 1951; s. Dean Sterling and Bettie Jean (Irby) M.; m. Jenifer Carole Fleagle, Mar. 14, 1981; children: Joelle, Rebecca, Scott. BS in Applied Math., U. Colo., 1974. Computer programmer Colo. Bureau of Investigation, Denver, 1974-78; systems analyst Boeing Computer Svcs., Seattle, 1978-82; pres. Raima Corp., Bellevue, Wash., 1982—. Author: Vista III Database Development System, 1987. Mem. Assn. for Computing Machinery. Republican. Mem. Evangelical Christian Ch. Office: Raima Corp 3245 146th Pl SE Bellevue WA 98007

MERIN, ROBERT LYNN, periodontist; b. L.A., Jan. 25, 1946; s. Marcus and Belle Merin; m. Barbara Rosen, June 27, 1971; children: Lori, Kimberly. DDS, UCLA, 1970; MS, Loma Linda U., 1972. Chief periodontal svc. Mather Air Force Hosp., Sacramento, 1972-74; pvt. practice, Woodland Hills, Calif., 1974—; chmn. dental staff Humana-West Hills (Calif.) Hosp., 1982-84; lectr. UCLA Sch. Dentistry, 1970, 74—. Author: (with others) Glickman's Clinical Periodontics, 1978, 84, 88; contbr. articles to profl. jours. Active UCLA Dental Scholarship and Loan Com., 1984—; cons. L.A. Olympic Com., 1984. Mem. ADA, Am. Acad. Periodontics, Calif. Soc. Periodontists, San Fernando Valley Dental Soc. (mem. polit. action com. 1988), UCLA Dental Alumni Assn. (pres. 1979-80, bd. dirs. 1970—), UCLA Apollonians (pres. 1983-86). Office: 6342 Fallbrook Ave #101 Woodland Hills CA 91367

MERIWETHER, MARGARET KATHERINE, historian; b. Lodi, Calif., July 22, 1921; d. George M. and Theresa L. (Dillonberg) Gannon; m. Richard Derling Meriwether, Nov. 18, 1945; children—Thomas Joseph, Theresa Lois. Cert. tchr. Calif. Elem. tchr., Glendale, Calif., 1943-45; docent Gamble House, Pasadena, Calif., 1969-74, organizer Greene & Greene Library, 1969-70, chmn., 1970-74; research historian Pasadena Cultural Heritage Com.; vol. reference dept. Pasadena Pub. Library, 1974—; cons. archtl. history Pasadena. Founding mem. Friends of Pasadena Pub. Library, bd. dirs., 1974-75. Recipient Pasadena Pub. Library and Cultural Heritage Com. spl. award for extraordinary service, 1982, Pasadena Heritage cert. appreciation, 1983. Mem. Gamble House Docent Council, Soc. Archtl. Historians (So. Calif. chpt.), Pasadena Heritage, Pasadena Assistance League, Alpha Chi Omega. Republican. Roman Catholic. Club: Annandale Golf (Pasadena). Author bibliographies and indexes on Pasadena history and architecture. Home: 1055 Stoneridge Dr Pasadena CA 91105

MERKEL, ALFRED WILLIAM, printing executive; b. Lafayette, Ind., Mar. 29, 1929; s. Charles Daniel and Lillian Mae (Bennett) M.; m. Marlowe Marcia Graves, Sept. 2, 1955; children: Jennifer, Todd, Carolyn. BS, Purdue U., 1952. Indsl. engr. R.R. Donnelly, Crawfordsville, Ind., 1952-53; v.p. sch. div. Jostens, Mpls., 1958-72; v.p. Am. Can Co., Indpls., 1972-75; pres. GTE-Directories Press (formerly Times Mirror Press), Los Angeles, 1975—. Area chmn. United Way, Los Angeles, 1983; mem. ALISO-PICO Businessmen's Council, Los Angeles, 1981—. Served to capt. USAF, 1953-58. Mem. Printing Industries So. Calif. (pres. 1980, Man of Yr., 1980), Printing Industries of Am. (vice chmn. 1983—). Lutheran. Club: Oakmont (Glendale, Calif.),. Office: GTE Directories Press 1115 S Boyle Ave Los Angeles CA 90023

MERKEL, KURT DWIGHT, surgeon; b. Lemmon, S.D., June 6, 1952; s. Sheldon Done and Lavinia Eva (Winter) Peters; m. Margaret Mary Sullivan, June 29, 1979; children: Thomas Sheldon , Tyler John. BS in Biochemistry magna cum laude, U. Wash., 1974; MD cum laude, St. Louis U., 1980; MS in Orthopedics, U. Minn., 1985. Diplomate Am. Bd. Orthopedic Surgery. Resident Mayo Clinic, Rochester, Minn., 1980-84, chief resident orthopedics, 1984-85; chief dept. orthopedics and orthopedic surgery Fairbanks Clinic, Fairbanks, Alaska, 1985—; co-dir. Fairbanks Sports Medicine Clinic, 1985—; cons. in field. Contbr. numerous articles to profl. jours. Orthopedic Research and Edn. Found. grantee, 1982-83; recipient Stinchfield award Hip Soc., 1984. Fellow Am. Acad. Othopedic Surgery, Am. Coll. Sports Medicine, Alpha Omega Alpha; mem. AMA, Fairbanks Med. Soc., Alaskan Soc. Orthopedic Surgery, U. Alaska Fairbanks Athletic Dept. (Silver Bear award 1986). Roman Catholic. Lodge: Elks. Office: Fairbanks Clinic 1867 Airport Rd Fairbanks AK 99701

MERKEL, MILES ADAIR, electrical engineer; b. Schnecksville, Pa., Sept. 1, 1929; s. Walter Charles and Bernice Alice (Ridenbaugh) M.; m. Elizabeth June Dietrich, Sept. 14, 1951; 1 child, David Alan. BSEE, Pa. State U., 1953. Registered profl. engr., Pa., Ariz. Chief R&D Nat. Security Agy., Japan, 1960-64; chief radio wave propagation predictions Nat. Security Agy., Ft. Meade, Fla., 1964-67; chief computer systems devel. Nat. Security Agy., Ft. Meade, 1967-68; sr. sci. advisor Syracuse (N.Y.) U., 1971-73; chief electromagnetics engring. office U.S. Army, Sierra Vista, Ariz., 1974-88; v.p. engring., co-owner, chmn. bd. QO, Inc., Sierra Vista, 1988—; ind. govt. contractor, 1988—; with Internat. Radio Consultative Com., 1974—. Author: Smooth in the Saddle, 1973. With USN, 1947-49. Mem. Nat. Writers Club (profl.), Elks. Republican. Lutheran. Home and Office: 2240 Golf Links Rd Sierra Vista AZ 85635

MERKERT, GEORGE L., JR., orthopedic surgeon; b. Mpls., Apr. 9, 1925; s. George LeRoy and Mary Elizabeth (Craig) M.; m. Karin Inger, Sept. 16, 1979; children: George L., Craig Napier, Thomas Whitney, Jon Walter. MD, U. Louisville, 1948. Diplomate Am. Bd. Orthopaedic Surgery. Intern rotating Ancker Hosp., St. Paul, 1948-49, resident in gen. surgery, 1949-50; resident in gen. surgery Grad. Sch. Orthopaedic Surgery U. Minn., 1953-54; pres. Merkert Carlton Waldron Mahony Orthopaedic Assn., Colorado Springs, Colo., 1955—. Served to lt. USN, 1950-55. Mem. Am. Acad. Orthopaedic Surgeons, Am. Acad. Cerebral Palsy, Am. Coll. Surgeons, Western Orthopaedic Assn., Rocky Mountain Trauma Soc., AMA, Broadmoor Golf Club. Republican. Presbyterian. Home: 3229 Leslie Dr Colorado Springs CO 80909 Office: Merkert Carlton Waldron Orthopaedic Assn 801 N Cascade Colorado Springs CO 80903

MERKES, DENNIS BRADFORD, infosystems specialist, minister; b. Chgo., Oct. 10, 1943; s. Marshall Pierre and Jean LaBelle (McIntyre) M.; m. Nancy Diane Burton, June 17, 1962; children: John Robert, Kevin Burton, DeAnne Janelle. BS in Electronic Engring., Northrop U., 1964; MDiv, Bethel Theol. Sem., San Diego, 1985; postgrad., Nat. U., Vista, Calif., 1988—. Ordained to ministry Baptist Ch., 1980. Engr. Pacific Telephone Co., L.A., 1964-67; bus. system specialist Bell Telephone Labs., Holmdel, N.J., 1967-69; cons. analyst NCR Corp., San Diego, 1969—; assoc. pastor Bethel Bapt. Ch., Edcondido, Calif., 1983-85, Trinity Bapt. Ch., Poway, Calif., 1988—; instr. So. Calif. Bible Coll., San Diego, 1986, So. Bapt. Sem. Extension, Escondido, 1986. Patentee in field. Mem. Am. Schs. Oriental Rsch., Biblical Archaeological Soc. Republican. Office: Trinity Bapt Ch 14315 Garden Rd Poway CA 92064

MERLINO, GARY CHARLES, air traffic control specialist, coach; b. Atlantic City, Sept. 29, 1955; s. Salvatore Charles and Dorothea Henrietta (Eickenberg) M.; m. Lisa Farraday Smith, May 28, 1983. AA, St. Petersburg (Fla.) Jr. Coll., 1984. Cert. air traffic controller specialist, FAA. Usher Atlantic City Conv. Hall, 1971-74; summer relief mgr. Russ Miller Records and Tapes, Inc., Margate, N.J., 1973-76; store mgr. Scott's Restaurant Co., Ltd., St. Petersburg, 1976-78; asst. store mgr. Eckerd Drug Co., St. Petersburg, 1978-80; store mgr. Cost Plus, Inc., Largo, Fla., 1980-81; asst. store mgr. Olson Electronics, St. Petersburg, 1981-82; electronics salesperson Couch's Inc., Gainesville, Fla., 1982-83; mgr. dept. Service Mdse. Co., Inc., St. Petersburg, 1983-86; air traffic controller Natrona County Internat. Airport, Casper, Wyo., 1986—. Canvasser Dem. com. Pinellas County, 1984; bd. dirs. Pinellas Park (Fla.) Little League, 1984, Babe Ruth Baseball League, umpire in chief; official high sch. football and basketball. Mem. Nat. Air Traffic Controllers Assn. Episcopalian. Home: 4821 S Ash Casper WY 82601 Office: Natrona County Internat Airport 7710 Fuller St Casper WY 82604

MERLINO, LAWRENCE UBALDO, educational administrator; b. Seattle, Feb. 22, 1933; s. Ubaldo Nicholas and Catherine (Pesce) M.; m. Billie-Marie Gannon, Dec. 26, 1959; children: Mark L., Wendy Ann Merlino Standaert. BA, U. Wash., 1956; MA in Phys. Edn., U. Calif., Berkeley, 1958. Tchr. phys. edn. San Jose (Calif.) Sch. Dist., 1959-62; coord. athletics, phys. edn. and health Federal Way (Wash.) Sch. Dist., 1963-75, prin. Continuation High Sch., 1975—. With USN, 1950-54. Mem. Federal Way Prins. Assn. (pres. 1988-89), Elks. Democrat. Roman Catholic. Home: 29866 12th Ave SW Federal Way WA 98023 Office: Continuation High Sch 31455 28th Ave S Federal Way WA 98003

MERLO, HARRY ANGELO, forest products executive; b. Stirling City, Calif., Mar. 5, 1925; s. Joseph Angelo and Clotilde (Camussa) M.; 1 son, Harry A. B.S., U. Calif.-Berkeley, 1949, postgrad., 1949. Vice pres. Rockport Redwood Co., Cloverdale, Calif., 1967; v.p. No. Calif. div. Ga.-Pacific Corp., Samoa, Calif., 1967-69; v.p. Western lumber div. Ga.-Pacific Corp., Portland, Oreg., 1969-71, exec. v.p. Western timber, plywood and lumber operations, 1971-73; pres., chmn. bd. La.-Pacific Corp., Portland, 1973—; adv. bd. Sch. Bus. Adminstrn. U. Calif., Berkeley; bd. dirs. World Forestry Ctr., Whitman Industries. Mem. Pres.'s Council, Columbia Pacific council Boy Scouts Am.; former mem. nat. adv. council Salvation Army; trustee Hugh O'Brian Youth Found., Oreg. Mus. Sci. and Industry, Goodwill Industries; past chmn. bd. Am. Acad. Achievement; Western fin. chmn. U.S. Olympic commn.; chmn., adv. bd. Salvation Army, Oreg.; bd. dirs. Marshall U. Soc. Yeager Scholars. Served to lt. USMCR. Named Man of Year Ga.-Pacific Corp., 1969; recipient Golden Plate award Am. Acad. Achievement, 1974; Horatio Alger award, 1980, Gold award for forest products industry The Wall St. Transcript, 1982, 83, Disting. Service award La. Tech. U., 1984, Aubrey Watzek award Lewis and Clark Coll., 1984, Citizen of Merit award Assoc. Builders and Contractors, 1986, Piemontese Del Munde award, 1986, Merit award Calif. Parks & Recreation Soc., 1988. Mem. Calif. Redwood Assn. (past pres., dir.), Am. Paper Inst. (dir.), Knights of the Vine. Clubs: Founders (bd. dirs.), Waverly Country, Arlington, Multnomah Athletic, Ingomar, West Hills Racquet. Office: La-Pacific Corp 111 SW 5th Ave Portland OR 97204

MEROLA, ANTHONY KEVIN, protective services official; b. Chgo., July 16, 1950; s. Anthony Augustus and Magdeline Koneta (Bottells) M. BA, U. Wash., 1974; cert. pub. adminstrn., U. So. Calif., 1984. Correctional officer U.S. Dept. Justice, Bur. Prisons, L.A., 1981-85, supervisory legal tech., 1985-86, sr. case mgr., 1986—. 2nd Lt. U.S. Army, 1972-73. Mem. Reserve Officers Assn., Fraternal Order of Police. Republican. Roman Catholic. Home: 114 2d St Seal Beach CA 90740 Office: Fed Bur Prisons 535 N Alameda St Los Angeles CA 90053

MERRELL, RAYMOND WELDON, surgeon, consultant; b. Williamsport, Pa., Feb. 11, 1951; s. George Wilson Merrell and Mary Jane (Billman) Bowen; m. Eileen Marie Broscoe, June 25, 1976; children: Jonathan Riley, Gregory Raymond, Justin Edward. BS, Pa. State U., 1970; MD, Jefferson Med. Coll., Phila., 1974. Diplomate Am. Bd. Urology. Surg. intern NYU/St. Vincent's Hosp., N.Y.C., 1974-75, surg. resident, 1975-76; urologic surg. resident Geisinger Clinic, Danville, Pa., 1976-79; fellow in pediatric urology Hosp. for Sick Children, Toronto, Ont., Can., 1979-80; clin. instr. U. Toronto, 1979-80; urology cons. Ont. Crippled Children, Toronto, 1979-80; urologic surgeon Meml. Hosp., Yakima, Wash., 1980—; pres. Urology Assocs., Yakima, 1984—, Merj Properties, Yakima, 1985—. Contbr. articles to profl. jours. Mem. adv. bd. Multiple Sclerosis Soc., Yakima, 1982—; bd. dirs. Cen. Wash. Kidney Soc., Yakima, 1982-87; sec., bd. dirs. Sta. KYVE Pub. TV, Yakima, 1985—. Fellow ACS, Phila. Coll. of Physicians; mem. Am. Urologic Assn., Am. Med. Soc., Yakima County Med. Soc., Yakima Tennis Club, Washington Athletic Club, Rotary. Office: Urology Assocs 306 S 12th Ave Ste 12 Yakima WA 98902

MERRELL, ROBERT BRUCE, oil company executive; b. Brigham City, Utah, Dec. 20, 1945; s. Elliott Hepworth and Doris (Jensen) M.; BS in Indsl. Engring., U. Utah, 1969, MEA, 1973; m. Lynne McDermott, Apr. 4, 1968; children: Melissa Ann, Jason Matthew, David Bruce, Jeffrey Todd. Sales rep. Shell Oil Co., Portland, Oreg., Seattle, 1969-70, 72-74, head office rep., Houston, 1974-75; v.p., treas., dir. Lilyblad Petroleum Co., Tacoma, 1975-77, also bd. dirs.; dir. mktg. Pacific No. Oil Corp., Seattle, 1975-77, exec. v.p., gen. mgr., 1977, chmn. pres., chief exec. officer, 1989—, also dir. pres., chief exec. officer Pacific No. Marine Corp., 1980-83. Mem. exec. bd. dirs. Chief Seattle council Boy Scouts Am., 1984—; bd. dirs. Seattle Urban League, Sea Fair; chmn. Latter-day Sts. relationship com., 1984-87. Served to capt. USAR, 1970-71. Decorated Bronze Star. Recipient Council Merit award Boy Scouts Am., 1985. Mem. Seattle C. of C. Mormon. Clubs: Washington Athletic, Columbia Tower (Seattle); Overlake Golf and Country (Bellevue, Wash.); Mercer Island Country (Wash.). Office: Pacific No Oil Corp 100 W Harrison N Tower #200 Seattle WA 98119

MERRELL, SAMUEL TAYLOR, manufacturing company executive, engineer; b. Casa Grande, Ariz., Sept. 4, 1942; s. Francis Cady Merrell and Margaret (Lewis) Towner; m. Marsha Johnson, Oct. 1, 1966 (div. Feb. 1972); m. Sandra Lee Caldwell, Feb. 11, 1980; children: Steven Caldwell, Ashley Margaret. BSME, U. Calif., Berkeley, 1966; MBA, U. So. Calif., 1972. Design engr. aerospace div. Northrop Co., Hawthoren, Calif., 1966-72; mgr. data processing Litton Co., L.A. and S.C., 1972-75; salesman System Software & Mfg. Systems, L.A., 1975-87; exec., owner Mann Aircraft Forming Co., Compton, Calif., 1987—; engring. and mfg. systems cons., L.A., 1970-75, 80-87. PTA scholar, 1960, State of Calif. scholar, 1960. Mem. Am. Prodn. and Inventory Control Soc. (cert. in prodn. and inventory mgmt.), Computer and Automated Systems Assn., Soc. Mfg. Engrs., Kappa Delta Rho. Office: Mann Aircraft Forming Co 15314 S Avalon Blvd Compton CA 90220

MERRICK, GRETCHEN SMITH, civil engineer; b. Evansville, Ind., Apr. 26, 1960; d. William Harold and Marjorie (Waller) Smith; m. Daniel Smith Merrick, July 12, 1986. BECE, Vanderbilt U., 1982; MSCE, San Jose (Calif.) State U., 1986. Registered profl. engr., Calif. Mem. staff engr. Sci. Svc., Inc., Redwood City, Calif., 1982-84; civil engr. San Jose (Calif.) Bldg. Dept., City of Morgan Hill (Calif.) Bldg. Dept., 1989—; lectr. San Jose State U., 1984-85; cons. San Jose State Found., 1984-86. Mem. ASCE (v.p. San Jose Tech. group 1987—), Tau Beta Pi, Chi Epsilon. Office: City Morgan Hill Bldg Dept 17555 Peak Ave Morgan Hill CA 95037

MERRICK, LEW, mechanical engineer; b. Washington, Oct. 29, 1953; s. Ivan Edward and Barbara Alice (Jones) M.; m. Sharon Ann Bisnett, Apr. 1, 1983; children: Shawna Lynn, Heather Alyse. Registered profl. engr. Engr. The Boeing Co., Seattle, 1978-81; sr. engr. Martin Marietta, New Orleans, 1981-82; consulting engr. Tangent Engring., Lynnwood, Wash., 1982—. Mem. ASME, Am. Soc. Metals, Forth Interest Group, C User's Group, German Machinist's Guild.

MERRILL, CHARLES MERTON, U.S. judge; b. Honolulu, Dec. 11, 1907; s. Arthur M. and Grace Graydon (Dickey) M.; m. Mary Luita Sherman, Aug. 28, 1931 (dec.); children: Julia Booth Stoddard, Charles McKinney. AB, U. Calif., 1928; LLB, Harvard, 1931. Bar: Calif. 1931, Nev. 1932. Sole practice Reno, 1932-50; judge Nev. Supreme Ct., 1951-59, chief justice, 1955-56, 59; judge U.S. Ct. of Appeals (9th cir.), San Francisco, 1959-74, sr. judge, 1974—. Mem. ABA, State Bar Nev. (gov. 1947-50), Am. Law Inst. (council 1960—). Office: US Ct Appeals PO Box 547 San Francisco CA 94101

MERRILL, DARWIN LEE, air force officer; b. Oakland, Calif., Mar. 2, 1947; s. Linden Ray and Donna Mae (Jensen) M.; m. Victoria Elena Gomez, Sept. 4, 1971; children: Steven Ray, Katherine Elizabeth, Cristina Elena; m. Kelly Sue Allred, Aug. 30, 1986; 1 child, Michael David. BA, Brigham Young U., 1973; M in Human Relations, U. Okla., 1984. Commd. USAF, advanced through grades to maj., 1983; transp. officer USAF, Seymour Johnson AFB, N.C., 1973-75, Howard AFB, Republic of Panama, 1975-78; chief, spl. security USAF, March AFB Riverside, Calif., 1979-81; intelligence officer USAF, Misawa AFB, Japan, 1981-84; staff officer Electronic Security Command USAF, San Antonio, 1984-85, chief ops. 6906 Electronic Security Squadron, 1985-86; comdr. Det. 1 Pacific Electronic Security div. USAF, Yokota AB, Japan, 1986—. Lay leader Mormon Ch., Misawa, 1982-83; coach San Antonio West Little League, 1983. Mem. Air Force Assn. Home: PSC Box 548 APO San Francisco CA 96293

MERRILL, FRANK HARRISON, data processing executive, consultant; b. Pitts., June 20, 1953; s. Edgar Frank and Harriet Margaret (Gallagher) M.; m. Rita Alice Mae Murray, May 27, 1977; 1 child, Laura Dawn. BSMetE, Colo. Sch. Mines., 1971-76; M of Computer Info. Systems, U. Denver, 1988. Cert. systems profl. Metall. engr. Inspiration Copper Co., Miami, Ariz., 1979-80, Cominco Am., Inc., Bixby, Mo., 1980-81; programmer, analyst M.L. Foss, Inc., Denver, 1981-83, Titsch & Assocs., Denver, 1983; data processing mgr. PBI/BAXA, Inc., Denver, 1983-86; owner (systems cons.) Dynamic Solutions, Denver, 1986—; cons. in field, Denver, 1985—; instr. continuing edn. User's Group, Denver, 1985—. Adult leader Boy Scouts Am., Denver and Globe, Ariz., 1973-88; chmn. Marriage Encounter Interfaith Bd., Denver. Served to 2d lt. U.S. Army, 1977-79. Mem. Assn. Systems Mgmt. (profl., sec. Mile-Hi chpt. 1989), Colo. Pick Users' Group (edn. chmn. 1984—), Info. Systems Security Assn. Republican. Free Methodist (nominating com. 1989, God and Service award 1984). Club: Rocky Mountain Wanderers (coord). Lodge: SAR.

MERRILL, HARVIE MARTIN, manufacturing executive; b. Detroit, Apr. 26, 1921; s. Harvie and Helen (Nelson) M.; m. Mardelle Merrill; children—Susan, Linda. B.S. in Chem. Engring, Purdue U., 1942. Devel. engr. Sinclair Refining Co., 1946-47; research and gen. mgr. 3M Co., St. Paul, 1947-65; v.p. fabricated products Plastics div. Stauffer Chem. Co., N.Y.C., 1965-69; with Hexcel Corp., San Francisco, 1969-86, pres., chief exec. officer, 1969-86, chmn. bd., 1976-88; chmn. Nimbus Inc., Rancho Cordova, Calif.; bd. dirs. TIS Mortgage/Investment Co., Corp. Capital Preffered Fund, Fibreboard Corp., Concord, Calif., Fireboard Corp. Trustee Grace Cathedral, San Francisco. Served with USAF, 1942-46. Clubs: Pacific-Union, Bohemian (San Francisco); Links (N.Y.C.). Home: 1170 Sacramento St San Francisco CA 94108 Office: 650 California St Ste 1401 San Francisco CA 94108

MERRILL, ROBERT EDWARD, special machinery manufacturing company executive; b. Columbus, Ohio, Oct. 21, 1933; m. Donna Rae Bernstein, Mar. 19, 1967; children—Robert Edward, Aaron Jay, Jonathan Cyrus, Raquel Naomi. MBA, Pepperdine U.; Pres., PSM Corp., San Jose, Calif., 1974—. Served with AUS, 1950-51; Korea. Patentee in pneumatic applications for indsl. press machinery. Home: 858 Fieldwood Ct San Jose CA 95120

MERRILL, THOMAS SELFRIDGE, clinical psychologist; b. Honolulu, Feb. 17, 1940; s. William Dickey and Evelyn Merriman (Selfridge) M.; m. Kathleen Morrissey, Jan. 16, 1965; children—Lisa Lani, Kirsten Elizabeth, Kimberly Alexander. B.A., U. Colo., 1963; M.Ed., U. Hawaii, 1977; Ph.D., U. Tex., 1981. Lic. psychologist, Hawaii; diplomate Am. Bd. Med. Psychotherapists, Am. Bd. Psychotherapy, Am. Acad. Pain Mgmt. Div. adminstrv. mgr. Kaiser Aluminum and Chem. Corp., Oakland, Calif., 1965-68; mktg./advt. mgr. Trans Internat. Airlines, Transamerica Corp., Alameda, Calif., 1968-70; sr. v.p. Fawcett McDermott Cavanagh Advt., Honolulu, 1970-77; dir. Peck, Sims, Mueller Advt.; pvt. practice cons., Austin and Honolulu, 1977—; clin. psychologist in pvt. practice, Honolulu, 1981—; founder, pres. Hawaii Mental Health Ctr; v.p., bd. dirs., treas. Ptnrs. in Health, Honolulu; v.p., bd. dirs. Hawaii Epilepsy Soc.; appt. state bd. licensing psychologists, 1988—; trustee Hawaiian Mission Children's Soc. Mem. Am. Psychol. Assn., Hawaii Psychol. Assn. (pres. 1984-85, Disting Svc. award 1989), Am. Group Psychotherapy Assn., Am. Soc. Clin. Hypnosis, Soc. Exptl. and Clin. Hypnosis, Running Psychologists, Am. Soc. Composers and Publishers, Am. Acad. Neuropsychologists, Am. Coll. Forensic Psychologists, Biofeedback and Behavioral Medicine Soc. of Hawaii (pres. 1988—). Club: Outrigger Canoe (Honolulu). Composer music and lyrics including Bottles & Cans, 1973. Home: 2657 Terrace Dr Honolulu HI 96822 Office: 1441 Kapiolani Blvd Ste 909 Honolulu HI 96814

MERRITT, JOSHUA LEVERING, JR., engineering executive, consultant; b. Balt., July 28, 1931; s. Joshua Levering Sr. and Sarah Ethel (Sparks) M.; m. Eleanor Grace Williams , June 26, 1954; children: Nancy Lynn Mann, Debra Sue Stevens, Steven Edward. BSCE, Lehigh U., 1952; MSCE, U. Ill., 1955, PhD in Engring., 1958. Registered civil, structural, geotech. engr., Calif.; registered civil and structural engr., Nev.; registered structural engr., Ill.; registered profl. engr., N.M. Rsch. asst., civil engr. U. Ill., Urbana, 1952-54, rsch. assoc., civil engr., 1954-58, asst. prof. civil engring., 1958-60, assoc. prof., 1960-66, prof., 1966-69; mgr. hard rock silo devel. TRW, San Bernardino, Calif., 1968-70; mgr. facility engring. TRW, 1970-71; pres. Merritt Cases, Inc., Redlands, Calif., 1971—; dir. Redlands ops. The BDM Corp., 1986—; cons. in field, Urbana, 1958-68. Fellow ASCE (local and nat. com.); mem. ASTM, Am. Underground Space Assn., Structual Engrs. Assn. of So. Calif., Am. Soc. for Engring. Edn., The Concrete Soc., Soc. of Am. Mil. Engrs., Internat. Soc. for Rock Mechanics, Internat. Soc. for Soil Mechanics and Found. Engrs., Seismol. Soc. Am., Am. Concrete Inst., Earthquake Engring. Rsch. Inst., Nat. Rsch. Coun. (mem. U.S. nat. com. on rock mechanics), Sigma Xi, Phi Kappa Phi, Chi Epsilon. Presbyterian. Home: 657 E Palm Ave Redlands CA 92374-6274 Office: The BDM Corp 25837 Business Ctr Dr Redlands CA 92374

MERRITT, KENNEDY WOOD, dentist; b. Clovis, N.Mex., Sept. 5, 1947; s. Dean Franklin and Chaney Katherine (Miller) M.; m. Marsha Kay Foster, Aug. 30, 1969; children: Kendra, Kyleigh, Janna. BA, U. N.Mex., 1969; MA, Ea. N.Mex. U., 1971; DDS, U. Mo., Kansas City, 1978. Tchr. English and history Marshall Jr. High Sch., Clovis, 1969-73; pvt. practice, Clovis, 1978—; instr. anatomy Ea. U., Clovis, 1980-86; vice chmn. dental staff Clovis High Plains Hosp., 1985—. Chmn. dental div. Curry County chpt. United Way, Clovis, 1980, 82, chmn. profl. div., 1981; mem. spl. com. N.Mex. Mental Resources, 1982; active Clovis High Plains Hosp. Community Assocs., 1983—; mem. adminstrv. bd. 1st United Meth. Ch., 1980—. Fellow Am. Coll. Dentists, 1987; named Dir. of Yr., Curry County Jaycees, 1981, Officer of Yr., Curry County Jaycees, Pres. of Quarter N.Mex. Jaycees, 1983, Outstanding Jaycee N.Mex. Jaycees, 1984. Mem. ADA (conv. subchmn. 1984, hospitality chmn. nat. meeting 1985), Curry-Roosevelt Dental Soc. (v.p. 1980-82), N.Mex. Dental Assn. (chmn. state conv. 1988), Am. Bd. Assn. Dental Examiners, N.Mex. Bd. Dental Examiners (pres., bd. dirs. 1982—), Am. Assn. Gnathological Orthpedics, U. N.Mex. Alumni Assn., Ea. N.Mex. U. Alumni Assn. (bd. dirs. 1983-84), Clovis C. of C. (bd. dirs. 1982-85), Duke City Study Club, Clovis Exec. Club. Democrat. Home: 121 Tanning Way Clovis NM 88101 Office: PO Box 1869 1620 Main Clovis NM 88101

MERROW, TONI SUE, public relations specialist, consultant; b. Springfield, Mo., Mar. 24, 1940; d. Haldene Kemp and Ruth Darlene (Jordan) Holt; m. Maesil LeGrand Merrow, May 13, 1961 (dec.); children: Dene O., Scott J., Regina L. Haney. Student pub. schs., Denver. Exec. sec. Colo. Brick Co., Denver, 1959-60; sec. Stanley Aviation, Denver, 1960-61; sec. to service specialist Ford Motor, Tractor div., Denver, 1961-77; sec. to v.p. advt. communications KWAL Paints, Inc., Denver, 1979-84; sec., asst. to v.p. Intermountain Network, Denver, 1985-88; customer service rep. Waste Mgmt.-Aurora, Denver, 1988—; pub. relations cons. The Osburn Band, Denver, 1977—. Vice pres. Hallet Sch. PTA, Denver, 1971-73; active various charitable orgns.; mem., pub. relations cons. Blue Knights Drum and Bugle Corps Parents Orgn., Littleton, 1983-84; historian, pub. relations cons. Highland High Sch. Booster Assn., Thornton, 1983-84. Cert. of Commendation, City of Thornton, 1975. Mem. Nat. Assn. Female Execs., Scholastic Gold Key. Club: Thornton Women's. Avocations: antiques; geneology; reading; camping. Home: 2502 E 90th Pl Thornton CO 80229 Office: Waste Mgmt-Aurora 3995 Nome St Denver CO 80239

MERSEL, MARJORIE KATHRYN PEDERSEN, lawyer; b. Manila, Utah, June 17, 1923; d. Leo Henry and Kathryn Anna (Reed) Pedersen; A.B., U. Calif., 1948; LL.B., U. San Francisco, 1948; m. Jules Mersel, Apr. 12, 1950; 1 son, Jonathan. Admitted to D.C. bar, 1952, Calif. bar, 1955; Marjorie Kathryn Pedersen Mersel, atty., Beverly Hills, Calif., 1961-71; staff counsel Dept. Real Estate State of Calif., Los Angeles, 1971—. Mem. Beverly Hills Bar Assn., Trial Lawyers Assn., So. Calif. Women Lawyers Assn. (treas. 1962-63), Beverly Hills C. of C., World Affairs Council. Clubs: Los Angeles Athletic, Sierra. Home: 13007 Hartsook St Sherman Oaks CA 91403 Office: Dept Real Estate 107 S Broadway Los Angeles CA 90012

MERSEREAU, JOANNA HAYES, graphic artist; b. Strawn, Ill., July 12, 1928; d. Fred Elmer Hayes and Lillie May Polenz; m. John DeWitt, June 11, 1950 (div. 1974); children: Anne Elizabeth, Juanita Louise, Guy Matthew. AA, Blackburn Coll., 1948; student, U. Ill., 1949-51. Staff artist Press-Enterprise, Riverside, Calif., 1955-64, Riverside County Schs., 1967-88; gallery owner Riverside, 1986—; v.p. Watercolor West Redlands, Calif.,

1969-80; artist in residence Na Bolom Studies, Inst. of Sci., Mex., 1986-87, 89. Bd. dirs. Riverside Art Mus., 1985-86. Democrat. Home: 4290 University Ave Riverside CA 92501

MERTA, PAUL JAMES, cartoonist, photographer, engineer, restaurateur, real estate developer; b. Bakersfield, Calif., July 16, 1939; s. Stanley Franklin and Mary Ann (Herman) M.; AA, Bakersfield Jr. Coll., 1962; BS in Engrng., San Jose State Coll., 1962. Cartoonist nat. mags., 1959—; civilian electronics engr. Air Force/Missiles, San Bernardino, Calif., 1962-65; electronics countermeasures engr., acquisition program mgr. Air Logistics Command, Sacramento, 1965—; TV film animator, producer, owner Merge Films, 1965—; photographer, owner The Photo Poster Factory, Sacramento, 1971—; owner restaurant La Rosa Blanca, Sacramento, 1980—; ptnr. Kolinski and Merta Hawaiian Estates, 1981—; polit. cartoonist Calif. Jour., 1958-59, Sacramento Union Newspaper, 1979—, Sacramento Legal Jour., 1979. Home: 4831 Myrtle Ave #8 Sacramento CA 95841 Office: 1005 12th St Sacramento CA 95814

MERWIN, EDWIN PRESTON, health planning executive; b. Revere, Mass., Oct. 13, 1927; s. George Preston and Edith Charlotte (Miller) M.; m. Marylynn Joy Bicknell, Nov. 3, 1979; 1 son by previous marriage, Ralph Edwin; stepchildren: Charles John Burns, Patrick Edward Burns, Stephen Allen Burns. BS, U. So.Calif., 1955, postgrad. Law Sch., 1955-57; postgrad., San Fernando Valley State Coll., 1965-66; M in Pub. Health (USPHS fellow), U. Calif. at Berkeley, 1970; PhD, Brantridge Forest (Eng.), 1971. Tng. officer Camarillo (Calif.) State Hosp., 1961-66; asst. coordinator Mental Retardation Programs, State of Cal., Sacramento, 1966-67; project dir. Calif. Council Retarded Children, Sacramento, 1967-69; asst. dir. Golden Empire Comprehensive Health Council, Sacramento, 1970-76, health care cons., 1976-77; gen. ptnr. EDRA Assocs., 1976—; cons. Calif. Dept. Health, 1977-78; cons. Calif. Office Statewide Health Planning and Devel., 1978-79; chief Health Professions Career Opportunity Program State of Calif., Sacramento, 1979-81; chief Health Personnel Info. and Analysis Sect., Office of Statewide Health Planning and Devel., 1981-82, asst. div. chief div. Health Professions Devel., 1982-84, asst. dep. dir., 1984-86; project dir. Alzheimers Disease Insts., Calif., 1986-87; chief demonstration project sect. div. Health Projects and Analysis, 1987-89, chief policy analysis and professsions devel. sect., 1989—; tchr. Ventura (Calif.) Coll., 1962-66, Merritt Coll., Oakland, Calif., 1969; sr. adj. prof. Golden Gate U., 1976—; lectr. continuing edn. program U. Calif. at Berkeley; instr. Los Rios Community Coll. Dist., 1982—; cons. NIMH, HEW, Calif. Assn. Health Facilities. Mem. health adv. council San Juan Sch. Dist., 1972-73; treas. Calif. Camping and Recreation Council, 1972-73. Bd. dirs. Sacramento Rehab. Facility, 1970-86, v.p., 1973-76, bd dirs. Sacramento Vocational Services, 1986—. Recipient Pres.'s award Golden Gate U., 1982. Mem. Am. Assn. Mental Deficiency, Calif. Pub. Health Assn., Sacramento Mental Health Assn., Sacramento Assn. Retarded (life mem., dir., service award 1984), Nat. Assn. for Retarded Children, DAV (life), Am. Legion, Marines Meml. Assn. (life), AAAS, SCAPA Praetors. Founder, editor: T. Patrick Heck Meml. Case Studies, 1982; co-author textbook: Written Case Analysis, 1982; contbr. articles to profl. lit. Home: 8008 Archer Ave Fair Oaks CA 95628 Office: 1600 9th St Sacramento CA 95814

MERYHEW, VERN ARTHUR, engineering executive; b. Agra, Kans., May 28, 1933; s. Nivas Lavern Meryhew and Ethel (Burton) Whitish; m. Sharie Karen Meryhew, July 12, 1957 (div.); children: Brad Allen, Pamela Ann Hudgins; m. Joan C. Meryhew, Sept. 26, 1970; children: Sheryl Ann, Sarah Kay. Student, Highline Coll., Seattle, 1966-69. Drafting mgr. The Boeing Co., Seattle, 1966-69, adminstr., 1971-80, engrng. mgr., 1980—; real estate developer, Seattle, 1969—. Leader Boy Scouts Am., Seattle 1968-72. Mem. Boeing Mgmt. Assn.

MESEC, DONALD FRANCIS, psychiatrist; b. Waukegan, Ill., Aug. 29, 1936; s. Joseph Mesec and Johanna (Setnicar) M.; m. Francesca Auditore, June 20, 1964 (div. 1987); 1 child, Steven Francis; m. Patricia Guitteau, Mar. 27, 1988. B.S. cum laude, U. Notre Dame, 1958; M.D., N.Y. Med. Coll., 1963. Diplomate Am. Bd. Psychiatry and Neurology. Resident in psychiatry and neurology N.Y. Med. Coll.-Manhattan State Hosp., N.Y.C., 1964-67; chief of service Manhattan Psychiat. Ctr., N.Y.C., 1970-76, dir. psychiat. research, 1974-75, dir. Meyer Manhattan Alcohol Rehab. Ctr., 1975; med. dir. Meyer Day Ctr., N.Y.C., 1976-77; staff psychiatrist Asheville VA Hosp., N.C., 1977-78; practice medicine specializing in psychiatry, Phoenix, 1978—; instr. clin. psychiatry Columbia U., N.Y.C., 1972-77; dir. psychiat. edn. St. Joseph's Hosp., Phoenix, 1982—, co-dir. pain program, 1982—, vice chmn. dept. psychiatry, 1984—, chmn. dept. psychiatry, 1987—. Served with USPHS, 1963-64. Mem. New York County Med. Soc., Ariz. Med. Assn., Maricopa County Med. Soc., Ariz. Psychiat. Soc., AMA, Am. Psychiat. Assn.,Am. Acad. Clin. Psychiatrists. Office: 222 W Thomas Rd Phoenix AZ 85013

MESOJEDNIK, JOANN MARIE, real estate broker; b. Ellensburg, Wash., Nov. 23, 1938. Student, Central Wash. U., 1956-57. Cert. real estate brokerage mgr., Wash. Sec., adminstrv. asst. R.A. Swanson Co., Olympia, Wash., 1965-78; adminstrv., designated broker James W. Hodges Inc., Realtors, Olympia, 1978-83; assoc. broker Virgil Adams Real Estate, Inc., Olympia, 1983—; pres. Multiple Listing Svc. Olympia, 1980-81. Pres. Olympia unit Am. Cancer Soc., 1988—. Mem. Nat. Assn. Realtors, Wash. Assn. Realtors (bd. dirs. 1984-88), Olympia-Thurston County Bd. Realtors (pres. 1984, Realty Achievement award 1982, Realtor of Yr. award 1984), Multiple Listing Sales Assn. (pres. Olympia 1988), Olympia-Thurston County C. of C. (trustee 1985-88, Top 10 Bus. Vol. of Yr. award 1988), Kiwanis. Republican. Methodist. Home: 6024 Blvd Ext Rd SE Olympia WA 98503 Office: Virgil Adams Real Estate Inc 806 E State Ave Olympia WA 98501

MESQUITA, ROSALYN ESTHER, artist, educator; b. Belen, N.Mex., Aug. 21, 1935; d. Trinidad Jose and Margaret Oliva (Aragon) Anaya; m. Theodore Richard Mesquita, Jan. 14, 1956; children: John, Richard, Larry, Thresa. BA, Calif. State U., Northridge, 1974; MFA, Calif. State U., Irvine, 1976. Cert. community coll. credential, Calif. Prof. Los Angeles City Coll., Van Nuys, Calif., 1965-81; curator State of N.Mex., Santa Fe, 1968-72; lectr. Los Angeles Hist. Soc., 1978—; prof. Pasadena (Calif.) City Coll., 1981—; lectr. Non Govtl. Orgn. UN Planning Com., Nairobi, Kenya, and N.Y., 1985—; curator, participant Am. Women in Art, UN World Conf., Nairobi, 1985; curator Mus. Natural History, Los Angeles, 1978. Lectr. Los Angeles BiCentennial and 1985 Olympic Com., 1976-84. Recipient Col.-Aide-De Camp award Gov. David F. Cargo, 1972; Ford Found. fellow, 1975. Mem. Coll. Art Assn., Nat. Womens Caucus for Art (affirmative action officer 1980-83, honorarium 1983), Hispanic Faculty Assn. (treas. 1980—), Assn. Latin Am. Artists (pres. 1982—), Los Angeles La Raza Faculty Assn. (sec. 1979-85). Democrat. Roman Catholic. Home: 13426 Vanowen St Van Nuys CA 91405 Office: Pasadena City Coll 1570 Colorado Blvd Pasadena CA 91106

MESSER, DONALD EDWARD, theological school president; b. Kimball, S.D., Mar. 5, 1941; s. George Marcus and Grace E. (Foltz) M.; m. Bonnie Jeanne Nagel, Aug. 30, 1964; children—Christine Marie, Kent Donald. B.A. cum laude Dakota Wesleyan U., 1963; M. Divinity magna cum laude Boston U., 1966, Ph.D., 1969. L.H.D. (hon.), Dakota Wesleyan U., 1977. Asst. to commr. Mass. Commn. Against Discrimination, Boston, 1968-69; asst. prof. Augustana Coll., Sioux Falls, S.D., 1969-71; assoc. pastor 1st United Methodist Ch., Sioux Falls, 1969-71; pres. Dakota Wesleyan U., Mitchell, S.D., 1971-81, The Iliff Sch. Theology, Denver, 1981—. Author: Christian Ethics and Political Action, 1984, Contemporary Images of Christian Ministry, 1989. Contbr. articles to Face To Face, The Christian Century, The Christian Ministry. Active Edn. Commn. of U.S., 1973-79; co-chmn. Citizens Commn. Corrections, 1975-76; vice chmn. S.D. Commn. on Humanities, 1979-81. Dempster fellow, 1967-68; Rockefeller fellow, 1968-69. Mem. Soc. Christian Ethics, Am. Acad. Religion, Assn. United Methodist Theol. Schs. (v.p. 1986—). Democrat. Office: Iliff Sch Theology Office of Pres 2201 S University Blvd Denver CO 80210

MESSEX, CHARLES LEE, pilot; b. Cin., Mar. 29, 1930; s. Leland C. and Gladys (Reinhardt) M.; m. Anita Sherlock, Oct. 27, 1950; children: Naomi K., Michael L., Martha J. BGE, U. Nebr., 1964. Commd. 2nd lt. USAF, 1950; advanced through grades to maj. 1966; assigned to U.S., Japan, Vietnam, Okinawa; retired 1970; charter pilot Exec. Air Corp., Spokane, Wash., 1971-76; chief corp. pilot ACME Concrete Co., Spokane, Wash., 1976--. Contbr. articles to various publs. Chmn. Citizens Organized to Protect Soc., Medical Lake, Wash., 1982, Citizens For Clean Air, Spokane, 1988--. Decorated Silver Star, D.F.C. with oak leaf cluster. Mem. Aircraft Owners and Pilots Assn., Exptl. Aircraft Assn., Air Commando Assn. Republican. Anglican. Home: S 15615 Salnave Rd Cheney WA 99004

MESSIER, DENNIS RICHARD, pharmacist; b. Charles City, Iowa, July 24, 1944; s. Richard Frank and Elizabeth Mary (Nimick) M.; m. Joy Annette Houser, Mar. 4, 1944; children: Justine Lynn, Christian Richard. AA, Mason City Jr. Coll., 1964; BS in Pharmacy, U. Iowa, 1969; MBA, U. Phoenix, 1986. Registered pharmacist, Iowa, Ariz. Intern U. Iowa Hosps. and Clinics, Iowa City, 1969-70, clin. pharmacist, 1969-74; dir. pharmacy Schoitz Meml. Hosp., Waterloo, Iowa, 1974-80; dir. pharm. svcs. Tucson Med. Ctr., 1981--; assoc. in pharmacy practice U. Ariz., Tucson, 1981--; presenter in field; mem. nat. adv. coun. pharmacy programs Voluntary Hosps. Am., 1984--, mem. western regional adv. coun. 1986-87, mem. multidisciplinary task force for physician dispensing, 1987--; mem. adv. com. for pharmacy technician program Pima Community Coll., 1986--. Contbr. articles to profl. jours. Named Iowa Hosp. Pharmacist of Yr., 1980, Ariz. Hosp. Pharmacist of Yr., 1987; recipient Leadership award McKesson County, 1986; Health Profl. scholar, 1967-69. Mem. Am. Soc. Hosp. Pharmacists, Ariz. Soc. Hosp. Pharmacists (bd. dirs. 1983-87, bd. pharmacy task force for hosp. rules and regulations rev. 1986--), So. Ariz. Soc. Hosp. Pharmacists (bd. dirs. 1981, 83-87, pres. 1985). Home: 361 N Calle Agua Verde Tucson AZ 85715 Office: Tucson Med Ctr 5301 E Grant Rd Tucson AZ 85715

MESSNER, KATHRYN HERTZOG, civic worker; b. Glendale, Calif., May 27, 1915; d. Walter Sylvester and Sadie (Dinger) Hertzog; B.A., UCLA, 1936, M.A., 1951; m. Ernest Lincoln, Jan. 1, 1942; children—Ernest Lincoln, Martha Allison Messner Cloran. Tchr. social studies Los Angeles schs., 1937-46; mem. Los Angeles County Grand Jury, 1961. Mem. exec. bd. Los Angeles Family Service, 1959-62; dist. atty.'s adv. com., 1965-71, dist. atty.'s adv. council, 1971-82; mem. San Marino Community Council; chmn. San Marino chpt. Am. Cancer Soc.; bd. dirs. Pasadena Rep. Women's Club, 1960-62, San Marino dist. council Girl Scouts U.S.A., 1959-68, Am. Field Service, San Marino, 1983—; pres. San Marino High Sch. PTA, 1964-65; bd. mem. Pasadena Vol. Placement Bur., 1962-68; mem. adv. bd. Univ. YWCA, 1956—; co-chmn. Dist. Atty.'s Adv. Bd. Young Citizens Council, 1968-72; mem. San Marino Red Cross Council, 1966—, chmn., 1969-71, vice chmn., 1971-74; mem. San Marino bd. Am. Field Service; mem. atty. gen.'s vol. adv. com., 1971-80; bd. dirs. Los Angeles Women's Philharm. Com., 1974—, Beverly Hills-West Los Angeles YWCA, 1974-85, Los Angeles YWCA, 1975-84, Los Angeles Lawyers Wives Club, 1974—, Pacificulture Art Mus., 1976-80, Reachout Com., Music Center, Vol. Action Center, West Los Angeles, Calif., 1980-85, Stevens House, 1980—, Pasadena Philharm. Com., 1980-85, Friends Outside, 1983—, Internat. Christian Scholarship Found., 1984—; hon. bd. dirs. Pasadena chpt. ARC, 1978-82. Recipient spl. commendation Am. Cancer Soc., 1961; Community Service award UCLA, 1981. Contbr. articles to profl. jours. Mem. Pasadena Philharmonic, Las Floristas, Huntington Meml. Clinic Aux., Nat. Charity League, Pasadena Dispensary Aux., Gold Shield (co-founder), Pi Lambda Theta (sec. 1983-89), Pi Gamma Mu, Mortar Bd., Prytanean Soc. Home: 1786 Kelton Ave Los Angeles CA 90024

MESTAS, JUAN EUGENIO, academic administrator; b. Havana, Cuba, Sept. 6, 1942; s. Juan A. and Amparo (Alvarez) M. BA, U. P.R., 1966; MA, SUNY, Stony Brook, 1974, PhD, 1985. Chmn., dept. P.R. studies SUNY, Stony Brook, 1974-76; dir., upward bound program San Jose State U., 1976-82; dir., ednl. opportunity program Calif. State U., Long Beach, 1983-85, dir., ednl. access svcs., 1985—; conducted numerous profl. devel. seminars in edn. Editorial bd.: Nat. Coun. of Ednl. Opportunity Assn. Jour., 1986-88; editor: La Escalera Jour., 1967-74, Guajana, 1962-66. Bd. dirs. Abrazar, Inc., Westminster, Calif., 1988—, League of United Latin Am. Citizens Head Start, Inc., Long Beach, Calif., 1986-87. Fellow Am. Coun. Edn., 1989—. Mem. Western Assn. of Ednl. Opportunity Personnel (pres. 1983-84, Steve Holeman Meml. award 1985), Nat. Coun. Ednl. Opportunity Assn. (bd. dirs. 1982-88), Raza Advocates for Change in Higher Edn., League of United Latin Am. Citizens. Office: Calif State U LA3-201 CSULB Long Beach CA 90840

MESTAS, PATRICK MARIO, engineer; b. Greeley, Colo., Nov. 29, 1943; s. Manual and Grace (Montoya) M; m. Angelita Belen Vasquez, Dec. 2, 1961; children: Santano Patrick, Sergio Peter, Sarena Leeann. BSCE, Colo. State U., Ft. Collins, 1971. Registered profl. engr., Colo. Head draftsman, survey party chief Parker & Underwood, Inc., Greeley, 1961-66; project/design engr. M&I, Inc., Ft. Collins, 1966-71; engrng. dept., dir. Hogan & Olhausen, Inc., Loveland, Colo., 1971-80; owner Delgado & Mestas, Inc., Ft. Collins, 1980-81; prodn. mgr., sr. design engr. Cornell Consulting Co., Ft. Collins, 1981-82; sr. project engr. Tri Consultants, Inc., Denver, 1982-84; project mgr. Greiner Engring., Denver, 1984-88; project mgr. engring. Merrick & Co., Denver, 1989—. Co-author: (software) Earthwork, 1981, Open Channel, 1981, Cantilever Beam, 1981; author (database) Utility Facilities Management, 1985. Scoutmaster, Boy Scouts Am., Greeley, 1965-66; assoc. mem. Spl. Dists. Assn., Denver, 1986-88. Mem. Home Builders Assn., Loveland Baseball Assn., Apple Club, Sigma Tau, Chi Epsilon. Republican. Roman Catholic. Home: 3112 Duffield Ave Loveland CO 80538

MESTER, ROBERT LOYD, engineer; b. Dayton, Ohio, Dec. 31, 1948; s. Lloyd Henry and Trilla Rite (Elfrink) M.; m. Mary Jane Scholl, Aug. 7, 1971; children: Amy, Erin, Benjamin. Student, Miami U., Oxford, Ohio, 1971-72, U. Redlands, 1988—. Field engr. RCA Service Co., Cin., 1972-73; systems engr. Asyst, Inc., Cin., 1974-75; field engr. Nat. Advanced Systems, San Diego, 1976-81, tech. support specialist, 1981-87, staff engr., 1987-88, product mgr., 1988—. Edn. dir. Penasquitas Luth. Ch., San Diego, 1985-87; congregation chmn. Messiah Luth. Ch., Cin., 1981. With USMC, 1967-71. Mem. Assn. of Field Service Mgrs. Republican. Lutheran. Home: 14292 Barrymore St San Diego CA 92129 Office: Nat Advanced Systems 9535 Waples St San Diego CA 92121

METCALF, MELLY, financial planner; b. Vallejo, Calif., Apr. 12, 1948; d. Chai Jill and Jane (Yee) Tom; m. Michael F. Metcalf, Feb. 13, 1973 (div. 1979). BA, U. Calif., Berkeley, 1969; MBA, Golden Gate U., 1982. Speech and lang. pathologist San Francisco Unified Schs., 1973-74, Old Adobe Union Sch., Petaluma, Calif., 1974-76, Marin County Schs., San Rafael, Calif., 1976-82; dir. advt U. Calif. San Francisco Alumni Pubs., 1982-83; free-lance portfolio mgr. San Francisco, 1982-83; account exec. Equitec Securities Co., San Francisco, 1983-84; fin. planner Ind. Planning Corp., San Francisco, 1984—. Mem. Peninsula Symphony Guild, Foster City, Calif. 1988—. Mem. AAUW (treas 1986-88), Internat. Assn. Fin. Planners, Inst. Cert. Fin. Planners (cert.). Democrat. Congregationalist. Lodge: Rotary. Home: 818 N Delaware San Mateo CA 94401 Office: Ind Planning Corp 1255 Post Ste 700 San Francisco CA 94109

METHENITIS, TIMOTHY SCOTT, printing executive; b. Evergreen Park, Ill., July 23, 1958; s. Thomas Anthony and Barbara Ann (Prosser) M. BS in Mktg., Ind. U., 1980, MBA in Internat. Bus., 1982. Sales rep. R.R. Donnelley & Sons, Stanford, Conn., 1982-83, Tampa, Fla., 1983-84, Atlanta, 1984-86, Irvine, Calif., 1987; regional v.p. western sales Arcata Graphics Corp., San Mateo, Calif., 1987—. Mem. Book Builders West. Republican. Roman Catholic. Office: Arcata Graphics 2929 Campus Dr San Mateo CA 94403

METHVEN, MARGARET PETERSON, speech pathologist, former school principal; b. Norfolk, Va., Dec. 24, 1918; d. Ward E. and Marguerite (Helm) Peterson; BA, Washburn U., Topeka, 1940; MA, U. Denver, 1960, EdD, 1976; cert. clinical competence in speech Am. Spl. Lang Hearing Assn.; m. William Charles Methven, Jan. 2, 1947: children: William Charles, Robert Ward. High sch. tchr., Burlingame, Kans., 1940-42; speech/lang. specialist Boettcher Sch. Physically Handicapped and Fairmont Sch., Denver Public Schs., 1959-88; pvt. practice, Englewood, Colo.; past prin. Force Elem. Sch.; prin. Barnum Elem. Sch. Rep. Denver Area Panhellenic. Mem. Am. Speech and Haring Assn., Colo. Speech and Hearing Assn. (past pres.), Nat. Orgn. Legal Problems Edn., Denver Pub. Schs. Women in Adminstrn., Denver Elem. Prins. Assn., Kappa Delta Pi, Delta Kappa Gamma (pres. 1978-80, State Parliamentarian 1979—), Alpha Phi., Phi Delta Kappa. Presbyterian.

METRICK, DENNIS LAWRENCE, court administrator, consultant; b. Phila., Oct. 11, 1942; s. George and Marie Metrick; m. Catherine Ann Moynihan, Sept. 4, 1967; children: Brian Paul, Sean Christopher, Claudine Marcel. BA, LaSalle U., 1964; MA, Pa. State U., 1967, PhD, 1968. Assoc. prof. Marietta (Ohio) Coll., 1968-73; mgmt. analyst State of Pa., Phila., 1974-75; ct. planner Phila. Ct., 1975-79; ct. adminstr. Delaware County Ct., Media, Pa., 1979-87, 2d Jud. Dist. Ct., Reno, Nev., 1987; cons. Computility PNR Assocs., Phila., 1979-87; part-time instr. Temple U., Villanova U., Phila., 1975-79; tchr. Inst. Ct. Mgmt., Denver, Colo., 1979-87; speaker in field; advisor Wallingford (Pa.) Mid. Sch., 1984. Contbr. articles to profl. jours. Mem. com. Rep. Party, Media, Pa., 1979-87; soccer coach Wallingford, Pa., 1985-87. Fellow Pa. State U., 1967-68, Inst. Ct. Mgmt., 1976-78. Mem. ABA, Pa. Trial Ct. Adminstrs. (pres. 1986-87), Pa. Assn. Adminstrn. Spl. Cts., Nat. Jud. Planning Council (mem. exec. com. 1980-83), Nat. Assn. Ct. Mgrs. Home: 7950 Oak Creek Dr Reno NV 89511 Office: 2d Jud Dist Ct 75 Court St Reno NV 89501

METTLER, ROBERT L., department store executive. Formerly pres., chief exec. officer L.S. Ayres, Indpls.; pres., chief exec. officer Robinson's, L.A., 1987—. Office: Robinson's 600 W Seventh St Los Angeles CA 90017 *

METTLER, RUBEN FREDERICK, electronics and engineering company executive; b. Shafter, Calif., Feb. 23, 1924; s. Henry Frederick and Lydia M.; m. Donna Jean Smith, May 1, 1955; children: Matthew Frederick, Daniel Frederick. Student, Stanford U., 1941; BSEE, Calif. Inst. Tech., 1944, MS, 1947, PhD in Elec. and Aero. Engring, 1949; LHD (hon.), Baldwin-Wallace Coll., 1980; LLD, John Carroll U., 1986. Registered profl. engr., Calif. Assoc. div. dir. systems research and devel. Hughes Aircraft Co., 1949-54; spl. cons. to asst. sec. def. U.S. Dept. Def., 1954-55; asst. gen. mgr. guided missile research div., tech. supr. Atlas, Titan, Thor and Minuteman programs Ramo-Wooldridge Corp., 1955-58; exec. v.p., then pres. TRW Space Tech. Labs. (merger Thompson Products and Ramo-Wooldridge), 1958-65; pres. TRW Systems Group, 1965-68; asst. pres. TRW Inc., 1968-69, pres., chief operating officer, 1969-77, chmn. bd., chief exec. officer, 1977-88, also bd. dirs.; bd. dirs. Bank Am. Corp., Merck & Co., Japan Soc. Inc.; mem. Pres. Reagan's Commn. Exec. Exchange, Adv. Council on Japan-U.S. Econ. Rels., Pres.'s Blue Ribbon Def. Panel, 1969-70; vice chmn. Def. Industry Adv. Council, 1964-70, chmn. Pres.'s Task Force on Sci. Policy, 1969-70; cons. Hughes Aircraft Co., Dept. Def., 1954—. Author: reports on airborne electronic systems; patentee interceptor fire control systems. Nat. campaign chmn. United Negro Coll. Fund, 1980-81; chmn. Nat. Alliance Bus., 1978-79; co-chmn. 1980 UN Day, Washington; chmn. bd. trustees Calif. Inst. Tech.; trustee Com. Econ. Devel., Cleve. Clinic Found.; bd. dirs. Nat. Action Council for Minorities in Engring. Served with USNR, 1942-46. Named one of Outstanding Young Men of Am., U.S. Jr. C. of C., 1955, So. Calif.'s Engr. of Year, 1964; recipient Meritorious Civilian Service award Dept. Def., 1969, Nat. Human Relations award NCCJ, 1979, Excellence in Mgmt. award Industry Week Mag., 1979, Disting. Service award Calif. Inst. Tech., 1966. Fellow IEEE, AIAA; mem. Sci. Research Soc. Am., Bus. Roundtable (chmn. 1982-84), Conf. Bd. (trustee 1982—), Bus. Council (vice chmn. 1981-82, chmn. 1986-87), Nat. Acad. Engring., The Japan Soc. (bd. dirs.), Sigma Xi, Eta Kappa Nu (Nation's Outstanding Young Elec. Engr. 1954), Tau Beta Pi, Theta Xi. Clubs: Cosmos (Washington); Union, 50 (Cleve.). Home and Office: TRW Inc 1900 Richmond Rd Cleveland OH 44124 also: TRW Space & Def Sector 1 Space Park Redondo Beach CA 90278

METWALLY, ANNA-MARIE BOOTH, lawyer; b. Gary, Ind., Feb. 2, 1946; d. Lavaughn Venchael and Georgia (Morris) Booth; m. Hany Metwally, Oct. 9, 1984. BA, NYU, 1969; JD, Emory U., 1974. Bar: Ga., 1974, D.C., 1976. Assoc. Huie, Brown & Ide, Atlanta, 1974-75; legal aide Lt. Gov. Ga., Atlanta, 1975; asst. gen. counsel U.S. Brewers Assn., Washington, 1975-77; counsel to the dir. Office Adminstrn. Legal Service Corp., Washington, 1977-78; atty. office community investment Fed. Home Loan Bank Bd., Washington, 1978-79; legis. asst. U.S. Sen. Bill Bradley, Washington, 1979-82; sole practice Washington, 1982-83; dir. govt. relations AT&T, San Francisco, 1983—. Bd. dirs. Legal Assistance to Elderly, 1984-87, Internat. Vis. Ctr., San Francisco Planning and Urban Rsch. Assn.; pres. 2945 Pacific Homeowners Assn., 1986-87; commr. San Francisco Arts Commn., 1986-88. Mem. ABA, Nat. Bar Assn., Oakland C. of C. (govt. affairs com.), San Francisco C. of C. (pub. affairs com.), Alameda County Taxpayers Assn., Mark Hopkins Profl. women's Assn. (core mem.), San Francisco City Club (gov. 1988—). Democrat. Home: 698 Regis Ct Benicia CA 94510 Office: AT&T 353 Sacramento Suite 1600 San Francisco CA 94111-3678

METZ, MARY SEAWELL, college president; b. Rockhill, S.C., May 7, 1937; d. Columbus Jackson and Mary (Dunlap) Seawell; m. F. Eugene Metz, Dec. 21, 1957; 1 dau., Mary Eugena. B.A. summa cum laude in French and English, Furman U., 1958; postgrad., Institut Phonetique, Paris, 1962-63, Sorbonne, Paris, 1962-63; Ph.D. magna cum laude in French, La. State U., 1966; H.H.D. (hon.), Furman U., 1984; LL.D. (hon.), Chapman Coll., 1985; D.L.T. (hon.), Converse Coll., 1988. Instr. French La. State U., 1965-66, asst. prof., 1966-67, 1968-72, assoc. prof., 1972-76, dir. elem. and intermediate French programs, 1966-74, spl. asst. to chancellor, 1974-75, asst. to chancellor, 1975-76; prof. French Hood Coll., Frederick, Md., 1976-81, provost, dean acad. affairs, 1976-81; pres. Mills Coll., Oakland, Calif., 1981—; vis. asst. prof. U. Calif.-Berkeley, 1967-68; mem. commn. on leadership devel. Am. Council on Edn., 1981—, adv. council SRI, 1985—, adv. coun. Grad. Sch. Bus. Stanford U.; assoc. Gannett Ctr. for Media Studies, 1985—; bd. dirs. PG&E, Pacific Telesis, PacTel & PacBell, Rosenberg Found., Union Bank. Author: Reflets du monde francais, 1971, 78, Cahier d'exercices: Reflets du monde francais, 1972, 78, (with Helstrom) Le Francais a decouvrir, 1972, 78, Le Francais a vivre, 1972, 78, Cahier d'exercices: Le Francais a vivre, 1972, 78; standardized tests; mem. editorial bd.: Liberal Edn., 1982—. NDEA fellow, 1960-62, 1963-64; Fulbright fellow, 1962-63; Am. Council Edn. fellow, 1974-75. Mem. Western Coll. Assn. (v.p. 1982-84, pres. 1984-86), Assn. Ind. Calif. Colls. and Univs. (exec. com. 1982), Nat. Assn. Ind. Colls. and Univs. (govt. relations adv. council 1982-85), So. Conf. Lang. Teaching (chmn. 1976-77), World Affairs Council No. Calif. (dir. 1984—), Bus.-Higher Edn. Forum, Women's Forum West, Women's Coll. Coalition (exec. com. 1984—), Phi Kappa Phi, Phi Beta Kappa. Office: Mills Coll Office of Pres Oakland CA 94613

METZGER, JOHN PETER, writer, communications executive; b. N.Y.C., Dec. 13, 1958; s. Howell Peter and Frances Braden (Windham) M.; m. Suzanne Franklin, July 14, 1985. Student, U. Colo. Sch. Mines, 1977-81. Exec. editor Soldier of Fortune mag., Boulder, Colo., 1980-86; combat corr. Soldier of Fortune mag., Cen. Am., 1983-84; editor Archtl. and Engring. Systemsmag., Ft. Collins, Colo., 1987-88; assoc. editor Asbestos Issues Software in Healthcare mag., 1987-88; owner Metzger Assocs., Boulder, 1988-89; account exec. Carl Thompson Assocs., Boulder, 1989—. Mem. Am. Motorcycle Assn. Democrat. Episcopalian. Home: 1344 Kilkenny Boulder CO 80303 Office: Carl Thompson Assocs 75 Manhattan Dr Boulder CO 80303

METZGER, ROBERT OWEN, banking consultant, educator, writer; b. N.Y.C., Oct. 22, 1939; s. Homer P. and Catherine Dale (Owen) M.; m. Dorothee Benkenstein, Apr. 25, 1968; 1 child, Joelle Laurence Owen. BS in Econs., U. Md. Overseas Coll., 1963; PMD, Harvard U., 1969; PhD in Bus. Adminstrn., U. Beverly Hills, 1981. Staff exec. IT&T, 1970-72; chief exec. officer Faber Merlin Ltd., Hong Kong, 1973; sr. mgr. McSweeney & Assocs., Newport Beach, Calif., 1974-75; founder, chmn., mag. prin. Metzger & Assocs., Santa Ana, Calif., 1976-88; adj. prof. mgmt. and orgn. Grad. Sch. Bus. Adminstrn. U. So. Calif., Los Angeles, 1984-88; assoc. dir. Ctr. for Ops. Mgmt., Edn. and Tng., 1986-88; sr. v.p. Furash & Co., Washington D.C., 1988—. Author: Organizational Issues to Strategic Planning in the Commercial Banking Industry, 1981, Consulting to Management, 1983, Profitable Consulting: Guiding America's Managers into the Next Century, 1988; editorial rev. bd. and contbr. editor: Fin. Mgrs. Statement Quar., Orgn. and Group Studies, Bankers Monthly; editorial rev. bd.: Jour. Retail Banking, Jour. Mgmt. Cons.; contbr. numerous articles on bank mgmt. to profl. jours. Mem. corp. solicitation com. Nat. Kidney Found. Served with USAF, 1958-62. Mem. Inst. Mgmt. Cons., Acad. Mgmt. (exec. com. mgmt. cons.

div.), Hon. Order Ky. Col. Berkshire Sch. Alumni Assn. (founder, pres. So. Calif. chpt.), Astron. Soc. Pacific., Acad. Mgmt. Cons. (managerial div., exec. com.). Club: Harvard Bus. Sch. So. Calif. Home: 3933 Ivy Terrace Ct NW Washington DC 20007

METZGER, VERNON ARTHUR, educator; b. Baldwin Park, Calif., Aug 13, 1918; s. Vernon and Nellie C. (Ross) M.; B.S., U. Calif., Berkeley, 1947, M.B.A., 1948; m. Beth Arlene Metzger, Feb. 19, 1955; children—Susan, Linda, 1 step-son, David. Estimating engr. C. F. Braun & Co., 1949; prof. mgmt. Calif. State U. at Long Beach, 1949—, founder Sch. Bus.; mgmt. cons., 1949—. Mem. Fire Commn. Fountain Valley, Calif., 1959-60; pres. Orange County Democratic League, 1967-68; mem. State Dept. mgmt. task force to promote modern mgmt. in Yugoslavia, 1977; mem. State of Calif. Fair Polit. Practices Commn., Orange County Transit Com. Served with USNR, 1942-45. Recipient Outstanding Citizens award Orange County (Calif.) Bd. Suprs. Fellow Soc. for Advancement of Mgmt. (life; dir.); mem. Acad. Mgmt., Orange County Indsl. Relations Research Assn. (v.p.), Beta Gamma Sigma, Alpha Kappa Psi, Tau Kappa Upsilon. Home: 1938 Balearic Dr Costa Mesa CA 92626 Office: 1250 Bellflower Blvd Long Beach CA 90804

METZLER, JERRY DON, nursing administrator; b. Mishawaka, Ind., Mar. 6, 1935; s. Gerald Donald and Cleota Christabell (Dowell) M.; m. Dorothy J. Masters, Aug. 18, 1962. BS, Ariz. State U., 1962, MEd, 1967; BS, San Diego State U., 1973; MS, U. Ariz., Tucson, 1980. Sci. tchr. Washington Sch., Sanger, Calif., 1963-68; tchr. biology San Jacinto (Calif.) High Sch., 1968-70; staff nurse Maricopa County Hosp., Phoenix, 1973-76; staff nurse St. Luke's Hosp., Phoenix, 1976-77; nursing instr., dept. head Gila Pueblo Coll., Globe, Ariz., 1977-78; nurse educator, asst. dir. nursing USPHS Indian Hosp., Tuba City, Ariz., 1980-84; asst. nursing svc. mgr. Phoenix Indian Med. Ctr., 1984-85; pub. health educator Phoenix Indian Med. Ctr., 1985-88; dir. nursing USPHS Indian Hosp., Dwyhee, Nev., 1988—. Served with USN, 1956-60, USPHS, 1980—; Mem. Res. Officers Assn., Am. Nurses Assn., Am. Assn. Critical Care Nurses. Republican. Methodist. Lodge: Masons. Home: PO Box 160 Owyhee NV 89832 Office: USPHS Indian Hosp Owyhee NV 89832

METZLER, PAUL RAYMOND, electrical engineer, consultant; b. St. Louis, Sept. 19, 1949; s. Raymond Herman and Rita Fanny (Morton) M.; m. Barbara Mary Dolan, May 18, 1974 (div. Dec. 1986); children: Tammi Marie, Julie Lynne, Brian Keith; m. Roxy Susan Clark, Dec. 20, 1988. BSEE, U. Mo., Rolla, 1973. Registered profl. engr., Tenn., Nev. Elec. engr. Titanium Pigment div. NL Industries, St. Louis, 1974-76, Reynolds Elec. & Engring. Co., Inc., Las Vegas, Nev., 1983-88; sr. elec. engr. Carborundum Environ. Systems div. Kennecott Corp., Knoxville, Tenn., 1976-8l; instrument and control project engr. Chem. Separations Corp., Knoxville, 198l-82; cons. engr. PM Engring. Assocs., Knoxville, 1982-84; quality control engr. C.R. Fedrick, Inc., Kaneohe, Hawaii, 1988—. Mem. Illuminating Engring. Soc. N.A. (assoc.), Instrument Soc. Am. (assoc.), Silver State Computer Users Group (v.p. 1984-86, librarian 1986-88). Home: 1375 Komo Mai Dr Pearl City HI 96782-2243 Office: CR Fedrick Inc PO Box 1276 Kaneohe HI 96744

METZNER, RICHARD JOEL, psychiatrist, educator; b. Los Angeles, Feb. 15, 1942; s. Robert Gerson and Esther Rebecca (Groper) M.; B.A., Stanford U., 1963; M.D., Johns Hopkins U., 1967; m. Linda Susan Nordlinger, Sept. 22, 1968; children—Jeffrey Anthony, David Jonathan. Intern, Roosevelt Hosp., N.Y.C., 1967-68; resident in psychiatry Stanford U. Med. Center, 1968-71; staff psychiatrist div. manpower and tng. NIMH-St. Elizabeths Hosp., Washington, 1971-73; chief audiovisual edn. system VA Med. Center Brentwood, Los Angeles, 1973-79, chmn. VA Dist. 26 Ednl. Task Force, 1976-78; asst. prof. psychiatry UCLA Neuropsychiat. Inst., 1973-80, asso. clin. prof., 1980—, lectr. Sch. Social Welfare, 1975-84; pvt. practice medicine specializing in psychiatry, Bethesda, Md., 1972-73, Los Angeles, 1973—; dir. Western Inst. Psychiatry, Los Angeles, 1977—; pres. Psychiat. Resource Network, Inc., 1984—; Served with USPHS, 1968-71. Recipient 6 awards for film and videotape prodns., 1976-80; diplomate Am. Bd. Psychiatry and Neurology (cons. 1974-78, producer audiovisual exam. programs 1975-77). Mem. Am. Psychiat. Assn., So. Calif. Psychiat. Soc., Mental Health Careerists Assn. (chmn. 1972-73), AAAS, Am. Film Inst., Phi Beta Kappa. Democrat. Jewish. Contbr. numerous articles to profl. publs., 1963—; producer, writer numerous ednl. films and videotapes, 1970—; developer videoscan treatment technique in psychiatry. Home and Office: 2711 Forrester Dr Los Angeles CA 90064

MEUNIER, ROBERT RAYMOND, research electrical engineer, optical engineer; b. Hollywood, Calif., Mar. 27, 1957; s. Raymond Robert and Anna Marie (Rapp) M. Student, Calif. State Poly. U., Pomona, Pasadena City Coll. Assoc. engr. Jet Propulsion Lab., Pasadena, Calif., 1984-85; research engr. Rockwell Internat., Seal Beach, Calif., 1985—. Mem. Laser Inst. Am., Soc. Photo-optical Instrumentation Engrs., Los Angeles Collegiate Council (alumnus), Inter Organizational Council (founder, chmn. 1981-82), Sigma Pi. Republican. Roman Catholic. Office: Rockwell Internat 2600 Westminster Blvd PO Box 3644 Seal Beach CA 90740

MEURLOTT, CONSUELO DINNEEN, realtor; b. Portland, Oreg., Mar. 14, 1929; d. Lawrence Ignatius and Marcella Marie (Larkins) Dinneen; m. Byron Emile Eluene Meurlott, Apr. 21, 1951; children: Byron Thomas, Marcelle Louise, Vince Paul, Anne Duvauchelle, Michelle Marie. BA in Social Sci., Marylhurst Coll., 1950; postgrad., Portland State U., 1956; student in real estate, Portland Community Coll., 1980; diploma, Grad. Realtor Inst., 1988. Licensed realtor. Personnel asst. Lipman Wolfe & Co., Portland, 1950-51; substitute tchr. St. Lawrence Sch., Portland, 1952; realtor Frazier Realty, Lake Oswego, Oreg., 1980-84, Coldwell Banker, Lake Oswego, 1984—. Vol. Marylhurst (Oreg.) Coll., 1951, cancer drive, Lake Oswego, 1976, March of Dimes, Lake Oswego, 1978; v.p. Jr. C. of C., Lake Oswego, 1956-57. Mem. Portland Million Dollar Realty Club, Clackamas County Million Dollar Club, Clackamas County Bd. of Realtors, Quarterback Club, Women's Devel. Com. (Marylhurst) (pres. 1978-79), Coldwell Banker 200% Club. Republican. Roman Catholic. Office: Coldwell Banker 366 3d St Lake Oswego OR 97034

MEYE, ROBERT PAUL, seminary dean; b. Hubbard, Oreg., Apr. 1, 1929; s. Robert and Eva (Pfau) M.; m. Mary Cover, June 18, 1954; children—Marianne Meye Thompson, Douglas, John. B.A., Stanford U., 1951; B.D., Fuller Theol. Sem., 1957, Th.M., 1959; D.Theol. magna cum laude, U. Basel, Switzerland, 1962. Prof. No. Bapt. Theol. Sem., Lombard, Ill., 1962-77, dean, 1971-77; dean Sch. Theology, Fuller Theol. Sem., Pasadena, Calif., 1977—, prof. N.T. interpretation, 1977—. Contbr. articles to profl. jours. Served to lt. (j.g.) USN, 1951-54, Korea. Am. Assn. Theol. Schs. grantee, 1970-71; 75-76. Mem. Am. Acad. Religion, Studiorum Novi Testamenti Societas, Soc. Bibl. Lit., Inst. Bibl. Research, Christianity Today Inst. Republican. Home: 1170 E Rubio St Altadena CA 91001 Office: Fuller Theol Sem 135 N Oakland St Pasadena CA 91101

MEYER, BENNY LEE, systems engineer; b. Redding, Calif., Sept. 7, 1939; s. Chester Bryant and Evlyn May (Lord) M.; m. Darleen Ellen Bauer, July 18, 1959 (div. Mar. 1983); children: Kimberley May, Lance Allen; m. Marguerite McInnish, May 29, 1983. BA in Maths., Calif. State U., Chico, 1961. Systems analyst NASA, Ames Rsch. Ctr., Moffet Field, Calif., 1961-66, Mellonics div. Litton Industries, Sunnyvale, Calif., 1966-72; site mgr. The Aerospace Corp., Buckley, Colo., 1972-88; sr. systems engr. IBM Corp., Boulder, Colo., 1988—. Democrat. Home: 149 S Fraser Circle Aurora CO 80012

MEYER, D. ALLEN, policy consultant; b. Fond du Lac, Wis., Oct. 12, 1941; s. William Edward and Catherine Angela (Hareid) M.; m. June 2l, 1975. SB, MIT, 1963; postgrad., U. Wis., 1963-65, George Washington U., 1968. Rsch. analyst Wis. Indsl. Commn., Madison, 1965-67; mgmt. analyst AID, Washington, 1967-68; sec. Dir.'s Rev., Office Mgmt. and Budget, W, 1968-72, policy analyst, examiner human resource programs, 1972-8l, chief income maintenance, 1981-85; cons., project mgr. Inst. for Human Svcs. Mgmt., Phoenix, 1985—; lectr. Old Dominion U., Norfolk, Va., 1978-85; policy adviser Bruce Babbitt Presdl. Campaign, Phoenix, 1987-88; editorial cons. S.W. Inst. for Rsch. on Women, Phoenix and Tucson, 1988. Contbg. author: Women in the Arizona Economy, 1986. Treas. Crosswoods Community Assn., McLean, Va., 1977. Recipient Presdl. commendation, 1975, Exemplary Svc. award Indochinese Refugee Task Force, 1976, Sr. Exec. Svc. award Office Mgmt. and Budget, 1983. Mem. Am. Soc. for Pub. Adminstrn. (program com. 1983).

MEYER, EDMOND GERALD, energy and natural resources educator, former chemistry educator; b. Albuquerque, Nov. 2, 1919; s. Leopold and Beatrice (Ilfeld) M.; m. Betty F. Knobloch, July 4, 1941; children: Lee Gordon, Terry Gene, David Gary. B.S. in Chemistry, Carnegie Mellon U., 1940, M.S., 1942; Ph.D. (research fellow), U. N.Mex., 1950. Chemist Harbison Walker Refractories Co., 1940-41; instr. Carnegie Mellon U., 1941-42; asst. phys. chemist Bur. Mines, 1942-44; chemist research div. N.Mex. Inst. Mining and Tech., 1946-48; head dept. sci. U. Albuquerque, 1950-52; head dept. chemistry N.Mex. Highlands U., 1952-59; dir. N.Mex. Highlands U. (Inst. Sci. Research), 1957-63; dean N.Mex. Highlands U. (Grad. Sch.), 1961-63; dean Coll. Arts and Sci., U. Wyo., 1963-75, v.p., 1974-80, prof. energy and natural resources, 1981-87, prof. and dean emeritus, 1987—; exec. cons. Diamond Shamrock Corp., 1980; chmn. Carbon Fuels Corp., 1981—; dir. Am. Nat. Bank, Laramie, 1980—; Sci. adviser Gov. Wyo.; cons. Los Alamos Nat. Lab., NSF, HHS, GAO, Diamond Shamrock Corp., Wyo. Bancorp.; contract investigator Research Corp., Dept. Interior, AEC, NIH, NSF, Dept. Energy, Dept. Edn.; Fulbright exchange prof. U. Concepcion, Chile, 1959. Co-author: Chemistry-Survey of Principles, 1963, Legal Rights of Chemists and Engineers, 1977, Industrial Research & Development Management, 1982; Contbr. articles to profl. jours. Served with USNR, 1944-46. Recipient Disting. service award Jaycees. Fellow AAAS, Am. Inst. Chemists (treas.); mem. Asso. Western Univs. (chmn. 1973-74), Am. Chem. Soc. (councillor), Chilean Chem. Soc., Biophys. Soc., Council Coll. Arts and Scis. (pres. 1971, sec.-treas. 1972-75, dir. Washington office 1973), C. of C. (pres. 1984), Sigma Xi. Home: 1058 Colina Dr Laramie WY 82070 Office: U Wyo Coll Arts & Sci Laramie WY 82071

MEYER, HENRY HUNTER, business educator; b. Hollywood, Calif., Oct. 29, 1936; s. Henry DeNorville and Kathleen Marjorie (Hunter) M.; m. Hallie Hyde Will, July 1, 1967 (dec. 1984); m. Pamela Lynn Geist, Nov. 22, 1987; children: Richard, Russell, Nicholas, Stephanie. BA, Claremont McKenna Coll., 1959; M in Pub. Adminstrn., U. So. Calif., 1969, PhD, 1975. Owner, mgr. H.D. Meyer & Sons, Inc., Newport Beach, Calif., 1961-66; assoc. dir. Inst. U. So. Calif., L.A., 1966-70; prof. Calif. State U., Fullerton, 1970-74; adviser Govt. of Singapore, 1975-79; asst. acad. v.p. U. So. Calif., 1979-81; prof. bus. San Diego State U., 1981-84; prof. Chapman Coll., Orange, Calif., 1984—; owner, mgr. Tex. Air Salvage, Inc., Houston, 1987—. Contbr. articles on mgmt. to various publs. With U.S. Army, 1959-61. Mem. Am. Soc. Pub. Adminstrn. (pres. Sacramento chpt. 1974), Personnel and Pub. Relations Assn. Republican. Methodist.

MEYER, IVAH GENE, social worker; b. Decatur, Ill., Nov. 18, 1935; d. Anthony and Nona Alice (Gamble) Viccone; A.A. with distinction, Phoenix Coll., 1964; B.S. with distinction, Ariz. State U., 1966, M.S.W., 1969; postgrad. U.S. Internat. U.; m. Richard Anthony Meyer, Feb. 7, 1954; children—Steven Anthony, Stuart Allen, Scott Arthur. Social worker Florence Crittendon Home, Phoenix, 1969-70; social worker Family Service of Phoenix, 1970-73; faculty asso. Ariz. State U., 1973; field supr. Pitzer Coll., Claremont, Calif., 1977—; social worker Family Service of Pomona Valley, Pomona, Calif., 1975—; field supr. Grad. Sch. Social Services, U. So. Calif., 1978—; pvt. practice Chino (Calif.) Counseling Center. Lic. clin. social worker, Calif. Mem. Nat. Assn. Social Workers, Acad. Cert. Social Workers. Republican. Roman Catholic. Home: 778 Via Montevideo Claremont CA 91711 Office: 12632 Central Ave Chino CA 91710

MEYER, JAMES HENRY, university chancellor emeritus; b. Fenn, Idaho, Apr. 13, 1922; s. Carl A. and Anita (de Coursey) M.; m. Mary Regan, Aug. 20, 1980; children by previous marriage: Stephen J., Susan T., Gary C., Joan K., Teresa A. B.S. in Agr, U. Idaho, 1947; M.S. in Nutrition (fellow Wis. Alumni Research Found.), U. Wis., 1949, Ph.D., 1951. Research asst. U. Wis., 1949-51; faculty U. Calif., Davis, 1951—; prof. animal husbandry U. Calif., 1960—, chmn. dept., 1960-63; dean U. Calif. (Coll. Agr. and Environment), 1963-69, chancellor univ., 1969-87; Mem. Commn. Undergrad. Edn. in Biology, 1964-69. Editorial bd.: Jour. Animal Sci, 1961-65. Mem. Western Coll. Sr. Accrediting Commn., 1982-88, Western Schs. Accrediting Comm., 1987— . Served with USMCR, 1942-46. Recipient Am. Feed Mfr.'s award in nutrition, 1960. Mem. AAAS, Am. Soc. Animal Prodn., Nat. Assn. State Univs. and Land Grant Colls., Western Coll. Assn. (exec. com. 1971-74), Sigma Xi.

MEYER, JOHN BERNARD, public relations executive; b. St. Louis, July 22, 1933; s. Bernard Charles and Virginia Marie (Hetherington) M.; m. Alberta Ruth Krohn, June 13, 1957; children: Margaret, Chrystal, Kathleen, Jennifer, Victoria. Student, So. Meth. U., 1951-53. TV network news corr. CBS News, Washington, 1962-75; anchor, corr. Mut. Radio Network, Washington, 1975-77; nat. dir. communications Gen. Aviation Mfrs. Assn., Washington, 1977-81; dir. corp. pub. relations Gates-Lear Jet Corp., Wichita, Kans., 1981-85; mgr. corp. pub. relations The Garrett Corp., L.A., 1985-87; mgr. pub. relations Allied Signal Aerospace Co., Tucson, 1987—. Editor: Civil Aviation-Fuel Crisis, 1974 (Aviation/Space Writers award, 1975); producer: General Aviation Benefits, 1978 (Aviation/Space Writers award, 1979). Bd. dirs. Tucson-Pima Arts Council, 1987—, Ariz. Council Econ. Edn., Tucson, 1987-88, Tucson Symphony Orch., 1988—; v.p., bd. dirs. Aviation/Space Writers Nat. Found., 1987—, Tucson Bus. Com. Arts, 1989—. Mem. Aviation/Space Writers Nat. Found. (bd. dirs. 1987—, Pub. Relations Soc. Am. (Tucson chpt. pres. 1985), Aviation/Space Writers Assn. (Golden Quill award 1988), Tucson Met. C. of C. Democrat. Lutheran. Home: 815 W Valle DeLoro Tucson AZ 85737 Office: Allied Signal Aerospace Co Airesearch Tucson Div 11100 N Oracle Rd Tucson AZ 85737

MEYER, JOHN CONRAD THEODORE, electronics engineeer; b. Sioux City, Iowa, July 7, 1940; s. Sigmond John and Loretta Wilheminia (Mosch) M.; m. Janet Irene Kivley, Aug. 4, 1962; children: Melina Marie, Carin Ann. BS in Electronics, Chapman Coll., 1987. Enlisted USN, 1958-61, 63-80; with Valco Electronics Co., Pleasant Hill, Calif., 196l-62, Western Electric Co., Bakersfield, Calif., 1962; technician Lockheed Co., Palo Alto, Calif., 1962-63; sr. field rep. GTE, Needham, Mass., 1980-8l; field task supr. GTE, Colorado Springs, Colo., 1982—; sr. engr. Eldyne, Virginia Beach, Va., 198l-82. Mem. Armed Forces Communications and Electronics Assn., Amateur Radio Relay League. Republican. Lutheran. Home: 1240 Charwest Dr Woodland Park CA 80863 Office: GTE 1925 Aerotech Dr Ste 224 Colorado Springs CO 80916

MEYER, JOSEPH B., state attorney general; b. Casper, Wyo., 1941; m. Mary Orr; children: Vincent, Warren. Student, Colo. Sch. Mines; BA, U. Wyo., 1964, JD, 1967; postgrad., Northwestern U., 1968. Dep. county atty. Fremont County, Wyo., 1967-69; ptnr. Smith and Meyer, 1968-71; asst. dir. legis. svc. office State of Wyo., Cheyenne, 1971-87, atty. gen., 1987—; conductor numerous govt. studies on state codes including Wyo. probate, criminal, state adminstrn., banking, domestic rels., game and fish, state instn., employment security, worker's compensation, motor vehicle, others; conductor legis. rev. of adminstrv. rules; negotiator with Office of Surface Mining for Wyo. state preemption; instr. Wyo. Coll. Law, fall 1986; lectr. Rocky Mountain Mineral Law Found., 1977. Bd. dirs. Cheyenne Jr. League, 1982-85, Jessup PTO, 1980-81; instr. Boy Scouts Am. Mem. Rotary. Congregationalist. Office: Atty Gen's Office 123 Capitol Bldg Cheyenne WY 82002

MEYER, LINDA DOREEN, writer; b. Santa Barbara, Calif., Apr. 2, 1948; d. John Floyd and Dorothy Lucidie (Baker) Potter; m. Donald Lee Meyer, Sept. 6, 1969; Joshua Scott, Matthew Sean. BA, San Jose State U., 1971. Pres. Charles Franklin Press, Edmonds, Wash., 1979—. Mem. Nat. Writers Club, Pacific NW Writers Conf. Office: PO Box 524 Lynnwood WA 98036-0524

MEYER, M. E. JOSEPH, III, small business owner; b. Ft. Campbell, Ky.; s. Milton Edward Jr. and Mary Charlotte (Kramer) M. BA in Humanities, U. Colo., 1974; cert. massage therapy, Boulder Sch. Massage Therapy, 1980; student, Rolf Inst., Boulder, Colo., 1982, Hakomi Inst., Boulder and Munich, 1982-84. Ski instr. various resorts including Geneva Basin, Squaw Pass, Arapaho Basin, Keystone, Colo., 1967-71; instr. guitar Musikschule Schöneberg, West Berlin, Federal Republic of Germany, 1977-81; instr. guitar (docent) Conservatory in West Berlin, 1978-81; freelance massage therapist, instr. Oslo, Aspen (Colo.), Copenhagen, Stockholm, others, 1981-85; fgn. editor Aspen Daily News, 1986; instr. German Colo. Mountain Coll., Aspen, 1986-87; dir., loan officer Centennial Mortgage Investments, Englewood, Colo., 1986-87; dir., owner Aspen Therapeutic Massage Assocs., Englewood, 1986—; dir. massage therapy Greenwood Athletic Club, Englewood, 1987—; massage therapist, cons. Aspen Valley Hosp., 1986—; translator World Cup Ski Races, Aspen, 1986-87. Contbr. articles to profl. jours.; scriptor, actor instructional video The Swedish Massage, 1987. Mem. Clean Air Adv. Bd., Aspen, 1985-87; ski guide Blind Outdoor Leadership Devel., Aspen, 1985-87. Mem. Am. Massage Therapy Assn., Hakomi Inst., S. Met. Denver C. of C., Boulder Sch. of Massage Therapy Alumni Assn., Cherry Creek Chorale, Aspen Resort Assn., Mensa, Greenwood Athletic Club. Republican. Home: 6006 S Holly St #283 Englewood CO 80111 Office: Aspen Therapeutic Massage 5801 S Quebec St Englewood CO 80111

MEYER, MADELINE ANNA, librarian; b. Great Bend, Kans., Mar. 26, 1948; d. George Albert and Anna Millicent (Noel) M. Student, Cambridge U., Eng., 1967-68; BA, Valparaiso U., 1970; MA, U. Denver, 1981. Libr. Denver Pub. Library, 1971-76; lease records mgr. Vantage Cos., Dallas, 1976-77; libr. Lytham-St. Annes Coll., St. Annes-on-Sea, Lancashire, Eng., 1977-78; lease records asst. J. Grynberg & Assocs., Denver, 1978-79; travel cons. Free Spirit Travel, Aurora, Colo., 1979-82; libr. Aurora Pub. Library, 1982-83; customer svc. rep. Western Air Lines, Denver, 1983-85; libr. Mesa (Ariz.) Pub. Library, 1985-87, Scottsdale (Ariz.) Pub. Library, 1987—. Dep. registrar Election Com., Phoenix, 1985—. Mem. Ariz. State Library Assn., Nat. Mgmt. Assn., Cen. Ariz. Tall Soc. Democrat. Lutheran. Office: Scottsdale Pub Libr 3839 Civic Ctr Pla Scottsdale AZ 85251

MEYER, MARK WARREN, marketing and sales executive; b. Durand, Wis., June 28, 1954; s. Warren A. Meyer and Renee A. (Thibodeau) Busseau; m. Christine Ann Nielsen, Apr. 21, 1979; children: Adrienne Nicole, Gregory Matthew. BSBA, Calif. State U., Long Beach, 1977. Dist. mgr. sales Randomex, Inc., Signal Hill, Calif., 1978-82; regional mgr. mktg. and sales Redmond, Wash., 1982-87; v.p. mktg. and sales Coresoft Corp., Seattle, 1987—. Pres. English Hill Homeowners Assn., Redmond, 1987-88. Mem. Wash. Software Assn., Theta Chi Alumni Assn. (pres. 1980-82). Home: 13821 174th Pl NE Redmond WA 98052 Office: Coresoft Corp 514 2d Ave N Seattle WA 98119

MEYER, MAUREEN CATHERINE, nurse; b. Cleve., Feb. 19, 1944; d. Anthony A. and Agnes (Murphy) Zaher; m. Donald J. Meyer, Jan. 2, 197l; children: Pamela Althea, Nicholas Bernhart. BS, Chapman Coll., 1982. RN, Ohio, Calif. Emergency-recovery room nurse Mercy Hosp., Toledo, 1964-66; cardiovascular nurse Drs. Navarre and Cordillo, Toledo, 1966-69; psychiat. nurse VA Hosp., West Los Angeles, Calif., 1969-70; insvc. nurse Brotman Hosp., Culver City, Calif., 1970-75; Lamaze instr. Kaiser Hosp., L.A., 1977-80; owner Child's Place Nursery Sch., 1980; lectr. Community Cancer Control, L.A., 1980-81; head instr. Pacific Coast Coll., L.A., 1981-85; pvt. duty nurse Assoc. Nurses, L.A., 1985-86; coord. invitro fertilization Century City Hosp., L.A., 1986—. Pres. Culver City Mid. Sch. PTA, 1982, La Ballona Elem. Sch. PTA, 1984; founding mem., advisor Culver City High Sch. Health Clinic, 1987. Mem. Rotary Ann (pres. Culver City 1988). Republican. Roman Catholic. Home: 4913 Maytime Ln Culver City CA 90230 Office: Century City Hosp 2070 Century Park E Los Angeles CA 90067

MEYER, NATALIE, state official; b. Henderson, N.C., May 20, 1930; d. Ranie Thomas and Mary Osborne (Johnson) Clayton; m. Harold Meyer, June 17, 1951; children—Mary, Becky, Amy. Student, U. No. Iowa, 1951. Formerly tchr. pub. schs. Jefferson County, Colo.; past tchr. and prin. Ascension Luth. Ch. Midweek Sch.; past leasing mgr. for office comple; sec. of state State of Colo., Denver, 1982—. Past vice chairperson Arapahoe County Republicans, Colo.; mgr. Senator Bill Armstrong's 1974 Fifth Congl. Campaign; exec. dir. Pres. Reagan's 1976 Colo. Campaign; dir. Ted Strickland's 1978 Gubernatorial Race; mgr. Phil Winn's race for Rep. state chmn., 1980; author, adminstr. Colo. program for Rep. legis. races, 1980, other statewide campaign plans; coordinator Draft Phil Winn effort. Office: Colo State Dept 1560 Broadway Ste 200 Denver CO 80202

MEYER, NICHOLAS JOSEPH, dentist; b. Chgo., Aug. 12, 1953; s. Raymond Joseph and Frances Therese (McInerney) M.; m. Nancy Lynn Macenas, Oct. 21, 1983; children: Allison, Ashley. BA, Lewis U., 1975; DDS, Loyola U., 1979. Pvt. practice dentistry Phoenix, 1979—. Contbr. articles to profl. jours. Fellow Internat. Coll. Craniomandibular Orthopaedics; mem. Am. Acad. Forensic Sci., ADA, Ill. Dental Soc. Home: 5801 N 12th Pl Phoenix AZ 85014 Office: 1222 E Missouri Phoenix AZ 85014

MEYER, RICHARD E(DWARD), music, film and video producer/executive, former advertising and cosmetics executive; b. Cin., May 8, 1939; s. Joseph H. and Dolores C. (Daley) M.; m. Julia I. Kallish; children: Donna, Valerie. AB in Journalism, Advt. and Mktg. with honors, U. Mich., 1961. Mgr. auto staff advt. dept. Chgo. Tribune, 1961-63; account supr., v.p. London & Assos., Chgo., 1963-64; founder, pres., chmn. bd. Meyer & Rosenthal, Inc. (formerly Richard E. Meyer, Inc.), Chgo., 1965-74; exec. v.p., gen. mgr. Jovan Inc., Chgo., 1974-75; pres., chief operating officer Jovan Inc., 1975-79, pres., chief exec. officer, 1980-85; pres., chief exec. officer Yardley of London, Lancaster, 1980-85, Beecham Cosmetics, 1980-85, Omni Cosmetics, 1980-85, Parfums Hermes U.S.A., 1980-85; pres., chmn. bd. Red Entertainment Inc., Chgo., 1983-86, Red Label Records Inc., Chgo., 1983-86; past pres. Fragrance Found., 1985. Writer, producer various feature videos/films including Super Bowl Shuffle (RIAA Gold and Platinum awards 1986, Grammy nominee 1986,87), Mike Ditka's Grabowski Shuffle (RIAA Gold and Platinum video awards, 1987); patentee various product designs. Recipient numerous awards N.Y. Advt. Club, Chgo. Advt. Club, Designers and Art Dirs., TV commls., Print Casebook, First Advt. Agy. Network; recipient Communication Arts awards Printing Industry Am., Mktg. Achievement award Am. Mktg. Assn., Chgo. Mem. NARAS, Am. Film Inst., Acad. Motion Picture Arts and Scis., Delta Upsilon (trustee 1961—, alumni corp. pres. 1965-68). Clubs: U. Mich. of Chgo.

MEYER, RODNEY JAY, food products executive; b. Kennewick, Wash., Apr. 12, 1957; s. Paul Jay and Joanne Marie (Hughes) M.; m. Cynthia Ann Leeser, Apr. 8, 1978; children: Angela Marie, Alica Ann. Student, Ea. Wash. U., 1975. Clk. Safeway, Cheney, Wash., 1975; mgr., buyer Tri-City Foods, Pasco, Wash., 1973-85; gen. mgr. Brown & Cole, Ferndale, Wash., 1985—. Chmn. United Way, Ferndale, 1987-88; v.p. Tri-City (Wash.) Water Follies, 1985; bd. dirs. City of Blaine (Wash.) Adv. Com., 1989. Named among top grocery stores in nation for mdse., Progressive Grocery Mgr., Ferndale, Wash., 1987, Best Hawaiin Days Thriftway Stores, Thriftway Associated Grocers, Ferndale, 1986-88, Best Coca-Cola Display in Nation, Coca-Cola Nat., Ferndale, 1988. Mem. Toastmasters, Rep. Nat. Com., Thriftway Planning Com. Republican. Home: 1218 Woburn Bellingham WA 98225 Office: Brown and Cole 638 Peace Portal Dr Blaine WA 98230

MEYER, ROGER PAUL, physician; b. Atlanta, Mar. 30, 1950; s. Leonard Arthur and Janet Elanor (Miller) M.; m. Debra Dawn Rowe, May 6, 1978; children: Seth E., Hilary R. BA in Psychology (hons.), U. N.C., 1972; MD, Medicl Coll. of Ga., 1976; postgrad., U. New Mex., Albuquerque, 1980. Physician in pvt. practice Carson Medical Group, Carson City, Nev., 1980--; chief of staff Carson Tahoe Hosp., Nev., 1986-87; v.p. Nev. Physicians Rev. Orgn., 1987. Govtl. affairs commn. Nev. State Med. Assn., Reno, 1984--. Fellow: Am. Coll. of Obstetricians and Gynecologists; mem. Am. Fertilism Soc. Democrat. Jewish. Office: Carson Med Group 1200 N Mountain St Carson City NV 89703

MEYER, SALLY CAVE, personnel director; b. Coulee Dam, Wash., Oct. 20, 1937; d. Verl Edwin and Etha Laree (Moore) Cave; m. Ronald Lee Meyer, July 27, 1957; children: John Lee, Deanna Meyer Brayton, Michael Ron, Geri Anne, Deborah Sue. BA, Wash. State U., 1959, postgrad., 1986. Cert. tchr., Wash. Tchr. English Colfax (Wash.) High Sch., 1959-60; tchr. Pasco (Wash.) High Sch., 1961-62, Chief Joseph Jr. High Sch., Richland, Wash., 1968-69; instr. Columbia Basin Community Coll., Pasco, 1962-70; mem. staff Wash. State U., Pullman, 1955-61, 71-77, dir. faculty, adminstrv., and profl. personnel, 1977—, acting dir. affirmative action program, 1986-87; coordinator Nat. Faculty Exchange Wash. State U., 1986—; dep. chmn.

Wash. State Employees Combined Fund Drive, 1987—, state steering commn., 1989—. Sec. Camp Fire Girls Am., Pullman, 1979-82; mem. Wash. State U. Pres.'s Commn. on of Status Women, 1985-88. Mem. NW Women's Studies Assn., Coll. and Univ. Personnel Assn., Nat. Assn. Female Execs., Lakewood Research Tng. Group, Wash. State U. Alumni Assn., Phi Delta Kappa. Office: Wash State U French Adminstrn 446 Pullman WA 99164-1049

MEYER, THOMAS ROBERT, television product executive; b. Buffalo, Apr. 20, 1936; s. Amel Robert and Mildred Lucille M.; m. Dawn E. Shaffer, 1985. Student Purdue U., 1953-55, Alexander Hamilton Inst. Bus., 1960-62, West Coast U., 1969-72; B in Math., Thomas Edison State Coll., 1988. Sect. chief wideband systems engring. Ground Elec. Engring. and Installation Agy., Dept. Air Force, 1960-66; product mgr., systems engr. RCA Corp., Burbank, Calif., 1966-71; systems cons. Hubert Wilke, Inc., L.A., 1971-72; product mgr. Telemation, Inc., Salt Lake City, 1972-77; v.p. engring. Dynair Electronics, San Diego, 1977—. Recipient Bronze Zero Defects award Dept. Air Force, 1966. Fellow Soc. Motion Picture and TV Engrs. (chmn. subcom. digital control, co-chmn. SMPTE/European Broadcast Union task force for remote control); sr. mem. Soc. Broadcast Engrs.; mem. Computer Soc. of IEEE, Am. Electronics Assn., Tau Beta Pi. Research and publs. on color TV tech. and optics, TV equipment and systems, application of computer to TV systems. Office: Dynair Electronics PO Box 84378 San Diego CA 92138

MEYER, URSULA, library director; b. Free City of Danzig, Nov. 6, 1927; came to U.S., 1941; d. Herman S. and Gertrud (Rosenfeld) M. BA, UCLA, 1949; M.L.S., U. So. Calif., 1953; postgrad., U. Wis., 1969. Librarian Butte County (Calif.) Library, 1961-68; asst. pub. libraries div. library devel. N.Y. State Library, Albany, 1969-72; coordinator Mountain Valley Coop. System, Sacramento, 1972-73; chmn. 49-99 Coop. Library System, Stockton, Calif., 1974-85; dir. library services Stockton-San Joaquin County Pub. Library, 1974—. Higher Edn. Title II fellow, 1968-69. Active Freedom to Read Found. Mem. ALA (council 1979-83, chmn. nominating com. 1982-83, legis. com. 1985-87), Calif. Library Assn. (pres. 1978, council 1974-82), Am. Assn. Pub. Adminstrs., Sierra Club. AAUW, LWV, Common Cause. Lodges: Rotary, Soroptimists. Office: Stockton-San Joaquin County Pub Libr 605 N El Dorado St Stockton CA 95202

MEYER, WENDELL JAMES, city official; b. Waterloo, Iowa, Aug. 13, 1933; s. Fred W.G. and Velma Dorothy (Meier) M.; m. Sharon Barbara Pazul, Nov. 19, 1955; children—Randell Scott, Rolin Shawn. BS in Elec. Engring., Valparaiso U., Ind., 1955; postgrad. U. Chgo., 1956, UCLA, 1957-59; MS in Bus. Adminstrn., Calif. State U.-L.A., 1966. Engring. supr. Aerojet-Gen., Azusa, Calif., 1956-61, mem. corp. staff, 1961-63, mgr. adminstrv. svcs., 1963-70; mgr. data processing Aerojet Electro Systems, Azusa, 1970-74; asst. gen. mgr. info. svcs. City of L.A., 1974-77, gen. mgr. info. svcs., 1977—; advisor Mt. San Antonio Jr. Coll., West Covina, Calif., 1968-72; founding chmn. Ctr. for Info. Resource Mgmt., Calif. State U.-L.A., 1982-84. Pres. Glendora Youth Basketball, Calif., 1971-72, Grace Luth. Ch.; v.p. Glendora Unified Sch. Dist., 1972-76; v.p. San Gabriel Valley Regional Occupation Program, West Covina, Calif., 1974-75. Mem. Soc. Info. Mgmt. (exec. com. So. Calif. chpt. 1983-84), Beta Gamma Sigma. Republican. Lutheran. Club: Equestrian Trails (pres. 1983-85). Home: 1760 Hollyhill Ln Glendora CA 91740 Office: LA Info Svcs 200 N Main St Los Angeles CA 90012

MEYER, WILLIAM STEVEN, transportation engineer; b. Moscow, Idaho, Mar. 28, 1959; s. William Leroy and Sharon Lee (Bromet) M.; m. June Marie Openshaw, Sept. 5, 1986; 1 child, William Ryan. BS, U. Idaho, 1982. Registered profl. engr., Utah. Project engr. Gilbert Western Corp., Salt Lake City, 1982-84; field engr. Utah Dept. Transp., Salt Lake City, 1985, civil engr., 1985-86; city transp. engr. City of Sandy (Utah), 1986-87; dep. city transp. engr. City of Salt Lake City, 1987—. Mem. Inst. Transp. Engrs. (assoc., sec. Utah chpt. 1987-88, treas. 1988-89, 1989-90), Am. Planning Assn. Home: 460 E Spring Creek Dr Bountiful UT 84010 Office: Salt Lake City Div Transp 333 South 200 East Ste 201 Salt Lake City UT 84111

MEYER, WILLIAM TIMOTHY, service company executive; b. Grahamstown, South Africa, Apr. 20, 1940; came to Canada in 1959; s. Timothy and Annette Edith (Wakeford) M.; m. Myrna Christena Mackinnon, Aug. 24, 1963; children: Timothy, Andrew, Alexandra. BS in Geology, McGill U., 1963; MS in Engring., U. Calif., Berkeley, 1965; PhD in Geochemistry, U. London, 1974. Lectr. Imperial Coll. Sci. and Tech., London, 1969-74; chief geochemist Cities Svc. Minerals Co., Tulsa, 1974-78; v.p. Barringer Resources, Inc., Golden, Colo., 1978-84; exec. v.p., pres. Barringer Labs., Inc., Golden, 1984—; dir. St. George Minerals, Inc., Vancouver, B.C., Can., Carterra, Inc., Denver. Regional editor Jour. of Geochemical Exploration, 1972-75. Presbyterian. Home: 14382 W Virginia Dr Lakewood CO 80228 Office: Barringer Geosvcs Inc 15000 W 6th Ave Ste 300 Golden CO 80401

MEYER, WILLIAM TRENHOLM, defense consulting company official, real estate executive, former army officer; b. Ancon, C.Z., May 28, 1937; s. Trenholm Jones and Virginia Blanche (Morgan) M.; m. Erna Charlotte Albert, Dec. 14, 1961; children: Cynthia L., Bonnie A., Christopher T., Tori L. BS, U. Nebr., 1965; grad. U.S. Army Command and Gen. Staff Coll., 1973. 2d lt. U.S. Army, 1961, advanced through grades to lt. col., 1976, ret., 1981; sr. engr. ManTech Internat. Corp., Sierra Vista, Ariz., 1981-82; mgr. field ops. RCA, Sierra Vista, 1982-88; chief exec. officer MYCO, 1989; gen. ptnr., dir. Southwestern Investment Ltd. Partnership, Sierra Vista, 1983-89; mgr. advanced devel. GE, 1989—. Sustaining mem. Republican Nat. Com., 1983—. Named to Mil. Intelligence Hall of Fame, 1989. Mem. Assn. Old Crows (regional dir. 1984-87, chpt. pres. 1983-84, Internat. Electronic Warfare-Intelligence medal 1983), Armed Forces Communications and Electronics Assn., Ret. Officers Assn., Assn. U.S. Army. Roman Catholic. Clubs: Kings Tennis (pres. 1980, 87, 88), Aquatic (pres. 1981) (Sierra Vista). Home: 1902 San Diego Circle Sierra Vista AZ 85635 Office: GE 2700 Fry Blvd Ste B-3 Sierra Vista AZ 85635

MEYERDING, EUGENE VILLAUME, surgeon; b. St. Paul, Aug. 2, 1924; s. Edward August and Eugenie M. (Villaume) M.; m. Patricia Page Elliott, May 19, 1950; children: Page Meyerding Berkowitz, Elliott Eugene, Eugene Villaume Jr. BS, U. Minn., 1945, MD, 1946. Diplomate, Am. Bd. Surgery. Intern Anchor Hosp., St. Paul, 1949; resident in gen. surgery Tripler Gen. Hosp., Honolulu, 1949-52; med. officer U.S. Army, 1947-49; med. officer USAF, Honolulu, 1949-52, Biloxi, Miss., 1952-55; pvt. practice Medford, Oreg., 1955—. Contbr. articles to med. jours. Maj. USAF, 1952-55. Fellow ACS; mem. Oreg. Med. Assn., Jackson County Med. Soc. Office: Meyerding Surg Assocs 2931 Doctors Park Dr Medford OR 97504

MEYERS, BONNIE, health care administrator; b. Wausau, Wis., July 1, 1948; d. Alvin William Blank and Erma Laura (Preuss) Wirt; m. Edward H. Meyers (div. 1972); children: Carmen, Edward. Assoc. Nursing, NCTI, Wausau, Wis., 1976; BS in Nursing, Ariz. State U., 1980, MS, 1982, postgrad., 1982. Flight nurse Samaritan Health Services, Phoenix, 1977-78; critical care nurse Good Samaritan Hosp., Phoenix, 1976-81; research asst. Ariz. State U., Tempe, 1980; assist. dir. quality assurance Good Samaritan Hosp., Phoenix, 1981; cons. Ariz. Hosp. Assn., Phoenix, 1982; nursing dir. St. Lukes Med. Ctr., Phoenix, 1982-88; dir. of mergers/acquisitions St. Josephs Hosp. Med. Ctr., Phoenix, 1988-89, dir. bus. devel., 1989—; mem. adj. faculty Ariz. State U., Tempe, 1986—; lectr. Am. Cancer So., Phoenix, 1982. Editorial reviewer Addison-Wesley Pub. Co. Pres. bd. trustees Ariz. Nurses Polit. Action Com., Phoenix, 1986-87; founder, dir. Free Hypertension Screening Clinic, Wausau, Wis., 1976; participant Med. Group Project, Honduras, Central Am., 1986; healthcare legislation cons. Ariz. Congl. Del., Washington, 1986—; regional coordinator Campaign 1986, Tempe, 1986. Mem. Am. Coll. Healthcare Execs., Valley Leadership Alumni Assn., Greater Phoenix Area Health Care Found., Heart Mus. Found., Sigma Theta Tau (pres. 1983-84). Republican. Office: St Josephs Hosp Med Ctr 350 W Thomas Rd Phoenix AZ 85013

MEYERS, BRADLEY EDWARD, electro-optical company executive; b. Milw., July 29, 1941; s. Alfred Arthur and Mabel Ann (Heidtman) M.; m. Nancy E. Flowers, July 29, 1972; children: Clint, Mathew, Rebecca. Student, U. Wis., Milw., 1962-64. Sales mgr. Roemer-Karrer Research Equip., Milw., 1965-70, Explosives Corp. Am., Issaquah, Wash., 1970-72; pres. Control Dynamics/Sea-Mech Corp., Seattle, 1972-76, B.E. Meyers and Co., Inc., Redmond, Wash., 1976—. Patentee in field. Mem. Am. Soc. Naval Engrs., Internat. Soc. Optical Engrs., Internat. Chiefs of Police, Infrared Info. Analysis. Office: BE Meyers & Co Inc 17525 NE 67th Ct Redmond WA 98052

MEYERS, DIANA LEE, public relations executive; b. Bremerton, Wash., July 27, 1937; d. Albert Earl and Evelyn Francis (Baldorf) Clark; m. Philip J. Meyers, Oct. 1, 1965 (div. 1976). BA in English and History, U. Calif., Santa Barbara, 1960. Office mgr. Alfred Millard Hist. Research, Santa Barbara, 1959-64; adminstrv. asst. Puritan Cos., Santa Barbara, 1964-75; ops. officer MacElhenny/Levy Real Estate, Santa Barbara, 1975-76; pub. relations officer Cancer Found. Santa Barbara, 1976-84; owner, mgr. Diana L. Meyers Cons. Svcs.., Santa Barbara, 1984—. Contbr. articles to profl. jours. Mem. publicity com. Tres Condados coun. Girl Scouts U.S., Santa Barbara, 1988—. Mem. Nat. Soc. Fund Raising Execs. (publicity and nat. philanthropy day coms. 1987-88), Santa Barbara Assocs. (bd. dirs. 1988—), Santa Barbara C. of C., AAUW (named gift award 1981), Santa Barbara Advt. Club (Silver medal 1987), Univ. Club. Republican. Unitarian. Home: 537 Mills Way Goleta CA 93117 Office: 928 Carpinteria St Ste 10 Santa Barbara CA 93103

MEYERS, HOWARD CRAIG, lawyer; b. Chgo., Nov. 15, 1951; s. Spencer M. and Joyce L. (Dresdner) M.; m. Susan M. Plimpton, July 1, 1977 (div. Jan. 1979); m. Sonia Marlowe-Marais, Dec. 30, 1980. BA in English, Ariz. State U., 1973, JD, 1977. Bar: Ariz. 1977. Assoc. Law Office of Powell B. Gillenwater, Phoenix, 1977-79; ptnr. Gillenwater & Meyers, Phoenix, 1980-81, Davis & Meyers, Phoenix, 1982-86; pres. Ultra Companies Ltd., Scottsdale, Ariz., 1987-88; of counsel Lancy, Scult & McVey, Phoenix, 1988—; v.p., sec. Mail-More, Inc., Phoenix, 1987—. Mem. ABA, State Bar Ariz., Maricopa County Bar Assn., Internat. Council of Shopping Ctrs., Plaza Club. Republican. Home: 6711 E Camelback Rd #65 Scottsdale AZ 85251 Office: Camelback Esplanade 2425 E Camelback Ste 880 Phoenix AZ 85016

MEYERS, JEANNE FRANKLIN, art dealer; b. L.A., Aug. 8, 1944; d. Maymard and Charlotte (Weinberg) F; children: Lucas, Elissa. BA, U. Calif., 1965; MS, U. South Calif., 1968. Dir. Bornstein Gallery, Santa Monica, 1985-87; owner Meyers Bloom Gallery, Santa Monica, 1987—; bd. dirs. Modern & Contempary Art Coun. Bd. dirs. Venice Art Walk, L.A. County Mus. Art. Mem. Santa Monica Art Dealer Assn. Jewish. Office: Meyers Bloom Gallery 2112 Broadway Santa Monica CA 90404

MEYERS, RICHARD STUART, college president; b. Chgo., Sept. 6, 1938; m. Yasuko Kamata, Sept. 15, 1965; children—Anne Akiko, Toni Takiko. B.M., DePaul U., 1961; M.S., U. So. Calif., 1963, Ph.D., 1971. With Inglewood Unified Sch. Dist., Calif., 1967-68; with Dept. Def. Overseas Sch. System, Tokyo, 1964-67; jr. and sr. high sch. tchr. Palos Verdes Peninsula Unified Sch. Dist., Palos Verdes, Calif., 1962-64; instr. media coordinator Grossmont Coll., El Cajon, Calif., 1968-72; dean instrn. Cerro Coso Community Coll., Ridgecrest, Calif., 1972-75, pres., 1975-78; sec. to bd. trustees, supt. and pres. Pasadena City Coll., Calif., 1978-83; pres. Western Oreg. State Coll., Monmouth, 1983—; speaker; cons. Contbr. articles to profl. jours. Bd. dirs. United Way, Salem, Oreg., 1984—; mem. Oreg. Internat. Trade Commn., 1983—, bd. dirs. Oreg. Symphony Assn., 1985—. Fulbright scholar, Egypt, 1975. Fellow Am. Leadership Forum; mem. Am. Assn. State Colls. and Univs., Pi Gamma Mu. Republican. Presbyterian. Lodge: Rotary. Home: 395 College St S Monmouth OR 97361 Office: Western Oreg State Coll 345 N Monmouth Ave Monmouth OR 97361

MEYERS, ROBERT ALLEN, scientist, publisher; b. L.A., May 15, 1936; s. Jack B. Meyers and Pearl (Cassell) Sorkin; m. Roberta Lee Hart, June 24, 1961 (div. 1976); children: Tamara, Robert Jr.; m. Ilene Braun, Feb. 17, 1977; children: Jennifer, Jacqueline. BA, San Diego State U., 1959; PhD, UCLA, 1963. Mem. faculty Calif. Inst. Tech., Pasadena, 1963-64; rsch. scientist Bell & Howell Rsch. Ctr., Sierra Madre, Calif., 1965; project mgr. TRW Def. & Space, Redondo Beach, Calif., 1966-81; bus. area mgr. TRW Energy Group, Redondo Beach, 1981-86; mgr. process devel. TRW Def. & Space, Redondo Beach, 1986—; del. U.S.-USSR Working Group, Washington and Moscow, 1973-80; chmn. adv. bd. Guide to Nuclear Power Tech., N.Y.C., 1982-84. Author: Coal Desulfurization, 1977; editor: Coal Handbook, 1981, Coal Structure, 1982; editor-in-chief Encyclopedia of Physical Science and Technology, 1987—; inventor in field. Mem. Am. Chem. Soc., Am. Inst. Chem. Engrs. Home: 3715 Glen Eagles Dr Tarzana CA 91356 Office: TRW Def & Space One Space Pk Redondo Beach CA 90278

MEYERS, ROGER J., business owner; b. Feb. 15, 1955; Married; 2 children. BFA, NYU, 1977. Owner AM PM Telegram, Beverly Hills, Santa Monica and West Los Angeles; owner, founder Am. Telegram. Mem. NYU Alumni Assn. Mailing: 270 N Canon #1167 Beverly Hills CA 90210

MICELI, MOTHER IGNATIUS, missionary sister; b. N.Y.C., Mar. 14, 1918; d. Joseph and Cecelia (Torre) M. BS, Regis Coll.; MEd, Loyola U., New Orleans; M Religious Edn., Seattle U.; postgrad., U. Denver, 1968-69. Coordinator religious programs All Souls Ch., Englewood, Colo., 1968-71, dir. home instr. for adults, 1971-72, dir. adult edn., 1972—; dir. religious edn. Assumption, Welby, Colo., 1973-77, Holy Cross, Thornton, Colo., 1971-73; instr. religion various missions, 1968—. Author: (poems) Leaves Of Thought, 1980, Random Thoughts and Meditations, 1968, Colorado and St. Francis Xavier Cabrini, M.S.C. Mem. Internat. Bibl. Assn., Religious Edn. Assn. U.S., Religious Edn. Assn. Can., Kappa Delta Pi. Home: Cabrini Shrine Golden CO 80401 Office: All Souls Ch Religious Edn Office 435 Pennwood Circle Englewood CO 80110

MICHAEL, DEBORAH JANE, dentist; b. Middle Village, N.Y., Oct. 18, 1961; d. George Anthony and Theresa Margaret (Badia) M.; m. James Kevin Murphy, Nov. 21, 1987. BS, SUNY, Stony Brook, 1983; DDS, U. Tex., Houston, 1987. Commd. 2d lt. U.S. Army, advanced through grades to capt., 1987—; resident in gen. dentistry U.S. Army, Ft. Carson, Colo., 1987-88; dentist Camp Casey Dental Clinic U.S. Army, San Francisco and Korea, 1988—. Mem. ADA, Am. Assn. Women Dentists, Tex. Assn. Women Dentists (v.p. 1986-87), Acad. Gen. Dentistry, Delta Sigman Delta. Lutheran. Office: Camp Casey Dental Clinic 10th Med Detachment Dental Svc APO San Francisco CA 96224

MICHAEL, JERROLD MARK, public health specialist, university dean, educator; b. Richmond, Va., Aug. 3, 1927; s. Joseph Leon and Esther Leah M.; m. Lynn Y. Simon, Mar. 17, 1951; children: Scott J., Nelson L. B.C.E., George Washington U., 1949; M.S.E., Johns Hopkins U., 1950; M.P.H., U. Calif., Berkeley, 1957; Dr. P.H., Mahidol U., 1983; Sc.D., Tulane U., 1984. Commd. ensign USPHS, 1950, advanced through grades to rear adm., asst. surgeon gen., 1966; ret. 1970; dean, prof. pub. health Sch. Pub. Health, U. Hawaii, Honolulu, 1971—; Bd. dirs. Nat. Health Council, 1967-78, Nat. Center for Health Edn., 1977—; mem. nat. adv. council on health professions edn., 1978-81; chmn. bd. dirs. Kuakini Med. Ctr., Honolulu; sec., treas. Asia-Pacific Acad. Consortium Pub. Health. Contbr. articles to profl. jours.; assoc. editor Jour. Environ. Health, 1958—, Asia-Pacific Jour. of Pub. Health, 1986—. Served with USNR, 1945-47. Recipient J.S. Billings award for mil. medicine, 1964, Walter Mangold award, 1961, gold medal Hebrew U. of Jerusalem, 1982, chair in pub. health named in his honor, 1985; decorated D.S.M., others; awarded Comdr. of the Royal Order of the Elephant, King of Thailand, 1987. Fellow Am. Public Health Assn.; mem. Am. Acad. Health Adminstrn., Am. Soc. Cert. Sanitarians, Nat. Environ. Health Assn., Am. Acad. Environ. Engrs. Democrat. Jewish. Club: Masons. Office: 1960 East-West Rd Honolulu HI 96822

MICHAEL, WAGIH H., financial executive; b. El Fashn, Bini Suif, Egypt, Sept. 29, 1944; came to U.S., 1970; s. Habib Girgis and Samira (Nakla) M.; m. Nagat W. Michael, Aug. 30, 1971; children: Dahlia N., David W. B in Communications, Ain Shams U., Cairo, Egypt, 1964; MBA, Calif. Coast U., 1984, PhD, 1986. Acct. Abdul Monim Ali Said, Binisuif, Egypt, 1963-65; asst. chief acct. El Fashn (Egypt) City Council, 1965-66; internal auditor Arab Foreign Trade Co., Cairo, Egypt, 1966-70; bus. mgr. Clinca De Salud, Brawley, Calif., 1970-75; finance dir. United Health Ctrs., Parlier, Calif., 1975-79; tech. assistance dir. Calif. Health Fedn., Fresno, 1979-81; fin. cons. Saudi MedCenter Ltd., Riyadh, Saudi Arabia, 1981-85; exec. dir. Buttonwillow (Calif.) Health Ctr., Inc., 1985—; sec./treas. Internat. Shared Svcs., Plymouth Meeting, Pa., 1982-84, Hou-Len Med. Enterprises, Dallas, 1982-88, Green Horizons Holding, Inc., Dallas, 1982-88. Contbr. various articles to profl. jours. Mem. Am. Mgmt. Assn., Calif. Health Fedn., Nat. Assn. Community Health Ctrs., Assoc. Calif. Health Ctrs., Inc., Healthcare Fin. Mgmt. Assn., So. Calif. Pub. Health Assn., Am. Coll. Healthcare Execs., Lions. Democrat. Coptic Orthodox. Home: 1913 Deerfield St Bakersfield CA 93312

MICHAELS, PATRICK FRANCIS, broadcasting company executive; b. Superior, Wis., Nov. 5, 1925; s. Julian and Kathryn Elizabeth (Keating) M.; A.A., U. Melbourne, 1943; B.A., Golden State U., 1954; Ph.D., London U., 1964; m. Paula Naomi Bowen, May 1, 1960; children—Stephanie Michelle, Patricia Erin. War corr. CBS; news editor King Broadcasting, 1945-50; war corr. Mid-East Internat. News Service, 1947-49; war corr. MBS, Korea, 1950-53; news dir. Sta. WDSU-AM-FM-TV, 1953-54; fgn. corr. NBC, S. Am., 1954-56; news dir. Sta. KWIZ, 1956-59; commentator ABC, Los Angeles, 1959-62; fgn. corr. Am. News Services, London, 1962-64; news commentator McFadden Bartell Sta. KCBQ, 1964-68; news commentator ABC, San Francisco, 1968-70; news dir. Sta. KWIZ, Santa Ana, Calif., 1970-74, station mgr., 1974-81; pres. Sta. KWRM, Corona, Calif., Sta. KQLH, San Bernardino, Calif., 1981-88; chmn. Michaels Media, Corona del Mar, Calif., 1988—. Bd. dirs. Econ. Devel. Corp. Mem. Nat. Assn. Broadcasters (bd. dirs.), Calif. Broadcasters Assn. (v.p.), Am. Fedn. TV and Radio Artists, Orange County Broadcasters Assn. (pres.), Sigma Delta Chi (ethics com.). Republican. Clubs: Rotary, Balboa Bay (bd. govs.), South Shore Yacht, Internat. Yachting Fellowship of Rotarians (staff commodore). Home: 4521 Cortland Dr Corona Del Mar CA 92625

MICHAELSON, PETER FREDERICK, lawyer; b. Schenectady, N.Y., Apr. 20, 1957; s. Alvin and Helen (Samuels) M.; m. Mary Therese Casey, July 27, 1985. BA, Pa. State U., 1979; JD, U. Denver, 1982; postgrad., U. Houston, 1987. Bar: Colo. 1982, U.S. Dist. Ct. Colo. 1982. Atty. Law Office of J. Wallace Wortham, Jr., Denver, 1982-84; dep. dist. atty. 5th Jud. Dist., Breckenridge, Colo., 1984-86, chief dep. dist. atty., 1986-88; dist. atty. 5th Jud. Dist., Breckenridge, 1989—; prosecutor, Frisco, Colo., 1985-89; mem. Juvenile Diversion Adv. Bd., Breckenridge, 1988. Author: On a Ledge Sitting Sideways, 1979; editor: The Daily Collegian, 1977-78; contbr. articles to profl. jours. Mem. adv. bd. Alpine Counseling Ctr., Breckenridge, 1986—; mem. Advocates for Victims of Assault, Breckenridge, 1984-86; committeeman Dem. Nat. Com., Blue River, Colo., 1988; player, coach Pumpkin Bowl, Inc., Breckenridge, 1984—. Mem. Summit County Bar Assn. (law day dir. 1986), Colo. Bar Assn., Continental Divide Bar Assn., Nat. Dist. Attys. Assn. Jewish. Office: Office of Dist Atty PO Box 488 Breckenridge CO 80424

MICHALIK, JOHN JAMES, bar association executive; b. Bemidji, Minn., Aug. 1, 1945; s. John and Margaret Helen (Pafko) M.; m. Diane Marie Olson, Dec. 21, 1968; children: Matthew John, Nicole, Shane. BA, U. Minn., 1967, JD, 1970. Legal editor Lawyers Coop. Publishing Co., Rochester, N.Y., 1970-75; dir. continuing legal edn. Wash. State Bar Assn., Seattle, 1975-81, exec. dir., 1981—. Mem. Am. Soc. Assn. Execs., Nat. Assn. Bar Execs., Am. Mgmt. Assn., Am. Judicature Soc. Lutheran. Club: Seattle Coll. Office: Wash State Bar Assn 2001 6th Ave 500 Westin Bldg Seattle WA 98121-2599

MICHALSON, EDGAR L., agricultural economics-rural sociology educator; b. Salem, Oreg., Dec. 13, 1929; s. Theodore Jr. and Clara Heldora (Scheweland) M.; m. Evangaline Bernice Olsen, Dec. 28, 9159; children: Erik Theodore, Arne Edward, Anne-Marie Elise. BS, Oreg. State U., 1956; MS, Pa. State U., 1959, PhD, 1963. Rsch. assoc. Pa. State U., University Park, 1961-63; agrl. economist USDA, Pullman, Wash., 1963-69; assoc. prof. Wash. State U., Pullman, 1963-69; assoc. prof. agrl. econs. and rural sociology U. Idaho, Moscow, 1969-74, prof., 1974—, resource economist, 1969-74, agrl. economist, 1974—; cons. Idaho Dept. Pub. Lands, 1970, Gary Operating Co., 1972, Coeur d'Alene Indian Tribe, 1977, Blue Sky Advs., 1982. Mem. Idaho Gov.'s Ad Hoc Adv. Com. on Wild and Scenic Rivers; treas. Idaho Inst. on Christian Edn. Mem. Am. Econ. Assn., Am. Agrl. Econs. Assn., Am. Water Resources Assn., Western Agrl. Econs. Assn., So. Agrl. Econs. Assn., Columbia River Soc. Rural Mgrs. and Appraisers (sec.-treas. 1970-72), SCSA (treas. Inland Empire chpt.), Masons, Kiwanis (pres. Moscow 1983-84). Lutheran. Office: U Idaho Dept Agrl Econs Moscow ID 83843

MICHEAU, JACK BRADFORD, lawyer; b. Aberdeen, Wash., Nov. 4, 1955; s. Donald Gene and Patricia (Hedrick) M.; m. Lynn Marie Bishop, Sept. 4, 1982. BS in Forestry, Wash. State U., 1978, BA in Sociology, 1979; JD, U. Wash., 1983. Bar: Wash. 1983, U.S. Dist. Ct. (we. dist.) Wash. 1983. Assoc. Law Offices J.K. Hallam, Aberdeen, 1983-84; ptnr. Copland and Micheau, Aberdeen, 1985—. Legal advisor Am. Days Com., 1987, 88, Shoalwater Tribal Ent. Bd., 1987; bd. dirs., officer Twin Harbors council Boy Scouts Am., 1986—. Mem. ABA, Wash. Bar Assn., Grays Harbor County Bar Assn., Jaycees. Democrat. Methodist. Office: Copland & Micheau 218 N Broadway Box 343 Aberdeen WA 98520

MICHEL, GARY SOLOMON, mechanical engineer; b. Balt., May 14, 1962; s. Carlo and Esther (Putzrath) M. BSME, Va. Poly. Inst. and State U., 1985; MBA, U. Phoenix, 1989. Rsch. engr. Harry Diamond Labs., Adelphi, Md., 1981-84; application engr. Ingersoll-Rand Co., Chgo., 1985-87; sales engr. Ingersoll-Rand Co., Denver, 1987—; distbn. product mgr. Ingersoll-Rand Co., Charlotte, N.C. Mem. ASME, Wings Club, Tau Kappa Epsilon (dist. v.p., pres. bd. dirs.). Jewish. Office: Ingersoll-Rand Co PO Box 240203 Charlotte NC 28224

MICHEL, VICTOR JAMES, JR., retired librarian; b. St. Louis, Feb. 2, 1927; s. Victor James and Bernadette (Fox) M.; student St. Louis U., 1946-48; m. Margaret A. Renaud, Feb. 3, 1951; children: Dennis W., Daniel J., Catherine A., Denise M. Asst. librarian McDonnell Aircraft Corp., St. Louis, 1948-55; mgr. Anaheim (Calif.) Information Center, Electronics Ops., Rockwell Internat. Corp., 1955-84; pres. V.J. Michel Inc., Grass Valley, Calif., 1986—; sec. Placentia Devel. Co., 1964-71. Charter mem. Placentia-Tlaquepaque Sister City Orgn., 1964-84; founder, pres. Placentia chpt. St. Louis Browns Fan Club. Planning commr., Placentia, Calif., 1957-60, city councilman, 1960-70, vice-mayor, 1960-64, mayor, 1964-68. Trustee Placentia Library Dist., 1970-79, pres., 1974-79; city historian, Placentia, 1976-84, city treas., 1980-84; chmn. Placentia Fine Arts Commn., 1978-80. Served from pvt. to staff sgt. AUS, 1945-46. Named Placentia Citizen of Yr., 1979. Mem. Placentia C. of C. (v.p. 1960), Placentia Jaycees (hon. life), Calif., Orange County (pres. 1976) library assns. Democrat. Roman Catholic. Club: West Atwood Yacht (hon. yeoman emeritus with citation 1970, ship's librarian). Author: Pictorial History of the West Atwood Yacht Club, 1966; Placentia—Around the World, 1970; also articles in profl. jours. Home: 107 Bernadine Ct Grass Valley CA 95949

MICHELSEN, THEODORE WILLIAM, marketing professional; b. Bklyn., Nov. 24, 1944; s. Warren Gerard and Maude Leanore (Smith) M.; m. Carol Lynn Steinkraus, June 18, 1967; children: Janet Lynn, Jennifer Lynn. BS in Chemistry, Rensselaer Poly. Inst., 1967, PhD in Inorganic Chemistry, 1971. Research chemist Manville Sales Corp., Denver, 1970-77, sr. research chemist, 1977-79, project. mgr., 1979-81, research mgr., 1981-83, mgr. mktg. engring. services, 1983-86, v.p., dir. research engring. services, 1986—; instr. Roofing Industry Ednl. Inst., Englewood, Colo., 1985—, Better Understanding of Roofing Systems Inst., Denver, 1983—. Mem. editorial bd. Internat. J. Roofing Tech. Mem. Ch. council Luth. Ch. Resurrection, Denver, 1975-80, chmn. Christian edn., 1978-80. Mem. Am. Chem. Soc., Asphalt Roofing Mfr's. Assn. (roofing systems tech. com. 1983—, built-up roofing com. 1983—, chmn. built-up roofing com. 1986—). Club: Rocky Mountain 99ers (Denver) (v.p. 1983-84, pres. 1984-85). Home: 1812 S Yank Ct Lakewood CO 80228 Office: Manville Sales Corp PO Box 5108 Denver CO 80217-5108

MICHELSON, DOUGLAS JEROME, metal dealer, former state senator; b. Albuquerque, Feb. 17, 1942; s. Jack and Mildred (Bell) M. Student U. Ariz., 1959-61; B.S., U. N.Mex., student Indsl. Coll. Armed Forces, 1970. Civilian sales research and product devel. Sunbell Corp., Albuquerque, 1963-67, v.p., 1967-69, v.p. fin. and capital expenditure, 1969-71; with Rembrandt Investments, Albuquerque, 1972-76; owner, metal dealer Michelson Metals, 1976—; mem. N.Mex. Senate, 1972-76, vice chmn. pub. affairs com. Mem.

N.Mex. Amigos. Democrat. Jewish. Home: 611 Lead SW #307 Albuquerque NM 87102 Office: 1503 Central St NW Ste 2 Albuquerque NM 87104

MICK, COLIN KENNEDY, information scientist; b. Lansing, Mich., Jan. 17, 1941; s. Allan H. and Lucille (Kennedy) M.; m. Ulla Kasperski, June 24, 1966. BA, U. Alaska, 1963; MA, Stanford U., 1969, PhD, 1972. Writer Jessen's Weekly, Fairbanks, Alaska, 1962-64; news editor U. Alaska, 1964-67; computer cons. Stanford U., Palo Alto, Calif., 1969-71; rsch. assoc. Stanford U., Palo Alto, 1972-75; pres. Applied Communications Rsch., Palo Alto, 1974-79; exec. dir. Decision Info. Svcs., Palo Alto, 1979-89; v.p., gen. mgr. svcs. div. Landuest Group, Santa Clara, Calif., 1989—; exec. dir. Open Token Found., Santa Clara, 1989—. Exec. producer program Understanding Personal Computers, 1982-85; author: Working Smart, 1984, Mastering Your Money, 1986. Mem. Gov.'s Task Force on Energy Extension, Sacramento, Calif., 1977-79; coord. College Terrace Residential Assn., Palo Alto, 1979—. 1st lt. U.S. Army, 1964-66. Office: 3375 Scott Blvd Ste 206 Santa Clara CA 95054

MICKEL, BUCK, construction company executive; b. Elberton, Ga., Dec. 17, 1925; s. James Clark and Reba (Vaughn) M.; m. Minor Herndon, May 2, 1946; children: Minor M. Shaw, Buck Alston, Charles Clark. BSCE, Ga. Inst. Tech., 1947; PhD (hon.), Erskine Coll., 1975. With Daniel Internat. Corp., Greenville, S.C., 1948—, chmn., 1974—; pres. Fluor Corp., Irvine, Calif., 1984-86; vice chmn. Fluor Corp., Irvine, 1986—, also dir.; vice chmn. U.S. Shelter Corp., Greenville, also bd. dirs.; chmn., bd. dirs. R.S.I. Corp., Greenville, 1978—; bd. dirs. Textile Hall Corp., Duke Power Co., Charlotte, C&S Corp., Atlanta, Monsanto Co., St. Louis, Liberty Corp., Greenville, Nat. Intergroup, Pitts., J.P. Stevens & Co., N.Y.C. Life trustee Converse Coll., 1964—, Clemson U., S.C., 1975—; mem. adv. bd. U. S.C. Bus. Sch., Columbia, S.C. Found. Ind. Colls., Columbia, James F. Brynes Internat. Ctr., Columbus, 1984—; bd. dirs. S.C. Bus. Week, S.C., 1985. Served to lt. C.E., U.S. Army; Korea. Named Citizen of Yr. Wofford Coll., Spartanburg, S.C., 1978; Disting. Salesman, Sales & Mktg. Execs., Greenville, 1975; inducted into S.C. Bus. Hall of Fame, 1986; First Institutional Advancement award Clemson U., 1986. Mem. S.C. State C. of C. (Businessman of Yr. 1983), U. S.C. Alumni Assn. (hon.). Republican. Baptist. Clubs: Augusta Nat. Golf; Collins Creek Gun., Commerce, Cotillion; Greenville Country, Green Valley Country (Greenville). Home: 415 Crescent Ave Greenville SC 29605 Office: US Shelter Corp PO Box 1089 Greenville SC 29602

MICKELSON, ROBERT EUGENE, real estate developer; b. Sioux Falls, S.D., Feb. 25, 1924; s. Walter Lavant and Ethel Edna (Mann) M.; m. Mary Lou Cleave, Jan. 20, 1951 (div. 1978); m. Joan Donaldson, Feb. 14, 1980; 1 child, Marc. BBA, U. Minn., 1948; MBA, Harvard U., 1950. Pres. Edelweiss Ski Wear, Tacoma, 1950-67, Alpental Land Co., Tacoma, 1967-72, Whittakers Chalet, Tacoma, 1967-72; owner, broker Mickelson Realty & Devel., Sun Valley, Idaho, 1972—; cons., Am. Dist. Telegraph, N.Y.C., 1978, Palm Beach, N.Y.C., 1979, Sun Valley Co., 1979; bd. dirs., Mountain State Savs. Bank, Sun Valley. Bd. dirs., Sun Valley Water and Sewer Dist., 1976-84. Mem. Rotary. Home: PO Box 1476 Sun Valley ID 83353 Office: Mickelson Realty Devel 260 1st Ave N Ketchum ID 83340

MIDDAUGH, LAURA GENE, lawyer; b. Chgo., Aug. 8, 1949; d. Charles William and Esta (Rader) M.; m. Steve Kuberski, Aug. 24, 1976 (div. 1984); m. Adam Kline, June 25, 1989. BA in Psychology, U. Calif., Santa Cruz, 1971; AS in Nursing, Cabrillo Coll., Capitola, Calif., 1974; JD cum laude, U. Puget Sound, 1983. Bar: Wash., U.S. Dist. Ct. (we. dist.) Wash. Asst. clin. nursing coordinator Stanford Hosp., Palo Alto, Calif., 1977-79; asst. head nurse Providence Med. Ctr., Seattle, 1979-80; assoc. Cromwell, Mendoza & Belur, Seattle, 1983—. Vol. Seattle King County Vol. Lawyers, Seattle, 1983-88, Forgotten Children's Fund, Seattle, 1987—, Swedish Hosp. Sustaining Care, Seattle, 1988—. Mem. Seattle King County Bar Assn. Office: Cromwell Mendoza & Belur 6300 Southcenter Blvd Ste 206 Seattle WA 98188

MIDDLEBROOK, GRACE IRENE, nurse, educator; b. L.A., Mar. 5, 1927; d. Joel P. and Betty (Larson) Soderberg; dip. West Suburban Hosp., 1950; BS in Nursing, Wheaton Coll., 1951; MEdn Ariz. State U., 1965, EdD, 1970; m. Albert William Middlebrook, July 7, 1950; children: Alberta Elizabeth, Jo Anne. Office nurse, Dr. G.A. Hemwall, Chgo., 1950-51; supr. Bates Meml. Hosp., Bentonville, Ark., 1955-58; instr. Sparks Meml. Hosp. Sch. Nursing, Ft. Smith, Ark., 1959-61; instr., coord. med.-surg. nursing Sch. of Nursing, Good Samaritan Hosp., Phoenix, 1961-64, asst. dir. Sch. Nursing, 1964-73, dir. edn. and tng., 1968-80; corp. dir. edn. Samaritan Health Svc., Phoenix, 1969—; adj. prof. Samaritan Coll. Nursing, Grand Canyon Coll. Mem. speakers bur. Sch. Career Days, 1970—. Recipient award for leadership co-op programs Phoenix Union High Sch., 1980, Sammy award Samaritan Health Svc. and Samaritan Med. Found., 1981. Mem. Ariz. Nurses in Mgmt. (bd. dirs. 1983-85), Am. Hosp. Assn., Nat. League Nursing, Ariz. League for Nursing, Adult Edn. Assn., Ariz. Heart Assn. (instr.), Pi Lambda Theta, Kappa Delta Pi, Sigma Theta Tau. Home: 4242 N 15th Dr Phoenix AZ 85015 Office: Samaritan Health Svc Edn Ctr 1500 E Thomas Rd Phoenix AZ 85014

MIDDLETON, ANTHONY WAYNE, JR., urologist, educator; b. Salt Lake City, May 6, 1939; s. Anthony Wayne and Dolores Caravena (Lowry) M.; BS, U. Utah, 1963; MD, Cornell U., 1966; m. Carol Samuelson, Oct. 23, 1970; children: Anthony Wayne, Suzanne, Kathryn, Jane, Michelle. Intern, U. Utah Hosps., Salt Lake City, 1966-67; resident in urology Mass. Gen. Hosp., Boston, 1970-74; practice urology Middleton Urol. Assos., Salt Lake City, 1974—; mem. staff Primary Children's Hosp., staff pres., 1981-82; mem. staff Latter-Day Saints Hosp., Holy Cross Hosp.; assoc. clin. prof. surgery U. Utah Med. Coll., 1977—; vice chmn. bd. govs. Utah Med. Self-Ins. Assn., 1980-81, chmn. 1985-87. Bd. dirs. Utah chpt. Am. Cancer Soc., 1978-86; bishop Ch. Jesus Christ Latter-day Saints; vice chmn. Utah Med. Polit. Action Com., 1978-81, chmn., 1981-83; chmn. Utah Physicians for Reagan, 1983-84; mem. U. Utah Coll. Medicine Dean's Search Com., 1983-84; bd. dirs. Utah Symphony, 1985—. Served as capt. USAF, 1968-70. Mem. ACS, Utah State Med. Assn. (pres. 87-88), Am. Urologic Assn.(socioecons. com. 1987—), AMA, Salt Lake County Med. Assn. (sec. 1965-67, pres. liaison com. 1980-81, pres.-elect 1981-83, pres. 1984), Utah Urol. Assn. (pres. 1976-77), Salt Lake Surg. Soc. (treas. 1977-78), Am. Assn. Clin. Urologists, Phi Beta Kappa, Alpha Omega Alpha, Beta Theta Pi. Republican. Contbr. articles to profl. jours. Home: 2798 Chancellor Pl Salt Lake City UT 84108 Office: 1060 E 1st S Salt Lake City UT 84102

MIDDLETON, JAMES ARTHUR, oil and gas company executive; b. Tulsa, Mar. 15, 1936; s. James Arthur and Inez (Matthews) M.; m. Victoria Middleton; children: Robert Arthur, James Daniel, Angela Lynn. B.A., Rice U., 1958, B.S. in Mech. Engring., 1959. With Atlantic Richfield Co., 1959—; design engr. Dallas, 1962-67; tech. planner 1967-69; mgr. shale devel. Grand Junction, Colo., 1969-72; mgr. engring. dept. Los Angeles, 1972-74; mgr. Prudhoe Bay project Pasadena, Calif., 1974-80; v.p., mgr. corp. planning Los Angeles, 1980-81; pres. ARCO Coal Co., Denver, 1981-82; sr. v.p. ARCO Oil and Gas Co., Dallas, 1982-85, pres., 1985—, sr. v.p. parent co., 1981-87, exec. v.p. parent co., 1987—, also bd. dirs.; bd. dirs. First RepublicBank Dallas. Mem. Ctr. for Strategic and Internat. Studies (CSIS)-Dallas Round Table, Am. Enterprise Forum, Chief Execs. Round Table; corp. rep. Circle Ten council Boy Scouts Am.; bd. dirs. United Way Met. Dallas, Dallas Council on World Affairs. Served to 2d lt. C.E., AUS, 1959-60. Mem. Soc. Petroleum Engrs. of AIME, Tex. Mid-Continent Oil and Gas Assn., Am. Petroleum Inst., Rocky Mountain Oil and Gas Assn. Clubs: Dallas Petroleum, Tower, Northwood. Office: Arco Oil & Gas Co 1601 Bryan Dallas TX 75201 also: Atlantic Richfield Co 515 S Flower St Los Angeles CA 90071

MIDDLETON, LOWELL GLENN, bank executive; b. Des Moines, May 31, 1948; s. Forrest Glenn and Melva L. (Miller) M.; m. Kathryn Sue Sirwaitis, Nov. 28, 1968; children: Trisha, Suzanne, Erin. BS, Ariz. State U., 1971. Sr. v.p. Security Pacific Bank, Phoenix, 1973—; vice-chmn., bd. dirs. Consumer Credit Councilors of Ariz., Phoenix, 1983—; bd. dirs. Credit Data Southwest, Phoenix; assoc. mem. Robert Morris and Assocs. Mem. Am. Bankers Assn. (region 6B council 1988—), Ariz. Bankers Assn. (chmn. consumer credit com. 1985). Republican. Roman Catholic. Office: Security Pacific Bank PO Box 2511 Phoenix AZ 85002

MIDDLETON, ROBERT GORDON, engineer, lecturer, author; b. Watsonville, Calif., May 31, 1908; s. Winton Gordon and Carrie (Leonard) M.; student U. Calif., 1928-31, U. Conn., 1944, N.Y. U., 1945; m. Teresa Emilson, June 29, 1940. Lectr., chief field engr. Simpson Electric Co., Chgo., 1954-57; internat. dir. tech. div. Radio Electronic TV Sch., Inc., Detroit, 1957-60. Mem. IEEE (life), Nat. Ret. Tchrs. Assn., Friends of U. Calif. at Santa Cruz Library. Club: Elks. Author 100 tech. books, the latest including: Transistor TV Servicing Guide, 1969; Transistor Color TV Servicing Guide, 1969; Tape Recorder Servicing Guide, 1970; Using Scopes in Color TV, 1970; Color-TV Waveform Analysis, 1970; Using Scopes in Transistor Circuits, 1970; Electronic Organ Servicing Guide, 1971; Audel's Television Service Manual, rev. edit., 1977; Audel's Radioman's Guide, rev. edit., 1977; Basic Electricity, 1974; Digital Equipment Servicing Guide, 1975; Handbook of Electronic Circuit Design, 1978; Handbook of Electronic System Design, 1978; Handbook of Audio Circuit Design, 1978; Acoustic Troubleshooting of Audio Systems, 1979; Understanding Microprocessors, 1980; Effectively Using the Oscilloscope, 1981; Understanding Digital Logic Circuits, 1982; Digital Logic Tests and Analysis, 1982; New Ways to Use Test Meters, 1983; New Digital Troubleshooting Techniques, 1984; Troubleshooting Electronic Equipment without Service Data, 1984; New Handbook of Troubleshooting Techniques for Microprocessors and Microcomputers, 1985; Designing Electronic Circuits, 1985, Handbook of Electronic Tables and Formulas, 1986, Rob Middleton's Handbook of Electronic Time-Savers and Shortcuts, 1987, How to Use DC Voltmeters, 1988, How to Read Oscilloscope Waveforms, 1988. Address: PO Box 594 Santa Cruz CA 95061

MIDDLETON, VINCENT FRANCIS, manufacturing company executive; b. N.Y.C., June 24, 1951; s. Vincent Aloysius and Mary Hilda (LeHane) M.; m. Collette Carolyn Peters, July 26, 1986. BSCE cum laude, So. Meth. U., 1974; MBA in Mgmt. summa cum laude, Golden Gate U., 1986. Registered profl. civil engr., Calif. Sr. structural engr. Bechtel, Inc., San Francisco, 1974-77; project mgr. Fisher Devel., Inc., San Francisco, 1977-80; mgr. projects Ecodyne Corp., Santa Rosa, Calif., 1980-81, dir. constrn., 1981-84; mgr. engring. and constrn. Custodis-Ecodyne, Inc., Santa Rosa, 1984-86; mgr. devel. and constrn. Custodis-Ecodyne Inc., Santa Rosa, 1986-87, v.p., gen. mgr., 1987—; researcher, regional v.p. Cottrell Cos., Inc., 1988—. Bd. dirs. Jr. Achievement, Sonoma County, Calif., 1986—. Engring. scholar So. Meth. U., Dallas, 1969; Tex. Pub. Works scholar, 1973. Mem. ASCE, Am. Concrete Inst., Nat. Asbestos Coun., Cooling Tower Inst., Mensa. Republican. Roman Catholic. Home: 260 Pacific Heights Dr Santa Rosa CA 95403 Office: Custodis-Ecodyne Inc PO Box 1267 Santa Rosa CA 95402

MIDDLETON-KEIRN, SUSAN, anthropology educator; b. Piqua, Ohio, Mar. 30, 1943; d. John Adlard and Alma Marguerite (Fischer) M. BA, U. Fla., 1967, MA, 1970, PhD, 1975. Mem. faculty Jacksonville (Ala.) State U., 1975-81; vis. lectr. Calif. State U., Turlock, 1981-82, asst. prof., 1982-83, assoc. prof., 1983-88, prof. anthropology, 1988—. Contbr. articles to scholarly jours. Mem. Am. Ethnol. Soc., Popular Culture Assn., Am. Culture Assn., So. Anthropol. Soc., Calif. Women in Higher Edn. (statewide exec. v.p. 1985-87, dir. project on multicultural perspectives in univ. curricula 1985-87, Outstanding Woman of Yr.1987), Am. Anthropol. Assn., Phi Beta Kappa, Lambda Alpha. Office: Calif State U 801 Monte Vista Ave Turlock CA 95380

MIDDLEWOOD, MARTIN EUGENE, technical communications specialist, writer, consultant; b. Galesburg, Ill., Mar. 21, 1947; s. Martin and Bernetta Maxine (Henderson) M.; m. Mona Marie Jarmer, Sept. 10, 1971; children: Erin, Martha, Emily, Margaret. BA, Eastern Wash. U., 1973, MA, 1980. Writer tech. manuals Tektronix, Inc., Beaverton, Oreg., 1976-77, tech. writer, 1977-79, sr. tech. writer, 1979-82, supr. pub. relations, 1982-84, mgr. pub. relations, 1984-85; mgr. mktg. communications Tektronix, Inc., Vacouver, Wash., 1985-87; account exec. The Waggener Group, Portland, Oreg., 1987—; chmn. adv. bd. sci. and tech. writing, Clark Coll., Vancouver, 1984—; owner communications cons. firm, Vancouver, 1978—. Author: (ednl. brochure series) Oscilloscope Measurements, 1979 (award of excellence Willamette Valley chpt. Soc. Tech. Communication, 1980); contbr. articles to profl. jours. Served with USMC, 1967-70. Recipient Cert. Recognition Clark Coll., Vancouver, 1984, 86; award of Excellence Pacific N.W. chpt. Internat. Assn. Bus. Communicators, 1985. Mem. Soc. Tech. Communication (sr.; pres. Willamette Valley chpt. 1983-85, award of recognition 1986, chpt. pub. achievement award 1985, 2 awards of distinction 1981). Home: 1107 SE 98th Ave Vancouver WA 98664 Office: The Waggener Group 6915 SW Macadam Ave Ste 300 Portland OR 97219

MIDGETT, MATTHEW EDWARD, marketing executive; b. Downey, Calif., Sept. 8, 1954; s. Jack Edward and Jeri (Peshek) M. BA in Journalis with honors, BA in Geography, Calif. State U., Long Beach, 1980. Dir. pub. rels. Samuel Merritt Hosp., Oakland, Calif., 1980-82; v.p. client svcs. Aclemir Communications, Beverly Hills, Calif., 1982-84, J. Pinto and Assocs., La Jolla, Calif., 1984-86; pres. Pacific Resource Communications, Cardiff-By-the-Sea, Calif., 1986—; cons. San Diego County Med. Soc., Am. Acad. Ophthalmology, San Francisco, 1984—. Mem. San Diego Assn. Advt. Agencies (v.p. 1987), Med. Mktg. Assn., Art Deco Preservation Soc. Republican. Office: Pacific Resource Communications 2533 S Hwy 101 #250 Cardiff by the Sea CA 92007

MIDKIFF, ROBERT RICHARDS, banker; b. Honolulu, Sept. 24, 1920; s. Frank Elbert and Ruth (Richards) M.; m. Evanita Sumner, July 24, 1948; children: Mary Lloyd, Robin Starr, Shelley Sumner, Robert Richards Jr., David Wilson. BA, Yale U., 1942; grad. Advanced Mgmt. Program, Harvard U., 1962. Asst. sec. Hawaiian Trust Co., 1951-56, asst. v.p., 1956-57, v.p., 1957-65; dir. Am. Factors, Ltd., 1954-65; v.p. Amfac, Inc., 1965-68; exec. v.p., dir. Am. Security Bank, Honolulu, 1968-69, pres., dir., 1969-71; pres., dir. Am. Trust Co. Hawaii, Honolulu, 1971—; chmn. bd. Bishop Trust Co. Ltd., Honolulu, 1984—; bd. dirs. Persis Corp., Honolulu, Kuakini Found., Honolulu. Co-chmn. Gov.'s Archtl. Adv. Com. on State Capitol, 1960-65; co-chmn. Gov.'s Adv. Com. on Fine Arts for State Capitol, 1965-69; past chmn., bd. dirs. Hawaii Visitors Bur.; past pres., bd. dirs. Downtown Improvement Assn.; bd. dirs. Lahaina Restoration Found., Samuel N. and Mary Castle Found., Atherton Family Found., Friends of Iolani Palace, Honolulu, 1972-79; past chmn. Profit Sharing Research Found., Aloha United Way, Honolulu, 1982, Hawaii Visitors Bur., Honolulu, 1964-66. 1st lt. AUS, 1943-46. Mem. Council on Founds., Employee Stock Ownership Plan Assn. Am. (bd. dirs.), Profit Sharing Council Am., Profit Sharing Research Found. (past. chmn.), Pacific Club, Waialae Golf Club, Oahu Country Club, Phi Beta Kappa. Democrat. Episcopalian. Office: Am Fin Svcs 841 Bishop St #1203 Honolulu HI 96813

MIEL, VICKY ANN, municipal government executive; b. South Bend, Ind., June 20, 1951; d. Lawrence Paul Miel and Virginia Ann (Yeagley) Hernandez. BS, Ariz. State U., 1985. Word processing coordinator City of Phoenix, 1977-78, word processing adminstr., 1978-83, chief dep. city clk., 1983-88, city clk. dir., 1988—; assoc. prof. Phoenix Community Coll., 1982-83, Mesa (Ariz.) Community Coll., 1983; speaker in field, Boston, Santa Fe, Los Angeles, N.Y.C. and St. Paul, 1980—. Author: Phoenix Document Request Form, 1985, Developing Successful Systems Users, 1986. Judge Future Bus. Leaders Am. at Ariz. State U., Tempe, 1984; bd. dirs. Fire and Life Safety League, Phoenix, 1984. Recipient Gold Plaque, Word Processing Systems Mag., Mpls., 1980, Green Light Productivity award City of Phoenix, 1981, Honor Soc. Achievement award Internat. Word Processing Assn., Willow Grove, Pa., 1981. Mem. Assn. Info. Systems Profls. (internat. dir. 1982-84), Internat. Inst. Mcpl. Clks. (cert.), Am. Records Mgrs. Assn., Assn. Image Mgmt., Am. Soc. Pub. Adminstrs., Am. Mgmt. Assn. Lodge: Soroptimists. Office: City of Phoenix 251 W Washington Phoenix AZ 85003

MIELKE, CLARENCE HAROLD, JR., hematologist; b. Spokane, Wash., June 18, 1936; s. Clarence Harold and Marie Katherine (Gillespie) M.; B.S., Wash. State U., 1959; M.D., U. Louisville, 1963; m. Marcia Rae, July 5, 1964; children—Elisa, John, Tina. Intern, San Francisco Gen. Hosp., 1963-64; resident in medicine Portland VA Hosp., 1964-65, San Francisco Gen. Hosp., 1965-67; fellow in hematology U. So. Calif., 1967-68; teaching fellow, asst. physician, instr. Tufts-New Eng. Med. Center Hosps., Boston, 1968-71; sr. scientist Med. Rsch. Inst., San Francisco, 1971—; chief hematology Presbyn. Hosp., San Francisco, 1971—; asst. clin. prof. medicine U. Calif. Sch. Medicine, San Francisco, 1971-80, assoc. clin. prof., 1979—, dir. Inst. Cancer Research; trustee, bd. dirs. Med. Research Inst. San Francisco. NIH grantee, 1973-88; dir. emeritus Inst. Cancer Rsch.,; trustee emeritus, bd. dirs. Med. Rsch. Inst., 1988—. Fellow ACP, Internat. Soc. Hematology, Am. Coll. Angiology; mem. Am. Soc. Internal Medicine, Internat. Soc. Thrombosis and Hemostasis, Am. Heart Assn., N.Y. Acad. Scis., AMA, San Francisco Med. Soc., Am. Thoracic Soc., AAAS, Internat. Soc. Angiology. Editor emeritus, Jour. Clin. Aphersis, 1981; contbr. chpts. to books, articles to med. jours. Office: Inst Cancer Rsch 2200 Webster St San Francisco CA 94115

MIELKE, FREDERICK WILLIAM, JR., retired utility company executive; b. N.Y.C., Mar. 19, 1921; s. Frederick William and Cressida (Flynn) M.; m. Lorraine Roberts, 1947; children: Bruce Frederick, Neal Russell. A.B., U. Calif., 1943; J.D., Stanford U., 1949. Bar: Calif. 1950. Law clk. to Assoc. Justice John W. Shenk, Calif. Supreme Ct., 1949-51; with Pacific Gas and Electric Co., San Francisco, 1951-86; exec. v.p. Pacific Gas and Electric Co., 1976-79, chmn. bd., chief exec. officer, 1979-86, now bd. dirs.; bd. dirs. Pacific Gas Transmission Co., SRI Internat., Edison Electric Inst., 1979-82. Trustee Stanford U., 1977-87, Golden Gate U., 1977-79; mem. adv. council Stanford Grad. Sch. Bus.; bd. dirs. Calif. C. of C., 1979-85, San Francisco C. of C., 1977-79, Ind. Colls. No. Calif., 1969-79; chmn. bd. United Way of Bay Area, 1986-88. Served with USN, 1943-46. Mem. ABA, Calif. Bar Assn., Pacific Coast Elec. Assn., Pacific Coast Gas Assn. Club: Electric of San Francisco. Office: Pacific Gas and Electric Co 245 Market St San Francisco CA 94106 *

MIES, WILLARD ESDOHR, newsletter editor; b. Chgo., Jan. 27, 1947; s. Willard G. and Grace A. (Esdohr) M.; m. Julia S. Harding, Oct. 6, 1979; 1 child, Virginia. BA, U. Ariz., 1969; MA, Stanford U., 1970. Reporter San Diego Union, 1970-71; assoc. editor Walker's Weekly Newsletter, San Francisco, 1971-74; exec. news editor Pulp & Paper mag., San Francisco, 1974—; editor Pulp & Paper Week newsletter, San Francisco, 1979—; editorial dir. Nonwoven's World Mag., 1987—. Author, editor numerous books and articles on paper industry. Mem. Stanford Alumni Assn., Soc. Profl. Journalists, Sigma Delta Chi. Home: 6201 Contra Costa Ave Oakland CA 94618 Office: Miller Freeman Publs Inc 500 Howard St San Francisco CA 94618 *

MIGLIETTA, JOSEPH HENRY, semiconductor process engineer; b. New Brunswick, N.J., Dec. 6, 1959; s. Joseph Henry and Elvira Leanor (Abadia) M. BS in Chem. Engring., U. Fla., 1985. Research assoc. Coll. Engring. U. Fla., Gainesville, 1983-85; ops. engr. Silicon Systems, Tustin, Calif., 1985—. Mem. RS/1 Users Group, Am. Inst. Chem. Engrs. Republican. Roman Catholic. Home: 224 Collins Ave Newport Beach CA 92662 Office: Silicon Systems 14351 Myford Rd Tustin CA 92680

MIHALY, EUGENE BRAMER, consultant, executive, writer; b. The Hague, Netherlands, Nov. 11, 1934; s. Eddy and Cecile (Bramer) Kahn; 1 stepson, Eugene Mihaly; m. Linda Davis, Oct. 7, 1978; children: Lisa Klee, Jessica; 1 stepson, Russell C. DuBrow. A.B. magna cum laude, Harvard U., 1956; Ph.D., London Sch. Econs. and Polit. Sci., 1964. Aviation/space editor Hartford (Conn.) Courant, 1960-61; internat. economist AID, Washington, 1964-65; dep. dir. Peace Corps, Tanzania, 1966, dir., 1967-68; dep. dir. East Asia/Pacific bur. Peace Corps, Washington, 1969, dir. office program devel., evalutaion and research, 1969-70; asso. dir. Inst. Internat. Studies, U. Calif., Berkeley, 1970-72; pres. Mihaly Internat. Corp., 1972—; adv. bd. World Resources Inst.; mem. U.S. nat. com. Pacific Econ. Coop. Author: Foreign Aid and Politics in Nepal: A Case Study, 1965; contbr.: Political Development in Micronesia, 1974, Management of the Multinationals, 1974; also articles to various publs. Bd. dirs. Internat. Vol. Services Inc., Foster Parents Plan, Inc.; trustee World Affairs Council No. Calif., World Without War Council; pres. Pacific-Indonesia C. of C.; dep. chmn. Nigeria-U.S. Bus. Council. Served to lt. (j.g.) USNR, 1956-59. Mem. Soc. Internat. Devel., Amnesty Internat., Signet Soc., Com. Fgn. Relations. Clubs: Harvard (N.Y.C. and San Francisco). Home: 18 Manzanita Pl Mill Valley CA 94941 Office: 116 Caledonia St Sausalito CA 94965

MIHAN, RICHARD, dermatologist; b. Los Angeles, Dec. 20, 1925; s. Arnold and Virginia Catharine (O'Reilly) M.; student U. So. Calif., 1945; M.D., St. Louis U., 1949. Rotating intern Los Angeles County Gen. Hosp., 1949-51, resident in dermatology, 1954-57; practice medicine specializing in dermatology, Los Angeles, 1957—; clin. prof. dept. medicine, dermatology and syphilology U. So. Calif. Served as lt. (j.g.) M.C., USNR, 1951-53, ret. as lt. comdr. Diplomate Am. Bd. Dermatology. Fellow ACP; mem. Internat. Soc. Tropical Dermatology, Soc. Investigative Dermatology, Pacific Dermatologic Assn. (exec. bd. 1971-74), Calif. Med. Assn. (chmn. dermatologic sect. 1973-74), AMA, Los Angeles Dermatol. Soc. (pres. 1975-76), Am. Acad. Dermatology, L.A. Acad. Medicines (pres. 1988-89). Office: 1245 Wilshire Blvd Los Angeles CA 90017

MIHELISH, GARY LEE, dentist, insurance consultant; b. Missoula, Mont., Mar. 14, 1942; s. Frank Daniel and Marjorie Lowave (Winschell) M.; m. Sandra Kay Miller, Aug. 15, 1965; children: Kurt, Kyle. BS in Pre-Medicine, Mont. State U., 1964; DMD, U. Oreg., 1968. Dental officer Indian Health Service, Lame Deer, Mont., 1969-71; supervising dentist hygiene dept. Carroll Coll., Helena, Mont., 1972-80; pvt. practive dentistry Helena, 1971—; cons. Blue Cross/Blue Shield, Helena, 1987—; bd. dirs. Dirs. Valley Bank, Shodair Children's Specialty Hosp. With USPHS, 1968-71. Recipeint Vol. Service award U.S. Swimming Assn., 1986. Mem. Mont. Dental Assn. (pres. 1982-83), Nat. Fedn. Scholastic Officials Assn. (bd. dirs. 1986—). Lutheran.

MIKALOW, ALFRED ALEXANDER, II, deep sea diver, marine surveyor; b. N.Y.C., Jan. 19, 1921; student Rutgers U., 1940; MS, U. Calif., Berkeley, 1948; MA, Rochdale U. (Can.), 1950; m. Janice Brenner, Aug. 1, 1960; children: Alfred Alexander, Jon Alfred. Owner Coastal Diving Co., Oakland, Calif., 1950—, Divers Supply, Oakland, 1952—; dir. Coastal Sch. Deep Sea Diving, Oakland, 1950—; capt. and master rsch. vessel Coastal Researcher I; mem. Marine Inspection Bur., Oakland. marine diving contractor, cons. Mem. adv. bd. Medic Alert Found., Turlock, Calif., 1960—. Lt. comdr. USN, 1941-47, 49-50. Decorated Purple Heart, Silver Star. Mem. Divers Assn. Am. (pres. 1970-74), Treasury Recovery, Inc. (pres. 1972-75), Internat. Assn. Profl. Divers, Assn. Diving Contractors, Calif. Assn. Pvt. Edn. (no. v.p. 1971-72), Authors Guild, Internat. Game Fish Assn., U.S. Navy League, U.S. Res. Officers Assn., Tailhook Assn., Explorer Club (San Francisco), Calif. Assn. Marine Surveyors (pres. 1988—), Masons, Lions. Author: Fell's Guide to Sunken Treasure Ships of the World, 1972; (with H. Rieseberg) The Knight from Maine, 1974. Office: 320 29th Ave Oakland CA 94601

MIKEL, THOMAS KELLY, JR, laboratory administrator; b. East Chicago, Ind., Aug. 27, 1946; s. Thomas Kelly and Anne Katherine (Vrazo) M.; B.A., San Jose State U., 1973; M.A., U. Calif.-Santa Barbara, 1975. Asst. dir. Santa Barbara Underseas Found., 1975-76; marine biologist PJB Labs., Ventura, Calif., 1976-81; lab. dir. CRL Environ., Ventura, 1981-88; lab. dir. ABC Labs, Ventura, 1988—; instr. oceanography Ventura Coll., 1980-81. With U.S. Army, 1968-70. Mem. Assn. Environ. Profls., Soc. Population Ecologists, ASTME (rsch. contbr. 10th ann. symposium 1986). Biol. coord.Anacapa Underwater Natural trail U.S. Nat. Park Svc., 1976; designer ecol. restoration program of upper Newport Bay, Orange County, Calif., 1978; rsch. contbr. 3d Internat. Artificial Reef Conf., Newport Beach, Calif., 1983, Ann. Conf. Am. Petroleum Inst., Houston. Democrat.

MIKHAIL, MARY ATTALLA, computer systems development executive; b. Cairo, Eqypt, Apr. 2, 1945; came to U.S., 1980.; d. Attalla Shehata and Soad (Kamel) Abd-El-Malek; m. Ibrahim Fahmy Mikhail, May 1 ,1967; 1 child, Ireny. BS in Math. and Physics, U. Assiut, Egypt, 1965; MS in Math. and Computer Sci., U. Clausthal, Fed. Republic Germany, 1973; PhD in Math., U. Tuebingen, Fed. Republic Germany, 1976. Lectr. Math. Inst., Assiut, Egypt, 1965-67; from instr. to asst. prof. Math. Inst., Tuebingen, Fed. Republic Germany, 1973-78; cons., project mgr. Datel, Fed. Republic Germany, 1978-80; planner, systems analyst C.F. Braun, Alhambra, Calif., 1980-82; optic dept. mgr. Burroughs Corp., City of Industry, Calif., 1982-87; project mgr. continuous transaction processing Unysys Corp., Mission Viejo, Calif., 1987—. Contbr. articles to profl. jours. Mem. IEEE (standards for software error, faults and failures com., standards for quality metrics com.), Am. Mgmt. Assn. Mem. Coptic Orthodox Ch.

MIKKELSEN, RICKI BARNER, educational administrator; b. Sanger, Calif., Nov. 7, 1944; d. Ed B. and Verdanel (Phillips) Barner; m. Donald Eugene Mikkelsen, Dec. 9, 1942. BA in Social Scis., Calif. State U., 1966; MA in Adminstrn., Calif. Luth. U., 1974. Tchr., Simi Valley Unified Sch. Dist., Calif., 1966-69; resource tchr. Timbe Sch. Dist., Newbury Park, Calif., 1969-74; gifted resource specialist Conejo Valley Unified Sch. Dist., Thousand Oaks, Calif., 1974-75, early childhood edn. program coord., 1975-78; tchr. ctr. coord. Ventura County Supt. Schs. Office, Ventura/Santa Barbara, Calif., 1978-81; diagnostic ctr. dir. Calif. Luth. U., Thousand Oaks, 1981-82, asst. dean continuing edn., spl. programs, 1981-87, pres. materials workshop, 1987—; cons., lectr. in field. Mem. Assn. Supervision and Curriculum Devel., Assn. Continuing Higher Edn. (past regional pres.), Am. Assn. Higher Edn., AAUW (bd. dirs.), Am. Soc. Trainers and Developers, Conejo Future Found. (chmn. bd. dirs.), Creative Options (co-chmn.), Internat. Reading Assn., Ventura County Reading Assn. (bd. dirs.), Assn. Adult and Continuing Edn. and Coun. for Continuing Edn. Unit, Bullock's Adv. Bd., Phi Delta Kappa, Delta Kappa Kappa. Home: 461 S Havenside Newbury Park CA 91320 Office: Calif Luth Coll Thousand Oaks CA 91360

MIKLOS, MARK ANTHONY, avionics systems engineer; b. Pitts., Mar. 7, 1952; s. Anthony Richard and Regina Louise (Thomas) M.; m. Elinor Marie Lillie, Aug. 2, 1987; children: Christopher, Brian. BS in Internat. Affairs, U.S. Air Force Acad., 1974; MS in Systems Mgmt., U. Southern Calif., 1981. Commd. USAF, 1974, advanced through grades to capt., resigned, 1981; avionics systems engr. Rockwell Internat., Downey, Calif., 1981—. Republican. Roman Catholic. Home: 25 Candlewood Way Buena Park CA 90621 Office: Rockwell Internat 12214 Lakewood Blvd Downey CA 90241

MIKOTA, WENDY LYNNE, teacher; b. Vancouver, Wash., Jan. 22, 1949; d. Max Mayer and Theresa Elizabeth (Simon) Kessler; m. Roger Joseph Mikota, Mar. 12, 1972; children: Kindra Bethany, Joshua Mayer. BE, Cen. Wash. State U., 1971; BA, Portland State U., 1975; MA in Counseling, Lewis and Clark Coll., 1988. Tchr. Vancouver Sch. Dist., 1972-75, 78—; counselor Vancouver Sch. Dist., 1988-89; therapist Cath. Community Svcs., 1988-89. Faculty rep. Parent-Tchr. Assn., Vancouver, 1984; active Student at Risk, Vancouver, 1988. Mem. PTA (1988 Elsie Johnson award), Wash. State Sch. Counselors Assn., Southwest Wash. Assn. Young Children. Jewish. Home: 12501 NW 17th Ave Vancouver WA 98685

MIKULKA, BOHUSLAV EDUARD, battery separators company executive; b. Velka Bystrice, Czechoslovakia, Apr. 7, 1925; s. Bohuslav and Anna (Langer) M.; B.S., U. Tharandt, Eberswalde, Germany, 1942-44; postgrad. U. Brno, Czechoslovakia, 1945-48; M. Forest Engring., Hochschule fur Bodenkultur, Vienna, Austria, 1951; Ph.D., Swiss Fed. Inst. Tech., Zurich, 1955, Inst. Wood Tech., Munich and Braunschweig, Germany, 1955; m. Maja Doris Eimer, July 25, 1956; 1 dau., Ann Elizabeth. Came to U.S., 1955, naturalized, 1961. Research assoc. Swiss Fed. Inst. Tech., 1951-55; with Temple Industries, Inc., Diboll, Tex., 1956-65; with Evans Products Co., Evanite, Inc., 1965—, dir. research and devel., mgr., Doswell, Va., 1969-71, mgr. tech. and engring. center, Corvallis, Oreg., 1971-77, dir. tech., 1977-79, v.p., dir. tech., dir. licensing, 1979—. Mem. tech. com. Insulation Bd. Inst., 1959-60; pres. Student Assn. Brno, 1947-49, Czechoslovakia Student Assn., Zurich, 1951-55, U. Free Europe, Strasbourg, France, 1953-55. Mem. Forest Products Research Soc., Nat. Particleboard Assn. (tech. com. 1964-65), Am. Hardboard Assn. (tech. com. 1971—). Home: 2917 NW Angelica Corvallis OR 97330

MILAM, BOBBY EUGENE, insurance executive; b. McCrory, Ark., July 16, 1945; s. John Wesley and Eleasin Ann (Williamson) M.; m. Billie Jean Williams, Jan. 1970 (div. 1974); m. Karen Sue Terry, May 10, 1975; 1 child, Matthew Joseph. Grad. high sch., Swayzee, Ind. Adjuster George A. White-Custard Agys., Marion, Ind., 1967-69; adjuster Transamerica Ins. Co., Jackson, Mich., 1969-71, claims mgr., 1971-74; br. claims mgr., then regional claims mgr. Transamerica Ins. Group, St. Louis, 1980-85; v.p. claims Transamerica Ins. Group, L.A., 1985—. With U.S. Army, 1963-66. Mem. CPCU Soc., Elks, Masons, Shriners. Republican. Home: 6318 Capricorn Ave Agoura Hills CA 91301 Office: TransAm Ins Group 6300 Canoga Ave Woodland Hills CA 91367

MILANI, MICHELLE MARIE, entrepreneur; b. Omaha, Dec. 17, 1953; d. Douglas Pasquale and Philomena (Baum) M. BSc in Acctg., U. Santa Clara, Calif., 1976; postgrad., Golden Gate U. Sr. lending officer Bank of Am., Santa Clara, 1974-83; v.p. fin. and adminstrn. T.M.E., Inc., Santa Clara, 1983-85. Mem. Rep. Nat. Com., Washington, 1982—. Mem. Am. Soc. Interior Designers, Ducks Unltd. Roman Catholic. Home and Office: 2815 Lantz Ave San Jose CA 95124

MILANOVICH, NORMA JOANNE, occupational educator; b. Littlefork, Minn., June 4, 1945; d. Lyle Albert and Loretta (Leona) Drake; m. Rudolph William Milanovich, Mar. 18, 1943; 1 child, Rudolph William Jr. BS in Home Econs., U. Wis., Stout, 1968; MA in Curriculum and Instrn., U. Houston, 1973, EdD in Curriculum and Program Devel., 1982. Instr. human services U. Houston, 1971-75; dir. videos project U. N.Mex., Albuquerque, 1976-78, dir. vocat. edn. equity ctr., 1978-84, asst. prof. tech. occupational edn., 1982—, coord. occupational vocat. edn. programs, 1983-85, dir. consortium rsch. and devel. in occupational edn., 1984-89; pres. The Alpha Connection, Inc., Albuquerque, 1989—; adj. instr. Cen. Tng. Acad. Dept. Energy, Wackenhut; adj. faculty So. Ill. U., Lesley Coll., Boston. Author: Handbook for Vocational-Technical Certification in New Mexico, 1985, Model Equitable Behavior in the Classroom, 1983, Frustration Is..., We The Arcturians, 1989; editor: A Handbook for Handling Conflict in the Classroom, 1983, Choosing What's Best for You, 1982, Starting Out...A Job Finding Handbook for Teen Parents, Going To Work...Job Rights for Teens, Modeling Equitable Behavior in the Classroom, 1988. Bd. dirs. Albuquerque Single Parent Occupational Scholarship Program, 1984-86; del. Youth for Understanding Internat. Program, 1985-89; tour dir. Interatn. Studies Tours Abroad to Japan, Austria, Korea, Mex., India Australia, New Zealand and Germany, 1984-88; mem. adv. bd. Southwestern Indian Poly. Inst., 1984-88; com. mem. Region VI Consumer Exchange Com., 1982-84. Grantee N.Mex. Dept. Edn., 1976-78, 78-86, 83-86, HEW, 1979, 80, 81, 83, 84, 85, 86, 87, JTPA Strategic Mktg. Plan. Mem. NAFE, Am. Vocat. Assn., Vocat. Edn. Equity Coun., Nat. Coalition for Sex Equity Edn., Am. Home Econs. Assn., Inst. Noctic Scis., N.Mex. Home Econs. Assn.Am. Soc. for Tng. and Devel., N.Mex. Vocat. Edn. Assn., N.Mex. Coun. on Vocat Edn., Greater Albuquerque C. of C., Phi Delta Kappa, Phi Upsilon Omicron, Phi Theta Kappa. Democrat. Roman Catholic.

MILAVSKY, HAROLD PHILLIP, real estate executive; b. Limerick, Sask., Can., Jan. 25, 1931; s. Jack and Clara Milavsky. B in Commerce, U. Sask., Saskatoon, Can., 1953. Chief acct., treas., controller Loram Internat. Ltd. div. Mannix Co. Ltd., Calgary, Alta., Can., 1956-65; v.p., chief fin. officer Power Corp. Devels. Ltd., Calgary, Alta., Can., 1965-69; exec. v.p., bd. dirs. Great West Internat. Equities Ltd. (name now Trizec Corp. Ltd.), Calgary, Alta., Can., 1969-76; former pres., now chmn., chief exec. officer, bd. dirs. Trizec Corp. Ltd., Calgary, Alta., Can., 1976—; bd. dirs. Trizec Corp. related cos., Brascan Ltd., Toronto, Can., Carena-Bancorp Inc., Toronto, The Rouse Co., Columbia, Md., Ernest C. Hahn Inc., San Diego, London Life Ins. Co., London, Bramalea Ltd., Toronto, Hees Internat., Toronto, Biotech. Internat. Can. Inc., Calgary, Coscan Devel. Corp., Toronto, Saskatchewan Oil & Gas Corp., Regina, Nova Corp. Alberta, Calgary, Amoco Can., Calgary, Internat. Trade Adv. Com., Toronto. Dir. Terry Fox Humanitarian Award Program; past dir. Conf. Bd. Can.; past gov., Acctg. Edn. Found. Alta.; mem. Chancellor's Club, U. Calgary. Fellow Inst. Chartered Accts. Alta.; mem. Inst. Chartered Accts. Sask. and Alta., Can. Inst. Pub. Real Estate Cos. (past pres., bd. dirs.), Can. C. of C. (past chmn.), Internat. Profl. Hockey Alumni (founder). Clubs: Petroleum, Ranchmen's, Glenmore Racquet (Calgary). Office: Trizec Corp Ltd, 700 2nd St SW #3000, Calgary, AB Canada T2P 2W2

MILBERY, JAMES MARTIN, production engineer; b. Providence, R.I., June 13, 1949; s. James Martin and Carolyn Marie (Whittaker) M.; m. Rene Irma O'Neill, Sept. 20, 1980; children: Genevieve, Joshua, Trevor. BA in History, U. R.I., 1967; AS in Electronics, Long Beach City Coll., 1978; MA in Mgmt., U. Redlands, 1987. Journeyman electronics mechanic Dept. Navy, Long Beach, Calif., 1975-81; quality assurance specialist Dept. Def., Inglewood, Calif., 1981-82; quality test engr. Hughes Aircraft, Torrance, Calif., 1982-84; mem. tech. staff Rockwell Internat., Seal Beach, Calif., 1984—. Served with USN, 1971-75. Mem. Nat. Mgmt. Assn. Mormon. Home: 6890 E 11th St Long Beach CA 90815-4934 Office: Rockwell Internat PO Box 3644 Seal Beach CA 90740-7644

MILDON, JAMES LEE, author, photojournalist; b. San Francisco, Jan. 5, 1936; s. James Lee and Jeannette Marie (Balandras) M.; B.A. cum laude, Calif. State U. at San Francisco, 1963; M.A., U. Nev. at Reno, 1970; m. Marie Roberta Wilson, Sept. 17, 1958; children—Laura Marie Jeannette. Owner Jim Mildon: Images, Ink, Reno, 1969—; v.p. Frank & Mildon, Assos., Reno, 1971—; mgmt. cons. Western Electric Co., 1972; devel. cons. Vacation Plan Ltd., 1971—; instr. photojournalism U. Nev., 1974-83. Served with Army Security Agy., AUS, 1959-60. Mem. Profl. Photographers Assn. Am., Nat. Profl. Photographers Assn., Phi Kappa Phi, Alpha Kappa Nu, Beta Phi Gamma. Author: (with others) Portland, The City Across the River, 1972. Pub., editor, co-author: My World to Share, 1982. Illustrator: Newswriting: From Lead to 30, 1977. Address: 9135 Spearhead Way Reno NV 89506

MILDWURM, RUTH ANN, teacher; b. San Francisco, Feb. 20, 1952; d. John R. and Ruth (Crews) Smith; m. Alan W. Mildwurm, Dec. 21, 1975; children: Jessica, Rebecca, Jason. BA, U. San Francisco, 1974; cert. in teaching, 1975. Tchr. St. Anselm Sch., Diocese of Oakland, Kentfield, Calif., 1975-78, St. Agnes Sch., Concord, Calif., 1978-80. Mem. AAUW (cultural affairs rep. San Ramon, Calif. chpt. 1987--). Republican. Home: 10015 Toby Rd San Ramon CA 94503

MILES, DOUGLAS IRVING, clergyman, pastor; b. Balt., Apr. 10, 1949; s. Walter Arthur Harris and Odessa Roberta (Southers) Miles; m. Rosanna White, Nov. 14, 1971; children: Harvey Eugene, Dante Kwiyisi. BA, Johns Hopkins U., 1970; MA in Theology, St. Mary's Sem., Balt., 1981; DD, Va. Coll. and Sem., 1980. Community organizer Neighborhood Action Group, Balt., 1968-70; asst. pastor St. Mark's United Meth. Ch., Balt., 1970-71; dir. consultation and edn. Provident Community Mental Health Ctr., Balt., 1971-72; co-dir. Inst. Constrn., Balt., 1972-74; branch mgr. First Nat. Bank Md., Balt., 1974-75; dir. United Way Cen. md., Balt., 1975-76; community relations officer Mass Transit Adminstrn., Balt., 1976-78; pub. relations dir. Project P.L.A.S.E., Balt., 1978-80; pastor Brown's Meml. Bapt. Ch., Balt., 1973-88, Calvary C.M.E. Ch., Pasadena, Calif., 1988-89, Greenwood C.M.E. Ch., Memphis, 1989—. Pres. Interdenominational Ministerial Alliance, Balt., 1985-87; exec. com. mem. Baltimoreans United in Leadership Devel., 1982-88; 2nd. v.p. Balt. NAACP, 1983-84; sec. Interdenominational Ministerial Alliance, Pasadena, Calif., 1988—. Recipient PLAQUE Pub. Spirit award People Not Politics, 1982, Outstanding Leadership award Bapt. Ministers Conf., 1985, Outstanding Service award Park Heights Community Corp., 1987, Outstanding Leadership award Ainsworth Paint & Chem. Corp., 1986. Mem. Progressive Nat. Bapt. Collentica (instr. 1983-88), Hampton Inst. Minister's Conf. (bd. dirs. 1988—), NAACP (2nd v.p., 1983-84), So. Calif. Annual Conf. CMB (dir. evangelism 1988—), Interdenominational Ministerial Alliance (sec. 1988—), Fulton Heights Club (pres. 1973, 80). Democrat. Baptist.

MILES, LAWRENCE EDWARD, naval officer; b. Salina, Kans., July 8, 1955; s. Lewis George and Phyllis Roberta (Blank) M. BA, Lewis and Clark Coll., 1977; MA, U. Kans., 1982. Tchr. elem. schs. Olathe, Kans., 1980-81; chemist Hercules Inc., DeSoto, Kans., 1981-82; commd. ensign USN, 1982, advanced through grades to lt., 1985; substance abuse counselor USN, Guam, 1984-85. Mem. Am. Chem. Soc., U.S. Naval Inst. Republican. Mem. Ch. of Christ. Home: 2521 N Brynwood Santa Ana CA 92701

MILES, SAMUEL ISRAEL, psychiatrist; b. Munich, Mar. 4, 1949; came to U.S., 1949; s. Henry and Renee (Ringel) M.; m. Denise Marie Robey, June 26, 1977; children: Jonathan David, Justin Alexander. BS, CCNY, 1970; MD, N.Y. Med. Coll., 1974; PhD, So. Calif. Psychoanalytic Inst., 1986. Diplomate Am. Bd. Psychiatry and Neurology. Intern D.C. Gen. Hosp., Washington, 1974-75; resident in psychiatry Cedars-Sinai Med. Ctr., Los Angeles, 1975-78; practice medicine specializing in psychiatry Los Angeles, 1978—; ind. med. examiner Calif. Dept. Indsl. Relations, 1984—; asst. clin. prof. psychiatry UCLA Sch. Medicine, 1978—; attending psychiatrist Cedars-Sinai Med. Ctr., 1978—, co-chmn. utilization rev. and quality assurance com. dept. psychiatry, 1984—, mem. in-patient adv. com., 1983-85, 87— psychiatry adv. com., 1984-86; attending psychiatrist Brotman Med. Ctr., Culver City, Calif., 1978—; faculty mem. So. Calif. Psychoanalytic Inst., 1986—. Fellow Am. Acad. Psychoanalysis, Am. Orthopsychiat. Assn.; mem. Acad. Psychiatry and the Law, So. Calif. Psychiat. Soc. (council rep. 1985-88, chair pvt. practice com. 1988-89), So. Calif. Soc. Adolescent Psychiatry (treas. 1980-81), So. Calif. Psychoanalytic Inst. (pres. clin. assocs. orgn. 1981-82). Jewish. Office: 8631 W 3d St #425E Los Angeles CA 90048

MILGRIM, DARROW A., insurance agent, recreational and educational consultant; b. Chgo., Apr. 30, 1945; s. David and Miriam (Glickman) M.; m. Gail de Boers (div. 1978); m. Laurie Stevens, Apr. 15, 1984; children: Derick, Jared. BA, Calif. State U., San Bernardino, 1968; postgrad., U. So. Calif., 1972. Accredited ins. advisor; cert. sch. adminstr. Tchr. Rialto (Calif.) Unified Sch. Dist., 1969-70, Las Virgines Unified Sch. Dist., Westlake Village, Calif., 1970-78; instr. Calif. State U., Northridge, Calif., 1980-84; ins. agt. Speare Ins. Co., Santa Monica, Calif., 1984—; bd. dirs. Calamigos Star C Ranch Summer Camp, Malibu, Calif, Calimagos Environ. Edn. Ctr., Malibu, Wilderness Inst., Los Angeles. Editor: Legislation and Regulations for Organized Camps, 1987. Pres. Calif. Camping Adv. Council, Long Beach, 1985-87; bd. dirs. Calif. Collaboration for Youth, Sacramento, 1985—, Indep. Camp Nat. Adv. Commn., Sickle Cell Disease Research Found. Camp, Los Angeles, 1985—; commr. dept. parks & recreation City of Agoura Hills (Calif.), 1987—; cons. So. Calif. Children's Cancer Services, Los Angeles, 1986—. Mem: Am. Camping Assn. (bd. dirs. So. Calif. sect., regional honor, 1986, vice chmn. nat. legis. com. Martinsville, Ind., 1980—). Office: Speare and Co Ins Brokers 2600 Colorado Ave #100 Santa Monica CA 90404

MILKS-MARTIN, MARTE ELIZABETH, contractor; b. Lansing, Mich., July 4, 1951; d. Malcolm Leonard and June Elizabeth (McIntosh) Milks; m. William Arden Martin, July 4, 1986; children: Jesse Cheyenne, Taylor Lansing. BFA, Mich. State U., 1975; postgrad., Lansing Community Coll., 1975-80, Coll. of Martin, Kentfield, Calif., 1985--. Community planner State of Mich. Dept. Labor, Lansing, 1976-77; exec. dir. Lansing Art Gallery, 1977-80; owner Milks Painters & Decorators, San Anselmo, Calif., 1980—; cons. Willilam A. Martin, Gen. Contractor, Ross, Calif., 1986--, Lansing Art Gallery & Art Ctr., 1980-81. Active various polit. campaigns, various charitable orgns. Grantee City of Lansing, 1977-80, Nat. Endowments for Arts, 1979, Oldsmobile, 1979, Mich. Mus. Assn., 1979. Mem. Am. Trade Assn., League Women Voters, Humane Farming Assn. Democrat. Office: Milks Painters & Decorators PO Box 2669 San Anselmo CA 94960

MILLAGE, STEVE ALAN, manufacturing executive; b. Charleston, Ill., Mar. 4, 1951; s. Leo and Eleanor Josephine (Taylor) M.; m. Patricia DeRuyter, Aug. 14, 1987. BA, Eastern Ill. U., 1975. Dist. mgr. Teledyne-McKay, Portland, Oreg., 1979-80, Cleve., 1980-81; sr. dist. mgr. Teledyne-McKay, Chgo., 1981-83; Western regional mgr. Teledyne-McKay, L.A., 1983-84, sales mgr., 1984-87, nat. accounts mhr., 1987—. Mem. Am. Welding Soc. (chmn. Long Beach/Orange County chpts. 1987-89, chmn. liason com. with internat. welding show 1989—), Sigma Tau Gamma (pres. interfraternity coun. 1971-72). Office: Teledyne McKay 19913 Beach Blvd Ste 131 Huntington Beach CA 92648

MILLAR, WILLIAM STUART, aerospace educator; b. Pasadena, Calif., Mar. 22, 1939; s. David Nielson and Jean Borland (Wyper) M.; m. Bonnie Jean Morris, July 10, 1959; children: Catherine, Alan, Heather. AA, Pasadena CityColl., 1959; AS, Glendale (Calif.) Coll., 1961; BA, BS, Moody Inst., Chgo., 1965; MA Philosophy & Religion, Coll. Notre Dame, Belmont, Calif., 1984. Lic. airline pilot, flight navigator. Aircraft maintenance inspector Butler Aviation, Chgo., 1964-66; charter pilot Kenmore Air Harbor, Seattle, 1966-68; airline pilot Pan Am. Airlines, San Francisco, 1968-87; aero instr. City Coll. San Francisco, 1970-78, aero chmn., 1978—; aerospace edn. cons., 1980—; gunmaker Scottish Pistols Mus. Replicas. Educator Presbyn. Ch., San Mateo, Calif., 1980—. Mem. Airline Pilots Assn., Am. Sci. Assn., Am. Fedn. Tchrs., Arm and Armour Soc. London, Firearms Engravers Guild Am. Republican. Office: City Coll San Francisco San Francisco Internat Airport San Francisco CA 94128

MILLARD, CHARLES ALLEN, manufacturing executive; b. Flint, Mich., Nov. 24, 1942; s. William Pierce and Mary (Allen) M.; m. Christine Takahashi, Mar. 21, 1975; 1 child, Charles Allen Jr. BA in Physics, Vanderbilt U., 1968; MS, Naval Postgrad., Monterey, Calif., 1976; MS in Bus., Cen. Mich. U., 1982. Enlisted USMC, 1962, commd. 2d. lt., 1968, advanced through grades to major, 1978, ret., 1982; sr. analyst FMC Corp., Santa Clara, Calif., 1983; system enging. mgr. FMC Corp., Santa Clara, 1984-85, tech. planning mgr., 1986-87, bus. ops. mgr., 1988, ops. rsch. and system analysis mgr., 1989—. Author numerous tech. reports. Active Dist. Planning Commn., San Jose, Calif., 1984. Decorated Meritorious Service medal. Mem. Mgmt. Sci. Inst., Ops. Research Soc., Mil. Ops. Research Soc. (group chmn. 1978). Republican. Lutheran. Office: FMC Corp 881 Martin Ave Santa Clara CA 95052

MILLARD, GEORGE RICHARD, bishop; b. Dunsmuir, Calif., Oct. 2, 1914; s. George Ellis and Constance (Rainsberry) M.; m. Mary Louise Gessling, June 29, 1939; children: George, Martha, Joseph. A.B., U. Calif.-Berkeley, 1936; B.D., Episcopal Theol. Sch., Cambridge, Mass., 1938; S.T.M., Pacific Sch. Religion, 1958; D.D., Ch. Div. Sch. Pacific, 1960; M.A., U. Santa Clara, 1983. Ordained to ministry Episcopal Ch. as priest 1938. Asst. in Episc. Ch., N.Y.C., 1938-39, Waterbury, Conn., 1930-40; rector in Episc. Ch., Danbury, Conn., 1940-50, Alameda, Calif., 1951-59; suffragan bishop Episc. Diocese Calif., 1960-76; bishop of San Jose, 1969-76; exec., venture in mission program, exec. council Episc. Ch., 1977-78; bishop in charge Am. Chs. in Europe, 1978-80, bishop in charge ch. divinity sch. pacific exec. office for alumni/ae affairs, 1978-80; dean Convocation of Oakland, Calif., 1957-60; chmn. dept. missions Diocese Calif., 1958-60; mem. Joint Commn. on Structure, Episc. Ch., 1967-76; pres. bd. Strong Environ. Ctr. Chmn. Maria Kip Orphange; chmn. devel. program U. Calif. at Berkeley Student Coop. Assn., 1966; coordinator Ch. Div. Sch. Pacific Alumni Affairs, 1986-88.

MILLARD, JAMES MICHAEL, oral surgeon; b. San Bernardino, Calif., Sept. 16, 1945; s. Joseph Eugene and Patricia Isabel (Gormley) M.; m. Nancy Jeanne Bedwell, June 15, 1968; children: Timothy, Meridith, Megan, Matthew. DDS, UCLA, 1970. Resident in oral and maxillofacial surgery Highland Hosp., Oakland, Calif., 1973-77; pvt. practice oral and maxillofacial surgery, Wenatchee, Wash., 1977-78; pvt. practice, Spokane, Wash., 1978—; cons. VA Med. Ctr., Spokane, 1979—. Capt. USAF, 1970-73. Fellow Am. Assn. Oral Maxillofacial Surgeons, Am. Coll. Oral Maxillofacial Surgeons; mem. ADA, Wash. State Dental Assn., Spokane Dist. Dental Soc. (pres. 1988—), Wash. State Soc. Oral Maxillofacial Surgeons, Western Soc. Oral Maxillofacial Surgeons, Rotary. Republican. Roman Catholic. Home: 8928 Day Rd E Mead WA 99021 Office: 123 Francis W Spokane WA 99205

MILLARD, KENNETH REIMANN, SR., architect; b. Salt Lake City, May 26, 1930; s. Vern Bryan and Laura Aurelia (Reimann) M.; m. Patricia Jordan Walton, Nov. 25, 1958 (div. Feb. 1977); children: Kenneth Reimann Jr., Vern Dyke, John Walton, Patricia Jacqueline, Jennifer Michelle; m. Carolyn Lee Sorensen, Dec. 29, 1977; children: Noel Yvette, Lee Sorensen, Mark Hugh. BFA, U. Utah, 1954, BArch., 1958; student, U. Wash., 1954-55; M in Regional Planning, Cornell U., 1960. Registered architect, Utah, Calif., Ariz., Nev. Dir. planning and engring. Provo (Utah) Mcpl. Corp., 1960-61; dir. planning S.W. Snohomish County (Wash.) Joint Planning Council, 1962; sr. planner Williams & Mocine, San Francisco, 1963-64; constrn. supr. Mormon Ch., France and Belgium, 1964-66; resident architect Nauvoo (Ill.) Restoration, 1966-67; pres. Millard Cons., Salt Lake City, 1967—; adj. prof. Brigham Young U., Provo, 1968-78. Author/editor Master Plans for numerous municipalities., counties, and Great Salt Lake, 1960—, Land Development Code for Utah Counties and Municipalities (annual edits.), 1973—. City councilman N. Salt Lake City Corp., 1984—. Served with U.S. Army, 1956-57. Mem. AIA, Am. Inst. Cert. Planners, Rotary (pres. Sugar House club 1989-90,, Nat. Assn. Ptnrs. Ams. (pres.), Utah-Bolivia Ptnrs. (pres. 1988-90). Republican. Mormon. Home: 745 Independence Way North Salt Lake UT 84054 Office: Millard Cons 2200 S 9th East St Salt Lake City UT 84106-1836

MILLARD, LAVERGNE HARRIET, free-lance artist; b. Chgo., July 8, 1925; d. Lewis and Julia (Smolk) Bassmire; student Chgo. Art Inst., 1937-39; m. Samuel Costales, 1943 (div. 1957); m. Bailey Millard, Mar. 9, 1958 (div.); children—Bryan Lewis Costales, Julianne, Juanita Crump, Candace Lynn Millard. Cocktail waitress Verdis, Grant Street, Concord, Calif., 1955-61; mgr. used book shop Joyce Book Shop, Concord, 1964-79, seller art works, own prints; freelance artist, 1979—. Recipient ribbons local fairs, art shows. Republican. Copyright holder for pastel art work. Home and Office: 1890 Farm Bureau Rd Apt 11 Concord CA 94519

MILLARD, MALCOLM STUART, lawyer; b. Highland Park, Ill., Mar. 22, 1914; s. Everett L. and Elizabeth (Boynton) M.; m. Sally Metzger, Sept. 15, 1976 (dec. Dec. 1986); 1 child, Anne W. Benjamin. BA, Harvard U., 1936; JD, Northwestern U., 1939. Bar: Ill. 1939, Calif. 1951. Ptnr. Farr & Millard, Carmel, Calif., 1951-55, Millard, Tourangeau, Morris & Staples, P.C., Carmel, 1955—; dir. Leslie Salt Co., 1975-81. Trustee Community Hosp. of Monterey Peninsula, 1982—, Monterey Inst. Fgn. Studies, 1955-76; pres. Community Chest of Monterey Peninsula, 1958. Served to lt. USN, 1943-46. Mem. Monterey Inst. Internat. Relations (hon. lifetime trustee 1982—), Ill. State Bar, Calif. State Bar, Monterey County Bar Assn. (pres.), Old Capital Club, Harvard Club. Office: Millard Tourangeau Morris & Staples PO Box 5427 Carmel CA 93921

MILLARD, NEAL STEVEN, lawyer; b. Dallas, June 6, 1947; s. Bernard and Adele (Marks) M.; m. Holly Ann Hinman, Dec. 30, 1970. BA cum laude, UCLA, 1969; JD, U. Chgo., 1972. Bar: Calif. 1972, U.S. Dist. Ct. (cen. dist.) Calif. 1973, U.S. Tax Ct. 1973, U.S. Ct. Appeals (9th cir.) 1987. Assoc. Willis, Butler & Schiefly, Los Angeles, 1972-75; ptnr. Morrison & Foerster, Los Angeles, 1975-84, Jones, Day, Reavis & Pogue, Los Angeles, 1984—; instr. Calif. State Coll., San Bernardino, 1975-76; lectr. Practising Law Inst., N.Y.C., 1983—, Calif. Edn. of Bar, 1987—. Mem. citizens adv. com. Los Angeles Olympics, 1982-84; trustee Altadena (Calif.) Library Dist., 1985-86; bd. dirs. Woodcraft Rangers, Los Angeles, 1982—, pres., 1986-88. Served to capt. U.S. Army, 1970-72. Mem. ABA, Calif. Bar Assn., Los Angeles County Bar Assn. (trustee 1985-87), Pub. Counsel (bd. dirs. 1984-87), U. Chgo. Law Alumni Assn. (So. Calif. chpt. bd. dirs. 1981—), Phi Beta Kappa, Pi Gamma Mu, Phi Delta Phi. Club: Altadena Town and County. Office: Jones Day Reavis & Pogue 355 S Grand Ave Ste 3000 Los Angeles CA 90071

MILLEGAN, ROBERT ALLEN, small business owner; b. Washington, Sept. 22, 1949; s. Lloyd Sidney and Ellen Eudora (Woodworth) M.; m. Lynn Louise Goldsmith, Dec. 20, 1968 (div. Sept. 1973); children: Laurie Corina, Julia Selina; m. Mary Johanna Hale, Feb. 14, 1987. Grad. high sch., McMinville, Oreg. Owner Long Hair Music Faucet, Portland, Oreg., 1967-71; clk. King Harvest Natural Foods, Portland, 1971-73; with sales div. Sound/Video Unltd., Portland, 1975-83, All Star Video, Eugene, Oreg., 1983-84, Applianced Video Store, Eugene, 1984-85; owner Video Audio Ventures, Eugene, 1984-85; owner, mktg. dir. Video Audio Systems, Eugene, 1985—. Office: 2911 W 11th Eugene OR 97402

MILLER, ALAN NORMAN, educator; b. N.Y.C., May 12, 1946; s. Edward Robert and Irene Lenore (Goodstein) M.; m. Cheryl Linda Goldfarb, Apr. 14, 1974; 1 child, Emily Sloan. BA, Temple U., 1968; BS, U. N.H., 1970; MBA, Syracuse U., 1972; MPhil., CUNY, 1980, PhD, 1981. Lectr. in mgmt. SUNY, New Paltz, 1973-75; mentor Empire State Coll., 1974-75; asst. prof. mgmt. U. Nev., Las Vegas, 1978-83, assoc. prof. mgmt., 1983-88, prof. mgmt., 1988—; chmn. Newcomers Task Force and Site Selection Com. Western Acad. of Mgmt., mem. program com., 1985-87, mem. program com. Behavior div., 1987-89. Reviewer manuscripts Jour. Applied Psychology and Jour. Managerial Issues; contbr. articles to profl. jours. Pres. Quail Summit Property Owners Assn., Inc. Henderson, Nev. 1987-89; mem. adv. com. The Quality and Productivity Inst. of So. Nev., 1985-88. Rsch. grantee Interstate Bankk Inst., 1988-89. Mem. Am. Psychol. Assn., Soc. for Indsl. and Organizational Psychology, Acad. of Mgmt., Phi Kappa Phi. Office: U Nev 4505 Maryland Pkwy Las Vegas NV 89154

MILLER, ANN KRISTINE, architect; b. Richmond, Va., Mar. 13, 1951; d. Archie W. and Lois (Miller) M. AB, U. Calif., 1973, MArch, 1980; MArch, Harvard U., 1984. Designer ROMA, San Francisco, 1974-75; urban designer Skidmore Owings & Merrill, San Francisco, 1978-79; architect Edward Larrabee Barnes, N.Y.C., 1980-82; project arch./planner The Austin Co., Irvine, Calif., 1985-87; project arch./urban designer Barton Myers Assocs., Los Angeles, 1987—. Mem. Forum for Architecture and Urban Design. Home: 1817 Edgecliffe Dr Los Angeles CA 90026

MILLER, ANNE KATHLEEN, training company executive and technical marketing consultant; b. Denver, Sept. 15, 1942; d. John Henry and Kathryn Elizabeth (Doherty) Meyer; m. Edgar Earle Miller, Aug. 20, 1966 (div. Aug. 1976); children: Sheila Anne, Rebecca Elizabeth; m. Warren Ross Landry, Dec. 11, 1982. BS in Chemistry, St. Mary Coll., Leavenworth, Kans., 1964. Cert. jr. coll., secondary tchr., Calif. Lectr. San Jose (Calif.) U., 1978-82; product mgr. Jasco Chem., Mountain View, Calif., 1979-82; v.p., gen. mgr. Micropel, Hayward, Calif., 1982-84; product mgr. Cambridge Instruments, Santa Clara, Calif., 1984-86; product mktg. mgr. KLA Instruments, Santa Clara, 1986-87; pres., owner Meyland Enterprises, Redwood City, Calif., 1987—, Semiconductor Svc. Tng. Orgn., Redwood City, Calif., 1988—. Inventor formation of optical film. Mem. Soc. Photo Optical Instrumentation Engrs., Am. Chem. Soc., Semiconductor Industry Equipment Materials Inst., Am. Electronics Assn. Office: Meyland/Semiconductor Svcs 735 Hillcrest Way Redwood City CA 94062

MILLER, ANTHONY DOUGLAS, data processing executive; b. Springfield, Ohio, Sept. 9, 1958; s. Edward and Latisha Lou (Zink) M. AA in Bus. Adminstrn., West L.A. Coll., Culver City, 1987; student, Calif. State U., Northridge, 1987—. Operator, programmer Gillespie Furniture, Co., L.A., 1979, programmer, analyst, 1979-80, sr. applications programmer, 1980-81; systems analyst Compex Systems, Inc., Culver City, 1981-84, data processing mgr., 1984—. Mem. COMMON.

MILLER, ARJAY, university dean; b. Shelby, Nebr., Mar. 4, 1916; s. Rawley John and Mary Gertrude (Schade) M.; m. Frances Marion Fearing, Aug. 18, 1940; children: Kenneth Fearing, Ann Elizabeth (Mrs. James Olstad). B.S. with highest honors, UCLA, 1937; LL.D. (hon.), 1964; postgrad., U. Calif.-Berkeley, 1938-40; LL.D. (hon.), Washington U., St. Louis; LL.D., Whitman Coll., 1965, U. Nebr., 1965, Ripon Coll., 1980. Teaching asst. U. Calif. at Berkeley, 1938-40; research technician Calif. State Planning Bd., 1941; economist Fed. Res. Bank San Francisco, 1941-43; asst. treas. Ford Motor Co., 1946-53, controller, 1953-57, v.p., controller, 1957-61, v.p. finance, 1961-62, v.p. of staff group, 1962-63, pres., 1963-68, vice chmn., 1968-69; dean Grad. Sch. Bus., Stanford U., 1969-79, emeritus, 1979—; Mem. Econ. Policy Council UNA.; former chmn. Automobile Mfrs. Assn., Econ. Devel. Corp. Greater Detroit; councillor The Conf. Bd.; past chmn., life trustee Urban Inst.; mem. Public Adv. Commn. on U.S. Trade Policy, 1968-69, Pres.'s Nat. Commn. on Productivity, 1970-74. Trustee Andrew W. Mellon Found., Eisenhower Exchange Fellowship, Brookings Instn., Internat. Exec. Service Corps; bd. dirs. Wm. and Flora Hewlett Found., UN Assn. U.S., S.R.I. Internat.; former pres. Detroit Press Club Found.; former chmn. Bay Area Council. Served from pvt. to capt. USAAF, 1943-46. Recipient Alumnus of Year Achievement award UCLA, 1964; Distinguished Nebraskan award, 1968; Nat. Industry Leader award B'nai B'rith, 1968. Presbyterian. Clubs: Pacific Union, Bohemian.

MILLER, B. J., feature film distributing company executive; b. Cleve., Nov. 13, 1958; d. Lester Theodore and Edith Frances (Dressel) M.; m. Paulo Carlos de Oliveira, July 14, 1984. AB magna cum laude, Brown U., 1980. Pres., owner Gingham Girls & Guys, Cleve., 1972-77; music parlegal Mitchell, Silberberg & Knupp, L.A., 1981; asst. Sotheby Parke Bernet, L.A., 1982; dir. music contracts adminstrn. Columbia Pictures, L.A., 1982-84; dir. adminstrn. Kodiak Films, L.A., 1985-87; v.p. corp. projects Skouras Pictures, Inc., L.A., 1987—. Mem. Women in Film Internat. (steering com., festival liaison person 1985-87), Am. Film Mktg. Assn. (outreach com. 1986-87), NAFE. Office: Skouras Pictures Inc 1040 N Las Palmas Ave Hollywood CA 90038

MILLER, BARBARA STALLCUP, medical foundation administrator; b. Montague, Calif., Sept. 4, 1919; d. Joseph Nathaniel and Maybelle (Needham) Stallcup; m. Leland F. Miller, May 16, 1946; children—Paula Kay, Susan Lee, Daniel Joseph, Alison Jean. B.A., U. Oreg., 1942. Women's editor Eugene (Oreg.) Daily News, 1941-43; law clk. to J. Everett Barr, Yreka, Calif., 1943-45; mgr. Yreka C. of C., 1945-46; Northwest supr. Louis Harris and Assocs., Portland, Oreg., 1959-62; dir. pub. relations and fund raising Columbia River council Girl Scouts U.S.A., 1962-67; pvt. practice pub. relations cons., Portland, 1967-72; adviser of student publs., asst. prof. communications U. Portland, 1967-72, dir. pub. relations and info., asst. prof. communications, 1972-78, dir. devel., 1978-79, exec. dir. devel., 1979-83; assoc. dir. St. Vincent Med. Found., 1983-88; dir. planned giving Good Samaritan Found., 1988—. Pres. bd. dirs. Vols. of Am. of Oreg., Inc., 1980-84, pres. regional adv. bd., 1982-84; chmn. bd. dirs. S.E. Mental Health Network, 1984-88, Oreg. Black History Project; nat. bd. dirs. Vols. of Am., Inc., 1984—. Recipient Presdl. Citation, Oreg. Communicators Assn., 1973, Matrix award, 1976, 80, Miltner award U. Portland, 1977. Mem. Nat. Assn. Hosp. Devel., Nat. Soc. Fundraising Execs., Women in Communications (NW regional v.p. 1973-75), Nat. Fedn. Press Women, Oreg. Press Women (dist. dir.), Pub. Relations Soc. Am. (dir. local chpt.), Oreg. Fedn. Womens Clubs (communications chmn. 1978-80), Alpha Xi Delta. Unitarian. Clubs: Portland Zenith (pres. 1975-76, 81-82), City Club of Portland. Contbr. articles to profl. jours. Home: 1706 SW Boca Ratan Dr Lake Oswego OR 97034 Office: 1015 NW 22d Ave Portland OR 97210

MILLER, BETH, Spanish and Portugese educator; b. Chgo., Jan. 13, 1941; d. Bert and Anita (Lome) Kurti; 1 child, Samantha. Postgrad., U. Madrid, 1960-61; BA summa cum laude, Northwestern U., 1962; MA, U. Calif., Berkeley, 1965, U. Calif., Berkeley, 1973. Asst. prof. Spanish and French SUNY, New Paltz, 1968-69; instr., asst. prof. Rutgers U., New Brunswick, N.J., 1969-76; assoc. prof. U. So. Calif., Los Angeles, 1976—, chmn. dept. Spanish and Portugese, 1977-78; cons. Guggenheim Found., Nat. Endowment for Humanities, U. Calif. Press. Author: La Poesia Constructiva de Jaime Torres Bodet, 1974, Mujeres en la Literatura, 1978, Rosario Castellanos: Una Conciencia Feminista en Mexico, 1983, 26 Autoras del Mexico de Hoy, 1978, Uma Consciencia Feminista: Rosario Castellanos, 1987: editor: Women in Hispanic Literature: Icons and Fallen Idols, 1982; translator: Siete poetas nortemericanas, 1977; assoc. edito Melus, 1977; mem. editorial bd. Caribe, Latin Am. Lit. Rev. Mem. Venice Town Council, Calif., 1987-88. Grantee Rutgers U., 1972-75, U. So. Calif., 1974-75, Del Amo Found., 1976-77, Am. Council Learned Socs., 1979, Colo. Endowment for Humanities, 1985; grantee in aid Am. Council Learned Socs., 1987; Nat. Women's Assn. fellow; Fulbright-Hays Commn. sr. fellow, 1985, 86. Mem. Latin Am. Studies, AAUW (award 1986). Inst. Internat. Lit. Iberoamericana, Am. Tchrs. Spanish and Portugese, Pacific Coast Council Latin Am. Studies. Home: 36 Navy St Apt 7 Venice CA 90291 Office: U So Calif Dept Spanish and Portuguese Los Angeles CA 90089

MILLER, BILL, management and marketing consultant; b. Jersey City, Mar. 6, 1933; Children: Valerie, Lynn, Lori, Michael, Billy Joe. MBA, La Jolla U., 1980. Cert. (life) coll. level tchr. psychology, bus. mgmt. and mktg., mgmt. orgn. and human relations, Calif. Enlisted USMC, 1948, ret., 1967; instr. karate, judo and mob control N.J. and Calif. Police Depts.; dist. sales mgr. Syntex Labs., Palo Alto, Calif., 1968-75; owner, pres. Bill Miller and Assocs., Inc., 1976—, Mgmt. Dynamics; cons. to mgmt. in healthcare, exec. search; presenter mgmt. seminars; instr. psychology, bus. mgmt. and mktg., mgmt. orgn. and human relations U. Calif.-La Jolla and Nat. U., San Diego. Sponsor, founder Ann. Rancho Bernardo (Calif.) Half Marathon. Home: 12696 Pacato Circle N Rancho Bernardo CA 92128

MILLER, BLAKE DELANE, marketing professional; b. Santa Monica, Calif., July 15, 1957; s. Robert Delane Miller and Florence Elizabeth (Kiessig) Jacobs; m. Jeryl Ann Byerly, Dec. 27, 1980; children: Luke Edward Christian, Blake Andrew Phillip. BS, UCLA, 1980; MS, Stanford U., 1982. Mktg. mgr. Hewlett Packard, McMinnville, Oreg., 1982-84, Marcom mgr., 1984-85; markets mgr. Hewlett Packard, Vancouver, Wash., 1985-87; product line mgr. Hewlett Packard, Vancouver, 1987—. Coach local YMCA, mem. bd. mgrs.; tchr. local Sunday sch. Mem. Stanford Alumni Assn. Republican. Mem. Christian Ch. Office: Hewlett Packard 18110 SE 34th St Camas WA 98607

MILLER, CAROLE ANN LYONS, editor, publisher, advertising specialist; b. Newton, Mass., Aug. 1, 1943; d. Markham Harold and Ursula Patricia (Foley) Lyons; m. David Thomas Miller, July 4, 1978. BA, Boston U., 1964; bus. cert., Hickox Sch., Boston, 1964; cert. advt. and mktg. profl. UCLA, 1973; cert. retail mgmt. profl. Ind. U., 1976. Editor Triangle Topics, Pacific Telephone, L.A.; programmer L.A. Cen. Area Speakers' Bur., 1964-66; mng. editor/mktg. dir. Teen mag., L.A. and N.Y.C., 1966-76; advt. dir. L.S. Ayres & Co., Indpls., 1976-78; v.p. mktg. The Denver, 1978-79; founder, editor, pub. Clockwise mag., Ventura, Calif., 1979-85; mktg. mgr., mgr. pub. rels. and spl. events Robinson's Dept. Stores, L.A., 1985-87, v.p. Harrison Svcs., L.A., 1987—; instr. retail advt. Ind. U., 1977-78. Mem. Fashion Group. Recipient Pres.'s award Advt. Women of N.Y., 1974; Seklemian award 1977; Pub. Svc. Addy award, 1978. Mem. Advt. Women N.Y., Advt. Club L.A., Ventura County Profl. Women's Network (founding), UCLA Alumni Assn. Editor: Sek Says, 1979. Home: 2554 Spinnaker Ave Port Hueneme CA 93041 Office: 8511 Washington Blvd Culver City CA 90232

MILLER, CAROLINE BAYEUX, human resources consultant; b. Miami, Fla., Oct. 4, 1926; d. Robert Monfort and Harriet (Perkins) M. Student, DePauw U., 1946-48; BS, U. Cin., 1962; postgrad. in arbitration, U. Mich., 1976, U. Wis., Milw., 1975. Instr. Cin. Bell Tel. Co., 1953-55, supr., 1955-56, staff writer, 1956-60, pers. mgr., 1961-84; ind. human resources cons. Santa Fe, 1986—; co-designer, developer info. and referral for Santa Fe County, 1988. Bd. dirs. Santa Fe Community Found., Vis. Nurse Svc. Santa Fe; grant writer, St. Elizabeth Shelter, Santa Fe; pres. Santa Fe Habitat for Humanity; active Affordable Housing Roundtable, Mayor's Affordable Housing Task Force, Community Devel. Loan Fund, Wheelwrigth Mus., N.Mex. Nature Conservancy, Native Plant Soc., Interfaith Coun., Guadalupe Historic Found., Friends of Santa Fe Libr. Democrat. Episcopalian.

MILLER, CHARLES DALY, business executive; b. Hartford, Conn., 1928; married. Grad., Johns Hopkins U. Sales mgr. Yale & Towne Mfg. Co., 1955-59; asso. Booz, Allen & Hamilton, 1959-64; with Avery Internat. Corp., Pasadena, Calif., 1964—, group v.p., 1969-72, exec. v.p. ops., 1972-75, pres., 1975-77, chief exec. officer, 1977—, now also chmn., dir. Office: Avery Internat Corp 150 N Orange Grove Blvd Pasadena CA 91103

MILLER, CLARA BURR, educator; b. Higganum, Conn., July 19, 1912; d. Eugene Orlando and Mabel (Clark) Burr; m. James Golden Miller, Sept. 19, 1942; children: Clara Elizabeth, Eugenia Manelle. BA, Mt. Holyoke Coll., 1933; MA, Columbia U., 1942. Cert. tchr., Conn., Pa., N.J., Ariz. Tchr. Suffield (Conn.) Jr. High Sch., 1934-36, Rockville (Conn.) High Sch., 1936-41, Buckeley High Sch., Hartford, Conn., 1941-42, Pitts. Schs., 1952-55, Winchester-Thurston Sch., Pitts., 1955-58, Vail-Deane Sch., Elizabeth, N.J., 1959-69, Kingman (Ariz.) High Sch., 1971-76; mem. res. faculty Mohave Community Coll., Kingman, 1978—; pres. bd. edn., clk. Mohave Union High Sch. Dist. 30, 1982—; v.p., bd. dirs. Mohave Mental Health Clinic, 1982—. Author: Trails, Rails and Tales, 1981, (with others) Short Stories, 1984. Bd. dirs. No. Ariz. Comprehensive Guidance Ctr., Flagstaff, 1985—, Kingman Aid to Abused People; sec. Good Samaritan Assn., Inc., Kingman, 1979—; pres., Ch. Women United, 1972-74, Presbyn. Women, 1987, elected elder session Kingman Presbyn Ch., 1986—; mem. Mohave County Community Action Bd., Western Ariz. Coun. Govts.; coord. League Friendship Indians & Ams., 1981—. Recipient Nat. Community Svc. award Mohave County Ret. Tchrs. Assn., 1987; named one of Women Making History Kingman Multi-Club Com., 1985. Mem. NEA, Ariz. Edn. Assn., AAUW (pres. 1979-81), Ariz. Sch. Bds. Assn., Soc. Profl. Journalists, Footprinters. Democrat. Home: 2629 Mullen Dr Kingman AZ 86401

MILLER, CONNIE SUE, nurse; b. Springfield, Ill., May 22, 1961; d. John Jr. and Mildred Ruth (Sager) Fletcher; m. Stephen Eugene Miller, Apr. 3, 1982. Assoc. degree in Nursing, Ill. Ea. Community Coll., 1982. RN, Wyo., Ill. Staff nurse Richland Meml. Hosp., Olney, Ill., 1983-86, W. Park Hosp., Cody, Wyo., 1986—. Home: 496 Rd 2AB Cody WY 82414

MILLER, CYNTHIA LYNETTE, travel agency executive; b. Denver, Mar. 23, 1959; d. Frederick Leroy and Barbara Ellen (Grimm) Brown; m. Delbert Wayne Miller, Aug. 17, 1980; children: Devon Wade, Calen Dale. AA in Bus., Diablo Valley Coll., 1979; BS magna cum laude, San Francisco State U., 1981. Mem. sales staff Am. Airlines, San Jose, Calif., 1978-85, Pacific Southwest Airlines, San Jose, 1983-84; owner, mgr. Friendship Travel, Fremont, Calif., 1984—; cons., Calico Corners, Fremont, 1981—. Coord., John Knox Presbyterian Ch., Dublin, Calif., 1987. Mem. Airline Reporting Corp., Internat. Airline Travel Agts. Republican. Office: Friendship Travel 39184 Fremont Blvd Fremont CA 94538

MILLER, DALE E., management consultant; b. Cashmere, Wash., May 20, 1941; s. Glen W. and Vivian B. (Barden) M.; m. Leslee Batchelder, Dec. 31, 1967; children: Damon J., Cameron T. BA, U. Puget Sound, 1964; MArch, U. Wash., 1970. Tchr. Academie de Gardiner, Paris, 1964-66, Peterson's Sch. of Bus., Seattle, 1966-68; archtl. designer M.I.T.V., Seattle, 1968-69, Roland Terry & Assocs., Seattle, 1969-70; coordinator Environ. Works, Seattle, 1970-73; mgr. Office Housing Planning, Seattle, 1973-75; dir. Mount Baker Neighborhood Devel., Seattle, 1975-78; community, econ. devel. cons. The Phoenix Group, Seattle, 1978-89; exec. dir. Clearwater Econ. Devel. Assn., Lewiston, Idaho, 1989—; tchr. Seattle U., 1979-80, N.W. Owner Builder Ctr., Seattle, 1982-85. Co-author: (book) Home Renovation, 1983. Pres. Maprona Neighborhood Devel., Seattle, 1980-89; bd. dirs. Group Health Co-op, Seattle, 1973-78, U. Dist. Devel., Seattle, 1970-73. With U.S. Army, 1959-60. Recipient Environ. Design award, Seattle/King County Bd. Realtors, Seattle, 1970, Nat. Pub./Pvt. Ptnrships. award, HUD, Washington, 1985. Mem. Am. Planning Assn., (assoc. mem.) AIA, Am. Assn. Cert. Rev. Appraisers and Mortgage Underwriters. Democrat. Home: 1537 38th Ave Seattle WA 98122 Office: Clearwater Econ Devel Assn 1626 B 6th Ave N Lewiston ID 83501

MILLER, DAVID JULIAN, psychologist, training executive, educator; b. Berkeley, Calif., Mar. 9, 1952; s. Shully Leon and Anna Elizabeth (Julian) M. Cert., U. Paris, 1972; BA in Psychology, U. Calif., Berkeley, 1974; MS in Psychology, U. Wis., 1976; EdD in Ednl. Psychology, U.S. Internat. U., 1989. Instr. psychology, counselor Imperial Valley Coll., Imperial, Calif., 1976-79; instr. psychology San Diego State U., 1979; dean students Grossmont Coll., San Diego, 1979-80; corp. tng. mgr. Gt. Am. Bank, San Diego, 1981—; adj. prof. psychology Nat. U., San Diego, 1981—; cons. to govt. and pvt. orgns., Calif., Ariz., 1979—; speaker in field. HEW grantee, 1979. Mem. Am. Psychol. Assn. (assoc.), Am. Soc. for Tng. and Devel., Orgn. Devel. Network, San Diego Personnel and Guidance Assn. (bd. dirs. 1981-84), Greater San Diego Bus. Assn. (bd. dirs. 1984-87). Home: 1542 Bridgeview Dr San Diego CA 92105 Office: Great American Bank 401 W 24th St National City CA 92050

MILLER, DAVID WALTER, lawyer; b. San Francisco, Oct. 23, 1957; s. Walter and Judith Kay (Waxman) M.; m. Leslye Mayling Louie, Aug. 10, 1986. BA in Polit. Sci., U. Calif., Davis, 1980; JD, Santa Clara U., 1986. Bar: Calif. 1987; U.S. Dist. Ct. (no. dist.) Calif. 1987. Law clk. Calif. Supreme Ct., San Francisco, 1986-87, rsch. atty., 1987; assoc. Murphy, Weir & Butler, San Francisco, 1987-88; atty. Hewlett-Packard Co., Palo Alto, Calif., 1988—. Editor-in-chief Santa Clara Law Rev., 1985-86; co-author: Bay Area Corporate Non-Cash Contributions: Programs and Policies for the 80's. Public affairs fellow No. Calif. Coro Found., 1982. Mem. ABA, Calif. Bar, San Francisco Bar Assn., Barristers Club San Francisco. Office: Hewlett Packard Co 3000 Hanover MS 20BQ Palo Alto CA 94304

MILLER, DUANE DAVID, entrepreneur; b. Phoenix, Apr. 5, 1930; s. Cecil Harold Sr. and Phyllis Josephine (Hickey) M.; m. Beverly Josephine Lockett, Jan. 17, 1953; children: Katherine, Susan, Leslie, Ben. BS in Agr., U. Ariz., 1951. Ptnr. Miller Bros., Sedona, Ariz., 1950—; v.p. Coconino Cattle Co. (Babbitt Ranches), Sedona, 1951—; pres. Sedona Racquet Club, 1973—, Millco Constrn. Co., Sedona, 1975—; gen. ptnr. Miller Family Partnership, Sedona, 1975—; bd. dirs., mem. exec. com. Valley Nat. Bank, Phoenix, Valley Nat. Corp.; bd. dirs. CO Livestock Corp.; state committeeman Ariz. Stabilization and Conservation Commn., 1970-73. Pres., bd. dirs. Minors Union High Sch. Bd., Cottonword, Ariz., 1958-68, Yavapai Jr. Coll. Bd., Prescott, Ariz., 1968-76, Ariz. State Parks Bd., Phoenix, 1965—, Ariz. Cattle Industry Rsch. and Edn. Found., 1983—; bd. dirs. U. Ariz. Found., 1985—; mem. Govs. Blue Ribbon Com. Correction Instn., 1974-78. Mem. Ariz. Cattle Growers Assn. (numerous offices), Farm Bur. Assn., Internat. Coun. of Shopping Ctrs., Ariz. Realtors Assn., Fairfield Country Club, Forest Highlands Country Club, Plaza Club, Mt. Oyster Club, Continental Country Club. Republican. Episcopalian. Office: Miller Bros 100 Racquet Rd Sedona AZ 86336

MILLER, EDMUND KENNETH, electrical engineer; b. Milw., Dec. 24, 1935; s. Edmund William and Viola Louise (Ludwig) M.; m. Patricia Ann Denn, Aug. 23, 1958; children: Kerry Ann, Mark Christopher. BSEE, Mich. Tech. U., 1957; MS in Nuclear Engring., U. Mich., 1958, MSEE, 1961, PhD in Elec. Engring., 1965. Rsch. assoc. U. Mich., Ann Arbor, 1965-68; sr. scientist MB Assocs., San Ramon, Calif., 1968-71; group leader engring. rsch. div. Lawrence Livermore Lab., Livermore, Calif., 1971-78, leader engring. rsch. div., 1978-83, leader nuclear energy systems div., 1983-85; regents prof. elect. and computer engring. U. Kans., 1985-87; mgr. electromagnetics Rockwell Sci. Ctr., Thousand Oaks, Calif., 1987-88; dir. electromagnetics rsch. operation Gen. Rsch. Corp., Santa Barbara, Calif., 1988—. Editor: Time Domain Measurements in Electromagnets, 1985. Contbr. numerous articles to profl. jours. Singer Lyra Male Chorus, Ann Arbor, Mich., 1966-68, Livermore Civic Chorus, 1969-71. Fellow IEEE, mem. Am. Phys. Soc., Optical Soc. Am., Acoustical Soc. Am., Am. Soc. Engring. Edn., Electromagnetics Soc. (past bd. dirs.) Internat. Sci. Radio Union (chmn. U.S. Commn. A), Applied Computational Electromagnetics Soc. (past pres.). Office: Gen Rsch Corp 5383 Hollister Ave Santa Barbara CA 93111

MILLER, EDWARD JOHN, dentist; b. Philipsburg, Mont., Mar. 5, 1955; s. John Lee and Anne (Bigar) M.; m. JoLynne Johnson, Aug. 14, 1976; children: John Lee, Jessi Anne. BS in Zoology, Mont. State U., 1977; DDS, U. Minn., 1980. Gen. practice dentistry Anaconda, Mich., 1981—; dentist Anaconda Job Corps, 1982-85; tchr. dental hygiene Carroll Coll., Helena, Mont., 1983-84; missionary Christian Med. Soc., Richardson, Tex., 1982, 86. U. Minn. fellow, 1978; recipient research grantee U. Minn., 1979. Mem. AMA, ADA, Mont. Dental Assn. (v.p. 1983-84, 84-85), Anaconda Jaycees (pres. 1988—), Elks, Kiwanis. Roman Catholic. Home: 1719 W Park Anaconda MT 59711 Office: 115 W Commercial Anaconda MT 59711

MILLER, ELVA RUBY CONNES (MRS. JOHN R. MILLER), civic worker; b. Joplin, Mo.; d. Edward and Ada (Martin) Connes; student Pomona Coll., part-time, 1936-56; m. John R. Miller, Jan. 17, 1934 (dec. Nov. 1968). Entertainer various night clubs, supper clubs, also Hollywood Bowl, 1967; TV appearances; rec. artist Capitol Records, 1966—, Amaret Records, 1969—; appeared in motion pictures. Active Girl Scouts U.S.A., 1933-58; hon. mem. Mayor's Com. for Sr. Citizens, L.A., 1966; mem. Disabled Am. Vets., Comdrs. Club, Music Ctr. L.A. County. Recipient awards including Thanks badge Girl Scouts U.S.A., 1956, Key to City, Mayor San Diego, 1967, plaque Dept. of Def. for trip to Vietnam, 1967. Mem. Gen. Alumni Assn. U. So. Calif. (life). Republican. Presbyterian. Home: 9585 Reseda Blvd Northridge CA 91324

MILLER, EMERSON WALDO, accountant, tax, financial, business and management consultant; b. Green Island, Jamaica, W.I., Jan. 27, 1920; s. Adolphus Eustace and Catherine Sarah (Dixon) M.; m. Olive Claire Ford, Apr. 10, 1945; children—Cheryll, Hellena, Emerson, Oliver, Donald, Selwyn. Student U. Toronto, (Ont., Can.), 1938-41, U. Calif.-Berkeley, 1950-61. Came to U.S., 1950, naturalized, 1957. Cost accountant Poierier & McLane Corp., N.Y.C., 1941-42; prin. Emerson Miller & Co., Kingston, Jamaica, 1942-49; lectr. accounting and bus. law Jamaica Sch. Commerce, Kingston, 1945-48; tax examiner, conferee Internat. Revenue Service, San Francisco, 1963-64; chief financial and accounting aspects transp. and communications services programs Gen. Services Adminstrn., San Francisco, 1965-70, chief maj. segment financial mgmt. activities, 1970-84; prin. Emerson W. Miller Tax, Fin., Bus. and Mgmt. Services, 1984—; instr. govt. accounting, 1966-69. Fed. Govt. Accountants Assn. rep. mgmt. improvement com. Fed. Exec. Bd., San Francisco, 1973-74. Chmn. credit com. VARO Fed. Credit Union, San Francisco, 1969-81, treas., dir., 1981—. Recipient Disting. Service award Toastmasters Internat., 1968, Commendable Service award Gen. Services Adminstrn., 1968, Spl. Achievement award, 1969; Faithful Service award VARO-SF Fed. Credit Union, 1974. Mem. Am. Accounting Assn., Nat. Assn. Accountants, Fed. Govt. Accountants Assn. (chpt. pres.), Am. Mgmt. Assn., Financial Mgmt. Assn., Brit. Inst. Mgmt., Am. Judicature Soc., Royal Econ. Soc. (Cambridge), U. Calif. Alumni Assn., Internat. Platform Assn., Acad. Polit. and Social Sci., AAAS, N.Y. Acad. Scis. Clubs: Toastmasters Internat. (ednl. v.p.), (San Francisco), No. Calif. Cricket (San Anselmo); Brit. Social and Athletic (Los Angeles). Home: 505 Coventry Rd Kensington CA 94707 Office: PO Box 471 Berkeley CA 94701

MILLER, EUGENE, retired chemical engineering educator; b. N.Y.C., Feb. 2, 1922; s. Benjamin and Emma A. (Goldberger) M.; m. Ruth Naomi Cooper, June 22, 1947; children: Lee R., Carey J. B ChemE, CUNY, 1944; M ChemE, Bklyn. Poly. Inst., 1947; PhD in ChemE, U. Del., 1949. Sr. devel. engr. MW Kellogg Co., N.Y.C., Jersey City, 1944-47, 49-52; chief rsch. labs. U.S. Army Missile Commd., Redstone Arsenal, Ala., 1952-57; dir. R&D Olin Corp., Marion, Ill., 1957-59; cons. Herrin, Ill., 1959-60; asst. tech. dir. Lockheed Propulsion Co., Redlands, Calif., 1960-65, mgr. propulsion systems rsch. div., 1965-67; mgr. Propulsion Mech. Systems Space Systems Lockheed Missile and Space Co., Sunnyvale, Calif., 1967-69; pres. Browning Arms Co., Morgan, Utah, 1969-73; prof. chem. engring. U. Nev., Reno, 1973-83, prof., chmn. dept. chem. engring., 1983-85, prof. emeritus, 1985—. Mem. Am. Inst. Chem. Engrs., Am. Chem. Soc., Tau Beta Pi, Phi Kappa Phi, Phi Lambda Upsilon, Sigma Xi. Home: PO Box 4361 Incline Village NV 89450 Office: U Nev Dept Chem and Metal Engring Mackay Sch Mines Reno NV 89557

MILLER, FRANKLIN EMRICK, software engineer; b. Greenville, Ohio, Aug. 12, 1946; s. Rollin Linde and E. Evelyn (Emrick) M.; m. Sandra Lewis, Dec. 20, 1969; children: William Rollin, Rose Mary. BS, Otterbein Coll., 1969; MEd in Ednl. Psychology and Counseling, Wayne State U., 1975; PhD, U. Denver, 1984. Lic. pvt. pilot FAA. Commd. U.S. Air Force, 1969, advanced through grades to capt.; space surveillance officer, Maine, 1970-71, Thule, Greenland, 1971-72; chief instr./systems analyst, Correlation Ctr., McGuire AFB, N.J., 1972-73; site space surveillance officer, Aviano, Italy, 1973-75; chief support programming unit, Colo., 1975-79; chief applications support programming, South Australia, 1979-81, ret., 1988; software engr. Aerojet Electro Systems Corp., Aurora, Colo., 1981-88. Bd. dirs., Aurora Community Mental Health Ctr., 1976-79; vol. counselor Comitis Crisis Ctr., YMCA, Aurora, 1976-78. Mem. Am. Psychol. Assn., Phi Delta Kappa. Republican. Author: The Preliminary Online Rorschach Test Manual, 1980; contbr. article to profl. jour. Office: The Aerospace Corp PO Box 92957 Los Angeles CA 90009

MILLER, FREDERICK HARRY, architect; b. Cin., June 21, 1927; s. George and Libbye (Leitz) M.; m. Gene Ann Ach, Nov. 22, 1950 (div. 1984); children: Kay Eugenia, Mark Ach; m. Shahla Zand, Apr. 24, 1977 (divorced). BArch, U. Cin., 1953. Registered architect, Calif. Estimator Frank Messer & Sons, Cin., 1947-48; cons. site design Cin. Metro Housing Authority, Cin., 1948-51; owner, chief exec. George Miller & Sons Gen. Contractors, Cin., 1952-62, Fred Miller Bldg Co., Cin., 1962-77, Fred Miller, Architect, Encino, Calif., 1988—; pres. Alof, Inc., Cin., 1961-66; chief architect David Haber & Assoc. Architects, L.A., 1978-88; art dir. Baja Okla. Film Prodn. Co., L.A., 1988. Cons. N.Avondale Neighborhood Assn., Cin., 1964-75. Mem. U. Cin. Alumni Assn., SCARAB (hon.), Sierra Club, Great Books Club (treas. 1968-70). Republican. Jewish. Office: Fred Miller Architect 4924 Gloria Ave Encino CA 91436

MILLER, GARY EVAN, graphic designer; b. Kansas City, Mo., Dec. 11, 1962; s. Francis Marion and Rose Marie (Frogge) M.; m. Amy Virginia Berry, Feb. 1, 1986. BFA in Visual Communications, U. Kans., 1984. Designer United Telecommunications, Mission Hills, Kans., 1984-85, Steve Nelson Design, Roeland Park, Kans., 1985; art dir. PCG Mktg. Communications, Beverly Hills, Calif., 1985-86; creative dir. Husberg Communications, Scottsdale, Ariz., 1986-87; pres. The M Group Graphic Design, Inc., Phoenix, 1987—; cons., Pub. Rels. Soc. Am., Phoenix, 1986. Grantee Graphic Arts Tech. Found., Pitts., 1981-84. Mem. L.A. Art Dirs. Club, Western Art Dirs. Club, Phoenix Soc. Communicating Arts. Office: M Group Graphic Design Inc 3930 E Camelback Rd Ste 204 Phoenix AZ 85016

MILLER, GARY GEORGE, credit bureau executive, marketing consultant; b. Pasadena, Calif., Jan. 12, 1948; s. Geo. Lane and Evelynn (Pringle) M.; m. Susan Anne Salvage, Jan. 1, 1980. BBA, U. Tex., 1970; M of internat. mgmt., Am. Grad. Sch. Internat. Mgmt., 1973. Internat. mktg. specialist agrl. machinery div. FMC, Jonesboro, Ark., 1974; sales rep. MBA tng. program Met. Life Ins., Torrance, Calif., 1975-76; mktg. cons. Carrigan, Hoffman & Assoc., Honolulu, 1976-77, Miller Cons., Honolulu, L.A. and San Francisco, 1978-84; outreach worker Project Help!, San Francisco, 1984-85; mktg. rep. First Interstate Bank Alaska, Anchorage, 1985-87; gen. mgr. Credit Bur. Alaska, Anchorage, 1988—. Mem. Commonwealth North, Rotary. Office: Credit Bur Alaska 3003 Minnesota Dr Ste 300 Anchorage AK 99503

MILLER, GARY WYNN, architect; b. Blackfoot, Idaho, Sept. 12, 1954; s. Earl Jacob and Lenora (Marlow) M.; m. Sherri Lynn Higbee Miller, Sept. 28, 1977; children: Dustin Earl, Megan June, Jared Eugene, Narroge. BArch, Calif. Polytech. Inst., 1979. Registered architect, Calif. Draftsman Robert Miller & Assocs., Riverside, Calif., 1979-80; project mgr. Joseph E. Benadiman & Assocs., San Bernardino, Calif., 1980-84; exec. v.p. Roger L. Grucke & Assocs., Redlands, Calif., 1984-86; prin. Gary W. Miller Architects & Assocs., San Bernardino, 1986—. Mem. AIA, San Bernadino C. of C., Kiwanis. Republican. Mem. Ch. of Latter Day Saints. Office: 350 W 5th St Ste 208 San Bernardino CA 92401

MILLER, GEORGE, congressman; b. Richmond, Calif., May 17, 1945; s. George and Dorothy (Rumsey) M.; m. Cynthia Caccavo, 1964; children: George, Stephen. B.A., San Francisco State Coll., 1968; J.D., U. Calif., Davis, 1972. Legis. counsel Calif. senate majority leader 1969-73; mem. 94th-101st Congresses from 7th Calif. Dist.; chmn. subcom. on water and power resources, 1985—, subcom. on labor standards, 1979-84, select com. on children, youth and families. Chmn. Contra Costa County (Calif.) Dem. Cen. Com., 1969-70. Mem. Calif. Bar Assn. Club: Martinez Dem. (past pres.). Office: 2228 Rayburn House Office Bldg Washington DC 20515

MILLER, GEORGE DAVID, retired air force officer, marketing consultant; b. McKeesport, Pa., Apr. 5, 1930; s. George G. and Nellie G. (Cullen) M.; m. Barbara Aex; 1 son, George David; m. Barbara Aex. BS, U.S. Naval Acad., 1953; MS in Aerospace Engring, Air Force Inst. Tech., 1966; postgrad., Nat. War Coll., 1970-71. Commd. 2d lt. U.S. Air Force, 1953, advanced through grades to lt. gen., 1981; ops. officer, comdr. 22d Spl. Ops. Squadron, Nakhon Phanom Royal Thai AFB, Thailand, 1970-71; dep. comdr. for ops., vice comdr., comdr. 55th Strategic Reconnaissance Wing, Offutt AFB, Nebr., 1971-74; comdr. 17th Air div., 307th Strategic wing, U-Tapao Airfield, Thailand, 1974-75; asst. dep. chief staff ops. hdqrs. SAC, Offutt AFB,, Nebr., 1977-79; dep. dir. single integrated operational plan Joint Strategic Target Planning Staff, Joint Chiefs of Staff, 1977-79; dir. plans, dep. chief of staff ops., plans and readiness Hdqrs. USAF, Washington, 1979-80; asst. dep. chief staff ops., plans and readiness Hdqrs. USAF, 1980-81; vice comdr. SAC, Offutt AFB, Nebr., 1981-84; sec.-gen. U.S. Olympic Com., 1984-87; cons. Sports Mktg. and Def. Programs, 1984—. Trustee Morris Animal Found., vice chair pub. rels. com.; trustee U.S. Naval Acad. Found. Decorated D.S.M., Legion of Merit, D.F.C. with 3 oak leaf clusters, Air medal with 18 oak leaf clusters, others. Mem. Air Force Assn., Am. Legion, Masons, Scottish Rite, Shriners. Republican. Lutheran. Home: 240 Garfield St Denver CO 80206 Office: 601 E 18th St #200 Denver CO 80203

MILLER, GEORGIA ELLEN, business owner; b. Seattle; d. George Rynd Sr. and Mary Edith (Martin) M. BE, MEd, UCLA, 1934. Tchr. Punahou Sch., Honolulu, 1948-74; owner Miller's Bus. Svcs., Honolulu, 1975—. Dir. Waikiki Improvement Assn., Honolulu, 1980—; pres. Waikiki Resident's Assn., Honolulu, 1978—; sec. Waikiki Neighborhood Bd., 1908-86; county chmn. Oahu (Hawaii) Rep. Party, 1976. Mem. Bus. and Profl. Women (pres. 1973, legis. chair 1980, 88, state lobbyist 1988), AAUW, Alpha Chi Omega, Pi Lambda Theta. Mem. United Ch. of Christ. Home: 2457 Ala Wai Apt 3 Honolulu HI 96815 Office: Millers Bus Svcs 1720 Ala Moana Bldv Ste B4 C Honolulu HI 96815

MILLER, GERALD KEITH, electronics executive; b. Porterville, Calif., Jan. 19, 1947; s. Luten M. and Lola M. (Crossno) M.; m. Sandra J. Zeugin, Feb. 5, 1977; 1 child, Andrea N. AA, Solano Coll., 1966; postgrad., San Jose State U., 1966-68, San Diego State U., 1972-74. Engr. in tng. Naval Electronics Systems Command, Vallejo, Calif., 1966-71, electronics tech., 1974-77, supr. electronics tech., 1980—; tech. adviser air ops. staff Naval Air Sta., Bermuda, 1977-80; adv. bd. Bermuda Civil Aviation and Marine Services, 1977-80. Inventor in field; contbr. articles to profl. jours. Coach Bermuda Youth League, 1977-80. Served with USN, 1971-74. Republican. Lutheran. Club: Bermuda Golf (handicap com. 1977-80). Office: Naval Electronic Systems Command Vallejo CA 94592

MILLER, GILBERT D., small business owner; b. Brigham City, Utah, Oct. 21, 1947; s. Don C. and Sharon (Gilbert) M.; m. Lyle Ann Virgin, Dec. 16, 1980. BS, Utah State U., 1971, PhD, 1985—. Ptnr. Gilbert Dairy Farm, Corinne, Utah, 1971—; treas. Don Miller's Appliance Outlet, Inc., Corinne, 1976—; teaching asst. Utah State U., Logan, 1986—. Treas. Box Elder County Dem. Party, Brigham City, 1978-80; council mem. Utah State Dem. Party, Salt Lake City, 1978-80. Mem. Am. Econ. Assn., Am. Agrl. Econ. Assn., Grad. Student Assn. (pres. 1988%, exec. council 1986-88), Nat. Assn. Grad. and Profl. Students (reg. conf. coordiantor 1989). Democrat. Mem. Ch. of Jesus Christ of Latter Day Saints. Office: Economics Dept Utah State Univ Logan UT 84322-3530

MILLER, GREGORY ALEXANDER, school administrator; b. Ft. Bragg, N.C., Sept. 11, 1953; s. Shelton and Eucataz (Halstead) M.; m. Kathy Haskins, Dec. 16, 1977; children: Christopher, Matthew. BS in Biology, U. Alaska, Fairbanks, 1976, teaching cert., 1977; teaching cert., U. Alaska, Anchorage, 1985, MEd in Adminstrn., 1985. Tchr. Valdez (Alaska) City Schs., 1977-82, cross-country ski coach, 1978-82; tchr. Mat-Su Schs., Palmer, Alaska, 1983-88; prin. Skwentna (Alaska) Sch., 1988—; instr. Learn Not to Burn program, Nat. Fire Protection Assn. Supt. Fairview Loop Ch., Wasilla, Alaska, 1987-88. Mem. NEA (assembly rep., L.A., 1981), Nat. Assn. Elem. Sch. Prins., Valdez Edn. Assn. (pres. 1980-81). Republican. Baptist. Home: SR Box 5265 Wasilla AK 99687 Office: Skwentna Sch PO Box 17 Skwentna AK 99667

MILLER, HAROLD WILLIAM, nuclear geochemist; b. Walton, N.Y., Apr. 21, 1920; s. Harold Frank and Vera Leona (Simons) M. BS in Chemistry, U. Mich., 1943; MS in Chemistry, U. Colo., 1948, postgrad. Control chemist Linde Air Products Co., Buffalo, 1943-46; analytical research chemist Gen. Electric Co., Richland, Wash., 1948-51; research chemist Phillips Petroleum Co., Idaho Falls, Idaho, 1953-56; with Anaconda (Mont.) Copper Co., 1956; tech. dir., v.p. U.S. Yttrium Co., Laramie, Wyo., 1956-57; tech. dir. Colo. div. The Wah Chang Co., Boulder, Colo., 1957-58; analytical chemist The Climax (Colo.) Molybdenum Co., 1959; with research and devel. The Colo. Sch. of Mines Research Found., Golden, 1960-62; cons. Boulder, 1960—; sr. research physicist Dow Chem. Co., Golden, 1963-73; bd. dirs. Sweeney Mining and Milling Corp., Boulder; cons. Hendricks Mining and Milling Co., Boulder; instr. nuclear physics and nuclear chemistry Rocky Flats Plant, U. Colo. Contbr. numerous articles to profl. jours. Mem. Sigma Xi. Home and Office: Box 1092 Boulder CO 80306

MILLER, HERMAN KARL, JR., sales manager, marketing executive; b. Phila., June 5, 1944; s. Herman and Edna (Allen) M.; m. Janet Jackson, Feb. 15, 1963 (div. Aug. 1974); children: Robert K., Debra L.; m. Dianne Ams, Nov. 12, 1988. BA in Bus. Adminstrn., Temple U., 1961-66. Special sales rep. Metropolitan Life Ins., Phila., 1964-66; mgr. dist. sales Lees Carpets, Phila., 1966-69; mgr. regional comml. sales C.H. Masland Co., Carlisle, Pa., 1969-75; mgr. regional sales Comml. Carpet Corp., Los Angeles, 1975-77; mgr. div. sales Allen Test Products, Los Angeles, 1977-83; mgr. western dist. sales western Durabond Profl. Products div. Dap, Inc., La Mirada, Calif., 1983—. Football coach Jr. Am. Football, Mission Viejo, Calif., 1979-81. Democrat. Episcopalian. Home: 17241 Berlin Ln Huntington Beach CA 92649 Office: Dap Inc Durabond Profl Products Div 14370 Gannet St La Mirada CA 92649

MILLER, IRA, electrical engineer, integrated circuit design consultant; b. Ionia, Mich., Oct. 11, 1943; m. Carolyn H. McKellips; children: Jodi, Erica, Mike. BSEE, Mich. State U., 1971; MSEE, U. Ariz., 1986. Staff engr. Motorola, Inc., Phoenix, 1971-73, sr. mem. tech. staff, 1976—, mem. sci. adv. bd., 1986; design mgr. Teledyne, Inc., Mountain View, Calif., 1973-74; sr. staff engr. Gen. Instrument, Inc., Chandler, Ariz. 20 issued patents. Mem. IEEE (speaker at IEEE Custom Integrated Cir. Conf. 1984), Am. Radio Relay League. Republican. Office: Motorola Asic 1300 N Alma School Rd Chandler AZ 85224

MILLER, JAMES PATRICK, management consultant; b. Portland, Oreg., June 30, 1954; s. David S. and Lois E. (Neely) M.; m. Janice Marie Allard, Aug. 1, 1975; children: Teresa Ann, Courtney Elizabeth. Grad. high sch., Lake Oswego, Oreg., 1972. Account rep. Oreg. Bus., Portland, 1981-84; nat. account rep. Time Systems Inc., Phoenix, 1984—; cons. Gen. Motors, Motorola, U.S. West, Pacific Telesis. Republican. Lutheran.

MILLER, JEAN R., librarian; b. St. Helena, Calif., Aug. 4, 1927; d. William Leonard and Jean (Stanton) M. BA, Occidental Coll., 1950; MLS, U. So. Calif., Los Angeles, 1952. Base librarian USAF, Wethersfield, Eng., 1952-55; post librarian USMC Air Sta., El Toro, Calif., 1955-63; data systems librarian Autonetics (Rockwell), Anaheim, Calif., 1963-65; mgr. library services Beckman Instruments, Fullerton, Calif., 1966—; mem. adv. com. Library Technician Program, Fullerton Coll., 1969—. Author: (bibliography) Field Air Traffic Control, 1965, Electrical Shock Hazards, 1974. Chair Fullerton Are U. So. Calif. Scholarship Alumni Interview Program, Fullerton, 1974—. Mem. IEEE, So. Calif. Assn. Law Libraries, Med. Library Group of So. Calif., Spl. Libraries Assn. (pres. So. Calif. chpt. 1975-76, chair Sci./Tech. Div. 1985-86). Republican. Home: 17901 Chapman Ave 9C Orange CA 92669

MILLER, JERI LYNN, physical therapist; b. Montgomery, Ala., Mar. 23, 1957; s. Archie Lee Miller Jr. and Gloria May (Murdy) Hall. BS in Psych., U. So. Calif., L.A., 1975-81, MS in Phys. Therapy, 1981. Cert. registered phys. therapist. RPT staff St. Jude Hosp., Fullerton, 1980-82; RPT supr. Orange Coast Rehab. Ctr., Fountain Valley, 1982--; cons. Chevron, South Calif., 1983, Nautilus Aerobics Plus, South Calif. Author: (book) Take Care of Your Back. Mem. Am. Phys. Therapy Assn., Lead's Club. Democrat. Home: 223 Palos Verdes Dr Santa Ana CA 92704

MILLER, JIMMY HILBERT, history educator; b. Battle Creek, Iowa, Jan. 2, 1945; s. Walter Carl and Helen Irene (Adams) M.; m. Sylvia Aurora Lujan, Nov. 22, 1969; children: Walter Leonard, Brenda Suzanne. BA in History, N.Mex. State U., 1968, MA in History, 1970; PhD in History and Polit. Sci., No. Ariz. U., 1986. Instr. history N.Mex. State U., Las Cruces, 1970; instr. history San Juan Campus N.Mex. State U, Farmington, 1970-76, asst. prof. history, 1976-82; assoc. prof. history San Juan Coll., Farmington, 1982-87; instr. history No. Ariz. U., Flagstaff, 1983-84; prof. history San Juan Coll., Farmington, 1987—. Author: A Philadelphia Brahmin in Flagstaff: The Life of Harold Sellers Colton, 1988 (research award 1984); editor: San Juan Coll. N. Cen. Accrediting Assn. Self Study, 1988 (Downum award 1984); contbg. author: Liberty Gazette, Farmington, 1987—. Bd. dirs. San Juan County Econ. Opportunity Council, Farmington, 1972-75; chmn. San Juan County Dem. Ward, Farmington, 1978-80. Mem. Community Coll. Humanities Assn. (pres. S.W. div. 1985-87, Outstanding Service 1987, chmn. S.W. div. conf. 1987), N.Mex. Humanities Council (regional rep. 1979-83, project dir. 1972—), Phi Alpha Theta, Phi Kappa Phi, Phi Theta Kappa (hon. mem., chpt. sponsor, Outstanding Service 1988), Pi Gamma Mu. Methodist. Lodge: Civitan (pres. 1986-87, sec. Great S.W. dist. 1979-80, dist. Civitan Yr. 1979-80, club Civitan Yr. 1986). Home: 3900 Country Club Dr Farmington NM 87401 Office: San Juan Coll 4601 College Blvd Farmington NM 87401

MILLER, JOHN LESTER, electro-optical physicist; b. Pitts., July 6, 1959; s. John Albert and Anna May (Bolinsky) M.; m. Corinne Leslie Foster, Dec. 22, 1985. BS in Physics, U. So. Calif., L.A., 1981; MBA in Ops. Mgmt. with honors, Regis Coll., Denver, 1988. Telescope operator Griffith Obs., L.A., 1980-84; optical tech. Mt. Wilson & Palomar Obs., L.A., 1980-81; electro-optical engr. Rockwell Internat., L.A., 1981-84; research assoc. U. Hawaii, Mauna Kea Obs., Hilo, 1984-85; sr. sensor staff engr. Martin Marietta Astronautics, Denver, 1985—; cons. in field. Contbr. articles to profl. jours. Recipient Bausch & Lomb Sci. award, 1976. Mem. Soc. Photo Optical Instrumentation Engrs., Optical Soc. Am., Rocky Mt. Optical Soc. Republican.

MILLER, JOHN R., congressman; b. N.Y.C., May 23, 1938; m. June Marion Hamula. B.A., Bucknell U., 1959; M.A., Yale U., 1964, J.D., 1964. Bar: Wash. Asst. atty. gen. State of Wash., 1965-68; practice law 1968-72; pres. Seattle City Council, 1972-80; adj. prof. govt. law U. Puget Sound, 1981-84; mem. 99th-101st Congresses from 1st Wash. Dist., 1985—. Mem. Wash. State Bar Assn. Office: care Postmaster Office of Ho of Reps Washington DC 20515 *

MILLER, JON HAMILTON, forest products company executive; b. Des Moines, Jan. 22, 1938; s. Victor George and Virginia Adelaide (Hamilton) M.; m. Sydney Gail Fernald, June 4, 1966; children: Emily, Sara. AB in Econs., Stanford U., 1959, MBA in Mktg. and Fin., 1961. Asst. to pres. Boise (Idaho) Cascade Corp., 1961-62, prodn. service mgr., 1962-65; sr. v.p. bus. products and services and packaging Boise (Idaho) Cascade Corp., Portland, Oreg., 1971-74; exec. v.p. paper and paper products Boise Cascade Corp., Boise, Idaho, 1974-76; exec. v.p. timber/wood products/bldg. materials Boise Cascade Corp., 1976-78, pres. and chief operating officer, 1978—, also dir.; bd. dirs. Northwestern Mut. Life Ins. Co., St. Luke's Regional Med. Ctr., Idaho Power Co. Served with U.S. Army, 1959-60. Recipient Top Mgmt. award Sales & Mktg. Execs. of Boise, 1984; named Idaho Bus Leader of Yr. Alpha Kappa Psi, Idaho State U., 1986. Mem. Greater Boise C. of C. (pres. 1977); Bronco Athletic Assn. (bd. dirs. 1987—). Republican. Methodist. Clubs: Arid (Boise) (bd. dirs. 1987); Multnomah Athletic (Portland). Home: 3330 Mountain View Dr Boise ID 83704 Office: Boise Cascade Corp One Jefferson Sq Boise ID 83728 *

MILLER, JOSEPH EDWARD, JR., media company executive; b. Seattle, Jan. 4, 1945; s. Joseph Edward and Kathleen Bell (Campbell) M.; m. Ingrid Maria Exner, Mar. 5, 1965 (div. July 1972); 1 child, Nancy Marie; m. Barbara Leigh Gregson, May 25, 1986. AA, Montgomery Coll., 1974; BS, U. Md., 1976, MA, 1978. Mktg. mgr. Inst. Modern Lang., Silver Spring, Md., 1974-75; pres. JEMPRO Films Ltd., Silver Spring, 1975-79; writer/dir. WRAMC Inst. of Research, Washington, 1979-81; lobbyist The Am. Legion, Washington, 1981-86; ptnr. Miller-Gregson Prodns., Sherman Oaks, Calif., 1986—; cons. Renaissance Communications, Silver Springs, 1983-88, Loreen Arbus Prodns., L.A., 1988. Author: House on Thayer Hill, 1988. Orgn. fund raiser United Way, Washington, 1984-85; bd. dirs. Vietnam Veterans Inst., Washington, 1981—; With U.S. Army, 1962-72. Decorated Bronze Star, Air medal with oak leaf cluster, Purple Heart with oak leaf cluster; Recipient Honor award Assn. of Mil. Surgeons Internat., 1979, spl. recognition award Walter Reed Army Inst. of Research, 1981. Mem. Ind. Media Producers Assn., Alpha Sigm Lambda, Phi Kappa Phi, Phi Theta Kappa. Republican. Presbyterian. Office: Miller-Gregson Prodns 14827 Ventura Blvd Ste 207 Sherman Oaks CA 91403

MILLER, KENNETH A., manufacturing executive; b. Spokane, Wash., Feb. 9, 1944; s. Reuben A. Miller and Frances M. Kirlin; m. Andria J. Wright, May 16, 1964; children: Donald G., Janet E. BBA, Calif. State U., 1975, MS, 1979. V.p. gen. mgr. photo rsch. div. Kollmorgen, Burbank, Calif., 1981-88; dir. mfg. Photo Rsch., Burbank, 1973-79, v.p. mfg., 1979-80, v.p. mktg., 1980-87, v.p. product line mgr., 1985-87, pres., 1988—; standards writer Soc. Automotive Engrs., 1981-87, Electronic Industries Assn., 1984-87, ASTM, 1985-87; lectr. display engring. UCLA, 1984-86; guest lectr. various orgns., 1979—. Contbr. articles to profl. jours.; patentee small distance measure. Served as staff sgt. USAF, 1962-70. Mem. Soc. Info. Display, U.S. Nat. Com. Internat. Commn. on Illumination, Internat. Soc. Color Coun., Soc. Photo-Optical Instrumentation Engrs. Republican. Office: Photo Rsch 9330 DeSoto Ave Chatsworth CA 91311

MILLER, KENNETH EDWARD, mechanical engineer, consultant; b. Weymouth, Mass., Dec. 24, 1951; s. Edward Francis and Lena Joan (Trotta) M.; m. Florence Gay Wilson, Sept. 18, 1976; children: Nicole Elizabeth, Brent Edward. BSME, Northeastern U., 1974; MS in Systems Mgmt., U. So. Calif., 1982. Registered profl. engr., N.Y., N.H., Ariz., Nev.; registered land surveyor, Ariz. Test engr. Stone & Webster Engring., Boston, 1974-76; plant engr. N.Y. State Power Authority, Buchanan, 1976-80; maintenance engr. Pub. Service Co. of N.H., Seabrook, 1980-82; cons. engr. Helios Engring. Inc., Litchfield Park, Ariz., 1982-87; sr. supervisory service engr. Quadrex Corp., Coraopolis, Penn., 1987—. Republican. Roman Catholic. Home and Office: 131 W Elm St Pembroke MA 02359

MILLER, KENNETH RUSSELL, JR., insurance and real estate executive; b. Bellevue, Pa., Mar. 7, 1946; s. Kenneth R. Sr. and Velma Jean (Barto) M.; divorced. Registered rep. Nat. Assn. Securities Dealers; lic. broker, SEC. Announcer various radio and TV stas., Calif. and Idaho, 1967-70; mgr. Alltrans Trucking, Watsonville, Calif., 1970-72, Bekins Moving & Storage Co., Burlingame, Calif., 1972-73; ins. agt. Mass. Mut. Life Ins. Co., San Jose, Calif., 1973-79; prin. Personalized Estate Planners, Sunnyvale, Calif., 1979-81; ins., investment real estate investor Money Concepts/Santa Clara County, Sunnyvale, Calif., 1982—. Served as cpl. USMC, 1964-67, Vietnam. Mem. Internat. Assn. Fin. Planners, San Jose Life Underwriters Assn., San Jose Real Estate Bd. Assn. Lodge: Eagles. Home: 3765 SE 25th St Gresham OR 97080 Office: PO Box 826 Gresham OR 97030

MILLER, KENT DUNKERTON, physics and computer science educator; b. Duluth, Minn., Apr. 17, 1941; s. Paul Theodore and Melba D. (Dunkerton) M.; children: Kendra, Jeffrey. BA in Physics, Ariz. State U., 1964, MA in Physics, 1965. Physics tchr. Claremont (Calif.) Sch. Dist., 1964-79, computer instr., cons., 1979-86; astronomy tchr. Citrus Coll., Glendora, Calif., 1969-88, prof. physics, 1987—; computer edn. and staff devel. cons., So. Calif., 1980-85; planetarium presentor Citrus Coll., 1975-85. Recipient McLuhan Disting. Educator award Marshall McLuhan Ctr. on Global Communications, 1984. Mem. AAAS, NEA, Am. Assn. Physics Tchrs., Calif. Tchrs. Assn. Democrat. Presbyterian. Home: 1166 Eileen Ct Upland CA 91786 Office: Citrus Coll Foothill Blvd Glendora CA 91740-1899

MILLER, KEVIN WEBSTER, mechanical engineer; b. Seattle, Mar. 24, 1959; s. Robert Webster and Joann (Foster) M.; m. Lela Ann Gallentine, June 12, 1982. BS in Mech. Engring., Oreg. State U., 1982. Stock handler II Tektronix, Inc., Beaverton, Oreg., summers 1978-80; engring. tech. Mare Island Naval Shipyard, Vallejo, Calif., 1981, nuclear engr., 1982—. Mem. The Planetary Soc., Nat. Space Soc.

MILLER, LARRY H., automobile dealer, professional sports team executive; b. Salt Lake City; m. Gail Miller; 5 children. Formerly with auto parts bus., Denver and Salt Lake City; now owner auto dealerships, Salt Lake City, Albuquerque, Denver and Phoenix; part-owner Utah Jazz, NBA, Salt Lake City, 1985-86, owner, 1986—. Office: care Utah Jazz 5 Triad Ctr Ste 500 Salt Lake City UT 84180 *

MILLER, LAURIE, science editor; b. Fed. Republic Germany, May 7, 1960; came to U.S., 1961; d. Thomas Walter and Jacquelyn (Jolley) M. Student, U. Minn., 1979-80; BA in Psychology, Scripps Coll., 1983; postgrad., UCLA. Programmer specialist Control Data Corp., San Diego, 1982, asst. mgr. software retail store, 1983-84; support technician Ashton-Tate, Torrance, Calif., 1984, editor-in-chief, 1985-87; mgr. tech. pub. Ashton-Tate, Torrance, 1986-87; product mgr. Apple Products, Nantucket Corp., Los Angeles, 1987-88; sr. mktg. cons. Macintosh Market Launch Systems, Rancho Palos Verdes, Calif., 1988; pres. Miller Tech. Pub., Los Angeles, 1987—; ind. contractor, Calif. Tech. and devel. editor Addison-Wesley, Osborne/McGraw Hill, TAB books; contbr. feature articles to monthly mag., 1985—, computer product manuals, 1987—. Mem. Software Pubs. Assn., Los Angeles chpt. Soc. Tech. Communication, Apple Programmers/Developers Assn., Pi Beta Phi (asst. treas. 1980). Democrat. Methodist.

MILLER, LOIS BLAIN, elementary teacher; b. Safford, Ariz., Sept. 3, 1930; d. Orin Robert and Lenna Kathryn (Bryce) Blain; m. Robert Wayne Miller, Jan. 28, 1950; children: Marcella, Dawn, Lisa, Kathryn, Robert A. Diploma, Gila Jr. Coll., Thatcher, Ariz., 1949; BA, Ariz. State U., 1951; postgrad., Sacramento State U., 1954-88, U. Calif., Davis, 1954-88. Tchr. kindergarten, first grade North Sacramento (Calif.) Sch. Dist., 1953-58; tchr. kindergarten and first grade Rocklin (Calif.) Sch. Dist., 1962—. Author: (with others) Filling the Gaps, 1984. Pres. Early Childhood Assn., Tempe, Ariz., 1950-51. Mem. Calif. Tchrs. Assn. (past-pres. Rocklin chpt.), Delta Kappa Gamma. Republican. Mormon. Home: 3805 Clover Valley Rd Rocklin CA 95677 Office: Rocklin Sch Dist 5145 Topaz Ave Rocklin CA 95677

MILLER, MARC DOUGLAS, airline pilot; b. New Orleans, Oct. 28, 1953; s. Harold and Juliette (Graff) M.; m. Denice Kaye Duchemin, Apr. 24, 1983; children: Catherine Rachael, Audrey Rose. BS, Tulane U., 1975, MS, 1976. Lic. FAA airline transport pilot; cert. flight instr. Regional airline capt. Scheduled Skyways, Inc., Fayetville, Ariz., 1983-85; nat. airline capt. Am. West Airlines, Phoenix, 1985—. Percussionist Mesa (Ariz.) Symphony Orch., 1985—. Served to lt. USN, 1976-82; lt. comdr. USNR, 1983—. Mem. Aircraft Owners and Pilots Assn. Republican. Jewish. Home: 15 W Vinedo Ln Tempe AZ 85284 Office: Am West Airlines 222 S Mill Ave Tempe AZ 85281

MILLER, MARION, manufacturing company executive; b. Spokane, Wash., July 7, 1913; s. Herman Gottleib and Maud (Fyke) M.; m. Marylouise Page, July 24, 1942 (div. 1968); children: Michael Afton; m. Doris Marie Dilley, Nov. 29, 1986. Student, U. Wash., 1931-34. Farm mgr. Miller Bros. Farm, Greenacres, Wash., 1933-45; irrigation mgr. Armold & Jeffer, Spokane, 1946-47; pres. Anderson-Miller Mfg. Co., Spokane, 1947-68; mktg. specialist W.R. Ames, Milpitas, Calif., 1968-71; mfrs. agt., pres. Marion Miller & Assocs., Colorado Springs, Colo., 1971—; pres. Irrigation Industries, Colorado Springs, 1976-86. Inventor irrigation equipment accessories. Named Man of the Year Idaho Irrigation Equipment Assn., 1987. Mem. Irrigation Assn. (bd. dirs. 1949-51, v.p.1952, pres. 1953. Industry Achivement award 1982), Am. Soc. Agrl. Engrs. (v.p. NW chpt. 1947), Spokane Club, Kiwanis, Lions. Unitarian. Home: 815 Old Dutch Mill Rd Colorado Springs CO 80907 Office: Marion Miller & Assocs PO Box 790 Colorado Springs CO 80901

MILLER, MARK CHARLES, chef, restaurateur; b. Gardner, Mass., Feb. 25, 1949; s. John Charles and Marie Jeanette (Hebert) M. BA, U. Calif., Berkeley, 1970, postgrad. in anthropology, 1972-73. Chef Chez Panisse, Berkeley, 1975-79; chef, owner Fourth Street Grill, Berkeley, 1979-85; chef, owner, mgr. Santa Fe Bar and Grill, Berkeley, 1980-81, Coyote Cafe, Santa Fe, 1987--; bd. dirs. New Eng. Culinary Acad., Montpelier, Vt., 1985--; mem. exec. bd. Symposium on Am. Cuisine, Louisville, 1988--. Author: Coyote Cafe, 1989. Named One of Top 25 Food People, Cook's mag., 1985, One of Best Young Chefs Am., Food and Wine, 1985; recipient key to City of Dallas, 1987. Mem. Master Chefs, Am. Inst. Food and Wine. Democrat. Office: Coyote Cafe 132 W Water St Santa Fe NM 87501

MILLER, MARTHA GLENN, academic administrator, consultant; b. Roswell, N.Mex., Aug. 20, 1951; d. Frank Chester and Mary Elizabeth (Russell) M.; m. Robert John Cox (div. 1980); m. William Robert Claybaugh II, May 12, 1984; 1 child, William Robert III. BA, Ind. U., 1974; PhD, Harvard U., 1979. Asst. prof. Yale Sch. of Orgn. and Mgmt., New Haven, Conn., 1980-84, asst. dean, 1984-85, assoc. dean, 1985-86; asst. dean Anderson Grad. Sch. Mgmt. UCLA, Los Angeles, 1987—; lectr. Harvard U., Cambridge, Mass., 1979-80; sr. assoc. Good Measure, Inc., Cambridge, 1976—. Fellow Danforth Found., 1974-78; Disting. scholar Ind. U. and Gen. Motors Corp., Bloomington, 1970-74; recipient Disting. Alumna

Award, Ind. U., 1974. Mem. Am. Sociol. Assn., Internat. Jour. of Small Group Research, Phi Beta Kappa. Home: 1054 Sueno Ct Camarillo CA 93010 Office: UCLA Anderson Grad Sch Mgmt 405 Hilgard Av Los Angeles CA 90024-1481

MILLER, MAYNARD MALCOLM, geology educator, research facility director, explorer; b. Seattle, Jan. 23, 1921; s. Joseph Anthony and Juanita Queena (Davison) M.; m. Joan Walsh, Sept. 15, 1951; children: Ross McCord, Lance Davison. BS magna cum laude, Harvard U., 1943; MA, Columbia U., 1948; PhD (Fulbright scholar), Cambridge (Eng.) U., 1957; student, Naval War Coll., Nat. Security Seminar Air War Coll., Oak Ridge Inst. Nuclear Sci. Registered profl. geologist, Idaho. Asst. prof. naval sci. Princeton (N.J.) U., 1946; geologist Gulf Oil Co., Cuba, 1947; rsch. assoc., coordinator, dir. Office Naval Rsch. Am. Geog. Soc., N.Y.C., 1948-51; vis. staff scientist Swiss Fed. Inst. for Snow and Avalanche Rsch., Davos, 1952-53; instr. dept. geography Cambridge U., 1953-54; assoc. producer, field unit dir. film Seven Wonders of the World for Cinerama Corp., Europe, Africa, Middle East, 1954-55; rsch. assoc. Lamont Geol. Obs., N.Y.C., 1955-57; sr. scientist dept. geology Columbia U., N.Y.C., 1957-59; asst. prof. geology Mich. State U., East Lansing, 1959-61; assoc. prof. Mich. State U., Lansing, 1961-63, prof., 1963-75; prof. geology, dean Coll. Mines and Earth Resources, also dir. Glaciological and Arctic Environ. Scis. Inst. (founder of inst. at Mich. State U. 1960) U. Idaho, Moscow, 1975—; prin. investigator, geol. cons. numerous sci. contracts and projects for govt. agys., univs., pvt. corps., geographic socs., 1946—, including geophys. cons. U.S. Forest Svc., 1956, Nat. Park Svc., NASA, 1964-72, chief geologist Am. Mt. Everest Expdn., 1963, dir. Nat. Geographic Soc. Alaskan Glacier Commemorative Project, 1964-74, field leader Mt. Kennedy Yukon Meml. Mapping Expdn., 1965, Muséo Argentino de Ciencias Naturales, Inst. Geologico del Peru, 1949-50, missions to People's Rep. of China, 1981, 86, 88, expdns. to Himalayas, Nepal, 1963, 84, 87; cons. to USAF mission to Polar Sea, 1951, to USN arctic project for Office Naval Rsch., 1958, prin. investigator U.S. Naval Oceanographic Office Rsch. Alaska, 1967-68, 70-73; dir. lunar field sta. simulation program Boeing Co., 1959-60; exec. dir. Found. for Glacier and Environ. Rsch., Pacific Sci. Ctr., Seattle, 1955—, pres., 1955-80, trustee, 1960—, organizer, dir. Juneau (Alaska) Icefield Rsch. Program, 1946; cons. Dept. Hwys. State of Alaska, 1965; chmn., exec. dir. World Ctr. for Exploration Found., N.Y.C., 1968-71; dir., mem. adv. bd. Idaho Geol. Survey, 1975-88; chmn. nat. coun. JSHS program U.S. Army Rsch. Office and Acad. Applied Sci., 1982—; lectr. worldwide; disting. guest prof. dept. earth scis. Chanchun U., 1988. Co-author book on Alaskan glaciers; contbr. over 200 reports, sci. papers to profl. jours., 12 ency. articles, chpts. to books, monographs; producer, lectr. 16 mm. films and videos. Past mem. nat. exploring com., nat. sea exploring com. Boy Scouts Am., mem-at-large nat. coun.; mem. nat. adv. bd. Embry Riddle Aero. U.; bd. dirs. Idaho Rsch. Found.; past mem. adv. com. Nat. Parks and Monuments, Dept. Interior; adv. com. arctic and mountain equipment U.S. Army; past pres. Lansing UN Assn.; pres. state div. Mich. UN Assn., 1970-73; mem. Centennial Commn., Moscow, 1987-89. With USN, 1943-46, PTO, capt. USNR, 1966—. Decorated 11 battle stars; named Leader of Tomorrow Seattle C. of C. and Time mag., 1953, one of Ten Outstanding Young Men U.S. Jaycees, 1954; recipient commendation for lunar environ. study USAF, 1960, Hubbard medal (co-recipient with Mt. Everest expdn. team) Nat. Geographic Soc., 1963, Elisha Kent Kane Gold medal Geog. So. Phila., 1964, Karo award (with Mt. Kennedy expdn. team) Soc. Mil. Engrs., 1966, Franklin L. Burr award Nat. Geog. Soc., 1967, Outstanding Contbn. commendation Boy Scouts Am, 1970, Dedicated Svc. commendation plaque UN Assn. U.S.A., Disting Svc. field of geology commendation State of Mich. Legislature, 1975, Outstanding Citizen Svc. medal U.S. Army Rsch. Office, 1977, Outstanding Leadership in Minerals Edn. commendation Idaho Mining Assn., 1987; Grad. Residence fellow Cobia U., 1946-48; recipient numerous grants Artic Inst. N. Am., Geol. Soc. Am., Sigma Xi, Explorers Club, Am. Philos. Soc., Reader's Digest Found., DeWitt Wallace Found., Talbert Adams Found., Gulf Oil Corp., Union Oil Found., USAF, U.S. Dept. Interior, Mich. State U. Alumni Assn., NASA, NSF, 1948-89, ARO. Fellow Am. Geol. Soc., Arctic Inst. N.Am. Explorers Club; mem. AIME, Am. Geophys. Union, Am. Meterol. Soc., Internat. Glaciological Soc. (past councilor) N.Y. Acad. Scis., Am. Soc. Photogrammetry, ASME (hon. nat. lectr.), Am. Assn. State Geologists (hon.), Am. Assn. Amateur Oarsmen (life), Am. Alpine Club (past councilor, life mem.), Alpine Club (London), Appalachian Club (hon. corr.), Brit. Mountaineering Assn. (hon., past v.p.), Himalyan Club (Calcutta, India), English Speaking Union (nat. lectr.), Navy League, Naval Res. Assn. (life), Dutch Treat Club, Circumnavigators Club (life), Adventurers Club (medalist), Harvard Club (N.Y.C. and Seattle), Mining Club (N.Y.C.), Sigma Xi, Phi Beta Kappa (pres. Epsilon chpt. Mich. State U. 1969-70), Phi Kappa Phi. Republican. Methodist. Home: 514 E First St Moscow ID 83843 Office: U Idaho Coll Mines & Earth Resources Mines Bldg Rm 204 Moscow ID 83843

MILLER, MICHAEL JON, survey engineer, local government manager; b. Parkers Prairie, Minn., Mar. 17, 1950; s. Buford Kenneth and Gretchen Cena (Sharp) M.; m. Terry Lynn Peck, May 20, 1972; children: Livia Mica, David Peter. BS, U. Wis., Platteville, 1972; M of Pub. Adminstrn., Ariz. State U., 1988. Cert. profl. land surveyor, Wis., Ariz., soil tester, Wis. Chief of surveys Hovelsrud Cons. Assn., Richland Ctr., Wis., 1972-78; ops. mgr. Tech, Advisors, Inc., Phoenix, 1978-82; profl. surveyor Coe and Van Loo, Inc., Phoenix, 1982-83; survey engr. City of Phoenix, 1983—. Contbr. articles to profl. jours. Dep. registrar Dem. Party of Ariz., Phoenix, 1983—; clk. Phoenix Friends Meeting, 1985-86; recording clk. Intermountain Yearly Meeting of Religious Soc. of Friends, 1984-85. Fellow Am. Congress Surveying and Mapping (membership chmn. 1987-88); mem. Nat. Soc. Profl. Surveyors (gov. for Ariz. 1985—), Western Fedn. Land Surveyors (state del. 1988—), Ariz. Profl. Land Surveyors (sec. 1983-84, pres. 1985-86, Outstanding award 1981), Internat. Jugglers Assn. Club, Greater Ariz. Bicycle Assn. Club. Democrat. Home: 4026 E Campbell Phoenix AZ 85018

MILLER, MILTON DAVID, agronomist, educator; b. Melmont, Wash., Nov. 27, 1911; s. Milton and Katie Virginia (Manney) M.; m. Mary Eleanor McGraw, July 24, 1932; children: Mary Lee Varone, Judith Marie Zone. BS, U. Calif., Davis, 1935, MS, 1960. Cert. profl. agronomist; cert. profl. crop specialist. Extension agronomist U. Calif., Davis, 1936-74; tech. advisor Calif. Rice Research Bd., (disting. service award 1974), Yuba City, Calif., 1970-82; cons. World Bank, Romania, 1975, US Aid, Egypt, 1977. Served to lt. col. Q.M.C., 1941-46. Recipient Legion of Merit award U.S. Army, 1949. Fellow AAAS, Am. Soc. Agronomy, Am. Crop Sci. Soc.; mem. Sigma Xi, Alpha Zeta, Alpha Gamma Rho. Republican. Club: Commonwealth of Calif. Lodges: Rotary, Masons. Home: 624 Oak Ave Davis CA 95616

MILLER, NORMAN, psychology educator, researcher; b. N.Y.C., Nov. 29, 1933; s. Arthur and Pearl (Doudera) M.; divorced 1975; 1 dau., Carrie Ellen. B.A., Antioch Coll., Yellow Springs, Ohio, 1956; M.S., Northwestern U., 1957; Ph.D., 1959. Asst. prof. Yale U., New Haven, 1959-65; assoc. prof. U. Calif., Riverside, 1966-68; assoc. prof. U. Minn., Mpls., 1966-68, prof., 1968-70; prof. psychology U. So. Calif., Los Angeles, 1970—, now Mendel B. Silberberg prof. Jame McKeen Cattell fellow, 1978; Guggenheim fellow, 1984-85; Fulbright Research fellow Bar-Ilan U. Israel, 1984-85. Office: U So Calif Dept Psychology Univ Park Los Angeles CA 90089

MILLER, NORMAN CHARLES, JR., newspaper editor; b. Pitts., Oct. 2, 1934; s. Norman Charles and Elizabeth (Burns) M.; m. Mollie Rudy, June 15, 1957; children—Norman III, Mary Ellen, Teri, Scott. B.A., Pa. State U., 1956. Reporter Wall Street Jour., San Francisco, 1960-63; reporter Wall Street Jour., N.Y.C., 1963-64; bur. chief Wall Street Jour., Detroit, 1964-66; Washington corr. Wall Street Jour., 1966-72, Washington Bur. chief, 1973-83; nat. editor Los Angeles Times, 1983—. Author: The Great Salad Oil Swindle, 1965. Served to lt. (j.g.) USN, 1956-60. Recipient Disting. Alumnus award Pa. State U., 1978; George Polk Meml. award L.I. U., 1963; Pulitzer Prize, 1964. Roman Catholic. Club: Gridiron (Washington). Office: Los Angeles Times Times Mirror Sq Los Angeles CA 90036

MILLER, PATRICIA ANN, state official; b. Yuba City, Calif., Jan. 31, 1943; d. Monroe Albert and Esther Marie (Schoeniger) Behr; m. Frederic Joseph May, Dec. 30, 1965 (div. 1977); children: Cameron Douglas and Jennifer Marie (twins); m. Charles William Miller, Apr. 11, 1981; stepchildren: Michael, Kenneth, Cynthia Dibb, John. AA in English/Bus., Yuba Community College, 1962. Stenographer Calif. Dept. Fin., Sacramento, 1962-64; fgn. service Am. Embassy, Paris, 1965; stenographer Calif. Dept. Transp., Marysville, 1966-73, asst. info. officer, 1973-80, info. officer, 1980--. Publicity chmn. Am. Field Service, Yuba City, 1987, 88. Recipient Sustained Superior Accomplishment award Calif. Dept. Transp., 1987. Republican. Roman Catholic. Office: Calif Dept Transp 703 B St Marysville CA 95901

MILLER, PAUL ALBERT, diversified holding company executive; b. San Francisco, Oct. 30, 1924; s. Robert W. and Elizabeth (Folger) M.; children: Robert L., Charles B., Christian F., Gordon E., Alejandro C., Juan J. BA, Harvard U., 1946. Staff aide So. Calif. Gas Co., Los Angeles, 1948-52; treas., dir. Pacific Enterprises, San Francisco, 1952-58, v.p., treas., 1958-66, exec. v.p., 1966-68, pres., chief exec. officer, 1968-72, chmn. bd., chief exec. officer, 1972—; bd. dirs. Wells Fargo & Co., Wells Fargo Bank, Newhall Mgmt. Corp.; trustee Mut. Life Ins. Co. N.Y. Bd. dirs. Civic Light Opera Assn., Los Angeles World Affairs Council, United Way, Los Angeles, Calif. Bus. Roundtable ; trustee Am. Enterprise Inst., Washington, U. So. Calif.; dir. French Found. for Alzheimer Rsch. Served with U.S. Army, 1943-46. Mem. Calif. C. of C. (bd. dirs.). Clubs: Pacific Union, Bohemian (San Francisco); Brook, Racquet and Tennis (N.Y.C.); The Regency; Regency Whist. London, Portland; White's. Office: Pacific Enterprises 801 S Grand Ave Los Angeles CA 90017

MILLER, RALPH MENNO, minister, religious organization administrator; b. Hubbard, Oreg., Mar. 22, 1925; s. Samuel S. and Catherine (Hooley) M.; m. Evelyn Irene Whitfield, Feb. 23, 1947; children: Judith Karen, Donna Joyce. D of Ministry, Internat. Bible Inst. and Sem., 1985. Owner, operator M & M Logging, Sweet Home, Oreg., 1952-56; support person Children's Farm Home, Palmer, Alaska, 1956-58; pastor North Pole (Alaska) Assembly of God, 1959-68, Sitka (Alaska) Assembly of God, 1968-78; pioneer pastor Sand Lake Assembly of God, Anchorage, 1978-84; sec., treas. Alaska Dist. Assemblies of God, Anchorage, 1978—, presbyter, 1964—; gen. presbyter Gen. Council Assemblies of God, Springfield, Mo.; exec. presbyter Alaska Assemblies of God, Anchorage, 1978—; exec. dir. Alaska Ch. Builders, 1984—, Revolving Loan Fund, Anchorage, 1984—, Little Beaver Camp, Big Lake, Alaska, 1984—. Pres. PTA, North Pole, 1964-66. Republican. Home: 2111 Tasha Dr Anchorage AK 99502 Office: Alaska Dist Assemblies of God 1048 W Internat Airport Rd #101 Anchorage AK 99518

MILLER, RANDY SMARR, mortgage banking company executive; b. Ann Arbor, Mich., June 5, 1958; s. William G. and Frances Helen (Smarr) M. BS, U. So. Calif., 1980. Account supr. Wrather Corp., Beverly Hills, Calif., 1980-83, Health & Tennis Corp., Century City, Calif., 1983; account supr. Colwell Fin., L.A., 1984; v.p. fin. Nat. Home Equity Corp., Woodland Hills, Calif., 1984-88; pres. Prime Access Corp., Woodland Hills, 1986-88; chief fin. officer Nat. Comml. Equity Corp., Woodland Hills, 1986-88, Equity Asset Mgmt. Corp., Woodland Hills, 1986-88; pres. Am. Resource Mortgage Group, 1989—. Mem. Am. Mgmt. Assn. Home: 4775 Regalo Rd Woodland Hills CA 91364 Office: Nat Home Equity Corp 8100 Balboa Blvd Van Nuys CA 91406

MILLER, RICHARD ELIHU, radiologist; b. N.Y.C., Jan. 5, 1942; s. David and Lillian Gloria (Atlas) M.; m. Isabelle kColette Sarton, June 21, 1976; children: Daniel, Jonathan, Pascal. AB, U. Calif.-Berkeley, 1968; MA, U. Calif.-San Diego, 1971; postgrad., U. Paris South, 1973-76; Dr.med., Albert Einstein Coll. Medicine, 1978. Diplomate Am. Bd. Radiology. Resident in diagnostic radiology UCLA-Harbor Med Ctr., Kirkland, Wash., 1978-82, fellow in neuroradiology, 1982-83; staff radiologist Evergreen Hosp. Med. Ctr., Kirkland, Wash., 1983--, chief diagnostic imaging, 1986--. Mem. Am. Soc. Neuroradiology (sr.), Am. Coll. Radiology, Radiol. Soc. N.Am., Wash. State Radiol. Soc. Home: 11828 84th Ave NE Kirkland WA 98034 Office: Evergreen Hosp Med Ctr 13127 121st Way NE Kirkland WA 98034

MILLER, RICHARD FRANKLIN, teacher, researcher, educational administrator; b. San Francisco, Sept. 9, 1927; s. Henry G. and Hulda M. M. A.B., San Francisco State U., 1950; M.A., U. Calif.-Berkeley, 1964, Ed.D., 1970. Cert. secondary tchr., gen. supr. Calif. With San Francisco Unified Sch. Dist., 1956—, tchr. bus. edn., econs. and social studies Mission High Sch., 1967—, adminstr. career edn. program, 1970-80. Mem. San Francisco Symphony, Fine Arts Mus. Soc. Served to sgt., U.S. Army, 1952-54. Fellow in edn. U. Calif.-Berkeley, 1974-75. Mem. Assn. Supervision and Curriculum Devel., San Francisco Fedn. Tchrs., Phi Delta Kappa. Democrat. Unitarian. Office: 3750 18th St San Francisco CA 94114

MILLER, RICK H., youth organization executive director; b. Fullerton, Calif., Dec. 11, 1947; s. Emilio and Molly (Kaplan) M.; m. Esther Kleiman, June 14, 1969; children: Kimberly, Aaron. BA, Calif. State U., Fullerton, 1970. Ednl. dir. Boys Club of San Gabriel Valley, El Monte, Calif., 1970-73; exec. dir. Boys Club of Buena Park (Calif.), 1973-78; dir. govt. relations Boys Club of Am., Washington, 1978-83; exec. dir. Boys and Girls Clubs of Met. Phoenix, 1983—; staff asst. White House Presdl. Task Force, Washington, D.C., 1982; adj. faculty Ariz. State U., Tempe, 1985-86. Contbr. articles to numerous profl. jours. Chmn. Beautification Commn., Buena Park, 1977-78, United Way Delinquency Symposium, Phoenix, 1984, United Way Exec. Dirs. Assn., Phoenix, 1986-87; vice chmn. City Solicitation Bd., Phoenix, 1987—. Mem. Boys Club Profl. Assn. (bd. dirs. 1988—). Democrat. Jewish. Club: Soc. Am. Magicians. Office: Boys and Girls Clubs of Met Phoenix 2218 W Missouri Phoenix AZ 85015

MILLER, RITA SARAH K., public health administrator; b. Mt. Vernon, N.Y., Feb. 25, 1914; d. Samuel Abraham and Bertha (Shreero) Kaitz; m. Harry Miller, Apr. 21, 1948. BS, Adelphi U., 1946, MA, 1974. RN. Teaching supr. dept. nursing edn. U. Oreg. Med. Sch., Portland, 1946-48; pres. North Shore Sci. Mus., Plandome, N.Y., 1965-72; coord. emergency med. svcs. Nassau County Dept. Health, Mineola, N.Y., 1974-77, pub. health adminstr., 1977-88; developed pvt. buying office, Santa Fe, 1989—; mem. Coun. Internat. Rels. Vol. speaker N.Mex. AIDS Svcs.; vol. St. Elizabeth's Shelter, Santa Fe; mem. Wheelwright Mus. of Am. Indian, Santa Fe Opera Guild, Santa Fe Pub. Libr. Mem. Santa Fe C. of C. (women's div.), Santa Fe Sch. Am. Rsch. Democrat. Home: 1053 Buckman Rd Santa Fe NM 87501

MILLER, ROBERT, investment banker; b. L.A., Mar. 26, 1947; s. Robert Martin and Marion Elisabeth (Mills) M.; m. Amparo Jaramillo, Nov. 6, 1978; 1 child, Alicia. Ptnr. CaliforniaGroup, Newport, 1972—. Office: Calif Group 3931 MacArthur Blvd Ste 108 Newport Beach CA 92660

MILLER, ROBERT HYLAND, optical physicist; b. Balt.; s. Theodore Hyland and Emma Louise (Kahmer) M.; B.A. in Physics, Johns Hopkins U., 1962; M.S., Stevens Inst. Tech., N.J., 1968. Supr. lab. Keuffel & Esser Co., Morristown, N.J., 1962-72; tech. dir. Valtec Corp., Holliston, Mass., 1972-77; sr. research scientist Optical Coating Lab., Inc., 1977-80; sr. optical physicist Nanometrics, Sunnyvale, Calif., 1980-81; pres. Stanford Tech. Assoc., Santa Rosa, Calif., 1981-84; process devel. physicist 3M Co. (optical recording), Mountain View, Calif., 1984-88; thin film specialist 3M corp. rsch. labs., Mountain View, 1988—, cons. to cos. including LTV Corp., Allied Corp., Teledyne, and Siemens. Recipient Hon. Sci. award Bausch & Lomb, 1956. Mem. Optical Soc. Am., Am. Vacuum Soc., Materials Research Soc., Soc. Photo-Optical Instrumentation Engrs., IEEE, Mus. Soc. San Francisco. Home: 1816 Arroyo Sierra Ct Santa Rosa CA 95405 Office: 420 Bernardo Ave Mountain View CA 94043

MILLER, ROBERT JOSEPH, acting governor of Nevada, lawyer; b. Evanston, Ill., Mar. 30, 1945; s. Ross Wendell and Coletta Jane (Doyle) M.; m. Sandra Ann Searles, Oct. 17, 1949; children: Ross, Corrine. BA in Polit. Sci., U. Santa Clara, 1967; JD, Loyola U., Los Angeles, 1971. First legal advisor Las Vegas (Nev.) Met. Police Dept., 1973-75; justice of the peace Las Vegas Twp., 1975-78; dist. atty. Clark County, Las Vegas, 1979-86; lt. gov. State of Nev., 1987-89; acting gov. Nevada, 1989—. Chmn. Nev. Commn. on Econ. Devel., Carson City, 1987—, Nev. Commn. on Tourism, Carson City, 1987—; mem. Pres. Reagan's Task Force on Victims of Crime, 1982. Mem. Nat. Dist. Atty.'s Assn. (pres. 1984-85), Nev. Dist. Atty.'s Assn. (pres. 1979, 83). Democrat. Roman Catholic. Office: State of Nev Office of Gov Capitol Bldg Carson City NV 89710

MILLER, ROBERT L., bishop; b. Eagle Grove, Iowa, June 24, 1933; m. Doris Mandsager; children: Tedd, Darrell, Diane. BA, St. Olaf Coll. Pastor Luth. congregations, St. Louis Park, Minn., Riverside and Santa Barbara, Calif., First Luth. Ch., Fullerton, Calif.; bishop So. Calif. (East)-Hawaii Synod, Evang. Luth. Ch. in Am., Yorba Linda, Calif., 1988—. Office: Evang Luth Ch in Am 23655 Via Del Rio Ste B Yorba Linda CA 92686 *

MILLER, ROBERT SCOTT, not-for-profit organization administrator, social worker; b. Seattle, Dec. 12, 1947; s. Bert Lester and Carol Theresa (Gustafson) M.; m. Karen Ann Staake, Nov. 12, 1977; children: Sarah, Megan, Emily. BA in Sociology, Seattle Pacific U., 1970; AM in Social Work, U. Chgo., 1972; MA in Human Resources Mgmt., Pepperdine U., 1977. Registered counselor, Wash.; cert. social worker, Wash. Br. supr. Wash. State Dept. Social and Health Services, Oak Harbor and Anacortes, 1975-78; supr. casework Everett, 1973-75; lectr., coordinator rural community mental health project U. Wash., Seattle, 1978-83; exec. dir. Armed Services YMCA, Oak Harbor, 1984-86; area dir. United Way of Island County, Oak Harbor, 1986-88, exec. dir., 1988—; part-time instr. Chapman Coll., Orange, Calif., 1988—. Contbr. articles to profl. jours. Recipient outstanding service award Armed Services YMCA of U.S., Dallas, 1985, two program merit awards McDonald's Corp., Oak Harbor, 1986. Mem. Nat. Assn. Social Workers (bd. dirs. Wash. chpt. 1982-85), Wash. Assn. Social Welfare (pres. 1975-76), Acad. Cert. Social Workers, Bus. and Profl. Women (v.p. Oak Harbor chpt. 1985-86, pres. 1986-87), Internat. Platform Assn., Navy League, Wildlife Haven Water Assn. (pres. 1989—), Lions (sec. North Whidbey chpt. 1987-88, v.p. 1988-89, pres. 1989—). Lutheran. Home: 2450 S Rocky Way Coupeville WA 98239 Office: United Way of Island County Navy Family Svc Ctr Seaplane Base Bldg 20 PO Box 798 Oak Harbor WA 98277

MILLER, ROBERT TIMOTHY, distributing company executive; b. Oceanport, N.J., June 28, 1963; s. Daniel Ludrick and Isabel Dorcas (Lauterbach) M. BA in Polit. Theory, The Evergreen State Coll., Olympia, Wash., 1985, BS in Molecular Biology, 1985; postgrad., Wash. State U., 1987—. Software engr. Global Tech. Internat., Inc., Everett, Wash., 1985-87; sales mgr., tech. rep. Cosmologic, Pullman, Wash., 1987—. Patentee in field. Tektronix fellow, 1988. Democrat. Home: PO Box 2553 CS Pullman WA 99165-0933

MILLER, RONALD THOMAS, utility company executive; b. Burke, Idaho, Aug. 6, 1919; s. Dale D. and Mary E. (Dunphy) M.; m. Betty Loretta Bergman, Mar. 7, 1942; children—Mary L. (Mrs. John A. Rhine, Jr.), Margaret A. (Mrs. Jan E. Monroe). B.S., Oreg. State U., 1941. Registered profl. engr., Oreg. Insp. fed. diking project U.S. C.E., Deer Island, Oreg., 1941; with N.W. Natural Gas Co., Portland, 1947—; chief engr. N.W. Natural Gas Co., 1968-71, v.p. engring. and gas control, 1971-73, exec. v.p., 1973-75, pres., chief exec. officer, from 1975, also dir.; v.p., dir. Asso. Oreg. Industries, Blue Cross Oreg. Pres. Lake Oswego (Oreg.) P.T.A., 1963, Am. Field Service, Lake Oswego, 1966-67; bd. dirs. Portland Better Bus. Bur., Columbia-Pacific council Boy Scouts Am. Served to capt. C.E. AUS, 1942-47, PTO. Mem. Am. Gas Assn. (chmn. liquefied natural gas com. 1972-73, dir. 1979—), Am. Soc. M.E., Nat. Soc. Profl. Engrs., Profl. Engrs. Oreg. (award of merit 1968, chpt. sec. 1968), Pacific Coast Gas Assn. (gen. chmn. operating sect. 1972-73, dir. 1976—, 2d vice chmn. 1979—), Portland C. of C. (dir. 1979—), Alpha Sigma Phi. Republican. Roman Catholic. Clubs: Waverley Country (Portland); Arlington, Rotary. Office: NW Natural Gas Co 220 NW 2nd Ave Portland OR 97209 *

MILLER, ROY PHILLIP, bank executive; b. Windom, Minn., Oct. 31, 1945; s. Calvin Edward and Majorie (Hanson) M.; m. Mary Susan Berg, Oct. 1, 1977; children: Rachel, Allison, Katherine. BS, USAF Acad., 1967; MBA, Ariz. State U., 1979. Instr. piloting Sawyer Aviation, Phoenix, 1973-75; fin. planner Conn. Gen. Life Ins. Co., Phoenix, 1975-76; adminstrv. asst. Ariz. Corp. Commn., Phoenix, 1976-79; exec. dir. Mining Suppliers Trade Assn., Phoenix, 1979-82; v.p. First Interstate Bank, Phoenix, 1982-88; regietered rep. Stiteler Investment Co., Phoenix, 1988—. Mem. Arix. Acad., Phoenix, 1981—; chmn. Phoenix Civil Svc. Bd., 1982-83. Lt. col. USAFR, 1974—. Mem. Assn. for Corp. Growth, Ariz. Dept. Mines (bd. govs. 1987—), Western Pension Conf., Ariz. Econ. Forum (bd. dirs. 1982—), Mensa, Rotary (com. chmn. Phoenix chpt.). Republican. Lutheran. Home: 1529 W Virginia Ave Phoenix AZ 85007

MILLER, SAMUEL LEE, real estate executive; b. Maywood, Ill., Apr. 22, 1912; s. Samuel Lee and Clarissa (Buck) M.; PhB, U. Chgo., 1935; m. Sally Ann Walton, June 24, 1939 (dec.); 1 child, Sally Ann Roth; m. Irene A. Reed, 1973. Foreman mfg. Am. Can Co., Maywood, 1933-42; adminstrv. mgr. George S. May Co., San Francisco, 1942-47; gen. sales mgr. Hunt Foods and Industries, Fullerton, Calif., 1947-58; with H.M. Parker and Son, wholesale automobile parts co., 1958-68, v.p., gen. mgr., North Hollywood, Calif., 1962-68, bd. dirs., 1959-68; pres. Am. Parts Systems, Inc., North Hollywood, 1968-69, regional sales promotion mgr., 1970-71, gen. mgr., Fairfield, Calif., 1972-76; pres. Roth & Miller Realty, Inc., 1977-85. Mem. Masons, Theta Delta Chi. Republican. Methodist. Home: 248 Cheyenne Dr Vacaville CA 95688

MILLER, SAUL EDWARD, healthcare facility administrator; b. Memphis, Dec. 15, 1930; s. Levi Ervin and Ruth Mae (Ragsdale) M.; m. Carrie D. Turner, Jan. 15, 1956; children: Saul E., Darrell K., Cheryl D., Reginald W., Tammy E. BS in Computer Sci., Southern Ill. U., 1975, MS in Occupational Edn., 1978. Cert. tchr., Calif. Enlisted USAF, 1952, advanced through grades to chief master sgt., 1952-74, ret., 1977; computer adminstr. USAF, Omaha, 1952-77; computer systems mgr. Riverside (Calif.) Community Hosp., 1978-82, dir. hosp. systems, 1983--. Mem. Healthcare Info. and Mgmt. Soc. Democrat. Baptist. Home: 6246 Promontory Ln Riverside CA 92506 Office: Riverside Community Hosp PO Box 1669 Riverside CA 92502

MILLER, SELAINA AUNOA LEVI, employment and training executive; b. Apia, Western Samoa, May 5, 1946; came to U.S., 1962, naturalized, 1969; d. Arius and Avasa (Niu) Levi; m. Charles M. Miller, Dec. 14, 1974; 1 child, Jamila Atamai. AA, Chabot Coll., 1969; BA, Calif. State U., Hayward, 1971. Cert. tchr., Calif. Program developer/coordinator Alameda County Assn. Mentally Retarded, Oakland, Calif., 1969-71; program dir., tchr. Contra Costa Assn. Retarded/Richmond Calif. Sch. Dist., Walnut Creek, Calif., 1971-74; mgr. regional services MidWillamette Jobs Council, Pvt. Industry Council, Salem, Oreg., 1975—; mem. adv. bd. study on unemployment problems of Samoans, N.W. Regional edn. Lab., Portland, Oreg., 1982-83; participant vocation extern program for tchrs. and trainers Oreg. State U. and Oreg. Alliance for Program Improvement, Corvallis, 1985-86. Participant region 9-Oreg. Joint Action for Community Service, 1982-85; bd. dirs. Green Thumb Agy. for Older Workers, Oreg.-Wash., 1985-86, Community Action Orgn. Info. and Referral, Stayton, 1985-86; mem. community adv. bd. spl. programs for students Salem-Keizer Sch Dist., 1986-88, South Marion County Secondary Sch. Programs, 1987-88; active Metro Work Experience Coordinators Oreg., 1986-88, commn. bd. Mid-Willamette Child Care, 1988; mem. adv. bd. State of Oreg. Commn. for the Blind Summer Youth Program, 1989. Mem. Soc. for Training Devel., NAFE, Oreg. Employment and Tng. Assn. Avocations: sewing, gardening, swimming, volleyball, travel. Home: 18874 Old Mehama Rd SE Stayton OR 97383 Office: Mid Willamette Jobs Coun 1495 Edgewater NW Ste 225 Salem OR 97304

MILLER, STANLEY RAY, sound system consultant; b. Lincoln, Neb., Oct. 25, 1940; s. Maurice Winston and Blanche Fern (Mosier) M.; div.; children: Cordie Lynne, Neil Andrew. BA, Kearney State Coll., 1965. Founder, pres., chief exec. officer Stanal Sound Ltd., Hollywood, Calif., 1962—; lectr. in field at numerous colls.; cons., trainer Altec Sound Contractor, JBL SND Contractors. Cons. engr./audio mixer for sound systems and concerts; chief live concert mixing engr. for Neil Diamond, 1969—; designed, manufactured, and toured large sound systems, worldwide 1964—; has toured sound systems for Simon & Garfunkel, Johnny Cash, Christy Minstrels, Young Americans, Bill Cosby, Mac Davis, Dolly Parton, Pink Floyd, Bob Dylan, John Denver, The Osmond Bros., Donnie & Marie Osmond, Tom Jones and Englebert Humperdink, 1964—; dir. sound svcs. at the Universal Amphitheatre, Greek Theatre, Pantages Theatre, and Wilshire Theatre, Henry Fonda Theatre, Fiddler's Green; supplied sound systems for Papal visit L.A., Sept. 1987; sound designer audio systems for Rep. Nat. Conv., 1984, 88; responsible for functional design of more than ten different models of Yamaha Sound Mixing Consoles, and numerous other Yamaha, JBL products for Concert Sound Industry. Mem. Audio Engring Soc. (nat. convs.), Profl. Entertainment Prodn. Soc. (treas.), Elks. Republican. Lutheran. Home: 3336 Primera Ave Hollywood CA 90068 Office: Stanal Sound Ltd 7351 Fulton Ave North Hollywood CA 91605

MILLER, STEPHEN ALLAN, accountant; b. Salt Lake City, Dec. 8, 1950; s. Loren Deane and Wilburta (Tainter) M.; m. Mary Cynthia Lynch, Mar. 4, 1975 (div. 1988); children: Allan Thrall, Ehran Hale. BA, U. Denver, 1972; MS, Colo. State U., 1984. CPA, Colo. County assessor Larimer County, Ft. Collins, Colo., 1984, mgr. records, 1979-82, mgr. adminstrn., 1982—; pvt. practice Ft. Collins., 1984—. Campaign mgr. Com. to Elect Bob Schaffer for Senate, Ft. Collins, 1988; coord. Larimer Co. United Way, Ft. Collins, 1981-82. Served to lt. USN, 1972-78. Mem. AICPA's, Colo. Soc. CPA's, Govt. Fin. Officers Assn., Assn. of Records Mgrs. and Adminstrs. Republican. Methodist. Office: Larimer County 200 W Oak St Fort Collins CO 80522

MILLER, STEPHEN RICHARD, sales executive; b. L.A., Jan. 23, 1948; s. Bill Carl and Eleanore (Gabel) M.; m. Margaret Geanne McCurry, Feb. 24, 1971; children: Joellen Marie, W. Brian. BA in Sociology, Azusa Pacific U., 1971. Reg. sales mgr. AT&T, Cypress, Calif., 1972--. Fund raiser United Way, San Jose, Calif., 1976-77, San Jose Jr. Achievement, 1976-78; bd. dirs. Steve Russo Orgn., L.A., 1988. Mem. Masons. Republican. Baptist. Home: 1367 Rapidview Dr Walnut CA 91789 Office: AT&T 6300 Gateway Dr Cypress CA 90630

MILLER, STEVE, television director, producer; b. L.A., Sept. 13, 1951; s. Nathan H. and Shirley Ann (Watstein) M.; m. Lee Keiter, June 22, 1975; children: Jeffrey, Brian, David. BA in Telecommunications, U. So. Calif., 1973. Producer, dir. TV program: The Love Report, Eye on Hollywood, Entertainment Tonight, Christmas Eve at the Music Ctr., Dads, The Car Man, Together with Shirley and Pat Boone, Summer Faire, The Voyager Spacecraft Meets Saturn; dir. home videos Shape Up with Arnold Schwarzenegger, Mickey, Donald, Goofy & Friends, How to Use Your IBM PC; dir., producer commls. and corp. videos; contbr. articles to profl. jours. Mem. Dirs. Guild Am., Acad. TV, Arts and Scis.

MILLER, STEVE, nurse practitioner; b. N.Y.C., June 19, 1950; s. Charles and Thelma (Yorowsky) M.; m. Glenys Owen, Aug. 14, 1988. AAS, Orange County Community Coll., Middletown, N.Y., 1968; BA, NYU, 1972; MS in Nursing, Pace U, 1976; postgrad., Kennedy Western U. RN practitioner, N.Y., Hawaii; bd. cert. hypnotherapist. Counselor, advocate Deaf Svcs., Inc., N.Y.C., 1976-78; psychiat. intake worker Arden Hill Hosp., Goshen, N.Y., 1978-81; nurse Columbia Presbyn. Med. Ctr., N.Y.C., 1981-83; dir. Critical Care, Inc., Chester, N.Y., 1982-87, RTR Assocs., Kailua, Hawaii, 1987—; nurse practitioner Crisis Response Systems Project, Honolulu, 1987—. Author: (workshop) Evaluating the Deaf Client, 1976. With USAR. Mem. Am. Acad. Physicians Assts. (assoc.), Am. Guild Profl. Hypnotherapists, Hawaii Nurses Assn., Hawaii Svcs. on Deafness, Aloha State Assn. of Deaf. Home: PO Box 1618 Kailua HI 96734 Office: Crisis Response Systems 924 Self Ln Honolulu HI 96819

MILLER, SUSAN ALICE, school principal; b. McCook, Nebr., Mar. 11, 1947; d. Boyd and Angela E. (Skinner) Ready; m. J. John Miller, July 19, 1969 (div. Dec. 1977). BS, U. Nebr., 1969, MEd, 1978; postgrad., U. Colo., currently. Cert. sch. adminstr., Colo. Tchr., team leader Lincoln (Nebr.) Pub. Schs., 1970-78; tchr., asst. prin. Aurora (Colo.) Pub. Schs., 1978-80; tchr. Cherry Creek Pub. Schs., Englewood, Colo., 1980-81; dir. children's ministries Faith Presbyn. Ch., Aurora, 1981; dir. Christian edn. Cherry Hills Community Ch., Littleton, Colo., 1982-84; founder Cherry Hills Christian Sch., Englewood, 1984-85, prin., 1985—. Mem. Assn. Supervision and Curriculum Devel., Nat. Assn. Elem. Sch. Prins., Phi Delta Kappa. Office: Cherry Hills Christian Sch 3651 S Colorado Blvd Englewood CO 80110

MILLER, THOMAS CECIL, private investigator; b. Los Angeles, Jan. 27, 1951; s. Thomas Cecil Miller and Oetta Elizabeth (Buckman) Harrison; m. Michele Marie Autin, Aug. 23, 1986. BA in History and Journalism, Metro State Coll., 1974; BA in Classical Langs., U. Denver, 1985; MA in English, Middlebury Coll., 1985; postgrad., U. Denver, 1989. Freelance writer, journalist Denver; prin. Investigative Reporting Services, Denver, 1983—; Tchr. creative writing and mag. editing Avapapoe Community Coll., 1985-88, Met. State Coll., 1987-88; founder Pearl St. Press, 1988. Author numerous poems. Pub. relation dir. John Fuhr for Gov., Colo., 1982; del. Denver County Reps., 1984, alt., 1986. Mem. Profl. Pvt. Investigators Assn. Colo., Colo. Press. Assn., World Assn. of Detectives, Denver C. of C. Roman Catholic. Office: Investigative Reporting Svcs PO Box 10844 Denver CO 80209

MILLER, THOMAS EUGENE, legal editor, writer; b. Bryan, Tex., Jan. 4, 1929; s. Eugene Adam and Ella Lucille (Schroeder) M. BA, Tex. A&M U., 1950; MA, U. Tex., 1956, JD, 1966; postgrad. U. Houston, 1957-58, U Calif., 1983. Bar: Tex. 1966. Rsch. technician M.D. Anderson Hosp., Houston, 1956-58; claims examiner trainee Soc. Security Adminstrn., New Orleans, 1964; trademark examiner trainee Dept. Commerce, Washington, 1966; editor Bancroft-Whitney Co., San Francisco, 1966—. Author book under pseudonym. Contbg. mem. Dem. Nat. Com., 1981-89; mem. Common Cause, People for the Am. Way. Decorated Medal of Honor. Fellow Internat. Biog. Assn. (life, dep. dir. gen.), Am. Biog. Inst. (life, mem. rsch. bd. advisors; recipient Grand Amb. of Achievement award, adv. rsch. bd.), World Lit. Assn., World Inst. of Achievement; mem. ABA, Nat. Trust for Hist. Preservation, Tex. Bar Assn., Mus. Soc., Am. Wildlife Found., World Affairs Coun. No. Calif., Internat. Platform Assn., Nat. Writers Club, Press Club, Commonwealth Club, Phi Kappa Phi, Psi Chi, Phi Eta Sigma. Methodist. Home: 2293 Turk Blvd Apt 5 San Francisco CA 94118 Office: Bancroft-Whitney Co 3205 Van Ness Ave San Francisco CA 94109

MILLER, VICTORIA LOREN, designer, art director; b. San Francisco, May 25, 1957; d. Leon and Malvina (Hoffman) M. BFA, UCLA, 1979; postgrad., Art Ctr. Coll. Design, Pasadena, Calif., 1979, 80, UCLA, 1980-82, Otis/Parsons, L.A., 1981. Designer Bright and Assocs., L.A., 1979-80, Richard Runyon Design, L.A., 1980-83; art dir. Grey Entertainment Media, Santa Monica, Calif., 1984; prin. Victoria Miller Design, Santa Monica, Calif., 1984—; freelance art dir. Backer Spielvogel Bates, L.A., 1987-88; designer Sussman/Prejza & Co., Santa Monica, 1984, Scott Medrick and Assocs., L.A., 1988-89. Designer label Grand Cru Vineyards (Clio award 1985); pub. corp. identity system Am. Corp. Identity, Letterheads 5. Mem. Art Dirs. Club (L.A.). Republican. Jewish. Home and Office: 1350 Midvale #8 Los Angeles CA 90024

MILLER, WARREN EDWARD, political scientist; b. Hawarden, Iowa, Mar. 26, 1924; s. John Carroll and Mildred Ovedia (Lien) M.; m. Ruth S. Jones, May 1981; children by previous marriage: Jeffrey Ralph, Jennifer Louise. B.S., U. Oreg., 1948, M.S., 1950; Ph.D., Maxwell Sch. Citizenship and Public Affairs, Syracuse U., 1954; Ph.D. (hon.), U. Goteborg, Sweden, 1972. Asst. study dir. Survey Research Ctr., Inst. Social Research, U. Mich., 1951-53, study dir., 1953-56, research assoc., 1956-59, program dir., 1959-68, research coordinator polit. behavior program, 1968-70, prin. investigator nat. election studies, 1977—; dir. Ctr. Polit. Studies, Inst. Social Research, 1970-81; program dir. Ctr. Polit. Studies, 1982—; asst. prof. polit. sci. Ctr. Polit. Studies, Inst. Social Research, 1956-58, asso. prof., 1958-63, prof., 1963—, Arthur W. Bromage prof. polit. sci., 1981-82; prof. polit. sci. Ariz. State U., 1981—; fellow Center Advanced Study in Behavioral Scis., 1961-62; exec. dir. Inter-univ. Consortium for Polit. and Social Research, 1962-70, assoc. dir., 1978—; vis. prof. U. Tilburg, Netherlands, 1973, U. Geneva, 1973, European U. Inst., Florence, Italy, 1979; vis. Disting. prof. Ariz. State U., 1981; trustee Inst. Am. Univs., 1970—; Regents' prof., Ariz. State U., 1988—. Author: (with others) books including The Voter Decides, 1954, American Voter, 1960, Elections and the Political Order, 1966, (with T.E. Levitin) Leadership and Change: Presidential Elections from 1952-1976, 1977, (with M.K. Jennings) Parties in Transition, 1986, Without Consent, 1988, (with others) The American National Election Studies Data Sourcebook, 1952-1978, 1980, The American National Election Studies Data Sourcebook, 1952-86; contbr. (with others) articles to profl. publs.; editorial bd.: (with others) Am. Polit. Sci. Rev, 1966-71, Computers and the Humanities, 1969-71, Social Science History, 1976—, Social Science Rev., 1973; editorial adv. bd.: (with others) Sage Electoral Studies Yearbook, 1974. Served with USAAF, 1943-46. Recipient Disting. Alumnus award Maxwell Sch. Citizenship and Public Affairs, Syracuse U., 1974, Disting. Faculty Achievement award U. Mich., 1977. Fellow AAAS; mem. Am. Polit. Sci. Assn. (pres. 1979-80), Internat. Polit. Sci. Assn. (coun. 1969-73), M.W. Polit. Sci. Assn., Internat. Soc. Polit. Psychology, So. Polit. Sci. Assn., Social Sci. History Assn. (pres. 1979-80). Office: Ariz State U Dept Polit Sci Tempe AZ 85287-2001

MILLER, WENDELL SMITH, chemist, consultant; b. Columbus, Ohio, Sept. 26, 1925; s. Wendell Pierce and Emma Josephine (Smith) M.; m. Dorothy Marie Pagen, Aug. 18, 1949; children: William Ross, Wendell Roger. BA, Pomona Coll., 1944; MS, UCLA, 1952. Chemist U.S. Rubber Co., Torrance, Calif., 1944; sr. chemist Carbide & Carbon Chemicals Corp., Oak Ridge, 1944-48; ptnr. Kellogg & Miller, Los Angeles, 1949-56; patent coordinator Electro Optical Systems, Inc., Pasadena, Calif., 1956-59; v.p. Intertech. Corp. optical and optoelectronic system devel., North Hollywood, Calif., 1960-66, dir., 1966—; assoc. Ctr. for Study Evolution and Origin of Life, UCLA. Commr. Great Western Council Boy Scouts Am., 1960-65. Served with AUS, 1944-46. Decorated Army Commendation medal. Mem. Los Angeles Patent Law Assn., IEEE, AAAS, 20th Century Round Table, Sigma Xi, Phi Beta Kappa, Pi Mu Epsilon. Numerous patents in field. Home: 1341 Comstock Ave Los Angeles CA 90024

MILLER, WILFRED STARE, family practitioner; b. Decatur, Ill., May 9, 1931; s. Wilfred S. Miller and Cecile B. (King) Corzine; children by previous marriage: Mark Lee, Steven Dale, Wendy Sue, Bruce Allen, Jeffrey Brian; Mavis A. Veile, 1984. BS, Ill. Wesleyan U., 1952; MD, U. Ill., 1956. Diplomate, Am. Bd. Family Practice. Intern Deaconess Hosp., Spokane, Wash., 1956-57; resident Pierce County Hosp., Tacoma, 1960-61; physician Whitefish (Mont.) Clinic, 1961-65; ptnr. Family Physicians Clinic, Whitefish, 1965—; pres. med. staff, North Valley Hosp., 1966-67, 85-86. Maj., USANG, 1961-66. Mem. Am. Acad. Family Practice, Flathead Med. Soc. (pres. 1970-71), Jaycees (pres. 1964-65), Toastmasters, Rotary (pres. 1986-87). Home: PO Box 1327 Whitefish MT 59937 Office: Family Physicians Clinic 401 Baker St Whitefish MT 59937

MILLER, WILLIAM CLARE, test engineering manager; b. Des Moines, July 19, 1940; s. Dale Randolph Miller and Edith Patricia (Cremer) Mesecher; m. Sandra Frances Bauman, July 18, 1941; children: Mitzi, Mark R., Matthew W., Monique. BSEE, U. Ariz., 1966; MBA, U. Santa Clara, 1970. Product engr. Fairchild Semiconductor, Shiprock, N.Mex., 1966-67; sect. head TTL production Signetics, Sunnyvale, Calif., 1967-69, quality assurance mgr., 1969-71, with mil aero mktg. dept., 1971-73; ops. mgr. Precision Monolithics Inc., Santa Clara, Calif., 1973-75; logic test engring. mgr. Nat. Semiconductor, Santa Clara, Calif., 1975-80, memory test mgr., 1980-81, CMOS test engring. mgr., 1981-84, ASIC test engring. mgr., 1985—. Served with USAF, 1958-62. Republican. Congregationalist. Home: 1453 Menorca Ct San Jose CA 95120 Office: Nat Semiconductor 2900 Semiconductor Dr San Jose CA 95051

MILLER, WILLIAM ELWOOD, mining company executive; b. Bend, Oreg., May 9, 1919; s. Harry Adelbert and Sarah (Heyburn) M.; B.A., Stanford, 1941, M.B.A., 1947; m. Constance Alban Crosby, July 2, 1955; children—William, Constance, Harold, Mary, Sarah Crosby, Charles Crosby, Helen, Harry. Owner and operator Central Oregon Pumice Co., Bend, 1948—; pres. The Miller Lumber Co., Bend, The Miller Ranch Co., Bend. Commr., City of Bend, 1959-62, mayor, 1960. Bd. dirs. Central Oreg. Coll.; pres. Central Oreg. Coll. Found., 1956-57; dir. Central Oregon Coll. Area Ednl. Dist., 1961-65, chmn., 1964-65; bd. govs. Ore. Dept. Geology and Mineral Industries, 1971-75. Served with A.C., USNR, 1942-45. Decorated D.F.C., Air medal. Mem. Central Oreg. (v.p. 1954), Bend (pres. 1954) chambers commerce, Kappa Sigma. Republican. Episcopalian. Rotarian (dir. Bend 1955-56). Club: Bend Golf. Home: 527 NW Congress St Bend OR 97701 Office: #1 NW Greenwood Ave Bend OR 97701

MILLER, WILLIAM FREDERICK, research company executive, computer science educator; b. Vincennes, Ind., Nov. 19, 1925; s. William and Elsie M. (Everts) M.; m. Patty J. Smith, June 19, 1949; 1 son, Rodney Wayne. Student, Vincennes U., 1946-47; B.S., Purdue U., 1949, M.S., 1951, Ph.D., 1956; D.Sc., 1972. Mem. staff Argonne Nat. Lab., 1955-64, assoc. physicist, 1956-59, dir. applied math. div., 1959-64; prof. computer sci. Stanford U., Palo Alto, Calif., 1965—; Herbert Hoover prof. pub. and pvt. mgmt. Stanford U., 1979—, assoc. provost for computing, 1968-70, v.p. for research, 1970-71, v.p., provost, 1971-78; mem. Stanford Assocs., 1972—; pres., chief exec. officer SRI Internat., Menlo Park, Calif., 1979—; chmn. bd., chief exec. officer SRI Devel. Co., Menlo Park, David Sarnoff Research Ctr., Inc., Princeton, N.J.; prof. lectr. applied math. U. Chgo., 1962-64; vis. prof. math. Purdue U., 1962-63; vis. scholar Center for Advanced Study in Behavioral Scis., 1976; bd. dirs. Fireman's Fund Ins. Co., Ann. Revs. Inc., Varian Assos. Inc., 1st Interstate Bancorp, 1st Interstate Bank of Calif., Pacific Gas and Electric Co.; mem. computer sci. and engring. bd. Nat. Acad. Sci., 1968-71; mem. Nat. Sci. Bd., 1982-88; mem. corp. com. on computers in edn. Brown U., 1972-79; mem. policy bd. EDUCOM Planning Council on Computing in Edn., 1974-79, chmn., 1974-76; ednl. adv. bd. Guggenheim Meml. Found., 1976-80; com. postdoctoral and doctoral research staff NRC, 1977-80. Assoc. editor: Pattern Recognition Jour, 1968-72, Jour. Computational Physics, 1970-74. Served to 2d lt. F.A. AUS, 1943-46. Fellow IEEE, Am. Acad. Arts and Scis., AAAS; mem. Am. Math. Soc., Am. Phys. Soc., Soc. Indsl. and Applied Math., Assn. Computing Machinery, Nat. Acad. Engring., Sigma Xi. Office: SRI Internat 333 Ravenswood Ave Menlo Park CA 94025

MILLER, WILLIAM HUGHES, theoretical chemist, educator; b. Kosciusko, Miss., Mar. 16, 1941; s. Weldon Howard and Jewel Irene (Hughes) M.; m. Margaret Ann Westbrook, June 4, 1966; children: Alison Leslie, Emily Sinclaire. B.S., Ga. Inst. Tech., 1963; A.M., Harvard U., 1964, Ph.D., 1967. Jr. fellow Harvard U., 1967-69; NATO postdoctoral fellow Freiburg (Germany) U., 1967-68; asst. prof. chemistry U. Calif.-Berkeley, 1969-72, assoc. prof., 1972-74, prof., 1974—; fellow Churchill Coll., Cambridge (Eng.) U., 1975-76. Recipient Ann. prize Internat. Acad. Quantum Molecular Sci., 1974; Alfred P. Sloan fellow, 1970-72; Camille and Henry Dreyfus fellow, 1973-78; Guggenheim fellow, 1975-76; Alexander von Humboldt-Stiftung U.S. Sr. Scientist award, 1981-82; Ernest Orlando Lawrence Meml. award, 1985. Fellow AAAS., Am. Phys. Soc.; mem. Internat. Acad. Quantum Molecular Sci., Nat. Acad. Sci. Office: U Calif Dept Chemistry Berkeley CA 94720

MILLER, ZOYA DICKINS (MRS. HILLIARD EVE MILLER, JR.), civic worker; b. Washington, July 15, 1923; d. Randolph and Zoya Pavlovna (Klementinovska) Dickins; grad. Stuart Sch. Costume Design, Washington, 1942; student Sophie Newcomb Coll., 1944, New Eng. Conservatory Music, 1946; grad. Internat. Sch. Reading, 1969; m. Hilliard Eve Miller, Jr., Dec. 6, 1943; children: Jeffrey Arnot, Hilliard Eve III. Fashion coordinator, cons. Mademoiselle mag., 1942-44; instr. Stuart Summer Sch. Costume Design, Washington, 1942; fashion coordinator Julius Garfinckel, Washington, 1942-43; star TV show Cowbelle Kitchen, 1957-58, Flair for Living, 1958-59; model mags. and comml. films, also nat. comml. recs., 1956—; dir. program devel. Webb-Waring Lung Inst., Denver, 1973—. Mem. exec. com., bd. dirs. El Paso County chpt. Am. Lung Assn., 1954-63; mem. exec. com. Am. Lung Assn. Colo., 1965-84, bd. dris. 1965-87, chmn. radio and TV council, 1963-70, mem. med. affairs com., 1965-70, pres., 1961-68, procurer found. funds, 1965-70; developer nat. radio ednl. prodns. for internat. use Nat. Tb and Respiratory Disease Assn., Am. Lung Assn., 1963-70, coordinator statewide screening programs Colo., other states, 1965-72; chmn. benefit fund raising El Paso County Cancer Soc., 1963; founder, coordinator Colorado Springs Debutante Ball, 1967—; coordinator Nat. Gov.'s Conf. Ball, 1969; mem. exec. com. Colo. Gov.'s Comprehensive Health Planning Council, 1967-74, chmn., 1972-73; chmn. Colo. Chronic Care Com., 1969-73, chmn. fund raising, 1970-72, chmn. spl. com. congressional studies on nat. health bills, 1971-73; mem. Colo.-Wyo. Regional Med. Program Adv. Council, 1969-73; mem. Colo. Med. Found. Consumers Adv. Council, 1972-78; mem. decorative arts com. Colorado Springs Fine Arts Ctr., 1972-75; founder, state coordinator Nov. Noel Pediatrics Benefit Am. Lung Assn., 1973-87; founder, state pres. Newborn Hope, Inc., 1987—. Recipient James J. Waring award Colo. Conf. on Respiratory Disease Workers, 1963; Zoya Dickins Miller Vol. of Yr. award established Am. Lung Assn. of Colo., 1979; Nat. Pub. Relations award Am. Lung Assn., 1979, Gold Double Bar Cross award, 1980, 83; named Humanitarian of Yr., Am. Lung Assn. of Colo., 1987. Lic. pvt. pilot. Mem. Nat. (chmn. nat. father of year contest 1956-57), Colo., El Paso County (pres. 1954, TV chmn. 1954-59) cowbelle assns., Colo. Assn. Fund Raisers. Club: Broadmoor Garden (ways and means chmn. 1967-69, civic chmn. 1970-71, publicity chmn. 1972, awards chmn. 1987—, spl. events chmn. 1988) (Colorado Springs, Colo.). Contbr. articles, lectures on health care systems and fund raising. Home: 74 W Cheyenne Mountain Blvd Colorado Springs CO 80906

MILLER-DAVIDSON, MOLLY ANN, sales executive, consultant; b. St. Paul, Dec. 26, 1952; d. Willard V. and A. Florence (Selander) Miller. Student, Wayne State U., 1976. Nat. sales dir. Paper Co., Seattle, 1983-85; nat. dir. sales and mktg. The Gifted Line, Sausalito, Calif., 1985-86; writer, cons. gift and stationery industries San Francisco, 1986—; show dir. DesignFocus, San Francisco, 1987—. Contbg. editor: Giftware News Mag., 1987—. Mem. People for the Am. Way, 1986—. Mem. Am. Jewish Congress, Am. Jewish Com., ACLU. Democrat. Office: 2181 Greenwich St San Francisco CA 94123

MILLICAN, NANCY JO, electronics executive; b. Oklahoma City, Sept. 13, 1941; d. Reese Frank Galyon and Oma Juanita (Bowyer) Cline; m. Donald L. Millican, June 1, 1963 (div. Apr. 1986); children: David Reese, Mark Louis. AA in Gen. Bus., College of the Desert, Joshua Tree, Calif., 1987; postgrad., Calif. State U., San Bernardino, 1987, Calif. State U., Palm Desert, 1988; BBA, Nat. U., San Diego, 1988. Personnel sec. Moore Bus. Forms, Fullerton, Calif., 1963-66; exec. sec. Douglas Missile & Space Systems, Huntington Beach, Calif., 1966-67; bookkeeper Katum, Longmont, Colo., 1975-76; gen. mgr., chief exec. officer A.D.P. Mfg. Co., Yucca Valley, Calif., 1981—; chief exec. officer MECA, Yucca Valley, Calif., 1976—. Chmn. Ednl. TV (channel 6), Longmont, 1973-76; pres. Suncountry Community Assn., Yucca Valley, 1986—. Fellow Am. Mgmt. Assn.; mem. LWV (chmn. children's code 1975), Beta Sigma Phi, Zeta Zeta (pres. 1975), Xi Omecron Psi (pres. 1979). Presbyterian. Home: 627 S Geronimo Trail Yucca Valley CA 92284 Office: MECA 56677 Sunset Ave NBU 8419 Yucca Valley CA 92284

MILLIKEN, JOHN GORDON, research economist; b. Denver, May 12, 1927; s. William Boyd and Margaret Irene (Marsh) M.; m. Marie Violet Machell, June 13, 1953; children: Karen Marie, Douglas Gordon, David Tait, Anne Alain. B.S., Yale U., 1949, B.Eng., 1950; M.S., U. Colo., 1966, D.B.A., 1969. Registered profl. engr., Colo. Engr. U.S. Bur. Reclamation, Denver, 1950-55; asst. to plant mgr. Stanley Aviation Corp., Denver, 1955-56; prin. mgmt. engr., dept. mgr. Martin-Marietta Aerospace Div., Denver, 1956-64; mgmt. engr. Safeway Stores, Inc., Denver, 1964-66; sr. research economist, prof., assoc. div. head U. Denver Research Inst., 1966-86; pres. Univ. Senate, 1980-81; prin. Milliken Chapman Research Group, Inc., Littleton, Colo., 1986-88, Milliken Research Group, Inc., Littleton, 1988—; vis. fellow sci. policy research unit U. Sussex, Eng., 1975-76; dir. Sci. Mgmt. Corp., Cogenco Internat., Inc., LIK Securities, Inc.; cons. mgmt. engr. Author: Aerospace Management Techniques, 1971, Federal Incentives for Innovation, 1974, Recycling Municipal Wastewater, 1977, Water and Energy in Colorado's Future, 1981, Technological Innovation and Economic Vitality, 1983, Metropolitan Water Management, 1981, Water Management in the Denver, Colorado Urban Area, 1988; contbr. articles to profl. jours. Bd. dirs. Southeast Englewood Water Dist., 1962—, South Englewood San. Dist., 1965—, South Suburban Met. Recreation and Park Dist., 1971—; chmn. Democratic Com. of Arapahoe County, 1969-71, 5th Congl. Dist. Colo., 1972-73, 74-75; mem. exec. com. Colo. Faculty Adv. Council, 1981-85; mem. Garrison Diversion Unit Commn., 1984; trustee Colo. Local Govt. Liquid Asset Trust, 1986—. Served with M.C. AUS, 1945-46. Recipient Adlai E. Stevenson Meml. award, 1981. Mem. Acad. Mgmt., Nat. Assn. Bus. Economists, Yale Sci. and Engring. Assn., Am. Water Works Assn., Sigma Xi, Tau Beta Pi, Beta Gamma Sigma, Sigma Iota Epsilon. Congregationalist. Home and Office: 6502 S Ogden St Littleton CO 80121

MILLION, HERBERT ARTHUR, computer company executive, consultant; b. Berry, Ky., Jan. 25, 1928; s. Harry Thompson and Mary Geneva (Chasteen) M.; m. Mary Kathleen Borders, May 27, 1950; children: Lisa, Jay, Kody, Kelly. Student, Eastern Ky. Coll., 1946-48; BS, Pa. State U., 1956; MS, McGill U., Montreal, Que., Can., 1962; MBA, George Washington U., 1965. Commd. 2d lt. USAF, 1953, advanced through grades to col., 1970; comdr. 10th Weather Squadron USAF, Udorn, Thailand, 1969-70; dep. chief staff Air Weather Service USAF, Scott AFB, Ill., 1970-74; com. 6th Weather Wing and Air Force Global Weather Cen. USAF, Omaha, 1974-76; mgr. bus. devel. Ford Aerospace, Palo Alto, Calif., 1976-81; mgr. activity Ford Aerospace, Colorado Springs, Colo., 1981-84; sr. dir. Unisys Corp., Camarillo, Calif., 1984—; program and cons. dir. Unisvs Australia Post, Melbourne, 1987-88. Contbr. articles to mil. meteorol. pubs. Scoutmaster Boy Scouts Am., Trenton, Ill., 1967-69. Decorated Legion of Merit (2), Bronze Star. Mem. Am. Meteorology Soc., Air Traffic Controllers Assn., Armed Forces Communications and Electronic Assn., Air Force Assn., Ret. Officers Assn. Home: 4588 Kenneth Ave Santa Maria CA 93455 Office: Unisys 5151 Calle Ruiz Camarillo CA 93010

MILLIONIG, HANS FREDERICK, mechanical engineer; b. Kingston, N.Y., Nov. 20, 1960; s. Henry Frederick and Carolyn Broadhead (Shults) M.; m. Janet Elizabeth Twarog, Oct. 8, 1983; l child, Michael Hans. BSME, Clarkson U., 1982. Lic. engr. in tng. Svc. engr. Flopetrol-Johnston-Schlumberger, Houston, 1982-85; sales engr. W.S. Shamban & Co., Santa Monica, Calif., 1985-87, product engr., 1987—. Deacon Woodland Hills (Calif.) Presbyn. Ch., 1988—. Mem. Soc. Automotive Engrs., Mariners Club. Republican. Home: 50ll Calderon Rd Woodland Hills CA 91364 Office: WS Shamban & Co 295l 28th St Santa Monica CA 90405

MILLMAN, JEROME ISRAEL, anesthesiologist; b. Detroit, Apr. 19, 1934; s. Sara (Michaels) M.; m. Audrey Lois Sinclair, Aug. 23, 1955 (div. 1965); children: Elissa Sheryl, Martin Neil; m. Felicitas Aquirre dela Cruz, Oct. 6, 1976. BS, U. Mich., 1955, MD, 1960. Intern Detroit Receiving Hosp., 1960-61; resident in anesthesiology U. Mich. Med. Ctr., Ann Arbor, 1961-63; practice medicine specializing in anesthesiology Centinela Hosp., Inglewood, Calif., 1977—. Home: 1625 Indiana Ave South Pasadena CA 91030

MILLS, CAROL LEA TOWNSEND, child care volunteer; b. Denver; d. Charles Leon and Mary Louise (Holter) Townsend; m. Kris Arvid Mills, Sept. 17, 1977; children: Sara Kristine, Katherine Lea. BS in Early Childhood Edn., Colo. State U., 1976. Asst. dir. Toddle Inn Day Care, Denver, 1976; tchr. New Horizons Preschool, Durango, Colo., 1976-77; receptionist Dr. McCanlies DDS, Durango, Colo., 1977-78; vol. Childcare, Boulder City, Nev., 1978—. Leader Girl Scouts U.S.A., Boulder City, 1987—; v.p. PTA, Boulder City, 1988, pres. 1988—; child check supr. Andrew Mitchell Elem. Sch., Boulder City, 1987—, tchr. aide, 1986—. Mem. AAUW (v.p. 1988-90). Home: 1515 Dorothy Dr Boulder City NV 89005

MILLS, CAROL MARGARET, trucking company executive; b. Salt Lake City, Aug. 31, 1943; d. Samuel Lawrence and Beth (Neilson) M.; BS magna cum laude, U. Utah, 1965. With W.S. Hatch Co., Woods Cross, Utah, 1965—, corp. sec., 1970—, traffic mgr., 1965-70, dir. publicity, 1974—; dir. Hatch Service Corp., Nat. Tank Truck Carriers, Inc., Washington; bd. dirs. Intermountain Tariff Bur. Inc., 1978—, chmn., 1981-82, 1986-87. Fund raiser March of Dimes, Am. Cancer Soc., Am. Heart Assn.; active senatorial campaign, 1976, gubernatorial campaign, 1984, 88, vice chair voting dist., 1988—; witness transp. com. Utah State Legislature, 1984, 85; mem. Pioneer Theater Guild, 1985—; apptd. by gov. to bd. trustee Utah Tech. Fin. Corp., 1986—, corp. sec., mem. exec. com., 1988—. Recipient service awards W. S. Hatch Co., 1971, 80, exec. com., 1988—; gov. apptd. Utah to bd. trustees Utah Tech. Fin. Corp., 1986; mem. Pioneer Theatre Guild, 1985—; v.i.p. capt. Easter Seal Telethon, 1989. Mem. Nat. Tank Truck Carriers, Transp. Club Salt Lake City, Am. Trucking Assn. (public relations council), Utah Motor Transport Assn. (dir. 1982—), Internat. Platform Assn., Beta Gamma Sigma, Phi Kappa Phi, Phi Chi Theta. Home: 77 Edgecombe Dr Salt Lake City UT 84103 Office: W S Hatch Co 643 S 800 W Woods Cross UT 84087

MILLS, DENISE YVONNE, librarian; b. Compton, Calif., July 19, 1946; d. Clifford Clinton and Lois Catherine (Eaton) Mills; children: Randall,

Marisa, Nicholas. BA in Sociology, Calif. State U., Long Beach, 1968; profl. diploma in elem. edn. U. Hawaii, 1976, MLS, 1980. Sch. librarian Stevenson Intermediate Sch., Honolulu, 1981-82, Bloomington (Calif.) High Sch., 1983—; librarian San Bernardino County Library, Fontana br., 1986—; instr. San Bernardino Valley Coll., 1987-88; rsch. sec. Johns Hopkins U., Balt., UCLA, U. Calif., Irvine, 1972-74. Mem. steering com. ednl. media task force San Bernardino County Supt. Schs., 1983-84; mem. Young Adult Svcs. Media Library Educators Network. Mem. ALA, Calif. Media Library Educators Assn., Am. Assn. Sch. Librarians. Republican. Presbyterian. Home: 6615 Churchill San Bernardino CA 92407

MILLS, DON HARPER, pathology and psychiatry educator; b. Peking, Republic of China, July 27, 1927; came to U.S., 1928; s. Clarence Alonzo and Edith Clarissa (Parott) M.; m. Lillian Frances Snyder, June 11, 1949; children: Frances Jo, Jon Snyder. BS, U. Cin., 1950, MD, 1953; JD, U. So. Calif., 1958. Diplomate Am. Bd. Law in Medicine. Intern L.A. County Gen. Hosp., 1953-54, admitting physician, 1954-57, attending staff pathologist, 1959—; pathology fellow U. So. Calif., L.A., 1954-55, instr. pathology, 1958-62, asst. clin. prof., 1962-65, assoc. clin. prof., 1965-69, clin. prof., 1969—, clin. prof. psychiatry and behavioral sci., 1986—; asst. in pathology Hosp. Good Samatarian, L.A., 1956-65, cons. staff, 1962-72, affiliating staff, 1972—; dep. med. examiner Office of L.A. County Med. Examiner, 1957-61; instr. legal medicine Loma Linda (Calif.) U. Sch. Medicine, 1960-66, assoc. clin. prof. humanities, 1966—; cons. HEW, 1972-73, 75-76, Dept. of Def., 1975-80; bd. dirs. Am. Bd. Law in Medicine, Inc., Chgo., 1980-86. Column editor Newsletter of the Long Beach Med. Assn., 1960-75, Jour. Am. Osteopathic Assn., 1965-77, Ortho Panel, 1970-78; exec. editor Trauma, 1964-88, mem. editorial bd., 1988—; mem. editorial bd. Aspects of Med. Practice, 1972—, Med. Alert Communications, 1973-75, Am. Jour. Forensic Medicine and Pathology, 1979-87, Hosp. Risk Control, 1981—; contbr. numerous articles to profl. jours. Fellow Am. Coll. Legal Medicine (pres. 1974-76, bd. govs. 1970-78, v.p. 1972-74, chmn. malpractice com. 1973-74, mem. jour. editorial bd. 1984—), Am. Acad. Forensic Scis. (pres. 1986-87, v.p. 1984-85, exec. com. 1971-74, gen. program chmn. 1966-67, chmn. jurisprudence sect. 1966-67, 73-74, mem. jour. editorial bd. 1965-79); mem. AMA (mem. jour. editorial bd. 1973-77), Calif. Med. Assn., L.A. County Med. Assn., AAAS, ABA, State Bar Calif., L.A. County Bar Assn., Am. Judicature Soc., Drug Info. Assn., Am. Soc. Hosp. Attys., Calif. Soc. Hosp. Attys. Office: 700 E Ocean Blvd Ste 2606 Long Beach CA 90802

MILLS, GLENN STERLING, electrical engineer; b. Lexington, Ky., Oct. 2, 1927; s. Otto and Mary (Walker) M.; m. Margaret Haynes, June 20, 1953; children: Michael David, Monte Dean, Melinda Kay. BSEE, U. Ky., 1953; MS, U. N.Mex., 1958. Registered profl. engr., N.Mex. Mem. tech. staff tester design and devel. div. Sandia Nat. Labs., Albuquerque, 1953—. With U.S. Army, 1945-47. Democrat. Baptist. Home: 8700 Princess Jeanne NE Albuquerque NM 87112 Office: Sandia Nat Labs Div 7265 PO Box 5800 Albuquerque NM 87185

MILLS, JAMES IAN, accountant; b. Hamilton, Ont., Can., Apr. 20, 1938; came to U.S., 1948; s. John and Jean P. (Kerr) M.; m. Lois Jean Mills, Mar. 12, 1966; children: Lesley Ann Blumenshine, Teresa Lynn, Shelly Dawn Jemmett. AA, Mt. San Antonio Jr. Coll., 1956; B in Econs. cum laude, Claremont McKenna Coll., 1958. CPA, Calif. Acct. Price Waterhouse & Co., Los Angeles, 1958-63; sr. acct. Price Waterhouse & Co., Santa Ana, Calif., 1963-65; prin. James I. Mills CPA, Santa Ana, 1965-71; shareholder, pres. James I. Mills An Accountancy Group, Laguna Beach, Calif., 1971—. Mem. Am. Inst. CPA's. Calif. Soc. CPA's. Democrat. Presbyterian. Home: PO Box 565 Laguna Beach CA 92652 Office: Laguna Beach CA 92652

MILLS, LAWRENCE, transportation company executive; b. Salt Lake City, Aug. 15, 1932; s. Samuel L. and Beth (Neilson) M.; BS, U. Utah, 1955, JD, 1956. Bar: Utah 1956, ICC 1961, U.S. Supreme Ct. 1963. With W.S. Hatch Co. Inc., Woods Cross, Utah, 1947—, gen. mgr., 1963—, v.p., 1970—, also dir.; dir. Nat. Tank Truck Carriers, Inc., Washington, 1963—, pres., 1974-75, chmn. bd., 1975-76; mem. motor carrier adv. com. Utah State Dept. Transp., 1979—; keynote speaker Rocky Mountain Safety Suprs. Conf., 1976. Del. to County and State Convs., Utah, 1970-72; v.p. Utah Safety Coun., 1979-82, bd. dirs., 1979—, pres., 1983-84; mem. Utah Gov's Adv. Com. on Small Bus.; capt. Easter Seal Telethon, 1989; state vice chmn. High Frontier, 1987—. Recipient Safety Dir., adv. com. Utah State Indsl. Commn., 1988—; award Nat. Tank Carriers Co., 1967, Trophy award W.S. Hatch Co., 1975. Mem. Salt Lake County Bar Assn., Utah Motor Transport Assn. (dir. 1967—, pres. 1974-76), Utah Hwy. Users Assn. (dir. 1981—), Indsl. Rels. Coun. (dir. 1974—), Utah Safety Coun. (bd. dirs. 1979—), Salt Lake City C. of C., U.S. Jaycees (life Senator 1969—, ambassador 1977—, pres. Utah Senate 1979-80, Henry Giessenbier fellow 1989), Nat. Petroleum Coun., Utah Associated Gen. Contractors (assoc. 1975-77, 88—), Silver Tank Club. Contbr. articles to legal publs. Home: 77 Edgecombe Dr Salt Lake City UT 84103 Office: 643 S 800 West Woods Cross UT 84087

MILLS, MARY ANNE, sales executive; b. Gary, Ind., Mar. 9, 1954; d. Frank and Marguerite Eloise (Schleicher) M. BS, U. Utah, 1978. Customer svc. mgr., inside sales mgr. Tote Cart Co., Rockford, Ill., 1978-82; purchasing/traffic mgr. Tote Cart Co., Rockford, 1982-85; sales mgr. Tote Cart Co., western U.S., 1986—; legis. asst. Rockford C. of C., 1985-86. Fundraising chmn. On the Waterfront Festival, Rockford, 1985, 86, Campaign/Senator Joyce Holmberg, Rockford, 1984. Mem. Friends of the Libr. (editor newsletter), Eagle Valley Arts Council (Vail, Colo.). Office: PO Box 3042 Vail CO 81658

MILLS, ROSALIE JANE GREGORY, clergyperson; b. Ottumwa, Iowa, Aug. 24, 1947; d. Robert Todd and Margaret Kathryn (Bentzinger) Gregory; m. Larry Eugene Mills, Mar. 30, 1973; 1 child, Jason Novell. BS, U. Tex., Austin, 1970; MS Edn., So. Ill. U., 1974; student, Fuller Theol. Sem., Pasadena, 1985-87. Ordained elder, A.M.E. Zion Ch., 1986; notary pub., Calif. Adminstrv. sec. Coldwell Banker, L.A., 1978-84; office mgr. Lincoln Property Co., L.A., 1984—; assoc. pastor 1st A.M.E. Zion Ch., Pasadena, Calif., 1983—; also dir. Christian edn. 1st A.M.E. Zion Ch.; sec. L.A. dist. Ministerial Alliance, A.M.E. Zion Ch., 1986—. Mem. NAFE, Nat. Notary Assn. Democrat. Home: 628 Alexander Apt 6 Glendale CA 91201 Office: Lincoln Property Co Ste 4270 444 S Flower St Los Angeles CA 90071

MILNE, JAMES CAIRNDAIE, small business owner, engineer; b. Glasgow, Scotland, Feb. 16, 1925; came to U.S., 1947; s. William and Jesse Jane (MacKay) M.; m. Gretchen Blaesing, June 3, 1950 (div. Apr., 1957); children: Will, Liz, Mary; m. Eleanor E. Stahli, Oct. 1, 1960; 1 child, Victoria. BS, Glasgow U., Scotland, 1945. Reg. profl. engr., Oreg. Project coord. Hoffman Constrn. Co., Portland, Oreg., 1947-53; pres., owner Milne Constrn. Co., Portland, 1953—; bd. dirs. Hampton Lumber Co. Portland, Oreg., Standard Ins. Co., Portland, Benson Industries, Portland. Inventor: Method of Making Mausoleum Structures, 1962; patentee in field. Trustee, First Presbyterian Ch., Portland, 1976-79, 1985-88, San Francisco Theological Seminary, San Anselmo, Calif., 1978—. Midshipman Royal Navy, 1945-46. Mem. Am. Soc. Civil Engrs., Structural Engrs. of Oreg., Assoc. Gen. Contractors of Oreg., Waverley Country Club. Office: Milne Constrn Co Inc PO Box 2740 1312 SW 16th Portland OR 97208

MILNER, CLYDE A., II, historian; b. Durham, N.C., Oct. 19, 1948; s. Charles Fremont and Eloyse (Sargent) M.; m. Carol Ann O'Connor, Aug. 14, 1977; children: Catherine Carol, Charles Clyde. AB, U. N.C., 1971; MA, Yale U., 1973, MPhil, 1974, PhD, 1979. Admissions counselor Guilford Coll., Greensboro, N.C., 1968-70; acting instr. Yale U., New Haven, Conn., 1974-75; research fellow McNickle Ctr., Chgo., 1975-76; instr. Utah State U., Logan, 1976-79, asst. prof., 1979-82, assoc. prof., 1982-88, prof., 1988—. Author: With Good Intentions, 1982; editor Major Problems in the History of the American West, 1989; assoc. editor: The Western Historical Quarterly, 1984-87, co-editor, 1987-88, editor, 1988—; co-editor Churchmen and the Western Indians, 1985,. Recipient Paladen Writing award The Montana Mag. Western History, 1987, Faculty Svc. award Associated Students Utah State U., 1987, Outstanding Social Science Researcher award Utah State U., 1983. Mem. Western History Assn., Orgn. Am. Historians, Am. Folklore Soc., Phi Alpha Theta, Phi Beta Kappa. Society of Friends. Home: 203 Boulevard Logan UT 84321-4713 Office: Dept of History Utah State U Logan UT 84322-0710

MILO, KENNETH CLARK, optics consultant; b. Riverside, Calif., Oct. 15, 1928; s. Milo N. and Marjorie (Cummins) C. BSME, BS in Bus. Mgmt., U. Colo., 1952. Jr. engr. Ling Tempco Vought, Dallas, 1952-53; proj. engr., supr. Bourns, Inc., Riverside, Calif., 1956-58; proj. engr. SCM, Inc., Oakland, Calif., 1958-61; vol. Peace Corps, Bangladesh, 1961-63; NASA contract engr. Bourns, Inc., Riverside, Calif., 1964-67; proj. mgr. Deutsch Co., Banning, Calif., 1967-76; proj. engr. Hughes Aircraft Co., Irvine, Calif., 1977-84; design specialist ITT-Cannon, Fountain Valley, Calif., 1984-86; optics cons. ITT-Cannon, Irvine, Calif., 1986-. Patentee self-aligning fiber optic connector, elec. connector, optical finishing tool. Sgt. USAF, 1953-56. Mem. ASME, Soc. Photographic Instrumentation Engrs., Optical Soc. Am. Home: 3 Delanter Dr Irvine CA 92720

MILOSZ, CZESLAW, poet, author, educator; b. Lithuania, June 30, 1911; came to U.S., 1960, naturalized, 1970; s. Aleksander and Weronika (Kunat) M. M.Juris, U. Wilno, Lithuania, 1934; Litt.D. (hon.), U. Mich., 1977. Programmer Polish Nat. Radio, 1935-39; diplomatic service Polish Fgn. Affairs Ministry, Warsaw, 1945-50; vis. lectr. U. Calif., Berkeley, 1960-61; prof. Slavic langs. and lits. U. Calif., 1961-78, prof. emeritus, 1978—. Author: The Captive Mind, 1953, Native Realm, 1968, Post-War Polish Poetry, 1965, The History of Polish Literature, 1969, Selected Poems, 1972, Bells in Winter, 1978, The Issa Valley, 1981, Separate Notebooks, 1984, The Land of Ulro, 1984, The Unattainable Earth, 1985, Collected Poems, 1988. Recipient Prix Littéraire Européen Les Guildes du Livre, Geneva, 1953, Neustadt Internat. prize for lit. U. Okla., 1978, citation U. Calif., Berkeley, 1978, Nobel prize for lit., 1980; Nat. Culture Fund fellow, 1934-35; Guggenheim fellow, 1976. Mem. Am. Inst. Arts and Letters, AAAS, Polish Inst. Letters and Scis. in Am., PEN Club in Exile. Office: U Calif Dept Slavic Langs and Lits Berkeley CA 94720

MILSTEAD, JAMES EDWARD, entomologist; b. Chgo., May 26, 1927; s. Robert Irving and Gladys Evans (Kellogg) M.; m. Cleo deYonne Franklin, Oct. 24, 1948 (div. 1983); children: Jennifer, Kimberley, James, Jeffrey; m. Mary Leonora Bates, Sept. 22, 1984. BA, Fresno State Coll., 1951; MA, U. Calif., Berkeley, 1957, PhD, 1977. Cert. Agrl. pest control advisor. Technician Fresno (Calif.) Mosquito Abatement Dist., 1950-52; radiation control monitor Calif. Rsch. and Devel., Livermore, 1952-53; staff rsch. assoc. IV U. Calif., Berkeley, 1956—. With USMC, 1945-46, Republic of China. Recipient Spl. Merit award Coll. Agr. U. Calif., Berkeley, 1975, 80, 88. Mem. Entomol. Soc. Am., Soc. Invertebrate Pathology, Pacific Coast Entomol. Soc., Calif. Native Plant Soc., Port Costa Conservation Soc. Democrat. Home: 2311 Collins Ave Pinole CA 94564 Office: U Calif Berkeley CA 94720

MILTON, THEODORE ROSS, retired military officer, writer; b. Honolulu, Hawaii, Dec. 29, 1915; s. Alexander Mortimer and Theresa Marie (McKenna) M.; m. Grace Elizabeth Bailey, Jan. 2, 1942; children: Patricia Adele Milton Morgan, Theodore Ross Jr., Barbara Bayley Milton Harju. BS, U.S. Mil. Acad., 1940. Lic. mil. pilot. Commd. 2d lt. U.S. Air Corps, 1940; advanced through grades to gen. U.S. Air Corps then USAF, 1940-71; formerly U.S. rep. to NATO Mil. Com., 1940-74; v.p. bd. editors US Strategic Inst., Waltham, Mass., 1976—; bd. dirs. Boston U. Sch. Communications, USAF Falcon Found., USAF Sci. Adv. Board. Contbg. Air Force Mag., 1974—; contbr. articles to profl. jours., mags., newspapers. Republican. Roman Catholic. Clubs: Army and Navy (Arlington, Va.); Garden Gods (Colorado Springs). Home: 14460 B Club Villa Pl Colorado Springs CO 80921

MIN, CLYDE GORDON, hotel executive; b. Hilo, Hawaii, Nov. 7, 1949; s. Samuel and Flora (Chee) M.; m. Hilda Maya Matsuda, May 9, 1981; children: Christina Maya, Christopher Kaonohi. BBA, U. Hawaii, 1971. Asst. mgr., restaurant mgr. Hawaiian Regent Hotel, Honolulu, 1972-76; asst. food and beverage mgr. Regent of Kuala Lumpur, Malaysia, 1976-77, Regent of Manila Hotel, 1977-80; exec. asst. mgr. Regent of Fiji Hotel, 1980-82, gen. mgr., 1982-85; gen. mgr. Regent of Bangkok (Thailand) Hotel, 1985-87; mng. dir. Hotel Hana-Maui, Hawaii, 1987—. Mem. Maui Hotel Assn. (bd. dirs. 1988—), TIM Internat. (pres. 1973-74), Chaine de Rotisseurs Confrerie, Am. Co. of C. Thailand, Fiji Inst. Mgmt., Rotary. Home and Office: Hotel Hana Maui PO Box 8 Hana HI 96713

MINAMI, ISAMU, farmer; b. Guadalupe, Calif., July 21, 1922; s. Henry Yaemon and Kuni (Yamasaki) M.; student Santa Maria (Calif.) Jr. Coll., 1942; m. Grace Misao Yamamoto, May 6, 1950; children: Sammy Yahe, Susan Kuniye. Engaged in vegetable farming, Guadalupe, 1944—; owner Security Farms, 1944—; past pres., bd. dirs. Santa Barbara County Fair Bd. Bd. dirs. Santa Maria Assn. Retarded, Boys Club Santa Maria Valley; past bd. dirs. bldg. fund Sisters Hosp., Santa Maria; mem. comdr.'s liaison group Vandenburg AFB; bd. regents Santa Clara U.; mem. subcom. Calif. State Bd. Food and Agr.; mem. Santa Maria Valley Water Study Com.; bd. dirs. Marian Hosp. Found.; mem. community adv. com. Valley Community Hosp.; past mem. spl. adv. com. Senator S.I. Hayakawa of Calif. Mem. Nisei Farmers League, United Fresh Fruit Assn., Iceberg Lettuce Research Assn. (dir.), Grower-Shippers Assn. (bd. dirs., past pres.), Western Growers Assn. (dir.), Calif.-Ariz. Growers Assn. (dir.), Calif. Farm Bur. Assn., Calif. C. of C., Santa Barbara County Taxpayers Assn., Santa Maria Valley C. of C. (dir.; Citizen of Year award 1980), Santa Maria Valley Developers (dir.), Friends of Santa Barbara County, Japan Am. Soc. So. Calif., Japanese Am. Citizens League, Santa Maria Valley Farmers Assn. (past pres.). Republican. Buddhist. Clubs: Guadalupe Rotary, 36th Congl., Republican Century, Santa Maria Elks. Office: PO Box 818 Guadalupe CA 93434

MINAR, PAUL GERALD, interior designer; b. Phoenix, July 12, 1932; s. Aaron Crowther and Ione Anna (Schmid) Mortensen. Student, Ariz. State U., 1950-54, John F. Kennedy U., 1978-80, Antioch West U., 1980; BA in Communication, U. Honolulu (formerly Golden State U.), 1989. Sound effects technician, TV stage mgr. Sta. KHJ-AM-TV, L.A., 1955-63; displayer W.&J. Sloane Furniture Co., Beverly Hills, Calif., 1963-66, Bullock's Dept. Store, L.A., 1966-68, Macy's Dept. Store, San Francisco, 1968-70; interior designer Lloyd's Furniture Co., San Diego, 1970-71, Bonynge's Furniture Co., Oakland, Calif., 1971-72, Breuner's Furniture Co., Oakland, 1972-74; design cons. The Other Artist, San Francisco, 1974—; v.p. Unrofet Inc., San Rafael, Calif., 1980—. Writer, producer (documentary) The Modern Nursing Home, 1959. Vol. talent agt. San Francisco Symphony Black and White Ball, 1983. Mem. Am. Soc. Interior Designers, Golden Gate Bus. Assn. (vol. talent agt. 1986, Mem. of Month award 1985, svc. awards 1985-87), Inst. Noetic Scis. Democrat. Roman Catholic. Home: 2030 Franklin St #303 San Francisco CA 94109 Office: The Other Artist 3200 Buchanan St San Francisco CA 94123

MINDELL, EARL LAWRENCE, nutritionist, author; b. St. Boniface, Man., Can., Jan. 20, 1940; s. William and Minerva Sybil (Galsky) M.; came to U.S., 1965, naturalized, 1972; BS in Pharmacy, N.D. State U., 1963; PhD in Nutrition, Pacific We. U., 1985; m. Gail Andrea Jaffe, May 16, 1971; children: Evan Louis-Ashley, Alanna Dayan. Pres. Adanac Mgmt. Inc., 1979—, Compact Disc-Count, Inc.; instr. Dale Carnegie course; lectr. on nutrition, radio and TV. Mem. Beverly Hills, Rancho Park, Western Los Angeles (dir.) regional chambers commerce, Calif., Am. pharm. assns., Am. Acad. Gen. Pharm. Practice, Am. Inst. for History of Pharmacy, Am. Nutrition Soc., Internat. Coll. Applied Nutrition, Nutrition Found., Nat. Health Fedn., Am. Dieticians Assn., Orthomolecular Med. Assn., Internat. Acad. Preventive Medicine. Clubs: City of Hope, Masons, Shriners. Author: Earl Mindell's Vitamin Bible, Earl Mindell's Vitamin Bible for your Kid, Earl Mindell's Quick and Easy Guide to Better Health, Earl Mindell's Pill Bible, Earl Mindell's Shaping Up with Vitamins, Earl Mindell's Unsafe At Any Meal; columnist Let's Live mag., The Vitamin Supplement (Can.), The Vitamin Connection (U.K.); contbr. articles on nutrition to profl. jours. Home: 709 N Hillcrest Rd Beverly Hills CA 90210 Office: 10739 W Pico Blvd West Los Angeles CA 90064

MINDRUM-LOGAN, SYLVIA ANN, watercolor artist, educator; b. Cin., Apr. 20, 1955; d. Gordon Melvin and Carmen Doris (Torres) Mindrum; m. Ronald Brian Logan, Nov. 1, 1980; Elizabeth Michelle, Christopher Scott. Student, Coe Coll., Cedar Rapids, Iowa, 1973-75, Edgecliff Coll., Cin., 1976. Artist Anchorage Times, 1981; owner, operator The Graphics Co., Anchorage, 1981-83; art dir. New Vistas Acad., Chandler, Ariz., 1987—; art resource Anchorage Infant Tng. Ctr., 1982-84, Scales Sch., Tempe, Ariz., 1988; pvt. art tchr., Chandler, 1987—. Exhibited in group show at All Alaska Juried Art Show, 1981, 82, Don Ruffin Meml. Juried Show, 1988. Chairperson Neighborhood Blockwatch, Chandler, 1987-88. Fellow Tempe Art League. Democrat. Home: 321 E Tremaine Ave Gilbert AZ 85234

MINER, DENNIS GENE, nurse; b. Chgo., Aug. 29, 1950; s. Paul Edward and Bobbie Jean (strunk) M.; m. Pamela Joy Lehman, Sept. 15, 1973; children: Jennifer Jean, Dena Rae. BS, U. Ill., 1978; A in Nursing, Elgin (Ill.) Community Coll., 1980. RN, Ill. Staff nurse operating rm. Michael Reese Hosp. and Med. Ctr., Chgo., 1980-82, asst. head nurse operating rm., 1982-84; nurse clinician peri-operative St. Vincent Med. Ctr., Toledo, 1984-87; operating rm. and post anesthetic recovery rm. supr. Sierra View Dist. Hosp., Porterville, Calif., 1987—; mem. contbg. faculty Med. Coll. of Ohio, Toledo, 1984-87; mem. adj. faculty St. Vincent Sch. of Nursing, Toledo, 1985-87; mem. adv. bd. Michael J. Owens Coll., Toledo, 1985-87. Mem. editorial bd. A.O.R.N. Jour., 1986; contbr. articles to profl. jours. With USN, 1971-75. Mem. Assn. Operating Rm. Nurses. Home: 2151 Tomah Porterville CA 93257 Office: Sierra View Dist Hosp 465 W Putnam Portersville CA 93257

MINER, PAUL DOUGLAS, city official; b. Salt Lake City, Mar. 15, 1935; s. Lyndon Leroy and Margaret (Young) M.; m. Mary Louise Thomson, Sept. 1, 1956; children: David, Steven, Lynda. BSBA, U. Ariz., 1957, MPA, 1964. Mgr. Havasu Spring Resort, Parker, Ariz., 1957-58; office mgr. Sun Valley Bakery, Phoenix, 1958-59; pers. analyst City of Tucson, 1959-66, pers. dir., 1966—. Bd. dirs. YWCA, 1970-78, YMCA, 1976-78, Tucson Ctr. for Women and Children, 1985—, Urban League, Tucson, 1978-86; mem. pers. com. Girl Scouts U.S., 1986—. Mem. Am. Soc. Pers. Assn., Internat. Assn. Pension Adminstrs., Nat. Pub. Employers Labor Rels. Assn., Ariz. Indsl. Rels. Assn. (bd. dirs. 1985), Tucson Pers. Assn. (bd. dirs. 1968-78, past pres.), Western Region Pub. Employers Assn. (bd. dirs. 1986—). Home: 1911 Calle Mecedora Tucson AZ 85745

MINETA, NORMAN YOSHIO, congressman; b. San Jose, Calif., Nov. 12, 1931; s. Kay Kunisaku and Kane (Watanabe) M.; children: David, K., Stuart S. B.S., U. Calif.-Berkeley, 1953. Agt./broker Mineta Ins. Agy., San Jose, 1956—; mem. adv. bd. Bank of Tokyo in Calif., 1961-75; mem. San Jose City Council, 1967-71; vice mayor San Jose, 1969-71, mayor, 1971-75; mem. 94th-101st Congresses from 13th Calif. dist., 1975—, chmn. House Com. on Pub. Works and Transp., subcom. surface transp.; mem. Com. on Sci., Space and Tech., Select Com. on Intelligence 94th-98th Congresses, dep. Dem. whip; chmn. fin. com. Santa Clara County Council Chs., 1960-62; commr. San Jose Human Relations Commn., 1962-64, San Jose Housing Authority, 1966—. Precinct chmn. Community Theater Bond Issue, 1964; mem. spl. gifts com. Santa Clara County council Boy Scouts Am., 1967; sec. Santa Clara County Grand Jury, 1964; bd. dirs. Wesley Found., San Jose State Coll., 1956-58, Pacific Neighbors, Community Council Cen. Santa Clara County, Japan Soc., San Francisco, Santa Clara County chpt. NCCJ, Mexican-Am. Community Services Agy.; mem. exec. bd. No. Calif.-Western Nev. dist. council Japanese Am. Citizens League, 1960-62, pres. San Jose chpt., 1957-59; bd. regents Smithsonian Instn., 1979—; chmn. Smithsonian vis. com. for Freer Gallery, 1981—. Served to lt. AUS, 1954-56. Mem. Greater San Jose C. of C., Nat. Assn. Indsl. Ins. Agts., Calif. Assn. Indsl. Ins. Agts., San Jose Assn. Indsl. Ins. Agts. (dir. 1960-62), North San Jose Optimists Club (chpt. pres. 1956-58), Jackson-Taylor Bus. and Profl. Assn. (dir. 1963). Methodist. Office: 2350 Rayburn House Office Bldg Washington DC 20515

MINGER, TERRELL JOHN, management company executive; b. Canton, Ohio, Oct. 7, 1942; s. John Wilson and Margaret Rose M.; BA, Baker U., 1966; MPA, Kans. U., 1969; Urban Exec. Program, M.I.T., 1975; Loeb fellow Harvard U., 1976-77; Exec. Devel. Program, Stanford U., 1979; MBA, U. Colo., 1983; m. Judith R. Arnold, Aug. 7, 1965; 1 child, Gabriella Sophia. Asst. dir. admissions Baker U., 1966-67; asst. city mgr. City of Boulder, Colo., 1968-69; city mgr. City of Vail, Colo., 1969-79; pres., chief exec. officer Whistler Village Land Co., Vancouver, B.C., Can., 1979-81; v.p., gen. mgr. Cumberland S.W. Inc., Denver, 1981-83; exec. asst., dep. chief of staff to Gov. Colo., 1983-87; pres., chief exec. officer Sundance (Utah) Inst. for Resource Mgmt., 1986—; pres., chief exec. officer Sundance Enterprises Ltd., 1988—; adj. prof. grad. sch. pub. affairs U. Colo., 1983—; bd. dirs. Colo. Open Lands, Inc., 1986—. Spl. del. UN Habitat Conf. Human Settlements; founder Vail Symposium; co-founder, bd. dirs. Colo. Park Found., 1985—. Nat. finalist White House Fellowship, 1978; named one of B.C.'s Top Bus. Leaders for the '80's, 1980. Mem. Urban Land Inst., Colo. Acad. Pub. Adminstrn. (charter, founding mem. 1988), Colo. City Mgmt. Assn., Internat. City Mgrs. Assn. (Mgmt. Innovation award 1974-76), Western Gov.'s Assn. (staff coun., chmn. adv. com. 1985-86). Editor: Vail Symposium Papers, 1970-79; author, editor: Growth Alternatives for Rocky Mountain West, 1976; Future of Human Settlements in the West, 1977. Club: Denver Athletic. Home: 785 6th St Boulder CO 80302 Office: Sundance Enterprises RR3 Box A-3 Sundance UT 84604

MINGES, PHILIP SEMON, III, publicist; b. Charleston, S.C., July 18, 1952; s. Philip Semon and Patricia (Bayman) M. BA in English, The Citadel, 1974; MA in Lit., U. Dallas, 1975. Editor Wing Publs., Columbia, S.C., 1975-76; English tchr. Carson Long Inst., New Bloomfield, Pa., 1977; lit. agt. Curtis Brown Ltd., N.Y.C., 1978-80; mng. editor After Dark mag., N.Y.C., 1980-81; editor Chelsea House Publs., N.Y.C., 1982-84; entertainment editor The Advocate, Los Angeles, 1985-86; publicist Davidson & Choy Publicity, Los Angeles, 1986-88, Solters, Roskin, Friedman, Los Angeles, N.Y.C., 1988—. Editor: Masterworks of Children's Literature (8 vols.), 1983; contbr. to lit. jours. Democrat. Office: Solters Roskin Friedman 5455 Wilshire Blvd Los Angeles CA 90036

MINHINNETT, THOMAS EDWARD, fire department administrator; b. Calgary, Alta., Can., Jan. 7, 1929; s. George Thomas and Mabel Gertrude (Sanderson) M.; m. Delores Etteline Smith, May 10, 1952; children: Glen Thomas, Marlene Delores. Diploma in Pub. Adminstrn., Mount Royal Coll., 1978. Joined Calgary Fire Dept., 1951, fire chief, 1983-88. Mem. Alta. Provincial Fire Chiefs Assn., Can. Assn. Fire Chiefs, Internat. Assn. Fire Chiefs (Can. div. provincial v.p.), Nat. Fire Protection Assn. (dir. Fire Service sect.). Conservative. Anglican. Lodge: Masons.

MINICHIELLO, STEVEN MARK, architect; b. Concord, N.H., June 16, 1955; s. Thomas Joseph and Catherine Marie M.; m. Joan Marie McEvey, May 26, 1984. Student, Conn. Coll., New London, 1974-76; BS in Architecture, U. Ariz., 1983. Designer draftsman Dickson, Holden & Assocs., Concord, N.H., 1978-79; cost control and design Peterson Tiffany Constrn., Tucson, 1983-85; ind. architect Ind. Designs, Tucson, 1985-86; mapper drafter City of Mesa Engring. Div., 1986; arch. draftsman Robert J. Schill Architects, Phoenix, 1986-87; civil engring. draftsman B&R Engring., Sun Lake, Ariz., 1987-88; engring. plans technician Ariz. Dept. of Transp., Phoenix, 1988; planner asst. City of Phoenix Planning Dept., 1988—. Mem. AIA, Ariz. Pub. Employees Assn., Am. Fedn. of State, County and Mcpl. Employees. Republican. Episcopalian. Office: City of Phoenix Planning 125 E Washington Phoenix AZ 85004

MINKLER, JOHN ARCHER, career military officer; b. Everett, Wash., Sept. 2, 1938; s. John Henry and Helen Alice (Mortland) M.; m. Donna Belle Becker, Nov. 1960 (div. July 1988); children: Scott Laurence, Douglas John; m. Gayle Frances Gryphan, July, 1988. BS, Oreg. State U., 1974; MBA, So. Ill. U., 1988. Commd. USAF, 1961, advanced through grades to lt. col., 1979; aerial navigator flight examiner 41st Mil. Airlift Squadron USAF, Charleston AFB, S.C., 1961-67; aerial navigator flight examiner 45th Mil. Airlift Squadron USAF, McGuire AFB, N.J., 1967-68, air nat. guard liaison officer 170th Aeromed. Airlift Group, 1968-72; combat gunship navigator 16th Spl. Ops. Squadron USAF, Ubon AB, Thailand, 1972-73; instr., navigator, computer svcs. mgr. 86th Mil. Airlift Squadron USAF, Travis AFB, Calif., 1975-77, instr., navigator, res. forces liaison officer 60th Mil. Airlift Wing, 1979-81, airfield mgr. 60th Airbase Group, 1981—. Mem. rev. com. Farifield (Calif.) Suison Sch. Bd. Facilities, 1977; charter patron Travis AFB Hist. Soc., 1983—. Decorated DFC; recipient 11 air medals, 1969-73; 36 awards. Mem. Am. Assn. Airport Execs., Airlift Assn., Southwest Assn. Airport Execs., Aircraft Owners & Pilots Assn., United Svcs. Orgn. (bd. dirs. Travis ABF 1985—), Travis AFB Aero Club (pres. 1985-88), The Cousteau Soc. (charter mem.), Beta Gamma Sigma. Republican. Methodist. Home: 349 Timber Dr Vacaville CA 95688-2141 Office: USAF 60th Air Base Group/OT Travis AFB CA 94535-5000

MINNEMAN, STEVEN ALAN, company executive; b. L.A., Oct. 6, 1948; s. John Jesse and Esther Annette (Lange) M. BS in Engring., U.S. Air Force Acad., 1970. Software engr. Digital Telephone Systems, Novato, Calif., 1977-80; software supr. Digital Telephone Systems, 1980-83; mgr. software devel. Harris DTS Div., Novato, 1983-85, Fujitsu America, San Jose, 1985-86; mgr. software sys. Fujitsu America, 1986-87; mgr. devel. planning Fujitsu Network Switching, San Jose, 1987—; vice chmn. ANSI, N.Y.C., 1987—. Capt. USAF, 1970-77. Decorated Air medals (9), DFC (2). Republican. Home: 1415 Kansas St San Francisco CA 94107 Office: Fujitsu Network Switching 3055 Orchard Dr San Jose CA 95134

MINNER, WARREN ANDREW, structural engineer, consultant; b. Bakersfield, Calif., Jan. 14, 1928; s. Wilford Ashton and Esther May (Pantel) M.; m. Marjorie Claire Olmstead, Mar. 21, 1953; children: Pamela Jean, William Allen, Andrew Michael, Laura Jo, Joyce Louise. BS in Civil Engring., U. Calif., Berkeley, 1951. Registered profl engr., Calif. Jr. engr., draftsman Kaiser Engrs., Oakland, Calif., 1951-53, Rickett & Reaves, Civil Engrs., Bakersfield, Calif., 1953-54; structural engr. S.B. Barnes & Assocs., L.A., 1954-57, Kern Engring. Corp., Bakersfield, 1957-58; pub. works engring. Kern County Dept. of Public Works, Bakersfield, 1958; cons. structural engr. Warren A. Minner, Structural Engrs., Bakersfield, 1959-73, Minner, Creswell & Davis, Structural Engrs., Bakersfield, 1974-77; cons. structural and civil engring. Minner & Davis, Structural and Civil Engrs., Bakersfield, 1978—. Chmn. YMCA Bd. Dirs., Bakersfield, 1965—; mem., chmn. Bd. Bldg. Appeals, Bakersfield, 1966—; mem. Bd. Bldg. Appeals, Kern County, Calif., 1982—. With U.S. Army, 1945-47. Fellow ASCE (branch pres. 1976); mem. Structural Engrs. Assn. of So. Calif., Am. Concrete Inst., Consulting Engrs. Assn. of Calif., Lions (pres. Bakersfield chpt. 1959-66), Engrs. Club (pres. 1967), Y's Men Club (sec. 1989). Democrat. Presbyterian. Home: 2413 Hasti Acres Dr Bakersfield CA 93309 Office: Minner & Davis Engrs 1716 Oak St Bakersfield CA 93301

MINNIE, MARY VIRGINIA, social worker, educator; b. Eau Claire, Wis., Feb. 16, 1922; d. Herman Joseph and Virginia Martha (Strong) M. BA, U. Wis., 1944; MA, U. Chgo., 1949, Case Western Reserve U., 1956. Lic. clin. social worker, Calif. Supr. day care Wis. Children Youth, Madison, 1949-57; coordinator child study project Child Guidance Clinic, Grand Rapids, Mich., 1957-60; faculty, community services Pacific Oaks Coll., Pasadena, Calif., 1960-70; pvt. practice specializing in social work various cities, Calif., 1970-78; cons., educator So. Calif. Health Care, North Hollywood, Calif., 1978—; med. social worker Kaiser Permanente Home Health, Downey, Calif., 1985-87; assoc. Baby Sitters Guild, Inc., 1987—; cons. Home Health, 1987—; pres. Midwest Assn. Nursery Edn., Grand Rapids, 1958-60; bd. dirs., sec. So. Calif. Health Care, North Hollywood; bd. dirs., v.p. Baby Sitters Guild Inc., South Pasadena; cons. project Head Start Office Econ. Opportunity, Washington, 1965-70. Mem. Soc. Clin. Social Workers, Nat. Assn. Social Workers, Nat. Assn. Edn. Young Children (1960-62). Democrat. Club: Altrusa (Laguna Beach, Calif.) (pres. 1984-87). Home and Office: 1622 Bank St S Pasadena CA 91030

MINOR, CAROLYN ANN, educational administrator consultant; b. Memphis; d. Lucius Minor and Carrie David (Ayers) Haynes. AA, Los Angeles City Coll., 1961; BA, L.A. State Coll., 1963; MA, Calif. State Coll., 1971; EdD, Calif. Coast U., 1983. Lic. tchr., supr. elem., community coll., adminstr. Tchr. Compton (Calif.) Unified Sch. Dist., 1963-68, asst. prin., 1968-70, Title 1 supr., 1970-71; dr. of fed. and state projects Del Paso Heights (Calif.) Sch. Dist., 1971-73; ednl. adminstrn. cons. Calif. State Dept. Edn., Sacramento, 1973—; edn. program cons. on migrant edn., Calif. Process Follow Through Modeland the child devel. div.; assisted dists. with in-service activities for problem solving. Co-author: I Am a Black Woman Who, 1977; editor: Nat. Assn. Univ. Women Bull. and Jours., 1986-89, Putting It Together With Parents; contbr. School-Age Program Quality Rev. Document: Latchkey, 1988; contbr. articles for profl. jours. Active NAACP. Recipient Sacramento County Office of Edn. Career Mentor Program award, Tony Davis Meml. award of merit, Community Service Nat. Assault on Illiteracy Program award for outstanding service, cert. merit Sacramento Black Women's Network, woman of the yr. Nat. Assn. Univ. Women; named to Sacramento's 100 Most Influential Blacks, Observer Newspapers. Mem. Nat. Assault Illiteracy Program, Assn. Calif. Sch. Adminstrs., Black Advs. State Svc., Black Am. Polit. Assn. Calif., Black Women's Network, Calif. Assn. Compensatory Edn. (regional rep.), Calif. Statehouse Children & Youth (Sacto county catylst), Nat. Brotherhood Skiers, Sacto Black C. of C. (edn. chmn.), Phi Delta Kappa, Alpha Kappa Alpha, Gamma Phi Delta (educator of Yr.). Democrat. Club: Camellia City Ski. Lodge: Soroptimist Internat. Home: Capitol Terrace Condominiums 200 P St #A-21 Sacramento CA 95814 Office: Calif State Dept Edn 721 Capitol Mall 560 J St Ste 220 Sacramento CA 95814

MINSHEW, LISA MICHELLE, political aide; b. L.A., June 21, 1966; d. Robert LaVon and Ann (Leveen) M. Student, Oxford (Eng.) U., 1987; BA, Claremont McKenna Coll., 1988; postgrad., Harvard U., 1988-89. Intern, rsch. asst. Office Presdl. Personnel The White House, Washington, 1985-86; campaign mgr. Bosshard for State Assembly, Santa Cruz, Calif., 1986; legal rsch. asst., polit. aide Bosshard Law Offices, Santa Cruz, 1987. Rsch. cons., campus campaign dir. Bush for Pres., Claremont and Huntington Beach, Calif. and Washington, 1988. Mem. Phi Beta Kappa, Claremont Republican Club. Baptist. Home: 102 Via Novella Aptos CA 95003

MINTON, PAUL ARTHUR SEVERIN, technology company executive; b. Paris, July 30, 1957; came to U.S. in 1958; s. Wilfred Max Mortimer and Florence Anita (Schrey) M.; m. Judith Lynne Cromie, June 25, 1983. BA, U. Md., 1979; MA, Stanford U., 1982. Lab technician NIH, Bethesda, Md., 1973-75; cons. Bethesda, Md., 1978-79, Palo Alto, Calif., 1984-85; adminstrv. aide Dept. of the Air Force, Washington, 1976-78; founder EarthData Corp., Stanford, Calif., 1984-85; v.p. Edison Systems Corp., San Francisco, 1985—; instr. Dept. Math. U. Md., College Park, 1980, Stanley Kaplan Ednl. Ctr., Palo Alto, 1981-85; program mgr. Stanford U., 1984. Editor and co-author AGSAT: Remote Sensing in Agriculture, 1984. Hoopes Fellow Md. Acad. Scis., Balt., 1975, doctoral fellow Stanford Bus. Sch., 1981, 82, 83. Mem. AAAS. Office: Edison Systems Corp 379 Oyster Pt Blvd South San Francisco CA 94080

MINTUN, SUSAN MAY, dental assistant; b. Detroit, Nov. 30, 1951; d. Louis Joseph and Margaret (Wenner) Yuhasz; m. Michael P. Rhodes, Dec. 11, 1970 (div. 1982); children: Trina Lynn, Heather Marie; m. Tom L. Mintun, Mar. 25, 1983. AA, Monroe (Mich.) Community Coll., 1982; cert. dental assisting, Andon Coll., 1985. Quality assurance technician Daniel Internat., Monroe, 1982-84; dental asst. Dr. Earl L. Haller, DDS, San Jose, Calif., 1986—. Mem. Am. Dental Asst's Assn. Roman Catholic.

MINTY, KEITH LARRY, medical services corporation executive; b. Roseburg, Oreg., Mar. 1, 1933; s. John Raymond and Vivian Melba (Adams) M.; m. Mary Louise Davis, May 4, 1953; children: Ronald, Karen, Gary. Enlisted airmen USAF, 1952—, advanced to master sgt., ret., 1978; bus. mgr. Taylor Knudson & Lum Profl. Assn., Las Vegas, Nev., 1978—, Nev. MRI Assocs., L.P., Las Vegas, 1987—, Palomino-Tonopah Assocs., Las Vegas, 1987—; dir., treas. Nev. MRI Assocs., Inc., Las Vegas, 1987—; mgmt. com., mem. Palomino-Tonopah Assocs., Las Vegas, 1987—. Decorated Air Force Commendation medal with 2 oak leaf clusters, Bronze Star. Republican. So. Baptist. Office: Taylor Knudson & Lum Profl 2020 Palomino Ln #100 Las Vegas NV 89030

MINTZ, RONALD EARL, artist, art conservator, chromotechnics scientist; b. Rocky Mount, N.C., Jan. 21, 1926; m. Mildred Tilson, Dec. 18, 1948; children—Richard, Robert. A.B., U. N.C., 1948; student under Griesche and Liese, London and Garmische-Oberammergau, 1953-56; M.S., George Washington U., 1964; Ph.D., Jackson State U., 1975. Dep. commr. revenue State of N.C., Greenville, 1950-52; artist, art conservator, Washington, 1956-58, various locations, Tex., Fla., Maine, Wash., Ala., Nebr. and Calif., 1958-74; prin. firm Macropaedia Conservation, conservation hist. and artistic works, Chapel Hill, N.C., 1974-80; exhibited in one man shows, Chapel Hill, 1978, 80, Seattle, 1981-84; exhibited in group shows, Bellevue, Wash., 1982, New Orleans, 1982-83, Palm Beach, Fla., 1982-83. Helped establish N.C. State Mus. Art, 1949-51. Served to col. USAF, 1951-74. Decorated Legion of Merit, Meritorious Service medal. Developer abstract art form technique of Chromoformism. Currently semi-retired, engaged in rsch. to prepare a new type of artist index reference work for collectors, dealers, etc. Address: 14510 SE 167th St Fairwood Greens Renton WA 98058

MINUDRI, REGINA URSULA, librarian, consultant; b. San Francisco, May 9, 1937; d. John C. and Molly (Halter) M. B.A., San Francisco Coll. for Women, 1958; M.L.S., U. Calif.-Berkeley, 1959. Reference librarian Menlo Park (Calif.) Pub. Library, 1959-62; regional librarian Santa Clara County (Calif.) Library, 1962-68; project coordinator Fed. Young Adult Library Services Project, Mountain View, Calif., 1968-71; dir. profl. services Alameda County (Calif.) Library, 1971, asst. county librarian, 1972-77; library dir. Berkeley Pub. Library, 1977—; lectr. U. San Francisco, 1970-72, U. Calif., Berkeley, 1977-81; cons., 1975—. Mem. ALA (pres. 1986-87, exec. bd. 1980-89, council 1979-88, Grolier award 1974), Calif. Library Assn. (pres. 1981, council 1965-69, 79-82), LWV (dir. Berkeley chpt. 1980-81). Author: Getting It Together, A Young Adult Bibliography, 1970; contbr. articles to publs. including School Library Jour., Wilson Library Bulletin. Office: Berkeley Pub Libr 2090 Kittredge St Berkeley CA 94704

MINZNER, DEAN FREDERICK, aviation company executive; b. Winchester, Mass., July 20, 1945; s. Frederick Louis and Winifred (Hughes) M.; B.A., Franklin and Marshall Coll., 1967; M.B.A., Columbia U., 1972. Dist. exec. Greater N.Y. councils Boy Scouts Am., N.Y.C., 1972-76; sales exec. Coast Avia, Long Beach, Calif., 1976-78, Performance Aircraft, Inc., Hayward, Calif., 1978; owner, pres. Western Aviation Consultants, Inc., Hayward, 1978-82, Cal-Pacific Assocs., Inc., Hayward, 1979—, Cal-Pacific Enterprises, Hayward, 1982—. Mem. Assn. M.B.A. Execs., Columbia U. Grad. Sch. Bus. Alumni Assn., Aircraft Owners and Pilots Assn. Office: PO Box 6206 Hayward CA 94540

MIRARCHI, ALBERT ROBERT, health facility administrator; b. Newark, Oct. 5, 1945; s. Salvatore M. and Connie (Mastrangelo) M.; m. Phyllis M. Galvin, June 9, 1968; children: Steven, Stacey, Kevin. BS in Acctg., Monmouth Coll., 1973, MBA, 1978. Audit staff acct. Price Waterhouse & Co., Newark, 1973-74; controller Jersey Shore Med. Ctr., Neptune, N.J., 1974-80; chief fin. officer Defiance Hosp., Ohio, 1980-81; asst. adminstr., chief fin. officer Portsmouth (Va.) Psychiatric Ctr., 1981-83; adminstr. Columbia (Mo.) Ctr. for Psychiatry, 1983-86, Hosp. Corp. Am., Houston, 1985-86; v.p. fin., treas. Penrose/St. Francis Healthcare Systems, Colorado Springs, Colo., 1986—; cons. in foeld. Mem. com. Boy Scouts Am., Colorado Springs, 1988, asst. Webelos leader, 1986; m em. youth council St. Patrick's Ch., Colorado Springs, 1988. Fellow Healthcare Fin. Mgmt. Assn.; mem. Nat. Assn. Accts. Roman Catholic. Office: Penrose/St Francis Healthcare Systems 2215 N Cascade Colorado Springs CO 80907

MIRASSOU, DANIEL PATRICK, vineyard executive; b. San Jose, Calif., Jan. 2, 1945; s. Edmund A. and Mildred K. (Denevan) M.; divorced; children: Marcel, Maximilian. Student of Viticulture, Fresno State U., 1963-65. With Mirassou Sales Co., San Jose, 1963—, pres., 1982—; with San Vicente Vineyards, San Jose, 1963—, pres., 1982—; with Mirassou Enterprises, San Jose, 1963—, pres., 1982—. Judge Orange County Fair, 1982—. Mem. Calif. Wine Inst. (pub. rels. and advt. com. 1986—), Monterey Wine Country Assocs., Santa Clara Winegrowers Assn. (pres. 1970), Monterey Winegrowers Coun. (pres. 1974), San Jose C. of C., Santa Clara C. of C., Brotherhood Knights Vine. Home and Office: Mirassou Vineyards 3000 Aborn Rd San Jose CA 95135

MIRELS, HAROLD, aerospace engineer; b. N.Y.C., July 29, 1924; s. Hyman and Lily (Efron) M.; m. Nell Segal, Oct. 4, 1953; children: Lily, Laurence Franklin, Jeremy Mark. BSME, Cooper U., 1944; MSME, Case Inst. Tech., 1949; PhD in Aero. Engring., Cornell U., 1953. Sect. head NACA, Cleve., 1944-57; br. chief NASA, Cleve., 1957-61; dept. head Aerospace Corp., El Segundo, Calif., 1961-78, assoc. dir., 1978-84, prin. scientist, 1984—. Co-inventor continuous wave chem. laser. Recipient Tech. Achievement award Cleve. Tech. Socs., 1960. Fellow AIAA (Fluid and Plasmadynamics award 1988), Am. Phys. Soc.; mem. Nat. Acad. Engring. Home: 3 Seahurst Rd Rolling Hills Estates CA 90274 Office: The Aerospace Corp Aerophysics Lab PO Box 92957 Los Angeles CA 90009

MIRES, RONALD E., communications executive; b. Port Huron, Mich., July 31, 1930; s. Charles Edical and Ella Etta (Frink) M.; m. Nancy Jane O'Hara, July 12, 1952; children: Geoffrey, Ronald II, Scott. Student, Port Huron Jr. Coll., 1949-50, Mich. State U., 1950, Syracuse U., 1951. Announcer, disc jockey Sta. WTTH Radio, Port Huron, 1948-50, news dir., asst. mgr., 1955-61; accouncer WKAR/WKAR-FM, E. Lansing, Mich., 1950, WILS, Lansing, Mich., 1950; news dir. WHAM, Rochester, N.Y., 1961-63, WBZ, Boston, 1963-65, KYW, Phila., 1965-68, KPIX-TV, San Francisco, 1968-73; news dir. KGTV, San Diego, 1973-83, asst. gen. mgr., 1985-86; v.p. news McGraw-Hill Broadcasting Co., San Diego and N.Y.C., 1983-85; v.p., gen. mgr. KERO-TV, Bakersfield, Calif., 1987—; broadcast judge Hearst Found. Journalism Awards Program, San Francisco. Bd. dirs. Golden Empire Gleaners, Kern View Found., United Way of Kern County, all in Bakersfield. With USAF, 1951-55. Recipient Disting. Service award in Journalism Sigma Delta Chi, 1982. Mem. Nat. Assn. Broadcasters, Nat. Assn. TV Program Execs., Radio/TV News Dirs. Assn., Soc. Profl. Journalists, Associated Press Broadcasters (bd. dirs.), Bakersfield Better Bus. Bur. (bd. dirs.), Rotary, Stockdale Country Club, Petroleum Club, Masons. Methodist. Office: Sta KERO-TV 321 21st St Bakersfield CA 93301

MIRKIN, I. MIRK, management consultant; b. Bronx, N.Y., Jan. 19, 1927; s. Louis and Anna Esther (Friedman) M.; m. Marcia Elicie Hirschhorn, June 20, 1954; children: Karen, Stephen, Philip, Judith. AB, Rutgers U., 1950; PhD, Burton Coll., 1958. Merchandising exec. L. Bamberger & Co., Newark, N.J., 1950-53; sr. exec. Saks & Co., N.Y.C., 1953-60, Zodys Dept. Stores, L.A., 1960-61; exec. v.p. Harwin & Co., Sherman Oaks, Calif., 1961-62, Mirimar Enterprises, Sherman Oaks, 1962-74; chief exec. officer Mirkin & Assocs., North Hollywood, Calif., 1974-80, Mirimar Enterprises, Sherman Oaks, 1980—; cons. Soc. Plastics Engrs., L.A., 1974, Mktg. Coun. Engrs., San Francisco. Editor: The Pitcairn Island Cookbook; contbr. articles on bus. trends to newspapers and periodicals. Chmn. Young Democrats, Plainfield, N.J. 1948-50; candidate City Coun. Mem. B'nai B'rith (Disting. Svc. award L.A. and Beverly Hills chpt.). Home: 13416 Magnolia Blvd Sherman Oaks CA 91423

MIRKO, ROSEMARY NATALYA, insurance broker, exotic automobile repair shop owner; b. Hawthorne, Calif., Jan. 22, 1958; d. Samuel Douglas Smeltzer and Mary Lou (Carter) Doty; m. Albert Francis Mirko, Dec. 27, 1987. AA, El Camino Coll., Torrance, Calif., 1982. Asst. mgr. Dauer Chiropractic, Manhattan Beach, Calif., 1977-79; acct. mgr. Southwest Savs., Los Angeles, 1979-80, Countrywide Funding, Los Angeles, 1980-81; acct. exec. Cal-Surance Assocs., Torrance, 1981-86; mktg. mgr. Alexander & Alexander, San Jose, Calif., 1986-87; mktg. v.p. Compro Ins. Svcs., San Jose, 1987-88; owner Mirko Auto Ltd., Santa Clara, Calif., 1985—; systems rep. ARC/AMS, Boston, 1984-86; team mgr. Mirko Racing; indep. ins. cons., Monterey, Calif., 1984-86, Winn & Co., Hollister, Calif., 1986, Cal-Surance Assocs., Torrance, 1985-86, Saliba-Charter, Los Angeles, 1984-86. Organizer Friends of Madrona Marsh, Torrance, 1975. Mem. Mensa, Sports Car Club of Am., Chartered Property Casualty Underwriters (cert., soc. mem.), Internat. Motorsports Assn. Home and Office: Mirko Auto Ltd 1945 Grant St Santa Clara CA 95050

MIRSALIS, JON CARL, toxicologist; b. Cleve., Nov. 27, 1952; s. Augustine and Blanche (Bredenberg) M. BS in Zoology, Kent (Ohio) State U., 1975; MS in Genetics, N.C. State U., 1977, PhD in Toxicology, 1979. Diplomate Am. Bd. Toxicology. Postdoctoral fellow Chem. Industry Inst. Toxicology, Research Triangle Park, N.C., 1979-81; cellular geneticist SRI Internat., Menlo Park, Calif., 1981-82, program dir., 1982-85, dept. dir., 1985—. Contbr. numerous articles to profl. jours. Mem. Environ. Mutagen Soc. (fin. com. 1983-84), Fifth Internat. Conf. on Environ. Mutagens (treas. 1986-89), Genetic and Environ. Toxicology Assn., Soc. for Cinephiles (pres. 1981-82). Office: SRI Internat 333 Ravenswood Ave Menlo Park CA 94063

MISA, KENNETH FRANKLIN, management consultant; b. Jamaica, N.Y., Sept. 24, 1939; s. Frank J. and Mary M. (Soszka) M.; BS cum laude in Psychology, Fairfield U., 1961; MS in Psychology, Purdue U., 1963; PhD in Psychology (Fellow 1963-66), St. John's U., 1966. Staff psychologist Rohrer, Hibler & Replogle, Los Angeles, 1966-67; assoc. A.T. Kearney, Inc., Los Angeles, 1968-71, sr. assoc., 1972-74, prin., 1975-78, v.p., partner, 1979-86; pres. HR Cons. Group, 1987—. Cert. mgmt. cons.; lic. psychologist, Calif. Mem. Am. Psychol. Assn., Calif. State Psychol. Assn., Los Angeles County Psychol. Assn., Am. Soc. for Tng. and Devel., Human Resources Planning Soc., Acad. of Mgmt., Indsl. Relations Research Assn. Internat. Assn. Applied Psychology, World Affairs Council of Los Angeles, Town Hall of So. Calif., Glendale C. of C. Republican. Roman Catholic. Clubs: Jonathan. Home: 924C S Orange Grove Blvd Pasadena CA 91105 Office: HR Cons Group 100 N Brand Blvd Ste 200 Glendale CA 91203

MISER, WILLIAM FREDERICK, physician, military officer; b. Welch, W.Va., Mar. 16, 1957; s. William George and Jeanetta M. (Rutledge) M.; m. Debra Krotz, June 23, 1979; children: Jenna, Jessica. BS in Biology, Wheaton Coll., 1979; MD, Ohio State U., 1982. Commd. capt. U.S. Army, 1982; intern Eisenhower Med. Ctr., Ft. Gordon, Ga., 1982-83, resident in family practice, 1983-84, chief resident, 1984-85; staff physician Reynolds Army Hosp., Ft. Sill, Okla., 1985-86, chief family practice clinic, 1986-88; faculty devel. fellow Madigan Army Med. Ctr., Tacoma; instr. Am. Heart Assn., Lawton, Okla., 1985-88, ACLS, Tacoma. Fellow Acad. Family Practice; mem. Uniformed Services Acad. Family Practice (major 1989), Alpha Omega Alpha. Republican.

MISHLER, DWAYNE EDWARD, teacher; b. San Bernardino, Calif., May 20, 1954; s. Russell Edward and Wanda Joyce (Flanders) M.; m. Janet Loyse McMillan, Aug. 14, 1976. BA, Calif. Bapt. Coll., 1978; postgrad., Fresno Pacific, 1980—. Cert. elem. tchr., cert. spl. edn. tchr., Calif. Tchr. Woodville (Calif.) Union Sch. Dist., 1978—. Umpire Visalia (Calif.) Girl's Softball, 1981—. Mem. Woodville Tchrs. Assn. (pres. 1987-88), Tulare/Kings Tchrs. Assn. (treas. 1987—). Democrat. Baptist. Home: 633 W Iris Visalia CA 93277 Office: Woodville Union Sch Dist 16541 Rd 168 Porterville CA 93257

MISHLOVE, JEFFREY, psychologist, television host; b. Fond du Lac, Wis., Dec. 4, 1946; s. Hyman and Rose (Rogow) M. BA, U. Wis., 1969; M in Criminology, U. Calif., Berkeley, 1972, PhD, 1980. Lic. psychologist, Calif. Pvt. practice clin. psychology San Rafael, Calif., 1986—; host, producer series Thinking Allowed TV, 1986—; chmn. bd. dirs. Thinking Allowed Prodns., Berkeley. Author: The Roots of Consciousness, 1975, Psi Development Systems, 1983. Pres. Spectrum Found., San Rafael, 1981—. Mem. Am. Psychol. Assn., Parapsychol. Assn., Assn. of Media Psychologists, Am. Soc. Psychol. Rsch. Assn. for Past-Life Rsch. and Therapy. Home: 48 St Francis Ln San Rafael CA 94901

MISKIMON, ROBERT MURRAY, JR., health association administrator; b. Richmond, Va., Aug. 18, 1943; s. Dr. Robert Murray Miskimon and Elizabeth Wallace (Blanton) Starbuck; m. Christine M. Madsen, Sept. 1966 (div. Jan. 1989); 1 child, Mae Martyn. AB, U. Richmond, 1966. Reporter Daily News of Virgin Islands, St. Thomas, 1967-68; editor, writer The Associated Press, New Haven, 1968-70; mng. editor Los Altos (Calif.) News, 1970-72; reporter, editor Salinas (Calif.) Californian, 1972-73; mng. editor Carmel (Calif.) Pine Cone, 1973-75, 81-85, Seaside (Calif.) Post News-Sentinel, 1975-81; pub. info. officer Community Hosp. of the Monterey (Calif.) Peninsula, 1985-89; dir. publs. Calif. Assn. Hosps. and Health Systems, Sacramento, 1989—. Mem. Hosp. Pub. Rels. and Mktg. Soc. (area coord. 1988-89), Soc. of the Cin. Club, Richmond, 1973—. Democrat. Episcopalian. Home: 1628 14th St Sacramento CA 95814 Office: Calif Assn Hosps and Health Systems 1050 20th St Sacramento CA 95812

MISKUS, MICHAEL ANTHONY, electrical engineer, consultant; b. East Chicago, Ind., Dec. 10, 1950; s. Paul and Josephine Miskus; BS, Purdue U., 1972; AAS in Elec. Engring. Tech., Purdue U., Indpls., 1972; cert. mgmt. Ind. U., 1972, Ind. Central Coll., 1974. Cert. plant engr.; m. Jeannie Ellen Dolmanni, Nov. 4, 1972. Service engr. Reliance Electric & Engring. Co., Hammond, Ind., 1972-73; maintenance supr., maintenance mgr. Diamond Chain Co./AMSTED Industries, Indpls., 1973-76; primary and facilities elec. engr. Johnson & Johnson Baby Products Co., Park Forest South, Ill., 1976-81; prin. Miskus Cons., indsl./comml. elec. cons., 1979—; plant and facilities engring. mgr. Sherwin Williams Co., Chgo. Emulsion Plant, Chgo., 1981-85; with Miscon Assocs., Riverside, Calif., 1985—; acting dir. plant and facilities engring. Bourns Inc., 1982—; instr., lectr. EET program Moraine Valley Community Coll., Palos Hills, Ill., 1979; instr. cert. program plant engring. U. Calif.; lectr. energy engring., bldg. automation systems Prairie State Coll., Chicago Heights, Ill., 1980—; mem. adj. faculty, faculty adv. bd. Orange Coast Coll., Costa Mesa, Calif.; commr. Riverside Energy Commn., 1988—; mem. Elec. Industry Evaluation Panel. Mem. faculty adv. bd. Moraine Valley Community Coll., 1980—. Mem. IEEE, Am. Inst. Plant Engrs. (pres. Pomona chpt. 1989—), Assn. Energy Engrs., Assn. Energy Engrs. (sr., So. Calif. chpt.), Illuminating Engring. Soc. N.Am., Internat. Platform Assn., Riverside C. of C. Club: Purdue of Los Angeles. Office: Miscon Assocs PO Box 55353 Riverside CA 92517

MISRA, RAGA KUMAR, aerospace engineer; b. Chandausi, India, Mar. 2, 1946; came to U.S., 1974.; s. Brij Nandan and Champa Misra; m. Kamlesh Dhiman, Dec. 19, 1987. BS in Physics, Agra U., India, 1963; MS in Physics, Birla Inst. Tech. and Sci., India, 1966, MS in Tech., 1968; MS in Mgmt., UCLA, 1984. Registered profl. engr., Calif., N.J., N.Y. Project leader Marconi Co., Stevenage, Eng., 1971-74; chief engr. Norsal Industries, Islip, N.Y., 1974-76; sr. staff engr. Litton Systems, Morris Plains, N.J., 1976-78; chief analyst Gen. Dynamics Co., Pomona, Calif., 1978—; cons. Upsystems Internat. Alta Loma, Calif., 1983—; owner Misra Enterprises, Alta Loma, 1982—. Contbr. articles to profl. jours. Active Soc. Preservation Hist. Architectures, San Bernardino, Calif., pres., 1988—. Recipient Gold Medal, Gov. Uttar Pradesh, India, 1963. Mem. IEEE, Am. Def. Preparedness Assn. Democrat. Hindu. Lodge: Old Crows. Home: 10421 Hidden Farm Rd Alta Loma CA 91701 Office: Gen Dynamics PO Box 2507 Pomona CA 91769

MITCHAM, RICHARD I., architect; b. San Bernardino, Calif., Nov. 1, 1923; s. DeWitt and Eva Mae (Sheppard) M.; m. Mary Theretta Catland, June 21, 1947; children: Marsha Amiel, Tod, Mark, Lucy Quesada, Jon, Lori Spatafore. AA, San Bernardino Valley Coll., 1946; BArch, U. So. Calif., 1950. Registered architect, Calif. Job capt. Kistner, Wright & Wright, L.A., 1946-50; pvt. practice San Bernardino, 1950-53; from project architect to dir. consulting svcs. William Pereira and Charles Luckman, L.A., 1953-72; chief architect Hugh Gibbs and Donald Gibbs, FAIA, Long Beach, Calif., 1961-62; from exec. architect to dir. pub. svcs. Daniel, Mann, Johnson & Mendenhall, L.A., 1960-74; pvt. practice Alhambra, Calif., 1974-77; assoc. architect Ruhnau-Evans-Ruhnau Assocs., Riverside, Calif., 1977-78; pres., chief executive officer Rima Group, L.A., 1978-83; dist. architect San Diego Unified Sch. Dist., 1983-85; prin. RMCA, Crestline, Calif., 1985—. Sgt. U.S. Army, 1943-46. Mem. AIA, Construction Specifications Inst. Republican. Home and Office: 774 Berne Dr Box 2260 Crestline CA 92325

MITCHELL, ANDREA L., librarian; b. Kalamazoo, Mich., Dec. 24, 1946; d. Allen Warren Mitchell and Ruth Alice (Remynse) Parker. BA in Social Scis., U. Calif., Berkeley, 1970, MLS, 1979. Librarian, dir. alcohol rsch. library Alcohol Rsch. Group, Med. Rsch. Inst. San Francisco, Berkeley, 1971—; cons. Nat. Inst. on Alcohol Abuse and Alcoholism, Rockville, Md., 1984-86, Office for Substance Abuse Prevention, Rockville, 1987—. Mem. Calif. Prevention Network (bd. dirs.), Substance Abuse Librarians and Info. Specialists (chair 1979-83, editor 4th edit. directory, editor quar. newsletter). Office: Alcohol Rsch Group 1816 Scenic Berkeley CA 94709

MITCHELL, CHARLES SUMMERS, gastroenterologist; b. New Albany, Miss., Jan. 22, 1934; s. Charles Mitchell and Dorothy Vernon (Beaty) M. BS, Spring Hill Coll., Mobile, Ala., 1956; MD, U. Miss., 1960. Diplomate Am. Bd. Internal Medicine. Intern Vanderbilt U., Nashville, 1960-61, resident in internal medicine, 1961-63, chief med. resident, 1963-64; fellow in gastroenterology Good Samaritan Hosp., VA Hosp., Phoenix, 1967-69; pvt. practice Phoenix, 1969—; mem. staff Good Samaritan Hosp., Phoenix, St. Luke's Hosp., Scottsdale (Ariz.) Meml. Hosp., Humana Hosp., Phoenix;

researcher in field. Contbr. numerous articles to profl. mags. With USPHS, 1964-67. Mem. AMA, Ariz. Med. Assn., Maricopa County Med. Assn., Phoenix Soc. Gastroenterology, Am. Gastroenterology Assn., Am. Soc. Gastroenterology Endoscopy, Alpha Omega Alpha, Ariz. Club, Mansion Club. Democrat. Home: 7629 E Foothills Dr S Paradise Valley AZ 85253 Office: 926 E McDowell Rd Ste 214 Phoenix AZ 85006

MITCHELL, EARL DEAN, corporate executive; b. Mishawaka, Ind., Sept. 27, 1939; s. Kenneth Earl and Mabel Ester (Florence) M. BA, Pasadena (Calif.) Playhouse, 1959. Cert. travel cons. Entertainment advisor USAF, Izmir, Turkey, 1960-61; on-air TV personality USAF, Germany, 1962; unit producer U.S. Dept. Def., various locations, 1963; pvt. practice as travel guide 1964-65; dir. North Am. ops. Trans-Australia Airlines, Melbourne, 1966-70; lectr. Australian Tourist Commn., 1970-71; dir. ops. Holiday Tours, Inc., San Francisco, Honolulu, 1971-83, dir. orientation services, v.p., 1983-85; pres., chief exec. officer Earl Dean Mitchell, Inc., 1985—; cons. Spire Prodns., London, 1988—, FM TV Prodns., Melbourne, 1985—; bd. dirs. Scott Hughes, Inc., Sunnyvale, Calif. Mem. Am. Soc. Travel Agts., Pacific Area Travel Assn. Republican. Mem. Unity Ch. of Hawaii. Home: 411 Hobron Ln #3812 Honolulu HI 96815 Office: Diamond Head Tours Inc 2222 Kalakaua Ave Honolulu HI 96815

MITCHELL, EVA PURNELL, industrial hygienist; b. New Orleans, Jan. 4, 1953; d. Sam and Isabell (Batton) Purnell; m. Tyrone Anthony Mitchell, Nov. 26, 1977; children: Melissa E., Monica T. BA in Biology, Tulane U., 1975. Clk., typist VA Regional Office, New Orleans, 1971-73, U.S. Pub. Health Hosp., New Orleans, 1973-75; quality control tech./supr. Am. Cynamid Chem. Co., Westwego, La., 1975-81; real estate sales assoc. Latter & Blum Inc., New Orleans, 1981-85; indsl. hygienist OSHA, U.S. Dept. Labor, San Diego, 1985-88, Naval Med. Clin., San Diego, 1988—; real estate sales assoc. Southland Ptnrs., Inc., San Diego, 1989—. Recipient Million Dollar award, New Orleans Bd. Realtors, 1985. Mem. Am. Indsl. Hygiene Assn. Democrat. Baptist. Home: 8725 Sparren Way San Diego CA 92129 Office: Occupational Health IH Dept Bldg 14 NASNI San Diego CA 92135-5153

MITCHELL, GENEVA BROOKE, hypnotherapist; b. Ringgold, Tex., Feb. 15, 1929; d. Roy Banks and Willie Jewel (Lemons) Shaw; m. Roy David Mitchell, Nov. 30, 1947; children: Ronald, Donald, Joel, Pamela, Annette. Cert. master hypnotist Hypnosis Tng. Inst., Los Angeles, 1980, cert. hypnotherapist, 1983; cert. in advanced investigative and forensic hypnosis Tex. A&M U., 1982; postgrad, Am. Inst. Hypnosis, 1989—. Chiropractic asst. Alamogordo, N.Mex., 1962-79; hypnotherapist Alamogordo Hypnosis and Counseling Ctr., 1980—; mgr. Shaw Mobile Home Park, 1986—; mng. ptnr. Shaw, Mitchell & Mallory, Albuquerque, 1986, mgr., 1987-88; hypnotherapist M&M Horses Corp., Tularosa, N.Mex., 1985—; owner A New Image Hypnosis Ctr., Albuquerque; pres. N.Mex. Chiropractic Aux., 1984-85; mem. Am. Council Hypnotist Examiners, 1980-85; hypnotist for tape series; instr. New Forever Trim Weight Loss Program. Charter pres. La Sertoma, Alamogordo, 1957; pres. Oregon sch. PTA, Alamogordo, 1958, La Luz Sch. Parents Club, N.Mex., 1962; sec. N.Mex. Jr. Rodeo Assn., 1964; co-founder Pre-Sch. La Luz, 1969; mem. N.Mex. Gov.'s Council on Youth, 1969; bd. dirs. Otero County Jr. Rodeo Assn., N.Mex., 1968; dir. self-hypnosis sch. Recipient Speakers award Life Found., 1984. Mem. Am Assn. Profl. Hypnotherapists, Ladies for Life (appreciation award 1984), N.Mex. Ladies Life Fellowship (pres. 1983, bd. dirs. 1985), S.W. Hypnotherapy Examining Bd. Avocations: golf; painting; swimming; martial arts. also: A New Image Hypnosis Ctr 10201 Montgomery NE Albuquerque NM 87111

MITCHELL, HARRY E., mayor, educator; b. Phoenix, July 18, 1940; s. Harry Casey and Irene Gladys (Childres) M.; m. Marianne Prevratil, May 5, 1962; children—Amy, Mark. B.A., Ariz. State U., 1962, M.P.A., 1981. Tchr. Tempe High Sch., Ariz., 1964—; councilman City of Tempe, 1970-76, vice mayor, 1976-78, mayor, 1978—. Bd. dirs. Tempe Sister City; trustee Tempe St. Lukes Hosp., Rio Salado Devel. Dist.; state rep. Sister Cities Internat., Washington; mem. Ariz. State U. Liberal Arts Alumni Adv. Bd., Adv. Council Ctr. Pub. Affairs, Ariz. Commn. Post Secondary Edn.; mem. Nat. League Cities Resolutions Com.; exec. com. League Ariz. Cities; bd. dirs. Ariz. Mcpl. Water Users. Recipient Disting. Service award Tempe Jaycees, Pub. Programs Disting. Achievement award, Ariz. State U. Mem. Ariz. State U. Alumni Bd. (chmn.), Ariz. State U. Advanced Pub. Exec. Program. Democrat. Roman Catholic. Office: City of Tempe 31 E 5th St Tempe AZ 85281 *

MITCHELL, ISAAC EARL, motel owner and manager; b. Leesburg, Ohio, Apr. 16, 1914; s. Isaac Vernon and Mae (Moore) M.; m. Alice Fitzpatrick (div.); children: Alice Earlene, Junia Mae, Barbara Jean. BA, Ohio Wesleyan U., 1937; BE, U. Cin., 1938, MEd, 1939. Tchr. San Bernardino, Calif., 1945-75; owner, mgr. Sherwood Forest Motel, Garberville, Calif., 1975—. Home and Office: Sherwood Forest Motel 814 Redwood Dr Garberville CA 95440

MITCHELL, JAMES DWIGHT, rural development company executive, priest; b. Long Beach, Calif., May 24, 1945; s. William B. and Lucille A. (Fennert) M.; adopted children: Ariel J., Libardo, Uriel J. AA in Bus. Adminstrn., Ventura Coll., 1966; PCU, N.Mex. State U., 1966; postgrad. in theology, Cristo Sacerdote, La Ceja, Colombia, 1970-72, Sem. San Carlos, San Gil, Colombia, 1973-74. Ordained priest Roman Cath. Ch., 1974. Mgr. small bus., Oxnard, Calif., 1961-66; vol. Peace Corps, Colombia, 1966-69; regional dir. Adult Edn. by Radio, Santander, Colombia, 1969-73; pastor Florian and Cite Parish, Santander, 1973-80; founder, dir. El Camino Sch. for Leadersship, Barbosa, 1973-84; coord. Hispanic Outreach,St. John's, Vancouver Archdiocese of Seattle, 1985-86; pres. El Camino Devel. and Ednl. Fund, Inc., Seattle, 1987—; adult edn. advisor Colombian Ministry Edn., 1982-86; cons. Diocese of Socorro y San Gil, Colombia, 1974—, Fundacion Comunidad El Camino, Colombia, 1984—; guest speaker Cath. chs. and orgns., 1987—; rep. Archdiocesan Adv. Com. for Hispanics, Seattle, 1984-86. Author manuals and booklet. Regional promotor community action groups, Santander, 1966-70; vol. fire fighter, Battle Ground, Wash., 1985-86; bd. dirs. Cath. Community Svcs., Vancouver, Wash., 1986. Named Educator of Yr., Colombian Ministry Edn., 1983; award Beyond War, 1988; numerous grants from U.S. and European orgns. Mem. U.S. Cath. Mission Assn., K.C. (chaplain), Rotary (hon. Port Hueneme, Calif.). Democrat. Home: PO Box 58182 Tukwila WA 98138-1182 Office: El Camino Fund 15144 65th Ave Ste 409 Seattle WA 98188-2519

MITCHELL, JOHN CHARLES, educator; b. Balt., Sept. 18, 1947; s. Albert Gray and Helen Clark (Northrop) M.; m. Beverly Adele Nutt, Dec. 20, 1969; children: David Alan, Donna Christine, Steven Charles. BA, Calif. State U., Long Beach, 1969. Cert. tchr., Calif. Tchr. Riverside (Calif.) Unified Sch. Dist., 1970-73; tchr., dist. coord. Glendora (Calif.) Unified Sch. Dist., 1973-76; tchr. math., basketball coach Sierra Plumas Joint Unified Sch. Dist., Downieville, Calif., 1976—; instrumental music judge, So. Calif. Sch. Band and Orch. Assn., Pasadena, 1974-76; music festival judge, Calif. Music Edn. Assn., Chester, 1982. Author curriculum guide. Chmn. bd. dirs., Sierra County Waterworks Dist., Calpine, Calif., 1980—; chief, Calpine Vol. Fire Dept., 1982. Mem. Sierra Plumas Tchrs. Assn. (pres. 1981-83), Riverside County Music Educators Assn. (pres. 1971-73), Nat. Coun. Tchrs. Math., NRA, Sierra Valley Fish and Game Club (sec.-treas. 1976-79). Republican. Home: PO Box 9 Calpine CA 96124

MITCHELL, JOSEPH NATHAN, real estate company executive; b. Winnipeg, Man., Can., Oct. 10, 1922; came to U.S., 1931, naturalized, 1936; s. Edward David and Anna (Copp) M.; m. Beverly Edna Henigson, Oct. 27, 1946; children: Jonathan Edward, Jan Ellen, Karin Helene. Student, UCLA, 1940-42. Pres. Beneficial Standard Corp. and Beneficial Standard Life Ins. Co., 1967-85; chmn., chief exec. officer EDM Equities, Inc., 1985-89; pres. Am. Investors and Cons., 1988—; mem. internat. bd. Ampal-Am. Israel Corp., N.Y.C.; dir. Pacific Enterprises, mem. compensation com., exec. com.; v.p. Jackson-Mitchell Pharms., Inc., Santa Barbara, Calif.; exec. com. Los Angeles Children's Bur. Found., 1988—; chmn. Mayor's Task Force-Capital Financing Subcom., 1988-89. Chmn. Los Angeles Appeal, State of Israel Bonds, 1967, also past mem. exec. com., cabinet; mem. Mayor's Steering Com. on Urban Coalition, Mayor's Ad Hoc Com. on Aging, 1980, Los Angeles Citizens Olympic Adv. Commn., 980-81, Dist. Atty.'s Adv. Council, Greater Los Angeles Urban Coalition, Los Angeles Mayor's Fin. Task Force; past mem. bd. dirs., exec. com., nat. campaign cabinet United Jewish Appeal; chmn. exec., investment, fin., planning, bldg., endowment funds, nominating and resource devel. com. Cedars-Sinai Med. Ctr., also chmn. exec. personnel com., bd. dirs.; past mem. exec. com. Jewish Fedn.-Council Greater Los Angeles; bd. dirs., past v.p., gen. chmn. United Jewish Welfare Fund, 1952; trustee, mem. adv. bd., past v.p. Jewish Community Found.; bd. dirs. ops. mgmt. council United Way, 1972-73, also mem. exec. com.; chmn. United Crusade Los Angeles, Music Ctr. Unified Fund Campaign, 1981; trustee, sec.-treas. Edward D. and Anna Mitchell Family Found.; vice chmn. bd. govs. Performing Arts Council, 1980-81; chmn. Los Angeles C. of C., 1979. Served with AUS, 1942-46, ETO. Mem. Am. Technion Soc. (past nat. v.p., bd. govs.), U.S. C. of C., Calif. C. of C., Calif.-Israel C. of C., Los Angeles C. of C. (bd. dirs., chmn., pres. 1977), Calif. Roundtable (bd. dirs.). Clubs: Hillcrest Country (Los Angeles) (past treas., dir.), Los Angeles (Los Angeles); Tamarisk Country (Palm Springs, Calif.). Office: 6222 Wilshire Blvd #450 Los Angeles CA 90048

MITCHELL, JOSEPH PATRICK, architect; b. Bellingham, Wash., Sept. 29, 1939; s. Joseph Henry and Jessie Delila (Smith) M.; student Western Wash. State Coll., 1957-59; B.A., U. Wash., 1963, B.Arch., 1965; m. Marilyn Ruth Jorgenson, June 23, 1962; children—Amy Evangeline, Kirk Patrick, Scott Henry. Asso. designer, draftsman, project architect Beckwith Spangler Davis, Bellevue, Wash., 1965-70; prin. J. Patrick Mitchell, AIA & Assoc./Architects/Planners/Cons., Kirkland, Wash., 1970—. Chmn. long range planning com. Lake Retreat Camp, 1965—; bldg. chmn. Northshore Baptist Ch., 1980—, elder, 1984—; mem. bd. extension and central com. Columbia Baptist Conf., 1977-83. Cert. Nat. Council Archtl. Registration Bds. Mem. AIA, Constrn. Specification Inst., Interfaith Forum Religion, Art, and Architecture, Nat. Fedn. Ind. Bus., Unltd. Hydroplane Hall of Fame Mus. Christian Camping Internat., Woodinville C. of C. Republican. Office: 12620 120th Ave NE Ste 208 Kirkland WA 98033

MITCHELL, KATHLEEN ANN, illustrator, graphic designer; b. Cin., July 27, 1948; d. Gerald Paige and Velma Alice (Bleier) Clary; m. Terence Nigel Mitchell, Feb. 2, 1977; 1 child, Jessica Rose. BSc in Design, U. Cin., 1971. Graphic designer Lippincott & Margulies, N.Y.C., 1971, Allied Internat., London, 1972, Moura-George Briggs, London, 1973-75; art dir., photographer Phonograph Record Mag., Los Angeles, 1976-77; ptnr. Walter Morgan Assocs., Santa Monica, Calif., 1977-80; illustrator Artists Internat., Los Angeles and N.Y.C., 1983—. Illustrator: The Snow Queen, 1982, Jane Eyre, 1983, Once Upon A Cat, 1983, Alice in Wonderland, 1986, The Wizard of Oz, 1986, A Bible Alphabet, 1986, The Secret Garden, 1986, The Christmas Cat, 1988, Timimoto, 1988, The Story of Christmas, 1989, Silent Night, 1989. Democrat. Home: 828 21st St #6 Santa Monica CA 90403

MITCHELL, KENNETH REECE, theologian, family therapist; b. Cin., June 7, 1930; s. Ernest Reece and Louise Gibson (Phillips) M.; m. Judith Bard, July 11, 1953; children: David, Susan, Catherine. AB, Princeton U., 1952, BD, 1955; PhD, U. Chgo., 1965. Ordained to ministry Presbyn. Ch., 1955. Pastor Calvary Presbyn. Ch., St. Louis, 1956-58; asst. prof. Vanderbilt U., Nashville, 1962-65; dir. religion and psychiatry Menninger Found., Topeka, 1965-76; dean U. Dubuque (Iowa), 1976-80; Schultz prof. pastoral theology Eden. Sem., Webster Grove, Mo., 1980-85; chmn. Northwest Council for Theol. Studies, Seattle, 1985–; Fulbright prof., Nijmegen, Netherlands, 1972. Author: Psychological and Theological Relationships in Multiple Staff Ministry, 1964, Hospital Chaplain, 1967, Multiple Ministries, 1988; co-author: All Our Losses, All Our Griefs, 1985. Mem. Am. Assn. Pastoral Counselors (diplomate), Soc. for Pastoral Theology.

MITCHELL, KIM WARNER, materials scientist; b. Wells, Nev., July 26, 1950; s. Kirk Richard and Gladys Marie (Whiteside) M.; m. Brenda Carol Nowlin, Apr. 15, 1978; 1 child, Jason Wesley. BS in Applied Physics with honors, Calif. Inst. Tech., 1972; MS in Materials Sci., Stanford U., 1974, PhD in Materials Sci., 1976. Mem. tech. staff Sandia Nat. lab., Albuquerque, 1976-78; mgr. program office Solar Energy Rsch. Inst., Golden, Colo., 1978-82; sr. sci. adv. ARCO Solar, Inc., Camarillo, Calif., 1982—. Co-patentee in field. Mem. IEEE, Am. Phys. Soc., Am. Vacuuum Soc. Home: 13238 Mission Tierra Way Granada Hills CA 91344 Office: ARCO Solar Inc 4650 Adohr Ln Camarillo CA 93010

MITCHELL, LARRY ROBERT, investment broker; b. Sutton, W.Va., July 27, 1952; s. Roland Adair and Eugie Marie (Wilson) M.; m. Susan Arlene Deacon, Aug. 19, 1978; children: Jeremy Scott, Brandon Jay. AA, Ohio Valley Coll., Parkersburg, W.Va., 1972; BBA, Harding U., Searcy, Ark., 1974. Owner CB Sales, Williamstown, W.Va., 1975; asst. mgr. Tri-County Datsun/Imports, Youngstown, Ohio, 1976-77; v.p. Gardening Equipment Corp., New Castle, Pa., 1978-80; exec. v.p. Gardening Equipment Corp., Youngstown, 1981-83; territory mgr. Homelite div. Textron Corp., Cin., 1984; sales rep. Don Jacobs Oldsmobile/Honda, Lexington, Ky., 1983, Good News Books, Scottsdale, Ariz., 1983; registered rep. Dean Witter Reynolds, Mesa, Ariz., 1983-84; investment broker Rauscher Pierce Refsnes, Sun City, Ariz., 1984—; cons. in field, 1984—; instr. Ariz. State U., 1988—. Block chmn. Am. Cancer Soc., Phoenix, 1987; deacon Ch. of Christ, 1985—. Republican. Office: Rauscher Pierce Refsnes 10211 W Thunderbird Blvd Sun City AZ 85351

MITCHELL, ROBERT CAMPBELL, nuclear engineering executive; b. West Point, N.Y., Mar. 28, 1940; s. Herbert V. and Beatrice Cheeseman (Campbell) M.; m. Mardeene Burr, Aug. 19, 1963 (div. Dec. 1983); children: Wendolyn, Dawnelle; m. Patricia Johnson, Aug. 17, 1987. BEE, Stevens Inst. Tech., 1962; MEE, Rensselaer Poly. Inst., 1965. Registered profl. engr., Calif. Design engr. Knolls Atomic Power Lab., Schenectady, N.Y., 1962-65, sr. reactor operator, 1965-67; prin. tng. engr. Nuclear Energy Div. Gen. Electric Co., San Jose, Calif., 1967-72, project engr., 1972-75, mgr. advanced projects, 1975-77, project mgr., 1977-87, licensing mgr., 1987—. Contbr. articles to profl. jours. Nominee White House fellow Gen. Electric Co., San Jose, 1973. Mem. Elfun Soc. Republican. Episcopalian. Home: 1011 Foothill Dr San Jose CA 95123-5302 Office: Gen Electric Co 175 Curtner Ave San Jose CA 95124

MITCHELL, ROBERT R., retired banker; b. 1923; married. Grad., Pacific Coast Sch. Banking, 1960; grad. exec. program, Stanford U., 1972. With U.S. Nat. Bank Oreg., Portland, 1945—, mgr. Lombard-Emerald br., 1959-62, mgr. Hollywood br., 1962-66, mgr. met. br., 1966-68, v.p. mgr. N.W. region, 1968-69, sr. v.p., mgr. orgn. and personnel div., 1969-71, sr. v.p., mgr. br. banking group, 1971-73, exec. v.p. gen. banking, 1973-74, pres., 1974-87, vice chmn., 1987, dir.; vice chmn., dir. U.S. Bancorp; ret. 1988. Office: US Nat Bank Oreg 111 SW 5th Ave PO Box 4412 Portland OR 97208

MITCHELL, TANDIE VERA, wilderness expedition and horseriding academy administrator; b. Carlisle, Pa., Nov. 12, 1942; d. Charles Howard and Vera Oleta (Gadberry) M.; m. Donald Jerry Bain (div. May 1978); Robert Kugler, David, Dean; m. Robert Anthony Astenius, Jan. 1, 1981. AA, Long Beach City Coll., 1973; BA, Calif. State U., Long Beach, 1976. Cert. community clin. psychology, Calif. Originator, producer, concert fundraiser, ops. dir. Snow Summit Jr. Race Team, Big Bear Lake, Calif., 1981; press dir. Snow Summit Women's Pro Ski Racing Tour, Big Bear Lake, 1981; co-founder, cons. S.M.A.R.T. Assocs., Long Beach, Calif., 1978—; pres. Adventure Expeditions of the Wilderness, Inc., Big Bear Lake, 1983—, All Terrain Vehicle Riding Acad., Big Bear Lake, 1985—. Editor: Guide to High Country Life, 1982; contbr. articles to profl. jours. Co-chmn. publicity com. City Council Candidate, Long Beach, 1977; planning com. coordinator Long Beach Commn. Status Women, 1975: adminstr. youth employment program Voter Edn. Project, Long Beach, 1975; yoga instr. Parks and Recreation Dept., Big Bear Lake, 1981. Mem. Am. Diabetes Assn. (support group facilitator 1988), Specialty Vehicle Inst. Am. (ATV instr. 1985—). Republican. Home: Adventure Expeditions of Wilderness Inc PO Box 3084 Big Bear Lake CA 92315

MITCHELL, THOMAS MERLIN, mechanical engineer; b. Sault Ste Marie, Mich., Oct. 27, 1947; s. Merlin M. and Bertha (Shoberg) M.; m. Marcia Ann Young, Aug. 30, 1969; children: Amy Gail, Cara Melinda, Julia Diane, Lindsey Vivian, Joshua Thomas. Student, Lake Superior State Coll., 1965-67; BSME, Mich. Tech. U., 1969. Registered profl. engr., Mich. Mech. engr. Mare Island Naval Shipyard, Vallejo, Calif., 1969-71, Kincheloe AFB, Sault Ste. Marie, 1971-75; utility engr. 8th Army, Uijongbu, Korea, 1975-76; supervisory engr. Kincheloe AFB, 1976-77; staff mech. engr. Hdqrs. USAFE, Ramstein AFB, Fed. Republic Germany, 1977-81; dep. base civil engr. Wurtsmith AFB, Oscoda, Mich., 1981-86, Elmendorf AFB, Anchorage, 1986—. Mem. Nat. Soc. Profl. Engrs., Zweibrucken (Fed. Republic Germany) Hockey Club, U.S. Ambassadors Hockey Club. Home: 10411 High Bluff St Eagle River AK 99577 Office: 21 CSG/DE Elmendorf AFB AK 99506

MITCHELL, WAYNE LEE, educator, social worker; b. Rapid City, S.D., Mar. 25, 1937; s. Albert C. and Elizabeth Isabelle (Nagel) M.; B.A., U. Redlands (Calif.), 1959; M.S.W., Ariz. State U., 1970, Ed.D., 1979. Profl. social worker various county, state, and fed. agencies, 1962-70, Bur. Indian Affairs, Phoenix, 1970-77, USPHS, 1977-79; asst. prof. Ariz. State U., 1979-84; with USPHS, Phoenix, 1984—. Bd. dirs. Phoenix Indian Community Sch., 1973-75; bd. dirs. Phoenix Indian Center, 1974-79, Community Service award, 1977; mem. Phoenix Area Health Adv. Bd., 1975; mem. Community Behavioral Mental Health Bd., 1976-80; lectr. in field. Bd. dirs. Central Ariz. Health Systems Agy.; mem. Fgn. Relations Com. Phoenix. Served with USCG, 1960-62. Recipient Community Service award Ariz. Temple of Islam, 1980. Mem. UN Assn., Nat. Assn. Social Workers, Am. Orthopsychiat. Assn., NAACP, Internat. Platform Assn., Asia Soc., U.S.-China Assn., Kappa Delta Pi, Phi Delta Kappa, Chi Sigma Chi. Congregationalist. Democrat. Contbr. articles to publs. Home: PO Box 9592 Phoenix AZ 85068 Office: 3738 N 16th St Phoenix AZ 85016

MITCHELL, WILLIAM LOUIS, art director; b. Memphis, Sept. 27, 1960; s. Don Louis and Edith Gayle (Wey) M. Cert., Embry Riddle U., 1979. Graphic artist The Label Factory, Inc., Santa Ana, Calif., 1980-81; graphic designer Vita-Fresh, Inc., Garden Grove, Calif., 1982-83; creative dir. Ad-Lib Mktg., Inc., Irvine, Calif., 1983-88; art dir. ANAgraph, Inc., Costa Mesa, Calif., 1988—; speaker, Fashion Inst. Design, Costa Mesa, 1979—. Republican. Eastern Orthodox. Home: 169 E 23d St Costa Mesa CA 92627

MITIO, JOHN, III, state agency administrator; b. Michigan City, Ind., Jan. 15, 1950; s. John Mitio Jr. and Bonnie Gloria (Pearce) Morse; m. Judy Sena, Nov. 25, 1971 (div. 1985); m. Gail Stefl, Sept. 5, 1987; 1 child, Kevin Michael. AA in Liberal Arts, N.Mex. State U., Alamogordo, 1976; BA in Anthropology, N.Mex. State U., Las Cruces, 1979. Engr. aide U.S. Civil Service, Alamogordo, 1974-75, Dynalectron Corp., Alamogordo, 1976; law enforcement campus police N.Mex. State U., Las Cruces, 1977-79; eligibility worker human svcs. dept. State of N. Mex., Albuquerque, 1984-86; medicaid planner human svcs. dept. State of N. Mex., Santa Fe, 1986—. Sgt. USAF, 1969-73, 1st lt., 79-83. Decorated Nat. Def. Svc. medal, Armed Forces Expeditionary medal, Air Force Overseas Svc. medal, Air Force Good Conduct medal. Mem. Planetary Soc., World Future Soc. Republican. Roman Catholic. Home: 2054 Placita de Quedo Santa Fe NM 87505 Office: NMex Dept Human Svcs Pera Bldg 500 Paseo de Peralta Santa Fe NM 87503

MITRANO, JOSEPH CHARLES, school principal; b. Rochester, N.Y., Sept. 22, 1940; s. Charles V. and Anna Marie (Robinson) M. BA, St. John's Coll., 1963; MA, U. Detroit, 1967; STB, U. Toronto, Ont., Can., 1969; EdS. Cert. tchr., adminstr., Calif., ednl. specialist. Tchr. Cath. Cen. Sch., Detroit, 1965-70, counselor, 1970-75; dean St. John Fisher Coll., Rochester, 1976-84, tchr., 1980-84; counselor U. Toronto, 1985-86; prin. Bishop O'Dowd High Sch., Oakland, Calif., 1986—; bd. dirs. Elan Engring., Novi, Mich., Fred M. Tinker, Inc., Fairport, N.Y. Mem. Assn. Secondary Sch. Prins., Nat. Assn. Sch. Pers. Adminstrs., Calif. Adminstrs. Assn., Basilian High Sch. Prins. (pres.), Oakland C. of C. Roman Catholic. Office: Bishop O'Dowd High Sch 9500 Stearns Ave Oakland CA 94605

MITTAL, MANMOHAN, electronics, computer-aided design engineer; b. Muzaffarnagar, India, Sept. 5, 1950; came to U.S., 1981; s. Kedar Nath and Prakash (Wati) M.; m. Shashi Rani, Jan 28, 1976; children: Vivek, Vibhav. BSEE, Inst. Tech., Varanasi, India, 1971; MASEE, U. Ottawa, Ont., Can., 1981; PhD in Elec. and Computer Engring., Wash. State U., 1984. Electronics engr. IIMS, BHU, Varanasi, 1971-73; design engr. Bharat Heavy Elecs. Ltd., Haridwar, India, 1973-79; grad. rsch./teaching asst. Wash. State U., Pullman and U. Ottawa, 1979-84; DA mgr. CAE design automation Silicon Systems, Inc., Tustin, Calif., 1984-88; mgr. standard cell design automation Vitesse Semiconductor Corp., Camarillo, Calif., 1988—; sole proprietor Am. Softfirm Integrators, Irvine, Calif., 1986—. Contbr. tech. papers to profl. jours. U. medal Inst. Tech., BHU, India, 1972; fellow U. Ottawa, 1979-81; grantee Wash. State U., 1981-84. Mem. IEEE (sr., sec. exec. com. Orange County chpt. 1985—, mem. tech. program com., custom integrated cirs. conf. 1988—, bipolar circuits and tech. conf. 1985—), N.Y. Acad. Scis., Assn. Computing Machines, Sigma Xi, Tau Beta Pi. Hindu. Office: Vitesse Semiconductor Corp 741 Calle Plano Camarillo CA 93010

MITTELMAN, PHILLIP SIDNEY, university administrator; b. N.Y.C., Sept. 28, 1925; s. Joseph F. and Rose (Brooks) M.; m. Myra I. Schoenfeld, Apr. 10, 1948; children: Vicki, David. BS in Physics, Rensselaer Poly. Inst., 1945; PhD in Physics, Rensselaer Poly. Inst., 1953; MA in Physics, Harvard U., 1947. Mgr. physics and math United Nuclear Corp., Elmsford, N.Y., 1953-66; pres., chmn. Math. Application Group, Elmsford, 1966-86; dir. lab. for tech. in art UCLA, 1986—. Fellow AAAS; mem. Nat. Computer Graphics Assn. (past pres.). Home: 257 S Barrington Los Angeles CA 90049 Office: UCLA Murphy Rm 265A Los Angeles CA 90024

MIURA, MIKE YUKO, design engineer; b. Wahiawa, Hawaii, Oct. 11, 1931; s. Thomas Mitsuo and May Shizue (Ishida) M.; m. Janet Akemi Fukusaki, Dec. 29, 1964; children: Kurtis Yukio, Kyle Masami. BSCE, U. Hawaii, 1954. Registered profl. engr., Hawaii. Asst. hwy. engr. Calif. Div. Hwys., Stockton, 1954-56; topog. surveyor C.E., U.S. Army, Libya, North Africa, 1957-58; civil engr. III, Ter. Hawaii, Honolulu, 1959; constrn. mgmt. engr. USN, Pearl Harbor, Hawaii, 1960, project mgr. pub. works ctr., 1985-88; project dir. Wilson Okamoto & Assocs., Honolulu, 1988—; head hwy. design engr. Hawaii Dept. Transp., Honolulu, 1960-85; trustee State Employees Retirement System, Honolulu, 1984-85. Pres. Hongwanji Mission Sch. PTA, Honolulu, 1975-76; mem. adv. bd. Hawaii Coastal Zone Mgmt., Honolulu, 1979; bd. dirs. Aiea Neighborhood No. 20, Hawaii, 1977—, chmn. 1987—; chmn. Selective Service Draft Bd. No. 5, Aiea, 1983—; mem. adv. coun. cen. dist. State Dept. Edn., 1986-87. Mem. ASCE, Am. Fedn. State, County and Mcpl. Employees, Am. Soc. Mil. Engrs., AFL-CIO, Hawaii Govt. Employees Assn. (state pres., sci. and profl. bargaining unit 13, 1982-85). Democrat. Home: 99-656 Aliipoe Dr Aiea HI 96701 Office: 460 Lagoon Dr Honolulu HI 96819

MIX, TERRY PLATT, banker; b. Moscow, Idaho, June 2, 1940; s. Gainford William and Rachel (Belle) M.; m. Judith Joan Mix, Sept. 15, 1962 (div. 1984); 1 child, Michelle; m. Ann Larner, Oct. 12, 1985. BA in Agrl. Sci., U. Idaho, 1963. Regional credit supr., br. mgr. Seafirst Bank, Seattle, 1967-84, sr. v.p., region mgr., 1984—. Bd. dirs. Jr. Achievement, Everett, Wash., 1982-83. Capt. U.S. Army, 1963-67, Vietnam; col. Wash. Army N.G. Mem. Lynnwood C. of C. (pres. 1977-78), Rotary. Home: 7028 168th St SW Lynnwood WA 98037

MIXON, WEHLAN EUGENE, communication systems specialist; b. Big Lake, Tex., Nov. 1, 1952; s. William Eugene and Lois Lea (Felkins) M.; m. Lee Ellen Egger, Sept. 1, 1979; 1 child, Alexis Andrea. AA in Bus. Adminstrn., Ventura Coll., 1972; BS in Tech. Edn., Oklahoma City U., 1977; MBA, Calif. Luth. U., 1981. Engr. GTE, Santa Monica, Calif., 1982-83; sr. engr. GTE, Thousand Oaks, Calif., 1983-86; staff analyst GTE, Thousand Oaks, 1986-88, mgr. network planning, 1989—. Sgt. USAF, 1973-81. Scholarship recipient Lions Club, Santa Paula, Calif., 1970. Republican. Home: 2624 Gemini Ct Camarillo CA 93010 Office: GTE Calif 1 GTE Pl Thousand Oaks CA 93162

MIYAHIRA, SARAH DIANE, university dean, psychologist, educator; b. Wailuku, Maui, Hawaii, May 13, 1948; d. Ronald Takayoshi and Bertha Asae (Nagagaki) M.; m. Justin Masakatsu Koizumi, Sept. 7, 1974; 1 child, Jason Miyahira. BA, U. Hawaii, 1970; MA, Ohio State U., 1973, PhD, 1976. Lic. psychologist, marriage, family and child counselor, Calif. Postdoctoral trainee L.A. Dept. Mental Health, 1977; staff psychologist counseling svcs.

U. So. Calif., L.A., 1978-8l; lectr. L.A., 1978-80; assoc. dir. counseling svcs. T, L.A., 1981-83, dir., 1983-85; dean student svcs. Honolulu Community Coll., 1985-88; dean student affairs and open grants East-West Ctr., Honolulu, 1988—; psychotherapist, orgnl. behavior cons., L.A., 1979-85; mem. bd. behavioral sci. examiners State of Calif., 198l-84, mem. accreditation team postsecondary edn. com., 198l; mem. adv. com. Ctr. for Non-Profit Mgmt., L.A., 1984-85; com. mem. Commn. on Status of Women, U. Hawaii, Honolulu, 1987. Mem. steering com. Asian Pacific Women's Network, L.A., 1980; bd. dirs. Asian Pacific Am. support group U. So. Calif., 1983-85; mem. scholarship com. Japanese Am. Citizens League, San Francisco, 1984-85; mem. nominating com. YWCA, Honolulu, 1986-88. Mem. Am. Psychol. Assn. (bd. ethnic minority affairs 1986-88, chmn. 1988, mem. ethics com. 1989), Soc. for Study Ethnics and Minority Issues, Am. Assn. for Counseling and Devel., Am. Coll. Personnel Assn., Am. Soc. for Personnel Adminstrs. Home: 5943 Kalanianaole Hwy Honolulu HI 96821 Office: East-West Ctr 1777 East-West Rd Honolulu HI 96848

MIYAMURA, WAYNE MAMORU, instrument technician; b. Wailuku, Hawaii, Aug. 12, 1950; s. Hikoki and Saeko (Go) M. AA in Sci., Community Coll. of the Air Force, Lackland AFB, Tex., 1977; BBA, U. Hawaii, 1972. Electronic technician Adrian's T.V. & Sound Engr., Wailuku, 1978; office equipment technician Bus. Equipment Co., Wailuku, 1978-81; instrument technician Hawaiian Comml. and Sugar Co., Paunene, 1982—. Served with USAF, 1973-77. Mem. The Future Soc.

MIYASAKI, SHUICHI, lawyer; b. Paauilo, Hawaii, Aug. 6, 1928; s. Torakichi and Teyo (Kimura) M.; m. Pearl Takeko Saiki, Sept. 11, 1954; children—Joy Michiko, Miles Tadashi, Jan Keiko, Ann Yoshie. B.S.C.E., U. Hawaii-Honolulu, 1951; J.D., U. Minn., 1957; LL.M. in Taxation, Georgetown U., 1959; grad. Army War Coll., 1973. Bar: Minn. 1957, Hawaii 1959, U.S. Supreme Ct. 1980. Examiner, U.S. Patent Office, 1957-59; dep. atty. gen. State of Hawaii, 1960-61; mem., dir., treas. Okumura Takushi Funaki & Wee, Honolulu, 1961—; atty. Hawaii Senate, 1961, chief counsel ways and means com., 1962, chief counsel judiciary com., 1967-70; civil engr. Japan Constrn. Agy., Tokyo, 1953-54; staff judge adv., col. USAR, Ft. DeRussy, Hawaii, 1968-79; local legal counsel Jaycees, 1962. Legis. chmn. armed services com. C. of C. of Hawaii, 1973; instl. rep. Aloha council Boy Scouts Am., 1963-78; exec. com., sec., dir. Legal Aid Soc. Hawaii, 1970-72; state v.p. Hawaii Jaycees, 1964-65; dir., legal counsel St. Louis Heights Community Assn., 1963, 65, 73; dir., legal counsel Citizens Study Club for Naturalization of Citizens, 1963-68; life mem. Res. Officers Assn. U.S. Served to 1st lt., AUS, 1951-54. Decorated Meritorious Service medal with oak leaf cluster. Mem. ABA, Hawaii Bar Assn., U.S. Patent Office Soc., Hawaii Estate Planning Council, Phi Delta Phi. Clubs: Rotary, Central YMCA, Waikiki Athletic, Army Golf Assn. Lodges: Elks. Address: 1552 Bertram St Honolulu HI 96816

MIYATA, KEIJIRO, culinary art educator; b. Tokyo, Mar. 8, 1951; came to U.S., 1967; s. Yataro Miyata and Hekkiken (Liu) Choy; m. Connie Joyce Nelson, Mar. 8, 1976; children: Michelle, Kelly, Adam. Assoc. in Occupational Study, Culinary Inst. Am., Hyde Park, N.Y., 1973. Cert. exec. chef; cert. culinary educator. Garde mgr. Mid-Pacific Country Club, Kailua, Hawaii, 1972; working chef Waikiki Yacht Club, Honolulu, 1972-74, Sagano Japanese Restaurant, New Rochelle, N.Y., 1974-76; asst. pastry chef Rye Town (N.Y.) Hilton Hotel, 1976-77; working chef The Explorer, Everett, Wash., 1977-79; exec. chef Holiday Inn, Everett, 1979-81, Mill Creek (Wash.) Country Club, 1981; culinary art instr. Everett Community Coll., 1981-85, North Seattle (Wash.) Community Coll., 1985—; cons. Chalon Corp., Redmond, Wash., Chiang-Mai Restaurant, Mukilteo, Wash., 1988. Recipient Gold awards Am. Culinary Fedn., Oreg. State Chef's Assn., Portland, 1983, Gold and Bronze medals World Culinary Olympic, Frankfurt, Germany, 1984, 88, Grand Champion award U.S. Nat. Ice Carving Contest, N.Y.C., 1986, 2d place award All Japan Ice Carving Assn., Asahikawa, 1988, Ednl. Excellence award Oreg. and Wash. Community Coll. Couns., 1988. Mem. Wash. State Chef's Assn. (bd. mem. 1982, 83, 86, 87, 88, cert. chmn. 1986—, Chef of Yr. 1986). Office: N Seattle Community Coll 9600 College Way N Seattle WA 98103

MIYAWAKI, EDISON HIROYUKI, health care executive, physician; b. Honolulu, Feb. 6, 1929; s. Kazumi and Fujiko (Ishikawa) M.; m. Sallie Yashiki, Oct. 5, 1956; 1 child, Edison Kazumi. BS, Loyola U., L.A., 1952; MD, George Washington U., D.C., 1972. Intern George Washington U. Med. Ctr., Washington, 1972-73; chmn., pres., chief exec. officer The Family Health Inc. (dba Nuuanu Hale Hosp.), Honolulu, 1973—; bd. dirs. The Family Health, Inc., Honolulu, 1973—, Enterprise Bank of Bellevue, Wash., 1988—. Author: Nerve Endings in the Human Heart, 1968; Am. Heart Assn. award, 1969. Trustee Loyola Marymount U. L.A., 1986—; mem. Commn. on Future of Loyola-Marymount, 1987—, Hawaii Criminal Justice Commn., Honolulu, 1987, 88. Named Disting. Alumni, Loyola-Marymount U., L.A., 1987; recipient William Beaumount Med. Soc. award, 1982, The Howard F. Kane-A.F.A. King Med. award. Mem. N.Y. Acad. Scis., Loyola Marymount U. Alumni Assn. (pres. 1980—), Kalia Lions, (bd. dirs. 1985-87), Honolulu Country Club, Plaza Club, Kansas City Chiefs Club. Home: 1010 Wilder Ave PH-E Honolulu HI 96822 Office: The Family Health Inc Nuuanu Hale Hosp 2900 Pali Hwy Honolulu HI 96817

MIYAZAWA, YASUO SCOTT, chemical company consultant; b. Tokyo, June 3, 1948; came to U.S. 1971; s. T. and M. (Kunihiro) M.; m. Kayoko Nakagome, June 28, 1975; 1 child, Hiroyuki. Student, Aoyamagakuin U., Tokyo, 1971, Calif. Coll. Dental Tng., L.A., 1973. Indsl. chemicals div. BASF Ag., Ludwigshafen, Fed. Republic Germany, 1979-80; indsl. chemicals div. BASF Japan, Tokyo, 1980, engring plastic group leader, asst. mgr., 1980-82; engring. plastic dept. leader Mitsibishi Yuka-Badische, Tokyo, 1982-84; v. p., dir. Yazaki USA, Dallas, 1984-86; pres. SeedTech, L.A., 1986—. Mem. Soc. Plastic Industries. Home: 28039 Ridgebrook Ct Rancho Palos Verdes CA 90274 Office: SeedTech 1518 W 10th St San Pedro CA 90732

MIZE, ROBERT HERBERT, JR., bishop; b. Emporia, Kans., Feb. 4, 1907; s. Robert Herbert and Margaret Talman (Moore) M. B.A., U. Kans., 1928 grad. Gen. Theol. Sem., N.Y.C., 1932, S.T.D., 1960. Vicar ch. missions Episcopal Ch., Hays Kans., 1932-41, Wakeeney, Kans., 1941-45; founder, dir. St. Francis Boys' Homes, Ellsworth and Salina, Kans., 1945-60; bishop of Damaraland Anglican Ch., Windhoek, Southwest Africa, 1960-68, asst. bishop, Gaberone, Botswana, 1968-70, 73-76; vicar Trinity Episcopal Ch., Marshall, Mo, 1970-73; assisting bishop Episcopal Ch. Diocese of San Joaquin, Fresno, Calif., 1978-88; dir. Gen. Theol. Seminary's Assoc. Mission, Hays, 1933-41; vicar St. Raphael's Episcopal Ch., Oakhurst, Calif., 1977-81. Mem. Phi Beta Kappa, Sigma Delta Chi, Phi Delta Theta. Office: Episcopal Diocese of San Joaquin 4159 E Dakota Ave Fresno CA 93726

MIZEL, LARRY A., housing construction company executive; b. 1942; married. BA, U. Okla., 1964; JD, U. Denver, 1967. Chmn. bd., chmn. exec. com., dir. MDC Holdings Inc., 1972—. Office: MDC Holdings Inc 3600 S Yosemite St Denver CO 80237 •

MIZER, RICHARD ANTHONY, senior engineer; b. San Francisco, Jan. 7, 1952; s. Conrad Xavier and Sally Jo (Hagan) M. BA in Bioengring. and Econs., U. Calif., San Diego, 1977. Founding ptnr. Microdoctors, Palo Alto, Calif., 1974—; mgr., ptnr. K-Family Corp., Fremont, Calif., 1977-78, Restaurants Unique Inc., Mountain View, Calif., 1980-83; mgr. engring. Pacific Bell, San Ramon, Calif., 1983—. Mem. security staff Republican Task Force, San Francisco, 1984, tech. staff U.S. Olympic Com., Los Angeles, 1984. Roman Catholic. Office: Pacific Bell 2600 Camino Ramon 3S450 San Ramon CA 94583

MIZNER, CHARLENE DINO, nurse; b. Johnson City, N.Y., Apr. 22, 1955; d. Charles Micheal and Mary Ann (Valusek) Dino; m. Richard Leo Mizner, Dec. 18, 1986; 1 child, Kristi Lee. AAS, Mohowak Valley Community Coll., 1976; BS in Nursing, SUNY, Utica, 1978. R.N., Calif. Commd. 1st lt. U.S. Air Force, 1980, advanced through grades to capt., 1982; res. USAF, 1987; staff nurse USAF, March AFB,, Calif., 1980-82; staff nurse, Azores, Portugal USAF, 1982-83; charge nurse USAF, Carswell AFB, Tex., 1983-86, Griffiss AFB, N.Y., 1986-87; charge nurse U.S. Air Force, Castle AFB, Calif., 1987—; staff nurse Mercy Hosp., Merced, Calif., 1987—. Mem. Nat. League Nursing, Air Force Assn., Officers Club. Republican. Roman Catholic. Office: Mercy Hosp 2740 M St Merced CA 95348

MIZOKAMI, IRIS CHIEKO, mechanical engineer; b. Honolulu, Oct. 19, 1953; d. Takeo and Muriel Yae (Maeda) M.; m. Joseph John Nainiger, Nov. 27, 1976 (div. June 1987). BSME, Case Inst. Tech., 1975. Project engr. Aluminum Co. of Am., Cleve., 1975-77; engr. machine, tool and die dept. Chevrolet-Parma, Ohio, 1977-81; engr. facilities Pearl Harbor (Hawaii) Naval Shipyard, 1988—. Vol. Manor Care Nursing Home, N. Olmsted, Ohio, 1986-87. Mem. Soc. Women Engrs., ASME, Eta Kappa Nu, Chopin. Mormon. Home: 1927 Uluwehi Pl Honolulu HI 96822 Office: Pearl Harbor Naval Shipyard PO Box 400 Pearl Harbor HI 96860

MOAK, RICHARD JOHN, protective services official; b. Cleve., Dec. 12, 1947; s. Glenn Duntlin and Yolanda (Apicella) M.; m. Laura Hall, Oct. 3, 1982 (div. May, 1985); m. Chang Soon Kim, Mar. 14, 1988. Student, U. Vienna, Austria, 1968-69; BA in German, Wabash Coll., 1970; MA in German, U. So. Calif., 1973, ABD, 1976. Life teaching cert. Adminstrv. asst. U. So. Calif., L.A., 1975-76; dep. sheriff L.A. County Sheriff's Dept., 1976-83, sgt., 1983—. Contbr. articles to profl. jours. Nat. Def. Edn. Act fellowship, U. So. Calif., 1970-73. Mem. Peace Officers Assn. of L.A. County, Calif. Peace Officers Assn., Women Peace Officers Assn., Internat. Police Assn., Cousteau Soc., Planetary Soc., Mensa, Tau Kappa Epsilon. Republican. Home: PO Box 55362 Valencia CA 91385 Office: LA County Sheriffs Dept 211 W Temple St #448 Los Angeles CA 90012

MOATS, HAROLD, manufacturing company representative; b. Oreg. City, Oreg., Sept. 29, 1939; s. Everett Elmer Moats and Nancy Ann (Engle) Downs; m. Carole Marie Bresee, Dec. 27, 1958; children: Robert John, Michele Rae, Anne-Marie, Karen Lynne. Student, Portland State U., 1962-69. Technician Tektronix, Inc., Beaverton, Oreg., 1962-68; electrical engr. Tektronix, Inc., Beaverton, 1968-72; product specialist Bourns, Inc., Riverside, Calif., 1972-73; sales mgr. Bourns, Inc., Riverside, 1973-75; ptnr. Electronic Sources, Inc., Portland, Oreg., 1975-86; majority ptnr. Electronic Engring. Sales, Portland, 1986—; bd. chmn. Northcon, Portland, 1988—. With USN, 1958-62. Mem. Electronic Reps. Assn. (bd. chmn. Cascade chpt. 1988-89). Republican. Roman Catholic. Home: 10085 SW Serena Way Tigard OR 97224 Office: Electronic Engring Sales 17020 SW U Boones Ferry Rd Portland OR 97224

MOBERLY, LINDEN EMERY, educational administrator; b. Laramie, Wyo., Jan. 4, 1923; s. Linden E. and Ruth (Gathercole) M.; B.S., Coll. Emporia, 1952; M.S., Kans. State Tchrs. Coll., 1954; m. Viola F. Mosher, Apr. 29, 1949. Tchr. sci., Florence, Kans., 1952-54, Concordia, Kans., 1954-56, Grand Junction, Colo., 1957-60; asst. prin. Orchard Mesa Jr. High Sch., Grand Junction, 1960-66, prin., 1967-84; field cons. Nat. Assn. Secondary Sch. Prins., 1985—. Served to sgt. USMC, 1941-46. Recipient Outstanding Secondary Prin. award Colo. Assn. Sch. Execs., 1978. Mem. NEA, Nat. Assn. Secondary Prins. (dir. 1979-83), Colo. Edn. Assn. (dir. 1968-71), Colo. North Central Assn. Colls. and Secondary Schs., Colo. Assn. Secondary Sch. Prins. (dir. 1974-77), Lions, Sons of the Revolution. Home: 2256 Kingston Rd Grand Junction CO 81503

MOBLEY, KAREN RUTH, art gallery director; b. Cheyenne, Wyo., Aug. 26, 1961; d. David G. and Marlene G. (Franz) M. BFA, U. Wyo., 1983; MFA, U. Oka., 1987. Sales assoc. Morgan Gallery, Kansas City, Mo., 1984-85; grad. asst. U. Okla. Mus. Art, Norman, 1985-87; dir. Univ. Art Gallery N.Mex. State U., Las Cruces, 1988—; guest artist Okla. City Community Coll., 1986. Paintings exhibited in numerous exhibitions including Art West Open Competition, 1987. Named Outstanding Young Women Am. Mem. Am. Assn. Mus., Mountain Plains Mus. Assn., NMex. Mus Assn., Coll. Art Assn., Phi Bets Kappa, Phi Kappa Phi. Home: PO Box 3817 UPB Las Cruces NM 88003 Office: U Art Gallery NMex State U Box 30001 Las Cruces NM 88003

MOCKEL, DENNIS EDWARD, engineer; b. Oakland, Calif., Sept. 4, 1952; s. Donald Joseph and Margaret Mary Mockel. AS, BS, Oreg. Tech. U., 1974. Engr. Diablo Systems/Xerox, Hayward, Calif., 1974-79; staff engr. PRIAM, San Jose, Calif., 1979-88; owner DME Cons., Pleasanton, Calif., 1988—. Office: DME 4509 Carver Ct Pleasanton CA 94566

MODROW, DOUGLAS KEVIN, mining processing executive; b. Tacoma, Nov. 10, 1958; s. Ronnie Dean and Ruth Charlene (Walker) M.; m. Marie Celeste Collopy, Feb. 1, 1986. BS in Metall. Engring., U. Idaho, 1982. Supt. yard dept. ASARCO, Tacoma, 1982-83; supt. anode plant ASARCO, Hayden, Ariz., 1983-85, supt. acid plant, 1985-86, tech. engr., 1986-88, mgr. tech. svcs., 1988—. Mem. AIME, Rotary (bd. dirs. Kearny, Ariz. 1988-89), Elks (exalted ruler Kearny 1986-87, trustee 1987-89). Home: 1150 W Santo Domingo Cir Tucson AZ 85704 Office: ASARCO 64 Asarco Ave Hayden AZ 85235

MODUGNO, RON STEVEN, sales executive; b. Sept. 7, 1952; s. Sam Frank and Pearl (Ditomaso) M.; m. Lisa Ann Charlton, Nov. 12, 1977; children: Kevin, Daniel, Steven. Student, U. So. Calif., 1970-72; BS in Indsl. Engring., Calif. State U., Northridge, 1975, postgrad., 1982-84. With San Fernando (Calif.) Elec. Mfg., 1971-88, inside sales mgr., 1976-78, key accounts mgr., 1978-80, western regional sales mgr., 1980-82, asst. gen. sales mgr., 1982-85, nat. sales mgr., 1985-88; account exec. Gtel Bus. Systems, Thousand Oaks, Calif., 1988-89; nat. sales mgr. KBI, Valencia, Calif., 1989—; mem. Exhibits com. Wescon Shows, L.A., 1977-84, chmn. 1984. Fundraising chmn. Valencia YMCA, 1988, nation chief indian guides. Mem. IEEE (electromech. chpt., sec. 1987), Valencia C. of C., Santa Clarita Valley C. of C., Lancaster (Calif.) C. of C. Home: 23637 Via Corsa Valencia CA 91355

MODUGNO, VICTOR JOSEPH, actuary; b. N.Y.C., Sept. 27, 1949; s. Joseph and Romola (Erriquez) M. BA magna cum laude, Queens Coll., Flushing, N.Y., 1971. Actuarial assoc. Met. Life. Ins. Co., N.Y.C., 1971-80; asst. actuary Pacific Mut. Life Ins. Co., Newport Beach, Calif., 1980-86; actuary Exec. Life Ins Corp. subs. 1st Exec. Corp., Los Angeles, 1986—. Fellow Soc. Actuaries; mem. Am. Acad. Actuaries, Los Angeles Actuaries Club. Republican. Roman Catholic. Home: 140 The Village #407 Redondo Beach CA 90277 Office: Exec Life Ins Co 11444 W Olympic Blvd Los Angeles CA 90064

MOE, ANDREW IRVING, veterinarian; b. Tacoma, Jan. 2, 1927; s. Ole Andrew and Ingeborg (Gordham) M.; BS in Biology, U. Puget Sound, 1949; BA, Wash. State U., 1953, DVM 1954; m. Dorothy Clara Becker, June 25, 1950; children: Sylvia Moe McGowan, Pamela Moe Barker, Joyce. Meat cutter Art Hansen, Tacoma, 1943-48; gen. practice as veterinarian Baronti Vet. Hosp., Eugene, Oreg., 1956-57; veterinarian, regulatory Calif. Animal Health br. Calif. Dept. Food and Agr. Resident veterinarian II, Modesto, Calif., 1957-64, acting veterinarian-in-charge Modesto Dist. Office (veterinarian III), 1976-77. Watersafety instr. ARC, 1958-61. Capt., Vet. Corps., 1954-56, 62; comdr. 417th Med. Svc. Flight Res. (AFRES), 1965-66, 71-73; lt. col. Biomed. Scis. Corps USAF, ret., 1982. Recipient Chief Veterinarian badge, 1975. Mem. Am., Calif., No. San Joaquin (pres. 1979) vet. med. assns., Calif. Acad. Vet. Medicine (charter), Res. Officers Assn. (life), Ret. Officers Assn. (life), Assn. Mil. Surgeons U.S., U.S. Animal Health Assn., Sons of Norway, Masons (Illustrious Master Modest coun. 1983, Allied Masonic degrees), Shriners, Theta Chi. Alpha Psi. Lutheran (del. 102d Synod 1961). Home: 161 Norwegian Ave Modesto CA 95350 Office: 1620 N Carpenter Rd Ste D48 Modesto CA 95351

MOE, DOUGLAS EDWIN, professional basketball coach; b. Bklyn., Sept. 21, 1938; m. Jane Twisdale; 2 children. Student, U. N.C. Player Italian Basketball League, Padua, 1965-67; player Am. Basketball Assn., New Orleans, 1967-68, Oakland, 1968-69; player Carolina Cougars, Am. Basketball Assn., 1969-70, Va. Squires, Am. Basketball Assn., 1970-72; coach San Antonio Spurs, NBA, 1976-80, Denver Nuggets, 1980—. Mem. All-Star Team, 1968-70, Championship Team, Am. Basketball Assn., 1969. Named National Basketball Association coach of the year, 1988. Office: Denver Nuggets McNichols Sports Arena 1635 Clay St Denver CO 80204 •

MOELLER, JAMES, state judge; b. Valley, Nebr., Nov. 14, 1933; s. Hans and Marie Grace (Shumaker) M.; m. Nancy Lee Kiely, Dec. 16, 1961; children: Amy Jo, Linda Anne. BA, Nebr. Wesleyan U., 1954; JD with high distinction, George Washington U., 1959. Bar: Ariz. 1959, U.S. Dist. Ct. Ariz. 1959, U.S. Ct. Appeals (9th cir.) 1961. Assoc. Lewis and Roca, Phoenix, 1959-64, ptnr., 1964-70; ptnr. Moeller Hover Jensen & Henry, Phoenix, 1970-77; judge Maricopa County Superior Ct., Phoenix, 1977-87; justice Ariz. Supreme Ct., Phoenix, 1987—. Editor-in-chief George Washington U. Law Rev., 1958-59. Bd. dirs. Found. for Blind Children, Scottsdale, Ariz., 1964-70, Ariz. Found. Prevention of Blindness, Phoenix, 1966-70; Rep. committeeman, Phoenix and Scottsdale, 1965-69. Served with U.S. Army, 1954-56. Mem. ABA, Am. Judicature Soc., Ariz. Bar Assn., Maricopa County Bar Assn. Methodist. Office: Ariz Supreme Ct 201 West Wing Capitol Bldg Phoenix AZ 85007

MOELLER, KENNETH PAUL, architect; b. Escondido, Calif., Dec. 19, 1953; s. Floyd A. and Helen L. (Posey) M.; m. Marianne Tanner, Dec. 30, 1976; children: Allisyn, Paul, Michelle. B. in Acctg., Ariz. State U., 1978, BArch., 1981. Registered architect, Ariz., Calif. Architect Drover Welch & Lindlan, Phoenix, 1982-84; prin. Moeller & Assocs., Phoenix, 1985-87; assoc. Deems Lewis McKinley, San Diego, 1987-88, Delawie Bretton Wilkes, San Diego, 1988—. Scoutmaster Boy Scouts Am., Ecinitas, Calif., 1988. Mem. AIA, Nat. Coun. Archtl. Registration Bds. Republican. Mormon. Home: 989 Olive Crest Dr Encinitas CA 92024 office: Delawie Bretton Wilkes 2827 Presidio Dr San Diego CA 92110

MOELLER, ROBERT CHARLES (BUD MOELLER), management consultant; b. Washington, Sept. 5, 1954; s. Charles Edward and Ann Joan (Federico) M.; m. Carol Elizabeth Buchanan, June 19, 1976; children: Melaine Elizabeth, Robert Kehne. BChemE, Ga. Inst. Tech., 1976; MBA, Harvard U., 1978. Cons. ERT, Concord, Mass., 1977-78; assoc. Booz, Allen & Hamilton, Bethesda, Md., 1978-81, sr. assoc., 1981-83; prin. Booz, Allen & Hamilton, San Francisco, 1983-88, v.p., 1988—; chmn. bd. dirs. Nat. Capital YFC, Olney, Md., 1981-83. Contbr. articles to energy pubs. Chmn. bd. dirs. East Bay Youth for Christ, Concord, Calif., 1983—; mem. Rep. Presdl. Task Force, Washington, 1984-86; adv. Montgomery County (Md.) Health Dept., 1981. Mem. Am. Inst. Chem. Engrs., Ferrari Owners Club, Mensa. Republican. Mem. Evangelical Free Ch. Club: HBS (San Francisco). Home: 610 Castlerock Rd Walnut Creek CA 94598 Office: Booz Allen & Hamilton 555 Montgomery St San Francisco CA 94111

MOERNER, WILLIAM ESCO, physicist; b. Pleasanton, Calif., June 24, 1953; s. William Alfred and Bertha Frances (Robinson) M.; m. Sharon Judith Stein, June 19, 1983. BS in Physics, Elec. Engring., Washington U., St. Louis, 1975, AB in Math., 1975; MS in Physics, Cornell U., 1978, PhD in Physics, 1982. Langsdorf engring. fellow Washington U., St. Louis, 1971-75; NSF grad. fellow Cornell U., Ithaca, N.Y., 1975-78; rsch. asst. Cornell U., 1978-81; mem. rsch. staff IBM Rsch. Div., Almaden, San Jose, Calif., 1981-88; mgr. IBM Rsch. Div., Almaden, San Jose, 1988—. Patentee, strain-sensitive spectral features detection method, device; author, editor: Persistent Spectral Hole-Burning: Science and Applications, 1988; contbr. articles to tech. publs. Tenor, San Jose Symphonic Choir, 1983—; ofcl. observer, Am. Radio Relay League, Santa Clara Valley, Calif., 1987—. Named Outstanding Young Elec. Engr., Eta Kappa Nu, 1984. Mem. IEEE (sr., treas. Lasers and Electro-Optics Soc. ann. meeting 1989), Am. Chem. Soc., Am. Phys. Soc., Optical Soc. Am., IBM Amateur Radio Club (pres. 1987-88). Democrat. Office: IBM Rsch Ctr K32 802 (D) 650 Harry Rd San Jose CA 95120-6099

MOES, ROGER ALLEN, JR., electrical engineer; b. Harvey, Ill., June 19, 1963; s. Roger Allen Sr. and Joyce Alice (Klooster) M.; m. Barbara Jean Kingma, Dec. 29, 1983. BS in Elec. Engring., Purdue U., 1985. Engr. Boeing Electronics, Seattle, 1985—. Mem. Internat. Soc. for Hybrid Microelectronics. Republican. Home: 1512 220th Pl NE Redmond WA 98053 Office: Boeing Electronics PO Box 24969 Seattle WA 98124

MOESLEIN, FRANK ADOLF, banker, accountant; b. N.Y.C., Oct. 11, 1943; s. Joseph and Rosa (Zoeller) M.; m. Imelda M. Hutchinson, Sept. 24, 1966. BBA, Manhattan Coll., 1966. CPA, N.Y. Audit mgr. Coopers and Lybrand, White Plains, N.Y., 1966-75; dep. controller Bankers Trust Co., N.Y.C., 1975-84; sr. v.p., controller Wells Fargo Bank, San Francisco, 1984—. With U.S. Army, 1966-68, Vietnam. Mem. AICPA, N.Y. Soc. CPAs, Fin. Execs. Inst. Republican. Roman Catholic. Office: Wells Fargo & Co 525 Market St San Francisco CA 94163

MOFFAT, RICHARD HOWE, judge, lawyer; b. Salt Lake City, Dec. 17, 1931; s. David Howe and Muriel (Dods) M.; m. Ann Hope Williamson, June 18, 1955; children: Kathleen Ann, Barbara Lynne, David Richard. BS, U. Utah, 1953; JD, Stanford U., 1956. Bar: Utah 1956. Mng. ptnr., pres. Moffat, Welling & Paulsen and predecessor, Salt Lake City, 1956-85; judge 5th Cir. Ct. Utah, Murray, 1985-86, 3d Dist. Ct. Utah, Salt Lake City, 1986—; chmn. Jud. Removal Commn., Salt Lake City, 1980-8l. Mem. Salt Lake County Bd. Adjustment, 1980-85, Utah Bd. Water Resources, 1982-85. Mem. ABA, Utah State Bar (commr. 1975-8l), Salt Lake County Bar Assn. (pres. 1969-70, exec. com. 1968-8l), Cottonwood Country Club. Democrat. Office: 3d Dist Ct Utah 240 East 4th South Salt Lake City UT 84111

MOFFATT, DAVIS FRANKLIN, electronics executive; b. Joplin, Mo., Jan. 24, 1937; s. Edwin Luther and Lelah Faye (Davis) M.; m. Mary Lucille Barnett, June 22, 1957; children: Theressa, Edwin, Kevin, Linda. BSEE, Okla. State U., 1963. Tech. field rep. Philco, Phila., 1961; systems engr. Bendix, Ann Arbor, Mich., 1961-62; project engr. Collins Radio Co., Cedar Rapids, Iowa, 1962-72; program mgr. Recognition Equipment, Irving, Tex., 1972-73; v.p. engring. Specialty Instruments, Irving, 1973; dept. mgr. Rockwell Internat., Richardson, Tex., 1974-79; founder, pres., chief exec. officer Stratotech Corp., Richardson, 1979-85; pres. Continental Woodcraft Co., Waxahachie, Tex., 1985; pres., chief exec. officer Harbor Utility Service Bodies, Brea, Calif., 1985—; bd. dirs. Microcomp Enterprises, Richardson, Advanced Vehicle Design, Brea. Patentee in field. Sgt. Richardson Police Reserves, 1968-75. Named Officer of Yr. Richardson, Police, 1968. Republican. Mem. Christian Ch. Home: 3361 Antler Rd Ontario CA 91761

MOFFATT, HUGH MCCULLOCH, JR., hospital administrator, physical therapist; b. Steubenville, Ohio, Oct. 11, 1933; s. Hugh McCulloch and Agnes Elizabeth (Bickerstaff) M.; m. Ruth Anne Colvin, Aug. 16, 1958; children: David, Susan. AB, Asbury Coll., 1958; cert. in phys. therapy, Duke U., 1963. Lic. in phys. therapy and health care adminstrn., Alaska. Commd. officer USPHS, 1964, advanced through grades to capt.; therapist USPHS, N.Y.C., 1964-66, Sitka, Alaska, 1970-72; therapist cons. USPHS, Atlanta, 1968-70; clinic adminstr. USPHS, Kayenta, Ariz., 1972-73; hosp. dir. USPHS, Sitka, 1973-78; therapist cons. Idaho Dept. Health, Boise, 1966-68; contract health officer USPHS, Anchorage, 1978—; therapist cons. Our Lady of Compassion Care Ctr., Anchorage, 1979—, Alaska Native Med. Ctr., Anchorage, 1988—. With U.S. Army, 1955-57. Mem. Am. Phys. Therapy Assn., Commd. Officers Assn. USPHS, Res. Officers Assn., Ret. Officers Assn., Am. Assn. Individual Investers, Am. Assn. Ret. Persons, Eagles.

MOFFATT, KATY (KATHERINE LOUELLA MOFFATT), musician, vocalist, songwriter; b. Ft. Worth, Nov. 19, 1950; d. Lester Huger and Sue-Jo (Jarrott) M. Student, Sophie Newcomb Coll., 1968, St. John's Coll., 1969-70. Rec. artist Columbia Records, 1975-79, Permian/MCA Records, 1982-84, Enigma Records, L.A., 1985, Wrestler Records, L.A., 1987-88. Folksinger, Ft. Worth, 1967-68; musician, vocalist, songwriter, rec. artist for: film Billy Jack, 1970; TV prodn. asst. film, Sta.-KIII, Corpus Christi, 1970, TV audio engr., Sta.-KRIS, Corpus Christi, 1970; musician, vocalist in blues band, Corpus Christi, 1970; receptionist, bookkeeping asst., copywriter, announcer, Sta.-KFWT, Ft. Worth, 1971, musician, vocalist, songwriter, Denver, 1971-72, on tour, 1973, 75—, Denver, 1974, on tour, 1976-79, European tour, 1977, Can. tour, 1984-85, on tour in Europe and U.S., 1985-88; spl. guest vocalist appearance: film Hard Country, 1981; albums include Katy, 1976, Kissin' In The California Sun, Am. release, 1977, internat. release, 1978, A Town South of Bakersfield, 1985, Walkin' on the Moon, European release, 1988, U.S. release, 1989; singles include Take it as it Comes, 1981, Under Loved and Over Lonely, 1983; songs include The Magic Ring, 1971; Gerry's Song, 1973, Kansas City Morning, 1974, Take Me Back To Texas, 1975, (Waitin' For) The Real Thing, 1975, Didn't We Have Love,

1976, Kissin' in the Calif. Sun, 1977, Walkin' on the Moon, 1989. Named One of 4 Top New Female Vocalists, Cashbox Singles Awards, 1976, One of 3 Top New Female Vocalists; recipient Record World Album awards, 1976. Mem. Am. Fedn. Musicians, AFTRA.

MOFFATT, MINDY ANN, teacher, educational and research consultant; b. Mpls., Aug. 3, 1951; d. Ralph Theron and La Vone Muriel (Bergstrom) M. Student, UCLA, 1972-73; BA, Calif. State U., Fullerton, 1975, postgrad. Cert. elem. tchr., Calif. Tchr. early childhood edn. program Meadows Elem. Sch., Valencia, Calif., 1977-78; tchr. United Parents Against Forced Busing, Chatsworth, Calif., 1978-80; founding tchr. Gazebo Two Sch. for Young Gifted and Creative Children, Summerville, S.C., 1980-81; tchr. Anaheim Union High Sch. Dist., Anaheim, Calif., 1981—, mentor, tchr., 1985-88; cons. writing project U. Calif., Irvine, 1982—; textbook cons. McDougal, Littell & Co., Evanston, Ill., 1984-86; facilitator Summer Tech. Tng. Inst., Irvine, 1987. Author: The Gifted and Talented Education Way to English, 1984; co-author: Practical Ideas for Teaching Writing as a Process, 1986, 87. Mem. Friends of the River, San Francisco, Handgun Control, Inc., Washington; active The Nature Conservancy, Arlington, Va.; sponsor English Council Orange County. Mem. NEA, Calif. Assn. Tchrs. of English, NOW, Nat. Coun. Tchrs. English, Nat. Writing Project, Sierra Club, Friends of the River, Handgun Control Inc. Democrat. Unity Ch. of Truth. Club: Our Ultimate Recreation (Orange County, Calif.) (social com. chairperson 1983, backpacking chairperson 1983).

MOFFATT, ROBERT HENRY, accountant, publisher, writer, consultant; b. Montreal, Que., Can., June 30, 1930; came to U.S., 1968, naturalized, 1973; s. James Bigelow and Edwige Edith M.; m. Hannelore Mann, Jan. 7, 1989. Student Loyola Coll., Montreal, Que., 1948-52, Acadia U., 1962, UCLA, 1970, 72. Lic. in air navigation, Can.; enrolled agt., Dept. Treasury. Mng. editor, pub. Kings-Annapolis Wings, 1961-66; pres., Valley Pubs. Ltd., Kingston, N.S., Can., 1961-67 exec. dir. Maritime Motor Transport Assn. and editor Maritime Truck Transport Rev., Moncton, N.B., Can., 1967-68; dir. spl. products div. Wolf-Brown Inc., Los Angeles, 1968-77; newsletter pub, writer, 1980—; pvt. practice acctg., tax acctg., Los Angeles, 1970—. Columnist, author editorials in mags. Clk., author constn. Village of Greenwood, N.S., 1961-63; chmn. bd. commrs., 1963-66; publicity chmn. Voluntary Econ. Planning Program, province N.S., 1965-66. Served to lt. Can. Air Force, 1954-60. Mem. Nat. Assn. Enrolled Agts. (newsletter editor, bd. dirs.), Nat. Soc. Pub. Accts (accredited in taxation), Calif. Soc. Enrolled Agts., Temple of Set, Inc. (bd. dirs.) Home: 7509 W 88th St Los Angeles CA 90045 Office: 8939 S Sepulveda Blvd Ste 430 Los Angeles CA 90045

MOFFETT, FRANK CARDWELL, architect, civil engineer, real estate developer; b. Houston, Dec. 9, 1931; s. Ferrell Orlando and Jewell Bernice (Williams) M.; BArch, U. Tex., 1958; m. Annie Doris Thorn, Aug. 1, 1952 (div.); children: David Cardwell (dec.), Douglas Howard; m. Darlene Adele Alm Sayan, June 7, 1985 (div.). Architect with archtl. firms, Seattle, Harmon, Pray & Detrich, Arnold G. Gangnes, Ralf E. Decker, Roland Terry & Assocs., 1958-64; ptnr. Heideman & Moffett, AIA, Seattle, 1964-71; chief architect Wash. State Dept. Hwys., Olympia, 1971-77, Wash. State Dept. Transp., 1977-87; owner The Moffett Co., Olympia, 1974—; founder, treas. TAA, Inc., Olympia, 1987—; advisor Wash. State Bldg. Code Adv. Council, 1975—; instr. civil engring. tech. Olympia Tech. Community Coll., 1975-77; adv. mem. archtl. barriers subcom. Internat. Conf. Building Ofcls.; archtl. works include hdqrs. Gen. Telephone Directory Co., Everett, Wash., 1964; Edmonds Unitarian Ch., 1966; tenant devel. Seattle Hdqrs. Office, Seattle-First Nat. Bank, 1968-70; Wash. State Dept. Transp. Area Hdqrs. Offices, Mt. Vernon, Selah, Raymond, Colfax and Port Orchard 1973-87; Materials Lab., Spokane, Wash., 1974; Olympic Meml. Gardens, Tumwater, Wash., 1988; archtl. barriers cons. State of Alaska, 1978. Chmn. Planning Commn. of Mountlake Terr., Wash., 1963, 64, mem., 1961-67; mem. State of Wash. Gov.'s Task Force on Wilderness, 1972-75, Heritage Park Task Force, Olympia, Wash., 1986—; trustee Cascade Symphony Orch., 1971; incorporating pres. United Singles, Olympia, 1978-79. With USN, 1951-54. Registered architect, Alaska, Calif., Wash., profl. engr., Wash.; cert. Nat. Council Archtl. Registration Bds., U.S. Dept. Def., Fallout Shelter Analysis, environ. engring. Mem. AIA (dir. S.W. Wash. chpt. 1980-82, pres.-elect 1985, pres. 1986, dir. Wash. council 1986, architects in govt. nat. com. 1978-87), Am. Public Works Assn., Inst. Bldgs. and Grounds, ASCE, Constrn. Specifications Inst., Am. Arbitration Assn. (invited panelist), Gen. Soc. Mayflower Descs. (gov. Wash. Soc. 1982-83), Nat. Huguenot Soc. (pres. Wash. Soc. 1981-83, 85-87), Olympia Geneal. Soc. (pres. 1978-80), SAR (state treas. 1984-85), SCV, Sons and Daus. of Pilgrims, (gov. Wash. Soc. 1984), Order of Magna Charta, Rotary (pres. Edmonds, 1969-70), Olympia, Coll. Club of Seattle, Olympia Yacht Club, Olympia Country and Golf Club. Co-author: An Illustrated Handbook for Barrier-Free Design, 2d edit., 1984, 3d edit., 1987. Republican. Unitarian. Home: PO Box 2422 Olympia WA 98507 Office: PO Box 2422 Olympia WA 98507

MOFFETT, JONATHAN PHILLIP, drummer, musical director, songwriter; b. New Orleans, Nov. 17, 1954; s. Eddie Vernon and Elnora (Dillon) M.; m. Rhonda Catherine Bartholomew, June 26, 1976; children: Tamara Renee, Julian Ryann. Grad. high sch., New Orleans. Drummer, vocalist Patti Austin, Los Angeles, 1982; drummer Cameo Tour, Altanta, 1982, 83, 86, Lionel Richie, Los Angeles, 1983; drummer, mus. dir. Michael Jackson and the Jackson's Victory Tour, Los Angeles, 1984; drummer Madonna, Los Angeles, 1985-87, Tina Marie, Los Angeles, 1986; drummer, mus. dir. Jermaine Jackson, Los Angeles, 1986-87; drummer The Jacksons Tour, Los Angeles, 1979, 81, 84, Elton John World Tour, 1988; recorded with Julian Lennon, Peter Cetera, Marilyn Martin, The Jacksons, Kenny Loggins, Chico DeBarge. Designer (drum equipment sculpture) Victory Tour Set, 1984; appeared on TV and in videos with Marilyn Martin, Tony Terry, The Kane Gang, Isacc Hayes, Rick James, Cameo, Madonna's Virgin Tour video, Madonna's Ciao Italia Tour video; producer, writer song All Dressed Up for film soundtrack Coming to America; Elton John Album, 1989, Madonna Album, 1989. Mem. Musician's Union. Democrat. Roman Catholic.

MOFFETT, PATRICIA ELLA, sales executive; b. Honolulu, Jan. 29, 1955; d. George Harry and Stephanie Rose (Straszewski) M.; m. Alan G. Simons, Mar. 1, 1975 (div. Oct. 1980). Grad., high sch., Santa Ana, Calif. Office mgr. Trig Tek Inc., Anaheim, Calif., 1978-80; adminstrv. asst. Stanford Applied Engring. Co., Costa Mesa, Calif., 1980-81; sales adminstr. Bertagni Electroacoustic Systems, 1981-84; sales engr. Nat. Tech. div. Helix, Irvine, Calif., 1984-89; sales mgr. USA PC World div. Helix Cirs., Scarborough, Ont., Can., 1989—. Dist. distbn. mgr. Daffodil Days program Orange County chpt. Am. Cancer Soc., 1987-89. Mem. Calif. Circuits Asssn., Inst. for Interconnecting and Packaging Electronics Circuits, Tech. and Mktg. Rsch. Coun. Democrat. Baptist. Office: PC World div. Helix Circuits 16601 Armstrong Ave Irvine CA 92714

MOFFETT, STEPHEN, engineer. BS, U. Ariz., 1983. Engr. electronic equipment design Westinghouse Corp., Richland, Wash., 1983-85, Varian Corp., Salt Lake City, 1985—. Contbr. articles to profl. jours; patentee for vision systems. Office: Varian 1678 S Pioneer Rd Salt Lake City UT 84104

MOFFITT, THOMAS LYNN, aerospace company official; b. L.A., Feb. 3, 1940; s. Calvin B. and Elizabeth L. (Coval) M.; m. Penelope A. Moffitt, July 4, 1964 (dec. Feb. 1973); children: Darla, Denise, Thomas, Elizabeth; m. Carolyn Grooms Moffitt, Nov. 25, 1983; 1 child, Jeffrey L. BA in Bus., Calif. State U., L.A., 1967. Sales rep. Ducommon Metals Co., Calif., 1961-69; mgr. indsl. sales Tectonics, Inc., Ann Arbor, Mich., 1969-75, E.C. De Young, Inc., Riverside, Calif., 1975-80; sales exec. Sta. WHIM, Providence, Calif., 1980-85, Sta. WEWO, Laurinburg, N.C., 1983-86; sales mgr. BFM Transport Dynamics, Inc., Santa Ana, Calif., 1986—. Bd. dirs. YMCA, Riverside, 1976-79, Laurinburg, 1984-86. Served with USMC, 1957-61. Mem. Aerospace Bearing Assn., Acad. Country Music, Broadcast Music, Songwriters Guild Am., BFM Transport Dynamics Mgmt. Assn. (bd. dirs. 1987-88), Country Music Assn., Am. Legion. Office: BFM Transport Dynamics Inc 3131 Segerstrom St Santa Ana CA 92704

MOFFORD, ROSE, governor; b. Globe, Ariz., June 10, 1922; m. T.R. Mofford (div.). Attended pub. schs. Sec. to Joe Hunt, Ariz. State Treas., 1941-43, Ariz. State Tax Commr., 1943-54, Wesley Bolin, Ariz. Sec. of State, 1954-55; asst. sec. of state State of Ariz., Phoenix, 1955-75; asst. dir. of revenue State of Ariz., 1975-77, sec. of state, 1977-88, governor, 1988—. Democrat. Office: Office of Gov 1700 W Washington St Phoenix AZ 85007 *

MOGENSEN, ARIE PAUL, geologist; b. Ogden, Utah, May 3, 1933; s. Svend Aage and Matilde (Van De Graaft) M; m. Bernadine Boyd, Apr. 12, 1969; children: Barrie Kaye, Kurt Evan. BS, Utah State U., 1955; MS, U. Wyo., 1959. Geologist Bear Creek Mining Corp., Denver, 1960-61; div. geologist Kennecott Copper Corp., various locations, 1961-78; cons. geologist Eureka, Utah, 1978; chief mine geologist to mgr. spl. project Gold Fields Mining Corp., Denver, 1978—. Contbr. articles to profl. jours. Mem. Joab County Planning Commn., Nephi, Utah, 1976-78; bd. dirs. Mineral Exploration Coalition, Denver, 1988-89. With U.S. Army, 1955-57. Mem. NRA, Am. Inst. Mining Engrs., Can. Inst. Mining, Soc. Econ. Geologists, Masons. Home: 28757 Clover Ln Evergreen CO 80439

MOGG, DONALD WHITEHEAD, chemist; b. La Grange, Ill., Feb. 11, 1924; s. Harold William and Margaret (Whitehead) M.; B.S., Allegheny Coll., 1944; postgrad. Harvard U., 1946-47. Asst. chemist Gt. Lakes Carbon Corp., Morton Grove, Ill., 1947-48, chemist, 1948-53, research chemist, 1953-56, project supr., 1956-59, sect. head, 1959-63; sect. head Gt. Lakes Research Corp., Elizabethton, Tenn., 1963-66; research and devel. mgr. bldg. products div. Grefco, Inc., Torrance, Calif., 1966-68, corp. research and devel. mgr., 1968-72, group mgr., 1972-81, sr. research assoc., 1981-82. Served with U.S. Army, 1944-46. Mem. Am. Chem. Soc., AAAS, Phi Beta Kappa, Phi Kappa Psi. Presbyterian. U.S. and fgn. patentee in field of bldg. products. Home: 3823 Ingraham St Apt B202 San Diego CA 92109

MOHABIR, VISHUNDYAL RAMOTAR, accountant; b. Georgetown, Guyana, Mar. 23, 1951; came to U.S., 1969; s. Ramotar and Maywattee (Harricharran) M.; m. Bibi Shamuene Udit, June 28, 1975; children: Rosanne, Danielle. Assoc., Washington Bus. Inst., N.Y.C., 1972; BS, St. Francis Coll., Bklyn., 1976. Cert. tax preparer. Asst. mgr. Schuman Motors Inc., Bklyn., 1970-72; mgr., acct. Schuman Motors Inc., 1973-78; staff acct. Braverman & Fagan Accountancy, L.A., 1973-84; controller First Transtate Fin. Group, Encino, Calif., 1985-86; pres. Tiffany Accountancy Corp., Inglewood, Calif., 1987—. Home: 4570 W 134th St Hawthorne CA 90250

MOHANTA, SAMARESH, manufacturing company executive; b. Burdwan, Bengal, India, July 15, 1949; came to U.S. 1970; s. Radha Shyam and Amiya Bala (Mohanta) M.; m. Aparna Mukhopadhyay, Feb. 20, 1975; children: Labonee, Imone. B.Tech. with hons., Indian Inst. Tech., 1970; MASc, U. Waterloo, Ont., Can., 1972; PhD, U. Waterloo, 1975. Registered profl. engr. Postdoctoral fellow U. Waterloo, 1975, research assoc., 1975-76; electrochem. engr. HSA Reactors, Toronto, Ont., Can., 1976-78; mgr. process design HSA Reactors, 1978-81, sr. corp. devel. engr., 1981-82; mgr. electrochem. engring. Durachell, Inc., Missisauga, Ont., 1982-87; owner Elchem Technologies, Missisauga, 1987; dir. engring. Aquanautics Corp., Alameda, Calif., 1987—; researcher U. Waterloo, 1975-76. Contbr. articles to profl. jours.; patentee in field. NRC fellow, 1975-76, others. Mem. Electrochem. Soc. (exec. com. Can. sect. 1982-86), Toastmasters. Office: Aquanautics Corp 980 Atlantic Ave #101 Alameda CA 94501

MOHLER, DANIEL BARTLEY, lawyer; b. Berwyn, Ill., Sept. 8, 1938; s. Sidney Eli and Mary Louise (Murray) M.; m. Barbara Jean Hauck, July 20, 1985. BA, Mich. State U., 1961; LLB, Indiana U., 1964. Bar: Colo., Idaho 1965. Law clk. Supreme Ct. Idaho, Boise, 1964-66; dep. dist. atty. Dist. Atty., 4th Dist., Colorado Springs, Colo., 1966-67; asst. city atty. City of Colorado Springs, 1966-67; pvt. practice Colorado Springs, 1968-77; tennis profl. Rancho Bernardo Inn., San Diego, Calif., 1978-84; real estate broker Watt Industries, Calif., 1979-84; pvt. practice law Colorado Springs, 1985—; cons. appeals for various lawyers, Colorado Springs, 1985—. Author, photogrpher (slide show) Wandering Thru Nepal, 1988. Dist. atty. candidate, Colorado Springs, 1972. Mem. ABA, Colo. Bar Assn., El Paso County Trial Lawyers, U.S. Profl. Tennis Assn. Office: 108 E Cheyenne Rd Colorado Springs CO 80906

MOHOLY, NOEL FRANCIS, clergyman; b. San Francisco, May 26, 1916; s. John Joseph and Eva Gertrude (Cippa) M.; grad. St. Anthony's Sem., Santa Barbara; S.T.D., Faculte de Theologie, Universite Laval, Quebec, Que., Can., 1948. Joined Franciscan Friars, 1935; ordained priest Roman Catholic Ch., 1941; tchr. fundamental theology Old Mission Santa Barbara, 1942-43, sacred theology, 1947-58; tchr. langs. St. Anthony's Sem., 1943-44; Am. adminstr. (handling affairs of the cause in U.S.) Cause of Padre Junipero Serra, 1950-55, vice postulator, 1958—; retreat master San Damiano Retreat, Danville, Calif., 1964-67. Mem. Ann. Assay Commn. U.S. Mint, 1964. Occupied numerous pulpits, assisted in several Franciscan Retreat Houses; condr. series illustrated lectrs. on cause of canonization of Padre Junipero Serra to students of all Franciscan study houses in U.S., summer 1952, also speaker in field at various clubs of Serra Internat. in U.S., Europe and Far East, on NBC in documentary with Edwin Newman, Padre Serra, Founding Father, 1985, PBS on Firing Line with William F. Buckley: Junipero Serra—Saint or Sinner, 1989, CBS, ABC broadcasts and conducted own local TV series. Exec. dir., treas. Old Mission Restoration Project, 1954-58; mem. Calif. Hist. Landmarks Adv. Com., 1962-71, Calif. Hist. Resources Commn., 1971-76, Calif. Bicentennial Celebration Commn., 1967-70; pres. Serra Bicentennial commn., 1983-86. Nat. and internat. authority on mariology, Calif. history (particularly history of Father Serra). Decorated Knight comdr. Order of Isabella the Catholic. Pres. Father Junipero Serra 250th Anniversary Assn., Inc., 1964—. Named hon. citizen Petra de Mallorca, 1969, Palma de Mallorca, 1976; recipient Cross of Merit Sovereign Mil. Order of Knights Malta, 1989. Mem. Mariol. Soc. Am., Native Sons Golden West, Associacion de los Amigos de Padre Serra, K.C., Calif. Missions Study Assn. Author: Our Last Chance, 1931; Saint Irenaeus; the Father of Mariology, 1952; The California Mission Story, 1975; The First Californian, 1976; co-author (with Don DeNevi) Junipero Serra, 1985; producer phonograph records Songs of the California Missions, 1951, Christmas at Mission Santa Barbara, 1953, St. Francis Peace Record, 1957; producer The Founding Father of the West, 1976. Home: St Boniface Friary 133 Golden Gate Ave San Francisco CA 94102 Office: Serra Cause Old Mission Santa Barbara CA 93105-3697

MOHR, JOHN LUTHER, biologist, environmental consultant; b. Reading, Pa., Dec. 1, 1911; s. Luther Seth and Anna Elizabeth (Davis) M.; m. Frances Edith Christensen, Nov. 23, 1939; children: Jeremy John, Christopher Charles. A.B. in Biology, Bucknell U., 1933; student, Oberlin Coll., 1933-34; Ph.D. in Zoology, U. Calif. at Berkeley, 1939. Research asso. Pacific Islands Research, Stanford, 1942-44; research asso. Allan Hancock Found., U. So. Calif., 1944-46, asst. prof., 1946-47, asst. prof. dept. biology, 1947-54, asso. prof., 1954-57, prof., 1957-77, prof. emeritus, 1977—, chmn. dept. 1960-62; marine borer and pollution surveys harbors So. Calif., 1948-51, arctic marine biol. research, 1952-71; chief marine zool. group U.S. Antarctic research ship Eltanin in Drake Passage, 1962, in South Pacific sector, 1965; research asso. malacology Los Angeles County Mus. of Natural History; research deontology in sci. and academia, problems with offshore drilling discharges and oil spill dispersants, 1978—; researcher on parasitic protozoans of anurans, crustaceans, elephants; analysis of agy. and industry documents, ethics and derelictions of steward agy., sci. and tech. orgns. as they relate to offshore oil activities, environ. effects of oil spill dispersants and offshore oil industry discharges. Mem. Biol. Stain Commn., 1948—, trustee, 1971-81, emeritus trustee, 1981—, v.p., 1976-80; bd. dirs. Calif. Natural Areas Coordinating Council. Recipient Guggenheim fellowship, 1957-58. Fellow AAAS (council 1964-73), So. Calif. Acad. Sci., Sigma Xi (exec. com. 1964-67, 68, 69, chpt.-at-large bd. 1968-69); mem. AAUP, Marine Biol. Assn. U.K. (life), Am. Soc. Parasitologists, Western Soc. Naturalists (pres. 1960-61), Soc. Protozoologists, Am. Soc. Tropical Medicine and Hygiene, Am. Soc. Zoologists, Ecol. Soc. Am., Planning and Conservation League, Calif. Native Plants Soc., Am. Inst. Biol. Scis., L.A. Macintosh Group, Natural Resources Def. Coun., Save San Francisco Bay Assn., So. Calif. Soc. of Parasitologists, Common Cause, Huxleyan, Phi Sigma, Theta Upsilon Omega, Sierra Club. Democrat. Home: 3819 Chanson Dr Los Angeles CA 90043-1601

MOHR, MARCIA SCHLATHER, actress; b. Boston, Feb. 3, 1930; d. Abraham and Etta Toby (Goldberg) Goodman; m. Kenneth O. Schlather, June 23, 1951 (div. 1964); children: Laura Lee Schlather Jones, Marc David, Dale Frederick. BS in Speech, Syracuse U., 1951. Appeared in films Jaws, The Front, Goodbye Columbus; TV: Superior Court, Divorce Court, Archie Bunker's Place, General Hospital; Theater (L.A.): Kvetch, Inquest, Baal, Pericles Berlin in the East, Beaux Arts Ball, A Short Circuit, (N.Y.) The Harold Arlen Songbook, Saga of Richard Nixon, Blood Wedding, Three Penny Opera, The Seagull, Madonna in the Orchard, White Whore & The Bit Player, Soon, Jack, November. Founder Miami Jewish Home for Aged, Fla., 1988; patron Odyssey Theatre Found., L.A., 1984-88; mem. Friends of Jeffrey Ballet, L.A.C.M.A. Mem. Actor's Equity Assn. (We. adv. bd. 1985—), SAG, AFTRA, Am. Inst. Wine & Food., Marina City Club, Sports Club (L.A.). Home: 42 Sea Colony Dr Santa Monica CA 90405 Office: Atkins and Assocs Agy 303 S Crescent Hgts Blvd Los Angeles CA 90048

MOHR, SELBY, retired ophthalmologist; b. San Francisco, Mar. 11, 1918; s. Selby and Henrietta (Foorman) M.; AB, Stanford U., 1938, MD, 1942; m. Marian Buckley, June 10, 1950; children—Selby, John Vincent, Adrianne E., Gregory P. Asst. resident in ophthalmology U. Calif. Hosp., 1942-43; pvt. practice ophthalmology, San Francisco, 1947-88; mem. past pres. med. staff Marshall Hale Meml. Hosp.; mem. staff Mt. Zion Hosp., St Francis Meml. Hosp. Dir. Sweet Water Co., Mound Farms, Inc., Mound Farms Oil & Gas, Inc. Lt. (j.g.) USNR, 1943-46; PTO. Diplomate Am. Bd. Ophthalmology. Fellow Am. Acad. Ophthalmology and Otolarngology; mem. AMA, Calif., San Francisco Med. Socs., Pan-Pacific Surg. Soc., Pan-Am. Assn. Ophthalmology, Pacific Coast Oto-Ophthalmol. Soc., Pan-Am. Med. Soc. Home: 160 Sea Cliff Ave San Francisco CA 94121 Office: 450 Sutter St San Francisco CA 94108

MOHR, SIEGFRIED HEINRICH, mechanical and optical engineer; b. Vöhrenbach, Baden, Fed. Republic Germany, Sept. 20, 1930; came to U.S., 1958.; s. Adolf and Luise (Faller) M.; m. Gloria P. Vauges, Apr. 25, 1959 (div. 1972); children: Michael S., Brigitte M.; m. Jeani Edith Hancock, Mar. 24, 1973; 1 child, Suzanne A. Diplom-Ingenieur, Universität Stuttgart, Fed. Republic Germany, 1957; MS in Optical Engring., SUNY, 1971. Thesis researcher Daimler Benz AG, Stuttgart, 1957; design engr. Russell, Birdsall & Ward B & Nut Co., Port Chester, N.Y., 1958-59; devel. engr. IBM Advanced Systems Devel. div., San Jose, Calif., 1960-64; rsch. engr., inventor Precision Instrument Co., Palo Alto, Calif., 1964-67; prin. engr. RCA Instructional Systems, Palo Alto, 1967-70; rsch. engr., scientist Singer Simulation Products, Sunnyvale, Calif., 1971-73; project leader Dymo Industries Tech. Ctr., Berkeley, Calif., 1973-77; leader, adv. rsch. & devel. NCR Corp. Micrographic Systems Div., Mountain View, Calif., 1977—; translator for books in English, French and German; corr., writer for European jazz publs. Patentee, author in field. Bicycle activist League of Am. Wheelmen, Balt., 1975—; del. mem. U.S. Del. ISO Conf., Paris, 1988. Mem. Assn. Info. and Image Mgmt., Internat. Soc. Optical Engring. Roman Catholic. Home: 3311 Benton St Santa Clara CA 95051

MOHRDICK, EUNICE MARIE, nurse, health educator; b. Alameda, Calif.; d. Walter William and Eunice Marie (Connors) M. BS in Nursing Edn., U. San Francisco, 1955; MA in Edn. spl interest, San Francisco State Coll., 1967; Pub. Health Cert., U. Calif., San Francisco, 1968; EdD, Western Colo. U., 1977. RN, Calif. Nurse, supr. St. Mary's Hosp., San Francisco, 1943-45, supr., instr., 1955-60, 62-65; asst. dir. nursing, tchr. nursing history St Mary's Coll. of Nursing, San Francisco, 1953-55; tchr. home nursing Mercy High Sch., San Francisco, 1960-61; tchr. Health, Family Life San Francisco Unified Schs., 1968-83; tchr. Holistic Health Contra Costa Coll., 1981-86; cons. pvt. practice Albany, Calif., 1986—; tchr. El Cerrito (Calif.) Senior Ctr., 1986-88. Author: Elementary Teacher Handbook, How to Teach Sex Education, Grades, 4,5,6, 1977. Mem. Madonna Guild, San Francisco, 1986—, Half Notes' Singing Club to Sick and Spl. Needy, 1970—. Recipient Title I Grant U. Calif. San Francisco, 1968, Workshop Grant for Culture Inter-relationship Study, Singapore, UNESCO, Washington U., St. Louis, 1973. Mem. AAUW, San Francisco State U. Alumna, U. San Francisco Nursing Alumni (charter mem., bd. dirs. 1974-88), Mensa. Republican. Roman Catholic. Home & Office: 555 Pierce St #129 Albany CA 94706

MOHRMANN, SISTER CORINNE MARIE, education executive; b. San Jose, Calif., Dec. 11, 1944; d. Walter Ferdinand and Dorothy Elizabeth (LaFrance) M. BA in Human Devel., Pacific Oaks Coll., 1972, MA in Human Devel., 1976. Tchr. St. Elizabeth's Day Home, San Jose, Calif., 1962-63, St. Francis Day Home, San Francisco, 1966-68, St. Vincent's Day Home, San Francisco, 1969-70; program dir. St. Vincent's Day Home, 1976-81, exec. dir., 1981—; tchr. Holy Family Day Home, San Francisco, 1969-70; kindergarten tchr. Divine Providence Day Home, Las Vegas, 1971; exec. dir. Divine Providence Day Home, 1972-76; guest speaker Japanese Social Worker's Conv., San Francisco, 1984, 86, 88, 89. Mem. Urban Strategies Coun., Oakland, 1988—; presenter League of Women Voters, 1988—; mem. child devel. div. adv. com. State Dept. Edn., 1985—, peer program quality reviewer, 1989; bd. dirs. Merritt Coll. Adv. Bd., 1984—. Democratic. Roman Catholic. Office: St Vincent's Day Home 1086 8th St Oakland CA 94607

MOIRAO, DANIEL R., educator; b. Oakland, Calif., Mar. 31, 1952; s. Manuel Joseph and Anna G. (Zuniga) M.; m. Anita Louise Stakenburg, June 16, 1979; children: Jacqueline Christine, Jennifer Margaret. BA, U. Calif., Davis, 1974; MS, Calif. State U., Hayward, 1980. Cert. tchr. k.- community coll., Calif., 1975; Sch. administrn. credential, Calif., 1979. Tchr. Tracy (Calif.) Pub. Schs., 1975-76; tchr. San Ramon VAlley Unified Sch., Danville, Calif., 1976-80, prin., 1980-86; dir., coordinatior Calif. Sch. Leadership Acad., Hayward, 1986-87; asst. supt. Pittsburg (Calif.) Unified Sch. Dist., 1987—; cons. Riverside (Calif.) County Office of Edn. Co-author: Enhancing Student Success Positive School Climate, 1987. Named Outstanding Tchr., San Ramon Valley Dist., 1977. Mem. Assn. of Calif. Sch. Adminstrs. (pres. 1987), Am. Assn. Sch. Adminstrs., Assn. for Supervision and Curriculum Devel., Nat. Assn. Elementary Sch. Prins., Phi Delta Kappa, Toastmasters (Best Speaker Area 5, 1986). Roman Catholic. Home: 110 Danforth Ct Danville CA 94526 Office: Pittsburg Unified Sch Dist 2000 Railroad Ave Pittsburg CA 94565

MOISE, STEVEN KAHN, lawyer; b. Lubbock, Tex., July 28, 1944; s. Joseph J. and Marguerite K. M.; m. Beth Maxwell, June 2, 1968; children: Adam, Grant. BA, U. Colo., 1966, JD, 1969. Bar: Colo. 1969, N.Mex. 1971. Assoc. Rothgerber, Appel & Powers, Denver, 1969-71; assoc. Sutin, Thayer & Browne, Albuquerque, 1971-74, ptnr., 1974—, bd. trustees, 1980—, mem., pres., chief exec. officer, 1984-88, chmn., 1989—. Bd. dirs. U. Colo. Found., Boulder, 1971—, trustee, 1988—, Sch. Law Alumni Bd. U. Colo. , 1985—; sec. Albuquerque All Seasons Corp., 1986-88, N.Mex. Amigos, 1986—, Albuquerque Community Found., 1981—, pres., 1984-88, Albuquerque Econ. Devel./Indsl. Found. Albuquerque, 1988—. Mem. ABA, N.Mex. Bar Assn., Colo. Bar Assn., Albuquerque Bar Assn. Democrat. Jewish. Home: 6611 Guadalupe Trail NW Albuquerque NM 87107 Office: Sutin Thayer & Browne PO Box 1945 Albuquerque NM 87103

MOK, MARY WHUN-WA, pathologist; b. Chgo., Apr. 1, 1947; d. Wa To and Victoria (Kiang) M.; m. William Thomas Malcolm, July 1, 1987. BA, U. Calif., Berkeley, 1968; MD, U. Calif., Davis, 1976. Diplomate Am. Bd. Pathology, Anatomic and Clinical Pathology. Pathology resident L.A. County Harbor, UCLA Med. Ctr., Torrance, Calif., 1976-80; cytopathology fellow Montefiore Hosp. and Med. Ctr., Bronx, N.Y., 1980-81; pathologist, co-dir. of lab. Pioneer Hosp., Mullikin Med. Ctr., Artesia, Calif., 1981-82; acting asst. prof. of Pathology, staff Pathologist LAC-Harbor, UCLA Med.Ctr., Torrance, 1982-83; pathologist DSA Med. Svcs. Inc., Panorama City, Calif., 1983-86, Cigna Healthplans of Calif., L.A., 1986-89, Kaiser Bellflower (Calif.) Med. Ctr., 1989—. Musician Palos Verdes (Calif.) Symphonic Band. Fellow Am. Soc. Clin. Pathologists, Coll. Am. Pathologists; mem. Am. Contract Bridge League, Phi Beta Kappa. Office: Kaiser Permanente Bellflower Med Ctr 2400 E Rosecrans Ave Bellflower CA 90706

MOLACEK, KATHRYN ANN, realtor, marketing executive; b. Long Beach, Calif., Mar. 10, 1944; d. Owen Frank Joyce and Carolyn Viola (Robson) Holmes; m. Cletus Frank Molacek, Mar. 24, 1963; children: Edward S., Michele Ann. Student, Long Beach Bus. Coll., 1963, Orange Coast Coll., 1976. Cert. dental asst., x-ray technician; lic. real estate sales. Office mgr. Donald J. Holm, DDS, Long Beach, Calif., 1966-69, Larry Hampsten, DDS, Irvine, Calif., 1976-78; tchr. Ariz. Med./Dental Colls., Phoenix, 1979; office mgr. James Sido, DDS, Scottsdale, Ariz., 1979-81; regional sales mgr.

Contact Staffing of Am., Phoenix, 1981-85; dir. mktg. Contract Personnel Systems, Inc., Phoenix, 1985—; realtor Chelsey Realty, Phoenix, 1988—; pvt. practice benefit cons., Scottsdale, 1985—; cons. Physician Fin. Svc., Inc., Phoenix, 1981—, Corp. Pers. Svcs., Inc., Phoenix, 1986—, Haulen, Inc., Phoenix, 1986—. Mem. N.W. Theater Project, Phoenix, 1987-88. Recipient Cert. of Distingushed Vol. Svc. Fountain Valley (Calif.) Sch. Dist., 1974-76. Mem. North Valley C. of C., Am. Soc. Profl. and Exec. Women, Phoenix Bd. Realtors, Chelsey Realty Pres.'s Roundtable, Harbor Dental Assts. Soc. (pres. 1975-76, friendship award 1972), So. Calif. Dental Assts. Soc. (state del. 1974-76). Republican. Roman Catholic. Office: Chelsey Realty/Internat Inc 515 E Carefree Hwy Phoenix AZ 85029

MOLBEGOTT, MARK ROBERT, social worker, marriage-family-child counselor; b. Bronx, N.Y., Jan. 25, 1952; s. Sidney and Pauline (Rosen) M.; m. Sharon Arlene Roffman, Aug. 23, 1981. BA in Psychology, SUNY, Stony Brook, 1973; MA in Psychology, Temple U., 1976; postgrad. in psychology, U.S. Internat. U., 1979. Lic. marriage, family and child counselor, Calif. Client care worker Woodhaven Ctr., Temple U., Phila., 1975-76; family counselor San Diego Youth and Community Svcs., 1977-78, asst. program dir., 1978-86; social worker IV and V, San Diego County Child Protection Svcs., San Diego, 1986-88, sr. protective svcs. worker, 1988—; marriage and family counselor, San Diego, 1980—; group counselor Parents United, San Diego, 1985-87, Daus.-Sons United, San Diego, 1987—. N.Y. State Regent's scholar, 1969. Mem. Am. Assn. for Marriage and Family Therapy (clin.), Calif. Assn. Marriage and Family Therapists (clin.), Calif. Profl. Soc. on Abuse of Children (life charter), San Diego Community Child Abuse Coordinating Coun., Rancho Penasquitos Tennis Assn. (sec. 1988—). Democrat. Office: Child Protection Svcs 6950 Levant St San Diego CA 92111

MOLDOVAN, GEORGENE, emergency physician; b. Trenton, N.J., Oct. 13, 1951; d. George and Eleanor (Wynn) Moldovan; m. Walter C. Monegan, Mar. 17, 1983; children: Sierra Elizabeth, Haleyne Victoria. BS in Chemistry, U. Del., 1972; MD, U. Pitts., 1976. Diplomate Am. Bd. Emergency Medicine. Resident in surgery Stanford U., 1976-77; dir. emergency rm. Alaska Hosp., Anchorage, 1978-85; med. dir. Municipality of Anchorage Emergency Med. Svcs., 1984-86, Girdwood (Alaska) Emergency Med. Svcs., 1983-85; clin. faculty U. Alaska, Anchorage, 1960—; dir. Northcare, Anchorage, 1984—; clin. specialist faculty Stanford U. Hosp., 1987—. Fellow Am. Coll. Emergency Physicians; mem. Alaska Med. Assn., Assn. Emergency Med. Physicians. Office: Northcare 4001 Lake Otis Pkwy Anchorage AK 99508

MOLINA, JOHN FRANCIS, chemist; b. Jamaica, N.Y., Jan. 4, 1950; s. Joseph Robert and Lee Marie (Salvatore) M.; m. Leslie Barbara Swartz, Jan. 8, 1973; children: Joseph Robert II, Lisa Nicole. BS in Chemistry, Northeastern U., Boston, 1973; PhD in Chemistry, U. New Orleans, 1977. Rsch. chemist Celanese Rsch. Co., Summit, N.J., 1979-81; group leader analytical svcs. Apollo Techs., 1981-83; mgr. lab. ops. At Sea Incineration, 1983-85; mgr. field analytical svcs. OH Material Corp., Findlay, 1985-86; exec. v.p. ops., dir. lab. Hager Labs., Englewood, Colo., 1987—; chem. cons. Booz Allen & Hamilton, Florham Park, N.J., 1979-81, N.Y. Testing, Westbury, N.Y., 1983-85. Crime watch coord. Tuxedo Park Neighborhood Assn., South Orange, N.J., 1979-83; mgr. Findlay Youth Baseball League, 1985. Mem. Am. Chem. Soc., Soc. for Applied Spectroscopy, Am. Inst. Chemists, N.Y. Acad. Scis., Alpha Theta Epsilon (award of honor 1976). Republican. Roman Catholic. Home: 4896 E Costilla Pl Littleton CO 80122-2324

MOLISANI, JOHN JOSEPH, JR., sales executive; b. Buffalo, Mar. 1, 1962; s. John Joseph and Gloria Frances (Nowakowski) M. BS in Computer Engring., Tulane U., New Orleans, 1984. Tech sales support Micrognosis, Inc., L.A., 1987-89; assoc. account exec. Micrognosis, Inc., 1989—; field staff Ch. of Scientology, L.A., 1988—; pub. registrar South Bay Dianetics Ctr., Manhattan Beach, Calif., 1988—. Author: Night Shadows, 1989 (novel). 1st lt. USAF, 1984-87. Mem. Internat. Assn. Scientologists, Tulane U. Alumni Assn. (activities com. chmn. 1988-89). Ch. of Scientology. Home: 327 Avenue G Redondo Beach CA 90277 Office: Micrognosis Inc 1525 Aviation Blvd Apt A120 Redondo Beach CA 90278

MOLL, DIANA CAROLYN, artist, graphic designer, painter; b. Summit, N.J., Apr. 21, 1958; d. John Lewis and Isabell Mary (Sieber) M.; m. Johnny Stewart Simmons, May 30, 1986. BA in Art, U. Calif., Santa Cruz. Night mgr. Cymbaline Records, Santa Cruz, Calif., 1981-84; wine bottler Smothers Winery, Scotts Valley, Calif., 1984-85; personal asst. Lou Harrison, Composer, Aptos, Calif., 1985-87; designer, artist Lizard Graphics, Santa Cruz, Calif., 1984—. Programer Sta. KUSP, Santa Cruz, 1982; bd. exec. Nuclear Weapons Freeze of Santa Cruz County, 1988; acting chair Gamelan Tatri Ratri, Santa Cruz, 1988. Recipient project grant, Cultural Coun. of Santa Cruz County, 1987; trust grant, Santa Cruz County Hist. Preservation Trust, 1987. Democrat. Office: Lizard Graphics PO Box 8291 Santa Cruz CA 95061

MOLLAN, DONNA LEA PACE, teacher, innkeeper; b. Phoenix, Dec. 27, 1936; d. James Donald and Sylvia Vena (Fanning) Pace; children: Vincent Kelly, Cheryl Lorraine Mollan Gundersen. AA, Phoenix Coll., 1957; BA, Chico State Coll., 1959; postgrad., Calif. Luth. Coll., 1975. Cert. elem. tchr., Calif. Tchr. Wilson Elem. Sch., Gridley, Calif., 1960-61, Clarksburg (Calif.) Unified Sch. Dist., 1961-62, Washington Unified Sch. Dist., West Sacramento, Calif., 1964-67, Tehachapi (Calif.) Unified Sch. Dist., 1967-70, Pleasant Valley Sch. Dist., Camarillo, Calif., 1970-88; owner, mgr. Embrionics Learning Ctr., Ventura, Calif, 1977-78; child abuse, neglect found. ednl. svcs., Van Nuys, Calif., 1978; travel researcher Calif. Luth. Coll., Thousand Oaks, 1977, Goddard Coll., Plainfield, Vt., 1985. Author: If You Knew You Had a Choice, The Not Quite Christmas Flight, The Year Without Santa Clause, The Christmas Witch, The Teapot Without a Lid. Mem. Hart for Senator campaign, 1986; chairperson fund-raiser Sedona Hopi Days, 1989. Mem. Sedona Oak Creek C. of C., Nat. Ednl. Assn. (life mem.), Calif. Tchrs Assn., Pleasant Valley Edn. Assn. (sec. 1976-77, pres. 1977-79), Channel Islands Svc Ctr. (chairperson 1978-79, we honor our own 1986), Bus. Profl. Women (publicity chairperson 1986), Sedona Innkeepers Assn., Sedona Bed and Breakfast Innkeepers Guild, Alpha Phi Gamma. Office: Sipapu Lodge 65 Piki Dr Sedona AZ 86336

MOLLON, ROGER KEVIN, computer company executive; b. Highland Pk., Mich., June 23, 1952; s. Leslie and Margaret Ann (Shawcross) M.; m. Barbara Ann Scoppa, Apr. 27, 1974; children: Scott Kevin, Anthony Jacob. BSE in Mech. Engring., U. Mich., 1974. Registered engr.-in-tng., 1974. Analytical engr. Pratt & Whitney Aircraft Co., East Hartford, Conn., 1974; design analysis engr. Ford Motor Co., Dearborn, Mich., 1975-79; corp. CAD-CAM scientist Mfg. & Cons. Svcs., Costa Mesa, Calif., 1979-81; dir. software ops. Graftek, Inc., Boulder, Colo., 1981-83; v.p. tech. Graftek, Inc., Boulder, 1983-87; v.p. advanced devel. Unisys CAD-CAM, Inc., Boulder, 1987—. Fund raiser Am. Cancer Soc., Lafayette, Colo., 1986; cubmaster pack 79 Boy Scouts Am., Lafayette, 1987; asst. cubmaster, Boulder, 1988. Mem. ASME, Soc. Automotive Engrs., Soc. Mfg. Engrs., Assn. for Computing Machinery, IEEE, Phi Eta Sigma, Pi Tau Sigma. Republican. Roman Catholic.

MOLT, CYNTHIA MARYLEE, author, publisher; b. Sierra Madre, Calif., Nov. 1, 1957; d. Lawrence Edward and Evelyn Mary (Novak) Molt. BA in English Lit., Calif. State U., Long Beach, 1980. Mng. editor Assoc. Graphics, Arts and Letters, Monrovia, Calif., 1981-87, pub., sr. and mng. editor, 1987—, authenticator, 1981—; author McFarland and Co., Inc., Pubs., Jefferson, N.C., 1988—. Author: Gone With the Wind: A Complete Reference, 1989; author, editor mag. The Wind, 1981—, Calif. Film, 1987—; spl. corr. Monrovia News-Post, 1985; corr. G.W.T.W. Collector's Club Newsletter, 1979-82, Monrovia Rev., 1975. Vol. adminstrv. asst. student activities Monrovia High Sch., 1976. Mem. Gone with the Wind Soc. (pres. 1985—), Vivien Leigh Fan Club (pres. 1987—), Clark Gable Fan Club (pres. 1987—), Grace Kelly Fan Club (pres. 1987—). Republican. Roman Catholic. Home and Office: 364 N May Ave Monrovia CA 91016

MOLTENI, BETTY PHILLIPS, painter; b. Norfolk, Va., Dec. 15, 1913; d. William Henry and Margaret (Brownley) Phillips; A.B., Coll. William and Mary, 1938; student art U. Nev., Reno, 1966-71; m. Peter G. Molteni, Jr., July 22, 1939; children—Peter G. III, Margaret Elizabeth, Christopher Phillips, Marianne Stephanie. Founder, chmn. Armed Forces Art Show Hawaii, 1962; one woman shows Artist Co-op., Reno, 1978, 81, Mother Lode Nat. Art Exhbn., Sonora, Calif., 1977, 79, Delta Art Assn. Show, Antioch, Calif., 1978; exhibited group shows Nev. Women Art Show Las Vegas, 1976, Nat. League Am. Pen Women, Salt Lake City, 1973, Sacramento, 1978, Washington, 1984, Lodi Art Ann., Acampo, Calif., 1979, 84, Tahoe Erhman Mansion Arts Festival, 1979-80, Sierra Nev. Mus., 1983, Nev. Watercolor Soc., 1984, New Artists Gallery, Celebration Watercolor Las Vegas Art Mus., 1986, Brewery Art Ctr., Carson City, Nev., 1986, 2d nat. miniature show Furman U., S.C.; represented in pvt. collections, also Sierra Nev. Mus. Art, Reno. Bd. dirs. Nev. Art Gallery, 1975-78; del. Sierra Arts Assembly, 1977-78, 80-81. Mem. Nat. League Am. Pen Women (v.p. 1973, treas. Reno br. 1979, pres. 1980, state pres. 1982-84), Soc. Western Artists, Latimer Art Club (art scholarship chmn. 1986, pres. 1971, treas. 1978), Carson City Alliance (charter), Nev. Artists Assn., Nev. Art Gallery, Sierra Arts Assembly, Artist Co-op. (charter, v.p. 1983), Sierra Nevada Mus. Arts Aux., Reno Philharmonic League, Cath. Daus. Republican. Roman Catholic. Home: 1130 Alpine Circle Reno NV 89509

MOLTENI, RICHARD ALOYSIUS, pediatrician, neonatologist; b. Teaneck, N.J., Nov. 11, 1944; s. Henry Albert and Dorothy Marie (Lewis) M.; m. Joyce Helene Toth, Aug. 17, 1968; children: Michael Patrick, Ann. BS in Biology, Fairfield (Conn.) U., 1966; MD, Med. Coll. of N.J., 1970. Resident in pediatrics U. Colo. Health Scis., Denver, 1970-73, chief resident in pediatrics, 1975-76, fellow neonatal medicine, 1976-78, instr. pediatrics dept., 1975-78; asst. prof. pediatrics John's Hopkins Hosp., Balt., 1978-84, assoc. prof. pediatrics, 1984-86; chief pediatrics Balt. City Hosp., 1984-85; vice chmn. pediatrics dept. U. Utah Med. Sch., Salt Lake City, 1986—; neonatal cons. Project HOPE, Poland, Costa Rica and People's Republic of China, 1984—. Contbr. articles to profl. jours. Maj. U.S. Army, 1973-75. Fellow Am. Acad. Pediatrics, Subsect. Perinatal and Neonatal Medicine; mem. Western Soc. for Pediatric Rsch., Dist. VIII Perinatal. Democrat. Roman Catholic. Home: 1522 S Roxbury Rd Salt Lake City UT 84108 Office: U Utah Med Ctr Neonatal Div 50 N Medical Dr Salt Lake City UT 94132

MOMMAERTS, WILFRIED FRANCIS HENRY MARIA, physiologist, educator; b. Broechem, Belgium, Mar. 4, 1917; came to U.S., 1948, naturalized, 1956; s. Hendrik David and Maria (van Damme) M.; m. Elizabeth Barbara Batyka, July 29, 1944 (dec.); children—Robert Wilfried Anthony, Edina Maria, Quentin Francis. Student, U. Leiden, Netherlands, 1934-39; Ph.D., Kolozsvar, Hungary, 1943; Dr. honoris causa, U. Dijon, 1976. Faculty Am. U., Beirut, 1945-48, Duke U., 1948-53, Western Res. U., 1953-56; coordinator Commonwealth Fund Med. Curriculum Expt., 1955-56; spl. Rockefeller fellow U. Coll., London, 1956; prof. medicine, physiology, dir. L.A. County Heart Assn. Cardiovascular Rsch. Lab. U. Calif., 1956-87; emeritus prof. UCLA, 1987-88, chmn. dept. physiology, 1966-87; Mem. Roger Wagner L.A. Master Chorale.; Commonwealth Fund fellow Centre des Recherches sur les Macromolecules, Strasbourg, 1963-64; chmn. physiology tng. com. NIH, 1967-71; vis. prof. U. Dijon, 1973-74; Mem. Internat. Commn. on Genetic Experimentation, 1980—; researcher Max Planck Inst. for Med. Rsch., Heidelberg, Fed, Rep. Germany. Author: Muscular Contraction, a Topic in Molecular Physiology, 1950; contbr. articles to profl. jours. Recipient award for outstanding contbn. to sci. knowledge Los Angeles County Heart Assn., 1967, award of merit, 1972; Samuel Racz medal, Budapest, 1985, Alexander von Humboldt award, 1986. Mem. Am. Physiol. Soc., Am. Soc. Biol. Chemists, Biophys. Soc., Am. Acad. Arts and Scis., Royal Belgian Acad. Medicine, Hungarian Physiol. Soc. (hon.), others. Office: U Calif Dept Physiology 405 Hilgard Ave Los Angeles CA 90024-1751

MOMPER, ARTHUR WILLIAM, real estate executive; b. Albuquerque, July 15, 1950; s. James A. and Wilma Joanne (Craigmile) M.; m. Robyn A. Wagner, Aug. 14, 1981. BS in Psychology, Okla. State U., Stillwater, 1972. Owner RCA Contractors, Denver, 1973-75; assoc. Crown Realty, Englewood, Colo., 1975-79, Re/Max Realty, Englewood, 1979-81; co-owner Re/Max Execs., Inc., Littleton, Colo., 1981-85; pres. Re/Max Execs., Inc., Littleton, 1986-87, mng. broker, owner, 1987; chmn., pres., owner, broker Re/Max Action, Inc., Littleton, 1988—; bd. dirs. Tencore, Inc., Littleton, Equisource, Inc., Littleton. Mem. Nat. Assn. Realtors, Colo. Assn. Realtors, Douglas Elbert Bd. Realtors, Real Estate Nat. Mktg. Inst., Employee Relocation Coun. Republican. Office: Re/Max Action Inc 2690 E County Line Rd Littleton CO 80126

MONAGHAN, JAMES EDWARD, JR., political consultant; b. South Bend, Ind., Mar. 31, 1947; s. James Edward and Marion (Currigan) M., m. Carol Lynn Foster; children: James Edward III, Brian Foster. BS, Colo. State U., 1971; cert. in environ. mgmt., Harvard U., 1976. Press sec. Coloradans for Lamm, Denver, 1974; asst. to gov. for natural resources State of Colo., Denver, 1975-78; campaign mgr. Coloradans for Lamm/Dick, Denver, 1978; dir. intergovtl. relations State of Colo., 1979-83; energy dir. Western Govs. Policy Office, Denver, 1979; asst. to the dir. U.S. Synthetic Fuels Corp., Washington, 1980; campaign mgr. Coloradans for Lamm/Dick, Denver, 1982; pres. Monaghan & Assocs., Denver, 1983—, Strategies West, 1984—; dir. Western Interstate Nuclear Bd., Denver, 1975-80; gov.'s alternate Western Govs. Policy Office, 1977-83; staff chmn. energy and natural resources com. Nat. Govs. Assn., Washington, 1978-79; bd. dirs. Limited Term Mcpl. Fund, Santa Fe, 1985—. Democrat. Roman Catholic. Office: Monaghan & Assocs 1225 17th St #1650 Denver CO 80202

MONARCHI, DAVID EDWARD, management scientist, information scientist, educator; b. Miami Beach, Fla., July 31, 1944; s. Joseph Louis and Elizabeth Rose (Muller) M.; BS in Engring. Physics, Colo. Sch. of Mines, 1966; PhD (NDEA fellow), U. Ariz., 1972; 1 son by previous marriage, David Edward. Asst. dir. of Bus. Rsch. Div., U. Colo., Boulder, 1972-75, asst. prof. mgmt. sci./info. systems, 1972-75, assoc. prof. mgmt. sci. and info. systems, 1975-84; assoc. dir. Bus. Rsch. Div., 1975-80, dir. Div. Info. Sci. Rsch., 1982-84; prin. investigator of socio-econ. environ. systems for govtl. agys., and local govt. orgns., State of Colo., also info. systems for pvt. firms, 1972-77. Mem. Gov.'s Energy Task Force Com., 1974. Mem. IEEE, Inst. for Mgmt. Sci., Assn. Computing Machinery, Am. Assn. Artificial Intelligence. Contbr. numerous articles on socio-econ. modeling and artificial intelligence to profl. jours. Home: 32 Benthaven Pl Boulder CO 80303 Office: U Colo Grad Sch Bus Boulder CO 80309

MONDAVI, ROBERT GERALD, winery executive; b. Virginia, Minn., June 18, 1913; s. Cesare and Rosa (Grassi) M.; m. Marjorie Declusin, 1940 (div.); 3 children: Robert, Timothy, Marcia; m. 2nd, Margrit Biever, 1980. BA, Stanford U., 1936. Dir. Sunny St. Helena Wine Co., St. Helena, Calif., 1937-45; v.p., gen. mgr., Charles Krug Winery, St. Helena, 1943-67; pres. Robert Mondavi Winery, Oakville, Calif., from 1967, now chmn. Office: Robert Mondavi Winery PO Box 403 Oakville CA 94558 *

MONE, LOUIS CARMEN, clin. social worker; b. Bklyn., July 10, 1936; s. Louis Anthony and Carmella (Guidone) M.; BA, U. Ariz., 1962; MSW, Rutgers U., 1965; PhD in Clin. Social Work, 1985. Diplomate Am. Bd. Clin. Socal Workers, m. Elinor Sypniewski, Sept. 28, 1958; children: Marc, Lisa. Detention supr. Pima County Detention Home, Tucson, 1959-60; social worker N.J. Neuro-Psychiat. Inst., Princeton, 1961-63; psychiat. social worker Alcoholism Treatment Ctr., Roosevelt Hosp. Metuchen, N.J., 1963-66; caseworker Family Counseling Svc. of Somerset County, Bound Brook, N.J., 1965-67, group cons., 1965-69; prin. psychiat. social worker Raritan Bay Mental Health Ctr., Middlesex County Mental Health Clinic, Perth Amboy, N.J., 1966-69; social work cons. Borough of Spotswood, Spotswood (N.J.) Pub. Schs., 1967-69; pilot project dir., group therapist Heart Assn. Middlesex County, Edison, N.J., 1968-69; chief psychiat. social worker Insts. Religion and Health, N.Y.C., 1969-71; pvt. practice adolescent and adult psychotherapy, marriage and family counseling, East Brunswick, N.J., 1965-71, Del Mar, Calif., 1972-78, individual, marriage, family and child therapy, San Diego, 1973-78, La Jolla, Calif., 1978-86, San Diego, Del Mar, Calif., 1986—; instr. nursing programs Rutgers U., New Brunswick, N.J., 1970; dir. profl. svcs. Family Svcs. Assn. San Diego, 1971-75; instr. Calif. Sch. Profl. Psychology, 1974, 76-80; assoc. prof. San Diego U., 1989. With AUS, 1955-57. Mem. Am. Group Psychotherapy Assn., Nat. Assn. Social Workers, San Diego Group Psychotherapy Soc., Calif. Soc. for Clin. Soc. Work, Delta Chi. Author: Private Practice: A Professional Business. Home: 40 Kingston Ct S Corondao Cays CA 92118 Office: 3555 5th Ave San Diego CA 92103

MONFORT, ELIAS RIGGS, III, management consultant; b. Chgo., Sept. 6, 1929; s. Elias Riggs and Elizabeth (Sebald) M.; B.S., Purdue U., 1952; m. Hathalie Jean Ward, June 8, 1957; children—Stephen, Scott, Jonathan, Christoper. Liaison engr. Douglas Aircraft Co., Santa Monica, Calif., 1952; internat. regional mgr. Cessna Aircraft Co., Wichita, Kans., 1958-64; long-range planning service Stanford Research Inst., Sunnyvale, Calif., 1964-77, strategic mgmt., 1978-87; mng. prin. Monfort Mgmt., 1988—. Bd. regents Cogswell Engring. Coll. Served to capt. USAF, 1952-57; Korea. Mem. Soc. Automotive Engrs., Exptl. Aircraft Assn., Internat. Aerobatic Club, Corp. Planners Assn. (founding), Planning Forum (contbg. editor). Republican. Episcopalian. Clubs: Sequoia Woods Golf and Country. Home: 1609 Honfleur Dr Sunnyvale CA 94087

MONFORT, KENNETH, cattle production and meat processing company executive; b. 1928. Mem. Colo. Ho. of Reps., 1965-69; pres. Monfort of Colo. Inc., Greeley, 1969—, co-chmn., sr. v.p., 1976, pres., chief exec. officer, 1980—, also bd. dirs.; now pres., chief operating officer ConAgra Redmeat Cos. Office: ConAgra Redmeat Cos care Shirley Bernhart 1930 AA St Box G Greeley CO 80632 *

MONFORT, RICHARD L., meat packaging and distribution company executive; b. 1954. Student, U. No. Colo. Cattle buyer Monfort of Colo., Inc., Greeley, 1974-79, v.p. fed. cattle procurement, 1979-81, group v.p. cattle products, beef slaughter, group v.p., product sales, 1983-84, exec. v.p., 1984-87, chief oper. officer, from 1984, pres., 1987—, also bd. dirs. Office: Monfort of Colo Inc 1930 AA St Box G Greeley CO 80632 *

MONGE, JULIUS EDWIN, resort management company executive; b. Waukegan, Ill., Jan. 27, 1939; s. Julius John and Yolanda (Fiorentini) M.; m. Rose Ellen Furlan, Aug. 20, 1960; children: Julius J., Michele L., Michael E. BS in Gen. Engring., U. Ill., 1960; MS in Mgmt., Advanced Mgmt. Inst., Lake Forest, Ill., 1972; postgrad. advanced mgmt., Harvard U., 1979. V.p. mktg. for N.Am., Internat. Harvester Co., Chgo., 1960-82, Fiat Allis, Carol Stream, Ill., 1982-83; exec. v.p., ptnr. Summit Ridge, Inc., Breckenridge, Colo., 1983—; pres., ptnr. Summit Ridge Sports, Inc., Breckenridge, 1985—; treas., ptnr. Peerless Maintenance & Svc., Inc., Breckenridge, 1987—; pres. SCI Mgmt. Co., Inc. (Bartlett Enterprises), Breckenridge, 1988—; bd. dirs. Nat. Reservations Network, Travel & Tours, Inc., Breckenridge. Bd. dirs. Backstage Theatre, Breckenridge, 1985—. Named One of 50 for Colo., Colo. Assn. Commerce and Industry, 1988. Mem. Continental Industry Mgrs. Assn. (bd. dirs. 1980-81), Breckenridge Resort C. of C. (bd. dirs. 1985). Home: PO Box 1586 Breckenridge CO 80424 Office: SCI Mgmt Co Inc PO Box 188 Breckenridge CO 80424

MONIZ-JENKINS, ROHNA MAE, probation official; b. Hayward, Calif., Dec. 6, 1942; d. Thomas Lester Moniz and Virginia Ruth (Twiggs) Kephart; m. Daniel Carl Fiore, Jan. 16, 1977 (div. Mar. 1979); children: David Daniel Maury, Dana Leon Fiore; m. Leonard Cecil Jenkin, Feb. 2, 1983. AA, Chabot Community Coll., Hayward, 1973; BA in Correctional Counseling, Calif. State U., Hayward, 1976. Photographer Tampa Tribune, 1967-69; photo tech. Bennetts Photo Svcs., Hayward, 1969-72; intake clk. M-2 Sponsors, Hayward, 1973-74; dir. prison program 7th Step Found., Hayward, San Leandro, Calif., 1977-82; house mgr. Vols. Am. Work Furlough, Oakland, 1982, Mens Crisis Home, Hayward, 1983; with customer svc. dept. AT&T, Pleasanton, Calif., 1983, Sun Diamond Growers, San Ramon, Calif., 1984; dep. probation officer Alameda County Probation Dept., Oakland, 1984—. Served with USN, 1962-64. Mem. Assn. Rsch. and Enlightenment (study group 1984—). Democrat. Christian Scientist. Office: Alameda County Probation Dept 400 Broadway PO Box 2059 Oakland CA 94604-2059

MONK, GREGORY BRITTAIN, artist, business owner; b. San Francisco, Dec. 28, 1942; s. John Clarkson and Barbara (Brittain) M.; m. Yvonne Adele Jones, Mar. 30, 1974 (div. Jan. 1987). AA, City Coll., San Francisco, 1963; BA in Econs., San Francisco State U., 1965. Freelance actor and extra various mediums Calif. and Hawaii, 1961-88; salesman, mgr. San Francisco Luggage Co., 1961-65; computer programmer Western Union, Mahwah, N.J., 1969-72; owner Gregory Monk - Wood and Glass, Sausalito, Calif., 1973-74, G. Brittain M. Co., Haleiwa, Hawaii, 1975-80, Greg Monk Stained Glass, Aiea, Hawaii, 1981—. Artist (stained glass designs) Maka Koa, 1981 (1st prize 1982), Flowing, 1984; glass artist (TV show) Portraits of Paradise, 1988. Sgt. USMC, 1966-68. Mem. Assn. Hawaii Artists, Stained Glass Assn. Hawaii (founder 1979, pres. 1979-81, treas. 1982-83), Glass Art Soc., Arts Council Hawaii, Hawaii Craftsmen, Pacific Handcrafters, Honolulu Acad. Arts, Screen Extras Guild, The Contemporary Mus. Democrat. Club: Toastmaster. Office: Greg Monk Stained Glass 98-027 Hekaha St Aiea HI 96701

MONROE, GERI LEE, automobile dealership official; b. Chgo., Oct. 1, 1948; d. Ottie C. Sizemore and Evelyn E. (Anderson) McCans; m. Elliot Eugene Monroe, Feb. 3, 1968 (div. 1975); children: Robert Blaine, Arlene Diane, Marlene Ann. Grad., high sch., Long Beach, Calif. Collection mgr. Citicorp Person to Person, Orange, Calif., 1976-78; credit rep. Gen. Mtrs. Acceptance Corp., Westminster, Calif., 1978-85; collection mgr. Cal Worthington Ford Inc., Long Beach, 1985—. Republican. Roman Catholic. Office: Cal Worthington Ford Inc 2850 Bellflower Blvd Long Beach CA 90815

MONROE, JANICE KATHLEEN, nurse; b. Longview, Wash., Nov. 21, 1952; d. Cedric Dale and Florence Paulene (Prichard) Bundy; m. Dean Collen Monroe, Dec. 4, 1974; stepchildren: James, Nathan, Rick, Tony, Paul. Assoc. Nursing, Central Oreg. Community Coll., 1988. Lic. practical nurse, Oreg. Staff nurse Pioneer Meml. Hosp., Prineville, Oreg., 1987-. Foster mother Grizzly Mountain Girls Ranch, 1985--. Democrat. Baptist. Home: Grizzley Star Rte Madras OR 97741

MONROE, ROBERT RAWSON, engineering and construction executive; b. Oakland, Calif., Sept. 25, 1927; s. Robert Ansley and Muriel Estelle (Burnham) M.; m. Charlotte Boies Anderson, Oct. 16, 1951; children: Robert Anderson, Nancy Lynn Monroe Sims, Susan Leslie Monroe Gordon. BS in Naval Sci., U.S. Naval Acad., 1950; MA in Internat. Rels., Stanford U., 1962. Commd. ensign USN, 1950, advanced through grades to vice-admiral, 1977; dir. Navy Systems Analysis USN, Washington, 1972-73; comdr. South Atlantic Force USN, 1973-74, comdr. Operational Test and Evaluation Force, 1974-77, dir. Def. Nuclear Agy., 1977-80, dir. Navy Rsch., Devel., Test and Evaluation, 1980-83, ret., 1983; sr. v.p., mgr. def. and space Bechtel Nat., Inc., San Francisco, 1984—; mem. nat. security adv. Bd., Los Alamos (N.Mex.) Nat. Lab., 1983-88, tech. evaluation panel, U.S. Dept. Energy, 1983-88, engring. adv. com., Oak Ridge (Tenn.) Nat. Lab., 1986—; bd. advisers, Office Technology Assessment, Washington, 1987—, Nat. Contract Mgmt. Assn.; mem. task forces, Def. Sci. Bd., Washington, 1983—; mem. of corp., Charles Stark Draper Lab., Cambridge, Mass., 1983—. Decorated DSM with Gold Star, Legion of Merit, Bronze Star medal, Legion of Honor (France). Mem. Nat. Security Indsl. Assn., Soc. Am. Mil. Engrs., Am. Def. Preparedness Assn., Am. Inst. Astronautics, U.S. Naval Inst., World Trade Club. Home: 10 Mountain View Pl Lafayette CA 94549 Office: Bechtel Nat Inc PO Box 3965 San Francisco CA 94119

MONROE, STANLEY EDWIN, surgeon; b. Bangor, Mich., June 26, 1902; s. Samuel E. and Ella (Monroe) M.; AB, U. Mich., 1925; MD, U. Chgo./Rush Med. Coll., 1936; m. Ruth Williams, June 14, 1932 (dec. 1981); m. 2d, Flora Doss, Aug. 6, 1982. Intern, Evanston (Ill.) Hosp., 1935-36, resident surgeon, 1936-37, asst. surgeon, 1940-41; clin. asst. surgeon Northwestern U., 1938-39, instr. surgery, 1940-41; asst. to Dr. Frederick Christopher, 1937-41; chief surgery VA Hosp., Tucson, 1947-49; surgeon ARAMCO, Saudi Arabia, 1950; pvt. practice, Chula Vista, Calif., 1952-82; staff Paradise Valley Hosp., Mercy Hosp. (San Diego); founder Monroe Clinic. Maj. AUS, 1942-47, PTO. Diplomate Am. Bd. Surgery. Fellow Soc. for Academic Achievement, Internat. Coll. Surgeons; mem. Soc. Gen. Surgeons of San Diego, Am. Med. Writers Assn., Assn. Mil. Surgeons, Am. Soc. Abdominal Surgeons (founding), Alpha Omega Alpha, Phi Beta Pi. Author: Medical Phrase Book with Vocabulary (also Spanish edit.). Office: 2 Palomar Dr Chula Vista CA 92011

MONROE, STEPHEN NOEL, federal agency executive; b. Leavonworth, Wash., Oct. 26, 1957. BA in Polit. Sci., BA in Liberal Arts, BA in Econs., BBA, Wash. State U., 1980; postgrad., U. Wash., 1981-82. Transit operator

Metro Transit of King County, Seattle, 1983—; arbitrator Better Bus. Bur. Seattle, 1982—; bd. dirs. Head Start/parent orgn. Highline, 1987—. Mem. youth devel panel United Way King County, 1987—; mem. candidate evaluation com. Mcpl. League King County, 1988; coach football Cen. Area Youth Assn., Seattle, 1987; coach basketball Hazel Valley Hornets, Seattle, 1987-88, Mt. View Tigers, 1988-89; Student Book Corp. Wash. State U., Pullman, 1977-78. Winner numerous awards, 1980-88. Mem. Nat. Panel Consumer Arbitrators, Poetry Soc. Am., Pacific NW Writers Conf., Acad. Polit. Sci. Republican. Office: PO Box 66681 Seattle WA 98166

MONS, ROBERT EMMETT, investment banker, securities trader; b. N.Y.C., Oct. 7, 1960; s. Robert Emmett Sr. and Grace Elizabeth (McLaughlin) M.; m. Prudence Elizabeth Vanderveer, July 15, 1984; children: Jennifer Louise, Robert Emmett. BS, Jacksonville U., 1983. Lic. securities dealer. V.p. securities sales Drexel Burnham Lambert, Beverly Hills, Calif., 1984-87; v.p. instl. trading Sutro & Co. Inc., Los Angeles, 1987-88; sr. ptnr., mng. dir. E&M Assocs., affiliate Morgan Olmstead, Los Angeles, 1988; sr. analyst Jadenburg Thalmann and Co., Inc. (merger E&M Assocs.), Los Angeles, 1988—; bd. dirs. Asset Growth Inc., Los Angeles, others. Com. mem. ERAS Found., West Los Angeles, 1988. Mem. Sports Club Los Angeles, Tennis Place (Los Angeles). Republican. Roman Catholic. Office: Ezra & Assoc c/o Morgan Olmstead 1000 Wilshire Los Angeles CA 90017

MONSEN, ELAINE RANKER, nutritionist, educator, editor; b. Oakland, Calif., June 6, 1935; d. Emery R. and Irene Stewart (Thorley) Ranker; m. Raymond Joseph Monsen, Jr., Jan. 21, 1959; 1 dau., Maren Ranker. B.A., U. Utah, 1956; M.S. (Mead Johnson grad. scholar), U. Calif., Berkeley, 1959, Ph.D. (NSF fellow), 1961; postgrad. NSF sci. faculty fellow, Harvard U., 1968-69. Dietetic intern Mass. Gen. Hosp., Boston, 1956-57; asst. prof. nutrition, lectr. biochemistry Brigham Young U., Provo, Utah, 1960-63; mem. faculty U. Wash., Seattle, 1963—; prof. nutrition and medicine U. Wash., 1984—, prof. nutrition, adj. prof. medicine, 1976-84, chmn. div. human nutrition, dietetics and foods, 1977-82, mem. Council of Coll. Arts and Scis., 1974-78, mem. U. Wash. Press com., 1981—; chmn. Nutrition Studies Commn., 1969-83; vis. scholar Stanford U., 1971-72; mem. sci. adv. com. food fortification Pan-Am. Health Orgn., São Paulo, Brazil, 1972; tng. grant coordinator NIH, 1976—. Editor Jour. Am. Dietetic Assn., 1983—; author research papers on lipid metabolism, iron absorption. Bd. dirs. A Contemporary Theatre, Seattle, 1969-72; trustee, bd. dirs. Seattle Found., 1978—, vice chmn., 1987—; pres. Seattle bd. Santa Fe Chamber Music Festival, 1984-85. Grantee Nutrition Found., 1965-68, Agrl. Research Service, 1969—, Center Research Oral Biology, 1970-72. Mem. Am. Inst. Nutrition, Am. Soc. Clin. Nutrition (sec. 1987—), Am. Dietetic Assn., Soc. Nutrition Edn., Am. Soc. Parenteral and Enteral Nutrition, Wash. Heart Assn. (nutrition council 1973-76), Phi Beta Kappa, Phi Kappa Phi. Office: U Wash Dept Human Nutrition DL-10 Seattle WA 98195

MONSON, DAVID SMITH, business manager, former congressman; b. Salt Lake City, June 20, 1945; s. Smith Weston and Dorothy (Brammer) M.; m. Julianne Johnson, Feb. 4, 1971; children: David Johnson, Traci Lyn, Marianne, Kari, Smith Douglas. BS in Acctg., U. Utah, 1970. C.P.A., Utah. Acct. Elmer Fox and Co., Salt Lake City, 1970-72; auditor State of Utah, Salt Lake City, 1973-76; lt. gov. State of Utah, 1977-84; mem. 99th Congress 1985-87; mem. exec. com. Nat. Conf. Lt. Govs., 1978-84 mem. State Bd. Regents, 1981-84. Bd. dirs. Utah Soc. to Prevent Blindness, 1976-83; chmn. Utah Cancer Crusade, 1979-80; chmn. bd. Salt Lake County unit Am. Cancer Soc., 1980-81; govt. group chmn. United Way, 1979, assoc. campaign chmn., 1981, campaign chmn., 1982; treas. Utah Rep. party, 1975-76; trustee Ballet West, 1977-81, Travis Found., 1977-84; bd. dirs. Osmond Found., 1982-84. Recipient Outstanding Young Man Am. award, 1977, 81; named One of 3 Outstanding Young Men Utah Jaycees, 1980-81. Mem. Council State Govts. (v.p. Western conf. 1974-75). Republican. Mem. Ch. Jesus Christ Latter Day Saints. Home: 792 Northview Dr Salt Lake City UT 84103 Office: 445 E 200 S #44 Salt Lake City UT 84111

MONSON, THOMAS SPENCER, church official, publishing company executive; b. Salt Lake City, Aug. 21, 1927; s. George Spencer and Gladys (Condie) M.; m. Frances Beverly Johnson, Oct. 7, 1948; children—Thomas L., Ann Frances, Clark Spencer. B.S. with honors in mktg, U. Utah, 1948; M.B.A., Brigham Young U., 1974, LL.D. (hon.), 1981. With Deseret News Press, Salt Lake City, 1948-64; mgr. Deseret News Press, 1962-64; mem. Council Twelve Apostles, Ch. of Jesus Christ of Latter Day Saints, 1963—, bishop, 1950-55; pres. Canadian Mission, 1959-62; chmn. bd. Deseret News Pub. Co., 1977—; dir. Beneficial Life Ins. Co., Key Bank of Utah, Deseret Mgmt. Corp., Continental Western Life Ins. Co., Western Am. Life Ins. Co.; pres. Printing Industry Utah, 1958; bd. dirs. Printing Industry Am., 1958-64; mem. Utah exec. bd. U.S. West Communications. Mem. Utah State Bd. Regents; nat. exec. bd. Boy Scouts Am.; Trustee Brigham Young U.; mem. 1st Presidency The Ch. of Jesus Christ of the Latter Day Saints, 1985—, council Twelve Apostles, 1963-85. Served with USNR, 1945-46. Recipient Recognition award, 1964, Disting. Alumnus award U. Utah, 1966; Silver Beaver award Boy Scouts Am., 1971; Silver Buffalo award, 1978. Mem. Utah Assn. Sales Execs., U. Utah Alumni Assn. (dir.), Salt Lake Advt. Club, Alpha Kappa Psi. Club: Exchange (Salt Lake City). Office: LDS Ch 47 East S Temple St Salt Lake City UT 84111 *

MONTAG, DAVID MOSES, computer company executive; b. Los Angeles, Apr. 30, 1939; s. Gustave and Esther (Kessler) M.; student UCLA, 1957-61; m. Beverly Edythe Bowden, Sept. 24, 1967; children: Daniel Gershon, Esther Yael, Michael Menachem. Tech. writer L.H. Butcher Co., Los Angeles, 1961; phys. sci. lab. technician East Los Angeles Coll., Monterey Park, 1961—, planetarium lectr., 1963—; owner EDUCOMP, Monterey Park, Calif., 1980—; mktg. cons. Aquinas Computer Corp.; ednl. cons. for computer-assisted instrn. Bd. dirs. Or Chadash, Inc., Monterey Park, 1968—; v.p., bd. dirs. Coll. Religious Conf., 1968—. Mem. Assn. of Orthodox Jewish Scientists, Laser Inst. Am., AIAA. Home: 729 N Spaulding Ave Los Angeles CA 90046 Office: Box 384 Monterey Park CA 91754

MONTAGUE, FRANK, hospital administrator, consultant; b. Phila., Mar. 4, 1935; s. John and Mary (Cleary) M.; m. Patsy R., Dec. 20, 1960 (div. 1979); children: Matthew, Mary, Mark; m. Sue S., June 19, 1982. BA, LaSalle Coll., Phila., 1956; MA, U. Iowa, 1984. Commd. USAF, 1957; advanced through grades to capt. USAF Med. Services Corp., 1957-67, resigned, 1967; asst. adminstr. St. Lawrence Hosp., Lansing, Mich., 1967-69; cons. mgr. A.T. Kearney, Chgo. and N.Y.C., 1969-73; exec. dir. Wausau (Wis.) Med. Ctr., 1973-76; cons. A.J.J. Rourke, Inc., Harrison, N.Y., 1976-80; pres. Family Hosp. and Nursing Home, Milw., 1980-86; exec. dir. Rancho Encino Hosp., Encino, Calif., 1986—; pres. Comprehensive Health Engring. and Safety, Inc., Milw., 1983-86; chmn. bd. F.H. Physicians Assocs., Inc., Milw., 1984-86; adj. prof. U. Wis. Sch. Bus., 1985. Author: Measuring Hospital Utlization, 1865. Mem. Am. Coll. Health Care Execs., Am. Hosp. Assn., Encino C. of C. (bd. dirs. 1988), Tuckaway Country Club (Franklin, Wis.), Milw. Athletic Club. Home: 18957 Plummer St Northridge CA 91324

MONTAGUE, GARY LESLIE, newspaper advertising executive; b. Mullan, Idaho, Apr. 4, 1939; s. William Bryan and Gladys Viola (Finkbeiner) M.; m. Dorothy Barclay, Feb. 14, 1959 (div. 1973); children: Teresa Montague Scofield, Douglas; m. Mikael Jones, Mar. 13, 1982. Student, Am. Press Inst. Columbia U., 1973, Cen. Wash. U., 1977. Classified advt. rep. The Wenatchee World, 1957-71, classified advt. mgr., 1971—; mem. arts adminstrn. and advt.; cons. and lectr. in field. Chmn. Wash. State Arts Commn., Olympia, 1985-88, commr., 1974-78, 82-88; trustee Wash. State Arts Alliance Found., 1981-88, Western States Arts Found., Santa Fe, N.M., 1982-88; pres. Cen. Wash. Hosp. Found., Wenatchee, 1987-88, Wenatchee Area Visitor and Conv. Bur., 1980-81, Allied Arts Council of North Cen. Wash., 1973-74, Music Theater of Wenatchee, 1970-71, Wenatchee Valley Dance Found., Gallery '76 art gallery Wenatchee Valley Coll.; commr. City of Wenatchee Arts Commn., 1975-78; exec. com. Wash. State Rep. Cen. Com., 1975-77. Mem. Assn. Newspaper Classified Advt. Mgrs., Western Classified Advt. Assn., Pacific Northwest Assn. of Newspaper Classified Advt. Mgrs. (pres. 1981-82), Wenatchee Area C. of C. (pres. 1978-79). Mem. Unity Ch. Lodge: Rotary. Club: Applarians. Home: 2142 Sunrise Circle Wenatchee WA 98801 Office: World Pub Co 14 N Mission Wenatchee WA 98801

MONTAGUE, SIDNEY JAMES, real estate developer; b. Denver, Oct. 3, 1950; s. Jerome Edward and Donna Sherrill (Nixon) M.; m. Linda Marie Meyers, May 22, 1982 (div. 1986); m. Mary Fancis Terry, Dec. 26, 1987; stepchildren: Jonathan Ramsey Shockley, Britt Elizabeth Shockley. BA in Econs., Midland Luth. Coll., Fremont, Nebr., 1972. Loan counselor Am. Nat. Bank, Denver, 1972-74; loan officer First Nat. Bank Denver, 1974-79; exec. v.p. Buell Devel. Corp., Denver, 1979-84; v.p. The Writer Corp., Denver, 1985-86; pres. Mondevco Inc., Littleton, Colo., 1986-87; devel. mgr. Perini Land & Devel. Co., Phoenix, 1987—. Active Central Ave. Assn., Phoenix, 1987, Valley Partnership, Phoenix, 1987;vol. Andre House, Phoenix, 1987. Mem. Urban Land Inst., Internat. Council Shopping Ctrs. Republican. Office: Perini Land & Devel Co 1807 N Central Ave Phoenix AZ 85004

MONTANA, JOSEPH C., JR., professional football player; b. New Eagle, Pa., June 11, 1956; s. Joseph C. Montana, Sr., and Theresa M.; m. 1st, Kim Monses, 1975 (div.); m. 2nd, Cass Castillo (div. 1983); m. 3rd, Jennifer Wallace, 1984; 2 children, Alexandra, Elizabeth. B.B.A. in Mktg., U. Notre Dame, 1978. Quarterback San Francisco 49ers, 1979—; mem. Super Bowl Championship Team, 1982, 85, 89; played in Pro Bowl, 1982-85. Author (with Alan Steinberg): Cool Under Fire, 1989. Named Most Valuable Player Super Bowl, 1982, 85. Office: care San Francisco 49ers 711 Nevada St Redwood City CA 94061 *

MONTANDON, CHARLOTTE SCHWARZ, language educator; b. Vienna, Austria, Apr. 25, 1930; came to U.S., 1951.; d. Franz and Cecilia (Urban) Schwarz. MA, U. Kans., 1952; PhD, U. Vienna, 1953; postgrad., Stanford U., 1961-63. Cert. tchr., supr., Calif. Instr. German Wash. State U., Pullman, 1953-54; instr. English Ft. Lewis Coll., U. Puget Sound, Taocoma, 1955-56, U. Idaho, Lewiston, 1956-57; instr. German and English Calif. Community Coll. San Jose City Coll., 1958—; instr. German Calif. Community Coll., De Anza Community Coll., Cupertino, 1965—; chmn. dept. San Jose City Coll., 1964-74, project dir. Writing Across the Curriculum, 1988-89. Fulbright scholar, 1951-52; Goethe Inst. study grantee, Munich, Fed. Republic Germany, 1981. Office: San Jose City Coll 2100 Moorpark St San Jose CA 95128

MONTANO, DANIEL JOSEPH, art director; b. Longmont, Colo., June 15, 1961; s. Joseph Alex and Mary O. (Alvarado) M. BFA in Graphic Design, Colo. State U., 1983. Art dir. Lamm Gubernatorial Campaign, Denver, 1982, Roy Advt., Inc., Frisco and Vail, Colo., 1983-84, Grant and Ptnrs., Inc., Denver, 1984; creative dir., pres. Daniel Montano's Inc., Denver, 1984—; instr. honorarium U. Colo., Denver, 1988. Art dir. Pena Mayoral Campaign, Denver, 1984. Named Outstanding Community Leader, Am. Biographical Inst., 1981-82; recipient award of Excellence, Art Dir. Club Denver, 1983; Masons scholar, 1979-83. Mem. Minority Enterprise, Inc., Hispanic C. of C. Democrat. Roman Catholic. Home: PO Box 175 Erie CO 80516 Office: Daniel Montano's Inc 1616 17th St Ste 371 Denver CO 80202

MONTANO, SUSANA MARIA, human resources executive; b. Long Beach, Calif., Oct. 31, 1947; d. James McCoy and Amalia Alma (Moreno) M.; m. William Fenton Moore, June 8, 1968 (div. Oct. 1972); m. Larry Eugene Smith, Oct. 16, 1982 (div. Apr. 1989). AA, Santa Barbara City Coll., 1967; BA, Calif. State U., Long Beach, 1975; M in Human Relations in Edn., Calif. State U., San Francisco, 1976. Mem. labor relations staff Hughes Aircraft Co., Fullerton, Calif., 1978-85; dir. human resources Eastman, Inc., Long Beach, 1985-87; human resources supr. Burger King Corp., Ft. Valley, Calif., 1987-89; human resources mgr. MDT Biologic, Rancho Dominguez, Calif., 1987—. Active spl. olympics, Gardena, Calif.; bd. dirs. Assn. Retarded Citizens, 1982. Mem. Am. Bus. Women's Assn. (corres. sec. 1987), Assn. Hispanic Profls. in Edn. Democrat. Roman Catholic. Office: MDT Biologic 19645 Rancho Way Rancho Dominguez CA 90220-6039

MONTERO, DARREL MARTIN, sociologist, educator; b. Sacramento, Mar. 4, 1946; s. Tony and Evelyn (Hash) M.; m. Tara Kathleen McLaughlin, July 6, 1975; children: David Paul, Lynn Elizabeth, Laura Ann, Emily Kathryn. AB, Calif. State U., 1970; MA, UCLA, 1972, PhD, 1974. Postgrad. researcher Japanese-Am. Research Project UCLA, 1971-73, dir. research, 1973-75; assoc. head Program on Comparative Ethnic Studies, Survey Research Ctr. UCLA, 1973-75; asst. prof. sociology Case Western Res. U., Cleve., 1975-76; asst. prof. urban studies, research sociologist Pub. Opinion Survey, dir. urban ethnic research program U. Md., College Park, 1976-79; assoc. prof., dir, urban ethnic research program Ariz. State U., Tempe, 1979—; cons. rsch. sect. Viewer Sponsored TV Found., Los Angeles, Berrien E. Moore Law Office, Inc., Gardena, Calif., 1973, Bur. for Social Sci. Research, Inc., Washington, Friends of the Family, Ltd., Nat. Sci. Found. Author: Japanese Americans: Changing Patterns of Ethnic Affiliation Over Three Generations, 1980, Urban Studies, 1978, Vietnamese Americans: Patterns of Resettlement and Socioeconomic Adaptation in the United States, 1979, Social Problems, 1988; mem. editorial bd. Humanity and Society, 1978—; contbr. articles to profl. jours. Served with U.S. Army, 1966-72. Mem. Am. Sociol. Assn., Am. Assn. Pub. Opinion Research (exec. council, standards com.), Am. Ednl. Research Assn., Council on Social Work Edn., Soc. Study of Social Problems, D.C. Sociol. Soc., Am. Soc. Pub. Adminstrn., Nat. Assn. Social Workers, Pacific Sociol. Assn. Home: 1444 W Kiva Ave Mesa AZ 85202 Office: Ariz State U Sch Social Work Tempe AZ 85281

MONTGOMERY, DOUGLAS CARTER, industrial engineering educator; b. Roanoke, Va., June 5, 1943; s. Gordon Ashby and Gladys (Reed) M.; m. Martha Ellen Price, Aug. 7, 1965 (div. July 1982); children: Meredith, Colin, Neil. BSIE, Va. Poly. Inst., 1965, MS, 1967, PhD, 1969. Prof. indsl. systems engring. Ga. Inst. Tech., Atlanta, 1969-84; prof. mfg. engring., dir. indsl. engring. U. Wash., Seattle, 1984-88, John M. Fluke disting. prof. mfg. engring., 1985-88; prof. indsl. and mgmt. systems engring. Ariz. State U., Tempe, 1988—; cons. IBM, various locations, 1976—, Coca-Cola Co., Atlanta, 1970-84, Boeing Electronics Co., Seattle, 1984—, other mfg. companies. Author 6 books including: Intoduction to Statistical Quality Control, 1985, Design and Analysis of Experiments, 2d edition, 1984. Named John M. Fluke Disting. Prof. of Mfg. U. Wash., 1985. Mem. Inst. Indsl. Engrs., Soc. Mfg. Engrs., Am. Statistical Assn., Am. Soc. Quality Control, Ops. Research Soc. Am. Home: 3841 E Talowa St Phoenix AZ 85044 Office: Ariz State U/Coll Engring Dept Indsl & Mgmt Systems Engring Tempe AZ 85287

MONTGOMERY, GERALD WILLIAM, clergyman, consultant; b. Wright County, Minn., Apr. 29, 1939; s. Joseph Arthur and Marie Maude (Ritter) M.; m. Ruth Ann Huntsinger, Dec. 30, 1960; children—Lisa, Eric. B.A., Macalester Coll., 1961; Ph.D., Calif. Coast U., 1976; postgrad. United Theol. Sem. Twin Cities, 1965-67, Vancouver Sch. Theology, 1982, Claremont Sch. Theology, 1983, Pacific Sch. of Religion, 1988, San Francisco Sch. of Theology, 1988. Ordained to ministry United Ch. of Christ, 1984; reporter UPI, Mpls., 1960; reporter, editor St. Paul Pioneer Press, 1960-69; mng. editor Port Angeles Daily News, Wash., 1969; reporter The Seattle Times, 1969-72; dir. King County Wash. Emergency Med. Services, 1973-75; pres. Communications Assn., Seattle, 1976-78; dir. communications URS Engrs., Seattle, 1978-81; owner Montgomery Communications, Seattle, 1980-83; pastor Shepherd of the Lakes, Tacoma, 1983-87; sr. pastor First Congl. Ch., Oakland, 1987-88; adj. prof. bus. adminstrn. Central Wash. U., Edmonds, 1983; pres. Minn. Rescue and First Aid Assn., 1966; mem. exec. com. Am. Heart Assn. Wash., 1973-83; mem. No. Calif. Conf. United Ch. of Christ, 1987—; chaplain Olympia Police Dept. Author: The Selling of You, 1980, Are You Man Enough, 1973. Served with USNR, 1960-66. Robert Wood Johnson Found. grantee in emergency med. services, 1974.

MONTGOMERY, JAMES FISCHER, savings and loan association executive; b. Topeka, Nov. 30, 1934; s. James Maurice and Frieda Ellen (Fischer) M.; m. Linda Jane Hicks, Aug. 25, 1956; children: Michael James, Jeffrey Allen, Andrew Steven, John Gregory. B.A. in Acctg., UCLA, 1957. With Price, Waterhouse & Co., C.P.A.'s, Los Angeles, 1957-60; controller Conejo Valley Devel. Co., Thousand Oaks, Calif., 1960; asst. to pres. Gt. Western Fin. Corp., Beverly Hills, Calif., 1960-64; fin. v.p., treas. United Fin. Corp., Los Angeles, 1964-69, exec. v.p., 1969-74, pres., 1975; pres. Citizens Savs. & Loan Assn., Los Angeles, 1970-75; chmn., chief exec. officer, dir. Gt. Western Fin. Corp., also Great Western Bank, Beverly Hills, 1975—. Served with AUS, 1958-60. Office: Gt Western Fin Corp 8484 Wilshire Blvd Beverly Hills CA 90211

MONTGOMERY, JAMES PATTON, III, writer, producer; b. Akron, Ohio, Mar. 2, 1955; s. James Patton Jr. and Anne Therese (Benko) M. BA in Drama and Communications, U. Portland, 1976. Big band/classical music disc jockey Sta. KWHO-AM-FM, Salt Lake City, 1976-80; asst. promotion dir. Sta. KUTV-TV, Salt Lake City, 1976-80; writer, co-host PM Mag. Utah, Salt Lake City, 1979-85; freelance writer, producer Portland, Oreg., 1985—. Mem. exec. bd. Utah Spl. Olympics, Provo, 1982-85. Recipient regional Emmy Acad. TV Arts and Scis., 1978, 81, 16 other national and regional awards. Mem. Portland Advt. Fedn.

MONTGOMERY, KENT ROBERT, military officer; b. Rantoul, Ill., July 21, 1961; s. Robert Knox and Lois Ann (Ehrich) M. BS in Aerospace Engring., U. Ariz., 1984. Commnd. capt. USAF, 1984; chief, B-1B terrain following engring. USAF, Edwards AFB, Calif., 1985—. Mem. Air Force Assn. Republican. United Methodist. Home: 41 F St Edwards AFB CA 93523 Office: 31st Test and Evaluation Squadron Edwards AFB CA 93523

MONTGOMERY, MICHAEL BRUCE, lawyer, consultant; b. Santa Barbara, Calif., Sept. 12, 1936; s. Clair Gruwell Montgomery and Florence Louise (Moran) Quigley; m. Pamela L. Wood, July, 1958 (dec. Aug. 1961); children: Michael, Megan; legally separated. BS, UCLA, 1960; LLB, U. So. Calif., 1963. Bar: Calif., Hawaii, Fla. Staff atty. div. hwys. State of Calif., Sacramento and L.A., 1965; assoc. Martin & Flandrick, San Marino, Calif., 1965-66; owner, pres. Michael B. Montgomery, L.C., Pasadena, Calif., 1966—; agy. atty. Huntington (Calif.) Park Redevel. Agy., 1988—, Walnut (Calif.) Improvement Agy., 1988—, South El Monte (Calif.) Improvement Agy., 1988—; spl. counsel County of San Bernardino, Calif., 1988—, City of Irwindale, Calif., 1988—. Contbr. numerous articles to profl. jours. Chmn. Calif. Rep. Party, 1977-79; mayor City of South Pasadena, 1980-81; chmn. Calif. Electoral Coll., Sacramento, 1980; commr. Calif. Fair Polit. Practices Commn., 1985-89. Sgt. U.S. Army, 1954-57, ensign USNR, 1960. Mem. Calif. Bar Assn., Fla. Bar Assn., Hawaii Bar Assn., United Sport Fishermen Internat. (pres. 1987—), Jonathan, Plaza, Elks. Office: 215 N Marengo 2d Fl Pasadena CA 91101

MONTGOMERY, MICHAEL DAVIS, advanced technology company executive; b. San Luis Obispo, Calif., June 4, 1936; s. Herold Ray and Elva Dee (Davis) M.; m. Rita Martin, Dec. 28, 1957 (div. Sept. 1975); children: Jeanne, Gwen, Michele. MSEE, Stanford U., 1959; PhD, U. N.Mex., 1967. Group leader Max Planck Inst. for Astrophysics, Munich, 1974-76; group leader advanced concepts Los Alamos (N.Mex.) Nat. Labs., 1976-83; program mgr. for simulation Maxwell Labs. Inc., San Diego, 1983-84, dep. for DNA programs, 1984-85, v.p. rsch. and devel., 1986—. Assoc. editor Jour. Geophys. Research; contbr. articles to sci. jours. Served to lt. comdr. USN, 1959-62. Recipient Sr. Scientist award Alexander Von Humboldt Found., 1972. Mem. AAAS, Am. Phys. Soc., Phi Beta Kappa, Sigma Xi, Tau Beta Pi. Home: 13906 Mira Montana Dr Del Mar CA 92014 Office: Maxwell Labs 8888 Balboa Ave San Diego CA 92123

MONTGOMERY, PARKER GILBERT, merchant banker; b. Norwood, Mass., July 30, 1928; s. Spencer Bishop and Eleanor Carrie (Gilbert) M.; children: Parker Jr., Carol, John B., William W., Kathryn. A.B., Harvard U., 1949, LL.B., 1953. Bar: Mass. 1953, N.Y. 1956. Assoc. Heminway & Barnes, Boston, 1953; assoc. Dewey, Ballantine, Bushby, Palmer & Wood, N.Y.C., 1956; with Baker, Weeks & Co., investment bankers, N.Y.C., 1957; pvt. practice law N.Y.C., Mt. Kisco, 1957-59, 61-63; spl. asst. to sec. state Dept. State, 1959-61; founder Cooper Labs., Inc., Palo Alto, Calif., 1958; chmn. bd., pres. The Cooper Cos., Inc.; chmn. Cooper Devel. Co., Cooper LaserSonics, Inc. Councilman Town of Bedford, 1971-75; vice-chmn. Presdl. Task Force on Internat. Pvt. Enterprise, 1983-84; bd. dirs. Santa Barbara Med. Found. Clinic, Music Acad. West. Lt. USNR, 1945-46, 54-55. Mem. Coun. Fgn. Rels. (N.Y.C.), Econ. Club (N.Y.), Harvard Club (N.Y.C), Pacific Union Club, Metro Club, River Club (N.Y.C.), Royal Thames Yacht Club, Bedford Golf and Tennis Club, The Valley Club of Montecito. Office: Cooper Devel Co 455 Middlefield Rd Mountain View CA 94043

MONTGOMERY, RICHARD ALAN, sales executive; b. Arlington Heights, Ill., Sept. 5, 1949; s. Charles Gaylord and Luva (Snider) M. BS in Communications, U. Tenn., 1974. Account exec. John M. Rose Advt., Knoxville, Tenn., 1974-75, Metcalfe-Cook & Smith Advt., Nashville, 1975-77, Sta. WTVF-TV, Nashville, 1977-78; div. mgr. Showbiz, Inc., Nashville, 1978-81; sales supr. Multimedia Program Prodns., Nashville, 1981-83; v.p., western regional mgr. Paramount TV, Los Angeles, 1983—. Served with USNG, 1970-78. Mem. Nat. Assn. TV Program Execs., Jr. C. of C. Republican. Methodist. Office: Paramount TV 5555 Melrose Ave Los Angeles CA 90038

MONTGOMERY, ROBERT LOUIS, chemical engineer; b. San Francisco, Nov. 20, 1935; s. Louis Clyde and Fay Elythe (Myers) M.; m. Patricia Helen Cook, Mar. 17, 1962; children: Cynthia Elaine, Jeanette Louise, Cecelia Irene, Howard Edwin. BS in Chemistry, U. Calif., Berkeley, 1956; PhD in Phys. Chemistry, Okla. State U., 1975. Registered profl. engr., Kans., Tex., Colo. Phys. chemist U.S. Bur. Mines, Reno, 1956-62; NSF predoctoral fellow Okla. State U., Stillwater, 1963-66; sr. engr. Boeing Co., Wichita, Kans., 1966-75; postdoctoral fellow Rice U., Houston, 1975-77, sr. research assoc., 1982-84; tech. data engr. M.W. Kellogg Co., Houston, 1977-82; staff engr. Martin Marietta, Denver, 1984—. Contbr. articles to profl. jours. Mem. Am. Chem. Soc., Profl. Engrs. Colo., Am. Soc. for Metals, AIAA, Sigma Xi. Lodge: Moose. Home: 9933 Fairwood St Littleton CO 80125 Office: Martin Marietta Astronautics Group PO Box 179 Denver CO 80201

MONTGOMERY, SETH DAVID, lawyer; b. Santa Fe, Feb. 16, 1937; s. Andrew Kaye and Ruth (Champion) M.; m. Margaret Cook, Oct. 29, 1960; children: Andrew Seth, Charles Hope, David Lewis. AB, Princeton U., 1959; LLB, Stanford U., 1965. Bar: N.M. 1965. Ptnr. Montgomery & Andrews, P.A., Santa Fe, 1965—; bd. dirs. 1st Interstate Bank Santa Fe; vis. instr. U. N. Mex. Sch. Law, Albuquerque, 1970-71; chmn. N. Mex. adv. council Legal Services Corp., Santa Fe, 1976-. Bd. visitors Stanford U. Sch. Law, 1967-70, 82-85; pres., chmn. Santa Fe Opera, 1981-86; pres. Santa Fe Opera Found., 1986-89; chmn., vice chmn. Sch. Am. Research, Santa Fe, 1985-89; bd. dirs. New Vistas, Santa Fe, 1986—. Lt. (j.g.) USN, 1959-62. Named Citizen of Yr. Santa Fe C. of C., 1986. Fellow Am. Coll. Trial Lawyers, Am. Coll. Probate Counsel, Am. Bar Endowment (bd. bar commrs., bd. dirs. N.Mex. chpt. 1986—, sec., treas. N.Mex. chpt. 1988-89); mem. ABA, Supreme Ct. Hist. Soc. (N.Mex. membership chmn. 1985—). Democrat. Office: Montgomery & Andrews PA 325 Paseo de Peralta Santa Fe NM 87504-2307

MONTGOMERY, TED MONROE, optometrist; b. Las Vegas, N. Mex., Oct. 15, 1954; s. Charles M. and Anna Mae (Jameson) M. BS in Math., N. Mex. Highlands U., 1975; BS in Visual Sci., So. Calif. Coll. Optometry, 1977, OD, 1979. Lic. optometrist, Calif., N. Mex. Staff optometrist Family Health Program, Fountain Valley, Calif., 1979-83, area chief optometrist, 1983—. Mem. Phi Kappa Phi. Office: Family Health Program 9930 Talbert St Fountain Valley CA 92708

MONTHAN, DORIS BORN, writer, editor; b. Manitowoc, Wis., May 26, 1924; d. Edgar Jacob and Linda Sophia (Vogt) Born; m. Guy Monthan Jr.; 1 child, William Edgar. Student, U. Ariz., 1943-44, NYU, 1948-49, Columbia U., 1950-51, No. Ariz. U., 1976, 82. Women's editor Tucson Daily Citizen, 1944-45; section editor Women's Wear Daily, N.Y.C., 1945-46; assoc. editor Simplicity Mag., N.Y.C., 1949-51; advtg. mgr. Crown Sleep Shops, Pasadena, Calif., 1953-67; editor-in-chief Northland Press, Flagstaff, Ariz., 1970-72; editor mus. notes Mus. of No. Ariz., Flagstaff, 1972-75; freelance writer, editor Flagstaff, 1975—. Author (book): The Thief, 1961, R.C. Gorman: The Lithographs, 1978; (with others): Art and Indian Individualists, 1975, Nacimientos, 1979, The Pueblo Storyteller, 1986. Panelist Ariz. Commn. on the Arts, Phoenix, 1982—. Mem. Soc. Southwestern Authors, No. Ariz. Alumnae Club of Kappa Kappa Gamma (Alumnae Achievement award 1984, pres. 1986—). Democrat. Episcopalian. Home and Office: PO Box 1698 Flagstaff AZ 86002

MONTOYA, LINDA FRASER, violinist, flower stylist; b. Wenatchee, Wash., Apr. 30, 1941; d. William Oscar Gordon and Gladys Margarite Helmick; m. Jesse E. Montoya, Mar. 20, 1964 (div. 1968); 1 child, Jesse David. Diploma in violin, Curtis Inst. of Music, Phila., 1957, 61; performers cert., Ind. U., Bloomington, 1963. Pvt. music studio Wenatchee, 1964—; instr. Wenatchee Valley Coll., 1964—. Active Wenatchee Fine Arts. Recipient 1st Pl. String Div., Soloist with Spokane Symphony Orch., 1957, 2nd Pl. winner Merriweather Post Competition, soloist with Wash. D.C. Symphony Orch., 1960, Phila. Youth Competition Top 2, Phila., 1960. Mem. Wenatchee Music Tchrs. (pres.), Wash. State Music Tchrs. Assn., Mu Phi Epsilon, St. Cecilia's Guild. Republican. Episcopalian. Home: 1020 Russell St Wenatchee WA 98801

MONTOYA-MAESTAS, MARY KAREN, speech and language pathologist; b. Espanola, N.Mex., Sept. 9, 1960; d. Armando and Roberta (Valdez) M.; m. Ernest Maestas, June 18, 1988. BA, N.Mex. State U., 1982, MA, 1984. Speech-lang. clinician Speech and Hearing Ctr. N.Mex. State U., Las Cruces, N.Mex., 1980-84, grad. asst., 1983-84; speech-lang. intern William Beaumont Army Med. Ctr., El Paso, Tex., 1984; speech-lang. pathologist Expanola Schs., 1985—; adminstrv. svc. aide Los Alamos (N.Mex.) Nat. Lab., summers 1979-81. Adrian Berryhill scholar, 1983. Mem. Am. Speech-Lang-Hearing Assn., N.Mex. State U. Alumni Assn. Roman Catholic. Home and Office: PO Box 424 Espanola NM 87531

MONTRONE, PAUL MICHAEL, diversified company executive; b. Scranton, Pa., May 8, 1941; s. Angelo H. and Beatrice M. (Giancini) M.; m. Sandra R. Gaudenzi, May 30, 1963; children: Michele Marie, Angelo Henry, Jerome Lawrence. B.S. in Accounting magna cum laude, U. Scranton, 1962; Ph.D. in Fin., Econs. and Ops. Research, Columbia U., 1965. Ops. analyst Office Sec. Def., Washington, 1965-67; v.p. Penn-Dixie Industries, N.Y.C., 1967-69; exec. v.p., chief fin. officer Wheelabrator-Frye Inc., Hampton, N.H., 1970-83; exec. v.p. Signal Cos., Inc., La Jolla, Calif., 1983-85; pres. Engineered Products Group Signal Cos., Inc., Hampton, N.H., 1983-85; exec. v.p. fin. and adminstrn. Allied-Signal Inc., Morristown, N.J., 1985-86; pres. The Henley Group Inc., LaJolla, Calif., 1986—, also bd. dirs.; pres. Henley Mfg. Corp., Hampton, N.H.; dir. ICI Ams. Inc. Adv. dir. Met. Opera Assn.; mem. dean's adv. council Bus. sch. Columbia U., N.Y.C. Served to capt. U.S. Army, 1965-67. Roman Catholic. Clubs: Brook, University (N.Y.C.); Bald Peak Colony (Melvin Village, N.H.); Lyford Cay (Nassau, Bahamas). Home: Great Hill Hampton Falls NH 03844 Office: The Henley Group Inc 11255 N Torrey Pines Rd La Jolla CA 92073 *

MONTROSE, DONALD W., bishop; b. Denver, May 13, 1923. Student, St. John's Sem., Calif. Ordained priest Roman Cath. Ch., 1949. Aux. bishop Roman Cath. Ch., Los Angeles, 1983; bishop Diocese of Stockton, Calif., 1985—. Office: Diocese of Stockton 1105 N Lincoln St Stockton CA 95203 *

MONTROSS, SUSAN KAY, nurse; b. Sacramento, June 6, 1962; d. Bill Gene and Frances Earlene Jamison; m. Mark Leslie Beatty, June 21, 1982 (div. Aug. 1984); m. Dean Floyd Montross, Aug. 18, 1985; 1 child, Michael Dean. AS in Nursing, Pacific Union Coll., 1982. Cert. in cancer chemotherapy. Private duty nurse's aid, Glendale, Calif., 1982; lead RN Hanford (Calif.) Community Hosp., 1982-85; office mgr. Dr. James A. Sadoyama, Loma Linda, Calif., 1985-86; home visiting nurse Nat. In-Home Health, Redlands, Calif., 1986-87; staff RN orthopaedics Loma Linda U. Med. Ctr., 1987-88; pvt. duty RN Am. Home Care, Fresno, Calif., 1988—; pvt. practice nursing, Fresno, 1988—. Seventh-day Adventist.

MOOD, ROBERT GIBBS, III, geophysical services company official; b. Wichita, Kans., Apr. 16, 1945; s. Robert Gibbs Jr. and Elizabeth Delalle (Toomey) M.; m. Gayle Eileen Darroch, Dec. 29, 1969 (div. Mar. 1973); m. Judith Diane Currie, Aug. 18, 1973. AB in Microbiolgy, Ind. U., 1968. Project adminstr. Geophys. Svc. Inc., Verplank, N.Y., 1973-76; country adminstr. Geophys. Svc. Inc., Kerman, Iran, 1976-78; sr. buyer Geophys. Svc. Inc., Dallas, 1979-81; mgr. logistics Geophys. Svc. Inc., Anchorage, 1981—. Vestryman St. Marys Ch., Anchorage, 1985. Served to lst lt. U.S. Army, 1968-72. Mem. Geophys. Soc. Alaska. Office: Halliburton Geogphs Svc Inc 5801 Silverado Way Anchorage AK 99518

MOODY, BLAIR EDWIN, forester; b. Milw., Nov. 5, 1950; s. Frederick Edwin and Elizabeth Moody; m. Carol Ann Cameron, Mar. 21, 1987; stepchildren: Catherine Ann, Christine Marie. BS in Forestry, No. Ariz. U., 1976. Logyard mgr. S.W. Forest Industries, Flagstaff, Ariz., 1977, contract pulpwood logging supr., 1977-81, contract adminstr., 1981-85; logging mgr. Stone Forest Industries, Medford, Oreg., 1985—. Scoutmaster Cub Scouts Boy Scouts Am., Flagstaff, 1977; vol. Big Bros./Big Sisters, 1973-75, bd. dirs., 1977-84, pres. 1983; mem. allocations com. bd. United Way, Medford, Oreg., 1988—; bd. dirs. Jackson County United Way, 1989—; mem. community rels. adv. bd. So. Oreg. State Coll., 1989—. Mem. Soc. Am. Foresters (chpt. chmn. 1983, sec., treas. Siskiyou chpt. 1989—), Am. Forestry Assn., So. Oreg. Timber Industries Assn., No. Ariz. U. Alumni Assn. (pres. forestry sch. 1984-85), Model RR Club. Republican. Home: 1148 Todd Circle Medford OR 97504 Office: Stone Forest Industries 7975 11st St White City OR 97503

MOODY, GEORGE FRANKLIN, banker; b. Riverside, Calif., July 28, 1930; s. William Clifford and Mildred R. (Scott) M.; m. Mary Jane Plank, Jan. 19, 1950; children: Jeffrey George, Jane Ellen Moody Fowler, John Franklin, Joseph William. Student, Riverside City Coll., 1948-50; grad. with honors, Pacific Coast Banking Sch., 1963. Bus. officer U. Calif., Riverside, 1950-52; with Security Pacific Nat. Bank, Los Angeles, 1953—, dir. personnel, v.p., 1970-71, sr. v.p. inland div. adminstrn., 1971-73, exec. v.p., 1973-78, vice chmn., 1978-80, pres., chief exec. officer, 1985; pres., chief operating officer Security Pacific Corp., Los Angeles, 1985—, also bd. dirs. Chief prin. officer, mem. nat. bd. govs., ARC, chmn. exec. com. 1979-80; bd. dirs. Found., U.S. Olympic Com., chmn. Western region, 1981-84; trustee Calif. Neighborhood Housing Service Found., Jr. Achievement So. Calif.; trustee, mem. exec. com. Pomona Coll.; pres. Los Angeles area council Boy Scouts Am., 1980—; past bd. dirs. Los Angeles Music Ctr. Operating Co., Los Angeles United Way, Calif. Econ. Devel. Corp.; past. bd. dirs., past v.p. Hollywood Presbyn. Med. Ctr., Calif. Econ. Devel. Corp.; past chmn. Music Ctr. Unified Fund, Invest-In-Am.; past trustee Calif. Mus. Found., Com. for Econ. Devel., Washington; past. mem. bd. govs. Calif. Community Found.; bd. dirs. John Douglas French Found. for Alzheimers Disease; pres. L.A. area C. Of C. Assocs. Mem. Los Angeles C. of C. (past pres.), U.S. C. of C. (bd. dirs.), Colorado River Assn. (pres.), Am. Bankers Assn. (bd. dirs.), Calif. Bankers Assn., Assn. Res. City Bankers, Merchants and Mfrs. Assn. (past chmn.), Performing Arts Council (former gov.), Calif. Club, Los Angeles Country Club, Hacienda Golf Club. Republican. Office: Security Pacific Corp 333 S Hope St Los Angeles CA 90071 *

MOOK, WALTER RAYMOND, environmental engineer; b. New Brunswick, N.J., June 28, 1931; s. W. Raymond and Rayone Alice (Dietrich) M.; m. Jeanne Noel Cunningham, Apr. 17, 1954; children: Pamela Ann Foley, Robert Brian, Kenneth Allan. BSME, Stevens Inst. Tech., 1953; M Engring., U. Redlands, 1972. Standards engr. Sandia Corp., Albuquerque, 1953-55; mem. tech. staff Ramo-Wooldridge Corp., Inglewood, Calif., 1959-60, Space Tech. Labs., Inglewood, 1960-61, TRW Systems, Inglewood, 1961-72; dir. tech. svcs. Statewide Air Pollution Rsch. Ctr., Riverside, Calif., 1972-73; dir. adminstrv. svcs. San Bernardino County (Calif.) Environ. Improvement Agy., 1974-79; exec. officer San Bernardino County Air Pollution Control Dist., Victorville, Calif., 1979—; chmn. Calif. Desert Air Working Group, San Bernardino, 1983—. Bd. dirs., Redlands (Calif.) Baseball for Youth, 1968-78. Lt. (j.g.) USNR, 1955-59. Mem. Calif. Air Pollution Control Officers Assn. (pres.-elect 1988-89), Air and Waste Mgmt. Assn., Assn. Local Air Pollution Control Ofcls., Tau Beta Pi. Republican. Home: 114 Anita Ct Redlands CA 92373 Office: Air Pollution Control Dist San Bernardino County 15428 Civic Dr Victorville CA 92392

MOOMJIAN, CARY AVEDIS, JR., lawyer, drilling executive; b. Albany, N.Y., June 8, 1947; s. Cary A. and Ruth (Michaél) M.; m. Laurian Sue Ingram, Aug. 11, 1984; 1 child, Chad Andrew. BA, Occidental Coll., 1969; JD, Duke U., 1972. Bar: Calif. 1972, U.S. Dist. Ct. (cen. dist.) Calif. 1972. Assoc. McCutchen, Black et al., Los Angeles, 1972-76; counsel, v.p., dir. Santa Fe Drilling Co., Alhambra, Calif., 1976—. Chmn. Santa Fe Internat. Corp. Polit. Action Com., Calif., 1985—. Mem. ABA, Maritime Law Assn. U.S. (proctor), Internat. Assn. Drilling Contractors (dir.), Nat. Ocean Industries Assn., Duke Law Alumni Council (trustee 1984—). Republican. Club: Bicycle (charter) (Bell Gardens, Calif.). Office: Sante Fe Drilling Co 1000 S Fremont Ave Alhambra CA 91802

MOON, MARJORIE RUTH, former state treasurer; b. Pocatello, Idaho, June 16, 1926; d. Clark Blakeley and Ruth Eleanor (Gerhart) M. Student, Pacific U., 1944-46; A.B. in Journalism cum laude, U. Wash., 1948. Reporter Pocatello Tribune, 1944, Caldwell (Idaho) News-Tribune, 1948-50; Salt Lake City bur. chief Deseret News, Boise, Idaho, 1950-52; owner, operator Idaho Pioneer Statewide (weekly newspaper), Boise, 1952-55; founder, pub. Garden City (Idaho) Gazette, 1954-68; partner Sawtooth Lodge, Grandjean, Idaho, 1958-60; ptnr. Modern Press, Boise, 1958-61; treas. State of Idaho, Boise, 1963-86; owner, pub. Kuna-Melba News, 1987—, Valley News, Meridian, Idaho, 1988—. Chmn. Idaho Commn. on Women's Programs, 1971-74; del. Dem. Nat. Nominating Conv., 1972, 76, 80, 84; Dem. candidate Lt. Gov., Idaho, 1986; mem. Idaho Comn. for the Blind, 1987—; sec.-treas. Kuna C. of C., 1987-88. Named Idaho Statesman of Yr. Pi Sigma Alpha of Idaho State U., 1989. Mem. Nat. Assn. State Treas. (sec.-treas. 1976-78, regional v.p. 1978-79, 84-85), Nat. Fedn. Press Women, Idaho Press Women (past pres.). Congregationalist. Clubs: Soroptimists (Boise) (pres. club 1971-73), Women's Ltd. (Boise) (pres. 1984, dir. 1983-84). dir.). Office: PO Box 207 Boise ID 83701

MOON, WILLIAM LAWRENCE, electrical engineer; b. Kenniwick, Wash., May 8, 1958; s. William R. and Barbara A. (Hills) M. BSEE magna cum laude, U. Lowell, 198l; MSEE, U. So. Calif., 1983, MBA, 1989. Project engr. Hughes Aircraft Co., L.A., 1981—; owner, mgr. Dive Trip & Instrn. Co., L.A., 1983—. Contbr. numerous articles to scuba diving publs. Mem. dean's adv. bd U. So. Calif., L.A., 1987. Hughes Aircraft Co. fellow, 198l. Mem. Nat. Assn. Underwater Instrs., Hughes Aircraft Scuba Club (v.p. 1982-85, pres. 1986—), Eta Kappa Nu. Office: Hughes Aircraft Co E4/M121 PO Box 902 El Segundo CA 90245

MOONEY, JOHN MURRAY (JAY MOONEY), mechanical engineer; b. Butte, Mont., Feb. 15, 1928; s. Albert S. and Johanna (Murray) M.; m. Bernice Elizabeth Maher,June 9, 1952; children Julie, John, Mary, Anne, Jim. BS in Mech. Engring., U. Utah, 1952. Research Sci. NACA (now NASA) Edwards AFB, Edwards, Calif., 1952; flight test engr. Cessna Aircraft, Wichita, Kans., 1953; project officer USAF Spl. Weapons Comd., Albuquerque, 1954-56; co-owner & mgr. Butte Aero. Sales & Svc., Butte, Mont., 1956-64; flight test engr. USAF Edwards AFB, Edwards, 1964-65; gen. aviation. ops. inspector FAA Gen. Aviation Dist. Office, Ontario, Calif., 1966; FAA Airspace Systems Inspection Pilot Procedures Spec. LAX FIFO, Los Angeles, 1967-77; FAA Air Carrier Ops. Instector NM-FSDO-67, Salt Lake City, Utah, 1978—. 1st Lt., USAF, 1954-56. Recipient James McGean: Outstanding Athlete and Scholar, Judge Meml. High, Salt Lake City 1946; DOT/FAA Spl. Ach. Award, NATI Program, Salt Lake City 1984-85. Mem. Aircraft Owners & Pilots Assn., Utah Pilots Assn. Republican. Roman Catholic.

MOORE, BEVERLY BARRETT, library director; b. Evanston, Wyo., Mar. 17, 1934; d. James Henry and Louise (Miller) Barrett; m. James O. Moore, Oct. 6, 1957 (div. Sept. 1967); children: Louis Barrett, Ann Louise Cushman. AA, Hutchinson Jr. Coll., 1954; BA, U. No. Colo., 1957; MLS, Denver U., 1970. Br. librarian Pueblo (Colo.) Library Dist., 1966-70; documents librarian U. So. Colo., Pueblo, 1970-74, head catalog librarian, 1974-76, library dir., 1976—; co-chair Colo. Acad. Library com., 1982-88; treas. Arkansas Valley Regional Library Services System, 1984—. Editor: Colorado Academic Master Plan, 1988. Mem. Colo. Library Assn. (pres. 1985), ALA, LWV, AAUW, Beta Phi Mu. Democrat. Congregationalist. Home: 1719 Jerry Murphy Rd Pueblo CO 81001 Office: U So Colo Libr Office of Dir Pueblo CO 81001-4901

MOORE, BRUCE WALLACE, county official; b. LaJolla, Calif., Feb. 23, 1937; s. George R. and Katherine E. M.; BS summa cum laude, Calif. State U., Fresno, 1970, MBA with distinction, 1970; m. Verna Christoffersen children: Katherine, Laura, Ian. Asst. mgr. Fresno (Calif.) Flood Control Dist., 1972-73; dep. exec. dir. Fresno Housing Authority, 1973-75, exec. dir., 1975-77; exec. dir. Monterey County (Calif.) Housing Authority, 1977—. Mem. Monterey County Housing Coun. Served with Army N.G., 1959. Mem. Nat. Assn. Housing and Redevel. Ofcls. (past pres. Pacific S.W. region), No. Calif. Exec. Dirs. Assn. (past v.p.), Housing Law Inst. (v.p.), Housing for the Homeless, Inc. Lodge: Rotary. Office: 123 Rico Salinas CA 93907

MOORE, CARLETON BRYANT, geochemistry educator; b. N.Y.C., Sept. 1, 1932; s. Eldridge Carleton and Mabel Florence (Drake) M.; m. Jane Elizabeth Strouse, July 25, 1959; children—Barbara Jeanne, Robert Carleton. B.S., Alfred U., 1954, D.Sc. (hon.), 1977; Ph.D., Cal. Inst. Tech., 1960. Asst. prof. geology Wesleyan U., Middletown, Conn., 1959-61; mem. faculty Ariz. State U., Tempe, 1961—; prof., dir. Ctr. for Meteorite Studies Ariz. State U., Regents' prof., 1988—; vis. prof. Stanford U., 1974; Prin. investigator Apollo 11-17; preliminary exam. team Lunar Receiving Lab., Apollo, 12-17. Author: Cosmic Debris, 1969, Meteorites, 1971, Principles of Geochemistry, 1982, Grundzügeder Geochemie, 1985. Editor: Researches on Meteorites, 1961, Jour. Meteoritical Soc.; contbr. articles to profl. jours. Fellow Ariz.-Nev. Acad. Sci. (pres. 1979-80), Meteoritical Soc. (life hon., pres. 1966-68), Geol. Soc. Am., Mineral. Soc. Am., AAAS (council 1967-70); mem. Geochem. Soc., Am. Chem. Soc., Am. Ceramic Soc., Sigma Xi. Home: 507 E Del Rio Dr Tempe AZ 85282 Office: Ariz State U Ctr for Meteorite Studies Tempe AZ 85287

MOORE, DAVID ALLISON, insurance company executive; b. McNarry, Ariz., Oct. 23, 1934; s. Sam Allison Moore and Geneva Evelyn (Bingham) Vaughn; m. Diane Louise, July 7, 1984; m. Lucinda Lynn Biles Moore, Dec. 26, 1960 (dec. 1980);. BA, N.Mex. State U., Las Cruces, 1967; MA, U. Calif., Irvine, 1972, PhD, 1974. Tchr. Irvine Unified Sch. Dist., Calif., 1970-77; fin. planner Pacific Mutual, Newport Beach, Calif., 1977—; sr. ptnr. Exemplar Fin. Ins. Svcs., Costa Mesa, Calif., 1987—; mem. Orange County Life Underwriters; cons. Roberts Protection. Author: Contemporary Peruvian Short Stoooory 1974, One Pocket 1987; contbr. articles to profl. jours. With USAF 1956-60. Recipient Carl A. Tyre grant New Mex. State U., Las Cruces 1967. Mem. Acad. Magical Arts, Irvine Lions Club, Costa Costa Mesa C. of C., Phi Kappa Phi. Republican. Home: 21081 Chubasco Ln Huntington Beach CA 92646 Office: Exemplar Fin & Ins Svcs 2850 Mesa Verde E Ste 111 Costa Mesa CA 92626

MOORE, DAVID AUSTIN, pharmaceutical company executive, consultant; b. Phoenix, May 8, 1935; s. Harry Theodore and Helen Ann (Newport) M.; divorced, Austin Newport, Cornelia Christina, Christopher Robinson. G-rad. high sch., Glendale, Ariz. Pres., owner Phoenix, 1969-71, Biol. Labs. Ltd., Phoenix, 1972-78; pres., co-owner Am. Trace Mineral Rsch. Corp., Phoenix, 1979-83; pres., owner Biol. Mineral Scis., Ltd., Phoenix, 1979-82; rsch. dir., pres., owner Nutritional Biols. Inc., Phoenix, 1979-83; nutritional dir.-owner Nutritional Biol. Rsch. Co., Phoenix, 1984-85; rsch. dir., product formulator Nutrition and Med. Rsch., Scottsdale, Ariz., 1986—; biochem. cons. Nutripathic Formulas, Scottsdale, 1975-88. Inventor first computer-ized comprehensive hair analysis interpretation, 1976. Recipient Plaque Am. Soc. Med. Techs., 1982, Mineralab Inc., 1976. Office: Nutrition and Med Rsch 13041 N 35th Ave Ste C-5 Phoenix AZ 85029

MOORE, DAVID HENRY, real estate developer, consultant; b. Cranbrook, B.C., Can., Oct. 9, 1936; s. Henry Headley and Katherine Alberta (Cameron) M.; m. Sylvia Louise West, Oct. 11, 1964 (div. 1984); children: Elizabeth, Douglas; m. Linda Joan Crutchfield, Feb. 14, 1986. BS in Forestry, U. Idaho, 1963; postgrad., Simon Fraser U., Burnaby, B.C., 1968-69, U. Denver, 1983-84. Gen. mgr. Edgewater (B.C.) Sawmills, 1963-66; sr. project supr. Crown Zellerbach, Vancouver, B.C., 1966-70, dir. long range planning, 1970-74; mgr. comml. div. Daon Corp., Vancouver, 1974; gen. mgr. Eddy Harware Co., Bathurst, N.B., Can., 1974-75; prin. David H. Moore & Assocs., Vancouver, 1975-76; pres. Edgewater Devels., 1976-81; devel. mgr. Dueck Group, Aurora, Colo., 1981—; instr. East Kootenay Community Coll., Cranbrook, 1978-81. Spokesman Aurora Agenda 21, 1987-88; active City of Aurora task forces; dir. various MP campaigns, B.C., 1969, 71; del. Can. polit. conv., Ottawa, Ont., 1969. Mem. Urban Land Inst., Xi Sigma Pi. Office: Dueck Group 15701 E 1st Ave Ste 200 Aurora CO 80011

MOORE, DIANNE LEA, word processing company owner; b. North Tonawanda, N.Y., Jan. 30, 1949; d. Donald Robert and Dorothy (Ghise) Wilke; m. William Lewis Tremont, Aug. 21, 1966 (div. Apr. 1973); children: Eric, Michelle; m. Allen Charles Moore, July 11, 1981. AA, Scottsdale Community Coll., 1978; student, Ariz. State U., 1978-81. Powder paint troubleshooter McGraw Edison, Phoenix, 1980-81; v.p., mgr. Cereus Recording, Tempe, Ariz., 1981—; adminstrv. asst. McKesson, Phoenix, 1982-83; owner, mgr. Cereus Letter Processing, Tempe, 1983—. Pres. Aid Assn. for Luths. br. 5555, Scottsdale. Mem. Soc. Profl. Audio Recording Svcs., Nat. Fedn. Ind. Businessmen, Better Bus. Bur., U.S. C. of C. Democrat. Office: Cereus Letter Processing 1733 E McKellips Ste 7 Tempe AZ 85281

MOORE, DONALD WALTER, educator; b. Culver City, Calif., June 9, 1942; s. Raymond Owen amd Jewel Elizabeth (Young) M.; m. Dagmar Ulbrich, Mar. 28, 1968; 1 child, Michael. AA, L.A. Valley Coll., 1967; BA in History, Calif. State U., Northridge, 1970; MA in Learning Disability, Calif. State U., 1973; MLS, U. So. Calif., 1974. Part time librarian L.A. Pierce Coll., Woodland Hills, Calif., 1974—; instr. vocat. edn. act program L.A. Trade Tech. Coll., 1978-80, pres.'s staff asst., 1983-87; instr. learning skills L.A. City Coll., 1987-88, dir. amnesty project, 1988—. Author: Cavalrymen, 1983; contbr. fiction, articles, revs. to various publs. Mem. Ednl. Writers Am., Co. Mil. Historians, U.S. Horse Cavalry Assn., Little Big Horn Assn. Republican. Roman Catholic. Office: AmnestyProgram LA City Coll 855 N Vermont Ave Los Angeles CA 90029

MOORE, DUDLEY SHIELDS, dentist; b. Sandusky, Ohio. AB in Chemistry, Maryville Coll., 1942; DDS, Ind. U., 1944; postgrad., U. Calif., 1956, Northwestern U., 1958-59. Private practice dentistry 1947-56, private practice oral surgery, 1956-82, private practice oral and maxillo-facial surgery, 1982-88, cons., 1988—; adminstr. Barlyn Hosp., 1959-78, U. So. Calif., 1947-48; instr. clin. U. Pacific, San Francisco, Calif., 1971-73; bd. dirs. Delta Dental Plan Calif.; mem. adv. hosp. bd. State of Calif., 1967-74, health facilities licensing adv. bd. State of Calif., 1974-78; guest lectr. Dental Study Group Mex., 1949, So. Calif. Dental Assn., 1949; guest clinician Armed Forces Desert Dental Soc., 1964, Calif. Dental Assn., 1952, 59, Mexican Dental Assn., 1953. Contbr. articles to profl. jours. Rep. institutional Boy Scout Am., 1962-64, Sacramento Sheriff's Air Squadron, 1984—; bd. trustees Santa Rosa Pub. Library, 1956-73, also pres. 1963-73; mem. Sonoma County Citizens Com. to Upgrade Gen. Plan, citizens adv. com. Santa Rosa Jr. Coll., blue ribbon com. to assist U. Calif. Site Selection, Pierre Fauchard Acad.; bd. govs. Empire Coll. Law; co-chmn. Calif. Dentists Reagan-Bush; chmn. Republican Cen. Com. Sonoma County, 1961-68, Sonoma County Californians Sen. Murphy, 1966; vice chmn. 1st Congl. Dist. Republican Com. Calif., 1961-68; mem. Republican State Cen. Com. Calif., 1961-66. Served to capt. U. S. Army, 1942-47, capt. USAR, 1947-48, capt. Air Nat. Guard, 1948-50, lt. col. USAFR, 1956-80. Named Eagle Scout, Boy Scouts Am., 1935. Fellow Am. Coll. Dentists, Assn. Oral and Maxillo-Facial Surgeons, Internat. Assn. Oral Surgeons, Royal Soc. Health; mem. Calif. Dental Assn. (pres. 1972-73, bd. dirs. 1976-82, chmn. polit. action com. 1973-76 and numerous other coms.), Jaycees (past pres., JCI senator), Calif. Library Assn., Am. Dental Assn. (del. 1969-78, alternate del. 1964-68), Fed. Dentaire Internat., No. Calif. Soc. Oral Surgeons, Alumni U. of Pacific (assoc.), Alumni U. Calif. Dental Schs. (assoc.), Redwood Empire Dental Soc. (various positions), Delta Sigma Delta. Clubs: St. Francis Yacht, Sacramento Yacht. Lodges: Mason, Shriners, Rotary, Order DeMolay (chmn. adv. bd. Santa Rosa chpt.). Home: 930 Commons Dr Sacramento CA 95825

MOORE, ELIZABETH JANE, banker; b. Long Branch, N.J., Dec. 14, 1940; d. Robert William and Ruth Elizabeth (Dunphy) Marton; m. Gerard George Moore, Mar. 3, 1962; children: Christine Marie, Stephanie Ann, Gerard Marton, Paul Henry George, Barbara Jean. BBA, U. Phoenix, 1987. Charge card specialist Valley Nat. Bank, Phoenix, 1971-74, corp. trust specialist, 1974-80; sec., trust specialist Valley Nat. Bank, Prescott, Ariz., 1980-84, 84-86, trust adminstr., trust officer, 1986, asst. v.p., 1989—. Active Dem. Com., Eatontown, N.J., 1966-67; bd. dirs. Cen. Yavapai County (Ariz.) Fire Dist., 1988—, clk. 1989—; bd. dirs. Yavapai Humane Soc., 1989—, Vol. Firefighter's Relief and Pension Fund, 1989. Mem. Nat. Assn. Bank Women, Ariz. Assn. Legal Secs. (conv. chmn. 1986, nominations chmn. 1985-86), Yavapai County Legal Secs. Assn. (treas. 1983-85, gov. 1985-86), U. Phoenix Network for Profl. Devel. (chartered), Soroptimists. Office: Valley Nat Bank Trust Dept 117 E Gurley St Ste 204 Prescott AZ 86301

MOORE, EVIA BRIGGS, librarian; b. Ripley, Miss., Jan. 18, 1943; d. Vance and Ruby (Braddock) Simelton; m. Henry Earl Briggs, Nov. 12, 1970 (dec. 1973); m. Jones Ambrose Moore, Jr., July 3, 1975; 1 child, Robert Vance. BA, Tougaloo (Miss.) Coll., 1965; MLS, Syracuse U., 1970; postgrad., U. Wis., 1973. Elem. tchr. Jackson (Miss.) Pub. Schs., 1965-66; acquisitions librarian Tougaloo Coll., 1966-74; asst. prof. Jackson State U., 1974-75; librarian San Joaquin Delta Coll., Stockton, Calif., 1977—; librarian cons. Prentiss (Miss.) Inst., 1974-75. Chmn. youth concert Stockton Symphony League, 1987-88; mem. scholarship com. Stockton chpt. Links, Inc., 1980—. Am. Missionary Assn. fellow, N.Y.C., 1969-70, U. Wis. fellow, 1972-73; recipient Tougaloo Coll. Alumni award Jackson/Tougaloo Alumni Club, 1968. Mem. Calif. Library Assn., Delta Kappa Gamma, Phi Delta Kappa, Delta Sigma Theta (pres. Stockton chpt. 1984-86), AAUW, ALA. Democrat. Methodist. Home: 3805 Hatchers Circle Stockton CA 95209 Office: San Joaquin Delta Coll 5151 Pacific Ave Stockton CA 95207

MOORE, GARY EDWARD, dentist; b. Boise, Idaho, May 15, 1935; s. Donald Edward and Audrey (Heap) M.; children: Cheri, Margaret, Loretta, Michael. Student, U. Idaho, 1953-54; BA, Coll. of Idaho, 1958; DDS, Marquette U., 1962. Pvt. practice Roseburg, Oreg., 1964—. Youth program chmn. Presbyn. Ch.; scoutmaster, packleader Boy Scouts of Am.; advisor Mercy Med. Ctr. Edn. Coun.; mem. YMCA, Umpqua Community Coll. Scholarship Bd. Capt. USAF, 1962-64. Mem. ADA, Oreg. Dental Assn. (bd. trustees 1971-72, exec. com. 1975, dental ins. com. 1975), Umpqua Dental Soc. (pres. 1970), Am. Soc. of Dentistry for Children(cert. of merit), Acad. Gen. Dentistry, Grad. Study Club (pres. 1982—), G.E.M. Ceramic Dental Lab. Home: 12 Spyglass Ln Roseburg OR 97470 Office: 1122 NW Garden Valley Blvd Roseburg OR 97470

MOORE, GEORGE EAGLETON, history professor; b. Osaka, Japan, Mar. 25, 1927; s. Lardner Wilson and Grace (Eagleton) M.; m. Velora Ruth Hieb, Aug. 22, 1953; children: Robert Wallace, Martha Ann, James Kennon. BA, U. Calif., Berkeley, 1951, MA, 1959; PhD, U. Calif., 1966. Tchr. Salinas (Calif.) Elem. Sch. Dist., 1954-56, Piedmont (Calif.) Unified Sch. Dist., 1956-62; prof. history dept. San Jose (Calif.) State U., 1964-86, chair history dept., 1986—; chair acad. senate San Jose State U., 1973-74, 86-87. 1st lt. M.I. Corps, U.S. Army, 1945-48. Mem. Assn. for Asian Studies, Asian Studies on the Pacific Coast., Piedmont Tchrs. Assn. (pres. 1960-61), Sigma Nu. Democrat. Presbyterian. Home: 35 Rincon Rd Kensington CA 94707 Office: San Jose State U 1 Washington Sq San Jose CA 95192

MOORE, GEORGE EUGENE, surgeon; b. Minn., Feb. 22, 1920; s. Jesse and Elizabeth (MacRae) M.; m. Lorraine Hammell, Feb. 22, 1945; children—Allan, Laurie, Linda, Cathy, Donald. B.A., U. Minn., 1942, M.A., 1943, B.S., 1944, B.M., 1946, M.D., 1947, Ph.D. in Surgery, 1950. Intern surgery U. Minn. Hosps., 1946-47; med. fellow gen. surgery 1947, dir. tumor clinic, 1951-53; sr. research fellow USHPS, 1947-48; faculty U. Minn. Med. Sch., 1948-53, cancer coordinator, 1951-53; chief surgery Roswell Park Meml. Inst., Buffalo, 1953-72; dir. Roswell Park Meml. Inst., 1953-67; dir. pub. health research N.Y. State Health Dept., Albany, 1967-73; clin. prof. surgery State U. N.Y. at Buffalo, 1962-73, also prof. research biology, 1955-69; dir. surg. oncology Denver Gen. Hosp., 1973—; prof. surgery U. Colo., 1973—. Author: Diagnosis and Localization of Brain Tumors, 1950, Cancerous Diseases, 1970; contbr. 660 articles to profl. jours. Recipient Outstanding Citizen award Buffalo Evening News, 1958; Outstanding Sci. Achievement award, 1959; Distinguished Achievement award Modern Medicine mag., 1962; Chancellor's medal U. Buffalo, 1963; Charles Evans Hughes award pub. adminstrn. Albany, 1963; Bronfman prize Am. Pub. Health Assn., 1964. Mem. Soc. U. Surgs., Halsted Soc., Am. Surg. Assn.,

Colo. Oncology Found. (pres.). Home: 12048 Blackhawk Dr Conifer CO 80433 Office: Denver Gen Hosp 645 Bannock St PO Box 1806 Denver CO 80204

MOORE, GORDON E., electronics company executive; b. San Francisco, Jan. 3, 1929; s. Walter Harold and Florence Almira (Williamson) M.; m. Betty I. Whittaker, Sept. 9, 1950; children: Kenneth, Steven. B.S. in Chemistry, U. Calif., 1950; Ph.D. in Chemistry and Physics, Calif. Inst. Tech., 1954. Mem. tech. staff Shockley Semicondr. Lab., 1956-57; mgr. engring. Fairchild Camera & Instrument Corp., 1957-59, dir. research and devel., 1959-68; exec. v.p. Intel Corp., Santa Clara, Calif., 1968-75; pres., chief exec. officer Intel Corp., 1975-79, chmn., chief exec. officer, 1979-87, chmn., 1987—; dir. Micro Mask Inc., Varian Assocs. Inc., Transamerica Corp. Fellow IEEE; mem. Nat. Acad. Engring., Am. Phys. Soc. Office: Intel Corp 3065 Bowers Ave Santa Clara CA 95051

MOORE, INA MAY, artist, art educator; b. Hayden, Ariz., Feb. 20, 1920; d. Jonathan L. and Filomena A. (Salmon) Booth; m. Minton I. Moore, Aug. 7, 1942. BA in Edn., U. Ariz., 1936; MA in Art Edn., Ariz. State U., 1964. Instr. watercolor Phoeniz Art Mus., 1967-87, Phoenix Coll., 1979—. Artist watercolor paintings and sculptures. Mem. Westerners, Phoenix 1956. Mem. Ariz. Watercolor Assn. (past pres. Phoenix chpt. 1963), Ariz. Artists Guild (Grumbcher award 1988), Contemporary Club. Democrat. Episcopalian. Home: 5718 N 10th Ave Phoenix AZ 85013

MOORE, JACK ARTHUR, health care company executive; b. Palo Alto, Calif., Feb. 10, 1949; s. Arthur and Juanita (Hunt) M.; m. Phylis Caul (div. 1974); m. Karen Lynn Russell. AS, Can. Coll., Redwood City, Calif., 1975. Survey technician NOAA/U.S. Dept. Commerce, Seattle, 1976; sr. data technician Geometrics, Inc., Sunnyvale, Calif., 1977-84; v.p. Witmoore Group/AMEDIC-USA, Phoenix, 1984—. With USAF, 1968-72, Vietnam. Democrat. Office: Witmoore Group 3702 E Roeser Rd Ste 27 Phoenix AZ 85040

MOORE, JAMES DALE, mechanical engineer, inventor; b. Seattle, Jan. 9, 1931; s. Frank Charles and Sarah E. (Jameson) M.; m. Lois Claire, Mar. 22, 1952; children: Allison Suzanne, Meredithe Elise. BSME, U. Wash., 1952; MSME, U. So. Calif., 1958; postgrad., UCLA, 1960. Registered profl. mechanical engr. Calif. Field engr. Union Oil Co. Calif., Santa Paula, 1952-56; design engr. Cal. Tech. Coop. Wind Tunnel, Pasadena, 1956-58; engr. project Hughes Aircraft Co., Culver City, Calif., 1958-64; dir. Mattel Inc., Hawthorne, Calif., 1964-74; v.p. Ryan Engring., Beverly Hills, Calif., 1974-78; pres. Moore Assocs., Palos Verdes, Calif., 1978—; cons. Aerospace Corp., El Segundo, Calif., 1981—; asst. prof. U. So. Calif., Los Angeles, 1971-86; presenter mgmt. seminar AMA, Los Angeles, 1969, also instr. N.Y.C., 1968. Contbr. articles to profl. jours. Patentee for toys, bicycles, consumer products. Founder 4th City Rancho Palos Verdes, 1970. Served to cpl. U.S. Army, 1953-54, Korea. Recipient Achievement award NASA 1987. Fellow IEEE; mem. AIAA (chmn. design engring. tech. com. 1987—), ASME (chmn. 1976), Los Angeles County Mus. Republican. Methodist. Home: 6810 Locklenna Ln Palos Verdes CA 90274

MOORE, JANICE MARIE, interior designer; b. St. Edward, Nebr., Oct. 4, 1940; d. Jacob and Helen (Arney) Kaufmann; m. Byron K. Moore, Dec. 30, 1968. BS with distinction, U. Nebr., 1963-67; postgrad., Kearney State Coll., 1968, 69, 70, 86, U. Wyo., 1983, 84, 85. Cert. home econs. tchr., Nebr., Wyo. Receptionist personnel dept. Mut. Omaha, 1960-63; orientation counselor U. Nebr., Lincoln, 1965-67; tchr. Beatrice (Nebr.) Sr. High Sch., 1967-68, Grand Island (Nebr.) Sr. High Sch., 1968-73; fashion coordinator Hoyland-Swanson, Grand Island, 1973-83; decorator Decorating Den, Casper, Wyo., 1983-84; dept. mgr. The Bon, Casper, 1983-84; fashion cons. Doncaster, Rutherfordton, N.C., 1983—; interior designer House of Stewart, Casper, 1984—; adv. bd. Natrona County High Sch., Casper, 1987—; community coll., Grand Island, 1981-83. Active Heart Fund, Grand Island, 1980-82; Red Cross, Grand Island, 1980-82; Grand Island Edn. Assn., 1968-83; Nat. Hist. Preservation, 1988. Named Disting. Nebraskan U. Nebr., 1967. Mem. Am. Soc. Interior Designers, Interior Design Soc. (nat. juror bd. 1987—), Mortar Bd. (sec. 1966), Illuminating Engrs. Soc., Phi Upsilon Omicron (v.p. 1964), Omicron Nu, Alpha Lambda Delta. Republican. Lutheran. Home: 3400 Stagecoach Dr Casper WY 82604 Office: House of Steward 800 W Collins Casper WY 82601

MOORE, JOHN ASHTON, zoo director; b. Inglewood, Calif., May 23, 1940; s. Ashton Edward and Maddie Ruth (Eaves) M.; m. Edna Louise Hotchkiss, June 25, 1959; children—Linda Marie, Theresa Ruth. Student, Mt. San Antonio Coll., 1960-61; grad., Jessup A.I. Tech. Sch., 1961. Mgr. Movieland Animal Park, Bloomington, Calif., 1964-65; curator birds Balt. Zoo, 1965-67, asst. dir., 1967-71; dir. Salisbury (Md.) Zoo, 1971-72, Audubon Park, New Orleans, 1972-77; dir. Rio Grande Zool. Park, Albuquerque, 1977—; cons. wildlife research, zoos. King, Crew of Tucks, New Orleans; Mem. part time faculty Johns Hopkins U., Balt., 1968-71, research asso., 1971-78; pioneer in hand rearing of Kagu; first western hemisphere captive breeding of Kagu. Contbr. articles to profl. jours. Recipient avicultural achievement award Peter Scott, Slimbridge, Eng., 1971. Fellow Am. Assn. Zool. Parks and Aquariums (profl. fellow); mem. La. Fedn. Zoos (past pres.), Internat. Crane Found. (hon. life). Club: Exchange. Office: Rio Grande Zool Pk 903 10th St SW Albuquerque NM 87102

MOORE, JOHN D., consultant; b. Mt. Pleasant, Iowa, Apr. 7, 1937; s. Burris P. and Esther I. (Copenhaver) M.; m. Karen K. Kriegel, June 19, 1957; children: Charles A., Michael J., Susan K., David J. AB, Muscatine Community Coll., 1961; BBA, Augustana Coll., 1966; postgrad. U. Iowa, 1966-68. Office mgr. Stanley Engring., Muscatine, Iowa, 1956-64; pers. mgr. Oscar Mayer & Co., Davenport and Perry, Iowa, 1964-68; Midwest regional mgr. A. S. Hansen, Lake Bluff, Ill., 1968-73; legal adminstr. Gardner, Carton & Douglas, Chgo., 1973-78, Heller Ehrman White & McAuliffe, San Francisco, 1978-84; v.p. and dir. Hildebrandt, Inc., Walnut Creek, Calif., 1984—. Pres., Libertyville (Ill.) High Sch. Bd., 1974, Libertyville Ecumenical Council, 1975; bd. dirs. Libertyville YMCA, 1969-71. Recipient Muscatine Disting. Service award, 1963; named Outstanding State V.P., Iowa Jaycees, 1964; Outstanding Nat. Dir., U.S. Jaycees, 1965. Mem. Assn. of Legal Adminstrs. (regional v.p. 1977-78, nat. v.p. 1979-81, nat. pres. 1982-83), Am. Mgmt. Assn., Adminstrv. Mgmt. Soc., Found. Assn. of Legal Adminstrs. (pres. 1986-88), Golden Gate Assn. Legal Adminstrs. Republican. Methodist. Home: 2632 Quiet Place Dr Walnut Creek CA 94598 Office: 2855 Mitchell Dr Suite 130 Walnut Creek CA 94598

MOORE, JOHN PORFILIO, federal judge; b. Denver, Oct. 14, 1934; s. Edward Alphonso Porfilio and Caroline (Carbone) Moore; m. Joan West, Aug. 1, 1959 (div. 1983); children—Edward Miles, Joseph Arthur, Jeanne Kathrine; m. Theresa Louise Berger, Dec. 28, 1983; 1 stepchild, Katrina Ann Smith. Student, Stanford U., 1952-54; BA, U. Denver, 1956, LLB, 1959. Bar: Colo. 1959, U.S. Supreme Ct. 1965. Asst. atty. gen. State of Colo., Denver, 1962-68, dep. atty. gen., 1968-72, atty. gen., 1972-74; U.S. bankruptcy judge Dist. of Colo., Denver, 1975-82; judge U.S. Dist. Ct. Colo., Denver, 1982-85, U.S. Ct. Appeals for 10th Cir., Denver, 1985—; instr. Colo. Law Enforcement Acad., Denver, 1965-70, State Patrol Acad., Denver, 1968-70; guest lectr. U. Denver Coll. Law, 1978. Committeeman Arapahoe County Republican Com., Aurora, Colo., 1968; mgr. Dunbar for Atty. Gen., Denver, 1970. Mem. ABA, Colo. Bar Assn., Denver Bar Assn. Roman Catholic. Office: US Ct Appeals C-438 US Courthouse 1929 Stout St Denver CO 80294

MOORE, JUDITH MARIE, nurse; b. Evanston, Ill., June 2, 1947; d. Herbert Potter and Irene Ellen (Wagner) M.; BS, Loma Linda (Calif.) U., 1970. Mem. staff White Meml. Med. Center, L.A., 1970-80, coord. edn. tng. MacPherson Applied Physiology Lab., 1979-80; critical care nurse Critical Care Svcs., Inc., L.A. 1980; dir. health edn. and rehab. tng. St. Helena Hosp. and Health Ctr., Deer Park, Calif., 1981—; bd. dirs. Napa County chpt. Am. Heart Assn., 1980—, McDougall program, 1981-86; speaker in field. Mem. Am. Assn. Critical Care Nurses, Am. Heart Assn., Calif. Soc. Cardiac Rehab. Seventh-day Adventist. Home: PO Box 154 Deer Park CA 94576 Office: St Helena Hosp and Health Ctr Deer Park CA 94576

MOORE, JUSTIN EDWARD, data processing executive; b. West Hartford, Conn., June 17, 1952; s. Walter Joseph and Victoria Mary (Calcagni) M. BS in Mgmt. Sci., Fla. Inst. Tech., 1974. Systems assoc. Travelers Ins., Hartford, Conn., 1974-77; data processing programmer R.J. Reynolds Inc., Winston-Salem, N.C., 1977-78; programmer, analyst Sea-Land Service, Elizabeth, N.J., 1978-79; mgr. market analysis Sea-Land Service, Oakland, Calif., 1979-82; asst. v.p., dir. application systems Fox Capital Mgmt. Corp., Foster City, Calif., 1982-86; mgr. bus. services dept mktg. and pricing Am. Pres. Cos., Ltd., Oakland, 1987-88, dir. mktg. and pricing systems, 1988—. Democrat. Roman Catholic. Home: 5214 Jomar Dr Concord CA 94521 Office: Am Pres Cos Ltd 1800 Harrison St Oakland CA 94612

MOORE, MARGARET PERLIN, financial services company executive, business consultant; b. Chgo., June 15, 1935; d. Clarence Arthur Perlin and Helen Ilene (Gragg) Alltop; m. Jimmy Nelson Moore, Oct. 29, 1955; 1 child, Marcia Moore King. Student, U. Ill., 1953-56; BS, U. Balt., 1973; M of Adminstrv. Sci., Johns Hopkins U., 1977. Audit supr. First Nat. Bank Md., Balt., 1973-76; sr. auditor Comml. Credit Co., Balt., 1976-78; divisional adminstr. Monumental Life Ins. Co., Balt., 1978-83; dir. programs MBR Internat., Inc., Tustin, Calif., 1983-85; v.p., bd. dirs. Topmast, Inc., Temecula, Calif., 1985—; treas., bd. dirs. Calmoc Enterprises, Inc., Temecula; founder Speedy Tax, Temecula. Creator Sommelier's Choice varietal wine jelly. Sec. City Incorp. Com., Rancho, Calif., 1988; bd. dirs. Sam Hicks Monument Pk. Found., Temecula, 1988—. Named Spouse of Yr. Rancho Temecula Murrieta Kiwanis Club, 1987. Mem. Inland Soc. Tax Cons., So. Calif. Culinary Guild, Temecula Valley C. of C., Rancho Temecula Exch. Club (sec., treas. 1987—), Temecula Valley Wine Soc., DAR, Alpha Delta Pi (chpt. advisor). Republican. Home: 41747 Borealis Dr Temecula CA 92390 Office: Topmast Inc 42143-F Avenida Alvarado Temecula CA 92390

MOORE, MARY FRENCH (MUFFY MOORE), potter, community activist; b. N.Y.C., Feb. 25, 1938; d. John and Rhoda (Teagle) Walker French; B.A. cum laude, Colo. U., 1964; m. Alan Baird Minier, Oct. 9, 1982; children—Jonathan Corbet, Jennifer Corbet, Michael Corbet. Ceramics mfr., Wilson, Wyo., 1969-82, Cheyenne, Wyo., 1982—; commr. County of Teton (Wyo.), 1976-83, chmn. bd. commrs., 1981, 83, mem. dept. public assistance and social service, 1976-82, mem. recreation bd., 1978-81, water quality adv. bd., 1976-82. Bd. dirs. Teton Sci. Sch., 1968-83, vice chmn., 1979-81, chmn., 1982; bd. dirs. Teton Energy Council, 1978-83; mem. water quality adv. bd. Wyo. Dept. Environ. Quality, 1979-83; Democratic precinct committeewoman, 1978-81; mem. Wyo. Dem. Central Com., 1981-83; vice chmn. Laramie County Dem. Central Com., 1983-84, Wyo. Dem. nat. committeewoman, 1984-87; chmn. Wyo. Dem. Party, 1987—; del. Dem. Nat. Conv., 1984, 88, mem. fairness commn. Dem. Nat. Com., 1985, vice-chairwoman western caucus, 1986—; chmn. platform com. Wyo. Dem. Conv., 1982; mem. Wyo. Dept. Environ. Quality Land Quality Adv. Bd., 1983-86; mem. Gov.'s Steering Com. on Troubled Youth, 1982, dem. nat. com. Compliance Assistance Commn., 1986-87; exec. com. Assn. of State Dem. Chairs, 1989—; legis. aide for Gov. Wyo., 1985, 86; project coord. Gov.'s Com. on Childrens' Svcs., 1985-86; bd. dirs. Wyo. Outdoor Coun., 1984-85. Recipient Woman of Yr. award Jackson Hole Bus. and Profl. Women, 1981. Mem. Jackson Hole Art Assn. (bd. dirs., vice chmn. 1981, chmn. 1982), Pi Sigma Alpha. Home: 8907 Cowpoke Rd Cheyenne WY 82009

MOORE, MELVIN G., school system administrator; b. Snow, Okla., Jan. 14, 1944; s. Manuel G. and Millie K. (Crownover) M.; m. Merlene S. Klinge, Feb. 24, 1962; (div. Dec. 1979); children: Torri Lynn Moore Wilson, Michael Trevor; m. Christine B. Levak, June 21, 1982; 1 child, Lyndsey Laura Victoria. BS, Oreg. Coll of Edn., Monmouth, 1967, MS, 1971; PhD, U. N.C., Chapel Hill, 1977. Cert. tchr., adminstr. Tchr. Dallas Pub. Schs., Dallas, Oreg., 1968-70; instr., teaching research div. OSSHE, Monmouth, 1971-72; asst. to dir., tech. assistance devel. systems U. N.C., Chapel Hill, 1972-74; adminstrv. intern, bur. of edn. for handicapped U.S. Office of Edn., Washington, 1974-75; research asst. U. N.C., Chapel Hill, 1975-76; asst. research prof. to assoc. research prof. OSSHE, Monmouth, 1976-79; dir. clin. svcs. Ea. Oreg. Hosp. & Tng. Ctr., Pendleton, 1980; dir. special edn. Hillsboro Union High Sch. Dist., 1980—; program dir. Marion County Mental Health Div., Salem, Oreg., 1977-79; asst. dir. WESTAR, U. Wash., Seattle, 1977-78, dir., 1979-80. Contbr. articles to profl. jours. Bd. dirs. Coalition in Oreg. for Parent Edn., Salem, 1986—; legis. com. Confederation of Oreg. Sch. Adminstrs., Salem, 1987—; adv. bd. Oreg. Adv. Coun. for Handicapped Children, Salem, 1988—, Tualatin Valley Mental Health Dept., Portland, 1984—. Recipient Exemplary Service award, Coalition in Oreg. for Parent Edn., Salem, 1988, Recognition of Service award, Portland Tech. Edn. Consortium, 1988. Mem. Coun. of Exceptional Children (gov. 1970-71), Assn. for Retarded Citizens, Confederation of Oreg. Sch. Adminstrs. (pres. 1986-87), Assn. for Supervision and Curriculum Devel. Democrat. Home: 5205 SW 49th Dr Portland OR 97221 Office: Hillsboro Union High Sch 645 NE Lincoln Hillsboro OR 97124

MOORE, MICHAEL EDWARD, health care facility administrator; b. Cin., Mar. 22, 1948; s. Edward Thornton and Mary Lou (Johnston) M.; m. Rebecca Doerr, Sept. 7, 1968; 1 child, Kelly. BSBA, U. Cin., 1974; MS in Healthcare Planning, Calif. State U., Sacramento, 1976. Assoc. adminstr. Community Hosp. Sacramento, 1974-76; adminstr. Pulmonary Medicine Assn., Sacramento, 1976-83; chief adminstrv. officer Sutter Hosps. Found., Sacramento, 1983—. Mem. adv. com. Calif. Polit. Action Com., 1986-88. Mem. Nat. Assn. Hosp. Devel. (bd. dirs. 1987-88), Sacramento C. of C., Active 20-30 (bd. dirs. 1980-81), Rotary (pres. 1985-86). Democrat. Presbyterian. Office: Sutter Hosps Found 2800 L St Sacramento CA 95816

MOORE, MITCHELL DEE, naval officer; b. Salt Lake City, Apr. 4, 1947; s. Val Clair and Beverly Dean (Maughan) M.; m. Deborah Dianne Pierce, Aug. 27, 1971; children: Sean, Candice, Aaron, Kimberly, Darcy. BS, U.S. Naval Acad., 1969. Commd. ensign USN, 1969; advanced through grades to comdr. to date, officer programs dept., head Navy Recruiting Dist. Portland, 1976-79; officer program trainer Command Orientation Unit, Orlando, Fla., 1979-80; student replacement pilot tng. VA-122 Lemoore, Calif., 1980-81; A7E pilot, maintenance/safety officer, VA-25 1981-83, A4 adversary instr. pilot, ops./adminstrn. officer VA-127, 1983-85; commanding officer Navy Recruiting Dist. Albuquerque, 1985-87, Navy Recruiting Dist. San Francisco, Oakland, Calif., 1987—. Active Boy Scouts Am. Recipient Navy Commendation medal, Meritorious Svc. medal. Mem. Assn. Naval Aviators, U.S. Naval Acad. Alumni Assn. Republican. Mormon. Home: 1212 Summit View Dr Concord CA 94521 Office: Navy Recruiting Dist San Francisco 1500 Broadway Oakland CA 94612

MOORE, MONICA MARGARET, real estate appraiser; b. East St. Louis, Ill., Mar. 12, 1942; d. Howard R. and Lela Catherine (Howard) M.; m. David Grover Fish, Jan. 8, 1977; stepchildren: David Joseph, Mary Kathryn, Robert Norman. BEd, Webster U., 1964; MS, So. Ill. U., 1970. Cert. tchr., Mo. Music tchr. East St. Louis Schs., 1964-70; social worker Children & Family Services, East St. Louis, 1970-73; administrator Sr. citizen Program, Lewis County, Wash., 1973-74, County of Orange, Calif., 1974-77; pres., chief exec. officer Fish & Moore Appraisers Inc., Corona Del Mar, Calif., 1977—. Chmn. 15th and 20th Coll. Reunion Webster U., 1979-84. Mem. Soc. Real Estate Appraisers (vice chmn. internat. chpt. services com. 1987—, vice gov. dist. 5 1983-88, treas. Calif. legis. steering com. govtl. regulation of appraiser 1985—), Sigma Alpha Iota. Democrat. Presbyterian. Home and Office: Fish & Moore Appraisers Inc 429 Marigold Ave Corona Del Mar CA 92625

MOORE, PHYLLIS CLARK, librarian; b. Binghamton, N.Y., Jan. 31, 1927; d. John Oscar and Gladys Jeanette (Tilbury) Clark; BA, Hartwick Coll., 1949; MS in Libr. Sci., Syracuse U., 1954 ; PhD, U. Wis., 1971; LittD, Colo. State U., 1973; DLS (hon.) Marquis Giuseppe Scicluna Internat. U., Malta, 1987; m. R(oberts) Scott Wellington Moore, Sept. 14, 1954 (dec. 1979); m. Donald S. Wolfe, Feb. 16, 1988. Librarian Free Library Phila., 1954-57; Librarian-adminstr. GS-9 main reference/Interloan Center, dir. 22 spl. services libraries mt. Stuttgart, Fed. Republic Germany, U.S. Govt. Spl. Services Europe, 1957-62; dept. Head young adult, fine arts, audiovisual, reference Yonkers (N.Y.) Pub. Library, 1962-67; dir. Hastings-on-Hudson (N.Y.) Pub. Library, 1967-68; cons. audio-visual services Westchester County (N.Y.) Library System, 1968-72; dir. Falls Church (Va.) Pub. Library, 1972-77; city librarian Alameda Free Library; library supr. Ojai (Calif.) Unified Sch. Dist., 1984-87; library cons., Ojai Valley Estates, 1987—; research dir. Underwater Sealabs, Bremerhaven, W. Ger., 1960-61; tech. advisor Community Action Program Yonkers, N.Y., 1965-68. Chancel choir Ojai Presbyn. Ch. Active Nat. Humane Soc., Recording Service for Visually Handicapped. Mem. ALA (exec. council 1975-79), Internat. Oceanographic Found., Nat. Assn. Sch. and Media Librarians, Mask and Lute (pres. 1974), Nat. Health and Welfare Assn. (exec. bd.), Defenders of Wildlife (adv. council), Greenpeace, U.S.A., Bay Area Library and Info. System (chairperson 1978-79), Audio Philharmonic Soc. (pres. 1983-84), Ojai Valley Hist. Mus., Ojai Art Ctr. Author: Beneath the Sea, 1974; Command Performance, 1975; Blues in the Bibliotheque, 1979; A Catchy Title, 1980; Beyond the Blues, 1981; Girls of Yesteryear, 1983-84 (nat. TV prodn. award). Contbr. articles to profl. publs. Home: 25 Juniper Ln Ojai CA 93023 Office: 1975 Maricopa Hwy Ste 25 Ojai CA 93023

MOORE, RANDOLPH GRAVES, real estate company executive; b. Honolulu, Feb. 12, 1939; s. Howard Hoffman and Mary May (Phillips) M.; m. Lynne Johnson, Nov. 8, 1979; children: Allison, Juliet. BA, Swarthmore Coll., 1961; MBA, Stanford U., 1963. Vol. Peace Corps, Brenerville, Liberia, 1963-65; fin. analyst Castle & Cooke, Inc., Honolulu, 1966-70, treas., 1970-74, group controller, 1974-77; from sr. v.p. to exec. v.p. Oceanic Properties, Inc., Honolulu, 1977-84, pres., 1984-86; pres. Molokai Ranch, Ltd., 1986-89; chief exec. officer Kanedre Ranch Co., 1989—. Home: 2447 Makiki Heights Dr Honolulu HI 96822

MOORE, ROGER A., banker; b. Hardin County, Ohio, Sept. 30, 1941; s. Carl H. and Lillian Louise (Gossard) M.; m. Kaye E. Smith, Nov. 24, 1961; children: Kendra K., Karen R., Molly M. BSBS, Ohio No. U., 1964; MBA, U. Va., 1977. From mgmt. trainee to v.p. Huntington Nat. Bank, Columbus, Ohio, 1963-78; v.p., regional mgr. Crocker Bank, San Francisco, 1978-86; pres., chief exec. officer East County Bank, Antioch, Calif., 1986—; instr. Am. Inst. for Banking, Columbus, 1974-78. Named Trustee of Yr. Haviland Civic Assn., Columbus, 1966, 68. Mem. Antioch C. of C. (various offices 1986—), Rotary, Masons. Republican. Office: East County Bank 315 G St PO Box 619 Antioch CA 94509

MOORE, SIDNEY DWAYNE, engineering executive, inventor; b. Monahans, Tex., June 2, 1938; s. Sidney Augusta and Florence Elizabeth (Van Loh) M.; m. Peggy Caffey, June 11, 1959; 1 child, Adam C. Student, Pratt Inst., 1956-57; BFA, U. Tex., 1963; MFA, R.I. Sch. of Design, Providence, 1965. Pvt. practice artist N.Y.C., 1965-69; asst. prof. Drexel U., Phila., 1969-74; owner, operator Camera Craft Photo-Tech Ctr., Prescott, Ariz., 1974-86; engring. mgr. Bushnell Div., Bausch & Lomb, San Dimas, Calif., 1986—; teaching fellow R.I. Sch. Design, Providence, 1963-65. Inventor, microcomputer-controlled rangefinding and aiming-compensating device for projectile firing apparatuses, microcontroller-controlled active reticle for microscopes, and locking device for binocular focusing mechanism. With U.S. Army, 1958-60. Mem. NASA Indsl. Applications Ctr. (assoc.), Soc. Advancement Materials & Process Engring., Internat. Soc. for Optical Engring., Am. Soc. Design Engrs.

MOORE, STANLEY W., political science professor; b. Camden, N.J., Feb. 11, 1937; s. Frank Stafford and Alma Beatrice (Law) M.; m. Nancy Joan Crawford, Sept. 1, 1961; children: David Crawford, Andrea Katrina, Stanley Edward Stafford Moore, Beth. AB magna cum laude, Wheaton (Ill.) Coll., 1959; MA and PhD in Govt., Claremont (Calif.) Grad. Sch., 1971. Asst. prof. polit. sci. Calif. State U.-Stainslaus, Turlock, 1967-69, Monterey (Calif.) Inst. for Internat. Studies, 1969-72; vis. assoc. U. Redlands, Calif., 1972-73; assoc. prof. Pepperdine U., Malibu, Calif., 1973-79, prof. polit. sci., 1979—. Author: A Child's Political World: A Longitudinal Perspective, 1985; contbr. articles to profl. jours. Mem. CROP Walk Com., Thousand Oaks, Calif., 1979—; scoutmaster Troop 761 Boy Scouts Am., 1981—; mem. Ventura County Air Pollution Control Bd., 1981—, Ventura County Beyond the Yr. 2,000 Commn., 1988—; appointed by Calif. Senate as Ctr. for Edn. in Pub. Affairs, 1986—; bd. dirs. Calif. Bicentennial Found. for U.S. Constn., 1988—; commr. Calif. Bicentennial Commn., 1988—; mem. Nat. Dem. Party, Calif. Dem. Party, Conejo Valley (Calif.) Dem. Party. Cleve. Found. grantee 1977, Spencer Found. of Chgo. grantee, 1979, 81; recipient BSA medal of honor for saving life, 1989. Fellow Am. Sci. Affiliation; mem. Am. Polit. Sci. Assn., Western Polit. Sci. Assn., So. Calif. Polit. Sci. Assn. (pres. 1988—), So. Calif. Soc. for Internat. Devel. (pres. 1988—), Internat. Studies Assn., Internat. Security Studies Subsect., Sierra, Aubudon Soc., Nature Conservancy, Nat. Wildlife Fedn. Presbyterian (elder). Home: 1756 Campbell Ave Thousand Oaks CA 91360 Office: Pepperdine U Dept Polit Sci Malibu CA 90265

MOORE, TERRY W., real estate developer; b. Ft. Worth, July 27, 1949; s. Bill and Sue M.; m. Sandra Lynne McElvany, Dec. 3, 1977. BBA, Okla. U., 1971; MBA, So. Meth. U., Dallas, 1973. comml. loan officer Bank of Am., San Diego, 1973-77; corp. planner Nat. Pen Corp., San Diego, 1977-79; pres. Handy Hardware, Norman, Okla., 1980-85; prin. Terry Moore Cons., San Diego, 1985-87; ptnr. Devel. Systems, San Diego, 1987—. Mem. Cert. Comml. Investment. Office: Devel Systems 3665 Kearny Villa #355 San Diego CA 92123

MOORE, TERRY WILLIAM, psychologist; b. Columbus, Ohio, Apr. 4, 1946; s. George F. and Kathryn V. (Harrison) M.; m. Conny J. Loach, June 21, 1969; 1 child, Lara Christy. BA, Ohio State U., 1969; MA, U. Wyo., 1974, PhD, 1982. Counselor vocat. rehab. Ohio State Reformatory, Mansfield, Ohio, 1969-71, City of Mansfield, 1971-72, Laramie County Community Coll., Cheyenne, Wyo., 1973-74; psychotherapist Washington County Mental Health Ctr., Marietta, Ohio, 1974-75, S.E. Wyo. Mental Health Ctr., Laramie, Wyo., 1975-84; outpatient clin. dir. Coconino Community Guidance Ctr., Flagstaff, Ariz., 1984-87, psychologist, 1987—; adj. prof. Union Grad. Sch., Cin., 1986-88; cons. Vocat. Rehab., Flagstaff, 1988—; mem. assoc. staff Flagstaff Med. Ctr., 1988—, Charter Psychiat. Hosp., Phoenix, 1988—. Trustee Federated Community Ch., Flagstaff, 1987, 88. U. Wyo. scholar, 1982. Mem. Am. Psychol. Assn., Ariz. Psychol. Assn. (bd. dirs. Flagstaff chpt. 1988), Assn. Clin. Mental Health Counselors, Phi Kappa Phi. Democrat. Office: Coconino Community Guidance Ctr 823 N San Francisco St Flagstaff AZ 86001

MOORE, WILEY LYNN, transportation executive; b. Warrensburg, Mo., Sept. 29, 1946; s. Abe Leslie and Laurene (Fuel) M.; m. June Feragen, Sept. 17, 1984; 1 child, Colby Lauren. BS in Chemistry, U. Mo., 1968. Capt. Continental Airlines, L.A., 1983-85; airbus capt. Continental Airlines, Denver, 1985—. Lt. comdr. USN, 1968-78. Republican. Home: 4868 Beach Dr Seattle WA 98116

MOORE, WILLIAM BYRON, real estate executive; b. Hutchinson, Kans., Apr. 18, 1925; s. Claude Sorency and Barbara Morma (Mitchell) M. BS, U. Colo., 1946. Jr. test engr. Pratt & Whitney, Hartford, 1946-47; engr. Spencer Chem. Co., Pitts., 1948-57; engring. mgmt. Spencer Chem. Co., Orange, Tex., 1958-64; project coordinator Gulf Oil Co., London, 1964-65; ops. mgr. Kuwait Chemicals, 1968-70; chemicals adv. Iberian Gulf Oil, Reston, Va., 1972-79; mgr., cons. Gulf Oil Real Estate, Pitts., 1979-81; mgr. area projects Gulf Oil Real Estate, Denver, 1982-83; v.p. BetaWest Properties, Inc., Denver, 1984—; bd. dirs. Fairfax County Vocat. Pres. Am. Sch. Bd. Kuwait, 1966-70. With USN, 1944-46. Mem. Urban Land Inst., Colo. Nat. Assn. Realtors, Real Estate Inst., Nat. Assn. Corp. Real Estate Execs. (bd. dirs. 1988—). Home: 6240 South Iola Way Englewood CO Office: BetaWest Properties Inc 1999 Broadway Suite 200 Denver CO

MOORE, WILLIAM JAMES, newspaper editor; b. Corpus Christi, Tex., Oct. 7, 1943; s. Edwin R. and Mary Wilson (Clokey) Ross M.; m. Ann Sare Bancroft, May 2, 1976; 1 child, Matthew. BA in Communication and Polit. Sci., Stanford U., 1965, MA in Communication, 1966. Reporter Ariz. Daily Star, Tucson, Ariz., 1962; editor Stanford (Calif.) Daily, 1964; reporter San Francisco Chronicle, 1967-79; news editor Oakland (Calif.) Tribune-Eastbay Today, 1979-81; met. editor Sacramento Bee McClatchy Newspapers, 1982, editor Forum, 1982—. Press asst., vol. Robert F. Kennedy Presdl. campaign, San Francisco, 1968; vol. VISTA, San Juan, P.R., 1966-67. Served with USCGR, 1967-73. Democrat. Office: Sacramento Bee PO Box 15779 Sacramento CA 95852

MOORE, WILLIAM JOSEPH, management executive; b. Banks, Oreg., Dec. 3, 1923; s. Charles Windsor and Eva Belle (Schulmerich) M.; m. Mary Louise Talcott, Nov. 3, 1945; children: Jeffry Talcott, William Andrew, Colleen Louise. BS In Aero. Engring., U. Colo., 1957. Commd. 2d lt. USAF, 1944, advance through grades to lt. col., 1964, navigator, meteorologist, mil. pilot, 1944-58; pilot, aero engr., comdr. flight test engring. div., USAF, Patterson AFB, Ohio, 1958-63; staff officer Hdqrs. Air Force Systems Command, Andrews AFB, Md., 1963-64, advisor, evaluator, test pilot, 1964-65; ret. USAF, 1965; pilot United Airlines, 1965-68, capt., pilot, 1969-84; 1st v.p., co founder, dir. Moore Nat. Lease Corp., Portland, Oreg., 1972-82; dir. Resource Systems Corp., Portland, Oreg., 1988—. Mem. Am. Meteorol. Soc., Airline Pilots Assn., Air Force Assn., Tau Beta Pi, Phi Delta Theta. Republican. Episcopalian. Home: 31655 Arbor Glen Loop Wilsonville OR 97070

MOORE, WILLIS HENRY ALLPHIN, state official; b. N.Y.C., Dec. 14, 1940; s. Carl Allphin and Mary Catherine (Moody) M.; children: Patrick Kakela, Michael Kirby, Catherine Malia. BA Letters, U. Okla., 1962; MEd in Adminstrn., U. Hawaii, 1971. Teaching asst. dept. history U. Hawaii, 1962-64; dir. edn. Bernice P. Bishop Museum, Honolulu, 1967-76; pres. Hawaii Geog. Soc., Honolulu, 1976-78, exec. sec., chief cartographer, 1978—; mem. Hawaii Com. for Humanities, 1976—; producer, narrator film-lecture programs Nat. Aududon Soc. and travelogue forums; instr. in Hawaiian culture and Hawaiian studies Hawaii Loa Coll. and U. Hawaii system, 1970—, Chaminade U. of Honolulu, 1987—; lectr. in field. Co-author/co-editor: Hawaii Parklands; contbr. articles to Honolulu Advertiser, Pacific Daily News, Guam, Pacific Mag., Honolulu Star-Bull. U.S. Info. Svc. Honolulu Reception Ctr. escort, 1962—. Mem. N.Am. Cartographic Info. Soc., Am. Museums Assn., Pacific Sci. Assn., Hawaii Mus. Assn. (pres. 1972-74), Pacific Area Travel Assn., Hawaii Pub. Radio, Am. Guild Organists (v.p. Hawaii chpt.), Sierra Club (chmn. Hawaii chpt. 1973-75), Hawaiian Hist. Soc., Honolulu Press Club, NSAL Club (Honolulu). Office: PO Box 1698 Honolulu HI 96806

MOORHEAD, CARLOS J., congressman; b. Long Beach, Calif., May 6, 1922; s. Carlos Arthur and Florence (Gravers) M.; m. Valery Joan Tyler, July 19, 1969; children: Theresa, Catharine, Steven, Teri, Paul. B.A., UCLA, 1943; J.D., U. So. Calif., 1949. Bar: Calif. 1949, U.S. Supreme Ct. 1973. Pvt. practice law Glendale, Calif., 1949-72; dir. Lawyers Reference Service, Glendale, 1950-66; mem. 93d-101st congresses from 22d Dist. Calif., Judiciary Com., Energy and Commerce Com.; dean Calif. Rep. Delegation. Pres. Glendale Hi-Twelve Club; mem. Verdugo Hills council Boy Scouts Am.; mem. Calif. Assembly, 1967-72; mem. Calif. Law Revision Commn., 1971-72; pres. 43d Dist. Republican Assembly, Glendale Young Republicans; mem. Los Angeles County Rep. Central Com., Calif. Rep. Central Com.; dean Calif. Congresional Rep. Delegation; pres. Glendale La Crescenta Camp Fire Girls, Inc. Served to lt. col. AUS, 1942-46. Recipient Man of Yr. award USO, 1979. Mem. Calif. Bar Assn., Angeles County Bar Assn., Glendale Bar Assn. (past pres.), Glendale C. of C., Masons, Shriners, Lions, Moose, VFW. Presbyterian. Office: US Ho of Reps 2346 Rayburn House Office Bldg Washington DC 20515

MOORHEAD, RUTH ANNE, small business owner; b. Deer Park, Calif., Mar. 17, 1948; d. Lowell O. "Peter" and Anne (Rowell) M. BA, U. Calif., Davis, 1971. Typist U. Calif., Davis, 1971-77; typist Walla Walla (Wash.) Community Coll., 1980-85, instr., 1982-85; instr. Idaho State U., Pocatello, 1986—; direct mail specialist 1987—. Author: (poetry collection) Sand Ripples, 1974. Dir., creator Womenspace, Walla Walla, 1980-85. Mem. Blue Mountain Audubon Soc., Walla Walla (pres. 1981-83), Nature Study Soc. Am., Portneuf Valley Audubon Soc. (membership chmn. 1986—), Wheatland Wheelers Bicycling Club (bd. dirs. 1979-85). Home: 1425 E Hayden St Pocatello ID 83201

MOORHOUSE, DOUGLAS CECIL, engineering consulting company executive; b. Oakland, Calif., Feb. 24, 1926; s. Cecil and Lynda (Roe) M.; BS in Civil Engring., U. Calif., Berkeley, 1950, postgrad., 1961; student Advanced Mgmt. Program, Harvard U., 1973; m. Dorothy Johnson; children: Scott, Jan. Research and resident engr. State of Calif. Div. Hwys., 1950-59; dir. San Diego office Woodward-Clyde & Assos., 1959-62; pres. Woodward-Moorhouse & Assos., 1962-73; pres., chief exec. officer Woodward-Clyde Cons., San Francisco, 1973-87; chief exec. officer, chmn. bd. dirs. Woodward-Clyde Group Inc., 1988—. Trustee, World Coll. West; mem. adv. com., dept. engring. U. Calif. Berkeley. Pres. Hazardous Waste Action Coalition, 1988-89. Served with inf. U.S. Army. Mem. Nat. Acad. Engring., ASCE (Wesley W. Horner award 1979). Office: Woodward-Clyde Group Inc 600 Montgomery St 30th Fl San Francisco CA 94111

MORAIN, MARY STONE DEWING, association executive; b. Boston, Mar. 18, 1911; d. Arthur S. and Frances (Hall Rousmaniere) Dewing; student Radcliffe Coll., 1930-33; BS, Simmons Sch. Social Work, 1934; MA, U. Chgo., 1937; cert. social work U. So. Calif., 1941; m. Lloyd L. Morain, July 6, 1946. Social worker, Calif., N.Y.C., 1941-45; tchr. social scis. Keuka Coll., N.Y., 1945-46; v.p. LWV, Boston, 1946-53; bd. dirs., v.p. Planned Parenthood League Mass., 1948-52; bd. dirs., pres. Planned Parenthood Assn. San Francisco, 1953-60; bd. dirs. Internat. Humanist and Ethical Union, 1953-65; bd. dirs., v.p. Assn. Vol. Sterilization, 1963-77, 79—, UNESCO Assn. U.S.A., 1977—, Monterey YWCA, 1975-80, UN Assn. San Francisco, 1961-69; pres. Internat. Soc. Gen. Semantics, 1976-85, v.p. mem. 1985—; bd. dir. Tor House Found., 1984—. . Fellow World Acad. Art and Sci.; mem. Am. Assn. Social Workers. Club: Altrusa. Author: (with Lloyd Morain) Humanism as the Next Step, 1954; contbr. articles to profl. jours. Editor: Teaching General Semantics, 1969; Classroom Exercises in General Semantics, 1980; Bridging Worlds through General Semantics, 1984; Enriching Professional Skills Through General Semantics, 1986. Home: PO Box 7190 Carmel CA 93921 Office: PO Box 2469 San Francisco CA 94126

MORALES, ARMANDO, psychotherapist, educator; b. Los Angeles, Sept. 18, 1932; s. Roberto Torres and Lupe (Acevedo) M.; m. Rebecca Gonzales, Aug. 27, 1955 (div. Apr. 1980); children: Roland Victor, Gary Vincent. AA, East Los Angeles Jr. Coll., 1955; BA, Los Angeles State Coll., 1957; MSW, U. So. Calif. Sch. Social Work, 1963, DSW, 1971. Diplomate Am. Bd. Clin. Social Work. Gang group worker Los Angeles Times Boys Club, 1954-57; sr. dep. probation officer Los Angeles County Probation Dept., 1957-63, Las Palmas Sch. for Girls, Los Angeles County Probation Dept., 1963-66; supervising psychiat. social worker, mental health cons. Los Angeles County Dept. Mental Health, 1966-71; prof., chief clin. social work dept., dir. Spanish speaking psychosocial clinic, dir. intern tng. program Neuropsychiat. Inst. UCLA Sch. Medicine, 1971—; cons. Calif. Youth Authority, East Los Angeles, 1977—; speaker in field. Author: Ando Sangrando: A Study of Mexican American-Police Conflict, 1972, Social Work: A Profession of Many Faces, 1977, 80, 83, 86, 89; co-editor The Psychosocial Development of Minority Group Children, 1983; composer ethnic songs. pres. Western Ctr. on Law and Poverty, Inc., Los Angeles, 1975-77, bd. dirs., 1968-78; vice chmn. Citizens Adv. Council, Calif. Dept. Mental Health, 1977-82. Served as sgt. USAF, 1951-54. Appointed to Pres.' Commn. on Mental Health Task Panel on Legal and Ethical Issues, 1977-78; fellow NIMH, 1962, 69, 77; named Far East Air Force Bantamweight Champion, 1952, 53. Mem. Nat. Assn. Social Workers (cert.), Trabajadores de La Raza, Council on Mental Health Western Interstate Commn. for Higher Edn., 1976-78 (chmn.), Commn. Human Relations (commr., v.p. 1975-78). Democrat. Roman Catholic. Office: UCLA Sch Medicine Neuropsychiatric Inst 760 Westwood Pla Los Angeles CA 90024

MORAN, ELIZABETH JANE, educational administrator; b. Greenville, Miss., Sept. 30, 1918; d. Robert Harold and Jane Hoisington (Griffin) Crawford; m. R. Richard Moran Jr., Aug. 11, 1940 (div. Oct. 1978); children: R. Richard III, Linda Jean Moran Kelley, Jocelyn Kay Moran Jackson, Marcia Elizabeth Moran Ahlansberg. BA, Ind. U., 1942; MA, San Jose State U., 1963. Tchr. South Bend (Ind.) Pub. Schs., 1943-45, Los Gatos (Calif.) Pub. Schs., 1959-60; assoc. prof. Santa Clara (Calif.) U., 1963—, dir. faculty devel. and grad. fellowships, 1978-86, dir. Teaching and Learning Ctr., 1986—; tchr. Peace Corps, San Jose State U., 1965. Elder 1st Presbyn. Ch., Palo Alto, Calif., 1983-86, chair Adult Study Com., 1983-86. Fellow Danforth Found. Stanford U., 1971-72, assoc., 1977-86; grantee Eli Lilly Found., 1975. Mem. AAUW (research fellow 1983), African Lit. Assn., Mortar Bd., Phi Beta Kappa (sec. Santa Clara U. chpt. 1984-86, pres. No. Calif. 1974-75, sec. Western Dist. United Chpts. 1979-85, chair 1985—, chpt. pres. 1977-79, 81-83). Presbyterian. Home: 933 College Dr San Jose CA 95128 Office: Santa Clara U Dept English Santa Clara CA 95053

MORAN, FRANCIS JOSEPH, JR., marine engineer; b. Greenwich, Conn., Jan. 18, 1937; s. Francis Joseph and Emma Elizabeth (Babcock) M.; m. Barbara Carol Bastian, June 30, 1962 (div. 1979); children: Douglas, Robert, Katherine Lee; m. Patricia Anne Kane, May 17, 1979; stepchildren: Maureen Quillen, Wendy Lynn Taylor, Sandra Lee Taylor. BS in Engring., U.S. Naval Acad., 1958; BS in Marine Engring., Webb Inst., Glen Cove, N.Y., 1968, MS in Naval Architecture, 1968; postgrad., Diablo Valley Coll., 1984. Cert. tchr., Calif. Commd. ensign USN, 1958, advanced through grades to commander, ret., 1978; v.p., dir. west coast div. Epoch Engring., Inc., Gaithersburg, Md., 1978-83; gen. ptnr. Moran and Dobie, Concord, Calif., 1983-84; program mgr. prodn. work control systems and cost analysis Merit Systems, Inc., Bremerton, Wash., 1984-87; sr. engr. Merit Systems, Inc., Bremerton, 1987—. Patentee in field. Active Nat. Taxpayers Union, Washington, 1988—, Calif. Tax Reduction Movement, 1988—. Decorated Navy Commendation medal, Navy Spl. Ops. medal, Nat. Defense medal. Mem. Soc. Naval Architects and Marine Engrs., Am. Soc. Naval Engrs. Roman Catholic. Home: 1774 Thornwood Dr Concord CA 94521

MORAN, GENE, information systems designer; b. Portsmouth, Va., Dec. 29, 1963; s. Earnest Eugene and Dianna Marie (Vandehey) M. BA in Systems Analysis, Linfield Coll., McMinnville, Oreg., 1986. Project asst. ABA Groups, Hermosa Beach, Calif., 1986; asst. projcet mgr. ABA Groups, Hermosa Beach, 1986; data base adminstr. Info. Resources Inc./ABA Groups, Manhattan Beach, Calif., 1986-87; field supr., Nat. Product Library Info. Resources Inc./ABA Groups, Manhattan Beach, 1987—; group product sales mgr. Dbase products Ashton-Tate, Torrance, Calif., 1988—. Mem. Pi Kappa Alpha (sgt. of arms 1984-86, grounds security 1986). Home: 22912 Maple Ave #4 Torrance CA 90505

MORAN, SHEILA KATHLEEN, theatrical producer; b. Norwalk, Conn.; d. Edmond Joseph and Alice Marie (Laux) M.; m. John Joseph Reynolds, Apr. 2, 1987. BA, Manhattanville Coll., Purchase, N.Y. Sportswriter, reporter AP, N.Y.C., 1969-71, N.Y. Post, N.Y.C., 1972-76, L.A. Times, 1976-80; actress, freelance writer L.A., 1981—; producer Evensong Assocs., Los Angeles, 1987—. Vol. VA Hosp., L.A., 1987—. Mem. AFTRA, Screen Actors Guild, Actors' Equity Assn. Democrat. Roman Catholic.

MORAN, THOMAS HARRY, university administrator; b. Milw., Oct. 21, 1937; s. Harry Edward and Edna Agnes Moran; BS, U. Wis., 1964, MA, 1972, PhD, 1974; m. Barbara Ellen Saklad, June 10, 1969; children: David Thomas, Karen Ellen. Dir. capital budgeting Wis. Dept. Adminstrn., 1962-64; exec. dir. Wis. Higher Ednl. Aids Bd., 1964-69; spl. cons. tax policy Wis. Dept. Revenue, 1973-74; dep. dir. Wis. Manpower Coun., Office of Gov., 1974-76; v.p. bus. and fin., treas. U. Detroit, 1976-78; exec. assoc. v.p. health affairs U. So. Calif., L.A., 1979-87; v.p. bus. affairs, 1988—. USN fellow, 1957-59; U.S. Office Edn. rsch. fellow, 1973. Mem. Am. Assn. Higher Edn., Phi Kappa Phi. Office: U So Calif 349 Adminstrn Bldg University Park Los Angeles CA 90007

MORAND, BLAISE E., bishop; b. Tecumseh, Ont., Can., Sept. 12, 1932. Ordained priest Roman Cath. Ch., 1958. Ordained coadjutor bishop Diocese of Prince Albert, Sask., Can., 1981, bishop, 1983—. Office: 1415 4th Ave W, Prince Albert, SK Canada S6V 5H1 *

MORBY, JACK JERALD, JR., infosytems specialist; b. White Salmon, Wash., Jan. 17, 1952; s. Jack Jerald Sr. and Mildred May (White) M.; m. Dian Marie Kinzey, Dec. 17, 1983. BA in Math., Wash. State U., 1974. Systems analyst trainee Systems Engring. & Computer Svcs., Portland, Oreg., 1974-75; with Oreg. Health Scis. U., Portland, 1975—, acting data processing mgr., 1981-82, project mgr. hosp. info. systems, 1982—. Race chmn. John Craig Meml. Cross-Country Ski Race, Oreg. Nordic Club, Sisters, Oreg., 1983; stewardship chmn. Community Ch. of Cedar Hills, Portland, 1988. Fellow Data Processing Mgmt. Assn., Oreg. Health Scis. U. Mgmt. Soc.; mem. Project Mgmt. Inst. (treas. 1988—), Oreg. Nordic Club (pres. Portland chpt. 1981-82), Bill Koch Youth Ski League (chmn. Portland chpt. 1980-81), Elks. Republican. Home: 11905 SW Douglas Portland OR 97225

MORE, VISHWAS DATTAG, laboratory administrator; b. Kolhapur, India, July 5, 1936; came to U.S., 1958; s. Dattagi Jagtap and Parvati M.; m. Sheila More, Sept. 30, 1958; children: Anil, Sanjiv, Dev, Sonya. BS, U. Mich., 1951, MS, 1953. Project engr. Air Conditioning Corp., Bombay, India, 1958-62; mech. engr. Abbott Lab., North Chgo., Ill., 1962-66; plant engr. Argonne (Ill.) Nat. Lab. U. Chgo., 1966-74; chief engr. Posotron Electron Project U. Calif., Stanford U., 1974-78; project mgr. Cell Culture Lab. U. Calif., 1979-80; plant engr., head dept. Lawrence Lab. U. Calif., Berkeley, 1978-83, project mgr., 1982-83, project mgr. Ctr. for Advanced Materials, 1984—; cons. to various other nat. projects funded by Fed. Govt. Fund raising host for U.S. Senator Pete Wilson; mem. Rep. Presdl. Task Force, Senatorial Inner Cir., 1989. Mem. Prominent Indians in Am. (exec. v.p. 1982). Hindu. Home: 506 Tahos Rd Orinda CA 94563 Office: U Calif Lawrence Berkeley Lab Berkeley CA 94720

MOREHEAD, DOUGLAS CHARLES, property management executive; b. St. Joseph, Mo., June 18, 1946; s. Raymond Warren and Dorothy M. (Gurley) M.; m. Susan Starr, May 12, 1984. BS, Ariz. State U., 1971. Mgr. Hyatt Hotels Corp., Anaheim, Calif., 1968-70; ptnr. Timely Products Corp., Anaheim, 1970-74; regional mgr. R&B Enterprises, L.A. and Houston, 1974-82; pres. property mgmt. Triton Nat. Co., Irvine, Calif., 1983-88; pres. Optima Capital Mgmt., Inc., Irvine, 1988—. Chmn., founder No-Name Invitational Charity Golf Tournament, Palm Springs, Calif., 1983—; bd. dirs. Aid to the Adoption of Spl. Kids. Mem. Bldg. Owners and Mgrs. Assn. Orange County, Comml. Indsl. Devel. Assn., Masons. Republican. Presbyterian. Home: 425 Via Lido Nord Newport Beach CA 92663

MORELAND, RONALD WILLIAM, insurance company executive; b. Decatur, Ill., Dec. 14, 1940; s. John William and Susan Irene (Daniels) M.; m. Jean Ann Cloyd, June 15, 1963 (div. 1976); children: Michael, Susan; m. Randi Elaine Thompson, June 3, 1984; 1 child, Lindsey. BEd, Eastern Ill. U., 1962; MEd, U. Ill., 1963. CLU. Group mgr. Prudential Ins. Co., Chgo., 1963-68; regional mgr. Prudential Ins. Co., San Francisco, 1968-71; dir. group ins. Prudential Ins. Co., Newark, 1971-73, N.Y.C., 1973-78; v.p. group ins. Prudential Ins. Co., Los Angeles, 1978-83; exec. v.p. Transamerica Occidental Life Ins. Co., Los Angeles, 1983-88; pres. Western Ops. Equicor, Los Angeles, 1988—. Mem. Wilshire County Club. Clubs: Jonathan (Los Angeles); Beverly Hills Country (Cheviot Hills, Calif.). Office: 3435 Wilshire Blvd Los Angeles CA 90010

MORELLI, ROBERT HASTINGS, management; b. San Mateo, Calif., Mar. 25, 1947; s. Ernest Edward and Mary Ella (Hodges) M.; m. Val May Klemzak, June 14,. AA, Coll Redwoods, 1972; BA, Humboldt State U., 1975. Re-devel. acct. Eureka Redevel. (Calif.) Agy., 1975-76; fin. housing officer Eureka Redevel. Agy., 1976-78; asst. exec. dir. Housing Authorities, Eureka, 1978-82, exec. dir., 1982—; cons. HUD, Eureka, 1986—. Mem. City of Eureka Housing Adv. Bd., 1987-88, Humboldt County Habitat for Humanity. Mem. No. Calif. Execs. Dirs. Assn., Nev. Exec. Dirs. Assn., Nat. Assn. of Housing and Redevel. Officials, Rotary. Democrat. Office: Housing Authorities 735 W Everding St Eureka CA 95501

MORENO, FERNANDO, infosystems specialist; b. Juan Aldama, Mex., May 13, 1946; came to U.S., 1962; s. Federico Moreno and Esperanza (Rodrigues) Rangel; m. Carol L. Berry, Aug. 18, 1973; children: Michael Alan, Debra Gaumont, Brian James. BA in Gen. Scis., Roosevelt U., Chgo., 1975. Team leader Fin. Info. Svcs., Chgo., 1973-78; mgr. Covia, Englewood, Colo., 1978—; owner, founder Moreno Enterprises, Ltd., Chgo., 1981—, Micro Computes Plus, Aurora, Colo., 1987—. Cons. Hispanic Assn. Career Advancement, Chgo., 1987—. With U.S. Army, 1965-67. Democrat. Roman Catholic. Home: 5773 S Killarney Way Aurora CO 80015 Office: Covia Denver Tech Ctr 5350 S Valentia Way Englewood CO 80111

MORENO, MANUEL D., bishop. Educ. Univ. of Calif., Los Angeles, St. John's Sem., Camarillo, Calif. Ordained priest Roman Cath. church, 1961. Ordained aux. bishop of Los Angeles, titular bishop of Tanagra, 1977; installed as bishop of Tucson, 1982. Office: 192 S Stone Ave PO Box 31 Tucson AZ 85702 *

MORENO, MICHAEL ANTHONY, loan officer, sales contractor; b. Los Angeles, Aug. 16, 1958; s. Gilbert Lopez and Jenny (Olivas) M. BA, Calif. State Polytechnic U., 1982. Lic. real estate sales, vehicle lic. sales, Calif. With The Broadway, Montclair, Calif., 1981-84; asst. div. mgr. electronics, then major appliance sales Montgomery Ward, Montclair, 1984-87; sales contractor to Los Angeles companies Golden State Wrecker Sales, Santa Ana, Calif., 1987-88; ind. sales contractor Tow Industries, Inc., Los Angeles, 1988; loan officer Transactions Plus, Brea, Calif., 1988, sr. loan officer, 1989—; v.p. in charge new accounts East San Gabriel Valley, 1989—, San Bernardino and Riverside counties, 1989—. Active Community Action Com., Montclair, Calif., 1985— (chmn. 1986, vice-chmn. 1987, liason to Athletic Adv. Com. 1986—). Mem. Am. Mgmt. Assn. (invited), Riverside Tow Truck Assn. (assoc.), Calif. Tow Truck Assn. (San Bernardino, Riverside and Los Angeles chpts), Bldg. Industry Assn. (rep. So. Calif. chpt.), Pomona Valley Bd. Realtors (rep.), Inland Empire West Bd. Realtors (rep.). Republican. Home: 9607 Bolton Ave Montclair CA 91763-2204 Office: Transactions Plus 595-C Tamarack Ave Brea CA 92622

MORENO, RICHARD MILLS, fire chief; b. Tucson, June 30, 1938; s. Fred Elias and Lupe (Mills) M.; m. Yolanda Bertha Rodriquez, Sept. 3, 1960; children—Richard, Robert, Sonya, Rene. B.A, U. Ariz., 1976. With Tucson Fire Dept., 1959—, fire chief, 1982—; mem. adj. faculty Nat. Fire Acad. Md., 1978-79. Contbr. articles to profl. jours. Tng. chmn. Tucson Boy Scouts. Served with USMC, 1956-59. Mem. Internat. Fire Chiefs Assn., Nat. Fire Protection Assn., Ariz. Fire Chiefs Assn. Democrat. Roman Catholic. Club: Centurions. Office: Tucson Fire Dept 265 S Church St Tucson AZ 85701 *

MORENO, STEVEN AUGUST, geologist; b. Chgo., Sept. 11, 1954; s. August Stephan and Dorothy Ester (Mickelsen) M.; m. Joanna Lucy Hamilton, Dec. 13, 1980. BS in Geology, U. Ill., Chgo., 1977; postgrad., Colo. Sch. Mines, Golden, 1988--. Computer geologist Cities Service, Tulsa, 1977-79, Houston Oil & Minerals, Denver, 1979-81; div. geologist Comtek Resources, Denver, 1981-82; pres. Moreno-Smith Software, Denver, 1980-86; computer geologist Earth Tech. Corp., Golden, 1983-84; sr. computer geologist Barringer Geoservices, Inc., Golden, 1984--. Author: Geology, 1985, Ground Water Hydrology, 1987. Mem. Internat. Assn. Math. Geologists, Am. Assn. Petroleum Geologists, Rocky Mt. Assn. Geologists. Office: Barringer Geosvcs Inc 15000 W 6th Ave Golden CO 80401

MOREY, CHARLES LEONARD, III, theatrical director; b. Oakland, Calif., June 23, 1947; s. Charles Leonard Jr. and Mozella Kathleen (Milliken) M.; m. Mary Carolyn Donnet, June 10, 1973 (div. 1975); m. Joyce Miriam Schilke, May 29, 1982; 1 child, William. AB, Dartmouth Coll., 1969; MFA, Columbia U., 1971. Artistic dir. Peterborough (N.H.) Players, 1977-88, Pioneer Theatre Co., Salt Lake City, 1984—; adj. asst. prof. theatre U. Utah, Salt Lake City, 1984—. Actor: N.Y. Shakespeare Festival, Playwrights Horizons, New Dramatists, ARk Theatre Co., Ensemble Studio Theatre, Cubiculo, Folger Theatre, Syracuse Repertory Theatre, Theatre by Sea, others; plays acted in and directed include: Cyrano de Bergerac, Death of a Salesmand, Arms and the Man, Midsummer Night's Dream, Harvey, Charley's Aunt, Arsenic and Old Lace, Shirley Basin, Amadeus, Room Service, Flea in her Ear, Bing and Walker, Eminent Domain, Philadelphia Story, Streetcar Named Desire, Sleuth, Of Mice and Med, Matchmaker, Devil and Daniel Webster, Jungle of Cities, Fugue, Woyzeck, Julius Caesar, Idle Hands Macbeth, Booth Brothers, In the Shadow of the Glen, The Tempest, Henry V, One Flew Over the Cuckoo's Nest, Our Town Twelfth Night Night Thoreau Spent in Jail, Holiday, Private Lives, the Sunshine Boys, Glass Menagerie, Birthday Party; TV appearances include: Young Maverick, Edge of Night, World Apart, Our Town. Recipient Best Dir. award Desert News, 1986, Best Dir. award Utah Holiday Mag., 1987. Mem. Arts Leadership Com., Soc. Stage Dirs. and Choreographers, AEA, SAG, Am. Fedn. TV and Radio Artists, Salt Lake City C. of C. Democrat. Episcopalian. Home: 1803 Yale Ave Salt Lake City UT 84108 Office: Pioneer Theatre Co U Utah Salt Lake City UT 84112

MOREY, ROBERT HARDY, communications executive; b. Milw., Sept. 5, 1956; s. Lloyd W. and Ruby C. (McElhaney) M. AA, Ricks Coll., 1978; BA, Brigham Young U., 1983. Program dir. Sta. KABE-FM, Orem, Utah, 1982-83, sales mgr., 1983; nat. mgr. ops. Tiffany Prodns. Internat., Salt Lake City, 1983-84; account exec. Osmond Media Corp., Orem, 1984; corp. sec., bd. dirs. Positive Communications, Inc., Orem, 1984—, chief exec. officer, 1987—; gen. mgr. Sta. KSRR, Orem, 1985—; pres. K-Star Satellite Network, Orem, 1986—; guest lectr. various colls. and univs., 1981—. Chmn. Rep. voting dist., Orem, 1984. Recipient Community Service award Utah Valley Community Coll., 1983; named one of Outstanding Young Men in Am. U.S. Jaycees, 1983. Mem. Rotary. Mormon. Home: 1200 N Terr Apt 228 Provo UT 84604 Office: Sta KSRR 1400 W 400 N Orem UT 84507

MORFORD, STEVEN DOUGLAS, financial executive; b. Nampa, Idaho, Dec. 9, 1949; s. Robert Byron and Kay (Schimmels) M.; m. Janice May Saari, Aug. 28, 1970; children: Scott Robert, Matthew Douglas, Kira Leigh. BS, U. Oreg., 1971, JD, 1977, MBA, 1979, BA (hon.), 1972. Tax mgr. Deloitte Haskins and Sells, Phoenix, 1979-83; tax supr. Ariz. Pub. Svc. Co., Phoenix, 1983-87; corp. tax mgr. Pinnacle West Capital Corp., Phoenix, 1987—; cons. in field. Mem. exec. bd. United Christian Youth Camp, Prescott, Ariz., 1983-88; bd. dirs. Scottsdale (Ariz.) Arts Ctr. Assn., 1982-86. Mem. AICPA, Western Pension Conf., Ariz. Soc. CPA's. Republican. Home: 5102 E Kings Ave Scottsdale AZ 85254 Office: Pinnacle West Capital Corp 2828 N Central Ave Phoenix AZ 85004

MORGAN, AUDREY, architect; b. Neenah, Wis., Oct. 19, 1931; d. Andrew John Charles Hopfensperger and Melda Lily (Radtke) Anderson; m. Earl Adrian Morgan (div.); children: Michael A., Susan Lynn Heiner, Nancy Lee, Diana Morgan Lucio. B.A., U. Wash., 1955. Registered architect, Wash.; cert. NCARB. Project mgr. The Austin Co., Renton, Wash., 1972-75; med. facilities architect The NBBJ Group, Seattle, 1975-79; architect constrn. rev. unit Wash. State Dept. Social and Health Services, Olympia, 1979-81; project dir., med. planner John Graham & Co., Seattle, 1981-83; pvt. practice architecture, Seattle, 1983—, also health care facility cons., code analyst. Contbr. articles to profl. jours. and govt. papers; prin. works include quality assurance coordinator for design phase Madigan Army Med. Ctr., Ft. Lewis, Wash.; med. planner and code analyst Rockwood Clinic, Spokane, Wash., Comprehensive Health Care Clinic for Yakima Indian Nation, Toppenish, Wash.; med. planner facilities for child, adult, juvenile and forensic psychiatric patients., States of Wash. and Oreg. Cons. on property mgmt. Totem council Girl Scouts U.S.A., Seattle, 1969-84, troop leader, cons., trainer, 1961-74. Mem. AIA (subcoms. codes and standards, health planning, vice-chair mental health com., 1987—, nat. com. on architecture for health 1980—, and numerous other coms., founding mem. Wash. council AIA architecture for health panel 1981—, recorder 1981-84, vice chmn., 1987, chmn. 1988, bd. dirs. S.W. Wash. chpt. 1983-84), Nat. Fire Protection Assn., Soc. Am. Value Engrs., Am. Hosp. Assn., Assn. Western Hosps., Wash. State Hosp. Assn., Seattle Womens Sailing Assn., Audubon Soc., Alpha Omicron Pi. Lutheran. Clubs: Coronado 25 Fleet 13 (Seattle) (past sec., bull. editor); GSA 25 Plus. Home and Office: 4216 Greenwood Ave N Seattle WA 98103

MORGAN, CHARLES EDWARD PHILLIP, banker; b. Wichita, Kans., Nov. 3, 1916; s. Wells C. Morgan and Mary E. (Brown) Allredge; m. Elizabeth Ann Brown, Oct. 14, 1943 (div. Dec. 1972); children—Valerie Donahue, Renee Tompkins. Student U. Wichita, 1935; student bus. adminstrn., U. Calif.-Berkeley, 1963. Teller First Nat. Bank, Santa Fe, 1938-42; safety officer Libby-McNeil-Libby, Sacramento, 1946-48; from teller to v.p./br. mgr. Wells Fargo Bank, Sacramento, 1948-76; sr. v.p. Capitol Bank of Commerce, Sacramento, 1976—. Served to 1st lt. USAF, 1942-45. Democrat. Mem. Christian Ch. Lodges: Masons, Shriners, Elks. Home: 6371 Granger's Dairy Dr Sacramento CA 95831

MORGAN, DAVID ALLEN, electronic engineer; b. Sidney, Neloraska, June 1, 1962; s. Richard Denis and Gerda Dorene (Foged) M.; m. Ann Marie Zollman, June 7, 1986. BS in Elec. Engring., Colo. State U., 1984. Engr. NCR VLSI Processor Products, Colo. Springs, Colo., 1984-85, NCR Digital Signal Processing, Fort Collins, Colo., 1985-87; engr., project leader NCR Computer Aided Design, Fort Collins, 1987—. Mem. IEEE, NCR Golf Club (organizer 1987—). Office: NCR Microelectronics Div 2001 Donfield Ct Fort Collins CO 80525

MORGAN, DAVID FORBES, minister; b. Toronto, Ont., Can., Aug. 3, 1930; came to U.S., 1954; s. Forbes Alexander and Ruth (Bamford) M.; m. Delores Mae Storhaug, Sept. 7, 1956; children—Roxanne Ruth, David Forbes II. BA, Rocky Mt. Coll.; ThB, Coll. of the Rockies, M.Div.; post-grad. Bishop's Sch. Theology; LittD (hon.), Temple Coll., 1956, D.C. Nat. Coll. Ordained priest. Pres., Coll. of the Rockies, Denver, 1960-73; prior Order of Christ Centered Ministries, Denver, 1973—; canon pastor St. John's Cathedral, Denver, 1982—; bd. dir. Alpha Inc., Denver, 1981—. Author: Christ Centered Ministries, A Response to God's Call, 1973; Songs with A Message, 1956. Clubs: Oxford, Denver Botanic Garden. Home: 740 Clarkson Denver CO 80218 Office: St Johns Cathedral 1313 Clarkson Denver CO 80218

MORGAN, DOUGLAS HENES, plastic surgeon; b. Berkeley, Calif., June 4, 1926; s. Frank Mattison and Mabel Evelyn (Kennedy) M.; m. Adrienne Atwood, July 13, 1957; children: Pamela Ann, Hillary Jean. AB, U. So. Calif., 1949, BS, 1950, DDS, 1955. Pvt. practice dentistry specializing in oral and maxillofacial surgery La Crescenta, Calif., 1969—; pres. Tempormand Joint Research Found., La Crescenta, 1966—; founding dir. T.M.J. Clinic White Med. Ctr., Los Angeles, 1968—. Contbr. articles to profl. jours. Served with Mcht. Marine Cadet Corps, USNR, 1944-46. Fellow Internat. Coll. Cramiomandibulan Orthopaedic (founder), Dental Soc. Anesthesiology; mem. ADA, Fedn. Dentaine Internat. Republican. Congregationalist. Lodge: Masons. Home: 1700 Lila Ln La Canada Flintridge CA 91011 Office: 3043 Foothill Blvd La Crescenta CA 91214

MORGAN, EVAN LOEW, interior designer; b. N.Y.C., Nov. 14, 1929; d. Arthur Warner And Zoë Loew; m. John Wiley Morgan Jr., June 5, 1954; children: Julie, Kym. Student, Ariz. State U., 1947-48, 69-75, Scottsdale (Ariz.) Community Coll., 1974-75; BS in Art, Lady Cliff Coll., Highland Falls, N.Y., 1977. Set designer Disney Prodns., Glendale/Burbank, Calif., 1979-82; interior designer, co-mgr. La Mirage Interiors, Rancho Mirage, Calif., 1983-87; interior designer, owner House of Morgan Interiors, Cathedral City, Calif., 1987—; vis. lectr. U. N.C., 1965-68; vis. instr. Lady Cliff Coll., 1975-78, Ariz. State U., Tempe, 1969-75, Scottsdale Community Coll., 1973-75, Orange County Community Coll., Middletown, N.Y., 1975-78. Contbr. articles to numerous newspapers and mags. Vol. instr. Fashion INst. Tech., N.Y.C., 1976-78, Fashion Inst. Design Merchandise, Los Angeles, 1979-82. Mem. Am. Soc. Interior Designers (v.p. Palm Springs chpt. 1987-88), Nat. Soc. Interior Designers (pres. Ariz. chpt. 1972-74, bd. dirs., First place award Internat. Fabric Fair 1971), (affiliate) AIA. Office: 68895 Perez Rd #23 Cathedral City CA 92234

MORGAN, FREDERICK WILLIAM, air force officer; b. Seattle, Oct. 2, 1943; s. Jacob Jesse and Violet Marie (Nord) M.; m. Victoria Milanda Koren, Feb. 4, 1967; children: Christopher Frederick, Elizabeth Rachelle, Milan James. BBA, U. Wash., 1965; MS in Pub. Rels., Am. U., 1972; grad. with honors, Def. Info. Sch., 1966; grad., Air Command & Staff Coll., 1979, Air War Coll., 1983. Commd. 2d lt. USAF, 1965, advanced through grades to col., 1965-86; info. officer USAF, various locations in U.S., Libya, 1965-73; spl. asst. for B-1 info. USAF, Wright-Patterson AFB, Ohio, 1973-77; dep. chief pub. info. div. USAF, Ramstein Air Base, Fed. Republic Germany, 1977-79, chief pub. affairs 86th Tactical Fighter Wing, 1979-81, dep. dir. pub. affairs, 1983-86; dir. pub. affairs Third Air Force USAF, RAF Mildenhall, Eng., 1981-83; dir. office pub. affairs USAF, L.A., 1986—. Editor various spl. interest newspapers, 1964-81. Vol. Annandale (Va.) Christian Community for Action, 1971-73; publicity chmn. Va. sect. Christian Family Movement, Annandale, 1972-73. Named one of Outstanding Young Men of Am., 1969. Mem. Pub. Rels. Soc. Am. (accredited, dir. govt. sect.), Aviation-Space Writers Assn., Air Force Assn., NRA, Calif. Rifle and Pistol Assn., Arnold Air Soc. (chpt. sec. 1963-64), Scabbard and Blade (chpt. sec. 1964-65). Roman Catholic. Home: 15 Stonewood Ct San Pedro CA 90732 Office: USAF Office Pub Affairs Western Region 11000 Wilshire Blvd Ste 10114 Los Angeles CA 90024-3602

MORGAN, JACK M., lawyer; b. Portales, N.Mex., Jan. 15, 1924; s. George Albert and Mary Rosana (Baker) M.; BBA, U. Tex., 1948; LLB, 1950; m. Peggy Flynn Cummings, 1947; children: Marilyn, Rebecca, Claudia, Jack. Admitted to N.Mex. bar, 1950; sole practice law, Farmington, N.Mex., 1956—; mem. N.Mex. State Senate, 1973-88 . Served with USN, 1942-46. Mem. Am. Bar Assn., N.Mex. Bar Assn., S.W. Regional Energy Council (past chmn.), Kiwanis, Elks. Republican. Office: PO Box 2151 Farmington NM 87499

MORGAN, JACOB RICHARD, cardiologist; b. East St. Louis, Ill., Oct. 10, 1925; s. Clyde Adolphus and Jennie Ella Henrietta (Van Ramshorst) M.; m. Alta Eloise Ruthruff, Aug. 1, 1953; children: Elaine, Stephen Richard. BA in Physics, BBA, U. Tex., 1953; MD, U. Tex., Galveston, 1957. Diplomate Am. Bd. Internal Medicine, Am. Bd. Cardiology. Ensign USN, 1944, advanced through grades to capt., 1969; intern U.S. Naval Hosp., Oakland, Calif., 1957-58; chief medicine U.S. Naval Hosp., Taipei, Republic of China, 1962-64; internal medicine staff San Diego, 1964-67, chief cardiology, 1969-73; ret. 1973; dir. medicine R.E. Thomas Gen. Hosp., El Paso, Tex., 1973-75; asst. clin. prof. medicine U. Calif., San Diego, 1970-73; prof. medicine, assoc. chmn. dep. Tex. Tech U. Sch. Medicine, Lubbock and El Paso, 1973-75; pvt. practice National City, Calif., 1976—; dir. cardiology Paradise Valley Hosp., National City, 1976-88; presenter in field. Contbr. articles on cardiology to sci. jours. Recipient Casmir Funk award, 1972. Fellow ACP, Am. Coll. Cardiology, Am. Coll. Chest Physicians, Am. Heart Assn. (coun. on clin. cardiology). Home: 9891 Edgar Pl La Mesa CA 92041 Office: 2409 Plaza Blvd National City CA 92050

MORGAN, JAMES EDWARD, project engineering executive; b. New Orleans, July 8, 1932; s. William Henry Morgan and Mary Elizabeth (Hall) McMurry; m. Sharon Morgan. BS, Va. Polytech. Inst. and State U., 1961; MS, West Coast U., L.A., 1978. Customer engr. IBM, Richmond, Va., 1956-59, 1959-61; with technical staff Sandia Corp., Albuquerque, 1961-62; project engr. Gen. Dynamics, Rancho Cucamonga, Calif., 1962—; Albu; adminstrv. chmn. combat system com., Am. Soc. Naval Engring., Alexandria, Va., 1980-84. Author: (computer program) Solution of Infrared Range Equation with Altitude as Variable, 1968; (book) Anatomy of A Marketing Failure- The SST, 1977. With USN, 1951-55. Mem. IEEE, Am. Def. Preparedness Assn. Home: 9760 Flying Mane Ln Alta Loma CA 91701 Office: Gen Dynamics Valley Systems 11000 E 4th St Rancho Cucamonga CA 91730

MORGAN, JAMES LAROY PETE, investment executive; b. Carterville, Mo., May 20, 1932; s. James Laroy Sr. and Ferne (Gladden) M.; m. Linda Dian Stair, Sept. 1, 1951 (div. 1971); children: Janet Lyn, Mark David; m. Sara Sue Naragon, Oct. 20, 1973. BSBA, Southwest Mo. State U., Springfield, 1956. Regional sales mgr. The Maytag Co., Kansas City, Mo., 1959-67; regional v.p. The Denver Corp., 1967-71, Mass. Co. Distbn., Phoenix, 1971-79; pres., chief exec. officer Maricopa Properties Inc., Phoenix, 1979-81; industry mgr. Mountain Bell Telephone Co., Phoenix, 1981-84; pres., chief exec. officer Internat. Insignia Inc., Paradise Valley, Ariz., 1984-88; securities prin. Stifel-Nicholaus & Co., St. Louis, 1985—. Served to maj. USAF, 1951-71. Mem. Sigma Tau Gamma. Republican. Lodge: Masons. Home: 5914 E Cactus Wren Rd Paradise Valley AZ 85253

MORGAN, JEROME GRAYSON, JR., urologist; b. Cin., Nov. 27, 1937; s. Jerome Grayson Sr. and Harriet (Jacobs) M.; m. Janice Morgan, Nov. 11, 1966 (div.); children: Scott, Sean. BS, U. Cin., 1959, MD, 1963. Intern Highland Hosp., Oakland, Calif., 1963-64; resident in surgery Highland Hosp., Oakland, 1966-67; resident in urology U. Ill. Hosp., Chgo., 1976-70; pvt. practice urologist Santa Rosa, Calif., 1971—; assoc. prof. U. Calif., San Francisco, 1976—. Pres. Am. Cancer Soc., 1978-80. With USAR, 1986—. Mem. Am. Urologic Assn. (nat. and western sects.), Calif. Med. Assn., Sonoma County Med. Assn., No. Calif. Urologic Assn., Airplane Owners and Pilots Assn., South Rosa C. of C. Republican. Mem. Church of Religious Science. Home: 6598 Bridgewood Dr Santa Rosa CA 95409 Office: 4720 Hoen Ave Santa Rosa CA 95405

MORGAN, JIM LEE, business educator; b. Little Rock, Apr. 14, 1943; s. James Charles and Lois Marie (McPherson) M.; BS, BA, U. Ark., 1961, MEd, 1968; MPA, U. So. Calif., 1980. Asst. city mgr. City of Beverly Hills, Calif., 1972-74; dir. Human Service Planning, Simi Valley, Calif., 1975-76; prof. bus. and mgmt. West Los Angeles Coll., 1975—, pres. acad. senate, 1975—; lectr. in field. Bd. advisors U. So. Calif. Traffic Safety Center, 1974-75; bd. dirs. Beverly Hills Chamber Orch., 1973-75, West Los Angeles chpt. ARC, 1972-75; founder, hon. chmn. Ann. Festival of Arts, City of Beverly Hills, 1972-75; founding mem. Research Coordinating Forum of Ventura County, 1976—; v.p. dist. senate Los Angeles Community Coll., 1978-80; treas. Acad. Senate, Calif. Community Colls., 1980-81, fin. task force commn. Chancellor's Office, 1980—. Served to capt. USAF, 1967-72. Decorated Air Force Commendation medal; honored by Jim Lee Morgan Day, City of Beverly Hills, Apr. 14, 1974; named Air Force Systems Command Personnel Officer of the Yr., 1970. Mem. Internat. City Mgrs. Assn., So. Calif. Assn. Human Resources Dirs., Am. Soc. Planning Ofcls., Am. Mgmt. Assn., Phi Delta Kappa, Blue Key, Beta Gamma Sigma. Author: Social Planning for the City, 1975; Business of Management, 1982; Study Guide to Management, 1982; editor Community Services Newsletter, 1974-75, Customer Relations: Policy and Procedures, 1975, Human Services Directory, City of Simi Valley, 1976, Rev. mag., 1972-74. Home: 2601 E 19th St Apt #5 Signal Hill CA 90804 Office: West Los Angeles Coll 4800 Freshman Dr Culver City CA 90230

MORGAN, JOAN MARIE, teacher; b. Kansas City, Mo., July 17, 1933; d. Alpha George and Eleanor Marie (Higgins) Carter; m. Robert Hantla, June 19, 1954 (div. June 1974); children: Jeff, Shawn, Dennis, Becky; m. Elbridge Sawyer Morgan, May 26, 1978. BS, U. Kans., 1954; MA, Ariz. State U., 1965, cert., 1970. Tchr. Saquaro High Sch., Scottsdale, Ariz., 1964-78, South Jr. High Sch., Colorado Springs, Colo., 1978-81, Harrison High Sch., Colorado Springs, 1981-84, Sierra High Sch., Colorado Springs, 1984—; bd. dirs. State Literacy Bd., Denver. Mem. NEA, Pikes Peak Edn. Assn., Colo. Reading Assn. (sec. 1980-82), International Reading Assn. Democrat. Home: 566 Potter Dr Colorado Springs CO 80909 Office: Sierra High Sch 2150 Jet Wing Dr Colorado Springs CO 80916

MORGAN, JOHN DERALD, electrical engineer; b. Hays, Kans., Mar. 15, 1939; s. John Baber and Avis Ruth (Wolf) M.; m. Elizabeth June McKneely, June 23, 1962; children: Laura Elizabeth, Kimberly Ann, Rebecca Ruth, John Derald. BSEE, La. Tech. U., 1962; MS, U. Mo., Rolla, 1965, hon. doctorate in elec. engring., 1987; Ph.D., Ariz. State U., 1968. Registered profl. engr., Mo., N.Mex. Elec. engr. Tex. Eastman div. Eastman Kodak Co., 1962-63; instr. U. Mo., Rolla, 1963-65, Ariz. State U., 1965-68; asso. prof. elec. engring. U. Mo., Rolla, 1968-72; Alcoa Found. prof. elec. engring. U. Mo., 1972-75, chmn. elec. engring., 1978-85, assoc. dir. Ctr. Internat. Programs, 1970-78, Emerson Electric prof., 1975-85; dean engring. N.Mex. State U., 1985—; cons. to industry. Author: Power Apparatus Testing Techniques, 1969, Computer Monitoring and Control of Electric Utility Systems, 1972, Control and Distribution of Megawatts Through Man-Machine Interaction, 1973, Electromechanical and Electromagnetic Machines and Devices, 1986; also articles. Pres. bd. trustees First Meth. Ch., Rolla, 1971-73; pres. adminstrv. bd. First United Meth. Ch. Rolla, 1978-79; v.p., mem. bd. adminstrn. People to People, 1976; bd. dirs., cubmaster Ozarks dist. Boy Scouts Am., 1968-79, asst. dist. commr., 1971-73, cubmaster YUCCA coun., 1986—, coun. commr., 1989—; dist. chmn. Meramec dist., 1978-80; bd. dirs. Mo. Partners of the Americas. Recipient Scouters Key award Ozarks council Boy Scouts Am., 1971, District award of merit Ozarks council Boy Scouts Am., 1977, Silver Beaver award Ozarks council Boy Scouts Am., 1982; T.H. Harris scholar, 1959-61; John H. Horton scholar, 1961-62. Fellow IEEE (chmn. internat. practices subcom. 1972-79, sec. PSE com., vice chmn., chmn. 1979-85, chmn. ednl. resources subcom. 1973-78, selected award of Merit St. Louis sect., Educators award St. Louis sect., honor award St. Louis sect., Centennial award 1984); mem. Am. Soc. Engring. Edn., NSPE (bd. govs., nat. dir.), N.Mex. Soc. Profl. Engrs., ASTM, Profl. Engrs. in Edn., Sigma Xi, Tau Beta Pi, Eta Kappa Nu, Omicron Delta Kappa, Phi Kappa Phi. Home: 2425 Janet Ann Ln Las Cruces NM 88005 Office: NMex State U Main Campus Coll Engring PO Box 30001 Dept 3449 Las Cruces NM 88003

MORGAN, KATHLEEN LAUREL, fashion consultant; b. L.A., Oct. 27, 1944; d. Edward Frazier Jr. and Wilma Anne (Paxton) Curtiss; m. Chase Morgan, Sept. 30, 1967; children: Matthew, Adam. BA, UCLA. Buyer Judy's, Inc., L.A., 1965-68; fashion coord. J.W. Robinson's, L.A., 1974-75; ind. fashion cons. Sherman Oaks, Calif., 1975—. Bd. dirs. Nine O'Clock Players, Hollywood, Calif., 1976—; mem. Assistance League So. Calif., Hollywood, 1976—. Mem. L.A. Country Club, Jonathan Club. Republican. Presbyterian. Home and Office: 3520 Loadstove Dr Sherman Oaks CA 91403

MORGAN, L. ROBERT, management consultant; b. Phila., Jan. 27, 1937; s. Maxwell and Nan (Cohen) M.; m. Delores Martha Vohs, June 2, 1962; children: Phillip, Daniel, Reisa. BA, Whittier Coll., 1958; MBA, Ind. U., 1959. Cert. real estate appraiser. Project mgr. mktg. rsch. Union Oil Co. Calif., L.A., 1960-63; salesman, sales mgr., profit ctr. mgr. D & B subsidiaries, L.A., Houston, 1964-73; dir. acquisitions, new bus. devel. D & B subsidiaries, Chgo., 1973-74; v.p. Rocliff Assocs., Inc., Chgo., 1974-75; pres., chief exec. officer Morgan & Assocs., Inc., L.A., 1975—, Morgan Lewis Co., L.A., 1988—; adj. prof. sch. bus. U. So. Calif., L.A., 1962-68; bd. dirs. Lifeline Healthcare Group Ltd., Naturade Inc.; asst. sec./treas. Helionetics Inc. Editorial staff Jour. Mktg., 1960-67. Pres. Oak Brook Little League, Oak Brook, Ill., 1977; v.p. Houston Tennis Assn., 1971; dir. polit. direct mail Com. to Re-elect the Pres., Washington, 1972; advisor Internat./Trade U.S. Dept. Commerce, Washington, 1981-87. Tennis scholar Whittier Coll., 1956-58, acad. scholar Ind. U., 1958-59. Mem. Nat. Assn. Real Estate Appraisers, L.A. Petroleum Club, Manhattan Beach Club. Republican. Jewish. Office: Morgan & Assocs Inc 900 Wilshire Blvd Ste 1424 Los Angeles CA 90017

MORGAN, MARK QUENTEN, astronomer, astrophysics educator; b. Topeka, Dec. 27, 1950; s. Walter Quenten and Barbara Gene (Haynes) M. BA in Astronomy, San Diego State U., 1972; PhD in Astronomy, U. Addison, Ont., Can., 1976. Jet engine and power plant engr. N.Am. Aviation, Palmdale, Calif., 1966-68; astron. observer San Diego State U., 1970-74; engr., solar observer U. Md.-Clark Lake Radio Obs., Borrego Springs, Calif., 1978-82; engr., lectr. Sci. Atlanta, San Diego, 1979—. Inventor continuous wave laser, 1965, high intensity sound acoustic screening system, 1979. Mem. Inst. Environ. Scis., Acoustic Soc. Am., Astrophys. Soc. Am., Union Concerned Scientists, Planetary Soc. Home: 2351 Boundary St San Diego CA 92104 Office: Sci Atlanta 4255 Ruffin Rd San Diego CA 92123

MORGAN, NEIL, author, editor, lecturer, columnist; b. Smithfield, N.C., Feb. 27, 1924; s. Samuel Lewis and Isabelle (Robeson) M.; m. Caryl Lawrence, 1945 (div. 1954); m. Katharine Starkey, 1955 (div. 1962); m. Judith Blakely, 1964; 1 child, Jill. A.B., Wake Forest Coll., 1943. Columnist San Diego Daily Jour., 1946-50; columnist San Diego Evening Tribune, 1950—, asso. editor, 1977-81, editor, 1981—; syndicated columnist Morgan Jour., Copley News Service, 1958—; lectr.; cons. on Calif. affairs Bank of Am., Sunset mag. Author: My San Diego, 1951, It Began With a Roar, 1953, Know Your Doctor, 1954, Crosstown, 1955, My San Diego 1960, 1959, Westward Tilt, 1963, Neil Morgan's San Diego, 1964, The Pacific States, 1967, The California Syndrome, 1969, (with Robert Witty) Marines of the Margarita, 1970, The Unconventional City, 1972, (with Tom Blair) Yesterday's San Diego, 1976, This Great Land, 1983; contbr.: non-fiction articles to Nat. Geog., Esquire, Redbook, Reader's Digest, Holiday, Harper's, Travel and Leisure, Ency. Brit. Served to lt. USNR, 1943-46. Recipient Ernie Pyle Meml. award, 1957, Bill Corum Meml. award, 1961, Disting. Service citation Wake Forest U., 1966; Grand award for travel writing Pacific Area Travel Assn., 1972, 78, Fourth Estate award San Diego State U., 1988; co-recipient Ellen and Roger Revelle award, 1986; named Outstanding Young Man of Year San Diego, 1959. Mem. Authors Guild, Am. Soc. Newspaper Editors, Soc. Profl. Journalists, Explorers Club, Soc. of Am. Travel Writers, Bohemian Club, Cuyamaca Club, Phi Beta Kappa, Omicron Delta Kappa. Home: 7930 Prospect Pl La Jolla CA 92037 Office: PO Box 191 San Diego CA 92112

MORGAN, RAYMOND SCOTT, finance executive; b. Santa Barbara, Calif., Aug. 31, 1949; s. Royald Raymond and Georgianna (Scott) M.; m. Sandra Ellain Knudsen, Jan. 12, 1974 (div. 1986); m. Sharon Kay Sprague, Sept. 17, 1988. BA in Econs., U. Calif., Santa Barbara, 1972; MS in Mgmt., MIT, 1976. Analyst Bankers Trust Co., N.Y.C., 1976-77; mgr. treasury planning and analysis Tiger Internat. div. Flying Tiger, Los Angeles, 1977-82; dir. domestic airline fin. McDonnell-Douglas Corp., Long Beach, Calif., 1982-86, dir. market securities investment, 1986-88, dir. spl. fin. products, 1988—. Contbr. articles to profl. jours. Mem. Phi Beta Kappa. Episcopalian. Office: McDonnell Dougals Fin 340 Golden Shore Long Beach CA 90802

MORGAN, REBECCA QUINN, state senator; b. Hanover, N.H., Dec. 4, 1938; d. Forrest Arthur and Rachel (Lewis) Quinn; m. James C. Morgan, June 10, 1960; children: J. Jeffrey, Mary Frances. BS, Cornell U., 1960; MBA, Stanford U., 1978. Trustee Palo Alto (Calif.) Bd. of Edn., 1973-78; asst. v.p. Bank of Am., Sunnyvale, Calif., 1978-80; county supr. County of Santa Clara, San Jose, Calif., 1980-84; senator State of Calif., Sacramento, 1984—; mem. exec. com. Calif. Leadership, Sacramento, 1987—. Mem. adv. bd. YWCA, Palo Alto, 1983—, Palo Alto Adolescent Services, 1975—, Pub. Service Ctr., Stanford, Calif., 1985—, Interplast, Palo Alto, 1984—. Named Calif. Legislator of Yr. Sch. Bd. Assn. of Sacramento, 1987, Legislator of Yr. Calif. Assn. for the Edn. of Young Children, 1988, Woman of Achievement Santa Clara County, 1983. Mem. Calif. Elected Women's Assn. (bd. dirs. 1973—). Republican. Office: State Capitol #4090 Sacramento CA 95814

MORGAN, RONALD LEE, toxicologist; b. Enterprise, Oreg., May 8, 1952; s. Earl Edward and Margaret Grace (Henderson) M.; m. Adele Ganjeloo, Oct. 10, 1980 (dec. May 1981); m. Sofya Yatskar, Dec. 29, 1982; 1 child, Becky Rose. BA with high distinction, Central Wash. U., Ellensburg, 1974, BS in Chemistry, 1975; PhD in Pharmacology, Wash. State U., 1979. Postdoctoral rsch. assoc. U. Calif., San Francisco, 1979-80, postdoctoral fellow, 1980-81; toxicologist Stauffer Chem. Co., Richmond, Calif., 1981-83, sr. toxicologist, 1983-88; staff toxicologist State Calif. Dept. Food and Agr., Sacramento, 1988—. Contbr. articles to profl. jours.; patentee in field. Recipient Sci. award Bausch and Lomb, Inc., Ellensburg, 1970; Am. Soc. Pharmacology travel fellow, Pullman, Wash., 1978, NIH fellow, San Francisco, 1980. Mem. Soc. Toxicology, Soc. Comparative Ophthalmology, No. Calif. Soc. Toxicology. Democrat. Jewish. Home: 3909 Boatwright Dr Concord CA 94519 Office: Dept Food and Agr 1220 N St Rm A430 Sacramento CA 95814

MORGAN, SHIRLEY ANN, marketing and advertising consultant; b. Prineville, Oreg., Sept. 16, 1947; d. Vernon David McCallister and Betty Faye (Dory) Hurt; m. Gary Morgan, Sept. 10, 1968 (div. Mar. 1973); 1 child, Shelly Marie Erickson. Student communications, Marylhurst Coll., 1984—. Mktg. dir. Bucher Realty, Beaverton, Oreg., 1978-79; account exec. Gerber Advt., Portland, Oreg., 1979-81; mktg. coordinator McDonald's Corp., Portland, 1981-84; market supr. Bernstein Advt., Kansas City, Kans., 1984-85; owner, mgr. Shirley Morgan Enterprises, Rhododendron, Oreg., 1985—. Com. chmn. Young Life, Portland, 1980; bd. dirs. Hoodland Fire Dept., Rhododendron, 1985—. Recipient cert. of appreciation Multiple Sclerosis Found., Portland, 1980. Mem. Mt. Hood C. of C., Rhododendron Women's Club, Toastmasters. Republican. Evangelical. Home and Office: 71145 E Faubion Loop Rhododendron OR 97049

MORGAN, STANLEY CHARLES, plastic and reconstructive surgeon; b. Phoenix, July 23, 1935; s. Fred Charles and Hazel (King) M.; m. Doris Anne Duke, Sept. 8, 1956; children: Pamela Anne, Cheryl Lynn, Mark Thomas. BS, U. Ariz.; MD, St. Louis Sch. Medicine. Diplomate Am. Bd. Plastic Surgery. Intern UCLA Ctr. Health Svcs., 1961-62, resident plastic surgery, 1966-68; resident gen. surgery Wadsworth Vets. Hosp., L.A., 1962-66; practice medicine specializing in plastic surgery Pasadena, Calif., 1970—; asst. clin. prof. U. So. Calif. Sch. Medicine, Los Angeles, 1981—, UCLA Ctr. Health Scis., 1970-81. Lt. col. U.S. Army, 1968-70. Fellow ACS, Am. Soc. Plastic and Reconstructive Surgeons, Am. Soc. Aesthetic Plastic Surgery, Calif. Soc. Plastic Surgeons. Office: 10 Congress St Ste 407 Pasadena CA 91105

MORGAN, STEPHEN AVERY, software consultant; b. New Rochelle, N.Y., May 11, 1951; s. Evans Gates and Josephine (Field) M.; m. Debra Sue Burrows, Jan. 2, 1988. BA, San Francisco State U., 1976. Ptnr. Silver Lining Entertainment, San Rafael, Calif., 1976-80; account exec. Wells Mgmt. Corp., San Francisco, 1980-81, dir. ins., 1981-82; ptnr. Hawthorn Group, San Francisco, 1982-87; software cons. McCormack and Dodge, Los Angeles, 1987—. Home: 2106 Clark Ln Redondo Beach CA 90278

MORGAN, THOMAS PHELPS, political consultant; b. Roswell, N.Mex., Feb. 15, 1952; s. Harold Maurice and Iverna (Phelps) M.; m. Celeste Ann Colberg (div.); m. Alison Mimm Kirk. BA, U. New Mex., 1974. State campaign dir. Pres. Ford Com., Little Rock, Ark., 1976; field dir. Holleman for Congress, Wynne, Ark., 1976; exec. dir. N.Mex. Rep. Legis. Campaign Com., Albuquerque, 1977-80; campaign mgr. Sego for Gov., Albuquerque, 1981; polit. dir. Colo. Reps., Denver, 1981-85; campaign dir. Mercer for Gov., Albuquerque, 1985-86, Citizens for Fair and Sensible Liability Laws, Phoenix, 1986; pres. Axtech Laser Data, Inc., Albuquerque, 1987-89; polit. dir. GOPAC, Wash., 1987—. Author: Incumbent's Manual, 1982; liasion producer (movie) GOPAC. Deacon La Mesa Presby. Ch., Albuquerque, 1978. Mem. Am. Assn. Polit. Cons. Office: GOPAC 440 1st NW Ste 300 Washington DC 20001

MORGAN, TIMOTHY STEWART, architect; b. Berwyn, Ill., June 21, 1947; s. Howard Pendleton and Rachel (Stewart) M.; m. Lucinda Mary Bellmar, Dec. 28, 1975. Student, U. Ill., 1965-69; BArch, Ariz. State U., 1971. Architect in tng. Eichsteadt/Narcisi, Roselle, Ill., 1967-68; airport planner United Airlines, Des Plaines, Ill., 1969-70; architect in tng. Richard John Frank, A.I.A., Denver, 1971-72; project architect, assoc. Seracuse Lawler and Ptnrs., Denver, 1972-78; project mgr. Cillessen Constrn. Co., Golden, Colo., 1978-81; pres. Heskin/Morgan Architects, Westminster, Colo., 1981-87, Architecture Unltd., Brighton, Colo., 1987—; chmn. archtl. control com., Van Aire Skyport, Brighton, Colo., 1982—, pres., 1989; sec., treas. Stratton Bancshares, Inc., Stratton, Colo., 1984—. Mem. Adams County New Denver Airport Task Force, Brighton, 1989. Am. Field Svc. Americans Abroad to Australia award, 1963-64. Mem. Internat. Conf. Bldg. Officials, Fly in For Lunch Bunch. Office: Architecture Unltd 15615 Elk Circle Hanger 1 Van Air Skyport Brighton CO 80601

MORGAN, WALTER RAY, aeronautical engineer; b. Mt. Airy, N.C., Jan. 25, 1947; s. James Mahlon and Lena Louise (Gibson) M.; m. Linda Kay Levi, May 30, 1968; children: Wendy Kay, Cheryl Ann. BS in Aero. Engring., N.C. State U., 1968. Sr. design engr. Lockheed Aircraft, Burbank, Calif., 1968-80; mgr. research/devel. facility AeroVironment, Inc., Simi Valley, Calif., 1980—; cons. in field. Contbr. articles to profl. jours. Mem. Soaring Soc. Am., U.S. Hang Gliding Assn., Model Aircraft Assn.

MORGAN, WILLIAM ROBERT, lawyer; b. Arkansas City, Kans., Jan. 6, 1924; s. Louis and Betty (Starner) M.; m. Willa June Hall, Mar. 11, 1945; children: Marilyn, Robert. A.A., Arkansas City Jr. Coll., 1942; postgrad., U. Okla., 1942-43, Susquehanna U., 1943; B.A., Stanford U., 1948, LL.B., 1949. Bar: Calif. 1949, U.S. Supreme Ct. 1953. Assoc. Johnson, Morgan, Thorne, Speed & Bamford, San Jose, Calif., 1949-52; founder, ptnr. Morgan, Beauzay, Hammer, Ezgar, Bledsoe & Rucka (and predecessors), San Jose, 1952-78; sr. ptnr. Morgan & Assocs., San Jose, 1978—; pres., chmn. bd. Triton Corp.; owner, operator Stas. KRAD and KJRL, Okla. Author: Chairman Mao's Big Red Book, 1976, Justin Morgan, Founder of the Breed, 1987, Morgan Horse of the West, 1985, The Perfect Horse, 1989; editor Labor Code Annotated, 1960—. Chmn. San Jose Fine Arts Commn., 1960-63; chmn., bd. dirs. Triton Mus. Art, 1963; mem. cen. com. Santa Clara County Dem. Com., 1958-60, campaign mgr. numerous Calif. Dems.; mem. San Martin Planning Commn., 1981, Calif. Jud. Coun., 1980-83; Gideon elder Presbyn. Ch.; appointee Regents Selection Adv. Com. State of Calif.

With U.S. Army, 1943-46. W. Robert Morgan day proclaimed on March 14, 1972 by resolution of Calif. Senate. Mem. ABA (Bus. Frauds and Their Complexities 1986), Calif. Bar Assn. (bd. govs. 1977-80), Santa Clara County Bar Assn. (pres.), Santa Clara County Bar Assn. (pres. sr. lawyers club 1986-87), Calif. State Bar (v.p. 1979-80, exec. bd. law office mgmt. sect. 1980—), Assn. Trial Lawyers Am. (jud. council), Internat. Acad. Trial Lawyers (past pres., past sec., Am. nat. dir.-at-large, editor Twenty-Four Dramatic Cases 1974), Am. Law Inst., Am. Bd. Profl. Liability Attys., Am. Law Inst., No. Calif. Morgan Horse Clubs, Geranium Soc., Lloyd's of London. Presbyterian (elder). Clubs: Masons, Shriners (v.p. club), Eastern Star, Rotary, Kiwanis. Home: 9500 New Ave PO Box 1507 Gilroy CA 95020 Office: Morgan & Assocs 1651 N 1st St San Jose CA 95112

MORGANTE, SAMUEL, marketing executive; b. Jamestown, N.Y., Feb. 1, 1953; s. Charles Joseph and Fannie D. (Cirincione) M.; m. Margaret M. Keegan, July 25, 1981; 1 child, Samuel. BA, SUNY, Binghamton, 1975; MBA, Columbia U., 1983. Sr. staff N.Y. State Legislature, Albany, 1975-81; asst. v.p. N.Y. State Urban Devel. Corp., N.Y.C., 1983-84; mgr. fin. Guaranty Div., Corroon and Black Corp., San Francisco, 1984-86; asst. v.p. mktg. dir. Capital Guaranty Ins. Co., San Francisco, 1986—. N.Y. State field ops. coord. Kennedy for Pres., N.Y.C., 1980. Mem. Calif. Soc. of Mcpl. Analysts (chmn. program), San Francisco Mcpl. Forum, Commonwealth Club of Calif., Northern Calif. Columbia U. Alumni. Democrat. Roman Catholic. Home: 4409 Harbord Dr Oakland CA 94618 Office: Capital Guaranty Ins Co Steuart Tower 22d Fl 1 Market Pla San Francisco CA 94105

MORGART, ROBERT ALLEN, financial consultant; b. Johnstown, Pa., Aug. 10, 1943; s. Robert Custer and Bettie (Keener) M. BA, U. Pitts., 1966, MA, 1968, MEd, 1972, postgrad., 1972-76. Foreman, systems analyst Jones & Laughlin Steel Corp., Pitts., 1967-68; teaching fellow U. Pitts., 1971-74; comml. liaison, bus. planner U.S. Dept. State, Pitts. and Washington, 1969; asst. prof. Oakland U., Rochester, Mich., 1974-76, Pepperdine U., Los Angeles, 1976-78; pres. Goram Corp., Detroit, 1978-81; sr. fin. cons. Merrill Lynch, Santa Fe, N.Mex., 1982—; cons. Calif. State Dept. Edn., Los Angeles, 1977, Mingi Corp., Carson, Calif., 1978—, Ford Motor Co., Dearborn, Mich., 1980. Author: (with others) Alienation in an Educational Context, 1974, The Federal Politics of Busing, 1974; TV Programs Work and Welfare Reform, 1976, Sex Roles, Schools and the Labor Market, 1976, ABC TV program Work and Welfare Reform, 1976. Bd. dirs. Santa Fe Council for the Arts, 1986—; v.p., treas. Hammer of Thor Found, 1986—; fund raiser Ctr. for Contemporary Arts, Santa Fe, 1984—, Santa Fe Animal Shelter, 1985—; mem. Sangre de Christo Animal Protection, 1987—, Nature Conservancy Greenpeace Union of Concerned Scientists. Mem. Nat. Assn. Securities Dealers, Nat. Futures Assn., Council on Econ. Priorities, The Trinity Forum, Action Linkage, Defenders of Wildlife Club, World Wildlife Fund, Sierra Club, The Club of El Gancho, Phi Eta Sigma, Phi Theta Kappa. Democrat. Presbyterian. Home: 1810 Calle de Sebastian Santa Fe NM 87501 Office: Merrill Lynch 123 E Marcy St Santa Fe NM 87501

MORGENROTH, EARL EUGENE, entrepreneur; b. Sidney, Mont., May 7, 1936; s. Frank and Leona (Ellison) M.; m. Noella Nichols, Aug. 2, 1958; children: Dolores Roxanna, David Jonathan, Denise Christine. BS, U. Mont., 1961. From salesman to gen. mgr. Sta. KGUO-Radio, Missoula, Mont., 1958-65; sales mgr. Sta. KGUO-Radio, KTUM-TV, KCFW-TV, Missoula, Butte, Kalispell, Mont., 1965-66; gen. mgr. Sta. KGUO-Radio, KTUM-TV, KCFW-TV, Missoula, Butte, Kalispell, 1966-68, Sta. KCOY-TV, Santa Maria, Calif., 1968-69; v.p., gen. mgr. Western Broadcasting Co., Missoula, 1966-69, gen. mgr., pres., 1969-81; gen. mgr., pres. numerous cos., Mont., Calif. Idaho, P.R., Ga., 1966-84; pres., chmn. Western Broadcasting Co., Missoula, 1981-84, Western Communications, Inc., Reno, 1984—; chmn. Western Fin., Inc., Missoula Music Ctr., Inc., Dickinsons Music Ctr., Inc., Big Sky Music Ctr., Inc.; prin. Western Investments, Reno, 1984—; bd. dirs. Mont. Naturals Inc. Active Bank Bd. State of Mont., Helena; trustee U. Mont., 1985—; commencement speaker U. Mont., 1988. Served with U.S. Army, 1954-57. Named Boss of Yr. Santa Maria Valley J.C.s, 1968. Mem. U. Mont. Century Club (pres.), Missoula C. of C. (pres.), Rocky Mountain Broadcasters Assn. (pres.). Republican. Methodist. Home: 3525 Brighton Way Reno NV 59806

MORGENSTERN, ALAN LAWRENCE, psychiatrist; b. Bklyn., Dec. 21, 1933; s. David Jacob and Lillian (Stoneberg) M.; m. Ann Rubenstein, Mar. 29, 1960 (div. 1984); children: David, Fred. BA, Cornell U., 1954; MD, Duke U., 1959. Diplomate Am. Bd. Psychiatry and Neurology. Intern Duke U. Hosp., Durham, N.C., 1959-60; resident to chief resident U. Colo. Med. Ctr., Denver, 1960-63; instr., clin. prof. Oreg. Health Services U., Portland, 1965—; sr. registrar Tavistock Clinic, London, 1972-73; chmn. Psychiatry dept. Good Samaritan Med. Ctr., Portland, 1976-87; cons. FAA, Seattle, 1965—, Nat. Inst. Mental Health, Bethseda, Md., 1973-75, Oreg. Episcopal Sch., Portland, 1986-87. Contbr. articles to profl. jours. Served to capt. USAF, 1963-65. Recipient Psychiat. Writing award Colo. Psychiat. Assn., 1964; travel-study fellow WHO, 1972. Mem. Oreg. Psychiat. Assn., Oreg. Psychoanalytic Found., Oreg. Med. Assn. Democrat. Jewish. Club: Multnomah Athletic, Portland. Home: 7929 SW Ruby Terr Portland OR 97219 Office: 1220 SW Morrison St Portland OR 97205

MORHART, JUDSON ADAM, school administrator; b. Little Rock, Ark., Nov. 1, 1943; s. Frank Elbert and Henrietta (Hafner) M.; m. Judith Ann Jurgensen, June 17, 1967; children: Jason, Amy. BA in Geography, Hastings Coll., 1965; MA in Ednl. Tech., San Jose State U., 1971; MA in Ednl. Adminstrn., Columbia U., 1983. Cert. sch. adminstr. Asst. principal Pueblo Junior High Sch., Los Alamos, N. Mex., 1968-80; principal Pueblo Junior High Sch., Los Alamos, 1980-81, Pinon Elementary Sch., Los Alamos, 1982-84; dir. of instrn. Los Alamos Schs., 1984—; cons. New Mexico State Dept. of Edn., Sante Fe, 1986-88. Contbr. articles to profl. jours. Bd. Dirs. Los Alamos Pub. Access Channel 8, RSVP Board. Mem.(bd. dirs.) C. of C., Los Alamos, ASCD (Assn. for Supervisory and Curricular Dev.), N. Mex. Sch. Adminstrn., N. Mex. ASCD, N. Mex. Computer Users in Edn., N. Mex. Council for the Soc. Studies. Club: Rotary Internat., Los Alamos. Home: 1666 Camino Uva Los Alamos NM 87544 Office: Los Alamos Schs 751 Trinity Dr Los Alamos NM 87544

MORIARTY, DONALD PETER, II, engineering executive, military officer; b. Alexandria, La., Jan. 26, 1935; s. Donald P. and Catherine G. (Stafford) M.; children by previous marriage: Erin, Donald P. III; m. Diana Mary Blackburn, Feb. 4, 1984. BS, La. State U., 1957; MA, Fla. Atlantic U., 1973; diploma, U.S Army Comdr. and Gen. Staff Coll., 1977. Commd. 2d lt. U.S. Army, 1957, advanced through grades to lt. col., 1978; artillery officer U.S. Army, various, 1957-74; head tactical plans sect. Army Air Def. Command, Darmstadt, Federal Republic of Germany, 1975-77; dir. C3I div. Army Air Def. Ctr., Ft. Bliss, Tex., 1977-80; retired Army Air Def. Ctr., 1980; sr. system engr. Hughes Aircraft Co., Fullerton, Calif., 1980-82, mgr. engr. design dept., 1982-84, project mgr., 1984—; U.S. Army Rep. to Tactical Airpower Com. NATO hdqrs., Brussels, 1977-79, Tri-Service Group on Air Def., NATO, 1978-80, Air Def. Electronic Equipment Com., NATO, 1978-80; lead systems engr. Hughes Aircraft Co., Fullerton, 1980-83; Strategic Def. Initiative Program Coordinator Systems Div. Hughes Aircraft Co., 1985-87; mgr. Tac Def. and Tac Command Control Program, Systems Div., GSG, Hughes Aircraft Co., 1987—. Author: The U.S. Army Officer as Military Statesman, 1973. Parade chmn. South Fla. Fair Assn., West Palm Beach, 1971; staff commr. Boy Scouts Am., Kaiserslautern, Federal Republic of Germany, 1974-76; sr. warden Episcopal Ch., Kaiserslautern, 1975, Wiesbaden, Federal Republic of Germany, 1977, Placentia, Calif., 1985-88. Decorated Vietnamese Cross of Gallantry with Palm, Air medal with two oak leaf clusters, Bronze Star with one oak leaf cluster, Legion of Merit; recipient Wood Badge award Boy Scouts Am., Newburgh, N.Y., 1969. Mem. AIAA, Assn. U.S. Army, Armed Forces Com.-Elect Assn., Am. Electronics Assn., SAR, Gen. Soc. Mayflower Descendants, Phi Alpha Theta, Acacia. Republican. Home: 626 E Riverview Ave Orange CA 92665 Office: Hughes Aircraft Co 1901 W Malvern St Fullerton CA 92634

MORIARTY, JOHN, opera administrator; b. Fall River, Mass., Sept. 30, 1930; s. John J. and Fabiola Marie (Ripeau) M. MusB summa cum laude, New Eng. Conservatory, 1952. Artistic adminstr. Opera Soc. of Washington, 1960-62, Santa Fe Opera, N.Mex., 1962-65; dir. Wolf Trap Co., Vienna, Va., 1972-77; chmn. Boston Conservatory Opera Dept., 1973—, prin. condr. Central City Opera, Denver, 1978—, artistic dir., 1982—; panelist Nat. Inst. Music Theater, 1985, 86, 87, Conn. Arts Council, 1982, 84; adjudicator various contests including Met. Opera auditions, 1965—. Author: Diction, 1975. Trustee Boston Concert Opera. Recipient Frank Huntington Beebe award, Boston, 1954, Disting. Alumni award New Eng. Conservatory Alumni Assn., 1982, Gold Chair award Cen. City Opera House Assn., 1988. Mem. Nat. Opera Assn., Sigma Alpha Iota, Delta Omicron, Pi Kappa Lambda. Office: Boston Conservatory Music 8 the Fenway Boston MA 02215 also: Cen City Opera House Assn 621 17th St #1601 Denver CO 80293 also: New Eng Conservatory Opera Dept 290 Huntington Ave Boston MA 02155

MORIGUCHI, TOMIO, gift and grocery store executive; b. Tacoma, Apr. 16, 1936; s. Fujimatsu and Sadako (Tsutakawa) M.; m. Lovett Keiko Tanaka, Nov. 15, 1969; children: Tyler Minoru, Denise Ritsuko. BSME, U. Wash., 1961. With missile div. Boeing Co., Seattle, 1961-62; with Uwajimaya Inc., Seattle, 1962—; pres. Uwajimaya Inc., 1965—; bd. dirs. Seafirst Corp., Seattle 1st Nat. Bank, Wash. Energy Co. Bd. dirs. Wash. Inst. Applied Tech., Seattle, Seattle Found., Leadership Tomorrow, Pacific Celebration; mem. Wash. Econ. Devel. Bd., Wash. Adv. Council on Internat. Trade and Devel.; v.p., bd. dirs., past chmn. Nikkei Concerns, Inc.; treas. Nat. Japanese Am. Citizens League, 1974-76; trustee Seattle Community Coll. Dist., 1985—, also past chmn.; past chmn. Chinatown-Internat. Dist. Preservation and Devel. Authority; bd. dirs., past pres. Internat. Dist. Improement Assn., many others. Recipient Outstanding Vol. Civic Leadership award Four Seasons Hotel, Seattle, 1987; named Alumni Legend, U. Wash., 1987. Mem. Seattle C. of C. (past v.p.), Internat. Dist. Econ. Assn. (v.p., past pres.), Japan Am. Soc. State Wash. (pres. 1985), Rotary. Office: Uwajimaya Inc 519 6th Ave S Seattle WA 98104

MORIKAWA, DAN KAZUO, leasing company executive; b. Honolulu, June 12, 1954; s. Minoru and Wakayo (Baba) M. Owner Buggin Hawaii, Honolulu, 1976-80, Environ. Plus, Honolulu, 1980--; pres., chief exec. officer, bd. dirs. Zaitek Corp., Honolulu, 1985--; pres., bd. dirs. Akowai Devel., Honolulu, Shayna of Hawaii Japan, Honolulu, Hoonani Corp., Honolulu, 1380 Akowai Corp., Honolulu, RE/MAX Profls., Honolulu and Kailua, Hawaii. Office: Zaitek Corp 1088 Bishop St Ste 1207 Honolulu HI 96813

MORIMOTO, AKIKO CHARLENE, educator; b. Los Angeles, May 2, 1948; d. Satosu Don and Midori Jean (Ohira) M. B, Calif. State U., Los Angeles, 1971. Cert. secondary tchr., Calif., adult edn. tchr., Calif. Tchr. Los Angeles City Schs., 1972-77; instr. U. Calif., San Diego, summers 1983-85; tchr. Vista (Calif.) Unified Sch. Dist., 1977—; cons. San Diego Area Writing Project, La Jolla, Calif., 1981—; bd. dirs. Greater San Diego Council Tchrs. of English; table leader Calif. Assessment Program-Writing, San Diego, 1987—, Calif. Lit. Project, 1988—. Co-author: (with others) Foundations of Art Education, 1973; editor (dist. lit. mag.) Visions of Our Youth, 1986, 87. Mem. Old Globe Theatre, San Diego, 1985—. Named Vista Mentor Tchr. Vista Unified Sch. dist., 1986-89. Mem. Calif. Assn. Tchrs. of English (Excellence in Classroom award 1988), Assn. San Diego Educators of Gifted, Calif. Assn. of Gifted, Nat. Council Tchrs. of English, Nat. Writing Project, Greater San Diego Council Tchrs. English (Excellence in Classroom award 1988), Calif. Reading Assn., Greater San Diego Reading Assn. Democrat. Home: 704 C-6 Regal Rd Encinitas CA 92024 Office: 740 Olive Ave Vista CA 92083

MORIMOTO, CARL NOBORU, computer system engineer; b. Hiroshima, Japan, Mar. 31, 1942; came to U.S., 1957, naturalized, 1965; s. Toshiyuki and Teruko (Hirano) M.; m. Helen Kiyomi Yoshizaki, June 28, 1969; children: Matthew Ken, Justin Ray. B.A., U. Hawaii, 1965; Ph.D., U. Wash., 1970. Research assoc. dept. chemistry Mich. State U., East lansing, 1970-72; postdoctoral fellow dept. biochemistry and biophysics Tex. A&M U., College Station, 1972-75; sr. sci. programmer Syntex Analytical Instruments Inc., Cupertino, Calif., 1975-78; prin. programmer analyst, software engring. mgr. Control Data Corp., Sunnyvale, Calif., 1978-83; mem. profl. staff Space System div. Gen. Electric Co., San Jose, Calif., 1983—. Mem. Am. Crytallographic Assn., Assn. Computing Machinery, Am. Chem. Soc., Sigma Xi. Am. Baptist. Home: 4003 Hamilton Park Dr San Jose CA 95130

MORIOKA, JUNE MEIKO MIURA, college administrator; b. Wahiawa, Hawaii, Apr. 19, 1935; d. Thomas Mitsuo and May Shizue (Ishida) Miura; m. Thomas Tadayoshi Morioka, June 2, 1962; children: Mark Mitsuo, Tammy Yukiko. BSN, U. Hawaii, 1957, MEd, 1972. RN, Hawaii; cert. community coll. tchr.; med. asst., Hawaii. Staff nurse Kapiolani Maternity Hosp., Honolulu, 1955-58; hear nurse Kaiser Med. Ctr., Honolulu, 1958-59, supr., 1959-60, clin. isnt., 1960-62; tchr. Kapiolani Tech. Sch., Honolulu, 1962-67; program coord. Kapiolani /community Coll., Honolulu, 1967—; mgr. Physicians Exch. Honolulu, 1979—, cons., 1980-83. Coord. Blood Bank Hawaii, 1979—. Named an Outstanding Med. Asst. of Yr., The Sorrel Waxman, 1984. Mem. Hawaii Nurses Assn. (chmn. 1959), Hawaii Soc. Med. Assts. (pres. 1983), Nat. Orgn. Women Execs., U. Hawaii Sch. Nursing Alumni Assn. Home: 37 California Ave Wahiawa HI 96786 Office: Physicians Exch Honolulu 1360 S Beretania St Ste 301 Honolulu HI 96814

MORISHITA, AKIHIKO, trading company executive; b. Osaka, Japan, Oct. 14, 1941; came to U.S., 1981; s. Sueyoshi and Toshiko Morishita; m. Fumiko Okamura; children: Shizuko, Kumiko. BA in Econs., Wakayama U., Wakayama, Japan, 1965. Mgr. Hanwa & Co. Ltd., Osaka, 1965-80; cons. oil dept. Pacific Southwest Trading Co., San Diego, 1981-82; exec. Pacific Marine Bunkering, Inc., L.A., 1982—. Mem. The Assoc. Club (Tex.), L.A. Oilmen's Club. Home: 4610 Don Pio Dr Woodland Hills CA 91364

MORITA, JAMES MASAMI, banker, lawyer; b. Kealakekua, South Kona, Hawaii, July 18, 1913; s. Ushima and Kichi (Yamamoto) M.; m. Aiko Nagakura, Jan. 12, 1957; children: Caryn Sami, Marie Michiko. B.A., U. Hawaii, 1936; LL.B., Georgetown U., 1940; grad., Stonier Grad. Sch. Banking, 1970. Bar: Hawaii, D.C. 1940, U.S. Supreme Ct. 1949. Partner firm Fukushima & Morita, Honolulu, 1941-50; 1st asst. pub. prosecutor Honolulu, 1951-52; atty. City-County Honolulu, 1953-55, spl. counsel, 1956-57; atty. Morita, Kamo & Sakai, Honolulu, 1960-70; chmn. bd., chief exec. officer City Bank; Chmn. bd., pres. CB Bancshares, Inc.; bd. dirs. Citibank Properties, All Hawaii Investment Corp., New Otani Kaimana Beach Hotel, Tony Hawaii Corp, Pacific Olds GMC, Pacific Nissan, Kanebo Cosmetics Hawaii, Inc., Huntington Beach Imports, Tony Calif., Ltd. Nat. trustee Nat. Jewish Hosp. and Research Ctr., 1977, Hawaii Loa Coll., 1980; active Boy Scouts Am.; mem. campaign exec. com. Japanese Cultural Ctr. Hawaii. Decorated Order of Rising Sun 3d class (Japan); recipient Outstanding award Nat. Jewish Hosp., 1976; recipient 75th Anniversary Rainbow award to disting alumni U. Hawaii, 1982, Freedom Symbol award Sertoma Club, 1983. Mem. Bar Assn. Hawaii, Am. Bankers Assn. (Stonier adv. bd.), Hawaii Bankers Assn. (pres. 1988—), Mid-Pacific Alumni Assn., Georgetown U. Alumni Assn., Japan-Hawaii Econ. Council, Japan-Am. Soc. Honolulu., Hawaii Soc. Corp. Planners, Hawaii C. of C. (bd. dirs), U. Hawaii Alumni Assn. Democrat. Clubs: Waialae Country, 200, Honolulu Country, U. Hawaii Pres.'s, Plaza, Mid-Pacific, All Winners, Mynah. Office: City Bank 810 Richards St Box 3709 Honolulu HI 96811

MORITA, RICHARD YUKIO, microbiology and oceanography educator; b. Pasadena, Calif., Mar. 27, 1923; s. Jiro and Reiko (Yamamoto) M.; m. Toshiko Nishihara, May 29, 1926; children—Sally Jean, Ellen Jane, Peter Wayne. B.S., U. Nebr., 1947; M.S., U. So. Calif., 1949; Ph.D., U. Calif., 1954. Postdoctoral fellow U. Calif., Scripps Inst. Oceanography, 1954-55; asst. prof. U. Houston, 1955-58; asst. prof., assoc. prof. U. Neb., 1958-62; prof. microbiology and oceanography Oreg. State U., Corvallis, 1962—; program dir. biochemistry NSF, 1968-69; cons. NIH, 1968-70; researcher in field. Contbr. articles to sci. lit. Patentee in field. Served with U.S. Army, 1944-46. Grantee NSF, 1962—, NIH, 1960-68, NASA, 1967-72, Office Naval Research, 1966-70, Dept. Interior, 1968-72, NOAA, 1975-82, Bur. Land Mgmt., 1982, EPA, 1986—; recipient awards including King Fredericus IX Medal and Ribbon, 1954, Sr. Queen Elizabeth II Fellowship, 1973-74, Hotpack lectr. and award Can. Soc. Mem. Am. Soc. Microbiology (Fisher award). Office: Oreg State U Dept Microbiology Corvallis OR 97331

MORITZ, WILLIAM ERNEST, software systems engineer; b. Cleve., Dec. 5, 1948; s. Ernest William and Rita (Behrens) M.; m. Evelyn Flynn, Dec. 30, 1978; children: Danny, Alison. BS in Chemistry, Kent State U., 1972; MS in Computer Sci, U. Colo., 1980. Rsch. chemist Internat. Liquid Crystal Co., Cleve., 1971-76; rsch. asst. U. Colo., Boulder, 1976-80; sr. programmer Burroughs, Inc., Denver, 1980-83; sr. software engr. Ball Aerospace Systems Group, Boulder, 1983—. Bd. dirs. Community Parenting Ctr., Boulder, 1986—. Recipient award of excellence NASA, 1979. Mem. Assn. for Computing Machinery, Ada Spl. Interest Group. Home: 4140 N 26th St Boulder CO 80304 Office: Ball Aerospace Systems Group Box 1062 Boulder CO 80306

MORLEY, JEFFREY JOSHUA, cosmetic dentist; b. Los Angeles, Apr. 25, 1953; s. David and Reneé M. Student, Santa Monica (Calif.) Coll., 1970-71, Calif. State U., Northridge, 1971-72; Degree, Calif. State U., San Jose, 1972-73; DDS, U. Pacific, San Francisco, 1976. Pvt. practice dentistry Novato, Calif., 1976-81; sr. ptnr. Ctr. Cosmetic Dentistry, San Francisco, 1981-83, prin. sr. dentist, 1983—; co-founder Ctr. Cosmetic Dentistry, San Francisco, 1981; advisor Press Report, Atlanta, 1988—, Cosmetic Dentistry for the General Practitioner, Atlanta, 1988—. Contbr. numerous articles to profl. jours. Mem. Am. Acad. Cosmetic Dentistry (accredited, co-founder 1983, pres.-elect, v.p. 1984-86, pres. 1987—), Esthetic Dentistry Research Group. Office: 1648 Union St San Francisco CA 94123

MORLEY, STEVEN ALLAN, engineering company executive; b. San Bernardino, Calif., Dec. 27, 1956; s. Richard Allan Morley and Norma Ruth (White) Gregory; m. Judith Margaret Ward, June 25, 1983; 1 child, Amanda Ruth. BSEE, U. Calif., Irvine, 1978; MSEE, Stanford U., 1980. Engr. Hughes Aircraft Co., Fullerton, Calif., 1978-80; engring. mgr. Linkabit Corp., San Diego, 1980-85, Qualcomm, Inc., San Diego, 1985—. Patentee in field. Republican. Pentecostal. Home: 10990 Red Rock Dr San Diego CA 92131 Office: Qualcomm Inc 10555 Sorrento Valley Rd San Diego CA 92121

MORO, MICHAEL JOSEPH, test engineer; b. Akron, Ohio, Jan. 25, 1949; s. Adam and Louetta Jane (Hofstetter) M.; m. Karen Lorraine Gaskin, Dec. 19, 1969; children: Sean Eric, Kelli Lyn. BS, Ariz. State U., 1987. Electronics technician U.S. Navy, 1969-73, Interstate Electronics, Anaheim, Calif., 1974-77; flight data engr. Garrett Engine Div., Phoenix, 1977—. Mem. Soc. Flight Test Engrs., Soc. Automotive Engrs., Instrument Soc. Am. Republican. Baptist. Home: 3232 N 63d Pl Scottsdale AZ 85251 Office: Garrett Engine Div PO Box 5217 MS 129 Phoenix AZ 85010

MORPHESIS, JAMES GEORGE, artist; b. Phila., Aug. 26, 1948; s. George Spiros and Bettie (Sarikianos) M., m. Melody Ann Poltroneri, May 26, 1988. BFA, Temple U., 1970; MFA, Calif. Inst. Arts., Valencia, 1972. Instr. Otis/Parsons Inst., Los Angeles, 1977-83, Immaculate Heart Coll., Los Angeles, 1974-76, Los Angeles City Coll., Los Angeles, 1974-80; dept. chmn. Calif. Bapt. Coll., Riverside, 1977-78; instr. Los Angeles Pierce Coll., Woodland Hills, Calif., 1978-79, 82, Calif. State U., Northridge, Calif., 1979-80; freelance artist 1983—; art dir. Master Graphics, Inc., Phila., 1966-68. One man shows include Los Angeles County Mus. Art, 1987, Tortue Gallery, Santa Monica, Calif, 1987, Marianne Deson Gallery, Chgo., 1987, Freidus/Ordover Gallery, N.Y.C., 1983; exhibited in group shows at Abstract Expressionism and After, San Francisco Mus. Modern Art, 1987, Security Pacific Nat. Bank's Gallery at the Plaza, 1985, Emanuel Walker/Atholl McBean Galleries, San Francisco Art Inst., 1985, L.A. County Mus. Art, 1987. Recipient Biennial grant Louis Comfort Tiffany Found., N.Y.C., 1986, Young Talent Purchase award Los Angeles County Mus. Art, 1983, Calif. Small Images Exhibition award Calif. State U., 1971, Nathan Margolis Meml. Painting award, Temple U., Phila., 1970. Mem. Coll. Art Assn. Am. Democrat. Greek Orthodox. Home: 118 S Hobart Blvd Los Angeles CA 90004

MORRICE, RUTH FILL, educator, writer, consultant; b. Tonawanda, N.Y., Feb. 15, 1914; d. William Louis Allen and Grace Lillian Maude (Bates) Fill; m. Charles Elmer Conklin, Dec. 8, 1930; 1 dau., Mary Ruth Fill Conklin Mailey; m. John Buchan Morrice, Oct. 19, 1946; children: John Fill Morrice, Christina Forbes Morrice Reynolds, Eleanor Wylde Morrice, George Niven Morrice. BA, Boston U., 1942, MA, 1943, postgrad., 1945-47; postgrad., Monterey Coll., San Jose State U., U. Calif.-Santa Cruz, U. Calif.-Berkeley. Asst. to English dept. Boston U., 1942-47; tchr. Hinsdale (Ill.) High Sch., 1943-45, head dept. English; instr. English Coll. William and Mary, Williamsburg, Va., 1947; instr. English and creative writing Culver Stockton Coll., Canton, Mo., 1948-49; faculty English and social studies Hartnell Coll., Salinas, Calif., 1967; teaching prin., counselor Olympia Sch., San Benito County, Calif., 1969-70; spl. tchr. Pacific Grove (Calif.) Unified Sch. Dist., 1964-76; ednl. cons., counselor, Carmel, Calif.; free lance writer, artist; sec. to Edward Rowe Snow, 1946, 47. Author: The Poetry of George Santayana, 1943, A Definition of the Novel 1920 to present, 1981, A Study of Santayana and Ruskin, 1981, ...Personal Biography, 1981; editor: A Pilgrim Returns to Cape Cod (Edward Rowe Snow), 1946-47, Photographs and Thoughts from My Journeying in the Orient, 1979. Bd. dirs., supt. Bible Sch., Tustin (Calif.) Congl. Ch., 1964; den mother, pack and dist. leader San Fernando Valley council Boy Scouts Am.; mem. sch. bd. Montague Sch., Los Angeles; active parent groups, Heart Fund, ch. and other choirs. Mem. AAUP, Coll. English Assn. (sec. to treas. 1947-48), Nat. Tchrs. Assn., Calif. Tchrs. Assn., Alpha Phi. Republican. Congregationalist. Home and Office: 3508 Trevis Way Carmel CA 93923

MORRIN, VIRGINIA WHITE, educator; b. Escondido, Calif., May 16, 1913; d. Harry Parmalee and Ethel Norine (Nutting) Rising; B.S., Oreg. State Coll., 1952; M.Ed., Oreg. State U., 1957; m. Raymond Bennett White, 1933 (dec. 1953); children: Katherine Anne, Marjorie Virginia, William Raymond; m. 2d, Laurence Morrin, 1959 (dec. 1972). Social caseworker Los Angeles County, Los Angeles, 1934-40, 61-64; acctg. clk. War Dept., Ft. MacArthur, Calif., 1940-42; prin. clk. USAAF, Las Vegas, Nev., 1942-44; high sch. tchr., North Bend-Coos Bay, Oreg., 1952-56, Mojave, Calif., 1957-60; instr. Antelope Valley Coll., Lancaster, Calif., 1961-73; ret., 1974. Treas., Humane Soc. Antelope Valley, Inc., 1968—. Mem. Nat. Aero. Assn., Calif. State Sheriffs' Assn. (charter assoc.), Oreg. State U. Alumni Assn. (life). Mailing: 3153 Milton Dr Mojave CA 93501

MORRIS, BENJAMIN FRANKLIN, JR., civil engineer; b. Chincoteaque, Va., Jan. 11, 1948; s. Benjamin Franklin and Helen Louise (Morgan) M.; m. Valerie Lynell Fink, Dec. 9, 1970; children: Benjamin Franklin III, Tamara Shawn. BCE, Va. Mil. Inst., 1971. Resident engr. VA, Washington, 1971-75; maintenance engr. VA, La Jolla, Calif., 1975-78; dir. engring. Scripps Clinic and Rsch. Found., La Jolla, 1978--. Contbr. articles to profl. publs. Co-chmn. fund raising Jaycees-Muscular Dystrophy Found., Encinitas, Calif., 1975; cubmaster Encinitas area Boy Scouts Am., 1984-86, asst. scoutmaster, 1986-88. Mem. ASCE (assoc. mem., pres. assoc. mem. forum 1978, chmn. western regional younger mem. council 1979, chmn. younger mem. com. on publs. 1980-83, nat. Alfred Nobel joint prize com. 1982-84, com. on sects. and dist. council 1988--; Outstanding Assoc. Mem. award western region 1978, Edmund Friedman Young Engr. award 1979), Am. Soc. Hosp. Engrs., Va. Mil. Inst. Alumni Assn. (pres. 1983-87). Republican. Roman Catholic. Home: 2002 Cumbre Ct Carlsbad CA 92009 Office: Scripps Clinic Rsch Found 10666 N Torrey Pines Rd La Jolla CA 92037

MORRIS, BRADLEY THOMAS, surgeon; b. Berwyn, Ill., Aug. 11, 1947; s. Donald and Grace (Keashly)M.;m. Veronica Ann Cudell, Jan. 20, 1973; children: Andrew, Megan, Keely, Madeline. BS, Beloit Coll., Wis., 1969; MD, U. Wis., 1973. Intern San Joaquin Gen. Hosp., Stockton, Calif., 1973-74; resident in otolaryngology U. Wis. Hosp., Madison, 1974-78; physician Western Mont. Clinic, Missoula, 1978—; pres. Western Mont. Clinic Bldg. Corp., Missoula, 1985—, MSB Inc., Missoula, 1984—. Fellow ACS, Am. Acad. Facial Plastic and Reconstructive Surgery, Am. Bd. Otolaryngology, Head and Neck Surgery. Home: 535 Evan Kelly Rd Missoula MT 59802 Office: Western Montana Clinic 515 W Front St Missoula MT 59802

MORRIS, DAVID JOHN, mining engineer, consultant, mining executive; b. Seattle, May 6, 1945; s. Jack Abraham and Alice Jean (Hanson) M.; m. Melania F. Kearney, July 28, 1978; children: Whitney Elizabeth, Benton James, Sienna Elise. BA in Math. and Physics, Whitman Coll., 1968; BS in Mining Engring., Columbia U., 1968. Registered profl. engr., Colo., Utah, Wash. Mining engr. Union Oil of Calif., Los Angeles, 1968-69; mining engr. John T. Boyd Co., Denver, 1974-76, sr. mining engr., 1976-78, v.p., mgr., 1978—; mng. ptnr. Palmer Coking Coal Co., Black Diamond, Wash., 1976-82, pres. Pacific Coast Coal Co., Black Diamond, 1982—. Mem. Bd. Overseers Whitman Coll., Walla Walla, Wash., 1986—, chmn. Rep. camapign for Whitman, Denver, 1985. Served as lt. USN, 1969-74, Vietnam. Henry Krumb scholar Columbia U., N.Y.C., 1967-68. Mem. NSPE, Soc. Mining Engrs. (admissions com. 1985—, Howard Eavenson award com. 1984—), Western Rugby Football Union (sec. 1980), Denver Country Club, Broadmoor Golf Club, Rotary. Republican. Home: 3711 E Madison Seattle WA 98112 Office: Pacific Coast Coal Co Inc PO Box 450 Black Diamond WA 98010

MORRIS, DAVID LENNOX, II, marketing and insurance executive; b. Indpls., Apr. 9, 1946; s. David Lennox and Clara Rose (Hess) M. BS, Ind. U., 1969. Dir. safety Baldwin and Lyons, Indpls., 1971-77; risk adminstr. City of Pasadena, Calif., 1977-78; risk mgr. Fleetwood Enterprises, Riverside, Calif., 1978-79; sr. analyst Atlantic Richfield Co., Los Angeles, 1980-85; sr. v.p. Pacific Mktg. Systems Ltd., Anaheim, Calif., 1985—; corp. ins. mgr. Am. Contracting Services, Inc., Anaheim, 1987-88; v.p. Earthquake Mut. Ins. Co., Costa Mesa, Calif., 1988—. Mem. Pasadena Tournament of Roses, 1978—. Served to 1st lt. U.S. Army, 1969-71, Vietnam. Decorated Bronze Star; named an Assoc. in Risk Mgmt., Ins. Inst. Am., 1981. Mem. Ind. Motor Truck Assn. (chmn. 1973-74), Risk and Ins. Mgmt. Soc. Republican. Home: 19974 Ridge Manor Way Yorba Linda CA 92686 Office: Earthquake Mut Ins Co 3183 C Airway Ave Costa Mesa CA 92626

MORRIS, DONALD CHARLES, real estate developer; b. Iowa City, Nov. 15, 1951; s. Lucien Ellis and Jean (Pinder) M.; m. Barbara Louise Small, Apr. 28, 1973 (div. Apr. 1980); m. Jana Susan Moyer, Aug. 28, 1982; children: Alexander Charles, Elisa Jean. Student, Cantab Coll., Toronto, Can., 1970-71; BSC, U. Guelph, Guelph, Can., 1974; MSC, U. Guelph, 1975; PhD, U. B.C., Vancouver, 1978. Instr. U. B.C., Vancouver, 1975-77; pres. Morley Internat., Inc., Seattle, 1976-81; self-employed Comml. Investment Real Estate, Seattle, 1981-83; v.p., regional mgr. DKB Corp., Seattle, 1983-86; pres. Morris Devel. Svcs., Inc., Seattle, 1986—, Washington Group, Inc., Seattle, 1986—; bd. dirs. Preservation Action, Washington. Dir. Preservation Action, Washington, 1985—; mem. Nat. Trust for Hist. Preservation. Mem. Seattle King County Bd. Realtors (legis. com.), Wash. Assn. Realtors, Nat. Assn. Realtors, Pioneer Square Assn. Seattle, Pioneer Square Property Owners Assn. Seattle, Meydenbauer Yacht Club. Office: Wash Group Morris Devel 85 S Main St Seattle WA 98104

MORRIS, ELIZABETH TREAT, physical therapist; b. Hartford, Conn., Feb. 20, 1936; d. Charles Wells and Marion Louise (Case) Treat; BS in Phys. Therapy, U. Conn., 1960; m. David Breck Morris, July 10, 1961; children: Russell Charles, Jeffrey David. Phys. therapist Crippled Children's Clinic No. Va., Arlington, 1960-62, Shriners Hosp. Crippled Children, Salt Lake City, 1967-69, Holy Cross Hosp., Salt Lake City, 1970-74; pvt. practice phys. therapy, Salt Lake City, 1975—. Mem. Am. Phys. Therapy Assn., Am. Congress Rehab. Medicine, Salt Lake Area C. of C., Friendship Force Utah, U.S. Figure Skating Assn. Home: 4177 Mathews Way Salt Lake City UT 84124 Office: 2178 So 900 East Ste 3 Salt Lake City UT 84106

MORRIS, ELLIOT MICHAEL, gastroenterologist; b. Glen Cove, N.Y., Feb. 27, 1956; s. Alexander and Frances (Riefberg) M.; m. Marie Buron, Feb. 28, 1988. BS-MD, Albany Med. Coll., 1980. Diplomate Am. Bd. Internal Medicine, Am. Bd. Gastroenterology. Resident U. N.Mex. Hosp., Albuquerque, 1980-83; fellow gastroenterology Duke U. Med. ctr., Durham, N.C., 1984-86; clin. asst. prof. medicine U. Ariz. Med. Ctr., Tucson, 1986-87; pvt. practice Tucson, 1987-89, Missoula, Mont., 1989—. Office: Western Montana Clin 501 W Broadway Missoula MT 59801

MORRIS, JACQUELYN MCCOY, university library administrator; b. Columbus, Ohio, June 14, 1942; d. Donald Richard and Jeanne (Clark) McCoy; m. Richard David Morris, Mar. 19, 1960; children: Patricia A., Michelle A. BA cum laude, Syracuse U., 1971, MS in Library Sci., 1972. Asst. librarian SUNY, Syracuse, 1972-79; head reference div. Albert Mann Library, Cornell U., Ithaca, N.Y., 1979-82; assoc. dean of library U. Pacific, Stockton, Calif., 1982-86; library dir. Occidental Coll., Los Angeles, 1986—; dir. N.Y. Libraries Instructional Clearinghouse, SUNY, Syracuse, 1974-79; cons. U.S. Presdl. Council Environ. Quality, 1980. Author: Library Searching—Research and Strategies, 1978, Teaching Library Skills for Academic Credit, 1985, ACRL College Library Standards, 1986. Bd. dirs Tierra del Oro council Girl Scouts N.Am., cen. Calif., 1985-86. Recipient Chancellors award, SUNY, 1978. Mem. Am. Library Assn. (chmn. com.), Calif. Library Assn., AAAS, 49/99 (mem. exec. council, bd. dirs. 1984-86), Phi Alpha Theta, Beta Phi Mu. Office: Occidental Coll M N Clapp Libr 1600 Campus Rd Los Angeles CA 90041

MORRIS, JEFFREY ALLAN, aerospace executive; b. Half Day, Ill., Jan. 13, 1949; s. Russell Arthur and LaVerne Isabel (Halvorsen) M.; m. Leslie Marie Daynard, Aug. 28, 1971 (div. Dec. 1981); 1 child, Courtney Lyn. BS in Indsl. Engring., U. Ill., 1973; BSBA, U. Redlands, 1979. Liaison engr. aircraft div. Northrop Corp., Hawthorne, Calif., 1973-76, sr. liaison engr. aircraft div., 1976-80, dep. program dir. Korean F-5 coproduction aircraft div., 1980-84, program dir. Korean F-5 coproduction aircraft div., 1984-87; mgr. program adminstrn. Electronics Systems div. Northrop Corp., Anaheim, Calif., 1987—. With USAF, 1967-73. Mem. Airplane Owners & Pilots Assn., Northrop Mgmt. Club. Home: 16182 Mt Lowe Circle Fountain Valley CA 92708 Office: Northrop Corp Electronics Systems div 500 E Orangethorpe Ave Hawthorne CA 90250

MORRIS, JEFFREY LEE, data processing executive; b. Anaheim, Calif., Dec. 8, 1959; s. Phillip Elliot and Kathleen Francis (Martin) M.; m. Jackie Lynn Sharp, Feb. 19, 1977; children: Jeffrey Loren, Jennifer Lynn, Jessica Nicole. Cert. in law enforcement, Orange County (Calif.) Sheriff's Acad., 1981. Computer operator Global Data Corp., Anaheim, 1977-79; supr. data processing Knott's Berry Farm, Inc., Buena Park, Calif., 1979—; cons. ops. documentation, 1987-88; res. officer Orange (Calif.) Police Dept., 1981-84. Scoutmaster Boy Scouts Am., Anaheim, 1983-88; mem. Orange Citizens Steering Com. for Schs., 1987; ednl. and legis. liaison Crescent Sch., Anaheim, 1988. Recipient community svc. award Assn. Calif. Sch. Adminstrs., 1988, Appreciation award, 1988. Mem. Assn. for Computer Ops. Mgmt., Knott's Berry Farm Mgmt. Club. Republican. Lutheran. Home: 138 N Wade Circle Anaheim CA 92807 Office: Knott's Berry Farms Inc 8039 Beach Blvd Buena Park CA 90620

MORRIS, JOHN PHILIP, mechanical engineer; b. Aurora, Colo., Mar. 18, 1958; s. Victor Burton and Shirley Romayne (Hamm) M.; m. Maureen Mulligan, May 24, 1986. BS, Colo. State U., 1982, MS, 1988. Registered profl. engr., Colo.; cert. energy mgr., 1986. Engr. Facilities Svcs., Colo. State U., Ft. Collins, 1983—. Mem. Assn. Energy Engrs., ASME, ASHRAE. Baptist. Office: Colo State U Facilities Svcs N Fort Collins CO 80523

MORRIS, JOHN THEODORE, planning official; b. Denver, Jan. 18, 1929; s. Theodore Ora and Daisy Allison (McDonald) M.; B.F.A., Denver U., 1955; m. Dolores Irene Seaman, June 21, 1951; children—Holly Lee, Heather Ann, Heidi Jo, Douglas Fraser. Apprentice landscape architect S.R. DeBoer & Co., Denver, summer 1949, planning technician (part-time), 1954-55; sr. planner and assoc. Trafton Bean & Assocs., Boulder, Colo., 1955-62; prin. Land Planning Assocs., planning cons., Boulder, 1962-65; planning dir. and park coordinator Boulder County, 1965-67; sch. planner Boulder Valley Sch. Dist., 1967-84, also dir. planning and engring., 1967-84, supr. facility improvement program, 1969-84; pvt. sch. planning cons., 1984—; cons. U. Colo. Bur. Ednl. Field Services, 1974. Bd. dirs. Historic Boulder, 1974-76; mem. parks and recreation adv. com. Denver Regional Council Govts., 1975-84. Served with USCG, 1950-53. Mem. Am. Inst. Cert. Planners, Am. Planning Assn., Council of Ednl. Facility Planners Internat. Home and Office: Jamestown Star Rt 7647 N 32d St Boulder CO 80302

MORRIS, KARLENE EKSTRUM, interior design educator; b. Kimball, S.D., Mar. 4, 1938; d. Carl Leonard and Caren (Johnson) Ekstrum; m. Robert Swift Morris, July 30, 1965; 1 child, Ingrid Caren. BS, S.D.State U., 1960; MA, Calif. State U.-Long Beach, 1964; postgrad., UCLA, Calif. State U. Tchr. Woodrow Wilson High Sch., L.A., 1960-61, Pioneer High Sch., Whittier, Calif., 1961-66; instr. Mt. San Antonio Coll., Walnut, Calif., 1966--; developer interior design program San Antonio Coll., 1971—. Recipient Outstanding Home Econs. Dept. award Chancellors Office L.A. Community Colls., 1984; grantee Illuminating Engrs. N.Am., 1987. Mem. Am. Home Econs. Assn. (treas. 1986--), Am. Soc. Interior Designers, Internat. Soc. Interior Designers, Interior Design Educators Council. Republican. Lutheran. Home: 3643 Yorkshire Rd Pasadena CA 91107

MORRIS, MARC, lawyer; b. Bklyn., Apr. 6, 1953; s. Edward and Lillian (Stone) M. BS, Boloit COll., 1975; JD, New England Sch. Law, 1979; LLM, Boston U., 1980. Bar: Mass. 1979, U.S. Dist. Ct. Mass. 1979, U.S. Ct. Appeals (1st cir.) 1979, Colo. 1981, U.S. Dist. Ct. Colo. 1981. Ptnr. Shaw, Spangler & Roth, Denver, 1981—. Mem. ABA, Colo. Bar Assn., Assn. Trial Lawyers Am. Jewish. Home: 6355 W Portland Pl Littleton CO 80123 Office: Shaw Spangler & Roth 1700 Broadway Denver CO 80290

MORRIS, ROBERT ALBERT, physicist; b. Aurora, Ill., Sept. 24, 1913; s. Maynard Owen and Leone (Funk) M.; m. Ruth Elizabeth Goodwin, May 16, 1942; children: Jeffrey, Christopher. BS in Physics, U. Mich., 1935; postgrad., U. Rochester, 1936-40. Rsch. asst. Eastman Kodak Co., Rochester, N.Y., 1935-42; tech. assoc. Eastman Kodak Co., Rochester, 1945-74; cons., prin. Robert A. Morris Assocs., San Diego, 1978—. Contbg. author: Progress in Photography, 1950, 2d edit., 1954, Television Engineering, 1986; contbr. articles to tech. publs. Fellow Soc. Motion Picture and Television Engring.; mem. Optical Soc. Am., Soc. Imaging Sci. and Tech., Phi Beta Kappa, Phi Kappa Phi. Home: 17637 Pomerado Rd San Diego CA 92128

MORRIS, ROBERT STEVEN, newspaper publisher; b. Princeton, N.J., Nov. 20, 1951; s. Mac Glenn and Janelle (Connevey) M.; 1 child, Manley Wessling. BA, Davidson Coll., 1974. Asst. retail mgr. Kansas City (Mo.) Star, 1974-78; major accounts mgr. N.Y. Daily News, N.Y.C., 1978-81; advt. dir. Denver Post, 1981-85; v.p. advt. Detroit Free Press, 1985-86, Denver Post, 1986-87; pub. L.A. Daily News, 1987—. Inventor inventory print availability technique, 1985; contbr. articles to newspapers. Bd. dirs. Urban League of Denver, 1986-87. Mem. Internat. Newspaper Advt. and Mktg. Execs. (bd. dirs. 1986—, chmn. retail com. 1986—), Young Pres.'s Orgn. Presbyterian. Office: Los Angeles Daily News 21221 Oxnard St Woodland Hills CA 91367

MORRIS, TAMMY MYNETTA, aerospace company executive; b. Arcadia, Calif., Feb. 25, 1959; d. Harold Johnston and O. Ruth (Hatton) M. BA in Tech. Writing, Calif. State U., Long Beach, 1981, MA in Computer Documentation, 1983. Hardware tech. writer Beckman Instruments Inc., Fullerton, Calif., 1983-84; tng. instr., writer TRW, Redondo Beach, Calif., 1984-85, hardware tech. writer, 1985-87, mgr. tech. documentation, sect. head tech. documentation, 1987—; instr. Golden West Coll., Huntington Beach, Calif., 1987—. Musician Pacific Wind Ensemble, Long Beach, Calif., 1987—. Named Charter mem. Nat. English Honor Soc. Mem. Soc. for Tech. Communications (lectr. 1986), IEEE Computer Soc., Assn. for Computing Machinery, Calif. Assn. Faculty in Tech. and Profl. Writing (lectr. 1984-87, bd. dirs. 1986), Jaycees, Sigma Alpha Iota. Lodge: Job's Daughters. Home: PO Box 1091 Palos Verdes Estates CA 90274 Office: TRW One Space Park 04/1699 Redondo Beach CA 90278

MORRISON, DAVID SCOTT, orthopaedic surgeon; b. Wilker-Barre, Pa., Jan. 16, 1953; s. Philip and Carolyn M.; m. Charlotte Kriske, Oct. 1987. BA in Physics, Coll. Holy Cross, 1975; MD, Columbia U., 1979. Diplomate Am. Bd Orthopaedic Surgeons, Nat. Bd. Med. Examiners, Calif., N.Y., Utah. Intern surgery U. Utah Med. Ctr., Salt Lake City, 1979-80, resident surgery, 1980-81; resident orthopaedic surgery Columbia Presbyn. Med. Ctr., N.Y.C., 1981-83, Helen Hayes Hosp., N.Y. State Rehab. Hosp., West Haverstraw and N.Y.C., N.Y., 1982; fellow in orthopaedic surgery Columbia Presbyn. Med. Ctr., N.Y.C., 1983-85; vis. clin. fellow orthopaedic surgery Coll. Physicians and Surgeons Columbia U., Columbia Presbyn. Med. Ctr., N.Y.C., 1982; vis. clin. fellow in shoulder and elbow surgery Columbia U., N.Y.C., 1984; instr. clin. orthopaedic surgery UCLA, 1985, U. Calif., Irvine, 1985; physician So. Calif. Ctr. Sports Medicine, Long Beach, 1986—; vis. clin. prof. orthopaedic surgery III Internat. Course for Continued Edn. Arthroscpy and Servico de Ortopedia e Traumatologia, Sao Paulo, Brazil, 1987. Office: So Calif Ctr Sports Medicine 2760 Atlantic Ave Long Beach CA 90806

MORRISON, EDWARD F, retail executive; b. Balt., Oct. 10, 1949; s. Edward F. and Ida Thelma (Putman) M.; m. Marcy L. Morrison, Oct. 17, 1981; 1 child, Erica Lynn. Gen. mgr. Holiday Inn, various locations, 1967-79; chief engr. Anthony B. Cassedy & Assocs., Ridgefield, Conn., 1979-84; v.p., ops. mgr. pharmacy div. Fred Meyer Inc., Portland, Oreg., 1984—; mgmt. cons. London Rubber Co., 1980, Am. Savs. and Loan, Phoenix, Salt Lake City, Portland, 1981-83. Bd. dirs. Arthritis Found., Portland, 1988. Office: Fred Meyer Inc 3800 SE 22nd Ave Portland OR 97221

MORRISON, FRANCIS MARTIN, real estate broker; b. Phila., Nov. 14, 1936; s. Francis Joseph and Beatrice (Solimeo) M.; m. Janice Norlyn Busk, June 30, 1956 (div. Mar. 1978); children: Bruce, Rebecca Randolph, Valerie; m. Shirley Leone Sink, Mar. 31, 1978; stepchildren: John, Jeffrey. Student, various colls., 1954-80. Commd. U.S. Army, advanced through grades, chief warrant officer; shipping and receiving mgr. Sears Roebuck & Co., Sierra Vista, Ariz., 1977-78; real estate salesman Sierra Vista Realty, Century 21, El Dorado, Sierra Vista, 1978-85; real estate broker Realty World, Andy Anderson Realty, Sierra Vista, 1985—. Contbr. articles to profl. jours. Precinct committeeman Ariz. Rep. Party, Sierra Vista, 1979—, area chmn., 1981-88, state alt. del., Phoenix, 1988; dep. registrar Cochise County, Ariz., 1979—; v.p. Ariz. State Bowling Assn. Mem. Ariz. Assn. Realtors (dir. 1987—, exec. com. 1988-89, regional v.p. 1989—, Hon. Soc. 1987), Nat. Assn. Realtors, Cochise Bd. Realtors (pres. 1988-89, dir. 1980—), 82d Airborne Div. Assn., Vietnam Helicopter Pilots Assn., Elks (com. chmn. 1988—). Republican. Roman Catholic. Home: 5137 Calle Virada Sierra Vista AZ 85635 Office: Realty World 1723 S Hwy 92 Sierra Vista AZ 85635

MORRISON, GUS (ANGUS HUGH MORRISON), mayor, engineer; b. Buffalo, Sept. 13, 1935; s. John Weir and Mary (Norton) M.; m. Joy Rita Hallenbarter, Feb. 7, 1959; children: Frank, Gloria, Heather. Technician Bell Aircraft Corp., Niagara Falls, N.Y., 1956-58; technician Lockheed Missiles and Space Corp., Sunnyvale, Calif., 1958-63, test. engr., 1963-78, group engr., 1978-86, dept. mgr., 1986—. Mayor Fremont, Calif., 1985—, council mem., 1978-85, planning commr., 1977-78; bd. dirs. Tri City Ecology Ctr., 1976—. Served with USN, 1953-56. Democrat. Roman Catholic. Office: Office of Mayor 39700 Civic Center Dr Fremont CA 94538

MORRISON, JOHN GILL, communications executive; b. Upham, N.D., Feb. 22, 1914; s. Claude Collins and Ann Louise (Gill) M.; m. Mary Lou Thompson, Aug. 17, 1940; children: Randolph, Malcolm, Mark, Timothy. BA, U. N.D., 1939, BS, 1940; MD, U. Chgo., 1942. Chmn. bd. Calif. Blueshield, San Francisco, 1960-63; pres. Alameda/Contra Costa Med. Assn., Oakland, Calif., 1961-62, Calif. Med. Assn., San Francisco, 1968-69; council Am. Med. Assn., Chgo., 1970-76; pres., chief exec. officer Audio Digest Fdn., Glendale, Calif., 1973-86; bd. dirs. Am. Sound and Video Corp., Detroit, 1981—; cons. in field. Lt. USN, 1942-48. Mem. Carmel Golf and Country Club. Republican. Home and Office: 450 Hampton Rd Piedmont CA 94611

MORRISON, LINDA LEE, teacher, department chairman; b. Oak Park, Ill., July 21, 1951; d. Richard Edward and Betty Joyce (Engel) M.; m. Bruce Alan Shipman, July 26, 1975; 1 child, Brian Alan. BA, U. Ill., 1973. Cert. tchr., Calif. Travel writer Chgo. Conv. & Tourism Bur., 1973-74; assoc. mgr. Prudential Ins., Chgo., 1974-78; pub. account rep. CNA Ins., Chgo., 1978-81; prodn. dir. Coverdell Ins., Atlanta, 1981-84; tchr. Salesian High Sch., Richmond, Calif., 1985-86; tchr., dept. chmn. John Muir Jr. High Sch., San Leandro, Calif., 1986—. Vol. Children's Meml. Hosp., Oakland, Calif., 1988. Mem. Nat. Council Tchrs. of English, Calif. Assn. Tchrs. English, U. Ill. Alumni Assn., Phi Beta Kappa, Phi Kappa Phi.

MORRISON, MIKE WADE, infosystems specialist, consultant; b. Charlotte, N.C., July 18, 1965; s. Oriville Wilbur Harless and Carol Luis (Soots) M.; m. Sandie Lynn, Aug. 31, 1985. Student, Polamar Coll., 1982. Graphic designer Yuma Daily Sun, 1985-86; personal computer coordinator Yuma Regional Med. Ctr., 1986-88; owner, operator Computers Plus, Yuma, Ariz., 1988—. Pres. Smart Users Group, Yuma, 1987-88. Jehovah's Witness. Home: 550 Robin Ln #42 Yuma AZ 85364

MORRISON, MURDO DONALD, architect; b. Detroit, Feb. 21, 1919; s. Alexander and Johanna (Macaulay) M.; B.Arch., Lawrence Inst. Tech., 1943; m. Judy D. Morrison; children from previous marriage—Paula L., Reed A., Anne H. Individual practice architecture, Detroit, 1949, Klamath Falls, Oreg., 1949-65, Oakland, Calif., 1965-78; partner Morrison Assocs., San Francisco, 1978-85, Burlingame, Calif., 1985—; v.p. Lakeridge Corp., 1968—; chmn. Oreg. Bd. Archtl. Examiners, 1961-65, chmn., 1964. Mem. Town Council Klamath Falls, 1955-57; co-chmn. Oakland Pride Com., 1968-77; mem. Redwood City (Calif.) Gen. Plan Com., 1986. Served with USN, 1943-46. Recipient Progressive Architecture award, 1955, Alumni of Yr. award Lawrence Inst., 1965. Mem. AIA (treas. East Bay, chmn. Oakland chpt.). Presbyterian. Clubs: Commonwealth, Bombay Bicycle Riding. Architect: Gilliam County Courthouse (Progressive Architecture design award), 1955, Chiloquin (Oreg.) Elem. Sch., 1963, Lakeridge Office Bldg., Reno, 1984, Provident Cen. Credit Union Bldg., Monterey, Calif., 1986, The McCosker Corp. Office Bldg., Oakland, Calif., 1986, others. Home: 3645 Jefferson Ave Redwood City CA 94062 Office: 1110 Burlingame Ave Burlingame CA 94010

MORRISON, ROBERT THOMAS, engineering consultant; b. Manson, Iowa, June 4, 1918; s. Charles Henry and Ida Magdeline (Fuessley) M.; m. Callie Louise Warren, July, 25, 1942; children: Linda Ann, Allan Charles, Janis Lou. BS in Mech. Engring., Iowa State U., 1942; MS in Engring., U. Calif., Los Angeles, 1961. Engr. Gen. Electric Co., Schenectedy, N.Y., 1942-45; sales engr., inventory supr. Gen. Electric Supply Corp., Omaha, 1945-50; pres. Morrison Mfg. Co., Omaha, 1950-52; elec. system designer Douglas Aircraft, Long Beach and Santa Monica, Calif., 1952-58; system engr., proposal mgr. Rockwell Internat., Downey, Seal Beach, Anaheim, Calif., 1958-81; freelance cons. Garden Grove, Calif., 1981—; originator, coordinator system engring. program West Coast U., Los Angeles, 1963-71, assoc. dir. devel., 1972. Author: Proposal Manager's Guide, 1972, Proposal Style Guide, 1988, Proposal Publications Guide, 1988. Lay Minister Crystal Cathedral, Garden Grove, 1980—; Garden Grove Energy Commn., 1982-85, Garden Grove Planning Commn., 1960-61; com. chmn. March of Dimes, Orange County, 1973-75; pres. Meth. Men, Garden Grove, 1964, 65. Recipient Apollo Achievement award NASA, 1970, Apollo-Soyuz Test Project award NASA, 1975, Space Shuttle Approach and Landing Test award NASA, 1978. Mem. Assn. Profl. Cons., World Future Soc., Inst. Mgmt. Scis., Ops. Research Soc. Am. Republican. Lodge: Mason. Clubs: Toastmasters (Long Beach, Calif.), Palm Springs Tennis.

MORRISON, ROGER BARRON, geologist; b. Madison, Wis., Mar. 26, 1914; s. Frank Barron and Elsie Rhea (Bullard) M.; BA, Cornell U., 1933, MS, 1934; postgrad. U. Calif., Berkeley, 1934-35, Stanford U., 1935-38; PhD, U. Nev., 1964; m. Harriet Louise Williams, Apr. 7, 1941; children: John Christopher, Peter Hallock and Craig Brewster (twins). Geologist U.S. Geol. Survey, 1939-76; vis. adj. prof. dept. geoscis. U. Ariz., 1976-81, Mackay Sch. Mines, U. Nev., Reno, 1984—; cons. geologist Morrison and Assocs., 1978—; prin. investigator 2 Landsat-1 and 2 Skylab earth resources investigation projects NASA, 1972-75. Fellow Geol. Soc. Am.; mem. AAAS, Internat. Assn. Quaternary Research (past mem. Holocene and pedology commns.), Am. Soc. Photogrammetry, Am. Soc. Agronomy, Soil Sci. Soc. Am., Internat. Soil Sci. Soc., Am. Quaternary Assn., Sigma Xi, Colorado Mountain Club. Author 2 books, co-author one book; editor 1 book; co-editor 2 books; also co-editor Catena, 1973—; contbr. more than 100 articles to profl. jours. Home and Office: 13150 W 9th Ave Golden CO 80401

MORRISON, SHARON LYN, health association administrator; b. Agenda, Kans., Nov. 4, 1937; d. Walter R. and Helen M. (Doupnik) Thompson; m. Raynor L. Morrison, Aug. 22, 1966; 1 child, Lynn A. BS in Nursing, U. Kans., 1959. RN. Supr., instr. internal medicine/neurology unit U. Kans. Med. Ctr., 1959-66; staff and pvt. duty nurse med./surgical unit Southwestern Hosp., Lawton, Okla., 1966; store mgr. MAAG Rod and Gun Club, Taipei, Taiwan, 1968-69; staff and charge nurse Coronary Care Unit, Balt., 1970-71; nurse surveyor Dept. Social Health Svcs., Olympia, Wash., 1972-75, specialty cons., complaint investigator, 1975-76, validation surveyor, 1975-80; program integrity mgr., coord. legal affairs Assn. Health Facilities Licensing & Cert. Dirs., Olympia, Wash., 1981-83, mgr. nursing home survey program, 1983-88; with div. med. assistance Assn. Health Facilities Licensing & Cert. Dirs., Olympia, 1986-88; also bd. dirs. Assn. Health Facilities Licensing & Cert. Dirs.; mem. elective hospitalization home health program Med. Intensive and Hosp. Rehab. Program, Olympia, Wash., 1988—; rep. 4-state mgmt. group Region X, Olympia, 1986—; mem. work group Inst. of Medicine Nat. Acad. Scis., 1985. Vol. Capital Lakefair, Olympia. Mem. Assn. Health Facilities Licensing and Cert. Dirs. (bd. dirs. 1986—), Selah Shrine, Ladies of the Nile. Republican. Presbyterian. Office: Dept Social Health Svcs Div Med Assistance MS HA-11 Olympia WA 98504

MORRISON, SID, congressman, orchardist; b. Yakima, Wash., May 13, 1933; s. Charles Freeman and Anne Helen (Fornfeist) M.; m. Marcella Britton, June 19, 1955; children: Wally, Mary Anne, Linda, Doris. Student, Yakima Valley Coll., 1950-51; B.S. in Agr., Wash. State U., 1954. Orchardist Morrison Fruit Co., Inc., Wash., 1956—; mem. 97th-101st Congresses from 4th Dist. Wash., 1981—, whip for Rep. freshmen, 1981-82, asst. regional whip, 1983-88. Mem. Wash. Ho. of Reps., 1967-74, Wash. State Senate, 1975-80; chmn. Wash. State Apple Commn.; mem. Dept. Agriculture Rsch. Adv. Com.; pres. Wash. State Peach Council. With U.S. Army, 1954-56. Mem. Wash. State Hort. Assn. (bd. dirs.), Grange, Rotary. Office: US Ho Reps 1434 Longworth House Office Bldg Washington DC 20515

MORRISON, VIRGINIA KATHRYN, music educator; b. Santa Rita, N.Mex., Sept. 28, 1946; d. Harland Spencer and Laura Myrtle (Carr) Smith; m. Robert William Morrison, Sept. 2, 1967; 1 child, Pamela Gayle. B of Music, N. Mex. State U., 1970; M of Music, Eastern N.Mex. U., 1985. Tchr. N.Mex. high schs., 1970-78; office mgr. Holland Corp., Roswell, N.Mex., 1981-87; tchr, Mesa Middle Sch., Roswell, 1985-87, Floyd (N.Mex.) Sch., 1987-88. Dir. Enchanters, Roswell, 1980-87. Mem. Am. Choral Dirs. Assn., Mus. Educators Nat. Conf. Office: Floyd Schs PO Box 75 Floyd NM 88118

MORRISON, WILLIAM CHARLES, business and personal education seminar instructor; b. Plainfield, N.J., May 26, 1952; s. Edward Richard and Eileen Linton (Hannah) M. Grad. high sch., Port Jefferson, N.Y.; cert. jewelry design, Charles Adler Sch., Manhattan, 1974; cert. gemologist, Gemilogical Inst. Am., Santa Monica, Calif., 1972. Lapidary, jeweler Ecolin Inc., Stony Brook, N.Y., 1970-72; mgr., jeweler Guys & Dolls, Port Jefferson, 1972-74; owner, jeweler William C. Morrison & Assoc., Santa Cruz, Calif., 1974-78; oriental art restoration, jeweler The Gallery Ltd., Maui, Hawaii, 1978-80; owner, jeweler William C. Morrison Custom Design, Maui, 1980-85; instr. P.S.I. World Seminars, San Rafael, Calif., 1985—; exec. coord. P.S.I. World Seminars, San Rafael, 1986—; options for youth instr. Hollywood High Options for Youth, L.A., San Rafael, 1987—; seminar instr. Mountain Bell, Denver, 1988, Las Vegas Bd. Realtors, 1988, Chevron USA, San Francisco, 1988. Exec. officer Men's Leadership, San Francisco, 1986—. Democrat. Episcopalian. Office: PSI World Seminars 10 N San Pedro Rd Ste 207 San Rafael CA 94901

MORRISON, WILLIAM FOSDICK, electrical company executive; b. Bridgeport, Conn., Mar. 14, 1935; s. Robert Louis and Helen Fosdick (Mulroney) M.; m. E. Drake Miller, Dec. 14, 1957 (div. Sept. 1972); children: Donna Drake, Deanne Fosdick, William Fosdick; m. Carol Ann Stover, Nov. 20, 1972. BA in Econs., Trinity Coll., Hartford, Conn., 1957. Mgr. purchasing dept. Westinghouse Electric Co., Lima, Ohio, 1960-68; mgr. mfg. Westinghouse Electric Co., Upper Sandusky, Ohio, 1969; gen. mgr. Westinghouse Electric Co., Gurabo, P.R., 1970-71; mgr. tng. Westinghouse Electric Co., Pitts., 1972-84; program mgr. Westinghouse Electric Co., Sunnyvale, Calif., 1984—. Author: The Pre-Negotiation Planning Book, 1985; contbr. articles to profl. jours. Bd. dirs. Valley Inst. of the Theatre Arts, Saratoga, Calif., 1986. Served to capt. USAFR, 1958-64. Named Man of the Yr. Midwest Lacrosse Coaches Assn., 1983, recipient Service award U.S. Lacrosse Assn., 1982. Mem. Nat. Assn. Purchasing Mgmt. (pres. Lima chpt. 1966-67, dir. nat. affairs 1967-68, dist. treas. 1968-70). Club: Sunnyvale Golf

Assn. (vice-chmn. 1985, chmn. 1986). Lodge: Elks. Home: 3902 Duncan Pl Palo Alto CA 94306 Office: Westinghouse Electric Co 401 E Hendy Ave Sunnyvale CA 94088

MORRISSEY, JOHN CARROLL, lawyer; b. N.Y.C., Sept. 2, 1914; s. Edward Joseph and Estelle (Caine) M.; m. Eileen Colligan, Oct. 14, 1950; children: Jonathan Edward, Ellen, Katherine, John, Patricia, Richard, Brian, Peter. B.A. magna cum laude, Yale U., 1937, LL.B., 1940; J.S.D., N.Y. U., 1951; grad., Command and Gen. Staff Sch., 1944. Bar: N.Y. State 1940, D.C. 1953, Calif. 1954, U.S. Supreme Ct. 1944. Asso. firm Dorsey and Adams, 1940-41, Dorsey, Adams and Walker, 1946-50; counsel Office of Sec. of Def., Dept. Def., Washington, 1950-52; acting gen. counsel def. Electric Power Adminstrn., 1952-53; atty. Pacific Gas and Electric Co., San Francisco, 1953-70; asso. gen. counsel Pacific Gas and Electric Co., 1970-74, v.p., gen. counsel, 1975-80; individual practice law San Francisco, 1980—; dir. Gas Lines, Inc. Bd. dirs. Legal Aid Soc. San Francisco; chmn. Golden Gate dist. Boy Scouts Am., 1973-75; commr. Human Rights Commn. of San Francisco, 1976-89, chmn., 1980-82; chmn. Cath. Social Service of San Francisco, 1966-68. Served to col. F.A. U.S. Army, 1941-46. Decorated Bronze star. Mem. Calif. Conf. Public Utility Counsel, Am. Bar Assn., San Francisco Bar Assn., Fed. Power Bar Assn., Pacific Coast Electric Assn., Pacific Coast Gas Assn., Econ. Round Table of San Francisco, World Affairs Council, San Francisco C. of C., Calif. State C. of C., Electric Club, Serra Club, Commonwealth Club, Yale Club of No. Calif., Pacific-Union Club, Sometimes Tuesday Club, Phi Beta Kappa. Roman Catholic. Home: 2030 Jackson St San Francisco CA 94109 Office: 215 Market St Ste 215 San Francisco CA 94106

MORROW, CHERYLLE A., accountant, consultant; b. Sydney, Australia, July 3, 1950; came to U.S., 1973; d. Norman H. and Esther A. E. (Jarrett) Wilson. Student U. Hawaii, 1975; diploma Granville Tech. Coll., Sydney, 1967. Acct., asst. treas. Bus. Investment, Ltd., Honolulu, 1975-77; owner Lanikai Musical Instruments, Honolulu, 1980-86, Cheryllе A. Morrow Profl. Svcs., Honolulu, 1981—; fin. managerial cons. E.A. Buck Co., Inc., Honolulu, 1981-84; contr., asst. trustee THC Fin. Corp., Honolulu, 1977-84, bankruptcy trustee, 1984—; panel mem. Chpt. 7 Trustees dist. Hawaii U.S. Depart. Justice, 1988—. Mem. Small Bus. Hawaii PAC, Lanikai Community Assn., Arts Coun. Hawaii, vol., mem. Therapeutic Horsemanship for Handicapped, Small Bus. Adminstrn. (women in bus. com. 1987—). Mem. Australian-Am. C. of C. (bd. dir. 1985—, corp. sec. 1986—, v.p. 1988—), NAFE, Pacific Islands Assn. Women (corp./treas. 1988—). Avocations: reading, music, dancing, sailing, gardening.

MORROW, MAUREEN JANE, interior designer; b. Clinton, Iowa; d. Joseph Kenneth and Rosena Viola (Henricksen) Melvin; m. James Richard Morrow, June 15, 1963; children: Colleen Renée, Kent Richard. AA, Mount Saint Clare, Clinton, Iowa, 1959; BA, U. Iowa, 1961; MS, Calif. Poly. U., 1983. Instr. art Santa Maria (Calif.) Elem Sch. Dist., 1961-63, tchr., 1963-67; cons. interior design Design Collaboration, Santa Maria, 1980-88; instr. design Allan Hancock Coll., Santa Maria, 1983-85, Calif. Polytech. State U., San Luis Obispo, 1984-86; designer, ptnr. Coastal Design Assocs., Santa Maria, 1988—. Coordinator hist. preservation Hart Home, Santa Maria Valley Hist. Soc., 1983—. Mem. Cen. Coast Interior Designers (sec. 1987-88, bd. dirs. 1986-88), Am. Soc. Interior Designers, Inst. Bus. Designers. Club: Minerva (Santa Maria). Office: Coastal Design Assocs 327 E Plaza Dr #4 Santa Maria CA 93454

MORROW, RICHARD TOWSON, lawyer; b. Glendale, Calif., Aug. 3, 1926; s. Ray Leslie and Marion Elizabeth (Towson) M.; m. Virginia Alice Kaspar, June 28, 1947; children—Kathleen Ann, Randall Ray, Nancy Lynn. Student, Occidental Coll., 1944-45; B.A., UCLA, 1947; LL.B., U. So. Calif., 1950. Assoc. Musick & Burrell, Los Angeles, 1950-53; lawyer Walt Disney Prodns., Burbank, Calif., 1953-64, v.p., 1964-69, v.p., gen. counsel, 1969-85, dir., 1971-84; ptnr. Hufstedler, Miller, Kaus & Beardsley, Los Angeles, 1985—; trustee Roy Disney Family Found., Burbank. Pres., bd. dirs. Glendale YMCA, Calif.; mem. adv. bd. Glendale Salvation Army. Served to lt. (j.g.) USNR, 1944-46. Mem. ABA (chmn. corp. law dept. com. 1982-84, council bus. law sect. 1984-88), Calif. Bar Assn., Los Angeles County Bar Assn. (trustee 1975-77, Outstanding Corp. Counsel award 1984-85), Glendale Bar Assn. Republican. Presbyterian. Clubs: Calif., Chancery (Los Angeles); Lakeside Golf (North Hollywood, Calif.); Pauma Valley Country. Home: 1422 N Central Ave Glendale CA 91202 Office: Hufstedler Miller Kaus & Beardsley 355 S Grand Ave 45th Fl Los Angeles CA 90071-3107

MORROW, THOMAS ALEXIS, computer-aided manufacturing applications engineering consultant; b. Phila., Dec. 11, 1946; s. Clifford and Florence (Riley) M.; m. Nancy Amacner, Feb. 26, 1966 (div. 1970); children: Eric Thomas, Christine; m. Elaine Susan Riegel, Nov. 1, 1978; children: Aarin Leigh, Waren Zachary. AA in Phys. Sci., Mira-Costa Jr. Coll., 1974; BA in Phys. Sci., Calif. State U.-Chico, 1976. Mgr. Beich Mobile Home Pk., Chico, Calif., 1976-77; lab. asst. Calif. State U.-Chico, 1976-77; resdl. energy analyst N.E. Wash. Rural Resources, Colville, Wash., 1978; programmer Colmac Ind., Colville, 1979-83; CAD/CAM engr. Vanguard Technologies Corp., Golden, Colo., 1983. Contbr. articles to profl. jours; patentee in field. With U.S. Army, 1964. Mem. Toastmasters (pres. club 3636 1985). Office: Vanguard Techs PO Box 567 Golden CO 80402

MORROW, WINSTON VAUGHAN, lawyer; b. Grand Rapids, Mich., Mar. 22, 1924; s. Winston V. and Selma (von Egloffstein) M.; m. Margaret Ellen Staples, June 25, 1948; children: Thomas Christopher, Mark Staples. AB cum laude, Williams Coll., 1947; JD, Harvard U., 1950. Bar: R.I. 1950. Assoc. atty. Edwards & Angell, Providence, 1950-57; exec. v.p., asst. treas., gen. counsel, bd. dirs. Avis, Inc. and subs., 1957-61; v.p., gen. mgr. Rent A Car div. Avis, Inc., 1962-64, pres., bd. dirs., 1964-75; chmn., chief exec. officer, bd. dirs. Avis, Inc. and Avis Rent A Car System, Inc., 1965-77; chmn., pres., bd. dirs. Teleflorists Inc. and subs., 1978-80; pres. Ticor, Los Angeles, 1981—, chief exec. officer, 1984—, also bd. dirs.; pres., chief exec. officer New TC Holding Corp., 1983—, also bd. dirs.; chmn., chief exec. officer Ticor Title Ins. Co., 1982—, also bd. dirs.; chmn. Ticor Realty Tax Services, also bd. dirs.; bd. dirs. S&L Holdings, Inc., MPB Corp.; mem. Pres.'s Industry and Govt. Spl. Travel Task Force, 1968, travel adv. bd. U.S. Travel Service, 1968-76, Los Angeles City-wide Airport Adv. Com., 1983-85; co-chmn. Los Angeles Transp. Coalition. Mem. juvenile task force Nat. Council Crime and Delinquency, 1985-86, Los Angeles Mayor's Bus. Council, 1983-86, Housing Roundtable, Washington, 1983-85; bd. dirs. Police Found., Washington, 1983—; trustee Com. for Econ. Devel., Washington, 1987—. Served as technician, M.C. AUS, 1943-46. Decorated Stella Della Solidarieta Italy, Gold Tourism medal Austria). Mem. Fed. Bar Assn., R.I. Bar Assn., Car and Truck Rental and Leasing Assn. (nat. pres. 1961-63), Los Angeles Area C. of C. (bd. dirs. 1983-88), Calif. Bus. Roundtable, Pacific Union Club, Bald Peak Colony Club, Racquet and Tennis Club, Williams Club, Internat. Club, Calif. Club, L.A. Tennis Club, Lincoln Club, Centre Santa Ana Club, Phi Beta Kappa, Kappa Alpha. Home: 8306 Wilshire Blvd Ste 1033 Beverly Hills CA 90211 also: Cushing Corners Rd Freedom NH 03836 Office: 6300 Wilshire Blvd Ste 2100 Los Angeles CA 90048

MORSE, BRUCE WARREN, scientist; b. Phoenixville, Pa., Feb. 22, 1957; s. William Frederick and Sylvia (Cathro) M.; m. Beth Ann Murphy, Sept. 5, 1981; children: Jessica, Sarah. BS, U. Del., 1980; MS, U. Minn., 1982, PhD, 1984. Rsch. asst. U. Minn., St. Paul, 1980-84, rsch. assoc., 1984-85; sr. scientist Autometric, Inc., Denver, 1985-88, prin. scientist, 1988—. Contbr. articles to profl. jours. Rsch. grantee Dept. Agr., 1985—, Dept. Interior, 1985—, Dept. Energy, 1988. Mem. Internat. Symposium on Advanced Tech. in Natural Resource Mgmt. (exec. com. 1987—), Am. Soc. Photogrammetry and Remote Sensing (reviewer 1988—), Automated Mapping/Facility Mgmt. Assn. Office: Autometric Inc 165 S Union Blvd St 902 Lakewood CO 80228-2214

MORSE, CARLTON E., author; b. Jennings, La., June 4, 1901; s. George Albert and Ora Anna (Grubb) M; m. Patricia Pattison DeBall, Sept. 23, 1928; 1 child, Mary Noel. Student, U. Calif., 1919-22. Newspaperman Sacramento Union, 1920-22; with various San Francisco newspapers, Seattle Times; writer NBC, from 1930; creator, writer radio series One Man's Family, 1932-59, I Love a Mystery, 1939-42, 43-44, His Honor, the Barber, 1945-46, The Woman in My House, 1951-59, Family Skeleton, 1953-54. Author: Killer at the Wheel, 1987, A Lavish of Sin, 1987, Stuff the Lady's Hatbox, 1988. Address: care Seven Stones Press Star Rte Box 50 Woodside CA 94062 *

MORSE, CHALMERS INGERSOLL, hotel executive; b. Chgo., Mar. 31, 1950; s. Charles Hosmer Jr. and Vesta Putnam (Culbertson) M.; m. Sylvia Page Lilley, Aug. 24, 1974 (div. Dec. 1985); 1 child, Chalmers Ingersoll Jr. AS in Hotel Mgmt., Paul Smith's Coll., 1971. Asst. mgr. Smoke Tree Ranch, Palm Springs, Calif., 1971-77; mgr. catering sales Westin Galleria Plaza, Houston, 1977-79, mgr. front office, 1979-81; exec. asst. mgr. Adam's Mark Hotel, Kansas City, Mo., 1981-85; v.p., gen. mgr. Silvertree Hotel, Snowmass Village, Colo., 1985--. Del. Pitkin County Rep. Com., Aspen, Colo., 1988; treas. Christ Episcopal. Mem. Colo.-Wyo. Hotel Assn., Lodging Assn. Snowmass Village (v.p. 1985-87,. Republican. Home: 115 Maringale Pl Snowmass Village CO 81615 Office: Silvertree Hotel 100 Elbert Ln Snowmass Village CO 81615

MORSE, LOWELL WESLEY, banking executive; b. West Palm Beach, Fla., May 1, 1937; s. Alton and Blanche (Yelverton) M.; B.S., U. Santa Clara, 1968; grad. Def. Lang. Inst., Monterey, Calif., 1959; m. Vera Giacalone, June 22, 1958; children—Lowell Wesley, Stephen D., Michael S. Russian linguist U.S. Army Security Agy., 1957-60; asst. city mgr. City of Pacific Grove (Calif.), 1961-66; city mgr. Town of Los Altos Hills (Calif.), 1967-69; chmn. Morse & Assos., Inc., Carmel, Calif., 1972—; founder, dir. Plaza Bank of Commerce, San Jose, 1979—. Served with U.S. Army, 1957-60. Home: PO Box 222980 Carmel CA 93922 Office: 26619 Carmel Center Pl Ste 201 Carmel CA 93923

MORSE, MARJORY HELEN, teacher, small business owner; b. Fargo, N.D., Jan. 18, 1929; d. Clarence R. and Helen Elizabeth (Bowman) Jacobsen; m. Stanley Allen Morse, Aug. 10, 1958; children: Kimberly Ann, Kandice Lynn. BA, U. N.D., 1950; MusB, MacPhail Mus. Coll., 1954. Cert. secondary tchr., N.D., Mont. Tchr. English, music Northwood (N.D.) Pub. Schs., 1950-52, Dickinson (N.D.) Pub. Schs., 1952-53; tchr. English Great Falls (Mont.) High Sch., 1954-62, substitute tchr., 1962-88; owner, operator Kitchen Kapers Catering Service, Great Falls, 1984—; supt. home arts Mont. State Fair, Great Falls, 1985—; dir. choir 1st United Meth. Ch., Great Falls, 1969-82; pvt. tchr. music, Great Falls, 1954—. Mem. AAUW (pres. Great Falls br. 1968-70, Mont. state pres. 1982-84), Bus. and Profl. Women's Club (Woman of Achievement 1986), Phi Beta Kappa. Mem. United Ch. Christ. Lodge: Order Eastern Star. Home: 802 E 50th St Great Falls MT 59405

MORSE, SCOTT DAVID, agricultural trade executive, consultant; b. Sacramento, Dec. 6, 1950; s. David Comestock and Jane Berenice (Derr) M. BSFS in Internat. Econs., Georgetown U., 1974, MSFS in Internat. Trade, 1983. Adminstrv. asst. nat. security coun. Exec. Office of The Pres. of U.S., Washington, 1972-73; internat. trade specialist Calif. Farm Bur. Fedn., Berkeley, Calif., 1975-76; mgr. commodity svc. div. Calif. Farm Bur. Fedn., 1977-81; agrl. trade cons. Patton, Boggs & Blow, Washington, 1983; v.p. agribus. BankAm. World Trade Corp., San Francisco, 1984-85; pres. Morse Mcht. Agribus., San Francisco, 1985—; adj. lectr. Santa Clara U., 1988—; cons. in field. Contbr. over a dozen articles to profl. jours. Mem. Am. Soc. Agrl. Cons. (cert.), Internat. Trade Coun. (bd. dirs. 1987—0, Internat. Mgrs. Assn. (bd. dirs., treas. San Francisco area 1986—), San Francisco Bay Club, Georgetown Club (bd. dirs.), Gergetown U. Alumni Assn. Office: Morse Mcht Agribus 700 Montgomery St Ste 305-A San Francisco CA 94111-2104

MORTELL, ROBERT THOMAS, aerospace and electronics company executive; b. Brookhaven, N.Y., June 6, 1946; s. Frank and Catherine Gretchen (Schellhammer) M.; m. Jacqueline Mary Corvaia, Nov. 1, 1969 (div. 1986); 1 child, Angela. BA, N.Y. Inst. Tech., 1974. Sr. analyst Grumman Aerospace, Bethpage, N.Y., 1974-80; mgr. program planning Grumman Aerospace, St. Augustine, Fla., 1980-86; staff mgr. bus. ops. McDonnell Douglas, Monrovia, Calif., 1986-88; mgr., cost mgmt. McDonnell Douglas Electronic Systems Co., Huntington Beach, Calif., 1989—. Treas. Big Bros./Big Sisters, St. Augustine, 1986. With USAF, 1963-67. Mem. Sertoma (treas. St. Augustine chpt. 1983, sec. 1984). Republican. Presbyterian. Home: PO Box 436 Monrovia CA 91017

MORTENSEN, SUSAN MARIE, manufacturing company executive; b. Portland, Oreg., Jan. 24, 1950; d. Leslie Dean Mortensen and Kathryn Merdell Huff; m. José Garcia Ruiz, Oct. 25, 1986. BA, U. Portland, 1972. Advt. dir. B.A.C. Inc., Portland, 1972-76, v.p., 1976-81; exec. dir. Econ. Devel. Assn. Skagit County, Inc., Mt. Vernon, Wash., 1982-86; mgr. Sugiyo U.S.A., Inc., Anacortes, Wash., 1986-87, exec. dir., 1987—. Active Skagit County Tourism Task Force., Washington, 1984; rep. Team Wash. Asian Mission, Japan, 1986; ambassador Wash. Partnership for Econ. Devel., 1984—. Mem. Japan-Am. Soc., Econ. Devel. Execs. Wash. (bd. dirs. 1985—), Anacortes C. of C. Jansen Found. grantee, 1985, Team Wash. Dept. Trade, 1985, Local Devel. Fund Matching Dept. Com. Devel., Washington, 1986.

MORTENSEN, THOMAS GILBERT, account manager; b. Elkhorn, Wis., May 9, 1951; s. Gilbert Harold and Doris Lillian (Christiansen) M.; m. Geraldine Orgill, June 6, 1981; children: Heather, Darren. BEE, U. N. Mex., 1974, MEE, 1980. Analyst E-Systems, Dallas, 1974-76; analyst research inst. U. Dayton, Albuquerque, 1977-79; scientist Jaycor, Albuquerque, 1979-81; region analyst Cray Research, Inc., Albuquerque, 1981-87, account mgr., 1987—. Republican. Lutheran. Office: Cray Rsch Inc 8500 Menaul St Ste A225 Albuquerque NM 87112

MORTENSON, MARVIN WARD, human resources director; b. Sioux Rapids, Iowa, Nov. 21, 1936; s. Elder Wilhelm and Sylvia Ann (Ross) M.; m. Gloria Kay Simpson, June 12, 1960; children: Michele Marie, Jayma Doreè, Christin Kayle. BA, Buena Vista Coll., 1960. Mgr. loan dept. Crocker Bank, Lompoc, Calif., 1960-66; mgr. employee rels. ITT Fed. Electric Corp., Paramus, N.J., 1966-72; mgr. laying hens Jerimison Farms, Mineota, Minn., 1970-72; owner, operator Western Auto Store, Carson City, Nev., 1978-82; mgr. employment and svcs. ITT, Van Nuys, Calif., 1972-78; dir. human resources IDEA Courier (formerly Alcatel Info. Systems), Tempe, Ariz., 1982—; Mem. Gov.'s Com. on Employment Handicapped, Phoenix, 1982-86; chmn. Mayor's Com. on Employment Handicapped, Tempe, 1985-87; bd. dirs. Tempe Ctr. for the Handicapped, 1985-87; crisis counselor Grace Community Ch., Tempe, 1984-86; mem. Valley of the Sun United Way, Phoenix and Tempe, 1982-87. Democrat. Mem. First Christian Disciples of Christ Ch. Home: 4133 Ashurst Dr Phoenix AZ 85044

MORTKOWITZ, BARBARA, office interiors and furniture designer, importer; b. Erding, Fed. Republic Germany, Oct. 5, 1946; came to U.S., 1951; d. Michael and Maria (Scheinmann) M. BA, San Jose State U., 1969; postgrad., Coll. Arts and Crafts, Oakland, Calif., 1973-75, U. Calif. Extension, Berkeley, 1981-85. Nat. cert. interior design qualifications. Designer Environ. Design & Rsch., San Francisco, 1973-75, Henry Conversano & Associates, Oakland, 1975-76, FACS FOR Offices, San Francisco, 1976-80, Reel Grobman & Assocs., —, 1980-83; prin. Barbara Mortkowitz Planning & Design & Sources in Design, Sausalito, Calif., 1983—. Work pub. in Interior Design mag., Interiors mag. Vol. tour leader Marin Civic Ctr., San Rafael, Calif., 1985; vol. Marin Arts Coun., Bus. Vols. for Arts; mem. Citizens Ambassador Program. Recipient award for project of yr. Chem. Bank, San Francisco, 1986. Mem. Inst. Bus. Designers (bd. dirs. San Francisco 1976-82, pub. rels. v.p. 1981-82). Office: 4000 Bridgeway Ste 301 Sausalito CA 94965

MORTON, CARL, obstetrician-gynecologist; b. Detroit, Apr. 17, 1938; s. David G. and Goldie (Jacobs) M.; m. Sharon Cecelia Boyer, Oct. 15, 1966; children: Joshua Paul, Goldie Melissa. BA, U. Mich., 1960; MD, Wayne State U., 1965. Diplomate Am. Bd. Ob-Gyn. Intern Sinai Hosp., Detroit, 1965-66; resident ob-gyn. William Beaumont Hosp., Royal Oak, Mich., 1966-69; practice medicine specializing in ob-gyn. Southfield, Mich., 1971-72, Honolulu, 1972—. Maj. U.S. Army, 1969-71. Fellow Am. Coll. Ob-Gyn.; mem. Hawaii Med. Assn., Honolulu County Med. Soc., AMA, Pacific Coast Fertility Soc., Am. Inst. Ultrasound in Medicine. Office: 1319 Punahou St Ste 980 Honolulu HI 96826-1079

MORTON, CHARLES BRINKLEY, bishop, former state legislator; b. Meridian, Miss., Jan. 6, 1926; s. Albert Cole and Jean (Brinkley) M.; m. Virginia Roseborough, Aug. 26, 1948; children—Charles Brinkley, Mary Virginia. JD with distinction, U. Miss., 1949; MDiv optime merens, U. South, 1959, DD, 1982. Bar: Miss. 1949, Tenn.; ordained to ministry Protestant Episcopal Ch. as deacon and priest, 1959. Sole practice Senatobia, Miss., 1949-56; mem. Thomas & Morton, Senatobia, Miss., 1952-56, Miss. Ho. of Reps., 1948-52, Miss. Senate, 1952-56; priest-in-charge Ch. of Incarnation, West Point, Miss., 1959-62; rector Grace-St. Luke's Ch., Memphis, 1962-74; dean Cathedral of Advent, Birmingham, Ala., 1974-82; bishop Episcopal Diocese of San Diego, 1982—. Contbr. articles to law and hist. jours. Mem. Miss. Commn. Interstate Coop., 1952-56, Miss. State Hist. Commn., 1952-56; chmn. bd. Bishop's Sch., La Jolla, Calif., Episcopal Community Services, San Diego; trustee Berkeley Div. Sch., Yale U.; active numerous civic and cultural groups. Served with AUS, World War II, Korea; col., chaplain Res. ret. Decorated Silver Star, Bronze Star medal with cluster, Purple Heart, Combat Inf. Badge; recipient Freedoms Found. Honor medal, 1967, 68, 72. Mem. Mil. Order World Wars, Am. Legion (past post comdr.), Phi Delta Phi, Tau Kappa Alpha, Omicron Delta Kappa, Phi Delta Theta. Lodge: Rotary. Office: St Paul's Ch 2728 6th Ave San Diego CA 92103

MORTON, DONALD LEE, surgery educator; b. Richwood, W.Va., Sept. 12, 1934; s. Howard Jennings and Mary Gertrude (Boggs) M.; m. Wilma Miley (dec. Aug. 1982); children: Diana Lynn, Laura Ann, Donald Jr., Christen Helene. BA, U. Calif., Berkeley, 1955; MD, U. Calif., San Francisco, 1958. Diplomate Am. Bd. Surgery, Am. Bd. Thoracic Surgery; lic. surgeon Calif. State Bd. Med. Examiners. Intern U. Calif. Med. Ctr., San Francisco, 1958-59, resident in surgery, 1959-60, surg. fellow, 1962-66; clin. assoc. surgeon Nat. Cancer Inst., NIH, Bethesda, Md., 1960-62; sr. investigator Nat. Cancer Inst., NIH, Bethesda, 1966-69, sr. surgeon, head tumor immunology sect., 1969-71; chief surgery VA Hosp., Sepulveda, Calif., 1971-74, chief oncology sect., surg. services, 1974-81; prof. surgery, chief surg. oncology div. UCLA, 1971—, chief gen. surgery div., 1977-82; hon. med. staff surgery Cedars-Sinai Med. Ctr., Los Angeles, 1981—; mem. immunology adv. segment Nat. Cancer Inst., 1969-71, search com., 1974, bd. sci. counselors, 1974-78, surg. oncology research devel. subcom. 1979-84; mem. com. for objective 6 Nat. Cancer Plan, 1971, chmn. surg. onconolgy research program planning, 1974; sci. adv. council Cancer Research Inst. 1974, bd. sci. advisors, 1974-80; sci. adv. bd. Wash. U., St. Louis, 1974-80; exec. policy com. Jonsson Comprehensive Cancer Ctr., UCLA, 1981—, ad hoc peer rev. com. 1984—. Mem. editorial bd. Jour. Nat. Cancer Inst., Jour. Surg. Oncology, Seminars in Oncology, Jour. Surg. Research, Surgery, Cancer Immunology and Immunotherapy; editorial adv. bd. Cancer Research, Clin. Orthopaedics Related Research. Served with USPHS, 1960-69. Recipient Superior Service award HEW, 1970, Esther Langer award U. Chgo., 1978, Golden Scalpel Teaching Excellence award, 1983-84, Cancer Immunology award Cancer Research Inst. Mem. AAAS, ACS, AMA, Am. Assn. Cancer Edn., Am. Assn. Cancer Research, Am. Assn. Thoracic Surgery, Am. Assn. Immunologists, Am. Radium Soc., Am. Soc. Exptl. Pathology, Am. Soc. Clin. Oncology (chmn. nominating com. 1976-77), Am. Soc. Microbiology, Am. Surg. Assn., Assn. Acad. Surgery, Bay Surg. Soc., Los Angeles County Med. Assn., Los Angeles Surg. Soc., Naffziger Surg. Soc., Pacific Coast Surg. Assn., Pan-Pacific Surg. Assn., Physician's Aid Assn., Reticuloendothelial Soc., Societe Internationale de Chirurgie, Soc. Head and Neck Surgeons, Soc. Surg. Oncology (ad hoc com. clin. research 1976-81, chmn. govt. relations com. 1978-81, long range planning com. 1981-84, exec. com. 1981-82, clin. research and govt. relations com. 1984-85), Soc. Univ. Surgeons, Transplantation Soc., Western Med. Research Assn., Western Thoracic Surg. Soc., Am. Coll. Chest Physicians. Office: UCLA Sch Medicine Div Surg Oncology Louis Factor Bldg Los Angeles CA 90024

MORTON, HENRIETTA OLIVE, academic administrator; b. Elbert, Colo., May 22, 1937; d. Henry Oliver and Mary Irene (Wasson) Pearson; m. Wayne Wilbur Morton, Dec. 29, 1956 (div. Aug. 1987); children: Lonnie Wayne, Vicki Rae. BA in Adult Edn. Adminstrn., Loretta Heights Coll., 1984. Supr. of community edn. and adminstrn. Colo. Northwestern Com. Coll., Steamboat Springs, Colo., 1975-80; dir. of community edn. Colo. Mountain Coll., Steamboat Springs, Colo., 1980—; mchts. coun. mem. Steamboat Chamber Resort Assn., 1985—, econ. devel. coun. mem. V.p., treas. Routt County Sch. Dist. RE-1, 1967-75; vice-chair Rep. Party, 1988—. Mem. Colo. Assn. Sch. Bds. (honor roll 1975), Mountain Plains Adult Edn. Assn., Nat. Coun. Community Svcs. and Continuing Edn., Internat. Toastmistress Club. Republican. Home: PO Box 771948 Steamboat Springs CO 80477 Office: Colo Mountain Coll PO Box 775288 Steamboat Springs CO 80477

MORTON, HUGHES GREGORY, real estate development executive; b. St. Joseph, Mo., Aug. 11, 1923; s. William Marmaduke and Jeanette (Hughes) M.; B.S., Wharton Sch. U. Pa., 1947; postgrad. UCLA, 1949-50; children: William Marmaduke II, Hughes Gregory, Mary Gladys. Lic. real estate broker Calif. Divisional personnel dir. Carnation Co., Los Angeles, 1950-52; contractors rep. Calif. Portland Cement Co., Los Angeles, 1959-64; v.p. Western Fed. Savs. & Loan Assn., Los Angeles, 1964-70; owner Morton and Assos., Beverly Hills, Calif., 1970—.Served as lt. (j.g.) USNR, 1941-46. Mem. Internat. Assn. Real Estate Appraisers. Office: PO Box 69421 Los Angeles CA 90069

MORTON, IRA L., advertising and public relations executive; b. Chgo., May 29, 1921; s. Jacob David and Esther (Kabrin) Lifschutz; m. Beryl Schubert, Dec. 28, 1952; children: Debra Morton Gelbart, Joel David. BS in Journalism, U. Ill., 1944. Lic. real estate broker, Ariz. With Time, Inc., Chgo., 1944-46; account exec. Jones Frankel Advt. Co., Chgo., 1946-49; founder, pres. Ira Morton Advt., Phoenix, 1961—. Author: The Red Grange Story, 1953, The Galloping Ghost, 1981; syndicated newspaper column, 1950-52; columnist Phoenix Gazette, 72-74; radio feature A Name to Remember, 1981—. Chmn. Communications North Phoenix Corp. Ministry, 1974-77. Served with U.S. Army, 1942-43. Mem. Nat. Acad. TV Arts and Scis. (life, pres. Phoenix chpt. 1970-71), U. Ill. Alumni Assn. Home: 8332 N 8th Ave Phoenix AZ 85021 Office: Ira Morton Advt 49 E Thomas Rd Phoenix AZ 85012

MORTON, ROBERT ARTHUR, travel agency owner; b. Buffalo, Sept. 2, 1942; s. Arthur M. and Elizabeth Mary (Mudie) M.; m. Georgia Ann Horvath, Aug. 16, 1969. BA, Bucknell U., 1964; MBA, U. Pa. Wharton Sch., 1966. Mgr. budgets American Airlines Inc., N.Y.C., 1966-71; cost and systems controller Princeton U., Princeton, N.J., 1971-77; v.p. fin. Hickory Farms of Ohio Inc., Maumee, Ohio, 1978-81; dir. fin. and acctg. Taco Tico Inc., Wichita, Kans., 1982-83; controller Western Systems Inc., Agana, Guam, 1984-85; pres. Uniglobe Airpark Travel Inc., Scottsdale, Ariz., 1986—; Bd. dirs. Jr. Achievement of Northwest Ohio, Toledo, 1981. Served to capt. U.S. Army, 1966-69. Office: Uniglobe Airpark Travel Inc 7335 E Acoma Dr Ste 201 Scottsdale AZ 85260

MORTON, S. BRUCE, aerospace company executive; b. Phila., Sept. 13, 1944; s. Mark and Ruth Morton. BA in Aero. Engring., NYU, 1966; MS in Mech. Engring., U. Pa., 1968. Design engr. Gen. Electric Co., Phila., 1966-76; program mgr. Gen. Electric Co., Valley Forge, Pa., 1976-78, mgr. aerospace mktg., 1978-84; dir. bus. devel. Avco Everett (Mass.) Rsch. Lab., 1984-86; mgr. strategic planning and mkt. rsch. Rockwell Internat., Anaheim, Calif., 1986—; . Mem. IEEE, AIAA. Office: Rockwell Internat 3370 Miraloma Ave Anaheim CA 92803

MORTVEDT, HOWARD WILLIAM, optometrist, consultant; b. Everett, Wash., Nov. 16, 1942; s. Howard Jacob and Emily Elizabeth (Webber) M.; m. Susan Burness, Apr. 6, 1968 (div. 1974); 1 child, Sonja Heidi; m. Betti-Jo Busch, Dec. 17, 1983; children: Janna, Jeff. AAS, Everett Jr. Coll., 1963; BA in Biology, Pacific Luth. U., 1966; OD, Pacific U., 1973. Owner Marysville (Wash.) Optometric Clinic, 1974—; contact lens clin. investigator, 1981—; cons. vision Hewlett-Packard, Lake Stevens, Wash., 1981—, Bayliner Marine Corp., Arlington, Wash., 1984—. Served with U.S. Army, 1966-69, Vietnam. Mem. Wash. Optometric Assn. (trustee 1986-89, chmn. peer rev. 1987—, Award of Merit 1987, 88), Snohomish County Optometric Soc. (pres. 1979-81, Award of Merit 1980, 81), Marysville C. of C. Baptist. Lodge: Rotary. Home: 4117 79th Pl NW Marysville WA 98270 Office: Marysville Optometry Clinic 1720 Grove Marysville WA 98270

MORVICE, MARK DONALD, mechanical engineer; b. Rockford, Ill., Nov. 25, 1958; s. Donald C. and Donna M. (Wolfram) M. BME, Marquette U., 1980; MBA, Seattle U., 1988. Facilities equipment engr. Boeing Comml. Airplanes, Renton, Wash., 1980-86, facilities engring. supr., 1986—. Mem. ASME (assoc.), Marquette Club Western Wash. (bd. dirs. 1982—). Office: Boeing Comml Airplanes PO Box 3707 M/S 63-32 Seattle WA 98124

MOSBY, DOROTHEA SUSAN, municipal official; b. Sacramento, Calif., May 13, 1948; d. William Laurence and Esther Ida (Lux) M. AA in Sociology, Bakersfield (Calif.) Coll., 1966-69; BS in Recreation, San Jose State U., 1969-72; MA in Pub. Adminstrn., Calif. State U. Dominguez Hills, Carson, 1980-82. Asst. dept. personnel officer San Jose Parks and Recreation Dept., 1972-73, neighborhood ctr. dir., 1973-74; sr. recreation leader Santa Monica Recreation and Parks Dept., 1974-76, recreation supr., 1976-83, bus. div. head, 1983-88; bus. adminstr. Santa Monica Cultural & Recreation Svcs., 1988-89; with Santa Monica City Employees Fed. Credit Union, 1988—; bd. dirs, officer Santa Monica City Employees Fedn. Credit Union, 1980—, pres. 1986, 87; mem. citizens adv. com. Los Angeles Olympic Organizing Com., 1982-84. Mem. choir, flute soloist Pilgrim Luth. Ch., Santa Monica, 1974—, treas.Luth. ch. council, 1984-86; vol. driver XXIII Olympiad, Los Angeles, 1984; contbr. local housing assistance U.S. Olympic Com., Los Angeles, 1984; mem. adv. com. Windsor Sq. Hancock Park Hist. Soc., Los Angeles, 1983, dir. Christmas carolling, 1980—, chmn. Olympic com., 1984, bd. trustees, 1984—, chmn. pub. programs, 1985, co-chmn. pub. programs, 1986, co-vice chair, 1987, chmn., 1988, 89—. Mem. Calif. Park and Recreation Soc. (bd. dirs. 1979-82, 86), Nat. Recreation and Park Assn., Mgmt. Team Assocs. (sec., treas. 1978-83), Chi Kappa Rho (pres. 1986), Pi Alpha Alpha. Home: 1134 Chelsea Ave Apt C Santa Monica CA 90403 Office: Cultural & Recreation Svcs 1685 Main St Santa Monica CA 90401

MOSCICKI, JOHN MARTIN, management development consultant; b. Clinton, Ind., Nov. 9, 1951; s. Martin C. and Yvonne E. (Uhrin) M.; m. Anne Marie Teters, May 31, 1986. BS, Fla. State U., 1973, MS, 1977; PhD, Columbia U., 1982. Instrnl. systems design engr. Grumman Aerospace, Bethpage, N.Y., 1978-79; sr. rsch. mgr. Xerox Learning Systems, Stamford, Conn., 1979-83; ptnr. Keilty, Goldsmith & Boone, La Jolla, Calif., 1984—. Designer, exec. producer Internactive Video Feedback System, 1984; co-inventor, patentee in field. Home: 127 Marietta Dr San Francisco CA 94127 Office: Keilty Goldsmith & Boone 1298 Prospect St La Jolla CA 92037

MOSCON, JOE DAVID, material handling executive; b. Santa Rosa, Calif., Sept. 24, 1952; s. Joe D. and Ruby (Peters) M.; m. Cindy (divorced); children: Joseph James, Angelina M.; m. Susanne Dawn, Jan. 15, 1981; children: Nicholas A., Frederick A., Daniel A., Stephen L. Student, Santa Rosa Jr. Coll., Yuba Coll. Svc. engr. Hyster Co./Fabtek, Healdsburg, Calif., 1978-80; gen. mgr. Roach & Assoc., Healdsburg, 1981-85, Atlas Lift Truck/Intl., Vallejo (Calif.) and Chgo., 1985—. Mem. Material Handling Equipment Distrbn. Assn. Office: 9775 Dawn Way Windsor CA 95492

MOSELEY, JOHN TRAVIS, university administrator, research physicist; b. New Orleans, Feb. 26, 1942; s. Fred Baker and Lily Gay (Lord) M.; m. Belva McCall Hudson, Aug. 11 1964 (div. June 1979); m. Susan Diane Callow, Aug. 6, 1979; children: Melanie Lord, John Mark, Stephanie Marie, Shannon Eleanor. BS in Physics, Ga. Inst. Tech., 1964, MS in Physics, 1966, PhD in Physics, 1969. Asst. prof. physics U. West Fla., Pensacola, 1968-69; sr. physicist SRI Internat., Menlo Park, Calif., 1969-75, program mgr., 1976-79; vis. prof. U. Paris, 1975-76; assoc. prof. U. Oreg., Eugene, 1979-81, dir. chem. physics inst., 1980-84, prof. physics, 1984—, head physics dept., 1984-85, v.p. rsch., 1985—; bd. dirs. Oreg. Resource and Tech., Portland; mem. com. on Atomic and Molecular Sci., 1983-85. Contbr. numerous articles to profl. jours. Mem. So. Willamette Rsch. Corridor, Eugene, 1985—, Lane Econ. Devel. Com., Eugene, 1988—; bd. dirs. Eugene/Springfield Metro Partnership, 1985—, Oreg. Bach Festival, Eugene, 1987—. Rcipient Doctoral Thesis award Sigma Xi, 1969; Fulbright fellow, 1975; numerous rsch. grants, 1969—. Fellow Am. Physical Soc.; mem. Am. Chem. Soc., Am. Assn. for Advancement Sci., Am. Assn. Univ. Prof. Office: U Oreg 110 Johnson Hall Eugene OR 97403

MOSER, DEAN JOSEPH, accountant; b. San Francisco, Apr. 5, 1942; s. Joseph Edward and Velma Ida (Cruz) M.; B.S., U. San Francisco, 1964, postgrad. Law Sch., 1964-66; MA in taxation, Golden Gate U., 1988; m. Michele Patrice Cicerone, June 16, 1963; children—Jay, Lynele, Todd. CPA, Calif.; cert. fin. planner; lic. real estate broker, Calif. Owner, acct. DJM Bookkeeping Service, 1962-65; asst. controller Dymo Industries, Internat., Berkeley, Calif., 1965-67; mgr. taxes Arthur Andersen & Co., San Francisco, 1967-76; owner, mgr. Contadora Ltd., Novato, Calif., 1981—, Esprit Realty Co., Novato, 1981—; Dean J. Moser Accountancy Corp., Novato, 1981—, Stellar Properties; gen. ptnr. Galli Sq.; founding dir., treas., chief fin. officer Novato Nat. Bank, NorthBay Bancorp. Asst. scout master Boy Scouts Am.; past bd. dirs. Novato Human Needs Center. C.P.A., Calif. Mem. Calif. Soc. CPA's, Am. Inst. CPA's. Republican. Roman Catholic. Club: Rotary (Paul Harris fellow, pres. Ignacio and pres. Marin pres.'s council). Office: 94 Galli Dr Novato CA 94949

MOSES, EDWARD CROSBY, painter; b. Long Beach, Calif.; s. Alfonsus Lemuel and Olivia (Branco) M.; m. Avilda Peters, Aug. 11, 1959; children: Cedd, Andrew. BA, U. Calif., L.A., 1954, MA, 1956. lectr. painting, drawing UCLA, 1961, 75-76, U. Calif., Irvine, 1969-72, Bakersfield Coll., Calif., 1977; guest lectr. Oberlin Coll., Wichita Art Mus., Cranbrook Inst. Numerous one-man shows, 1958—, latest include Andre Emmerich Gallery, N.Y.C., 1974-75, Los Angeles County Mus. Art, 1976, Smith-Anderson Gallery, Palo Alto, Calif., Tex. Gallery, Houston, 1979, High Mus. Art, Atlanta, 1980, Dorothy Rosenthal Gallery, Chgo., 1982, Janus Gallery, L.A., 1982, Bernard Jacobson Gallery, L.A., 1983, Dorothy Rosenthal Gallery, Chgo., 1982—, L.A. Louver Gallery, Venice, 1985-89, Galeria Joan Pratt, N.Y.C., 1989, Galerie Georges Lavrov, Paris; exhibited numerous group shows, 1958—, latest include Corcoran Gallery Art, Washington, 1979, High Mus., 1980, San Francisco Mus., 1980, San Francisco Art Inst., 1981, Mus. Modern Art, Paris, 1982, L.A. Mcpl. Gallery, 1982, Mus. Contemporary Art, L.A., 1983, 86, Nat. Gallery Art, Washington, 1984, Nat. Gallery of Modern Art, 1988, Smithsonian Instn., 1986, Galerie Koltontorvet, Copenhagen; represented in permanent collections U. Calif. Art Mus., Berkeley, Seattle Art Mus., San Francisco Art Mus., Mus. Modern Art, N.Y.C., San Francisco Art Inst., Chgo. Art Inst., Hirshhorn Mus., Phila., Akron Art Inst., Ohio, Harvard U., Cambridge, Mass., Yale U., New Haven, Walker Art Mus., Mpls., Corcoran Gallery Art, Whitney Mus. Am. Art, N.Y.C., Mus. Modern Art, N.Y.C., Los Angeles County Mus. Art, Nat. Mus. Am. Art at Smithsonian Inst., Washington, Phila. Mus. Art. Served with USN, 1944-46. Recipient Tamarind fellowship in lithography, 1968, Art in Pub. Places award Calif. Arts Coun., 1987; NEA grantee, 1976; Guggenheim fellow, 1980. Office: Los Angeles Louver Gallery 55 N Venice Blvd Venice CA 90291

MOSES, ELBERT RAYMOND, JR., speech and dramatic arts educator; b. New Concord, Ohio, Mar. 31, 1908; s. Elbert Raymond Sr. and Helen Martha (Miller) M.; m. Mary Miller Sterrett, Sept. 21, 1933 (dec. Sept. 1984); 1 child, James Elbert (dec.); m. Caroline Mae Entenman, June 19, 1985. AB, U. Pitts., 1932; MS, U. Mich., 1934, PhD, 1936. Instr. U. N.C., Greensboro, 1936-38; asst. prof. Ohio State U., Columbus, 1938-46; assoc. prof. Ea. Ill. State U., Charleston, 1946-56; asst. prof. Mich. State U., E. Lansing, Mich., 1956-59; prof. Clarion (Pa.) State Coll., 1959-71, chmn. dept. speech and dramatic arts, 1959—, emeritus prof., 1971—; Fulbright lectr. State Dept. U.S. Cebu Normal Sch., Cebu City, Philippine Islands, 1955-56; vis. prof. phonetics U. Mo., summer 1968; hon. sec.'s advocate dept. of aging State of Pa., Harrisburg, 1980-81. Author: Guide to Effective Speaking, 1957, Phonetics: A History and Interpretation, 1964, Three Attributes of God, 1983, Adventure in Reasoning, 1988; contbr. articles to profl. jours. Del. 3d World Congress Phoneticians, Tokyo, 1976; mem. nat. adv. com. fgn. students and tchrs. HEW; del. to Internat. Congress, Soc. Logopedics and Phoniatre, Vienna, 1965; liaison rep. to Peace Corps; pres. County Library Bd.; past exec. dir. Clarion County United Way; commr. Boy Scouts Am., 1976-77; pres. Venango County Adv. Coun. for Aging, 1978-79. Maj. AUS, 1942-46, Lt. USAR, ret. Mem. Hospitaller Order of St. John of Jerusalem, Knights Hospitaller, Chevalier, Knightly and Mil. Order of St. Eugene of Trebizond, Sovereign and Mil. Order os St. Stephen the Matyr (comdr.), Knightly Assn. of St. George the Matyr, l'Ordre des Chevaliers du Sinai, Hist. File, Rotary (pres. 1966-67, dist. gov. 1973-74), VFW (comdr.), Am. Legion (comdr.), Order of Eastern Star (worthy patron 1964-80), Order of White Shrine of Jerusalem, Lions (treas. 1986-88), Phi Delta Kappa (Svc. Key 1978). Republican. Methodist. Home: 2001 Rocky Dells Dr Prescott AZ 86303

MOSES, GAARD HOPKINS, graphic artist; b. Binghamton, N.Y., June 6, 1945; s. Ben Hopkins and Elizabeth (Hopkins) M.; m. Mary Lynn Patton, July 25, 1985; 1 child, Merritt. Student, Syracuse U., 1965-68, U. Grenoble, 1966-67. Owner, pres. Gaardgraphic, Aspen, Colo., 1969—; prof. skier pro free style cir., 1970-74. Office: Gaardgraphic 800 S Alps Rd Box 21 Aspen CO 81612

MOSHER, LAREY LAVERNE, graphic artist; b. Council Bluffs, Iowa, Nov. 3, 1951. Student, Sacramento State U., De Anza Jr. Coll., Palo Alto, Calif., Sacramento City Coll., Consumnes Jr. Coll., Sacramento, Calif. Asst. editor Music Phaze mag., Sacramento, Calif., 1977-80; graphic artist Palo Alto, Calif., 1980-84; art. dir. Portable Puppeteers, Sacramento, Calif., 1984-85; art. dir., prodn. mgr. P&G Products, Lake Arrowhead, Calif., 1985—; graphic artist, camera man CNW TV sta., Lake Arrowhead, Calif., 1986-87. Graphic designer Twin Peaks Summerfest Com., 1985, 87. Mem. Screen Printing Assn. Internat., Nat. Assn. Die Makers and Die Cutters, Graphic Arts Assn., Elks (chaplain 1989—). Home: PO Box 1454 Blue Jay CA 92317

MOSHER, SALLY EKENBERG, lawyer; b. N.Y.C., July 26, 1934; d. Leslie Joseph and Frances Josephine (McArdle) Ekenberg; m. James Kimberly Mosher, Aug. 13, 1960 (dec. Aug. 1982). MusB, Manhattanville Coll., 1956; postgrad., Hofstra U., 1958-60, U. So. Calif., 1971-73; JD, U. So. Calif., 1981. Bar: Calif., 1982. Musician, pianist, tchr. 1957-74; music critic Pasadena Star-News, 1967-72; mgr. Contrasts Concerts, Pasadena Art Mus., 1971-72; rep. Occidental Life Ins. Co., Pasadena, 1975-78; v.p. James K. Mosher Co., Pasadena, 1961-82, pres., 1982—; pres. Oakhill Enterprises, Pasadena, 1984—; assoc. White-Howell, Inc., Pasadena, 1984—. Contbr. articles to various publs. Bd. dirs. Jr. League Pasadena, 1966-67, Encounters Concerts, Pasadena, 1966-72, U. So. Calif. Friends of Music, Los Angeles, 1973-76, Pasadena Arts Council, 1986—, pres., 1989—; v.p., bd. dirs. Pasadena Chamber Orch., 1986—, pres., 1987-88; mem. Calif. 200 Council for Bicentennial of U.S. Constn., 1987—; commr. Endowment Adv. Commn., Pasadena, 1988; bd. dirs. Calif. Music Theatre, 1988, Pasadena Hist. Soc., 1989—. Manhattanville Coll. hon. scholar, 1952-56. Fellow Fellows of Contemporary Art (Los Angeles); mem. ABA, Calif. Bar Assn., Los Angeles Bar Assn., Pasadena Bar Assn., Nat. Assn. Realtors, Am. Assn. Realtors, Calif. Assn. Realtors, Pasadena Bd. Realtors, Assocs. of Calif. Inst. Tech., Kappa Gamma Pi, Mu Phi Epsilon, Phi Alpha Delta. Republican. Club: Athenaeum. Home: 1260 Rancheros Rd Pasadena CA 91103 Office: 711 E Walnut St Ste 407 Pasadena CA 91101

MOSHER, WILLIAM EUGENE, real estate development executive; b. Denver, Oct. 22, 1950; s. Henry Camp Mosher and Carolyn (Kirkham) Ducaj; m. Marianne Sherman, July 19, 1986; children: Christianne Kathryn, Elizabeth Carolyn. BA, Willamette U., 1972; MS, U. Ariz., 1976. Asst. mgr. Fred Meyer, Inc., Portland, Oreg., 1973-74; urban resource specialist City of Tucson, 1976-79; sr. project mgr. Downtown Devel. Corp., Tucson, 1979-80, exec. dir., 1980-; bd. dirs. Pima County Real Estate Research Council, Tucson, 1988--. Pres. Ariz. Childrens Home Assn., 1986-87; treas. Ariz. Theatre Co., 1988-. Baxter scholar Willamette U., 1971. Democrat. Home: 2742 E Devon St Tucson AZ 85716

MOSK, STANLEY, state justice; b. San Antonio, Sept. 4, 1912; s. Paul and Minna (Perl) M.; m. Edna Mitchell, Sept. 27, 1937 (dec.); 1 child, Richard Mitchell.; m. Susan Hines, Aug. 27, 1982. Student, U. Tex., 1931; Ph.B., U. Chgo., 1933; postgrad., U. Chgo. Law Sch., 1934; JD, Southwestern U., 1935; postgrad., Hague Acad. Internat. Law, 1970; LL.D., U. Pacific, 1970, U. San Diego, 1971, U. Santa Clara, 1976, Calif. Western U., 1984, Southwestern U., 1987. Bar: Calif. 1935, U.S. Supreme Ct. 1956. Practiced in Los Angeles until 1939; exec. sec. to gov. Calif., 1939-42; judge Superior Ct. Los Angeles County, 1943-58; pro tem justice Dist. Ct. Appeal, Calif., 1954; atty. gen. Calif, also head state dept., justice, 1959-64; justice Supreme Ct. Calif., 1964—; mem. Jud. Council Calif., 1973-75, Internat. Commn. Jurists. Chmn. San Francisco Internat. Film Festival, 1967; mem. Dem. Nat. Com., Calif., 1960-64; bd. regents U. Calif., 1940; pres. Vista Del Mar Child Care Service, 1954-58; bd. dirs. San Francisco Law Sch., 1971-73, San Francisco Regional Cancer Found., 1980-83. Served with AUS, World War II. Recipient Disting. Alumnus award U. Chgo., 1958. Mem. Nat. Assn. Attys. Gen. (exec. bd. 1964), Western Assn. Attys. Gen. (pres. 1963), ABA, Calif., Los Angeles, Santa Monica, San Francisco bar assns., Am. Legion, Manuscript Soc., Calif. Hist. Soc., Am. Judicature Soc., Inst. Jud. Adminstrn., U. Chgo. Alumni Assn. No. Calif. (pres. 1957-58, 67), Order of Coif, Phi Alpha Delta. Mem. B'nai B'rith. Clubs: Hillcrest Country (Los Angeles); Commonwealth, Golden Gateway Tennis (San Francisco); Beverly Hills Tennis. Office: Calif Supreme Ct 350 McAllister St #4250 San Francisco CA 94102 also: Calif Supreme Ct Sacramento CA 95814

MOSKOW, KEITH GEOFFREY, architect; b. Boston, Feb. 18, 1960; s. Michael B. and Donna B. (Melnick) M. BA, Dartmouth Coll., 1983; MArch, U. Pa., 1986. Boat builder K.G.M. Boatworks, Boston, 1983-84; archtl. designer Dunn Brady Assocs., Vineyard Haven, Mass., 1985, Robert Stern Architects, N.Y.C., 1986-87, Barton Phelps Architect, Los Angeles, 1988—. Recipient hon. mention Mcpl. Art Soc. N.Y.C., 1987, L.A. West Coast Gateway, N.Y. Waterfront Mcpl. Art Soc., Thesis prize (2d place) Lewis E. Dales traveling fellowship U. Pa. Grad. Sch. Architecture. Office: Barton Phelps Architect 5514 Wilshire Blvd Los Angeles CA 90036

MOSLEIN, FRANK A., banker, accountant; b. N.Y.C., Oct. 11, 1943; s. Joseph and Rosa (Zoeller) M.; m. Imelda M. Hutchinson, Sept. 24, 1966. BBA, Manhattan Coll., 1966. CPA, N.Y. Audit mgr. Coopers & Lybrand, White Plains, N.Y., 1966-75; dep. controller Bankers Trust Co., N.Y.C., 1975-84; sr. v.p., controller Wells Fargo Bank, San Francisco, 1984-- . With U.S. Army, 1966-68, Vietnam. Men, AICPA, N.Y. State Soc. CPA's, Fin. Execs. Inst. Republican. Roman Catholic. Office: Wells Fargo Bank 525 Market St San Francisco CA 94163

MOSLEY, JERALD LEE, lawyer; b. Mexico City, July 16, 1949; s. Ramon Thomas and Frances (Smith) M. BA in Religion, Loma Linda U., 1971; BA in Philosophy, Western Ill. U., 1972; MA in Philosophy, U. of Calif., Davis, 1976, PHD in Philosophy, 1979; JD, UCLA, 1982. Bar: Calif. 1982. Atty./assoc. Carter & Mosley, Pasadena, Calif., 1983-87, atty./ptnr., 1987—. Contbr. articles to profl.jours. Mem. Am. Philos. Assn., ABA, Calif. State Bar Assn., Los Angeles County Bar Assn., Pasadena Bar Assn. Home: 372 S Santa Anita Ave Pasadena CA 91107 Office: Carter & Mosley 301 Colorado Blvd Ste 504 Pasadena CA 91101

MOSQUEIRA, CHARLOTTE MARIANNE, dietitian; b. Los Angeles, July 26, 1937; d. Leo and Magdalene Tollefson; B.S., St. Olaf Coll., 1959; postgrad. U. Oreg. Med. Sch., 1959-60; M.A., Central Mich. U., 1980; children—Mark, Michael. Chief clin. dietitian, asst. dir. food service Queen of Angels Hosp., Los Angeles, 1968-70; asst. dir. food service Presbyn. Hosp. Ctr., Albuquerque, 1970-73; dir. food service Holy Cross Hosp., Salt Lake City, 1973-77; dir. dietetics Riverside Meth. Hosp., Columbus, Ohio, 1977-79; dir. nutrition and food service Fresno (Calif.) Community Hosp. and Med. Ctr., 1980-84; mem. faculty Dept. Enology and Food Sci., Calif. State U., Fresno, 1984—. Mem. Am. Soc. for Hosp. Food Service Adminstrs., Am. Dietetic Assn., Calif. Dietetic Assn., AAUW. Republican. Lutheran. Club: Community Vocal Chorale.

MOSS, CHARLES NORMAN, physician; b. Los Angeles, June 13, 1914; s. Charles Francis and Lena (Rye) M.; A.B., Stanford U., 1940; M.D., Harvard U., 1944; cert. U. Vienna, 1947; M.P.H., U. Calif.-Berkeley, 1955; Dr.P.H., UCLA, 1970; m. Margaret Louise Stakias; children—Charles Eric, Gail Linda, and Lori Anne. Surg. intern Peter Bent Brigham Hosp., Boston, 1944-45, asst. in surgery, 1947; commd. 1st lt. USAF, M.C., USAAF, 1945, advanced through grades to lt. col., USAF, 1956; Long course for flight surgeon USAF Sch. Aviation Medicine, Randolph AFB, Tex., 1948-49, preventive medicine div. Office USAF Surgeon Gen., Washington, 1955-59; air observer, med., 1954, became sr. flight surgeon 1956; later med. dir., Los Angeles div. North Am. Rockwell Corp., Los Angeles; chief med. adv. unit Los Angeles County, now ret. Decorated Army Commendation medal (U.S.); Chinese Breast Order of Yun Hui. Recipient Physicians Recognition award AMA, 1969, 72, 76, 79, 82. Diplomate in aerospace medicine and occupational medicine Am. Bd. Preventive Medicine. Fellow Am. Pub. Health Assn., AAAS, Am. Coll. Preventive Medicine, Royal Soc. Health, Am. Acad. Occupational Medicine, Western Occupational Med. Assn., Am. Assn. Occupational Medicine; mem. AMA, Mil. Surgeons U.S., Soc. Air Force Flight Surgeons, Am. Conf. Govt. Hygienests, Calif. Acad. Preventive Medicine, (dir.), Aerospace Med. Assn., Calif., Los Angeles County med. assns., Assn. Oldetime Barbell and Strongmen. Research and publs. in field. Home: 7714 Cowan Ave Los Angeles CA 90045

MOSS, DEBRA LEE, school counselor; b. L.A., June 15, 1952; d. Boris and Mildred Rose (Volk) Elkin; m. Donald Alan Moss, July 29, 1973; children: Ryan Adam, Lauren Nicole, Rebecca Anne. BA in Psychology, UCLA, 1973; MA in Spl. Edn., Calif. State U., L.A., 1977. Cert. elem. tchr. severely handicapped, learning handicapped and jr. coll. tchr., Calif. Tchr. spl. edn. UCLA Neuropsychiat. Inst., 1972-75, demonstration tchr., coord., 1975-78; edn. specialist Harbor Regional Ctr. for Developmentally Disabled, Torrance, Calif., 1978-82; ednl. cons. North L.A. Regional Ctr. for Developmentally Disabled, Panorama City, Calif., 1982-87; behavior specialist L.A. Unified Sch. Dist., 1987—; hon. lectr. West Valley Occupational Ctr., 1986—; tutor spl. edn., L.A., 1973—; behavior specialist to families, 1985—. Contbr. articles to profl. jours. Mem. Am. Assn. on Retardation, Nat. Assn. for Autistic Children and Adults, Coun. for Exceptional Children. Democrat. Jewish. Office: LA Unified Sch Dist Valley Spl Edn Svc Unit 6505 Zelzah St Reseda CA 91335

MOSS, DOUGLAS MABBETT, military officer; b. Washington, Mar. 21, 1954; s. Lon Harold and Mildred (Mabbett) M. BS in Nuclear Engring., Ga. Inst. Tech., 1976, MS in Mech. Engring., 1981. Teaching asst. Ga. Tech. Mech. Engr. Dept., Atlanta, 1976-77; commd. 2d lt. USAF, 1976, advanced through grades to maj., 1988; instr. pilot 71st Flying Tng. Wing USAF, Vance AFB, Okla., 1977-82; F-15 fighter pilot 18th Tactical Fighter Wing USAF, Kadena AFB, Japan, 1982-84; test pilot 6510 Test Wing USAF, Edwards AFB, Calif., 1984-88; tactical weapons officer USAF, Osan AFB, Korea, 1988-89; instr. test pilot USAF Test Pilot Sch., Edwards AFB, Calif., 1989—; project test pilot T-46 Test Force, Edwards AFB, 1986-87; project mgr. Advanced Tactical Fighter, Edward AFB, 1985-88. Mem. Soc. of Exptl. Test Pilots, Martin-Baker Tie Club, Smithsonian Air and Space Soc., Air Force Assn., Order of the Daedalians. Home: 1020 Palm Ln Redondo Beach CA 90278 Office: 7AF/DOOW APO San Francisco CA 96570

MOSS, (MORTON) HERBERT, newspaper columnist, editor, poet; b. N.Y.C., Mar. 21, 1914; s. Carl and Rose (Schnur) M.; student Columbia U., 1930-32; m. Ruth Miller, Feb. 19, 1939; 1 son, Eric. Sports writer N.Y. Post, N.Y.C., 1932-37, Internat. News Service, N.Y.C., 1937-40; sports editor, columnist Los Angeles Examiner (now Herald Examiner), 1941-61, asst. sports editor, columnist, 1962-68, TV editor, columnist, 1969-77, news wire editor, 1978-79. Mem. Nat. Acad. TV Arts and Scis., Los Angeles World Affairs Council, Greater Los Angeles Press Club, Poetry Soc. Am., Acad. of Am. Poets. Represented in Best Sports Stories, E.P. Dutton & Co., Inc., 1952, 1960, 61, 62, 64, 65, 66, 67. Author: In Sight of the Invisible, 1987; contbr. articles to various mags.; contbr. poetry to mags. Lyric, Ariz. Quar., Coastlines, Am. Poet, Global Architecture, also anthologies The Golden Year, 1960, The Various Light, 1964, Ipso Facto, 1975. Creator Simplified Five, the boxing scoring system adopted by Calif. State Athletic Commn., 1960-70. Home: 1909 N Normandie Ave Los Angeles CA 90027

MOSS, JAMES R., educational administrator, educator; b. Salt Lake City, Apr. 23, 1942; s. Rex F. and Ione (Naegle) M.; m. LaVelle Ridd, July 6, 1965; children: James Jr., John, David, Daniel, Jefferson, Jared, Rachelle. BS, U. Utah, 1966; JD, Stanford U., 1969; AS (hon.), U. Tech. Coll., 1985. Supr. Latter Day Saints Ch. Edn. System, Epsom, Surrey, Eng., 1969-71; div. coordinator Latter Day Saints Ch. Edn. System, London, Eng., 1971-73, Los Angeles, 1973-75; prof. Brigham Young U., Provo, Utah, 1975-86; supt. pub. instrn. State Utah, Salt Lake City, 1986—; mem. Western Interstate Commn. for Higher Edn., Denver, 1986; bd. dirs. Far West Lab. U.S. Dept. Edn., San Francisco, 1987—. Author/editor: The International Church, 1982, Truth Will Prevail, 1987; contbr. articles to mags. and chpts. to books. Mem. Utah Ho. of Reps., Salt Lake City, 1983-86, Utah Jud. Conduct Commn., Salt Lake City, 1983-86; chmn. Utah Jud. Reform Task Force, Salt Lake City, 1985-86; mem. exec. com. Western States Conf. of State Legislators, 1983-86. Mem. MENSA, Phi Alpha Theta, Pi Sigma Alpha, Phi Kappa Phi. Office: Utah State Office Edn 250 E 500 S Salt Lake City UT 84111

MOSS, MARVIN LYNNE, school superintendent; b. Ogden, Utah, May 27, 1930; s. George Lynne and Veda Victoria (Fernilius) M.; m. Barbara Jen Albee, Dec. 11, 1948 (div. June 1978); children: Linda K., Stephen C., Collen R., Joel B., Larry D., Pamela G., Vicki M., Michelle T.; m. Dixie Lee Miller, Aug. 5, 1978. BA, U. Nev., 1952, MEd, 1962, EdD, 1982. Salesman Standard Stations Inc., Reno, 1954-55; tchr. Washoe County Sch. Dist., Spark, Nev., 1955-58; elem. sch. prin. Washoe County Sch. Dist., Reno, 1958-66, program devel. specialist, 1966-69, adminstrv. asst. curriculum, 1969-78, assoc. supt., 1978-83, supt., 1983—; chair Coll. Edn. Adv. Com., Reno, 1976—. Fin. chmn. Girls Scouts U.S., Reno, 1969-71; v.p. Sierra Nevada Council Boy Scouts Am., Reno, 1984—; dir. Econ. Devel. Authority, Reno, 1983—. Col. USAR, 1952-54, Korea. Named Nev. Outstanding Educator Nev. State Edn. Assn., 1971, Educator of Yr., Phi Delta Kappa, 1984. Mem. Nev. Assn. Sch. Adminstrs. (pres. 1969-71), Am. Assn. Sch. Adminstrs., Internat. Reading Assn., Rotary Club. Office: Washoe County Supt Schs 425 E 9th St Reno NV 89520

MOSS, STEVEN DAVID, police officer, consultant, educator; b. San Diego, Apr. 21, 1955; s. David Lee and Patricia Ann (Hizer) M.; m. Lesli Kay Lord, Oct. 24, 1981; children: Adam Christopher, Ryan Andrew. BS, Nat. U., San Diego, 1981, MBA, 1986. Police officer San Diego Police Dept., 1978—; instr. San Diego Community Colls., 1982—, San Diego Law Enforcement Tng. Ctr., 1982—; gen. ptnr., chief exec. officer C&M Collision Analysis, San Diego, 1982—; instr. Riverside Acad. Justice, Calif., 1988—. Author: Basic Collision Analysis and Scene Documentation, 1983. Mem. Internat. AAAS, Southwestern Assn. Tech. Investigators, Inc., Mcpl. Motorcycle Officers Assn., Chi Phi.

MOSSMAN, THOMAS MELLISH, JR., television manager; b. Honolulu, Nov. 20, 1938; s. Thomas Mellish and Marian (Ledwith) M.; m. Leonore Jean Stapleton, Aug. 25, 1960; children: Thomas M. III, James Michael. Student, U. Hawaii, 1954-57; BA, U. Denver, 1958, MA, 1965. Producer-dir. KRMA-TV, Denver, 1960-64, KCET-TV, Los Angeles, 1964-72; pres. Mosaic Films, Los Angeles, 1972-73; prodn. and operations dir. KLCS-TV, Los Angeles, 1973-78, station mgr., 1978-87; dept. dir. Archdiocese of Los Angeles, 1987—; instr. Calif. State U., Northridge, 1981—. Mem. Acad. TV Arts & Sciences, Dirs. Guild Am., Assn. Visual Communicators, Nat. Fedn. Local CAble Programmers. Episcopalian. Office: Archdiocese Los Angeles 1520 W Ninth St Los Angeles CA 90015-1194

MOST, JOHN ANTHONY, physician; b. Dubuque, Iowa, Aug. 12, 1928; s. George Henry and Mary Caroline (Fay) M.; children: John George, Wiliam Andrew, Sara Ann, Gregory Patrick Joseph, Ann Caroline. Student, Loras Coll., Dubuque, 1946-49; MD, St. Louis U., 1953. Diplomate Nat. Bd. Med. Examiners, Am. Bd. Family Practice. Surg. intern Univ. Hosp., Little Rock, 1953-54; resident surgery U.S. Naval Hosp., Chelsea, Mass., 1960-61; pvt. practice Carlsbad, N.Mex., 1961-; mem. staff Guadalupe Med. Ctr., Carlsbad; mem. assoc. faculty N.Mex. State U., Carlsbad. Bd. dirs. N.Mex. Lung Assn., Albuquerque; past pres. Boys' Club, Carlsbad; past chmn. bd. trustees Guadalupe Med. Ctr., Carlsbad. Lt. comdr. USNR, 1954-61. Fellow Am. Acad. Family Physicians (past state pres.); mem. Am. Soc. Law and Medicine, Hasting Ctr. (assoc.), Thoracic Soc. (past v.p.). Republican. Roman Catholic. Home: 1133 Tracy Pl Carlsbad NM 88220 Office: Med Arts Bldg Carlsbad NM 88220

MOSTART, GUUS LAURENT MARIE (AUGUST MOSTART), artistic director; b. Den Haag, The Netherlands, Mar. 1, 1951; s. August Constant Marie Joseph Armani and Betty Jacoba Maria (Noordman) M. BA in Medicine, U. Amsterdam, The Netherlands, 1971; diploma in stage mgmt., London Opera Centre, 1975. Gen. trainee The Netherlands Opera, Amsterdam, 1973-74, asst. dir., 1975-77, artistic dir., 1986-88; touring throughout U.K. 1977-85; staff dir. Glundebourne Festival Opera, U.K., 1977-79, assoc. dir., 1979-85, prodn. dir., 1980-85, dep. to artistic dir., 1984-84; artistic dir. Vancouver (B.C.) Opera Assn., Can., 1989—. Dir. operas Le Docteur Miracle (debut), 1977, L'isola Disabitata, 1982, Ariodante, 1985, and many other prodns. Office: Vancouver Opera Assn, 1132 Hamilton St, Vancouver, BC Canada V6B 2S2

MOSTELLER, (MARY) DEE, business consultant, freelance writer, editor; b. San Antonio, Apr. 14, 1942; d. Charles Dee and Elsie (McRorey) M. BA in English Lit., Hardin-Simmons U., 1964, postgrad., 1965. Reporter, feature writer Abilene (Tex.) Reporter News, 1960-65; writer, account exec. Beals Adv. Agy., Oklahoma City, 1965-67; account exec., internat. specialist Friedlich, Fearon, et al., N.Y.C., 1967-71; pvt. practice as bus. cons. N.Y.C., 1971—; freelance writer and editor, 1971—; cons. bus. to various orgns. including Dow Jones, Mead Corp., 1971—; editor, site devel. coordinator Tropical Marine Expdn. Soc., Oakland, Calif., 1988—; bd. dirs. Calif. Avionics Labs., Campbell, 1987—. Co-author: Trapunto, 1977; editor: Marine Invertibrates, 1984; author, tech. editor Pub. Broadcasting System TV series on aviation weather, 1975-77 (Internat. Aviation and Space Writers award, 1976); author, programmer multimedia show on aviation, 1976 (Internat. Aviation and Space Writers award, 1976). Mem. Contra Costa County Women's Network, 1988—; editor, bd. dirs. Older Women's League, Calif., 1987—; active pub. relations and promotion Multiple Sclerosis Soc., Okla., 1960-65, recipient Outstanding Svc. award, 1965. Mem. Nat. Assn. Underwater Instrs. (Outstanding Svc. award 1983), Ninety-Nines (nat. publicity chmn. 1969-70). Home and Office: 40 Avalon Ct Walnut Creek CA 94595

MOSTELLER, JAMES WILBUR, III, data processing executive; b. Ft. Riley, Kans., June 21, 1940; s. James Wilbur, Jr., and Ruth Renfro (Thompson) M.; B.S. in Econs., Rensselaer Poly. Inst., 1962; M.B.A., Temple U., 1971; m. Sandra Josephine Stevenson, Oct. 13, 1962; children—Margaret, Steven, Michael. Data processing systems analyst, Philco-Ford, Ft. Washington, Pa., 1966-69; data processing analyst and supr., Merck Sharp & Dohme, West Point, Pa., 1969-75, dir. mgmt. info. systems KELCO div. Merck and Co., San Diego, 1975-87; dir. info. mgmt. Advanced Systems div. United Technologies, San Diego, 1987-88; computer scientist Navy Personnel Research and Devel. Ctr., San Diego, 1988—. Bd. dirs. New Horizons Montessori Sch., Ft. Washington, Pa., 1974-75; leader youth programs North County YMCA, 1977-81; mem. San Diego Research Park Com., 1978-86; trustee San Diego Space and Sci. Found., 1985—. Served with USN, 1962-66; mem. Res. 1966—. Cert. in data processing. Mem. Data Processing Mgmt. Assn., Assn. Systems Mgmt., Naval Reserve Assn., Beta Gamma Sigma, Sigma Alpha Epsilon (chpt. pres. 1961-62). Office: Navy Pers Rsch and Devel Ctr San Diego CA 92152-0068

MOSTOFI, KHOSROW, political scientist, educator; b. Tehran, Iran, July 8, 1921; came to U.S., 1949; s. Mostafa and Nasrin (Djam) M.; m. Nesrin Imamverdi, Aug. 18, 1960; 1 dau., Simin S. (dec.). B.A., U. Tehran, 1944; M.A., U. Utah, 1957, Ph.D., 1958, grad. cert. in public adminstrn., 1965. Instr. langs. Ministry Edn., Tehran, 1944-49; asst. U. Utah Inst. Govt., Salt Lake City, 1956-58; mem. faculty Dept. Polit. Sci. U. Utah, 1960—, prof. polit. sci., 1970—, prof. emeritus, 1987—, dir. Middle East Ctr., 1967-83, staff specialist Middle East Ctr., 1987—, coordinator Arab Devel. Program, 1976-81; pres. Western Asian Trade and Investment Corp., 1983-87, Am. Found. for islamic Studies, 1978-89; dir. Am. Center Iranian Studies, Tehran, summer 1970; instr. polit. sci. Portland (Oreg.) State U., 1958-59, asst. prof., 1959-60; cons. div. of higher edn. U.S. Dept. Edn., 1968-70, 76; co-sponsor, organizer Internat. Conf. on Islam, Iran, and Pakistan, 1975, Internat. Conf. on Higher Edn. and Devel. in Arab World, 1978; sponsor, organizer Internat. Conf. on Comparative Law, 1977. Author: Parsee Nameh, rev. edit, 1969, Aspects of Nationalism: A Sociology of Colonial Revolt, 1964; contbr. to: Ency. Britannica, 1974, 83, 87, Studies in Art and Literature of the Near East, 1974. Trustee Internat. Visitors-Utah Council, 1984-87. Recipient disting. service award Utah Acad. Scis., Arts and Letters, 1983, Service award World Trade Assn. of Utah, 1981. Fulbright-Hayes fellow, 1965-66; mem. Am. Inst. Iranian Studies (trustee), AAUP, Western Polit. Sci. Assn., Middle East Inst., Middle East Studies Assn., Ctr. Arabic Studies Abroad (bd. dirs. 1970-83), Pi Sigma Alpha, Phi Kappa Phi. Moslem. Home: 2481 E 1300 S Salt Lake City UT 84108 Office: U Utah Dept Polit Sci Salt Lake City UT 84112

MOTE, CLAYTON DANIEL, JR., mechanical engineer, educator; b. San Francisco, Feb. 5, 1937; s. Clayton Daniel and Eugenia (Isnardi) M.; m. Patricia Jane Lewis, Aug. 18, 1962; children—Melissa Michelle, Adam Jonathan. B.Sc., U. Calif., Berkeley, 1959, M.S., 1960, Ph.D., 1963. Registered profl. engr., Calif. Asst. specialist U. Calif. Forest Products Labs., 1961-62; asst. mech. engr. 1962-63; lectr. mech. engring. U. Calif., Berkeley, 1962-63, asst. prof., 1967-69, asst. research engr., 1968-69, asso. prof., asso. research engr., 1969-73, prof., 1973—, vice chmn. mech. engring. dept., 1976-80, 83-86, chmn. mech. engring. dept., 1987—; research fellow U. Birmingham, Eng., 1963-64; asst. prof. Carnegie Inst. Tech., 1964-67; vis. prof. Norwegian Inst. Wood Tech., 1972-73, vis. sr. scientist, 1976, 78, 80, 84, 85; cons. in engring. design and analysis; sr. scientist Alexander Von Humboldt Found., Fed. Republic Germany, 1988. Contbr. articles to profl. jours.; patentee in field. NSF fellow, 1963-64; recipient Blackall award ASME, 1975, Disting. Teaching award U. Calif., 1971, Pi Tau Sigma Excellence in teaching award U. Calif., 1975, Humboldt Prize, Fed. Republic Germany, 1988. Fellow ASME (v.p. environ. and transp. 1986-90, nat. chmn. noise control and acoustics 1980-84, chmn. San Francisco sect. 1978-79), U.S. Nat. Acad. Engring., Internat. Acad. Wood Sci.; mem. Am. Soc. Biomechanics, Forest Products Research Soc., AAAS, Orthopaedic Rsch. Soc., Internat. Soc. Skiing Safety (v.p., sec. 1977-85, bd. dirs. 1977—, chmn. sci. com. 1985—), AIAA, ASTM (com. on snow skiing F-27 1984-87, chmn. new projects subcom.) Acoustical Soc. Am., Sigma Xi, Pi Tau Sigma, Tau Beta Pi. Office: U Calif Dept Mech Engring Berkeley CA 94720

MOTIL, JOSEPH SYLVESTER, senior chemist, optometrist; b. Stockett, Mont., May 29, 1910; s. Josef and Veronica Motil; m. Margaret Elaine Colton, July 15, 1939; children: William J., Joseph A. Student, Carroll Coll., 1932; AA, Vallejo Coll., 1949; BS and OD, Chgo. Coll. Optometry, 1951. Registered Optometrist, Mont., Ariz. Carpenter Frank Robbins Constrn., Stockett, 1933-37; carpenter, mine electrician Great Northern Coal Co., Giffen, Mont., 1937-41; machinist supr. USN, Vellejo, Calif., 1941-48; sr. chemist Goodyear Aerospace, Litchfield Park, Ariz., 1951-75; cons. Bronstein Labs., Phoenix, 1967. Inventor in field. Recipient Invention award Goodyear Aerospace Co., Litchfield Park, 1967. Mem. Cen. Chem. Soc., Am. Chem. Soc., Am. Optometric Assn., Ariz. Optometric Assn., Bola Tie Soc., Am. Electroplaters Soc. Democrat. Roman Catholic. Club: Tempe (Ariz.) Bus. and Profl. Men's. Lodge: KC. Home: 611 E Fairmont Tempe AZ 85282 Office: 1761 E Warner Ste A-9 Tempe AZ 85284

MOTT, JUNE MARJORIE, teacher, consultant, elected official; b. Faribault, Minn., Mar. 8, 1920; d. David C. and Tillie W. (Nelson) Shifflett; B.S., U. Minn., 1943, M.A., 1948; m. Elwood Knight Mott, Oct. 18, 1958. Tchr. high schs. in Minn., 1943-46, 48-53, 54-57; script writer, Hollywood, Calif., 1953-54; tchr. English, creative writing and journalism Mt. Miguel High Sch., Spring Valley, Calif., 1957-86, chmn. English dept., 1964-71, chmn. Dist. English council, 1967-68; mem. Press Bur., Grossmont (Calif.) High Sch. Dist., 1958-86; elected to Grossmont Union High Sch. Gov. Bd., 1986—; scriptwriter TV prodn. Lamp Unto My Feet, Jam Dandy Corp.; free-lance writer, Cons. travel writer, photographer; editor, publ Listening Heart, 1989. Vice chmn. polit. action San Diego County Regional Resource Ctr., 1980-81; pub. rels. chmn. Lemon Grove Luth. Ch., 1962-78, 89—; mem. Grossmont Edn. Fund Bd., 1986—. Writing project fellow U. Calif., San Diego, 1978; named Outstanding Journalism Tchr., State of Calif., Outstanding Humanities Tchr., San Diego County, Tchr. of Yr. for San Diego County, 1978. Mem. Nat. Council Tchrs. English, Nat. Journalism Assn., NEA, AAUW, Assn. Supervision and Curriculum Devel., Calif. Assn. Tchrs. English, Calif. Tchrs. Assn., So. Calif. Journalism Assn., San Diego County Journalism Educators Assn. (pres. 1975-76), Grossmont Edn. Assn. (pres. 1978-80), Greater San Diego Council Tchrs. English, Nat. Writers Club, Am. Guild Theatre Organists, Calif. Sch. Bd. Assn., Calif. Retired Tchrs. Assn. (chairwoman 1987-89, pres. chpt. #69 1989—), Nat. Sch. Bds. Assn., Kiwanis, Sigma Delta Chi. Democrat. Club: Order Eastern Star. Author, editor in field. Home and Office: 2883 New Jersey Ave Lemon Grove CA 92045

MOTT, ROBERT CLAUDE, data processing executive; b. Seattle, July 14, 1953; s. Harold Arthur and Bonnie (Wray) M.; m. Beverly Anita Monjay, Feb. 14, 1974 (div. 1982); m. Mary Kathleen Dunne, Sept. 14, 1984; children: Joey, Julie. AA, Shoreline Community Coll., Seattle, 1975; BS, Seattle Pacific U., 1977; M. Software Engring., Seattle U., 1987. Programmer Sears Roebuck & Co., Seattle, 1977-79; systems analyst GTE, Everett, Wash., 1979-83; systems programmer GTE Data Services, Everett, 1983-86, sr. systems programmer, 1986—. Mem. Computer Measurement Group, SHARE. Home: 13917 Club Way Arlington WA 98223

MOTTEK, CARL T., hotel company executive; b. 1928. With Hilton Hotels Corp., 1951—, dir. food and beverage ops., from 1964, v.p., 1965-68, sr. v.p. food and beverage ops., 1968-73, sr. v.p. so. region, 1973-85, exec. v.p., also pres. div. Hilton Hotels, 1985—, also bd. dirs. Office: Hilton Hotels Corp 9336 Santa Monica Blvd Beverly Hills CA 90210 *

MOTTER, RICHARD CHARLES, realtor; b. Seattle, Aug. 13, 1938; 0. Frederick Rudolph Motter and Pearl Elizabeth (Piper) Motter Gerow; children: Teresa Lynn, Karen Louise, Kirsten Diane Motter Clark, Richard Charles Jr. Grad. high sch., Bremerton, Wash. Enlisted USCG, 1956, advanced through grades to commdr., 1977, retired, 1978; assoc. broker, sales assoc. John L. Scott Real Estate, Seattle, Bellevue, 1978-80; assoc. broker, br. mgr. Sherwood & Roberts, Inc., Burien and Renton, Wash., 1980-81; assoc. broker Pacific Coast Realty, Seattle, 1981-86, William A. Fazekas Realtor, Seattle, 1986-88, Windermere Real Estate, Seattle, 1988; maintenance mgr. Desert Hot Springs (Calif.) Spa Hotel, 1988—. Active real estate craft adv. bd. Renton Vocat. Tech. Sch., 1987—; co-chmn. legis. campaign Bob Eberle, 1964; treas. fund raising com. to elect Bob Eberle to Congress, 1981. Mem. Chief Warrant & Warrant Officers Assn. USCG, Res. Officers Am., Ret. Officers Am., Nat. Assn. Realtors, Wash. Assn. Realtors, Seattle King County Bd. Realtors, Pacific N.W. Warrant & Chief Warrant Officer Club (Seattle pres. 1978-79), Great Lakes Warrant & Chief Warrant Officer Club (Cleve. pres. 1975-76), Rotary (sec. Seattle chpt. 1987—, Dist. Gov. Cert. Appreciation). Office: Desert Hot Springs Spa Hotel 10805 Palm Dr Desert Hot Springs CA 92240

MOTTER, ROBERTA LEE, marketing executive; b. Honolulu, Mar. 8, 1936; d. Donald and Florence B. Reed; children: Edwin, Lori, Lisa. Student, Cornell U., 1956, George Washington U. Office mgr. Fisher Constrn. Co., Honolulu, 1960-61; paymaster computer specialist Gate City Steel, Omaha, 1961-64; accounts receivable supr. Mayflower Hotel, Washington, 1966-67; computer specialist, personnel dir. Alan M. Voorhees & Assocs., Mclean, Va., 1985—; adminstrv. mgr. Planning Rsch. Co. Computer Ctr., 1972-73; conversion specialist Medenco, Inc., 1973-74; personnel dir., office mgr. Summit Ins. Co. N.Y., Houston, 1974-75; dir. adminstrv. svcs. N.Y. State Ins. Dept. Liquidation Bur., 1975-80; supervisory procurement analyst Gen. Svcs. Adminstra., Arlington, Va., 1980-84; pres. Contacts Unlimited, Inc., Orangevale, Calif., 1985—. Mem. Labor Com., vice chmn. Taste of Am. Mem. Women in Info. Processing, Am. Soc. Personnel Adminstrs., Adminstrv. Mgmt. Soc. (bd. dirs. 1980-82), Wash. Purchasing Mgmt. Assn., Internat. Platform Assn., Hawaii State Soc., Nat. Assn. Profl. Saleswomen, Community Entrepreneurs Orgn., Sacramento Valley Mktg. Assn., Nat. Procurement Mgmt. Assn., Sales Mktg. Profl. Svcs. Assn., Beta Sigma Phi, Xi Gamma Alpha, Xi Gamma Beta. Office: Contacts Unltd Inc 9198 Greenback Ln Ste 116 Orangevale CA 95662

MOTULSKY, ARNO GUNTHER, geneticist, physician, educator; b. Fischhausen, Germany, July 5, 1923; came to U.S., 1941; s. Herman and Rena (Sass) Molton; m. Gretel C. Stern, Mar. 22, 1945; children: Judy, Harvey, Arlene. Student, Cen. YMCA Coll., Chgo., 1941-43, Yale U., 1943-44; BS, U. Ill., 1945, MD, 1947. Diplomate Am. Bd. Internal Medicine, Am. Bd. Med. Genetics. Intern, fellow, resident Michael Reese Hosp., Chgo., 1947-51; staff mem. charge clin. investigation dept. hematology Army Med. Service Grad. Sch., Walter Reed Army Med. Ctr., Washington, 1952-53; research assoc. internal medicine George Washington U. Sch. Medicine, 1952-53; from instr. to assoc. prof. dept. medicine U. Wash. Sch. Medicine, Seattle, 1953-61, prof. medicine, prof. genetics, 1961—; head div. med. genetics, dir. genetics clinic Univ. Hosp., Seattle, 1959—, Children's Med. Ctr., Seattle, 1966-72; dir. Ctr. for Inherited Diseases, Seattle, 1972—; attending physician Univ. Hosp., Seattle; cons. Pres.'s Commn. for Study of Ethical Problems in Medicine and Biomed. and Behavioral Research, 1979-83; cons. various coms. NRC, NIH, WHO, others. Editor Am. Jour. Human Genetics, 1969-75, Human Genetics, 1969—, Progress in Med. Genetics, 1974—. Commonwealth Fund fellow in human genetics Univ. Coll., London, 1957-58; John and Mary Markle scholar in med. sci., 1957-62; fellow Ctr. Advanced Study in Behavioral Scis., Stanford U., 1976-77, Inst. Advanced Study, Berlin, 1984. Fellow A.C.P.; mem. Internat. Soc. Hematology, Am. Fedn. Clin. Research, AAAS, Genetics Soc. Am., Western Soc. Clin. Research, Am. Soc. Human Genetics, Am. Soc. Clin. Investigation, Am. Assn. Physicians, Nat. Acad. Scis., Inst. of Medicine, Am. Acad. Arts and Scis. Home: 4347 53d Ave NE Seattle WA 98105 Office: U Wash Div Med Genetics Seattle WA 98195

MOTZER, PAUL D., clergyman, counselor; b. Dahlgren, Ill.; s. Narvel Darvin and Evelyn Louise (Jenner) M.; m. Elizabeth Caroline Petersen, June 1, 1966 (div. 1980); children: Timothy Paul, Julie Elizabeth Loftis, David Edwin; m. Irene Frances Koteles, June 28, 1980. BA, McKendree Coll., 1957; postgrad., Edentheological Sem., 1960; MDiv., Garrett Theological Sem., 1962; postgrad., Fielding Inst., 1978-79; D of Ministry, Nat. Christian U. Mo., 1980. Ordained to ministry United Meth. Ch., 1962. Commd. capt. USAF, 1966, advanced through grades to lt. col., 1987; base protestant chaplain Air Def. Command, Hamilton AFB, Calif., 1966-69; remote sites chaplain Alaskan Air Command, Alaska, 1969-70; base protestant chaplain, hosp. chaplain Air Force Logistics Command, Tinker AFB, Okla., 1970-73; sr. protestant chaplain USAF Europe, Zweibrucken AFB, Fed. Republic of Germany; base protestant chaplain Air Tng. Command, Randolph AFB, Tex., 1976-80; sr. protestant chaplain Pacific Air Command, Kusan AFB, Republic of Korea, 1980-81; base and sr. protestant chaplain SAC, Vandenberg AFB, Calif., 1981-83, base hosp. chaplain, 1981-86; ret. USAF, Vandenberg AFB, Calif., 1987; pastoral counselor Santa Maria, Calif., 1987—; conducts seminars and workshops, U.S., Europe, Republic of Korea, 1970—; marriage and family course tchr. Los Angeles Met. Coll., Kunsan, Republic of Korea, 1980; psychology guest lecturer various univs., 1973-76. Contbr. articles to profl. jours. Active Drug and Alcohol Evaluation and Rehab. Com., Vandenberg AFB, 1970-87, Santa Barbara County Alcoholism Adv. Bd., 1988—; bd. dirs. Nat. Coun. on Alcoholism, Santa Maria, 1985-87. Mem. Internat. Transactional Analysis Assn., Retired Officers Assn., Am. Psychotherapy Assn. (diplomate), Am. Assn. for Counseling and Devel., Assn. for Religious Values in Counseling, Am. Mental Health Assn., Ministerial Assn., Santa Maria Valley Ministerial Assn. (v.p. 1984-87), Masons, Lions (pres. 1962-64). Democrat. Home: 1114 River Birch Ct Santa Maria CA 93454

MOUCK, NORMAN GARRISON, JR., retired college president; b. Omaha, Sept. 9, 1928; s. Norman Garrison and Madge Arvilla (Bossoh) M.; m. Dorothy Margaret Davis, Jan. 3, 1949; children: Susan Gayle, Richard Forrest, Teresa Joann. BS, Edinboro (Pa.) State Coll., 1953; MEd, UCLA, 1956, postgrad., 1956-58, 65-67; M of Basic Sci., U. Colo., 1960. Instr. math., then asst. prof. Santa Barbara (Calif.) City Coll., 1961-66, dir. research, 1966-68; instr. math. Coll. of the Canyons, Valencia, Calif., 1979-82, v.p., 1968-79, pres., 1979, 82-83; lectr. U. Calif., Santa Barbara, 1965-66; cons. Stanford U. Sch. Math. Study Group, 1963-64, Coll. of the Canyons, 1983. Co-author: (textbooks) Mathematics Through Science, 1964, Elementary Algebra for College Students, 1968. Active United Crusade, Canyon County, Calif., 1972-74. Served with U.S. Army, 1946-53, Korea. Mem. AAAS, Math. Assn. Am., U.S. Ski Assn. (chmn. Far West div., mem. Far West competition bd., chmn. Masters Series Ski Racing), Phi Delta Kappa. Democrat. Presbyterian. Lodges: Kiwanis (internat. life mem. 1973, disting. pres. local chpt. 1978-79). Home: PO Box 3648 Incline Village NV 89450

MOULTON, KENNETH, restaurant owner; b. London, Eng., Mar. 10, 1957; came to U.S., 1957; s. Eric Walter and Helen M.; m. Marie Eriksson Moulton, Jan. 10, 1987. BS in TV/Communications, Oreg. State, 1979. Gen. mgr. Grand Am. Fare, Santa Monica, Calif., 1980-83; gen. mgr. Marix Tex Mex, W. Hollywood, Calif., 1984-86; mgr. Restaurant Enterprises Group, Seattle, 1986--. Mem. Kappa Delta Rho (v.p. 1978-79). Republican. Methodist. Home: 2711 72d Ave SE Mercer Island WA 98040

MOULTON, WILLIAM ALFRED, insurance executive, underwriter, lawyer; b. Letha, Idaho, May 26, 1931; s. William Mareshal and Irma Mae (Wilson) M.; m. Margaret Ellen Figgat, Aug. 20, 1952 (div. Apr. 1988); children: Valerie Ann, Bradford W., Jennifer Lee, Steven D.; m. Alicia Eugenia Roqueni, May 10, 1988. AA, Boise (Idaho) Jr. Coll., 1951; BA in Law, U. Mont., 1954; postgrad., Golden Gate Coll., 1957-58. Pres., chief exec. officer Security Title Ins Co., Boise, 1958-66, First Am. Title of Wash., Seattle, 1971-76; regional v.p., counsel First Am. Title Ins. Co., Boise, 1976-77; v.p., asst. gen. counsel St. Paul Title Ins. Co., 1978-79; pres., chief exec. officer Fidelity Title Co., Ontario, Oreg., 1977-86; mgr. cartographics div. Boise Cascade Corp., 1981-86; v.p., regional counsel Am. Title Ins. Co., San Diego, 1987-88; sr. underwriter, v.p. Fidelity Nat. Title Co., Irvine, Calif., 1988—. State treas. Idaho Easter Seal Soc., Boise, 1962; pres. Boise Better Bus. Bur., 1963; bd. dirs. Seattle Better Bus. Bur., 1973-74. Lt. comdr. USNR, 1954-57, 66-71. Decorated Legion of Honor, Cross of Honor. Mem. Calif. Land Title Assn. (edn. com.), Wash. Land Title Assn. (pres. 1974-75), Idaho Land Title Assn. (v.p. 1964-65), Lions (pres. Boise chpt. 1964), Masons, Phi Delta Phi. Republican. Episcopalian. Home: 30041 Tessier St #236 Laguna Niguel CA 92677 Office: Fidelity Nat Title Ins Co 2100 SE Main St Irvine CA 92714

MOUNDS, LEONA MAE REED, teacher; b. Crosby, Tex., Sept. 9, 1945; d. Elton Phillip and Ora Lee (Jones) Reed; m. Aaron B. Mounds Jr., Aug. 21, 1965 (div.); 1 dau., Lisa Nichelle. BS in Elem. Edn., Bridgewater State Coll., 1973; MA in Mental Retardation, U. Alaska, 1980. Cert. tchr. Alaska, Colo., Tex., Mass., cert. adminstrv. prin. Tchr., Sch. Dist.# 11, Colorado Springs, Colo., 1973-75; tchr. Anchorage Sch. Dist., 1976-78, 80—, mem. maths. curriculum com., reading contact tchr., mem. talent bank. Tchr. Del Valle (Tex.) Sch. Dist., 1979-80. Bd. dirs. Urban League, 1974; 1st v.p. PTA, Crosby, Tex.; del. Tex. Dem. Conv., 1980, dist. 13 chmn.; mem. Women League Voters, Alaska Women Polit. Caucus; Dem. Com., Anchorage; bd. dirs. C.R.I.S.I.S. Inc.; tchr. religious edn., lay Eucharist minister St. Martin De Pores Roman Cath. Ch., St. Patrick's Ch.; pres. Black Educators of Pike Peak Region, 1974; mem. NAACP, Coun. for Exception Children. With USAF, 1964-66. Alaska State Tchr. Incentive grantee, 1981, Ivy Lutz scholar, 1972. Mem. NEA (human rels. coord. Alaska chpt., region 6 bd. dirs., bd. dirs Alaska chpt., vice-chmn. women's caucus), Anchorage Edn. Assn. (minority chmn. 1982—, mem. black caucus polit. action com., v.p. programs 1986-88), Anchorage Edn. Assn. (v.p. programs com. 1986-87, women's caucus), Assn. Supervision and Curriculum Devel., Alaska Women in Adminstrn.

MOUNT, ROBERT ARL, microbiologist, medical laboratory executive; b. Niles, Calif., Dec. 31, 1943; s. James Merle and Norma Belle (Springfield) M.; m. Madeleine J. Ehrlich, June 19, 1966; children: Monica, Aaron, Kimberly. BA, U. Calif., Berkeley, 1966; MA, San Jose State U., 1970. Lab. mgr. Community Hosp., Santa Rosa, Calif., 1970-74; pres. Redwood Med. Lab., Santa Rosa, Calif., 1974—; asst. prof. Sonoma State U., Cotati, Calif., 1984. Mem. Am. Soc. Microbiology. Democrat. Home: 1377 Wikiup Dr Santa Rosa CA 95401 Office: Redwood Med Lab 1166 Montgomery Dr Santa Rosa CA 95405

MOWBRAY, JOHN CODE, judge; b. Bradford, Ill., Sept. 20, 1918; s. Thomas John and Ellen Driscoll (Code) M.; m. Kathlyn Ann Hammes, Oct. 15, 1949; children: John, Romy, Jerry, Terry. B.A., Western Ill. U., 1940, L.H.D. (hon.), 1976, LL.D. (hon.), 1977; LL.D. (hon.), Far Eastern Civil Affairs Tng. Sch., Northwestern U., 1945; D.J. cum laude, U. Notre Dame, 1949; LL.D. (hon.), U. Nev., 1978. Bar: Nev. 1949, Ill. 1950. Dep. dist. atty. Clark County, Las Vegas, Nev., 1949-53; U.S. referee Fed. Cts. in Nev., 1955-59; dist. judge for Nev. 1959-67; justice Nev. Supreme Ct., Carson City, 1967—, chief justice, 1986—; founder 1st pub. defender program in Nev., 1967; mem. faculty Nat. Coll. State Judiciary, 1967. V.p. Boulder Dam Area council Boy Scouts Am., 1960-70; bd. dirs. Nev. Area council, 1967—; pres. City of Hope, 1963-64, NCCJ, 1965-66; v.p. YMCA, 1964—; chmn. Nev. Commn. on Bicentennial U.S. Constitution, 1986; nat. trustee Freedoms Found. Valley Forge, Pa. Served to maj. AUS, 1942-46, PTO. Recipient Outstanding Alumni award Western Ill. U., 1971, Equal Justice award Western regional dept. NAACP, 1970, Minuteman award SAR, 1982, Silver Antelope award Boy Scouts Am., 1983, Jurist of Yr. award Nev. Trial Lawyers Assn., 1986, Judicial Officer of Yr. award State Sheriff and Police Assn., 1986; Mowbray Hall, Western Ill. U. named in his honor, 1974. Mem. ABA, Nev. Trial Lawyers Assn. (Jurist of Yr. award 1986), Am. Judicature Soc., State Sheriff and Police Assn. (Jud. Officer of Yr. award 1986), SAR (pres. Nev. 1969-70, Nat. Gen. MacArthur medal 1971, nat. trustee 1971—), VFW. Clubs: Rotarian (hon.), Elk. Home: 189 Lake Glen Dr Carson City NV 89701 Office: Nev Supreme Ct 100 N Carson St Carson City NV 89710

MOWER, MONTE J., electrical engineer, communications consultant; b. Ogden, Utah, Feb. 2, 1956; s. Horace and Wanda Jennie (Sharp) M.; m. Tamera Ann Hansen, Mar. 20, 1980 (div. Nov. 1987); children: Tara, Branden; m. Cynthia High, Nov. 22, 1988. BSEE, Brigham Young U., 1986. Field svc. engr. Hewlett-Packard Co., Salt Lake City, 1978-80; avionics-radio technician Cen. Utah Avionics, Provo, 1980; field svc. mgr. SOS Computer Systems, Provo, 1980-82; mfg. test technician WICAT, Provo, 1982-83; svc. technician, cons. Brigham Young U., Provo, 1984-86; tech. svcs. engr., cons. ATN, Inc., Provo, 1986-87; project engr. Hart Sci. Co., Provo, 1987-88; systems engr. Gen. Data Systems, Salt Lake City, 1988; owner, mgr. Mower Cons., Provo, 1988—; cons. Digital Air Systems, Provo, 1987-88. Mem. Utah County Amateur Radio Emergency Svcs., 1984, Utah County Sheriff's Communication Aux. Team, 1987—. Mormon. Office: 137 North 900 West Provo UT 84601

MOWLES, RICHARD GLEN, financial company executive; b. Camp White, Oreg., Aug. 7, 1944; s. Stanley James and Georgia Marie (Gilliam) M.; m. Denice A. Patterson, Mar. 16, 1968; children: Richard II, Deanna, Kimberlee. Student, Am. River Coll., 1965. Underwriter N.Y. Life Ins. Co., San Diego, 1969; v.p., dir. div. ITT Fin. Co., Denver, 1970-87; v.p., mgr. area Barclays Am. Fin. Corp., Denver, 1987—; bd. dirs. Ariz. Consumer Fin. Assn., Colo. Consumer Fin. Assn., Idaho Consumer Fin. Assn. Served with U.S. Navy, 1965-69, Vietnam. Republican. Home: 5164 S Laredo Way Aurora CO 80015

MOXLEY, ALLEN VINCENT, insurance agent, underwriter, consultant; b. Rutland, Vt., July 10, 1938; s. Alfred Victor and Betty Jane (Eldred) M.; m. Sharon Marie Hart, May 29, 1964; children: Jeff Edward, Van Allen, Shauna Lynn. Student in bus., Brigham Young U., 1959-60; CLU, Am. Coll., 1981. Gen. agt. Occidental Life Ins. Co., Scottsdale, Ariz., 1963-73; field agt. Northwestern Mutual Life, Salt Lake City, 1973-87; asst. to gen. agt. Mass. Mutual Life, Newport Beach, Calif., 1987—. Fellow Life Underwriter Tng. Coun. (moderator 1985-86); mem. Am. Soc. CLU, Nat. Assn. Life Underwriters, Orange County Assn. Life Underwriters, Valley Assn. Life Underwriters (pres. 1981-82), Rotary (founder Sandy, Utah club 1986, officer and bd. dirs. various clubs 1968—). Republican. Mormon. Office: Mass Mutual Life PO Box 1434 Newport Beach CA 92663

MOYA, JOHN GASTELO, SR., realtor, retired union official; b. Globe, Ariz., May 6, 1926; s. Angel Samaniego and Teresa (Gastelo) M.; m. Lola Calles, Aug. 18, 1945; children: John Jr., Irene, Ernie, Frankie, RoseAnn, Fred, Peter, Lola, Joey, Michael. Bus. mgr., sec./treas. Laborers' Union Local 383, Phoenix, 1982-83, acting bus. mgr., sec./treas., 1983-86; realty assoc. Gene Clements Realty Better Homes and Gardens, Phoenix, 1987—. Patient care attendent Ariz. Bridge for Ind. Living, Phoenix, 1987—. Mem. Phoenix Bd. Realtors. Democrat. Mem. Pentecostal Ch. Home: 4731 N 61st Ave Phoenix AZ 85033

MOYA, PATRICK ROBERT, lawyer; b. Belen, N.Mex., Nov. 7, 1944; s. Adelicio E. and Eva (Sanchez) M.; m. Sara Dreier, May 30, 1966; children: Jeremy Brill, Joshua Dreier. AB, Princeton U., 1966; JD, Stanford U., 1969. Bar: Calif. 1970, Ariz. 1970, D.C. 1970, U.S. Dist. Ct. (no. dist.) Calif. 1970, U.S. Ct. Claims 1970, U.S. Tax Ct. 1970, U.S. Ct. Appeals (D.C. cir.) 1970, U.S. Supreme Ct. 1973. Assoc. Lewis and Roca, Phoenix, 1969-73, ptnr., 1973-83; sr. ptnr. Moya, Bailey, Bowers & Jones, P.C., Phoenix, 1983-84; ptnr., mem. nat. exec. com. Gaston & Snow, Phoenix, 1985—; instr. sch. of law Ariz. State U., 1972; bd. dir. Bobby McGee's U.S.A., Inc., 1982-86. Mem. bd. adjustment Town of Paradise Valley, Ariz., 1976-80, chmn. 1978-80, councilman 1980-82; bd. dir. Phoenix Men's Arts Coun., 1973-81, pres. 1979-80; bd. dirs. The Silent Witness, Inc., 1979-84, pres., 1981-83; pres. Enterprise Network, Inc., 1989—; bd. dirs. Phoenix Little Theatre, 1973-75; Interfaith Counseling Svc., 1973-75; Rep. Precinct Committeeman, 1975-77, dep. voter registrar Maricopa County, 1975-76; mem. Gov.'s Adv. Com., Ariz. and Mex., Ariz. Corp. Commn. Adv. Com. on Capital Formation; bd. dirs. The enterprise Network, Inc., 1989—. Mem. ABA, Los Abogados Hispanic Lawyers Assn., Nat. Assn. Bond Lawyers, Ariz. Bar Assn., Maricopa County Bar Assn., Paradise Valley Country Club, Univ. Club (Phoenix). Office: 4722 N 24th St Ste 400 Phoenix AZ 85016

MOYA, SARA DREIER, municipal government official; b. N.Y.C., June 9, 1945; d. Stuart Samuel and Hortense (Brill) Dreier; m. P. Robert Moya, May 30, 1966; children: J. Brill, Joshua D. BA, Wheaton Coll., Norton, Mass., 1967; postgrad., Mills Coll., Oakland, Calif., 1967-68. Mem. Paradise Valley (Ariz.) Town Coun., 1986—; pres. Ctr. for Acad. Precosity, Ariz. State U., Tempe, 1987—; dir. Valley Leadership, Inc., Phoenix, 1988—. Mem. Citizens Adv. Bd. Paradise Valley Police Dept., 1984-86; chair Maricopa Assn. Govts. Task Force on Homeless, 1989. Mem. Ariz. Women in Mcpl. Govt. (sec. 1988—, bd. dirs. 1986—), Maricopa Assn. Govts. (regional coun. 1988—), Paradise Valley Country Club. Republican. Home: 5119 E Desert Park Ln Paradise Valley AZ 85253 Office: Town Paradise Valley 6401 E Lincoln Dr Paradise Valley AZ 85253

MOYER, ALAN DEAN, newspaper editor; b. Galva, Iowa, Sept. 4, 1928; s. Clifford Lee and Harriet (Jacques) M.; m. Patricia Helen Krecker, July 15, 1950; children: Virginia, Stanley, Glenn. BS in Journalism, U. Iowa, 1950. Reporter, copy editor Wis. State Jour., Madison, 1950-53; reporter, photographer Bartlesville (Okla.) Examiner-Enterprise, 1953; telegraph editor Abilene (Tex.) Reporter-News, 1954-55; makeup editor Cleve. Plain Dealer, 1955-63; mng. editor Wichita (Kans.) Eagle, 1963-70; exec. editor Wichita Eagle and Beacon, 1970-73; mng. editor Phoenix Gazette, 1973-82, Ariz. Republic, 1982-89; ret. 1989; pres., dir. Wichita Profl. Baseball, Inc., 1969-75; mem. jury Pulitzer Prizes, 1973-74, 85, 86, 88. Mem. AP Mng. Editors Assn. (dir. 1973-78), Am. Soc. Newspaper Editors, Wichita Area C. of C. (dir. 1970-72), Sigma Delta Chi. Office: 120 E Van Buren St Phoenix AZ 85004

MOYER, CRAIG ALAN, lawyer; b. Bethlehem, Pa., Oct. 17, 1955; s. Charles Alvin and Doris Mae (Schantz) M.; m. Candace Darrow Brigham, May 3, 1986; 1 stepchild, Jason; 1 child, Chelsea A. BA, U. So. Calif., L.A., 1977; JD, U. Calif., L.A., 1980. Bar: Calif. 1980, U.S. Dist. Ct. (cen. dist.) Calif. 1980. Assoc. Nossaman, Krueger et al, L.A., 1980-83, Finley, Kumble et al, Beverly Hills, Calif., 1983-85; ptnr. Demetriou, Del Guercio & Lovejoy, L.A., 1985—; instr. Air Resources Bd. Symposium, Sacramento, 1985—, U. Calif., Santa Barbara, 1989—; lectr. Hazmat Conf., Long Beach, Calif., 1986—, Pacific Automotive Show, Reno, Nev., 1989—. Contbr. articles to profl. jours. Pres. Calif. Pub. Interest Rsch. Group, L.A., 1978-80. Mem. ABA, Calif. Bar Assn. (natural resources sect.), L.A. County Bar Assn. (environ. law sect., chmn. legis. com.), Tau Kappa Epsilon (pres. L.A. chpt. 1975-76, Outstanding Alumnus 19830. Republican. Office: Demetriou Del Guercio et al 649 S Olive St Ste 500 Los Angeles CA 90014

MOYER, GARY THOMAS, lawyer; b. Somerville, N.J., Nov. 2, 1959; s. Samuel Harvey and Agnes Margaret (Gore) M.; 1 child, Grayson I. BS in Acctg., Ariz. State U., 1981; JD, U. San Diego, 1986, LLM in Taxation, 1989. Bar: Calif. 1986. Agt. IRS, Van Nuys, Calif., 1981-82; facilities and fin. analyst MIA-Com Linkabit, San Diego, 1983-84; sr. acct. Jennings & Campbell, La Jolla, Calif., 1985; tax atty. J.E. Schneider, Inc., San Diego, 1986; ptnr. Schneider, Moyer & Lee, San Diego, 1987-89, Ferris & Britton, San Diego, 1989—. Tax advisor Vol. Income Tax Assistance Program for Elderly and Economically Underprivileged, Van Nuys, 1981-82. Mem. ABA (taxation sect., estate planning, trust and probate sect.), San Diego County Bar Assn. (taxation sect., estate planning, trust and probate sect.), Centre City Assn. (govtl. relations com.), Calif. State Bar, San Diegans Inc. Democrat. Roman Catholic. Office: Ferris & Britton 1855 1st Ave Ste 300 San Diego CA 92101

MOYER, HARLAN ERNEST, technical corporation executive; b. Napa, Calif., 1926; grad. U. Nev., 1952. Pres. CH2M Hill, Inc., Corvallis, Oreg.; pres. CH2M Hill Calif., Inc., CH2M Hill Southeast, Inc., CH2M Hill Va., Inc., CH2M Hill Northwest, Inc., CH2M Hill Central, Inc., CH2M Hill N.Y., Inc. Mem. ASCE, Nat. Soc. Profl. Engrs. Office: CH2M Hill Inc PO Box 22508 Denver CO 80222 *

MOYER, JAMES WORDEN, manufacturing company executive; b. San Jose, Calif., Nov. 26, 1948; s. Lane Walker and Priscilla Anne (Tracey) M. BS in Chemistry, Sonoma State U., 1972; PhD in Pharmacology, U. Calif.-San Francisco, 1985. Tchr., dept. head Nyeri (Kenya) High Sch., 1972-74; rsch. asst. dept. pharmacology U. Calif.-San Francisco, 1979-84; dir. rsch. Digital Cardiovascular Instruments, Berkeley, Calif., 1985--. Contbr. articles to profl. publs. Mem. AAAS, Assn. Computing Machinery, N.Am. Soc. Pacing and Electrophysiology. Home: 3885 18th St San Francisco CA 94114 Office: Digital Cardiovascular Instruments 1780 4th St Berkeley CA 94710

MRACKY, RONALD SYDNEY, management consultant; b. Sydney, Australia, Oct. 22, 1932; came to U.S., 1947, naturalized, 1957; s. Joseph and Anna (Janousek) M.; student English Inst., Prague, Czechoslovakia, 1943-47; grad. Parsons Sch. Design, N.Y.C., 1950-53; postgrad. NYU, 1952-53; m. Sylvia Frommer, Jan. 1, 1960; children: Enid Hillevi, Jason Adam. Designer D. Deskey Assocs., N.Y.C., 1953-54; art dir., designer ABC-TV, Hollywood, Calif., 1956-57; creative dir. Neal Advt. Assocs., Los Angeles, 1957-59; pres. Richter & Mracky Design Assocs., Los Angeles, 1959-68; pres., chief exec. officer Richter & Mracky-Bates div. Ted Bates & Co., Los Angeles, 1968-73, pres., chief exec. officer Regency Fin., Internat. Fin. Services, Beverly Hills, Calif., 1974-76; sr. ptnr. Sylron Internat., Los Angeles, 1973—; mgmt. dir. for N.Am. Standard Advt.-Tokyo, Los Angeles, 1978—; chief. exec. officer Standard/Worldwide Cons. Group, Los Angeles and Tokyo, 1981—; cons. in field; exec. dir. Inst. for Internat. Studies and Devel., Los Angeles, 1976-77. Bd. dirs. Dubnoff Ctr. for Child Devel. and Ednl. Therapy, Los Angeles, John Wayne Cancer Clinic/UCLA; bd. dirs., chmn. exec. com. Calif. Chamber Symphony Soc., Los Angeles. Served with U.S. Army, 1954-56. Mem. Am. Mktg. Assn., Los Angeles Publicity Club (com. mem.), Toluca Lake C. of C. Contbr. articles to profl. jours. Recipient nat. and internat. awards design and mktg. Office: 3855 Lankershim Blvd Universal City CA 91604

MRUVKA, ALAN SCOTT, cable network executive; b. N.Y.C., Dec. 1, 1957; s. Murray and Ruth (Bialach) M. Student, U. Miami, Pratt Inst. Pres. A.M. Properties, Seacaucus, N.J., 1983—; chmn., co-founder Movietime Channel Inc., Hollywood, Calif., 1984—; chmn. Movies USA Inc., Atlanta, 1989—; bd. dirs. Radis Inc. Bd. dirs. Beverly Hills-Cannes Sister City Com., Calif., 1988—; mem. exec. com. Corey Davis for Gov. Republican. Jewish. Office: Movietime Channel Inc 1800 N Vine St Hollywood CA 90028

MUCCILLI, JAY EDWARD, psychologist; b. Duluth, Minn., July 22, 1941; s. Eddie Ormando and Edythe Marie (Stortz) M.; m. Jessie M. Lomoro, Aug. 6, 1965 (div. 1974); children: Lisa, Nicholas, Marcus; m. Alta Jean Merriam, June 21, 1980. BA, U. Minn., 1963; postgrad., George Washington U., 1963-65; MA with honors, U. Colo., 1967, PhD with honors, 1979. Lic. psychologist, marriage, family and child counselor, Calif. Sch. psychologist Boulder (Colo.) Valley Sch. Dist., 1966-67; assoc. dir. counseling svcs. U. Santa Clara (Calif.), 1968-70, acting asst. prof. ednl. psychology, 1969-70, guest prof. Grad. Sch., 1973-79; dir., co-founder Therapeutic Homes, Inc. (now called Community Devel. Svcs.), San Jose, Calif., 1971-73; psychologist, coord. acute psychiat. inpatient units Santa Clara Valley Med. Ctr. and County Hosp., San Jose, 1970-74; pres., co-founder Inst. for Human Svcs., San Jose, 1972-76; clin. psychologist psychiat. dept. Kaiser Permanente Med. Ctr., Santa Clara, 1974-77; pvt. practice San Jose, 1976-1986, Los Gatos, Calif., 1983—; clin. psychologist El Camino Health Ctr., Sunnyvale, Calif., 1969-70; asst. clin. prof. dept. psychiatry Stanford (Calif.) U. Sch. Medicine, 1973-79; chief psychologist psychiat. dept. Kaiser Permanente Med. Ctr. and Hosp., San Jose, 1977-83; mem. instnl. rev. bd. Inst. for Psychosocial Interaction, Palo Alto, Calif., 1981-85; oral exam. commr. psychology exam. com. Calif. Bd. Med. Quality Assurance, 1988, also cons. to numerous agys., 1970--. Pres., co-founder Found. To Aid Minorities in Human Svc. Careers, San Jose, 1972-76;; bd. dirs. Bill Wilson Ctr., Santa Clara, 1977-80. George Washington U. fellow and scholar, 1964-65; USPHS-NIMH fellow, 1965-66; U. Colo. scholar and fellow, 1966-67. Mem. Am. Psychol. Assn., Calif. State Psychol. Assn. (Santa Clara County rep., bd. dirs., Outstanding Grad. Educator award 1986), Santa Clara County Psychol. Assn. (pres. 1986, Outstanding Psychologist award 1987), Am. Psychology and Law Soc., Psi Chi. Office: 405 Alberto Way Ste 4 Los Gatos CA 95032

MUCE, PAUL MAXIMILIAN, finance executive; b. Palermo, Italy, Sept. 4, 1940; came to U.S., 1968; s. Nicola and Antonina (Alaimo) M.; m. Josephine LoCicero, Oct. 28, 1965 (div. Feb. 1988); children: Antonella S., Nick P., Rosalie E., Sasha J., Lana R.; m. May 1988. BSBA, U. Palermo, Italy, 1964; student, NYU, 1964; BSBA, U. Beverly Hills, 1983, MBA, 1984. Mgr. export dept. I.D.O.S. Spa, Palermo, Italy, 1965-68; asst. corp. comptroller Diversa Graphics Inc., N.Y.C., 1968-74; regional comptroller ITT Corp., N.Y.C., 1974-85; v.p. fin. Del Piso Brick & Tile Corp., Anaheim, Calif., 1985—. Leader Catholic Youth Orgn., Palermo, 1955-60. Served with Italian Artillery, 1965-66. Mem. Fin. Exec. Inst. Republican. Roman Catholic. Home: 4922 Kermath Placentia CA 92670 Office: Del Piso Brick & Tile Corp 1635 S State College Blvd Anaheim CA 92806

MUCHMORE, DON MONCRIEF, museum administrator; b. Wichita, Kans., Dec. 26, 1922; s. Floyd Stephen and Ivy Fay (Campbell) M.; m. Virginia Gunn, June 18, 1949 (div. Dec. 1978); children—Melinda, Marcia. B.A., Occidental Coll., Los Angeles, 1945; postgrad., U. So. Calif. Law Sch., 1945; postgrad. polit. sci., UCLA. Intern Nat. Inst. Pub. Affairs, Washington, 1944; exec. asst. to congressman Washington, 1946-48; teaching asst. UCLA, 1949-50; mem. faculty San Diego State U., 1950-51; asst. prof., adminstr. Calif. State U.-Long Beach, 1951-56; spl. asst. to supt. pub. instrn. Calif. Dept. Edn., Sacramento, 1956-57; exec. mus. dir. Calif. Mus. Sci. and Industry, Los Angeles, 1957-62, 82-88; exec. v.p., chief exec. officer Calif. Mus. Found., Los Angeles, 1957-62, 82—; dep. dir. Calif. Dept. Fin., Sacramento, 1960; vice chancellor Calif. State Colls. and Univs. System, Long Beach, 1962-64; sr. v.p., exec. asst. to chmn. and chief exec. officer Calif. Fed. Savs. and Loan Assn., Los Angeles, 1964-82; chmn. bd. dirs., chief exec. officer Opinion Research of Calif., Opinion Surveyors, The State Poll & Market Surveys, Inc., Long Beach, 1948-71, also M-R Assocs. campaigns; cons. in pub. opinion, mus. mgmt. and fund raising, 1948-71; cons. DMM & Assocs., Long Beach, 1981—; mem. Inst. Mus. Services, 1983-88; bd. dirs. Sci. Mus. Film Collaborative, 1982-88. Chmn. bd. Campbell Found., Long Beach, 1956—; mem./chmn. 4 Presdl. commns., 1970-82. Elks nat. scholar. Mem. Am. Assn. Mus., Calif. Mus. Assn. (pres. 1960, bd. dirs. 1982-88), Assn. Sci. and Tech. Ctrs. (bd. dirs. 1982-88), Am. Assn. Pub. Opinion Rsch., Am. Polit. Sci. Assn., AAAS. Club: Jonathan (Los Angeles). Home: 4225 Virginia Vista Long Beach CA 90807 Office: Calif Mus Found Calif Mus Sci and Industry 700 State Dr Los Angeles CA 90037

MUCHMORE, PATRICK WAYNE, engineering contracting company executive; b. Vancouver, Wash., Feb. 13, 1955; s. Alva A. and Eilene Geneviva (Pratt) M.; m. Patricia Ann Welch, June 30, 1979; children: Kindy Ann, Tracy Lynn. Cook Rock Creek Country Club, Portland, Oreg., 1974-75; drill operator A&W Rock Drilling Co., Newburg, Oreg., 1975-76, constrn supt., 1976-78; constrn supt. Capital Devel. Co., Olympia, Wash., 1978-81; pres. Zycom Inc. div. Capital Devel., Olympia, 1981-83; co-owner, v.p. Hpt Corp., Olympia, 1983-85; owner, mgr. Patrick W. Muchmore-Gen. Engring. Contractor, Antioch, Calif., 1985—. Republican. Methodist. Home and Office: 3934 Rocky Point Dr Antioch CA 94509

MUCHNIC, SUZANNE, art critic, educator, lecturer; b. Kearney, Nebr., May 16, 1940; d. Walter Marian Ely and Erva Nell Liston; m. Paul D. Muchnic, 1963; B.A., Scripps Coll., 1962; M.A., Clarement Grad. Sch., 1963. Art instr. Weber State Coll., Ogden, Utah, 1972-73; art history instr. Los Angeles City Coll., 1974-82; editor for So. Calif., Artweek, 1976-78; art critic Los Angeles Times, 1978—; art criticism instr. Claremont Grad. Sch., 1984. Author: Tim Nordin retrospective catalogue, 1982, Martha Alf retrospective catalogue, 1984, Mark Lere Catalogue, 1986, catalogue essay Taiwan Mus. of Art, 1988. Recipient Disting. Alumna award Claremont Grad. Sch., 1982, Disting. Alumna award Scripps Coll., 1987. Mem. Coll. Art Assn., Internat. Assn. Art Critics. Office: Los Angeles Times Times-Mirror Sq Los Angeles CA 90053

MUCKLER, JOHN, professional hockey coach; b. Midland, Ont.; m.; 5 children. Professional hockey player, Ea. Hockey League, Baltimore, also Long Island Duck; coach, gen. mgr. Long Island Ducks; coach, gen. mgr. New York Rangers affiliate team, Am. Hockey League, Providence, R.I.; formerly head coach Minnesota North Stars; with Edmonton Oilers, 1981—, formerly co-coac, head coach, 1989—. Office: Edmonton Oilers, Northlands Coliseum, Edmonton, AB Canada T5B 4M9 *

MUDD, JOSEPH DELBERT, accountant; b. Wheatridge, Colo., Sept. 10, 1964; s. John William and Alberta Marie (Guzman) M.; m. Lyn Beyer, Aug. 27, 1988. AA, Otero Jr. Coll., 1984; BS, Colo. State U., 1987. Auditor State of Colo., Denver, 1987--. Mem. Nat. Assn. Accts. Republican. Roman Catholic.

MUEHLBAUER, RENICE ANN, public relations consultant, writer; b. Milw., Jan. 2, 1947; d. Fredrick and Lucia (Stewart) Fregin; m. Thomas George Muehlbauer, July 5, 1968; children: Jennifer Jean, Whitney Susan. BA, U. San Diego, 1988, postgrad., 1989—. Pres. Chubby Bumpkins, Inc., Houston, 1980-82; contracts adminstr. Gulf States Computer Svcs., Houston, 1980-82; pres. RAM Prodns., Houston, 1981-82, Pizza Internat., Inc., Houston, 1982-84; contracts adminstr. First Alliance Corp., Houston, 1982-85; freelance pub. rels. cons., San Diego, 1985—. Tutor U. San Diego Writing Ctr., 1987—; founder, dir. pub. relations-tng. Montgomery County (Tex.) Crisis Action Line, Houston, 1979-84; founder, v.p., bd. dirs. Montgomery County Rape Crisis Coalition, 1982-84, speaker, 1982-84; speaker Trauma Rape Coalition, 1982-84; mem. prodn. com. Community Women Together, Montgomery County, 1980-82; pres. Living Arts Council, Houston, 1980-81. Named Woman of Yr. YWCA, 1981, 82. Mem. Am. Assn. Bus. Women (dir. activities Houston chpt. 1983-84), Bus. Women's Forum (dir. community awareness Houston chpt. 1982-83), Assn. Women Bus. Owners, Lions (hon.), Phi Alpha Delta.

MUELLER, MICHELLE MARIE, technical communications executive; b. Madison, Wis., June 15, 1954; d. Neil Edward and Maura Kay (Smith) M.; m. Michael Gault, Sept. 7, 1984; 1 stepchild, Gina Marlena. B.A., Eastern Mich. U., 1974; M.A., Morehead State U., 1975; postgrad., U. Mich., 1977-78; M.B.A., Syracuse U., 1985. Radio-TV/Producer WEMU-FM, WUOM-FM, Ann Arbor, Mich., 1972-78; instr. U. Mich., Ann Arbor, 1976-78; mgr. tech. communication Bendix Co., Southfield, Mich., 1978-81; dir. advt. and pub. relations E.F. Hutton Life Ins., La Jolla, Calif., 1981-83; v.p. pub. relations Knoth & Meads Advt./Pub. Relations, San Diego, Calif., 1983-85; asst. v.p. ops. support services M/A-COM Govt. Systems, San Diego, 1985—; instr. San Diego State U., U. Calif.-San Diego, 1981—; instr. U. Mich., Easter Mich. U., Moorehead State U., San Diego State U., 1974—; promotions dir. Artrain, San Diego, 1983. Author cookbook Recipes by the Dozen, 1987; contbr. articles to profl. jours. Mem. Women in Communications (v.p. programs 1983, pres. 1984, v.p. profl. devel. 1981, Woman of Achievement award 1984)), Pub. Relations Soc. Am. (v.p. promotion 1983, v.p. profl. devel. 1984, sec. 1985), San Diego C. of C., Oceanside Econ. Devel. Council, PR Club San Diego, Soc. for Tech. Communications (Outstanding Presentation award 1980), Phi Kappa Phi, Alpha Epsilon Rho. Roman Catholic. Office: 3033 Science Park Rd San Diego CA 92121

MUGLER, LARRY GEORGE, regional planner; b. Chgo., June 22, 1946; s. Warren Franklin and Elaine Mae (Mittag) M.; m. Judy Ann Allison, Aug. 3, 1968; children: Jonathan, Allison. BSCE, Northwestern U., 1968; postgrad., Evang. Theol. Sem., 1969-70; MS in Urban and Regional Planning, U. Wis., 1972. Planning analyst State of Wis., Madison, 1970-72; dir. community devel. Cen. Okla. Econ. Devel. Dist., Shawnee, 1972-74; planner Denver Regional Council of Govts., 1974-80, dir. environ. services, 1980-83, dir. devel. services, 1983—. Contbr. chpt. in book. Pres. bd. dirs. Leawood Met. Recreation and Park Dist., Littleton, Colo., 1978—. Named one of Outstanding Young Men in Am., Jaycees, 1974; Lasker Found. fellow, 1971. Mem. Am. Planning Assn., ASCE (subcom. chmn. 1985-86, 88-89). Republican. Methodist. Office: Denver Regional Coun Govts 2480 W 26th Ave Ste 200B Denver CO 80211

MUH, ROBERT A., investment banker; b. N.Y.C., Jan. 7, 1938; s. Irving and Frieda (Glenn) M.; m. Berit C. Spant, Dec. 19, 1968; children: Alison, Carrie. BS, MIT, 1959; MBA, Columbia U., 1961, MPhil, 1965. Cons. McKinsey & Co., N.Y.C., 1966-69; investment banker Newburger, Loeb & Co., N.Y.C., 1970-72, Fin. Svcs. Internat., L.A., 1973-76, Bear, Stearns & Co., L.A. and San Francisco, 1977-87; with Fin. Svcs. Internat., San Francisco, 1987—; dir. Far West Fin., L.A., Frontier Ins., Monticello, N.Y., Transcisco Industries, San Francisco, MIT, Cambridge. 1st Lt. U.S. Army. Mem. World Trade Club, Bankers Club.

MUHLEBACH, RICHARD FRANK, management and development company executive; b. San Francisco, July 16, 1943; s. Frank Joseph and Flora Delores (Luglini) M.; m. Maria Delia Rivera, Nov., 1964; children: Kathy, Eric. BA, San Francisco State U., 1968; AA, Golden West Coll., 1972. Cert. property mgr., shopping ctr. mgr., real property adminstr. Caseworker Alameda County Welfare Dept., Oakland, Calif., 1968-69; v.p. The Lusk Co., Irvine, Calif., 1969-76, Tishman West Mng. Corp., Orange, Calif., 1976-80; pres. TRF Mgmt. Corp., Bellevue, Wash., 1980—; v.p. The Rainier Fund, Inc., Bellevue, 1984—; instr. Orange Coast Coll., Costa Mesa, Calif., 1976-80, Internat. Coun. Shopping Ctrs., N.Y.C., 1980—, N.W. Ctr. for Profl. Edn., Bellevue, 1980—. Contbr. articles to profl. jours. With USNG, 1965-71. Mem. Inst. Real Estate Mgmt (instr. 1980—, r.v.p. 1987-88), Real Estate Educators Assn. (pres. 1989, v.p. 1988), Internat. Real Estate Mgmt. (v.p. western Wash. chpt. 1984, pres. 1985). Home: 17910 NE 125th St Redmond WA 98052 Office: TRF Mgmt Corp 12400 SE 38th St Bellevue WA 98006

MUIA, CARL JOSEPH, mechanical engineer; b. Pitts., May 6, 1938; s. Carl and Minne (Rizzo) M.; m. Charlotte Ruth amideon, Sept. 2, 1961; children: Tina, Louise, Gina Marie. BSME, Carnegie Inst. Tech., 1960. Maintenance engr. Wheeling Steel, Steubenville, Ohio, 1960-61; engr. Boeing Co., Seattle, L.A., New Orleans, 1961-65, Westinghouse Co., Balt., 1965-66; chief exec. officer Engring. Corp. Am., Seattle, 1966—. Res. police detective King County Police, Seattle, 1975—. Mem. Nat. Tech. Svcs. Assn., Wash. Assn. Temp. Svcs. (treas. 1987-88). Office: Engring Corp Am 2705 California Ave SW PO Box 16438 Seattle WA 98116

MUJUMDAR, VILAS SITARAM, structural engineer, construction management consultant; b. Indore, India, June 26, 1941; s. Sitaram and Kamala (Kulkarni) M.; m. Ingrid M. Dietrich, Mar. 1, 1969. BSc, Vikram U., India, 1961; MS, U. Roorkee, India, 1962; MBA, U. Santa Clara, Calif., 1980. Registered profl. engr., U.S., Can., U.K.; registered structural engr., Calif. Design engr. U.S.D. & Co., India, 1962-65, Donovan H. Lee & Ptnrs., London, 1965-66; asst. chief engr. Francon & Spancrete Ltd., Montreal, Can., 1966-68; gen. mgr., dir. engring. Modular Constructors, Woburn, Mass., 1968-70; sr. project engr., tech. mgr. LeMessurier Assocs., Cambridge, Mass., 1970-74; v.p. Precast Systems Cons., Woburn, 1974-77; prin. structural engr. Ecodyne Corp., Santa Rosa, Calif., 1977-79; v.p. Foster Engring., Inc., San Francisco, 1979-81, 3D/Internat. Inc., Houston, 1981-85; pres. VSM Assocs., Santa Rosa, Calif., 1985—; dir. U.S. Tech. Corp., Mich.; mem. various tech. coms. nat. orgns. Inventor pre-cast concrete bldg. systems; contbr. articles to profl. jours. Merit scholar Govt. India, 1957-62, Gold medal. Fellow Inst. Structural Engrs.; mem. ASCE, Am. Concrete Inst., Prestressed Concrete Inst., Structural Engrs. Assn. of No. Calif., Beta Gamma Sigma (hon. soc.). Home: 2120 Parrish Dr Santa Rosa CA 95404 Office: 5979 Commerce Blvd Ste 2 Rohnert Park CA 94928

MUKAI, ROBERT KENGI, sound and lighting engineer; b. Vincenza, Italy, Mar. 19, 1962; came to U.S., 1963; s. Thomas Mamoru and Mihoko (Sato) M.; m. Nancy Ann Baldwin, June 23, 1984. Grad. high sch., Redondo Beach, Calif. Asst. auto mechanic, head auto mechanic John's 76 Auto Service, Redondo Beach, 1980-82, 84-87; technician Audio Visual Hdqrs. Corp., Inglewood, Calif., 1982-84; sound and lighting engr. Century Plaza Hotel, Century City, Calif., 1987—; regional v.p. A.L. Williams Ins. Svcs., Pasadena, Calif., 1984—; cameraman, sound and lighting engr., New Life Cable TV Show, Redondo Beach, 1985-87. Republican. Office: 1327 Post Ave Ste F Torrance CA 90501

MULENBURG, GERALD MARTIN, aerospace engineer; b. Granite Falls, Minn., Nov. 20, 1938; s. Martin and Amanda Bergquist; m. Judith Ann McGuire, Mar. 17, 1981; children: Kristen Luann, Kathryn Elizabeth. BSME, Okla. State U., 1967; MS in Aerospace Engring. with distinction, Air Force Inst. Tech., Dayton, Ohio, 1969; MS in Systems Mgmt., U. So. Calif., 1971. Registered engr., Calif. Enlisted USAF, 1956, advanced through grades to capt., aerospace engr., 1956-77, ret., 1977; rsch. lab. mgr. Stanford U., Palo Alto, Calif., 1977-79; engr. aerospace facilities USN, Alameda, Calif., 1979-84, program mgr., 1986-89; pvt. cons. practice, Lafayette, Calif., 1984-85; asst. dir. Lawrence Hall of Sci. U. Calif., Berkeley, 1985-86; engr. rsch. facilities NASA/Ames Rsch. Ctr., Mountain View, Calif., 1989—. Contbr. numerous articles to profl. jours. and confs. Mem. AIAA, McClellan Soc. Profl. Engrs., Toastmasters, Pi Tau Sigma. Republican. Home: 1201 Park Ave Alameda CA 94501 Office: NASA Ames Rsch Ctr Code SL MS 239-7 Moffett Field CA 94035

MULGAONKAR, RANJIT P., marketing manager; b. Kolhapur, Maharashtra, India, Oct. 24, 1957; s. Pandurag and Kamal (Joshi) M.; m. Dana R. Mulgaonkar, Mar. 28, 1987. Diploma in Electronics and Telecommunication Engring., Govt. Poly., Poona, India, 1978; MS, Va. Poly. Inst., 1983. Software engr. Vicom Systems Inc., San Jose, Calif., 1983-84; from software engr. to project leader TAU Corp., Los Latos, Calif., 1984-87; product mgr. Recognition Concepts Inc., Incline Village, Nev., 1987—. Contbr. articles to profl. jours. Cunningham Found. fellow ,1983. Home: PO Box 8919 Incline Village NV 89450 Office: Recognition Concepts Inc PO Box 8570 Incline Village NV 89450

MULICK, EDWARD JAMES, orthodontist; b. Missoula, Mont., June 2, 1938; s. Edward Claude Mulick and Neta I. (McFadden) Marolich; m. Jeanne Mae Christison, Aug. 13, 1960; children: Edward Michael, Susan Marie, Michelle Ann, Michael John, Patrick Sean. BS, Gonzaga U., 1960; DDS, Creighton U., 1963; MS, U. Nebr., 1970. Gen. practice dentistry Priest River, Idaho, 1963-68; practice dentistry specializing in orthodontics Boise, Idaho, 1970—; cons. Boise State U. Vocat. Sch., 1978—, Am. Inst. Health, Boise, 1986—. Mem. ADA, Am. Assn. Orthodontists, Idaho Dental Assn. (pres. 1986), SW Idaho Dist. Dental Assn. (pres. 1982-83), Idaho State Orthodontic Assn. Republican. Roman Catholic. Lodge: Kiwanis (pres. 1976). Home: 4001 Del Monte Boise ID 87304 Office: Boise Orthodontic Assocs 7373 Emerald Boise ID 87304

MULKEY, JUDY CARMEN, nurse; b. Farmington, N.M., July 23, 1959; d. Maclovio Robert and Isa (Garcia) Gurule; m. Phillip Martin Elze, Nov. 1, 1975 (div. 1985); children: Veronica, Misty; m. Wylie Daniel Mulkey, Feb. 21, 1987. Student, San Juan Coll., Farmington, N.M., 1982; A.Nursing, N.M. Jr. Coll., Hobbs, 1986. Nurse San Juan Reg. Med. Ctr., Farmington, N.M., 1982-83, Good Samaritan Village, Hobbs, N.M., 1984-86; nurse, minor emergency clinic nurse Notre Vista Med. Ctr., Hobbs, 1984-86; nurse hosp. float pvt. duty Med. Personnel Pool, Colorado Springs, 1986-88; nurse psych., charge Mountain View Care Ctr., Colorado Springs, 1988—. Mem. Health Occupations (treas. 1979-80). Democrat. Roman Cathlic. Home: 217 S 11th St Colorado Springs CO 80904 Office: 1901 N Union Blvd Ste 202 Colorado Springs CO 80909-1830

MULLARKEY, MARY J., state supreme court justice; b. New London, Wis., Sept. 28, 1943; d. John Clifford and Isabelle A. (Steffes) M.; m. Thomas E. Korson, July 24, 1971; 1 child, Andrew Steffes Korson. BA, St. Norbert Coll., 1965; LLB, Harvard U., 1968. Bar: Wis. 1968, Colo. 1974. Atty.-advisor U.S. Dept. Interior, Washington, 1968-73; asst. regional atty. EEOC, Denver, 1973-75; 1st atty. gen. Colo. Dept. Law, Denver, 1975-79, solicitor gen., 1979-82; legal advisor to Gov. Lamm State of Colo., Denver, 1982-85; ptnr. Mullarkey & Seymour, Denver, 1985-87; justice Colo. Supreme Ct., Denver, 1987—. Recipient Alumni award St. Norbert Coll., De Pere, Wis., 1980. Mem. ABA, Colo. Bar Assn., Colo. Women's Bar Assn. (recognition award 1986), Denver Bar Assn. Office: Colo Supreme Ct 2 E 14th Ave Denver CO 80203

MULLEN, JOHN HAROLD, III, accountant; b. Shields, Ill., Feb. 14, 1951; s. John Harold Jr. and Charlotte (Romney) M.; m. Jana Rae Low, Apr. 25, 1976; children: John, Kathleen, Nathan, Charles, Lauren. Student, Ariz. State U., 1969-70; BS in Acctg., Brigham Young U., 1975; MBT, U. So. Calif., 1979. CPA, Tex., 1977. Missionary Ch. of Jesus Christ of Latter Day Saints, Saniago, Chile, 1970-72; various positions KMG Main Hurdman, Midland, El Paso, Tex., 1976-82; ptnr. KMG Main Hurdman, Midland, 1982-84; nat. dir. personal fin. planning KMG Main Hurdman, N.Y.C., 1984-86; ptnr. in charge KMG Main Hurdman, Irvine, Calif., 1986-87; ptnr. Peat, Marwick, Main & Co., Costa Mesa, Calif., 1987—. Contbr. articles to profl. jours. Scouting coordinator Orange V ward Boy Scouts Am. Mem. Am. Inst. CPA's, Calif. Soc. CPA's, N.Y. State Soc. CPA's, Tex. Soc. CPA's. Republican. Lodge: Rotary (chmn., career info., 1987—, bd. dirs. 1988—) (Newport/Irvine, Calif.), (bd. dirs. 1981, 83) (Midland).

MULLEN, THOMAS JOHN, business owner; b. Grand Island, Nebr., Sept. 17, 1945; s. Paul Raymond and Jacquelyn Jo (Moore) M.; m. Cheri Annette Poncelow, May 26, 1968 (div. Sept. 1979); 1 child, Robin Jeannette; m. Martha Evelyn Moulton, Feb. 14, 1981; 1 child, Gordon Sadler. Student, Hastings (Nebr.) Coll., 1963-66, U. Colo., 1970-74. Field supr. Colo. Mcht. Police, Inc., Denver, 1974-76, supr. ops., 1976-82, mgr. guard div., 1982-83; mgr. ops. Wells Fargo Guard Service, Inc., Denver, 1983; owner, pres. Mullen Security & Investigations, Inc., Denver, 1983—. Candidate State Legislature, Denver, 1980; mem. Adhoc Com. on State Licensing, Denver, 1982-83. Served with USAF, 1966-70. Mem. Am. Soc. for Indsl. Security, Mountain Air Ranch Club, Rotary (Wheatridge), Masons (master 1987). Presbyterian. Office: Mullen Security & Investigations Inc 7100 Broadway #3J Denver CO 80221

MULLEN, THOMAS PATRICK, academic administrator; b. Wenatchee, Wash., May 10, 1938; s. Thomas Lyle and Ruth Genevive (Green) M. BA, Whittier Coll., 1960; MA, U. Minn., 1970, PhD, 1971. Cert. prof. Tchr. Anaheim (Calif.) Union High Sch., 1960-68; instr. U. Minn., 1968-71, U. Calif., 1970; asst. prof. Ariz. State U., Tempe, 1971-73, Bemidji (Minn.) State U., 1973-75; prof. edn. Calif. State U., San Bernardino, 1975—; dir. Calif. State Learning Ctr., 1988—, cons. City and County Schs., San Bernardino, 1975—. Author study skills; contbr. articles to profl. jours. Bd sec. Family Service Assn., San Bernadino, Calif., 1986-88. Mem. Arrowhead Reading Council, Calif. Reading Assn., Internat. Reading Assn., Nat. Social Sci. Assn. (adv. bd.). Democrat. Home: 5875 N Riverside Ave Rialto CA 92376 Office: Calif State U 5500 State University Pkwy San Bernardino CA 92407

MULLER, JEROME KENNETH, art dealer, editor, psychologist; b. Amityville, N.Y., July 18, 1934; s. Alphons and Helen (Haberl) m.; m. Nora Marie Nestor, Dec. 21, 1974. BS, Marquette U., 1961; postgrad., Calif. State U., Fullerton, 1985-86; MA, Nat. U., San Diego, 1988; postgrad., Newport Psychoanalytic Inst., 1988—. Comml. and editorial photographer N.Y.C., 1952-55; mng. editor Country Beautiful mag., Milw., 1961-62, Reprodns. Rev. mag., N.Y.C., 1967-68; editor, art dir. Orange County (Calif.) Illustrated, Newport Beach, 1962-67, art editor, 1970-79, exec. editor, art dir., 1968-69; owner, chief exec. officer Creative Services Advt. Agy., Newport Beach, 1969-79; founder, chief exec. officer Mus. Graphics, Costa Mesa, Calif., 1978—; tchr. photography Lindenhurst (N.Y.) High Sch., 1952-54; tchr. comic art U. Calif., Irvine, 1979; guest curator 50th Anniversary Exhbn. Mickey Mouse, 1928-78, The Bowers Mus., Santa Ana, Calif., 1978; organized Moving Image Exhbn. Mus. Sci. and Industry, Chgo., Cooper-Hewitt Mus., N.Y.C., William Rockhill Nelson Gallery, Kansas City, 1981; collector original works of outstanding Am. cartoonists which are exhibited at major mus. One-man shows include Souk Gallery, Newport Beach, 1970; Author: Rex Brandt, 1972; contbr. photographs and articles to mags. Served with USAF, 1956-57. Recipient two silver medals 20th Ann. Exhbn. Advt. and Editorial Art in West, 1965. Mem. Am. Assn. Profl. Hypnotherapists, Internat. Psychohistorical Assn., Newport Harbor Art Mus., Mus. Modern Art (N.Y.C.), Met. Mus. Art, Art Mus. Assn. Am., Laguna Beach Mus. Art, Newport Harbor C. of C., Alpha Sigma Nu. Clubs: Los Angeles Press, Orange County Press. Home: 2438 Bowdoin Pl Costa Mesa CA 92626 Office: PO Box 10743 Costa Mesa CA 92627

MULLIGAN, MARTIN FREDERICK, clothing executive, professional tennis player; b. Sydney, Australia, Oct. 18, 1940; s. Frederick William and Marie Louise (Tome) M.; m. Rossella Rita Labella, Sept. 19, 1969 (div. Mar. 1980); children: Monica, Martin Thomas. Winner Tennis Singles Championships of Australia, 1952, 53, 55, 56, 57, 58; mem. Davis Cup team Australia, 1959, 60; winner Australian Hard Court Singles and Doubles tournaments, 1960, 64; finalist Wimbledon Singles tournaments, 1962—; winner Italian Open Singles tournaments, 1963, 65, 67; co-organizer Italian Open tournament, Rome, 1972-73; winner German Open Singles tournament, 1963; winner singles and doubles titles Monte Carlo Championships, 1964; coach Italian Davis Cup team, 1966-76; winner, Davis Cup tournament, 1976; winner Spanish Open tournament, 1966, 67, Swedish Open tournament, 1966, 67, Austrian Open tournament, 1966, 67, Champion Cup tournament, 1966, 67; promotional cons. Alpina Australian Mfg. Co., 1973-74; cons. and internat. promotion mgr. Diadora Co., 1973-78; internat. promotion mgr. FILA-Italy Sportswear, 1976-1978, v.p. of internat. promotion and pub. relations, 1979—; negotiated contracts between FILA and various sports profls. and celebrities. Ranked Number 3 in World in Tennis, 1967, ranked 5 times in world's top 10 tennis players. Office: FILAsports Inc 821 Indstrial St San Carlos CA 94070

MULLIKIN, HARRY LAVERNE, hotel executive; b. Hot Springs, Ark., Apr. 27, 1927; s. Carlton and LeVerne (Harper) Mahone; m. Judith Ann Thomas, July 25, 1970; children: Michael, Patricia, Scott, Kelly. Student, Wash. State Coll., 1947, U. Wash., Seattle, 1949. Resident mgr. Davenport Hotel, Spokane, 1953-57; gen. mgr. Olympic Hotel, Seattle; with Westin Hotel Co., Seattle, from 1961, sr. v.p., then exec. v.p., 1970-73, pres., 1973-77, chief exec. officer, 1977-89, chmn., 1981-89, pres., 1982-84, also dir.; chmn. Hilton Internat. Co., N.Y.C., 1987; dir. UAL, Inc., United Airlines, SeaFirst Corp., Seattle-First Nat. Bank. Bd. dirs. Virginia Mason Hosp. Served with USAAF, World War II. Recipient Golden Plate award Internat. Foodservice Mfrs. Assn., 1972; Man of Year award Pa. State U., 1975; Alumni Achievement award Wash. State U., 1976. Mem. Am. Hotel and Motel Assn. (past pres., past chmn.), Nat. Restaurant Assn. (past dir.). Republican. Roman Catholic. Clubs: Seattle Golf (Seattle), Seattle Yacht Bohemian, Rainier (Seattle). Office: Westin Hotels & Resorts The Westin Bldg 2001 6th Ave Seattle WA 98121 *

MULLINEX, TRAVIS, food company executive. Pres., chief operating officer Tri/Valley Growers, Inc., San Francisco. Office: Tri/Valley Growers Inc 1255 Battery St San Francisco CA 94120 *

MULLINNIX, STAN WARREN, jeweler; b. Casper, Wyo., May 22, 1953; s. Johny Warren and Lois Mae (Sauter) M.; m. Sherri Austin, June 15, 1975. BA in Philosophy, U. Wyo., 1975. Mgr. Okes Jewelers, Casper, 1975-79; gen. ptnr. S.W. Mullinnix, Jeweler, Douglas, Wyo., 1979-88; owner S.W. Mullinnix, Jeweler, Douglas, 1988—. Designer and artist numerous medallions. Chmn. Bd. Adjustments, Douglas; bd. dirs. Small Bus. Devel. Ctr. East Wyo. Coll. Mem. Jewelers of Am., Jewelers Vigilance Com., Mont.-Wyo. Jewelers Assn., Rotary. (pres. Douglas chpt. 1988-89). Office: SW Mullinnix Jeweler 1954 E Richards Douglas WY 82633

MULLINS, ANNA CARROLLE, hospital administrator; b. Mayfield, Ky., Oct. 29, 1945; d. Louis and Opal (Rowland) M. AD in Nursing, Paducah Community Coll, 1968; BSN, U. Calif, San Francisco, 1969; MSN, U. Calif, 1971, Dr. Nursing Sci, 1975. Reg. profl. nurse. Head nurse Mayfield (Ky.) Hosp., 1968; charge nurse Unity Hosp., San Francisco, 1971-74; clin. nurse IV U. Calif. Hosps., San Francisco, 1974-77; assoc. dir. edn. and research U. Calif. Hosps., 1977-78; dir. nursing 1978-82; asst. adminstr. nursing Children's Hosp., San Francisco, 1982-83; asst. v.p. 1983-86, chief ops. officer, 1986; chief ops. officer Seton Med. Ctr. and St. Catherine Hosp., Daly City and Half Moon Bay, Calif., 1986-89; chief exec. officer Seton Med. Ctr. and St. Catherine Hosp., Daly City and Half Moon Bay, 1989—; clin. prof., U. Calif. Sch. Nursing 1977—; adj. prof. nursing, San Francisco State U. 1977—. Contbr.: Instl. Rev. Bds., 1981; contbr. articles to profl. jours. Mem. Aldersgate United Meth. Ch., San Rafael, 1985-87; Christian edn. com., Mill Valley, Calif., 1978-79; vol. Marin Co. Heart Assn. Crusade, San Rafael, 1977-83. Named Tchr. of Yr. Adminstr., U. Calif., San Francisco, 1985-86. Mem. Calif. League Nursing (chmn. nominating com. 1983-85), Calif. Soc. Nursing Svc. Adminstrs. Democrat. Home: 125 Holmes Ave San Rafael CA 94903 Office: Seton Med Ctr 1900 Sullivan Ave Daly City CA 94015

MULLINS, JOSEPH JOHNSON, JR., lawyer; b. Birmingham, Ala., Nov. 13, 1929; s. Joseph Johnson and Sarah (Nabors) M.; m. Genevieve Townsend, Jan. 27, 1957 (div. 1962); 1 child, Melinda; m. Evelyn H. Tittmann, Aug. 21, 1969; children: Cerianne, Margarethe. BA, Washington and Lee U., 1952; LLB, Harvard U., 1955. Bar: Ala. 1955, N. Mex. 1960. Bd. dirs. Rodey, Dickason, Sloan, Akin & Robb, Albuquerque, 1966--. Mem. ABA. Democrat. Methodist. Home: 910 Sierra Pl SE Albuquerque NM 87108

MULLINS, RUTH GLADYS, nurse; b. Westville, N.S., Can., Aug. 25, 1943; d. William G. and Gladys H.; came to U.S., 1949, naturalized, 1955; student Tex. Womans U., 1961-64; BS in Nursing, Calif. State U.-Long Beach, 1966; MNursing, UCLA, 1973; m. Leonard E. Mullins, Aug. 27, 1963; children: Deborah R., Catherine M., Leonard III. Pub. health nurse, L.A. County Health Dept., 1967-68; nurse Meml. Hosp. Med. Center, Long Beach, 1968-72; dir. pediatric nurse practitioner program Calif. State U., Long Beach, 1973—, asst. prof., 1975-80, asso. prof., 1980-85, prof., 1985—; health svc. credential coord. Sch. Nursing, chmn., 1979-81, coord. grad. programs, 1985—; mem. Calif. Maternal, Child and Adolescent Health Bd., 1977-84; vice chair Long Beach/Orange County Health Consortium, 1984-85, chair 1985-86. Tng. grantee HHS, Calif. Dept. Health; cert. pediatric nurse practitioner. Fellow Nat. Assn. Pediatric Nurse Assos. and Practitioners (exec. bd., pres. elect); mem. Am. Pub. Health Assn., Assn. Faculties Pediatric Nurse Practitioner Programs, Calif. Assn. Pediatric Nurse Practitioners and Assocs., Am. Assn. U. Faculty, Ambulatory Pediatric Assn. Democrat. Methodist. Author: (with B. Nelms) Growth and Development: A Primary Health Care Approach; contbg. author: Quick Reference to Pediatric Nursing, 1984; asst. editor Jour. Pediatric Health Care. Home: 6382 Heil Ave Huntington Beach CA 92647 Office: Calif State U Dept Nursing 1250 Bellflower Blvd Long Beach CA 90802

MULLIS, KARY BANKS, biochemist; b. Lenoir, N.C., Dec. 28, 1944; s. Cecil Banks Mullis and Bernice Alberta (Barker) Fredericks; m. Richards Dorothy Train, June 15, 1964 (div. Feb. 1972); 1 child, Louise; m. Cynthia Ann Gibson, May 25, 1976 (div. Dec. 1985); children: Christopher, Jeremy. BS in Chemistry, Ga. Inst. Tech, 1966; PhD in Biochemistry, U. Calif., Berkeley, 1973. Lectr. biochemistry U. Calif., Berkeley, 1972; postdoctoral fellow U. Calif., San Francisco, 1977-79, U. Kans. Med. Sch., Kansas City, 1973-76; scientist Cetus Corp., Emeryville, Calif., 1979-86; dir. molecular biology Xytronyx, Inc., San Diego, 1986-88; cons. Eastman Kodak, Angenics, Inc., Specialty Labs, Inc., Amersham, Inc. and various others, Calif., 1988—. Contbr. articles to profl. jours.; patentee in field. Mem. Am. Chem. Soc., Inst. for Further Study (pres. 1983—). Home and Office: 6767 Neptune Pl Apt#4 La Jolla CA 92037

MULLISEN, RONALD STEPHEN, mechanical engineering educator, consultant; b. N.Y.C., Jan. 5, 1947; s. Charles Fredrick and Marie (Gron) M.; m. Claire Gibson, June 11, 1977; children: Luke, Emily. BSME, Calif. Poly State U., 1969, MEngring, 1977; PhD, Colo. State U., 1983. Registered profl. engr., Calif. Cons. 1974-77; tchr. Calif. Poly. State U., San Luis Obispo, 1977-86, prof. mech. engring., 1986—. Author: Experiments in Heat Transfer, 1986. Served to capt. USMC, 1969-74, Vietnam. Recipient Excellence in Teaching award TRW, 1986; Disting. Tchr. award Calif. Poly. State U., 1988. Mem. ASME. Home: 2375 Crest Ave Los Osos CA 93402 Office: Calif Poly State U Dept Mech Engring San Luis Obispo CA 93407

MULTANEN, JACQUELINE MAY, educational administrator, consultant; b. Eureka, Calif., June 20, 1935; d. Michael Joseph and May Elizabeth (Holm) Sintic; m. William Multanen, Sept. 2, 1956; children: Tuija, Pirkko. BA, Calif. State U., Fresno, 1957; MEd, U. La Verne, 1979. Life gen. secondary teaching credential, Calif. Tchr. Antelope Valley Union High Sch. Dist., Lancaster, Calif., 1961-78; v. prin. Palmdale (Calif.) High Sch., 1979--. Bd. dirs. Antelope Valley Arts Council. Mem. Am. Soc. for Curriculum Devel., Am. Assn. Sch. Adminstrs., Am. Assn. U. Women, Antelope Valley Coll. Intercultural & Women's Studies (adv. bd.), Delta Kappa Gamma (cons. 1971). Republican. Home: 43917 Elm Ave Lancaster CA 93534 Office: Palmdale High Sch 2137 E Ave R Palmdale CA 93550

MULTER, MICHAEL M., foundation administrator; b. New Haven, Oct. 30, 1936; s. Herman David and Jeannette Roslyn (Katz) M.; m. Frances Fannie Kollin, Aug. 14, 1960 (div. 1971); 1 child, Stephen Kollin; m. Linda Paulette Hanks, Nov. 18, 1979. BA, U. Ariz., 1957; BS, NYU, 1960; MS, Ariz. State U., 1963; PhD, U.S. Internat. U., 1979. Assoc. research biochemist U. Calif., San Diego, 1965-76; sr. research biochemist Calbiochem-Behring, La Jolla, Calif., 1977-78; dir. cancer research Rees-Stealy Research Found., San Diego, 1978-80; cons. M3 Assocs., San Diego, 1980-84; exec. dir. Psoriasis Research Inst., Palo Alto, Calif., 1984-87; dir. devel. Rehab. Mental Health Svcs, San Jose, 1987—. Editor, Basic Mountaineering, 1972; contrib. articles to profl. publs. Co-founder San Diego Mountain Rescue Team, 1967; mem., subcom. chair San Diego Com. Emergency Med. Care, 1968-72; cons. eleemosynary objectives, 1985—; bd. dirs. Colyer Inst. 1982--, Nat. Mountain Rescue Assn., 1969-71, Project Concern Internat., 1983-84. With U.S. Army 1957-60. Recipient 5 awards for saving human life, State of Calif., San Diego, Imperial, Riverside, and Mono Counties, 19k;68-71; recipient, Outstanding Service award, Nat. Mountain Rescue Assn., 1970. Mem. Nat. Soc. Fund Raising Execs. (cert., bd. dirs. 1985—, cert. fund raising exec. 1986, founding mem. Silicon Valley chpt., pres. 1985-87), Pub. Relations Soc. Am., Gilbert and Sullivan Soc. (bd. dirs. San Jose chpt. 1988—), Am. Alpine Club. Democrat. Jewish.

MULVANEY, DONALD MURPHY, physician; b. Fort Collins, Colo., Oct. 31, 1947; s. Charles Seldon and Oreline M.; m. Mary Lynn Glasscock, Apr. 25, 1987; stepchildren: Julie, Raymond Korte. BA, U. Colo., Boulder, 1969; MD, U. Colo., Denver, 1973. Diplomate Am. Bd. Family Practice. Intern Good Samiritan Med. Ctr., Phoenix, 1973-74, resident, 1976-78, assoc. dir. family practice residency, 1978—. Served to lt. comdr. USPHS, 1974-76. Fellow Am. Acad. Family Physicians, Ariz. Acad. Family Practice (pres. 1985-86); mem. Soc. Tchrs. Family Medicine, Phi Beta Kappa, Alpha Omega Alpha. Democrat. Roman Catholic.

MULVIHILL, PETER JAMES, fire protection engineer; b. Honolulu, Jan. 24, 1956; s. James H. and Jane A. (Norton) M. BSCE, Worcester (Mass.) Poly. Inst., 1978. Sr. engr. Indsl. Risk Insurers, San Francisco, 1978-84; fire protection engr. Aerojet Gen. Corp., Sacramento, 1984-87, Reno (Nev.) Fire Dept., 1987—; instr. part-time Truckee Meadows Community Coll., Reno, 1988—. Commr. Gov.'s Blue Ribbon Commn. to Study Adequacy of State Regulations Concerning Highly Combustible Materials, Carson City, Nev., 1988. Mem. Soc. Fire Protection Engrs., No. Nev. Fire Marshal's Assn., Nat. Fire Protection Assn., Calif. Fire Chief's Assn. (fire prevention officers sect. No. div.). Office: Reno Fire Dept 200 Evans Ave Reno NV 89501

MUMME, STEPHEN PAUL, political science educator; b. Phoenix, Nov. 6, 1948; s. James Horace and Vida Faye (Robinson) M.; m. Valerie Joan Assetto, June 6, 1987. BA, Ariz. State U., 1973, MA, 1975; PhD, U. Ariz., 1982. Vis. prof. U. Ariz., Tucson, 1982; cons. John Muir Inst., Tucson, 1982-83; asst. prof. polit. sci. Colo. State U., Ft. Collins, 1983-87, assoc. prof., 1987—; mem. editorial bd. ann. edits. Dushkin Press., Sluice Docks, Conn., 1986—; cons. Latin Am. Inst., U. N.Mex., Albuquerque, 1987—; mem. adv. bd. Transboundary Resources Ctr., Albuquerque, 1987—. Co-author: Statecraft, Domestic Politics and Foreign Policy Making, 1988; mem. editorial bd. Bull. Mcpl. Fgn. Policy, 1987—; contbr. articles to profl. jours. Mem. Larimer County Dem. Com., 1983—; del. county and state Dem. convs., 1988. With U.S. Army, 1968-71, Vietnam. Recipient faculty svc. award Hispanic Student Svcs., 1988; Bank Am. fellow Ctr. U.S.-Mex. Studies, 1981. Mem. Am. Polit. Sci. Assn., Latin Am. Studies Assn., Western Polit. Sci. Assn., Rocky Mountain Coun. on Latin Am. (pres. 1987-88), Borderlands Scholars Assn. (adv. coun. 1985-88). Democrat. Methodist. Home: 1504 Constitution Ave Fort Collins CO 80521 Office: Colo State U Dept Polit Sci Fort Collins CO 80523

MUNDELL, DAVID EDWARD, leasing company executive; b. Montreal, Que., Can., Dec. 27, 1931; s. Charles D.T. and Elise Warden (Dunton) M.; m. Willa Price McReynolds, July 25, 1969; children: David Edward (dec.), Elise Mundell. Diploma, Royal Mil. Coll. Can., 1953; B Engring., McGill U., 1954; MBA, Harvard, 1957. Research and devel. DuPont of Can., 1957-59; pres. Can.-Dominion Leasing Corp., Ltd., Toronto, 1959-65; exec. v.p. U.S. Leasing Corp., 1965-68; pres. U.S. Leasing Internat. Inc., San Francisco, 1968-88, chief exec. officer, 1976—, chmn., 1988—, also bd. dirs.; advisor Orix Corp., Tokyo. Lt. Royal Canadian C.E., 1951-57. Mem. Villa Taverna Club, Pacific-Union Club, Toronto Golf Club. Office: US Leasing Internat Inc 733 Front St San Francisco CA 94111

MUNDHENK, DENNIS EDGAR, civilian military official; b. Dayton, Ohio, May 13, 1938; s. Harold Robert and Ethel Lucille (Mishler) M.; m. Anita Louise Gruber, July 30, 1960; children: Brian David, Kent Eugene. BS, U. Dayton, 1960; MBA, Auburn U., 1974; grad., Air Command and Staff Coll., Montgomery, Ala., 1974. Cert. profl. contracts mgr. Mail clk. U.S. Postal Svc., Dayton, 1957-61, 64-66; contract specialist Wright Patterson AFB, Dayton, 1966-73; chief policy and compliance div. White Sands Missile Range, N.Mex., 1974-83, chief equipment contracting br., 1987—; dir. purchasing Armed Forces Recreation Ctr., Europe, 1983-86. Treas. Temple Bapt. Ch., Las Cruces, N.Mex., 1989—. Officer U.S. Army, 1961-64, Fed. Republic Germany. Mem. Nat. Contracts Mgmt. Assn. (sec. 1987, v.p. 1988, pres. 1989—), Am. Def. Preparedness Assn., Alpha Kappa Psi. Home: 1045 Jasmine Dr Las Cruces NM 88005 Office: Contracting Directorate STEWS-PR-ME White Sands Missile Range NM 88002-5201

MUNEKUNI, YOSHIHIDE, automotive executive. Pres. Am. Honda Motor Co., Inc., Gardena, Calif. Office: Am Honda Motor Co Inc 100 W Alondra Blvd Gardena CA 90248 *

MUNGER, CHARLES GALLOWAY, retired metal processing company executive; b. L.A., Dec. 29, 1912; s. Charles U. and Lena (Galloway) M.; m. Maryann Hickson, June 26, 1936; children: Patricia Ann, Charles Loyd. BA, Pomona Coll., 1935; postgrad., Claremont Coll., 1939-40. Registered profl. engr. Calif. Chemist Am. Concrete & Steel Pipe Co., 1935; chief chemist Am. Pipe & Constrn. Co. (formerly Am. Concrete & Steel Pipe Co.); dir. rsch. Amercoat Corp. (formerly Am. Pipe & Constrn. Co.); v.p. rsch. & mfg. Amercoat Corp., pres., v.p. internat., cons. coatings & corrosion, 1988—. Author: Corrosion Prevention by Protective Coatings, 1985; contbr. articles to profl. jours. Patentee in field. Bd. dirs. Fallbrook (Calif.) Hosp. Found., 1988—, Casa Colina Rehab. Hosp., Pamona, 1960-80, also pres. Fellow Am. Inst. Chemists; mem. Nat. Assn. Corrosion Engrs. (pres. 1963, corrosion specialist), Am. Chem. Soc., Am. Chem. Soc. Div. Organic Coatings and Plastics, Wash. Paint Tech. Group, Steel Structures Painting Council, Nat. Rsch. Council (com. problems inert gas systems for cargo tank atmosphere control), Steel Structures Painting Council (John d. Keane award merit 1986), Rotary. Republican. Home and Office: 3210 Sage Rd Fallbrook CA 92028

MUNK, FRANK, political science educator; b. Kutna Hora, Czechoslovakia, May 26, 1901; came to U.S., 1939; s. Alfred and Marie (Mautner) M.; m. Nadezda Prasilova, July 18, 1925; children: Michael, Suzanne. MA, U. Prague, Czechoslovakia, 1922; ScD, U. Prague, 1936; postgrad., Harvard U., 1931-33, Columbia U., 1931-33. Lectr. Reed Coll., Portland, Oreg., 1939-41, prof. polit sci., 1946-65, prof. emeritus, 1965—; lectr. U. Calif., Berkeley, 1941-44; prof. Portland State U., 1965-83, prof. emeritus, 1983—; dir. tng. UN Relief and Rehab. Adminstrn., 1944-46; advisor intellectual coop. Radio Free Europe, Munich, 1958-60; research assoc. Fgn. Policy Research Inst. U. Pa., Phila., 1962-65; dean NW Inst. Internat. Relations, 1947-56; dir. Zagreb Inst. Cen. European Studies, 1967-68; vis. prof. sci. U. Wash., Seattle, 1952, Coll. Europe, Bruges, Belgium, 1961-62, U. Zabreb, Yugoslavia, 1967-68; USIA univ. lectr. French and German univs., 1961-62. Author: The Economics of Force, 1940, The Legacy of Nazism, 1943, Atlantic Dilemma, 1964, others; contbg. editor Dictionary of Polit. Sci., 1964; commentator world affairs KOIN-TV, Portland, 1962-67. Chmn. Portland Com. Fgn. Relations, 1986-88; chmn. sect. polit. sci. World Congress Czechoslovak Soc. Arts and Scis., Toronto, Can., 1984, speaker European conf. Switzerland, 1983; trustee Starr King Sch. Ministry, Berkeley, 1944-47. Research fellow Rockefeller Found., 1931-33, Atlantic Inst., Paris, 1961-62; recipient Lit. of Scholarship Gold medal Commonwealth Club Calif., 1944, Edn. in World Affairs Nat. Community award Fgn. Policy Assn., 1957; named 1st Citizen World Affairs Council Oreg., 1973. Mem. Inst. Strategic Studies, NW Polit. Sci. Assn. (pres. 1968-69), World Affairs Council Oreg. (bd. overseers 1985-89). Home: 3808 SW Mt Adams Dr Portland OR 97201

MUNK, LINDA FRANCIS, realtor; b. Yuma, Ariz., May 14, 1940; d. Francis Horan and Dorothy Louise (McCaw) Johnson; m. Gary Eldroe Munk, Aug. 11, 1962; children: Annalisa, Rolf Nikolas. BE, U. Ariz., 1962. Cert. kindergarten-primary tchr. Ariz. Tchr. Yuma Sch. Dist. #1, 1963, 68-69, 70-79, 81, Tucson (Ariz.) Sch. Dist. #1, 1962-63, USAF Dependent Kindergarten, Rhein Main AFB, Fed. Republic Germany, 1964-66, St. Francis Cath. Sch., Yuma, 1982-84; with real estate sales Century 21 Gary Munk & Assocs., Yuma, 1983—. Treas. Yuma Ballet Theatre Inc., 1980—; bd. dirs. Children's Research Ctr., Tucson, 1987-88; pres. bd. Yuma Aquatics Swim Team. Mem. Yuma Bd. Realtors, U. Ariz. Alumni Assn. (nat. bd. dirs. 1985—, pres.-elect1988), Assist. League (v.p. 1970), Yuma Panhellenic, Delta Gamma. Republican. Episcopalian. Home: 523 E Pal Verde Yuma AZ 95365 Office: Century 21 Gary Munk & Assoc 1595 S 1st Ave Yuma AZ 85264

MUNK, WALTER HEINRICH, geophysics educator; b. Vienna, Austria, Oct. 19, 1917; came to U.S., 1933; m. Edith Kendall Horton, June 20, 1953; children: Edith, Kendall. BS, Calif. Inst. Tech., 1939, MS, 1940; PhD, U. Calif., 1947; PhD (hon.), U. Bergen, Norway, 1975, Cambridge (Eng.) U., 1986. From asst. prof. to prof. geophysics Scripps Inst. Oceanography U. Calif. San Diego, La Jolla, 1947—. Contbr. over 180 articles to profl. jours. Recipient Gold medal Royal Astron. Soc., 1968, Capt. Robert Dexter Conrad award Dept. Navy, 1978; named Calif. Scientist of Yr., Calif. Mus. Sci. and Industry, 1969; fellow Guggenheim Found., 1948, 55, 62, Overseas Found., 1962, 81-82, Fulbright Found., 1981-82, Nat. Medal Sci., 1985; Sr. Queen's fellow, 1978. Fellow Am. Geophys. Union (Maurice Ewing medal 1976, William Bowie medal 1989), AAAS, Am. Meteorol. Soc. (Sverdrup Gold medal 1966), Accoustical Soc. Am., Marine Tech. Soc.; mem. Nat. Acad. Scis. (Agassiz medal 1976, chmn. ocean studies bd. 1985-88), Am. Philos. Soc., Royal Soc. London (fgn. mem.), Deutsche Akademie der Naturforscher Leopoldina, Am. Acad. Arts and Scis. (Arthur L. Day medal 1965), Am. Geol. Soc. Office: U Calif San Diego Scripps Inst Oceanography A-025 La Jolla CA 92093

MUNN, LYNN ELIZABETH, medical center manager; b. Tripoli, Libya, Mar. 14, 1958; (parents Am. citizens); d. Robert Henderson and Ethel Marie (Bianucci) M. Student, U. Calif., San Diego, 1975-77; BA in Internat. Rels., Brigham Young U., 1979; postgrad., George Mason U., 1981-83; MBA, Calif. State U., Long Beach, 1985—. Staff asst. Heritage Found., Washington, 1980-81; confidential asst. exec. secretariat U.S. Dept. Edn., Washington, 1982-83; spl. asst. Bur. Justice Stats., U.S. Dept. Justice, Washington, 1983-85; adminstrv. analyst sch. bus. adminstrn. Calif. State U., Long Beach, 1985-89; med. ctr. mgr. FHP, Inc., Long Beach, 1989—. Author: (monograph) The Annual Insider, 1980. Vol. reader Va. Dept. Visually Handicapped, 1983-85; pres. Huntington Beach (Calif.) Relief Soc., 1987-88; vol. Steve Horn for Congress Campaign, Long Beach, 1988. Grad. fellow Brigham Young U., 1979. Mem. Pi Sigma Alpha. Republican. Mormon. Home: 508 Utica Ave Huntington Beach CA 92648 Office: FHP Inc Long Beach Sr Ctr 628 Alamitos Ave Long Beach CA 90802

MUNN, WILLIAM CHARLES, II, psychiatrist; b. Flint, Mich., Aug. 9, 1938; s. Elton Albert and Rita May (Coykendall) M.; student Flint Jr. Coll., 1958-59, U. Detroit, 1959-61; M.D., Wayne State U., 1965; m. Deborah Lee Munn, 1983; children by previous marriage—Jude Michael, Rachel Marie, Alexander Winston. Intern David Grant USAF Med. Center, Travis AFB, Calif., 1965-66; resident in psychiatry Letterman Army Hosp., San Francisco, 1967-70; practice medicine, specializing in psychiatry, Fairfield, Calif., 1972—; chief in-patient psychiatry David Grant Med. Center, 1970-71, chmn. dept. mental health, 1971-72; psychiat. cons. Fairfield-Suisun Unified Sch. Dist., 1971—, Fairfield Hosp. and Clinic, 1971, N. Bay Med. Ctr.(formerly Intercommunity Hosp.), Fairfield, 1971—, Casey Family Program, 1980—, Solano County Coroner's Office, 1981; asst. clin. prof. psychiatry U. Calif., San Francisco, 1976—; cons. Vaca Valley Hosp., Vacaville, Calif., 1988—, VA Hosp., San Francisco, 1976, David Grant USAF Hosp., 1976. Served to maj., M.C., USAF, 1964-72, flight surgeon, chief public health, chief phys. exam. center McGuire AFB, N.J., 1966-67. Diplomate Am. Bd. Psychiatry and Neurology (examiner). Mem. Am. Psychiat. Assn., No. Calif. Psychiat. Soc., E. Bay Psychiat. Assn. Home: 450 Ridgewood Dr Martinez CA 94553 Office: 1245 Travis Blvd Ste E Fairfield CA 94533

MUNNICH, JOSEPH EDWARD, tourist railway consultant; b. Swanton, Ohio, Sept. 13, 1932; s. Charles and Leila (Gaiman) M.; m. Frances Katherine Searcy; children: Christopher, Susan, Teresa. Student, U. Toledo, 1956-58, Am. U., 1969. Ins. broker Wright Russell & Bay Co., Toledo, 1961-67; ch. adminstr. St. Paul's Luth. Ch., Toledo, 1968-80; pres. Toledo Lake Erie & Western R.R., 1978-81, Heritage R.R. Co., 1981-83; sr. ptnr. Centennial Rail, Ltd., Denver, 1981—. Author: Steam Locomotives in the United States, 1985, Historic Diesels in the United States, 1988; editor Trainline mag., 1979—. Sgt. USAF, 1951-55. Nat. Assn. Ch. Bus. Adminstrs. fellow, 1971. Mem. Tourist Ry. Assn. (bd. dirs. 1984—), Nat. Ry. Hist. Soc. (editor newsletter Intermountain chpt. 1987—), Colo. Ry. Mus. Republican. Lutheran. Home: 3641 S Yampa St Aurora CO 80013 Office: Centennial Rail Ltd PO Box 24841 Denver CO 80224

MUNNINGER, MICHAEL JOSEPH, architect; b. Albany, N.Y., Aug. 24, 1948; s. Karl Otto and Margaret Josephine (Craugh) M.; m. Kathryn Denmark, Feb. 10, 1979; children: Lisa, John Karl, Michael, Suzanne, Paul, Mark. BArch, U. Tex., 1971; postgrad., Ariz. State U., Phoenix, 1976-77. Registered architect, Ariz., Calif.; lic. real estate salesman, Ariz. Founder, ptnr. Archtl. Alliance, Phoenix, 1974—. Contbr. articles to mags., newspapers. Active Boys Club Met. Phoenix, Ariz. Hunter Safety Instr. Program, Nat. Trust Hist. Preservation; mem. City of Phoenix Visual Improvement Com. Recipient 2d prize Art by Architects, 1982, Most Beautiful Home award Phoeniz mag., 1982, Visual Improvement award, City of Phoenix, 1984. Mem. Phoenix C. of C., Ariz. Indsl. Devel. Assn. Home: 10001 N 132d St Scottsdale AZ 85259

MUNOZ, ALBERT ANTHONY, aerospace engineer; b. L.A., July 2, 1965; s. Elias Alvarez and Soledad (Molinar) M. BA in Aerospace Engring., UCLA, 1988. Engring. aide NASA, Edwards, Calif., 1987-88; mem. tech. staff Hughes Aircraft, L.A., 1988—. Precinct leader Dem. Com., L.A., 1988. Mem. Delta Delta (athletic chmn. 1985-86). Roman Catholic. Home: 2448 Hancock St 2 Los Angeles CA 90031

MUÑOZ, DEBORAH LYNN, financial company executive; b. L.A., Apr. 7, 1956; d. J. Louis and Dorothy (Blough) M.; m. Gary Aaron Young, sept. 10, 1978 (div. July 1988). BA Sociology, Social Work, Whittier Coll, 1978, MBA in Fin., 1986. Sr. auditor Security Pacific Bank, L.A., 1978-80, audit officer, 1980-82, asst. audit, 1982-84, asst. v.p., auditor, 1984-86; v.p., audit mgr. Gt. Western Fin. corp., Northridge, Calif., 1986—. Recipient Young Career Woman award South Pasadena Bus. & Profl. Women, 1985. Mem. Inst. Internal Auditors (cert. internal auditor chmn.; v.p. 1988—). Republican. Methodist. Office: Gt Western Fin Corp 9401 Oakdale Ave Chatsworth CA 91311

MUNOZ, JOHN JOSEPH, construction executive; b. Salinas, Calif., Jan. 18, 1932; s. John Fernando and Naomal (Smith) M.; m. Phyllis Taylor, Feb. 6, 1961 (div. 1978); children: Sam, Kathy, Toni; m. Rachel Canales, Nov. 24, 1979; children: Michelle, Monique. AA, Allan Hancock Coll., 1956; student, San Jose State U., 1981, Western Sierra Law Sch. Ops. mgr. So. Pacific Milling Co., Santa Maria, Calif., 1971-77; cons. Govt., Venezuela, 1977-78; fleet supt. Granite Rock Co., San Jose, Calif., 1978-80; plant mgr. Granite Constrn. Co., Greenfield, Calif., 1980-85; mgr. transpn. Ball, Ball & Brosmer Inc., Danville, Calif., 1985-86; ops. mgr. Sorrento Ready Mix Co., Del Mar, Calif., 1986—; bd. dirs. Sorrento Ready Mix Inc., 1986—; cons. Dept. Agrl. Devel., Maricaibo, Venezuela, 1976—. Commr. Planning Commn., Greenfield, Calif., 1982-85; mem. fund raising com. Broccoli Festival, Greenfield, 1983-85; dir. Soledad Prison Vocat. Tng., 1982-85. Lt. U.S. Army, 1950-52, Korea. Mem. Am. Concrete Inst., Calif. Trucking Assn., Los Californianos, Rotary, Lions, Elks. Republican. Home: 10283 Hwy 76 Pala CA 92059 Office: Sorrento Ready Mix Co 3505 Carmel Valley Rd Del Mar CA 92014

MUÑOZ, ROBERT R., library science educator; b. Corpus Christi, Tex., Nov. 20, 1942; s. Manuel S. and Juanita R. M. AA in Bus. Adminstrn., Rio Hondo Coll., 1970; BA in History, Whittier Coll., 1972; MLS, Calif. State U., Fullerton, 1973. Cert. elem. and community coll. tchr., Calif., elem. tchr., Nev., Latin Am. Studies, Whittier Coll. Athlete tutor, acad. coordinator Whittier (Calif.) Coll., 1970-72; educator, librarian Herlong (Calif.) Elem. Sch. Dist., 1973-84; educator Lassen Community Coll., Herlong, 1982-83; pres., bus. edn. cons. Robert R. Muñoz, Inc., Reno, 1984—; educator Washoe County Sch. Dist., Reno, 1986-88; English as a second lang. instr. Truckee Meadows Comm. Coll., Reno, 1988—; chief negotiator Herlong Tchrs. Assn., 1976,81; pres., 1982; basketball coach Herlong High Sch. Dist., 1976-82; home tchr. for the terminally ill, Herlong Elem. Sch. Dist., 1980; mgmt. trainee, bus. cons., educator USPS, Reno. EEO/AA activist, human rights activist, Calif., Nev., 1965—; v.p. Sierra Fed. Credit Union, Herlong, 1978; coach Jr. Olympics, Herlong, 1981; timer, judge N.Am. Boxing Fedn., 1987. Served with USAF, 1961-67. Recipient Outstanding Student award, Rio Hondo Coll., 1970. Mem. Omega Delta Kappa. Roman Catholic. Home: 2406 Marjay Ct Reno NV 89512

MUNRO, MICHAEL DONALD, military officer; b. Kindley AFB, Bermuda, May 6, 1953; (parents Am. citizens); s. Donald M. and Marilyn Barbara (Ravenelle) M. AAS in Criminology, U. Md., 1978; BA in Sociology, SUNY, Plattsburg, 1981; MA in Mgmt., Embry-Riddle U., 1986; PhD, U. Denver, 1988. Commd. 2d lt. USAF, 1976, advanced through grades to capt., 1985; chief security adminstr. Plattsburg AFB, N.Y., 1979-81; ICBM launch officer Grands Forks AFB, N.D., 1981-83, ICBM flight comdr., 1984-86; satellite officer Colorado Springs, Colo., 1986-87; chief satellite officer U.S. Space Command, Colorado Springs, 1987; chief U.S. Space Def. Ops. Ctr., Colorado Springs, 1988—; cons. 1980 Winter Olympics, Lake Placid, N.Y., 1979-80; dir. Grand Forks City Govt., 1986. Contbr. articles to profl. jours. Mem. Pike's Peak Rodeo Com., Colorado Springs, 1987. Recipient Scholastic Achievement award Boeing Aerospace, 1988; named Outstanding Young Man Grand Forks County, 1985. Mem. Profl. Rodeo Cowboys Assn. (judge 1987-88, cons. 1987, announcer 1988—), Assn. Govt. Execs., Crewmembers Assn. (pres. 1985-86), Grand Forks C. of C. Republican. Roman Catholic. Home: 8255 Camfield Circle Colorado Springs CO 80920 Office: Hdqrs US Space Command J350 Cheyenne Mountain CO 80920

MUNRO, RALPH DAVIES, state government official; b. Bainbridge Island, Wash., June 25, 1943; s. George Alexander and Elizabeth (Troll) M.; m. Karen Hansen, Feb. 17, 1973; 1 son, George Alexander. BA in History and Edn. (scholar), Western Wash. U. Successively indsl. engr. Boeing Co.; sales mgr. Continental Host, Inc.; asst. dep. dir. ACTION Agy.; spl. asst. to gov. of Wash.; gen. mgr. Tillicum Enterprises & Food Services Co.; dir. Found. for Handicapped; pres. Northwest Highlands Tree Farm; now sec. of state State of Wash. Chmn. community service com. Seattle Rotary Club 4; founder 1st pres. Rotary Youth Job Employment Center, Seattle. Named Man of Yr. Assn. Retarded Citizens, Seattle, 1970. Mem. Nat. Assn. Secs. State, Nat. Assn. Retarded Children, Wash. Historic Mus. (dir.), Wash. Trust Historic Preservation (founder), Nature Conservancy. Republican. Lutheran. Office: Sec of State Legislature Bldg AS22 Olympia WA 98504

MUNROE, DONNA SCOTT, information and management consultant, statistician; b. Cleve., Nov. 28, 1945; d. Glenn Everett and Louise Lenox (Parkhill) S.; m. Melvin James Ricketts, Dec. 23, 1968 (div. Aug. 1979); 1 child, Suzanne Michelle; m. Peter Carlton Munroe, Feb. 14, 1981. BS in Sociology, Portland (Oreg.) State U., 1976, BS in Philosophy, 1978, MS in Sociology, 1983. Lectr. Portland State U., 1977-79; writing, editorial cons. Worth Pubs., N.Y.C., 1978-79; statis. cons. Oreg. U. Sch. Health Sci. and Morrison Ctr. for Youth and Family Svcs., Portland, 1979-82; tech. writer Equitable Savs & Loan, Portland, 1981-82; mgr. acct. and projects. Electronic Data Systems, Portland, 1982-87; sr. mgmt. cons. to govt. div. Computer Mgmt. Systems, Inc., Portland, 1987—. Mem. Am. Mgmt. Assn., Sigma Xi, City Club of Portland. Democrat. Episcopalian. Home: 1435 SW Harrison Portland OR 97201 Office: Computer Mgmt Systems Inc 0234 SW Bancroft Portland OR 97201

MUNROE, LYDIA DARLENE, jeweler, travel industry executive; b. San Diego, July 9, 1933; d. Daniel O. and Bertha E. (Smith) Thayer; m. H. Flack Jr., July 29, 1949 (div. 1953); children: Debrha Flack Miller, Mona Lynn Flack Pietz; m. Don Evan Heath, Oct. 13, 1953 (dec. 1968); 1 child, Daniel Evan; m. Duskin M. Shears, July 24, 1969 (dec. 1982); m. Albert G. Munroe, Nov. 26, 1982. Student, Sweetwater Adult Edn. Coll. With accounts receivable, payroll Burtrum Yacht Co., Miami, Fla., 1954-55; gen. bookkeeper Stafford and Gardner, 1955-56; bookkeeper, switch bd. operator William Creek Copper Mines, 1956-57; with Brisbane (Australia) and Wonderlick, 1957; small bus. owner, miner Coober Pedy South Australia Opal Fields, 1957-72; small bus. owner Down Under Opal, Seattle, 1972-88; tour guide, itinerary planner to Australia, 1982—; lectr. on Opals. Author: Pricing Opal. Active Widowed Info. and Cons. Services. Mem. Maplewood Gem Club (rep. to regional gem show com., dealer chairwoman 1988), West Seattle Gem Club (treas., show chairwoman), N.W. Opal Assn. (v.p., pres., show dealer chairwoman, chairwoman edn. com.), Puyallup Valley Gem Club, OES Juanita Chpt., Am. Mineral Gem Suppliers Assn., Greater Seattle C. of C. Home: 716 SW 179th Ct Seattle WA 98166

MUNSON, LUCILLE MARGUERITE (MRS. ARTHUR E. MUNSON), real estate broker; b. Norwood, Ohio, Mar. 26, 1914; d. Frank and Fairy (Wicks) Wirick; R.N., Lafayette (Ind.) Home Hosp., 1937; A.B., San Diego State U., 1963, student Purdue U., Kans. Wesleyan U.; m. Arthur E. Munson, Dec. 24, 1937; children—Barbara Munson Papke, Judith Munson Andrews, Edmund Arthur. Staff and pvt. nurse Lafayette Home Hosp., 1937-41; indsl. nurse Lakey Foundry & Machine Co., Muskegon, Mich., 1950-51, Continental Motors Corp., Muskegon, 1951-52; nurse Girl Scout Camp, Grand Haven, Mich., 1948-49; owner Munson Realty, San Diego, 1964—. Mem. San Diego County Grand Jury, 1975-76, 80-81, Calif. Grand Jurors Assn. (charter). Home: 5765 Friars Rd Apt 200 San Diego CA 92108 Office: 2999 Mission Blvd # 102 San Diego CA 92109

MUNSTERTEIGER, KAY DIANE, speech language pathologist; b. Newcastle, Wyo., June 2, 1956; d. Donald Francis and Janice Mathilda (Emerson) M. BS, U. Wyo., 1978; MS, U. Nev., Reno, 1980. Speech lang. pathologist No. Nev. Speech lang. Clinic, Reno, 1980-82, Washakie County Sch. Dist. 1, Worland, Wyo., 1982—; pvt. practice speech pathologist Worland, 1982—; speech lang. pathologist, cons. Washakie County Sch. Dist. 2, Tensleep, Wyo., 1984-85; speech lang. pathologist Spl. Touch Presch., Worland, 1985-86; bd. dirs. Spl. Touch Presch./Children Resource Ctr., 1987—; bd. examiners Speech Pathology and Audiology, 1988—. Mem. Pub. Sch. Caucus. Mem. NEA, State Edn. Assn., Am. Speech Lang. Hearing Assn., Wyo. Speech Lang. Hearing Assn., Nat. Stuttering Project, Pub. Sch. Caucus, Assn. Childhood Edn. Internat., Phi Kappa Phi. Democrat. Roman Catholic. Office: Washakie County Sch Dist # 1 800 S 17th Worland WY 82401

MUNTZ, ERIC PHILLIP, aerospace engineering and radiology educator, consultant; b. Hamilton, Ont., Can., May 18, 1934; came to U.S., 1961, naturalized, 1985; s. Eric Percival and Marjorie Louise (Weller) M.; m. Janice Margaret Furey, Oct. 21, 1964; children: Sabrina Weller, Eric Phillip. B.A.Sc., U. Toronto, 1956, M.A.Sc., 1957, Ph.D., 1961. Halfback Toronto Argonauts, 1957-60; group leader Gen. Electric, Valley Forge, Pa., 1961-69; assoc. prof. aerospace engring. and radiology U. So. Calif., Los Angeles, 1969-71, prof., 1971-87, chmn. aerospace engring., 1987—; cons. to aerospace and med. device cos., 1967—; mem. rev. of physics (plasma and fluids) panel NRC, Washington, 1983-85. Contbr. numerous articles in gas dynamics and med. diagnostics to profl. publs., 1961—; patentee med. imaging, isotope separation, nondestructive testing. Mem. Citizens Environ. Adv. Council, Pasadena, Calif., 1972-76. U.S. Air Force grantee, 1961-74, 82—; NSF grantee, 1970-76, 87—; FDA grantee, 1980-86. Fellow AIAA (Aerospace Contbn. to Soc. award 1987); mem. Am. Assn. Physicists in Medicine. Episcopalian. Home: 1560 E California Blvd Pasadena CA 91106 Office: U So Calif University Pk Los Angeles CA 90089-1191

MUNTZNER, GREGORY CHARLES, military officer; b. Bklyn., July 26, 1952; s. Eugene Clement and Stellamarie (Bernard) M. BA in Econs., N.C. State U., 1974; MBA in Systems Mgmt., U. N.D., 1977; student, Def. Systems Mgmt. Coll., Ft. Belvoir, Va., 1985. Commd. 2d lt. USAF, 1974, advanced through grades to maj., 1986; chief of program support div. Dep. for Launch Systems, L.A. AFB, 1986, chief of program analysis div., 1986-87; advanced Upper Stages Project mgr. Upper Stages Program Office, L.A. AFB, 1987-88; asst. dep. program dir. Medium Launch Vehicles Office, L.A. AFB, 1988; project mgr. Small Launch Vehicles Office, L.A. AFB, 1989—. Pres., chmn. Partridge Berry Hills Assn., Nashua, N.H., 1982, 83; v.p. Gramercy Gardens Home Owners Assn., Torrance, Calif., 1988-89, pres., 1989—. Mem. Air Force Assn. Roman Catholic. Home: 2721 Gramercy Ave #7 Torrance CA 90501 Office: Space Systems Div-CLM PO Box 92960 Los Angeles CA 90009-2960

MUNZ, LARRY MARTIN, educational administrator; b. Prescott, Ariz., May 23, 1940; s. Martin Henry and Dorothy (Draper) M.; m. Carol Jean Blackburn, Jan. 7, 1962 (div. 1984); 1 child, Laurence Blackburn; m. Cynthia Deanne Hardy, Mar. 17, 1984; 1 child, Megan Elise. BS, Oreg. State U., 1962; MA, U. Redlands, 1971. Cert. tchr., adminstr., Calif. Tchr. San Bernardino (Calif.) City Unified Sch. Dist., 1963-64, Redlands (Calif.) Unified Sch. Dist., 1964-71; cons. San Bernardino County Schs., 1971, coordinator, 1974-87; dir. San Jacinto-Moreno Valleys Regional Occupational Program, Hemet, Calif., 1971-72; coordinator Riverside (Calif.) County Schs., 1972-74; supt. Colton-Redlands-Yucaipa Regional Occupational Program, 1987—; asst. prof. Calif. State U.-San Bernardino, 1975-86. Pub., Calif. Jour. Vocat. Edn., 1987-88. Bd. dirs. Redlands Bicycle Classic, 1986-88;mem. membership drive com. Redlands YMCA, 1986-88; chair Redlands Historic and Scenic Preservation Com., 1987—. Mem.Calif. Assn. Vocat. Adminstrs. (pres. 1986-87), Assn. Calif. Sch. Adminstrs. (rep. 1985-86; Outstanding Vocat. Adminstr. 1983), Calif. Assn. Regional Occupational Ctrs.-Programs (So. Calif. rep. 1988-90), Am.Vocat. Assn., Phi Delta Kappa, Kiwanis. Republican. Office: Colton Redlands Yucaipa Regional Occupational Program 105 Tennessee St Redlands CA 92373

MUNZER, ANNETTE ELIZABETH, artistic director; b. Washington, Aug. 19, 1944; d. Edward Norman and Mary Elizabeth (Snider) M.; divorced 1977; children: Edward, Aaron. AB, Syracuse U., 1966; MA, U. Okla., 1970. Anthropologist U. Alaska, College, Alaska, 1970-77; art research librarian Phoenix Art Museum, 1978-80, curator, collections, edn., 1981-85; exec. dir. Tucson Festival Soc., 1985—. Mem. Internat. Festivals Assn., Am. Assn. of Museums, Am. Assn. for State and Loal History. Home: 8122 E Estes Ln Tucson AZ 85710

MURAD, EMIL MOISE, company executive; b. Detroit, May 10, 1926; s. Max Moise and Jean Grace (Esquith) M. AB, U. So. Calif., 1949, MS, 1951. Rsch. scientist Nat. Aircraft Corp., Burbank, Calif., 1952-56; prin. scientist Gen. Dynamics Corp., Rochester, N.Y., 1957-59; aerospace scientist N.Am. Rockwell (name now Rockwell Internat.), Anaheim and Downey, Calif., 1959-68; pres. Quantadyne Assocs., Inc., Huntington Beach, Calif., 1968—. Sgt. AUS, 1944-46, PTO. Mem. IEEE. Libertarian. Office: Quantadyne Assocs Inc 924 Hancock Ave Ste 8 West Hollywood CA 90069

MURDOCK, DAVID H., diversified company executive; b. Los Angeles, Apr. 10, 1923. Chmn. Cannon Mills Co., Kannapolis, N.C., 1982-86, chief exec. officer, 1982-84; now sole proprietor, chmn., chief exec. officer Pacific Holding Corp., Los Angeles, Calif.; chmn., chief exec. officer Castle & Cooke, Inc., Los Angeles, 1985—, also bd. dirs. Served with USAAF, 1941-45. Office: Castle & Cooke Inc 10900 Wilshire Blvd Los Angeles CA 90024 also: Pacific Holding Co 10900 Wilshire Blvd Ste 1600 Los Angeles CA 90024 *

MURDOCK, PAMELA ERVILLA, wholesale travel company executive, retail travel company executive; b. Los Angeles, Dec. 3, 1940; d. John James and Chloe Conger (Keefe) M.; children—Cheryl, Kim. BS, U. Colo., 1962. Pres., Dolphin Travel, Denver, 1972-87; owner, pres. Mile Hi Tours, Denver, 1974—, MH Internat., 1987—. Named Wholesaler of Yr., Las Vegas Conv. and Visitors Authority, 1984. Mem. Am. Soc. Travel Agts., Colo. Assn. Commerce and Industry, Nat. Fedn. Independent Businessmen, NAFE, Internat. Platform Assn. Republican. Office: Mile Hi Tours Inc 2120 S Birch Denver CO 80222

MUREZ, MELANIE GOODMAN, translation company executive; b. L.A., May 11, 1954; d. Max A. and Marlyene (Monkarsh) Goodman; m. James Douglas Murez, Sept. 20, 1953. BA cum laude, UCLA, 1974, MA, 1977, PhD, 1988. Tchr. Temple Emmanuel, L.A., 1974-76; new accounts rep. 1st L.A. Bank, 1975-76; instr. UCLA, 1976-81, Concorde Internat. High Sch., L.A., 1981-82; mgr. L.A. Olympic Orgn. Com., 1982-84; pres. Lang. Svcs. Internat., L.A., 1984—; customer svc. rep. TWA, L.A., 1981; tour guide JetAmerica, L.A., 1981. Mem. Los Angeles-Bordeaux Sister City Com., 1976. Mem. So. Calif. Translators and Interpreters Assn., Citroen Car Club Am. Democrat. Jewish. Home: 804 Main St Venice CA 90291 Office: Language Svcs Internat 8801 Sepulveda Blvd Los Angeles CA 90045

MURILLO, LOUIS MARIN, JR., health program administrator; b. L.A., Feb. 3, 1949; s. Louis Marin and Antonia (Juarez) M.; m. Roberta Lee Shakespeare June 29, 1973; children: Andrea, Danae, Brett. AA, Rio Hondo Junior Coll., Whittier, Calif., 1973; BS, Long Beach State Coll., 1975; MPA, San Jose State Coll., 1984. Recreation therapist VA, Long Beach, Calif., 1975-79; recreation dir. VA, Temple, Tex., 1979-81, Sepulveda, Calif., 1981-82, Palo Alto, Calif., 1982-85; mental health program coord. El Dorado County Mental Health, South Lake Tahoe, Calif., 1986—; cons. Murillo & Co., L.A., 1975-79; dist. dir. VA, Sepulveda, Calif., 1981-82; regional dir. VA, Palo Alto, Calif., 1982-85. Author: (with others) NHCU Guidelines, Veterans' Administration, 1977, Standards of Practice, Therapeutic Recreation, Nat. Recreation and Park Assn., 1981. Mem. Recreation Commn. Temple (Tex.) Parks and Recreation, 1980; Recreation Commn. Palo Alto (Calif.) Parks and Recreation, 1984. Mem. Am. Soc. Pub. Adminstrs., Nat. Recreation and Parks Assn., Calif. Park & Recreation Soc. (pub. rels. dir. 1983-85). Democrat. Roman Catholic. Home: PO Box 612781 South Lake Tahoe CA 95761 Office: Mental Health El Dorado County PO Box 797 South Lake Tahoe CA 95705

MURINO, CLIFFORD JOHN, atmospheric & oceanic research institute executive; b. Yonkers, N.Y., Feb. 10, 1929; s. Vincent Joseph and Marie (Fuccillo) M.; m. Janet Rosalie Spallino, Dec. 28, 1954 (div. Dec. 1983); children: John Clifford, Carolyn Ruth, Kathryn Marie; m. Fryne Irene White, Jan.28, 1984. BS, St. Louis U., 1950, MA, 1954, PhD, 1957. Mem. faculty Parks Coll. Aero. Tech., Cahokia, Ill., 1954-60; prof. meteorology St. Louis U., 1960-75, v.p., 1969-75; div. dir. Nat. Ctr. Atmospheric Research, Boulder, Colo., 1975-80; pres. Deseert Research Inst., Reno, 1980-83, pres., bd. dirs. Found., 1982-83; pres. Univ. Corp. for Atmospheric Research, Boulder, 1983--, Bd. dirs. Found., 1986--. Co-author: Weather Motions from Space, 1969; contbr. numerous articles to sci. jours. Mem. Nev. Gov.'s Adv. Com., 1980-83, Reno Mayor's Adv. Com., 1982-83; trustee Nev. Devel. Authority, 1981-83. Recipient sustained superior performance award NSF, 1969; NSF research grantee, 1965-66, NOAA research grantee, 1966. Fellow Am. Meteorol. Soc. (pres. 1985); mem. Elks Club, Sigma Xi, Pi Mu Epsilon. Home: 1590 S Bradley Dr Boulder CO 80303 Office: Univ Corp for Atmospheric Rsch PO Box 3000 Boulder CO 80307-3000

MURKOWSKI, FRANK HUGHES, senator; b. Seattle, Mar. 28, 1933; s. Frank Michael and Helen (Hughes) M.; m. Nancy R. Gore, Aug. 28, 1954; children—Carol Victoria Murkowski Sturgulewski, Lisa Ann Murkowski Martell, Frank Michael, Eileen Marie Murkowski Van Wyke, Mary Catherine, Brian Patrick. Student, Santa Clara U., 1952-53; BA in Econs, Seattle U., 1955. With Pacific Nat. Bank of Seattle, 1957-58; with Nat. Bank of Alaska, Anchorage, 1959-67; asst. v.p., mgr. Nat. Bank of Alaska (Wrangell br.), 1963-66; v.p. charge bus. devel. Nat. Bank of Alaska (Wrangell br.), Anchorage, 1966-67; commr. dept. econ. devel. State of Alaska, Juneau, 1967-70; pres. Alaska Nat. Bank of the North, Fairbanks, 1971-80; U.S. Senator from Alaska, 1981—; mem. Energy and Natural Resources Com.; ranking mem. Vets. Affairs Com.; mem. Fgn. Relations Com., Intelligence Com., Indian Affairs Com., Intelligence Com. former vice pres. B.C. and Alaska Bd. Trade; Rep. nominee for U.S. Congress from Alaska, 1970. Served with USCGR, 1955-57. Mem. Am. Legion, Polish Legion Am. Vets., AMVETS, Ducks Unltd., NRA, Res. Officer's Assn., Army-Navy Club, Pioneers of Alaska, Tower Club, Shilla Club, Internat. Alaska Nippon Kai, Capital Hill Club, Alaska Geographic Soc., Army Athletic Club, Alaska World Affairs Coun., Congl. Staff Club, AAA, Fairbanks Hist. Preservation Found., Coalition Am. Vets., Alaska Native Brotherhood, Diamond Athletic Club, Nat. Wildlife Fedn., Nat. Mining Hall of Fame, Naval Athletic Assn., Am. Bankers Assn, Alaska Bankers Assn. (pres. 1973), Young Pres.'s Orgn., Alaska C. of C. (pres. 1977), Anchorage C. of C. (dir. 1966), B.C. C. of C., Fairbanks C. of C. (dir. 1973-78). Clubs: Elks, Lions, Washington Athletic. Office: US Senate 709 Hart Senate Bldg Washington DC 20510

MURNEY, DONALD WILLIAM, finance company executive; b. Chgo., June 30, 1960; s. John Thomas and Mary Lou (Molnor) M.; m. Michele Diane Maszk.. Student, Scottsdale Coll., 1982-83, Fayetteville State, 1979-80. Loan officer Coury Fin. Svcs., Inc., Mesa, Ariz., 1984-85; investment cons. Coury Fin. Svcs., Inc., Mesa, 1985-86, v.p., 1986-88, sr. v.p., 1988—; cons. Mercury Investments, Phoenix, 1986—; bd. dirs. Coury Real, East Valley Ptnrship., Mesa. Focus 2000 Senator. Mem. Exec. Resources Networking (bd. dirs. 1989—), Mortgage Bankers Assn. Democrat. Roman Catholic. Office: Coury Fin Group 4710 E Falcon Dr Ste 209 Mesa AZ 85205

MURPHEY, ROBERT WILLIAM, publishing company executive, educator; b. Oakland, Calif., Oct. 30, 1933; s. John Patrick and Alice Julia (Knudsen) M.; m. Kay Louise Wandmaker, Apr. 13, 1957; children: Diane Murphey Henderson, Karen, Maureen, John. AA, Coll. San Mateo, 1954; BA, San Jose State U., 1956, MS, 1957; postgrad., Iowa State U., 1964. Mgmt. position Pacific Bell Co., Oakland and San Francisco, Calif., 1957-65; dist. mgr. Pacific Bell Co., San Diego, 1965-85; owner, pub. Fireside Pubs., San Diego, 1984—; faculty Chapman Coll., San Diego, 1986-88, prof., 1988—, faculty mem., Grossmont Coll., El Cajon, Calif., 1986—, Southwestern Coll., Chula Vista, Calif., 1986-87. Author: Methods and Procedures of Handling Employee Grieviences, 1957. Pres. Home of Guiding Hands, Lakeside, Calif., 1972-74, Home of Guiding Hands Found., 1975; 1st v.p. Cystic Fibrosis, San Diego, 1985; officer Grossmont Coll. Academic Senate, 1988—. Mem. Am.'s Finest City Dixieland Jazz Soc., Faculty Assn. Calif. Community Colls., Pi Kappa Alpha (pres. alumni 1957). Republican. Lutheran. Home and Office: 6490 Lake Shore Dr San Diego CA 92119

MURPHY, BLANCHE M(AXINE), speech pathologist; b. Shandon, Ohio, Oct. 22, 1916; d. Elmer P. and Margaret (Hayes) Heitfield. A.A., Ventura Coll., 1954; B.A. in Speech Therapy, L.A. State U., 1956; M.A. in Edn., U. Santo Tomas (Philippines), 1970; M.A. in Counseling Psychology, Ball State U., 1975. Lic. speech pathologist, Calif.; m. Harry Blaisdell Murphy, Aug. 24, 1952. Tchr., Santa Paula (Calif.) Sch. Dist., 1954-55, speech therapist, 1956-57; speech therapist Oxnard (Calif.) Sch. Dist., 1957-58, Ventura County (Calif.) Schs., 1958-61, Dept. Def. Dependent Schs., Clark Air Base, Philippines, 1961-70; speech pathologist Dept. Def. Dependent Schs., European Area, Sembach, Fed. Republic of Germany, 1970-77, Dept. Def. Dependent Schs., Okinawa, Japan, 1977—; speaker edn. seminars, in-svc. tng. Pacific Area Command Air Force, 1963-70; condr. workshops for Am. tchrs. Am. Sch., Saigon, Socialist Rep. of Viet Nam, 1963. Recipient Outstanding Contbn. award as sec. of conf. European Coun. Parents and Students, 1977, Rotary scholar Ventura Coll., 1954. Mem. NEA, Am. Speech and Hearing Assn. (cert. clin. competence in speech pathology 1969),

Calif. Speech and Hearing Assn., Am. Personnel and Guidance Assn., Overseas Edn. Assn., Coun. for Exceptional Children, Phi Delta Kappa, Pi Lambda Theta. Episcopalian. Author: Speech Improvement for First Grade Children, 1970; Speech Improvement of the Primary School Child Through Ear Training Techniques, 1975. Home: 279 E Elfin Green Port Hueneme CA 93041 Home: 1804 Parkside Terr, Okinawa Japan

MURPHY, CAROLYN JO, hotel executive; b. Chgo., Nov. 12, 1953; d. Roy William and Ruth Joyce (Staley) M.; m. Dennis Rowan, July 17, 1979 (div. Oct. 1985). BA in Psychology, Calif. State U., Chico, 1975. Dir. human resources Aircoa, Concord-Hilton, Calif., 1982-85; regional dir. Aircoa, Concord-Hilton, 1983-85; dir. human resources Pleasanton Hilton (Calif.) Hotel, 1985-87; regional dir. human resources Hotel div. Duffel Fin. Constrn. Co., Newark, Calif., 1987—; assoc. cons. labor rels. D.N. Cornford, San Francisco, 1982—. Mem. Am. Soc. Personnel Adminstrs., No. Calif. Human Resources Coun., Newark C. of C. Republican. Home: 108 Cordova Way Concord CA 94520 Office: Newark Fremont Hilton 39900 Balentine Dr Newark CA 94560

MURPHY, DENNIS FRANCIS, oil company executive; b. San Francisco, Dec. 5, 1954; s. Francis Joseph and Ann (Casey) M.; m. Mahgie Dean, March 3, 1984. BSCE, Santa Clara U., 1977; MSCE, Stanford U., 1978. Registered civil engr., Calif. Oil co. exec. Exxon Co., USA, Calif., 1978—. Co-author: Directions in Construction Management, 1980. Mem. ASCE, Soc. Petroleum Engrs. Democrat. Roman Catholic. Home: 2155 9th Ave San Francisco CA 94116

MURPHY, FRANCIS SEWARD, journalist; b. Portland, Oreg., Sept. 9, 1914; s. Francis H. and Blanche (Livesay) M.; BA, Reed Coll., 1936; m. Clare Eastham Cooke, Sept. 20, 1974. With The Oregonian, Portland, 1936-79, TV editor, Behind the Mike columnist, 1952-79. Archeol. explorer Mayan ruins, Yucatan, Mex., 1950—, mem. Am. Quintana Roo Expdn., 1965, 66, 68. With AUS, 1942-46. Author: Dragon Mask Temples in Central Yucatan, 1988. Mem. Royal Asiatic Soc., Royal Hong Kong Jockey Club, City Club (bd. govs. 1950, 64-66), Explorers Club, Am. Club of Hong Kong. Democrat. Congregationalist. Home: 4213 NE 32d Ave Portland OR 97211 also: 1102 Tavistock, 10 Tregunter Path, Hong Kong Hong Kong

MURPHY, FRANKLIN DAVID, physician, educator, publisher; b. Kansas City, Mo., Jan. 29, 1916; s. Franklin E. and Cordelia (Brown) M.; m. Judith Joyce Harris, Dec. 28, 1940; children: Joyce Murphy Dickey, Martha (Mrs. Craig Crockwell), Carolyn (Mrs. Ross Speer), Franklin. A.B., U. Kans., 1936; M.D., U. Pa., 1941. Diplomate: Am. Bd. Internal Medicine. Intern Hosp. U. Pa., 1941-42, instr., 1942-44; instr. medicine U. Kans., 1946-48, dean Sch. Medicine, assoc. prof. medicine, 1948-51, chancellor, 1951-60; chancellor UCLA, 1960-68; chmn. bd., chief exec. officer Times Mirror Co., 1968-81, chmn. exec. com., 1981-86; trustee J. Paul Getty Trust; dir. emeritus Times-Mirror Co. Chmn. Kress Found., Nat. Gallery of Art.; trustee Los Angeles County Mus. Art. Served to capt. AUS, 1944-46. Named One of Ten Outstanding Young Men U.S. Jr. C. of C., 1949; recipient Outstanding Civilian Service award U.S. Army, 1967. Fellow A.C.P.; mem. Phi Beta Kappa, Sigma Xi, Alpha Omega Alpha, Beta Theta Pi, Nu Sigma Nu. Episcopalian. Home: 419 Robert Ln Beverly Hills CA 90210 Office: Times Mirror Co Times Mirror Sq Los Angeles CA 90053

MURPHY, FREDERICK VERNON, research physicist; b. Washington, Mar. 26, 1938; s. Frederick Vernon and Margery (Cannon) M.; m. Fayne Chupack, June 30, 1965; children: Frederick S., Matthew B. BS in Physics, Georgetown U., 1959; MA, Princeton U., 196l, PhD, 1967. Instr. Princeton (N.J.) U., 1966-67; rsch. assoc. U. Calif., Santa Barbara, 1967-75; engring. mgr. Varian Assocs., Inc., Palo Alto, Calif., 1975-80, 1985-; rsch. scientist Telesensory Systems, Inc., Mountain View, Calif., 1980-83. Contbr. articles to sci. jours.; patentee computed tomography scanner collimator. Mem. Am. Vacuum Soc., Am. Assn. Physicists in Medicine. Democrat. Roman Catholic. Home: 430 Sherwood Way Menlo Park CA 94025 Office: Varian Assocs Inc 6ll Hansen Way Palo Alto CA 94303

MURPHY, JOHN THOMAS, lawyer; b. Pierre, S.D., July 20, 1932; s. Bernard J. and Gertrude (Loner) M.; LL.B., U. S.D., 1957; m. Rose Marie Cogorno. Admitted to S.D. bar, 1957, Calif. bar, 1962; practiced Stockton, Calif., 1965-75, Modesto, Calif., 1975—; atty. Office Gen. Counsel Q.M. Gen. Dept. of Army, 1957-58; asst. chief counsel Sharpe Army Depot, 1958-63, gen. counsel, 1963-65; assoc. Short, Short, Scott & Murphy, and predecessor firm, 1965-68; partner Hulsey, Beus, Wilson, Scott & Murphy, Stockton, 1968-70. Sec. Golden Bear Assn. Beagle Clubs. Bd. dirs. Delta-Stockton Humane Soc., 1970-75; bd. govs. Calif. Trout Inc. Mem. State Bar Calif., Assn. Trial Lawyers Am., Calif. Trial Lawyers Assn., Beta Theta Pi, Phi Delta Phi. Republican. Episcopalian. Clubs: Commonwealth, Stockton Beagler's (sec., dir.), Am. Kennel (Beagle adv. com. 1984-86). Home: 2162 Parkridge Dr Modesto CA 95355 Office: 1104 12th St Modesto CA 95353

MURPHY, LEWIS CURTIS, lawyer, former mayor of Tucson; b. N.Y.C., Nov. 2, 1933; s. Henry Waldo and Elizabeth Wilcox (Curtis) M.; m. Carol Carney, Mar. 10, 1957; children—Grey, Timothy, Elizabeth. B.S. in Bus. Adminstrn, U. Ariz., 1955, LL.B., 1961. Bar: Ariz. bar 1961. Individual practice law Tucson, 1961-66; trust officer So. Ariz. Bank & Trust Co., 1966-70; atty. City of Tucson, 1970-71; mayor 1971-87; mem. law firm Schroeder & Murphy, Tucson, 1978-88; trustee U.S. Conf. Mayors, 1978-87, chmn. transp. com., 1984-87; mem. pub. safety steering com. Nat. League Cities, 1973-87, mem. transp. steering com., 1973-87; v.p. Central Ariz. Project Assn., 1978; bd. dirs. Interwest Bank. of Ariz., Community Food Bank. Mem. adv. bd. Ariz. Cancer Ctr., 1988—. Served with USAF, 1955-58. Mem. Ariz. Bar Assn., Pima County Bar Assn., Ariz. Acad. Republican. Presbyterian.

MURPHY, MARY ANN, human services administrator; b. Salt Lake City, Feb. 13, 1943; d. Wallace L. and Irene (Hummer) Matlock; m. Robert A. Glatzer, Dec. 31, 1977; children: Gabriela, Jessica, Nicholas. BA, U. Wash., 1964; MS, Ea. Wash. U., 1975. House counselor Ryther Child Ctr., Seattle, 1966-67; tchr. presch. Head Start, L.A. and Seattle, 1967-70; tchr. presch. Children's Orthopedic Hosp., Seattle, 1970-71, Washington, 1971-72; mem. faculty Ea. Wash. U., Cheney, 1973-82; exec. dir. Youth Help Assn., Spokane, Wash., 1983-88; mgr. regional ctr. for child abuse and neglect Deaconess Med. Ctr., Spokane, 1988—; pres. Wash. State Alliance for Children, Youth & Families, Seattle, 1985-87; chair Gov.'s Juvenile Justice Adv. Commn., Olympia, Wash., 1987—, Spokane Prevention of Child Abuse and Neglect Coun., Spokane, 1988—. Bd. dirs. Vols. of Am., Spokane, 1985—. Mem. DSHS (regional adv. com. 1986—, oversight com. div. children and family svcs. 1987—), Children's Interagency Coordinating Commn., Head Start Policy Adv. Coun. Home: W 1950 Clarke Ave Spokane WA 99201 Office: Deaconess Med Ctr W 800 Fifth Ave Spokane WA 99210

MURPHY, MICHAEL BROCK, architect; b. Lincoln, Nebr., Sept. 29, 1946; s. Edward Preston and Pauline (Brock) M.; m. Cheryl Elizabeth Leprich, Sept. 21, 1986. AA in Architecture, Pasadena City Coll., 1966; BArch, Ariz. State U., 1969. Vol. VISTA, Denver, 1969-70; assoc. architect Anderson, Barker, Rinker, Denver, 1970-75; prin. architect Barker, Rinker, Seacat, Denver, 1975-81; instr. design U. Colo., Denver, 1978-84; prin., owner Michael Murphy Architect, Denver, 1981-83; v.p., dir. design H.O.H. Assocs. Inc., Denver, 1983-86; prin., owner Michael Murphy Architecture, Denver, 1986—; Guest juror Design Com. Am. Soc. Landscape Architects, 1986; design critic U. Colo. 1978-84, mem. curriculum devel. com. 1978; judge Colo. Carpenter's Apprenticeship, 1978. Works include Denver Community Design Ctr, 1970; co-author: Design Studio Curriculum, 1978-84. Mem. AIA (Denver chpt. edn. com.). Methodist. Office: 4100 E Mississippi Ste 1400 Denver CO 80222

MURPHY, PHYLISS PETERS, infosystems specialist, consultant; b. Quincy, Ill., Dec. 3, 1941; d. Ray E. and Helen Kathleen (Gray) Peters; m. Michael P. Murphy, Aug. 22, 1961 (div. 1983); 1 child, Michael Murphy; m. Van Lynn Swearingen, Jan. 7, 1989; 1 child, Sharon Edwards. Student, Stephens Coll., 1960-61, Ill. Coll., 1961-62; BBA, Western Ill. U., 1968; postgrad., DePaul U., 1970-72. Dir. Consumer Systems, Inc., Oak Brook, Ill., 1972-79; v.p. CBM, Inc., Schaumburg, Ill., 1979-81; pres. P. Murphy & Assoc., Inc., Burbank, Calif., 1981—; exec. v.p. EDPMA, Inc., Burbank, Calif., 1985—. Mem. Nat. Assn. Computer Cons. Bus. (charter, mem. exec. com. 1986-89), So. Calif. Bus. Assn. (charter, pres. 1986-88, treas. 1988—), Toluca Lake C. of C. Home: 13229 Morrison Ave Sherman Oaks CA 91423

MURPHY, STEPHEN EUGENE, dentist; b. Cin., Sept. 14, 1945; s. William Smith and Orla (Deyton) M.; m. Phyllis Jane Johnson, Dec. 21, 1968; children: Timothy Scott, Shanna Jo. DMD, U. Ky., Lexington, 1970. Commd. 2d lt., rotating intern USPHS, Anchorage, 1970-71; dental assoc. Dr. Keith McCavit, Palmer, Alaska, 1971-72; gen. practice dentistry Alaska Bush, Alaska, 1972-74, Glenn Allen, Alaska, 1974-80, Sutherlin, Oreg., 1980—. Mem. ADA, Oreg. Dental Soc., Umpqua Dental Soc. (pres. 1984-85). Republican. Lodge: Lions (v.p. Sutherlin chpt. 1988—). Office: 311 E Central Sutherlin OR 97479

MURPHY, STEVEN R., auto finance company executive; b. Ogden, Utah, Dec. 18, 1939; s. Patrick B. and Mary Alice (Wardley) M.; m. Marlene Murphy, Mar. 10, 1968; children: Kevin Patrick, Brian Timothy. BS in Bus., Calif. State U., Hayward, 1968. Pres., founder First Leasing Corp., Alameda, Calif., 1970-85; group exec. western territory Marine Midland Automotive Fin. Corp., San Leandro, Calif., 1985—; Bd. dirs. Alameda Bancorp, Alameda 1st Nat. Bank, 1974-85. Mem. Nat. Vehicle Leasing Assn. (pres. 1980-81, Clemens-Pender award 1987, Murphy Cup named in his honor), Calif. Bankers Assn. (chmn. leasing com. 1981).

MURPHY, TERENCE MARTIN, botany educator; b. Seattle, July 1, 1942; s. Norman Walter and Dorothy Louise (Smith) M.; m Judith Baron, July 12, 1969; 1 child, Shannon Elaine. BS, Calif. Inst. Tech., 1964; PhD, U. Calif. San Diego, La Jolla, 1968. Sr. fellow dept. biochemistry U. Wash., Seattle, 1969-70; asst. prof. botany U. Calif., Davis, 1971-76, assoc. prof., 1976-82, prof., 1982—, chmn. dept. botany, 1986-89. Author: Plant Molecular Development, 1988; N.Am. exec. editor, N.Am. office, Physiologia Plantarum, 1988—; contbr. articles to profl. jours. Mem. AAAS, Am. Soc. Plant Physiologists, Am. Soc. Photobiology, Internat. Soc. Plant Molecular Biology, Scandinavian Soc. Plant Physiology. Home: 725 N Campus Way Davis CA 95616 Office: U Calif Dept Botany Davis CA 95616

MURPHY, TERESA HODES, nursing service executive; b. Kansas City, Mo., Nov. 28, 1955; d. Richard Erb and Barbara Marie (Altman) Hodes; m. Rick S. Murphy. Apr. 23, 1988. BS in Biology magna cum laude, Regis Coll., 1978; BS in Nursing, U. Colo., Denver, 1980; MBA, U. Phoenix, Denver, 1987. RN. Nurse Denver Gen. Hosp., 1980-82, asst. head nurse, 1982-86; head nurse Rose Med. Ctr., Denver, 1986-87; br. dir. Favorite Nurses, Denver, 1987—. Contbr. papers to nursing jours. Mem. Nat. Orgn. Female Execs., Network for Profl. Devel. Roman Catholic. Home: 840 S Lima Aurora CO 80012 Office: Favorite Nurses 425 S Cherry #100 Denver CO 80222

MURPHY, THOMAS JOSEPH, bishop; b. Chgo., Oct. 3, 1932; s. Barthomew Thomas and Nellie M. AB, St. Mary of the Lake Sem., 1954, STB, 1956, MA, 1957, STL, 1958, STD, 1960. Ordained priest Roman Cath. Ch., 1958. Various positions with Archdiocese of Chgo.; bishop of Great Falls-Billings Mont., 1978-87; coadjutor archbishop of Seattle 1987—; coadjutor archibishop, Seattle. Office: Archdiocese of Seattle 910 Marion St Seattle WA 98104

MURPHY, THOMAS JOSEPH, naval officer; b. Schenectady, N.Y., Sept. 8, 1955; s. Joseph Leo and Marian Elizabeth (Murphy) M.; m. Rosanne Mohn, May 16, 1981; 1 child, Thomas J. Jr. BS in Chem. Engring., Northwestern U., 1977; MME, Naval Postgrad. Sch., 1987. Registered profl. engr., Calif. Commd. ens. USN, 1977, advanced through grades to lt. comdr., 1987; assignments include diving officer USS Florikan; exec. officer USS Moctobi; ship supt. USS McClosky; now ship supt. USS Pigeon, Long Beach, Calif. Mem. Am. Soc. Naval Engrs. Republican. Roman Catholic. Office: Long Beach Naval Shipyard Code 33810 Long Beach CA 90822

MURRAY, CONNEL LYLE, advertising and public relations executive, consultant; b. Lompoc, Calif., Feb. 22, 1928; s. Connel Victor and Mary Mandilla (Hostetler) M.; m. June Louise White, Jan. 9, 1954; children: Corinne Louise, Erin Lucille, Connel Raymond, Alison Reita. Student, Lewis and Clark Coll., 1945, 47; BA, San Francisco State Coll., 1954. Pub. relations account exec. Fred Gray & Assocs., San Francisco, 1954-55; v.p., owner Mitchell, Murray & Horn Pub. Relations, San Francisco, 1955-57; newswriter KRON-TV, San Francisco, 1957; account exec. various advt. cos., Calif., 1957-68; pres. Murray/Bradley Advt. and Pub. Relations, Anchorage, 1968-86, The Murray Group, Inc., Seattle, 1986--; cons. Bradley Advt., Anchorage, 1986--. Pres. YMCA, Anchorage, 1976; mem. found. bd. Evergreen State Coll., Olympia, Wash., 1987--. With USN, 1945-47. Recipient North Star award Alaska Visitors Assn., Juneau, 1976. Mem. Am. Assn. Advt. Agys. (Wash. chmn. 1986), Pub. Relations Soc. Am. (accredited, bd. govs. 1972--), Anchorage Yacht Club. Libertarian. Office: The Murray Group 1904 3d Ave Ste 425 Seattle WA 98101

MURRAY, DAVID IRVIN, service executive; b. Pitts., Aug. 19, 1949; s. Irvin Andrew and Mary Elizabeth (Kohle) M.; m. Susan Aline Van Cura, Nov. 26, 1976; children: Nichole Elizabeth, RoseMary Elizabeth. BA, Ind. U. of Pa., 1971; MA, W.Va. U., 1972. Procurement analyst Westinghouse Electric, Pitts., 1973-75; regional v.p. Hertz Corp., Millbrae, Calif., 1975-87; sr. v.p., owner Nat. Car Rental, Burlingame, Calif., 1987—; bd. dirs. Calif. Catrala, Sacramento. Democrat.

MURRAY, JO BUMBARGER, public relations executive; b. Scotland County, N.C., Oct. 8, 1945; d. Paul William and Sara (Ward) B.; m. Cecil Lawrence Murray, July 12, 1967 (div. 1979); m. Harre Wilkins Demoro, Mar. 1, 1986. BA, Mich. State U., 1967. Writer Del. River Port Authority Log, Camden, N.J., 1968-69; assoc. editor Oakland (Calif.) Tribune, 1972-81; prin. Jo Murray Pub. Relations, Oakland, 1981—. Recipient writing award State Bar Calif., 1975, feature writing award Press Club San Francisco, 1975, Best Pub. Service Reporting In-State award Sigma Delta Chi N.J. chpt., 1968, Best News Writing Phila. area award Sigma Delta Chi Phila. chpt., 1968. Mem. Pub. Relations Soc. Am. (chair profl. devel. com. East Bay chpt. 1985, sec. 1986, v.p. 1987, pres. 1988), Alameda/Contra Costa County Bench/Bar Com. (chmn. 1981), Bay Area Electric RR Assn. Democrat. Club: Lakeview (Oakland). Office: 4100 Redwood Rd Ste 200 Oakland CA 94619

MURRAY, JOHN ROBERTS, physicist; b. Camp White, Oreg., Aug. 8, 1943; s. John Lewis and Cherry Mary (Roberts) M.; m. Gwynedd Morgan Davis, July 1976; children: David James, Catherine Ann. SB, MIT, 1965, PhD, 1970. Laser devel. physicist Lawrence Livermore (Calif.) nat. Lab., 1972—. Topical editor Jour. Optical Soc. Am., 1984—. Capt. U.S. Army, 1970-72. Mem. Optical Soc. Am. Home: 605 Camino Amigo Danville CA 94526 Office: Lawrence Livermore Nat Lab Box 5508 L-490 Livermore CA 94550

MURRAY, KATHLEEN ELLEN, editor; b. Chgo., Feb. 23, 1946; d. John Joseph and Marie Agnes (Stoltzman) M.; B.A., Calif. State U., Sacramento, 1973; A.A., Am. River Coll., 1968. File clk. Allstate Ins. Co., Sacramento, 1964-66; clk. typist Calif. Hwy. Patrol, Sacramento, 1968-69; copy editor Sacramento Bee, 1971—; instr. Calif. State U., Sacramento, 1975-76. Newspaper Fund intern, scholar, 1971. Club: Sacramento Press. Home: PO Box 606 Nevada City CA 95959

MURRAY, ROBERT BRUCE, theatre administrator; b. Evanston, Ill., Apr. 8, 1932; s. Robert Wolcott and Hazel (Clayton) M.; m. Erika Grob, Oct. 19, 1957 (dec. Feb. 1986); children: Christopher (dec.), Timothy, Molly, Gideon. BS, U. Wis., 1954; MFA, Yale U., 1961. Program dir. Aspen (Colo.) Inst. For Humanistic Studies, 1961-65; assoc. prof. dept. drama Emerson Coll., Boston, 1965-72; dir. City of Salem (Mass.), 1972-78, Aspen Community Sch., 1978-83; exec. dir. Wheeler Opera House, Aspen, 1983—; bd. dirs. League Hist. Am. Theatres, Washington, 1984—. Playwright: The Good Lieutenant, 1963 (PBS-TV award 1965), Donner, 1973 (Rockefeller Found. award 1975), Salem Chronicles, 1974 (U.S. Park Service award 1976). Mem. Hist. Salem Inc., 1970-76; bicentennial dir. City of Salem, 1973-77; pres. Aspen Hist. Soc., 1980-81; bd. mem. Mountain Valley Devel. Services, 1981—. Named Playwright in Residence Yale U., John Golden Found., 1963-65; recipient Bristol Myers Drama award, N.Y.C., 1963, Rockefeller Drama award Rockefeller Found., U. Calif. Davis, 1973. Office: Wheeler Opera House 320 E Hyman Ave Aspen CO 81611

MURRAY, ROBERT EMMET, illustrator; b. Cedar Rapids, Iowa, Dec. 2, 1945; s. Charles Emmet and Frances Josephine (Rompotl) M.; m. Mary Lacey Dixon, Sept. 27, 1975; 1 child, Michael. BA, U. Iowa, 1968. Artist Accent Graphics, Phoenix, 1971-73; audio-video mgr. U-Haul Internat., Phoenix, 1973-77; illustrator Broadway Southwest, Mesa, Ariz., 1979-81; pvt. practice Scottsdale, Ariz., 1977-79, 82—. With U.S. Army, 1969-70, Vietnam. Episcopalian. Home and Office: 11228 E Laurel Ln Scottsdale AZ 85259

MURRAY, STEPHEN DOUGLAS, airline pilot; b. Decatur, Ill., May 26, 1944; s. Robert Thomas and Jean Elizabeth (Horne) M.; m. Deborah Jean Waer, Feb. 16, 1980 (div. 1984); 1 child, Krista Marie. BS, Benedictine Coll., 1966; postgrad., Naval Air Tng. Command Sch., 1968. Commd. 2nd lt. USMC, 1967, advanced through grades to lt. col., 1978, resigned, 1978; with USMCR, 1981-84; pilot Western Airlines, L.A., 1979-80, Air Calif., Newport Beach, 1981-87; pilot, capt. Am. Airlines, Dallas, 1987—; capt. Air Spur Helicopters, L.A., 1983-84; transport pilot USN Blue Angels, 1976-78. Decorated 40 Air medals, Disting. Flying Cross. Mem. SAR, Marine Corps Res. Officers Assn., Airline Pilots Assn., Allied Pilots Assn. Roman Catholic. Home: 4435 E Ocean Blvd #16 Long Beach CA 90803 Office: Am Airlines 32 Skypark Cir Newport Beach CA 92714

MURRAY, WALTER ALLAN, JR., lawyer; b. Riverside, Calif., June 17, 1943; s. Walter Allan Sr. and Edna Marie (Freeman) M.; . Carol Gene Hamilton, Dec. 22, 1967 (dec. Feb. 1984); 1 child, Walter Allan III; m. Ellen Denise Lipske, Nov. 18, 1987. Student, San Bernardino Valley Coll., Calif., 1961-64; BA in Polit. Sci., San Diego State U., 1966; JD, Baylor U., 1971. Bar: Calif. 1974, Wyo. 1981. Pvt. practice Rialto, Calif., 1974-81; pros. atty. Natrona County, Casper, Wyo., 1981-82; dep. pub. defender State of Wyo., Casper, 1982-84; judge State of Wyo., Gillette, 1984-88; pvt. practice Casper, 1988—; ct. commr. Mcpl. Ct. San Bernardino, Fontana, Calif., 1974-81; juvenile ct. referee Superior Ct. of San Bernardino, 1974-81; commr. Dist. Ct. 6th Dist., Gillette, 1984—. BD. dirs. Pub. Utilities Commn., Rialto, 1975-78. Recipient Resolution of Appreciation, City of Rialto, 1975. Mem. Am. Legion (judge advocate 1976-81, 86-88, Citation of Appreciation 1981), Vietnam Vets. (bd. dirs. Gillette chpt. 1988), VFW. Democrat. Office: 200 N Wolcott Ste 302 Casper WY 82601 also: 400 Kendrick Ste 304 Gillette WY 82716

MURREN, DOUGLAS EDWARD, pastor; b. Wenatchee, Wash., July 16, 1951; s. Virgil Edward and Gloria Mae (Humphres) M.; m. Debra Jean Landin, Mar. 27, 1971; children: Matthew Douglas, Raissa Anne. BA in Religion, Seattle Pacific U. Lic. pastor Internat. Ch. Foursquare Gospel. Asst. pastor Bethesda Christian Ctr., Wenatchee, 1974-79; founding pastor Eastside Christian Communion, Bellevue, Wash., 1979-80, Eastside Foursquare Ch., Kirkland, Wash., 1981—; conf. speaker, cons. various orgns. Poland, USSR, Norway, Fed. Republic Germany, Haiti, and U.S.; supt. div. Foursquare Gospel Ch., N. King County, Wash., 1985—. Author: Iceman, 1986; editor Pastoral Resource, 1986—; host (radio show) Growing Together; contbr. articles to profl. jours. Office: Eastside Foursquare Ch PO Box 536 Kirkland WA 98083-0536

MURRISH, RICHARD EUGENE, mechanical engineer; b. Holdrege, Nebr., May 15, 1949; s. Richard DeVern and Mae Marie (Bergman) M.; m. Beverly Jean Gross, Aug. 14, 1971; 1 child, Kiptara Marie. Student, USAF Acad., 1967-68; BSME, U. Nebr., 1972. Design engr. Boeing Military Aircraft Co., Wichita, Kans., 1972-74; CAD/CAm specialist Boeing Comml. Aircraft Co., Seattle, 1974-79; mgr. computer graphics Kenner Products, Cin., 1979-84; CIM mgr. Sci. Applications Internat. Corp., La Jolla, Calif., 1984-85; pres. Technology Mgmt. Svcs., Seattle, 1985—. Contbr. articles to profl. jours. Mem. AIAA, Puget Sound Engring. Council, IEEE, Computer Automated Systems Assn. (chmn. 1983-84), Soc. Mfg. Engrs. Office: Tech Mgmt Svcs PO Box 7372 Seattle WA 98133

MURTAGH, CHRISTOPHER MATTHEW, fuel company executive; b. N.Y.C., Dec. 28, 1955; s. John Patrick and Doris Mary (Peterson) M.; m. Polly Mary Karadontes, May 25, 1980; 1 child, Andrew. Student, Steven's Inst. Tech., N.J. Inst. Tech. Sales rep. G.A. Fleet Assocs., Harrison, N.Y., 1977-79; dist. sales mgr. Fairbanks Morse Pump Div., Kansas City, Kans., 1979-81; N.Y.C. comml. sales mgr. Aurora Pump, N. Aurora, Ill., 1981-84; mgr. bldg. trades market Paco Pump, Inc., Oakland, Calif., 1984-87, North Am. regional mgr., 1987—. Patrol leader Boy Scouts Am., N.J., 1967. Mem. Am. Soc. Plumbing Engrs., Nat. Fire Protection Assn., Am. Soc. Sanitary Engrs., Phila. Engrs. Club (guest speaker 1988). Republican. Roman Catholic. Home: 951 Maricaibo Pl San Ramon CA 94583 Office: Paco Pump Inc 845 92d Ave Oakland CA 94623

MUSACCHIO, THEODORE ALPHONSUS, international business consultant; b. Fresno, Calif., Aug. 11, 1934; s. Anthony and Constance (Ambrogio) M.; B.A., Fresno State Coll., 1956; postgrad. U. Calif. Sch. Law-San Francisco, 1959-61; m. Darlene June Mirigian, Mar. 20, 1955; 1 child, Kirk Anthony. Exec. trainee Bank of Am., NT & SA, Fresno, 1956-59; exec. Wells Fargo Bank, San Francisco, 1961-64; adminstrv. v.p. Columbus Savs. & Loan Assn., San Francisco, 1964-72; sr. v.p. Imperial Savs. and Loan Assn., San Francisco, 1972-76; dir., pres., chief exec. officer Columbus-Marin Savs. and Loan Assn., TAM Fin. Corp., Marcent Fin. Corp. and Columbus Fin. Corp., 1976-85; chmn. bd. and chief exec. officer KTM Corp., 1986—. Mem. exec. com. Boys' Towns of Italy, 1965—; pres. San Francisco Columbus Day Celebration, 1968. Mem. Fin. Instns. Mktg. Assn. (charter), Musicians' Union, Internat. Assn. Machinists, Am. Savs. and Loan Inst. (past pres. San Francisco chpt.), Il Cenacolo, Order Sons of Italy in Am., Italian Fedn. Calif. (past bd. dirs.), Sigma Pi. Clubs: Commonwealth of Calif., Family, Villa Taverna (San Francisco). Lodges: Masons (32 deg.), Shriners. Home and Office: 130 El Dorado Ct San Bruno CA 94066

MUSHEN, ROBERT LINTON, ophthalmologist; b. Klamath Falls, Oreg., Mar. 4, 1943; s. Samuel Albert and Beulah (Gore) M.; m. Deborah Campbell, July 5, 1969 (div. 1987); children: Melanie, Gregory, Timothy; m. Geraldine Kay Geise, Apr. 29, 1988. BSChemE (Nat. Merit scholar), Stanford U., 1964; MD, U. Oreg., 1968. Intern, Santa Clara Valley Med. Center, San Jose, Calif., 1968-69; resident in ophthalmology Brooke Army Med. Center, San Antonio, 1972-75; chief service Kerrville (Tex.) VA Hosp., 1975-76; mem. staff Madigan Army Med. Center, Tacoma, 1976-77; chief of staff and eye service Kadlec Hosp., Richland, Wash., 1977—; pres. Richland Eye Clinic, 1977—; cons. in field. Served with M.C., U.S. Army Res., 1969-75. Recipient award Oreg. Mus. Sci. and Industry, 1960; Nat. Eye Found. fellow, 1974-75. Mem. A.C.S., Am. Acad. Ophthalmology, Am. Intraocular Implant Soc., Soc. Eye Surgeons, AMA, Wash. Med. Assn., Wash. Acad. Ophthalmology, Benton-Franklin County Med. Soc., Alpha Omega Alpha. Republican. Co-author: Neuroanatomy Guide, 1967; contbr. articles to med. jours. Inventor bifocal trial lens. Home: 1302 Brentwood Richland WA 99352-9699 Office: Richland Eye Clinic 948 Stevens Dr Richland WA 99352

MUSIHIN, KONSTANTIN K., electrical engineer; b. Harbin, China, June 17, 1927; s. Konstantin N. and Alexandra A. (Lapitsky) M.; came to U.S., 1967, naturalized, 1973; ed. YMCA Inst., 1942, North Manchurian U., 1945, Harbin Poly. Inst., 1948; m. Natalia Krilova, Oct. 18, 1964; 1 son, Nicholas. Asst. prof. Harbin Poly. Inst., 1950-53; elec. engr. Moinho Santista, Sao Paulo, Brazil, 1955-60; constrn. project mgr. Caterpillar-Brazil, Santo Amaro, 1960-61; mech. engr. Matarazzo Industries, Sao Paulo, 1961-62; chief of works Vidrobras, St. Gobain, Brazil, 1962-64; project engr. Brown Boveri, Sao Paulo, 1965-67; sr. engr. Kaiser Engrs., Oakland, Calif., 1967-73; sr. engr. Bechtel Power Corp., San Francisco, 1973-75; supr. power and control San Francisco Bay Area Rapid Transit, Oakland, 1976-78; chief elec. engr. L.K. Comstock Engring. Co., San Francisco, 1978-79; prin. engr. Morrison Knudsen Co., San Francisco, 1979-84; prin. engr. Brown and Caldwell, Cons. Engrs., Pleasant Hill, Calif., 1984-85; cons. engr. Pacific Gas and Electric Co., San Francisco, 1986—. Registered profl. engr., Calif., Colo., N.Y., N.J., Pa., Ill., Wash. Mem. IEEE (sr.), Instrument Soc. Am. (sr.), Am. Mgmt. Assn., Nat., Calif. socs. profl. engrs., Nat. Assn. Corrosion Engrs., Instituto de Engenharia de Sao Paulo. Mem. Christian Orthodox Ch.

Clubs: Am.-Brazilian, Brit.-Am. Home: 320 Park View Terr Unit 207 Oakland CA 94610

MUSSELWHITE, EDWIN A., management consulting company executive; b. Miami, Fla., Jan. 21, 1940; s. Thomas A. and Edna B. W.; BS, Northwestern U., 1964; m. Linda Silvestrini, 1984; Kenneth, Thomas, Zachary. Mktg. rep. IBM, Chgo., 1964-68, exec. staff asst., 1968, br. sales mgr., Aurora, Ill., 1968-69; dir. profl. personnel Leasco Systems Corp., Oakbrook, Ill. 1969-70; co-founder, exec. v.p. Deltak, Inc., Oakbrook, Ill., 1970-76; pres. Systems Growth Inst., Santa Cruz, Calif., 1976-82; v.p. Zenger-Miller, Inc., Cupertino, Calif., 1982—, also chmn. bd. dirs.; cons. mgmt. to IBM, Gen. Electric Co., Fireman's Fund Ins. Co., Stanford U., TRW, others; guest lectr. at univs.; mem. bd. advs.; Center for Orgn. and Mgmt. Devel., San Jose State U. Served as sgt. U.S. Army, 1964. Mem. Am. Soc. Tng. Devel., Orgn. Devel. Network. Co-author: Toward Excellence, 1983, How To Get The Most Training, 1987; contbg. author: Everybody Wins, 1976; Interpersonal Dimensions, 1981; producer over 2000 hours of video-based instrn. in mgmt. devel, data processing and sales skills, 1973—. Office: Zenger-Miller Inc 10201 Torre Ave Cupertino CA 95014

MUSSER, C. WALTON, physical scientist, consultant; b. Mt. Joy, Pa., Apr. 5, 1909; s. Ezra Nissley and Cora Grace (Weidman) M.; m. Edna Mae Hoak, June 23, 1937; children—Lila Darle (Mrs. Richard Hackman), Yvonne Duane (Mrs. Harold Graham), Stanley Walton. Student, Chgo. Tech. Coll., 1926-28, Leavitt Sch. Psychology, 1928-29, Wharton Sch. Fin. and Commerce, 1929-30, U. Pa., 1930-32, MIT, 1957. Chief engr. product devel. Indsl. Improvement Corp., Phila., 1936-41; rsch. adviser Dept. Def., 1941-56; pres., dir. rsch. Sci. Rsch., Inc., Glenside, Pa., 1945-52; pvt. practice cons., adviser in rsch. and devel. 1936—. Holder of over 162 U.S. Patents in 32 different classes and more than 60 patents in over 28 countries. Recipient Exceptional Civilian Service award for First Working Recoilless Weapon, Sec. of War, 1945; John C. Jones medal for Disting. Svc., Am. Ordnance Assn., 1951; Machine Design award ASME, 1968; named to Ordnance Hall of Fame, 1976. Mem. Acad. Applied Scis., Am. Def. Preparedness Assn. (hon. life), Nat. Soc. Profl. Engrs., Sigma Xi. Address: 1206 Lela Ln Santa Maria CA 93454

MUSSMAN, WILLIAM EDWARD, III, lawyer; b. San Francisco, Jan. 31, 1951; s. William Edward and Janet Jonn (Skittone) M.; m. Carol Lynne Johnson, Jan. 9, 1988; BS, Stanford U., 1973; JD, U. Calif.-San Francisco, 1976. Bar: Calif. 1976, U.S. Dist. Ct. (no. dist.) Calif. 1976,, U.S. Dist. Ct. (cen. dist.) Calif. 1982, U.S. Supreme Ct., 1986, U.S. Ct. Appeals (9th cir.) 1987. Assoc. Lasky, Haas, Cohler & Munter, San Francisco, 1980-82, Pillsbury, Madison & Sutro, San Francisco, 1982-84; assoc. Carr & Mussman, San Francisco, 1984—. Missionary Ch. Jesus Christ Latter Day Sts., Tokyo, 1977-78. Mem. ABA, San Francisco Bar Assn., Latter Day Saints Bus. Club (pres. 1982-84), Brigham Young U. Mgmt. Soc. (bd. dirs., 1984-88, v.p. 1984-86, pres. 1986-87), Stanford Alumni Assn. (life), Tau Beta Pi. Office: Carr & Mussman 3 Embarcadero Ctr Ste 1060 San Francisco CA 94111

MUSTACCHI, PIERO, physician, educator; b. Cairo, Egypt, May 29, 1920; came to U.S., 1947; naturalized, 1952; s. Gino and Gilda (Rieti) M.; m. Dora Lisa Ancona, Sept. 26, 1948; children—Roberto, Michael. BS in Humanities, U. Florence, Italy, 1938; postgrad. in anatomy, Eleve Interne, U. Lausanne, Switzerland, 1938-39; MB, ChB, Fouad I U., Cairo, Egypt, 1944, grad. in Arabic lang. and lit., 1946; D Medicine and Surgery, U. Pisa, 1986; D Honoris Causa, U. Aix-Marseilles, France, 1988. Lic. physician Egypt, 1946. Diplomate, Am. Bd. Internal Medicine. House officer English Hosp., Ch. Missionary Soc., Cairo, Egypt, 1945-47; clin. affiliate U. Calif., San Francisco, 1947-48; intern Franklin Hosp., San Francisco, 1948-49; resident in pathology U. Calif., San Francisco, 1949-51; resident in medicine Meml. Ctr. Cancer and Allied Diseases, N.Y.C., 1951-53; research epidemiologist Dept. HEW, Nat. Cancer Inst., Bethesda, Md., 1955-57; cons. allergy clinic U. Calif., San Francisco, 1957-70, clin. prof. medicine and preventive medicine, 1970—, head occupational epidemiology, 1975—, head div. internat. health edn. dept. epidemiology and internat. health, 1985—; med. cons., vis. prof. numerous ednl. and profl. instns. including U. Calif.-San Francisco, U. Marseille, 1981, 82, U. Pisa, Italy, 1983, U. Gabon, 1984, U. Siena, Italy, 1985, U. Calif.-San Francisco Ctr. for Rehab. and Occupational Health, 1984—, Work Clinic, 1975—; cons. numerous govtl. agys. throughout the world. Contbr. chpts. to books, articles to profl. jours. Editorial bd. Medecine d'Afrique Noire, Ospedali d'Italia. Served with USN, USPHS, 1953-55. Decorated Order of Merit (Italy), Ordre de la Legion d'Honneur (France), Medal of St. John of Jerusalem, Sovereign Order of Malta, Order of the Republic (Egypt); Scroll, Leonard da Vinci Soc., San Francisco, 1965; award Internat. Inst. Oakland, 1964; Hon. Vice Consul. Italy, 1971—. Fellow Am. Soc. Occupational Medicine, ACP; mem. AAAS, Am. Soc. Environ. and Occupational Health, Am. Assn. Cancer Research, Calif. Soc. Allergy and Immunology, Calif. Med. Assn., San Francisco Med. Soc., West Coast Allergy Soc. (founding mem.), Mexican Congress on Hypertension (corr.), Assn. Internationale pour la Recherche Medicale et l'Edn. Continue (U.S. rep.). Democrat. Clubs: Villa Taverna (San Francisco), Accademia Italiana della Cucina. Home: 3344 Laguna St San Francisco CA 94123 Office: U Calif Parnassus Ave San Francisco CA 94143

MUSTAFA, MOHAMMAD GHULAM, biochemistry educator; b. Dhaka, Bangladesh, Mar. 1, 1940; came to U.S., 1963, naturalized, 1978; s. Mohammad and Quamerunnesa Yaseen; m. Sultana Begum Mustafa, Nov. 6, 1969; 1 child, George E. BS, Dhaka U., 1960, MS summa cum laude, 1962; MA, U. Calif., Berkeley, 1966; PhD, SUNY, Albany, 1969. Asst. research biochemist U. Calif., Davis, 1969-73, asst. adj. prof., 1973-75; adj. asst. prof. UCLA, 1975-78, assoc. prof. in residence, 1978-79, assoc. prof., 1979-84, prof. environ. and occupational health sci., 1984—. Co-editor: Biomedical Effects of Ozone, 1983; mem. editorial bd. Toxicology and Indsl. Health, Princeton, N.J., 1984—; contbr. articles to profl. jours. Recipient Research Career Devel. award NIH, 1976-81; grantee NIH, 1970—. Mem. Am. Chem. Soc., Am. Coll. Toxicology, Air Pollution Control Assn., AAAS, N.Y. Acad. Sci., Sigma Xi. Democrat. Muslim. Home: 10534 Louisiana Ave Los Angeles CA 90025 Office: UCLA Sch Pub Health 405 Hilgard Ave Los Angeles CA 90024

MUSTAIN, ROY W., aeronautical engineer; b. San Diego, Dec. 13, 1914; s. Anton Mustain and Elizabeth Torres; m. D.L. Mustain Pritchard, Oct. 28, 1938; 4 children. Student, L.A. City Coll., U. So. Calif., UCLA, Calif. State U., Long Beach, Saddleback Coll. Engr. tech. N.Am. Aviation, L.A., 1946-52; rsch. engr. Internat. Rectifier, El Segundo, Calif., 1952-54; dynamics engr. Northrop Aircraft, L.A., 1954-62, McDonnell Douglas Astronautics, Huntington Beach, Calif., 1962-74; dynamics engr., engring. specialist, mem. tech. staff Rockwell Internat., Downey, Calif., 1974—; vice-chmn., sec. SAE com. G-5 on Aerospace Shock & Vibration, 1955-83. Contbr. articles to profl. jours. Home: PO Box 1179 El Toro CA 92630-1179 Office: Rockwell Internat Mail Sta AB62 12214 Lakwood Blvd Downey CA 90242

MUTSCHLER, HERBERT FREDERICK, librarian; b. Eureka, S.D., Nov. 28, 1919; s. Frederick and Helena (Oster) M.; m. Lucille I. Gross, Aug. 18, 1945; 1 dau., Linda M. B.A., Jamestown Coll., 1947; M.A., Western Res. U., 1949, M.S., 1952. Tchr. history high sch. Lemmon, S.D., 1947-48; asst. librarian Royal Oak (Mich.) Library, 1952-55; head librarian Hamtramck (Mich.) Library, 1955-56; head public services Wayne County Library System, Wayne, Mich., 1956-59; asst. county librarian Wayne County Library System, 1960-62; dir. King County Library System, Seattle, 1963—; library bldg. cons. Wayne County Library, 1956-62, Wash. State Library, 1966—; cons. Salt Lake County Library, Pierce County Library, North Olympic Library; lectr. U. Wash. Sch. Librarianship, 1970-71; bldg. cons. Hoquiam (Wash.) Library, Olympic (Wash.) Regional Library. Contbr. articles profl. jours. Served with AUS, 1941-45; to capt. 1950-52. Decorated Silver Star, Bronze Star with cluster, Purple Heart. Mem. ALA (councilor at large 1965-69, chpt. councilor 1971-75, pres. library adminstrv. div. 1974-75), Pacific N.W. Library Assn., Wash. Library Assn. (exec. bd. 1964-65, 69-71, pres. 1967-69). Republican. Lutheran. Club: City, Municipal League. Lodge: Kiwanis. Home: 5300 128th Ave SE Bellevue WA 98006 Office: 300 8th Ave N Seattle WA 98109

MYBECK, RICHARD RAYMOND, lawyer; b. Chgo., Dec. 5, 1928; s. Walter Raymond and Genevieve Lucille (Carlsten) M.; m. Betty Jane Engle, Aug. 23, 1952; children: Walter R. II, Wendy Sue, Lucinda Jeanne, Amanda Jane, (dec.), Candace Christine, Sara Melinda. BSChE, Purdue U., 1950; BS in Engring. Law, Ind. U., 1953, JD, 1953. Bar: Ind. 1953, Wis. 1954, Ill. 1962, Ariz. 1973; registered patent atty., patent agt., Can. Patent trainee, atty. Allis Chalmers Mfg. Co., West Allis, Wis., 1953-57, patent atty., 1957-62; atty. Koehring Corp., Milw., 1957; patent atty. Armour and Co., Chgo., 1962-71; sr. patent atty. Greyhound Corp., Chgo., Phoenix, 1971-77; sr. counsel Armour Pharmaceutical Co., Phoenix, Scottsdale, Ariz., 1977-81; pvt. practice Scottsdale, 1981—; pres., bd. dirs. Farmakeia, Inc., Scottsdale. Councilman Town of Paradise Valley, Ariz., 1988—, commr., chmn. planning and zoning commn., 1981-88, mem. chmn. bd. adjustment, 1974-81. Named to Hall of Fame Oak Park (Ill.) Youth Baseball, 1987; recipient Degentesh award Forest Park (Ill.) VFW, 1969. Mem. ABA, Ariz. Bar Assn. (chmn. various sects.), Ill. Bar Assn., Wis. Bar Assn., Elks, Masons, Tau Kappa Epsilon, Sigma Delta Kappa. Methodist. Home: 4901 E Tomahawk Tr Paradise Valley AZ 85253 Office: Myback Law Office 8010 E Morgan Tr Ste 10 Scottsdale AZ 85258-1234

MYER, NANCY ELIZABETH, medical librarian; b. Normal, Ill., Nov. 15, 1942; d. Kenneth Otho and Mary Elizabeth (Cox) M. AB, Ind. U., 1965, MLS, 1971. With VA, 1971—; chief librarian VA Med. Ctr., Albuquerque, 1982—. Vol. Tucson Big Sisters, 1976-80; Chaco Culture Nat. Hist. Park, 1986—. Mem. Med. Library Assn., N. Mex. Library Assn., Nat. Speleological Soc. (sec.-treas. local chpt. Sandia Grotto 1985), Enchanted Lens Camera Club (pres. 1986-88), Phi Beta Kappa, Beta Phi Mu. Democrat. Office: VA Med Ctr Libr Svc 142D 2100 Ridgecrest Dr Albuquerque NM 87108

MYERS, AL, realtor property manager, mayor; b. Oakland, Calif., Aug. 6, 1922; s. Alvi A. and Emma (Thoren) M.; student Oreg. Inst. Tech., 1940-41; m. Viola Doreen Wennermark, Sept. 11, 1954; children: Susan Faye, Pamela Ann, Jason Allen. Supt.'s asst. Aluminum Co. Am., Troutdale, Oreg., 1942-44; asst. mgr. Western Auto Supply Co., Portland, 1944-46; owner, operator Al Myers Auto & Electric, Gresham, Oreg., 1946-53; realtor, broker Al Myers Property Mgmt., 1954—; v.p., sec. Oreg. Country, Inc.; faculty Mt. Hood Community Coll. Chmn., Indsl. and Econ. Devel. Com. for Multonomah County, Oreg. Real Estate Ednl. Program, 1961. Mayor Gresham, Oreg., 1972—. Pres. East Multonomah County Dem. Forum, 1965—, mem. exec. com., 1958—. With AUS, 1943. Mem. Portland Realty Bd., Nat. Assn. Real Estate Bds., Christian Bus. Men's Com. Internat., Internat. Platform Assn., Rho Epsilon Kappa (pres. Oreg.). Mem. Evang. Ch. (trustee, treas.). Home: 935 NW Norman Ave Gresham OR 97030 Office: 995 NE Cleveland Ave Gresham OR 97030

MYERS, BARTON, architect; b. Norfolk, Va., Nov. 6, 1934; s. Barton and Meeta Hamilton (Burrage) M.; m. Victoria George, Mar. 7, 1959; 1 child, Suzanne Lewis. BS, U.S. Naval Acad., 1956; MArch with honors, U. Pa., 1964. Commd. 2d lt. USAF, 1956, resigned, 1961; architect Louis I. Kahn, Phila., 1964-65, Bower, Fradley, Phila., 1967-68; architect, prin. A.J. Diamond & Barton Myers, Toronto, Ont., Can., 1968-75; architect, prin. Barton Myers Assocs., Toronto, 1975—, Los Angeles, 1981—; disting. vis. prof. Ariz. State U., Tempe, 1986—; sr. prof. UCLA, 1981—; Thomas Jefferson Prof. U. Va., Charlottesville, 1982; vis. prof., lectr., Harvard U., U. Pa., other univs. U.S. and Can., 1968—. Prin. works include Myers Residence, Toronto (Ont. Assn. Architects Toronto Chpt. Annual Design award, 1971, Can. Housing Design Council award, 1971), Wolf Residence, Toronto (Architectural Record: Record Houses of 1977, Twenty-Five Yrs. of Record Houses, 1981), Housing Union Bldg., Edmonton (Can. Housing Design Council award, 1974, Design in Steel award, 1975), Citadel Theatre, Edmonton (City of Edmonton Design award, 1978, Stelco Design award, 1978), Seagram Mus., Waterloo, Ont., (Gov. Gen.'s Medal for Architecture, 1986), Howard Hughes Ctr. Master Plan and Wang Tower, Los Angeles, 1986, Phoenix Mcpl. Govt. Ctr. (Winning Competition Entry 1985), Portland Ctr. for the Performing Arts, Portland (Progressive Architecture Design award, 1984), Art Gallery Ont. expansion (Winning Competition Entry, 1987), Film and Drama Facility York U., Toronto, 1987, theater and concert hall Cerritos Ca. Community Arts Ctr., 1987, UCLA Housing and Commons, 1987, others. Fellow Royal Archtl. Inst. Can.; mem. AIA, Soc. Archtl. Historians, Royal Can. Acad. Art, Tau Sigma Delta. Office: Barton Myers Assocs Inc 6834 Hollywood Blvd Los Angeles CA 90028 also: 322 King St, West Toronto, ON Canada M5V 1J2

MYERS, BILL RALPH, real estate developer and investor; b. Lincoln, Nebr., Apr. 30, 1944; s. Ralph Francis and Dorothy Delia (Gates) M.; m. Carolyn Coke, Jan. 1962 (div. Jan. 1972); children: Gregory, Eric; m. Sandra Lee Morrison, Aug. 3, 1973; children: Tracy, Jennifer. BS, U. Colo., 1971. CPA, Colo.; lic. real estate broker, Ariz. Auditor, acct. Ernst & Ernst, 1971-73; audit mgr. Gates Rubber Co. and subs., Denver and Colorado Springs, 1973-81; v.p., treas., controller Oxford Properties, Inc., Denver, 1981-83; v.p. Alpert Corp., Denver, 1983-86, Dawson Cos., Scottsdale, Ariz., 1986—. Bd. dirs. Colorado Springs Boy's Club, 1979-81. Mem. Colo. Soc. CPAs. Republican. Methodist. Home: 5901 E Windrose Dr Scottsdale AZ 85254 Office: Dawson Cos 7400 E McCormick Pkwy Scottsdale AZ 85254

MYERS, BRADLEY LAWRENCE, electrical and electronics engineer; b. Lynwood, Calif., Jan. 27, 1961; s. Larry Dean and Jill Elaine (Ostler) M. BS in Elec. and Electronics Engring., Calif. State U., Chico, 1984. Control systems engr. Rexnord/Mathews Conveyor, Chico, 1984-85; custom products engr. Bently Nev. Corp., Minden, 1985-87, mfg. engr., 1987, prodn. supr., 1987—. V.p. Carson City (Nev.) Jaycees, 1986-87, state dir., 1987-88, dir., 1988—; v.p., MBA assoc. U. Nev., Reno, 1988-89. Mem. IEEE. Office: Bently Nev Corp 1617 Water St Minden NV 89423

MYERS, CONNIE JEAN, real estate; b. Portland, Oreg., Mar. 16, 1946; d. Thomas Arthur and Jennie Maifair (Saunders) M. BS, Oreg. State U., 1968. Asst. controller Builders Resources Corp., San Mateo, Calif., 1971-73; controller Little & Blackwell, Menlo Park, Calif., 1973-76; v.p. Landsing Property Corp., Menlo Park, 1976-82; v.p. reg. ptnr. Landsing Property Corp., Denver, 1982-85; cons. Denver, 1985; sr. v.p. De Anza Assets, Inc., Beverly Hills, Calif., 1985-87; v.p., dir. of asset mgmt. Holden Real Estate, Inc., L.A., 1987-88; pres. The RIM Co. Comml. Properties Group, Lynnwood, Wash., 1988—. Author: (procedure manuals) Apartment and Mobilehome Communities, 1986, General Management, Leasing & Marketing, Maintenance & Disaster. Mem. Inst. of Real Estate Mgmt. (cert. property mgr. 1980), Internat. Council of Shopping Ctrs., Colo. State Bd. of Real Estate (broker 1983), Wash State Bd. of Real Estate (broker 1989) Seattle/King County Assn. Realtors (affiliate). Republican. Office: The RIM Co 18631 Alderwood Mall Blvd Ste 201 Lynnwood WA 98037

MYERS, DENNIS GILLFORD, marketing professional; b. Canton, Ohio, Apr. 15, 1953; s. Kenneth and Margaret (Wallace) M.; m. Teresa Rose DiCarlo, Nov. 25, 1972; children: Michelle Lynn, April Marie. AA, Oreg. Coast Coll., 1971-73; AS in Respiratory Therapy, Blair Coll., 1974. Respiratory therapist McKenzie-Willamette Hosp., Springfield, Oreg., 1978-79; asst. mgr. Singer Machine Co., Eugene, Oreg., 1979-80; respiratory therapist Sacred Heart Gen. Hosp., Eugene, 1980-88; mktg. rep. Linde Home Care Med. Services, Eugene, 1988—; computer online specialist CompuServe; owner, pres. Infotrac Consulting Svcs., Springfield, 1984—. Adv. bd. Home BusinessLine newsletter. Active Metro Area Planning Adv. Com., 1982-83, 85-87, Willamalane Budget Com., 1983-84, Springfield Citizen Involvement Com., 1980-83, Lane County Citizen Involvement Program, 1979-81; mem. adv. com. Sr. & Disabled Svcs., 1989—. Mem. World Future Soc. (coordinator Oreg. chpt.), Northwest Info. Profls. (bd. dirs.), Am. Home Bus. Assn. (bd. dirs., editor newsletter). Democrat. Home: 5780 North E St Springfield OR 97478

MYERS, DONNA MARIE, aerospace executive; b. San Francisco, Sept. 30, 1956; d. Woodrow and Patricia Chiyoko (Chun-Fat) Boettcher; m. Michael Glen Myers, July 21, 1979. BS in Chemistry, San Jose State U., 1979; MBA, Pepperdine U., 1986. Aerospace engr. Rocketdyne, Rockwell Internat., Canoga Park, Calif., 1979-87, assoc. program mgr., 1987—.

MYERS, DOUGLAS GEORGE, zoo administrator; b. Los Angeles, Aug. 30, 1949; s. George Walter and Daydeen (Schroeder) M.; m. Barbara Firestone Myers, Nov. 30, 1980; children: Amy, Andrew. BA, Christopher Newport Coll., 1981. Tour and show supr. Annheuser-Busch (Bird Sanctuary), Van Nuys, Calif., 1970-74, mgr. zool. ops., 1974-75, asst. mgr. ops., 1975-77, mgr. ops., 1977-78; gen. services mgr. Annheuser-Busch (Old Country), Williamsburg, Va., 1978-80, park ops. dir., 1980-81; gen. mgr. wild animal park Zool. Soc. San Diego, 1981-83, dep. dir. ops., 1983-85, exec. dir., 1985—; cons. Econ. Research Assocs., Los Angeles, 1981. Chmn. San Pasqual-Lake Hodges Planning Group, Escondido, Calif., 1982; exec. com. Cen. Balboa Park Assn., San Diego, 1986-87. Profl. fellow Am. Assn. Zool. Parks & Aquariums, Internat. Union Dirs. Zool. Gardens; mem. Internat. Assn. Amusement Parks and Attractions, Internat. Assn. Quality Circles, Calif. Assn. Zoos and Aquariums (chmn. 1986—). Lodge: Rotary. Office: Zool Soc San Diego PO Box 551 San Diego CA 92112

MYERS, DOUGLAS SCOTT, advertising executive; b. Quincy, Ill., Aug. 31, 1954; s. Frank Earl and Joanna Mae (Boss) M.; m. Lisa Marie Hilton, Oct. 11, 1986; 1 child, Ariel Terisse. BBA, U. Ariz., 1977. Account exec. Film Creations, Ltd., Tucson, 1979-80; exec. v.p. GEO & Assocs. Advt., Tucson, 1980-82; producer, dir. Taylor Advt., Tucson, 1982-85; producer, dir., writer Duval Advt., Tucson, 1985-86; pres. Hilton & Myers Advt., Tucson, 1986—. Bd. dirs. Ariz. Dance Theatre, Tucson, 1984-86. Mem. Tucson Advt. Club (Tucson Topps award), Phoenix Advt. Dirs. (Prisma award 1986). Office: Hilton & Myers Advt 325 W Franklin Tucson AZ 85701

MYERS, DOWELL, urban planning educator; b. Miami, Fla., Oct. 10, 1950; s. Gates and Ruth (Dowell) M.; m. Susan Marie Tuemmler, July 3, 1983; children: Benjamin Briggs, Jesse Austin. BA, Columbia U., 1972; MCP, U. Calif., Berkeley, 1975; PhD, MIT, 1981. Asst. prof. U. Cin., 1980-81, U. Tex., Austin, 1981-85, U. Wis., Madison, 1985-88; assoc. prof. urban planning U. So. Calif., L.A., 1988—; pres. Benchmark Real Estate Forecasts, Inc., Madison, 1987-88. Contbr. articles to profl. jours. rsch. grantee NSF, HUD. Mem. Am. Plannning Assn., Am. Real Estate Soc., Population Assn. Am. Home: 1184 Morada Pl Altadena CA 91001 Office: Sch Planning U So Calif Los Angeles CA 90089

MYERS, ELIZABETH ROUSE, management consultant; b. Grand Island, Nebr., July 14, 1923; d. William Wayne Rouse and Lulu Zella Trout; m. Richard Roland Myers, June 25, 1943; children: Diane Marie Berndt, Richard Wayne. Student, Kearny State Tchrs. Coll., Nebr., 1942-43. Draftsman Borg-Warner Corp., Kalamazooo, 1944; acct. CFI Steel Corp., Pueblo, Colo., 1950-52; sec., treas. Standard Paint, Yakima, Wash., 1954-86; pres. Pied Piper Childrens Books, Yakima, Wash., 1985—; federal oil leases 1980—; docent Yakima Valley Mus. & Gilbert House, Wash. 1984—. Editor: High Sch. Paper. Tchr., Supt. First Presbyn. ch., Yakima Wash. 1958-70; Bd. Parent Tchrs.; bd. dirs. teen chmn. YWCA. Mem. Gilbert House & Yakima Valley Mus. (awarded Doll 1985, Show 1986,. Republican. Presbyterian. Home: 106 N 25th Ave Yakima WA 98902

MYERS, ELMER, psychiatric social worker; b. Blackwell, Ark., Nov. 12, 1926; s. Chester Elmer Myers and Irene (Davenport) Lewis; widowed; children: Elmer Jr., Keith, Kevin. BA, U. Kans., 1951, MA, 1962; student, U. Calif., Santa Barbara, 1977-78. Psychiat. social worker Hastings (Nebr.) State Hosp., 1960-62; psychiat. social worker State of Calif., Sacramento, 1962-75, supr. psychiat. social worker, 1975-80; supr. psychiat. social worker Alta Calif. Regional Ctr., Sacramento, 1980-85; exec. dir. Tri-County Family Services, Yuba City, Calif., 1966-69; cons. to 3 convalescent Hosps., Marysville, Calif., 1969-71; lectr. Yuba Coll., Marysville, 1971-76; assoc. prof. Calif. State U., Chico, 1972-73; cons. in field, Marysville, 1985—. Juror Yuba County Grand Jury, Marysville, 1965, 87-88; sec. Y's Men's Club, Yuba City, 1964-65; chmn. Tri-County Home Health Agy., Yuba City, 1974-76; vice-chmn. Gateway Projects, Inc., Yuba City, 1974-75; bd. dirs. Yuba County Truancy Bd., Marysville, 1964-67; bd. dirs. Golden Empire Health Systems Agy., Sacramento, 1972-76; bd. dirs. Youth Services Bur., Yuba City, 1967; bd. dirs. Bi County Mental Retardation Planning Bd., Yuba City, 1972; bd. dirs. Yuba County Juvenile Justice Commn., Marysville, 1982—; bd. dirs. Am. Cancer Soc., Marysville, 1985—; bd. dirs. Yuba County Rep. Cen. Com., 1983—. Recipient Cert. Spl. Recognition Calif. Rehab. Planning Project, 1969, Cert. Spl. Recognition State of Calif., 1967; Cert. Spl. Recognition Alta Calif. Regional Ctrs., 1985. Mem. Nat. Assn. Social Workers (cert.), Kern County Mental Health Assn. (chmn. 1978-79). Lodge: Rotary (bd. dirs. Marysville club 1975-76). Home and Office: 3920 Hwy 20 Marysville CA 95901

MYERS, GAIL ANDERSEN, author, journalist; b. Hartford, Conn., Oct. 14, 1933; d. H. Viggo Andersen and Greta (Sigourney) Andersen-Berendt; m. Robert Glenn Myers Jr., June 18, 1955; children: Abigail A., Melissa M. Smith, John F. (dec.). BA in English, Conn. Coll. Women, 1955. Cert. elem. tchr., N.J. Editorial asst. Oak Leaves, Oak Park, Ill., 1956-57; elem. tchr. Madison Coop. Nursery, Madison, N.J., 1972-74; free-lance writer Poway, Calif., 1974—; workshop leader Phila. Writers' Conf., 1984. Author A World of Sports for Girls, 1981, Fun Sports for Everyone, 1985 (selection Jr. Lit. Guild); contbr. articles to mags. and newspapers. Mem. AAUW, Nat. League Am. Pen Women (pres. Phila. chpt. 1983-85, speaker San Diego workshop 1987), Scribblers (chmn. 1988). Republican. Presbyterian. Club: Welcome Wagon (pres. Rancho Bernardo chpt. 1986). Home and Office: 13331 Tining Dr Poway CA 92064

MYERS, GENE JAY, trainer, adult educator; b. Springfield, Mass., Apr. 19, 1931; s. Elbryn Howard and Miriam Kraybill (Bard) M.; B.A., Pa. State U., 1952; m. Norma Lee Barrett, Sept. 23, 1972. Prin., sr. trainer N.W. Social Systems, Seattle, 1969-74; mgr. tng. Westinghouse Hanford Co., Richland, Wash., 1974-78; nat. seminar adminstr. Pacific Inst., Seattle, 1978-80; instructional design and implementation specialist corp. tng. Morrison-Knudsen Co., Inc., Boise, Idaho, 1980-83; pres. Gene Myers Seminars, 1983—; adj. faculty Western Wash. U.; vocat. instr. Columbia Basin Coll. (Pasco, Wash.). Active Boy Scouts Am., named Commr. of Year, Inland Empire council, 1967, mem. Order of Arrow, 1968. Mem. Am. Soc. Tng. and Devel., Internat. Platform Assn. Episcopalian. Author: Old Style Sioux Costumes, 1968. Office: 3910 Buckingham Pl Boise ID 83704

MYERS, GREGORY EDWIN, aerospace engineer; b. Harrisburg, Pa., Jan. 1, 1960; s. Bernard Eugene and Joyce (Calhoun) M.; m. Susan Ann Hayslett, Dec. 30, 1983; 1 child, Kimberly. BS in Aerospace Engring., U. Mich., 1981; MS in Aerospace Engring., Air Force Inst. Tech., 1982. Aerospace engr. Sperry Comml. Flight Systems group Honeywell, Inc., Phoenix, 1987—. Capt. USAF, 1981-86. Recipient Certs. of Recognition and Appreciation Lompoc Valley Festival Assn., Inc., 1983, Arnold Air Soc. (comdr. 1979). Mem. AIAA. Lutheran. Office: Honeywell Inc Sperry Comml Flight Systems Group 21111 N 19th Ave Phoenix AZ 85036

MYERS, JAMES DAVID, municipal government official; b. Salt Lake City, Sept. 16, 1944; s. James William and Pauline (Winsor) M.; m. Carmen Kay Forsland, Mar. 28, 1979 (div.); stepchildren: James Christopher, Jesse Robin; m. Cleo Ester Evitt, Sept. 20, 1986; stepchild: Jennifer Michelle. Student, U. Calif., Berkeley, 1965; BSBA, Calif. State U., Chico, 1969; MPA, Golden Gate U., 1979. Mgr. Unishops, Inc. (Monte Mart), Del Rey Oaks, Calif., 1968-69; acct.-adminstrv. asst. City of Pacific Grove, 1969-79; mgr. Monterey Regional Waste Mgmt. Dist., Marina, Calif., 1979—; dir., sec. Monterey Fed. Credit Union, 1979—, vice chmn., 1986-87, chmn. supervisory com., 1976-87. Mem. Monterey County Solid Waste Adv. Com., Salinas, Calif., 1979—; dir. Ecology Action of Monterey Peninsula, 1979-82, Milne Home, Residential Treatment Facility for Boys, Carmel Valley, Calif., 1985-87. Sgt. USAF, 1966-72. Mem. Nat. Solid Waste Mgmt. Assn., Calif. Resource Recovery Assn., Governmental Refuse Collection and Disposal Assn. (dir. No. Calif. chpt. 1988—, internat. landfill gas steering com., 1984—, internat. conf. chmn. 1989), Commonwealth Club (San Francisco), Marines' Meml. Club (San Francisco). Democrat. Office: Monterey Regional Waste PO Box 609 Marina CA 93933

MYERS, JEFFREY DONALD, entrepreneurial inventor; b. Phoenix, Mar. 11, 1955; s. Donald Dean and Joan (Lillevig) M.; m. Kim Webber, Mar. 12, 1982. Student, Scottsdale Community Coll., 1974-76, Ariz. State U., 1977-79. Pres. Commerce Fin. Group Ltd., 1981-86, JDM Interests Ltd., Scottsdale, Ariz., 1985—, Miidea Co., Paradise Valley, Ariz., 1986—, What a Character Co., Paradise Valley, 1988—; owner Little Folks Pub., Scottsdale, Ariz., 1986—; pres. Wax Bean Prodn., Scottsdale, 1986—; pres., chief exec. officer Vasco, Charlotte, N.C., 1987—; owner JDM Pub., Scottsdale, 1987—; pres. Nat. Crazemaker Studio, Scottsdale, 1988—. Author: Don't Leave that

Leaf, Boy Who Lost Sight of His Kite, Two Kings; co-inventor internat. lic. characters, Wexler (Little Buddy) and Friends, Desert Dog, Prickly Bear, Wild Hares and Surf Newts from Mars; songwriter: Just Pick One and Dance; creator: photogun, no logo. Mem. exec. coun. Phoenix Boys and Girls Clubs. Mem. Phoenix C. of C., Scottsdale C. of C., Licensing Industry Merchants Assn., Nashville Songwriters Assn., Ariz. Songwriters Assn., Sigma Alpha Epsilon. Republican. Home: PO Box 12485 Phoenix AZ 85267 Office: JDM Interests Ltd 7898 E Acoma Ste 209 Scottsdale AZ 85260

MYERS, PAUL REED, educational psychologist, consultant, trainer; b. Fresno, Calif., Aug. 31, 1948; s. Walter Joseph and Norma (Schneider) M.; m. Donna Jean Stokes, Jan. 23, 1971; children: Eric, Judson, Brent, Shelley, Grant, Rebecca, Jeff, Cindy. BA magna cum laude, Calif. State U., Fresno, 1973; MA, Brigham Young U., 1981; postgrad., Utah State U., 1983, U. No. Colo., 1984. Standard teaching credential, Calif.; basic profl. cert., Utah. Camp commr. Boy Scouts Am., Fresno, 1970-73; custodian Fresno Unified Sch. Dist., 1973-74, tchr. adult spl. edn., 1974-79; dir. tng. programs ARC, Fresno, 1976-79; rsch. intern spl. edn. dept. Brigham Young U., Provo, Utah, 1979-80; profl. coord. staff devel. Utah State Tng. Sch., American Fork, 1980-82; dir. rehab. svcs. C.U.E., Provo, 1982-85; pres. South Valley Tng. Co., Inc., Sandy, Utah, 1985—, How-to Tng. & Resources Co., Orem, Utah, 1988—. Pres. bd. dirs. Alpine House for Mentally Ill, Provo, 1982-84, Utah County South unit ARC, 1984-85; bishop LDS Ch., Orem, 1985—; chmn. troop com. 445, Boy Scouts Am., Orem, 1985-89; v.p. bd. dirs. Kids on Move, Inc., Orem, 1986—; coach Babe Ruth Baseball League, Orem, 1988-89; mem. think tank Alpine Sch. Dist., Orem, 1988. Mem. Assn. for Persons with Sevre Handicaps, Assn. for Retarded Citizens (bd. dirs. 1982), Am. Soc. for Tng. and Staff Devel., Utah Assn. Rehab. Facilities (chmn. tng. com. 1982-83, pres.-elect 1983, award of appreciation 1982), Athletic Congress, Phi Kappa Phi. Republican. Home: 294 North 400 West Orem UT 84057 Office: South Valley Tng Co Inc 455 West 9160 South Sandy UT 84070

MYERS, PERDITA HORN, teacher; b. Orange, Calif., Aug. 3, 1932; d. Robert Goodlin and Gertrude Beatrice (McKinley) Horn; m. Orville Myers, June 26, 1960; children: Roberta, Paula. BA, Pomona Coll., Claremont, Calif., 1954. Tchr. Burbank (Calif.) High Sch., 1956-58; asst lighting dir. Olesen Co., Hollywood, Calif., 1958-60; substitute tchr. various sch. dists., Calif., 1960-62, Orange, Calif., 1984--. Drama coord. Pomona Coll., Claremont, Calif., 1962-63; dir. Civic Light Opera, Burbank, Calif., 1958-59; judge Community Players, Santa Ana, Calif., 1969-72. Mem. AAUW (named Gift Honoree, 1978), Phi Beta Kappa. Republican. Presbyterian.

MYERS, PHILLIP FENTON, business executive; b. Cleve., June 24, 1935; s. Max I. and Rebecca (Rosenbloom) M.; m. Hope Gail Strum, Aug. 13, 1961. B.I.E., Ohio State U., 1958, M.B.A., 1960; D.B.A., Harvard U., 1966. Staff indsl. engr. Procter & Gamble Co., Cin., 1958; sr. cons. Cresap, McCormack & Paget, N.Y.C., 1960-61; staff assoc. Mitre Corp., Bedford, Mass., 1961; cons. Systems Devel. Corp., Santa Monica, Calif., 1963-64; corp. asst. long range planning Electronic Specialty Co., Los Angeles, 1966-68; chmn. Atek Industries, 1968-72; pres. Myers Fin. Corp., 1973—, Steel Fuels Corp., 1976-77; chmn. Amvid Communication Services, Inc., 1975-79, Gen. Hydrogen Corp. Am., 1976-79, Omni Resources Devel. Corp., 1979-83; chmn., pres. Am. Internat. Mining Co., Inc., 1979-83; pres. Whitehall Internat. Mgmt. Co., Inc., 1982—, Global Bond Mktg. Services, Inc., 1987—; gen. ptnr. Pacific Internat. Devel. Co., 1985—; founding dir. Warner Ctr. Bank, 1980-83; lectr. bus. adminstrn. U. So. Calif., Los Angeles, 1967-74; prof. Pepperdine U. Grad. Sch. Bus. Adminstrn., 1974-81. Trustee, treas. Chamber Symphony Soc. Calif., 1971-78; pub. safety commr. City of Hidden Hills, Calif., 1977-83, chmn., 1982-83; co-chmn. budget adv. com. Las Virgenas Sch. Dist., 1983-86; mem. Mayor's Blue Ribbon Fin. Com., 1981-82; mem. dean's select adv. com. Coll. Engring., Ohio State U., 1984—; mem. state exec. com. Calif. Libertarian Party, chmn. region 61. Served to capt. USAF, 1958-60. Ford Found. fellow, 1961-64. Mem. Harvard Bus. Sch. Assn., Ohio State Alumni Assn. Club: Harvard of So. Calif. (bd. dirs. 1970-74, treas. 1971-73). Home and Office: 5819 Fitzpatrick Rd Ste 1000 Calabasas CA 91302

MYERS, ROBERT DAVID, lawyer; b. Springfield, Mass., Nov. 20, 1937; s. William and Pearl (Weiss) M.; m. Judith G. Dickenman, July 1, 1962; children—Mandy Susan, Jay Brandt, Seth William. A.B., U. Mass., 1959; J.D., Boston U., 1962. Bar: Ariz. bar 1963. Practice in Phoenix, 1963—; mem. firm Hofmann, Salcito, Stevens & Myers, 1966—; pro tem judge Superior Ct. of, Maricopa County, Ariz., Ct. Appeals; Chmn. com. on exams. and admissions Ariz. Supreme Ct., 1974-75, chmn. com. on character and fitness, 1975-76, mem. multi-state bar exam. com., 1976—. Pres. Valley of Sun chpt. City of Hope, 1965-66, Community Orgn. for Drug Abuse Control, 1972-73, Valley Big Bros., 1975; chmn. Mayors Ad Hoc Com. on Drug Abuse, 1974-75; bd. dirs. Maricopa County Legal Aid Soc., 1978, Phoenix Jewish Community Center; sec. Jud. Selection Adv. Com. of City of Phoenix. Mem. Ariz. Bar Assn. (gov., com. chmn., sect. pres.), Maricopa County Bar Assn. (dir., pres. 1979-80), Assn. Trial Lawyers Am. (nat. chmn. gov.), Ariz. Trial Lawyers Assn. (pres., dir., co-editor Newsletter), Phoenix Trial Lawyers Assn. (pres., dir.), Western Trial Lawyers Assn. (pres. 1977), Am. Arbitration Assn. (nat. panel arbitrators), Am. Judicature Soc. (spl. merit citation outstanding service improvement of adminstrn. justice 1986), Am. Bd. Trial Advocates. Office: Hofmann Salcito Stevens & Myers 302 E Coronado St Phoenix AZ 85004

MYERS, ROBERT JOSEPH, telecommunications systems consultant; b. Lima, Ohio, Apr. 27, 1922; s. John Henry and Edna Ann (Hill) M.; children: Bruce, Nancy, John, Robert, Daniel. Student, Iowa State U., 1943, Cornell U., 1944-46, NYU, 1947-48. With U.S. Dept. of Justice, Washington, 1940-41, Engring. and Rsch. Corp., Riverdale, Md., 1941-42; project engr. TV, computers, simulators, teletype Office Naval Rsch. & Devel., Sands Point, N.Y., 1946-48, USN Mus. Sci. and Industry, Rockefeller Ctr., N.Y.C., 1946-48; we. dist. mgr. TV transmission div. Allen B. DuMont Labs., Clifton, N.J., 1948-56; pres., gen. mgr., owner, cons. Indsl. TV, L.A., Calif., 1956--; founder, pres. cons. Crest TV, Century City, Calif., 1964--; cons. in field. Inventor in field--TV broadcasting stas., microwave TV relay systems. Mem. Gov.'s Adv. Commn. for Ednl. TV in Calif., 1960. Served with USN, 1942-47. Home: 2131 Fox Hills Dr Los Angeles CA 90025 Office: Crest TV 67607 Century City Sta Los Angeles CA 90067-0607

MYERS, STEVEN BRETT, accountant, company executive; b. Washington, Ind., Apr. 15, 1960; s. Ralph Gale and Marcella Ann (Hunter) M.; m. Michelle Renee Miller, July 7, 1984 (div. Mar. 1987); 1 child, Ashley Ann. Student, Lincolnland Community Coll., Springfield, Ill., 1978-80; BSBA in Acctg., Ill. Coll., 1983. Office mgr. Western Energy Inc., Loveland, Colo., 1983-85; contr. Gold, Inc. (doing bus. as Goldbug), Denver, 1985-89, dir. computer ops., 1989—. Mem. Delta Mu Delta. Home: 13400 Albrook Dr Apt A314 Denver CO 80239 Office: Gold Inc 4999 Oakland St Denver CO 90239

MYERS MEDEIROS, PATRICIA JO, entrepreneur; b. Cairo, Ill., July 24, 1942; d. Leon Lester and Thelma Elizabeth (Frey) Jones; m. Zan Albert Myers, Mar. 30, 1967 (div. Jan. 1983); 1 child, Zan Robert; m. Gene Alexander Medeiros, Dec. 31, 1988. Student, Sawyer Sch. Computer Sci., North Hollywood, Calif., 1961, Living Waters Bible Coll., Pasadena, Calif., 1975, Narramore Found. Psychology, Rosemead, Calif., 1980, Richards Hairmasters U., Ontario, Calif., 1988. Computer scientist C. F. Braun Internat., Alhambra, Calif., 1965-67, Fluor Corp., Irvine, Calif., 1967-70; psychol. counselor Living Waters, Pasadena, 1973-76, Christian Ctr., Arcadia, Calif., 1977-86; real estate investor Upland, Calif., 1983-88; tchr. personal enrichment clubs and classes Narramore Christian Found., Rosemead, 1979-85; investor Valencia and Upland, Calif., 1983—; tchr. counselor tng. seminars Narramore Found., Rosemead, 1980-89, fin. freedom seminars various locations, 1983-89, Richards Hairmasters U., Ontario, Calif., 1988. Mem. Rep. Senatorial Inner Circle, Upland, 1985-88; mem. Dare Program-Dare to Keep Kids Off Drugs, Upland, Valencia, 1985; supporter Handicap Children Through Upland, Valencia, Ontario and San Bernardino (Calif.) Police, 1985-88; active ARC.

MYHREN, TRYGVE EDWARD, communications company executive; b. Palmerton, Pa., Jan. 3, 1937; s. Arne Johannes and Anita (Blatz) M.; m. Carol Jane Enman, Aug. 8, 1964; children: Erik, Kirsten, Tor; m. 2d Victoria Hamilton, Nov. 14, 1981; 1 stepdau., Paige. B.A. in Philosophy and Polit. Sci., Dartmouth Coll., 1958, M.B.A., 1959. Sales mgr., unit mgr. Procter and Gamble, Cin., 1963-65; sr. cons. Glendinning Cos., Westport, Conn., 1965-69; pres. Auberge Vintners, 1970-73; exec. v.p. Mktg. Continental, Westport, 1969-73; v.p., gen. mgr. CRM, Inc., Del Mar, Calif., 1973-75; v.p. mktg. Am. TV and Communications Corp., Englewood, Colo., 1975-78, sr. v.p. mktg. and programming, 1978-79, exec. v.p., 1980, pres., 1981, chmn. bd., chief exec. officer, 1982-88; pres. Myhren Media, 1989—; v.p. Time Inc., N.Y.C., 1981-86; treas., vice chmn., then chmn. bd., mem. exec com. Nat. Cable TV Assn., Washington, 1982—; mem. FCC Adv. Com. on HDTV, 1987—; bd. dirs. Turner Broadcasting, Atlanta, NovaNet Inc., Englewood, Advanced Mktg. Systems Inc., La Jolla. Vice chmn. Pub. Edn. Coalition; mem. Colo. Forum, 1984—, chmn. higher edn. com., 1986; bd. dirs., founder Colo. Bus. Com. for the Arts, 1985—; mem. exec. council Found. for Commemoration U.S. Constn., 1987—; mem. Nat. GED Task Force, 1987—. Served to lt. (j.g.) USN, 1959-62. Recipient Disting. Leader award Nat. Cable TV Assn., 1988. Mem. Cable TV Adminstrn. and Mktg. Soc. (pres. 1978-79, Grand Tam award 1985), Dartmouth Assn. Gt. Divide (trustee 1982-85), Cable Adv. Bur. (founder 1978). Episcopalian.

MYLES, ALLEN HAROLD, SR., industrial relations specialist; b. Montgomery, Ala., May 8, 1937; s. Leonard and Adell (Jackson) M.; m. Lorene Dixon, Feb. 2, 1957; children: Cheryl La-Kay Reddick, Kevin Gregory, Allen Harold Jr., Michael Edwin. AA, AS in Acctg., Southwestern Coll., Chula Vista, Calif., 1975; BSBA, Coll. Nortre Dame, Belmont, Calif., 1980; MBA, Coll. Nortre Dame, 1983. Enlisted USN, 1955, advanced through ranks to master chief petty officer, 1967; supr., mgr. USN, Milton, Fla., 1965-69, Iwakuni, Japan, 1970-73, Mountain View, Calif., 1975-79; ret. USN, 1979; gen. foreman Nat. Semiconductor Corp., Santa Clara, Calif., 1980-85; supr. Dept. Def., San Bruno, Calif., 1985—. Tchr. Bapt. Sunday sch. Mem. NAACP, Masons. Democrat. Home: 2148 Muirwood Ct San Jose CA 95132

MYLES, MARGARET JEAN, hospital supplies buyer, real property appraiser; b. Detroit, Oct. 26, 1952; d. William Thompson and Patricia (Maclean) M. Student, Western Mich. U., 1973, Oakland U., 1974; AA, Coast Line Coll., 1986. Unit sec. Hoag Meml. Hosp., Newport Beach, Calif., 1976-80, buyer, 1981-86; real estate appraiser P.M. Myles & Assocs., Irvine, Calif., 1980—. Home: 120 A Carriage Dr Santa Ana CA 92707 Office: PM Myles & Assocs 25 Mandrake Way Irvine CA 92715

MYREN, ALBEN THEODORE, industrial engineer, air pollution consultant; b. Oak Park, Ill., Dec. 2, 1944; s. Alben Theodore and Leola Carolyn (Tews) M.; m. Ilse Margrethe Jensen, Oct. 20, 1969; children: Alben Theodore, Jebadiah T., Orion B., Thyer L. BS in Animal Sci., U. Ill, 1967; postgrad., U. No. Iowa, 1972-74, U. Mont., 1974-78. Indsl. engr. Rath Packing Co., Waterloo, Iowa, 1969-74; v.p. ops. Inter Mountain Ambient, Missoula, Mont., 1977—. With U.S. Army, 1967-69. Office: Inter Mountain Ambient PO Box 5106 Missoula MT 59806

MYRTLE, ROBERT CHARLES, public administration educator; b. London, Ont., Can., Jan. 1, 1940; came to U.S., 1956; s. Raymond I. and Lillian C. (Martin) M.; m. Alice E. Dietz, Dec. 20, 1969; 1 child, Robert James. AA, Compton Coll., 1963; BS, Calif. State U., 1965; MPA, U. So. Calif., 1972, D of Pub. Adminstrn., 1975. Prodn. mgr. Interchem. Corp., L.A., 1960-65; mgmt. analyst Dept. Adoptions, L.A., 1967-69; hosp. adminstr. Dept. Hosps., L.A., 1969-75; asst. prof. U. So. Calif., L.A., 1975-83, assoc. prof., 1983—; chmn. bd. Sr. Care Action Network, Long Beach, Calif., 1982—, Bd. Health and Human Svcs., Long Beach, 1982—; vice-chmn. Hosps. Commn., L.A., 1983—. Author: Managing Public Systems, 1980, Public Personnel Adminstration, 1984; contbr. articles to profl. jours. Mem. City of Long Beach Strategic Planning Com., 1983-84. With U.S. Army, 1965-67, Fed. Republic Germany. USPHS fellow Dept. Health and Human Svcs., 1970-72. Mem. Am. Soc. Tng., Acad. of Mgmt., Am. Coll. Healthcare Execs., Am. Mktg. Assn. Office: U So Calif Sch Pub Adminstrn Los Angeles CA 90089-0041

NAAR, JOSEPH THOMAS, film producer; b. San Diego, Apr. 25, 1925; s. Richard and Sara (Meyer) N.; m. Dolores Naar Nemiro (div. 1979); children: Peter, Sharman, Andrew; m. Barbara Rand Naar, Dec. 31, 1983. BA in Lit., UCLA, 1950. Agt. William Morris Agy., Los Angeles, 1950-55; assoc. producer Universal, Los Angeles, 1956-62; with ind. motion picture prodn. sect. Am. Internat. Pictures, Los Angeles, 1963-70; agt., v.p. Creative Mgmt. Assn., Los Angeles, 1971-74; TV producer Spelling Goldberg, Los Angeles, 1975-84; sr. v.p. Blake Edwards TV, Los Angeles, 1985-86; with ind. prodn. devel. sect. Orion Pictures, Los Angeles, 1987; ind. film producer Joseph T. Naar Prodns., Los Angeles, 1988—. Producer: (movies) Blacula, All-Am. Boy, (TV) Starsky and Hutch (People's Choice award, 1978, 79), GE Theater, Checkmate, Schlitz Playhouse, Chrysler Theater; co-creator: Hart to Hart, Patrol Torpedo Boats. Served with U.S. Navy, 1943-46. Decorated Silver Star, Presdl. citation.

NACHMAN, RICHARD JOSEPH, management executive; b. Washington, Sept. 18, 1944; s. Joseph Frank and Rosemary (Anderson) N.; m. Nancy Ruth Hodgson, Feb. 4, 1966 (div. Oct. 1975); children: Russell J., Kirk L.; m. Christina Maria Schulz, Jan. 2, 1979; 1 child, William C. Hoff. BA, U. Colo., 1968. Program dir. mgmt. edn. Grad. Sch. Bus. U. Mich., Ann Arbor, 1968-70; dir. Ctr. Mgmt. and Tech. Programs Sch. Bus. U. Colo., Boulder, 1970-74; pres. Mgmt. Rsch. Corp., Loveland, 1974—, RJN and Assocs., Loveland, 1977—. Contbr. articles to profl. publs.; producer seminars, video tng. materials The Art of Negotiating, The One Minute Manager, Japanese Manufacturing Techniques, World Class Manufacturing. Mem. Fellowship of Cos. for Christ. Republican.

NACHT, SERGIO, biochemist; b. Buenos Aires, Apr. 13, 1934; came to U.S., 1965; s. Oscar and Carmen (Scheiner) N.; m. Beatriz Kahan, Dec. 21, 1958; children: Marcelo H., Gabriel A., Mariana S., Sandra M. BA in Chemistry, U. Buenos Aires, 1958, MS in Biochemistry, 1960, PhD in Biochemistry, 1964. Asst. prof. biochemistry U. Buenos Aires, 1960-64; asst. prof. medicine U. Utah, Salt Lake City, 1965-70; rsch. scientist Alza Corp., Palo Alto, Calif., 1970-73; sr. investigator Richardson-Vicks Inc., Mt. Vernon, N.Y., 1973-76; asst. dir., dir. rsch. Richardson-Vicks Inc., Mt. Vernon, 1976-83; dir. biomed. rsch. Richardson-Vicks Inc., Shelton, Conn., 1983-87; v.p. rsch. and devel. Advanced Polymer Systems, Redwood City, Calif., 1987—; lectr. dermatology dept. SUNY Downstate Med. Ctr., Bklyn., 1977-87. Contbr. articles to profl. jours.; patentee in field. Mem. Soc. Investigative Dermatology, Soc. Cosmetic Chemists (award 1981), Dermatology Found., Am. Physiological Soc., Am. Acad. Dermatology. Democrat. Jewish. Home: 289 Quinnhill Ave Los Altos CA 94022

NACHT, STEVE JERRY, geologist; b. Cleve., July 8, 1948; s. Max and Elfrida (Kamm) N.; m. Patricia Katherine Osicka, Aug. 3, 1976; 1 child, David Martin. BS in Geology, Kent State U., 1971, MS in Geology, 1973; Ms in Environ. Scis., Cleve. State U., 1979. Registered geologist, S.C., Va., environ. assessor, Calif.; cert. geologist, Ind.; lic. drinking water treatment class III, Ohio. Geologist Cleve. Utilities Dept., 1974-78; geologist, hydrologist Dalton, Dalton & Newport, Cleve., 1979-82; prin. scientist Lockheed-Emsco, Las Vegas, Nev., 1983-86; sr. geologist, project mgr. Earth Tech. Inc., Long Beach, Calif., 1986-87; sr. geologist, project mgr. The MARK Group, Las Vegas, 1987—, dir. waste tech. Contbr. articles to profl. jours. Mem. AAAS, Am. Inst. Profl. Geologists (cert.), Assn. Ground Water Scientists and Engrs. (jour. reviewer), Assn. Engring. Geologists, ASTM (com. mem. groundwater, chmn. sect., chmn. ground water monitoring, well maintenance, rehab. and abandonment sect.). Home: 4184 Del Rosa Ct Las Vegas NV 89121 Office: The MARK Group 2300 Paseo Del Prado D108 Las Vegas NV 98102

NADDEO, FRANK C., sales executive; b. Huntington Park, Calif., Feb. 4, 1947; s. Joseph Ralph and Frances Pauline (Fergurski) N.; married, July 8, 1973, (div. Feb. 1975); m. Carole Lee Sands, Nov. 11, 1978. Cert., Don Martin Sch. Radio and TV, Hollywood, Calif., 1970; AA, Coll. of the Redwoods, 1974. Lic. 1st class radio telephone. Sr. communication coordinator Crocker Nat. Bank, San Francisco, 1974-75; dir. KOLO-TV, Reno, Nev., 1975-76; prin. Stone Svcs., Ltd., Lagunitas, Calif., 1976; prodn. mgr. KOBI-TV, Medford, Oreg., 1976-78; prodn. asst. KFMB-TV, San Diego, 1978-79; nat. sales mgr. Swiss Colony Stores, Inc., Monroe, Wis., 1979-85; dir. ops., west 1 Potato 2, Inc., Colorado Springs, 1985-86; dir. ops. Co. West, Inc., Colorado Springs, 1986-88; nat. sales mgr. Comstock Creations, Inc., Durango, Colo., 1988-89; pvt. practice mktg. and retail cons., Durango, 1989—; health cons., Grand Rapids, Mich., 1983-85. Author, editor: (internal tng. manuals), Sales, Operations and OSHA Procedures, 1983-89. With USN, 1964-67, Pacific, Hawaii, Vietnam. Mem. Am. Mgmt. Assn., U.S. Golf Assn. Republican. Office: PO Box 5075 Durango CO 81301

NADELL, ANDREW THOMAS, psychiatrist; b. N.Y.C., Nov. 3, 1946; s. Samuel Tyler and Bertha Elaine (Trupine) N. MA, Columbia U., 1968; MSc, U. London, 1973; MD, Duke U., 1974. Diplomate Am. Bd. Psychiatry and Neurology. Resident in psychiatry U. Calif., Davis, 1974-77; clin. instr. psychiatry Stanford (Calif.) U. Sch. Medicine, 1979-84, clin. asst. prof. psychiatry, 1984—. Fellow Royal Soc. Medicine; mem. Am. Psychiat. Assn., Am. Assn. History of Medicine, Am. Osler Soc., Bay Area History Medicine Soc. (sec. 1984-88, v.p. 1988—), Soc. for Social History Medicine, Assn. Internat. de Bibliophilie, Soc. Internat. d'Histoire de la Médecine, Stanford U. Libraries Assocs. (adv. council 1988—). Clubs: University (San Francisco); Grolier (N.Y.C.); Roxburghe, Colophon, Commonwealth, Book of Calif. (San Francisco). Office: 1828 El Camino Real Burlingame CA 94010

NADLER, GEORGE L., orthodondist; b. Bklyn., Jan. 13, 1939; s. Rudolph M. and Hannah (Helfman) N.; m. Essie Rubinstein, Jun4 4, 1961; children: Rudolph M, Eric Marc. Student, Bkly. Coll., 1956-59; DDS, NYU Coll. of Dentistry, 1963, postgrad., 1966-70. Diplomate Am. Bd. Orthodontia, 1979. Intern L.I. Coll. Hosp., Bklyn., 1963-64; pvt. practice Bklyn., 1966-70, Tucson, Ariz., 1970—; cons. El Rio Health Ctr., Tucson, 1973—. Contbr. articles to profl. jours. Cons. Ariz. Crippled Children Svc., Tucson, 1973—. With USPHS, 1964-66. Fellow NIH, 1961, 62. Mem. ADA, Ariz. Dental Assn., So. Ariz. Dental Assn., Am. Assn. Orthodontists, Pacific Coast Orthodontic Assn., Ariz. Orthodontic Study Club, Tucson Orthodontic Study Club, Tucson Orthodontic Soc. (pres. 1980-81), Ariz. State Orthodontic Soc. (pres. 1988—), Angle Orthodontic Soc., Golden Key, Skyline Country Club, Omicron Kappa Upsilon. Home: 6822 N Longfellow Rd Tucson AZ 85718 Office: 5610 E Grant Rd Tucson AZ 85712

NADLER, GERALD, industrial engineering educator; b. Cin., Mar. 12, 1924; s. Samuel and Minnie (Krumbein) N.; m. Elaine Muriel Dubin, June 22, 1947; children: Burton Alan, Janice Susan, Robert Daniel. Student, U. Cin., 1942-43; BSME, Purdue U., 1945, MS in Indsl. Engring, 1946, PhD, 1949. Registered profl. engr., Mo., Wis. Instr. Purdue U., 1948-49; asst. prof. indsl. engring. Washington U., St. Louis, 1949-52, assoc. prof., 1952-55, prof., head dept. indsl. engring., 1955-64; prof. U. Wis., Madison, 1964-83, chmn. dept. indsl. engring., 1964-67, 71-75; prof., chmn. dept. indsl. and systems engring. U. So. Calif., L.A., 1983—, IBM prof. engring. mgmt., 1986—; v.p. Artcraft Mfg. Co., St. Louis, 1956-57; dir. Intertherm Inc., St. Louis, 1969-85; pres. Planning, Design, and Improvement Methods Group, L.A., 1980—; vis. prof. U. Birmingham, Eng., 1959, Waseda U., Tokyo, 1963, Ind. U., 1964, U. Louvain, Belgium, 1975, Technion-Israel Inst. Tech., Haifa, 1976; speaker in field. Author: Work Design: A Systems Concept, 1970, (with J. T. Johnston and J. E. Bailey) Design Concepts for Information Systems, 1975, (with M. Norton and W.C. Bozeman) Student Planned Acquisition of Required Knowledge, 1980, The Planning and Design Approach, 1981; contbr. numerous articles to profl. jours.; reviewer books, papers, proposals. Pantentee ultrasonic measurement of body movements. Mem. Ladue Bd. Edn., St. Louis County, 1960-63; acting exec. dir. Higher Edn. Coordinating Coun. Met. St. Louis, 1962-63; chmn. planning com. Wis. Regional Med. Program, 1966-69, mem. steering com., 1969-73. Served with USN, 1943-45. Recipient Gilbreth medal Soc. Advancement Mgmt., 1961; Editorial award Hosp. Mgmt. Mag., 1966; Disting. Engring. Alumnus award Purdue U., 1975; Inst. Indsl. Engrs. Book of Yr. award, 1983. Fellow AAAS, Inst. Indsl. Engrs. (pres. 1989—); mem. Am. Soc. Engring. Edn., Inst. Mgmt. Scis., AAUP, Nat. Acad. Engring., World Future Soc., Japan Work Design Soc. (hon. adv. 1968—), Coun. Understanding of Tech. in Human Affairs (bd. dirs.), Sigma Xi, Alpha Pi Mu (nat. officer), Pi Tau Sigma, Omega Rho, Tau Beta Pi. Office: University Park GER 240 Los Angeles CA 90089-0193

NADY, JOHN, electronics company executive; b. Agfalva, Hungary, Feb. 13, 1945; came to U.S., 1951; s. John and Hermine Nady. BSEE, Calif. Inst. Tech., 1968; MSEE, U. Calif., Berkeley, 1968. Elec. engr. Lawrence Radiation Lab., Livermore, 1966-71, Westinghouse Corp., Oakland, Calif., 1971-72; owner, chief exec. officer Nady Systems, Inc., Oakland, Calif., 1976—, Club Omni, Inc., Oakland, Calif., 1985—. Patentee in field. Mem. Nat. Assn. Broadcasters, Audio Engring. Soc., Nat. Assn. Music Merchants. Office: Nady Systems Inc 1145 65th St Oakland CA 94608

NAEGELE, JOSEPH LOYOLA, SR., lawyer; b. San Francisco, July 19, 1955; s. Charles Frederick and Rosemary Cecilia (Ledogar) N.; m. BeaLisa Elizabeth Sydlik, Feb. 21, 1981; children: Joseph Loyola Jr., Elizabeth Anne. BA, U. Calif., Davis, 1977; JD, U. Calif., San Francisco, 1981. Bar: Calif. 1982. Legal intern U.S. Congress, Washington, 1976; legal extern Calif. Ct. Appeals, San Francisco, 1980; law clk. U.S. Dist. Ct., San Francisco, 1981, Sacramento Dist. Atty.'s Office, Sacramento, 1982; tchr. St. Francis High Sch., Sacramento, 1982; atty. Law Offices of Jack Komar, San Jose, Calif., 1983-85; ptnr. Naegele & Naegele, San Jose, 1985—; prof. Lincoln Law Sch., San Jose, 1983-85. Mem. Santa Clara County Bar Assn., Calif. Trial Lawyers Assn., Santa Clara County Trial Lawyers Assn., St. Thomas Moore Soc., Barristers Club. Roman Catholic. Home: 1105 Loupe Ave San Jose CA 95121 Office: 111 W St John St Ste 650 San Jose CA 95113-1105

NAFF, ROBERT BURNS, management consultant; b. Anchorage, Dec. 23, 1944; s. Robert Burns and Ferol Genevieve (Weber) N.; m. Cristina Bueno, Dec. 10, 1971; 1 child, Robert Brian. BBA, Columbia Pacific U., 1988. Technician RCA Service Co., Cherry Hill, N.J., 1966-67; mgr. ops. Page Communications, Vienna, Va., 1967-73; mgr. employee relations Page Communications, Vienna, 1973-75, Computer Sci. Corp., Falls Church, Va., 1975-77, ITT Corp., Fed. Republic of Germany, 1977-79; mgr. employee relations ITT/FSI, Colorado Springs, Colo., 1979-86, mgr. quality assurance, 1986-87; pres. Mgmt. Recruiters of Lynnwood (Wash.), 1987—; chmn. supervisory com. Credit Union, Colorado Springs, 1982—. Served with U.S. Army, 1963-66, Vietnam. Mem. Armed Forces Communications and Electronics Assn. Republican. Episcopalian. Home: 691 Grey Eagle Circle S Colorado Springs CO 80919

NAFZIGER, SANFORD ERNEST, transportation executive; b. Salem Oreg., Jan. 4, 1953; s. William Edgar and Shirley Adel (Roth) N.; m. Susan Carol Lunoe, Jan. 28, 1978; 1 child, Sarah. AA, Green River Community Coll., Auburn, Wash., 1974; student, Christian Heritage Coll., San Diego, 1974-77; BS, Western Bapt. Coll., Salem, 1984. Air traffic controller FAA, Ephrata, Wash., 1977-79, Walla Walla, Wash., 1979-81, Salem, 1981-87, Gt. Falls, Mont., 1987—. Mem. Nat. Air Traffic Controllers Assn. Republican. Home: 2736 Carmel Great Falls MT 59404 Office: FAA Air Traffic Control Tower Gt Falls Internat Airport Great Falls MT 59404

NAGEL, JANET IRENE, banker; b. Am. Fork, Utah, July 17, 1953; d. Robert George and Nina Lucille (Webb) N. BA with honors, Calif. State U., Fullerton, 1984. Cert. elem. tchr. Comml. and savs. teller Union Bank, Orange, Calif., 1971-72; note teller Union Bank, Fullerton, 1972-75, utility service clk., 1975-76, asst. ops. officer, 1976-77; installment loan officer Lloyds Bank Calif. (now Sanwa Bank Calif.), 1977-79, asst. mgr., comml. loan officer, 1979-82; ind. bank examiner Janet I. Nagel, Inc., Irvine, Calif., 1985—. Vol. Big Sisters Orange County, Garden Grove, Calif., 1973-82. Mem. Nat. Assn. Bank Women (bd. dirs. Orange County chpt. 1980), Golden Key Honor Soc. Republican. Presbyterian.

NAGEL, JEROME KAUB, architect; b. Denver, Dec. 26, 1923; s. Fritz Andrew and Josephine (Gaylord) N.; m. Cynthia Fels, Sept. 1, 1951; children—Peter Barry, James Gaylord. B.Arch., Yale U., 1949. Registered architect, Colo. Prin. J.K. Nagel Architect, Denver, 1953-61, Rogers & Nagel, Denver, 1961-66, Rogers, Nagel, Langhart, Architects, 1966-77, Interplan Inc., 1969-77; pres. Nagel Investment Co.; dir. Bank Western, Denver, Field Devel. Corp., Denver. Mem. Colo. Hwy. Commn., chmn., 1982-83; bd. dirs. Planned Parenthood Fed. Am. Inc., N.Y.C., 1974-78, Rocky Mountain Planned Parenthood, Denver, 1972-76, Colo. chpt. ARC,

1957-60, 80-81, Denver Santa Clus Shop, 1987—; mem. panel arbitrators Am. Arbitration Assn., 1962—; chmn. Colo. Bicycle Adv. Bd. Served to 1st lt. AC U.S. Army, 1943-45. Decorated D.F.C., Air medal with 11 oak leaf clusters. Mem. AIA (nat. life; sec. chpt. 1960-61, pres. 1962-63), Denver Country (bd. dirs. 1983-86), University (bd. dirs. 1962-66) Mile High, Rotary. Republican. Episcopalian. Home: 67 Eudora St Denver CO 80220

NAGEL, RONALD CURTIS, electrical engineer; b. Park Ridge, Ill., June 29, 1961; s. Robert Ira and Edda (Hoerer) N. BSEE, U. Ariz., 1986. Intern engr. GTE R & D Labs., Phoenix, 1980, Motorola Microsystems, Scottsdale, Ariz., 1981-82, IBM, Tucson, 1983, Computer Automation, Tucson, 1983; cons. Nagel Electronics, Chgo., 1984—; engr. Zenith Corp., Chgo., 1985; engr., project leader NATO program Motorola GEG, Tempe, Ariz., 1986—. Active Nat. Rep. Com., Washington, 1987—. Mem. IEEE, Mensa, Rod and Gun Club Tucson, Phi Eta Sigma, Tau Beta Pi. Jewish. Home: 2853 S El Marino Mesa AZ 85202 Office: Motorola GEG 8201 E McDowell Scottsdale AZ 85252

NAGER, STEVE (ACE), international marketing company executive, chemist; b. N.Y.C., Mar. 26, 1949; s. Murray and Judy (Von) N.; divorced; children: Eric Channing, Chanelle. BS in Chemistry, Bklyn. Coll., 1964; MA in Chemistrymagna cum laude, CUNY, 1965; diploma in space sci., NASA, 1965, PIB, NYU, 1975; MBA in Internat. Mktg., Fordham U., 1975; PhD in ChemE, Applied Rsch. Inst., Netherlands, 1988. Lic. chemistry tchr. Internat. area mgr. Mobil Oil Co., N.Y.C., 1968-75; v.p. Carbonit, Netherlands, 1975-77; gen. mgr. Mitsui, Houston, 1977-80; dir. Sobin Trading, Houston, 1980-82; pres. Nager Internat., Houston, 1982-85, San Diego, 1985—. Vol. pub. spl. assignments Space & Def. Systems, USAF, Grumman Aerospace, NASA, DOD, CIA. Recipient cert. Internat. Exec. Assoc., 1970, Am. Mgrs. Assn. award, 1968, Spl. award Chem. Mktg. Rsch. Assn.,1975, plaque CIA, 1975. Mem. Mensa, Phi Betta Kappa, Kappa Delta Pi, Sierra Club, Libertarian, Humanist. Home and Office: 3050 Rue D'Orleans Ste #318 San Diego CA 92110

NAGER, (HARVEY) STEVEN, marketing professional, chemist; b. N.Y.C., Mar. 26, 1944; s. Murray and Judy (Von) N.; divorced; children: Eric Channing, Chanelle. BS in Chemistry, Bklyn. Coll., 1964; MA in Chemistry magna cum laude, CUNY, 1985; diploma in space sci., NASA, 1965; PIB, NYU, 1975; MBA in Internat. Mktg., Fordham U., 1975; PhD in ChemE, Netherlands Rsch. Inst., 1988. Cert. chemistry tchr., N.Y. Internat. area mgr. Mobil Oil Co., N.Y.C., 1968-75; v.p. Carbonit, Netherlands, 1975-77; gen. mgr. Mitsui, Houston, 1977-81; pres. Nager Internat., Houston, 1981—; spl. assignments Space & Def. Systems, USAF, Grumman Aerospace, NASA, Dept Def., CIA. Recipient cert. Internat. Exec. Assn., 1970, Am. Mgmt. Assn., 1968, Spl. award Chem. Mktg. Rsch. Assn., 1973, plaque Chem. Industry Assn., 1975. Mem. Sierra Club (San Diego, trip dir.), Libertarian Club, Torrey Pines Club (San Diego, bd. dirs.), Mensa, Phi Beta Kappa, Kappa Delta Pi. Home: 3050 Rue D'Orleans San Diego CA 92110

NAGHDI, PAUL MANSOUR, engineering educator; b. Tehran, Iran, Mar. 29, 1924; came to U.S., 1944, naturalized, 1948; s. G. H. and A. (Momtaz) N.; m. Patricia Spear, Sept. 6, 1947 (dec. Mar. 15, 1975); children: Stephen, Suzanne, Sondra. B.S., Cornell U., 1946; M.S., U. Mich., 1948, Ph.D., 1951; DSc. (hon. causa), Nat. U. of Ireland, Dublin, 1987. From instr. to prof. engring. mechanics U. Mich., 1949-58; prof. engring. sci. U. Calif., Berkeley, 1958—, chmn. div. applied mechanics, 1964-69; Miller prof. Miller Inst. Basic Sci., 1963-64, 71-72; cons. theoretical and applied mechanics 1953—; Mem. U.S. Nat. Com. on Theoretical and Applied Mechanics, 1972-84, chmn., 1979-80; mem. gen. assembly Internat. Union Theoretical and Applied Mechanics, 1978-84. Served with AUS, 1946-47. Recipient Disting. Faculty award U. Mich., 1956, George Westinghouse award Am. Soc. Engring. Edn., 1962; Guggenheim fellow, 1958. Fellow ASME (chmn. applied mechanics div. 1971-72, Timoshenko medal 1980, hon. mem. 1983), Acoustical Soc. Am., Soc. Engring. Sci. (dir. 1963-70, A.C. Eringen medal 1986); mem. Nat. Acad. Engring., Soc. Rheology, Sigma Xi. Home: 530 Vistamont Ave Berkeley CA 94708

NAGLESTAD, FREDERIC ALLEN, legislative advocate; b. Sioux City, Iowa, Jan. 13, 1929; s. Ole T. and Evelyn Elizabeth (Erschen) N.; student (scholar) U. Chgo., 1947-49; m. Beverly Minnette Shellberg, Feb. 14, 1958; children—Patricia Minnette, Catherine Janette. Pub. affairs, pub. relations, newscaster, announcer KSCJ-radio, Sioux City, Iowa, 1949-51; producer, dir., newscaster, announcer WOW-TV, Omaha, 1953-57; program mgr. WCPO-TV, Cin., 1957-58; mgr. KNTV-TV, San Jose, Calif., 1958-61; owner Results Employment Agy., San Jose, 1961-75; legis. advocate Naglestad Assocs., Calif. Automotive Wholesalers Assn., Air Quality Products, Calif. Assn. Wholesalers-Distbrs., State Alliance Bd. Equalization Reform, Quakemaster, many others, 1969—. Pres. Calif. Employment Assn., 1970-72. Asst. concertmaster Sioux City Symphony Orch., 1945-47. Sgt. AUS, 1951-53. Recognized for outstanding contbn. to better employment law, Resolution State Calif. Legislature, 1971. Office: 3991 Fair Oaks Blvd Sacramento CA 95864

NAGURSKI, JAN STEPHEN, controller; b. Long Beach, Calif., Sept. 23, 1944; s. Stephen and Edna Mae (Hart) N.; m. Bernadette Esther Barrett, Apr. 23, 1976; children: Mark, Brian, Kevin. BA in English, Calif. State U., Long Beach, 1967; degree in civilian club mgmt. with honors, Air Force Inst. Tech., Wright-Patterson AFB, Ohio, 1971; MBA, Pepperdine U., 1983. Commd. 2d lt. USAF, 1967, advanced through grades to capt., 1970, resigned, 1975; acct. Sta. WBAP/KSCS, Ft. Worth, 1975-76; mgmt. acct. Adria Ltd., Strabane, Ireland, 1976-78; gen. mgr. Bundoran (Ireland) Holidays, 1978-81; corp. fin. planning mgr. Luxfer USA, Riverside, Calif., 1981-87; controller Superform USA, Inc., Riverside, 1987—; cons., controller Superform USA, Riverside, 1985—; instr. acctg. community colls. Author, editor newsletter Smudgepot, 1984-86. Cubmaster Boy Scouts Am., Canyon Lake, Calif. Recipient Gold Medal Menu award Nat. Restaurant Assn., Ft. Worth, 1973. Mem. Nat. Assn. Accts. (pres. 1985-86), Data Processing Mgmt. Assn., Inst. Adminstrv. Acctg., U.K. Republican. Roman Catholic. Office: Superform USA Inc 6825 Jurupa Ave PO Box 5375 Riverside CA 92517-5375

NAGY, BARTHOLOMEW STEPHEN, geochemist, educator; b. Budapest, Hungary, May 11, 1927; came to U.S., 1948, naturalized, 1955; s. Stephen and Mary (Mueller) N.; m. Marjorie Lois Bibey, Feb. 1, 1952; 1 dau., Erika Anne; m. Lois Anne Brach, Aug. 10, 1967; 1 child, Yvonne Maria. Student, Peter Pazmany U., Budapest, 1945-48; M.A., Columbia U., 1950; Ph.D., Pa. State U., 1953. With Stanolind Oil & Gas Co., Tulsa, 1953-55; supr. geophys. research Cities Service Research & Devel. Co., Tulsa, 1955-57; assoc. prof. Fordham U., 1957-65; vis. assoc. prof. U. Calif., San Diego, 1963-65, assoc. research geochemist, 1965-68; prof. geoscis. U. Ariz., Tucson, 1968—; mem. adv. bd. Lunar Sci. Inst., 1972; researcher petroleum and organic geochemistry, X-ray crystallography and analytical chemistry, carbonaceous meteorites. Author 3 books, articles in field.; editor-in-chief Jour. Precambrian Research. Mem. Geochem. Soc. (counselor 1961-64), Am. Chem. Soc., Internat. Soc. for Study of Origin of Life. Home: 245 Greenock Dr Tucson AZ 85737 Office: U Ariz Lab Organic Geochemistry 522 Gould-Simpson Bldg Tucson AZ 85721

NAGY, MELINDA MCCORKLE, communications executive; b. Seattle, Oct. 2, 1959; d. Richard Dwight and Colleen Constance (Chowning) McC.; m. Andras Miklos Nagy, Sept. 3, 1988. Student, U. Wash., 1978-80, Stirling (Scotland) U., 1981-82; BA in Communications, Wash. State U., Pullman, 1983. Account exec. Jay Rockey Pub. Relations, Seattle, 1983-86; asst. v.p., mgr. corp. communications Wash. Mut. Savs. Bank, Seattle, 1986—. Vol. Children's Hosp., Seattle, 1987—. Mem. Pub. Relations Soc. Am. (2 Totem awards 1985, 1 Totem award 1987). Office: Wash Mut Savs Bank 1201 Third Ave Seattle WA 98101

NAHAT, DENNIS F., artistic director, choreographer; b. Detroit, Feb. 20, 1946; s. Fred H. and Linda M. (Haddad) N. Hon. degree, Juilliard Sch. Music, 1965. Prin. dancer Joffrey Ballet, N.Y.C., 1965-66; prin. dancer Am. Ballet Theatre, N.Y.C., 1968-76; founder, artistic dir. Cleve. Ballet, 1976—. Prin. performer Broadway show Sweet Charity, 1966-67; choreographer Two Gentlemen of Verona (Tony award 1972), 1969-70; (ballet) Celebrations and Ode (resolution award 1985), 1985; founder Sch. of Cleve. Ballet, 1972, Cleve. Ballet, 1976; founder, artistic dir. San Jose Cleve. Ballet, 1985. Grantee Nat. Endowment Arts, 1978, Andrew Mellon Found., 1985. Office: Cleve San Jose Ballet 1 Playhouse Sq 1375 Euclid Ave Cleveland OH 44115 also: San Jose Cleve Ballet PO Box 1666 San Jose CA 95109 *

NAHMAN, NORRIS STANLEY, electrical engineer; b. San Francisco, Nov. 9, 1925; s. Hyman Cohen and Rae (Levin) N.; m. Shirley D. Maxwell, July 20, 1968; children: Norris Stanley, Vicki L., Vance W., Scott T. B.S. in Electronics Engring, Calif. Poly. State U., 1951; M.S.E.E., Stanford U., 1952; Ph.D. in Elec. Engring, U. Kans., 1961. Registered profl. engr., Colo. Electronic scientist Nat. Security Agy., Washington, 1952-55; prof. elec. engring., dir. electronics rsch. lab. U. Kans., Lawrence, 1955-66; qci. cons., chief pulse and time domain sect. Nat. Bur. Standards, Boulder, Colo., 1966-73; chief time domain metrology, sr. scientist Nat. Bur. Standards, 1975-83, group leader field characterization group, 1984-85; v.p. Picosecond Pulse Labs, Inc., Boulder, 1986—; prof., chmn. dept. elec. engring. U. Toledo,, 1973-75;; prof. elec. engring. U. Colo.,, Boulder,, 1966—; disting. lectr., prin. prof. Centre Nat. d'Etude des Telecommunications Summer Sch., Lannion, France, 1978; disting. lectr. Harbin Inst. Tech., Peoples Republic China, summer 1982; mem. faculty NATO Advanced Study Inst., Castelvecchio, Italy, 1983, Internat. Radio Sci. Union/NRC; chmn. internat. intercommn. group Waveform measurements 1981—, chmn. Commn. A, 1985-86. Contbr. rsch. articles profl. jours.; patentee in field. Asst. scoutmaster Longs Peak coun. Boy Scouts Am., 1970-73, 75—. With U.S. Mcht. Marine, 1943-46, U.S. Army, 1952-55. Ford Found. faculty fellow MIT, 1962; Nat. Bur. Standards sr. staff fellow, 1978-79; recipient Order of Arrow Boy Scouts Am., 1976. Fellow IEEE (Andrew H. Chi award for best tech. paper 1984), Internat. Sci. Radio Union; mem. Instrumentation and Measurement Soc. of IEEE (editorial bd. Trans., 1982-86, Tech. Leadership and Achievement award 1987), Am. Assn. Engring. Edn., Sigma Pi Sigma, Tau Beta Pi, Eta Kappa Nu, Sigma Tau, Sigma Xi, Am. Radio Relay League Club (life). Office: PO Box 44 Boulder CO 80306

NAKAGAWA, ALLEN DONALD, radiologic technologist; b. N.Y.C., Mar. 14, 1955; s. Walter Tsunehiko and Alyce Tsuneko (Kinoshita) N. BS in Environ. Studies, St. John's U., Jamaica, N.Y., 1977; MS in Marine Biology, C.W. Post Coll., 1980. Cert. radiologic technologist, fluoroscopy, Calif. Research asst. environ. studies St. John's U., 1976-78; lab. asst. Bur. Water Surveillance, Nassau Co. of Health Dept., Wantaugh, N.Y., 1978; clin. endocrinology asst. U. Calif. VA Hosp., San Francisco, 1981-83; student technologist St. Mary's Hosp., San Francisco, 1985-86; radiologic technologist Mt. Zion Hosp., San Francisco, 1986-88. Contbr. articles to profl. jours., chpts. to books. Recruiting chmn. hunger project C.W. Post Coll., 1979. Mem. Calif. Soc. Radiologic Technologists (San Francisco and state chpts.), Calif. Marine Mammal Ctr., AAAS, Am. Registry Radiol. Technologists (cert.), Calif. Acad. Scis., Planetree Health Resource Ctr., ACLU, Sigma Xi. Democrat. Methodist. Home: 1251-8 Ave Apt 7 San Francisco CA 94122 Office: U Calif Dept Radiology 3d Ave at Parnassus San Francisco CA 94143

NAKAHATA, TADAKA, retired consulting engineer, land surveyor; b. Kauai, Hawaii, Nov. 24, 1924; s. Tadao and Yae (Ohta) N.; BS in Civil Engring., U. Hawaii, 1951; m. Clara S. Sakanashi, June 23, 1956; children—Leanne A. Nikaido, Holly E. Chung, Merry Y. Engr./surveyor B.H. McKeague & Assos., Honolulu, 1951-55, Harland Bartholomew & Assos., Honolulu, 1955-56, Paul Low Engring. Co., Honolulu, 1956-59, Nakahata, Kaneshige, Imata & Assos., 1959-63; owner T. Nakahata, Honolulu, 1964-83, ret., 1983; mem. Hawaii Bd. Registration of Architects, Engrs. and Land Surveyors, 1980-83. With AUS, 1946-47. Mem. ASCE, Am. Congress Surveying and Mapping, Nat. Soc. Profl. Engrs. Mem. Makiki Christian Ch.

NAKAMURA, HIROMU, psychologist; b. L.A., Nov. 6, 1926; s. Genjiro and Misao (Kamura) N.; AB, U. Redlands, 1948; MA, UCLA, 1951; PhD, U. So. Calif., 1973; m. Tamaye Yumiba, Mar. 27, 1955; children: Glenn Vernon, Colleen Patricia. Clin. psychology intern Massillon (Ohio) State Hosp., 1951-52; clin. psychologist Patton (Calif.) State Hosp., 1952-58; clin. psychologist Lanterman State Hosp. and Developmental Ctr. (formerly Pacific State Hosp.), Pomona, Calif., 1958—, program dir., 1971—. Mem. Am., Calif. psychol. assns., Am. Assn. Mental Deficiency, AAAS, Am. Pub. Health Assn., Nat. Geographic Soc., Town Hall Calif., L.A. World Affairs Coun., World-wide Acad. Scholars, N.Y. Acad. Scis., Psi Chi. Presbyterian. Home: 3861 Shelter Grove Dr Claremont CA 91711 Office: PO Box 100 Pomona CA 91769

NAKAMURA, YUKIO, engineer; b. Kurume, Japan, Jan. 5, 1930; came to U.S., 1930; s. Jingo N.; m. Alyce Sumiko Yuzuki, July 18, 1954; children: Jeffrey, Kathy, Lori, Kari. BSME, UCLA, 1951; MSME, U. So. Calif., L.A., 1956. Registered profl. engr., Calif. Engr. Byron Jackson Co., Vernon, Calif., 1951, 53-56, N.Am. Aviation Co., Downey, Calif., 1956-57, 59-60; cons. Rhodes E. Rule, L.A., 1957-58; engr. Airite Products Co., L.A., 1958-59; sr. engring. specialist Aerojet Gen. Co., Azusa, Calif., 1960-71; program mgr. Jet Propulsion Lab., Pasadena, Calif., 1971—. Patentee in field. Author tech. reports, papers. Cpl., U.S. Army, 1951-53. Grantee, NSF, 1974, 76. Mem. Am. Def. Preparedness Assn., AIAA, Assn. U.S. Army. Republican. Buddhist. Home: 12213 Ramona Blvd El Monte CA 91732 Office: Jet Propulsion Lab 4800 Oak Grove Dr Pasadena CA 91109

NAKANISHI, DON TOSHIAKI, educator, writer; b. L.A., Aug. 14, 1949; s. Dick Tsugio and Eva Miyoko (Harada) N.; m. Marsha J. Hirano; 1 child, Thomas. BA, Yale U., 1971; PhD, Harvard U., 1978. Prof. UCLA, 1982—. Home: 4501 Berkshire Ave Los Angeles CA 90032

NAKANO, KENNETH RIKUJI, real estate and travel exec.; b. Hilo, Hawaii, Nov. 10, 1915; s. Genatro and Takiyo (Kawakami) N.; ed. Waseda Internat. Inst., Tokyo; polit.-economy certificate, Waseda U., 1938; Ph.D., H.H.D., St. John's Theol. Sem.; m. Ellen Nakatani, June 12, 1942; 1 dau., Judith. Chmn. Nakano Ken Realty (Tokyo) Inc.; sales coordinator, travel cons. Travel Booking, Inc.; v.p. Internat. Bus. Service Co. Ltd., Tokyo, Hawaii Jet Travel, Inc.; prin. broker Cen. Pacific Kosan, Inc., Honolulu; dir. Hawaiian Lanes Inc., Banpo Shoji Co. Tokyo Inc. Mem. Honolulu City Traffic Commn., 1953, Honolulu City Rent Control Commn., 1957; bd. govs. Goodwill Industries, Honolulu; mem. Honolulu chpt. Nat. Crime and Delinquency. Assn.; mem. rural dist. bd. mgrs. YMCA; exec. bd. Aloha council Boy Scouts Am. Recipient Lions Internat. Charter-Monarch 25 Yr. award, 1971, Humanitarian award Mountain Dist., 1984; cert. of distinguished service strengthening ties State of Calif. and Hawaii, County of Los Angeles, 1973; lic. minister Ho. of God Ch. and Bible Sch. Inst. Mem. Honolulu C. of C., Pacific Air Travel Assn., Am. Soc. Travel Agts., Honolulu Bd. Realtors, Nat. Assn. Realtors, Navy League U.S. (life), Philippine Shrine Assn. of Saigon Shrine Oasis, Smithsonian Assocs. Clubs: Lions, Masons, K.T., Shriners, Honolulu Press. Home and Office: PO Box 245 Waianae HI 96792

NAKASHIMA, DEBORAH LEE, college official; b. Stuttgart, Fed. Republic of Germany, Aug. 21, 1959; parents Am. citizens; d. Marion Thomas and Jane Toshie (Kuwada) Thornburg; m. Wade Kiyoshi Nakashima, Feb. 24, 1985; children: Matthew M., Lindsey M. AA in Liberal Arts, Leeward Community Coll., 1980; BS in Human Devel., U. Hawaii, 1982. Paraprofl. Komo Mai-Leeward Community Coll., Pearl City, Hawaii, 1980-81; tchr. Hawaii Child Ctr. of Salt Lake, Honolulu, 1981-83; admissions counselor Hawaii Pacific Coll., Honolulu, 1983-85, acad. advisor, office mgr., 1985—; cons. Noevir, Inc., Honolulu, 1988—. Recipient Staff Recognition award Hawaii Pacific Coll., 1986, Cert. Appreciation, 1987, 88. Democrat. Home: 351A Olomana St Kailua HI 96734 Office: Hawaii Pacific Coll 1060 Bishop St Penthouse Honolulu HI 96813

NAKASHIMA, PATRICIA HATSUYE, educational association administrator; b. Tulelake, Calif., Jan. 24, 1943; d. Harry and Kayo (Shimada) N. BA, San Jose State U., 1964; MA, Stanford U., 1965. Cert. secondary tchr. Dept. head Bret Harte Jr. High Sch., San Jose, Calif., 1967-73, John Steinbeck Jr. High Sch., San Jose, Calif., 1980-83; dept. head Henry T. Gunderson High Sch., San Jose, Calif., 1983-85, faculty rep., 1985-86; affiliate rep. Calif. Fgn. Lang. Tchrs. Assn., San Jose, 1986-87, 2d v.p., 1987—; curriculum cons. State Dept. Edn. Calif., 1986-87; mem. adv. panel Title II, Pub. Law 98-377 Calif. Post-Secondary Edn. Commn., 1985-88, reader grant proposals, 1985-88. Co-chmn. W. Buddist Sangha, San Jose, 1968-69; advisor San Jose Young Buddhist Assn., 1970-80. Mem. NEA, Am. Assn. Tchrs. French, Calif. Tchrs. Assn., San Jose Tchrs. Assn. (faculty rep. 1977-79), Fgn. Lang. Assn. Santa Clara County (pres. 1985-86), Delta Kappa Gamma. Office: Gunderson High Sch 622 Gaundabert Ln San Jose CA 95136

NAKATANI, CLIFFORD YOSHIHARU, publishing executive, consultant; b. San Francisco, Apr. 6, 1941; s. Roy Y. and Haruko Nakatani; m. Betty T. Yamasaki, Dec. 20, 1963; children: Lamont, Martin. BFA, Utah State U., 1963. Asst. art dir. Deseret News Pub., Salt Lake City, 1964-73; art dir. Walker Scott Dept. Stores, San Diego, 1973-74; art. dir., prodn. mgr. Marcoa Pub., Inc., San Diego, 1974-84; prodn. mgr. Registry Pub., Inc., El Cajon, Calif., 1984-87; mgmt. cons. Windsor Publs., Northridge, Calif., 1987-88, Wildlife Edn. Ltd., San Diego, 1988—; advisor San Diego community Coll. Arts, 1974-86. Recipient Merit award Am. Advt. Fedn., 1969, Simpson Paper Co., 1979, Excellence award Simpson Paper Co., 1981, Grand award Seklemian Awards, N.Y.C., 1974. Buddhist. Home: 5754 Amaro Dr San Diego CA 92124

NAKAUCHI, EDWARD MITSUO, electronics engineer, consultant; b. Phila., Sept. 17, 1946; s. Hidemitsu and Hatsue (Tadokoro) N.; m. Linda S. Mulherin, Oct. 4, 1969; children: Michael, Caryn, Pamela. AA, cert. tech., Orange Coast Coll., 1966; BSEE cum laude, Northrop U., 1969. Engr. Advanced Kinetics, Costa Mesa, Calif., 1969-70, Electronic Memories, Hawthorne, Calif., 1970-71, Pertec Bus. Systems, Irvine, Calif., 1971-74; mgr. HTL-K West, Santa Ana, Calif., 1974-77; sr. engr. Basic Four, Tustin, Calif., 1977-83; mgr. Century Data Systems, Anaheim, Calif., 1983-85; pvt. practice cons. Westminster, Calif., 1985-89; sr. tech. specialist Northrop Corp., Pico Rivera, Calif., 1989—; cons. in field. Advisor Explorer Scouts, Tustin, 1982; cubmaster, Webelos leader Cub Scouts, Westminster, 1979, 80, 81; commr. Boy Scouts Am., Orange County, Calif., 1981; olympics chmn. Girl Scouts U.S., Garden Grove, Calif., 1983, 84, 85. Mem. IEEE (chmn. 1983-84, Outstanding Svc. award 1984, Speaker and Com. award 1986), EOS/ESD Assn., Tau Beta Pi. Republican. Home: 14772 Forrest Ln Westminster CA 92683

NALLE, C(HARLES) ALEXANDER, real estate consultant; b. Santa Ana, Calif., Sept. 13, 1938; s. Charles Crawford and Florence Sophia (Brownridge) N.; m. Dorothy Anne Peterson, Sept. 3, 1961; children: Anna Beck, Heather Brownridge Nalle. BFT, Claremont (Calif.) Men's Coll., 1956-58; BA, Mex. City Coll., Mex. DF, 1961; BFT, AGSIM, Phoenix, 1966. Sales engr. Caterpillar Tractor Co., Peoria, Ill., 1966-69; dir. Latin Am. Challenge-Cook Bros., Inc., Industry, Calif., 1969-78; comml. real estate assoc. W.H. Daum & Staff, Newport Beach, Calif., 1978-83, Coldwell Banker, Santa Ana, Calif., 1983—; bd. dirs. Orange County Pub. Facility Corp., Santa Ana; mem. Orange County Assessment Appeals Bd. Chmn. Santa Ana Redevel. Commn., 1973-84; mem. Commn. of the Californians, Sacramento, 1970-80, Goodwill Industries of Orange County, 1984—; bd. dirs. Bowers Mus., Santa Ana, 1981-85; mem. Orange County Sheriffs Adv. Coun., Santa Ana, 1986—, Orange County Pioneer Coun., Santa Ana, 1983—. Capt. USMC, 1961-64. Mem. Rotary Club Santa Ana, La Grulla Legal Affairs (Ensenada, Mex.), Viaje de Portola (Orange County). Republican. Baptist. Office: Coldwell Banker 2333 N Broadway Santa Ana CA 92706

NALTY, DAMON GENE, history, department chairman, educator; b. Omaha, July 27, 1930; s. John Patrick and Esther Alta (Barnes) N.; m. Anna Helen Curry Nalty, Dec. 29, 1962; children: Mary Bustamante, Erin Faso, Audrey, John, William. AB in history, St. Mary's Coll., Moraga, Calif., 1952; MA in history, U. of San Francisco, 1956; Edn. in instrn. tech., USC, 1972. Tchr. Serra High Sch., San Mateo, Calif., 1955-57; tchr. Campbell High Sch. Dist., Campbell, Calif., 1957-59; asst. headmaster Woodside Priory Sch., Portola Valley, Calif., 1960-67; prof. San Jose State U., San Jose, Calif., 1967—; chairman, Dept. of Soc. Sci. San Jose State U., San Jose, 1987—. Editor: profl. jour. Social Studies Review, 1981—; author: book, Analysis of the Social Sciences, 2nd edition 1987. Mem. sch. bd., Moreland Sch. Dist. San Jose, 1973—. Recipient Hilda Tauba Award, Calif. Council for the Social Studies, 1984. Home: 849 Rockwood Dr San Jose CA 95129 Office: San Jose State U One Washington Sq San Jose CA 95192-0121

NAMIAS, JEROME, meteorologist; b. Bridgeport, Conn., Mar. 19, 1910; s. Joseph and Saydie (Jacobs) N.; m. Edith Paipert, Sept. 15, 1938; 1 child, Judith Ellen. Student, MIT, 1932-34, M.S., 1941; M.S., U. Mich., 1934-35; Sc.D. (hon.), U. R.I., 1972, Clark U., 1984. Research asst. Blue Hill Meteorol. Obs., Milton, Mass., 1933-35; research assoc. MIT, Boston, 1936-41, Woods Hole (Mass.) Oceanographic Inst.; mgr. extended forecast br. U.S. Weather Bur., Washington, 1941-64; assoc. dir. Nat. Meteorol. Ctr., 1964-66, chief extended forecast div., 1966-71; vis. scientist NYU, N.Y.C., 1966; research meteorologist Scripps Inst. Oceanography, La Jolla, Calif., 1968—; vis. scholar Rockefeller Study and Conf. Center, Bellagio, Italy, 1977; frequent cons. USAAF, USN; developer of system for extending time range of gen. weather forecasts up to a season. Author: An Introduction to the Study of Air Mass and Isentropic Analysis, 1936, Extended Forecasting by Mean Circulation Methods; monograph, 1947, Thirty-Day Forecasting, 1953; Short Period Climatic Variations, Collected Works of Jerome Namias, 1934-74, 1975-82, 83, Namias Symposium Volume, 1986; also tech. articles to sci. jours.; Editorial bd.: Geofisica Internacional, Mexico. Recipient Meisinger award Am. Meteorol. Soc., 1938; citation for weather forecasts North African invasion Sec. of Navy, 1942; Dept. Commerce Meritorious Service award, 1950; Rockefeller Pub. Service award, 1955; award for extraordinary sci. accomplishment Am. Meteorol. Soc., 1955; Sverdrup Gold medal Am. Meteorol. Soc., 1981; Gold medal for distinguished achievement Dept. Commerce, 1965; Chancellor's Assocs. award excellence in research U. Calif.-San Diego; Compass award for research Marine Tech. Soc., 1984; Rossby fellow Woods Hole (Mass.) Oceanographic Instn., 1972. Fellow Am. Geophys. Union, Washington Acad. Scis., AAAS, Am. Meteorol. Soc. (councilor 1940-42, 50-53, 60-63, 70-73), Explorers Club, Am. Acad. Arts and Scis., Royal Meteorol. Soc. Great Britain (hon. mem.), Nat. Acad. Sci. Home: 240 Coast Blvd 2C La Jolla CA 92037 Office: Scripps Inst Oceanography Poss Bldg A-024 La Jolla CA 92093

NANCE, ANCIL KENNINGTON, photographer; b. Hong Kong, China, June 5, 1941; came to the U.S., 1945; s. Ancil Benwes and Elizabeth (Kennington) N.; m. D. Nance; children: Lisa R., Ben Wes. BA, Portland State Coll., 1964; MS, Portland State U., 1971. Tchr. Portland (Oreg.) Pub. Sch., 1964-73; owner Ancil Nance Photographs, Portland, 1973--, North Paranoid Climbing Sch., Portland, 1973-75; photographer staff Oreg. Mag., Portland, 1975-78. Artist, photographer numerous posters. Mem. Am. Assoc. Mag. Photographers. Democrat. Home: 2526 SW Custer Port OR 97219 Office: Ancil Nance Photographs 600 SW 10th #530 Portland OR 97205

NANCE, JAMES WESLEY, mechanical engineer; b. Ardmore, Okla., Feb. 7, 1956; s. James Winfield and Lina Jane (Bigelow) N. BSMe, U. Okla., 1979. Assoc. engr. Lockheed Austin Div., Austin, Tex., 1983-86; engring. asst. Mobil Oil Co., Lindsay, Okla., summer 1977; quality engr. John Deere & Co., Waterloo, Iowa, 1982. Advisor, Nat. Jr. Achievement, Waterloo, Iowa, 1982. Mem. Am. Soc. Quality Control, Nat. Mgmt. Assn., Tech. Soc. Republican. Home: 5944 S Datura St #4 Littleton CO 80120

NANCE, JOHN JOSEPH, lawyer, writer; b. Dallas, July 5, 1946; s. Joseph Turner and Margrette (Grubbs) N.; m. Benita Ann Priest, July 26, 1968; children: Dawn Michelle, Bridgitte Cathleen, Christopher Sean. BA, So. Meth. U., 1968, JD, 1969. Bar: Tex. 1970. Newspaper reporter, broadcaster, newsman Various papers and sta's., Honolulu and Dallas, 1957-66; anchorman Sta. WFAA-Radio, Dallas, 1966-70; newsman including on camera Sta. WFAA-TV, Dallas; airline pilot Braniff Internat. Airways, Dallas, 1975-82, Alaska Airlines, Inc., Seattle, 1985—; pvt. pratice, atty. Dallas, 1970—; chmn., pres. Exec. Transport, Inc., Tacoma, 1979-85; chmn., chief exec. officer EMEX Corp., Kent, Wash., 1987—; profl. speaker Human Mgmt., 1984—; airline safety, advocate Ind. Cons., Broadcast Analyst, nationwide, 1986—, earthquake preparedness spokesman Ind. Cons., Broadcast Analyst, nationwide, 1987—; dir. steering com. Found. for Issues Resolution in Sci. Tech., Seattle, 1987—; speaker Northwestern Transp. Ctr. Deregulation and Safety Conf., 1987. Author: On Shaky Ground, 1988, Blind Trust, 1986 (Wash. Gov's. award 1987), Splash of Colors, 1984; Co-author Transportation Deregulation in the U.S., 1988. Pres. Fox Glen Homeowner's Assn., Tacoma, 1974-77; cons. Congl. Office Tech. Assessment, Tacoma, 1987; witness numerous air safety hearings, U.S. Congress, Washington,

1986-88; mem. bd. St. Charles Borromeo Sch., Tacoma, 1975-78. Lt. col. USAF, 1970-75, lt. col. res. 1975—. Named Airline Safety Man of Year Wash. State Div. of Aeronautics, , 1987. Mem. ABA, Tex. Bar Assn., Author's Guild Am., Nat. Speakers Assn., Am. Mgmt. Assn., Res. Officers Assn. Home: 4512 87th Ave W Tacoma WA 98466 Office: EMEX Corp PO Box 5476 Kent WA 98064

NANCE, ROBERT LEWIS, oil company executive; b. Dallas, July 10, 1936; s. Melvin Renfro Nance and Ruth Natlie (Seibert) Nowlin; m. Penni Jane Warfel; children: Robert Scott, Amy Louise, Catherine Leslie. BS, So. Meth. U., 1959. V.p. geology Oliver & West Cons., Dallas, 1960-66; ptnr. Nance & Larue Cons., Dallas, 1966-69; pres. Nance Petroleum Corp., Billings, Mont., 1969—; bd. dirs. First Interstate Bank, Billings, Rimrock Bank, Billings; chmn. bd. Rocky Mountain Coll., Billings. Council pres. Am. Luth. Ch., Billings, 1980; trustee, vice chmn. Deaconess Med. Ctr., Billings. Recipient Hall of Fame award Rocky Mountain Coll. Alumni, 1987, Disting. Svc. Trusteeship, Assn. Governing Bds. Univs. Colls., 1988. Mem. Am. Assn. Petroleum Geologists, Indep. Petroleum Assn. Am. (v.p. Mont. chpt. 1975), Indep. Petroleum Assn. Mountain States (v.p. Mont. 1977-79), Mont. Petroleum Assn., Hilands Golf Club, Yellowstone Country Club, Billings Petroleum Club. Office: Nance Petroleum Corp 550 N 31st St PO Box 7168 Billings MT 59103

NANCE, SANDRA JUNE TADDIE, immunohematology research associate, educator; b. Balt., Nov. 21, 1953; d. John Anthony and Elizabeth Arlene (Warfel) Taddie; m. Robert Daniel Nance, May 2, 1982; 1 child, Danielle Elizabeth; stepchildren: Christa Darleen, Amy Rebecca. BS, Ind. U. of Pa., 1975; MS in Pathology, U. Md., 1982. Lic. clin. immunohematology tech., Calif., 1981, med. tech., Am. Soc. Clin. Pathologists, 1975, spl. in blood banking, Am. Soc. Clin. Pathologists, 1979. Instr. U. Md., Balt., 1979-80, grad. student researcher pediatric research dept., 1979-80; lead tech. Johns Hopkins Blood Bank, Balt., 1979-81; research tech. ARC Blood Svc., L.A., 1981-85; faculty research assoc. ARC Blood Servicew, L.A., 1985—; speaker numerous confs. Contbr. articles to prof. jours.; editor: Methods in Immunohematology, 1988, Immune Destruction of Red Blood Cells, 1989. Ch. tchr. St. Peter's by the Sea Presby. ch., Rancho Palos Verdes, 1987-88. Recipient Alpha Mu Tau Scholarship award, Md. Sco. Med. Tech., 1978, Hyland Therapeutics Scholarship Honorarium, Travenol Labs, Inc., 1978. Mem. Am. Soc. Clin. Pathologists, Am. Assn. Blood Banks (annual seminar com. 1986—, chmn. 1988—, scientific program abstract reviewer 1986—, Found. Rsch. Grant award 1989), L.A. Serum Cell Soc., Invitational Conf. of Investigative Immunohematologists, ARC Monocyte Monolayer Assay Working Group, Calif. Blood Bank Soc. (scientific program com. 1982-84, 1986-88, administrv. program com., 1982-83, publs. com. 1986-89, abstract review com. 1986-87). Democrat. Presbyterian. Office: ARC Blood Services 1130 S Vermont Ave Los Angeles CA 90006

NANDA, VED PRAKASH, law educator; b. Gujranwala, India, Nov. 20, 1934; came to U.S., 1960; s. Jagan Nath and Attar (Kaur) N.; m. Katharine Kunz, Dec. 18, 1982; 1 child, Anjali. MA, Punjab U., 1952; LLB, U. Delhi, 1955, LLM, 1958; LLM, Northwestern U., 1962; postgrad., Yale U., 1962-65. Asst. prof. law U. Denver, 1965-68, assoc. prof., 1968-70, prof. law, dir. Internat. Legal Studies Program, 1970—, Thompson G. Marsh prof. law, 1987—; vis. prof. coll. law U. Iowa, Iowa City, 1974-75, U. San Diego, 1979, Fla. State U., 1973; disting. vis. prof. internat. law Chgo. Kent Coll. Law, 1981, Calif. Western Sch. Law, San Diego, 1983-84; distin. vis. scholar sch. law U. Hawaii, Honolulu, 1986-87; cons. Solar Energy Rsch. Inst., 1978-81, Dept. Energy, 1980-81. Author: (with David Pansius) Litigation of International Disputes in U.S. Courts, 1987; editor: Water Needs for the Future, 1977, (with M. Cherif Bassiouni) A Treatise on International Criminal Law, 2 vols., 1973, (with others) Global Human Rights, 1981, The Law of Transnational Business Transactions, 1981, World Climate Change, 1983, (with George Shepherd) Human Rights and Third World Development; editorial bd. Jour. Comparative Law; adv. bd. Jour. Legal Edn. Co-chmn. Colo. Pub. Broadcasting Fedn., 1977-78; mem. Gov.'s Commn. on Pub. Telecommunications, 1980—. Mem. World Assn. Law Profs. (pres. 1987—), UN Assn. (v.p. Colo. div. 1973-76, pres. 1986-88), Am. Assn. Comparative Study Law (bd. dirs. 1980—), Am. Soc. Internat. Law (v.p. 1987-88, exec. coun. 1969-72, 81-84), Assn. Am. Law Schs., U.S. Inst. Human Rights, Internat. Law Assn. (mem. exec. com. 1986—), Colo. Coun. Internat. Orgns. (pres. 1988—), Assn. U.S. Mems. Internat. Inst. Space Law (bd. dirs., mem. exec. com.), Order St. Ives (pres.), Denver Athletic Club, Rotary. Office: U Denver Coll Law 1900 Olive St Denver CO 80220

NANEY, DAVID GLEN, tax consultant; b. Bakersfield, Calif., Apr. 21, 1952; s. Glen Tillman and Olivia Mae N.; children—David Tillman, Michael Christian, Timothy Donovan. AA, Bakersfield Coll., 1972; BA, UCLA, 1974; JD, Loyola U., 1977. Bar: Calif. 1977, U.S. Dist. Ct. (ea. dist.) Calif. 1980, U.S. Dist. Ct. (cen. dirs.) Calif. 1981.Atty. firm Freeman, Freeman & Smiley, L.A., 1978-80; ptv. practice law, Bakersfield, 1980-86; v.p. Cemco Corp.; exec. v.p. Cemland Dev., 1986; v.p. Kern Valley Tank Lines, 1986-87; v.p., corp. sec. legal dept. Lenders Auto Acceptance Corp., 1987-88; asst. v.p. legal dept. Lendco Acceptance Corp.; sr. cons. DuCharme, McMillen and Assocs., Inc., 1988—; former judge pro tempore West Kern Mcpl. Ct. Dist., other Kern County Justice Cts.; prof. law Bakersfield Coll.; legal adviser CAP; instr. in estate planning. Mem. scholarship com. Bakersfield Coll. Mem. UCLA Alumni Assn., Bakersfield Coll. Alumni Assn., Lions, Phi Alpha Delta. Republican. Author (with Douglas K. Freeman): How to Incorporate a Small Business, 1978. Office: DuCharme McMillen & Assocs Inc 5655 Lindero Canyon Rd #222 Westlake Village CA 91362

NANKIN, PABLO, surgeon; b. Mexico City, Sept. 4, 1944; came to U.S., 1976; s. Abraham and Sara (Brener) N.; m. Jan. 7, 1967; children: Jody, Stephanie, Jenifer, Tamara. BS, Colegio Cristobal, Mexico, 1960; MD, U. Mexico, 1967. Intern Reddy Meml. Hosp., Montreal, Que., Can., 1965-66; resident in vascular surgery Jewish Gen. Hosp., Montreal, 1966, Mt. Sinai Hosp., Chgo., 1966-71; chief resident Michael Reese Hosp., Chgo., 1971-72; surgeon specializing in vascular diseases Los Angeles, 1979—. Contbr. articles to profl. jours. Mem. Denton Cooley Soc., Soc. Clin. Vascular Surgery, AMA, Los Angeles County Med. Soc. Office: 4231 E 3d St Los Angeles CA 90063

NANNEY, HERBERT BOSWELL, musician, educator; b. Whittier, Calif., Aug. 1, 1918; s. Leslie Carson and Edna (Thornburgh) N.; m. Jean Duncan, Aug. 1, 1947; 1 child, Duncan Leslie. BA, Whittier Coll., 1940; artists diploma, Curtis Inst. Music, Phila., 1947, Paris Conservatory, 1946; MA in Music, Stanford U., 1951. Organist First Meth. Ch., Pasadena, Calif., 1937-40; organist, choir dir. Jenkintown, Pa., 1941-42; asst. organist Stanford (Calif.) Univ., 1940-41; mem. faculty Stanford (Calif.) U., 1947-85, prof. music, 1952-85, univ. organist, 1947-85, prof. music and univ. organist emeritus, 1985—; organist First Congl. Ch., Los Angeles, summer 1942; organist, choir dir. Episcopal Cathedral, Paris, 1945; minister of music Ninth Presbyn. Ch., Phila., 1946-47; cons. First Congl. Chs., Santa Cruz and Oakland, Calif., 1956-57, St. Mark's Episcopal Ch., Palo Alto, Calif., 1984-85, St. Denis Cath. Ch., Menlo Park, Calif., 1980-87. Composer: Sonata for Organ, 1940, Trio for Oboe, Viola and Piano, 1950, Contata-The Creation, 1951. Mem. exec. bd. Santa Clara County chpt. Nat. Council Alcoholism, San Jose, Calif., 1976-79. Served with U.S. Army, 1942-46, ETO. Herbert Nanney organ scholarship named in his honor Stanford Univ., 1987. Mem. Am. Guild Organists (chmn. Far Western region 1975-81, nat. council 1975-81, program chmn. nat. conv. 1984), Coll. Music Soc., Am. Musicol. Soc., Music Tchrs. Assn. Calif. Democrat. Presbyterian. Home: 4271 N 1st St #33 San Jose CA 95134 Office: Stanford U Dept Music Stanford CA 94305

NANTO, ROXANNA LYNN, career planning administrator, consultant; b. Hanford, Calif., Dec. 17, 1952; d. Lawson Gene Brooks and Bernice (Page) Jackson; m. Harvey Ken Nanto, Mar. 23, 1970; 1 child, Shea Kiyoshi. A, Chemeketa Community Coll., 1976; B, Idaho State U., 1978. PBX operator Telephone Answer Bus. Svc., Moses Lake, Wash., 1965-75; edn. coord. MimiCassia Community Edn., Rupert, Idaho, 1976-77; office mgr. Lockwood Corp., Rupert, Idaho, 1977-78; cost acct. Keyes Fibre Co., Wenatchee, Wash., 1978-80; acctg. office mgr. Armstrong & Armstrong, Wenatchee, Wash., 1980-81; office mgr. Cascade Cable Constrn. Inc., East Wenatchee, Wash., 1981-83; interviewer, counselor Wash. Employment Security, Wenatchee, 1983-84; pres. chief exec. officer Regional Health Care Plus, East Wenatchee, 1986—; dist. career coord. Eastmont Sch. Dist., East Wenatchee, 1984—; prin. Career Cons., 1988—; speaker No. Cen. Washington Profl. Women, Wenatchee, 1987; cons., speaker Wash. State Sch. Dirs., Seattle, 1987; speaker Wenatchee C. of C., 1989; sec. Constrn. Coun. of No. Cen. Washington, Wenatchee, 1981-83; bd. dirs. Gen. Vocat. Adv. Bd., Wenatchee, 1986-88, Washington Family Ind. Program, Olympia, 1989—. Mem. at large career Women's Network, 1984—, mem. Econ. Devel. Coun. of No. Cen. Washington. Mem. Nat. Assn. of Career Counselors, Nat. Assn. Pvt. Career Cons; fellow Dem. Women Club. Home: 704 NE Larch Ct East Wenatchee WA 98802 Office: Eastmont Sch Career Ctr 955 NE 3d St East Wenatchee WA 98802

NAPOLES, VERONICA KLEEMAN, graphic designer, consultant; b. N.Y.C., July 9, 1951; d. Florencio Andres and Elena (Colomar) N.; m. Michael Jeffrey Kleeman, May 5, 1985; 1 child, Samuel Andres. BA, U. Miami, 1972; BArch, U. Calif., Berkeley, 1979. Account supr. Marsh & McLennan, Miami, Fla., 1974-76; designer Mus. of Anthropology, San Francisco, 1977-79; project dir. Landor & Assocs., San Francisco, 1979-81; prin. Communications Planning, Kentfield, Calif., 1981—; bd. dirs. Mind Fitness, Mill Valley, Calif., Main Arts Coun.; instr. U. Calif.-Berkeley, San Francisco, 1983—, Sonoma State U., Santa Rosa, Calif., 1983-84; tchr. Dynamic Graphics Ednl. Found., San Francisco. Author: Corporate Identity Design, 1987; contbr. articles to profl. jours. Bd. dirs. Marin Arts Coun. Recipient Bay Area Hispanic Bus. Achiever award, 1988, Design award PRINT, 1988. Mem. Am. Inst. Graphic Arts, Women in Communications. Office: Communications Planning 100 Upper Briar Rd Kentfield CA 94904

NAPOLIELLO, DANIEL ANDREW, nurse administrator; b. Omaha, Sept. 27, 1944; Ceasare Dan and Therese Mary (Sierszynski) N.; m. Sally Ann Rodak, Jan. 7, 1967; children: John, Ann Marie, Michael. Diploma in nursing, St. Joseph Hosp., Omaha, 1965; BS in Nursing, U. S.C., 1975; MEd, Chapman Coll., 1977. Commd. U.S. Army, 1964; advanced through grades to capt. Nurse Corps U.S. Army; chief nurse 8th combat support hosp. Nurse Corps U.S. Army, Fort Ord, Calif., 1975-77, resigned, 1977; comdr. USPHS, 1988—; dir. nursing Indian Hosp. USPHS, Rosebud, S.D., 1977-78, Winnebago, Nebr., 1984-87; assoc. hosp. dir. nursing edn. USPHS, Balt., 1978-81, evening supr. nursing, coord. quality assurance, 1981-84; area hosp. nursing cons. Phoenix Area Indian Health Svc., 1987—; mem. USPHS Nursing Continuing Edn. Rev. Com., Rockville, Md., 1979-81, 88—, Indian Health Svc. Nursing Profl. Splty. Group, Rockville, 1984—, Ind. Health Svc. Coun. of Nursing, 1987—, chmn., 1988—. Asst. scoutmaster Sioux council Boy Scouts Am., S.D., 1977-78, Wood Badge 1981, scoutsmaster Balt. council, Md., 1978-81, asst. dist. commr. Prairie Gold Area council, Iowa, 1982-87, Theodore Roosevelt Council, Ariz., 1987—; chmn. Dist. Health and Safety Com., 1978-81; cubmaster, 1985—; CPR Instr. ARC, 1982-87; mem. Nebr. State Hist. Soc., Union Pacific R.R. Hist. Soc. Decorated Vietnam Cross of Gallantry Unit citation, USPHS Achievement medal; recipient Merit award Boy Scouts Am., 1984, Vigil Honor, 1987, Souters Key, 1985,. Mem. Am. Nurses Assn., Nebr. Nurses Assn., Balt. Commd Officers Assn. Chpt. of USPHS (nurse officers rep. 1980, v.p. 1981), Aberdeen Area Council on Nursing (pres. 1986-87), Nat. Model Railroaders Assn., Nat. Scout Collectors Soc., Camerail Club. Democrat. Roman Catholic. Home: 10031 N 47th Ave Glendale AZ 85302

NARDOZZA, RANDY JAMES, wallcovering installation company owner; b. Hackensack, N.J., Mar. 3, 1956; s. James Anthony and Maye (Salmon) N.; m. Debora Lee Gallanda, Oct. 21, 1984. Student, U. Oreg., 1974-77, U. Ariz., 1987—. State lic. contractor, Ariz. With sales Norton Stores, Inc., Paramus, N.J., 1977-79; proprietor Randy J. Nardozza/Wallcovering Installation, Little Ferry, N.J., 1979-86, Tucson, 1986—. Mem. Ariz. Lic. Contractors Assn. Republican. Roman Catholic. Home and Office: 8421 E Tourmaline Dr Tucson AZ 85715

NARITA, HIRO, cinematographer; b. Seoul, Republic of Korea, June 26, 1941; came to Japan, 1945, came to U.S., 1957; s. Masao Morikawa and Masako (Kojima) Morikawa ; m. Barbara Parker, Sept. 9, 1971. BFA in Design, San Francisco Art Inst., 1964. V.p. Pictures & Words, Berkeley, Calif., 1972—; lectr. Mill Valley Film Festival, 1984, Hawaii Internat. Film Festival, 1984. Dir. photography for films: Farewell to Manzanar, 1976 (Emmy award nomination 1976), Never Cry Wolf, 1983 (Best Cinematography, 1983), Solomon Northup's Odyssey, 1984, Go Tell It On The Mountain, 1985, Fire With Fire, 1985, Amerika, 1987. Served with U.S Army, 1964-66. Mem. Internat. Assn. Theatrical Stage Employees (cert.). Office: Pictures and Words 1807B Fourth St Berkeley CA 94710

NARRAMORE, RANDY EARL, protective services official; b. Fullerton, Calif., Oct. 16, 1948; s. Charles Earl and Geraldine (Peterson) N.; m. Marie Edith Seuss, Dec. 5, 1970; 1 child, Ben. AS, Grossmont Coll., El Cajon, Calif., 1973; BS, San Diego State U., 1976; student police adminstrn., FBI Nat. Acad., 1985. Chief detectives El Cajon (Calif.) Police Dept., 1970-88; chief of police Ridgecrest (Calif.) Police Dept., 1988—; instr. Police Sci. Grossmont Coll., El Cajon, Calif., 1975-88, Bakersfield (Calif.) Coll., 1988—. Bd. dirs. Coun. on Substance Abuse, Ridgecrest, Calif., 1988—. Mem. Kern County Police Chiefs' Assn., Calif. Chiefs of Police Assn., Internat. Chiefs Police, Police Officers Rsch. Assn. Calif., Footprinters. Republican. Home: 1219 Mayflower Cir Ridgecrest CA 93555

NARULA, MOHAN LAL, realtor; b. Ferozepur, India, Feb. 2, 1939; came to U.S., 1962; s. Ram Dyal and Pemeshwari Narula; m. Sylvia Conway, Aug. 31, 1968; children: Rabinder, Rajinder. BS, Panjab U., India, 1960; BSME, Calif. Poly. State U., San Luis Obispo, 1965; MS in Engring., Calif. State U., Northridge, 1970. Engr. Abex Corp., Oxnard, Calif., 1965-69; salesman, realtor Walker & Lee, Oxnard, Calif., 1970-73; owner, realtor Narula Co. Realtors, Oxnard, Calif., 1973—. Mem. Cert. Comml. Investment Mem. (designate 1979), Oxnard Harbor Bd. Realtors (mem. profl. standard com. 1980—), Los Angeles Cert. Comml. Investment Mem. (bd. dirs., treas. 1985). Home: 2830 W Hill St Oxnard CA 93033 Office: Narula Co Realtor 3201 Samuel Ave Ste 7 Oxnard CA 93033

NASER, JOSEPH ALBERT, II, project manager; b. Chgo., Feb. 23, 1947; s. Joseph Albert and Faye Janice (Mickens) N. BS in Engring., Northwestern U., 1969; MS in Nuclear Engring., U. Calif., Berkeley, 1971, PhD in Nuclear Engring., 1976; MS in Computer Sci., Stanford U., 1985. Co-op technician Argonne (Ill.) Nat. Lab., 1966-69, resident student assoc., 1971-73; project mgr. Electric Power Research Inst., Palo Alto, Calif., 1974—; vis. prof. engring. U. Calif., Berkeley, 1980. Contbr. numerous articles to profl. jours. Fellow AEC, 1969-72. Mem. Am. Nuclear Soc., Am. Assn. for Artificial Intelligence. Office: Electric Power Rsch Inst 3412 Hillview Ave PO Box 10412 Palo Alto CA 94303

NASH, ANNE ELIZABETH, health facility administrator; b. L.A., Jan. 2, 1940; d. Armand Casimir and Peggee Anne (Bennett) Feichtmeir; m. James P. Nash, Oct. 6, 1973; 1 child, Jason Patrick. BA in Internat. Relations, Stanford U., 1962. Bus. mgr. James P. Nash, M.D., Templeton, Calif., 1986—. Bd. dirs. Camp Fire Girls, Paso Robles (Calif.) Rep. Women Rederated; chmn. Doug Beckett Campaign, San Luis Obispo County, Oak Hills Homeowners Assn., Career Day, Flamson Middle Sch.; mem. San Luis Obispo County Med. Aux. Recipient Service to Children award Paso Robles Pub. Schs., 1987. Mem. AAUW (bd. dirs.), Paso Robles Hist. Soc., Paso Robles C. of C., Stanford Alumni Assn.San Luis Obispo North County Symphony Guild, Paso Robles Golf and Country Club, DAR, Kappa Kappa Gamma. Republican. Home: 485 Ambush Tr Paso Robles CA 93446 Office: James P Nash MD 959 Las Tablas Rd Templeton CA 93465

NASH, BEVERLY EILENE, French and theology educator; b. Chinook, Mont., June 8, 1944; d. Oscar Charles and Dorothy Marie (Rost) Gratton; m. Michael Murray Nash, June 11, 1966; children: Francis Michael, Robert Charles, Maria Kathryn, Steven Donald. BA in French, Carroll Coll., Helena, Mont., 1966. Tchr. French and English Hellgate High Sch., Missoula, Mont., 1966-67; tchr. enrichment program Wis. Correctional System, Oregon, 1971-72; tchr., substitute and enrichment programs Deer Lodge (Mont.) Elem., 1974-75; mem. staff Holy Rosary Parish, Bozeman, 1983-85; tchr. French and theolgy Butte (Mont.) Cen. High Sch., 1985—, chmn. fgn. lang. dept., 1986—; vol. tchr. Bozeman, Mont., Missoula, Mont., Tallahassess, Fla., Deer Lodge, Mont.;mem. cirriculum com. Butte Cen. High Sch., 1986—, theology dept. com., 1986—. Lay Missionary Cath. Diocese of Helena, 1963, 65, Grail Lay Women's Organ., San Jose, Calif., 1965; vol. Homebound program, Washington, 1966, GlenMary Home Missions, Eaton, Ohio, Longfellow Sch., Bozeman, 1983-86; den mother Cub Scouts Am., Bozeman, 1977-80; den leader Campfire Orgn., Bozeman, 1978-79; lector and choir mem. Holy Rosary Parish, 1984-86, children's liturgy cons., 1983-86; choir mem. St. Ann Parish, Butte, 1987—. Cert. in religious edn. Cath. Diocese of Helena, 1988. Mem. Nat. Cath. Edn. Assn., Mont. Student Edn. Assn. (state sec. 1965-66), Pacific N.W. Coun. Foreign Languages, Mont. Assn. of Language Tchrs. Club: Investment (Bozeman). Lodge: Lioness. Office: Butte Cen High Sch 9 S Idaho Butte MT 59701

NASH, PHILIP LUTHER, industrial real estate broker; b. Birmingham, Ala., Jan. 11, 1959; s. Luther William and Annie Laura (Bean) N. BA, Calif. State U., Los Angeles, 1984. Broker Investment Property Services, Glendale, Calif., 1987—. Editor, contbr. newsletter Industrial Report, 1987. Mem. Am. Indsl. Realtors Assn., Rotary (pres.), Toastmasters Internat., Glendale C. of C. Republican. Mem. Evangelical Ch. Home: 4240 Sarah St #24 Burbank CA 91505 Office: Investment Property Svcs 300 W Glen-Oaks #100 Glendale CA 91202

NASH, RICHARD EUGENE, aerospace engineer; b. San Diego, Feb. 18, 1954; s. Clifford Arthur Jr. and Dorothy Fay (Johnson) N.; m. Lynn Elora Martin, Aug. 5, 1978. BSCE, U. Ky., 1981; MCE, U. So. Calif., 1988. Registered profl. civil engr., Calif., 1985. Mem. tech. staff Rockwell Internat., Downey, Calif., 1982—, lead engr. space shuttle propulsion systems, 1986-88; engr. Nat. Aero-Space Plane, Fullerton, Calif., 1988—; pvt. practice civil engring., Buena Park, Calif., 1985—. Scoutmaster Boy Scouts Am., Covington, Ky., 1972-74, Williamstown, Ky., 1976-82, asst. scoutmaster, Ft. Hood, Tex., 1975-76. Recipient Eagle Scout award Boy Scouts Am., 1972; named to Hon. Order of Ky. Cols. 1985. Mem. NSPE, Nat. Mgmt. Assn. (cert. profl. mgr.), Nat. Eagle Scout Assn. (advisor 1983), Chi Epsilon. Republican. Office: Rockwell Internat Space Transp and Systems Div 12214 Lakewood Blvd Downey CA 90241

NASKY, H(AROLD) GREGORY, lawyer; b. Titusville, Pa., June 9, 1942; s. Harold G. and Majella Marie (Beck) N.; m. Rosanne Guson, July 22, 1967. AB, St. Bonaventure U., 1964; JD, U. Notre Dame, 1967. Assoc. Eaton & Hill, Warren, Pa., 1967-68, Vargas, Bartlett & Dixon, Reno, 1972-73; ptnr. Vargas & Bartlett, Las Vegas, Nev., 1974—, mng. ptnr., 1981—; corp. sec. Showboat, Inc. (NYSE-SBO), Las Vegas, 1978—, bd. dirs. 1983—. Legal advisor Nev. Dance Theatre, Las Vegas, 1977—, bd. dirs. 1988—; legal com. Nev. Resort Assn., Las Vegas, 1978-85; life mem. Rep. Nat. Com., Washington, 1984—; bd. dirs. Boulder Dam Council Boy Scouts Am., Las Vegas, 1986—; del. People to People Citizen Ambassador Program, People's Republic China, 1985, New Zealand/Australia, 1987. Served to capt. JAGC, U.S. Army, 1968-72, Vietnam. Decorated Bronze Star, 1970. Mem. ABA, Pa. Bar Assn., State Bar Nev. (chmn. fee dispute com. 1983—, exec. com. mem. Gaming Law Sect. 1985—), Am. Soc. Corp. Secs., Notre Dame Alumni Assn. (pres. Las Vegas chpt. 1978-79). Office: Vargas & Bartlett 300 S 4th St #500 Las Vegas NV 89101

NASO, VALERIE JOAN, automobile dealership executive, travel company operator, photographer, writer; b. Stockton, Calif., Aug. 19, 1941; d. Alan Robert and Natalie Grace (Gardner) McKittrick Naso; m. Peter Joralemon, May 31, 1971 (div.). Student pub. schs., Piedmont, Calif. Cert. graphoanalyst. Pres., Naso Motor Co. (formerly Broadway Cadillacs, Oakland, Calif.) Bishop, Calif., 1964—; owner, operator Wooden Horse Antiques, Bishop, 1970-82; editor, writer, photographer Sierra Life Mag., Bishop, 1980-83; freelance artist, writer, photographer, 1975—; owner, operator Boredom Tours, Bishop, 1981—; owner, sole photographer, Renaissance Photography, N.Y.C. and Bishop, Calif., 1982—, Keyboard Colors, 1986; cons. graphoanalyst. Fiction, non-fiction work pub. in Horse and Horseman, Am. Horseman, Cameo Mag., Desert Mag., Sierra Life Mag. Mem. Authors Guild, Inc., Authors League Am., Am. Film Inst., Archives of Am. Art, Bishop C. of C., Victorian Soc. Am. (Manhatten chpt.), Nat. Trust for Hist. Preservation, Nat. Rifle Assn., Beethoven Soc. Clubs: Cadillac LaSalle; Wagner Soc. (N.Y.C.). Home: 220 E 54th St Apt 9A New York NY 10022 Office: 783 N Main St Bishop CA 93514

NATHANSON, GERALD, retail stores executive. Past pres. Pay'N Save Corp., Seattle; now vice chmn., chief exec. officer PNS Inc. subs. Pay'n Save Corp., Seattle. Office: PNS Inc 4045 Delridge Way SW Seattle WA 98146 *

NATHANSON, PHILIP, healthcare consultant; b. Oakland, Calif., July 21, 1941; s. Ralph and Miriam Gertrude (Cushman) N.; m. Vicky Boretz, June 20, 1964; children: Laura H., Joshua J. AB, U. Calif., Berkeley, 1963. With Social Security Adminstrn., Balt. and San Francisco, 1964-76; dir. gen. policy Social Security Adminstrn., Balt., 1977-78; regional adminstr. Health Care Financing Adminstrn./HHS, San Francisco and Chgo., 1978-86; dir. health standrads and quality bur. Health Care Financing Adminstrn./HHS, Balt. and Washington, 1982-86; corp. dir. clin. cost effectiveness program Am. Med. Internat., Inc., Beverly Hills, Calif., 1986-88; pres. Nathanson Healthcare Consulting Group, Inc., Pacific Palisades, Calif., 1988—. Contbr. articles to profl. jours. Home and Office: Nathanson Healthcare Cons 11696 Michael Ln Pacific Palisades CA 90272

NATHANSON, THEODORE HERZL, aeronautical engineer; architect; b. Montreal, Que., Can., Apr. 20, 1923; came to U.S., 1949; naturalized, 1983; s. Henry and Minnie (Goldberg) N.; student McGill U., 1940-42; SB in Aero. Engring., MIT, 1944; MArch, Harvard U., 1955. Research engr. Noorduyn Aviation Ltd., Montreal, 1944-45; stress engr. Canadair Ltd., Montreal, 1945-46; structural engr. A.V. Roe (Can.) Ltd., Malton, Ont., 1946-47; with Mies van der Rohe, Chgo., summer 1949, R. Buckminster Fuller, Forest Hills, N.Y., summer 1951; cons. engr. and architect, Montreal, Boston, Los Angeles, 1955—; mem. tech. staff Rockwell Internat., 1979—, structural analysis and advanced design Space Transp. Systems div., Downey, Calif., 1979-86, mission ops. and advanced concepts Space Sta. Systems div., 1986-87, space sta. elec. power system Rocketdyne div., Canoga Park, Calif., 1987—; lectr. architecture, McGill U., 1967-68. Fellow Brit. Interplanetary Soc.; mem. Order Engrs. Que., Order Architects Que., Soc. Am. Registered Architects, Nat. Soc. Profl. Engrs., AIAA, Royal Archtl. Inst. Can., Nat. Mgmt. Assn., Copley Soc. of Boston, MIT Club of So. Calif. (bd. govs.), Can. Soc. (Los Angeles). Projects and models included in group shows: Mus. Fine Arts, Springfield, Mass., 1961, N.Y. World's Fair, 1965, Winterfest, Boston, 1966, Boston Artists' Project '70. Jewish. Home: 123 S Figueroa St Apt 231A Los Angeles CA 90012 Office: 6633 Canoga Ave Canoga Park CA 91303

NATHWANI, BHARAT NAROTTAM, pathologist, consultant; b. Bombay, Jan. 20, 1945; came to U.S., 1972; s. Narottam Pragji and Bharati N. (Lakhani) N. MBBS, Grant Med. Coll., Bombay, 1969, MD in Pathology, 1972. Asst. prof. pathology Grant Med. Coll., 1972; fellow in hematology Cook County Hosp., Chgo., 1972-73; resident in pathology Rush U., Chgo., 1973-74; fellow in hematopathology City of Hope Med. Ctr., Duarte, Calif., 1975-76, pathologist, 1977-84; prof. pathology, chief hematopathology U. So. Calif., L.A., 1984—; cons. Norris Cancer Hosp., L.A., 1986—. Contbr. numerous articles to profl. jours. Recipient Grant award Nat. Libr. Medicine, Bethesda, Md., 1986. Mem. AAAS, Internat. Acad. Pathology, Am. Soc. Clin. Pathology, Am. Soc. Hematology, Am. Soc. Oncology. Office: U So Calif Sch Medicine HMR 204 2025 Zonal Ave Los Angeles CA 90033

NATKIN, LEONARD JAY, software engineer; b. Chgo., Sept. 19, 1951; s. Howard Phillip and Elinore Nora (Rabin) N.; m. Oct. 10, 1980 (div. Nov. 1984); 1 child, David Clement; m. Linda Joyce Sherman, Dec. 1, 1984; children: Tanya Nicole, Danielle Renee. Software techniques engr. Honeywell Info. Systems, Phoenix, 1980-84; group leader software support Lockheed Space Ops. Co., Vandenberg AFB, Calif., 1984-86; software engr. Computer Tech. Assocs., Inc., Ridgecrest, Calif., 1986--, Colorado Springs, Colo., 1986--. Recipient Cert. of Appreciation Grumman Tech. Services Inc., , 1986, Team award Lockheed Space Ops. Co., 1986. Republican. Office: Computer Tech Assocs Inc 7150 Campus Dr Ste 100 Colorado Springs CO 80920

NAUGHTEN, ROBERT NORMAN, pediatrician; b. Stockton, Calif., Oct. 13, 1928; s. Norman Stafford and Junetta (Doherty) N.; m. Ann Louise

Charkins, June 26, 1954; children: Robert James, Annette Marie Naughten-Dessel, Patricia Louise. AA, San Jose City Coll., San Jose, Calif., 1948; BA, U. Calif., Berkeley, 1950; MA, Stanford U., 1955; MD, Hahnemann U., 1959. Lic. physician and surgeon, Calif. Intern Highland-Alameda County Hosp., Oakland, Calif., 1959-60; research fellow Nat. Cancer Inst., Stanford, Calif., 1960-61; resident pediatrics Stanford Med. Ctr., 1961-63; pvt. practice pediatrics Los Gatos, Calif., 1963—; instr. Santa Clara Valley Med. Ctr., San Jose, 1963—, Dept. of Pediatrics, Stanford, 1963-73; cons. drug abuse San Jose Police Dept., 1963-68; cons. child abuse Dist. Atty., San Jose, 1984—. Contbr. articles to profl. jours. Bd. dirs., v.p. Outreach and Escort, Inc., San Jose, 1985-88. Named Alumnus of Yr. San Jose City Coll., 1967, Chef of the West Sunset Mag., 1989; fellow Coll. of Physicians, Phila., 1986. Mem. AMA, Calif. Assn., Santa Clara Med. Assn. (v.p. 1986-88), Am. Acad. Pediatrics, Am. Acad. Allergy and Clin. Immunology, Calif. Alumni Assn. (Berkeley), Stanford Alumni Assn., Commonwealth Club (San Francisco). Democrat. Roman Catholic. Home: 13601 Riverdale Dr Saratoga CA 95070 Office: 360 Dardanelli Ln Ste 2B Los Gatos CA 95030

NAUMER, HELMUTH JACOB, museum administrator; b. Santa Fe, May 7, 1934; s. Helmuth and Tomee (Reuter) N.; m. Mary Ann Singleton, Sept. 3, 1957 (div. Feb. 1966); children: Karina Anne, Helmuth Karl; m. Carolyn Palmer, Oct. 9, 1966 (div. Nov. 1986); children: Kirsten Anne, Tatiana Elizabeth. BA, U. N.Mex., 1957; postgrad., U. Minn., 1958. Mgr. Taos Ski Valley, N.Mex., 1958-59; archaeologist Town Creek Indian Mound, Mt. Gilead, N.C., 1959-60; dir. Charlotte Nature Mus., N.C., 1960-62; exec. dir. Fort Worth Mus. Sci. and History, 1962-76, Pacific Sci. Ctr., Seattle, 1976-79; exec. dir., pres. San Antonio Mus. Assn., 1979-86; pres. Mus. N.Mex. Found., 1986-87; officer cultural affairs State of N.Mex., 1987—; chmn. print media sect. White House Conf. on Children, 1970-71; mem. panel Nat. Endowment for Arts, 1973-76, NEH, 1971-72, Smithsonian Conf. Museums and Edn., Tex. Arts and Humanities Commn., Nat. Inst. Mus. Services, 1984-88; speaker Australian Mus. Assn.; mem. Commn. on Mus. for a New Century, 1982-84. Author: Of Mutual Respect and Other Things, 1977; contbr. articles to profl. jours. Bd. dirs. High Frontier, 1978-85, Dallas-Fort Worth Council Sci. Engring. Socs., 1971-73; internat. bd. trustees Turkish Mus., 1984; bd. trustees Inst. Mus. Services, 1988—. Recipient Elsie M.B. Naumberg award Natural Sci. for Youth Found., 1968; Glenda Morgan award for excellence Tex. Hist. Commn., 1986. Mem. Am. Assn. Mus. (chmn. various coms., various offices 1960—), Mt. Plains Mus. Assn. (regional rep.), Tex. Assn. Mus. (pres. 1969, 71), Art Mus. Assn. (bd. dirs.), Am. Assn. Youth Mus. (pres. 1969, 71), Tex. Inst. Small Mus. Republican. Home: Rte 3 Box 105 Santa Fe NM 87501

NAUMER, JANET NOLL, library director; b. Phila., May 26, 1933; d. Ray Clifford and Julia Barton (Coffey) N.; m. Carlos Naumer, Sept. 30, 1960 (div. 1972); 1 child, Mark. BA in Journalism, Pa. State U., 1955; MA, U. Denver, 1968; PhD in Edn., U. Colo., 1978. Media specialist Santa Fe Sr. High Sch., 1968-69; edn. specialist Inst. Am. Indian Arts, Santa Fe, 1969-73; instr. U. N.Mex., Albuquerque, 1973-74; media specialist Kubasaki High Sch., Zukeran, Okinawa, Japan, 1974-75; asst. prof. grad. sch. libr. and info. mgmt. U. Denver, 1977-83; dir. libr. and media ctr. Porterville (Calif.), 1983—; cons. Colo. State Library, Denver, 1981, 83. Author: Media Center Management With an Apple II, 1984; contbr. articles to profl. jours. Bd. dirs. Porterville Hist. Mus., 1986—. No. Calif. Community Colls. rsch. grantee, 1985-86; named innovator of Yr., Kern Dist. League for Innovation, 1988. Mem. ALA, Assn. Ednl. Communications and Tech., Calif. Tchrs. Assn., Phi Delta Kappa, Beta Phi Mu, Theta Sigma Phi. Democrat. Home: 33368 Tule Oak Dr Springville CA 93265

NAYLOR, FRANKLIN LLEWELLYN, JR., financial advisor; b. Arlington, N.J., July 17, 1910; s. Franklin Llewellyn Sr. and Mary H. (Fliedner) N.; m. Edna Anabel Woglom, Sept. 7, 1932 (dec. 1978); children: Marjorie Evelyn Glidden, Franklin III, Virginia Irene Hubacek; m. Louella Roger Sanderson, July 26, 1986. Registered profl. engr., gen. bldg. contractor, real estate broker, Calif.; lic. ins. agt., Ariz.; registered fin. adviser SEC. Engaged in various engring. capacities, 1928—; cons. indsl. engr., 1946—; formerly with Indsl. div. S.S. White Dental Mfg. Co., Breeze Corp., Inc., Walker-Turner Corp., Aluminum Co. Am., also U.S. Spring and Bumper Co., Lockhead Aircraft Corp., Pacific div. Bendix Aviation Corp., Grand Central Aircraft Co.; v.p. Baker and Weikel engrs., after 1948; pres. Naylor Engring. & Research Corp., Los Angeles; mng. gen. agt. Nat. Old Line Ins. Co.; pres. Am. Pacific Life Ins. Co., Honolulu, after 1964; owner, operator Ariz. Chem. & Engring. Co., Tucson and Phoenix, Naylor & Assocs., estate and bus. cons., Tucson and Phoenix; lectr. estate preservation and tax planning, also investment planning for retirement; instr. Tucson and Phoenix secondary schs., Burbank and Glendale Unified Sch. Dists., Calif., 1939—, Ariz. Jr. Colls., Ariz. State Colls. Author: Aluminum and Its Alloys; co-author several books on supervisory devel. Contbr. articles to maj. trade jours. Pres. Glendale-Burbank Joint Carpentry Apprentice Com., 1948; mem. War Prodn. Bd., World War II; chmn. trade adv. com. for sheet metal workers Nat. Def. Com., 1943-45, employer rep. trade com. for drafting, lofting and pattern makers, 1943-45.; mem. SCORE, Hattiesburg, Miss., 1987—; vice chmn. Small Bus. Execs. Clearing House; mem. Internat. Exec. Service Corps.; pres. Greater Phoenix Republican Club, 1962. Mem. AMSE (life, bd. dirs. profl. mgmt. div.), Am. Ordnance Assn., Bldg. Contractors Assn. Calif., Soc. Advancement Mgmt., Glendale C. of C., Am. Arbitration Assn. (nat. panel arbitrators), Hammond Organ Soc. (pres. Tucson 1955), AIM, Hawaii C. of C. (aero affairs com., vocat. edn. and manpower com., indsl. devel. com.), NSPE, Nat. Travel Club, Presidents Club, Phoenix Execs. Club, Statesman's Club, Hattiesburg (Miss) Country. Office: F Naylor & Assocs 1334 W Mulberry Dr Phoenix AZ 85013-4029 Address: 107 Greenwood Pl Hattiesburg MS 39401

NAZZARO, DAVID ALFRED, sales executive; b. Malden, Mass., Sept. 15, 1940; s. Alfred Anthony and Louise (Cunningham) N.; m. Jane Valentine, June 26, 1971; one child, David Thomas. BME, U.S. Mcht. Marine Acad., 1962; MS, Columbia U., 1965; MBA, Pepperdine U., 1975. Regional mgr. Turbo Power and Marine Systems div. United Tehcnologies, Hardford, Conn., 1965-74; mgr. bus. devel S & Q Corp., San Francisco, 1974-78; v.p. and gen. mgr. Con-Val, Oakland, Calif., 1978-85; pres. and chief exec. officer Dasa Controls, Belmont, Calif., 1985-87; mgr. bus. devel Johnson Controls, Inc., San Francisco, 1987--. Contbr. papers to profl. publs. Bd. dirs. Clearview Homeowners Assn., San Mateo, 1976; pres. St. Bartholomew's Parish Council, San Mateo, 1986. Lt. USNR, 1963-69. Sr. Mem. Instrument Soc. Am. (pres. No. Calif. Sec. 1987-88); mem. ASME, Am. Water Works Assn., Elks, Jaycees, St. Bartholomew's Mens Club (pres. 1977). Home: 30 Tollridge Ct San Mateo CA 94402 Office: Johnson Controls Inc 50 Park Ln Brisbane CA 94005

NEAL, JAMES WEATHERLY, investment banker; b. Greensboro, N.C., Nov. 6, 1956; s. James Weatherly and Mildred (Hartzoge) N.; m. Suzanne Jarema, Sept. 15, 1979; children: James Weatherly III, Winston Dwyer. BS, U. N.C., 1978; MBA, U. Chgo., 1983. V.p. Salomon Bros., L.A., 1983-87; mng. dir. Bear, Stearns & Co. Inc., L.A., 1988—. Mem. exec. com. Pres.'s Invitational Golf Tournament, Children's Bur. L.A., 1989. Mem. Sleepy Hollow Country Club (Scarborough, N.Y.), Regency Club (L.A.). Home: 11827 Kearsarge St Los Angeles CA 90049 Office: Bear Stearns & Co Inc 1800 Century Park East Los Angeles CA 90067

NEAL, ROBERT EUGENE, JR., financial and legal printing executive; b. Lebanon, Ind., Aug. 22, 1944; s. Robert Eugene and Ruth Winifred (Medsker) N.; A.B., Wabash Coll., 1966; postgrad. Butler U., 1967-68; m. Gretchen Ann Rolfe, June 21, 1975; children—Patricia Lee, Lisa Lyn, David Christopher. With R. R. Donnelley & Sons, Chgo., 1966-69, exec. salesman, 1968-69; with Arcata Corp., Menlo Park, Calif., 1970-76, mgr. corp. planning and devel., 1975-76; Bowne & Co., Inc., 1976-83; pres. Bowne of San Francisco, Inc., 1979-83; pres. Pandick, San Francisco, 1983-86; exec. v.p. Pandick Calif., Inc., 1986—; pres. S&G Press, Inc.; mng. ptnr. Corp. Fin. Assocs. of San Ramon, Calif. Mem. Am. Soc. Corp. Secs., Assn. Corp. Growth, Printing Industries No. Calif. Republican. Clubs: Kiwanis, Tennis (San Francisco); Round Hill Golf and Country (Alamo, Calif.); Commonwealth of Calif. Home: 3570 Deer Crest Dr Danville CA 94526 Office: 25377 Huntwood Ave Hayward CA 94544

NEAL, TIMOTHY ROBERT, organization executive; b. Lynwood, Calif., Oct. 26, 1951; s. Warren Robert and Marjorie May (Cuddigan) N.; m. Marsha Flynn, Apr. 15 1971 (div. 1979); children: Brian Robert, Katherine Louise, Jennifer Marie; m. Jo Ann Kenworthy, June 26, 1981; 1 child, Nicolas Simon Cooper. BS, U. San Francisco, 1980. Cert. fund raising practitioner. Purchasing agt. Zynolyte Paint Products, Compton, Calif., 1971-75; fin. mgr. GM, San Francisco, 1975-81; dist. exec. Boy Scouts Am., Visalia, Calif., 1981-84; dist. exec. Boy Scouts Am., San Mateo, Calif., 1984-86, fin. dir., 1986-88; sr. dist. exec. Boy Scouts Am., Modesto, Calif., 1988—. Scoutmaster Boy Scouts Am., Downey, Calif., 1971, cubmaster, Hanford, Calif., 1982; vol. San Francisco Bay area United Way, 1988. Recipient Profl. Circle award Boy Scouts Am., 1985, Fellowship honor, 1988. Republican. Home: 3113 Village Park Ct Turlock CA 95380 Office: Boy Scouts Am 1324 Celeste Dr Modesto CA 95355

NEAL-RICKER, NORMA CANDACE, construction engineer; b. Berkeley, Calif., Aug. 19, 1947; d. Charles Edward and Norma Alice (Davidson) Neal; m. Frederick Augustin Ricker; children: Candace Victoria, Chelsea Elizabeth. BS, Oregon State U., 1969; MBA, Golden Gate U., 1977; postgrad exec. program, Stanford U., 1988. Personnel mgmt. Bechtel Group of Cos., Sn Francisco, 1969-73, contracts mgr., 1973-78, bus. devel. exec. rep., 1978-84, project mgr. exec. rep., 1984—. Bd. dirs. Marin YMCA, San Rafael, Calif., 1976—. Named Outstanding Young Career Woman, Bus. and Profl. Women, San Francisco, 1970. Mem. Commercial Club, Commonwealth Club. Republican. Episcopalian. Home: 88 Monte Vista Rd Fairfax CA 94930 Office: Bechtel Inc PO Box 3965 San Francisco CA 94119

NEARING, RICHARD CARL, artist; b. Toledo, Aug. 11, 1923; s. Carl Theodore and Gertrude Ellen (Morgan) N.; m. Barbara Jean Crosley, Dec. 30, 1946; children: Sherry DeWilde, Nancy Gail, Richard David. Student, Miami U., Oxford, Ohio, 1941-42, 46-47. Mgr. gen. sales Action Equipment Co., Phoenix and Tucson, 1974-77; mfrs. rep. Century Agts., Inc., Tempe, Ariz., 1977-83; owner, artist Heritage Gallery of Art, Tempe, 1983-86; artist, co-owner Country Palette and Heritage Framers, Inc., Tempe, 1986—; instr. art Country Palette and Heritage Framers, Inc., Tempe, 1986—. Dist. scout chmn. Boy Scouts Am., Tempe, 1977-78; mem. Ariz. Ctr. Reverse the Arms Race, Phoenix, 1984—. Served to cpl. USAC, 1943-45, 50-51, PTO. Mem. Ariz. Artist Guild, Tempe Art League, Inc. (treas. 1986-88, pres. 1988—), Mesa Art League, Ironwood Soc. Democrat. Lodge: Lions (treas. Garwood, N.J. chpt. 1965-70). Home: 1807 E Loma Vista Dr Tempe AZ 85282

NEEB, MARTIN JOHN, media executive; b. Austin, Texas, Aug. 16, 1933; s. Martin Jacob and Vera (Basilius) N.; m. Barbara Ann Brauer, Aug. 25, 1956; children: Douglas Martin, John Martin, Kristina. BA, Concordia Theol. Sem, St. Louis, 1955, MDiv in Theology, 1958; MA, St. Louis U., 1959; PhD, Northwestern U., 1967; grad. exec. mgmt. program, U. Pa., 1983. Gen. mgr. sta. WNUR-FM, Northwestern U., Evanston, Ill., 1965-67; dir. pub. rels., assoc. prof. speech Concordia Coll., Chgo., 1959-67; exec. sec. and gen. mgr. Luth. TV, St. Louis, 1967-78; dir. broadcast div. Franciscan Communications Ctr., L.A., 1978-81; exec. dir. univ. communications and gen. mgr. sta. KPLU-FM, Pacific Luth. U., Tacoma, 1981—; former bd. dirs. Luth. Film Assocs., Templeton Found. Adv. Com.; former bd. dirs., Arthritis Found., U.S. Cath. Conf. Commucications Com. Finalist White House fellowship, 1966, fellow Northwestern U., 1965-66, recipient Nat. TV Emmy Awards, 1974, 77, Gabriel awards, various other media awards from N.Y. Film and TV Festival, Columbus Film Festival, TV Bur. Advt., Freedoms Found., San Francisco Internat. Film Festival, Am. Film Festival, Advt. Club of L.A., Faith and Freedom award Religious Heritage Am., 1985; named One of Outstanding Young Men Am., Jr. C. of C., 1967. Mem. Religious Pub. Rels. Assn. (bd. dirs., nat. awards chmn.), Internat. TV Assn., Pub. Rels. Soc. Am., Nat. Protestant Broadcasters (pres. 1982), Parkland/Spanaway C. of C. (bd. dirs.), City Club Ta;coma (program chmn. 1984). Lutheran. Home: 18109 28th Ave E Tacoma WA 98445 Office: Pacific Luth U Tacoma WA 98447

NEECE, OLIVIA HELENE, interior designer; b. Los Angeles, Jan. 3, 1948; d. Robert and Beatrice Pearl Ernst; m. Huntley Lee Bluestein, 1967 (div. 1974); children: Melissa Dawn, Brendon Wade; m. Anthony Ray Neece, Mar. 20, 1977. Student, U. So. Calif., 1966-69, 86—; cert. interior design, UCLA, 1972-75. Cert. Nat. Council Interior Design Qualification; lic. gen. contractor Calif. Staff designer Frances Lux Designs, Los Angeles, 1974; project designer Yates Silverman Inc., Los Angeles, 1974-77; owner Olivia Neece Planning & Design, Tarzana, Calif., 1977-86; v.p. project devel. Design Services/Aircoa, Englewood, Colo., 1986-87; v.p. project adminstrn. Hirsch-Bedner Assoc., Santa Monica, Calif., 1987-88; treas./sec. Eon Corp/Ernst, Luce, Neece Assocs., Los Angeles, 1980—; owner Olivia Neece Planning & Design, Tarzana, 1988—; speaker in field; instr. UCLA Extension Program, 1981-83. Co-author: A Step by Step Approach to Hotel Development, 1988; conbtr. articles to profl. jours. Vol. restoration San Diego RR Mus., 1985-88. Recipient Holiday Inn Devel. award, Foster City, Calif., 1986, Warwick, R.I., 1988, 1st and 2d place awards Lodging Hospitality Designers Circle, 1987, Gold Key award Russell St. Inn, 1986. Mem. Inst. Bus. Designers (v.p., bd. dirs.), Am. Soc. Interior Designers (1st place award portfolio competition 1974), Illumination Engring. Soc. (1st place residential design 1982), Am. Hotel and Motel Assn., Los Angeles County Mus. Art (charter mem.), Decorative Arts Coun. Office: Olivia Neece Planning & Design 18200 Rosita St Tarzana CA 91356

NEEDHAM, ROBERT BENNETT, military officer, chaplain; b. Chgo., July 22, 1936; s. Robert Leonard and Grace Irene (Bennet) N.; m. Barbara Jean Ferguson, Sept. 9, 1961; children: Bethel Kristina, Rebekah Dawn, Sharon Grace, Rachel Melissa. BA in Biology, Reed Coll., 1962; M in Div., Westminster Theol. Sem., 1966; MA in Nat. Security Affairs, Naval Postgrad. Sch., 1979. Ordained to ministry Reformed Presbyn. Ch., 1967; cert. specialist strategic planning and internat. security USN, 1979. Pastor Reformed Presbyn. Ch., Muscle Shoals, Ala., 1966-67, View Crest Community Ch., Eighty Four, Pa., 1967-71; commd. lt. USN, 1968, advanced through grades to comdr.; squadron chaplain USN, San Diego, 1972-74; staff chaplain USN, Lemoore, Calif., 1974-77; squadron and staff chaplain USN, Charleston, S.C., 1979-83, sr. chaplain, 1983-84; group chaplain Marine Aircraft Group 16 USN, Tustin, Calif., 1984-88; command chaplain USS Tarawa USN, 1988—. Pres. Sandhurst Civic Assn., Charleston, 1982; exec. v.p. Charleston Clean City Commn., 1983; chmn. bd. dirs. Charleston Christian Sch., 1980-84. Mem. Officers Christian Fellowship (nat. bd. dirs. 1984—), Joint Svcs. Conf. on Profl. Ethics, Internat. Motor Car Club. Republican. Clubs: Packard Auto Classics (Oakland, Calif.), Packards Internat. (Santa Ana, Calif.). Home: 538 Hibiscus Ct Chula Vista CA 92011 Office: USS Tarawa (LHA-1) FPO San Francisco CA 96622-1600

NEELY, JAMES DENNIS, specialty gas manufacturing executive; b. Beaver Falls, Pa., May 7, 1952; s. Robert Paul and Margaret Evelyn (Smith) N. Student, Pa. State U., 1971-73, U. Hawaii, 1973-75. Entomologist Dept of Def. Kaneohe Marine Corp. Air Sta., Kailua, Hawaii, 1975-80; gen. mgr., v.p. W.A. Flick Co (The Brit. Oxygen Corp.), Honolulu, 1984-85; tech. rep. Gaspro (Airco, The Brit. Oxygen Corp.), Honolulu, 1985—. Fund raiser Aloha United Way, Honolulu, 1987—; bd. dirs. Hale Kipa Youth Shelters, Honolulu, 1984—, Hawaii Youth Shelter Vol. Program, Honolulu, 1987; mem. Hoopono adv. bd. State Found. for the Rehab. of the Blind, 1989—. Recipient Thomas Jefferson award Am. Inst. Pub. Service, 1988. Mem. Entomol. Soc. Am., Australian Am. C. of C. (Hawaiian chpt.). Democrat. Presbyn. Home: 46316 Ahui Nani Pl Kaneohe HI 96744

NEERHOUT, JOHN, JR., petroleum company executive; b. 1931. BSME, U. Calif., 1953. With Bechtel Petroleum, Inc. (now Bechtel, Inc.), San Francisco, 1966—; pres. Bechtel Petroleum, Inc. (now Bechtel, Inc.), 1983-86, also dir. Bechtel Group, Inc. Office: Bechtel Inc PO Box 3965 San Francisco CA 94119

NEFF, JAMES DENNIS, manufacturing company executive, consultant; b. Ft. Wayne, Ind., Aug. 24, 1937; s. James Marion and Margaret Ann (Lynch) N.; m. Jeanette Ann Day, Apr. 8, 1966; children: Bryan James, Julie Ann, Sarah Lynn. Student, Purdue U., 1955-57; BSME, U. Ill., 1959; MBA, Ind. U., 1963. Sr. mktg. analyst Allison div. Gen. Motors Corp., Indpls., 1963-67; mgr. Merwins Internat. Harvester Truck Dealership, St. Croix, V.I., 1967-68; sr. v.p. Hexcel Corp., Dublin, Calif., 1968—; coll. instr. V.I., 1967-68. Served with U.S. Army, 1960. Mem. Aerospace Industries Assn., Am. Def. Preparedness Assn. (bd. dirs. 1975), Soc. Advancement of Material and Process Engring. (presenter). Office: Hexcel Corp 11555 Dublin Blvd Dublin CA 94568

NEFF, WILLIAM MEDINA, biology educator; b. San Francisco, Oct. 27, 1929; s. Benjamin Henry and Ruth Marion (Medina) N.; m. Joan MacIntyre Frisbie, July 18, 1952; children: Harold, Susan Janet, Patricia (dec.). AB, Stanford U., 1951, PhD, 1958. Assoc. prof. Knox Coll., Galesburg, Ill., 1956-68, Chico (Calif.) State Coll., Ill., 1968-70; instr. biology San Francisco City Coll., 1970—; rsch. assoc., Argonne Nat. Lab., Lemont, Ill., 1961-62. Mem. AAAS, Western Soc. Naturalists, Calif. Acad. Scis., Call Apple. Democrat. Office: San Francisco City Coll 50 Phelan Ave San Francisco CA 94112

NEFF-SINCLAIR, JAN A., software engineer; b. Chgo., Sept. 12, 1957; d. Jerome Price and Joan Ruth (McKeown) Neff. Student, Ill. Inst. Technology, Chgo., 1975-78, De Anza Coll., Cupertino, Calif., 1980-81, San Diego Community Coll., 1985-89. Computer programmer Cortron Div. Ill. Tool Works, Inc., Elmhurst, 1977-78; systems programmer Olivetti Advanced Technology Ctr., Cupertino; software engr. Lomac Corp., San Jose, Calif., Shasta Gen. Systems, Sunnyvale, Omex, Santa Clara, Calif.; sr. software project engr. Metacomp, Inc., San Diego, 1983-86; prin. programmer analyst Fusitsu Systems Am., Inc., San Diego, 1986—. Mem. NAFE, Mensa, Theatre Goers of San Diego, Athletic Singles Assn. Libertarian. Home: 9528 Miramar Rd #8 San Diego CA 92126

NEGRIN, ALAN EDWARD, telecommunications company executive; b. Bronx, N.Y., June 23, 1938; s. David and Lillian (Emanuel) N.; m. Patricia Townsend, Mar. 1, 1962; children: Anthony, Katherine. BSEE, U. Calif., Berkeley, 1960; MSEE, Stanford U., 1964. Electronics engr. Gen. Dynamics Corp., San Diego, Calif., 1960-62; mgr., office systems Xerox Corp., Palo Alto, Calif., 1964-79; v.p. Harris Digital Telephone Systems, Novato, Calif., 1979-84; pres. Elan Digital Systems, Palo Alto, 1984-86; exec. v.p. Optilink Corp., Petaluma, Calif., 1987—; dir. Optilink Corp., Petaluma, 1987—, Elan Digital Systems, Ltd., Crawley, Sussex, U.K., 1976—. Contbr. articles to profl. jours. Office: Optilink Corp 1310C Redwood Way Petaluma CA 94952

NEHAMEN, CLIFFORD ALVIN, finance executive; b. L.A., Sept. 10, 1948; s. Norman and Edith (Gootman) N.; m. Gail Ann Olken, July 15, 1973; children: Marc, Megan. Degree in Indsl. Arts, Santa Monica City Coll., Calif., 1968; BSBA, Woodbury Coll., 1970; student, UCLA, 1978. Cert. credit mgmt. Sr. asst. mgr. Household Fin. Corp., various, 1971-74; collection mgr. Fireside Thrift and Loan, various, 1974-76; credit mgr. Forecast Lighting Co., Inglewood, Calif., 1976-80; dir. corp. credit Hoffinger Ind. Inc., Rancho Cucamonga, Calif., 1980—. Pres. City of Hope, Rancho Cucamonga, 1986; coach Citrus Little League, Rancho Cucamonga, 1983. Recipient Disting. Chmn. award, N.Y. Credit Assn.; named Fin. Mgr. of Yr., N.Y. Credit Assn., 1987, 88. Mem. N.Y. Credit Assn. (chmn. 1983-88, legis. com. 1984-87). Office: Hoffinger Industries Inc 10959 Jersey Blvd Rancho Cucamonga CA 91730

NEHER, RAYMOND EDWIN, soil scientist; b. McCune, Kans., Feb. 5, 1925; s. Eli Edwin and Myra Sybil (Lange) N.; m. Marjorie Anne Roepke, Oct. 28, 1950; 1 dau., Elizabeth Anne. BS, Kans. State U., 1950; student Cornell U., 1965, N.Mex. State U., 1966. Cert. soils scientist Southwest Engrs.; cert. soils specialist Dona Ana County, N.Mex. Student asst. Agronomy Dept., Kans. State U., 1946-50; soil scientist trainee U.S. Dept. Agr., Emporia, Kans., 1950, soil scientist, 1950-53; self-employed rancher, farmer, Manhattan, Kans., 1953-56; soil scientist, party leader, Mountainair, N.Mex., 1956-60, Lordsburg, N.Mex., 1960-63, Taos, N.Mex., 1963-66, Las Cruces, N.Mex., 1966-77, Truth or Consequences, N.Mex., 1977-79, area soil scientist Soil Conservation Service, U.S. Dept. Agr., Las Cruces, 1979-83, Dona Ana County Survey and Engring. Dept., N.Mex., 1984-87; dir. Dona Ana County Flood Commn., 1987—. Served with USNR, 1944-46. Registered Soil Scientist, soil classifier, soil specialist. Mem. Soil Conservation Soc. Am. (past pres.), Am. Soc. Agronomy, Soil Sci. Soc. Am., Soil Sci. Soc. N.Mex. (past pres.). Methodist (lay speaker). Clubs: Kiwanis, Mesilla Valley Radio, Voz Vaqueros, The Singing Men of Las Cruces. Contbr. articles to U.S. Dept. Agr. and univs. Home: 1930 E Madrid Ave Las Cruces NM 88001

NEIDERT, KALO EDWARD, educator; b. Safe, Mo., Sept. 1, 1918; s. Edward Robert and Margaret Emma (Kinsey) N.; m. Stella Mae Vest, June 22, 1952; children—Edward, Karl, David, Wayne, Margaret. B.S. in Bus. Adminstrn. with honors, Washington U., St. Louis, 1949, M.S. in Bus. Adminstrn, 1950; postgrad., U. Minn., 1950-54. C.P.A., Nev. Mem. faculty U. Minn., 1950-54; mem. faculty U. Miss., 1954-57, U. Tex., Austin, 1957-61, Gustavus Adolphus Coll., St. Peter, Minn., 1961-62, U. Nev., Reno, 1962—; prof. acctg. and info. systems U. Nev., 1962—; auditor Washoe County Employee Fed. Credit Union, 1969-82, dir., treas., 1982-86. Author: Statement on Auditing Procedure in Decision Tree Form, 1974. Asst. scoutmaster local Boy Scouts Am.; Bd. dirs. Tahoe Timber Trails, 1980-82, treas., 1981-82, v.p. fin., 1982-84; Bd. dirs. St. Johns Child Care Center, 1982-84. Mem. Am. Inst. C.P.A.'s, Assn. System Mgmt. (treas. Reno chpt. 1984—), Am. Acctg. Assn., Am. Econ. Assn., Fin. Mgmt. Assn., Nev. Soc. C.P.A.'s, Western Fin. Assn., Beta Alpha Psi, Beta Gamma Sigma. Presbyterian. Club: Odd Fellows. Home: 2300 Balsam St Reno NV 89502 Office: Coll Bus Adminstrn Univ Nev Reno NV 89557

NEIL, JESSIE PRUITT, businesswoman, civic worker; b. Pasadena, Calif., Oct. 20, 1927; d. Cecil D. and Jessie (Parsons) Pruitt; BA, U. So. Calif., 1950; m. Edmund R. Neil, Mar. 24, 1956; children: Edmund R. II, Jessica R., Richard William. Dir. design Leland Gardens Bldg. Corp., 1950-56; sales dir. Washington Sq. Bldg. Corp., 1950-52; pres. Barrett Devel. Corp., 1951-70; sec. Reliance Bldg. Corp., 1951-68; self-employed home designer, 1953; sec. So. Counties Escrow, 1956-77; pres. Futuramic Homes, Inc., 1956-68, Desert and Delta Safaris, Inc., Desert and Delta Safaris Pty. Ltd., Botswana, Africa, Desert and Delta Air Svcs., Mokoro Holdings Ltd., Maun Properties. Founder Cardiac League, Guild of Huntington Meml. Hosp., 1963; pres. Cardiac League, 1966-68, pres. Women's Council, 1967; v.p. San Marino League, 1968-73; pres. docent council Pasadena Art Mus., 1971-72; mem. Costume Council L.A. County Mus.; assoc. U. So. Calif.; patron, mem. membership council Pasadena Art Mus.; mem. Founders L.A. Music Ctr.; hon. life mem. Arcadia Meth. Hosp.; Blue Ribbon 400 of L.A. Music Ctr. Recipient graphics award Pasadena Arts Council, 1968; Eve award. Mem. World Affairs Council, Internat. Platform Assn., Fellows Pasadena Art Mus., Assistance League So. Calif., Nine O'Clock Players, Delta Zeta. Home: 301 Hermosa St South Pasadena CA 91030 Office: Pvt Bag 10, Maun Botswana

NEILSEN, ELEANOR JO, sales executive; b. L.A., Sept. 29, 1911; d. Frank Luther and Annie Marie Manley. AA, Compton Jr. Coll., 1932; student, UCLA, 1932-33. Office mgr. Point Mugu Resort, Oxnard, Calif., 1941-43; co-owner Neilsen Tire Co., Ventura, Calif., 1944-60; mgr., buyer Community Meml. Hosp. & Gift Shop, Ventura, 1961—; pres. Bus. & Profl., Ventura Calif. 1949-50; mem. Ventura Adv. Com., 1953. Supt. Home Econ. County Fair, Ventura, 1951-60; bd. dirs. Aux. Community. Mem. Saticoy Country Club. Home: 2135 Hilcrest Dr Ventura CA 93001 Office: Community Meml Hosp Bent at Loma Vista Ventura CA 93001

NEILSON, JOHN WILBERT TENNANT, research company executive, consultant, educator; b. Oakland, Calif., May 9, 1944; s. Donald Wilbert Tennant and Mary Vera (Peart) N.; divorced; children—Sean Wilbert Tennant, Kimberly Mary. B.S. in Edn., So. Oreg. State Coll., 1969, M.S. in Gen. Studies, 1972. Registered sanitarian trainee Oreg. State Dept. Health, 1973. Dept. chmn. Days Creek (Oreg.) High Sch., 1969-70; chmn. biology dept. South Umpqua High Sch., Myrtle Creek, Oreg., 1970-75; microbiologist, chemist Umpqua Research Co., Myrtle Creek, Oreg., 1973-76, field rep., 1976-78; prof. sci. Lane Community Coll., Eugene, Oreg., 1976-78; salesman Jewett Office Supply, Medford, Oreg., 1978-80, Truscott Office Products, Medford, 1978-82, chief exec. officer pres. Neilson Research Medford, 1976—; lab. analyst, cons. drinking water. Served with U.S. Army, 1962-65, USAR, 1976—. Mem. Am. Soc. Microbiology, Am. Water Works Assn., Assn. Ofcl. Analytical Chemists, Water Pollution Control Fedn. Republican. Episcopalian. Club: Rotary. Author: Northwestern CB Log Book, 1976. Office: 446 Highland Dr Medford OR 97504

NEILSON, ROBERT MCKENZIE, JR., materials scientist; b. Buffalo, July 1, 1949; s. Robert McKenzie and Jean E. (Feist) N.; m. Georgette P. Mullen, May 22, 1971 (div. May 1984); 1 child, Robert McKenzie III; m. Laurel Kim Moncur, Dec. 22, 1984; 1 child, Amber. B Engring. Sci., SUNY, Stony Brook, 1971, MS in Materials Sci., 1973, MS in Indsl. Mgmt., 1979. Sci. assoc. Brookhaven Nat. Lab., Upton, N.Y., 1974-82; sr. scientist EG&G Idaho, Inc., Idaho Falls, 1982-88, rsch. and devel. mgr., 1988—; cons., Idaho Falls, 1983—; lectr. ASME, N.Y.C., 1978-82; U.S. rep. IAEA, Vienna, Austria, 1980. Editor Jour. Nuclear and Chem. Waste, 1980-83; contbr. articles to profl. jours.; patentee tritum waste disposal field. Bd. dirs. Bonneville County unit Am. Cancer Soc., 1984—; mem. Idaho Innovation Ctr., 1988—. Recipient R & D 100 award R & D mag., 1988. Mem. Am. Ceramic Soc., Am. Soc. for Metals (bd. dirs. local chpt. 1980-82), Am. Nuclear Soc. (standards com. 1981—), ASTM (C-28 com. 1986—), U.S. Power Squadron (sec. Patchogue, N.Y. 1980-82), Idaho Falls Ski Club, Tau Beta Pi. Republican. Episcopalian. Office: EG&G Idaho Inc PO Box 1625 Idaho Falls ID 83415

NEIMANN, ALBERT ALEXANDER, statistician, consultant; b. Torrington, Wyo., Nov. 29, 1939; s. Alexander and Lydia (Temple) N.; m. Barbara Jean (Maw), May 6, 1962; children: Debbie, Todd, Amy, Kelly. BA, Willamette U., 1967. Mathematician Keyport (Wash.) Naval Torpedo Sta., 1968-70; math. statistician Concord (Calif.) Naval Weapons Sta., 1970-85, engring. statistician, 1985—. Mgr. Little League Baseball, Antioch, Calif., 1977-84, Little League Softball, Antioch, 1984-87; Sunday sch. tchr. Grace Bapt. Ch., 1979—; statistician Antioch High Sch., 1985—. With USAF, 1961-65. Recipient performance award Concord Naval Weapons Sta., 1979, 88. Mem. Am. Statis. Assn., Math. Assn. Am., Am. Soc. for Quality Control, Nat. Coun. Tchrs. Math.

NEIPLING, LAWRENCE EDWARD, marketing executive, engineering consultant; b. Nov. 24, 1953; s. Lawrence Edward and Joan (Nolen) N.; m. Apr. 9, 1977. BS in Mech. Engring., Calif. State U., Long Beach, 1976, MS in Mech. Engring., 1979, cert. supervision, 1984; MBA with honors, Nat. U., 1988. Registered profl. engr., Calif.; lic. bldg. contractor, Calif.; cert. jr. coll. tchr., Calif. Design engr. Rockwell Internat., L.A., 1976-77, Hughes Co., L.A., 1977-78; project engr. Dana Corp., Irvine, Calif., 1978-81; product mgr. Smith Internat., Irvine, Long Beach, Calif., 1981-86, London, 1981-86; mgr. internat. mktg. Shamban Internat., Santa Monica, Calif., 1986--; solar advisor Harbor (Calif.) Coll., 1980; instr. Cerritos (Calif.) Coll., 1982. Patentee choke control system. Mem. ASME (assoc.), Pi Tau Sigma. Home: 43471 Clubhouse Dr Lakewood CA 90712 Office: Shamban Internat 24412 S Main St Carson CA 90745

NELIPOVICH, SANDRA GRASSI, artist; b. Oak Park, Ill., Nov. 22, 1939; d. Alessandro and Lena Mary (Ascareggi) Grassi; m. John Nelipovich Jr., Aug. 19, 1973. BFA in Art Edn., U. Ill., 1961; postgrad., Northwestern U., 1963, Gonzaga U., Florence, Italy, 1966, Art Inst. Chgo., 1968; diploma, Accademia Universale Alessandro Magno, Prato, Italy, 1983. Tchr. art Edgewood Jr. High Sch., Highland Park, Ill., 1961-62, Emerson Sch. Jr. High Sch., Oak Park, 1962-77; batik artist Calif., 1977—; illustrator Jolly Robin Publ. Co., Anaheim, Calif., 1988—; supr. student tchrs., Oak Park, 1970-75; adult edn. tchr. ESL, ceramics, Medinah, Ill., 1974; mem. curriculum action group on Human Dignity, EEO workshop demonstrator, Oak Park, 1975-76; guest lectr. Muckenthaler Ctr., Fullerton, Calif., 1980, Niguel Art Group, Dana Point, Calif., 1989; fabric designer for fashion designer Barbara Jax, 1987. One-woman shows include Lawry's Calif. Ctr., Los Angeles, 1981-83, 1982, Whittier (Calif.) Mus., 1985-86, Anaheim (Calif.) Cultural Ctr., 1986-88, Ill. Inst. Tech., Chgo., 1989; also gallery exhibits in Oak Brook, Ill., 1982, La Habra, Calif., 1983; represented in permanent collections McDonald's Corp., Oak Brook, Ill., Glenkirk Sch., Deerfield, Ill., and in galleries in Laguna Beach, Calif., Maui, Hawaii; illustrator for Jolly Robin Pub. Co., Anaheim, 1988—; poster designer Saratoga Fine Arts Show, 1989. Recipient numerous awards, purchase prizes, 1979—. Mem. AAUW (hospitality chmn. 1984-85), Oak Park Art League, Orange Art Assn. (jury chairperson 1980), Anaheim Art Assn., Muckenthaler Ctr. Circle. Roman Catholic. Club: Anaheim Hills Women's. Home and Office: 5922 Calle Cedro Anaheim CA 92807

NELL, JAMES LEO, hospital administrator; b. N.Y.C., Oct. 4, 1948; s. Sidney Watts and June Sybil (Suesskind) n.; m. Patricia Jean Falkowski, May 11, 1974; children: Daniel Alexander, Christopher Eric. BA, Rutgers U., 1970; MHA, U. Mich., 1972. Staff specialist N.J. Hosp. Assn., Princeton, N.J., 1972-75; asst. dir. N.J. Hosp. Assn., Princeton, 1975-78; dir. Monmouth-Ocean Hosp. Shared Services Assn., Wall Twp., N.J., 1978-79; pres. S. Cen. Mich. Hosp. Council, Lansing, 1979-83, Seattle Area Hosp. Council, 1983—; mem. steering com. Community Obsterics Referral Program, Seattle, 1985—, State Issues Forum, Washington, 1986—; mem. adminstrv. com. Found. Health Care Quality, Seattle, 1988—. Pres. Rep. Club, Matawan, N.J., 1978-79. Lt. USAFR, 1972-80. Mem. Allied Hosp. Assn. (mem. com.), Am. Hosp. Assn., Am. Soc. Assn. Execs., Am. Coll., Healthcare Execs., Rotary. Office: Seattle Area Hosp Coun 190 Queen Anne North Seattle WA 98109

NELLI, JOHN DAVID, health facility administrator; b. Glendale, Calif., Oct. 30, 1952; s. Andrew Edward and Hope (Merian) N.; m. Karen Elaine Adamson, Apr. 17, 1982; 1 child, Hilary Caroline. BA, Pepperdine U., 1974, MA in Psychology, 1975. Counselor, program dir. Teen Challenge, Los Angeles, 1975-77; adminstr. Waxtec Industry, Canoga Park, Calif., 1977-83, The Lighthouse, North Hollywood, Calif., 1983—. Mem. Pres. Council Calif. Reps., 1982—. Mem. Calif. Orgn. Residential Care Operators, Calif. Assn. Residential Homes, Wisdom Seekers (pres. 1984-85), Unison Software Club. Mem. Assembly of God Ch. Home: 513 Cumberland Rd Glendale CA 91202 Office: The Lighthouse 10406 Magnolia Blvd North Hollywood CA 91601

NELMS, SHERYL LYNNE, writer; b. Marysville, Kans., Dec. 3, 1944; d. Edwin Andrew and Margaret Eva (Smith) Nelms; m. Edward Floyd Baker, Aug. 9, 1963 (div. 1984); children: Julie Lynne, Benjamin Edward, David Alan; m. Danny Clayton Pennington, June 3, 1986. BS, S.D. State U., 1979. Cert. nursery sch. tchr., Ariz.; lic. ins. agt., Ariz. With Kelly Svcs., Hurst, Tex., 1983, Tucson, 1986-87; with N & N Life Investors, Hurst, 1983-85; ins. adjustor Va. Life Ins. Co., Ft. Worth, 1985-86; ins. sales agt. A.L. Williams/Milico, Tucson, 1986-87, United of Omaha/Mil. Sales, Tucson, 1987-88; counsellor Non-Commd. Officers Assn./Acad. Life, Tucson, 1988; with Landscapes by Susanna, Las Cruces, N.Mex., 1989—. Author poetry books: Their Combs Turn Red in the Spring, 1984, Sunrust, 1987, The OKeto Yahoos, 1989; contbr. articles, short stories, poetry to various publs. Bd. dirs. Trinity Arts Council, Bedford, Tex., 1980-84. Mem. Western Writers Am., Nat. League Am. Pen Women, Okla. Writers Fedn. (bd. dirs. 1980-86), Soc. Southwestern Authors, Pi Gamma Mu, Kappa Delta Pi, Phi Upsilon Omicron. Republican.

NELSON, ALVIN JOHN, computer information scientist, software publisher; b. Ronan, Mont., July 19, 1935; s. Alvin John and Eva (Leishman) N.; m. GaNene Rowbury, Nov. 2, 1955; children: Beryl, Alan, Eric, Carla, Evan. BS, Brigham Young U., 1959; MS, Stanford U., 1964. Dynamicist Lockheed Missile and Space Co., Sunnyvale, Calif., 1961-64; ops. research analyst Stanford Research Inst., Menlo Park, Calif., 1964-65; various teaching positions Mont., 1965-71; sr. analyst Aetna Life & Casualty, Hartford, Conn., 1971-74; tech. staff mem. Mitre Corp., Washington, 1974-76; prin. info. sci. specialist EG&G Idaho, Inc., Idaho Falls, 1976—; stats. cons. Stanford Research Inst., 1965-66, Rogers Bros. Seed Co., Idaho Falls, 1982-85; math. coordinator Idaho Falls Ctr. for Higher Edn., 1983—. Treas. Idaho Falls Opera Theatre, 1980-81, pres., 1983-84, artistic dir., 1984-85, bd. dirs., 1988—. Sci. faculty fellow NSF, 1969. Mem. Phi Kappa Phi. Mormon. Home: 245 E 18th St Idaho Falls ID 83404 Office: Magistor Ltd PO Box 3005 Idaho Falls ID 83403-3005

NELSON, ANNA MARGARET, realtor; b. Blair, Nebr., Mar. 16, 1928; d. Theodore Marcus and Serena (Christensen) Hansen; m. Harold Ellsworth Nelson, Feb. 17, 1950 (dec.); children: Karl Marcus, Dale Ellsworth, Bruce harold, Gary newgard, Sue Leigh. Student, Dana Coll., 1945-46, 52, Mankato State Tchrs. Coll., 1948-49. Cert. elem. tchr. Elem. tchr. Blooming Prairie, Minn., 1948-50, Blair, 1953-56; realtor, sales rep. Lakewood Villa, Tacoma, 1973-75, Hawkins-Poe, Gig Harbor, Wash., 1975-79; br. mgr., relocation dir. Victor L. Lyon Realtors, Gig Harbor, 1979-86; relator, sales rep. Coldwell Banker, Gig Harbor, 1986—, sales mgr., 1987—. Mem. Realtors Nat. Mktg. Inst. (cert. residental broker, specialist), Tacoma Pierce County Bd. Realtors (edn. chmn.). Republican. Lutheran. Home: 4513 35th Ave Ct NW Gig Harbor WA 98335 Office: Coldwell Banker 2801 Hollycroft Gig Harbor WA 98335

NELSON, AUDREY IRENE, interior designer; b. Cleve., Apr. 11; d. Clyde Allen Davis; m. Robert A. Nelson (div. 1971); children: Bruce, Susan, Robin, Scot, Mark, Lori. Student, Cleve. Inst. Art, 1948, Ohio State U., 1952; AA, UCLA, 1960. Prin. Mediterrain Design Studio, Pacific Palisades, Calif., 1964-66; designer, store planner, buyer Breuners Furniture, Los Angeles, 1972-80; importer Mex. artifacts 1980-85; travel cons. Tradewinds Travel, Palm Desert, 1985—; freelance comml. set designer, Los Angeles, 1976—. Mem. Rep. Womens Group, Los Angeles, 1967; vol. UCLA Med. Ctr., 1967, Desert Hosp., Palm Springs, Calif., 1979. Mem. Nat. Soc. Interior Designers, Palm Springs C. of C., Palm Desert C. of C. Roman Catholic. Home: 516 Sunset Way Palm Springs CA 92263

NELSON, BRYAN H(ERBERT), speech pathologist; b. Yakima, Wash., July 3, 1956; s. Herbert B. and Marilyn A. (Cupper) N.; m. Linda K. Miller, June 16, 1979; children: Christofer A., Bryanne E. BEd, Ea. Wash. U., 1977, MS in Speech Pathology, 1978. Speech pathologist Ednl. Service Dist. 101, Spokane, Wash., 1978-83, coordinator speech pathology, 1983-84, coordinator inservice tng., 1985; processor fruit broker Herb Nelson Inc., Yakima, 1985-88; C.D.S./preschool project coord.ood edn. Selah (Wash.) Sch. Dist., 1988—; guest lectr. Ea. Wash. U., Cheney, 1984-85; chmn. very spl. arts festival Ednl. Service Dist 101, 1985, on-site coordinator IDEAS conv., 1983. Bd. dirs., chair citizens adv. bd. Yakima Vocat. Skill Ctr., 1988-89; Yakima Vocat. Coop. gen. adv. com.; mem. allocation panel United Way, Yakima, 1974. Lodge: Lions. Home: 700 Mapleway Rd Selah WA 98942 Office: Selah Sch Dist PO Box 610 Selah WA 98942

NELSON, CAROLYN JEAN, realtor; b. Upland, Calif., Jan. 22, 1957; d. Jacob and Alida Klaaasje (Rodenhuis) Heida; m. David Seymour Nelson, Aug. 2, 1980; children: Erik, Aaron. Student, Mt. San Antonio Coll., 1975-77, Boise State U., 1977-81; grad., Acad. Real Estate, Boise, Idaho, 1985. Lic. real estate saleswoman, Idaho. Realtor Coldwell Banker, Boise, 1986, Holland Realty, Boise, 1987—. Vol. Boise Little Theatre, 1981-82, Idaho Hist. Soc., Boise, 1984-87; clk. Ada County Election Bd., 1981-85; pres. Idaho Hist. Aux., 1986; vol. for Guardian ad Litem Child Advocacy Program. Mem. Nat. Assn., Realtors, Idaho Assn. Realtors, Idaho Assn. Realtors, Boise Bd. Realtors (profl. standards com.), Ada County Multiple Listing Assn., Idaho Geneal. Soc., Nite-Lites Club. Republican. Office: Holland Realty 4720 Emerald St Ste 116 Boise ID 83706

NELSON, CAROLYN MARIE, artist; b. Oak Park, Ill., Jan. 4, 1945; d. Carl Lewis and Mary Wilma (Clark) Eilers; m. Michael Woodrick, June 5, 1970 (div. Sept. 1977); children: Katrina, Matthew; m. Stephen Paul Nelson, Aug. 31, 1985. Student, Palm Beach Art Inst., West Palm Beach, Fla., 1962-65, Palm Beach Jr. Coll., Lake Worth, Fla., 1964-65, Maude King Sch. Art, West Palm Beach, Fla., 1959-69, Cerritos (Calif.) Coll., 1987. Owner, instr. art sch. and gallery, Lake Park, Fla., 1972-80; artist, instr. Scottsdale (Ariz.) Ctr. of Arts, 1982; artist Contracting Agys., Los Angeles, 1983-85; asst. dir. fine art Adamson-Duvannes Galleries, Los Angeles, 1985-86; artist, dir. Gateways to History, Los Angeles, 1986—; art dir. Studio 3, Lake Park, Fla., 1974-80; artistic dir. Steve's Stitchery, Los Angeles, 1988—. Artist cartoons AMA, 1976, typography Christmas in Dixie parade float (trophy 1978), painting NASA, 1977, graphics Kenyatiq U. Narobi, 1979, Getty Oil Co., 1984, Medical Illustrating, 1989. Fellow Los Angeles County Mus., Gallery One Guild (v.p. 1977-78). Lutheran. Home: 10912 E Hopland St Norwalk CA 90650

NELSON, CHARLES ROBERT, financial planner; b. Philippines, Jan. 14, 1930; m. Beverly Ann Nelson, May 17, 1980. V.p., mgr. Paine Webber Jackson and Curtis, Newport Beach, Calif., 1972-73, Bache Halsey Stuart, Tucson, 1973-77; owner, mgr. King Of The North, Irvine, Calif., 1978-84; owner, mgr. Nelson Fin., Laguna Hills, Calif., 1983-84; gen. mgr. First Liberty Securities, Carlsbad, Calif., 1984-86; sr. ptnr. Nelson Fin. Assocs., Laguna Niguel, Calif., 1986—. Mem. planning adv. com. Orange County Hosp., 1979; bd. dirs., v.p. Palm Desert Resort Country Club Homeowner's Assn., 1982-83; mem. bd. mgrs. South Coast YMCA, 1988; vol. bus editor Dana Point/Laguna Niguel News. Mem. Internat. Assn. Fin. Planners, Alpha Delta Phi. Club: Marbella Country (San Juan Capistrano, Calif.). Lodge: Rotary. Office: Nelson Fin Assocs 27782 El Lazo Ste B Laguna Niguel CA 92677

NELSON, CHRISTOPHER ARNOLD, computer sales support representative; b. Santa Monica, Calif., Aug. 16, 1952; s. Theodoret Arnold and Donna Mae (Norem) N.; m. Kathleen Mary Fields, Aug. 21, 1976; children: Heather Kristine, Steven Christopher Owen. BA in Biology, Calif. State U., 1975. Ops. foreman Disneyland, Anaheim, Calif., 1970-77; client rep. Sci. Dynamics Corp., Torrance, Calif., 1978-83, tng. mgr., sales adminstr., 1984-87; rep. sales support SMS, Long Beach, Calif., 1987—; adminstr. of sales Sci. Dynamics Corp., Torrance, Calif., 1987-88; owner Can'd Software Consulting, Anaheim, Calif., 1986—. Republican. Lutheran. Home: 729 Alvy St Anaheim CA 92802 Office: Shared Medical Systems 3901 Via Oro Ave 110 Long Beach CA 90810

NELSON, CLIFFORD L(EE), JR., company official; b. South Bend, Ind., Feb. 12, 1936; s. Clifford Lee and Margaret (Toops) N.; m. Doris Ann Huber, Aug. 23, 1958; children: Catherine Lynn and Christina Lee (twins), Clifford Lee III. BA, Washington and Jefferson Coll., 1958. Life ltd. svc. teaching credential, Calif. Sales coord. Jessop Steel Co., Washington, Pa., 1958-60; sales engr. Wah Chang Corp., Albany, Oreg., 1960-63; sales engr. metals div. Stauffer Chem. Co., Richmond, Calif., 1963; sr. govt. accounts rep. traffic control materials div. 3M Co., Sacramento, 1964--, field sales trainer, 1967-76. Bd. dirs. Retreat Ministries, Inc., Orange, Calif., 1980--; ruling elder, clk. of session 1st Presbyn. Ch., Orange, 1982-85; gift chmn. class of 1958, Washington and Jefferson Coll., 1983--; bd. dirs. Sr. Citizens Community Ctr., Orange, 1985-87; pres. Sister City Assn., Orange, 1989--. Named Jaycee of Yr., Orange Jaycees, 1967. Mem. Am. Pub. Works Assn. (assoc., equipment com. 1982-85), Maintenance Supts. Assn. Calif. (life, bd. dirs. 1984-85), Orange County Traffic Engrs. Coun. (bd. dirs. 1979-80), Riverside-San Bernardino Traffic Engrs., Rotary (pres. Orange chpt., 1989—, Rotarian of Yr. award 1985). Republican. Home: 1448 N Pine St Orange CA 92667 Office: 3M Co 1010 Hurley Way Sacramento CA 95825

NELSON, DANNY ROBERT, systems engineer; b. Amery, Wis., Jan. 31, 1959; s. Robert Martin and Clarice Sophie (Thaemert) N. AS, Rochester Community Coll., 1983; BEE, U. So.Colo., 1986; postgrad, U. Colo., 1987—. Cert. tech. engr. Electronic lab. technician IBM, Rochester, Minn., 1982-83, NASA, Pueblo, Colo., 1983-84; quality engr. Data Control Corp., Mpls., 1984-86; prodn. engr. Sperry Corp., Pueblo, Colo., 1986-87; systems engr. UNISYS Corp., Pueblo, 1987—. Served to sgt. USAF, 1977-80, with Res. 1980—. Mem. IEEE, Soc. of Quality Assurance, So. Colo. Runners Assn. Office: UNISYS Corp 5 William White Blvd Pueblo CO 81001

NELSON, DARRYL JAMES, small business owner; b. Detroit, Nov. 9, 1950; s. Herschell James Burns and Madeline Veronica Zidick. Student, Whittier Coll. Warehouseman E.D. Bullard & Co., City of Industry, Calif., 1969-72, C Hagar & Sons Hinge Mfg. Co., City of Industry, 1972-73; mgr. shipping, receiving Rutland Tool & Supply Co., Pico Rivera, Calif., 1974-76, mgr. wholesale traffic, 1983—; owner, mgr. Reno (Nev.) Prospector's Supply Co., 1984—. Mem. Nev. Prospectors, Comstock Prospectors, Motherlode Miners, E Clampus Vitus, Reno C. of C., Winners Circle Breakfast Club (bd. dirs., chmn. Welcome Com.). Home: 311 19th St Sparks NV 89431 Office: 315 Claremont St Reno NV 89502

NELSON, DONALD ARVID (NELLIE NELSON), professional basketball coach; b. Muskegon, Mich., May 15, 1940. Student, U. Iowa. Player NBA teams, Chgo. Zephyrs, 1962-63, Los Angeles Lakers, 1963-65, Boston Celtics, 1965-76; from asst. to head coach Milw. Bucks NBA, 1976-87, also dir. player personnel; exec. v.p., part owner Golden State Warriors, NBA, Oakland, Calif., from 1987; mem. Nat. Basketball championship teams, 1966, 68, 69, 74, 76; head coach Golden State Warriors, 1988—, now also gen. mgr. Named Coach of Yr. NBA, 1983, 85. Office: care Golden State Warriors Oakland Coliseum Arena Oakland CA 94621 *

NELSON, DREW VERNON, mechanical engineering educator; b. Elizabeth, N.J., Oct. 11, 1947; s. Andrew K. and Myra G. (Kempson) N. BSME, Stanford U., 1968, MSME, 1970, PhDME, 1978. Research asst. Stanford U., Calif., 1971-74, asst. prof., 1978-83, assoc. prof., 1983—; engr. Gen. Electric Co., Sunnyvale, Calif., 1975-76, sr. engr., 1977-78; cons. in field. Co-editor: Fatigue Design Handbook, 1989; contbr. articles to profl. jours.; inventor Optical Stress Determination Systems. Recipient Spergel Meml. award for Most Outstanding Paper, 32nd Internat. Wire and Cable Symposium, 1984. Mem. ASTM, Soc. Automotive Engrs., Am. Acad. Mechanics, Sigma Xi, Tau Beta Pi. Home: 840 Cabot Ct San Carlos CA 94070-3464 Office: Stanford U Dept Mech Engring Stanford CA 94305-4021

NELSON, ESTHER ROWENA, retired educator; b. Prospect Park, Pa., Feb. 26, 1930; d. Oscar Severine and Helen Rowena (Davidson) N. BS, U. Pa., 1951; MS, U. Ill., 1961. Recreation leader Dept. Recreation, City of Denver, 1951-52; recreation leader Dept. Recreation, City of Phila., 1953-56, ctr. dir., 1956-59; farmer Vanel Ranch, Oakdale, Calif., 1961-63, 87—; phys. edn. tchr. Lincoln Unified Sch. Dist., Stockton, Calif., 1963-87, dept. exec., 1968-87, head badminton coach, 1974-85; asst. athletic dir. Lincoln Unified Sch. Dist., Stoockton, Calif., 1974-87; basketball ofcl. various high schs. and colls., Phila. and Cen. Calif., 1951—. Mem. San Joaquin Athletic Assn. (Gold Pass award 1987), Mother Lode Club Mineral Soc. Home and Office: PO Box 142 Oakdale CA 95361

NELSON, GEORGE N., petroleum company executive; b. Kansas City, Mo., Oct. 11, 1932; s. Claude and Hazel M. (Smith) N.; m. Cynthia M. Buck; children: Christopher, Georgianne, Stephanie, Amy. BS in Indsl. Mgmt. Engring., U. Okla., 1955; postgrad. in mgmt., MIT, 1983. Petroleum engr. Magnolia Petroleum Co., Okla., Tex. and La., 1955; from drilling engr. to prodn. engr. to prodn. foreman Mobil Oil Co. Venezuela, 1955-61; from prodn. supr. to project engr. to supt. marine terminal and tank farm Superior Oil Co. Venezuela, Lake Maracaibo, 1961-65; project engr. J.F. Pritchard and Co., Kansas City, Mo., 1965; sr. prodn. engr. Arabian Am. Oil Co., Saudi Arabia, 1966; from sr. engr. to sr. supervising engr. to supt. tech. services to mgr. ops. Oasis Oil Co. of Libya, Inc., Tripoli, 1968-75; mgr. prodn. planning British Petroleum of Alaska, Inc., San Francisco, 1975; field mgr. Prudhoe Bay Sohio Alaska Petroleum Co., Anchorage, 1977, asst. gen. mgr. ops., 1978, v.p. ops., 1981; pres. Standard Alaska Prodn. Co./BP Exploration, Anchorage, 1982—. Mem. adv. bd. Alaska Ctr. for Internat. Bus. Devel., U. Alaska, 1986—; chmn. bd. trustees Govt. Council on Local Hire, Anchorage, 1986; trustee Alaska Pacific U., 1988; bd. dirs. Boys and Girls Club Alaska, Anchorage, 1981—, Alaska Ctr. for Performing Arts, 1988. 2d lt. C.E. U.S. Army, 1957-58. Recipient Alaska Native Community award Alaska Fedn. Natives, 1983, Cert. Appreciation, Gov. of Alaska, 1984, Outstanding Service award NANA Region, 1984, 85, Pub. Service award Municipality of Anchorage, 1986, Cert. Appreciation, Anchorage Star of North C. of C., 1986, Outstanding Service award Alaska chpt. Associated Gen. Contractors Am., 1986, Outstanding Achievement in Environ. Protection award Nat. Environ. Devel. Assn., 1987, Disting. Services award Alaska State C. of C., 1987, Outstanding Service award Alaska Assn. Secondary Prins., 1987, Man and Youth award Boys and Girls Club Alaska, 1988. Mem. Alaska Oil and Gas Assn. (exec. com. 1981-88, bd. dirs. 1981-88, pres. bd. dirs. 1985, 88), Petroleum Club, Tau Beta Pi, Sigma Tau. Democrat. Office: Standard Alaska Prodn Co 900 E Benson Blvd PO Box 196612 Anchorage AK 99519-6612

NELSON, HARRY, anthropologist, educator; b. Hazleton, Pa., Nov. 13, 1915; s. Abram and Anna (Rosenthal) N.; m. Donna Granger, June 28, 1956 (div. 1978); m. Sandra Quint, Sept. 23, 1985. BS, Bloomsburg (Pa.) U., 1939; MA, Columbia U., 1941; PhD, U. Calif., Berkeley, 1953. Instr. Santa Monica (Calif.) Coll., 1956-65; prof. emeritus Foothill Coll., Los Altos, Calif., 1965-86. Author: (filmstrip) Fossil Man, 1969; co-author: (book) Atlas of Human Evolution, 1979, Introduction to Physical Anthropology, 1985, 4th rev. edit., 1988, Understanding Physical Anthropology and Archeology, 1984, 3d rev. edit., 1987. Served to capt. U.S. Army, 1942-46. Fellow Am. Anthrop. Assn., Am. Assn. Phys, Anthropology, N.Y. Acad. Sci., Calif. Acad. Scis., Southwest Anthrop. Assn.; mem. San Francisco Rose Soc. (cons.). Democrat. Jewish. Home and Office: 535 Dewey Blvd San Francisco CA 94116

NELSON, JACK RUSSELL, university administrator; b. Portland, Oreg., Dec. 18, 1929; s. George Bahn and Elsa Margaret (Hamilton) N.; m. Bonita Casey, June 17, 1951; children: Richard Meredith, Ronald Gregory, Robert Geoffrey. B.A., Pacific Union Coll., 1952; M.B.A., UCLA, 1957, Ph.D., 1962. Chief accountant St. Helena Sanitarium and Hosp., 1951-53; mgr. Modesto City Hosp., 1954-55; assoc. prof. Andrews U., 1959-61; from asst. prof. to prof. U. Minn. Sch. Bus., 1961-70; asst. to pres. U. Oreg., 1966-67; vice provost, prof. U. Colo., Boulder, 1970-71; assoc. provost U. Colo., 1971-72, v.p., 1972-74, exec. v.p., 1974-78, acting chancellor, 1977, chancellor, 1978-81, dean Coll. Bus. and Adminstrn., 1989—; pres. Ariz. State U., Tempe, 1981-89; bd. dirs. Del. E. Webb Corp. Contbr. articles to profl. jours. Mem. Am. Econ. Assn. Office: U Colo Coll Bus and Adminstrn Boulder CO 80309

NELSON, JAMES AUGUSTUS, II, real estate executive, architect, banker; b. Damrascotta, Maine, July 26, 1947; s. Robert Maynard and Margret Rebbeca (Harmision) N.; m. Linda Ray, Aug. 15, 1975 (div. 1985); m. Tina Nides, Oct. 22, 1986; 1 child, Jennifer Alexandria. BArch, Columbia U., 1973, MBA, 1974. Resident v.p. Citibank, N.Y.C., 1974-77; group v.p. Bank of Am., San Francisco, 1977-82; assoc. John Portman and Assocs., Atlanta, 1983-85; pres. J.A. Nelson and Assocs., L.A., 1986-88; dir. real estate planning and devel. MCA Devel. Co., L.A., 1988—. Author: Banker's Guide to Construction, 1978, Doing Business in Saudi Arabia, 1979. Chmn. Laurel Canyon Coalition, L.A.; pres. Laurel Canyon Area Assn.; chmn. planning com. Hillside Fedn., L.A.; v.p. Lookout Mountain Assocs., L.A.; treas. Hollywood Heritage. Mem. L.A. Athletic Club. Home: 8306 Grandview Dr Los Angeles CA 90046 Office: MCA Devel Co 100 Universal City Pla Universal City CA 91608

NELSON, JAMES F., judge, religious organization administrator. BS, U. Calif., LLB, Loyola U., Los Angeles. Bar: Calif. 1954. Judge, Los Angeles Mcpl. Ct. Chmn. Baha'i Faith Nat. Spiritual Assembly Bahais of the U.S., Wilmette, Ill. Office: US Courthouse 110 N Grand Ave Los Angeles CA 90012 *

NELSON, JAN ANDERS, computer company executive, artist; b. Houston, July 18, 1952; s. Eugene Bernard and Doris Mae (Thorpe) N.; m. Connie Jean Jennings, June 18, 1974; children: Natalie Jean, Reid Anders, Maja Sophia. BA, Midland Luth. Coll., 1974; postgrad., Creighton U., 1974, NYU, 1977; MA, U. Wis., 1977. Instr. art U. Wis. Ext., Madison, 1977, Ft. Steilacoom (Wash.) Community Coll., 1977-78, Tacoma Community Coll., 1978-80; exec. v.p., bd. dirs., prin. Data Tech Reliance, Inc., Federal Way, Wash., 1980—; bd. dirs. Rubatino Labs., Inc., Federal Way. Exhibited in numerous group shows. Chmn. Madison Area Referendum to Stop Hwy., 1978. Lutheran. Office: Data Tech Reliance Inc 33901 9th Ave S Federal Way WA 98003

NELSON, KENNETH ARTHUR, electrical engineer; b. Coeur d'Alene, Idaho, Apr. 18, 1942; s. Elton Arthur and Maxine Edna (Barnes) N.; m. Sharon Fay Paynter, Sept. 2, 1962; children: Neva Kenine, Krena Krista, Kelina Kara, Kimberly Kay. BSEE, U. Idaho, 1965; cert., Alaxander Hamilton Inst., 1970. Registered profl. engr., Calif. With GE, various locations, 1965-75; sr. mfg. engr. Jenn-Air Corp., Indpls., 1975-79; plant engr. A.O. Smith Corp., Newark, Calif., 1979-82; dir. facilities Memorex Corp., Santa Clara, Calif., 1982-88; with Scenic Mgmt. Corp., Livermore, Calif., 1988—; instr. Profl. Engring. Inst., San Carlos, Calif., 1985-88; founder Scenic Mgmt., Livermore, Calif., 1986—. Inventor in field. Mem. IEEE, Am. Soc. Metals Internat. Republican. Lutheran. Home: 1289 N Vasco Rd Livermore CA 94550

NELSON, LARRY BRUCE, pharmaceutical engineer, consultant; b. Galesburg, Ill., Aug. 27, 1949; s. Ralph Theodore and Juanita Maxine (Smith) N.; m. Salleelu Kafka, June 28, 1969; children: Michel, Laurel, Grant. BSBA, Ill. Wesleyan U., 1971; BSEE, Mont. State U., 1975. Design engr. Summit-Dana Corp., Bozeman, Mont., 1975-80; project engr. Summit-Dana Corp., Bozeman, 1980-83; validation engr. Skyland Scientific Svcs., Bozeman, 1984-86, project mgr., 1986-88, supr. engring, 1988—. Mem. Internat. Soc. Pharm. Engrs. (speaker 1988), Parenteral Drug Assn., Bozeman Airtelemetry Soc. (pres. 1978, 83, 88, 89). Office: Skyland Scientific Svcs 2311 S 7th Ave Bozeman MT 59715

NELSON, LAWRENCE OLAF, administrative educator; b. Hartford, Conn., Feb. 1, 1926; s. Lawrence Olaf and Gerda Amelia Elizabeth (Hanson) N.; m. Kathleen Alice Brito, Aug. 26, 1950; children: Scott Laurence, Adam Foster. B.S., Central Conn. State U., 1949; M.A., U. Conn., 1953; Ph.D., Mich. State U., 1960. Tchr. pub. schs. Stamford, Conn., 1949-52; asst. dir. U. Conn., 1952-55; asst. to pres. State Coll., Moorhead, Minn., 1956-57; dean of adminstrn. State Coll., 1957-58; cons. Office of Edn., HEW, Washington, 1960; mem. faculty Purdue U., Lafayette, Ind., 1960-74; adminstrv. dean Purdue U., 1967-74; dean Purdue U. (Ft. Wayne Campus), 1969-70, asst. to provost, 1974; prof. higher edn., dean continuing edn. U. Ariz., Tucson, 1974-81; prof. ednl. founds., adminstrn. and higher edn. U. Ariz., 1974—; cons. in field. Mem. planning com. Ind. Gov.'s Regional Correction Center, 1969-71; mem. adv. panel Ind. Higher Edn. Telecommunications System, 1971-74; adv. bd. Midwestern Center, Nat. Humanities Series, 1972-74; mem. Ind. Com. for Humanities, 1972-74, Tucson Com. on Fgn. Relations, 1975-85; bd. dirs. Continuing Edn. for Deaf, 1975-81, Ariz. Consortium for Edn. in Social Services, 1977-81. Author: Cooperative Projects Among Colleges and Universities, 1961. Mem. Am. Assn. Higher Edn., Assn. Continuing Higher Edn., Nat. Assn. Student Personnel Administrators, NEA, Nat. Univ. Continuing Edn. Assn., Nat. Coun. Profs. of Ednl. Adminstrn., Nat. Univ. Extension Assn. (award 1971, dir. 1978-80), Phi Delta Kappa, Epsilon Pi Tau, Delta Chi. Clubs: Kiwanis of Greater Lafayette (pres. 1967), Kiwanis of Moorhead (dir. 1957-58), Rotary of Tucson (dir. 1979-80, pres. 1980-81). Home: 1330 Indian Wells Rd Tucson AZ 85718 Office: U Ariz 629 Edn Bldg Tucson AZ 85721

NELSON, LINDA MARIE, counselor; b. Fukuoka, Kyushu, Japan, Dec. 29, 1955; came to U.S., 1958; d. Julio and Tomiko (Yamamoto) Carrillo; m. Gillard Gunshi Matsumiya, June 1, 1975 (div. 1981); 1 child, Sibyl Matsumiya; m. Carl Russell Nelson, Feb. 14, 1982; 1 child, Christina Nelson. BA in Psychology, U. Hawaii-Manoa, Honolulu, 1977; MA in Communication, U. Hawaii, 1980, postgrad., 1986—. Assoc. realtor H.K. Horita Realty, Kalihi, Hawaii, 1978-80, realtor, broker, 1980—; substitute tchr. Hawaii Dept. Edn., 1978—, counselor intern, 1986—; pres. Am. Field Service, Wahiawa, Hawaii, 1972-73. Home: 94-1505 Waipio Uka St #B-103 Waipahu HI 96797 Office: Herbert K. Horita Realty Inc 2024 N King St Honolulu HI 96819

NELSON, MANFRED R., surgeon; b. Jackson, Wyo., Mar. 29, 1933; s. Neal Valdez and Ilena (Richardson) N.; m. Inga-Lena Carlstrom, Aug. 30, 1956, (div. 1976); m. Carol Croft, Oct. 4, 1977; children: Rachel Lynn, Rebecca, Jeanette, Mark, Sarah. Student, Brigham Young U., 1951-53, U. Wyo., 1956, U. Utah, 1957-58; MD, George Washington U., 1962. Diplomate Am. Bd. Med. Examiners. Enlisted USAF, 1962, advanced through grades to col., ret., 1982; intern Latter-Day-Saints Hosp., Salt Lake City, 1962-63; flight surgeon USAF Hosp. S. Ruislip, London, 1963-66; residency in gen. surgery Wilford Hall USAF Med. Ctr., Lackland AFB, Tex., 1966-71; med. officer, gen. surgery USAF, various locations, 1971-82; gen. surgeon student health ctr., Brigham Young U., Provo, Utah, 1982-86; staff physician Timpangos Community Mental Health Ctr., Provo, 1986-87; gen. surgeon White Mountain Community Hosp., Springerville, Ariz., 1987—. Mem. AMA, Ogden Surg. Soc., Collegium Aesculapium (exec. com. 1982-85), Ariz. Med. Assn., Utah Med. Assn. Republican. Mormon. Home: PO Box 700 Eagar AZ 85925 Office: Round Valley Med Clin PO Box 71 Springerville AZ 85938

NELSON, MARK DANIEL, chiropractor; b. Mpls., Aug. 6, 1959; s. Gerald Daniel and Arlene Marie (Leisz) N.; m. Cindy Lou Cashman, Mar. 21, 1980 (div. June 1985); 1 child, Erick Daniel. Student, Coll. St. Thomas, 1977-79; D in Chiropractic Medicine, Northwestern Coll., Mpls., 1983. Clinic dir., owner Granite Bay Chiropractic Clinic, Roseville, Calif., 1983—; indsl. cons. Athletes in Industry, Roseville, 1987—; disability evaluator Calif. Chiropractic Found., Sacramento, 1986—. Mem. Sacramento Valley Chiropractic Soc. (pres. 1987—), Rotary Club (charter). Republican. Baptist. Office: Granite Bay Chiropractic Clinic 5420 Douglas Blvd Roseville CA 95661

NELSON, MARTHA JANE, magazine editor; b. Pierre, S.D., Aug. 13, 1952; d. Bernard Anton and Pauline Isabel (Noren) N. BA, Columbia U., 1976. Mng. editor Signs: Jour. of Women in Culture, N.Y.C., 1976-80; sr. editor Ms. Mag., N.Y.C., 1980-85; editor-in-chief Women's Sports and Fitness Mag., Palo Alto, Calif., 1985-88; exec. editor Savvy, 1989—. Editor: Women in the American City, 1980; contbr. articles to profl. jours. Bd. dirs. Painting Space 122, N.Y.C., 1982-85, Urban Athletic Assn. Mem. Am. Soc. Mag. Editors, Western Pubs. Assn. Office: 3 Park Ave New York NY 10016

NELSON, MARVIN RAY, life insurance company executive; b. Thornton, Iowa, Aug. 29, 1926; s. Clarence Anton and Rose Bessie (Nicolet) N.; m. Juanita Mae Brown, May 26, 1951; children: Nancy, Kenneth. BS, Drake U, 1951. Actuary Security Mut. Life Ins. Co., Lincoln, Nebr., 1951-58; assoc. actuary Life Ins. Co. N.Am., Phila., 1958-59; group actuary Bankers Life of Nebr., Lincoln, 1959-66; actuary Mut. Service Life Ins. Co., St. Paul, 1966-68; sr. v.p. Horace Mann Educators Corp., Springfield, Ill., 1968-77; sr. v.p. Security Life of Denver, 1977-83, exec. v.p., 1988—; pres., chief oper. officer, dir., mem. investment com. Midwestern United Life Ins. Co., Denver, 1983—. Bd. dirs., treas. Ft. Wayne Urban League, 1983-87; bd. dirs. Taxpayers Research Assn., Ft. Wayne, 1984-88. Served with U.S. Army, 1946-47. Fellow Soc. Actuaries; mem. Am. Acad. Actuaries, Phi Kappa Phi. Home: 7636 Windford Parker CO 80134 Office: Security Life of Denver Ins Co 1290 Broadway Denver CO 80203

NELSON, MARY CARROLL, artist, author; b. Bryan, Tex., Apr. 24, 1929; d. James Vincent and Mary Elizabeth (Langton) Carroll; m. Edwin Blakely Nelson, June 27, 1950; children: Patricia Ann, Edwin Blakely. BA in Fine Arts, Barnard Coll., 1950; MA, U. N.Mex., 1963. Juror Am. Artist Golden Anniversary Nat. Art Competition, 1987, N.Mex. Arts and Crafts Fair, 1989, Don Ruffin Meml. Exhibition, Ariz., 1989; moderator Harwood Found. Art History Conf., 1987; curator Shrines, 1988. Group shows include: Southwestern Watercolor Soc., Dallas, N.Mex. Watercolor Soc., N.Mex. State Fair, N.Mex. Mus. Fine Arts Biennial, 1987; represented in pvt. collections in: U.S., Fed. Republic of Germany, Eng. and Australia; author: American Indian Biography Series, 1971-76, (with Robert E. Wood) Watercolor Workshop, 1974, (with Ramon Kelley) Ramon Kelley Paints Portraits and Figures, 1977, The Legendary Artists of Taos, 1980, (catalog) American Art in Peking, 1981, Masters of Western Art, 1982, Connecting, The Art of Beth Ames Swartz, 1984, (catalog) Layering, An Art of Time and Space, 1985, (catalog) Layering/Connecting, 1987; contbg. editor Am. Artist, 1976—, Southwest Art, 1987—. Mem. Albuquerque Arts Bd., 1984-88. Mem. Soc. Layerists in Multi-Media (founder 1982), Albuquerque Mus. Found., Nat. Fedn. Press Women, N.Mex. Press Women. Home: 1408 Georgia St NE Albuquerque NM 87110

NELSON, MARY RUTH, realtor; b. Chgo., July 14, 1952; d. Charles Robert and Pauline (Cober) Wark; m. Monty Gene Nelson, Nov. 18, 1972; 1 child, Monty Gene II. Student, William Woods Coll., 1970-71, Prairie State Coll., 1971-72, San Diego City Coll., 1972-79. Lic. realtor, Hawaii. Teller Imperial Savs., San Diego, 1972-75, Gt. Western Savs., San Diego, 1975-76; teller, receptionist San Diego County Credit Union, 1976-77; owner Pony Expression Photography, San Diego, 1979-83; grounds and house keeper Bradys, San Diego, 1982-83; rental agt. asst. NoeLani Condo Resort, Maui, Hawaii, 1984; rental agt. Honokowai Condo Resort, Maui, 1984-86, Polynesian Shores Resort, Maui, 1987—. Mem. Maui Bd. Realtors, Inc., Hawaii Assn. Realtors (assoc.). Home and Office: 3975 Honoapii Lani Rd Lahaina HI 96761

NELSON, MICHAEL A., land development company executive; b. Portland, Oreg., Oct. 7, 1943; s. John Tony and Verena M. (Gaspard) N.; m. Ethel F. Jenson, July 20, 1963; 1 child, John. BS in Geography, Portland State U., 1969. Vice pres. United Homes Corp., Portland, 1969-72; pres. Dimension Homes, Inc., Portland, 1972-84; v.p. BenjFran Devel., Inc., Portland, 1984-87; pres. BenjFran Devel., Inc., 1987—. Bd. dirs. Greater Hillsboro Area Found.; mem. Portland Solar Access Task Force, Metro Portland Solar Access Task Force, Tualatin Valley Econ. Devel. Council. Mem. Bldg. Owners and Mgrs. Assn., urban Land Inst., Nat. Assn. Home Bldrs., Nat. Assn. Indsl. and Office Parks (pub. affairs dir.), Homebuilders Assn. Met. Portland, Sunset Corridor Assn. (bd. dirs.), Greater Hillsboro Area C. of C. Office: BenjFran Devel Inc 501 SE Hawthorne St #295 Portland OR 97214

NELSON, MICHAEL BERNARD, nuclear engineer; b. Phoenix, June 25, 1951; s. James Joseph and Roberta Christine (Dekle) N.; m. Cynthia Ann Currie, Oct. 9, 1976. BS in Biol. Sci., U. Ariz., 1974, BS in Nuclear Engring., 1976. Cert. engr.-in-tng., Ariz. Nuclear engr. Am. Atomics Corp., Tucson, 1976-77, Bechtel Power Corp., L.A., 1978-79; field nuclear engr. Bechtel Power Corp., Phoenix, 1979-82; nuclear engr. Ariz. Pub. Svc. Co., Phoenix, 1982—. Mem. Am. Nuclear Soc. (assoc., treas. Phoenix 1982), ASME (assoc.). Democrat. Home: 810 W Glenn Dr Phoenix AZ 85021-8639 Office: Ariz Pub Svc Co MS7434 PO Box 52034 Phoenix AZ 85072-2034

NELSON, NANCY ELEANOR, pediatrician, educator; b. El Paso, Apr. 4, 1933; d. Harry Hamilton and Helen Maude (Murphy) N. B.A. magna cum laude, U. Colo., 1955, M.D., 1959. Intern, Case Western Res. U. Hosp., 1959-60, resident, 1960-63; practice medicine specializing in pediatrics, Denver, 1963—; assoc. clin. prof. U. Colo. Sch. Medicine, Denver, 1977-88, clin. prof., 1988—, asst. dean Sch. Medicine, 1982-88, assoc. dean, 1988—. Mem. Am. Acad. Pediatrics, AMA, Denver Med. Soc. (pres. 1983-84), Colo. Med. Soc. (bd. dirs. 1985-88). Home: 1265 Elizabeth Denver CO 80206 Office: 4200 E 9th Ave Denver CO 80262

NELSON, NEVIN MARY, interior designer; b. Cleve., Nov. 5, 1941; d. Arthur George Reinker and Barbara Phyllis (Gunn) Parks; m. Wayne Nelson (div. 1969); children: Doug, Brian. BA in Interior Design, U. Colo., 1964. Prin. Nevin Nelson Design, Boulder, Colo., 1966-70, Vail, Colo., 1970—; program chmn. Questers Antique Study Group, Boulder, 1969. coordinator Bob Kirscht for Gov. campaign, Eagle County, Colo., 1986; state del. Repub. Conv., 1986, 88; county coordinator George Bush for Pres. campaign, 1988; social chmn. Eagle County Reps. Mem. Am. Soc. Interior Designers. Episcopalian. Club: Pro Denver. Home: Box 1212 Vail CO 81658 Office: 2271 N Frontage Rd W Vail CO 81657

NELSON, NOELLE CROSS, psychologist; b. N.Y.C., Oct. 21, 1947; d. Frank Bradley III and Suzanne (De St. Gilles) N. BA, UCLA, 1967; doctorat, U. Paris Sorbonne, 1972; MA, U.S. Internat. U., 1984, PhD, 1988. Staff therapist West Valley Psychological Clinic, Tarzana, Calif., 1987—; cons., coach communications. Mem. Am. Psychol. Assn., Calif. State Psychol. Assn., Nat. Speakers Assn., Am. Soc. Trial Cons., Psi Chi. Office: West Valley Psychol Clinic 18455 Burbank Blvd #406 Tarzana CA 91356

NELSON, PAUL WILLIAM, real estate broker; b. Mpls., Mar. 7, 1952; s. William H. and Jean (Darrington) N.; m. Jill Brownson, Oct. 18, 1986. BS, U. Colo., 1974. Lic. real estate broker, Colo. Advt. dir. Denver Beechcraft, 1976-77; real estate broker Coldwell Banker, Grand Junction, Colo., 1977—; bd. dirs. Colo. Assn. Realtors, Denver, 1981-83. City council mem. Grand Junction, 1985—; mem. Downtown Devel. Authority, Grand Junction, 1985—; bd. dirs. Mesa County Planning Commn., Grand Junction, 1980-85. Recipient Citizen Service award Mesa County, Colo., 1985. Mem. Grand Junction Bd. Realtors (bd. dirs. 1981-83). Republican. Lodge: Rotary. Office: Coldwell Banker Box 3117 Grand Junction CO 81502

NELSON, PAULA MORRISON, educator; b. Memphis, Mar. 26, 1944; d. Fred Ford and Julia (Morrison) Bronson: m. Jack Marvin Nelson, July 13, 1968; children: Eric Allen, Kelly Susan. BS, U. N. Mex., 1967; MA, U. Colo., Denver, 1985. Physical edn. tchr. Grant Union Sch. Dist., Sacramento, Calif., 1967-68; physical edn. tchr. Denver Pub. Schs., 1968-74, with program for pupil assistance, 1974-80, chpt. 1 reading specialist, 1983—; tchr. ESL Douglas County Pub. Schs., Parker, Colo., 1982-83; demonstration tchr. Colo. Edn. Assn., 1970-72; curriculum com. mem. Denver Pub. Schs., 1970-72, Douglas County Accountability Com., Castle Rock, Colo., 1986-88. Co-author: Gymnastics Teacher's Guide Elementary Physical Education, 1973; producer: slide shows Brotherhood, 1986, We the People...Our Dream Lives On, 1987. Pub. Edn. Coalition grantee, Denver, 1987, 88, Rocky Mountain Global Edn. Project grantee, Denver, 1987, Wake Forest Law Sch. grantee, Winston-Salem, N.C., 1988. Mem. Windstar Found., Colo. Council Internat. Reading, Internat. Reading Assn., Nat. Soc. for the Study of Edn. Republican. Methodist. Home: 10488 E Meadow Run Parker CO 80134

NELSON, RANDALL ERLAND, surgeon; b. Hastings, Nebr., Dec. 28, 1948; s. Marvin Erland and Faith Constance (Morrison) N.; m. Carolyn Joy Kaufman, Feb. 28, 1976. BS in Chemistry cum laude, So. Nazarene U., 1971; MD, U. Nebr., 1975; MS in Surgery, U. Ill., Chgo., 1979. Diplomate Nat. Bd. Med. Examiners, Am. Bd. Surgery. Intern in gen. surgery Strong Meml. Hosp., Rochester, N.Y., 1975-76; resident in gen. surgery U. Rochester Affiliated Hosps., 1976-78, Rush-Presbyn.-St. Luke's Med. Ctr., Chgo., 1978-81; gen. surgeon Surg. Group San Jose, Calif., 1981—; instr. gen. surgery U. Rochester Sch. Medicine and Dentistry, 1975-78, Rush Med. Coll., Chgo., 1978-80; adj. attending surgeon Rush-Presbyn.-St. Luke's Med. Ctr., 1980-81. Mem. Rep. Nat. Com., Washington, 1984—. Fellow ACS, Southwestern Surg. Congress; mem. AMA, Calif. Med. Assn., Santa Clara County Med. Soc., San Jose Surg. Soc., U.S. C. of C., Circle-K Club, Commonwealth Club Calif., Phi Delta Lambda. Republican. Office: Surg Group of San Jose 2101 Forest Ave Ste #124 San Jose CA 95128-1489

NELSON, RICHARD BURTON, patent consultant; b. Powell, Wyo., Dec. 10, 1911; s. Severt A. and Sedona Lenora (Fesenbeck) N.; m. Maxine Caroline George, Feb. 25, 1950 (div. June 1963); 1 child, Anna Afton Ghandour; m. Pauline Wright, Dec. 29, 1969. Student, San Diego State Coll., 1930-32; BS in Physics with honors, Calif. Inst. Tech., 1935; PhD, MIT, 1938. Registered patent agt. Physicist R.C.A. Mfg. Co., Harrison, N.J., 1938-41, Nat. Research Council, Ottawa, Ont., Can., 1941-42; research assoc. G.E. Research Lab., Schenectady, 1942-50; div. mgr. Varian Assocs., Palo Alto, Calif., 1960-63, chief engr., 1963-74, patent agt., 1974-77, cons., 1977—; bd. dirs. 1st Nat. Bank, Powell, Lovell (Wyo.) Nat. Bank, 1st Co., Powell. Author of numerous tech. papers; patentee in field. Fellow IEEE; mem. N.W. Wyo. Community Coll. Assocs. Club: Los Altos Golf and Country. Home and Office: 27040 Dezahara Way Los Altos Hills CA 94022

NELSON, RICHARD HENRY, county government official; b. Am. Fork, Utah, Aug. 22, 1949; s. Ray Conder and Affra (McNeill) N.; m. Marilyn Bradford, Apr. 24, 1972; children: Melissa, Caroline, Kristen, Susanna. Bachelors, Brigham Young U., 1973; Masters, Ohio State U., 1974. Cert. assoc. fin. planner. Human resources asst. Wasatch Front Regional Coun., Bountiful, Utah, 1974-76; exec. dir. Davis County Dept. of Employment and Tng., Farmington, Utah, 1976—; dir. Community Investment Corp., Farmington, 1984—; cons. Native Am. Devel. Corp., Fort Duchesne, Utah, 1989—; exec. sec. Davis County Pvt. Industry Coun., Farmington, 1989—. Dir. Davis County Coordinating Coun., Farmington, 1984—, Voluntary Action Ctr., Salt Lake City, 1974-76. Mem. Utah Assn. Pvt. Industry Couns. (dir. 1984—), Mountainwest Venture Group, Nat. Assn. County Employment and Tng. Adminstrn., Nat. Assn. Pvt. Industry Couns., Nat. Alliance Bus. Republican. Mormon. Home: 248 E 600 N Kaysville UT 84037 Office: Davis County Dept Employ 200 W 225 S Farmington UT 84025

NELSON, ROBERT M., astronomer; b. Los Angeles; s. Steve and Margaret (Yeager) N.; m. Carolyn Valley (div.); children: Tom, Chet; m. Marguerite Renner. BS, CUNY, 1966; MA, Wesleyan U., Middletown, Conn., 1969; PhD, U. Pitts., 1977. Research assoc. Jet Propulsion Lab., Pasadena, Calif., 1978-80, sr. scientist, 1980—; producer weekly sci. radio show Sta. KPFK, 1980—. Vice chmn. Pasadena Dem. Club, 1984—; mem. Calif. Dem. State Cen. Com., 1984—; chmn. Dem. 41st Assembly Dist. Calif.; commr. Pasadena Pub. Utilities, 1984—. Mem. AAAS, Am. Astron. Soc. (press officer div. planetary scis. 1983-86), Am. Geophys. Union, Internat. Astron. Union, So. Calif. Fedn. Scientists (co-chmn. 1981—). Home: 775 N Mentor Ave Pasadena CA 91104 Office: Jet Propulsion Lab 4800 Oak Grove Dr Pasadena CA 91103

NELSON, ROBERT MARTIN, electrical engineer, educator; b. Superior, Wis., Nov. 19, 1954; s. Roy Martin and Delores Helen (Carlson) N.; m. Mary Ellen Deja, Aug. 21, 1982; 1 child, Paul Robert. BA in Mathematics, Northland Coll., 1977; MSEE, Washington State U., 1981; PhD in Elec. Engring., North Dakota State U., 1987. Teaching asst. dept. of mathematics Washington State U., Pullman, 1977-78, research, teaching asst. dept. of elec. engring., 1978-81; tech. staff Bell Telephone Lab., Indpls., 1981-83; teaching asst. dept. elec. engring. North Dakota State U., Fargo, 1983-87; asst. prof dept. elec. engring. U. Idaho, Moscow, 1987—. Recipient Outstanding Young Elec. Engring. Prof., North Dakota State U., Fargo Chpt. Eta Kappa Nu, 1987, Alumni award for Faculty Excellence, Alumni Assn., Moscow, 1987. Mem. IEEE, Am. Soc. Engring. Edn. Office: U Idaho Dept Elec Engrs Moscow ID 83843

NELSON, ROBERT WILLIAM, real estate executive; b. Eugene, Oreg., May 29, 1942; s. Roy Robert and Alta (Peterson) N.; divorced; 1 child, Erin Michele. BS in Mgmt., Oreg. State U., 1965; MBA in Real Estate, U. Oreg., 1972. Lic. real estate investment broker. Real estate investor Nelson, Taylor & McCulley, Inc., Eugene, 1968-72; instr. real estate Lane Community Coll., Eugene, 1972—; pres., broker Robert W. Nelson, Real Estate Cons., Inc., Eugene, 1974—; expert witness to value Oreg. Tax Ct. and Lane County Circuit Ct., 1979—; ptnr., broker, exchange cons. PACWEST Real Estate Investments, 1984—. Author: Real Estate Law, 1974, Real Estate Finance, 1974, Real Estate Practices, 1974, Tax Deferred Exchanges, 1977. Active Bus. Adv. Counsel, Lane Community Coll., 1975—. Lt. USN, 1965-68. Named Realtor of Yr. Eugene Bd. Realtors, 1983. Mem. Soc. Real Estate Appraisers (nat. grad. fellow 1983), Brokers Million Dollar Club (pres. 1986, 89—), Comml. Investment Div. (pres. 1972), Downtown Athletic Club, Elks. Methodist. Office: PACWEST Real Estate Investments 540 Oak St Ste B Eugene OR 97401

NELSON, ROY G., pediatrician; b. Hinsdale, Ill., Nov. 9, 1951; s. Gunnar H. and Ingrid (Anderson) N.; m. Nancy G. Brackett, Dec. 23, 1973; children: Lisa, Julie, Kevin. BA in Chemistry, Union Coll., Lincoln, Nebr. 1974; MD, Loma Linda U., 1977. Intern Loma Linda (Calif.) U. Med. Ctr. 1978, resident, 1979-81; pvt. practice pediatrics and adolescent medicine Flatirons Med. Ctr., Boulder, Colo., 1981—; chmn. dept. pediatrics Boulder United Med. Staff, 1983-84; cons. Boulder and Weld County Health depts. 1982-85, Martin Luther Home, 1982-84; bd. dirs. CompreCare. Mem. sch. bd. Boulder Jr. Acad., 1982-89; mem. Boulder County Child Abuse Team 1982-85. Home: 633 Sunnyside St Louisville CO 80027 Office: Flatirons Med Group 350 Broadway Ste 130 Boulder CO 80303

NELSON, RUSSELL MARION, surgeon, educator; b. Salt Lake City Sept. 9, 1924; s. Marion C. and Edna (Anderson) N.; m. Dantzel White Aug. 31, 1945; children: Marsha Nelson McKellar, Wendy Nelson Maxfield Gloria Nelson Irion, Brenda Nelson Miles, Sylvia Nelson Webster, Emily Nelson Wittwer, Laurie Nelson Marsh, Rosalie Nelson Ringwood, Marjorie Nelson Helsten, Russell Marion, Jr. B.A., U. Utah, 1945, M.D., 1947 Ph.D. in Surgery, U. Minn., 1954; Sc.D. (hon.), Brigham Young U., 1970. Diplomate: Am. Bd. Surgery, Am. Bd. Thoracic Surgery (dir. 1972-78). Intern U. Minn. Hosps., Mpls., 1947; asst. resident surgery U. Minn. Hosps. 1948-51; first asst. resident surgery Mass. Gen. Hosp., Boston, 1953-54; sr. resident surgery U. Minn. Hosps., Mpls., 1954-55; practice medicine (specializing in cardiovascular and thoracic surgery), Salt Lake City, 1959-84; staff surgeon Latter-day Saints Hosp., Salt Lake City, 1959-84; dir. surg. research lab. Latter-day Saints Hosp., 1959-72, chief cardiovascular-thoracic surg. div., 1967-72, also bd. govs., 1970—, vice chmn., 1979-89; staff surgeon Primary Children's Hosp., Salt Lake City, 1960; attending in surgery VA Hosp., Salt Lake City, 1955-84, Univ. Hosp., Salt Lake City, 1955-84; asst. prof. surgery U. Utah Med. Sch., 1955-59, asst. clin. prof. surgery, 1959-66, asso. clin. prof. surgery, clin. prof., 1966-69, research prof. surgery, 1970—; staff services Utah Biomed. Test Lab., 1970-84; dir. tng. program cardiovascular and thoracic surgery at Univ. Utah affiliated hosps., 1967-84; mem. policyholders adv. com. New Eng. Mut. Life Ins. Co., Boston, 1976-80. Contbr. articles to profl. jours. Mem. White House Conf. on Youth and Children, 1960; Bd. dirs. Internat. Cardiology Found.; bd. govs. L.D.S. Hosp., 1970—, Deseret Gymnasium, 1971-75, Promised Valley Playhouse, 1970-79. Served from 1st lt. to capt. M.C. AUS, 1951-53. Markle scholar in med. scis., 1957-59; Fellowship of Medici Publici U. Utah Coll. Medicine, 1966; Distinguished Alumni award, 1967; Gold Medal of Merit, Argentina, 1974. Fellow A.C.S. (chmn. adv. council on thoracic surgery 1973-75), Am. Coll. Cardiology, Am. Coll. Chest Physicians; mem. Am. Assn. Thoracic Surgery, Am. Soc. Artificial Internal Organs, AMA, Dirs. Thoracic Residencies (pres. 1971-72), Utah Med. Assn. (pres. 1970-71), Salt Lake County Med. Soc., Am. Heart Assn. (exec. com. cardiovascular surgery 1972, dir. 1976-78, chmn. council cardiovascular surgery 1976-78), Utah Heart Assn. (pres. 1964-65), Soc. Thoracic Surgeons, Soc. Vascular Surgery (sec. 1968-72, pres. 1974), Utah Thoracic Soc., Salt Lake Surg. Soc., Samson Thoracic Surg. Soc., Western Soc. for Clin. Research, Soc. U. Surgeons, Am., Western, Pan-Pacific surg. assns., Inter. Am. Soc. Cardiology (bd. mgrs.), Phi Beta Kappa, Sigma Xi, Alpha Omega Alpha, Phi Kappa Phi, Sigma Chi. Mem. Ch. of Jesus Christ of Latter-day Saints (pres. Bonneville Stake 1964-71, gen. pres. Sunday sch. 1971-79, regional rep. 1979-84, Quorum of the Twelve Apostles 1984—). Home: 1347 Normandie Circle Salt Lake City UT 84105 Office: 47 E S Temple Salt Lake City UT 84150

NELSON, SANDRA LEE, realtor; b. Wilkensburg, Pa., July 5, 1947; d. Richard David and Hazel Louise (Painter) Thornton; m. Larry Dean Nelson, Mar. 1, 1970 (div. Dec. 1986); children: Kristina Dawn, Amy Josephine, Rebecca Lyn, Julie Anne. BA, Amb. Coll., Bricketwood, Eng., 1969; student, Century 21 Real Estate Sch., San Gabriel, Calif., 1984. Real estate agt. Century 21 Val Realty, Arcadia, Calif., 1984; realtor Anthony & Co. Realtors, Arcadia, 1984-88, Douglas Brooker & Assocs., 1988—. Mem. Calif. Assn. Realtors, Women's Club (pres. 1976-77, advisor 1977-80). Office: Douglas Brooker & Assocs 817 S 1st Ave Arcadia CA 91006

NELSON, SARAH MILLEDGE, archaeology educator; b. Miami, Fla., Nov. 29, 1931; d. Stanley and Sarah Woodman (Franklin) M.; m. Harold Stanley Nelson, July 25, 1953; children: Erik Harold, Mark Milledge, Stanley Franklin. BA, Wellesley Coll., 1953; MA, U. Mich., 1969, PhD, 1973. Instr. archaeology U. Md. extension, Seoul, Republic Korea, 1970-71; asst. prof. U. Denver, 1974-79, assoc. prof., 1979-85, prof. archaeology, 1985—, chair dept. anthropology, dir. women's studies program, 1985-87; vis. asst. prof. U. Colo., Boulder, 1974. Mem. com. on scholarly communication with teh Poeple's Republic China, Nat. Acad. Scis., 1988; active Earthwatch, 1989. Grantee Southwestern Inst. Research on Women, 1981, Acad. Korean Studies, Seoul, 1983, Internat. Cultural Soc. Korea, Seoul, 1986. Fellow Am. Anthrop. Assn.; mem. Soc. Am. Archaeology, Assn. Asian Studies, Royal Asiatic Soc., Sigma Xi (sec.-treas. 1978-79), Phi Beta Kappa. Democrat. Home: 4970 S Fulton St Englewood CO 80111 Office: U Denver Dept Anthropology Denver CO 80208

NELSON, TERRY JAMES, organization executive; b. Sioux Falls, S.D., Jan. 11, 1950; s. Harvey Laun and Dorothy Ann (Cody) N.; m. Deborah Jo Wallace, Dec. 21, 1972. BA, Augustana Coll., Sioux Falls, 1972; M of Mgmt., U. Phoenix, 1989. Program dir. YMCA Met. Denver, 1973-79, exec. dir. Schlessman br., 1979-81, Jeffco br., 1981-; pres., chief exec. officer Colo. Carriages, Ltd., Denver, 1982-85. V.p. alumni coun. Augustana Coll., 1979-81; com. chmn. Holy Shepherd Luth. Ch., Lakewood, Colo., 1987-88, vice chmn. coun., 1988—, pres., 1989—. Recipient Adminstrv. Exec. award YMCA U.S.A., 1986. Mem. Lakewood C. of C., Kiwanis. Office: Jeffco Family YMCA 11050 W 20th Ave Lakewood CO 80215

NELSON, VALERIE JOY, newspaper editor; b. Seattle, Oct. 1, 1956; d. William Eugene Nelson and Marguerite Joy (Best) Peterson; m. Steven Decker Clow, April 26, 1985; 1 child: Gillian Hannah Clow. BA, U. So. Calif., 1979. Copy editor Los Angeles Herald Examiner, 1980-81, asst. news editor, 1982-84, news editor Style sect., 1984-86, dep. editor Style sect., 1986-87, editor Style sect., 1987-88; founder, editor Nelson Gray Communications, Los Angeles, 1988—; asst. editor Valley View and Calendar sect. Los

Angeles Times, 1988—. Asst. press aide to U.S. Rep. James H. Quillen, Washington, 1979. Recipient page design award Soc. Newspaper Design, 1986. Mem. Sigma Delta Chi. Republican. Home: 5410 Columbus Ave Van Nuys CA 91411 Office: Los Angeles Times 20000 Prairie Chatsworth CA 91311

NELSON, WILLARD GREGORY, veterinarian, mayor; b. Lewiston, Idaho, Nov. 21, 1937; s. Donald William and Eve Mae (Boyer) N.; m. Mary Ann Eklund, Apr. 3, 1965 (div.); children: Elizabeth Ann, John Gregory. BS in Premedicine, Mont. State U., 1959; DVM, Wash. State U., 1961. Lic. veterinarian, Wash., Oreg., Idaho, Mont. Pvt. practice vet. medicine, Kuna, Idaho, 1963-66; asst. to dir. Idaho Dept. Agr., Boise, 1966-78; asst. chief Idaho Bur. Animal Health, 1978-80, chief, 1980-81; adminstr., state veterinarian Idaho Div. Animal Industries, 1981—; mayor City of Kuna (Idaho), 1984—; chmn. Idaho Gov.'s Human and Animal Health Consortium, 1983—. Kuna city councilman, 1964-68, pres. Planning and Zoning Commn., 1968-72; mem. bd. trustees Joint Sch. Dist. 3, 1970-71, pres., 1972-76; mem. adv. bd. Mercy Med. Hosp., Nampa, Idaho, 1986—; mem. adv. com. Wash., Oreg., Idaho Coll. Vet. Medicine, 1983—. Served as capt. U.S. Army Vet Corps, 1961-63; lt. col. Idaho Army N.G., 1979-88, col., 1988—. Mem. Idaho Vet. Med. Assn. (v.p. 1987, pres.-elect 1988, pres. 1989, Idaho Veterinarian of Yr. 1989), S.W. Idaho Vet. Med. Assn., U.S. Animal Health Assn. (chmn. anaplasmosis com. 1987—), AVMA (mem. coun. on pub. health and regulatory medicine 1988—, pres. nat. assembly 1988), Western States Livestock Assn., Am. Legion. Lutheran. Club: Lions (Kuna). Home: 793 W 4th Kuna ID 83634 Office: 2270 Old Penitentiary Rd Boise ID 83702

NELSON, WILLIAM RANKIN, surgeon; b. Charlottesville, Va., Dec. 12, 1921; s. Hugh Thomas and Edith (Rankin) N.; m. Nancy Laidley, Mar. 17, 1956 (div. 1979); children: Robin Page Nelson Russel, Susan Kimberly Nelson Wright, Anne Rankin Nelson Cron; m. Pamela Morgan Phelps, July 5, 1984. BA, U. Va., 1943, MD, 1945. Diplomate Am. Bd. Surgery. Intern Vanderbilt U. Hosp., Nashille, 1945-46; resident in surgery U. Va. Hosp., Charlottesville, 1949-51; fellow surg. oncology Meml. Sloan Kettering Cancer Ctr., N.Y.C., 1951-55; instr. U. Colo. Sch. Medicine, Denver, 1955-57; asst. clin. prof. U. Colo. Sch. Medicine, 1962-87, clin. prof. surgery, 1987—; asst. prof. Med. Coll. Va., Richmond, 1957-62; mem. exec. com. U. Colo. Cancer Ctr. Contbr. articles to profl. jours. Capt. USAAF, 1946-48. Recipient Nat. Div. award Am. Cancer Soc., 1979. Fellow Am. Coll. Surgeons (bd. govs. 1984--); mem. Soc. Surgical Oncology (pres. 1975-76), Soc. Head and Neck Surgeons (pres. 1986-87), Am. Cancer Soc. (pres. Colo. div. 1975-77, profl. edn. com.) , Internat. Soc. Surgery, Am. Soc. Clinical Oncology, Western Surgical Assn., Univ. Club, Rotary. Republican. Presbyterian. Office: 2005 Franklin St #180 Denver CO 80205

NEMETH, JOHN LOUIS, electronics design executive; b. Perth Amboy, N.J., Sept. 2, 1950; s. John Louis and Irene Julia (Hudanish) N. Student, Bell Labs., 1970. Draftsman Bell Telephone Labs., Holmdel, N.J., 1968-74, Parsons, Brinkerhoff, Tudor-Bechtel, Atlanta, 1974-75; designer Burr-Brown Corp., Tucson, 1975—. Author: U-100, 1985, Where No Man Has Gone Before, 1988. Office: Burr-Brown Corp 6730 S Tucson Blvd Tucson AZ 85706

NEMETZ, NATHANIEL THEODORE, lawyer, former chief justice British Columbia; b. Winnipeg, Man., Can., Sept. 8, 1913; s. Samuel and Rebecca (Birch) N.; m. Bel Newman, Aug. 10, 1935; 1 son, Peter Newman. B.A. with 1st class honors, U. B.C., 1934; LL.D. (hon.), Notre Dame, Nelson, B.C., 1972, U. B.C., 1975, Simon Fraser U., 1975, U. Victoria, 1976. Bar: Created King's Counsel 1950. Spl. counsel Public Utilities Commn., 1958-61; spl. counsel to cities of Vancouver, Burnaby, New Westminster, Can., 1959-63; justice Supreme Ct. B.C., 1963-68, Ct. Appeal, 1968-73; chief justice B.C. Supreme Ct., 1973-78, B.C., 1979-88; mem. Royal Commn. to investigate election irregularities, 1965; arbitrator fishing, lumber and hydro industries West Coast shipping dispute, 1966-73; chmn. Legal Conf., Stanford U., 1986; co-chmn. 1st Can.-Australasian Legal Conf., Canberra, Australia, 1988; mem. appeal bd. Can.-U.S. Free Trade Agreement; chmn. Japan-Can. Coal Dispute Arbitration, 1988; hon. consul Singapore, 1989. Contbr. articles in field to profl. publs. Mem. senate, chmn. bd. govs. U. B.C., 1957-68, chancellor, 1972-75; chmn. Can. edn. del. to China, 1974; Chmn. Univ. Dist. Sch. Bd., 1957-59; hon. chmn. Crusade Against Cancer, 1988; hon. trustee B.C. Govt. Ho. Found., 1988; founder Freeman City of Vancouver, 1988. Named hon. fellow Hebrew U., Jerusalem, 1976; recipient award Can. Council Christians and Jews, 1958; Great Trekker award U.B.C., 1969; Beth Emeth Brotherhood award, 1969; Canada medal, 1967; award of distinction U. B.C. Alumni, 1975; Queen Elizabeth medal, 1977, Alumni award U. B.C., 1988; Nathan T. Nemetz chair in Legal History created in his honor U. B.C., 1988. Mem. Can. Jud. Council (exec. 1973—, vice chmn. 1988), Can. Bar Assn., Faculty Assn. U. B.C. (hon.), Alumni Assn. U. B.C. (pres. 1957). Jewish. Clubs: Faculty (U. B.C.); Vancouver (Vancouver), University (Vancouver) (pres. 1961-62).

NEMIR, DONALD PHILIP, lawyer; b. Oakland, Calif., Oct. 31, 1931; s. Philip F. and Mary (Shavor) N.; AB, U. Calif. at Berkeley, 1957, JD, 1960. Admitted to Calif. bar, 1961; sole practice San Francisco, 1961—; pres. Law Offices Donald Nemir. Bd. dirs. Summit Found., Redwood City, Calif. 1980—. Mem. ABA (litigation com.), Calif. State Bar Assn. (litigation com.). Phi Delta Phi. Club: Univ. (San Francisco). Office: 2 Embarcadero Ctr Ste 740 San Francisco CA 94111

NEMIRO, BEVERLY MIRIUM ANDERSON, writer, educator; b. St. Paul, May 29, 1925; d. Martin and Anna Mae (Oshanyk) Anderson; m. Jerome Morton Nemiro, Feb. 10, 1951 (div. May 1975); children: Guy Samuel, Lee Anna, Dee Martin. Student Reed Coll., 1943-44; B.A., U. Colo., 1947; postgrad., U. Denver. Tchr., Seattle Pub. Schs., 1945-46; fashion coordinator, dir. Denver Dry Goods Co., 1948-51; fashion model, Denver, 1951-58, 78—; fashion dir. Denver Market Week Assn., 1952-53; free-lance writer, Denver, 1958—; moderator TV program Your Preschool Child, Denver, 1955-56; instr. writing and communications U. Colo. Denver Ctr., 1970—, U. Calif., San Diego, 1976-78, Met. State Coll., 1985—; dir. pub. relations Fairmont Hotel, Denver, 1979-80; free lance fashion and TV model; author: The Complete Book of High Altitude Baking, 1961, Colorado a la Carte, 1963, Colorado a la Carte, Series II, 1966, (with Donna Hamilton) The High Altitude Cookbook, 1969, The Busy People's Cookbook, 1971 (Better Homes and Gardens Book Club selection 1971), Where to Eat in Colorado, 1967, Lunch Box Cookbook, 1965, Complete Book of High Altitude Baking, 1961, (under name Beverly Anderson) Single After 50, 1978, The New High Altitude Cookbook, 1980. Co-founder, pres. Jr. Symphony Guild, Denver, 1959-60; active Denver Art Mus., Denver Symphony Guild. Recipient Achievement Rewards for Coll. Scientists, Sante Fe Opera, Denver Ear Inst., Top Hand award Colo. Authors' League, 1969, 72, 79-82, 100 Best Best Books of Yr. award N.Y. Times, 1969, 71; named one of Colo.'s Women of Yr., Denver Post, 1964. Mem. Pub. Relations Soc. Am., Am. Soc. Journalists and Authors, Nat. Writers Club, Colo. Authors League (dir. 1969—), Authors Guild, Authors League Am., Friends Denver Library, Sigma Delta Chi, Kappa Alpha Theta. Address: 420 S Marion Pkwy Apt 1003 Denver CO 80209

NEMIROFF, MAXINE CELIA, museum curator, director, educator; b. Chgo., Feb. 11, 1935; d. Oscar Bernard and Martha (Mann) Kessler; m. Paul Rubenstein, June 26, 1955 (div. 1974); children: Daniel, Peter, Anthony; m. Allan Nemiroff, Dec. 24, 1979. BA, U. So. Calif., 1955; MA, UCLA, 1974. Sr. instr. UCLA, 1974—; dir., curator art gallery Doolittle Theater, Los Angeles, 1985-86; leader of worldwide art tours; cons. L'Ermitage Hotel Group, Beverly Hills, Calif., 1982—, Broadway Dept. Stores, Southern Calif., 1979—, Security Pacific Bank, Calif., 1978—; art chmn. UCLA Thieves Market, Century City, 1960—, Los Angeles Music Ctr. Mercado, 1982—; lectr. in field. Apptd. bd. dirs. Dublin (Calif.) Fine Arts Found., 1989. Named Woman of Yr. UCLA Panhellenic Council, 1982, Instr. of Yr. UCLA Dept. Arts, 1984. Mem. Los Angeles County Mus. Art council art mus., UCLA Art Council, UCLA Art Council Docents, Alpha Epsilon Phi (alumnus of yr. 1983). Democrat. Jewish.

NEPTUNE, JOHN ADDISON, chemistry educator, consultant; b. Barnesville, Ohio, Nov. 27, 1919; s. George Addison and Lola Mae (Skinner) N.; m. Ruth Elizabeth Dorsey, Aug. 24, 1947; 1 child, Benjamin. B.S. summa cum laude, Muskingum Coll., 1942; M.S., U. Wis., 1949, Ph.D., 1952. Instr. chemistry Muskingum Coll., New Concord, Ohio, 1943-44, 45-48; foreman Tenn. Eastman Corp., Manhattan Project, 1944-45; asst. prof. chemistry Bowling Green State U., Ohio, 1949-50; instr. pharm. chemistry U. Wis.-Madison, 1952-55; asst. prof. chemistry San Jose State U., Calif., 1955-58, assoc. prof., 1958-61, prof., 1961—, chmn. dept., 1973-86; cons. FMC Corp., Crown-Andersen Corp. Mem. Am. Chem. Soc., AAUP. Methodist. Home: 50 Cherokee Ln San Jose CA 95127 Office: San Jose State U Dept Chemistry San Jose CA 95192

NERO, ANTHONY VINCENT, JR., physicist; b. Salisbury, Md., Apr. 11, 1942; s. Anthony V. Nero and Anna Elizabeth Coladonato. BS summa cum laude, Fordham U., 1964; PhD in Physics, Stanford U., 1971. Rsch. fellow physics dept. Fordham U., summers 1962-63; grad. rsch. asst. Nuclear Physics Lab., Stanford (Calif.) U., 1966-70; postdoctoral rsch. fellow Kellogg Radiation Lab., Calif. Inst. Tech., Pasadena, 1970-72; asst. prof. physics Princeton (N.J.) U., 1972-75; physicist applied sci. div. Lawrence Berkeley (Calif.) Lab., 1975—, leader indoor radon group, 1980-86, sr. scientist, 1986—, dep. leader indoor environ. program, 1986—; visitor nuclear power div. Electric Power Rsch. Inst., summers 1974-75; phys. sci. officer Non-Proliferation Bur., ADCA, 1978; lectr. dept. mech. engring. U. Calif., Berkeley, 1979, lectr. energy and resources program, 1980, lectr. Sch. Pub. Health, 1989—; mem. adv. com. 3d Internat. Conf. on Indoor Air Quality and Climate, Stockholm, 1984, symposium organizer, rapporteur for radon 4th Conf., Berlin, 1987; mem. various adv. and rev. panels EPA, 1984—; mem. program com. 4th Internat. Symposium on Natural Radiation Environ, Lisbon, 1987. Author: A Guidebook to Nuclear Reactors, 1979; co-author: Instrumentation for Environmental Monitoring, Vol. 1, 1983, Radon and Its Decay Products in Indoor Air, 1988; contbr. articles to profl. and popular publs., chpts. to books. Gen. Motors Corp. nat. scholar, 1960-64; NSF undergrad. summer rsch. fellow, 1962, 63, NSF grad. fellow, 1964-68. Fellow Am. Physics Soc. (panel on pub. affairs 1981-83, Leo Szilard award for Physics in the Pub. Interest 1989, exec. com. forum on physics and society 1988—); mem. AAAS, Health Physics Soc., Air Pollution Control Assn., Fedn. Am. Scient ists, Nat. Council on Radiation Protection and Measurements (sci. coms. on radon measurements and control of radon and its products in residences), Phi Beta Kappa, Sigma Xi. Home: 2738 Benvenue Ave Berkeley CA 94705 Office: Lawrence Berkeley Lab 1 Cyclotron Rd Bldg 90 Rm 3058 Berkeley CA 94720

NERO, PETER, pianist, conductor, composer, arranger; b. N.Y.C., May 22, 1934; s. Julius and Mary (Menasche) N.; m. Marcia Dunner, June 19, 1956; children—Beverly, Jedd; m. Peggy Altman, Aug. 31, 1977. Ed., Juilliard Sch., N.Y.C. Nat. tour with Paul Whiteman on TV and in concert, 1953-57, appearances concert halls, theatres, colls., TV and supper clubs throughout U.S., Eng., France, Holland, Italy, Scandinavia, 1962—; appeared at Grand Gala du Disque, Amsterdam, The Netherlands, 1964, five TV specials on, BBC-TV; arranged, appeared and recorded with Boston Pops Orch.; music dir., Philly Pops Orch., 1979—; recording artist for, RCA Victor, Arista Records, Crystal Clear Records, Columbia; albums include Peter Nero Now; appeared in film Sunday in New York; composer: condr. more than 150 symphony orchs., 1971—. Honored by Internat. Soc. Performing Arts Adminstrs., 1986. Office: care Columbia Artists Mgmt Inc 4605 Lankershim Blvd #421 North Hollywood CA 91602 *

NERO, ROBERT ANTHONY, data processing executive; b. Cleve., Mar. 4, 1946; s. Harold Alfred and Carolyn Elizabeth (Parker) N.; m. Mary Jo Strozdas, Sept. 13, 1969; children: Patrick, Peggy, Peter. BA, U. Dayton, 1968; MS, Mich. State U., 1970. Ops. rsch. analyst Mead Corp., Dayton, Ohio, 1971-73; acct. exec. ADP Network Svcs., Dayton, 1973-76; sr. dist. mgr. ADP Network Svcs., Dearborn, Mich., 1976-82; regional v.p. ADP Network Svcs., Chgo., 1982-83, v.p. sales, mktg., 1983-85; v.p. worldwide sales Mead Data Cen., Dayton, 1985-88; pres. Boole & Babbage N.Am., Sunnyvale, Calif., 1988—; v.p., gen. mgr. Info. Tech. div. Goal Sytems Internat., Columbus, Ohio, 1989—. bd. dirs. Jr. Achievement, 1987-88; coach St. Michaels Sch., 1981-85. Capt. USAR, 1970-77. Mem. Am. Mgmt. Assn., Info. Industry Assn. (mktg. com. chmn., 1987-88)., Nat. Cash Register Country Club. Republican. Roman Catholic. Home: 616 Murrell Dr Kettering OH 45429 Office: Boole & Babbage N Am 510 Oakmead Pkwy Sunnyvale CA 94086

NESBITT, LISA DANIEL, marketing consultant; b. Great Lakes, Ill., Dec. 31, 1953; d. Lewis Holberg and Irene (Bronnais) D.; m. Stephen Lane Nesbitt; children: John Daniel, Stephen Blake. BA, Stanford U., 1976; MBA, U. Calif., Berkeley, 1981. Assoc. Econs. Research Assocs., San Francisco, 1976-79; mktg. coordinator Wells Fargo Bank, San Francisco, 1979-81; sr. prodn. mgr. Security Pacific Nat. Bank, Los Angeles, 1981-85; mgr. First Interstate Bank Calif., Los Angeles, 1985-88; mktg. cons. First Interstate Bancorp, Los Angeles, 1988—. Presch. coordinator Brentwood Presbyn. Ch., Los Angeles, 1988-89. Mem. Stanford Profl. Women, Jr. League Los Angeles. Republican. Presbyterian. Home: 460 22nd St Santa Monica CA 90402 Office: First Interstate Bancorp 707 Wilshire Blvd Los Angeles CA 90017

NESBITT, PAUL EDWARD, historian, author, educator; b. Balt., Dec. 25, 1943; s. William Ervin and Margaret Caroline (Shaw) N.; m. Donna Jean Coppock, Aug. 15, 1966 (dec. 1972); children: Erik-Paul A., Janelle M., m. Pamela Jean Lichty, May 25, 1974 (div. 1983); m. Anita Louise Wood, Dec. 8, 1984 (div. 1989). AB, U. Wash., 1965; MA, Wash. State U., 1968, PhD (hon.), 1970; PhD, U. Calgary, 1972. Reader in Anthropology, U. Wash., 1965, grad. research-tchr. Wash. State U., 1966-68, instr., Tacoma Community Coll., Wash., 1968-69; grad. research-tchr. U. Calgary, Alta., Can., 1969-71; exec. Hudson's Bay Co., Calgary, 1971; prof. Western Oreg. U., Monmouth, 1971-74; state historian State of Calif., Sacramento, 1974—; dir. Am. Sch. of Interior Design, San Francisco, 1974, HBC Bow Fort Research, Morley, Alta., 1970-71; instr. Am. River Coll., Sacramento, 1980-86; exec. mgr. Calif. State Govt. United Way Campaign, 1986, 87; designer, cultural research cons. pvt. contracts western states, 1960—. Contbr. articles to prof. jours. Fellow Am. Anthropl. Assn.; mem. Calif. Hist. Soc., Am. Inst. of Interior Designers (profl. 1974-77, bd. dirs. energy planning and devel. cos.), AIA (Cen. Valley chpt. 1975-77). Office: PO Box 942896 Sacramento CA 94296-0001

NETHERCOTT, NEAL C., utilities company executive; b. Jackson, Wyo., Mar. 7, 1946; s. Moy Emerson and Erma Lucille (Chambers) N.; m. Sharon Kay Dockham, June 24, 1966; children: Neal Cole, Cade James. Grad. high sch., Jackson; lineman tng., Casper (Wyo.) Coll., 1975. Apprentice lineman Lower Valley Power and Light, Jackson, 1972-75, lineman, 1975-77, foreman, 1977-83, supt., 1983-87, ops. mgr., 1987—, safety dir., 1983—, apprentice trainer, 1988—; bd. dirs. Boise (Idaho) Coll., 1988—. Firefighter Jackson Vol. Fire Dept., 1980-84, 2nd lt., 1984-86, 1st. lt., 1986—, capt. emergency response team, 1986-88, mem., 1988—. With USAF, 1968-72, Vietnam. Home: PO Box 2120 Jackson WY 83001 Office: Lower Valley Power & Light PO Box 572 Jackson WY 83001

NETZ, PAMELA BELPORT, restaurant executive; b. Manhasset, N.Y., Oct. 23, 1954; d. Daniel Carl Erdman and Wynette Maude (Miller) N. Student, Pima Community Coll., 1982-85. Lic. real estate agt. Bookkeeper, catering cons. Continental Cuisine Caterers, Tucson, 1973-75; restaurant mgr. Benjee's Restaurant, Tucson, 1972-77; wine-catering hostess Old Pueblo Club, Tucson, 1975-77; property mgr. Fidelity Realty, Tucson, 1977-80, J. C. Harry & Assocs., Tucson, 1980-82; owner, comptroller Coffee, Etc., Inc., Tucson, 1982—; cons. Cafe Magrite, Tucson, 1987-89, Continental Cuisine Caterers, Tucson, 1973-75. Supporting mem. KXCI Pub. Radio, Tucson, 1986-88, Invisible Theatre, Tucson, 1988-89. Mem. Resource Exchange (sec. spl. events com. 1987-88). Democrat. Presbyterian. Home: 110 N Cherry Ave Tucson AZ 85719 Office: Coffee Etc Inc 2830 N Campbell Ave Tucson AZ 85719

NETZEL, PAUL ARTHUR, fund raising management executive, consultant; b. Tacoma, Sept. 11, 1941; s. Marden Arthur and Audrey Rose (Jones) N.; BS in Group Work Edn., George Williams Coll., 1963; m. Diane Viscount, Mar. 21, 1963; children: Paul M., Shari Ann. Program dir. S. Pasadena-San Marino (Calif.) YMCA, 1963-66; exec. dir. camp and youth programs Wenatchee (Wash.) YMCA, 1966-67; exec. dir. Culver-Palms Family YMCA, Culver City, Calif., 1967-73, vice-chmn., bd. mgrs., 1989—; v.p. met. fin. devel. YMCA Met. Los Angeles, 1973-78, exec. v.p. devel., 1979-85; pres. bd. dirs. YMCA Employees Credit Union, 1977-80; chmn. N.Am. Fellowship of YMCA Devel. Officers, 1980-83; adj. faculty U. So. Calif. Coll. Continuing Edn., 1983-86, Loyola Marymount U., Los Angeles, 1986—; chairman, chief exec. officer Netzel/Steinhaus and Assocs., Inc., 1985—; pvt. practice cons., fund raiser. Pres. bd. Culver City Guidance Clinic, 1971-74; mem. Culver City Bd. Edn., 1975-79, pres., 1977-78; mem. Culver City Edn. Found., 1982—; bd. dirs. Los Angeles Psychiat. Service; mem. Culver City Council, 1980-88, vice-mayor, 1980-82, 84-85, mayor, 1982-83, 86-87; mem. Culver City Redevel. Agy., 1980-88, chmn., 1983-84, 87-88, vice chmn, 1985-86; bd. dirs. Los Angeles County Sanitation Dists., 1982-83, 85-87; bd. dirs. western region United Way, 1986—; chmn. bd. dirs. Calif. Youth Model Legislature, 1987—. Recipient Man of Year award Culver City C. of C., 1972; trustee Washington Med. Ctr. 1988—. Mem. Nat. Soc. Fund Raising Execs. (bd. dirs. 1989—, vice-pres. bd. dirs. Greater Los Angeles chpt. 1986-88, pres. bd. dirs. 1989—, Profl. of Yr. 1983). Roman Catholic. Clubs: Los Angeles Athletic, Rotary (bd. dirs. Los Angeles chpt. 1989—), Mountain Gate Country. Address: Netzel Steinhaus & Assocs 9696 Culver Blvd Ste 204 Culver City CA 90232

NEU, CARL HERBERT, JR., management consultant; b. Miami Beach, Fla., Sept. 4, 1937; s. Carl Herbert and Catherine Mary (Miller) N.; BS, MIT, 1959; MBA, Harvard U., 1961; m. Carmen Mercedes Smith, Feb. 8, 1964; children—Carl Bartley, David Conrad. Indsl. liaison officer MIT, Cambridge, 1967-69; coord. forward planning Gates Rubber Co., Denver, 1969-71; pres., co-founder Dyna-Com Resources, Lakewood, Colo., 1971-77; pres., founder Neu & Co., Lakewood, 1977—; mng. dir. Pro-Med Mgmt. Systems, Lakewood, 1981—; lectr. Grad. Sch. Pub. Affairs, U. Colo. Denver, 1982-84. Mem. exec. coun. Episcopal Diocese Colo., 1974; mem. Lakewood City Coun., 1975-80, pres., 1976; chmn. Lakewood City Charter Commn., 1982, Lakewood Civic Found., Inc., 1986—; pres. Lakewood on Parade, 1978, bd. dirs., 1978-80; pres. Classic Chorale, Denver, 1979, bd. dirs., 1978-83; pres. Lakewood Pub. Bldg. Authority, 1983—. With U.S. Army, 1961-67. Decorated Bronze Star medal, Army Commendation medal; recipient Arthur Page award AT&T, 1979; Kettering Found. grantee, 1979-80. Mem. World Future Soc., Internat. City Mgrs. Assn., Lakewood/So. Jefferson County C. of C. (bd. dirs. 1983—, chmn. 1988, chmn. 1987-88), Jefferson County C. of C. (chmn. 1988). Republican. Episcopalian. Contbr. articles to profl. jours. Home: 8169 W Baker Ave Lakewood CO 80227

NEU, ROGER JOHN, real estate company executive; b. Long Beach, Calif., Apr. 11, 1944; s. John F. and Phyllis A. (Wetzel) N.; m. Marilyn Jean Albertson, Sept. 11, 1965; children: Randall J., Carter P. BS, U. Oreg., 1968. Asst. appraiser Carl Trowbridge & Assoc., Portland, Oreg., 1968-70; researcher real estate Pacific Research Assoc., Portland, 1970; ptnr., real estate appraiser Younger & Neu, Portland, 1970-82; pres. Allied Real Estate Appraisers Inc., Portland, 1982-84; v.p. Schnitzer Investment Corp., Portland, 1985—; tchr. Portland Community Coll., 1972-76; presenter seminars in field. Chmn. Oreg. chpt. Nat. Multiple Sclerosis Soc., Portland, 1976; chmn. bd. trustees 1st United Meth. Ch., Portland, 1988. Mem. Am. Inst. Real Estate Appraisers, Nat. Assn. Corp. Real Estate Execs., Portland C. of C., Rotary. Republican. Home: 6055 SW 90th Portland OR 97223 Office: Schnitzer Investment Corp 3200 NW Yeon Portland OR 97210

NEUBAUER, JAMES EMMANUEL, real estate developer; b. Sterling, Colo., Dec. 6, 1952; s. John and Patricia (Westland) N.; m. Pamela Dee Fisher, Nov. 27, 1976; children: Heather, Jonathan. Student, Stanford U., 1977, Northwestern U., 1977. V.p. Continental Bank, Phoenix, 1974-78; exec. v.p. P.F. West Inc., Tucson, 1978-85, pres., 1985—. Pres. Tucson Boys Chorus, 1984—; bd. dirs. Pima County (Ariz.) Research Council, 1984—. Mem. Southern Ariz. Home Builders Assn. Republican. Episcopalian. Clubs: Toastmasters (Phoenix), U. Ariz. Presidents. Office: PF West Inc 5995 E Grant Rd Tucson AZ 85712

NEUENSCHWANDER, BETTY JEAN, laboratory administrator, medical technologist; b. Oi-Mura, Japan, Nov. 12, 1948; came to U.S., 1951; d. William Rudolph and Saiko (Takayama) Perkov; m. Leon Fredric Neuenschwander, Aug. 12, 1972; children: Jennifer Lee, Douglas Darwin. BS in Med. Tech., Calif. State U., L.A., 1971; postgrad. bus. adminstrn., U. Idaho, 1988—. Registered med. technologist Coll. Am. Pathologists. Intern, med. technologist So. Calif. (Kaiser) Permanente, L.A., 1971-72; dep. head chemistry, alt. asst. lab. mgr. West Tex. Hosp., Lubbock, 1972-75; med. technologist Gritman Meml. Hosp., Moscow, Idaho, 1980-86; lab. mgr. Pullman (Wash.) Meml. Hosp., 1986—, lab. adminstrv. dir., 1989—. Mem. Moscow Centennial Com., 1986-88. Mem. Am. Soc. Clin. Pathologists, Am. Soc. for Med. Technology, Am. Soc. Med. Technologists (registered), Calif. Clin. Lab. Technologists. Democrat. Roman Catholic. Office: Pullman Meml Hosp Washington Ave Pullman WA 99163

NEUFELD, TIMOTHY LEE, lawyer; b. Glendale, Calif., Apr. 23, 1947; s. Stanley and Marie E. (Scott) N.; m. Naomi Das, Nov. 27, 1971; children: Pamela, Katherine. AB, Brown U., 1969; JD, Boston U., 1975. Bar: Calif. 1975. Assoc. Richards, Watson & Gershon, L.A., 1975-80, ptnr., 1980—. Lt. (j.g.) USN, 1969-72. Mem. State Bar Calif., L.A. County Bar Assn. Presbyterian. Office: Richards Watson & Gershon 333 S Hope St Los Angeles CA 90071

NEULREICH, ROBERT JOSEPH, regional manager; b. Milw., June 28, 1925; s. Walter F. and Anna M. (Kohar) N.; m. Fern A. Stevens, Nov. 9, 1946 (dec. July 21, 1987); 1 child, Judith Ann. BA, Augustana Coll., 1940. Mgr. Sears, Roebuck and Co., Tucson, 1957-68; Western states regional mgr. Sears, Roebuck and Co., 1968-77; group mgr. SW Group, 1977-82; regional mgr. Angels-Oles Wickes Group, 1982—. Sgt. U.S. Army, 1943-45. Mem. Oasis, Eagles. Republican. Episcopalian. Home: 4041 E Becker Ln Phoenix AZ 85028

NEUMAN, RICHARD BURTON, sales agent; b. Oakland, Calif., Mar. 1, 1940; s. Charles Burton and Virginia Louise (Jones) N.; m. Diana Alice Wilde, Aug. 12, 1967; children: David Wilde, Caroline Wilde. BS, U. Calif., Berkeley, 1961; MBA, U. So. Calif., L.A., 1966. Retail store employee, corp. buyer Safeway Stores, Inc., Oakland, 1957-70; regional sales mgr. Agripac, Inc., Salem, Oreg., 1970-73; we. region sales mgr. Stokley Van Camp, San Jose, Calif., 1973-75; account exec. E.A. Durell & Co., Inc., San Francisco, 1975-83; exec. v.p. Sheridan-Durell, Inc., Walnut Creek, Calif., 1983-84; owner R. B. Neuman, Inc., Orinda, Calif., 1984—. Pres. Orinda Youth Assn., 1983; troop com. Boy Scouts Am., Orinda, 1979-89. Lt. U.S. Army, 1962-64. Mem. The Foodsters (pres. 1981-82), Sun Valley Gang, No. Calif. Frozen Food Coun., Orinda Country Club. Republican. Office: R B Neuman Inc 89 Orinda Way Ste 4 Orinda CA 94563

NEUMAN, TED, state senator; b. Great Falls, Mont., Apr. 19, 1946; s. Earl and Lucille (Dixon) N.; m. Stevie May Lahti, Dec. 36, 1968; children: Stacie, Ty, Matt. BS in Bus., Mont. State U., 1968; postgrad., USAF Acad. Mil. Sci., Knoxville, 1980. Pres. Neuman Ranch Co., Vaughn, Mont., 1968—; owner Dracht Function Cattle Co., Sun River, Mont., 1980—; ptnr. High Plains Prodn. Co., Power, Mont., 1983—; U.S. senator from Mont. 1984—; dir. Sun River Ditch Co., Vaughn, Mont., 1974—; cons., advisor Western Petroleum Marketers Assn., Bozeman, Mont., 1988—. Contbr. articles tp profl. jours. Chmn. Mont. Job Coordinating Council, Helena, 1987—, Cascade County (Mont.) Planning Bd., 1978; vice chmn. 5-State Legis. Counsil, Helena, 1987—, Bus. and Industry Commn.; mem. Mont. Water Devel. Council, 1982—; supr. Cascade County Conservation Dist., 1970-86. Served to capt. Mont. Air N.G., 1968-88. Named Outstanding Supr. Soil Conservation Svc., 1980. Mem. Air N.G. Officers Assn., Nat. Conf. State Legislators (vice chmn. food and nutrition council 1984), Western States Hwy. Transp. Assn., Mont. Grain Growers Assn., Monts. Stock Growers Assn., Mont. Farm Bur., Elks, Phi Sigma Kappa. Democrat. Lutheran. Home: 639 US Hwy 89 Vaughn MT 59487 Office: PO Box 87 Vaughn MT 59487

NEUMANN, ALFRED KURT, public health physician, educator; b. Milw., July 25, 1930; s. Alfred P. and Hannah A. (Lange) N.; B.A., U. Wis., 1952, M.A., 1955; M.D., NYU, 1958; M.P.H., Harvard U., 1960; m. Charlotte Grantz, Sept. 10, 1959; children—Frederick, Peter, Daniel. Diplomate Am. Bd. Preventive Medicine. Intern, Kings County Gen. Hosp., Bklyn., 1958-59; resident in preventive medicine Mass. Dept. Pub. Health-Harvard U., 1960-62; gen. practice medicine, Marathon, Wis., 1959; pub. health physician

Mass. Dept. Pub. Health, 1960-61, asst. med. dir., 1961-65; instr. Tufts U. Sch. Medicine, Boston, 1963-65; dir. Health Dept. Brookline (Mass.), 1964-65; lectr. Johns Hopkins U., Balt., 1965-68; asst. prof. UCLA, 1968-71, assoc. prof., 1972-76, prof. Sch. Pub. Health, 1977—, dir. preventive medicine residency program, 1986—, assoc. dean of students, sch. pub. health, 1988—; vis. prof. People's Republic China, 1983, 85, 86; officer rural health project Narangwal, India, 1965-68; prin. investigator, co-dir. Danfa Comprehensive Rural Health Project, Ghana, 1970-79; cons. World Bank, WHO, UNFPA, Am. Pub. Health Assn.; chmn. Internat. Health Adv. Com., Project Concern Internat.; sec., bd. dirs. New Era Found. for Internat. Devel., Inc., N.Y.C. Fellow Soc. Applied Anthropology, Am. Pub. Health Assn.; mem. Wis. Acad. Sci., Arts and Letters, African Studies Assn., Internat. Health Soc. (pres. 1985-86), Delta Omega. Baha'i. Contbr. articles to profl. jours. Home: 520 20th St Santa Monica CA 90402 Office: UCLA Sch Pub Health Rm 36-081CHS Los Angeles CA 90024-1772

NEUMANN, HARRY, philosophy educator; b. Dormoschel, Germany, Oct. 10, 1930; came to U.S., 1937, naturalized, 1948; s. Siegfried and Frieda (Lion) N.; m. Christina Sopher, Sept. 25, 1959. B.A., St. John's Coll., 1952; M.A., U. Chgo., 1954; Ph.D., Johns Hopkins U., 1962; postgrad., U. Heidelberg, Germany, 1956-58. Mem. faculty Mich. State U., 1962-63, Lake Forest Coll., 1963-65; prof. philosophy, and govt. Claremont Grad. Sch. Scripps Coll., Claremont, Calif., 1966—; research assoc. Rockefeller Inst., N.Y.C., 1963. Contbr. articles profl. jours. Mem. nat. adv. bd. Am. Security Council, U.S. Def. Com. Served with AUS, 1954-56. Classical Philosophy fellow Center Hellenic Studies, Dumbarton Oaks, Washington, 1965-66; research fellow Salvatori Center for the Study of Individual Freedom in the Modern World, 1970; research fellow Earhart Found., 1973-74, 78, 82, 86. Mem. Am. Security Coundil (U.S. Def. com.), N.Am. Nietzsche Soc., Univ. Centers Rational Alternatives, Univ. Profs. for Acad. Order, John Brown Cook Assn. for Freedom (advisor). Home: Scripps Coll Claremont CA 91711

NEUMANN, LON RICHARD, audio engineer; b. Glendale, Calif., Jan. 18, 1949; s. Leonard A. Neuman and Lois Mae Fischer. Recording technician Wally Heider Recording, Hollywood, Calif., 1975-78; lead engr. Nova Sound Labs., L.A., 1978; audio engr. Enactron Studios, North Hollywood, Calif., 1979-80; remote recording engr. Record Plant Studios, Hollywood, 1980-81; tech. dir. Stevie Wonder's Studio, L.A., 1981-83; chief technician Everything Audio, Encino, Calif., 1983-84; field service engr. Mitsubishi Profl. Audio, San Fernando, Calif., 1984-86, Sony Profl. Audio, Burbank, Calif., 1986-88; dist. sales mgr. Sony Profl. Audio, Burbank, 1988—; guest lectr. UCLA, 1984-86; lectr. seminar Audio Engring. Soc. Conv., 1988; audio engr. Stevie Wonder Comes Home. Recipient 1st Annual Recording and Sound award, Pro Sound News, 1978. Mem. Audio Engring. Soc. Home: 13571 Rye St #3 Sherman Oaks CA 91423-3143 Office: Sony Profl Audio 2820 W Olive Ave Ste A Burbank CA 91505

NEUMANN, NANCY RUTH, studio teacher; b. L.A., Feb. 1, 1948; d. Robert Thomas and Frances Elizabeth (Gold) Andersen; m. Bernd Fritz Dietmar Neumann, June 26, 1971; children: Peter, Christina, Linda, Christoph, Karin. BA, U. Calif., Riverside, 1969; MA, Sorbonne U., Paris, 1971; credentials, Calif. State U., San Bernardino, 1985. Cert. community coll. tchr., various subjects, Calif., studio tchr., Calif. Missionary, reading instr. Maroua, Cameroon, Africa, 1971-73; instr. Pasadena City Coll., 1974-75; secondary tchr. Riverside (Calif.) Christian Sch., 1985-86; studio tchr. Paramount Studios, Hollywood, Calif., 1986, MGM - Lorimar Prodns., Culver City, Calif., 1986-89, Hollywood Studios, Hollywood, 1986-88, Vista Films, Culver City, 1986, Universal Studios, Universal City, Calif., 1986-88, R.J. Louis Prodns., Burbank, Calif., 1987, Michael Landon Prodns., Culver City, 1987-88, Carsey-Werner Prodns., L.A., 1988, Bob Booker Prodns., Hollywood, 1988—; instr. Riverside Community Coll., 1988; pvt. tutor, Riverside, L.A., 1987-89; drama coach, Magnolia Ave. Baptist Ch., Riverside, 1988-89, Grace Church, Riverside, 1981-82. Author: several plays, 1981-89; writer 70 songs, 1968—. Active supporter Congl. Campaign (Stark), San-Bernardino/Riverside, 1985, 88; coach for mock trial, Riverside Christian High Sch., 1985-86; choir dir. Riverside Christian Sch., 1985-86; Sunday sch. tchr., Vineyard Christian Fellowship, Riverside, 1983, Magnolia Ave. Baptist Ch., Riverside, Grace Church, Riverside, Harvest Christian Fellowship, Riverside. Recipient award in fgn. languages, Bank of Am., Riverside, 1965, Sons of Norway Study Scholarship, Sons of Norway, 1967. Mem. Nat. Assn. Christian Educators, Internat. Alliance of Theatre and State Employees, Sons of Norway, Delta Phi Alpha. Republican. Home: 1787 Prince Albert Dr Riverside CA 92507 Office: Bob Booker Prodns 6605 Eleanor Los Angeles CA 90038

NEUMEISTER, DANIEL PAUL, hospital administrator; b. San Diego, Dec. 14, 1954; s. Fred Wilhelm and Frances Lois (Laubmayer) N.; m. Kim Diane Parker, May 22, 1977; children: Lisa, Megan. BS in Mgmt., San Diego State U., 1977; MHA, Trinity U., 1979. Adminstrv. asst. Grossmont Dist. Hosp., La Mesa, Calif., 1979-82; asst. adminstr. Salinas (Calif.) Valley Meml. Hosp., 1982-84, assoc. exec. dir., 1985—. Mem. Am. Coll. Health Care Execs., Calif. Hosp. Assn. (com. on vol. service 1985-88), Hosp. Council No. Calif. (hosp. billing task force 1988), Region One Tumor Registry Council. Office: Salinas Valley Meml Hosp 450 E Romie Ln Salinas CA 93901

NEUVILLE, PAUL JOSEPH, software engineer and analyst; b. Portland, Oreg., Dec. 22, 1959; s. James Thomas and Patricia Jeanne (Limbach) N.; m. Anahita Esmaili. BS in Computer Sci., Portland State U., 1983. Programmer, analyst ADP, Portland, 1985-88; software engr. Wyatt Co., Portland, 1988—; cons. P & A Neuville Software Co., Beaverton, Oreg., 1987—. Grant scholar Portland State U., 1982. Office: Westcoast Software 1211 SW 5th 1250 Portland OR 97005

NEVILLES, JOHN ELLSWORTH, business machines company executive, consultant; b. Mpls., Jan. 24, 1940; s. Wilbur E. and Phillis A. N.; m. Amelia Carbajal, Feb. 2, 1959; children—John, Sonya. A.B.A., St. Philips Coll., 1974. Personnel specialist, resource planner U.S. Army, 1958-78; indsl. engr. IBM, Tucson, 1978-80, sr. recruiting specialist, 1981, mgr. quality svcs., 1982-86, mgr. quality tech. ops., 1986-88; pres., cons. TQM Consulting Svc., 1989—; total quality mgmt. cons., 1988—; lectr. career planning, quality assurance, statis. quality control, continuous flow mfg. Adv. mem. Job Corps, Tucson Skills Ctr. Author: Processing Guide Quality Information, 1986, Decision Guide for Choosing Control Charts, 1985, Total Quality Management For The Service Organization, 1989. Decorated Bronze Star. Mem. Am. Soc. Quality Control, Am. Statis. Assn., Am. Soc. Tng. and Devel., Nat. Assn. Trade Tech. Schs. (cert.), VFW, Am. Legion. Democrat. Roman Catholic. Home: 3225 S Eastview Tucson AZ 85730

NEVIN, CROCKER, investment banker; b. Tulsa, Mar. 14, 1923; s. Ethelbert Paul and Jennie Crocker (Fassett) N.; m. Mary Elizabeth Sherwin, Apr. 24, 1952 (div. 1984); children: Anne, Paul, Elizabeth, Crocker; m. Marilyn Elizabeth English, Nov. 3, 1984; 1 child, Jennie Fassett. Grad. with high honors, St. Paul's Sch., 1942; A.B. with high honors, Princeton U., 1946. With Vick Chem. Co., 1949-50, John Roberts Powers Cosmetic Co., 1950-52; with Marine Midland Grace Trust Co. of N.Y., 1952—, exec. v.p., 1964-66, pres., 1966-70, chmn. bd., chief exec. officer, 1968-73; also dir.; vice chmn. bd. Evans Products Co., N.Y.C., 1974-76, Drexel Burnam Lambert Co., investment bankers, N.Y.C., 1976-88; chmn. bd., chief exec. officer CF & I Steel Corp., Pueblo, Colo., 1985—; dir. Medco Containment Services Inc., Magnatck, Inc., BOC Group PLC; bd. govs. U.S. Postal Svc. Chmn. exec. com. ACCION Internat. Lt. (j.g.) AC USN, 1942-46. Clubs: Links (N.Y.C.), N.Y. Yacht (N.Y.C.); Blind Brook. Home: 62 E 91st St New York NY 10028

NEVIN, DAVID WRIGHT, real estate broker; b. Culver City, Calif., July 27, 1947; s. Wilbur D. and Anita J. (Hulderman) N.; m. Shirley Grimes, Nov. 12, 1977; children: Jenny, David Wright Jr. BA, Calif. State Poly. U., 1974. Rural manpower asst. employment devel. State Calif., Riverside, 1970-74; personnel mgr. Lindsay Olive Growers, Calif., 1974-79; employee relations mgr. Morton Salt Co., Newark, Calif., 1979-80; real estate salesman Valley Realty, Fremont, Calif., 1980, The Property Professionals, Fremont, Calif., 1980-85; owner Nevin & Nevin, Inc., 1984-88; dir., officer CitiBrokers Real Estate, Inc., 1986—; co-owner Brokers Exchange, Inc., 1985-86. Sustaining mem. Republican Nat. Com., Washington, 1984; mem. Presdl. Task Force, Washington, 1984. Served with U.S. Army, 1967-69. Mem. Nat. Assn. Realtors, Calif. Assn. Realtors, Realtors Nat. Mktg. Inst. (real estate brokerage council), Internat. Real Estate Fedn., So. Alameda County Bd. Realtors (local govt. relations com. 1983-86). Mem. Assemblies of God. Ch. Home: 40670 Marino Way Fremont CA 94539 Office: CitiBrokers Real Estate Inc 39650 Liberty St Ste 100 Fremont CA 94538

NEVINS, DONALD JAMES, agricultural educator; b. San Luis Obispo, Calif., July 6, 1937; s. Vernon James and Elizabeth N.; m. Sylvia Ann Nelson, Aug. 25, 1962; children: Jennifer, Stephanie. BS, Calif. Poly. U., 1959; MS, U. Calif., Davis, 1962, PhD, 1965. Postdoctoral fellow U. Colo., Boulder, 1965-67; asst. prof. botany Iowa State U., Ames, 1967-70, assoc. prof., 1970-74, prof., 1974-84; prof., chmn. dept. plant, physiologist vegetable crop dept. U. Calif., Davis, 1984—. Editor: Tomato Biotechnology, 1987; contbr. articles to profl. jours. Mem. Am. Chem. Soc., Am. Soc. Horticult. Scis., Scandinavian Soc. Plant Physiology, Am. Soc. Plant Physiology. Lutheran. Home: 607 Estrella St Davis CA 95616 Office: U Calif Dept Vegetable Crops Davis CA 95616

NEW, ROSETTA HOLBROCK, home economics educator, nutrition consultant; b. Hamilton, Ohio, Aug. 26, 1921; d. Edward F. and Mabel (Kohler) Holbrock; m. John Lorton New, Sept. 3, 1943; 1 son, John Lorton Jr. BS, Miami U., Oxford, Ohio, 1943; MA, U. No. Colo., 1971; PhD, Ohio State U., 1974. Cert. tchr., Colo. Tchr. English and sci. Monahans (Tex.) High Sch., 1943-45; emergency war food asst. U.S. Dept. Agr., College Station, Tex., 1945-46; dept. chmn. home econs., adult edn. Hamilton (Ohio) Pub. Schs., 1946-47; tchr., dept. chmn. home econs. East High Sch., Denver, 1948-59, Thomas Jefferson High Sch., Denver, 1959—; mem. exec. bd. Denver Pub. Schs.; also lectr.; exec. dir. Ctr. Nutrition Info. U.S. Office of Edn. grantee, 1971-73. Mem. Am. Home Econs. Assn., Am. Vocat. Assn., Ohio State U. Assn., Ohio State Home Econs. Alumni Assn., Fairfield (Ohio) Hist. Soc., Republican Club of Denver, Internat. Platform Assn., Phi Upsilon Omicron. Presbyterian. Lodges: Daughters of the Nile, Order of Eastern Star, Order White Shrine of Jerusalem. also: 615 Crescent Rd Hamilton OH 45013

NEWACHECK, DAVID JOHN, lawyer; b. San Francisco, Dec. 8, 1953; s. John Elmer and Estere Ruth Sybil (Nelson) N. AB in English, U. Calif., Berkeley, 1976; JD, Pepperdine U., 1979; MBA, Calif. State U., Hayward, 1982; LLM in Tax, Golden Gate U., 1987. Bar: Calif. 1979, U.S. Dist. Ct. (no. dist.) Calif. 1979, U.S. Ct. Appeals (9th cir.) 1979, U.S. Supreme Ct. 1984, Washington D.C. 1985. Tax cons. Pannell, Kerr and Forster, San Francisco, 1982-83; lawyer, writer, editor Matthew Bender and Co., Oakland, 1983—; tax cons., Walnut Creek, Calif., 1983—; bd. dirs. Aztec Custom Co., Orinda, Calif., 1983—; cons. software Collier Bankruptcy Filing System, 1984. Author/editor (treatises) Ill. Tax Service, 1985, Ohio State Taxation, 1985, N.J. Tax Service, 1986, Pa. Tax Service, 1986, Calif. Closely Held Corps., 1987, Texas Tax Service, 1988, Bender's Federal Tax Service, 1989; author: (software) Tax Source 1040 Tax Preparation, 1987; Texas Tax Service, 1988. Mem. youth com. Shepherd of the Valley Luth. Ch., Orinda, 1980-85, ch. coun., 1980-82. Mem. ABA, State Bar Assn. Calif., Alameda County Bar Assn., U. Calif. Alumni Assn., U. Calif. Band Alumni Assn., Mensa. Republican. Club: Commonwealth (San Francisco). Home: 21 Tappan Ln Orinda CA 94563-1310 Office: Matthew Bender & Co 2101 Webster St Oakland CA 94612

NEWBERG, DOROTHY BECK (MRS. WILLIAM C. NEWBERG), portrait artist; b. Detroit, May 30, 1919; d. Charles William and Mary (Labedz) Beck; student Detroit Conservatory Music, 1938; m. William C. Newberg, Nov. 3, 1939; children: Judith N. Bookwalter, Robert Charles, James William, William Charles. Trustee Detroit Adventure, 1967-71, originator A Drop in Bucket Program for talented inner-city children. Bd. dirs. Bloomfield Art Assn., 1960-62, trustee 1965-67; bd. dirs. Your Heritage House, 1972-75, Franklin Wright Settlement, 1972-75, Meadowbrook Art Gallery, Oakland U., 1973-75; bd. dirs. Sierra Nevada Mus. Art, 1978-80. Recipient Heart of Gold award, 1969; Mich. vol. leadership award, 1969. Mem. Sierra Art Found., Birmingham Soc. Women Painters. Home: 2000 Dant Blvd Reno NV 89509

NEWBERG, ELLEN JOYCE, library administrator; b. Wellman, Iowa, Sept. 29, 1941; d. Carl Clarence and Elda Grace (White) Herr; m. Alan Keith Newberg, June 11, 1965. B.A., Sioux Falls Coll., 1962; M.L.S., U. Ill., 1963. Asst. dir. library Sioux Falls Coll., S.D., 1963-66; library cataloger U. Wyo., Laramie, 1966-67, U. Oreg., Eugene, 1967-69; asst. library dir. Rocky Mountain Coll., Billings, Mont., 1969-73; head tech. services library Parmly Billings Library, 1973-82, dir., 1982-88; dir. Kitsap Regional Library, 1989—; Western Library Network retrospective conversion trainer, Mont., 1981-82; OCLC installation trainer Dowling Coll. Library, Oakdale, N.Y., 1978-79. Contbr. articles to profl. jours. Recipient Great Performance in the Library award Exxon, 1985. Mem. ALA, Wash. Library Assn., Pacific Northwest Library Assn. (Mont. rep. 1980-82, joint planning team 1981-82). Avocations: gourmet cooking; gardening; hiking. Office: Kitsap Regional Libr 1301 Sylvan Way Bremerton WA 98310-3498

NEWBERG, WILLIAM CHARLES, stock broker, real estate broker, automotive engineer; b. Seattle, Dec. 17, 1910; s. Charles John and Anna Elizabeth (Anderson) N.; B.S. in Mech. Engring., U. Wash., 1933; M. in Mech. Engring., Chrysler Inst. Engring., 1935; LL.B. (hon.), Parsons Coll., 1958; m. Dorothy Beck, Nov. 3, 1939; children—Judith N. Newberg Bookwalter, Robert Charles, James William, William Charles. Salesman, Am. Auto Co., Seattle, 1932-33; student engr. Chrysler Corp., Detroit, 1933-35, exptl. engr., 1935-42, chief engr. Chgo. plant, 1942-45, mem. subs. ops. staff, Detroit, 1945-47, pres. airtemp. div., Dayton, Ohio, 1947-50, v.p., dir. Dodge div., Detroit, 1950-51, pres. Dodge div., 1951-56, group v.p., Detroit, 1956-58, exec. v.p., 1958-60, pres., 1960; corp. dir. Detroit Bank & Trust, Detroit, 1955-60; corp. cons., Detroit, 1960-76; realtor Myers Realty, Inc., Reno, 1976-79; owner Bill Newberg Realty, 1979—; account exec. Allied Capital Corp., Reno, 1980—; chmn. Newberg Corp., 1982. Elder, St. John's Presbyterian Ch., Reno, 1976—; exec. bd. Detroit Area council Boy Scouts Am., 1955-74, Nev. Area council Boy Scouts Am., 1976—; Mich. state chmn. March of Dimes, 1967-68. Mem. Soc. Automotive Engrs., Am. Def. Preparedness Assn. (life), Automotive Orgn. Team (life), U. Wash. Alumni Assn. (life), Newcomen Soc., Franklin Inst., Alpha Tau Omega. Clubs: Bluecoats of No. Nevada, Prospectors, Harley Owners Group, Goldwing Road Riders, Rider Motorcycle Touring, Internat. Retreads. Lodge: Elks. Home: 2000 Dant Blvd Reno NV 89509

NEWBERRY, ALAN JOHN HESSON, chief superintendent of schools; b. Victoria, B.C., Can., Sept. 4, 1937; s. John Harold Newberry and Hazel Margaret Hesson; children: Alison, Graham; m. Janet Christina (McIntosh); children: Christina, Andrea, Alison, Graham. BA, U. Victoria, 1969; MEd, U. Portland, Oreg., 1971; EdD, Ind. U., 1975. Cert. tchr., B.C., Alta., Can. Tchr. Victoria, 1959-60; prin. Sooke Schs., 1961-68, supr., 1968-75; supt. schs. Ministry Edn., Victoria, 1975-79, exec. dir., 1979-85; chief supt. schs. Calgary (Alta.) Bd. Edn., 1985—. Home: 260 Canterville Dr SW, Calgary, AB Canada T2W 3X2 Office: Calgary Bd Edn, 515 Macleod Tr SE, Calgary, AB Canada T2G 2L9

NEWBERRY, CONRAD FLOYDE, aerospace engineering educator; b. Neodesha, Kans., Nov. 10, 1931; s. Ragan McGregor and Audra Anitia (Newmaster) N.; m. Sarah Louise Thonn, Jan. 26, 1958; children: Conrad Floyde Jr., Thomas Edwin, Susan Louise. A.A., Independence Jr. Coll., 1951; B.Engring. in Mech. Engring. (Aero. Sequence), U. So. Calif., 1957; M.S. in Mech. Engring., Calif. State U., Los Angeles, 1971, M.A. in Edn., 1974; D.Environ. Sci. and Engring., UCLA, 1985. Registered profl. engr., Calif., Kans., N.C., Tex. Mathematician Los Angeles div. N.Am. Aviation Inc., 1951-53, jr. engr., 1953-54, engr., 1954-57, sr. engr., 1957-64; asst. prof. Calif. State Poly. U., Pomona, 1964-70, assoc. prof., 1970-75, prof. aerospace engring., 1975—; staff engr. EPA, 1980-82. Recipient John Leland Atwood award Am. Inst. Aeronautics and Astronautics/Am. Soc. Engring. Edn. Fellow Inst. Advancement Engring., Brit. Interplanetary Soc.; assoc. fellow AIAA (dep. dir. edn. region VI 1976-79, dep. dir. career enhancement 1982—); mem. Am. Acad. Environ. Engrs. (cert. air pollution control engr.), Am. Soc. Engring. Edn. (chmn. aerospace div. 1979-80, div. exec. com. 1976-80, exec. com. ocean and marine engring. div. 1982-86), ASME, Am. Meteorol. Soc., Nat. Soc. Profl. Engrs., Soc. Naval Architects and Marine Engrs., Am. Helicopter Soc., Air Pollution Control Assn., Inst. Environ. Scis., Exptl. Aircraft Assn., Water Pollution Control Fedn., Soc. Automotive Engrs., Nat. Assn. Environ. Profls., AAAS, Am. Soc. Pub. Adminstrn., Tau Beta Pi, Sigma Gamma Tau, Kappa Delta Pi. Democrat. Mem. Christian Ch. (Disciples of Christ). Home: 861 Kenwood St Upland CA 91786 Office: Calif State Poly U 3801 W Temple Ave Pomona CA 91768

NEWBIGGING, WILLIAM, publisher, journal executive; b. Toronto, Ont., Can., Feb. 3, 1939; s. William and Dorothy (Ridge) N.; children—William, Patricia, Scott, Dorothy, Ty. Jr. reporter Edmonton Jour., Alta., Can., 1957-65; city editor Edmonton Jour., 1965-67, news editor, 1967-71, asst. to pub., 1971-73, v.p., pub., 1982—; exec. to pub. Ottawa Citizen, Ont., 1973-74; bus. mgr. Ottawa Citizen, 1974-76, gen. mgr., 1976-78, v.p., pub., 1978-81; dir. Can. Press, Newspaper Mktg. Bur. Mem. Can. Daily Newspaper Pubs. Assn. (bd. dirs.). Anglican. Clubs: Edmonton, Centre, Windermere. Home: 108 Westbrook Dr, Edmonton, AB Canada T6J 2E1 Office: Edmonton Jour, PO Box 2421, Edmonton, AB Canada T5J 2S6

NEWBURY, F(RANK) RON(ALD), credit union executive; b. Whitefish, Mont., May 4, 1957; s. Frank J. and Carol Louise (Hedman) N.; m. Cynthia Kay Riley, Feb. 20, 1978 (div. 1981); 1 child, Peter Verner; m. Melinda Lou Nick, Jan. 1, 1983 (div. 1987); 1 child, F. Brandon Tyler. Grad. high sch., Whitefish. Property mgr. Happ Real Estate, Kalispell, Mont., 1976; mgr. No. Nordic Ski Ctr., Whitefish, 1976-77; bldg. contractor Whitefish, 1977; asst. mgr. Western Bldg. Ctrs., Whitefish, 1977-80; loan officer, compliance officer Whitefish Credit Union, 1980--. Co-founder, sr. editor Whitefish Mag.; contbr. articles to newspapers. Republican candidate Mont. Ho. of Reps., 1984, 88; mem. Whitefish City and County Planning Bd., 1985--, Pacific Power and Light Citizens Panel, Flathead Valley, Mont., 1987--; co-chmn. Whitefish Forward Group, 1987--; mem. bus. adv. panel Flathead Valley Coll., Kalispell, 1988; mem. Nordic support crew, 1980 Winter Olympics. Rotary fellow, India, 1987. Mem. Whitefish C. of C. (bd. dirs. 1986--, past pres.), Rotary Internat., Whitefish Soccer Club (pres. 1981-83), Moron Majority Ski Club. Home: W Blanchard Lake Box 1927 Whitefish MT 59937-1927 Office: Whitefish Credit Union 418 2d St Box 37 Whitefish MT 59937-0037

NEWBY, JILL JEANINE, airline pilot; b. Mpls., Oct. 8, 1960; d. Clinton Warner and Betty Jane (Mandelcorn) Erickson; m. Thomas William Newby, Jr., Oct. 18, 1986. BS in Aviation Adminstrn., U. N.D., 1983. Flight coord. Fed. Express Corp., Memphis, 1982-83; flight instr. U. N.D., Grand Forks, 1982-83; ramp handler Fed. Express Corp., L.A., 1984-85; flight instr. Gunnell Aviation, Santa Monica, Calif., 1984-85; with pub. rels. U. N.D., Grand Forks, 1983-84; reservation sales agt. Northwest Airlines, L.A., 1984-85; pilot Desert Sun Airlines, Long Beach, Calif., 1985, United Airlines, L.A., 1985—. Vol. speaker Career Days L.A. Pub. Schs., 1988. Mem. Airline Pilots Assn., Internat. Soc. Women Airline Pilots, Aircraft Owners and Pilots Assn., U. N.D. Flying Team, Alpha Eta Rho. Democrat. Lutheran.

NEWELL, MICHAEL STEPHEN, finance company executive; b. Denver, Dec. 22, 1949; s. Henry Michael and Marlene (McRae) N.; m. Linda Margaret Wolfe, Sept. 19, 1987: 1 child, Katherine Margaret; children from previous marriage: Troy, Angela, Michael, Jennifer. Grad., Denver Police Acad., 1972; CO Real Estate Lic., Real Estate Prep., 1977. Cert. peace officer, Colo. Police officer Denver Police Dept., 1972-79; prin. Michael Newell & Assocs., Denver, 1979-82; sr. account exec. Am. Protection Industries, Los Angeles, 1982-84; chief exec. officer Newco Financial, Huntington Beach, Calif., 1984—; chmn. The Newco Internat. Group/Newco Fin., Huntington Beach; founder, bd. dirs. EDEN Philanthropic Found., Fountain Valley, Calif., VALUES Self Improvement Program, Fountain Valley; co-founder, bd. dirs. Self-Love, Sexuality & Spirituality seminars, Fountain Valley; bd. dirs. Lifesong Self-Esteem workshops, Huntington Beach. Founder, bd. dirs. Law Enforcement Support Assn., Denver, 1981. Served with U.S. Army, 1968-71, Viet Nam. Decorated Bronze Star, Viet Svc. medal with clusters; recipient numerous civilian/police awards Denver Police Dept. Republican. Mem. Religious Sci. Ch. Office: The Newco Internat Group 18627 Brookhurst St Ste 415 Fountain Valley CA 92708

NEWHART, BOB, entertainer; b. Oak Park, Ill., Sept. 29, 1929; m. Virginia Quinn, Jan. 12, 1963; 4 children. BS, Loyola U., Chgo., 1952. Law clk. U.S. Gypsum Co.; copywriter Fred Niles Film Co.; performer Dan Serkin TV show, 1957; appeared on Jack Paar Show, 1960; TV performer numerous guest appearances, 1961—; star TV series Bob Newhart Show, 1971-78, Newhart, 1982—. Rec. artist (album) Button Down Mind on TV; royal command performance, London, 1964, appeared in films Hot Millions, 1968, Catch 22, 1970, Cold Turkey, 1971, First Family, 1980, Little Miss Marker, 1982; TV films include Thursday's Game, 1978, Marathon, 1980. Served with U.S. Army, 1952-54. Recipient Emmy award, 1961, Peabody award, 1961, Sword of Loyola award, 1976. Office: care David Capell 2121 Ave of the Stars #1240 Los Angeles CA 90067

NEWHOFF, STANLEY NEAL, advertising executive; b. Bronx, N.Y., Jan. 31, 1944; s. Norman and Daisy (Weiss) N.; m. Hayde Mathilde Stekkinger, June 16, 1969 (dec. Nov. 1984); children: Michelle Hayde, Angela Robin. BA in English, UCLA, 1967. Columnist UCLA Daily Bruin, 1963-64; tabulator, asst supr., asst. dir. corp. communications Audience Studies, Inc., Los Angeles, 1964-65; English tchr. Beit Safer Tichon Makief High Sch., Qiryat Gat, Israel, 1969-70; advt. copywriter Doyle Dane Bernbach; Foote, Cone & Belding and others, Los Angeles, 1970-74; v.p., creative dir. Basso Boatman, Inc., Newport Beach, Calif., 1976-79; prin., pres. Lerner-Newhoff Advt., Los Angeles, 1974-76, Stanley Newhoff & Assocs., Irvine, Calif., 1979-81, Newhoff & Prochnow, Inc., Costa Mesa, Calif., 1981-85; prin., chmn. Newhoff & Russakow, Inc., Newport Beach, 1985-87; exec. v.p., creative dir. Todd Hughes & Meren, Irvine, 1987—. Contbr. articles on advt. to publs. Mem. Med. Mktg. Assn., Irvine Edn. Found. (founding, pres.), Nat. Energy Research Info. Inst. (mem. founding task force), Mensa. Republican. Jewish. Home: 21 Silkberry Irvine CA 92714 Office: Todd Hughes & Meren 17780 Fitch St #165 Irvine CA 92714

NEWKIRK, JOHN JORDAN, computer company executive; b. Nov. 21, 1961; s. John B. and Carol (Jordan) N. Student, U. Denver, 1978; BSEE, Rensselaer Poly. Inst., 1983. Founder, owner, pres. Colo. Computer Assocs., Inc., Evergreen, Colo., 1983--; cons. Codman & Shurtleff, Inc. a Johnson & Johnson Corp., 1986--. Tech. editor, columnist Healthcare Computing and Communications; author software PowerMenu and Diskman. Winner Colo. Philharm. Young Artists Competition, 1981. Mem. Pi Mu Epsilon. Mem. Christian Ch. Office: Colo Computer Assocs Inc 6851 Hwy 73 Evergreen CO 80439

NEWKIRK, RAYMOND LESLIE, management consultant; b. Shreveport, La., July 13, 1944; s. Raymond Clay and Dorothy Emily (Parker) N.; m. Felicisima Guese Calma, Jan. 19, 1985. AA, Dayton Community Coll., 1973; BS in Behavioral Sci., N.Y. Inst. Tech., 1976; MS in Philosophy, Columbia Pacific U., 1980, PhD in Behavioral Sci., 1982; postgrad., Saybrook Inst. Chief exec. officer, cons. Newkirk & Assocs., Ft. Lauderdale, Fla., 1980-84; head dept. ADP Royal Saudi Naval Forces, Jeddah, 1984-86; pres., cons. Internat. Assn. Info. Mgmt., Santa Clara, Calif., 1984; cert. quality analyst Quality Assurance Inst., Orlando, Fla., 1986—; prin. cons. Info. Impact Internat., Nashville, 1988—; exec. dir. Systems Mgmt. Inst., Pleasant Hill, Calif., 1988—. Author: Chronicles of the Making of A Philosopher, 1983; contbr. articles to profl. jours. Speaker, mem. Union for Concerned Scientists, San Francisco, 1988. Fellow Brit. Inst. Mgmt.; mem. Assn. Systems Mgmt., Assn. Profl. Cons., Planetary Soc., Columbia Pacific Alumni Assn. (pres. Mid-east chpt. 1985), Phi Theta Kappa (Outstanding scholar award 1973). Roman Catholic. Home: 837 Treehaven Ct Pleasant Hill CA 94523

NEWLAND, RUTH LAURA, small business owner; b. Ellensburg, Wash., June 4, 1949; d. George J. and Ruth Marjorie (Porter) N.; m. Thomas Arnold, Oct. 18, 1979 (div. Nov. 1986). BA, Cen. Wash. State Coll., 1970, MEd, 1972; EdS, Vanderbilt U., 1973; PhD, Columbia Pacific U., 1981. Tchr. Union Gap (Wash.) Sch., 1970-71; ptnr. Newland Ranch Gravel Co. (div. Beazers of London), Yakima, Wash., 1970—, Arnold Artificial Limb Co., Yakima, 1981-86; owner, pres. Arnold Artificial Limb Inc., Yakima, Richland, Wash., 1986—; ptnr. Newland Ranch, Yakima, 1969—. George Washington scholar Masons, Yakima, 1967. Mem. NOW, Am. Orthotic and

Prosthetic Assn., Vanderbilt U. Alumni Assn., George Peabody Coll. Alumni Assn., Columbia Pacific U. Alumni Assn. Democrat. Seventh-Day Adventist. Home: 2004 Riverside Rd Yakima WA 98901-9539 Office: Arnold Artificial Limb 9 S 12th Ave Yakima WA 98901

NEWLIN, DOUGLAS RANDAL, marketing communications manager; b. Denver, Mar. 26, 1940; s. Loren Randall and Nola Berneice (Paris) N.; m. Sandra Temple, June 22, 1968; children: Jason Britt, Jeremy Owen. BS in Journalism, U. Colo., 1968. Advt. prodn. mgr. Am. Sheep Producers Council, Denver, 1968-70; promotion dir. Sta. KLZ-AM-FM, Denver, 1970-71; account mgr. Curran-Morton Advt., Denver, 1971-72; advt. and sales promotion specialist Gates Rubber Co., Denver, 1972-78; mktg. communications mgr. Hewlett Packard Co., Ft. Collins, Colo., 1978—; vis. lectr. U. Colo., Boulder, 1972-73, statis. quality control course George Washington U., Washington, 1984. Author hardware and software catalogs, 1984—; contbr. articles to profl. jours. Pres. Lake Sherwood Homeowners Assn., Ft. Collins, 1982; treas. Lake Sherwood Lake Com., Ft. Collins, 1983-85. Served with U.S. Army, 1959-61. Recipient Gold Key award Bus. and Profl. Advt. Assn., 1976. Democrat. Home: 4112 Mount Vernon Ct Fort Collins CO 80525 Office: Hewlett Packard Co 3404 E Harmony Rd Fort Collins CO 80525

NEWMAN, CAROL L., lawyer; b. Yonkers, N.Y., Aug. 7, 1949; d. Richard J. and Pauline Frances (Stoll) N. A.B./M.A. summa cum laude, Brown U., 1971; postgrad. Harvard U. Law Sch., 1972-73; J.D. cum laude, George Washington U., 1977. Bar: D.C., 1977, Calif., 1979. With antitrust div. U.S. Dept. Justice, Washington and Los Angeles, 1977-80; assoc. Alschuler, Grossman & Pines, Los Angeles, 1980-82, Costello & Walcher, Los Angeles, 1982-85, Rosen, Wachtell & Gilbert, 1985-88, ptnr., 1988—; adj. prof. Sch. Bus., Golden Gate U., spring 1982. Candidate for State Atty. Gen., 1986. Mem. ABA, State Bar Calif., Los Angeles County Bar Assn., Order of Coif, Phi Beta Kappa.

NEWMAN, CYNTHIA (CYNTHIA LADEN), brokerage house executive; b. N.Y.C., Dec. 20, 1960; d. Burton S. Laden and Florence (Baum) Morel; m. Robert Neil Newman, May 15, 1986. BA, U. Vt., 1981. Sales asst. Merrill Lynch Pierce Fenner & Smith, N.Y.C., 1981-82; account exec., v.p. Merrill Lynch Pierce Fenner & Smith, L.A., 1989—, Drexel Burnham Lambert, Beverly Hills, Calif., 1982-89. Office: Merrill Lynch Pierce Fenner & Smith 400 S Hope St #300 Los Angeles CA 90071

NEWMAN, DENISE BARB, data processing executive; b. Denver, Apr. 7, 1953; d. Denver Mann and Peggy Lee (Hoskins) Barb; m. George Elliott Newman, July 30, 1983; 1 child, David Elliott. BA in Speech Pathology and Audiology cum laude, San Francisco State U., 1977; MBA, U. Denver, 1981. Tutor, Learning Ctr. San Francisco State U., 1975-76, mgr. Learning Ctr., 1976-77; speech pathology asst. Robt. G. Weiland Sch., Denver, 1978-79; lease analyst Enserch, Denver, 1980-81, Mobil Oil Co., Denver, 1981-82; mgr. land records Samson Resources Co., Denver, 1982-84; pres. Computer Rental Time, Inc., Denver, 1984-85, Bakersfield, Calif., 1985-88. Mem. Network, Kern Ind. PC User's Group (bd. dirs. 1985—), Sunset Beach & Racquet Club. Republican. Episcopalian.

NEWMAN, DENISE MARIE, manufacturing company executive; b. Pitts., Apr. 21, 1952; d. Harold Lloyd and Stella (Saladiack) Newman; m. Rich Schwartz. BA, S.W. Mo. State U. Bartender Westin Hotel, Kansas City, Mo., 1973-77; asst. to v.p. sales Giltspur, Garden Grove, Calif., 1977-81; sr. account exec. The Exhibit Pl., Garden Grove, 1981-89, exec. v.p., 1989—; dietary cons. Internat. Ins. Natural Health Scis., Huntington Beach, 1978; dir. The Exhibit Pl. Active various polit., charitable orgns. including Green Peace, People for the Ethical Treatment Animals, Physicians Com. For Responsible Medicine. Mem. Med. Mktg. Assn., Internat. Exhibitors Assn., Internat. Health Care Assn., Sales and Mktg. Execs., Women in Sales, Orange County World Trade Assn., Sierra Club. Office: The Exhibit Pl 12442 Knott St Garden Grove CA 92641

NEWMAN, EDGAR LEON, historian, educator; b. New Orleans, Jan. 21, 1939; s. Isidore and Anna (Pfeifer) N.; children: Jonathan, Suzanne. BA, Yale U., 1962; PhD, U. Chgo., 1969. Assoc. prof. N.Mex. State U., Las Cruces, 1969-75, asst. prof. history, 1975—; lectr. U. Peking, 1985; bd. dirs., speaker Am. Congress on Bicentennial of French Revolution of 1989. Fulbright fellow, 1965-66; Am. Philos. Soc. fellow, 1971; Nat. Endowment for Humanities fellow, 1975-76. Mem. Western Soc. for French History (pres. 1977-78), Société d'histoire de la Révolution de 1848 (mem. comité directeur), Soc. Scis. History Assn., French Hist. Studies Assn., Am. Hist. Assn. Editor: Historical Dictionary of France from the 1815 Restoration to the Second Empire. Office: NMex State U Box 3-H Las Cruces NM 88003

NEWMAN, GLEN CARROLL, superintendent of schools; b. Guthrie, Okla., July 20, 1935; s. Nathaniel Clark and Evelyn Irene (Miller) N.; m. Nancy Jo Kennedy, Feb. 24, 1961; 1 child, Geoffrey William. BA, Cen. State U., Edmond, Okla., 1955; MA in Teaching, U. Redlands, 1966; MA, Calif. State U., Fullerton, 1969; EdD, U. So. Calif., 1978. Tchr. Hemet (Calif.) Unified Sch. Dist., 1956-58, 61-74, dir. spl. svcs., 1974-78; dist. supt. schs. Menifee Union Sch. Dist., Sun City, Calif., 1978—; instr. U. Calif. Extension, Riverside, 1969-70, Calif. State U. Extension, San Diego, 1970-71; NDEA cons. in English, Calif. Dept. Edn., 1969-71; cons. on lang. arts Riverside County Interns, 1970. Bd. dirs. Hemet Hosp. Found., 1987—; vice chmn. Sun City-Menifee Valley Community Plan Adv. Com., 1988-89. Recipient award of appreciation and leadership Riverside County Governance Coun., 1985. Mem. Am. Assn. Sch. Adminstrs., Assn. Supervision and Curriculum Devel., Assn. Calif. Sch. Adminstrs. (chmn. supt.'s com. region 12, 1988—), Riverside County Reading Assn. (pres. 1975-78), Rotary (pres. Sun City 1984-85), Phi Delta Kappa. Home: 26570 Vassar St Hemet CA 92344 Office: Menifee Union Sch Dist 28125 Bradley Rd Ste 210 Sun City CA 92381

NEWMAN, JAMES, financial journalist; b. Covington, Okla., Apr. 24, 1932; s. James Austin and Olive Elizabeth (Adair) N. BA, Westminster Coll., 1952. Bus. editor AP, Washington, 1974-76; bus. reporter NBC, N.Y.C., 1976-79; pres. Newman Econs., L.A., 1979-81; bus. reporter Sta. KTLA-TV, L.A., 1981-82, CBS, L.A., 1982-83; bus. corr. Satellite News Channel ABC, N.Y.C., 1983-84; bus. corr. Sta. KFWB, L.A., 1984—. Cpl. U.S. Army, 1952-54. Recipient Janus award Mortgage Bankers, Washington, 1974, Bus. Reporting award L.A. Press Club, 1982. Mem. Overseas Press Club, Sigma Delta Chi. Home: PO Box 1246 Beverly Hills CA 90213 Office: Westinghouse Broadcasting 6232 Yucca Hollywood CA 90028

NEWMAN, JAMES, marketing professional; b. New Brunswick, N.J., Apr. 12, 1961; s. Arthur and Katherine Elizabeth (Kolb) N.; m. Teri Lynn Nebron, June 3, 1984. BS, U. Nev., 1984, MS, 1985. Bus. devel. assoc. U. Nev. Reno, 1987; mktg. mgr. Carisonite Internat. Corp., Carson City, Nev., 1987—; v.p. Zunini-Newman Inc., Reno Nev. 1984—. Coach, former bd. mem. Am Youth Soccer Orgn., Sparks Nev. 1981—. Republican. Office: Zunini Newman Inc 1092 S Virginia St Reno NV 89502

NEWMAN, KATHARINE DEALY, writer, consultant; b. Phila., Aug. 17, 1911; d. Creswell Victor and Harriet Elizabeth (Hetherington) Dealy; m. Morton Newman, May 11, 1946 (div. 1968); children: Deborah Silverstein, Blaze. BS in Edn. summa cum laude, Temple U., 1933; MA in English, U. Pa., 1937, PhD in English, 1961. Cert. secondary and coll. English educator, Commonwealth of Pa. Tchr. Phila. High Schs., 1933-46, 49-50; asst. prof. U. Minn., Mpls., 1946-47, Temple U. Community Coll., Phila., 1959; assoc. prof. Moore Coll. Art, Phila., 1961-63; tchr. Abington (PA.) High Sch., 1963-67; prof. West Chester (Pa.) State U., 1967-77; cons. Inst. for Ethnic Studies West Chester U., 1975-77; exch. prof. Cheyney State (Pa.) U., 1971; cons. in field. Author: The Gentleman's Novelist: Robert Plumer Ward, 1765-1946, 1961, The American Equation: Literature in a Multi-Ethnic Culture, 1971, Ethnic American Short Stories, 1975, Never Without a Song: The Years and Songs of Jennie Hess Devlin 1865-1952, 1989, (introduction) The Girl of the Golden West, 1978; contbr. articles to profl. jours. Named Outstanding Bd. Mem. Jr. League, 1987; Coordinating Coun. Literary Mags. Editor fellow, 1980. Mem. Modern Lit. Assn. (emeritus mem.), Philogical Assn. Pacific Coast, Soc. for the Study of Multi-Ethnic Lit. of U.S. (founder, officer 1973, editor newsletter 1973-77, editor MELUS jour. 1977-81, editor emeritus 1983—, Contbn. award 1982), Inst. for Ethnic Studies (founder, chmn. 1975-77), Episc. Svc. Alliance (co-founder 1978, bd. dirs. 1978-87, v.p. 1982, 86, pres. 1983, 84, cert. appreciation 1987). Democrat. Home: 6232 B Warner Ave Huntington Beach CA 92647

NEWMAN, LLOYDE MARRI, buyer; b. Portland, Oreg., June 28, 1953; d. Robert Lloyd and Ailsa Andrea (Bynon) Bloodworth; m. Bruce Joseph Newman, June 28, 1953. BA, Fairhaven Coll., 1975; postgrad., Liberty U., 1987—. Office asst. Western Wash. U., 1975-77; buyer S. Puget Sound Community Coll., Olympia, Wash., 1978—; piano instr. Olympia, Wash., 1979—; sec. Olympia (Wash.) Music Tchrs., 1987—; exec. com. mem. Combined Fund Drive, Olympia, 1986—. Course marshall Olympia Women Trials/Marathon, 1984; mem. Encore Wash. Ctr. for Performing Arts, Olympia, 1987; voter registrar Thurston County, Olympia, 1983—. Recipient Award of Excellence Gov. of Wash., 1987, 88, Award of Merit Gov. of Wash., 1986. Mem. Purchasing Assn. Community Colls., Wash. Music Tchrs. Assn. (sec. 1987—). Republican. Assembly of God. Office: Puget Sound Community Coll 2011 Mottman Rd SW Olympia WA 98502

NEWMAN, MARC ALAN, electrical engineer; b. Jasper, Ind., Nov. 21, 1955; s.Leonard Jay and P. Louise (Shainberg) N.; m. Shelley Jane Martin, Aug. 13, 1977. BSEE, Purdue U., 1977, MSEE, 1979. Sr. elec. engr. Sperry Corp. Flight Systems, Phoenix, 1979-85; staff engr. Motorola Inc., Tempe, Ariz., 1985-88, Quincy St. Corp., Phoenix, 1988-89; sr. staff scientist Motorola Inc., Chandler, Ariz., 1989—; prolog expert Motorola Inc., Tempe and Chandler, 1985—. Mem. IEEE, Am. Assn. Artificial Intelligence, Ariz. Artifical Intelligence Assn. (founder), Internat. Platform Assn., Phi Sigma Kappa, Eta Kappa Nu. Home: 1539 N Hobson Mesa AZ 85203 Office: Motorola Inc 1300 N Alma Sch Rd Chandler AZ 85224

NEWMAN, MICHAEL LOUIS, casino dealer; b. San Diego, Oct. 9, 1940; m. Paul Ann Eskenasy, Jan. 7, 1973; children: Nathene Eden, Ben Jordan. BA, Occidental Coll., L.A., 1962; MA, U. Nev., 1986, postgrad., 1987—. Casino dealer Dunes Hotel, Las Vegas, 1970—; freelance writer, Las Vegas, 1966—; instr. U. Nev., Las Vegas, 1986—. Editor: Think Jazz, 1976-77; columnist Gambling Times Magazine, 1977-78; author: Dealer's Special, 1979; contbr. articles to popular newspapers and mags. Harcourt, Brace and World fellow, 1968. Mem. Sigma Tau Delta, Phi Kappa Phi. Democrat. Jewish. Home: 5212 Valley Glen St Las Vegas NV 89119 Office: U Nev English Dept 4505 Maryland Pkwy Las Vegas NV 89154

NEWMAN, MICHAEL RODNEY, lawyer; b. N.Y.C., Oct. 2, 1945; s. Morris and Helen Gloria (Hendler) N.; m. Cheryl Jeanne Anker, June 11, 1967; children—Hillary Abra, Nicole Brooke. BA, U. Denver, 1967; JD, U. Chgo., 1970. Bar: Calif. 1971, U.S. Dist. Ct. (cen. dist.) Calif. 1972, U.S. Dist. Ct. (no. dist.) Calif. 1975, U.S. Dist. Ct. (so. dist.) Calif. 1979, U.S. Dist. Ct. (ea. dist.) Calif. 1983, U.S. Ct. Appeals (9th cir.) 1974, U.S. Tax Ct. 1979, U.S. Supreme Ct. 1978. Assoc., David Daar, 1971-76; ptnr. Daar & Newman, 1976-78, Miller & Daar, 1978-88, Miller & Daar & Newman, 1988—; judge pro tem L.A. Mcpl. Ct., 1982—, L.A. Superior Ct., 1988—. Lectr. Eastern Claims Conf., Eastern Life Claims Conf., Nat. Health Care Anti-Fraud Assn., AIA Conf. on Ins. Fraud; mem. L.A. Citizens Organizing Com. for Olympic Summer Games, 1984, mem. govtl. liaison adv. commn. 1984; mem. So. Calif. Com. for Olympic Summer Games, 1984; cert. ofcl. Athletics Congress of U.S., co-chmn. legal com. S.P.A-T.A.C, chief finish judge. Recipient NYU Bronze medal in Physics, 1962, TAC Disting. Svc. award, 1988, Maths. award U.S. Navy Sci., 1963. Mem. ABA (multi-dist. litigation subcom., com. on class actions), Los Angeles County Bar Assn., Conf. of Ins. Counsel, So. Pacific Assn. (bd. dirs.). Office: 11500 W Olympic Blvd Ste 600 Los Angeles CA 90064

NEWMAN, PAUL HAROLD, data processing manager; b. Washington, Apr. 25, 1933; s. Simon M. and Sarah (Herman) N.; m. Joyce Reid, Apr. 12, 1958; children: Kurt, Scott, Amy. BS, Antioch Coll., 1956. Research scientist Am. Inst. for Research, Pitts., 1956-60; research engr. Boeing Co., Seattle, 1960-61; br. mgr. Systems Devel. Corp., Colorado Springs, Colo., 1961-73; systems design mgr. Wash. Dept. Social and Health Services, Olympia, 1973-75, asst. chief office info. services, 1975-80, mgr. systems engring., 1980-85, chief office info. services, 1985-87, mgr. software technology, 1987—. Precint com. man Dem. Party, Tacoma, 1980—. Home: 6004 Hillcrest Dr SW Tacoma WA 98499 Office: Wash Dept Social and Health Svcs Mail Sta OB-12 Olympia WA 98504

NEWMAN, PHILIP JAY, language and history educator; b. N.Y.C., July 16, 1935; s. Joseph Eisen and Norma (Berger) N.; m. Phyllis George, Dec. 20, 1958; children: Mitchell Lewis, Elissa Michelle. AA, U. Calif., Berkeley, 1955; BA, UCLA, 1957; MA, Calif. State U.-Northridge, 1969. Cert. tchr., Calif. Tchr., dept. chmn. Monroe High Sch., L.A., 1963—; instr. L.A. Valley Coll., Van Nuys, 1972—. Precint worker L.A. Dem. Com., 1960—; del., translator Office of Ams. Trip to Nicaragua, Santa Monica, 1987. NDEA fellow, 1963. Mem. Am. Fedn. Tchrs., United Tchrs. L.A. (founding mem., mem. polit. action com.), Fgn. Lang. Tchrs. L.A. (v.p. 1978-80), Phi Beta Kappa. Jewish. Home: 16733 Calahan St Sepulveda CA 91343 Office: James Monroe High Sch 9299 Haskell Ave Sepulveda CA 91343

NEWMAN, SHELLEY JANE, mechanical engineer; b. Plymouth, Ind., Nov. 9, 1957; d. Hubert Lincoln and Alice Louise (Miller) Martin; m. Marc Alan Newman, Aug. 13, 1977. BSME, Purdue U., 1979. Sr. engr. Sperry Flight Systems, Phoenix, 1979-85; engring. project leader Motorola Govt. Electronics Group, Tempe, Ariz., 1985—. Named Hoosier scholar, Ind., 1975-79, Jaycees scholar, Plymouth, Ind., 1975-79. Mem. ASME. Office: Motorola Govt Elec Group 2100 E Elliot Rd Tempe AZ 85282

NEWMAN, STUART THEODORE, aerospace engineer; b. Hollywood, Calif., June 25, 1954; s. Victor Herbert Newman and Debra Doris (Morrow) Farrell; m. Janet Sanchez, Dec. 20, 1986 (div. 1989). BS, UCLA, 1976. Systems engr. Hughes Aircraft, Fullerton, Calif., 1983-86, project engr., 1984-87, project head, 1987—; exec. producer, gen. ptnr. Bullseye Entertainment Group, North Hollywood, Calif., 1987—; pres. STUN Enterprises, Inc., Irvine, Calif., 1987—. Lt. USN, 1976-83, lt. comdr. USNR, 1988—. Mem. Naval Res. Assn., U.S. Naval Inst., Project Mgmt. Inst., Naval Sailing Assn. (instr.). Republican. Jewish. Home: 4900 E Chapman Ave Unit 3 Orange CA 92669 Office: Hughes Aircraft PO Box 3310 Fullerton CA 92634

NEWMARK, LEONARD DANIEL, linguistics educator; b. Attica, Ind., Apr. 8, 1929; s. Max Jacob and Sophie (Glusker) N.; m. Ruth Broessler, Sept. 16, 1951; children: Katya, Mark. A.B., U. Chgo., 1947; M.A., Ind. U., 1951, Ph.D., 1955. Instr. English U. Ill., Urbana, summer 1951; vis. asst. prof. linguistics U. Mich., Ann Arbor, summer 1961; assoc. prof. English Ohio State U., 1954-62; assoc. prof. linguistics Ind. U.-Bloomington, 1962-63; prof. linguistics U. Calif.-San Diego, La Jolla, 1963—, chmn. dept., 1963-71, 79-85, head program in Am. lang. and culture, 1979-84. Author: Linguistic History of English, 1963, Spoken Albanian, 1981, Standard Albanian, 1982; inventor memory aid device. Mem. Linguistics Soc. Am. Home: 2643 St Tropez Pl La Jolla CA 92037 Office: U Calif San Diego La Jolla CA 92093

NEWQUIST, DONALD STEWART, designer, technical director, consultant; b. Frankfort, Ky., May 25, 1953; s. Edward Wallace N. and Jeanne Gayle (Utterback) Caddy; m. Linda Susan Carter, Oct. 10, 1987. BA, Centre Coll. of Ky., Danville, 1975; MA, U. Nev., Las Vegas, 1979; postgrad., U. Nev., 1987—. Grad. fellow Ctr. Coll. of Ky., 1975-76; grad. teaching asst. U. Nev., Las Vegas, 1976-78; instr. tech. theater Clark County Community Coll., N. Las Vegas, Nev., 1978-80; tech. supr. City of Las Vegas Cultural Div., 1979—; adminstr. Las Vegas Civic Ballet, 1988—; Tech. dir. USAF Base Talent Show, Davis-Monthan AFB, Ariz., 1986, 87; tech. cons. USAF Recreation Ctr., Nellis AFB, Nev., 1982-85; resident designer, Ecdysis Dance Theater, Las Vegas, 1980-84; mem. Lorenzi Park Amphitheater Task Force, Las Vegas, 1988. Designer: stage renovation, Reed Whipple Cultural Ctr., 1981; stage addition, Charleston Heights Arts Ctr., 1980. Lic. lay reader, Christ Episcopal Ch., Las Vegas, 1981—. Mem. U.S. Inst. for Theater Tech., Illuminating Engring. Soc. of N.Am. (sect. treas., bi-regional conf. com.). Republican. Office: Las Vegas Cultural Div 749 Veterans Memorial Dr Las Vegas NV 89101

NEWQUIST, HARVEY PAUL, high technology writer; b. Utica, N.Y., Dec. 28, 1950; s. Harvey Paul and Patricia Mary (Starr) N. BA, U. Notre Dame, 1980. Advt. mgr. The O'Malley Corp., Phoenix, 1980-82; mktg. mgr. Phaze Info. Machines, Scottsdale, Ariz., 1982-84; editor/analyst DM Data, Scottsdale, 1984-87; columnist Music Tech. Mag., Los Angeles, 1987—; Editor AI Trends, Scottsdale, 1985—; contbg. editor Computerworld, 1986—, Artificial Intelligence Expert/Miller-Freeman, San Francisco, 1987—; pres. Relayer Group Prodns., Scottsdale, 1984—. Mem. Artificial Intelligence East (chmn. 1987).

NEWSTADT, DAVID ROLAND, food company executive; b. N.Y.C., Mar. 19, 1930; s. Herbert Morris and Evelyn (Bleckerman) N.; m. Millicent R. Brown, Nov. 23, 1952; children—A. Todd, Tracy Heather. A.B. magna cum laude, Syracuse U., 1951; M.B.A., NYU, 1957. With Johnson & Johnson, 1955-58, 61-73, various product mgmt. positions to dir. mktg., 1961-69, gen. mgr. dental div., domestic operating co., 1969-71, v.p., mem. mgmt. bd. domestic operating co., 1971-72; pres. Johnson & Johnson Dental Products Co., 1972-73; asst. account exec. Compton Advt., 1958-59, account exec., 1959-61; with CPC Internat. Inc., 1974-85; pres., chief exec. officer Sun-Diamond Growers Calif., Pleasanton, 1986-87; chmn., pres., chief exec. officer S.B. Thomas, Inc. affiliate CPC N.Am., 1974-78; pres. Consumer Devel. unit CPC N.Am., 1978-81; v.p. CPC Internat. Inc., 1978-85; pres. Best Foods U.S. unit CPC N.Am., 1981-84; exec. v.p. Best Foods N.Am. div. CPC Internat. Inc., Englewood Cliffs, N.J., 1984-85; bd. dirs. GoodMark Foods Inc., Raleigh, N.C., Internat. Food and Beverages, Irvine, Calif. Served to lt. (j.g.) USNR, 1951-55. Mem. Am. Mgmt. Assn. (pres. assn.), NYU Grad. Sch. Bus. Alumni Assn. (bd. dirs. 1977—, past pres.), Phi Beta Kappa, Psi Chi. Republican. Jewish. Office: Sun-Diamond Growers Calif 1050 S Diamond St Stockton CA 95201

NEWSTEAD, ROBERT RICHARD, urologist; b. Detroit, Sept. 16, 1935; s. Oran Henry and Agnes Audery (Lewandowski) N.; m. Marie Carmela LiPuma, Aug. 5, 1961; children: Elizabeth Marie, Peter Joseph, Angela Agnes, Paul Michael. Student, Coll. Idaho, 1955-57, Quincy Coll., 1957-58; MD, Loyola U., Chgo., 1963. Intern Walter Reed Gen. Hosp., Washington, 1963-64; resident U. Iowa, Iowa City, 1967-71; urologist Urology Clinic Yakima, Wash., 1971-84, pres., 1984—; chief of surgery St. Elizabeth Med. Ctr., Yakima, 1980-81, Yakima Valley Hosp., 1978-79. Bd. dirs. St. Elizabeth Found., Yakima, 1983—, The Capital Theater, 1987—, Boy Scouts Am., Yakima, 1982-86. Capt. U.S. Army, 1962-67. Fellow Am. Cancer Soc., Iowa City, 1969-70, Am. Cancer Soc., 1961; named one of Outstanding Young Men Am., 1968. Fellow Am. Bd. Urology, ACS, Am. Urol. Assn., Wash. State Urol. Bd.; mem. AMA, Rubin Flocks Soc. (pres. 1985-86), Yakima Surgical Soc. (pres. 1982-83), Yakima County Med. Soc. (pres. 1988—), Rotary. Roman Catholic. Home: 814 Conestoga Blvd Yakima WA 98908 Office: Urology Clinic Yakima 206 S 11th Ave Yakima WA 98902

NEWTON, CHARLES ALLEN, computer systems engineer; b. Duluth, Minn., Apr. 11, 1938; s. Eldred Charles and Margaret Louise (Paulson) N.; m. Vera Ann Glose, Sept. 5, 1964; children: Teresa Yvonne, Catherine Leslie, Pamela Louise. AB in Math., San Diego State Coll., 1965; MS in Info. and Computer Sci., Ga. Inst. Tech., 1968. Engr. aide Convair Astronautics, San Diego, 1958-60; commd. 2d lt. USAF, 1961, advanced through grades to lt. col., 1977, navigator, 1960-71, sr. program mgr., 1971-74, command and control specialist, 1974-83, ret., 1983; sr. program mgr. Ramtek Corp., Napa, Calif., 1983—; prof. math., computer sci. Napa Valley Community Coll., 1986—; dir. sales and mktg. Ramtek Corp., Napa, 1988—; bd. dirs. Deltek Systems Incorp. Pres. PTA Am. Sch., Oslo, 1982. Decorated DFC Air medal. Mem. Assn. Computing Machinery, Am. Mensa, Air Force Assn., Armed Force Communications and Electronics Assn., Retired Officers Club. Republican. Presbyterian. Lodge: Rotary. Home: 3591 Twin Oaks Dr Napa CA 94558

NEWTON, CHARLES WILLARD, educator, retired army officer; b. Longmont, Colo., May 9, 1929; s. Joseph Guy and Violet (Weathers) N.; m. June Ann Debarbieris, Aug. 4, 1956; children; C. Christopher, Catherine E., Cynthia L., Craig J. BA, U. Calif., Berkeley, 1950; MA, Ariz. State U., 1973. Commd. 2d lt. U.S. Army, 1950, advanced through grades to lt. col., 1967, served in various locations,, 1967-71, ret., 1971; tchr. Tempe (Ariz.) High Sch., 1971—. Named High Sch. Journalism Tchr. of Yr. Ariz. Newspapers Assn., 1979. Mem. Soc. Profl. Journalists, NEA, Ret. Officers Assn. Republican. Roman Catholic. Office: Tempe High Sch 1730 S Mill St Tempe AZ 85281

NEWTON, EUGENIE VINCENTIA, human resources executive; b. Coronado, Calif., June 27, 1946; d. Roy Arthur and Mary Elizabeth (Irwin) N. BA in Polit. Sci., San Diego State U., 1968; MA in Psychology, Profl. Sch. Psychol. Studies, 1985. Mgr. trainee, tng. dir. Sears Roebuck & Co., San Diego, 1968-71, asst. personnel dir., 1974-75, dir. regional affirmative action, 1974-75, dir. personnel, 1975-79; owner, mgr. Crowne-Abra Employment AGy., San Diego, 1979-81; dir. personnel Mesa Vista Hosp., San Diego, 1981-83; dir. human resources Vista Hill Found., San Diego, 1983-84ž, v.p. human resources, 1984--; cons., San Diego, 1988--. Bd. dirs., sec. Terrasanta Community Coun., 1973-74; mem. edn. adv. com. Southwestern Community Coll. Dist., 1975-76; mem. regional affirmative action clearinghouse San Diego County Human Rels. Commn., 1975-76; mem. women's opportunity week subcom. San Diego Mayor's Adv. Com. on Status of Women, 1980; mem. Women's Career Devel. Coun., 1978-80, Big Sister League, 1981; mem. adv. com. Children's Learning Ctr., 1982-88; mem. compensation task force San Diego and Imperial County Hosp. Coun., 1985-87. Mem. Calif. Hosp. Personnel Mgmt. Assn. (pres. San Diego chpt. 1986, treas. 1987). Democrat. Home: 3265 Erie St San Diego CA 92117

NEWTON, LINDA DIANE, interior designer; b. Springfield, Ill., Sept. 16, 1963; d. Robert George and Sharon Kaye (Christian) Hanson; m. Edward Allen Newton, May 30, 1987. BS in Interior Design, U. Wis., 1986. Cons. Cedar Corp., Menomonie, Wis., 1985-86; mgr. sales Marble & Tile Imports, Emeryville, Calif., 1986-88; interior designer Hernikl & Assocs., Walnut Creek, Calif., 1988—. Mem. Am. Soc. Interior Designers. Republican. Lutheran. Home: 201 Sunwood Meadows Pl San Jose CA 95119 Office: Hernikl & Assocs 144 Mayhew Way Walnut Creek CA 94596

NEWTON, RAY CLYDE, university administrator; b. Denver, Colo., Sept. 26, 1935; s. Louis Weiss and Thelma (Sipe) N.; m. Patricia Rae (Boekhaus), Dec. 27, 1956; children: Sheri D., Lynn D., William L. (dec.). Grad., Kans. State U., Ft. Hays, 1957; postgrad., S.D. State U., 1959-61, U. Tex., 1970-72. Tchr., chmn. English dept. LaCrosse (Kans.) High Sch., 1957-59; mem. faculty N.Mex. Highlands U., Las Vegas, 1961-63, instr., asst. dean students, 1963-73, dir. pub. info. and pubs., adminstrv. asst. to pres., 1965-73, asst. prof., then assoc. prof. journalism, 1965-73; mem. faculty No. Ariz. U., Flagstaff, 1973—, prof. journalism, asst. dean creative and communication arts, 1984-87, dean, 1987-88, asst. to pres., 1988—; dir. bilingual mass media program N.Mex. Highlands U., 1972-73; corr. Sta. KGGM-TV, Albuquerque, 1966-71; cons. in field to newspapers and mcpl. govts. Author: (with Newsom and Wellert) Media Writing, 1984; contbr. articles and revs. to profl. jours. and popular mags. Mem. adminstrv. bd. Trinity Heights Meth. Ch.; mem. exec. council Grand Canyon council Boy Scouts Am.; bd. dirs. Flagstaff Festival of the Arts; ex-officio bd. dirs. Ariz. Alliance for Arts Edn. Grantee Rotary Found. 1968, Danforth Found., 1969-70; Walter fellow U. Tex., 1971-72; named Journalism Prof. of Yr., Ariz. Newspaper Assn., 1984, Disting. Faculty mem. No. Ariz. U., 1984; recipient Nat. Teaching award Poynter Inst. Media Studies, St. Petersburg, Fla., 1985. Mem. Assn. Edn. Journalism/Mass Communication, Am. Soc. Journalism Sch. Adminstrs., Am. Soc. Newspaper Editors (mem. minorities edn. com.), Ariz. Press Assn. (mem. bd. dirs., chmn. edn. com.), Western Social Scis. Assn. (v.p. 1979-80, mem. exec. council, editorial bd.), Am. Assn. Higher Edn., Inter-Am. Press Assn., 1st Amendment Coalition (past bd. dirs.), Soc. Profl. Journalists, Coll. Sports Info. Dirs. Assn., Flagstaff C. of C., Phi Eta Sigma, Lambda Iota Tau, Phi Delta Kappa, Pi Rho Sigma, Phi Kappa Phi, Kappa Tau Alpha. Lodge: Kiwanis. Home: 1520 Appalachian Flagstaff AZ 86004 Office: No Ariz U Office of Pres Box 4092 Flagstaff AZ 86011

NEWTON, STANLEY BARCLAY, automobile executive; b. Worcester, Mass., Apr. 23, 1946; s. Stanley and Barbara Louise (Clark) N.; m. Karen Mary Rizzuto, Apr. 9, 1966; children: Lynette Marie, Kim Michelle. Assocs. in Acctg., New England Sch. Acctg., Worcester, 1966. Staff acct. Tupper Moore & Co. CPA, Worcester, 1966-69; office mgr. Muzi Ford, Needham, Mass., 1969-73; bus. mgr. Kelly Buick Co. Inc., Worcester, 1973-76, Al Ives Chevrolet, Worcester, 1976-80; treas. Holmes Tuttle Ford, Tucson, 1980-88, v.p. fixed ops., 1988—. Bd. dirs. Loshe Br. YMCA, Tucson, 1985—; cons. Jr. Achievement, Tucson, 1980-1983. Served with USAR, 1966-72. Republican. Club: Skyline (Tucson), Pueblo. Lodge: Kiwanis (pres. Worcester chpt. 1979). Office: Holmes Tuttle Ford 800 E Broadway PO Box 2552 Tucson AZ 85702

NEY, JAMES WALTER EDWARD COLBY, English language educator; b. Nakaru, Kenya, July 28, 1932; s. Reginald Osborne and Elizabeth Grace Colby (Aikins) N.; m. Joan Marie Allen, June 12, 1954; children: Cheryl Lyn, James Allen Colby, Peter Cameron. A.B., Wheaton Coll., 1955, A.M., 1957; Ed.D., U. Mich., 1963. Cons. Dade County (Fla.) schs., 1961-62; mem. Faculty U. Ryukyus, Okinawa, 1962-64, Mich. State U., 1964-69; mem. faculty Ariz. State U., Tempe, 1969—; prof. English Ariz. State U., 1974—; vis. prof. U. Montreal, 1962, George Peabody Coll., Nashville, 1965, U. Hawaii, 1967, Western N.Mex. U., 1971; pres. Ariz. Bilingual Council, 1973-74; appointed to council on practice The Am. Assn. Nurse Anesthetists, 1976-83. Author: Readings on American Society, 1969, Exploring in English, 1972, Discovery in English, 1972, American English for Japanese Students, 1973, Linguistics, Language Teaching and Composition in the Grades, 1975, Semantic Structures for the Syntax of the Modal Auxiliaries and Complements in English, 1981, Transformational Grammar: Essays for the Left Hand, 1989, others. Instr. workshop Community Assn. Inst. Tech. Writing, 1988; cons. TESL and bilingual edn. with Sta. KFYI, 1986-88. Mem. Am. Linguistic Assn., MLA, Nat. Council Tchrs. English, Can. Linguistic Assn., Am. Assn. Nurse Anesthetists (council on practice), Nat. Assn. Fgn. Student Affairs. Office: Ariz State U English Dept Tempe AZ 85287

NEY, MICHAEL JAMES, lawyer; b. Oakland, Calif., Nov. 20, 1943; s. George William and Monica Patricia (Ford) N.; m. Jamie Sue Deren, July 13, 1968; children: Molly, Deren. B of Sci. and Commerce, Santa Clara U., 1965; JD, John F. Kennedy U., 1971. Bar: Calif. 1972, U.S. Dist. Ct. (no. dist.) Calif. 1972. Dept. dist. atty. County of Alameda, Oakland, 1972-73; assoc. Helzel, Leighton, Brunn & Deal, Oakland, 1973-75; ptnr. McNamara, Houston, Dodge, McClure & Ney, Walnut Creek, Calif., 1975—. Mem. ABA, Calif. Bar Assn., Contra Costa Bar Assn. (chmn. landslide com. 1987-88). Roman Catholic. Home: 1031 Via Nueva Lafayette CA 94549 Office: McNamara Houston Dodge McClure & Ney 1211 Newell Ave Walnut Creek CA 94596

NEYLON, MARTIN JOSEPH, bishop; b. Buffalo, Feb. 13, 1920; s. Martin Francis and Delia (Breen) N. PhL, Woodstock Coll., 1944, ThL, 1951; MA, Fordham U., 1948. Ordained priest Roman Cath. Ch., 1950. Bishop Roman Cath. Ch., 1970; mem. Soc. of Jesus; tchr. Regis High Sch., N.Y.C., 1952-54; master Jesuit novices Poughkeepsie, N.Y., 1955-67; chaplain Kwajalein Missile Range, Marshall Islands, 1967-68; superior Residence for Jesuit Students, Guam, 1968-70; coadjutor bishop Caroline and Marshall Islands, 1970-80; Vicar apostolic 1971—; residential bishop New Diocese of Carolines-Marshalls, 1980—. Address: PO Box 250, Truk 96942, Federated States of Micronesia

NG, FRANCIS KAM-CHUNG, auditor; b. Hong Kong, Oct. 11, 1958; came to U.S., 1980; s. Pun Wah and Wai Man (Poon) N. AA, Mt. Hood Community Coll., 1982; BS, Portland (Oreg.) State U., 1985. CPA, Mo. Mem. ADP staff Environ. Testing Group, Portland, 1985; acctg. intern United Telephone Co. N.W., Hood River, Oreg., 1985-86, reports acct., 1986-88; intermediate auditor United Telecommunication Inc., Kansas City, Mo., 1988—.

NG, LAWRENCE MING-LOY, pediatric cardiologist; b. Hong Kong, Mar. 21, 1940; came to U.S., 1967, naturalized, 1977; s. John Iu-cheung and Mary Wing (Wong) N.; B.Med., U. Hong Kong, 1965, B.Surg., 1965; m. Bella May Ha Kan, June 25, 1971; children—Jennifer Wing-mui, Jessica Wing-yee. House physician Queen Elizabeth Hosp., Hong Kong, 1965-66, med. officer, 1966-67; resident physician Children's Hosp. of Los Angeles, 1967-68; resident physician Children's Hosp. Med. Center, Oakland, Calif., 1968-70, fellow in pediatric cardiology, 1970-72, now mem. teaching staff; practice medicine, specializing in pediatrics and pediatric cardiology, San Leandro, Calif., 1972—, Oakland, Calif., 1982—; chief of pediatrics Oakland Hosp., 1974-77; chief of pediatrics Vesper Meml. Hosp., 1977-79, sec. staff, 1984, v.p. staff, 1985; chief pediatrics Meml. Hosp., San Leandro, 1986-88. Active Republican Party. Diplomate Am. Bd. Pediatrics. Fellow Am. Acad. Pediatrics; mem. AMA, Calif. Med. Assn., Am. Heart Assn., Los Angeles Pediatric Soc., East Bay Pediatric Soc., Smithsonian Assos., Nat. Geog. Soc., Orgn. Chinese Ams. (chpt. pres. 1984), Chinese-Am. Physicians Soc. (co-founder, sec. 1980, pres. 1983), Oakland Mus. Assns., Oakland Chinatown C. of C. (bd. dirs. 1986—). Buddhist. Club: Bay-O-Vista. Office: 345 9th St Ste 204-205 Oakland CA 94607 also: 1234 E 14th St Ste 401 San Leandro CA 94577

NGUYEN, ANN CAC KHUE, pharmaceutical and bioorganic chemist; b. Sontay, Vietnam; came to U.S., 1975; naturalized citizen; d. Nguyen Van Soan and Luu Thi Hieu. BS, U. Saigon, 1973; MS, San Francisco State U., 1978; PhD, U. Calif., San Francisco, 1983. Teaching and research asst. U. Calif., San Francisco, 1978-83, postdoctoral fellow, 1983-86; research scientist U. Calif., 1987—. Contbr. articles to profl. jours. Recipient Nat. Research Service award, NIH, 1981-83; Regents fellow U. Calif., San Francisco, 1978-81. Mem. Am. Chem. Soc., AAAS, Bay Area Enzyme Mechanism Group, Nat. Coop. Drug Discovery Group. Roman Catholic. Home: 1488 Portola Dr San Francisco CA 94127 Office: U Calif Dept Pharm Chemistry San Francisco CA 94143

NGUYEN, BICH TU, engineer; b. East Lansing, Mich., Mar. 21, 1958; s. Ban Tu Nguyen and Quy Thi Tran; m. Tu-Anh Hathi. BSEE, Cornell U., 1980; MSEE, U. Mich., 1981. Mem. tech. staff Bell Labs., Holmdel, N.J., 1980-83; rsch. engr. SRI Internat., Menlo Park, Calif., 1983—; cons. Make Systems, Mountain View, Calif., 1987-88. Patentee in field. Mem. IEEE, Eta Kappa Nu. Home and Office: SRI Internat 333 Ravenswood Ave EK-354 Menlo Park CA 94086

NGUYEN, DOAN, engineering specialist; b. Quangtri, Vietnam, Oct. 16, 1950; came to U.S., 1975; s. Bieu and Thi Thi Nguyen; m. Vinh Thi Tran, June 14, 1978; children: Johnkim Tran, Josephhung Tran, Maryann Tran. Student, Hue Med. U., Vietnam, 1975; BSEE, Calif. State U.-Fullerton, 1982, MSEE, 1985. Tchr. Jean D'Arc High Sch., Hue, Vietnam, 1972-75; nurse aid Casa Carlos Rehab. Ctr., Anaheim, Calif., 1976-77; community worker Garden Grove (Calif.) City, 1977-79; electronic technician Gen. Automation Corp., Anaheim, 1979-82; electronics instr. Nat. Inst. Tech., Cypress, Calif., 1982-83; chief engr. Westminster Engring. Corp., Anaheim, Calif., 1983-84; sr. engr. Northrop Electronics, Hawthorne, Calif., 1984-88; instr. in electronics Rancho Santiago Coll., Santa Ana, Calif., 1984-88; sr. project engr. GTE, Pomona, Calif., 1987; engr. specialist Tool Design Group, McDonnell Douglas, Long Beach, 1988--. Scout master Boy Scouts Am., Anaheim, 1980--; pres. Gia Dihh Lac Viet Brotherhood Family, Santa Ana, 1975-85. Mem. Nat. Soc. Profl. Engring. Roman Catholic. Home: 1605 N Huron Dr Santa Ana CA 92706

NGUYEN, LAN KIM, software engineer; b. Saigon, July 5, 1960; parents Hai Kim Dang and My Thi Nguyen. BSEE, Cornell U., 1983; MA in Physics, SUNY, Buffalo, 1985, MSEE, 1986. Software engineer McDonnell Douglas Astronautics, Huntington Beach, Calif., 1986—. scholar Cornell U., 1982-83. Mem. Eta Kappa Nu. Office: McDonnell Douglas Astronautics 5301 Bolsa Ave Huntington Beach CA 92647

NGUYEN, TANG DINH, data processing specialist; b. Hanoi, Vietnam, May 31, 1948; came to U.S., 1975; s. Tinh Van and Lien Thi N.; m. Xuan Mai, Dec. 6, 1973; children: Diana Kim Phung, Grace Kieu Loan, Charles Vinh Khang, Ann Marie Bao An, Jean Paul Vinh Phuc, Yvonne Ngoc Hanh. JD, U. Saigon, South Vietnam, 1971; postgrad., Pierce Coll., 1975, UCLA, 1986. V.p. An Giang Co., DaLat, South Vietnam, 1966-67; atty. Saigon Bar Assn., 1971-75; laborer Metex Partyline Inc., Canoga Park, Calif., 1975, prodn. mgr., 1975-79; test engr. AM Internat., Jacquard Systems, Newbury Park, Calif., 1979-81; project engr. 3M-Comtal, Altadena, Calif., 1981-82; mgr. large-scale integration lab. Pacesetter Systems Inc. (Siemens), Sylmar, Calif., 1982—; cons. ind. service in data processing field, Canoga Park, 1981-86. 2d sec. Vietnamese Assn., L.A., 1976-77. Mem. Vietnamese Lawyer Assn. Calif. Home: 22552 Napa St West Hills CA 91304 Office: Pacesetter System Inc 12740 San Fernando Rd Sylmar CA 91342

NGUYEN, TRUNG DUC, research scientist; b. Saigon, Vietnam, May 14, 1951; came to U.S., 1969; s. Ambrose Q. and Teresa T. Nguyen; m. Susan Bui, Apr. 5, 1975; children: Jason T., Jessica K. BSEE, U. Minn., 1973; MSEE, U. Santa Clara, 1974; PhD in Elec. Engring., Calif. Western U., 1980. Project engr. Systron Donner Corp., Van Nuys, Calif., 1975-79; engring. specialist Litton Data Systems, Van Nuys, 1979-83; sr. engr. Singer Co., Glendale, Calif., 1983-86; sr. tech. staff TRW, Redondo Beach, Calif., 1986-87; rsch. scientist Teledyne Systems Co., Northridge, Calif., 1987—. Contbr. articles on electronics to profl. jours. Mem. IEEE (sr.), Northridge Mgmt. Club. Home: 9430 Gierson Ave Chatsworth CA 91311 Office: Teldyne Systems Co 19601 Nordhoff St Northridge CA 91324

NI, WAYNE WEIJEN, telecommunications executive; b. Taipei, Taiwan, China, May 4, 1961; came to U.S., 1976; s. Fu Yuan and Suh Ling (Hwang) N. BA in Bus. Econs., U. Calif., Santa Barbara, 1983; MBA, Pepperdine U., 1989. Acct. Valley Provisions, Inc., Goleta, Calif., 1983-84; cost acct. Info. Magnetics, Inc., Goleta, 1984-85; chief acct. Goleta Valley Hosp., 1985-86; chief exec. officer NI Telecommunications, Inc., Santa Barbara, 1985—; corp. controller Signal Tech., Inc., Goleta, 1987—; cons., tax planning Wayne Ni Enterprises, Santa Barbara, 1982—. Mem. Am. Electronics Assn. Republican. Protestant. Home: 325-D Northgate Dr Goleta CA 93117 Office: Signal Tech Inc 5951 Encina Rd Goleta CA 93117

NIBECK, STUART NEIL, school system administrator; b. Fostoria, Ohio, Jan. 1, 1942; s. Ellsworth Charles and Josephine Elizabeth (Buaer) N.; m. Cecilia Grace Lively, Aug. 22, 1964; children: Melody Ann, Stuart Michael. BSBA, Kent State U., 1965; MBA, Oklahoma City U., 1968. Commd. 2d lt. USAF, 1967, advanced through grades to lt. col., 1983; br. chief, procurement officer USAF, Anchorage, 1972-76; div. chief, logistics plans officer USAF, Denver, 1976-80; inspector USAF, Riverside, Calif., 1980-81; dir. logistics plans USAF, Anchorage, 1981-88; ret. USAF, 1988; dir. purchasing Anchorage Sch. Dist., 1988—; adj. lectr., U. Alaska, Anchorage, 1983—. Editor: Salmon Recipes, 1988, Alaskan Halibut Recipes, 1989. Decorated Bronze Star medal. Home: 6920 Gemini Dr Anchorage AK 99504

NIBLEY, ROBERT RICKS, lawyer; b. Salt Lake City, Sept. 24, 1913; s. Joel and Teresa (Taylor) N.; m. Lee Allen, Jan. 31, 1945 (dec.); children—Jane, Annette. A.B., U. Utah, 1934; J.D., Loyola U., Los Angeles, 1942. Bar: Calif. bar 1943. Accountant Nat. Parks Airways, Salt Lake City, 1934-37, Western Air Lines, Los Angeles, 1937-40; asst. mgr. market research dept. Lockheed Aircraft Corp., Burbank, Calif., 1940-43; asso. firm Hill, Farrer and Burrill, Los Angeles, 1946-53; partner Hill, Farrer and Burrill, 1953-70, of counsel, 1971-78. Served from ensign to lt. comdr. USNR, 1943-46. Mem. Am., Los Angeles bar assns., Phi Delta Phi, Phi Kappa Phi, Phi Delta Theta. Club: California (Los Angeles). Home: 4860 Ambrose Ave Los Angeles CA 90027

NICE, CARTER, conductor, music director; b. Jacksonville, Fla., Apr. 5, 1940; s. Clarence Carter and Elizabeth Jane (Hintermister) N.; m. Jennifer Charlotte Smith, Apr. 4, 1983; children: Danielle, Christian. MusB, Eastman Sch. Music, 1962; MusM, Manhattan Sch. Music. Asst. condr., concert master New Orleans Philharm., 1967-79; condr., music dir. Sacramento Symphony, 1979—; music dir., conductor Bear Valley Music Fest., 1985—. Office: Sacramento Symphony Orch 77 Cadillac Dr #101 Sacramento CA 95825

NICE, DAVID CHARLES, educator; b. Colorado Springs, Colo., Oct. 30, 1952; s. Gerald William and Mary Jayne (Newman) N.; m. Ruth Ann Larson, June. BA, Washburn U., 1974; PhD, U. Mich., 1979. Asst. prof. Ind. U., 1979-80; asst. prof. U. Ga., Athens, 1980-85, assoc. prof., asst. dept. head, 1985-88; assoc. prof. Washington State U., Pullman, 1988—. Author: Federalism, 1987; mem. editorial bd. State and Local Govt. Rev., Athens, 1989—; contbr. articles to profl. jours. Fellow Earhart Found., Ann Arbor, Mich., 1987. Mem. Am. Polit. Sci. Assn., Midwest Polit. Sci. Assn., So. Polit. Sci. Assn., Nat. Assn. R.R. Passengers. Democrat. Lutheran. Office: Wash State U Poly Sci Dept Pullman WA 99164

NICE, JAMES WILLIAM, electronics educator; b. La Grande, Oreg., Apr. 10, 1948; s. Glenn Orvin and Jeana Mae (Sullivan) N.; m. Claudia Jo Salzer, Oct. 21, 1967; children: Laura Lee, Chandra Rae. AS in Bus. Mgmt., Mt. Hood Community Coll., Gresham, Oreg., 1979; student, Thomas A. Edison State Coll., 1988—; AS in Electronics Engring. Tech., ITT Tech. Inst., Portland, 1989. Enlisted USN, 1966, electronics technician, 1966-76, resigned, 1976; field service technician AM Corp., Portland, Oreg., 1976-78; sci. inst. technician State of Oreg., Portland, 1978-81; quality control mgr. Landa Inc., Portland, 1981-83; sr. electronics instr. ITT Tech. Inst., Portland, 1983—. Mem. Land Use Planning Bd., Gresham, 1977-78; chmn. budget com. Rockwood Water Dist., Gresham, 1982-86; mem. Multnomah County Mounted Sheriff Posse, Portland, 1988—. Mem. IEEE (assoc.), Nat. Assn. Radio and Telecommunications Engrs. Democrat. Mormon. Home: 815 SE 224th Ave Gresham OR 97030-2605 Office: ITT Tech Inst 6035 NE 78th Ct Portland OR 97218

NICHOLAS, DAVID RICHARD, lawyer, state senator; b. Gillette, Wyo., Mar. 2, 1941; s. Thomas Arthur and Mary Margaret (McKean) N.; B.A., Harvard Coll., 1963; J.D., U. Wyo., 1966; m. Karen Kay Brewer, Aug. 25, 1963; children—Kristin Kay, Alexander McKean. Admitted to Wyo. bar, 1967, U.S. Ct. Mil. Appeals, 1967; partner Corthell, King, McFadden, Nicholas & Prehoda, Attys., Laramie, Wyo., 1971—; instr. polit. sci. U. Wyo., Laramie, 1977-78, 83-84; mem. Wyo. Senate, Laramie, 1979-87, chmn. travel, recreation and wildlife com., mem. judiciary com. Justice of Peace, Albany County, Wyo., 1977-78; bd. dirs. Salvation Army, 1971-80, Cathedral Home for Children, 1975—, Sr. Ctr., 1975-81, Albany County Pub. Library, 1979-83; mem. Wyo. Council for Humanities, 1982-86, AOPA, 1983—; civilian aide to Sec. of Army, 1984—. Served to capt. Judge Adv. Gen.'s Corps, U.S. Army, 1967-71. Mem. ABA, Albany County Bar Assn., Wyo. Bar Assn. Republican. Club: Rotary (past pres.). Office: PO Box 1147 Laramie WY 82070

NICHOLAS, THOMAS PETER, library director, community television consultant, producer; b. Laramie, Wyo., Dec. 6, 1948; s. Thomas Lloyd Nicholas and Frances (Collins) Chambers; m. Tanya Michelle Villont; 1 child, Ja'el Michelle. AA in Fine Arts, Cabrillo Coll., 1970; BA in English, U. Colo., 1972; MS in Librarianship and Info. Sci., U. Denver, 1982. Real estate salesperson Sun Country, Lakewood, Colo., 1972-74; v.p. Nicholas Properties, Denver, 1971-77; libr. City of Aurora, Colo., 1975-80, system support mgr., 1981-83, dir. libr. and TV svcs., 1984—; pres. bd. Irving Libr. Network Inc., Denver, 1985—; advisor CL System Inc., Boston, 1985—. Exec. producer TV programs: Election Night 85 (Franny award 1986), Miss Plumjoy's Place, 1988 (Starwards 1988), Aurora's Can't Afford Not To, 1988 (Starwards 1988). Mem. exec. bd., chmn. Arapahoe Pub. Access to Librs., 1984-85; site coordinator Am. Cancer Soc., Aurora, 1988; adv. Youth at Risk, Aurora, 1989; bd. dirs. Cen. Colo. Libr. System, Lakewood, 1985-87; mem. exec. bd. Colo. Libr. Legis. Com., Denver, 1988—. Mem. ALA, Colo. Libr. Assn. (advisor 1982-83, Programming award 1982, 1st Colo. Childrens Program award 1983, 88), Nat. Assn. Telecommunications Officers and Advisors (regional pres. 1983-84, T.V. Program award 1986), Rotary (program chmn. 1987-88), Eastgate Lions Club (pres. 1989-90). Democrat. Greek Orthodox. Office: Dept Libr and TV Svcs 14949 E Alameda Dr Aurora CO 80012

NICHOLLS, CHRISTINA, nurse; b. The Netherlands, Jan. 17, 1947; came to U.S., 1968; d. Jacob Frans and Janette (Popping) Medema; m. G. Gary Nicholls, Oct. 9, 1982; 1 child, J.R.S. Anderson; 1 adopted child, Gabriel Aaron. Secondary degree, St. Thomas Bus. Coll., 1965; AA, Bellevue Community Coll., 1982; diploma in nursing, Wenatchee Valley Coll., 1987. RN, Wash. Hospital staff nurse Cen. Wash. Hosp., Wenatchee, Wash., 1987—; co-owner bed and breakfast establishment.

NICHOLS, ELIZABETH GRACE, nursing educator, administrator; b. Tehran, Iran, Feb. 1, 1943; came to U.S., 1964; d. Terence and Eleanor Denny (Payne) Quilliam; m. Gerald Ray Nichols, Nov. 20, 1965; children: Tina Lynn, Jeffrey David. B.S.N., San Francisco State U., 1969; M.S., U. Calif.-San Francisco, 1970, Dr. Nursing Sci., 1974. Staff nurse Peninsula Hosp., Burlingame, Calif., 1966-72; asst. prof. U. Calif.-San Francisco Sch. Nursing, 1974-82; chmn. dept. nursing Idaho State U., Pocatello, 1982-85; assoc. dean Coll. Health Scis. Sch. Nursing U. Wyo., Laramie, 1985—; cons. U. Rochester, N.Y., 1979, Carroll Coll., Mont., 1980, div. Nursing Dept. HHS, Washington, 1980, 84, 85, 86, 87, Stanford Hosp. Nursing Service, Calif., 1981-82, Ea. N.Mex. U., 1988. Contbr. articles on nursing to profl. jours. Mem. adv. bd. dirs. Ombudsman Service of Contra Costa Calif., 1979-82, U. Calif. Home Care Service, San Francisco, 1975-82, Free Clinic of Pocatello, 1984. Fellow Gerontol. Soc. Am., Am. Acad. Nursing; mem. Gerontol. Soc. Am. (chmn. clin. medicine section 1987), Am. Nurses Assn., Wyo. Nurses Assn., Idaho Nurses Assn. (dist. 51 adv. bd. dirs. 1982-84), Western Inst. Nursing (bd. govs.). Club: Oakland Ski (1st v.p. 1981-82). (Calif.). Office: U Wyo Sch Nursing Laramie WY 82071

NICHOLS, FRANK ANDREW, manufacturing executive; b. Madera, Calif., July 1, 1948; s. Carl Andrew and Marion Marie (Guillroy); m. Sharon Elizabeth Wilson, July 10, 1969 (div. Apr. 1982); children: Kendle, Samantha; m. Susan Elaine Graham, June 13, 1982 (div. Dec. 1987); children: Ashleigh, Brianna. BS in Mech. Engring., Calif. State U., Fresno, 1972. Registered profl. mech. engr., quality engr. Mech. engr. Pacific Missile Test Ctr., Pt. Muqu, Calif., 1972-77; gen. engr. Joint Cruise Missle Project Office, Washington, 1977-82; mgr. mktg. Aerojet Tactical Systems Co., Sacramento, 1982-85; mgr. mktg. program Eaton-Kenway, Salt Lake City, 1985-87; pres. Orion Services, Poway, Calif., 1987—. Mem. Am. Soc. Quality Control, Navy League, Am. Def. Preparedness Assn., Electronic Warfare Assn. Republican. Home: 13323 Rancho Penasquitos #D-102 San Diego CA 92129 Office: Orion Svcs 12915 Pomerado Rd #B Poway CA 92064

NICHOLS, HOWARD EUGENE, educational administrator; b. Bremerton, Wash., Oct. 10, 1940; s. Donald Lyford Nichols and Jean (Mercer) Fisher; m. Mary Elizabeth Hurlbut, Aug. 18, 1963 (div. July 1981); children: Elizabeth, Stephanie; m. Diana Frances Baglione, Dec. 27, 1981. BA, Stanford U., 1963. Asst. supt. Palo Alto (Calif.) Pvt. Schs., 1965-72, Harker Acad., San Jose, Calif., 1972-73; chmn., chief exec. officer Harker Acad. Found., San Jose, 1973—. Capt. U.S. Army, 1963-71. Mem. Masons, Shriners. Republican. Office: Harker Acad 500 Saratoga Ave San Jose CA 95129

NICHOLS, HUGH, university dean; b. Boise, Idaho, Dec. 5, 1936; s. Jack and Devere (Oliver) N.; m. Lauren Gayle Harrison, Dec. 16, 1983. BA, So. Oreg. Coll., 1961; ArtsD, U. Oreg., 1979. Asst. prof. English Lewis and Clark Coll., Lewiston, Idaho, 1971-77, assoc. prof. English, 1978-82, chair humanities div., 1976-83, prof., dean Sch. Arts and Scis., 1983—; chmn. Idaho Humanities Coun., 1989—. Office: Lewis and Clark State Coll Coll Arts and Scis Lewiston ID 83501

NICHOLS, IRIS JEAN, illustrator; b. Yakima, Wash., Aug. 2, 1938; d. Charles Frederick and Velma Irene (Hacker) Beisner; (div. June 1963); children: Reid William, Amy Jo; m. David Gary Nichols, Sept. 21, 1966. BFA in Art, U. Wash., 1978. Freelance illustrator Seattle, 1966-81; med. illustrator, head dept. illustration Swedish Hosp. Med. Ctr., Seattle, 1981-86; owner, med. and scientific illustrator Art for Medicine, Seattle, 1986—; part-time med. illustrator U. Wash., Seattle, 1966-67; part-time med. illustrator, graphic coord. dept. art The Mason Clinic, 1968-78; cons. Tech. Communications Cons., Seattle, 1983—; instr. advanced illustration Cornish Coll. Arts, Seattle, 1988—. Illustrator various books including Bryophytes of Pacific Northwest, 1966, Microbiology, Molecules, Microbes and Man, 1973, Microbiology, 1978, 3d rev. edit., 1983, Introduction to Human Physiology, 1980, The Microbial Perspective, 1982, Understanding Human Anatomy and Physiology, 1983, Human Anatomy, 1984 and children's books on various subjects; exhibited in group shows at Seattle Pacific Sci. Ctr., summer 1979, 82, Am. Coll. Surgeons (1st prize 1974), N.W. Urology Conf. (1st prize 1974, 76, 2d prize 1975). Pres. West Seattle Arts Coun., 1983; active Seattle Art Mus. Named to West Seattle High Sch. Alumni Hall of Fame, 1986, Matrix Table, 1986. Mem. Assn. Med. Illustrators (Murial McLatchie Fine Arts award 1981), Nat. Mus. Women in the Arts (Wash. state com., bd. dirs. 1987—), Women Painters of Wash. (pres. 1987-89), U. Wash. Alumni Assn., Lambda Rho (v.p. 1981-82), Alpha Chi Omega.

NICHOLS, ROBERT EDMUND, writer, editor, journalist; b. Daytona Beach, Fla., Feb. 14, 1925; s. Joe D. and Edna A. (Casper) N.; m. Diana R. Grosso; children by previous marriage: Craig S., Kim S., Robin K. Student, San Diego State Coll., 1942-43, St. John's Coll., 1944-45, George Washington U., 1948-49. Reporter San Diego Union, 1942-44; corr. Washington bur. N.Y. Herald Tribune, 1945-48, CBS, 1948-51, Time, Inc., 1951-61; contbg. editor, asst. edn. dir. Life mag., N.Y.C., 1951-52; corr. representing Time, Life, Fortune, Sports Illus. mags., San Diego area, 1952-61; Sunday editor San Diego Union, 1952-61; fin. editor Los Angeles Times, 1961-68, mem. editorial bd., 1965-68; spl. asst. to bd. govs. Fed. Res. System, 1968-70; v.p., dir. various editorial svcs. Bank of Am., 1970-85; prin. Robert E. Nichols Communications, San Francisco, 1985—. Writer, dir. film and radio documentaries. Recipient Loeb Newspaper Spl. Achievement award, 1963, Loeb award disting. fin. reporting, 1964. Fellow Royal Geog. Soc., Explorers Club; mem. Calif. Scholarship Fedn. (hon. life), Soc. Am. Bus. Editors and Writers (pres. 1967-68), U.S. Antarctic Expedition. Clubs: South Polar Press (Little Am. Antarctic); S.Am. Explorers (Lima). Home and Office: 38 Ord Ct San Francisco CA 94114

NICHOLSON, PAUL, theater executive. Gen. mgr. Oreg. Shakespearean Festival, Ashland. Office: Oreg Shakespearean Festival Office of Gen Mgr Box 158 Ashland OR 97520 *

NICHOLSON, TOM GEORGE, geologist, consultant; b. Casper, Wyo., Dec. 3, 1946; s. Tom George and Marie Gloria (Nicholas) N.; m. Sharren Marie Rogers, Dec. 20, 1968; children: Gretchen M., Amy R. AS in Geology, Casper Coll., 1968; BS in Geology, U. Wyo., 1972. Grade control engr. Kerr McGee Uranium, Casper, Wyo., 1972-73; staff geologist Am. Nuclear Corp., Casper, 1973-80; petroleum geologist Flory & Assocs., Gillette, Wyo., 1980-81, Dever Exploration, Casper, 1981-83, High Summit Oil & Gas, Evans, Colo., 1983-84; cons. geologist InterMountain Cons., Casper, 1984—. Mem. Am. Assn. Petroleum Geologists, Soc. Econ. Geologists, Wyo. Geologist Assn. (field conf. asst. 1983), Rocy Mountain Assn. Geologists. Republican. Home: 1906 Bonnie Brae Casper WY 82601 Office: InterMountain Geologists Casper WY 82601

NICHOLSON, WILL FAUST, JR., bank holding company executive; b. Colorado Springs, Colo., Feb. 8, 1929; s. Will Faust and Gladys Olivia (Burns) N.; m. Shirley Ann Baker, Nov. 26, 1955; children: Ann Louise Nicholson Naughton, Will Faust III. S.B., M.I.T., 1950; M.B.A., U. Denver, 1956. Vice pres. Van Schaack & Co., Denver, 1954-66; partner N. G. Petry Constrn. Co., Denver, 1966-70; sr. v.p. Colo. Nat. Bankshares, Inc., Denver, 1970-75; pres. Colo. Nat. Bankshares, Inc., 1975—, chmn. bd., chief exec. officer, 1985—; dir. Pub. Service Co. Colo. Mem. Denver Urban Renewal Authority, 1958-59; mem. Denver Bd. Water Commrs., 1959-65, pres., 1964, 65; bd. dirs. Boys Clubs Denver, Nat. Western Stock Show; bd. mgrs. Presbyn. Denver Hosp. Served with USAF, 1950-53. Mem. Assn. Bank Holding Cos. (dir. 1979-87, exec. com. 1980-85, vice chmn. 1981-82, chmn. 1983-84), Colo. Golf Assn. (bd. govs. 1973—), U.S. Golf Assn. (exec. com. 1974-82, v.p. 1978, 79, pres. 1980, 81). Republican. Episcopalian. Clubs: Denver Country (Denver), University (Denver), Denver (Denver), Castle Pines Golf (Denver); University (N.Y.C.); Augusta Nat. Golf; Royal and Ancient Golf (St. Andrews, Scotland). Home: 30 Cherry St Denver CO 80220 Office: Colo Nat Bankshares PO Box 5168 TA Denver CO 80217

NICK, LEWIN, magician; b. London, Feb. 14, 1952; s. Owen Michael and Jessie Blythe (Pringle) L.; m. Susan Mitchell Garfield, Dec. 15, 1973; children: Natasha Alexandra, Katrina Elizabeth. BA, Guild Hall Sch. Music and Drama, 1970. Actor, magician various, 1970—. Author: (book) Sleight of Crime, 1975; appeared TV showsAmazing Stories, Trapper John M.D., Misfits of Science, Dynasty, Alfred Hitchcock Presents, 1988; appeared TV movie, The Gambler; comedian, magician nat. comedy club circuit Harrah's, Caesars Palace, Las Vegas, Nev., The Magic Castle, London. Anglican. Office: Nick Lewin Prodns Inc 13906 Ventura Blvd #156 Sherman Oaks CA 91423

NICKEL, SUSAN EARLENE, physical education educator, financial analyst; b. Fort Madison, Iowa, June 27, 1951; d. Earl Dean and Irma Ellen (Ivins) N. BE, Northeast Mo. State U., 1973. Phys. edn. tchr. Ft. Madison (Iowa) Sr. High. Sch., 1974-79; phys. edn. specialist Los Angeles Unified Schs., 1979—; fin. planner, then mgr. Martin Fin. Svcs., Marina Del Rey, Calif., 1986—. Bd. dirs. Connexxus Womens' Ctr., Los Angeles, 1985-87, profl. women's facilitator, 1984—; vol. facilitator Los Angeles Womens' Ctr., 1981-84; vol. Spl. Olympics, U.S. Assn. for Blind Athletes, Exceptional Games, Women's Wheelchair Basketball Assn., all Los Angeles. Mem. Los Angeles Adapted Phys. Edn. Assn. (bd. dirs.), Calif. Assn. Health, Phys. Edn., Recreation and Dance, Bus. and Profl. Alliance, Nat. Assn. Female Execs. Office: Martin Fin Svcs 13160 Mindanao Way Marina Del Rey CA 90292

NICOLAI, EUGENE RALPH, investments consultant; b. Renton, Wash., June 26, 1911; s. Eugene George and Josephine (Heidinger) N.; student U. Wash., 1929, Whitman Coll., 1929-30; B.A., U. Wash., 1934; postgrad. Am. U., 1942; M.A., George Washington U., 1965; m. Helen Margaret Manogue, June 5, 1935; 1 son, Paul Eugene. Editor, U. Wash. Daily, Seattle, 1934; asst. city editor, writer, nat. def. editor Seattle Times, 1934-41; writer Sta. KJR, Seattle, 1937-39; writer, editor, safety edn. officer Bur. Mines, Washington, 1941-45; news dir. Grand Coulee Dam and Columbia Basin Project, Washington, 1945-50; regional info. dir. Bur. Mines, Denver and Pitts., 1950-55, asst. chief mineral reports, Washington, 1955-61, news dir. office of oil and gas, 1956-57; sr. info. officer, later sr. public info. officer Office Sec. Interior, Washington, 1961-71, staff White House Nat. Conf. on Natural Beauty, spl. detail to White House, 1971, ret.; now public relations cons., tech. editor, writer. Formerly safety policy adviser Interior Dept.; com. mem. Internat. Cooperation Year, State Dept., 1971. With George Washington U. Alumni Found.; founder, mng. dir. Josephine Nature Preserve; pres. Media Assocs. Bd. dirs. Wash. State Council on Alcoholism; adviser Pierce Transit Authority, Pierce County Growth Mgmt., Pierce County Ethics Commn. Named Disting. Alumnus, recipient Penrose award, both Whitman Coll., 1979. Mem. Nature Conservancy, Wash. Environ. Council, Nat. Audubon Soc. (Am. Belgian Tervuren dist. rep.), Crook County (Oreg.) Hist. Soc., Washington State Hist. Soc., Emerald Shores Assn, Sigma Delta Chi, Pi Kappa Alpha. Presbyn. Clubs: George Washington U., Purdy (pres.). Lodge: Masons. Author: The Middle East Emergency Committee; editor: Fed. Conservation Yearbooks. Home: North 9809 Seminole Dr Spokane WA 99208

NICOLATUS, STEPHEN JON, financial consultant; b. Salt Lake City, June 6, 1950; s. George Stephen and Viola (Kerikas) N. BS in Polit. Sci., U. Utah, 1975; MS in Agril. Econ., U. Ariz., 1977. Rsch. assoc. U. Ariz., Tucson, 1975-77; rsch. lab. asst. Utah Cooperative Assn., CENEX, Salt Lake City, 1977; rsch. assoc. Frank K. Stuart & Assocs., Salt Lake City, 1977-81, v.p., 1981-89; v.p. Stuart, Nicolatus & Peterson, Salt Lake City, 1989—; econs. faculty U. Phoenix, Salt Lake City, 1985—, area chair econs., 1987—. With USAFR, 1968-74. Mem. Am. Econ. Assn., Inst. Bus. Appraisers, Wasatch Front Econ. Forum. Greek Orthodox. Home: 939 Donner Way 103 Salt Lake City UT 84108 Office: Frank K Stuart & Assocs 136 E South Temple 1530 Salt Lake City UT 84111

NIDA, JILL BAILEY, teacher; b. Redwood City, Calif., May 5, 1963; d. Kenneth Alvin and Linda Joy (Smith) Bailey; m. Frederick Robert Nida, June 29, 1984. Student, U. Calif., Davis, 1982-84; BA in Anthropology, San Jose State U., 1985, teaching credential, 1986. Tchr. elem. sch. Gilroy (Calif.) Unified Sch. Dist., 1987—, bilingual-Spanish transition tchr., 1987-88, program quality reviewer, 1989—; mem. sch. site coun. Rod Kelley Sch., Gilroy, 1988—. Mem. NEA, Gilroy Tchrs. Assn., Beyond War. Democrat. Home: 9292 El Caminito St Gilroy CA 95020

NIEDERHOFER, ROBERT JUDE, sales executive; b. Cortland, N.Y., Aug. 4, 1950; s. LaVern Carl and Elizabeth Ann (Kahl) N.; m. Gloria Jean Schaut, Aug. 4, 1973 (div. Apr., 1986); children: Amy Marie, John Jude; m. Traci Helene Blaser, Nov. 15, 1987. BS, Gannon U., 1972. Reg. v.p. Nat. Assn. the Remodeling Industry, Arlington, Va., 1985—. Mem. Nat. Assn. the Remodeling Industry (cert. remodeler, pres. Sacramento, Calif. chpt., 1988, 89). Office: Sauder Bldg Products 1607-B O'Donnelly Way Orange CA 92667

NIELSEN, BOJE TURIN, landscape architect; b. Copenhagen, Oct. 9, 1944; came to U.S., 1946; s. Poul and Grete Turin; m. Carol Nielsen, 1981; 1 child, Kelsey. AS, Hudson Valley Community Coll., 1964; BS, U. Mass., 1975, M Landscape Architecture, 1978. Engr. Vappi & Co., Cambridge, Mass., 1965-68; interior designer Scandinavia House, Manchester, Vt., 1968-74; landscape architect Rio Grande Nat. Forest, Monte Vista, Colo., 1977, Tonto Nat. Forest, Phoenix, 1978-80, Deerlodge Nat. Forest, Butte, Mont., 1980—; chmn. bd. dirs. Urban Forest, Silver Bow County. Prin. works include Sheepshead Camp for Handicapped, 1982 (several awards), Georgetown Lake Recreation Area, I-15 Interstate Hwy. (U.S.D.A. cert. of merit), Red River Hist. Ranger Sta., Idaho. Recipient Green Leaf award Internat. Arborculture Soc., 1983. Mem. Am. Soc. Landscape Architects (chpt. bd. dirs. 1982—), Vintage D'Fenders (sec. 1985—), Butte C. of C. (com. chmn. 1982-84, cons. 1982, Arborculture Soc. award 1983). Lodge: Masons. Home: 1102 Waukesha Box 107 Butte MT 59703-0107 Office: Deerlodge Nat Forest 400 Main St Box 400 Butte MT 59073-0400

NIELSEN, BRANDOM KENT, pension fund administrator; b. Stockton, Calif., May 8, 1942; s. Roy Gilbert and Lucinda (Kuecks) N.; m. Susan Karen Rhodes, June 23, 1964; children: Erik Rhodes, Clover Elizabeth. BA, U. Wash., 1964. CLU. Various positions to regional group mgr. Prudential Ins. Co., L.A. and Seattle, 1964-74; various positions to dir. group pensions Prudential Ins. Co., Seattle and San Francisco, 1974-81; v.p. Frank Russell Trust Co., Tacoma, Wash., 1981-85; sr. v.p. Frank Russell Trust Co., Tacoma, 1985—. Vice chmn. devel. fund bd., U. Wash., Seattle. Mem. We. Pension Conf., U. Wash. Alumni Assn., Overlak Golf and Country Club. Republican. Presbyterian. Office: Frank Russell Trust Co 909 A St Tacoma WA 98402

NIELSEN, DONALD RODNEY, soil and water science educator; b. Phoenix, Oct. 10, 1931; s. Irven Roy and Irma Evelyn (Chase) N.; m. Joanne Joyce Locke, Sept. 26, 1953; children: Cynthia, Pamela, Barbara, Wayne, David. BS, U. Ariz., 1953, MS, 1954; PhD, Iowa State U., 1958; DSc (hon.), Ghent (Belgium) State U., 1986. Asst. prof. soil and water sci. U. Calif., Davis, 1958-63, assoc. prof., 1963-68, prof., 1968, dir. Kearney Found. of Soil Sci., 1970-75, assoc. dean, 1970-80, dir. Food Protection and Toxicology Ctr., 1974-75, chmn. dept. land, air and water resources, 1975-77, prof., 1968—, exec. assoc. dean Coll. Agrl. Environ. Scis., 1986-89, chmn. dept. agronomy and range sci., 1989—; cons. corps. and govtl. agys. Editor Nitrogen in the Environment; co-editor Water Resources Research, 1985-88; mem. editorial bd. Irrigation Sci., Jour. Soil Sci., Soil Sci., Outlook In Agrl., Soil and Tillage Research, contbr. articles to profl. jours. NSF fellow, 1965-66. Fellow Am. Geophys. Union, Soil Sci. Soc. Am. (pres. 1983-84), Am. Soc. Agronomy; mem. Sigma Xi, Phi Kappa Phi, Gamma Sigma Delta, Phi Lambda Upsilon, Alpha Zeta. Democrat. Home: 1004 Pine Ln Davis CA 95616 Office: U Calif/Dept Land Air & Water Resources Veihmeyer Hall Davis CA 95616 also: U Calif Dept Agronomy and Range Sci Hunt Hall Davis CA 95616

NIELSEN, JAMES WILEY, state senator; b. Fresno, Calif., July 31, 1944; s. Woodrow E. and Geraldine P. (Hudson) N.; B.S. in Agribus., Fresno State Coll.; m. Marilyn Nielsen; children: Prima, Brandi, Kelly, Chris. Farm mgr.; farmer; mem. Calif. Senate, minority leader, 1983-87; involved in library funding, edn. and welfare reform, econ. devel., rural aid, coll. support throughout Calif., 1983—. Chmn. Sacramento Valley Water Task Force. Named Agrl. Spokesman of Year, 1976; Legislator of Yr., Calif. Rifle and Pistol Assn., 1982, Calif. Bus. Edn. Assn., 1982, Calif. Ind. Producers Assn., 1983; Agrl. Leadership Program fellow, 1975-76. Mem. Council State Legislators, Farm Bur., Calif. Welfare Fraud Investigators Assn. (life mem.), Native Sons Golden West. Republican. Baptist. Home: 4990 Country Club Dr Rohnert Park CA 94928 Office: Office of the State Senate State Capitol Sacramento CA 95814

NIELSEN, JOHN DAVID, credit company executive; b. Pasadena, Calif., May 12, 1955; s. John Frances and Aileen Mae (Young) N. BA with distinction, Occidental Coll., 1977. Officer First Hawaiian Bank, Honolulu, 1977-86; br. mgr. officer First Hawaiian Credit Corp., Honolulu, 1986—. Pres. Hawaii Com. of U.S. Water Polo, Honolulu, 1981—. Mem. Am. Inst. Banking, Omicron Delta Epsilon. Home: 3200 Diamond Head Rd Honolulu HI 96815 Office: 4211 Waialae Ave Ste 107 Honolulu HI 96816

NIELSEN, LAURA CHRISTINE, investment company executive; b. Fairbanks, Alaska, Nov. 2, 1960; d. Raymond Elzworth Nielsen and Jacqueline Ann Marie (Harmon) Butler. Diploma in sci. and bus., Coll. of Marin, 1983; student, U. Calif., Berkeley, 1984. Office mgr. Suzanne Sammis Personal Mgmt. Co., Corte Madera, Calif., 1981-83; mktg. asst. pub. rels. dept. Investment Mortgage Internat., San Francisco, 1983-84; loan funder/closer 1st Calif. Mortgage Co., San Rafael; regional mgr. Desert Bay Investment Corp., Corte Madera, 1987—; office mgr. Smith-Thomas Investment Svcs., Inc., Corte Madera, 1987—; cons. real-corp. mortgage banking, San Francisco, 1985-87, Dan Dominguez Hi-Tech Leasing Co., Sausalito, Calif., 1987-89. Vol. pub. rels. com. Just Say No, 1987—, March of Dimes, 1988—, Just Say No to Drugs, Cystic Fibrosis Found., Oakland Athletics. Recipient telecommunications award Stanford U. Med. Ctr. Mem. Mensa. Republican. Roman Catholic. Home: PO Box 754 Tiburon CA 94920 Office: Smith-Thomas Investment Svcs Inc 770 Tamalpais Dr Ste #206 Corte Madera CA 94925

NIELSEN, STUART DEE, chemist; b. Green River, Wyo., Oct. 26, 1932; s. Julian Woodruff and Reva May (Stewart) N.; m. Lila Ellen Larett, June 10, 1954; children: Laura May, Martha Ellen, Karl Allen, Jennifer Marie, Isabelle Anne. BS, U. Wyo., 1954; PhD, U. Wash., 1962. Research chemist Rohm & Haas Co., Phila., 1962-66; research scientist Gen. Tire & Rubber Co., Akron, Ohio, 1966-78; chemist Los Alamos (N.Mex.) Nat. Lab., 1978—. Patentee in field. Scoutmaster Boy Scouts Am., Akron, 1970-78. Served with U.S. Army, 1954-56. Allied Chem. Co. fellow, 1960. Mem. Am. Chem. Soc., Soc. Applied Spectroscopy, Am. Indsl. Hygiene Assn., Sigma Xi. Mormon. Home: 114 Sherwood Blvd Los Alamos NM 87544 Office: Los Alamos Nat Lab Group HSE-9 MS K484 Los Alamos NM 87545

NIELSON, HOWARD CURTIS, congressman, educator; b. Richfield, Utah, Sept. 12, 1924; s. Herman Taylor and Zula May (Curtis) N.; m. Julia Adams, June 18, 1948; children: Noreen (Mrs. Stephen Astin), Elaine (Mrs. Stanley Taylor), John, Mary Lee (Mrs. Paul Jackson), James, Jean (Mrs. Clay Cundick), Howard Curtis. B.S. in Math, U. Utah, 1947; M.S. in Math, U. Oreg., 1949; M.B.A., Stanford U., 1956, Ph.D. in Bus. Adminstrn. and Statistics, 1958. Statistician C & H Sugar Refining Corp., 1949-51; research economist and statistician Stanford Research Inst., 1951-57; mem. faculty Brigham Young U., Provo, Utah, 1957-82; prof. statistics Brigham Young U., 1961-82, chmn. dept., 1960-63; sr. devel. engr. Hercules, Inc., 1960-66; dir. Center for Bus. and Econ. Research, 1971-72; sr. statistician, acting field mgr. C-E-I-R, Inc., 1963-64, mgr., cons., 1964-65; prin. scientist GCA Corp., 1965-67; dir. econ. research Eyring Research Inst., 1974-75; assoc. commr. higher edn. State of Utah, 1976-79; mem. 98th-101st Congresses from 3d dist. Utah; econ. adviser Kingdom of Jordan, Ford Found., 1970-71; prof. Am. U., Beirut, 1970; adj. prof. U. Utah, 1972-76. Author: The Efficiency of Certain Truncated Order Statistics in Estimating the Mean of Various Distributions, 1949, Population Trends in the United States Through 1975, 1955, The Hows and Whys of Statistics, 1963, Experimental Designs Used in industry, 1965, Membership Growth of the Church of Jesus Christ of Latter Day Saints, 1957, 67, 71, 75, 78, Evaluation of the Seven Year Plan for Economic Development in Jordan, 1971, Economic Analysis of Fiji, Tonga, Western and Am. Samoa, 1972; co-author: The Newsprint Situation in the Western Region of North America, 1952, America's Demand for Wood, 1954, also reports. Mem. Utah Gov.'s Econ. Research Adv. Council, 1967-72; Dir. bur. ch. studies Ch. of Jesus Christ of Latter-day Saints, 1958-63; research dir. Utah Republican Party, 1967-68; mem. Utah Ho. Reps., 1967-75, majority leader, 1969-71, speaker, 1973-75, mem. legis. budget-audit com., 1967-73, chmn., 1971-73, chmn. legis. council, 1973-75; mem. Utah Council Sci. and Tech., 1974-76; chmn. Utah County Rep. Com., 1979-81. Mem. Am. Statis. Assn. (pres. Utah 1964-65, nat. council 1967-70), Sci. Research Soc. Am., Order of Artus, Phi Beta Kappa, Sigma Xi, Pi Mu Epsilon, Sigma Pi Sigma, Phi Kappa Phi. Office: US Ho Reps 1122 Longworth Office Bldg Washington DC 20515

NIELSON, ROBERT LOUIS, physician, educator; b. Livingston, Mont., Feb. 22, 1925; s. Louis H. and Helen Barbara (Hoch) N.; m. Luella T. Rouse, Aug. 15, 1951 (div. 1978); children: Niels A., Peter C., John R., Karn L.; m. Barbara Gail Gilpatrick, May 26, 1979. Student, Mont. State U., Missoula, 1947; MD, Harvard U., 1951. Diplomate Am. Bd. Med. Examiners, Am. Bd. Internal Med., Am. Bd. Endocrinology. Intern King County Hosp., Seattle, 1951-52, resident in medicine, 1952-54; resident in medicine Seattle Vets. Hosp., Seattle, 1952-53; fellowship in endocrinology Mass. Gen. Hosp., Boston, 1954-56; instr. in medicine U. Wash., 1956-57, clin. asst. prof. of medicine, 1957-68, clin. assoc. prof., 1968-76, clin. prof., 1976—; staff physician Va. Mason Hosp., Seattle, 1957-87; med. dir. Med. and Health Edn. Assoc., Bellevue, Wash., 1987—; cons. in endocrinology Children's Orthopedic Hosp., Seattle, King County Hosp., Seattle; mem. sect. of endocrinology and metabolism Mason Clinic, Seattle, 1957--87, head sect., 1967-82. Contbr. articles to profl. jours. such as New Eng. Jour. Med. Bd. dirs. Am. Diabetes Assn., 1971-77, affiliate, 1969—, pres. 1972-74, 79-81, Va. Mason Research Ctr., 1981-84, Planned Parenthood, Seattle-King County; pres. Med. and Health Edn. Assn., 1977-87, Diabetic Trust Fund., Wash. Citizens for Abortion Choice; chmn. Am. Diabetes Assn., Western Regional Coordinating Group. 1980-82; med. dir. YMCA, Seattle, 1964-82, mem. camping com. Fellow Am. Coll. Physicians; mem. King County Med. Soc., Wash. State Med. Soc., AMA, Endocrine Soc., Am. Thyroid Assn., No. Pacific Soc. Internal Medicine. Home: 6842 29 St NE Seattle WA 98115 Office: Med and Health Edn Assn 10037 13 St NE Bellevue WA 98004

NIELSON, THEO GILBERT, law enforcement official, university official; b. Roosevelt, Utah, June 29, 1938; s. John Gilbert and Mazie (Alexander) N.; m. Martha Perez, May 22, 1961; children: Lucille Marie, Sherry Lou, Mark Andrew, Rex Alexander, Theo Gilbert Jr., Cristal Ina, Gregory Angus, Mazie Leah, Rosanna Alma. Grad., FBI Nat. Acad., 1970; BA, Ariz. State U., 1975, MS, 1977. Officer Univ. Police, Ariz. State U., Tempe, 1963-67, sgt., 1967-70, lt., 1970-79; chief police Douglas (Ariz.) Police Dept., 1979-82; div. adminstr. Ariz. Criminal Intelligence Systems Agy., Tucson, 1982-84; dir. campus safety and security No. Ariz. U., Flagstaff, 1984—. Mem. Am. Soc. for Indsl. Security (chmn. No. Ariz. chpt. 1987), Internat. Assn. Chiefs Police, Internat. Assn. Campus Law Enforcement Adminstrs., Ariz. Assn. Campus Law Enforcement (pres. 1989—). Republican. Mormon. Home: 2520 E Joshua Ln Flagstaff AZ 86004 Office: No Ariz U PO Box 5602 Flagstaff AZ 86011

NIEMAN, GLENDA LEAH, school counselor; b. Omaha, Nov. 16, 1944; d. Glenn Bert and Florence Elizabeth (Lee) N.; m. Carl Richard Johns, Nov. 21, 1973 (div. June 1976). AA, Phoenix Coll., 1964; BEd, No. Ariz. U., 1967; MEd, Ariz. State U., 1978; cert., Basic Inst. Reality Therapy, Tempe, Ariz., 1989. Cert. tchr., Ariz. Recreation leader Maricopa County Parks and Recreation Dept., Phoenix and Chandler, Ariz., 1963-68; residential, day camp dir. Phoenix YWCA, 1965-77; physical edn. tchr. Chandler Unifed Schs., 1967-77; counselor Chandler Jr. High, 1977-88; pvt. practice Chandler, 1988—; counselor Andersen Jr. High, Chandler, 1988—; cons. East Valley Charter Hosp., Chandler, 1988—; group facilitator, Anderson Jr. High, 1988—, Chandler Jr. High Sch., 1977-88; cons. workshops Chandler YMCA, 1988—. Artist numerous assn. logos. Bd. mgmt. Chandler Young Men's Christian Assn., 1981—; credit com. San Tan Credit Union, Chandler, 1979—. Recipient Svc. award, Women's Athlete and Recreation Assn., Phoenix, 1964. Mem. NEA, Ariz. Edn. Assn., Chandler Edn. Assn., Delta Psi Kappa, Delta Kappa Gamma. Baptist. Home: 2004 W Erie Chandler AZ 85224 Office: Andersen Jr High Sch 1255 N Dobson Rd Chandler AZ 85224

NIEMI, JANICE, state legislator, lawyer; b. Flint, Mich., Sept. 18, 1928; d. Richard Jesse and Norma (Bell) Bailey; m. Preston Niemi, Feb. 4, 1953 (divorced 1987); children—Ries, Patricia. B.A., U. Wash., 1950, LL.B., 1967; postgrad. U. Mich., 1950-52; cert. Hague Acad. Internat. Law, Netherlands, 1954. Bar: Wash. 1968. Assoc. firm Powell, Livengood, Dunlap & Silverdale, Kirkland, Wash., 1968; staff atty. Legal Service Ctr., Seattle, 1968-70; judge Seattle Dist. Ct., 1971-72, King County Superior Ct., Seattle, 1973-78; acting gen. counsel, dep. gen. counsel SBA, Washington, 1979-81; mem. Wash. State Ho. of Reps., Olympia, 1983-87, chmn. com. on state govt., 1984; mem. Wash. State Senate, 1987—; sole practice, Seattle, 1981—; mem. White House Fellows Regional Selection Panel, Seattle, 1974-77, chmn., 1976, 77; incorporator Sound Savs. & Loan, Seattle, 1975. Bd. dirs. Allied Arts, Seattle, 1971—, Ctr. Contemporary Art, Seattle, 1981-83, Women's Network, Seattle, 1981-84, Pub. Defender Assn., Seattle, 1982-84; bd. visitors dept. psychology U. Wash., Seattle, 1983-87, bd. visitors dept sociology, 1988— . Named Woman of Yr. in Law, Past Pres.'s Assn., Seattle, 1971; Woman of Yr., Matrix Table, Seattle, 1973, Capitol Hill Bus. and Profl. Women, 1975. Mem. Wash. State Bar Assn., Wash. Women Lawyers. Democrat. Office: 226 Summit Ave E Seattle WA 98102

NIEMI, ROBERT JOHN, bank operations manager; b. Lakeheath, Suffolk, Eng., Feb. 27, 1961; came to U.S., 1964; s. Robert Edward and Mary Louise (Lippert) N.; m. Paula MaryAnn Wright, Sept. 19, 1981. Student, Lorretto Heights Coll., 1979. Ops. mgr. First Colo. Bank & Trust, Denver, 1980-86, Littleton (Colo.) Nat. Bank, 1986—. Mem. Littleton Jaycees (treas. 1988, v.p. 1989, Presdl. awd. of honor 1988, Jaycee of Yr. 1988). Avocations: Russian history, piano. Office: Littleton Nat Bank 5734 S Prince St Littleton CO 80120

NIERENBERG, NORMAN, urban land economist, state official; b. Chgo., May 8, 1919; s. Isadore Isaac and Sadie Sarah (Dorfman) N.; m. Nanette Joyce Fortgang, Feb. 9, 1950; children: Andrew Paul, Claudia Robin. AA, U. Chgo., 1939; AB, Calif. State Coll., L.A., 1952; MA, U. So. Calif., 1956. Lic. real estate broker, Calif.; cert. supr. and coll. instr., Calif. Right-of-way agt. Calif. Dept. Transp., L.A., 1951-61, 85-88; sr. agt. Calif. Dept. Transp., San Francisco, 1988—; instr. UCLA, 1960-61, 67-75, 81-85; coord. dept. real estate div. continuing edn. U. Calif., Berkeley, 1961-64; coord. econ. benefits study Salton Sea Calif. Dept. Water Resources, L.A., 1967-68; regional economist L.A. dist. CE, 1970-75, chief economist, 1981-85; regional economist Bd. Engrs. for Rivers and Harbors, Ft. Belvoir, Va., 1975-81; chief economist Faculty Resource Oakland Project, Ford Found., U. Calif., Berkeley, 1962-64; project reviewer EPA, Washington, 1972-73. Editor: History of 82d Fighter Control Squadron, 1945; also contbr. articles to Way Nat. Mag., 1952-55. 1st lt. USAAF, 1942-46, ETO, lt. col. USAFR ret. Mem. NEA, Am. Econ. Assn., Calif. Tchrs. Assn., Calif. Assn. Real Estate Tchrs. (bd. dirs. 1962), L.A. Coll. Tchrs. Assn., Res. Officers Assn., Ret. Officers Assn., Omicron Delta Epsilon. Democrat. Jewish.

NIERENBERG, WILLIAM AARON, oceanography educator; b. N.Y.C., Feb. 13, 1919; s. Joseph and Minnie (Drucker) N.; m. Edith Meyerson, Nov. 21, 1941; children—Victoria Jean (Mrs. Tschinkel), Nicolas Clarke Eugene. Aaron Naumberg scholar, U. Paris, 1937-38; B.S., CCNY, 1939; M.A., Columbia U., 1942, Ph.D. (NRC predoctoral fellow), 1947. Tutor CCNY, 1939-42; sect. leader Manhattan Project, 1942-45; instr. physics Columbia U., 1946-48; asst. prof. physics U. Mich., 1948-50; assoc. prof. physics U. Calif. at Berkeley, 1950-53, prof., 1954-65; dir. Scripps Instn. Oceanography, 1965-86, dir. emeritus, 1986—; vice chancellor for marine scis. U. Calif. at San Diego, 1969-86; dir. Hudson Labs., Columbia, 1953-54; assoc. prof. U. Paris, 1960-62; asst. sec. gen. NATO for sci. affairs, 1960-62; spl. cons. Exec. Office Pres., 1958-60; sr. cons. White House Office Sci. and Tech. Policy, 1976-78. Contbr. papers to profl. jours. E.O. Lawrence lectr. Nat. Acad. Sci., 1958, Miller Found. fellow, 1957-59, Sloan Found. fellow, 1958, Fulbright fellow, 1960-61; mem. U.S. Nat. Commn. UNESCO, 1964-68, Calif. Adv. Com. on Marine and Coastal Resources, 1967-71; adviser-at-large U.S. Dept. State, 1968—; mem. Nat. Sci. Bd., 1972-78, 82-88, cons., 1988—; chmn. USNC/PSA, NRC, 1988—; mem. Nat. Adv. Com. on Oceans and Atmosphere, 1971-77, chmn., 1971-75; mem. sci. and tech. adv. Council Calif. Assembly; mem. adv. council NASA, 1978-83, chmn. adv. council, 1978-82; mem. council Nat. Acad. Scis., 1979—. NATO Sr. Sci. fellow, 1969; Decorated officer Nat. Order of Merit France; recipient Golden Dolphin award Assn. Artistico Letteraria Internazionale, Disting. Pub. Service medal NASA, 1982, Delmer S. Fahrney medal The Franklin Inst., 1987, Compass award Marine Tech. Soc., 1975. Fellow Am. Phys. Soc. (council, sec. Pacific Coast sect. 1955-64); mem. Am. Acad. Arts and Scis., Nat. Acad. Engring., Nat. Acad. Scis., Am. Philos. Soc., Am. Assn. Naval Architects, Navy League, Fgn. Policy Assn. (mem. nat. council), Sigma Xi (pres. 1981-82, Proctor prize, 1977). Club: Cosmos. Home: PO Box 8949 La Jolla CA 92038-8949 Office: U Calif Scripps Instn Oceanography A-021 La Jolla CA 92093

NIES, ALAN SHEFFER, pharmacology educator; b. Orange, Calif., Sept. 30, 1937; s. Arthur J. and Mary Dora (Sheffer) N.; m. Sally K. Goode; children: Lorrie Kathyrn, Craig Alan. BS, Stanford U., 1959; MD, Harvard Med. Sch., 1963. Intern King County Hosp., Seattle, 1963-64; resident U. Wash. Hosp., Seattle, 1964-66; fellow in clin. pharmacology Cardiovascular Research Inst. U. Calif., San Francisco, 1966-68; chief. clin. pharmacology Walter Reed Army Inst. Research, Washington, 1968-70; asst. prof. medicine and pharmacology Vanderbilt U. Sch. Medicine, Nashville, 1970-72, assoc. prof., 1972-76, prof., 1976; prof. pharmacology, head div. clin. pharmacology U. Colo., Denver, 1977—. Contbr. articles to numerous profl. jours. Served to major U.S. Army, 1968-70. Recipient Clin. Pharmacology award Burroughs Wellcome Fund, 1975. Mem. ACP, Am. Soc. Clin. Investigation, Assn. Am. Physicians, Am. Soc. Pharmacology and Exptl. Therapeutics, Western Assn. Physicians (sec., treas. 1983-86), Am. Soc. Clin. Pharmacology and Therapeutics (Rawls-Palmer Progress in Medicine award 1985). Home: 6146 S Fulton St Englewood CO 80111 Office: U Colo Sch Medicine Health Scis Ctr Dept Medicine Box C-237 Denver CO 80262

NIES, BOYD ARTHUR, hematologist, oncologist; b. Orange, Calif., Jan. 12, 1935; s. Arthur J. and Mary Dora (Sheffer) N.; m. Helen May Salter, July 28, 1957; children: Nancy, Linda, Boyd Jr. AB, Stanford U., 1956, MD, 1959. Diplomate Am. Bd. Internal Medicine, Am. Bd. Internal Medicine: Hematology, Med. Oncology. Intern UCLA, 1959-60, asst. resident, 1960-61; assoc. resident Wadsworth VA Hosp., L.A., 1961-62; clin. assoc. Nat. Cancer Inst., Bethesda, Md., 1962-64; fellow in hematology Stanford U., Palo Alto, Calif., 1964-65; pvt. practice internal medicine and hematology Redlands, Calif., 1965-68; pvt. practice hematology and med. oncology San Francisco, 1968—. Contbr. articles to profl. jours. Bd. dirs. First United Meth. Ch., Redlands, 1985-88, St. Bernardine Hosp., San Bernardino, Calif., 1975-77; bd. dirs. Riverside-San Bernardino Counties Blood Bank, 1984—, pres., 1988—. Surgeon USPHS, 1962-64. Fellow ACP; mem. AMA, Am. Soc. Internal Medicine, Am. Soc. Hematology, Am. Soc. Clin. Oncology, Internat. Soc. Hematology, Redlands Country Club, Redlands Swim and Tennis Club. Republican. Methodist. Home: 645 E Mariposa Dr Redlands CA 92373 Office: Inland Hematology Oncology Med Group Inc 399 E Highland Ave #201 San Bernardino CA 92404

NIESLUCHOWSKI, WITOLD S., cardiovascular and thoracic surgeon; b. Warsaw, Poland, Mar. 2, 1944; came to U.S., 1975; s. Stanislaw Leon and Izabela Anna (Swierczynska) N.; m. Bonnie Jean Thomas, Apr. 15, 1978; children: Jason Brian, Christopher Thomas, Megan Jean, Jennifer Anne. MD, Warsaw Med. Sch., 1967. With Akademicki Zwiazek Sportowy, Warsaw, 1961-75; cardiovascular surgeon Oxnard (Calif.) Hosp., 1975—. Mem. Oxnard Humanitarians, 1987—; bd. dirs. Am. Heart Assn., Camarillo, Calif., 1988—. Fellow ACS, Am. Coll. Cardiologists; mem. Soc. for Thoracic Surgeons. Club: Cabrillo Tennis (Camarillo). Office: 435 S D St #200 Oxnard CA 93030

NIGHTINGALE, R. LEE, federal agency administrator; b. Wichita, Kans., Dec. 15, 1954; d. L.D. and Barbara Louise (McClain) Figgins; m. William Boyd III, Dec. 30, 1982; 1 child, Theodore Jacob. BA, U. Kans., 1977.

Hydrologic technician U.S. Geol. Survey, Lawrence, Kans., 1975-78; personnel clk. U.S. Geol. Survey, Denver, 1978-79, position class specialist, 1979-80; personnel mgmt. specialist Office of Personnel Mgmt., Denver, 1980-81; personnel officer USDA Forest Service, Glenwood Springs, Colo., 1981-83; adminstrv. officer USDA Forest Service, Nemo, S.D., 1983-87, Bighorn Nat. Forest, Sheridan, Wyo., 1987-88, Tongass Nat. Forest, Ketchikan, Alaska, 1989—; chmn. exec. com. Regional Adminstrv. Team, 1987-88. Rep. Pres. Carters Adv. Com. on the Status of Women, Denver, 1980, Civil Rights Commn., Custer, S.D., 1986-87. Named one of Outstanding Young Women in Am., Jaycees, 1983, 87. Mem. Am. Soc. of Personnel Adminstrn. (treas. 1975-76), Bus. and Profl. Women (dir. young career woman prog. 1984-85, Young Career Women award for Western Colo. 1983), Fed. Employed Women (sec. 1980-81), Epsilon Sigma Alpha (dir. pub. relations 1982-83), Alpha Delta Pi. Democrat. Presbyterian.

NIGL, ALFRED JAMES, psychologist, author; b. Oshkosh, Wis., July 30, 1949; s. Alfred Joseph and Marion Jane (Roberts) N.; m. Terri S. Abbott, Feb. 19, 1982; children: William Scott, Geoffrey Alan, Brandon Abbott. BA in Psychology, U. Wis., 1971; MA in Clin. Psychology, U. Cin., 1973, PhD in Clin. Psychology, 1975. Diplomate Am. Acad. Behavioral Medicine; cert. Biofeedback Certification Inst. Am. Lic. psychologist, Wis., Calif. Clin. intern or grad. trainee Cin. Gen. Hosp., 1971, Rollman Psychiat. Clinic, Cin., 1971, U. Cin. Univ. Counseling Ctr., 1971, 73, U. Cin. Med. Ctr. Cen. Psychiat. Clinic, 1972, Cin. Ctr. Developmental Disorders, 1973-75, U. Cin. Crises Intervention Clinic, 1973-75, U. Cin. mental health program, 1974-75; acting dir. tng. and research, mental health program U. Cin. Student Health Program, 1974-75; cons. staff psychologist Psychol. and Mgmt. Cons. Services, S.C., Milw., 1975-76; cons. First Western Med. Group, So. Calif., 1986—, Sci. Trading Gmbh, Frankfurt, Fed. Republic Germany, 1981—; pres. Milw. Devel. Ctr., 1975-78; chief psychologist Jackson Psychiat. Ctr., Milw., 1978-80; dir. child and adolescent services Oxnard (Calif.) Mental Health Ctr., 1980-81; cons., dir. biofeedback Kaiser-Permanente Healthwise, 1982-83; dir. rehab. psychology Grossmont Dist. Hosp., 1983-85; pvt. practice psychology, 1985—; cons. Calif. Regional Ctrs. for Developmentally Disabled; staff psychologist Luth. Hosp. Milw., 1978-70, dept. psychiatry Waukesha Meml. Hosp., 1978-80; dir. biofeedback, family practice residency program Waukesha Meml. Hosp. affiliated with Med. Coll. Wis., 1980; adj. clin. prof. Grad. Sch. Pub. Health, San Diego State U., 1983—; pres. Biofeedback Soc. Wis., 1979-80. Bd. dirs. Big Bros./Big Sisters, Ventura County, Calif., 1981-82, Ventura County Rape Crisis Ctr., 1982. U. Cin. Gradn. sch. Council research grantee, 1974; Am. Psychol. Assn. Overseas travel grantee, 1982. Mem. Am. Acad. Behavioral Medicine, AAAS, Am. Psychol. Assn., N.Y. Acad. Scis., Acad. Psychosomatic Medicine, Biofeedback Soc. Am. (rep. to Council State Biofeedback Socs. 1980), Internat. Assn. Study of Pain, Ventura County Psychol. Assn. (bd. dirs. 1982-83). Author: (with Fischer-Williams and Sovine) A Textbook of Biological Feedback, 1981, revised 1986, The Development of Children's Understanding of Spatial Relations, vol. 62 of European Univ. Studies-Psychology, 1981, Biofeedback and Behavioral Strategies in Pain Treatment, 1984; research, publs. in field. Office: 1662 E Main St Ste 216 El Cajon CA 92021

NIJENHUIS, ALBERT, mathematician, educator; b. Eindhoven, Netherlands, Nov. 21, 1926; came to U.S., 1952, naturalized, 1959; s. Hendrik and Lijdia (Koornneef) N.; m. Marianne Dannhauser, Aug. 14, 1955; children: Erika, Karin, Sabien, Alaine. Candidaat, U. Amsterdam, Netherlands, 1947, Doctorandus, 1950, Doctor cum laude, 1952. Assoc. Math. Ctr., Amsterdam, Netherlands, 1951-52; asst. Inst. Advanced Study, Amsterdam, Netherlands, 1955; mem. Inst. Advanced Study, Amsterdam, 1953-55, 61-62; instr., rsch. assoc. U. Chgo., 1955-56; faculty U. Wash., Seattle, 1956-63, prof., 1961-63, affiliate prof., 1988—; prof. math. U. Pa., Phila., 1963-87, prof. emeritus, 1987—; Fulbright lectr. U. Amsterdam, 1963-64; vis. prof. U. Geneva, Switzerland, 1967-68, Dartmouth Coll., 1977-78; researcher and author publs. on subjects including differential geometry, deformation theory in algebra, combinatorics, especially tensors, holonomy groups, graded lie algebras, algorithms. Co-author: Combinatorial Algorithms, 1975, 78; editor: Jour. Algorithms. Postdoctoral fellow Princeton, 1952-53; Fulbright grantee, 1952-53, 63-64; Guggenheim fellow, 1961-62. Mem. Am. Math. Soc., Math. Assn. Am., Netherlands Math. Soc., Assn. for Computing Machinery, AAUP, Royal Netherlands Acad. Scis. (corr.). Office: U Wash Dept Math G N-50 Seattle WA 98195

NIJENHUIS, ALBERT, mathematics educator; b. Eindhoven, The Netherlands, Nov. 21, 1926; came to U.S., 1952; s. Hendrik and Lijdia (Koornneef) N.; m. Marianne Dannhauser, Aug. 14, 1955; children: Erika, Karin, Sabien, Alaine. Candidaat, U. Amsterdam, 1947, Doctorandus cum laude, 1950, Dr cum laude, 1952. Sci. assoc. Math. Ctr., Amsterdam, The Netherlands, 1951-52; asst. prof. math. U. Wash., Seattle, 1956-58, assoc. prof., 1958-61, prof., 1961-63, affiliate prof., 1988—; prof. math. U. Pa., Phila., 1963-87, prof. emeritus, 1987—; mem. Inst. for Advanced Study, Princeton, N.J., 1953-55, 61-62, asst.; vis. prof. U. Amsterdam, 1963-64, U. Geneva, 1967-68, Dartmouth Coll., Hanover, N.H., 1977-78; investigator Office Naval Rsch., Seattle, 1958-63, NSF, Phila., 1964-72. Author: Combinatorial Algorithms, 1975, 2d edit., 1978; contbr. numerous articles to math. jours. Fulbright grantee, 1952-53, 63-64; Guggenheim fellow, 1961-62. Mem. Am. Math. Soc. (life), Math. Assn. Am. (life), Royal Netherlands Acad. Scis. (corr.), Netherlands Math. Soc. Home: 13727 41st Ave NE Seattle WA 98125 Office: U Wash Dept Math GN-50 Seattle WA 98195

NILES, GEDDES LEROY, private investigator; b. Haines, Alaska, Oct. 31, 1926; s. Geddes William and Gladys Bell (McCormack) N.; m. Aline Terii Tehei, June 17, 1960; children: Diana Mareva Niles-Hansen, Stephen Lloyd Teva. BA, U. Calif., Berkeley, 1949. Investigator and hearing officer U.S. Civil Service Commn., San Francisco, 1955-62, Honolulu, 1962-78; pres. Niles Realty Ltd., Honolulu, 1979—; dir. The Niles Agy., Honolulu, 1983—. Mem. Neighborhood Bd., Kailua, Hawaii, 1979-80. Club: Iaorana Tahiti (Honolulu) (treas. 1985—). Office: 350 Ward Ave Suite 106 Honolulu HI 96814

NILLES, JOHN MATHIAS (JACK NILLES), futurist; b. Evanston, Ill., Aug. 25, 1932; s. Elmer Edward and Hazel Evelyn (Wickum) N.; m. Laila Padorr, July 8, 1957. BA magna cum laude, Lawrence Coll., 1954; MS in Engring., U. Calif., Los Angeles, 1964. Sr. engr. Raytheon Mfg. Co., Santa Barbara, Calif., 1956-58; section head. Ramo-Woodridge Corp., Los Angeles, 1958-59; project engr. Space Technology Lab., Los Angeles, 1960; dir. The Aerospace Corp., Los Angeles, 1961-67; sr. systems engr. TRW Systems, Los Angeles, 1967-69; assoc. group dir. The Aerospace Corp., Los Angeles, 1965-72; dir. interdisciplinary programs U. So. Calif., Los Angeles, 1972-81, dir. info. technology program, 1981-89; pres. JALA Assocs. Inc., Los Angeles, 1980—; dir., treas. Technology Transfer Soc., Los Angeles, 1975-80. Author: The Telecommunications Transportation Tradeoff, 1976, Exploring the World of the Personal Computer, 1982, Micros and Modem, 1983. Capt. USAF, 1954-56. Recipient Rod Rose award Soc. Research Adminstrators, 1976. mem. Assn. For Computing Machinery, IEEE Computer Soc., Inst. Mgmt. Sciences, Am. Assn. for the Advancement Science, World Future Soc., Calif. Yacht. Office: JALA Assocs Inc 971 Stonehill Ln Los Angeles CA 90049-4241

NINOS, NICHOLAS PETER, military officer, physician; b. Chgo., May 11, 1936; s. Peter Spiros and Ann (Lesczynsky) N.; m. Joyce Jean Brewer, Nov. 22, 1967; 1 child, Cynthia Suzanne. BA in Art, Bradley U., 1958, BS in Chemistry, 1959; MD, U. Ill., Chgo., 1963. Diplomate Am. Bd. Internal Med., Am. Bd. Cardiology, Am. Bd. Critical Care Medicne. Commd. 2d lt. U.S. Army, 1968, advanced through grades to col., 1979; intern Cook County Hosp., Chgo., 1963-64, resident in internal medicine, 1964-67, fellow in cardiology, 1967-68; chief dept. medicine U.S. Army Community Hosp. U.S. Army, Bremerhaven, Fed. Republic Germany, 1968-69, Wurzberg, Fed. Republic Germany, 1969-72; chief critical care Letterman Army Med. Ctr., San Francisco, 1976—; dep. commdr. med. commd. U.S. Army, USN Dept. Def., San Francisco and Oakland, Calif., 1988—; assoc. prof. medicine and surgery Uniformed Svcs. U. Health Scis., Bethesda, Md., 1981—; cons. U.S. Surgeon Gen., 1981—; chief resident physician internal medicine Kaiser Found. Hosp., San Francisco, 1973-74; lectr. in field. Author (jour.): Ethics, 1988; co-editor: Nutrition, 1988; mem. editorial bd. Jour. Critical Care Medicine, 1988—; illustrator: Medical Decision Making, 1988. Mem. Am. Heart Assn. Recipient Meritorious Svc. medal, Army Commendation medal, Army Forces Reserve medal; decorated oak leaf cluster. Mem. AMA, Soc. Critical Care Medicine (pres. uniformed svcs. sect. 1987—, Shubin/Weil award 1988), Advanced Heat Assn. (affiliate faculty San Francisco chpt.). Home: 535B Simonds Loop San Francisco CA 94129 Office: Letterman Army Med Ctr Box 1283 San Francisco CA 94129

NISH, ALBERT RAYMOND, JR., writing consultant, retired newspaper editor; b. San Bernardino, Calif., Mar. 16, 1922; s. Albert Raymond and Mabel Clair (Shay) N.; m. Lois Maxine Ringgenberg, June 21, 1942; children—Steven Raymond, Richard Henry, Kathleen Lorie Jenner. Student San Bernardino Valley Jr. Coll., 1939-41, U. Calif., Berkeley, 1941-42, Wash. State Coll., 1943; Am. Press Inst., 1977. Pony wire editor AP, San Francisco, 1941-42; reporter Chico Record, Calif., 1945-46, Berkeley Daily Gazette, Calif., 1946-48; valley editor Modesto Bee, Calif., 1948-60, asst. mng. editor, 1960-62, mng. editor, 1962-85. Served as fighter pilot USAAC, 1942-45, PTO. Decorated DFC. Mem. Soc. Profl. Journalists. Episcopalian.

NISHIGUCHI, DON JERRY, obstetrician, gynecologist; b. San Diego, Apr. 26, 1955; s. Toshio and Sue (Okamoto) N.; m. Cecelia M. Hann, Sept. 3, 1978; 1 child, Jessica Lee. BS, U. So. Calif., 1977; MS, U. Nev., 1980; MD, Ohio State U., 1984. Diplomate Am. Bd. Ob-Gyn. Rsch. assoc. Calif. Inst. Tech., Pasadena, 1977-79; intern Los Angeles County-U. So. Calif. Med. Ctr., L.A., 1984-85, resident in ob-gyn, 1985-87, chief resident, 1987-88; pvt. practice Valencia, Calif., 1988—. Contbr. articles to profl. jours. Samuel J. Roessler scholar, 1981-83; Sigma Xi rsch. grantee, 1980-81; Am. Cancer Soc. grantee, 1983-84. Mem. Internat. Corr. Soc. Ob-Gyn, Am. Coll. Ob-Gyn, L.A. Ob-Gyn Soc., Am. Fertility Soc., Landacre Soc., Sigma Xi. Office: Valancia Gynecology Assocs 23928 Lyons Ave Ste 202 Newhall CA 91321

NISHIKUBO, DUANE TAMOTSU, dentist; b. Los Angeles, Aug. 25, 1959; s. Thomas Tamotsu and Miyona (Okimoto) N.; m. Napaporn Jessie Lukanakul, Aug. 13, 1983; children: Jason Ben, Amanda Tanaporn. DMD, Washington U., St. Louis, Mo., 1987. Pvt. practice Palm Desert, Calif., 1987—. Mem. ADA, Calif. Dental Assn., Tri-County Dental Soc., Washington U. Dental Alumni Assn. Republican. Roman Catholic. Office: 73-925 Hwy 111 Ste A Palm Desert CA 92260

NISHIMURA, HOWARD ISAMU, accountant; b. Seattle, Aug. 31, 1936; s. Toshimi and Marumi (Hamada) N.; student Los Angeles City Coll., 1955-57; B.S., U. Calif. at Los Angeles, 1961; m. Hideko Omura, Aug. 11, 1963; children—Derek Isamu, Julia Miyuki. Mgr., Kenneth Leventhal & Co., C.P.A.s, Los Angeles, 1961-67; partner Furuta & Nishimura, C.P.A.s, Los Angeles, 1967-76; pres. Nishimura, Kojima & Sy, Los Angeles, 1978-79; commr. City of Los Angeles Community Redevel. Agy., 1978-84, treas., 1979-81, chmn., 1982-84; mem. community unit for participation in housing and urban devel. City Los Angeles, 1976-82; dir. Skid Row Devel. Corp., 1979—, SRO Housing Inc., 1984. Chmn., Little Tokyo Community Devel. Adv. Com., 1975-78; pres. So. Calif. Nisei Golf, 1974-78; mem. Nisei Week Festival Com., 1977—, chmn., 1980. C.P.A., Calif. Mem. Am. Inst. C.P.A.s, Calif. Soc. C.P.A.s, Los Angeles-Nagoya Sister City Affiliation (bd. dirs. 1981—, chmn. 1982), Japan-Am. Soc. So. Calif. Home: 3307 Landa St Los Angeles CA 90039 Office: 120 S San Pedro St Ste 523A Los Angeles CA 90012

NISHIOKA, TERUO (TED NISHIOKA), electrical engineer; b. Crystal City, Tex., Sept. 6, 1945; s. Kazuto Benjamin and Kofumi (Shinkawa) N.; m. Suzanne Nayeko Hayashi, June 24, 1978; 1 child, Stephanie. BSEE, Calif. State Poly. U., 1970. Engr. Salt River Project, Phoenix, 1970-72, Pacific Gas and Electric, San Francisco, 1972-74; power plant engr. Wismer and Becker, Sacramento, 1975-78; sr. elec. engr. Ariz. Pub. Svc., Phoenix, 1978—. Author: Underground Cable Thermal Backfill, 1981. Active Japanese-Am. Citizens League, Phoenix, 1978—; v.p. Ariz. Buddhist Ch., Phoenix, 1987-88, pres., 1989—. With U.S. Army, 1966-68. Mem. IEEE, Power Engring. Soc., Elec. Insulation Soc. Office: Ariz Pub Svc PO Box 53999 Sta 5360 Phoenix AZ 85072-3999

NISKANEN, PAUL MCCORD, travel company executive; b. Bend, Oreg., July 6, 1943; s. William Arthur and Nina Elizabeth (McCord) N.; m. Christine Campbell; 1 son, Tapio. Student U. Freiburg, W. Ger., 1963-64; B.A., Stanford U., 1965; M.B.A., U. Chgo., 1966. Fin. analyst Kimberly-Clark Corp., Neenah, Wis., 1966-68; bus. mgr. Avent Inc. subs. Kimberley-Clark Corp., Tucson, 1968-70; v.p., gen. mgr. Pacific Trailways Bus. Line, Portland, Oreg., 1970-81; chmn. bd., owner Niskanen & Jones, Inc., Moab, Utah, 1982—, Perspectives, Inc., Portland. Appointed consul for Finland, 1980—; Mem. Gov.'s Travel Adv. Com., Salem, Oreg., 1976-81; 1st pres. Oreg. Hospitality and Visitors Assn., Portland, 1977-78; bd. dirs. Suomi Coll., Hancock, Mich., 1981—; nat. co-chmn. Dole for Pres. Com., 1987; co-chmn. Vistory 88. Mem. Travel Industry Assn. Am., Am. Assn. Travel Agts., Pacific Northwest Travel Assn. (chmn. 1978-79), Scandinavian Heritage Found. (bd. dirs. 1984). Republican. Home: 4366 SW Hewett Blvd Portland OR 97221 Office: Niskanen & Jones Inc 452 N Main St Moab UT 84532

NITTA, EUGENE TADASHI, endangered species biologist; b. Lodi, Calif., Aug. 19, 1946; s. Kenji and Emiko (Taguchi) N.; m. Teresa Thelma Tanibe, Dec. 26, 1987; stepchildren: Sheri Y. Yamamoto, Tani-Lyn T. Yamamoto, Staci S. Yamamoto. BA, U. Calif., Santa Barbara, 1969. Observer Internat. Whaling Commn., Cambridge, England, 1972-75; marine mammal & endangered species program coord. Nat. Marine Fisheries Svc. S.W. region, NOAA, Terminal Island, Calif., 1976-79; protected species program coord. Nat. Marine Fisheries Svc. Pacific Area Office, NOAA, Honolulu, 1980—; instr. coll. continuing edn. U. Hawaii, Honolulu, 1988-89. Mem. Soc. for Marine Mammalogy (charter mem.), Am. Soc. Mammalogists. Democrat. Episcopalian. Office: Nat Marine Fisheries Svc 2570 Dole St Honolulu HI 96822

NITZ, FREDERIC WILLIAM, electronics company executive; b. St. Louis, June 22, 1943; s. Arthur Carl Paul and Dorothy Louise (Kahm) N.; m. Kathleen Sue Rapp, June 8, 1968; children: Frederic Theodore, Anna Louise. AS, Coll. Marin, 1970; BS in Electronics, Calif. Poly. State U., San Luis Obispo, 1972. Electronic engr. Sierra Electronics, Menlo Park, Calif., 1973-77, RCA, Somerville, N.J., 1977-79; engring. mgr. EGG-Geometrics, Sunnyvale, Calif., 1979-83; v.p. engring. Basic Measuring Insts., Foster City, Calif., 1983—; cons. in field, Boulder Creek, Calif., 1978—. Patentee in field. Bd. dirs. San Lorenzo Valley Water Dist., Boulder Creek, 1983—, Water Policy Task Force, Santa Cruz County, Calif., 1983-84. Served with U.S. Army, 1965-67. Democrat. Lutheran. Home: 12711 East St Boulder Creek CA 95006 Office: BMI 335 Lakeside Dr Foster City CA 94404

NITZEL, DONALD LEROY, teacher; b. Denver, May 23, 1947; s. Dale Kenneth John and Donna Jean (Williams) N.; m. Shanna Lea Powell, Dec. 3, 1966; children: Donald LeRoy, Dale Edward, Jessica Marie. BA, U. Kans., 1975; MBA, Nat. U., San Diego, 1981, teaching credential, 1989. Enlisted USN, San Diego, 1966, electrician, 1967-75; electrician USN, USS Crockett, Guam, 1971-72; commd. ensign USN, 1975, retired, 1987; salesman Radio Shack, San Diego, 1987-88; tchr. aide San Diego Unified Sch. Dist., 1988, substitute tchr., 1989—. Home: 2466 Calle Aguadulce San Diego CA 92139

NIX, DENNIS KEITH, editor; b. Long Beach, Calif., May 22, 1941; s. Ira and Gladys (McGavock) N.; m. Marilyn Schowengerdt, June 24, 1966; children: Ayn, Ali, Ami. BS, West Tex. State U., 1970. Tchr. Sunnyside Schs., Tucson, 1971-74; editor-pub. Tucson mag./Desert Silhouette Pub., Tucson, 1974-81; owner Pointe One Advt., Tucson, 1981-87; assoc. editor Fortuna Pub., Inc., Agoura Hills, Calif., 1987-88; publisher Bobit Pub., Redondo Beach, Calif., 1988—. Author: (with others) Teacher Abuse, 1986. Bd. dirs. 88-Crime, 1980-81, Tucson Conv. Bur., 1978-81, Mother Goose Parade, El Cajon, Calif., 1987; media rep. Jack Fitzgerald for Ariz. Senate, 1986; mem. Tucson Tomorrow Inc., 1987; organizing com. Tucson Meth. Ch., 1987, lay rep., 1987. With U.S. Army, 1964-68. Mem. Nat. Alarm Assn., Tau Kappa Epsilon (bd. alumni housing U. Ariz. 1986-87). Republican. Methodist.

NIX, NANCY JEAN, librarian, designer; b. Denver; d. James Frederik and Josephine (Britt) N. AB in History, U. So. Calif., L.A., 1959, MLS, 1960. Mem. guiding com. Art Assn. Egg and the Eye Gallery and Restaurant, 1973—; participant Arts & Humanities Symposium, Palm Desert, Calif., 1974; patron cultural symposium L.A. Garden Club, 1975. Recipient Kakan Monpyo award Ikenobo Ikebana Inst., 1988. Mem. Ikebana Internat. (bd. dirs. L.A. chpt. 1978-82, mem. chmn. 1980-82), Japanese Am. Citizens League. Republican. Jewish.

NIXON, ALAN CHARLES, chemist; b. Workington, Eng., Oct. 10, 1908; married; 2 children. B.Sc., U. Saskatchewan, 1929, M.Sc., 1931; Ph.D. in Chemistry, U. Calif.-Berkeley, 1934. Instr. chemistry U. Calif., 1934-36, research asso., 1936-37, 72—; research chemist Shell Devel. Co., Emeryville, Calif., 1937-54; research supr. Shell Devel. Co., 1954-70, cons., 1970—; sec. Calsec Cons., Inc., 1979-83, pres., 1982—; dir. Teck Research, Inc., Vancouver, B.C., Can., Moli Energy Ltd., Vancouver. Moderator, Arlington Community Ch., 1980; dir. No. Calif. conf. United Ch. of Christ; chmn. Council Sci. Soc. Pres., 1973-74. Recipient awards in field. Fellow AAAS, Am. Inst. Chemists; mem. Am. Chem. Soc. (pres. 1973, bd. dirs. 1972-74, councillor, Henry A Hill award 1984, Peterson award, 1989), AIAA, Combustion Inst., Catalysis Soc., Sierra Club, Sigma Xi, Alpha Chi Sigma. Home: 2727 Marin Ave Berkeley CA 94708 Office: care Wells Fargo Bldg Ste 511 2140 Shattuck Ave Berkeley CA 94704

NIXON, MARK D., marketing professional; b. Waco, Tex., Mar. 1, 1954; m. Dea Ferris, Jan. 3, 1976; 1 child, Joshua. BS, U. Nebr., 1976, MS in Indsl. Mgmt., Mgr. mktg. support Edgcomb Metals Co., Tulsa, 1977-83; pres. Am. Wusl Thermographers, Tulsa, 1983-87; v.p. mktg. music products div., gen. mgr. indsl. products div. Ultimate Support Systems, Fort Collins, Colo., 1988—; cons. in printing, recording, computers, travel. Methodist. Office: Ultimate Support Systems 2506 Zurich Dr Fort Collins CO 80522

NIXON, RAY, JR., data systems executive; b. Monterey, Calif., Dec. 11, 1956. Salesman John Fluke Mfg. Co., Inc., Everett, Wash., 1979-83; pres. Comdat, Inc., Everett, 1984-85, U.S. Data Systems, Inc., Mukilteo, Wash., 1986—. Office: US Data Systems Inc 405 Lincoln Ave Mukilteo WA 98275

NIZAMI, TARIQ AHMED, real estate developer; b. Karachi, Sind, Pakistan, Aug. 23, 1958; came to U.S., 1975; s. Zilley Ahmed and Birgis (Talat) N.; m. Moneeza Fatmi, July 12, 1987. BBA, Calif. State U., L.A., 1982. Ops. mgr. Mijobe Corp., Upland, Calif., 1977-80; sales mgr. Computer Valley, Walnut, Calif., 1980-83; product mgr. Calif. Switch & Signal, Gardner, Calif., 1983-85; gen. mgr. Computerland, Van Nuys, Diamond Bar, Calif., 1985-88; pres. N Enterprises, Inc., Brea, Calif., 1985—; cons. Computerland Corp., Hayward, Calif., 1984-86; pres. Ampak Investment Properties, Inc., Brea, Calif., 1986— , Lu/Pac Industries, Inc. Moreno Valley, Calif. 1987—, Lu/Pac Constrn. Inc., Moreno Valley, 1986—; bd. dirs. Ramada Inn, Cleve., Ohio. Van Nuys (Calif.) C. of C. award, 1984; AT&T, IBM sales awards, 1985. Mem. Leo Club, Lion Club (Pakistan). Republican. Muslim. Home: 1402 Valeview Dr Diamond Bar CA 91765 Office: Lu/Pac Three Pointe Drive #317 Brea CA 92621

NIZAMI, TARIQ AHMED, investment company executive; b. Karachi, Pakistan, Aug. 23, 1958; s. Zilley Ahmad and Birgis (Talat) N.; m. Moneeza Nizami, May 15, 1986. BS in Bus. Adminstrn., Calif. State U., L.A., 1981, MBA in Mktg., 1983. Product mgr. Cal Switch, Gardena, Calif., 1980-82; ops. mgr. Computer Valley, Walnut, Calif., 1982-84; prin., dir. Computerland, Diamond Bar, Calif., 1984—; Pres. Ampak Investments, Brea, Calif., N Enterprises, Inc., Brea, LU/PAC Industries, Inc., Moreno Valley, Calif. Republican. Muslim. Office: Three Pinte Dr Ste 317 Brea CA 92621

NIZZE, JUDITH ANNE, physician assistant; b. L.A., Nov. 1, 1942; d. Robert George and Charlotte Ann (Wise) Swan; m. Norbert Adolph Otto Paul Nizze, Dec. 31, 1966. BA, UCLA, 1966, postgrad., 1966-76; grad. physician asst. tng. program, Charles R. Drew Sch. Postgrad., L.A., 1979; BS, Calif. State U., Dominguez, 1980. Cert. physician asst., Calif. Staff rsch. assoc. I-II Wadsworth Vet. Hosp., L.A., 1965-71; staff rsch. assoc. III-IV John Wayne Clinic Jonsson Comprehensive Cancer Ctr., UCLA, 1971-78, sr. physician asst. Donald L. Morton prof., chief surg. oncology, 1983—; clin. asst. Robert S. Ozeran, Gardena, Calif., 1978; physician asst. family practice Fred Chasan, Torrance, Calif., 1980-82. Contbr. articles to profl. jours. Fellow Am. Acad. Physicians Assts., Am. Assn. Surgeons Assts.; mem. South Bay Physicians Asst. Assn., Am. Sailing Assn., Calif. Acad. Physicians. Republican. Presbyterian. Home: 13243-J Fiji Way Marina del Rey CA 90292 Office: UCLA Med Ctr John Wayne Clinic 10833 Le Conte Los Angeles CA 90024

NOBE, KENNETH CHARLES, agricultural economy educator; b. Venedy, Ill., Oct. 26, 1930; s. Elmer F. and Alvina (Froehke) N.; m. Hazel Leona McCullough, Oct. 22, 1949; children—Sandra, Jeffrey, Michael. B.S., So. Ill. U., 1953; M.S., Cornell U., 1954, Ph.D., 1959. Mktg. agt. Dept. Agr., Ithaca, N.Y., 1954-55; instr. Cornell U., 1955-56; economist Dept. Agr., Washington, 1958-61, USPHS, Denver, 1961-63, Dept. Interior, Washington, 1963-64; econ. cons. Harza Engring. Co. Internat., Lahore, West Pakistan, 1964-65; assoc. prof. econs. Colo. State U., Ft. Collins, 1966-69; prof. econs., chmn. econs. dept. Colo. State U., 1969-83, prof. agrl. econs., chmn. dept. agr. and resource econs., 1984-87, emeritus prof., 1987—; exec. v.p. RAD Internat. Inc., Ft. Collins, 1987—; chmn. exec. council Environ. Resources Center, 1970-71; dir. Internat. Sch. Econ. Devel. Studies, 1980-83; exec. dir. Internat. Sch. Agr. and Resource Devel., 1983-85; econ. adviser to dir. Water and Power Devel. Authority West Pakistan, 1964-65; cons. U.S. State Dept., AID, 1966, 76-88, Ford Found./India, 1980, World Bank, 1984-88, Food Agr. Organ. of UN, 1989; chmn. Western Agrl. Econs. Council, 1976-78; cons. Dept. Agr., Republic of Philippines, 1977. Served with USAF, 1948-50. Recipient Ill. State Farmer award Future Farmers Am., 1947, Disting. Service award Colo. State U., 1979. Mem. Am. Econs. Assn., Am. Agrl. Econs. Assn., Western Agrl. Econs. Assn., Soil Conservation Soc. Am., Internat. Assn. Agrl. Econs., Assn. Environ. and Resource Economists, Omicron Delta Epsilon. Home: 3510 Terry Ridge Rd Fort Collins CO 80524

NOBILE, ANN BUTTERFIELD, teacher; b. Battle Creek, Mich., May 2, 1934; d. Reynolds Hunt and Gertrude (Schwehn) Butterfield; m. Camille Rocco Nobile, Nov. 27, 1958; children: Michelle, Charles Hunt. BS, Central Mich. U., 1956; MA, Calif. State U., 1979. Kindergarten tchr. Royal Oak (Mich.) city schs., 1956-58, San Bernardino (Calif.) Unified Schs., 1958-59, 60-62, 1965—. Mem. San Bernardino Tchrs. Assn., Calif. Tchrs. Assn., Nat. Tchrs. Assn., Arrowhead Assn. for Edn. of Young Children, AAUW, Delta Kappa Gamma.

NOBLE, ALAN CHARLES, software engineer; b. Adelaide, Australia, Feb. 23, 1961; came to U.S., 1986; s. Douglas Charles and Pamela Ruth (Seidel) N. BE with honours, U. Adelaide, 1983; MS, Stanford U., 1988. Programmer Dai-ichi Kaden Office Automation, Ltd., Tokyo, 1983-84; programmer, tech. writer Interlang. Svc. Systems, Inc., Tokyo, 1984-85; tech. writer NEC Communication Systems, Abiko, Japan, 1985-86; analyst, programmer Creswick Data Systems, Sydney, Australia, 1986; software engr. Schlumberger Techs. Labs., Palo Alto, Calif., 1988-89; sr. software engr. Schlumberger Tech., ATE, San Jose, Calif., 1989—; freelance Japanese-English translator, 1982--. Vol. translator Stanford U. Hosp., 1987--. Conzinc Riotinto Australia Asian studies grantee, 1981; Frank Perry scholar, 1983. Mem. IEEE, A.C.M., Am. Assn. for Artificial Intelligence, Internat. Adventure Club (Tokyo, pres. 1985-86), JapAm. Club (pres. Palo Alto chpt. 1988—). Office: Schlumberger Techs ATE div 1601 Technology Dr San Jose CA 95110

NOBLE, CHARLES EDWARD, investment counselor; b. Boston, Sept. 18, 1930; s. Charles A. Jr. and Agnes (von Adelung) N. AB, Harvard U., 1952, MBA, 1954. Security analyst Bank of Calif., San Francisco, 1957-58; investment counselor Loomis Sayles & Co., San Francisco, 1958—, v.p., sr. mgr., bd. dirs., 1968—. Sgt. U.S. Army, 1954-56. Mem. Pacific Union Club, Bohemian Club, San Francisco Golf Club, Univ. Club. Republican. Episcopalian. Office: Loomis Sayles & Co #2 Embarcadero Ctr Ste 2900 San Francisco CA 94111

NOBLE, JOHN ROBERT, lawyer; b. New Orleans, Jan. 9, 1953; s. John Page Noble and Florence Velma (Drumm) Maness; children: Sean Robert, Michelle Marie, Douglas Bryan. AA in Social Sci., Golden West Coll., 1973; BA in Philosophy, Calif. State U., Fullerton, 1975; JD, Western State

U., 1978. Bar: Calif. 1979, U.S. Dist. Ct. (cen. dist.) Calif. 1982; lic. real estate broker, Calif.; cert. ground instr. Trial lawyer Stedman and Menicucci, Anaheim, Calif., 1979-81; ptnr. Noble and Kuzelka, Santa Ana, Calif., 1981-84; trial lawyer Harden C. Bennion and Assocs., L.A., 1984-86; mng. atty. Timothy C. Kuzelka, P.C., Santa Ana, 1986-88; trial lawyer Franklin J. Dimino, Inc. and Assocs., Santa Ana, 1988—; prof. evidence Am. Coll. Law, Brea, Calif., 1984-87. Mem. L.A. County Bar Assn., Orange County Bar Assn., Orange County Barristers, Orange County Ins. Def. Assn., Aircraft Owners and Pilots Assn. (participating atty. 1988—). Democrat. Office: Franklin J Dimino & Assocs 1633 E 4th St #120 Santa Ana CA 92701

NOBLE, PHILLIP RAY, radio station owner; b. Anna, Ill., Sept. 12, 1945; s. Loyde N. and Frances (Owen) N.; m. Lynn Birleffi, Apr. 25, 1987. BA in Tech. Journalism, Colo. State U., 1974. Reporter Sta. KYCU-TV, Cheyenne, Wyo., 1974-76; dir. news Sta. KRAE-Radio, Cheyenne, 1976-77; capitol correspondent Sta. KTWO-TV/Radio, Cheyenne, 1977-80; cons. mktg. Sta. KTAG-Radio, Cody, Wyo., 1981; cons. media Wyo. Dept. Health and Social Svcs., Cheyenne, 1983; owner/mgr. Blue Sky Broadcasting Inc., Cheyenne, 1983—; cons. media for various polit. candidates, Cheyenne, 1982—; participant Atlantic Exchange Program, Rotterdam, Holland, 1987. Mgr. campaign Gov. Ed Herschler Re-election Campaign, Cheyenne, 1982; chmn. Laramie County Tourism Bd., 1987-88; pres. Cheyenne Civic Ctr. Golden Star Bd., 1986-87; mem. Newcomer Soc., 1987-88. Served with U.S. Navy, 1963-66. Mem. Cheyenne C. of C. (pres. 1989), Nat. Fedn. Independent Bus. (Guardian), Wyo. Assn. Broadcasting (dir.), Sigma Delta Chi. Democrat. Home: 1018 W Pershing Blvd Cheyenne WY 82001 Office: Sta KLEN-FM 1416 Bradley Ave Cheyenne WY 82001

NOBLE, RICHARD LLOYD, lawyer; b. Oklahoma City, Oct. 11, 1939; s. Samuel Lloyd and Eloise Joyce (Millard) N. AB with distinction, Stanford, 1961, LLB, 1964. Bar: Calif. 1964. Assoc. firm Cooper, White & Cooper, San Francisco, 1965-67; assoc., ptnr. firm Voegelin, Barton, Harris & Callister, Los Angeles, 1967-70; ptnr. Noble & Campbell, Los Angeles, San Francisco, 1970—; dir. Langdale Corp., Los Angeles, Gt. Pacific Fin. Co., Sacramento; lectr. Tax Inst. U. So. Calif., 1970; Treas. Young Republicans Calif., 1960-62; Bd. govs. St. Thomas Aquinas Coll.; mem. Colo. River Bd. of Calif. Contbr. articles to legal jours. Recipient Hilmer Oehlman Jr. award Stanford Law Sch., 1962; Benjamin Harrison Fellow Stanford U., 1964. Mem. Am., Los Angeles, San Francisco bar assns., State Bar Calif., Pi Sigma Alpha, Delta Sigma Rho. Republican. Clubs: Commercial (San Francisco), Commonwealth (San Francisco); Stock Exchange (Los Angeles), Petroleum (Los Angeles); Beach Tennis (Pebble Beach, Calif.); Capitol Hill (Washington). Home: 2222 Ave of Stars Los Angeles CA 90067 Office: Noble & Campbell 888 W 6th St Los Angeles CA 90017

NOBLE, THOMAS CARL, JR., safety engineer; b. Kingman, Ariz., June 6, 1948; s. Thomas Carl and Opal Cathrine (Thomas) N.; m. Karen A. Phelps, Nov. 8, 1968 (div. June 6, 1975); 1 child, Kimberly T.; m. Cathryn Anne Sibley, Aug. 23, 1980; 1 child, Thomas Carl III. BS, SUNY, Albany, 1980; MS, U. So. Calif., 1982. Cert. safety mgr. Asst. IH officer USN, Pearl Harbor, Hawaii, 1978-80; safety and health dir. Safety Specialists Inc., Santa Clara, Calif., 1980-82; safety engr. Lockheed Missiles and Space Co., Sunnyvale, Calif., 1982-85; safety mgr. Physics Internat., San Leandro, Calif., 1985-88; staff engr. Lockheed Missles and Space Co., Sunnyvale, Calif., 1988—; indsl. hygienist Kairos Corp., Mountain View, Calif., 1980-85; chmn. 7th Internat. System Safety Conf., San Jose, Calif., 1985. Contbr. articles to profl. jours. Served with USNR, 1965—. Mem. System Safety Soc. (pres. No. Calif.), Am. Soc. Safety Engrs., Am. Pub. Health Assn., Nat. Safety Mgmt. Soc., World Safety Orgn. Republican. Home: 4686 Phebe Ave Fremont CA 94555 Office: Lockheed Missles & Space Co 1111 Lockheed Way Sunnyvale CA 96830

NOBLE, WALTER MORRIS HART, physician, educator; b. San Francisco, Mar. 24, 1933; s. Charles A. Jr. and Agnes (Von Adelung) N.; m. Winifred Brady, Sept. 21, 1962; children: Christopher (dec.), Morris, William. BA cum laude, Harvard U., 1954, MD, 1958. Diplomate Am. Bd. of Internal Med. Intern and resident U. N.C., 1958-60; resident San Francisco Gen. Hosp., 1962-63; resident H.C. Moffitt Hosp., San Francisco, 1963-64, instr. to clin. prof., 1964-83; acting chmn. dept. of medicine Children's Hosp., San Francisco, 1981-82, bd. dirs., 1984—. Sec., treas. Pacific Interurban Clin. Club, 1978-82, chmn. 1988-89; trustee Town Sch. San Francisco, 1966-84, Thacher Sch., Ojai, Calif., 1967-73; bd. govs. San Francisco Heart Assn. 1967-72. Capt. U.S. Army Med. Corps, 1960-62, Korea. Mem. AMA, San Francisco Med. Soc., ACP, Am. Soc. of Internal Med., Pacific Union (San Francisco), Calif. Tennis Club. Office: 3838 California St San Francisco CA 94118

NOCE, WALTER WILLIAM, JR., hospital administrator; b. Neptune, N.J., Sept. 27, 1945; s. Walter William and Louise Marie (Jenkins) N.; m. Cinda Ann Miller, Apr. 15, 1967; children: Krista Suzanne, David Michael. B.A., LaSalle Coll., Phila., 1967; M.P.H., UCLA, 1969. Regional coordinator USPHS, Rockville, Md., 1969-71; v.p. Hollywood Presbyn. Hosp., Los Angeles, 1971-75; sr. v.p. Hollywood Presbyn. Med. ctr., 1975-77; v.p. adminstrn. Huntington Meml. Hosp, Pasadena, Calif., 1977-83; pres., chief exec. officer St. Joseph Hosp., Orange, Calif., 1983—; pres. so. Calif. region St. Joseph Health System, 1987—; preceptor UCLA Health Services Mgmt. Program, 1977—; chmn. bd. Health Plan of Am., 1985—; chmn. Hosp. Coun. So. Calif., 1989. Exec. v.p. Mental Health Assn. in Los AngelesCounty, 1979-82; regional v.p. Calif. Mental Health Assn., 1982-83. W. Glenn Ebersole finalist Assn. Western Hosp., 1969; recipient USPHS letter commendation, 1971. Mem. Am. Coll. Hosp. Adminstrs., Am. Hosp. Assn., UCLA Hosp. Adminstrn. Alumni Assn. (pres. 1979-80), Pasadena C. of C. (v.p. 1980-82). Home: 20388 Via Marwah Yorba Linda CA 92686 Office: St Joseph Hosp 1100 W Stewart Dr Orange CA 92688

NODINE, RICHARD, designer, printmaker; b. Neptune, N.J., Aug. 2, 1944; s. Jean Holmes. Student, Parsons Sch. Design, 1963-67. Retail designer R.H. Macy, Inc., Monmouth, N.J., 1967-68, Newark, 1968-69, San Francisco, 1969-75; graphic designer R.H. Macy, Inc., N.Y.C., 1977; dir. graphic design R.H. Macy, Inc., San Francisco, 1977-87; prin. Pacific Design Group, San Francisco, 1987—. Recipient Award of Excellence Communication, Arts Mag. 19th ann. exhbn., 1978, 24th ann. exhbn., 1983, 26 ann. exhbn. 1985; Merit award N.Y. Art Dirs. Club, 1984, Distinctive Merit award, 1984, others. Mem. Am. Inst. Graphic Arts. Republican.

NOE, NORMAN D., insurance executive; b. Denver, July 5, 1931; s. Fred W. Noe and Maxine (Grout) Rhoads; m. Martha Strovers, Apr. 16, 1955; children: David C., Laura Jeane, Steven S. BA, Grinnell Coll., 1954; postgrad., Colo. U. Extension, 1962. Sports announcer Sta. KFKA Radio, Greeley, Colo., 1954-60; ins. sales Fred W. Noe, Insuror, Greeley, 1954-62; ptnr. Noe & Arnold Ins. Agy., Greeley, 1962-70; v.p. Bartels & Noe Agy., Inc., Greeley, 1970—, Ponderosa Mgmt., Inc., Littleton, Colo., 1986—; pres. Greeley-Weld Insurors, 1964-66; coordinator Greeley Pub. Schs. Ins. Program, Greeley, 1962-72. Pres., bd. dirs. Boys Club Greeley, 1963—; chmn. distbn. com. Greeley Area Found.; bd. dirs. Greeley Independence Stampede, 1980-85, United Way, Boy Scouts Am., County Fair, City Recreation, City Traffic, City Mus. Recipient Disting. Service award Greeley Jaycees, 1963, Outstanding State V.P. Colo. Jaycees, 1964, medallion Boys Club Am., 1977. Mem. Ind. Ins. Agts., Colo., Nat. Assn. Surety Bond Producers, Heritage Assn. No. Colo. (pres. Greeley chpt. 1980-87). Republican. Congregationalist. Lodges: Masons, Shriners, Elks, Moose. Home: 1721 Fairacres Dr Greeley CO 80632 Office: Bartels & Noe Agy PO Box B Greeley CO 80632

NOE, SALLY WOODWORTH (SARA NOE), teacher, local history researcher; b. Kansas City, Mo., Mar. 18, 1926; d. Hugh Johnson and Katharine (McAntire) Woodworth; m. Robert Clark Noe, Aug. 14, 1945; children: Katharine Merry, Thomas Clark, William Dean. BA, U. N.Mex., 1969, MA, 1984. Cert. tchr., N.Mex. Elem. tchr. Morenci Pub. Schs., Ariz., 1946-47; elem. tchr. Gallup-McKinley County Sch. Dist., N.Mex., 1955-56, tchr. Office Navajo Edn. Opportunity, Concentrated Employment Practice, 1968-69, tchr. secondary social studies, 1969-87, chmn. dept. social studies, 1977-87; social studies evaluator, N.Mex. schs., 1975—; instr. N.Mex. history U. N.Mex., Gallup, 1986—; cons. Harcourt, Brace, Jovanovich, 1985-86, Gallup-McKinley County Schs., 1988. Author N.Mex. Council for Social Studies and State N.Mex. Dept. Edn. unit for Native Am. history, 1979; author Gallup centennial calendar, 1981. Head rug clk. InterTribal Indian Ceremonial, Gallup, 1976—; bd. dirs. N.Mex. Law Related Edn.; regional dir. N.Mex. History Day; mem. com. Ft. Wingate Preservation Task Force, 1984, Com. on Status of History in N.Mex. Pub. Schs., 1984; participant Navajo Nation History and Govt. Inst., 1987; bd. dirs. Inter-Tribal Indian Ceremonial Assn., 1987—; presenter Colloquium for Research on Women C.R.O.W. U. N.Mex., 1988; mem. U. N.Mex. Centennial Com., 1988. Recipient 3d Place award High Sch. div. econs. Kazanjian Found., 1970, Tchr.'s medal Freedom Found. at Valley Forge, 1973, Inst. for Am. Indian History award Newberry Library, 1978, Dorothy Woodward award for Edn. Hist. Soc. N.Mex., 1987; Ethnic Am. Coe fellow Stanford U., Calif., 1979; S.W. Inst. Research on Women fellow U. Ariz., 1983; Spl. Programs in Citizenship Edn. fellow Wake Forest U. Sch. Law, 1985. Mem. AAUW, N.Mex. Council for Social Studies (pres. 1980-81), N.Mex. Hist. Soc. (presenter), Nat. Council Social Studies, N.Mex. Archeol. Soc. (cert. crew mem., presenter state meeting 1986), N.Mex. Soc. for Preservation History, Gallup Hist. Soc., Delta Kappa Gamma (pres. Gallup chpt. 1979-80), Alpha Delta Pi. Democrat. Episcopalian. Lodges: Order Eastern Star, PEO. Home: PO Box 502 1911 Mark St Gallup NM 87301 Office: Gallup High Sch PO Box 39 Gallup NM 87301

NOEGROHO, ESTER TIANA, architect; b. Semarang, Indonesia, Mar. 2, 1958; came to U.S., 1976; d. Moses S. and Christine (Liong) N.; m. Kornelius Tjandra Subadya, Dec. 10, 1983. BArch, U. So. Calif., 1982. Drafter S.P.I., Inglewood, Calif., 1982-83; drafter, designer Frank Nick and Assocs., Pasadena, Calif., 1983-84; designer, project mgr. Austin Field Fry and Barlow, L.A., 1984—. Congregationalist. Home: 285 Camino del Sol South Pasadena CA 91030

NOETH, LOUISE ANN, journalist; b. Evergreen Park, Ill., Nov. 17, 1954; d. Cy John and Alice Rose (Bobrovich) N. Editor Petersen Pub. Co., Inc., Calif., 1980; assoc. pub., editor Autoscene Mag., Westlake Village, Calif., 1981; investigative editor Four Wheeler Mag., Canoga Park, Calif., 1982—; cons. Sirit Am. World Speed Record Team, Pontiac Motor Div., others; mem. Green Mamba Racing Team, Reseda, Calif., 1978—, Spirit of Am. World Speed Racing Record; graphic art commns. for Ferro Corp., Crown Oldsmobile, Glendale Porsche-Audi, others. Editor Hot Rod Performance and Custom, 1979; contbr. articles to numerous automotive mags. Recipient Moto award in investigative news category, 1983-84, 86. Mem. Tallship Californian Quarter deck Comm., Oxnard C. of C., Edn. Comm. Youth Edn. Motivation Program,Internat. Motor Press Assn. (sec. 1986—), Specialty Equipment Market Assn. (pub. relations com. 1983, suspension and tire com. 1984-85), Am. Auto Racing Writers and Broadcasters Assn. Office: Landspeed Prodns 4260 S Harbor Blvd #A107 Oxnard CA 93035

NOGUCHI, HIDEO, insurance agency executive; b. Kyoto, Japan, Jan. 17, 1945; s. Tasao and Ishiko (Tsuji) N.; m. Eleanor Kazuko Horii, May 7, 1970; children—Mark H.Y., Mitchell H.Y. B.B.A., U. Hawaii, 1969. Buyer RCA Purchasing Co., Tokyo, 1969-73; ins. specialist Continental Ins. Agy., Honolulu, 1973-82; pres. Noguchi & Assocs., Inc., Honolulu, 1983—; cons. Recipient Nat. New Agt. Leadership award CNA Corp., 1974, Agt. of Yr. award Continental Ins. Agy., annually 1973-81, Key Club award CNA Co., 1975, 79-81. Mem. Nat. Assn. Life Underwriters, Honolulu Assn. Life Underwriters, Million Dollar Round Table. Lodge: Elks. Home: 3678 Woodlawn Terrace Pl Honolulu HI 96822 Office: 1314 S King St Ste 560 Honolulu HI 96814

NOGUCHI, THOMAS TSUNETOMI, author, pathologist; b. Fukuoka, Japan, Jan. 4, 1927; came to U.S., 1952; s. Wararu and Tomika Narahashi N. D of Medicine, Nippon Med. Sch., Tokyo, 1951; LLD (hon.), U. Brazil, Sao Paolo, Brazil, 1980; DSc (hon.), Worcester State Coll., 1985. Dep. med. examiner Los Angeles County Dept. Coroner, Los Angeles, 1961-67, coroner, 1967-82; prof. forensic pathology U. So. Calif., Los Angeles, 1982—. Author: Coroner, 1983 (N.Y. Times Bestseller 1984), Coroner At Large, 1985, (fiction) Unnatural Causes, 1988. Fellow Am. Acad. Forensic Sci. (chmn. sect. 1966); mem. Nat. Assn. Med. Examiners (pres. 1983), Calif. State Coroners Assn. (pres. 1974), World Assn. Med. Law (v.p.). Republican. Home: 1110 Avoca Ave Pasadena CA 91105 Office: U So Calif Med Ctr 1200 N State St Rm 2519 Los Angeles CA 90033-1084

NOLAN, BARBARA BRYANT, special educator; b. Schenectady, N.Y., July 21, 1953; d. John Walber and Patricia (Alvord) Bryant; m. Christopher Payne Nolan, July 03, 1981; children: Joseph, Daniel. BA, Beaver Coll., 1975; MEd, Temple U., 1977; MA, San Francisco State U., 1984. Cert. tchr. resource specialist. History, math tchr. Rebecca Gratz Alternative Sch., Phila., 1975-77; intensive studies tchr. Internat. Sch. of Bangkok, Bangkok, Thailand, 1977-79; spl. class tchr. Vallejo Unified Sch. Dist., Vallejo, Calif., 1979-83; resource specialist Vallejo Unified Sch. Dist., Vallejo, 1983—. Grantee Calif. Tchr. Instructional Improvement Program, 1984-87; named Educator of Yr., Vallejo Elks, 1988. Mem. bd. dirs. Calif Assn. of Resource Specialists (pres. 1987-88, outstanding contbn. award 1987); mem. State Adv. Com. on Special Edn., 1988—. Democrat.

NOLAN, BARRY HANCE, specialty catalog executive; b. Easton, Pa., Sept. 15, 1942; s. Arthur James Nolan and Marion (Hance) Slater; m. Janet Lynch, Mar. 20, 1971 (dec. Mar. 1981); 1 child, Tracy; m. Catherine McDermott, Feb. 19, 1983; children: Craig, Kelsey. AB in Econs., Princeton U., 1964; MBA, Columbia U., 1966. Account exec. Papert, Koenig, Lois Advt., N.Y.C., 1966-68; group mgr. new bus.'s Butterick div. Am. Can, N.Y.C., 1969-72; dir. mktg. planning Current Inc. subs. Deluxe Check Printers, Colorado Springs, Colo., 1973-77, v.p. mktg., 1977-79, pres., chief exec. officer, 1980—; asst. to pres. Pacific Water Works Supply Co., Seattle, 1979-80. Pres. bd. dirs. Pikes Peak br. Cystic Fibrosis Found., Colorado Springs, 1984—, nat. trustee-at-large, Washington, 1985—. Mem. Parcel Shippers Assn. (bd. dirs. 1987—). Republican. Presbyterian. Clubs: Cheyenne Mountain Country (Colorado Springs); Sahalee Country (Redmond, Wash.). Home: 35 Elm Ave Colorado Springs CO 80906 Office: Current Inc PO Box 2559 Colorado Springs CO 80901

NOLAN, DENNIS PAUL VINCENT, engineer; b. Detroit, Dec. 8, 1954; s. James Vincent and Anastasia Theresa (Kulick) N. BS in Fire Protection Engring., U. Md., 1977; MS in Systems Mgmt., Fla. Inst. Tech., 1979; cert. sch. offshore, U. Tex., 1981. Registered profl. engr., Calif. Assoc. engr. Boeing Aerospace Co., Kennedy Space Ctr., Fla., 1977-80; engr. Marathon Oil Co., Findlay, Ohio, 1980-83; sr. engr. Lockheed Missiles and Space Co., Vandenburg AFB, Calif., 1984-87; fire protection engr. Occidental Petroleum Corp., Los Angeles, 1987—. Mem. NSPE, Nat. Mgmt. Assn., Mil. Vehicle Collectors Club. Home: 24321 Friar St Woodland Hills CA 91367 Office: Occidental Petroleum Corp 10889 Wilshire Blvd Los Angeles CA 90024

NOLAN, JAMES MARTIN, structural engineer, consultant; b. Joliet, Ill., Feb. 25, 1950; s. Aloysius Edward and Marjorie Cecelia (Drauden) N.; m. Denise Dorothy Lavoie, Jan. 17, 1972; children: Tanya Marie, Shannon Kathleen. BS in Engring., U. Colo., 1973; postgrad., U. Colo., Denver, 1975-79, Calif. State U., Fullerton, 1974. Registered profl. engr., Colo., Kans., Mo., Iowa, Wyo., Okla., N.Mex., Calif., Ariz. Bridge engr. Colo. Dept. Hwys., Denver, 1975-78; structural engr. E.W. Peterson, Cons., Lakewood, Colo., 1978-80, HDR, Denver, 1980-82; v.p. KTN and Assocs., Lakewood, Colo., 1982-84; chief structural engr. CRS Sirrine, Inc., Denver, 1984-88; prin. Goodell-Nolan and Assocs. Inc., Englewood, Colo., 1988—; enging. cons. Englewood, Colo., 1984. Bd. dirs. Havana Water and Sanitation Dist., Denver, 1982—, Cherry Creek Vista Met. Recreation and Park Dist., Englewood, Colo., 1979-84; del. Rep. Caucus, Arapahoe County, 1984. Mem. ASCE, Am. Concrete Inst., Am. Cons. Engrs. Council. Home: 10806 E Maplewood Pl Englewood CO 80111 Office: Goodell-Nolan & Assocs Inc 3700 S Inca St Ste 2 Englewood CO 80110

NOLAN, PAUL T., telephone company executive. Pres. GTE NM Inc. formerly Gen. Tel. Co. of the N.W. Office: GTE NW Inc 1800 41st St PO Box 1003 Everett WA 98206 *

NOLL, CLIFFORD LESTER, manufacturing executive; b. Newark, June 10, 1926; s. Leroy Frederick and Mae Elizabeth (Search) N.; m. Muriel Sawyer Beck, Sept. 16, 1950; children: Thomas Abbott, Richard Sawyer, Bruce Clifford, William Search. BS in Engring., MIT, 1949. Engr. Foster Wheeler Corp., N.Y.C., 1951-55, Phila., 1955-59; mgr. Foster Wheeler Energy Corp., Kansas City, Mo., 1959-63, Denver, 1963-75, 1975-79, v.p., 1979—. Com. chmn. Boy Scouts Am. Littleton, Colo., 1964-72. Mem.ASME, Rocky Mountain Elec. League, Pacific Coast Elec. League. Republican. Office: Foster Wheeler Energy Corp Englewood CO 80112

NOLL, H. ELIZABETH, cardiologist; b. Pontiac, Mich., May 19, 1955; d. Page and Martha Elizabeth (Coen) N.; m. Reinaldo Beyer, Apr. 1, 1989. BA in Chemistry, U. Calif., San Diego, 1977; MD, UCLA, 1981. Diplomate Am. Bd. Internal Medicine and Cardiovascular Diseases, Nat. Bd. Med. Examiners. Resident in internal medicine Wadsworth VA Med. Ctr., L.A., 1981-84, cardiology fellow, 1984-86, clin. instr. cardiac electrophysiology, postgrad. scholar, 1986-87; staff cardiologist Sharp Rees-Stealy Med. Group, San Diego, 1987—. Fellow Am. Coll. Cardiology; mem. AMA, Am. Med. Women's Assn., Calif. Med. Assn., San Diego Med. Soc., ACP. Office: Sharp Rees Stealy Med Group 2001 4th Ave San Diego CA 92101

NOLL, WILLIAM NIVEN, insurance executive; b. Pasadena, Calif., June 1, 1942; s. William Albrecht and Barbara Jean (Niven) N.; m. Jane Ann Hall, Jan. 17, 1969; children: Jeremy Edward, Kristy Ann, Katy Ann. BA, Pepperdine U., 1969; MDiv, San Francisco Theol. Sem., 1971; MBA, Golden Gate U., San Francisco, 1973. Property/casualty underwriter Indsl. Indemnity Co., L.A., 1974-80; v.p. Swett & Crawford Grp. (Lloyds of London), L.A., 1981—. Author: Topical Index for the Bible, 1970, Riverine Warfare, 1980. Bd. trustees Trinity Bapt. Ch., Sunnyvale, Calif., 1970-73; mem. West Pasadena City Com., 1986—. Capt. U.S. Army, 1965-68. Decorated Purple Heart, Bronze Star, Air Medal, Presdl. Unit Citation, Army Commendation medal, Vietnam Cross. Mem. Ind. Ins. Agts. Assn., Spl. Surplus Lines Ins. Assn., Western Ins. Brokers Assn., Lloyds Minet Syndicate, Pacific Producers Re-Insurance, Pasadena Athletic Club, Kiwanis. Republican. Baptist. Home: 620 W California Blvd Pasadena CA 91105 Office: Swett & Crawford Group 3699 Wilshire Blvd 12th Fl Los Angeles CA 90010

NOLLETTE, LE ROY I., data processing executive; b. Brainard, Minn., July 25, 1941; s. LeRoy and Josephine (Ryan) N.; m. Julie Herrin, July 28, 1962; children: Linda Stevenson, Monica, Mia. BS in Mgmt. Devel., Maryhurst (Oreg.) Coll., 1980. Programmer/analyst Rayette Faberge', St. Paul, 1961-67; software tech. Consol. Freightways, Portland, Oreg., 1967-71; software engr. Tektronix Inc., Beaverton, Oreg., 1972-86; data processing cons. Sherwood, Oreg., 1986-87; data processing mgr. Metro Svc. Dist., Portland, 1987—. Democrat. Roman Catholic. Home: 1235 E Willamette Sherwood OR 97140 Office: Metro Svc Dist 2000 SW 1st Ave Portland OR 97201-5398

NOMBERG, BEVERLY REDNER, social worker, psychotherapist; b. Springfield, Mo., Dec. 12, 1942; d. Frederic Schofield and Agnes Lucille (Cunningham) Redner; div.; 1 child, Ilana Rebekah. BA, U. Mo., 1964; MSW, Adelphi U., 1968. Diplomate Acad. Cert. Social Workers. Social worker I, Family Service League, Huntington, N.Y., 1968-70; social worker II, Long Island Jewish Med. Ctr., New Hyde Park, N.Y., 1970-72; nephrology social worker N.Mex. Artificial Kidney Ctr., Albuquerque, 1977-88; psychotherapist Albuquerque Ctr. for Psychotherapy, 1980-86; social worker Profl. Stress Intervention, Albuquerque, 1986—; adoption cons. La Familia, Albuquerque, 1988—; employee assistance counselor Human Affairs Internat., Albuquerque, 1988—. Sec. bd. dirs. Jewish Family Services, 1986—. Mem. Nat. Assn. Social Workers (treas. 1979-82, Social Worker of the Year, N.Mex. chpt., 1981). Democrat. Jewish. Home: 405 Sierra SE Albuquerque NM 87108 Office: 1722 Lead SE Albuquerque NM 87106

NOMURA, MASAYASU, biological chemistry educator; b. Hyogo-Ken, Japan, Apr. 27, 1927; s. Hiromichi and Yaeko N.; m. Junko Hamashima, Feb. 10, 1957; children—Keiko, Toshiyasu. Ph.D., U. Tokyo, 1957. Asst. prof. Inst. Protein Research, Osaka (Japan) U., 1960-63; assoc. prof. genetics U. Wis., Madison, 1963-66, prof., 1966-70, prof. genetics and biochemistry, 1970-84, co-dir. Inst. for Enzyme Research, 1970-84; prof. biol. chemistry, Grace Bell chair U. Calif., Irvine, 1984—. Recipient U.S. Steel award in molecular biology Nat. Acad. Scis., 1971; recipient Acad. award Japanese Acad. Arts and Sci., 1972. Mem. Am. Acad. Arts and Scis., Nat. Acad. Scis., Royal Danish Acad. Scis. and Letters. Home: 26 Starlight Irvine CA 92715 Office: U Calif Dept Biol Chemistry Med Sci I D240 Irvine CA 92717

NONG, painter, sculptor; b. Seoul, Korea, Oct. 10, 1930; came to U.S., 1952, naturalized, 1958; Commr. Asian Art Commn., City and County of San Francisco, 1981-84. One-man exhbns. paintings and/or sculpture include Ft. Lauderdale (Fla.) Mus. Arts, Santa Barbara (Calif.) Mus. Art, Crocker Art Mus., Sacramento, Calif., 1965, Ga. Mus. Art, Athens, 1967, El Paso (Tex.) Mus. Art, 1967, Galerie Vallombreuse, Biarritz, France, 1970, Nat. Mus. History, Taiwan, 1971, Nihonbashi Gallery, Tokyo, Japan, 1971, Shinsegye Gallery, Seoul, Korea, 1975, Nat. Mus. Modern Art, Seoul, 1975, San Francisco Zool. Garden, 1975, Tongin Art Gallery, Seoul, 1978, Consulate Gen. Republic of Korea, Los Angeles, 1982, Choon Chu Gallery, Seoul, 1982, Mee Gallery, Seoul, 1984, 86, Leema Art Mus., Seoul, 1985, Tong-A Dept. Store, Taegu, Korea, 1986, Tongso Gallery, Masan, Korea, 1986, Han Kwang Art Mus., Pusan, Korea, 1986, Union de Arte, Bercelona, Spain, 1987, Acad. de Belles Arts, Sabadell, Spain, 1987, numerous group exhibits Mus. and Art Ctr., Douglaston, N.Y., 1961, Nat. Collection Fine Arts Smithsonian Instn., Washington, 1961, Mus. Fine Arts, Springfield, Mass., 1961, Conn. Acad. Fine Arts, Hartford, Conn., 1962, Charles and Emma Frye Art Mus., Seattle, 1962, The Denver Art Mus., 1965, Jersey City Mus., 1967, U. Santa Clara (Calif.) Mus., 1967, U. Calif., Berkeley, 1968, Maison de la Culture du Havre, Le Havre, France, 1970, Oakland (Calif.) Art Mus., 1971, Gallerie des Champs Elysees, Paris, 1971, Nat. Sculpture Soc., Lever House, N.Y.C., 1971, Taipei Provincial Mus., Republic of China, 1971, San Francisco Mus. Modern Art, 1972, Galerie Hexagramme, Paris, 1975, Galeria de Arte Misrachi, Mexico City, 1979, The Mun Ye Art Ctr., Seoul, 1986, Salon de Artistes Francais, Paris, France, 1971, Salon d'Automne, Paris, 1969-71, Salon Grands et Jeunes d'Aujourd'hui, Paris, 1971-77; represented in numerous permanent collections including, Santa Barbara Mus. Art, Anchorage (Alaska) Hist. and Fine Art Mus., Museo de Arte, Lima, Peru, Govt. Peru, Nat. Mus. History, Govt. of Republic of China, Oakland (Calif.) Art Mus., Ga. Mus. Art, Athens, Korean Embassy, Lima, Peru, Nat. Mus. of Modern Art, Nat. Mus. Korea, Govt. of Republic of Korea, Seoul, Kook Min U., Seoul, Nat. Gallery of Modern Art, New Delhi, India, Asian Art Mus. San Francisco, Govt. of People's Republic China, Beijing and Shanghaia, Palacio de la Zarzuela, Madrid, Palacio de la Moncloa, Madrid, The Korean Embassy, Madrid, Mus. Art de Sabadell, Spain, Mus. Nat. des Beaux-Arts, Monte Carlo, Monaco, others; author: Nong Questions, 1982. Chmn. San Francisco-Seoul Sister City Com., City and County San Francisco, 1981-84. Served with U.S. Army, 1956-59; Served with USAF, 1959-60. Recipient numerous awards including citations from Republic of Korea., Cert. Disting. Achievement State of Calif. Proclamation City and County of San Francisco. Home: 2938 Plaza Terrace Dr Orlando FL 32803

NONG, ANH THE, medicine educator; b. Haiphong, Socialist Republic of Vietnam, Oct. 25, 1940; came to U.S., 1972; s. Dang Van and Boi-Thuy (Lam) N.; m. Nhon T. Nguyen, June 27, 1980; children: Chantal, Dominique. MD, U. Saigon, Vietnam, 1970. Intern coll. of medicine U. Okla., Oklahoma City, 1972-75, asst. prof. medicine, 1975-80; assoc. prof. medicine U. Calif., L.A., 1980-85, prof. medicine, 1985-88; prof. med. U. Calif., Irvine, Calif., 1988—; dir. div. of gen. internal medicine, dept. of medicine San Bernardino (Calif.) Med. Ctr. Named Best Tchr. in Medicine, San Bernardino County Med. Ctr., Calif., 1981. Fellow Am. Coll. Physicians, Am. Acad. Family Physicians. Republican. Roman Catholic. Home: 209 E Sunset Dr S Redlands CA 92373 Office: San Bernardino Med Ctr 780 E Gilbert San Bernardino CA 92404

NOODLEMAN, JEFFREY SCOTT, radiologist; b. Mpls., May 24, 1953; s. Benny Norman and Esther (Gonor) N. Student with honors, Pasadena City Coll., 1973; BA in Chemistry summa cum laude, BS in Biol. Scis. summa cum laude, U. Calif., Irvine, 1975, MA in Chemistry, 1976; MD, Loyola U., Chgo., 1979. Diplomate Am. Bd. Radiology, Am. Bd. Nuclear Medicine, Am. Bd. Med. Examiners. Intern U. Calif. Irvine Affiliates, 1979-80; resident L.A. County— U. So. Calif. Med. Ctr., L.A., 1980-81, VA West L.A., 1981-86; physician Family Health Plan, Anaheim, Calif., 1986-89, Western

Roentgenologic Assocs., Canoga Park, Calif., 1989—. Mem. Am. Coll. Nuclear Physicians, Soc. Nuclear Medicine, Radiol. Soc. N.Am., Am. Roentgen Ray Soc., Phi Beta Kappa. Democrat. Home: 2131 S 5th Ave Arcadia CA 91006

NOONAN, CHARLES ANDREW, psychiatrist; b. Valparaiso, Ind., Sept. 8, 1949; s. Leo Charles and Bettie Jane (Barboul) N.; m. Jill Elizabeth Short, Dec. 2, 1967; children: Jennifer Marie, Benjamin Alexander, Jessica Faye. BS in Biology, Purdue U., 1971; MD, Ind. U., Indpls., 1975. Diplomate Am. Bd. Psychiatry and Neurology. Intern U. Calif. Davis Sacto Med. Ctr., Sacramento, 1976, resident in psychology, 1978; staff psychiatrist LaPorte County Community Mental Hosp., Ind., 1978-79, clin. dir., 1979-82; staff psychiatrist Calif. Med. Correctional Facility, Vacaville, Calif., 1982-83; pvt. practice Concord, Calif., 1983—; chmn. Dept. Psychiatry LaPorte Hosp., 1979-80; cons. psychiatry Health Analysis, San Jose, Oakland, San Mateo, Calif., 1983-85, Sierra Clinic, San Francisco, 1983-85, Contra Costa County Superior Cts., Martinez, Calif., 1983—, U.S. Dist. Ct., San Francisco, 1983—, Forensic Mental Health, Martinez, 1987—; med. dir. Behavioral Medicine Assocs., Concord, 1984-85; instr. cable TV program on hypnosis for stress and eating disorders Televents Cable TV, San Francisco, 1984-85, video tape tng. on stress mgmt. of U.S. probation officers, 1986; founder, med. dir. Serenity Eating Disorder program Mt. Diablo Hosp., Concord, 1984-87; radio interviewer on eating disorders Sta. KSBS, 1985-86. Editor: (newspaper column) Mental Health Corner, 1977-78. Adv. Bd. pub. opinion panel Sta. KRON-TV, San Francisco, 1983—; bd. dirs. Inst. for a Better Way, Berkeley, Calif., 1984—. Recipient Physicians Recognition award AMA, Washington, 1978, 81, 84. Mem. Am. Psychiatry Assn., C. of C., No. Calif. Psychiatric Soc., So. Calif. Med. Assn., Alameda Contra Costa Med. Assn, Purdue U. Alumni Assn., Ind. U. Alumni Assn. Roman Catholic. Home: 639 New Seabury Ct Walnut Creek CA 94598 Office: 2001 Salvio St Ste 22 Concord CA 94520

NOONAN, JOHN T., JR., federal judge, legal educator; b. Boston, Oct. 24, 1926; s. John T. and Maria (Shea) N.; m. Mary Lee Bennett, Dec. 27, 1967; children: John Kenneth, Rebecca Lee, Susanna Bain. B.A., Harvard U., 1946, LL.B., 1954; student, Cambridge U., 1946-47; M.A., Cath. U. Am., 1949, Ph.D., 1951, LHD, 1980; LL.D., U. Santa Clara, 1974, U. Notre Dame, 1976, Loyola U. South, 1978; LHD, Holy Cross Coll., 1980; LL.D., St. Louis U., 1981, U. San Francisco, 1985; student, Holy Cross Coll., 1980, Cath. U. Am., 1980, Gonzaga U., 1986, U. San Francisco, 1986. Bar: Mass. 1954, U.S. Supreme Ct. 1971. Mem. spl. staff Nat. Security Council, 1954-55; sole practice Boston, 1955-60; prof. law U. Notre Dame, 1961-66, U. Calif., Berkeley, 1967-86; judge U.S. Ct. Appeals (9th cir.), San Francisco, 1986—, chmn. religious studies, 1970-73, chmn. medieval studies, 1978-79; Oliver Wendell Holmes, Jr. lectr. Harvard U. Law Sch., 1972; chmn. bd. Games Research, Inc., 1961-76; Pope John XXIII lectr. Cath. U. Law Sch., 1973; Cardinal Bellarmine lectr. St. Louis U. Div. Sch., 1973. Author: The Scholastic Analyst of Usury, 1957; Contraception: A History of Its Treatment by the Catholic Theologians and Cononists, 1965; Power to Dissolve, 1972; Persons and Masks of the Law, 1976; The Antelope, 1977; A Private Choice, 1979; Bribes, 1984; editor: Natural Law Forum, 1961-70, Am. Jour. Jurisprudence, 1970, The Morality of Abortion, 1970. Chmn. Brookline Redevel. Authority, Mass., 1958-62; cons. Papal Commn. on Family, 1965-66, Ford Found., Indonesian Legal Program, 1968, NIH, 1973, NIH, 1974; expert Presdl. Commn. on Population and Am. Future, 1971; cons. U.S. Cath. Conf., 1979-86; sec., treas. Inst. for Research in Medieval Canon Law, 1970-88; pres. Thomas More-Jacques Maritain Inst., 1977—; trustee Population Council, 1969-76, Phi Kappa Found., 1970-76, Grad. Theol. Union, 1970-73, U. San Francisco, 1971-75; mem. com. theol. edn. Yale U., 1972-77; exec. com. Cath. Commn. Intellectual and Cultural Affairs, 1972-75; bd. dirs. Ctr. for Human Values in the Health Scis., 1969-71, S.W. Intergroup Relations Council, 1970-72, Inst. for Study Ethical Issues, 1971-73. Recipient St. Thomas More award U. San Francisco, 1974, Christian Culture medal, 1975, Laetare medal U. Notre Dame, 1984, Campion medal Cath. Book Club, 1987; Guggenheim fellow, 1965-66, 79-80, Laetare medal U. Notre Dame, 1984, Campion medal, 1987, Alemany medal W. Dom. Prov., 1988; Ctr. for advanced Studies in Behavioral Scis. fellow, 1973-74; Wilson Ctr. fellow, 1979-80. Fellow Am. Acad. Arts and Scis., Am. Soc. Legal Historians (hon.); mem. Am. Soc. Polit. and Legal Philosophy (v.p. 1964), Canon Law Soc. Am. (gov. 1970-72), Am. Law Inst., Phi Beta Kappa (senator United chpts. 1970-72, pres. Alpha of Calif. chpt. 1972-73). Office: US Ct Appeals PO Box 547 San Francisco CA 94101

NOONAN-DRACHKOVITCH, STEPHANIE ANN, television producer; b. Ft. Lewis, Wash., June 26, 1957; d. Richard Burke and Sandra Marie (Faroe) Noonan; m. Rasha Drachkovitch, Apr. 27, 1985; 1 child, Michael Ryan. Student, U. Nebr., Lewis and Clark Coll.; BA, U. Oreg., 1980. Assoc. producer Sta. KATU-TV, Portland, Oreg., 1979-81, Sta. WPVI-TV, Phila., 1981-82; exec. producer Sta. WCAU-TV, Phila., 1982-83; producer Telepictures Corp., Sherman Oaks, Calif., 1983-84; v.p. 44 Blue Prodns., San Francisco, 1984—. Recipient Gold medal Broadcast Promotion and Mktg. Execs., 1985, Silver medal Houston Internat. Film Festival, 1988; nominated for local Emmy award Nat. Acad. TV Arts and Scis. Phila. chpt., 1983. Mem. Women in Film, Am. Women in Radio and TV, Women in Communications. Office: 44 Blue Prodns Inc 1755 E Bayshore Rd Ste 7-B Redwood City CA 94063

NOPAR, ALAN SCOTT, lawyer; b. Chgo., Nov. 14, 1951; s. Myron E. and Evelyn R. (Millman) N. BS, U. Ill., 1976; JD, Stanford U., 1979. Bar: Ariz. 1979, U.S. Dist. Ct. Ariz. 1980, U.S. Ct. Appeals (9th cir.) 1980, U.S. Supreme Ct. 1982; CPA, Ill. Assoc. O'Connor, Cavanagh, Anderson, Westover, Killingsworth & Beshears P.A., Phoenix, 1979-85, ptnr., 1985-87; of counsel Tower, Byrne & Beaugureau, Phoenix, 1987-88, Minutillo & Gorman, San Jose, Calif., 1989—. Mem. Ariz. Rep. Caucus, Phoenix, 1984-88. Mem. ABA (bus. law sect., pub. contract law sect., forum com. on franchising), Ariz. Bar Assn. (corp. banking and bus. law sect.), Maricopa County Bar Assn. (corp. banking and bus. law sect.), Am. Inst. CPA's. Office: Minutillo & Gorman 55 S Market St Ste 1100 San Jose CA 95113

NORA, JAMES JACKSON, physician, author; b. Chgo., June 26, 1928; s. Joseph James and May Henrietta (Jackson) N.; m. Barbara June Fluhrer, Sept. 7, 1949 (div. 1963); children: Wendy Alison, Penelope Welbon, Marianne Leslie; m. Audrey Faye Hart, Apr. 9, 1966; children: James Jackson Jr., Elizabeth Hart Nora. AB, Harvard U., 1950; MD, Yale U., 1954; MPH, U. Calif., Berkeley, 1978. Assoc. prof. pediatrics Baylor Coll. Medicine, Houston, 1965-71; prof. genetics, preventive medicine and pediatrics U. Colo. Sch. Medicine, Denver, 1971—; dir. genetics Rose Med. Ctr., Denver, 1980—; dir. pediatric cardiology and cardiovascular tng. U. Colo. Sch. Medicine, 1971-78; mem. task force Nat. Heart and Lung Program, Bethesda, Md., 1973; cons. WHO, Geneva, 1983—; mem. U.S.-U.S.S.R. Exchange Program on Heart Disease, Moscow and Leningrad, 1975. Author: The Whole Heart Book, 1980, 2d rev. edit., 1989; (with F.C. Fraser) Medical Genetics, 1981, 3d rev. edit., 1989, Genetics of Man, 1986; (novels) The Upstart Spring, 1989, The PSI Delegation, 1989. Com. mem. March of Dimes, Am. Heart Assn., Boy Scouts Am. Served to lt. USAAC, 1945-47. Grantee Nat. Heart, Lung and Blood Inst., Nat. Inst. Child Health and Human Devel., Am. Heart Assn., NIH; recipient Virginia Apgar Meml. award. Fellow Am. Coll. Cardiology, Am. Acad. Pediatrics; mem. Am. Pediatric Soc., Soc. Pediatric Research, Am. Heart Assn., Teratology Soc., Transplantation Soc., Am. Soc. Human Genetics, Authors Guild, Authors League, Acad. Am. Poets. Democrat. Presbyterian. Club: Rocky Mountain Harvard (Denver). Home: 6135 E 6th Ave Denver CO 80220 Office: U Colo Sch Medicine A-007 4200 E 9th Ave Denver CO 80262

NORBY, ROCKFORD DOUGLAS, motion picture company executive; b. Silver City, N.Mex., June 28, 1935; s. John Rockford and Alice (Simons) N.; children: John Rockford II, Katherine Alice Laidley, James Randall. B.A. magna cum laude, Harvard U., 1957, M.B.A. with distinction (Baker scholar), 1959. Assoc. McKinsey & Co., Inc., N.Y.C., 1960-63, San Francisco, 1963-67; v.p. fin. Itel Corp., San Francisco, 1968-73; exec. v.p. Itel Corp., 1977-79; sr. v.p., chief fin. officer Syntex Corp., Palo Alto, Calif., 1979-85; pres. Lucasfilm, Ltd., 1985—; v.p. First Chgo. Corp., 1973-74; v.p. fin. Fairchild Camer & Instrument Corp., Mt. View, Calif., 1974-77; bd. dirs. New Horizons Savs. & Loan Assn., Pegasus Capital Corp. Bd. dirs. Marin Symphony, Marin Ballet, Mill Valley Film Festival; mem. Bay Area coun. Nat. Hispanic U. Recipient Decur award Harvard Coll., 1956. Mem. Sierra Club, Phi Beta Kappa. Democrat. Roman Catholic. Clubs: Olympic, Harvard, Harvard Bus. Sch. No. Calif. Home: 3055 Pacific Ave San Francisco CA 94115 Office: Lucasfilm Ltd Box 2009 San Rafael CA 94912 *

NORDAHL, JAMES H., nuclear fuels company executive; b. Billings, Mont., July 13, 1941; s. Harold F. and Mabel M. (Kloster) N.; m. Patty Jo Davis, June 16, 1963; children: Beth R., Steven T. BS in Chem. Engring., Mont. State U., 1963. Process engr. Gen. Electric Corp., Richland, Wash., 1963-68; mgmt. engr. Atlantic Richfield Co., Richland, 1968-72; mgmt. engr. nuclear fuel reprocessing div. Exxon Nuclear Co., Bellevue, Wash., 1972-76, with comml. dept. nuclear div., 1976-83, mgr. proposals nuclear div., 1983-84; mgr. bus. devel. Exxon Nuclear Internat., Brussels, 1984-86; mgr. site services Advanced Nuclear Fuels Corp., Bellevue, 1986-88, v.p. U.S. mktg., 1988—. Contbr. articles to profl. jours. Troop leader Boy Scouts Am., Richland, 1970-72; active local ch. council, Richland and Brussels. Mem. Am. Inst. Chem. Engrs. Republican. Lutheran.

NORDBY, GENE MILO, college administrator; b. Anoka, Minn., May 7, 1926; s. Bert J. and Nina Grace N.; m. Arlene Delores Anderson, Aug. 27, 1949 (dec. Nov. 1974); children: Susan Pamela, Brett Gene, Lisa Lea; m. Dusilla Anne Rycroft, July 8, 1975, (div. July, 1988). B.S. in Civil Engring, Oreg. State U., 1948; M.S. in Civil Engring., U. Minn., 1949, Ph.D. in Civil Engring., 1955. Registered profl. engr., Colo. Ariz., Okla. Grad. asst. U. Minn., 1948-50; structural designer Pfeiffer and Shultz (engrs.), Mpls., summer 1950; instr., then asst. prof. civil engring. U. Colo., 1950-56; asso. prof. civil engring., research engr. Joint Hwy. Research Project, Purdue U., 1956; engr. program dir. engring. scis. NSF, 1956-58; lectr. civil engring. George Washington U., 1956-58; prof. civil engring., head dept. U. Ariz., 1958-62; dir., then chmn. adv. com. Ariz. Transp. and Traffic Inst. at univ., 1959-62; prof. engring. U. Okla., 1962-77; dean U. Okla. (Coll. Engring.), 1962-70, v.p. for adminstrn. and fin., 1969-77; v.p. for bus. and fin., prof. civil engring. Ga. Inst. Tech., 1977-80; chancellor U. Colo., Denver, 1980-85; prof. civil engring. U. Colo., Denver and Boulder, 1985-86; prof. agrl. engring., head dept. U. Ariz., Tucson, 1986—; mem. Reinforced Concrete Research Council Engring. Found., 1954-60; trustee Frontiers of Science Found., 1963-70; pres. Tetracon Assos., Inc., 1968-86; cons. structural engring., research financing and programming, ednl. facilities planning and constrn., reinforced concrete, also higher edn. adminstrn., engring. program accreditation, NSF, 1984-87, panel engring. ctrs. of excellence, 1983-87; bd. dirs. Higher Edn. and the Handicapped, Am. Council on Edn., 1980-83; pres. Accreditation Bd. for Engring. and Tech., 1985-86, fellow; gen. chmn. Nat. Congress on Engring. Edn., Washington, 1986; commr. at large N. Cen. Assn. Schs. and Colls., 1988—. Co-author: Introduction to Structural Mechanics, 1960; Cons. editor, MacMillan Co., 1962-70. Bd. visitors Air Force Inst. Tech., 1985-87. Served with AUS, 1943-46. Recipient Citation for Service to State Okla. Ho. of Reps., 1977; recipient Linton E. Grinter Disting. Service award Accreditation Bd. for Engring. and Tech., 1982. Fellow ASCE (com. on engring edn., 1964-68, com. on research needs, 1965-70, com. on ednl. research, 1976-79, Edmund Friedman Profl. Devel. award 1982); mem. Am. Soc. Engring. Edn. (projects bd. 1969-70, chmn. Curtis W. McGraw award com. 1968, Dean's Inst. Com. 1966-69, Accreditation Process Com. 1979-81), Nat. Soc. Profl. Engrs., Am. Arbitration Assn., Am. Soc. Agrl. Engrs., Engrs. Council for Profl. Devel. (chmn. engring. edn. and accreditation com. 1970, dir. 1976-79, 83-87), Ariz. Soc. Profl. Engrs., Okla. Soc. Profl. Engrs. (dir. 1966-69), Nat. Assn. State Univs. and Land Grant Colls. (commn. edn. engring. profession 1966, 70-73), Engring. Colls. Adminstrv. Council (mem. exec. bd. 1966), Ga. Soc. Profl. Engrs. (bd. dirs. Atlanta chpt. 1978-79), Nat. Assn. Coll. and Univ. Bus. Officers (chmn. personnel com. 1977-79), Sigma Tau, Omicron Delta Kappa, Tau Beta Pi, Chi Epsilon. Club: Mason. Office: U Ariz 507 Shantz Bldg #38 Tucson AZ 85721

NORDGREN, WILLIAM BENNETT, engineering executive; b. Salt Lake City, Mar. 5, 1960; s. Kent Widstoe and Eliza (Schmuhl) N.; m. Carolyn B. Erickson, June 26, 1981; 1 child, William Tyson. BS, Brigham Young U., 1986, MS, 1989. Engr. Boeing Airplanes Co., Seattle, 1986-88; pres. CIM Engring. Assocs., Orem, Utah, 1988-89; v.p. Prodn. Modeling Corp., Orem, 1989—. Developer, polar coordinant mill. Mem. Soc. Mfg. Engrs. Republican. Mormon. Office: Prodn Modeling Corp 1834 S State St Orem UT 84058

NORDLUND, DONALD EUGENE, teacher; b. Waukegan, Ill., June 14, 1937; s. Ero Victor and Irya Silvia (Lineck) N.;m. Carol Ann Dandy, May 18, 1962 (div. Sept. 1983); children: Karen (dec.), Victor, Kristin; m. Barbara Ann Peak L'Ecuyer, Mar. 30, 1985; stepchildren: Jeanine, Lawrence, Paul, Julie, Anne. BA, Wabash Coll., 1959; MA, Ariz. State U., 1967. Tchr. Zion (Ill.) Pub. Schs., 1959-60, Waukegan (Ill.) Pub. Schs., 1960-61, Sierra Vista #97, Phoenix, 1962, Scottsdale (Ariz.) Unified #48, 1962—; coord. Nat. Bicentennial Competition the Constn. and Bill of Rights, Ariz., 1987—. Precinet committeeman Dem. Com., Scottsdale, 1972-80; bd. mem. Sister Cities, Scottsdale, 1985—; mem. Ariz. Close Up Adv. Bd., Phoenix, 1981—; Australian Am. exch. tchr. Sister Cities Internat., 1988. With USAR, 1957-63. Mem. Nat. Coun. Social Studies, Nat. Coun. Geographic Edn., Ariz. Coun. Social Studies (sec. 1984—), Am. Fedn. Tchrs., United Tchrs. Scottsdale (treas. 1970-72), Phoenix Rose Soc., Ariz. State U. Alumni Assn., Phi Kappa Psi, Masons. Democrat. Mem. United Ch. of Chirst. Home: 8433 E Angus Dr Scottsdale AZ 85251 Office: Coronado High Sch 2501 N 74th St Scottsdale AZ 85257

NORDMEYER, MARY BETSY, vocational specialist educator; b. New Haven, May 19, 1939; d. George and Barbara Stedman (Thompson) N. ABPhil, Wheaton Coll., Norton, Mass., 1960; MA, San Jose State U., 1968; AS in Computer Sci., West Valley Coll., 1985. Cert. tchr. spl. edn., Calif.; cert. secondary tchr., Calif. Instr. English Santa Clara (Calif.) Unified Sch. Dist., 1965-77, vocat. specialist, 1977—, dir. project work ability, 1984—. Author poetry, 1960, Career and Vocat. Edn. for Students With Spl. Needs, 1986; author/designer Career English, 1974, Career Information, 1975. Facilitator Project Work-Ability Region 5, 1985—; mem. community adv. com. Santa Clara Unified Sch. Dist. Recipient Outstanding Secondary Educator award, 1975, Award of Excellence, Nat. Assn. Vocat. Edn., 1984; named Tchr. of Yr. in Spl. Edn., Santa Clara Unified Sch. Dist., 1984-85. Mem. Calif. Assn. Work Experience Educators, Sierra Club, Epsilon Eta Sigma. Democrat. Home: 14920 Sobey Rd Saratoga CA 95070 Office: Santa Clara Unified Sch Dist 1889 Lawrence Rd Santa Clara CA 95052

NORDQUIST, JEFFREY SCOTT, mechanical engineer; b. Neptune, N.J., Mar. 5, 1963; s. Walter Reinhold and Nancy Jane (Galway) N. BS, U. Ill., 1985; MS, Stanford U., 1987. Research/devel. engr. Amoco Research Ctr., Naperville, Ill., 1982-83, 85; product engr. AT&T, Lisle, Ill., 1984; research engr. Stanford U., 1985-87; thermodynamics engr. Lockheed Missiles & Space Co., Sunnyvale, Calif., 1987—. Chevron scholar, 1982-83; First Chgo. scholar, 1981. Mem. ASME, AIAA, ASHRAE. Home: 255 S Rengstorff Ave #145 Mountain View CA 94040

NORDSTROM, BRUCE A., department store executive; b. 1933; married. BA, U. Wash., 1956. With Nordstrom, Inc., Seattle, 1956—, v.p., 1964-70, pres., 1970-75, chmn., 1975-77, co-chmn., 1977—, dir. Office: Nordstrom Inc 1501 5th Ave Seattle WA 98101 *

NORDSTROM, JAMES F., apparel company executive; b. 1940; married. BBA, U. Wash., 1962. Various positions Nordstrom, Inc., Seattle, 1960—, exec. v.p. 1975-78, pres., 1978—, also bd. dirs. Office: Nordstrom Inc 1501 5th Ave Seattle WA 98101 *

NORDSTROM, JANIS LYNN, litigation support specialist; b. Burbank, Calif., Jan. 9, 1952; d. Walter Boyd and Mary Louise (Metcalf) Crouch; m. Gordon Thomas Nordstrom, Dec. 16, 1978; children: Gregory James, Jeffrey Lee. AB in Russian Studies, U. Calif., Berkeley, 1974; MA, UCLA, 1975, PhD program, 1975-76. Manuscript editor, Russian translator Ctr. for Slavic Studies, Berkeley, Calif., 1973-74; prof. Russian lit. UCLA, 1975-76; editor. tech. translator Gardner & Anton, Beverly Hills, Calif., 1976-77; litigation support specialist Richard I. Fine, Esq., Los Angeles, 1977-82; pres. Leviathan Svcs., Los Angeles, 1983—; cons. IAM vs. OPEC lawsuit, Los Angeles, 1978-79, SEC vs. Rothschild class action litigation, Los Angeles, 1984-88. Contbr. article in Jour. Fgn. Affairs, 1979. Regents fellow U. Calif., 1974-75, 79. Mem. Calif. Lifetime Alumni Assn., Westlake Alumni Assn. Episcopalian. Home and Office: 1924 Fox Hills Dr Los Angeles CA 90025

NORDYKE, JAMES WALTER, economist, educator; b. Rock Springs, Wyo., June 21, 1930; s. Ray Beatty and Gracia Marie (Perry) N. B.A. with gt. distinction, Stanford U., 1952; M.A. (Sanxay fellow 1952-53, univ. fellow 1955-56), Princeton U., 1957, Ph.D., 1959. Rsch. asst. Princeton (N.J.) U., 1956-58; instr., then asst. prof. econs. Kenyon Coll., Gambier, Ohio, 1958-64; mem. faculty N.Mex. State U., Las Cruces, 1964—; prof. econs. N.Mex. State U., 1969—, chmn. dept., 1974-88. Author: International Finance and New York, 1976; co-author: Comparative Economic Systems, 3d edit, 1983. Served with AUS, 1953-55. Recipient Westhafer award excellence in teaching N.Mex. State U., 1973. Mem. Phi Beta Kappa, Phi Kappa Phi, Delta Sigma Pi. Home: 2035 Rentfrow Ave Las Cruces NM 88001 Office: NMex State U Dept Econs Box 3511 University Pk Las Cruces NM 88003

NOREEN, ROBERT GERALD, English educator; b. Gresham, Oreg., Jan. 2, 1938; s. Oscar Emmanual and Floella Marie (Jacobs) N.; m. Carole Ethel Stone, June 24, 1961 (div. 1978); children: Kirstin, Eric. AA, North Park Coll., 1958; BA, U. Chgo., 1960, MA, 1963, PhD, 1969. Instr., dir. composition Northwestern U., Evanston, Ill., 1965-68; asst. prof. Calif. State U., Northridge, 1968-71, assoc. prof., 1972-77, prof. English, 1978—; faculty English cons., chancellor's office, Calif. State U., Long Beach, 1988—; freelance writing cons., 1975—; chmn. English test devel. sect., Ednl. Testing Svc., Princeton, N.J., 1984—; mem. assessment program adv. bd., Calif. Bd. Edn., mem. writing skills adv. bd.; active state coms. on English as second lang., testing handicapped students, college freshman writing standards, computer bull. bds. Author: Saul Bellow: A Reference Guide, 1976; textbook editor: Perspectives for the '70s, 1970; contbr. essays to various publs. Mem. Con. on Coll. Communication and Composition, MLA, Nat. Coun. Tchrs. English, Calif. Assn. Tchrs. English, Sierra Club. Democrat. Episcopalian. Office: Dept English Calif State U 18111 Nordhoff St Northridge CA 91330

NOREEN, TERRY GENE, health and safety consultant; b. Walla Walla, Wash., May 21, 1946; s. Arthur Sanford and Norma Jean (Slater) N.; AS, Grossmont Coll., 1974; BA, San Diego State U., 1976; MS, Portland State U., 1980; m. Linda Lou Mays, May 2, 1965 (div. 1982); children: Holly, Tina, Terry Gene; m. Cindra L. Starmer, Dec. 9, 1983; children: Jennifer, Ryan, Erin, Jenice. Dir. data communications equipment Naval Communications Sta., San Diego, 1972-76; health and safety specialist Tidewater Barge Lines, Vancouver, Wash., 1976-82; health and safety cons. to marine and gen. industry, 1982—. Contbg. author trade jours. Mem. Clark County Sheriff Res., 1981; leader Boy Scouts Am., 1981-86. With USN, 1963-71. Cert. hazard control mgr.; lic. tankerman U.S. Mcht. Marine. Mem. Oil Chem. and Atomic Workers Union (shop steward 1978-80, health and safety steward 1979-82), Columbia River Boatman's Union (sec. 1977-78), Portland Shipyard Safety Council, Am. Soc. Safety Engrs., Auto Body Craftsmen's Soc. (co-dir. chpt. 1984-86, program dir. 1983-85, program dir. SW Wash. chpt. 1983-84, Wash. State health and safety dir. 1984-86), Nat. Fire Protection Assn., Am. Pub. Health Assn., Nat. Safety Mgmt. Soc., C. of C. U.S.A., Lions (bd. dirs. 1985). Mormon. Home: 25604 NE Manley Rd Battle Ground WA 98604 Office: 7622 NE 47th Ave Vancouver WA 98661

NOREN, PAUL HAROLD ANDREAS, retired clergyman; b. St. Paul, July 10, 1910; s. Andreas and Amanda Amelia (Olson) Noren; m. Linnea Swanson, Oct. 7, 1936 (dec.); children: Andrea Marie, Karen, Mary-Ellen Beth; m. Janice Herrick, Feb. 14, 1979; children: Craig Llewellyn, Karen, Brian Llewellyn. AB, Gustavus Adolphus Coll., 1931; MDiv, Augustana Theol. Sem., Rock Island, Ill., 1934; DD (hon.), Bethany Coll., Lindsborg, Kans., 1958. Ordained to Luth. ministry, 1934. Pastor St. Paul, 1934-38, Duluth, Minn., 1938-44, Mpls., 1944-53; sr. pastor Augustana Luth. Ch., Denver, 1953-68, Mt. Olivet Luth. Ch., Mpls., 1968-74; preacher biennial conv. Luth. Ch. in Am., Dallas, 1972, White House, 1969; mem. Bd. Christian Svc., Luth. Minn. Conf., 1938-41, chmn. budget com., 1940-51; mem. com. on liturgical theory and practice Augustana Luth. Ch., 1944-60, v.p. cen. conf., 1956-62, sec. Bd. Christian Higher Edn., 1952-62, chmn. joint com. on Luth. unity, 1961-62, mem. exec. bd., 1962-68, mem. commn. on Luth. chaplaincy for Colo. instns., 1961-62, v.p. Bd. Coll. Edn. and Ch. vocations, 1962-64, pres., 1964-66; mem. Bd. World Missions, 1968-70; del. Nat. Council of Chs., 1966; pres. Denver Area Council Chs., 1962-64; pres. Religious Council Human Rels. Met. Denver, 1965; pres. Colo. Council Chs., 1967; chaplain Colo. Senate, 1963-68, 81-82, Rep. Nat. Conv., 1964; chmn. Billy Graham Colo. Crusade, 1965, gen. chmn. Upper Midwest Crusade, 1973; exec. bd. Minn. Synod Luth. Ch. in Am., 1968-76; mem. exec. coun. Luth. Conf. Am., 1966-68. Author Profiles of the Passion, 1961; contbr. articles to profl. jours.; radio broadcaster, 1963-68, devotional telecast, 1968-78. Chmn. Gov.'s Com. on Respect for Law, 1964-68, Pres.'s Colo. Commn. Law Enforcement and Adminstrn. of Justice, 1966-68, Gov.'s Com. on Minorities and the Disadvantaged, 1968, Mt. Olivet Luth. Ch. Council, Mt. Olivet Sr. Citizen's Home, Mt. Olivet Careview Home, Mt. Olivet Rolling Acres and Sch. for Mentally Retarded, Cathedral of the Pines Youth Camp, Santal Mission Bd., 1970-72; mem. Mayor's Com. on City-Citizen Rels., 1965-68; trustee Swedish Med. Ctr., Englewood, Colo., 1953-68, Greater Mpls. Council Chs., 1948-53, v.p. 1952-53, chmn. weekly edn. for released time instrn. 1951-53; bd. dirs. Midland Luth. Coll., Fremont, Nebr., 1966-68. Recipient Disting. Alumni Citation Gustavus Adolphus Coll., 1962, Torch of Liberty award Anti-Defamation League of B'nai B'rith, 1964. Mem. Rotary, Kiwanis, Probus Club of Fullerton (Calif.), Sigma Tau. Home: 839 Glenwood Circle Fullerton CA 92632

NORKIN, MARK MITCHELL, sales executive; b. Whittier, Calif., Nov. 19, 1955; s. Cleo Donald and Carol Ann (Stewart) Mathis. Grad., Gemmological Inst. Am., 1976. Gemmologist Slavicks Jewelers, Newport Beach, Calif., 1976-77; apprentice Troy Sheet Metal Works, Montebello, Calif., 1977-79, journeyman, 1979-80, foreman, 1980-82, project engr., 1982-85, v.p. sales and engring., 1985—. Republican. Home: 1320 Wynn Rd Pasadena CA 91107 also: 13528 N 102d Pl Scottsdale AZ 85260 Office: Troy Sheet Metal Works 1026 S Vail Ave Montebello CA 90640

NORLING, BRIAN LEE, mechanical engineer; b. Mpls., Sept. 29, 1954; s. Ralph E. and Phylis M. (Benson) N.; m. Lori K. Nelsen; 1 child, Amber L. BSME, U. Wash., 1977; MBA with honors, Seattle U., 1987. Registered profl. engr., Wash. Design engr. Paccar, Renton, Wash., 1977-80, sr. design engr., 1980-82; sr. design engr. Sundstrand Data Control, Redmond, Wash., 1981-82, project engr., 1982-84, prin. engr., 1984-86, engring. supr. advanced tech., 1986-87; mgr. engring. advanced tech. Sundstrand Data Control, Redmond, 1987—; cons. inertial navigation and instrumentation projects. Patentee in field; inventor in field; contbr. articles to profl. jours. Active Mill Creek (Wash.) Community Assn. Mem. IEEE, Am. Mktg. Assn., Inst. Navigation. Office: Sundstrand Data Control 15001 NE 36th St Redmond WA 98073-9701

NORMAN, JOHN BARSTOW, JR., designer, educator; b. Paloa, Kans., Feb. 5, 1940; s. John B. and Ruby Maxine (Johnson) N.; B.F.A., U. Kans., 1962, M.F.A., 1966; m. Roberta Jeanne Martin, June 6, 1967; children—John Barstow III, Elizabeth Jeanne. Designer and illustrator Advt. Design, Kansas City, Mo., 1962-64; asst. instr. U. Kans., Lawrence, 1964-66; art dir. Hallmark Cards, Inc., Kansas City, Mo., 1966-69; instr. dept. art U. Denver, 1969-73, asst. prof., 1973-78, assoc. prof., 1978—, Disting. prof., 1980, chmn. design dept.; design cons. Mo. Council Arts and Humanities, 1966-67; cons. designer Rocky Mountain Bank Note Corp., Denver, 1971—, Signage Identity System, U. Dever; bd. dirs. communications U. Denver; dir. Internat. Design Conf. in Aspen Seminar Group; tech. cons. Denver Art Mus., 1974—, designed exhbns., 1974-75; adv., cons. Jefferson County (Colo.) Sch., System, 1976—; chmn. Design and Sculpture Exhbn., Colo. Celebration of the Arts, 1975-76; chmn. arts and scis adv. com., Career Edn. Adv. Bd., Denver Pub. Sch. System, 1976-77. One man shows include: Gallery Cortina, Aspen, Colo., 1983; commd. works include: Jedda, Saudi Arabia, Synegistics Corp., Denver, Gillette (Wyo.) Pub. Library; represented in permanent collections Pasadena Ctr. for the Arts, N.Y. Art Dirs. Club, Midland Art Council/Fiber Collection, Pasadena (Calif.) Ctr. for the Arts, 1984, N.Y. Art Dirs. Club, 1985 Midland Art Council/Fiber Collection, 1985, Geologic Soc. Am.; represented in traveling exhbns. Los Angeles Art Dirs. Show and N.Y. Art Dirs. Show, U.S., Europe, Japan, 1985; featured in Denver Post, 1984, Post Electric City Mag., 1984, Rocky Mt. News, 1984,

Douglas County Press, 1984, Mile High Cabel Vision, 1985, Sta. KWGN-TV, 1985, Les Krantz's Am. Artists, 1988, Illustrated Survey of Leading Contemporaries, 1988, U.S. Surface Design Jour., 1988; work represented in film collection Mus. Modern Art, N.Y.C.; selected fashion show designs displayed to Sister City dels., Denver, 1987. Recipient Silver Medal award N.Y. Internat. Film and Video Competition, 1976, Design awards Council Advancement and Support of Edn., 1969, 71, 73, 76, Honor Mention award Los Angeles Art Dirs. Club, 1984, Honor Mention award N.Y. Art Dirs. Club, 1984, 1st place Nat. Native Am. Wearable Art Competition, 1985, 5th place Nat. Wind Sail: Am. Banners Competition, Midland, Mich., 1985, also awards for surface designs in Colo. Ctr. for the Arts Wearable Art Competition, 1984-85, Foothills Art Gallery Nat. Wearable Art Competition, 1984-85, Fashion Group of Denver Competition, 1984-85. Mem. Art Dirs. Club Denver (ednl. liaison, 6 Gold medals 1974-82, Best of Show Gold medal 1983, Honor Mention award, 1984), Univ. Art Dirs. Assn. Home: PO Box 302 751 Willow Lake Dr Franktown CO 80116 Office: U Denver Sch Art 2121 E Asbury St Denver CO 80208

NORMAN, JOHN EDWARD, petroleum landman; b. Denver, May 22, 1922; s. John Edward and Ella (Warren) N.; m. Hope Sabin, Sept. 5, 1946; children—J. Thomas, Gerould W., Nancy E., Susan G., Douglas E. BSBA, U. Denver, 1949, MBA, 1972. Clk., bookkeeper Capitol Life Ins. Co., Denver, 1945-46; salesman Security Life and Accident Co., Denver, 1947; bookkeeper Central Bank and Trust Co., Denver, 1947-50; automobile salesman H.A. Hennies, Denver, 1950; petroleum landman Continental Oil Co. (name changed to Conoco Inc. 1979), Denver, 1950-85; ind. petroleum landman, 1985—. Lectr. pub. lands Colo. Sch. Mines, 1968-85; lectr. mineral titles and landmen's role in oil industry Casper Coll., 1969-71. Mem. Casper Mcpl. Band Commn., 1965-71, mem. band, 1961-71, mgr., 1968-71; former musician, bd. dirs. Casper Civic Symphony; former bd. dirs. Jefferson Symphony, performing mem., 1972-75. Served with AUS, World War II. Mem. Am. Assn. Petroleum Landmen (dir. at large, chmn. publs. for regional dir.), Wyo. Assn. Petroleum Landmen (pres.), Denver Assn. Petroleum Landmen, Rocky Mountain Oil and Gas Assn. (pub. lands com. 1981—), Rocky Mountain Petroleum Pioneers. Episcopalian (mem. choir, vestryman, past dir. acolytes). Club: Elks. Home and Office: 2710 S Jay St Denver CO 80227

NORMANDY, GEORGE MITCHELL, JR., electrical engineer; b. Decatur, Ga., Oct. 23, 1935; s. George Mitchell and Martha Randolph (Jones) M.; m. Marcia Del Farris, May 23, 1955 (div. Sept. 1969); children: Penny, Patricia, George III, Pamela, Paulette; m. Jean Edna Stolberg, Jan. 15, 1971; children: Jo Ann, John, Penny. AA in Phys. Sci, AA in Math., San Diego State U., 1977, BSEE, 1981; AA in Psychology, AS in Mfg. Tech., San Diego City Coll., 1984; postgrad., West Coast U., 1984-86. Registered profl. engr. Enlisted USN, 1954-69, resigned, 1969; with customer svc. Motor Machine Co., San Diego, 1969-80; engr. Gen. Atomic Co., San Diego, 1980-82; sr. engr. GA Techs. Inc. (name now Gen. Atomics), San Diego, 1982—. Mem. IEEE, Assn. Computing Machinery, Am. Nuclear Soc., Mensa. Republican. Lutheran. Home: 3842 Basilone St San Diego CA 92110 Office: Gen Atomics Box 85608 San Diego CA 92138

NORRIS, D. WAYNE, insurance and financial services company executive; b. Portland, Ind., Feb. 9, 1939; s. Leo D. and Mable L. (Miller) N.; m. Bonnie K. Smith, Mar. 6, 1965; children: Julia A., Elizabeth. Student, Ball State U., 1961-64. Chartered life underwriter. Gen. mgr. Am. Gen. Ins., Muncie, Inc., 1964-69; owner D. Wayne Norris CLU and Assocs., Muncie, 1969-73, Tucson, 1973—. Contbr. articles to profl. jours. Bd. dirs. Jr. Achievement Ariz., 1985—; life mem. Nat. Cowboy Hall of Fame, 1981—. Mem. Nat. Assn. Life Underwriters (pres. Ind. 1971-72, Underwriter of Yr. 1972, Nat. Quality award 1965), Am. Soc. CLUs (dir. Tucson 1975-79), Tucson Metro C. of C. (chmn. Los Compadres 1986-88), Nat. Assn. Securities Dealers, Plaza Club, Pima Early Rising Execs. (founder, past pres. 1975—). Avocations: writing, hiking. Office: D Wayne Norris CLU & Assocs 5620 N Kolb Rd #164 Tucson AZ 85715

NORRIS, DAVID OTTO, educator; b. Ashtabula, Ohio, Oct. 1, 1939; s. Otto Lee and Thelma Louise (Colledge) N.; m. Kay Linda Wilkinson, July 23, 1966; children: Sara Elizabeth, Linda Kay. BS, Baldwin-Wallace Coll., Berea, Ohio, 1961; PhD, U. Wash., 1966. Asst. prof. biology U. Colo., Boulder, 1966-70, assoc. prof. biology, 1970-76, prof. biology, 1976—; vis. assoc. prof. U. Calif., Berkeley, 1974; vis. prof. Oreg. State U., 1983-84. Author: (with others) General Biology Laboratory I, 2d ed., 1970, General Biology Laboratory II, 2d ed., 1971, Investigations for Practicing Biology, 1975, Vertebrate Endocrinology, 2d ed., 1985, Hormones and Reproduction in Fishes, Amphibians, and Reptiles, 1987, Identifying Plant Food Cells in Gastric Contents for Forensic Investigation, 1988; contbr. articles to profl. jours. Grantee NSF, 1968-70, 76-78, 79-83, Nat. Inst. Justice, 1984-86, Council on Research and Creative Work, 1967, 72, 76, 79, 84, NIH, 1968, 75, 79, 80, 85, 86. Mem. Am. Soc. Zoologists, Colo.-Wyo. Acad. Sci., Endocrine Soc., Herpetologists League, Soc. Study Amphibians and Reptiles, Sigma Xi. Office: U Colo Dept Environ Population and Organismic Biology Box B-334 Boulder CO 80309

NORRIS, JOAN LOUISE, occupational therapist; b. San Gabriel, Calif., Apr. 20, 1958; d. Ronald Charles and Virginia (Pytlinski) Sommerfield; m. Joseph Walter Norris, June 14, 1980. AA, Santa Barbara City Coll., 1978; BS, San Jose State U., 1980. Psychiatric occupational therapist Santa Barbara (Calif.) Cottage Hosp., 1981—, intern supr., 1985—. Mem. Occupational Therapy Assn. Calif. Democrat. Roman Catholic. Office: Santa Barbara Cottage Hosp PO Box 689 Santa Barbara CA 93102

NORRIS, PHILIP, brokerage executive; b. N.Y.C., Oct. 16, 1928; s. Claude Basil and Fannie Inez (Bell) N.; m. Rose Martin, Aug. 24, 1957 (div.); children: Laura Ashley Coats, Susan Martin Bradford, Philip Blair; m. Rebecca Snider, Oct. 1, 1977. BA, Claremont McKenna Coll., 1953. Account exec. Dean Witter & Co., Honolulu, 1960-66; Hawaii area mgr. E.F. Hutton & Co., Honolulu, 1966—; resident mgr. Prudential-Bache Securities, Honolulu, 1989—; mem. bus. conduct com. Nat. Assn. Securities Dealers, San Francisco, 1972-74. Bd. dirs. Downtown Improvement Assn., Honolulu, 1983—; vice chmn. Met. YMCA, Honolulu, 1985—; mem. bd. trustees Seabury Hall, Maui, Hawaii. Served to maj. USMC, 1954-60. Mem. Securities Industry Assn. (govt. relations com. 1980-87), Hawaii C. of C. (bd. dirs. 1985-88). Republican. Mem United Ch. Christ. Lodge: Rotary (pres. Honolulu club 1986-87, pres. Waikiki club 1966-67). Home: 3721 Kanaina Ave Apt 122 Honolulu HI 96813 Office: Prudential-Bache Securities 2 Waterfront Pla Ste #400 Honolulu HI 96813

NORRIS, WAYNE BRUCE, physicist; b. Passaic, N.J., Mar. 13, 1947; s. Harold Quittman and Helen Margaret (Currey) N.; m. Maryann Nora Cassidy, Apr. 17, 1971; children: Brian Eric, Zachary Thomas. BA in Physics, U. Calif., Santa Barbara, 1969; postgrad in human factors, U. Calif., 1976-77. Physicist Rockwell Internat. Sci. Ctr., Thousand Oaks, Calif., 1969-72; environ. test tech. Approved Engring. Test Labs., Chatsworth, Calif., 1972; computer programmer Jet Propulsion Lab., Pasadena, 1972-73; computer analyst Fed. Electric div. ITT, Vandenberg AFB, Calif., 1973-74, McGraw Hill, Santa Barbara, Calif., 1974; computer cons. various firms, 1974-85; environ. cons. Norris Assocs., Santa Barbara, 1975-78; diver/tender Oceaneering Internat., 1978; pres. Norris Airways, 1978-81, Gasohol Inc., 1979-82; physicist, mem. tech. staff Gen. Rsch. Corp., Santa Barbara, 1985—. Author: The Gasohol Primer, 1980, The Big Book of Photocopier Humor, 1984, You Don't Have to be Crazy to Work Here, But It Sure Helps, 1986. Mem. Santa Barbara Co. Grand Jury, 1977-78; pres., v.p., bd. dirs. MADD, Santa Barbara, 1982-88; candidate for U.S. Ho. of Reps. from 19th Congl. Dist. Calif., 1984, 86. Mem. IEEE, Santa Barbara Sci. and Engring. Council, Assn. Old Crows. Democrat. Home: 215 Palisades Dr Santa Barbara CA 93109-1943 office: Gen Rsch Corp 5383 Hollister Ave Santa Barbara CA 93111-2349

NORRIS, WAYNE OREN, corporate executive; b. Houston, Nov. 17, 1952; s. Oren Tom and Doris (Paker) N. BA in Acctg. and Theology, Houston Bapt. U., 1975; MBA in Fin., U. Houston, 1976. Auditor Houston Natural Gas Corp., 1975; contr. Gen. Homes, Inc., Houston, 1975-77, King-Wilkinson, Inc., Houston, 1977-78; pres. Norris & Assocs., Dallas, 1978-84; contr. Rollins Environ. Svcs., Inc., Baton Rouge, 1984-86; v.p., sec., treas. TSD Systems Corp., Bakersfield, Calif., 1986—, TSD Remedial Svcs. Corp., Bakersfield, 1988—. Named one of Outstanding Young Men of Am., 1983. Mem. Money Guild (mem. fin. outlook forum), Kiwanis. Repulican. Home: 2417 Mountain Oak Bakersfield CA 93111 Office: TSD Systems Corp 2000 Oak St Ste 2-A Bakersfield CA 93301

NORTH, WHEELER JAMES, marine ecologist, educator; b. San Francisco, Jan. 2, 1922; s. Wheeler Orrin and Florence Julia (Ross) N.; m. Barbara Alice Best, Apr. 25, 1964; children: Hannah Catherine, Wheeler Orrin. B.S. in Engring, Calif. Inst. Tech., 1944; M.S. in Oceanography, U. Calif. at San Diego, 1953; Ph.D., 1953. NSF postdoctoral fellow Cambridge (Eng.) U.; Electronics engr. U.S. Navy Electronics Lab., Point Loma, Calif., 1947-48; asst. research biologist Scripps Inst. Oceanography, U. Calif. at San Diego, 1953, Rockefeller postdoctoral fellow, 1955-56; asst. research biologist Inst. Marine Resources Scripps Inst. Oceanography, 1956-63; assoc. prof. Calif. Inst. Tech., Pasadena, 1963-70; prof. Calif. Inst. Tech., 1970—; Cons. marine biology U.S. Govt., State of Calif., San Francisco, Los Angeles, San Diego, numerous industries, 1957—; Phi Beta Kappa vis. scholar, 1973-74; mem. Calif. Adv. Commn., 1972-73, Nav. and Ocean Devel. Commn., 1973-76; dir. Marine Biol. Cons. Contbr. articles to profl. jours. Recipient NOGI award Underwater Soc. Am., 1975. Mem. Am. Littoral Soc. (James Duggan award), AAAS, Am. Soc. Limnology and Oceanography, Am. Soc. Zoology, Soc. Gen. Physiology, Calif. Acad. Sci., Fish Protective Assn. (dir.), N.Y. Acad. Sci., Am. Geophys. Union, Smithsonian Instn., Am. San Diego museums, Marine Tech. Soc., Western Soc. Naturalists, Calif. Soc. Profl. Engrs., Am. Zoomalac Soc., Internat. Oceanographic Found., Sigma Xi.

NORTHCRAFT, SHIRLEY LOUISE, educator; b. Eugene, Oreg., June 8, 1950; d. Robert Eugene and Aline Mae (Jennings) Kischel; m. Ronald Owen Northcraft, June 12, 1976; children: Lori Diane, Daniel Adam. BS in Elem. Edn., Western Oreg. State Coll., 1973; MS in Curriculum, Instrn., U. Oreg., 1975. Cert. tchr., Oreg. Tchr. Hucrest Elem. Sch., Roseburg, Oreg., 1972—; cons., participant revisions in curriculum materials, evaluation materials. Judge, cons., com. chair Jr. Miss Scholarship program, Roseburg, 1974—; bd. dirs. Doug County Schs. Fed. Credit Union, Roseburg, 1980-82. Fellow Oreg. State Schs. Standardization Cadre; mem. Altrusa, Roseburg Jaycettes, Alpha Delta Kappa (corr. sec.). Republican. Presbyterian. Home: 3128 NE Monterey Dr Roseburg OR 97470 Office: Hucrest Elem Sch 1810 NW Kline St Roseburg OR 97470

NORTHCUTT, HELENE LOUISE BERKING (MRS. CHARLES PHILLIP NORTHCUTT), artist, educator; b. Hannibal, Mo., July 6, 1916; d. Robert Stanley and Alice Lee (Adkisson) Berking; student Christian Coll., Columbia, Mo., 1932-33; B.S., U. Mo., 1939, A.M., 1940, Ed.D., 1959; m. Charles Phillip Northcutt, June 4, 1938 (dec.); children—John Berking, Francois Lee Northcutt Hedeen. Art tchr., supr. Oakwood High Sch. and Elem. Sch., 1937-39; tchr. jr. high sch. U. Mo. Lab. Sch., 1939-40; tchr. elem. art, Memphis, Mo., 1941; county fine arts supr., Ralls County, Mo., 1941-42; tchr. art high sch., Columbia, 1943-44; tchr. art jr. high sch., Hannibal, Mo., 1951-54; supr. art Ralls County Reorganized Sch. Dist. VI, New London, 1954-56; vis prof. U. Upper Iowa, 1956; instr. U. Mo., 1956-57; prof. art Eastern Mont. Coll. unit U. Mont., Billings, from 1957, now prof. emeritus, mem. grad. faculty; vis. prof. art U. B.C., Vancouver, 1965; cons. in curriculum in art edn.; cons. environ. edn., cons. on Indian edn., early childhood; exhibits fibers and paintings; state dir. Am. Art Week, Am. Artists Profl. League, 1963-65; exhibit chmn. E.M.C. Gallery Fine Arts; program chmn. Becky Thatcher council Girl Scouts U.S.A., 1946-48; bd. dirs., treas. United Christian Campus Ministry; bd. dirs. Growth Through Art. Recipient scholarship Delta Kappa Gamma, 1956-57; Nat. Press award Gen. Fedn. Women's Clubs, 1951; named Outstanding Honor Grad. U. Mo., 1968; citations for distinctive service Eastern Mont. Coll., Helene B. Northcutt Gallery named in her honor. Mem. Nat. Soc. Coll. Profs., AAUP, Mont. Edn. Assn. (past pres. Eastern Faculty unit; v.p. dept. higher edn. 1966-68, dept. pres. 1968-70) Nat., Mont. (sec. 1967-69) art edn. assns., AAUW (past chpt. pres.), Mont. Early Childhood Edn. Assn., Gen. Fedn. Women's Clubs (local past pres.), Delta Kappa Gamma (past chpt. pres., chmn. com., chmn. state world fellowship), Delta Phi Delta, Kappa Delta Epsilon. Methodist (mem. commn. higher edn. ministries, Yellowstone Conf.). Club: Eastern Montana College Faculty (Billings, Mont.). Author: Creative Expression, 1964; Competency base Module-Methods and Materials, 1974; contbr. to publs. in field; reviewer, editor manuscripts on art and art edn. Home: M-3 Timbers Townhomes 3224 Granger Ave E Billings MT 59102

NORTHRUP, SANDRA JOAN, nurse; b. Indpls., Apr. 22, 1938; d. Clifford LaVern and Christine (Cummingham) Cox; m. Carl Ellis, Feb. 14, 1958 (div. 1968); children: April Lyn, Ronald Murray, Judith Ann Ellis Berezyk; m. John Judson Northrup, Mar. 2, 1979. RN, Clark County (Nev.) Community Coll., 1973; student, U. Nev., 1973-76. Cert. home nurse, 1973. Staff nurse Univ. Med. Ctr., Las Vegas, Nev., 1976-77, Desert Springs Hosp., Las Vegas, 1977-79; supr., coordinator ins. Women's Hosp., Las Vegas, 1977-82; home health nurse Clark County Health Dist., Las Vegas, 1979-83; dir. nursing Tenn. State Prison, Nashville, 1983-85; cons. nursing State of Tenn., Nashville, 1985-86; crisis counselor, sr. psych. nurse State of Nev., Las Vegas, 1987—. Recipient Appreciation award ARC. Mem. Am. Nurses Assn., Nev. Nurses Assn., Phi Kappa Phi, Phi Lambda Alpha. Democrat. Baptist. Lodge: Order Ea. Star. Office: Crisis Unit Univ Med Ctr 1800 W Charleston Blvd Las Vegas NV 89106

NORTHRUP, WILLIAM STEPHEN, JR., television producer; b. South Kingstown, R.I., Aug. 18, 1946; s. William Stephen and Elizabeth (Northup) N.; m. Lynn Louise Henneberry, July 27, 1968. Grad., Northeast Broadcasting Sch., Boston, 1965; cert., Inst. for Orgn. Mgmt., Washington, 1975. News dir. Sta. WPRO, Providence, 1972-74; v.p. communications Providence C. of C., 1974-76; reporter Sta. WJAR-TV, NBC, Providence, 1977-81; asst. news dir. Sta. WLNE-TV, CBS, Providence, 1981-83, news dir., 1983-84; exec. producer news Sta. KHJ-TV, L.A., 1984--. Mem. Acad. TV Arts and Scis. (Emmy award 1986), Radio-TV News Assn. So. Calif. (judges search com. 1988--, Golden Mikew award 1986), Am. Film Inst. Episcopalian. Office: Sta KHJ-TV News 5515 Melrose Ave Los Angeles CA 90038

NORTON, CLIFF, real estate executive; b. Seattle, Dec. 20, 1926; s. Cyrus J.N. and Kathrine (Armstrong) N.; m. Brenda V. Haberlin, June 20, 1947; children: Robert, Virginia, Marlene, Constance. Cert. Real Estate Grad. Real Estate Inst., Green River Coll., Auburn, Wash., 1971-75. Ordained to ministry Presbyn. Ch., as deacon 1949, as elder 1953. Mgr. Safeway Stores, Inc., Seattle, 1944-56; prin. Cliff's Food Ctr., Seattle, 1956-66; br. exec. v.p., mgr. salesman John L. Scott Real Estate, Seattle, 1968—; pres., bd. dirs. SW Multiple Listing Service, Seattle, 1975-79. Pres. Internat. New Life Ministries, Seattle, 1986—; bd. dirs. Seattle Youth for Christ, 1971—; adv. bd. Union Gospel Mission, Seattle; missionary Homes Service. Mem. Assn. Realtors, Burien C. of C. (pres.). Republican. Office: John L Scott Real Estate PO Box 97015 Bellevue WA 98166

NORTON, DUNBAR SUTTON, economic developer; b. Hoquiam, Wash., Jan. 30, 1926; s. Percy Dunbar and Anna Fedelia (Sutton) N.; m. Kathleen Margaret Mullarky, Dec. 21, 1948; children: Priscilla K., Rebecca C., Jennifer A., Douglas S. Student, U. Oreg., 1946-48; diploma, U.S. Army Command & Gen. Staff, 1964. Commd. 2d lt. U.S. Army, 1944, advanced through grades to lt. col., ret., 1974; dir. econ. devel. dept. Yuma (Ariz.) County C. of C., 1974-83; exec. v.p. Lakin Enterprises, Yuma, 1983-87; owner Norton Cons., Yuma, 1987—; corp. mem. Yuma Econ. Devel. Corp., 1984—; bd. dirs. Yuma-La Paz County Vocat. Plan, Yuma. Mem. County of Yuma Indsl. Devel. Authority, 1984—; vice chmn. Yuman Main St. Bd., 1988—; chmn. fundraising com. Yuma Cross Pk. Coun., 1984-88, sec., 1988—; chmn. devel. com. Yuma County Airport Authority, 1985—. Decorated Legion of Merit, Bronze Star. Mem. Ariz. Assn. for Indsl. Devel. (bd. dirs. 1975-82, pres. 1982-83, Developer of the Yr. 1977), Yuma Edn. Bus. Alliance., Yuma Execs. Assn. (sec., treas., exec. dir.). Republican. Episcopalian. Home and Office: 11843 Calle Del Cid Yuma AZ 85365

NORTON, KAREN ANN, accountant; b. Paynesville, Minn., Nov. 1, 1950; d. Dale Francis and Ruby Grace (Gehlhar) N. BA, U. Minn., 1972; postgrad. U. Md., 1978; cert. acctg. U.S. Dept. Agr. Grad. Sch., 1978; postgrad. Calif. State Poly. U.-Pomona, 1984—. CPA, Md. Securities transactions analyst Bur. of Pub. Debt., Washington, 1972-79, internal auditor, 1979-81; internal auditor IRS, Washington, 1981; sr. acct. World Vision Internat., Monrovia, Calif., 1981-83, acctg. supr., 1983-87; sr. systems liaison specialist, Home Savs. Am., 1987—; cons. (vol.) info. systems John M. Perkins Found., Pasadena, Calif., 1985-86. Author (poetry): Ode to Joyce, 1985 (Golden Poet award 1985). Second v.p. chpt. Nat. Treasury Employees Union, Washington, 1978, editor chpt. newsletter; mem. M-2 Prisoners Sponsorship Program, Chino, Calif., 1984-86. Recipient Spl. Achievement award Dept. Treasury, 1976, Superior Performance award, 1977-78; Charles and Ellora Alliss scholar, 1968. Mem. Christian Ministries Mgmt. Assn., Nat. Assn. Accts. Mem. Covenant Ch. Avocations: chess, racquetball, whitewater rafting.

NORTON, MAXWELL VANKONYNENBU, university administrator; b. Modesto, Calif., July 13, 1954; s. Max C and Adrianna (VanKonynenburg) N.; m. Diane Karen Souza, July 21, 1959; children: Thys Albert, Linnea Bernice. BS, Calif. State U., Fresno, 1977, MS, 1979. With Konynenburg Farms, Salida, Calif., 1972-77; lectr. Calif. State U., Fresno, 1977-79; farmer Norton Enterprises, Salida, Calif., 1977-87; farm advisor U. Calif., Merced, 1979—; pres. U. Calif. Coop. Extension Acad. Assembly; chmn. Merced County Econ. Devel. Com.; mem. Merced High Sch. Agr. Adv. Com. Bd. dirs. Merced County Farm Bur., 1986-89. Calif. Agrl. Leadership Program fellow Agr. Edn. Found., Templeton, 1981-83. Mem. Internat. Soc. Hort. Sci., Internat. Dwarf Fruit Tree Assn., Am. Soc. Enology and Viticulture, Agrl. Leadership Assocs., Calif. Assn. Farm Advisors and Specialists, Merced County C. of C. (dir. 1988, 89, 90, 91, outstanding agriculturalist 1987), Elks. Republican. Home: 5865 Victoria Way Merced CA 95340 Office: U Calif Coop Extension 2145 Wardrobe Merced CA 95340

NORTON, PATRICIA LOUISE, mortgage company executive, realtor; b. Kansas City, Kans., June 17, 1943; d. Frank Royal and Mary Aline (Brown) O'Donnell; m. Roger David Witulski (div.); children: Daphne Laurel, Cynthia Kay, Linda Marie, Peter Anthony; m. Gerald Logan Norton, Jan. 8, 1983. Student, U. Denver, 1961-64. Lic. real estate broker, securities broker dealer. Pres. Quasar Mgmt., Denver, 1970-82; mortgage broker Wedgwood Realtors, Wheat Ridge, Colo., 1982-83; v.p. Colo. Mortgage Exchange, Englewood, Colo., 1983—; pres. Norton Real estate and Mortgage Investment Co., Denver, 1985—; sec. Wellton Mortgage Co., Englewood, 1987—. Pres. PTSA Merrill Middle Sch., Denver, 1981-83, Consumer Edn. Inst.; active Colo. Hist. Soc., 1987—, Denver Urban Forest, 1987—. Mem. Colo. Assn. Mortgage Brokers 9sec., edn. dir. 1988—), Denver Bd. Realtors, Young Mortgage Bankers Com. Republican. Office: 333 W Hampden Ave Englewood CO 80110

NORTON, PAUL RAYMOND, physicist; b. Mpls., Jan. 26, 1943; s. Raymond and Vivian Norton; m. Elyse June Meitzler, Aug. 21, 1976; children: Wynne, Andrew, Erik. AB, Carleton Coll., 1965; PhD in Physics, Syracuse U., 1970. Rsch. assoc. Syracuse (N.Y.) U., 1970-73; mem. tech. staff Bell Labs., Allentown, Pa., 1973-75, Murray Hill, N.J., 1975-76; prin. scientist Honeywell Rsch. Ctr., Bloomington, Minn., 1976-79; mem. tech. staff Santa Barbara Rsch. Ctr., Goleta, Calif., 1979-80, sect. head, 1980-85, dept. mgr., 1985-88, lab. mgr., 1988--. Contbr. articles to profl. jours.; patentee in field. Mem. AAAS. Office: Santa Barbara Rsch Ctr 75 Coromar Dr Goleta CA 93117

NORTON, (CHARLES) PHILIP, JR., real estate developer; b. L.A., Apr. 9, 1914; s. Charles Philip and Lalita (Legerton) N.; m. Lillian Marie Bergin, July 25, 1943; children: Charles Philip III, Candace. Student, U. So. Calif., 1934-36. With Philip Norton, Inc., L.A., 1933-42, 46-59, pres., 1959—; founding chmn. bd. Wilshire Nat. Bank, 1971—; bd. dirs. Bel Air Savs. and Loan Assn. Mem. bd. govs. L.A. Welfare Fedn., 1961-64. Mem. Calif. Real Estate Assn. (dir.), S. Bay Assn. Real Estate Bds. (vice chmn. 1938-39), Calif. Assn. Realtors, Riviera Tennis Club, Palos Verdes Estates Realty Bd. (past pres.), Investors League Am., L.A. Real Estate Bd. (pres. 1971. regional v.p. 1972), Shadow Mt. Racquet Club, Bel Air Bay Club, Phi Kappa Tau, Phi Mu Alpha. Home: 1621 Amalfi Dr Pacific Palisades CA 90272 Office: 11911 San Vicente Blvd Los Angeles CA 90049

NORTON, PHILIP HAYES, physician; b. Columbus, June 28, 1929; s. Kenneth Bain and Marion (Hayes) N.; m. Marion Martin, Apr. 29, 1960. BSBA, Ohio State U., 1952. Indsl. engr. Westinghouse Corp., Columbus, 1952-55; physician pvt. practice Denver, 1960—; bd. dirs. Aurora (Colo.) Presbyn. Hosp. Mem. Adams-Aurora Med. Soc., Cen. Colo. Acad. (pres. 1965), Mensa. Republican. Episcopalian. Home: 2800 S University #39 Denver CO 80210

NORWOOD, RONALD EUGENE, auditor, accountant; b. Cresent, Okla., Dec. 24, 1952; s. Jimmie L. and Charlene L. (House) N.; m. Cathyn Lynn Reed, Nov. 20, 1971 (div. 1976); children: Katrina, LaFrances, Portia. AS, Enid (Okla.) Bus. Coll., 1974; BS, Phillips U., 1979. Jr. acct. Phillips Petroleum Co., Bartlesville, Okla., 1974-75; fin. dir. Operation Uplift, Inc., Enid, 1976-79; cons. Nash and Assocs., Tulsa, 1979-80; acct. EDA Corp., Stillwater, Okla., 1980-81, Mitchelll Cos., Tulsa, 1981-83; cons. Hill Constrn., Enid, 1983, De'Zanella by J. Scott, Oklahoma City, 1983; examiner, auditor Colo. Real Estate Commn., Denver, 1984—; rsch. analyst U.S. Dept. Labor, Washington, 1978. Sgt. U.S. Army, 1970-73. Named Young Bus. Man of Yr., State of Okla., 1978. Mem. Nat. Assn. Black Accts. Democrat.

NORWOOD, WILLIAM KNIGHT, dentist; b. Balt., June 26, 1928; s. William Knight and Mae Virginia (Cleaveland) N.; m. Irene Marie Alfke, Dec. 27, 1953; children: Susan, Geoffrey, Virginia, Kathryn. BS, Swarthmore, 1950; DDS, Northwestern U., 1954. Gen. practice dentistry Spokane, Wash., 1956--. Trustee, YMCA, Spokane, 1965-79; pres. Mead Sch. Bd., Spokane, 1968-72. LT. USN, 1954-56. Mem. Kiwanis (sec. Spokane chpt. 1959-67, pres. 1978-79, sec. 1987—). Republican. Episcopalian. Office: W 22 Central Spokane WA 99205

NOSLER, ROBERT AMOS, sports company executive; b. Ashland, Oreg., Apr. 21, 1946; s. John Amos and Louise (Booz) N.; m. Joan Kathleen Hilliard, July 15, 1967; children: Christie Lynn, Jill Ann, John Robert. Student, U. Oreg., 1965. V.p., gen. mgr. Nosler Bullets, Inc., Bend, Oreg., 1974-88; pres., chief exec. officer Nosler Bullets, Inc., 1988—. Editor: Nosler Reloading Manual #1, 1976. Bd. dirs. Bend C. of C., 1984-88, treas., 1988; chmn. Central Oreg. Welcome Ctr. Steering Com., 1988. With USN, 1966-70. Recipient Pres.'s award Bend C. of C., 1984, 87. Mem. Nat. Reloading Mfrs. Assn. (dir. 1982-86, pres. 1984-86), Greater Bend Rotary (dir. 1989). Republican. Lutheran. Office: Nosler Bullets Inc 107 SW Columbia Bend OR 97702

NOTEWARE, MARGUERITE SMITH, speech and langauge specialist; b. Stockton, Calif., Aug. 25, 1928; d. James Arthur and Florence Marion (Williams) Smith; m. Warren Douglass Noteware, July 22, 1951; children: James Douglass, Brian Arthur, Frederick Harold. BA, U. Pacific, 1950, MA, 1970. Cert. tchr. elem. and jr. high schs., Calif. Elem. sch. tchr. Stockton Unified Sch. Dist., 1950-51, speech and lang. specialist, 1970—; elem. sch. tchr. Isleton (Calif.) Sch. Dist., 1951-52, 59-66; speech therapist San Joaquin (Calif.) County Schs., 1966-70; with Stockton Pupil Personnel Assn., 1973-87. Pres. bd. dirs. Stockton Camp Fire Girls (recipient Luther Halsey Gulick award 1970, bd. pres. 1969-70). Mem. AAUW, PEO, Delta Kappa Gamma, Phi Kappa Phi. Republican. Methodist. Home: 1615 Sheridan Way Stockton CA 95207

NOTEWARE, WARREN DOUGLASS, commissioner, civil engineer; b. Stockton, Calif., Aug. 29, 1925; s. Harold Douglass and Esther (Ulrey) N.; m. Marguerite Smith, July 22, 1951; children: James Douglass, Brian Arthur, Frederick Harold. BSCE, Stanford U., 1949. Registered civil engr., Calif. Owner Diversified Farming Operation, Isleton, Calif., 1959-70, Noteware and Assocs., Isleton and Manteca, Calif., 1953-76; pres. Associated Engrs. and Planners, Manteca, 1976-82; mem. staff Water Resources Control Bd., Sacramento, 1982-84; commr. Calif. Energy Commn., Sacramento, 1984—. Designer Calvary AOG Ch., 1982, gymnasium and classrooms St. Anthony's Ch., 1973, Manteca News Bldg., 1975, San Joaquin Farm Bur. Bldg., 1972. Served with USN, 1944-46. Mem. NSPE, Assn. Energy Engrs. Republican. Methodist. Office: Calif Energy Cmmn 1516 9th St Sacramento CA 95814

NOTHMANN, RUDOLF S., legal researcher; b. Hamburg, W.Ger., Feb. 4, 1907; came to U.S., 1941, naturalized, 1943; s. Nathan and Henrietta G. (Heymann) N. Referendar, U. Hamburg, 1929, Ph.D. in Law, 1932; postgrad. U. Liverpool Law Sch. (Eng.), 1931-32. Law clk. Hamburg Cts., 1929-33; export, legal adviser, adviser ocean marine ins. various firms, Ger., Eng., Sweden, Calif., 1933-43, 46-47; instr. fgn. exchange, fgn. trade Extension div. UCLA, 1947-48, vis. assoc. prof. UCLA, 1951; asst. prof. econs. Whittier Coll., 1948-50, assoc. prof., 1950-51; contract work U.S. Air Force, U.S. Navy, 1953-59; contract negotiator space projects, space and missile systems orgn. U.S. Air Force, Los Angeles, 1959-77; pvt. researcher in internat. comml. law, Pacific Palisades, Calif., 1977—. Served with U.S. Army, 1943-45; ETO. Recipient Gold Tape award Air Force Systems Command, 1970. Mem. Internat. Bar Assn. (vice chmn. internat. sales and related comml. trans. com. 1977-82), Am. Econ. Assn., Calif. Bar Assn. (internat. law sect.), Am. Soc. Internat. Law. Author: The Insurance Certificate in International Ocean Marine Insurance and Foreign Trade, 1932; The Oldest Corporation in the World: Six Hundred Years of Economic Evolution, 1949. Club: Uebersee (Hamburg). Home: PO Box 32 Pacific Palisades CA 90272

NOTKIN, DAVID, computer science educator; b. Syracuse, N.Y., Jan. 1, 1955; s. Herbert and Isabell (Schulman) N.; m. Catherine Vaughn Tuttle, July 3, 1988. ScB in computer sci., Brown U., 1977; PhD in computer sci., Carnegie-Mellon U., 1984. Assoc. prof. computer sci. U. Wash., Seattle, 1984—. Contbr. articles to profl. jours. Named NSF Presdl. Young Investigator, 1988, others. Mem. IEEE, Assn. Computing Mechanism, Sigma Xi. Democrat. Jewish. Home: 4412 Corliss Ave N Seattle WA 98103 Office: U Washington Dept Computer Sci Seattle WA 98195

NOVICK, JUDITH ANN, transportation executive; b. El Paso, Feb. 15, 1948; d. Jehiel and Dorothy Ruth (Selicovitz) Novick; m. Jonas Simonis, May 13, 1988; 1 son, Darren Scott. BS in Edn., So. Ill. U., Carbondale, 1970; MEd, Nat. Coll. Edn., 1974; MBA, St. Mary's Coll., Moraga, Calif., 1984. Asst. credit mgr. States Steamship, San Francisco, 1976-78; asst. traffic mgr. Lykes Bros., Seattle, 1979; asst. mktg. mgr. Barber Lines, Houston, 1980-81; pricing mgr. So. Pacific Internat., San Francisco, 1981; mgr. internat. Star Shipping, San Francisco, 1981-84, line mgr., 1984-87; dist. educator Equal Rights Ammendment, Evanston, Ill., 1973-74. Republican. Jewish. Home: 4606 SW 319th St Federal Way WA 98023

NOVIE, MARY KELTZ, manufacturing company executive; b. Lawrence, Kans., Mar. 23, 1949; d. Harold L. and Dorothy C. (Cohen) Keltz; m. Jan Novie, July 7, 1972 (div. Feb. 1983). BA, Colo. Coll., 1971. Sales rep. Livingston's, San Francisco, 1971, buyer, 1972-80, mdse. mgr., 1981-84; v.p. Circa Corp., San Francisco, 1985—. Grantee Ford Found., 1971. Mem. Fashion Group (past treas., past program chmn.), Friends of Ethnic Art, Women's Profl. Network. Democrat. Club: Commonwealth (San Francisco). Office: Circa Corp 2300 Harrison St San Francisco CA 94110

NOWINSKI, STUART ALAN, chemist, educator; b. Colorado Springs, Colo., Oct. 28, 1953; s. Stanley Anthony and Beatrice Ellen (Merefield) N. BS in Chemistry, Calif. State U., Long Beach, 1975, MS in Chemistry, 1987. Cert. secondary phys. sci. tchr. Analytical chemist U.S. Borax and Chem., Wilmington, Calif., 1976-78; tchr. chemistry and advanced placement chemistry San Marino (Calif.) High Sch., 1978-85; tchr. chemistry Pasadena (Calif.) City Coll., 1985; tchr. chemistry and advanced placement chemistry Los Alamitos (Calif.) High Sch., 1985-87; instr. chemistry Pasadena (Calif.) City Coll., 1987-88, Glendale (Calif.) City Coll., 1988—; mem. Tchr. Preparation and Assessment Adv. Panel State of Calif. Recipient PTSA Service award, San Marino, Calif., 1983; DOE research grantee, 1985. Mem. Am. Chem. Soc. (exec. com. So. Calif. sect. 1982-85, chmn. ednl. affairs com. So. Calif. sect. 1983-85, Chemistry Tchr. of Yr. award So. Calif. sect. 1984, Western Regional Teaching award 1984), Calif. Assn. Chemistry Tchrs. (treas. So. sect. 1983-86), Nat. Sci. Tchrs. Assn., State of Calif. Single Subject Credential Review Bd., Calif. State U. Long Beach Secondary Edn. Adv. Com., Phi Lambda Upsilon. Republican. Roman Catholic. Home: 1444 Sepulveda St San Pedro CA 90732

NOWLIN, JANET, utilities executive, data processing executive; b. Buffalo, July 16, 1953; d. Sam Angelo and Josephine (Sciolino) Conti; m. Harry Wayne Nowlin, Nov. 30, 1973 (div. Oct. 1988); 1 child, Wesley Wayne. Student, Phoenix Coll., 1972-73; cert., IBM Tech., 1986. Cert. data processor and programmer. Supr. data processing Levitz Furniture, Phoenix, 1970-74; mgr. data processing dept. Ariz. Water Co., Phoenix, 1974—, cons., 1984. Mem. Data Processing Mgmt. Assn., Postal Customer Council, Beta Sigma Phi (sec. 1985-86). Republican. Roman Catholic. Home: 4019 W Meadow Glendale AZ 85308 Office: Ariz Water Co 2612 N 16th St Phoenix AZ 85006

NOYCE, ROBERT NORTON, electronics company executive; b. Burlington, Iowa, Dec. 12, 1927; s. Ralph B. and Harriet (Norton) N.; m. Ann S. Bowers; children: William B., Pendred, Priscilla, Margaret. BA, Grinnell Coll., 1949; PhD, MIT, 1953. Rsch. engr. Philco Corp., Phila., 1953-56, Shockley Semicondr. Lab., Mountain View, Calif., 1956-57; founder, dir. rsch. Fairchild Semicondr., Mountain View, 1957-59; v.p., gen. mgr. Fairchild Semicondr., 1959-65; group v.p. Fairchild Camera & Instrument, Mountain View, 1965-68; founder, pres. Intel Corp., Santa Clara, Calif., 1968-75; chmn. Intel Corp., 1968-75, vice chmn., 1979—; pres., chief exec. officer Sematech, Austin, Tex., 1988—. Patentee in field. Trustee Grinnell Coll., 1962—. Recipient Stuart Ballentine award Franklin Inst., 1967, Harry Goode award AFIPS, 1978, Nat. Medal of Sci., 1979, Nat. Medal of Tech. Pres. of U.S., 1987, Harold Pender award U. Pa., 1980, John Fritz medal, 1989; named to Nat. Bus. Hall of Fame, 1989. Fellow IEEE (Cledo Brunetti award 1978, medal of honor 1978, Faraday medal 1979); mem. Nat. Acad. Engring., AAAS, Nat. Acad. Sci. Office: Sematech 2706 Montopolis Dr Austin TX 78741

NOYES, H(ENRY) PIERRE, physicist; b. Paris, Dec. 10, 1923; s. William Albert and Katharine Haworth (Macy) N.; m. Mary Wilson, Dec. 20, 1947; children—David Brian, Alan Guinn, Katharine Hope. B.A., Harvard U., 1943; Ph.D., U. Calif., Berkeley, 1950. Physicist MIT, 1943-44, U. Calif., Berkeley, 1949-50; Fulbright fellow U. Birmingham, Eng., 1950-51; asst. prof. U. Rochester, N.Y., 1951-55; group leader Lawrence Livermore Lab., 1955-62; Leverhulme lectr. U. Liverpool, Eng., 1957-58; adminstrv. head theory sect. Stanford Linear Accelerator Center, 1962-69; asso. prof. Stanford U., 1962-67, prof., 1967—; vis. scholar Center Advanced Study Behavioral Scis., Stanford, 1968-69; cons. in field. Author papers in field. Chmn. Com. for Direct Attack on Legality of Vietnam War, 1969-72; mem. steering com. Faculty Political Action Group, Stanford U., 1970-72; mem. policy com. U.S. People's Com. on Iran, 1977-79. Served with USNR, 1944-46. Fellow NSF, 1962; Fellow Nat. Humanities Faculty, 1970; recipient Alexander von Humboldt U.S. Sr. Scientist award, 1979. Mem. Alternative Natural Philosophy Assn. (pres. 1979-87, 1st alternative natural philosopher award 1989), Am. Phys. Soc., AAAS, Sigma Xi. Home: 823 Lathrop Dr Stanford CA 94305 Office: Stanford U/Stanford Linear Accelerator Ctr PO Box 4349 Stanford CA 94305

NOZAKI, ERIKO SATO, nurse; b. Yokohama, Japan, Nov. 1, 1956; came to U.S., 1959; d. Isamu and Yoko Jane (Watanabe) Sato; m. Ken Andrew Nozaki, Mar. 27, 1983; children: Matthew, Akira. Assoc. Sci. in Nursing, Pacific Union Coll., 1978; BS in Pub. Health, Loma Linda U., 1980, BS in Nursing, 1982. RN, Calif. Health educator Loma Linda (Calif.) Community Hosp., 1979; ICU nurse Loma Linda U., 1979-83, Glendale (Calif.) Adventist Med. Ctr., 1983; ICU nurse Mercy Gen. Hosp., Sacramento, 1984—, admiting discharge planning, 1988—. Mem. Am. Assn. Critical Care Nurses.

NTESO, TŠEPO OBED, computer scientist; b. Leribe, Lesotho, Oct. 1, 1944; came to U.S., 1971; s. Lekokoto Elliot and Mamoahloli (Flora) N.; m. Jane Mookho Manyeli, Aug. 31, 1968; children: Teboho Derek, Thato Yevette. BSEE, U. Alta., Can., 1968; MSEE, Carleton U., Ottawa, Can., 1972. Jr. programmer Computer Machinery Corp., Santa Monica, Calif., 1972-74; sr. programmer Transaction Tech. Inc., Los Angeles, 1974-77, Data Gen., Anaheim, Calif., 1977-80; computer scientist McDonnel Douglas Astronautics, Monrovia, Calif., 1980-82; software engr. Tylan Corp., Carson, Calif., 1982-87; sr. software engr. Emulex Corp., Costa Mesa, Calif., 1987—. Mem. AAAS, N.Y. Acad. Sci., Planetary Soc.

NULL, PAUL BRYAN, minister; b. Oakland, Calif., May 7, 1944; s. Carleton Elliot and Dorothy Irene (Bryan) N.; m. Renee Yvonne Howell, Aug. 23, 1969; children: Bryan Joseph, Kara Renee. BS, Western Bapt. Coll., 1973; MDiv, Western Conservative Bapt. Sem., 1979. Ordained to ministry Bapt. Ch., 1982. Asst. pastor Bethel Bapt. Ch., Aumsville, Oreg., 1972-74, sr. pastor, 1974-87; sr. pastor The Calvary Congregation, Stockton, Calif., 1987—; trustee Conservative Bapt. Assn. of Oreg., 1982-85, mem. Ch. extension com., 1975-85. Radio show commentator Food for Thought, 1987. Panel mem. Presdl. Anti-Drug Campaign, 1984. Served with U.S. Army, 1965-67. Named Outstanding Young Man Am., 1979. Mem. Conservative Bapt. Assn. of Am., Kiwanis, Lions, Delta Epsilon Chi. Home: 2202 Moutauban Ct Stockton CA 95210 Office: The Calvary Congregation 703 E Swain Rd Stockton CA 95207

NUNIS, RICHARD ARLEN, amusement parks executive; b. Cedartown, Ga., May 30, 1932; s. Doyce Blackman and Winnie E. (Morris) N.; 1 child, Richard Dean. B.S. in Edn, U. So. Calif., 1954. With The Walt Disney Co., 1955—; dir. ops. Disneyland, Calif., 1961-68; chmn. park ops. com. Disneyland, 1968-74; corp. v.p. Disneyland Ops., 1968—, Walt Disney World, Orlando, Fla., 1971—; exec. v.p., then pres. Walt Disney Attractions and Disneyland Internat., 1972—; mem. exec. com. Walt Disney Co.; dir. Sun Bank Inc., Orlando, Fla. Mem. exec. com. Pres.'s Council for Internat. Youth Exchange; bd. dirs. Give the Kids the World; co-chmn. Orange County Com. on Children. Named first acad. All-Am., U. So. Calif., 1952. Mem. Fla. C. of C. (bd. dirs.), Fla. Coun. of 100. Republican. Office: 1313 Harbor Blvd Anaheim CA 92803 also: 1675 Buena Vista Dr Lake Buena Vista FL 32830

NUNN, CANDY LEE, human resources executive; b. San Francisco, Mar. 10, 1946; d. Richard E. and Hazel M. (Spelts) N. BS, Western Coll., Salem, Oreg., 1969; MA, U. Calif., Sacramento, 1972. Cert. jr. coll. instr., Calif. Dean Bapt. U. Am., Atlanta, 1973-76; prof. L.A. Bapt. Coll., 1976-81; mgr. human resources Hughes Aircraft Co., El Segundo, Calif., 1981—; cons.; presenter seminars. Mem. Am. Productivity Assn., Mgmt. Club El Segundo. Republican. Baptist. Office: Hughes Aircraft Co PO Box 92919 Airport Sta Los Angeles CA 90009

NUNN, CHERYL LEE, financial advisor; b. San Bernardino, Calif., Oct. 16, 1954; d. John William and Eura Jean Zylstra; m. Robert H. Nunn (div. 1979); children: Dawn Susan, Heather Deneal. BS in Fin., Brigham Young U., 1983. V.p. Coordinated Fin. Mgmt., Irvine, Calif., 1983-86; pres. Capital Mgmt. Group, Laguna Niguel, Calif., 1986—. Author newspaper column The Beacon, 1986; contbr. articles to profl. jours. Mem. Internat. Assn. Fin. Planning (v.p. Irvine chpt. 1981-88), Inst. Cert. Fin. Planners, Nat. Fedn. Rep. Women. Mormon. Office: Capital Mgmt Group 30101 Town Center Dr Ste 202-B Laguna Niguel CA 92677

NUNN, G. RAYMOND, history educator; b. Pirbright, Surrey, Eng., May 18, 1918; came to U.S., 1951; s. Alfred Gerald Cole and Sybil Amy (Bolton) N.; m. E. Margaret Brown,. BA honours, U. London, 1951, Dip. Librarianship, 1952; MA, U. Mich., 1954, PhD Far Eastern studies, 1957. Head Asia Library Univ. Mich. Library, Ann Arbor, 1951-61; instr. history Univ. Mich., Ann Arbor, 1959-61; prof. history U. Hawaii, Honolulu, 1961-64, prof. history and Asian studies, 1964--, dir. research collections East-West Ctr., 1961-64. Author: Asia and Oceania, A Guide to Archival and Manuscript Sources in the U.S. Maj. inf., Indian Army, 1940-47. Ford Found. fellow, 1956. Mem. Internat. Assn. Orientalist Librarians (pres. 1976-80). Episcopalian. Home: 2631 Ferdinand Ave Honolulu HI 96822 Office: U Hawaii SHAPS 1890 East West Rd Honolulu HI 96822

NUNN, LESLIE EDGAR, lawyer; b. Evansville, Ind., Oct. 10, 1941. BA, U. Evansville, 1964; JD, U. Denver, 1967. Bar: Colo. 1967, N.Mex. 1977. Lawyer, adminstr. Navajo Tribe of Indians, 1973-76; sole practice, Silverton and Cortez, Colo., 1977-78; ptnr. Nunn & Dunlap, Farmington, N.Mex., 1978-84; sole practice, Denver, 1984-87, Burlington, Colo., 1987—. Served with JAGC, USAF, 1967-73. Mem. ABA, Colo., N.Mex., S.W. Colo., San Juan County, Navajo Nation bar assns., World Peace Through Law Assn., World Assn. Lawyers (world chmn. law and agr. com.). Decorated Bronze Star. Contbr. articles to legal jours. Home: 5807 County Rd 47 Burlington CO 80807 Office: 415 14th St Burlington CO 80807

NUNZ, GREGORY JOSEPH, aerospace engineer; b. Batavia, N.Y., May 28, 1934; s. Sylvester Joseph and Elizabeth Marie (Loesell) N.; m. Georgia Monyea Costas, May 30, 1958; children: John, Rebecca, Deirdre, Jaimie, Marta. B. Chem. Engring., Cooper Union, N.Y.C., 1955; postgrad., U. So. Calif., L.A., 1957-62, Calif. State U., Northridge, 1957-62. Mem. tech. staff Rocketdyne div. Rockwell, Canoga Park, Calif., 1955-65, Aerospace Corp., El Segundo, Calif., 1965-70, Jet Propulsion Lab., Pasadena, Calif., 1970-72; chief. monoprop. engring. Bell Aerospace Corp., Buffalo, N.Y., 1972-74; group supr. comb. devices Jet Propulsion Lab., Pasadena, 1974-76; asst. div. leader, program/project mgr. Los Alamos (N.Mex.) Nat. Lab., 1977—; instr. No. N.Mex. Community Coll., Los Alamos, 1978-80; assoc. prof. electronics Los Angeles Pierce Coll., Woodland Hill, Calif., 1961-72; div. head sciences, adj. prof. math. U. N.Mex., Los Alamos, 1980—. Author: Electronics in Our World, 1972; co-author: Electronics Mathematics, Vol. I, II, 1967; contbr. articles to profl. jours.; inventor smallest catalytic liquid NZH4, rocket engine, co-inventor first monoprop/biprop bimodal rocket engine. Mem., investigator Am. Soc. for Psychic Research, So. Calif. chpt., 1970-72; mem. Aerial Phenomena Research Orgn., LA., 1975. Fellow AIAA (assoc.); mem. Tech. Mktg. Soc. Am., Math. Assn. Am., ARISTA, Shrine Club, Masons, Ballut Abyad Temple. Republican. Messianic Jewish. Home: 109 Piedra Dr Los Alamos NM 87544 Office: Los Alamos Nat Lab PO Box 1663 MS D 441 Los Alamos NM 87545

NUSBAUM, DANIEL MICHAEL, humanities, educator; b. Los Angeles, Aug. 27, 1946; s. Robert Abram and Ruth Lillian (Sperling) N.; m. 1968 (div. 1974); 1 child, Micah Robert. BA in English, SUNY, Buffalo, N.Y., 1968; MS in English, State U. Coll., Buffalo, 1970. Cert. tchr. secondary schs. and community coll. Calif., secondary schs. N.Y. Musician various bands, We. N.Y. and So. Calif., 19604-87; substitute tchr. Los Angeles County, Calif., 1972-87; English instr. Los Angeles City Coll., 1987—. Author: essays on edn. and polit reform 1981-87, Teaching in Prison, 1982. Elected intern rep. Buffalo Tchr. Corps., N.Y., 1969; candidate state supr. of pub. instrn. in Calif. 1982, 86, Los Angeles City Sch. Bd. 1983. Named Mus. Artist-in-Residence Calif. Arts Coun., L.A., 1976. Home: 1918 N Taft Ave Los Angeles CA 90068 Office: Los Angeles City Coll 855 N Vermont Ave Los Angeles CA 90029

NUSS, RODNEY GEORGE, military officer; b. New Orleans, Apr. 8, 1952; s. George Leonard and Mildred Lucille (Butman) N.; m. Betty Jane Carpenter, Nov. 22, 1972 (div. Feb. 1984); m. Annette Marie Marandino, Feb. 16, 1985; 1 child, Andrew Joseph. BS in Math. cum laude, Tulane U., 1974; MS in Ops. Rsch., Air Force Inst. Tech., 1984. Commd. 2d lt. USAF, 1974, advanced through grades to maj., 1985; dep. fin. officer 29th Tng. Wing USAF, Craig AFB, Ala., 1974-76; comptroller 12th Missile Warning Group USAF, Thule Air Base, Greenland, 1976-77; missile launch officer 341st Strategic Missile Wing USAF, Malmstrom AFB, Mont., 1978-82; chief plans tech. testbed Process Analysis Br. USAF, Offutt AFB, Nebr., 1984-87, chief ballistic missile evaluation, 1988; chief ICBM Performance div. USAF, Vanderberg AFB, Calif., 1988—. Mem. Am. Assn. for Artificial Intelligence. Republican. Roman Catholic. Home: 744 Cagney Way Lompoc CA 93436 Office: Air Force Operation Test & Evaluation Ctr/OL-BC Vandenberg AFB CA 93437-5000

NUTT, NAN, church administrator; b. Pasadena, Calif., Dec. 25, 1925; d. Paul Geltmacher and Estelle Boggs (Love) White; m. David Ballard Norris, Jan. 8, 1944 (div. 1966); children: Teresa, Anita, Carol, Steven; m. Evan Burchell Nutt, July 14, 1969. AA, Chaffee Jr. Coll., Calif., 1967; BA, Pomona Coll., 1969. Adminstrv. asst to dept. head sch. elec. engring. U. Tenn., Knoxville, 1952-53; adminstrv. asst. to minister of ch. edn. United Congl. Ch., Claremont, 1955-62; adminstrv. asst. to personnel dir. Pomona Coll., Claremont, 1962-63; bus. mgr. 1st Congl. Ch., Long Beach, Calif., 1982-86, ch. adminstr., 1986—. Chmn. Nat. Women's Polit. Caucus, Tucson, 1972, nat. rep., Ariz., 1973-79, chmn. greater Long Beach, 1981, vice chmn., Calif.; pres. Coalition for ERA, Ariz., 1973-79; commr. Cultural Heritage Commn., Long Beach, 1985-87, chair 1987—. Democrat.

NUTTER, CHRISTOPHER GLENN, naval aviator officer; b. Lakewood, Ohio, Mar. 20, 1954; s. Elmer Glenn and Sally Osborne (Johnson) N.; m. Kuniko Tanaka, May 20, 1978; children: Christopher Kenji, William Satoshi. BS in Indsl. Mgmt., Purdue U., 1976; MBA, Webster Coll., 1980; MS in Aero. Engring., Naval Postgrad. Sch., Monterey, Calif., 1986. Advanced jet flight instr. USN, Beeville, Tex., 1979-80; tactical jet pilot USN, Lemoore, Calif., 1981-; civilian flight instr. USN, 1980-. Contbr. articles to profl. jours. Mem. AIAA. Office: VA97 FPO San Francisco CA 96601

NYE, BRIAN ADAMS, securities trader, accountant, real estate developer; b. Boise, Idaho, Nov. 4, 1956; s. William A. and Mary Loa (Layne) N.; married. BBA, Idaho State U., 1979. CPA, Idaho. Acct. Coopers & Lybrand, Boise, 1979-83; controller Chandler Corp., Boise, 1983-84; ptnr. Brian Nye & Assocs. P.A., Boise, 1984—; pres. NICOM Properties, Boise, 1984—; v.p., bd. dirs. Margenes, Inc., Boise, 1985—; stockbroker Dean Witter Reynolds, Inc., Boise, 1989—; account exec. Dean Witter Reynolds, 1988—; prin. Mountain West Communications, Inc. Supporter LeRoy for Gov., Boise, 1986; v.p. Idaho Shakespeare Festival, 1984-85. Named one of Outstanding Young Men, 1984; Buttrey Food Stores fellow, 1979-80. Mem. Am. Inst. CPA's. Idaho Soc. CPA's, Sales and Mktg. Execs., Boise C. of C. (vice chmn. 1984-85). Republican. Methodist. Lodge: Rotary (local pres. 1985-86). Home: 7552 Thunder Mountain Dr Boise ID 83709

NYE, ERIC WILLIAM, educator; b. Omaha, July 31, 1952; s. William Frank and Mary Roberta (Lueder) N.; m. Carol Denison Frost, Dec. 21, 1980. AB, St. Olaf Coll., 1974; MA, U. Chgo., 1976, PhD, 1983; postgrad., Queens' Coll., Cambridge, England, 1979-82. Tutor in coll. writing com. U. Chgo., 1976-79, teaching intern, 1978; supr., tutor in Am. Lit. Cambridge U., England, 1979-82; asst. prof. English U. Wyo., Laramie, Wyo., 1982-89, assoc. prof. English, 1989—; honorary visiting fellow U. Edinburgh (Scotland) Inst. for Advanced Studies in the Humanities, 1987; guest lectr. NEH Summer Inst., Laramie, Wyo., 1985, Carlyle Soc. of Edinburgh, 1987, Wordsworth Summer Conference, Grasmere, England, 1988. Contbr. articles and reviews to profl. jours. Mem. Am. Friends of Cambridge U. Named Nat. Merit Scholar St. Olaf Coll., 1970-74; recipient Grad. Fellowship, Rotary Found., 1979-80, grant U. Wyo., 1984-85, Am. Coun. of Learned Socs., 1988, Disting. Alumnus award, Lincoln (Neb.) E. High Sch., 1986. Mem. Modern Language Assn., Assn. for Documentary Editing, Bibliographical Soc. London, Assn. for Computers and the Humanities, Assn for Literary and Linguistic Computing, Coleridge Soc. (life), Friends of Dove Cottage (life), Charles Lamb Soc., Carlyle Soc., Rsch. Soc. for Victorian Periodicals, The Victorians Inst., The Tennyson Soc., Am. Acad. of Religion-Soc. of Biblical Lit., Penn Club (London), Queens' Coll. Club (Cambridge), Phi Beta Kappa. Home: 1628 Kearney St Laramie WY 82070 Office: Dept English U Wyo Box 3353 Univ Station Laramie WY 82071

NYE, W. MARCUS W., lawyer; b. N.Y.C., Aug. 3, 1945; s. Walter R. and Nora (McLaren) N.; m. Eva Johnson; children: Robbie, Stephanie, Philip, Jennifer. BA, Harvard U., 1967; JD, U. Idaho, 1974. Bar: Idaho 1974, U.S. Dist. Ct. Idaho 1974, U.S. Ct. Appeals (9th cir.) 1980. Ptnr. Racine, Olson, Nye, Cooper & Budge, Pocatello, Idaho, 1974—; vis. prof. law U. Idaho, Moscow, 1984. Fellow ABA (house dels. 1988—), Am. Bar Found.; mem. Idaho State Bar (commr. 1985—, pres. bd. commrs., 1987-88), Idaho Ins. Def. Counsel Assn. (pres. 1982), Idaho State Centennial Found. (commr. 1985—), 6th Dist. Bar Assn. (pres. 1982), Am. Bd. Trial Advocates (adv. 1988—). Home: 173 S 15th Pocatello ID 83201 Office: Racine Olson Nye Cooper & Budge PO Box 1391 Pocatello ID 83201

NYERGES, CHRISTOPHER JOHN, author, educator; b. Pasadena, Calif., Jan. 11, 1955; s. Frank and Marie N.; m. Dolores Miller. Cert. Cherokee literacy instr. Field guide White Tower Inc. & Survival Services, Los Angeles, 1974—; outdoor columnist Pasadena Star News, Knight-Ridder paper, Pasadena, 1976—; syndicated columnist Copley papers, San Diego, 1978-83, Gannet papers, Washington, 1978-81; sales mgr. Survival Services, Newspaper Syndication, Los Angeles, 1978-85; hiking instr. Pasadena City Coll., 1980—, wilderness survival instr.; "Perspective" columnist Foothill paper, Knight Ridder paper, Arcadia, Calif., 1985—; tchr. Am. Indian religion, City of Pasadena Recreation dept., 1975—, tchr. Writing for Pub., Glendale City Coll., 1985; tchr. for special populations adult div. Escalon Inc., Pasadena, 1986-88. Author: Guide to Wild Food, 1978, Urban Wilderness, 1980, Wild Greens and Salads, 1982; editor of "Lament", 1988—. Named Citizen of Yr. Citizens Com. Right to Keep and Bear Arms, 1986-87. Mem. Internat. Assn. Egyptologists, Mensa, NRA. Home: PO Box 42152 Los Angeles CA 90042

NYHAN, WILLIAM LEO, pediatrician, educator; b. Boston, Mar. 13, 1926; s. W. Leo and Mary (Cleary) N.; m. Christine Murphy, Nov. 20, 1948; children: Christopher, Abigail. Student, Harvard U., 1943-45; M.D., Columbia U., 1949; M.S., U. Ill., 1956, Ph.D., 1958; hon. doctorate, Tokushima U., Japan, 1981. Intern Yale U.-Grace-New Haven Hosp., 1949-50, resident, 1950-51, 53-55; asst. prof. pediatrics Johns Hopkins U., 1958-61, assoc. prof., 1961-63; prof. pediatrics, biochemistry U. Miami, 1963-69, chmn. dept. pediatrics, 1963-69; prof. U. Calif., San Diego, 1969—; chmn. dept. pediatrics U. Calif., 1969-86; mem. FDA adv. com. on Teratogenic Effects of Certain Drugs, 1964-70; mem. pediatric panel AMA Council on Drugs, 1964-70; mem. Nat. Adv. Child Health and Human Devel. Council, 1967-71; mem. research adv. com. Calif. Dept. Mental Hygiene, 1969-72; mem. med. and sci. adv. com. Leukemia Soc. Am., Inc., 1968-72; mem. basic adv. com. Nat. Found. March of Dimes, 1973-81; mem. Basil O'Connor Starter grants com., 1973—; mem. clin. cancer program project rev. com. Nat. Cancer Inst., 1977-81; vis. prof. extraordinario U. del Salvador (Argentina), 1982. Author: (with E. Edelson) The Heredity Factor, Genes, Chromosomes and You, 1976,Genetic & Malformation Syndromes in Clinical Medicine, 1976, Abnormalities in Amino Acid Metabolism in Clinical Medicine, 1984, Diagnostic Recognition of Genetic Disease, 1987; editor: Amino Acid Metabolism and Genetic Variation, 1967, Heritable Disorders of Amino Acid Metabolism, 1974; mem. editorial bd. Jour. Pediatrics, 1964-78, King Faisal Hosp. Med. Jour., 1981-85, Western Jour. Medicine, 1974-86, Annals of Saudi Medicine, 1985—; mem. editorial com. Ann. Rev. Nutrition, 1982-86; mem. editorial staff Med. and Pediatric Oncology, 1975-83. Served with U.S. Navy, 1944-46; U.S. Army, 1951-53. Nat. Found. Infantile Paralysis fellow, 1955-58; recipient Commemorative medallion Columbia U. Coll. Physicians and Surgeons, 1967. Mem. AAAS, Am. Fedn. Clin. Research, Am. Chem. Soc., Soc. Pediatric Research (pres. 1970-71), Am. Assn. Cancer Research, Am. Soc. Pharmacology and Exptl. Therapeutics, Western Soc. Pediatric Research (pres. 1976-77), N.Y. Acad. Sci., Am. Acad. Pediatrics (Borden award 1980), Am. Pediatric Soc., Am. Inst. Biol. Scis., Soc. Exptl. Biology and Medicine, Am. Soc. Clin. Investigation, Am. Soc. Human Genetics (dir. 1978-81), Inst. Investigaciones Citologicas (Spain; corr.), Biochem. Soc., Société Française de Pediatrie (corr.), Sigma Xi, Alpha Omega Alpha. Office: U Calif San Diego Dept Pediatrics La Jolla CA 92093

NYIRI, JOSEPH ANTON, sculptor, art educator; b. Racine, Wis., May 24, 1937; s. Joseph Anton Nyiri and Dorothy Marion (Larson) Zink; m. Laura Lee Primeau, Aug. 29, 1959 (dec. Mar. 1982); children: Krista, Nicole, Page; m. Melissa Trent, July 28, 1985. BA, U. Wis., 1959, MS, 1961. Tchr. art Madison (Wis.) Sch. Dist., 1959-62; art cons. San Diego Unified Schs., 1962-65, dist. resource tchr., 1965-73, regional tchr. occupational art, 1973-76, mentor tchr., 1985—; sculptor San Diego, 1962—, fine arts cons., 1966—; head dept. art edn. Serra High Sch., San Diego, 1976—; head dept. art edn. San Diego City Schs., 1976—, mentor tchr., 1985—; instr. art U. Calif. at San Diego, LaJolla, 1967-80, San Diego State U. Extension, 1969—; fine art restorer, 1963—, lectr. art and art edn., 1963—. Exhibited sculpture in numerous one-man, two-person, juried and invitational shows, 1960—, U. Mex.-Baja Calif., 1983. Active Art Guild San Diego Mus. Art. Sgt. Wis. NG, 1955-61. Named One of 3 Tchrs. of Yr. San Diego County, 1983, One of Outstanding Art Tchrs. in U.S. RISD, 1984; recipient Pacific Inst. Creativity award, 1969. Mem. Arts/Worth: Nat. Coun. Art (charter), Allied Craftsmen San Diego. Democrat. Mem. Christian Ch. Home: 3525 Albatross St San Diego CA 92103 Office: Serra High Sch 5156 Santo Rd San Diego CA 92124

NYMAN, CARL JOHN, JR., university dean and official; b. New Orleans, Oct. 21, 1924; s. Carl John Sr. and Dorothy (Kraft) N.; m. Betty Spiegelberg, July 15, 1950; children: Gail Katherine, John Victor, Nancy Kraft. B.S., Tulane U., 1944, M.S., 1945; Ph.D., U. Ill., 1948. Jr.

technologist Shell Oil Co., Wilmington, Cal., 1944; instr. chemistry U. Ill., 1948, Wash. State U., Pullman, 1948-50; asst. prof. Wash. State U., 1950-55, assoc. prof., 1955-61, prof., 1961-88, prof. emeritus, 1988—, acting dean grad. sch., 1968-87, dean and vice provost for rsch. emeritus grad. sch., 1988—; vis. asst. prof. Tulane U., summer 1950; vis. fellow Cornell U., 1959-60, Imperial Coll. Sci. and Tech., 1966-67; Chmn. acad. coun. ctr. grad. study, Richland, Wash., 1968-70, N.W. Assn. Colls. and Univs. for Sci., 1969; mem. Gov.'s Adv. Coun. on Nuclear Energy. Author: (with G.B. King and J.A. Weyh) Problems for General Chemistry and Qualitative Analysis, 4th edit, 1980, (with R.E. Homm) Chemical Equilibrium, 1967, (with W.E. Newton) Procs. of the 1st Internat. Conf. Nitrogen Fixation; Contbr. articles to profl. jours. Mem. Am. Chem. Soc. (chmn. Wash.-Idaho border sect. 1961-62), AAAS, Sigma Xi, Phi Lambda Upsilon, Alpha Chi Sigma, Omicron Delta Kappa. Home: NW 1320 Orion Dr Pullman WA 99163

NYMAN, DAVID HAROLD, nuclear engineer; b. Aberdeen, Wash., May 21, 1938; s. Carl Victor and Elsie Ingagord (Laaksonen) N.; m. Lawana Flora Rice, July 19, 1939. Assoc., Grays Harbor Coll., 1958; BSMetE, U. Wash., 1961, MSMetE, 1963. Engr. Gen. Electric Co., Richland, Wash., 1963-68; engrng. specialist United Nuclear Corp., New Haven, 1968-73; mgr. Westinghouse Hanford subs. Westinghouse Corp., Richland, 1973—. Contbr. articles to profl jours. Mem. ASTM (chmn. F-28 Robotics mem. com. 1986-87), Robotics Internat. of Soc. Mfg. Engrs. (div. chmn. 1985-86, tech. v.p. 1986-88), Robots West Conf. (adv. com. 1984, vice-chmn. 1986, Pres.'s award 1989), Am. Nuclear Soc. (vice-chmn. tech. program com. 1986-87), Am. Soc. Metals., Columbia Basin Dog Tng. Club (pres. 1982-84), Richland Kennel Club, West Highland White Terrier Club of Puget Sound, West Highland White Terrier Club Am. (obedience com. 1982-88, judge tracking dog excellent tests). Republican. Lutheran.

NYMAN, KENNETH BRESEE, small business owner; b. Portland, Oreg., Feb. 3, 1925; s. Carl Axel and Esther O. (Swensen) N.; m. Alice Eleanor Osmondeen, May 7, 1947; children: Brenda, Douglas, Gwendolyn. Grad. high sch., Portland. Office mgr. Johnson Lieber Co., Portland, 1947-78; acct. Russan's Inc., Portland, 1979; chief fin. officer Clear Creek Mut. Telephone Co., Oregon City, 1979-89; owner Nyman Sprinklers, 1989—. Pres. Zion Luth Ch., 1962-63, St. Matthew Luth. Ch., 1977-78. With U.S. Army, 1943-46, South Pacific. Mem. Adminstrv. Mgmt. Soc. (pres. 1973-74), East Side C. of C. (bd. mem. 1958). Republican. Home: 5135 SW Murray Blvd Beaverton OR 97005-3612

NYQUIST, MAURICE OTTO, federal parks agency manager and scientist; b. Fairmont, Minn., May 30, 1944; s. Carl Arthur and Wilda Yvette (Freitag) N.; m. Mary Maud Magee, Aug. 8, 1977; children: Gretchen, Beth. BS in Biology, Hamline U., 1966; MA in Biology, Mankato State U., 1968; PhD in Zoology, Wash. State U., 1973. Asst. prof. zoology Wash. State U., Pullman, 1973-74; scientist Nat. Park Service, Lakewood, Colo., 1974-76, mgr., 1979—; cons. Ch2M-Hill, Seattle, 1972-73. Dir. prodn. interactive computer exhibit on remote sensing for Denver Mus. Nat. History; contbr. sci. articles to profl. jours. Bd. dirs. Nat. Park Service Equal Employment Opportunity Com., Denver, 1981, chmn., 1982. Recipient Mgrs. award Nat. Park Service, Lakewood, 1981, Performance Commendation award, 1988; research grantee Nat. Rifle Assn., 1972. Mem. Am. Soc. Photogrammetry and Remote Sensing (exec. com. and bd. dirs. 1988-90, asst. dir. remote sensing applications div. 1985-87, dir. 1987—), Am. Congress on Surveying and Mapping Joint Satellite Mapping and Remote Sensing Com., The Wildlife Soc., GRASS Users Group (steering com. 1986—), ELAS Users Group (co-chair 1985-86, chmn. 1986-87), Sigma Xi. Office: Nat Park Svc GIS-WASO PO Box 25287 Denver CO 80225-0287

NYSTROM, CLAIR KARL, electronics engineer, educator; b. Havre, Mont., June 19, 1947; s. Karl A. and Ruth (Cooper) N.; m. Linda L. Haines, Aug. 18, 1968. BS in Indsl. Edn., Walla Walla Coll., 1971; postgrad., Northern Mont. Coll., 1988. Owner, prin. avionics shop, Dillingham, Alaska, 1971-74; electronics, auto mech. instr. Dillingham High Sch., 1973-74; electronics technician Radio Shack, Havre, 1977-78; avionics mechanic Farrell Aircraft Svc., Havre, 1978-79; biomed. electronics technician Northern Mont. Hosp., Havre, 1979-83; electronics field svc. engr. Picker Internat., Havre, 1983—; electronics instr. Northern Mont. Coll., Havre, 1984—. Lectr., asst. community health programs Havre Seventh-Day Adventist Ch., 1984—, elder, deacon, tchr., 1984—. Mem. Soc. Mech. Engrs. Republican. Home: 403 19th St Po Box 1 Havre MT 59501 Office: No Mont Coll PO Box 7751 Havre MT 59501

NYSTROM, LAURA STERNBERG, infosystems specialist; b. Columbus, Ga., Oct. 17, 1941; d. Mark S. and Irma Corinne (Ottenheimer) S.; m. Walther Nystrom, June 27, 1965 (div. 1980); children: Per Arne, Ellen Rebecca. BA, Smith Coll., 1963. Editorial asst. Gregg div. McGraw-Hill Book Co., N.Y.C., 1963-65; admissions asst. Vassar Coll., Poughkeepsie, N.Y., 1965-66; tech. writer Mohawk Data Services, Los Gatos, Calif., 1979-82, IBM, Poughkeepsie, San Jose, 1966-71; info. developer IBM, San Jose, 1982—. Staff asst. Cancer Support and Edn. Ctr., Menlo Park, Calif., 1985-87. Office: IBM 555 Bailey Ave San Jose CA 95161-9023

OAKERSON, JAMES F., retired auditorium manager, director of stage productions; b. Zwolle, La., Oct. 7, 1921; s. Edna (Thompson) Oakerson; m. Hope Oakerson (div.); 1 child, James N.; m. Ora Fern (div. 1978); children—Sharon Ann Cleaver, Mary Alice Pounds, Edna Robinson. Ed., Jefferson Bus. Coll., U. Idaho; grad. Radar Sch., Firefighting Sch, Communications Sch. Oceanside. Head sound Mcpl. Auditorium, Shreveport, La., 1946-50; head electrician CBS, Burbank, Calif., 1953-61; stage mgr. Shrine Auditorium, Los Angeles, 1961-76, auditorium mgr., 1976-88; tchr. Scotish Rite Temple, Los Angeles, 1983, 84; lighting design for various operas and religious TV. Served to radio tech. 2d class USN, 1942-45; PTO. Mem. Am. Soc. Lighting Dirs., Internat. Auditorium Mgrs. Assn., Al Malaikah Stagecraft (capt. 1984—, dir. 1981 conv.). Lodges: Shrine (dir. 1974, 75, 80, 81), Royal Order Of Jesters. Home: 1558 Dahlia Circle Corona CA 91720 Office: Shrine Auditorium 649 W Jefferson Blvd Los Angeles CA 90007

OAKES, DAVID WAYNE, software company executive, consultant; b. Lockport, N.Y., Sept. 5, 1954; s. Lester Murrell and Rosemary Catherine (Mosure) O.; m. Pamula Jean Mosher, June 22, 1974 (div. 1984); m. La Donna Joan Johnson, Mar. 31, 1984; children: Chantil Marie, Tianna Marie, David Wayne II, Joshua Clayton. AA in Bus. Adminstrn., Santa Ana Coll., 1976, AA in Mgmt. Info. Sci., 1977; cert. data processing, MTI Bus. Coll., 1978; postgrad., Calif. State U., San Bernadino, 1988—. Jr. programmer Compusource, Anaheim, Calif., 1979; mgr. data processing Serec Calif., City of Industry, 1979; systems analyst Profl. Bus. Mgmt., Westminster, Calif., 1980-81; pres. Do Software, Rialto, Calif., 1980--; owner, mgr. product devel. and support A.D.P.S., Torrance, Calif., 1981-82; instr. Calif. Coll. Tech., Anaheim, 1982-83; sr. tech. analyst CSC Compufact, Garden Grove, Calif., 1983--. With USMC, 1972-74. Mem. Am. Prodn. and Inventory Soc., Am. Mgmt. Assn., U.S. Chess Fedn. Democrat. Roman Catholic. Office: Do Software 460 S Primrose Ave Rialto CA 92376

OAKES, TERRY LOUIS, retail clothing store executive; b. Denver, June 12, 1953; s. Robert Walter and Stella Marie (Ray) O.; m. Cynthia Alison Bailey, Jan. 10, 1981; 1 child, Madeleine Bailey. BBA, So. Meth. U., 1975. Dept. mgr. Woolf Bros., Dallas, 1975-76; buyer I.K.O. Dry Goods, Denver, 1976-79, gen. sales mgr., 1979-81, exec. v.p., mdse. mgr., 1981-86; nat. sales mgr. Fresh Squeeze div. Bayly Corp., Denver, 1986-88; owner, mgr. Bolderdash, Denver, 1988—. Democrat. Presbyterian. Home: 5332 S Geneva Way Englewood CO 80111 Office: Bolderdash 2817 E 3d Ave Denver CO 80206

OAKS, DALLIN HARRIS, clergyman; b. Provo, Utah, Aug. 12, 1932; s. Lloyd E. and Stella (Harris) O.; m. June Dixon, June 24, 1952; children: Sharmon, Cheri Lyn, Lloyd D., Dallin D., TruAnn, Jenny June. B.A. with high honors, Brigham Young U., 1954, LL.D., 1980; J.D. cum laude, U. Chgo., 1957; LL.D. (hon.), Pepperdine U., 1982. Bar: Ill. 1957, Utah 1971. Law clk. to Supreme Ct. chief justice Earl Warren, 1957-58; with firm Kirkland, Ellis, Hodson, Chaffetz & Masters, Chgo., 1958-61; mem. faculty U. Chgo. Law Sch., 1961-71, assoc. dean and acting dean, 1962, prof., 1964-71, mem. vis. com., 1971-74; pres. Brigham Young U., Provo, Utah, 1971-80; also prof. law J. Reuben Clark Law Sch., 1974-80; justice Utah Supreme Ct., 1981-84; mem. Council of Twelve Apostles Ch. Jesus Christ of Latter-day Saints, 1984—; asst. states atty. Cook County, Ill., summer 1964; legal counsel Bill of Rights com. Ill. Constl. Conv., 1970. Author: (with G.G. Bogert) Cases on Trusts, 1967, 78, (with W. Lehman) A Criminal Justice System and The Indigent, 1968, The Criminal Justice Act in the Federal District Courts, 1969, (with M. Hill) Carthage Conspiracy, 1975, Trust Doctrines in Church Controversies, 1984, Pure in Heart, 1988; editor: The Wall Between Church and State, 1963. Mem. Wilson council Woodrow Wilson Internat. Center for Scholars, 1973-80; trustee Intermountain Health Care Inc., 1975-80; mem. adv. com. Nat. Inst. Law Enforcement and Criminal Justice, 1974-76; bd. dirs. Rockford Inst., 1980—, Notre Dame Center for Constl. Studies, 1977-80; bd. dirs. Pub. Broadcasting Service, 1977-84, chmn., 1980-85. Fellow Am. Bar Found. (exec. dir. 1970-71); mem. ABA (mem. com. to survey legal needs 1971-78, mem. cons. panel on advanced legal and jud. edn. 1978-80), Am. Assn. Presidents Ind. Colls. and Univs. (pres. 1975-78, dir. 1971-78), Nat. Assn. Ind. Colls. and Univs. (dir. 1977-79), Order Coif. Mem. Ch. of Jesus Christ of Latter-day Saints (regional rep. 1974-80; past 1st counselor Chgo. South Stake). Address: 47 E S Temple St Salt Lake City UT 84150

OAKS, M. MARLENE, minister; b. Grove City, Pa., Mar. 30, 1940; d. Allen Roy and Alberta Bell (Pinner) Eakin; m. Lowell B. Chaney, July 30, 1963 (dec. Jan. 1977); children: Christopher Allen, Linda Michelle; m. Harold G. Younger, Aug. 1978 (div. 1986); Gilbert E. Oaks, Aug. 3, 1987. BA, Calif. State U., L.A., 1972. Ordained to ministry Ch. Religious Sci., 1978. Educator Whittier (Calif.) Sch. Dists., 1972-74, Fullerton (Calif.) Coll., 1974-75, Garden Grove (Calif.) Sch. Dist., 1974-78; minister, founder Community Ch. of the Islands now Ch. of Religious Sci., Honolulu, 1978-80; minister Ch. of Divine Sci., Pueblo, Colo., 1980-83; minister, founder Ch. Religious Sci., Palo Alto, Calif., 1983-86; minister Ch. Religious Sci., Fullerton, 1986—; workshop leader Religious Sci. Dist. Conv., San Jose, Calif., 1985, Internat. New Thought Alliance Conference, Las Vegas, 1984, Calgary, Alta., Can., 1985, Washington, 1988, Golden Valley Unity Women's Advance, Mpls., 1986, 87, Qume Corp., San Jose, 1985. Author: (books) Old Time Religion is a Cult, 1985, Beyond Forgiveness, 1985, Stretch Marks On My Aura, 1987; contbr. articles to profl. jours. Del. Soviet and Am. Citizens Summit Conf., 1988, 89. Mem. Fullerton Interfaith Ministerial Assn. (sec., treas. 1987—), United Clergy of Religious Sci., Internat. New Thought Alliance (pres. Orange County chpt.), Soroptimists (chmn. com. internat. coop. and goodwill, 1987-88), Kappa Delta Pi. Republican. Office: First Ch Religious Sci 117 N Pomona Fullerton CA 92632

OBAL, MICHAEL WALTER, air force officer, engineer; b. Ft. Monmouth, N.J., Dec. 9, 1952; s. Michael and Stephanie Martha (Jaritz) O.; m. Margaret Mary Lang, Sept. 4, 1976; children: Michael, Christopher. BS in Engrng., Stevens Inst. Tech., 1974, MS in Engrng., 1975; M in Bus., Wright State U., 1979; grad., USAF Test Pilot Sch., Edwards AFB, Calif., 1980; PhD, Ga. Inst. Tech., 1986. Cert. flight instructor. Enlisted USAF, 1975, advanced through grades to maj., 1986; systems vibration engr. flight dynamics lab. USAF, Wright Patterson AFB, Ohio, 1975-79; laser flight test engr. weapons lab. USAF, Kirtland AFB, N.Mex., 1980-82; lead airframe systems engr. B-2 combined test force USAF, Edwards AFB, 1986—. Contbr. articles to profl. jours. Mem. AIAA, Soc. Flight Test Engrs., Air Force Assn. Republican. Roman Catholic. Home: 6733 Doolittle Dr Edwards AFB CA 93523 Office: USAF 6520 Test Group/ENAE Edwards AFB CA 93523

OBANDO, NANCY MORENO, speech-language pathologist; b. Maywood, Calif., Oct. 26, 1952; d. Martin Gardea and Ana Maria (Adame) Moreno; 1 child, Janelle Obando. BS in Communication, Loma Linda U., 1974; postgrad., Calif. State U., 1976-83; MS in Ednl. Computing, Pepperdine U., 1986. Cert. speech-lang. pathologist. Speech-lang. pathologist Riverside (Calif.) Unified Sch. Dist., 1974, Century West Rehab. Svcs., Los Angeles, 1982-83, Med. Therapeutic Cons. Svc., Los Angeles, 1984-85, Therapeutic Cons. Svcs., Sherman Oaks, Calif., 1988—, Marianne Dunn & Assocs., North Hollywood, Calif., 1988—, Los Aangeles County Office Edn., Downey, Calif., 1974—; pvt. practice lang. cons., Glendale, Calif., 1987—. Bd. dirs., A-plus Children's Ctr., Glendale, 1987—. Mem. Am. Speech-Lang. Hearing Assn., Nat. Network Hispanic Women, Assn. Mexican-Am. Educators, Inc., Calif. Speech Lang. Hearing Assn. Democrat. Seventh-day Adventist. Home: 134 Maynard St Glendale CA 91205 Office: Los Angeles Co Office Edn 9300 E Imperial Hwy Downey CA 90242

OBERG, STEPHANIE JEANNE, materials scientist; b. Mpls., Jan. 28, 1963; d. Gustav Robert and Mary (Flesner) O. BS in Materials Sci. and Engrng., MIT, 1984; MS in Materials Sci. and Engrng., Stanford U., 1987. Mem. tech. staff Watkins Johnson Co., Palo Alto, Calif., 1984—. Mem. Electrochem. Soc., Laser Inst. Am., Amnesty Internat. Democrat. Office: Watkins-Johnson Co 3333 Hillview Ave Palo Alto CA 94306

OBERHEIM, THE BARON (TIMOTHY MICHAELS DRIESEL), musical concert artist; b. Lock Haven, Pa., Oct. 1, 1951. Student, Mansfield (Pa.) State U., 1969; student (summers), Chatauqua Inst., N.Y., 1969-73; MusB, U. Rochester, 1971; Diploma, Mozarteum, Salzburg, Austria, 1975. Mem. Oberlin (Ohio) Opera Theatre, 1972; artist in residence Univrsitetet Kursverksamheten, Stockholm, Sweden, 1975-77; mem. San Francisco Opera Ctr., 1985-87; Bd. dirs. Driesel Painting, Lancaster Productions, Imagine Nine, Inc., Peacequake, Inc., CANUSA Entertainment Productions Ltd., The Actors' Workshop Ltd. Tenor soloist with Indianapolis Symphony, Louisville Symphony, Cleveland Symphony and Columbus Symphony, concert performances in San Francisco and Stockholm and other European cities, toured with celebrated Czech guitarist Josef Holecek, 1975-80, with the Italian Opera dell'Barga, 1975; many concerts and performances in operatic roles in San Francisco area. Mem. U.S. Cultural Exchange, United Nations Assn., UNESCO, Clinton County Coun. of Arts, People to People Internat., Promoting Enduring Peace, Nat. Trust for Hist. Preservation; founder scholarship Lock Haven Music Club. Recipient Excellence in Music award, Chautaqua Inst. Music, 1973, Honorary Diploma, Cambridge, England, 1977, plaque Outstanding Arts Achievements, Internat. Biographical Ctr., England. Mem. Nat. Fed. Music Clubs (Honorary Peace through Music Citation 1976), Pa. Fed. Music Clubs (Outstanding Recitals award 1973, Excellence in Arts citation 1975), The Lock Haven Music Club, Internat. Soc. Chamber Music, Internat. Sóc. Contemporary Music, Royal Swedish Chamber Music Soc., Goethe Society of Stockholm, AFTRA, Actors Equity, National Thespians Soc., AAAS, N.Y. Acad. Scis., Nat. Hist. Soc., Swedish Rikonserter, AGMA. Office: The Baron Oberheim Timoth Michaels Driesel 1516 Oak St Ste 11 Alameda CA 94501

OBERSTEIN, MARYDALE, geriatric specialist; b. Red Wing, Minn., Dec. 30, 1942; d. Dale Robert and jean Ebba-Marie (Holmquist) Johnson; children from previous marriage: Kirk Robert, Mark Paul; m. William Bruce Oberstein, June 19, 1972; children: MaryJean, Brennon. Student, U. Oreg., 1961-62, Portland State U., 1962-64, Long Beach State U., 1974-76. Cert. geriatric specialist, Calif. Florist, owner Sunshine Flowers, Santa Ana, Calif., 1982—; pvt. duty nursing aide Aides in Action, Costa Mesa, Calif., 1985-87; owner, adminstr. Lovelight Christian Home for the Elderly, Santa Ana, 1987—; activity dir. Bristol Care Nursing Home, Santa Ana, 1985-88; nursing home activist to reform laws to force bad homes out, 1984-86; founder, tchr. hugging classes/healing therapy, 1987—; bd. dir. Orange County Coun. on Aging, 1984—. Chairperson Helping Hands, 1985—, Woman Aglow Orange County, 1985—, Pat Robertson Com. 1988, Orange County Bush for Pres. campaign, 1988. Recipient Carnation Silver Bow Carnation Svc. Co., 1984-85; named Woman of Yr. Kiwanis, 1985; honored AM L.A. by Calif. Lt. Gov. McCarthy, 1984. Mem. Calif. Assn. Residential Care Homes, Orange County Epilepsy Soc. (bd. dirs. 1986—), Calif. Assn. Long Term Facilities. Home: 2722 S Diamond Santa Ana CA 92704 Office: Lovelight Christian Home for Elderly 2306 W Avalon Santa Ana CA 92706

OBERTI, SYLVIA MARIE ANTOINETTE, rehabilitation counselor and administrator, career advisor, textile consultant; b. Fresno, Calif., Dec. 29, 1952; d. Silvio Lawrence and Sarah Carmen (Policarpo) O. B.A. in Communicative Disorders, Calif. State U.-Fresno, 1976, M.A. in Rehab. Counseling, 1977. Lic. vocat. cons., Calif.; cert. rehab. counselor Commn. Rehab. Counselors; cert. life tchr. community coll. Rehab. counselor intern Calif. Dept. Rehab., Fresno, 1977; vol. counselor Fresno Commn. Aging, 1976-77; rehab. counselor trainee traumatic injury ward, Fresno Community Hosp., 1976-77; sr. rehab. cons. Crawford Rehab. Services, Inc., Emeryville, Calif., 1978-80; vocat. rehab. counselor Rehab. Assocs., Inc., San Leandro, Calif., 1980-81; owner, textile cons. Rugs and Carpets of the Orient, Oakland, Calif., 1979—; adminstr., counselor Oberti & Lohr, Oakland and San Jose, Calif., 1981-83; exec. dir. Oberti Co., Oakland, San Francisco and San Jose, 1983—; cons. to industry, ins. cos., disabled; tchr. job seeking skills to the disabled. Bd. dirs., treas. Pacific Basin Sch. Textile Arts, 1982-86; active Calif. Assn. Physically Handicapped, Inc., 1976—, Bay Area Profl. Women's Network, 1979—. HEW grantee, 1976-77. Mem. Am. Personnel and Guidance Assn., Am. Rehab. Counseling Assn., Calif. Assn. Rehab. Profls., Indsl. Claims Assn., Internat. Round Table Advancement of Counseling, Nat. Rehab. Assn., Nat. Rehab. Counseling Assn., Nat. Vocat. Guidance Assn., LWV, Women Entrepreneurs. Office: 2169 Union St San Francisco CA 94123 Office: 3629 Grand Ave Suite 101 Oakland CA 94610

OBLAD, ALEXANDER GOLDEN, chemistry educator, research chemist; b. Salt Lake City, Nov. 26, 1909; s. Alexander H. and Louie May (Brewster) O.; m. Bessie Elizabeth Baker, Feb. 23, 1933; children: Alex Edward, Elizabeth (Mrs. D. Sonne), Virginia Oblad Christensen, John R.B., Hayward B., Jean Rio B.(Mrs. S. Calder). B.A. in Chemistry, U. Utah, 1933, M.A. in Phys. Chemistry, 1934, D.Sc. (hon.), 1980; Ph.D. in Phys. Chemistry, Purdue U., 1937, D.Sc. (hon.), 1959. Research chemist Standard Oil Co., Whiting, Ind., 1937-42, Magnolia Petroleum Co., Dallas, 1942-43; sect. leader Magnolia Petroleum Co., 1943-46, chief chem. research, 1946; head indsl. research Tex. Research Found., Dallas, 1947; dir. chem. research Houdry Process Corp., Marcus Hook, Pa., 1947-52; assoc. mgr. research and devel. Houdry Process Corp., 1952-55, mgr., 1955, v.p., dir., 1955-57; v.p. research and devel. M.W. Kellogg Co., N.Y.C., 1957-66, v.p. research and engrng. devel., 1966-69; v.p. IRECO Chems., Salt Lake City, 1969-70; prof. metallurgical and fuels engrng. U. Utah, 1969-75, disting. prof. metallurgical and fuels engrng., 1975—, prof. chemistry, 1975—; assoc. dean U. Utah Coll. of Mines, 1970-72, acting dean, 1972-75; co-founder, dir. Ireco Chemicals Co., Salt Lake City, 1958-72, 74-75; mem. Sec. of Interior's Saline Water Conversion Adv. Com., Office of Saline Water, Washington, 1959-61; mem. fossil energy research working group Dept. Energy, 1980-82. Mem. editorial bd.: Catalysis Revs., Fuel Processing Tech, 1976—; mem. internat. adv. bd.: Ency. of Chem. Processing and Design, 1973—; contbr. numerous articles on phys. chemistry, catalysis, petroleum chemistry and chem. engrng. to tech. and sci. jours.; patentee in field. Mem. alumni research council Purdue Research Found., Lafayette, Ind., 1960-63; chmn. sustaining membership campaign Orange Mountain council Boy Scouts Am., 1966-67; mem. adv. council Brigham Young U., Provo, Utah, 1962-81; mem. nat. adv. council U. Utah, 1962-77, Dixie Coll., 1987—; bd. dirs. Internat. Congress on Catalysis, 1956-65. Recipient First Purdue Chemist's award, 1959, Distinguished Alumni award U. Utah, 1962. Mem. Am. Chem. Soc. (mng. editor publs. div. petroleum chemistry 1857-69, sec. treas. div. petroleum chemistry 1952-54, div. petroleum chem. 1956 , E.V. Murphree award 1969), Am. Inst. Chem. Engrs., AAAS, Calif. Catalysis Soc., Western States Catalysis Soc., Rocky Mountain Fuel Soc., Nat. Acad. Engrng., Am. Inst. Chemists (Chem. Pioneer award 1972), Utility Shareholders Assn. Utah (trustee 1980—), Sigma Xi, Phi Lambda Upsilon, Sigma Pi Sigma, Phi Kappa Phi, Tau Beta Pi. Mormon. Home: 1415 Roxbury Rd Salt Lake City UT 84108 Office: U Utah 302 Browning Mineral Sci Bldg Salt Lake City UT 84112

OBNINSKY, VICTOR PETER, lawyer; b. San Rafael, Calif., Oct. 12, 1944; s. Peter Victor and Anne Bartholdi (Donston) O.; m. Clara Alice Bechtel, June 8, 1969; children: Mari, Warren. BA, Columbia U., 1966; JD, U. Calif., Hastinas, 1969. Bar: Calif. 1970. Sole practice, Novato, Calif., 1970—; arbitrator Marin County Superior Ct., San Rafael, 1979—; superior ct. judge pro tem, 1988-89. lectr. real estate and ptnrship. law. Author: The Russians in Early California, 1966. Bd. dirs. Calif. Young Reps., 1968-69, Richardson Bay San. Dist., 1974-75, Marin County Legal Aid Soc., 1976-78; baseball coach Little League, Babe Ruth League, 1970-84; mem. nat. panel consumer arbitrators Better Bus. Bur., 1974-88; leader Boy Scouts Am., 1970-84; permanent sec. Phillips Acad. Class of 1962. Mem. State Bar Calif., ABA, Marin County Bar Assn. (bd. dirs. 1985-87, treas. 1987-88, pres.-elect 1989), Phi Delta Phi, Phi Gamma Delta. Russian Orthodox. Club: Commonwealth (San Francisco). Home: 6 Mateo Dr Tiburon CA 94920 Office: 2 Commercial Blvd Suite 103 Novato CA 94948-5068

OBRENTZ, HOWARD, transportation executive; b. Bklyn., Aug. 31, 1926; s. Max and Florence (Price) O.; m. Dec. 1950 (div. 1983); children: Maxanne, Lindsay, David, Marla. AB, Riddle Coll., 1948; BBA, U. Balt., 1950. Owner Coll. Bowl Inc., Balt., 1950-55; west coast rep. Sacony, 1955-70; v.p. sales, mgr. Paddle & Saddle, 1970-75; div. mgr. Airport Limousine, 1975-80; gen. mgr. Golden State Limousine, Santa Clara, Calif., 1980-81; pres., chief exec. officer Corp. Transp. Svc. Inc., San Jose, Calif., 1982—. With USNR, 1944-46, PTO. Mem. Nat. Com. to Preserve Social Security and Medicare. Republican. Jewish. Home: 18850 Newsom Ave Cupertino CA 95014 Office: Corp Transp Svc Inc 7280 Blue Hill Dr Ste 3 San Jose CA 95129

O'BRIEN, HAROLD ALOYSIUS, JR., nuclear chemist, physics researcher, consultant; b. Dallas, May 17, 1936; s. Harold Aloysius and Adelaide (Esser) O'B.; m. Ann Akard, Aug. 22, 1958; children: Walter, Sheri, Matthew. BA, U. Tex., 1959; MS, N.Mex. State U., 1961; PhD, U. Tenn., 1968. Hon. diplomate Am. Bd. Sci. in Nuclear Medicine. Rsch. scientist Oak Ridge (Tenn.) Nat. Lab., 1962-68; mem. rsch. staff Los Alamos Nat. Lab., 1968-74, 86—, asssoc. group leader, 1974-80, group leader, 1980-85; vis. scientist Lawrence Berkeley (Calif.) Lab., 1985-86, Lawrence Livermore (Calif.) Lab., 1985-86, U. Calif., Davis, 1985-86; bd. dirs. Am. Bd. Sci. in Nuclear Medicine, 1976-85, pres., 1983-85; bd. dirs. Rho Med, Inc., Albuquerque, Radiopharm. Sci. Coun., 1981-86; mem. subcom. on nuclear and radio chemistry NAS-NRC, 1974-78; mem. spl. study sect. NIH, 1976. Contbr. numerous articles to profl. jours., chpts. to books; patentee in field. Chmn. N.Mex. Radiation Tech. Adv. Coun., Santa Fe, 1974-85. Mem. Am. Chem. Soc. (exec. com. 1981-84), AAAS, Soc. Nuclear Medicine (trustee 1975-76, bd. dirs. Edn. and Rsch. Found. 1985—). Home: 107 La Senda Rd Los Alamos NM 87544 Office: Los Alamos Nat Lab Physics Div MS D449 PO Box 1663 Los Alamos NM 87545

O'BRIEN, JACK GEORGE, artistic director; b. Saginaw, Mich., June 18, 1939; s. J. George and Evelyn (MacArthur Martens) O'B. A.B., U. Mich., 1961, M.A., 1962. Asst. dir. APA Repertory Theatre, N.Y.C., 1963-67; asso. dir. APA Repertory Theatre, 1967-69; worked with San Diego Nat. Shakespeare Festival, 1969-82, A.C.T., 1970-80, Loretto Hilton, 1975, Ahmanson, Los Angeles, 1978-80, San Francisco Opera, Houston Grand Opera, Washington Opera Soc., N.Y.C. Opera. Lyricist: Broadway prodn. The Selling of the President, 1972; dir.: on Broadway Porgy and Bess (Tony award 1977), Most Happy Fella, Street Scene; others; artistic dir.: Old Globe Theatre, San Diego, 1981; (Tony award nominee for direction Porgy and Bess 1977). Mem. Actors' Equity, Am. Soc. Composers and Performers, Soc. Stage Dirs. and Choreographers, Dirs. Guild Am. *

O'BRIEN, JOHN CONWAY, economics educator, writer; b. Hamilton, Lanarkshire, Scotland; s. Patrick and Mary (Hunt) O'B.; m. Jane Estelle Judd, Sept. 16, 1966; children: Kellie Marie, Kerry Patrick, Tracy Anne, Kristen Noël. B in Commerce, U. London, 1952, cert. in German lang., 1954; AM, U. Notre Dame, 1959, PhD, 1961. Cert. tchr., Scotland. Tchr. Scottish High Schs., Lanarkshire, 1952-56; instr. U. B.C., Can., 1961-62; asst. prof. U. Saskatchewan, Can., 1962-63, U. Dayton, Ohio, 1963-64; assoc. prof. Wilfrid Laurier U., Ont., Can., 1964-65; from asst. to full prof. Econs. and Ethics Calif. State U., Fresno, 1965—; vis. prof. U. Pitts., 1969-70, U. Hawaii, Manoa, 1984; keynote speaker Wageningen Agrl. U., The Netherlands, 1987; presenter Schmoller Symposium, Heilbronn am Neckar, Fed. Republic Germany, 1988, paper The China Confucius Found. and "2540" Conf., Beijing, 1989; active rsch. U. Göttingen, Fed. Republic Germany, 1987; acad. cons. Cath. Inst. Social Ethics. Author: Karl Marx: The Social Theorist, 1981, The Economist in Search of Values, 1982, Beyond Marxism, 1985; editor Internat. Rev. Econs. and Ethics, Internat. Jour. Social Econs., Festschrift in honor of George Rohrlich, 3 vols., 1984, Festschrift in honor of Anghel N. Rugina, parts I and II, 1987; translator econ. articles; contbr. numerous article to profl. jours. With British Royal Army Service Corps, 1939-46, ETO, NATOUSA, prisoner of war, Germany. Recipient GE Corp. award Stanford U., 1966. Fellow Internat. Inst. Social Econs. (mem. council, program dir. 3d World Cong. Social Econs., Fresno, 1973, keynote speaker 4th cong., Toronto, 1986); mem. Assn. Social Econs. (dir. west region 1977—, pres.-elect 1989-90, program dir. conf. 1989), Western Econ.

Assn. (organizer, presenter 1989), History of Econs. Soc., Soc. Reduction Human Labor (mem. exec. com.), Internat. Soc. Intercommunications of New Ideas. Roman Catholic. Home: 2733 W Fir Ave Fresno CA 93711 Office: Calif State U Dept Econs Fresno CA 93740

O'BRIEN, JOHN WILLIAM, JR., investment management company executive; b. Bronx, N.Y., Jan. 1, 1937; s. John William and Ruth Catherine (Timon) O'B.; B.S., MIT, 1958; M.S., UCLA, 1964; m. Jane Bower Nippert, Feb. 2, 1963; children—Christine, Andrea, Michael, John William III, Kevin Robert. Sr. asso. Planning Research Corp., Los Angeles, 1962-67; dir. fin. systems group Synergetic Scis., Inc., Tarzana, Calif., 1967-70; dir. analytical services div. James H. Oliphant & Co., Los Angeles, 1970-72; chmn. bd., chief exec. officer, pres. O'Brien Assos., Inc., Santa Monica, Calif., 1972-77; v.p. A.G. Becker Inc., 1977-81; chmn., chief exec. officer Leland O'Brien Rubinstein Assos., 1981—. Served to 1st lt. USAF, 1958-62. Recipient Graham and Dodd award Fin. Analysts Fedn., 1970. Mem. Delta Upsilon. Home: Box 3159 Blue Jay CA 92317 Office: Leland O'Brien Rubenstein Assocs 523 W 6th St Ste 220 Los Angeles CA 90014

O'BRIEN, KERAN, physicist; b. Bklyn., Nov. 5, 1931; s. Raymond Keran and Mary Josephine (Marache) O'B.; m. Barbara Hope Zwickel, May 5, 1961; children: David Keran, Judith Nancy. BS, Fordham U. Physicist U.S. Dept. Energy, Environ Measurements Lab., N.Y.C., 1953-61, mem. prin. staff, 1961-81, dir. radiation physics, 1981-87; cons. Sedona, Ariz., 1987—; cons. SSC Cen. Design Group, Berkeley, 1987—, FAA, Oklahoma City, 1985—, Woods Hole Oceanographic Inst., Mass., 1988—, Dept. Energy, Washington, 1988—; adj. prof. physics No. Ariz U., Flagstaff, 1988—. Mem. editorial bd. Radiation Protection Dosimetry, 1987—; contbr. articles to profl. jours., chpts. to books. Fellow Am. Nuclear Soc. (Outstanding Svc. award 1976); mem. Am. Physics Soc., Am. Geophys. Union, Am. Archael. Inst., Radiation Rsch. Soc. Home: PO Box 967 Sedona AZ 86336 Office: No Ariz U Coll Arts and Sci PO Box 6010 Flagstaff AZ 86011-6010

O'BRIEN, KEVIN CHARLES, research engineer; b. Pitts., Dec. 30, 1957; s. Charles James and Minerva A. (Mars) O'B.; m. Ann Marie Poydock, Oct. 9, 1982; 1 child, Michael James. BS in Polymer Engring., Case Western Res. U., 1979, MS in Macromolecular Engring., 1981, PhD in Macromolecular Engring., 1984. Grad. fellow Case Western Res. U., Cleve., 1979-82, staff technician I, 1982-84; postdoctoral research assoc. dept. chem. engring. U. Tex., Austin, 1984-85; project leader Dow Chem. USA, Walnut Creek, Calif., 1985-89; product devel. engr. Raychem Corp, Menlo Park, Calif., 1989—. Contbr. articles to profl. jours.; patentee in field. Instr. religious edn. Newman Cath. Ctr. U. Tex., Austin, 1985; indsl. mentor Industry Initiatives for Sci. and Math. Edn., 1987-88. B.F. Goodrich fellow, 1981. Mem. Am. Phys. Soc., Am. Chem. Soc., Materials Research Soc., N.Am. Membrane Soc., Sigma Alpha Epsilon.

O'BRIEN, MICHAEL F., retail executive; b. Cleve., Apr. 1, 1944; s. James Leo and Donna M. (Frame) O'B.; m. Jean Ellen; children: Jeffrey, Timothy, Patrick. BA, U. Charleston, 1966. Salesman photo div. Honeywell Inc., L.A., 1966-68; pres. Flags Photo Ctrs., Inc., L.A., 1968—. Active arts council Pasadena (Calif.) Jr. Colls. Mem. Pasadena Mental Health Assn., Photo Mktg. Internat. Assn. (Territorial V.p. of Yr. award 1987), So. Calif. Photo Mktg. Assn., University Club, Elks Lodge. Home: 1500 Pegfair Estates Dr Pasadena CA 91103 Office: Flags Pasadena Photo 509 E Walnut St Pasadena CA 91101

O'BRIEN, RAYMOND FRANCIS, transportation executive; b. Atchison, Kans., May 31, 1922; s. James C. and Anna M. (Wagner) O'B.; m. Mary Ann Baugher, Sept. 3, 1947; children: James B., William T., Kathleen A., Christopher R. B.S. in Bus. Adminstrn., U. Mo., 1948; grad., Advanced Mgmt. Program, Harvard, 1966. Accountant-auditor Peat, Marwick, Mitchell & Co., Kansas City, Mo., 1948-52; controller-treas. Riss & Co., Kansas City, Mo., 1952-58; regional controller Consol. Freightways Corp. of Del., Indpls., also, Akron, Ohio, 1958-61; with Consol. Freightways, Inc., San Francisco, 1961—; controller-treas. Consol. Freightways, Inc., 1962-63, v.p., treas., 1963-67, v.p. finance, 1967-69, exec. v.p., 1969-75, pres., 1975—, chief exec., 1977, chmn., chief exec. officer, 1979, also dir., pres. motor carrier subs., 1973-75; dir. Consol. Freightways Corp. of Del., CF Data Services, Inc., CF Land Services, Inc., Canadian Freightways Ltd., Canadian Freightways Eastern Ltd., CF Air Freight Inc., Transcan Corp., Union Bank, Watkins-Johnson, Inc., CF Ocean Services; past chmn., now dir. Western Hwy. Inst. Former mem. bus. adv. bd. Northwestern U., U. Calif., Berkeley; chmn. bd. trustees St. Mary's Coll.; bd. dirs. Charles Armstrong Sch. Served to 1st lt. USAAF, 1942-45. Mem. Am. Trucking Assn. Clubs: Pacific Union, World Trade, Commonwealth (San Francisco); Palo Alto Hills Golf and Country, Burning Tree Country, Menlo Country, Congressional Country, Firestone Country. Home: 26347 Esperanza Dr Los Altos Hills CA 94022 Office: Consol Freightways Inc PO Box 10340 Palo Alto CA 94303

O'BRIEN, ROBERT MULLINGS, physician, surgeon; b. Rutland, Vt., Nov. 10, 1932; s. John Emmett and Christine (Mullings) O'B.; m. Carol Selzer, Sept. 4, 1954 (div. 1973); children: Terri, Stephen, Kelli; m. Barbara Ann O'Brien, June 29, 1974; 1 child, Kevin. BS, St. Michael's Coll., Winooski, Vt., 1954; MD, U. Vt., 1958. Diplomate Am. Bd. Surgery. Intern Buffalo Gen. Hosp., 1958-59; commd. lt. USN, 1959, advanced through grades to capt.; resident in gen. surgery Naval Hosp., Great Lakes, Ill., 1962-66; resident in thoracic surgery Naval Hosp., San Diego, 1968-70; comdg. officer 1st Hosp. Co., Vietnam, 1967; staff surgeon gen. and thoracic surgery Nat. Naval Med. Ctr., Bethesda, Md., 1975-77; chief of surgery U.S. Naval Hosp., Camp Pendleton, Calif., 1977-80, regional health care coordinator, 1980, dir. clin. services, 1980-81; comdg. officer Naval Regional Med. Ctr., Naples, Italy, 1981-83; chief surgery VA Hosp., Livermore, Calif., 1984-85; practice medicine specializing in gen. and thoracic surgery Vets. Home of Calif., Yountville, 1984-88, Phila., 1988—. Decorated Legion of Merit with Combat V. Fellow Am. Coll. Physician Execs.; mem. Am. Acad. Med. Dirs., Am. Soc. Mil. Surgeons of U.S., Profl. Ski Instrs. Am. (assoc. cert.). Republican. Roman Catholic. Office: Knights & Red Lions Rds Ste 301 Philadelphia PA 19114

O'BRIEN, ROBERT S., state official; b. Seattle, Sept. 14, 1918; s. Edward R. and Maude (Ransom) O'B.; m. Kathryn E. Arvan, Oct. 18, 1941 (dec. June 1984). Student public schs. With Kaiser Co., 1938-46; restaurant owner 1946-50; treas. Grant County, Wash., 1950-65, State of Wash., 1965-89; chmn. Wash. State Fin. Com., 1965-89, Wash. Public Deposit Protection Commn., 1969-89, Wash. Public Employees Retirement Bd., 1969-77, Law Enforcement Officers and Firefighters Retirement System, 1971-77, Wash. State Investment Bd., 1981-89; retired 1989; mem. Wash. Data Processing Adv. Bd., 1967-73, Gov.'s Exec. Mgmt. and Fiscal Affairs Com., 1978-80, Gov.'s Cabinet Com. on Tax Alternatives, 1978-80; trustee Wash. Tchr.'s Retirement System, 1965-89. Recipient Leadership award Joint Council County and City Employees-Fedn. State Employees, 1970, Eagles Leadership award, 1967. Mem. Nat. Assn. State Auditors, Comptrollers and Treasurers (pres. 1977), Nat. Assn. Mcpl. Fin. Officers, Nat. Assn. State Treasurers, Western State Treasurers Assn. (pres. 1970), Wash. County Treas. Assn. (pres. 1955-56), Wash. Assn. Elected County Ofcls. (pres. 1955-58), Olympia Area C. of C., Soap Lake C. of C. (pres. 1948). Democrat. Clubs: Elks (hon. life); Moose, Eagles, Lions, Olympia Yacht, Olympia Country and Golf; Empire (Spokane); Wash. Athletic (Seattle). Address: 3618 Plummer SE Olympia WA 98503

OBRIEN, SEAN LELAND, paramedic; b. Long Beach, Calif., Sept. 28, 1966; s. Dan Leland and Suzanne Louise (Dollar) O. Assoc. in Paramedicine, Tucson Med. Ctr., 1986. Emergency med. technician Metro Medic Ambulance, Tucson, 1984-85; paramedic Rural Metro Fire Dept., Tucson, 1985—; v.p. Seatbelt Com. of Ariz., Tucson, 1986—; drowning cons. Ariz. Drowning Com. of Tucson, 1988—; med. cons. Rural Metro Fire Dept., 1985—. Instr. CPR, ACLS, Am. Heart Assn. Republican. Roman Catholic. Office: Rural Metro Fire Dept 490 W Magee Tucson AZ 85704

O'BRIEN, SHARON ANN, nurse aide; b. Newark, July 10, 1951; d. Joseph William Fay and Emma (Rose) Sackmann; m. Warren Edward O'Brien, Dec. 28, 1974; children: Jodi Lynn, Francis Warren. Cert. Nurses Aide, Crossmont Health Occupat. Coll, 1988. Nurses aide Toms River Conv., N.J., 1978, Bayview Conv., Bayville, N.J., 1979-81, Spring Valley Conv., Calif., 1982-83, Friendship Manor, Lakeside, Calif., 1983, Calif. Spl. CAre, La Mesa, Calif., 1984-86; nurses aide, mem. nursing pool Nurses Network, La Jolla, Calif., 1988—. Mem. Bowling League, Moose (mem. publicity Lemon Grove chpt. 1983-85, asst. guild 1985). Democrat. Roman Catholic.

O'BRIEN, SUE, journalist; b. Waukon, Iowa, Mar. 6, 1939; d. John Gordon and Jean (Schadel) O'B.; children—Peter, Sarah, Andrew. B.A., Grinnell Coll., 1959; M.P.A., JFK Sch. Govt., Harvard U., 1985. Reporter, KTLN/KTLK Radio, Denver, 1968-70; anchor, reporter KBTR-AM, Denver, 1970-73; anchor, reporter, commentator KOA-AM/TV, Denver, 1973-75; corr. NBC Radio, N.Y.C., 1975-76; news dir., exec. editor KOA AM/FM/TV, Denver, 1976-80; press sec. Gov. Colo., Denver, 1980-85; campaign mgr. Roy Romer 1985-86; asst. city editor The Denver Post, 1987-88; assoc. prof. journalism Sch. Journalism & Mass Communication, U. Colo., Boulder, 1988—; adj. assoc. prof. U. Colo. Grad. Sch. Pub. Adminstrn., 1986—. Chmn., Christian Social Relations div. Episcopal Diocese Colo., 1964-68; chmn., editor Colo. Journalism Rev., 1974-75; press sec. Coloradans for Lamm/Dick, 1982. Recipient Headliner award Women in Communications Colo., 1972, Big Hat award U. Colo. Soc. Profl. Journalists, 1973, Alumni award Grinnell Coll., 1974. Mem. Soc. Profl. Journalists (v.p. 1977-78), Radio and TV News Dirs. Assn., Mortar Bd., Phi Beta Kappa. Democrat. Episcopalian. Club: Denver Press. Home: 17 Ogden St Denver CO 80218 Office: U Colo Sch Journalism and Mass Communication Box 287 Boulder CO 80309

O'BRIEN, THOMAS JOSEPH, bishop; b. Indpls., Nov. 29, 1935. Grad., St. Meinrad Coll. Sem. Ordained priest Roman Catholic Ch., 1961. Bishop of Phoenix 1982—. Office: 400 E Monroe Phoenix AZ 85004 *

O'BYRNE, PAUL J., bishop; b. Calgary, Alta., Can., Dec. 21, 1922. Ordained priest Roman Catholic Ch., 1948; bishop of Calgary 1968—. Office: Cath Pastoral Care Ctr, 1916 2d Ave SW Room 205, Calgary, AB Canada T2S 1S3 *

O'CALLAGHAN, J. PATRICK, newspaper publisher; b. Mallow, Ireland, Oct. 8, 1925; imigrated to Can., 1959, naturalized, 1964; s. Michael Joseph and Marguerita (Hayes) O'C.; children: Patrick, Michael, Sean, Brendan, Fiona. Student, Christian Brothers Sch., Limerick, Ireland, 1931-32, Cotton Coll., Eng. Reporter, deskman English newspapers 1947-53; asst. editor Liverpool (Eng.) Echo, 1953-59; mng. editor, asst. pub. Red Deer Advocate, Alta., 1959-68; asst. to pub. Edmonton Jour. (Alta.), 1968, pub., 1976-82; exec. editor Southam News Svcs., Ottawa, Ont., Can., 1969-71; exec. asst. to mng. dir. Southam Press Ltd., 1971-72; v.p., pub. Windsor Star (Ont.), 1972-76; pub. Edwardian Jour., 1976-82, Calgary (Alta.) Herald, from 1982. Served with RAF, 1943-47. Mem. Can. Daily Newspaper Pubs. Assn. (past pres.), Can. Press (chmn.), Commonwealth Press Union, Internat. Press Inst., Am. Press Inst. Roman Catholic. Home: 1002 639-14 Ave SW, Calgary, AB Canada Office: Ryerson Poly Inst, Sch Journalism, 350 Victoria St, Toronto, ON Canada M5B 2K3

O'CASEY, SEAN, hypnotherapist; b. Washington, Jan. 6, 1942; s. Edward L. Casey and Eleanor Dorothea (Basterl) Cacioppo. BS, SUNY, Albany, 1988. Enlisted USAF, 1960, advanced through grades to sr. master sgt., 1977, ret., 1980; mgr. photographic dept. Walgreen Co., Albuquerque, 1982-87; dir. O'Casey Inst. of Hypnotherapy, Albuquerque, 1987-88; hypnotherapist A to Z Profl. Hypnosis, Albuquerque, 1988—; cons., seminar leader Combined Therapeutics Wellness Ctr., Albuquerque, 1987—. Author: Hypnosis for Everyone: Especially You!, 1988. Mem. Am. Council Hypnotist Examiners, Southwest Hypnotherapists Examining Bd., Assn. to Advance Ethical Hypnosis, Internat. Soc. for Profl. Hypnosis, Am. Legion, Retired Enlisted Assn., Am. Assn. Behavioral Therapists, Mensa. Republican. Home: 3300 Morris NE #2 Albuquerque NM 87111 Office: A to Z Prof Hypnosis 2632-E Pennsylvania St NE Albuquerque NM 87110

OCCHIATO, MICHAEL ANTHONY, city official; b. Pueblo, Colo.; s. Joseph Michael and Joan Occhiato; m. Peggy Ann Stefonowicz, June 27, 1964 (div. Sept. 1983); children: Michael, James, Jennifer; m. Patsy Gay Payne, June 2, 1984; children: Kim Carr, Jerry Don Webb. BBA, U. Denver, 1961; MBA, U. Colo., 1984; postgrad., U. So. Colo. Sales mgr. Tivoli Brewing co., Denver, 1965-67, acting brewmaster, prodn. control mgr., 1967-68, plant mgr., 1968-69; adminstrv. mgr. King Resources Co., Denver, 1969-70; ops. mgr. Canners Inc., Pepsi-Cola Bottling Co., Pueblo, 1970-76; pres. Pepsi-Cola Bottling Co., Pueblo, 1978-82; gen. mgr. Pepsi-Cola Bottling Group div. PepsiCo., Pueblo, 1982, area v.p., 1982-83; ind. cons. Pueblo, 1983—; pres. Ethnic Foods Internat. dba Taco Rancho, Pueblo, Colo. mem. council City of Pueblo, 1978—, pres. 1986—; mem. bd. health, 1978-80, regional planning commn., 1980-81, Pueblo Action Inc., 1978-80, Pueblo Planning and Zoning Commn., 1985; chmn. Pueblo Area council Govts., 1980-82; mem. Pueblo Econ. Devel. Corp., 1983-85; chmn. fundraising Pueblo chpt. Am. Heart Assn., 1983—; bd. dirs. El Pueblo Boys Ranch, 1971-73. Served to lt. USN, 1961-65. Mem. So. Colo. Emergency Med. Technicians Assn. (pres. 1975), Pueblo C. of C. Lodge: Rotary. Home: 11 Harrogate Terr Pueblo CO 81001 Office: City of Pueblo 1 City Hall Pl Pueblo CO 81003

OCCHIPINTI, CARL JOSEPH, broadcasting executive; b. New Orleans, Feb. 11, 1931; s. Victor and Anne (Maenza) O.; m. Ila M. Fanning, Nov. 22, 1939; children—Vickie, Michael, Diane. B.S., U. Wyo., 1956. Bus. and advt. mgr. Laramie (Wyo.) Newspapers, Inc., 1957-63; gen. mgr. Sta. KTVS-TV, Sterling, Colo., 1963-75; gen. mgr., v.p. Wyneco Communications, Inc., including Stas. KYCU-TV, Cheyenne, Wyo., KSTF-TV, Scottsbluff, Nebr., KTVS-TV, Sterling, Colo., 1975-86; gen. mgr. Sta. KGWN TV Cheyenne, 1986—, Sta. KSTF TV, Scottsbluff, Nebr., 1986—, Sta. KTVS TV, Sterling, Colo., Sta. KGWC TV, Casper Wyo., 1986—, STa. KGWL TV., Lander-Riverton, Wyo., Sta. KGWR TV, Rock Springs, Wyo., 1986—. With USAF, 1950-53. Mem. Wyo. Assn. Broadcasters Assn., Rocky Mountain Broadcasters Assn., Advt. Assn. Denver, Colo. Broadcasters Assn. (past v.p.), Am. Legion, Cheyenne C. of C. (past 1st v.p.). Roman Catholic. Clubs: Rotary, Cheyenne Country, Sterling Country, Elks. Office: Sta KGWN-TV 2923 E Lincolnway Cheyenne WY 82001

OCHOA, JAMES EDWARD, educational administrator; b. L.A., Apr. 18, 1950; s. Alex Cano and Sarah (Rodriguez) O.; m. Rosella Sherman, Sept. 5, 1981; children: Melissa Rose, Sarah Alexandra. BA in Econs., Western N.Mex. U., 1972, BA in Elem. Edn., 1978, MA in Sch. Adminstrn., 1978. Cert. elem. tchr. and adminstr., N.Mex. Tchr. Belen (N.Mex.) Jr. High Sch., 1978-81, prin., 1985-87; tchr. Rio Grande Elem. Sch., Belen, 1981-85; dir. pers. and fed. programs Belen Consol. Sch. Dist., 1987—; speaker, lectr., presenter edn. and civic groups, 1985—. Active Youth Wellness Com., Belen, 1986—, Resource Devel. and Plans Com., Belen, 1987—; bd. dirs. Valencia County Literacy Coun., Belen, 1987—. 1st lt. USMC, 1973-75, maj. USMCR. Mem. N.Mex. Sch. Pers. Dirs. Assn., Res. Officers Assn., VFW. Republican. Roman Catholic. Office: Belen Consol Schs 520 N Main St Belen NM 87002

OCHOA, MARIAELENA LOPEZ, counselor, teacher; b. Reedley, Calif., Sept. 26, 1947; d. Ventura Cortina and Ruth (Acosta) Lopez; m. Alberto Monroy Ochoa, Apr. 7, 1973; children: Yolanda, Anjelica, Javier. BA in Math., UCLA, 1970; MS in Edn., U. So. Calif., 1972; PhD in Counseling Edn., U. Mass., 1981. Tchr. math San Benito High Sch., Hollister, Calif., 1972-73; counselor advocate program U. Mass., Amherst, 1974-75; counselor Sweetwater Union High Sch., National City, Calif., 1975—, tchr. advanced math., 1980—. Mem. Com. on Chicano Rights, National City, 1976—. Named Counselor of Yr., Alba "80" Soc., 1988. Mem. Assn. Mex.-Am. Educators (Educator of Distinction South Bay chpt. 1987), Calif. Sch. Guidance Assn. Democrat. Roman Catholic. Office: Sweetwater Union High Sch 2900 Highland Ave National City CA 92050

OCHS, GARY LEE, chemical research consultant; b. Escondido, Calif., Nov. 4, 1949; s. Clarence Conrad and Darlene Raye (Dyckman) O.; m. Elizabeth Woodard Otto, Dec. 23, 1971. AA, Palomar Community Coll., 1969; BS, U. Calif., Riverside, 1971. Chemist Twin City Testing and Engring., St. Paul, 1972-76; dir. field svcs. Corning Labs., Cedar Falls, Iowa, 1976-79; project mgr. York Rsch. Cons., Denver, 1979-83, program mgr., 1983-85, v.p., 1985-86; mgr. Ochs Oil Co., San Marcos, Calif., 1986—. Sec. Cedar Falls (Iowa) Community Theater Bd. Dirs., 1977-79; pres., bd. dirs. Palisades Point Homeowners Assn., 1988-89. Recipient Order of the Arrow award Boy Scouts Am., 1966; named Scout of Yr. troop 729 Boy Scouts Am., 1963, 66. Mem. Am. Chem. Soc., Air Pollution Control Assn., Assn. Energy Engrs., Air Pollution Control Assn. Micro-computer Users Group (sec. 1984-85). Roman Catholic. Office: Ochs Oil Co 145 Via Vera Cruz San Marcos CA 92069

OCKEY, RONALD J., lawyer; b. Green River, Wyo., June 12, 1934; s. Theron G. and Ruby O. (Sackett) O.; m. Arline M. Hawkins, Nov. 27, 1957; children—Carolyn S. Ockey Baggett, Deborah K. Ockey Christiansen, David, Kathleen M. Ockey Hellewell, Valerie, Robert. B.A., U. Utah, 1959, postgrad. 1959-60; J.D. with honors, George Washington U., 1966. Bar: Colo. 1967, Utah 1968, U.S. Dist. Ct. Colo. 1967, U.S. Dist. Ct. Utah 1968, U.S. Ct. Appeals (10th cir.) 1969, U.S. Ct. Claims 1987. Missionary to France for Mormon Ch., 1954-57; law clk. to judge U.S. Dist. Ct. Colo., 1966-67; assoc. ptnr., shareholder, v.p., treas., dir. Jones, Waldo, Holbrook & McDonough, Salt Lake City, 1967—; mem. Utah Ho. Reps., 1988—; lectr. in securities, pub. fin. and bankruptcy law. State govtl. affairs chmn. Utah Jaycees, 1969, state del. 1980-82, 84-86; del. Rep. Convs., 1972-74, 1976-78, 1980-82, 84-86, del. Salt Lake County Rep. Conv., 1978-80, 88; sec. Wright for Gov. campaign, 1980; legis. dist. chmn. Utah Rep. Party, 1983-87; trustee Food for Poland, 1981—. Lt. U.S. Army, 1960-66; to capt. Judge Adv. Gen. USAR, 1966-81. Mem. ABA(various coms.), Utah State Bar Assn. (various coms.), Nat. Assn. Bond Lawyers (chmn. com. on state legislation 1982-85), George Washington U. Law Alumni Assn. (bd. dirs. 1981-85), Order of Coif, Salt Lake Rotary, Phi Delta Phi. Contbr. articles on law to profl. jours.; mem. editorial bd. Utah Bar Jour., 1973-75; mem. staff and bd. editors George Washington Law Rev., 1964-66. Home: 4502 Crest Oak Cir Salt Lake City UT 84124 Office: 1500 First Interstate Pla Salt Lake City UT 84101

O'CONNELL, JAMES STAPLETON, JR., public relations executive; b. Boston, May 30, 1950; s. James Stapleton and Mary Agnes (Kelly) O.; m. Betsy Ellen Gee, June 19, 1971; children: Matthew James, Mary Kathleen, Michael Thomas. AB, Dartmouth Coll., 1971; MA, U. Wis., 1975. Asst. dir. of devel. Lincoln Ctr. for the Performing Arts, N.Y.C., 1975-77; mng. dir. Civic Ctr. of Greater Des Moines (Iowa), 1977-80, Des Moines Community Playhouse, 1980-82; event coord. Gammage Ctr. Ariz. State U., Tempe, 1982-83; dir. adminstrn. Ariz. State U. Pub. Events, Tempe, 1983-84, exec. dir., 1984—; cons. Found . Arts in Iowa, 1980; mem. adv. com. Ctr. for Arts Adminstrn. U. Wis., 1976-80, chmn. 1978-80; mem. theater/dance panel Iowa Arts Coun., 1979-80, theater panel Ariz. Commn. on Arts, 1985-86. Mem. planning com. All-Am. City Celebration , Des Moines, 1977; mem. Phoenix Super Bowl Task Force, 1985, 87—; mem. negotiating team to bring N.F.L. Cardinals from St. Louis to Ariz., 1987-88; site coord. Visit of Pope John Paul II to Ariz., 1987. Grad. fellow U. Wis., 1973-75; recipient Excellence in Acting award Drama Workshop, Des Moines, 1979-80, Marcus Heiman award Dartmouth Coll., 1972. Mem. Assn. Performing Arts Presenters, Western Alliance of Arts Adminstrs. (bd. dirs. 1986-87), Internat. Assn. Auditorium Mgrs. Home: 2112 E Tulane Dr Tempe AZ 85283 Office: Ariz State U Pub Events Tempe AZ 85287

O'CONNELL, MICHAEL KEHOE, investment banker; b. Washington, May 2, 1938; s. Walter Francis and Majel (Kehoe) O'C.; m. Judith Grant Shepard, June 6, 1965 (div. 1977); children: Michael Courtney, Robin Shepard; m. Marie Louisa Freyvogel Camarama, May 15, 1980; 1 stepchild, Christopher Freyvogel. BA, Yale U., 1961. Sr. assoc. Eastman Dillon Union Securities, N.Y.C., 1963-69; pres., owner M.K. O'Connell, Inc., N.Y.C., 1969-72; v.p. William D. Witter, Inc., N.Y.C., 1972-74, Chem. Bank, N.Y.C., 1974-79; dep. mng. dir. Chem. Bank Internat., Ltd., London, 1979-84; mng. dir., owner Equitable Capital & Securities, Ltd., London, 1984—, Fin. Pacific Co., L.A., 1987—; bd. dirs. First Residential Devels., Inc., London. With U.S. Army, 1961-62. Mem. Suningdale Golf, Annabels, Aspinals. Republican. Roman Catholic. Office: Fin Pacific Co 1801 Century Pk E Los Angeles CA 90153

O'CONNOR, BRIAN JOHN, banker; b. Aurora, Ill., Oct. 17, 1955; s. Charles Andrew and Charlene (Quinn) O'C. BS in Finance, Drake U., 1977; MA in Internat. Econs., Am. Grad. Sch. Internat. Mgmt., Glendale, Ariz., 1978. Ops. mgr. Walter E. Heller & Co., Phoenix, 1978-82; regional mgr. Allegheny Internat. Corp., Phoenix, 1982-83; v.p. Boettcher & Co., Phoenix, 1983-87; mng. gen. ptnr. CMC Partners, Ltd., Phoenix, 1987—; sr. v.p. Capital Mkts. Corp., Phoenix, 1988—; owner, officer, bd. dirs. Salt Lake City Trappers, Inc.; bd. dirs. Pocatello Giants, Inc. Republican. Roman Catholic. Home: PO Box 323 Phoenix AZ 85001 Office: CMC Ptnrs Ltd 2198 E Camelback Rd Ste 335 Phoenix AZ 85016

O'CONNOR, CHRISTINE ANN, city official; b. Bklyn., May 26, 1949; d. Michael and Patricia (Reilly) O'C.; m. John J. Dillon, June 18, 1975 (div. 1987). BA, SUNY-Brockport, 1971, MA, 1973; postgrad., U. Ariz., 1973-77. Tech. asst. Tucson Library, 1977-79; rsch. analyst Budget and Rsch. Dept. City of Tucson, 1979-80, mgmt. analyst, 1980-81; mgmt. info. adminstr., comdr. Police Dept., City of Tucson, 1981-82, tech. svcs. bur. adminstr., comdr., 1982—. Am. Pub. Works Assn. Bicentennial fellow, 1974. Mem. Am. Mgmt. Assn., Police Mgmt. Assn. Home: 7320 San Anna St Tucson AZ 85704 Office: Tucson Police Dept PO Box 1071 Tucson AZ 85702-1071

O'CONNOR, HUBERT PATRICK, bishop; b. Huntingdon, Que., Can., Feb. 17, 1928; s. Patrick Joseph and Mary Stella (Walsh) O'C. B.A., St. Patrick's Coll., Ottawa, 1952; L.S.T., Holy Rosary Scholasticate, Ottawa, 1956. Joined Congregation Missionary Oblates Mary Immaculate, 1948; ordained priest Roman Cath. Ch., 1955; mem. staff Holy Rosary Scholasticate, 1956-61; pastor St. John's Parish, Lillooet, B.C., 1967-68; prin. Cariboo Indian Residential Sch., Williams Lake, B.C., 1961-67; sec.-treas. Order Oblates Mary Immaculate in B.C., Vancouver, 1968-71; dir. St. Paul's Provincial House, 1968-71, Western region Oblate Fathers Indian-Eskimo Commn., 1968-71; bishop Diocese of Whitehouse, Y.T., Can., 1971-86, Diocese of Prince George, B.C., Can., 1986—; nat. dir. Cath. Women's League Can., 1973-78; chmn. Missions Commn., Can. Conf. Cath. Bishops. Club: K.C. (state chaplain B.C. and Yukon).

O'CONNOR, JUNE ELIZABETH, religious studies educator; b. Chgo., June 3, 1941; d. Philip Kevin and Eva Marie (Ennis) O'C.; m. Harry Hood, Aug. 11, 1973; 1 child, Meagan Hood. BA in English Lit., Mundelein Coll., 1964; MA, Marquette U., 1966, Temple U., 1972; PhD, Temple U., 1973. Instr. theology Mundelein Coll., Chgo., 1965-69, Temple U., Phila., 1970-73; asst. prof. religion U. Calif., Riverside, 1973-79, assoc. prof., 1979—, chmn. program in religious studies, 1985—; instr. theology Rosary Coll., River Forest, Ill., 1971; cons. William H. Sadlier Pubs., N.Y., 1971-81. Author: The Quest for Political and Spiritual Liberation: A Study in the Thought of Sri Aurobindo Ghose, 1977; assoc. editor Jour. Religious Ethics, 1978-82, mem. editorial bd. 1982-85; contbr. articles to profl. jours. Grantee U. Calif., Riverside, 1975—. Mem. Am. Acad. Religion (pres. Western region 1984-85, v.p., program chmn. 1983-84, mem. nat. com. on edn. study of religion), Soc. Christian Ethics (bd. dir. 1979-83, chmn. Pacific sect. 1977-78, vice chmn., program chmn. 1976-77), Coll. Theology Soc., Danforth Found. (assoc.), Pacific Coast Theol. Soc., Soc. Values in Higher Edn. Office: U Calif Program Religious Studies Riverside CA 92521

O'CONNOR, MAUREEN, mayor; b. San Diego, July 14, 1946; d. Jerome and Frances O'Connor; m. Robert O. Peterson, 1977. B in Psychology and Sociology, San Diego State U., 1970. Tchr., counselor Rosary High Sch., 1970-71; council mem. City of San Diego, 1971-79, dep. mayor, 1976, mayor, 1986—; with Calif. Housing Fin. Agy., 1977-79; mem. Met. Transit Devel. Bd., 1976-81; port commr. San Diego, 1980-85; mem. Rules, Legis., and Intergovtl. Relations com.; chmn. pub. services and safety com. 1974-75; mem. League Calif. Cities' Com. on Human Resources Devel., Natl League Cities' Manpower and Income Support com.; mem. mayor's crime commn. Roman Catholic. Office: City of San Diego 202 C St San Diego CA 92129 *

O'CONNOR, ROBERT JEROME, power company executive; b. Uniontown, Wash., Aug. 23, 1927; s. Eugene Joseph and Kathryn (Lunders) O'C.; m. Margaret Jean Carter, Aug. 27, 1950; children: Mary Sue, John

Carter. B.S. in Elec. Engring., U. Idaho, 1951. With GE, Schenectady, N.Y., 1951-52; with Idaho Power Co., Boise, 1952—, various positions, 1952-70, vice pres., asst. to pres., 1970-72, sr. v.p. adminstrn., 1972-76, exec. v.p. ops., 1976-81, pres., chief operating officer, 1981-85, pres., chief exec. officer, 1985-87, chmn., chief exec. officer, 1987—, also bd. dirs.; bd. dirs. Key Bank Idaho, Boise. Mem. Boise Planning and Zoning Commn., 1963-67; bd. dirs. St. Lukes's Regional Med. Ctr.; exec. com. Idaho Council on Econ. Edn., 1983—. Served with U.S. Army, 1946-48. Mem. Idaho Assn. Commerce and Industry (chmn. bus. week 1979), Boise C. of C. (exec. com.). Republican. Roman Catholic. Lodge: Rotary. Home: 710 Ranch Rd Boise ID 83702 Office: Idaho Power Co 1220 Idaho St PO Box 70 Boise ID 83707 *

O'CONNOR, RUTH ELKINTON, real estate executive, consultant; b. Oakland, Calif., May 19, 1927; d. Alfred Cope and Anna (Lydia) Elkinton; m. Roger Edward O'Connor, Oct. 12, 1950; children: Bruce E., Colleen, Lynn, Michael, John E. AA, U. Calif., 1949. Salesman Ruth Hendrickson, Realtor, Honolulu, 1966-68; salesman, broker John D. McCurry, Realtor, Honolulu, 1968-76; prin. broker O'Connor Realty, Honolulu, 1976-80; owner, pres. R.E.O. Inc., Honolulu, 1980—; owner Ga. Manor Nursing Home, Amarillo, Tex., 1981—; pres. Farm and Land Brokers, Honolulu, 1972; mem. profl. standards com. Grievance Honor Bd., Honolulu, 1983-85. Editor: Friends of Samoa, 1979. Recipient Exchangor of the Yr. award The Investment Group, Realtors, 1968, Councelor of the Yr. award The Investment Group, Realtors, 1969, Arts Council award Govt. of Am. Samoa, 1980. Mem. Honolulu Bd. Realtors (dir. 1970-72), Hawaii Bd. Realtors, Nat. Assn. of Realtors (real estate aviation cpt.), Internat. Real Estate Fedn., Nat. Assn. Female Execs., Pan Pacific S.E. Asian Women (life), Arts Council (dir. 1976-79), The Ninety-Nines (Hawaii del. 1985, Silver Wings), Profl. Assn. Diving Instrs., Tex. Nursing Home Assn., Am. Nursing Home Assn., Am. Health Care Assn., Berkeley City Club, Outrigger Canoe, Berkeley City Club, Alpha Omicron Pi. Mem. Soc. of Friends. Club: Outrigger Canoe. Office: REO Inc 417 Kanekapolei St Ste 103 Honolulu HI 96815

O'CONNOR, WILLIAM MICHAEL, ombudsman; b. Norfolk, Va., Nov. 29, 1942; s. William and Geneva (Harmon) O'C.; m. Betty Metzler, June 15, 1965 (div.); m. Catherine E. Katsel, Sept. 28, 1979; 1 child, Geneva Maureen. AA, Shoreline Community Coll., 1969; BA in Sociology, Cen. Wash. U., 1971; MS in Mgmt., Alaska Pacific U., 1986; postgrad., Nova U., 1987-88. Lic. nursing home adminstr. Police officer City of Mountlake Terrace, Wash., 1969-70; counselor Shoreline Ct. Probation, Seattle, 1970-79; exec. dir. Older Alaskans Program, Anchorage Salvation Army, 1979-83; ombudsman for older Alaskans State of Alaska, Anchorage, 1983—; mgmt. cons. Mental Health North, Seattle, 1975-78, Snohomish County Probation, Everett, Wash., 1978, Anchorage Salvation Army, 1985-88, R.P. Kinney Engring., Anchorage, 1986-87. Author: Alcohol Diagnosis in the Court System, 1975. Chmn. Eagle River (Alaska) Rd. Commn., 1985-86, dist. 15 Alaska Dem. Com., 1987. Sgt. U.S. Army, 1965-68. Mem. Data Processing Mgmt. Assn., Am. Mgmt. Assn., Alaska Project Dirs. Assn., Elks, Lions. Roman Catholic. Office: Office Older Alaskan Ombudsman 3601 C St Ste 380 Anchorage AK 99503-5209

O'CONNOR, WILLIAM STEWART, retail executive; b. Jacksonville, Fla., Dec. 14, 1953; s. Charles John and Sylvia Carolyn (Tint) O'C. BS, Pa. State U., 1975; MA in Edn., Kent State U., 1977. Instr., speech cons. Ft. Lauderdale (Fla.) Oral Sch. for the Deaf, 1975-76; instr., speech therapist Calif. Sch. for the Deaf, Riverside, Calif., 1977-79; program dir., cons. deaf-blind program Jefferson County Schs., Louisville, 1979-81, media programmer, specialist deaf-blind program, 1979-81, instr., cons. adult edn. program, 1979-81; sales assoc., area mgr. Saks Fifth Ave., Palo Alto, Calif., 1981-83; asst. store mgr., store mgr. Johnston & Murphy Co., Portland, Oreg., 1983; dept. mgr., area mgr. I. Magnin & Co., Costa Mesa, Calif., 1983-88; asst. store mgr. Gump's, Beverly Hills, Calif., 1988-89; fur salon mgr. I. Magnin & Co., L.A., 1989—. Author, dir., producer, actorvideotape workshops instructional sign lang., 1980. Active One in Long Beach (Calif.), BA Long Beach, 1987-88. Democrat. Episcopalian. Home: 1136 N Larrabee Apt 207 Los Angeles CA 90069 Office: I Magnin & Co 3240 Wilshire Blvd Beverly Hills CA 90010

OCZON, ARNEL MIRAFLORES, electrical engineer; b. Sasebo, Japan, Dec. 14, 1962; s. Leonardo Enerio and Arsenia (Miraflores) O. BSEE, U. N.Mex., 1984; MSEE, Stanford U., 1986. Mem. tech. staff Sandia Nat. Labs., Albuquerque, 1985—. Republican. Roman Catholic. Office: Sandia National Labs PO Box 5800 Div 9132 Albuquerque NM 87185

ODA, MARGARET YURIKO, educational administrator; b. Hakalau, Hawaii, Mar. 26, 1925; d. Satoru and Satoyo Kurisu; m. Glenn K. Oda (dec.); 1 child, Marjorie. B.Ed., U. Hawaii, 1947; M.A., Mich. State U., 1950; Ed.D., U. Hawaii, 1977. Tchr. Hilo Intermediate Sch., Hawaii, 1951, counselor, 1951-52, 53-56, vice prin., 1956-63; prin. Hakalau-Honomu-Pepeekeo, Hilo, 1963-66; dir. gen. edn. State Dept. Edn., Honolulu, 1965-76; prin. Kaiser High Sch., Honolulu, 1978-82; supt. Honolulu Sch. Dist., Honolulu, 1982-84; state dep. supt. Hawaii State Dept. Edn., Honolulu, 1984-87, dist. supt., 1987—; mem. Western Regional Adv. Panel Coll. Bd., 1984-86, Northwest Regional Ednl. Lab. Adv. Bd., Portland, Oreg., 1984-85, exec. bd. Chief State Sch. Officers Study Commn., 1985-86; coordinator State Edn. Policy Seminars, 1984-86. Bd. dirs. Hawaii Heart Assn., Honolulu, 1979-84, Honolulu Community Theatre, 1972-75, Honpa Hongwanji Buddhist Orgn., 1984—, Pan Pacific Found., 1982—, Jr. Achievement 1986-88; bd. trustees Kuakini Med. Devel., Honolulu Acad. of Arts, Hawaii Pub. Sch. Found.; bd. dirs., sec. Japanese Cultural Ctr. Hawaii; vice-chairperson, bd. dirs. Pacific Cultural Ctr.. Fellow Ctr. for Study Edn. Yale U., 1973. Mem. Am. Assn. Sch. Adminstrs., Nat. Assn. Secondary Sch. Prins., Pi Lambda Theta. Club: Japanese Women's Soc. (pres. 1983-85). Office: Honolulu Dist Supr Office 4967 Kilauea Ave Honolulu HI 96816

ODA, YOSHIO, physician, internist; b. Papaaloa, Hawaii, Jan. 14, 1933; s. Hakuai and Usako (Yamamoto) O.; AB, Cornell U., 1955; MD, U. Chgo., 1959. Intern U. Chgo. Clinics, 1959-60; resident in pathology U. Chgo., 1960-62, Queen's Hosp., Hawaii, 1962-63, Long Beach (Calif.) VA Hosp., 1963-65; resident in allergy, immunology U. Colo. Med. Center, 1966-67; pvt. practice, L.A., 1965-66; pvt. practice internal medicine, allergy and immunology, Honolulu, 1970—; asst. clin. prof. medicine U. Hawaii, Honolulu, 1970—. Maj., AUS, 1968-70. Diplomate Am. Bd. Internal Medicine. Mem. ACP, Am. Acad. Allergy. Office: Piikoi Med Bldg 1024 Piikoi St Honolulu HI 96814

ODEGAARD, CHARLES EDWIN, history educator; b. Chicago Heights, Ill., Jan. 10, 1911; s. Charles Alfred and Mary (Cord) O.; m. Elizabeth Jane Ketchum, Apr. 12, 1941 (dec. 1980); 1 child, Mary Ann Quarton. A.B., Dartmouth Coll., 1932, LL.D., 1959; M.A., Harvard U., 1933, Ph.D., 1937; L.H.D., Lawrence Coll., 1951; LL.D., Miami U., Oxford, Ohio, 1955, U. B.C., Can., 1959, Gonzaga U., 1962, UCLA, 1962, Seattle U., 1965, U. Mich., 1969; Litt.D., U. Puget Sound, 1963. Asst. in history Radcliffe Coll., 1935-37; from instr. to prof. U. Ill., 1937-48; exec. dir. Am. Council Learned Soc., Washington, 1948-52; prof. history, dean Coll. Lit. Sci. and Arts U. Mich., Ann Arbor, 1952-58; pres. U. Wash., Seattle, 1958-73; pres. emeritus, prof. higher edn. U. Wash., 1974—, prof. biomed. history, 1975—; mem. U.S. Nat. Commn. UNESCO, 1949-55, advisor U.S. del. 5th Gen. Conf., Florence, Italy, 1950; chmn. Commn. Human Resources and Advanced Tng., 1949-53, pres. Internat. Council of Philosophy and Humanistic Studies, 1959-65; mem. adv. com. cultural info. USIA, 1955-62, Western Interstate Com. on Higher Edn., 1959-70, Citizens Com. on Grad. Med. Edn., 1963-66, Nat. Adv. Health Counci USPHS, 1964-68, Nat. Adv. Health Manpower, 1965-67, NEH, 1966-72, Study Commn. Pharmacy, 1973-75; mem. Macy Study Commn. on Acad. Psychiatry, 1978-79. Author: Fideles and Vassi in the Carolingian Empire, 1945; Minorities in Medicine, 1977, Area Health Education Centers, 1979, Dear Doctor: A Personal Letter to a Physician, 1986; contbr. articles on mediaeval history and higher edn. to profl. jours. bd. regents Uniformed U. Health Scis., 1973-80; chmn. Wash. State Bd. Continuing Legal Edn., 1976-79. Served from lt. (j.g.) to lt. comdr. USNR, 1942-46. Recipient Medal of Merit State of Wash., 1989. Mem. Am. Council on Edn. (dir., chmn. 1962-63), Am. Hist. Assn., NAS, Mediaeval Acad. Am., Tchrs. Ins. and Annuity Assn. (dir. 1963-69, trustee 1970-86, coll. retirement equity fund 1970-86), Inst. Medicine, Phi Beta Kappa, Phi Eta Sigma, Beta Theta Pi. Clubs: Rainier, Seattle Yacht, University (Seattle); Cosmos (Washington); Bohemian (San Francisco). Lodge: Rotary. Office: U Wash 222 Miller Hall Seattle WA 98195

ODELL, JOHN H., construction company executive; b. Toledo, Oct. 31, 1955; s. John H. and Doris Irene (Haskell) O. BS in Environ. Design, U. Miami, Oxford, Ohio, 1977. Staff architect Richard Halford and Assocs., Santa Fe, 1978-79; ptnr. B.O.A. Constrn., Santa Fe, 1980-84; assoc. Stanley Design Works, Santa Fe, 1984-85; owner John H. Odell Constrn., Santa Fe, 1985—. Musician Santa Fe Community Orch., 1982, Huntington Community Orch., Huntington, W.Va., 1972-73. Mem. AIA (assoc., treas., bd. dirs. Santa Fe chpt. 1988, mem. liaison Nat. Design Com., 1987—), Home Builders Assn. Home: PO Box 2967 Santa Fe NM 87504 Office: John H Odell Constrn 236 Montezuma Suite 22 Santa Fe NM 87501

O'DELL, RONALD LUTHER, real estate developer; b. Friendship, Ohio, Apr. 16, 1939; s. Luther Benton and Farrel Della (Beekman) O'D.; m. Carole Anne Ries, June 28, 1971. BSEE, Milw. Sch. Engring., 1960. Cons., exec. officer Woodstone Inc., Sunnywood Devel. Corp., Woodland Park, Colo., 1972—; asst. instr. Milw. Sch. Engring., 1959-60; project engr. Gen. Motors AC Electronics Div., Milw., 1960-62; space defense ops. analyst Gen. Electric Corp., Syracuse, N.Y. and Colo., 1962-70; cons. broker Mills Land Co. (div. Woodland RE), Woodland Park, Colo., 1970-74; pres., chief exec. officer Sunnywood Devel. Corp., Woodland Park, 1972—, Woodstone, Inc., Woodland Park, 1985—; cons., analyst Information Bldg. Assn., Woodland Park, 1987—; bd. dirs. Woodstone, Inc., Woodland Park,, Sunnywood Devel. Corp., Woodland Park. Precinct com. Teller County, Colo. Democratic Party, 1972-78, county and state del., 1974, 76, 78. Home: 150 Apache Trail Woodland Park CO 80863

ODEN, WILLIAM EVERT, management consultant; b. Chickasha, Okla., Feb. 20, 1944; s. William Evert Oden and Geneva Pauline (Forbes) Hannah; m. Joan Carol Wise, Aug. 3, 1968; children: Ryan William, Carol Eileen. BS, Okla. State U., 1967, MS, 1972. Informational rep. Okla. Indsl. Devel. and Parks Dept., Oklahoma City, 1967-68; internat. student advisor Okla. State U., Stillwater, 1968-70; resource devel. specialist Tex. Agrl. Extension Svc., College Station, 1972-73; fed.-state coordinator Tex. Parks and Wildlife Dept., Austin, 1973-75; county planning coordinator Tex. Dept. Community Affairs, Austin, 1975-77; fin. planner Fin. Adv.Svcs., Austin, 1977-79; v.p. external affairs Loretto Heights Coll., Denver, 1979-81; pres., owner TMI-Tng., Denver, 1981—. Author booklets on money mgmt. Bd. dirs. Denver Boys, Inc., 1981-82, Community Resources, Inc., Denver, 1985—. Named to Outstanding Young Men Am., 1981. Mem. Am. Soc. Tng. and Devel., Am. Mgmt. Assn., Rotary, Delta Tau Delta. Presbyterian. Office: TMI-Tng 3793 E Mineral Pl Littleton CO 80122

ODERMATT, DIANA BIRTWISTLE, educational administrator, educational consultant; b. Hollywood, Calif., Nov. 25, 1938; d. Harold Jr. and Mary H. (Wilson) Birtwistle; m. Robert Allen Odermatt, June 9, 1960; children: Kristen Ann, Kyle David. BA, Mills Coll., 1960. Statis. asst. Inst. Human Devel., U. Calif., Berkeley, 1960-62; from admissions counselor to dean admissions and fin. aid Mills Coll., Oakland, Calif., 1978-86; asst. dir. devel. Head-Royce Sch., Oakland, 1986-87, dir. devel., 1987—; cons. Western Region Coll. Bd., 1986—. Contbr. articles to profl. pubs. Mem. Council for the Advancement and Support of Edn. (commn. on enrollment), Jr. League-Oakland-East Bay. Home: 39 Drury Ln Berkeley CA 94705 Office: Head Royce School 4315 Lincoln Ave Oakland CA 94602

ODERMATT, ROBERT ALLEN, architect; b. Oakland, Calif., Jan. 3, 1938; s. Clifford Allen and Margaret Louise (Budge) O.; m. Diana Birtwistle, June 9, 1960; children: Kristin Ann, Kyle David. B.Arch., U. Calif.-Berkeley, 1960. Registered architect, Calif., Oreg., Nev., Colo. cert. Nat. Council Archtl. Registration Bds. Draftsman Anderson Simonds Dusel Campini, Oakland, 1960-61; architect James R. Lucas, Orinda, Calif., 1961-62, ROMA Architects, San Francisco, 1962-76; architect, pres. ROMA Architects, 1976-84; prin. ROMA Design Group, San Francisco, 1962—. Prin. designer (comprehensive plan), Grand Canyon Nat. Park, 1977, Yosemite Nat. Park, 1987, prin. planner (devel. plan); prin.-in-charge: Hotel Complex, Westin Hotel, Vail, Colo., 1982, U.S. Embassy, Manama, Bahrain, Kaanapali Resort Master-Plan, 1987, Las Manamas Resort, San Diego, 1988, Master-Plan U. Calif., Berkeley, 1988; U.S. Design in Am. Program, Sofia, Bulgaria. Mem. Oakland Mayors Com. on High Density Housing, 1982; prin. charge U.S. Embassy, Bahrain. Fellow AIA (dir. East Bay chpt. 1969-71, pres. 1980-81, dir. Calif. council 1979-81, nat. dir. 1983-86, nat. v.p. 1986-87). Office: ROMA Design Group 1420 Sutter St San Francisco CA 94109

ODGEN, VALERIA M., non-profit foundation administrator; b. Okanogan, Wash., Feb. 11, 1924; d. Ivan Bodwell and Pearle (Wilson) Munson; m. Daniel Miller Odgen Jr., Dec. 28, 1946; children: Janeth Lee Ogden Martin, Patricia Jo Ogden Hunter, Daniel Munson. BA, Wash. State U., 1946. Exec. dir. Potomac Council Camp Fire, Washington, 1964-68, Ft. Collins (Colo.) United Way, 1969-73, Designing Tomorrow Today, Ft. Collins, 1973-74, Poudre Valley Community ED, Ft. Collins, 1975-77; pres. Valeria M. Odgen Tng., Washington, 1977-82; exec. dir. Nat. Capital YWCA, Washington, 1981-84; nat. field cons. Camp Fire, Inc., Vancouver, Wash., 1984-85; exec. dir. Clark County YWCA, Vancouver, 1985—; lectr. in field.; pres. elect nat. bd. Assn. Vol. Adminstrn., Boulder, Colo., 1984—; mem. adj. faculty pub. adminstrn. program Lewis and Clark Coll. Portland (Oreg.) State U., 1979—, Pvt. Industry Council, Vancouver, 1984—, Wash. State Voluntary Action Council, Olympia, 1987—. County V chair Larimer County Dem. Party, Ft. Collins, 1974-75; mem. precinct com. Clark County Democrats, Vancouver, 1986—. Named Citizen of Yr. Ft. Collins Bd. of Realtors, 1973. Mem. Nat. Assn. YWCA ED, Women in Action, Nat. Mortar Bd. Found. (treas. 1987—), Phi Beta Kappa. Unitarian. Home: 3118 Royal Oaks Dr Vancouver WA 98662 Office: Clark County YWCA 1115 Esther Vancouver WA 98660

ODGERS, JAYME, artist; b. Butte, Mont., Aug. 24, 1939; d. Rupert Archibald and Nell (Wyatt) O. BA with great distinction, Art Ctr. Coll. Design, L.A., 1963. Asst. Paul Rand, Weston, Conn., 1964-66; self-employed artist L.A., 1967—; instr. Art Ctr. Coll. Design, L.A., 1968-73, Calif. Inst. Arts, Valencia, Calif., 1976-78, Otis-Parsons Sch. Design, L.A., 1989. With USAAF, 1963-68. Recipient Gold medals N.Y. Art Dirs. Club, N.Y.C., 1970, L.A. Art Dirs. Club, 1971, Silver Internat. award Typomundus, Switzerland, 1968; Fulbright scholar, 1966. Mem. Am. Inst. Graphic Arts (bd. dirs. L.A. chpt. 1988). Democrat. Home: 6636 Iris Dr Los Angeles CA 90068

ODGERS, RICHARD WILLIAM, lawyer; b. Detroit, Dec. 31, 1936; s. Richard Stanley and Elsie Maude (Trevarthen) O.; m. Gail C. Bassett, Aug. 29, 1959; children: Thomas R., Andrew B. AB, U. Mich., 1959, JD, 1961. Bar: Calif. 1962. Assoc. Pillsbury, Madison & Sutro, San Francisco, 1961-69, ptnr., 1969-87; exec. v.p., gen. counsel, sec. Pacific Telesis Group, 1987—. Served with USNR. Fellow Am. Bar Found., Am. Judicature Soc., Am. Coll. Trial Lawyers; mem. ABA, Am. Law Inst., San Francisco Bar Assn. Clubs: Olympic, Pacific-Union, City (San Francisco). Office: Pacific Telesis Group 130 Kearny St San Francisco CA 94108

O'DONNELL, MARLENE G., construction company executive; b. San Francisco, July 21, 1988; d. Edgar M. and Cathrine Barbara (Carlomagno) Donahoo; m. Lloyd A. Mannon, Nov. 16, 1958 (div. 1964); m. Chester R. O'Donnell, Dec. 18, 1965; children: Michael L., Kraig C., Jeffrey P., Todd C., Shawna C. Student, Foothill Jr. Coll., 1958-60. Office mgr. Blue Haven Pools, Sunnyvale, Calif., 1963-72; bookkeeper O'Donnell Plastering, Inc., Santa Clara, Calif., 1972-80; owner, v.p. O'Donnell Plastering, Inc., 1980--; v.p. Builders Exchange State Fund Bd., Santa Clara, 1983--. Mem. Nat. Assn. Women in Constrn. (trustee, past officer Santa Clara chpt.). Office: O'Donnell Plastering Inc 2318 Lafayette St Santa Clara CA 95050

O'DONNELL, PATRICK BERNARD, photographer, educator; b. Omaha, May 22, 1941; s. Patrick Albert and Martha (Peterson) O'D.; m. Margaret Carol Williamson, Aug. 19, 1967; children: Kevin, Ryan, Steven. AA, Cerritos Coll., 1961; BA, Calif. State U., Long Beach, 1964. Cert. tchr. Calif. Staff photographer Daily News, Whittier, Calif., 1963-68, Orange Coast Daily Pilot, Costa Mesa, Calif., 1968-83; lectr. Calif. State U., Fullerton, 1983—; freelance photojournalist; project chmn. historic front-page project Calif. State U-Fullerton, 1987. Dem. precinct chmn. Whittier, Calif., 1964. With USAF, 1965-66. Mem. Calif. Faculty Assn., AAUP, Calif. Press Photographers Assn. (pres. 1987—), Nat. Press Photographers Assn. (chmn. flying short course 1986), Orange County Press Club (bd. dirs. 1969-72, pres. 1972-73, Sky Dunlap awd. 1980). Home: 10840 El Mar St Fountain Valley CA 92708 Office: Calif State U Fullerton CA 92634

O'DONNELL, WILLIAM RUSSELL, state senator; b. Quincy, Mass., Jan. 16, 1951; s. Alfred Joseph and Ruth Irene (McCausland) O.; m. Mary Hogan, June 13, 1976; children: Meagan, Patrick, Kevin, Colleen, Kyle. BS in Bus. and Econs., U. Nev., Las Vegas, 1979. Patrolman Las Vegas Met. Police, 1973-74; realtor Coldwell-Banker, Las Vegas, 1988—; pres. Computer System Concepts, Las Vegas, 1980—; Nev. state senator 1987—. Nev. state assemblyman, Las Vegas, 1985-86; alt. legis. commn. Nev., 1987-89; majority Whip Rep. Party Nev., 1989; mem. Nev. Child Watch Adv. Bd., Assn. for the Handicapped, Pro-Life Nev., Citizens for Responsible Govt.; pres. Sect. 10 Homeowners Assn., Las Vegas, 1986—, Spring Valley Town Bd., 1984—; bd. dirs. Home of the Good Shepherd, St. Rose de Lima Hosp., 1985—. Mem. Las Vegas Bd. Realtors, Rotary. Republican. Roman Catholic. Office: Office of the State Senate State Capitol Carson City NV 89710 also: O'Donnell Bus Ctr 2995 S Jones Blvd Las Vegas NV 89102

O'DONNELL, WILLIAM THOMAS, radar systems marketing executive; b. Latrobe, Pa., Feb. 22, 1939; s. William Regis and Kathryn Ann (Coneff) O'D.; m. Judith Koetke, Oct. 1, 1965; children: William Thomas, William Patrick, Allison Rose, Kevin Raymond. Student Eastern N.Mex. U., 1958-61; student in mktg. John Carroll U., 1961-65, Ill. Inst. Tech., 1965-66; BSBA, U. Phoenix, 1982, MBA with distinction, 1984. Various sales positions Hickok Elec. Instrument Co., Cleve., 1961-65, Fairchild Semicondr., Mpls., 1965-67; Transitron Semicondr., Mpls., 1967-69; Burroughs Corp., Plainfield, N.J., 1967-71; mktg. mgr. Owens-Ill. Co., 1972-73, v.p. mktg. Pantek Co., subs. Owens-Ill. Co., Lewistown, Pa., 1973-75, v.p. mktg., nat. sales mgr., Toledo, 1975-76; mktg. mgr., nat. sales mgr. Govt. Electronics div. group Motorola Co., Scottsdale, Ariz., 1976-80, U.S. mktg. mgr. radar positioning systems Motorola Govt. Electronics Group, 1981—; gen. mgr. J.K. Internat., Scottsdale, 1980-81; mgmt. cons. Pres. Cambridge Group, 1987—; adj. prof. Union Grad. Sch.; guest lectr. U. Mich. Grad. Sch. Bus. Adminstrn.; instr., chair strategic mgmt. U. Phoenix, 1988, pres. faculty, 1989—; Scottsdale Community Coll., Paradise Valley Community Coll.; area chair-gen. mgmt. Union Grad. Sch. Maricopa Community Coll., U. Phoenix. Chmn., Rep. Precinct, Burnsville, Minn., 1968-70; city fin. chmn., Burnsville; dir. community devel. U.S. Jaycees, Mpls., 1968-69; mem. Scottsdale 2000 Com. Served with USAF, 1957-61. Recipient Outstanding Performance award Maricopa Community Coll. System, 1987, Faciliation award, Maricopa Community Coll., Citation for Faciliation Ability U. Phoenix, 1986; named Hon. Citizen, Donaldsville, La., 1978; others. Mem. Phoenix Execs. Club, Am. Mktg. Assn., U. Phoenix Faculty Club (pres. 1988-89), recipient Presdl. Designation award, officer, pres. 1988-89), North Cape Yacht Club, Scottsdale Racquet Club, Toftnees Country Club. Roman Catholic. Home: 8432 E Belgian Tr Scottsdale AZ 85258

O'DOWD, DONALD DAVY, university president; b. Manchester, N.H., Jan. 23, 1927; s. Hugh Davy and Laura (Morin) O'D.; m. Janet Louise Fithian, Aug. 23, 1953; children: Daniel D., Diane K., James E., John M. BA summa cum laude, Dartmouth Coll., 1951; postgrad. (Fulbright fellow), U. Edinburgh, Scotland, 1951-52; MA, Harvard U., 1955, PhD, 1957. Instr., asst. prof. psychology, dean freshmen Wesleyan U., Middletown, Conn., 1955-60; assoc. prof., prof. Wesleyan U., 1960, dean Univ., 1960-65, provost, 1965-70; pres. Oakland U., Rochester, Mich., 1970-80; exec. vice chancellor SUNY, Albany, 1980-84; pres. U. of Alaska Statewide System, 1984—. Bd. dirs. Research Found. SUNY, State Univ. Constrn. Fund, N.Y. Sea Grant Inst., Albany Symphony Orch.; pres. Capital Repertory Theatre Co. Served with AUS, 1945-47. Carnegie Corp. fellow, 1965-66. Mem. Am. Psychol. Assn., AAAS, AAUP, Am. Assn. Univ. Adminstrs., Phi Beta Kappa, Sigma Xi. Office: U Alaska Mus 907 Yukon Dr Fairbanks AK 99775 *

OEHNINGER, DANIEL SCOTT, military officer; b. Dallas, May 27, 1954; s. James Richard and Mary Louis (Kastens) O.; m. Wendy Iris Norton, Dec. 5, 1976; children: Brandy Leigh, Benjamin James. Student, U. Wash., 1980, Roosevelt U., 1983. Enlisted USMC, 1971, advanced through grades to capt.; armorer USMC, Okinawa, Japan, 1972-73, Marine Barracks, Long Beach, Calif., 1973-74; embassy guard Marine Security Guard Battalion, Darkar, Senegal, 1974-75, Geneva, 1975-76; interrogator, interpreter 19th ITT, Camp Pendleton, Calif., 1976-78; pilot comdr. Assault Amphibian Detachment, Kaneohe, Hawaii, 1981-84; selection officer USMC, St. Louis, 1984-85; combat cargo officer USS Guam LPH-9, Norfolk, Va., 1985-87; logistics officer Schs. Battalion, Camp Pendleton, 1987—. Chmn. activity Combined Fed. Campaign, Camp Pendleton, 1987-88; mem. Boy Scouts Am. Mem. Marine Corps Assn. Republican. Lutheran. Home: 2619 Joann Dr Oceanside CA 92056 Office: USMC Marine Corps Base Schools BN S-4 Camp Pendleton CA 92056

O'FARRELL, DAVID JOHNSTON, information systems specialist, accountant; b. Tacoma, Aug. 3, 1948; s. Duane Dunlap and Dorothy (Johnston) O'F.; m. Nancy Jane Wiloth, June 24, 1977; 1 child, Jay Johnston. BA, Whitman Coll., 1971; MBA, Colo. State U., 1977. Acctg. supr. Hewlett-Packard Co., Loveland, Colo., 1977-79; acctg. mgr. Hewlett-Packard Co., Everett, Wash., 1980-83, info. systems specialist, 1983-88; programming supr. Fin. Systems, Loveland, Colo., 1989—. Chmn. Marysville (Wash.) Gen. Adv. Council on Vocat. Edn., 1986-88. Recipient Vocat. Sch. Edn. Recognition award Marysville Sch. Dist., 1987. Mem. Nat. Assn. Accts., Beta Gamma Sigma, Alpha Iota Delta. Avocations: flying, skiing, amateur radio. Home: 2527 Courtland Ct Fort Collins CO 80526 Office: Hewlett-Packard Co PO Box 301 Loveland CO 80539

OFFICER, JAMES EOFF, anthropologist; b. Boulder, Colo., July 28, 1924; s. Forrest Irving and Josephine Emma (Eoff) O.; m. Roberta Mitzel, Feb. 22, 1946; children: Sarah Jean, James Robert. AB, U. Ariz., 1950, PhD, 1964. Radio announcer Kansas City, Kans. and Phoenix, 1942-45; radio announcer, writer various stas. Tucson, 1946-50; intern Dept. State, Washington, 1950-51; info. attache U.S. Embassy Dept. State, Santiago, Chile, 1951-53; radio and TV announcer, writer various stas. Tucson, 1953-60; assoc. commr. Bur. Indian Affairs, Washington, 1961-67; adminstrv. asst. to sec. Dept. Interior, Washington, 1967-69; prof. anthropology U. Ariz., Tucson, 1969—; U.S. rep. Interam. Indian Inst., Mexico City, 1966-78; bd. dirs. Ariz./Mex. Commn., Tucson, 1976-80. Author: Hispanic Arizona, 1987 (S.W. Books award Border Regional Libr. Assn. 1988), Arizona's Hispanic Perspective, 1981, Anthropology and the American Indian, 1973; collaborator (book) The Hodges' Ruin. Active Tucson-Guadalajara Sister City Commn., 1974-80, Tucson-Pima County Hist. commn., 1989; precinct committeeman Dem. Com., Tucson, 1970-72; bd. dirs. Ariz. Hist. Soc., 1985—, Hospitality Internat. Tucson, 1971-78. Staff sgt. U.S. Army, 1945-46. Recipient Best Article on Ariz. History award Ariz. Hist. Found., Phoenix, 1988. Fellow Am. Anthrop. Assn. (program chmn. 1974), Soc. Applied Anthropology (chmn. local arrangements 1972), Pacific Coast Coun. on Latin Am. Studies (bd. govs. 1987—), Tucson Press Club (bd. dirs. 1956-59), Rotary (historian Tucson club 1978—). Home: 621 N Sawtelle Ave Tucson AZ 85716 Office: U Ariz Dept Anthropology Tucson AZ 85721

OFFUTT, SUSAN DENISE, market researcher; b. Kansas City, Mo., Dec. 31, 1953; d. George Dennis and Susan Elizabeth (Ohrazda) O.; m. Glenn Edward Miller, Dec. 29, 1979. BS, Mo. Western State U., 1975; MS, Emporia State U., 1983. State data coordinator Purex Corp., Carson, Calif., 1978; market research mgr. Purex Corp., Carson, 1978-79, group mgr. research and info. svcs., 1980-85; mktg. mgr. Van de Kamp's Holland Dutch Bakery, Los Angeles, 1985-87; acct. mgr. A.C. Nielsen Co., Santa Ana, Calif., 1987—. Mem. Friends of the Marsh, Torrance, Calif., 1980. Named Outstanding Young Mgr. Purex Corp., 1982. Mem. AAUW (v.p. 1986-88). Episcopalian. Home: 3527 Cricklewood St Torrance CA 90505 Office: AC Nielsen Co 4 Hutton Centre Dr Ste 700 Santa Ana CA 92707

OGAWA, KENNETH MIKIO, dentist; b. Tokyo, Feb. 9, 1961; s. Richard Toshiyuki and Clara Ann (Dally) O. Student, Apollo Coll. of Beauty, St. Louis, 1981, Big Rig Truckdriving, St. Louis, 1981; DMD, Washington U.,

St. Louis, 1986. Sales rep. Euclid Records, Inc., St. Louis, 1984-86; dental officer Navajo Area Indian Health Service, Shonto, Ariz., 1986—. Author: Q, 1985; producer, writer (film) The Big Tree, 1987. Active with Jews for Jesus, Columbia, Mo., 1981. Mem. ADA, Acad. Dentistry for Handicapped. Democrat. Home: Box 7397 Shonto AZ 86054

OGBORN, MICHAEL JAMES, lawyer, educator; b. Sioux Falls, S.D., July 21, 1947; s. Robert James and Kathryn Agnes (Murray) O.; m. Jill Brooks Argetsinger, Nov. 15, 1967; children: Sarah Anne, Matthew Robert. BA, U. S.D., 1969, JD, 1972. Bar: S.D. 1972, U.S. Dist. Ct. S.D. 1972, Nebr. 1974, U.S. Dist. Ct. Nebr. 1974, U.S. Ct. Appeals (9th cir.) 1975, Colo. 1975, U.S. Dist. Ct. Colo. 1975, U.S. Ct. Appeals (8th and D.C. cirs.) 1977, U.S. Ct. Appeals (5th cir.) 1981, U.S. Ct. Appeals (6th and 11th cirs.) 1982, U.S. Ct. appeals (10th cir.) 1986. Gen. counsel All-Am. Transport Inc., Sioux Falls, 1972-74; assoc. Nelson & Harding, Lincoln, Nebr., 1974-75, ptnr., 1975-84; ptnr. Nelson & Harding, P.C., Denver, 1984-88, Heron, Buychette, Ruckert & Rothwell, Denver, 1988—; lectr. Transp. Law Inst., Denver, 1979-85; adj. prof. law U. Denver, 1987—; bd. cons. Eno Found. for Transp. Inc., Westport, Conn., 1986—; spl. asst. atty. gen. State of Mont., 1987—. Contbr. articles to legal publs. Pres. Colo. Youth Symphony Orgns. Assn., Denver, 1986—. Mem. ABA, Assn. Trial Lawyers Am., Nebr. Bar Assn. (sect. chmn.), Colo. Bar Assn., S.D. Bar Assn., Transp. Lawyers Assn. (pres. 1988—, Disting. Svc. award 1987), Colo. Assn. Corp. Counsel, Assn. Transp. Practitioners, Can. Transp. Lawers Assn., Colo. Assn. Commerce and Industry, Denver C. of C. Republican. Episcopalian. Office: Heron Buychette Ruckert & Rothwell 2600 Mannville Pla Denver CO 80202-3357

OGDEN, DALE FRANCIS, management consultant; b. Balt., Sept. 17, 1951; s. Robert B. and Anna E. (Carl) O.; m. Sylvia Matani, Nov. 14, 1979 (div. Sept. 1986); m. Colleen J. Salese, Jan. 20, 1989. BA in Math., Towson State U., 1975. Field rep. Equifax Svcs., Balt., 1974-76; math tchr. Balt. City Pub. Schs., Balt., 1974-76; actuary Md. Automobile Ins. Fund, Annapolis, Md., 1976-80; mgr. Peat Marwick Main & Co, N.Y.C., 1980-83; exec. v.p. Kramer Capital Cons., Greenwich, Conn., 1983-87; pres. Dale F. Ogden & Assocs., San Pedro, Calif., 1988—. Contbr. articles to publs. Mem. Casualty Actuarial Soc. (assoc.), Soc. of Actuaries (assoc.), Am. Acad. Actuaries, Internat. Actuarial Assn., Soc. Ins. Accts. Republican. Office: Dale F Ogden and Assocs 3620 Almeria St San Pedro CA 90731

OGDEN, DANIEL MILLER, JR., government official, educator; b. Clarksburg, W.Va., Apr. 28, 1922; s. Daniel Miller and Mary (Maphis) O.; m. Valeria Juan Munson, Dec. 28, 1946; children: Janeth Lee Martin, Patricia Jo Hunter, Daniel Munson. BA in Polit. Sci., Wash. State U., 1944; MA, U. Chgo., 1947, PhD, 1949. From instr. to assoc. prof. Wash. State U., Pullman, 1949-61; staff asst. resources program U.S. Dept. Interior, 1961-64; asst. dir. U.S. Bur. Outdoor Recreation, 1964-67; dir. budget U.S. Dept. Interior, Washington, 1967-68; dean Coll. Humanities and Social Scis. Colo. State U., Ft. Collins, 1968-76; disting. vis. prof. Lewis and Clark Coll. and Portland (Oreg.) State U., 1977-78; dir. Office of Power Mktg. Coordination U.S. Dept. Energy, 1978-84; mgr. Pub. Power Coun., Portland, Oreg., 1984-88, ret., 1988; mem. profl. staff Com. Interstate and Fgn. Commerce, U.S. Senate, 1956-57; spl. asst. to chmn. Dem. Nat. Com., 1960-61; lectr. Exec. Seminar Ctrs., U.S. Office Personnel Mgmt., 1966—. Co-author: Electing the President, rev. edit., 1968, American National Government, 7th edit., 1970, American State and Local Government, 5th edit., 1972, Washington Politics, 1960. Committeeman Wash. Dem. Cen. Com., 1952-56; chmn. Whitman County Dem. Cen. Com., 1958-60. Served with inf. U.S. Army, 1943-46. Mem. Phi Beta Kappa, Phi Kappa Phi, Pi Sigma Alpha, Sigma Delta Chi. Mem. Unitarian Ch. Home: 3118 NE Royal Oaks Dr Vancouver WA 98662

OGDEN, JAMES RUSSELL, marketing executive, educator; b. Paris, Ill., Nov. 4, 1954; s. Russell Lee and Marianne (Johnson) O.; children: David James, Anne Marie, Kari Kristine. B of Bus. Edn., Eastern Mich. U., 1978; MS, Colo. State U., 1981; PhD, U. No. Colo., 1986. Grad. fellow Colo. State U., Ft. Collins, 1979-81, asst. mgr. family housing, 1979-81; placement counselor U. No. Colo., Greeley, 1981-83, mktg. instr., 1982-83; sr. ptnr. J.R. Ogden & Assocs., Alamosa, Colo., 1982—; assoc. prof. mktg. Adams State Coll., Alamosa, 1983—; interim dir. Small Bus. Devel. Ctr., Adams State Coll., 1988—. Textbook reviewer, editorial cons. Merrill Pub. Co., Allyn & Bacon Inc., Richard Irwin Inc.; contbr. articles to profl. jours. Treas. Com. to Elect Jorge Amaya County Commr., Colo., 1985, Bob Pastore for Senate Com.; senator Assoc. Student and Faculty Senate, Adams State Coll., 1984-85; bd. dirs. Alamosa Personnel Bd., 1986-88, Alamosa County Devel. Corp., 1987—, Alamosa Tourism Com., 1988—,trustee bd. dirs. Creede Repertory Theater; expert witness in tourism and mktg. State of Colo. Recipient award for Excellence in Econ. Edn. Freedom Found. Valley Forge, 1986. Mem. Internat. Platform Assn., Am. Advtg. Fedn. (advisor 1987—), Nat. Assn. Student Personnel Adminstrs., Am. Mktg. Assn., Western Mktg. Educators Assn. (paper reviewer), Acad. Mktg. Sci., Pueblo (Colo.) Advt. and Mktg. Assn., Acad. for Health Service Mktg., Alamosa C. of C. (pres., bd. dirs. 1986—), U.S. Jaycees (named One of Outstanding Young Men in Am.), Elks, Masons (jr. steward), Alpha Kappa Psi (dist. dir. 1985—), Phi Delta Kappa. Democrat. Office: Adams State Coll Sch Bus Alamosa CO 81102

OGDEN, JEAN LUCILLE, sales executive; b. Chgo., Jan. 20, 1950; d. George William and Mary Elizabeth (MacKenzie) Anderson; m. Michael Jude Ogden, Aug. 27, 1977 (div. Dec. 1983). BA with honors, U. Calif., Santa Barbara, 1971. Sales rep. Am. Hosp. Supply Co., Irvine, Calif., 1975-77, Abbott Labs., HPD, L.A., 1977-78, Gillette Co., Albququerque, 1978-79, Unitek Corp., Monrovia, Calif., 1979-86, Nat. Patent Dental Products, San Diego, 1986-87; area mgr. Branson Ultrasonics Corp., L.A., 1987—. Mem., co-chair Nat. Multiple Sclerosis Soc., San Diego, 1983—; mem. Am. Cancer Soc., San Diego, 1985—, Zool. Soc., San Diego, 1984-85. Named one of Outstanding Young Women in Am., 1984. Mem. Med. Mktg. Assn., Salesmasters Albuquerque, Soroptimists Internat. (officer Carlsbad and Oceanside, Calif. chpt. 1983-86), Alpha Phi (house corp. bd. Long Beach chpt. 1974-75, chpt. advisor 1975-76). Republican. Home: 2634 Levante St Rancho La Costa CA 92009 Office: Branson Ultrasonics Corp 12955 E Perez Pl City of Industry CA 91746

OGDEN, MYRON WALDO, retired educational administrator; b. Cambridge, Mass., July 8, 1917; s. Waldo M. and Florence (Newton) O.; B.S. in Edn., Boston U., 1949; M.S. in Spl. Edn., U. Wash., Seattle, 1966; children—David M., Darren R. Instr. history Peninsula Coll., Port Angeles, Wash., 1967-70; dir. adult edn. Neah Bay (Wash.) Schs., 1969-70, dir. spl. edn., 1973-76, ret., 1976. Rep. Sch. Community Council, 1970-76. Mem. NEA, Wash., Clallam County (past pres.) edn. assns., Pi Gamma Mu, Phi Delta Kappa. Home: Belvedere 702 35th Ave Seattle WA 98122

OGDEN, RALPH, lawyer; b. Chgo., Jan. 19, 1946; s. Ralph Parsons and Shirley May (Walker) O.; m. Anne Wilcox, Jan. 31, 1981; children: Helen Wilcox, Christopher T. Wilcox. BA, Butler U., 1967; JD magna cum laude, Ind. U., 1978. Bar: Ind. 1978, U.S. Dist. Ct. (so. dist.) Ind. 1978, U.S. Ct. Appeals (7th cir., 1978, U.S. Supreme Ct. 1982, U.S. Ct. Appeals (10th cir.) 1983, Colo. 1984, U.S. Dist. Ct. Colo. 1984, U.S. Ct. Appeals (4th cir.) 1985. V.p., gen. mgr. Ogden Engring. Corp., Schererville, Ind., 1967-71; sr. planner Met. Manpower Commn. City of Indpls., 1971, acting dir. Mayor's Commn. on Youth, 1972-74; asst. dir. Div. Occupational Tng. Ind. Dept. Pub. Instrn., Indpls., 1974-75; reporter juvenile justice div. Ind. Judicial Study Commn., Indpls., 1976-78; pubs. coord. Ind. Jud. Ctr., Indpls., 1978; ptnr. Wilcox and Ogden, Indpls., 1979-83, Denver, 1983—; chmn. screening com. Ind. Civil Liberties Union, Indpls., 1978-79; gen. counsel and bd. dirs. Social Health Assn. of Ind. Inc., Indpls., 1981-83. Co-chair Urban Walls Task Force, Indpls., 1972-74; mem. adv. com. Ind. Arts Commn., Indpls., 1972-73. Mem. Ind. Bar Assn., Colo. Bar Assn., Denver Bar Assn., Assn. Trial Lawyers Am., Sierra Club (sec., legal chair Ends Mills Group 1986-88), Mt. Vernon Country Club. Democrat. Home: 21579 Cabrini Blvd Golden CO 80401 Office: Wilcox & Ogden 1120 Lincoln Ste 1306 Denver CO 80203

OGG, WILSON REID, poet, curator, publisher, lawyer, educator; b. Alhambra, Calif., Feb. 26, 1928; s. James Brooks and Mary (Wilson) O. Student Pasadena Jr. Coll., 1946; A.B., U. Calif. at Berkeley, 1949, J.D., 1952; Cultural D in Philosophy of Law, World Univ. Roundtable, 1983. Assoc. trust Dept. Wells Fargo Bank, San Francisco, 1954-55; admitted to Calif. bar; pvt. practice law, Berkeley, 1955-78; real estate broker, cons., 1974-78; curator-in-residence Pinebrook, 1964—; owner Pinebrook Press, Berkeley, Calif., 1988—; research atty., legal editor dept. of continuing edn. of bar U. Calif. Extension, 1958-63; psychology instr. 25th Sta. Hosp., Taegu, Korea, 1954; English instr. Taegu English Lang. Inst., Taegu, 1954. Trustee World U., 1976-80; dir. admissions Internat. Soc. for Phil. Enquiry, 1981-84; dep. dir. gen. Internat. Biographical Centre, Eng., 1986—; dep. gov. Am. Biographical Inst. Research Assn., 1986—. Served with AUS, 1952-54. Cert. community coll. instr. Recipient 5th Prize for poem "My Cat and I" Am. Poetry Assn., 1987. Fellow Internat. Acad. Law and Sci.; mem. ABA, State Bar Calif., San Francisco Bar Assn., Am. Arbitration Assn. (nat. panel arbitrators), World Univ. Round Table, World Future Soc. (profl. mem.), AAAS, Am. Assn. Fin. Profls., Am. Soc. Psychical Research, Calif. Soc. Psychical Study (pres., chmn. bd. 1963-65), Soc. for Phys. Research (London), Parapsychol. Assn. (asso.), 999 Soc., Internat. Soc. Unified Sci., Worldwide Acad. Scholars, Am. Acad. Polit. and Social Sci., World Acad. Arts and Culture, Inc., Artists Embassy Internat., Internat. Platform Assn., Intertel, Ina Coolbrith Circle, Cincinnatus Soc., Minerva Soc., Am. Legion, VFW, Mensa, Lawyers in Mensa, Psychic Sci. Spl. Interest Group, Am. Legion, VFW. Unitarian. Mason, Elk. Clubs: Faculty (U. Calif.), City Commons (Berkeley); Press (San Francisco); Commonwealth of Calif.; Town Hall Calif. Author, illustrator: My Escaping Self, 1988, Suns Without End, 1988; author: Love's Cradle, 1988, We Hatch Our Embryo, 1988; editor: Legal Aspects of Doing Business under Government Contracts and Subcontracts, 1958, Basic California Practice Handbook, 1959; contbr. numerous articles profl. jours; contbr. poetry to various mags. including American Poetry Anthology Vol. VI Number 5, Hearts on Fire: A Treasury of Poems on Love, Vol. IV, 1987, New Voices in American Poetry, 1987, The Poetry of Life A Treasury of Moments An. Poetry Anthology, Vol. VII, 1988. Home: 1104 Keith Ave Berkeley CA 94708-1607 Office: 8 Bret Harte Way Berkeley CA 94708-1611

OGILVY, DAVID WALLACE, banker; b. Washington, D.C., May 18, 1945; s. Lester Edwin and Margaret Virginia (Stauffer) O.; m. Mary Skiles Dunlap, Jan. 20, 1973. BA, Washington and Lee U., 1963; M in Internat. Mgmt., Am. Grad. Sch. Internat. Mgmt., Glendale, Ariz., 1972. Asst. cashier Bank of Am. Nat.Trust & Savs. Assn., Los Angeles, 1973-75; asst. v.p. Lawrence Systems, Phoenix, 1976-77; v.p. The Ariz. Bank, Phoenix, 1977-81, Valley Nat. Bank Ariz., Phoenix, 1981—; bd. dirs. Ariz. Dist. Export Council, Phoenix; mem. World Bus. Adv. Council Am. Grad. Sch. Internat. Mgmt., Glendale, Ariz., 1984—. Bd. dirs. Men's Arts Council Phoenix Art Mus., 1978—, mem. Citizen's Bond Com., Phoenix, 1988; bd. dirs. The Luke's Men St. Luke's Hosp., Phoenix. Served as sgt. U.S. Army, 1968-71. Mem. Valley Field Riding and Polo Club, Paradise VAlley Country Club. Republican. Episcopalian. Club: Paradise Valley (Ariz.) Country. Office: Valley Nat Bank Ariz 201 N Central Ave Phoenix AZ 85004

OGLE, KATHY MULLER, hydrologist; b. Sheridan, Wyo., Jan. 18, 1951; d. Simon and Winnifred Ester (Williams) Muller; m. Philip Ray Ogle, Jan. 24, 1981; 1 child, Raymond Paul. BS, Mont. State U., Bozeman, 1973; MS, N.Mex. Sch. Mines and Tech., 1982. Registered hydrologist, Wyo. Engr. II Banner Engring., Laramie, Wyo., 1981; hydrologist Wyo. Dept. Environ. Quality, Cheyenne, 1981-84, rep. mine ops., 1984-85; cons. Muller-Ogle Hydrology Cons., Cheyenne, 1985-88; hydrologist U.S. Geol. Survey, Cheyenne, 1988—. Mem. State Mus. Vols., Cheyenne, 1982-88, past bd. dirs. Mem. Am. Geophys. Union, Nat. Water Well Assn. (mem. edit. bd. 1984—), LWV (bd. dirs. 1986-88). Home: 6146 Kevin Ave Cheyenne WY 82009 Office: US Geol Curvey 2617 E Lincolnway Cheyenne WY 82001

OGLE, MADELINE ANN BRIGHT, realtor, investment counselor; b. Fresno, Calif., Jan. 5, 1926; m. Dale A. Mart (dec.); m. George H. Sciaroni (dec.); m. Richard P. Bright (div.); m. Jerome C. Ogle. Student, Fresno State U., 1956-58; BA, San Francisco State U., 1959; postgrad., Coll. of San Mateo, 1969-71. Cert. investment counselor, 1979. Asst. mgr. customer relations Sears and Roebuck Co., 1954-55; Bookkeeper, clk. Innes Reliable Leather Goods, 1955-56; bookkeeper Langendorf Bakeries, 1956; ins. clk. Assigned Risk, San Francisco, 1959-60; owner Madeline's Dog Salon and Boutique, Santa Clara, Calif., 1961-86; assoc. realtor Santa Rosa, Calif., 1979. Mem. Friend's of Trition Mus., 1975-77; Citizen's Adv. Bd., Santa Clara, 1971; mem. Hist. Preservatin Comn., 1971—, chmn. Goals Comn.; lobbyist Target State Lic. for dog grooming, Calif. Recipient Contributions to City of Santa Clara award, 1969. Mem. State of Calif. Dept. Real Estate, United Dog Groomers, Inc. (v.p. 1966-71), Soroptimists Internat. of Santa Clara (mayor's rep. 1971, chmn. community services com., fundraiser 1982), Santa Clara Women's Club, Calif. Fedn. of Women's Club,. Home: 2772 Canterbury Dr Santa Rosa CA 95405 Office: The Madson Group Inc 321 S Main St Ste 522 Sebastopol CA 95472

OGLE, RONALD EUGENE, bar/legal association administrator; b. Oak Park, Ill., Aug. 14, 1951; s. Eugene Harold Ogle and Eleanor Jean (Weckel) Smith; m. Ann Bast, Aug. 19, 1972 (div.); m. Donna Marie Moscatello, Aug. 9, 1980. BS in Indsl. Mgmt., Purdue U., 1972; JD, Wayne State U., 1977. Bar: Mich. 1977. Patent atty. Burton, Parker, Schramm, Mt. Clemens, Mich., 1977-78; atty. Renfrew, Moir, Miskin, Stover, Royal Oak, Mich., 1978; adminstr. dept. head Fluid Components, Inc., San Marcos, Calif., 1978—; sec. Fluid Components Internat. Inc., U.S. Virgin Islands, 1986—. Mem. ABA, San Marcos C. of C. (dir. 1983—, treas. v.p. ops. 1988), Mich. Bar Assn., Instrument Soc. of Am. Republican. Roman Catholic. Office: Fluid Components Inc 1755 La Costa Meadows Dr San Marcos CA 92069

OGLESBY, CLARKSON HILL, civil engineering educator, writer; b. Clarksville, Mo., Nov. 9, 1908; s. Edwin Bright Oglesby and Frances Lewis Thomas; m. Ardis May Hansen, June 8, 1938; children: Virginia Lee Hancock, Judith Lynne Donaghey, Marjorie Kay Zellner. AB in Engring., Stanford U., 1932, degree in civil engring., 1936. Registered civil engr., Calif. Draftsman to engr. State of Ariz. Dept. Transportation, Phoenix, 1928-41; constrn. engr. Vinson and Pringle, Phoenix, 1941-43; acting asst. prof. civil engring. Stanford (Calif.) U., 1943-46, asst. prof., 1946-48, assoc. prof., 1947-52, prof., 1952-74; cons. Calif. Toll Bridge Author, San Francisco, 1948; prof., cons. in constrn. mgmt. Cath. U., Chile, U. New South Wales, Australia and U. Cape Town, South Africa. Author: Highway Engineering, 1952, 4th rev. edit., 1982, Methods Improvement, 1972, Productivity Improvement in Construction, 1988; also articles. Mem. Nat. Acad. Engring., ASCE (hon., Peurifory award Constrn. Rsch. 1988), NSPF (Outstanding Constrn. Educator 1984), Phi Beta Kappa, Sigma Xi, Tau Beta Pi. Democrat. Congregationalist. Home: 850 Webster St #923 Palo Alto CA 94301 Office: Stanford U Dept Civil Engring Stanford CA 94305

OGLESBY, MYRNA LEE, lawyer; b. Ukiah, Calif., Sept. 29, 1935; d. Earl Victor and Ruby Alice (Phillips) Snook; m. Neal Vernon Oglesby, June 13, 1964; children: Keith, Deborah, Gerald, Donald, Linda. Bar: Calif. 1983. Ptnr. Rawles, Hinkle, Carter, Behnke & Oglesby, Ukiah, Calif., 1985—; asst. prof. Sonoma State Coll. extension, Rohnert Park, Calif., 1986-87. Active Ukiah Bus. and Profl. Women, 1986—; hearing officer Mendocino County Dept. Mental Health; hospice bd. dirs. Project Sanctuary Resource Coun.; bd. dirs. Geriatric Task Force, In-Home Health Svcs., Community Care Mgmt. Mem. Mendocino County Bar Assn. (bd. dirs. lawyer referral service com. 1985—), State Bar Calif., Calif. Women Lawyers, ABA. Democrat. Baptist. Office: Rawles Hinkle Carter & Behnke & Oglesby 169 Mason St Ste 300 Ukiah CA 95482

OGLESBY, RICHARD JAMES, IV, anesthesiologist; b. Springfield, Ill., Apr. 21, 1947; s. Richard James III and Yolande (Perkins) O.; 1 child, Richard James V; m. Donna K. Harbert, July 26, 1988; 1 stepchild, Brian A. Johnston. Student, Elizabethtown Community Coll., 1973-76; BS, U. Louisville, 1978, MD, 1982. Resident in anesthesia U. Hosp., Louisville, 1982-85; anesthesiologist, dir. dept. anesthesiology and dept. respiratory therapy West Park Hosp., Cody, Wyo., 1985-87; anesthesiologist, dir. dept. anesthesiology Meml. Hosp., Rawlins, Wyo., 1988—. Capt. U.S. Army, 1967-73, Vietnam. Decorated Bronze Star with oak leaf cluster, Army Commendation medal, Air medal with cluster, Vietnam Cross of Gallantry; named Ky. Col. Commonwealth of Ky., 1987. Mem. AMA, Wyo. Med. Soc., Am. Soc. Anesthesiologists, Am. Soc. Regional Anesthesia, Wyo. Ambulance and Emergency Med. Svcs. Assn., VFW, Ducks Unltd., Vietnam Helicopter Pilots Assn., Wilderness Med. Soc., Tex. Jack Assn., Olive Glenn Country Club, Lions, Masons, Elks, Phi Kappa Phi (hon. soc.), Phi Delta Epsilon. Republican. Episcopalian. Home: 2222 Dunblane Dr Rawlins WY 82301 Office: Carbon County Meml Hosp Rawlins WY 82301

O'GORMAN, KEVIN CHRISTOPHER, marketing professional; b. Newark, May 30, 1955; s. Patrick James and Jo Anne (Ryan) O'G. Bachelor's degree, U. Vt., 1979; MA in Counseling and Psychology, Antioch U., 1981. Cons., therapist Champlain Valley Inst., Burlington, Vt., 1980-83; project dir. market research ComputerLand Corp., Hayward, Calif., 1983-84; corporate account mgr. ComputerLand Corp., San Francisco, 1984-87; dir. mktg. and sales Personal Tech. Corp., Palo Alto, Calif., 1987—. Mem. Am. Soc. Tng. Devel., Nat. Speaker's Assn. Office: Personal Tech Corp 550 S California Ave Palo Alto CA 94306

O'GREEN, FREDERICK WILBERT, multi-industry company executive; b. Mason City, Iowa, Mar. 25, 1921; s. Oscar A. and Anna (Heikkinen) O'G.; m. Mildred G. Ludlow, Mar. 21, 1943; children: Susan Renee, Jane Lynn O'Green Koenig, John Frederick, Eric Stephen. Student, Mason City Jr. Coll., 1939-40; BS in Elec. Engring., Iowa State U., 1943; MS in Elec. Engring., U. Md., 1949; LLD (hon.), Pepperdine U., 1977. Project engr. Naval Ordnance Lab., White Oak, Md., 1943-55; dir. Agena D project Lockheed Aircraft Co., Sunnyvale, Calif., 1955-62; v.p. Litton Industries, Inc., Beverly Hills, Calif., 1962-66, sr. v.p., 1966-67, exec. v.p., 1967-72, pres., 1972-81, chmn., 1981-88, chief exec. officer, 1981-87, also dir., chmn. exec. com., 1988—. Served with USNR, 1945. Recipient Meritorious Civilian Service award U.S. Navy, 1954; Outstanding Achievement award Air Force Systems Command, 1964; Disting. Achievement citation Iowa State U., 1973; Energy Exec. of Yr. award Third World Energy Engring. Congress, 1980. Mem. AIM, AIAA, U.S. C. of C., Assn. U.S. Army, Phi Kappa Psi, Phi Mu Alpha. Republican. Lutheran. Office: Litton Industries Inc 360 N Crescent Dr Beverly Hills CA 90210 *

O'HAGAN, WILLIAM GORDON, automotive repair shop owner; b. Allentown, N.J., Oct. 12, 1943; s. Forrest Allen and Voncile Arline (Linton) O'H.; m. Marcia Helen Beck, Aug. 12, 1947 (div. Oct. 1985). Grad. high sch., Azusa, Calif., 1962. Owner Richfield Oil Co., Baldwin Park, Calif., 1970-72; mgr. Am. Teaching Aids, Covina, Calif., 1972-88; owner Bill's Auto Repair Co., Covina, 1988—. Block commander Neighborhood Watch, Covina. Republican. Baptist. Home: 125 N Houser Dr Covina CA 91722 Office: Bills Automotive 635 E San Bernardino Rd Covina CA 91723

O'HAIR, SUSAN ELINOR, educator; b. San Francisco, July 13, 1939; d. Donald Leigh O'Hair and Jane Elinor (Larsen) Hudkins. BA, Calif. State U., Sacramento, 1961. Cert. gen. edn. tchr. (life). Tchr. Redondo Beach (Calif.) City Schs., 1961-65; tchr. San Ramon (Calif.) Valley Unified Sch. Dist., 1965-67, librarian, 1967-69, tchr., 1969-77, tchr. English and World History, 1977—. Author: Best Loved Contemporary Poem, 1979. Vice chmn. San Ramon Valley Arts Council, Danville, 1978-81; bd. dirs. San Ramon Library Found., 1985. Named Mentor Tchr. San Ramon Valley Unified Sch. Dist., Danville, 1985, Tchr. of Month Pine Valley PTA, San Ramon, 1985, Tchr. of the Yr. SRVUSD, 1988. Mem. AAUW (pres. local br. 1970—), NEA (life), Calif. Tchrs. Assn. (legis. chmn. 1985-86, pres. Contra Costa County chpt. 1971-72, state council rep. 1972-75, We Honor Ours award 1975), Calif. Tchrs. English, Nat. Assn. Tchrs. English (del.), Delta Kappa Gamma. Democrat. Methodist. Clubs: Red Barn (San Ramon); Tao House (Danville). Home: 401 Blanco Ct San Ramon CA 94583-2001

O'HALLORAN, (LAVERNE M.) KATHLEEN (MRS. JOHN R. O'HALLORAN, JR.), real estate broker; b. Laurium, Mich., Nov. 15, 1921; d. Joseph Wilfred and Della K. (Gervais) Shaffer; student Fond Du Lac Comml. Coll., 1938-40, Fresno City Coll., 1965-66; m. John Richard O'Halloran, Jr., July 15, 1942; children: Sheila Ann O'Halloran Stoll, Gregory, Michael, Maureen O'Halloran Benelli, Sean, Margaret. Co-owner Hamlin Hotel, San Francisco, 1946-48, Lazy F Guest Ranch, Ellensburg, Wash., 1948-50; owner, broker Kathy O'Halloran Realty, Fresno, 1980—; pres. C & R Investments, 1974-75; broker Settlers Real Estate, Inc., Fresno, 1975-80. Charter mem. Infant of Prague Adoption Agy. Aux., 1954—, sec., 1955; mem. Mayor's Com. for Community Devel., 1963-64; charter mem. Nat. Mus. of Women in the Arts; pres. Sacred Heart Mothers Club, 1959; pres. Calif. Citizens for Decent Lit., 1961-63, Central Calif. Citizens for Decent Lit., 1959-64; precinct chmn. Goldwater campaign, 1964; chmn. Fresno County United Republicans Calif., 1962; area coordinator Clean Campaign Ballot Initiative, 1966; candidate Fresno City Council, 1961; mem. Women's League of Fresno Arts Center, 1976—, St. Agnes Service Guild, 1983—, Fresno Fiber Guild, 1985—. Mem. Fresno Bd. Realtors, Nat. Assn. Real Estate Bds. Roman Catholic. Home: 3503 N Bond St Fresno CA 93726 Office: 3503 N Bond St Fresno CA 93726

O'HARE, SANDRA FERNANDEZ, educator; b. N.Y.C., Mar. 19, 1941; d. Ricardo Enrique and Rosario de Los Angeles (Arenas) Fernandez; m. S. James O'Hare, Oct. 12, 1963; children: James, Richard, Michael, Christopher. BA, Marymount Coll., 1962; MA, U. San Francisco, 1980. Instr. adult edn. Guam, 1964-66, Spanish Speaking Ctr., Harrisburg, Pa., 1977-79; tchr. Colegio Salesiano, Rota, Spain, 1973, 84, Alisal Sch. Dist., Salinas, Calif., 1979-81, Liberty Sch., Petaluma, Calif., 1981-85, Cinnabar Sch., Petaluma, 1985—; instr. Santa Rosa (Calif.) Jr. Coll., 1982-83; mem. math. curriculum com. Sonoma County Office Edn., Santa Rosa, 1988. Translator: Isabel la Catolica, 1962. Vol., ARC, Harrisburg, 1975, Boy Scouts Am., Petaluma, 1983, Mechanicsburg, Pa., 1974, Monterey, Calif., 1971. Mem. Calif. Assn. Bilingual Educators, NEA, AAUW (chmn. ednl. founds. program 1985-86), Club Hispano-Americano Petaluma (pres. 1987—). Roman Catholic. Home: 1289 Glenwood Dr Petaluma CA 94954

OHARENKO, MARIA T., public relations official; b. Louvain, Belgium, Dec. 25, 1950; came to U.S., 1951; d. Vladimir and Lubomyra (Kotz) O. BS, Northwestern U., 1972, MS, 1973. Pub. info. officer U.S. AEC, ERDA, Dept. Energy, Argonne and Chgo., Ill., 1973-79; pub. info. and news media advance officer U.S. Dept. Energy, Washington, 1980-81; corp. pub. info. mgr. Northrop Corp., Los Angeles, 1981—. Mem. Aviation/Space Writers Assn., Women in Communications, Soc. Profl. Journalists. Ukrainian Catholic. Office: Northrop Corp 1840 Century Park E Los Angeles CA 90067

OHGI, TOM IWAO, small business owner; b. San Francisco, June 11, 1928; s. Frank Matasuke and Lucy Shizue (Okuma) O.; m. Irene Ayako Ono, Oct. 28, 1962; children: Elizabeth Hideko, Kenneth Akitoshi. BS, U. Calif., Berkeley, 1956. Registered sanitarian, Calif. Pub. health sanitarian L.A. City Health Dept., 1956-64, sanitarian, 1964-70, sr. sanitarian, 1970-81, sr. sanitarian specialist, 1981-87; owner, operator Vista (Calif.) Oriental Gift Shop, 1987—; tchr. East Los Angeles Community Coll., 1977-78. Mem. Asian Pacific Legal Def. and Edn. Fund Inc., 1985—. With U.S. Army, 1951-53, Fed. Republic Germany. Recipient Merit award Fin. Programs Inc., 1972. Mem. AARP, L.A. County Pub. Health Sanitarians Assn., Akebono Bonsai Soc. Calif. (Outstanding mem. 1979), SanPu Kai, Bonsai Internat. Home: 4858 Glenhaven Dr Oceanside CA 92056 Office: Vista Oriental Gift Shop 135 Hillside Terr Vista CA 92084

OHLFS, MARY IRENE, community volunteer; b. Oxnard, Calif., May 18, 1923; d. Michael Gustav and Elizabeth Theresa (Godde) Vujovich; m. Fabian Henry Ohlfs, June 20, 1960; 1 child, Michael Jeffrey. BA, Mt. St. Mary's Coll., L.A., 1946. Teen-age recreation, playground dir. Oxnard Recreation Dept., 1946-48; field dir. Girl Scouts U.S., Ventura County, Calif., 1949-54; social worker Ventura County Welfare Dept., 1954-60. Vol. West Valley Rep. Women, Saratoga, Calif., 1965—, Santa Clara County Girl Scouts, 1965—, Boy Scouts Am., 1965—. Recipient Marillac Svc. award Santa Clara County Cath. Social Svcs. Aux., 1979, Alumnae Svc. award Mt. St. Mary's Coll., 1972. Mem. AAUW, Mt. St. Mary's Coll. Alumni Assn., Native Daus. of Golden West, Young Ladies Inst., Santa Clara Univ. Catala Club. Roman Catholic. Home: 13923 Malcolm Ave Saratoga CA 95070

OHNSTAD, TERRY MICHAEL, publishing executive; b. Breckenridge, Minn., Apr. 6, 1949; s. Oliver Alexander and Maxine Vivian (McCready) O.; m. Barbara Ann Rector, June 19, 1976; children: Kyle, Erin. BS in Math., U. S.D., 1971, MBA, 1972. Credit analyst Am. Express Co., Denver, 1973;

instr. Dakota State Coll., Madison, S.D., 1975-77; account mgr. Burroughs Corp., Mpls., 1977-83; sales rep. Hewlett-Packard Co., Englewood, Colo., 1983-89; v.p. Peak to Peak mag., 1989—. Tribal chief YMCA Indian Guides, Littleton, Colo., 1987. Home: 7467 S Washington St Littleton CO 80122

OHYAMA, HEIICHIRO, music educator, violist, conductor; b. Kyoto, Japan, July 31, 1947; came to U.S., 1970; s. Heishiro and Sumi (Ohara) O.; m. Gail Jean Allen; 1 child, Shinichiro Allen Ohyama. Assocs. degree, Guildhall Sch. Music and Drama, London, 1970. Instr. N.C. Sch. Arts, Winston-Salem, 1972-73; prof. music U. Calif.; Santa Barbara, 1973—; prin. violist Los Angeles Philharm., 1979—, asst. conductor, 1987—; music dir. Santa Barbara Chamber Orch., 1983—, Crossroads Chamber Orch., Santa Monica, Calif., 1981—; artistic dir. La Jolla (Calif.) Chamber Music Festival, 1986—; conductor Round Trip Music Festival, 1983—, N.W. Chamber Orch., 1985-87; vis. lectr. Ind. U., Bloomington, 1972-73. Appearances at Marlboro Music Festival, Vt., 1972-76, Santa Fe Chamber Music Festival, 1977-85, Round Top Music Festival, Tex., 1983—, La Jolla (Calif.) Chamber Music Summer Fest., 1986—; various recordings. Receipient award Young Concert Artist N.Y., 1974. Home: 2878 Angelo Dr Los Angeles CA 90077 also: LA Philharm Assn 135 N Grand Ave Los Angeles CA 90012

O'KANE, PATRICK ALAN, engineer; b. Oxnard, Calif., Dec. 12, 1947; s. William Harold and Ellen Louise (Hoecker) O'K.; m. Lois Elizabeth Whittenburg, Nov. 9, 1968; children: Frith Estella, Drew Everett. BS, U. Calif., Berkeley, 1971, MS, 1972. Engr. Naval Missile Ctr., Point Mugu, Calif., 1972-75, Naval Ship Weapon Systems Engr. Sta., Port Hueneme, Calif., 1975-79; radar systems analyst PAVE PAWS System Programming Agy., Beale AFB, Calif., 1979-84; engr. Twelfth Coast Guard Dist., Alameda, Calif., 1984-85; tech. group mgr. XonTech, Inc., Lafayette, Calif., 1985—. Mem. Phi Beta Kappa. Home: 8532 Terrace Dr El Cerrito CA 94530 Office: 3746 Mt Diablo Blvd Ste 215 Lafayette CA 94549

O'KEEFE, KEVIN CHARLES, aerospace engineer; b. Phila., Nov. 13, 1958; s. Joseph and Joan MAry (Semon) O'K. BA in Biology/Bio-Physics, U. Pa., 1979; MS in Optics, U. Rochester, 1982; postgrad, UCLA, 1988—; research asst., U. Pa. Vet. Sch., Phila., 1978-79, Scheie Eye Inst., Phila., 1980; sr. project engr., Hughes Aircraft Co., Los Angeles, 1982—. Mem. AAAS, Optical Soc. of Am., Am. Physical Soc., Phi Kappa Sigma. Home: 231 MAryland St El Segundo CA 90245 Office: Hughes Aircraft PO Box 902 M/S E-54/F212 El Segundo CA 90245

OKERMAN, JOHN LIESTER, school administrator; b. Billings, Mont., June 10, 1943; s. Andrew Victor and Hazel Isabelle (Vance) O.; m. Leslie Adele Garretson, Nov. 22, 1969; children: Kristen Randalle, Todd Andrew. BA in Phys. Edn., U. Wash., 1966, MS in Phys. Edn., 1967, sch. adminstr. credential, 1982. Cert. tchr., sch. adminstr., Wash. Salesman Brown & Bigelow, Seattle, 1970-71; tchr. elem. schs. Issaquah (Wash.) Sch. Dist., 1971-82, asst. prin. various schs., 1982—; assoc. ski instr., Ski Acres (Wash.) Ski Sch., 1971—. Bd. dirs., Toys for Tots Run, Seattle, 1981—; tchr., St. John's Epis. Ch., Seattle, 1982-88; scoutmaster, Woodinville (Wash.) area Boy Scouts Am., 1988. 1st lt. USMC, 1967-70, Vietnam; to lt. col. Res., 1970—. Mem. Nat. Assn. Secondary Sch. Prins., Am. Assn. Sch. Adminstrs., Profl. Ski Instrs. Am., Marine Corps Res. Officers Assn. (pres. Seattle chpt. 1985-86). Republican. Home: 17027 NE 160th Pl Woodinville WA 98072 Office: Echo Glen Sch 565 NW Holly St Issaquah WA 98027

OKIMOTO, DANIEL IWAO, political science educator; b. Santa Anita, Calif., Aug. 14, 1942; s. Tameichi and Kirie (Kumagai) O.; m. Nancy Elizabeth Miller, Jan. 27, 1970; children: Saya Elizabeth, Kevin Jun. BA, Princeton U., 1965; MA, Harvard U., 1967; PhD, U. Mich., 1977. Assoc. prof. Stanford (Calif.) U., 1978—; Co-dir. N.E. Asia-U.S. Forum on Internat. Policy, StAnford, 1984—; adv. coun. Princeton (N.J.) U. Dept. Politics, 1988—. Author: Between Hiti and the Marker; editor: The Political Economy of Japan, 1988; co-editor: Inside the Japanese System, 1988. Exec. dir. U.S.-Japan Legislator's Com., Stanford, 1986—; mem. Coun. on Fgn. Rels., N.Y.C., 1978—. Mellon fellow Aspen Inst., 1978, Nat. fellow Hoover Instn., 1980-81. Mem. World Affairs Coun. No. Calif., Am. Polit. Sci. Assn., Assn. for Asian Studies. Democrat. Office: Stanford U Dept Polit Sci Stanford CA 94305

OKINO, GARY HARUJI, city official; b. Honolulu, Jan. 2, 1942; s. Shigeo and Helene Yaeko (Teramoto) O.; m. Pearl Takako Kimata, June 24, 1967; children: Paul Takaji, Michael Haruo. BA, U. Hawaii, 1966. Planner City and County of Honolulu, 1967—. Nat. bd. dirs. Am. Youth Soccer Orgn., Hawthorne, Calif., 1988-89, Hawaii dir., 1981-88. Home: 98-1315 Kaonohi St Aiea HI 96701 Office: Am Youth Soccer Orgn 5403 W 138th St Hawthorne CA 90251

OKUMA, ALBERT AKIRA, JR., architect; b. Cleve., Feb. 10, 1946; s. Albert Akira Sr. and Reiko (Suwa) O.; m. Janice Shirley Bono, July 17, 1971; children: Reiko Dawn, Benjamin Scott. BS in Archtl. Engring, Calif. Poly. State U., San Luis Obispo, 1970, BArch, 1975. Registered architect, Calif. Architect USN, Point Mugu, Calif., 1975-76; designer Wilson Stroh Wilson Architects, Santa Paula, Calif., 1976-79; architect, project mgr. W.J. Kulwiec AIA & Assocs., Camarillo, Calif., 1979-83, Wilson & Conrad Architects, Ojai, Calif., 1983-84, Dziak, Immel & Lauterbach Services Inc., Oxnard, Calif., 1984-85; ptnr. Conrad & Okuma Architects, Oxnard, 1985—; commr. Calif. Bd. Archtl. Examiners, 1985—. Treas. Spiritual Assembly Baha'is of Ventura, Calif., 1978-79, 84, 86—; treas.'s rep. Nat. Spiritual Assembly Bahai's U.S., Wilmette, Ill., 1981—; treas. Parents and Advocates for Gifted Edn., 1988-89. 1st lt. U.S. Army, 1971-73. Mem. AIA (chpt. bd. dirs. 1976-79, 81—, chpt. sec. 1981, v.p. 1982, pres. 1983.), Internat. Conf. Bldg. Offcls., Nat. Trust Hist. Preservation, Constrn. Specifications Inst., Design Methods Group. Office: Conrad & Okuma Architects 183 Montgomery Ave Oxnard CA 93030

OKUMURA, WINIFRED ELSA, air force logistics manager; b. Framingham, Mass., Apr. 18, 1947; d. Judson Grant and Henrietta (Young) Boughton; m. Richard Minori Okumura, Apr. 24, 1976. BA in Sociology, U. N.H., 1972, MEd in Counseling, 1974; MBA, Calif. State U., Sacramento, 1982. Logistics mgmt. specialist USAF Sacramento Air Logistics Ctr., McClellan Air Force Base, Sacramento, 1977-82; sr. logistics planner USAF Hdqrs. Air Force Logistics Command, Dayton, Ohio, 1982-86; chief aeronautical equipment logistics USAF Aeronautical Systems Div., Dayton, 1986-87; chief strategic defense weapons logistics USAF Hdqrs. Space Div., L.A. Air Force Base, Calif., 1987-89; assoc. dir. logistics plans USAF Hdqrs. Pacific Air Force, Hickam Air Force Base, Hawaii, 1989—; mem. Dept. Defense Exec. Leadership Demonstration Program, 1986-87, Logistics Civilian Career Enhancement Program, 1983—; speaker profl. societies; adminstrv. chmn. 2nd Space Logistics Symposium, 1988. Contbr. articles to profl. jours. Activities coord. Buckeye Trail Assn., Dayton, 1984-87. Mem. Soc. Logistics Engrs. (cert. profl. logistician, internat. field award for logistics planning 1985), Am. Defense Preparedness Assn. Home: 94-44a Hiawale Loop Mililani HI 96789 Office: Hdqrs PACAF Air Forces Logistics Plans Hickam AFB HI 96853-5000

OLAH, GEORGE ANDREW, chemist, educator; b. Budapest, Hungary, May 22, 1927; came to U.S., 1964, naturalized, 1970; s. Julius and Magda (Rasznai) O.; m. Judith Agnes Lengyel, July 9, 1949; children: George John, Ronald Peter. PhD, Tech. U. Budapest, 1949; DSc hon. causa, U. Durham, 1988. Mem. faculty Tech. U. Budapest, 1949-54; asso. dir. Cen. Chem. Rsch. Inst., Hungarian Acad. Scis., 1954-56; rsch. scientist Dow Chem. Can. Ltd., 1957-64, Dow Chem. Co., Framingham, Mass., 1964-65; prof. chemistry Case-Western Res. U., Cleve., 1965-69, C.F. Mabery prof. rsch., 1969-77; Donald P. and Katherine B. Loker disting. prof. chemistry, dir. Hydrocarbon Rsch. Inst., U. So. Calif., L.A., 1977—; vis. prof. chemistry Ohio State U., 1963, U. Heidelberg, Germany, 1965, U. Colo., 1969, Swiss Fed. Inst. Tech., 1972, U. Munich, 1973, U. London, 1973-79, L. Pasteur U., Strasbourg, 1974, U. Paris, 1981; hon. vis. lectr. U. London, 1981; cons. to industry. Author: Friedel-Crafts Reactions, Vols. I-IV, 1963-64, (with P. Schleyer) Carbonium Ions, Vols. I-V, 1969-76, Friedel-Crafts Chemistry, 1973, Carbocations and Electrophilic Reactions, 1973, Halonium Ions, 1975, (with G.K.S. Prakash and J. Somer) Superacids, 1984; (with G.K.S. Prakash, R.E. Williams, L.D. Field and K. Wade) Hypercarbon Chemistry, 1987; also chpts. in books, numerous papers in field; patentee in field. Recipient Leo Hendrik Baekeland award N.J. sect. Am. Chem. Soc., 1966, Morley medal Cleve. sect., 1970; Alexander von Humboldt sr. U.S. scientist award, 1979; Guggenheim fellow, 1972, 88, Calif. Scientist Yr. award, 1989. Fellow Chem. Inst. Can., AAAS; mem. Nat. Acad. Scis., Italian Nat. Acad. Scis., Ital Chem. Soc. (hon.), Am. Chem. Soc. (award petroleum chemistry 1964, award synthetic organic chemistry 1979, Roger Adams award in organic chemistry, 1989), German Chem. Soc., Brit. Chem. Soc. (Centenary lectr. 1978), Swiss Chem. Soc., Sigma Xi. Home: 2252 Gloaming Way Beverly Hills CA 90210 Office: U So Calif Dept Chemistry Los Angeles CA 90007

OLAH, GEORGE JOHN, financial company executive; b. Budapest, Hungary, June 17, 1954; came to U.S. in 1964; s. George Andrew and Judith Agnes (Lengyel) O.; m. Salli Marjorie Smith, Sept. 25, 1982. BS in Acctg., Case Western Reserve U., 1978; MBA, U. So. Calif., 1989. Sr. acct. Fremont Gen. Corp., Los Angeles, 1980-82; mgr. investment acctg. The Holden Group, Los Angeles, 1982--. Mem. Beta Theta Pi (sec. 1972-74). Home: 3662 Meadville Dr Sherman Oaks CA 91403

OLANDER, DONALD EDGAR, chemist, engineering executive; b. Chgo., Aug. 12, 1929; s. Albert Edgar and Abbie (Snyder) O.; m. Dayle Neva Roberts, June 22, 1950 (div. Jan. 1973); children: Mark, Eric, Lauren, Paul, Lisa; m. Geraldine June Frere, Feb. 25, 1975; children: Russell, Basilio, Kimberly, Bebe. BS in Chemistry, Northwestern U., 1951; MS in Chemistry, St. Louis U., 1955; PhD in Engring., Calif. Coast U., 1980. Chemist Mallinckrodt Co., St. Louis, 1951-53; project engr. Universal Match Corp., Ferguson, Mo., 1959-67; engr., quality control mgr. Aerojet-Gen. Co., Nimbus, Calif., 1959-67; staff scientist Explosive Tech., Fairfield, Calif., 1967-69; v.p. Networks Electronic Corp., Chatsworth, Calif., 1969-72; staff scientist Hi-Shear Tech. Corp., Torrance, Calif., 1979-87; chief scientist, tech. dir. Hi-Shear Propulsion div. Hi-Shear Tech. Corp., Sparks, Nev., 1987—. Patentee in field; contbr. articles to profl. jours. Asst. scoutmaster Boy Scouts Am., Fair Oaks, Calif., 1959-65; active Fair Oaks Presbyn. Ch., 1959-71. Mem. ASTM, Am. Chem. Soc., Am. Def. Preparedness Assn. Home: 3240 Cashill Blvd Reno NV 89509 Office: Hi-Shear Tech Corp 204 Edison Reno NV 89502

OLBRANTZ, JOHN PAUL, museum administrator, art historian; b. Tacoma, June 19, 1950; s. Walter John and Theresa Christine (Hill) O.; m. Pamela Ann Southas, Apr. 12, 1980; children: Aaron Michael, Sarah Jessica. B.A., Western Wash. U., 1972; postgrad. U. Calif.-Santa Barbara, 1973-74; MA, U. Wash., 1976; study cert. in arts adminstrn. and mgmt. U. Calif.-Berkeley, 1984. Dirs. Bellevue Art Mus., Wash., 1976-85, San Jose Mus. Art, Calif., 1985-87; dep. dir. Watcom Mus. History and Art, Wash., 1987—; regional rep. Art Mus. Assn., 1982—; Exhbns. arranged: Eye for Eye: Egyptian Art and Inscriptions, 1978; Glen Alps: A Retrospective, 1980; Israel in Antiquity, 1980; 5,000 Years of Faces, 1982; Dale Chihuly: A Decade of Glass, 1984, Two Centuries of Afro-American Art, 1985, Robert Sperry: A Retrospective, 1986, FOCUS: Seattle, 1987, Robert Colescott: A Retrospective, 1987 . David Gray grantee U. Calif.-Santa Barbara, 1974; J. Paul Getty Trust scholar, 1984. Mem. Archaeol. Inst. Am. (v.p. 1978-79, pres. 1979-80), Am. Research Ctr. in Egypt, Am. Assn. Mus., Internat. Council Mus. Democrat. Roman Catholic. Home: 2112 Ontario St Bellingham WA 98226 Office: Whatcom Mus History and Art 121 Prospect St Bellingham WA 98225

OLBRECHTS, GUY ROBERT, electrical engineer, consultant; b. Mechelen, Belgium, May 22, 1935; came to U.S., 1967, naturalized, 1978; s. Alphonse and Blanche (Van Coolput) O.; m. Andree Julia Van Nes, Oct. 19, 1961; children: Philippe, Ingrid, Dominique. Ingenieur civil electricien Catholic U. Leuven, Belgium, 1960; MBA, Seattle U., 1976. Lead engr. Ctr. D'Etudes Nucleaires, Mol, Belgium, 1962-65; quality control mgr., chief engr. for magnetics Sprague Electromag., Ronse, Belgium, 1965-67; sr. engr. Boeing Co., Seattle, 1967-79; sect. mgr. data systems engring. and product support Sundstrand Data Control Corp., Redmond, Wash., 1979-88; project engr. memory systems Sundstrand Data Control; propr., cons., designer Gentronics, Bellevue, Wash., 1970—. Patentee gyro wheel speed modulator, 1981, integrated strapdown/airdata sensor system, 1981, slow-acting phase-locked loop, 1983. Served as cpl. Belgian Army, 1961-62. Recipient inventor award Boeing Co., 1978. Republican. Roman Catholic. Home: 4809 116th Ave SE Bellevue WA 98006 Office: Sundstrand Data Control Corp 15001 NE 36th Stark Redmond WA 98073-9701

OLBRICH, STEVEN EMIL, farmer; b. Chgo., Nov. 24, 1938; s. Emil Jacob and Mary Jo (Merchant) O.; m. Janice Pui Jun Yee, June 17, 1968; children: Rachel, Benjamin, Nathanel, Joshua. BS, U. Wis., 1965; MS, U. Hawaii, 1968; PhD, U. Mo., Columbia, 1972. Dairy extension specialist U. Hawaii, Honolulu, 1973-79; owner, operator Huanui Dairy, Waianae, Hawaii, 1979—, Olbrich Farms, Chatfield, Minn., 1985—; mem. U.S./China Session in Industry, Trade and Econ. Devel., Beijing, China, 1988; v.p. faculty senate Coll. Tropical Agr. U. Hawaii, pres., 1979. Contbr. articles to sci. jours. Pres. Palolo (Hawaii) PTA, 1977-79. With U.S. Army, 1962-64. Mem. Hawaii Farm Bur. Fed., 50th State Dairy Farmers' Coop. (pres. 1989, bd. dirs. 1986-88), Hawaii Feed Coop. (treas. bd. dirs. 1986—), Hawaii Dairy Herd Improvement Assn. (pres. 1989, bd. dirs. 1983-87), Hawaii Milk Mktg. Coop. (pres. bd. dirs. 1986), Sigma Xi, Gamma Sigma Delta. Office: PO Box 627 Waianae HI 96792

OLCOTT, JOANNE ELIZABETH, naval officer; b. Portland, Oreg., May 12, 1958; d. Richard Hutton and Eleanor (Looker) O. BS, Oreg. State U., 1980; postgrad. in sci., Naval Postgrad. Sch., 1987—. Commd. ensign U.S. Navy, 1980, advanced through grades to lt., 1985; oceanographic watch officer, Guam, 1981-82, Antigua, W.I., 1982-84; adminstrv. officer, Antigua, 1983-84; ops. officer, 1984-85, chief testing mgmt. sect., 1985-87, Salt Lake City; with mil. entrance processing sta., Salt Lake City. Mem. Nat. Assn. Female Execs., Kappa Delta. Republican. Episcopalian. Avocations: athletics, reading. Office: NPS SMC 1409 Monterey CA 93944

OLDEMEYER, ROBERT KING, retired seed company executive; b. Brush, Colo., Sept. 23, 1922; s. Clarence Lester and Gayle Esther (King) O.; m. Shirley Faye Schlessinger, May 24, 1944; children: G. Janine Hill, Kristin Kay Moyer. BS, Colo. State U., 1947; MS, U. Wis., 1948, PhD, 1950. Plant breeder Great Western Sugar Co., Longmont, Colo., 1950-60, chief plant breeder, 1960-67, sta. dir., 1967-69, dir. seed devel., 1969-74, dir. plant breeding, 1975-85; dir. ops. Hilleshog Mono-Hy Inc., Longmont, 1985-89. Served to 1st lt. U.S. Army, 1943-47, ETO. Republican. Mem. United Ch. Christ. Lodge: Rotary (bd. dirs.). Home: 530 Gay St Longmont CO 80501 Office: Hilleshog Mono-Hy Inc 11939 Sugarmill Rd Longmont CO 80501

OLDEN, ROBERT M., recruitment company executive, writer; b. Westville, N.J., Sept. 2, 1948; s. Frederick Milton and Mae Belle (Koger) O.; m. Lillian Grace Fittz, June 21, 1969; children: Robin, Randy, Ryan, Robbie. BA in Humanities, Biola Coll., 1970; MA in Religious Edn., Talbot Sem., 1973. Missionary, adminstr., educator, writer Soc. for Internat. Ministries Internat., Cochabamba, Bolivia, 1973-85; elem. tchr. L.A. Unified Sch. Dist., 1985-86; recruitment and tng. coord. Polly's Inc., Santa Fe Springs, Calif., 1986—. Contbr. articles to profl. jours. Mem. Am. Soc. for Tng. and Devel. Republican. Mem. Soc. of Friends. Office: Polly's Inc 14325 Iseli Rd Santa Fe Springs CA 90670

OLDERMAN, GERALD MYRON, medical device company executive; b. N.Y.C., July 16, 1933; s. Cass and Hilda (Klein) O.; m. Myrna Ruth Schwartz, Aug. 3, 1958; children: Sharon, Neil, Lisa. BS in Chemistry, Rensselaer Poly Inst., 1958; MS Phys. Chemistry, Seton Hall U., 1971, PhD, 1972. Research chemist Nat. Cash Register, Dayton, Ohio, 1958-61; tech. mgmt. positions Johnson & Johnson, New Brunswick, N.J., 1961-75, v.p. rsch. and devel. Surgikos div., 1975-78; v.p. rsch. and devel. Am. Convertors div. Am. Hosp. Supply Corp., Evanston, Ill., 1978-85; v.p. internat. rsch. and devel. Pharmaseal div. Baxter Healthcare Corp., Valencia, Calif., 1985—; bd. dirs. Am. Convertors. Served with USMC, 1954-56. Recipient Robert Wood Johnson medal, Johnson & Johnson, 1969. Fellow Am. Inst. Chemists; mem. Assn. Advancement Med. Instrumentation, Assn. Nonwovens Industry (bd. dirs., corp. rep. 1986, 87), Nat. Fire Protection Assn. (industry rep.), Am. Soc. Artificial Internal Organs. Home: 17300 Citronia St Northridge CA 91325 Office: Pharmaseal 27200 N Tourney Rd Valencia CA 91355

OLDHAM, MAXINE JERNIGAN, real estate broker; b. Whittier, Calif., Oct. 13, 1923; d. John K. and Lela Hessie (Mears) Jernigan; m. Laurance Montgomery Oldham, Oct. 28, 1941; 1 child, John Laurence. AA, San Diego City Coll., 1973; student Western State U. Law, San Diego, 1976-77, LaSalle U., 1977-78; grad. Realtors Inst., Sacramento, 1978. Mgr. Edin Harig Realty, LaMesa, Calif., 1966-70; tchr. Bd. Edn., San Diego, 1959-66; mgr. Julia Cave Real Estate, San Diego, 1970-73; salesman Computer Realty, San Diego, 1973-74; owner Shelter Island Realty, San Diego, 1974—. Author: Jernigan History, 1982, Mears Geneology, 1985, Fustons of Colonial America, 1988. Mem. Civil Service Commn., San Diego, 1957-58. Mem. Nat. Assn. Realtors, Calif. Assn. Realtors, San Diego Bd. Realtors, San Diego Apt. Assn., Internationale des Professions Immobilieres (internat. platform speaker), DAR, Colonial Dames 17th Century, Internat. Fedn. Univ. Women. Republican. Roman Catholic. Avocations: music, theater, painting, geneology, continuing edn. Home: 3348 Lowell St San Diego CA 92106 Office: Shelter Island Realty 2810 Lytton St San Diego CA 92110

OLDHAM, SUSAN LORAIN, chemical engineer; b. L.A., Aug. 29, 1954; d. Leonard and Harriet Howard; m. Paul Oldham, June 26, 1976; 1 child, Jennifer. BA in Chemistry, U. Calif., Irvine, 1976; MSChemE, U. So. Calif., 1982. Assoc. engr. McDonnell Douglas Aircraft Co., Huntington Beach, Calif., 1976-78; rsch. chemist CIBA Geigy Co., Fountain Valley, Calif., 1978-80; sr. staff engr. Hughes Aircraft Co., El Segundo, Calif., 1980—. Contbr. articles to profl. jours.; patentee method of fabricating composite of encapsulated articles, fiber reinforced syntactic foam, method to prepare epoxy, silicone compounds, allyl-terminated silicone compounds, also others. Recipient cert. of achievement YWCA, L.A., 1985. Mem. Am. Chem. Soc., Soc. Plastics Engrs., Soc. for Advancement Materials and Process Engring. (vice chmn. 1984-85 L.A. chpt., chmn. 1985-86, jr. nat. bd. dirs. L.A. chpt. 1986-87, sr. nat. bd. dirs. 1987-88). Democrat. Office: Hughes Aircraft Co PO Box 902 El/F157 El Segundo CA 90245

OLDHAM, WILLIAM GEORGE, electrical engineering and computer science educator; b. Detroit, May 5, 1938; s. William D. and Freada (Howes) O.; m. Nancy Dereich; children: Katherine Ann, William James. B.S., Carnegie Mellon Inst., 1960, M.S., 1961, Ph.D., 1963. Staff scientist Siemens-Schuckert, Erlangen, W.Ger., 1963-64; mem. faculty elec. engring. and computer scis. dept. U. Calif., Berkeley, 1964—, prof., 1972—, dir. Electronics Research Lab., 1985—; project mgr. Intel Corp., Santa Clara, Calif., 1974-75. Author: An Introduction to Electronics, 1972, Electrical Engineering, An Introduction, 1984. NSF fellow, 1970; Guggenheim fellow, 1985-86. Fellow IEEE; mem. Nat. Acad. Engring. Office: U Calif Berkeley Dept Elec Engring & Computer Scis Berkeley CA 94720

OLDROYD, ROLAND KENDAL, pharmacist, farmer; b. Salt Lake City, Sept. 2, 1939; s. Roland A. and Belva Faye (Herbert) O.; m. Judith Innes, July 20, 1966 (div.); m. Carole Lucille Bird, July 1, 1988. BS in Pharmacy, U. Utah, 1965. Registered pharmacist, Utah. Farmer Old Mill Orchards & Nurseries, Glenwood, Utah, 1973—; pharmacist, owner, mgr. S.O.S. Drug Co., Springville, Utah, 1985—. Mayor Town of Glenwood (Utah), 1980-86. Mem. Rotary (pres. Springville 1988), Sigma Nu. Office: SOS Drug Co 214 S Main St PO Box 149 Springville UT 84663

OLDSHUE, PAUL FREDERICK, financial executive; b. Chgo., Nov. 4, 1949; s. James Young and Betty Ann (Wiersema) O.; m. Mary Elizabeth Holl, July 12, 1975; children: Emily Jane, Andrew Armstrong. Abigail Anne. BA, Williams Coll., Williamstown, Mass., 1971; MBA, NYU, 1978. With Chem. Bank, N.Y.C., 1973-78, asst. sec., 1976-78; with Orbanco Fin. Svc. Corp., 1978-83, v.p., treas., 1980-83; exec. v.p. Oreg. Bank, Portland, 1984-88; v.p. syndications & participations PacifiCorp Fin. Inc., 1988—. Mem. Fin. Execs. Inst. Republican. Club: Founders (Portland).

O'LEARY, CHARLOTTE MAE, retail computer executive, fruit packaging/shipping executive; b. Ontario, Oreg., Dec. 18, 1942; d. Harold A. and Mabel (Marcum) Warren; m. James Ernest O'Leary, Aug. 16, 1962; children: James II, Shelley Renáe, Shawna Lenáe. AS, Treasure Valley Community Coll., 1980. Head draftsman Interstate Engring. Co., Ontario, 1978-80; owner, operator House of Computers, Ontario, 1980—, Hudco Engring., Ontario, 1980-84; gen. mgr. Gem Fruit, Inc., Emmett, Idaho, 1987—, also sec. bd. dirs.; agt. Western Union, Ontario, 1983—; instr. computers, small bus. adminstrn., Treasure Valley Community Coll., Ontario, 1986. Pres. Ontario Downtown Merchants Assn., 1986-88; mem. adv. com. bus. dept. Ontario High Sch. Named Nat. Top Dealer Datasphere, Inc., 1984. Mem. Phi Theta Kappa. Office: House of Computers 249 S Oregon St Ontario OR 97914 also: Gem Fruit Inc PO Box 308 1750 Hwy 52 Emmett ID 83617

O'LEARY, GEORGE PATRICK, scientific computer consultant; b. Watertown, Minn., Sept. 27, 1942; s. George F. and Maria (Schultz) O'L.; m. Loretta Theresa Donegan, Aug. 29, 1964; children: Heather, Kaeley. BA in Physics, Yale U., 1964, MS in Physics, 1966, PhD in Physics, 1969. Asst. prof. Oreg. Grad. Ctr., Beaverton, Oreg., 1969-72; engring. cons. Floating Point Systems Inc., Beaverton, 1971-73, v.p. engring., 1973-81, v.p. European ops., 1981-83, pres., chief operating officer, 1986-87, also bd. dirs.; pvt. practice cons. Portland, Oreg., 1983-85; pres., chief exec. officer Accufiber Inc., Vancouver, Wash., 1985-86; bd. dirs. Archinetics, Portland, Microcosm, Beaverton. Chmn. Oreg. Art Inst., Portland, 1986—. Clubs: Portland Golf, University.

O'LEARY, PEGGY RENÉ, accountant; b. Billings, Mont., Dec. 6, 1951; d. Paul Eugene and Norma Dean (Metcalf) O'L.; m. Kim Patric Johnson, Mar. 19, 1983. BS, Mont. State U., 1976. CPA, Mont. Staff acct. Peat Marwick Main, Billings, 1976-80; dir. fin. Billings Clinic, 1980—. Div. leader youth support campaign YMCA, Billings, 1987-88, bd. dirs., 1988—, sec. bd., 1989. Mem. Billings C. of C. (sch. tax com. 1982-88), Pink Chips Investment Club (treas. 1987-88). Republican. Roman Catholic. Home: 4565 Pine Cove Rd Billings MT 59106 Office: Billings Clinic 2825 8th Ave N Billings MT 59107

OLES, DOUGLAS STUART, lawyer; b. Seattle, Nov. 10, 1954; s. Stuart G. and Ilse (Hanewald) O.; m. Laura Treadgold, Dec. 18, 1979. AB in History with honors and distinction, Stanford U., 1976; JD with honors, U. Wash., 1979. Bar: Wash. 1979, U.S. Dist. Ct. (we. dist.) Wash. 1979. Law clk. to judge U.S. Dist. Ct. (we. dist.) Wash., Seattle, 1979-81; assoc. Oles, Morrison, Rinker, Stanislaw & Ashbaugh, Seattle, 1981-87; ptnr. Oles, Morrison & Rinker, Seattle, 1988—. Exec. editor U. Wash. Law Rev., 1978-79. Mem. Diocese Olympia Council, Western Wash., 1985-89. Mem. ABA, Wash. State Bar Assn., Seattle King County Bar Assn., Japanese Am. Soc. for Legal Studies, Phi Beta Kappa. Episcopalian. Club: Rainier (Seattle). Office: Oles Morrison & Rinker 3300 Columbia Ctr Seattle WA 98104-7007

OLES, STUART GREGORY, lawyer; b. Seattle, Dec. 15, 1924; s. Floyd and Helen Louise (La Violette) O.; B.S. magna cum laude, U. Wash., 1947, J.D., 1948; m. Ilse Hanewald, Feb. 12, 1954; children—Douglas, Karl, Stephen. Admitted to Wash. bar, 1949, U.S. Supreme Ct. bar, 1960; dep. pros. atty. King County (Wash.), 1949, chief civil dept., 1949-50; gen. practice law, Seattle, 1950—; sr. partner firm Oles, Morrison & Rinker and predecessor, 1955—. Chmn. Seattle Community Concert Assn., 1955; pres. Friends Seattle Pub. Library, 1956; mem. Wash. Pub. Disclosure Commn., 1973-75; trustee Ch. Div. Sch. of Pacific, Berkeley, Calif., 1974-75; mem. bd. curators Wash. State Hist. Soc., 1983; mem. Seattle Symphony Bd.; pres. King County Ct. House Rep. Club, 1950, U. Wash. Young Rep. Club, 1947; Wash. conv. floor leader Taft, 1952, Goldwater, 1964; Wash. chmn. Citizens for Goldwater, 1964; chmn. King County Rep. convs., 1966, 68, 76, 84, 86, 88, Wash. State Rep. Conv., 1980. Served with USMCR, 1943-45. Mem. Seattle, King County, Wash., Am. (past regional vice chmn. pub. contract law sect.) bar assns., Order of Coif, Scabbard and Blade, Am. Legion, Phi Beta Kappa, Phi Alpha Delta. Episcopalian (vestryman, lay-reader). Clubs: Rainier, Seattle Yacht, Beavers. Home: 5051 50th Ave NE #40 Seattle WA 98105 Office: Oles Morrison & Rinker 701 Fifth Ave Ste 3300 Seattle WA 98104

OLFMAN, LORNE, information systems analyst, educator; b. Calgary, Alta., Can., Nov. 29, 1948; came to U.S., 1983; s. Hymie and Sara Frances (Martin) O.; m. Darlene May Puhach, Dec. 30, 1981. BS in Computing Sci., U. Calgary, 1970, MA in Econs., 1980; MBA, Ind. U., 1986, PhD in Bus.

Mgmt. Info. Systems, 1987. Computer programmer Bercov Computer Cons. Ltd., Calgary, 1969-71; teaching asst. Dept. Econs. U. Calgary, 1973-74; economist Transport Can. Air Adminstrn., Edmonton, Ottawa and Toronto, Alta. and Ont., Can., 1973-80; planning analyst B.C. (Can.) Telephone Co., Vancouver, 1981-83; instr. Sch. Bus. Ind. U., Bloomington, 1983-86; research assoc. Devel. Tng. Ctr., Bloomington, 1986-87; asst. prof. Info. Sci. Dept. Claremont (Calif.) Grad. Sch., 1987—. Assoc. editor: Jour. Bus. and Econs. Perspectives, 1988—; contbr. articles to profl. jours. Ind. U. fellow, 1983-86, IBM fellow, 1985, Richard D. Irwin fellow, 1986-87. Mem. Assn. Computing Machinery, Inst. Mgmt. Scis., IEEE Computer Soc., Decision Scis. Inst. Office: Claremont Grad Sch Info Sci Dept Claremont CA 91711-6190

OLIPHANT, CHARLES ROMIG, physician; b. Waukegan, Ill., Sept. 10, 1917; s. Charles L. and Mary (Goss) R.; student St. Louis U., 1936-40; M.D., 1943; postgrad. Naval Med. Sch., 1946; m. Claire E. Canavan, Nov. 7, 1942; children: James R., Cathy Rose, Mary G., William D. Intern, Nat. Naval Med. Ctr., Bethesda, Md., 1943; pvt. practice medicine and surgery, San Diego, 1947—; pres., chief exec. officer Midway Med. Enterprises; former chief staff Balboa Hosp., Doctors Hosp., Cabrillo Med. Ctr.; chief staff emeritus Sharp Cabrillo Hosp.; mem. staff Mercy Hosp., Children's Hosp., Paradise Valley Hosp., Sharp Meml. Hosp.; sec. Sharp Sr. Health Care, S.D.; mem. exec. bd., past. comdr. San Diego Power Squadron. Charter mem. Am. Bd. Family Practice. Served with M.C., USN, 1943-47. Fellow Am. Geriatrics Soc., Am. Acad. Family Practice, Am. Assn. Abdominal Surgeons; mem. AMA, Calif. Med. Assn., Am. Acad. Family Physicians (past pres. San Diego chpt., del. Calif. chpt.), San Diego Med. Soc., Public Health League, Navy League, San Diego Power Squadron (past comdr.), SAR. Clubs: San Diego Yacht, Cameron Highlanders. Home: 4310 Trias San Diego CA 92103

OLIPHANT, ERNIE L., safety educator, public relations executive, consultant; b. Richmond, Ind., Oct. 25, 1934; d. Ernest E. and Beulah A. (Jones) Reid; m. George B. Oliphant, Sept. 25, 1955; children—David, Wendell, Rebecca. Student, Earlham Coll., 1953-55, Ariz. State U., 1974, Phoenix Coll., 1974-78. Planner, organizer, moderator confs., programs for various women's clubs, safety assns., 1971-86; nat. field coordinator Operation Lifesaver, Inc., 1986—; assoc. dir. Operation Lifesaver Nat. Safety Council, Phoenix, 1978-86; cons. Fed. R.R. Adminstrn.; lectr. in field.; adviser Am. Ry. Engring. Assn., Calif. Assn. Women Hwy. Safety Leaders, numerous others. Mem. R.R./Hwy. grade crossing com. Ariz. Corp. Commn.; mem. transp. and system com. Ariz. Gov.'s Commn. on Environment; mem. Ariz. Gov.'s Council Women for Hwy. Safety; mem. motor vehicle traffic safety at hwy.-r.r. grade crossings com., roadway environment com., women's div. com. Nat. Safety Council; mem. Phoenix Traffic Accident Reduction Program; task force mem. U.S. Dept. Transp. on Grade Crossing Safety. Recipient Safety award SW Safety Congress, 1973; citation of Merit Adv. Commn. on Ariz. Environment, 1974; Gov.'s award for hwy. safety, 1978; Gov.'s Merit of Recognition Outstanding Service in Hwy. Safety, 1980. Mem. Assn. R.R. Editors, Nat. Assn. Female Execs., Inc., Pub. Relations Soc. Am., R.R. Pub. Relations Assn., committees Nat. Acad. Scis. (dir. transp. research, planning, adminstrn. of transp. safety com., r.r.-hwy. grade crossing safety com.), Women's Transp. Seminar, Ariz. Fedn. Women's Clubs (named pres. of yr. 1968), Ariz. Safety Assn. (safety recognition award 1975), Gen. Fedn. Women's Clubs (internat. bd. dirs.), Nat. Assn. Women Hwy. Safety Leaders, Soc. Govt. Planners, Inc., Phi Theta Kappa. Republican. Quaker. Author of tech. publs.

OLIVA, STEPHEN EDWARD, resource conservationist; b. San Rafael, Calif., Jan. 31, 1946; s. George Verdelli Jr. and Dorothy Margaret (Austin) O.; m. Susan Rebecca Ellis, May 5, 1984; 1 child, Stephanie Rebecca. BA, U. Calif., Santa Barbara, 1972; postgrad. in law, U. of the Pacific, 1988—. Naturalist Calif. Dept. Transp., Sacramento, 1976-76; planner Calif. Energy Commn., Sacramento, 1976, Calif. Air Resources Bd., Sacramento, 1976-79; spl. asst. to sec. The Resources Agy., Sacramento, 1979-80; spl. asst. Calif. Dept. Conservation, Sacramento, 1980, mgr. land conservation unit, 1981-87; spl. asst. Calif. Dept. Forestry, Sacramento, 1980-81; chief Office Land Conservation Calif. Dept. Conservation, Sacramento, 1987—; mem. governing bd. Calif. Tahoe Regional Planning Agy., South Lake Tahoe, 1979-81; mem. policy adv. com. Sacramento County Local Agy. Formation Commn., 1988—. Served with U.S. Army, 1966-68, Vietnam. Mem. ABA-LSD, Assn. Environ. Profls., Am. Soc. Pub. Adminstrs, Assn. Am. Geographers, Capital Athletic Club. Democrat. Office: Office Land Conservation 1516 9th St Rm 400 Sacramento CA 95819

OLIVE, JAMES AUSTIN, pathologist; b. Fayette, Ala., Nov. 7, 1943; s. W.D. and Hazel (Waldrop) O.; m. Mary Elizabeth Heutess; 1 child, James Austin. BS, U. Ala., 1965; DMD, U. Ala., Birmingham, 1970, MD, 1978. Diplomate Am. Bd. Pathology; lic. physician La., Ala., Wis., Ariz.; dentist, Miss., Ala., La. Resident in clin. pathology Univ. Hosp., Birmingham, 1970-73; asst. dir. haematology and coagulation labs., sr. attending staff U. Ala. Hosps., Birmingham, 1973-76; physician-in-charge pediatric section comprehensive hemophilia clinic, sr. med. staff, asst. dir. dept. hemotherapy Charity Hosp. La. at New Orleans, 1978-80; dir. blood bank, sr. attending staff Milw. County Med. Complex, 1980-84; med. dir. United Blood Services Ariz., Scottsdale, 1984-87; v.p. med.-tech. ops., med. dir. cen. reference lab. and viral marker testing Blood Systems, Inc., Scottsdale, 1984—; cons. staff Birmingham VA Hosp., 1973-76, health services found. U. Ala., Birmingham, 1978; sr. attending staff Froedtert Meml. Luth. Hosp., 1981-84; clin. asst. prof. dept. pathology Med. Coll. Wis., 1984—, asst. prof., 1980-84; clin. assoc. prof. dept. oral diagnosis/medicine/radiology sch. dentistry La. State U., 1980; lectr. in field. Contbr. articles to profl. jours. Organizer AIDS Task Force State of Ariz., 1985—; bd. dirs. Great Lakes Hemophilia Found., 1981-84. Mem. AMA, Ariz. Med. Assn. (edn. com. 1986—), Am. Assn. Blood Banks (inspector 1981-84, component therapy com. 1981-84), So. Med. Assn., Am. Soc. Clin. Pathologists, Am. Blood Resources Assn., South Cen. Assn. Blood Banks (sci. com. 1987—, apheresis com., 1985-86, Am. Soc. Histocompatibility and Immunogenetics, Internat. Soc. Blood Transfusion, N.Y. Acad. Scis., AAAS, Delta Sigma Delta. Home: 7607 E Onyx Ct Scottsdale AZ 85258

OLIVER, DAN DAVID, banker; b. Walla Walla, Wash., Mar. 11, 1952; s. Harold Allen and Nydia Jane (Munns) O.; children: Anna Mary, Whitney Leigh. BA, Wash. State U., 1974; MBA in Taxation, Golden Gate U., 1979; JD, Western State U., 1978; grad. in trust specialization, Pacific Coast Banking Sch., 1987. Tax acct. John F. Forbes & Co., San Francisco, 1979-81; cat skinner James Francis Munns Farms, Inc., Prescott, Wash., 1981-82; law clk. Sherwood, Tugman, Gose & Reser, Walla Walla, 1975-79; v.p. and legal officer Baker-Boyer Nat. Bank, Walla Walla, 1982—; vice chmn. bd. Elite Turf Farm, Inc., Richland, Wash., sr. v.p. and sec., 1988—; bd. dirs. Kent Land Co., Walla Walla. Chmn. bd. Prescott (Wash.) Sch. Dist., 1986; officer Walla Walla Valley Estate Planning Council, treas. 1987-88, sec. 1988-89, v.p., 1989—; mem. Nat. Arbour Day Found. Named to Outstanding Young Men of Am., Montgomery, Ala. 1985. Mem. Am. Bankers Assn., Wash. Bankers Assn., Sigma Alpha Epsilon (recorder 1971-72), Walla Walla Exchange Club. Republican. Roman Catholic. Office: Baker-Boyer Nat Bank Main and 2d Sts Walla Walla WA 99362

OLIVER, FRANK SOMMARS, environmental sciences, geologist; b. Auburn, Calif., July 27, 1948; s. Henry William and Luella Maude (Hanson) O. B, Eastern Washington U., 1982. Field asst. Minatome Corp., Spokane, Wash., 1978, Stan Ponsness Assoc., Coeur D'Alene, Idaho, 1978; student aide interim U.S. Bureau of Mines (W.F.O.C.), Spokane, Wash., 1979-82; tech. temporary U.S. Bureau of Mines (W.F.O.C.), Spokane, 1982-83; contract geologist U.. Borax Exploration, Spokane, 1984; bookkeeper Samhi Corp., Santa Maria, Calif., 1984-88; tech. U.S. Bureau of Mines (S.L.C.R.C.), Salt Lake City, 1988-89, physical sci., 1989—. With U.S. Army, 1967-70, Vietnam. Mem. Nat. Rifle Assn., Am. Legion, W.P. and C. Club (Spokane) (pres. 1983—). Republican. Office: US Bur of Mines (SLCRC) 729 Arapeen Dr Salt Lake City UT 84108

OLIVER, GEOFF SCOT, military officer; b. Denver, May 21, 1957; s. Raymond Curtis and Lu Elizabeth (Eubanks) O.; m. Yolanda Portal, June 16, 1984. BS, U. Colo., 1980; MBA, Nat. U., 1989. Commd. 2d. lt. USAF, 1980, advanced through grades to capt., 1984; student navigator 451st Flying Tng. Squadron, Mather AFB, Calif., 1980-81; student weapon systems officer 310th Tactical Fighter Tng. Squadron, Luke AFB, Ariz., 1981-82; weapon systems officer 613th Tactical Fighter Squadron, Torrejon AB, Spain, 1982-83, 526th Tactical Fighter Squadron, Ramstein AB, Fed. Republic of Germany, 1983-85; course mgr. 449th Flying Tng. Squadron, Mather AFB, 1986-88; flight examiner 323d Flying Tng. Wing, Mather AFB, 1988—. Mem. AIAA, Nat. Geographic Soc., Airplane Owners and Pilots Assn. Office: 323d Flight Tng Wing/DOV Mather AFB CA 95655

OLIVER, JANICE CAROLINE YEE, dentist; b. Castro Valley, Calif., Nov. 25, 1961; d. Kenneth Kwock Sang and Vicenta Chan She (Leong) Yee; m. Richard N. Oliver III, June 23, 1985. BS in Dental Sci., DDS, U. Calif., San Francisco, 1986; postgrad., Calif. State U., Fullerton, 1987—. Assoc., office adminstr. Thomas M. Boone DDS, Stanton, Calif., 1987—. Mem., potter Calif. State-Fullerton Arboretum; mem. Friends Fullerton Library. Mem. ADA, Calif. Dental Assn., Orange County Dental Soc., U. Calif.-San Francisco Alumni Assn. (chief editor Sch. Dentistry Class of '86 newsletter 1986—), Psi Omega Beta. Democrat. Office: Thomas M Boone DDS 12075 Beach Blvd Stanton CA 90680

OLIVER, JOHN EDWARD, banking consultant; b. Bedford, Eng., Apr. 14, 1951; came to U.S., 1978; s. Fred K. and Marjorie F. (Brown) O.; m. Jacqueline L. Alcock, Oct. 7, 1972; 1 child, Sophie Rose. Student, Mander Coll., Bedford, 1968-71. Cert. U.K. Inst. Bankers. Mgr.'s asst. Nat. Westminster Bank, Bedford, 1971-73; credit analyst Kleinwort Benson Ltd., London, 1973-76; mktg. coord. Amex Bank Ltd., London, 1976-78; v.p. Continental Ill. Energy Devel. Corp., Houston, 1978-85; pres. Laurel Mgmt. Systems Inc., San Francisco, 1986—; banking cons. Kansallis-Osake-Pankki, London, 1985—; bank edn. cons. Bank Am., San Francisco, 1986—. Author banking tng. programs. Office: Laurel Mgmt Systems Inc 1275 Market St Ste 1300 San Francisco CA 94103

OLIVER, JOYCE ANNE, journalist, editorial consultant; b. Coral Gables, Fla., Sept. 19, 1958; d. John Joseph and Rosalie Cecile (Mack) O. BA in Communications, Calif. State U., Fullerton, 1980, postgrad. sch. mgmt., 1988. Corp. editor Norris Industries Inc., Huntington Beach, Calif., 1979-82; pres. J.A. Oliver Assocs., La Habra Heights, Calif., 1982—; corp. editorial cons. Norris Industries, 1982, Better Methods Cons., Huntington Harbour, Calif., 1982-83, Summit Group, Orange, Calif., 1982-83, UDS, Encinitas, Calif., 1983-84, ALS Corp., Anaheim, Calif., 1985, Gen. Power Systems, Anaheim, 1985, MacroMarketing, Costa Mesa, Calif., 1985-86, PM Software, Huntington Beach, Calif., 1985-86, CompuQuote, Canoga Park, Calif., 1985-86, Nat. Semicondr. Can. Ltd., Mississauga, Ont., Can., 1986, Frame Inc., Fullerton, Calif., 1987-88, The Johnson-Layton Co., Los Angeles, 1988-89, Corp. Research Inc., Chgo., 1988; mem. Research Council of Scripps Clinic and Research Found., 1987-89. Contbr.: Cleve. Inst. Electronics publ. The Electron, spl. feature editor, 1988—; contbg. editor Reseller Management mag. (formerly Computer Dealer mag.), 1987-89; also contbr. to Can. Electronics Engring. Mag., PC Week, The NOMDA Spokesman, Entrepreneur, Adminstrv. Mgmt., High-Tech Selling, Video Systems, Tech. Photography, Computing Canada, Stores. Mem. Internat. Platform Assn., IEEE, Soc. Photo-Optical Instrumentation Engrs., Inst. Mgmt. Scis., Nat. Writers Club (profl.), Internat. Mktg. Assn., Soc. Profl. Journalists. Republican. Roman Catholic. Office: JA Oliver Assocs 2045 Fullerton Rd La Habra Heights CA 90631

OLIVER, JOYCE FRIZZELL, writer; b. Balt., Sept. 6, 1935; d. Roscoe Shipley and Ruth Evelyn (Donaldson) Frizzell; m. Frederic Joseph Jones, June 14, 1958 (div. 1978); 1 child, Lisa Karen Jones Huntington; m. Bill Erwin Oliver, Aug. 7, 1982. BS in English Edn., Towson (Md.) State U., 1958; MA in English, NYU, 1965. Research editor Grolier Inc., N.Y.C., 1959-63; research asst. Lenox Hill Hosp., N.Y.C., 1967-69; market research analyst Ruder & Finn Inc., N.Y.C., 1969-72, v.p. research, 1972-75; life ins. broker various cos., San Francisco, 1978-81; communications specialist Syntex Corp., Palo Alto, Calif., 1981-82, mgr. adnt. prodn., 1982-85, med. writer, 1985—; leader seminars. Author: (text) Citizenship Education, 1966; editor: Johnny Tremaine, 1966; editor various newsletters. Recipient 2 Indsl. Design awards Health Scis. Communications Assn., 1989. Mem. Am. Med. Writers Assn. (1st pl. award John Muir Med. Film Festival 1983), Peninsula Profl. Women's Network. Republican. Home: 115 16th Ave San Mateo CA 94402

OLIVER, MARY LOU, city official; b. Midland, Mich., Feb. 9, 1941; d. William Charles and I. Flora (Ahern) Goggin; m. Donald Bruce Oliver, Oct. 28, 1967; children: Stephen, Patricia. BA in Comml. Art, Marygrove Coll., Detroit, 1963; BA in Edn., U. Mich., 1964. Tchr. South Lyon (Mich.) Community Sch., 1964-69; mem. coun. City of San Ramon, Calif., 1983—, mayor, 1985; dir. Dougherty Regional Fire Authority; commr. San Ramon Redevel. Agy. Pres. Homeowners Assn. Twin Creek, San Ramon, 1979-81; founder San Ramon Incorporation Com., 1982. Named Woman of Distinction, Soroptimist Internat., San Ramon, 1985. Mem. AAUW (community area rep. 1985—). Republican. Office: City of San Ramon 2222 Camino Ramon San Ramon CA 94583

OLIVER, PAT PHILLIPS, publisher, editor, writer; b. Crown Point, Ind.; d. John Adam and Anna (Kindness) Patterson; student U. Chgo., 1941, Ind. U., 1938-40; m. Charles Everett Phillips, Jr., Sept. 17, 1941 (div.); children: Anne, Jill, Candace, Pamela; m. 2d, Eddie Oliver, Feb. 2, 1963 (dec.). Columnist, feature writer Ind. newspapers, nat. mags., 1935-40; women's editor, feature writer Burbank (Calif.) Daily Rev., 1953-57, Hollywood (Calif.) Citizen-News, 1957-63; mng. editor, exec. editor Palm Springs Life mag., 1964-79, Palm Springs Pub. Relations, 1980-85; lifestyle editor Indio (Calif.) Daily News, 1985-87; owner, pub. Palm Springs Personages, 1982—. Mem. Theta Sigma Phi. Clubs: Desert Press, Hollywood Women's Press, Palm Springs Women's Press (founding, Lifetime Achievement in Journalism award 1986). Office: PO Box 1004 Palm Springs CA 92263

OLIVER, ROBERT WARNER, economics educator; b. Los Angeles, Oct. 26, 1922; s. Ernest Warner and Elnore May (McConnell) O.; m. Darlene Hubbard, July 1, 1946; children: Lesley Joanne, Stewart Warner. A.B., U. So. Calif., 1943, A.M., 1948; A.M., Princeton U., 1950, Ph.D., 1958. Teaching asst. U. So. Calif., 1946-47; instr. Princeton U., 1947-50, Pomona Coll., Claremont, Calif., 1950-52; asst. prof. U. So. Calif., Los Angeles, 1952-56; economist Stanford Research Inst., South Pasadena, Calif., 1956-59; mem. faculty dept. econs. Calif. Inst. Tech., 1959-88, prof. econs., 1973-88, prof. emeritus, 1988—; urban economist World Bank, Washington, 1970-71; cons. Brookings Instn., 1961, OECD, Paris, 1979; vis. prof. U. So. Calif., 1985; vis. scholar Pembrook Coll., Cambridge U., Eng., 1989. Author: An Economic Survey of Pasadena, 1959, International Economic Cooperation and the World Bank, 1975, Bretton Woods, A Retrospective Essay, 1985, Oral History Project The World Bank, 1986; contbg. author: Encyclopedia of Economics, 1981. Mem. Human Relations Com. City of Pasadena, 1964-65, Planning Commn., 1972-75; bd. dirs. Pasadena City Council, 1965-69, mem. Utilities Adv. Commn., 1984-88, Strategic Planning Com., 1985; pres. Pasadena Beautiful Found., 1972-74; bd. dirs. Pasadena Minority History Found., 1984—. Lt. (j.g.) USN, 1942-46. Social Sci. research fellow London Sch. Econs., 1954-55; Rockefeller Found. fellow, 1974; Danforth assoc., 1981; recipient Outstanding Teaching award, 1982, Master of the Student Houses, 1987; Hon. Alumnus, 1987—. Mem. Internat. Inst. Strategic Studies, Calif. Seminar on Internat. Security and Fgn. Policy, Am. Econs. Assn., Royal Econs. Assn., Com. on Fgn. Relations, Western Econs. Assn., Phi Beta Kappa, Phi Kappa Phi, Delta Tau Delta. Democrat. Methodist. Club: Athenaeum. Home: 3197 San Pasqual Pasadena CA 91107 Office: 1201 California Blvd Pasadena CA 91125

OLIVER, STEPHEN CHARLES, educational administrator; b. Tulsa, Apr. 14, 1960; s. James Donald and Ann Marie (Skelton) O. Student, U. Tulsa, 1978-80; BA cum laude, Georgetown U., 1982. Instr., br. mgr. Jhoon Rhee Inst., Washington, 1980-82; head instr. Am. Karate Schs., Washington, 1982-83; br. mgr. Nautilus of West, Denver, 1983; chief exec. officer, pres. Am. Achievement Schs., Denver, 1983—; bd. dirs. Ednl. Fin., Inc., Denver, Ednl. Funding Co., U.S. Martial Arts, Washington. Pub. relations dir. Project Concert, Tulsa, 1975-80. Republican. Home: 24107 Genesee Trail Rd Golden CO 80401 Office: Am Achievement Schs DBA Mile High Karate 7857 W Jewell Lakewood CO 80226

OLLSON, MICKEY LOUIS, zoo owner; b. Phoenix, May 12, 1941; s. William Archie and Edith Iris (Curnow) O.; m. Donna Marie Ollson, Dec. 5, 1965 (div. Feb. 1975); children: Micalin, Louis Michael. AA, Phoenix Coll., 1961; BS, Ariz. State U., 1963. Owner, dir. Ollson's Exotic Animal Farm, Glendale, Ariz., 1965-83, Wildlife World Zoo, Glendale, 1983—. Contbr. articles to profl. publs. Mem. Am. Assn. Zool. Parks and Aquariums (profl.), Am. Fedn. Aviculture (v.p. 1976-77), Am. Game Bird Fedn. (bd. dirs. 1988—, pres. 1984-89, Outstanding Mem. of Yr. award 1968), Internat. Soc. Zooculturists (charter; treas. 1987-88), Am. Pheasant and Waterfowl Soc. (bd. dirs. 1972-78), Avondale-Goodyear-Litchfield Park C. of C. (bd. dirs. 1985-88), Kappa Sigma (pres. Rho chpt. 1964). Republican. Office: Wildlife World Zoo 16501 W Northern St Litchfield Park AZ 85340

OLMAN, MARYELLEN, human resources administrator; b. Grand Rapids, Mich., Dec. 24, 1946; d. Norman Adolph and Mary Irene (McCarthy) Olman; m. Richard Isaac Fine, Nov. 25, 1982; 1 child, Victoria Elizabeth. B.A. in Community Service, Mich. State U., 1968. Legis. researcher Hon. Gerald R. Ford, U.S. Ho. of Reps., 1969-71; spl. asst. Hon. Jack F. Kemp, U.S. Ho. of Reps., 1971-74; personnel analyst Los Angeles City Housing Authority, 1975-78; profl. placement rep. Gen. Telephone of Calif., Santa Monica, 1978-81, mgmt. staffing adminstr., 1981-84. Mem. Los Angeles Internat. Visitors Assn., 1982—; mem. founders circle Los Angeles Music Ctr. Mem. Am. Soc. Personnel Adminstrs., Coll. Placement Council, Western Coll. Placement Assn., Personnel and Indsl. Relations Assn. Republican. Home: 5331 Horizon Dr Malibu CA 90265

OLMSTED, JANICE ELIZABETH, surgical technologist; b. Spokane, Wash., Dec. 22, 1939; d. Garth Joseph and Jeanette Leola (Nixon) Botts; m. George Britton, Sept. 8, 1969 (div. July 1979); children: Scott, Shannon, Duane, Erich; m. James Allen Olmsted, July 14, 1979. Diploma in practical nursing, Sacred Heart Sch. Nursing, 1959; student, North Seattle Jr. Coll., 1976. Surg. technologist Sacred Heart Med. Ctr., Spokane, 1961-72, Holy Family Hosp., Spokane, 1972-74; surg. asst. Group Health Coop. Puget Sound, Seattle, 1974—. Pres. Audubon Elem. PTA, Spokane, 1965, Westview Pre Sch. PTA, Spokane, 1969. Fellow Nat. Surg. Asst. Assn. (pres. 1987-88), Nat. Assn. Surg. Technologists (bd. dirs. 1983-88), Assn. Surg. Technologists (1st asst. legis. com. chairperson). Roman Catholic. Home: 9217 210th Pl SE Shohomish WA 98290 Office: Assn Surg Technologists 8207 Shaffer Pkwy Littleton CA 80127

OLMSTED, MAXINE BLAKEMORE, writer; b. Seattle, Dec. 18, 1907; d. John Flick and Cassa Geneva (Illsley) Blakemore; B.A. in Drama, U. Wash., Seattle, 1931; m. Joel Burleson Olmsted, Sept. 5, 1931; children—Cassa Blakemore, Spalding Maxine. Pub. relations dir. United Cerebral Palsy Assn. Central Ariz., 1957-59, Maricopa County and Ariz. assns. mental health, 1959-61, Ariz. Assn. Crippled Children and Adults, 1962-64, Phoenix Jewish Community Center, 1965-68, Ariz. Commn. Arts and Humanities, 1969-70; Maricopa County coordinator Ariz. Commn. Arts and Humanities for dance/movement in elementary schs., 1970-79; author histories of Phoenix and Scottsdale for photography book Phoenix: 1870-1970, 1970; also articles, stories; editor Ariz. Dance Guild News, 1974-79; leading actor in documentary film The Desert Speaks (Golden Eagle award 1978). Recipient various service citations. Mem. Screen Actors Guild, AFTRA, Nat. League Am. Pen Women, Ariz. Dance Arts Alliance (a founder), Artes Bellas (a founder), Phoenix Art Mus., Scottsdale Center for Arts, Ariz. Humane Soc. Republican. Episcopalian. Address: 8531 N 11th Ave Phoenix AZ 85021

OLNEY, KATHRYN LOUISE, magazine research director; b. Upperdarby, Pa., Dec. 9, 1955; d. Edward Stuart and Marilyn (Patterson) O.; m. Clifford Jay Bell, June 16, 1979; 1 child, Lindsay Olney-Bell. BA, Purdue U., 1978. Library assoc. DePaul U., Chgo., 1978-79, U. of Pacific, Stockton, Calif., 1979-81; cons. Mother Jones mag., San Francisco, 1982-83, research dir., 1984—; researcher California mag., San Francisco, 1983-84. Home: 4222 26th St San Francisco CA 94131 Office: Mother Jones Mag 1663 Mission St San Francisco CA 94103

OLONA, MICHAEL DAVID, assistant vice president administration; b. Midwest City, Okla., Sept. 8, 1952; s. Orlando and Melba (Dimas) O.; m. Majella Hoffman, Mar. 21, 1987; 1 child, Geralyn. BBA, U. N. Mex., 1979, MPA, 1983. Asst. v.p. adminstrn. ABQ Tech. Vocat. Inst., Albuquerque, N. Mex., 1976—; pres. N. Mex. Pub. Sch. Instr. Authority, ABQ, 1987-88. With U.S. Army, 1972-75. Mem. Nat. Assn. Accts. Democrat. Roman Catholic. Home: 6104 Kearny Trail NW Albuquerque NM 87120 Office: ABQ TVI 525 Buena Vista SE Albuquerque NM 87106

OLPIN, ROBERT SPENCER, art history educator; b. Palo Alto, Calif., Aug. 30, 1940; s. Ralph Smith and Ethel Lucille (Harman) O.; m. Mary Florence Catharine Reynolds, Aug. 24, 1963; children: Mary Courtney, Cristin Lee, Catharine Elizabeth, Carrie Jean. BS, U. Utah, 1963; AM, Boston U., 1965, PhD, 1971. Lectr. art history Boston U., 1965-67; asst. prof. U. Utah, Salt Lake City, 1967-72, assoc. prof., 1972-76, prof., 1976—, chmn. dept., 1975-82, dir. art history program, 1968-76, 83—, dean Coll. Fine Arts, 1987—; cons. curator Am. and English art Utah Mus. Fine Arts, 1973—. Grantee U. Utah, 1972, 85, Utah Mus. Fine Arts, 1975, Utah Bicentennial Commn., 1975, Ford Found., 1975; trustee Salt Lake Art Ctr., 1979, Utah Endowment for Humanities, 1985-86. Mem. Archives Am. Art Smithsonian Instn., Coll. Art Assn. Am., Mid-Am. Coll. Art Assn., Utah Acad. Scis. Arts Letters, Utah Art History Assn., Assn. Historians Am. Art, Utah Heritage Found., Phi Kappa Phi, Sigma Nu. Republican. Mormon. Author: Alexander Helwig Wyant, 1836-92, 1968, Mainstreams of American Architecture, 1973, American Painting Around 1850, 1976, Art-Life of Utah, 1977, Dictionary of Utah Art, 1980, A Retrospective of Utah Art, 1981, Waldo Midgley: Birds, Animals, People, Things, 1984, A Basket of Chips, 1985, The Works of Alexander Helwig Wyant, 1986. Home: 887 Woodshire Ave Murray UT 84107 Office: U Utah Dept Art Salt Lake City UT 84112 *

OLSEN, ALFRED JON, lawyer; b. Phoenix, Oct. 5, 1940; s. William Hans and Vera (Bearden) O.; m. Susan K. Smith, Apr. 15, 1979. B.A. in History, U. Ariz., 1962; M.S. in Acctg, Ariz. State U., 1964; J.D., Northwestern U., 1966. Bar: Ariz. 1966, Ill. 1966; C.P.A., Ariz., Ill. cert. tax specialist. Acct. Arthur Young & Co., C.P.A.s, Chgo., 1966-68; dir. firm Ehmann, Olsen & Lane (P.C.), Phoenix, 1969-76; dir. Streich, Lang, Weeks & Cardon (P.C.), Phoenix, 1977-78; v.p. Olsen-Smith, Ltd., Phoenix, 1978—. Bd. editors: Jour. Agrl. Law and Taxation, 1978—, Practical Real Estate Lawyer, 1983—. Mem. Phoenix adv. bd. Salvation Army., 1973-81. Fellow Am. Coll. Probate Counsel, Am. Coll. Tax Counsel; Mem. Central Ariz. Estate Planning Council (pres. 1972-73), State Bar Ariz. (chmn. tax sect. 1977-78), ABA (chmn. com. on agr., sect. taxation 1976-78, chmn. CLE com. sect. taxation 1982-84), Am. Law Inst. (chmn. tax planning for agr. 1973—), Nat. Cattlemen's Assn. (tax com. 1979-88), Internat. Acad. Estate and Trust Law (academician), Sigma Nu Internat. (pres. 1986-88). Office: 3300 Liberty Bank Pla 301 E Virginia Ave Phoenix AZ 85004

OLSEN, ARTHUR ROBERT, economist, educator, author; b. Bklyn., Dec. 1, 1910; s. Martin and Clara Anita (Hansen) O.; m. Helen Marie Fehleisen, June 25, 1938; 1 dau., Karen Marie Steadman. B.S., NYU, 1939, A.M., 1940, Ed D., 1942. Prin. Elwood Sch., L.I., N.Y., 1935-37; asst. prin., instr. No. Merrick Sch., L.I., 1937-43; instr. Pratt Inst., N.Y.C., 1943-44; statistician Rayonier Inc., N.Y.C., 1944-47; prof. Western Ill. U., 1947-70, now emeritus; disting. adj. prof. econs. Ariz. State U., 1981-82; economist, author Southwestern Publ. Co., Cin., 1957—; del. U.S. Nat. Commn. UNESCO, economist S.W. Mo. Council on Econ. Edn.; bd. dirs. Ill. Council Econ. Edn.; bd. dirs. Community Edn. project, Macomb, Ill., 1957-59; past dir. and moderator WKAI Round Table of the Air. Mem. Rep. Presdl. Task Force, 1982; v.p. Sun City Agrl. Club, 1982. Served with USNG, 1930-33. Recipient Alumnus of Yr. award SUNY, 1978; Vesterheim fellow Norwegian Am. Mus., 1987, Joint Council Econ. Edn. fellow, 1960. Mem. NEA (life), Am. Econ. Assn. (life), Ill. Council Social Studies (past pres.), Smithsonian Assocs., Nat. Geog. Soc., Phi Delta Kappa, Kappa Delta Pi, Omicron Delta Epsilon. Republican. Protestant. Clubs: N.Y.U., Sun City Country. Lodge: Masons (33d degree). Author: (with T.J. Hailstones), Economics, 10th edit., 1985; Economic Institutions, 1958; Readings on Marriage and Family Relations, 1953; Economics Transparancies, 1973; Beat the Market, 1973; contbr. articles to profl. jours. Home and Office: 9232 107th Ave Sun City AZ 85351

OLSEN, CARL MARK, recruiting company executive, consultant; b. Manhattan, Kans., Oct. 22, 1931; s. John Carl and Veva (Shaw) O.; m. Connie B. Stocking, Sept. 20, 1958 (div. 1974); m. Janet C. Knouse; children:

Richard, Devon, Deanna, Sue, John, Elizabeth. BS, Mont. State U., 1955, MS, 1957; postgrad., UCLA, 1957-60; PhD, U. Calif., Berkeley, 1964. Rsch. technician U. Calif., Berkeley, 1960-64; dir. biol. rsch. Litton Industries, Palo Alto, Calif., 1964-65, gen. mgr., 1965-67; dir. applications rsch. Varian Assoc., Palo Alto, 1967-70; dir. mktg. Zoecon Corp., Palo Alto, 1970-74; gen. mgr. Zoecon Corp., Palo Alto and Dallas, 1974-79; pres., chief exec. officer Retro-Tek, Sunnyvale, Calif., 1979-80; chief operating officer OMAC Corp., San Jose, Calif., 1980-81; v.p., ptnr. Korn/Perry, Palo Alto, 1981-83; sr. v.p., ptnr. Boyden Internat., Menlo Park, Calif., 1983—. Trustee Mountain View (Calif.) Sch. Bd., 1966-70. Republican. Episcopalian. Office: Boyden Internat 3000 Sand Hill Rd Menlo Park CA 94025

OLSEN, DANIEL PAUL, computer systems professional; b. Butte, Mont., May 31, 1952; s. Paul B. and Rose Patrica (Roe) O.; m. Barbara Diane Nelson, May 28, 1983; children: Lisa Lynn, Christina Danielle, Ashley Dyan. Student, Mont. State U., 1970-72; BS in Computer Sci., U. Mont., 1975; postgrad., Mont. Coll. Mineral Sci. and Tech., 1977—. Cert. data processor. Programmer Mont. Power Co., Butte, 1976-77, systems programmer, 1977-78, sr. systems programmer, 1978-83, sr. system support analyst, 1983, supr. prime services, 1983-88, supr. network support, 1988—; adj. instr. Mont. Coll. of Mineral Sci. and Tech., butte, 1977-79. Pres. Echo Lake (Mont.) Homeowners Assn., 1981—. Mem. Assn. Cert. of Computer Profls., Nat. Prime Computer Users Group (sec./treas. 1989—), Nat. Prime Users Group. Home: PO Box 524 Butte MT 59703-0524 Office: Mont Power Co 40 E Broadway Butte MT 59701

OLSEN, DAVID MAGNOR, science educator; b. Deadwood, S.D., July 23, 1941; s. Russell Alvin and Dorothy M. Olson; m. Muriel Jean Bigler, Aug. 24, 1963; children: Merritt, Chad. BS, Luther Coll., 1963; MS in Nat. Sci., U. S.D., 1967. Instr. sci., math. Augustana Acad., Canton, S.D., 1963-66; instr. chemistry Iowa Lakes Community Coll., Estherville, Iowa, 1967-69; instr. chemistry Merced (Calif.) Coll., 1969—, instr. astronomy, 1975—, div. chmn., 1978-88. Bd. trustees Merced Union High Sch. Dist., 1983—, pres. 1986-87; mem. exec. bd. Merced Coll. Found. Mem. Am. Chem. Soc., Astron. Soc. of the Pacific, NEA, Calif. Tchrs. Assn., Planetary Soc., L5 Soc., Merced Coll. Faculty Assn. (pres. 1975, treas. 1980—), Track Club (mem. exec. bd. 1981), M Star Lodge (pres. Merced club 1981), sons of Norway (v.p. 1983). Democrat. Lutheran. Home: 973 Idaho Dr Merced CA 95340 Office: Merced Coll 3600 M St Merced CA 95340

OLSEN, HARRIS LELAND, real estate executive; b. Rochester, N.H., Dec. 8, 1947; s. Harries Edwin and Eva Alma (Turmelle) O.; m. Mimi Kwi Sun Yi, Mar. 15, 1953; children: Garin Lee, Gavin Yi. AS, SUNY, Albany, 1983, BS, 1988; postgrad., U. Honolulu, U. Hawaii. Enlisted USN, 1967; served in various nuclear power capacities USN, Conn., 1971-76, Hawaii, 1976-87; ret. USN, 1987; v.p. Asian Pacific Electricity, Honolulu, 1988—, Kapano Land Assocs., Honolulu, 1988—, Waiono Land Corp., Honolulu, 1981—; staff cons., Mariner-Icemakers, Honolulu, 1982-84, Transpacific Energy Corp., Honolulu, 1982-84; sr. cons. Western Rsch., Honolulu, 1984-87; quality assurance cons., Asian Pacific, Inc., Honolulu, 1987-88. Inventor, alternate power supply system; contbr. articles to profl. publs. Head coach USN Men's Softball, Honolulu, 1978-79; pres. Pearl Harbor (Hawaii) Welfare and Recreation Com., 1983-84. Mem. USCG Aux., Delta Epsilon Sigma. Democrat. Buddhist. Home: 94-1025 Anania Circle Wahiawa HI 96789 Office: Waiono Land Corp 3652 1750 Kalakaua Ave Honolulu HI 96826

OLSEN, JANUS FREDERICK, III, library director; b. Portland, Oreg., Jan. 4, 1942; s. Janus Frederick and Edna Mae (Petersen) O.; BFA, U. S.D., 1964; postgrad. Luther Theol. Sem., St. Paul, 1964-65; MLS, U. Western Ont. (Can.), 1971; m. Doris Marie Scheetz, Apr. 19, 1974. Successively reference librarian, head cataloging and tech. processing, field coord. in-svc. tng. pub. and instl. librarians, cons. to tribal, pub., organizational, sch. and govt. libraries, acting asst. dir., acting dir. S.D. State Library Commn., Pierre, 1971-73; dir. Mitchell (S.D.) Pub. Library, 1973-80; dir. Alexander Mitchell Pub. Library, Aberdeen, S.D., 1980-86, Natrona County Pub. Library, Casper, Wyo., 1986—. S.D. Interium Documents Study Commn., 1972, Mitchell Prehistoric Indian Village Commn., 1974-75; chmn. Davison County Centennial Commn., 1975; edn. chmn. Mitchell Bicentennial Commn., 1975-77; pres. Mitchell Area Arts Council, 1976; pres. Aberdeen Area Arts Coun., 1985, Brown County Hist. Mus. and Mus. Found., 1986. Served with arty. U.S. Army, 1965-67. Mem. Am. Library Assn., S.D. Library Assn. (pres. 1977, chmn. centennial com. 1981—, chmn. ad hoc com. on state union catalog of audio-visual materials), Mountain Plains Library Assn. (exec. bd. 1977), Can. Library Assn., Corn Palace Reading Coun. (pres. 1975), Mitchell Right-to-Read Com., Aberdeen Assn. Adminstrs. (sec.), Oscar Howe Cultural Ctr., Mitchell C. of C., Internat. Soc. Artists, Am. Legion. Lutheran. Contbr. articles in field to profl. jours. Home: 1280 Bretton Dr Casper WY 82609 Office: 307 2d St Casper WY 82601 *

OLSEN, MURRAY R., manufacturing systems analyst; b. Ogden, Utah, May 26, 1953; s. J. Keith and VerNona (Murray) O.; m. Janalee Foster, May 14, 1983. AS, Weber State Coll., 1972, BA in History, 1976, BA in Econs., 1977; MPA, Brigham Young U., 1982. Asst. mgmt. asst. Williams Internat., Ogden, 1977-78, analyst coord., 1978-79, supr. computer ops., 1979-83, system analyst, 1983—; advisor Weber County Sch. Dist., Ogden, 1988—. Asst. scoutmaster troop 411, Boy Scouts Am., Harrisville, Utah, 1987—; mem. Ogden-Weber Area Vocat. Ctr., 1987—, Data Processing Employer Adv. Coun., chmn., 1989, Weber County Sch. Vocat. Adv. Com., 1988-89, young alumni coun. Weber State U., Ogden, 1988—. Mem. Am. Prodn. and Inventory Control Soc. (cert., sec. 1988-89), Soc. Mfg. Enging. (sr.). Republican. Mormon. Home: 558 W Harrisville Rd Ogden UT 84404

OLSEN, ROBERT ARTHUR, finance educator; b. Pittsfield, Mass., June 30, 1943; s. Arthur Anton and Virginia O.; B.B.A., U. Mass., 1966, M.B.A., 1967; Ph.D., U. Oreg., 1974; m. Maureen . Joan Carmell, Aug. 21, 1965. Security analyst Am. Inst. Counselors, 1967-68; research assoc. Center for Capital Market Research, U. Oreg., 1972-74; asst. prof. fin. U. Mass., 1974-75; prof. fin. Calif. State U., Chico, 1975—; cons. bus. feasibility studies for Stinson, Isom Assocs. & Career Assocs., Calif. State U., Chico, Endowment Fund, U.S. Forest Service. Stonier Banking fellow, 1971-72; Nat. Assn. Mut. Savs. Banks fellow, 1975-76; scholar Stanford U., Decision Research, Inc., 1986. Recipient Research award Calif. State U.-Chico, 1983, 86, Profl. Achievement award, 1985. Mem. Am. Fin. Assn., Fin. Execs. Inst., Western Fin. Assn. (Trefftzs award 1974), Southwestern Fin. Assn., Fin. Mgmt. Assn., Eastern Fin. Assn., Sierra Club. Contbr. articles to profl. jours. Office: Calif State U Sch Bus Chico CA 95929

OLSON, A. MAX, insurance broker; b. Hubbard, Oreg., Nov. 5, 1935; s. Gust Olaf and Helen Marie (Clagett) O.; m. Priscilla Gwen English, Oct. 5, 1957; children: Virginia, Alan. BS in Bus., Portland State U., 1961. Claims adjuster, spl., agt, broker Ins. Cos., Wash., Alaska, 1961—; v.p. Pippel Ins. Agy. Inc., Palmer, Alaska, 1971—. Pres. Matanuska-Susitna Borough Sch. Bd., Palmer, Alaska, 1980-86; dir. Alaska Assn. Sch. Bds., 1987. Mem. Ind. Ins. Agts. Am. (state nat. dir. Alaska 1985—, Dimock award 1984, Schweir award 1986), Alaska Ind. Ins. Agts. and Brokers (pres. 1976), Anchorage Ind. Ins. Agts. Assn. (pres. 1971). Republican. Roman Catholic. Home: PO Box 864 Palmer AK 99645-0864

OLSON, CHRISTI ANN, telecommunication consultant; b. Spokane, Wash., Apr. 14, 1956. BA, U. Calif., Davis, 1980; MS, Golden Gate U., 1988; postdoctoral, Fielding Inst., 1989—. Project engr. Harris Corp., San Carlos, Calif., 1982-83; sr. engr. Pacific Bell, San Francisco, 1983-85, group project mgr., 1985-87; pres., owner Comprehensive Design, Oakland, Calif., 1988—; adj. prof. Golden Gate U., 1986—; program advisor extended edn. program San Francisco State U., 1987—. Mem. Saybrook Soc., Bay Area Orgn. Devel. Network, Women in Telecommunications (bd. dirs. San Francisco chpt. 1984-86). Democrat. Roman Catholic. Office: Comprehensive Design 460 A Santa Clara Ave Oakland CA 94610

OLSON, CRAIG ALAN, investment banker; b. Sumter, S.C., Apr. 13, 1960; s. Harold Gordon and Velma Jean (Hanna) O. BA, U. Wash., 1983. Assoc. Drexel Burham Lambert, Seattle, 1983-85, v.p., 1986, 1st v.p., 1987; 1st v.p. corp. services Bateman Eichler, Hill Richards, Seattle, 1988—; bd. dirs. Met. Prodns., 1986-88, Nicholson Systems Seattle, Wash., 1985-88. Pres. Young Rep., 1981-82, sec. Scoliosis Found., 1981-82; bd. dirs. U. Wash., 1982; chpt. advisor Sigma Chi fraternity, Seattle, 1988. Mem. Seattle Bus. Exchange, Rainier Club, Seattle Yacht Club, Washington Athletic Club, Seattle Bachelor Club. Republican. Presbyterian. Office: Bateman Eichler Hill Richards 600 University St Ste 2010 Seattle WA 98101

OLSON, DAVID L., marketing professional; b. Rockford, Ill., June 22, 1937; s. Delbert D. and Lenore B. (Brown) O.; m. Susan C. Babbe, Feb 2, 1964; children: Daniel S., Kari L. BA, San Diego State, 1964. Mktg. dir. Swartz-Linkletter Co., San Diego, 1962-69; v.p. mktg. and group v.p. U.S. Fin., San Diego, 1969-73; exec. v.p. Fla. Land Co., Winter Park, 1973-75; v.p. mktg. U.S. Home Corp., Denver, 1975-79; pres. Olson Mktg. Group, Inc., Denver, 1979—; assoc. cons. Stone Inst., mem. Trends and Strategies Editorial Adv. Bd.; founder, pres. Sales and Mktg. Coun., Denver; founder, chmn. Major Achievers in Merchandising Excellence, Denver; adv. bd. Real Estate and Constrn. U. Denver; lectr. in field. Contbr. articles to various publs. Mem. Nat. Assn. Home Builders (Sales and Mktg. Man of Yr.), Home Builder Assn. of Metro. Denver (Mktg. Man of Yr.), Denver Homebuilders Assn. (Person of Yr.), Soc. of Builder Mktg. Specialists (advisor). Office: Olson Mktg Group Inc 8400 E Prentice Ave Ste 435 Englewood CO 80111

OLSON, DAVID LEROY, university dean; b. Oakland, Calif., Mar. 17, 1942; s. Roy Theodore and Adelia H. (Gustafson) O.; m. Judith Ellen Perrine, Sept. 15, 1963; children: Katherine Louise, Eric Gustaf, Ivan Carl, Anna Christina. BS in Phys. Metallurgy, Wash. State U., 1965; PhD in Materials Sci., Cornell U., 1969; postgrad., Ohio State U., 1972. Registered profl. engr., Colo. Mem. tech. staff Tex. Instruments, Dallas, 1969-70; postdoctoral rsch. assoc. Ohio State U., Columbus, 1970-72; asst. prof. Colo. Sch. Mines, Golden, 1972-75, assoc. prof., 1975-78, prof. metall. engring., 1978—, dean rsch., 1986—, v.p. rsch. devel., 1986—; bd. dirs. Am. Welding Inst., Knoxville, Tenn.; vis. sr. scientist SIN TEF at Norwegian Inst. Tech., 1979; cons. in field. Contbr. articles to profl. jours.; patentee in field. Chmn. materials adv. group com. on Marine Structures, Marine Bd. Nat. Acad. Sci., Washington, 1983—. Amoco Found. awardee, 1982; Ohio State U. postdoctoral fellow, 1971-72. Fellow ASM; mem. Am. Welding Soc., Am. Nuclear Soc., Alpha Sigma Mu, Tau Beta Pi, Sigma Xi, APS, AIME, Am. Ceramic Soc., Nat. Assn. Corrosion Engrs., ASAS, ASTM, Kiwanis (pres. 1981-82). Home: 13943 W 20th Pl Golden CO 80401 Office: Colo Sch of Mines 1500 Illinois St Golden CO 80401

OLSON, DENNIS ISACK, finance professional; b. Fergus Falls, Minn., Oct. 6, 1938; s. Isack and Laura (Kuchenbacher) O.; m. Eleanor Ann Johnson, Mar. 13, 1965; children: Curtis, Douglas, Daniel. BA in Anthropology, U. Minn., 1966. Radar technician USAF, Mpls., 1963-65; missionary Wycliffe Bible Translators, U.S. and S. Am., 1965-82; literacy worker Wycliffe Bible Translators, Globe, Ariz., 1982-88; office mgr. Wycliffe Bible Translators, Thornton, Colo., 1988—; mem.exec. com. No. Am. br. Summer Inst. Linguistics, Thornton, 1986—; bd. dirs. Su Camino Internat., Colorado Springs, Colo., 1983-88. With USAAF, 1956-60. Democrat. Baptist.

OLSON, ELAINE MARY, computer engineer; b. Hackensack, N.J., Dec. 24, 1952; d. Walter John and Frances May (Maguire) Kiernan; m. Maynard Gerald Olson, June 27, 1987. BA in Math., Montclair (N.J.) State Coll., 1975. Computer programmer Bell Telephone Labs., Holmdel, N.J., 1977-80; computer engr. U. Hawaii Inst. for Astronomy, Kula, 1980—; cons. in field. Active Maui Community Theater, Wailuku, Hawaii. Recipient Group Achievement award NASA, 1988. Mem. Digital Equipment Corp. User Soc., Hawaii Govt. Employees Assn. Office: U Hawaii PO Box 209 Kula HI 96790

OLSON, GALE KRISTEN, educator, athletic coach; b. West Point, N.Y., May 16, 1960; d. Kenneth William and Carol Alice (Herbener) O. BA in Chemistry, U. Ariz., 1985, BS in Secondary Edn., 1985; MS in Secondary Edn., No. Ariz. U., 1987. Cert. tchr., Ariz. Substitute tchr. Ampitheater Sch. Dist., Tucson, 1983-85; tchr. math. and computer sci.; volleyball, basketball coach Willcox Pub. Sch. Dist., Willcox, Ariz., 1985-88; 5th grade tchr. Dr. Daniel Bright Elem. Sch., Cottonwood, Ariz., 1988--; ; coordinator for No. Ariz. U. Preprofl. Skills Test (PPST) Navajo Workshop, summer, 1988. Mem. NEA, Ariz. Edn. Assn., Jr. Woman's Club. Republican. Lutheran. Home: PO Box 445 Sedona AZ 86336 Office: Dr Daniel Bright Elem Sch 1500 Montetessero Cottonwood AZ 83623

OLSON, GARY ROBERT, banker; b. Milw., May 9, 1946; s. Ward Louis and Mary Jane (Brown) O.; m. Mia Kristina Sohn, Feb. 26, 1972; children: Kristin Anne, Brian Ward. Student, Loyola U., Rome, 1966-67; AB, Marquette U., 1968; M Internat. Mgmt., Am. Grad. Sch. Internat. Mgmt., Glendale, Ariz., 1973. Instr. Sogang Jesuit U., Seoul, 1968-70, Hankuk U. Fgn. Studies, Seoul, 1971-72; grad. asst. Am. Grad. Sch. Internat. Mgmt., 1972; credit analyst Chase Manhattan Bank, N.A., N.Y.C. and Tokyo, 1973-75; asst. treas. Chase Manhattan Bank, N.A., N.Y.C., 1975-77; 2d v.p. Chase Manhattan Bank, N.A., Madrid, 1977, Paris, 1977-80; v.p., mgr. Regional Banking Office Chase Manhattan Bank, N.A., Chgo., 1980-83; v.p., regional mgr. Case Nat. Corp. Svcs., San Francisco, 1983-87; sr. v.p. Chase Bank Ariz., Phoenix, 1987—. Advisor English program USIS, Seoul, 1969; campus rep. Am. Grad. Sch. Internat. Mgmt., 1986-87, domestic counselor Thunderbird Sch., 1989; vol. Spl. Olympics, Phoenix, 1988; fund drive capt. Phoenix Econ. Growth Corp., 1988. Mem. Robert Morris Assocs. (assoc.), Econ. Club Phoenix, World Trade Club. Republican. Roman Catholic. Office: Chase Bank Ariz 4000 N Central Ave Phoenix AZ 85012

OLSON, GERALD THEODORE, educational consultant; b. Rockford, Ill., Mar. 10, 1928; s. Ernest Hjalmer and Irma Lena (Widgren) O.; B.S., U. San Francisco, 1953; M.A., San Francisco State U., 1960; M.Ed., U. So. Calif., 1964; Ph.D., U. Calif., Berkeley, 1974; m. Jean Vujovich, Aug. 28, 1949; children—Gerald Theodore, Kathleen Elaina Olson Groves, John Ernest, Carol Frances Olson Love. Counselor, tchr., dir. student activities Canyon High Sch., Castro Valley, Calif., 1964-70, also lectr. Calif. State U., Hayward, 1971-72 and instr. Chabot Coll., Hayward, 1964-73; cons. counseling and guidance Colo. Dept. Edn., Denver, 1973; cons. career, vocat. counseling and guidance, ednl. services group Los Angeles County Office of Supt. Schs., 1973—. Served with USMC, 1946-49, with Army Res. and Calif. Army N.G., 1950-81. Cert. secondary sch. teaching, secondary sch. adminstrn., gen. pupil personnel services, community coll., marriage, family and child counseling, Calif. Contbr. articles to profl. jours. NDEA scholar, 1963-64; NIMH trainee, 1971-72; decorated Meritorious Service medal USAR, 1981. Mem. Am. Psychol. Assn., Western Psychol. Assn., Calif. Career Edn. Assn. (pres. 1986-87), Calif. Assn. for Counseling and Devel. (editor Compass newsletter 1982-83, 86-87, pres. 1984-85), Calif. Assn. Measurement and Evaluation in Guidance (pres. 1981-82). Democrat. Home: 3366 Tempe Dr Huntington Beach CA 92649 Office: 9300 E Imperial Hwy Downey CA 90242-2890

OLSON, HILDING HAROLD, surgeon, educator; b. Burlington, Wash., Apr. 30, 1916; s. Adolph and Gerda (Gerdin) O.; m. Donna D. Anderson, Aug. 14, 1943; children: Sheila K. Richardson, Susan L. LeClerq, Daniel L. BS, U. Wash., 1939; MD, U. Oreg., 1943. Diplomate Am. Bd. Surgery. Intern King County Hosp., Seattle, 1944-45, resident, 1945-51, attending surgeon, 1951—; clin. prof. surgery U. Wash., Seattle, 1964-87, emeritus, 1987—; mem. staff Providence Med. Ctr., Harborview Med. Ctr., Swedish Hosp. Med. Ctr., Univ. Hosp.; teaching fellow Dept. Anatomy, U. Oreg., 1940-43; dir. surgical clerkship program U. Wash. Dept. Surgery, 1954-73; dir. residency program Providence Med. Ctr., U. Wash. Dept. Surgery, 1976-87. Contbr. numerous articles to profl. jours. Served with U.S. Army, 1941-43, 46. Recipient Outstanding Teacher award U. Wash. Sch. Medicine, 1985; fellow Am. Cancer Soc., 1950. Fellow Am. Coll. Surgeons; mem. AMA, Western Surg. Assn., Pacific Coast Surg. Assn. (pres. 1982-83), North Pacific Surg. Assn., Seattle Surg. Soc. (pres. 1975), Internat. Soc. Surgeons, King County Med. Assn., Pan Pacific Surg. Assn. Home and Office: 401 100th Ave NE #317 Bellevue WA 98004

OLSON, JANICE LYNN, real estate executive; b. Washington, Feb. 13, 1946; d. Charles Arthur and Jean Elizabeth (Mudd) O.; divorced; 1 child, Robert. Dir. mktg. Homart Devel. Co., San Bernardino, Calif., 1974-76; property mgr. Homart Devel. Co., Brea, Calif., 1976-82; dir. pub. affairs. Homart Devel. Co., Chgo., 1982-85; gen mgr. Homart Devel. Co., Mesa, Ariz., 1985—. Contbr. articles to profl. jours. Active Mesa Growth Com., 1988—; pres. Mesa unit, bd. dirs. Am. Cancer Soc., 1987—. Recipient Jake award Am. Cancer Soc., 1987. Mem. Internat. Coun. Shopping Ctrs. Office: Homart Devel Co 2104 Fiesta Mall Mesa AZ 85202

OLSON, JERRY STEPHEN, research electrical engineer, musician; b. Cleve., Feb. 28, 1951; s. Robert Louis and Frances Elizabeth (Jenkin) O.; m. Judith Lynn James, Sept. 12, 1987. BSEE, U. Cin., 1974. Sr. mem. tech. staff Micro Power Systems, Inc., Santa Clara, Calif., 1974-82; staff engr. Nat. Semicondr. Corp., Santa Clara, 1982; rsch. engr. SERA Solar Corp., Santa Clara, 1982—; prin. tuba Fremont (Calif.)-Newark Symphony, 1978—, San Jose (Calif.) Mcpl. Band, 1985—, Berkeley (Calif.) Symphony Orch., 1986—; cons. Citel Corp., Santa Clara, 1980-83; cons., vendor Stanford U., 1985-87. Mem. Internat. Congress Bldg. Ofcls. (profl.), Am. Fedn. Musicians, Tubists Universal Brotherood Assn., Internat. Trombone Assn. Democrat. Office: SERA Solar Corp 3151 Jay St Santa Clara CA 95054-3308

OLSON, JOHN DAVID, tax consultant; b. Everett, Wash., May 29, 1944; s. John Howard and Barbara (Woodard) O.; m. Christine Estelle Pearson, Aug. 12, 1978; children: Eric, Justin. AA, Everett (Wash.) Community, 1968; BA, Western Wash. State U., 1970. Truck driver Scott Paper Co., Everett, 1965-66; night mgr. Safeway Stores, Everett, 1966-70; tax auditor Wash. Dept. of Revenue, Seattle, 1970-75; audit supr. Wash. Dept. of Revenue, Everett, 1975-81; chief of audit Wash. Dept. of Revenue, Olympia, 1981-86; tax cons., ptnr. Dowell & Assocs., Mercer Island, Wash., 1986—; exec. com. mem., Multi-State Tax Commn., Boulder, Colo., 1984-86, audit com. mem., 1984-86; exec. com. mem. Wash. Career Execs. Program, Olympia, 1983-86. Bd. dirs. Wash. State Employees Credit Union, Olympia, 1983-89, chmn. of bd. 1986. With U.S. Army, 1962-65. Recipient Career Exec. of Yr. nomination, State of Wash., 1986. Republican. Home: 9644 65th Ln SE Olympia WA 98503 Office: Dowell & Associates PO Box 1400 Mercer Island WA 98040

OLSON, KENNETH PAUL, rehabilitation counselor; b. Providence, June 26, 1935; s. Gustave Frederick and Beatrice Evelyn (Backstrom) O.; m. Judith Luellan Hazard, Nov. 12, 1965; children: Glenn Edward Johnson. BA in Sociology, U. Denver, 1960; MA in Sociology, U. Colo., 1973. Cert. rehab. counselor, vocational specialist. Exec. dir. Goodwill Industries, Colorado Springs, Co., 1960-65, San Francisco, 1965, Ft. Worth, 1966-70; counselor II Colo. Div. Rehab., Colorado Springs, 1972-83; pres. Olson Vocational Svcs., Colorado Springs, 1983—; vocational expert Social Security Adminstn., Denver, 1984—; rehab counselor U.S. Dept. Labor, Denver, 1984-89. V.p. Bus. Arts Ctr., Manitou Springs, 1988-89; councilman Manitou Springs, 1975-78; mem. Econ. Devel. Com., Manitou Springs, 1984-86; chmn. Health Adv. Coun., Pikes Peak Region, 1979-80; commr. Commn. for Rehab. Counselor Cert., 1979-85, Bd. for Rehab. Cert., 1984-86. Fellow Nat. Rehab. Counseling Assn.; mem. Colo. Rehab. Counseling Assn. (pres. 1979, named counselor of yr. 1976), Great Plains Rehab. Assn. (pres. 1982-83), Colo. Rehab. Assn., Colo. Vocational Evaluation Work Adjustment Assn., Colorado Springs C. of C., Manitou Springs C. of C. (pres. 1986), Pla. Club. Home: PO Box 215 Manitou Springs CO 80829 Office: Olson Vocat Svcs 701 S Cascade Ave Colorado Springs CO 80903

OLSON, LLOYD WILLIAM, forester, Christmas tree grower; b. Centralia, WA, Oct. 24, 1932; s. Lloyd Raymond and Kathryn Agnew (Scales) O.; m. Lucile Ann Pond, Nov. 3, 1962; children: Daniel Lee, Joseph Peter, Patrick William. BS in Forest Mgmt., U. Wash., 1954; postgrad., U. Alaska, 1973-78. Forester U.S. Forest Service, Vancouver (Wash.), Klamath Falls, (Oreg.), 1954-67, Joseph, Oreg., 1967-71, Juneau, Alaska, 1971-77, Washington, 1979-87; forester Crestwood (Oreg.) Farms, 1987—. Mem. Soc. Am. Foresters, Am. Fisheries Soc., Am. Forestry Assn., Oreg. Small Woodlands Assn. Republican. Presbyn. Home and Office: Crestwood Farms 17054 S Harding Rd Oregon City OR 97045

OLSON, MARIAN KATHERINE, federal agency administrator, publisher, information broker; b. Tulsa, Oct. 15, 1933; d. Sherwood Joseph and Katherine M. (Miller) Lahman; BA in Polit. Sci., U. Colo., 1954, MA in Elem. Edn., 1962; EdD in Ednl. Adminstrn., U. Tulsa, 1969; m. Ronald Keith Olson, Oct. 27, 1956. Tchr. public schs., Wyo., Colo., Mont., 1958-67; teaching fellow, adj. instr. edn. U. Tulsa, 1968-69; asst. prof. edn. Eastern Mont. State Coll., 1970; program assoc. research adminstrn. Mont. State U., 1970-75; on leave with Energy Policy Office of White House, then with Fed. Energy Adminstrn., 1973-74; with Dept. Energy, and predecessor, 1975—, program analyst, 1975-79, chief planning and environ. compliance br., 1979-83; regional dir. Region VIII Fed. Emergency Mgmt. Agy., 1987—; pres. Solar Sense of Colo., Lawyers' Rsch., Bannack Pub. Co. Lawyers Rsch. Contbr. articles in field. Grantee Okla. Consortium Higher Edn., 1969, NIMH, 1974. Mem. Am. Soc. for Info. Sci., Am. Assn. Budget and Program Analysis, Women in Energy, Internat. Assn. Ind. Pubs., Kappa Delta Pi, Phi Alpha Theta, Kappa Alpha Theta. Republican. Home: 707 Poppy Dr Brighton CO 80601 Office: FEMA Denver Fed Ctr Bldg 710 PO Box 25267 Denver CO 80225-0267

OLSON, MARTEEN LESLIE, nurse; b. Oct. 12, 1948; d. Margaret Holcombe; m. Larry Wood Olson, Aug. 23, 1968; children: Tiffany, Lisa. BS in Nursing, U. Pa., 1972, MS in Nursing, 1974; EdD, U. Houston, 1982. Instr. Parkland Coll., Champaign, Ill., 1974-75, Bethany Gynecologists and Obstetricians, Phoenix, 1975-80; mem. faculty Ariz. State U., Tempe, 1975-80; dean, prof. Grand Canyon Coll., Phoenix, 1981-88, Samaritan Coll. Nursing, Phoenix, 1981—; instr. Grand Canyon Coll., summers 1978-80; cons. Baylor U., Waco, Tex., 1986, Samaritan Health Service, Phoenix, 1986. Contbr. articles to profl. jours. Mem. Am. Nurses' Assn., Nat. League for Nursing (cons. 1986), Ariz. Nurses' Assn. (cons. 1987), Ariz. Coun. on Nursing Edn., Ariz. Statewide Coun. on Nursing (chairperson 1987—). Baptist.

OLSON, RHONDA SANDERS, graphic designer; b. Elmhurst, Ill., Nov. 4, 1961; d. Ronald Edward and Patricia Mae (West) SAnders; m. Scot Vernon Olson, Oct. 26, 1985. BA in Communication, Ariz. State U., 1983. Producer, dir. Sta. KAET-TV, Tempe, Ariz., 1982-85; graphics dir. Sta. KPNX-TV, Phoenix, 1985-87; owner, designer Rhonda Graphics, Inc., Phoenix, 1987—; co-organizer computer graphics seminars Nat. Acad. TV Arts and Scis., Phoenix, 1987-88. Created pub. svc. announcements for Am. Cancer Soc., 1988. Mem. Nat. Computer Graphics Assn., Broadcast Designers Assn., Phoenix Soc. of Communicating Arts (Prisma Merit 1986), Spl. Interest Group for Computer Graphics (SIGGRAPH). Republican. Baptist. Office: Rhonda Graphics Inc 2235 W Alice Phoenix AZ 85021

OLSON, RICHARD DEAN, pharmacology educator; b. Rupert, Idaho, June 22, 1949; s. Emerson J. and Thelma Maxine (Short) O.; m. Carol Ann Dyba, Jan. 5, 1974; children: Stephan Jay, David Richard, Jonathan Philip. BS, Coll. Idaho, 1971; postgrad., Idaho State U., 1972-74; PhD, Vanderbilt U., 1978. Instr. Vanderbilt U., Nashville, 1980-81, asst. prof., 1982, head pediatric clin. pharmacology unit, 1982; asst. prof. U. S. Ala., Mobile, 1982-83; acting asst. prof. U. Wash., Seattle, 1984-85, research assoc. prof., 1985—; v.p. Olson, Wong and Walsh Labs., Inc., Lindenhurst, Ill., 1987—; chief cardiovascular pharmacology research VA Med. Ctr., Boise, Idaho, 1984—; hon. dir. cardiovascular research lab. Capital Inst. Medicine, Beijing, Peoples Republic of China, 1986; investigator Am. Heart Assn., Nashville, 1981, NIH, Mobile, 1982; bd. dirs. Idaho affiliate Am. Heart Assn. Contbr. articles to profl. jours. Pres. Fellowship Crusade for Christ, Inc., Nampa, Idaho, 1986. Grantee Am. Heart Assn., 1981, 83, 84, 86, 88, Am. Fedn. Aging Research, Inc., Boise, 1985; VA Merit Review grantee, 1985, 88; NIH trainee, 1975-78; NIH New Investigator 1982; fellow, Am. Fedn. Aging Research, Inc. 1985—, NIH U. Colo., Denver, 1978-80. Mem. AAAS, N.Y. Acad. Scis., Am. Soc. Pharmacology and Exptl. Therapeutics, Am. Heart Assn., Am. Fedn. for Clin. Research, Sigma Xi. Home: 425 N Benewah Nampa ID 83651 Office: VA Med Ctr #151 500 W Fort St Boise ID 83702

OLSON, RICHARD THOMAS, lawyer; b. Yakima, Wash., Oct. 7, 1939; s. Richard Theodore and Virginia Rae (Symonds) O.; m. Carol Anne Weeks, Dec. 2, 1967; 1 child, Katherine Louise. BA in Econs., U. Wash., 1961, JD, 1966. Bar: Wash. 1966. Assoc. Moriarty Olson & Campbell, Seattle, 1966-68, ptnr., 1969-70; ptnr. Moriarty, Mikkelberg, Broz, Wells & Fryer, Seattle, 1971-85, Reed, McClure, Moceri, Thonn & Moriarty, Seattle, 1985—. Bd. dirs. Glaser Found., Seattle, 1975—, Episcopal Charities Appeal, Seattle,

1987—. Capt. U.S. Army, 1961-63, Res. ret. Mem. ABA, Wash. State Bar Assn., Phi Delta Phi (internat. pres. 1981-83), Rainier Club, Rotary (sec. 1986-88). Republican. Home: 6490 NE Monte Vista Bainbridge Island WA 98110 Office: Reed McClure Moceri Thonn & Moriarty 701 5th Ave Seattle WA 98104

OLSON, ROBERT HOWARD, lawyer; b. Indpls., July 6, 1944; s. Robert Howard and Jacquline (Wells) O.; m. Diane Carol Thorsen, Aug. 13, 1966; children: Jeffrey, Christopher. BA in Govt. summa cum laude, Ind. U., 1966; JD cum laude, Harvard U., 1969. Bar: Ohio 1969, Fla. 1980, U.S. Dist. Ct. (no. dist.) Ohio 1970, U.S. Dist. Ct. (no. Dist.) Ind. 1970, U.S. Dist. Ct. (so. Dist.) Ohio 1971, U.S. Supreme Ct. 1973, Ariz. 1985. Assoc. Squire, Sanders & Dempsey, Cleve., 1969, 70-71, 76-81, ptnr., 1981—, ptnr., Phoenix, 1985—; sr. law clk. U.S. Dist. Ct., No. Dist. Ind. 1969-70; chief civil rights div. Ohio Atty. Gen.'s Office, Columbus, 1971-73, chief consumer protection, 1973-75, chief counsel, 1975, 1st asst. (chief of staff), 1975-76; instr. Law Sch., Ohio State U., Columbus, 1974; mem. Cen. Phoenix com. to advise city council and mayor, 1987—; bd. trustees Orpheum Theater Found., 1989—, Ariz. Ctr. Law Pub. Interest, 1989—; bd. dirs., sec. Orpheum Theater Found., 1989—, The Ariz. Ctr. for Law in the Pub. Interest, 1989—. Author monograph on financing infrastructure, 1983; also law rev. articles on civil rights, consumer protection. Treas. Alfred for Mayor Campaign, Shaker Heights, Ohio, 1983; bd. dirs. 1st Unitarian Ch. Phoenix, v.p., 1987-89. Mem. Greater Cleve. Bar Assn. (sec. health law sect. 1984), Am. Acad. Hosp. Attys., Ariz. State Bar Assn., Fla. State Bar Assn., Ohio State Bar Assn., Phi Beta Kappa. Democrat. Home: 5201 E Paradise Dr Scottsdale AZ 85254 Office: 201 N Central Ave Suite 2200 Phoenix AZ 85073

OLSON, RODNEY ELLSWORTH, bacteriologist, business owner; b. Mt. Vernon, Wash., Nov. 12, 1912; s. Charles Eugene Theodore and Angelika Lydia Louise (Anderson) O.; m. Eleanor Olive Englund, Sept. 11, 1943; children: Randall John, Rosalind Louise Spitzer, Suzanne Andrea Appelo, Stanton Charles Gustavus. BS, Wash. State U., 1936. Bacteriologist Skagit Co. Dairymen's Assn., Mt. Vernon, 1936-66; owner Olson Dairy Equipment Co., Mt. Vernon, 1966-81; pres. Olson-McNair Equipment Co., Inc., Mt. Vernon, 1980—; owner Valley Farm Ctr., Mt. Vernon, 1981—, Valley R. V., Mt. Vernon, 1986—. Commr. Skagit Valley Hosp. and Health Ctr., 1955—. Mem. C. of C., Theta Xi Fraternity (pres. 1935-36). Republican. Lutheran. Lodge: Rotary (Mt. Vernon) (bd. mem. 1955-65). Home: 1686 Britt Rd Mount Vernon WA 98273 Office: Olson-McNair Equipment Co Inc 235-7 N 1st St Mount Vernon WA 98273

OLSON, RONALD CHARLES, aerospace executive; b. Sioux Falls, S.D., Jan. 23, 1937; s. Arthur Helmer and Myrtle Esther (Gustafson) O.; m. Barbara Jean Newcomb, Apr. 7, 1957; children: Bradley Charles, Jodi Lynn. AA, North Idaho Coll., 1956; BS in EE, U. Idaho, 1958; grad. sr. exec. mgmt. program, MIT, 1988. Design engr. Boeing Aerospace, Seattle, 1958-72, engring. mgr., 1973-83, chief engr., 1983-84, program mgr., 1985—; mem. engring. adv. bd. U. Idaho Coll. Engring., Moscow, 1988—. Recipient Gen. Ira C. Eaker, Air Force Assn., Vandenburg AFB, 1985. Mem. Boeing Mgmt. Assn. (sec. 1981-85), Big Band Dance Club (instr. 1980-85), Elks. Republican. Home: 1123 E Laurel St Kent WA 98031 Office: Boeing Aerospace PO Box 3999 Seattle WA 98124

OLSON, STEVEN STANLEY, social service executive; b. Longview, Wash., Aug. 5, 1950; s. Robert Martin and Martha Virginia (Duffin) O.; m. Jane Leslie Dailey, May 22, 1981; 1 child, Derek Thomas Dailey. BA, Wash. State U., 1972; MEd, Auburn U., 1977; postgrad., Seattle U., 1981-83. Cert. rehabilitation mgmt. Agrl. extensionist Action/Peace Corps, Popayan, Colombia, 1972-73; supr. Stonebelt Ctr. for the Mentally Retarded, Bloomington, Ind., 1974; adjustment counselor Exceptional Industries, Bowling Green, Ky., 1974-75; vocat. evaluator Exceptional Industries, 1975-76; alcohol counselor E. Ala. Mental Health, Opelika, 1976; intern Auburn Univ./Ptnrs. of the Americas, Guatemala City, Guatemala, 1976; planner, researcher Marion County Mental Health, Salem, Oreg., 1977-79; assoc. dir. Reliable Enterprises, Centralia, Wash., 1979-80; exec. dir. Reliable Enterprises, 1980—; v.p. govt. affairs Rehabilitation Enterprises Wash., Olympia, 1984-86, chair regional rep., 1986-89; treas. Assn. for Retarded Citizens Wash., Olympia, 1983-85, govt. affairs chairperson, 1983-89. Contbr. articles to Vocat. Evaluation and Work Adjustment Bull., 1976, Rehab. World, 1977. Treas. Communities United for Reponsible Energy, Lewis County, Wash., 1979—; vice chairperson Wash. Solar Coun., Olympia, Wash., 1980-83; co-chair Early Childhood Help Orgn., Olympia, 1988. Mem. Am. Assn. Mental Retardation, Assn. for Severely Handicapped, Wash. Assembly for Citizens with Disabilities, Alliance for Children, Youth, and Family. Home: 4333 Maytown Rd SW Olympia WA 98502 Office: Reliable Enterprises 1500 Lum Rd Centralia WA 98531

OLSON, THOMAS JON, computer engineer; b. Virginia, Minn., Aug. 24, 1953; s. Robert James and Gwendolyn Lynette (Hansen) O. BSME, N.D. State U., 1975; MSME, U. Wis., 1977. Registered profl. engr., Minn., N.D. Sr. prin. engr. Honeywell, Inc., Mpls., 1977-84; pres. Olson Computer Systems, Mpls., 1984-87; engring. mgr. Impell Computer Systems subs. Combustion Engring., Berkeley, Calif., 1987-88; mgr. hardware products SysScan, Inc., Cueprtino, Calif., 1988—. Inventor method and apparatus for power load shedding. Communications spl. dep. Hennepin County sheriff's radio and water patrol divs., Mpls., 1979-87; bd. dirs. Mpls. Vocal Consort, 1985—. Mem. Soc. Mfg. Engrs. (sr.), ASME (young engr. of the year 1983). Republican. Lutheran. Home: 505 Shell Pkwy #1306 Redwood City CA 94065 Office: SysScan Inc 1601 S Saratoga-Sunnyvale Rd Cupertino CA 95014

OLSON, TIMOTHY ALLAN, state official; b. Portland, Oreg., July 1, 1952; s. Lloyd Gordon and Emily Pauline (Winchester) O. BA, U. Calif., Santa Barbara, 1977. Dir. internat. program Calif. Energy Commn., Sacramento, 1978—. Democrat. Home: 1712 42d St Sacramento CA 95819 Office: Calif Energy Commn 1516 Ninth St Sacramento CA 95814

OLSON, WILLIAM HERBERT, nuclear medicine physician, administrator; b. Sioux City, Dec. 3, 1925; s. Victor L. and Leona (Hewitt) O.; m. LuEtta Brunn, Sept. 4, 1949; children—Daniel John, Susan Louise. B.A., Sioux Falls Coll., 1949; M.D., State U. Iowa, 1953. Diplomate Am. Bd. Internal Medicine, Am. Bd. Nuclear Medicine. Resident in internal medicine Seaside Meml. Hosp., Long Beach, Calif., 1954-55, Long Beach VA Hosp., 1955-57; practice medicine specializing in internal medicine, Long Beach, 1958-67; dir. dept. nuclear medicine Long Beach Community Hosp., 1967—, chief of staff, 1985-87; cons. nuclear medicine Long Beach VA Hosp., 1958-72; clin. instr. medicine U. Calif.-Irvine, 1962—. Contbr. articles to profl. jours. Ruling elder Convenant Presbyn. Ch., Orange, Calif., 1981. Served with UASSF, 1944-46. Fellow ACP.; mem. Long Beach Soc. Internal Medicine (pres. 1967). Republican. Home: 4609-8 Via La Paloma Orange CA 92669 Office: Long Beach Community Hosp 1720 Termino Ave Long Beach CA 90804

OLSON, WILLIAM MICHAEL, real estate company official, consultant; b. Allentown, Pa., Apr. 14, 1959; s. Robert Sylvan and Mary Jane (Hineman) O.; m. Kathleen Marie Knebel, Jan. ll, 1986. BS cum laude, Ariz. State U., 1982. Cert. shopping ctr. mgr., property mgr., mktg. dir. Internat. Coun. Shopping Ctrs. Regional property and leasing mgr. Del E. Webb Corp., Phoenix, 1982-86; v.p. property mgmt. Wolfswinkel Group, Inc., Mesa, Ariz., 1986-88; regional leasing and ops. mgr. Rouse Co., Phoenix, 1988—. Mem. Inst. Real Estate Mgmt. (cert. property mgr.), Soc. Real Property Administrs., Bldg. Owners and Mgrs. Assn. (bd. dirs. Phoenix 1988-89), Realtor Assocs., Ariz. State U. Alumni Assn., Golden Key. Republican.

OLSON, WILLIAM THOMAS, educator, consultant; b. Coeur d'Alene, Idaho, May 1, 1940; s. William Anthony and Julia Glenn (Hunter) O.; BA, U. N.Mex., 1968; postgrad. U. Va., 1968-72; m. Diana Jean Dodds, Aug. 22, 1962; children: Kristin Ann (dec.), Kira Lynn. Intelligence agt. U.S. Army, 1962-65; asso. editor Newspaper Printing Corp., Albuquerque, 1965-66; news and pub. affairs dir. Sta. KUNM-FM, U. N.M., 1966-68; news person KOAT-TV, Albuquerque, 1968; news dir. WCHV Radio, Charlottesville, Va., 1968-69; moderator, producer Radio-TV Center, U. Va., 1969-73; columnist The Jefferson Jour., Charlottesville, Va., 1972; instr. history U. Va., 1971-73; information specialist Wash. State U. Cooperative Ext. Service, Pullman, 1973-77, instr. Sch. Communications, 1976-77, asst. program dir., info. officer Wash. Energy Ext. Service, 1977-79; dir. Spokane County Head Start, 1979-84; adminstr. Community Colls. of Spokane, 1984—, critical Thinking Project, 1988—; pres. Effective Mgmt. Systems, 1987—. Dir. Ryegrass Sch., Spokane, 1978-84. Bd. dirs. Charlottesville-Albemarle Mental Health Assn., 1969-72; bd. dirs. Charlottesville-Albemarle chpt. ACLU, 1969-71, Spokane chpt., 1983-88; mem. adv. bd. Spokane Pub. Radio, 1983—; pres. Charlottesville-Albemarle Human Relations Council, 1970-71; chairperson Pullman area chpt. ACLU, 1976-79, chmn., 1976-78; dir. Connoisseur Concerts Assn., 1983-86, pres. 1985-86; dir. West Cen. Community Devel. Assn., pres., 1985-86; dir. Spokane Community Ctrs. Found., 1986—; mem. Mayor's budget com. City of Spokane, 1988-89. Served with AUS, 1962-65. Mem. Nat. Council for Resource Devel., Nat. Head Start Dirs. Assn. (region V steering com. chmn. 1981-82, regional sec. 1980). Author TV documentary (with Ken Fielding): The Golden Years?, 1973; film (with B. Dale Harrison and Lorraine Kingdon) New Directions Out of the Culture of Poverty, 1974. Home: E 2018 14th Ave Spokane WA 99202 Office: N 2000 Greene St MS 2010 Spokane WA 99207

OLUM, PAUL, mathematician, former university president; b. Binghamton, N.Y., Aug. 16, 1918; s. Jacob and Rose (Citlen) O.; m. Vivian Goldstein, June 8, 1942 (dec. Mar. 1986); children—Judith Ann, Joyce Margaret, Kenneth Daniel. A.B. summa cum laude, Harvard, 1940, Ph.D. (NRC predoctoral fellow 1946-47), 1947; M.A., Princeton, 1942. Theoretical physicist Manhattan Project, Princeton, 1941-42, Los Alamos Sci. Lab., 1943-45; Frank B. Jewett postdoctoral fellow Harvard, 1947-48, Inst. Advanced Study, 1948-49; mem. faculty Cornell U., Ithaca, N.Y., 1949-74, prof. math., 1957-74, chmn. dept., 1963-66, trustee, 1971-75; prof. math., dean Coll. Natural Scis. U. Tex. at Austin, 1974-76; prof. math., v.p. for acad. affairs, provost U. Oreg., Eugene, 1976-80, acting pres., 1980-81, pres., 1981-89; mem. Inst. Advanced Study, 1955-56; on leave at U. Paris (France) and Hebrew U., Jerusalem, 1962-63; vis. prof. U. Wash., 1970-71. Author monograph, research articles on algebraic topology. Mem. adv. com. Office Ordnance Research, NRC, 1958-61. NSF fellow Stanford, 1966-67. Mem. Am. Math. Soc., AAUP, Math Assn. Am., Phi Beta Kappa, Sigma Xi. Office: U Oreg Main Campus Office of Pres Eugene OR 97403-1226

OLZAK, RICHARD ALBERT, manufacturing executive; b. Ellwood City, Pa., Mar. 30, 1938; s. Albert Frank and Lillian Emma (Lersch) O.; m. Myrna Ann DeGraw, Sept. 22, 1962; children: Eric, Gretchen, Katrin. Grad. high sch., Ellwood City. Pattern maker Nat. Plumbing Fixtures, Ellwood City, 1956-64; die setter Mathew's Conveyer Co., Ellwood City, 1964-66; model maker Boeing Airplane Co., Seattle, 1966-70; from precision assembler to mfg. engr. Sundstrand Data Control, Redmond, Wash., 1971—. Mem. Electronic Mfrs. Assn. Office: Sundstrand Data Control 15001 NE 36 St Redmond WA 98073

O'MALLEY, EDWARD PAUL, physician, consultant; b. Hudson, N.Y., May 30, 1926; s. Thomas Patrick and Helen Mary (Cornell) O. BS, St. John's U., Bklyn., N.Y., 1949; MS, Loyola U., Chgo., 1952, PhD, 1954; MD, SUNY, Bklyn., 1958. Psychiat. cons. dept. of corrections N.Y.C., 1962-68; psychiatrist Cath. Charities, N.Y.C., 1963-68; dir. of mental health Suffolk County Govt., Hauppauge, N.Y., 1968-70; commr. of mental health Orange County, Goshen, N.Y., 1970-72; dir. drug abuse services State of N.Y., Bronx, 1972-78; lic. sch. psychiatrist N.Y.C. Bd. of Edn., 1962-82; chief psychiatry services VA, Huntington, W.Va., 1982-86; med. cons. State of Calif., San Diego, 1986—, psychiat. cons. dept. of corrections, 1987—; asst. prof. psychiatry N.J. Med. Sch., Newark, 1975—; examiner Am. Bd. of Psychiatry and Neurology, Los Angeles, 1980; assoc. prof. psychiatry U. Calif., San Diego, 1980—; prof. psychiatry Marshall U. Sch. of Medicine, Huntington, 1982-86; dir. com. on sea cadets Navy League, San Diego, 1987—. Contbr. articles to profl. jours. Bd. dirs. Suffolk Community Council, Hauppauge, 1968-70, United Fund of Long Island, Huntington, 1968-70. Served to capt. USN, 1978-81. Scholar N. Y. State Coll., 1946-49, SUNY Joseph Collins Med. Sch., 1955-58; Teaching and Research fellow Loyola U., 1952-54. Fellow Am. Psychiat. Assn.; mem. San Diego Psychiat. Soc., Soc. of Med. Cons. to the Armed Forces, Soc. of Military Surgeons of U.S.A., N.Y. Celtic Med. Soc. Roman Catholic. Home: 3711 Alcott St San Diego CA 92106

O'MALLEY, PETER, professional baseball club executive; b. N.Y.C., Dec. 12, 1937; s. Walter F. and Kay (Hanson) O'M.; m. Annette Zacho, July 10, 1971; children: Katherine, Kevin, Brian. B.S. in Econs, U. Pa., 1960. Dir. Dodgertown, Vero Beach, Fla., 1962-64; pres., gen. mgr. Spokane Baseball Club, 1965-66; v.p. Los Angeles Dodgers Baseball Club, 1967-68, exec. v.p., from 1968; pres. Los Angeles Dodgers, Inc., 1970—. Bd. dirs. L.A. Police Meml. Found., L.A. World Affairs Council, Jackie Robinson Found.; vice chmn. bd. govs. L.A. Music Center Performing Arts Council; trustee Little League Found., Washington, Knudsen Found., L.A. Mem. L.A. Area C. of C. (bd. dirs.). Office: LA Dodgers 1000 Elysian Park Ave Los Angeles CA 90012 also: Dodger Stadium Los Angeles CA 90012

OMAN, RICHARD GEORGE, museum curator; b. Salt Lake City, Oct. 15, 1945; s. Dorse Miles and Margaret (Call) O.; m. Susan Staker, May 31, 1970 (div. 1983); children: Sarah Elizabeth, Nathan Bryan, Bevin Marie; m. Pamela Fillmore, Oct. 4, 1984; children: Emily Anne, Lisa Meleana. AA, Big Bend Community Coll., 1965; BA in History, Brigham Young U., 1970; BA in Art History, U. Wash., 1971, postgrad., 1971-75. Dir. audio-visual sect. Seattle Art Mus., 1973-75; mgr. mus. sect., hist. dept. Ch. of Jesus Christ of Latter-day Saints, Salt Lake City, 1975-86; curator acquisitions Mus. Ch. History and Art, Salt Lake City, 1986—; high priest missionary to Quebec and Ontario, 1965-67; v.p., Import Broker, Salt Lake City, 1984—; instr. Brigham Young U., Provo, 1979; cons., Utah State Hist. Soc., Salt Lake City, 1980—, Utah Endowment for Humanities, Salt Lake City, 1981; bd. dirs., Utah Children's Mus., Salt Lake City, 1981-83. Contbg. author: Arts and Inspiration, 1980, Utah Folk Art, 1980; contbr. articles to numerous publs. Asst. commr., Salt Lake City area Boy Scouts Am., 1979-82; chmn. Cen. City Parks Com., Salt Lake City, 1980-83; cons. L.D.S. Hosp. Found., Salt Lake City, 1984; cons., judge, Dixie Coll. Ann. Art Exhbn., St. George, Utah, 1987-89, Springville (Utah) Mus. Art; cons. art mus., Brigham Young U., 1984-87; mem. sesquicentennial com., Mormon Ch., Salt Lake City, 1980. Mem. Utah Mus. Assn. (pres. 1979-81), Am. Assn. State and Local History, Am. Assn. Mus., Mormon History Assn. Republican. Mem. Reorganized Ch. of Jesus Christ of Latter-day Saints. Home: 3266 Bon View Dr Salt Lake City UT 84109 Office: Mus Ch History and Art 45 N West Temple St Salt Lake City UT 84109

OMENN, GILBERT STANLEY, university dean, physician; b. Chester, Pa., Aug. 30, 1941; s. Leonard and Leah (Miller) O.; m. Martha Darling; children: Rachel Andrea, Jason Montgomery, David Matthew. A.B., Princeton U., 1961; M.D., Harvard U., 1965; Ph.D. in Genetics, U. Wash., 1972. Intern Mass. Gen. Hosp., Boston, 1965-66; asst. resident in medicine Mass. Gen. Hosp., 1966-67; research assoc. NIH, Bethesda, Md., 1967-69; fellow U. Wash., 1969-71, asst. prof. medicine, 1971-74, assoc. prof., 1974-79, Howard Hughes med. inst., 1976-77, prof., 1979—, prof. environ. health, 1981—, chmn. dept., 1981-83, dean Sch. Pub. Health and Community Medicine, 1982—; bd. dirs. Rohm & Haas Co., Amgen, Ecova Corp., BioTechniques Labs. Inc., Immune Response Corp., Clean Sites, Inc.; White House fellow/spl. asst. to chmn. AEC, 1973-74; assoc. dir. Office Sci. and Tech. Policy, The White House, 1977-80; assoc. dir. human resources Office Mgmt. and Budget, 1980-81; vis. sr. fellow Wilson Sch. Pub. and Internat. Affairs, Princeton U., 1981; sci. and pub. policy fellow Brookings Instn., Washington, 1981-82; cons. govt. agys., Lifetime Cable Network; mem. environ. adv. com. Rohm & Haas, Rene Dubos Ctr. for Human Environments, AFL-CIO Workplace Health Fund. Co-author: Clearing the Air, Reforming the Clean Air Act, 1981. Editor: (with others) Genetics, Environment and Behavior: Implications for Educational Policy, 1972; Genetic Control of Environmental Pollutants, 1984; Genetic Variability in Responses to Chemical Exposure, 1984, Environmental Biotechnology: Reducing Risks from Environmental Chemicals through Biotechnology, 1988; editorial bd., assoc. editor Cancer Rsch. Environ. Biotech., 1988, Am. Jour. Med. Genetics, Cancer Research, Environmental Research, Am. Jour. Preventive Medicine, Am. Jour. Health Promotion; contbr. articles on cancer prevention, human biochem. genetics, prenatal diagnosis of inherited disorders, susceptibility to environ. agts., cancer prevention, clin. medicine and health policy to profl. publs. Mem. President's Council on Spinal Cord Injury; mem. Nat. Cancer Adv. Bd., Nat. Heart, Lung and Blood Adv. Council, Wash. State Gov.'s Commn. on Social and Health Services, Ctr. for Excellence in Govt.; chmn. awards panel Gen. Motors Cancer Research Found.; chmn. bd. Environ. Studies and Toxicology, Nat. Rsch. Coun.; mem. Bd. Health Promotion and Disease Prevention, Inst. Medicine; mem. adv. com. Woodrow Wilson Sch., Princeton U.; trustee Pacific Sci. Ctr., Fred Hutchinson Cancer Research Ctr., Seattle Symphony Orch., Seattle Youth Symphony Orch., Seattle Chamber Music Festival, Santa Fe Chamber Music Festival; chmn. rules com. Democratic Conv., King County, Wash., 1972. Served with USPHS, 1967-69. Recipient Research Career Devel. award USPHS, 1972; White House fellow, 1973-74. Fellow ACP, Hastings Ctr.; mem. White House Fellows Assn., Am. Soc. Human Genetics, Western Soc. Clin. Research, Soc. Study Social Biology, Inst. Medicine of Nat. Acad. Sci. Jewish. Home: 5100 NE 55th Seattle WA 98105 Office: U Wash Dean Sch Pub Health SC-30 Seattle WA 98195

OMHOLT, BRUCE DONALD, product designer, mechanical engineer, consultant; b. Salem, Oreg., Mar. 27, 1943; s. Donald Carl and Violet Mae (Buck) O.; m. Mavis Aronow, Aug. 18, 1963 (div. July 1972); children—Madison, Natalie; m. 2d, Darla Kay Faber, Oct. 27, 1972; 1 son, Cassidy. B.S.M.E., Heald Coll. Engring., San Francisco, 1964. Real estate salesman R. Lea Ward and Assocs., San Francisco, 1962-64; sales engr. Repco Engring., Montebello, Calif., 1964; in various mfg. engring. and mgmt. positions Ford Motor Co., Rawsonville, Saline, Owosso and Ypsilanti, Mich., 1964-75; chief engr. E. F. Hauserman Co., Cleve., 1975-77; dir. design and engring. Am. Seating Co., Grand Rapids, Mich., 1977-80; pres. Trinity Engring., Grand Rapids, Mich., 1980-81, Rohnert Park, Calif., 1981—; 1986 U.S. Patent For Vertical Mitre Machine; cons. mfg. U.S., fgn. patentee carrier rack apparatus, motorcycle improvements, panels.

OMURA, JIMMY KAZUHIRO, electrical engineer; b. San Jose, Calif., Sept. 8, 1940; s. Shomatsu and Shizuko Dorothy (Takesaka) O.; divorced; children: Daniel, Dawn. B.S., MIT, 1963, M.S., 1963; Ph.D. (NSF fellow 1963-66), Stanford U., 1966. Research engr. Stanford Research Inst., 1966-69; mem. faculty UCLA, 1969—; founder, chmn. bd. Cylink Corp., Sunnyvale, Calif., 1983—; cons. to industry and govt. Co-author: Principles of Digital Communication and Coding, 1979, Spread Spectrum Communications, Vols. I, II, III, 1985; contbr. articles profl. jours. NSF grantee, 1970-78. Fellow IEEE (info. theory group). Office: Cylink Corp 110 S Wolfe Rd Sunnyvale CA 94086

OMURO, ERIC MITSUO, computer executive, consultant; b. Honolulu, Dec. 9, 1960; s. Wayne Shigeo and Ruth Masuko (Kochi) O.; m. Deborah Lum, Jan. 23, 1988. BS, U. Hawaii, 1982. Software devel. mgr. Hewlett-Packard, MRIC, Cupertino, Calif., 1982-88; v.p. ops. Complimate, Cupertino, 1988—; owner Omuro Enterprises, Sunnyvale, Calif., 1986—. Mem. Data Processing Mgmt. Assn. Republican. Office: Complimate Inc 20430 Town Ctr #5J2 Cupertino CA 95014

O'NAN, LAWRENCE WAYNE, fundraising executive; b. Grand Junction, Colo., Mar. 11, 1944; s. Lawrence Amos and Ida Frances (Garner) O'N.; m. Patricia Ellen Menghini, May 2, 1970; children: Caroline Irene, Jessica Leigh. AA, Mesa Coll., 1964; BS in English Edn., U. Colo., 1966; cert. completion, Inst. Biblical Studies, 1970. Sign artist O'Nan Signs, Grand Junction, 1962-66; student counselor Campus Crusade for Christ, San Bernadino, Calif., 1966-68; music adminstr. Campus Crusade for Christ, San Bernadino, 1968-72, dir. devel., 1972-84; v.p. stewardship strategies Mgmt. Devel. Assocs., Orange, Calif., 1984—; pres. Andy Ant Prodns., Inc., Lakewood, Colo., 1986—. Author: Giving Yourself Away, 1984; creator Andy Ant Books, 1987. Chmn. bd. Judson Bapt. Ch., San Bernadino, 1986-88. Mem. Am. Profl. Resources (bd. dirs. 1986—), Nat. Network of Youth Ministers (chmn. bd. San Diego chpt. 1988, chmn. bd. Asia Impact 1989—). Republican. Office: Mgmt Devel Assocs 1744 W Katella Ste 22 Orange CA 92667

ONDRIK, JEANENE CAPSHAW, realtor; b. Dallas, Nov. 6, 1946; d. David Herman and Pauline (Myers) Capshaw; m. Michael Anthony Ondrik, Jan. 28, 1967; 1 child, David Anthony. BA, Ind. U., 1969; MBA, U. Phoenix, Albuquerque, 1988. Research assoc. Ind. U., Bloomington, 1969-76; instr. natural childbirth Monroe County Childbirth Assn., Bloomington, 1976-78; nutrition counselor Nutri-Health, Albuquerque, 1983-84; adminstr. Nuclear Pharmacy, Inc., Albuquerque, 1985-86; realtor Hooten/Stahl, Inc., Albuquerque, 1988--. Sec. bd. dirs. N. Mex. Boys and Girls Ranch, Belen, 1982-88; finance dir., alumni advisor, program dir., seminar counselor N. Mex. leadership seminar Hugh O'Brian Found., 1982--; recognition liaison person Eisenhower PTO, Albuquerque, 1988--. Mem. Albuquerque Bd. Realtors, Women's Council Realtors, Network for Profl. Devel., Nat. Fedn. Women's Clubs (N. Mex. pub. affairs chmn. 1982-84), Woman's Club (pres. 1980-82). Office: Hooten Stahl Inc 2051 Wyoming NE Albuquerque NM 87112

O'NEAL, HARRIET ROBERTS, psychologist, psycholegal consultant; b. Covington, Ky., Dec. 28, 1952; d. Nelson E. and Georgia H. (Roberts) O'N.; m. Michael Coy Acree, Oct. 5, 1985 (div. Dec. 1986). Student, U. Paris Sorbonne, 1972; BA in Psychology, Hollins Coll., 1974; JD, U. Nebr., 1978, MA in Psychology, 1980, PhD in Psychology, 1982. Program dir., therapist Richmond Maxi Ctr., San Francisco, 1979-81; clin. coordinator, therapist Pacifica (Calif.) Youth Service Bur., 1981-83; staff psychologist Kaiser-Permanente Med. Ctr., Walnut Creek, Calif., 1983—; psycholegal cons., Nebr., Calif., 1987—; oral exam commr. Calif. Bd. Behavioral Sci. Examiners, Sacramento, 1982—; pvt. practice psychotherapy, Pleasant Hill, Calif., 1985—, Lafayette, Calif., 1987—; psycholeg.l cons., presenter San Francisco State U., 1980, U. Calif., San Francisco, 1980, VA Med. Ctr., San Francisco, 1983. Cons. Nebr. Gov.'s Commn. on Status of Women, 1975, 78. NIMH fellow, 1974-79. Mem. Am. Psychol. Assn., Calif. Psychol. Assn., Phi Beta Kappa, Psi Chi. Club: Commonwealth (San Francisco). Home: 286 Park Lake Circle Walnut Creek CA 94598 Office: Kaiser-Permanente Med Ctr Mental Health Dept 1425 S Main St Walnut Creek CA 94596

O'NEIL, MARGARET CLARE, nurse; b. Grangeville, Idaho, Nov. 1, 1957; d. Lewis Kelsey and Edith Linnea (Ranstrom) Smith; m. Douglas M. O'Neil, June 7, 1980; children: Michael Keith, Trevor Kellen, Megan Kathleen. BSN, Idaho State U., 1980. RN, Wash. Staff nurse St. Patrick's Hosp., Missoula, Mont., 1980-87, Kittitas Valley Community Hosp., Ellensburg, Wash., 1987—. Mem. Am. Nurses Assn., Wash. State Nurses Assn., Order of Eastern Star, Alpha Chi Omega. Republican. Lutheran. Office: Kittitas Valley Community Hosp 603 Chestnut St Ellensburg WA 98826

O'NEILL, MICHAEL FOY, business educator; b. Milw., Apr. 16, 1943; s. Edward James and Marcellian (Wesley) O'N.; m. Karen Lynn Shoots, June 13, 1968; children: Kristine, Brenna. BBA, Ohio State U., 1966; PhD in Bus. Adminstrn., U. Oreg., 1978. Cons. Robert E. Miller and Assocs., San Francisco, 1969-73; mem. faculty Calif. State U., Chico, 1971-73, 1980—, U. Oreg., Eugene, 1974-77, U. Ariz., Tucson, 1977-79; pres. Decision Sci. Inst., Atlanta, 1986-87, v.p., 1985-86. Contbr. articles to profl. jours. Served with U.S. Army, 1962-68. Recipient Dean's Research award Calif. State U. Chico, 1981. Home: 2819 North Ave Chico CA 95926 Office: Calif State U Dept Fin and Mktg Chico CA 95926

O'NEILL, NORAH ELLEN, airline pilot; b. Seattle, Aug. 23, 1949; d. John Wilson and Bertha Ellen (Moore) O'N.; m. Scott Reynolds, Jan. 31, 1970 (div. Apr. 1973); m. Scott Edward Byerley, Jan. 29, 1983; children: Cameron, Bren Maxey. Student, U. Calif., Santa Barbara, 1967-68, San Diego State U., 1868-70; BS in Profl. Aeros., Embry-Riddle Aero. U. Lic. airline transport pilot (comml., instrument instr.). Flight instr. Reynolds Aviation, Anchorage, 1973; flight instr. Alaska Cen. Air, Fairbanks, 1973-74, mail, commuter, medivac pilot, 1974-76; DC-8 pilot Flying Tigers, Los Angeles, Seattle, N.Y.C., 1976-80; 747 pilot Flying Tigers, Los Angeles, 1980—. Mem. Airline Pilots Assn., Women Airline Pilots Soc. (co-founder 1978, v.p. 1979-80), The 99's (hon.). Home: PO Box 1504 Walla Walla WA 99362 Office: Flying Tigers 7401 World Way W Los Angeles CA 90009

O'NEILL, PETER SMITH, development company executive; b. Flushing, N.Y., Mar. 24, 1937; s. Donald Derickson and Elizabeth (Smith) O'N.; m.

Mary Leslie, Apr. 2, 1960 (div. 1981); children: Karen, Cissy, Derick, Megan; m. Barrie Connolly, Nov. 27, 1983. Sales engr. Aluminum Co. of Am., Chgo., 1959-63; sr. v.p. Boise (Idaho) Cascade Corp., 1965-76; owner, operator Rapon Investments, Inc., Boise, 1971-84; dir. Sat. Corp. & Aragon, Dania, Fla., 1972-86; ptnr., founder Louie's Pizza & Italian Restaurant, Boise, 1983-87; creator, owner River Run Devel. Co., Boise, 1977-86, pres., chief exec. officer, 1986—; pres. Columbia-Willamette Devel. Co., Portland, Oreg., 1988—. Chmn. bd. dirs. Boise Redevelopment Agy., 1984-87; bd. dirs. Boise Future Found., 1983—; past mem. policy adv. for Joint Ctr. for Urban Studies of MIT and Harvard U.; bd. trustees Nat. Housing Ctr. Council; active various charitable orgns. Mem. World Bus. Council, Urban Land Inst., Chief Exec. Orgn., Arid Club. Office: Columbia-Willamette Devel 920 SW Third Ave Ste 100 Portland OR 97204 also: River Run Devel Co 671 E River Park Ln Ste 200 Boise ID 83706

O'NEILL, SALLIE BOYD, educator, business owner; b. Ft. Lauderdale, Fla., Feb. 17, 1926; d. Howard Prindle and Sarah Frances (Clark) Boyd; AA, Stephens Coll., 1945; m. Roger H. Noden, July 8, 1945; children: Stephanie Ann Ballard, Ross Hopkins Noden; m. Russell R. O'Neill, June 30, 1967. Course coord. UCLA Extension, 1960-72, specialist continuing edn. dept. human devel., acad. appointment, 1972-83; pres. Learning Adventures, Inc., 1985-86; v.p., chief fin. officer The Learning Network, Inc., 1985-86; ednl. cons., 1986—. Sculptor, 1987—. Bd. dirs. Everywoman's Village, Vn Nuys, 1988—; mem. friends of the ctr. for the study of women and women's studies UCLA. HEW Women's Edn. Equity grantee, 1976-77. Mem. Nat. Univ. Continuing Edn. Assn., Women in Bus. Inc. (v.p., bd. dirs. 1976-77, 86-87). Democrat. Home: 15430 Longbow Dr Sherman Oaks CA 91403

O'NEILL, TIMOTHY THOMAS, moving and storage executive; b. Portland, Oreg., Aug. 18, 1934; s. Peter Francis and Lucile (Antoinette) O'N.; m. Cynthia Jo Barrows, Aug. 4, 1962; children: Catherine, Elizabeth. BSc, Santa Clara U., 1956. Mgmt. trainee Sears Roebuck, Portland, 1956; pres. O'Neill Transfer Co., Inc., Portland, 1958—; cons. Cert. Moving Consultants, Portland, 1982—; mem. Oregonian Bus. Forum, Portland, 1988-89. Sec. Northwest Indsl. Neighborhood Assn., Portland, 1980-82. 1st Lt. U.S. Army, 1956-58. Mem. Metro. Bus. Assn., Oreg. Draymen and Wholesale Assn. (pres. 1973-74), Portland C. of C., Delta Nu Alpha, Elks. Republican. Roman Catholic. Office: O'Neill Transfer Co Inc 2233 NW 22d Ave Portland OR 97210

ONGARO, MARIO PETER, priest; b. Verona, Italy, Apr. 7, 1926; came to U.S., 1947; s. Giuseppe and Giulia (Bonfante) O. BA, Athenaeum of Ohio, 1951; MA, Xavier U., 1961; MLS, U. Mich., 1964. Ordained priest Roman Cath. Ch., 1951; lic. psychologist, Ohio. Pastoral ministry Pala Indians, San Diego, 1956-58; instr. classics Sacred Heart Sem., Monroe, Mich., 1952-56, instr. philosophy classics, 1961-64; instr. classics Sacred Heart Sem., Cin., 1958-61, sch. counselor, 1964-68; adminstr. Comboni Mission Ctr., Cin., 1968-83; psychologist, educator Casa Comboni, Los Angeles, 1983-87; vice provincial superior Provincial Hdqrs., Cin., 1987—, dir. personnel, 1981—; mem. com. re-writing constitutions Comboni Missionaries, Rome, 1976-79, provincial counselor, 1979-84. Mem. Am. Psychol. Assn., Ohio Psychol. Assn., Am. Orthopsychiat. Assn., Soc. Personality Assessment. Home and Office: 8108 Beechmont Ave Cincinnati OH 45255

ONGCAPIN, JENNIFER FLORENDO, dentist; b. Manila, May 2, 1960; came to U.S., 1972.; d. Leopoldo T. and Eleanor (Florendo) O. BA in Psychology, UCLA, 1983; DDS, U. of the Pacific, 1986. Pvt. practice dentistry, L.A., 1986—. Mem. ADA, L.A. Dental Soc. Office: 579 S Fairfax Ave Los Angeles CA 90036

ONO, JON RYOICHI, lawyer; b. Honolulu, July 11, 1946; s. Nobuichi and Mutsuko (Yano) O.; m. Yvonne M.H. Sue, Aug. 10, 1969; children: Yvette Mei, Kelvin Nobuichi. BA, U. Hawaii, 1968; JD, U. San Francisco, 1971. Bar: Hawaii 1971, U.S. Dist. Ct. Hawaii 1971, U.S. Ct. Appeals 1971, U.S. Supreme Ct. 1982. Dep. pros. atty. Office Pros. Atty. County Hawaii, Hilo, 1971-74, first dep. pros. atty., 1974-78; pros. atty. Office Pros. Atty. County Hawaii, 1978—; lectr. U. Hawaii, Hilo Coll., 1973-84. Served to 1st lt. U.S. Army, 1968-72. Mem. Hawaii Pros. Attys. Assn. (past pres.), Hawaii State Bar Assn., Hawaii County Bar Assn. (pres. 1980), Nat. Dist. Attys. Assn., Nat. Orgn. for Victimes Assistance, Phi Delta Phi. Democrat. Lodge: Lions. Office: Office Pros Atty 34 Rainbow Dr Hilo HI 96720

ONOROFSKI, MARK ALAN, construction company executive; b. Denver, Sept. 6, 1950; s. Peter Paul and Emaline Loretta (Ellerman) O.; m. Susan Adair Fowler, Apr. 25, 1976; 1 child, Jaime Lynn. BS, Colo. State U., 1974. Constrn. engr. Climax (Colo.) Molybdenum Co., 1976-79; gen. contractor Denver, 1979-83; constrn. engr. Stapleton Internat. Airport, Denver, 1983-85; v.p. constrn. Custom Bldrs. and Remodlers, Inc., Leadville, Colo., 1986—. Home: 6900 W Quincy Ave 5A Littleton CO 80123 Office: Custom Bldrs Rem Inc PO Box 906 Leadville CO 80461

ONOROFSKIE, STEPHEN ANTHONY, construction company executive; b. Denver, July 16, 1947; s. Peter Paul and Emaline Lorreta (Ellerman) O.; m. Deborah Jean Spies, May 28, 1977; children: Stephenie, Angela. EM, Colo. Sch. of Mines, Golden, 1970, MS, 1971. Project engr. Cleveland Cliffs Iron Co., Ishpeming, Mich., 1968; surveyor A.A. Engrs., Denver, 1969; project engr. Consolidated Coal Co., Pinckneyville, Ill., 1970; devel. engr. Amay Inc., Climay, Colo., 1971-76, formean, 1976-86; pres. Custom Builders and Remodelers, Inc., Leadville, Colo., 1986—. Chmn. Am. Cancer Soc., Leadville, 1973; sec. Annunciation Ch. Parrish Coun., Leadville, 1986—; pres. Sylvan Lakes Water & Sanitation Dist., 1984-88. Mem. Colo. Sch. Mines Alumni Assn., Scabbarh and Blade, Sigma Gamma Epsilan, Tau Beta Pi, Sigma NU, BPEO. Democrat. Roman Catholic. Home: 136 Shadow Valley Dr Leadville CO 80461 Office: Custom Bldrs Rem Inc PO Box 906 Leadville CO 80461

ONSKT, NANCY RAE, systems engineer; b. Findlay, Ohio, Apr. 17, 1939; d. Raymond E. and Bonita M. (Leary) O. Student U. Toledo, 1966, Owens Tech. Coll., 1972. Order entry supr. Four-Phase, Cupertino, Calif., 1974-76; mgr. mktg. systems, Fairchild, San Jose, Calif., 1976-81; sr. product mgr. Savin, Sunnyvale, Calif., 1981-82; MIS mgr. Inmac Corp., Santa Clara, Calif., 1982-85; system engr. Hewlett-Packard, Santa Clara, 1985—; systems cons. System Application Computer Svcs., Santa Clara, 1976—. Mem. NOW, Assn. System Mgmt., Summit Orgn., Women's Found., Women's Entrepreneur Assn. Democrat. Roman Catholic. Home: 2404 Golf Links Circle Santa Clara CA 95050

ONSTOTT, EDWARD IRVIN, research chemist; b. Moreland, Ky., Nov. 12, 1922; s. Carl Ervin and Jennie Lee (Foley) O.; m. Mary Margaret Smith, Feb. 6, 1945; children—Jenifer, Peggy Sue, Nicholas, Joseph. B.S. in Chem. Engring., U. Ill., 1944, M.S. in Chemistry, 1948, Ph.D. in Inorganic Chemistry, 1950. Chem. engr. Firestone Tire & Rubber Co., Paterson, N.J., 1944, 46; research chemist Los Alamos Nat. Lab., 1950—, now cons. Patentee in field. Served with C.E., AUS, 1944-46. Fellow AAAS, Am. Inst. Chemists; mem. Am. Chem. Soc., Electrochem. Soc., N.Y. Acad. Scis., Internat. Assn. Hydrogen Energy, Rare Earth Research Confs., Izaak Walton League. Republican. Methodist. Home: 225 Rio Bravo Los Alamos NM 87544 Office: Los Alamos Nat Lab MS Los Alamos NM 87545

O'PATRY, DAVID JOSEPH, obstetrician, gynecologist, educator; b. Cleve., Feb. 19, 1942; s. John Joseph and Rose O'Patry; divorced; children; Bryan, Sean, Kelley, Megan, Daryn, Courteney. BS, Capital U., 1965; MD, Ohio State U., 1969. Commn. ensign USN, 1968, advanced through grades to comdr., 1975, resigned, 1977; intern U.S. Naval Hosp., San Diego, 1969-70, resident in ob-gyn., 1970-73, staff physician, 1975-77; staff physician U.S. Naval Regional Med. Ctr., Guam, 1973-75; staff physician Kaiser Permanente Med. Ctr., San Diego, 1977—, asst. chief ob-gyn., 1982-86; asst. prof. dept. ob-gyn. U. Calif. Med. Ctr., San Diego, 1985—; pres. Prosperity Dynamics, San Diego, 1976—. Fellow Am. Coll. Ob-Gyn. Republican. Office: Kaiser Permanente Med Ctr 8010 Parkway Dr La Mesa CA 92041

OPITZ, JOHN MARIUS, clinical geneticist, pediatrician; b. Hamburg, Germany, Aug. 15, 1935; came to U.S., 1950, naturalized, 1957; s. Friedrich and Erica Maria (Quadt) O.; m. Susan O. Lewin; children: Leigh, Teresa, John, Chrisanthi, Felix. BA, State U. Iowa, 1956, MD, 1959; DSc (hon.), Mont. State U., 1983; MD (hon.), U. Kiel, Fed. Republic of Germany, 1986. Diplomate Am. Bd. Pediatrics, Am. Bd. Med. Genetics. Intern, State U. Iowa Hosp., 1959-60, resident in pediatrics, 1960-61; resident and chief resident in pediatrics U. Wis. Hosp., Madison, 1961-62; fellow in pediatrics and med. genetics U. Wis., 1962-64, asst. prof. med. genetics and pediatrics, 1964-69, assoc. prof., 1969-72, prof., 1972-79; dir. Wis. Clin. Genetics Ctr., 1974-79; clin. prof. med. genetics and pediatrics U. Wash., Seattle, 1979—; adj. prof. medicine, biology, history and philosophy, vet. rsch. and vet. sci. Mont. State U., Bozeman, 1979—; adj. prof. pediatrics, med. genetics U. Wis., Madison, 1979—; coordinator Shodair Mont. Regional Genetic Svcs. Program, Helena, 1979-82; chmn. dept. med. genetics Shodair Children's Hosp., Helena, 1983—; Farber lectr. Soc. Pediatric Pathology, 1987. Author 12 books; founder, editor-in-chief Am. Jour. Med. Genetics, 1977—; mng. editor European Jour. Pediatrics, 1977-85; contbr. numerous articles on clin. genetics. Mem. German Acad. Scientists Leopoldina, Am. Soc. Human Genetics, Am. Pediatric Soc., Soc. Pediatric Rsch., Am. Bd. Med. Genetics, Birth Defects Clin. Genetic Soc., Am. Inst. Biol. Scis., Am. Soc. Zoologists, AAAS, Teratology Soc., Genetic Soc. Am., European Soc. Human Genetics, Soc. Study Social Biology, Am. Acad. Pediatrics, German Soc. Pediatrics (corr.), Western Soc. Pediatrics Research, Italian Soc. Med. Genetics, Sigma Xi. Democrat. Roman Catholic. Home: 579 2d St Helena MT 59601 Office: Shodair Children's Hosp 840 Helena Ave Helena MT 59601

OPPEDAHL, JOHN FREDRICK, newspaper editor; b. Duluth, Minn., Nov. 9, 1944; s. Walter H. and Lucille (Hole) O.; m. Alison Owen, 1975 (div. 1983); m. Gillian Coyro, Feb. 14, 1987. B.A., U. Calif., Berkeley, 1967; M.S., Columbia U., 1968. Reporter San Francisco Examiner, 1967; reporter Detroit Free Press, 1968-75, city editor, 1975-80, exec. city editor, 1981, exec. news editor, 1981-82, asst. mng. editor, 1983; nat. editor, asst. mng. editor Dallas Times Herald, 1983-87; mng. editor/news L.A. Herald Examiner, 1987-89; mng. editor Ariz. Republic, Phoenix, 1989—. Mem. Am. Soc. Newspaper Editors, AP Mng. Editors. Home: 4565 E Lafayette Blvd Phoenix AZ 85018 Office: 120 E Van Buren Phoenix AZ 85004

ORAM, JOSEPH B., physician; b. Stowe, Pa., Oct. 3, 1925; s. Harold Joseph and Georgia Mary (Reger) Oram; m. Louise Catherine Papp, Nov. 14, 1970; children: Susannah Yost, John Joseph. Asst. clin. prof. dept. medicine U. Calif. Med. Ctr., San Francisco, 1962-72; coun. mem. for profl. svc. commn. Calif. Soc. Internal medicine, San Francisco, 1976-77; pres. East Bay Soc. Internal Medicine, Oakland, Calif., 1977-78; chmn. dept. Med. Vesper Meml. Hosp., San Leandro, Calif., 1978-79; chmn. various coms. Med. Vesper Meml. Hosp., 1964—; mem. med. staff Physicians Community Hosp, Humana Hosp. Asst. coach Alameda (Calif.) Soccer Team, 1980-81, sponsor, asst. coach Little League Baseball Team, Alameda, 1984—. Mem. Calif. Med. Soc., Alameda Contra Costa Med. Soc. Democrat. Methodist. Clubs: Commonwealth (San Francisco); Harbor Bay Isle (Alameda). Lodges: Shriners, Masons. Home: 1306 Sherman St Alameda CA 94501 Office: 237 Estudillo Ave San Leandro CA 94577

ORDYNSKY, GEORGE, optometrist; b. Feldsberg, Austria, June 20, 1944; came to U.S. 1952; s. Viacheslav Leonidovich and Galina Alexandrovna (Plutalov) O.; m. Carol-Lyn Grace Freeark, Jan. 29, 1968; 1 child, Lara. BS, U. Colo., 1969; MA, Webster U., St. Louis, 1977; OD, So. Coll. Optometry, 1983; postgrad. U. So. Calif., 1972-73. Physicist, project officer Space and Missile Sys. Orgn., L.A., 1969-73; commd. USAF, 1966, advance through grades to capt., 1980; optometrist Noble Army Hosp., Ft. McClellan, Ala., 1983-86; chief optometry Eye Clinic Anniston (Ala.) Army Depot, 1984-86; cons. indsl. vision Ft. Huachuca & Yuma Proving Ground, Ariz., 1986—; cons. eye safety Occupational health Clinic, Ft. Huachuca, 1986—; chief optometry Yuma Proving Ground Clinic, 1986—, R.W. Bliss Army Hosp., Ft. Huachuca, 1986—. Capt. U.S. Army, 1983-86, maj. U.S. Army, 1986—. Decorated Air Force Commendation medal. Fellow Am. Coll. Optometric Physicians; mem. So. Ariz. Optometric Soc. (bd. dirs. 1988—), Sigma Alpha Sigma, Beta Sigma Kappa. Republican. Eastern Orthodox Ch. Avocations: chess, astronomy. Home: 15 Sonoita Patagonia AZ 85624 Office: MEDDAC PO Box 975 Fort Huachuca AZ 85613-0975

O'REILLY, JOHN F., lawyer, state agency administrator; b. St. Louis, July 23, 1945; s. John Francis and Marie Agnes (Cooney) O'R.; m. Rene E. Lee, June 24, 1967; children: Molly, Bryan, Erin, Timothy. BS, St. Louis U., 1967, JD cum laude, 1969; MBA cum laude, U. Nev., Las Vegas, 1974. Bar: Mo. 1969, U.S. Dist. Ct. Nev. 1972; lic. real estate broker. Auditor, tax acct. Ernst & Whinney, St. Louis, 1966-69; pres. Keefer, O'Reilly & Ferrario, Las Vegas, Nev., 1972—; atty. Nev. Gaming Commn., Las Vegas, 1983—, chmn., 1986—; pres., bd. dirs. Nev. Fed. Credit Union, Las Vegas, 1974-86. Editor-in-chief Communique mag., 1983. Alt. mcpl. judge City of Las Vegas, 1975-86; mem. adv. bd. Boulder Dam council Boy Scouts Am., Las Vegas, 1977—; mem. Nev. Gaming Policy Com., Las Vegas, 1983—; pres. adv. bd. Bishop Gorman High Sch., Las Vegas, 1986—. Served to capt., mil. judge USAF, 1969-73. Mem. ABA, Mo. Bar Assn., Nev. Bar Assn., Clark County Bar Assn. (pres. 1984), So. Nev. Home Builders Assn. (Homer award 1986), Las Vegas C. of C., Knights of Malta, Breakfast Exch. Club, Boys and Girls Club. Democrat. Roman Catholic. Office: Keefer O'Reilly & Ferrario 325 S Maryland Pkwy #1 Las Vegas NV 89101

O'REILLY, THOMAS JOSEPH, accountant; b. Pitts., Dec. 10, 1958; s. William Joseph and Mary Elizabeth (Huber) O. BSBA, Robert Morris Coll., 1981. Acctg. clk. Westinghouse Electric Supply Co., Pitts., 1981-82; acctg. analyst Westinghouse Electric Supply Co., Dammam, Saudi Arabia, 1982-84; adminstrv. trainee Westinghouse Electric Supply Co., Santa Clara, Calif., 1984-85; br. asst. Westinghouse Electric Supply Co., San Dimas, Calif., 1985-86; adminstrv. mgr. Westinghouse Electric Supply Co., Palm Springs, Calif., 1986-87; acct. Tenen Cooper and Co., Palm Springs, Calif., 1987—. Mem. Vol. Fire Dept. Craton, Pa., 1977. Mem. Mensa. Home: 528 S Camino Real #2 Palm Springs CA 92262

O'REILLY, THOMAS MARK, real estate executive, lawyer; b. Cleve., Apr. 10, 1944; s. Wilfred Phillip and Mary Alice (Conger) O. BA, Middlebury Coll., 1966; JD, U. Denver, 1974; MS, U. Vt., 1982. Bar: Colo. 1974. Pvt. practice Denver, 1974-76; atty. Forest Oil Corp., Denver, 1976-77; dir. pub. affairs U.S. Ski Assn., Denver, 1977-79; mgr. Sherburne Corp., Killington, Vt., 1979-81; v.p. Talley Properties, Ltd., Denver, 1983-85, Mission Viejo Co., Denver, 1986—. Bd. dirs. Colo. Ski Mus., Vail , Colo., 1987—. Capt. USAF, 1967-71. Mem. Colo. Bar Assn., Colo. Assn. Homebuilders, Rocky Mountain Middlebury AlumniAssn. (bd. dirs. 1975—). Home: 619 S Race St Denver CO 80209 Office: Mission Viejo Co 8822 S Ridgeline Blvd Highlands Ranch CO 80126

O'REILLY, WENDA BREWSTER, writer, researcher; b. Frankfurt, Fed. Republic of Germany, Mar. 29, 1948; d. William Russell Brewster and Harriet Stimson Bullitt; m. James Patrick Brewster O'Reilly, July 18, 1981; children: Andrea Mariele, Noelle Christine, Mariele Angelica. BA in Psychology, U. Wash., 1975; MEd, Harvard U., 1977; MA, Stanford U., 1977, PhD in Edn., 1983. Gen. asst. King Broadcasting Co., Seattle, 1965-66; media buyer Benton & Bowles Advt. Agy., N.Y.C, 1967-68; acct. exec. Young & Rubicam Advt. Agy., Milan, 1969-70; advt. producer McCann-Erickson Advt. Agy., Milan, 1971-73; researcher, scholar Inst. for Research on Women and Gender Stanford (Calif.) U., 1983—; exec. dir. The Birth Place, Menlo Park, Calif., 1985-87; guest lectr., seminar leader in women in mgmt., communications and childbirth isssues, 1979—; statis. analyst and research asst., Stanford U., 1978-81. Author: The Beautiful Body Book, 1984; contbr. chpts. to books, articles to profl. jours. V.p., bd. dirs. Calif. Assn. Free-standing Birth Ctrs., 1986-88. Grantee William H. Donner Found. Mem. Mid-peninsula Access Corp. (founding bd. dirs. Calif. chpt., v.p., founding bd. dirs. 1986-87). Democrat. Episcopalian.

OREN, JOSEPH, transportation executive; b. Bucharesti, Romania, Apr. 21, 1945; came to U.S., 1987; s. Tobias and Reghina (Askenazy) Grunberg; m. Shoshana Rosenbaum, Aug. 4, 1968; children: Eiran, Ami. BA, Bar-Ilan U., Ramatgan, Israel, 1982. Enlisted Israel Air Force, 1964, advanced through grades to lt. col., resigned, 1987; gen. mgr. Israel Aircraft Svcs., USA, 1987-88, pres., 1988—; spl. cons. Plastab Industries Holon, Israel, 1973-87, Int. Logistics Systems Ltd., Tel Aviv 1987—. Jewish.

OREŠKOVICH, MARY JO, school system administrator; b. Butte, Mont., Aug. 24, 1944; d. Joseph A. and Nora D. (Kuburich) O. BS, Mont. State U., 1966; MEd, U. Mont., 1972. Tchr. Anaconda (Mont.) Schs., 1966-78, fed. aid and labor rels. coord., 1978-82, supr. schs., 1982—; guest instr. negotiations, U. Mont., Missoula, Mont., 1983, 84. Mem. Fin. Task Force, 1981; bd. dirs. Hearst Free Library Bd., Anaconda, 1986—; rep. Mont. Bd. of Personnel Appeals, Helena, Mont., 1978-80. Mem. Am. Chem. Soc., Soroptimist Internst., Delta Kappa Gamma. Democrat. Serbian Orthodox. Office: Anaconda Schs 1510 W Park Anaconda MT 59711

ORGAN, DEBBIE JARIE, nurse; b. Artesia, N.Mex., Sept. 18, 1945; d. James Morgan and Georgia Pauline (Duggar) Brewton; m. Leslie Lee Organ, July 27, 1972; 1 child, Cory Alyn. Assoc. in Nursing, Ea. N.Mex. U., 1981. RN, N.Mex. Nurse St. Mary's Hosp., Roswell, N.Mex., 1981-87, Chaves County Home Health Svcs., Roswell, 1987—. Author numerous poems. Sec. Parkview PTA, 1987—; tchr. Sunday Sch., Highland Bapt. Ch. Mem. N.Mex. Bapt. Nursing Fellowship (treas.). Home: 1607 W Hendricks St Roswell NM 88201

ORIARD, MICHAEL VINCENT, writer, educator; b. Spokane, Wash., May 26, 1948; s. Marcel Hubert and Ronda Albertine (O'Leary) O.; m. Julie Voelker, June 14, 1971; children: Colin Vincent, Alan Joseph. BA, Notre Dame, 1970; postgrad., U. Wash., 1971; PhD, Stanford U., 1976. Profl. football player Kansas City (Mo.) Chiefs, 1970-74; asst. prof. Am. lit. Oreg. State U., Corvallis, 1976-81, assoc. prof., 1981—; vis. prof. U. Stuttgart, Fed. Republic of Germany, 1982. Author: Dreaming of Heroes, 1982, The End of Autumn, 1982; numerous essays and articles. Awarded postgrad. fellowship Nat. Collegiate Athletic Assn., 1970, Danforth Found., 1970, Nat. Endowment for the Humanities, 1984. Mem. Modern Lang. Assn., Am. Studies Assn., N.Am. Soc. for the Study of Sport History, Sport Lit. Assn., Phi Beta Kappa. Home: 3010 NW McKinley Dr Corvallis OR 97330 Office: Oreg State U Dept English Corvallis OR 97331

O'RIORDAN, JOHN FRANCIS, research chemical engineer; b. Phila., July 16, 1957; s. Joseph Patrick and Anna Catherine (Connor) O'R.; m. Kathi Anne Threeton., Apr. 29, 1989. BSChemE, Bucknell U., 1979; MS, Northwestern U., 1980, PhD, 1986. Software engr. Digital Devices, Inc., Line Lexington, Pa., 1978; rsch. asst. Aalborg (Denmark) U., 1980, Northwestern U., Evanston, Ill., 1980-85; rsch. engr. COBE Labs., Inc., Lakewood, Colo., 1986—. Contbr. articles to profl. jours. NIH fellow, 1985-86. Mem. Biomed. Engring. Soc., Am. Chem. Soc., Am. Inst. Chem. Engrs., AAAS, Internat. Soc. on Oxygen Transport to Tissue, Toastmasters, Sierra Club. Office: Cobe Labs Inc 1201 Oak St Lakewood CO 80215

ORMAN, ARTHUR ALLEN, educator; b. Mpls., June 18, 1932; s. Joseph M. and Sylvia C. (Landy) O.; m. Sylvia Florenia Mangum, April 4, 1958 (div. Oct. 1988). BA, Ariz. State U., 1956, MA, 1957. Cert. tchr. Tchr. Pomona (Calif.) Unified Schs., 1957-58, Flagstaff (Ariz.) High Sch., 1958-59, Phoenix Union High Sch. Dist., 1959-64; prof. of English Phoenix Coll., 1965-87, prof. of English emeritus, 1988—. Served with U.S. Army, 1953-55. Republican. Office: Phoenix Coll 1202 W Thomas Rd Phoenix AZ 85013

ORMAN, JOHN LEO, software engineer, writer; b. San Antonio, Mar. 19, 1949; s. Alton Woodlee and Isabel Joan (Paproski) O. BS in Physics, N.Mex. Inst. Mining & Tech., 1971, BS Math., MS Physics, 1974. Rsch. asst. N.Mex. Inst. Mining & Tech., Socorro, 1967-74; computer programmer State of N.Mex., Santa Fe, 1974-76; computer analyst Dikewood Corp., Albuquerque, 1976-83; nuclear engr. Sandia Nat. Labs., Albuquerque, 1983-88, software engr., 1988—. Author numerous poems. Recipient grad. fellowship NSF, 1971-74, 2d place N. Mex. State Poetry Soc. Mem. IEEE Computer Soc., Am. Assn. Physics Tchrs., Assn. for Computing Machinery, Nat. Writer's Club (poetry award 1987), Southwest Writers Workshop (3d place award non-fiction 1987), N.Mex. Mountain Club. Home: 8611 Los Arboles NE Albuquerque NM 87112 Office: Sandia Nat Labs Org 2825 PO Box 5800 Albuquerque NM 87185

ORME, MAYNARD EVAN, broadcasting executive; b. Fresno, Calif., Dec. 7, 1936; s. Otis Lowe and Lila (Morton) O.; m. Joan Frances King, Apr. 2, 1966; children: Jennifer Ariana, Juliana Alaire. MusB, U. Calif., Berkeley, 1961; MA in Theatre Arts, UCLA, 1967, PhD in Edn., 1978. Cert. community coll. tchr., Calif. Research asst. Instructional Media Ctr. Dept. Edn. UCLA, 1965-66; producer-dir., instructional TV coordinator, news dir. Sta. KVCR-TV San Bernardino (Calif.) Valley Coll., 1966-68; learning resources coordinator, dir. Sta. KCET-TV, Los Angeles, 1968-73; gen. mgr., dir. media services, exec. dir. Sta. KTEH-TV, San Jose, Calif., 1973-86; exec. dir. Oreg. Pub. Broadcasting, Portland, 1986—; mem. TV adv. com. Calif. State Instructional TV, 1977-82, chmn. 1979-80. Vice chmn. San Jose Police Activities League, 1982-83, chmn., bd. dirs. 1983-85. Served to capt. U.S. Army, 1961-66. Mem. Assn. Calif. Pub. TV Stas. (pres. 1982-86), Calif. Media and Library Educators Assn., Nat. Acad. TV Arts and Scis., Pacific Mountain Network (bd. dirs. 1981-88, v.p. 1984-88, chmn. 1986-88), Calif. Pub. Broadcasting Commn. (chmn. TV adv. com. 1978-79), Pub. Broadcasting Service (bd. dirs. 1984—, chmn. membership com. 1985-86, vice chmn. bd. 1987-89, satellite interconnection com. 1987—, mem. exec. com.), UCLA Doctoral Alumni Assn., Big C Soc., Los Gatos Athletic Assn. (v.p. 1975, pres. 1976, bd. dirs.), West Valley Joggers and Striders, Order of Golden Bear, Phi Delta Kappa, Alpha Epsilon Rho. Home: 2726 SW Riven Dell Dr Lake Oswego OR 97034-7390 Office: Oreg Pub Broadcasting 7140 SW Macadam Ave Portland OR 97219

ORMISTON, PATRICIA JANE, educator; b. Flint, Mich., Aug. 22, 1938; d. Elmer A. and Katheryn Lucille (Day) Knudson; m. Lester Murray Ormiston, June 13, 1964; 1 child, Brian Todd. BS, Minot State U., 1962; postgrad., U. Mont., 1963, Mont. State U., 1963, Western Mont. Coll., 1987. Elem. tchr. Lowell Sch., Gt. Falls, Mont., 1958, Webster Sch., Williston, N.D., 1958-59, Plaza (N.D.) Pub. Sch., 1959-61, Cen. Sch., Helena, Mont., 1962-63, Elrod Sch., Sch. Dist. 5, Kalispell, Mont., 1963—. Vol. Conrad Mansion Restoration, Kalispell, 1976—; presenter 34th ann. conv. Lit. Base Reading Internat. Reading Assn., New Orleans, 1989. Named Tchr. of Yr., Kalispell Sch. Dist. 5, 1986; Chpt. 2 grantee, 1987-88; Gertrude Whipple Profl. Devel. grantee IRA, 1988. Mem. NEA, Mont. Edn. Assn., Kalispell Edn. Assn. (bldg. rep. 1987-88), Internat. Reading Assn., Phi Delta Kappa, Delta Kappa Gamma. Home: Box 64 Kalispell MT 59901 Office: Sch Dist 5 Elrod Sch 34 Ave and 4th St W Kalispell MT 59901

OROLOGAS, GUS NICHOLAS, military officer; b. San Francisco, June 18, 1953; s. George Epamenondas and Elpiniki (Kariotoglos) O.; m. Julie Cowley McDonnel, Oct. 15, 1977; children: Jason Alexander, Alexis Celeste. AA, Coll. of Marin, Kentfield, Calif., 1973; BA in Zoology, Humboldt State U., 1976. Commd. ensign USN, 1976, advanced through grades to lt. comdr., 1986; planner cruise missile mission USN, Honolulu, 1981-84; flag sec. strike ops. USN, Subic Bay, Republic of Philippines, 1984-87; mgr. reserve program USN, Whidbey Island, Wash., 1987—. Greek Orthodox. Office: VA 128 NAS Whidbey Island Oak Harbor WA 98278

ORONA, ERNEST JOSEPH, real estate and construction company executive; b. Belen, N.Mex., Oct. 5, 1942; s. Joseph B. and Melinda (Sanchez) O.; B.A. in Latin Am. Affairs and Spanish, U. N.Mex., 1968; m. Margaret M. Guinan, Aug. 22, 1964; children—Mary Melinda, Marie-Jeanne. Vol. community devel. Peace Corps, Colombia, S. Am., 1962-64; instr. Peace Corps tng. U. Mo., Kansas City, summer 1964, Baylor U., Waco, Tex., summer 1965, also U. Ariz., N.Mex. State U., Las Cruces, 1966, U. N.Mex., Albuquerque, 1966; exec. dir. Mid-Rio Grande Community Action Project, Los Lunas, N.Mex., 1965-66; community devel. cons. Center for Community Action Services, Albuquerque, 1967-68; project dir. Peace Corps Tng. Center, San Diego State U., Escondido, Calif., 1968-70; propr., developer GO Realty and Constrn. Co., Albuquerque, 1970—; pres. La Zarzuela de Alburquerque; pres. Benchmark Real Estate InvestmentInc. Mem. Albuquerque Sister Cities. Mem. Nat. Bd. Realtors, Albuquerque Bd. Realtors, Albuquerque C. of C., Albuquerque Com. on Fgn. Relations. Roman Catholic. Home: 908 Sierra Dr SE Albuquerque NM 87108 Office: GO Realty & Constrn Co 10601 Lomas NE Ste 112 Albuquerque NM 87112

OROSCO, JESÚS LINARES, labor union administrator; b. Oakland, Calif., Oct. 28, 1953; s. Manuel Ordunez and Concepción Linares Orosco; m.

Alicia N. Ribeiro; children: Jesús Andres, Anahi Andrea, Alexis Mixtli. Student, San Jose State U., 1971-74; BA in Mgmt., St. Mary's Coll. of Calif., Moraga, 1987. Pres. Internat. Fedn. Profl. and Tech. Engrs., Milpitas, Calif., 1983—. Bd. dirs. Santa Clara Ctr. for Occupational Health, San Jose, Calif., 1987—, Silicon Valley Toxic Coalition, San Jose, 1987—; mem. local 189 Workers Edn. Mem. Amnesty Internat., Nat. Writers Union. Democrat. Roman Catholic. Home: 3058 Armdale Ct San Jose CA 95148 Office: TIU IFPTE 500 E Calaveras Blvd #205 Milpitas CA 95035

O'ROURKE, EUGENE LAWRENCE, public utility executive; b. San Antonio, Aug. 12, 1929; s. Lawrence F. and Rose (Lackey) O'R.; m. Marilyn Jean Rickert, June 25, 1955; children—Ronald E., Kenneth R., Craig A. B.S. in Mech. Engring., UCLA, 1955. V.p. So. Calif. Gas Co., Los Angeles, 1964—. Pres. Newport Harbor Union High Sch. Dist., 1964. Served with U.S. Army, 1952-54. Mem. Am. Gas Assn. (chmn. ops. sect.), Pacific Coast Gas Assn., Town Hall, Orange County World Affairs Council, Balboa Bay Club, Masons, Los Angeles Club (pres. 1986). Republican. Presbyterian. Home: 1039 Tiller Way Corona Del Mar CA 92625 Office: So Calif Gas Co 810 S Flower St Los Angeles CA 90017

O'ROURKE, PATRICK J., university administrator. Chancellor U. Alaska, Fairbanks, 1983—. Office: U Alaska Office of Chancellor Fairbanks AK 99775-0500 *

ORR, DAVID WILLIAM, real estate company executive, forester; b. Portland, Oreg., Jan. 15, 1950; s. Samuel Robert and Florence (Lewis) O.; m. Sally Muriel Tyson, July 14, 1973; children: Tammy Cho, Crystal Cho. BS in Forest Mgmt., Oreg. State U., 1972; MA in Internat. Relations, Salve Regina Coll., 1987; postgrad., U.S. Naval War Coll., Newport, R.I., 1986-87. Cert. forester, Alaska. Forester State of Alaska, Anchorage, 1977-86, 88—; pres. Foraker Enterprises, Inc., Anchorage, 1978-87; cons. Forest Resources Unltd., Anchorage, 1976-80. Contbr. articles to profl. jours.; columnist The Anchorage Times. Mem. Resource Devel. Council Alaska, Anchorage, 1985-88; del. Reps. Alaska, Anchorage, 1978, 82. Maj. USMCR, 1971—. Recipient Adm. Richard G. Colbert Meml. prize U.S. Naval War Coll., 1987, ICS Disting. Essay on Nat. Strategy award, 1987. Mem. Res. Officer Assn. Alaska (v.p. 1984-87), Marine Corps Res. Officer Assn. (pres. 1986-88), Elks. Methodist. Home and Office: 16361 Sandpiper Dr Anchorage AK 99516

ORR, NANCY LYNNE, computer engineer; b. Chattanooga, July 16, 1955; d. Martin Post and Evelyn (Timberlake) O.; m. Maxim Geoffrey Holloway, Aug. 8, 1988. BSEE, Memphis State U., 1977; MS in Computer Sci., U. Utah, 1989. Elec. engr., prin. programmer UNISYS Corp., Salt Lake City, 1978—; cons. Becton-Dickinson, Inc., Salt Lake City, 1978-79. Author: A Method for Evaluation of Graphics Coprocessors for Personal Computers, 1989. Vol. Splore, Salt Lake City, 1984—. Mem. Tau Beta Pi, Phi Kappa Phi, Alpha Lambda Delta, Wasatch Mountain club.

ORRAS, GEORGE L., social worker; b. Chincoteeque, Va., Mar. 4, 1952; s. George and Elsie (Hill) O. BA in Sociology, U. S. Fla., 1974; MSW, Ariz. State U., 1976; PhD in Social Work, U. So. Calif., 1983. Psychotherapist Tri City Mental Health, Mesa, Ariz., 1976-78; social worker for handicapped Phoenix High Sch., 1978-80; instr. U. So. Calif., Los Angeles, 1981-82; emergency room social worker Long Beach (Calif.) Meml. Hosp., 1982-84; pvt. practice in psychotherapy Long Beach, 1983—; clin. program dir. outstretch services Coll. Hosp., Cerritos, Calif., 1983—; cons., stress reduction Cen. Ariz., Phoenix, 1978-80; cons. tng., Phoenix, 1978-80; cons., developer Crisis Response Unit, Cerritos; cons. Orange County Hotline, Los Alamitos, Calif., 1985—; practitioner hypnosis, Los Angeles, 1985—. Bd. dirs. Long Beach Drug Prevention, 1986—; bd. dirs. Turn Est, Venice, Calif., 1986—. Fellow Soc. Clin. Social Workers; Mem. Nat. Assn. Social Workers, Omicron Delta Kappa. Democrat. Roman Catholic. Office: Coll Hosp 10802 College Pl Cerritos CA 90701

ORSTEN, GEORGE S. F., engineer; b. Vienna, Austria, Aug. 16, 1930; came to U.S., 1940; s. Paul George and Hildegard E. (Vulda) O.; m. L. Revea Orsten, June 17, 1957. Sr. engr. The Martin Co., Denver, 1956-59; rsch. engr. Ball Bros. Rsch., Boulder, Colo., 1959-62; dir. engring. T.E.C., Boulder, 1962-63; sr. engr. Veeder Industries, Mass., 1963-66; rsch. engr. Harvard U., Cambridge, Mass., 1966-67; lectr., rsch. engr. dept. physics U. Mass., Amherst, 1967-84; mgr. spl. programs Millitech Corp., South Deerfield, Mass., 1982-87; staff scientist Lockheed Missiles & Space Co., Palo Alto, Calif., 1987—.

ORTEGA, RUBEN BAPTISTA, police chief; b. Glendale, Ariz., July 17, 1939; s. Epifanio Dominguez and Clara (Baptista) O.; B.S. in Criminal Justice and Police Adminstrn., No. Ariz. U., 1980; m. Nellie Ann Alvarado, Nov. 23, 1958; children—Karen Ann, Jeffrey Randal. With Phoenix Police Dept., 1960—, police chief, 1980—; instr. Phoenix Police Regional Tng. Acad., 1969-73; cons. Juvenile Crime Prevention Task Force, Phoenix, 1975-79. Bd. dirs. NCCJ, 1979-81. Recipient Outstanding Community Service awards Am. Legion, 1979, also others. Mem. Ariz. Organized Crime Prevention Council, Ariz. Law Enforcement Office Adv. Council, Internat. Assn. Chiefs of Police. Roman Catholic. Office: City of Phoenix Police Dept 620 W Washington St Phoenix AZ 85003 *

ORTEGO, GILDA BAEZA, librarian; b. El Paso, Tex., Mar. 29, 1952; d. Efren and Bertha (Singh) Baeza; m. Felipe de Ortego y Gasca, Dec. 21, 1986. BA, Tex. Woman's U., 1974; MLS, U. Tex., 1976; cert., Hispanic Leadership Inst., 1988. Libr. pub. svcs. El Paso Community Coll., 1976-77; ethnic studies librarian U. N.Mex., Albuquerque, 1977-81; br. head librarian El Paso Pub. Library, 1981-82, dep. head librarian Mex.-Am. Svcs., 1982-84; librarian Mex.-Am. Studies U. Tex. Library, Austin, 1984-86; librarian Phoenix Pub. Library, 1986—; sec. bd. Unlimited Potential Inc., Phoenix, 1987-89; speaker and cons. in field. Editor jour. La Lista, 1983-84; indexer Chicano Periodical Index, 1981-86; reviewer jour. Voice for Youth Advocates, 1989—; contbr. articles to profl. jours. Mem. ALA, Ariz. State Library Assn. (pres. svcs. Spanish speaking Roundtable 1989), Reforma (pres. El Paso chpt. 1983), MUJER Inc. (treas. 1988—), Hispanic Leadership Inst. Alumni Assn. Home: 5038 S Hardy #2120 Tempe AZ 85282 Office: Phoenix Pub Libr Harmon Br 411 W Yavapai Phoenix AZ 85003

ORTEN, CATHERINE GRACE, educational administrator; b. Denver, Mar. 17, 1953; d. Albert John and Elizabeth (Menning) Brandsma; m. Russell Sage Orten, Sept. 12, 1975. BA with distinction, U. Colo., 1975, MA, 1982. Statis. analyst office instnl. rsch. and acad. planning U. Colo., Boulder, 1975-85, asst. dir. admissions, 1985—; cons. tech. com. Colo. Commn. Higher Edn., Denver, 1988; cons. data bases Nat. Ctr. Ednl. Mgmt. Statistics, Boulder, 1985. Nennsberg Meml. Found. scholar, 1973-74, Regents and Pres. Found. scholar, 1971-75. Mem. Am. Assn. Collegiate Registrars and Admissions Officers, Assn. Instnl. Researchers, Phi Beta Kappa. Republican. Lutheran. Office: U Colo Campus Box 7 Boulder CO 80309

ORTEZ, GEORGE H., photojournalist; b. Apr. 10, 1929; m. Joan K. Ortez. Freelance photojournalist; former mem. White House Press Corps, Washington; former mem. Dept. Interior Bur. Indian Affairs, Washington; photojournalist News Photo, Spanaway, Wash. Contbr. numerous photos Am. Indian Archives, 1970—. Mem. Photographer's Assn. Inc., White House News Photo Assn., Capital City Press Club, Lions Club. Home: 13013 224 St E Graham WA 98338-8944 Office: News Photo 19614 Mountain Hwy E Spanaway WA 98387

ORTIZ, ANTONIO IGNACIO, public relations executive; b. Mexico City, Feb. 22, 1961; s. Antonio and Sylvia (Vega) O.; m. Socorro Chinolla, June 12, 1982. B in Bus., Baja State U., Tijuana, Calif., 1984. With acctg. dept. Bank of the Atlantic, Tijuana, 1979-83; mgr. Aldaco, Tijuana, 1983-84; dir. pub. rels. Oh! Laser Club, Tijuana, 1984-88, Iguanas, Tijuana, 1988—; cons. DDBSA Corp., Chula Vista, Calif., Calif. Alson Ltd., San Diego, Exim Trading Co., San Diego, R.P. Noble Enterprises, La Tolla, Ca.; dir. pub. rels. R. Noble Enterprises. Home: PO Box 1859 San Ysidro CA 92073 Office: Exim Trading Corp PO Box 5108 San Ysidro CA 92073

ORTON, KAY THURGOOD, energy conservation specialist; b. Salt Lake City, Feb. 26, 1957; d. Dean Barton and Ann Louise (Miller) T.; children: Casey Arthur Orton, Kelly Dean Orton. Student, Brigham Young U., 1975-78, U. Utah, 1982-85. Cert. energy auditor. Interior designer R.C. Willey Home Furnishings, Salt Lake City, 1977-79; energy auditor Weatherization prog., Davis County Human Svcs., Farmington, Utah, 1985-88; energy conservation specialist Davis County Human Svcs., Farmington, 1988—. Office: Davis County Human Svcs 225 S 200W Box 685 Farmington UT 84025

ORULLIAN, B. LARAE, banker; b. Salt Lake City, May 15, 1933; d. Alma and Bessie (Bacon) O.; cert. Am. Inst. Banking, 1961, 63, 67; grad. Nat. Real Estate Banking Sch., Ohio State U., 1969-71. With Tracy Collins Trust Co., Salt Lake City, 1951-54; sec. to exec. sec. Union Nat. Bank, Denver, 1954-57; exec. sec. Guaranty Bank, Denver, 1957-64, asst. cashier, 1964-67, asst. v.p., 1967-70, v.p., 1970-75, exec. v.p., 1975-77, also bd. dirs.; pres., chief exec. officer, dir. The Women's Bank N.A., Denver, 1977-88, chair, chief exec. officer, dir., 1989—, Equitable Bankshares of Colo., 1980—; vice chmn. Equitable Bank Littleton; vice chmn. bd., dir. Colo. and N.Mex. Blue Cross/Blue Shield, lectr. Nat. treas. Girl Scouts U.S.A., 1981, 1st. nat. v.p., chair exec. com., 1987—; bd. dirs., chair fin. Rocky Mountains Health Care Corp. Named to Colo. Women Hall of Fame, 1988. Mem. Bus. and Profl. Women Colo. (3d Century award 1977), Inst. for Better Govt. (bd. dirs.), Colo. State Ethics Bd., Denver C. of C. (bd. dirs., chair state and local affairs), Am. Inst. Banking, Am. Bankers Assn. (mem. adv. bd. Community Bankers Coun.), Nat. Assn. Bank Women, Nat. Women's Forum, Com. of 200, Denver Partnership. Republican. Mormon. Home: 10 S Ammons St Lakewood CO 80226

ORUND, VALDEK JAAN, mechanical engineer; b. Estonia, USSR, July 4, 1922; s. Jaan and Johanna O.; MSME, Tallinna Politehniline Inst., 1941; came to U.S., 1950, naturalized, 1963; m. Katharina Baumstark, Aug. 13, 1966. Engr., Shaffer Tool Works, Brea, Calif., 1952-69; product engring. mgr. Rucker Co., Brea, 1969-77; chief engr. R&D N.L. Shaffer, N. L. Industries, Inc., Brea, 1977-82, engring. specialist, 1982—. Mem. ASME, Computer Soc. of IEEE (affiliate mem.), Soc. Exptl. Stress Analysis, Am. Soc. Metals, AIME, Soc. Mfg. Engrs., Robotics Internat. Republican. Lutheran. Patentee in field.

ORWOLL, REBECCA LYNN, physician; b. Camden, N.J., May 10, 1949; d. Walter and Patricia Anne (Page) Schroth; m. Eric S. Orwoll, 1970 (div. 1988); children: Benjamin, Katherine. AB cum laude, U. Mich., 1970; MA, U. Md., 1973; BS, Portland State U, ., 1975; MD magna cum laude, U. Oreg., Portland, 1979. Diplomate Am. Bd. Intern, resident, fellow Oreg. Health Scis. U., Portland, 1979-84; pvt. practice Portland, Oreg., 1984—; clin. instr. Oreg. Health Scis. U., Portland, 1985—. Mem. AMA, Am. Soc. Clin. Oncology, Am. Heart Assn. (mem. council), Oreg. Med. Soc., Multnomah County Med. Soc., Alpha Omega Alpha. Democrat. Unitarian. Office: Hematology Clin 510 NE 49 Ste 421 Portland OR 97213

OSAKODA, RONALD TOSHIO, insurance company official; b. Wailuku, Hawaii, Nov. 23, 1956; s. Jack Toshio and Peggy Fumiko) Sato) O.; m. Sheilah Mae Nakanishi, Mar. 18, 1976; children: Andrea Toshie Alana, Amber Fumie Maile, Holly May Kuulei. Grad., high sch., Wailuku. Mem. wash crew Maui Meat Co., Kahului, Hawaii, 1975, truck driver, 1975-76, meat cutter, 1976-79; meat cutter Star Supermarket, Kahului, Hawaii, 1979-85; agt. lst Ins. Co. Hawaii, Kahului, 1985--. Solicitor Maui United Way, 1986-87. Mem. Profl. Ins. Agts. Assn., Ind. Ins. Agts. Assn., Maui Assn. Life Underwriters, lst Ins. Agts. Assn. Office: lst Ins Co Hawaii PO Box 308 Kahului HI 96732

OSBERG, RICHARD HENRY, educator; b. Boston, Jan. 25, 1947; s. Calvin John and June Sheldon (Lander) O.; m. Sally Anne Reeves, Sept., 1969; 1 child, Jerusha Hope. BA, Dartmouth Coll., 1969; MA, Claremont (Calif.) Grad. Sch., 1971, PhD, 1975. Asst. prof. Hamilton Coll., Clinton, N.Y., 1978-82; assoc. prof. english lit. Santa Clara (Calif.) U., 1982—. Author: Sir Gawain and the Green Knight, 1989; contbr. articles to profl. jours. Concert adv. com. San Jose (Calif.) Symphony Orchestra, 1988—. NEH fellow, 1981. Mem. MLA, Medieval Acad. Am. Episcopalian. Home: 1251 Yosemite Ave San Jose CA 95126 Office: Santa Clara U The Alameda Santa Clara CA 95053

OSBORN, BERT LEROY, lawyer; b. Ephrata, Wash., Feb. 11, 1950; s. Bert and Thaddene (Jennings) O.; m. Suzan Kay McMillon, 1971; children: Shannon, Jacquelynne. BA, Whitman Coll., 1972; JD, U. Idaho, 1975. Bar: Idaho, 1975, U.S. Dist. Ct Idaho 1975. Sole practice Payette, Idaho, 1975—; mem. rules com. Idaho Supreme Ct., Boise, 1986-87. Author: Freefire Zone: Vietnam, 1985. Mem. Idaho Trial Lawyers, Idaho State Bar Assn. (pro bono 1980—), 3d Dist. Bar Assn. (pres. 1983), Lions. Home: 315 N 20th St Payette ID 83661 Office: 26 S 9th St Payette ID 83661

OSBORN, JAMES R., pest control company executive; b. Phoenix, Apr. 24, 1939; s. John Ellis and Jean Elizabeth (Cunningham) O.; m. Margee Ann Blackstone, 1964 (div. 1966); m. Gail Elizabeth Tunstall, 1968; 1 child, Jennifer. Pres. Paratex Paramount, Seattle, 1962—, Paratex Internat. Inc., Seattle, 1987—, Paratex-Morgan Inc., Seattle, 1988—. With USMC. Mem. Nat. Pest Control Assn. (regional bd. dirs.), Seattle Execs. Assn. (pres.), Millionaire Club (pres.), Rotary. Office: Paramount Svcs Inc Box C-81420 Seattle WA 98108

OSBORN, LYNDA RUTH, mechanical engineer, consultant; b. Denver, Feb. 19, 1958; d. Luther Johnson and Nancy Elise (Kofoed) Fuller; m. Steven George Osborn, Aug. 7, 1982 (div. Nov. 1987). BSME, Colo. State U., 1981. Registered profl. engr., Colo. Engr. EMC Engrs., Inc., Denver, 1981-84; project engr. BHCD Engrs., Inc., Denver, 1984-85; product mgr. Tri Fund Research, Inc., Denver, 1985-87; engring. cons. Lynda Osborn Cons. Engring., Denver, 1987—; guest lectr. U. Colo., 1987. Co-author: PC DOE User's Manual, 1985. Mem. ASHRAE (Rocky Mountain chpt. editor 1986-1987, sec. 1987-1988, v.p. 1988). Republican. Methodist. Office: 5353 W Dartmouth Ste 506 Denver CO 80227

OSBORNE, GAYLE ANN, corporate executive; b. Bossier City, La., Feb. 1, 1951; d. Walker Henry and Marjorie Evelyn (Cook) Pyle; m. Paul A. Huelsman, June 28, 1969 (div. Jan. 1976); children: Ginger, Paula; m. Luther L. Osborne, Sept. 10, 1976; stepchildren: David Brett, Darren. Sales assoc. Model City Real Estate, Midwest City, Okla., 1972-73; mgr. adminstrn. Equipment Renewal Co., Oklahoma City, 1973-76, Gulfco Industries, Inc., Casper, Wyo., 1976-77; v.p. B&B Tool and Supply Co., Inc., Casper, Wyo., 1977, 79, 81, pres., 1978, 80, 82—; ptnr. Williston, N.D., 1983—, Osborne Leasing Co., Casper, Wyo., 1977—; pres. BOP Repair & Machine, Inc., Casper, Wyo., 1981—; ptnr. Pronghorn Trap and Skeet, Casper, Wyo., 1986—. Mem. Casper Petroleum Club, Nat. Skeet Shoot Assn., Amature Trapshooting Assn., Casper Skeet Club. Democrat. Office: B&B Tool & Supply Co Inc PO Box 2974 Casper WY 82602

OSBORNE, RONALD DRAKE, health services management executive; b. Wheeling, W.Va., Mar. 20, 1941; s. William Thornton and Earnestine V. (Drake) O.; m. Linda Kay Bach, Jan. 4, 1964; children: Keri Lin, Keith Evan. BA, Ohio State U., 1963. Personnel devel. asst. Gen. Tel. Calif., Santa Monica, 1970-72, manpower planning adminstr., 1972-73; mgr. personnel devel. Blue Cross of So. Calif., Hollywood, 1973-75; coord. nat. health ins., v.p. corp. planning Blue Cross Assn., Chgo., 1975-81; v.p. cost containment Blue Cross-Blue Shield Ill., Chgo., 1982-84; v.p. contracting St. Joseph Health System, Orange, Calif., 1984-87; pres. Medworth Futures Inc., Brea, Calif., 1987; chief operating officer Beech St. Inc., Irvine, Calif., 1987-89; chief exec. officer Nat. Specialty Networks, Inc., 1989—. Bd. dirs. Pilgrimage Family Therapy Ctr., Orange, 1986—, Opportunity Internat., Inc., Oakbrook Ill., 1989; elder United Presbyn. Ch. Lt. Comdr. USN, 1964-70. Home: 106 S Flower Hill Brea CA 92621 Office: Beech Street Inc #3 Ada Irvine CA 92718

OSBORNE-MACGREGOR, VIRGINIA, nurse; b. Racine, Wis., Sept. 22, 1952; d. Lucien and Patton (FitzGerald) Osborne; m. Paul Donald Macgregor, Aug. 11, 1980; children: Kipp Osborne, Duncan Paul. A in Nursing, Elgin (Ill.) Community Coll., 1978; student, U. Wis., 1970-72; BSN, Mesa State Coll., Grand Junction, Colo., 1989. RN, Colo. Nurse Craig Meml. Hosp., Steamboat Springs, Colo., 1978-80, Little Wranglers ABC Ranch, Steamboat Springs, 1980-81, Routt Meml. Hosp., Steamboat Springs, 1981-82, 88—, Dr. Donald Tomlin, Ob-Gyn., Steamboat Springs, 1981-82, Mt. Med. Assocs., Steamboat Springs, 1982-84, Home Health Care, Steamboat Springs, 1984-85, N.W. Colo. Vis. Nurses Assn., Steamboat Springs, 1985—; cons. Holistic Health Ctr., Steamboat Springs, 1987-88; nurse inservice lectr. The Playworks, 1985-86. Vol. Soda Creek Elem. Sch., Steamboat Springs, 1986—, The Playworks, 1985-86, Steamboat Springs Winter Sports Club, 1987—. Mem. Am. Nurses Assn., Am. Wholistic Nurses Assn. Democrat. Office: NW Colo Vis Nurses Assn 136 6th St Steamboat Springs CO 80477

OSBY, ROBERT EDWARD, protective services official; b. San Diego, Oct. 29, 1937; s. Jesse William and Susie Lillian (Campbell) O.; m. Clydette Deloris Mullen, Apr. 11, 1961; children: Daryl Lawrence, Gayle Lorraine. AA in Fire Sci., San Diego Jr. Coll., 1970; BA in Mgmt., Redlands U., 1985. Recreation leader San Diego Parks and Recreation Dept., 1955-58; postal carrier U.S. Postal Service, San Diego, 1958-59; fire fighter San Diego Fire Dept., 1959-67, fire engr., 1967-71, fire capt., 1971-76, fire bn. chief, 1976-79; fire chief Inglewood (Calif.) Fire Dept., 1979-84, San Jose (Calif.) Fire Dept., 1985—. Served to 2d lt. Calif. NG, 1960-65. Mem. Calif. Met. Fire Chiefs (chmn. 1987—), Internat. Assn. Black Firefighters (regional dir. 1974-77), Brothers United (pres. 1972-75). Democrat. Home: 7196 Queensbridge Way San Jose CA 95120 Office: San Jose Fire Dept 4 N 2d St Ste 1100 San Jose CA 95113

O'SCANNLAIN, DIARMUID FIONNTAIN, judge; b. N.Y.C., Mar. 28, 1937; s. Sean Leo and Moira (Hegarty) O'S.; m. Maura Nolan, Sept. 7, 1963; children: Sean, Jane, Brendan, Kevin, Megan, Christopher, Anne, Kate. AB, St. John's U., 1957; JD, Harvard U., 1963. Bar: Oreg. 1965, N.Y. 1964. Tax atty. Standard Oil Co. (N.J.), N.Y.C., 1963-65; assoc. Davies, Biggs, Strayer, Stoel & Boley, Portland, Oreg., 1965-69; dep. atty. gen. Oreg., 1969-71; public utility commr. of Oreg., 1971-73; dir. Oreg. Dept. Environ. Quality, 1973-74; sr. ptnr. Ragen, Roberts, O'Scannlain, Robertson & Neill, Portland, 1978-86; judge, U.S. Ct. Appeals (9th cir.), San Francisco, 1986—; cons. Office of Pres.-Elect and mem. Dept. Energy Transition Team (Reagan transition), Washington, 1980-81; chmn. com. adminstrv. law Oreg. State Bar, 1980-81. Mem. council of legal advisers Rep. Nat. Com., 1981-83; mem. Rep. Nat. Com., 1983-86, chmn. Oreg. Rep. Party, 1983-86; del. Rep. Nat. Convs., 1976, 80, chmn. Oreg. del., 1984; Rep. nominee U.S. Ho. of Reps., First Congl. Dist., 1974; team leader Energy Task Force, Pres.'s Pvt. Sector Survey on Cost Control, 1982-83. Maj. USAR, 1955-78. Mem. Fed. Energy Bar Assn., ABA, Multnomah Club, Nat. Lawyers Club. Roman Catholic. Home: 2421 SW Arden Rd Portland OR 97201 Office: US Ct Appeals Pioneer Courthouse 555 SW Yamhill St Portland OR 97204-1396

OSGOOD, FRANK WILLIAM, urban and economic planner; b. Williamston, Mich., Sept. 3, 1931; s. Earle Victor and Blanche Mae (Eberly) O.; children: Ann Marie, Frank William Jr. BS, Mich. State U., 1953; M in City Planning, Ga. Inst. Tech., 1960. Prin. planner Tulsa Met. Area Plnning Commn., 1958-60; sr. assoc. Hammer & Co. Assocs., Washington, 1960-64; econ. cons. Marvin Springer & Assocs., Dallas, 1964-65; sr. assoc. Gladstone Assocs., Washington, 1965-67; prof. urban planning Iowa State U., Ames, 1967-73; pres. Frank Osgood Assoc./Osgood Urban Research, Dallas, 1973-84; dir. mktg. studies MPSI Americas Inc., Tulsa, 1984-85, Comarc Systems/Roulac & Co., San Francisco, 1985-86; pres. Osgood Urban Research, Millbrae, Calif., 1986—; adj. prof. U. Tulsa, 1974-76; lectr. U. Tex., Dallas, 1979, 83. Author: Control Land Uses Near Airports, 1960, Planning Small Business, 1967, Continuous Renewal Cities, 1970; contbr. articles to profl. jours. Chmn. awards Cub Scouts Am., Ames, 1971-73; deacon Calvary Presbyn. Ch., San Francisco, 1987—. 1st lt. USAF, 1954-56. Recipient Community Leaders and Noteworthy Americans award 1976. Mem. Am. Planning Assn. (peninsula liason, No. Calif. sect., Calif. chpt., 1987, dir. N.Cen. Tex. sect., Tex. chpt., 1983), Am. Inst. Planners (v.p. Okla. chpt. 1975-77), Okla. Soc. Planning Cons. (sec.-treas. 1976-79), Urban Land Inst. Republican. Presbyterian. Club: Le Club. Home and Office: 12 Elder Ave Millbrae CA 94030

OSGUTHORPE, SUSAN GALE LIKINS, nurse adminstrator; b. Salt Lake City, July 8, 1948; d. Corwin Hale and Virginia Louise (Snyder) Likins; m. Steven Garn Osguthorpe, Jan. 29, 1983. BS in Nursing cum laude, U. Utah, 1971, MS in Nursing, 1981. Staff nurse Holy Cross Hosp., Salt Lake City, 1971-73, Sisters of Mercy Hosp., Buffalo, 1973, St. Joseph's Hosp., Syracuse, N.Y., 1973-74; staff nurse Holy Cross Hosp., Salt Lake City, 1974-75, supr., 1975-81, critical care nurse clinician, 1981-82, clin. dir. critical care svcs., 1982-84; clin. dir. critical care Virginia Mason Hosp., Seattle, 1984—; mem. clin. faculty Weber State Coll., 1980-84, U. Utah, 1982-84, u. Wash., 1986—; Mem. healthside com. Wash. Heart Assn., 1984—. Named Outstanding Young Woman of Am., 1981. Mem. Am. Heart Assn., Am. Assn. for Critical Care Nurses (Puget Sound chpt.), Am. Assn. for Critical Care Nurses, Am. Nurses Assn., Sigma Theta Tau (Gamma Rho chpt., ann. rsch. award 1982), Alpha Lambda Delta. Republican. Congregationalist. Home: 5808 E Mercer Way Mercer Island WA 98040 Office: Virginia Mason Hosp 925 Seneca St Seattle WA 98111

O'SHEA, SCOTT MICHAEL, regional sales manager; b. Burlingame, Calif., Feb. 14, 1958; s. John E. and Norma Jane (Shuttleworth) O'S. BA in Mktg., S.D. State U., 1980. Sales rep. Durkee Foodservice, Pleasanton, Calif., 1980-81; territory mgr. Durkee Foodservice, 1982-83, dist. mgr., 1983-85, regional mgr., 1985—. Mem. AMA. Republican. Roman Catholic. Home: 2161 Filbert San Francisco CA 94123

OSHINS, RICHARD ALAN, lawyer; b. Bklyn., Dec. 31, 1941; s. Benjamin Morris and Ruth S. (Schlossberg) O.; m. Carol L. Bernstein, Aug. 14, 1966; children: Steven, Jason. BS, Am. U., 1963; JD, St. John's Law Sch., 1966; MBA in Taxation, U. Calif., Berkeley, 1968; LLM in Taxation, George Washington U., 1970. Bar: D.C. 1970, N.Y. 1972. Law clk. U.S. Ct. Claims, Washington, 1969-70; atty. Tax Legis. Counsel Dept. of Treasury, Washington, 1970-71; assoc. Lionel, Sawyer, Collins & Wartman, Las Vegas, 1971-72; pvt. practice Las Vegas, 1973; ptnr. Singer & Oshins, Las Vegas, 1973-74, Goodman, Oshins, Brown & Singer, Las Vegas, 1974-87, Rudiak, Oshins, Segal & Larsen, Las Vegas, 1987—; lectr. in field. Contbr. articles to profl. jours. Mem. ABA, Nev. Bar Assn. (chmn. continuing legal edn. com. 1973-75, 77-79, tax com. 1975), D.C. Bar Assn., S. Nev. Estate Planning Council. Office: Rudiak Oshins Segal Larsen 720 S Fourth St #200 Las Vegas NV 89109

OSHMAN, M(ALIN) KENNETH, electrical engineer; b. Kansas City, Mo., July 9, 1940. AB, Rice U., 1962, BSc, 1963; MSc, Stanford U., 1965, PhD, 1967. Mem. tech. staff Sylvania Elec. Products, 1963-69; formerly pres. Rolm Corp., Santa Clara, Calif.; pres., chief exec. officer Echelon, 1988—. Mem. IEEE, Nat. Acad. Engring. Office: Echelon 727 University Ave Los Gatos CA 95030 *

OSSERMAN, ROBERT, mathematician, educator; b. N.Y.C., Dec. 19, 1926; s. Herman Aaron and Charlotte (Adler) O.; m. Maria Anderson, June 15, 1952; 1 son, Paul; m. Janet Adelman, July 21, 1976; children—Brian, Stephen. B.A., NYU, 1946; postgrad., U. Zurich, U. Paris; M.A., Harvard U., 1948, Ph.D., 1955. Teaching fellow Harvard U., 1949-52, vis. lectr., research assoc., 1961-62; instr. U. Colo., 1952-53; mem. faculty Stanford U., 1955—, prof. math., 1966—, chmn. dept. math., 1973-79, Mellon Prof. Interdisciplinary Studies, 1987—; mem. NYU Inst. Math. Scis., 1957-58, Math. Scis. Research Inst., Berkeley, Calif., 1983-84 head math. br. Office Naval Research, 1960-61; researcher and author publs. on differential geometry, complex variables, differential equations, especially minimal surfaces, Laplace operator, isoperimetric inequalities, ergodic theory. Author: Two-Dimensional Calculus, 1968, A Survey of Minimal Surfaces, 1969, 2d edit., 1986. Fulbright lectr. U. Paris, 1965-66; Guggenheim fellow, 1976-77; vis. fellow U. Warwick, Imperial Coll., U. London. Mem. Math. Assn. Am., Am. Math. Soc. Office: Stanford U Math Dept Stanford CA 94305

O'STEEN, VAN, lawyer; b. Sweetwater, Tenn., Jan. 10, 1946; s. Bernard Van and Laura Emelyne (Robinson) O.; m. Deborah Ann Elias, May 18, 1974; children—Jonathan Van, Laura Ann. B.A., Calif. Western U., 1968; J.D. cum laude, Ariz. State U., 1972. Bar: Ariz. 1972, U.S. Dist. Ct. Ariz. 1972, U.S. Ct. Appeals (9th cir.) 1973, U.S. Supreme Ct. 1975. Staff atty. Maricopa Legal Aid Soc., Phoenix, 1972-74; atty. Bates & O'Steen, Legal

Clinic, Phoenix, 1974-77; atty. O'Steen Legal Clinic, Phoenix, 1977-80; mng. ptnr. Van O'Steen and Ptnrs., Phoenix, 1980—; pres. Van O'Steen/Lawyer Mktg. Group, Inc., Phoenix, 1985—. Author numerous self-help legal books. Founding dir. Ariz. Ctr. for Law in the Pub. Interest, 1974-80. Served with USNR, 1963-69. Mem. ABA (chmn. spl. com. delivery legal services 1982-85), Am. Legal Clinic Assn. (pres. 1979), Assn. Trial Lawyers Am. Democrat. Address: 3605 N 7th Ave Phoenix AZ 85013

OSTENDORF, FREDERICK OTTO, real estate executive, former county official; b. Milw., May 24, 1913; s. Frederick and Emily (Smith) O.; AA, Glendale Coll., 1933; BA, UCLA, 1937; MA in Sociology, U. So. Calif., 1949, cert. in real estate, 1954; m. Beryl Louverne Bell, May 29, 1941 (dec. Mar. 1986); children: Frederick Otto, Margaret Ann. With Los Angeles County Probation Dept., 1939-73, cons. juvenile delinquency, 1948-51, adult investigator, 1951-61, hearing officer juvenile traffic Superior Ct., 1961-63, adult supervision officer, 1964-73; owner Ostendorf Properties, LaCanada, Calif., 1959—. Cub scout commr. Boy Scouts Am., La Canada, 1952-54. Served to lt. USNR, 1942-46; lt. comdr. Res. ret. Named Outstanding Older Am., La Canada City Council-L.A. County Bd. Suprs., 1980. Mem. Crescenta-Canada Art Assn. (past pres.), Naval Res. Assn. (charter mem.; past pres. Rose Bowl chpt.), Alpha Kappa Delta, Toastmasters (pres. 1967, 75, 87, Disting. Toastmaster award 1980), Descanso Garden Guild Club (docent La Canada 1973-79, lectr. 1975, tour dir. 1978-79), Leisure Club (pres. 1980-81). Author: The Art of Retirement, 1980. Home: 1084 Inverness Dr Flintridge CA 91011

OSTER, JEFF LYNN, infosystems specialist; b. Glendale, Calif., July 9, 1946; s. Betty (Genest) O.; m. Beverly S. Beaton, Oct. 30, 1978; children: Bryan, Graham, Sarah, Anne. Student, Glendale Coll., 1964-66, San Jose State U., 1966-68. Sales mgr. Burroughs Corp., San Jose, Calif., 1968-71, Memorex Corp., Santa Clara, Calif., 1971-76; regional mgr. Verbatim Corp., Sunnyvale, Calif., 1976-85; pres. Interloc Info. Systems, Glendale, 1985—. Republican. Presbyterian. Office: Interloc Info Systems 1800 Victory Blvd Glendale CA 91201

OSTER, MICHAEL CROLY, insurance executive; b. Los Angeles, Nov. 1, 1944; s. Otto and Irene Evelyn (Croly) O.; m. Linell Ruth Rynkiewicz, Oct. 1, 1985. BS with honors, Calif. State U., Long Beach, 1969. CLU; cert. ins. cons. Engring. cost data analyst McDonnell-Douglas Aircraft Corp., Long Beach, 1966-70; mktg. rep. Continental Can Co., Los Angeles, 1970-72; v.p. mktg. Calif. Casualty Mgmt. Co., San Mateo, 1972-79; exec. v.p. Frank B. Hall & Co., San Francisco, 1979—. Contbr. articles to profl. jours. Mem. Bay Area Council. Staff sgt. USAFR, 1966-72. Recipient Gov.'s Commendation Medal, State of Calif., 1967. Mem. Commonwealth Club, Lahaina Yacht Club (Maui, Hawaii), Grand Banks Cruising Club, San Francisco Bay Club, Olympic Club, South Beach Yacht Club. Office: Frank B Hall & Co One Market Pla Ste 2100 Spear Tower San Francisco CA 94105

OSTERMAN, CONSTANTINE E., Canadian provincial government minister; b. Acme, Alta., Can., June 23, 1936; m. Joe Osterman, Oct. 30, 1954; children: Theo, Kurt, Kim, Kelly, Joe Jr. MLA representing Three Hills constituency Alta. Legis. Assembly, 1979-82, 82-85, 86—, party whip, mem. edn. caucus and agr. caucus coms., 1979-82, Minister of Consumer and Corp. Affairs, mem. social planning com. of cabinet, cabinet/caucus com. on legis. rev., agr. caucus com., 1982-85, Minister of Social Services and Community Health, 1986, Minister Social Services, mem. social planning, energy, met. affairs and mgmt. policy coms. of cabinet, 1986—; served select legis. com. to rev. surface rights issue, lead role in passing of Surface Rights Act, 1983. Active exec. bds. local ch., home and sch. assns., Carstairs, Alta., 1958—, surface rights area; commr., charter mem. Alta. Human Rights Commn., 1973-78; pres. Can. Assn. Statutory Human Rights Agys. Office: Ministry Social Svcs, 424 Legislature Bldg, Edmonton, AB Canada T5K 2B6

OSTERMAN, JULIE MARIE, financial executive; b. San Mateo, Calif., July 15, 1963; d. George Frederick and Kathleen Irene (Davi) O'Brien; m. Peter Michael Osterman, July 26, 1986; 1 child, Chase Michael. Cert., Skyline Coll., San Bruno, Calif., 1987. Acct. Genstar, Inc., San Mateo, 1981-84, EPR/CRSS, Inc., San Francisco, 1984-85, Rudolph & Sletten, Inc., Foster City, Calif., 1985-86; contr. Control Systems Specialists, San Mateo, 1986—. Roman Catholic. Office: Control System Specialists 800 S Amphlett Blvd San Mateo CA 94402

OSTERMILLER, JOHN VICTOR, real estate company executive; b. Lincoln, Nebr., Nov. 4, 1910; s. John and Louise (Bernhardt) O.; m. Margaret Ellen Kerr, June 17, 1934; children: Karen Rea, John Kerr. Student, U. Nebr., 1927-28; BS, Colo. State U., 1932. Tchr. vocat. agr., pub. sch. Colo., 1934-42; agrl. fieldman Gt. Western Sugar Co., Brush, Colo., 1942-49; asst. mgr. Gt. Western Sugar Co., Brush and Ft. Morgan, 1949-57; mgr. Gt. Western Sugar Co., Longmont, Colo., 1957-63; agrl. mgr. Gt. Western Sugar Co., Ft. Morgan, 1963-70, N.E. Colo. asst. dist. agrl. mgr., 1970-73; v.p. Gt. Western Sugar Export Co., 1973-75; mgr. farm and ranch dept. Crown Realty Co., Denver, 1975-78, Carriage House Realtors, Ft. Morgan, 1978-83, Realty Assocs., Ft. Morgan, 1984-87, Accent Real Estate, Ft. Morgan, 1987—. Contbr. articles to profl. jours. Instr. Adult Edn., Yuma, Colo., 1935-38, Brush, 1938-42. Rep. precinct committeeman, Morgan County, 1950-57, 64-74, Boulder County, 958-63; mem. St. Vrain Valley Sch. Bd., Longmont, 1961-63; bd. dirs. Brush Civic Club, 1944-50, Ft. Morgan Heritage Found., pres. 1969-75; bd. dirs., pres. Colo. State U. Found., 1973-86. Mem. Ft. Morgan C. of C. (dir. 1965-69, pres. 1968), Colo. State U. Alumni (dir. 1971-82, pres. 1975-76), Am. Sugar Beet Soc. Technologists, Masons, Lions, Alpha Tau Alpha, Lamda Gamma Delta, Sigma Phi Epsilon. Presbyterian. Home: 4 Yates Terr Fort Morgan CO 80701

OSTLER, RUSSELL HAWS, automotive industry professional; b. Provo, Utah, June 5, 1944; s. Don M. and Eva (Haws) O.; m. Henrica L. Day, May 2, 1963; children: Toby Alan, Tracy Anne. Cert., UCLA, 1973. With Chrysler Motors, Calif., 1976-83; mem. tng. staff Chrysler Motors, Salt Lake City, 1983-85; supr. tng. Chrysler Motors, Livermore, Calif., 1985—; cons., Auto Tech. Assoc., Hayward, Calif., 1985—; adviser, Chabot Coll., Hayward, 1985—. Pres., Calif. Fine Art League, 1987; v.p. Mayor's Com. of Arts, 1988. Mem. Soc. Automotive Engrs., Automotive Svc. Excellence Assn., Manteca (Calif.) C. of C., Eagles. Republican. Roman Catholic. Office: Chrysler Motors Corp 151 F Lindbergh Ave Livermore CA 94550

OSTOP, RONALD LEE, utilities executive; b. Washington, Pa., Sept. 7, 1947; s. Anthony and Mildred Barbara (Zaculek) O. BEE, Cleveland State U., 1970, MChemE, 1974. Registered profl. engr., Colo., Ohio. Dist. chief div. surveillance Ohio Environ. Protection Agy., Twinsburg, Colo., 1970-75; mgr. div. environ. services Colorado Springs (Colo.) Dept. Utilities, 1975—; mgr. Energy & Environ. Scis., ADA Technologies, Inc., 1989—. Chmn. Pikes Peak Area Council Govts. (air quality com., 1985-87). Mem. IEEE, NSPE, Nat. Assn. Environ. Profls., Utility Air Regulatory Group (chmn. 1984—), Air Pollution Control Assn. Home: 13120 Murphy Rd Elbert CO 80918 Office: Colorado Springs Dept Utilities 304 Inverness Way S Englewood CO 80112

OSTRANDER, CHRISTOPHER TAYLOR, food products company executive; b. Mt. Kisco, N.Y., Oct. 1, 1957; s. F. Taylor and Ruth Valerie (Kashuk) O.; m. Stephanie Anne Kearns; children: Galen O'Toole, Nikita Christephan. Student, Coll. of Atlantic, 1977-79. Field technician AMAX, Inc., Denver, 1975, 79; co-owner, mgr. Sunflour Natural Foods Bakery, Bar Harbor, Maine, 1980; regional coord. Rene Dubos Ctr. for Human Environ., Bronx, N.Y., 1981; co-owner, co-mgr. Santa Cruz (Calif.) Trucking, 1983-85, Third Planet Produce, Santa Cruz, 1985-87; pres. Organic Matters, Inc., Watsonville, Calif., 1987—. Democrat. Office: Organic Matters Produce Co 303-A Salinas Rd Watsonville CA 95000

OSTROGORSKY, MICHAEL, historian, archaeologist; b. Hamilton, Ont., Can., Sept. 11, 1951; came to U.S., 1952; s. William and Hedy Ostrogorsky. BA, Boise State Coll., 1973; MA, San Francisco State U., 1976; postgrad., U. Idaho, 1981-85. Cons., ptnr. Idaho Archaeol. Cons., Boise, 1976-80; instr. history U. Alaska, Dillingham, 1985; historian Nat. Park Svc., Anchorage, 1986, Alaska Office History and Archaeology, Anchorage, 1987—; freelance cons., 1981-85. Contbr. articles to archaeol. and hist. jours. Cons. N.W. Office, Sierra Club, Seattle, 1984, mem. exec. com. Alaska chpt., 1987-89, chmn., 1988-89; bd. dirs. Alaska Ctr. for Environ., Anchorage, 1989—. Whittenberger Found. fellow, 1982-83, John Calhoun Smith fellow, 1983-84; Charles Redd Ctr. grantee Brigham Young U., 1987. Mem. Am. Hist. Assn. (Beveridge grantee 1982), Soc. for Hist. Archaeology, Western History Assn., Nat. Trust for Historic Preservation, Phi Alpha Theta. Democrat. Home: PO Box 241453 Anchorage AK 99524

OSWALD, THERESE ANNE, nurse; b. Lynwood, Calif., Nov. 4, 1960; d. Andrew and Mary Louise (Keolker) O. AA in Nursing, Harbor Coll., Wilmington, Calif., 1982; BS in Nursing, Calif. State U., 1987. Registered nurse, Calif. Nurse Torrance (Calif.) Hosp., 1982—; preceptor, lead person Torrance Meml. Hosp., 1988—; med. asst. So. Calif. Regional Occ. Ctr., Torrance, 1977-78; candy striper Bay Harbor Hosp., Harbor City, Calif., 1974-76. First Class Scout Sr. Girl Scouts U.S., Rolling Hills, Calif., 1972-76. Mem. MENSA, Alpha Gamma Sigma. Office: Torrance Meml Hosp 3330 Lomita Blvd Torrance CA 90509

OSWALT, MARCIA JANE, educational administrator; b. Oregon City, Oreg., Aug. 24, 1937; d. Nolan Raymond and Helen Marian (Wilson) Yoder; m. Reed Edward Oswalt, June 9, 1962; children: Aaron J., Eric N. BS in Edn., Western Oreg. State Coll., 1958; MA, U. Denver, 1961, postgrad., 1961-62; postgrad. in adminstrn., Lewis and Clark Coll., 1985. Cert. tchr., adminstr. Oreg., Alaska. Tchr. elem. schs. Parkrose Sch. Dist., Portland, Oreg., 1958-59; instr. Oreg. Coll. Edn. (name now Western Oreg. State Coll.), Monmouth, 1959-64; storekeeper Kadiak Fisheries, Ouzinkie, Alaska, 1964-67; tchr. elem. schs. Kodiak Island Borough Sch. Dist., Port Lions, Alaska, 1967-76, Kodiak, Alaska, 1976-85; tchr. jr. high sch. Kodiak Island Borough Sch. Dist., Kodiak, 1985-87; prin. Peterson Elem. Sch. and Chiniak Elem. Sch., Kodiak, 1987--. Mem. Kodiak Arts Council, 1985--. Mem. Nat. Assn. Elem. Prins., Assn. for Supervision and Curriculum Devel., Alaska Assn. Elem. Prins., AAUW (pres. Alaska div. 1984-86), Kodiak Hist. Soc. Home: 3601 Monashka Bay Rd PO Box 722 Kodiak AK 99615 Office: Peterson Elem Sch 722 Mill Bay Rd Kodiak AK 99615

OTANI, MICHAEL NOBURU, small business owner; b. Seattle, July 17, 1955; s. David Naomi and Sylvia Michiko (Nomura) O. BS, U. Wash., 1977. Estimator Proctor Sales Inc., Seattle, 1978-80; sales person Wallace and Wheeler Inc., Bellevue, Wash., 1980-81; estimator Washington Air Reps Inc., Seattle, 1981-85; owner, operator Air Commodities Inc., Seattle, 1985—. Active Mcpl. League, Seattle, 1984-86. Mem. ASHRAE (assoc.), Seattle Jaycees (Outstanding Pres. 1984-85, internat. senator), Wash. Athletic Club. Home: 6209 52d St NE Seattle WA 98115

OTERO, ENRIQUE FRANCISCO, systems programmer; b. Mantua, Cuba, Mar. 9, 1946; came to U.S., 1961; s. Ofelio E. and Nieves M. (Pitaluga) O. BS in Engring., Calif. State U., L.A., 1969; MS in Computer Sci., U. So. Calif., 1972; MBA, Pepperdine U., 1988. Programmer, analyst Atlantic Richfield Co., L.A., 1968-77, systems programmer, 1977-85; systems programmer So. Calif. Gas Co., L.A., 1986—. Mem. IEEE, Assn. for Computing Machinery. Democrat. Roman Catholic. Home: 1900 N Vine St APT 202 Los Angeles CA 90068 Office: So Calif Gas Co 1801 S Atlantic Blvd 711-B Monterey Park CA 91754

OTHELLO, MARYANN CECILIA, management consultant; b. N.Y.C., Oct. 23, 1946; d. Alphonse Reasum and Edith (Atwater) Othello. BS, St. Paul's Coll., Lawrenceville, Va., 1968; MS, Columbia U., 1972. Cert. adoption specialist. Family therapist crisis intervention Dept. Social Svcs., N.Y.C., 1968-72; dir. treatment team Abbott House, Irvington, N.Y., 1972-73; unit chief Manhattan State Psychiat. Facility, N.Y.C., 1973-75; asst. dir., dir. social svcs. St. Peter's Sch., Peekskill, N.Y., 1975-77; dir. Patchwork Svcs. for Children, Santa Ana, Calif., 1977-78; dir. adult and geriatric svcs. Cen. City Community Mental Health, L.A., 1978-79; trainer, facilitator Lifespring, Inc., San Rafael, Calif., 1978-80; sr. mgmt. cons. Nelson Cons. Group, Inc., Mpls., 1980—; cons. Calif. Dept. Edn., 1977; field instr. casework Hunter Coll. Sch. Social Work, N.Y.C., 1975-77; adj. instr. U. So. Calif., L.A., 1977-78; specialist career devel. Goal for It, L.A., 1977-82; mgmt. devel. cons. Mgmt. Dynamics, Irvine, Calif., 1980-82. Contbr. articles to profl. jours.; was interviewed twice on radio talk show As It Is, U. Calif., Irvine. Bd. dirs., presenter humanitarian awards L.A. Commn. on Assaults Against Women, 1985-87; facilitator Ch. of Religious Scis., Huntington Beach, Calif., 1981-83, NAACP, Urban League. Named one of Outstanding Young Women of Am., 1976, 81; N.Y. State Regent scholar, 1968; Marie Antoinette Canon fellow Columbia U., 1972. Fellow Child Welfare League Am. (Adoption Specialist plaque 1976-89); mem. NAFE, Smithsonian Inst., Nat. Soc. for Historic Preservation, Wadsworth Antheneum, Nat. Trust for Hist. Preservation, Assn. for Female Execs. Office: Nelson Cons Group Inc 14001 Ridgedale Dr Ste 300 Minneapolis MN 55343

OTIS, KATHERINE MARIE, auditor, consultant; b. Columbus, Ohio, Sept. 22, 1958; d. Gordon Edward and Marlene Mary (Allix) O. BSBA, Cen. Mo. State U., 1980. With Farmers Ins. Group, 1980—; home office auditing specialist Farmers Ins. Group, L.A., 1987-88, home office EDP auditor, 1988—; beauty cons. Mary Kay Cosmetics, Simi Valley, Calif., 1988—. Big sister Big Sister/Bros. Am., Thousand Oaks, Calif., 1987. Mem. Inst. Internal Auditors. Roman Catholic. Office: Farmers Ins Group 4680 Wilshire Blvd Los Angeles CA 90010

OTOSHI, TOM YASUO, electrical engineer; b. Seattle, Sept. 4, 1931; s. Jitsuo and Shina Otoshi; m. Haruko Shirley Yumiba, Oct. 13, 1963; children: John, Kathryn. BSEE, U. Wash., 1954, MSEE, 1957; m. Haruko Shirley Yumiba, Oct. 13, 1963. With Hughes Aircraft Co., Culver City, Calif., 1956-61; mem. tech. staff Jet Propulsion Lab., Calif. Inst. Tech., Pasadena, 1961—; cons. Recipient NASA New Tech. awards. Mem. I Cantori and The Early Music Ensemble., IEEE (sr., editorial bd. Transactions on Microwave Theory and Techniques), Sigma Xi. Contbr. articles to profl. jours; composer works include I Cantori, Early Music Ensemble, patentee in field. Home: 3551 Henrietta St La Crescenta CA 91214 Office: Jet Propulsion Lab 4800 Oak Grove Dr Pasadena CA 91109

OTT, WENDELL LORENZ, art museum director, artist; b. McCloud, Calif., Sept. 17, 1942; s. Wendell and Rose (Jacob) O. Student, San Francisco Art Inst., 1960-61, 62-63; B.A., Trinity U., San Antonio, 1968; M.F.A., U. Ariz., 1970; postgrad., Mus. Mgmt. Inst., U. Calif., 1984. Asst. dir. Roswell (N.Mex.) Mus. and Art Center, 1970-71, dir., 1971-86; dir. Tacoma Art Mus., 1986—; chmn. Roswell Humanities Series, 1972-73; instr. N.Mex. Mil. Inst., Roswell; mem. visual arts adv. com. Coll. of Santa Fe, 1985; grant reviewer Inst. Mus. Services, Washington, 1983. One man exhbns. include, Trinity U., 1967, 68, Men of Art Guild, San Antonio, 1967, 68, David Orr's Gallery, Roswell, 1976, G.W.V. Smith Art Mus., Springfield, Mass.; group exhbns. include Tex. Painting and Sculpture, Dallas Mus. Fine Arts, 1966, Witte Meml. Mus., San Antonio, 1967, 68, 1st ann. S.W. Arts Festival, Tucson, 1969, Graphics 69, Western N.Mex. U., 1969, 11th Ariz. ann. Phoenix Art Mus., 1969 (purchase awards), 9th ann., Security, Colo., 1969, 5th invitational Yuman Art Center, Yuma, Ariz., 1970, Juarez (Mexico) Mus. Art and History, 1973. Served with AUS, 1964-66. Mem. Am. Assn. Museums (MAP surveyor mus. assessment program 1984), Tacoma Zoo Soc. (bd. dirs.). Lodge: Rotary. Home: 10513 107th St Ct SW Tacoma WA 98498 Office: Tacoma Art Mus 12th & Pacific Tacoma WA 98402

OTTER, CLEMENT LEROY, lieutenant governor; b. Caldwell, Idaho, May 3, 1942; s. Joseph Bernard and Regina Mary (Buser) O.; m. Gay Corinne Simplot, Dec. 28, 1964; children: John Simplot, Carolyn Lee, Kimberly Dawn, Corinne Marie. BA in Polit. Sci., Coll. Idaho, 1967; PhD, Mindanao State U., 1980. Mgr. J.R. Simplot Co., Caldwell, Idaho, 1971-76, asst. to v.p. adminstrn., 1976-78, v.p. adminstrn., 1978-82, internat. pres., from 1982, now v.p.; lt. gov. State of Idaho, Boise, 1987—. Mem. Presdl. Task Force AID, Washington, 1982-84; com. mem. invest tech. devel. State Adv. Council, Washington, 1983-84; mem. exec. council Bretton Woods Com., 1984—; mem. U.S. C. of C., Washington, 1983-84. Mem. Young Pres.' Orgn., Sales and Mktg. Execs., Idaho Assn. Commerce and Industry, Idaho Agrl. Leadership Council, Idaho Ctr. for Arts, Idaho Internat. Trade Council, Pacific N.W. Waterways Assn., N.W. Food Producers, Ducks Unltd. Republican. Roman Catholic. Clubs: Arid, Hillcrest Country. Lodge: Moose, Elks. Office: Office of the Lt Gov State House Rm 225 Boise ID 83702 *

OTTLEY, JEROLD DON, choral conductor, educator; b. Salt Lake City, Apr. 7, 1934; s. Sidney James and Alice (Warren) O.; m. JoAnn South, June 22, 1956; children: Brent Kay, Allison. B.A., Brigham Young U., Provo, Utah, 1961; M.Mus., U. Utah, 1967; Fulbright study grantee, Fed. Republic Germany, 1968-69; D.M.A. (grad. teaching fellow), U. Oreg., 1972. Tchr. public schs. Salt Lake City area, 1961-65; mem. faculty U. Utah, 1967—, asst. prof. music, 1971-78, adj. assoc. prof. music, 1978-81, adj. prof. music, 1981—; assoc. conductor Salt Lake Mormon Tabernacle Choir, 1974-75, conductor, 1975—; also guest conductor throughout U.S. Recording artist, CBS Masterworks. Past mem. gen. music coms. Mormon Ch., cultural arts com. Salt Lake City C. of C. (Honors in the Arts award), past bd. advs. Barlow Endowment Music Composition. Served with U.S. Army, 1957-59. Faculty Study grantee U. Utah, 1972. Mem. Am. Choral Dirs. Assn., Am. Choral Found., Master Tchr. Inst. Arts. (past trustee). Office: Mormon Tabernacle Choir 50 E North Temple Salt Lake City UT 84150

OTTO, B. MARIE, educational administrator, educational consulting company executive; b. Houston, July 11, 1930; d. Robert Lillard and Bertha Irene (Allen) Davis; m. Robert Lee Otto, Jan. 7, 1950; children: Lois Ann Otto Buschmann, Barbara Jeane Otto Hunt, Robert Lee Jr. Student, Tex. Christian U., 1947-49, Hardin-Simmons U., summers 1947, 49, 54; BA in Speech, Drama and Edn., Sul-Ross State U., 1954; postgrad., U. Wyo., U. Calif., Santa Barbara, UCLA, Calif. State U., Northridge, Calif. State U., Fullerton; MA, Calif. State U., Long Beach, 1967. Lic. tchr., Tex., secondary tchr., Wyo., Calif.; lic. psychologist; lic. marriage and family counselor. Tchr. high schs., Tex., Wyo. and Calif., 1956-64; tchr., counselor Excelsior High Sch., Norwalk, Calif., 1964-66; counselor Neff High Sch., La Mirada, Calif., 1966-69; psychologist Huntington Beach (Calif.) Union High Sch. Dist., 1969-74, project mgr., dir. pupil pers., 1974-80, asst. supt., 1980-84, supt., 1984-88, supt. emeritus, 1988—; v.p. Poole-Young-Koehler Assocs. Inc., Long Beach, 1964-79; pvt. practice marriage and family counselor, Fountain Valley, Calif., 1970—; pres. Marie Ottos Assocs., Fountain Valley, 1979—; supr. student tchrs. Chapman Coll., Santa Ana, Calif., 1988—. Mem. Fountain Valley Human Svcs. Com., Huntington Beach Human Resources Commn., state planning com. Girl Scouts U.S., Worland, Wyo., 1959-61; pres. Spl. Edn. Local Plan Orgn., 1983-84; bd. dirs. Humana Hosp. Huntington Beach, Golden West Coll. Found., Huntington Beach, Huntington Beach Community Clinic, Orange County chpt. ARC, Santa Ana, Calif, No on Drugs, 1988—. Recipient plaque Fountain Valley Human Svcs. Com., 1979, Spl. Edn. Local Plan Orgn., 1984; named Woman of Yr., Soroptimists, Westminster, 1984, Disting. Alumnus, Grad. Sch. Edn. Calif. State U., Long Beach, 1988. Mem. Nat. Assn. Sch. Psychologists (pres. Orange County chpt. 1974-75, plaque 1975), Phi Kappa Phi. Home: 16689 Mt Hoffman Circle Fountain Valley CA 92708 Office: Huntington Beach High Sch Dist 10251 Yorktown Ave Huntington Beach CA 92646

OTTO, GEORGE JOHN, investment banker; b. San Francisco, June 8, 1904; s. Paul O. and Emma (Shanstrum) O.; m. Marie Kendrick, Oct. 10, 1933; children—Marie L., Elizabeth A., Susan. A.B., U. Calif. at Berkeley, 1926. Bond salesman Mitchum Tully & Co., 1926-35; partner Irving Lundborg & Co., San Francisco, 1935-70; vice chmn. bd. dirs. Clark Dodge Co., Inc., San Francisco, 1970-74; v.p. Kidder Peabody & Co., 1974—; dir. Schlage Lock Co.; gov. Stock Exchange Firms; pres. Pacific Coast Stock Exchange, chmn. San Francisco div. Active local council Girl Scouts U.S.A.; trustee World Affairs Council; bd. dirs. Internat. Hospitality Center, Columbia Park Boys Club, Golden Gate Coll., No. Calif. Soc. for Prevention Blindness, San Francisco Ladies Protection and Relief Soc., Palace Fine Arts League. Mem. Investment Bankers Assn. Am. (v.p., gov. Calif. group; past gov.), Brit. Am. C. of C. (dir.). Clubs: Bond (San Francisco) (pres. 1947), Bohemian (San Francisco) (sec., dir. 1956-57), San Francisco Golf (San Francisco), Pacific Union. Home: 2701 Pierce St San Francisco CA 94123 Office: 555 California St San Francisco CA 94104

OTTO, JEFFERY LEE, pharmaceutical company executive; b. Colorado Springs, Colo., Aug. 4, 1955; s. Carlyle Leonard and Lelia Irene (Carr) O. BA in Chemistry, U. Colo., 1977, PhD in Analytical Chemistry, 1981. Sr. rsch. analyst Cord Labs., Broomfield, Colo., 1982-85, mgr. analytical rsch. and devel., 1985-89; dir. analytical rsch. and devel. Cord Labs., Broomfield, 1989—. Named Eagle Scout Boy Scouts Am., 1969. Mem. Am. Chem. Soc., Rocky Mountain Chromatography Discussion Group. Republican. Lutheran. Home: 7514 Queen Circle Arvada CO 80005 Office: Cord Labs 2555 W Midway Boulder CO 80020

OTUS, SIMONE, public relations executive; b. Walnut Creek, Calif., Jan. 10, 1960; d. Mahmut and Alexa (Artemenko) O. BA, U. Calif., Berkeley, 1981. Account exec. Marx-David Advt., San Francisco, 1981-82; freelance writer Mpls. and San Francisco, 1982-83; account exec. D'Arcy, MacManus & Masius, San Francisco, 1983; account supr. Ralph Silver Assocs., San Francisco, 1984-85; ptnr., co-founder Blanc & Otus Pub. Relations, San Francisco, 1985—. Office: Blanc & Otus Pub Rels 40 Gold St San Francisco CA 94133

OUGHTON, THOMAS VICTOR, engineer; b. Denver, Oct. 12, 1951; s. Victor William and JoAnne (Speicher) O.; m. Kelly Ann Gomer, June 14, 1980; children: Kevin Thomas, Theodore Powell. BS in Engring. Physics, U. Colo., 1975. Researcher U. Colo. Health Scis. Ctr., Denver, 1976-81; engring. programmer UNISYS, Thorton, Colo., 1981—. Republican. Club: Star Prowlers (Broomfield, Colo.) (treas. 1983), Star Fleet (Arvada, Colo.) (sec. 1988—). Office: UNISYS 9351 Grant St #500 Thornton CO 80229

OVERALL, JAMES CARNEY, JR., pediatrics educator; b. Nashville, Sept. 27, 1937; s. James Carney and Evelyn Byrd (Duncan) O.; m. Marie Kathryn Pauli, Aug. 14, 1965; children: David, Paul. BS, Davidson Coll., 1959; MD, Vanderbilt U., 1963. Cert. pediatrics. Intern Vanderbilt U. Hosp., Nashville, 1963-64; resident Columbia Presbyn. Med. Ctr., N.Y.C., 1964-66; research assoc. Nat. Inst. Child Health, Bethesda, Md., 1966-68; instr. pediatrics Rochester, N.Y., 1968-70; asst. prof. pediatrics, microbiology U. Utah Sch. Med., Salt Lake City, 1970-74, assoc. prof. pediatrics, microbiology, 1974-79, prof. pediatrics, 1979—, prof. pathology, 1981—; chief pediatrics infectious diseases Univ. Utah Sch. Med., 1970—; bd. govs. Primary Children's Med. Ctr., Salt Lake City, 1976-78; dir. virology course U. Utah Sch. Med., 1980—; vice chmn. pediatrics dept. U. Utah Sch. Med., 1982—; dir. diagnostic virology lab., 1981—. Contbr. chpts. to textbooks, articles to profl. jours. vice moderator Holladay United Ch. Christ, Salt Lake City, 1982-85. Served to lt. comdr. USPHS, 1966-68. Recipient Investigator award Howard Hughes Med. Inst., 1974-80. Mem. Am. Pediatric Soc., Soc. Pediatric Research, Am. Soc. Virology. United Ch. of Christ. Home: 382 L St Salt Lake City UT 84103 Office: Univ Utah Sch Med Dept Pediatrics Salt Lake City UT 84132

OVERALL, MANARD, manufacturing executive, electrical engineer; b. St. Louis, Sept. 20, 1939; s. Walter and Emma O.; 1 child, Marc Allen. Student, U. Md., 1969-71; BS in Elec. Engring., Hampton U., 1973; MBA, Fairleigh Dickenson, 1977. Enlisted USCG, 1957, aviation electronics technician CPO, 1957-67; chief warrant officer U.S. Army, 1967-77; mktg. engr. Tex. Instruments Digital Systems, Austin, 1979-81; mgr. bus. devel. telecommunications Tracor, Austin, Tex., 1979-81; dir. mktg. & program mgmt. Modular Power Systems, Austin, 1981-85; engring. projects mgr. power conversion div. Eldec Corp., Lynnwood, Wash., 1986-88; mgr. applications engring. display products Eldec Corp., Lynnwood, 1988—; prin. Mgmt. Objectives (bus. consulting), Austin, Tex., 1982-85. Mem. Leadership Austin , Tex., 1983; treas. Mt. Zion Baptist Ch. Brotherhood, Seattle, 1987—. Decorated with 2 Bronze Stars, U.S. Army, Vietnam, 1968, 1970, Legion of Merit, U.S. Army, 1977. Mem. Puget Sound Black Engrs. (pres. 1988—). Home: PO Box 126 Lynnwood WA 98046 Office: Eldec Corp Display Products M/S 80 PO Box 100 Lynnwood WA 98046

OVERHOLT, MILES HARVARD, cable television consultant; b. Glendale, Calif., Sept. 30, 1921; s. Miles Harvard and Alma Overholt; A.B., Harvard Coll., 1943; m. Jessie Foster, Sept. 18, 1947; children—Miles Harvard, Keith Foster. Mktg. analyst Dun & Bradstreet, Phila., 1947-48; collection mgr. Standard Oil of Calif., Los Angeles, 1948-53; br. mgr. RCA Service Co., Phila., 1953-63, ops. mgr. Classified Aerospace project RCA, Riverton, N.J.,

1963; pres. CPS, Inc., Paoli, Pa., 1964-67; mem. pres.'s exec. com. Gen. Time Corp., Mesa, Ariz., 1970-78; gen. mgr., dir. service Talley Industries, Mesa, 1967-78; v.p., gen. mgr. Northwest Entertainment Network, Inc., Seattle, 1979-81; mcpl. cable cons., 1981—. Served with USMCR, 1943-46. Decorated Bronze Star, Purple Heart (two). Mem. Assn. Home Appliance Mfrs., Nat. Assn. Microwave Distbn. Service Cos. Editor, publisher Mcpl. Cable Regulation Newsletter. Club: Harvard (N.Y.C.). Home: 8320 Frederick Pl Edmonds WA 98020 Office: NW Entertainment Network 4517 California Ave SW Ste B Seattle WA 98116

OVERMYER, VINCENT SHEARER, marketing executive; b. Burbank, Calif., July 11, 1957; s. Robert D. Overmyer and Phylis Jean (Brown) Petersen; m. Rosala May Parker, July 17, 1987; children: Allison M., Melanie May. BS, U. Colo., 1981. Sales Cimarron Bldg. Co., Riverside, Calif., 1987-88; mktg. mgr. Premier Inc., L.A., 1988—. Mem. Nat. Pool and Spa Inst., Seven Hills Golf Club. Republican. Methodist. Office: Premier Inc 303 S Andrita Los Angeles CA 90065

OVERSON, BRENT C., municipal official, former state senator; b. Nephi, Utah, Apr. 18, 1950; s. Fay Dean and Elda Rae (Huntsman) O.; m. Joanne Robison, Nov. 18, 1971; 3 children. A.A., U. Md., 1978; B.S. in Fin., U. Utah, 1982. Lic. real estate broker. Sales agt., office mgr. Envirowest Realty, Inc., Salt Lake City, 1978-82, 85-87; v.p. real estate and devel. Trailside Gen. Stores, Bountiful, Utah, 1982-85; mem. Utah Senate, 1983-86; chief dep. assessor, Salt Lake County, 1987—. Served with USN, 1972-78. Mem. Nat. Assn. Realtors, Internat. Assn. Assessing Officers (bd. dirs. Utah chpt.) Republican. Mormon. Office: N 2300 2001 S State Salt Lake City UT 84190-1300

OVERTON, EDWIN DEAN, campus minister, educator; b. Beaver, Okla., Dec. 2, 1939; s. William Edward and Georgia Beryl (Fronk) O. B.Th., Midwest Christian Coll., 1963; M.A. in Religion, Eastern N.Mex. U., 1969, Ed.S., 1978; postgrad. Fuller Theol. Sem., 1980. Ordained to ministry Christian Ch., 1978. Minister, Christian Ch., Englewood, Kans., 1962-63; youth minister First Christian Ch., Beaver, Okla., 1963-67; campus minister Central Christian Ch., Portales, N.Mex., 1967-68, Christian Campus House, Portales, N.Mex., 1968—; tchr. religion, philosophy, counseling Eastern N.Mex. Univ., Portales, 1970—, campus minister, Christian Campus House, 1968—, dir., 1980—; farm and ranch partner, Beaver, Okla., 1963—. State dir. Beaver Jr. C. of C., 1964-65; pres. Beaver High Sch. Alumni Assn., 1964-65; elder Cen. Christian Ch., Portales, N.Mex., 1985-88; chmn. Beaver County March of Dimes, 1966; pres. Portales Tennis Assn., 1977-78. Mem. U.S. Tennis Assn. Republican. Club: Lions. Home: 1129 Libra St Portales NM 88130 Office: 223 S Ave K Portales NM 88130

OVERTON, JOHN FARRELL, electronic manufacturing executive, educator; b. San Francisco, Dec. 26, 1950; s. John J. and Lavaughn F. (Schaaf) O.; m. Merry Linda Reinke, Dec. 27, 1969; children: Shane Kelly, Todd Allan. BA, San Francisco State U., 1977; MBA, Golden Gate U., 1987. Electronics tchr. Buschser High Sch., Santa Clara, Calif., 1978; service station mgr. Chevron, Pacifica, Calif., 1978; supr. technicians Varian Assocs. EIMAC div., San Carlos, Calif., 1978-83; product assurance engr. Varian Assocs. EIMAC div., San Carlos, 1983-86, product assurance mgr., 1986-87, div. mfg. mgr., 1987--. Served with USAF, 1969-76. Mem. Electronics Assn., Soc. Mfg. Engrs., Golden Gate Alumni Assn., Shriners, Masons, Eastern Star. Home: 35233 Severn Dr NewarK CA 94560 Office: Varian EIMAC Div 301 Industrial Way San Carlos CA 94070

OVERVOLD, ROBERTA JOYCE (ROBBI OVERVOLD), interior and product designer; b. Watertown, S.D., Apr. 17, 1934; d. Clifford Harland and Lilly Louise (Reinecke) O. Student, U. So. Calif., 1952-54, U. So. Calif., 1954-55, N.D. State U., 1957; BFA, U. So. Calif., 1959. Staff designer Coleman's, Fargo, N.D., 1955-57, Southland Interiors, Lomita, Calif., 1959-61, Frank Bros., Long Beach, Calif., 1961-66; owner, designer Robbi Overvold Interior Design, Seal Beach, Calif., 1966-70; interior designer, buyer Crossroads, Whittier, Calif., 1970-74; dir. design, interior designer, buyer Nerlands Home Furnishings, Kahului and Wailea, Hawaii, 1974-80; dir. design C.S. Wo & Sons, Lahaina, Hawaii, 1980-81; owner, designer Robbi Overvold A.S.I.D., Maalaea Village, Hawaii, 1980—. Designer: (rugs) Sun and Moon, Unika Vaev of Danmark, 1964, Aurora, Moreddi of Copenhagen 1964. Co-chmn. U. So. Calif. Blood Drive, Los Angeles, 1953; cellist Fargo-Moorhead Symphony Orch., 1950-52, 54-57, U. So. Calif. Symphony Orch., Light Opera Orch., Chamber Ensemble, 1952-54, 57-59; v.p. U. So. Calif. Sch. Fine Arts, 1958-59; bd. dirs. Pat Nixon Days Parade, Cerritos, Calif., 1969, Maui Symphony Orch., 1984; bd. dirs., chmn. memberships Maui Philharm. Soc., 1980. Recipient Gold Key award Calif. Design VIII Nat. Home Fashions League, Pasadena, 1962, Gold Medallion Apt. House of Yr. Calif. State Dept. Water and Power, North Hollywood, Calif. 1971. Mem. Am. Soc. Interior Designers (cert.), Nat. Council for Interior Design Qualification, Wailea Shopping Village Merchants Assn. (pres., bd. dirs. 1980), Am. Cetacean Soc. (bd. dirs. 1980), Seal Beach Yacht Club (mem. race and protest coms. 1965-73, Commodore's award 1964, 65, 66, 67, 68, 70, 71, 72, 73), Mu Phi Epsilon Hon. Music Soc. Republican. Methodist. Home and Office: Maalaea Kai 307 PO Box YYY Maalaea Village HI 96793

OVESON, W. VAL, state lieutenant governor, accountant; b. Provo, Utah, Feb. 11, 1952; s. Wilford W. and LaVon Oveson; m. Emilee Nebeker, Sept. 1, 1973; children: Polly, Libby, Peter, Benjamin. Student, U. Utah, 1973-74; BS in Acctg., Brigham Young U., 1976. CPA, Utah. Acct. Squire and Co., Orem, Utah, 1975-79; pvt. practice acctg. Squire and Co., Orem, 1979-80; state auditor State of Utah, Salt Lake City, 1981-84, lt. gov., 1985—; mem. dist. export council U.S. Dept. Commerce, 1985—; bd. examiners, 1981-84; chmn. State Records Com., 1981-84. Bd. dirs., unit campaign dir. United Way of Greater Salt Lake, 1985-86; trustee Travis Found., 1985—; treas. Utah County Rep. Party; mem. State Platform Com., 1982, 84; exec. com. Utah State Rep. Party, 1981—. Mem. Nat. Conf. Lt. Govs., Am. Inst. CPA's (mem. governing council 1986), Utah Assn. CPA's (Pub. Service award 1984). Republican. Mormon. Home: 2125 S 900 E Bountiful UT 84010 Office: Lt Govs Office 203 State Capitol Salt Lake City UT 84114

OWEN, AMY, library director; b. Brigham City, Utah, June 26, 1944; d. John Wallace and Bertha (Jensen) O. BA, Brigham Young U., 1966, MLS, 1968. Systems libr. Utah State Libr., Salt Lake City, 1968-72, dir. reference svcs., 1972-74, dir. tech. svcs., 1974-81, dep. dir., 1981-87, dir., 1987—; serials com. chmn. Utah Coll. Libr. Coun., Salt Lake City, 1975-77, exec. sec., 1978-84, coun. mem. 1987—; mem. staff Gov.'s Utah Systems Planning Task Force, Salt Lake City, summer 1982; staff liaison Utah Gov.'s Conf. on Libr. and Info. Svcs., 1977-79; mem. pres.'s adv. panel Baker & Taylor Co., Somerville, N.J., 1977-78; mem. rev. panel Nat. Commn. Libr. and Info. Svcs., 1985. Contbr. chpts. to books, also contbg. author various manuals; cons. and trainer in field. Coun. mem. Utah Endowment for Humanities, 1986—, vice chmn., 1987—, chair, 1988—; trustee Bibliographic Ctr. for Rsch., 1987—, pers. com., 1988—, chmn. pers. com., 1989—, nominating com., 1984; mem. nominations com. Chief Officers of State Libr. Agys., 1987-88, stats. com., 1988—, state info. policy workshop com., 1988; mem. conf. program com. Fedn. of State Humanities Couns., 1988; mem. coop. pub. libr. data system task force Nat. Commn. on Libr. and Info. Svcs., 1988—; grant rev. panelist NEH, 1988, panel mem. reading and discussion groups, 1988; regional project mgmt. bd. mem. Intermountain Community Learning and Info. Ctr. Project, 1987—. Mem. Utah Libr. Assn. (pres. 1978-79, exec. bd. 1976-80, Spl. Recognition award 1989), Mountain Plains Libr. Assn. (rec. sec. 1979-80, fin. com. 1982-84, Disting. Svc. award 1989), ALA (bd. dirs. ASCLA div. 1984-86, fin. com. 1984-86, planning, orgn. and bylaws com. 1981-85, SLAS program com. 1984-86, pres. program com. 1986, exec. bd. mem., 1988—; clene roundtable mem. com. 1984-86, nominations com. 1986—, nat. adv. com. office communications svcs., voices and visions project; LITA div. Satellite Conf. Task Force mem. 1982; PLA div. editor column. 1987—, PLA div. goals, guidelines & standards com., ALA Office for Research coop. pub. libr. data system adv. com., ALA Office for communications svcs., Voices and Visions project nat. adv. com.), Phi Kappa Phi, Alpha Lambda Delta. Home: 4786 Naniloa Dr Salt Lake City UT 84117 Office: Utah State Libr 2150 S 300 W Ste 16 Salt Lake City UT 84115

OWEN, CAROL THOMPSON, artist, educator; b. Pasadena, Calif., May 10, 1944; d. Sumner Comer and Cordelia (Whittemore) Thompson; m. James Eugene Owen, July 19, 1975; children: Kevin Christopher, Christine Celese. Student, Pasadena City Coll., 1963; BA with distinction, U. Redlands, 1966; MA, Calif. State U., L.A., 1967; MFA, Claremont Grad. Sch., 1969. Cert. community coll. instr., Calif. Head resident Pitzer Coll., Claremont, Calif., 1967-70; instr. art Mt. San Antonio Coll., Walnut, Calif., 1968—; dir. coll. art gallery Mt. San Antonio Coll., 1972-73. Group shows include: Covina Pub. Library, 1971, U. of Redlands, 1964, 65, 66, 70, 78, 88, Am. Ceramic Soc., 1969, others. Mem. Calif. Scholarship Fedn., Faculty Assn. Mt. San Antonio Coll., Coll. Art Assn. Am., Calif. Tchrs. Assn., Friends of Huntington Library, L.A. County Mus. Art, Heard Mus. Assn., Sigma Tau Delta. Republican. Presbyterian. Home: 534 S Hepner St Covina CA 91723 Office: Mt San Antonio Coll Grand Ave Walnut CA 91789

OWEN, FRANK ELLWOOD, JR., chemical engineer; b. Tacoma, Wash., July 4, 1923; s. Frank Ellwood and Margaret Isabelle (McNaughton) O.; m. Betty Eileen Corey, Sept. 18, 1948; children: Philip Corey, Margaret Eileen Mercer. BS in Chem. Engring., U. Wash., 1948. Various positions Gen. Electric Co., Richland, Wash., 1948-65; sr. radiol. engr., sr. health physicist United Nuclear Inc., Richland, 1965-73; prin. engr. Wash. Pub. Power Supply System, Richland, 1973-83; tech. leader Battelle Northwest, Richland, 1983—. Served with USN, 1943-46, PTO. Fellow Health Physics Soc. Home: 1030 Birch Richland WA 99352 Office: Battelle NW Battelle Blvd Richland WA 99352

OWEN, HERBERT RODNEY, infosystems specialist; b. Bremerton, Wash., Oct. 10, 1935; s. Herbert Harry Owen and Maude Winona (Byington) Garner; children: Jeffrey Rod, Perry Jay. BSCE, Walla Walla Coll., 1962; BS in Phys. Scis., Wash. State U., 1973; M in Internat. Mgmt., Am. Grad. Sch. Internat. Mgmt., 1974. ADP intern Mgmt. Engring. Tng. Agy., Rock Island, Ill., 1963-64; ADP dir. Naval Sta., Keflavik, Iceland, 1968-70; ADP project mgr. Naval Ships System Command, Bremerton, 1970-74; supr. systems analyst Naval Supply Depot, Subic Bay, Philippines, 1975-79; ADP coordinator Far East Engring. Dist., Seoul, Republic of Korea, 1981-83; ADP security officer Trident Tng. Facility, Bangor, Wash., 1979-81, 83-85; ADP dir. Commdr. Fleet Activities, Okinawa, Japan, 1985-89; dep. dir. Infosystems Command, Fort Ord, Calif., 1989—. Bus. mgr. Northwest Chess Mag. Mem. U.S. Chess Fedn. (sr. tournament dir.), Wash. Chess Fedn. (bd. dirs.), Am. Bowling Assn. (regional pres.). Republican. Clubs: Flying (Keflavik), Toastmasters. Office: Navy Air Facility Kadena ADP Commdr Fleet Activities Okinawa Seattle WA 98770-1150

OWEN, JEFFREY LYNN, communications executive; b. San Francisco, Mar. 11, 1951; s. Adele Cruz (Liebers) O.; m. Elizabeth S. Wosman, July 29, 1972 (div. 1978); children: Gregory, Rebecca; m. Karen Lee Nelson, June 26, 1987. AA, Skyline Coll., 1980. Apprentice carpenter Standard Builders, San Francisco, 1978-80; mgr. So. City Camera Store, San Francisco, 1980; communication system rep. Pacific Tele., San Francisco, 1980-83; telecommunications cons. engr. Crocker Bank, San Francisco, 1983-84; sr. project mgr. Wells Fargo Bank, San Francisco, 1984-86; asst. v.p., mgr. 1st Interstate Bank, L.A., 1986-89, Hughes Aircraft Co., Long Beach, Calif., 1989—; instr. Golden Gate U., San Francisco, 1985-86. Pres. Newport Heights Homeowners Assn., Long Beach, Calif., 1987; active Am. Diabetes Assn., L.A., 1984—. Staff sgt. USMC, 1968-77. Mem. Am. Mgmt. Assn. (assoc.), Friends of Photography, Calumet Photography Soc. Republican. Roman Catholic. Home: 6141 Anthony Ave Garden Grove CA 92645 Office: Hughes Aircraft Co PO Box 9399 Bldg C06 MS 2034 Long Beach CA 90810

OWEN, WILLIAM FREDERICK, engineering and management consultant; b. Pontiac, Mich., July 27, 1947; s. Webster Jennings and Elizabeth (Hayes) W.; m. Delores T. Owen, Mar. 30, 1974 (div. Dec. 1978); m. Janice L. Pierce, July 29, 1983. BS, Mich. Tech. U., 1972; MS, U. Mich., 1973; PhD, Stanford U., 1978. Research engr. Neptune Microfloc, Corvallis, Oreg., 1973-75, process applications engr., 1975-76; process applications engr. Dr. Perry McCarty, Stanford, Calif., 1976-78; sr. engr. Culp/Wesner/Culp, Cameron Park, Calif., 1978-82; pres. Owen Engring. and Mgmt. Cos., Denver, 1982—. Author: Energy in Wastewater Treatment, 1982, Turbo Mainenance Manager. Del. People-to-People, People's Republic China, 1986. Served with USN, 1965-68. Recipient Local Govt. Innovations award Denver Regional Council Govt., 1983, Boettcher Innovations award Denver Regional Council Govt., 1984, Energy Innovations award Colo. Council Energy Ofcls., 1983. Club: Pinehurst Country (Denver). Home: 3829 S Chase St Denver CO 80235 Office: Owen Engring and Mgmt Cons Inc 5353 W Dartmouth Ave Denver CO 80227

OWENS, BUCK (ALVIS EDGAR, JR.), singer, musician, songwriter; b. Sherman, Tex., Aug. 12, 1929; s. Alvis Edgar and Maicie A.; m. Bonnie Owens, 1947 (div. 1955); children: Buddy, Mike; m. Phyllis Owens (div. 1972); 1 son, John; m. Jennifer, 1978. Attended pub. schs., Mesa, Ariz. Pres. Buck Owens Prodns.; owner Radio stas. KUZZ-AM-FM, Owens Enterprises, Bakersfield, Calif., KNIX AM/FM Radio, Phoenix. Rec. artist, Capitol Records, 1958-76, 88—, Warner Bros. Records 1976-80; star syndicated TV shows Buck Owens Ranch Show; leader, Buck Owens' Buckaroos Band, 1960—; star of TV show Hee Haw, 1969-86. Records include Under Your Spell Again, Above and Beyond, Excuse Me, I Think I've Got a Heartache, Fooling Around, Under the Influence of Love, My Heart Skips a Beat, Act Naturally, Waitin' in the Welfare Line, Sam's Place, How Long Will My Baby Be Gone, Tall Dark Stranger, Too Old to Cut the Mustard, Rollin' in My Sweet Baby's Arms, The Kansas City Song, We're Gonna Get Together, others. Recipient Instrumental Group of Year award Country Music Assn., 1967-68; named Artist of Decade Capitol Records, Country Artist of Year for 5 consecutive years Billboard, Cash Box and Record World; awarded 28 consecutive No. 1 records. Office: Buck Owens Prodns 3223 Sillect Ave Bakersfield CA 93308

OWENS, GARY, radio and television performer, author; b. Mitchell, S.D., May 10; s. Bernard and Vennetta Owens; m. Arleta Lee Markell, June 26; children: Scott Michael, Christopher Dana. Student (Speech scholar), Dakota Wesleyan U., Mitchell; student, Mpls. Art Inst. With KMPC, Los Angeles, 1962-82; with KPRZ, Los Angeles, 1982—; With KFI, Los Angeles, 1986—; pres. The Foonman & Sons, Inc.; radio host Gary Owens Music Weekend, Lorimar Telepictures, 1987—; v.p., nat. creative dir. Gannett Broadcasting, 1984. Radio performer, 1955—; nat. creative dir., Golden West Broadcasters, 1981-82; syndicated radio show The G.O. Spl. Report, from 1969; host: world-wide syndicated show Soundtrack of the 60's, 1981—, Biff Owens Sports Exclusive, 1981—; USA Today, Mut. Broadcasting System, 1982—; performer, writer: world-wide syndicated show Sesame St, 1969—, Electric Co, 1969—, Dirkniblick (Mathnet) CTW, 1988; numerous animated cartoons including Dyno-Mutt, ABC-TV, 1975, Roger Ramjet, 1965, Space Ghost, 1968, Perils of Penelope Pitstop, 1970, Square One, 1987, also over 1400 animated cartoons including Godzilla's Power Hour, 1979, Space Heroes, 1981, Mighty Orbots, 1984, World's Greatest Adventures, 1986, Garfield, Cops; appeared: in films The Love Bug, 1968, Prisoner of Second Ave., 1975, Hysterical, 1982, Nat. Lampoon's European Vacation, 1985, I'm Gonna Get You Sucka, 1988, Kill Crazy, 1988, How I Got Into College, 1988, Say Bye Bye, 1989, others; performer: Rowan and Martin's Laugh-in, 1968-73; TV host: Gong Show, ABC-TV, 1976, Monty Pythons Flying Circus, 1975; regular performer: TV Games People Play, 1980-81, Breakaway, 1983; author: Elephants, Grapes and Pickles, 1963; 12 printings The Gary Owens What To Do While Your're Holding the Phone Book, rev, 1973, A Gary Owens Chrestomathy, 1980; author: (screenplay) Three Caraway Seeds and an Agent's Heart, 1979; columnist: (screenplay) Radio and Records newspaper, 1978—, Hollywood Citizen-News, 1965-67, Hollywood mag., 1983—, The Daily News, 1981—; rec. artist (screenplay), MGM, ABC, Epic, Warner Bros., RCA, Reprise, Decca. Chmn. Multiple Sclerosis dr. Los Angeles, 1972; chmn., grand marshall So. Calif. Diabetes Dr., 1974—; mayor City of Encino, Calif., from 1972; bd. govs. Grammy awards, 1968—, Emmy awards, 1972; adv. bd. Pasadena (Calif.) City Coll., 1969—, Sugar Ray Robinson Youth Found., 1971—; mem. nat. miracle com. Juvenile Diabetes Found., 1981—, nat. com. for Carousel Ball Children's Diabetes Found. Denver; radio adv. bd. U. So. Calif., 1980—; hon. chmn. Goodwill Industries Sporting Goods Dr., 1986, chmn. 1986 campaign.; bd. dirs. D-Fy (anti-drug org.), D.A.R.E. (drug education program) Los Angeles Police Dept., 1986; announcer (for homeless in Am.) Comic Relief, 1987-88, 89—. Named outstanding radio personality in U.S., 1965-79, top Radio Personality in World, Internat. Radio Forum, Toronto, 1977, Man of Yr. All-Cities Employees Assn., City of Los Angeles, 1968, Top Radio Broadcaster, Nat. Assn. Broadcasters, 1986, Radio Man of Yr. Nat. Assn. Broadcasters, 1986; recipient Distinguished Service award Hollywood Jaycees, 1966, David award, 1978, Hollywood Hall of Fame award, 1980, Am. award Cypress Coll., 1981, Carbon Mike award Pacific Broadcasters, 1987, 5 Grammy nominations, Emmy award for More Dinosaurs, 1986; Star on Hollywood Walk of Fame, 1981; honored by U.S. Dept. Treasury, 1985. Hon. mem. No. Calif. Cartoonists Assn.; mem. Cartoonists and Artists Profl. Soc. Office: 610 S Ardmore Los Angeles CA 90005 *

OWENS, ROBERT PATRICK, lawyer; b. Spokane, Wash., Feb. 17, 1954; s. Walter Patrick and Cecile (Phillippay) O.; m. Robin Miller, Aug. 12, 1978; children: Ryan Barry, Meghan Jane. BA, Wash. State U., 1976; JD, Gonzaga U., 1981; LLM in Admiralty Law, Tulane U., 1983. Bar: Wash. 1982, Alaska 1984, U.S. Dist. Ct. (ea. dist.) Wash. 1982, U.S. Dist. Ct. Alaska 1984, U.S. Ct. Appeals (5th cir.) 1983. Assoc. Groh, Eggars & Price, Anchorage, 1983-88; mng. atty. Taylor & Hintze, Anchorage, 1988—. Coord. supplies Insight Seminars, Anchorage, 1985-86. Mem. ABA (Dist. 27 rep., young lawyers div. 1988—), Alaska Bar Assn., Wash. State Bar Assn., Anchorage Bar Assn. (pres. young lawyers Sect. 1986-88), Alaska Fly Fishers, Phi Alaska Delta. Democrat. Roman Catholic. Office: Taylor & Hintze 303 K St Ste 603 Anchorage AK 99501

OWENS, ROBERT PHILLIP, police official; b. Stamford, Conn., Sept. 12, 1931; s. Robert Evan and Ann (Humphreys) O.; children—Steven, Olga. B.S. Police Adminstrn., Calif. State U.-Los Angeles, 1968; M.B.A., Pepperdine U., 1973. With Los Angeles County Sheriff's Dept., Los Angeles, 1954-67; chief police San Fernando City, Calif., 1967-70, Oxnard Police Dept., Calif., 1970—; cons. U.S. Dept. Justice, 1977-81, Office Criminal Justice Planning Calif., 1977—, Ind. U., 1974-78. Served with USMC, 1949-53. Named Outstanding Law Enforcement Officer, Calif. Trial Lawyers Assn., 1984; recipient Oxnard trophy Greater Oxnard C. of C, 1983. Mem. Nat. Orgn. Victim Assistance (bd. dirs. 1981—). Republican. Unitarian. Lodge: Rotary (pres. 1975-76). Office: Oxnard Police Dept 251 C St S Oxnard CA 93030

OWENS, WARNER BARRY, physical therapist; b. Detroit, Apr. 29, 1939; s. Wendell Lee and Flora Lucille (Maddox) O.; m. Frances Hutton, June 11, 1960 (div. May 1973); children—Jeffrey, Karen; m. Sandra Irene Olstyn, Nov. 16, 1974. B.S., UCLA, 1962. Staff phys. therapist Valley Phys. Therapy Ctr., Van Nuys, Calif., 1962-63; chief phys. therapist St. Joseph Med. Ctr., Burbank, Calif., 1963-70, dir. rehab., 1970—, bd. dirs. Credit Union, 1974-76, 83-86, pres., 1986—; exec. v.p. Therapeutic Assocs. Inc., Van Nuys, 1970—; dir. Tetrad and Assocs., Van Nuys, 1972—; co-dir. Barry-Boyd Leasing Ltd., Van Nuys, 1978—; mem. admissions com. phys. therapy option Calif. State U.-Northridge, 1976—. Childrens Hosp. Sch. Phys. Therapy Kate Crutcher scholar, 1961; recipient Outstanding Contbn. to Profession award Calif. State U.-Northridge, 1983. Mem. Am. Phys. Therapy Assn. (chmn. jud. com. 1981-82), Am. Coll. Sports Medicine, Phys. Therapy Dirs. Forum, Internat. Wine and Food Soc. (bd. dirs. San Fernando Valley 1979—, pres. 1980). Republican. Home: 3680 Alomar Dr Sherman Oaks CA 91423 Office: Therapeutic Assocs Inc 15216 Vanowen St Ste 2D Van Nuys CA 91405

OWENS, (DOUGLAS) WAYNE, congressman; b. Panguitch, Utah, May 2, 1937; m. Marlene Wessel; 5 children. Grad., U. Utah, JD, 1964. Mem. Congress, 1972-74; sole practice Salt Lake City and Washington, 1974, 78-80; pres. Montreal Mission for Ch. of Jesus Christ of Latter-Day Saints, Que., Can., 1974-78; mem. 100th, 101st Congresses from 2d Utah dist., mem. interior and insular affairs com., judiciary com., fgn. affairs com., Dem. steering and policy com.; adminstrv. asst. Sen. Edward Kennedy, 1969. Coordinator western states Roberty Kennedy for Pres., 1968, Edward Kennedy for Pres., 1980; candidate for U.S. Senate, 1974, for gov. of Utah, 1984. Named one of 200 Leaders for the Future, Time Mag., 1974. Office: Office of House Mems care The Postmaster Washington DC 20515

OWINGS, MARGARET WENTWORTH, conservationist, artist; b. Berkeley, Calif., Apr. 29, 1913; d. Frank W. and Jean (Pond) Wentworth; m. Malcolm Millard, 1937; 1 child, Wendy Millard Benjamin; m. Nathaniel Alexander Owings, Dec. 30, 1953. A.B., Mills Coll., 1934; postgrad., Radcliffe Coll., 1935. One-woman shows include Santa Barbara (Calif.) Mus. Art, 1940, Stanford Art Gallery, 1951, stitchery exhbns. at M.H. De Young Mus., San Francisco, 1963, Internat. Folk Art Mus., Santa Fe, 1965. Commr. Calif. Parks, 1963-69, mem., Nat. Parks Found. Bd, 1968-69; bd. dirs. African Wildlife Leadership Found., 1968-80, Defenders of Wildlife, 1969-74; founder, pres. Friends of the Sea Otter, 1969—; chair Calif. Mountain Lion Preservation Found., 1987; trustee Environmental Def. Fund, 1972-83; Regional trustee Mills Coll., 1962-68. Recipient gold medal, Conservation service award Dept. Interior, 1975, Conservation award Calif. Acad. Scis., 1979, Am. Motors Conservation award, 1980, Joseph Wood Krutch medal Humane Soc. U.S., 1980, Nat. Audubon Soc. medal, 1983, A. Starker Leopold award Calif. Nature Conservancy, 1986. Home: Grimes Point Big Sur CA 93920

OWNBEY, LENORE F. DALY, real estate investment specialist; b. Fremont, Nebr., Feb. 24; d. Joseph E. and Anna R. (Godel) Daly; m. Amos B. Ownbey, June 18, 1948; children: Kenton, Stephen. BBA, U. Nebr. Cert. comml. investment mem. Real estate and comml. investment specialist Denver, 1976—; lectr. in field. Writer, speaker Investment, Business and Personal Skills, Motivational and Inspirational. Mem. Nat. Speakers Assn., Colo. Chpt. Nat. Speakers Assn., Internat. Platform Assn., Denver Bd. Realtors, Colo. Assn. Realtors, Nat. Assn. Realtors, Realtors Nat. Mktg. Inst. (Cert. Comml. Investment Mem. Colo.-Wyo. chpt. #6), Real Estate Educators Assn., Colo. Real Estate Educators Assn.

OXFORD, RICHARD O., manufacturing executive; b. El Paso, Tex., Nov. 19, 1937; s. Orrville O. and Elizabeth (Gladney) O.; m. Isabel M. Oxford, Dec. 29, 1962; children: Sidney, Sandra. BS, U. So. Calif., 1959, MBA, 1962. Assoc. Kintner Assocs., L.A., 1962-64; project leader Transam. Rsch. Corp., L.A., 1964-66; assoc. McKinsey & Co., L.A., 1966-68; pres. Dial Industries, Inc., L.A., 1968—; bd. dirs. Chartwell Corp., L.A. Inventor in field. Mem. Soc. Plastics Industry, Nat. Housewares Mfg. Assn., Univ. So. Calif. MBA A ssn., Jonathan Club (sec. 1985-86, pres. 1986-87). Democrat. Home: 2248 N New Hampshire Ave Los Angeles CA 90027

OYAMADA, PAUL HERBERT, dentist, consultant; b. Portland, Oreg., Oct. 19, 1921; m. Alice Yasuko Sono, Nov. 7, 1953; 1 child, Debra Kay. DMD, U. Oreg., 1950. Pvt. practice Portland, 1952—; dental cons. John Hancock Group, 1974—, Blue Cross-Blue Shield, 1977—, Washington Nat. Ins., 1985—, Prin. Mut. Des Moines, 1985—, Portland. Capt. U.S. Army, 1950-52, Korea. Fellow Am. Coll. Dentists (sect. chmn.), Internat. Coll. Dentists; mem. Oreg. Dental Assn. (pres. 1973-74, del. to ADA, 1978-83), Multnomah Dental Soc. (pres. 1969-70), Delta Sigma Delta Bldg. Corp. (pres. 1983—), Roseway Lions (pres. 1956). Avocation: fishing. Office: 6510 NE Siskiyou St Portland OR 97213

OZANICH, CHARLES GEORGE, real estate broker; b. Fayette County, Pa. Aug. 11, 1933; s. Paul Anthony and Alma Bertha (Sablotne) O.; student Am. River Coll., Sierra Coll.; m. Betty Sue Carman, Feb. 20, 1955; children—Viki Lynn, Terri Sue, Charles Anthony, Nicole Lee. Owner, broker Terrace Realty, Basic Realty, Grass Valley, Calif., 1971—. Mem. Grass Valley Vol. Fire Dept., 1965—. Served with USAF, 1951-55; Korea. Decorated Bronze Star with three oak leaf clusters, Korean Presdl. citation, UN citation. Mem. Neveda County Bd. Realtors (dir. 1973-74). Lodges: Masons, Shriners. Nat. champion Truck Drivers Roadeo class 5 semi-trailer 18 wheeler div., 1954. Home: 15053 Chinook Ln Grass Valley CA 95945 Office: 10113 Alta Sierra Dr Suite 100 Grass Valley CA 95945

PABST, THOMAS CHARLES, entrepreneur; b. Lynwood, Calif., Mar. 13, 1947; s. Robert Franklin Pabst and Beverley (Travis) Weinstein; m. Becky Rae Olson, Oct. 21, 1981, (div. Dec. 1988). BA, U. N.Mex., 1971. Product sales mgr. Chemrite Corp., L.A., 1971-75; mgr. sales tng. Bio-Dynamics/BMC, Indpls., 1975-81; pres., owner Prestige Travel, Inc., Portland, Oreg., 1981-88; asst. to pres. No. Capital Corp., Portland, 1988—; cons. Topaz

Travel Mgmt., Portland, 1985-88; bd. dirs. Prestige Travel, Inc., Portland. Named Rookie Driver of Yr., Sports Car Club Am., 1987. Mem. Metro Travel Group (pres. 1985-86), Bus. Travel Network (bd. dirs. 1984-87), Multnomah Athletic Club (com. chmn. 1986-87), Team Continental (pres. 1987). Republican. Lutheran. Home: 3550 S W Woods Portland OR 97221 Office: No Capital Corp 4380 SW Macadam #370 Portland OR 97201

PACE, EUGENE CHARLES, agricultural developer, retail executive; b. Wilkes-Barre, Pa., May 26, 1940; s. George Davenport and Regina (Hahn) P.; m. Emilie King, June 1968 (div. June 1982). JD, Western State U., Fullerton, Calif., 1979. Bar: Calif. 1980. Pres., chief exec. officer Gemini Fin. Corp., Los Angeles, 1968-76, U.S. Agrl. Devel., Irvine, Calif., 1980—; chmn., chief exec. officer Golden Beverage Co., Irvine, 1984—; bd. dirs. Riverside (Calif.) Bancorp; v.p. Thrift Assn. Bancorp, Riverside, 1986—; cons. Mesa Grande Land and Devel., Irvine, 1979-81. Contbr. articles to profl. jours. Mem. ABA, Calif. Bar Assn., Assn. for Corp. Growth. Republican. Office: US Agrl Devel Corp 18831 Von Karman Ste 350 Irvine CA 92715

PACE, JOHN DANIEL, service executive; b. Ellwood City, Pa., July 7, 1953; s. John P. and Concetta M. (Santillo) P.; m. Patricia M. Matthews, Apr. 19, 1975; children: Adam J., Allyson M. BS, Slippery Rock (Pa.) U., 1975. Tchr. Diocese of Pitts., Beaver Falls, Pa., 1975-77; account mgr. ServiceMaster East, Bridgeville, Pa., 1977-81; master coordinating mgr. ServiceMaster East, Bridgeville, 1981-83, mgmt. rep., 1983-85; v.p. ServiceMaster East, Wayne, Pa., 1986-88; pres. ServiceMaster West, Irvine, Calif., 1988—; mem. long-range planning group ServiceMaster, Downers Grove, Ill., 1986—. Republican. Roman Catholic. Home: 22861 Pocetas Mission Viejo CA 92692 Office: ServiceMaster West Mgmt 17310 Redhill Ave Suite 300 Irvine CA 92714

PACE, RICHARD, writer, director; b. N.Y.C., Mar. 2, 1947; s. Thomas F. and Ann T. (Guarino) Paccione. BA in Philosophy, Wagner Coll., 1968. News dept. apprentice ABC-TV, N.Y.C., 1968-70; copywriter Cinemagic Distrbs., N.Y.C., 1970-73; sr. v.p. Samuel Botero Assocs., Inc., N.Y.C., 1974-82; dir. Sanuel Botero Assocs., Inc., N.Y.C., 1978—; pub. relations dir. Beverly Hills (Calif.) Hotel, 1982-83; exec. producer Pace Prodns. Co., Los Angeles, 1983—. Mem. Am. Edn. Soc. (bd. dirs. 1983—), Nat. Speech Assn., Los Angeles C. of C., Am. Film Inst., Toastmaster Internat. Club: Cavendish Bridge (Los Angeles).

PACELA, ALLAN FRED, publisher, editor; b. Chgo., Oct. 5, 1938; s. John Paul and Eleanor M. (Sorge) P.; children from previous marriage: Elizabeth Jean, David Allan, John Allan; m. Ramona Bachich, Feb. 14, 1987. BSEE, MIT, 1960; MS in Math., U. Miami, Coral Gables, Fla., 1962; D of Med. Engring., Ind. No. U., 1971. Sr. scientist Lear Siegler Med. Lab., Santa Monica, Calif., 1963-64; chief research scientsit Beckman Instruments, Fullerton, Calif., 1964-72; pres., gen. mgr. Interscience Tech. Corp., Brea, Calif., 1972—; editor, pub. Quest Pub. Co., Brea, 1970—; tech. and editorial cons. Inventor Bilateral Impedance Plethysmograph. Mem. IEEE, Assn. for the Advancement of Med. Instrumentation. Office: Quest Pub Co 1351 Titan Way Brea CA 92621

PACHON, CARRIE WEAVER, librarian; b. Pocatello, Idaho, Dec. 26, 1945; d. Elmer Dever and Pearl (Cutting) Weaver; m. Harry Peter, Mar. 16, 1968; 1 child, Marc Harry. BA, Calif. State U., L.A., 1972; MS, U. So. Calif., 1974. Reference librarian L.A. County Pub. Library, 1974; adminstrv. asst. Lansing (Mich.) Parks and Recreation, 1975-76; cons. Applied Mgmt. Systems, Silver Spring, Md., 1977; reference librarian Fairfax (Va.) County Pub. Library, 1978, children's librarian, 1979-81, regional children's librarian, 1981-83, br. mgr., 1983-88; coord. Downey (Calif.) City Library, 1987-88; asst. city librarian Commerce (Calif.) Pub. Library, 1988—. Bd. dirs. First River Farm Assn. Mem. ALA, Calif. Library Assn. (staff orgn. roundtable 1987-88), Library Adminstrn. and Mgmt. Assn., Pub. Library Assn., Fairfax County Library Employees Assn. (pres., treas. 1982-85). Home: 2354 N Indian Hill Blvd Claremont CA 91711 Office: Commerce Pub Library 5655 Jillson Commerce CA 90040

PACHON, HARRY PETER, educator; b. Miami, Fla., June 4, 1945; s. Juan and Rebeca (Perez) P.; m. Carrie Weaver, Mar. 16, 1968; 1 child, Marc. BA, Calif. State U., Los Angeles, 1967, MA, 1968; PhD, Claremont (Calif.) Grad. Sch., 1973. Adminstrv. aide U.S. Ho. of Reps., Washington, 1977-81; assoc. prof. CUNY, 1981-86; Kenan prof. politics Pitzer Coll., Claremont, 1987—; cons. Ford & Carnegie Founds., U.S. A.I.D. Co-author: Hispanics in the U.S., 1985; contbr. articles to profl. jours. NEH fellow, 1973-74, Nat. Assn. Schs. Pub. Affairs and Adminstrn. postdoctoral fellow, 1976-77. Mem. Am. Polit. Sci. Assn., Am. Soc. Pub. Adminstrs., Nat. Assn. Latino Elected and Appointed Officials (exec. dir.). Democrat. Home: 1050 N Mills Claremont CA 91711 Office: Pitzer Coll Claremont CA 91711-6110

PACHT, JORY ALLEN, geologist; b. Madison, Wis., Oct. 23, 1951; s. Asher Roger and Perle (Landau) P. BS, Ohio U., 1973; MS, U. Wyo., 1976; PhD, Ohio State U., 1979. Cert. flight instr., competition and airshow aerobatic pilot. Well site geologist Sentry Engring., 1973-74; teaching asst. U. Wyo., 1975-76, Ohio State U., 1976-78; asst. prof. geology Kent State U., 1979; rsch. geologist ARCO Oil & Gas Co., Dallas, 1980, sr. rsch. geologist, 1980-88, prin. rsch. geologist, 1988; instr. geology U. Tex.-Dallas, 1982-88; sr. scientist RPI Internat., Boulder, Colo., 1988—; owner Pacum Aerobatics. Hill fellow U. Wyo., 1975. Contbr. articles to profl. jours. Mem. Am. Assn. Petroleum Geologists (Grant-in-Aid com. 1989), Soc. Econ. Paleontologists and Minerologists, Geol. Soc. Am., Internat. Assn. Sedimentologists, Dallas Geol. Soc., Gulf Coast Soc. Econ. Paleontologists and Mineralogists (rsch. conf. com., Disting. Svc. cert. 1982), Internat. Club Aerobatic (pres. chpt. 24, contest dir. 1987). Office: 2845 Wilderness Pl Boulder CO 80301

PACIFIC, JOSEPH NICHOLAS, JR., educator; b. Honolulu, Oct. 27, 1950; s. Joseph Nicholas Sr. and Christine Mary (Mondelli) P.; m. Paulette Kay Miller, July 7, 1975. BA in Math., BS in Biology, BSEE, Gonzaga U., 1974; MMSc in Clin. Microbiology, Emory U., 1978. Cert. tchr., Hawaii, Wash. Research specialist Ctr. Disease Control, Atlanta, 1978-82; supr. Joe Pacific Shoe Repair, Honolulu, 1983; lab. technician Mont. State U., Bozeman, 1984; sci. tchr. Hawaii Preparatory Acad., Kamuela, 1985-87; unit mgr. Hawaii Med. Service Assn., Honolulu, 1987-88; tchr. biology St. Andrew's Priory Sch., Honolulu, 1988—. Mem. Internat. Platform Assn., Nat. Registry Microbiologists, Sigma Xi, Pi Mu Epsilon, Phi Sigma, Kappa Delta Pi, Alpha Sigma Nu. Home: 2013 Kaola Way Honolulu HI 96813 Office: St Andrew's Priory Sch 224 Queen Emma Sq Honolulu HI 96813

PACK, PHOEBE KATHERINE FINLEY, civic worker; b. Portland, Oreg., Feb. 2, 1907; d. William Lovell and Irene (Barnhart) Finley; student U. Calif., Berkeley, 1926-27; B.A., U. Oreg., 1930; m. Arthur Newton Pack, June 11, 1936; children: Charles Lathrop, Phoebe Irene. Layman referee Pima County Juvenile Ct., Tucson, 1958-71; mem. pres.'s council Menninger Found., Topeka; mem. Alcoholism Council So. Ariz., 1960—; bd. dirs. Kress Nursing Sch., Tucson, 1957-67, Pima County Assn. for Mental Health, 1958—, Ariz. Assn. for Mental Health, Phoenix, 1963—, U. Ariz. Found., Casa de los Niños Crisis Nursery; co-founder Ariz.-Sonora Desert Mus., Tucson, 1975—, Ghost Ranch Found., N.Mex.; bd. dirs. St. Mary's Hosp., Tucson, Tucson Urban League, Tucson YMCA Youth Found. Mem. Mt. Vernon Ladies Assn. Union (state vice regent, 1962-84),Mt. Vernon One Hundred (founder), Nature Conservancy (life), Alpha Phi. Home: Villa Compana Apt 415 6653 E Carondelet Dr Tucson AZ 85710

PACKARD, CLAYTON JAMES, towing company official; b. Portland, Oreg., Sept. 3, 1956; s. Dexter Fordyce and Dorothy Maxine (Baker) P.; m. Catherine Jane Packard, Apr. 2, 1977 (div. June 1983); children: Brian James, Jadia Marie; m. Lynette Kay Cruikshank, Aug. 6, 1988. Student, Portland Community Coll., Oreg., 1987--. Tow truck driver Nine-T-Nine Towing, Tigard, Oreg., 1984-87, Buck's Towing, Portland, Oreg., 1988, Handy Andy's Towing, Portland, 1988—. With USAF, 1974-82. Republican. Home: 9980 SW Greenburg Rd Tigard OR 97223 Office: Handy Andy's Towing 7991 SW Capitol Hwy Portland OR 97219

PACKARD, DAVID, manufacturing company executive, electrical engineer; b. Pueblo, Colo., Sept. 7, 1912; s. Sperry Sidney and Ella Lorna (Graber) P.; m. Lucile Salter, Apr. 8, 1938 (dec., 1987); children: David Woodley, Nancy Ann Packard Burnett, Susan Packard Orr, Julie Elizabeth Stephens. B.A., Stanford U., 1934, M.E.E., 1939; LLD (hon.), U. Calif., Santa Cruz, 1966, Catholic U., 1970, Pepperdine U., 1972; DSc (hon.), Colo. Coll., 1964; LittD (hon.), So. Colo. State Coll., 1973; D.Eng. (hon.), U. Notre Dame, 1974. With vacuum tube engring. dept. Gen. Electric Co., Schenectady, 1936-38; co-founder, ptnr. Hewlett-Packard Co., Palo Alto, Calif., 1939-47, pres., 1947-64, chief exec. officer, 1964-68, chmn. bd., 1964-68, 72—; U.S. dep. sec. defense Washington, 1969-71; dir. Genetech, Inc., 1981—; bd. dirs. Caterpillar Tractor Co., 1972-83, Chevron, 1972-85; chmn. Presdl. Commn. on Def. Mgmt., 1985-86; mem. White House Sci. Council. Mem. President's Commn. Personnel Interchange, 1972-74, Trilateral Commn., 1973-81, Dirs. Council Exploratorium, 1987; pres. bd. regents Uniformed Services U. of Health Scis., 1975-82; mem. U.S.-USSR Trade and Econ. Council, 1975-82; trustee The Ronald Reagan Presdl. Found., 1986—; mem. bd. overseers Hoover Instn., 1972—; bd. dirs. Nat. Merit Scholarship Corp., 1963-69; dir. Found. for Study of Presdl. and Congl. Terms, 1978—, Alliance to Save Energy, 1977-87, Atlantic Council, 1972-83, (vice chmn. 1972-80), Am. Enterprise Inst. for Public Policy Research, 1978—, Nat. Fish and Wildlife Found., 1985-87, Hitachi Found. Adv. Council, 1986—; trustee Herbert Hoover Found., 1974—, dir. Wolf Trap Found.; vice chmn. The Calif. Nature Conservancy, 1983—; trustee Stanford U., 1954-69, (pres. bd. trustees 1958-60), Hoover Instn., The Herbert Hoover Found.; mem. Dir.'s Council Exploratorium, 1987. Decorated Grand Cross of Merit Fed. Republic of Germany, 1972, Medal Honor Electronic Industries, 1974; numerous other awards including Silver Helmet Def. award AMVETS, 1973, Washington award Western Soc. Engrs., 1975, Hoover medal ASME, 1975, Gold Medal award Nat. Football Found. and Hall of Fame, 1975, Good Scout award Boy Scouts Am., 1975, Vermilye medal Franklin Inst., 1976, Internat. Achievement award World Trade Club of San Francisco, 1976, Merit award Am. Cons. Engrs. Council Fellows, 1977, Achievement in Life award Ency. Britannica, 1977, Engring. Award of Distinction San Jose State U., 1980, Thomas D. White Nat. Def. award USAF Acad., 1981, Disting. Info. Scis. award Data Processing Mgmt. Assn., 1981, Sylvanus Thayer award U.S. Mil. Acad., 1982, Environ. Leadership award Natural Resources Def. Council, 1983, Dollar award Nat. Fgn. Trade Council, 1985. Fellow IEEE (Founders medal 1973); mem. Nat. Acad. Engring. (Founders award 1979), Instrument Soc. Am. (hon. lifetime mem.), Wilson Council, The Bus. Roundtable, Bus. Council, Am. Ordnance Assn. (Crozier Gold medal 1970, Henry M. Jackson award 1988, Nat. Medal Tech. 1988, Presdl. Medal of Freedom 1988), Sigma Xi, Phi Beta Kappa, Tau Beta Pi, Alpha Delta Phi (Disting. Alumnus of Yr. 1970). Clubs: Bohemian, Commonwealth, Pacific Union, World Trade, Engrs. (San Francisco); The Links (N.Y.C.); Alfalfa, Capitol Hill (Washington). Office: Hewlett-Packard Co 1501 Page Mill Rd Palo Alto CA 94304

PACKARD, MARC DAVID, accountant; b. Lewiston, Maine, Apr. 27, 1960; s. Frank Edwin P. and Elaine (Hobson) Weston; m. Sally Ann, Oct. 8, 1983; children: Michelle Kayleen, Katelyn Rose. BSBA, Bryant Coll., 1981. CPA, Calif. Staff acct. Mills and Mills Accts., Laguna Beach, Calif., 1981-84; acct. Patterson Accountancy, San Clemente, Calif., 1984-88; pres., acct. M. David Packard, Accountancy Corp., Laguna Hills, Calif., 1988—. Mem. Exchange Club (Laguna Beach chpt. pres. 1986-87, bd. dirs. 1983-86), Calif. Soc. CPAs. Office: M David Packard Accounting 23195 La Cadena Ste 103 Laguna Hills CA 92653

PACKARD, ROBERT GOODALE, III, planner; b. Denver, Apr. 12, 1951; s. Robert and Mary Ann (Woodward) P.; m. Jane Ann Collins, Aug. 25, 1973; children: Jessica Nelson, Robert Gregg. BA, Willamette U., 1973; M in Urban and Regional Planning/Community Devel., U. Colo., 1976. Project mgr. Environ. Disiciplines, Inc., Portland, Oreg., 1973-75; asst. dir. planning Portland Pub. Schs., 1976-78; dir. planning Bur. of Parks, Portland, 1978-79; dir. planning and urban design Zimmer Gunsul Frasca, Portland, 1979-81, dir. project devel., 1981-84, mng. ptnr., 1984—; pres. Art Celebration, Inc. 1986-88. Co-author: The Baker Neighborhood/Denver, 1976. Contbr. articles to profl. jours. Mem. City of Portland Waterfront Commn., 1982-83; mem. Mayor's Task Force for Joint Use of Schs., Portland, 1979-80; mem. Washington Park Master Plan Steering com., Portland, 1980-81; bd. dirs. Washington Park Zoo, 1983-86, pres. Arts Celebration Inc./Artquake, 1986—. New Rose Theatre, 1981-83; dir., pres. Grant Park Neighborhood Assn., Portland, 1981-83. Recipient Spl. Citation, Nat. Sch. Bds. Assn., 1978; Meritorious Planning Project award Am. Planning Assn., 1980, Nat. Am. Planning Assn., 1981; Meritorious Design award Am. Soc. Landscape Architects, 1981; Honor award Progressive Arch., 1983. Mem. AIA (assoc.), Am. Planning Assn., Soc. Mktg. Profls. Clubs: Oreg. Road Runners, City. Home: 3313 SW Fairmount Blvd Portland OR 97201 Office: Zimmer Gunsul Frasca Ptnrship 320 SW Oak Ste 500 Portland OR 97204

PACKARD, RONALD, congressman; b. Meridian, Idaho, Jan. 19, 1931; m. Jean Sorenson, 1952; children: Chris, Debbie, Jeff, Vicki, Scott, Lisa, Theresa. Student, Brigham Young U., 1948-50, Portland State U., 1952-53; D.M.D., U. Oreg., Portland, 1953-57. Gen. practice dentistry Carlsbad, Calif., 1959-82; mem. 98th-101st Congresses from 43d Dist. Calif. Mem. Carlsbad Sch. Dist. Bd., 1960-72; bd. dirs. Carlsbad C. of C., 1972-76; mem. Carlsbad Planning Commn., 1974-76, Carlsbad City Coun., 1976-78; Carlsbad chmn. Boy Scouts Am., 1977-79; mayor City of Carlsbad, 1978-82; mem. North County Armed Svcs. YMCA, North County Transit Dist., San Diego Assn. Govts., Coastal Policy Com., Transp. Policy Com.; pres. San Diego div. Calif. League of Cities. Served with Dental Corps USN, 1957-59. Republican. Mormon. Office: 316 Cannon House Office Bldg Washington DC 20515

PACKER, MARK BARRY, lawyer, financial consultant; b. Phila., Sept. 18, 1944; s. Samuel and Eve (Devine) P.; AB magna cum laude, Harvard U., 1965, LLB, 1968; m. Donna Elizabeth Ferguson, July 2, 1967; children—Daniel Joshua, Benjamin Dov, David Johannes. Bar: Wash. 1969, Mass. 1971. Assoc. Ziontz, Pirtle & Fulle, Seattle, 1968-70; ptnr. Millhouse Nelle & Packer, Bellingham, Wash., 1972-82, pvt. practice, Bellingham, 1982—; bd. dirs., corp. sec., trustee No. Sales Co., Inc., 1977—; bd. dirs., corp. sec., gen. counsel Dr. Cookie Inc., 1981—. Mem. Bellingham Planning and Devel. Commn., 1975-84, chmn., 1977-81, mem. shoreline subcom., 1976-82; pres. Congregation Beth Israel, Bellingham, 1980-82, chmn. rabbi search com., 1986-87, scroll reader ba'al k'riah, 1982-87; mem. Bellingham Mcpl. Arts Commn., 1986—, landmark rev. bd., 1987—; treas. World Affairs Coun. N.W. Wash., 1985-88, pres., 1988—; chmn. Bellingham campaign United Jewish Appeal, 1979—; bd. dirs. Whatcom Community Coll. Found., 1989; lit. tutor Whatcom Lit. Coun., 1988—. Recipient Blood Donor award ARC, 1979, 8-Gallon Pin, 1988. Mem. ABA (sec. urban, state and local govt. law, commn. land use, planning and zoning, sec. real property probate and trust), Wash. State Bar Assn. (sec. environ. and land use law). Republican. Home: 208 S Forest St Bellingham WA 98225 Office: 1501 Eldridge Ave Bellingham WA 98225

PACKHAM, EDWARD RICHARD, holding company executive; b. Rupert, Idaho, Aug. 21, 1930; s. Edward Francis and Estella (Judd) P.; m. Sara Lynn Turner, June 17, 1959 (div. 1972); children: Richard T., Trent T., Laura, Mindy; m. Beverly A. Oder, June 29, 1973; stepchildren: Pamela, Bruce, Paul, Bryan. BS in Chem. Engring., U. Idaho, 1955; MBA, Northwestern U., 1958; student, U. Colo., 1948-50. Research engr. Wilson & Co., Chgo., 1958-60; prodn. engr. The Dow Chem. Co., Midland, Mich., 1960-72; v.p. ops. Mich. Nat. Leasing Co., Detroit, 1973-75; exec. v.p., chief operating officer First Ala. Leasing Co., Montgomery, 1975-77; v.p., chief operating officer First Security Leasing Co., Salt Lake City, 1977-80; pres. Western Oil & Mining, Inc., Provo, Utah, 1980-83; cons., owner Capital West Cons., Provo and Portland, 1983-86; pres. Telergy Inc., Portland, Oreg., 1987—. Author book: Born of the Spirit, 1979. Missionary Ch. of Jesus Christ of Latter Day Saints, 1950-52, bishop, Mich., 1960-62, stake pres., 1968-72. Republican. Mem. Ch. of Jesus Christ of Latter Day Saints. Office: Telergy Inc 10260 SW Greenburg Rd #1100 Portland OR 97223

PACKWOOD, BOB, senator; b. Portland, Oreg., Sept. 11, 1932; s. Frederick William and Gladys (Taft) P.; m. Georgie Ann Oberteuffer, Nov. 25, 1964; children: William Henderson, Shyla. A.B., Willamette U., 1954; LL.B., NYU, 1957; LL.B. (hon.), Yeshiva U., 1982, Gallaudet Coll., 1983. Chmn. Multnomah County Rep. Cen. Com., 1960-62; mem. Oreg. Legislature, 1963-69; U.S. senator from Oreg. 1969—, chmn. small bus. com., 1981-84, chmn. commerce com., 1981-85; chmn. fin. com. U.S. Senate, Washington, 1985-86. Mem. Internat. Working Group of Parliamentarians on Population and Devel., 1977; mem. Pres.'s Commn. on Population Growth and the Am. Future, 1972; chmn. Nat. Rep. Senatorial Com., 1977-78, 81-82; bd. dirs. NYU, 1970; bd. overseers Lewis and Clark Coll., Portland, 1966. Named One of Three Outstanding Young Men of Oreg., 1967; Portland's Jr. 1st Citizen, 1966; Oreg. Speaker of Yr., 1968; recipient Arthur T. Vanderbilt award NYU Sch. Law, 1970; Anti-Defamation League Brotherhood award, 1971; Torch of Liberty award B'nai B'rith, 1971; Richard L. Neuberger award Oreg. Environ. Council, 1972; Conservation award Omaha Woodmen Life Ins. Soc., 1974; Monongahela Forestry Leadership award, 1976; Solar Man of Yr., Solar Energy Industries Assn., 1980; Guardian of Small Bus. award Nat. Fedn. Ind. Bus., 1980; Forester of Yr., Western Forest Industries Assn., 1980; Am. Israel Friendship award B'nai Zion, 1982; Grover C. Cobb award Nat. Assn. Broadcasters, 1982; Religious Freedom award Religious Coalition for Abortion Rights, 1983; 22d Ann. Conv. award Oreg. State Bldg. and Constrn. Trade Council, 1983, United Cerebral Palsy Humanitarian award, 1984, Am. Heart Assn. Pub. Affairs award, 1985, Margaret Sanger award, Worth His Wheat in Gold award Planned Parenthood Assn., 1985, Worth his Wheat in Gold award for leadership on tax reform Gen. Mills., 1986, Am. Assn. Homes for the Aging for Outstanding Service in cause of elderly, 1987, NARAL award for congrl. leadership, 1987, numerous others. Mem. Oreg. Bar Assn., D.C. Bar Assn., Beta Theta Pi. Office: US Senate 259 Russell Senate Bldg Washington DC 20510

PADGETT, DON K., banker; b. Mar. 29, 1949; married; three children. BBA in Fin. and Acctg., Ea. N.Mex. U., 1971; student, U. Okla. Successively asst. nat. bank examiner, nat. bank examiner, examiner in charge Office of Comptroller of Currency, Regional Adminstr. of Nat. Banks, Denver, 1971-82; pres., chief exec. officer Fidelity Nat. Bank subs N.Mex. Banquest Corp., Albuquerque, 1982-84; sr. v.p., credit adminstrn. First Nat. Bank in Albuquerque subs. N.Mex. Banquest Corp., 1984, exec. v.p. comml. group, 1984—; exec. v.p. First Nat. Fin. Corp.; instr. tng. courses. Office: NMex Banquest Corp 2700 Yale Blvd SE Albuquerque NM 87106

PADGETT, FRANK DAVID, associate state supreme court justice; b. Vincennes, Ind., Mar. 9, 1923. LLB, Harvard U., 1948. Bar: Hawaii 1949, U.S. Supreme Ct. 1967. Assoc., then ptnr. Robertson, Castle & Anthony, Honolulu, 1949-66; ptnr. Padgett & Greeley, Honolulu, 1966-67, Padgett, Greeley & Marumoto (and predecessor firms), Honolulu, 1968-74; assoc. judge Intermediate Ct. Appeals State Hawaii, Wailuku and Maui, 1980-82; assoc. justice Hawaii Supreme Ct., Honolulu, 1982—. Mem. ABA, Hawaii Bar Assn., Assn. Trial Lawyers Am. Office: Supreme Ct Hawaii PO Box 2560 Honolulu HI 96804

PADILLA, ANDY, utilities company representative; b. Albuquerque, Nov. 30, 1947; s. Guermillo Padilla and Charlotte (Moya) Olguin; m. Rosa Dolores Lopez, Mar. 15, 1969; children: Shawn Renee, Martinique Chrishanna. BSBA, U. Albuquerque, 1980; postgrad., N.Mex. Highlands U., 1980-81. Radio dispatcher So. Union Gas Co., Albuquerque, 1969-70, field draftsman, 1970, engring. technician, 1971, line spotter, 1971-72; jr. estimator Pub. Svc. Co. N.Mex., Albuquerque, 1973-75, estimator, 1976-78, cost engr., 1979-80, cost analyst, 1981-82, sr. auditor, 1983-88; gas agt. Gas Co. N.Mex., Truth or Consequences, 1988--. With USN, 1965-68, Vietnam. Mem. Am. Assn. Cost Engrs. (cert., bd. dirs. 1980, 84, pres. 1986, regional rep. 1987), Order of Engr. Jehovah's Witness. Home: 208 Camino de Cielo Truth or Consequences NM 87901 Office: Gas Co NMex PO Box 970 Truth or Consequences NM 87901

PADRO, PETER LOUIS, JR., theologian, historian, consultant; b. Bronx, N.Y., Apr. 6, 1945; s. Peter and Florence P.; m. Ramona James, June 26, 1971; children: Peter Jason, Daniel Ross. Student St. Benedict's Sem., 1965-71; MDiv, Fuller Theol. Sem., 1984. Ordained to ministry Spanish Reform Ch., 1974. Pastor Calvary Chapel, Hawaiian Gardens, Calif., 1973, Grace Orthodox Presbyn. Ch., Carson, Calif., 1980-81, 1st Bapt. Ch. Carson, 1981-83, Inglewood (Calif.) Friends Ch., 1989—; dir. Libr. Padro y Navarro, Carson, 1986—; cons. Fedn. Anti-Communist Entities Latin Am., Buenos Aires, 1985—. Fellow Caribbean Hist. Assn. (sec. 1983—); mem. Nat. Assn. Profl. Journalists, Interam. Fedn. Journalists. Home: 2721 Monroe St Carson CA 90810

PADVE, MARTHA BERTONNEAU, arts administrator, fundraiser; b. Scobey, Mont., Feb. 22; d. Henry Francis and Marie (Vaccaro) Bertonneau; m. Jacob Padve, May 9, 1954 (div. 1980). Student, Pasadena Jr. Coll., 1938-40; cert., S.W. U. Bus. Coll., L.A., 1940-41, Pasadena Inst. for Radio, 1946-47; student, Claremont Colls., 1972-74, U. So. Calif., 1983-84, Community Coll., Pasadena, 1987-88. Ptnr., bus. mgr. restaurant devel. ventures, Pasadena, 1940-50; club dir. Red Cross, Nfld., Can., 1944-45; leading roles Penthouse Theatre, Altadena, Calif., 1946-48; club dir. armed forces spl. svcs. Red Cross, Austria, 1949-52; head dept. publs. Henry E. Huntington Libr., San Marino, Calif., 1953-57; cons. art planning Model Cities program, Omaha, 1975; founding instr. contemporary art collecting class, 1979-80; dir. devel. Bella Lewitzky Dance Found., L.A., 1980-81; instr. Art. Ctr. Coll. Design, Pasadena, 1981-82, assoc. dir. devel., 1981-83; instr. Coll. Continuing Edn. U. So. Calif., L.A., 1983-84; urban planning and arts cons. The Arroyo Group, Pasadena, 1979—; cons. in field, 1984—; developer edn. program Mus. Contemporary Art, L.A., 1984-86. Contbr. articles to newspapers. Trustee, v.p. Pasadena Art Mus., 1967-74; co-chmn. bldg. fund Norton Simon Mus. Art, Pasadena 1968-70; chmn. Pasadena Planning commn., 1973-81; vice-chmn. Pasadena Design Review commn., 1974-78; founding chmn. So. Calif. Fellows of Contemporary Art, 1976-78; mem. adv. com. U. So. Calif. art galleries, 1976-82, UCLA oral history program contemporary art, 1983—; chmn. audit com. L.A. County Grand Jury, 1986-87. Named Woman of the Yr., Pasadena Women's Civic League, 1980; recipient Gold Crown award Tenth Muse, Pasadena Arts Coun., 1983, Commendation awards Pasadena City Dirs., 1975, 80, 82, 83, Commendation award L.A. County Bd. Suprs., 1987, Graphic Arts award Southern Calif. Fellows Contemporary Art, 1978. Mem. Calif. Inst. Tech. Assocs. Republican. Roman Catholic. Home and Office: 80 N Euclid Ave Pasadena CA 91101

PAGANI, ALBERT LOUIS, aerospace system engineer; b. Jersey City, Feb. 19, 1936; s. Alexander C. and Anne (Salvati) P.; m. Beverly Cameron, Feb. 23, 1971; children: Penelope, Deborah, Michael. BSEE, U.S. Naval Acad., 1957; MBA, So. Ill. U., 1971. Commd. 2d lt. USAF, 1957, advanced through grades to col., 1978; navigator USAF, Lake Charles, La., 1957-63; pilot USAF, McGuire AFB, N.J., 1963-65; command pilot USAF, Anchorage, Alaska, 1965-68; mgr. airlift USAF, Saigon, Socialist Republic of Vietnam, 1968-69; chief spl. missions USAF, Scott AFB, Ill., 1969-74; commd. tactical airlift group USAF Europe, Mildenhall, Eng., 1974-76; dep. comdr. Rhein Main Air Base USAF Europe, Frankfurt, Fed. Republic Germany, 1976-78; chief airlift mgmt. USAF Military Airlift Command, Scott AFB, Ill., 1978-81, dir. tech. plans and concepts, 1981, dir. command and control, 1982-85; ret. 1985; sr. staff engr., dep. program mgr. Lockheed Missile and Space Co., Sunnyvale, Calif., 1985—. V.p. Cath. Ch. Council, Mildenhall, 1974, pres., 1975. Decorated Legion of Merit, Bronze Star, Air medal, Vietnam Cross of Gallantry. Mem. Nat. Def. Transp. Assn., Soc. Logistics Engrs., Air Force Assn., Armed Forces Communication and Electronics Assn., Air Lift Assn., Daedalions, Mensa. Home: 41090 Driscoll Terr Fremont CA 94539 Office: Lockheed Missile & Space Co Advanced Programs 69-90 1111 Lockheed Way Sunnyvale CA 94539

PAGANI, BEVERLY DARLENE, government administrator; b. Compton, Calif., Aug. 29, 1937; d. Donald Marshell Cameron and Irene Von (Kirkendoll) Good; m. Albert Louis Pagani, Feb. 21, 1971; children: Penelope Collins, Deborah Anne, Michael Stuart. BS, So. Oreg. Coll., 1967; MBA, So. Ill. U., Edwardsville, 1972. Cert. cost analyst. Enlisted USAF, 1959, advanced through grades to capt., 1962, resigned, 1971; chief mgmt. analysis USAF, Mildenhall, Eng., 1974-76; personnel classifier USAF, Scott AFB, Ill., 1979-80; housing mgmt. analyst USAF, Scott AFB, 1980-81, cost analyst, 1981-85; chief manpower analyst USN, Moffett Field, Calif., 1985—; chief mgmt. support office Army Aviation Research and Tech. Activity, Moffett Field, Calif., 1986-88; project control mgr. NASA-AMES Rsch.

Ctr., Moffett Field, Calif., 1988—. Mem. Soc. of Logistic Engrs., Inst. of Cost Analysts, Am. Soc. Mil. Comptrollers. Republican. Roman Catholic. Office: US Army Aviation Rsch & Te AIASA-AMES Rshc Ctr Moffett Field CA 94503-1099

PAGANO, THOMAS GEORGE, accountant; b. Hollister, Calif., Sept. 13, 1951; s. Peter Eugene and Marjorie Maxine (Lange) P.; m. Mary Kay Taylor, Sept. 13, 1980; 1 child, Amy Elizabeth. BS in Commerce, Santa Clara U., 1973. CPA, Wash. Staff acct. Ernst and Ernst, Tacoma, 1975-78, Johnson and Carr, P.S., Tacoma, 1979-82; ptnr. Johnson, Stone, Deaton, Pagano and Co., Tacoma, 1982—. Chmn. audit com. United Way, Pierce County, Wash., 1983; mem. fin. com. St. Leo's Parish, Tacoma, 1973—, mem. council, 1976-78, 85-86; bd. dirs. Christian Counseling Service, Tacoma, 1987—. Recipient Community Service award United Way, Pierce County, 1983, Disting. Service award Nat. Assn. Accts., Tacoma, 1983. Mem. Am. Inst. CPAs, Wash. Soc. CPAs (com. chmn. 1985), Assn. Regional Acctg. Firm. Roman Catholic. Clubs: Tacoma, Tacoma Lawn and Tennis. Home: 740 N Stadium Way Tacoma WA 98403 Office: 820 A St Tacoma WA 98402

PAGE, ALINE HAMMOND, insurance agency executive; b. Sacramento, Jan. 17, 1946; d. Gordon Miller and Yvonne (Peterson) H. Student, UCLA. Office mgr. Dr. Richard H. Gahm, Thousand Oaks, Calif., 1963-380; owner, agt. Ins. Dimensions, Thousand Oaks, 1980—. Bd. dirs. Southeast YMCA. Mem. Nat. Assn. Life Underwriters, NASD, Ventura County Life Underwriters, Soroptimist (pres. Thousand Oaks 1985-87). Office: Ins Dimensions 3625 Thousand Oaks Blvd Ste 224 Westlake Village CA 91362

PAGE, CURTIS MATTHEWSON, minister; b. Columbus, Ohio, Oct. 24, 1946; s. Charles N. and Alice Matthewson P.; m. Martha Poitevin, Feb. 12, 1977; children: Allison, Charles, Abigail. BS, Ariz. State U., 1968; M in Div., San Francisco Theol. Sem., 1971, D in Ministry, 1985. Ordained to ministry, 1971. Pastor Ketchum (Idaho) Presbyn. Ch., 1972-80, Kirk O'The Valley Presbyn. Ch., Reseda, Calif., 1980—; bd. dirs. Express Pub., Ketchum, 1977—, Mary Magdalene Home, Reseda, 1987—; moderator Kendall Presbytery, 1978; chmn. com. on preparation for the ministry, San Fernando, Calif., 1988. Chmn. Ketchum City Zoning Commn., 1979-80; Dem. precinct committeeman, Ketchum, 1978; mem. Ketchum Master Planning Commn., 1974; co-chmn. Voice Community Orgn. in San Fernando Valley, 1988—. Home: 19955 Lanark Canoga Park CA 91306 Office: Kirk O' The Valley Presbyn 19620 Vanowen Reseda CA 91335

PAGE, LARRY WALDRON, building contractor; b. Ogden, Utah, Aug. 28, 1955; s. Joseph K. and Elaine (Waldron) P.; m. Rouda Johnson, June 15, 1977; children: Amy Marie, Meisha, Nathan, Mindy. Student, Weber State Coll., 1976-82. Owner, mgr. Page Drywall, Kaysville, Utah, 1980—; pres. Pacor, Inc., Kaysville, 1982—. Scoutmaster, Kaysville area Boy Scouts Am., 1987. Mem. Nat. Small Bus. United. Republican. Mormon. Home: 680 E 700 N Kaysville UT 84037

PAGE, LESLIE ANDREW, medical supply company executive; b. Mpls., June 5, 1924; s. Henry R. and Amelia Kathryn (Steinmetz) P.; m. DeEtte Abernethy Griswold, July 6, 1952 (div. Sept. 1975); children: Randolph, Michael, Kathryn, Caroline; m. Mary Ellen Decker, Nov. 26, 1976. BA, U. Minn., 1949; MA, U. Calif., Berkeley, 1953; PhD, U. Calif., 1956. Asst. microbiologist, lectr. U. Calif., Davis, 1956-61; microbiologist, research leader Nat. Animal Disease Ctr., USDA, Ames, Iowa, 1961-79; ret. 1979; med. text cons. Bay St. Louis, Miss., 1979-85; pres. Steri-Derm Corp., Escondido, Calif., 1987--. Editor: Wildlife Diseases, 1976, Jour. Wildlife Diseases, 1965-68; contbr. numerous articles on infectious diseases to profl. jours. Pres. Garden Island Community Assn., Bay St. Louis, 1980-81; chief commr. East Hancock Fire Protection Dist., Bay St. Louis, 1982-83; sec., treas. Woodridge Escondido Property Owners Assn., 1986-88. With AUS, 1943-46, ETO. Fellow Am. Acad. Microbiology; mem. Wildlife Disease Assn. (pres. 1972-73, Disting. Service award 1980), Am. Soc. for Microbiology, Zool. Soc. San Diego, Sigma Xi, Phi Zeta (hon.). Home and Office: 1723 Cypress Point Glen Escondido CA 92026

PAGE, PETER CROZER, real estate executive; b. Bryn Mawr, Pa., May 21, 1946; s. Richard Kremer and Martha (Rivinus) P.; m. Rosa Rajkovic, Sept. 5, 1975 (div. Oct. 1982); m. Maryjo Austin, Feb. 14, 1986. BA in Am. Lit., Middlebury Coll., 1968; PhD in English, Ind. U., 1976, cert. in applied linguistics, 1976. Cert. real estate agt., broker,. Asst. instr. English Ind. U., Bloomington, 1975-76; instr. U. N.Mex., Albuquerque, 1976-80, asst. prof., 1980-84; real estate sales Coldwell Banker Comml. Real Estate, Albuquerque, 1984-87; pres. Tesch, Page & Lott Comml. Brokerage, Albuquerque, 1987—. Pres., editorial bd. Artspace Southwestern Quarterly of the Arts, 1980-81, v.p., 1979-81; contbg. author Poe Studies, 1980, Black and Write mag., 1981, S.W. Conceptions, 1982; co-author: College Writing, 1981. Bd. dirs. Albuquerque Leasing Info. Network, 1988; active Internat. Council Shopping Ctrs. Democrat. Episcopalian. Home: 421 Amherst SE Albuquerque NM 87106 Office: Tesch Page & Lott Comml Brokerage 1000 2d St NW Albuquerque NM 87102

PAGE, SUSAN, management consultant, writer; b. Cleve., June 16, 1943; d. Edwin H. and Helen E. (Taggart) Hammock; m. Mayer Shacter, June 14, 1981. BA, Oberlin Coll., 1965; MDiv, San Francisco Theol. Sem., 1977. Program assoc. Protestant Campus Ministry, Washington U., St. Louis, 1965-67; tng. dir. World Council of Chs.-New Zealand Project, Aukland, 1974; dir. womens programs U. Calif.-Berkeley, 1970-74; exec. dir. Care Ctr. Crisis Hotline, Lafayette, Calif., 1976-79; mgmt. cons. Oakland, Calif., 1979--. Author: If I'm So Wonderful, Why Am I Still Single?, 1988. Pres. bd. dirs. Huichol Ctr., Oakland, 1980--; founding pres. bd. dirs. Battered Women's Alternatives, Walnut Creek, Calif., 1979-83. Mem. Nat. Writers Union, Am. Craft Council. Democrat.

PAGE, THOMAS ALEXANDER, utility executive; b. Niagara Falls, N.Y., Mar. 24, 1933; m. Evelyn Rainnie, July 16, 1960; children: Christopher, Catherine. B.S. in Civil Engring, Purdue U., 1955, M.S. in Indsl. Administrn, 1963. Registered profl. engr., N.Y. C.P.A., Wis., Tex. Comptroller, treas. Wis. Power & Light Co., Madison, 1970-73; treas. Gulf States Utilities Co., Beaumont, Tex., 1973-75, sr. v.p. fin., 1975, exec. v.p., 1975-78, also bd. dirs.; exec. v.p., chief operating officer San Diego Gas & Electric Co., 1978-81, pres., chief exec. officer, 1981—, chmn., 1983—, also bd. dirs., 1979—. Mem. Dane County Bd. Suprs., Wis., 1968-72. Served to capt. USAF, 1955-57. Home: 1904 Hidden Crest Dr El Cajon CA 92020 Office: San Diego Gas & Electric Co 101 Ash St San Diego CA 92101 *

PAGET, JOHN ARTHUR, mechanical engineer; b. Ft. Frances, Ont., Can., Sept. 15, 1922; s. John and Ethel (Bishop) P.; B.Applied Sci., Toronto, 1946; m. Vicenta Herrera Nunez, Dec. 16, 1963; children—Cynthia Ellen, Kevin Arthur, Keith William. Chief draftsman Gutta Percha & Rubber, Ltd., Toronto, Ont., 1946-49; chief draftsman Viceroy Mfg. Co., Toronto, 1949-52; supr., design engr. C.D. Howe Co. Ltd., Montreal, Que., Can., 1952-58, sr. design engr. Combustion Engring., Montreal, 1958-59; sr. staff engr. Gen. Atomic, Inc., La Jolla, 1959-81. Mem. ASME, Am. Inst. Plant Engrs., Soc. Mfg. Engrs., Profl. Engrs. Ont., Soc. for History Tech., Inst. Mech. Engrs., Soc. Am. Mil. Engrs., Newcomen Soc., Brit. Nuclear Energy Soc. Patentee in field. Home: 3183 Magellan St San Diego CA 92154 Office: PO Box 427 Nestor CA 92053

PAGLIOTTI, DOUGLAS ALICK, stage manager; b. Santa Barbara, Calif., Jan. 1, 1958; s. Angelo and Barbara (Becker) P. AA, Allen Hancock Coll., Santa Monica, Calif., 1978; BFA, Webster Coll., St. Louis, 1980. Stage mgr. Denver Ctr. Theatre Co., 1980-81; prodn. stage mgr. Old Globe Theatre, San Diego, 1981—; tchr. San Diego State U., U. Calif., San Diego; guest lectr. in field. Stage mgr. world premiere Into The Woods; exec. producer TV Am. Playhouse, The Skin of Our Teeth. Mem. Actors and Stage Mgrs. Union, Actors Equity Assn. Home: 3359 Meade Ave San Diego CA 92116 Office: Old Globe Theatre PO Box 2171 San Diego CA 92112

PAI, PAUL TSU-CHIANG, automotive executive; b. Taichung, Republic of China, Nov. 30, 1941; came to U.S., 1970; s. Liang and Shui-Ze Pai; m. Lee-Shieh Hsueh, Jan. 26, 1971; children: Edwin P., Doris J. BA, Tamkung U., 1965; MA, N.E. Mo. State U., Kirksville, 1972; postgrad., U. Mo. Salesman Econo-Auto Ctr., Riverside, Calif., 1977-79, Honda Cars of Corona, Calif., 1979-81; owner Best Oriental Imports, Riverside, 1981; salesman Jim Glaze Invc., Redlands, Calif., 1981-83, Tom Bell Toyota, Redlands, 1983-85; mgr. Tom Bell Chevrolet, Redlands, 1987—; owner Suntron Co., Riverside, 1986—; lectr. Calif. State U., San Bernardino, 1988—; cons. Vichen Corp., Montebello, Calif., 1987. Mem. Honda Dealers of U.S., Mazda Dealers of U.S. Office: Calif State U 5500 University Pkwy San Bernardino CA 92407-2397

PAINE, THOMAS OTTEN, electrical engineer, space foundation executive; b. Berkeley, Calif., Nov. 9, 1921; s. George Thomas and Ada Louise (Otten) P.; m. Barbara Helen Taunton Pearse, Oct. 1, 1946; children: Marguerite Ada, George Thomas, Judith Janet, Frank Taunton. A.B. in Engring, Brown U., 1942; M.S. in Phys. Metallurgy, Stanford, 1947; Ph.D., Stanford U., 1949. Research assoc. Stanford, 1947-49; with Gen. Electric Co., 1949-68, 70-76, GE Research Lab., Schenectady; mgr. center advanced studies Santa Barbara, Calif., 1963-68; v.p., group exec. power generation 1970-73, sr. v.p. sci. and tech., 1973-76; pres., dir. Northrop Corp., Los Angeles, 1976-82; chmn. Thomas Paine Assocs., Los Angeles, 1982—, Nat. Commn. on Space, 1984-86; dep. adminstr., then adminstr. NASA, 1968-70; dir. NIKE, Quotron Systems, Orbital Scis. Contbr. articles to tech. publs.; co-inventor lodex R magnets. Bd. dirs. Pacific Forum, Honolulu, Planetary Soc., Pasadena. Served to lt. USNR, World War II. Decorated Submarine Combat insignia with stars, USN Commendation medal; grand ufficiale della Ordine al Merito Italy; recipient Distinguished Service medal NASA, 1970, Apollo Achievement award, Disting. Pub. Service Medal, 1986, Washington award Western Soc. Engrs., 1972; John Fritz medal United Engring. Socs., 1976; Faraday medal Inst. Elec. Engrs., London, 1976; Humanitarian award NCCJ; John F. Kennedy award Am. Astronautical Soc., 1987, Konstantin Tsiolkovskii medal, USSR, 1987. Fellow AIAA; mem. Nat. Acad. Engring., N.Y. Acad. Scis., Am. Phys. Soc., IEEE, U.S. Naval Inst., Am. Astronautical Soc. (John F. Kennedy Astronautics award 1987), Sigma Xi. Clubs: Explorers (N.Y.C.), Lotos (N.Y.C.), Sky (N.Y.C.); Cosmos (Washington), Army and Navy (Washington); Calif., Regency (Los Angeles). Home: 765 Bonhill Rd Los Angeles CA 90049 Office: Thomas Paine Assocs 2401 Colorado Ave #178 Santa Monica CA 90404

PAINTER, LOUIS JOSEPH, statistician, consultant; b. Phila., Feb. 17, 1931; s. John William and Agnes (Montag) P.; m. Sigrid Maria Dejas, May 12, 1956; children: Michael, Kerstin, Steven, Brita. B in Chem. Engring., Cath. U. Am., 1952; MA in Stats., U. Calif., Berkeley, 1963. With Chevron Rsch. Co., Richmond, Calif., 1952-61, 63-86, rsch. statitician, 1963-67, sr. rsch. assoc., 1971-86; cons., owner Statis. PLUS, San Rafael, Calif., 1986—; cons. Coordinating Rsch. Coun., Atlanta, 1986-88, Nat. Inst. Petroleum and Energy Rsch., Bartlesville, Okla., 1986—, Am. Petroleum Inst., Washington, 1987—, U. Calif., Berkeley, 1988—. Contbr. numerous articles to profl. jours. Mem. Am. Statis. Assn., ASTM (chair 1983—, Achievement award 1987). Democrat. Roman Catholic. Home: 637 Kernberry Dr San Rafael CA 94903 Office: Statis PLUS 637 Kernberry Dr San Rafael CA 94903

PAL, DEEPAK, electrical engineering; b. Taunggyi, Burma, Feb. 21, 1963; came to U.S., 1976.; s. Brum and Tripta (Soni) P.; m. Annu Kanotra, Mar. 12, 1987. BEE, U. Ill., 1984; MEE, Cornell U., 1985. Tech. staff, computer devel. AT&T, Bell Labs., Naperville, Ill., 1985-87; pres., cons. DPL, Inc., Bolingbrook, Ill., 1987; MTS-5 firmware dept. GTE, CSC, Phoenix, 1987—. Recipient Apache Quality award Large Computer Devel., AT&T-Bell Labs, 1986. Home: 220 W Bell Rd #1056 Phoenix AZ 85023 Office: GTE-CSC 2500 W Utopia Rd Phoenix AZ 85027

PALACIOS, PEDRO PABLO, lawyer; b. Santo Tomas, N.Mex., June 29, 1953; s. Luis Flores and Refugio (Hernandez) P.; m. Kelle Haston, July 2, 1983; children: Pedro Pablo II, Charles Rey, Jose Luis. BA, Yale U., 1975; JD, U. N.Mex., 1979. Bar: N.Mex. 1979. Pvt. practice Las Cruces, N.Mex., 1983—. Mem. N.Mex. State Bar Assn. Democrat. Roman Catholic. Home: PO Box 16335 Las Cruces NM 88004 Office: 500 S Main #305 Las Cruces NM 88004

PALAZZO, ROBERT P., lawyer, accountant; b. L.A., Apr. 14, 1952; s. Joseph Francis and Muriel Palazzo. BA in Econs., UCLA, 1973; MBA, U. So. Calif., 1976, JD, 1976; postgrad., U. Oxford, 1979. CPA Calif., Nev., Colo.; Bar: Calif. 1976, U.S. Dist. Ct. (so. dist.) Calif. 1977, U.S. Tax Ct. 1977, U.S. Ct. Appeals (9th cir.) 1978, U.S. Supreme Ct. 1980. Assoc. Graham & James, L.A., 1976-78; ptnr. Rader, Cornwall, Kessler & Palazzo CPAs, L.A., 1978-81, Palazzo & Kessler, attys at law, L.A., 1978-81; sole practice L.A., 1981—; judge pro tem L.A. Mcpl. Ct., 1982—; bd. dirs. Cons. Am. Oil Co., Fin. Systems Internat. Inc., Adventures Prodns., Inc.; alumni advisor UCLA, 1977-81, mem. adv. and scholarship com., 1978-81. Contbg. editor: The Gun Report; contbr. articles to profl. jours. Founder Ohio History Flight Mus.; bd. dirs. Calif. Cancer Found., L.A., 1978—, pres., 1979-80; pres. Calif. Cancer Found., 1979-80. Mem. L.A. County Bar Assn. (arbitration com.), Italian Am. Lawyers Assn. (bd. govs. 1980-88, 1st v.p. 1984-88), Nat. Acad. Recording Arts and Scis., Century City Bar Assn. (vice-chmn. estate planning, trust and probate com. 1979-80), Am. Numismatic Assn. (dist. rep. Carson City 1981-82, L.A. 1982-83), Omicron Delta Epsilon, Beta Alpha Psi (pres. 1972), Pi Gamma Mu, Phi Alpha Delta, Zeta Phi Eta. Office: 3002 Midvale Ave #209 Los Angeles CA 90034

PALCULICH, JERRY GINA, educator; b. Kagoshima, Kyushu, Japan, Oct. 1, 1954; came to U.S., 1958.; d. Roger Dempsey and Michiko (Sasaki) Putnam; m. Michael Anthony Palculich, Aug. 7, 1971; children: Jean Marie, Michael Anthony. Student, Palomar Coll., San Marcos, Calif., 1981. Classroom aide Fallbrook (Calif.) Union Elem. Sch. Dist., 1980-83, outdoor edn. asst., 1984--. Mem. AEOE, Nat. Audubon Soc., Am. Mus. Natural History, The Nature Conservancy. Republican. Home: 1205 Peppertree St Fallbrook CA 92028 Office: DeLuz Ecology Ctr 321 N Iowa St Fallbrook CA 92028

PALEN, JOSEPH WILLIAM, chemical process research company executive; b. Springfield, Mo., June 4, 1935; s. John Carlyle and Jean Allen (Gravely) P.; m. Louise Kibler, Sept. 13, 1956 (div. 1977); children: Patti, Joni, James; m. Kasdina Kasdan, June 4, 1977; children: Indradini, Indrasto, Indrastati. BS in Chem. Engring., U. Mo., 1957; MS in Chem. Engring., U. Ill., 1965; PhD in Chem. Engring., Lehigh U., 1988. Process design engr. Phillips Petroleum Co., Bartlesville, Okla., 1957-63; rsch. engr. Heat Transfer Rsch., Inc., Alhambra, Calif., 1965-68; asst., then assoc. tech. dir. Heat Transfer Rsch., Inc., Alhambra, 1968-86, prin. staff cons., 1988—. Patentee in field; editor: Heat Exchanger Sourcebook, 1986; contbr. to tech. publs. Lectr., UNESCO, Yugoslavia, 1981. Fellow Am. Inst. Chem. Engrs. (lectr. internat. heat transfer conf. 1986); mem. Am. Sci. Affiliation, Gideons, Tau Beta Pi. Democrat. Baptist. Home: 2445 E Del Mar St Pasadena CA 91107 Office: Heat Transfer Rsch Inc 100 S Fremont St Alhambra CA 91802

PALM, NANCY CLEONE, medical center administrator, radiography technologist; b. Portland, Oreg., July 8, 1939; d. Oscar Emanuel and Hallie Vernice (Thurber) Palm. Student U. Oreg. Sch. Radiology, 1957; grad. Hosp. Corpswave, Hosp. Corps Sch., Great Lakes (Ill. Naval Base, 1958; grad. X-ray Tech., Sch. Radiology, Bremerton, Wash. Naval Base, 1961. Lic. radiography technologist, Oreg. Chief radiography technologist New Lincoln Hosp., Toledo, Oreg., 1961-63; sr. radiography technologist Gresham (Oreg.) Gen. Hosp., 1963-65; chief radiography technologist Neurol. Clinic, Portland, Oreg., 1965-79; head bookkeeper Rinehart Clinic, Wheeler, Oreg., 1979-80; owner, gen. mgr. San Dune Motel, Manzanita, Oreg., 1971-83; bus. agt. Rinehart Found., Inc., Manzanita, 1983—; owner Sears & Roebuck Catalog Store, Nehalem, Oreg., 1979-81; adminstrn. mgr. Rinehart Found., Inc. (Nehalem Bay Med. Ctr.), Manzanita and Garibaldi, Oreg., 1980—. Sponsor Willamette council Campfire Girls, Inc., 1982-84. Served with USN, 1958-61. Fellow Nat. Coll. Radiography Technologists; mem. Oreg. Med. Group Mgmt. Assn., Nat. Assn. Female Execs., Am. Registry Clin. Radiography Technologists (nat. dir. 1970-76, trustee 1972-74, sec. 71-72, pres. 72-74; Citation award 1970, Disting. Service award 1971, 73, Order of Golden Ray 1974, founder Margaret Harris Award Competition 1973). Republican. Presbyterian. Home: 423 Dorcas Ln PO Box 262 Manzanita OR 97130 Office: PO Box 580 Manzanita OR 97130

PALMER, BEVERLY BLAZEY, psychologist, educator; b. Cleve., Nov. 22, 1945; d. Lawrence E. and Mildred M. Blazey; m. Richard C. Palmer, June 24, 1967; 1 child, Ryan Richard. PhD in Counseling Psychology, Ohio State U., 1972. Lic. clinical psychologist, Calif. Adminstrv. assoc. Ohio State U., Columbus, 1969-70; research psychologist Health Services Research Ctr. UCLA, 1971-77; commr. pub. health Los Angeles County, 1978-81; pvt. practice clin. psychology Torrance, Calif., 1985—; prof. psychology Calif. State U., Dominguez Hills, 1973—. Reviewer manuscripts for numerous textbook pubs; contbr. numerous articles to profl. jours. Recipient Proclamation County of Los Angeles, 1972, Proclamation County of Los Angeles, 1981. Mem. Am. Psychol. Assn. Office: Calif State U Dept Psychology Carson CA 90747

PALMER, BOB GENE, traffic safety educator; b. Hallowell, Kans., Oct. 28, 1932; m. Carolyn K. Boggess, Feb. 27, 1954; children: Vicki Palmer Banks, Kenna Palmer O'Hara, Sherri Palmer Wilson, Flint. BS, Kans. State U., 1953, MS, 1961. Cert. tchr., Calif. Adminstr. Miami (Okla.) Unified Sch. Dist., 1958-64; dir. traffic safety edn. Fullerton (Calif.) Union High Sch. Dist., 1964-79; ind. cons. various agys. and sch. dists., Fullerton, 1979-84; pres., chief exec. officer Traffic Safety Educators Inc., Corona, Calif., 1984—; cons. Riverside (Calif.) Office Traffic Safety, 1979—. Patentee traffic safety range tng. device; author tng. manual. Liaison officer West Point (N.Y.) Acad., 1971—; mem. Acad. Congl. Rev. Bd., Fullerton, 1978-86. With U.S. Army, 1954-58, Korea. Mem. Calif. Assn. Safety Educators, Res. Officers Assn. (chpt. pres. 1960-62), Am. Legion, Rotary (Paul Harris fellow 1989), Elks, Masons. Office: Traffic Safety Educators Inc 180 N Joy St Corona CA 91719

PALMER, CHARLES RAY, graphics arts executive; b. New Orleans, Oct. 17, 1940; s. Zack and Amy Cecile P.; m. Jeanette Francis Smith, Oct. 24, 1964; 1 child, Bridgette Latrice. AA in Art, Southwest City Coll., 1975; BA in Art with honors, Calif. State U., Dominguez Hills, 1979. Binderyman System Devel. Corp., Santa Monica, Calif., 1964-66; duplicator operator System Devel. Corp., Santa Monica, 1966-73, Northrop Corp., Hawthorne, Calif., 1973-75; printing press operator Northrop Corp., Hawthorne, 1975-79, visual aid artist, 1979-83, graphics prodn. control specialist, 1983-87, graphic art service mgr., 1987—; ltd. partnership, Crenshaw Graphics, L.A., 1979-82. With USAF, 1960-64. Mem. Am. Legion. Democrat. Roman Catholic. Home: 7630 S Cimarron St Los Angeles CA 90047 Office: Northrop Corp One Northorne Ave Orgn/Zone 1150/87 Hawthorne CA 90250

PALMER, CHRISTOPHER MASSEY, geologist; b. Princeton, N.J., May 3, 1951; s. Walter Madison and Elenore Justine (Epps) P.; m. Ann C. Sjolander, Sept. 6, 1980. BA, Calif. State U., Fresno, 1975, MA, 1978. Registered geologist, Calif.; cert. engring. geologist, Calif.; registered environ. assessor, Calif. Staff geologist Twining Labs., Fresno, 1979-82; project geologist Emcon Assocs., San Jose, Calif., 1982-85; sr. engring. geologist J.V. Louney Assocs., Palo Alto, Calif., 1985-86; sr. program geologist Ensco Environ. Svcs., Fremont, Calif., 1986—; instr. U. Santa Calif., Santa Cruz, 1988. Mem. Geological Soc. Am., Assn. Engring. Geologists, Nat. Water Well Assn., Internat. Assn. Engring. Geologists. Democrat. Episcopalian. Home: 1345 Kimberly Ave San Jose CA 95118 Office: Ensco Environ Svcs Inc 41674 Christy St Fremont CA 94538

PALMER, CLINTON SCOTT, marketing consultant; b. Clinton, Iowa, Mar. 9, 1954; s. Clinton Duane and Dorothy Hazel (Johnson) Palmer; m. Julie Anne Allen, Nov. 6, 1976 (div. 1988); 1 child, Brynne Lorraine; m. Cathy Marie Greer, Oct. 1, 1988. BA, UCLA, 1976. Urban planner Jack Raub Co., Costa Mesa (Calif.) and Denver, 1976-82; pres. Palmer Mktg. Group, Corona Del Mar, Calif., 1982—; cons. Garbe Mfg. Co., La Habra, Calif., 1984-87, W. Coast Pub. Co., Costa Mesa, 1988—. Mem. Citizens for Traffic Solutions, Irvine, Calif., 1988. Mem. Bldg. Industry Assn., Indsl. League Orange County. Republican. Methodist. Office: Palmer Mktg Group 2816 E Coast Hwy Ste E Corona Del Mar CA 92625

PALMER, COLETTE DORAIS, sales and marketing professional; b. Orange, Calif., Mar. 5, 1963; d. Joseph Gerard and Fleur Ange (Forest) Dorais; m. Michael Dean Palmer, June 15, 1986. BA in English, U. Calif., Irvine, 1986. With sales and mtkg. dept. Integrate Comml. Applications, Tustin, Calif., 1986-87; product mgr. Microsystems Engring., Hoffman Estates, Ill., 1987-88; with sales and mktg. dept. State of the Art, Costa Mesa, Calif., 1989—. Mem. Christian Businessman's Assn. Office: State of the Art 3545 Howard Way Costa Mesa CA 92626-1418

PALMER, CURTIS HOWARD, diversified company executive, lawyer; b. Oakland, Calif., 1908; s. Howard H. and Catherine May (Larkin) P.; m. Helen Hayes, Apr. 8, 1936. LL.B., U. Calif., 1932. Sole practice 1932-35; tax counsel Calif. Bd. of Equalization, 1935-43; gen. counsel Alfred Hart, Los Angeles, 1943-60; exec. officer City Nat. Bank, Beverly Hills, Calif., 1960-75, chmn. bd., 1975; chmn. bd. Arden Group, Inc., Beverly Hills, 1976—; dir. Internat. Aluminum Corp.; chmn. bd. dirs. Arden Group Inc. Office: Arden Group Inc 9595 Wilshire Blvd Ste 411 Beverly Hills CA 90012

PALMER, DAVID, writer; b. Tucson, Dec. 9, 1941; s. Maxwell R. and Zeta G. P.; m. Mary C. McGovern, Nov. 8, 1986; children: David, Vicki, Brian, Jennifer, Anthony. Student, Yale U., 1963, U. Ariz., 1971. Mgr. CTI, Inc., Tucson, 1978-83; adminstrv. dir. The Authors Resource Ctr., Tucson, 1984-85; pres. Taliesin & Co., Tucson, 1984—; editor Tucson Weekly, 1985—; sr. reporter Grassroots Rsch., San Francisco, 1989—; pres., dir. Entrepreneur Forum, Tucson, 1984—. Author: Tucson, 1988; contbr. articles to profl. jours. Mem. Soc. Southwestern Authors, Internat. Entrepreneurs Network, Digital Equipment Computer Users Soc., So. Ariz. Hiking Club, Yale Alumni Assn. Office: Taliesin & Co 8645 E Hawthorne Tucson AZ 85710-1724

PALMER, EVERETT VERNON, industrial engineer; b. Jackson, Mich., Jan. 31, 1948; s. Everett Otto and Helen Carol (Fisher) P.; divorced; children: Andra Rochelle, Lance Vernon; m. Mary Ann Galati, July 30, 1983. AA, Jackson Community Coll., 1969; MD, Northern Mich. U., 1971; postgrad., Central Mich. U., 1972-76, Maynard Inst., 1973. Cert. indsl. engr., Mich. Tchr. Cass City (Mich.) Pub. High Schs., 1971-73; indsl. engr. Walbro Corp., Cass City, 1973-77; prodn. mgr. Walbro Corp.-Walbro de Mexico, Nogales, Ariz., and Mex., 1977-79; prodn. supt. Samsonite Corp./Samson, Nogales, 1980-82; plant mgr. Cambion (Midland Ross) Cambion de Mex., Nogales, and Mex., 1982-84; mfg. mgr. SFE-West Cap de Mex., Nogales, and Mex., 1984-86; process engring. mgr. Tusonix Inc./Temsa, Tuscon, 1986-89, plant mgr., 1989—. Head coach, bd. dirs. Say Cayetano Little League, Rio Rico, Ariz., 1980—. Mem. Assn. Maquiladoras of Sonora, Ducks Unltd., NRA. Roman Catholic. Office: Tusonix/Temsa PO Box 2302 Nogales AZ 85628

PALMER, JUDITH, artist; b. Oakland, Calif., Dec. 10, 1934; d. Bean Mark and Laurinne (Mattern) P.; m. Robert Ballard Herschler, Aug. 1, 1959 (div. Nov. 1981); children: Matthew, Mark, Sarah, Stephen; m. Ben Frank Stoltzfus, Nov. 8, 1975. BA, U. Calif., Berkeley, 1957; MA, Claremont Grad. Sch., 1971. Photoetching series include Surfaces, 1986, Constructions, 1987, Assemblages, 1987, Romoland, 1988. Recipient Purchase Prize Galleries Elect, Venice, Calif., 1987, printmaking award Artists' Liaison, Los Angeles, 1986, 87, Jurors award Dulin Gallery, Knoxville, Tenn., 1987. Mem. Los Angeles Printmakers Soc. Studio: U Calif 2040 Arroyo Dr Riverside CA 92506

PALMER, MARK ANDREW, software engineer, county official; b. Roswell, N.Mex., Oct. 6, 1959; s. George Richard and Helen (Glancy) P.; m. Janice Marie Cesena, Jan. 23, 1988. AS Computer Programming, Solano Community Coll., 1985; BA in Math., San Jose State U., 1987. Engring. and sci. programmer Ford Aerospace Corp., Sunnyvale, Calif., 1984-86; programmer, analyst Ford Aerospace Corp., San Jose, Calif., 1986-88; data base analyst Stanislaus County, Modesto, Calif., 1988-89; sr. software engr. Ford Aerospace Corp., Sunnyvale, Calif., 1989—. With USN, 1978-84. Republican. Baptist. Home: 1521 Atteboro Ct Modesto CA 95351

PALMER, PATRICIA ANNE, marketing professional, consultant; b. Tacoma, Wash., Mar. 6, 1940; d. Theodore Roosevelt Benson and Grace Katherine (Hiscox) Davenport; m. Chester William Palmer Jr., Dec. 21, 1969 (div. Apr. 1979); children: Shandy Lee Palmer Simchen, Coelleen Patricia Palmer Warfe. BS with high honors, So. Ill. U., 1977; MS, Evergreen State

Coll., 1982. Succesively programmer II, programmer III, computer specialist I, computer specialist II, info. systems asst. mgr., info systems mgr. dept. transp. State of Wash., Olympia, 1969-83; v.p., mgr. tech. support Seafirst Bank, Seattle, 1983-87; regional systems engr. Amdahl, Bellevue, Wash., 1987—; bd. dirs. Olympia Tech. Community Coll.; cons. Thousand Trails, Bellevue, 1986. Editor newsletter Assn. Data Processing Mgrs., 1977-80. Captain membership drive YMCA, Olympia, 1979; counselor Christian Broadcasting Network 700 Club, Kirkland, Wash., 1987. Fellow Fed. Dept. Transp., 1980. Mem. Facts for Freedom, Nat. Fedn. Decency. Republican. Office: Amdahl 10900 NE 4th Ste 1600 Bellevue WA 98004

PALMER, PAUL EDWARD, communications executive; b. York, Pa., Nov. 18, 1942; s. Daniel Isaih Palmer and Eleanor (Beard) Wolff; m. Margaret Ann Strong, Oct. 2, 1965; children: Paul Joseph, Wendy Suzanne, Caroline Marie. BA in Speech Radio/TV, U. Md., 1964. With Sta. WBAL Radio, Balt., 1964-65; account exec. Sta. KDKA Radio, Pitts., 1965-68, RAR, Chgo., 1968-70; sales mgr. Sta. WIND Radio, Chgo., 1970-72; v.p., gen. mgr. Sta. KFMB AM-FM, San Diego, 1972—; pres. Sun Mountain Broadcasting, Inc., San Diego, 1985—. Mem. Assn. Ind. Met. Stas. Home: 2915 Woodford Dr La Jolla CA 92037 Office: Sta KFMB AM-FM 7677 Engineer Rd San Diego CA 92111

PALMER, ROBERT LEWIS, lawyer; b. Seattle, June 24, 1910; s. Lewis Crosby and E. Claire (Howard) P.; m. Elizabeth Campbell, Feb. 20, 1936 (dec. Feb. 1984); children: Sally Reed, Joan Long. BA, U. Wash., 1932, JD, 1935. Bar: Wash. 1935. Assoc. Stratton & Kane, Seattle, 1935; ptnr. LeSourd & Patten and predecessors, Seattle. Served to lt. USNR, 1943-53. Decorated Air medal. Mem. ABA, Seattle Bar Assn., King County Bar Assn., Wash. State Bar Assn., University Club (Seattle), Seattle Golf Club (pres. 1956), Seattle Tennis Club, Phi Gamma Delta. Republican. Home: The Highlands Seattle WA 98177 Office: LeSourd & Patten 2400 Columbia Ctr 701 5th Ave Seattle WA 98104-7005

PALMER, VINCENT ALLAN, construction consultant; b. Wausa, Nebr., Feb. 18, 1913; s. Victor E. and Amy (Lindquist) P.; AA, Modesto Jr. Coll., 1933; BSCE, U. Calif., Berkeley, 1936; m. Louise V. Cramer, Mar. 12, 1938 (dec. June 1979); children: Margaret, Georgia, Vincent Allan; m. 2d, Hope Parker, Jan. 23, 1982. Constrn. engr. Kaiser Engrs., 1938-63, constrn. mgr., 1963-69, mgr. constrn., 1970-75, project mgr., 1975-76; project mgr. reef runway Universal Dredging Corp., Honolulu, 1975-76; pvt. practice constrn. cons., Walnut Creek, Calif., 1976—. Mem. ASCE (life), Project Mgmt. Inst., Monterey Bay Aquarium, Sierra Club. Clubs: San Francisco Press; Tattersall's (Sydney, Australia). Home and Office: 1356 Corte Loma Walnut Creek CA 94598

PALMIERI, RODNEY AUGUST, state agency administrator, pharmacist; b. Santa Rosa, Calif., July 12, 1944; s. August John and Olga (Giusti) P.; m. Phyllis Scott, Aug. 14, 1965; children: Christopher August, Joshua Scott. AA, Santa Rosa Jr. Coll., 1964; B of Pharmacy, U. Colo., 1968. Pvt. practice pharmacy, Santa Rosa, 1968-71; pharm. cons. State of Calif., San Jose, 1971-75; chief pharm. cons. State of Calif., Sacramento, 1975-80, sr. mgr., 1980—; prin. Cold Springs Cons., Placerville, Calif., 1984—. Weblos leader Boy Scouts Am., 1976-77, scoutmaster, 1977-82; referee, coach El Dorado (Calif.) Youth Soccer League, 1977-83. Mem. Rho Chi (pres. 1967-68), Phi Delta Chi. Office: Cold Springs Cons 2900 Cold Springs Rd Placerville CA 95667

PALOMBI, BARBARA JEAN, psychologist; b. Rockford, Ill., May 28, 1949; d. Frank and Vira Lavina (Gornet) P. BA, Luther Coll., Decorah, Iowa, 1971; MA, Pacific Lutheran U., Tacoma, Wash., 1974; PhD, Mich. State U., 1987. Career counselor Wright State U., Dayton, Ohio, 1974-77; asst. dean, dir. U. Calif., Irvine, 1977-80; grad. asst. Mich. State U., E. Lansing, 1980-83, clin. intern, 1983-84; clin. intern Colo. State U., Fort Collins, 1984-85; psychologist Ariz. State U., Tempe, 1985—; cons. in field. Contbr. articles and papers to profl. jours. Mem. U.S. Wheelchair Olympic Team, 1976, U.S. Wheelchair Team to the Interna.t Stoke-Mandelville Games, 1979; alternative mem. U.S. Wheelchair Olympic Team, 1980; U.S. rep. Internat. Symposium on Sports, Physical Edn. and Recreation for the Handicapped, UNESCO, 1982. Grantee Nat. Sci. Found., U. Calif., 1977, 79; named Outstanding Handicapped Citizen Rock County 1982, Handicapped Profl. Woman of the Yr. Western Region, 1987. Mem. Am. Assn. Counseling and Devel. (Glen E. Hubele Nat. Grad. Student Research award 1988), Am. Coll. Personnel Assn. (bd. dirs. Div. VII-Counseling, mem. Div. VIII-Wellness, Burns B. Crookston Research award 1988, Commn. VII Grad. Student Research award 1988). Democrat. Home: 1140 E Marny Tempe AZ 85281 Office: Ariz State U Counseling & Consultation Tempe AZ 85287

PAMPLIN, ROBERT BOISSEAU, JR., agricultural company executive, minister, writer; b. Augusta, Ga., Sept. 3, 1941; s. Robert Boisseau and Mary Katherine (Reese) P.; m. Marilyn Joan Hooper; children: Amy Louise, Anne Boisseau. Student in bus. adminstrn. Va. Poly. Inst., 1960-62; BSBA, Lewis and Clark Coll., 1964, BS in Acctg., 1965, BS in Econs., 1966, MBA, U. Portland, 1968, MEd, 1975, LLD (hon.), 1972; MCL, Western Conservative Bapt. Sem., 1978, DMin, 1982, PhD, Calif. Coast U., DHL (hon.), Warner Pacific Coll., 1988; cert. in wholesale mgmt. Ohio State U., 1970; cert. in labor mgmt., U. Portland, 1972; cert. in advanced mgmt., U. Hawaii, 1975; DD (hon.), Judson Baptist Coll., 1984; DBA (hon.), Marquis Giuseppe Scicluna Internat. U. Found., 1986; LittD (hon.), Va. Tech. Inst. and State U., 1987, LHD (hon.), Warner Pacific Coll., 1988. Pres. R.B. Pamplin Corp., Portland, Oreg., 1964—; chmn. bd. Columbia Empire Farms, Inc., Lake Oswego, Oreg., 1976—; pres. Twelve Oaks Farms, Inc., Lake Oswego, 1977—; dir. Mt. Vernon Mill Inc.; lectr. bus. adminstrn. Lewis and Clark Coll., 1968-69; adj. asst. prof. bus. adminstrn., U. Portland, 1973-76; pastor Christ Community Ch., Lake Oswego, Oreg. lectr. in bus. adminstrn. and economics, U. Costa Rica, 1968, Va. Tech. Found., 1986, dir. R.B. Pamplin Corp., Ross Island Sand & Gravel Co. Author: Everything is Just Great, 1985, The Gift, 1986, Another Virginian: A Study of the Life and Beliefs of Robert Boisseau Pamplin, 1986, (with others): A Portrait of Colorado, 1976, Three in One, 1974, The Storybook Primer on Managing, 1974, One Who Believed, 1988; editor Oreg. Mus. Sci. and Industry Press, 1973, trustee, 1971, 74—; editor Portrait of Oregon, 1973, (with others) Oregon Underfoot, 1975. Mem. Nat. Adv. Council on Vocat. Edn., 1975—; mem. Western Interstate Comm. for Higher Edn., 1981-84; co-chmn. Va. Tech. $50 million Campaign for Excellence, 1984-87, Va. Tech. Found., 1986—, Albert Einstein Acad. Bronze medal, 1986, Va.-Oreg. State Scholarship Commn., 1974—, chmn., 1976-78; mem. Portland dist. adv. council SBA, 1973-77; mem. Rewards Review Com., City Portland, 1973-78, chmn., 1973-78; mem. bd. regents U. Portland, 1971-79, chmn. bd., 1975-79, regent emeritus, 1979—; trustee Lewis and Clark Coll., 1980-84, 85, Oreg. Epis. Schs., 1979. Named disting. alumnus, Lewis and Clark Coll., 1974; recipient Air Force ROTC Disting. Service award, USAF, 1974, Albert Einstein Acad. Bronze medal, 1986; Va. Tech Coll. of Bus. Adminstrn. renamed R.B. Pamplin Coll. of Bus. Adminstrn. in his honor; Western Conservative Bapt. Sem. Lay Inst. for Leadership, Edn., Devel. and Research named for R.B. Pamplin, Jr., 1988. Mem. Acad. Mgmt., Delta Epsilon Sigma, Beta Gamma Sigma, Sigma Phi Epsilon, Waverley Country Club, Arlington, Multnomah Athletic Club, Capitol Hill Club, Rotary. Republican. Episcopalian.

PAN, HERMES, choreographer; b. Memphis, Dec. 10, 1910; s. Pantelis and Mary (Huston) Panagiotopulos. Studies with, Miss Georgia Brown's Pvt. Sch., Nashville. Choreographer films and TV 1933-86. Dancer Broadway musicals, 1927-30; choreographer: (mus. films) Flying Down to Rio, 1933, The Gay Divorcee, 1934, Top Hat, 1935, I Dream Too Much, 1935, Swing Time, 1936, Shall We Dance, 1937, Damsel in Distress (Oscar award), 1937, Carefree, 1938, The Story of Vernon and Irene Castle, 1939, That Night in Rio, 1941, Moon Over Miami, 1941, Rise and Shine, 1941, Song of the Islands, 1942, My Gal Sal, 1942, Sweet Rosie O'Grady, 1943, Pin-Up Girl, 1944, Irish Eyes Are Smiling, 1944, Blue Skies, 1946, The Shocking Miss Pilgrim, 1947, I Wonder Who's Kissing Her Now, 1947, The Barkleys of Broadway, 1949, Let's Dance, 1950, Excuse My Dust, 1951, Lovely to Look At, 1952, Kiss Me Kate, 1953, The Student Prince, 1954, Jupiter's Darling, 1955, Hit the Deck, 1955, Meet Me in Las Vegas, 1956, Silk Stockings, 1956, Pal Joey, 1957, Porgy and Bess, 1959, Can-Can, 1960, Flower Drum Song, 1961, My Fair Lady, 1964, Finian's Rainbow, 1968, Darling Lili, 1969, Lost Horizon, 1973, (TV spls.) An Evening With Fred Astaire (Emmy award), 1961, Sounds of America, Star-Time Academy Award of Songs, Remember How Great, Frances Langford Show. Recipient Emmy award Nat. Acad. TV Arts and Scis., 1958, 59, Nat. Film award for Achievement in Cinema, 1980, Joffrey Ballet award, 1986. Roman Catholic. *

PAN, JEH-NAN (JACK PAN), statistician, engineer; b. Dachen, Zehjiang, People's Republic of China, Feb. 18, 1954; s. Shan-Ming ans Ying-Mei (Hsieh) P.; m. Sherrie Tsai Pan, June 9, 1984; 1 child, Carol Kaiting. BS, Nat. Kaohshing (Republic of China) Normal U., 1976; MS in Indsl. Engring., Tex. Tech U., 1980, PhD in Indsl. Engring. and Stats., 1984. Math. tchr. Da-De High Sch., Taichung, Republic of China, 1976-78; indsl. engr. Am. Pharmaseal Corp., San Marcos, Calif., 1980-81, Roberts Consol. Industries, City of Industry, Calif., 1981-83; part-time instr. Tex. Tech U., Lubbock, 1983-84; statistician, sr. engr. relay div. Leach Corp., L.A., 1985-89, chief statistician, 1989—; adj. assoc. prof. Calif. State U., Northridge, 1985-86, Dominguez Hills, 1988—, U. So. Calif., L.A., 1986-87; cons. in field. Mem. Am. Soc. for Quality Control (awards 1981, 86), Ops. Research Soc. Am., Nat. Mgmt. Assn., Inst. Indsl. Engrs. Home: 4420 Elenda St Culver City CA 90230 Office: Leach Corp 5915 Avalon Blvd Los Angeles CA 90003

PANASCI, NANCY ERVIN, speech pathologist, cookbook writer, communications consultant; b. Fairborn, Ohio, Mar. 24, 1954; d. Lindsay James and Frances E. (Erickson) Ervin; m. Ernest James Panasci, Aug. 7, 1976; children: Caitlin Alba, Adele Frances, Carissa Anne. BS, Colo. State U., 1976; MA, Cath. U., Washington, 1979. Tchr. Montessori Sch., Rome, N.Y., 1971-72, Fairfax (Va.) Sch. Dist., 1976-77; speech pathologist Littleton (Colo.) Pub. Schs., 1979—; communication cons. speech pathology Trial Attys., Denver, 1986—. Com. chairperson Jr. League Denver, 1982—. Named Best Cook in West, Rocky Mountain Newspaper, Denver, 1982. Mem. Am. Speech Hearing Lang. Assn. (cert. clin. competence 1980), Colo. Speech Hearing Assn. (com. chairperson 1982-86), Valley Club (Aurora, Colo.), Racquet World Club (Englewood, Colo.). Roman Catholic. Home: 5191 S Hanover St Englewood CO 80111 Office: Littleton Pub Schs Littleton CO 80120

PANDOLF, VICTORIA ANN, refrigerated foods executive; b. Cannonsburg, Pa., Dec. 20, 1938; d. Richard B. and Helen (Staron) Milliken; m. Donald Winter, May 17, 1956 (div. June 1967); children: Donald R. and Ronald O. (twins); m. John Frank Pandolf, June 17, 1967. Student, American River Jr. Coll., Sacramento, 1968-69; mgmt. cert., Calif. State U., Sacramento, 1986. Gen. officer worker Seafarer's Internat. Union, Richmond, Calif., 1962-66; with shipping and receiving dept. Bercut-Richards Packing Co., Sacramento, 1966-76; mgr. warehouse office Borden Foods, Inc., Sacramento, 1976-79; warehouse mgr. Sacramento Foods, Inc., 1979-86; mgr. Sierra Cold Storage, Sacramento, 1986—. Mem. Internat. Assn. Refrigerated Warehouses, Exec. Women's Internat., Nat. Women's Polit. Caucus. Democrat. Presbyterian. Office: Sierra Cold Storage 426 N 7th St Sacramento CA 95814

PANECALDO, LORETO ANTONIO, III (TONY PANECALDO), personnel director; b. Yuba City, Calif., June 19, 1948; s. Loreto Antonio and Marjorie Isabelle Sarmento Thayer; AA, Yuba Coll., 1969. Floral designer and decorator, owner, gen. mgr. Tony Panecaldo III, Florist, Gridley, Calif., 1977-86; exec. sec., adminstrv. asst. Jay D. Roberts, MD, 1988; dir. personnel, A Profl. Corp. 1988—. councilman City of Gridley, 1976-80, mayor, 1978-80. Chmn., Butte County Republican Cen. Com., 1974-78; mem. Calif. Rep. Cen. Com., also mem. exec. com., platform com., 1978; mem. Calif. Rep. Assembly, alt. del. Rep. Nat. Conv., 1976; bd. dirs. Gridley Hospice of Love. Mem. Butte County Hist. Soc. (dir.), Bidwell Mansion Restoration Assn., Bidwell Mansion Cooperating Assn., Gridley Art League, Commonwealth Club, Order of DeMolay (life), Masons. Home: 1800 Hazel St Gridley CA 95948 Office: 1448 The Esplanade Chico CA 95926 also: PO Box 5408 Chico CA 95927

PANELLI, EDWARD ALEXANDER, associate justice; b. Santa Clara, Calif., Nov. 23, 1931; s. Pilade and Natalina (Della Maggiora) P.; m. Lorna Christine Mondora, Oct. 27, 1956; children: Thomas E., Jeffrey J., Michael P. BA cum laude, Santa Clara U., 1953, JD cum laude, 1955, LLD (hon.), 1986; LLD (hon.), Southwestern U., L.A., 1988. Bar: Calif. 1955. Ptnr. Pasquinelli and Panelli, San Jose, Calif., 1955-72; judge Santa Clara County Superior Ct., 1972-83; assoc. justice 1st Dist. Ct. of Appeals, San Francisco, 1983-84; presiding justice 6th Dist. Ct. of Appeals, San Jose, 1984-85; assoc. justice Calif. Supreme Ct., San Francisco, 1985—; instr. Continuing Legal Edn., Santa Clara, 1976-78. Trustee West Valley Community Coll., 1963-72; trustee Santa Clara U., 1963—, chmn. bd. trustees, 1984—. Recipient Citation, Am. Com. Italian Migration, 1969, Community Legal Services award, 1979, 84, Edwin J. Owens Lawyer of Yr. award Santa Clara Law Sch. Alumni, 1982, Merit award Republic of Italy, 1984. Mem. ABA, Nat. Italian Bar Assn. (inspiration award 1986), Calif. Trial Lawyers Assn. (Trial Judge of Yr. award Santa Clara County chpt. 1981), Calif. Judges Assn. (bd. dirs. 1982), Jud. Coun. Calif.(vice-chair 1989—). Republican. Roman Catholic. Office: Supreme Ct Calif 350 McAllister St San Francisco CA 94102

PANETTA, LEON EDWARD, congressman; b. Monterey, Calif., June 28, 1938; s. Carmelo Frank and Carmelina Maria (Prochilo) P.; m. Sylvia Marie Varni, July 14, 1962; children: Christopher, Carmelo, James. B.A. magna cum laude, U. Santa Clara, Calif., 1960, LL.B., J.D., 1963. Bar: Calif. bar 1965, U.S. Supreme Ct. 1965, U.S. Dist. Ct. (no. dist.) Calif. 1965, U.S. Ct. Appeals 1965. Legis. asst. to U.S. Sen. Thomas Kuchel, Washington, 1966-69; dir. U.S. Office Civil Rights, HEW, Washington, 1969-70; exec. asst. to Mayor of N.Y.C., 1970-71; ptnr. Panetta, Thompson & Panetta, Monterey, 1971-76; mem. 95th-101st Congresses from 16th Calif. Dist., 1977—, Calif. dist. chmn. budget com., mem. Ho. of Reps. adminstrn. com., dep. majority whip agr. com. for budget issues, mem. select com. on hunger. Author: Bring Us Together, 1971. Counsel Monterey Regional Park Dists.; counsel NAACP, 1971-76; bd. trustees U. Santa Clara Law Sch.; founder Monterey Coll. Law; mem. Monterey County Dem. Cen. Com., 1972-74; v.p. Carmel Valley Little League, 1974-75. Served with AUS, 1964-66. Recipient Lincoln award NEA, 1970, Disting. Service award NAACP, 1972, Bread for World award, 1978, Nat. Hospice Orgn. award, 1984, Golden Plow award Am. Farm Bur. Fedn.; named Lawyer of Yr. Law Sch. U. Santa Clara, 1970. Mem. Calif. Bar Assn. Roman Catholic. Office: Cannon House Office Bldg Rm 339 Washington DC 20515

PANG, HERBERT GEORGE, ophthalmologist; b. Honolulu, Dec. 23, 1922; s. See Hung and Hong Jim (Chuu) P.; student St. Louis Coll., 1941; BS, Northwestern U., 1944, MD, 1947; m. Dorothea Lopez, Dec. 27, 1953. Intern Queen's Hosp., Honolulu, 1947-48; postgraduate course ophthalmology N.Y.U., Med. Sch., 1948-49; resident ophthalmology Jersey City Med. Ctr., 1949-50, Manhattan Eye, Ear, & Throat Hosp., N.Y.C., 1950-52; practice medicine specializing in ophthalmology, Honolulu, 1952-54, 56—; mem. staffs Kuakini Hosp., Children's Hosp., Castle Meml. Hosp., Queen's Hosp., St. Francis Hosp.; asst. clin. prof. ophthalmology U. Hawaii Sch. Medicine, 1966-73, now asso. clin. prof. Cons. Bur. Crippled Children, 1952-73, Kapiolani Maternity Hosp., 1952-73, Leahi Tb. Hosp., 1952-62. Capt. M.C., AUS, 1954-56, Diplomate Am. Bd. Ophthalmology. Mem. AMA, Am. Acad. Ophthalmology and Otolaryngology, Assn. for Rsch. Ophthalmology, ACS, Hawaii Med. Soc. (gov. med. practice com. 1958-62, chmn. med. speakers com. 1957-58), Hawaii Eye, Ear, Nose and Throat Soc. (pres. 1960), Pacific Coast Oto-Ophthalmological Soc., Pan Am. Assn. Ophthalmology, Mason, Shriner, Eye Study Club (pres. 1972—). Home: 346 Lewers Rd Honolulu HI 96815 Office: Pane Eye Clinic 1374 Nuuanu Ave Honolulu HI 96817

PANIKAR, SURESH KRISHNAKUTTY, manufacturing executive; b. Bombay, Oct. 29, 1951; came to U.S., 1975; s. Krishna Kutty and Padma (Nair) P.; m. Marla E. Athanasopoulos, Sept. 25, 1982. BS, Calicut (India) U., 1975; MS, Oreg. State U., 1978. Lectr. Oreg. State U., Corvallis, 1976-77, systems engr., 1977-78; systems design engr. Zilog Inc., Cuperino, Calif., 1978-80; dir. computer systems engring. Televideo Systems, Inc., Sunnyville, Calif., 1980-83; v.p. engring. Molecular Computer, San Jose, Calif., 1983-84; pres., chief operating officer, v.p. engring. Unilogic, OSM, Fremont, Calif., 1984-86; pvt. practice cons. Los Gatos, Calif., 1986—; with mktg. dept. Priam Corp., San Jose, 1988—. Mem. IEEE, Assn. of Computing Machines. Democrat. Hindu. Office: Priam Corp 20 W Montague Expressway San Jose CA 95134

PANKOVE, JACQUES ISAAC, physicist; b. Chernigov, Russia, Nov. 23, 1922; came to U.S., 1942, naturalized, 1944; s. Evsey Leib and Miriam (Simkine) Pantchechnikoff; m. Ethel Wasserman, Nov. 24, 1950; children: Martin, Simon. B.S.E.E., U. Calif., Berkeley, 1944, M.S.E.E., 1948; Ph.D. in Physics, U. Paris, 1960. Mem. tech. staff RCA Labs., Princeton, N.J., 1948-70; physicist, fellow RCA Labs., 1970-85; prof. U. Colo., Boulder, 1985—, Hudson Moore Jr. Univ. prof., 1989—, program mgr. materials and devices Ctr. for Optoelectronic Computing Systems, 1986—; disting. rsch. fellow Solar Energy Rsch. Inst., 1985—; vis. McKay lectr. U. Calif., Berkeley, 1968-69; vis. prof. U. Campinas, Brazil, 1975; Disting. vis. prof. U. Mo. at Rolla, 1984; Hudson Moore Jr. prof. computer engring., 1989—; participant NAS sci. exchange program with: Romania, 1970, Hungary, 1972, Yugoslavia, 1976. Mem. hon. editorial bd. Solid State Electronics, 1970—, Solar Energy Materials, 1984—, Optoelectronics, 1986—; regional editor Crystal Lattice Defects and Amorphous Materials, 1984—; author: Optical Processes in Semiconductors, 1971, 75; editor: Electroluminescence, 1977, Display Devices, 1980, Hydrogenated Amorphous Silicon, 1984; author: (ednl. film) Energy Gap and Recombination Radiation, 1962; laser sculpture, Bklyn. Mus., 1968; contbr. articles to sci. jours.; organizer sci. confs.; patentee in field. Trustee Princeton Art Assn., 1970-82; mem. Experiment-in-Arts-and-Tech., Berkeley, 1968-69. Served with U.S. Army, 1944-46. Recipient RCA achievement awards, 1952, 53, 63; David Sarnoff scholar, 1956. Fellow IEEE (J.J. Ebers award 1975, assoc. editor Jour. Quantum Electronics 1968-77), Am. Phys. Soc.; mem. Nat. Acad. Engring. (hon.), Electrochem. Soc., Sigma Xi. Home: 2386 Vassar Dr Boulder CO 80303 Office: U Colo Dept Elec Engring Boulder CO 80309-0425 also: Solar Energy Rsch Inst 1617 Cole Blvd Golden CO 80401

PANNARALE, LUIS STEPHEN, principal; b. Virginia, Minn., June 4, 1948; s. Joseph Edward and Eileen (Scheel) P.; m. Sandra Jan Smith, May 5, 1973; children: Katherine Ann, Bridget Ashlee. AA, Fresno City Coll., 1973; BA in English, Fresno State U., 1975; MA in Edn., Pacific Coll., 1978. Jr. high tchr., v.p. Central Unified Sch. Dist., Fresno, Calif., 1976-86, high sch. athletic dir., 1986-87, elem. prin., 1987—. Scoutmaster Boy Scouts Am., Fresno, 1976-86. With USN, 1967-71, Vietnam. Mem. Assn. Calif. Sch. Adminstrs., Calif. Sch. Leadership Acad. (assoc.), Classic Thunderbird Internat., Central Calif. Thunderbird Club. Democrat. Roman Catholic. Home: 4185 N Katy Ave Fresno CA 93722 Office: Biola Preshing Elem Sch 4885 N Biola Fresno CA 93722

PANNER, OWEN M., United States district judge; b. 1924. Student, U. Okla., 1941-43, LL.B., 1949. Atty. Panner, Johnson, Marceau, Karnopp, Kennedy & Nash, 1950-80; judge U.S. Dist. Ct. Oreg., Portland, 1980—. Office: US Dist Ct 602 US Courthouse 620 SW Main St Portland OR 97205

PANTELL, ROBERT HOWARD, pediatrician, educator; b. N.Y.C., Oct. 6, 1945; s. Milton and Rose Katharyn (Rappaport) P.; m. Marcia Ruth Snell, Oct. 30, 1971 (div. 1980); m. Maureen Theresa Shannon, Aug. 29, 1982; children: Matthew Shannon, Gregory Michael, Megan Elizabeth. BA, Columbia U., 1965; MD, Boston U., 1969. Resident in pediatrics U. N.C., Chapel Hill, 1969-72; pediatrician, med. dir. Community Health Clinics, Nampa, Idaho, 1972-74; Robert Wood Johnson Found. clin. scholar Stanford (Calif.) U., 1974-77; asst. prof. med. U. S.C., Charleston, 1977-80; assoc. prof., dir. div. gen. pediatrics U. Calif.-San Francisco, 1980—; cons. for fed. and pvt. founds. Author: Taking Care of Your Child, 1977, 2d edit., 1982, trans. to Japanese, 1982, Spanish, 1983 (Book of Yr. award Am. Med. Writers Assn. 1978); author, editor: Parents' Pharmacy, 1982, Pediatrics: A Study Guide, 1987; contbr. articles to profl. publs. Grantee HHS, David and Lucile Packard Found., Nat. Ctr. Health Svcs. Rsch., others. Fellow Am. Acad. Pediatrics; mem. Ambulatory Pediatric Assn. (bd. dirs. 1988). Home: 2039 Broderick St San Francisco CA 94115 Office: U Calif 400 Parnassus Ave San Francisco CA 94143

PANTI, MILAN, investment banker and financial planner, consultant; b. Milw., Oct. 23, 1951; s. Pero and Smilja Pantich; m. Linda Drobac, Sept. 9, 1978 (div. Oct. 1984); m. Sherry Cochran, Dec. 24, 1986; 1 child, Lovey. Student bus. and fin., U. Wis., Milw., 1972; student bus. law, Marquette U., 1976. Owner, operator Milan's Balkan Inns, Milw., 1975-80; exec. food and beverage dir. Holiday Inn Corp., Chgo., 1980-84; exec. v.p. Wrigley-Four-Ten Corp., Chgo., 1984-85; dir. ops. Hilton Hotel Corp., Las Vegas, Nev., 1985-87; investment banker and fin. planner I.D.S./Am. Express, 1987—. Author: Hotel Operations, 1983, Budgeting Hotels, 1984, Food and Beverage Operations, 1984, Close to the Edge, 1985. Bd. dirs. Chgo. Conv. Bur., 1978-84, Congl. Adv. Bd., Washington, 1980—, Presdl. Task Force, 1980—, Chgo. Devel. Authority, 1984, Near North Entertainment Coun., Chgo., 1985; mem. election com. Cook County Rep. Com., 1984. Named Man of Yr., Ill. Businessmen's Assn., 1983. Mem. Nat. Restaurant Assn., Nat. Hotel Assn. (Mgr. of Yr. award 1984), Internat. Hotel Execs. Assn. Serbian Orthodox. Home: 2578 Pera Circle Las Vegas NV 89121

PAOLI, MARILYN SUE TATRO, insurance agent; b. Boise, Idaho, Nov. 26, 1949; d. Don A. and Katherine S. (Smith) Tatro; m. Robert N. Paoli, Jan. 11, 1972 (dec. 1983); children: Lisa, Juliana. BS, U. Nev., 1981. Supr. taxation dept. State of Nev., Carson City, 1973-79, sr. mgmt. analyst budget div., 1979-82; agt. State Farm Ins., Carson City, 1982—. Named Young Bus. Mgr. of Yr., Carson City Jaycees, 1987, C. of C. Woman of Yr., 1988, Bd. Realtors Affiliate of Yr., 1987. Mem. Carson City C. of C. (bd. dirs. 1986-89), Nat. Assn. Life Underwriters, Builders Assn. Western Nev., Carson, Douglas and Lyon Bd. Realtors, Soroptimist (pres. 1987-88). Republican. Roman Catholic. Office: Marilyn Paoli Ins 321 W Winnie Ln Ste 106 Carson City NV 89703

PAOLINO, JOHN JULIAN, utilities executive; b. Florence, Colo., Oct. 27, 1938; s. John Benjamin Paolino and Albena Frances (Nogavica)Wylie; m. Barbara Alice Cage, June 18, 1960 (div. 1974); children: Kris Anthony, Tish Marie, Dana Leigh. BA in Phys. Edn., U. No. Colo., 1959, MA in Ednl. Psychology, 1960. Cert. tchr., Colo.; cert. community col.. tchr., Ariz. Commd. 2d lt. USAF, 1959, advanced through grades to lt. col., 1976; served as pilot tng. officer USAF, various locations, 1960, 61; mem. faculty USAF Acad. USAF, 1972-76, sta. in Vietnam, 1964-65, ret., 1980; mgmt. cons. Beardsley & Assocs., San Jose, Calif., 1981-85; adminstr. Ariz. Pub. Svc. Co., Phoenix, 1985--; mem. adj. faculty Rio Salado Community Coll., Phoenix, 1985--, Ariz. State Coll., Tempe, 1978-80. Mem. Assn. for Quality and Participation (pres. 1987-88), Air Force Assn. (v.p. 1986-88), Order of Daedalians. Republican. Roman Catholic. Home: 1914 E Watson Dr Tempe AZ 85283

PAPA, ANTHONY JOSEPH, recording sound engineer, producer; b. Camden, N.J., June 14, 1947; s. John and Jean (Caparolla) P.; divorced; children: Anna Marie, Terasa Lee; m. Lauren Michelle Papa, June 5, 1988; 1 child, Matthew Derek. BS, Rutgers U., 1969, MA, 1971. Owner, engr., producer MSI, Pennsauken, N.J., 1971-78; chief engr., mgr. Scotti Bros. Entertainment, L.A., 1978—; proprietor Sound Consortium, L.A., 1983—. Fundraiser Greenpeace, L.A., 1987-89. Recipient Gold Records, RIAA, 1985-88, Platinum Record, 1984, Golden Reel, 1985, Platinum 45, 1988. Office: Scotti Bros Entertainment 2114 Pico Blvd Santa Monica CA 90404

PAPAY, MICHAEL LAWRENCE, aerospace engineer; b. Zanesville, Ohio, July 11, 1964; s. Harry Lawrence and Jean Marie (Spann) P.; m. Amanda Lee Shorter, July 25, 1987. BS in Aerospace and Ocean Engring. cum laude, Va. Poly. Inst. and State U., 1986. Mem. tech. staff TRW Inc., San Bernardino, Calif., 1986—. Mem. AIAA (career enhancement com.), Sigma Gamma Tau. Home: 1400 Barton Rd 2806 Redlands CA 92373

PAPE, THOMAS EMIL, marketing professional, consultant; b. Redbud, Ill., Apr. 28, 1959; s. Gilbert Raymond and Delphine (Hehrtens) P. BA, So. Ill. U., 1981. Cert. energy auditor, Ill., residential conservation svc. trainer, Calif., master water auditor. Energy cons. VISTA, Carbondale, Ill., 1979-80; design cons. Applied Alternatives, Desoto, Ill., 1980-83; energy auditor DMC Energy Inc., Springfield, Ill., 1981-83, field cons., 1983-84; project supr. DMC Energy Inc., Santa Monica, Calif., 1984-85; mktg. rsch. cons. DMC Energy Inc., L.A., 1985-88; conservation specialist City of Pasadena,

Calif., 1988—; mem. solar speaker bur. Ill. Dept. Energy and Natural Resources, 1979-82. Mem. Assn. Profl. Energy Mgrs. Roman Catholic. Home: 2303 Carnegie Ln #G Redondo Beach CA 90278

PAPEN, FRANK O'BRIEN, banker, former state senator; b. Dec. 2, 1909; m. Julia Stevenson; 1 child, Michele Papen-Daniel. LLD (hon.), N.Mex. State U., 1988. Dir. First Nat. Bank Dona Ana County, Las Cruces, N.Mex., 1957-60, exec. v.p., 1957-60, pres., 1960-71, chmn. bd. dirs., chief exec. officer, 1971-82, 88—, pres., chmn. bd. dirs., 1982-87; mem. Ho. of reps. State of N.Mex., 1957-58, senator, 1969-84; vice-chmn. 12 regional adv. com. on banking practices and policies, 1965-66; mem. adv. com. on fed. legis., 1966; mem. N.Mex. State Investment Council, 1963-67; mem. N.Mex. Dept. Devel. Adv. Council, 1967-68; mem. steering com. Edn. Commn. States; mem. Albuquerque dist. adv. council SBA; pres. N.Mex. State U. Pres. Assocs. Mem. N.M. Ho. of Reps., 1957-58 (chmn. legis. fin. com. and legis. sch. study com.), N.M. State Senate, 1969-84. Recipient Citizen of Yr. award N.Mex. Assn. Realtors, 1966, Branding Iron award N.Mex. State U., 1977, The Pres.'s award for Service N.Mex. State U., 1983, Regent's medal N.Mex. State U., 1985, N.Mex. Sch. Banking Leadership award, 1987, Bob Haynsworth Sportsmanship award Sunland Park Race Track, 1987. Mem. Am. Bankers Assn. (savs. bond chmn. N.Mex. 1964-66), N.Mex. Bankers Assn. (pres., mem. exec. com. 1965-66), Las Cruces C. of C. (past pres.). Democrat. Lodges: Kiwanis, KC. Office: PO Box FNB Las Cruces NM 88004

PAPEN, JULIA STEVENSON, food products company executive; b. Beaufort, S.C., May 21, 1910; d. Carl Frederick and Emma Stevenson; m. Frank O'Brien Papen, Apr. 22, 1942; 1 child, Michele Papen-Daniel. BA magna cum laude, U. S.C., 1931. Office mgr. Longview (Tex.) Coca-Cola Bottling Co., 1931-41, v.p., dir., 1960—; gen. mgr. Las Cruces (N.Mex.) Coca-Cola Bottling Co., 1941-44; office mgr. Frank O. Papen Ins. Agy., Las Cruces, 1944-57. Gov. appointed Regent N.Mex. State U., 1976-82; mem. Las Cruces Womens' Improvement Assn., Dona Ana Arts Council, Las Cruces, 1975-88; bd. dirs. Las Cruces Symphony Assn., 1983—. Named to Order of Holy Sepulchre Pope Pius XII, 1960. Mem. AAUW, Phi Beta Kappa, Beta Gamma Sigma. Democrat. Roman Catholic. Home and Office: 1857 Paisano Rd Las Cruces NM 88005

PAPENTHIEN, KEITH ERIC, merchant marine officer; b. Stockton, Calif., May 30, 1959; s. Richard Papenthien and Carole (Gott) Dennis; m. Kristine Marie Barcott, Oct. 14, 1988; children: Stevie, Ann, Noel. Commd. 2d lt. USCG, 1987, advance through grades to capt., 1987—. With USN, 1979-82. Recipient Meritorious Advancement. Mem. Inland Boatmans Union of Pacific. Republican. Office: Knappton Maritime Alaskan Way Seattle WA 98121

PARADISE, PHYLLIS ELIZABETH, nurse; b. Fennimore, Wis., Feb. 13, 1922; d. Wesley Arthur and Minerva Aurelia (Riley) Walker; m. Robert Earl Finn, Aug. 12, 1944 (div.); children: Bernard Robert Paradise, Sheri Anne Jones, Melanie Marcella Nieman; m. Henry Melvin Paradise, Sept. 24, 1953; children: Penny Aurelia Grace Paradise Jacobson, Henrietta Charlotte, Wesley John. Diploma in nursing, Meth. Kahler, Rochester, Minn., 1943. Registered nurse. Staff clin. nurse Dept. Health and Human Services, Nev., Okla., Nebr. and N.Mex., 1953-85; staff nurse Quality Care Agy., Albuquerque, 1986—; retired but active 1985—. Treas. N.Mex. Mus. Natural Hist., Albuquerque, 1987-88. Mem. Nat. Assn. Retired Fed. Employees. Republican. Methodist.

PARADY, JOHN EDWARD, information systems executive, consultant; b. Inglewood, Calif., Sept. 26, 1939; s. Raymond Oliver and Ella Louise (Timm) P.; m. Barbara Lyn Pettit, Aug. 13, 1966; chidlren: John, Renee, Stacy. BS, Calif. State U., Los Angeles, 1966; MS, U. So. Calif., 1969. Cert. data processing. Dir. info. systems Weyerhauser Co., Tacoma, Wash., 1975-82; exec. dir. McKenna, Conner & Cuneo, Los Angeles, 1982-83; sr. v.p. Bank of Am., San Francisco, 1983-85, Ticor, Los Angeles, 1985-88; exec. v.p. Pacific Stock Exchange, Los Angeles, 1988—; pvt. practice cons., Los Angeles, 1986—; mem. The Research Bd., N.Y.C., 1983-86; bd. dirs. The Ctr. for Info. Systems Research, Cambridge, Mass., 1977-85. Served to 2d lt., U.S. Army, 1959-64. Republican. Mormon. Home: 1004 Vista Del Valle La Canada CA 91011 Office: 233 S Beaudry Ave Los Angeles CA 90012

PARASKA, WILLIAM FRANK, air force officer; b. Cleve., Oct. 18, 1948; s. Frank William and Anne Rosemarie (Tomko) P.; m. Susan Elizabeth Rowe, May 10, 1975; children: Margo Elaine, David Leland. BA, Kenyon Coll., 1970; MA, U. Nebr., Lincoln, 1981. Commd. 2d lt. USAF, 1970, advanced through grades to lt. col., 1987; mem. communications staff USAF, Omaha and Belleville, Ill., 1971-84; with NATO squadron command USAF, Kindsbach, Fed. Republic Germany, 1984-87; systems architect hdqrs. U.S. Space Command USAF, Colorado Springs, Colo., 1987—. Den leader, Colorado Springs area Boy Scouts Am., 1988—; mem. covenant com., Mountain Shadows Homeowners Assn., Colorado Springs, 1989. Mem. Armed Forces Communications Electronics Assn. (exec. bd.). Republican.

PARDEW, DONALD AMBROSE, service company executive; b. L.A., Oct. 8, 1951; s. Ambrose Thacker and Dethba Lee (Criss) P.; m. Trina Marie Sabin, June 25, 1972 (div. 1974); m. Lilian Julia Marks, Aug. 1, 1981; 1 child, Michelle Julia. Student, Los Beach City Coll., 1973-75. Asst. mechanic Pardew's Flying Svc., Long Beach, Calif., 1969-71; with A.M.C. Cycle Safety Corp., Long Beach, Calif., 1972-75; mechanic Downey (Calif.) Volkswagen, 1977-78, Timmon's Volkswagen, Long Beach, 1978-79, Rushak Volkswagen, Culver City, Calif., 1979-81; researcher Civil War Aviation, Long Beach, 1982-84; aviation researcher World Aviation Corp., Long Beach, 1984-86, Lakewood, Calif., 1986-87; owner, mgr. Pardew's Volkswagen, Lakewood, 1987--. Mem. Aircraft Pilots Assn. (cert. pvt. pilot), Hist. Preservation Assn., Civil War Times Assn., CSA (mem. White House of Confederacy). Home and Office: 5428 Fidler Ave Lakewood CA 90712

PARDEW, THOMAS EUGENE, mechanical engineer; b. Portland, Oreg., Mar. 9, 1946; s. James Maurice and Anna Louise (Bonner) P.; m. Elaine Michelle Pandapas, Nov. 16, 1969; children: Kevin James, Michael Joseph. BSME, N.J. Inst. Tech., 1968. Cert. engr.-in-tng. Maintenance engr. FMC Corp., Carteret, N.J., 1968-69; quality control supr. Skyline Corp., McMinville, Oreg., 1975, prodn. supr., 1976; project engr. Evanite Fiber Corp., Corvallis, Oreg., 1979-81, plant engr., 1981-85, plant supt., 1985-88, mgr. mfg. engring., 1988—; owner, mgr. Dr. Tom's Travelling Tune-Up, Dallas, Oreg., 1975-79. Soccer coach Kids, Inc., Dallas, 1985-87; asst. cub master Boy Scouts Am., Dallas, 1986, chmn. transp. and advancement, 1988. Mem. TAPPI, Am. Paper Inst., Soc. Mfg. Engrs., Sports Car Club Am., Pi Kappa Phi. Home: 11805 Orrs Corner Rd Dallas OR 97338 Office: Evanite Fiber Corp PO Box E Corvallis OR 97339

PAREDES, BERT (NORBERT PAREDES), computer systems engineer; b. Frankfurt, Fed. Republic Germany, Dec. 27, 1947; s. George and Elfriede (Kleebach) P.; m. Linda L. Stubblefield, July 5, 1968 (div. 1986); m. Katherine Blacklock, Feb. 4, 1989. BS in Computer Sci., SUNY, Albany, 1970; postgrad., U. Colo., 1977-78. Enlisted U.S. Army, 1970, programmer/analyst, 1970-79, resigned, 1979; staff engr. Martin Marietta Denver Aerospace div., 1979-81; sr. staff engr. Martin Marietta Advanced Launch Systems, 1984—; regional analyst, mgr. Gould Computer Systems, Denver, 1981-84; mgr. tech. analysis and support Denelcor, Inc., Aurora, Colo., 1984; Pres., chief exec. officer A.C.T., Inc., Denver, 1982-84. Contbr. articles to profl. jours. Vol. cons. Opera Colo., Denver, 1982—. Nat. Merit scholar, 1966. Mem. Assn. Computing Machinery, Armed Forces Communications and Electronics Assn., Am. Rose Soc., Mensa, Denver Mus. Natural History, Denver Bot. Gardens. Libertarian. Lutheran. Home: 6859 N Beaver Run Littleton CO 80125 Office: Martin Marietta Astronautics PO Box 179 Denver CO 80201

PARENT, NANCY L., lawyer; b. Antioch, Calif., June 23, 1940; d. Edward N. and Grace L. (Simpson) P. AB, U. Calif., Berkeley, 1962; postgrad., San Jose State U., 1963; JD, U. Calif., San Francisco, 1970. Cert. secondary edn. tchr. Tchr. Pittsburg Unified Sch. Dist., Pittsburg, Calif., 1963-67; editor Bancroft Whitney Co., San Francisco, 1970-73; dep. city atty. City of San Jose, Calif., 1973-76; pvt. practice Pittsburg, 1976—. Editor: California Jurisprudence, 2nd edit. Trustee Pittsburg Unified Sch. Dist., 1976-81; council mem. City of Pittsburg, 1984—, mayor, 1985 and 1989. Named Citizen of Yr. Pittsburg C. of C., 1983. Mem. State Bar Calif., Contra Costa County Bar, Soroptimist Internat. Pittsburg, Bus. and Profl. Women (pres. Pittsburg and East County chpt. 1966). Democrat. Office: 64 E 4th St Pittsburg CA 94565

PARENTE, EMIL J., chemical engineering executive; b. N.Y.C., Aug. 2, 1930; m. Phyllis Sara Gordon, Mar. 15, 1970; children: Victoria Rebecca, Stephen Raphael. BSChemE, Cooper Union, 1953; MSChemE, NYU, 1957. Process engr. Vitro Corp. Am., 1953-54; from process engr. to project mgr. Fluor, Singmaster & Breyer Inc., 1954-63; from project mgr. to v.p., gen. mgr. petroleum chem. div. sales The Ralph M. Parsons Co., 1963-78; v.p., then sr. v.p. sales Fluor Corp., 1978-82; sr. v.p., gen. mgr. advanced tech. div. and telecommunications div. Fluor Corp., Irvine, Calif., 1982-84; pres. Fluor Tech. Inc., Irvine, 1984-86; pres. govt. sector Fluor Daniel, Inc., Irvine, 1986—; lectr. on energy and synthetic fuels. Contbr. papers to profl. jours. Mem. Am. Inst. Chem. Engrs., Am. Petroleum Inst., U.S. C. of C. (energy com. 1981-84), U.S.-Arab C. of C. (bd. dirs. 1975-78). Office: Fluor Corp 3333 Michelson Dr Irvine CA 92730

PARENTI, KATHY ANN, interior designer; b. Gary, Ind., Sept. 24, 1957; d. Lee Everett Huddleston and Barbara Elizabeth (Daves) Tilley; m. Michael A. Parenti, Mar. 31, 1979. Student, Ind. U., Gary, 1977; cert., U. Nev., Las Vegas, 1978; diploma, Interior Design Inst., Las Vegas, 1984. Office mgr. Realty Execs., Las Vegas, 1977-78, Jet Set Internat., Las Vegas, 1978-79; bookkeeper Las Vegas Water Dist., 1979-80; supr. Circus Circus Hotel, Las Vegas, 1980-87; owner Interior Views, Las Vegas, 1984-87; sales rep. Win-Glo Window Coverings, 1987-88; owner Dimension Design, 1988—. Mem. Las Vegas C. of C., Women's Council (membership com.), Internat. Brotherhood of Teamsters, Chauffeurs, Warehousemen, and Helpers of Am. Republican.

PARIS, EDWARD MARVIN, educational institutional researcher; b. Denver, Oct. 7, 1951; s. Marvin E. and Winifred A. (West) P.; m. Carol L. Powell, Aug. 2, 1975; 1 child, Julia. BA, U. Colo., Boulder, 1973, MPA, 1979; postgrad., U. Colo., Denver. Adminstrv. officer Colo. Dept. Revenue, Denver, 1979-80, Colo. Dept. Social Svc., Denver, 1980; budget analyst U. Colo., Boulder, 1980-84; instnl. researcher U. Colo., Colorado Springs, 1984—; cons. in information systems, Colorado Springs. Mem. Assn. Instnl. Rsch. (mem. workshop selection com. for nat. conv. 1989). Roman Catholic. Home: 2614 Farragut Circle Colorado Springs CO 80907 Office: U Colo Colorado Springs PO Box 7150 Colorado Springs CO 80933-7150

PARIS, JAMES LEE, educator; b. Bozeman, Mont., Nov. 20, 1943; s. Cecil R. and Ethlyn L. (Wagner) P.; m. Maida M. Bickle, June 1, 1963; children: Debrorah L. Paris McCulogh, Robert J. BA in Social Studies Edn., Mont. State U., 1966; MA in Elem. Edn., No. Mont. Coll., 1977. Tchr. Scobey (Mont.) High Sch., 1966-69, Sch. Dist. No. 1, Great Falls, Mont., 1969--; co-owner Lawman's Supply Co., Great Falls, 1978-84; owner, mgr. apts. Great Falls, 1972-88; negotiations cons. numerous sch. dist., Mont., 1968-80. Co-chmn. Daniels County campaign Knutson for Ho. Reps., 1968; campaign worker D olezal for Senate Com., Great Falls, 1988. Recipient cert. of appreciation Sch. Dist. No. 1, 1987, Good Apple award 1988. Mem. NEA (mem. com. 1983-85), Mont. Edn. Assn. (numerous coms. 1968-85), Great Falls Edn. Assn. (numerous coms. 1974-85, Silver Key award 1976-78), Masons, Elks. Democrat. Lutheran. Office: East Jr High Sch 4040 Central Ave Great Falls MT 59405

PARIS, SANFORD PHILIP, industrial park developer; b. Chgo., Sept. 14, 1937; s. Oscar L. and Irene Ida (Feldman) P.; m. Eileen Goldman, July 4, 1960 (widowed Nov. 1981); children: Russell H., Jodi H.; m. Carolyn Nowabielsky, June 7, 1987. BS in Acctg., UCLA, 1959; LLB, South Western Law Sch., L.A., 1963. Owner Paris Indsl. Parks, L.A., 1967--; acct. Seidman & Seidman, L.A., 1965-67; corp. atty. ARCS Mortgage, Inc., Canoga Park, Calif., 1976-87; bd. dirs. Tarzana Regional Med. Ctr. Pres., bd. dirs. L.A. Hdqrs. City Assn., 1986-87, Valley Industry & Commerce Assn., L.A., 1988--; mem. L.A. City Bd. Library Commrs., 1985--. Capt. U.S. Army, 1963-65. Named Man of Yr., Anti-Defamation League, 1987. Mem. State Bar Assn. Calif., L.A. County Bar Assn., San Fernando Bar Assn. Democrat. Jewish. Office: Paris Indsl Parks 16501 Ventura Blvd Ste 402 Encino CA 91436-2001

PARK, EDWARD CAHILL, JR., physicist; b. Wollaston, Mass., Nov. 26, 1923; s. Edward Cahill and Fentress (Kerlin) P.; m. Helen Therese O'Boyle, July 28, 1951. AB, Harvard U., 1947; postgrad., Amherst Coll., 1947-49; PhD, U. Birmingham, Eng., 1956. Instr. Amherst (Mass.) Coll., 1954-55; mem. staff Lincoln Lab., Lexington, Mass., 1955-57, Arthur D. Little, Inc., Cambridge, Mass., 1957-60; group leader electronic systems Arthur D. Little, Inc., Santa Monica, Calif., 1960-64; sr. staff engr., head laser system sect. Hughes Aircraft Co., Culver City, Calif., 1964-68; sr. scientist Hughes Aircraft Co., El Segundo, Calif., 1986-88; mgr. electric optical systems sect. Litton Guidance and Control Systems, Woodland Hills, Calif., 1968-70; sr. phys. scientist The Rand Corp., Santa Monica, 1970-72; sr. scientist R&D Assocs., Marina Del Rey, Calif., 1972-1986, cons., 1986—. Contbr. articles to profl. jours.; patentee in field. Served to 1st lt. USAAF, 1943-46. Grantee Dept. Indsl. and Sci. Research, 1953. Fellow Explorers Club (sec. So. Calif. chpt. 1978-79); mem. IEEE, Optical Soc. Am., Armed Forces Communications and Electronics Assn., Assn. Old Crows, Sigma Xi. Democrat. Clubs: 20-Ghost (Eng.), Harvard (So. Calif.). Home and Office: 932 Ocean Front Santa Monica CA 90403

PARK, HOWARD MITCHELL, priest; b. International Falls, Minn., Jan. 27, 1922; s. Mike and Lydia (Pullianen) P.; m. Shirley Danielson, Sept., 1952; children: Sharman, Diedre, Karl, Erik, Kirsten; m. Dorothy Lew Wallace, July, 1983. Student, U. Alaska, 1950-52, U. B.C., 1952-56; BS, SUNY, Albany, 1974; diplomate in divinity, Ch. Divinity Sch. of the Pacific, 1981. Ordained priest Episcopal Ch., 1982. Engr. Dept. Aviation, Terr. of Alaska, 1951-53; project engr. Morrison-Knudsen Co., 1950-60; v.p., gen. mgr. Saunders, Inc., Anchorage, 1961-65, No. Ventures, Inc., Anchorage, 1961-65; mgr. heavy constrn. Braund, Inc., Anchorage, 1968-73; spl. asst. Occupational Safety and Health Adminstrn., State of Alaska, Anchorage, 1973-74, Dept. Health, State of Alaska, Anchorage, 1974-75; vicar St. Barnabas Mission Ch., Mt. Shasta, Calif., 1982—; chmn. Commn. on Stewardship, Episcopal Diocese No. Calif., 1983-85. Served to 1st lt. USAF, 1942-50, ETO. Decorated D.F.C., Purple Heart with cluster, Air medal with 18 clusters; recipient Presdl. citation with cluster, 1944-45. Mem. Order St. Luke (chaplain 1985-88). Democrat. Lodges: Shriners, Masons. Office: St Barnabas Episcopal Ch PO Box 1350 Mount Shasta CA 96067

PARK, MARY SOONMIE, computer services professional; b. Seoul, Korea, Mar. 5, 1956; came to U.S., 1962; d. Kyung June and Bokhie Lee (Lee) P.; m. Hong Michael Kim, Dec. 29, 1980; children: Andrew K., Alexander T. BA in Econs., U. Wash., 1978; MBA, U. Puget Sound, 1980. Systems analyst, programmer Boeing Comml. Airplane Co., Renton, Wash., 1978-83; sr. systems analyst Boeing Computer Svcs., Bellevue, Wash., 1983-85; mgr. advanced systems devel. Boeing Computer Svcs., Bellevue, 1985—; cons. bus. Jr. Achievement, Seattle, 1988—. Active in Puget Sound SANE, Seattle, 1985—; del. Presdl. Reception Korean Embassy, 1985. Roman Catholic.

PARK, WEE WUONE, architect, concert pianist; b. Seoul, Republic of Korea, Aug. 20, 1931; came to U.S., 1954; s. Yong Kwan and Eun Kyung (Kim) P. BS, U. Wyoming, 1959; MA, Harvard U., 1964; M. Performing Arts, U. Paris, 1970. Registered architect, Colo. Concert pianist Denver, Paris, 1950—; chief design architect Stapleton Internat. Airport Paul Reddy Architect Group, Denver, 1970-79; pres. Wee Park & Co. Architects, Denver, 1979—; pres. Wee Park & Co. Architects, Denver, 1979—. Pres. Men's Orgn. Denver Symphony, 1975, I Pagliacci opera group, Denver, 1980; bd. dirs. Denver Symphony Assn., 1976; founding bd. mem. Opera Colo., Denver, 1982; v.p. Denver Civic Ballet, 1978-80, bd. dirs., 1980. Capt. Republic of Korea Air Force, 1950-53. Recipient Medal of Honor Republic of Korea, 1950. Mem. Denver Athletic Club, Denver Press Club. Republican. Office: 1751 Franklin St Denver CO 80218

PARKER, BRIAN PRESCOTT, forensic scientist; b. Norfolk, Va., Aug. 31, 1929; s. Milton Ellsworth and Louise Randall (Smith) P.; B.S. in Quantitative Biology, M.I.T., 1953; J.D., Northwestern U., 1957; M.Criminology, U. Calif., Berkeley, 1961, D.Criminology, 1967; m. Sonia Garcia Rosario, Dec. 23, 1960; children—Robin Marie, Augustin Keith. Research asst. U. P.R. Med. Sch., 1961; cons. P.R. Justice Dept., 1961-63; spl. asst. FDA, Washington, 1964; lectr., then asst. prof. criminology U. Calif., Berkeley, 1964-70; sr. criminalist, then sr. forensic scientist Stanford Research Inst., Menlo Park, Calif., 1971-73; prof. forensic sci. and criminal justice Calif. State U., Sacramento, 1973—; prof. emeritus, 1988—; project dir. phys. evidence Dept. Justice, 1969-70; vis. fellow Nat. Police Research Unit, Australia, 1985; vis. prof. Elton Mayo Sch. Mgmt., South Australia Inst. Tech., 1985. Fellow Am. Acad. Forensic Scis.; mem. Am. Acad. Polit. and Social Sci., Am. Chem. Soc., Acad. Criminal Justice Scis., Calif. Assn. Criminalists, Forensic Sci. Soc. London. Co-author: Physical Evidence in the Administration of Criminal Justice, 1970, The Role of Criminalistics in the World of the Future, 1972; asso. editor Law, Medicine, Science—and Justice, 1964; contbr. to Ency. Crime and Justice, 1983. Home: 5117 Ridgegate Way Fair Oaks CA 95628 Office: 6000 J St Sacramento CA 95819

PARKER, C. RICHARD, company executive; b. Houston, Sept. 28, 1939; s. Charles Robert and Evelyn Louise (Donaldson) P.; m. Linda Rolls, Sept. 12, 1970 (div. 1980); children: Christian Holt, Richard Jason, Jacqueline Marie. BA in Psychology, UCLA, 1970; MA in Orgn. Devel., Pepperdine U., 1973. Dir. mktg. and ops. Am. Clinic Enterprises, Beverly Hills, Calif., 1973-80; internal mgmt. cons. Blue Cross-Blue Shield, N.Y.C. and Woodland Hills, Calif., 1980-83; v.p. corp. productivity Ticor, L.A., 1984-85; mgmt. cons. L.A., 1986-88; dir. ops. Nadel Partnership Inc., L.A., 1988—; bd. dirs. Carter Holdings, Santa Monica, Calif. Vol. Brentwood Boys Club, L.A., 1983; mem. Town Hall Calif., L.A., 1988-89. Mem. Rotary (treas. West Los Angeles, Calif. 1984-85). Republican. Roman Catholic. Home: 5ll Geneva St Glendale CA 91206 Office: Nadel Partnership Inc 1990 S Bundy Dr Los Angeles CA 90025

PARKER, CATHERINE SUSANNE, psychotherapist; b. Norwood, Mass., Nov. 4, 1934; d. George Leonard and Hazel Olga (Remmer) P. BA, Bates Coll., 1956; MSW, U. Denver, 1961. Lic. social worker, Colo. Social worker Taunton (Mass.) State Hosp., 1956-59; social worker Ft. Logan Mental Health Ctr., Denver, 1961-66, clin. team leader, 1966-72; dir. adult services Western Inst. Human Resources, Denver, 1973-74; pvt. practice psychotherapy Denver, 1974—; instr. U. Denver, 1977-79; workshop facilitator Arapahoe Community Coll., 1986—. Mem. Nat. Assn. Social Workers, Acad. Cert. Social Workers (cert.), Internat. Transactional Analysis Assn. Home: 6453 S Downing St Littleton CO 80121 Office: Denver Mental Health 165 Cook St Suite 100 Denver CO 80206

PARKER, CHARLES EDWARD, lawyer; b. Santa Ana, Calif., Sept. 9, 1927; s. George Ainsworth and Dorothy P.; m. Marilyn Esther Perrin, June 23, 1956; children—Mary, Catherine, Helen, George. Student, Santa Ana Coll., U. So. Calif.; J.D., S.W. U.-La. Bar: Calif. 1958, U.S. Dist. Ct. (cen. dist.) Calif. 1958, U.S. Supreme Ct. 1969, D.C. 1971, U.S. Dist. Ct. (no. and so. dists.) Calif. 1981. Prof. law Western State U., Fullerton, Calif., 1973-83; spl. counsel Tidelands, First Am. Title Co., 1980-82; dir. First Am. Fin. Corp., 1981-82. Served to sgt. U.S. Army, 1951-53. Mem. ABA (com. improvement land records, sect. real property), Orange County Bar Assn., Calif. Bar Assn., D.C. Bar Assn. Club: Santa Ana Kiwanis, Lodge: Elks (Santa Ana). Contbr. articles in field to profl. jours. Office: 18101 Charter Rd Villa Park CA 92667

PARKER, CONNIE ALLEN, marina executive; b. San Francisco, Jan. 2, 1940; s. Harold Chester and June Marie (Pridgeon) P.; m. Karen Kay Hamilton (div. May 1978); children: Jeffrey Allen, Matthew Charles, Jennifer Ann, Katherine Louise. BS, Portland State Coll., 1961. Commd. ensign USNR, 1961, advanced through grades to lt. comdr.; line officer USNR, various locations, 1961-71; resigned USNR, 1971; chief engr. Helmsey-Spear Calif., Los Angeles, 1971-73; v.p. Cushman & Wakefield Oreg., Portland, 1973-87. Chmn. Pete Ward Baseball Clinic, Portland, 1988. Mem. University Club. Home: 2020 SW Salmm #104 Portland OR 97205

PARKER, DAVID GENE, professional baseball player; b. Jackson, Miss., June 9, 1951; m. Kelleye Crockett; children: Danielle, David II. With Pitts. Pirates, 1973-82, Cin. Reds, 1983-87; with Oakland A's, 1987—; Nat. League player in All-Star Game, 1977, 79, 80, 81, 85, 86. Named Most Valuable Player Nat. League, 1978; named Nat. League Player of Yr., Sporting News, 1978; winner Gold Glove, 1977-79. Address: care Oakland As Oakland-Alameda County Stadium Oakland CA 94621 *

PARKER, JILL KENNEDY, educator; b. Sendai, Japan, Dec. 5, 1949; d. John Edward and Olive June (Hesser) Kennedy; m. Henry Raymond Parker, Nov. 10, 1972; children: Kelly, Daniel. BA, Cameron U., 1972; postgrad., U. Portland, 1985-86. Cert. tchr., Idaho. Substitute tchr. Lawton (Okla.) Pub. Schs., 1972-73, Boise (Idaho) Pub. Schs., 1973-79, 1988-89; teaching asst. Skinner Montessori Sch., Boise, 1984-85; primary tchr. Tng. Montessori Edn. Ctr., Portland, Oreg., 1985-86; lead tchr. Tom Thumb Montessori Sch., Boise, 1986—. Mem. N.Am. Montessori Tchrs. Assn., Assn. Montessori Internat. (primary diploma). Home and Office: 724 Warm Springs St Boise ID 83712

PARKER, JOHN HAVELOCK, Canadian provincial official; b. Didsbury, Alta., Can., Feb. 2, 1929; s. Bruce T. and Rose H. P.; m. Helen A. Panabaker, 1955; children: Sharon, Gordon. B.Sc. in Engring. Geology, U. Alta., Edmonton, 1951. Mng. engr. Norman W. Byrne, Ltd., Uranium City and Yellowknife, N.W.T., Can., 1951-63; pres. Precambrian Mining Services Ltd., 1964-67; councillor Town of Yellowknife, 1959-63, mayor, 1964-67; councillor N.W.T., 1967-74, dep. commr., 1967-79, commr., 1979-89; chmn. Sci. Inst. N.W.T., Arctic Inst. N.Am. Mem., vice chmn. Duke of Edinburgh's Award in Can.; past mem. senate Univ. Alb.; patron Tree of Peace, Yellowknife; vice-prior St. John Ambulance for N.W.T. Decorated knight Order of St. John; named to Order of Can. Fellow Arctic Inst. N.Am. (chmn.); mem. Can. Inst. Mining and Metallurgy, Assn. Profl. Engrs. Alta., Sci. Inst. N.W.T., Royal Can. Geog. Soc. (bd. dirs.).

PARKER, JOHN HOWARD, state official; b. Wash., July 16, 1950; s. Lewis and Kathleen P.; m. Cynthia Parker, 1976. AA, Butte Coll., Pentz, Calif., 1970; BA, Calif. State U., Chico, 1976. Program review analyst Calif. Dept. Fin., Sacramento, 1977-84; microcomputer resource coordinator State Tchrs. Retirement Sys., Sacramento, 1985-87, chief mgmt. and cons. svcs., 1987; ptnr. Investors Retirement Info. Svc., Sacramento, 1987-88. Contbg. analyst, author, editor Pub. Departmental. Reports, 1977-84. Dept. chmn. State Employee's United Way campaign, Sacramento, 1987; charter mem. Monterey Bay (Calif.) Aquarium, 1985—; assoc. Smithsonian Instn., Wash. D.C., 1982. Served with U.S. Army, 1970-72. Mem. Acad. Polit. Sci., Ctr. for Study of Presidency. Office: State Tchrs Retirement System 7667 Folsom Blvd Sacramento CA 95826

PARKER, JOHN WILLIAM, pathology educator, investigator; b. Clifton, Ariz., Jan. 5, 1931; s. Vilas William and Helen E. Parker; m. Barbara A. Atkinson, June 8, 1957; children: Ann Elizabeth, Joy Noelle, John David, Heidi Susan. BS, U. Ariz., 1953; MD, Harvard U., 1957. Diplomate Am. Bd. Pathology. Clin. instr. pathology U. Calif. Sch. Medicine, San Francisco, 1962-64; asst. prof. U. So. Calif. Sch. Medicine, Los Angeles, 1964-68, assoc. prof., 1968-75, prof., 1975—, vice chmn. dept. pathology, 1985—; assoc. dean sci. affairs U. So. Calif., 1987-89; co-chmn. 15th Internat. Leucocyte Culture Conf., Asilomar, Calif., 1982; chmn. 2nd Internat. Lymphoma Conf., Athens, Greece, 1981; bd. dirs. ann. meeting Clin. Applications of Cytometry, Charleston, S.C. Founding editor (jour.) Hematological Oncology, 1982—; assoc. editor Jour. Clin. Lab. Analysis, 1985—; co-editor: Intercellular Communication in Leucocyte Function, 1983; contbr. over 150 articles to profl. jours., chpts. to books. Named sr. oncology fellow Am. Cancer Soc., U. So. Calif. Sch. Medicine, 1964-69, Nat. Cancer Inst. vis. fellow Walter and Eliza Hall Inst. for Med. Research, Melbourne, Australia, 1972-73. Fellow Coll. Am. Pathologists, Am. Soc. Clin. Pathologists, Royal Soc. Medicine; mem. Am. Assn. Pathologists, Am. Soc. Hematology, Internat. Acad. Pathology, Phi Beta Kappa, Phi Beta Pi. Republican. Office: U So Calif Sch Medicine EDM 186 2025 Zonal Ave Los Angeles CA 90033

PARKER, JUDITH, television writer, producer; b. Boston; d. Paul and Lenore (Duboff) P.; m. John Robert Peaslee. BA, UCLA, 1975, postgrad., 1977-80. Ind. scriptwriter, producer L.A., 1974—; dir. motion pictures and mini-series NBC Television, L.A., 1978-79; sr. exec. in charge creative affairs Orion Pictures, L.A., 1979-80; writer, co-producer series L.A. Law 20th Century Fox Television-NBC, L.A., 1988-89; creator, supervising producer pilot episode-Studio 5B Lorimar Television-ABC, L.A., 1988; judge, Emmy award panel, Acad. Television Arts and Scis., L.A., 1976—; lectr. Cal. Arts, San Francisco State U., San Jose State Coll., 1976-87; participant Am. Film Inst. Womens Directing workshop, 1987. Scriptwriter: Miles to Go Before I Sleep, 1974 (Christopher award), Choices, 1986, Are You in The House Alone?, 1978; scriptwriter, co-producer: First Affair, 1983 (Bronze Halo award, So. Calif. Picture Coun.), others. Adminstr. Open Door Program of Writers Guild of Am. West, L.A., 1977-79. Mem. Writers Guild Am. West, Acad. Television Arts and Scis.

PARKER, KIMBERLEE ANN, landscape contractor; b. Hollywood, Calif., Sept. 21, 1954; d. Donald Duane and Enice Elenor (Quirk) P.; m. Peter Charles Herrera, Oct. 4, 1986. Salesperson Juster's Clothing Store, Mpls., 1972-74; clk. N.Am. Employment, Mpls., 1974-78; with sales, design rep. Interior Landscape Co., San Jose, Calif., 1978-80; owner Kim Parker Assocs., Inc., San Jose and Milpitas, Calif., 1980—; speaker various seminars. Contbr. articles to profl. jours. Recipient numerous awards for landscape design & plumbing installation. Mem. Am. Soc. Architects, Am. Soc. Interior Designers, Calif. Landscape Contractors Assn., Inst. Bus. Designers, No. Calif. Profl. Plantscape Assn., Am. Soc. Landscape Architects, Milpitas C. of C., San Jose C. of C. Office: Kim Parker Assocs Inc 430 Evans Rd Milpitas CA 95035

PARKER, MICHAEL DAVID, computer scientist, consultant; b. Ft. Wayne, Ind., Feb. 27, 1954; s. Milton Duane and Katherine Elizabeth (Sours) P. BS in Systems Engring., U. Ariz., 1976, MS in Computer Science, 1977. Systems programmer Grumman Data Systems, Oxnard, Calif., 1978-80; project mgr. Omnidata, Thousand Oaks, Calif., 1980-82; test specialist Raytheon Data Systems, Thousand Oaks, 1982-83; lead designer Logicon, San Diego, 1983-85; computer security mgr. Gen. Dynamics, San Diego, 1985-86; pres. MDPC, San Diego, 1986—. Office: MDPC PO Box 261369 San Diego CA 92126-0993

PARKER, RICHARD W., entrepreneur, real estate developer; b. Charleston, S.C., Oct. 10, 1945; s. Waynard Hugh and Kathleen (Brown) P.; m. Linda Kay Fuxa, June 4, 1966; children: Tricia Kay, Adam Frederick. Grad. high sch., Lafayette, Colo. Owner, mgr. Parker Joint Ventures, Longmont, Colo., 1970—, Parker's Outfitters Ltd., Longmont, 1986—; constrn. cons., estimator Parker Realty Inc., Longmont, 1970—, owner, mgr., 1981—. Mem. Longmont City Coun., 1980-82; bd. dirs. Longmont Hosp., 1986—. With U.S. Army. Named Contractor of Yr. Pub. Works Assn. Wyo. and Colo., 1981. Mem. Nat. Assn. Securities Dealers (regulatory securities prin.), Real Estate Securities Syndication Inst., Foxhill Country Club (Longmont). Home: 440 Golden Ln Longmont CO 80501 Office: 1350 Florida Ave Ste 4 Longmont CO 80501

PARKER, THEODORE CLIFFORD, electronics engineer; b. Dallas, Oreg., Sept. 25, 1929; s. Theodore Clifford and Virginia Bernice (Rumsey) P.; B.S.E.E. magna cum laude, U. So. Calif., 1960; m. Jannet Ruby Barnes, Nov. 28, 1970; children—Sally Odette, Peggy Claudette. Vice pres. engring. Telemetrics, Inc., Gardena, Calif., 1963-65; chief info. systems Northrop-Nortronics, Anaheim, Calif., 1966-70; pres. AVTEL Corp., Covina, Calif., 1970-74, Aragon, Inc., Sunnyvale, Calif., 1975-78; v.p. Teledyne McCormick Selph, Hollister, Calif., 1978-82; sr. staff engr. FMC Corp., San Jose, Calif., 1982-85; pres. Power One Switching Products, Camarillo, Calif., 1985-86; pres. Condor D.C. Power Supplies, Inc., 1987-88, pres. Intelligence Power Tech. Inc., Camarillo, 1988—. Mem. IEEE (chmn. autotestcon '87), Am. Prodn. and Inventory Control Soc., Am. Def. Preparedness Assn., Armed Forces Communications and Electronics Assn., Nat. Rifle Assn. (life), Tau Beta Pi, Eta Kappa Nu. Home: 1290 Saturn Ave Camarillo CA 93010 Office: Intelligence Power Tech Inc 829 Flynn Rd Camarillo CA 93010

PARKER, THOMAS A., school district superintendent; b. Watseka, Ill., July 21, 1940; s. Elbert C. and Anna M. (Illif) P.; divorced; children: Michele, Troy. BS, Ill. State U., 1962; MS, U. Ill., 1967, EdD, 1976. Cert. tchr., supt., Ill., Ariz. Dir. choirs Mattoon (Ill.) High Sch., 1962-64; dir. choral music Proviso West High Sch., Hillside, Ill., 1964-68, dean students, 1968-69; asst. prin. Proviso East High Sch., Maywood, Ill., 1969-77; supt. United Twp. High Sch., East Moline, Ill., 1977-84, Tempe (Ariz.) Union High Sch., 1984—. Mem. adv. com. Coll. Edn., selection com. Ariz. State U., Tempe, 1986—; chmn. exec. bd. Ariz. Edn. Info. System, Tempe, 1986-87; adv. Mayor's Youth Council, Tempe, 1985-86. Named Vol. of Yr. Tempe Leadership, 1988. Mem. Am. Assn. Sch. Adminstrs., Ariz. Sch. Adminstrs., Maricopa County Supts. Assn. (treas. 1986-87, pres. 1987-88), Tempe C. of C. (bd. dirs. 1987-89). Office: Tempe Union High Sch Dist 500 W Guadalupe Rd Tempe AZ 85283

PARKER, TIMOTHY ERWIN, title officer; b. Albuquerque, Dec. 15, 1953; s. Earl B. and Frances E. (Day) P. AA, Casper Coll., 1973; BS, U. Wyo., 1976. Abstracter Deister, Ward & Witcher, Inc., Casper, Wyo., 1977-79; ops. asst. McAdams, Roux, O'Connor Assocs., Inc., Denver, 1980-82, title examiner, 1983-87; title officer Security Title Guaranty Co., Denver, 1983—. Author short story. Democrat. Home: 1540 S Albion St Apr 205 Denver CO 80222 Office: Security Title Guaranty Co 3575 Cherry Creek Dr N Ste 210 Denver CO 80209

PARKER, VICTORIA L., video dating services company executive; b. New London, Conn.; d. Harvey and Mickey (Loukakis) Jeske; m. Robert Parker, Apr. 7, 1966 (div. Nov. 1968). Student, San Jose State Coll., 1964-66. Sec. Calif. Blue Shield, San Francisco, 1966-70; flight attendant Trans Internat. Airlines, Oakland, Calif., 1970-73; waitress Host Internat., Emeryville-Huntington Beach, Calif., 1973-76, MGM Grand and John Ascuaga's Nugget, Reno and Sparks, Nev., 1976-83; mgr. Am. Millionaires Club, Newport Beach, Calif., 1983-84; mgr. sales and mktg. Great Expectations, L.A., San Diego, Washington, 1984-87; owner, mgr. Great Expectations, San Diego and Dallas, 1987—. Mem. Kona Kai Club (Shelter Island). Home: 7585 Country Club Dr La Jolla CA 92037 Office: Great Expectations 3465 Camino del Rio S San Diego CA 92108

PARKER, WILLIAM ELBRIDGE, consulting civil engineer; b. Seattle, Mar. 18, 1913; s. Charles Elbridge and Florence E. (Plumb) P.; m. Dorris Laurie Freeman, June 15, 1935; children—Dorris Laurie, Jane Elizabeth. B.S., U.S. Naval Acad., 1935. Party chief King County Engrs., 1935-39; exec. sec., cons. engr. State Wash., 1946-49; city engr., chmn. Bd. Pub. Works, City of Seattle, 1953-57; cons. City of San Diego, 1957; ptnr. Parker-Fisher & Assocs., 1958-66; cons. engr. Minish & Webb Engrs., Seattle, 1966-70; city engr. City of Bremerton (Wash.), 1970-76; owner Parker & Assocs., Seattle, 1976—. Served to capt. C.E.C., USNR, 1939-45, 51-53. Named to Broadway Hall of Fame. Registered profl. engr., Wash. Mem. Am. Pub. Works Assn., U.S. Naval Inst., Pioneers of State Wash. (pres.), U.S. Naval Acad. Alumni Assn., Club: College (Seattle). Lodges: Masons, Shriners.

PARKER, WILLIS LAMONT, publishing consultant; b. Keokuk, Iowa, Oct. 14, 1904; s. Early Spring and Charlotte Jane (Robinson) P.; student Columbia, 1922-26; m. Grace Eleanor Evans, June 23, 1930 (dec. Sept. 1976); children: Sarah Martha, Daniel Evans (dec.). With Guaranty Trust Co., N.Y.C., 1927-30; free-lance editor, N.Y.C., 1930-44; mem. editorial staff U.S. Armed Forces Inst., Washington, 1944-45; with Pitman Pub. Co., N.Y.C., 1945-51, W. W. Norton and Co., N.Y.C., 1951-59; mng. editor Chandler Pub. Co., San Francisco, 1960-71; now pub. cons. Mem. Phi Gamma Delta. Home and Office: 454 Pope St San Francisco CA 94112

PARKHURST, LAWRENCE GLENN, management specialist; b. Buffalo, Oct. 31, 1940; s. Glenn Henry and Margaret Noreen (heckathorn) P.; m. Mary Ann Kneeshaw, Oct. 7, 1967; 1 child, Richard Lawrence. Student, No. Ariz. U., 1961; AA, San Diego Mesa Coll., 1965; student., San Diego State U., 1976. Lic. contractor. Bldg. insp. Mercy Hosp., San Diego, 1964-65; title engr. Safeco Title Ins. Co., San Diego, 1965-67; bldg. inspector County of San Diego, 1967-79; owner, cons. L.G. Parkhurst Gen. Contractor, San Diego, 1979—; gen. mgr. R. & W. Gen. Contractor, San Diego, 1982-87; founder, chief exec. officer Phoenix Co., San Diego, 1987—. Pres. Lakeside Am. Little League, Calif., 1978-82, bd. dirs. Mem. Am. Soc. Profl. Estimators, Nat. Assn. Gen. Contractors, Am. Concrete Inst., Am. Mgmt. Assn., Assoc. Bldg. Contractors San Diego. Republican. Home: 5818 Arboles St San Diego CA 92120 Office: Phoenix Co 4901 Morena Bldg #126 San Diego CA 92117

PARKINSON, JOSEPH L., electronics company executive, lawyer; b. San Antonio, Aug. 6, 1945; s. Douglas R. and Jane E. (Peck) P.; child by previous marriage, Jay Curtis. BA, Columbia Coll., 1967; JD, Tulane U., 1971; LLM in Taxation, NYU, 1972. Bar: La. 1971, Idaho 1975. Law clk. to judge U.S. Ct. Appeals (5th cir.), New Orleans, 1972-73; asst. prof. law Tulane U., New Orleans, 1973-74; cons. Baker & McKenzie, N.Y.C., 1974-75; asst. prof. law NYU, 1974-75; assoc. Moffatt, Thomas, Barrett & Blanton, Boise, Idaho, 1975-77; ptnr. Lloyd & Parkinson, Boise, 1978-80, Parkinson, Lojek & Penland, Boise, 1980-84; pres. Micron Tech., Inc., Boise, 1980-85, chmn., chief exec. officer, 1985—; bd. dirs. Sematech, Austin, Tex., Standard Microsystems, Long Island, N.Y. Trustee Boise State U. Found., 1985—; bd. dirs. Idaho Health Facilities Authority, Boise, 1986—. Mem. Semiconductor Industry Assn. (bd. dirs. 1988—), Arid Club, Crane Creek Country Club. Office: Micron Tech Inc 2805 E Columbia Rd Boise ID 83706

PARKINSON, MARIA LUISA, entertainment employment executive; b. Burbank, Calif., July 27, 1951; d. Roy Wilbur (Parky) and Serafina Antonia (Sorzano) P. AA, Pasadena City Coll., 1973; student, Acad. Stage and Cinema Arts, Los Angeles, 1973-76, The Living History Center, Augoura, Calif. Career counsleor Apple One Employment Agy., Marina Del Rey, Calif., 1977-80; career counselor Good People, Inc., Los Angeles, 1980-83, Friedman Personnel Agy., Inc., Los Angeles, 1983-84; owner Parkinson Entertainment Agy., Hollywood, Calif., 1984—; lectr. in field, 1978—. sponser Latin Legal Ctr., Santa Monica, 1987—; charter mem. Mus. Contemporary Art. Mem. Am. Film Inst., Women in Show Bus. (publicity chair), Acad. Sci. Fiction, Fantasy and Horror Films, Hollywood C. of C. (exec. com.), Entertainment Council, 1984—, Bd. Govs. Count Dracula Soc. Democrat. Roman Catholic. Office: Parkinson Entertainment Agy 6525 Sunset Blvd 3d Fl Hollywood CA 90028

PARKINSON, THOMAS BRIAN, marketing executive; b. Lytham- St. Annes, Lancashire, Eng., Oct. 14, 1935; came to U.S., 1966; s. Alfred and Marjorie (Wright) P.; m. Margaret Moore, Oct. 12, 1957; children: Karen, Lynn, Stephen David. Cert. Mech. Engring., Harris Coll. Further Edn., Preston, Lancashire, Eng., 1962. Apprentice tool maker English Electric Co. Ltd., Preston, Lancashire, Eng., 1951-57; designer aircraft structure British Aircraft Corp., Warton, Lancashire, Eng., 1957-63, stress engr. aircraft, 1963-66; stress engr. aircraft Douglas Aircraft Co., Long Beach, Calif., 1966-76, sales engr. commercial mktg., 1976-78, project mgr. commercial mktg., 1978-85, sales mgr. commercial mktg. Pacific and Asia, 1985—. Commr. Planning Commn., City of Huntington Beach (Calif.), 1975-77, Underground Utilities Commn., Huntington Beach, 1975-77; chmn. City Charter Revision Com., Huntington Beach, 1977; campaign mgr. Com. to Re-Elect Jerry Matney, Huntington Beach, 1973. With Royal Navy, 1953-55. Mem. Instn. Engring. Designers (assoc.), Pacific Area Travel Assn. (chmn. rsch. authority, bd. dirs. 1983-85, award of merit 1985). Episcopalian. Home: 9042 Annik Dr Huntington Beach CA 92646 Office: Douglas Aircraft Co 3855 Lakewood Blvd Long Beach CA 90846

PARKOS, GREGORY T., diversified industry executive; b. Somerville, Mass., Mar. 11, 1930; s. Theodore K. and Mary (Diomandes) P.; m. Joan McDonough, 1977; children: January, Jaclyn. BSBA, Bryant Coll., 1950, DSc in Bus. Adminstrn. (hon.), 1988; MBA, Boston U., 1951. Vice pres. Rosbro Plastics, Pawtucket, R.I., 1957-65; v.p. H-F Livermore Co., Boston, 1965-68; pres. Am. Chem. Corp., Providence, 1968-74, CPL Corp, Providence, 1974-79; exec. v.p. Whittaker Corp., Los Angeles, 1979-86, pres., chief operating officer, 1986—. Bd. trustees, Bryant Coll., Smithfield, R.I. Served as spl. agt. Counter Intelligence Corps, U.S. Army, 1951-53, U.S. Fgn. Svc., 1953-56. Greek Orthodox. Lodge: Masons. Office: Whittaker Corp 10880 Wilshire Blvd Los Angeles CA 90024

PARKS, DANIEL W., design engineer; b. San Diego, Dec. 28, 1942; s. Roy Robert and Georgia Lee (Beckner) P.; m. Sheila Kaye Mayse, Dec. 20, 1965;children: Michelle, Theodore, William, Jarrod. Designer Cubic Corp., San Diego, 1967-68, Sylvania, Mt. View, Calif., 1968-70, Spectral Dynamics, San Diego, 1970-71, Digital Devel., San Diego, 1970-71, Rockwell Internat., Cedar Rapids, Iowa, 1972-74, UTL Corp., Dallas, 1976-80, No. Telecom., Dallas, 1976-80; mech. engr. OAI, Hartshorne, Okla., 1980-85; design engr. Honeywell, Albuquerque, 1985--. Inventor: Optical Disk Media Devel., 1986; high density packaging design, adv. air data computer. With USN, 1962-66. Mem. Am. Mensa. Republican. Mem. Ch. of Christ. Office: Honeywell 9201 San Mateo Blvd NE Albuquerque NM 87124

PARKS, DONALD LEE, mechanical engineer, human factors engineer; b. Delphos, Kans., Feb. 23, 1931; s. George Delbert and Erma Josephine (Boucek) P.; student Kans. Wesleyan U., 1948-50; BSME, Kans. State U., 1957, BS in Bus. Adminstrn., 1957, MS in Psychology, 1959; m. Bessie Lou Schur, Dec. 24, 1952; children: Elizabeth Parks Anderson, Patricia, Donna, Charles, Sandra. Elem. tchr., 1950-51; with Kans. State U. Placement Svc., 1957-59; human factors engr., systems engr. Boeing Co., Seattle, 1959—, sr. specialist engr., 1972-74, sr. engring. supr., 1974—; cons., lectr. in field; participant workshops on guidelines in profl. areas, NATO, NSF, Nat. Acad. Sci., NRC. Mem. Derby (Kans.) Planning Commn., 1961-62, chmn., 1962; del. King County (Wash.) Republican Conv., 1972; mem. sci. com. Internat. Transp. Ctr. With AUS, 1952-54. Mem. Human Factors Soc. (Puget Sound Pres.'s award 1969), Assn. Aviation Psychologists, ASME, Am. Psychol. Assn., Midwestern Psychol. Assn., Elks. Presbyterian. Contbr. numerous articles to tech. jours., chpts. to books. Home: 6232 127th Ave SE Bellevue WA 98006

PARKS, GERALD THOMAS, JR., lawyer, business executive; b. Tacoma, Wash., Feb. 25, 1944; s. Gerald Thomas and Elizabeth (Bell) P.; m. Susan Simenstad, July 22, 1967; children—Julie, Christopher; m. 2d, Bonny Kay O'Connor, Jan. 15, 1979, children: Garrett, Ardrienne. BA in Polit. Sci., U. Wash., 1966; JD, U. Oreg., 1969. Bar: Wash. 1969. Assoc. Graham & Dunn, 1972-77, ptnr., 1977-82; sole practice, 1982—; sec., treas. Holaday-Parks Fabricators, Inc., 1972-78, v.p., gen. mgr. (named changed to Holaday-Parks, Inc.), 1978-84; pres., chief exec. officer, 1984—. Served to lt. with USN, 1969-72. Mem. Wash. State Bar Assn. Clubs: Seattle Yacht, Broadmoor Golf, Seattle Tennis. Office: 616 1st Ave Lowman & Hanford Bldg 6th Fl Seattle WA 98104

PARKS, HARRISON ALAN, mathematician; b. Berkeley, Calif., Sept. 8, 1944; s. Robert Monroe and Mildred Rebecca (Washburn) P.; m. Mary Renee Fischer, Apr. 2, 1966; 1 child, Rebecca Anne. BA, UCLA, 1965; MA, U. Southern Calif., 1969, PhD, 1974. Math analyst Lockheed Calif. Co., Burbank, 1966-70; teaching asst. U. Southern Calif., Los Angeles, 1970-74; project mgr. Hughes Aircraft Co., El Segundo, Calif., 1974—. Democrat. Home: 890 N Bundy Dr Los Angeles CA 90049 Office: Hughes Aircraft Co PO Box 902 El Segundo CA 90245

PARKS, MICHAEL, journalist; b. Detroit, Nov. 17, 1943; s. Robert James and Rosalind (Smith) P.; m. Linda Katherine Durocher, Dec. 26, 1964; children: Danielle Anne, Christopher, Matthew. AB, U. Windsor, Ont., Can., 1965. Reporter Detroit News, 1962-65; corr. Time-Life News Service, N.Y.C., 1965-66; asst. city editor Suffolk Sun, Long Island, N.Y., 1966-68; polit. reporter, foreign corr. The Balt. Sun, Saigon, Singapore, Moscow, Cairo, Hong Kong, Peking, 1968-80; foreign corr. Los Angeles Times, Los Angeles, Peking, Johannesburg, Moscow, 1980—. Recipient Pulitzer Prize, 1987. Club: Foreign Corr. (Hong Kong). Home: Sadova-Samotechnaya 12/24, Kv 37, Moscow USSR Office: L A Times Times Mirror Sq Los Angeles CA 90053

PARKS, RICHARD DEE, theater director; b. Omaha, Aug. 29, 1938; s. Charles and Josephine Marie-Rose P. B.A., San Jose State U., 1961; M.A., U. Wash., 1963; postgrad. Stanford U. Tchr. San Jose State U., 1964-65; tchr. oral interpretation Stanford U., 1965-66; tchr. San Jose State U., 1966-71, B.F.A. program U. Wash., 1971-72; dir. theatre San Jose State U., 1972-79, coordinator performance area, 1979—, coordinator auditions, 1975—, chmn. performance area, coordinator M.F.A. performance degree program, 1983—; exchange prof. Ventura Coll., spring 1982; exec. dir. Actors Symposium of Hollywood; actor, dir., producer; sr. producer Star Weekend projects NBC, 1978—; cons. profl. and community theatre orgns.; interim coordinator theatre arts grad. program, 1977-78; producer, dir., dialects coach San Jose Civic Light Opera; research cons. Ednl. Films of Hollywood; cons. Monterey Peninsula's 4th St. Playhouse; cons., dir. Gen. Electric Sales Conf., Pajaro Dunes, 1983, Lockheed Missles and Space Co., 1987—; mem. adv. council sta. KRON-TV, San Francisco. Winner New Play Directing award Am. Coll. Theatre Festival Region I, 1975. Mem. Calif. Ednl. Theatre Assn. (exec. sec.-treas. 1978-80), AAUP, Calif. Assn. Am. Conservatory Theatre, Am. Coll. Theatre Festival, Am. Film Inst., Dramatists Guild, Authors League Am., Women's History Resources, Nat. Women's History Project, Brit. Am. Clubp, San Jose Players. Episcopalian. Author: How to Overcome Stage Fright, 1978; American Drama Anthology, 1979; (plays) Charley Parkhurst Rides Again!, 1978, Wild West Women, 1980, Ken Kesey's Further Inquiry, 1980; (book) Career Preparation for the TV-Film Actor, 1981; (play) stage adaptation of Tandem Prodns. Facts of Life, 1982; (teaching supplement) Calendar of American Theatre History, 1982; The Role of Myth in Understanding Amber in the Ancient World, 1983; (textbook) Oral Expression, 1985, 2d. rev. edit., 1986, 3rd rev. edit., 1989. Office: San Jose State U Theater Arts Dept San Jose CA 95192

PARKS, RICHARD KEITH, social worker; b. Rock Springs, Wyo., Oct. 13, 1947; s. Keith Andrew and Mildred Ann (Matkovich) P.; m. Debra D. Thomas, Sept. 21, 1968 (div. Nov. 1971); m. Alberta Dea Henderson, Feb. 26, 1974; children: Heather, Richell. AA, Western Wyo. Coll., 1969; BSW, U. Wyo., 1985; MSW, Denver U., 1988. Owner, mgr. Rich's Britches, Rock Springs, 1974-76; asst. mgr. Wyo. Bearing, Rock Springs, 1976-82; residential counselor Southwest Wyo. Rehab. Ctr., Rock Springs, 1983-85; community care worker, therapist Southwest Counseling Svc., Rock Springs, 1985—; program mgr. Transitional Living Ctr., 1985-87; workshop presenter in field, 1986. Vol. counselor Sweetwater Crisis Intervention Ctr., Rock Springs, 1973-83, bd. dirs., 1979-83; v.p. Downtown Mchts. Assn., 1975. Mem. Nat. Assn. Social Workers, Am. Pub. Welfare Assn., Alumni Assn. U. Wyo. Congregationalist.

PARMA, FLORENCE VIRGINIA, magazine editor; b. Kenilworth, N.J., Aug. 30, 1940; d. Howard Frank and Mildred Faye (Lister) von Finkel; m. Wilson Henry Parma, June 15, 1973 (div. Aug. 1986). Studies with pvt. tutor, Chaumont, France, 1961-62; student, NYU, 1962-63. Copywriter Schless & Co., N.Y.C., 1963-65; editor, researcher Barchas Lab., Stanford, Calif., 1969-73; adminstrv. exec. Crater Inc., Honolulu, 1974-79; mgr., editor Off Duty mag., Honolulu, 1979—. Editor: Welcome to Hawaii Guide, 1985—; co-editor: Serotonin and Behavior, 1972; freelance columnist. Republican. Episcopalian. Home: 3711 Anuhea St Honolulu HI 96816

PARMENTER, DEBORAH LYNN, military officer; b. Patrick AFB, Fla., Apr. 26, 1963; d. Vernon Franklin and Linda Faye (Brookins) P. BSEE with high honors, U. Fla., 1986. Bookkeeper Stevenson Constrn. Co., Starke, Fla., 1981-87; commd. 2nd lt. USAF, 1987; student Undergra. Space Tng. USAF, Denver, 1987-88; mgr. staellite ops. USAF, Onizuka AFB Sunnyvale, Calif., 1988—. Recipient Scholarship award, Fla. Acad. Scholars Fund, Gainesville, 1981-86. Mem. IEEE, Golden Key, Phi Kappa Phi, Tau Beta Pi, Eta Kappa Nu. Democrat. Baptist.

PARMENTIER, JOHN THOMAS (JACK PARMENTIER), management consultant; b. Wilmington, Del., May 1, 1934; s. Marceau Roger and Louise Ann (Richardson) P.; m. Dorothy Mae Roberts,. BA in Biology, Muhlenberg Coll., Allentown, Pa., 1956. Materials engr. Glenn L. Martin Co., Balt., Denver, 1956-63; specification writer Martin Co., Denver, 1963-76; launch site rep. Martin Marietta Corp., Kennedy Space Ctr., Fla., 1977-85; chief- configuration mgmt. Martin Marietta Corp., Denver, 1977-85; mgr. configuration and data mgmt. Martin Marietta Denver Aerospace, 1985-87, Martin Marietta Space Systems, Denver, 1987—; pres. WPM Racing Enterprises, Inc., Lakewood Colo., 1985--. Author: Contbr. articles to profl. jours., 1963. Deacon Our Saviours Reformed Ch., Lakewood Colo., 1980; Elder Our Saviours Reformed Ch., Lakewood Colo., 1982. Recipient Honors Night award Martin-Marietta 1963. Mem. Am. Def. Preparedness Assn. (chpt. v.p. 1988-), Airforce Assn., Nat. Republican. Office: Martin Marietta Space Systems 12999 Deer Creek Canyon Rd Littleton CO 80127

PARNELL, RICHARD MICHAEL, consulting company executive; b. Kansas City, Kans., Aug. 14, 1956; s. Raymond Oliver and Lila Lee (Harris) P.; m. Darlene Gay Marie Burke, Aug. 29, 1981; children: Jonathan Ray, Zachary Lee, Brianna Joy. BSBA in Mktg., Cen. Mo. State U., 1979. Dist. mgr. Wire Rope Corp. Am., St. Joseph, 1979-84; gen. mgr. River Rigging & Supply Inc., Camas, Wash., 1984-86; pres. Wire Rope & Rigging Cons. Inc., Vancouver, Wash., 1986—, U.S. Bus. Svcs. Inc., Vancouver, 1988—. Author: Crane and Rigging Management, 1988; author video tapes in field. Chmn. maj. funds Boy Scouts Am., Vancouver, 1986—; trustee Leadership Scholarship Cen. Mo. State U., Warrensburg, 1985—. Mem. Am. Soc. Safety Engrs. Republican. Home: 3508 E 13th St Vancouver WA 98661

PARONI, GENEVIEVE MARIE SWICK, educator; b. Eureka, Nev., July 27, 1926; d. William Jackson and Myrtle Rose (Smith) S.; m. Walter Andrew Paroni, Dec. 26, 1954; 1 child, Andrea Marie. BA, U. Nev., Reno, 1948; MEd, U. Idaho, 1978; postgrad., MIT, Oreg. State U., U. Oreg., U. Wash., Ft. Wright Coll., U. Portland. Cert. elem. and secondary sect., Nev. Tchr., vice prin. Eureka County High Sch., 1948-66; assayer Eureka Corp. Mine, 1958; coast geodetic U.S. Govt., Eureka, 1950's; tchr., facilitator Dist. #393, Wallace, Idaho, 1968—; gov. library bd. State of Nev., Carson City, 1950; regional dir. NSTA, Idaho, Panhandle, 1982—; chmn. in service adv. State Dept. Edn., Boise, Idaho, 1980-83; commr. State Sci. Commn., State Dept. Edn., Boise, 1981-82; mem. Idaho Sci. Curriculum Guide Com., 1987. Contbr. history articles to profl. jours. Active Wallace City Council, 1970-80; library bd. mem. Wallace Pub. Library, 1983—; precinct chmn. Republicans, Wallace, 1970-80; bd. dirs. Greater Wallace, 1980—. Grantee Idaho Power, 1985; named Outstanding Tchr., Dist. #393, 1975. Mem. NEA, Idaho Edn. Assn., Wallace Edn. Assn. (sec. 1970's), AAUW (pres. 1970's), Bus. and Profl. Women Assn. (v.p. Nev. chpt. 1953-55), Delta Kappa Gamma (pres. 1980-82), Phi Delta Kappa. Epsicopalian. Lodge: Pythian Sisters (Grand Guard, 1950), Order of Eastern Star (matron Nev. chpt.). Office: Sch Dist #393 River St PO Box 500 Wallace ID 83873

PARR, JAMES ALLAN, literature professor; b. Ritchie County, W.Va., Oct. 7, 1936; s. James William and Virginia Alice (Bragg) P.; m. Carmen Salazar, Aug. 19, 1968 (div. 1980); 1 child, Jacqueline; m. Patricia Catherine Brinck, June 28, 1985. BA, Ohio U., 1959, MA, 1961; PhD, U. Pitts., 1967. Prof., chmn. Murray (Ky.) State U., 1964-70; prof. U. So. Calif., Los Angeles, 1970—. Author: Don Quixote: An Anatomy of Subversive Discourse, 1988; editor: Critical Essays on Juan Ruiz de Alarcon, 1972, (jour.) Bulletin of the Comediantes, 1973—. Recipient Phi Beta Kappa award, Ohio U., 1960, Mellon fellowships, U. Pitts., 1961-63, Del Amo fellowship, U. So. Calif., Los Angeles, 1977, 84. Mem. Modern Lang. Assn., Calif. Foreign Lang. Tchrs. Assn. (1st v.p.), Internat. Assn. Hispanists. Home: 421 Elmwood Dr Pasadena CA 91105

PARRIE, TRAUTE LYNN NYE, civil engineer, firefighter; b. Laramie, Wyo., June 23, 1959; d. John Ronald Nye and Elizabeth Irene (Small) Ferguson; m. Michael David Parrie, Sept. 3, 1977; children: Lindsay Elizabeth, Zachary David. BSCE with honors, U. Wyo., 1982. Draftsman Marker Assoc., AIA, Casper, Wyo., 1977; constrn. worker Gentry Constrn., Laramie, 1981; layout person Kloefkorn Balard Constrn., Casper, 1983; inspector U.S. Forest Service, Encampment, wyo., 1984; civil engr. U.S. Forest Service, Saratoga, Wyo., 1985—; firefighter U.S. Forest Service, 1985—. Mem. Iron Skull Honor Soc., Tau Beta Pi, Phi Kappa Phi. Republican. Episcopalian. Home: Box 296 Saratoga WY 82331 Office: US Forest Svc Box 249 Saratoga WY 82331

PARRILL, SHARON GAYLE, interior designer; b. Denver, May 8, 1945; d. Albert Allen and Lorene Francis (Mock) Depew; m. Robert Lee Parrill Sr., July 30, 1960; children: Deborah Anne Parrill Swatzell, Robert Lee

Jr. Owner, prin. Sharon Parrill Interior Design, Denver, 1983-86; interior designer Design House, Beverly Hills, Calif., 1986—. Baptist. Home: 3939 E 2d St A Long Beach CA 90803 Office: Design House 345 N Palm Dr #6 Beverly Hills CA 90210

PARRINGTON, MARK, healthcare executive; b. Topeka, Kans., Jan. 23, 1948; s. Thomas Richard and Valencia Claire (Baeten) P.; m. Ethel Virginia Moore, Aug. 10, 1973; children: Shannon Michelle, Allison Nicole. BA, U. Okla., 1974; MHA, Va. Commonwealth U., 1977. Asst. dir. corp. planning Fairfax Hosp. Assn., Falls Church, Va., 1977-79; v.p. corp. planning Sutter Health, Sacramento, 1979-88, v.p. strategy support group, 1988—; trustee Sutter Solano Med. Ctr., Vallejo, Calif., 1985-87. Bd. dirs. Family Svc. Agy., Sacramento, 1983—. With U.S. Army, 1970-71. Mem. Soc. for Healthcare Planning and Mktg., Acad. for Health Svcs. Mktg., Am. Mktg. Assn., Healthcare Forum, World Future Soc. Republican. Roman Catholic. Home: 7790 Dutra Bend Dr Sacramento CA 95831 Office: Sutter Health 2800 L St Sacramento CA 95816

PARRIS, JIM RAY, accountant; b. Ft. Smith, Ark., Apr. 28, 1949; s. Ray Howell and JoAnne Elizabeth (Stingley) P.; m. Cruz Ann Pena, Mar. 16, 1974; children: Jamie Louise, Jason Ray. BS, Okla. State U., 1977. CPA, Okla. Compt. Osage Fed. Grants and Contracts, Pawhuska, Okla., 1978-79; ptnr. Lowrey, Eubank, Coates & Parris, CPA's, Ponca City, Okla., 1980-81; acctg. mgr. Mertz, Inc., Ponca City, 1982-83; auditor Osage Nation of Okla., awjisla, 1983-84; chief br. trust fund acctg. Bur. Indian Affairs, Dept. Interior, Albuquerque, 1985—. With USN, 1973-76. Recipient Jaycee of Month award, Jaycee of Quarter award, Presdl. award of honor Ponca City Jaycees, 1981. Mem. AICPA, Okla. Soc. CPA's. Democrat. Roman Catholic. Office: Bur Indian Affairs PO Box 1067 Albuquerque NM 87103

PARRIS, PATRICIA ELIZABETH (PATTY PARRIS), actress; b. Columbus, Ohio, Oct. 22, 1950; d. Howard Lindsey and Bernice Claire (Rogers) P. BA, Brenau Coll., Gainesville, Ga., 1972. Over 200 voice-overs and cartoon voices including Bambi, Mary Poppins, Cinderella; co-star films including Robotics, Mgr. of the Yr.; TV appearances include Knots Landing, My Husband is Missing; active in cartoons, voice-overs, radio and TV with cos. Hanna Barbera, Disney, Dic, Marvel, NBC, ABC and CBS. Recipient 20 Gold and Platinum records Buena Vista/Walt Disney Prodns. Mem. AFTRA, Screen Actors Guild, Sierra Club. Presbyterian.

PARRISH, GEORGE R(ODERICK), architectural specifications writer; b. Litchfield, Minn., Apr. 19, 1943; s. Clarence Lestor and Georgia Jane (Fitze) P.; m. Donna Jean Sjogren, June 11, 1966; children: Catherine Jeneen Connelly, Robert Thomas, Michelle Marie. Student, U. Minn., 1962-63, Winona State Coll., 1964-66, Roosevelt U., 1982. Cert. constrn. specifier. Archtl. draftsman Setter Leach & Lindstrom, Inc., Mpls., 1966-68, Armstrong, Schlichting, Torseth & Skold, Inc., Mpls., 1968-72; chief specifications writer and archtl. draftsman Chapman Desai Sakata, Inc., Honolulu, 1972-88, sr. assoc., 1983-88; prin. specifications cons. G. Parrish Services, Kailua, Hawaii, 1981—; guest speaker U. Hawaii Sch. Architecture; guest instr. Earle M. Alexander, Ltd. Author/editor (computer program package) Office Cost Control System, 1982, 4th rev. edit., 1984. Mem. New Eng. Hist. Geol. Soc., Internat. Platform Assn., Constrn. Specifications Inst. (v.p. Honolulu chpt. 1985-86, pres. 1986-87, Certificate of Appreciation for Ednl. Service 1979, Certificate of Appreciation 1980, 1981, Pres'. Cert. Appreciation, 1987). Roman Catholic. Home and Office: 647 N Kainalu Dr Kailua HI 96734

PARRISH, NORMAN CHARLES, technical consultant, mechanical engineer; b. Los Angeles, Feb. 28, 1912; s. George Cornelius and Estella Nancy (Lay) P.; m. Margaret Pierce Smith (div. Nov. 1969); 1 child, Candace Parrish Peterson; m. Dorothy Dalley Caswell, Jan. 16, 1976; stepchildren: Thomas Caswell, James Caswell, Dennis Caswell. AA, Los Angeles City Coll., 1933; BSME, U. So. Calif., 1942, MS, 1965. Rsch. engr. Lockheed Aircraft Co., Burbank, Calif., 1937-42; dir. Parlin Engring. Co., Hawthorne, Calif., 1943-46; field tech. cons. So. Calif. Edison Co., L.A., 1946-48; preliminary design engr. Northrop Aircraft Co., Hawthorne, 1947-54; research engr. Lockheed Missiles & Space Co., Sunnyvale, Calif., 1955-60; mem. tech. staff Hughes Aerospace Co., El Segundo, Calif., 1960-65; staff scientist Lawrence Berkeley (Calif.) Lab, 1966-81; ret. 1981, tech. cons., 1981—; cons. U.S. Dept. Energy, 1975-80, Nat. Bur. Standards, 1975-80, SEC, San Francisco, 1979-80; chmn. Nat. Def. Exec. Res., San Francisco, 1979—. Author: Micro Diaphragm Pressure Transducers, 1964, Proc. Hawaii Inventors Conference, 1978, Successful Inventing, 1988; co-author: Inventors Source Book, 1978. Mem. Am. Soc. for Metals, Nat. Congress Inventor Orgns. (pres. 1983—), Inventors of Calif. (bd. dirs. 1979—). Home: 215 Rheem Blvd Moraga CA 94556

PARROTT, DENNIS BEECHER, sales executive; b. St. Louis, June 13, 1929; s. Maurice Ray and Mai Ledgerwood (Beecher) P.; m. Vivian Cleveland Miller, Mar. 24, 1952; children: Constance Beecher, Dennis Beecher, Anne Cleveland. BS in Econs., Fla. State U., Tallahassee, 1954; postgrad. Princeton U., 1964; MBA, Pepperdine U., 1982. With Prudential Ins. Co. Am., 1954-74, v.p. group mktg., L.A., 1971-74; sr. v.p. Frank B. Hall Cons. Co., L.A., 1974-83; v.p. Johnson & Higgins, L. A., 1983—; speaker in field. Chmn. Weekend with the Stars Telethon, 1976-80; chmn. bd. dirs. United Cerebral Palsy/Spastic Children's Found. Los Angeles County, 1979-82, chmn. bd. govs., 1982-83; bd. dirs. Nat. United Cerebral Palsy Assn., 1977-82, pres., 1977-79; mem. community adv. council Birmingham High Sch., Van Nuys, Calif., 1982-85 ; sect. chmn. United Way, Los Angeles, 1983-84; bd. dirs. The Betty Clooney Found. for Brain Injured, 1986-88; mem. com. to fund an endowed chair in cardiology at Cedars-Sinai Med. Ctr., 1986-88; adv. council Family Health Program Inc., 1986-88. Served to 1st lt. AUS, 1951-53. C.L.U. Mem. Am. Soc. C.L.U.s, Internat. Found. Employee Benefits, Merchants and Mfrs. Assns. 44th Annual Mgmt. Conf. (chmn. 1986), Employee Benefits Planning Assn. So. Calif. Republican. Presbyterian. Clubs: Los Angeles, Woodland Hills Country, Jonathan (Los Angeles). Office: 2029 Century Park E One Century Pl Los Angeles CA 90067

PARRY, ATWELL, JR., state senator, retailer; b. Ogden, Utah, June 14, 1925; s. John Atwell and Nina Virginia (McEntire) P.; m. Elaine Hughes, Feb. 6, 1946; children—Bonnie, Michael, Jay, Donald, David, Delbert, Kent. Student pub. schs., Nampa, Idaho. Salesman, King's Packing Co., Nampa, 1947-54, credit mgr., 1954-55; plant mgr. Stone Poultry Co., Nampa, 1955-56; salesman Nestle Chocolate Co., 1956-64; owner, mgr. Melba Foods, Idaho, 1964-82; mem. Idaho Senate, 1981—; bd. dirs. Western Idaho Tng. Ctr., 1987—; chmn. Senate Finance Com. and co-chmn. Joint Fin. and Appropriations Com., 1987—; chmn. Idaho State Bd. for Nat. Ctr. for Constl. Studies, 1988—. Bd dirs. Alcohol Treatment Ctr., Nampa, 1978-82; mem. adv. bd. Mercy Med. Ctr., Nampa, 1976—; mem. Melba City Council, 1971-74. Recipient Silver Beaver award Boy Scouts Am., 1959, Service award Mercy Med. Ctr. Republican. Mormon.

PARRY, BARBARA JEAN, clinical psychologist; b. Culver City, Calif., June 14, 1956; d. James Thomas and Elsie (Matovich) P.; (div. Dec. 1985). BA, San Diego State U., 1978; MA, Calif. Sch. Profl. Psychology, 1982, PhD, 1985. Lic. clin. psychologist. Psychol. intern Ceres (Calif.) Sch. Dist., 1980-81, Adult Day Treatment of Stanislaus County, Modesto, Calif., 1981-82, Modesto Counseling Ctr., 1982-83, Geropsychiat. Outreach Program, Modesto, 1983-84; clin. psychologist Stockton Devel. Ctr., State of Calif., 1984-86, Haynes Enterprises, Lodi, Calif., 1985-88; clin. psychologist, owner San Joaquin Counseling Svcs., Stockton, 1985—; resource therapist Stanislaus County Alzheimers Disease & Related Disorders Orgn., Modesto, 1983-85; presenter for LIFE series St. Joseph's Hosp., Stockton, 1988—. Mem. Am. Psychol. Assn., Calif. State Psychol. Assn., Delta Psychol. Assn. Office: San Joaquin Counseling Svcs 829 Rosemarie Ln Stockton CA 95209

PARRY, PETER LARSON, park superintendent; b. Morgantown, W.Va., Oct. 6, 1931; s. Vernon Frank and Roma (Larson) P.; BS, Colo. State U., 1954; m. Joyce Glen, Mar. 7, 1957; children: Christy, Frank (dec.), Michael (dec.). Ranger, Nat. Pk. Svc., 1956-75, supt. Arches and Canyonlands Nat. Parks, Moab, Utah, 1975-86. Served with USAF, 1954-56. Recipient Spl. Achievement award Nat. Pk. Svc., 1974, Meritorious Svc. award Dept. Interior, 1984. Mem. Canyonlands Nat. History Assn. (vice chmn. bd. dirs. 1987—), Canyonlands Field Inst. (chmn. bd. dirs. 1988—), Am. Legion, C. of C., Rotary. Office: 400 Marcus Ct Moab UT 84532

PARRY, ROBERT TROUTT, economist; b. Harrisburg, Pa., May 16, 1939; s. Anthony C. and Margaret R. (Troutt) P.; m. Brenda Louise Grumbine, Dec. 27, 1956; children: Robert Richard, Lisa Louise. BA magna cum laude, Gettysburg (Pa.) Coll., 1960; MA in Econs, U. Pa., 1961, PhD, 1967. Asst. prof. econs. Phila. Coll. Textiles and Sci., 1963-65; economist Fed. Res. Bd., Washington, 1965-70; v.p., chief economist Security Pacific Nat. Bank, Los Angeles, 1970-76, sr. v.p., chief economist, 1976-81, exec. v.p., chief economist, 1981-86; pres., chief exec. officer Fed. Res. Bank San Francisco, 1986—; dir. Nat. Bur. Econ. Research; mem. adv. bd. Pacific Rim Bankers Program; adv. bd. Ctr. for Fin. and Real Estate, adv. bd. Ctr. for Fin. System Research, Ariz. State U.; mem. policy adv. bd. Ctr. for Real Estate & Urban Econs., U. Calif., Berkeley; dir. San Francisco Bay Area Coun.; chmn. Bay Area Econ. Forum; mem. exec. bd. Boy Scouts Am., 1988—; lectr. Pacific Coast Banking Sch., 1976-78; mem. mng. com. Nat. Ctr. on Fin. Services U. Calif., Berkeley, policy adv. bd. Ctr. for Real Estate and Urban Econs. U. Calif., Berkeley. Contbr. articles to profl. jours. Mem. bd. trustees Calif. Bicentennial Found. for U.S. Constn.; mem. exec. bd. Boy Scouts Am. NDEA fellow, 1960-63. Mem. Nat. Assn. Bus. Economists (pres. 1979-80), Am. Bankers Assn. (chmn. econ. adv. com.), Calif. Bankers Assn. (bd. dirs. 1982-83), Am. Econs. Assn., Western Econs. Assn. Home: 90 Overhill Rd Orinda CA 94563 Office: Fed Res Bank San Francisco PO Box 7702 San Francisco CA 94120

PARSAYE, KAMRAN, data processing executive; b. Tehran, Iran, Mar. 3, 1954; came to U.S., 1977; s. Vadji and Caehri Parsaye; m. Jenny Parsaye. BS in Math., King's Coll., London, 1976, MS in Math., 1977; PhD in Computer Sci., UCLA, 1981. Computer scientist Hewlett-Packard Labs., Palo Alto, Calif., 1981-83; pres. Silegic, Inc., L.A., 1983-84, IntelligenceWare, Inc., L.A., 1984—; mem. investigation panel on artificial intelligence rsch. U.S. Congress, 1983; chmn. expert systems UNIFORUM Unix Conf., Dallas, 1985; mem. program com. Assn. Computing Machinery, Database Conf., Miami, Fla., 1985, Very Large Data Bases conf., Kyoto, Japan, 1986. Author: Expert Systems for Experts, 1988, Intelligent Database, 1989; contbr. numerous articles to profl. jours. Mem. IEEE (chmn. expert systems COMPCON conf. 1984-85, program chmn. Expert Systems in Govt. conf. 1986, editorial bd. Expert mag. 1986—, Outstanding Session award 1985). Office: IntelligenceWare Inc 9800 S Sepulveda Blvd Ste 730 Los Angeles CA 90045

PARSLOW, PHILIP LEO, film producer, film company executive; b. South Gate, Calif., Aug. 2, 1938; s. Richard Nelson Parslow Sr. and Evelyn Inez (Holz) Abell; m. Gelena Lea Wilson, Feb. 14, 1962; 1 child, Eric Christopher. BA in ECons., UCLA, 1960. Prin. Philpar Films Ltd., Inc., Los Angeles, 1972—; assoc. producer The Paper Chase, 1972-73 (3 Oscars), An Enemy of the People, 1979; producer, assoc. producer Love Story, 1972-73; producer The Underground Man, 1973, The Master Gunfighter, 1975; v.p. prodn. Tom Laughlin's Billy Jack Prodns., Culver City, Calif., 1974-76, Steve McQueen's Solar Prodns., Culver City, 1976-79. Producer TV shows including Dynasty, 1979-82, Love for Rent, 1982-83, A Doctor's Story, 1984-85 (Helen Hays Nat. Media award 1988), Murder Ordained, 1986-87 (TV Guide Judith Crists Top Ten 1987, N.Y. Times Best of Best 1987), The Father Clements Story (Christopher medal 1988, Ceba award 1988), Falcon Crest, 1988—; co-producer Right of Way, 1983-84, (Ace award); exec. producer Women of Valor, (Best Drama Am. Women), 1985-86. Served to capt. U.S. Army, 1960-66, with res. Recipient Best Drama award Nat. Media Awards, 1985. Mem. Dirs. Guild of Am., Producers Guild of Am. Republican. Episcopalian.

PARSONS, GEORGE HOWLAND, investment company executive; b. Seattle, July 13, 1910; s. Reginald H. and Maude (Bemis) P.; m. Elizabeth McDonald, June 28, 1934;. BA, U. Wash., 1933; MBA, Harvard U., 1935. Treas. Retail Svc. Bur., Seattle, 1935-43; with acct. dept. Boeing Co., Seattle, 1943-45; treas. Parsons, Hart & Co., Seattle, 1945—, pres., 1955—; treas. Hillcrest Corp., Seattle, 1945--, pres., 1955--. Bd. dirs. Seattle coun. Campfire Girls, 1935-88, Boy Scouts Am., Seattle, 1938—. Mem. Honolulu Outrigger Canoe Club, The Pacific Club, Waialae Country Club, Medford Ore Club, Rogue Valley Golf Club, Seattle Golf Club, Seattle Yacht Club, Kiwanis. Republican. Episcopalian. Office: Hillcrest Corp 2303 Seattle Towers Seattle WA 98101

PARSONS, JONATHAN WAYNE, aerospace company information systems executive; b. Washington, Oct. 19, 1955; s. James Melvin Parsons and Geraldine Ann (Yates) Lovett; m. Barbara Anderson, Feb. 14, 1985; 1 child, Julia Mianna. BSBA, U. Redlands, 1987. Missionary Ch. of Jesus Christ of Latter-Day Saints, Honolulu, 1980-82; sr. ptnr. Parsons Plumbing, El Paso, Tex., 1983-84; cons. Parand Devel., San Diego, 1984-85; mgmt. info. systems specialist Info. Resource Mgmt. Gen. Dynamics/Convair, San Diego, 1985-87; chief systems Subcontract Mgmt./Convair, San Diego, 1987—; chmn. Local Area Networks standards com. Convair, San Diego, 1986-87; cons. Integrated Product Assurance Program, San Diego, 1987-88. Coach Pop Warner Football, Mira Mesa, Calif., 1986-88, Am. Youth Soccer Orgn., Mira Mesa, 1988; Explorer leader Boy Scouts Am., Mira Mesa, 1988. Mem. Am. Nat. Standard Inst., SHARE IBM Users Group, USENIX Unix Tech. Group. Republican. Reorganized Ch. of Jesus Christ of Latter-day-Saints. Office: Gen Dynamics/Convair PO Box 85377 MZ 92-8080 San Diego CA 92138

PARSONS, LEE ROY, sales executive; b. Casper, Wyo., Feb. 6, 1937; s. William N. and Vi (Chaney) P.; m. Maryann Snodgrass, Aug. 12, 1959 (div. 1960); m. Edith M. Hambrick, July 12, 1967. Student, Santa Monica City Coll., 1957-58; cert., Alexander Hamilton Inst., 1964. Regional mgr. Moore's Bldg. Supply co., Roanoke, Va., 1967-78; v.p. ops. Fullerton Lumber Co., Mpls., 1978-79; dir. purchasing Wholesale Bldg. Products Co., Nashville, 1979-82; gen. mgr. Aluminum Products Co. Inc., Rural Hall, N.C., 1982-86, Lester Home Ctr., Martinsville, Va., 1986-87; systems cons. Computerland, Roanoke, 1988—. Patentee barbeque basting device. With USN, 1955. Mem. Roanoke Valley Freight Claims Assn. (pres. 1967), Nat. Exchange Club, Moose. Republican. Methodist. Home: 3234 Ledgewood Ave SW Roanoke VA 24018

PARSONS, THOMAS SAMUEL, university administrator; b. Niles, Mich., Mar. 24, 1924; s. Cecil Bernard and Dorothy May (Elder) P.; m. Sara Bedell Perry, Dec. 18, 1968; children: Timothy Dion, Pamela Lynn. AB, U. Mich., 1950, MS, 1952, PhC, 1962. Registered psychologist, Ill. Research dir. Charles S. Mott Found., Flint, Mich., 1952-63; lectr., research assoc. U. Mich., Ann Arbor, 1953-63; research dir. Joint Youth Devel. Commn., Chgo., 1963-64; owner, cons. Community Edn. Assocs., Park Forest, Ill., 1964-67; assoc. dean Pub. Services, dir. Ctr. Community Devel. Calif. State U., Humboldt, 1967-87, dir. emeritus, 1987—. Editor: The Tolowa Language, 1984, Handbook of Community Development and Services, 1984; contbr. articles to profl. jours.; producer Again A Person I've Become, 1982. Bd. dirs. Am. Lung Assn. Calif., Oakland, 1985-87, pres. 1982-83; pres. United Way of Humboldt, Eureka, Calif., 1983-84. Served to staff sgt. USAAF, 1942-45, ETO. Decorated D.F.C. Air medal with three oak leaf clusters; recipient Innovation award Nat. U. Extension Assn., Am. Coll. Testing Program, 1973, Community Devel. Achievement award Community Devel. Soc., 1984; Joint Resolution of Commendation Calif. State Legislature, 1987, Calif. State U. Chancellor's Spl. Appreciation award, 1987, Disting. Svc. to Community Devel. award. Nat. U. Continuing Edn. Assn., 1989. Mem. Am. Sociol. Assn., Am. Psychol. Assn., Internat. Soc. Polit. Psychology, Nat. U. Continuing Edn. Assn. (chmn. community devel. div. 1979-80, Innovation in Community Devel. award 1980, Spl. Program award 1983, Philip E. Frandson award 1986), 8th Air Force Hist. Soc. (life), 2d Air Div. Assn., Phi Delta Kappa (life), Phi Kappa Phi (life). Democrat. Episcopalian. Home: 2091 Black Fox Dr NE Atlanta GA 30345

PARSONS, WILLIAM FINTAN, engineer; b. Ontario, Can., Mar. 9, 1960; came to U.S., 1962; s. Frank Watson and Kathleen (McCauliffe) P.; m. Bridget Ann O'Connor, Aug. 24, 1985; children: Sarah Marie, Jon William. BS, Mich. State U., 1982; MBA, Nat. U., 1987. Sr. engr. electronics div. Northrop Corp., Hawthorne, Calif., 1983—. Mem. Soc. Packaging and Handling Engrs. Republican. Roman Catholic. Home: 411 S Pacific Hwy Redondo Beach CA 90277 Office: Northrop Electronics Div 2301 W 120th Org H561 Hawthorne CA 90250

PARTAIN, ROBERT MERRILL, construction company executive; b. San Diego, Mar. 10, 1952; s. Charles Reed and Dorothy (Hogan) P.; m. Lyndia Dianne Campbell, Apr. 15, 1972; children: Robert Merrill Jr., William Charles. AA, San Diego City Coll., 1972. Cert. millman journeyman, Calif.; cert. real estate agt., Calif. Asst. job supt. Charles Partain Gen. Contracting, El Cajon, Calif., 1970; inhouse draftsman and apprentice Valley Cabinet Shop, El Cajon, 1970-72; millman, apprenticed journeyman Am. Mill & Mfg., Chula Vista, Calif., 1972-74; owner, operator Bob Partain Custom Cabinets, Santee, Calif., 1974-79; v.p. new constrn. R&B Plumbing Inc., Santee, 1978-81; owner, operator R&B Solar Co., Santee, 1981-85; v.p. new constrn. Maio Plumbing, Heating, Solar Inc., San Diego, 1985-87; v.p. sales and mktg. Total Living Cabinets, San Marcos, Calif., 1987—; owner, operator B&D Constrn., Santee, 1975—. Mem. Bldg. Industry Assn. (sec., treas. 1988-89, bd. dirs. 1988), Kiwanis (1st v.p. Santee chpt. 1986), Elks. Home: 11825 Handrich Dr San Diego CA 92131 Office: Total Living Cabinets 1355 Descanso Ave San Marcos CA 92069

PARVIS, AZAR-MEHR, prosthodontist; b. Iran, July 9, 1937; came to U.S., 1962; s. Mahmood and Ozra (Asgari) A.; m. Han Young Pak, Dec. 1963; children: Shahin, Arlssn. DMD, Tehran U., 1960; cert. prosthodontics, NYU, 1965; postgrad., U. Mich., 1967. Asst. dean Sch. Dentistry Mashad U., Iran, 1968-70; assoc. prof. prosthodontics Nat. U. Iran, Tehran, 1970-82, chmn. dept. prosthodontics, 1970-82; clin. assoc. prof. prosthodontics NYU, N.Y.C., 1982-84; clin. assoc. prof. dept. of advanced prosthodontics Univ. So. Calif., Los Angeles, 1984--; pres. Wilshire Dental Group, Los Angeles, 1984--. Contbr. articles in field to dental jours. Mem. ADA, Am. Acad. Group Practice, Am. Assn. Group Practice Mgrs.,. Office: Wilshire Dental Group 2975 Wilshire Blvd Ste 400 Los Angeles CA 90010

PASARI, RON, manufacturing executive; b. Udaipur, Rajasthan, India, July 22, 1946; came to U.S., 1968; s. Hanuman Prasad and Kala P.; m. Carole Price, May 29, 1973; 1 child, Jae Ryan. BTech., Indian Inst. Tech., Bombay, Maharashtra, 1968; MBA, U. Pitts., 1969. Sr. systems analyst Exxon Co., Houston, 1969-73; sr. fin. analyst Petty Ray Geophysical, Houston, 1974-75; dir. fin. planning Datapoint Corp., San Antonio & Sunnyvale, Tx, Calif., 1975-80; mgr. fin. planning Apple Computer, Cupertino, Calif., 1980-81; fin. & adminstn. mgr. Apple Computer, Singapore, 1981-84; ops. mgr. Apple Computer, Mexico City, 1984-85; mgr. internat. logistics Apple Computer, Cupertino, Calif., 1985-88; fin. mgr. Apple Computer, Cupertino, 1988—; lectr. U. Houston, 1970-72. Home: 22776 Mercedes Rd Cupertino CA 95014

PASCAL, CRAIG ALBERT, construction company executive; b. Pueblo, Colo., May 4, 1943; s. Lloyd Richard and Florence Maxine (Sarten) P.; m. Judi Ann Anderson, Dec. 22, 1962; children: Noelle, Matthew, Rebecca. Student, Phillips U., Enid, Okla., 1961-62, Colo. U., 1963-64. V.p. Haco Contractors, Inc., Golden, Colo., 1961-75; pres. Haco Contractors, Inc., Golden, 1975—. Mem. Colo. Contractors Assn. (pres. 1983, contractor of yr. 1984), Assoc. Gen. Contractors (nat. dir. 1987—). Republican. Office: Haco Contractors Inc 18610 W Hwy 72 Golden CO 80403

PASCO, DUANE NOBLE, artist; b. Seattle, May 14, 1932; s. Duane Noble Doolittle and Della Artiel (Turner) Pasco; m. Katie Marie McAuliffe, Mar. 4, 1967: children: Shelley, John, Amy; m. Audrey Stenvahl, 1957 (div. 1963); children: Audrey, Brian. Grad. high sch., Seattle. Tchr. Alaska Native Brotherhood, Ketchikan, 1971, K'San Village, Hazelton, B.C., Can., 1969-71, Evergreen State Coll., Olympia, Wash., 1971, Native Cultural Ctr., Sitka, Alaska, 1977, Totem Heritage Ctr., Ketchikan, 1978, 80, Kitenmax Sch. N.W. Art, K'San Village, Hazelton, 1983, U. Wash., 1984, 85, 86, Ketchikan Community Coll., 1984, U. Alaska, 1985; cons. Nat. Park Svc., Sitka Nat. Hist. Park (Alaska), 1978, Nat. Native Indian Artists' Symposium, Vancouver, B.C., 1983. artist in residence Pacific Sci. Ctr., Seattle, 1985. Group shows include Seattle Ctr., 1980, 82, 83, State Capitol Mus., Olympia, Wash., 1981, Field Mus. Natural History, Chgo., 1982, Robert Adams Gallery, San Francisco, 1982, Pacific Sci. Ctr., Seattle, 1982, Stonington Gallery, Seattle, 1983, Oreg. Mus. for Sci. and History, Portland, 1983, Gallery Mack, Seattle, 1984, Scanlon Gallery, Ketchikan, Alaska, 1985, Quintna's Gallery, Portland, 1986, 87, 88, Partlow Gallery, Olympia, 1986, Bellevue (Wash.) Art Mus., 1987, Snow Goose Gallery, Seattle, 1988, Marianne Partlow Gallery, Olympia, Wash., 1988; represented in permanent collections Alaska State Mus., Juneau, U. B.D. Mus. Anthropology, Vancouver, U. Tokyo, Wash. State Hist. Mus., Seattle; vis. artist S.E. Alaska Indian Coun., Sitka, 1979; contbr. articles in field to profl. jours. Sgt. U.S. Army, 1957-60, Korea. Recipient 1st Place award Edmonds Art Festival, 1967; study grantee Alaska State Coun. for the Arts, Anchorage, 1984, Inst. Alaska Native Arts, Juneau, 1984, Nat. Endowment for the Arts, Washington, 1985. Home and Office: 19330 Widme Rd Poulsbo WA 98370

PASCOE, PATRICIA HILL, writer, state legislator; b. Sparta, Wis., June 1, 1935; d. Fred Kirk and Edith (Kilpartrick) H.; m. D. Monte Pascoe, Aug. 3, 1957; children: Sarah, Ted, Will. BA, U. Colo., 1957; MA, U. Denver, 1968, PhD, 1982. Tchr. Sequoia Union High Sch. Dist., Redwood City, Calif. and Hayward (Calif.) Union High Sch. Dist., 1957-60; instr. Met. State Coll., Denver, 1969-75; instr. Denver U., 1975-77, 81, research asst. bur. ednl. research, 1981-82; tchr. Kent Denver Country Day, Englewood, Colo., 1982-84; freelance writer Denver, 1985—; commr. Edn. Commn. of the States, Denver, 1975-82. Contbr. articles to numerous publs. and jours. Pres. East High Sch. PTSA, Denver, 1984-85, Moore Budget Adv. Com., Denver, 1966-72; mem. legis. chair Colo. U. Alumni Bd., Boulder, 1987—; del. Dem. Nat. Conv., San Francisco, 1984. Mem. Common Cause (bd. dirs. Denver chpt. 1986—), Modern Language Assn., SDX/Soc. Profl. Journalists, Phi Beta Kappa. Presbyterian. Home: 744 Lafayette St Denver CO 80218

PASHAYAN, CHARLES, JR., congressman; b. Fresno, Calif., Mar. 27, 1941; s. Charles and Lillie P. B.A., Pomona Coll., 1963; J.D., U. Calif., 1968; M.Litt., Oxford U., 1977. Bar: Calif. 1969, D.C. 1972, U.S. Supreme Ct. 1977. Spl. asst. to gen. counsel HEW, Washington, 1973-75; with 96th-101st Congresses from 17th Calif. Dist., 1975—. Capt. Strategic Intelligence U.S. Army, 1969-70. Mem. Fresno County Bar Assn., Royal Inst. Internat. Affairs, Internat. Inst. Strategic Studies. Republican. Office: 203 Cannon House Office Bldg Washington DC 20515

PASKEWITZ, BILL, JR, artist, educator; b. N.Y.C., Aug. 5, 1953; s. William and Emily (Gulden) P.; m. Victoria Joyce Ryan, Nov. 18, 1984. Student, Calif. Inst. Arts, Valencia, 1973-74; BFA, Cooper Union, 1975; MFA, Queens Coll., 1976-78. Head silkscreen dept. Motivational Design & Mktg., Irvine, Calif., 1979-80; instr. creative art workshops Newport Harbor Art Mus., Newport Beach, Calif., 1979-81, Irvine Valley Coll., 1979-88, Irvine Fine Art Ctr., 1980-85, Cypress (Calif.) Coll., 1986-87, Cerritos Coll., Norwalk, Calif., 1988; adj. lectr. Golden West Coll., Huntington Beach, Calif., 1980-86, Orange Coast Coll., Costa Mesa, Calif., 1986-88; coord., instr. studio painting, drawing and art history Las Positas Coll. (formerly Chabot Coll.), Livermore, Calif., 1988—. One-man shows Contemporary Art Gallery, N.Y.C., 1972, Queens Coll., 1977, Jacques Seligmann Gallery, 1978, West Coast Gallery, Newport Beach, 1980, Irvine Fine Art Ctr., 1981, James Turcotte Gallery, L.A., 1984, Laguna Moulton Gallery, Laguna Beach, Calif., 1988, Orange Coast Coll. Art Gallery, 1987; exhibited in group shows Columbus (Ohio) Mus. Art, 1978, Newport Harbor Art Mus., 1979, Laguna Art mus., Laguna Beach, 1986, 87, also numerous galleries, 1975—. Mem. Coll. Art Assn. Am. Office: Las Positas Coll Art Dept 3033 Collier Canyon Rd Livermore CA 94550

PASQUARELLA SMITH, JOSEPH EDWARD, bank executive; b. L.A., Feb. 23, 1953; s. J.A. and M. (Smith) Pasquarella. BA in Psychology, Calif. State U.-L.A., 1977. Ops. mgr. BankAm. Corp., Pasadena, Calif., 1980—. Office: BankAm Corp 101 S Marengo Ave Pasadena CA 91122

PASQUINI, KEITH ALAN, commercial printing company executive; b. Sacramento, July 29, 1951; s. Orland Fredrick and Helen Mae (Perry) P.; m. Jo-Ellen Marie Waters, Sept.7, 1974; children: Keith Alan Jr., Alicia. AA, Modesto Jr. Coll., 1971; BS, Calif. Poly. State U., 1974. With customer svc. dept. Cal Cen. Press, Sacramento, 1974-78, estimator, 1978-84, sales rep., 1984-85, regional sales mgr., 1985—; instr. Printing Industries No. Calif., Sacramento, 1987. Mem. 20-30 Club. Democrat. Roman Catholic. Home: 9 Sage River Cir Sacramento CA 95831 Office: Cal Cen Press 2629 5th St Sacramento CA 95818

PASSMORE, JAN WILLIAM, insurance company executive; b. Winchester, Ind., Nov. 5, 1940; s. Gale Orth and Helen Louise (Hoskinson) P.; student Nebr. State U., 1959-61; B.S., Ball State U., 1963; m. Pamela Boa, Feb. 14, 1964. With Aetna Life & Casualty, 1964-75, Western region dir., San Jose, Calif., 1972-75; broker, Sanders & Sullivan, San Jose, 1975-78, partner, 1978-80, pres., 1980-81; pres., chief exec. officer Corroon & Black, San Jose, 1981-88, chmn. 1988—; chmn. nat. adv. council INA Marketdyne, 1980-82; chmn. Nat. Producer's Council Cigna Corp., 1983-86; chmn. Aetna Life & Casualty Regional Adv. Council, 1982-84, 87-89. Chmn. bd. Goodwill Industries, 1978-80, 86-89; pres. Boy Scouts Am., 1981-83; bd. dirs. Music and Arts Found., 1980-85, Alexian Bros. Hosp. Found., 1978-85; chmn. bd. Hope Rehab., 1985-87; chmn. bd. dirs. Santa Clara County United Way; mem. San Jose Trolley Commn.; chmn. bd. trustees Alum Rock Meth. Ch.; nat. council rep. Boy Scouts Am., 1985, 86, 87, 88, 89. Recipient Silver Beaver award, Benefactors award Boy Scouts Am., Mayoral Proclamation City of San Jose, Suprs. Proclamation County of Santa Clara, Proclamation from Calif. State Assembly; named Citizen of Yr., Aetna Life & Casualty Co., 1975, Disting. Citizen of Yr. Santa Clara County, 1985; INA-Marketdyne Golden Circle, 1977-82, 87. Mem. Western Assn. Ins. Brokers (trustee 1987-89), Nat. Assn. Ind. Ins. Agts. Republican. Methodist. Clubs: San Jose Country (treas., bd. dirs.), Sainte Claire, Spartan Found., Pres.'s Council San Jose State U., Aetna Life and Casualty Gt. Performers, Masons, Shriners, Kiwanis (pres. Mechanicsburg, Pa. chpt. 1969, lt. gov. Pa. 1970-72, pres. San Jose chpt. 1986). Home: 16371 Aztec Ridge Dr Los Gatos CA 95032 Office: 1735 Technology Dr San Jose CA 95110

PASSMORE, MICHAEL FORREST, environmental administrator; b. Oroville, Calif., July 9, 1947; s. Audley Forrest and Betty Beryle (Elkin) P.; m. Laura Ann Travis, Sept. 7, 1968 (div. 1985); children: Travis Forrest, Robert Bryan: m. Elise Jean Bechtold, Nov. 9, 1985; 1 child, Heather Elise. BS, Oreg. State U., 1974, MS, 1977; PhD, Tex. A&M U., 1981. Research asst. Oreg. State U., Corvallis, 1974-77, research assoc., 1977; grad. fellow Rob and Bessie Welder Wildlife Found., Sinton, Tex., 1977-80; wildlife biologist Environ. Resources Br. U.S. Army Corps Engrs., Walla Walla, Wash., 1980-87; asst. chief U.S. Army Corps Engrs., Walla Walla, 1986-87, chief, 1987—; master bird bander Fish and Wildlife Service, 1981—; citizen ambassador, wildlife biology del. People-to-People Internat., China, 1987; cert. wildlife biologist, 1987—. Co-author manual: Raptors on COE Lands, 1986; contbr. articles to profl. publs. Coach youth sports, 1984--; mem. com. Walla Walla Parks Aviary Devel., 1983; vol. Boy Scouts Am., Walla Walla, 1986--. Mem. Wildlife Soc. (mem. spl. award com. 1987-88), Wilson Ornithol. Soc., Western Bird Banding Assn., Nat. Mil. Fish and Wildlife Assn., Northwest Scie. Assn. Methodist. Home: 1146 Sturm Ave Walla Walla WA 99362 Office: US Army Corp Engrs Bldg 602 Walla Walla WA 99362

PASTERNAK, DERICK PETER, internist; b. Budapest, Hungary, Apr. 21, 1941; s. Leslie Laszlo and Hedvig Eva (Hecht) P.; came to U.S., 1956, naturalized, 1962; BA, Harvard U., 1963, MD cum laude, 1967; MBA, U. N.Mex., 1985; m. Nancy Jean Clark, June 6, 1969; children: Kenneth Zoltan, Katherine Renee, Sarah Marie. Intern, jr. resident Bronx Municipal Hosp., N.Y.C., 1967-69; resident in internal medicine U. Calif. Hosps., San Francisco, 1971-73; mem. staff Lovelace Med. Center, Albuquerque, 1973—, med. dir. quality assurance program, 1976-80; med. dir. Lovelace Med. Found., 1980-86, pres., chief exec. officer, 1986—; pres. N.Mex. PSRO, Inc., 1980-82; clin. assoc. prof. medicine U. N.Mex. Referee U.S. Soccer Fedn. Served to capt. M.C., AUS, 1969-71. Decorated Bronze Star, Army Commendation Medal. Diplomate Am. Bd. Internal Medicine. Fellow AMA, Am. Coll. Physicians, Am. Coll. Physician Execs.; mem. AMA, N.Mex. Med. Soc. (councillor), Greater Albuquerque Med. Assn. Office: 5400 Gibson Blvd SE Albuquerque NM 87108

PASTIN, MARK J., ethics educator; b. Ellwood City, Pa., July 6, 1949; s. Joseph and Patricia Jean (Camenite) P.; m. Joanne Marie Reagle, May 30, 1970 (div. Mar. 1982); m. Carrie Patricia Class, Dec. 22, 1984. BA summa cum laude, U. Pitts., 1970; MA, Harvard U., 1972, PhD, 1973. Asst. prof. Ind. U., Bloomington, 1973-78, assoc. prof., 1978-80; prof., dir. Ariz. State U., Tempe, 1980—; founder, bd. CTG, Inc., Tempe, 1983—; adv. bd. Euro-Pacific Investments, San Diego, 1988—; dir. Sandpiper Group, Inc., N.Y.C., 1987—; chmn. bd. Council Ethical Orgns., Phoenix, 1986—; cons. Southwestern Bell, St. Louis, 1987—; vis. faculty U. Mich., Ann Arbor, 1978, Harvard U., 1980. Author: Hard Problems of Management, 1986; editor: Public-Private Sector Ethics, 1979; columnist Rethink-City Bus. Jour., 1986. Founding bd. mem. Tempe Leadership, 1985—; bd. mem. Ctr. for Behavioral Health, Phoenix, 1986—, Tempe YMCA, 1986—; mem. Clean Air Com., Phoenix, 1987—. Nat. Sci. Found. fellow, Cambridge, Mass., 1971-73; Nat. Endowment for the Humanities fellow, 1975; Exxon Edn. Found. grant, 1982-83. Mem. Strategic Mgmt. Soc. (invited presenter 1985), Am. Soc. Assn. Execs. (invited presenter 1987-88), Bus. Ethics Soc. (founding bd. mem. 1983), Found. Ethical Orgns. (chmn. 1988), Phi Beta Kappa. Club: Harvard (Ariz.). Home: 4435 S Rural Rd #351 Tempe AZ 85282 Office: Lincoln Ctr Ethics Ariz State U BAC 543 Tempe AZ 85287

PASTORIA, DEBORAH ANN, writer; b. Grosse Pointe, Mich., Mar. 21, 1954; d. Anthony and Frances (Mazzara) P. Student, U. Mich., 1972-74; BA in Fine Arts, UCLA, 1978. Freelance writer 1978-79; bus. mgr. Hal Kern Accountancy Corp., L.A., 1979-8l, Creative Fin. Svcs., Beverly Hills, Calif., 198l-83; TV prodn. assoc. Stephen J. Cannel Prodns., Hollywood, Calif., 1983-84; various position including mgr. spl. projects Walt Disney Co., Burbank, Calif., 1984-86, mgr. corp. mktg., 1986-88; freelance writer Santa Rosa, Calif., 1989—. Writer teleplay for episode What's Happening, 1978. Leader Girl Scouts U.S.A., Beverly Hills, 198l. Mem. Assn. for Responsible Communication.

PASTREICH, PETER, orchestra manager; b. Bklyn., Sept. 13, 1938; s. Ben and Hortense (Davis) P.; m. Jamie Garrard Whittington; children by previous marriages: Anna, Milena, Emanuel, Michael. A.B. magna cum laude, Yale Coll., 1959; postgrad., N.Y. U. Sch. Medicine, 1959-60; studied trumpet, with Robert Nagle at Yale U., with Raymond Sabarich, Paris. Asst. mgr. Denver Symphony, Balt. Symphony; Mgr. Greenwich Village Symphony, N.Y.C., 1960-63; gen. mgr. Nashville Symphony, 1963-65, Kansas City Philharmonic, 1965-66; asst. mgr., mgr. St. Louis Symphony, 1966-78, exec. dir., 1966-78; exec. dir. San Francisco Symphony, 1979—; instr. orch. mgmt. Am. Symphony Orch. League; bd. dirs. Nat. Com. for Symphony Orch. Support; founder San Francisco Youth Orch.; rep. planning and constrn. Davies Symphony Hall, San Francisco Symphony, 1980. Author: TV comml., 1969 (CLIO award); contbr. articles to various newspapers. Mem. recommendation bd. of the Avery Fisher Artist Program, Yale U. Council com. on music; past mem. adv. panel Nat. Endowment for the Arts, co-chmn. music panel, 1985; founding mem. bd. dirs. St. Louis Conservatory, mem. policy com. Maj. Orch. Mgrs. Conf., chmn., 1980; bd. dirs. Laumeier Sculpture Park, St. Louis, Stern Grove Festival, San Francisco Conv. and Visitors Bur.; chmn. fund campaign French-Am. Internat. Sch., San Francisco. Served with U.S. Army, 1960. Recipient First Disting. Alumnus award Yale U. Band, 1977, cert. Merit Yale Sch. Music, 1984. Mem. Am. Symphony Orch. League (dir., chmn., former chmn. task force on mgmt. tng.; mem. exec. and long-range planning com., chmn. standing com. on adminstrv. policy), Assn. Calif. Symphony Orchs. (dir.), Bankers Club of San Francisco. Club: Yale (N.Y.C.). Office: San Francisco Symphony Davies Symphony Hall San Francisco CA 94102

PATCHETT, LARRY GLENN, audio engineer, artist, researcher, writer; b. Tulsa, Okla., Dec. 17, 1953; s. Jay Glenn Patchett and Jerry Joanne (Hill) Hurley. BS in Music/Media with honors, U. Colo., Denver, 1980. Pres. Nomad Prodns. & Sound, Denver, 1980—; audio cons. Sta. KDBI-TV, Broomfield, Colo. Assoc. producer pub. TV series including Who's Taking The Heat, 1984 (Emmy award); editor of sound installation: Denver Art Museum, Native American Stories, Poems, Speeches, Prayers, 1988; post prodn. audio mgr. First Films, Inc., Denver, 1987-88, also three feature films including "Mind Killer", 1987-88; audio artist Denver Art Mus., 1988. Guest lectr. U. Colo., Denver, 1986, 88; vol. cameraman Sta. KDBI-TV , Broomfield, Colo., 1982—; sch. bus driver Assn. for Retarded Citizens, Littleton, Colo., 1981. Mem. Nat. Hist. Soc., Colo. Hist. Soc.

PATE, CHRISTINE VETTER, judge; b. San Diego, Sept. 27, 1943; d. William Paul and Ethel Marguerite (Waters) Vetter; m. William Craig Pate, Oct. 30, 1966; children: William C., Bryan L., David G., Douglas F. BA, U. Calif., 1965; JD, U. San Diego, 1969. Bar: Calif., U.S. Dist. Ct. (so. dist.) Calif. 1970. Shareholder Jennings, Engstrand & Henrikson, San Diego, 1970-88; judge Superior Ct. of San Diego, 1988—; bd. dirs. San Diego Law Ctr. Bd. dirs. San Diego Vol. Lawyers, 1984-87. Mem. State Bar Assn. Calif. (dist. rep. 1983-86), Calif. Judges Assn., San Diego County Bar Assn. (dir., v.p., sec.), Lawyers Club of San Diego (pres.), Rotary. Republican. Roman Catholic. Office: Superior Ct 220 W Broadway San Diego CA 92101

PATEL, ASHOK C., civil engineer; b. Changa, Gujarat, India, Dec. 29, 1948; came to U.S., 1971; s. Chunibhai H. and Chanchalben (Bhailalbhai) P.; m. Rita A. Jashbhai, Dec. 14, 1974; children: Amil, Jason. BCE, Sardar P. U., India, 1970; MCE in Water Resources, Brigham Young U., 1972. Registered profl. civil engr., Ariz.; profl. land surveyor, Ariz. Surveyor Utah County Surveyors, Provo, 1971; staff engr. Parker & Assocs., Denver, 1972; design engr. PRC Engring., Phoenix, 1972-76, project engr., 1976-80, assoc. v.p., 1980-84; v.p. Coe & Van Loo Cons. Engrs., Phoenix, 1984-85, sr. v.p., 1985—. Mem. citizen's bond com. Storm Sewers for City of Phoenix, 1974. Mem. ASCE, Ariz. Floodplain Mgmt. Assn., Ariz. Hydrological Soc., Ariz. Cons. Engrs. Assn. Democrat. Hindu. Home: 2120 E Cactus Wren Dr Phoenix AZ 85020 Office: Coe & Van Loo Cons Engrs 4550 N 12th St Phoenix AZ 85014

PATEL, RAMESH HIRABHAI, service executive; b. Asta, Gujarat, India, Nov. 5, 1954; came to U.S., 1966; s. Hirabhai V. and Jeliben Patel; m. Hina R. Vithalbhai, Apr. 20, 1978; children: Dipali R., Mitesh R. AA in Bus. Adminstrn., San Francisco City Coll., 1975; student, So. Oreg. State Coll., 1985—. Acctg. clk. Topps & Trowsers, San Francisco, 1978-79; owner Sis-Q Motel, Medford, Oreg., 1980-88, Royal Crest Motel, Medford, 1988—. Republican. Hindu. Home and Office: 411 E Barnett Rd Medford OR 97501

PATEL, SUDHIR, service executive; b. Samthan, Gujarat, India, Dec. 11, 1961; came to U.S., 1979; s. Nagin Khushal and Lalita (Mangubhai) P.; m. Rita Kantilal, May 29, 1985. BS in Biochemistry, Purdue U., 1984, MS in Indsl. Mgmt., 1985. Desk clk. Sagamore Inn, Lafayette, Ind., 1982-83, gen. mgr., 1984-86; asst. mgr. Wendys REstaurant, Seymour, Ind., 1986; fin. cons. First Investors Corp., N.Y.C., 1986-87; mgr. Westminster (Calif.) Motor Inn, 1987-88; owner Arco AM/PM, Bonita, Calif., 1988—; rsch. asst. Purdue U., West Lafayette, Ind., 1983-84. Mem. Internat. Soc. Financiers. Republican. Hindu. Office: Arco AM/PM 4498 Bonita Rd Bonita CA 92002

PATERSON, ROBERT LAMB, university official, biologist; b. Charlottesville, Va., Jan. 25, 1947; s. Robert L. and Margaret (Echols) P.; m. Margaret Scharpf, Nov. 19,1976; children: Jane, Katharine. BS, U. Miami, 1969; MS, Central Mich. U., 1975; PhD, Va. Poly. Inst. and State U., 1981. Tchr. math., sci. and phys. edn. Dade County Schs., Miami, Fla., 1969-73; instr. Cen. Mich. U., Mt. Pleasant, 1975-77, Radford U., Va., 1980; asst. prof. biology Frostburg State Coll., Md., 1981-83; mgr. acad. computing Pacific Luth. U., Tacoma, Wash., 1984-88, dean for computing, 1989--. Contbr. articles to ornithol. jours. Research grantee, 1976-83. Mem. Educom, Ducks Unltd. (area chmn. 1986-87). Office: Pacific Luth U Computer Ctr Tacoma WA 98447

PATI, ABHAY KUMAR, publisher, physician; b. Calcutta, India, Jan. 6, 1954; came to U.S., 1981; s. Sudarsan and Sabitri P. B in Allopathic and Ayurvedic Medicine and Surgery, J.B. Bay State Ayurvedic Med. Coll., Calcutta. Publisher Holistic Health Jour., Millvalley, Calif., 1982-86, Health World, Burlingame, Calif., 1987—. Office: Health World 1477 Rollins Rd Burlingame CA 94010

PATIL, HANUMANT RUDRABHAT, electronics executive; b. Agraharamuchadi, Karnataka, India, Apr. 9, 1934; came to U.S., 1962; s. Rudrabhat A. and Shanta R. (Shanta Naik) P.; m. Lata Patil, Dec. 11, 1967; 1 child, Vikram. BS,, Karnataka U., Dharwad, India, 1957, MS, 1961. Rsch. assoc. Cornell U., Ithaca, N.Y., 1969-71, MIT, Cambrdige, Mass., 1972-73; mem. tech. staff Hewlett-Packard Co., Palo Alto, Calif., 1973-77; sec., mgr. Hewlett-Packard Co., Colorado Springs, Colo., 1978-83; sec., mgr. Hewlett-Packard Co., Palo Alto, 1893-87, dir. electronics packaging lab., 1988--.

PATINO, DOUGLAS XAVIER, foundation administrator; b. Calexico, Calif., Apr. 11, 1939; s. Jose Luis and Maria Teresa (Seymour) P.; m. Barbel Wilma Hoyer, Aug. 13, 1970; 1 child, Viktor Xavier. AA, Imperial Valley Coll., 1960; BA, Calif. State U., San Diego, 1962, MA, 1966; PhD, U.S. Internat. U., 1972. Deputy dir. Sacramento Concilio, Inc., Sacramento, Calif., 1968-69; v.p. student affairs U. So. Colo., Pueblo, 1973-75; dep. dir. for planning and rev. svc. br. to dir. Calif. Employment Devel. Dept., 1975-83; dir. Ariz. Dept. of Econ. Security, Phoenix, 1983-87; pres., chief exec. officer Marin Community Found., Larkspur, Calif., 1987—; commr. Wm. T. Grant Found, 1986. Mem. Sec. of Dept. of Labor Task Force, Ariz., 1985-86, Staff Adv. Com. of the Human Resource Com., Nat. Gov. Assn., Ariz., 1983-86, Jr. League of Ariz., Phoenix, 198-586; bd. dirs. Calif. Leadership, Mountain View, Calif., 1985—, Ariz. Assn. Bus., 1984; chair U.S. Savings Bond Drive for State of Calif., 1982; trustee Nat. Hispanic U., Oakland, Calif., 1987—. Recipient Disting. Performance award, Nat. Alliance of Bus., Washington, 1985, Superior Svc. Mgmt. award, Am. Soc. Pub. Adminstrn., 1985, Humanitarian award, Los Padrinos, Inc., 1981, Small and Minority Bus. award for the State of Calif. 1982, Disting. Alumni award, Calif. Jr. Community Coll. Assn., Sacramento, 1982, Silver Spur award, Nat. Fedn. of Charros in Guadalajaro, Jalisco, Mex., 1974, Calif. Community Svc. award, Former Gov. Ronald Reagan, Sacramento, 1973. Mem. Ind. Sector, Hispanics in Philanthropy, No. Calif. Grantmakers, Am. Pub. Welfare Assn. (bd. dirs., Leadership award 1987), Rotary. Office: Marin Community Found 110 Larkspur Landing Cir Ste 365 Larkspur CA 94939

PATINO, ISIDRO FRANK, law enforcement educator; b. San Antonio, Mar. 10, 1943; s. Isidro F. and Maria (Narro) P.; m. Karin I. Schutt, Aug. 5, 1966 (div. 1985); children: Michael, Rebecca, Karleen. BS, Calif. State U., L.A., 1973. Records comdr. Placentia (Calif.) Police Dept., 1980-85; asst. dean Criminal Justice Tng. Ctr. Golden West Coll., Huntington Beach, Calif., 1986—. Mem. Calif. Law Enforcement Assn. of Records Suprs. (pres. so. chpt. 1985-87, state pres. 1986-87), Calif. Acad. Dirs. Assn. (vice-chmn. 1987-88, chmn. 1988-89), Acad. Criminal Justice Scis., Western and Pacific Assn. Criminal Justice Educators, Calif. Assn. Adminstrn. of Justice Educators, Calif. Peace Officers Standards and Tng. Basic Course Consortium (chmn. instrn. com. 1987-88), World Future Soc. Roman Catholic.

PATMORE, ALAN BARRY, financial executive, consultant; b. Vancouver, B.C., Can., Oct. 28, 1940; came to U.S., 1965; s. Alan Max and Geraldine (Jorgenson) P.; m. Carole L. Patmore, Dec. 28, 1963; children: Suzanne D., Alan R. B in Commerce, U. B.C., Vancouver, 1964; MBA, Columbia U., 1965. Form mgr. to ptnr. Arthur Andersen & Co., San Francisco, 1969-78; from ptnr. to mng. ptnr. Arthur Andersen & Co., Seattle, 1978-88, Andersen Cons. mng. ptnr. N.W., 1988—; cons. with over 100 major cos. on effective use of info. tech.; lectr. on info. tech. Author: Strategic Information Planning, 1985. Bd. dirs. San Mateo (Calif.) Suicide Prevention Ctr., 1975-78, Wash. Children's Home Soc., Seattle, 1981-85, Eastside Cath. High Sch., Bellevue, 1983—, pres. bd. 1987-88. Mem. Bellevue Athletic Club, Cen. Park Tennis Club (Bellevue), Columbia Tower Club (Seattle). Home: 10015 SE 25th Bellevue WA 98004 Office: Arthur Andersen & Co 801 2d Ave Seattle WA 98104

PATMORE, GERALDINE MARY (BOBBE PATMORE), realtor, real estate developer; b. Vancouver, B.C., Can.; came to U.S., 1968; d. Oscar Andrew and Geraldine Mary (Whalen) Jorgenson; m. Alan Max Patmore; children: Alan Barry, Paul Richard (dec.), Rosemary Anne Marta. Student, U B.C., Vancouver, Marylhurst Coll. Realtor George Beebe Co., Palm Springs, Calif., 1971-75; v.p. realtor Frank Bogert Co., Palm Springs, Calif., 1975-77; realtor West World Properties, Palm Springs, Calif., 1978-87; dir. sales Golden Mile Investment Co., Palm Springs, Calif., 1987—; pres. Patmore Assocs. Real Estate Investments, Palm Springs, 1989—. Charter mem. Child Help-USA (bd. dirs., desert chpt. 1976-80), Palm Springs; v.p. Humane Soc. Desert, Palm Springs, 1984-86; bd. dirs. SPCA-Animal Samaritans, Palm Springs, 1986—. Named Liaison Officer for work on sister city program between U.S. and Can. City of Palm Springs, 1973—. Mem. Palm Springs C. of C. (charter mem. sister city program 1972—), Nat. Bd. of Realtors (mem. Palm Springs Bd. Realtors 1972—), Internat. Council Shopping Ctrs. Roman Catholic. Clubs: Racquet (Palm Springs,Calif.), Vancouver Lawn Tennis and Badminton (B.C.). Home: 1466 Plato Circle Palm Springs CA 92264 Office: Golden Mile Investment Co 559 S Canyon Dr Ste B 212 Palm Springs CA 92264

PATRICK, LESLIE DAYLE, hydrologist; b. Grand Island, Nebr., Nov. 20, 1951; d. Robert Norman and Charlotte Ruth (Thomas) Mayfield; m. Jeffrey Rogan Patrick, July 1, 1972. BA in Geology, U. Alaska, Anchorage, 1975. Hydrologist water resources div. U.S. Geol. Survey, Anchorage, 1975—. Mem. Alaska Groundwater Assn. (sec./treas. 1980). Office: US Geol Survey Water Resources Div 4230 University Dr Ste 201 Anchorage AK 99508-4664

PATRINOSTRO, FRANK S., communications company executive, consultant; b. Tampa, Fla., July 23, 1929; s. Anthony and Dora (Maggio) P. BJ, U. Miami, 1954. Mgr. sales western region Sci. Press, Ephrata, Pa., 1965-68; exec. dir. Assn. for Library Automation Rsch. Communications, Tempe, Ariz., 1968-76; mgr. western region Control Data Technotec, San Jose, Calif., 1976-80; pres. Tech. Communications Assocs., Sunnyvale, Calif., 1981—. Author: Software Development Documentation, 6 vols., 1987; contbr. numerous articles to profl. publs. Mem. Soc. for Tech. Communications. Home: 575 E Remington Dr Apt 5F Sunnyvale CA 94086 Office: Tech Communications Assocs 1250 Oakmead Pkwy Ste 210 Sunnyvale CA 94086

PATSCHECK, KELLY RAE, real estate broker; b. Orange, Calif., Sept. 4, 1962; d. Raymond Ralph and Jean Etta (Grossman) P. BSBA, U. So. Calif., 1984. Sales rep. Coldwell Banker Comml. Real Estate, Riverside, Calif., 1985—. Mem. Internat. Coun. Shopping Ctrs. Republican. Office: Coldwell Banker 3750 University Ave #250 Riverside CA 92501

PATTEN, RICHARD E., microfilm company executive; b. Seattle, May 17, 1953; s. Donald Wesley and Lorraine Louise (Kienholz) P.; m. Monica Rose Bourg, Mar. 20, 1976; children: Richard Douglas, Wesley Bourg, Melinda Rose. BA, U. Wash., 1976. Exec. v.p. Microfilm Svc. Co., Seattle, 1976-84, gen. mgr., 1985-87, chmn. bd., 1988—. Candidate U.S. Congress, Wash., 1982; deacon Bethany Bapt. Ch., Seattle, 1983-86. Mem. Nat. Micrographics Assn. (pres. N.W. chpt. 1979-80, bd. dirs. 1978-79), Assn. Image and Info. Mgmt. (chmn. svc. co. 1987), Assn. Records Mgrs. and Adminstrs., Wash. Athletic Club, Rotary. Republican. Baptist. Home: 7012 NE 161st Bothell WA 98011 Office: Microfilm Svc Co 13540 Lake City Way NE Seattle WA 98125

PATTERSON, DALE RICHARD, musician, retired English teacher; b. Trinidad, Colo., Oct. 4, 1928; s. Dale O. and Evaline Ann (Tureck) P.; m. Elisabeth Ann Milton, Nov. 24, 1954; children: Mark Allan, Craig Stuart. BA, U. No. Colo., 1951; MA, U. Chgo., 1959. Life teaching cert., Colo. Tchr. English Carl Sandburg High Sch., Orland Park, Ill., 1954-56, Evanston (Ill.) Twp. High Sch., 1956-63; tchr. Englisth, English dept. chmn. Jefferson County Pub. Schs., Colo., 1963-86; musician variety of big bands, small groups and symphony orchs. Chgo., N.Y., Denver, N.Mex., Ariz., Wis., Nebr. and Kans., 1942—. Cpl. U.S. Army, 1952-54. Mem. Denver Musicians Assn.

PATTERSON, DANIEL WILLIAM, dentist; b. Minot, N.D., Aug. 12, 1948; s. Girdell William and Fern Lemay (Sullivan) P.; m. Gloria Jean Eckert, Oct. 9, 1982. DDS, Northwestern U., 1972; Alumnus degree (hon.), U. Colo., 1977. Dentist Dan L. Hansen, DDS, P.C., Lakewood, Colo., 1974-75; pvt. practice dentistry Littleton, Colo., 1975—; clin. instr. dept. applied dentistry U. Colo., 1981-84, lectr., 1983. Mem. edit adv. panel Dental Econs. Jour., 1981, contbr. articles., 1983. Active Chatfield Jaycees, Littleton, 1976-81; vocal soloist, mem. Denver Concert Chorale, 1978-82. Lt. USN, 1968-74. Mem. ADA, Met. Denver Dental Soc., Acad. Gen. Dentistry, Colo. Dental Assn. (Pres.'s Honor Roll 1982-84), Am. MENSA, Ltd., Columbine Mchts. Assn., Sedalia (Colo.) Wild Game. Lutheran. Home: 6984 Fargo Trail Littleton CO 80125 Office: 7660 S Pierce St Littleton CO 80123

PATTERSON, DARWIN DANIEL, utility executive; b. Phoenix, Feb. 3, 1949; s. Albert Daniel and Lorraine Idel (Caviness) P.; m. Diana Paulette Chapman, Feb. 13, 1970 (div. 1974); m. Frances Shirlene Brown, Nov. 15, 1974; 1 child, Lea Ann. AAS, Northland Pioneer Coll., Showlow, Ariz., 1981; BS, Ottawa U., Phoenix, 1989; DD (hon.), Universal Life Coll., Modesto, Calif., 1978, HHD (hon.), 1979. Asst. mgr. Regal Oil Co., Phoenix, 1968-69; parts mgr. Salmi Corp., Scottsdale, Ariz., 1971-72; truck driver Ariz. Welding Co., Phoenix, 1972-73; fuel handler Salt River Project, Phoenix, 1973-74, aux. tender, 1974-75, asst. control operator, 1975-77; control operator Salt River Project, St. Johns, Ariz., 1977-80, asst. shift supr., 1980-82, shift supr., 1982—. Active St. Johns Airport Com., 1982, Navajo County Library Bd., St. Johns, 1984-86; mem. Concho (Ariz.) Fire Dept., 1984. Sgt. USAF, 1969-71. Mem. St. Johns Flyers (officer 1982-83, pres. 1983-84). Republican. Mormon. Home: HC 30 Box 3151 Concho AZ 85924

PATTERSON, DAWN MARIE, educator, consultant; b. Gloversville, N.Y., July 30; d. Robert Morris and Dora Margaret (Perham) P.; m. Robert Henry Hollenbeck, Aug. 3, 1958 (div. 1976); children: Adrienne Lyn, Nathaniel Conrad. BS in Edn., SUNY, Geneseo, 1962; MA, Mich. State U., 1973, PhD, 1977; postgrad., U. So. Calif. and Inst. Ednl. Leadership. Librarian Brighton (N.Y.) Cen. Schs., 1962-67; asst. to regional dir. Mich. State U. Ctr., Bloomfield Hills, 1973-74; grad. asst. Mich. State U., East Lansing, 1975-77; cons. Mich. Efficiency Task Force, 1977; asst. dean Coll. Continuing Edn., U. So. Calif., Los Angeles, 1978-84; dean continuing edn. Calif. State U., Los Angeles, 1985—; pres. Co-Pro Assocs. Mem. Air Univ. Bd. Visitors, 1986—, Commn. on Extended Edn. Calif. State U. Calif., 1988—; Hist. Soc., Los Angeles Town Hall, Los Angeles World Affairs Council. Dora Louden scholar, 1958-61; Langworthy fellow, 1961-62; Edn. Professions Devel. fellow, 1974-75; Ednl. Leadership Policy fellow, 1982-83. Mem. AAUW (pres. Pasadena br. 1985-86), Am. Assn. Adult and Continuing Edn. (charter), Nat. Univ. Continuing Edn. Assn., Calif. Coll. and Mil. Educators Assn. (pres.), Los Angeles Airport Area Edn. Industry Assn. (pres. 1984), Kappa Delta Pi, Phi Delta Kappa. Republican. Unitarian. Club: Fine Arts of Pasadena. Lodge: Zonta. Office: 5151 State University Dr Los Angeles CA 90032

PATTERSON, DENNIS GLEN, Canadian government official, lawyer; b. Vancouver, B.C., Can., Dec. 30, 1948; common law wife: Marie Uviluq; children: Bruce, George, Jessica, Alexander. BA with distinction, U. Alta., Edmonton, 1969; LLB, Dalhousie U., Halifax, N.S., 1972. Bar: N.S., 1972, B.C. 1974. Exec. dir. Maliiganik Tukisinniavik, Iqaluit, N.W.T., Can., 1975-81; mem. legis. assembly, Iqaluit Govt. of N.W.T., Yellowknife, 1979-87, minister edn., 1981—, minister aboriginal rights and constl. devel., 1981-87, minister responsible for women, 1985; also minister of the executive, minister responsible for: intergovernmental affairs, office of devolution, Sci. Inst.; chmn. Cabinet, priorities and planning com., polit. and constitutional devel. com.; dep. chmn. fin. mgmt. bd. Office: Govt of NWT, PO Box 1320, Yellowknife, NT Canada X1A 2L9

PATTERSON, GARY KENT, chemical engineer, educator; b. Springfield, Mo., Dec. 10, 1939; s. Efton William and Freda (Young) P.; m. Barbara Ruth Lay, June 3, 1960; children: Sean Kent, Kelly Erin, Paul Brian. BS in Chem. Engring., Mo. Sch. Mines, 1960; MS in Chem. Engring., U. Mich., 1961; PhD in Chem. Engring., U. Mo., 1966. Profl. engr., Mo. Engr. trainee Procter and Gamble, St. Louis, 1959; devel. engr. Pitts. Plate Glass Chem. Div., Akron, Ohio, 1960, Esso Research Labs., Baton Rouge, 1961-63; asst. prof. chem. engring. U. Mo., Rolla, 1966-69, assoc. prof. chem. engring., 1969-78, prof. chem. engring., 1978-84; prof., head chem. engring. U. Ariz., Tucson, 1984—; research engr. Lawrence Livermore Labs., Livermore, Calif., 1977; cons. in field. Contbr. articles to profl. jours. Mem. Am. Inst. Chem. Engrs., Am. Chem. Soc., Am. Inst. Physics (Soc. of Rheology), Am. Soc. for Engring. Educators, Kiwanis (bd. dirs. 1980-84), Sigma Xi. Office: U Ariz Dept Chem Engring Tucson AZ 85721

PATTERSON, LUCILLE GREMILLION, foundation administrator, dietitian; b. New Orleans, Jan. 20, 1938; d. Seltz Gabriel and Elmira Cecile (Alexander) Gremillion; m. William Earl Patterson, Mar. 26, 1966 (div. Aug. 1984); 1 child, Ross Alexander. BS, La. State U., 1959; MS, Purdue U., 1972. Dietetic intern Vanderbilt U. Hosp., Nashville, 1961; clin. dietitian USAF Hosp., Maxwell AFB, Montgomery, Ala., 1961-62; chief dietitian, cons. to tactical air command surgeon USAF Hosp., Langley AFB, Hampton, Va., 1962-64; dir. of dietetics, cons. to Pacific air command surgeon USAF Hosp., Tachikawa AB, Tachikawa, Japan, 1964-68; dir. of dietetics, cons. to strategic air command surgeon USAF Hosp., Offutt AFB, Omaha, 1968-70; course supr. USAF Sch. of Health Care Sci., Dept. Biomedical Scis., Wichita Falls, Tex., 1972-77; dir. of dietetics, cons. to Pacific air command surgeon USAF Hosp., Clark AB, Philippines, 1977-79; dir. of dietetics, cons. to air tng. command surgeon USAF Med. Ctr., Keesler AFB, Biloxi, Miss., 1979-84; pres. Wildwood Resources, Inc., Wildwood Child Care Food Program, Englewood, Colo., 1984—; cons. in nutrition with USAF. Advisory bd. Big Bros./Big Sisters of YMCA, Colorado Springs, Colo., 1988-89. Mem. Am. Dietetic Assn., Colo. Dietetic Assn., Plaza Club (vice chair, soltero com. 1988-89), Going Concern (membership com., social com. 1988-89), Omicron Nu. Republican. Episcopalian. Home: 4765 Farthing Dr Colorado Springs CO 80906 Office: Wildwood Resources Inc 6143 S Willow Dr Englewood CO 80111

PATTERSON, MICHAEL CLARKE, funeral director; b. Long Beach, Calif., May 30, 1944; s. Delevon C. and Ella D. (Duis) P.; m. Eileen L. Knudsen, Mar. 11, 1973; 1 child, Denise. AA in Mortuary Sci., U. Minn., 1968; BSBA, U. Nebr., 1969. Lic. embalmer, funeral home dir., Wyo., Nebr. Funeral dir. Gering (Nebr.) Meml. Chapel, 1970-71, Colyer Funeral Home, Torrington, Wyo., 1971-75; ptnr., mgr. Colyer Funeral Home, 1975-83, owner, mgr., 1983—; coroner, Goshen County, Wyo., 1982—. Vice pres. Goshen County Econ. Devel. Corp., 1988, Joint Powers Bd. Eastern Wyo. Coll. Fitness and Wellness Ctr., 1989—. Ensign USN, 1969-70. Mem. Wyo. Funeral Dirs. Assn. (bd. dirs. 1988), Order of Golden Rule (state chmn. 1988—), Rotary, Masons, Shriners. Republican. Episcopalian. Home: Drawer A Torrington WY 82240 Office: Colyer Funeral Home 2935 Main St Torrington WY 82240

PATTERSON, RONALD GILBERT, quality manager; b. Cozad, Nebr., Aug. 20, 1932; s. Milo Thomas and Ethel Marie (Cochran) P.; m. Jane G. Hart, July 16, 1955; children: John G., Thomas E., Laurie A., Robert D., Keith H., Michele. BSEE, U. Wash., 1961; MS in Mgmt., Naval Postgrad. Sch., 1977. Commd. USN, 1961, advanced to comdr., ret., 1980; project engr. quality assurance Gen. Atomics, Inc., San Diego, 1980-83, mgr. fusion and advanced tech., 1983--; mem. adj. faculty vocat. edn. Palomar Coll., 1982--. Contbr. articles to profl. jours. Decorated Navy Commendation medal. Mem. Am. Soc. Quality Control (membership chmn. 1982-84). Republican. Methodist. Home: 14238 El Topo Dr Poway CA 92064 Office: Gen Atomics 10955 John Jay Hopkins Dr San Diego CA 92121

PATTERSON, SETH LYNN, cement company executive; b. Lamar, Colo., Feb. 15, 1953; s. Richard Harlan and Muriel Irene (Rodgers) P.; m. Patricia Lynn Alvine, June 14, 1980; children: Andrea Lynn, Eric Michael, Bryce Christian. BS in Acctg., U. Colo., 1975. CPA Colo., Nebr. Sr. acct. Deloitte Haskins & Sells, 1975-80; audit mgr. Deloitte Haskins & Sells, Denver, 1980-86; controller Ideal Basic Industries, Inc., Denver, 1986—; adj. prof. acctg. Buena Vista Coll., Council Bluffs, Iowa, 1979. Mem. employers adv. coun. U. Colo. Bus. Sch., 1985-86; vol. fundraising div. Denver Symphony Corp., 1985. Mem. Am. Inst. CPA's, Colo. Soc. CPA's., Fin. Execs. Inst., Portland Cement Assn. (fin. and adminstrv. exec. com). Democrat. Office: Ideal Basic Industries Inc 950 17th St Denver CO 80202

PATTERSON, WILLIAM ROBINSON, surgeon; b. Belfast, No. Ireland, Jan. 4, 1935; came to U.S., 1937; s. William John and Jane (Robinson) P.; m. Joan Tempel, Dec. 27, 1959 (div.); m. Donna Radford, July 14, 1985; children: William, Robin, Thomas. BS, Ohio State U., 1956, MD, 1960. Diplomate Am. Bd. Orthopedic Surgery. Resident in orthopedic surgery U. Mich., Ann Arbor, 1967; pvt. practice Grand Junction, Colo., 1967—; bd. dirs. Cen. Bank, Grand Junction. Chief of staff St. Mary's Hosp., Grand Junction, 1985. Capt. USAR, 1962-64. Fellow Am. Acad. Orthopedic Surgeons, Western Orthopedic Assn.; mem. AMA, Orthopedics Overseas. Republican. Presbyterian. Home: 662-26 Rd Grand Junction CO 81506 Office: 550 Patterson Rd Grand Junction CO 81506

PATTI, ANDREW S., consumer products company executive. Pres., chief oper. officer The Dial Corp., Phoenix; pres. Armour Internat. Co., Phoenix. Office: The Dial Corp Greyhound Tower Phoenix AZ 85077 *

PATTISON, NEAL ALLEN, newspaper editor; b. Canton, Ohio, Dec. 18, 1952; s. William Hoffman Pattison and Martha A. (Harper) Nystrom; divorced. BS in Journalism, Ohio U., 1974. Reporter-editor Daily Herald, Delphos, Ohio, 1973; reporter Carroll County Times, Westminster, Md., 1974-75; reporter-editor Bristol (Va.) Herald-Courier, 1975; news editor feature Roanoke (Va.) Times, 1975-78; assignments editor Ariz. Republic, Phoenix, 1978-82; asst. mng. editor Spokane Spokesman-Rev., 1982—; instr. journalism Gonzaga U., Spokane, 1984-87; co-chmn. Newspaper Design LTD regional workshop, Wash. State U.; site chmn. AP Execs. of Wash. and Oreg., 1986. Active Spokane Food Bank, 1987—; co-chmn. Minorities in Western Newspapers conf., 1989. Mem. Bench-Bar-Press Com., Soc. Newspaper Design (bd. dirs. N.W. region 1988—), Nat. Audubon Soc. Democrat. Office: Spokesman-Rev W 999 Riverside Spokane WA 99201

PATTNI, ARUN KUMAR, electrical engineer; b. Zanzibar, Tanzania, Dec. 7, 1940; came to U.S., 1962; s. C. R. and Mode C. P. BEE, N.Mex. State U., 1965. Engr. Phys. Sci. Lab., University Park, N.Mex., 1975-84; high-power microwave projects engr. Phys. Sci. Lab., 1984--. Co-author tech. papers for profl. confs., reports and studies in field; contbr. articles to profl. jours., conf. proceedings. Mem. IEEE, Assn. Old Crows, Am. Def. Preparedness Assn., Blue Key, Eta Kappa Nu, Tau Beta. Home: 2020 Jordan St Las Cruces NM 88001 Office: Phys Sci Lab Stewart St University Park NM 88003

PATTON, AUDLEY EVERETT, retired business executive; b. Eve, Mo., Nov. 9, 1898; s. Charles Audley and Letitia Virginia (Earhart) P.; B.S. in Indsl. Adminstrn., U. Ill., 1921, M.S. in Bus. Orgn. and Operation, 1922, Ph.D. in Econs., 1924; m. Mabel Dickie Gunnison, Aug. 5, 1930 (dec. Feb. 1976); 1 dau., Julie Ann Patton Watson; m. 2d, Mary Ritchie Key, June 24, 1977. Auditor, Mfg. Dealers Corp., Cambridge, Mass., 1921; instr. econs. public utilities U. Ill., Champaign-Urbana, 1924-25, asst. prof. econs. Coll. Commerce and Bus. Adminstrn., 1925-26; asst. to pres. Chgo. Rapid Transit Co., Chgo. South Shore & South Bend R.R. Co., Chgo. North Shore & Milw. R.R. Co., Chgo. Aurora & Elgin R.R. Co., 1926; asst. to pres. Public Service Co. No. Ill., Chgo., 1926-43, sec., 1928-52, asst. treas., 1928-44, v.p., 1943-53; v.p., dir. No. Ill. Gas Co., Aurora, 1953-54; v.p. Commonwealth Edison Co., Chgo., 1952-63, ret., 1963; asst. to pres. Presbyn-St. Luke's Hosp., Chgo., 1963-65; former v.p., dir. Big Muddy Coal Co.; past dir. Gt. Lakes Broadcasting Co., Chgo., Chgo. & Ill. Midland Ry. Co., Allied Mills, Inc., Chgo., Am. Gage & Machine Co., Elgin, Ill., HMW Industries, Inc., Stamford, Conn. Treas., Katherine Kreigh Budd Meml. Home for Children, Libertyville, Ill., 1929-36; mem. adv. com. on pub. utilities U. Ill., 1937-40, mem. gen. adv. com., 1943-46. Bd. dirs. Am. Cancer Soc. Ill. div., 1948-76, pres., 1957-59, chmn. bd., 1959-62, mem. fin. com., 1970-76; bd. dirs. Civic Fedn. Chgo., 1945-63, v.p., 1954-63; bd. dirs. South Side Planning Bd. Chgo., 1950-58; bd. dirs., mem. exec. com. Ill. C. of C., 1957-61; trustee Kemper Hall Sch. for Girls, Kenosha, Wis., 1929-37, Highland Park (Ill.) Hosp., 1946-51, Christine and Alfred Sonntag Found. for Cancer Research, 1965-81. Recipient Am. Cancer Soc. medal, 1951. Mem. U. Ill. Found., U.S. Men's (dir. 1958-62, v.p. 1960-65), Midwest (dir. 1956-60) curling assns., OX5 Aviation Pioneers (life mem.), Beta Gamma Sigma, Phi Eta, Delta Sigma Pi, Phi Kappa Phi, Delta Chi. Episcopalian. Clubs: Tower (Chgo.); Univ. Chgo. (bd. dirs. 1944-46, treas. 1945-46); Chgo. Curling (pres. 1956-57) (Northbrook, Ill.). Contbr. articles to profl. jours. Home and Office: 14782 Canterbury Tustin CA 92680

PATTON, COLLEEN PENNOCK, nurse; b. Twin Falls, Idaho, Oct. 31, 1926; d. James Everett and Rachael Alta (Powell) Pennock; m. William Wheeler Patton, Feb. 24, 1961; children: Sharon Lee Patton Williams, Julia Ellen Patton Cramer. RN diploma, Holy Cross Hosp. Sch. Nursing, 1948; student, Emory U., 1960, Ricks Coll., 1976. Nurse Holy Cross Hosp., Salt Lake City, 1950, U.S. VA Hosp., Atlanta, 1960-66, ARC, Idaho Falls, Idaho, 1971—; vol. nurse Pub. Health Dept., Idaho Falls, 1971—. Served to capt. USAF, 1957-59. Mem. Am. Nurses Assn., Med. Aux. Relief Soc. (councilor Idaho Falls chpt. 1982-85). Republican. Mormon. Home: 1854 Tiffany Dr Idaho Falls ID 83404

PATTON, DAVID WAYNE, healthcare executive; b. Utica, N.Y., June 15, 1942; s. Dale Willard and Eleanor (Miller) P.; BS, Ariz. State U., 1964; MHA, U. Minn., 1966; MA, Claremont U., 1989; m. Karmen Louise Rames, June 12, 1965; children—Jodi Lynn, Steven Wayne. Asst. adminstr. Maricopa County Gen. Hosp., Phoenix, 1969-71; adminstr. Holy Rosary Hosp., Miles City, Mont., 1971-74; exec. dir. St. Luke's Hosp., Aberdeen, S.D., 1974-79; pres., chief exec. officer Parkview Episcopal Med. Ctr., Pueblo, Colo., 1979-84; pres. Community Health Corp. and Riverside (Calif.) Community Hosp., 1984—. Bd. dirs. San Louis Valley Health Maintenance Orgn., 1982-84. Served to capt. USAF, 1966-69. Fellow Am. Coll. Healthcare Execs. (regent 1976-79); mem. Am. Acad. Med. Adminstrs. Am. Hosp. Assn., Calif. Hosp. Assn., Young Pres.' Orgn. (Inland Empire chpt.), Riverside C. of C. (bd. dirs. 1986—, pres. 1988-89), Victoria Club, Monday Morning Club, Raincross Club. Republican. Presbyterian. Home: 2596 Raeburn Dr Riverside CA 92506 Office: 4445 Magnolia Riverside CA 92501

PATTON, GEORGE HOMER, advertising executive; b. Grove City, Pa., Dec. 25, 1913; s. William Howard and Elizabeth Ann (Dobie) P.; m. Audrey Terry, (div. 1950); Children: George, Mary; m. Carol Louise Kramer, Oct. 19, 1974; children: Lynda, Sandy, Julie. BSC, Grove City Coll., 1938. Account exec. Tullis Co., Los Angeles, 1946-48, Roche & Eckhoff, Los Angeles, 1948-51; pres. George Patton Advt., Los Angeles, 1951—. Chmn. publicity Meals for Millions, Los Angeles, 1963; mem. publicity com. Foster Children, Los Angeles, 1974; bd. dirs. San Fernando Valley Symphony Orch., Los Angeles, 1970. Served to lt. comdr. USN, 1942-45. Mem. Advt. Ind. Emergency Relief Fund., Am. Legion. Republican. Presbyterian. Club: So. Calif. Advt. Tennis Soc. Lodge: Masons.

PATTON, RICHARD WESTON, mortgage company executive; b. Evanston, Ill., Sept. 26, 1931; s. Robert Ferry and Sue Buckley P.; m. Lynda A. Kruse, Feb. 2, 1971; 1 child, Robert Weston. B.A., Amherst Coll., 1954. Sales engr. Thermo Fax Sales Corp., Chgo., 1958-60; account exec. Nat. Mortgage Investors, Inc., Chgo. and Pasadena, Calif., 1960-66; asst. v.p. Nat. Mortgage Investors, Inc., 1966-67, v.p., 1967-69, exec. v.p., 1969-73, pres., chief exec. officer, dir., 1973-84, vice-chmn. bd., 1984—; pres., chmn. exec. com., dir. Ocean Park Restaurant Corp., Santa Monica, Calif., 1977-88; dir. Century Fed. Savs. and Loan Assn., Cenfed Corp. Bd. dirs. Pasadena Boys' Club, 1963-66; mem. steering com. Amherst Coll. Capital Fund Drive, 1963-66; bd. dirs. Opera Assocs., 1984—. Served with USMCR, 1955-58. Mem. Calif. Savs. and Loan Assn. League, U.S. League Savs. Assns., Amherst Coll. Alumni Assn. (bd. dirs. 1963—, pres. 1977-79, 86-89), Overland Club (sec., dir.), Kronenstadt Ski Club (past pres.). Office: NMI Mortgage Co PO Box 90307 Pasadena CA 91109

PAUL, DAVID PATRICK, insurance company executive; b. Minot, N.D., July 12, 1959; s. Herbert Lawrence and Doloris (Sawatzke) P.; m. Joanne Francis Kochis, May 4, 1985. BS in Agrl. Econs., N.D. State U., 1981. Field underwriter Fed. Crop Ins. Corp., Billings, Mont., 1981-86; field statistics coordiantor Fed. Crop Ins. Corp., 1986-88, dir., 1988; dir. St. Paul Compliance Office, Eagan, Minn., 1988—. Mem. liturgy com. St. Patrick's Ch., Billings, 1988-89, lector and Eucharistic minister, 1988—. Recipient Superior Svc. award, USDA, 1985. Office: Saint Paul Compliance Office Yankee Sq I Office Bldg 3440 Federal Dr Eagan MN 55122

PAUL, GEORGE C., small business owner; b. Denver, Oct. 18, 1921; s. Clarence Leroy and Dorothy (Curtis) P.; m. Lillian Skinner, Jan. 15, 1943 (div. Nov. 1956); 1 child, Robert Curtis; m. Edna Louise Fragale, Apr. 22, 1958. AA, Mesa Jr. Coll., 1941; BS in Mktg., U. Denver, 1946. Sales rep. Morey Mercantile Co., Denver and Albuquerque, 1947-52; advt. specialist Mountain States Tel. & Tel., N.Mex., 1952-64; sales rep. Starline Printing, Albuquerque, 1964-71, McGraw-Hill Publs., San Antonio, 1971-72; co-owner Bus. Graphics, Inc., Albuquerque, 1972-76; sales rep. Xerox Corp., Albuquerque, 1976-77; N.Mex. sales rep. Fed. Envelope, div. of Champion Internat., Albuquerque, 1977-87; owner Plastikoil Binding of the S.W., Albuquerque, 1987—; liaison officer, Air Force Acad., Albuquerque, 1962-64. Maj. USAF, 1942-45, North Africa. Decorated Silver Star, Air medal with seven clusters, Purple Heart. Mem. Albuquerque Tip Club, Masons, Shriners. Republican. Home: 7805 Am Heritage NE Albuquerque NM 87109 Office: Plastikoil of the SW Inc 3100 E Pan American Fwy NE Albuquerque NM 87107

PAUL, JODY, computer information scientist; b. Bklyn., June 22, 1955. BS in Math., UCLA, 1978, MS in Computer Sci., 1980, PhD in Computer Sci., 1988. Mem. tech. staff Hughes Research Labs., Malibu, Calif., 1978-80; rsch. scientist Bell Labs., N.J., 1980-82; computing specialist Hughes Aircraft, L.A., 1982-83, cons. knowledge engr., 1983—; computer scientist The Rand Corp., Santa Monica, Calif., 1984—; lectr. computer sci. dept., UCLA, 1988—, instr. UCLA extension, 1986—. Contbr. articles to profl. jours. Mem. IEEE, Assn. for Computing Machinery, Am. Assn. Artificial Intelligence, Assn. for Computers and Humanities, Upsilon Pi Epsilon (computer sci. honor soc.), Phi Mu Epsilon (math. honor soc.). Home: 1117 12th St Ste 3 Santa Monica CA 90403 Office: The Rand Corp 1700 Main St Santa Monica CA 90406

PAUL, LARRY ANTHONY, architect; b. Cleve., Nov. 19, 1946; s. Valerian Anthony and Bette Mae (Kramer) P.; m. Linda Christine Fields, Jan. 24, 1970 (div. 1976); 1 child, Avrielle; m. Susan Money Quarnstrom, June 20, 1987; 1 child, Nicholas. B Arch, U. So. Calif., 1967; M Arch, Ohio State U., 1970; D Archtl. Design, UCLA, 1975; PhD in Communications, San Francisco State U., 1977. Registered architect, Calif., Hawaii. Planner Land Devel. Planning, Inc., San Francisco, 1970-73; sr. designer Environ. Design Works, Honolulu, 1973-75; asst. dir. Undercover Graphics, Inc., Berkeley, Calif., 1975-77; project mgr. Archimedia Corp., San Francisco, 1977-85; v.p. Measure of Man Assocs., San Francisco, 1985-87; pres. L.A. Paul & Assocs., San Francisco, 1987—; cons. Inst. Childhood Resources; commr. Calif. Bd. Archtl. Examiners, Sacramento, 1985—, Fairfax (Calif.) Design Rev. Bd., 1984. Editor periodical Archimedia, 1982 (award 1985). Bd. dirs. Mill Valley Film Festival, Calif., San Francisco Toy Mus., 1986—. Capt. USAF, 1970-74. U. So. Calif. fellow, 1970; recipient 1st Place award San Francisco Art Festival, 1975, Pacific Coast Builders Conf., 1984. Mem. AIA (1st Prize 1980), Nat. Council Archtl. Registration Bds., Resource Inst. (bd. dirs. 1979—), Olympic Club, Tiburon Club (bd. dirs. 1988—), Tiburon Lodge. Republican. Roman Catholic. Office: Measure of Man Assocs 1829 Union St San Francisco CA 94123

PAUL, MALCOLM DAVID, Plastic and reconstructive surgery; b. Balt., Nov. 8, 1943; s. William and Rose (Friedman) P.; m. Pamela Sisk Paul, May 15, 1981; children: Stephen, Scott, Jacquie, Matthew. BS, U. Md., 1965; MD, U. Md., Balt., 1969. Cert. Am. Bd. Plastic Surgery, 1976. Intern Mt. Sinai Hosp., N.Y.C., 1969-70, resident, 1970-71; resident George Washington U., Washington, 1971-75; practice medicine specializing in plasic surgery Fountain Valley, Calif., 1975—; asst. clin. prof. plastic surgery U. Calif., Irvine, 1976—. Author:. Mem. Am. Soc. Plastic and Reconstructive Surgery, Am. Soc. Aesthetic Plastic Surgery, Am. Bd. Plastic Surgery. Republican. Jewish. Office: Malcolm D Paul MD 11100 Warner Ave #218 Fountain Valley CA 92708

PAUL, RICHARD DAVID, manufacturing executive, retired military officer; b. Revere, Mass., Nov. 25, 1935; s. Samuel and Marion (McNeil) P.; m. Marilyn Ann Lanzo, Dec. 6, 1956; children: Beth J. Wolpman, Brenda L. Asmus. BS in Pub. Rels., Boston U., 1957; MS in Govt., Webster U., 1975; postgrad. in sr. exec. fellow program, Harvard U., 1982. Commd. lt. USAF, 1957, advanced through grades to col.; served as navigator various posts, 1959-64; instr. Squadron Officer's Sch., Maxwell AFB, Ala., 1964-65; gen.'s aide de camp Air U., Maxwell AFB, Ala., 1965-68; asst. exec. officer, mil. polit. affairs officer USAF hdqrs., Washington, 1968-70; group exec. officer 504 Tactical Air Support Group, Cam Ranh Bay, South Vietnam, 1970-71; WG exec. 374 Tactical Aircraft Wing, Taiwan, 1971-73; staff exec. officer, tng. officer Scott AFB, Ill., 1973-76; exec. officer Hdqrs. Air Force Recruiting Svc., Randloph AFB, Tex., 1975-76, Air Force Mil. Tng. Ctr., Lackland AFB, Tex., 1976-79; wing comdr. Air Force Basic Tng. Sch., Tex., 1979-81; wing comdr. 323 Flying Tng. Wing, Mather AFB, Calif., 1981-83, ret., 1983; dir. mktg. Deutsch Metal Components, Gardena, Calif., 1984—. Pres. PTA, Alexandria, Va., 1968; mem. exec. com. United Way, Sacramento, 1981-83. Decorated D.F.C., Legion of Merit. Mem. Air Force Assn., Soc. Aerospace Engrs. (assoc.), ASTM (assoc.), Boston U. Alumni, Sigma Alpha Epsilon. Republican. Office: Deutsch Metal Components 14800 S Figueroa St Gardena CA 90248

PAUL, ROBERT JAQUISH, financial executive; b. Ontario, Oreg., Mar. 10, 1922; s. Herbert Brooks and Dorothy Dean (Jaquish) P.; m. Ruth Elaine Fowler, Dec. 4, 1926; children: Lawrence Eugene, Jody Lynne Paul Brodston. BA, U. Denver, 1947, MA, 1955. Tchr., coach Denver Pub. Schs., 1947-80; pres., chmn. funding and financing Polaris Mining-Pub. Co., Denver, 1965-70; chief exec. officer Belvoir Ptnrs., Inc., Denver, 1984-89, B&P Co., Lakewood, Colo., 1970—; chief fin. officer Transam Petroleum Corp., Lakewood, 1989—; chief fin. officer Transam. Petroleum Co.(pub. co., holding co. and devel.), 1989—. Pres. bd. dirs. Applewood Homeowners Assn., Golden, Colo., 1964-65; scoutmaster Boy Scouts Am., Denver, 1955; asst. dir. Rep. Party of Jefferson County (Colo.), 1964; bd. dirs. Bonvue Water Dist., Lakewood, 1975-76; mem. County Sheriffs of Colo., Jefferson County, 1988. Mem. Rotary. Presbyterian. Home: 105 S Garland St Lakewood CO 80226 Office: Belvoir Ptnrs Inc 5299 DTC Blvd Ste 700 Aurora CO 80226

PAULAKOVICH, DONNA FRANCES, hotel housekeeping executive; b. Kansas City, Kans., Mar. 6, 1938; d. Bronco and Frances (Horvat) Dodig; children: Kenneth, Christopher, Ann. AA, Donnelly Coll., 1978. Mgmt. trainee Westin Hotel-Crown Ctr., Kansas City, Mo., 1978-80; asst. housekeeper Westin Hotel-Crown Ctr., 1980-81; asst. dir. housekeeping Westin Hotel-Ariz. Biltmore, Phoenix, 1981-82; dir. housekeeping Ariz. Biltmore, Phoenix, 1982-85; dir. housekeeping svcs. Chgo. Hilton and Towers, 1985-86; dir. housekeeper Boca Raton Hotel and Club, Boca Raton, Fla., 1986-87; dir. housekeeping svc. Caesar's Palace Hotel, Las Vegas, Nev., 1987—. Mem. Nat. Exec. Housekeeper Assn. (pres. Valley of Sun chpt. 1985). Roman Catholic. Office: Caesars Palace 3750 Las Vegas Blvd S Las Vegas NV 89109

PAULING, LINUS CARL, chemistry educator; b. Portland, Oreg., Feb. 28, 1901; s. Herman Henry William and Lucy Isabelle (Darling) P.; m. Ava Helen Miller, June 17, 1923 (dec. Dec. 7, 1981); children: Linus Carl, Peter Jeffress, Linda Helen, Edward Crellin. B.S., Oreg. State Coll., Corvallis, 1922, Sc.D. (hon.), 1933; Ph.D., Calif. Inst. Tech., 1925; Sc.D. (hon.), U. Chgo., 1941, Princeton, 1946, U. Cambridge, U. London, Yale U., 1947, Oxford U., 1948, Bklyn. Poly. Inst., 1955, Humboldt U., 1959, U. Melbourne, 1964, U. Delhi, Adelphi U., 1967, Marquette U. Sch. Medicine, 1969; L.H.D., Tampa U., 1950; U.J.D., U. N.B., 1950; LL.D., Reed Coll., 1959; Dr. h.c., Jagiellonian U., Montpellier (France), 1964; D.F.A., Chouinard Art Inst., 1958; also others. Teaching fellow Calif. Inst. Tech., 1922-25, research fellow, 1925-27, asst. prof., 1927-29, assoc. prof., 1929-31, prof. chemistry, 1931-64; chmn. div. chem. and chem. engring., dir. Calif. Inst. Tech. (Gates and Crellin Labs. of Chemistry), 1936-58, mem. exec. com., bd. trustees, 1945-48; research prof. (Center for Study Dem. Instns.), 1963-67; prof. chemistry U. Calif. at San Diego, 1967-69, Stanford, 1969-74; pres. Linus Pauling Inst. Sci. and Medicine, 1973-75, 78—, research prof., 1973—; George Eastman prof. Oxford U., 1948; lectr. chemistry several univs. Author several books, 1930—, including How to Live Longer and Feel Better, 1986. Contbr. articles to profl. jours. Fellow Balliol Coll., 1948; Fellow NRC, 1925-26; Fellow John S. Guggenheim Meml. Found., 1926-27; Recipient numerous awards in field of chemistry, including; U.S. Presdl. Medal for Merit, 1948, Nobel prize in chemistry, 1954, Nobel Peace prize, 1962, Internat. Lenin Peace prize, 1972, U.S. Nat. Medal of Sci., 1974, Fermat medal, Paul Sabatier medal, Pasteur medal, medal with laurel wreath of Internat. Grotius Found., 1957, Lomonosov medal, 1978, U.S. Nat. Acad. Sci. medal in Chem. Scis., 1979, Priestley medal Am. Chem. Soc., 1984, award for chemistry Arthur M. Sackler Found., 1984, Chem. Edn. award Am. Chem. Soc., 1987. Hon., corr., fgn. mem. numerous assns. and orgns. Home: Salmon Creek 15 Big Sur CA 93920 Office: Inst Sci & Medicine 440 Page Mill Rd Palo Alto CA 94306 *

PAULSEN, SUZANNE MARGARET, psychiatrist, pathologist; b. Great Falls, Mont., Sept. 15, 1932. BS in Pharmacy, U. Wash., 1954, MD, 1959. Diplomate Am. Bd. Psychiatry, Am. Bd. Pathology. Intern Jackson Meml. Hosp., Miami, 1959-60, resident in anatomic pathology, 1960-62; resident in clin. pathology U. Oreg. Health Sci. Ctr., Portland, 1962-64, resident in psychiatry, 1974-77; practice medicine specializing in pathology Terre Haute, Ind., 1964-66; practice medicine specializing in psychiatry Portland, 1977--; clin. instr. pathology Ind. State U. Sch. Nursing, 1964-66; pathologist Good Samaritan Hosp., Portland, 1966-74, supr. residents, 1966-74, dir. med. tech. tng., 1972-74. Mem. Oreg. Med. Assn., Multnomah County Med. Soc., Am. Psychiat. Assn., Oreg. Psychiat. Assn. (sec. 1984-85), Oreg. Pathologists Assn. Home and Office: 2831 NW Westover Rd Portland OR 97210

PAULSON, A. B., writer, educator; b. St. Paul, Mar. 13, 1944; s. Arthur H. and Alma Marie P.; m. Karen Kondrad, Sept. 3, 1967 (div. Sept., 1985); 1 child, Phoebe. AB, U. Chgo., 1966, AM, 1967; PhD, SUNY, Buffalo, 1974. Instr., asst. prof. Dartmouth Coll., Hanover, N.H., 1972-81; asst. prof. Hamilton Coll., Clinton, N.Y., 1981-85; asst. prof. Portland State U., Oreg., 1985-87, assoc. prof., 1987--. Author: Watchman Tell Us of the Night, 1987. Mem. MLA, Associated Writing Programs. Office: Portland State U Dept English Box 751 Portland OR 97207

PAULSON, DAVID LEWIS, architect, educator; b. Heron Lake, Minn., May 5, 1931; s. Sylvanus and Adela (Pietsch) P.; m. Joy Lois Larsen, Sept. 10, 1956; children: Martha Mary, Sarah Katherine, Joseph David. BA, U. Minn., 1953, BArch with distinction, 1955; MArch, Harvard U., 1957. Archtl. draftsman R.V. McCann, Mpls., 1953-56, Carl Koch & Assocs., Cambridge, Mass., 1956; archtl. designer Easton & Assocs., Architects, Boulder, Colo., 1957-81; instr. U. Colo., Boulder, 1957-59, asst. prof., 1959-66, assoc., 1966-67, prof., 1971—; assoc. prof. U. Conn., Storrs, 1966-67; vis. prof. Nat. U. Fine Arts, Tokyo, 1981-82; mem. archtl. control com. Denver Tech. Ctr., 1970-75, 80-83; design cons. Boulder Pub. Library, 1972. Contbr. articles, book revs. to profl. publs. Bd. dirs., v.p., pres. Help for Boulder, Inc., 1968-78; mem. Citizens Com. for Housing and Devel., Boulder, 1974-76; chmn. Bd. Zoning Adjustment, Boulder, 1970-73. Fisher Traveling scholar, 1968; Japan Soc. for Promotion of Sci. fellow, 1981; U.S. Japan Friendship Commn. rsch. grantee, 1982. Mem. AIA, AIA Colo., Assn. Asian Studies, Am. Fedn. Tchrs., Internat. Ho. Japan, Univ. Club, Alpha Rho Chi. Democrat. Home: 1517 48th St Boulder CO 80303 Office: U Colo Coll Environ Design Campus Box 314 Boulder CO 80309

PAULSON, HELEN ELIZABETH, hypnotherapist, artist; b. San Francisco, Feb. 12, 1919; d. Clayton French and Alvera Elizabeth (Miller) Richards; m. John Nicolay Paulson Jr., Aug. 18, 1940 (div. May 27, 1981); children: John Nicolay III, Robert Peter, Lisa Marie. BA in Psychology with distinction, Stanford U., 1939. Cert. Am. Coun. Hypnotist Examiners. Psychol. examiner, vocat. counselor Jr. Counseling Svc., USES, San Francisco, 1940-41; freelance artist and photographer 1952-77; tchr. art adult edn. pub. schs. Poughkeepsie, N.Y., 1953-56, Campbell, Calif., 1957-60; gallery dir. Mendocino (Calif.) Art Ctr., 1975-76; adminstr. Evergreen Resource Conservation Dist., San Jose, Calif., 1981-84; instr. self-hypnosis DeAnza Coll., Cupertino, Calif., 1981-83; pvt. practice hypnotherapy and graphology Los Gatos, Calif., 1982—; guest lectr. civic, cultural and profl. orgns., 1980—. Numerous-one-woman shows, Calif., N.Y., 1952-77; represented in numerous pvt. collections. Vol., a founder Suicide and Crisis Svc., San Jose, 1968-71. Mem. Am. Handwriting Analysis Found. (cert.), AAUW, Orchesis, Ram's Head, Assn. for Rsch. and Enlightenment, Phi Beta Kappa. Mem. Soc. of Friends. Office: PO Box 2032 Los Gatos CA 95031

PAULSON, HOWARD EUGENE, engineer; b. Seattle, Apr. 12, 1941; s. Arne Walter and Virginia May (Pommer) P.; m. Roberta Bell Graham, Apr.

11, 1960; children: Kenneth John, Jennifer Louise, Stephen Andrew. Student, Whitman Coll., 1959-62, 69-70, Wash. State U., 1979—. Lithographer Inland Printing, Walla Walla, Wash., 1960-62; with sales Sears Roebuck & Co., Walla Walla, 1962-63, Huntington Office Supply, Walla Walla, 1963-65; draftsman Key Equipment Co., Milton-Freewater, Oreg., 1965-68, design engr., 1968-73; applications engr. Key-Electrosonic, Milton-Freewater, 1973-75; ptnr. Kemp Constrn. Co., Milton-Freewater, 1975-78; design engr. Key Tech., Inc., Milton-Freewater, 1978-86, project engr., 1986—. Commr. City of Milton-Freewater Planning Commn., 1982-85, vice-chmn., 1986-87, chmn., 1988—. Mem. Nat. Inst. for Cert. in Engring. Techs. (cert.), Elks. Republican. Presbyterian. Home: 1318 Davis St Milton-Freewater OR 97862 Office: Key Tech Inc 517 N Elizabeth Milton-Freewater OR 97862

PAULSON-EHRHARDT, PATRICIA HELEN, laboratory administrator; b. Moses Lake, Wash., June 10, 1956; d. Luther Roanoke and Helen Jane (Baird) Paulson; m. Terry Lee Ehrhardt, Mar. 12, 1983. Student, Pacific Luth. U., 1974-76; BS in Med. Tech., U. Wash., 1976; BS in Biology, MS in Biology, Eastern Wash. U., 1982. Med. technologist Samaritan Hosp., Moses Lake, 1979-81; lab. supr. Moses Lake Clinic br. Wenatchee Valley Clinic, 1983-87; with Kalispell (Mont.) Regional Hosp., 1987-88; client svcs. rep. Mont. Pathology Assocs. Med. Lab., Kalispell, 1988—; mem. med. lab. tech. adv. com. Wenatchee (Wash.) Valley Coll., 1984-85, chmn., 1985-86. Mem. Flathead Valley Community Band, 1987—. Mem. Am. Soc. Med. Technologists (hematology judge 1986 Wash. State Student Bowl), Wash. State Soc. Med. Techologists (coordinator sci. assembly small lab. 1986), Wash. Assn. Diabetic Educators, Am. Soc. Clin. Pathologists (cert.), Pan Players Flute Soc., AAUW, Flathead Tennis Assn., Sigma Xi, Kappa Delta (pledge class pres. 1976). Republican. Lutheran. Club: Moses Lake Volleyball Assn. (pres. 1985-86). Lodge: Rotary (active wive's br. Moses Lake, 1985). Home: 3270 Airport Rd Kalispell MT 59901

PAUMIER, KAY ELLEN, public relations consultant; b. Elmhurst, Ill., Oct. 11, 1944; d. Charles Joseph and Jeannette Rose (Durr) P. BA, St. Joseph's Coll., Orange, Calif., 1969. Cert. elem., secondary tchr., lifetime, Calif. Researcher, writer Indsl. Indemnity Co., San Francisco, 1972-74; adminstr. Legal Aid Soc., San Francisco, 1974-76; asst. account exec. Ruder & Finn Pub. Relations, San Francisco, 1976-79; account exec. Russom & Leeper Pub. Relations, San Francisco, 1979-83; v.p. D-A-Y Pub. Relations, Los Altos, Calif., 1983-87; founder, pres. Communications Plus, Mountain View, Calif., 1987—. Editor: (book) Games Children Should Play, 1980. Recipient Market Support First Prize award No. Calif. chpt. Pub. Rels. Soc. Am., 1983, Honorable Achievement award No. Calif. chpt. Pub. Rels. Soc. Am., 1981. Mem. Peninsula Mktg. Assn., Toastmasters (awards 1980-86). Democrat. Office: Communications Plus 145 Centre St Mountain View CA 94041

PAUP, MARTIN ARNOLD, real estate and securities investor; b. Seattle, Aug. 30, 1930; s. Clarence Jacob and Emaline Ethel (Lodestein) P.; m. Mary Jean Iske, Apr. 4, 1959; children: Barbara Ann Paup Soriano, Jennifer Marie, Elizabeth Paup Gail. BS, U. Wash., 1952. Indsl. engr. Boeing Airplane Co., Seattle, 1954-60; owner Coopers Unfinished Furniture, Seattle, 1960-63; claims rep. Unigard Ins., Seattle, 1963-66; asst. benefits mgr. Equitable Life Assurance, Seattle, 1966-85; owner Paup Ventures, Seattle, 1974--, Paup Investment Co., Seattle, 1963--, Ella Paup Properties, Seattle, 1963--. Bd. dirs. Denny Regrade Property Owners' Assn., Seattle, Denny Regrade Bus. Assn., Seattle, First Ave. Assn., Seattle. Seattle Dept. Community Devel. grantee, 1980. Mem. Greenwood C. of C., Stanwood Camano Yacht Club, Seattle, Enological. Democrat. Roman Catholic. Home: 2021 1st Ave Ste G-4 Seattle WA 98121 Office: Paup Co 2021 1st Ave G-4 Seattle WA 98121

PAUTLER, CRAIG THOMAS, corporate professional; b. Buffalo, N.Y., Jan. 26, 1948; s. Elmer E. and Evelyn Marie (Rainey) P.; m. Bonnie Lou Boeldt, Nov. 26, 1983; children: Michelle Christine, Megan Suzzane. Assoc., Miami (Fla.) Dade Jr. Coll., 1970; BSEd., Fla. Atlantic U., 1972. Head pro and mgr. No. Wildwood (N.J.) Tennis Club, 1973; tennis por Dorado Beach Hotel, Puerto Rico, 1973-74, dir. tennis, 1974-77; dir. tennis Cerromar Beach Hotel, Puerto Rico, 1974-77, Little Dix Bay Hotel, British Virgin Islands, 1974-77, Caneel Bay Hotel, St. John, U.S. Virgin Islands, 1974-77, Mauna Kea Beach Hotel, Kamuela, Hawaii, 1977-82; pres. Craig T. Pautler, Inc., Kamuela/Scottsdale, Ariz., 1982—; bd. dirs. U.S. Sports Devel., Inc., Kentfield, Calif.; tennis adv. bd., Adidas, 1979—, Joe Lampe's Tennis Ranch, Scottsdale, 1985—; dir. tennis Mauna Lani Bay Hotel, Kamuela, Hawaii, 1982—, Hyatt Regency Waikaloa (Hawaii), 1988—, Kiahuna Tennis Club, Poipu Beach, Kauai, 1988—; dir. of sports, Crescent Hotels, Phoenix, 1984-87; tennis adv. Boast Sportswear, Palm Beach, Fal., 1983—. Chmn. Hotel Industry Charity Walk, Hawaii, 1981-84. Recipient Court of the Year. award of excellence, Tennis Industry, Mauna Lani Bay, Tennis Garden, 1988, Tennis Industry Mag., 1988. Fellow, U.S. Tennis Assn. (facilities com. mem., N.Y. 1986—). Office: Craig T Pautler Inc PO Box 1434 Kamuela HI 96743

PAVELKA, RONALD GENE, sales executive; b. Los Angeles, June 16, 1956; s. Ronald George and Alberta Marie (George) P.; m. Jane Katherine Stiitz, June 20, 1981; 1 child, Cristina Katherine. Grad. high sch., Villa Park, Calif. V.p. JBL, Inc., Orange, Calif., 1980-83; regional sales mgr. Sherwood Scuba, Irvine, Calif., 1983—; pres. Sports Mktg. Group, Santa Rosa, Calif., 1985—. Author: NAUI Advanced Text, 1988. Mem. Nat. Assn. Underwater Instrs., Profl. Assn. Diving Instrs. Republican. Lutheran. Home and Office: PO Box 246 Cloverdale CA 95425

PAVESE, RICHARD FRANCIS, plastic and reconstructive surgeon; b. N.Y.C., Mar. 5, 1948; s. Frank Anthony and Jacqueline (Aiello) P.; m. Mary Beth Luther, Jan. 11, 1976; children: Edward, Lisa. BA in Biology, Coll. City of N.Y., 1967; MD, U. Ariz., Tucson, 1973. Diplomate Am. Bd. Plastic Surgery. Intern in gen. surgery Vanderbile Hosp., Nashville, 1973-74; resident plastic surgery Boston U. Hosp., 1974-77; plastic surgery residency tng. Phoenix, 1977-79; fellowship plastic surgery Tulane U., New Orleans, 1979-80; plastic surgeon Richard Pavese M.D., Tempe, Ariz., 1981—; pvt. practice Valley Inst. Plastic Surgery, Tempe, 1987—; med. dir. Tempe Surgical Ctr., 1988—. Mem. Am. Soc. Plastic & Reconstructive Surgeons, AMA, Maricopa County Med. Soc., Maricopa County Plastic Surgeons Soc. Home: 5501 N 67th Pl Paradise Valley AZ 85253 Office: Valley Inst Plastic Surgery 1847 E Southern Ave Tempe AZ 85282

PAVLICK, HARVEY NAYLOR, financial executive; b. San Francisco, May 29, 1942; s. Leopold Ferdinand and Anna Cathrine (Naylor) P. BA, San Francisco State U., 1965; MA, U. Chgo., 1968; D in Philosophy, Claremont Grad. Sch., 1974. Dir. annual fund Union Coll., Shenectady, N.Y., 1968-70; dir. corp. and found. funding U. Calif., Berkeley, 1975-78; prin. Hyde Park Properties, Ltd., San Francisco, 1979-83; pres. Am. Equity Council, Inc., Irvine, Calif., 1984—; chmn. bd. dirs. Investment Grade Real Estate Council, Inc., Irvine. Sponsor Friends Huntington Library, San Marino, Calif., 1986—, Children, Inc., Alexandria, Va., 1984—; mem. World Affairs Council of Orange County, Santa Ana, Calif., 1986; L.A. County Museum Art, 1988—. Mem. World Affairs Coun. L.A., Pi Sigma Alpha.

PAVLIK, NANCY, convention services executive; b. Hamtramck, Mich., July 18, 1935; d. Frank and Helen (Vorobojoff) Phillips; m. G. Edward Pavlik, June 30, 1956; children: Kathleen, Christine, Laureen, Michael, Bonnie Jean. Student, U. Ariz., 1956-80. Exec. sec. Mich. Bell, Detroit, 1951-56, RCA, Camden, N.J., 1956-58; owner, pres. Southwest Events Etc., Scottsdale, Ariz., 1969—. Chairwoman hopitality industry commn. Scottsdale City Coun., 1989—; bd. dirs. Scottsdale Curatorial Bd., 1987—. Mem. Soc. Incentive Travel Execs., Meeting Planners Internat., Am. Soc. Assn. Execs., Contact, Indian Arts and Crafts Assn., Scottsdale C. of C. (bd. dirs., tourism steering com. 1984-88), Contemporary Watercolorists Club. Democrat. Roman Catholic. Home: 7500 E McCormick Pkwy #33 Scottsdale AZ 85258 Office: SW Events Etc 8233 E Paseo Del Norte E-400 Scottsdale AZ 85258

PAWLYK, WILLIAM JOHN, computer services manager; b. Hoboken, N.J., Mar. 25, 1941; s. William and Margaret Elizabeth (Kolvek) P.; m. Jacqueline Loyacono, July 31, 1965 (div. 1981); children: John, Karen; m. Marguerite Kathleen Amstadt, Feb. 14, 1982; children: Brent, Chad, Seth. BS, U.S. Naval Acad., 1963; MBA, U. Pa., 1971. Naval officer Destroyers and Nuclear Submarines U.S. Navy, Washington, 1963-70; prodn. mgr. Naval Products Div. UNC Inc., Montville, Conn., 1972-74; asst. gen. mgr. Recovery Ops. UNC Inc., Wood River Junction, R.I., 1978; ops. mgr. Systems and Services Div. UNC Inc., Richland, Wash., 1978-80, planning mgr., 1980-85; prodn. mgr. Sandvik Spl. Metals Corp., Finley, Wash., 1974-78; mgr. ops. support, site plans Boeing Computer Services, Richland, Wash., 1985—; chmn. Tri-Cities Enterprise Assn., 1987—, Richland Small Bus. Task Force, 1986-87. Chmn. Richland Econ. Devel. Bd., 1986—; southcentral Wash. ombudsman Wash. Com. Employer Support of Guard & Reserve, 1988. Served to capt. USNR. Recipient Navy Commendation medal, Econ. Devel. Merit award Wash. chpt. Am. Planning Assn., 1987. Mem. Nat. Mgmt. Assn., Naval Reserve Officers Assn. (v.p. Tri-Cities chpt. 1980—), U.S. Naval Inst., Naval Submarine League, U.S. Naval League (pres. Columbia Basin Council 1987-88), Tri-Cities Indsl. Devel. Coun. (v.p. 1988—), U.S. Naval Acad. Alumni Assn. Club: Toastmasters. Home: 1775 Columbia Dr SE #212 Richland WA 99352 Office: Boeing Computer Svcs 825 Jadwin Ave Richland WA 99352 also: Tri-Cities Enterprise Ctr 2000 Logston Blvd Richland WA 99352

PAWULA, KENNETH JOHN, artist, educator; b. Chgo., Feb. 4, 1935; s. John and Clara (Brzezinski) P.; student Northwestern U., 1956, Art Inst. Chgo., 1956; B.F.A., U. Ill., 1959; M.A. in Painting, U. Calif., Berkeley, 1962. Graphic designer Motorola, Inc., Chgo., 1959-60; grad. asst. printmaking U. Calif., Berkeley, 1961-62, asso. in art, 1962-63; archaeol. delineator for Islamic excavation Am. Research Center, Egypt, 1964-65; instr. Sch. of Art, U. Wash., Seattle, 1965-67, asst. prof., 1967-73, asso. prof., 1974—; participant artist-in-residence program of Ecole Superieure Des Beaux-Arts D'Athenes at Rhodos Art Center, Greece, 1978; cons. to Wydawnictwo Interpress, Warsaw, Poland, 1978; mem. art jury ann. painting, drawing and sculpture show Art Mus. of Greater Victoria, Can., 1971, Unitarian Art Gallery, Seattle, 1968, Cellar Gallery, Kirkland, Wash., 1968, Lakewood Artist's Outdoor Exhibit, Tacoma, Wash., 1968; participant Painting Symposium, Janow Podlaski, Poland, 1977. One-man shows of paintings include: Univ. Unitarian Fine Arts Gallery, Seattle, 1970, Polly Friedlander Gallery, Seattle, 1970, Lynn Kottler Galleries, N.Y.C., 1971, U. Minn. Art Gallery, Mpls., 1971, Art Mus. of Greater Victoria, Can., 1972, Second Story Gallery, Seattle, 1972; group shows include: Worth Ryder Gallery, U. Calif., Berkeley, 1962, Seattle Art Mus., 1964, 70, 65, 66, Frye Art Mus., Seattle, 1966, San Francisco Art Ins., 1966, Henry Gallery, U. Wash., Seattle, 1966, 67, 70, State Capitol Mus., Olympia, Wash., 1967, Attica Gallery, Seattle, 1967, 69, Sec. of State's Office, Olympia, 1968, Eastern Mich. U., Ypsilanti, 1968, Rogue Gallery, Medford, Oreg., 1968, Marylhurst Coll., Oreg., 1968, Spokane Art Mus., 1968, Cheney Cowles Mus., Spokane, 1969, Jade Gallery, Richland, Wash., 1969, Alaska U., 1970, Polly Friedlander Gallery, Mpls., 1971, Anchorage Art Mus., 1972, U. Nev. Art Gallery, 1972, Juneau (Alaska) Art Mus., 1972, Springfield (Mo.) Art Mus., 1973, U. N.D., Grand Forks, 1974, Washington and Jefferson Coll., Washington, Pa., 1975, MacMurray Coll., Jacksonville, Ill., 1976, Gallery of Fine Arts, Eastern Mont. Coll., 1976, Inst. of Culture, Janow Podlaski, Poland, 1977, Seattle Arts Commn., 1978, Polish Cultural Center, Buffalo, 1979, Cabo Frio Internat. Print Biennial, Brazil, 1983, Sunderland (Eng.) Poly. U. Faculty Exchange Exhbn., 1984, Internat Art Biennial Mus. Hosio Capranica-Viterbo, Italy, 1985; represented in permanent collections: San Francisco Art Mus., Seattle Art Mus., Henry Gallery, U. Wash., Seattle, Highline Coll., Midway, Wash., Marylhurst Coll., Art Mus., Janow Podlaski, Poland, Tacoma Nat. Bank, Fine Arts Gallery of San Diego. Mem. Coll. Art Assn., AAUP. Home: 10037 NE 115th Ln Kirkland WA 98033 Office: U Wash Coll Arts & Scis Sch Art Seattle WA 98195

PAYMAR, JAMES EDWARD, television reporter, correspondent; b. Duluth, Minn., Nov. 19, 1950; s. Mandel and Freida (Finegold) P.; divorced; children: Sheryl, Joseph, Daniel. BS in History and Edn., U. Minn., Duluth, 1973. Anchor, reporter KNTV (ABC), San Jose, Calif., 1976-80, KOMO-TV (ABC), Seattle, 1980-81, WABC-TV (ABC), N.Y.C., 1981-82, KRON-TV (NBC), San Francisco, 1982-88; correspondent Fox TV, N.Y.C., 1988—; pres. Calif. News Svc., San Francisco, 1988. Recipient UPI awards 1980, 87 (Calif.), 1980 (nat.), Gabriel award, 1978, Am. Cancer Soc. award, 1978, Western Ednl. Telecommunications, 1977; recipient commendation City of San Jose, County of Santa Clara. Mem. Nat. Acad. TV Arts and Scis. (Emmy awards 1978, 79, 85), Sigma Delta Chi.

PAYNE, ANCIL HORACE, retired broadcasting executive; b. Mitchell, Oreg., Sept. 5, 1921; s. Leslie L. and Pearl A. (Brown) P.; m. Valerie Dorrance Davies, Apr. 6, 1959; children—Anne Sparrow, Alison Louise, Lucinda Catherine. Student, Willamette U., 1939-41, U. Oreg., 1941, U. Notre Dame, Ohio State U., 1943; B.A., U. Wash., 1947; postgrad., Am. U., 1950-51. Adminstrv. asst. to congressman Washington, 1949-52; gen. mgr. Martin Van Lines, Anchorage, 1952-56, Frontiers-Oreg. Ltd., Portland, Oreg., 1956-59; asst. v.p. bus. div. King Broadcasting Co., Seattle, 1959-63, v.p., 1963-70, exec. v.p., 1970-71, pres., 1971-87, also exec. com. bd. dirs.; chmn. bd. affiliates NBC, 1975-79; bd. dirs. Airborne Freight Co. Mem. Oreg. Bd. Higher Edn., 1966-70; bd. dirs. Seattle Symphony, Centrum Found., World Affairs, Oreg. Shakespeare Festival; trustee Whitman Coll. Served to lt. (j.g.) USNR, 1942-45, PTO. Mem. Seattle C. of C., Roundtable, Phi Beta Kappa, Alpha Delta Sigma. Episcopalian. Clubs: Monday, Rainier, Columbia Tower (bd. dirs.) (Seattle). Home: 1107 1st Ave Seattle WA 98101 Office: 1119 1st Ave #211 Seattle WA 98101 also: 333 Dexter Ave N Seattle WA 98109

PAYNE, BONNIE ANN, psychologist; b. Washington, July 14, 1944; d. Wesley St. John and Evelyn Alice (Hall) Bagby; m. Salvatore Spinella, Aug. 21, 1965 (div. Oct. 1976); 1 child, Alisa Marie Spinella; m. Richard Karl Payne, Aug. 2, 1980. BA, U. Calif., Berkeley, 1966, MSW, 1971; PhD, Inst. Transpersonal Psychology, Menlo Park, Calif., 1982. Lic. psychologist, clin. social worker. Dep. adult probation officer Santa Clara County Adult Probation Dept., San Jose, Calif., 1966-69; clin. social worker Family Svc. Assn., Palo Alto, Calif., 1971, Santa Clara County Mental Health Ctr., San Jose, 1973-75; coord. family treatment O'Connor Hosp. Pain Ctr., San Jose, 1979-80; pvt. practice clin. social work Palo Alto, 1978-82, Aoibashi Family Clinic, Kyoto, Japan, 1983; assoc. acad. dean Inst. Transpersonal Psychology, 1984-87; pvt. practice clin. social work Los Gatos, Calif., 1985—; adj. faculty Inst. Transpersonal Psychology, 1986—. Contbr. articles in field. Mem. Calif. Psychol. Assn., Nat. Social Workers Assn. (diplomate), Assn. for Transpersonal Psychology, Assn. for Advancement Counseling and Devel., Los Gatos Athletic Club. Democrat. Buddhist. Office: 825 Pollard Rd Ste 200 Los Gatos CA 95030

PAYNE, CARL ALLEN, gripman; b. Elizabeth, Pa., July 27, 1940; s. James McRuby and Alberta (Sweney) P. Grad. high sch., Elizabeth, Pa. Gripman San Francisco Mcpl. Railways, 1962—; good will ambassador City and County of San Francisco, 1977—. Cpl. USMC, 1958-62. Recipient Citizen's Meritorious Conduct award San Francisco Police Dept., 1973, 74, Respect for Law Commendation Optimist Internat., 1974. Mem. Am. Fedn. TV and Radio Artists, Masons. Democrat. Methodist. Office: San Francisco Mcpl Railways 1201 Mason St San Francisco CA 94501

PAYNE, CURTIS MARION, geologist, miner; b. La Ceiba, Honduras, May 4, 1952; came to U.S., 1952; s. Donald Edward and Marjorie Ann (Curtis) P.; m. Margaret Anderson Miller, July 23, 1981; children: Dustin Edward, Jennifer Ann. BS, Auburn U., 1974; MS, S.D. Sch. Mines and Tech., 1979. Field geologist, lab instr. Auburn (Ala.) U., 1972-73; temp. geologist Rocky Mountain Energy Co., Wheatridge, Colo., 1974-76; geologist Homestake Mining Co., Lakeridge, Colo., 1977-79; geologist I Amoco Minerals Co., Englewood, Colo., 1979-81; sr. geologist Battle Mountain Exploration Co., Reno, Nev., 1981—. Mem. KNPB Channel 5, Reno, 1988. Mem. NRA, The Mineralogical Record, Geol. Soc. Nev., Auburn Geol. Soc. (treas. 1974), Nat. Muzzleloading Rifle Assn., Lake's Crossing Muzzle Loaders; subscriber Soc. Econ. Geologists. Republican. Methodist. Home: 10515 Palm Springs Dr Sparks NV 89436 Office: Battle Mountain Exploration Co 220 S Rock Blvd # 15 Reno NV 89502

PAYNE, DANIEL FRANKLIN, broadcasting entrepreneur; b. Los Angeles, Aug. 7, 1945; s. William Franklin and Patricia Jean (Gordon) P. Student U. Mont., 1962, Calif. Western U., 1963, U. Ga., 1964, U. Denver, 1965, George Washington U., 1966, UCLA, 1967, Loyola Law School, 1968; M.B.A. Calif. Coast U., 1976, Ph.D. in Bus., 1978. Pres., owner Design Trust and World in Water Corp., 1969-73; west coast mgr. Arbitron/Control Data, 1973-76; mktg. mgr. Dickinson Communications, Huntington Beach, Fountain Valley and Westminster, Calif., 1976-78; dir. franchising, gen. mgr. Six Star Cablevision Co., Los Angeles, N.Y.C. and Chgo., 1978-81; pres., chief exec. officer Internat. CableSystems, Inc., Beverly Hills, Calif., 1981-83; founder, gen. ptnr. Am. TV Network, owners TV channels in Anchorage, Durango, Colo. Coos Bay, Oreg., Maui, Hawaii, Cheyenne, Wyo., Hilo, Hawaii, Eureka, Calif., Reading, Calif., 1979—; co-founder Internat. Football League, owner Hawaiian Warriors Football Team, Honolulu, 1985, owner, founder Discount Travel of Los Angeles and Glendale; owner Priceless Places, Paige One Designs, bd. dirs. So. Calif. Archtl. Preservation, 1987—; owner, architect, builder Rivendell Retreat Compound. Mem. Calif. Rare Fruit Growers Assn., Mensa. Libertarian. Home: Rivendell Retreat 1870 Burnell Dr Los Angeles CA 90065 Office: PO Box 1211 Glendale CA 91209

PAYNE, KEVIN JOSEPH, association executive; b. Yonkers, N.Y., Mar. 5, 1953; s. Joseph F. and Maureen L. (Delahanty) P.; m. Pamela Jane Groves, Oct. 18, 1980; children: Ashley Marie, Rebecca Fields. Student, LeMoyne Coll., Syracuse, N.Y., 1971-73, SUNY, Purchase, 1975-76. Asst. news dir. Radio Sta. WLNA-WHUD, Peekskill, N.Y., 1975-83; news corr. Radio Sta. WOR-AM, N.Y.C., 1980-83; news anchor Radio Sta. WCBS-FM, N.Y.C., 1982-83; news dir. Radio Sta. KVMT-FM, Vail, Colo., 1983-84; dir. chamber services Vail Resort Assn., 1984-85; exec. dir. Avon Beaver Creek (Colo.) Resort Assn., 1985—; bd. dirs. World Ski Championships Organizing Com., Am. Ski Classic, Vail, 1984—. Bd. dirs. Bravo! Colo. Performing Arts Found., Vail, 1987—, Internat. Sculpture Arts Ctr., Avon/Beaver Creek, 1986—, Eagle County Transit Commn., 1987—, Vail Soccer Club Inc., 1983—, Vail/Eagle Valley Arts Council, 1986. Recipient Regents scholarship N.Y. State, 1971,. Mem. Rocky Mountain Ski Writers (assoc.). Clubs: Homestead Ct., Singletree Golf (Edwards, Colo.). Lodge: Vail/Eagle Valley Rotary (bd. dirs. 1986-87). Home: #16 Arlington Pl Box 2119 Avon CO 81620

PAYNE, PHILIP W., biophysicist; b. New Castle, Ind., Feb. 26, 1950; s. Robert Hedges and Esther Lois (Lamb) P.; m. Caroline Lelear, May 27, 1978. BA, Pomona Coll., 1971; PhD, Princeton U., 1976. Rsch. assoc. U. N.C., Chapel Hill, 1976-77; asst. prof. chemistry U. Hawaii, Honolulu, 1977-84; sr. computational chemist SRI Internat., Menlo Park, Calif., 1985-88, cons., 1988—; scientist Protein Design Labs., Menlo Park, 1988—; mem. study sect. Nat. Cancer Inst., Bethesda, Md., 1986. Author: Protein Engineering: Strategic Issues and Technical Perspectives, 1986; contbr. articles to profl. jours. Bd. dirs., sec. Cupertino (Calif.) Nazarene Ch., 1988. NIH grantee, 1987. Mem. AAAS, Am. Phys. Soc., Am. Chem. Soc. (grantee 1980), Protein Soc., N.Y. Acad. Scis. Office: Protein Design Labs 3181 Porter Dr Palo Alto CA 94304

PAYNE, RAYMOND LEE, JR., lawyer; b. Kansas City, Mo., Nov. 7, 1927; s. Raymond Lee and Erma Elizabeth (Whitaker) P.; m. Betty Joyce Billingsley, 1948; children—Raymond Lee, Janifer H. Payne Cohn, Gregory M.; m. Kathleen Marie Wood, Dec. 14, 1957; m. Patricia Paschall Chancellor, June 17, 1977. B.S., U. Denver, 1959, J.D., 1960. Bar: Colo. 1960; cert. hotel/motel adminstr. Assoc. Harding & Herman, Denver, 1960-62; assoc. Tilly & Skelton, Denver, 1962-66; sole practice, Denver, 1966-67; ptnr. Safran & Payne and predecessors, Denver, 1968-78; sole practice, Denver, 1978—; sec., dir. Commerce Motor Hotel Corp., Adventure Travel Corp., ptnr. Cameron Assocs.; Chmn. bd. S.W. Denver Community Mental Health Services, 1960-74; bd. dirs. Denver Bar Assn. Credit Union, 1979-89, chmn. loan com., 1982, pres., 1983-84; chmn. Downtown Dem. Forum. Served with AUS, 1946-47. Mem. Colo. Bar Assn., Denver Bar Assn., Colo.-Wyo. Hotel/Motel Assn. (bd. dirs.), Am. Arbitration Assn., City of Denver Club, Toastmasters, Masons. Democrat. Home: 9200 Cherry Creek South Dr Denver CO 80231 Office: 8000 E Girard Ave South Tower Ste 415 Denver CO 80231

PAYZANT, THOMAS, school superintendent. Supt. schs. City of San Diego. Office: San Diego Unified Sch Dist 4100 Normal St San Diego CA 92103 *

PAZ SOLDÁN, MIGUEL MATEO, financial/tax planner; b. Lima, Peru, Feb. 11, 1945; came to U.S., 1968; s. Fernando and Elsa Ricardina (Estrada) P.; m. Harriet Sue Skousen; children: Michelle, Monica, Miguel Jr., Manuel, Marcy, Marc, Marcella, Melinda, Melissa, Myra. BS in Chemistry and Microbiology, Ariz. State U., 1980; M of Internat. Mgmt., Am. Grad. Sch. Internat. Mgmt., Glendale, Ariz., 1982. Chemist Motorola Inc., Phoenix, 1980-82; fin. planning, adminstrv. mgr. Motorola Inc., Mesa, Ariz., 1984-85; process engineer Motorola Inc., Mesa, 1983-84, 85-86; mgr. fin. and tax planning M.P.S. Acctg. and Tax Services, Chandler, Ariz., 1986—. Cubmaster Boy Scouts Am., Chandler, Ariz., 1980—. Mem. Electrochem. Soc., Am. Chem. Soc., Internat. Platform Assn. Republican. Mormon. Home and Office: MPS Acctg & Tax Svcs 22231 S 118th St Chandler AZ 85249

PEACH, JUDITH ELAINE, aerospace engineer; b. Ft. Belvoir, Va., Oct. 20, 1955; d. Robert Malcolm and May Evelyn (Boone) P. BS in Aerospace Engring. cum laude, U. Tenn., 1977; MS in Engring., UCLA, 1982. Rsch. asst. U. Tenn., Knoxville; project test engr. Arnold Rsch. Orgn., Arnold AFB, Tenn.; mem. tech. staff, project engr. The Aerospace Corp., 1986-88; mgr. advanced satellite control sys. The Aerospace Corp., L.A., 1988—; pres. The Aerospace Women's Com., 1989—. Mem. Manhattan Athletic Club, Air Force Assn., Am. Mgmt. Assn., Internat. Found. Telemetry (chair tech. session 1989), Women Mgmt.

PEACHES, DANIEL, government official; b. Kayenta, Ariz., Sept. 2, 1940; s. Henry and Adelaide (Donald) P.; m. Carolotta Boone, Sept. 15, 1955; children: Ivis, Aarow, Thaddeus, Shawna. BS in Polit. Sci., No. Ariz. U., 1967; postgrad., U. N.Mex.; LLd, Navajo Community Coll., 1975. Staff adminstr. Navajo Nation, Window Rock, Ariz., 1971-83; scholarship officer Navajo Nation, 1973-78, dep. dir. office of legis. affairs, 1988—; state legislator State of Ariz., Phoenix, 1975-85; bus. instr. Leupp Sch., Ariz., 1987-88; bus./govt. cons. Kayenta, Ariz., 1985-87; chmn. bd. regents Navajo Community Coll., 1988—. Pres. Navajo Mt. Soil & Water Conservation Dist., Kayenta, 1985—, Dineh Coop., Inc., Chiule, Ariz., 1975—, Navajo Community Coll., Tsaile, 1988—; sec. Northland Pioneer Coll., Holbrook, Ariz., 1985—; mem. Indian Commn. of Ariz., 1971-78, Nat. Adv. Council on Indian Edn., 1972-76, Higher Edn. Consortium, Washington, 1988—. Recipient Presdl. Commendation, Pres. Gerald Ford, 1976. Mem. Native Am. Cultural Exchange Ctr. (pres. 1988—). Republican. Presbyterian. Home: Wetherill Hill Dr PO Box 1801 Kayenta AZ 86033 Office: Northerland Pioneer College 1200 E Hermosa Dr Holbrook AZ 86025

PEAIRE, VICTORIA LYNN, marketing executive; b. Durand, Wis., Nov. 27, 1961; d. Fredrick and Brenda Lee (Bauer) Hineslev; m. David Wayne Peaire, Apr. 16, 1988. BA, U. So. Maine, 1984. Reporter, anchor Westbrook (Maine) Cablevision, 1983-84; asst. program coordinator Community Diabetes Control Program, Riverside, Calif., 1984-86; field rep. Am. Diabetes Assn., Riverside, Calif., 1986; account exec. PacifiCare Health Systems, Cypress, Calif., 1986-88; enrollment & mktg. rep. Ptnrs. Health Plan, San Bernardino, Calif., 1988—. Mem. Women in Communications, Inc., San Bernardino of C., Redlands C. of C., Nat. Assn. Female Execs., Am. Assn. Univ. Women, YMCA, U. So. Maine Alumni, Chi Delphia. Roman Catholic. Office: Ptnrs Health Plan 16855 W Bernardo Dr Ste 307 San Diego CA 92127

PEARL, JULIE CHAIKIN, lawyer; b. Detroit, May 23, 1960; d. Jack William and Faye (Chaikin) P. BA, Stanford U., 1981; MPA, Harvard U., 1986; JD, U. Calif., Hastings, 1987. Bar: Calif. 1988. Translator Internat. Interpreter's Svc., N.Y.C., 1981-82; founder, prin. artist Ont. Soft Sculpture Gallery, Toronto, Can., 1982-83; asst. to sr. producer ABC-News Nightline, London, 1986; spl. projects atty. Office Atty. Gen. of Calif., Sacramento, 1987-89, dep. atty. gen., 1989—. Author: Symposium 87: White-Collar Crime, 1988; contbr. numerous articles to profl. jours. Mem. ABA, Calif. Bar Assn., Amnesty Internat. Office: Atty Gen's Office 1515 K St Sacramento CA 95814

PEARLMAN, DANIEL LAWRENCE, advertising executive, public relations executive, sports marketing executive; b. N.Y.C., Aug. 13, 1946; s. Benedict and Muriel (Halpern) P.; m. Lynn Lubin, Oct. 10, 1970 (div. 1973). AB, UCLA, 1968, MBA, 1970. Account exec. Young and Rubicam, N.Y.C., 1970-73; account supr. Ogilvy and Mather, N.Y.C. and Los Angeles, 1973-77; v.p. Admktg. Inc., Los Angeles, 1977-79; sr. v.p. Carl Terzian Assoc., Los Angeles, 1979-83; pres., chief exec. officer Pearlman Wohl Inc., Los Angeles, 1983-87, Pearlman Group, Inc., Los Angeles, 1988—. Bd. dirs. Scopus Soc., Beverly Hills, Calif., Los Angeles Inst. Contemporary Art, Pres. Adv. Council City of Hope, Los Angeles. Recipient Andy award Denver Advt. Club, 1975, Lulu award Los Angeles Advt. Women Am., 1981. Mem. Los Angeles Advt. Club (Clio award 1979), Advt. Agy. Assn. Am., Pub. Relations Soc. Am. Home: 10450 Wilshire Blvd Los Angeles CA 90024 Office: Pearlman Group Inc 10000 Washington Blvd Suite N-220 Culver City CA 90232

PEARLMAN, MARION OLA, educational administrator, actress, consultant; b. Mechanicsville, N.Y., Dec. 24, 1920; d. Charles Forrest and Minnie (Mayhew) McBride; m. Albert M. Pearlman, June 9, 1963 (dec. Jan. 1985); 1 son, Michael Edward. B.S., SUNY-Buffalo, 1951; M.Ed., U. Ariz., 1959. Tchr., Pierce Creek Sch., Binghamton, N.Y., 1940-42; tchr. Skaneateles, N.Y., 1942-43; vacation relief agt., reservation clk., ticket agt., auditor, supr. sales control Am. Airlines, Buffalo, 1943-48; ins. analyst Aetna Casualty and Surety Co., Buffalo, 1948-49; tchr., Lancaster, N.Y., 1949-51, University Heights, Tucson, Ariz., 1951-59; Livingston, Calif., 1959-60; cons. elem. edn. County Office Edn., Napa, Calif., supr. Alum Rock Sch. Dist., San Jose, Calif., 1961-62; supr. schs. Nogales, Ariz., 1962-63; tch. Gump Sch. for retarded, blind, emotionally handicapped, deaf, trainable and educable retarded, 1964-78; prin. Valencia Sch., Sunnyside Unified Sch. Dist. #12, Tucson, 1978-83; pvt. cons., 1983—; tchr. spl. edn. Tokono O'otham High Sch., Parago Reservation; actress Sunset Years, Access TV, 1984—; lectr. Kans. State Tchrs. Coll., Emporia. Mem. exec. com. Tucson House for Retarded; bd. dirs. Beacon Found. for Mentally Retarded; active PTA, PTO; del. to Ariz. State Assembly. Cert. elem. tchr. Democrat. Jewish. Mem. NEA, Ariz. Edn. Assn., Tucson Edn. Assn., Sunnyside Adminstrs. Assn., AAUW (membership com., del. to nat. conv.), Phi Delta Kappa, Pi Lambda Theta.

PEARNE, GEORGE REGINALD, poet; b. 1948. BA in Geography, U. Utah, 1974. Cert. in secondary edn., Hong Kong. Instr. geography, history, English lang., antiques Chinese U. Hong Kong, 1980-87; poet Sunnymead, Calif., 1987—. Inventor ednl. games. Recipient Merit cert. for Distinction in Poetry Writing Coll. Ea. Utah, 1973, Appreciation, Devoted Sentiments and Apostolic Blessing of His Holiness Pope Paul VI, 1973, Plaudits from President Nixon, 1972, Gov. Utah, 1973, Prime Min. of New Zealand, 1975. Home: 23806 Wolcott Dr Sunnymead CA 92388

PEARSALL, ROSELLEN DEE, insurance executive; b. Ft. Dix, N.J., Aug. 15, 1945; d. Raymond Donald and Rosemary (Dannenberg) P. BS in Nursing, U. Ky., 1967. RN U. Ky. Med. Ctr., Lexington, 1967-68; RN Cardiac Care Unit Cedars of Lebanon Hosp., Los Angeles, 1968-69; rehab. nurse cons. Employers Ins. of Wausau, Los Angeles, 1969-76; asst. v.p. rehab. services Fremont Compensation Ins. Co., Los Angeles, 1976—; ins. adv. bd. Casa Colina Inc., Pomona, Calif., 1984—. Recipient Cert. Achievement in Bus. and Industry Los Angeles YWCAs, 1978, 80. Mem. Nat. Assn. Rehab. Profls. in the Pvt. Sector (legis. chair Calif.), Nat. Rehab. Assn. (pres. So. Calif. chpt. 1979-80, Outstanding Achievement award 1981), Rehab. Nurses Soc. (founding pres. 1972-74, Outstanding Services award 1980, Greatest Support award 1984-85), Ins. Rehab. Study Group. Club: Los Angeles Athletic. Office: Fremont Compensation Ins Co 1709 W 8th St Los Angeles CA 90017

PEARSE, LUCRETIA GROVER CRATER, radio reading service dir.; b. Dover, N.J., Aug. 7, 1933; d. Ronald David and Phyllis Ellen (Grover) C.; m. Frederic Montagu, Aug. 27, 1955 (div. Mar. 1971); children: Paul Grover, Elizabeth Crater. BA, Sweet Briar (Va.) Coll., 1955. Tchr. Livingstone (N.J.) Pub. Schs., 1966-67; sr. interviewer Div. of Employment Security State of Mass., Worcester, 1971-74; personnel generalist Data Gen. Corp., Southboro, Mass., 1974-76; field eligibility clk., operation coordinator Sun Sounds of Ariz., Phoenix, 1979-83, dir., 1983—. Assn. of Radio Reading Services (pres. 1988—, bd. dirs. 1986-88). Republican. Episcopalian. Office: Sun Sounds of Ariz 3124 E Roosevelt Phoenix AZ 85008

PEARSON, ALFRED S(TANLEY), JR., dentist; b. Seattle, Jan. 13, 1948; s. Alfred Stanley Sr. and Pauline Ruby (Antrim) P.; m. Janice Marie D'Arielli, Dec. 15, 1972; children: Cameron Jon, Christian Charles. BS, Wash. State U., 1970; DDS, U. Wash., Seattle, 1974. Pvt. practice Walla Walla, Wash., 1974—. Pres. Assumption Home and Sch., Walla Walla, 1986. Mem. ADA, Wash. State Dental Assn. Republican. Roman Catholic. Home: 733 Bryant St Walla Walla WA 99362 Office: 121 W Poplar Walla Walla WA 99362

PEARSON, ANTHONY ROBERT, securities executive; b. L.A., Jan. 10, 1939; s. Alberto Roy and Margaretha (Krohn) P.; m. Barbara Ann Laing, Mar. 1, 1960 (div. 1973); children: Andrew Rhodes, Wendy Laing; m. Barbara Ann Morton, May 11, 1973; children: Barbara Stone, David Shell, Joe Shell, Diane Campbell, Harold Shell. Student, Oreg. State Coll., 1957-58, Pasadena (Calif.) City Coll., 1958-60, U. So. Calif., 1960-65, UCLA, 1960-65. Sales mgr. Peason Trucking, L.A., 1960-68; acct. exec. Paine Webber, L.A., 1968-73; pres. Petrovest, L.A., 1976-82, Pearson Petroleum, L.A., 1982-83; acct. exec. Bateman Eicher, Century City, Calif., 1983-84; v.p. investment Drexel Burnham, Beverly Hills, Calif., 1984-88, Smith, Barney, Harris & Upham, Beverly Hills, 1988—; lectr. UCLA, Santa Monica Coll.; cons. in field. With USN. Mem. Jonathan Club, Lahaina Yacht Club, Dana Point Yacht Club, Masons, Shriners. Republican. Episcopalian. Home: 220 S Arden Los Angeles CA 90004 Office: Smith Barney Harris & Upham 9346 Civic Ctr Dr Los Angeles CA 90213

PEARSON, BRYAN GEOFFREY, airline executive; b. Ipswich, Eng., Nov. 19, 1931; came to U.S., 1952; s. Cyril Victor Bolton and Dorothy Constance (Edwards) P.; m. Ursula Margarete Gadischke, July 14, 1956 (div. 1968); children: Michael Grant, Erika Margarete; m. Celestine Aimee Turi, Dec. 29, 1976; children: Teri'i Victor, Tamara Dorothy. Ed., Framlingham (Eng.) Coll. Resident mgr. Maui Beach Hotel, Moorea, Tahiti, 1971-73; gen. mgr. Moana Hotel, Moorea, 1973-74, Maui Beach Hotel, Moorea, 1975-76; regional sales mgr. Sanico Chem. Co., Honolulu, 1977-80; v.p. sales, mktg. Island Airlines Hawaii, Honolulu, 1980-83, Pacific Air Express, Honolulu, 1983-84; v.p. cargo Mid Pacific Airlines, Honolulu, 1984-88; mng. dir. Pacific Islands Airlines subs. Continental Airlines, Honolulu, 1988-89; dir. cargo Hawaiian Airlines, Honolulu, 1989—. Appeared under stage name of Bryan Grant in West End of London Prodns. of Charlesy Aunt, Mrs. Dot and First Person Singular, 1950-52. Mem. San Francisco Air Freight Assn., L.A. Air Freight Assn., Nat. Def. Transp. Assn., Indsl. Traffic Assn. Hawaii, U.S. Navy League, Brit. Commonwealth Club Hawaii (v.p.), La Mariana Sailing Club, Elks. Republican.

PEARSON, DAVID S., hotel manager; b. Portland, Oreg., Apr. 9, 1942; s. Samuel S. and Barbara E. (Olson) P.; children: Lisa Claire, Jennifer. BS, U. N.Mex., 1966. Gen. mgr. Ramada Inns, several locations, 1966-68, Howard Johnson's, Albuquerque, 1968-72; income auditor Salishan Lodge, 1973-76; travelling supr. Thunderbird/Red Lion, Pacific N.W., 1976-78; gen. mgr., regional supr. Ambassador Inn's, S.W., 1978-81; gen. mgr. TraveLodge, Corpus Christi, Tex., 1981-83; regional mgr. TrustHouse Forte Internat. (TraveLodge), S.W. and Rocky Mountains, 1983—. Office: Trust House Fortel 2028 E Fremont St Las Vegas NV 89101

PEARSON, JAMES EDWARD, anesthesiologist; b. Grand Junction, Colo., Aug. 3, 1956; s. Thomas Harris and June Elizabeth (Cook) P. BA, U. Colo., 1978, MD, 1982. Diplomate Am. Bd. Med. Examiners. Resident in anesthesiology Stanford Med. Ctr., Calif., 1986; pvt. practice anesthesiology San Francisco, 1986—; cons. anesthesiologist Interplast, Palo Alto, Calif., 1986—; chmn. dept. anesthesiology St. Rose Hosp., Haywood, Calif. Contbr. articles to profl. jours. Mem. Am. Soc. Anesthesiology, Calif. Soc. Anesthesiology, Soc. for Anesthesia in Developing Countries, Peninsula Sportsman's Club, Mortar Bd., Phi Beta Kappa. Republican. Office: 1259 El Camino #330 Menlo Park CA 94025

PEARSON, JOHN, mechanical engineer; b. Leyburn, Yorkshire, U.K., Apr. 24, 1923; came to U.S., 1930, naturalized, 1944; s. William and Nellie Pearson; m. Ruth Ann Billhardt, July 10, 1944; children—John, Armin, Roger. B.S.M.E., Northwestern U., 1949, M.S., 1951. Registered profl. engr., Calif. Research engr. Naval Ordnance Test Sta., China Lake, Calif., 1951-55, head warhead research br., 1955-58, head solid dynamics bd., 1958-59, head detonation physics group, 1959-67; head detonation physics div. Naval Weapons Ctr., China Lake, Calif., 1967-83, sr. research scientist, 1983—; cons., lectr. in field; founding mem. adv. bd. Ctr. for High Energy Forming, U. Denver; mem. bd. examiners Sambalpur U., India, 1982-83. Author: Explosive Working of Metals, 1963; Behavior of Metals Under Impulsive Loads, 1954; contbr. articles to profl. publs; patentee impulsive loading, explosives applications. Charter mem. Sr. Exec. Service U.S., 1979. Served with C.E., U.S. Army, 1943-46. Recipient L.T.E. Thompson medal, 1965, William B. McLean medal, 1979, Superior Civilian Service medal U.S. Navy, 1984, Haskell G. Wilson award, 1985, cert. of recognition Sec. Navy, 1975, Merit award Dept. Navy, 1979, cert. of commendation Sec. Navy, 1981. Fellow ASME; mem. Am. Soc. Metals, Am. Phys. Soc., N.Y. Acad. Scis., AIME, NSPE, Fed. Exec. League, Sigma Xi, Tau Beta Pi, Pi Tau Sigma, Triangle. Home and Office: 858 N Primavera Rd PO Box 1390 Ridgecrest CA 93555

PEARSON, KEITH LAURENCE, environmental scientist; b. Chgo., Apr. 1, 1929; s. Victor R. and Ingeborg E. (Olson) P.; m. Ellen M. O'Dell, May 28, 1955; 1 child, Brian V. BA, Augustana Coll., 1951; MA, U. Ariz., 1965, PhD, 1969. Asst. prof. U. Wis., Superior, 1967-68; assoc. prof. No. Ariz. U., Flagstaff, 1968-76; environ. analyst Bur. Land Mgmt., Washington, 1976-78; environ. planner Bur. Land Mgmt., Phoenix, 1979—. Author: The Indian in American History, 1973; contbg. author: A Slice of Life, 1975; contbr. articles to profl. jours. Fellow Am. Anthropol. Assn.; mem. Soc. for Applied Anthropology. Democrat. Episcopalian. Home: 12634 N Rosewood Ave Phoenix AZ 85029

PEARSON, KORT VICTOR, manufacturing executive; b. Newport Beach, Calif., Dec. 20, 1960; s. Victor LLoyd and Marylin (Willats) P.; m. Kymberly Lynn Moll, May 16, 1986; 1 child, Kristopher. BA, Ea. Wash. U., 1982. Owner, pres. Full Phase Prodns., Commerce, Calif., 1981—; v.p., gen. mgr. Colonial Dames Co., Ltd., Commerce, 1986—, also bd. dirs., 1988—; bd. dirs. Laguna Riviere Hotel, Laguna Beach, Calif., 1989—. Republican. Office: Colonial Dames Co Ltd 6820 E Watcher St Commerce CA 90040

PEARSON, MARTHA ELISABETH, teacher; b. Pasadena, Calif., July 28, 1944; d. Ira Emil and Jaunita Ruth Kelley; m. Lynn Allen Pearson, July 22, 1966; children: Andrew Allen, Robert Anthony. AA, Pasadena City Coll., 1966; BA, Pasadena Coll. (now Point Loma Nazarene Coll.), 1969. Cert. elem. and secondary tchr., Calif. Tchr. elem. La Rosa Sch., Temple City, Calif., 1969-72; tchr. substitute Temple City Schs., 1972-73, Santee and Lakeside Sch. Dists., Calif., 1973-74; tchr. Playmate Presch., La Mesa, Calif., 1974-76; tchr. elem. El Cajon (Calif.) Valley Christian Sch., 1978-80, Hesperia (Calif.) Sch. Dist., 1980—; tutor reading Powerline Program, Santee, 1973-77; facilitator Project WILD, 1984—. Co-author sci. lab. curriculum, 1971. Bd. dirs. High Desert Youth Soccer League, Apple Valley, Calif., 1986-88, Hesperia (Calif.) Ch. Nazarene, 1985-88, Victorville (Calif.) Nazarene, 1983-85; mem. Hesperia Jr. High Sch. Roadrunner Parent Tchr. Orgn., 7th Grade Basketball Team. Grantee Hesperia Sch. Dist., 1983, 87. Mem. Mountain Desert Reading Council, Hesperia Educators Assn. (site rep. 1988-89). Republican. Office: Cottonwood Sch 8850 Cottonwood Hesperia CA 92345

PEARSON, RICHARD JARVIS, diversified manufacturing company executive; b. Chgo., June 3, 1925; s. Andrall E. and Dorothy M. (MacDonald) P.; m. Janice Lee Pope, Mar. 2, 1951; 1 child, Douglas R. BA, U. So. Calif., 1946; MBA, Harvard U., 1947. Dir. mktg. Bireley's, Hollywood, Calif., 1947-55; dir. mktg. Forest Lawn Meml. Park, Glendale, Calif., 1955-57, Revell, Inc., Venice, Calif., 1957-60; dir. mktg. Avery Label Co., Monrovia, Calif., 1960-64, v.p., gen. mgr., 1964-70; group v.p. Avery Internat., San Marino, Calif., 1970-76, exec. v.p., 1976-81; exec. v.p., chief operating officer Avery Internat., Pasadena, Calif., 1981-83, pres., chief operating officer, 1983—; bd. dirs. Ameron, Inc., Monterey Park, Calif., Ducommun, Inc., Los Angeles. Chmn. United Way, 1982-83; bd. dirs. Boy Scouts Am., 1983-84; bd. dirs. Am. Heart Assn., 1986—; trustee Ponoma Coll., 1988—. Served to lt. (j.g.) USN, 1946. Mem. Merchants and Mfrs. Assn. (bd. dirs. 1986—). Republican. Presbyterian. Clubs: Annandale, Calif., PGA West. Home: 1046 Oak Grove Pl San Marino CA 91108 Office: Avery Corp 150 N Orange Grove Blvd Box 7090 Pasadena CA 91103

PEASE, CAROL HELENE, oceanographer; b. Bay City, Mich., Dec. 29, 1949; d. George Olson and Mernabelle Hattie (Laabs) P.; m. Alexander Jeffrey Chester, June 16, 1974 (div. May, 1978). Student, U. Mich., 1968-71; BS in Math., U. Miami, 1972; MS in Phys. Oceanography, U. Wash., 1975, MS in Meteorology, 1981; postgrad., U. Wash., Seattle, 1985. Rsch. asst. Arctic ice dynamics joint expt. U. Wash., Seattle, 1972-75; oceanographer Pacific Marine Environ. Lab., Nat. Oceanic and Atmospheric Adminstrn., Seattle, 1975-78, sea ice project leader, 1978—. Contbr. articles to profl. jours. Mem. Arboretum Found., Seattle, 1975—, Seattle Art Mus., 1978—, Nat. Women's Polit. Caucus, Seattle, 1984—; sustaining mem. Friends of KUOW, KCTS Found., Seattle, 1978, 82. Recipient performance awards NOAA, 1977, 82, 85, 87, 88, Adminstr.'s award, 1988. Mem. AAAS, Assn. Women in Sci., Am. Geophys. Union, Am. Meteorol. Soc. (session chair symposium meterology and oceanography N.Am. high latitudes 1984, mem. standing com. on polar meteorology and oceanography 1985—, chmn. 1987—, session chair, co-convener conf. on polar meteorology and oceanography 1988), Corinthian Yacht Club (Seattle), Valkyrien (sec. 1978-81), Daus. Norway. Clubs: Corinthian Yacht (Seattle). Lodges: Valkyrien (sec. 1978-81), Daughters of Norway. Office: Pacific Marine Environ Lab 7600 Sand Point Way NE Seattle WA 98115

PEASE, JANINE BERNADETTE, college president; b. Nespelem, Wash., Sept. 17, 1949; d. Benjamin and Margery Louise (Jordan) P.; m. Sam V. Windy Boy, Jr., July 23, 1975 (div. Jan. 1983); children: Roses, Vernon. BA in Sociology, Cen. Wash. U., 1970, BA in Anthropology, 1970; MEd in Higher Edn., Mont. State U., 1987. Dep. dir. Wash. Gov. Youth Commn., Olympia, Wash., 1971; tutor counselor Big Bend Community Coll., Moses Lake, Wash., 1971-72; women's counselor Navajo Community coll., Many Farms, Ariz., 1972; upward bound dir. Big Bend Community Coll., Moses Lake, 1972-75; adult edn. dir. Crow Tribal Cen. Edn., Crow Agy., Mont., 1975-79; edn. evaluator Fort Belknap (Mont.) Indian Community, 1979-80; Indian careers dir. Eastern Mont. Coll., Billings, 1981-82; pres. Little Big Horn Coll., Crow Agy., 1982—; bd. dirs. Am. Indian Higher Edn. Com., Washington, 1985—; mem. Coll. Bd. Minority Concerns, N.Y.C., 1988—. County chair Bighorn County Dems., Hardin, Mong., 1983-88; coordinator Native Ams. for ACtion Now, Crow Agy., 1988-89. Fellow Mont. State U. Tribal Coll. Devel., Bozeman, Mont., 1985-88; Assn. for Am. Indian Affairs, No. Lights Inst. (bd. dirs. 1987—), Nighthawks. Democrat. Baptist. Office: Little Big Horn Coll PO Box 370 Crow Agency MT 59022

PEAT-HANNA, RICHARD SAMS, marketing executive; b. Porum, Okla., Feb. 5, 1942; s. Charles Vester and Grace Helen (Price) Hanna; m. Patricia Wells, June 20, 1970 (div. Oct. 15, 1971); m. Margaret Elizabeth, July 25, 1977; children: Jeanette Daunyelle, Sasha Deanne. Mgmt. tng. analyst State of Calif., Sacramento, 1971-73; counselor Sacramento City Coll., 1974-75, mgr., 1975-76; mgr. employee devel. Hastings Corp., Stanford, Calif., 1976-79; sales rep. Neutrogena Corp., Los Angeles, 1979-82, western region sales mgr., 1982—. Regional v.p., Young Republicans, Calif., 1968. Mem. Steering Com. Peace & Freedom Party, Calif., 1970; fund raiser Dem. party, Calif., 1972. Served with USAF, 1960-64. Democrat. Home: 129 Riviera Dr Oceanside CA 92054

PECCORINI, FRANCISCO LETONA, retired philosopher, educator; b. San Miguel, El Salvador, Nov. 27, 1915; came to U.S., 1962, naturalized, 1976; s. Miguel Vinerta and Julia (Letona) P.; m. Teresa Samayoa; 1 stepdau., Teresa Moran Enneman. Ph. Licentiate, Colegio de San Francisco Javier, Burgos, Spain, 1943; Ph.D., Pontifical U. Comillas, Santender, Spain, 1958. Tchr. San Jose High Sch., San Salvador, 1943-47; writer Estudios Centro Americanos, San Salvador, 1947-52; editor mag. Estudios Centro Americanos, 1952-55; prof. philosophy U. Deusto, Bilbao, Spain, 1956-58, Nat. U., San Salvador, 1959-62; asst. prof. U. San Diego, 1963-66; mem. faculty Calif. State U., Long Beach, 1966—, prof. philosophy, 1972-86, prof. emeritus, 1986. Author: A Method of Self-Orientation to Thinking, 1970, La Voluntad del Pueblo en la Emancipación de El Salvador, 1972, From Gentile's "Actualism" to Sciacca's "Idea," 1981, On to the World of Freedom. A Kantian Meditation on Finite Selfhood, 1982, Selfhood as Thinking Thought in The Work of Gabriel Marcel, 1987; also articles: Mem. Nat. Acad. Historia of San Salvador, Acad. Lang. El Salvador, Medieval Acad. Am., Medieval Assn. Pacific, Am. Philos. Assn., Inst. for Ency. of Ultimate Reality and Meaning (Toronto). Office: Calif State U Dept Philosophy Long Beach CA 90840 *Died, June 5, 1989.*

PECHET, JOY ELIZABETH, project planner, business owner, real estate salesman; b. Seattle, July 9, 1954; d. Meleo Samuel and Adelle (Bornstein) P.; m. Gregory Paul Archer, Sept. 4, 1984 (div. Feb. 1988). BS in CE, MIT, 1977. Intern Carnegie Endowment for Internat. Peace, Washington, 1978-79; transp. analyst Automated Scis. Group, Inc., Silver Spring, Md., 1979-80; civil engr. U.S. Dept. Transp., Cambridge, Mass., 1980; real estate analyst Parkland Construction Co., Marlboro, Mass., 1982-84; program analyst Rockwell Internat., El Segundo, Calif., 1984-85; mem. computer staff Hughes Aircraft Co., El Segundo, 1985-87; sr. project planner Euro Disneyland, Paris, 1987—. Political Sci. Dept. fellow MIT, 1977; Urban Planning Dept. fellow and grantee MIT, 1977. Club: MIT. Home: 2718 Centrania St Lakewood CA 90712 Office: Walt Disney Imagineering 1401 Flower St Glendale CA 91201

PECK, CHARLES KARL, JR., writer, producer; b. N.Y.C., Apr. 1, 1921; s. Charles K. and Lena (Molnar) P. BA, U. N.C., 1942; MFA, Yale U., 1948. Screenwriter, producer 1951—; prin. Charles Peck Prodns., Los Angeles, 1960—. Producer, writer: (films) The Basketball Fix, 1951, Yankee Buccaneer, 1952, Seminole, 1953 (Acad. award nomination 1954), The Warrior, 1955, The Key, 1955, Clash by Night, 1956, Matador, 1960, others, (TV spls.) Philco Playhouse (Emmy award nomination 1962), Omnibus, 1958, others, (Broadway prodns.) Break It Up, 1951, When in Rome, 1953, High Heels, 1957, Christine, 1960, La Strada, 1970, (off-Broadwat prodns.) Terrific, 1983, Today Tomorrow and Yesterday, 1984, (London prodns.) Roar of the Dove, 1960, Finale, 1964, Love Life Again; creator: (TV series) Paris Precinct, 1954, The Lawyer, 1963, The Challenger, 1969, Caribe, 1972, others; contbr. to TV series The Defenders, Ben Casey (Emmy award nomination 1952), East Side, West Side, (TV films) True Confessions, 1983, Visible Proof, 1985, (TV pilot) Island Force One, 1987; author: No Place for a Hero, Duiler, 1971. Served with OSS, 1942-45, col. USAFR, 1947-80. Office: 6310 San Vincente Blvd Ste 407 Los Angeles CA 90048

PECK, DONALD HARVEY, chiropractor; b. Oak Park, Ill., July 18, 1945; s. Donald Ray and Dorothy Sylvia (LaFlamme) P.; m. Mary Evelyn Lamb, June 15, 1964 (div. 1971); children: Donald Lee, Nancy Ellen; m. Cheryl Jean Cox, July 7, 1973; children: Richard Krom Watkins Jr., Bradley Alan, Steven Edward. AA, Mt. San Antonio Coll., 1966; DC, Palmer Coll. of Chiropractic, 1970. Diplomate Nat. Bd. Chiropractic Examiners. Engring. technician Besteel Corp., Industry, Calif., 1965-66, City of Ontario, Calif., 1966-67; supr. Mercy Hosp., Davenport, Iowa, 1967-70; pvt. practice chiropractor San Bernardino and Redlands, Calif., 1971-81; pvt. practice chiropractics Cottonwood, Ariz., 1981—; instr. Yavapai Coll. Clarkdale, Ariz., 1982-86. Scoutmaster Grand Canyon Coun. Boy Scouts Am., Cottonwood, Az., 1974—, Calif. Inland Empire Coun. Boy Scouts Am., Redlands, 1974—; regional commr. Am. Youth Soccer Orgn., Cottonwood, 1977-88 (regional commr. 1984-88); chief instr. Ariz. Game and Fish Dept., Cottonwood, 1983—. Recipient Award of Merit Boy Scouts Am., 1980, Silver Beaver award, 1988; named Vol. of Yr. Verde Valley C. of C., 1987. Mem. Kiwanis (bd. dirs. 1985-87), Order of Arrow (com. advisor 1989—). Republican. Office: 703 S Main St Cottonwood AZ 86326

PECK, ELLIE ENRIQUEZ, state administrator; b. Sacramento, Oct. 21, 1934; d. Rafael Enriquez and Eloisa Garcia Rivera; m. Raymond Charles Peck, Sept. 5, 1957; children—Reginaldo, Enrico, Francisca Guerrero, Teresa, Linda, Margaret, Raymond Charles, Christina. Student polit. sci. Sacramento State U., 1974. Tng. services coordinator Calif. Div. Hwys., Sacramento, 1963-67; tech. and mgmt. cons., Sacramento, 1968-78; expert examiner Calif. Personnel Bd., 1976-78; tng. cons. Calif. Personnel Devel. Center, Sacramento, 1978; spl. cons. Calif. Commn. on Fair Employment and Housing, 1978; community services rep. U.S. Bur. of Census, No. Calif. counties, 1978-80; spl. cons. Calif. Dept. Consumer Affairs, Sacramento, 1980-83, project dir. Golden State Sr. Discount Program, 1980-83; asst. chief of staff and dir. spl. programs for Calif. Lt. Gov., 1983—; mem. Sacramento Community Services Planning Council, 1987—; chairperson Calif. Suprs.' Forum, 1966. Trustee, Stanford Settlement, Inc., Sacramento, 1975-79, hon. life trustee, 1979—; bd. dirs. Sacramento Emergency Housing Center, 1974-77; v.p. Comision Femenil Nacional, Inc., 1987—; del. Democratic Nat. Conv., 1976; mem. exec. bd. Calif. Dem. Central Com. Recipient numerous awards, including Outstanding Community Service award Comuicaciones Unidos de Norte Atzlan, 1975, 77, Outstanding Service award, Chicano/Hispanic Dem. Caucus, 1979, Vol. Service award Calif. Human Devel. Corp., 1981, Democrat of Yr. Sacramento County Dem. Com., 1987, Outstanding Advocate Calif. Sr. Legis., 1988. Mem. Nat. Women's Polit, Caucas, Mexican-Am. Polit Assn, Ombudsman Assn. (advocacy award), Hispanic C. of C. Club: Hispanic Dem. Sacramento County (v.p. 1982-83). Author U.S. Office Consumer Edn. publ., 1982, Calif. Dept. Consumer Affairs publ., 1981. Home: 2667 Coleman Way Sacramento CA 95818

PECK, JEFFREY WAYNE, broadcast sales executive; b. Culver City, Calif., Sept. 9, 1941; s. Melva (Bess) P. BS in Bus. Adminstrn., U. So. Calif., 1965. Account exec. Sta. KHJ, Los Angeles, 1972-78, mgr. nat. sales, 1978-79, sales mgr., 1979-81; gen. mgr. Sta. KPRI/KOGO, San Diego, 1981-82, Sta. KNAC, Long Beach, Calif., 1983-84; gen. sales mgr. Sta. KHJ, Los Angeles, 1984-86; pres. United Broadcast Sales, Redondo Beach, Calif., 1986—; cons. Sta. KIFM San Diego Radio, 1981-82. Co-author: (self-help cassette) Run for Your Life, 1973. Served with U.S. Army, 1966-68. Republican. Office: United Broadcast Sales 420 S Francisca Redondo Beach CA 90277

PECK, MARGO STUDENT, nursing educator; b. Düsseldorf, Fed. Republic Germany, Feb. 8, 1959; d. Richard Allen and Elaine Ossette (Solberg) Student; m. Jeffrey Scott Peck, Aug. 1, 1981; 1 child, Andrea Lynn. BA in Communication Arts, Pacific Lutheran U., 1981. Pub. relations San Mateo (Calif.) County Transit, 1980; newspaper reporter The Vidette, Montesano, Wash., 1981; nursing edn. asst. Cen. Wash. Hosp., Wenatchee, Wash., 1983—; bd. dirs. Apple Valley Credit Union, Wenatchee, 1985-87. Mem. Career Women's Network, Am. Assn. Univ. Women. Republican. Lutheran. Office: Cen Wash Hosp 1300 Fuller St Wenatchee WA 98801

PECK, MARIE JOHNSTON, Latin American area studies consultant; b. New Haven, Aug. 15, 1932; d. James Howard and Marie Anna Christina (Voigt) Johnston; m. Austin Monroe Peck, July 9, 1952 (div. 1959). AS, Larson-Quinnipiac, 1952; BA, U. N.Mex., 1968, PhD, 1974. Writer, coord. bilingual edn. coll. edn. U. N.Mex., Albuquerque, 1976-78; pres., owner Southwestern Images, Inc., Shawnee Mission, Kans., 1978—; Vis. scholar U. N.Mex., Albuquerque, 1983; vis. instr. Wofford Coll., Spartanburg, S.C., 1984; adj. instr. humanities Johnson County Community Coll., Overland Park, Kans., 1985-86, coord. Brown V. Topeka Conf., 1986; cons. Brown V. Topeka Project, Merriam, Kans., 1984-88; bd. dirs. Op. SER, Colorado Springs, Colo., Midcoast Radio, Inc., Kansas City; curriculum writer Albuquerque Pub. Schs., 1980-81. Contbr. articles to profl. jours. Mem. Internat. Trade Task Force Greater Kansas City. Fulbright scholar, 1981-82; Fgn. Lang. fellow HEW, 1967-71, Rsch. fellow Orng. Am. States, 1970. Mem. MLA, Latin Am. Studies Assn., Am. Assn. Tchrs. Spanish and Portugese, Midwest Assn. for Latin Am. Studies, Nat. Women's Studies Assn., Internat. Rels. Coun. (speakers bur. Kansas City 1986—), Internat. Trade Club Kansas City, Silicon Prairie Tech. Assn. Kansas City, Pacific Coast Coun. on Latin Am. Studies, Phi Beta Kappa. Home and Office: 209 Girard SE #6 Albuquerque NM 87106

PECK, PAMELA IRENE, banker; b. Paynesville, Minn., July 20, 1955; d. Walter Lowell and Rosemary Ann (Thielen) D.; m. William Thomas Hunter,

June 4, 1976 (div. June, 1987); 1 child, Sean Thomas; m. Howard Thomas Peck, June 10, 1989. Student, Coll. of St. Benedict, 1973-75. Sr. account exec. Data Protection Inc., North Hollywood, Calif., 1977-86; asst v.p. Southwest Bank, Vista, Calif., 1986-89; asst. v.p. fin. svcs. Bank of San Diego Datacorp, 1989—; guest speaker Simi Valley (Calif.) Unified Schs., 1988—; guest lectr. AAUW, Simi Valley Unified Sch. Dist. Sci. Conf., 1989. Mem. Nat. Assn. Bank Women, Les Amis du Vin. Republican. Roman Catholic. Office: Bank of San Diego North Hollywood CA 91607

PECK, RAYMOND CHARLES, SR., driver and traffic safety research specialist; b. Sacramento, Nov. 18, 1937; s. Emory Earl and Margaret Helen (Fiebiger) P.; m. Ellie Ruth Enriquez, Sept. 5, 1957; children: Teresa M. Peck Montijo, Linda M. Peck Heisler, Margaret H. Peck Ryzak, Raymond C., Christina M. BA in Exptl. Psychology, Calif. State U., Sacramento, 1961, MA in Exptl. Psychology, 1968. Jr. rsch. tech. Calif. Dept. Motor Vehicles, Sacramento, 1962-63, asst. social rsch. analyst, 1963-64, staff rsch. analyst, 1967-71, sr. rsch. analyst, program mgr., 1971-80, rsch. program specialist II, 1980, acting, chief rsch., 1980-81, rsch. program specialist II, 1981-84, chief of rsch., 1984—; cons. to Computing and Software, Inc., Mentoris Co., Sims & Assocs., Pub. Systems, Inc., Planning Rsch. Corp., Nat. Pub. Svcs. Rsch. Inst., Dunlap & Assocs., Sacramento Safety Council, Nat. Safety Council, Boston U., Sch. Pub. Health, Vt. Alcohol Rsch. Ctr.. Chmn. com. on operator regulation Transportation Rsch. Bd., Nat. Acad. Scis., 1976-82. Recipient Met. Life award of Hon., Nat. Safety Council, 1970, Met. Life Cert. of Commendation, 1972, A.R. Lauer award Human Factor Soc., 1981, award of Hon., award of Merit Traffic Safety Evaluation Rsch. Rev., 1983. Mem. Am. Statis. Assn., Western Psychol. Assn. Democrat. Contbr. articles to profl. jours.; editorial adv. bd. Jour. Safety Research, Accident Analysis and Prevention, Traffic Safety Evaluation Research Rev., Abstracts and Revs. in Alcohol and Driving. Home: 2667 Coleman Way Sacramento CA 95818 Office: Calif Dept Motor Vehicles 2415 First Ave Sacramento CA 95818

PECK, SHARON RAE, educator; b. Pasadena, Calif., Dec. 1, 1950; d. William Jason and Florine (Feinstein) Alexander; m. Stephen John Peck, Aug. 17, 1974. BA in Home Econs., Fresno U., 1973. Tchr. learning handicapped Visalia (Calif.) Unified Sch. Dist., 1980—; swimming tchr. Spl. Olympics, Visalia, 1986. Mem. Prevent Unwanted Pet Population, Visalia, 1988; treas. Ducks Unltd.-Happy Honkers, Tulare, Calif., 1986-87. Mem. NEA, Calif. Tchrs. Assn., Visalia Unified Tchrs. Assn. (rep. 1986-88). Democrat. Jewish. Office: Golden West High Sch 1717 N McAuliff Visalia CA 93291

PECKHAM, ROBERT FRANCIS, U.S. district judge; b. San Francisco, Nov. 3, 1920; s. Robert F. and Evelyn (Crowe) P.; m. Harriet M. Behring, Aug. 15, 1953 (dec. Apr. 1970); children: Ann Evelyn, Sara Esther; m. Carol Potter, June 9, 1974. A.B., Stanford U., 1941, LL.B., 1945; postgrad. in law, Yale U., 1941-42; LL.D., U. Santa Clara, 1973. Bar: Calif. 1945. Adminstrv. asst. to regional enforcement atty. OPA, 1942-43; pvt. practice Palo Alto and Sunnyvale, 1946-48; asst. U.S. atty., 1948-53, chief asst. criminal div., 1952-53; mem. firm Darwin, Peckham & Warren, San Francisco, Palo Alto and Sunnyvale, 1953-59; judge Superior Ct., Santa Clara County, Calif., 1959-66; presiding judge Superior Ct., 1961-63, 65-66; U.S. dist. judge No. Dist. Calif., 1966—, chief judge, 1976-88; trustee Foothill Coll. Dist., 1957-59, pres., 1959; mem. bd. visitors Stanford Law Sch., 1969-75, chmn., 1971-72; sr. mem. Am-Asia Law Del. of Asia Found., 1984-85, 87. State chmn. adv. bd. Friends Outside; coun. mem. Friends of Bancroft Libr., 1981-87. Recipient Brotherhood award NCCJ, 1968; recipient award for alt. dispute resolution leadership Ctr. for Pub. Resources, 1984, award for written scholarship, 1985. Fellow Am. Bar Found.; mem. ABA (chmn. Nat. Conf. Fed. Trial Judges 1983-84, ho. of dels. 1984—), U.S. Jud. Conf. (exec. com. 1987—), Fed. Bar Assn., San Francisco Bar Assn., Santa Clara County Bar Assn., Am. Law Inst., Am. Judicature Soc., Soc. Calif. Pioneers (bd. govs. 1984-87) Calif. Hist. Soc. (trustee 1974-78), Council Stanford Law Socs. (chmn. 1974-75), U.S. Dist. Ct. for No. Dist. Calif. Hist. Soc. (chmn. 1979—), World Affairs Coun. (trustee 1979-85), Asia Found. (sr. mem. Am.-Asia law del. 1984-85), Phi Beta Kappa, Phi Delta Phi. Office: US Dist Ct 450 Golden Gate Ave PO Box 36060 San Francisco CA 94102

PECKNER, DONALD, lawyer, engineer; b. N.Y.C., Mar. 15, 1928; s. Irvin Mortimer and Natalie (Breitman) P.; m. Doris Rosalind Bernstein, June 14, 1953; children: Lloyd Michael, Nancy Tina, Amy Beth. B in Metall. Engring., Polytech. Inst. Bklyn., 1949; MS, U. Pitts., 1968; JD, Loyola U., L.A., 1976. Engr. Westinghouse Electric Corp., Pitts., 1952-59; assoc. editor Reinhold Pub. Co., N.Y.C., 1959-64; dir. tech. communications dept. Climax Molybdenum Co., N.Y.C., 1964-69; asst. to v.p. resch. dept. Whittaker Corp., L.A., 1969-72; cons. TechCom, Santa Monica, Calif., 1972-76; assoc. Irwin, Hale & Jacobs, L.A., 1976-78; pvt. practice Marina Del Rey, Calif., 1978—; Editor: book Encyclopedia of Engineering Materials, 1963, Strengthening of Metals, 1965, Handbook of Stainless Steels, 1977; contbr. articles to profl. jours. Cpl. U.S. Army, 1950-52, Korea. Mem. ABA, Am. soc. for Metals (chpt. chmn. 1968-69), L.A. County Bar Assn., Calif. Bar Assn. Democrat. Office: 4720 Lincoln Blvd #250 Marina Del Rey CA 90292

PEDERSEN, JOY SUSAN, success consultant, lecturer; b. Denville, N.J., Nov. 6, 1955; d. Harris Raymond and Gerd Marion (Jensen) P. Student, County Coll. Morris, Randolph, N.J., 1973, 74, Profl. Sch. Bus., Union, N.J., 1975; cert., First Sch. Paralegal Studies, Fairfield, N.J., 1978; student, UCLA, 1980-81. Cert. paralegal. Researcher Free Pub. Library, Parsippany-Troy Hills, N.J., 1971-75; paralegal Alfred F. Carolonza, Jr., Milburn, N.J., 1976-79; publicist IFI Scope III, Hollywood, Calif., 1980; cons., lectr. Express Success, West Hollywood, Calif., 1981—; publicist, Paramount Pictures Corp., Los Angeles, 1980-85; bur. chief PM Mag., Lost Angeles, 1986-88; cons., owner Pedersen Pub. Relations, West Hollywood, 1985-88. Vol. Olympic Organizing Com., Los Angeles, 1983, 84. Mem. Acad. TV Arts and Scis., Women in Show Bus. (v.p. 1982-83), Book Publicists of So. Calif., The Publicists Guild, Inst. Noetic Sciences. Home: 907 Green Pond Rd Rockaway NJ 07866 Office: Express Success 8539 Sunset Blvd Ste 4112 West Hollywood CA 90069

PEDERSEN, MARTIN ALBERT, consulting engineer, surveyor; b. Rawlins, Wyo., Dec. 2, 1946; s. Rasmus and Ella (Rasmussen) P.; m. Karen Louise Bond, Aug. 26, 1967 (div. 1978); children: David Frank, Jennifer Louise; m. Patricia Ann Smith, Mar. 1, 1980; 1 child, Hans Rasmus. Student, U. Wyo., 1965. Registered land surveyor, Wyo., Mont., Idaho, Nev., Ariz., N.Mex., N.D., S.D., Colo. Surveyor Robert Jack Smith & Assocs., Rawlins, 1966-75, prin., 1975—. Scoutmaster Boy Scouts of Am., Rawlins, 1969-75, dist. chmn., 1975-81; head Rawlins Search and Rescue Dive Team, 1984; mem., past chmn. Rawlins Carbon County Airport Bd.; elder Christ Luth. Ch., Rawlins, 1985-88; treas. Christ Luth. Ch. Mem. Wyo. Assn. Cons. Engrs. and Surveyors (pres. 1978), Profl. Land Surveyors Wyo. (pres. 1980-81), Am. Congress Surveying and Mapping, Wyo. English Soc. (sec.-treas. 1988—), Ducks Untld. (chmn. Rawlins chpt.). Lodge: Elks. Home: 207 E Heath Rawlins WY 82301 Office: Robert Jack Smith Assocs Inc 1015 Harshman Box 1104 Rawlins WY 82301

PEDERSEN, PAUL ANDREAS, JR., law enforcement manager; b. Berkeley, Calif., Aug. 4, 1949; s. Paul Andreas and Phyllis (Bowman) P.; m. Vanita Taylor, June 24, 1972; children: Kate, Mark. BA, U. Ariz., 1972; MA, St. Mary's Coll., Moraga, Calif., 1980. Cert. Peace Officer, Ariz. Dep. sheriff Pima County Sheriff's Dept., Tucson, 1972-77, sgt., 1977-86, lt., 1986—; assessor Commn. on Accreditation for Law Enforcement, Washington, D.C., 1983—. Contbr. numerous articles to profl. jours. Bd. dirs. We the People of Ariz., Tucson, 1986—, Tucson Boys Chorus, 1985-87. Maj. USAR, 1972—. Mem. Internat. Assn. of Chiefs of Police, Criminal Intelligence Adv. Council, Am. Soc. for Indsl. Security (vice-chmn. so. Ariz. chpt. 1987). Republican. Office: Pima County Sheriff's Dept 1801 S Mission Rd Tucson AZ 85713

PEDERSEN, ROGER ARLEN, electronic technician; b. Yankton, S.D.; s. Arlen Peter and Darlene June (Brockman) P.; m. Betty Jane Krueger, June 17, 1983; 1 child, Megan Sue. Cert. tng., USAF, 1983. Electronic tech. Pacific Missile Test Ctr. USN, Point Mugu, Calif., 1984—. With U.S. Army, 1978-82. Office: Dept Navy Range Ops Code 3281.2 Point Mugu CA 93042

PEDERSON, PETER ORLO, fire department chief; b. Los Angeles, July 2, 1934; s. Orlo G. and Iola (Wilson) P.; m. Betty Lou Pederson, Nov. 27, 1954; children—David, Chris. BA, Calif. State U.-Long Beach, 1957; MS, Pepperdine U., 1978. Bn. chief L.A. County Fire Dept., 1973-80, asst. fire chief, 1980-81; fire chief Salt Lake City Fire Dept., 1981—. With USN, 1952-54. Mem. Nat. Fire Protection Assn., Internat. Assn. Fire Chiefs, Western Fire Chiefs Assn., Metro Fire Chiefs Assn. Lodge: Rotary. Office: Salt Lake City Fire Dept 315 E 2d St S Salt Lake City UT 84111

PEDERSON, RAYMOND SVEND, dentist; b. Alameda, Calif., Feb. 9, 1931; s. Svend and Elizabeth (Sorensen) P.; m. Gail Yvonne MacDonald, May 2, 1981; children: Richard, Linda, Pamela, Christian, Stephen, Anne. DDS, U. So. Calif., 1956. Lic. dentist, Calif. Gen. practice dentistry Bakersfield, Calif., 1958--; pres. United Found. Med. Care, 1984-88. Mem. Rotary, Elks. Republican. Home and Office: 1729 26th St Bakersfield CA 93301

PEDOLSKY, ALAN ROBERT, federal agency administrator; b. Bronx, N.Y., Aug. 14, 1946; s. Hyman and Hannah (Weisner) P.; m. Joan Kathleen Anderson, July 21, 1979; stepchildren: Stacie L. Allen, Michael D. Warwas. BA, Long Island U., 1968. Tchr. Blkyn. Sch. Spl. Children, 1969-70; vol. U.S. Peace Corps., Kabul, Afghanistan, 1970-71; revenue officer IRS, N.Y.C., 1972-73, New Rochelle, N.Y., 1973-74, Tucson, 1974—; instr. IRS, Phoenix, 1983—. Jewish. Office: IRS 300 W Congress Tucson AZ 85701

PEDRETTI, DONALD LEE, communications systems engineer; b. Port Hueneme, Calif., Mar. 8, 1954; s. Charles Donald and Irene Anna (Hansen) P.; m. Linda Maxine Goldstein, Jan. 17, 1981; children: Robyn Sarah, Donald Henry. AA, Pierce Coll., Woodland Hills, Calif., 1977; student, Calif. State U., Northridge, 1978. Digital elec. tech. Fed. Elec. Corp./J.P.L., Pasadena, 1980-85; communications systems tech. OAO Corp./J.P.L., Pasadena, 1985—. Recipient JPL/IPC Uranus Encounter Achievement award, Jet Propulsion Lab., 1986. Home: 11020 Cohasset St Sun Valley CA 91352

PEDRIE, DOUGLAS ROSS, oil company executive; b. Denver, Dec. 7, 1954; s. Robert Joseph and Ethel Mae (Dieter) P.; m. Denise Davis, Aug. 4, 1979. BSBA in Fin., U. Northern Colo., 1977; MBA in Fin., U. Denver, 1979. Credit and fin. analyst First Nat. Bancorp., Denver, 1978-81; pres., owner Big Valley Resources, Inc., Colo. Springs, Colo., 1982-87; pres. Bison Petroleum Co., Denver, 1987--; shareholder, dir. Equity Internat. Bank, Ltd. Mem. Black Forest Inst. (bd. dirs.). Lutheran. Home: 1260 Big Valley Dr Colorado Springs CO 80919 Office: Bison Petroleum Co Inc 999 18th St Ste 3300 Denver CO 80202

PEEBLES, CAROL LYNN, immunology researcher; b. Wellington, Kans., Jan. 20, 1941; d. Harry Alexander and Phyllis Dorothy (Pyle) P. BA, Kans. State Coll. of Pittsburg, 1962, MS, 1964; cert. med. technology, St. Francis Hosp., Wichita, Kans., 1965. Med. technologist St. Francis Hosp., Wichita, 1965-74; lab. supr. allergy and immunology Scripps Clinic and Rsch. Found., La Jolla, Calif., 1974-77; sr. rsch. asst. autoimmune disease ctr. Scripps Clinic and Rsch. Found., La Jolla, 1982—; lab. supr. rheumatology lab. U. Colo. Health Scis. Ctr., Denver, 1977-82; cons., Vitrotech Labs., Carlsbad, Calif., 1987—, Miragen, San Diego, 1988—. Author workshop manual; contbr. articles to sci. publs. Mem. Am Rheumatism Assn., AAAS, Am. Soc. Microbiology, Am. Soc. Med. Tech., Am. Soc. Clin. Pathology. Office: Scripps Cinic Rsch Found 10666 N Torrey Pines Rd La Jolla CA 92037

PEEBLES, HERBERT ELMER, college administrator; b. Buffalo, May 30, 1943; s. Elmer Alton and Gladys Mae (Murray) P.; m. Alice Goertz, Nov. 23, 1963; children: Brent H., Lisa Renee. BS in Math. and Edn., Goshen Coll., 1966; student Purdue U., 1967-68; MA in Math., U. Notre Dame, 1970; DA in Math., Idaho State U., 1973. Tchr. math. Goshen Community Schs., Ind., 1966-69; instr. math. U. Notre Dame, Ind., 1970-71; assoc. prof. math. St. Bonaventure U., N.Y., 1973-79; div. chairperson sci. and math. Lorain County Community Coll., Elyria, Ohio, 1979-85; v.p. instrn. Collin County Community Coll., McKinney, Tex. 1985-87; v.p. acad. affairs Clark County Community Coll., Las Vegas, Nev., 1987—; workshop leader Ctr. Occupational Research and Devel., Waco, Tex., 1983—; lectr., 1983—. Contbr. articles to profl. jours. Mem. Assn. Computing Machinery, Am. Mus. Natural Hist., Am. Math. Assn. Two Yr. Colls. Presbyterian.

PEEBLES, LUCRETIA NEAL DRANE, educational administrator; b. Atlanta, Mar. 16, 1950; d. Dudley Drane and Annie Pearl (Neal) Lewis; divorced; 1 child, Julian Timothy. BA, Pitzer Coll., 1971; MA, Claremont Grad. Sch., 1973, PhD, 1985. Special edn. tchr. Marshall Jr. High Sch., Pomona, Calif., 1971-74; high sch. tchr. Pomona High Sch., 1974-84; adminstr. Lorbeer Jr. High Sch., Diamond Bar, Calif., 1984—; co-dir. pre-freshman program, Claremont (Calif.) Coll., 1974; dir. pre-freshman program, Claremont Coll., 1975; cons., Claremont, 1983—. Author: Negative Attendance Behavior: The Role of the School, 1985. Active Funds Distbn. Bd.-Food for All, 1987—, Funds Distbn. Task Force-Food for All, 1986. Named Outstanding Young Career Woman Upland Bus. and Profl. Women's Club, 1978-79; Stanford U. Sch. Edn. MESA fellow, 1983, Nat. Sci. Found. fellow, 1981, Calif. Tchrs. Assn. fellow, 1979, Claremont Grad. Sch. fellow, 1977-79. Mem. Assn. Calif. Sch. Adminstrs. (Minigrant award 1988), Assn. for Supervision and Curriculum Devel., Nat. Assn. Secondary Sch. Principals, Pi Lambda Theta. Democrat. Am. Baptist. Home: 725 Mansfield Dr Claremont CA 91711 Office: Lorbeer Jr High Sch 501 S Diamond Bar Blvd Diamond Bar CA 91765

PEEK, LARRY DAVID, product development engineer, computer and peripheral applications specialist; b. Ottumwa, Iowa, Jan. 25, 1949; s. Joseph LaVerne and Mildred Jane (Duncan) P.; m. Lucille Ruth Babcock, Mar. 23, 1970; children: Kathleen Ann, Nikoljas Joseph Wilbert. Grad. tech. high sch., Des Moines, 1967. Field repairman IBM Field Engring., Des Moines, 1967-68; with bus. report depts. Dunn & Bradstreet, Des Moines, 1969-70; with stock dept. Mercy Hosp., Des Moines, 1970-77; mgr. Radio Shack, Hayward, Calif., 1977-78; repairman Diablo Systems, Hayward, 1978-82; with applications specialist dept. Xerox Corp., Fremont, Calif., 1982-87, with product devel. dept., 1987—; leader Repair Ctr. Quality Circle, Hayward, 1978-82; div. rep. Multi-Nat. Tool Com., Webster, N.Y., 1982—. Author: Interfacing Micro/Mini Computers, 1982. System ops. dir. San Lorenzo (Calif.), Bapt. Computer Ministry, 1983—; dir. Bapt. Repertory Arts Theatre, San Lorenzo, 1984—; citizen rep. Civic Adv. Bd. KRON-TV, San Francisco, 1986—. Served with U.S. Army, 1968-69. Home: 560 Blossom Way Hayward CA 94541 Office: Xerox Corp 901 Page Ave Fremont CA 94537

PEEK, MERL BICKNELL, lawyer, retired oil company executive; b. Tecumseh, Nebr., Apr. 2, 1914; s. Charles William and Effa M. (Bicknell) P.; m. Carol Jean Wherry, Feb. 6, 1943; children: Jeffrey M., Elizabeth S. Peek Larson-Hays, Emery J. Kling. BA, Peru State U., 1935; JD, Georgetown U., 1948. Bar: Nebr. 1948, Ill. 1956, Calif. 1962. Tchr., athletic coach various high schs., 1935-41; asst. to Sen. Wherry of Nebr. U.S. Senate, Washington, 1945-48; exec. dir. Republican Valley Conservation Assn., McCook, Nebr., 1948-49; asst. exec. dir. Nat. Reclamation Assn., Washington, 1950-51; atty., Office Chief Counsel IRS, Washington, 1951-52; trial atty. IRS, St. Paul, 1953-55; mem. legal dept. Universal Oil Products Co., Des Plaines, Ill., 1955-66; corp. sec. Universal Oil Products Co., 1966-79; ret. 1979. Bd. dirs. Clearbrook Ctr. Found., Rolling Meadows, Ill., 1977-79; founding pres. Oakton Community Coll. Found., Des Plaines, 1977-79; founding pres. Concerned Advisors, Inc., Green Valley, Ariz., 1984, bd. dirs., 1988-; pres. Community Coordinating Council, Green Valley, 1986-87; chmn. project for incorporation of Green Valley, 1988-89; Pima County Bd. adv. com., 1985-86. Recipient Silver Beaver award Boy Scouts Am., Des Plaines, 1981. Mem. Kiwanis. Presbyterian. Home: 3161 S Calle Madrid Green Valley AZ 85614

PEER, RAKESH, civil engineer; b. Srinagar, Kashmir, India, May 9, 1961; came to U.S. 1984; s. Autar Kishen and Krishna (Tickoo) P. BS in Civil Engring., Kashmir U., India, 1981; MBA, San Jose State U., 1987. Civil engring. supr. Elec. Constrn. Co., Tripoli, Libya, 1981-84; teaching asst./reader Sch. of Bus., San Jose State U., 1985-87; projects coordinator Contrn. Mgmt. Assocs., San Jose, 1987—; cons. in field. Contbr. articles to profl. jours. Mem. Am. Soc. Profl. Estimators, ASCE, Am. Assn. Cost Engrs., Constrn. Mgmt. Assn. Am., Constrn. Specifications Inst., Assn. MBA Execs., Leo Club (treas. 1979-80). Office: Construction Mgmt Assocs 2216 The Alameda Santa Clara CA 95050

PEERY, J. CRAIG, psychologist; b. Salt Lake City, Apr. 21, 1945; s. Joseph Smith and Phyllis (Evans) P.; m. Irene Weiss, June 21, 1969; children: Joseph, Christie, Samuel. BA, Columbia U., 1970, MA, 1973, PhD, 1973. Research scientist N.Y. Psychiat. Inst. and Research Found. for Mental Hygiene, N.Y.C., 1970-73; asst. prof. family and human devel. Utah State U., Logan, 1973-80, assoc. prof., 1980; assoc. prof. family scis. Brigham Young U., Provo, Utah, 1980-85, prof., 1985—, dir. Program for Optimal Devel., 1985—; spl. asst. to chmn. U.S. Senate Labor and Human Resources Com., Washington, 1980-82; staff assoc. U.S. Senate Subcom. for Family and Human Services, 1983-84; mem. several nat. adv. panels on children, adolescents, families. Editor: Music and Child Development, 1987. Com. mem. Utah Symphony. Mem. AAAS, Soc. Research in Child Devel., Am. Psychol. Assn., Nat. Council on Family Relations, Southwestern Soc. for Research in Child Devel., Utah Acad. Scis. Arts & Letters, Am. Orthopsychiat. Assn., Sigma Xi, Phi Kappa Phi. Mem. Ch. Jesus Christ of Latter Day Saints. Cons. editor and contbr. articles to profl. jours; contbr. chpts. to books. Office: Brigham Young U 1000 SWKT Provo UT 84602

PEEVEY, MICHAEL R., electric company executive; b. N.Y.C., Feb. 8, 1938; s. Willard Michael Bliss and Miriam Gardiner (Cooke) Bliss Peevey; m. Lauretta Ann Peevey, Mar. 17, 1961 (div. 1976); children: Darcie Ann, Maria Beth; m. Carole Jean Liu, May 27, 1978; 1 child, Jared Liu. BA in Econs., U. Calif.-Berkeley, 1959, MA in Econs., 1961. Economist U.S. Dept. Labor, Washington, 1961-65; coord. community programs Inst. Indsl. Rels., U. Calif.-Berkeley, 1969-70; dir. rsch. Calif. Labor Fedn., AFL-CIO, 1971-73, 65-69; pres. Calif. Coun. for Environl./Econ. Balance, San Francisco, 1973-84; v.p. So. Calif. Edison Co., Rosemead, 1984-85, sr. v.p., 1985-86, exec. v.p., 1986—. Bd. dirs. Calif. Housing Fin. Agy., Sacramento, 1984-86; mem. Commn. to Rev. the Master Plan for Higher Edn., Calif., 1985—; trustee Calif. State U. and Colls., 1977-85, Joint Coun. on Econ. Edn., N.Y., 1969-85; mem. Gov.'s Infrastructure Rev. Task Force, Sacramento, 1983-84; bd. govs. Econ. Literacy Coun. of Calif., 1982—; bd. visitors Calif. Maritime Acad., 1980-83; mem. steering com. State Solid Waste Mgmt. Bd., 1980-83; commr. Nat. Commn. on State Workmen's Compensation Laws, Washington, 1971-72; bd. dirs. Consumer Fedn. Calif., 1972-78; co-chmn. Citizens for Adequate Energy, 1979-82. Mem. Indsl. Rels. Rsch. Assn., World Trade Club, Sutter Club, Calif. Club. Democrat. Episcopalian. Office: So Calif Edison Co 2244 Walnut Grove Ave Rosemead CA 91770

PEIFFER, ELIZABETH ANNE, computer systems consultant, auditor; b. Syracuse, N.Y., Dec. 5, 1954; d. Robert Victor and Marion Alice (Jagelle) P.; m. Gerald Lee Brickey, June 9, 1978 (div. Apr. 1989). BA in Econs., Acctg. and Psychology Magna Cum Laude, Coll. Holy Cross, 1976. CPA, Oreg., Ill.; cert. info. systems auditor. Mem. audit staff Arthur Young & Co., Chgo., 1976-78; sr. auditor, computer auditor Arthur Young & Co., Portland, Oreg., 1978-80; corp. auditor EDP Orbanco Fin. Services Corp., Portland, Oreg., 1980-82, systems audit mgr., 1982-83, asst. v.p., asst. dir. auditing, 1983-84; computer audit mgr. Coopers & Lybrand, Portland, 1984-88, computer auditor, cons. mgr., 1988—; instr. Concordia Coll., Portland, 1986-87; cons. 1000 Friends of Oreg., Portland, 1981; lectr. in field. Developer, editor EDP ednl. materials. Econ. adviser Portland Energy Commn., 1980; fundraiser Northwest Artists Workshop, Portland, 1984; adviser St. Mary's Acad., Portland, 1986—. Mem. AICPA, Inst. Internal Auditors (bd. dirs. 1988—), Oreg. Soc. CPA's (chair 1987-88, bd. dirs. 1988—), EDP Auditors Assn. (chpt. pres. 1985-86, regional asst. v.p. 1986-88, regional v.p. 1988—), Oreg. Accts. for the Pub. Interest (bd. dirs. 1979-81), Phi Beta Kappa. Office: Coopers & Lybrand 2700 1st Interstate Tower Portland OR 97201

PEIRANO, LAWRENCE EDWARD, civil engineer; b. Stockton, Calif., May 13, 1929; s. Frank Lloyd and Esther Marie (Carigiet) P.; m. Mary Ellen Alabaster, July 26, 1952; children: Thomas Lawrence, Ellen Marie. BSCE, U. Calif., Berkeley, 1951, MSCE, 1952. Registered profl. engr., Calif., Nev.; diplomate Am. Acad. Environ. Engrs. Assoc. civil engr. Calif. Div. Water Resources, 1952-53; with Kennedy/Jenks/Chilton, Inc. (formerly Kennedy Engrs. Inc.), San Francisco, 1955—, project mgr., 1960—, v.p., chief environ. engr., 1974—, dir. ops., 1979—, sr. v.p., regional mgr., 1986—, also chmn. bd. dirs.; spl. lectr. san. engring. U. Calif., Berkeley, 1976. Served with U.S. Army, 1953-55, Korea. James Monroe McDonald scholar, 1950-51. Fellow ASCE; mem. Water Pollution Control Fedn., Am. Water Works Assn., Cons. Engrs. Assn. Calif., Internat. Assn. on Water Pollution Research and Control, Sierra Club, Far West Ski Assn., U. Calif. Alumni Assn., Tau Beta Pi, Chi Epsilon. Republican. Roman Catholic. Home: 3435 Black Hawk Rd Lafayette CA 94549 Office: Kennedy Jenks Chilton 657 Howard St San Francisco CA 94105

PEIRCE, JAMES MARK, realtor; b. Ft. Wayne, Ind., Dec. 25, 1956; s. Clyde Raymond and Hilda Frances (Sellers) P.; m. Vikki Lynn Vinton, Aug. 14, 1982. BA, Manchester Coll., 1979; MBA, U. Phoenix, 1986. Realtor Rousseau Realtors, Ft. Wayne, 1979-80; ops. mgr. Greyhound Lines Inc., Indpls., 1980-83; ops. control supr. Greyhound Lines Inc., Phoenix, 1983-85; realtor Russ Lyon Realty Co., Phoenix, 1986—. Pres. Mi Casa Home Owners Assn., 1985. Mem. Nat. Assn. Realtors, Ariz. Assn. Realtors, Phoenix Bd. Realtors. Republican. Office: Russ Lyon Realty Co 2036 E Camelback Rd Phoenix AZ 85016

PELATT, LAURENCE R., small business owner; b. Billings, Mont., Apr. 21, 1954; s. George H. and Mary H. P.; m. Deanne M., July 16, 1977; children: Kevin, Scott. BBA, Ea. Mont. Coll., Billings, 1976. Br. mgr. Builders Mart Inc., Sheridan, Wyo., 1976-79; lumber broker N. Pacific Lumber Co., Portland, Oreg., 1979-82; regional sales mgr. Workmans Forest Products, Clackamas, Oreg., 1982-84; gen. sales mgr. T.K. Forest Products, Beaverton, Oreg., 1984-485; pres., owner Columbia Wood Products, Beaverton, 1985—. Office: Columbia Wood Products Inc PO Box 1758 Beaverton OR 97075

PELLEGRINI, ALEX ALFRED, printmaker; b. San Francisco, Dec. 23, 1944; s. Alexander Joseph and Rose Marie (Ratto) P.; m. Leslie Roberta Richards, Dec. 11, 1982. MEd, U. San Francisco, 1968, MA in Psychology, 1970; MA in English Lit., U. Santa Barbara, 1973; MFA, U. Nev., 1975. Cert. secondary sch. tchr., Calif. English tchr., head counselor San Francisco Unified Sch. Dist., 1968-72; probation officer San Francisco Juvenile Hall, 1972-74; psychology asst. Learning for Living, San Francisco, 1974-77; head counselor Quest House, San Francisco, 1977-81; masseur San Francisco Sch. Massage, 1982-88; chief printmaker Ft. Mason, San Francisco, 1984—; cancer therapist St. Francis Hosp., San Francisco, 1988—; chmn. Massage Therapists of San Francisco, 1986-87. Artist in residence Hatley-Martin Gallery, San Francisco, 1985; author: (poetry) Belladona, 1984, Hearts of Fire, 1986; poetry editor San Francisco Quarterly, 1980-83.

PELLERITO, JOHN THOMAS, JR., physician; b. Detroit, June 8, 1949; s. John T. and Lucy M. (Bolone) P. BS in Pharmacy, Wayne State U., 1971-75, MD, 1983. Pharmacist Detroit Gen. Hosp., 1973-78; physician Urgent Care/ER, Tuson, 1984—; physician pvt. practice Tuson, 1988—. Capt. USAR, 1984—. Mem. AMA, Am. Soc. of Internists, Am. Coll. of Physicians, Pima Med. Assn., Ariz. Med. Assn. Home: 6911 S Vereda De Las Casitas Tucson AZ 85746 Office: 4462 E Fifth St Tucson AZ 85711

PELLONE, DAVID THOMAS, controller; b. Ashtabula, Ohio, Mar. 15, 1944; s. Frank Joseph and Shirley Edna (Foster) P.; m. Sunny Jewel Unfug, May 28, 1977; children: Todd Gary, Michelle Christine. BBA in Indsl. Mgmt., Kent State U., 1967; MBA in Acctg. and Fin., U. Santa Clara, 1973. Product supr., indsl. engr. Owens Corning Fiberglass, Santa Clara, Calif., 1970-72; line contr. Fairchild Semiconductor, Mountain View, Calif., 1973-74; corp. contr. Cermetek, Inc., Mountain View, 1974-76; with 3M Co., Ventura, Calif., 1976-83; cons. J&P Assocs., Menlo Park, Calif., 1983-84; area fin. mgr. GenRad, Inc., Milpitas, Calif., 1984-86; v.p., contr. Genus, Inc., Mountain View, 1986—. With U.S. Army, 1967-69. Mem. Am. Mgmt. Assn., Am. Acctg. Assn., Inst. Internal Auditors, Inst. Indsl. Engrs. (sr.),

Churchill Club, Commonwealth Club (Calif.). Republican. Episcopalian. Office: Genus Inc 515 Ellis St Mountain View CA 94043

PELOSI, NANCY, congresswoman; b. Balt., 1941; d. Thomas J. D'Alesandro Jr.; m. Paul Pelosi; children: Nancy Corinne, Christine, Jacqueline, Paul, Alexandra. Grad., Trinity Coll. Former chmn. Calif. State Dem. Com., 1981; committeewoman Dem. Nat. Com., 1976, 80, 84; elec. to U.S. Congress from 5th dist. Calif. 1987; fin. chmn. Dem. Senatorial Campaign Com., 1987. Office: Offices of House Mems care The Postmaster Washington DC 20515

PELOTTE, DONALD EDMOND, bishop; b. Waterville, Maine, Apr. 13, 1945; s. Norris Albert and Margaret Yvonne (LaBrie) P. AA, Eymard Sem. and Jr. Coll., Hyde Park, N.Y., 1965; BA, John Carroll U., 1969; MA, Fordham U., 1971, PhD, 1975. Ordained priest Roman Cath. Ch., 1972. Provincial superior Blessed Sacrament, Cleve., from 1978; ordained coadjutor bishop Diocese of Gallup, N.Mex., 1986—; nat. bd. dirs. Maj. Superiors of Men, Silver Spring, Md., 1981—, Tekakwitha Conf., Great Falls, Mont., 1981—. Author: John Courtney Murray: Theologian in Conflict, 1976. 1st native Am. bishop. Mem. Cath. Theol. Soc. Am., Am. Cath. Hist. Soc. Address: Coadjutor Bishop of Gallup PO Box 1317 Gallup NM 87301 *

PELTASON, JACK WALTER, university chancellor; b. St. Louis, Aug. 29, 1923; s. Walter B. and Emma (Hartman) P.; m. Suzanne Toll, Dec. 21,1946; children: Nancy Hartman, Timothy Walter H., Jill K. BA, U. Mo., 1943, MA, 1944, LLD (hon.), 1978; AM, Princeton U., 1946, PhD, 1947; LLD (hon.), U. Md., 1979, Ill. Coll., 1979, Gannon U., 1980, U. Maine, 1980, Union Coll., 1981, Moorehead (N.D.) State U., 1980; LHD (hon.), 1980, Ohio State U., 1980, Mont. Coll. Mineral Scis. and Tech., 1982, Buena Vista Coll., 1982, Assumption Coll., 1983, Chapman Coll., 1986, U. Ill., 1989. Asst. prof. Smith Coll., Mass., 1947-51; asst. prof. polit. sci. U. Ill., Urbana, 1951-52, assoc. prof., 1953-59, dean Coll. Liberal Arts and Scis., 1960-64, chancellor, 1967-77; vice chancellor acad. affairs U. Calif., Irvine, 1964-67, chancellor, 1984—; pres. Am. Coun. Edn., Washington, 1977-84; Cons. Mass. Little Hoover Commn., 1950. Author: The Missouri Plan for the Selection of Judges, 1947, Understanding the Constitution, 11th edit, 1988, Federal Courts in the Political Process, 1957, (with James M. Burns) Government by the People, 13th edit, 1987, Fifty-eight Lonely Men, 1961, also articles, revs. Recipient James Madison medal Princeton U., 1982. Fellow Am. Acad. Arts and Scis.; mem. Am. Polit. Sci. Assn. (council 1952-54), Phi Beta Kappa, Phi Kappa Phi, Omicron Delta Kappa, Alpha Phi Omega, Beta Gamma Sigma. Home: 6 Gibbs Ct Irvine CA 92715 Office: U Calif Irvine Office of the Chancellor Campus Dr Irvine CA 92717

PELTIER, GARY LEE, education educator; b. Elsie, Mich., Nov. 2, 1936; s. Howard J. and Ruth A. (Parks) P.; m. Doris M. Debar, Sept. 14, 1957 (dec. Oct. 1982); children: Lisa, Bryan; m. Barbara J. Hasleton, Feb. 14, 1987; children: Corrie, Lindsey, Stacey. BA, Mich. State U., 1958; MA, U. Ill., 1959, U. Denver, 1963; PhD, U. Denver, 1965. Cert. tchr., adminstr., Nev. Jr. high sch. tchr. Washoe County Sch. Dist., Reno, 1959-62; asst. prof. U. Nev., Reno, 1965-70, assoc. prof., 1970-74, prof., 1974—, chmn. dept. ednl. founds., 1968-74. Editor: Perspectives on Education, 1979, 4th edit., 1988; contbr. articles to ednl. jours. NDEA fellow, 1962-65. Mem. AAUP, Phi Delta Kappa. Democrat. Office: U Nev Reno NV 89557

PELTON, HAROLD MARCEL, mortgage broker; b. Montreal, Que., Can., Jan. 24, 1922; s. Grover Cleveland and Denise (Pigeon) P.; m. Frances Farley, June 1947 (div. 1968); children: Mary Virginia Joyner, Diane Jean Slagowski; m. Virginia L. King, July 11, 1970. Student, L.A. City Coll., 1948-49, Anthony Schs., Van Nuys, Calif., 1966. Lic. real estate real broker, Calif. Stockbroker, agt. Mitchum, Jones, Templeton Assurance Co., L.A., 1957-60; owner Assurance Investment Co., Van Nuys, Calif., 1960-65; sales syndicator TSI Investment Co., L.A., 1965-69; pres., owner Univest Co., Beverly Hills, Calif., 1970-72, Am. Oil Recovery, L.A., 1973-79; v.p. Newport Pacific Funding Co., Newport Beach, Calif., 1979-81; chmn. bd. dirs. TD Publs., El Toro, Calif., 1981-83; pres., broker HP Fin., Inc., Laguna Hills, Calif., 1983--. Contbg. editor Am. Oil Recovery newspaper, 1973-79; editor Trust Deed Jour., 1981-83. Served with U.S. Army, 1942-46, PTO. Mem. L. A. Mus. Art, Laguna Hills C. of C., Kiwanis, Toastmasters. Republican. Home: 24942 Georgia Sue Dr Laguna Hills CA 92653 Office: HP Fin Inc 23276 S Pointe Dr Ste 114 Laguna Hills CA 92653

PELTZER, ROBERT GERARD, electrical engineer; b. New Britain, Conn., Nov. 20, 1931; s. Julius and Natalie A. (Eggert) P.; m. Marilyn Alice Kerkhoff, Aug. 3, 1963; children: Gerard Robert, Katherine Rose. BS cum laude, U. Conn., 1957; MEE, U. Mich., 1961. Jr. engr., then engr. Bendix Systems, Ann Arbor, Mich., 1957-62; asst. research engr., then research engr. U. Mich., Ann Arbor, 1962-74; project engr. to co-prin. investigator U. Colo., Boulder, 1973-79; sr. staff engr., then engring. mgr. Martin Marietta Astronautics, Denver, 1979—. Contbr. articles to sci. publs. With USN, 1949-53. Recipient Spl. award, NASA, 1981. Mem. IEEE, Optimists, Eta Kappa Nu, Tau Beta Pi, Sigma Xi, Phi Kappa Phi. Republican. Roman Catholic. Home: 75 Ridge Rd Boulder CO 80303 Office: Martin Marietta Space Sys PO Box 179 Denver CO 80201

PEMBERTON, HELEN RENEE, design engineer; b. Pitts., Oct. 29, 1956; d. Alex Richard and Lillian Mae (Hallam) Smith; m. Terrence Jay Pemberton, July 4, 1981; 1 child, Trevor Jay. BS in Nuclear Engring., Pa. State U., 1978; MS in Engring., Calif. State U., Long Beach, 1989. Registered profl. engr., Calif. Test engr. Norfolk Naval Shipyard, Portsmouth, Va., 1978-80; cognizant test engr. Westinghouse Hanford, Richland, Wash., 1980-82; ind. engr. So. Calif. Edison, Rosemead, 1982-87; sr. design engr. Swedlow, Inc., Garden Grove, Calif., 1987—; rsch. asst. Innovative Nuclear Space Power Inst., Calif. State U., Long Beach, 1986, Oak Ridge Assoc. U., Tenn., 1977. Kunkle scholar, 1978; recipient Cert. Achievement YWCA, 1986. Mem. NAFE, Alpha Lambda Delta (v.p. 1977-78). Office: Swedlow Inc 12122 Western Ave Garden Grove CA 92641-2990

PENA, FEDERICO FABIAN, mayor, lawyer; b. Laredo, Tex., Mar. 15, 1947; s. Gustavo J. and Lucille P.; m. Ellen Hart, May 1988. BA, U. Tex., Austin, 1969, JD, 1972. Bar: Colo. 1973. Ptnr. Pena & Pena, Denver, 1973-83; mayor City and County of Denver, 1983—, re-elected for 2d term, 1987; mem. Colo. Gen. Assembly, 1979-83, ho. Dem. leader, 1981; mem. Colo. Bd. Law Examiners, Denver; assoc. Harvard Ctr. for Law and Edn., Cambridge, Mass. Named Outstanding House Dem. Legislator, Colo. Gen. Assembly, 1981. Roman Catholic. Office: City & County of Denver 350 City & County Bldg Denver CO 80202 *

PENA, MANUEL, JR., state senator; b. Cashion, Ariz., Nov. 17, 1924; s. Manuel and Elvira (Gomez) P.; student public schs.; m. Aurora Cruz, June 13, 1945; children: Yolanda, Mary, Henry, Steve, Patricia, Geraldine, Manuel III. Owner Pena Realty & Ins. Agy., Phoenix, 1951—; pres. Penasco, Inc.; mem. Ariz. state adv. com. U.S. Commn. Civil Rights, 1981—, Ariz. Ho. of Reps., Phoenix, 1967-72, Ariz. Senate, Phoenix, 1973—. Exec. sec. Ariz. Athletic Commn., 1964-66, 67-71; bd. dirs. Ariz. Consumers Coun., 1960—; commr. human relations City of Phoenix, 1967-71. Served with U.S. Army, 1945-46. Mem. Am. Legion (comdr.), VFW Post #3718. Democrat. Roman Catholic. Office: State Capitol Office State Senate Phoenix AZ 85007

PENCE, DORIS ELLEN, travel consultant; b. Oregon City, Oreg., Sept. 27, 1943; d. John Lewis and Marjorie C. (Schoenborn) Dunton; m. Donald R. Pence, Mar. 7, 1975; 1 child, Shirley Jean. Grad. high sch., Molalla, Oreg. Owner, mgr. Molalla Realty, Inc., 1975-87; cons. Molalla Travel Ctr., 1983—. Chairperson Molalla City Planning Commn., 1964-76; organist, Molalla Nazarene Ch. Mem. Clackamas County Realty Bd., Kiwanis. Home: PO Box 290 Molalla OR 97038 Office: Molalla Travel Ctr PO Box 290 Molalla OR 97038

PENCE, FRANCES BENEDICT, former educator; b. Hartford, Conn., Jan. 2, 1926; d. Ivan Howland and Hilda Frances (Pratt) Benedict; m. Roy James Pence, June 20, 1959; childrn: Jennifer Pence McManus, Robert, Richard, Roger. BA, Vassar Coll., 1947; MS, U. N.H., 1950; PhD, UCLA, 1956. Curator asst. N.Y. State Mus., Albany, 1951-52; lab. asst. UCLA, 1957, instr., 1957-58, asst. prof. med. ext., 1960-64; asst. prof. Calif. State U., Fresno, 1958-60,, L.A., 1961-63, 68-73. Author: Hair Structure as a Generic Characteristic in Bats, 1957. Trustee sch. bd. Paradise (Calif.) Unified Sch. Dist., 1976-81, pres., 1977-78;trustee Butte County Bd. Edn., Oroville, Calif., 1982—, pres. 1986-88; pres. bd.dirs. Meals on Wheels, Paradise, 1984—; pres. adminstrv. bd. Paradise United Meth. Ch., 1986—; adv. bd. extended opportunity program and svcs. Butte Community Coll., Oroville, 1986—; observer chmn. LWV, Butte county, 1985-87; active Council on Aging, Paradise, 1986—; bd. dirs. Calif. County Bds. Edn., 1987—, Edn. Congress Calif., 1987-89, EdSource, 1987-89. Fulbright fellow, 1955-56. Mem. AAUW (pres. Paradise br. 1983-85, edn. and legis. rep., edn. chair Calif. div. 1987-89), Calif. Elected Women's Assn. for Edn. and Rsch., Calif. Sch. Bds. Assn. (mem. del. assembly 1987—). Democrat.

PENCE, JERRY DONNELLY, insurance company executive; b. Bisbee, Ariz., June 25, 1938; s. D. K. and Vivian (Farrar) P.; m. Angela Briseño, June 26, 1965; children: Erik David, Daniel Kirk, Angelica Michelle, Jerry Benjamin. BA, U. Ariz., 1960; BD, Princeton Theol. Sem., 1963, Master of Divinity, 1963; MS, U. Calif., San Jose, 1969. Pastor Stewart Meml. Presbyn. Ch., San Francisco, 1965-67; co-dir. The St. Mark Community, San Jose, 1968-69; mass media researcher Internat. Rsch. Assocs., Mexico City, 1969-74; mktg. dir. Organizacion Radio Formula, Mexico City, 1974-78; agt. N.Y. Life, Tucson, 1978-84; co-owner Internat. Ins. Assocs., Inc., Tucson, 1984—. Contbr. articles to various Presbyn. publs. Vol. campaign to elect Robert Kennedy, 1968. Work study fellow United Presbyn. Ch., Mexico City, 1963-65. Mem. Nat. Assn. Life Underwriters, Tucson Rod and Gun Club. Democrat. Home: 11650 E Speedway Tucson AZ 85748 Office: Internat Ins Assocs 5447 E 5th St Ste 200 Tucson AZ 85711

PENCE, LAWRENCE CYRUS, surgeon; b. Spokane, Wash., July 21, 1910; s. Cyrus Griswold and Ollie Jane (Rounds) P.; m. Christine A. Snow (div. Mar. 1973); children: Sally Ann, Judith B., Robert L., Christopher C.; m. Maurine A. LeSeur, Aug. 31, 1973. MA, Stanford U., 1932, MD, 1936. Diplomate Am. Bd. Surgery. Intern San Francisco Gen. Hosp., 1935-36; resident in pathology Stanford Sch. Med. Lane Hosp., San Francisco, 1936-37; resident in gen. surgery Los Angeles Gen. Hosp., 1937-39; surgeon, gen. practice medicine Spokane (Wash.) hosp., 1940-42; surgeon U.S. Army 31st Portable Surg. Hosp., PTO, 1942-45; surgery dept. chief U.S. Army Baxter Gen. Hosp., Spokane, 1945-46; surgeon, gen. practice medicine Spokane (Wash.) hosp., 1946-82; cons. Wash. State Dept. Soc. Health Services, Spokane, 1982-84, Armed Forces Exam. Sta., Spokane, 1984—; dir. med. edn. St. Luke's Hosp. Spokane, 1946-65; mem. Project Hope, Cen. and So. Am., 1962, 64-66; surgeon and comdr. reserves 85th Gen. Hosp. , Spokane, 1952-70; surgeon Direct Relief Internat., Cen. Am. and Carribean, 1974, 76, 80. Contbr. articles to sci. jours. Mem. St. Luke's Found. Fellow ACS; mem. St. Luke's Hosp. Found.; Rotary (pres. Spokane chpt. 1974) (recipient Paul Harris award, 1976). Home: 907 S Azalea Dr Spokane WA 99204

PENDELL, SUE DAVIS, speech communication educator; b. Baton Rouge, Dec. 16, 1946; d. Frank B. and Elizabeth (Young) Davis. BS, Fla. State U., 1966; MA, Auburn U., 1970; PhD, U. Utah, 1976. Instr. speech U. Wis., La Crosse, 1971-73; asst. prof. speech communication, dir. speech extension U. Mo., Columbia, 1976-79; asst. then assoc. prof. speech communication Colo. State U., Ft. Collins, 1979—; faculty rep. Colo. Bd. Agr., 1988—. Author: (with others) Speech Coursebook, 1986; contbr. articles to profl. jours. Cons. Ft. Collins Area United Way, 1986-88, bd. dirs., 1988—. Mem. Environ. Design Rsch. Assn., Internat. Communication Assn., Speech Communication Asn., Soc. for Study Symbolic Interaction, Western Speech Communication Assn., Phi Kappa Phi. Office: Colo State U Dept Speech Communication 302 WH Fort Collins CO 80523

PENDER, DOUGLAS HOWARD, social service administrator; b. Auburn, N.Y., Jan. 1, 1934; s. Howard Douglas and Mary Elizabeth (Schetrompf) P.; m. Crystle Fayne Klein, Feb. 12, 1956; children: Helen Elizabeth Wood, Judith Fayne Walker. BA, Idaho State U., 1961; DD (hon.), Universal Life Ch., 1979. Dir. Mohave Co. Community Action Agy., Kingman, Ariz., 1970-71, Hualapai Com. Action Agy., Peach Springe, Ariz., 1971-76; career counselor Ariz. Army N.G., Kingman, 1976-80; human service worker Ariz. Dept. Econ. Security, Lake Havasu City, 1980-86; pres. Concepts Beyond, Lake Havasu City, 1986—; bd. dirs. Graphoanalytics, Lake Havasu, 1986—. Pub. Hualapai Times, 1973. Served with Ariz. N.G., 1971-80. Mem. Am. Assn. Counseling and Devel., Nat. Career Devel. Assn., Am. Rehab. Counselors Assn. Republican. Presbyterian. Lodges: Shriners (sec. treas. Lake Havasu City club 1982-84), Masons. Home: 457 Sunfield Dr Lake Havasu City AZ 86407 Office: GraphoAnalytics Inc 1990D McCulloch Blvd Suite 265 Lake Havasu City AZ 86403

PENDERGHAST, THOMAS FREDERICK, business educator; b. Cin., Apr. 23, 1936; s. Elmer T. and Dolores C. (Huber) P.; BS, Marquette U., 1958; MBA, Calif. State U., Long Beach, 1967; D in Bus. Adminstrn. Nova U., 1987; m. Marjorie Craig, Aug. 12, 1983; children: Brian, Shawna, Steven, Dean, Maria. Sci. programmer Autonetics, Inc., Anaheim, Calif., 1960-64; bus. programmer Douglas Missile & Space Ctr., Huntington Beach, Calif., 1964-66; computer specialist N.Am. Rockwell Co., 1966-69; asst. prof. Calif. State U., Long Beach, 1969-72; assoc. prof. Sch. Bus. and Mgmt., Pepperdine U., Los Angeles, 1972—; spl. adviser Commn. on Engring. Edn., 1968; v.p. Visual Computing Co., 1969-71; founder, pres. Scoreboard Animation Systems, 1971-77; exec. v.p. Microfilm Identification Systems, 1977-79; pres. Data Processing Auditors, Inc., 1981—; data processing cons. designing computer system for fin. health and mfg. orgns., 1972—. Mem. Orange County Blue Ribbon Com. on Data Processing, 1973; mem. Orange County TEC Policy Bd., 1982-87. Served to lt. USNR, 1958-60. Cert. in data processing. Mem. Users of Automatic Info. Display Equipment (pres. 1966). Author: Entrepreneurial Simulation Program, 1988. Home: 17867 Bay St Fountain Valley CA 92708

PENDLAY, JAMES RALPH, physics technician; b. L.A., Mar. 26, 1945; s. Oliver Scott Pendlay and Wilhelmina Mae (Rosendale) Walker; m. Gloria Szymanski, Mar. 10, 1975. Student, U. Calif., Riverside, 1963-68. Technician U. Bristol, Eng., 1974-84; lab. specialist physics dept. Calif. Inst. Tech., Pasadena, 1985—. Office: Calif Inst Tech 1201 E California Blvd 106-38 Pasadena CA 91125

PENDLETON, ALAN R., conservation agency executive; b. Riverside, Calif., May 26, 1940; s. Roy Clayton and Carolyn (Parker) P.; m. Joyce Ellen Edwards, Aug. 22, 1964; 1 child, David. AB, U. Calif., Berkeley, 1961; JD, U. Calif., San Francisco, 1969. Bar: Calif. Tchr. Anderson Valley Sch. Dist., Boonville, Calif., 1970; atty. San Francisco Bay Conservation and Devel. Commn., 1971-76, chief regulatory functions, 1976-81, dep. dir., 1981-83, exec. dir., 1983—; bd. dirs. East Brothers Light Station, Richmond, Calif., Flowerlane, Inc., Oakland, Calif.; mem. environ. com. 9th Dist. Ct. Calif., 1985—. Contbr. articles to profl. jours. Mem. Save San Francisco Bay Assn., Berkeley. Lt. USAF, 1962-67. Mem. Bay Area Planning Dirs. Assn. (bd. dirs. 1987—), Calif. Bar Assn., Sierra Club. Office: San Francisco Bay Conservatory & Devel Commn 30 Van Ness Ave Rm 2011 San Francisco CA 94102

PENDLETON, OTHNIEL ALSOP, fund raiser, clergyman; b. Washington, Aug. 22, 1911; s. Othniel Alsop and Ingeborg (Berg) P.; m. Flordora Mellquist, May 15, 1935; children: John, James (dec.), Thomas, Ann, Susan. AB, Union Coll., Schenectady, N.Y., 1933; BD, Eastern Bapt. Theol. Sem., 1936; MA, U. Pa., 1936, PhD, 1945; postgrad., Columbia U., 1937-38. Ordained to ministry Bapt. Ch., 1936. Pastor chs. Jersey City, 1935-39, Phila., 1939-43; dean Sioux Falls Coll., S.D., 1943-45; fund raiser Am. Bapt. Ch., N.Y.C., 1945-47; fund-raiser Mass. Bapt. Ch., Boston, 1947-54; fund-raiser Seattle, Chgo., Boston, Washington, N.Y.C. and Paris, France, 1955-64, Westwood, Mass., 1971-84; staff mem. Marts & Lundy, Inc., N.Y.C., 1964-71; lectr. Andover-Newton Sem., Newton, Mass., 1958, Boston U. Sch. Theology, 1958, Harvard U., Cambridge, Mass., 1977-84. Author: New Techniques for Church Fund Raising, 1955, Fund Raising: A Guide to Non-Profit Organizations, 1981; contbr. articles in field to profl. jours. Address: 529 Berkeley Ave Claremont CA 91711

PENHARLOW, DAVID PAUL, electrical engineer; b. Lackawanna, N.Y., July 20, 1943; s. Walter and Helen (Ross) P.; m. Julie Linden; 1 child, Jason. BEE, Calif. Poly. Inst., 1966. Instrumentation engr. Boeing Corp., Seattle, 1966-70, Lockheed Corp., Burbank, Calif., 1970-74; engring. supr. Hughes Helicopter, Culver City, Calif., 1974-80; engring. mgr. Loral Data Systems, San Diego, 1980-82, Aydin Vector, Newtown, Pa., 1982—; guest lectr. U. Tenn. Space Inst., Tullahoma, 1985, 86, 87. Contbr. articles to profl. publs. Staff sgt. USNG, 1964-72. Mem. Soc. Flight Test Engrs. Republican.

PENIKETT, ANTONY DAVID JOHN, politician; b. Nov. 14, 1945; s. Erik John Keith and Sarah Ann (Colwell) P.; m. Lula Mary Johns, 1974; children—John Tahmoh, Sarah Lahlil, Stephanie Yahsan. Exec. asst. to nat. leader New Dem. Party, Ottawa, Ont., Canada, 1975-76, nat. pres., 1981-85, fed. councillor, 1973—; leader New Dem. Party, Whitehorse, Y.T., Canada, 1980—; campaign mgr. New Dem. Party, N.W.T., Canada, 1972; city councillor City of Whitehorse, Y.T., Canada, 1977-79; elected mem. Yukon Legis. Assembly, 1978—; opposition leader Yukon Legis. Assembly, Y.T., Canada, 1982-85; elected govt. leader Yukon Terr. Yukon Legis. Assembly, 1985—. Author (film): The Mad Trapper, 1972; La Patrouille Perdue, 1974. Mem. Christian Socialist Ch. Home: PO Box 4584, Whitehorse, YK Canada Y1A 2R8 Office: Yukon Territorial Govt, PO Box 2703, Whitehorse, YK Canada Y1A 2C6 *

PENISTON, EUGENE GILBERT, psychologist; b. Osceola, Iowa, June 23, 1931; s. Milton James and Delia B. (Youing) P.; m. Helen M. Kerr, Oct. 16, 1959; children: Denise R., Eugene Lyle. BA, Cen. State U., Wilberforce, Ohio, 1953; MS, S.D. State U., 1962; EdD., Okla. State U., 1972. Am. Bd. Med. Psychotherapy; lic. clin. psychologist, S.D. Chief sch. psychologist Clarance (N.Y.) Pub. Schs., 1965-69; chief psychology svc. tng. ctr. Va. State Hosp., Petersburg, 1972-75; assoc. prof. Va. State U., Petersburg, 1975-76; mental health cons. HHS, USPHS, Roosevelt, Utah, 1976-79; cons. clin. psychologist Redfield (S.D.) State Hosp., HHS, USPHS, 1976-81; clin. psychologist VA Med. Ctr., Ft. Lyon, Colo., 1981—; profl. adv. coun., Am. Bd. Med. Psychotherapists, Nashville, 1986—. Editorial cons. and mem. of editorial bd. for jours. and newsletters in field; contbr. articles to profl. jours. Mem. Human Rights Commn. Ark. Valley Community Ctr. for the Handicapped and Retarded Persons, Inc., La Junta, Colo., 1988—. Lt. U.S. Army, 1953-56. Recipient Spl. Contribution award, VA Med. Ct., Ft. Lyon, 1983. Mem. Am. Psychol. Assn. (divs. 17 counseling psychology, 13 cons. psychology), N.Y. Acad. Scis., Phi Delta Kappa (Outstanding Achievement award, 1988, treas. 1984-88). Lutheran. Home: 1919 Cimarron Ave La Junta CO 81050 Office: Psychology Svc 116B VA Med Ctr Fort Lyon CO 81038

PENMAN, BRIAN EDWARD, radio personality; b. Wilkensburg, Pa., Aug. 1, 1959; s. Edward John and Dorothy May (Smead) P.; m. Melisa Joan Felty, Sept. 27, 1980; 1 child, Kurtiss William. Student, Los Medanos Community Coll., Pittsburg, Calif., 1978; student, Ohlone Community Coll., Fremont, Calif., 1982-83. Maintenance engr. Clear Pane Window Cleaning, Concord, Calif., 1975-83; welder C.M. Farr Constrn. Co., San Ramon, Calif., 1979-82; air personality Sta. KLOQ, Merced, Calif., 1982-83, Sta. KSTN, Stockton, Calif., 1983-84, Sta. KWUN, Concord, 1984-85, Sta. KITS-FM, San Francisco, 1985-86, Sta. KIOI-FM, San Francisco, 1986-89, Stas. KKIS and KXXX-FM, San Francisco, 1989—. Bd. regents communications dept. Ohlone Community Coll., 1986—; media liaison Walk Am., San Francisco area March of Dimes, 1986; vol. Jerry Lewis Telethon, Oakland, Calif., 1988. Mem. M.H. DeYoung-Steinhart Aquarium. Republican. Office: Sta KIOI-FM 700 Montgomery St San Francisco CA 94111

PENNELL, BRUCE JAMES, development association executive; b. Newport, Wash., Nov. 25, 1946; s. Keith James and Selma Elaine (Schibsby) P.; m. Sharilee Horgdal, Sept. 6, 1968 (div. 1977); children: Hope Elizabeth, Joshua James. BS, Eastern Wash. U., 1969. Dep. dir. Okanogan (Wash.) Community Action, 1976-78; interim dir. N. Central Wash. Supervised Skills, Wenatchee, 1978-79; chief exec. office NE Wash. Rural Resource Devel. Assn., Colville, 1979—; sole practice community devel. cons. Chmn. Partnership for Rural Improvement, Pullman, Wash., 1982-87, Rural Wash. Task Force, 1983-84; chmn. com. Gov.'s Task Force on Hunger, Seattle, 1986—. Served with USN, 1969-73. Democrat. Congregationalist. Office: NE Wash Rural Resource Devel N 320 Main Colville WA 99114

PENNELL, MICHAEL NEALE, real estate executive; b. Tokyo, Mar. 12, 1936; s. Elmer Lewis and Frances (Colt) P.; m. Joan Glinski, Oct. 15, 1961 (div. Oct. 1971); 1 child, Michele Elizabethe. BA, U. Wyo., 1958; JD, U. Calif., Hastings, 1966. Subrogation asst. State Compensation Ins. Fund, San Francisco, 1967-68; real estate exec. shopping ctr. devel. and leasing div. F.W. Woolworth Co., 1968-69; corp. trial counsel Western regional office Sears, Roebuck & Co., 1969-75; assoc. Fagan, Klugman, Monroe & Edell, Beverly Hills, Calif., 1975-76, Bollington, Pennell, Stilz & Bloeser, Woodland Hills, Calif., 1976-81, Morganstern, Mann & Smith, Beverly Hills, 1981-82, Dunford & Pennell, Hollywood, Calif., 1982-83; exec. v.p. NAVESCO Corp., Culver City, Calif., 1983-84; chief operating officer, broker Mike Glickman Realty, Inc., Woodland Hills, 1984—; chief fin. officer Choice Escrow, Encino, Calif., 1988, Homeowners Fin., Encino, 1988, Homeowners Ins., Encino, 1988, Integrated Acctg., Encino, 1988. Lt. USNR, 1958-63. Mem. Calif. Bar Assn., Calif. Assn. Realtors, Nat. Assn. Realtors, San Fernando Bd. Realtors, L.A. Bd. Realtors, Simi Bd. Realtors, Conejo Bd. Realtors, Burbank Bd. Realtors, Real Estate Brokerage Coun., Mulholland Tennis Club. Office: Mike Glickman Realty 19836 Ventura Blvd Woodland Hills CA 90069

PENNER, JAMES R., finance executive; b. Helena, Mont., Mar. 28, 1946; s. Robert Isaac and Elsie Ann (Jorgenson) P.; m. Barbara Jean Hanson, June 24, 1968; children: Brett Edward, Julie Michelle. BS in Acctg., U. Mont., 1968; MBA, Columbus Coll., 1979. Chartered fin. analyst. Acct. Investors Diversified Svcs., Mpls., 1968-74; chief auditor Callaway Gardens, Pine Mountain, Ga., 1974-79; pvt. investor LaCrosse, Wis., 1979-80; investment officer First Interstate Bank, Billings, Mont., 1980-84; investment officer Mont. Bd. Investments, Helena, 1984-89, chief investment officer, 1989—. Bd. dirs. St. John's Lutheran Home, Billings, 1984; treas. Helena Youth Choirs, Helena, 1989; pres. Our Redeemer's Lutheran Ch., Helena, 1987. Named Outstanding Jaycee, Harris County Jaycees, Pine Mountain, 1978. Mem. Barbershop Chorus (Helena chpt. pres. 1988-89). Home: 1601 Highland Helena MT 59601 Office: Montana Bd Investments 555 Fuller Helena MT 59620

PENNINGTON, BRUCE WILSON, II, service company executive; b. Washington, June 29, 1947; s. Bruce Wilson and Twila Dean (Reid) P.; m. Karen Baptist, Aug. 14, 1974 (div. Jan. 1976); m. Cynthia Ann Haseltine; children: Brandie Ann, Lynette Ann, Travis Bruce. AA in Bus., Los Angeles Valley Jr. Coll., Van Nuys, Calif., 1977; BA in Mgmt., U. Redlands, 1984. Electronic technician Singer-Librascope Co., Glendale, Calif., 1969-71; mgr. prodn. test Terminal Data Corp., Van Nuys, Calif., 1971-74; field engr. Terminal Data Corp., Woodland Hills, Calif., 1974-77, western regional svc. mgr., 1977-82, sr. tech. specialist, 1983-84; dir. product support Terminal Data Corp., Moorpark, Calif., 1985—; tech. specialist Datapraphix, San Diego, 1982-83; v.p. Terminal Data Svc. Corp., Moorpark, 1985—. With U.S. Army, 1964-69, Vietnam. Mem. Amateur Radio Relay League, Amateur Satellite Corp. Republican. Baptist. Office: Terminal Data Svc Corp 5898 Condor Dr Moorpark CA 93021-2601

PENNISI, VINCENT RAYMOND, plastic surgeon; b. Jamaica, N.Y., May 13, 1923; s. Vincenzo Pennisi and Mary (Carmela) Sorrentino; m. Madeline Heckeri; children: Madeline Mary Fendler, Vincent Peter, Vinette Marie Ramsay. BS, L.I. U., 1943; DDS, St. Louis U., 1946; MD, Georgetown U., 1950. Intern Mary Immaculate Hosp.; resident in plastic surgery Bronx Vets. Hosp. and St. Francis Meml. Hosp.; pvt. practice San Francisco, 1958—; pres. med. staff St. Francis Meml. Hosp., San Francisco, 1967-69, pres., trustee, 1982-84, past dir. plastic surgery and residency program and burn ctr., dir. Subcutaneous Mastectomy Data Evaluation Ctr.; cons. Letterman Army Med. Ctr. Served to capt. U.S. Army, 1956-58. Fellow Am. Coll. Surgeons; Mem. AMA, Calif. Med. Assn., Am. Assn. Plastic Surgeons, Am. Soc. Plastic and Reconstuctive Surgeons. Office: 490 Post St #723 San Francisco CA 94102

PENNOCK, BRADFORD LEE, electronics engineer; b. Stockton, Calif., Dec. 21, 1952; s. Jerry Pennock and Mable Sheets; m. Suzy Schussler, July 23, 1988. BS in Electronics, Ariz. State U., 1976; AA in Music, Phoenix Coll., 1979. Musician several bands, Phoenix, 1976-79; v.p. Audio and Design/Calrec, Belfair, Wash., 1981-86; pres. BP Electronics and Design,

Bozeman, Mont., 1987—; musician Max Delay Band, Bozeman, 1987—. Asst. engr. sound effects movie Tron, 1975; producer numerous records and tapes. Democrat. Office: BP Electronics and Design 34 W Main Bozeman MT 59715

PENNY, LAURA JEAN, librarian; b. Union City, Tenn., June 25, 1956; d. Glen Jones and Harriet Smith (Gould) P. BS in Econs., Lambuth Coll., 1978; MLS, U. Ariz., 1980. Asst. librarian local history and genealogy Pikes Peak Library Dist., Colorado Springs, Colo., 1981-84; info. officer Inmos Corp., Colorado Springs, 1984-86; dir. library Colo. State Hosp., Pueblo, 1987—. Author: A Tempstuous Voyage, 1987, Abstracts of Strafford County, 1987, Abstracts of Washington County, 1988. Pres. El Paso County Democratic Women's Club, Colorado Springs, 1986-87; chmn. El Paso County Democratic Com., 1987—. Mem. Colo. Council Library Devel., Pikes Peak Genealogical Soc. (editor 1985-87). Methodist. Home: 910 Tenderfoot Hill Rd #101 Colorado Springs CO 80906 Office: Colo State Hosp 1600 W 24th St Pueblo CO 81003

PENTZ, EDWIN LESTER, JR., wine broker; b. Chambersburg, Pa., Aug. 5, 1942; s. Edwin Lester and Grace (Lambert) P.; m. Janet Sachiko Hirata, Dec. 24, 1963; children: Nastasya Sachiko, Shelley Ayame. BA, Am. River Coll., Sacramento, 1972. Sales rep. McKesson Liquor Co., Honolulu, 1965-68; dist. mgr. Paul Masson Vineyards, Sacramento, 1968-72; regional mgr. Browne Vintners, San Francisco, 1972-74; div. mgr. Sonoma Vineyards, Chgo., 1974-75; nat. sales mgr. Chevalier Imports, Chgo., 1975-77; v.p. sales and mktg. Park Benziger Co., Yonkers, N.Y., 1977-81; pres. Great Am. Wine Co., Greenwich, Conn., 1981-86, Sogeri, U.S.A., Inc., Honolulu, 1985--, E L P Enterprises, Inc., Honolulu, 1986--. Author: The Wilson Saga, 1985, The Kaslovi Deception, 1986. Cpl. USMC, 1960-64. Mem. Chaine des Rotisseurs, Confrerie du Medoc et Bontemps, Austraila/Am. C. of C. (mem. program com.), Hawaii C. of C., Knights of the Vine (master comdr. Republican. Office: E L P Enterprises Inc PO Box 61446 Honolulu HI 96839-1446

PENTZ, PERI DIANE, computer consultant; b. Mpls., May 14, 1958; d. James Joseph and Peri (Norton) P. BA in Econs., U. San Francisco, 1980, MA in Econs., 1987. Mem. bank mgmt. staff Bank of Am., San Francisco, 1980-85; computer cons. City and County of San Francisco, 1985-88; trust mgr. Bank of Calif., San Francisco, 1988—; computer cons. various small bus., San Francisco, 1984—. Photographer: Reflections, 1986. Computer cons. Self Help for the Elderly, San Francisco; computer operator Hunger Project, San Francisco, 1987; computer operator and trainer for AIDS Project, San Francisco, 1987-88. Mem. Am. Mgmt. Assn., Commonwealth Club, Women in Bus. Democrat. Home: 194 23d Ave San Francisco CA 94121 Office: Bank of Calif 400 California St San Francisco CA 94102

PENWELL, CLIFFORD FORREST, company executive; b. Burbank, Calif., Oct. 23, 1952; s. Clifford R. and Mildred (Monaco) P.; m. Alice P. Perazzo, June 1, 1975. BA in English, U. Nev., Las Vegas, 1975, MA in English, 1978. Mem. prodn. personnel Las Vegas Rev.-Jour., 1973-75; grad. instr. English U. Nev., Las Vegas, 1975-77; dir. publicity, advt. Flamingo Capri Hotel, Las Vegas, 1977-78; civilian editorial advisor U.S. Mil., Fed. Republic Germany, 1978-80; vol., rep. Emissaries of Divine Light, Eng., Fed. Republic Germany, Republic South Africa, Can., U.S., 1980-85; dir. ground ops., editor EDL, Inc., Loveland, Colo., 1985—; historian Friends of Library, Las Vegas, 1977-78; editorial advisor Found. House Publs., Loveland, 1988; co-dir. Sunrise Ranch Writers Conf., Loveland, 1988. Founding editor (academic jour.) Freshman English Resource Notes, 1975-78; ghostwriter numerous articles, 1972—. Mem. State Dem. Caucus Cen. Com.,voter registrar, Las Vegas, 1972; Dem. student lobbyist, Washington, 1972. Mem. Loveland Repeater Assn. Mem. Emissaries of Divine Light Ch. Home and Office: EDL Inc 5569 N County Rd 29 Loveland CO 80537

PENWELL, JONES CLARK, real estate appraiser, consultant; b. Crisp, Tex., Dec. 19, 1921; s. Clark Moses and Sarah Lucille (Jones) P.; B.S., Colo. State U., 1949; m. A. Jerry Jones, July 1, 1967; children—Dale Maria, Alan Lee, John Steven, Laurel Anne, Tracy Lynn. Farm mgmt. supr. Farmers Home Adminstrn., Dept. Agr., 1949-58; rancher 1958-61; real estate appraiser/realty officer Dept. Interior, Tex., Calif., Ariz., Colo., Washington, 1961-78, chief appraiser Bur. Reclamation, Lakewood, Colo., 1978-80; ind. fee appraiser, cons., 1980—. Served with USN, 1940-46. Accredited rural appraiser; cert. review appraiser; recipient Outstanding Performance awards U.S. Bur. Reclamation, 1964, 75, 80. Mem. Am. Soc. Farm Mgrs. and Rural Appraisers, Internat. Right-of-Way Assn., Nat. Assn. Rev. Appraisers (regional v.p. 1978-79), Jefferson County Bd. Realtors. Democrat. Presbyterian. Clubs: Elks, Rotary, Mt. Vernon Country. Author: Reviewing Condemnation Appraisal Reports, 1980; The Valuation of Easements, 1980. Home and office: 10100 W 21st Pl Lakewood CO 80215

PEPLAU, HILDEGARD ELIZABETH, nursing educator; b. Reading, Pa., Sept. 1, 1909; d. Gustav and Ottylie (Elgert) P. Diploma, Pottstown Hosp. Sch. Nursing, 1931; BA, Bennington Coll., 1943; MA, Columbia U., N.Y.C., 1947, EdD, 1953; cert., William Alanson White Inst., 1953; DSc (hon.), Alfred U., 1970, Duke U., 1974, Columbia U., 1983, Rutgers U., New Brunswick, N.J., 1985; Doctor of Nursing Sci. (hon.), Boston Coll., 1972; Doctor of Humane Letters (hon.), U. Indpls., 1987. RN, N.J., Calif. Exec. officer Coll. Health Svc., Bennington (Vt.) Coll., 1938-43; dir. grad. program psychiatric nursing Tchrs. Coll., Columbia U., N.Y.C., 1948-53; exec. dir. Am. Nurses' Assn., Kansas City, 1969-70; dir. grad. program psychiatric nursing Rutgers U., New Brunswick, N.J., 1955-74; prof. emerita Rutgers U., New Brunswick, 1974—. Author: Interpersonal Relations in Nursing, 1952; contbr. numerous articles to profl. publs. and jours., 1942—. 1st lt. Nurse Corps, U.S. Army, 1943-45. Mem. Am. Nurses' Assn., Am. Acad. Nursing, Internat. Council Nurses (3rd v.p. 1977-81, bd. dirs. 1973-77), Nat. League Nursing. Democrat. Lutheran. Home: 14024 Otsego St Sherman Oaks CA 94123-1225

PEPPER, DAVID M., physicist, educator, author, inventor; b. Los Angeles, Mar. 9, 1949; s. Harold and Edith (Kleinplatz) P. BS in Physics summa cum laude, UCLA, 1971; MS in Applied Physics, Calif. Inst. Tech., 1974, PhD in Applied Physics, 1980. Mem. tech. staff Hughes Research Labs., Malibu, Calif., 1973-87, sr. staff physicist, 1987—; adj. prof. math. and physics Pepperdine U., Malibu, 1981—. Co-author: Optical Phase Conjugation, 1983, Laser Handbook Vol. 4, 1985, Physics and Applications of Spatial Light Modulators, 1989; guest editor Soc. Photo-Optical Engring. Instrumentation Jour. 1982 (Rudolf Kingslake award 1982); guest editor IEEE Jour. Quantum Electronics, 1989—; contbr. numerous articles to profl. tech. jours. and periodicals including Scientific American; patentee in field. Mem. Sons and Daughters of 1939 Club, 2d Generation of Martyrs Meml., Mus. Holocaust. NSF trainee Calif. Inst. Tech., 1971; Howard Hughes fellow Hughes Aircraft Co., 1973-80; recipient Hughes Research Labs. Publ. of Yr., 1986. Mem. AAAS, IEEE, Am. Phys. Soc., Optical Soc. Am., Sigma Xi (v.p. 1986-87, chpt. pres. 1987-88), Sigma Pi Sigma. Jewish. Office: Hughes Rsch Labs RL 65 3011 Malibu Canyon Rd Malibu CA 90265

PEPPER, JOHN ROY, oil and gas executive; b. Denver, Feb. 24, 1937; s. Wesley Wayne and Lucille (Stith) P.; m. Sallie K. Force, Dec. 13, 1958 (div. July 1970); m. Judithea Lawrence, Sept. 24, 1977; stepchildren: Sarah Douglas-Broten, Kenneth R. Douglas. BBA, U. Denver, 1961; postgrad., UCLA, 1962, U. Denver, 1965. Analyst Texaco, Inc., Los Angeles, 1962-63; landman Texaco, Inc., Bakersfield, Calif., 1963-65; prin. John Pepper, Landman, Denver, 1965-75; owner, operator John R. Pepper Oil & Gas Co., Denver, 1975—; bd. dirs. Trans-Telecom, Miami, Fla.; cons. Organizer Friends of Bob Crider campaign, Denver, 1985. Mem. Ind. Petroleum Assn. Mountain States, Ind. Petroleum Assn. of Ams. (pub. lands com. 1968-74), Kenosha Trout Club (chmn. first aid and fish procurement coms. 1974-82). Republican. Lutheran. Home: 6161 S Forest Ct Littleton CO 80121 Office: John R Pepper Oil & Gas Co 1800 Glenarm Pl Denver CO 80202

PEPPER, WILLIAM CHARLIE, computer specialist; b. Anderson, S.C., Dec. 9, 1948; s. James Herbert Pepper and Annie Mae (Ford) Klingler. AA, Anderson Coll., 1969; BA in Math., Clemson (S.C.) U., 1975. Tchr. secondary edn. Anderson Sch. Dist. 1, Piedmont, S.C., 1975-76; computer operator Dresser Industries, Belton, S.C., 1976-78; computer programmer State of N.C., Raleigh, 1978-80; programmer analyst Fed. Res. Bank, San Francisco, 1980-82; cons. Traidigm Internat., San Francisco, 1983—. Democrat. Baptist. Office: Triadigm Internat 345 California St #1220 San Francisco CA 94109

PEPPERCORN, JOHN EDWARD, chemical company executive; b. Hutchinson, Kans., Sept. 3, 1937; s. John Edward and Lorena Fay (Hirt) P.; m. Mary Claire Purcell, July 25, 1961; children: Michael Edward, Mark Purcell. BSBA, U. Kans., 1960; grad. Tuck Exec. Program, Dartmouth Coll., 1978. Mgr. plastic sales Gulf Oil Chems., Houston, 1966-69, mktg. mgr., 1973-77, v.p. U.S. plastics, 1977-81, v.p. aromatics and derivatives, 1981-83; gen. mgr. Gulf Plastic Products Co., Morristown, N.J., 1969-72; v.p. domestic mktg. Gulf Oil Products, Houston, 1983-85; v.p., gen. mgr. aromatics Chevron Chem. Co., Houston, 1985; sr. v.p. indsl. chems. Chevron Chem. Co., San Francisco, 1985-86, sr. v.p., 1986—. Served to capt. U.S. Army, 1960-61. Mem. Soc. Plastic Industry (bd. dirs. 1978-81), Flexible Packaging Assn. (bd. dirs. 1980-82). Office: Chevron Chem Co 575 Market St San Francisco CA 94105 *

PEQUEGNAT, LINDA HAITHCOCK, biologist, researcher; b. Bedford, Ind., Oct. 27, 1931; d. Fred Daniel Haithcock and Virginia Lee (Menaugh) Arnold; m. Willis Eugene Pequegnat, Nov. 22, 1957; children: Marina Lynn, William Gordon. BA, Pomona Coll., 1953; MS, Scripps Inst. Oceanography, 1957; PhD, Tex. A&M U., 1970. Rsch. scientist radiobiol. lab. U. Tex., Austin, 1953-54; lab. technician Scripps Inst. Oceanography, La Jolla, Calif., 1954-57; lectr., rsch. scientist dept. oceanography Tex. A&M U., College Station, 1974-81, curator systematic collection marine organisms, 1974-81; rsch. scientist Tereco Corp., College Station, 1970-83; pvt. practice cons. rsch. scientist La Jolla, 1983—; cons. rsch. scientist LGL Ecol. Rsch. Assocs., Bryan, Tex., 1983-87. Co-editor: Biota of the West Flower Garden Bank, 1974; mem. editorial bd. Jour. of Biol. Oceanography, 1979—. Pres. Family Planning Clinic, Bryan, 1966-68. NSF fellow, 1955; Pomona Coll. scholar, 1950-53. Mem. Am. Soc. Limnology and Oceanography, Soc. of Systematic Zoology, Am. Soc. Zoologists, Crustacean Soc., Western Soc. Naturalists, Honor Soc. of Phi Kappa Phi, Calif. Scholarship Fedn. (life), AAUW (pres., v.p. Bryan chpt. 1967-72). Democrat. Unitarian. Home and Office: 8463 Paseo Del Ocaso La Jolla CA 92037

PERALA, SUSAN MARIE, advertising company executive, bookkeeper; b. Portland, Oreg., Dec. 11, 1943; d. Everett Joseph and Cleo Ann (Wiesendanger) Gottschalk; m. Gene A. Perala, June 21, 1963; 1 child, Dennis. BA, U. Oreg., 1961; postgrad., Portland State U., 1962. Bookkeeper McCoys Bookkeeping Svc., Portland, 1961-63; office mgr., bookkeeper Branch & Bauer Advt., Portland, 1964-74, Al Bauer Advt., Portland, 1980—. Mem. Rocky Butte Little League, Portland, 1974-78, Parkrose Jr. High Parent Group, Portland, 1970; pres., treas. Jr. C. of C., 1965-70. Mem. Tyee Yacht Club. Office: Al Bauer Advt 2470 NW Westover Rd Portland OR 97210

PERALTA-RAMOS, LEE GAMBLE, architectural and interior designer; b. St. Louis, Aug. 5, 1952; d. James Carr and Dorothy Lee (Wharton) Gamble; m. A.H. Peralta-Ramos, May 31, 1975 (div. 1989); children: Lindsey Elise, Ashley Elizabeth. BS, Skidmore Coll., 1974; degree in Interior Design, N.Y. Sch. Interior Design, 1976. Asst. buyer Abraham & Strauss, Bklyn., 1974-75; mgr. Trevi Co., Pitts., 1975; buyer Saks Fifth Ave., N.Y.C., 1975-77; pres. West Wind Designs, Cody, Wyo., 1977—; owner Southfork Expdns. Ltd., Cody, 1987—; cons. design Wyo. Waterfowl Park, Cody, 1984-86, bd. dirs. Mem. Zoo Mont. (bd. dirs. 1985—). Republican. Presbyterian. Office: Solitary Ventures Inc PO Box 2045 Cody WY 82414

PERATA, KATHY LOIS, food company executive; b. Malden, Mass., Dec. 9, 1945; d. Malcolm Gordon and Evelyn Maude (Elliott) MacDonald; m. Michael Vail Sr., Mar. 17, 1963 (div. 1978); children: Michael David Jr., Carol Ann; m. George Alfred Perata, May 6, 1979; (foster children) Thomas, Charles, Maggie, Kate, Gary, Shannon. Diploma, Aragon High Sch., San Mateo, Calif., 1963. Cert. adult edn. tchr., Calif. Cake decorating tchr. San Carlos (Calif.) Recreation Ctr., 1970-76, San Mateo Recreation Ctr., 1970-80, Burlingame (Calif.) Recreation Ctr., 1971-79; tchr. adult edn. San Mateo and Burlingame, 1973-77; owner, pres. Kathy's Kreative Kakes, San Mateo, 1975—; speaker in field. Founder, mem. San Mateo County Foster Parents Assn., 1968, Calif. State Foster Parents Assn., Santa Rosa, 1968. Named Foster Mother of Yr., San Mateo County Foster Parents Assn., 1975. Mem. San Mateo C. of C., Redwood City C. of C., South San Francisco C. of C. Methodist. Home: 404 W 37th Ave San Mateo CA 94403 Office: Kathy's Kreative Kakes 631 S B St San Mateo CA 94401

PERCY, HELEN SYLVIA, physician; b. Atlanta, May 7, 1923; d. George L. and Sophia (Toulchin) P.; 1 child, Valentina Stewart-Annor. BS, U. San Francisco, 1951; MD, Med. Coll. Pa., 1958. Diplomate Am. Bd. Family Practice. Intern Harbor Gen. Hosp., Torrance, Calif., 1958-59; resident Harbor Gen. Hosp., Torrance, 1959; physician Maui Med. Group, Lahaina, Hawaii, 1968—; asst. prof. medicine U. Hawaii, Honolulu, 1978—. Chair adv. bd. Maui Community Health Ctr., 1986-89; v.p. Maui AIDS Found., 1986-89. Mem. AMA, Maui County Med. Soc. (councilor 1988—), Hawaii Med. Assn. Democrat. Buddhist. Office: Maui Med Group 130 Prison St Lahaina HI 96761

PERCY, LEE EDWARD, motion picture film editor; b. Kalamazoo, Feb. 10, 1953; s. Richard Noyes and Helen Louise (Sheffield) P. Student, Goodman Sch., Chgo., 1971, Juilliard Sch., 1972; AB, U. Calif., Santa Cruz, 1977. Radio news reporter McGovern Campaign, Chgo., 1972; cons. Kjos Pub. Co., Chgo., 1973-74; dir. VisArt, Ltd., San Francisco, 1977; ind. film editor L.A., 1978—. Editor motion pictures Re-Animator, 1984, Kiss of the Spiderwoman, 1985, Slam Dance, 1987, Checking Out, 1988, Blue Steel, 1989. Mem. Editors Guild. Democrat. Mem. Ch. of Religious Science.

PERDUE, JAMES RICHARD (JIM PERDUE), communications company administrator; b. Cheshire, Ohio, Dec. 8, 1945; s. Dennis C. and Olivene M. (Lambert) P.; m. Michelle Y. Ament, Oct. 4, 1969; children: Nicholas Alexander, Monique Marie. ASEE magna cum laude, Victor Valley Coll., 1976; BSBA suma cum laudé, U. Redlands, 1986, postgrad., 1989—. Cert. tchr., Calif. With dept. communications tech. Contel, Barstow, Calif., 1965-68; with dept. def. communications Contel, Delta, Utah, 1968-72; with dept. research and devel. Contel, Victorville, Calif., 1973-84, network support superintendant dept. info. resources, 1984—; cons. Contel, San Jose, Calif., 1974-76. Pres. Parent-Tchrs. Group, Apple Valley, Calif., 1984; provider Child Abuse task force, Victorville, 1984—. Served as sgt. U.S. Army, 1966-68, Vietnam. Recipient Outstanding Contbns. to Data Processing award Victor Valley Coll., Victorville, Calif., 1976. Mem. Am. Mgmt. Assn., UCLA Alumni Assn., U. Redlands Alumni Assn., VFW, Am. Legion. Home: 18361 Chapae Ln Apple Valley CA 92307-4553 Office: Contel 16461 Mojave Dr Victorville CA 92392-3699

PEREGRINE, DAVID SEYMOUR, astronomer, consultant; b. Telluride, Colo., June 9, 1921; s. William David and Ella Bethea (Hanson) P. AB, UCLA, 1950; postgrad., U. Calif., Berkeley, 1956-59. Leadman N.Am. Aviation, Inglewood, Calif., 1940-44; sr. physicist N.Am. Aviation, Downey, Calif., 1960-66; photogrammetric cartographer U.S. Geol. Survey, Denver, 1950-56; exec. and sci. specialist space div., Chrysler Corp., New Orleans, 1966-68; cons. Denver, 1970—. Co-author: (environ. manuals) Mars, 1964, Venus, 1966. Served with U.S. Army, 1944-46, PTO. Mem. Am. Astron. Soc., Am. Soc. Photogrammetry, Sigma Xi. Home: 190 S Marion St Pkwy Denver CO 80209

PERELMAN, ALVIN H., physician; b. Montreal, Que., Can., May 29, 1952; s. Saul andPeggy (Morris) P; children: Corrie L., Robert A. BSc, McGill U., 1975; MD, U. Calgary, 1976. Intern Foothills Hosp., Calgary, Alta., Can., 1976-77, resident in pediatrics, 1977-78; pediatric endocrinology fellow Children's Hosp. of Calif., 1978-79, Harbor Gen. Hosp., Torrance, Calif., 1979-80; dir. pediatric endocrinology Phoenix Children's Hosp., 1987—. Mem. Am. Diabetes Assn., Lawson Wilkins Pediatric Endocrinology Soc. Jewish. Office: Phoenix Children's Hosp 909 E Brill St Phoenix AZ 85006

PEREYRA-SUAREZ, CHARLES ALBERT, lawyer; b. Paysandu, Uruguay, Sept. 7, 1947; came to U.S., 1954, naturalized, 1962; s. Hector and Esther (Enriquez-Sarano) P.-S.; m. Susan H. Cross, Dec. 30, 1983. BA in History magna cum laude, Pacific Union Coll., 1970; postgrad., UCLA, 1970-71; JD, U. Calif., Berkeley, 1975. Bar: Calif. 1975, D.C. 1980. Staff atty. Western Ctr. Law and Poverty, Inc., Los Angeles, 1976; trial atty. civil rights div. U.S. Dept. Justice, Washington, 1976-79; asst. U.S. atty., criminal div. U.S. Dept. Justice, Los Angeles, 1979-82; sr. litigation assoc. Gibson, Dunn & Crutcher, Los Angeles, 1982-84; sole practice Los Angeles, 1984-86; ptnr. McKenna, Conner & Cuneo, Los Angeles, 1986—. Democrat. Office: McKenna Conner & Cuneo 444 S Flower Los Angeles CA 90071

PEREZ, RICHARD LEE, lawyer; b. Los Angeles, Nov. 17, 1946; s. Salvador Navarro and Shirley Mae (Selbrede) P.; m. Janice May Smart, July 20, 1970; children: Kristina, Kevin, Ryan. BA, UCLA, 1968; JD, U. Calif., Berkeley, 1971. Bar: U.S. Dist. Ct. (no. dist.) Calif. 1974, U.S. Ct. Appeals (9th cir.) 1974, U.S. Dist. Ct. (ea. dist.) Calif. 1982, U.S. Dist. Ct. (no. dist.) Tex. 1984. Assoc. McCutchen, Doyle, Brown & Enersen, San Francisco, 1972-74, John R. Hetland, Orinda, Calif., 1974-75; ptnr. Lempres & Wulsfberg, Oakland, Calif., 1975-82, Perez & McNabb, Orinda, 1982—; speaker real estate brokerage and computer groups and seminars; mem. adv. bd. Computer Litigation Reporter, Washington, 1982-85, Boult Hall High Tech. Law Jour., 1984—. Assoc. editor U. Calif. Law Rev., 1970-71. Served to capt. U.S. Army, 1968-79. Mem. ABA, Alameda County Bar Assn., Contra Costa County Bar Assn. Office: Perez & McNabb 140 Brookwood Orinda CA 94563

PERHARLOW, DAVID PAUL, electrical engineer; b. Lackawanna, N.Y., July 20, 1943; s. Walter and Helen (Ross) P.; m. Julie Linden; 1 child, Jason. BEE, Calif. Poly. Inst., 1966. Instrumentation engr. Boeing Corp., Seattle, 1966-70, Lockheed Corp., Burbank, Calif., 1970-74; engring. supr. Hughes Helicopter, Culver City, Calif., 1974-80; engring. mgr. Loral Data Systems, San Diego, 1980-82, Aydin Vector, Newtown, Pa., 1982—; guest lectr. U. Tenn. Space Inst., Tullahoma, 1985, 86, 87. Contbr. articles to profl. jours. With USNG, 1964-72. Mem. Soc. Flight Test Engrs. Republican.

PERINI, PATRICK LEMOS, electrical engineer; b. Syracuse, N.Y., July 18, 1964; s. Jose and Maria (Lemos) P. BSEE, Syracuse U., 1985. Pre-profl. engr. IBM, Oswego, N.Y., 1983-84; elec. engr. Jet Propulsion Lab., Pasadena, Calif., 1985—. Mem. Nat. Space Inst., Planetary Soc., Tau Beta Pi. Home: PO Box 17313 Boulder CO 80308 Office: Jet Propulsion Lab 4800 Oak Grove Dr MS-300-241 Pasadena CA 91109

PERITO, JOSEPH GERALD, JR., educator, counselor, consultant; b. Denver, Feb. 9, 1927; s. Joseph and Rose (Comnillo) P.; B.A. in Music Edn., Denver U., 1950, M.A., 1955; Ed.D., U. No. Colo., 1967. Tchr. music Jefferson County (Colo.) Pub. Schs., Lakewood, 1950-57, supr. music, 1957-64, research specialist, 1964-65; prin. Carmody Jr. High Sch., Lakewood, 1965-78, adminstrv. asst. in central adminstrn., 1978-81; ednl. cons. in adminstrn., 1983—. Mem. Am. Ednl. Research Assn., Am. Acad. Polit. and Social Scis., Nat., Colo. assns. secondary sch. prins., Music Edn. Nat. Conf., Am. Choral Dirs. Assn., Am. String Tchrs. Assn., NEA, Colo. Edn. Assn., Kappa Delta Pi, Phi Delta Kappa. Home: 430 N Garrison St Denver CO 80226 Office: 430 N Garrison St Lakewood CO 80226

PERKIN, GORDON WESLEY, international health agency executive; b. Toronto, Ont., Can., Apr. 25, 1935; came to U.S., 1962; s. Irvine Boyer and Jean (Laing) P.; m. Elizabeth Scott, Dec. 21, 1957; children: Scott, Stuart. MD, U. Toronto, 1959. Asst. dir. clin. research Ortho Research Found., Raritan, N.J., 1962-64; assoc. med. dir. Planned Parenthood Fedn. Am., N.Y.C., 1964-66; program advisor Ford Found., N.Y.C., 1966-67; regional program advisor Ford Found., Bangkok, 1967-69, Rio de Janeiro, 1973-76; program officer Ford Found., N.Y.C., Mexico City, 1976-80; project specialist Ministry Fin. and Econ. Planning, Accra, Ghana, 1969-70; cons. World Health Orgn., Geneva, 1971-73; pres. Program for Appropriate Tech. in Health, Seattle, 1980—; affiliate prof. pub. health, U. Wash., Seattle. Contbr. numerous articles to profl. jours. Am. Pub. Health Assn. fellow, 1970. Mem. Planned Parenthood Fedn. Am. (bd. dirs. 1983—), Planned Parenthood Seattle-King County (bd. dirs. 1982—, mem. exec. com. 1983-86), Nat. Council for Internat. Health (bd. govs. 1984—), Nat. Acad. Scis. (com. mem. 1987—), Alan Guttmacher Inst. (bd. dirs. 1985—), Assn. Reproductive Health Profls., Alpha Omega Alpha Hon. Med. Soc. Office: PATH 4 Nickerson St Seattle WA 98109-1699

PERKINS, DALE WARREN, library director; b. Wichita, Kans., Feb. 27, 1933; s. Lawrence Waldo and Georgia (Powell) P.; m. Linda Ann Perkins, Aug. 14, 1960 (div. Feb. 1974); 1 child, Kerry; m. Barbara Lee Miller, Apr. 12, 1976. BA, Ball State U., 1958; MLS, Kansas State U., 1960. Libr. Mid-Columbia Regional Libr., Kennewick, Wash., 1960-62; dir. Baker (Oreg.) City Libr., 1962-65; field libr. Idaho State Libr., Boise, 1965-66; coord. Mountain Valley Libr. System, Sacramento, Calif., 1967-70; dir. San Luis Obispo (Calif.) City-County Libr., 1970—. Contbr. articles to profl. jours. With USAF, 1954-55. Mem. ALA, Calif. Library Assn., Calif. Inst. Libraries (past pres.). Democrat. Home: 741 Stratford Pismo Beach CA 93449

PERKINS, DOROTHY A., association executive; b. Weiser, Idaho, Aug. 13, 1926; d. Ross William and Josephine Stanford (Gwilliam) Anderson; m. Leonard Taylor Perkins, Nov. 16, 1948; children: Larry Taylor, Michael A., Drew A., Nancy. Grad. high sch., Boise, Idaho. Sec. Meadow Gold Dairies, Boise, 1944-46; sec. to supt. Idaho State Police, Boise, 1946-48, Idaho State Dept. Edn., Boise, 1952-56; sec. to maintenance engr. Idaho State Dept. Hwys., Boise, 1956-58; adminstrv. sec., asst. mgr. Casper (Wyo.) C. of C., 1962-72, exec. v.p., 1972—. Mem. Wyo. Ho. Reps., 1982—; pianist, organist, Casper Ch. Jesus Christ Latter Day Sts. Mem. Wyo. C. of C. Execs. (sec.-treas. 1978—, past pres.), Mountain States Assn. (bd. dirs. 1979—, past pres.), Wyo. Hwy. Users Found. (bd. dirs. 1978—). Republican. Home: 1014 Surrey Ct Casper WY 82609 Office: Casper Area C of C 500 North Ctr PO Box 399 Casper WY 82602 also: 1581 Nottingham Dr Casper WY 82609

PERKINS, DOUGLAS EDWARD, aviation executive; b. Cleve., Dec. 22, 1939; s. Frederic Douglas and Margaret (Straessley) P.; m. Maureen Alis Horan, Sept. 16, 1978. Student, Colo. Sch. Mines, 1957-63. Mining engr. U.S., Can., 1961-72; owner Douglas Aviation, 1969-74; cons. Aviation Ops. Consulting, Sedona, Ariz., 1972—; pres. Desert Pacific Airlines, Sedona, 1976-80, Oversea Air Transport Corp., Sedona, 1983—; ops. cons. for numerous domestic and internat. airlines, 1972—. Author: How to Start Up an Aircraft Part 135 Op., 1988, An Outline for Writing a Flight Operations Manual, 1982, numerous mag. articles. Precinct committeeman Yavapai County Rep. party; trustee/sec. Sedona Hist. Soc., Inc.; bd. dirs. Am. Youth Soccer Orgn., Verde Valley, 1984-86; maj. CAP, 1983—. Recipient Comdr's. Commendation award CAP, 1987. Republican. Home: 50 Park Cir PO Box 874 Sedona AZ 86336 Office: Oversea Air Transport Corp Sedona Airport PO Box 1292 Sedona AZ 86336

PERKINS, FLOYD JERRY, theology educator; b. Bertha, Minn., May 9, 1924; s. Ray Lester and Nancy Emily (Kelley) P.; m. Mary Elizabeth Owen, Sept. 21, 1947 (dec. June 1982); children: Douglas Jerry, David Floyd, Sheryl Pauline; m. Phyllis Geneva Hartley, July 14, 1984. AB, BTh, N.W. Nazarene Coll., 1949; MA, U. Mo., 1952; MDiv, Nazarene Theol. Sem., 1952; PhD, U. Witwatersrand, Johannesburg, South Africa, 1974. Ordained to Christian ministry, 1951. Pres. South African Nazarene Theol. Sem., Florida Transvaal, Africa, 1955-67; pres. Nazarene Bible Sem., Lourenzo Marques, Mozambique, 1967-73, Campinas, Brazil, 1974-76; prof. missions N.W. Nazarene Coll., Nampa, Idaho, 1976; prof. theology Nazarene Bible Coll., Colorado Springs, Colo., 1976—; chmn., founder com. higher theol. edn. Ch. of Nazarene in Africa, 1967-74; sec. All African Nazarene Mission Exec., 1967-74; ofcl. Christian Council Mozambique, 1952-74. Author: A History of the Christian Church in Swaziland, 1974. Served with USN, 1944-46. Mem. Am. Schs. Oriental Research, Am. Soc. Missiology, Assn. Evan. Missions Profs. Republican. Office: Nazarene Bible Coll 122 Chapman Dr Colorado Springs CO 80935

PERKINS, HENRY LEE, mortgage company executive; b. Oakland, Calif., Aug. 30, 1958; s. Henry J. and Mattie Louise (Coleman) P.; m. Patricia Ann Sheppard-Perkins, Mar. 6, 1982; children: Enree Havier, Enjoli Gabrielle. AA in Bus. Adminstrn., Coll. Alameda, Calif., 1981; student, Golden

State Sch. Theology. Lic. real estate agent, Calif. Loan clk. Wells Fargo Bank, Oakland, Calif., 1979-82; loan analyst Transam. Mortgage Co., San Francisco, 1982-83; loan processor Great Western Savs., San Francisco, 1983-84; br. mgr. Greater Suburban Mortgage Co., Alameda, 1984-88; v.p., mortgage banker Am. Suburban Mortgage, Oakland, 1988—; dir. music Pleasant Grove Bapt. Ch., 1976-84, associated minister, 1984—. Mem. Nat. Assn. Real Estate Brokers, Calif. Assn. Real Estate Brokers, Oakland Bd. Realtors, Associated Real Property Brokers (pres. 1989-90), Calif. State Young Adult Conv. (2d v.p. 1987, 1st v.p. 1988, Outstanding Young Man of Yr. 1980, Outstanding Youth of Yr. 1979). Democrat. Home: 4150 Maynard Ave Oakland CA 94605 Office: Am Suburban Mortgage Inc 7700 Edgewater Dr Ste 600 Oakland CA 94621

PERKINS, JOHN PRESTON, infosystems specialist, consultant; b. Eugene, Oreg., Feb. 19, 1956; s. John Alex and Barbara Lee (Reynolds) P.; m. Dianne Marie English, Aug. 19, 1979; 1 child, Preston. Student, Oreg. Inst. Tech., 1976-77, Cen. Oreg. Community Coll., 1978-79; AA Bus. Equipment System Tech., Mount Hood Community Coll., 1988. Gen. laborer Hudspeth Saw Mill, Prineville, Oreg., 1981-82; with svc. dept. City Abilene (Tex.), 1982-84; cons. Prineville, 1984-87; assoc., cons. Access Techs. Group, Portland, Oreg., 1987—, Direct Access Systems, Portland, 1988—; cons. Access Reservations Network, Portland, 1988—. Patentee automotive field, 1987. Recipient 2d place entrepreneurship award State Oreg. Distributive Edn. Club, 1987. Mem. Moose. Republican. Baptist. Office: Direct Access Systems 16219 NE Glisan Portland OR 97230

PERKINS, KENT, television and movie producer; b. Alexandria, La., Feb. 11, 1948; s. Dee M. Jr. and M. Elaine (Posey) P.; m. Ruth Buzzi, Dec. 10, 1978. BA in English and Psychology, North Tex. State U., 1970; MA, Tex. Wesleyan Coll., 1972. Pres. Tex. Talent, Inc., Los Angeles, 1978—; producer NBC, Burbank, Calif., 1987—; assoc. dir. Northwest Bankshares, Ft. Worth, 1972-83. Performed as actor in various Film and TV prodns. including "Nashville Palace", 1980, "Any Which Way You Can", 1980, "Buckaroo Banzai", 1986; author: (book) Once Upon a Crime, 1987, (screenplay) To Protect and Serve. Dir. Rep. Presdl. Task Force, Los Angeles, 1984; bd. dirs. Ft. Worth Rehab. Ctr., 1972-83. Mem. SAG, Writer's Guild of Am., Nat. Police Chief's Assn., Los Angeles C. of C., Rolls Royce Owners of Am. Lodge: Kiwanis Internat. Clubs: Am. Equestrian, Los Angeles Yacht. Office: NBC Burbank 3000 W Alameda Ste C-237 Burbank CA 91523 also: Bois d'arc Ranch Rte 1 Box 294 Caddo OK 74729

PERKINS, RICHARD BURLE, II, materials and processes engineer; b. Houston, May 25, 1960; s. Richard Burle I and Mariam (Jamail) P. BSChemE, U. Tex., Austin, 1983. Engr. Dresser Industries DiChem Div., Houston, 1979-82, Honeywell Satellite Systems, Phoenix, 1984—; chmn. electro static discharge control com. Honeywell Inc., Satellite Systems Div., Phoenix, 1985—. Pub. The Texzoni, Phoenix. State Rep. del., Austin, 1980, alt. del., 1982. Mem. Ariz. Tex. Execs. (pres. 1984, 87). Home: 6318 W Beverly Glendale AZ 85306

PERKINS, STEVEN CURTIS, law librarian, law educator; b. Cin., May 1, 1949; s. Denval and Mary Ruth (Ball) P.; m. Carol J. Fritzler-Becker, June 7, 1985; 1 stepchild, Vanessa Becker. BA in Fgn. Affairs magna cum laude, U. Cin., 1976, JD, 1979; MLL, U. Denver, 1983. Bar: Ohio 1979. Reference librarian U. Cin. Coll. of Law, 1979-82, U. Denver Coll. of Law, 1982-83; assoc. librarian U. Cin. Coll. of Law, 1983-84; librarian N.Y. Joint Internat. Law Program, N.Y.C., 1984-85; dir. library, asst. prof. law Western State U. Coll. of Law, Fullerton, Calif., 1985—; librarian collection Urban Morgan Inst. for Human Rights, Cin., 1979-85. Served with M.I. Corps, U.S. Army, 1968-71. Mem. ABA, Am. Assn. Law Libraries, So. Calif. Assn. Law Libraries, Am. Legal Studies Assn. Baptist. Home: 300 Canyon Country Rd Brea CA 92621 Office: Western State U Coll of Law 1111 N State College Blvd Fullerton CA 92631

PERKINS, TAMMY JO, municipal government official; b. Salem, Ohio, May 10, 1959; d. Glenn Wayne and Janet Elaine (Galbreath) P. BA, Drake U., 1981; MPA, U. Denver, 1982. Mgmt. intern City of Boulder, Colo., 1980; mgmt. intern City of Phoenix, 1982-83, mgmt. asst., 1983—; bd. dirs. City of Phoenix Deferred Compensation Bd., 1989—. Bd. dirs. Downtown Phoenix YMCA, 1986—; active Ariz. Women's Town Hall, Chandler, 1988, Valley Leadership, Phoenix, 1986-87. Mem. Am. Soc. Pub. Adminstrs., Ariz. City Mgmt. Assn. (exec. com. 1985), Ariz. Mcpl. Mgmt. Assts. Assn. (pres. 1985), Internat. City Mgmt. Assn., Renaissance Club, Phoenix City Club, Herberger Theatre Assocs. Republican. Methodist. Office: City of Phoenix 251 W Washington Phoenix AZ 85003

PERKINS, THOMAS JAMES, venture capital company executive; b. Oak Park, Ill., Jan. 7, 1932; s. Harry H. and Elizabeth P.; m. Gerd Thune-Ellefsen, Dec. 9, 1961; children: Tor Kristian, Elizabeth Siri. B.S.E.E., M.I.T., 1953; M.B.A., Harvard U., 1957. Gen. mgr. computer div. Hewlett Packard Co., Cupertino, Calif., 1965-70, dir. corp. devel., 1970-72; gen. partner Kleiner & Perkins, San Francisco, 1972-80; sr. partner Kleiner Perkins Caufield & Byers, San Francisco, from 1980; chmn. bd. Tandem Computers, Genentech; dir. Spectra Physics., Corning Glass Works, Collagen Corp., LSI Logic Corp., Hybritech Inc., Econics Corp., Vitalink Communications Corp. Author: Classic Supercharged Sports Cars, 1984. Trustee San Francisco Ballet, 1980—. Mem. Nat. Venture Capital Assn. (chmn. 1981-82, pres. 1980-81). Clubs: N.Y. Yacht, Links, Am. Bugatti (pres. 1983—). Office: Tandem Computers Inc 10435 N Tantau Ave Cupertino CA 95014-3548 also: Genentech Inc 460 Point San Bruno San Francisco CA 94080 *

PERKS, BENJAMIN WINWOOD, accountant; b. Springfield, Ohio, Feb. 24, 1942; s. Ben Wheldon and Nancy (Turner) P.; m. Sally West Morris, July 16, 1966; children: James Winwood, David Addison. BA, Denison U., 1964; JD, U. Cin., 1967, MBA, 1968; profl. acctg. program degree, Northwestern U., 1970. CPA, Ill., Ariz., Calif., Iowa, N.C. Staff acct., ptnr. Price Waterhouse, Chgo., 1968-83; mng. ptnr. Price Waterhouse, Tucson, 1983-87, Newport Beach, Calif., 1987—. Bd. dirs., mem. exec. com. Boy Scouts Am., Newport Beach, 1987, United Way, Newport Beach, 1988, campaign chmn., Tucson, 1986. Mem. AICPA, ABA. Office: Price Waterhouse 660 Newport Ctr Dr Ste 600 Newport Beach CA 92660

PERL, MARTIN LEWIS, physicist, educator; b. N.Y.C., June 24, 1927; s. Oscar and Fay (Rosenthal) P.; m. Teri Hoch, June 19, 1948; children: Jed, Anne, Matthew, Joseph. B.Chem. Engring., Poly. Inst. Bklyn., 1948; Ph.D., Columbia U., 1955. Chem. engr. Gen. Electric Co., 1948-50; asst. prof. physics U. Mich., 1955-58, asso. prof., 1958-63; prof. Stanford, 1963—. Author: High Energy Hadron Physics, 1975; contbr. articles on high energy physics and on relation of sci. to soc. to profl. jours. Served with U.S. Mcht. Marine, 1944-45; Served with AUS, 1945-46. Recipient Wolf prize in physics, 1982. Fellow Am. Phys. Soc.; mem. Nat. Acad. Scis., AAAS. Home: 3737 El Centro Ave Palo Alto CA 94306 Office: Stanford U Stanford Linear Accelerator Ctr Stanford CA 94305

PERLICK, NANCY BETH, health services executive; b. Chgo., Aug. 18, 1944; d. Gene Roland and Joanne Catherine (Olender) Perlick. BA in Social Sci., Russell Coll., 1969; BS in Nursing, U. San Francisco, 1970; MHA, U. Wash., 1983. Clin. nurse intern St. Mary's Hosp. and Med. Ctr., San Francisco, 1970; staff nurse St. Joseph's Hosp. and Med. Ctr., Phoenix, 1970-73; charge nurse Mercy Hosp., Bakersfield, Calif., 1973-74; supr. nurse Mercy Hosp. and Med. Ctr., San Diego, 1974-81; adminstrv. intern Harborview Med. Ctr., Seattle, 1982; adminstrv. asst. St. Joseph's Hosp. and Med. Ctr., Phoenix, 1983-84, adminstr. Barrow Neurol. Inst., 1984-85, v.p. Barrow Neurol. Inst. and Mental Health, 1986—; bd. dirs Ariz. Emergency Med. Systems, Inc., Phoenix, 1988, standing hosp. com.,1987, Mercy Hosp., 1983, v. chair 1988, St. John's Regional Med. Ctr., Oxnard, Calif., 1979-81; mem. Health Services Adv. Board-Sisters of Mercy, 1978-81, Grossmont (Calif.) Coll. Nursing Program Com., 1977-81, Cen. Ariz. Health Systems Agy. Contbr. articles to Jour. of Neurosurg. Nursing and other profl. jours. Bd. dirs. Ariz.-Mex. Commn., 1986, Cen. Ariz. Shelter Services, Phoenix, 1986, Community Housing Partnership, 1987, Human Devel. Council-Roman Catholic Diocese of Phoenix, 1986—, Phoenix Coalition for Health Care for the Homeless, 1986—, Soc. Justice Commn.-Sisters of Mercy, 1985, Soc. Justice Com.-Sisters' Council-Roman Catholic Diocese of Phoenix, 1986—, Tule Devel. Corp., Bakersfield, Calif., 1983-86, Soc. Concerns Commn.-Sisters of Mercy, 1980-81, Peace and Justice Commn.-Roman Catholic Diocese of San Diego, 1979-81. Mem. Sisters of Mercy of Burlingame, Calif., Am. Assn. Neurosci. Nurses, Am. Mgmt. Assn., Health Svcs. Rsch. Assn., Mental Health Adminstrs. Assn., Health Care Fin. Mgmt. Assn., NAFE, Nat. League of Nurses, Sigma Theta Tau (Beta Gamma chpt.). Office: St Josephs Hosp and Med Ctr 350 W Thomas Rd Phoenix AZ 85013

PERLIN, JOEL DAVID, financial consultant; b. Boston, May 4, 1950; s. Wilbur and Miriam (Sher) P.; m. Karla Ingrid Gustafson, Aug. 24, 1975 (div. 1980); m. Lesley Ronson, July 30, 1983. BS in Acctg., Southeast Mass. U., 1975; postgrad., U. Wis., 1980. Teller Baybank Merchants, N.A., New Bedford, Mass., 1972-75; asst. ops. officer Community Bank, L.A., 1976-77; v.p., controller Century Bank, L.A., 1977-81, Bank Beverly Hills (Calif.), 1982; v.p., cashier Mission Valley Bank, N.A., San Clemente, Calif., 1982-88; fin. cons. San Clemente, 1988—. Basketball coach Boys and Girls Club, San Clemente, 1986—. bd. dirs., 1984—; dir. San Clemente Ocean Festival, 1984-86; co-chmn. San Clemente Fiesta, 1985. Recipient Pres. Citation Am. Bankers Assn., 1984. Mem. San Clemente C. of C. (v.p., bd. dirs. 1984—), Rotary (pres., bd. dirs. San Clemente chpt. 1986-87, Internat. Svc. award 1987). Home and Office: 946 Avenida Presidio San Clemente CA 92672

PERLIS, MICHAEL FREDRICK, lawyer; b. N.Y.C., June 3, 1947; s. Leo and Betty F. (Gantz) P.; children—Amy Hannah, David Matthew; m. Angela M. Rinaldi, Dec. 23, 1988. B.S. in Fgn. Service, Georgetown U., 1968, J.D., 1971. Bar: D.C. 1971, U.S. Dist. Ct. D.C. 1971, U.S. Ct. Appeals 1971, D.C. Ct. Appeals 1971, Calif. 1980, U.S. Dist. Ct. (no. dist.) Calif. 1980, U.S Dist. Ct. (cen. dist.) Calif. 1985, U.S. Ct. Appeals (9th cir.) 1980, U.S. Supreme Ct., 1980. Law clerk D.C. Ct. Appeals, Washington, 1971-72; asst. corp. counsel D.C., Washington, 1972-74; counsel U.S. SEC, div. enforcement, Washington, 1974-75, br. chief, 1975-77, asst. dir., 1977-80; ptnr. Pettit & Martin, San Francisco, 1980-89; ptnr. Stroock & Stroock & Lavan, L.A., 1989—. adj. prof. Cath. U. Am., 1979-80. Mem. ABA (co-chmn. subcom. securities and commodities litigation 1982-83), D.C. Bar Assn., Calif. State Bar Assn., San Francisco Bar Assn. Office: Stroock & Stroock & Lavan 2029 Century Pk E Los Angeles CA 90067

PERLMUTTER, LEONARD MICHAEL, concrete construction company executive; b. Denver, Oct. 16, 1925; s. Philip Permutter and Belle (Perlmutter); m. Alice Love Bristow, Nov. 17, 1951; children: Edwin George, Joseph Kent, Cassandra Love. B.A., U. Colo., 1948, postgrad., 1948-50. Ptnr. Perlmutter & Sons, Denver, 1947-58; v.p. Prestressed Concrete of Colo., Denver, 1952-60; pres. Stanley Structures, Inc., Denver, 1960-83; chmn. bd. Stanley Structures, Inc., 1983-87; dir. Colo. Nat. Bankshares, Inc.; chief exec. officer Econ. Devel. Gov.'s Office State of Colo., 1987-88; chmn. bd. Colo. Open Lands, 1989—. Chmn. bd. U. Colo. Found., Boulder, 1979-81; dir. Santa Fe Opera Assn., N.Mex., 1976-85; v.p. Santa Fe Fedn., 1979-87; chmn. bd. Nat. Jewish Hosp.-Nat. Asthma Ctr., Denver, 1983-86; pres. Denver Symphony Assn., 1983-84, chmn. bd., 1985. Recipient Humanitarian Am. Jewish Com., 1981. Mem. Am. Concrete Inst., Prestressed Concrete Inst. (pres. 1977, dir. 1973-74). Club: Rolling Hills Country (Golden) (pres. 1966-68). Home: 15125 Foothill Rd Golden CO 80401 Office: LAP Inc 1515 Arapahoe Three Park Cen Ste 222 Denver CO 80202

PERLMUTTER, STEVEN BARRY, ophthalmologist; b. Bklyn., Jan. 5, 1955; s. Robert and Audrey Harriet (Boyarsky) P.; m. Nora Elizabeth Cone, June 18, 1981; children: David Zachary, Christopher Robert. AB, Sarah Lawrence Coll., 1976; MD, Washington U., 1980. Diplomate Am. Bd. Ophthalmology, 1986. Intern St. John's Mercy Med. Ctr., Creve Coeur, Mo., 1980-81; resident in ophthalmology Washington U., St. Louis, 1981-84; ophthalmologist Neumann Eye Inst., DeLand, Fla., 1984-85; med. dir. Omni Eye Svcs., Phoenix, 1985-88; ophthalmologist Southwestern Eye Ctr., Phoenix, 1988—; mem. quality assurance com. Glendale (Ariz.) Surgicenter, 1986-88. Bd. dirs. Temple Chai, Phoenix, 1987-88, Am. Cancer Soc., St. Louis, 1977-78. Fellow Am. Acad. Ophthalmology; mem. Am. Soc. Cataract and Retroactive Surgeons, Ariz. Med. Assn. (profl. affairs com. 1988), Maricopa County Med. Soc., Mansion Club. Jewish. Office: Southwestern Eye Ctr 3150 N 7th St Ste B Phoenix AZ 85014

PERRAULT, JACQUES, educator; b. Montreal, Quebec, Can., June 25, 1944; s. Jean-Paul and Irene (Girard) P.; m. Marcella Ann McClure, Mar. 1, 1974; stepchildren: Elissa, Sarah. BSc, McGill U., 1964; PhD, U. Calif., San Diego, 1972. Asst. prof. dept. microbiology and immunology Wash. U. Sch. of Medicine, St. Louis, 1977-84; assoc. prof. dept. of biology San Diego State U., 1984-88, prof. dept. of biology, 1988—. Contbr. articles to profl. jours. Recipient Research Career Devel. award, NIH, 1980-85; grantee, NIH, NSF, March of Dimes Defects Found., 1977—. Mem. AAAS, Am. Soc. Microbiology, Am. Soc. Virology, Gen. Soc. for Microbiology. Office: San Diego State U Dept of Biology San Diego CA 92182

PERRENOD, DOUGLAS ARTHUR, aerospace engineer; b. Weehawken, N.J., Sept. 13, 1947; s. George Edward and Eunice Lillian (Cohn) P. Student, Fla. Inst. Tech., 1968-72; B.A. in Interdisciplinary Sci. U. South Fla., 1973; postgrad. Calif. State U., 1982—; grad. engr. mgmt. cert. program Calif. Inst. Tech., 1987. Cert. glider flight instr. FAA. Engr. trainee NASA Kennedy Space Ctr., Fla., 1969-73; quality control engr. Pelletech Corp., Fontana, Calif., 1976-77; electronics specialist Gen. Telephone Co., San Bernardino, Calif., 1977-79; aerospace and project engr. Rockwell Internat., Downey, Calif., 1979-85, Lockheed Corp., Ontario, Calif., 1986-87, Lockheed Engring. Mgmt. Svc. Co., 1987, Eagle Engring., 1988—; aviation cons., owner-founder Flight Unltd., Long Beach, Calif.; mission pilot, project engr. Flight Level 500 High Altitude Soaring Project. Vol. mem. Orange County Human Services Agy., 1981-86; active Big Bros. of Am., 1978. Maj. USAF, 1973-75, maj. USAFR. Recipient Amelia Earhart award CAP, 1968, Manned Flight Apollo 11 medallion NASA, 1971, 1st Shuttle Flight award NASA, 1981, Aerospace Maintenance Officer of Yr. award USAFR, 1979; named to Engr. Honor Roll, Rockwell Internat., 1982. Mem. AIAA, Res. Officers Assn., Air Force Assn., Soaring Soc. Am., Toastmasters Internat., Speakers Bur. (Rockwell Internat.), Assoc. Glider Club of So. Calif., Long Beach Navy Aero. Club. Designer telescope mount for 1st astronomy obs. Fla. Inst. Tech., 1969. Home: 18511 Egret Bay Blvd #612 Houston TX 77058-3275

PERRIGO, LYLE DONOVAN, chemical engineer; b. San Antonio, Sept. 28, 1930; s. Lyle Donovan and Winniferd Marie (Eyrich) P.; m. Neoma Dalene Twing, Aug. 1, 1959; children: Juliann Marie, Susan Dalene, Lyle Donovan, Dale Benjamin. BA, BS, Rice Inst., 1953; MS, U. Idaho, 1961. Registered profl. engr., Calif. Engr. GE Co., Richland, Wash., 1956-65; rsch. engr. Battelle-NW, Richland, 1965-66, mgr., 1966-75, 78-81, project mgr., 1976-78; sect. mgr. Battelle Alaska Ops., Anchorage, 1981-83; sr. sci. dir. U. Alaska Found., Fairbanks, 1984-85, trustee, 1986—; dep. dir. Arctic Environ. Info. and Data Ctr., Anchorage, 1985-88; staff officer U.S. Arctic Rsch. Commn., Anchorage, 1986—; mem. Internat. Task Force on Nuclear Decontamination, 1960-68; pres., chmn. bd. Hunter Trans. Real Estate, Richland, 1966-74. Co-Author: Eldridge Larkins and Elizabeth Bledsoe and Their Descendants, 1969; author: Asa Flint Perrigo and Some of His Descendants, 1980. Mem. Wash. State-U.N.-Econ. and Social Commn. for Asia and the Pacific Trade Mission, 1975; trustee Columbia Basin Coll., Pasco, Wash., 1967-79; mem. Anchorage Hist. and Fine Arts Commn., 1988—. Lt. (j.g.) USN, 1953-56. Mem. Nat. Assn. Corrosion Engrs. (sect. trustee 1971-81, 82-85, 86-88, chmn. tech. practices com. 1985-87, Corrosion Engr. of Yr. award western region 1974), Alaska Acad. Engring. and Scis. (sec.-treas. 1986—), Masons. Republican. Home: 1921 Congress Circle Apt B Anchorage AK 99507 Office: US Arctic Rsch Commn 707 "A" St Anchorage AK 99501

PERRILLO, RICHARD JOHN, psychologist; b. N.Y.C., July 19, 1950; s. John and Rose (Pignone) P. BA, Cathedral Coll., 1972; MEd, Springfield Coll., Mass., 1973; PhD with distinction, U. Utah, 1978. Lic. clin. psychologist, Calif. Cons. psychologist Mgmt. Health & Devel., Century City and L.A., Calif., 1979-80; pvt. practice Beverly Hills, Calif., 1980—; cons. psychologist to numerous cos., 1979—. Contbr. articles to profl. jours. Mem. Am. Psychol. Assn., Calif. State Psychol. Assn., Div. I-Clin. Psychology, Psi Chi. Roman Catholic. Office: 255 S Elm Dr Beverly Hills CA 90212-4010

PERRIN, EDWARD BURTON, health services researcher, biostatistician, public health educator; b. Greensboro, Vt., Sept. 19, 1931; s. J. Newton and Dorothy E. (Willey) P.; m. Carol Anne Hendricks, Aug. 18, 1956; children—Jenifer, Scott. B.A., Middlebury Coll., 1953; postgrad. (Fulbright scholar) in stats, Edinburgh (Scotland) U., 1953-54; M.A. in Math. Stats, Columbia U., 1956; Ph.D., Stanford U., 1960. Asst. prof. dept. biostats. U. Pitts., 1959-62; asst. prof. dept. preventive medicine U. Wash., Seattle, 1962-65; asso. prof. U. Wash., 1965-69, prof., 1969-70, prof., chmn. dept. biostats., 1970-72, prof. dept. health services, 1975—, chmn. dept., 1983—; prof. (hon.) West China U. of Med. Scis., Szechwan, Peoples Republic of China, 1988—; clin. prof. dept. community medicine and internat. health Sch. Medicine, Georgetown U., Washington, 1972-75; dep. dir. Nat. Center for Health Stats., HEW, 1972-73, dir., 1973-75; research scientist Health Care Study Center, Battelle Human Affairs Research Centers, Seattle, 1975-76, dir., 1976-78; dir. Health and Population Study Center Battelle Human Affairs Research Centers, Seattle, 1978-83; sr. cons. biostats. Wash./Alaska regional med. programs, 1967 -72; biometrician VA Co-op Study on Treatment of Esophageal Varices, 1961-73; mem. Epidemiology and Disease Control Study Sect., NIH, 1969-73; chmn. health services research study sect., HEW, 1976-79; chmn. health services research and devel. field program rev. panel, VA, 1988—. Contbr. articles on biostats., health services and population studies to profl. publs.; mem. editorial bd.: Jour. Family Practice, 1978—. Mem. tech. bd. Milbank Meml. Fund, 1974-76. Recipient Outstanding Service citation HEW, 1975. Fellow AAAS, Am. Public Health Assn. (Spiegelman Health Stats. award 1970, program devel. bd. 1971, chmn. stats. sect. 1978-80, governing council 1983-85), Am. Statis. Assn. (mem. adv. com. to div. statis. policy 1975-77); mem. Inst. Medicine of Nat. Acad. Sci. (chmn. membership com. 1984-86, mem. bd. on health care services 1987—), Population Assn. Am., Biometrics Soc. (pres. Western N.Am. Region 1971), Inst. Math. Stats., Internat. Epidemiologic Assn., Sigma Xi, Phi Beta Kappa. Home: 4900 NE 39th St Seattle WA 98105 Office: U Wash Dept Health Svcs SC-37 Seattle WA 98195

PERRINE, JAY RANDAL, senior cost analyst; b. Trenton, N.J., Mar. 27, 1946; s. Henry Bergen Perrine and E. Marie (Cottrell) Dey; m. Madalyn Jo Frazzini, Nov. 30, 1975; 1 child, Danielle Thérèse Frazzini Perrine. BA, Goddard Coll., 1969; MA, Wash. U., St. Louis, Mo., 1975; postgrad., Santa Clara U., 1978-80. Interviewer N.J. Dept. of Labor, Burlington, 1969-70; asst. to adminstr. Downstate Med. Ctr., Brooklyn, 1970-72; sr. cost analyst Econ, Inc., San Jose, Calif., 1975—. Planning commr. and chmn. City of Campbell, Calif., 1984—. Democrat. Quaker. Office: Econ Inc 4020 Moor Park Ave Suite 216 San Jose CA 95117

PERRON, J. EDWARD, communications executive; b. Hastings, Minn., May 24, 1939; s. Karl Earl and Kathleen (Kennedy) P.; m. Judith Evans (div. 1966); 1 child, Michael. Acct. No. Pacific R.R., St. Paul, 1959-65; office mgr. Sorenson Equipment, Denver, 1965-67; with estimating and purchasing dept Mullins Neon, Denver, 1967-72; office and sales mgr. Acad. Signs, Denver, 1972-76; lease broker 3M Nat. Advt., Denver, 1976-81; ops. mgr. Gannett Outdoor Co. of Colo., Denver, 1981-84, mgr. dept. real estate and pub. affairs, 1984—; adviser Bd. Standards Bldg. Dept. City of Denver, 1988—. Recipient Pres.'s award Mile High Council on Alcoholism and Drug Abuse, 1988. Republican. Roman Catholic. Home: 6611 W Montana Pl Denver CO 80128

PERRY, ALICE HILLARY, engineer; b. San Francisco, Nov. 17, 1961; d. John Weir Perry and Laura Ann (Gotlieb) Shulgin. BS, Calif. State Polytechnic U., Pomona, 1985. Flight analysis engr. Gen. Dynamics, Rancho Cucamonga, Calif., 1986-. Mem. Nat. Mgmt. Assn. Democrat.

PERRY, ANTHONY FRANK, printing company executive; b. L.A., Oct. 23, 1965; s. Frank Guy and Verna Dean (Bland) P. Artist Thunderbird Printing Co., Inc., Reno, Nev., 1983-87; pres., chief exec. officer T-Bird Entertainment, Inc., Reno, 1987—. Lighting designer Sheep Dip Show, Reno Hilton, 1986, 87, 89. Mem. Nev. Repertory Co., 1983—. Mem. Reno Advt. Club. Roman Catholic. Home: 3395 Shawnee Circle Reno NV 89502 Office: T-Bird Entertainment Inc 425 Gentry Way Ste E Reno NV 89502

PERRY, BONNE LU, county public welfare administrator; b. Miles City, Mont., Mar. 26, 1929; d. Daniel Glenn and Mabel Jane (Scriven) Harris; adopted d. Albert Hartford and Bertha Gertrude (Erickson) P. Student, No. Mont. Coll., 1947-49; BA, U. Mont., 1951, postgrad., 1953-56; postgrad., Queens Coll., 1966. Tchr. English Whitefish (Mont.) High Sch., 1951-53; tchr. English and drama Great Falls (Mont.) High Sch., 1953-58; tchr. English Northport (N.Y.) High Sch., 1958-67; social worker Roosevelt County Dept. Pub. Welfare, Wolf Point, Mont., 1969-74; social worker supr. I Roosevelt, Sheridan, and Daniels Counties Dept. Pub. Welfare, Wolf Point, Mont., 1974-78; county dir. II Richland County Dept. Pub. Welfare, Sidney, Mont., 1978—. Author: (poetry) Winter, 1978. Mem. Mont. Pub. Welfare Assn., Am. Pub. Welfare Assn., Mont. County Dirs., Eastern Mont. Mental Health Assn., Community Health Mtg., U. Mont. Alumni Assn., Whitefish Edn. Assn. (pres. 1952-53), Alpha Phi. Democrat. Congregationalist. Lodges: Order of Eastern Star, PEO (recording sec. 1984-85. Home: 120 7th St SW Lot 25 Sidney MT 59270 Office: Richland County Dept Pub Welfare 221 5th St SW Sidney MT 59270

PERRY, DAVID NILES, public relations company executive; b. Utica, N.Y., Mar. 7, 1940; s. Francis N. and Marion H. P.; B.S., Utica Coll. Syracuse U., 1962; m. Jacqueline J. Adams, Dec. 21, 1962. Pub. affairs rep. Allstate Ins. Co., Pasadena, Calif., 1966-67; dir. press relations Los Angeles C. of C., 1968; rep. pub. relations Lockheed Propulsion Co., Redlands, Calif., 1968-70; mgr. pub. relations Bozell & Jacobs Inc., Los Angeles, 1970-73, Phoenix, 1971; pres. David Perry Pub. Relations Inc., Scottsdale, Ariz. Mem. Ariz. Gov.'s Commn. Ariz. environment, 1972—, Ariz. chpt. ARC. Served with USNR, 1962-65. Mem. Pub. Relations Soc. Am. (accredited) (dir. Phoenix chpt. 1975-82, pres. 1978). Office: 6819 E Diamond St Scottsdale AZ 85257

PERRY, ELIZABETH JEAN, educator; b. Shanghai, China, Sept. 9, 1948; came to U.S., 1962; d. Charles Elliot and Carey (Coles) P. BA, William Smith Coll., 1969; MA, U. Wash., 1971; PhD, U. Mich., 1978. Asst. prof. U. Ariz., 1977-78; asst. prof. U. Wash., 1978-81, assoc. prof., 1981-86, prof., 1986—; vis. assoc. prof. Harvard U., 1982-83; bd. dirs. Seattle China Coun. Author: Rebels & Revolutionaries, 1980, Chinese Perspectives, 1981, Political Economy Reform, 1985; rev. editor Modern China, 1987—. Recipient numerous rsch. grants, 1974-87. Mem. Internat. Studies Admissions Com. (chmn. 1987—), Assn. Asian Studies, Nat. Com. on U.S.-China Rels., China Coun. of Asia Soc. Democrat. Episcopalian. Office: U Wash Jackson Sch Dr-05 Seattle WA 98195

PERRY, J. RICHARD, infosystems specialist; b. South Bend, Ind., July 24, 1941; s. Owen B. and Florence I. (Reese) P.; m. Constance L. Van Buskirk, Dec. 22, 1962; children: Jeffrey Tod, Lonette K. BBA, Bradley U., 1963; MBA, Sangamon State U., Springfield, Ill., 1973. Cert. data processor. Div. mgr. Franklin Data Services Corp., Springfield, Ill., 1968-75; info. systems exec. State of Ill., Springfield, 1975-78; dir. mktg. systems Am. Express, N.Y.C., 1978-81; v.p., gen. mgr. Processing Mgmt. Systems Corp., Phoenix, 1981-87; br. mgr. Leardata Info. Services, Phoenix, 1987—. Vol. United Way, Springfield, 1973-74; elder Presbyn. Ch., Springfield, 1977—. Served to cpt. USAF, 1963-68. Mem. Assn. Records Mgrs., Assn. Info. and Image Mgmt., Pi Kappa Alpha. Home: 5201 E Crocus Dr Scottsdale AZ 85254 Office: Leardata Info Svcs 1661 E Camelback Rd Ste 250 Phoenix AZ 85016

PERRY, JAMES MITCHELL, psychological and management consultant; b. Santa Barbara, Calif., Dec. 28, 1951; s. I. Newton and Sally (Mitchell) P.; m. Sylvia Hillyer, Sept. 29, 1979; children: Marlowe Hillyer, Hayden Mitchell. BA, U. of the Pacific, 1973, MA, 1975, EdD, 1980. Entertainer, leader, musician 1970-75; staff counselor San Joaquin County Mental Health Svcs., Stockton, Calif., 1975-76; elem. sch. counselor Fillmore Sch., Stockton Sch. Dist., 1976-77; pvt. practice marriage and family therapist 1976; sr. devel. assoc. U. of the Pacific, Stockton, 1977-80; owner JM Perry Corp., Stockton, 1980—; pvt. practice psychotherapy 1986; founder, developer community devel. lecture series and interpersonal skills workshops. Contbr. articles to profl. pubs. Mem. Calif. Assn. Marriage and Family Therapists (past bd. dirs.), Bus. Execs. for Nat. Security. Home and Office: 205 E Magnolia St Stockton CA 95202

PERRY, JAMES WOOD, marketing professional; b. Marshall, Mo., Mar. 12, 1947; s. Charles Albert and Gertrude (Broer) P.; m. Cheryl Anne Greene, June 14, 1969 (div. Nov. 1976); children: David Babcock, Elizabeth Stevens. BS, Case Inst. Tech., Cleve., 1969. Mgr. systems mktg. Data Gen. Corp., Westboro, Mass., 1973-83; dir. distbn. mktg. Convergent Techs., Inc., San Jose, Calif., 1983—. Democrat. Office: Convergent Techs Inc 2700 North First St San Jose CA 95150

PERRY, JOHN VAN BUREN, historian, educator; b. Aberdeen, S.D., Feb. 7, 1928; s. Van Buren and Elise (Andersen) P.; B.Sc., No. State Coll., S.D., 1954; postgrad. Law Sch., N.Y. U., 1954-55; M.A., U. Calif., Berkeley, 1959; postgrad. U. So. Calif., 1965-66. Instr. history Calif. State Univ. Fresno and Sonoma, 1963-65; asst. prof. Kern Community Coll. Dist., Bakersfield and Porterville, Calif., 1969-71; prof. social scis. and humanities Central Wyo. Coll., Riverton, 1971-75; prof. history, humanities and social scis. Lake Tahoe Community Coll., South Lake Tahoe, Calif., 1975—, pres. faculty senate, 1979-80, senate sec., 1983-84, advisor Truman Scholarship, 1979—, chmn. student com., 1986—, founder/advisor Lambda Tau chpt. Alpha Gamma Sigma Soc.. Pres., Lake Tahoe Community Concert Assn., 1977-79, 81—, bd. dirs., 1975—, campaign mgr., 1979-81; pres. Arts in Action, 1973-75; del. Wyo. Council on Arts, 1972-75, Wyo. Council for Humanities, 1973-75; bd. dirs. Riverton Community Concert Assn., 1972-75, Assn. to Restore Tallac Sites, 1981-83; bd. dirs. Lake Tahoe Cultural Arts Alliance, 1981—, treas., 1982-84, 86—, co-pres., 1984-86. Served with USN, 1946-50. Root-Tilden fellow, 1954-55. Mem. Am. Hist. Assn., Community Coll. Humanities Assn., Mus. Soc. San Francisco, Los Angeles County Mus. Art, Met. Mus. N.Y.C., Am. Philatelic Soc., Smithsonian Instn. Club: Scottish Rite. Home: PO Box 14266 South Lake Tahoe CA 95702 Office: PO Box 14445 South Lake Tahoe CA 95702

PERRY, L. TOM, merchant, church official. Mem. Quorum of the Twelve, Ch. of Jesus Christ of Latter-day Saints, Salt Lake City; co-chmn. ZCMI, Salt Lake City. Office: LDS Church Quorum of the 12 50 E N Temple St Salt Lake City UT 84150 *

PERRY, LEE ROWAN, lawyer; b. Chgo., Sept. 23, 1933; s. Watson Bishop and Helen (Rowan) P.; m. Barbara Ashcraft Mitchell, July 2, 1955; children: Christopher, Constance, Geoffrey. B.A., U. Ariz., 1955, LL.B., 1961. Bar: Ariz. 1961. Since practiced in Phoenix; clk. Udall & Udall, Tucson, 1960-61; mem. firm Carson, Messinger, Elliott, Laughlin & Ragan, 1961—. Mem. law rev. staff, U. Ariz., 1959-61. Mem. bd. edn. Paradise Valley Elementary and High Sch. Dists., Phoenix, 1964-68, pres., 1968; treas. troop Boy Scouts Am., 1970-72; mem. Ariz. adv. bd. Girl Scouts U.S.A., 1972-74, mem. nominating bd., 1978-79; bd. dirs. Florence Crittenton Services Ariz., 1967-72, pres., 1970-72; bd. dirs. U. Ariz. Alumni, Phoenix, 1968-72, pres., 1969-70; bd. dirs. Family Service Phoenix, 1974-75; bd. dirs. Travelers Aid Assn. Am., 1985—; bd. dirs. Vol. Bur. Maricopa County, 1975-81, 83-86, pres., 1984-85; bd. dirs. Ariz. div. Am. Cancer Soc., 1978-80, Florence Crittenton div. Child Welfare League Am., 1976-81; bd. dirs. Crisis Nursery for Prevention of Child Abuse, 1978-81, pres., 1978-80. Served to 1st lt. USAF, 1955-58. Mem. State Bar Ariz. (conv. chmn. 1972), Am., Maricopa County bar assns., Phi Delta Phi, Phi Delta Theta (pres. 1954). Republican (precinct capt. 1970, chmn. Reps. for Senator De Concini 1976, 82, 88, precinct committeeman 1983-84). Episcopalian (sr. warden 1968-72). Clubs: Rotary (dir. 1971-77, pres. 1975-76), Plaza, Ariz. Office: Citibank Tower PO Box 33907 Phoenix AZ 85067

PERRY, MARY LYNN, arts administrator; b. Fredericksburg, Va., Oct. 26, 1954; d. James Beverly and Mary Ellen (Stone) P.; m. Scott Michael Lebar, Dec. 21, 1976; 1 child, Julia Mary. European concert tour, Shenandoah Coll., 1973; BA, U. Md., 1976; MA, George Washington U., 1983. Adminstrv. asst. Mus. of African Art, Washington, 1977-80; program asst. Smithsonian Instn., Washington, 1980-82; edn. specialist Smithsonian Instn., 1982-85; arts program coord. Sacramento Metro. Arts Commn., 1985—; cons. Nat. Mus. Natural History, New Delhi, India, 1984; instr. Calif. State U., Sacramento, 1988. Adv. bd. Sacramento Regional Getty Inst. for Educators on Visual Arts, Sacramento, 1987-88; steering com. Northern Calif. Partnership Project Arts Internat./Inst. Internat. Edn., 1987-89; pres. Sacramento Children's Mus., 1988, El Dorado Arts Coun., 1988, Sacramento Coun. for Internat. Visitors, 1988-89. Smithsonian Instn. Travel grantee to India, 1984. Mem. Am. Assn. Mus., Women's Heritage Mus. Project (area rep. 1985—), Anne Arundel County Women's Commn. (assoc. commr. 1984), Edn. Roundtable Sacramento (founder 1986), Phi Kappa Phi. Office: Sacramento Metro Arts Commn 800 10th St Ste 2 Sacramento CA 95814

PERRY, MERVYN FRANCIS, investment company executive; b. Brockton, Mass., Feb. 20, 1923; s. Mervyn Elsworth and Marie (Therrien) P.; m. Marian D. Sprong, June 9, 1949 (div. 1979); children: Richard Caverhill, Cynthia Perry Parr, Susan Perry Diette, Janet Perry Horton; m. Gayle A. Lenihan, Sept. 17, 1980. AB, Boston U., 1950, JD, 1951. Mgr. Conn. Gen. Life Ins. Co., Cleve., 1956-62; v.p., dir. Mass. Gen. Life Ins. Co., Boston, 1962-65; pres., chief exec. officer, dir. Mass. Co. Distbr., Inc., Boston, 1965-69; pres., chmn. bd., chief exec. officer Mass. Fund for Income, 1973-78; pres., chief exec. officer, dir. Mass. Co., Inc., 1969-77; chmn. bd., pres., chief exec. officer, dir. Freedom Fund, Inc.; pres., dir., chmn. bd. Massco Investment Mgmt. Corp., 1969-78; pres., chief exec. officer Ready Reserves Trust, 1975-78; chmn. bd., chief exec. officer Investment Mgmt. Assocs., Inc., Denver, 1978—. With USNR, 1942-45, PTO, with USAAF, 1946-48. Mem. Union Club (Boston), Univ. Club (Boston), Met. Club (Denver), Beaver Creek Club, Avon Co. Republican. Episcopalian. Home: 1934 Five Iron Dr Castle Rock CO 80104 Office: Investment Mgmt Assn Inc One Denver Tech Ctr 5251 Denver Tech Ctr Pkwy Ste 1210 Englewood CO 80111

PERRY, MICHAEL LAWRENCE, museum director; b. Nampa, Idaho, Jan. 6, 1946; s. Lowell Delmar and Lucy Dora (Lemon) P.; m. Sandra Lynne Miles, Dec. 13, 1968; children: Allyson, Justin, Adrienne. BS, U. Utah, 1971, MS, 1973. Animal care handler U. Utah, Salt Lake City, 1965-73, asst. curator, 1968-73, teaching fellow, 1969-73; dir. Dinosaur Natural History Mus., Vernal, Utah, 1973-81, Idaho Mus. Natural History, Pocatello, 1981-84, Mus. Western Colo., 1984—; cons. Idaho Assn. for Humanities, Pocatello, 1981-84; bd. dirs. Canyonlands Field Inst., Moab, Utah, 1985—. Co-author: Utah Birds, 1975; contbr. articles to profl. jours. Bd. dirs. Grand Junction (Colo.) Visitors and Conv. Bur., 1986, Grand Junction Downtown Assn., 1985. Recipient Leadership Achievement award Grand Junction Downtown Assn., 1985, Outstanding Employee award Utah Div. Parks and Recreation, 1979, Outstanding Pub. Service award Vernal C. of C., 1978, Outstanding Achievement award Salt Lake Tribune, 1980. Mem. Am. Assn. Mus., Mountain Plains Mus. Assn., Colo.-Wyo. Assn. Mus., Grand Junction C. of C., Sigma Xi. Republican. Mormon. Lodge: Lions. Home: 1909 Monument Canyon Dr Grand Junction CO 81503 Office: Mus of Western Colo 248 S 4th St Grand Junction CO 81501

PERRY, WILLIAM JOSEPH, food processing company executive; b. Sacramento, Calif., Nov. 4, 1930; s. Joseph Nasciemeto and Jennie (Nunez) P.; m. Beverly Ann Styes, Dec. 9, 1956 (div. May 1981); children: Katherine, Bill Jr., Kathleen, Barbara; m. Leslie Z. Blumberg, June 30, 1986. BS, U. Calif., Berkeley, 1953. Quality control supr. Stokely Van Camp, Oakland, Calif., 1953-54; plant mgr. Safeway Stores, Brookside div., Grandview, Wash., 1954-61, Gallo Winery, Modesto, Calif., 1961-62; gen. mgr. Bocca Bella Olive Assoc., Wallace, Calif., 1962-65; v.p. Early Calif. Ind., L.A., 1965-74, Fairmont Foods, Santa Ana, Calif., 1974-75; pres. Cal Agra Ind., Stockton, Calif., 1975-76; exec. v.p. Food Brokers Internat., L.A., 1976—; pres., co-owner Girards Fine Foods, Inc., L.A., 1981—; dir. Girards Fine Foods, L.A., 1981—, Food Brokers, Inc., L.A., 1976—, Cozad & Assoc. Ad Agy., Encino, Calif., 1985-87. Wrestling com., dir. protocol, L.A. Olympic Com., 1981-84. Mem. Nat. Food Brokers Assn., Assn. of Dressings and Sauces, Nat. Juice Processing Assn., Nat. Single Service Assn., Am. Chem. Soc., Westlake Tennis & Swim Club. Republican. Roman Catholic. Home: 9370 Flicker Way Los Angeles CA 90069 Office: Girards Fine Foods 5443 E Washington Blvd Los Angeles CA 90040

PERSCHBACHER, REX ROBERT, law educator; b. Chgo., Aug. 31, 1946; s. Robert Ray and Nancy Ellen (Beach) P.; m. Debbie Bassett Hamilton; children: Julie Ann, Nancy Beatrice. AB, Stanford U., 1968; JD, U. Calif., Berkeley, 1972. Bar: Calif. 1972, U.S. Dist. Ct. (no. dist.) Calif. 1973, U.S. Dist. Ct. (so. dist.) Calif. 1979, U.S. Ct. Appeals (9th cir.) 1980, U.S. Dist. ct. (ea. dist.) Calif. 1985. Law clk. to judge U.S. Dist. Ct. (no. dist.) Calif., San Francisco, 1973-74; asst. prof. law U. Tex., Austin, 1974-75; assoc. Heller, Ehrman, White & McAuliffe, San Francisco, 1975-78; asst. prof. law U. San Diego, 1978-79, assoc. prof. law, 1980-81; mem. faculty Inst. on Internat. and Comparative Law, London, 1984—; acting prof. law U. Calif., Davis, 1981-85, prof., 1988—; dir. clin. edn. U. Calif., Davis, rep.-at-large acad. senate, 1986—, law sch. rep., 1989—; vis. prof. law U. Santa Clara (Calif.), summer 1986. Co-author: Civil Procedure, 1967; contbr. articles to legal jours. Mem. site coun. West Davis Elem., Davis, 1985-86, chmn., 1986-87. Mem. ABA, Calif. Bar Assn., Am. Assn. Law Schs. Democrat. Office: U Calif Sch Law King Hall Davis CA 95616

PERSON, DONALD AMES, SR., pediatrician, rheumatologist; b. Fargo, N.D., July 17, 1938; s. Ingwald Haldor and Elma Wilhelmina (Karlstrom) P.; m. Blanche Durand, Apr. 28, 1962; children: Donald Ames Jr., David Wesley. Student, Gustavus Adolphus Coll., 1956-58, U. Minn., 1958-59; BS, U. N.D., 1961; MD, U. Minn., 1963. Intern Mpls.-Hennepin County Gen. Hosp., 1963-64; resident neurol. surgery Mayo Clinic and Mayo Grad. Sch. Medicine, Rochester, Minn., 1967, fellow in microbiology, 1968-70; rsch. asso. Baylor Coll. Medicine, Houston, 1971, Arthritis Found. fellow, 1972-74, mem. faculty, 1971-73, asst. prof. pediatrics, 1980-87, resident in pediatrics, 1978-80; asst. attending pediatrics Harris County Hosp. Dist., 1980-88; rheumatologist Tex. Children's Hosp., 1980-88, attending pediatrician, 1982-88; cons. Kelsey Seybold Clinic, 1980-88 ; cons. Houston Shrine Crippled Children's Hosp., 1983-88 , Houston Meth. Hosp., 1983-88 , St. Luke's Episc. Hosp., 1983-88 ; cons. Honolulu Shriner's Crippled Children's Hosp., 1988—; assoc. prof. clin. pediatrics U. Hawaii Sch. Medicine, Honolulu, 1988—, Uniformed Svcs. U. Health Scis., Bethesda, Md., 1989—; chief ambulatory pediatrics, Tripler Army Med. Ctr., Tripler AMC, Hawaii, 1988—, asst. chief dept. pediatrics, 1988—. Contbr. articles to profl. jours. Served with AUS, 1964-66, Arthritis Found. sr. investigator, 1975-77. Fellow Am. Acad. Pediatrics; mem. AAAS, Am. Fedn. Clin. Rsch., AMA, Am. Rheumatism Assn., Am. Soc. Microbiology, Soc. Pediatric Rsch., Am. Soc. Tropical Medicine and Hygiene, Arthritis Found. (dir., med. adv. bd.), Assn. Mil. Surgeons U.S., Harris County Med. Soc., Houston Acad. Medicine, Houston Pediatric Soc., Internat. Orgn. Mycoplasmologists, N.Y. Acad. Sci., N.D. Acad. Sci., Soc. Exptl. Biology and Medicine, So. Soc. Pediatric Rsch., S.W. Sci. Forum, Tex. Med. Assn., Tex. Pediatric Soc., Tex. Rheumatism Assn., Tissue Culture Assn., Honolulu Pediatric Soc., U.S. Fedn. Culture Collections. Mem. Evangelical Lutheran Ch. in Am. Home: 1321 Parks Rd Honolulu HI 96819-2126 Office: Tripler Army Med Ctr Tripler HI 96859-5000

PERSONS, JAMES ANDREW, personnel consultant; b. Cherry Point, N.C., Dec. 9, 1948; s. Walter David and Mary Ann (Frampton) P.; m. Nancy Ann Way, Dec. 2, 1978; children: Marcy Ann, Heather Susan, Jeffery Andrew, Wendy Colleen. BA in Polit. Sci., U. Calif., Irvine, 1981; postgrad., Western State U., 1982-84. Technical recruiter McDonnel Douglas, Long Beach, Calif., 1983-85, Magnavox Govt. Electronics, Torrance, Calif., 1985-86; technical staffing specialist semiconductor products div. Rockwell Internat., Newport Beach, Calif., 1987—; sr. advisor minority engring. program Calif. Poly. Inst., Pomona, 1986—; dir. minority engring. program U. Calif., Irvine, 1987—. Founder Minority Community Affairs Program, Santa Ana, Calif., 1980. Sgt. USAF, 1969-71. Home: 1540 Alexis Ave Anaheim CA 92802 Office: Rockwell Internat Rocketdyne div 6633 Canoga Ave Canoga Park CA 91303

PERTHOU, ALISON CHANDLER, interior designer; b. Bremerton, Wash., July 22, 1945; d. Benson and Elizabeth (Holdsworth) Chandler; m. A.V. Perthou III, Sept. 9, 1967 (div. Dec. 1977); children: Peter T.R., Stewart A.C. BFA, Cornish Coll. Arts, 1972. Pres. Alison Perthou Interior Design, Seattle, 1972—, Optima Design, Inc., Seattle, 1986—; treas. Framejoist Corp., Bellevue, Wash., 1973—; pres. Classics: Interiors & Antiques, Inc., 1988—; cons. bldg. and interiors com. Children's Hosp., Seattle, 1976—; guest lectr. U. Wash., Seattle, 1980-81. Bd. trustees Cornish Coll. Arts, Seattle, 1973-80, sec. exec. com., 1975-77; mem. procurement com. Patrons of N.W. Cultural and Charitable Orgn., 1985—. Mem. Am. Soc. Interior Design, Seattle Tennis Club (house and grounds com. 1974-75), City Club (Seattle). Office: 4216 E Madison St Seattle WA 98112

PESCE, GABRIEL VINCENT, civil engineer, educator; b. Staten Island, N.Y., Apr. 21, 1924; s. Vincent S. and Mary (Paratore) P.; m. Lois Jean Ballintine, June 30, 1950; children: Vincent, Mary Anne (dec.), David, Laurie, Barbara. BCE, Cornell U., 1949, MCE, 1951; ScB, Brown U., 1945; PhD in Archaeology, UCLA, 1986. Registered profl. engr., Calif. Hydraulic research engr. TVA, Knoxville, 1949-50; instr. Cornell U., Ithaca, N.Y., 1948-49, 50-53; prin. research engr. Republic Aviation Corp., Farmingdale, N.Y., 1953-56, Lockheed Aircraft, Marietta, Ga., 1956-57; v.p. Abex Aerospace, Oxnard, Calif., 1957-72; pres. G.V. Pesce & Assocs. Inc., Camarillo, Calif., 1972—; instr. Ventura (Calif.) Coll., 1974—; bd. dirs. Santa Anita Mut. Water Co., Gaviota, Calif. Patentee in field. Bd. dirs., v.p., Hollister Ranch Coop., Gaviota, 1982-86, Hollister Ranch Owners Assn., Gaviota, 1978. Served with USN, 1942-47; to lt. col. USAFR, 1949-76; ret. col. Mem. ASCE, Soc. Am. Mil. Engrs., Earthquake Engring. and Research Inst., Am. Geophys. Union, Calif. Land Surveyors Assn., Council Cons. Engrs., Ventura County Archaelogical Soc., Am. Water Works Assn., Navy League, Air Force Assn., Chi Epsilon. Republican. Roman Catholic. Home: PO Box 1528 Camarillo CA 93011-1528 Office: GV Pesce & Assocs Inc 541 Calle San Pablo Camarillo CA 93010

PESMAN, GERARD HYDE, land surveyor, civil engineer; b. Denver, Aug. 9, 1925; s. M. Walter and Elizabeth (Hyde) P.; m. Mary Smith, Oct. 1955 (div. 1971); children: Nancy, Jill, Diane, Kristin; m. Nancy Proctor, Feb. 12, 1975. BSCE, U. Colo., 1950; MSCE, U. Wash., 1952. Registered profl. engr., Colo., Utah, N.Mex. Instr. U. Colo., Boulder, 1953-55; cons. engr. and land surveyor Grand Junction, Colo., 1955-69; pres. Survey Engrs. Inc., Grand Junction and Aspen, Colo., 1969-86, USSV Inc.-Masters Ski Series, Boulder, 1980-86, G.H. Pesman Inc., Boulder, 1984—; constrn. engr. Vail (Colo.) Assocs., 1965-85; cons. Colo. Ski Areas, 1965—; expert witness Title USA, 1987; lectr. Rocky Mountain Lift Assn., 1983-88. With U.S. Army, 1943-46. Fellow Am. Congress Surveying and Mapping; mem. ASCE (chmn. surveying and mapping div. 1964), Profl. Land Surveyors Colo. (pres. 1971). Democrat. Unitarian. Home and Office: 1009 Vivian Cir Boulder CO 80303

PESSAGNO, RICHARD ANTHONY, nurse; b. Washington, June 27, 1960; s. Richard E. and Judith (Johnson) P. BS in Nursing, The Cath. U. Am., 1984. RN, Md., Calif., Colo., Va., Conn., Colo., NY. Commd. 2d lt. U.S. Army, 1984, advanced through grades to capt., 1987; clin. staff nurse Evans Army Hosp. U.S. Army, Fort Carson, Colo., 1984-85, perioperative educator, orthopedical surgical cons. Evans Army Hosp., 1985-87, clin. nurse mgr. Evans Army Hosp., 1987-88; AIDS nurse counselor Arlington (Va.) Co. Govtl. Basic Cardiac Life Support Provider, 1988—; bereavement team mem. Pike's Peak Hosp., Colorado Springs, Colo., 1984-86; instr. Assn. of Nurses in AIDS Care, 1985—. Presenter workshops on death and grief, 1987. Interpreter Pike's Peak Ctr. on Deafness, Colorado Springs, 1984-87; mem. So. Colo. AIDS Project, Colorado Springs, 1987. Mem. Am. Nurses Assn., Colo. Nurses Assn., Am. Assembly for Men in Nursing, Nat. Hospice Orgn., Assn. Nursing in AIDS Care. Democrat. Roman Catholic.

PESTA, BEN W., II, lawyer, writer; b. Hagerstown, Md., Oct. 15, 1948; s. Ben W. and Ethel Irene (Kirkpatrick) P.; m. Monique Raphel High, Dec. 24, 1987. AB, UCLA, 1969; JD, U. Calif., Berkeley, 1972. Assoc. pub. Weider Health & Fitness, Woodland Hills, Calif., 1984—. Editor: Esquire; assoc. editor Playboy, Rolling Stone, Sports, TV Guide, Cosmopolitan, L.A. Style; contbr. articles to profl. jours. Capt. USAF., 1973. Home: 431 S RexfordDr Beverly Hills CA 90212 Office: Weider Health & Fitness 21100 Erwin St Woodland Hills CA 91367

PETERS, ANN DEHUFF, pediatrician; b. Augusta, Ga., Mar. 22, 1915; d. John David and Elizabeth Wilson (Willis) DeHuff; m. Richard M. Peters, Oct. 2, 1946; children: Joan, Deborah, Barbara, Rick. BA cum laude, U. N.Mex., 1936; BS, Simmons Coll., 1937; M. in Social Work, Simmons Coll., Boston, 1938; MD cum laude, Wash. U., 1946. Lic. MD, Calif. From caseworker to case supr. The Children's Bur. of Indpls. Orphan Asylum, 1938-43; intern in obstetrics and gynocology John Hopkins U., Balt., 1946-47; med. rsch. asst. child devel. Fed. Security Agy., Washington, 1947-49; fellow in preventive medicine and neuropsychiatry Wash. U., St. Louis, 1949-51, instr., lectr., 1951-52; from instr. to clin. assoc. prof. dept. pediatrics U. N.C., Chapel Hill., 1953-69; pediatrician N.C. Meml. Hosp., Chapel Hill., 1953-69; day care coord. Children Hosp., San Diego, 1969-70; lectr., day care coord. San Diego (Calif.) State U., 1970-72, med. dir. Primary Nurse Practioner Program, 1974-79, from assoc. clin. prof. to clin. prof., 1971—, attending pediatrician, 1975—; dep. adminstr. St. Louis Study of Vision Testing Procedures, 1948-49. Contbr. numerous articles to profl. jours. Adv. com. day care N.C. State Bd. Pub. Welfare, 1963-68; elected mem. San Diego Head Start Program; cons. to com. on the presch. child, 1970-72; mem. steering com. on day care, 1983—. Recipient French Medal for scholar U. N.Mex., 1936. Fellow Am. Acad. Pediatrics (elected hon., cons.), Am. Orthopsychiatric Assn. (v.p. 1978-79, bd. dirs. 1979-83, pres.-elect 1980-81, pres. 1981-82), Am. Pub. Health Assn. (chmn. Com. Day Care 1962-68, mem. Early Child Carer Com. 1968-71); mem. Calif. Assn. for Edn. Young Children, Nat. Assn. Edn. Young Children (chmn. Health Commn. 1973-74, governing bd. 1979-83), Soc. Rsch. and Child Devel., San Diego Assn. Edn. Young Children, N.C. Pediatric Soc., San Diego Pediatric Soc. (Calif. chpt. III), Phi Kappa Phi, Alpha Omega Alpha, Delta Omega. Democrat. Home and Office: 233 Prospect St San Diego CA 92037

PETERS, BARBARA HUMBIRD, writer, editor; b. Santa Monica, Calif., Sept. 26, 1948; d. Philip Rising and Caroline Jean (Dickason) Peters. AA, Santa Monica Coll., 1971; BS, San Diego State U., 1976; postgrad. UCLA, 1981-82, 84. Gen. ptnr. Signet Properties, Los Angeles, 1971-85; tech. editor C. Brewer & Co., Hilo, Hawaii, 1975-76; editor The Aztec Engineer mag., San Diego, 1976-77; regional publicist YWCA, San Diego, 1977-78; campaign cons. Rep. Congl. and Assembly Candidates San Diego; Pollster, Los Angeles Times, 1983; pres. Humbird Hopkins Inc., Los Angeles, 1978—; pub. relations cons. ASCE, San Diego, 1975-76, Am. Soc. Mag. Photographers, San Diego, 1980. Author: The Layman's Guide to Raising Cane: A Guide to the Hawaiian Sugar Industry, 1975, The Student's Survival Guide, 1976, 2d edit. 1977. Council mem. Mayor's Council on Libraries, Los Angeles, 1969; mem. Wilshire Blvd. Property Owners Assn., Santa Monica, 1972-78; docent Mus. Sci. and Industry, Los Angeles, 1970; founding mem. Comml. and Indsl. Properties Assn., Santa Monica, 1982—. Recipient Acting award Santa Monica Coll., 1970. Mem. Internat. Assn. Bus. Communicators, Sales and Mktg. Execs. Assn. Avocations: travel, opera.

PETERS, DAVID MERRITT, member senatorial staff; b. Honolulu, Aug. 6, 1923; s. Charles Merritt and Mollie Kanani (Akana) P.; m. Joan Sabin, June 1, 1953 (dec. 1986); children: Lauren Peters Moriarty, David Merritt Jr., Diane. BS in Engring., U.S. Mil. Acad., 1946; MS in Journalism, U. Wis., 1961. Commd. 2d lt. U.S. Army, 1946; advanced through grades to col. U.S. Army, Korea and Vietnam; ret. U.S. Army, 1976; exec. asst. to U.S. Senator Daniel K. Inouye, Honolulu, 1976--. Decorated Silver Star, Legion of Merit with three oak leaf clusters, Bronze Star with V. Home: 1371 Kina St Kailua HI 96734 Office: 300 Ala Moana Blvd Ste 7325 Honolulu HI 96850

PETERS, DOUGLAS CAMERON, mining engineer, geologist; b. Pitts., June 19, 1955; s. Donald Cameron and Twila (Bingel) P. BS in Earth and Planetary Sci., U. Pitts., 1977; MS in Geology, Colo. Sch. Mines, 1981, MS in Mining Engring., 1983. Technician, inspector Engring. Mechanics Inc., Pitts., 1973-77. Research asst. Potential Gas Agy., Golden, Colo., 1977-78; geologist U.S. Geol. Survey, Denver, 1978-80; cons. Climax Molybdenum Co., Golden, 1981-82; cons., Golden, 1982-84; mining engr., prin. investigator U.S. Bur. Mines, Denver, 1984—; bur. rep. to Geosat Com., 1984—; program chmn. GeoTech Conf., Denver, 1984-88. Author: Physical Modeling of Draw of Broken Rock in Caving, 1984, Bur. Mines Articles and Reports; editor COGS Computer Contbns., 1986—, Coal Geology, 1988—; contbr. articles to profl. jours. Mem. Computer Oriented Geol. Soc. (charter, com. chmn. 1983—, pres. 1985, dir. 1986), Geol. Soc. Am., Rocky Mountain Assn. Geologists, Soc. Mining Engrs. (jr. mem.), Am. Assn. Petroleum Geologists (com. mem. 1984—), Am. Soc. Photogrammetry and Remote Sensing, Nat. Space Soc., EMD (astrogeology com., remote sensing com. 1989—), Colo. Mining Assn., Pitts. Geol. Soc. Republican. Office: US Bur Mines Denver Fed Ctr Box 25086 Bldg 20 Denver CO 80225

PETERS, LESLIE ANN, television and radio producer; b. Baytown, Tex., Mar. 17, 1961; d. Jack Lee and Barbara Marie (Jannopoulo) P.; m. Bradford Thomas Thornburgh, June 30, 1985. Student, U. Calif., San Diego, 1984. Gen. mgr. Sta. KSDT-FM, San Diego, 1982-84; sales rep. On Air mag., San Diego, 1984-85; news announcer Sta. KPBS-FM, San Diego, 1985-88; producer, dir. ITV-TV, San Diego, 1986-88; sr. assoc. producer St. KPBS-TV, San Diego, 1987-89; ind. producer and reporter CBS News and Nat. Pub. Radio, 1988—. Mem. NCCJ, 1989. Recipient Golden Mike award Radio, TV and Newscasters Assn., 1988, Spl. Event award Broadcast Industry Cong., 1988, Emmy, 1988; 1st place Huston Film Festival, 1989. Mem. Am. Women in Radio and TV (bd. dirs. San Diego chpt. 1985-86, sec. 1986-87). Democrat. Presbyterian. Home: 3131 Via de Caballo Encinitas CA 92024

PETERS, MICHAEL ARTHUR, plastic and reconstructive surgeon; b. Evergreen Park, Ill., June 21, 1943; s. Arthur Myron and Mary Ann (Bragiel) P.; m. Laurie Jean Smith, June 21, 1969; children: Jonathan and Michael (twins). BS, U. Notre Dame, 1965; MD, Northwestern U., 1969. Diplomate, Am. Bd. Plastic Surgery. Intern Northwestern U. Med. Ctr., Chgo., 1969-70, resident in gen. surgery, 1970-73, resident in plastic and reconstructive surgery, 1973-75; pvt. practice San Diego, 1975—; pres., Michael A. Peters Med. Clinic, Inc., San Diego, 1979—; assoc. clin. prof. plastic surgery, U. Calif. San Diego Med. Ctr., La Jolla, 1985—. Mem. admissions com. U. Calif. San Diego Med. Sch., 1982—, bd. dirs. Sch. Medicine Assocs, 1984—. Fellow ACS; mem. San Diego County Med. Soc., Calif. Med. Assn., AMA, San Diego Internat. Plastic Surgery Soc. (pres. 1986). Roman Catholic. Home: PO Box 1928 Rancho Santa Fe CA 92067 Office: 4103 3d Ave San Diego CA 92103

PETERS, RAYMOND EUGENE, computer systems company executive; b. New Haven, Aug. 24, 1933; s. Raymond and Doris Winthrop (Smith) P.; m. Mildred K. Mathers, July 14, 1978 (div. Nov. 1983). Student, San Diego City Coll., 1956-61; cert., Lumbleau Real Estate Sch., 1973, Southwestern Coll., Chula Vista, Calif., 1980. Lic. quality assurance engr. Founder, pub. Silhouette Pub. Co., San Diego, 1960-75; news dir. Sta. XEGM, San Diego, 1965-67; founder, chief exec. officer New World Airways, Inc., San Diego, 1969-75; news dir. Sta. XERB, Tijuana, Mex., 1973-74; co-founder, vice chmn. bd. San Cal Rail, Inc., San Diego, 1974-77; founder, pres. Ansonia Sta., micro systems, San Diego, 1986—; co-founder, dir. S.E. Community Theatre, San Diego, 1960-68; comdt. New World Aviation Acad., Otay Mesa, Calif., 1971-77; cons. Alpha Micro Videotrax Systems, Santa Anna, Calif., 1988—; bd. dirs. Greater San Diego Minority C. of C., 1987—. Author: Black Americans in Aviation, 1971, Profiles in Black American History, 1974, Eagles Don't Cry, 1988; founder, pub., editor Oceanside Lighthouse, 1958-60, , San Diego Herald Dispatch, 1959-60. Co-founder, bd. dirs. San Diego County Econ. Opportunity Commn., 1964-67; co-founder Edn. Cultural Complex, San Diego, 1966-75. With U.S. Army, 1950-53, Korea. Mem. Am. Soc. for Quality Control, Afro-Am. Micro Systems Soc. (exec. dir. 1987—), Negro Airmen Internat. (Calif. pres. 1970-75, nat. v.p. 1975-77), U.S. C. of C., Masons (grand master), Shriners (Disting. Community Svc. award 1975, Imperial Potentate). Republican. Unitarian. Home: 8410 El Paso St La Mesa CA 92042 Office: Ansonia Sta 1727 Sweetwater Rd Ste W National City CA 92050

PETERS, RAYMOND ROBERT, banker; b. Concord, Calif., Sept. 14, 1942; s. Robert V. and Pegi M. (Carr) P.; m. Nancy Choy; children: Angel, Ray, Matthew. BBA, U. Oreg., 1964. Head customer securities Bank of Am., San Francisco, 1969-71, Eurocurrency and fgn. exchange mgr., London, 1971-72, San Francisco, 1972-76, sr. v.p., head offshore funds, 1976-85, sr. v.p. head treasury, 1985-86; exec. v.p. Bank Am. Corp., 1987—; mem. fgn. exchange com. N.Y. Fed. Res. Bank, 1978-87, chmn., 1984-85; mem. Chgo. Merc. Exchange, 1987—; mem. Chgo. Bd. Trade, 1987—; cons. on fgn. currency, offshore banking matters U.S. Fed. Res., fgn. central banks. Served to lt. USN, 1964-68. Office: BankAm Treasury Div 555 California St Ste 3170 San Francisco CA 94104

PETERS, ROBERT WAYNE, insurance executive; b. LaPorte, Ind., Jan. 2, 1950; s. Harry Carl and Dorothy May (Fischer) P.; m. Frances Kay Cooley, Aug. 21, 1971; children: Carolyn Marie, Angela Lynn. BA, Purdue U., 1972. CLU. Mgr. pension adminstrn. Gen. Life Ins. Corp. Am., Milw., 1973-75; dir. qualified plan devel. Cen. Life Assurance Co., Des Moines, 1976-84; v.p. individual ops. First Farwest Ins. Co., Portland, Oreg., 1984—; lectr. various govt. agys. Contbr. articles to profl. jours. Mem. Am. Soc. of CLUs, Nat. Assn. Life Underwriters, Oreg. Accident Health Claims Assn., City Club of Portland, N.W. Vintage Thunderbird (v.p. 1988), Optimists (treas. West Des Moines, Iowa Club 1983-84). Office: First Farwest Ins Co 400 SW 6th Ave Portland OR 97204

PETERS, SASHA STRATTON, real estate officer; b. Zurich, Switzerland, Aug. 26, 1959; came to U.S. 1965.; d. Malte and Margo Whitney (Stratton) Peters; m. John Allen Parezo, Sept. 26, 1981 (div. 1987). BA in Genetics, U. Calif., Berkeley, 1981; MBA, U. So. Calif., 1989. Rsch. cons. Engring. Econs. Assocs., Berkeley, 1980; credit analyst Union Oil Co. Calif., San Francisco, 1981-83; investment analyst Damon Raike & Co., 1983-84, Bank of Am., 1984-85; acquisitions officer, also v.p. Karsten Realty Advisors, L.A., 1985—; cons. in field. Mem. New Commerce Assocs., Chi Omega. Office: Karsten Realty Advisors 12121 Wilshire Blvd #900 Los Angeles CA 90025

PETERSEN, DONALD LOREN, chemical company executive; b. Tama, Iowa, Sept. 29, 1936; s. Arthur Paul and MIldred Vera (Lacina) P.; m. Marilyn Kay Zeigler, Sept. 2, 1961 (div. Nov. 1980); children: Mark Lewis, Corinn Marie Petersen Topoleski, Michael Paul, Ronald Fray; m. Adrianne Kala Perelskin, May 9, 1981. BSME, Iowa State U., 1962. Test engr. USDA Forest Svc., Arcadia, Calif., 1962-65; prodn. dept. supr. Monsanto Co., Soda Springs, Idaho, 1965-71; wildfire div. mgr. Monsanto Co., Ontario, Calif., 1971—. Served with U.S. Army, 1957-58. Mem. Lions (v.p. 1966-70). Republican. Office: Monsanto Co 810 E Main St Ontario CA 91761

PETERSEN, FINN BO, oncologist, educator; b. Copenhagen, Mar. 26, 1951; came to U.S., 1983; s. Jorgen and Ebba Gjeding (Jorgensen) P.; m. Merete Secher Lund, Mar. 7, 1979; children: Lars Secher, Thomas Secher, Andreas Secher. BA, Niels Steensen, Copenhagen, 1971; MD, U. Copenhagen, 1978. Intern in internal medicine Copenhagen, 1978-79, resident in hematology, 1980-83; fellow oncology Fred Hutchinson Cancer Research Ctr. U. Wash., Seattle, 1983-85, assoc. researcher oncology, 1985-87, asst. mem. in clin. research, 1987—; asst. prof. Fred Hutchinson Cancer Research Ctr. U. Wash., 1988—. Author: Hematology, 1977; contbr. articles to profl. jours. Mem. AMA, AAAS, Danish Med. Assn., Assn. Gnotobiology, Exptl. Soc. Hematology. Office: U Wash Fred Hutchinson Cancer Research Ctr 1124 Columbia St Seattle WA 98104

PETERSEN, NORMAN WILLIAM, naval officer, engineering facility administrator; b. Highland Park, Ill., Aug. 26, 1933; s. Jens Edlef and Marie (Wenderling) P.; m. Ann Nevin, Aug. 24, 1956; children: Richard Nevin, Robert William, Thomas Marshall, Anita, David Arthur. BEE, U. N.Mex., 1956; MEE with distinction, Naval Postgrad. Sch., Monterey, Calif., 1962; postgrad., Harvard Bus. Sch., 1982. Registered profl. engr., Mass., Calif. Shops engr. Naval Station, Key West, Fla., 1956-59; personnel dir. Bur. Yards and Docks, Washington, 1959-60; pub. works officer Fleet Anti-Air Warfare Ctr., Dam Neck, Va., 1962-64; engring. coord. Southwest div. Naval Facilities Engring. Command, San Diego, 1964-66; exec. officer Amphibious Constrn. Battalion 1, San Diego, 1966-67; force civil engr. Comdr. Naval Air Force Pacific, San Diego, 1967-70; pub. works officer Naval Air Sta. Miramar, San Diego, 1970-73; exec. officer Pub. Works Ctr., Great Lakes, Ill., 1973-75; comdg. officer Navy Civil Engring. Rsch. Lab., Port Hueneme, Calif., 1975-78, Pub. Works Ctr. San Francisco Bay Area, Oakland, Calif., 1978-80; comptroller, programs dir. Naval Facilities Engring. Command, Washington, 1980-84; pub. works officer Pacific Missile Test Ctr., Point Mugu, Calif., 1984-86; deputy assoc. dir. for plant engring. Lawrence Livermore (Calif.) Nat. Lab., 1986—. Contbr. articles to profl. jours. Bd. dirs. CBC Fed. Credit Union, Port Hueneme, 1984-86, Ventura County United Way, Oxnard, Calif., 1976-78, strategic planning com., Camarillo, Calif., 1984-86; guest mem. Ventura County Assn. Govts., 1984-86. Decorated (twice) Legion of Merit; Gallantry Cross (Republic Vietnam). Mem. Am. Soc. Mil. Comptrollers, Soc. Am. Mil. Engrs., Assn. Phys. Plant Adminstrs. (affiliate), Navy League, Oxnard Gem and Mineral Soc. (2d v.p.), Sigma Xi, Lambda Chi Alpha. Office: Lawrence Livermore Nat Lab PO Box 808 L-657 Livermore CA 94550

PETERSEN, ROLAND, painter, printmaker; b. Endelave, Horsens, Denmark, 1926; came to U.S., 1928; m. Sharane Havlina, Aug. 12, 1950; children—Dana Mark, Maura Brooke, Julien Conrad, Karena Caia. B.A., U. Calif.-Berkeley, 1949, M.A., 1950; postgrad., Han Hofmann's Sch. Fine Arts, summers 1950-51, S.W. Hayter's Atelier 17, Paris, 1950, 63, 70, Islington Studio, London, 1976, The Print Workshop, London, 1980. Tchr. State Coll. Wash., Pullman, 1952-56; mem. faculty U. Calif. at Davis, 1956—, now prof. art. Exhibited one-man shows: Gump's Gallery, San Francisco, 1962, Staempfli Gallery, N.Y.C., 1963, 65, 67, Adele Bednarz Gallery, Los Angeles, 1966, 69, 70, 72, 73, 75, 76, Crocker Art Gallery, Sacramento, 1965, de Young Mus., San Francisco, 1968, La Jolla Mus., 1971, Phoenix Mus., 1972, Santa Barbara Mus., 1973, USIS sponsored touring one-man exhbn., Turkey, U. Reading, Eng., 1977, 80, U. Calif., Davis, 1978, Brubaker Gallery, Sarasota, Fla., 1979, Rorick Gallery, San Francisco, 1981, 82, 83, 84, 85, Himovitz-Salomon Gallery, Sacramento, 1987-88, Vandenwoude Tananbaum Gallery, N.Y.C., 1987-89, Harcourts Gallery, San Francisco, 1989; group shows including: Calif. Palace Legion of Honor, San Francisco Art Inst., 1962, Mus. Art, Carnegie Inst., Pitts., 1964, Obelisk Gallery, Washington, John Herron Art Inst., Indpls., 1964, Pa. Acad. Fine Arts, Phila., Crocker Art Gallery, Sacramento, 1965, 81, Art Inst. Chgo., 1965, Va. Mus. Fine Arts, Richmond, 1966, U. Ariz. Art Gallery, Tucson, 1967, Am. Cultural Center, Paris, 1971, Nat. Gallery, Washington, 1972, Otis Art Inst. Gallery, Los Angeles, 1974, Auerbach Fine Art Gallery, London, 1977, U. Wis., Madison, 1977, Bklyn. Mus., 1978, U. Ill., 1978, U. Nev., Las Vegas, 1980, Brubaker Gallery, Sarasota, Fla., 1983, U.S.A. World Print Council, San Francisco, Nat. Mus., Singapore, Nat. Gallery, Bangkok, Thailand, Amerika Haus, Berlin, Malmo Konsthall, Sweden, Museo Carrillo Gil, Mexico City, all 1984-86; represented in permanent collections: de Young Mus., San Francisco, San Francisco Mus. Modern Art, Va. Mus. Fine Arts, Richmond, Mus. Modern Art, N.Y.C., Phila. Mus. Art, Whitney Mus. Am. Art, Phoenix Mus., Santa Barbara Mus., Musée Municipal, Brest, France, Smithsonian Instn. Nat. Collection Fine Arts, others. Served with USN, 1944-46, PTO. Recipient numerous prizes and awards, 1950—; Guggenheim fellow, 1963; U. Calif. creative arts fellow, 1967, 70, 77; Fulbright grantee, 1970. Mem. Print Council Am., AAUP, San Francisco Art Assn., Calif. Soc. Printmakers. Office: U Calif Dept Art Davis CA 95616

PETERSEN, VERNON LEROY, communications and engineering corporation executive; b. Mason, Nev., Nov. 3, 1926; s. Vernon and Lenora Eloise (Dickson) P. Cert. naval architecture, U. Calif., 1944, cert. in plant engring., adminstrn. and supervision UCLA, 1977; cert. in real estate exchanging Orange Coast Coll., 1978. Registered profl. engr. ;children—Anne C., Ruth F. Chief, Philippines Real Estate Office, U.S. C.E., 1950-55; pres., gen. mgr. Mason Merc. Co., 1956-62; pres., gen. mgr. Mason Water Co., 1956-62; pres. Petersen Enterprises, Cons. Engrs., Nev. and Calif., Downey, 1962-79, Vernon L. Peterson, Inc., 1980—; pres., chief exec. officer Castle Communications Co. Inc., 1985—; Sta. KCCD-TV, 1985-89; installation mgr. Pacific Architects & Engrs., L.A. and Socialist Rep. of Vietnam, 1969-72, facilities engr., ops. supr., acting contract mgr. L.A. and Saudi Arabia, 1979-82; bldg. engr. Purex Co., Inc., Lakewood, Calif., 1975-79; lectr. plant engring., various colls. in Calif., 1975—. Candidate for U.S. Congress, 1956, del. Rep. State Conv., 1960-64. With AUS, 1944-47. Fellow Soc. Am. Mil. Engrs. (life mem.; named Orange County Post's Engr. of Year 1977, founder Da Nang Post 1969, Orange County Post 1977, pres. 1978-79, Red Sea Post, Jeddah, Saudi Arabia 1980), Internat. Platform Assn., Orange County Engr. Coun. (pres. 1978-79), Am. Inst. Plant Engrs. (chpt. 38 Engring. Merit award 1977-78), Soc. Women Engrs. (assoc.), AIAA. Mormon. Office: Castle Communications PO Box 787 Temecula CA 92390

PETERSON, ANTJE A., real estate broker; b. Oberstdorf, West Germany, Mar. 28, 1944; came to U.S., 1967; d. Peter G. and Gerda T. (Schmied) Alkemade; m. Daniel J. Coleman, July 20, 1971 (div. 1977); m. Thomas A. Peterson III, May 17, 1981. AA, Phoenix Coll., 1970; BA, Ariz. State U., 1972. Br. mgr. Deutsche Buch Gemeinschaft, Augsburg, West Germany, 1963-67; grad. tchng. asst. Ariz. State U., Tempe, 1973-75; jr. exec. Crown Crafts Internat., Phoenix, 1976-78; br. mgr. Gordon Bell Realty and Devel. Corp., Scottsdale, Ariz., 1978-80; pres., broker Sigma Real Estate, Inc., Scottsdale, 1980—; instr. Scottsdale Bd. Realtors, 1988—. Editor: SIGMA News, 1980—; contbr. articles to profl. jours. Bd. dirs. Ariz. Real Estate Edn. Found., 1989—; active Scottsdale Leadership, 1989—. Mem. CRB (pres. Grand Canyon chpt. 1989), Real Estate Brokerage Council (bd. govs. 1989—), Scottsdale Bd. Realtors (multiple listing service com. 1988—), Ariz. Assn. Realtors (bd. dirs. 1989—), Realtors Land Inst. (bd. dirs. 1989). Republican. Roman Catholic. Office: Sigma Real Estate Inc 14901 N Scottsdale Rd Ste 100 Scottsdale AZ 85254

PETERSON, ARTHUR MAURICE, franchising company executive; b. Centerville, S.D., Oct. 16, 1934; s. Arthur M. and Mursedus G. (Sorenson) P.; m. Carol L. Sigueido, May 27, 1957; children—Curt, Bryan, Kristin. With retail mgmt. and supervision Genesco, 1952-69; mdse. mgr. Kampgrounds of Am., Billings, Mont., 1969-72, v.p., 1972-76, sr. v.p., 1976-78, exec. v.p., chief operating officer, 1978-80, pres., chief exec. officer, 1980—. Regent Pacific Luth. U.; v.p., dir. Am. Recreation Coalition. Served with U.S. Army, 1957-59. Republican. Club: Yellowstone Country (Billings). Lodge: Rotary. Office: Kampgrounds of Am Box 30558 Billings MT 59114

PETERSON, BARBARA ANN, history educator; b. Portland, Oreg., Sept. 6, 1942; d. George Wright and Hope (Hamilton) Bennett; m. Frank Lynn Peterson, July 1, 1967. BA, BS, Oreg. State U., 1964; MA, Stanford (Calif.) U., 1965; PhD, U. Hawaii, Honolulu, 1978. Prof. history U. Hawaii, 1967—; sabbatical teaching Asian and African history and world problems Chapman Coll. World Campus Afloat, 1974; teaching European overseas exploration and expansion and colonialism, 1978; assoc. prof. continuing edn. and history U. Hawaii, Manoa, 1981; chmn. social scis. dept. Honolulu Community Coll., 1971-73, 75-76, asst. dean instruction, 1973-74. Author: Woman's Place is in the History Books, Her Story, 1620-1980, A Curriculum Guide for American History Teachers, 1980, America In British Eyes, 1988; Notable Women of Hawaii, 1984. Chairperson First Nat. Women's History Week, Hawaii, 1982; mem. State Commn. on Status of Women Bishop Mus. Coun. Recipient state proclamations Gov. Honolulu, Mayor City of Honolulu, Pres. U.S., Cert. Appreciation Lt. Gov.; Fulbright scholar Sophia U., 1967, Wuhan Univ., China, 1988-89; Woodrow Wilson fellow Princeton (N.J.) U., 1980. Mem. Am. Studies Assn., Fulbright Alumni Assn. Hawaii (pres. 1984—), Am. Hist. Assn. (numerous coms.), Hawaii Found. for History and Humanities (mem. editorial bd. 1972-73), Hawaii Found. for Women's History, Hawaiian Hist. Assn., AAUW, Nat. League Am. Pen Women (contest chairperson 1986). Home: 1341 Laukahi St Honolulu HI 96821

PETERSON, BARBARA JO, public relations counselor; b. San Diego, Aug. 21, 1943; d. Warner Ernest and Opal Oneida (Weeks) P. Student, U. Houston, 1966, U. Ghana, West Africa, 1970-71; BA, UCLA, 1972, MA, 1975, postgrad., 1977. Jr. publicist Maslansky/Koenigsberg Pub. Rels., L.A., 1980; publicist Mahoney/Wasserman Pub. Rels., L.A., 1980; account exec. Scanlon, Skalsky, Menken Pub. Rels., L.A., 1981; assoc. Henri Bollinger Pub. Rels., L.A., 1982-85; ptnr. Peterson and Fisher Pub. Rels., L.A., 1986—. Editor: (mag.) World Series of Poker, 1984—. Chancellor's fellow, UCLA, 1972. Mem. Women In Film, Publicists Guild of Am., Phi Beta Kappa, Phi Alpha Theta , Pi Gamma Mu. Republican. Greek Orthodox. Office: Peterson & Fisher Pub Rels 1800 N Argyle Ave Ste 407 Hollywood CA 90028

PETERSON, BROOKE ALAN, lawyer; b. Omaha, Dec. 6, 1949; s. Lloyd Earl and Priscilla Anne (Bailey) P.; m. Linda Jane Harlem, June 30, 1979 (div. 1980). B.A., Brown U., 1972; J.D., U. Denver, 1975. Bar: Colo. 1975, U.S. Dist. Ct. Colo. 1975. Assoc. Garfield & Hecht, Aspen, Colo., 1975-77, Robert P. Grueter, Aspen, 1977-78; ptnr. Wendt, Grueter & Peterson, Aspen, 1978-79; prin. Brooke A. Peterson, P.C., Aspen, 1979—; mcpl. judge, Aspen, 1980—. Chmn. election commn., Pitkin County, 1979—. Mem. ABA, Colo. Bar Assn. (bd. govs. 1984-86, exec. council 1986-87), Pitkin County Bar Assn. (pres. 1981-83), Am. Trial Laywers Assn., Colo. Trial Lawyers Assn. Avocations: skiing, surfing, softball, squash, music. Home: 0222 Roaring Fork Dr Aspen CO 81611 Office: 315 E Hyman Aspen CO 81611

PETERSON, CHARLES ERIC, senator, automotive executive; b. Ogden, Utah, June 4, 1914; s. Charles Eric and Dora Ann (Brown) P.; m. Harriet Robison, Oct. 4, 1935; children: Charlese, Joan P. Fisher, Kent D., Steven V. Student, Weber Coll., 1931-33; BA, U. Chgo., 1935; AA, Utah Tech. Coll., 1985. Personnel supr. Kimberly-Clark, Neenah, Wis., 1935-42, U.S. Steel Co., Provo, Utah, 1942-46; mgr. Barbizon Co., Provo, 1946-49; ptnr. Utah Office Supply, Provo, 1949-59; owner, mgr. Chuck Peterson Motors, Provo, 1959-84; senator State of Utah, Provo, 1984—; pres. Utah Auto Dealers, Salt Lake City, 1965. Speaker Utah Ho. of Reps., 1951-55; vice chmn. Utah Bd. Regents, 1969-79; pres. Utah C. of C., 1959, Utah Jaycees, 1957, Chgo. Mission Mormon Ch., 1980-83. Recipient Pub. Service award Brigham Young U., 1978, Presdl. citation Weber Coll., 1980, Quality Dealer award Time Mag., 1973; named Hon. Alumnus Brigham Young U., 1975, Citizen of Yr., Utah County, 1978. Republican. Clubs: Riverside Country, Brigham Young U. Cougar. Lodge: Kiwanis. Home: 2737 Edgewood Provo UT 84604

PETERSON, CHASE N., university president; b. Logan, Utah, Dec. 27, 1929; s. E.G. and Phebe (Nebeker) P.; m. Grethe Ballif, 1956; children: Erika Elizabeth, Stuart Ballif, Edward Chase. A.B., Harvard U., 1952, M.D., 1956. Diplomate: Am. Bd. Internal Medicine. Asst. prof. medicine U. Utah Med. Sch., 1965-67; assoc. Salt Lake Clinic; dean admissions and fin. aids to students Harvard U., 1967-72, v.p. univ., 1972-78; v.p. health scis. U. Utah, Salt Lake City, 1978-83, pres., 1983—. Home: 1480 Military Way Salt Lake City UT 84103 Office: U Utah Office of Pres Salt Lake City UT 84112

PETERSON, CHRIS ROBERT, research and development engineer; b. Camp LeJuene, N.C., Feb. 16, 1961; s. Robert Lance and Marilyn Jean (Daniel) P.; m. Babbett Lynn LaFavor, Oct. 18, 1986. BSEE, U. Calif., Irvine, 1983. Research and devel. engr. Ford Aerospace Corp., Newport Beach, Calif., 1983—. Mem. IEEE, Eta Cappa Nu. Republican.

PETERSON, CLIFFORD WILLIAM, retired merchant, consultant; b. Souris, N.D., Apr. 7, 1906; s. Henry William Peterson and Jennie Norgren; m. Myrtle E. Hanson, Oct. 31, 1930; children: Clifford William Jr., Karrol K. Student pub. schs., Detroit Lakes, Minn. Owner, mgr. Peterson's Ready to Wear, Plentywood, Mont., 1936-86; ret. Peterson's Ready to Wear, Plentywood, 1986; bd. dirs. Mont. Pioneer Manor, Plentywood. Mayor City of Plentywood, 1952-53; moderator ch. council First Congl. Ch., Plentywood; pres. Plentywood Athletic Club, 1958-59, Plentywood Booster Club, 1974-76; parade marshall Sheridan County Fair, 1978. Named Boss of Yr., Plentywood Jaycees, 1974, Disting. Svc. award, 1976. Mem. Masons, Lions (local pres. 1943-44). Republican. Home: 201 N Adams St Plentywood MT 59254

PETERSON, DARIL G., manufacturing company executive; b. Rockford, Ill., Feb. 22, 1946; s. Grant Ribble and Chrlotte E (Frink) P.; m. Peggy J. McWilliams, Feb. 26, 1966; children: Randall Brian, Brenda Ranea. AA, Glendale Community Coll., 1988. Prodn. control mgr. Sundstrand Machine Tool Co., Belvidere, Ill., 1966-73; prodn. mgr. Adapto, Inc., Goodyear, Ariz., 1971-79; plant mgr. Fuel Products div. Parker Hannifin Corp., Phoenix, 1979-88, ops. mgr. Aerospace Hydraulics div., 1988—. Mem. Pop Warner Farwest Football Assn., Tolleson, Ariz., 1976-81; mem. citizens adv. panel Maricopa Assn. Gov., Phoenix, 1980-82; bd. dirs. Holly Acres Flood Control Assn., Tolleson, 1979-82. Me. Soc. Mfg. Engrs., Am. Prodn. and Inventory Control Soc., Tolleson C. of C. Home: 10302 W Earll Phoenix AZ 85039 Office: Parker Hannifin Corp 18321 Jamboree Blvd Irvine CA 92715

PETERSON, DENNIS ROGER, physician; b. Salt Lake City, June 26, 1945; s. Joseph LeRoy and Nelda Kathryn (Pedersen) P.; m. Claudia Kirton, Apr. 2, 1975; children: Joseph Kirton, Merilee Kirton, Bryce Kirton, Anne-Marie. MD, U. Utah, 1972. Diplomate Am. Bd. Family Practice. Intern LDS Hosp., Salt Lake City, 1972-73; resident San Joaquin County Hosp. U. Calif., Davis, 1973-75; pres. Family Physicians Assoc., Bountiful, Utah, 1975—; chmn. dept. family practice Lakeview Hosp., Bountiful, 1977-79, 84-86. Contbr. articles to profl. jours. Scoutmaster Boy Scouts Am., Bountiful, 1987—. Mem. AMA, Utah Med. Assn. (recipient Outstanding Svc. award 1988). Mem. Ch. of Jesus Christ of Latter Day Saints. Office: Family Physicians Assoc 415 Medical Dr Bountiful UT 84010

PETERSON, EDWIN J., state supreme court justice; b. Gilmanton, Wis., Mar. 30, 1930; s. Edwin A. and Leora Grace (Kitelinger) P.; m. Anna Chadwick, Feb. 7, 1971; children: Patricia, Andrew, Sherry. B.S., U. Oreg., 1951, LL.B., 1957. Bar: Oreg. 1957. Asso. firm Tooze, Kerr, Peterson, Marshall & Shenker, Portland, 1957-61; mem. firm Tooze, Kerr, Peterson, Marshall & Shenker, 1961-79; assoc. justice Supreme Ct. Oreg., Salem, 1979—, chief justice, 1983—; mem. standing com. on fed. rules of practice and procedure, 1987—; bd. dirs. Conf. Chief Justices, 1985-87, 88—. Chmn. Portland Citizens Sch. Com., 1968-70; vice chmn. Young Republican Fedn. Orgn., 1951; bd. visitors U. Oreg. Law Sch., 1978-83, 87—, chmn. bd. visitors, 1981-83. Served to 1st lt. USAF, 1952-54. Mem. ABA, Am. Judicature Soc., Oreg. State Bar (bd. examiners 1963-66, gov. 1973-76, vice chmn. profl. liability fund 1977-78), Multnomah County Bar Assn. (pres. 1972-73), Phi Alpha Delta, Lambda Chi Alpha. Episcopalian. Home: 3365 Sunridge Dr S Salem OR 97302 Office: Oreg Supreme Ct Supreme Ct Bldg Salem OR 97310

PETERSON, ERIC MICHAEL, behavior therapist; b. Inglewood, Calif., Aug. 26, 1945; s. Eric Chandler and Betty Mae P.; m. Michelle Bernadetta Piquemal, Mar. 1, 1983; children: Matthew, Catherine. AA, El Camino Coll., 1965; BA, Am. Inst. Hypnotherapy, Santa Ana, Calif., 1984, PhD, 1986. Cons. Arby's Roast Beef Restaurants, Newport Beach, Calif., 1978-80, Taco Bell, Santa Ana, 1983-86; pvt. practice counseling Mission Viejo, Calif., 1981-83; pvt. practice behavior therapy Nederland, Colo., 1986—. With U.S. Army, 1965-67. Mem. Am. Bd. Hypnotherapy (cert.), Nat. Bd. Hypnotic Anaesthesiology (assoc.), Nat. Soc. Hypnotherapy (assoc.), Optimist Internat. (presd. citation 1969, 73, pres.). Home: PO Box 280 Nederland CO 80466 Office: 257 Alpine Dr Nederland CO 80466-0280

PETERSON, FRANK LYNN, geology educator, hydrogeology consultant; b. Klamath Falls, Oreg., May 8, 1941; s. Burton Henry and Elizabeth (Ritsch) P.; m. Barbara Bennett, July 1, 1967. B.A., Cornell U., 1963; M.S., Stanford U., 1965, Ph.D., 1967. Field geologist Climax Molydenum, Nev., 1963; teaching/research asst. Stanford U., Calif., 1963-67; asst. prof. geology U. Hawaii, Honolulu, 1967-71, assoc. prof., 1971-76, prof., 1976—; acting prof. Chapman Coll., 1973, U. Oreg., 1973, U. Colo., 1978; cons. on hydrogeology, 1967—. Co-author: Groundwater in Hawaii, 1981; Hawaii Geography, 1983; Volcanoes in the Sea, 1983; also numerous articles. Fellow Geol. Soc. Am; mem. Am. Geophys. Union, Nat. Water Well Assn., Am. Water Resources Assn., Assn. Engring. Geologists, Hawaiian Acad. Scis. Home: 1341 Laukahi St Honolulu HI 96821 Office: U Hawaii Dept Geology & Geophysics Honolulu HI 96822

PETERSON, GARY ANDREW, agronomics researcher; b. Holdrege, Nebr., Apr. 30, 1940; s. Walter Andrew and Evelyn Christine (Johnson) P.; m. Jacquelyn Charlene Flick, June 18, 1965; children: Kerstin, Ingrid. BS, U. Nebr., 1963, MS, 1965; PhD, Iowa State U., 1967. Research assoc. agronomy Iowa State U., Ames, 1964-67; prof. U. Nebr., Lincoln, 1967-84; prof. agronomy Colo. State U., Ft. Collins, 1984—. Assoc. editor Agronomy Jour., 1979-81, tech. editor, 1981-83, editor, 1984—; contbr. articles to profl. jours. and popular mags. Fellow Am. Soc. Agronomy (Ciba-Geigy Agr. Achievement award 1974), Soil Sci. Soc. Am. (Applied Research award 1987); mem. Soil Conservation Soc. Am. Republican. Office: Colo State U Dept Agronomy Fort Collins CO 80523

PETERSON, GEORGE ELLSWORTH, JR., financial executive; b. Bklyn., Apr. 15, 1937; s. George Ellsworth and Marjorie (Day) P.; A.B., San Francisco State Coll., 1960. Internal auditor, plant controller Crown Zellerbach Corp., San Francisco, Miami, Fla. and Newark, Del., 1963-72; internal auditor, controller, corp. center Planning Research Corp., Los Angeles, 1972-76; controller Casa Blanca Convalescent Homes, San Diego, 1976-78, Medevac Inc., emergency med. services, San Diego, 1978-79; pvt. practice fin. cons., 1979-80; dir. internat. acctg. Welton Becket Assocs., Santa Monica, Calif., 1981-83; bus. mgr. Buss, Silvers Hughes & Assocs., San Diego, 1984-85; controller Jerde Ptnrship. Inc., Los Angeles, 1985—. Served with U.S. Army, 1960-62. Mem. Newark C. of C. Episcopalian.

PETERSON, GREGORY WAYNE, chiropractor; b. Albert Lea, Minn., Mar. 30, 1955; s. Dewayne Roger and Janet Ruth (Throlson) P.; m. Elizabeth Anne Larson, Aug. 20, 1983; children: Kathleen, Michael. Grad., U. Minn., 1977; D of Chiropractic, Northwestern Coll. Chiropractic, Bloomington, Minn., 1985. Diplomate Nat. Bd. Chiropractic Examiners. Owner Federal Heights (Colo.) Chiropractic Clinic, 1985—. Fellow Internat. Acad. Clin. Acupuncture; mem. Colo. Chiropractic Assn., Internat. De Molay Found. (Chevalier 1974), Minn. De Molay (state master councillor 1972-75), Masons. Republican. Lutheran. Office: Fed Heights Chiropractic Clinic 1261 W 84th Ave Denver CO 80221

PETERSON, HOWARD COOPER, attorney, accountant; b. Decatur, Ill., Oct. 12, 1939; s. Howard and Lorraine (Cooper) P.; BEE, U. Ill., 1963; MEE, San Diego State Coll., 1967; MBA, Columbia U., 1969; JD, Calif. Western Sch. Law, 1983; LLM in Taxation NYU, 1985. Bar: Calif., cert. fin. planner.; CPA, Tex.; registered profl. Engr., Calif.; cert. neuro-linguistic profl. Elec. engr. Convair div. Gen. Dynamics Corp., San Diego, 1963-67, sr. electronics engr., 1967-68; gen. ptnr. Costumes Characters & Classics Co., San Diego, 1979-86; v.p., dir. Equity Programs Corp., San Diego, 1973-83; pres., dir. Coastal Properties Trust, San Diego, 1979—; chief fin. officer and dir. Imperial Screens of San Diego, 1977—, A.S.A.P. Ins. Svcs. Inc., 1983-85, Juno Securities, Inc., 1983—, Juno Real Estate, Inc., 1983—, Scripps Mortgage Corp., 1987—, Juno Transport Inc., 1988—, Heritage Transp. Mgmt. Inc., 1989—, Juno Transport Inc. 1988—, Heritage with sog. Mem. ABA, Interamerican Bar Assn., Nat. Soc. Public Accts., Internat. Assn. Fin. Planning, Assn. Enrolled Agts.

PETERSON, JAMES HILL, otolaryngology surgeon; b. Ovid, Colo., June 17, 1937; s. Arthur E. and Tressa (Hill) P.; m. Sylvia Ann Rigg, June 3, 1961; children: Anne-Marie, James Jr., Amanda. MD, U. Nebr., 1966. Diplomate Am. Bd. Otolaryngology. Intern Good Samaritan Hosp., Phoenix, 1966-67; Ear, Eye, Nose & Throat intern U. Kans. Med. Ctr., Kansas City, Kans., 1969-73; surgeon No. Colo. Ear, Eye, Nose & Throat Hosp., Greeley, Colo., 1973—. Served to capt. U.S. Army, 1967-69. Mem. Am. Acad. Otolaryngology. Republican. Club: Rotary. Office: 2528 16th St Greeley CO 80631

PETERSON, JAMES RICHARD, industrial water treatment company owner; b. Pueblo, Colo., Nov. 20, 1934; s. Carl William and Ruth Bertha (Handke) P.; m. Kathleen Maureen Meyer, May 31, 1962; children: James Conrad, Stephen lee. BS, U. N.Mex., 1958, postgrad., 1959. Mgr. Reliable Drugstore, Albuquerque, 1959-61; geologist N.Mex. State Hwy. Dept., Albuquerque, 1961-67; civil engr. Tex. Aeronautics Com., Austin, 1967-77; owner Peterson's Water Treatment Co., Albuquerque, 1977—. With U.S. Army, 1957-59. Mem. Optimist Club (pres. Albuquerque chpt. 1987-88). Republican. Home: 1804 Rita Dr NE Albuquerque NM 87106 Office: Petersons Water Treatment 4851 Ellison NE Bldg 3L Albuquerque NM 87109

PETERSON, JAMES ROBERT, accountant; b. Red Lake Falls, Minn., Dec. 29, 1958; s. Robert L. and Rose (Peterson) P.; m. Sherri L. Matthews, Mar. 21, 1987; 1 child, Sonia Marie. AA in Acctg., U. Minn., Crookston, 1979; BS in Acctg. and Computer Sci., Morehead State U., 1980. CPA Colo. Internat. auditor KN Energy Inc., Lakewood, Colo., 1981-84; mgr. acctg. systems and procedures KN Energy Inc., Lakewood, 1984—. Active Big Bros. Denver, 1985. Mem. Colo. Soc. CPAs, Denver Info. Expert Users

Group (chmn. 1988—), Van Gordon Investors (Lakewood) (pres. 1986-88). Home: 433 S Devinney St Lakewood CO 80228 Office: KN Energy Inc 12055 W Second Pl Lakewood CO 80228

PETERSON, JOHN DARGAVEL, travel company executive; b. L.A., Sept. 17, 1961; s. Arthur Robert and Jean (Dargavel) P. AA, Pepperdine U., 1980-82. Broker, estate specialist Fred Sands Realtors, Sherman Oaks, Calif., 1980-85; mgr. Ask Mr. Foster Travel, Woodland Hills, Calif., 1985-86; pres. Sable Travel Internat., Sherman Oaks, 1986—. Vice-pres. Friends of French Art, Beverly Hills, Calif., 1986. Mem. Original Tramp of London (exec. mem.), Heleana's (L.A.). Presbyterian. Home: 16987 Escalon Dr Encino CA 91436

PETERSON, KENT LEE, podiatrist; b. Ogden, Utah, June 24, 1954; s. Ralph J. and Ruth Evelyn (Sherman) P.; m. Karen Kristine Webb, Sept. 19, 1956; children: Katie Marie, Korey Brook. BS in Zoology, Brigham Young U., 1979, MS in Physiology, 1980; BMed. Sci., Calif. Coll. Podiatric Med., 1981, DPM, 1984. Resident in podiatric surgery VA Med. Ctr., Albuquerque, 1984-85; pvt. practice Prescott, Ariz., 1985—; clin. cons. Coll. Podiatric Medicine and Surgery, Des Moines, 1984-85. Scholar Case Western Res. U., 1972. Mem. Am. Podiatric Med. Assn., Am. Coll. Foot Surgeons (assoc.). Republican. Mormon. Office: Prescott Foot and Ankle Clin 1228 Willow Creek Rd Prescott AZ 86301

PETERSON, KEVIN BRUCE, newspaper editor, publishing executive; b. Kitchener, Ont., Can., Feb. 11, 1948; s. Bruce Russell and Marguerite Elizabeth (Hammond) P.; m. Constance Maureen Bailey, Feb. 11, 1975 (dec. May 1975); m. Sheila Helen O'Brien, Jan. 9, 1981. B.A., U. Calgary, Alta., Can., 1968. Chief bur. Calgary Herald, 1972-75, city editor, 1976-77, news editor, 1977-78, bus. editor, 1978, mng. editor, 1978-86, editor, asst. pub., 1986-87, gen. mgr., 1987-88, pub., 1989—; pres. Canadian U. Press, Ottawa, Ont., Can., 1968-69. Harry Brittain Meml. fellow Commonwealth Press Union, London, 1979. Mem. Can. Mng. Editors (bd. dirs. 1983-87), Am. Soc. Newspaper Editors, Horsemen's Benevolent and Protective Assn., Alta. Legis. Press Gallery Assn. (v.p. 1971-76). Clubs: Calgary Petroleum, Ranchmen's, 100-to-1 (Arcadia, Calif.). Office: Calgary Herald, 215 16th St SE, Calgary, AB Canada T2P 0W8

PETERSON, LEROY, educator; b. Fairfield, Ala., Feb. 15, 1930; s. Leroy and Ludie Pearl (Henderson) P.; m. Theresa Petite, Apr. 6, 1968 (div. Oct. 1984); children: Leroy III, Monica Teresa; m. Ruby Willodine Hopkins, July 21, 1985. Cert. in piano, Bavarian State Acad., Wuerzburg, Fed. Republic Germany, 1954; BS in Music Edn., Miami U., Oxford, Ohio, 1957. Life credential music tchr., Calif. Tchr. music Cleve. Pub. Schs., 1957-62, L.A. Unified Schs., 1963—. Composer song. With U.S. Army, 1952-54. Mem. Phi Mu Alpha Sinfonia. Democrat. Mem. Ch. of Christ. Home: 3730 Yuba River Dr Ontario CA 91761-0222 Office: Chester W Nimitz Jr High 6021 Carmelita Ave Huntington Park CA 90255

PETERSON, LOWELL, cinematographer; b. Los Angeles, Feb. 1, 1950; s. Lowell Stanley and Catherine Linda (Hess) P.; m. Deanna Rae Terry, Aug. 2, 1981. Student, Yale U., 1968-69; BA in Theater Arts, UCLA, 1973. Asst. cinematographer, Hollywood, Calif., 1973-83; camera operator, Hollywood, 1983—. Asst. cinematographer various prodns. including Blind Ambition, 1979, Hawaii Five-O, 1979-80, White Shadow, 1980-81, Lou Grant, 1981-82, Two of a Kind, 1982, Remington Steele, 1982-83, Something About Amelia, 1983; camera operator various prodns. including Tourist Trap, 1979, Newhart, 1983, Scarecrow and Mrs. King, 1983-85, Children in the Crossfire, 1984, Stranded, 1986, Knots Landing, 1986-87, Like Father Like Son, 1987, Star Trek: The Next Generation, 1987—; contbr. articles to Film Comment, 1974, International Photographer, 1984—. Mem. Soc. Motion Picture and TV Engrs., Internat. Photographers Guild, Los Angeles Music Ctr. Opera Guild, Friends of UCLA Film Archive, U.S. Chess Fedn. Home and Office: 3815 Ventura Canyon Ave Sherman Oaks CA 91423

PETERSON, LOWELL S., former state senator, rancher; b. Ogden, Utah, July 20, 1937; s. Rulon P. and Naomi (Skeen) P.; m. Kathleen Shurtleff, 1959; children—Dale Lowell, Laurie, Lisa, Lorna, Douglas Shurtleff, Mary Ann, Emily. B.S., Utah State U., 1961. Pres., Bar 70 Ranches, 1966-69; mng. ptnr. Peterson Bros. Herefords, 1971, mng. gen. ptnr., 1971—; mng. gen. ptnr. The Hayloft Restaurant, 1982—; mem. Utah Ho. of Reps. from Dist. 50, 1979-80, Utah State Senate, from Dist. 20, 1981-86. Commr. Weber County (Utah), 1987—; past pres. Utah State U. Young Republicans, Golden Spike Nat. Livestock Show. Mem. Utah Hereford Assn. (past pres., v.p.) Phi Kappa Phi. Republican. Mormon. Home: 4538 S 1725 W Roy UT 84067 Office: Weber County Commn 2510 Washington Blvd Ste 2M Ogden UT 84401

PETERSON, PHILIP EVERETT, legal educator; b. Galena, Ill., July 10, 1922; s. Everett Marvin and Marie Isabelle (Gleason) P.; m. Jeanne Rosanna Payette, Nov. 17, 1947; children—Christine Marie, Barbara Ellen, Claudia Ann, Patricia Eileen, Eric Karl, Kurt Kevin. Student, Loras Coll., 1948; B.S., U. Ill., 1950, J.D., 1952; LL.M., Harvard, 1958. Bar: Ill. bar 1951, Idaho bar 1955, U.S. Supreme Ct. bar 1958. Practice in Urbana, Ill., 1951-52; mem. faculty U. Idaho Law Sch., 1952-88, prof. law, 1961—, dean, 1962-67; legal cons., 1955—. Served with AUS, 1942-48; lt. col. USAF Res. Decorated Purple Heart, D.F.C. with cluster, Air medal with 3 clusters. Mem. Am., Ill., Idaho bar assns., AAUP. Home: 318 5th St Lewiston ID 83501

PETERSON, RICHARD ALLEN, furniture design executive; b. Chgo., July 29, 1955; s. Lawrence William and Marian (Malmquist) P.; m. Patricia Anne McLaughlin, Dec. 21, 1980; children: Christopher, Michael. B.A., So. Ill. U., 1980. Owner, mgr. Rick Peterson Design, Murphysboro, Ill., 1979-81; pres. Peterson Design Ltd., 1981—. Mem. Indsl. Designers of Am., Inst. of Bus. Designers (allied), Hayward C. of C. Republican. Methodist. Avocation: boating. Office: Peterson Design Furniture Inc 30962 San Benito Ct Hayward CA 94544

PETERSON, ROBERT GERALD, capital projects coordinator; b. Plentywood, Mont., May 29, 1949; s. Roger Gerald and Charlotte Clair (Robertson) P.; m. H. Susan, May 15, 1981; children: Gregory Michael Vaughan, Tracy Gayle Vaughan. BS in Math., U. Utah, 1971, BS in History, 1971, MS in Engring. Adminstrn., 1975. Analyst Labor Commercy Industry, Tonga, South Pacific, 1976-77; planner Kodiak (Alaska) Area Native Assn., Kodiak, 1978-80; dir. Puget Sound Assn. Cooperating Tribes, Suquamish, Wash., 1980-84; gen. mgr., adminstr. Suquamish Indian Tribe, Suquamish, 1984-87; prin., owner Milestones Consultant Group, Seattle, 1985—; mgmt. analyst Metro-Secondary, Seattle, 1988-89, capital projects coordinator, 1989—; bd. dirs. Western Wash. Indian Employment and Tng., Tacoma, Wash., 1984-87, Small Tribes of Western Wash., 1984-87, Cascadia Revolving Fund, Inc., 1989—. Co-author: Determining the True Cost of Contracting Federal Programs for Indian Tribes, 1987; contbr. articles to jours. Evaluation com. mem. Mcpl. League of King County, Seattl, 1988-89. Mem. Am. Inst. Cert. Planners. Home: PO Box 21541 Seattle WA 98111 Office: Metro 821 Second Ave MS 201 Seattle WA 98104

PETERSON, ROLAND OSCAR, electronics company executive; b. Bklyn., Jan. 18, 1932; s. Oscar Gustaf and Klara Ingegerd (Lindau) P.; m. Agnes Frances Walsh, Sept. 12, 1953; children: Joan, Lauren, Paul, Michael. BEE, Poly. Inst. N.Y., 1953, MEE, 1954. Registered profl. engr., N.Y. Research fellow Microwave Research Inst., Bklyn., 1953-54; sr. engr. Sperry Gyroscope Co., Great Neck, N.Y., 1956-60; with Litton Industries Inc., Woodland Hills, Calif., 1961—; v.p. advanced systems engring. Guidance and Control Systems div., Litton Industries Inc., Woodland Hills, Calif., 1973-76, v.p. bus. devel., 1976-77, pres., 1977-83; v.p. Litton Industries Inc., 1979-83; sr. v.p., group exec. Litton Industries Inc., Beverly Hills, Calif., 1983-88, pres., chief operating officer, 1988—. Regional chmn. Los Angeles United Way campaign , 1985-86. Served to 1st lt. U.S. Army, 1954-56. Recipient Disting. Alumni award Poly. Inst. N.Y., 1986. Mem. Am. Electronics Assn., Inst. Navigation (western regional v.p. 1975-76, Hays award 1982). Roman Catholic.

PETERSON, RONALD ARTHUR, emeritus business law educator; b. Valley, Nebr., June 21, 1920; s. Arthur Lawrence and Hazel McClellan (Foster) P.; m. Patricia Marguerite North, Aug. 29, 1942; children—Ronald, Kathleen, Patrick, James, John, Thomas, Mary, Joseph. B.A. in Poly. Sci., U. Omaha, 1943; J.D. in Law, Creighton U., 1948; postgrad. U. Wash., 1963-64. Bar: Nebr. 1948, Wash. 1949. Asst. prof. Seattle U., 1963-76, dir. legal studies, 1973-83, assoc. prof., 1976-84, prof. emeritus dept. bus. law, 1984—; dir., resident agt. Lesan Corp., Seattle. Mem. editorial bd. Introduction to Law and the Legal Process, 1980. Mem. Spl. Task Force on Legislation for Wash. system of pub. libraries, 1971-73; founding mem. Seattle Archdiocese Sch. Bd., Western Wash., 1969. Lt. USNR, 1943-46. Recipient Exemplary Tchr. award Alpha Kappa Psi, 1964. Mem. Am. Bus. Law Assn. (del. 1980), Pacific Northwest Bus. Law Assn. (pres. 1984-85), Seattle U. Alumni Assn. (Campus Svc. award 1989), Beta Gamma Sigma. Roman Catholic. Home: 1625 McGilvra Blvd E Seattle WA 98112

PETERSON, ROY OTTO, tax company executive; b. St. Paul, Jan. 20, 1916; s. John Charles and Selma Petterson; m. Elizabeth Kletzing, Dec. 27, 1941 (div. May 1972); children: Roger L., Janis J.; m. Marlene Booher, Dec. 29, 1973; stepchildren: Randall L., Ronald J. BBA, Fletcher Coll., 1940. Acct. Paper Calmenson Steel Co., St. Paul, 1940-41; cost acct. Nat. Gould Battery Co., St. Paul, 1941-42; agt. IRS, St. Paul, 1942-64; field agt, reviewer IRS, Long Beach, Calif., 1964-77; class instr. IRS, St. Paul, 1960-61; asst. group mgr. IRS, Long Beach, 1975, class instr., 1976-77; controller Super Screen, Inc., Long Beach, 1977-83; bus., tax cons. Super Screen, Inc., Long Beach., 1983—. asst. advisor Boy Scouts Am., St. Paul, 1955-59, advisor, 1960-63; ch. treas. Bethany Bapt. Ch., Long Beach, Long Beach, 1982-87. Recipient Service award Bethany Bapt. Ch., Long Beach, 1983. Mem. Christian Ministries Mgmt. Assn. Home and Office: 3040 Knoxville Ave Long Beach CA 90808

PETERSON, STANLEY LEE, engineering technician, artist; b. Viborg, S.D., Mar. 26, 1949; s. Norman and Neva Jean (Harns) P.; m. Katherine Anne Burnett. BFA, U. S.D., 1971. Artist W.H. Over Museum, Vermillion, S.D., 1971-72; graphic artist S.D. Pub. TV, Brookings, 1972-76; free lance artist San Francisco, 1976-77; engring. technician City of Tracy, Calif., 1977-85; artist Stanley Peterson Graphics, Los Banos, Calif., 1985—; contract engring. technician, system mgr. City of Tracy, 1985—; cons. in field. Artist/designer Nat. History Diorama, W.H. Over Museum, 1972. Democrat. Home: 427 N Santa Monica St Los Banos CA 93635 Office: City of Tracy 427 N Santa Monica St Los Banos CA 93635

PETEUIL, SHERYL ANN, nurse; b. Detroit, Dec. 13, 1953; d. John M. and Alfreda Gloria (Doskocz) P. Diploma in Nursing, Harper Hosp., 1979; BS, U. Phoenix, 1984; postgrad., U. Ariz., 1988—. RN, Mich., Ariz. Staff nurse ICU Cottage Hosp., Grosse Pointe Farms, Mich., 1975-80, William Beaumont Hosp., Royal Oak, Mich., 1980-81, Scottsdale (Ariz.) Meml. Hosp., 1981-82; supr. nursing, patient-staff educator Humana Hosp., Phoenix, 1982-87; asst. dir. nursing Navapache Hosp., Showlow, Ariz., 1987-88; staff nurse stepdown ICU-telemetry unit St. Mary's Hosp., Tucson, 1988—; coordinator Pulmonary Edn. Program, 1985. Active healthcare concerns, Ariz. State Legislature, 1982-85; adult vol. Girl Scouts U.S. Fellow Assn. Critical Care Nursing; mem. Pub. Health Assn., Am. Nursing Assn., Ariz. Runners Club. Democrat. Roman Catholic.

PETILLON, LEE RITCHEY, lawyer; b. Gary, Ind., May 6, 1929; s. Charles Ernest and Blanche Lurene (Mackay) P.; m. Mary Amme Leetpm, Feb. 20, 1960; children: Andrew G., Joseph R. BBA, U. Minn., 1952; LLB, U. Calif., Berkeley, 1959. Bar: Calif. 1960, U.S. Dist. Ct. (so. dist.) Calif. 1960. V.p. Creative Investment Capital, Inc., L.A., 1969-70; corp. counsel Harvest Industries, L.A., 1970-71; pres. Spring Fin. Svc., 1970-71; v.p., gen. counsel, dir. Tech. Svcs. Corp., Santa Monica, Calif., 1971-78; ptnr. Petillon & Davidoff, L.A., 1978—; lectr. Calif. State U. Seminars, Northridge, 1980-81; dir. Pub. Counsel, Dir. Westside Vol. Bur., 1981-84; chmn. Dispute Resolution Adv. Coun.,1988—. Chmn. Neighborhood Justice Ctr. Com., 1983-85, Middle Income Com., 1983-85; mem. Audit and Fin. Com., Bylaws Com., Election Com., State Bar Calif. task force on alternative dispute resolution, 1984-85.1st lt. USAF, 1952-54. Cert. of appreciation L.A. City Demonstration Agy., 1975, United Indian Devel. Assn., 1981, city of L.A. for Outstanding Vol. Svcs., 1984. Mem. ABA, L.A. County Bar Found. (dir. 1986—), State Bar of Calif. (pres. Pro Bono Svcs. award 1983), United Indian Devel. Assn. (cert. of appreciation), L.A. County Bar Assn. (law, tech. sect). Home: 1636 Via Machado Palos Verdes CA 90274 Office: Petillon and Davidoff 9841 Airport Blvd Ste 1500 Los Angeles CA 90045

PETRE, DONNA MARIE, county judge; b. Joliet, Ill., Apr. 21, 1947; d. James Jacob and Catherine (Hedrick) P.; m. Dennis Michael Styne, Sept. 4, 1971; children: Rachel Catherine, Jonathan James. BA, Clarke Coll., 1969; MA, Northwestern U., 1971; JD, U. Calif., San Francisco, 1976. Bar: Calif. 1976. Jud. clk. Calif. Ct. Appeals, San Francisco, 1976-77; instr. legal research and writing U. Calif. Hastings Coll. Law, San Francisco, 1976; dep. atty. gen. criminal appeals dept. State of Calif., San Francisco, 1977-80, consumer fraud dept., 1977-80; med. fraud dept. State of Calif., Sacramento, 1983-86; judge Yolo County Mcpl. Ct., Woodland, Calif., 1986—; mem. Marin County Bd. Suprs. Criminal Justice Commn., 1982; mem. adv. com. Jud. Coun. on Adminstrn. Justice in Rural Counties, 1988—. Mng. editor Hastings Constl. Law Quar., 1975-76. Mem., bd. dirs. Woodland Literacy Coun., 1986—. Mem. Calif. Judges Assn. (commn. studying problems with driving under the influence of alcohol and drugs), Yolo County Bar Assn., Women Lawyers Calif., AAUW, Bus. and Profl. Women's Assn. (co-chmn. legis. 1986—), LWV, Davis C. of C., Yolo C. of C., Woodland C. of C., West Sacramento C. of C., Davis Sci. Ctr. Republican. Office: Yolo County Mcpl Ct 725 Court St Woodland CA 95695

PETREE, JACK OTTO, writer, consultant; b. San Diego, Sept. 17, 1945; s. Jack and Lucille (Wollenburg) P.; m. Sally Delgado, Sept. 8, 1967; children: Jack Clayton, Simon Wesley. BA, Western Wash. U., 1971. Author: Advertising Your Financial Services, 1988; syndicated columnist: Advertising the Small Business, 1983-88; contbr. over 100 articles to mags. including Sports Illustrated, Small Bus. mag., Pool and Spa mag., Bus. Pulse, Home LIghting and Accessories, Western and English Fashions, Am. Nurseryman; contbr. short stories to Mike Shayne Mystery mag., Espionage mag. Served with USN, 1963-66. Lutheran. Home: 2955 Sunset Bellingham WA 98225

PETRICK, ALBERT HENRY, JR., insurance executive; b. Denver, Jan. 30, 1930; s. Albert H. and Ethel M. (Sale) P.; m. Dorothy W. Petrick, June 30, 1952; children: Randy, Tammy, Connie, Donna. BS, U. Denver, 1956. CLU, CPCU; chartered fin. cons. Agy. mgr. State Farm Ins. Co., Bloomington, Ill., 1954—. Mem. Colo. Assn. Life Underwriters (Colo. pres. 1970-71), No. Rocky Mountain CLU (pres. 1968), Gen. Agts. Mgrs. Assn. (pres. 1981). Republican. Home: 7326 E Soland Dr Scottsdale AZ 85253 Office: State Farm Ins Co 7975 N Hayden Rd Ste A-108 Scottsdale AZ 85258

PETRICK, DALE LEE, dentist; b. Bentleyville, Pa., Feb. 26, 1942; s. Stanley and Rose Ann (Cario) P. BS in Mech. Engring., Pa. State U., 1963; MS in Mgmt., Rensselaer Poly. Inst., 1970; DDS, UCLA, 1987. Assoc. scientist missiles ana space div. Lockheed, Sunnyvale, Calif., 1963-64; plant engr. Monsanto Co., Santa Clara, Calif. and Springfield, Mass., 1964-68; gas turbine engr. United Techs. Corp., Hartford, Conn., 1968-76; group leader long-distance bicycle tours Bike Centennial, Missoula, Mont., 1976-81; ski instr., program dir. Trapp Family Lodge Ski Touring Ctr., Stowe, Vt., 1977-81; assoc. dentist Dr. Larry Cohen, Oxnard, Calif., 1987-88; gen. practice dentistry Cathedral City, Calif., 1988—. Mem. Acad. Gen. Dentistry, ADA, Calif. Dental Assn. Democrat. Home: 67405 Rango Rd Cathedral City CA 92234 Office: 31855 Date Palm Dr Cathedral City CA 92234

PETRIE, ALLAN KENDRICK, insurance company executive; b. Buffalo, Mar. 14, 1928; s. William Alexander and Hazel Victoria (Ball) P.; student U. Idaho, 1948-50; MS in Program Mgmt., West Coast U., 1978. Vice pres. Western Internat. Ins. Brokers, Newport Beach, Calif., 1979-83; pres. Kendrick Ins. Offices, Inc., Redondo Beach, Calif., 1983—. Served to capt. U.S. Army, 1945-48. Mem. Am. Soc. Safety Engrs., Wine and Food Soc. So. Calif., Lambda Chi Alpha. Contbr. articles to mags. and newspapers. Home: 27808 Palos Verdes Dr E Rancho Palos Verdes CA 90274

PETRIE, DOROTHEA GRUNDY, producer, writer; b. Lawton, Okla.; d. Walter A. and June Marie (Leo) Grundy; m. Daniel Mannix Petrie; children: Daniel Jr., Donald Mark, Mary Susan and June Anne. Student, U. Iowa, 1943-44, Columbia U., 1944-45, Northwestern U., 1946-48. Actress NBC, CBS, ABC, N.Y.C. and Chgo., 1944-51; dir. theater dept. Creighton U., Omaha, 1948-49; casting dir. U.S. Steel Hour, N.Y.C., 1953-55; theatrical and lit. agent Lucy Kroll Agy., N.Y.C., 1956-58; prodn. assoc. Hal Cook Assocs., N.Y.C., 1963-65; co-owner D. Petrie Prodns., Los Angeles, 1988—; trustee Women in Film Found., Los Angeles. Author: Orphan Train, 1978 (Christopher award 1979, Writers Guild award 1979); producer: (TV films) Orphan Train, CBS, 1979, Angel Dusted, NBC, 1981, License to Kill, CBS, 1984 (Christopher award 1985), Picking Up the Pieces, 1985, Love is Never Silent, NBC, 1985 (Emmy award), Foxfire, CBS, 1987 (Humanitas award 1988, Monte Carlo Film Festival award 1988, Peabody award, Media Owl award), (theatrical prodn.) Catholics, 1983. Mem. Writers Guild Am., The Caucus of Producers, Writers and Dirs., TV Acad. Arts and Scis., Am. Film Inst., Producers Guild Am. Office: D Petrie Prodns 13201 Haney Pl Los Angeles CA 90049

PETRIE, LORETTA D. STEIGNER, college dean, English educator; b. Paterson, N.J., Nov. 22, 1928; d. George William and Lauretta (Seymour) Steigner; m. Stuart Allen Petrie, Jan. 19, 1951; children: Donald, Duane, Charles, Heidi. BA in English, U. Wash., 1965, MA in English, 1967, PhD in English, 1974. Instr. U. Wash., Seattle, 1967-71, U. Hawaii, Honolulu, 1971-78; asst. prof. Chaminade U. Honolulu, 1978-82, assoc. prof., 1982-86, prof. English, dean Coll. of Arts and Scis., 1986—; mem. exec. bd. Hawaii Com. for the Humanities, Honolulu, 1983—, chair, 1988—. Editor Chaminade Lit. Rev.; contbr. articles, reviews, poetry to lit. jours. Mem. Hawaii Literacy Arts Council (exec. bd. 1978-83, chair 1982), AAUW, Phi Beta Kappa. Democrat. Office: Chaminade U of Honolulu Coll Arts & Scis 3140 Waialae Ave Honolulu HI 96816

PETRILLI, JOHN ANTHONY, aerospace engineer; b. Pitts., May 4, 1949; s. Edmund Stephen and Ann Gloria (Swick) P. BS, U. Pitts., 1971; MA, Pa. State U., 1973. Cert. profl. estimator. Grad. asst. Pa. State U., University Park, 1971-73; indsl. engring. trainee Jones & Laughlin Steel Corp., Pitts., 1974-75, indsl. engr., 1975-76, sr. indsl. engr., 1976-80; sr. indsl. engr McDonnell Douglas Helicopter Co., Culver City, Calif., 1981-82, supr. indsl. engring., 1982-85; mgr. indsl. engring. McDonnell Douglas Helicopter Co., Culver City, 1985-86; mgr. program planning, Mesa, Ariz., 1986—. Mem. Nat. Estimating Soc., Mensa, McDonnell Douglas Helicopter Co. Mgmt. Club, McDonnell Douglas Helicopter Co. Gun Club, Phi Beta Kappa. Republican. Roman Catholic. Home: 6127 E Saddleback St Mesa AZ 85205 Office: McDonnell Douglas Helicopter Co 5000 E McDowell Rd Mesa AZ 85205

PETRINI, KAREN ANNE, auditor; b. Allentown, Pa., Feb. 14, 1962; d. Bart F. and Rosemary Ellen (DeRicci) P. BSBA, Old Dominion U., 1983; MBA, San Jose State U., 1986. Cred mktg. mgr. Miller & Rhoads, Richmond, Va., 1984-85; ind. mktg. cons. Cupertino, Calif., 1986-87; nat. mktg. mgr. Source Code, Inc., Palo Alto, Calif., 1987-89; sr. internal auditor Carter, Hawley & Hole, San Francisco, 1989—; mktg. cons., AT&T, Sunnyvale, Calif., 1986, Hewlett Packard, Cupertino, 1986-87. Mem. San Jose (Calif.) Symphonic Choir, 1988—; vol., Big Bros./Big Sisters, Belmont, Calif., 1988—. Mem. Peninsula Mktg. Assn. Republican. Roman Catholic. Home: 707 Continental Circle #524 Mountain View CA 94040 Office: Emporium-Capwell CHH Internal Audit 835 Market St 6th Fl San Francisco CA 94103-1803

PETRISOR, GREGORY CHRISTIAN, electrical engineer; b. Pasadena, Calif., Dec. 15, 1963; s. John William Petrisor and Nelda Yvonne (Perry) Sykes. BEE, U. So. Calif., 1986, MEE, 1987. Mem. tech. staff Hughes Aircraft Co., L.A., 1984—. Mem. IEEE, Toastmasters. Home: 435 S Virgil Ave #309 Los Angeles CA 90020 Office: Hughes Aircraft Co PO Box 902 MS-E52/C235 El Segundo CA 90245

PETRON, DONALD ROBERT, magazine editor; b. South Bend, Ind., Sept. 21, 1946; s. Robert Henry and Margaret Henrietta (Ostrowski) P.; m. Carmen Gloria Rodriguez, Feb. 15, 1969 (div. Nov. 1982); children: Gloria Louise, Margaret Evelyn. AA, Am. River Coll., 1974. Mcht. Kroger Co., South Bend, 1964-66; enlisted USAF, 1966, advanced through grades to master sgt., 1986, ret., 1986; electronic technician USAF Air Weather Svc., Southwestern U.S., 1966-71, Western U.S., 1972-74; technician, instr. USAF Royal Thai Air Base, Ubon, Thailand, 1971-72; instr. electronics Chanute Tech. Tng. Ctr., Rantoul, Ill., 1974-78; mgr. installations USAF Communications Command, Pacific area, 1978-84; dir. pub. rels. 1849th Electronic Installation Squadron USAF, Sacramento, 1984-86; writer, photographer Country Music Forum mag., Sacramento, 1986-87, editor, 1987-88; with Sacramento Army Depot, 1988—. Contbr. articles to profl. jours. Mem. Neighborhood Watch, North Highlands, Calif., 1982. Sgt. USAF, 1980-84. Mem. Air Force Assn., Non-Commd. Officers Club. Republican. Roman Catholic. Office: Sacramento Arym Depot Fruitridge Rd Sacramento CA 95813

PETROVSKY, FREDERIC ALAN, magazine publishing executive; b. Memphis, Apr. 20, 1958; s. Seymour and Bernice (Silverman) P.; m. Amy Jill Fann, Apr. 20, 1986; 1 child, Mara Erin. BA, U. Ariz., 1980, MFA, 1982. Staff writer, columnist Phoenix Jewish News, 1982-83; assoc. editor Scottsdale (Ariz.) Scene mag., 1982-84; mgr. media relations City of Scottsdale, 1984-86; v.p. communications Valley of the Sun United Way, Phoenix, 1986; dir. publs. Ariz. Office of Tourism, Phoenix, 1986-87; dir. communications, mktg. Phoenix Home and Garden mag., 1987—. Mem. Fiesta Bowl Publicity Com., Phoenix, 1988. Mem. Internat. Assn. Bus. Communicators (bd. dirs. Phoenix chpt. 1988—, Copper Quill Writing award 1987), Pub. Relations Soc. Am. Office: Phoenix Home & Garden Mag 3136 N Third Ave Phoenix AZ 85013

PETRUNCOLA, ALEXANDER DANIEL, computer engineer; b. Jersey City, N.J., Sept. 16, 1951; s. Alexander Charles and Joan Patricia (Lang) P.; m. Roxanne Orlando, Mar. 18, 1972; children: Alexander Anthony, Sarah Ann. BS in Engring., Calif. Inst. Tech., 1973; MS in Computer Sci., U. Calif., Berkeley, 1975. Mem. tech. staff Hewlett Packard, Cupertino, Calif., 1975-79; mgr. data communications Hewlett Packard, Cupertino, 1980; mem. tech. staff Elxsi, San Jose, Calif., 1980-89, Mips Computer Systems, Sunnyvale, Calif., 1989—. Mem. Assn. for Computing Machinery. Home: 347 El Molino Way San Jose CA 95119 Office: MIPS 930 Arques Ave Sunnyvale CA 94086

PETTERSEN, THOMAS MORGAN, acccountant, broadcast company executive; b. Poughkeepsie, N.Y., Nov. 9, 1950; s. Olsen Thomas and Reva Frances (Palmer) P. BS, SUNy at Albany, 1973. CPA, N.Y. Sr. acct. Arthur Andersen and Co., N.Y.C., 1973-76; sr. ops. auditor Gulf and Western Inc., N.Y.C., 1977, fin. analyst, 1978; adminstr. auditing NBC, N.Y.C., 1979; mgr. auditing NBC, Burbank, Calif., 1980, dir. auditing, 1981-88, dir. acctg. systems and ops. analysis, 1988—. Mem. AICPA, N.Y. State Soc. CPAs. Republican. Roman Catholic. Home: 217 1st Pl Manhattan Beach CA 90266 Office: NBC Inc 3000 W Alameda Ave Burbank CA 91523

PETTIGREW, STEVEN LEE, healthcare management company executive, consultant; b. Colorado Springs, May 8, 1949; s. Wesley N. and Mary Ellen (Howard) P.; m. Elise Woodcock, Dec. 12, 1987. BS in Mech. Engring., Colo. State U., 1972. Regional dir. Mgmt. Engring. Svcs. Assn. Program, Inc., Phoenix, 1972-76; v.p. Ariz. Hosp. Assn., Phoenix, 1976-79; corp. dir. Samaritan Health Svc., Phoenix, 1979—; lectr. Ariz. State U., Tempe, 1976-78. Contbr. articles to tech. publs. Bd. dirs. Hospice of Valley, Phoenix, 1981-88, pres. 1986-88, trustee endowment fund, 1983—. NSF rsch. grantee, 1971-72. Fellow Healthcare Info. and Mgmt. Systems Soc. (bd. dirs. 1980-81); mem. Healthcare Fin. Mgmt. Assn. (sr.), Inst. Indsl. Engrs. (sr.), Sigma Tau, Kiwanis (bd. dirs. Phoenix chpt. 1985-86, Spl. Svc. award 1986). Methodist. Office: Samaritan Health Svc 1441 N 12th St Phoenix AZ 85006

PETTINOTTI, JAMES WALTER, film and video producer, consultant; b. Merced, Calif., Jan. 27, 1932; s. Jack and Mary (Ramondini) P.; m. Janet Ann Holland, Aug. 10, 1954 (div. 1974); children: Laura, Grant; m. Norma Kanzler, Sept. 22, 1979. Student, Modesto Coll., 1950-51, 54-55. Mgr. Pinkerton Detective Agy., L.A., 1955-61; dist. sales mgr. Engelhard Industries, L.A., 1961-64; owner, mgr. Pettinotti Prodns., L.A., 1964-79; mng. dir.

Payson (Ariz.) C. of C., 1979-82, Pinetop (Ariz.) C. of C., 1982-87; owner, mgr. Internat. T.V. Prodns., Scottsdale, Ariz., 1987—. Sgt. USAF, 1950-54. Mem. Masons, Rotary. Republican. Home and Office: 5139 N Granite Reef Scottsdale AZ 85253

PETTIS, RONALD EUGENE, lawyer; b. Williston, N.D., Sept. 5, 1939; s. Elmer Roy and Hildur Ann (Olson) P.; m. T. Mary Whitehead, June 12, 1961; children: Anna T. Scott, Phillip A. BA, U. Idaho, 1961; JD, U. Calif., Berkeley, 1969. Bar: Calif. 1970, U.S. Dist. Ct. (cen. dist.) Calif. 1974, U.S. Supreme Ct. 1978. Assoc. Hennigan, Butterwick & Clepper, Riverside, Calif., 1971-74, ptnr., shareholder, 1974-79; ptnr., shareholder Butterwick, Bright, Pettis & Cunnison, Inc., Riverside, 1979-82; ptnr. Gray, Cary, Ames & Frye, San Diego, 1982—. Served to capt. USMC, 1961-66. Mem. ABA, Internat. Bar Assn., Rotary, Masons. Presbyterian. Office: Gary Cary Ames & Frye 1700 1st Interstate Plaza 401 B St San Diego CA 92101-4219

PETTIS, SHIRLEY MCCUMBER, former congresswoman; b. Mountain View, Calif.; d. Harold Oliver and Dorothy Susan (O'Neil) McCumber; m. John J. McNulty (dec.); m. Jerry L. Pettis (dec. Feb. 1975); m. Ben Roberson, Feb. 6, 1988; children: Peter Dwight, Deborah Neil Pettis Moyer. Student, Andrews U., U. Calif., Berkeley. Mgr. Magnetic Tape Diplicators, Hollywood, Calif., Audio-Digest Found., Los Angeles; sec.-treas. Pettis, Inc., Hollywood, 1958-68; mem. 94th-95th Congresses from 37th Calif. Dist., mem. interior com., internat. relations com. and edn. and labor com.; pres. Women's Research and Edn. Inst., 1979-81. Mem. Pres.'s Commn. on Arms Control and Disarament, 1980-83; bd. dirs. Kemper Group, 1979—. Mem. Nat. Women's Econ. Alliance Found., Capitol Hill Club (Washington), Congressional Club, Morningside Country Club.

PETTIT, GHERY DEWITT, veterinarian; b. Oakland, Calif., Sept. 6, 1926; s. Hermon DeWitt Pettit and Marion Esther (St. John) Menzies; m. Frances Marie Seitz, July 5, 1948; children: Ghery St. John, Paul Michael. BS in Animal Sci., U. Calif., Davis, 1948, BS in Vet. Sci., 1951, DVM, 1953. Diplomate Am. Coll. Vet. Surgeons (recorder 1970-77, pres., chmn. bd. dirs. 1978-80). Asst. prof. vet. surgery U. Calif., Davis, 1953-61; prof. vet. surgery Wash. State U., Pullman, 1961—; mem. Wash. State Vet. Bd. Govs., 1981-88, chmn., 1987; vis. fellow Sydney (Australia) U., 1977. Author/editor: Intervertebral Disc Protrusion in the Dog, 1966; cons. editoral bd. Jour. Small Animal Practice, Eng., 1970—; mem. editoral bd. Compendium on C.E., Lawrenceville, N.J., 1983-86, editoral rev. bd. Jour. Vet. Surgery, Phila., 1984-86, editor 1987—; contbr. articles to profl. jours., chpts. to books. Elder Presbyn. Ch., Pullman, 1967—. Served with USN, 1944-46. Recipient Norden Disting. Tchr. award Wash. State U. Class 1971, Faculty of Yr. award Wash. State U. Student Com., 1985. Mem. Am. Vet. Med. Assn., Sigma Xi, Phi Zeta, Phi Kappa Sigma (chpt. advisor 1981—). Republican. Office: Wash State U Vet Hosp Pullman WA 99164-6610

PETTIT, GHERY ST. JOHN, electronics engineer; b. Woodland, Calif., Apr. 6, 1952; s. Ghery DeWitt and Frances Marie (Seitz) P.; m. Marilyn Jo Van Hoose, July 28, 1973; children: Ghery Christopher, Heather Kathleen. BS in Electrical Engring., Wash. State U., 1975. Nuclear engr. Mare Island Naval Shipyard, Vallejo, Calif., 1975-76; electronics engr. Naval Electronic Systems Engring. Ctr., Vallejo, 1976-79; sr. engr. Martin Marietta Denver Aerospace, 1979-83; staff engr. Tandem Computers Inc., Santa Clara, Calif., 1983—. asst. cubmaster Boy Scouts Am., San Jose, Calif., 1985-86, cubmaster, 1986-88, asst. scoutmaster, 1988—. Mem. IEEE (sec. treas. EMC Soc. Littleton, Colo. chpt. 1983, sec, Santa Clara Valley chpt. EMC Soc. 1985-87, vice chmn. 1987-89, chmn. 1989—), Civil War Skirmish Assn. (nat. paymaster 1985—). Republican. Presbyterian. Office: Tandem Computers Inc 2550 Walsh Ave Santa Clara CA 95051

PETTIT, HENRY JEWETT, JR., editor, English language educator; b. Olean, N.Y., Dec. 8, 1906; s. Henry Jewett and Anne Benson (Edwards) P.; student Bucknell U., 1924-25; B.A., Cornell U., 1932, Ph.D., 1938; M.A., U. Oreg., 1934; m. Mary Madelyn Mack, July 18, 1927 (dec.); 1 dau., Judith Walsh; m. 2d, Gertrude Stockton Eckhardt, Apr. 9, 1977. Instr. English, U. Tulsa, 1934-36, Cornell U., Ithaca, N.Y., 1936-38, Yale, 1938-39; asst. prof. English, Beloit (Wis.) Coll., 1939-40; from assoc. prof. to prof. English, U. Colo., Boulder, 1940-72, prof. emeritus, 1972—, hon. keeper of rare books Norlin Library, 1950-62; vis. prof. U. Vt., summer 1958. Served with USNR, 1942-45. Recipient U. Colo. Faculty fellowships, 1948, 54, 60, 66, 69; Am. Philos. Soc. grantee, 1960, 66, 69; Am. Council Learned Socs. grantee, 1963. Mem. Modern Humanities Research Assn. (nat. sec. 1958-63), MLA (exec. sec. Rocky Mountain chpt. 1966-70), AAAS, Naval Res. Assn. Democrat. Clubs: Town and Gown (Boulder); Univ. (Denver). Author: A Bibliography of Young's Night-Thoughts, 1954; A Collection of English Prose, 1660-1800, 1962; The Correspondence of Edward Young 1683-1765, 1971; Annual Bibliography of English Language and Literature, 1942-52; A Dictionary of Literary Terms, 1951; The Authentic Mother Goose, 1960; mem. editorial bd. Western Humanities Rev., 1950-85, Colo. Quar., 1957-77; English Language Notes, 1963-74. Home: 1333 King Ave Boulder CO 80302

PETTITE, WILLIAM CLINTON, public affairs consultant; b. Reno, Nev.; s. Sidney Clinton and Wilma (Stibal) P.; m. Charlotte Denise Fryer; children—Patrick Keane, William Ellis, Joseph Clinton. Owner, Market Lake Citizen & Clark County Enterprise Newspapers, Roberts, Idaho, 1959-70, pub., 1959-61; publicity dir. Golden Days World Boxing Champs, Reno, 1970; public affairs cons., Fair Oaks, Calif., 1966—, owner PT Cattle Co., Firth, Idaho. County probate judge, Idaho, 1959-61; acting county coroner, 1960-61; sec., trustee Fair Oaks Cemetery Dist., 1963-72; bd. dir. Fair Oaks Water Dist., 1964-72, v.p., 1967-68, pres., 1968-70; dir., v.p. San Juan Community Svcs. Dist., 1962-66, 68-72; exec. sec. Calif. Bd. Landscape Architects, 1976-77.. Cons. Senate-Assembly Joint Audit Com. Calif. Legislature, 1971-73; exec. officer Occupational Safety and Health Appeals Bd., 1981-82; mem. regulatory rev. commn. Calif. FabricCare Bd., 1981-82; mem. Sacramento County Grand Jury, 1981-82, cons. bd. supvs. Sacramento County, 1985-86. Election campaign coord. for E.S. Wright, majority leader Idaho Senate, 1968, Henry Dworshak, U.S. Senator, 1960, Hamer Budge, U.S. Rep., 1960, Charles C. Gossett, former Gov. Idaho, 1959-74; asst. sgt. at arms Rep. Nat. Conv., 1956; chmn. Rep. County Cen. Com., 1959-61; del. Rep. State Conv., 1960. Chmn. Idaho County Centennial Commn., 1959-61. Recipient Idaho Centennial award, 1968, 69. Mem. Assn. Sacramento County Water Dists. (bd. dir. 1967-72, pres. 1970-72), No. Calif. Peace Officers Assn., Nat. Coun. Juvenile Ct. Judges (com. 1959-61), Sacramento Law Enforcement Adminstrs. Club. Author: Memories of Market Lake, Vol. I, 1965; A History of Southeastern Idaho, Vol. II, 1977, Vol. III, 1983; contbr. articles to newspapers, profl. jours. Home: PO Box 2127 Fair Oaks CA 95628 Office: 2631 K St Sacramento CA 95816

PETTY, DIANA M., social service agency executive; b. Eureka, Calif., Apr. 25, 1950; d. R.E. and Lena C. (Sequestri) P.; m. John P. Bosshardt. Student, Humboldt State U., 1968-72; BA, Calif. State U., Sacramento, 1975. Asst. sec. State Assembly, Sacramento, 1973-74; self-employed writer/pub. rels. cons. Sacramento, 1974-75; communications coord. Community Svcs. Planning Coun., Sacramento, 1975-78; staff writer Solem/Loeb & Assocs., San Francisco, 1978; exec. dir. Family Survival Project, San Francisco, 1978—; adv. panel mem. and contractor U.S. Congress Office of Tech. Contbr. articles to profl. jours and books; editor, co-author: Family Survival Handbook, 1979. Mem. Nat. Soc. Fund Raising Execs., Am. Soc. Aging. Office: Family Survival Project 425 Bush St Ste 500 San Francisco CA 94108

PETTY, DONALD GRIFFIN, research administrator; b. Montgomery, Ala., Nov. 4, 1949; s. William Henry and Ellen Marie (Ford) P.; m. Patricia Marie Sanchez, Sept. 1, 1984; 1 child, Zachary Allan. BS in Chemistry, Colo. State U., 1972; MA in Tech. Journalism, U. Colo., 1976; MBA, Regis Coll., 1988. Geochemist Hazen Research Inc., Golden, Colo., 1973-75; mktg. specialist Tech. Dynamics Corp., Denver, 1976-77; publ. specialist Community Coll. Denver, 1977-78; mktg. coordinator Micro Motion Inc., Boulder, Colo., 1978; project mgr. Solar Energy Research Inst., Golden, 1978-88; adminstr. Sch. Medicine U. Colo., Denver, 1988—; instr. Community Coll. Denver, Met. State Coll., 1977—. Pres., chmn. bd. Front Range Literacy Action, 1985—; Rep. precinct capt., Denver, 1984—. Named one of Outstanding Young Men Am., Jaycees, 1981. Mem. AAAS, Soc. Tech. Communication (sr.), Am. Chem. Soc., Am. Inst. Chemists. Republican.

PETTY, GUY JAMES, designer, scenic engineer, theatrical consultant; b. Pueblo, Colo., Sept. 8, 1951; s. Walter Lee and Anna Elizabeth (Kilsay) P.; m. Carla Rene Hord, Oct. 6, 1972. BS, U. So. Colo., 1973; postgrad., U. Wyo., 1973-75. Art dir., theater mgr. Lincoln Plaza, Oklahoma City, 1975-76; art dir. Design Concepts, Las Vegas, Nev., 1976-79; freelance art dir. The Design Table, Las Vegas, 1979-83, freelance art dir., producer, 1985—; art dir. Las Vegas Scenery Studios, 1983-85; cons. design Safari's, Las Vegas, Mitsui Greenland, Fukuoka, Japan, Maritz Communications, St. Louis; art dir. Englebert Humperdinck, Hollywood, Calif. Prin. works include: (concert tour) stage design Michael Jackson World Tour, 1979; (stage show) scenic design Mikado 20th anniversary, Tokyo, 1984, A Caesars Palace Christmas Show, Crystal Palace Hotel & Casino, Nassau, Bahamas, 1988, scenic design 10th Anniversary Sun city Extravaganza, South Africa, scenic design Celebration on Ice Bally's Hotel and Casino, Atlantic City; designs for John Denver, Loretta Lynn, Beach Boys, Gatlin Bros., Lou Rawls, Kenny Rogers, Robert Guillaume, Bobby Vinton, Supertramp, Mills Brothers, Della Reese shows; (ice stage show) scenic design New Fujiya Grand Opening, Atami, Japan, 1986; (trade show) exhibit design include Shell Oil Co., 1986, Mobil Oil Conv., Nat. Benefit Life, Deltona, Rodeo Am., Gulf State Toyota; scenic design local chpt. Muscular Dystrophy Assn., Las Vegas, 1983-85, United Cerebral Palsy, 1984; produced and directed 1987 Toyota Can. New Car Show, Am. Super Dream, Fugiya Hotel; projects include The Floorplan Library offering floorplan specifications for all Las Vegas theaters and conv. facilities. Recipient scholarship U. So. Colo., 1970-73, Best Show Design award Am. Water Exhibit, Las Vegas, 1984. Mem. Internat. Assn. Theatrical Stage Employees (Local 720). Home and Office: The Design Table 241 N Crestline Dr Las Vegas NV 89107

PETZEL, FLORENCE ELOISE, educator; b. Crosbyton, Tex., Apr. 1, 1911; d. William D. and A. Eloise (Punchard) P.; Ph.B., U. Chgo., 1931, A.M., 1934; Ph.D., U. Minn., 1954. Instr., Judson Coll., 1936-38; vis. instr. Tex. State Coll. for Women, 1937; asst. prof. textiles Ohio State U., 1938-48; asso. prof. U. Ala., 1950-54; prof. Oreg. State U., 1954-61, 67-75, 77, prof. emeritus, 1975—, dept. head, 1954-61, 67-75; prof., div. head U. Tex., 1961-63; prof. Tex. Tech U., 1963-67; vis. prof. Wash. State U., 1967. Effie I. Raitt fellow, 1949-50. Mem. Seattle Art Mus., Oreg. Art Mus., Textile Mus., Met. Opera Guild, San Francisco Opera Assn., Portland Opera Assn. Sigma Xi, Phi Kappa Phi, Omicron Nu, Iota Sigma Pi, Sigma Delta Epsilon. Author Textiles of Ancient Mesopotamia, Persia and Egypt, 1987; contbr. articles to profl. jours. Home: 625 NW 29th St Corvallis OR 97330

PEURA, EDWIN WALTER ARIEL, air force officer; b. Steubenville, Ohio, July 1, 1940; s. Edwin Tauno and Salme Kaarina (Taåhtivirta) P.; m. Marcia Marie Pexton, June 11, 1966. BS in Nuclear Physics, Ohio U., 1963; MA in Polit. Sci., Auburn U., 1977. Commd. 2nd lt. USAF, 1964, advanced through grades to col., 1985; project engr. nuclear power plant Hdqrs. Air Defense Command, Ent Air Force Base, Colo., 1964-68; advanced plans officer Hdqrs. Aerospace Defense Command, DCS Plans, Ent Air Force Base, 1969-73; mgr. countermeasures and satellite attack warning systems Space and Missile Systems Orgn., L.A., 1973-76; action office DCS plans and ops., directorate of plans Space and Defensive Forces div. Hdqrs. USAF, Washington, 1977-81; vis. fellow Am. Enterprise Inst. for Pub. Policy Research, Washington, 1981-82; mil. asst. to asst. dep. under sec. defense U.S. Office of the Sec. Defense, Washington, 1982-85; asst. dep. comdr. for plans and advanced programs Space Systems Div., AFB, L.A., 1985-89, chief of staff, 1989—. Author: Technical Evaluation of the PM-1 Nuclear Power Plant & Related Programs; co-author U.S. Arms Sales Policy Background and Issues. Decorated Meritorious Svc. medals, Def. Superior Svc. medal. Mem. Air Force Assn. (life), AIAA. Home: 5340 W 135th St Hawthorne CA 90250 Office: Space Systems Div AFSC Los Angeles AFB CA 90009

PFABE, PETER KENT, economist; b. St. Louis, Nov. 4, 1959; s. Eldon Max Pfabe and Dorothy Fieger (Traub) Kearney; m. JulianaPfabe. BS in Econs., USN Acad., 1982. Instr.sailing U.S. Naval Acad., Annapolis, Md., 1982; tng. officer Navy Fighter Weapons Sch. (Topgun), Miramar, Calif., 1987, USN Fighter Squadron 114, Miramar, Calif., 1985-88; v.p. A.B. Laffer Assocs., Lomita, Calif., 1988—. Mem. Young Ams. for Freedom, Sierra Madre, Calif., 1988. Lt. USN. Mem. U.S. Naval Acad. Alumni Assn., Naval Aviation Tailhook Assn. Republican. Roman Catholic.

PFAFFMANN, FREDERICK CARL, automotive executive; b. Peoria, Ill., Jan. 22, 1943; s. Karl and Marie (Rassi) P.; m. Christine Ellen Mason, May 25, 1968; children: Kendrick Alan, Garrick Mason. BA in Bus., Monmouth Coll., 1965; MBA, U. Denver, 1967. CPA, Colo. Acct. Arthur Young & Co., Denver, 1967-71; comptroller Summit County Devel. Co., Breckenridge, Colo., 1971-72; bus. mgr. Monarch Motors Ltd., Littleton, Colo., 1972-73; treas. Monarch Volvo-Mazda, Ltd., Littleton, 1973-85, pres., owner, 1985-88; treas., chmn. bd. dirs. The Upper Image, Ltd., Aspen, Colo., 1979—; v.p., bd. dirs. A Shore Thing, Ltd., Hilton Head, S.C., 1985—; treas., bd. dirs. Aspen (Colo.) Cruise Lines, Ltd., 1985—; ind. bus. cons. Littleton, 1988—. Bd. edn., St. Thomas More Ctr., Englewood, Colo., 1983-86, fin. adviser, 1988—. Mem. Littleton Kiwanis (bd. dirs. 1984—, pres. 1987-88). Republican. Roman Catholic.

PFEFFER, ANNE MILLAR, nurse; b. Jacksonville, Fla., Aug. 19, 1954; d. Robert Cameron and Ellen (Russell) Millar; m. Michael Peter Pfeffer, July 18, 1987; 1 child, Erin, Kyleen. Student, Fla. Jr. Coll., 1978. RN, Fla., Wash. Nurse St. Vincent Hosp., Jacksonville, 1978-80, Overlake Hosp., Bellevue, Wash., 1982—. Mem. Wash. State Nurses Assn. Presbyterian.

PFEIFFER, JOHN WILLIAM, publisher, management consultant; b. Wallace, Idaho, July 10, 1937; s. John William and Mary Loretta (Schmidt) P.; m. Sandra Lou Withee, 1964 (div. 1973); 1 child, Heidi Erika; m. Judith Ann Cook, Dec. 14, 1973; 1 child, Charles Wilson. B.A., U. Md., 1962; Ph.D. (fellow), U. Iowa, 1968; J.D., Western State U., 1982; DABS (hon.), Calif. Am. U., Escondido, 1980. Instr. U. Md., 1965-67; dir. adult edn. Kirkwood (Iowa) Community Coll., 1967-69; dir. ednl. resources Ind. Higher Edn. Telecommunications Systems, Indpls., 1969-72; pres. Univ. Assocs., San Diego, 1972—; adj. tchr. Ind. U., 1969-72, Purdue U., 1971-72. Author: Instrumentation in Human Relations Training, 1973, 2d edit., 1976, Reference Guide to Handbooks and Annuals, 1975, 2d edit., 1977, 3d edit., 1981, (with Goodstein and Nolan) Applied Strategic Planning, 1986; editor: A Handbook of Structured Experiences for Human Relations Training, 10 vols, 1969-85, The Annual Handbook for Group Facilitators, 10 vols, 1972-81, Group and Orgns. Studies Internat. Jour. for Group Facilitators, 1976-79, The Annual for Facilitators, Trainers and Consultants, 1982-89, Strategic Planning: Selected Readings, 1986, The Instrumentation Kit, 1988, Shaping Strategic Planning, 1988, Training Technology, 7 vols, 1988. Served with U.S. Army, 1958-62. Office: Univ Assocs Inc 8517 Production Ave San Diego CA 92121

PFEIFFER, ROBERT JOHN, business executive; b. Suva, Fiji Islands, Mar. 7, 1920; came to U.S., 1921, naturalized, 1927; s. William Albert and Nina (MacDonald) P.; m. Mary Elizabeth Worts, Nov. 29, 1945; children—Elizabeth Pfeiffer Tumbas, Margaret Pfeiffer Hughes, George, Kathleen. Grad. high sch., Honolulu, 1937; DSc (hon.), Maine Maritime Acad.; HHD (hon.), U. Hawaii; DHL (hon.), Hawaii Loa Coll. With Inter-Island Steam Navigation Co., Ltd., Honolulu; With (re-organized to Overseas Terminal Ltd. 1950); with (merged into Oahu Ry. & Land Co. 1954), 1937-55, v.p., gen. mgr., 1950-54, mgr. ship agy. dept., 1954-55; v.p., gen. mgr. Pacific Cut Stone & Granite Co., Inc., Alhambra, Calif., 1955-56, Matcinal Corp., Alameda, Calif., 1956-58; mgr. div. Pacific Far East Line, Inc., San Francisco, 1958-60; with Matson Nav. Co., San Francisco, 1960—; v.p. Matson Nav. Co., 1966-70, sr. v.p., 1970-71, exec. v.p., 1971-73, pres., 1973-79, chmn. bd., pres., chief exec. officer, 1984, chmn. bd. dirs., 1989—, chmn. bd., 1989—; v.p. The Matson Co., San Francisco, 1968-70; pres. The Matson Co., 1970-82; v.p., gen. mgr. Matson Terminals, Inc., San Francisco, 1960-62; pres. Matson Terminals, Inc., 1962-70, chmn. bd., 1970-79; chmn. bd. Matson Svcs. Co., 1973-79, Matson Agys., Inc., 1973-78; sr. v.p. Alexander & Baldwin, Inc., Honolulu, 1973-77; exec. v.p. Alexander & Baldwin, Inc., 1977-79, pres., 1979-80, chmn., pres., chief exec. officer, 1980-84, 89—, 1989—, also dir.; chmn. bd., pres., dir. A&B-Hawaii, Inc., 1988-89, chmn. bd., 1989—; bd. dirs. A&B Devel. Co. (Calif.), Inc., A&B Properties, Inc., McBryde Sugar Co. Ltd., First Hawaiian Inc., First Hawaiian Bank, Calif. and Hawaiian Sugar Co., WDCI, Inc., also pres.; mem. adv. bd. Pacific Resources, Inc.; mem. Gov.'s comm. on exec. salaries State of Hawaii, com. on jud. salaries; chmn., pres. A&B-Hawaii, Inc., 1988-89, chmn., 1989—. Past chmn. maritime transp. rsch. bd. Nat. Acad. Sci.; former mem. select com. for Am. Mcht. Marine Seamanship Trophy Award, commn. sociotech. systems NRC.; mem. adv. com. Joint Maritime Congress; trustee Pacific Tropical Bot. Garden, Bishop Mus., Pacific Aerospace Mus., also bd. dirs.; mem. Japan-Hawaii Econ. Coun., Army Civilian Adv. Group; vice-chmn. Hawaii Maritime Ctr.; chmn. A Commitee on Excellence (ACE), Hawaii; mem. adv. coun. Girl Scouts U.S. Coun. of the Pacific; bd. govs. Hugh O'Brian Youth Found.; mem. exec. com. Rsch. Round Table Alameda County chpt. Am. Heart Assn.; bd. govs. Japanese Cultural Ctr. Hawaii; mem. bd. nominators Am. Inst. for Pub. Svc.; mem. govs. commn. exec. salaries and com. jud. salaries State of Hawaii, Veterans Fgn. Wars U.S. Lt. USNR, World War II; comdr. Res. ret. Mem. Am. Inst. Pub. Svc. (mem. bd. nominators), Nat. Assn. Stevedores (past pres.), Internat. Cargo Handling Coordination Assn. (past pres. U.S. nat. com.), Propeller Club U.S. (past pres. Honolulu), Nat. Def. Transp. Assn., Conf. Bd., 200 Club, Long Beach C. of C., Portland C. of C., Oakland C. of C., Richmond (Calif.) C. of C., Seattle C. of C., Kauai C. of C., L.A. C. of C., San Francisco C. of C., Hawaii Island C. of C., Hawaii C. of C., Maui C. of C., Am. Bur. Shipping (bd. mgrs.), Aircraft Owners and Pilots Assn., VFW (life), Pacific Club, Outrigger club, Oahu Country Club (Honolulu), Maui Country Club (Hawaii), U. Hawaii Club, Pacific Union Club, Bohemian Club, World Trade Club (San Francisco), Masons, Shriners. Republican. Home: 535 Miner Rd Orinda CA 94563 Office: Alexander & Baldwin Inc 822 Bishop St Honolulu HI 96813

PFITZNER, KURT PATRICK, military officer; b. Sacramento, Calif., Jan. 7, 1958; s. Raymond Richard Pfitzner and Marion Anne (Luning) Jordahl. Diploma, FBI AntiSniper, San Angelo, Tex., 1978; BA, Angelo State U., 1982; diploma, Squadron Officer, Montgomery, Ala., 1986; post-grad., Webster U., 1987—. Enlisted USAF, 1977; policeman USAF, San Angelo, 1977-80; commd. USAF, 1982, advanced through grades to capt., 1987; student pilot USAF, Lubbock, Tex., 1983; officer in charge law enforcement USAF, Wichita Falls, Tex., 1983-85, sect. comdr. tech. tng. group, 1985-86; chief edn. Air Force Space Command USAF, Colorado Springs, Colo., 1986, protocol officer Air Force Space Command, 1986—; planning cons. U.S. Space Found., Colorado Springs, 1986; exec. chmn. Security Police Cadet Post, Wichita Falls, 1983. Instr. Peterson AFB Chapel, 1987; CPR instr. ARC, Wichita Falls, 1986, first-aid instr., 1986, swimming instr., 1986; CPR instr. Am. Heart Assn., 1981; vol. radio personality CARE Christian Radio, San Angelo, 1980; Sunday Sch. instr., Fain Presbyn. Ch., Wichita Falls, 1985. Named Officer of Yr. Hdqrs. Air Force Space Command, 1987. Mem. Air Force Assn., North Tex./So. Okla. Criminal Investigators Assn. Republican. Home: 2695 Haystack Dr Colorado Springs CO 80922 Office: AFSPACECOM/CP Peterson AFB CO 80914

PFLUEGER, JOHN MILTON, architect; b. San Francisco, Aug. 23, 1937; s. Milton Theodore and Genevive (Wendgard) P.; BS, Stanford, 1959, BArch, 1960; m. Lynne Williams, Jan. 23, 1963; children: Peter, John Thomas, Christopher Timothy. Pres., chief exec. officer Pflueger Architects, Inc., San Francisco, 1976; lectr. Urban Life Inst., U. San Francisco, U. Colo., 1978; campus architect U. San Francisco, Coll. of Holy Names, City Coll. San Francisco. Mem. planning com. San Francisco Downtown Assn., 1971-83. Lic. architect, Calif., Nev., Hawaii. Mem. AIA (pub. edn. com. No. Calif. chpt. 1970-79), NCARB, Constrn. Specifications Inst., Soc. Coll. and Univ. Planning, San Francisco Planning and Urban Renewal, Sierra Club, U.S. C. of C., Calif. Acad. Scis., Soc. Am. Mil. Engrs., Delta Tau Delta. Clubs: Olympic (bldg. com. 1973-78, properties commn. 1979-81), Family (San Francisco). Major works include: Cowell Hall, Calif. Acad. Scis. (Prestress Concrete Inst. award 1969), Creative Arts Extension, City Coll. San Francisco (AIA design excellence award 1974), Fish Roundabout, Calif. Acad. Scis., 1976, Natural Energy Office Bldg., 1977 (Honor award State of Calif.), Batmale Hall, City Coll. San Francisco, 1978, Calif. Farm Bur. Fedn., Sacramento, 1980 (Owens Corning, Dept. Energy and ASHRAE awards), San Jose State U. Library, 1982, Nev. Nat. Bank Hdqrs., Reno, 1982 (ASHRAE award), Performing Arts Ctr. and Fine Arts Mus., Sierra Arts Found., Reno; 8 major bldgs. at Stanford U., including Environ. Safety Facility, 1986; Co-Generation facility and Health and Recreation Ctr., U. San Francisco, 1987; rehabilitation Santa Rosa Ferry Boat, James Licks Bathhouse, 1981, Warfield Office Bldg. and Theater, 1985; major hosps. include Shriners Hosp. for Crippled Children, Walter Reed Army Med. Ctr. (Pre-Stressed Concrete Inst., Dept. Def. design awards 1980). Office: 165 10th St San Francisco CA 94103

PFORZHEIMER, HARRY, JR., oil consultant; b. Manila, Nov. 19, 1915; s. Harry and Mary Ann (Horan) P.; BS in Chem. Engring., Purdue U., 1938; postgrad. Case Inst. Tech., Law Sch., George Washington U., Case Western Res. U.; m. Jean Lois Barnard, June 2, 1945; children: Harry, Thomas. with Standard Oil Co. (Ohio), various locations, 1938-80, pres. White River Shale Oil Corp., 1974-76, v.p. Sohio Natural Resources Co., 1971-80, program dir. Paraho oil shale demonstration, Grand Junction, 1974-80; pres., chmn. bd., chief exec. officer Paraho Devel. Corp., 1980-82, sr. mgmt. advisor and dir., 1982-85, cons., 1985—; pres. Harry Pforzheimer Jr. and Assocs., 1983—; dir. IntraWest Bank Grand Junction; adj. prof. chem. engring. Cleve. State U. Contbr. articles to tech. and trade jours. Mem. planning adv. bd. St. Mary's Hosp. and Med. Ctr.; bd. dirs. Colo. Sch. Mines Research Inst.; mem. Petroleum Adminstrn. for War, Washington, 1942-45; chmn. Wayne N. Aspinall Found. Mem. Am. Inst. Chem. Engrs. (chmn. Cleve. 1955, gen. chmn. internat. meeting, Cleve. 1961), Am. Petroleum Inst., Am. Mining Congress, Colo. Mining Assn., Rocky Mountain Oil and Gas Assn., Denver Petroleum Club, Purdue Alumni Assn., Sigma Alpha Epsilon. Clubs: Army and Navy (Washington), Bookcliff Country, Rio Verde Country. Lodge: Kiwanis. Summer Home: 2700 G Rd #1-C Grand Junction CO 81506 Winter Home: 25604 Abajo Dr Rio Verde AZ 85255 Office: 743 Horizon Ct Grand Junction CO 81506

PFUND, EDWARD THEODORE, JR., electronics co. exec.; b. Methuen, Mass., Dec. 10, 1923; s. Edward Theodore and Mary Elizabeth (Banning) P.; B.S. magna cum laude, Tufts Coll., 1950; postgrad U. So. Calif., 1950, Columbia U., 1953, U. Calif., Los Angeles, 1956, 58; m. Marga Emmi Andre, Nov. 10, 1954 (div. 1978); children—Angela M., Gloria I., Edward Theodore III; m. Ann Lorenne Dille, Jan. 10, 1988. Radio engr., WLAW, Lawrence-Boston, 1942-50; fgn. service staff officer Voice of Am., Tangier, Munich, 1950-54; project. engr. Crusade for Freedom, Munich, Ger., 1955; project mgr., materials specialist United Electrodynamics Inc., Pasadena, Calif., 1956-59; cons. H.I. Thompson Fiber Glass Co., Los Angeles, Andrew Corp., Chgo., 1959, Satellite Broadcast Assocs., Encino, Calif., 1982; teaching staff Pasadena City Coll. (Calif.), 1959; dir. engring., chief engr. Electronics Specialty Co., Los Angeles and Thomaston, Conn., 1959-61; with Hughes Aircraft Co., various locations, 1955, 61—, mgr. Middle East programs, also Far East, Latin Am. and African market devel., Los Angeles, 1971—, dir. internat. programs devel., Hughes Communications Internat., 1985—. Served with AUS, 1942-46. Mem. Phi Beta Kappa, Am. Inst. Aeros. and Astronautics, Sigma Pi Sigma. Contbr. articles to profl. jours. Home: 25 Silver Saddle Ln Rolling Hills Estates CA 90274 Office: PO Box 92919 Airport Sta Los Angeles CA 90009

PFUNTNER, ALLAN ROBERT, medical entomologist; b. Buffalo, May 19, 1946; s. Robert James and Verna May (Colton) P.; m. Sri Hartini Hartono, Aug. 23, 1970; children: Nicolis Dean, Erin Tristina. BA in Biology, San Jose State U., 1969, MA in Biology, 1977. Sanitarian Monterey County Health Dept., Salinas, Calif., 1972-73; vector control asst. Santa Clara County Health Dept., San Jose, Calif., 1973-75; entomologist Northwest Mosquito Abatement Dist., Riverside, Calif., 1975-84; asst. mgr. West Valley Vector Control Dist., Chino, Calif., 1984-89, mgr., 1989—; cons., bd. dirs. Consol. Labs., Corona, Calif., 1984—. Contbr. articles to jours. Served with U.S. Army, 1969-72. Mem. Entomol. Soc. Am., Am. Mosquito Control Assn., Am. Registry Profl. Entomologists (cert.), Soc. Vector Ecologists. Democrat. Office: West Valley Vector Control Dist 13766 Arapahoe Chino CA 91710

PHAM, KINH DINH, electrical engineer, educator, administrator; b. Saigon, Republic of Vietnam, Oct. 6, 1956; came to U.S., 1974; s. Nhuong D.

and Phuong T. (Tran) P.; m. Ngan-Lien T. Nguyen, May 27, 1985. BS with honors, Portland State U., 1979; MSEE, U. Portland, 1982. Registered profl. engr., Oreg., Calif. Elec. engr. Irvington-Moore, Tigard, Oreg., 1979-80; elec. engr. Elcon Assocs., Inc., Beaverton, Oreg., 1980-87, sr. elec. engr., assoc. ptnr., 1987—; adj. prof. Portland (Oreg.) Community Coll., 1982—. Contbr. articles to profl. jours. Recipient Cert. Appreciation Am. Pub. Transit Assn. and Transit Industry, 1987. Mem. IEEE. Buddhist. Office: Elcon Assocs Inc 12670 NW Barnes Rd Portland OR 97229

PHELAN, PATRICK JOHN, research engineer; b. Upland, Calif., Feb. 16, 1959. BS, U. Calif., Riverside, 1981, MS, 1984, PhD, 1987. Research asst. U. Calif., 1981-87; sr. engr. materials and processing Rohr Industries, Inc., Riverside, 1987-88, sr. research engr., 1988—. Editor: Materials - Pathway to the Future, 1988; contbr. profl. jours. Research scholar U. Calif., 1981-87. Mem. AAAS, Am. Chem. Soc., Soc. for Advancement Material and Process Engring. (internat. treas. 1989—), Sigma Xi, Gamma Sigma Delta. Club: Newport Sailing (Newport Beach, Calif.). Home: 825 Spruce St Riverside CA 92507

PHELPS, DOUGLAS L., educator; b. Santa Monica, Calif., July 1, 1940; s. Harold Alvin and Elizabeth May (Stark) P.; m. Sandra Ann Greenberg, June 14, 1967 (div. 1978); m. Elma Carolyn Brown, Feb. 18, 1979. Student, El Camino Coll., 1963-64; BA in Drama, Long Beach (Calif.) State U., 1970; postgrad., No. Ariz. U., 1987—. Cert. tchr., Calif., Ariz. Tchr. drama Anaheim (Calif.) Unified Sch. Dist., 1969-78; tchr. drama Tuba City (Ariz.) Pub. Schs., 1979-83, lang. arts computer specialist, 1983-86, alternative edn. academic instr., 1986—; tech. dir., Studio Theatre, Calif. State U., Long Beach, 1967-69, Bob Baxter Banjo Band Bash, Northridge, Calif., 1974; dir. plays, various orgns. Vol., L.A. Theatre Assn., 1976-77; newsletter editor, Presbyn. Mission, Tuba City, 1984-85. With USAF, 1959-62. Mem. NEA, Tuba City Edn. Assn. (pres. 1986-87), Nat. Coun. Tchrs. English, Tchrs. of English to Speakers of Other Langs., Ariz. Edn. Assn., Tuba City Unified Sch. Edn. Assn. (grievance rep. 1979—). Republican. Home: Box 1574 Tuba City AZ 86045 Office: Tuba City Pub Schs Box 67 Tuba City AZ 86045

PHELPS, HARVEY WILLIAM, physician, former state senator; b. Pueblo, Colo., June 27, 1922; s. Harvey Jay and Honor Twinet (Wright) P.; B.S., Idaho State Coll., 1946; M.D., St. Louis U., 1949; m. Adah Lucile Godbold, Sept. 1, 1948; children—Castle Wright, Stuart Harvey, Martha Gail. Intern, Brooke Gen. Hosp., Fort Sam Houston, Tex., 1949-50; resident in internal medicine Fitzsimmons Gen. Hosp., Denver, 1951-54; practice medicine specializing in internal medicine, 1954—; commd. 1st lt. U.S. Army, 1949, advanced through grades to lt. col., 1961; chief med. service U.S. Army Hosp., Ft. MacArthur, Calif., 1955-57; asst. chief pulmonary disease service Fitzsimmons Gen. Hosp., Denver, 1958-59; chief dept. medicine U.S. Army Med. Center, Japan, 1959-62; cons. internal medicine to Surgeon, U.S. Army, Japan, 1959-62; cons. pulmonary disease Tri-Service, Japan, 1959-62; chief dept. medicine DeWitt Army Hosp., Fort Belvoir, Va., 1963-65; chief pulmonary disease service Valley Forge Gen. Hosp., Phoenixville, Pa., 1965-66, ret., 1966; dir. inhalation therapy St. Mary-Corwin Hosp. and Parkview Episcopal Hosp., Pueblo, Colo., 1966-78; Pueblo County coroner, 1967-76; cons. disease of the chest Colo. State Hosp., 1966-76; dir. So. Colo. State Coll. asso. degree program in respiratory therapy, 1971—; regent U. Colo., 1988—; mem. Colo. State Senate, 1976-85. Mem. Colo. State Air Pollution Variance Bd., 1967-76. Recipient James J. Waring award Am. Lung Assn., 1972. Fellow ACP, Am. Coll. Chest Physicians; mem. Colo. State Med. Soc. (del. 1970—, Community Service award 1980), Pueblo County Med. Soc., AMA. Democrat. Methodist. Clubs: Masons, Shriners, Vintage Motor of Am. Contbr. articles on respiratory disease to profl. jours. Home and Office: 2424 N Greenwood St Pueblo CO 81003

PHELPS, JAMES E., banker. Formerly pres. First Security Bank of Idaho, N.A., Boise, chmn. bd., 1984—. Office: 1st Security Bank Idaho PO Box 7069 Boise ID 83730 also: 1st Security Bank of Idaho NA 119 N 9th St Boise ID 83730 *

PHELPS, KENNETH HOWARD, JR., manufacturing executive; b. Glens Falls, N.Y., Nov. 17, 1942; s. Kenneth H. and Croke (Lange) P. BA, Western State Coll. Skier U.S. ski team, 1958-68; prodn. mgr. Lange Ski Boots, Broomfield, Colo., 1967-78; pres. Sanmarco Ski Boots, Aspen, Colo., 1978—; mem. U.S. Olympic ski team, 1968. Mem. Ski Industries of Am. Home: PO Box 4970 Aspen CO 81612

PHELPS, MARK STEVEN, health facility administrator; b. San Francisco, Aug. 13, 1947; s. Rodney Earl and Patricia Jean (Anderson) P.; m. Susan Loebig, Nov. 11, 1980. BA, Ft. Lewis State Coll., 1970; MA, U. No. Colo., 1980. With Peace Corps (Vista), 1966-68; state probation counselor Colo. Jud. Dept., Durango, 1970-78; psychotherapist Mental Health Ctr., Crescent City, Calif., 1978-80; supt. Kans. Correctional Facility, Atchison, 1980-85; chief exec. officer Children's Home of Stockton, Calif., 1985—; cons. juvenile justice to pub., pvt. agys., 1973—. Named Kans. Pub. Adminstr. of Yr. Am. Soc. Pub. Adminstrn., 1985, Adminstr. of Yr. Calif. Council for Exceptional Children. Mem. Am. Correctional Assn., Calif. Assn. Services for Children. Lodge: Rotary. Office: Childrens Home of Stockton PO Drawer R Stockton CA 95201

PHIBBS, HARRY ALBERT, interior designer, professional speaker, lecturer; b. Denver, Jan. 9, 1933; s. Harry Andrew and Mary May (Perriam) P.; m. Alice Conners Glynn, Oct. 23, 1957 (div. Jan. 1988); children: Kathleen Ann, Paul Robert, Mary Alice, Michael John, Peter James, Daniel Edward; m. Nevelle Haley Jones, Feb. 1988. B.A., U. Colo., 1954, B.F.A., 1957. Interior designer Howard Lorton, Inc., Denver, 1957-68; interior designer, v.p. Ronald Ansay Inc., Wheatridge, Colo., 1969-71; interior designer, pres. Phibbs Design Assos., Inc., Denver, 1972-78; interior designer, mgr. Howard Lorton, Inc., Colorado Springs, Colo., 1979—; pres. Interior Designers Housing Devel. Corp., 1969-72. Vice pres. Arvada (Colo.) Hist. Soc., 1973; bd. dirs. Colo. Opera Festival, also pres., 1986; bd. dirs. Downtown Colorado Springs, Inc., also pres., 1984. Served with U.S. Army, 1954-56. Fellow Am. Soc. Interior Designers (nat. pres. 1977); mem. Am. Arbitration Assn., Theta Xi (pres. Denver Area alumni club 1958-64). Democrat. Roman Catholic. Home: 902 Bayfield Way #101 Colorado Springs CO 80906 Office: 27 S Tejon St Colorado Springs CO 80903

PHIBBS, PHILIP MONFORD, university president; b. Bemidji, Minn., Oct. 2, 1931; s. Clifford Matthew and Dorothy Ethel (Wright) P.; m. Gwen Willis, Aug. 29, 1954; children: Kathleen, Jennifer, Diana, Dirk (dec.). B.A. with highest honors, Wash. State U., 1953; postgrad. (Rotary Found. fellow), Cambridge (Eng.) U., 1953-54; M.A., U. Chgo., 1956, Ph.D. (Edward Hillman fellow), 1957. Congl. fellow Am. Polit. Sci. Assn., Washington, 1957-58; instr. polit. sci. Wellesley Coll., 1961-63, asst. prof., 1963-68, assoc. prof., 1968-73, exec. v.p., 1968-73, acting pres., 1973; pres. U. Puget Sound, Tacoma, 1973—; Dir. Wellesley-Vassar Washington Internship Program, 1962-73; assoc. Danforth Found., 1963—; mem. Seattle Found., Seattle Com. on Fgn. Relations. Contbr. to publs. in field. Trustee Seattle Opera Assn., Pacific Sci. Ctr.; mem. Wash. Friends Higher Edn.; bd. govs. Greater Tacoma Community Found.; mem. Council Postsecondary Edn. State of Wash., 1974-79, Coll. Bd. Acad. Adv. Panel, 1982-85, Assn. Governing Bds. Univs. and Colls. Adv. Council of Pres., 1987—; mem. nat. task force Council for Advancement and Support of Edn., 1987-88. Fulbright grantee India, 1963; Rockefeller grantee India, 1966-67. Mem. Am. Council Edn. (bd. dirs., chmn. commn. internat. edn. 1984-86, chmn. undergrad. internat. edn. adv. com. 1987—), Assn. Am. Colls. (bd. dirs.), Am. Polit. Sci. Assn., Nat. Assn. Ind. Colls. and Univs. (chmn. 1982-83), Nat. Assn. Schs. and Colls. United Meth. Ch. (bd. dirs., chmn. pub. policy com. 1983-87, pres. 1985-86, univ. senate), Phi Beta Kappa, Phi Kappa Phi, Pi Sigma Alpha, Phi Kappa Delta. Office: U Puget Sound Office of Pres 1500 N Warner St Tacoma WA 98416

PHILBRICK, RALPH, botanist; b. San Francisco, Jan. 1, 1934; s. Howard R. and Elizabeth (Jauckens) P.; children—Lauren P. Lester, Winston H., Edward W. B.A., Pomona Coll., 1956; M.A., UCLA, 1958; Ph.D., Cornell U., 1963. Research assoc. Cornell U., 1957-63; assoc. in botany U. Calif., Santa Barbara, 1963-64; biosystematist Santa Barbara Botanic Garden, 1964-73, dir., 1974-87, biol. cons., 1987—; research assoc. U. Calif., Santa Barbara, 1964-82. Mem. Santa Barbara County Planning Commn., 1981-85. Mem. Sigma Xi, Phi Kappa Phi. Office: 29 San Marcos Trout Club Santa Barbara CA 93105

PHILEMONOFF, RON PAUL, company executive, management consultant; b. St. Paul Island, Alaska, Aug. 5, 1954; s. Terenty and Alexandra Alice (Kozloff) P.; m. Laurie Ellen Holmgren, Jan. 9, 1976; children: Erik Lawrence, Paul Thomas, Rachel Alexandra. B Tech. in Bus., U. Alaska, 1978. Equal employment opportunity officer Cook Inlet Native Assn., Anchorage, 1978-80, program planning asst., 1980-81; housing mgr. Aleutian Housing Authority, Anchorage, 1981-84; mgmt. cons. RPM Cons., Anchorage, 1984—; chmn. bd. Tanadgusix Corp., Anchorage, 1986—, also bd. dirs.; bd. dirs. St. Paul Island, Aleut Corp., Anchorage, The 2d Co., San Diego, Pribilof Bering Seafood, Ltd., Anchorage. Russian Orthodox. Office: Tanadgusix Corp 741 Sesame St Ste 201 Anchorage AK 99503

PHILIPPE, ROBERT SAM, real estate developer; b. Chgo., Oct. 22, 1949; s. Frank Philippe and Gertrude (Miller) Naster; m. Penny Lovely, Dec. 31, 1985; 1 child, Trevor F. Student, Western State Coll., 1967-68, Colo. U., 1969, Drake U., 1970. Lic. real estate broker. Chief exec. officer Equities Philippe, Frisco, Colo., 1981—, Masontown Devel. Co., Frisco, 1981—, Am. Barn Co., Frisco, 1981—; prin. Robert S. Philippe Spl. Projects Real Estate Brokerage Co., Frisco, 1981—; bd. dirs. Columbine Iron and Metal Co., Erie, Colo. Chmn. Amature High Altitude Observatory, Frisco; vice-chmn. Frisco Lakefront Commn.; mgr., gen. ptnr. Mt. Royal Lodge, Angler's Inn, Frisco; rep. Summit County Leadership Group, Summit County Econ. Devel. Co. Mem. Frisco Yacht Club (pres.). Republican. Office: Frisco Bay 303 Main St PO Box 67 Frisco CO 80443

PHILIPPILLAI, MARY RAJAPUSHPAM, nurse; b. Trincomal, Sri Lanka, Jan. 27, 1947; d. Augustinpillai Rajah and Theresammah (Ponnampalam) P.; m. Alan Francis Javel, Apr. 24, 1976; 1 child, Avril Therese. BS, Upsala Coll., E. Orange, N.J., 1984. Grad. nurse Beth Israel Med. Ctr., Newark, N.J., 1972-74; clin. nurse II U. Calif., San Francisco, 1974-78; staff nurse Mills Meml. Hosp., San Mateo, Calif., 1978-79, Royal Infirmary, Edinburgh, Scotland, 1980; relief charge nurse Watsonville (Calif.) Community, 1980; staff nurse St. Barnabas Med. Ctr., Newark, 1981-82; charge nurse Panorama Convalescent Ctr., Olympia, Wash., 1982-87; staff nurse St. Peter Hosp., Olympia, 1987—. Mem. advocations com. St. Michael's Ch., Olympia,, 1985—; mem. com. for bread for the world in dist. 3, Olympia, 1985—. Home: 6426 Woodard Bay Rd NE Olympia WA 98506

PHILLIPS, DARRELL, retail executive; b. Hamilton, Ohio, Oct. 7, 1956; s. Bill L. and Lois J. (Marcum) P. Student, Western State Coll., Gunnison, Colo., 1974-77; BSBA, U. No. Colo., Greeley, 1979. Sales rep. Econ. Lab., White Plains, N.Y., 1979, Color Tile, Inc., Denver, 1980-81; store mgr. Color Tile, Inc., Lake Charles, La., 1981-82; v.p. Phillips Stationers, Inc., Denver, 1982-87; pres. Pro-Dispatch Office Supply, Denver, 1988—. Mem. Nat. Office Produts Assn., Cherry Creek Sporting Club (Denver). Republican. Club: Cherry Creek Sporting (Denver).

PHILLIPS, DEBORAH LEE, nurse; b. East Liverpool, Ohio, June 10, 1950; d. Thomas Eugene and Phyllis May (Bair) P.; m. Craig S. Lanway, June 9, 1983; 1 child, Scott Phillip. Diploma in nursing, Presbyterian Hosp., Pitts., 1971; BA, St. Mary's Coll., Moraga, Calif., 1988. Staff nurse Presbyn. Hosp., Pitts., 1971; pub. health nurse Allegheny County Health Dept., Pitts., 1972; sr. staff nurse U.C. San Diego Hosp., 1972-73; staff nurse III Stanford Med. Ctr., Palo Alto, Calif., 1973-76; critical care supr. St. Lukes Hosp., San Francisco, 1976-79; pvt. practice nurse cons. Pleasanton, Calif., 1979—; wellness/cardiology dir. Valley Meml. Hosp., Livermore, Calif., 1982-88; program dir. Golden State Rehab. Hosp. (formerly San Ramon (Calif.) Rehab. Hosp.), 1989—. Mem. Am. Heart Assn. (com. chmn. 1981-82), Calif. Soc. Nursing Svc. Adminstrs., Diablo Valley Wellness Council, Am. Assn. Critical Care Nurses, No. Calif. Healthcare Mktg. Assn., Assn. Fitness in Bus., Commonwealth Club, Job's Daughters. Democrat. Home and Office: 4095 Suffolk Way Pleasanton CA 94566

PHILLIPS, DOUGLAS ALAN, teacher, consultant; b. Volga, S.D., Oct. 7, 1949; s. Alan and Carolyn Rae (Hook) P.; m. Marlene Francis Rydberg, Oct. 3, 1970; children: Christopher, Angela, Daniel. BS in Edn., No. State Coll., Aberdeen, S.D., 1971, MS in Edn., 1971; Cert. Edn. Adminstrn., U. Alaska, 1987. Cert. tchr., Alaska. Organizer low income community Interlakes Community Action Program, Sioux Falls, S.D., 1972-73; tchr. social studies Gettysburg (S.D.) Pub. Schs., 1973-75; tchr. social studies Brookings (S.D.) Pub. Schs., 1975-78, coordinator law related edn., 1977-78; social studies curriculum specialist S.D. div. Elem. and Secondary Edn., Pierre, 1978-81; coordinator social studies program Anchorage Sch. Dist., 1981—; lectr., cons. World Affairs, Nat. Bicentennial Program. Author: The Pacific Rim Region: Emerging Giant, 1988; ednl. designer Alaskan Sketches, Litterbits, South Dakota Adventures, Alaska Regional Geography; contbg. editor The Social Studies Teacher, 1988. Treas. Anchorage Sister Cities Commn., 1985; state coordinator Nat. Bicentennial Constn. and Bill of Rights Competition, 1987-88. Named Outstanding Young Educator, S.D. C. of C., 1977. Mem. Nat. Council for Geog. Edn. (exec. bd. 1986-88, chmn. K-12 com. 1987-88, Meritorious Teaching Achievement award 1983, Disting. Teaching Achievement award 1985), Nat. Council Social Studies (chmn. curriculum adv. com. 1982, steering com. 1985-86, nominations com. 1983-84, chmn. internat. action com., internat. activities com. 1987-88, presenter pacific rim conf. 1986-88, social edn. editorial bd. 1985-86), Alaska Council Social Studies (founder 1982, treas. 1986, Mr. Social Studies of Alaska 1988), S.D. Council Social Studies (founder 1978). Democrat. Methodist. Home: 2310 Paxson Anchorage AK 99504 Office: Anchorage Sch Dist PO Box 196614 Anchorage AK 99519-6614

PHILLIPS, EDWARD THOMAS, marketing professional, engineer; b. San Diego, Apr. 6, 1928; s. Walter Thomas and Anna Olivia (Sjaastad) P.; m. Elizabeth Florence Petersen, Sept. 1, 1951 (div. Sept. 1976); children: Anne Elizabeth Mellor, Steven Thomas, Cynthia Mary Orlando; m. Catherene Mary Brooks Tearnen, Nov. 12, 1976; children: Teresa Marie Howett, Thomas Patrick, Catherine Ann Martin, Paul Andrew. BEE with honors, U. Calif., Berkeley, 1949; MEE, U. Calif., 1950. Registered profl. engr., Calif. Various engring. positions Teledyne Ryan Electronics, San Diego, 1950-59, chief engring. design, 1959-65, dir. mktg., 1965-69; Washington rep. Teledyne Systems, Washington, 1969-73; v.p. govt. ops. Teledyne Inet, Torrance, Calif., 1986; v.p. advt. systems Calif. Microwave, Woodland Hills, 1987; pres., owner Engring. and Mktg. Service Inc., San Diego, 1973—; cons. in field. Lectr. on engring. careers Escondido (Calif.) High Sch., 1969. Mem. IEEE, Assn. Old Crows, Inst. Navigation, San Diego Yacht Club, Sigma Xi, Tau Beta Pi, Eta Kappa Nu. Republican. Home and Office: 2926 Kellogg St #B-11 San Diego CA 92106

PHILLIPS, ELIZABETH LOUISE (BETTY LOU PHILLIPS), author; b. Cleve.; d. Michael N. and Elizabeth D. (Materna) Suvak; m. John S. Phillips, Jan. 27, 1963 (div. Jan. 1981); children: Bruce, Bryce, Brian; m. 2d, John D.C. Roach, Aug. 28, 1982. B.S., Syracuse U., 1960; postgrad. in English, Case Western Res. U., 1963-64. Cert. elem. and spl. edn. tchr., N.Y. Tchr. pub. schs., Shaker Heights, Ohio, 1960-66; sportswriter Cleve. Press, 1976-77; spl. features editor Pro Quarterback Mag., N.Y.C., 1976-79; freelance writer specializing in books for young people, 1976—; bd. dirs. Cast Specialties Inc., Cleve. Author: Chris Evert: First Lady of Tennis, 1977; Picture Story of Dorothy Hamill (ALA Booklist selection), 1978; American Quarter Horse, 1979; Earl Campbell: Houston Oiler Superstar, 1979; Picture Story of Nancy Lopez, (ALA Notable book), 1980; Go! Fight! Win! The NCA Guide for Cheerleaders (ALA Booklist), 1981; Something for Nothing, 1981; Brush Up on Your Hair (ALA Booklist), 1981; Texas ... The Lone Star State, 1989, Who Needs Friends? We All Do!, 1989; also contbr. articles to young adult and sports mags. Mem. Soc. Children's Book Writers, Delta Delta Delta. Republican. Roman Catholic. Home: 4 Random Rd Cherry Hills Village CO 80110

PHILLIPS, ERIC, finance company executive; b. Los Angeles, June 12, 1955; s. George Harold and Miriam (Ciment) P.; m. Stephanie Ann Hayes, June 8, 1985; 1 child, Joseph Lawrence. MBA, Gonzaga U., 1976. Pres. West Valley Funding, Woodland Hills, Calif., 1978-81, Data Mortgage Credit Service, Encino, Calif., 1981—. Office: Data Mortgage Credit Svc 16400 Ventura Blvd Encino CA 91436

PHILLIPS, GENEVA FICKER, editor; b. Staunton, Ill., Aug. 1, 1920; d. Arthur Edwin and Lillian Agnes (Woods) Ficker; m. James Emerson Phillips, Jr., June 6, 1955 (dec. 1979). B.S. in Journalism, U. Ill., 1942; M.A. in English Lit., UCLA, 1953. Copy desk Chgo. Jour. Commerce, 1942-43; editorial asst. patents Radio Research Lab., Harvard U., Cambridge, Mass., 1943-45; asst. editor adminstrv. publs. U. Ill., Urbana, 1946-47; editorial asst. Quar. of Film, Radio and TV, UCLA, 1952-53; mng. editor The Works of John Dryden, Dept. English, UCLA, 1964—. Bd. dirs. Univ. Religious Conf., Los Angeles, 1979—. UCLA teaching fellow, 1950-53, grad. fellow 1954-55. Mem. Assn. Acad. Women UCLA, Friends of Huntington Library, Friends of UCLA Library, Renaissance Soc. So. Calif., Samuel Johnson Soc. of So. Calif., Assocs. of U. Calif. Press., Conf. Christianity and Lit., Soc. Mayflower Descs. Lutheran. Home: 213 First Anita Dr Los Angeles CA 90049 Office: UCLA Dept English 2225 Rolfe Hall Los Angeles CA 90024

PHILLIPS, JAMES NISHIMURA, video facsimile company executive; b. Tokyo, Mar. 26, 1964; came to U.S., 1970; s. Barney Louis and Kyoko (Nishimura) P.; m. Susan Ann Scollard, Sept. 7, 1985; 1 child, Jennifer Lynn. BSBA, U. So. Calif., 1985. Lic. real estate broker, Calif. Realtor assoc. Vance Otis Co., Hollywood, Calif., 1983-84; pres. Internat. Pin Corp., Playa Del Rey, Calif., 1984-86; mng. dir. Fukutoku USA, Inc., L.A., 1986-87; v.p. bd. dirs. Color Video Fax Corp., L.A., 1987-88; owner, real estate broker Jasco Investments, Playa Del Rey, 1985—; with Fukutoku USA, Inc., L.A., 1988—. Mem. U. So. Calif. Gen. Alumni Assn., Los Angeles County Mus. Art (charter), Delta Sigma Phi. Home: 8512 Tuscany Ave Apt 309 Playa Del Rey CA 90293 Office: Fukutoku USA Inc 11075 Santa Monica Blvd Ste 200 Los Angeles CA 90025

PHILLIPS, JAMES PAUL, aerospace company executive; b. Seminole, Okla., Jan. 26, 1935; s. Paul John and Lucy Alice (Waugh) P.; m. Alma Ayleen Howard, Nov. 29, 1957; children: Steven Paul, Janet Marcelle Phillips Melton. BS in Elec. Engring., U. Tex., 1958, MS in Elec. Engring., 1960. Engring. contbr. mil. electronics Gen. Electric Co., Syracuse, N.Y., 1960-65; mgr. tech. program avionic controls dept. Gen. Electric Co., Johnson City, N.Y., 1967-72; engring contbr. space systems div. LTV Corp., Grand Prairie, Tex., 1965-67; tech. mgr. Lockheed Missles & Space Co., Sunnyvale, Calif., 1972-81, program mgr. space systems div., 1981-85, v.p. programs, 1985-88, v.p., asst. gen. mgr. astronautics div., 1988—; adj. prof. Sch. Advanced Tech. SUNY, Binghamton, 1971-72. Mem. AIAA. Office: Lockheed Missiles & Space Co Astronautics div o/50-01 1111 Lockheed Way Sunnyvale CA 94089

PHILLIPS, JOHN P(AUL), neurosurgeon; b. Danville, Ark., Oct. 14, 1932; s. Brewer William Ashley and Wave Audrey (Page) P.; AB cum laude, Hendrix Coll., 1953; MD, U. Tenn., 1956; m. June Helen Dunbar, Dec. 14, 1963; children: Todd Eustace, Timothy John Colin, Tyler William Ashley. Intern, Charity Hosp. La., New Orleans, 1957; resident in surgery U. Tenn. Hosps., 1958; resident in neurol. surgery U. Tenn. Med. Units, 1958-62; practice medicine, specializing in neurol. surgery, Salinas, Calif., 1962—; chief of staff, chief of surgery Salinas Valley Meml. Hosp.; mem. staffs Community Hosp. Monterey Peninsula, U. Calif. Hosp., San Francisco; asst. clin. prof. U. Calif., 1962—. Commd. Ky. col. Diplomate Am. Bd. Neurol. Surgeons. Mem. ACS, Internat. Coll. Surgery, Harvey Cushing Soc., Congress Neurol. Surgery, Western Neurosurg. Assn., AMA, San Francisco Neurol. Soc., Pan Pacific Surg. Assn., Alpha Omega Alpha, Phi Chi, Alpha Chi. Home: 6 Mesa del Sol Salinas CA 93901 Office: 220 San Jose St Salinas CA 93901

PHILLIPS, JUDITH, real estate company executive; b. Denver, Mar. 3; d. Frank E. and Marjorie E. (Barclay) P. Student, U. Colo., Fullerton Jr. Coll., Colo. Mountain Coll., 1970-80. Lic. real estate broker, Colo. V.p. Vail (Colo.) Realty Inc.; broker Vail Assocs. Inc.; pres. JP Co., Vail, 1977-81, Denver Comml. Brokers, 1982-85; sr. mktg. exec. Previews Inc., Denver, 1985-87; pres. Estate Mktg. Group/Phillips Realty, Denver, 1987—; cons. Ridge at Castle Pines, Castle Rock, Colo., 1987—. Fundraiser Artreach, Denver, 1980-87; bd. dirs. Denver chpt. Cystic Fibrosis Found., 1987—, Colo. Spl. Olympics, 1988—; mem. exec. com. Colo. Spl. Olympics, 1987—. Recipient awards for lyrics Am. Song Festival, Nashville, 1977—, grand prize Am. Song Festival, 1981. Mem. Nat. Assn. Realtors, Colo. Assn. Realtors (edn. com. 1988—), Denver Bd. Realtors, Fedn. Internationale des Professions Immobilieres (pres. Colo. coun.), Citivan Club. Republican. Office: Estate Mktg Group 1021 S 9th Ave #127 Denver CO 80218

PHILLIPS, LOIS GAIL, exotic bird breeder; b. Detroit, June 21, 1939; d. John Patrick and Leona Victoria (Wagner) P.; BS in Chemistry, Fresno (Calif.) State U., 1962. Radiol. chemist Nat. Canners Assn., Berkeley, Calif., 1963-64; tchr. Progress Sch., Long Beach, Calif., 1966-67; vol. Peace Corps tchr., Nepal, 1967-69; univ. extension tchr. Nepal tng. programs, Davis, Calif., 1969-71; nursery employee Valley Gardens, Woodland, Calif., 1971-74, Farrell's Garden Center, Sonoma, Calif., 1974-75; mgr. 7-Eleven Store, Petaluma, Calif., 1977-85; chemist, Chem. Waste Mgmt. div., 1985-87, Clearwater Environ., Santa Rosa, 1987—; owner Bodega Birds, Petaluma. Bd. dirs. Sonoma County People Econ. Opportunity, 1978-83, sec. to bd., 1978-79. Mem. ACLU, Am. Fedn. Aviculture, Nat. Audubon Soc., Sierra Club. Home: 1821 Lakeville St Apt 55 Petaluma CA 94952 Office: 1791 Marlow Santa Rosa CA 95401

PHILLIPS, RICHARD A., distribution consultant; b. Oakland, Calif., Dec. 23, 1927; s. Ethan Allen and Helen Lucille (Struthers) P.; m. Barbara Joan Guthrie, June 4, 1950; children: Susan Joan Phillips Barker, Laurel Ann Phillips Nielsen, Allan Bruce. BS in Engring., USCG Acad., 1950. Contr., treas. Phillips & Edwards Electric Supply Co., San Francisco, 1954-63; treas. Phillips & Ober Electric Supply Co., San Francisco, 1963-84, Western Ind. Elec. Distbrs., San Mateo, Calif., 1984-87; cons. on wholesale distbn. San Mateo, 1987—. Contbr. numerous articles to Elec. Distbr. mag. Advisor, instr. Sequoia Jr. Sailing Club, Redwood City, Calif., 1957-87; treas. Hillcrest Chaplaincy and Ministries, San Mateo, 1985—, Baywood Park Improvement Assn., San Mateo, 1987—; chmn. adminstrn. coun. Crystal Springs United Meth. Ch., San Mateo, 1987—. Lt. USCG, 1950-54. Recipient award Elec. Mfrs. Assn., 1981, President's award Hillcrest Chaplaincy and Ministries, 1988. Mem. Nat. Assn. Elec. Distbrs. (hon. life, exec. com. 1983-85, Disting. Svc. award 1977), Sequoia Yacht Club (Redwood City, Armitage Meml. award 1980), Crystal Springers Square Dance Club (pres. 1985-86), Elks. Republican. Home and Office: 1675 Parrott Dr San Mateo CA 94402

PHILLIPS, TED RAY, advertising agency executive; b. American Falls, Idaho, Oct. 27, 1948; s. Virn E. and Jessie N. (Aldous) P.; m. Dianne Jacqulynne Walker, May 28, 1971; children—Scott, Russell, Stephen, Michael. B.A., Brigham Young U., 1972, M.A., 1974. Account exec. David W. Evans, Inc., Salt Lake City, 1972-75; dir. advt. Div. Continuing Edn., U. Utah, Salt Lake City, 1975-78; sr. v.p. Evans/Lowe & Stevens, Inc., Atlanta, 1978, exec. v.p., 1979; pres., chief exec. officer David W. Evans/Atlanta, Inc., 1979-80; dir. advt. O.C. Tanner Co., Salt Lake City, 1980-82; pres. Thomas/Phillips/Clawson Advt., Inc., Salt Lake City, 1982-86; pres. Hurst, Jarrard, Phillips, Salt Lake City, 1987—; advt. instr. div. continuing edn. Brigham Young U., 1983. Dir. publicity, promotion Western States Republican Con., 1976. Mem. Am. Advt. Fedn. (8 Best-in-West awards, 2 nat. Addy awards, Clio finalist 1984), Utah Advt. Fedn. (bd. dirs. 1976-78, 80-87, pres. 1984-85). Mormon. Home: 1094 E Gravel Hills Dr Sandy UT 84070 Office: Hurst & Phillips Advt & Pub Communications Inc 342 West 200 South Ste 200 Salt Lake City UT 84101

PHILLIPS, TEDDY STEVE, conductor, saxophone player, production company executive; b. Chgo., June 15, 1917; s. Steve and Kaliope P.; children: Jody, Teddy. Student U. Ill., 1935-39. Saxophone player with big bands, across country, 1940-45; staff musician Radio Sta. CBS, Chgo., 1944-45; condr. Teddy Phillips Orch., across country, 1945-55, 1957-62; prin. Teddy Phillips Show, Sta. WBKB-TV-ABC, Chgo., 1956-57; condr. Tedd Phillips and Orch., Ambassador Hotel, Los Angeles and Flamingo Hotel, Las Vegas, Nev., 1962-80, Statler Hotels, Aragon Ballroom, Chgo., Hilton Hotels, Chgo.; dir. Guy Lombardo Orch. and Royal Canadians, 1980—; pres. P&M Prodns., Woodland Hills, Calif., 1976—, Heads Hallmark Ltd.; TV producer Great Concert in the Sky; record producer; writer Do the Camel Hump?, Wishin; writer, arranger, conductor on tour Great Concert in the Sky, 1986—; producer, condr., writer Lion and the Turtle; pres. Nostalgic Records. Served with U.S. Army, 1940-41. Recipient Gould Tech.

Achievement award. Mem. Musicians Union. Greek Orthodox. Club: Masons. Home and Office: 23760 Oakfield Rd Hidden Hills CA 91302

PHILLIPS, THOMAS DAVID, JR., sales executive; b. Washington, Dec. 6, 1948; s. Thomas David and Eleanor (Hamilton) P.; m. Gaynell Reed, Sept. 3, 1987. AA, Southwood Jr. Coll., Salemburg, N.C., 1968; student, Kent State U., 1971. Asst. chemist Firestone Tire and Rubber Co., Akron, Ohio, 1971-74; plant mgr. Visu-Flex Corp., Pico Rivera, Calif., 1974-79; salesman Gen. Tire and Rubber Co., City of Industry, Calif., 1979-84; sr. sales rep. Igloo Corp.-Impact Extrusions, Orange, Calif., 1984-89; with Spartech Corp., Arlington, Tex., 1989—. Republican. Roman Catholic.

PHILLIPS, THOMAS KENT, minister; b. Corinth, Miss., Oct. 19, 1947; s. John Thomas and Dorothy Lorene (Conn) P.; m. Quida Jean Jobe, July 20, 1968; children: Cara Elizabeth, Molly Faith, Mathew Thomas. BA magna cum laude, U. Miss., 1970; MDiv, So. Bapt. Theol. Seminary, Louisville, Ky., 1974; DM, So. Bapt. Theol. Seminary, 1978. Ordained minister. Pastor Octuckalofa Bapt. Ch., Water Valley, Miss., 1969-70; street evangelist Walnut St. Bapt. Ch., Louisville, 1971; coordinator counseling and follow-up Billy Graham Evangelistic Assn., Mpls., 1975, dir. counseling, 1976-88, asst. and resident crusade dir., 1978-86, sr. crusade dir., 1987-88, program dir., 1987-89, dir. counseling and follow-up, 1989; doctoral cand. supr. So. Bapt. Theol. Seminary, Louisville, 1982—; founder ARISE, Tacoma, Wash., 1988-89; lectr. spiritual awakening, 1985-89. Author: Prescription for a Slumbering Church, 1988; editor 30 Discipleship Exercises, 1981, Teen Scene, 1982, Roots, 1983. Bd. dirs. Greater Tacoma (Wash.) Christian Outreach Fellowship, 1984-89; v.p. Follow-Up Ministries, 1985-89; bd. dirs. Creative Lifestyle Internat., 1988-89, Youth for Christ, 1989. Mem. N. Am. ch. Growth Soc., Evangelists Network. Baptist.

PHILLPOTT, REBECCA FOELBER, legislative aide, campaign consultant; b. Indpls., May 2, 1960; d. Herbert Lincoln and Margie ann (Mutscher) Foelber; m. Steven Walter Phillpott, June 8, 1985. Student in Polit. Sci., San Diego State U., 1978-83. Cons. campaign The San Diego Group, 1982-83, 84-85; cons. Campaign for Econ. Democracy, San Diego, 1983; cons. campaign State Assemblyman Jim Costa, Hanford, Calif., 1985—; field rep. State Assemblyman Jim Costa, Hanford, 1985-88; asst. account exec. pub. affairs Stoorza, Ziegaus & Metzger, San Diego, 1988—. Planning commr. City of Lamore, Calif., 1987-89; mem. adv. bd. Community Action Teen Pregnancy and Parenting Program County of King, Hanford, 1986-88; active on San Diego County Dem. Cen. Com., 1982-83. Named Outstanding Young Woman of Am. Jaycees, 1985. Mem. Kings County Alumnae Panhellenic, Lemoore Jr. Women, Alpha Gamma Delta. Lutheran.

PHILP, HEDLEY JAMES, accounting manager; b. Miami, Ariz., Mar. 18, 1943; s. Hedley James Sr. and SyMone Haroldine (Pilgrim) P.; m. Sharon Lynn Sonntag, Apr. 24, 1971; 1 child, David Brian. BS, Ariz. State U., 1968; postgrad., UCLA, 1969-70, Golden West Coll., 1979-83. Tchr. Compton (Calif.) High Sch. Dist., 1968-69; govt. bid coordinator Purex Corp., Carson, Calif., 1969-73; supr. cost acctg. Ansen Automotive div. Whittaker Corp., Gardena, Calif., 1973-75; dir. cost acctg. Appliance Inc. div. W.R. Grace, Harbor City, Calif., 1975-79; mgr. cost acctg. Narmco Materials div. Celanese, Anaheim, Calif., 1979-83; mgr. acctg. Huck Mfg. div. Fed. Mogul, Carson, 1983-88; mgr. acctg. Mennen div. Aromatic Industries, Anaheim, 1988—; cons. Calsonic Climate Control, Irvine, Calif., 1988—. Active Calif. Hist. Soc., Los Angeles and San Francisco, 1982—. Mem. Nat. Contract Mgmt. Assn., Inst. Cost Analysis (cert.), Am. Mgmt. Assn., Am. Philatelic Soc., Mex.-Elmhurst Soc. (v.p. 1973-76), Ariz. State Alumni Assn., UCLA Alumni Assn. Republican. Lodge: Masons. Home: 17901 Old Glen Ln Huntington Beach CA 92649

PHISUTHIKUL, CHAKORN, architect; b. Bangkok, Oct. 22, 1950; came to U.S., 1968; s. Termasak and Manie P.; m. Marilyn Heinemann, Aug. 10, 1986; children: Ava Mari, Andrew John. BS, B. Arch., Wash. Stae U., 1973; M. Arch., MIT, 1975. V.p. Habitat West Inc., Seattle, 1976--, developer, property owner, 1977--. Recipient Designer of Yr. award Qualified Remodeler & Community Renovator, 1987, Builder Our Environ. Seattle King Bd. Realtors, 1987. Home: 310 N 43d Seattle WA 98103 Office: Habitat West Inc 1000 Lenora St Ste 514 Seattle WA 98121

PI, WEN-YI SHIH, aircraft company engineer, researcher; b. Peiping, People's Republic of China, Feb. 28, 1935; came to U.S., 1959; d. Chih-Chuan and Hsiu-Yun (Yang) Shih; m. William Shu-Jong Pi, July 2, 1961; 1 child, Wilfred. BS, Nat. Taiwan U., Taipei, Republic of China, 1956; MS, Stanford U., 1961, PhD, 1963. Research assoc. Stanford (Calif.) U., 1963-64; engring. specialist Northrop Corp., Hawthorne, Calif., 1965-83, sr. tech. specialist, 1983—. Contbr. articles to profl. jours. Recipient Silver Achievement award Los Angeles YWCA, 1983; Amelia Earhart Scholar Zonta Internat., 1961-62. Fellow: AIAA (assoc.); mem. Sigma Xi. Office: Northrop Corp Aircraft Div One Northrop Ave Dept 3854/82 Hawthorne CA 90250-3277

PIATT, MARTY EUGENE, architect; b. Marysville, Calif., Oct. 21, 1958; s. Gale Dean and Joana Lee (Geniella) P. AS, Yuba Coll., Marysville, 1979. Lic. architect, Calif. Project designer, draftsman Key and Laughlin, Yuba City, Calf., 1978-80; project mgr., designer Saunders Constrn. Co., Yuba City, Calf., 1980; project capt. Gilbert Aja and Assocs., Laguna Hills, Calf., 1980-82; project mgr., designer Van Fossen and Ptnrs., Irvine, Calf., 1982-84; project mgr. Corbin, Yamafuji and ptnrs., Irvine, Calf., 1984-86; dir. prodn. Chris R. Stephens, Inc., Costa Mesa, Calf., 1986-87; project mgr. Burke, Lester and Assocs., Laguna Hills, Calf., 1987-88; architect Piatt et al, Laguna Niguel, Calif., 1988—. Home and Office: 45 Campton Pl Laguna Niguel CA 92677

PIAZZA, DUANE EUGENE, biomedical researcher; b. San Jose, Calif., June 5, 1954; s. Salvador Richard and Mary Bernice (Mirassou) P. BS in Biology, U. San Francisco, 1976; MA in Biology, San Francisco State U., 1986. Staff research assoc. I U. Calif., San Francisco, 1975-81; sr. research technician XOMA Corp., San Francisco, 1981-82; biologist II Syntex USA Inc., Palo Alto, Calif., 1982-85; pres., cons. Ryte For You, Oakland, Calif., 1985—; research assoc. I Cetus Corp., Emeryville, Calif., 1986—. CPR instr. ARC, San Francisco, 1980-86; instr., First Aid sta. vol., Santa Cruz, Calif., 1985-86; First Aid sta. vol. disaster action team ARC, Oakland, 1986—; branch chmn. disaster action team ARC, 1987-88. Mem. AAAS, Am. Soc. Microbiology, N.Y. Acad. Scis., Astron. Soc. Pacific. Republican. Roman Catholic. Home: 3755 Emerson Way Apt E Oakland CA 94610 Office: Cetus Corp 1400 53d St Emeryville CA 94608

PICCIRILLO, ANTHONY VITO, telecommunications executive; b. Pasadena, Calif., Nov. 20, 1953; s. Salvatore V. and Virginia A. (Brackley) P.; m. Sara Slayton Qua, Nov. 11, 1978; 1 child, Andrew Qua Piccirillo. BA, Trinity Coll., Hartford, Conn., 1975; MBA, Harvard U., 1978. Pension actuary Hartford Ins. Group, 1975-76; prin. Am. Mgmt. Systems, Inc., Arlington, Va., 1978-84; dir. strategic planning U S WEST Communications, Inc., Denver, 1985-87, dir. market planning, 1987-89; dir. bus. development U S WEST, Inc., Englewood, Colo., 1989—. Mem. Colo. Harvard Bus. Sch. Club, Denver Athletic Club. Home: 620 Williams St Denver CO 80218 Office: U S WEST Inc 7800 E Orchard Rd Ste 480 Englewood CO 80111

PICCONE, JOSEPH ANTHONY, industrial engineer; b. Louisville, Colo., Dec. 19, 1935; s. Joseph Piccone and Lucille Elizabeth (Johnson) Shepherd; m. Linda M. Ingemarson, July 28, 1955; children: Sharon Louise, Aaron Arthur. Student, U. Colo., 1963-65, Ariz. State U., 1965-66, Phoenix Coll., 1966-67, Glendale Community Coll., 1967-69. Methods engr. Martin Marietta Corp., Denver, 1957-64, Goodyear Aerospace Corp., Litchfield Park, Ariz., 1964-65; cost engr. Sperry Flight Systems, Phoenix, 1965-70; cons. engr. M.E.S.A. Program Inc., Phoenix, 1970-73; indsl. engr. Goodyear Aerospace Corp., Litchfield Park, 1973-76; mgmt. engr. St. Mary's Hosp., Tucson, Ariz., 1976-77; prin. Costcomp, Glendale, Ariz., 1988—; mgr. design devel. Bapt. Hosps. and Health Systems, Phoenix, 1977-88. Contbr. articles to profl. jours. Pres. St. Jerone's PTO, 1970; v.p. Washington Schs. PTA, Phoenix, 1969; mem. exec. com. Boy Scouts Am. Manzanita Sch., Phoenix, 1968; precinct cpt. Dem. party, Phoenix, 1969-72. Petty officer USNR, 1956-a64. Mem. Inst. Indsl. Engrs. (pres. 1980-81, v.p. 1979-80, dir. 1967-78, Excellence award 1978, 81), Soc. Health Systems, Healtcare Info. Mgmt. Systems Soc. Roman Catholic. Avocation: photography. Home: 5926 W Muriel Dr Glendale AZ 85308 Office: Costcomp 5932 W Bell Rd Ste D-106 Glendale AZ 85308

PICK, ARTHUR JOSEPH, JR., chamber of commerce executive; b. Louisville, Mar. 22, 1931. BS, U. Calif., Riverside, 1959; MA in Urban Studies, Occidental Coll., 1969. Mem. Riverside County Rep. Cen. Com., 1962-63; founding dir. Riverside Civic League, 1963, pres., 1964; resident mgr. J. Henry Helser & Co., Investment Mgrs., Riverside, 1965-72; exec. v.p. Greater Riverside C. of C., 1972—; sec., treas. Riverside Monday Morning Group, 1988—. Pres. Young Life Riverside, 1966-68; pres. Riverside Symphony Orch. Soc. 1966, 67, 68, 69; founding pres. Riverside Cultural Arts Coun., 1969; elected Riverside City Coun., 1967, re-elected, 1971; candidate assembly State of Calif. Legis., 1972; mem. adv. bd. Riverside Jr. League, 1975-79, LWV, 1976-80; v.p. The Friends of the Mission Inn, 1977-79; founding mem. exec. com. adv. bd., treas. Calif. Citrus Heritage Park, 1969—; founder Riverside Area Urban League. With U.S. Army, 1953-55. Named Outstanding Young Man of Am., Riverside Jaycees, 1966; recipient Disting. Service award Riverside Jaycees, 1966, Patron of Arts award Cultural Arts Council, 1977. Mem. Mayors and Councilmen Assn. Riverside County (pres. 1968-69), Inland Area Urban League (founder, bd. dirs., Pacesetter award 1982), U. Calif. Alumni Assn. Riverside (bd. dirs. 1981-87), Riverside Jaycees (life). Office: Greater Riverside C of C 4261 Main St Riverside CA 92501

PICK, JAMES BLOCK, university administrator; b. Chgo., July 29, 1943; s. Grant Julius and Helen (Block) P.; B.A., Northwestern U., 1966; M.S. in Edn., No. Ill. U., 1969; Ph.D., U. Calif., Irvine, 1974, C.D.P., 1980. C.S.P., 1985, C.C.P., 1986. Asst. research statistician, lectr. Grad. Sch. Mgmt. U. Calif., Riverside, 1975-84, dir. computing, adj. lectr., 1984—; co-dir. U.S.-Mex. Database Project, 1988—; mem. Univ. Commons Bd., 1982-86; cons. U.S. Census Bur. Internat. Div., 1978; mem. bd. govs. PCCLAS, 1989—. Trustee Newport Harbor Art Mus., 1981-87, 88—, chmn. permanent collection com., 1987-89. Mem. Assn. Computing Machinery, Assn. Systems Mgmt. (pres. Orange County chpt. 1978-79), AAAS, Am. Statis. Assn., Population Assn. Am., Internat. Union for Sci. Study of Population, Soc. Info. Mgmt. Clubs: Balboa Bay (Newport Beach); Standard (Chgo.). Author: Computer Systems in Business, 1986, Geothermal Energy Development Micromanual, 1986, Atlas of Mexico, 1989; condr. research in info. systems, population, environ. studies; contbr. sci. articles to publs. in field. Office: U Calif Grad Sch Mgmt Riverside CA 92521

PICKARD, BRIAN ALAN, lawyer; b. London, Ont., Can., June 10, 1952; came to U.S., 1975; s. Harold Alan and Pearl Victoria (Pudney) P. BA, U. Western Ont., 1974; MAM, Embry-Riddle Aero. U., 1977; JD, Western State U., 1980. Bar: Calif. 1981. With Pearpic Mgmt. Corp., London, Ont., 1973-75, mgmt. cons., 1977—; sole practice Fullerton, Calif., 1981—. Contbr. articles to profl. jours. Recipient Nat. Pilots Assn. Flight award, 1979, Am. Jurisprudence award, 1979, Best Advocate in Trial Practice award West Pub. Co., 1980. Mem. Calif. Trial Lawyers Assn., Orange County Trial Lawyers Assn., Assn. Trial Lawyers Am., Internat. Platform Assn., Alpha Eta Rho (v.p.). Republican. Club: Aviation Facilities Flying. Office: 170 S Main St Ste 100 Orange CA 92668

PICKARD, GARY LOUIS, electrical engineer, consultant; b. Norman, OK, Nov. 19, 1955; s. Porter Louis and Betty Jo (Harden) P.; m. Laurinda Naomi Bennett, Oct. 9, 1981; children: Bradley Louis, Krystal Lynn. BEE, U. Tex., 1979. Process control elec. engr. Ariz. Pub. Service, Phoenix, 1981-84; ptnr., cons. Pickard Systems, Wheat Ridge, Colo., 1984—. Mormon. Home: 10552 Garrison St Westminster CO 80020 Office: Pickard Systems 3914 Youngfield St Wheat Ridge CO 80033

PICKARD, MURPHY LEE, electrical engineer; b. Norman, Okla., Dec. 7, 1949; s. Porter Louis and Betty Jo (Harden) P. BEE, U. Tex., 1974. Sect. mgr. Baylor Coll. Medicine, Houston, 1974-78; project mgr. Wordstream Computer Products, Houston, 1978-79; owner Biomatrix, Jay, Okla., 1979-81; group leader Seismograph Service Corp., Tulsa, 1981-83; sr. ptnr. Pickard Systems, Wheat Ridge, Colo., 1983—. Inventor artificial heart valve tester, 1987. Mem. Eta Kappa Nu, Tau Beta Pi. Office: Pickard Systems 3914 Youngfield St Wheat Ridge CO 80036

PICKENS, ALEXANDER LEGRAND, education educator, university administrator; b. Waco, Tex., Aug. 31, 1921; s. Alex LeGrand and Elma L. (Johnson) P.; m. Frances M. Jenkins, Aug. 20, 1955. B.A., So. Methodist U., 1950; M.A., North Tex. State U., Denton, 1952; Ed.D., Columbia U., 1959. Tchr. art public schs. Dallas, 1950-53, Elizabeth, N.J., 1953-54; mem. faculty U. Mich. Coll. Architecture and Design, 1954-59, U. Ga., Athens, 1959-62, U. Hawaii Coll. Edn., Honolulu, 1962—; prof. edn. U. Hawaii Coll. Edn., 1968—, dir. coll. devel., 1984—, chmn. doctoral studies curriculum instrn., 1984—; dir. children's classes Ft. Worth Children's Museum, 1951-53; head art Nat. Music Camp, Interlochen, Mich., summers 1957-58, U. Oreg., Portland, summers 1959-60, 62; cons. youth art activities Foremost Dairies, 1964-74; cons. art films United World Films, 1970-75; art edn. cons. Honolulu Paper Co., 1970-76, Kamehameha Sch., Bishop Estate, 1978—. Exhibited ceramics, Wichita Internat. Exhbn., Syracuse (N.Y.) Nat. Exhbn., St. Louis Mus., Dallas Mus., San Antonio Mus., Detroit Art Inst., Hawaii Craftsmen, also others; editorial bd.: Arts and Activities mag, 1955-82; editor: U. Hawaii Ednl. Perspectives, 1964—; contbr. articles to profl. jours. Mem. adult com. Dallas County chpt. Jr. ARC, 1951-53; exec. com. Dallas Crafts Guild, 1950-53; v.p., publicity chmn. U. Ga. Community Concert Assn., 1960-62. Served with USAAF, 1942-44. Recipient award merit Tex. State Fair, 1957, All Am. award Ednl. Press Assn. Am., 1968, 70, 72, 75, 79, Bd. of Regents medal, 1989. Mem. Internat. Soc. Edn., NEA, Nat. Art Edn. Assn., AAUP, Phi Delta Kappa, Kappa Delta Pi. Address: 1471 Kalaepohaku St Honolulu HI 96816

PICKENS, ALLEN ARTHUR, accountant; b. Des Moines, Iowa, Nov. 29, 1940; s. Leo Arthur and Odessa Leona (Sly) P.; m. Dianne Patricia Gueliff, Feb. 15, 1969; children—Shawn, Courtney, Megan. B.S. in Bus. Adminstrn., Drake U., 1965. C.P.A., Hawaii, Guam. Acct. Pickens, Borja & Filush P.C. (rep. firm of Klynveld Peat Marwick Goerdler), Agana, Guam, 1965—, mng. ptnr. Guam office, Agana, 1975—; mng. ptnr. Pickens Borja & Filush, P.C., 1988—; instr. U. Guam, Am. Inst. Banking. Chmn. Territorial Bd. Pub. Accountancy, 1970-78; pres. Guam Growth Council, 1978-83; pres. USO, 1976-77; pres. Guam Soc. Cultural Exchange, 1979-80; pres., founder Jr. Achievement of Guam Inc., 1984-86. Served with USAF, 1958-62. Named Guam Person of Yr. 1979, Rotary Club of Tumon Bay. Mem. Am. Inst. C.P.A.s, Guam Soc. C.P.A.s (founder, pres. 1973-75), Assn. Govt. Accts., Am. Acctg. Assn., Navy League U.S. (pres. Guam 1978-79), Air Force Assn. (pres. Guam chpt. 1982-83), Guam C. of C. (chmn. 1982-84). Roman Catholic. Clubs: Rotary (Guam) (pres. 1975-76, 80-81).

PICKENS, STEPHEN MATTHEW, vice president finance; b. Phila., July 10, 1948; s. Edmund Julian and Marilyn (Miller) P.; m. Vicki Lynn (Bryce), Oct. 1, 1983; 1 child, Lauren Jayne. BA in Econ., Windham Coll., 1970. Br. mgr. Union Trust Co., Stamford, Darien, Conn., 1970-74; lease adminstr. Computer Investers Group, Stamford, 1974-75; br. mgr. Litton Industries Credit Corp., Stamford, 1975-76; sales mgr. Equico Lessors, San Francisco, 1976-77; asst. cashier Am. Bank & Trust, Walnut Creek, Calif., 1978; credit, fin. mgr. Commodore, Palo Alto, Santa Clara, Calif., 1978-80; v.p. fin. Calif. Group Svcs., San Francisco, 1980-88, Profl. Lease Mktg., Corte Madera, Calif., 1988—; cons. Aon Corp., Chgo., 1988—. Editor Windham College Economics Journal, 1968-70. Dir., treas. Market St. Railway Co., San Francisco, 1986—. Mem. Western Assn. Equipment Lessors. Republican. Congregationalist. Home: 272 Amber Dr San Francisco CA 94131

PICKERING, AVAJANE, specialized education facility executive; b. New Castle, Ind., Nov. 5, 1951; d. George Willard and Elsie Jean (Wicker) P. BA, Purdue U., 1974; MS in Spl. Edn., U. Utah, 1983, postgrad., 1985—. Tchr. Granite Community Edn., Salt Lake City, 1974-79; tchr. coordinator Salt Lake City Schs., 1975-85; co-dir., owner Specialized Ednl. Programming Service, Inc., Salt Lake City, 1976—; adj. instr. U. Utah, Salt Lake City, 1985—. Rep. del. Utah State Conv., also county conv.; vol. tour guide, hostess Temple Square, Ch. Jesus Christ of Latter-Day Saints, 1983—. Mem. Council for Exceptional Children, Assn. Children and Adults with Learning Disabilities, Delta Kappa Gamma. Home: 1595 S 2100 E Salt Lake City UT 84108 Office: 2022 S 2100 E Ste 201 Salt Lake City UT 84108

PICKERING, SCOTT N., soft drink company executive, accountant; b. Lawrence, Kans., Aug. 29, 1957; s. Alan J. and Charlotte S.; m. Susan Michelle Puype, Mar. 9, 1985. Student, U. Kans., 1975-76; BS, Ariz. State U., 1981. CPA, Ariz. Income tax preparer H&R Block, Inc., Mesa, Ariz., 1977; acct. U-Haul Internat., Inc., Phoenix, 1977-78; proposal analyst Motorola, Inc., Scottsdale, Ariz., 1979; staff acct. Price Waterhouse & Co., Phoenix, 1981-83, audit sr., 1983-84; dir. fin. and adminstrn. Valley Computer Systems, Inc., Phoenix, 1984-85; supr. planning and analysis Pepsi-Cola Co., Phoenix, 1985-86, mgr. planning and analysis, 1986—. Author fin. planning software. Cons. Jr. Achievement, Phoenix, 1989. Mem. AICPA, Ariz. Soc. CPA's. Republican. Office: Pepsi-Cola Co 4242 E Raymond St Phoenix AZ 85040

PICKETT, A(LBERT) DEAN, lawyer; b. Casper, Wyo., June 25, 1949; s. A. Foy and Esther Laurine (Nieman) P.; m. Lucinda Marie Wayne, July 3, 1971; children: Amanda Marie, Gregory Dean. BA, No. Ariz. U., 1971; JD with distinction, U. Ariz., 1974. Bar: Ariz. 1974, Wash. 1975. Assoc. Holesapple, Conner, Jones & Johnson, Tucson, 1978-79, Mangum, Wall, Stoops & Warden, Flagstaff, Ariz., 1980-83; ptnr. Mangum, Wall, Stoops & Warden, 1984--; legal counsel No. Ariz. U., 1981—; lectr. edn. law Ariz. Sch. Bds. Assn., 1983—. Chmn. Coconino County Republican party, 1986-88; trustee Mus. No. Ariz., 1983--; bd. dirs. Coconino County Acad. Decathlon, 1986--; pres. Flagstaff Federated Community Ch., 1987. Lt. USN, 1974-77. Mem. State Bar Ariz., Wash. State Bar Assn., Nat. Assn. Coll. and Univ. Attys., Nat. Sch. Bds. Assn. Council Sch. Attys., Coconino County Bar Assn., Malpais Kiwanis (pres. 1982-83). Presbyterian.

PICKETT, DAVID FRANKLIN, JR., aerospace company executive; b. Littlefield, Tex., May 3, 1936; d. David Franklin and Dottie Ardell (Britton) P.; m. B. Christine Klop, Aug. 21, 1971. AA, Del Mar Coll., Corpus Christi, 1960; BS in Chem., U. Tex., 1962, MA, 1965, PhD, 1970. Rsch. chemist Am. Magnesium Co., Snyder, Tex., 1969-70; chemist, chem. engr. Air Force Aero Propulsion Lab., Dayton, Ohio, 1970-78; sect. head Hughes Aircraft Co., El Segundo, Calif., 1978-84; asst. dept. mgr. Hughes Aircraft Co., El Segundo, 1984-86, dept. mgr., 1986—; ECS coordinator ann. battery conf. Calif. State U., Long Beach, 1987-89. Inventor preparation of nickel eelectrodes, 1974, prodn. of cadmium electrodes, 1975; author Ni Electrode, Nicd and Niltz Ell Technology Publications, 1978-88. With USN, 1955-57. Mem. Southern Calif./Nev. Electrochem. Soc. (sec. 1980-81, vice chmn. 1981-82, chmn. 1982-83), Am. Chem. Soc., Am. Inst. Aeronautics and Astronautics, Phi Lambda Upsilon. Baptist. Home: 4 Hilltop Circle Rancho Palos Verdes CA 90274 Office: Hughes Aircraft Co Space and Communications Grp 909 N Sepulveda Blvd El Segundo CA 90245

PICKLE, FRANKLIN PORTER, accountant; b. Taylor, Tex., June 21, 1924; s. Andrew Porter and Bertha Celia (Taulbee) P.; children: Mary Pickle Webster, David. BBA, Southwestern U., 1947; MBA, Tex. Tech. U., 1951. CPA, Tex., N.Mex. Office, credit mgr. Container Corp. Am., Ft. Worth, 1951-53; supv. billing assembly div. GM, Arlington, Tex., 1953-55; asst. to v.p., fin. Chance Vought Aircraft, Dallas, 1955-57; controller Trinity Steel Co., Dallas, 1957-59; auditor, SW region FAA, Ft. Worth, 1959-63; pvt. practice Arlington-Ft. Worth, 1963-73, Albuquerque, 1983—; staff acct. U.S. Maritime Adminstrn., Washington, 1978—. Comdr. USNR, 1942-45, PTO. Mem. AICPA (cons. com. on relations with fed. govt. 1965-67), N.Mex. Soc. CPAs (fed. taxation com. 1986-87, personal fin. planning com. 1987-88), Rio Grande Jazz Soc. (bd. dirs. 1987—), Naval Rsch. Assn., Masons, Shriners. Democrat. Methodist. Home and Office: 1913 Chandelle Loop NE Albuquerque NM 97112

PICKLE, JOSEPH WESLEY, JR., theology educator, clergyman; b. Denver, Apr. 8, 1935; s. Joseph Wesley and Wilhelmina (Blacketor) P.; m. Judith Ann Siebert, June 28, 1958; children—David E., Kathryn E., Steven J. B.A., Carleton Coll., Minn., 1957; B.D., Chgo. Theol. Sem., 1961; M.A., U. Chgo., 1962, Ph.D., 1969. Ordained to ministry Am. Baptist Conv., 1962. Asst. pastor Judson Meml. Ch., N.Y.C., 1959-60; from asst. prof. to prof. religion Colo. Coll., Colorado Springs, 1964—, acting dean summer session, 1969-70, chair dept. religion, 1972-84; cons. Colo. Humanities Program, Denver, 1975-82. Co-editor: Papers of the 19th Century Theology Group, 1978, 88. Bd. dirs., pres. Pikes Peak Mental Health Ctr., Colorado Springs, 1975; mem. Colo. Health Facilities Rev. Council, Denver, 1976-84, chmn., 1979-84; mem. Colo. Bd. Health, Denver, 1986—. Am. Baptist Conv. scholar, 1953-57; Fulbright-Hays fellow U. Tübingen, Ger., 1963-64; Danforth fellow, 1957-63; Malone Faculty fellow, Cairo, 1987. Fellow Soc. Values in Higher Edn.; mem. Am. Theol. Soc., Am. Acad. Religion, (region pres. 1983-84), Cath. Theol. Soc. Am., Phi Beta Kappa. Democrat.

PICKRELL, JACK EVON, accountant; b. Ottumwa, Iowa, Apr. 15, 1933; s. Robert Lee, Jr., and Emily Margaret (Merrill) P.; student Georgetown U., 1955-56, State U. Iowa, 1956, U. Md., 1957-58; BS in Acctg., Met. State Coll., Denver, 1980; m. Reiko Washizu, Feb. 6, 1959; 1 dau., Linda Reiko. Enlisted in U.S. Navy, 1950; served with USN, 1950-54, USAR, 1954-56, USNR, 1956-57, USAF, 1957-73, master sgt., 1968-73; ret., 1973; ops. mgr. Diamond Gas & Fuel Co., Englewood, Colo., 1973-76; gen. mgr. Alpine Pipe & Supply Co., Denver; pvt. practice pub. acct., Denver, 1977—. Decorated Bronze Star, Air Force Commendation medal with oak leaf clusters (3). Mem. U.S. Naval Cryptologic Vets. Assn., Better Bus. Bur. Greater Denver (arbitration judge). Republican. Home: 3065 Olive St Denver CO 80207 Office: 3390 Brighton Blvd Denver CO 80216

PICOULT, HARRIS M., small business owner; b. Albuquerque, Oct. 3, 1949; s. Charles and Mariam (Robbins) P.; m. Geraldine Cottle, June 6, 1974; children: Elizabeth Ann, Georgiana Lee. Grad., High sch., Albuquerque. Dist. mgr. Richman Bros. Co., Northridge, Calif., 1970-73; div. mgr. Southwest Leasing, Los Angeles, 1973-78; gen. mgr. Atlas Leasing Group, Los Angeles, 1978-86, Hoffman Leasing Co., Industry, Calif., 1986-89; owner Tri-City Bowl, Oregon City, Oreg., 1989—. Mem. Nat. Vehicle Leasing Assn. Republican. Jewish. Home: 3885 Rosepark Dr West Linn OR 97068

PIELE, PHILIP KERN, education infosystems educator; b. Portland, Oreg., May 14, 1935; s. Theodore R. and Helen D. (Hanson) P.; m. Sandra Jean Wright, Aug. 10, 1963; children: Melissa, Kathryn. BA, Wash. State U., 1957; student, U. Wash., 1960, San Jose State U., 1964; MS, U. Oreg., 1963, PhD, 1968. Asst. prof. dept. ednl. adminstrn. U. Oreg., Eugene, 1968-72, assoc. prof. dept. ednl. adminstrn., 1972-79, prof. dept. ednl. policy and mgmt., 1979—, dir. ERIC Clearinghouse on Ednl. Mgmt., 1969—; dir. numerous ednl. orgns. and coms., U. Oreg. Coll. Edn., Eugene, 1968—; vis. scholar Stanford U., 1984; exec. sec. Oreg. Sch. Study Council, 1980—; dir. Ctr. for Advanced Tech. in Edn., 1984—. Author numerous books, chpts., monographs; editor numerous books; contbr. articles to profl. jours. Bd. dirs. Oreg. Bach Festival, Eugene, 1980-83. 1st lt. U.S. Army, 1958-60. Mem. Nat. Orgn. on Legal Problems in Edn. (pres. 1977-78), Nat. Sch. Devel. Coun. (pres. 1985-86). Home: 455 Lochmoor Pl Eugene OR 97405 Office: ERIC Clearinghouse on Ednl Mgmt 1787 Agate St Eugene OR 97403

PIERCE, DEBORAH MARY, educator; b. Charleston, W. Va., Nov. 1, 1938; d. Edward Ernest and Elizabeth Anne (Trent) P.; m. Henry Matthew Armetta, Sept. 1, 1967 (div. 1981); children: Rosse Matthew Armetta, Stacey Elizabeth Pierce. Student, U. Tenn., 1956-59, Broward Jr. Coll., 1968-69; BA, San Francisco State U., 1977. Cert. elem. tchr., Calif. Pub. relations assoc. San Francisco Internat. Film Festival, 1965-66; account exec. Stover & Assocs., San Francisco, 1966-67; tchr. San Francisco Archdiocese Office of Cath. Schs., 1980—. Author: (with Frances Spatz Leighton) I Prayed Myself Slim, 1960. Pres. Mothers Alone Working, San Francisco, 1966, PTA, San Francisco, 1979, Parent Teacher Student Assn., San Francisco, 1984; apptd. Calif. State Bd. Welfare Community Rels., Com., 1964-66. Named Model of the Yr. Modeling Assn. Am., 1962. Mem. Peoples Med. Soc., Assn. for Research and Enlightenment, The Course in Miracles. Democrat. Episcopal.

PIERCE, FREDERICK WATSON, IV, real estate consultant; b. Elmhurst, Ill., July 27, 1962; s. Frederick Watson III and Diane (Tatlock) P. BS in

Fin. cum laude, San Diego State U., 1984, MBA in Real Estate Fin., 1988. Real estate appraiser Bank of Am., San Diego, 1983-84; dir. appraisal Goodkin/Cowan Inc., La Jolla, Calif., 1984-85; dir. real estate cons. Goodkin Group and Peat Marwick, La Jolla, Calif., 1985-88; mgr. real estate cons. Price Waterhouse, San Diego, 1988—; guest lectr. U. Calif. San Diego, 1988, faculty, 1989; guest lectr. San Diego Community Coll., 1986, Inst. Residential Mktg., San Diego, 1987-88; named to panel of experts Pacific Coast Builders Conf., 1987—. Speaker Calif. Jaycees, 1987. Named to Panel of Experts Pacific Coast Builders Conf., 1987-88. Mem. Bldg. Industry Assn. (speaker bur. 1988), Nat. Assn. Home Builders, Urban Land Inst. Assoc., Fin. Mgmt. Assn. Nat. Hon. Soc., Beta Gamma Sigma. Republican. Presbyterian. Club: Toastmasters (La Jolla) (ednl. v.p. local chpt 1985, Toastmaster of Yr. 1986). Office: Price Waterhouse 600 B St Ste 1600 San Diego CA 92101

PIERCE, GEORGE ADAMS, university official; b. Carlsbad, N.Mex., May 21, 1943; s. Jack Colwell and Shirley (Adams) P.; m. Margaret Mary Brakel, Feb. 10, 1980; children: Christopher, Catherine Rose. BA in Polit. Sci., Fairleigh Dickinson U.; MA in Polit. Sci., New Sch. Social Rsch.; PhD in Higher Edn., Claremont Grad. Sch. Asst. dir. promotion Afco, N.Y.C., 1969-71; dir. spl. programs U. Calif., Riverside, 1971-73; asst. to pres. Claremont (Calif.) Grad. Sch., 1973-75; asst. to pres. Seattle U., 1975-78, dir. planning, 1978-83, v.p. adminstrn., 1983-89; v.p. bus. and fin. Western Washington U., 1989—; chmn. regional review panel Truman Scholarship Found., 1977—. Chmn. Seattle Ctr. Adv. Commn., 1977-83; bd. dirs. N.W. Kidney Found., Seattle, 1986—. With USAF, 1963-65. Recipient Cert. Merit Riverside County Comprehensive Health Planning, 1972, Cert. Appreciation Office Mayor City of Seattle, 1983, Nat. Truman Scholarship Found., 1986. Mem. Am. Assn. Higher Edn., Assn. Instnl. Rsch. (regional pres. 1977—), Soc. Coll. and Planning, Cause, City Club (Seattle). Democrat. Roman Catholic. Office: Seattle U Broadway and Madison Sts Seattle WA 98122

PIERCE, GIFFORD DAVID, architect, educator; b. Worcester, Mass., Apr. 19, 1937; s. Harrison Hanson and Margaret (Gifford) P. BA, Yale U., 1959, BArch, 1964, MArch, 1964. Registered architect, Idaho, N.H., Mass. Instr. Sch. of Worcester (Mass.) Art Mus., 1969-70; asst. prof. Mont. State U., Bozeman, 1970-73; adj. prof. R.I. Sch. of Design, Providence, 1974-79; acting head, assoc. prof. Carnegie-Mellon U., Pitts., 1979-80; dept. chmn., prof. U. Idaho, Moscow, 1987—; pvt. practice architect, various cities in U.S., 1969—; instr. Groton Ctr. for the Arts, Groton, Mass., 1978. Contbr. numerous articles to profl. jours. and pubs. Planning coordinator Model Cities Commn., Worcester, 1968-70; planning bd. mem., Groton, 1981-87; mem. Downtown Devel. Task Force, Moscow, 1987—; Trustee Prichard Gallery, Moscow, 1987—. Served to 2d lt., 1959-61. Named HUD Residential Design winner Dept. HUD, Groton, 1979; recipient Honor award Pitts. chpt. AIA, 1980, Honor Design award N.E. Electric, Boston, 1985, Merit Desing award Roger Williams Coll., Briston, R.I., 1986. Mem. AIA, Assn. Collegiate Schs. of Arch, Nat. Council of Architecture Registrations Bds. Office: U Idaho Dept Architecture Moscow ID 83843

PIERCE, JAMES D(ENNIS), tax practitioner; b. L.A., Sept. 17, 1923; s. Dennis L. and Edna M. (James) P. AA, UCLA, 1947. Freelance writer Glendale, Calif., 1948-50; account exec. T.E. Parkhouse Advt., Glendale, 1951-54; investor, freelance writer Glendale, 1955-80, enrolled tax practitioner, fin. cons., 1981—; instr. Tax Counseling for the Elderly, Glendale, 1981—. Author: Adventures of Davy West, 1964, Shackle, 1965; contbr. articles to mags. Sgt. U.S. Army, 1942-45. Mem. Nat. Assn. Enrolled Agts., Calif. Soc. Enrolled Agts., Authors Guild of Authors League Am., Am. Legion. Republican. Office: 530 W Stocker St Glendale CA 91202

PIERCE, JAMES FRANKLIN, data systems consultant; b. Seaford, N.Y., Aug. 24, 1950; s. James Franklin and Marion April (Augustine) P.; m. Kit Lan Lee, July 4, 1980; 1 child, James Franklin. AAS, Olympic Coll., 1970; BSBA, U. Phoenix, 1984; BS, SUNY, 1984; MBA, U. Phoenix, 1986. Cert. systems profl. Cons. GTE-Informatics Co., N.Y.C., 1974-75, Frito-Lay Co., Dallas, 1976-77, Occidental Petroleum Co., Houston, 1977-78, Lockheed Missiles & Space Co., Sunnyvale, Calif., 1978-79; cons., owner Intel Corp., San Jose, Calif., 1979—. Mem. Republican Task Force. Mem. Assn. Systems Mgmt., ACM. Home and Office: 32807 Orick St Union City CA 94587

PIERCE, JEFFREY PAUL, engineer; b. Burbank, Calif., Aug. 27, 1963; s. Hubert Edward and Judith Jean (Heinecke) P. AS in Indsl. Tech., L.A. Valley Coll., 1984; BS in Indsl. Tech., Calif. State U., 1988. Cert. mfg. technologist, Calif. Producibility engr. Douglas Aircraft Co., Long Beach, Calif., 1987; methods engr. TRW Space and Defense Div., Redondo Beach, Calif., 1988—. Instr. Nat. Handicapped Sports and Recreation Assn. Mem. Soc. of Mfg. Engrs. (student vice chmn. 1987-88), TRW Bicycle Club, TRW Wilderness Club. Office: TRW 1 Space Park M3/1568 Redondo Beach CA 90278

PIERCE, JON PAGE, aluminum and chemical company executive, personnel administrator; b. Mobile, Ala., Oct. 26, 1940; s. Edwin Patterson and Teva (Jordan) P.; m. Sherry Kaye Hammack, July 18, 1964; children: Lesley, Julie, Brad. BS in Labor and Personnel Mgmt., U. Ala., 1963. Plant employee relations mgr. Kaiser Aluminum and Chem. Corp., Baton Rouge and Spokane, Wash., 1969-77; mgr. employee relations div. Kaiser Aluminum and Chem. Corp., Oakland, Calif., 1977-82, dir. compensation and benefits, 1982-85, personnel director, 1985-88, corp. officer, v.p. human resources, 1988—; instr. Dale Carnegie, Walnut Creek, Calif., 1979-80; adv. group Sr. Human Resources, San Francisco Bay, 1985-87. Bd. dirs., exec. com. United Crusade, Spokane, 1970-73, Baton Rouge, 1976; bd. dirs., mem. exec. com. Spokane C. of C., 1970-73, Jr. Achievement, 1970-73. Served to 1st lt. U.S. Army, 1963-65. Recipient Outstanding Alumnus award dept. mgmt. U. Ala., 1985. Mem. Western Pension Conf., Am. Mgmt. Assn., Am. Compensation Assn., Council on Employee Benefits, Sigma Chi (pres. 1962, Outstanding Mem. award 1963). Republican. Clubs: Sherwood Forest Country; Spokane; Lakeview (Oakland). Home: 8 Golden Hill Ct Walnut Creek CA 94596 Office: Kaiser Aluminum and Chem Corp 300 Lakeside Dr Oakland CA 94643

PIERCE, MONICA LU ANN, nurse; b. Granite City, Ill., Sept. 13, 1958; d. Lewis Ray and Peggy Ann (Stone) P. BSN, U. Tulsa, 1980; postgrad. in bus., Okla. State U., 1985-87. RN, Okla., Calif. Staff nurse Hillcrest Med. Ctr., Tulsa, 1980-83, asst. head nurse, 1983-87; staff nurse Hoag Meml. Hosp., Newport Beach, Calif., 1987—. Mem. Am. Assn. Critical Care Nurses (cert.), Nat. League for Nursing. Democrat. Jewish. Home: 18642 Libra Cir Huntington Beach CA 92646 Office: 301 Newport Blvd Newport Beach CA 92663

PIERCE, ROBERT L., petrochemical, oil and gas company executive. Chmn. and chief exec. officer Foothills Pipe Lines (Yukon) Ltd., Calgary, Alta., Can.; chmn. Pan-Alta. Gas.; dir. NOVA Corp. of Alta., Novacor Chemicals Ltd., Bank of N.S., Husky Oil Ltd. Mem. Can. C. of C. (bd. dirs.). Office: NOVA Corp Alta, 801 7th Ave SW PO Box 2535, Calgary, AB Canada T2P 2N6

PIERCE, SHANCY, casting director; b. L.A., Sept. 30, 1942; d. Warren Alfred and Loraine Rice (Potter) P. BA, Calif. State U., Northridge, 1979. Animation Walt Disney Studios, L.A., 1961-62; acctg. Universal Pictures, L.A., 1962-65; negative assembly Technicolor Studios, L.A., 1966-72; royalties ABC/Dunhill Records, L.A., 1970-72; talent coord. Dick Clark Teleshows, L.A., 1972-73; royalties Henry Mancini, L.A., 1973-75; TV spot buying rep. Salowitz Orgn., L.A., 1975-77; casting dir. Spungbuggy Works, L.A., 1977-82; owner Slate Please Casting, L.A., 1982—. Mem. Comml. Casting Dir. Assn. (sec. 1987—), Acad. of TV Arts and Scis., Calif. State U. Northridge Alumni Assn. (pres. 1986-87). Republican. Office: Slate Please Casting 3917 Riverside Dr 9109 Burbank CA 91505

PIERCY, GORDON CLAYTON, banker; b. Takoma Park, Md., Nov. 23, 1944; s. Gordon Clayton and Dorothy Florence (Brummer) P.; B.S., Syracuse U., 1966; M.B.A., Pace U., 1973; m. Roberta Margaret Walton, 1985; children: Elizabeth Anne, Kenneth Charles, Virginia Walton. Mgmt. trainee Suburban Bank, Bethesda, Md., 1962-66; mktg. planning asso. Chem. Bank, N.Y.C., 1966-70; sr. market devel. officer Seattle-First Nat. Bank, 1970-74; product expansion adminstr., mktg. planning mgr. Nat. BankAmericard, Inc., San Francisco, 1974-76; v.p., dir. mktg. Wash. Mut. Savs. Bank, Seattle, 1976-82; v.p., mktg. dir. First Interstate Bank of Wash. N.A., 1983-86; v.p. mktg., dir. Puget Sound Nat. Bank, Tacoma, 1986—. Mem. Am. Mktg. Assn., Bank Mktg. Assn., Mktg. Communications Execs. Internat., Seattle Advt. Fedn., Am. Bankers Assn. (retail electronic services and bank card div., exec. com.), Sigma Nu, Alpha Kappa Psi, Delta Mu Delta. Episcopalian. Home: 23632 SE 225th St Maple Valley WA 98038 Office: PO Box 2076 Tacoma WA 98401

PIERCY, JOHN PHILIP, environmental engineer; b. Monterey, Calif., May 24, 1931; s. Philip Henderson and Mary Fredrica (Fauth) P.; m. Edeltrand Margarete Wlosinski, Apr. 23, 1955; 1 child, Michael John. BCE, Santa Clara U., 1953; MS, U. Minn., 1962. Diplomate Am. Acad. Environ. Engrs. Commd. 1st lt. U.S. Army, 1960; sanitary engr. U.S. Army, France, 1953-56; asst. city engr. City of Tracy (Calif.), 1956-58; pub. works dir. City of Vacaville (Calif.), 1958-60; sanitary engr. U.S. Army, 1960-79; pub works asst. dir. City of Berkeley (Calif.), 1979-81; project mgr. Engring. Sci. Berkeley, Calif., 1981-82; chief engr. Brugge & Percy Assoc., Sacramento, Calif., 1982—; advance through grades to col. Brugge & Percy Assoc.; cons. in field, 1982--. Commr. Solid Waste Mgmt. Commn., Berkely, Calif., 1981-83. Col. U.S. Army, 1953-56, 1960-79. Fellow Am. Soc. Civil Engrs.; mem. Conf. Fed. Environ. Engrs. (pres. 1975-76), Soc. Am. Military Engrs, Kiwanis. Republican. Roman Catholic. Home: 1040 Park Hills Rd Berkeley CA 94708 Office: Brugge & Piercy Assoc 4647 American River Dr Sacramento CA 95864

PIERSON, PAUL EVERETT, seminary dean, history educator; b. L.A., Feb. 13, 1927; s. Daniel and Pearl Lena (Frost) P.; m. Rosemary Aliene Lucksinger, July 2, 1950; children: Stephen Paul, Kathryn Aliene, Stanley Frederick, David Jonathan. BS, U. Calif., Berkeley, 1949; BD, Princeton Theol. Sem., 1954, PhD, 1971. Ordained to ministry Presbyn. Ch., 1954. Engr. Colgate Palmolive Peet Co., Berkeley, 1950; asst. pastor First Presbyn. Ch., Orange, N.J., 1954-55; pastor Presbyn. Ch., Corumba, Brazil, 1957-60; vis. prof. Bapt. Sem. North, Recife, Brazil, 1969-70; prof. ch. history and missions Presbyn. Sem. North, Recife, 1961-70; prof. Evang. Sem., Lisbon, Portugal, 1971-73; pastor First Presbyn. Ch., Fresno, Calif., 1973-80; dean, prof. history Sch. World Mission Fuller Theol. Sem., Pasadena, Calif., 1980—. Author: A Younger Church, Themes From Acts. V. Chmn. bd. trustees Latin Am. Mission, Miami, Fla., 1984—; pres., mem. exec. coun. World Impact, L.A., 1978—; trustee Overseas Crusades, Milpitas, Calif., 1985—, Frontier Laborers, Denver, 1987—. With USNR, 1945-46. Mem. Am. Soc. Missiology, Assn. Prof. Missions. Democrat. Office: Fuller Theol Sem 135 N Oakland Pasadena CA 91182

PIES, RONALD E., city official; b. Rochester, N.Y., Mar. 21, 1940; s. Herman S. and Sylvia P.; m. Bernita Orloff, Aug. 27, 1964; children—Cara Jean, David Paul; B.S., Ariz. State U., 1963. Recreation leader City of Phoenix, Ariz., 1962-64; head recreation div. City of Scottsdale (Ariz.) Parks and Recreation Dept., 1964-69; dir. parks and recreation, City of Tempe, Ariz., 1969-84, community services dir., 1984—; guest lectr. Ariz. State U. Mem., pres. Kyrene Sch. Dist. Governing Bd., 1979-82. Chmn., bd. regents Pacific Revenue Sources Mgmt. Sch. NRPA; gen. chmn. Fiesta Bowl Soccer Classic, 1982—; founding mem. Tempe YMCA bd. mgrs.; appointed mem. Ariz. State Parks Bd., 1987—. Named Outstanding Young Man, Jaycees; recipient superior service mngt. award Am. Soc. for Pub. Adminstrn., Ariz. chpt., 1988 . Mem. Tempe C. of C., Ariz. Parks and Recreation Assn. (bd. dirs. 1986—, pres. adminstrs., Disting. Fellow award 1983), Nat. Recreation and Parks Assn., Sigma Alpha Epsilon. Club: Tempe Diablos. Office: 3500 S Rural Rd Tempe AZ 85282

PIETRZYK, DIANA LYNN, personnel director; b. Chgo., Dec. 13, 1956; d. John Richard and Beverly Ann (Mitchell) P. Student, Robert Morris Coll., 1975. Retail mgmt. various corps., Chgo., 1975-87; nat. account mgr. Adolph Coors Co., Golden, Colo., 1985-87, Laguna Hills, Calif., 1987-88; branch mgr. Adia Personnel Svcs., Anaheim, Calif., 1988—. Chmn. U.S. Ski Team Ednl. Found., Denver, 1984-87, Newport Beach, Calif., 1988; com. mem. Jr. League of Denver, 1986-87, Jr. League of Orange County, Newport Beach, Calif., 1988-89. Mem. Personnel and Indsl. Relations Assn., Anaheim C. of C., Young Republicans. Office: Adia Personnel Svcs 225 S Harbor 200 Ste 200 Anaheim CA 92801

PIETTE, LAWRENCE HECTOR, biophysicist, educator, university dean and official; b. Chgo., Jan. 4, 1932; s. Gerald John and Lillian (Bumgardner) P.; m. Mary Irene Harris, Aug. 15, 1957; children—Jeffrey, Martin. B.S., Northwestern U., 1953, M.S., 1954; Ph.D., Stanford U., 1957. Mgr. research biochemistry and biophysics Varian Assos., 1956-65; prof. biophysics U. Hawaii, 1965—, chmn. dept., 1968—, dir. Cancer Research Lab., 1970-84; exec. dir. Cancer Center Hawaii, 1974; Chmn. cancer adv. com., regional med. program, research com. Hawaii div. Am. Cancer Soc.; dean. Sch. Grad. Studies Utah State U., Logan, 1984—; assoc. v.p. research Utah State U., 1984—, prof. biochemistry, 1984—. Contbr. articles to profl. jours.; Asso. editor: Jour. Organic Magnetic Resonance. Mem. Am. Chem. Soc., Biophys. Soc., A.A.U.P. Home: 363 Boulevard Logan UT 84321

PIGOTT, CHARLES MCGEE, transportation equipment manufacturer; b. Seattle, Apr. 21, 1929; s. Paul and Theiline (McGee) P.; m. Yvonne Flood, Apr. 18, 1953. B.S., Stanford U., 1951. With PACCAR Inc, Seattle, 1959—, exec. v.p., 1962-65, pres., 1965-86, chmn., pres., 1986-87, chmn., chief exec. officer, 1987—, also bd. dirs.; dir. Boeing Co., Citibank/Citicorp, Chevron Corp. Pres. Nat. Boy Scouts Am., 1986-88, mem. exec. bd. Mem. Bus. Council. Office: PACCAR Inc 777 106th Ave NE PO Box 1518 Bellevue WA 98004 *

PIHLAJA, MAXINE MURIEL MEAD, orchestra executive; b. Windom, Minn., July 19, 1935; d. Julian Wright and Mildred Eleanor (Ray) Mead; m. Donald Francis Pihlaja, Jan. 4, 1963; children: Geoffrey Blake, Kirsten Louise, Jocelyn Erika. BA, Hamline U., 1957; postgrad., Columbia U., 1957-58. Group worker Fedn. of Chs., L.A., 1956; case worker St. John's Guild Floating Hosp. Ship, N.Y.C., 1957-59; Y-Teen program dir. YWCA, Elizabeth, N.J., 1957-60, Boulder, Colo., 1964-65; spl. svcs. program and club dir. U.S. Army, Ingrandes and Nancy, France, 1960-62; music buyer, salesperson Guinn's Music, Billings, Mont., 1977-78, N.W. Music, Billings, 1978-79; office adminstr. Am. Luth. Ch., Billings, 1979-84; mgr. Billings Symphony Soc., 1984—; substitute tchr. Community Day Care and Enrichment Ctr., Billings, 1971-76. Dir. handbell choir 1st Presbyn. Ch., Billings, 1972—, Am. Luth. Ch., 1981-84, 1st English Luth. Ch., 1982—; mem. Billings Symphony Chorale, 1965—, bellissimo!, 1983—. Mem. Nat. Soc. for Fund Raising Execs. (sec. Mont. 1988), Mont. Assn. Female Execs., Am. Guild of English Handbell Ringers (state chair 1988—), Mont. Assn. Symphony Orchs. (treas. 1987—). Lutheran. Office: Billings Symphony Orch 104 N Broadway Ste 403 PO Box 602 Billings MT 59103

PIIRTO, DOUGLAS DONALD, forester, educator; b. Reno, Nev., Sept. 25, 1948; s. Rueben Arvid and Martha Hilma (Giebel) P.; BS, U. Nev., 1970; MS, Colo. State U., 1971; PhD, U. Calif., Berkeley, 1977; m. Mary Louise Cruz, Oct. 28, 1978. Rsch. asst. Colo. State U., 1970-71, U. Calif., Berkeley, 1972-77; forester, silviculturist U.S. Dept. Agr., Forest Svc., Sierra Nat. Forest, Trimmer and Shaver Lake, Calif., 1977-85; assoc. prof. natural resources mgmt. dept. Calif. Poly. State U., San Luis Obispo, 1985—; researcher in field; instr. part-time Kings River Community Coll., Reedley, Calif. Registered profl. forester, Calif.; cert. silviculturist U.S. Forest Svc. Recipient Meritorious Performance and Profl. Promise award CalPoly, 1989. Mem. Soc. Am. Foresters, Am. Forestry Assn., Forest Products Rsch. Soc., Soc. Wood Sci. and Tech., Alpha Zeta, Xi Sigma Pi, Sigma Xi, Beta Beta Beta, Phi Sigma Kappa. Lutheran. Contbr. articles to sci. and forestry jours. Home: 7605 El Retiro Ave Atascadero CA 93422 Office: Calif Poly State U Dept Natural Resources Mgmt San Luis Obispo CA 93710

PIKE, DOUGLAS EUGENE, Indochina studies director; b. Cass Lake, Minn., July 27, 1924; s. Clarence Eugene and Esther (Jensen) P.; m. Myrna Louise Johnson, Sept. 15, 1956; children: Andrew Jefferson, Victoria Louise, Ethan Edward. BA, U. Calif., 1953; MA, Am. U., 1961; postgrad., MIT, 1963-64. Writer UN, Korea, 1950-52; fgn. service officer U.S. Govt. State Dept., Washington, Saigon, Hong Kong, Tokyo, and Taipei, Taiwan., 1958-82; dir. Indochina Studies Program, U. Calif., Berkeley, 1982—. Author: Viet Cong: The Organizational Techniques of the National Liberation Front of South Vietnam, 1965, War, Peace and the Viet Cong, 1969, History of Vietnamese Communism, 1978, PAVN: People's Army of Vietnam, 1986, Vietnam and the USSR: Anatomy of an Alliance, 1987; editor: Indochina Chronology, 1983—; contbr. numerous articles to profl. jours. Bd. dir. Vietnam Refugee Assn., Washington, 1975-82. Recipient Surperior Honor award, U.S. Info. Agy., 1976, Sec. Def. medal, U.S. Dept. Def., 1981. Mem. Author's Guild, Army-Navy Club (Washington), Fgn. Service Club, Faculty Club U. Calif. Methodist. Home: 2265 Alva Ave El Cerrito CA 94530 Office: U Calif 6701 San Pablo Ave Berkeley CA 94720

PIKE, GARY, public relations specialist; b. Sacramento, Calif., June 23, 1954; s. Leslie Harold and Doris Charmion (Parker) P. BA in Communications, Resource Mgmt., Calif. State U., Sacramento, 1977. Field services dir. Animal Protection Inst., Sacramento, 1977-78; adminstrv. analyst Calif. Conservation Corp., Sacramento, 1978; Great Lakes regional dir. Animal Protection Inst., Chgo., 1978-80; adminstrv. analyst Calif. Coastal Commn., San Francisco, 1980; dir. pub. relations Victoria's Secret, San Francisco, 1980-82; pres. Pike Communications, San Francisco, 1982—. Mem. Pub. Relations Soc. Am. (accredited), Pub. Relations Roundtable, Small Bus. Council, San Francisco C. of C., Ambassador Club. Democrat. Presbyterian. Office: Pike Communications 685 Market St Ste 300 San Francisco CA 94105

PIKE, ROBERT CLIFTON, real estate executive; b. Oakland, Calif., Dec. 8, 1936; s. Thomas Clifton and Nedra (Lamborn) P.; m. Deanna Lee Fulmer, June 21, 1959; 1 child, Ty Clifton. Student, Brigham Young U., 1954-55, Fresno (Calif.)Jr. Coll., 1959-60. With Nat. Literary Assocs., 1955-57, Chanslor & Lyon, Fresno, Calif., 1958-59, O'Dell Constrn. Co., Sanora, Calif., 1960-62; constrn. supr. various cos. various locations, 1962-74; with Red Carpet Realty, San Diego, 1975-78; office mgr. Realty World, San Diego, 1978-80; property mgr. E.R.A. United, San Diego, 1980-85; owner/mgr. 1st Coast Realty Svcs., Del Mar, Calif., 1985-88, Realty Club, San Diego, 1988—. Fund raiser Muscular Dystrophy Assn., San Diego, 1982. Recipient Community Achievement award, Lions, 1984-85, 82-84, others. Mem. San Diego Bd. Realtors, San Diego Apt. Owners Assn., Lions (pres. 1980-81). Office: Realty Club 9524 Kearny Villa Rd #201 San Diego CA 92126

PIKE, RONALD SCOTT, hospital executive; b. Pueblo, Colo., Feb. 12, 1949; s. Lisle Osborn and Hildred Eugene (Watkins) P.; m. Karen Louise Swartz, Aug. 13, 1972; children: Justin M., Ryan W. BA in Edn., So. Colo. State Coll., 1971; MA in Counseling, U. Colo., 1978; MA in Mgmt., U. Phoenix, Colorado Springs, Colo., 1989. Cert. tchr., Colo.; counseling cert. Tchr. Harrison Sch. Dist. #2, Colorado Springs, 1971-78, Pueblo (Colo.) Sch. Dist. #60, 1978-81; prodn. engr. CF&I Steel Corp., Pueblo, 1982; tchr. Acadamy Sch. Dist. #20, Colorado Springs, 1982-83; dir. edn. and training St. Mary-Corwin Hosp., Pueblo, 1983—. Bd. mem. Pueblo Sch. Dist. #60, 1987—, bd. pres., 1989; coun. mem. Pueblo Com. Coll. Vocation Adv., 1987—, Vocat. Edn. Pueblo Sch. Dist. #60, 1985-88; participant, grad. Leadership Pueblo, 1985. With USAR, 1971-77. Mem. Am. Soc. for Training and Devel., Am. Soc. Health Care Edn. and Training, Am. Assn. Sch. Adminstr., Colo. Wrestling Ofcls. Assn., Kiwanis, Pueblo. Republican. Baptist. Home: 5 Mayweed Ct Pueblo CO 81001

PILE, JOHN EDWARD, educational administrator; b. Charleston, W. Va., June 27, 1947; s. John Willis and Edith (Estep) P.; m. Barbara Charlotte Herold, Jan. 2, 1971; children: John Edward Jr., Jill Suzanne, Michael Wayne, Kari Willow. BS in Secondary Edn., Concord Coll., 1970; MA in Reading Edn., Marshall U., 1973, prin.'s cert., 1974. Cert. reading tchr., elem. prin., elem. tchr., social studies tchr., W. Va. Vol. VISTA, Washington, 1966-68; elem. tchr. Monroe County bd. Edn., Union, W. Va., 1971, 73-76; prin. Monroe County bd. Edn., Union, 1973-80; elem. tchr. Clay County Bd. Edn., Clay, W. Va., 1971-73; reading tchr. Fairbanks (Alaska) North Star Sch. Dist., 1980-83; prin. Emily Ivenoff Tieasuk Brown Elem. Sch., 1983—; pub. speaker Roast Internat., Fairbanks. Named Educator of Yr. State of Alaska PTA, 1989. Mem. Nat. Prins. Assn., Fairbanks Prins. Assn. (sec. 1986-87,), Rotary. Democrat. Methodist. Home: 2615 Lisa Ann Dr North Pole AK 99705 Office: PO Box 1250 Fairbanks AK 99707

PILKINGTON, MARCILLE, medical equipment manufacturing company executive; b. Lewiston, Idaho, Apr. 9, 1958; d. Howard Lawrence and Sophia Marguerite Jungert Pilkington. Co-owner Behrend's Interiors, Tucson, 1978-80; asst. mgr. Spaghetti Co., Tucson, 1980-82; bus. broker V.R. Bus. Brokers, Tucson, 1982-85; br. mgr. Harris Lanier, Tucson, 1985-86; asst. to pres. JMJ Co, Tucson, 1986—; program dir. Internat. Forums in Medicine, Tucson, 1987—, also bd. dirs. Author: (poetry) Ramblings of an Average American Woman, 1987. counselor Rape Crisis Ctr. of Ariz., 1982; advocate Girls Ranch of Ariz., 1984, 85. Recipient Pres.'s Honor Scholarship U.S. Govt., 1976, Ann. Sales award Jr. Bus. Brokers, 1983, 84. Mem. Meeting Planners Internat., Smithsonian Inst. Republican. Office: JMJ Co 1200 E Ajo Ste 109 Tucson AZ 85713

PILL, JEFFREY MACLIN, television and film producer; b. Le Mars, Iowa, Oct. 12, 1942; s. Edward and Dorothy (Kushner) P. BA, U. Iowa, 1964, MA, 1969. Producer/writer CBS News, Chgo., 1969-71; producer/dir./writer Sports Action Profile, Chgo., 1971-73, David Wolper Prodns., Los Angeles, 1974-78; series producer Alan Landsburg Prodns. "In Search of...", Los Angeles, 1978-80; sr. producer ABC News 20/20, N.Y.C., 1980-81; pres. Pill Enterprises, Inc., Los Angeles, 1981—. Author/editor: Larry Mahan's Rodeo, 1972. Served to lt. USNR, 1964-67. Mem. Nat. Acad. TV Arts and Scis., Writers Guild of Am. Home: 117 S Doheny Dr #209 Los Angeles CA 90048

PILLAR, CHARLES LITTLEFIELD, mining consultant; b. Denver, May 25, 1911; s. Charles and Alice May (Littlefield) P.; m. Elizabeth Reed Broadhead, Sept. 10, 1932 (div. May 1939); m. 2d Gwendola Elizabeth Lotz, Sept. 16, 1939; children: Ann, Catherine, Pamela. Engr. mines, Colo. Sch. Mines, 1935. Registered profl. engr., B.C., Ariz. Various positions in field, 1935-75; mine cons. Pillar, Lowell & Assocs., Tucson, Ariz., 1976-83; cons. Bechtel Corp., San Francisco, 1976-79, Fluor Corp., Redwood City, Calif., 1979-83; mem. Colo. Sch. Mines Rsch. Inst., Golden, 1975-83, pvt. practice Tucson, 1985-89; dir. Internat. Geosystems Corp., Vancouver, B.C. Contbr. articles to profl. jours. Capt. USAF, 1942-45. Mem. AIME (William Saunders Gold Medal award, Disting. mem. award), Can. Inst. Mining and Metallurgy, Profl. Engrs. B.C., U.S. Senatorial Club, Vancouver Club, Tucson Nat. Country Club. Republican. Episcopalian. Home: 9460 N Camino Del Plata Tucson AZ 85741 Office: Mining Cons 5115 N Oracle Rd Tucson AZ 85704

PILLING, STEVE PAUL, telecommunications consultant; b. Decatur, Ill., July 23, 1958; s. Frank E. and Lauri Lee (Riesland) P.; m. Patti Verna Crow, Apr. 20, 1985. BS, Millikin U., 1980; MBA, Nat. U., 1984. Sales rep. Burroughs Corp., Decatur, 1981, Starnet, San Diego, Calif., 1981-86; regional mgr. Com System, Newport, Calif., 1986; pres., cons. Telecom Cons., San Diego, 1986—; v.p. Le Tip, San Diego, 1982—. Mem. Soc. Telecommunications Cons., San Diego C. of C. Home: 5413 Escharchosa Ln San Diego CA 92124 Office: Telecom Cons 10615G Tierrasanta Blvd Ste 123 San Diego CA 92124

PILLOW, RANDOLPH PRESTON, medical consultant; b. Roanoke, Va., Jan. 18, 1921; s. Robert Allen and Caroline (Herr) P. BA, U. Va., 1942, MD, 1944. Diplomate Am. Bd. Internal Med. Intern Va. Mason Hosp., Seattle, 1944-45; resident U. Va. Hosp., Seattle, 1945-46; asst. to chief med. U. Va. Hosp., Charlottesville, 1948-49; physician and ptnr. The Va. Mason Clinic, Seattle, 1949-86; pres. of staff, Va. Mason Hosp., Seattle, 1960-61; clin. instr. U. Wash. Med. Sch., Seattle, 1950-86. Mem. Seattle Found., 1975—; v.p. Greater Seattle, 1966-68; bd. dirs. Japan Am. Soc., Seattle, 1988—. With M.C., U.S. Army, 1946-47, M.C., USAF, 1953. Fellow Am. Coll. Physicians; mem. Internat. Soc. Hemotology, King County Med. Soc., AMA, Wash. Athletic Club (pres. 1976-77), U. Club, Phi Beta Kappa, Alpha Omega Alpha. Home: 3801 E Highland Dr Seattle WA 98112 Office: PO Box 900 Seattle WA 98101

PIMIENTA, GILBERT, anesthesiologist; b. L.A., Mar. 14, 1957; s. Ruben G. and Esther (Ojeda) P. AA, El Camino Coll., 1977; BS, U. Calif., Irvine, 1979; MD, U. Calif., San Diego, 1984. Intern in internal medicine Good Samaritan Med. Ctr., Phoenix, 1984-85; resident in anesthesiology Maricopa County Med. Ctr., Phoenix, 1985-87; pvt. practice Phoenix, 1987--. Mem. AMA, Internat. Anesthesia Rsch. Soc., Am. Soc. Anesthesiologists. Home: PO Box 10332 Phoenix AZ 85064 Office: 2950 N 7th St Phoenix AZ 85014

PINDER, JOAN LOUISE, chemist; b. Whittier, Calif., Dec. 29, 1956; d. Robert Cecil and Lola Louise (Gray) P. Student, U. Manchester, Eng., 1977-78; BS in Chem. with honors, Calif. State U., San Luis Obispo, 1979; MBA, U. Phoenix, 1986. Assoc. staff Raychem Co., Menlo Park, Calif., 1979-82; product engr. Cybernex Co., San Jose, Calif., 1982-87; product mgr. Domain Tech. Co., Milpitas, Calif., 1987; mktg. mgr. Censtor Co., San Jose, 1988—. V.p., Colony Green Homeowners Assn., San Jose, 1987—. Mem. Am. Chem. Soc., Alpha Phi. Office: Censtor Co 530 Race St San Jose CA 95126

PINDER, MICHAEL JAMES, sales executive; b. Portland, Oreg., Dec. 7, 1958; s. Robert Harold and Joann Janet (Ellis) P. BS in Bus. Adminstrn., Portland State U., 1982. Salesperson The Unisource Corp., Portland, 1983—. Republican. Roman Catholic.

PINE, CHARLES JOSEPH, clinical psychologist; b. Excelsior Springs, Mo., July 13, 1951; s. Charles E. and LaVern (Upton) P.; m. Mary Day, Dec. 30, 1979; children: Charles Andrew, Joseph Scott, Carolyn Marie. BA in Psychology, U. Redlands, 1973; MA, Calif. State U.-Los Angeles, 1975; PhD, U. Wash., 1979; postdoctoral UCLA, 1980-81. Lic. psychologist, Calif. Psychology technician Seattle Indian Health Bd., USPHS Hosp., 1977-78; psychology intern VA Outpatient Clinic, Los Angeles, 1978-79; instr. psychology Okla. State U., 1979-80, asst. prof., 1980; asst. prof. psychology and native Am. studies program Wash. State U., 1981-82; dir. behavioral health services Riverside-San Bernardino County Indian Health Inc., Banning, Calif., 1982-84; clin. psychologist, clin. co-dir. Inland Empire Behavioral Assocs., Colton, Calif., 1982-84; clin. psychologist VA Med. Ctr., Long Beach, Calif., 1984-85; clin. psychologist, psychology coordinator Psychiatry div. VA Med. Ctr., Sepulveda, Calif., 1985—; clin. dir. Traumatic Stress Treatment Ctr., Thousand Oaks, Calif., 1985—; asst. clin. prof. UCLA Sch. Medicine, 1985—, Fuller Grad. Sch. Psychology, Pasadena, Calif., 1985—; mem. Los Angeles County Am. Indian Mental Health task force, 1987—. Editorial cons. White Cloud Jour., 1982-85; cons. Dept. Health and Human Services, USPHS, NIMH, 1980. Vol. worker Variety Boys Clubs Am., 1973-75; coach Rialto Jr. All-Am. Football League, 1974, Conejo Youth Flag Football Assn., Conejo Valley Little League. U. Wash. Inst. Indian Studies grantee, 1975-76, UCLA Inst. Am. Cultures grantee, 1981-82; fellow Menninger Found. Mem. Am. Psychol. Assn. (chair task force on service delivery to ethnic minority populations bd. ethnic minority affairs 1988—, bd. ethnic minority affairs 1985-87), Soc. Indian Psychologists (pres. 1981-83), Western Psychol. Assn., AAAS, Calif. State Psychol. Assn., N.Y. Acad. Sci., Soc. for Psychol. Study Ethnic Minority Issues (exec. com. 1987-88), Sigma Alpha Epsilon. Republican. Baptist. Contbr. psychol. articles to profl. lit. Home: 2379 Sirius St Thousand Oaks CA 91360 Office: VA Med Ctr Psychology Service 116B 16111 Plummer St Sepulveda CA 91343

PINEDA, MICHAEL EDWARD, teacher; b. National City, Calif., Jan. 30, 1949; s. Edward Eugene and Betty Ruth (Lewis) P.; m. Sandra Marie Clifton, Dec. 16, 1972. BA in Social Scis., San Diego State U., 1972, MEd, 1976, MS in Counseling, 1985. Tchr. learning handicapped San Diego Unified Sch. Dist., 1974; tchr. learning handicapped Sweetwater Union High Sch. Dist., Chula Vista, Calif., 1974-79, tchr. severely disturbed, 1980, resource specialist, 1980-85, coord. Plato Ind. Ctr., 1985-88, tchr. nonseverely handicapped, 1988—. Editor The Forum, 1979-83. Advisor Rotary Interact. Chula Vista High Sch., 1974-80. Mem. Council Exceptional Children (bd. mem. 1981-84, chmn. legis. action 1983-84), San Diego Assn. Counseling and Devel. (pres. 1985-86, bd. mem. 1983-85), Calif. Assn. Counseling and Devel., Assn. Calif. Sch. Adminstrs., Phi Delta Kappa, Mensa. Home: 4095 Bonita Rd #228 Bonita CA 92002 Office: Sweetwater Union High Sch 1130 5th Ave Chula Vista CA 92011

PINGS, ANTHONY CLAUDE, architect; b. Fresno, Calif., Dec. 16, 1951; s. Clarence Hubert and Mary (Murray) P.; m. Carole Clements, June 25, 1983. AA, Fresno City Coll., 1972; BArch, Calif. Poly. State U., San Luis Obispo, 1976. Lic. architect, Calif.; cert. Nat. Council Archtl. Registration Bds. Architect Aubrey Moore Jr., Fresno, 1976-81; architect, prin. Anthony C. Pings, AIA, Fresno, 1981-83, 86—, Pings-Taylor Assocs., Fresno, 1983-85. Prin. works include Gollaher Profl. Office (Masonry Merit award 1985, Best Office Bldg. award 1986), Fresno Imaging Ctr. (Best Institutional Project award 1986, Nat. Healthcare award Modern Health Care mag. 1986), Orthopedic Facility (award of honor Masonry Inst. 1987, award of merit San Joaquin chpt. AIA 1987). Mem. Calif. Indsl. Tech. Edn. Consortium Calif. State Dept. Edn., 1983, 84. Mem. AIA (bd. dirs. Calif. chpt. 1983-84, v.p. San Joaquin chpt. 1982, pres. 1983, Calif. Council evaluation team 1983, team leader Coalinga Emergency Design Assistance team). Democrat. Home: 4350 N Safford Ave Fresno CA 93704 Office: Anthony C Pings AIA 1640 W Shaw Ste 107 Fresno CA 93711

PINHOLSTER, MICHAEL DANIEL, dentist; b. Trenton, N.J., May 2, 1960; s. Daniel Elvin Pinholster and Lillian Teresa (Simmons) Richart; divorced. BS in Biology, N.Mex. State U., 1982; DDS, U. Mo., 1986. Gen. practice dentistry Sherwood Dental Ctr., Midland, Tex., 1986-87; prvt. practice dentistry Las Cruces, N. Mex., 1987--. Mem. ADA, N. Mex. Dental Assn. Republican. Methodist. Home: 301 N Roadrunner Pkwy #701 Las Cruces NM 88001 Office: Michael D Pinholster DDS 1201 Medical Park Dr Las Cruces NM 88005

PINNELL, ROBERT PEYTON, chemistry educator; b. Fresno, Calif., Dec. 5, 1938; s. Paul Peyton and Iris Ione (Shepherd) P.; m. Sharron Lyne Gregory, Aug. 18, 1962; children: Jason Peyton, Sabrina Lyne. BS, Calif. State U., Fresno, 1960; PhD, U. Kansas, 1964. Postdoctoral fellow U. Tex., Austin, 1964-66; asst. prof. chemistry Claremont (Calif.) McKenna Coll., Scripps Coll. and Pitzer Coll., 1966-72, assoc. prof., 1972-78, prof., 1978—, chmn. joint sci. dept., 1974-77; rsch. affilate Jet Propulsion Lab., 1986—, vis. assoc. prof. chemistry Calif. Inst. Tech., 1973-74. Postdoctoral fellow U. Calif. at Santa Barbara, 1980-81, NASA-Am. Soc. for Engring. Edn. fellow, 1982, 83, 86, 87. Mem. Nat. Sci. Tchrs. Assn., Am. Assn. for the Advancement Sci., Am. Chem. Soc., Calif. Assn. Chemistry Tchrs., Sigma Xi. Democrat. Office: Claremont McKenna Scripps & Pitzer Colls Joint Sci Dept Claremont CA 91711

PINNOW, ARNO LEE, quality assurance executive; b. Milw., July 21, 1941; s. Roy Lee and Lila Viola (Uphoff) P.; m. Leta Sheila Williams, Dec. 28, 1963; children: Christopher Gene, Marjorie Lee. BS in Chem. Engring., Ill. Inst. Tech., 1964. Registered profl. engr., Ill. Mgr. systems and tng. Amp-vial project Abbott Labs., North Chicago, Ill., 1971-72, mfg. quality mgr. Hosp. div., Rocky Mount, N.C., 1972-74, sect. mgr. quality audits, North Chicago, 1974-77, ops. mgr. quality evaluation, 1977-82; dir. quality assurance Hollister, Inc., Libertyville, Ill., 1981-85; mgr. quality engring. Advanced Cardiovascular Systems subs. Eli Lilly & Co., Temecula, Calif., 1985-88; mgr. quality assurance Medtronic Versaflex, San Diego, Calif., 1989—; dist. mgr. A.L. Williams Assocs., San Diego, 1988—; distbr., Nat. Safety Assocs., San Diego, 1988—; cons. in field, 1984-85, 88—. Patentee in field. Judge Sci. Fair Gurnee Schs., 1968-70; leader Boy Scouts Am., 1959-77; mem. ch. council Lutheran Chs., Waukegan, Ill., 1971-73, Rocky Mount, N.C., 1971-73, Fallbrook, Calif., 1989—; mem. Citizens Adv. Bd. Warren Twp. High Sch., Gurnee, 1979-81. Mem. Nat. Soc. Profl. Engrs. Calif. Soc. Profl. Engrs., Am. Soc. Quality Control, Am. Prodn. and Inventory Control Soc., Am. Inst. Chem. Engrs., Marquetry Soc. Am., Woodworkers Assn. N.Am., Pi Kappa Phi, Alpha Phi Omega. Lutheran. Avocations: woodworking, stained glass, construction, locksmithing, landscaping. Home: 1619 Ranchwood Ln Fallbrook CA 92028-4358

PINOLA, JOSEPH JOHN, banker; b. Pittston, Pa., May 13, 1925; m. Doris Jean Walker; children: Mary, James. B.A. in Econs, Bucknell U., 1949; postgrad., Dartmouth Coll., 1960; A.M.P., Harvard U., 1971; H.L.D., Wilkes Coll., 1978. With Bank of Am., 1953-76, sr. v.p., 1970-74, exec. v.p. N.Am. div., 1974-76; pres., dir. United Calif. Bank, 1976-77; dir. First Interstate Bancorp. (formerly Western Bancorp.), L.A., 1977—; chmn., chief exec. officer First Interstate Bancorp. (formerly Western Bancorp.), 1978—; bd. dirs. First Interstate Bank Wash., First Interstate Bank Calif., Lockheed Corp., SCEcorp, SCEcorp, So. Calif. Edison Co. Mem. adv. bd. Salvation Army, Los Angeles; campaign chmn. L.A. Area United Way, 1981-82; chmn. bd. govs. Music Ctr. L.A. County. With USNR. Mem. Assn. Res. City Bankers, Calif. Club, L.A. Country Club. Office: First Interstate Bancorp 707 Wilshire Blvd Los Angeles CA 90017

PINSON, LARRY LEE, pharmacist; b. Van Nuys, Calif., Dec. 5, 1947; s. Leland J.and Audrey M. (Frett) P.; m. Margaret K., Mar. 18, 1972; children: Scott C., Kelly E. AA, Am. River Coll., Sacramento, 1969; PharmD, U. Calif., San Francisco, 1973. Staff pharmacist/asst. dir. pharm. svcs. St. Mary's Hosp., Reno, 1973-77; chief pharmacist May Ang Base USAF, 1973-77; owner/chief pharmacist Silverada Pharmacy, Reno, 1979--; cons. pharmacist Physicians Hosp., 1974--, Reno Med. Plaza, 1973--; pharmacist coordinator Intensive Pharm. Svcs., 1986-87; cons. Calif. Dept. Health & Corrections, Susanville, 1975-76, Nev. Med. Care Adv. Bd., Carson City, 1984-87; provider and reviewer Nev. State Bd. Pharmacy, Reno, 1975-84; instr. We. Nev. Community Coll., 974-76; cons. Rural Calif. Hosp. Assn., 1973-74. Co-author: Care of Hickman Catheter, 1984. Mem. Nev. Arthritis Found.; bd. dirs. Am. Cancer Soc., 1986--; softball coach Reno/Sparks Recreation Dept.l 1973--; cubmaster Pack 153, Verdi, Nev. Recipient Bow of Hygeia award (Pharmacist of the Year), 1984. Mem. Nev. Pharmacists Assn. (pres. 1981-82), Am. Pharm. Assn., Nev. Profl. Standards Rev. Orgn., Greater Nev. Health Sys. Agy., Kappa Psi. Home: PO Box 478 Verdi NV 89439 Office: Silverada Pharmacy 2005 Silverada Blvd #160 Reno NV 89520

PINTA, WANDA BOHAN (MRS. R. JACK PINTA), home economist; b. Greenfield, Ia., Sept. 11, 1918; d. Edward Philip and Stella (Plymesser) Bohan; B.S., Ia. State U., 1943; postgrad. Los Angeles State Coll., 1956-59; m. R. Jack Pinta, Apr. 17, 1948 (dec. Sept. 1982). Tech. writer, editor Gen. Motors Corp., Milford, Mich., 1943-45; sr. home economist Los Angeles Dept. Water and Power, 1956-61, dir. home econs., 1961—, dir. ednl. services, 1981-86, ret., 1986. Sec. Assn. for UN, Des Moines, 1953-55. Mem. mayor's Community Adv. Com. Recipient Laura McCall Home Service Achievement award, 1960; acceptor Aham's Alma award, 1970-72. Mem. Am. (consumer interests com. 1968-70), Cal. (exec. council, pres. Los Angeles dist. 1966-67) home econs. assns., Los Angeles Home Economists in Bus., Elec. Women's Round Table (dir. 1974, nat. pres. 1978-80), Soc. Consumer Affairs Profls. in Bus. (sec. So. Calif. chpt. 1978-79), Los Angeles City/County Energy Edn. Council (communications chmn. 1981-83, pres. 1983-84), Calif. Energy Edn. Forum, LWV (exec. bd. Des Moines 1953-55), Los Angeles World Affairs Council, Town Hall, Ia. State U. Alumni Assn. Episcopalian. Mem. Order Eastern Star. Club: Pilot (pres. Van Nuys 1962-63). Home: 5744 Vantage Av North Hollywood CA 91607

PINTERPE, DOMINICK, company executive; b. Flint, Mich., May 9, 1942; s. Livio Giovanni Pinterpe and Annette (Grammatico) Iannetti; m. Judy Gaill Christine, Nov. 9, 1963; children: Maria, Diana. BS, Calif. State U., Long Beach, 1968; MBA, U. Laverne, 1984. Staff asst. Rockwell Internat., Downey, Calif., 1967-69; supr. Rockwell Internat., Downey, 1969-70, program adminstr., 1970-73, quality engr., 1973, supr., 1973-77, mgr. aerospace, resource mgmt., 1977—; owner Whirligig Retail Party Supplies, Cypress, Calif., Long Beach, 1979—; agt. Realty World, Cerritos, Calif., 1979—; pres. DAC Bus. Enterprises, Cerritos, 1986-87; cons. in field. Recipient Tech. Utilization award NASA, 1974. Mem. Nat. Mgmt. Assn. Republican. Roman Catholic. Home: 12460 Bingham St Cerritos CA 90701

PIOTRKOWSKI, DAVID THOMAS, electrical engineer; b. Cleve., Dec. 31, 1959; s. Jozef Anthony and Florence Marie (Arko) P. BS in Computer Info. Systems, Cleve. State U., 1984; BEE, U. Dayton, 1986. Program mgr. diagnostics and connectors, asst. program mgr. VHSIC Air Logistic Ctr. USAF, McClellan AFB, Calif., 1986—. Active Sacramento Zool. Soc., 1986—. Fast Track Engring scholarship Air Force Logistics Commd., Dayton, Ohio, 1985. Mem. IEEE, Assn. Old Crows. Roman Catholic. Office: USAF SM-ALC/MMEHTM McClellan AFB CA 95652 also: PO Box 511 North Highlands CA 95660

PIOTROWSKI, JOSEPH, human resources manager; b. Pottstown, Pa., Aug. 11, 1954; s. Chester and Catherine (Freeh) P.; m. Britta lee Jorstad, Dec. 3, 1983. BA in Journalism, U. S.C., 1976. Announcer Sta. WBUX, Doyelstown, Pa., 1976-79; indsl. liason O.I.C., Inc., Pottstown, Pa., 1976-79; recruiter I.E.S. of Tex., Inc., Ft. Washington, 1979-80; employment mgr. Bechtel Power Corp., San Francisco, 1980-87, Kirk Paper Co., Commerce, Calif., 1987-88; human resources mgr. Lockman and Assocs., Monterey Park, Calif., 1988—. Mem. NRA, Employment Mgmt. Assn., Commerce Sr. Rifle and Pistol Club. Republican. Office: Lockman and Assocs 249 E Pomona Blvd Monterey Park CA 91754

PIPAL, GEORGE HENRY, journalist; b. Lafayette, Ind., Oct. 14, 1916; s. Francis John and Belle (Kadavy) P.; m. Caroline Dunsmore, Aug. 17, 1946; children—John, Susan, Philip, Frank. B.A., U. Nebr., 1937; M.S., Columbia, 1939. Corr. various bureaus UPI, 1937-41; bur. mgr. UPI, Prague, 1946; mgr. for UPI, Eastern Europe, 1947, Germany, 1948; dir. European Services, 1949-51; gen. bus. mgr. Europe, Middle East, Africa, 1952-65; gen. sales exec. computer svcs. N.Y.C., 1966-68; gen. mgr. internat. features div. 1968-78; mng. dir. UPI (U.K.), Ltd., 1964-65; v.p. United Feature Syndicate, 1978-84, United Media Enterprises, 1985—. Served as lt. USNR, 1942-46. Mem. Sigma Delta Chi, Chi Phi. Club: Sonoma County Press (pres. 1986). Office: United Media 1 Snoopy Pl Santa Rosa CA 95403

PIPKIN, ALVA (CLAUDE), beverage company executive; b. Mulberry, Fla., Mar. 16, 1931; s. Edgar Holmes and Cleo Judson (Limeberger) P.; m. Lois Rhodes, Oct. 14, 1961; children: Stephen Rhodes, Amy Lois. BS in Acctg. and Econs. magna cum laude, Fla. So. U., 1953. Acct., supr. Chemstrand Corp., Pensacola, Fla., 1953-60; sr. auditor N.Y.C., 1960-65; audit mgr. Monsanto Co., St. Louis, 1965-68, systems mgr., 1968-72; asst. controller Iowa Beef Processors, Inc., Dakota City, Nebr., 1972-75, asst. v.p., asst. controller, 1975-78, asst. v.p., ops. controller, 1978-81; v.p., controller Adolph Coors Co., Golden, Colo., 1981—; bd. advisors Faulkner & Gray's Corp. Controller. Bd. dirs. Tech. Assistance Ctr., Denver, 1986—; mem. adv. bd. computer sci. and tech. info. systems Regis Coll., Denver, 1988; mem. adv. bd. Bus. Alumni U. Colo., 1986—. Mem. Planning Forum, Fin. Execs. Internat., Nat. Assn. Accts. (mem. rsch. com. 1989—), Controllers Council, Fin. Mgmt. Assn., Acad. Intergenerational Scholars (chmn. founding com. 1988—), Sigma Iota Epsilon (Businessman of Yr. 1987). Methodist. Home: 142 S Devinney St Golden CO 80401 Office: Adolph Coors Co 12th & Ford Golden CO 80401-1295

PIROSKO, CONNIE MARIAN, corporate professional; b. Cleve., Aug. 11, 1954; m. Michael E. Proulx, Sept. 9, 1952. BA, Ohio U., 1976; MA in Librarianship and Info. Mgmt., U. Denver, 1981. Libr. asst. Coll. of Law U. Denver, 1978-81; libr. Coll. of Law U. Denver, Denver, 1981-84, mgr., libr. and file svcs., 1984-87, asst. dir. adminstr., 1987—. Mem. Assn. Legal Adminstrs., Colo. Assn. Law Libraries (v.p. 1984 pres. 1986), Rocky Mountain Bus. Travelers Assn. Office: Holland & Hart 555 17th St Suite 2900 Denver CO 80202

PISANO, ROBERT RENO, architectural photographer; b. Lynn, Mass., Apr. 22, 1953; s. Reno Victor and Mary Antoinette (Votano) P.; m. Lani Elizabeth Doely, May 29, 1983 (div. 1986). Student, Boston U., 1971-75, U. Wash., 1977-79. Freelance archtl. photographer Seattle, 1980—. Contbr. photographs to profl. publs. Mem. Am. Soc. Mag. Photographers. Democrat. Home: 2817 Broadway E Seattle WA 98102 Office: 911 E Pike St #301 Seattle WA 91022

PISCIOTTA, SAMUEL JAMES, small business owner; b. Pueblo, Colo., Dec. 10, 1938; s. Sam Jr. and Eva May (Padula) P.; m. Cynthia Diane Garrett, Aug. 8, 1961; children: Samuel, Pamela, Richard, Michael. BA, Western State Coll., 1967. Pres., mgr. Pueblo (Colo.) Bus. Men's Club, Inc., DBA Capt. Sam's Family Athletic Club, Inc., 1961—. Co-founder, v.p. Pueblo Performing Arts Guild, 1986—. Named one of Outstanding Young Men of Am., 1970; recipient Bus. of Yr. awards Pueblo & S.E. Colo. Small Bus., 1988. Mem. Nat. Swim and Recreation Assn. (pres. 1976-77), Greater Pueblo Sports Assn., Pueblo Hall of Fame (co-founder 1972), Jaycees (state dir. 1973-75), Pueblo Bus. Exchange (co-founder 1982, pres. 1984), So. Colo. Better Bus. Bur. (co-organizer Pueblo office 1985—, 1st pres. 1987-88), Tau Kappa Epsilon. Republican. Lodge: Kiwanis (bd. dirs. 1986), Elks, Masons, Knight Templar, Royal Order of Jesters, Shriners, So. Colo. Consistory Ritualistic Team, Order of Quetzalcoatl & Dante Alighieri Soc. Home: 27 Pedregal Ln Pueblo CO 81005 Office: Capt Sam's Family Athletic Club Inc 1500 W 4th St Pueblo CO 81004

PISTILLI, LARRY STEVEN, management consultant; b. Evanston, Ill., June 8, 1947; s. Renaldo Joseph and Florence (Stempel) P.; m. Bonita Jean Sasso, May 17, 1986. BA, Edison State Coll., 1975, U. N.Y., Albany, 1977; PhD in Edn., U. N.Y., 1987, PhD in History, 1982. Ordained to ministry Eastern Orthodox Ch. Bishop Eastern Orthodox Cathedral ofJoliet, Ill., 1968-70; asst. to sherrif Will County Sheriff's Dept., Wilmington, Ill., 1970-74; mgr. indsl. devel. dept. Research Tech., Inc., Evanston, Ill., 1974-81; corp. fin. programmer Gen. Fin. Corp., Evanston, 1982-83; corp. time sharing analyst Square D Co., Palatine, Ill., 1983; corp. tng. coordinator Harris Corp., Palm Bay, Fla., 1984-86; reg. rep./spl. agt. Prudential, Orange, Calif., 1988—; bd. dirs. Faith Life Ch., Inc., Palm Bay, 1970—; research chmn. S. Orange County Computer Group, Fountain Valley, Calif., 1987—. Chairmn. Adv. Com. for Handicapped, City of Fountain Valley, 1987—; bd. dirs. City of Cresthill, Ill., 1967. With U.S. Army, 1964-67. Mem. DAV, Am. Ex-POW's, Kappa Beta Kappa (nat. pres. 1970-75), Epsilon Delta Chi, Kappa Delta Chi, Chuan Chi Assn. Assemblies of God.

PITCHER, DONALD ANTHONY, banker; b. Teaneck, N.J., Apr. 24, 1949; s. John Pitcher and Edith (Hoffeller) Ell; m. Deidre Virgina Ell, Mar. 11, 1978 (div. Jan., 1983); 1 child, Cheryl Lynn; m. Joan Karen Walz, Mar. 14, 1987. BS in Acctg., Fairleigh Dickinson U., 1975, MBA in Acctg. & Taxation, 1978. Various EDP clerical positons United Jersey Banks, Hackensack, N.J., 1972-75; EDP dept. supr. United Jersey Banks, Hackensack, 1975-76, customer support rep., 1976-77, staff acct., 1977-81, sr. cost analyst, 1981-82; mgr. cost acctg. United Jersey Banks, Princeton, N.J., 1982-83; v.p. acctg. & fin. United Jersey Banks, Princeton, 1983-87; project mgr. First Interstate Bank of Calif., L.A., 1987-88; v.p, controller Torrey Pines Bank, Solana Beach, Calif., 1988—. Treas. UJB FedPac & UJB Pac, Princeton, N.J., 1984-87. Staff Sgt., USAF, 1968-72. Mem. Nat. Assn. of Accts. (CMA dir. N. San Diego chpt. 1988-89, sec. 1989-90), Nat. Assn. Bank Cost Analysis (charter mem.), VFW, Am. Legion. Republican. Home: 1749 Avenida Vista Labera Oceanside CA 92056 Office: Torrey Pines Bank 265 Santa Helena Solana Beach CA 92056

PITCHER, HELEN IONE, advertising executive; b. Colorado Springs, Colo., Aug. 6, 1931; d. William Forest Medlock and Frankie La Vone (Hamilton) Tweed; m. Richard Edwin Pitcher, Sept. 16, 1949; children: Dushka Myers, Suzanne, Marc. Student, U. Colo., 1962-64, Ariz. State U., 1966, Maricopa Tech. Coll., 1967, Scottsdale Community Coll., 1979-81. Design draftsman Sundstrand Aviation, Denver, 1962-65; tech. illustrator Sperry, Phoenix, 1966-68; art dir. Integrated Circuit Engring., Scottsdale, Ariz., 1968-71, dir. advt., 1981—; advt. artist Motorola Inc., Phoenix, 1971-74; pres. Pitcher Tech. Pubs., Scottsdale, 1974-81. Profl. advisor Paradise Valley Sch. Dist., Phoenix, 1984—; mem. bd. advisors graphic arts dept. Ariz. State U., Tempe. mem. Nat. Audio Visual Assn., Bus. Profl. Advt. Assn. (treas. 1982-86), Direct Mktg. Club. Democrat. Mem. Ch. Christ. Office: Integrated Cir Engring Corp 15022 N 75th St Scottsdale AZ 85260

PITCOCK, JAMES KENT, oncologist; b. Tachikawa AFB, Japan, Nov. 18, 1951; s. James Kenneth and Helen (Robertson) P.; m. Mary Beth Veronica Bewersdorf, Sept. 22, 1984. Student, U. Houston, 1974; MD, Baylor U., 1979. Diplomate Am. Bd. Otolaryngology. Resident in gen. surgery Baylor Coll. Medicine, Houston, 1979-81, resident in otolaryngology, head and neck surgery, 1981-84; clinician Kelsey-Seybold Clinic, P.A., Houston, 1984-85; lectr. head and neck surgery Inst. Laryngology and Otology, U. London, 1985-86; instr., fellow head and neck surgery U. Chgo., 1986-88; asst. prof. div. otlaryngology, head and neck surgery U. Calif.-Irvine Med. Ctr., Orange, 1988—; dir. head and neck surg. oncology dept. U. Calif.-Irvine Med. Ctr., 1988—, Long Beach (Calif.) VA's Med. Ctr., 1988—. Author: Oral and Maxillofacial Trauma, 1989, Musculocutaneous Flap Reconstruction of the Head and Neck, 1989, Surgery of the Skull Base, 1989. Fellow Am. Acad. Otolaryngology, Head and Neck Surgery; mem. Am. Acad. Facial Plastic and Reconstructive Surgery, Soc. Univ. Otolaryngologist, ACS, Undersea Med. Soc., Trout Unltd., Oriole Soc. Office: U Calif Irvine Med Ctr 101 City Dr S Bldg 25 Orange CA 92668

PITKIN, ROY MACBETH, physician, educator; b. Anthon, Iowa, May 24, 1934; s. Roy and Pauline Allie (McBeath) P.; m. Marcia Alice Jenkins, Aug. 17, 1957; children: Barbara, Robert Macbeth, Kathryn, William Charles. B.A. with highest distinction, U. Iowa, 1956, M.D., 1959. Diplomate Am. Bd. Obstetrics & Gynecology, 1967. Intern King County Hosp., Seattle, 1959-60; resident in ob-gyn U. Iowa Hosps. and Clinics, Iowa City, 1960-63; asst. prof. ob-gyn U. Ill., 1965-68; assoc. prof. ob-gyn U. Iowa, Iowa City, 1968-72; prof. U. Iowa, 1972-87, head dept. ob-gyn, 1977-87; prof., chmn. dept. ob-gyn. UCLA, 1987—; mem. residency rev. com. ob-gyn, 1981-87, chmn. 1984. Editor-in-chief: Year Book of Obstetrics and Gynecology, 1975-86; editor-in-chief: Clinical Obstetrics and Gynecology, 1979; editor: Obstetrics and Gynecology, 1985. Contbr. articles to med. jours. Served to lt. comdr. M.C. USNR, 1963-65. NIH career awardee, 1972-77. Fellow Royal Coll. Obstetricians and Gynecologists (ad eundem); mem. AMA (Goldberger award in clin. nutrition 1982), Am. Coll. Obstetricians and Gynecologists, Am. Gynecol. and Obstet. Soc., Central Assn. Obstetricians and Gynecologists, Soc. Gynecologic Investigation (pres. 1985-86), Soc. Perinatal Obstetricians (pres. 1978-79). Presbyterian. Office: UCLA Sch Medicine Dept Ob-Gyn Los Angeles CA 90024-1740

PITRE, THOMAS JAMES, educator; b. Waterbury, Conn., Oct. 11, 1941; s. Thomas Matthew and Lydia Frances (Labrie) P.; m. Carolyn Jane Starbird, Nov. 25, 1981. BFA, San Francisco Art Inst., 1963; MA, San Francisco State U., 1971; PhD, Columbia Pacific U., 1986. Cert. adminstr., community coll. instr., adult edn. instr., Calif. Instr. Mt. View (Calif.) /Los Altos Adult Edn., 1974-87, Santa Clara (Calif.) Adult Edn., 1987—; prof. bus. City U., Santa Clara, 1986—; adj. faculty mem. Nat. Hispanic U., Oakland, Calif., 1986—, Nat. U., San Jose; faculty mentor Columbia Pacific U., San Rafael, Calif., 1986—; owner, gen. mgr. Thomas Pitre Assoc., San Jose, Calif., 1970—. Tech. adv. Explorer Scouts of Am., Oakland, 1986-87. Mem. Am. Soc. Tng. and Devel., Phi Delta Kappa, So. Alameda County Tech. Edn. Assn. (Pres. 1986). Democrat. Home and Office: 15149 Joanne Ave San Jose CA 95127

PITSKER, PETER BROKAW, management consultant; b. San Mateo, Calif., Mar. 14, 1933; s. John Raynold and Dorothy Louise (Brokaw) P.; m. Polly Drake DuBose, Aug. 30, 1958; children: Peter D., Amy F., Paul B., Jack. BSChemE, Stanford U., 1955. Refinery engr. Mobil Oil, Torrance, Calif., 1957-60; v.p. mktg. and sales Foxboro (Mass.) Co., 1960-72; mgr. N.Am. sales Mod Comp, Ft. Lauderdale, Fla., 1972-75; dir. mktg. and sales Gen. Automation, Anaheim, Calif., 1975-78; pres. North & Donahoe, Santa Ana, Calif., 1978-88, TechnoMgmt., Inc., San Juan Capistrano, Calif., 1988—; bd. dirs., founder Triconex, Irvine, Calif., 1985—; bd. dirs. Wonderware, Irvine; mem. adv. bd. ABR Corp., Laguna Hills, Calif., 1988—. Served with U.S. Army, 1955-57. Mem. Instrument Soc. Am. (sr.), Am. Inst. Chem. Engrs., Soc. Mfg. Engrs., Am. Electronics Assn., Orange County C. of C. Republican. Home: 31842 Aguacate Rd San Juan Capistrano CA 92675 Office: TechnoMgmt Inc PO Box 3934 Mission Viejo CA 92660-1934

PITT, WILLIAM ALEXANDER, cardiologist; b. Vancouver, B.C., Can., July 17, 1942; came to U.S., 1970; s. Reginald William and Una Sylvia (Alexander) P.; m. Judith Mae Wilson, May 21, 1965; children: William Matthew, Joanne Katharine. MD, U. B.C., Vancouver, 1967. Diplomate Royal Coll. Physicians Can. Intern, Mercy Hosp., San Diego, 1967-68, resident, 1970-71; resident Vancouver Gen. Hosp., 1968-70, U. Calif., San Diego, 1971-72; assoc. dir. cardiology Mercy Hosp., San Diego, 1972—; bd. trustees San Diego Found. for Med. Care, 1983—, pres., chmn. bd. trustees, 1986-88; bd. dirs. Mut. Assn. for Profl. Services, Phila., 1984—. Fellow Royal Coll. Physicians Can., Am. Coll. Cardiology (assoc.); mem. AMA,

Am. Heart Assn., Calif. Med. Assn., San Diego County Med. Soc., San Diego County Heart Assn. (bd. dirs. 1982-88). Episcopalian. Office: Mercy Cardiology Med Group 4077 5th Ave San Diego CA 92103

PITTER, KEIKO MURATA, academic administrator; b. Tokyo, Dec. 14, 1948; came to U.S., 1960; d. Minoru and Haruko (Matsubara) Murata; m. Richard Leon Pitter, Nov. 21, 1971 (div. 1988); children: Gregory, Jacqueline. BA, UCLA, 1970. Program analyst Jet Propulsion Lab., Pasadena, Calif., 1970-73, Tektronix, Inc., Beaverton, Oreg., 1974-77; owner, founder Pathways Elem. Sch., Cheverly, Md., 1981; instr. Truckee Meadows Community Coll., Reno, 1982-84, chmn. computer info. sci. dept., 1984-88, coordinator acad. computing, 1987—; lectr. Interface, The Computer Edn. Quarterly, Santa Cruz, Calif., 1988. Author: Using Appleworks, 1986, 2d edit., 1989, Using IBM Micro, 2d edit., 1986, 3d edit., 1989, Application Software Tutorial, 1988, Programming Logic and Design, 1988, others. Mem. Assn. Systems Mgmt. (pres. 1987—, Disting. Service award 1988), Data Processing Mgmt. Assn. (v.p. 1986-87), Assn. Computing Machinery, Nat. Bus. Edn. Assn. Home: 1240 Freddie Ct Reno NV 89503 Office: Truckee Meadows Community Coll 7000 Dandini Blvd Reno NV 89512

PITTMAN, PENDELL, III, communications executive; b. Dallas, Dec. 26, 1951; s. PenDell Jr. and Mary Elizabeth (Benson) P. BA in Music, Colo. State U., 1974; MM in Music, Cleve. Inst. Music, 1976; MA, Case Western Res. U., 1976; postgrad., UCLA, 1980-81. Producer film Uncle Josh Prodns., Loveland, Colo., 1968-70; adminstr. music EDL Inc., Loveland, 1976-84; adminstr. communication Emissary Found. Internat., Loveland, 1984—; v.p. ops. WorldView Corp., Denver, 1987-88; cons. Whole Health Inst., 1984—, Resaissance Bus. Assocs., 1985—, Renaissance Ednl. Assocs., 1986—; bd. dirs. WorldView. Assoc. producer, composer (video) Apocalype of Light, 1988; contbr. articles to profl. jours. Coordinator emergency Amateur Radio Emergency Service, Ft. Collins, Colo. 1987-88; dir. net Pacific Area Staff Nat. Traffic System, Boise, Idaho, 1986-87; cons., advisor Nat. Emergency Response Com., Newington, Conn., 1988. Mem. Am. Radio Relay League (officer pub. info. 1987—, Colo. sect., cert. merit, 1986, 87, pub. service honor roll 1987), Assn. Responsible Communication (dir. radio div. 1982—, bd. dirs., founder, treas., grantee 1986), Loveland Repeater Assn., Aikido-ki Loveland, Phi Mu Alpha (pres. 1972-73). Club: No. Colo. Amateur Radio (Ft. Collins coordinator emergency 1986-88). Home: Sunrise Ranch 5569 N County Rd 29 Loveland CO 80538 Office: WorldView Corp 1625 Larimer St Ste 3206 Denver CO 80202

PITTNER, KELLY CASAS, human resources professional; b. Lynwood, Calif., Mar. 29, 1961; d. Charles Frances and Bernice Corina (Walter) Casas; m. Ronald Ward Pittner, May 22, 1982. Mgr. human resources Tech. Magic, Inc., Irvine, Calif., 1979-85; mgr. profl. staffing Computer Assistance, Inc., Norwalk, Calif., 1985—; software cons., Computer Assistance, Inc., Marriott Hotels, Calif. Assn. Realtors. Mem. NAFE. Roman Catholic. Office: Computer Assistance Inc 12100 E Imperial Hwy Norwalk CA 90650

PITTS, JOANNE PATRICIA, software engineer, systems analyst; b. Riverside, Calif., Jan. 9, 1953; d. Otis Kemp and Margaret Louise (Schaffer) P. BA in Math., BS in Computer Sci., U. Calif., Irvine, 1974; MBA in Mgmt., Calif. State U., Fullerton, 1987; postgrad., U. So. Calif., 1987—. Computer programmer Rockwell Internat., Anaheim, Calif., 1974-76, Los Angeles, 1976-77; lead software engr. Anaheim, 1978—, Seal Beach, Calif., 1987—; software analyst Computer Sci. Corp., Santa Ana, Calif., 1977-78. Sponsor Immigration and Refugee Ctr. St. Anselm's, Garden Grove, Calif., 1979-82; soprano in ch. choir. Mem. Nat. Mgmt. Assn., Nat. Assn. Female Execs., Beta Gamma Sigma. Democrat. Episcopalian. Home: 12292 Lesley St Garden Grove CA 92640 Office: Rockwell Internat 2600 Westminster Blvd Mail Code SJ62 Seal Beach CA 90740

PITTS, MARTHA JEAN, social worker; b. Orleans, Vt., Feb. 1, 1943; d. Francis Nelson and Beryl Viola (Marshall) Rushlow; children: Randy, Craig, Shawn, Stacey, Diana. BA, Goddard Coll., Plainefield, Vt., 1973; postgrad., U. No. Colo., 1987—. Parent & child coord. Parent Child Ctr., Barton, Vt., 1967-69; family planning specialist Planned Parenthood of Vt., Burlington, 1969-71; vol. Planned Parenthood and Motherhood Project, Albuquerque, 1973-78; parent coord. Park Ave Preschool, Canon City, Colo., 1978-79; social worker Dept. Social Services, Canon City, 1980—; Dir. first planned parenthood clinic, St. Johnsbury, Vt., 1970; developer first college planned parenthood clinic, Lyndonville, Vt., 1971, Senior Express Transportation, Canon City, 1982; cons. Block Grant City Govt., Canon City, 1983-84. Fundraising chmn. Colo. Territorial Prison Mus., Canon City, 1987-88; campaign mgr. County Commr. Candidate, Canon City, 1988. Named Ford fellow, Ford Found., Newport, Vt., 1971, 72. Mem. Zonta Internat. (chmn. several programs, 1983—). Methodist. Home: 263 Glenmoor Rd Canon City CO 81212 Office: Dept Social Services Box 631 Canon City CO 81212

PITTS, WILLIAM CLARENCE, physicist; b. Seattle, Apr. 19, 1929; s. Clarence H. and Emily B. (Kepp) P.; m. Joanne R. Lawson, May 18, 1952 (dec. Jan. 1978); children: Starr R., Nancy H.; m. Patricia A. Kirkland, May 1, 1981. BS in Physics, U. Wash., 1951; postgrad., Stanford U., 1951-58. Rsch. scientist NACA/NASA, Moffett Field, Calif., 1951-88, Eloret Inst., Moffett Field, 1988—. Contbr. articles to profl. jours.; inventor two-force measuring balance. Office: NASA Ames Rsch Ctr Moffett Field CA 94035

PITZAK, AVERY NORMAN, geologist; b. Highland Park, Mich., Oct. 23, 1946; s. Irving and Mollie (Portner) P.; m. Susan Starr, June 24, 1969; 1 child, Sandra Beth. BSc in Geology, Wayne State U., Detroit, 1968, MSc in Geology, 1976. Geologist Exxon Co., U.S.A., Harvey, La., 1977-78; offshore geologist Exxon Co., U.S.A., New Orleans, 1978-79; prodn. geologist Husky Oil Co., Denver, 1979-82; devel. geologist Northwest Exploration Co., Denver, 1982-84; geol. and mktg. cons. M.A.R. Cons. Co., Aurora, Colo., 1984-88, pres., owner, 1988—. Contbr. articles to newspaper. Sgt. USAF, 1968-72. Office: Avery N Pitzak Cons Box 460297 Aurora CO 80015

PIZZO, JAMES RICHARD, educational administrator; b. San Jose, Calif., Mar. 22, 1926; s. Joseph Anthony and Josephine Margarette (Bonzani) P.; m. Evelyn Mary Caniparoli, Sept. 8, 1962; children: Theresa, Michael, Maria. AB, U. Portland, 1950, MEd, 1956. Cert. tchr., ednl. adminstr., Oreg. Tchr., swimming coach, counselor Lake Oswego (Oreg.) High Sch., 1952-58, vice prin., 1958-61; student counselor Oreg. State System Higher Edn., Eugene, 1961-63; dir. sch. rels. Oreg. State System Higher Edn., 1963-82, asst. vice-chancellor student svcs., 1982-88, asst. vice-chancellor acad. affairs, 1988—; exec. sec. Oreg. High Sch.-Coll. Rels. Coun., 1966-82; chmn. bd. dirs. Oreg. Career Info. System, 1978-79; trustee The Coll. Bd., 1978-82. Mem. editorial bd.: Mapping Your Education, 1965-81, Careers, 1971-73. Sgt. U.S. Army, 1944-46, PTO. Mem. Pacific Assn. Collegiate Registrars and Admissions Officers, Pacific Northwest Assn. Coll. Admissions Counselors (pres.), Sons of Italy in Am., K.C. Democrat. Roman Catholic. Home: 712 E 39th Pl Eugene OR 97405 Office: Oreg System Higher Edn PO Box 3175 Eugene OR 97403

PIZZORNO, JOSEPH EGIDIO, JR., college president; b. San Gabriel, Calif., Dec. 7, 1947; s. Joseph Egidio Sr. and Mary (Carmela) P.; m. Mavis Bonnar (div. Oct. 1983); 1 child, Raven Muir; m. Lara Elise Udell, Sept. 28, 1985. BS with Distinction, Harvey Mudd Coll., Claremont, Calif., 1969; Naturopathic Doctor, Nat. Coll. Naturopathic Medicine, Portland, Oreg., 1975. Research asst. Lockheed Aircraft, Ontario, Calif., 1968; research technologist U. Wash., Seattle, 1970-75; practice naturopathic medicine Seattle, 1975-80, practice midwifery, 1978-82; pres. John Bastyr Coll., Seattle, 1978—; pres. Council on Naturopathic Med. Edn., Portland, Oreg., 1985-87. Co-author: A Textbook of Natural Medicine, 1985; contbg. editor Let's Live mag., Los Angeles, 1987—; contbr. articles to profl. jours. Mem. Am. Assn. Naturopathic Physicians (bd. dirs. 1984—), Wash. Assn. Naturopathic Physicians (edn. dir. 1976), Seattle Midwifery Sch. (edn. com. 1978—), Northwest Sci. Fiction Soc. Libertarian. Office: John Bastyr Coll 144 NE 54th St Seattle WA 98105

PLACET, RONALD VINCENT, military officer; b. L.A., Aug. 9, 1959; s. Donald John Placet and Christine (Leon) Benadum; m. Cheryl Lynn Swanson, July 16, 1988. Student, Victor Valley Coll., 1977-79; BA in Polit. Sci., Calif. State U., Northridge, 1981; postgrad., U. Pacific, 1987—. Commd. 2d lt. USAF, 1981, advanced through grades to capt., 1985; stationed at USAF, Mather AFB, Calif., 1981-82; instr. electronic warfare systems USAF, Calif. and Mich., 1983-86; instr. Electronic Warfare Sch. USAF, Mather AFB, 1987-88, acting flight comdr., 1988, mgr. curriculum Hqtrs. Air Tng. Command, 1989—. Project officer United Way, Mather AFB, 1987; chairperson Mather AFB Blood Drive Orgn., 1987-88. Mem. ABA (student div.), Computers and the Law Assn., Air Force Assn., Res. Officers Assn., Assn. Old Crows. Roman Catholic. Home: 9750 Old Placerville Rd #198 Sacramento CA 95827 Office: 3305 Sch Squadron/Operating Location Alpha (Ol-A) Mather AFB CA 95655

PLAINER, TRUMAN DEAN, physician, ophthamologist; b. L.A., Feb. 14, 1934; s. Harry Anton and Johanna (Kruse) P.; m. Janice Lynne Huff, Aug. 30, 1986. BA, Pomona Coll., 1956; MD, Stanford U., 1960. Diplomate, Am. Bd. Ophthamology. Intern U.S. Naval Hosp., Oakland, Calif., 1960-61; resident in Ophthamology Health Sci. Ctr., UCLA, Jules Stein Eye Inst., 1963-67; pvt. practice Ophthamology Mesa, Ariz., 1967—; staff physician, Desert Samaritan Hosp., Mesa, Ariz., 1967—. Lt. U.S.N., 1960-64; col USAF active reserve, 1967-82. Mem. Ariz. Opthal. Soc. (pres. 1976-77), Phoenix Opthal. Soc. (pres. 1977-78). Office: Ophthamology Ltd 1450 S Dobson Rd #120 Mesa AZ 85202

PLAKE, CHARLES ROBERT, mortgage company executive; b. Beaumont, Tex., June 19, 1936; s. Charles Fairbank and Nettie Beatrice (Gary) P.; m. Verna YukYun Wong, May 2, 1958; children: Kenneth, Jennifer. BS, Ariz. State U., 1963; postgrad., Pacific Coast Banking Sch., 1982. V.p., mgr. First Internstate Bank, L.A., 1963-85; pres. Hacienda Mex. Food Products, Inc., City of Industry, Calif., 1985-87; owner, cons. Charles Plake & Assocs., Fullerton, Calif., 1987—; sr. v.p. SVS Mortgage Capital, Inc., Yorba Linda, Calif., 1988—; cons. ValuVision, L.A., 1988—. Pres. Norwalk (Calif.) Youth Football, 1967-71. Sgt. USAF, 1954-59. Mem. Lions, Rotary, Delta Sigma Pi. Republican. Home: 1732 Camino La Vista Fullerton CA 92633 Office: SVS Mortgage Capital Inc 4405 Manchester Ave Ste 203 Encinitas CA 92633

PLANCK, MICHEAL CHRISTOPHER, software engineer, entrepreneur; b. Dayton, Ohio, Aug. 19, 1962; s. Russell Edward and Sharon Ann (Wynne) P. BA in Philosophy, U. Ariz., 1989. Programmer Wilson Rsch. Group, Tucson, 1984-86; software engr. Wyko Corp., Tucson, 1986-88, Computer Output Processers and Engring., Tucson, 1988-89; v.p. software div. Micro Map, Inc., Tucson, 1989—. Author: computer game Emperor of Elishia, 1989. Inducted into Photonics Circle of Excellence, Photonics Spectre Mag., 1988. Democrat. Home: 1605-A E 9th St Tucson AZ 85719

PLANERT-GEFFEN, CHERYL DIANNE, dance therapist; b. Chgo., Dec. 21, 1948; d. George Raymond and Lila Louise (Frank) Planert; m. Jeffrey Alan Geffen, Sept. 20, 1981. BA, Wittenberg U., 1972; MA, Immaculate Heart Coll., Los Angeles, 1982. Registered by Acad. Dance Therapists; lic. marriage, family and child counselor. Dance/movement therapist Tierra del Sol Sch. for the Developmentally Delayed, Sunland, Calif., 1978-81; pvt. practice dance/movement therapist Los Angeles, 1982—; dance/movement therapist Stephen S. Wise Parenting Ctr., Bel Air, Calif., 1981—, Gateways Adolescent Inpatient Treatment Program, Los Angeles, 1987—, Sierra Rayole Hosp., Azusa, Calif., 1989—; instr. William Lyon U., Los Angeles, 1985—; guest lectr. U. Calif., Davis, 1985—. Mem. Am. Dance Therapy Assn. (nat. co-chair nat. conf. program com. 1987, editor newsletter 1981-86), Assn. Child Devel. Specialists, Assn. Marriage and Family Therapists. Home and Office: 1332 Linda Rosa Ave Los Angeles CA 90041

PLANK, WILLIAM EARL, professional buyer; b. Haily, Idaho, Apr. 5, 1938; s. Raymond Russell and Irene Marjorie (Fagen) P.; m. Janet Louise Cecil, Nov. 22, 1963 (div. 1977); 1 child, Tonya Jean. BS, Ariz. State U., 1960. Sr. trust acct. Transamerica Title, Phoenix, 1962-66; buyer Sperry Corp., Phoenix, 1966-86; sr. buyer Honeywell, Inc., Glendale, Ariz., 1986—; bd. dirs. Town Sq. Homeowners Assoc., Phoenix, 1988—. Sgt. U.S. Army, 1960-61. Recipient Outstanding Contribution to Problem Solving award NASA, 1988. Mem. Oriental Lodge, Scottish Rite, Internat. Supreme Council Order of DeMolay, Nat. Contract Mgmt. Assn., Phi Sigma Kappa, Alumni Assn. Ariz. State U. Republican. Home: 408 E Hartford Ave Phoenix AZ 85022 Office: Honeywell Inc 19019 N 59th Ave Glendale AZ 85308

PLANT, DENNIS ALAN, manufacturing executive, entrepreneur; b. Fremont, Calif., Oct. 11, 1959; s. Alan Dennis Plant and Connie Rose (Yorks) Gomez; m. Joanne Irene Parlos, Mar. 17, 1980 (div. June 1983); 1 child, Matthew Adam. Grad. high sch., San Lorenzo, Calif. With Oreg. State Hwy. Dept., Klamath Falls, 1977-79; field counselor Kirby Co., Klamath Falls, 1979-80; owner Super Sweeps, Klamath Falls, 1980-82, Basin Wood Heat, Klamath Falls, 1982-83, Dennis Plant Window and Covering Installations, Cathedral City, Calif., 1983-86, Vertical Visions, Cathedral City, 1986-87, Window Coverings West, Cathedral City, 1987—. Writer songs; inventor puzzle; contbr. articles to profl. jours. Republican. Office: Window Coverings West 68-615 Perez Rd Ste 8A Cathedral City CA 92234

PLATT, ELISABETH JOHNSON, fraternal organization administrator, instructor; b. Jamestown, N.Y., Nov. 12, 1924; d. Carl John Amandus and Esther Elisabeth (Stendahl) Johnson; widowed; children: Corlu Esther Mahan, Helen Marie Fortner. Student, Fillmore Coll., Buffalo, 1942-45; cert. RN, Buffalo Deaconess Hosp. Sch. Nursing, 1945. RN, Calif.; ordained ministry Internat. Ministerial Fellowship, 1984. Conf. coord. Women's Aglow, Calif., 1975-79; conf. coord., pres. Shalom Ctr., Calif., 1976—; organist, dir. music Presbyn. Ch. & So. Baptist, Calif., 1961-70. Mem. Calif. Nurses Assn. (founder, pres. dist. 13 1965-67). Home: 98 Melody Ln Morgan Hill CA 95037 Office: Shalom Ctr Inc PO Box 849 San Martin CA 95046

PLATT, JAMES ROBERT, manufacturing executive; b. Batavia, N.Y., Oct. 23, 1948; s. Robert John and Mildred J. (Foote) P.; m. Shelly A. Tunis, May 24, 1980; children: Shane Christopher, Tristan Robert. BS, SUNY, Brockport, 1970; MA, Ariz. State U., 1982. Cert. tchr., N.Y. Inside sales supr. Mallco Distbrs., Phoenix, 1972-77; grad. teaching asst. Ariz. State U., Tempe, 1978-79; sales rep. Wisco Equipment Co., Inc., Phoenix, 1979-82, sales mgr., 1984-88; sales rep. Clyde Hardware Co., Tucson, 1982-84; v.p. Wistech Controls, Phoenix, 1988—. Regents scholar, 1966-70. Mem. Instrument Soc. Am., Young Execs.-Fluid Power Distbrs. Assn., Am. Soc. Environ. History, Soc. Mfg. Engrs., Phi Alpha Theta. Office: Wistech Controls 4810 S 36th St Phoenix AZ 85040

PLATT, JOSEPH BEAVEN, former college president; b. Portland, Oreg., Aug. 12, 1915; s. William Bradbury and Mary (Beaven) P.; m. Jean Ferguson Rusk, Feb. 9, 1946; children: Ann Ferguson Walker, Elizabeth Beaven Garrow. BA, U. Rochester, 1937; PhD, Cornell U., 1942; LLD, U. So. Calif., 1969, Claremont McKenna Coll., 1982; DSc, Harvey Mudd Coll., 1981. Instr. physics U. Rochester, N.Y., 1941-43, from asst. prof. to prof., 1946-56, assoc. chmn. dept. physics, 1954-56; staff mem. radiation lab. MIT, Cambridge, 1943-46; pres. Harvey Mudd Coll., Claremont, Calif., 1956-76, now part-time sr. prof. physics; pres. Claremont U. Ctr., 1976-81; trustee Aerospace Corp., 1972-85, Consortium for Advancement of Pvt. Higher Edn., 1985—; chief physics br. AEC, 1949-51; cons. U.S. Office Ordnance Rsch., NSF, 1953-56; mem. com. on sci. in UNESCO, Nat. Acad. Scis.-NRC, 1960-62, mem. com. on internat. orgns. and programs, 1962-64; sci. advisor U.S. Del., UNESCO Gen. Conf., Paris, 1960, alt. del., 1962; mem. panel on internat. sci. Pres.'s Sci. Adv. Com., 1961; chmn. Subcom. on Sino-Am. Sci. Cooperation, 1965-79; trustee Analytic Svcs., Inc., chmn. 1958-89; mem. adv. com. on sci. edn. NSF, 1973-74, chmn., 1974; bd. dirs. Lincoln Found., 1979-85, Bell & Howell Corp., 1978-88, Am. Mut. Fund, 1981-88. Trustee China Found. for Promotion of Edn. and Culture, Carnegie Found. for Advancement Teaching, 1970-78; chmn. select com. Master Plan for Higher Edn. Calif., 1971-73; mem. Carnegie Coun. for Policy Studies in Higher Edn.; bd. dirs. L.A. World Affairs Coun., 1973-79. Fellow Am. Phys. Soc.; mem. IEEE, Automobile Club So. Calif. (bd. dirs. 1973—, chmn. bd. dirs. 1986-87), Calif. Club, Sunset Club, Town Hall Club, Twilight Club, Cosmos Club, Bohemian Club, Phi Beta Kappa, Sigma Xi, Phi Kappa Phi. Home: 452 W 11th St Claremont CA 91711

PLATT, WILLIAM RAYMOND, health care executive; b. L.A., Aug. 16, 1951; s. William Raymond and June Caroline (Robinson) P.; m. Tonya Susan Fuller, Nov. 11, 1970 (div. Oct., 1977); children: Joshua Adam, Zachery Tucker. BA, Brigham Young U., 1974; MPA, Calif. State U., Fullerton, 1976. Long range planning asst. City of Anaheim, Calif., 1975-76; planning analyst Anaheim Meml. Hosp., 1976-79, dir. program devel., 1979-83, dir strategic plannning, 1983-86, v.p. corp. devel., 1986—. Recipient Recognition award Calif. Community Hosp. Assn., 1979. Mem. Am. Mktg. Assn., Soc. for Hosp. Planning and Mktg. (mem. edit. com. 1980-81), So. Calif. Soc. Planning and Mktg. (bd. dirs. exec. com. 1980-82), Hosp. Coun. of So. Calif. (chmn. com. bus. coop. 1986—), Assn. Western Hosps. (chmn hosp. based planners com. 1978); nominee Am. Coll. Healthcare Execs., Annaheim C. of C., Fullerton C. of C. Democrat. Home: 17430 Bristlecone Ln Yorba Linda CA 92686 Office: Anaheim Meml Hosp 1111 W La Palma Ave Anaheim CA 92803

PLAYER, THERESA JOAN, lawyer; b. Great Lakes, Ill., Nov. 17, 1947; d. Heber and Rita Jane (Mulhulland) P. AB, San Diego State U., 1970; JD, UCLA, 1973. Bar: Calif. 1973, U.S. Dist. Ct. (so. dist.) Calif. 1973, U.S. Ct. Appeals (9th cir.) 1978. Staff atty. Legal Aid Soc., San Diego, 1974-78; ptnr. Meaney & Player, San Diego, 1979-80; clin. prof. law U. San Diego, 1980-83, clinic dir., 1983—; faculty mem. Nat. Inst. Trial Advocacy, San Diego, 1982—. Contbg. author: Every Woman's Legal Guide, 1980. Recipient Outstanding contribution award San Diego Vol. Lawyers, 1985. Mem. ABA, Criminal Def. Bar Assn., Women's Criminal Def. Bar Assn. (steering com. 1978-84, service award 1982), Calif. Attys. Criminal Justice, Lawyers Club. Democrat. Office: U San Diego Alcala Park San Diego CA 92110

PLEMING, LAURA CHALKER, educator; b. Sheridan, Wyo., May 25, 1913; d. Sidney Thomas and Florence Theresa (Woodbury) Chalker; B.A., Long Beach State Coll. (now Calif. State U., Long Beach), 1953, M.A. in Speech and Drama, 1954; postgrad. U. So. Calif., 1960-63; Rel.D., Sch. Theology, Claremont, Calif., 1968; m. Edward Kibbler Pleming, Aug. 25, 1938; children—Edward Kibbler, Rowena Pleming Chamberlin, Sidney Thomas. Profl. Bible tchr., 1953—; lectr. Calif. State U., Long Beach, 1960-66, U. So. Calif., 1963-65; Bible scholar for teaching Scriptures Program, First Ch. of Christ Scientist, Boston, 1970-75; free-lance Bible lectr., tchr., resource person for adult seminars, 1954—; active in summer teaching for young people, 1963-68, 86-87; tchr. adult edn. Principia Coll., summers 1969-71; tour lectr. to Middle East, yearly, 1974—; mem. archaeol. team, Negev, Israel. Mem. Am. Acad. Religion, AAUP, Soc. Biblical Lit. and Exegesis, Am. Schs. Oriental Research, Inst. Mediterranean Studies, Religious Edn. Assn., Internat. Congress Septuagint and Cognate Studies, Internat. Platform Assn., Phi Beta, Zeta Tau Alpha, Gamma Theta Upsilon. Republican. Christian Scientist. Author: Triumph of Job, 1979; editor Bibleletter Rev., 1968, 76, 81, 8-84.

PLETSCH, MARIE ELEANOR, plastic surgeon; b. Walkerton, Ont., Can., May 3, 1938; came to U.S. 1962; d. Ernest John and Olive Wilhemina (Hossfeld) P.; m. Ludwig Philip Breiling, Aug. 25, 1967; children: John, Michael, Anne. Dr. Med., U. Toronto, 1962. Diplomate Am. Bd. Plastic Surgery. Intern Cook County Hosp., Chgo., 1962-63, resident, gen. surgery, 1963-64; resident, gen. surgery St. Mary's Hosp., San Francisco, 1964-66; resident in plastic surgery St. Francis Hosp., San Francisco, 1966-69; practice med. specializing in plastic surgery Santa Cruz, Calif., 1969—; adminstr. Plasticenter, Inc., Santa Cruz, 1976-88, med. dir., 1987-88. Mem. Am. Soc. Plastic and Reconstructive Surgeons, Calif. Soc. Plastic Surgeons (mem. council 1986—, sec. 1989—), AMA, Calif. Med. Assn., Santa Cruz County Med. Soc. (bd. govs. 1983-88), Assn. Calif. Surgery Ctrs. (pres. 1988—). Roman Catholic. Office: Santa Cruz Can-Am Med Group 3003 Salisbury Ln Santa Cruz CA 95065

PLINE, DALE S., association administrator; b. 1938. BS, U. Idaho. Mgr. dairy farming ops. Larrydale Farms Inc., 1959-84; now pres. Dairymens Creamery Assn., also bd. dirs.; dir. Western Dairymen Coop. Inc., 1979-84. Mem. Idaho State Holstein Assn. (pres. 1965), Nat. Young Cooperators (sec. 1967, pres. 1968), N.W. Young Cooperators (pres. 1968), Idaho Dairymens Assn. (pres. 1974). Office: Dairymens Creamery Assn 5th & Albany Caldwell ID 83605 *

PLOEGER, JANICE ELIZABETH, political consultant; b. San Francisco, May 7, 1957; d. Richard Collins and Bonnie Marie (Daugherty) P. BS in Bus. and Mktg., San Diego State U., 1979. On-site cons. for market opinion rsch. re-election campaign Gov. Bill Clements, Austin, Tex., 1982, Senator Charles Percy, Chgo., 1983-84; dir. ops. polit. cons. div. Market Opinion Rsch., Detroit, 1984-85; on-site polit. cons. campaign for state assembly Chuck Quackenbush, San Jose, Calif., 1986-87, Brian Carroll, Riverside, Calif., 1988-89; fin. cons. Calif. Rep. Party, Sacramento, 1989—; chief staff Office Assemblyman Chuck Quackenbush, Sacramento, 1987-88, cons., 1988—. Chmn. bd. devel. Children's Home Soc., Santa Clara County, Calif., 1986-88, mem. Sacrement County, 1989; mem. Calif. Rep. Com., World Affairs Coun. No. Calif., 1988-89. Mem. NAFE. Congregationalist. Home: 4808B Sunset Terr Fair Oaks CA 95628 Office: Calif Rep Party 1228 N St #16 Sacramento CA 95814

PLOG, FRED, educator; b. Ft. Monmouth, N.J., July 19, 1944; s. Fred T. and Phyllis (Gessert) P.; m. Gayle Martha Gillham, Apr. 11,. BA in Econs., Northwestern U., 1966; MA in Anthropology, U. Chgo., 1968, PhD in Anthropology, 1969. Asst. prof. UCLA, 1969-72; assoc. prof. SUNY, Binghamton, 1972-75; prof. Ariz. State U., 1976-81, N.Mex. State U., Las Cruces, 1981—; pres. Past & Future, Inc., Las Cruces, N.Mex. 1979-. Author, editor 24 books; contbr. numerous articles to profl. jours. Fellow Am. Anthropol. Assn., Soc. for Am. Archaeology; mem. AAAS. Democrat. Roman Catholic. Home: 113 Lytton Circle Las Cruces NM 88001 Office: NMex State U Las Cruces NM 88003

PLOOG, HOLLI ILENE, electronics company executive; b. N.Y.C., Dec. 11, 1947; d. A.R. Goldin and Molly Beth (Greenberg) P.; m. Bertrand Charles Campbell, Nov. 20, 1941. BA, George Washington U., 1969; JD, Golden Gate U., 1980. Writer, prodn. assoc. Marvel Comics Group, N.Y.C., 1970-74; dir. Marin County Criminal Justice Dept., San Rafael, Calif., 1975-76, Marin County, San Rafael, Calif., 1976-80; atty. jud. coun. State of Alaska, Anchorage, 1980; legis. coun. State of Alaska, Juneau, 1981; ptnr. Dichter & Ploog Law Offices, 1981-84; dir. Anchorage Dept. Revenue, 1984-88; v.p. Lockheed Datacom Systems Corp., L.A., 1988—; bd. dirs. Nat. Coun. State Child Support Adminstrs., Washington, Nat. Child Support Enforcement Assn., Washington. Bd. dirs. Blood Bank Alaska, Anchorage, 1983-88; chair Alaska Women's Polit. Caucus, Anchorage, 1982-84; mem. state cen. com. Dem. Party, Anchorage, 1986-88; del. Dem. Party Conv., San Francisco, 1984. Mem. ABA, Alaska Bar Assn., Soroptomists. Democrat. Office: Lockheed Datacom Systems 818 W 7th Ste 801 Los Angeles CA 90017

PLOTKIN, ALLEN, aerospace engineering educator; b. N.Y.C., May 4, 1942; s. Oscar and Claire (Chasick) P.; m. Selena Berman, Dec. 18, 1966; children: Samantha Rose, Jennifer Anne. BS, Columbia U., 1963, MS, 1964; PhD, Stanford U., 1968. Asst. prof. aerospace engring. U. Md., College Park, 1968-72, assoc. prof., 1972-77, prof., 1977-85; prof. dept. aerospace engring. San Diego State U., 1985--, chmn. dept., 1985--; vis. assoc. Calif. Inst. Tech., Pasadena, 1975-76; cons. Naval Surface Weapons Ctr., White Oak, Md., 1981-84. Contbr. articles on aerodynamics, streamlining, propeller and wind tunnel to World Book Ency. Recipient Engring. Sci. award Washington Acad. Scis., 1981; rsch. grantee NASA, NSF; NASA-Am. Soc. Engring. Edn. summer faculty fellow, 1969-70. Fellow AIAA (assoc., assoc. editor jour. 1986—, Young Engr.-Scientist award Nat. Capital sect. 1976); mem. ASME, Soc. Naval Architects and Marine Engrs., Am. Helicopter Soc., Aerospace Dept. Chmn.'s Assn. (chmn. 1989-90), Sigma Xi, Tau Beta Pi. Democrat. Jewish. Home: 17364 St Andrews Dr Poway CA 92064 Office: San Diego State U Dept Aerospace Engring San Diego CA 92182

PLUM, RICHARD EUGENE, flight engineer; b. Alliance, Ohio, Feb. 24, 1928; s. Vernon and Mida Lucile (Halverstadt) P.; children: Pamela Sue Lachman, Patricia Ann Quaranto, Peggy Lynn, Richard John. Grad., Alliance High Sch. Cert. master aircraft mechanic, flight engr. Flight engr. Am. Airlines, Inc., Dallas, Ft. Worth, 1951—; check airman Am. Airlines,

Chgo., 1968-70. Served with USN, 1945-47. Recipient Top Gun award Western Fast Draw Assn., 1969. Mem. NRA, Calif. Rifle and Pistol Assn., World Fast Draw Assn. (chmn. 1984—, editor-pub. newsletter 1984—, Top Gun award 1988), Mid-Western Fast Draw Assn. (chmn. 1964-68, Mid-Am. champion 1967, Chgo. conf. champion 1968), Restless Guns. Republican. Home and Office: 16421 McFadden #350 Tustin CA 92680

PLUMB, JAN CHARLES, construction company executive, real estate broker, architectural designer; b. Glendale, Calif., Mar. 11, 1952; s. Gerald Barney and Lucille (Mortenson) P.; m. Frances Rae Jean Hanson, May 31, 1980; children: Chad, Tara, Bree, Brittany. BBA, Nat. U., 1986. Lic. gen. contractor, Calif. Carpenter Plumb Constrn., North Hollywood, Calif., 1967-70; v.p. Plumb Constrn., North Hollywood, 1973-78; pres. Plumb Constrn., San Diego, 1978-82; pres., owner Plumb Constrn., Encinitas, Calif., 1982—; supt. Eglet Constrn., Reseda, Calif., 1970-72; ptnr. J&J Constrn. Co., North Hollywood, 1972-73; owner, real estate broker Plumb Properties, Encinitas, Calif., 1984—; developer custom homes Fairbanks Ranch, 1987, Rancho La Cima Estates, 1988. Exec. sec. Cardiff (Calif.) 1st ward Ch. of Jesus Christ of Latter day Saints, 1982—; mem. Olivenhain Town Council, Encinitas, 1986—. Mem. Encinitas Contractors Assn., Encinitas Bd. Realtors, Carlsbad C. of C. (growth mgmt. com. 1982-86), Rotary. Republican. Office: Plumb constrn 1416 Rancho Encinitas Dr Olivenhain CA 92024

PLUMLEY, DONALD JACKSON, sales automation consultant; b. Pasadena, Calif., May 4, 1962; s. Don W. and Michiko (Kusayanagi) P.; m. Beth Ann Friedenberg, Jan. 17, 1987. BS in Physiology, U. Calif., Davis, 1985. Mktg. assoc. Entre Computer Ctr., Irvine, Calif., 1985-86; field sales engr. Honeywell, Inc., Orange, Calif., 1986-88; pres., founder SaleSolutions, Inc., Irvine, 1988—; cons. Honeywell, Inc., Orange and Freeport, Ill., McKinsey & Co., Inc., L.A., Bergen Brunswig, Orange. Office: SaleSolutions Inc 18552 MacArthur Blvd 395 Irvine CA 92715

PLUMMER, LAURA JEAN, nurse; b. Chgo., Dec. 19, 1956; d. Richard Cecil Davis and Bonnie Carol (Breischke) Nelson; m. Gregory S. Plummer, Sept. 8, 1979; children: Stephen Allen, Erin Kathleen. AA, Diablo Valley Coll., 1977; BS, Calif. State U., 1979. Staff nurse John Muir Hosp., Walnut Creek, Calif., 1979-83; asst. head nurse endocrine/renal unit John Muir Meml. Hosp., Walnut Creek, 1983-84, head nurse endocrine/renal unit, 1984-86; program coord. Metabolic Nutrition Program, Inc., Walnut Creek, 1986—; cons. Metabolic Nutrition Program, Inc., various locations, 1986—. Leader youth group, St. Luke's Lutheran Ch., Walnut Creek, 1980-82; bd. dirs. Diabetes Soc. Contra Costa, Walnut Creek, 1981-84; vol. Walnut Creek unit Am. Heart Assn., 1988. Office: Metabolic Nutrition Program Ste 120 112 La Casa Via Walnut Creek CA 94598

PLUMMER, MARCIE STERN, real estate executive; b. Plymouth, Mass., Oct. 28, 1950; d. Jacob and Rosalie (Adelman) Stern; m. John Dillon McHugh II, Oct. 8, 1974 (div.); 1 child, Joshua Stern; m. Louis Freeman Plummer Jr., Sept. 25, 1982; children: Jessica Price, Denelle Boothe. BA, Am. Internat. Coll., 1972, MA in Edn., 1973; postgrad., U. Conn., 1974; lic. real estate broker, Anthony Sch. Real Estate, Walnut Creek, Calif., 1985. Educator, chair dept. Windsor Locks (Conn.) Sch. Dist., 1972-74; educator, placement dir. Heald Bus. Coll., San Francisco, 1974-77; educator evening and day divs. Diablo Valley Coll., Pleasant Hill, Calif., 1975-77; real estate agt. Morrison Homes, Pleasant Hill, 1977-78; real estate agt., tract mgr. Dividend Devel., Santa Clara, Calif., 1978-81; real estate broker, owner The Preséd Co. Inc. subs. Better Homes Realty, Danville, Calif., 1981—. Better Homes Realty rep. for orgn. of Danville 4th of July Parade, 1984-88; publicist San Ramon Valley Little League, Alamo, Calif., 1986—; active Battered Women's Found., Contra Costa County, Calif., 1986—; active Rep. voter registration, Walnut Creek, Calif., 1987-88; mem. Civic Arts Coun., Walnut Creek, 1988—. Recipient numerous nat., state and regional awards in field. Mem. Bldg. Industry Assn. (Sales vol. award 1978-89), Sales & Mktg. Coun. (sponsor MAME awards banquet 1978-89, Gold sponsor 1986-88), Calif. Assn. Realtors, Contra Costa Bd. Realtors. Jewish. Home: 123 Erselia Trail Alamo CA 94507 Office: The Presèd Co Inc 360 Diablo Rd Danville CA 94526

PLUNKETT, JOSEPH CHARLES, electrical engineering educator; b. Centerville, Tenn., Dec. 3, 1933; s. Harold D. and Lorraine (Lewis) P. B.S., Middle Tenn. State U., 1964; B.S.E.E., U. Tenn., 1966; M.S.E.E., Ga. Inst. Tech., 1973; Ph.D., Tex. A&M U., 1978. Registered profl. engr., Mass. Devel. engr. Martin Marietta Co., Orlando, Fla., 1966-69; research engr. Raytheon Co., Wayland, Mass., 1969-71, IIT Research Inst., Annapolis, Md., 1971-72, Tex. A&M U., College Station, 1974-77; assoc. prof. elec. engring. Calif. State U.-Fresno, 1977-80, prof., 1980—, chmn. dept., 1980-84; cons. Author numerous articles in field. Served to capt. Ordnance Corps, USAR, 1958-66. Mem. IEEE, Nat. Soc. Profl. Engrs., N.Y. Acad. Scis., Sigma Xi, Eta Kappa Nu. Republican. Mem. Ch. of Christ. Office: Calif State U Fresno CA 93740

PLUTA, LEE J., manufacturing company executive; b. Newark, Aug. 10, 1944; s. Leon Michael and Virginia (Kucharski) P.; m. Carol Ann Bell, Apr. 11, 1964; children: Douglas W., Christine A., Sandra L. Student, E. Carolina Coll., Greenville, N.C., 1963. Mgr. plating dept. Mitronics-Varadyne, Murray Hill, N.J., 1964-71; tech. sales engr. Enthone Inc., West Haven, Conn., 1971-82; sr. sales engr. Electrochems., Youngstown, Ohio, 1982-83; mfg. mgr. Info. Memories Corp., Santa Clara, Calif., 1983-85; sr. sales engr. Electrochems., Youngstown, 1985-87; dir. engring./v.p. ops. Dynamic Disk Inc., Carlsbad, Calif., 1987-88; pres. Burton MagneKote Inc., Inglewood, Calif., 1988—. Chmn. sch. site coun. Marilyn Ave. Sch., Livermore, Calif., 1982-83. Mem. Am. Electro Plating Soc. Republican. Roman Catholic. Home: 12244 Creekside Ct San Diego CA 92131 Office: Burton MagneKote Inc 343 Glasgow Ave Inglewood CA 90301

PLUTCHAK, NOEL BERNARD, meteorologist, consultant; b. Green Bay, Wis., Dec. 14, 1932; s. Bernard Edward and Violet Marie P.; m. Sandra Kolvig (div.); 1 child, Channin. BS in Geology, U. Wis., 1960; MS in Meteorology, Fla. State U.u, 19674; postgrad., Oreg. State U. Research asst. Columbia U., Lamont Geol. Inst., Nyack, N.Y., 1960-64; dir. theoretical studies Bendix Marine Advisors, La Jolla, Calif., 1965-69; research assoc. U. So. Calif., Los Angeles, 1972-75; chief scientist Interstate Electronics, Ocean Engring. Div., Anaheim, Calif., 1975-83, Raytheon Svcs., Ocean Engring. Div., Ventura, Calif., 1984-87; chief exec. officer, chief scientist Active Leak Testing, Inc., San Pedro, Calif., 1987--. Inventor: EarthProbe process, patent 1988, (other patents in 1960's); contbr. articles to profl. jours. With USAF, 1952-56. Mem. Am. Geophys Union, Marine Tech. Soc., Experimental Aircraft Assn. Republican. Office: Active Leak Testing Inc 1300 S Beacon St Ste 120 San Pedro CA 90731

PLUTH, JOHN VICTOR, data processing executive; b. Cleve., Dec. 24, 1951; s. Elmer Victor and Marie (Parme) P.; m. Karen Anne Conklin, June 21, 1975. BS in Computer Sci., Ohio State U., 1973; MS in Computer Sci., U. Ariz., 1976. Cert. commodity trading advisor. Computer/stats. analyst Coll. Edn. Ohio State U., Columbus, 1973-76; cons. computer ctr. U. Ariz., Tucson, 1975-76; programmer/analyst Computing Assocs., Inc., Tucson, 1976-78; sr. analyst Control Data Corp., Tucson, 1978-80; programmer/analyst Halco Commodity Research, Dallas, 1980-86; software mfr. Halco Commodity Research, 1988—; hedging cons. Silver & Gold Assocs., Tucson, 1987—; software cons. Systems and Solutions, Tucson, 1986—, software mfr., 1988—. Author: Grand Canyon Echo, 1987. Active Sierra Club, Tucson, 1974-87, Legal Def. Fund, San Francisco, 1984-87, Nat. Resource Def. Coun., Washington, 1984-87, Ariz. Civil Liberties Union, Phoenix, 1985-86. Mem. Nat. Futures Assn. Home and Office: 10011 N Orange Ranch Rd Tucson AZ 85741

PLYMYER, JOHN ROBERT, professional association administrator; b. Emigsville, Pa., Oct. 21, 1931; s. Gordon Norris and Helen May (Eyler) P.; m. Lois Harwood, June 14, 1952; children: Thomas, John, Carol. BA in Edn., Calif. State U., 1956, MA in Elem. Edn., 1958. Cert. assn. exec. 1977. Tchr. Garden Grove (Calif.) Unified Sch. Dist., 1955-59, prin., 1961-62; vice-prin., curriculum coord. Los Alamitos (Calif.) Unified Sch. Dist., 1959-61; dir., customer svc. Crown Zellerbach Corp., L.A., 1962-69; dir., chpt. coord. Calif. Soc. CPAs, L.A., 1969-81, dir., member svc. dir., 1981-84; exec. dir. Wash. Soc. CPAs, Bellevue, Wash., 1984—. Author numerous articles in field. Candidate Garden Grove City Council, 1958; active Blue Ribbon Sch. Reorganization and Sch. Closure Com., Garden Grove, 1983. Mem. Am. Soc. Assn. Execs. (bd. dirs. 1988—), So. Calif. Soc. Assn. Execs. (pres. 1977-78, Exec. of Yr. award 1983), Washington Soc. Assn. Execs. (pres. 1987-88), Bellevue Athletic Club, Lakes Club, Rotary. Democrat. Episcopalian. Office: Wash Soc CPAs 902 140th Ave NE Bellevue WA 98005

POCHARDT-JOHNSON, CAROL ANNE, computer scientist; b. Lewiston, Idaho, Apr. 6, 1957; d. Arthur Ralph Noah and Wilma Jean (Wolfe) Pochardt; m. Karl Walter Johnson, May 20, 1979; 1 child, Katrina Grace. BSEE, U. Idaho, 1979; MS in Computer Sci., Wash. State U., 1987. Statis. programmer U. Idaho, Moscow, Idaho, 1979-80; systems programmer I Wash. State U. Computing Service Ctr., Pullman, 1980-83, systems programmer II, 1983-85, systems programmer III, 1985-88; mgr. network systems computing svc. ctr. Wash. State U., Pullman, 1988—. Mem. Pres.'s Commn. on the Status of Women, Pullman, 1988—, Latah County Humane Soc., Moscow, 1988. Mem. Nat. Assn. Female Execs., Wash. State Data Processing Mgrs. Lutheran. Clubs: Inland Empire Brittany (Spokane, Wash.)(v.p. 1986—), Palouse Hills Dog Fanciers (Pullman). Office: Wash State U Computing Svc Ctr Pullman WA 99164-1220

POCHINI, JUDY HAY, interior designer; b. Phoenix, Mar. 16, 1932; d. Cecil Clifford and Nadine Mary (Larimer) Cook; m. Gordon Eugene Hay, June 5, 1971 (dec. 1974); m. Robert Frank Pochini, Sept. 18, 1983. BA, U. Calif., Santa Barbara, 1953; MA in Journalism, U. Calif., Berkeley, 1965. Exec. sec. Mobil Oil Corp., Mpls., 1958-60, Kaiser Aluminum & Chem. Corp., Oakland, Calif., 1960-64; asst. trade publ. editor Sunset mag., Menlo Park, Calif., 1966-68, trade publ. editor, 1968-73; owner, home furnishings editor Lifestyle West, Walnut Creek, Calif., 1974-79; interior designer Berman's Drexel-Heritage, Oakland, 1979-85, Suburban House Drexel-Heritage, Concord, Calif., 1986-87; ptnr., interior designer Judy Hay Interiors, Lafayette, Calif., 1987—; mem. nat. consumer action panel Carpet & Rug Industry, Dalton, Ga., 1973-75; cons. in field. Contbr. articles to profl. jours. Mem. Am. Soc. Interior Designers (affiliate), Internat. Furnishings & Design Assn., Women in Communications Inc., Lakeview Club, Chi Omega. Republican. Mem. Unity Ch. Office: Judy Hay Interiors 47 Lafayette Circle Ste 167 Lafayette CA 94549

POCHOP, MARILYN ANN, nurse; b. Carson City, Nev., June 13, 1953; d. Stanley F. and Marilyn L. (Pruuett) Pochop Harper; m. Edmond James Miller, Aug. 4, 1980 (div. 1986); children: Chad Jason, Heather Nicole, Jamie Lyn. Assoc., Truckee Meadows Community Coll., Reno, 1983; student, Weber State U., 1989—. RN, Nev. Nurse St. Mary's Regional Med. Ctr., Reno, 1979-86, maternal outreach edn. coord., 1986-88, dept. mgr. labor, delivery and antepartum Birthing Ctr., 1988—; edutor, speaker in field. Mem. Am. Nurses Assn., Nat. Flight Nurses Assn. Democrat. Presbyterian. Home: 7477 Limestone Dr Reno NV 89511 Office: St Mary's Regional Med Ctr 235 W 6th St Reno NV 89520

POCKLINGTON, PETER H., business executive; b. Regina, Sask., Can., Nov. 18, 1941; s. Basil B. and Eileen (Dempsey) P.; m. Eva McAvoy, June 2, 1974; 4 children. Pres. Westown Ford, Tilbury, Ont., Can., 1967-69; pres. Chatham, Ont., 1969-71, Edmonton, Alta., Can., from 1971; now chmn. Pocklington Fin. Corp. Ltd., Edmonton; owner, gov. Edmonton Oiler Hockey Club, 1976—. Office: Pocklington Fin Corp Ltd, 2500 Sun Life Pl, 10123-99 St, Edmonton, AB Canada T5J 3H1 other: Edmonton Oilers, Edmonton, AB Canada T5B 4M9 *

PODBOY, JOHN WATTS, psychologist; b. York, Pa., Sept. 27, 1943; s. August John and Harriett Virginia (Watts) P.; 1 son, Matthew John. B.A., Dickinson Coll., 1966; M.S., San Diego State Coll., 1971; Ph.D., U. Ariz., 1973. Dir., Vets. Counseling Center, U. Ariz., Tucson, 1972-73; project dir. San Mateo County (Calif.) Human Relations Dept., Redwood City, 1974; staff psychologist Sonoma State Hosp., Eldridge, Calif., 1975-81; cons. clin. psychologist Comprehensive Care Corp., Newport Beach, Calif., 1974-75, Sonoma County (Calif.) Probation Dept., 1976-88; pvt. practice, 1982—; asst. prof. Sonoma State U., 1977-81; dir. Sonoma Diagnostic and Remedial Center, 1979-82. Chmn. San Mateo County Diabetes Assn., 1975. Served to lt. USNR, 1966-69. Fellow Am. Coll. Forensic Psychology, Am. Bd. Med. Psychotherapists (fellow); mem. Am. Psychol. Assn., Western Psychol. Assn., Redwood Psychol. Assn. (pres. 1983), Nat. Council Alcoholism, Nat. Rehab. Assn. Home: PO Box 488 Kenwood CA 95452

POETTMANN, FRED HEINZ, petroleum engineering educator; b. Germany, Dec. 20, 1919; s. Fritz and Kate (Hussen) P.; m. Anna Bell Hall, May 29, 1952; children—Susan Trudy, Phillip Mark. B.S., Case Western Res. U., 1942; M.S., U. Mich., 1944, Sc.D., 1946; grad., Advanced Mgmt. Program, Harvard U., 1966. Registered profl. engr., Colo., Okla. Research chemist Lubrizol Corp., Wickliffe, Ohio, 1942-43; mgr. production research Phillips Petroleum Co., Bartlesville, Okla., 1946-55; asso. research dir. Marathon Oil Co., 1955-72; mgr. comml. devel. Marathon Oil Co., Littleton, Colo., 1972-83; prof. petroleum engineering Colo. Sch. Mines, 1983—. Contbr. articles to numerous publs.; co-author, editor 9 books in field; patentee in field. Chmn. S. Suburban Met.Recreation and Park Dist., 1966-71; chmn. Littleton Press Council, 1967-71; bd. dirs. Hancock Recreation Center,Findlay, Ohio, 1973-77. Mem. Nat. Acad. Engring., Soc. Petroleum Engrs., Am. Inst. Chem. Engring., Am. Chem. Soc., Am. Petroleum Inst., Sigma Xi, Tau Beta Pi, Alpha Chi Sigma, Phi Kappa Phi, Pi Epsilon Tau. Republican. Home: 47 Eagle Dr Littleton CO 80123 Office: Colo Sch Mines Dept Petroleum Engring Golden CO 80401

POHLMAN, DAVID LAWRENCE, federal systems consultant; b. Detroit, May 17, 1944; s. Lawrence Luther and Lois Betty (Huffcut) P.; m. Diane Lee Ewing, Dec. 27, 1967 (div. Dec. 1980); children: Scott David, Anne Kiersten; m. Katherine Margaret Wattigney, Dec. ll, 1981; children: Ann Margaret Williams, David Joseph Williams. BS in Edn., Ohio U., 1967; MA in Psychology, U. No. Colo., 1977. Commd. officer USAF, 1967, advanced through grades to lt. col.; instr. pilot USAF, Chandler, Ariz., 1975-78, rsch. pilot., 1978-82; div. chief USAF, San Antonio, 1982-87; ret. 1987; tng. div. mgr. Gallegos Rsch. Group, Wheatridge, Colo., 1987-88; pres. Dave Pohlman Assocs., Aurora, Colo., 1988; mgr. fed. systems Andersen Cons., Denver, 1988—; com. chmn. Dept. Def., Washington, 1982-87, subcom. mem. industry panel, 1988—; subcom. mem. Intersvc.-Industry Tng. System, Orlando, Fla., 1987. Contbr. articles to profl. publs. Mem. Am. Edn1. Rsch. Assn., Am. Def. Preparedness Assn., Nat. Security Indsl. Assn., Air Force Assn., Aurora Athletic Club. Roman Catholic. Home: 2557 S Evanston St Aurora CO 80014 Office: Andersen Cons 717 17th St Ste 1900 Denver CO 80202

POIMIROO, JOHN ROBERT, marketing executive; b. San Mateo, Calif., Nov. 7, 1946; s. Maurice John and Irene Frances (Ducasse) P.; m. Joan Kathryn Poimiroo. AA, Coll. San Mateo, 1967; BA in Pub. Rels., San Jose State U., 1969; MA in Journalism, U. Colo., 1973. Grad. teaching asst. U. Colo., Boulder, 1972-73; dir. pub. rels. Lake Eldora Ski Area, Nederland, Calif., 1973-74; dir. mktg. Squaw Valley USA, Olympic Valley, Calif., 1974-75; gen. sales mgr. Marriott's Great Am., Santa Clara, Calif., 1975-81; v.p. Hoefer Amidei, San Francisco, 1981-82; group v.p. Ketchum Pub. Rels., San Francisco, 1982-85; v.p. mktg., pub. rels. Roaring Camp Inc., Felton, 1985-86; dir. mktg. Yosemite (Calif.) Park & Curry Co., MCA Inc., 1986—; Photographer various publicity photos; film maker (video clip) March. Moderator Candidates Night, Yosemite Nat. Park, 1987-88; cubmaster local pack. Boy Scouts Am. Mem. Calif. Travel Industry Assn. (v.p. 1988-89, 2nd v.p. 1987-88, pres. 1989—), So. Am. Travel Writers, Pub. Rels. Soc. Am., Soc. Profl. Journalists, U.S. Ski Writers Assn. Roman Catholic. Office: Yosemite Park & Curry Co PO Box 182 Yosemite CA 95389

POIRIER, RICHARD OVEILA, talent agent, personal manager, motion picture investment company executive; b. Boston, Dec. 10, 1947; s. Oveila A. and Evelyn G. (Sullivan) P. Student, George Washington U., 1968; diploma in Law, City of London Coll., 1969; BS summa cum laude, Boston U., 1976. Exec. producer Kaleidescope Records, Boston, 1979-81; acct., law office mgr. William R. Dickerson & Assocs., Los Angeles, 1981; artist royalty supr. Capitol and EMI Am. Records, Hollywood, Calif., 1981-83; dir. royalties Warner/Elektra/Atlantic Internat. Records, Warner Home Video, Burbank, Calif., 1983-86; pres. Richard Poirier and Assocs., Los Angeles, 1986—; cons. in field.; guest speaker various functions. Contbr. articles to Boston U. Pubs., The Daily Free Press, 1975-76. Mem. Ford Hall Forum, Boston, 1974-79, Boston Mus. Fine Art, 1973-79. With U.S. Army, 1967-69. Mem. Nat. Acad. Rec. Arts and Scis., Nat. Acad. Video Arts and Scis., Beverly Hills Bar Assn. (entertainment law sect., legis. com.), Music Industry Network, Hollywood C. of C., 5% Club of L.A., Mondrian Models and Photographers Club, The Actors Ctr., Club de L'Ermitage. Home: 11701 Oxnard St #1 North Hollywood CA 91606 Office: Richard Poirier & Assocs 3575 Cahuenga Blvd W #254 Los Angeles CA 90068

POIRIER, ROLAND LEONARD, management consultant; b. Gardner, Mass., July 28, 1941; s. Clarence and Irene (St. Cyr) P. BA, Georgetown U., 1963. With personnel dept. IBM, Gaithersburg (Md.), Atlantic City, 1964-69; rep. mktg. IBM, Los Angeles, San Francisco, 1964-71; sr. cons. Peat, Marwick, Main, Los Angeles, 1971-75; ptnr. Poirier, Hoevel & Co., Los Angeles, N.Y.C., Paris, 1975—; bd. dirs. Communications Bridge, Maga-Link, also sec. Served with USCGR, 1964-70. Mem. TV Acad., Calif. Exec. Recruiters Assn., Westside Shelter Coalition, Motion Picture and TV Controllers Assn. Democrat. Roman Catholic. Home: 110 Ocean Park Blvd Santa Monica CA 90405 Office: Poirier Hoevel & Co 12400 Wilshire Blvd Los Angeles CA 90025

POIROT, JAMES WESLEY, engineering company executive; b. Douglas, Wyo., 1931; m. Raeda Poirot. BCE, Oreg. State U., 1953. With various constrn. firms, Alaska and Oreg.; with CH2M Hill Inc., 1953—, v.p., Seattle and Atlanta, from 1967, chmn. bd., Englewood, Colo., 1983—; former chmn. CEO Western Regional Council, Design Profls. Coalition. Named ENR Constrn. Man of Yr., 1988. Fellow ASCE (chmn. steering com. quality manual from 1985, bd. dirs.); mem. Am. Cons. Engrs. Coun. (pres. 1989—). Office: CH2M Hill Inc 6060 S Willow Dr Englewood CO 80111

POLAKOFF, KEITH IAN, historian, university administrator; b. N.Y.C., Dec. 12, 1941; s. Irwin L. and Edna (Sopkin) P.; m. Carol J. Gershuny, June 21, 1964; children: Amy Ellen, Adam Matthew. BA magna cum laude, Clark U., 1963; MA, Northwestern U., Evanston, Ill., 1966, PhD, 1968. Lectr. Herbert H. Lehman Coll., CUNY, 1967-69; asst. prof. history Calif. State U., Long Beach, 1969-73, assoc. prof. 1973-78, prof., 1978—, assoc. dean instrnl. support Sch. Social and Behavioral Scis., 1980-81, assoc. dean ednl. policy, 1981-84, dean, 1985-86; dean Sch. Fine Arts, 1984-85, asst. v.p. acad. affairs, dean grad. studies, 1986—; mem. coun. Big West Conf. (formerly Pacific Coast Athletic Assn.), 1982—, Western Collegiate Athletic Assn., 1982-85. Author: The Politics of Inertia, 1973, (with others) Generations of Americans, 1976, Political Parties in American History, 1981; contbg. author: The Presidents: A Reference History, 1984; editor: The History Tchr., 1972-77, prodn. mgr., 1977-80. Mem., clk. bd. trustees Los Alamitos Sch. Dist., 1980-81; bd. dirs. Long Beach Opera Assn., 1981—, pres. 1982-83, treas., 1987-88. Avocations: travel, photography. Home: 2971 Druid Ln Los Alamitos CA 90720 Office: Calif State U 1250 Bellflower Blvd Long Beach CA 90840

POLAN, DAVID JAY, television company executive, lawyer; b. Chgo., Feb. 16, 1951; s. Julius and Jeanne Warsaw (Fox) P.; m. Terri Susan Lapin, Aug. 3, 1980; children: Adam Michael, Daniel Jacob, Jennifer Leigh. BA, U. Ill., 1972; JD, John Marshall Law Sch., Chgo., 1975. Bar: Ill. 1975, U.S. Dist. Ct. (no. dist.) Ill. 1975, U.S. Ct. Appeals (7th cir.) 1976. Atty., Pritzker & Glass, Ltd., Chgo., 1975-78, Barnett, Ettinger, Glass, Berkson & Braverman, Chgo., 1978-79; gen. mgr. Y.P. Aurora, Ltd., Ill., 1979-83; counsel, corp. sec. JP Communications Co., Tucson, 1981—; sta. mgr. KPOL-TV, Tucson, 1983-86, gen. mgr., 1986—; gen. counsel Northtown Bus Svc., Ltd., Lincolnwood, Ill., 1975-88; gen. ptnr. THC Ptnrs., Chgo., 1980—; co-owner LV Pictures, Las Vegas, 1984-86. Active Orchard Village Assn. for Handicapped, Skokie, Ill., 1981 , co-owner Rockford Lightning Continental Basketball Assn., 1986—; mem. Soviet Jewry commn., Jewish Fedn. So. Ariz., Tucson, 1984, leadership devel. program, 1984-87, chmn., 1985-87, bd. dirs., 1985—, active various coms.; mem. bd. Congregation Bet Shalom, 1984; assoc. mem. Hadassah, Tucson, 1984; mem. nat. com. for leadership devel. Coun. Jewish Fedn., 1986—, chmn. western area 1988—; bd. dirs. Jewish Family and Children's Svcs., 1986—, also sec. 1988—, Jewish Community Found., 1987—, Tucsonans Say No to Drugs, 1986-87, 88-Crime, 1986-89, treas. 1987. Recipient Community Svc. Award Jewish Fedn. So. Ariz., 1987—, Meritorious Svc. award, 1988, Gary I. Sarver Young Man of Yr. award, 1989. Mem. ABA, Davis-Mountain AFB Counties of 50, Volk Jewish Community Ctr. Club, Diehard Cubs Fan Club, Ventana Canyon Golf and Racquet Club. Office: Sta KPOL-TV Channel 40 2475 N Jack Rabbit Ave Tucson AZ 85745

POLAND, MERLE GORDON, electrical engineer; b. Eugene, Oreg., Mar. 26, 1909; s. Cortus Oscar and Lola Jane (Spurling) P;; m. Audrey Larie Dirr, Aug. 13, 1930; children: Shirley Jean Poland Slack, Janice Rae Poland Lee. BSEE, Wash. State U., 1930, MSEE, 1933. Cert. profl. elec. engr., Oreg. Elec. engr. Bell Telephone Labs., N.Y.C., 1930-32; elec. engr., sales Portland Gas & Coke Co., Oreg., 1935-38; elec. engr. Bonneville Power Adminstrn., Portland, 1938-44, 46-72, cons. elec. engring., 1975-77; cons. elec. engring. Commonwealth Assocs., Rio de Janeiro, Jackson, Mich., 1973-74, Burns and McDonnell, Kansas City, Mo., 1977-88. Served to lt. comdr. USNR, 1944-46. Mem. IEEE, NSPE, Bioelectromagnetics Soc. Democrat. Methodist. Home: 12660 SE Main Portland OR 97233

POLEN, DANNY BRENT, controller; b. Glen Dale, W.Va., Jan. 17, 1952; s. Carrell Lloyd and Iris Jean (Francis) P.; m. Margie Ellen Young, Dec. 4, 1971; children: Amy Marie, Molly Anne, Danny Brent. BA, W. Liberty State Coll., 1973. CPA, W.Va. Staff acct. Allied Chem., Moundsville, W.Va., 1974-77; bus. controller Allied Chem., W. Conshonocken, Pa., 1977-79; construction controller Autex Fiber, Nitro, W.Va., 1979; sr. internal auditor Union Carbide Corp., S. Charleston, W.Va., 1980-84; nat. account mgr. Union Carbide Corp., St. Petersburg, Fla., 1984-86; controller Union Carbide Corp., Oakland, Calif., 1986-88; div. mgr. Union Carbide Corp., Oakland, 1988—. Mem. Am. Inst. of CPA's, Nat. Rifle Assn., Fla. Inst. of CPA's, Calif. Inst. of CPA's, Rep. Exec. Com., Alpha Kappa Psi (treas. 1972-73). Republican. Methodist. Club: Demolay. Office: Union Carbide Corp 1171 Ocean Ave Oakland CA 94608

POLESON, KATHRYN LANE, dentist; b. Moscow, Idaho, Dec. 2, 1947; m. Thomas S. Dowdy. BS, U. Idaho, Moscow, 1970; DMD, Oreg. Sch. Dentistry, 1975. Vol. dentist Christian Missionaries, Lesotho, South Africa, 1974, Agy. for Internat. Dentistry, Cameroon, Africa, 1975; dental clinic coordinator Multnomah County Health, Portland, 1978-81; gen. dentist Army Dental Clinic, Frankfurt, Germany, 1981-84; pvt. practice Portland, 1985—; chmn. Internat. Relations Am. Student Dental Assn., 1973-75; instr. Oreg. Health Scis. Ctr., Portland, 1978-81; dentist Dammasch State Hosp., 1978-79, Wilsonville, Oreg., 1978-87. Aux. work, Oreg. Symphony Orch. Capt. U.S. Army 1975-77, maj. Res. 1983—. Fellow Acad. Gen. Dentistry; mem. ADA, Multnomah County Dental Soc., Oreg. Dental Assn., Wash. State Dental Assn. Office: 511 SW 10th Ste 802 Portland OR 97205

POLICASTRO, MARTHA JO, restaurateur; b. Shawnee, Okla., June 3, 1945; d. Joe Policastro and Martha Sue (Taylor) Finley. Student, N. Tex. State U., 1965-66. Flight attendant Am. Airlines, San Francisco, 1968-72, Republic Airlines, 1972-77; floor ops. mgr., staff recruitment and tng., with pub. relations and promotions dept. Scott's Seafood Restaurant, San Francisco, 1977-81; gen. mgr. Osteria Romana, San Francisco, 1982; with Bentley's Oyster Bar and Seafood Restaurant, San Francisco, 1983-86; with pub. relations dept., floor mgr. Cafe Royale, San Francisco; pres., founder Restii, Inc., San Francisco, 1986; owner Maltese Grill subs. Restii and MTP Enterprises, San Francisco, 1987—; founder Butterworks, Inc., 1985; cons. to David Keh on Safari Grill, N.Y.C.; speaker Golden Gate U., 1986-87. Food editor San Francisco mag., 1984-85. Dir., Christmas Eve Lunches for Homeless, San. Francisco Glide Meml. Ch., 1984, 85, 86; hon. dir. Cold Nights, Warm Hearts Benefit, San Francisco, 1987-88. Recipient award San Fransisco Bd. Suprs., Outstanding Svc. Merit award City of San Francisco, 1988. Mem. Internat. Food and Wine Soc., Telegraph Hill Club. Republican. Office: The Maltese Grill 20 Annie st San Francisco CA 94105

POLIS, SAMUEL, chemical company executive; b. Phila., Feb. 15, 1926; s. Abraham and Reba (Shalita) P.; m. Bette Jane Oaks, Dec. 27, 1950; children: Stephen Guy, Diane Gayle. BSChemE, U. Pa., 1950; MBA, U. Conn., 1980. Plastics engr. Naval Air Exptl. Sta., Phila., 1952-56; tech. svc. rep. flexible urethane foam Mobay Chem. Co., Pitts., 1956-60; mgr. urethane rsch. and devel. Olin Corp., New Haven, 1960-82; tech. dir. western region Crain Industries, Compton, Calif., 1982-87; ret. Crain Industries, Compton, 1987. Contbr. articles to profl. jours.; patentee in field. Served to capt. U.S. Army, 1944-45, ETO, 1950-52, Korea. Decorated Bronze Star medal with oak leaf cluster; recipient Superior Accomplishment award Naval Air Exptl. Sta. 1956. Mem. Soc. Plastics Industry (asst. chmn. flexible foam tech. com. 1968-69, chmn. 1970-71, 78-80), Am. Legion (vice comdr. Wilton, Conn. chpt. 1981-82). Home: 170 Grumman Hill Rd Wilton CA 06897

POLLACK, DANIEL, concert pianist; b. Los Angeles, Jan. 23, 1935. MS in Music, Juilliard Sch., 1957, Acad. Musik, Vienna, Austria, 1958. Asst. prof. U. Hartford, Conn., 1966-70; prof. piano U. So. Calif., Los Angeles, 1971—. Concert performances in U.S., USSR, Europe, Far East, South Am. Recipient prize Internat. Tschaikowsky Piano Competition, Moscow, USSR, 1958; Fulbright grantee, 1957-58; Martha Baird Rockefeller Found. grantee, 1963. Mem. Am. Fedn. Musicians, Kosciuszko Found., Chopin Found., Music Tchrs. Nat. Assn. (nat. exec. bd.). Office: U So Calif Dept Music Los Angeles CA 90089 *

POLLACK, DAVID ALAN, psychiatrist, psychiatry professor; b. Tulsa, Oct. 21, 1947; s. Simon and Roberta Muriel (Friedman) P.; m. Veda Kathryn Kerr, May 1, 1971; 1 child, Sasha. BA, Northwestern U., 1969; MD, Oklahoma Health Scis. Ctr., 1973. Psychiat. dir. Delannay Mental Health Ctr., Portland, Oreg., 1976-87; psychiat. cons. Conquest Ctr., Portland, 1983-86, Displaced Homemaker Program, Oregon City, 1986—; med. dir. Mental Health Svcs. West, Portland, 1987—; assoc. dir. Pub. Psychiat. Tng. Program, Portland, 1987—; psychiat. cons. Dammasch State Hosp., Wilsonville, Oreg., 1987—; adj. asst. prof. dept. psychiat. Oreg. Health Scis. U., Portland, 1987—. Contbr. articles to profl. jours. Founding mem. Disarmanent Media Network Oreg., Portland, 1982-86. Mem. Am. Psychiat. Assn., Physicians for Social Responsibility (v.p. Portland chpt. 1986—), Am. Assn. Community Psychiatrists. Democrat. Office: Mental Health Svcs West 710 SW 2d Portland OR 97204

POLLAK, JERRY LESLIE, architect; b. Chgo., Apr. 23, 1929; s. Emery P.; m. Marcia Kovenock, June 20, 1951; m. Michael, Shira, Oren. BArch, Ill. Inst. Tech., 1956. Registered architect, Calif., Nev. Staff planner City of San Bernardino, Calif., 1956-57; ptnr. Pollak-Jaharis Engring., San Bernardino, 1957-59; assoc. Victor Gruen Assocs., L.A., 1959-69; ptnr. Pollak, Barsochinni & Assocs., L.A., 1970-73; pres. Jerry L. Pollak AIA & Assocs., Sherman Oaks, Calif., 1973—; cons., expert witness in field. Sgt. U.S. Army, 1953-55, Korea. Mem. AIA, Am. Soc. Consulting Planners. Democrat. Jewish. Home and Office: 14319 Millbrook Dr Sherman Oaks CA 91423

POLLAR, ODETTE MARIE, business consultant; b. Oakland, Calif., July 10, 1955; d. Henry Armstead and Mary Ann (Marsh) P. BA, U. Calif., Irvine, 1977. Cert. community coll. instr.'s credential, Calif. Animal trainer Stanford U., Palo Alto, Calif., 1977-79; asst. instr. sports U. Calif., Berkeley, 1979; founder, dir. Time Mgmt. Systems, Oakland, Calif., 1979—; bd. dirs. Fredrick Gilbert & Assocs., Redwood City, Calif. Contbr. articles to profl. publs. Vol. animal handler San Francisco Zoo, 1980; vol., trainer Support Ctr., San Francisco, 1981—, Career Action Ctr., Palo Alto, 1984—. Mem. Nat. Speakers Assn., NAFE, Last Monday Club. Democrat. Home: 2648 8th Ave Oakland CA 94606 Office: Time Mgmt Systems 2640 8th Ave Ste C Oakland CA 94606

POLLARD, ERIC WILTON, retired naval officer, consultant; b. Alameda, Calif., May 18, 1917; s. Eric Wilton and Gladys (Gibson) P.; m. Caroline Walker, 1944 (div. 1945); 1 child, Eric Wilton III; m. Nanette De Lac, July 14, 1946; children: Line Maryvonne, Michelle. Grad., U.S. Naval Acad., 1941; postgrad., U.S. Naval War Coll., 1947, Naval Intelligence Sch., 1949-50. Commd. ensign USN, 1941, advanced through grades to capt., 1962; commdg. officer surveillance flights USN, Eastern Europe; attache U.S. Embassy USN, Tehran, Iran, 1950-53; exec. asst. to supreme allied comdr. NATO USN, Paris, 1961-63; counterinsurgency dir. Joint Chiefs of Staff USN, Washington, 1963-65; ret. USN, 1965; ops. exec. Standard Oil N.J., Saigon, Vietnam, 1965-67; founder, pres. Wilton Internat. Cons., Inc., N.Y.C. and Tehran, 1970-79, The Phoenix Challenge, Inc., 1983—. Decorated numerous medals, World War II. Mem. U.S. Naval Acad. Alumni Assn., Internat. Assn. Chiefs of Police, U.S. Tennis Assn., Army/Navy Country Club, Monterey Peninsula Yacht Club. Episcopalian. Home: 5136 N 31 Pl Phoenix AZ 85016 Office: Phoenix Challenge Inc 56 Biltmore Estates Phoenix AZ 85016

POLLARD, MELVIN EUGENE, aerospace engineer; b. Ash Grove, Mo., Dec. 11, 1937; s. F.W. and Grace Louise (Schneider) P.; m. Louise Kelley, Apr. 2, 1961. BS, USAF Acad., 1959; MS, Rochester Inst. Tech., 1971. Commd. 2d lt. USAF, 1959; instr. pilot air tng. command USAF, Webb AFB, Tex., 1959-66; fighter pilot air tactical command USAF, Davis-Monthan AFB, Ariz., 1966-67, 68-69; fighter pilot Pacific air forces USAF, Vietnam, 1967-68; devel. engr. systems command USAF, Westover AFB, mass. and Andrews AFB, Md., 1970-79; br. chief systems command USAF, Hill AFB, Utah, 1979-82; ret. USAF, 1982; quality engr. Lockheed Missiles & Space Co., Magna, Utah, 1982-83; dept. mgr. Computer Sci. Corp., Clearfield, Utah, 1983-84; aerospace engr. TRW, Inc., Ogden, Utah, 1984—. Decorated DFC, Air medal. Mem. Air Force Assn., USAF Acad. Assn. Graduates, Order Daedalians. Republican. Home: 1497 Cheever Ln Farmington UT 84025 Office: TRW Inc 1104 Country Hills Dr Ogden UT 84401

POLLARD, WILLIAM SHERMAN, JR., civil engineer, educator; b. Oak Grove, La., Jan. 1, 1925; s. William Sherman and Carrie Lois (Hornor) P.; m. Gloria Louise Ponder, June 29, 1946; children: William Sherman, III, Katherine Lynn. B.S. in Civil Engring, Purdue U., 1946, M.S., 1948. Instr. civil engring. Purdue U., 1948-49; instr. U. Ill., 1949-51, assoc. prof., 1951-55; with Harland Bartholomew & Assos., St. Louis, 1955-71; assoc. partner, chief civil engr. Harland Bartholomew & Assos., 1956-58; partner Harland Bartholomew & Assos., Memphis, 1958-71; head ops. Harland Bartholomew & Assos., 1958-60; head Harland Bartholomew & Assos. (Memphis office), 1960-71; pres. William S. Pollard Cons., Inc., Memphis, 1971-81; prof. civil engring. U. Colo., Denver, 1981—; adj. prof. urban planning Memphis State U., 1973-81; dir. Ctr. Urban Transp. Studies, U. Colo.; chmn. WKNO-TV, Memphis. Served with USMC, 1942-46. Named Distinguished Engring. Alumnus Purdue U., 1969. Fellow Am. Cons. Engrs. Council, ASCE (state of the art award 1970), Inst. Transp. Engrs.; mem. Am. Rd. Builders Assn., Nat. Soc. Profl. Engrs., Soc. Am. Mil. Engrs., Urban Land Inst., Transp. Research Bd., Lambda Alpha. Presbyterian. Clubs: Engrs, Summit. Lodge: Rotary (pres. 1979-80). Office: U Colo 1200 Larimer St Campus Box 113 Denver CO 80204-5300

POLLCHIK, ALLAN LEE, psychologist; b. Denver, Sept. 18, 1949; s. Morris and Helen Ruth (Perlmutter) P.; B.A., UCLA, 1971; M.A., Vanderbilt U., 1973, Ph.D., 1975. Intern, Langley Porter Neuropsychiat. Inst., U. Calif. Med. Sch., San Francisco, 1975-76; instr. San Diego State U., 1977—; clin., cons. psychologist El Camino Psychology Center, Oceanside, Calif., 1976-78; pres. Allan L. Pollchik, Ph.D., P.C., Oceanside, 1978—. Pres., Seawind/Oceanside Homeowners Assn., 1980. Nat. Merit scholar, 1967-71; NSF fellow, 1972-73; NIMH fellow, 1973-75. Mem. North County Psychol. Assn. (pres. 1980-81). Mem. Am. Psychol. Assn., Calif. Psychol. Assn., Interam. Soc. Psychology, Soc. Psychol. Study Social Issues, Zeta Beta Tau. Club: Oceanside Health. Home: 1138 Arden Dr Encinitas CA 92024 Office: 2101 El Camino Real Ste 203A Oceanside CA 92054

POLLEY, PATRICK WILLIAM, marketing professional; b. Sioux City, Iowa, Aug. 20, 1930; s. Raymond Louis and Margaret (Corrigan) ; m. Jacqueline Jane, June 28, 1952; children: Nancy, Patrick, Kevin. AA, Pasadena City Coll., 1951. Fin. reporter Dun & Bradstreet, Los Angeles, 1952-56; prodn. dir. Erwin, Wasey, Ruthrauff & Ryan Advt., Los Angeles, 1956-62; mktg. dir. Paterson Parchment Co., Los Angeles, 1962-65, Simpson Paper Co., Los Angeles, 1965-76; v.p. mktg. dir. Repap Sales, Los Angeles, 1976—. Office: Repap 2136 Country Club Dr Glendora CA 91740

POLLEY, TERRY LEE, lawyer; b. Long Beach, Calif., June 2, 1947; s. Frederick F. and Geraldine E. (Davis) P.; m. Patricia Yamanoha, Aug. 4, 1973; children: Todd, Matthew. AB, UCLA, 1970; JD, Coll. William and Mary, 1973. Bar: Calif. 1973, U.S. Tax Ct. 1974, U.S. Supreme Ct. 1987. Assoc. Loeb & Loeb, Los Angeles, 1973-78; ptnr. Ajalat & Polley, Los Angeles, 1978—; lectr. taxation law U. So. Calif. Author (with Charles R. Ajalat) California's Water's Edge Legislation, 1987; contbr. articles to profl. jours, legal jours.; editorial bd. William and Mary Law Rev. Mem. sch. bd. Greater Long Beach Christian Schs.; elder Grace Brethren Ch., Long Beach. Mem. ABA (sate and local tax com.), Calif. Bar Assn. (exec. com. taxation sect., steering com., property, sales and local tax com. taxation sect.), Los Angeles County Bar Assn. (chmn. and exec. com. taxation sect., chmn. state and local tax com. taxation sect.), Omicron Delta Epsilon. Democrat. Office: Ajalat & Polley 643 S Olive St Ste 200 Los Angeles CA 90014

POLLOCK, JOHN PHLEGER, lawyer; b. Sacramento, Apr. 28, 1920; s. George Gordon and Irma (Phleger) P.; m. Juanita Irene Gossman, Oct. 26, 1945; children: Linda Pollock Harrison, Madeline Pollock Chiotti, John, Gordon. A.B., Stanford U., 1942; J.D., Harvard U., 1948. Bar: Calif. 1949, U.S. Supreme Ct. 1954. Partner Musick, Peeler & Garrett, Los Angeles, 1953-60, Pollock, Williams & Berwanger, Los Angeles, 1960-80, Rodi, Pollock, Pettker, Galbraith & Phillips, Los Angeles, 1980—. Contbr. articles to profl. publs. Active Boy Scouts Am.; former trustee Pitzer Coll., Claremont, Calif., 1968-76; trustee Fletcher Jones Found., Good Hope Med. Found., Pacific Legal Found. Served with AUS, 1942-45. Fellow Am. Coll. Trial Lawyers; mem. ABA, Los Angeles County Bar Assn. (trustee 1964-66). Home: 30602 Paseo del Valle Laguna Niguel CA 92677 Office: 801 S Grand Ave Los Angeles CA 90017

POLLOCK, RICHARD EDWIN, former county administrator; b. Phila., Aug. 27, 1928; s. Ernest Edwin and Evelyn Marie (Scarlett) P.; student Armstrong Coll., 1947, U. Calif., Berkeley, 1949-51, 55; BA in Recreation, San Jose State U., 1961; postgrad. San Fernando Valley State U., 1969-70, U. Calif., Davis, 1963-77, UCLA, 1964, U. Calif., Santa Barbara, 1970, U. Redlands, 1979; m. Yvonne May Graves, Oct. 11, 1952; children: Colleen May, Karen Marie, Richard Irvin, Annette Yvonne, Mary Ann. Swim pool mgr. and instr. Berkley Tennis Club, 1955-56; police officer City of Berkeley, 1956; recreation and aquatic supr. Pleasant Hill (Calif.) Recreation and Park Dist., 1956-62; gen. mgr. Pleasant Valley Recreation and Park Dist., Camarillo, Calif., 1962-68; bldg. insp. Ventura County (Calif.), 1969-71; adminstr. Sacramento County-Carmichael Recreation and Park Dist., 1971-73; dir. parks and recreation Imperial County (Calif.), 1973-81; ret., 1981; mem. faculty Imperial Valley Jr. Coll., 1974—, others; aquatic cons., 1957—; real estate investor, 1984—; chmn. San Francisco Bay Area Conf. for Cooperation in Aquatics, 1958-59. Adviser/scoutmaster Desert Trails council Boy Scouts Am.; bd. dirs., instr. ARC; work with devel. disabled and handicapped children and adults; res. dep. Sheriff, 1981— Served from pvt. to lt. U.S. Army, 1951-55; Korea. Recipient recognition for 41 years vol. service ARC, 1978; registered recreator and park mgr.; cert. elem., secondary and community coll. tchr., Calif.; reg. hypnotherapist. Mem. Nat. Recreation and Park Assn., AAHPER, Calif. Park and Recreation Soc., Calif. County Dirs. Parks and Recreation Assn., Calif. Boating Safety Officers Assn., Aircraft Owners and Pilots Assn., Nat. Assn. Emergency Med. Technicians. Democrat. Mormon. Author: Bibliography: A Pool of Aquatic Sources, 1960. Home: PO Box 3011 El Centro CA 92244-3011

POLON, LINDA BETH, educator, writer, illustrator; b. Balt., Oct. 7, 1943; d. Harold Bernard and Edith Judith Wolff; m. Marty I. Polon, Dec. 18, 1966 (div. Aug. 1983); m. Robert Dorsey, Apr. 13, 1986 (Nov. 6, 1986). B.A. in History, UCLA, 1966. Elem. tchr. Los Angeles Bd. Edn., 1967—; writer-illustrator Scott Foresman Pub. Co., Glenview, Ill., 1979—, Frank Schaffer Pub. Co., Torrance, Calif., 1981-82, Learning Works, Santa Barbara, Calif., 1981-82; editorial reviewer Prentice Hall Pub. Co., Santa Monica, Calif., 1982-83. Author: (juvenile books) Creative Teaching Games, 1974; Teaching Games for Fun, 1976; Making Kids Click, 1979; Write up a Storm, 1979; Stir Up a Story, 1981; Paragraph Production, 1981; Using Words Correctly, 3d-4th grades, 1981, 5th-6th grades, 1981; Whole Earth Holiday Book, 1983; Writing Whirlwind, 1986; Magic Story Starters, 1987. Mem. Soc. Children's Book Writers. Democrat. Home: 1515 Manning Ave Apt 3 Los Angeles CA 90024 Office: L A Bd of Edn 980 S Hobart Blvd Los Angeles CA 90006

POLOVETS, ALEXANDER, editor, publisher; b. Moscow, USSR, July 12, 1935; naturalized U.S. citizen, 1983; s. Boris and Dina (Tsank) P.; widower; 1 child, Stanislav. Grad., Stanford Poligraphical Coll. of Moscow, 1951-55; M in Pub., Moscow Pub. Poligraphical Inst., 1958-64; M in Patent Info., Cen. Inst. Patent Studies, 1968-71. Supr. quality control Western Lithograph, 1976-80; founder, publisher Alamanac Press Russian-Am. Pub. Co., 1977—; pres. Almanac Enterprises, Inc., 1983—. Author: Fugitive Pachikhin, and Other Stories, 1987; publisher Underground Jokes (2 vol. anthology Soviet humor), Russian lang. suppliment for Isreal Today mag., 1978-80, and numerous others in Russian and English; publisher, editor-in-chief Panorama (nat. Russian lang. newspaper), 1980—, annual Russian Community Ref. Guide (Russian Yellow Pages); author 2 books; contbr. numerous articles in USSR and Am. Recipient Resolutions for contbns. to Almanac Panorama from Gov. Calif. Mem. Publicity Club of L.A., Press Club Greater L.A. Republican. Office: Almanac Press 501 S Fairfax Ave Ste 206 Los Angeles CA 90036

POLSGROVE, JOHN ALMUS WALKER, newspaper editor; b. San Antonio, Oct. 30, 1954; s. John Brooks and Juanita Joyce (Parker) P.; m. Mary Cristina Trujillo, May 25, 1985. AA, El Centro Coll., 1981; student, U. Ariz., 1984-87. Freelance writer Tucson, 1981-84; contbr. writer Ariz. Bus. Gazette, Phoenix, 1984-87; mng. editor Florence (Ariz.) Reminder, 1987--; aide to instr. U. Ariz., Tucson, 1985-87, vis. lectr. journalism dept., 1988--. Mem. adv. bd. Project Yes, Tucson, 1986-87. Mem. Ariz. Newspapers Assn., Ariz. Press Club, Tucson Press Club. Democrat. Home: 7932-98 E Colette Circle Tucson AZ 85710 Office: Florence Reminder 260 N Main St Florence AZ 85232

POLSON, DONALD ALLAN, surgeon; b. Gallup, N.Mex., May 12, 1911; s. Thomas Cress and Carrie Fern (Cantrall) P.; student Stanford U.; M.D., Northwestern U., 1936, M.Sc., 1947; m. Cecily, Lady Avebury, Nov. 9, 1946; 1 dau., Carolyn Kathleen. Intern, then resident in surgery St. Luke's Hosp., Chgo., 1936-38; practice medicine specializing in gen. surgery, Phoenix, 1947-83; formerly chmn. Drs. Polson, Berens & Petelin, Ltd.; chief staff Maricopa County Hosp., 1952-53, St. Joseph's Hosp., 1961; bd. dirs. Ariz. Blue Shield, 1950-55, pres., 1956. Served to col. M.C., AUS, World War II. Diplomate Am. Bd. Surgery. Mem. AMA, A.C.S., Ariz. Med. Assn. (dir. 1955-60), Maricopa County Med. Soc. (pres. 1954), Phoenix Surg. Soc. (pres. 1959), Alpha Omega Alpha, Nu Sigma Nu. Republican. Episcopalian. Clubs: Paradise Valley Country, White Mountain Country. Home: 7619 N Tatum Blvd Paradise Valley AZ 85253 Office: 550 W Thomas Rd Phoenix AZ 85013

POLSTON, WILLIAM THOMAS, corporate executive; b. Chgo., June 30, 1942; s. William T. and Dorothy (Vancura) P.; m. Barbara Plahętka; children: William Jr., Scott, Shawn, Kevin. AA, Coll. DuPage, LaGrange, Ill., 1968; BS, Roosevelt U., Chgo., 1975. Acct. Internat. Harvester, Chgo., 1960-66; controller, chief fin. officer Hammermill Paper Co., Chgo., 1966-76; exec. v.p., gen. mgr. Mills-Am. div. Stanwood, Chgo., 1976-78, Hanimex USA Inc., Elk Grove Village, Ill., 1978-83; pres., chief exec. officer Autocom Corp., Phoenix, 1983-85; pres., chief exec. officer Saranda Corp., Phoenix, 1985—, also bd. dirs.; bd. dirs. Hanimex USA Inc, Elk Grove Village. bd. mem. Tempe (Ariz.) Little League, 1985-88. Recipient honorable mention, Art Inst. of Chgo., 1975; named Man of the Year, Rotary Club, 1975. Office: Saranda Corp 4024 E Broadway Phoenix AZ 85040

POMEROY, LEASON FREDERICK, III, architect; b. Orange, Calif., May 9, 1937; s. Leason Fredrick Pomeroy Jr. and Dorothy (Finley) Kidd; m. Marlene Egerer, June 18, 1960; children: Joselyn Miller, Leason Pomeroy IV. AA, Orange Coast Coll., 1958; BS, Ariz. State U., 1961; BArch, U. So. Calif., 1965. Registered architect, Calif. Oreg., Wash., Nev., Utah., Mont., Ariz., Tex., Colo., Hawaii, Pa., N.J., Va., Ind., S.C., Fla., Md., Idaho. Architect Schwager-Desatof, Costa Mesa, Calif., 1961-65; pres. Leason Pomeroy and Assocs. Inc., Orange, 1965—. Bd. dirs. Orange County Devel. Corp., Newport Beach, Calif., 1985; trustee Orange YMCA, 1985. Served with U.S. Army, 1960-66. Recipient numerous design awards. Fellow AIA (design com. 1985-86, bd. dirs. Calif. council 1984-85; appreciation award 1982-85); mem. Orange County AIA (bd. dirs. 1982-83), Soc. Am. Regular Architects (spl. service award 1985-86), Internat. Council Shopping Ctrs., Urban Land Inst., Phi Delta Theta. Republican. Lodge: DeMolay. Office: Leason Pomeroy Assocs Inc 44 Plaza Sq Orange CA 92666 *

POMPEO, JOHN ANTHONY, musician; b. Saugus, Mass., Aug. 11, 1934; s. Giovanni Michaeli and Ellen Mary (Doherty) P.; children: Catherine Elisabeth, Stephen, John. Student, Boston Conservatory, 1947-49, Berklee Coll. Music, 1950-53. Musician, vibraphone George Shearing Quintet, N.Y.C., 1955-56, Johnny Smith Quartet, N.Y.C., 1956-57, Herbie Mann Sextet, N.Y.C., 1959-60; musician, drums Cal Tiader Quintet, San Francisco, 1961-66, Vince Guaraldi Trio, San Francisco, 1967, Cal Tiader Quintet, San Francisco, 1967-70, Charlie Byrd Trio, Washington, 1972-75; musician, percussion Shorenstien-Nederlander Theaters, San Francisco, 1975—; disk jockey Sta. KJAZ Radio, Alameda, Calif., 1962-70; contractor Concord Summer Festival, Concord, Calif., 1971-72, Concord Pavillion, 1973-76. Author: Jazz Phrasing for Mallets, 1960, Latin Guide for Drummers, 1963. Recipient Jammies award, Bay Area Musician magazine, 1984. Mem. Am. Fedn. Musicians, Percussive Arts Soc., NARAS. Democrat. Roman Catholic. Office: 228 Jones St San Francisco CA 94102

POMRANING, ALLEN NORWOOD, computer infosystems specialist, civil engineer; b. Lancaster, Pa., Oct. 29, 1954; s. Ken and Dolly Pomraning; m. Lois Pomraning Plummer, Jan. 2, 1977; 1 child, Joelle. BS in Civil Engring., Walla Walla Coll., 1980. Civil engr. Corp. of Engrs., Walla Walla, Wash., 1980-82, software engr., 1982-85, br. chief, info. mgmt. dept., 1985—; part-time instr. Walla Walla Coll., 1982—. Mem. sci. com. Walla Walla sch. dist., 1988; coach Walla Walla softball, 1986—. Mem. Data Processing Mgmt. Assn., ACSE (treas. 1984-85). Club: Blue Mt. Ski. Office: Corps of Engrs Info Mgmt Office City-County Airport Walla Walla WA 99362-9265

PONCE, JOHN JAY, journalist, political consultant; b. Whittier, Calif., Nov. 21, 1949; s. Victor Joseph and Margaret Eva (Tunberg) P.; m. Linda Renee Prideaux, Feb. 26, 1972; children: Nicholas Gordon, Crystal Marie. Ba in Communications, Calif. State U., Fullerton, 1971. Writer, photographer East Whittier Rev., 1969-70, Record-Gazette, Banning, Calif., 1975; writer, editor Call-Enterprises Newspapers, Bellflower, Calif., 1970-72, Contra Costa Times, Walnut Creek, Calif., 1972-73; news editor Valley Times, Walnut Creek, Calif., 1973-74; assoc. editor Town Crier, Idyllwild, Calif., 1975-78; mng. editor Valley News, Solvang, Calif., 1978; pub. Paonian Herald, Paonia, Colo., 1979-81; editor Humboldt Beacon and Satellite TV Week, Fortuna, Calif., 1982-86; writer, cons. forest products industries Fortuna, Calif., 1986--. Editor: Trees of San Jacintos, 1977, Tall Tree Forest, 1987. Mem. pub. info. com. Humboldt Hist. Soc., 1987--; Humboldt County Bd. Edn., Eureka, Calif., 1986--. Republican. Home: 3630 Newburg Rd Fortuna CA 95540 Office: Humboldt Bd Edn 901 Myrtle Ave Eureka CA 95501

PONCE DE LEON, JOSE-LUIS SIERRA, professor; b. Vigo, Spain, Sept. 23, 1931; came to U.S., 1960; s. Vicente Sierra and Amelia Ponce de Leon. JD, Universidad De Santiago De Compostela, Spain, 1953; student, Harvard U., 1956-57; PhD, Stanford U., 1966. Asst. prof. Stanford U., Stanford, Calif., 1966-72; prof. Calif. (Hayward) State U., 1973—. Author: La Novela Espanola De La Guerra Civil, 1971, El Arte De La Conversacion, 1986. Mem. MLA, Am. Assn. Tchrs. of Spanish and Portugese, Asociacion De Licenciados Y Doctores Espanoles En Los Estados Unidos. Democrat. Home: 1822A Church St San Francisco CA 94131 Office: Calif State U Hayward CA 94542

POND, L. PAGE, optometrist; b. Richmond, Va., Mar. 28, 1952; s. James Page and Daisy (Nash) P.; m. Kimberly Faris, Aug. 21, 1976; children: Matthew Page, Mark Jeffrey. BS in Psychology, Coll. of William & Mary, 1974; OD, Pacific U., 1978. Optometrist, clin. instr. Ferris State Coll., Big Rapids, Mich., 1978-79; optometrist Kaiser Permanente, Denver, 1979-80; pvt. practice optometry Aurora, Colo., 1980—; bd. dirs. Omni Eye Services, Denver. Mem. Am. Optometric Assn., Colo. Optometric Assn. (trustee 1987—), Beta Sigma Kappa. Club: Montbello Optimist (Denver) (v.p. 1983-84). Office: 1460 Chambers Rd Aurora CA 80011

PONDER, WILLIAM STANLEY, university administrator; b. San Diego, Sept. 12, 1949; s. William Bryant and Mary Louise (Parker) P.; m. Theresa Elizabeth Pinrey, July 18, 1976 (div. 1980); m. Deborah Millot, Dec. 22, 1982; children: Dana Michelle, Jordan Thomas. BA in Music, San Diego State U., 1972, MS in Counseling, 1983. Tchr. San Diego/Riverside Sch. Dist., 1973-77; dir. tng. Twelfth Night Repertory Co., San Diego, 1977-78; counselor Girls Club of Chula Vista, Calif., 1978-79; v.p. Telesis II of Calif., Inc., San Diego, 1979-83; sr. recruitment officer U. Calif.-Riverside, 1983-86, assoc. dir. Office of Admissions, 1986--; cons. State of Calif. Health Svc., Sacramento, 1982-83. Commr. City of San Bernardino Bldg. and Safety, 1987--. Recipient Pub. Svc. award Co. of San Diego, 1984; KPBS TV Svc. award, 1984. Mem. Third World Counselors Assn. (dir. 1983-86), Calif. Articulation Numbering Systems Council, Western Assn. Coll. Admissions Counselors, Nat. Assn. Coll. Admission Counselors, Calif. Black Faculty and Staff Assn., Rancho Mediterrian Club (Colton, Calif.). Democrat. Presbyterian. Home: 243 N Meridian Ave #115 San Bernardino CA 92410

PONTILLO, FRANK JOHN, data processing executive; b. Chgo., Feb. 5, 1939; s. Frank John and Dorothy Ann (Wseisbrodt) P.; m. Ruth Dimelis, Apr. 9, 1988. Student computer sci., Electronics Computer Prog.Inst, Chgo., 1966. Computer programmer Motorola Inc., Chgo., 1966-69; computer analyst Prudential Ins. Co., Phoenix, 1969-71; project leader 1st Nat. Bank Ariz., Tempe, 1971-74, sr. EDP auditor, 1974-76; EDP audit supr. Western Bancorp, Tempe, 1976-78, Patagonia Corp., Mesa, Ariz., 1978-80, Del E Webb Corp., Phoenix, 1980-85, Ariz. Dept. Econ. Security, Phoenix, 1985—. Author, editor: General Controls, 1974, Application and Department Controls, 1974. With USMC, 1958-61. Mem. EDP Auditors Assn. (cert., pres. Phoenix 1981-83, Auditor Yr. award 1984), Inst. Internat. Auditors (bd. govs. Phoenix 1979-81), Info. Sys. Security Assn. (cert., v.p. Phoenix 1986-88), Quality Assurance Assn., (cert.), Inst. Cert. Computer Profls. (Cert.). Home: 1440 S Parkcrest Mesa AZ 85206 also: 8530 N 22d Ave Apt 1032 Phoenix AZ 85021 Office: Ariz Dept Econ Security 1140 E Washington St Phoenix AZ 85034

POOL, ROBERT NORMAN, electrical designer; b. Santa Monica, Calif., Dec. 26, 1952; s. John Hampton and Olive Marie (Cammack) P. BA, Stanford U., 1974; cert., Multi-Amp Inst., Duncanville, Tex., 1983. Forestry technician U.S. Forest Svc., Pacific Southwest Range Experiment Sta., Berkeley, Calif., 1972-74; child care worker Clear Water Ranch, Philo, Calif., 1975-76; asst. tchr. Burt Children's Ctr., San Francisco, 1977; foreman, lineman Pacific Gas & Electric Co., San Francisco, 1977-81; lineman Alaska Electric Light & Power Co., Juneau, 1981; electrical designer, technician T.E. Neubauer & Assocs., S.S.& R., Juneau, 1983-88; distbn. designer Chugach Electric Assn., Anchorage, 1988—; co-owner Cedar Point Ranch, Mariposa, Calif., 1984—. Counselor, Awalt High Sch., Mountain View, CAlif., 1973-74; grant writer Freestone Wilderness Inst., San Francisco, 1977; shop steward Internat. Brotherhood Electrical Workers, Juneau, 1983-88. Democrat. Home: 3908 Turnagain Blcd E Anchorage AK 99517 Office: Chugach Electric Assn PO Box 196300 Anchorage AK 99519-6300

POOLE, ELLEN LOUISE, nurse; b. Omaha, Jan. 15, 1951; d. Robert Eugene Sr. and Claramerle (Butler) Benge; m. Timothy James Poole, May 31, 1975. BSN, Creighton U., 1973. RN, Ariz.; cert. crit. care nurse, post anesthesia nurse. Staff nurse Boswell Meml. Hosp., Sun City, Ariz., 1973-74, in-svc. educator, 1980-81, recovery rm. coord., 1981-83; staff nurse St. Luke's Hosp., Phoenix, 1974-80; clin. nurse III Maryvale Samaritan Hosp., Phoenix, 1983-87, Thunderbird Samaritan Hosp., Glendale, Ariz., 1987—; cons. Cactus Pine coun. Girl Scouts U.S., Ariz., 1985—. Mem. Ariz. Post Anesthesia Nurses Assn. (sec. 1986-88), Am. Soc. Post Anesthesia Nurses, Am. Assn. Crit. Care Nurses. Republican. Mem. Ch. Christ. Home: 5409 W Maui Ln Glendale AZ 85306

POOLE, HARRY WENDELL, county group probation counselor; b. Paces, Va., Jan. 29, 1953; s. Charlie Washington and Minnie Beatrice (Oliver) P. AA, Riverside Community Coll., 1981; BS, U. Redlands, 1983; MS, Calif. State U., Dominuez Hills, Calif., 1985. With payroll Kaiser Steel

Corp., Fontana, Calif., 1975-83; group counselor I Riverside County Probation, Riverside, Calif., 1983-86; group counselor II Riverside County Probation, 1986—; youth counselor Calif. Youth Authority, Chino, 1978. Democrat. Baptist. Office: Riverside County Probation 3933 Harrison St Riverside CA 92503

POOLE, HENRY JOE, JR., business executive; b. Rocky Point, N.C., July 5, 1957; s. Henry Joe Sr. and Marjorie (Morse) P.; m. Loretta Lynn Scott, Sept. 12, 1981; 1 child, Robert Howard. AA, Cypress Coll., 1977; student, San Diego State U., 1978, Calif. State U., Fullerton, 1978-79. Pres. Poole Ventura Inc., Ventura, Calif., 1979—. Inventor in field. Mem. ASME, Soc. of Mfg. Engrs., Am. Vacuum Soc., Am. Welding Soc. Office: Poole Ventura Inc 1860 Eastman Ave Ventura CA 93003

POOLE, ROBERT ANTHONY, journalist; b. St. Austell, Cornwall, Eng., Dec. 17, 1944; arrived in Can., 1977; m. Valerie Avril Taggart, Apr. 14, 1973; children—Claire Lucy, Emma Louise. Irish editor Press Assn., Belfast, Northern Ireland, 1970-77; gen. reporter Calgary Herald, Alta., Can., 1977-79; city editor Calgary Albertan, 1979-80; city editor Calgary Sun, 1980-81, mng. editor, 1981-84, editor-in-chief, 1984—. Office: Calgary Sun, 2615 12th St NE, Calgary, AB Canada T2P 7W9

POOLE, STEPHEN MICHAEL, materials manager, geotechnical and materials engineering consultant; b. Columbus, Ohio, Mar. 5, 1949; s. Kelmer Donald and Reda Melba (Billingsley) P.; m. Jacquelyn Kay Dean Poole, Sept. 5, 1970. BS in Civil Engring., Ohio U., 1973; M.S. in Civil Engring., Mich. State U., 1977. Lab. and field supr. Materials Testing Cons., Grand Rapids, Mich., 1974-75; project engr. McClelland Engrs., Houston, 1977-80; project supr. McClelland-Suhaimi, Ltd., Dammam, Saudi Arabia, 1980-82; geotechnical and material mgr. Lyon Assocs., Riyadh, Saudi Arabia, 1984-85; dir. cen. lab. Ministry of Def. and Aviation, Riyadh, 1984-85; dept. mgr. Testing Engrs.- San Diego, 1985-87; v.p. engring. ATL Testing Labs., Phoenix, Ariz., 1987; materials mgr. Deleuw, Cather Internat., Ltd., Khartowm, Sudan, 1987—. Mem. Am. Soc. Civil Engrs., Internat. Soc. of Soil and Found. Engrs. Republican. Methodist. Club: Am. (Khartoum). Home: 16025 N 4th Ave Phoenix AZ 85023 Office: Deleuw Cather Internat Ltd, P O Box 1396, Khartoum Sudan

POOLE-HENDERSON, H. SUSAN, manufacturing executive; b. Phila., Feb. 4, 1942; d. Roy Charles and Grace (Lucas) Fitzgerald; m. Fred Carpenter, June 10, 1966 (div. 1976); children: Paul Joseph, Patricia Janette, Fred Thomas; m. Andreu Austin Henderson II, Feb. 10, 1989. BS, Ohio State U., 1963; MBA, U. Calif., Berkeley, 1965. Adminstrv. specialist Ohio State U., Columbus, 1965-70; mng. ptnr. Profitmakers, Inc., Oakland, Calif., 1970-78; v.p. ops. Pierce Cons. Internat., Richmond, Calif., 1978-82; gen. mgr. ATA Industries, Oakland, 1982—; founder Expatriate Mgmt. Cons., Inc., 1980-82. Mem. Am. Mgmt. Assn., Nat. Bus. Profl. Women's Clubs Am. (pres. 1982-84), Nat. Negro Bus. Profl. Women's Clubs, Nat. Council Negro Am. Avocations: tennis, racquetball, violinist. Home: 7 Embarcadero W #108 Oakland CA 94607-4533 Office: ATA Industries Inc 4901 E 12th St Oakland CA 94601

POONJA, MOHAMED, management executive; b. Mombasa, Kenya, Nov. 8, 1948; came to U.S., 1984; s. Abdulrasul and Maleksultan (Dharsee) P.; m. Zaitun Virji, Feb. 24, 1979. Student, Inst. Chartered Accts., Dublin, Ireland, Chartered Assn. Cert. Accts., London; MS in Mgmt. and Organizational Behavior, U.S. Internat. U. CPA. Audit supr. Ernst & Whinney, Dublin, Ireland, 1966-72, Coopers & Lybrand, Dublin, 1973-76; group controller Diamond Trust of Kenya, Nairobi, 1976-78; chief operating officer Kenya Uniforms, Ltd., Nairobi, 1978-81; sr. mgr. Coopers & Lybrand, Calgary, Alta., Can., 1981-84; regional dir. Coopers & Lybrand, San Jose, Calif., 1984—. Mem. ABA, Brit. Inst. Mgmt., Am. Bankruptcy Inst., Assn. Insolvency Accts., Brit. Inst. Bankers, Calif. Bankers Assn., Rotary. Home: 630 Milverton Rd Los Altos CA 94022 Office: Coopers & Lybrand 10 Almaden Blvd Ste 1600 San Jose CA 95113

POOR, CLARENCE ALEXANDER, physician; b. Ashland, Oreg., Oct. 29, 1911; s. Lester Clarence and Matilda Ellen (Doty) P.; AB, Willamette U., 1932; MD, U. Oreg., 1936. Intern, U. Wis., Madison, 1936-37, resident in internal medicine, 1937-40, instr. dept. pathology Med. Sch., 1940-41, clin. instr., clin. asst. dept. internal medicine, 1942-44; practice medicine specializing in internal medicine, Oakland, Calif., 1944—; mem. attending staff Highland Alameda County Hosp., Oakland, 1949—; mem. staff Providence Hosp., Oakland, 1947—, pres. staff, 1968-69; staff mem. Samuel Merritt Hosp., Oakland, 1958—, also Peralta Hosp., 1968—. Mem. Nat. Council on Alcoholism, 1974—, bd. dirs. Bay Area, 1977—. Diplomate Am. Bd. Internal Medicine. Mem. Am., Calif., Alameda-Contra Costa med. assns., Alameda County Heart Assn. (trustee 1955-62, 72-82, pres. 1960-61), Calif. Heart Assn. (dir. 1962-72), Soc. for Clin. and Exptl. Hypnosis, Am. Soc. Clin. Hypnosis, San Francisco Acad. Hypnosis (dir. 1966—, pres. 1973). Home: 1241 West View Dr Berkeley CA 94705 Office: 400 29th St Oakland CA 94609

POORE, CAROL ANN, utility writer; b. Phoenix, May 7, 1958; d. Edgar Frederick and Mary Lou (Wood) White; m. David John Poore, Sept. 11, 1981. BS, Ariz. State U., 1980. High sch. tchr. Page, Ariz., 1979-80; advt. mgr., news reporter Lake Powell (Ariz.) Chronicle, Page, 1981-86; staff writer Salt River Project-Navajo Generating Sta., Page, 1986-88, Salt River Project-Water and Power, Phoenix, 1988—; prin., media cons. Carol Poore, Page and Phoenix, 1985—. Author: Parents Handbook for Happiness, 1985. Pub. rels. dir. Page United Way, 1987; mem. Mayor's Task Force Against Drug Abuse, Page, 1988—; cons. Supt.'s Forum Page Schs., 1987-88; bd. dirs. Coll. Pub. Programs Ariz. State U.; mem. parade mktg. com. Fiesta Bowl Parade, 1988-89, mem. corp. float sponsorship com., 1989—. Mem. Internat. Assn. Bus. Communicators Phoenix chpt., Lake Powell C. of C. (pub. rels. dir. 1984-88, bd. dirs. 1986-88), Tempe C. of C. (mem. pub. rels. and univ. rels. com.), Ariz. Press Club, Pi Beta Phi. Republican. Office: Salt River Project Water and Power PO Box 52025 Phoenix AZ 85072

POPE, BARBARA M. HARRAL, editor; b. Lubbock, Tex., Jan. 26, 1937; d. Leonard Paul and Olivette (Stuart) Harral; m. John Rowell Toman (div. 1963); 1 child, Stuart Rowell. BE, Tex. Christian U., 1959; MLS, U. Hawaii, 1968; postgrad., Golden Gate U., 1980-82. Tchr. pub. elem. schs., various cities, Tex. and Hawaii, 1959-66; contracts abstractor, indexer Champlin Oil Co., Ft. Worth, 1963-64; adminstrv. asst. engring. Litton Industries, Lubbock, Tex., 1964-65; mgr. rsch. library Hawaii Employers' Coun., Honolulu, 1968-72; rsch. cons. Thailand Hotel, Touche-Ross Assocs., Honolulu, 1974; dir. med. library U. S.D.-Sacred Heart Hosp., Yankton, 1977-79; editor, adminstrv. coord. book div. ABC-Clio, Inc., Santa Barbara, Calif., 1981-88; free-lance rsch./editorial cons. Albuquerque, 1988-89; instr. Santa Fe Community Coll., 1989—; ptnr. Broome-Harral, Inc., Adminstrv., Tech., & Ednl. Svcs., 1989—. Vol., contbr. Boy's Ranch, Amarillo, Tex., 1987—; mem. Lobero Theater Group, Santa Barbara, 1975-76; mem., treas. Yankton Med. Aux., 1977-79. Mem. ALA, Spl. Libraries Assn., Med. Libraries Assn., Am. Soc. Info., Sci., Tech. Cons. Inst., Tex. Christian U. Alumni Assn., Delta Delta Delta. Republican. Episcopalian. Home: 9300 Seabrook NE Albuquerque NM 87111 Office: PO Box 26356 Albuquerque NM 87125

POPE, DEAN A., county official; b. Vernal, Utah, May 23, 1956; s. Lynn M. and Amy (Gardner) P.; m. Dorothy Houston, Feb. 2, 1980; 2 children. BA cum laude, Utah State U., Logan, 1979. Pool mgr. Uintah County, Vernal, Utah, 1979-80; mgr. tng. Nowsco Svcs., Vernal, Utah, 1980-84; purchasing agt. Uintah County, Vernal, Utah, 1984—. Mem. Nat. Assn. Purchasing Mgrs. Republican. Office: Uintah County 152 E 100 N Vernal UT 84078

POPE, JANE LARUE, nurse educator; b. Boise, Idaho, July 17, 1929; d. James Alton and Luella (Sillivan) Weed; m. Henry Louis Pope Jr., Mar. 3, 1967 (dec. May 1986). Diploma in nursing, St. Marks Hosp., Salt Lake City, 1951; BS in Nursing, U. Utah, 1952; MS, U. Colo., 1960. RN, Utah, Calif., Ariz.; jr. coll. lifetime teaching credential, Calif. Nurse various hosps. in Utah and Idaho, 1952-58; instr. in psychiat. nursing Ariz. State U., Tempe, 1960-64; dir. of nursing Ariz. State Hosp., 1964-68; psychiat. nurse cons. Dept. Instns., Olympia, Wash., 1968; staff devel. project coord. Dept. Instns., Olympia, 1969-70; psychiat. nurse narcotic treatment project U. Calif., San Diego, 1974; program trainer health svcs. Atascadero (Calif.) State Hosp, 1977, dir. psychiat. nursing edn., 1978—; Nurse cons., reviewer Psychiatric Drug Guide, 1989. Contbr. articles to profl. jours. Grantee NIMH, 1965, 70. Republican. Episcopalian. Office: Atascadero State Hosp 10333 El Camino Real Atascadero CA 93423-7001

POPE, MARK L., computer information coordinator, university educator, consultant; b. St. Louis, Apr. 23, 1952; s. Marvin D. Williams and Ethyle R. (Ray) Harget. AB, U. Mo., 1973, MEd, 1974; student, Northwestern U., 1977-78; EdD, U. San Francisco, 1988. Nat. cert. counselor; nat. cert. career counselor; lic. psychol. asst. Drug abuse counselor Brotherhood Clinic Ill. Drug Abuse Program, Chgo., 1974-75; mental health worker, career counselor adolescent unit Northwestern Inst. Psychiatry, Chgo., 1975-76; career counselor, psychol. test cons. Meth. Youth Svcs., Chgo., 1976-77; rsch. interviewer, drug abuse counselor Cook County Treatment Alternatives to Street Crimes, Chgo., 1977-78; cons., pres. Data Psych Systems, N.Y.C. and San Francisco, 1978—; computer ops. mgr. Pacific Am. Group, San Francisco, 1981-83; supr. info. systems Bechtel Engring. & Constrn. Cos., San Francisco, 1983-87; software devel. editor Cons. Psychologists Press, Palo Alto, Calif., 1987—; dir., founder Horizons Profl. and Peer Counseling Svcs., Chgo., 1975-77; lectr. Cen. YMCA Community Coll. Dept. Psychology, Chgo., 1977-78, Northwestern U. Indsl. Engring. and Orgn. Devel. Dept., 1977-78, John F. Kennedy U. Career Devel. and Planning, Orinda, Calif., 1987—; adj. prof. Golden Gate U. Grad. Sch. Mgmt. Human Resource Mgmt., San Francisco, 1984—, U. San Francisco Info. Systems Mgmt., 1986—, counseling and edn. psychology, 1988—; career devel. cons. Pacific Bell, San Francisco, 1988—; human resources cons. Alpha Computer Svcs., San Rafael, Calif., 1988—; founder, organizer Counselors With Computers Conf., 1988—. Contbr. articles to profl. jours. Mem. collaborative planning com. U. San Francisco Sch. Edn., 1987-88, Mo. Gen. Assembly drug abuse adv. com., 1972-73; bd. dirs. Ill. Civil Liberties Union, Chgo., 1976-78; appointee Mo. Gov.'s Reorganization Commn., 1973. Mem. Am. Assn. Counseling and Devel. (mem. couseling software rev. bd. 1987—), Am. Psychol. Assn., Assn. for Computing Machinery, Assn. for Counselor Edn. and Supervision (co-chair internat. network 1988—, chair subcom. on internat. counselor edn. database 1986-88, mem. counseling and tech. network 1985—, counseling in bus. and industry network 1985—), Assn. for Measurement and Evaluation in Counseling and Devel., Bay Area Career Devel. Assn. (co-chair 1987—), Calif. Assn. for Counseling and Devel. (chair subcom. human rights com. 1986-88), Calif. Assn. Measurement and Evaluation in Counseling and Devel. (sec., treas. 1988-89, pres. elect 1989-90), Calif. Assn. Multi-Cultural Counseling, Calif. Career Devel. Assn. (profl. devel. chair 1988—), Computers in Psychology, Human Factors Soc., Nat. Career Devel. Assn., No. Calif. Assn. for Counseling and Devel., Phi Delta Kappa. Home: PO Box 1734 San Francisco CA 94101-1734 Office: Cons Psychologists Press 577 College Ave Palo Alto CA 94306

POPE, MAX LYNDELL, public utility official; b. Clinton, N.C., Nov. 5, 1932; s. William Walter and Maggie (Honeycutt) P.; B.A., Idaho State Coll., 1962; grad. U.S. Army Command and Gen. Staff Coll., 1977, Security Manpower Program, Indsl. Coll. Armed Forces, 1980; m. Sarah Jane Norris, Dec. 10, 1954. City mgr. City of Rangely (Colo.), 1963-66, City of Seaside (Oreg.), 1966-69, City of Pasco (Wash.), 1969-70; city adminstr. City of Coeur d'Alene (Idaho), 1971-72; planner State of Idaho, Boise, 1972-75; city adminstr. City of Woodburn (Oreg.), 1975-85; gen. mgr. Woodinville Water Dist., Wash., 1986—. Ordained elder Presbyn. Ch., 1958, elder, Woodburn, 1976—. Served with U.S. Army, 1953-56, 70-71. Recipient Distinguished Service award Rangely Jaycees, 1964. Mem. Internat. City Mgmt. Assn., Am. Soc. Public Adminstrn., Am. Public Works Assn., Internat. Union Local Authorities, Civil Affairs Assn., Res. Officers Assn., Woodinville C. of C., Woodburn C. of C. Clubs: Rotary, Gowen Field Officers, Elks. Home: 14206 NE 181st Pl Suite L203 Woodinville WA 98072 Office: 17238 Woodinville-Duvall Rd Woodinville WA 98072

POPE, PETER T., forest products company executive; b. 1934; married. B.A., Stanford U., 1957, M.B.A., 1959. With Pope & Talbot Inc., Portland, Oreg., 1960—, asst. sec., 1964-68, v.p., 1968-69, v.p., gen. mgr., 1969-71, chmn. bd., chief exec. officer, 1971—, also dir. Served with USAR, 1957-58. Office: Pope & Talbot Inc 1500 SW 1st Ave Portland OR 97201

POPE, ROBERT ALLEN, data processing executive, consultant; b. Whitewater, Wis., May 26, 1949; s. Donald Charles Pope and Roberta Carole (Cunneliff) Comstock; m. Debra Lynn Crombie, Apr. 16, 1973 (div.); 1 child, Karla Anne; m. Shirley Anne Droughn, Nov. 14, 1986; children: Tina Michelle Clatterbuck, Amy Marie Clatterbuck, Edward Shane Clatterbuck. Student, Walnut City (Calif.) Coll., 1976. Sr. statistician, jr. analyst Farmer Ins. Co., Los Angeles, 1969-74; chief statistician, sr. analyst Signal/Imperial Ins. Cos., Los Angeles, 1974-77; documentation mgr., sr. systems analyst Transit Casualty Ins. Co., Los Angeles, 1977-79; supr. ops. Showboat Hotel and Casino, Las Vegas, Nev., 1980-85; corp. data processing mgr. Exber Inc., Las Vegas, 1985—; cons. Riviera Hotel and Casino, Las Vegas, 1985-86, Alexis Park Hotel, Las Vegas, 1984-86. Regional pres. Calif. PTA for Deaf and Hearing Impaired, Los Angeles, 1974; 3d v.p., bd. dirs. John Tracy Clinic, Los Angeles, 1977-78; asst. Cubmaster Boy Scouts Am., Las Vegas, 1986-88. Lodge: Elks. Home: 3860 Azui Pl Las Vegas NV 89121 Office: Exber Inc 107 N 6th St Las Vegas NV 89101

POPE, THOMAS JAY, management consultant; b. Casper, Wyo., Sept. 21, 1930; s. Clifford Bardwell and Mildred Ethel (Stubbs) P.; m. Robina Marie Harbaugh, Apr. 18, 1954; children: Robert, David, Daniel. BSME, U. Wyo., 1955. Design engr. Westinghouse Electric Corp., Kansas City, Mo., 1955-58; div. mgr. Sundstrand Corp., Denver, 1958-71; gen. mgr. Am. Air Filter Co., Santa Paula, Calif., 1971-74; group pres. Pacific Sci. Co., Anaheim, Calif., 1974-86, Bus. Search, Carlsbad, Calif., 1986—. With USAF, 1950-53, Korea. Mem. Am. Soc. Mech. Engrs., Am. Mgmt. Assn. Republican. Congregationalist. Home: 399 Hillcrest Dr Leucadia CA 92024 Office: Bus Search Ste 104-128 6992 El Camino Real Carlsbad CA 92009

POPEJOY, WILLIAM J., savings and loan association executive; b. 1938; married. B.A., Calif. State U., 1961, M.A., 1962. Pres. Fed. Home Loan Mortgage Corp., 1971-74; pres. Am. Savs. & Loan Assn. subs. Fin. Corp. Am., Los Angeles, 1974-80; chmn., pres., chief exec. officer Am. Savs. & Loan Assn. subs. Fin. Corp. Am., Irving, Calif., 1984-89, also bd. dirs.; pres. Far West Savs. & Loan Assn., 1980-81; pres., chief fin. officer Fin. Fedn. Inc., Culver City, Calif., from 1981; chmn., pres., chief exec. officer Fin. Corp. Am., Irvine, 1984-89, also bd. dirs. Office: Fin Corp Am 18401 Von Karman Ave Irvine CA 92715 *

POPELKA, ROBERT JOSEPH, lawyer; b. Madison Lake, Minn., May 9, 1920; s. Charles Joseph and Gertrude Helen (Mape) P.; m. Dorothy Popelka; children—Robert, Robin, John, James, Mark (dec.). A.B., Coll. of St. Thomas, 1940; J.D., U. Calif., 1948. Bar: Calif. bar 1949. Practice law San Francisco, 1949-51; founder, sr. partner firm Popelka, Allard, McCowan & Jones, San Jose, Calif., 1951—. Served with USMC, 1942-46, PTO. Mem. ABA, Calif. Bar Assn., Am. Coll. Trial Lawyers, Trial Attys. Am. (v.p.), Am. Bd. Trial Advocates, Internat. Soc. Barristers, Internat. Acad. Trial Lawyers, Bencher, Inn of Ct. XII. Republican. Roman Catholic. Clubs: Sainte Claire of San Jose, San Jose Country; Thunderbird Country (Rancho Mirage, Calif.); Commonwealth of Calif. Home: 574 Kumquat Dr San Jose CA 95117 Office: Popelka Allard McCowan & Jones One Almaden Blvd 8th Fl San Jose CA 95115

POPKOFF, VALERIAN, engineering technician; b. Sept. 26, 1946; s. Boris Ivanovitch and Klaudia Ivanova Popkoff; m. Galina V. Popkoff, Feb. 18, 1968; 1 child, Boris. Diploma, Indsl. Tng. Ctr., San Francisco, 1963, U.S. Southeastern Sch., Ft. Gordon, Ga., 1966; student, U. Santa Clara, 1982. Electromechanical tech. Dalmo Victor Co. div. of Textron, Belmont, Calif., 1969-71, mfg. data equipment tech., 1974-86; communications data equipment tech. Vadic Corp., Mountain View, Calif., 1971-74; prototype technician Randtron Systems subs. Loral Corp., Menlo Park, Calif., 1987-89, mfg. supr., 1989—. Nat. adv. bd. Am. Security Council, Boston, Va., 1986. With U.S. Army, 1966-69. Office: Randtron Systems 130 Constitution Dr Menlo Park CA 94025

POPOVICH, STEVE S., computer company executive; b. Monessen, Pa., Feb. 21, 1932; s. John and Elizabeth (Martin) P.; m. Beverly Viola Thies, July 21, 1954; children: Steve J., Scott D., Todd T. BEE, U. Mich., 1959. Engr. Northrop Corp., Hawthorne, Calif., 1959-62, Control Data Corp., Mpls., 1962-69; dir. engring. Control Data Corp., 1969-74, v.p., 1983; sr. v.p. Calif. Computer Products, Anaheim, 1974-77; founder, pres., chief fin. officer Catas Corp., Tustin, Calif., 1977-79; founder, gen. mgr. advanced products lab. Control Data Corp., Colorado Springs, 1979-82; founder, pres. Optical Peripherals Lab., Colorado Springs, 1982; founder, pres., chief exec. officer Info. Storage, Inc., Colorado Springs, 1983--; presenter seminars on optical memory, 1983--. Contbr. articles to tech. publs. With USAF, 1951-55. Mem. IEEE, Soc. Profl. Indsl. Engrs., Country Club Colo., Plaza Club. Roman Catholic. Home: 375 Wedgewood Ct Colorado Springs CO 80906

POPP, DALE D., orthopedic surgeon; b. Tama County, Iowa, July 6, 1923; s. Herbert John and Millie (Rayman) P.; m. Dorothy L. Higgins (div. July, 1970); children: Mark, Craig, Gordon, Brian, Nancy, James, Melissa; m. Carla Jean Drobny, Aug. 27, 1970; 1 child (stepson) Gary. BA, U. Iowa, 1944, MD, 1947. Am. Bd. Orthopedic Surgeons. Orthopedic surgeon Spokane (Wash.) Orthopedic Clinic, 1954-82, Inland Medic Evaluations, Spokane, 1986-87. Capt. USAF, 1951-53. Mem. Am. Acad. Orthopedic Surgeons, North Pacific Orthopedic Soc., Western Orthopedic Assn., Spokane Surg. Soc. Republican.

POPPA, RYAL ROBERT, manufacturing company executive; b. Wahpeton, N.D., Nov. 7, 1933; s. Ray Edward and Annabelle (Phillips) P.; m. Ruth Ann Curry, June 21, 1952; children: Sheryl Lynn, Kimberly Marie. BBA, Claremont Men's Coll., 1957. Sales trainee IBM, L.A., 1957-59, sales rep., 1959-62, product mktg. rep., 1963, sales mgr., 1964-66; v.p., gen. mgr. Comml. Computers Inc., L.A., 1966-67; v.p. Greyhound Computer Corp., Chgo., 1967-68, pres., chief exec. officer, bd. dirs., 1969-70; pres., chief exec. officer, bd. dirs., mem. exec. com. Data Processing Fin. & Gen., Hartsdale, N.Y., 1970-72; exec. v.p., chief fin. officer, bd. dirs., mem. exec. com. Mohawk Data Sci. Corp., Utica, N.Y., 1972-73; chmn., pres., chief exec. officer Pertec Computer Corp., L.A., 1973-81, BMC Industries, Inc., St. Paul, 1982-85; pres., chmn., chief exec. officer Storage Tech. Corp., Louisville, Colo., 1985—; bd. dir. Western Digital Corp., Irvine, Calif.; founder Charles Babbage Inst.; past dir. Spacelabs, Inc. Trustee Claremont Men's Coll., Colo. Music Festival; mem. Chmn.'s Circle Colo. Reps.; past mem. Pres. Com. Nat. Medal of Sci. Recipient Exec. of Yr. award U. Colo. MBA Alum Assn., 1986, Community Svc. award Inst. Human Rels. Am. Jewish Com., 1980. Mem. World Bus. Coun., Chief Exec. Orgn., World Bus. Coun., Computer and Communications Industry Assn. (past bd. dirs., chmn., mem. exec. com.), Am. Electronics Assn. (past bd. dirs., mem. exec. com. Colo. chpt.), Electronic Mfrs. Club, Boulder Country Club, The Denver Club. Office: Storage Tech Corp 2270 S 88th St Louisville CO 80028-4315

PORAD, LAURIE JO, jewelry company official; b. Seattle, Dec. 19, 1951; d. Bernard L. and Francine J. (Harvitz) P. BA, U. Wash., 1974; postgrad., Seattle Pacific U., summers 1975-76. Cert. standard tchr., Wash. Substitute tchr. Issaquah (Wash.) Sch. Dist., 1974-77; with data processing dept. Ben Bridge Jeweler, Seattle, 1977-83, auditing mgr., 1983-87, systems mgr., 1987—; mem. adv. bd. computer sci. dept. Highline Community Coll., Midway, Wash., 1985—. Tchr. religion sch. Temple de Hirsch Sinai, Seattle, 1972-76, 84—, coord. computerized Hebrew learning ctr., 1987-88, coord. of religion sch. city facility, 1988—; tutor Children's Home Soc. Wash., Seattle, 1976-77. Mem. Assn. for Women in Computing (life mem., chmn. chpt. workshop 1985-88, nat. chpts. v.p. 1985-88, nat. pres. 1988—), A Singular Investment Club (Seattle). Home: 14616 NE 44th St Apt M2 Bellevue WA 98007 Office: Ben Bridge Jeweler PO Box 1908 Seattle WA 98111

PORCARO, MICHAEL FRANCIS, advertising agency executive; b. N.Y.C., Apr. 3, 1948; s. Girolamo M. and Marianna (DePasquale) P.; m. Bonnie Kerr, Apr. 7, 1972; children: Sabrina, Jon. BA in English, Rockford (Ill.) Coll., 1969. Broadcaster Sta. KFQD, Anchorage, 1970-71, Sta. KENI, Anchorage, 1972-73; v.p. ops. Cook Inlet Broadcasters, Anchorage, 1973-74; owner Audio Enterprises, Anchorage, 1974-75; asst. Alaska Pub. Broadcasting Commn., Anchorage, 1975-76; exec. dir. Alaska Pub. Broadcasting Commn., 1976-81; chief exec. officer, ptnr. Porcaro Blankenship Advt. Corp., Anchorage, 1981—; cons. Arco Alaska TV sta., Anchorage, 1981; expert witness U.S. Sen. Subcom. on Telecommunications, Washington, 1978. Mem. urban design commn. Municipality of Anchorage, 1988; mem. transition team Mayor of Anchorage, 1987-88; bd. dirs. Anchorage Glacier Pilots Baseball Club, 1987, 88. Recipient Silver Mike award Billboard mag., 1974, Bronze award N.Y. Film Critics, 1981, Best of North award Ad. Fedn. Alaska, 1982—, Addy award, 1985, Cable TV Mktg. award, 1986; Paul Harris fellow. Republican. Roman Catholic. Office: Porcaro Blankenship Advt 320 E 12th Ave Anchorage AK 99501

PORLIER, LINDA KAY, professional speaker, sales communications company executive; b. Seattle, Jan. 28, 1948; m. Terry Lamont Porlier, Sept. 21, 1967. BBA, U. Wash., 1970. Prin., POKO Internat., Ltd., Seattle, 1971-80; mgr., tng. exec. Dale Carnegie Courses, Seattle, 1980-84; ptnr. Porlier & Porlier, Mesa, Ariz., 1985—; cons. in communications, human relations, sales tng., improved decision making, career blueprinting and developing motivation by design, 1985—; profl. speaker and workshop presenter in field. Author: Living Over the Limit: The Credit Card Survival Kit, 1989. Sec., King County Republican Women's Commn. 1984; candidate for Wash. State Senate, 1982; Mem. Seattle C. of C. (roundtable facilitator 1986). Republican. Mem. Christian Ch. Lodge: Zonta (chmn. 1988—). Office: Porlier & Porlier 2051 S Dobson Rd Ste 5-215 Mesa AZ 85202

PORRERO, HENRY, JR., computer company executive; b. Upland, Calif., Aug. 16, 1967. AA, Chaffey Coll., 1970; BS, Calpoly Pomona U., 1973. Bus. mgr. Guy F. Atkinson Co., South San Francisco, 1973-83; controller Laird Constrn. Co., Inc., R. Cucamonga, Calif., 1983-85; pres., founder PLT Computer Systems, Inc., Upland, Calif., 1986—; fin. cons. Parrott & Wright Constrn., Corona, Calif., 1987—. Treas. Boy Scouts Am., Upland, 1987--. With USN,1966-69. Mem. Am. Legion, Friends Upland Library, Calif. Sheriffs Assn. Republican. Home: 1068 W 11th St Upland CA 91786

PORSCH, DENISE KELLER, public information/public relations executive, educator; b. Stockton, Calif., Apr. 27, 1957; d. Alebrt J. and Joycelyn J. Keller; married. AA, San Joaquin Delta Coll., Stockton, 1976; BA, Calif. State U., Chico, 1978; MA, Calif. State U., Stanislaus, Turlock, 1984. Media coord. Community Action Vols. in Edn., Chico, 1977-78; with Stockton News, 1978; reporter Lodi (Calif.) Life & Times, 1979-80; asst. pub. info. San Joaquin Delta Coll., 1980-88; pub. info. officer Cosumnes River Coll., Sacramento, 1988—; instr. Modesto (Calif.) Jr. Coll., 1986-87; publicity coord. Showcase Prodns., Stockton, 1980—. Mem. youth adv. bd. People to People Internat., Kansas City, 1985—. Mem. Sacramento Pub. Relations Assn. Office: Cosumnes River Coll 8401 Center Pkwy Sacramento CA 95823-5799

PORT, MIKE, professional baseball team executive; b. Los Angeles, Calif., July 24, 1945; m. Thaylea Port; children: Brian, Adam. B.B.A., Calif. Western U. Minor league infielder San Diego Padres, 1969; gen. mgr. Key West team, Fla. State League, 1969-79, Lodi team, Calif. league, 1970-71; dir. promotions San Diego Padres, 1972, minor league dir., 1973-77; dir. player personnel Calif. Angels, Anaheim, 1977-80, v.p., chief adminstrv. officer, 1980-84, sr. v.p., gen. mgr., 1984—. Office: Calif Angels 2000 State Coll Blvd Anaheim CA 92806 *

PORTER, ARTHUR WOODS, lawyer; b. Darien, Conn., Nov. 6, 1955; s. Arthur Leaholme and Margaret Jane (Woods) Porter. AB in Econs. magna cum laude, Boston U., 1979; JD, Am. U., 1982. Bar: Colo. 1983, U.S. Dist. Ct. Colo. 1983, U.S. Ct. Appeals (10th cir.) 1983. Assoc. Spurgeon, Haney & Howbert, P.C., Colorado Springs, Colo., 1982-85, Holland & Hart, Colorado Springs, 1985-88; spl. counsel Trott, Kunstle & Hughes, Colorado Springs, 1988; ptnr. Thomas & Porter, P.C., Colorado Springs, 1988—. Column editor The Colo. Lawyer, 1988—. Cons. to project bus. Jr. Achievement of Colorado Springs, 1984—, bd. dirs., 1987—, v.p. 1988—; bd. dirs. Colorado Pub. Expenditure Council, 1987-88. Recipient B V rating Martindale-Hubbell, 1985, Vigil Hon. Order of Arrow Boy Scouts Am., Bronze Palm; named Eagle Scout Boy Scouts Am.; rsch. grantee Am. U., 1980. Mem. ABA, Assn. Trial Lawyers Am., Colo. Bar Assn. (mem. exec.

council young lawyers div. 1987—), El Paso County Bar Assn., Colo. Trial Lawyers Assn., Nat. Inst. Trial Advocacy, Mortar Board. Methodist. Club: Plaza (Colorado Springs). Home: 29 Cragmor Village Rd Colorado Springs CO 80918 Office: Thomas & Porter PC 128 S Tejon Ste 402 Colorado Springs CO 80903

PORTER, BLAINE ROBERT MILTON, sociology educator; b. Morgan, Utah, Feb. 24, 1922; s. Brigham Ernest and Edna (Brough) P.; m. Elizabeth Taylor, Sept 27, 1943 (dec.); children—Claudia Black, Roger B., David T., Patricia A. Hintze, Corinna; m. Myrna Katherine Kennedy, Feb. 26, 1988. Student, Utah State U., 1940-41; B.S., Brigham Young U., 1947, M.A., 1949; Ph.D. (Grant Found. fellow family life edn. 1951-52), Cornell U., 1952. Instr. sociology Iowa State Coll., 1949-51; asst. prof. sociology and child devel. Iowa State U., 1952-55; prof., chmn. dept. human devel. and family relationships Brigham Young U., 1955-65; dean Brigham Young U. (Coll. Family Living), 1966-80, Univ. prof., 1980—; vis. prof., Fulbright research scholar U. London, 1965-66; vis. prof. U. Wurzberg, 1980, 81, 83. Editor: The Latter-day Saint Family, 1963, rev. edit., 1966; editor quar. jour.: Family Perspective, 1966-82; contbr. articles to profl. jours. Pres. elect Iowa Council Family Relations, 1954-55; pres. Utah Council Family Relations, 1957-58; chmn. sect. marriage counseling Nat. Council Family Relations, 1958-59, bd. dirs., 1957-60, exec. com., 1958-72, pres., 1963-64; bd. dirs. Am. Family Soc., 1975—. Served as pilot USAAF, 1942-45. Recipient Prof. of Year award Brigham Young U., 1964. Mem. Am. Home Econs. Assn. (vice chmn. sect. family relations and child devel. 1955-56), Am. Sociol. Assn. (sec. sect. on family 1964-67), Am. Assn. Marriage and Family Therapists, Am. Psychol. Assn., Soc. Research in Child Devel., Sigma Xi, Phi Kappa Phi (chpt. pres. 1969-71). Home: 1675 Pine Ln Provo UT 84604 Office: Brigham Young U 2240 SFLC Provo UT 84602

PORTER, DIXIE LEE, insurance executive, consultant; b. Bountiful, Utah, June 7, 1931; d. John Lloyd and Ida May (Robinson) Mathis. B.S., U. Calif. at Berkeley, 1956, M.B.A., 1957. Personnel aide City of Berkeley (Calif.), 1957-59; employment supr. Kaiser Health Found., Los Angeles, 1959-60; personnel analyst U. Calif. at Los Angeles, 1961-63; personnel mgr. Reuben H. Donnelley, Santa Monica, Calif., 1963-64; personnel officer Good Samaritan Hosp., San Jose, Calif., 1965-67; fgn. service officer AID, Saigon, Vietnam, 1967-71; gen. agt. Charter Life Ins. Co., Los Angeles, 1972-77, Kennesaw Life Ins. Co., Atlanta, from 1978, Phila. Life Ins. Co., San Francisco, from 1978; now pres. Women's Ins. Enterprises, Ltd.; cons. in field. Co-chairperson Comprehensive Health Planning Commn. Santa Clara County, Calif., 1973-76; bd. dirs. Family Care, 1978-80, Aegis Health Corp., 1977—, U. Calif. Sch. Bus. Adminstrn., Berkeley, 1974-76; mem. task force on equal access to econ. power U.S. Nat. Women's Agenda, 1977—. Served with USMC, 1950-52. C.L.U. Mem. C.L.U. Soc., U. Calif. Alumni Assn., U. Calif. Sch. Bus. Adminstrn. Alumni Assn., AAUW, Bus. and Profl. Women, Prytanean Alumni, The Animal Soc. Los Gatos/Saratoga (pres. 1987—), Beta Gamma Sigma, Phi Chi Theta. Republican. Episcopalian. Home and Office: PO Box 64 Los Gatos CA 95031

PORTER, JAMES STUART, JR., automation technologist; b. St. Louis, Feb. 1, 1948; s. James Stuart and Irene Janette (Hubert) P.; m. Diana Mae Saathoff, June 27, 1967 (div. Feb. 1974); m. Judy Ellen Rolwing, June 17, 1976; children: Michelle Ann, Jennifer Lynn. AS, ITT Tech. Inst., Indpls., 1967, Purdue U., Indpls., 1968; student, Casper Coll., Wyo., 1981-88; instr. cert., We. Wyo. Coll., 1986. Cert. electronics technologist. Distributor UPS, Indpls., 1966-68; customer engr. IBM, St. Louis, 1968-72, advanced customer service rep., 1972-76; advanced tech. rep. IBM, Casper, Wyo., 1976-81; pres., chief executive officer Express Bus. Systems, Casper, 1981—; ptnr. Express Automation, Casper, 1985-88; owner, mgr. Porter Properties, Casper, 1981—; cons. Express Automation, Casper, 1984-88. Author: Wilderness Survival, 1976; author, editor: Managing in the '80s, 1986; co-author: Introduction to Lotus 1-2-3, 1985. Scoutmaster, Boy Scouts Am., Evansville, Wyo., 1978-85, dist. commr., Casper, 1985—, dist. com., 1986—. Sgt. U.S. Army, 1968-70, Vietnam. Democrat. Roman Catholic. Home: 1500 Bellaire Dr Casper WY 82604

PORTER, KATHERYNE ADELADE, postmaster; b. Springerville, Ariz., May 13, 1934; d. Manning Lee Sr. and Rena Belle (Sudduth) Lewis; m. Walter Clyde Porter, July 28, 1950; children: Lynnda, Larry, Chris, Sandra, Sharon, Carla. Grad. high sch., Fence Lake, N.Mex., 1951. Postmaster U.S. Postal Service, Alpine, Ariz., 1984—. Republican. Home: Box 404 Alpine AZ 85920-0404 Office: US Postal Svc Alpine AZ 85920-9998

PORTER, LEONARD EDGAR, physics educator; b. New Limerick, Maine, Nov. 19, 1934; s. Oscar Byron and Ina Ellen (Hand) P.; m. JoAnn Maureen Johnson, Aug. 16, 1958; children: Laurie Maureen, Leonard Emerson. AB summa cum laude, Miami U., Oxford, Ohio, 1956; MS, U. Wis., 1961, PhD, 1965. Postgrad. researcher in physics U. Calif.-Riverside, 1965-66, asst. researcher, 1966-67; asst. prof. physics U. Mont., Missoula, 1967-73, assoc. prof., 1973-77, prof., 1977—, chmn. dept., 1976—, dir. Mont. Sci. Fair, 1974-85 ; mem. Assoc. Western Univs. vis. summer faculty Los Alamos Sci. Lab., 1969-72, Battelle Pacific N.W. Lab., 1973-74; Mt. States Energy Lab., 1989. Air Force summer faculty rsch. fellow, Air force Wapons Lab., 1988. Contbr. numerous articles, abstracts to profl. publs. Trustee Loyola Sacred Heart Found., Missoula, 1983-84; mem. Govs. Task Force on the Superconducting Supercollider, Helena, Mont., 1987-88. 1st lt. USMC, 1956-59. Mem. Am. Phys. Soc., Am. Assn. Physics Tchrs., Mont. Acad. Scis. (pres. 1980-81), Mont. Sci. Adv. Coun., Missoula Exchange Club (pres. 1978-79), Sigma Xi (pres. U. Mont. chpt. 1971-72). Republican. Unitarian. Office: U Mont Dept Physics and Astronomy Missoula MT 59812

PORTER, MAXON R., communications corporation executive; b. Reno, July 24, 1943; s. Maxon R. and Izola Mae (Barker) P.; m. Jane Elizabeth Jacobs, Aug. 2, 1963; children: Tamra Lynn, Jennifer Lynn. Grad. high sch., Carson City, Nev. Technician Nev. Bell, Reno, 1962-73, supr., 1973-82; supr. AT&T, Reno, 1982—, tchr., 1982-84. Instr. skiing Reno Recreation Program, 1961-74, head instr., 1974-85; asst. coach skiing Reno High Sch., 1985—. Fellow Profl. Ski Instr. Am. (assoc.), U.S. Ski Coaches Assn. (level 1 coach 1986—). Republican. Lutheran. Club: Toastmasters (pres. 1978). Home: 4090 Jasper Ln Reno NV 89509 Office: AT&T 150 E First St PO Box 1789 Reno NV 89501

PORTER, MICHAEL PELL, lawyer; b. Indpls., Mar. 31, 1940; s. Harold Troxel and Mildred Maxine (Pell) P.; m. Alliene Laura Jenkins, Sept. 23, 1967 (div.); 1 child, Genevieve Natalie; m. Janet Kay Smith Hayes, Feb. 13, 1983. Student, DePauw U., 1957-58; BA, Tulane U., 1961, LLB, 1963. Bar: La. 1963, U.S. Ct. Mil. Appeals 1964, N.Y. 1969, Hawaii 1971. Clk., U.S. Ct. Appeals (5th cir.), New Orleans, 1963; assoc. Sullivan & Cromwell, N.Y.C., 1968-71; assoc. Cades Schutte Fleming & Wright, Honolulu, 1971-74, ptnr., 1975—; mem. deans coun. Tulane Law Sch., 1981-88; dep. vice chancellor Episcopal Diocese Hawaii, 1980-88, chancellor, 1988—; chancellor Episcopal Ch., Micronesia, 1988—. Author: Hawaii Corporation Law and Practice, Nat. Corp. Law Series, 1989. Bd. dirs. Jr. Achievement Hawaii, Inc., 1974-84, Inst. Human Svcs., Inc., 1980-88; Hoa Kokua Hospice Vols., 1984-85; donor Michael P. and Janet K. Porter Dean's Scholastic award U. Hawaii Law Sch., 1977—. With JAGC, U.S. Army, 1963-66, Vietnam. Tulane U. fellow, 1981. Mem. ABA, Assn. Bar City N.Y., Hawaii State Bar Assn., Friends of U. Hawaii Law Sch. Republican. Club: Pacific (Honolulu). Office: Cades Schutte Fleming & Wright 1000 Bishop St Honolulu HI 96813

PORTER, PATRICIA JEAN, realtor; b. Kansas City, Mo., May 31, 1935; d. Percy Lee Jones and Eva Marie (Welch) Hedges; m. Robert Fred Porter, Mar. 21, 1952 (div. 1972); children: Linda Marie, Teri Sue, Jeri Lou. Grad., UCLA, 1965. Legal sec. Louis A. Sackin Assocs., Los Angeles, 1959-65; mgr. RSVP Realtors, Encino, Calif., 1969-82, Merrill Lynch Realty, Encino, 1982-85; owner The Producers, Encino, 1985-87; mgr. Mike Glickman Realty, Encino, 1987—. Mem. Calif. Assn. Realtors (bd. dirs. 1965-77), San Fernando Valley Bd. Realtors (bd. dirs. 1965-77), Encino C. of C. (bd. dirs. 1969-77). Republican. Office: Mike Glickman Realty 16830 Ventura Blvd Encino CA 91436

PORTER, STEPHEN CUMMINGS, research geology educator; b. Santa Barbara, Calif., Apr. 18, 1934; s. Lawrence Johnson Porter Jr. and Frances (Cummings) Seger; m. Anne Mary Higgins, Apr. 2, 1959; children: John, Maria, Susannah: BS, Yale U., 1955, MS, 1958, PhD, 1962. Asst. prof. geology U. Wash., Seattle, 1962-66, assoc. prof., 1966-71, prof., 1971—, dir. Quaternary Research Ctr., 1982—; mem. bd. earth scis. Nat. Acad. Sci., Washington, 1983-85; mem. advisory com., div. polar programs NSF, Washington, 1983-84; vis. fellow Clare Hall Cambridge (Eng.) U., 1980-81; guest prof. Academia Sinica, People's Republic of China, 1987—. Co-author: Physical Geology, 1987, The Dynamic Earth, 1989; editor: Late Quaternary Environments of the United States, 1983, (jour.) Quaternary Research, 1976—; assoc. editor (jour.) Radiocarbon, 1982—. Served to lt. USNR, 1955-57. Recipient Benjamin Silliman prize Yale U., New Haven, 1962, Willis M. Tate Lectr., So. Meth. U., Dallas, 1984; Fulbright-Hays Sr. Research fellow New Zealand, 1973-74. Fellow Geol. Soc. Am., Arctic Inst. N.Am. (bd. govs); mem. AAAS, Internat. Glaciol. Soc., Am. Quaternary Assn (council), Sigma Xi. Club: Am. Alpine (N.Y.C.). Home: 18034 15th Ave NW Seattle WA 98177 Office: U Wash Quaternary Rsch Ctr Seattle WA 98195

PORTER, VICKI SHARON, lawyer, educator; b. Chgo., July 29, 1955; d. Simon Seymore and Renee Marilyn (Rossman) P. BA, U. Colo., 1976; JD cum laude, U. Miami, Coral Gables, Fla., 1979. Bar: Colo. 1980, U.S. Dist. Ct. Colo. 1980, U.S. Ct. Appeals (10th cir.) 1983; lic. real estate broker. Pvt. practive law Denver, 1979—; assoc. Holmes & Starr PC, Denver, 1979-80, Sterling & Simon PC, Denver, 1980-82, Sweig & Pockross, PC, Denver, 1983-84, Robinson, Waters, O'Dorsio & Rapson, PC, Denver, 1984; dir., assoc. Sterling & Miller, PC, Denver, 1984-86; spl. counsel Massey Burke & Showalter, PC and predecessor firms, Denver, 1986—; instr. U. Miami, Coral Gables, 1978-79; lectr. U. Denver, 1987-88, prof. Arapahoe Community Coll., Littleton, Colo., 1988-89. Contbr. articles to profl. jours. Apptd. as panel bankruptcy trustee by U.S. Trustee Dist. Colo., 1983—. Mem. ABA (mem. cabinet young lawyers sect. 1987-89, co-author, editor A Desk-Side Guide to the Rules of Bankruptcy 1986, second edit. 1988, moderator ann. meeting, 1987, chairperson debtor-creditor relationships com. 1986—), Colo. Bar Assn. (chmn. young lawyers sect. 1985-86, del. to ABA 1988—, author, speaker), Denver Bar Assn., Colo. Women's Bar Assn. (girls just wanna have fun com. 1988—, speaker), Colo. Women's C. of C. (gen. counsel 1988—) Bar and Gavel, Omicron Delta Kappa. Democrat. Jewish. Office: Massey Burke & Showalter PC 518 17th St Ste 1100 Denver CO 80202

PORTER, WALTER THOMAS, JR., banker; b. Corning, N.Y., Jan. 8, 1934; s. Walter Thomas and Mary Rebecca (Brookes) P.; m. Dixie Jo Thompson, Apr. 3, 1959; children: Kimberlee Paige, Douglas Thompson, Jane-Amy Elizabeth. BS, Rutgers U., 1954; MBA, U. Wash., 1959; PhD, Columbia U., 1964. CPA, Wash., N.Y. Staff cons. Touche Ross & Co., Seattle, 1959-61; NDEA fellow Columbia U., 1961-64; dir. edn. Touche Ross & Co., N.Y.C., 1964-66; assoc. prof. U. Wash., 1966-70, prof., 1970-74; vis. prof. N. European Mgmt. Inst., Oslo, Norway, 1974-75; nat. dir. planning Touche Ross & Co., Seattle, 1975-78, dir. exec. fin. counseling, 1978-84, exec. v.p., mgr. pvt. banking, Rainier Nat. Bank, 1984-87, exec. v.p., mgr. capital mgmt. and pvt. banking, 1987-88, vice chmn. 1988-89; vice chmn. Security Pacific Bank Washington, 1989—; vis. lectr. taxation U. Wash., 1978-85, 1988—. Mem. Seattle adv. bd. Salvation Army, 1975-83; trustee Ryther Child Ctr., 1975-85, pres., 1979-81; trustee Lakeside Sch., 1977-87, treas., 1970-81, 1st v.p. 1982-84, pres. 1984-86; trustee Virginia Mason Rsch. Ctr., 1982-87, Mus. History and Industry, 1982-83, Va. Mason Med. Ctr., 1986—. Served with U.S. Army, 1955-57. Author: Auditing Electronic System, 1966; (with William Perry) EDP: Controls and Auditing, 1970, 5th edit., 1987; (with John Burton) Auditing A Conceptual Approach, 1974; (with D. Alkire) Wealth: How to Achieve It, 1976; Touche Ross Guide to Personal Financial Management, 1984, 3d edit., 1989; (with D. Porter) The Personal Financial Planner's Practice Sourcebook, 1986. Mem. Am. Inst. CPA's. Congregationalist. Club: Wash. Athletic, Sand Point Country. Office: Security Pacific Bank Wash 1301 5th Ave PO Box 3966 Seattle WA 98124

PORTEUS, JAMES OLIVER, physicist; b. Wilmington, Del., Oct. 25, 1929; s. James Ray and Dorothy Richardson (Newton) P.; m. Margaret Louise Morley, Oct. 24, 1953; children: Holly Anne Porteus Rous, Megan Jane Porteus Jones, Gwynne Cameron. BS, U. Del., 1951; PhD, Cornell U., 1958. Rsch. assoc. Cornell U., Ithaca, N.Y., 1958-59; rsch. physicist Naval Weapons Ctr., China Lake, Calif., 1959-70; head crystal physics br. Naval Weapons Ctr., China Lake, 1970-78, head quantum surface dynamics br., 1978—. Contbr. articles to profl. jours.; patentee in field. Mem. Am. Phys. Soc., Am. Vacuum Soc., Internat. Soc. for Optical Engring., Sigma Xi (pres., treas. China Lake chpt. 1972-73), Folk Dance Club (pres. 1978-79), Ski Club. Office: Naval Weapons Ctr Code 3817 China Lake CA 93555

PORTILLO, KIMBERLY JOY, industry training and career resource manager; b. Delta, Colo., July 14, 1962; d. Terrance Randy and Karen Ruth (Sebesta) Zortman; m. José Antonio Portillo, June 5, 1983; children: Taylor Anthony, Catherine Elizabeth, Jordan Randy. Grad. High Sch., Broomfield, Colo. Bookkeeper Colo. Aero Tech, Broomfield, 1981-84, receptionist, 1984-85, career advisor, 1985-87, mgr. industry tng.-career resource ctr., 1987—. Mem. Profl. Aviation Maintenance Assn., AMTECH. Office: Colo Aero Tech 10851 W 120th Ave Broomfield CO 80020

PORTIN, SHARON ROSE, sales executive; b. Portland, Oreg., Jan. 28, 1949; d. Henry Ernest and Florence Clara (Hinkel) P. BA, Seattle Pacific U., 1972. Continuing edn. specialist U. Wash., Seattle, 1977; instr. Shoreline Community Coll., Seattle, 1978-79; pvt. practice cons. Seattle, 1978-79; account mgr. Showtime, San Francisco, 1979, regional dir., 1981; regional dir. The Entertainment Channel, Showtime and The Movie Channel, L.A., 1981-82, dir. nat. accounts, 1982-86; dir. nat. sales Viewers Choice, L.A., 1986-87, v.p. nat. sales, 1987-88, v.p. sales and affiliate rels., 1988-. Bd. dirs. Nat. Acad. TV, Seattle, 1973-78. Named Young Career Woman, Bus. Am. Women, Wash., 1976, Ky. Col., Gov. of Ky., 1976; recipient ACE award Nat. Cable TV, 1975, 76, 77. Mem. So. Calif. Cable Assn. (com. mem.), Cable TV Mktg. and Adminstrn. (com. mem.), Women in Cable (bd. dirs. 1984-86), Bay Area Cable Club. Office: Viewers Choice 1888 Century Park E Ste 830 Los Angeles CA 90067

PORTNEY, JOSEPH NATHANIEL, aerospace executive; b. L.A., Aug. 15, 1927; s. Marcus and Sarah (Pilson) P.; m. Ina Mae Leibson, June 20, 1959; children: Philip, Jeffrey. BS, U.S. Naval Acad., 1952. Commd. 2d lt. USN, 1952, advanced through grades to capt., 1956, resigned, 1960; with Litton Systems, Inc., Woodland Hills, Calif., 1960—; project engr. Litton Aero Products Litton Systems, Inc., Woodland Hills, 1967-68, program mgr. Litton Aero Products, 1968-72, advanced program mgr. guidance and control systems, 1972-85, mgr. advanced programs guidance and control systems, 1985—. Patentee, solar compass; creator pilot and navigator calendar. Mem. Inst. of Navigation (exec. v.p. 1988-89, pres. 1989-90), U.S. Naval Acad. Alumni Assn. (trustee 1980-83). Jewish. Home: 4981 Amigo Ave Tarzana CA 91356 Office: Litton Systems Inc 5500 Canoga Ave Woodland Hills CA 91367

PORTUGAIS, HOWARD L., talent company executive; b. Chgo., June 20, 1939; s. Alex and Helen (Rosenberg) P. Student, U. Ill., 1958-62. Talent mgr. BNB Assocs., Beverly Hills, Calif., 1973-76; talent agent Creative Mgmt., Los Angeles, 1969-71, Internat. Famous, Los Angeles, 1971-73; talent mgr. Bernard Co., Los Angeles, 1976-79; talent agent Internat. Creative Mgmt., Los Angeles, 1980-82; talent mgr. Portugais Co., Los Angeles, 1982—; road mgr. Donovan tour, 1968; exec. cons. Consumer Buyline, Los Angeles, 1978-79. Fundraiser Last Chance for Animals, Los Angeles, 1986—; v.p. Los Angeles Pub. Library Adult Reading Program Literary Council. Mem. Acad. TV Arts and Scis., Acad. Rec. Arts and Scis., Nat. Acad. TV Arts and Scis., Zeta Beta Tau. Jewish. Home and Office: 2712 Nichols Canyon Rd Los Angeles CA 90046

PORTWOOD, PAMELA ANNE, writer, editor; b. Houston, Mar. 10, 1957; d. Silas Norman Lynn and Alice Anne (Stone) P.; m. Mark Wayne Taylor, June 30, 1981. BA with honors, English Rhodes Coll., Memphis, 1978; student, U. N.C., Greensboro, 1979; MA in Individual Studies, Memphis State U., 1982; MFA in Creative Writing, U. Ariz., 1985. Info. specialist II U. Ariz. Museum of Art, Tucson, 1987-88; freelance writer and editor Tucson, 1984—; cons. Tucson Community Cable Corp., 1988—, Law Offices of Waterfall, Economidis, Hanshaw & Villamana, Tucson, 1987. Author numerous poems; poetry editor: Clarion, Tucson, 1986—; columnist: Artspace, Albuquerque, 1985—; co-editor: Rebirth of Power, 1987; art critic numerous jours.; editor, writer: Envision, 1988—. Sponsor Save the Children, Westport, Conn., 1987—; mem. Amnesty Internat. USA, Washington, 1983—; vol. Am. Friends Service Com., Tucson, 1986-87. Grantee, Tucson Community Cable Corp., 1986. Mem. Soc. for Photographic Edn., Internat. Women's Writing Guild. Democrat. Office: 631 N Desert Ave Tucson AZ 85711

POSKANZER, ALAN MICHAEL, chemist electronics industry, executive; b. Albany, N.Y., June 1, 1947; s. Alfred Thomas Poskanzer and Beatrice (Sacherson) Martin; m. Carol Ann Huska, Aug. 24, 1968 (div. Oct. 1982); children: Alison Michele, Jessica Leigh; m. Linda Dianne May, Apr. 13, 1988. BS in Chemistry, Clarkson Coll. Tech., 1969, MS in Chemistry, 1971, PhD in Chemistry, 1974. Sr. research chemist Shipley Co., Inc., Newton, Mass., 1974-76; tech. dir. Morton/Thiokol Corp., Tustin, Calif., 1976-84; regional sales mgr. Enthone, Inc., Long Beach, Calif., 1984-86; cons. ChemProTech Enterprises, Dana Point, Calif., 1985—; pres. LinMar Tech., Inc., Dana Point, 1986—. Contbr. articles to profl. jours. Served to capt. USAR, 1970-83. Mem. Am. Chem. Soc., Am. Electroplaters Soc., Calif. Circuits Assn. (program chmn. 1986—, newsletter editor 1986—). Republican. Office: care ChemProTech 34184-B Coast Hwy 176 Dana Point CA 92629

POSNER, BARRY Z., management educator; b. Hollywood, Calif., Mar. 11, 1949; s. Henry and Delores Ann (Ginsberg) P.; m. Jacqueline Ann Schmidt, July 23, 1972; 1 child, Amanda Delores. BA, U. Calif., Santa Barbara, 1970; MA, Ohio State U., 1972; PhD, U. Mass., 1976. Prof. Santa Clara (Calif.) Univ., 1976—, dir. grad. edn., 1987—; dir. Share Data, Inc., Mt. View, Calif., 1983—; mng. dir. Kouzes Posner Internat., Inc., Santa Clara, 1987—; chmn. MTP, Inc., Sepulveda, Calif., 1987—. Author: (with others) The Leadership Challenge, 1987, (Book of the Year, Am. Council of Health Care Execs., 1989), Effective Project Planning and Management, 1988; contbr. articles to publs. Mem. Acad. Mgmt., Am. Psychological Assn., Orgn. Behavior Teaching Soc. (dir. 1982-86), Sigma Phi Epsilon (dir. 1972-82). Democrat. Jewish. Office: Leavey Sch Bus Adminstrn Santa Clara University Santa Clara CA 95053

POSNER, EDWARD CHARLES, communications engineer, educator; b. N.Y.C., Aug. 10, 1933; s. Gustave and Kate (Cohen) P.; m. Sylvia Kouzel, Apr. 26, 1956; children: Joyce K., Steven K. BA, U. Chgo., 1952, MS, 1953, PhD, 1957. Mem. tech. staff advanced studies Bell Labs., N.Y.C., 1956-57; research instr. math. U. Wis.-Madison, 1957-60; asst. prof. math. Harvey Mudd Coll., Claremont, Calif., 1960-61; with Jet Propulsion Labs., Pasadena, Calif., 1961—; researcher, mgr. Calif. Inst. Tech. Jet Propulsion Lab., Pasadena, 1961-78, mgr. telecommunications planning, 1978-83, chief technologist telecommunications and data acquistion, 1983-88; vis. prof. elec. engring. Calif. Inst. Tech., 1978—; cons. seismic signal processing, 1980—; mem. adv. bd. in communications Inst. Def. Analyses, Princeton, N.J., 1983-86; bd. dirs. Precision Vidwo Technologies Corp. Author: (with others) Introduction to Communications Science and Systems, 1980; editor: (with others) Studies in Combinatorics, 1970; translation editor: Road Traffic Control, 1977; patentee in field. Precinct chmn. Altadena Dem. Party, 1964; bd. dirs. Caltech Y, 1978-81. Fellow IEEE (gov. info. theory group); mem. Soc. Indsl. and Applied Math. (chmn. So. Calif. sect. 1967-68, 72-73), AAAS, Am. Math. Soc., Math. Assn. Am. Soc. Exploration Geophysicists, Skeptics, AIAA, Toastmasters (area gov. 1967-68). Sigma Xi, Phi Beta Kappa. Office: Jet Propulsion Lab 303-400 Telecommunication & Data Acquisition 4800 Oak Grove Dr Pasadena CA 91109

POSNER, LINDA ROSANNE, charity volunteer, educator; b. Rockford, Ill., Sept. 24, 1940; d. Lawrence George and Genevieve Annette (Reecher) Turnquist; m. Christian John Posner, Oct. 14, 1972; children: Katrina E., Christian L. BA, Rockford Coll., 1962; MEd, U. Md., 1970. Elem. sch. tchr. Elmhurst and Villa Park, Ill., 1962, 68; spl. edn. tchr. Christ Ch. Child Ctr., Bethesda, Md., 1970-72. Chmn. Heart Ball, 1988—, Golden Thimble IX, Hosp. of Good Samaritan, L.A., 1986-87, Heart of Gold recognition dinner; chmn. Am. Heart Assn. Greater L.A., 1983, now bd. dirs.; pres. St. Vincent Med. Ctr. Auxiliary, L.A., 1983-84; trustee St. Alban's Episc. Ch., L.A., 1985-87. Mem. U. So. Calif. Med. Faculty Wives (pres. 1986-87). Home: 1010 Harvard Ave Claremont CA 91711

POST, ALAN, economist, artist; b. Alhambra, Calif., Sept. 17, 1914; s. Edwin R. and Edna (Stickney) P.; m. Helen E. Wills, Nov. 21, 1940; 1 child, David Wills. AB, Occidental Coll., 1938; student Chouinard Inst. Art, 1938; MA, Princeton, 1940; LLD, Golden Gate U., 1972, Occidental Coll., 1974, Claremont Grad. Sch., 1978. In banking bus., 1933-36; instr. econs. Occidental Coll., 1940-42; asst. prof. Am. U., 1943; economist Dept. State, 1944-45; rsch. dir. Utah Found., 1945-46; chief economist, adminstrv. analyst State of Calif., 1946-50, state legis. analyst, 1950-77; cons. to commn. studying higher edn. Wells Commn., N.Y.; cons. Milton Eisenhower Com. Higher Edn. and State, 1964; mem. Nat. Com. Support of Public Schs., 1967; mem. nat. adv. panel Nat. Center Higher Edn. Mgmt. Systems, 1971-72; chmn. Calif. Gov.'s Commn. on Govt. Reform, 1978—; mem. faculty U. So. Calif. Grad. Sch. Public Adminstrn., 1978—; Regents' prof. U. Calif., Davis, 1983, vis. prof., 1984; spl. cons. Touche Ross and Co., 1977-87; cons., interim exec. dir. Calif. Commn. for Rev. of Master Plan for Higher Edn., 1985, vis. prof. U. Calif., Davis, 1984-85.; mem. adv. bd. Calif. Tomorrow nat. shows and one-man shows; dir. Crocker Art Gallery Assn., pres., 1966-67. Trustee. U. Calif. Art Mus., 1986—, mem. adv. com. on future ops. Coun. State Govts., 1965; bd. mgrs., pres. YMCA; bd. dirs. Sacramento Civic Ballet Assn.; trustee Calif. Coll. Arts and Crafts, 1982-86; chmn. Calif. State Task Force on Water Future, 1981-82, Sacramento Regional Found.; bd. dirs. Calif. Mus. Assn., 1983—, pres., 1976-77, Policy Analysis for Calif. Edn., 1985—, Senate Adv. Commn. on Control of Cost of State Govt., 1986—. With USNR, 1943-44. Mem. Nat. Acad. Public Adminstrn., Phi Beta Kappa, Kappa Sigma. Home: 1900 Rockwood Dr Sacramento CA 95864

POSTELLO, DOROTHY MARIE, personnel executive; b. Tyler, Minn., Jan. 1, 1941; d. Robert Ferdinand and Lena Christine (Schroeder) Westphal; m. Carl Joseph Postello, Sept. 22, 1963 (dec. Dec. 1984); stepchildren; Theresa, Deborah, David. Student, S.D. State U., 1959-60; bus. cert., Nettleton Bus. Coll., Sioux Falls, S.D., 1962; BS, Coll. of Notre Dame, Belmont, Calif., 1982, MBA, 1984. Lic. real estate agt., Calif. Receptionist Drs. Smith and Church, Sioux Falls, 1962-63; personal sec. Nev. Warehouse, Sparks, 1963-64; clk. Boy Scouts Am., Reno, 1964-67; confidential sec. H.D. Lee Co., South San Francisco, Calif., 1967-71; administrv. facilitator Internat. Paper Co., San Mateo, Calif., 1971-85; sales and svc. mgr. Unisource Corp., Dublin, Calif., 1985-86; with customer svc. dept. San Mateo Dist. Atty.'s Office, 1986-87; clerical supr. Family Ct. Svcs., Redwood City, Calif., 1987-88; personnel supr. Belmont Dept. Social Svcs., 1988—; owner, mgr. Dorothy's Wordprocessing, Foster City, Calif., 1987—; orgnl. cons. San Mateo County, Redwood City, 1987—, oral bd. interviewer, 1988—, personnel advisor, Belmont, 1988—. Vol. San Mateo Rep. Com., 1978-80; active young people's dept. Luth. Ch., Reno, 1964. Mem. Women in Mgmt., Delta Epsilon Sigma. Home: 1497 Marlin Ave Foster City CA 94404 Office: Dept Social Svcs 400 Harbor Blvd Belmont CA 94002

POSTER, CAROL, electronics executive, writer; b. N.Y.C., Aug. 5, 1956; d. William Shakespeare and Constance (Hammett) P.; m. David Chris Allen, July 1987. BA summa cum laude, Hollins Coll., 1977; postgrad., Ind.U., 1978-79, U. So. Miss., 1979, Athens, Greece, 1973-74. Founder, dir. Necessary Repertory, Roanoke, Va., 1976-77; dir. Almost Street Theatre, Salt Lake City, Utah, 1985-86, Off Broadway theatres, N.Y.C., 1977-78; assoc. instr. Ind. U. Dept. of English, Bloomington, Ind., 1978-79; teaching asst. U. So. Miss, Hattiesburg, 1979-80; software writer Cen. Data Corp., Rockville, Md., 1980-81; assoc. programmer Sperry Corp., Salt Lake City, Utah, 1981-83, sci. programmmer, 1983-84; owner Amaryllis Software, 1984—; judge Ariz. Authors Assn. poetry contest, 1987; lectr. various colls., univs., workshops, confs.; freelance writer, 1977—. Exec. editor: The Sports Guide, 1988—; author: Selected Poems of Jacques Prevert, (trans.), 1987, Deceiving the Worms, 1984, Black Bird, 1979, and numerous other poems and articles. Mem. Computer Profls. for Social Responsibility, 1986—, Greenpeace, 1984—, Zero Population Growth (officer), 1982—. Recipient 2d prize Utah Original Writing Competition, 1986, Excellence award Cen. Data Corp., 1981. Mem. IEEE, Assn. for Computing Machinery, Poets and Writers, Associated Writing Programs, Utah Blue Chips. Office: Amaryllis Software 535 Parkview Dr Park City UT 84060

POSTHUMA, HELEN MARIE, service executive; b. Bisbee, Ariz., Jan. 4, 1920; d. Harold Chamberlain and Harriet Elizabeth (Jones) Stull; m. Ynte Meindert Posthuma, June 28, 1941; children: Stephen Chamberlain, John Robert. BA in Spanish cum laude, Pomona Coll., 1941; postgrad., U. So. Calif., 1942. Tchr. Fontana (Calif.) Jr. High Sch., 1943; with rsch. dept. Aerojet Engring Co., Azusa, Calif., 1945; fashion model Copacabana Hotel, Rio de Janeiro, 1945; counselor Plaza Travel, Burbank, Calif., 1983—; bd. dirs. Art Ctr. Coll. Design, Pasadena, Calif. Mem. Huntington Meml. Clinic Aux., Pasadena, Altadena Guild Huntington Hosp. Mem. Am. Contract Bridge League, Pi Lambda Theta. Republican. Presbyterian. Home: 610 S Orange Grove Ave Pasadena CA 91105 Office: Plaza Travel 4020 W Magnolia Burbank CA 91505

POSTLER, J(ANICE) LYNN, chemical engineer; b. Cin., Oct. 21, 1956; d. John W. and Marian R. (Codnnors) P. BA in Zoology, Miami U., Oxford, Ohio, 1978; BS in Chem. Engring., U. Wash., 1984. Process engr., prodn. mgr. ITT Rayonier, Hoquiam, Wash., 1984-86; prodn. supt. ITT Rayonier, 1986--. Mem. Am. Inst. Chem. Engrs., Wash. Profl. Engrs. Soc., Toastmasters (sec.-treas. Aberdeen, Wash. chpt. 1988), Mountaineers Club, Tau Beta Pi. Home: 704 7th Ave Aberdeen WA 98520 Office: ITT Rayonier PO Box 299 Hoquiam WA 98550

POSTMA, CONNIE JANE, land development company executive; b. Sheldon, Iowa, Oct. 28, 1950; d. Clarence and Evelyn Dean (Wilts) P. BAE, Wayne State Coll., 1972. Cert. tchr., Calif. Tchr. Columbus, Nebr., 1972-75; loan processor Van Schaak Mortgage, Denver, 1975-76; loan officer Anaheim (Calif.) Savs., 1976-79; loan officer Home Fed. Savs., San Diego, 1979-80, major loan officer, corp. banking, 1980-84; sr. project mgr. Home Capital Devel. Group, San Diego, 1984—. Bd. dirs. United Cerebral Palsy Assn., San Diego; chmn. Celebrity Waiters Luncheon, 1984-88; prodn. asst. Telethon, 1984-88. Republican. Presbyterian. Office: Home Capital Devel Group 707 Broadway Ste 1017 San Diego CA 92101

POSTON, JIM BAECHLE, traffic engineer; b. Ft Leonard Wood, Mo., Sept. 9, 1956; s. Eddley Gray and Kiwako Poston; m. Patti, May 24, 1986. BSCE, U. idaho, Moscow, 1978. Registered profl. engr., Nev. City traffic engr. City of Kent, Wash., 1979-85, City of Las Vegas, Nev., 1988; system mgr. Las Vegas Area Computer Traffic System, 1985-89; city traffic engr. City of Reno, 1989—; lectr. U. Wash., Seattle, 1983-85. Recipient Cert. of Appreciation, Lions Club, 1985, Nat. U., 1986, Cert. of Recognition, Clark County Sch. Dist., 1988; State of Idaho scholar, 1974. Mem. inst. Transp. Engrs., Am. Pub. Works Assn., Mensa, U.S. Volleyball Assn. Libertarian. Home: PO Box 41092 Reno NV 89505 Office: Las Vegas Area Computer Traffic System 416 N 8th St Las Vegas NV 89101

POTASH, STEPHEN JON, international public relations specialist; b. Houston, Feb. 25, 1945; s. Melvin L. and Petrice (Edelstein) P.; m. Jeremy Warner, Oct. 19, 1969; 1 son, Aaron Warner. BA in Internat. Relations, Pomona Coll., 1967. Account exec. Charles von Loewenfeldt, Inc., San Francisco, 1969-74, v.p., 1974-80; founder, pres. Potash & Co., Pub. Rels., Oakland, Calif., 1980-87; cons. Am. Pres. Lines and Am. Pres. Cos., 1979-87; exec. dir. Calif. Coun. Internat. Trade, 1970-87; v.p. corp. communications Am. Pres. Cos., 1987—, Oakland, Calif. Bd. dirs. Calif. Council Internat. Trade, 1987—, Temple Sinai, Oakland, 1979-81. Mem. Pub. Rels. Soc. Am. (counselors acad.), Lakeview Club, Commonwealth Club of Calif. Office: Am Pres Cos 1800 Harrison St Oakland CA 94612

POTHIER, GERALD TELESPHORE, military officer; b. Gloucester, Mass., June 30, 1934; s. Gerald Peter and Mary Irene (Sears) P.; m. Shirley Elizabeth Luster, Feb. 15, 1953 (div. May 1978); children: Gerald William, Mark Stephen, Craig Michael; m. Theresa Estelle Karas, Feb. 17, 1984; children: Deborah Ann, Jason Fabian. Commd. 2d lt. USMC, 1966, advanced through grades to capt., 1969, ret., 1988; radio chief, communications chief, communications electronics officer USMC, various locations, U.S., Japan, Korea, Okinawa, Vietnam, Europe, 1951-84; communications-electronics chief Hdqrs Fleet Pacific Camp H.M. Smith USMC, Hawaii, 1984-88. Mem. Armed Forces Communications and Electronics Assn. (treas. 1981-82, v.p. 1982-83, pres. 1984, Exec. of Month award 1987), Marine Corps Mustang Assn., Ret. Officers Assn. Roman Catholic. Home: 1301 Waterside Blvd Monks Corner SC 29461

POTOCKI, JOSEPH EDMUND, marketing company executive; b. Jersey City, Jan. 31, 1936; s. Joseph and Estelle (Bielski) P.; m. Margaret Mary Shine, May 21, 1960; children: Joseph, Meg, David. BS, Seton Hall U., 1957. Asst. regional sales mgr. Gen. Mills Inc., Valley Stream, N.Y., 1960-67; group mgr. merchandising Warner Lambert Co., Morris Plains, N.J., 1967-84; dir. merchandising svcs. Beatrice Hunt/Wesson, Fullerton, Calif., 1974-83; pres., chief exec. officer Joseph Potocki & Assocs., Irvine, Calif., 1983—; pres. Mktg. Fulfillment Svcs., Tustin, Calif., 1985-87; bd. dirs. Schmidt Cannon, L.A.; chief exec. officer Clarke Hooper U.S.A., Irvine, 1987—; bd. dir. Clarke Hooper PLC, London; sec. Nat. Premium Sales Exec., Union, N.J., 1982-87. 1st lt. U.S. Army, 1957-59. Recipient Mktg. Motivator award L.A. Mktg. Exhbn., 1981, Mktg. Gold medal Am. Mktg. Assn. 1957. Mem. Promotion Mktg. Assn. (chmn. bd. dirs. 1977-79, v.p. West sect. 1980-87, Reggie award 1984, 85, 87), Promotion Mktg. Assn. Am. (bd. dir. exec. com. 1978-87, Chmn.'s Bowl 1979, Named to Chmn.'s Circle 1986), Nat. Premium Sales Execs. (dir. exec. com. 1980-87, Pres. award 1985). Republican. Roman Catholic. Home: 26952 Pueblo Nuevo Mission Viejo CA 92691 Office: Joseph Potocki & Assocs 30 Corporate Park Irvine CA 92714

POTTER, BEVERLY ANN, management psychologist, consultant, publisher; b. Summit, N.J., Mar. 3, 1944; d. Campbell McLeod and Alice Ceres (Modersohn) P. BA in Psychology, San Frascico State U., 1965, MS in Rehab. Coun., 1968; PhD in Counseling Psychology, Stanford U., 1974. Pres. Ronin Publ. Inc., Berkeley, Calif., 1984—, Profl. Workshops, Berkeley, Calif., 1976—, Books-By-Phone, Berkeley, Calif., 1984—. Author: Turning Around: Keys to Motivation and Produtivity, 1980; Beating Job Burnout, 1980; The Way of Ronin, 1984; Preventing Job Burnout: A Workbook, 1987. Activist City Task Force, Beverly, 1985-89. Ford Found. fellow, 1973. Mem. Nat. Speakers Assn., No. Calif. Book Publ. Assn. Office: Profl Workshops PO Box 1035 Berkeley CA 94701

POTTER, CHARLES ARTHUR, JR., trust company executive; b. St. Charles, Ill., July 25, 1925; s. Charles Arthur and Althea Mae (Whitney) P.; m. Joan Patricia Johnson, June 12, 1948; 1 child, Charles Arthur. Student, Western Mich. Coll., 1943, Officers Candidate Sch., U.S. Marine Corps, Quantico, Va., 1945; B.S., U. Ill., 1948, J.D., 1949; postgrad., Northwestern U., 1956. Bar: Ill. 1949. Mem. firm Gately & Burns, Chgo., 1949-50; spl. agt. FBI, Washington, Boston, N.Y.C. and Chgo., 1951-54; asst. trust officer Elmhurst Nat. Bank, Ill., 1955-59, United Calif. Bank, Los Angeles, 1959-61; v.p. trust officer First Am. Title and Trust Co., Santa Ana, Calif., 1961-68, also dir.; pres. First Am. Trust Co., Santa Ana, Calif., 1968—; treas., bd. dirs. Orange County Estate Planning Coun., 1966-69, Mansfield Ctr. Pacific Affairs, Helena, Mont., 1984-87; chmn. Nat. Def. U. Found., Washington, 1985-88; bd. dirs. Eldorado Bank, Tustin, Calif., First Am. Title Co. of Nev. Bd. dirs. Orange County Sports Celebrities, 1971-80, Providence Speech and Hearing Ctr., Orange County chpt. Multiple Sclerosis Soc., 1978—, Orange County area AMC Cancer Research Ctr., 1985—, Children's Hosp. Orange County Found., 1980—; mem. adv. bd. Salvation Army, Santa Ana, 1980—; trustee Calif. Med. Coll., U. Calif., Irvine, 1985—. Served with USMC, 1943-45. Recipient County of Los Angeles Cert. Commendation for pub. service, 1975. Mem. Soc. Former Spl. Agts. FBI (Western regional v.p. 1976-77), Calif. Bankers Assn. (chmn. trust div. 1982-83, dir. 1982-83), So. Calif. Trust Officers Assn. (pres. 1973-74), ABA, Ill. Bar Assn., Orange County Bar Assn., Def. Orientation Conf. Assn. (pres. 1982-84, dir., 1975—, chmn. 1985-86), Big Canyon Country Club (Newport Beach, Calif.), Indian Wells Country Club, Center Club (Costa Mesa, Calif.), PGA West Club (La Quinta, Calif.), Phi Delta Phi, Alpha Delta Phi. Home: 47 Pinewood St Irvine CA 92714 Office: 421 N Main St Santa Ana CA 92701

POTTER, CLAUDE EDWIN, accountant; b. York, Pa., Dec. 22, 1946; s. Edwin Wallace and Sara Jane (Baum) P.; m. Barbara Ann Johnson, May 10, 1969; children: Matthew Edwin, Deborah Lynne, Kimberly Ann. AA, Mt. San Antonio Coll., 1967; BS in Acctg., Calif. Poly. U., 1972; MBA, Long Beach State U., 1982. CPA, Calif. Staff acct. Deloitte Haskins & Sells, L.A., 1972-74, Erickson & Kaestner CPAs, Santa Ana, Calif., 1974-75; internal auditor Health Industries, Newport Beach, Calif, 1975-79; asst. controller Spancrete Calif., Irwindale, Calif., 1979-82; acctg. mgr. Internat. Customs Svcs., Long Beach, Calif., 1982-86; corp. controller United Concrete Cos., Irwindale, Calif., 1987--. Served with armed forces, 1967-69, Vietnam. Mem. Am. Inst. CPA's, Calif. Soc. CPA's. Republican. Home: 4572 Minuet Dr Huntington Beach CA 92649 Office: United Concrete Cos 13131 Los Angeles St Irwindale CA 91706

POTTER, DAVID ERIC, computer executive; b. San Jose, Calif., Sept. 12, 1949; s. Charles Devere and Ada (Ranelli) P.; m. Lauren Fins, Sept. 22, 1974; 1 child, Tracy Brianne. BA, U. Calif., 1971, MA, 1974, postgrad., 1978. Tng. instr. Intel Corp., Santa Clara, Calif., 1978-79; sales devel. mgr. Intel Corp., Santa Clara, 1979-80; pres., chief exec. officer Concurrent Sciences, Inc., Moscow, Idaho, 1980—. Contbr. articles to profl. jours. Mem. Assn. Computing Machinery, Internat. RMX User's Group (v.p. 1985-87). Home: 1191 Tolo Trail Moscow ID 83843 Office: Concurrent Scis Inc 105 S Washington Moscow ID 83843

POTTER, JEFFREY GALLANT, information systems officer; b. Monroe, Wis., Nov. 18, 1953; s. Ralph Edward and Athena (Stasnopolis) P.; m. Cathy Sue Stuessel, Aug. 3, 1974; children: Jason William, Jamie Len, Christine Marie. AS, Mt. San Antonio Coll., 1978; BS, Columbia Pacific U., 1988. Programmer Honeywell, West Covina, Calif., 1979-81; system analyst Bell and Howell, Pasadena, Calif., 1981-83, Structured Software & Systems, Laguna Hills, Calif., 1983-87; info. systems analyst Security Pacific, Glendale, Calif., 1987—. Author: (software) Telemetry Data Base, 1983; contbr. articles to profl. jours. Mgr. Diamond Bar Little League, 1988; coleader Girl Scouts Am. Republican. Greek Orthodox. Home: 512 Deep Hill Rd Diamond Bar CA 91765

POTTER, J(EFFREY) STEWART, property manager; b. Ft. Worth, July 8, 1943; s. Gerald Robert Potter and Marion June (Mustain) Tombler; m. Dianne Eileen Roberb, Dec. 31, 1970 (div. Aug. 1983); 1 child, Christopher Stewart. AA, San Diego Mesa Coll., 1967. Cert. apartment mgr., apartment property supr. Sales mgr. Sta. KJLM, La Jolla, Calif., 1964-67; mgr. inflight catering Host Internat., San Diego, 1967-69; lead aircraft refueler Lockheed Co., San Diego, 1969-70; mgr. property Internat. Devel. and Fin Corp., La Jolla, 1970-72; mgr. bus. property BWY Constn. Co., San Diego, 1972-73; mgr. residents Coldwell Banker, San Diego, 1973-74; mgr. Grove Investments, Carlsbad, Calif., 1974-76, Villa Granada, Villa Seville Properties Ltd., Don Cohn, Chula Vista, Calif., 1976-83; gen. mgr. AFL-CIO Bldg. Trades Corp., National City, Calif., 2983—. Fellow Nat. City C. of C., Toastmasters, Founding Families San Diego Hist. Soc., La Jolla Monday Night Club (treas. 1984-89). Roman Catholic. Home: 3245 Camino Ameca La Jolla CA 92037 Office: AFL-CIO Bldg Trades Corp 2323 D Ave National City CA 92050

POTTER, ROBERT L. ANDREW (BOB POTTER), solicitor, consultant; b. San Jose, Calif., May 24, 1932; s. Andrew Willis and May Verser P.; m. Peggy Ann (Joseph), July 29, 1978; children: Kevin David, Brian Lawrence, Kathryn May-Marie, Kirk Robert. AA in Bus. Adminstrn., Hartnell Coll., 1958; BS in Organizational Behavior, U. San Francisco, 1961. Asst. contr. Honolulu Oil Corp., San Francisco, 1959-60; mgmt. cons. Allstate Ins., Merced, Calif., 1960—; pres. R. Potter Consulting, Merced; cons. Mercy Hosp., Merced. Campaign mgr., cons. Am. Cancer Soc., Merced, Mariposa County; campaign mgr. Calif. State Assembly Seat, Merced, Stanislaus County, Ambassador Good Will Merced C. of C. Capt. USMC, 1950-55, Korea. Decorated Bronze Star, Purple Heart. Mem. Yosemite Corvett Club (treas.), Elks. Republican. Roman Catholic. Home: 2862 St Thomas Ct Merced CA 95348

POTTER, TELMA FARRUGIA, teacher, writer; b. Republic of Panama, Mar. 16, 1924; d. Luis Silverio and Teresa Maria (Ayala) Farrugia; m. Jack Warren Potter, Feb. 20, 1960. BA in Sociology, Linfield Coll., McMinnville, Oreg., 1950; MA in Clin. Psychology, McMurray Coll., Jacksonville, Ill., 1951. Tchr. Spastic Children's Found, Los Angeles, summers 1948-49; dir. pre-sch. Calif. Epileptic Soc., Los Angeles, 1951-52; tchr. Tracy Putnam Found., Los Angeles, 1952-53; social svc. aide United Cerebral Palsy Assn., Los Angeles, 1953-66; coord. Phoenix Products Warehouse, Los Angeles, 1967-68; office clk. Bank of Am., Los Angeles, 1968-75; vol. Hacienda-La Puente Sch., Calif., 1977—; tutor, speaker for handicapped 1977—. Editor: Elementary Problems in Chess, 1968; author poetry in Panamanian newspapers, 1971. Home: 1538 Summer Lawn Way Hacienda Heights CA 91745

POTTER, TIMOTHY DEAN, electronics executive; b. Walla Walla, Wash., Dec. 12, 1957; s. James Dean and Charlotte Claudette (Sherlock) P.; m. Teresa J. Blanco, June 16, 1984; children: Valarie, Windee, Angela. BS in Mktg., Oreg. State U., 1980. Sales engr. Barber Colman Co., Rockford, Ill., 1981-84; svc. mgr. G.J. Yamas Inc., Broderick, Calif., 1984-86; v.p. G.J. Yamas Inc., Broderick, 1987-88, Las Vegas, 1989—; educator, control systems seminars, 1985-88. Coach, Elk Grove (Calif.) Softball Assn., 1985-87, Sacramento County Softball, 1985-88, Southgate Parks and Recreation, Sacramento, 1985. Mem. ASHRAE (bd. dirs. 1989—), Assn. Profl. Energy Mgrs. (mem. com. 1986-87, award 1987), Assn. Energy Engrs., Sheet Metal and Air Conditioning Contractors Assn. Republican. Roman Catholic. Home: 1402 Sierra Vista Boulder City NV 89005 Office: GJ Yamas Inc 6245 Harrison Dr Ste 14 Las Vegas NV 89120

POTTINGER, KEVIN EARL, military officer; b. Tucson, Nov. 15, 1954; s. George Earl Pottinger and Deborah Marie (Dunseath) Blaich; m. Anne Colt Josephs, Aug. 26, 1978; 1 child, Patrick Kevin. BS in Geography, Ariz. State U., 1976. Commd. 2nd lt. USAF, 1977, advanced through grades to maj., 1988; served as F-4 pilot 21st TFTS USAF, George AFB, Calif., 1979; 512th TFS USAF, Ramstein AFB, Ger., 1979-81; F-16 pilot 4th TFS USAF, Hill AFB, Utah, 1982-85; Luke AFB, Ariz., 1985-88; 422 Test and Evaluation Squadron Nellis AFB, Nev., 1988—. Named One of Outstanding Young Men of Am., Jaycees, 1984. Mem. Daedalians. Republican. Roman Catholic. Office: 422 TES Nellis AFB NV 89115

POTTS, JON SELBY, quality and technical consultant; b. Portland, Oreg., Nov. 21, 1933; s. Selby and Joan Wilhemina (McGregor) P.; m. Nathalie Sawyer Smith, Dec. 20, 1957 (div. Aug. 1976); children: Kenneth Selby, James Harold; m. Sharon Lee Van Leuven, Mar. 10, 1984. BS in Chemistry, Brigham Young U., 1961; MS in Chemistry, U. N.H., 1963. Chemist UpJohn Co., Carwin Chem. div., North Haven, Conn., 1963-65; research and devel. chemist various cos., 1966-69; in air quality control dept. State Dept. Environ. Quality, Portland, 1970-72; chemist Masti-Kure Products Co., Norwich, 1973-74; elect. technician, mgr., engr. Tektronix, Inc., Beaverton, Oreg., 1975-86; pres. Quality Systems Inc., Oregon City, Oreg., 1986—; mem. adj. faculty Oregon Inst. Tech., Portland Community Coll. Contbr. aticles to profl. jours. Active Boy Scouts Am., 1964-68. With USAF, 1954-58. NDEA fellow, U. N.H., 1961. Mem. Am. Soc. Quality Control (cert.), Soc. Reliability Engrs., Soc. Plastics Engrs., Soc. Mfg. Engrs. (sr.). Republican. Morman. Office: Quality Systems Inc 15770 S Priscilla Ln Oregon City OR 97045

POTTS, SIMON, record company executive; b. Newcastle-upon-Tyne, Tyne and Wear, Eng., Jan. 26, 1953; came to U.S., 1987; s. Alan and Doreen Helen (Etheridge) P. Diploma in art and design, Newcastle Art Coll., 1972. Sales rep. ABC Records, London, 1978-79; promotion mgr. Arista Records, London, 1979, div. dir., 1980-85; mng. dir. Elektra Records, London, 1985-86; sr. divisional v.p. Capitol Records, Los Angeles, 1987—. Anglican. Home: 8700 Hollywood Blvd Los Angeles CA 90069 Office: Capitol Records 1750 N Vine St Los Angeles CA 90028

POULIN, DAVID PETER, SR., retail executive; b. Augusta, Maine, Aug. 8, 1946; s. Lucien Joseph Sr. and Fay (Bolduc) P.; m. Peggy Sykes, May 15, 1970; children: David Jr., Michael, Mark, Jeffrey, Samantha, Gregory. AA, Hartnell Coll., 1971. Bookkeeper Simonds Packing and Rubber Co., Augusta, 1965-67; clk. Longs Drugs., Salinas, Calif., 1970-73; jr. dept. mgr. Longs Drugs., Carmel, Calif., 1974-76, sr. dept. mgr., 1977-79; asst. mgr. Longs Drugs., Salinas, 1980-81; store mgr. Longs Drugs., North Salinas, Calif., 1982—. Served wtih U.S. Army, 1967-69. Republican. Roman Catholic. Club: Salinas Valley Fly Fisherman (pres. 1984-85). Home: 626 St Augustine Dr Salinas CA 93905 Office: Longs Drugs 110 E Laurel Dr Salinas CA 93906

POULOS, CLARA JEAN, nutritionist; b. L.A., Jan. 1, 1941; d. James P. and Clara Georgie (Creighton) Hill; PhD in Biology, Fla. State Christian U., 1974; PhD in Nutrition, Donsbach U., 1979; D in Nutritional Medicine, John F. Kennedy U., 1986; Cert. in Diabetes Edn.; m. Themis Poulos, Jan. 31, 1960. Dir. rsch. Leapou Lab., Aptos, Calif., 1973-76, Monterey Bay Rsch. Inst., Santa Cruz, Calif., 1976—; nutrition specialist, Santa Cruz, 1975—; dir. nutritional svcs., health enhancement, lifestyle planning, Santa Cruz, 1983—; instr. Santa Cruz Extention U. Calif. and Stoddard Assocs. Seminars; cons. Biol-Med. Lab., Chgo., Nutra-Med Rsch. Corp., N.Y., Akorn-Miller Pharmacal, Chgo., Monterey Bay Aquaculture Farms, Threshhold Lab., Calif., Resurrection Lab., Calif. Recipient Najulander Internat. Rsch. award, 1971, Wainwright Found. award., 1979, various state and local awards. Fellow Internat. Coll. Applied Nutrition, Am. Nutritionist Assn., Internat. Acad. Nutritional Consultants; mem. Am. Diabetes Assn. (profl., pres. Santa Cruz chpt., editor newsletter The Daily Balance Santa Cruz chpt., sec. No. Calif. chpt.), AAAS, Internat. Platform Soc., Am. Heart Assn., Am. Public Health Assn., Calif. Acad. Sci., Internat. Fishery Assn. (health asct.), Am. Women's Bowling Assn., MUSE- Computer Users Group.Clubs: Toastmistress, Quota. Author: Alcoholism - Stress - Hypoglycemia, 1976; The Relationship of Stress to Alcoholism and Hypoglycemia, 1979; assoc. editor Internat. Jour. Bio-social Research, Health Promotion Features; contbr. articles to profl. jours. Office: 1595 Soquel Dr Suite 222 Santa Cruz CA 95065

POULOS, DARWIN ROBERT, chemist; b. L.A., Mar. 22, 1959; s. Robert Annis and Victoria Mary (Baba) P.; m. Donna Elizabeth Long, Mar. 21, 1987. AS in Chem., W. Valley Coll., 1980, AA in Math., 1981; BS in Chem. Engring., U. Calif., 1982; MS in Chem. Engring., San Jose State U., 1985. Registered engr. Calif.; cert. tchr. Calif. Tchr. asst. W. Valley Coll., Saratoga, Calif., 1977-80; asst. rsch. Dept. Chmn. U. Calif., Berkeley, 1982; chemist formulation IBM Amaden Rsch. Ctr., San Jose, 1983-85; chemist rsch. Lifescan Inc., Mountain View, Calif., 1986—. Grantee NSF, 1976. Mem. Am. Chem. Soc. Republican. Lutheran. Office: Lifescan Inc 2443 Wyandotte St Mountain View CA 94043

POULSEN, KEILA DAUN, medical technologist; b. Idaho, Feb. 23, 1948; d. Norman Perry and Bernice Carolina (Johnson) Bingham; m. Dennis Taylor Poulsen, Jan. 17, 1970; children: Britt Bing, Drew Dennis. BS in Microbiology, Brigham Young U., 1970. Lic. med. technologist. Lab. asst. Latter Day Saints Hosp., Idaho Falls, 1969-70, med. technologist, 1970-75, supr. hematology, 1975—; cons. hematology Brigham Young U., Provo, Utah, 1982—; lectr. and presenter in field. Author: Hematology Procedures Lab. Text, Varient RBC Handout, Leukemia Book, Coagulation Seminar Handout; contbr. articles to profl. jours. Active Spl. Olympics, March of Dimes, Cancer Drive. Named Outstanding Young Woman Am., 1985. Mem. Am. Soc. Clin. Pathologists (cert. med. technologist, hematologists, hematologist specialist, Nat. Cert. Agy. (clin. lab. specialist, hematology lab specialist), Idaho Soc. Med. Technologists (Med. Technologist Yr. 1988), Women's Softball Assn. Republican. Mormon. Home: 477 N 3600 E Rigby ID 83442 Office: Ea Idaho Regional Med Ctr 3100 Channing Way Idaho Falls ID 83404

POURNELLE, JERRY EUGENE, author; b. Shreveport, La., Aug. 7, 1933; s. P. Eugene and Ruth (Lewis) P.: M. Roberta Jane Isdell, July 17, 1959; children: Alexander, Francis Russell, Phillip Eugene, Richard Stefan. BS, U. Wash., 1954, MS, 1957, PhD, 1964. Instr. U. Wash., Seattle, 1956-57; research engr., aviation psychologist Boeing Co., Seattle, 1958-64; mgr. spl. studies Aerospace Corp., San Bernardino, Calif., 1964; prof., dir. research inst. Pepperdine U., Los Angeles, 1965-69; exec. asst. to mayor City Los Angeles, 1969; author, lectr., cons. Studio City, Calif., 1970—; cons. Directorate of Plans USAF, 1968; chief cons. Profl. Educators Los Angeles, 1970; cons. to chancellor Calif. State Colls., 1970—. Author: Human Temperature Tolerance in Astronautic Environments, 1959, Stability and National Security, 1968, (with Stefan Possony) The Stategy of Technology, 1970, Congress Debates Viet Nam, 1971, The Right to Read, 1971, Red Heroin, Red Dragon, 1971; (with Larry Niven) The Mote in God's Eye, 1974, (with Larry Niven) Inferno, 1976; West of Honor, 1976, The Mercenary, 1977, High Justice, 1977, (with Larry Niven) Lucifer's Hammer, 1977, Janissaries, 1979, King David's Spaceship, 1980, (with Larry Niven) Oath of Fealty, 1981, Prince of Mercenaries, 1989, (with Roland Green) Janissaries: Clan and Crown, 1982, (with Dean Ing) Mutual Assured Survival, 1984, (with Larry Niven) Footfall, 1985, Legacy of Heorot, 1987, (with Roland Green) Storms of Victory, 1987; editor: 2020 Vision; sci. editor, columnist Galaxy Sci. Fiction, 1975-78, Byte mag., 1978—; (with John F. Carr) Black Holes, 1978, Endless Frontier, 1979, Survival of Freedom, 1982, Endless Frontier Vol. II, 1982, There Will Be War, 1983, Men At War, 1984, Blood and Iron, 1984, Day of The Tyrant, 1985, Warrior, 1986, Imperial Stars, 1986, Guns of Darkness, 1987, Imperial Stars: Republic and Empire, Vol. II; InfoWorld, 1986—, WAR WORLD, 1988, THERE WILL BE WAR: Call to Battle, 1988, Imperial Stars: Clash of Empire Vol. III, 1989, Armageddon!, 1989, Armageddon!, 1989, Endless Frontier, Vol. III, 1989. Scoutmaster Boy Scouts Am., 1958; chmn. bd. dirs. Seattle Civic Playhouse Assn., 1960-63; asst. chmn. San Bernardino County Rep. Com., 1964; assoc. dir. Sam Yorty for Mayor Campaign, 1969; bd. dirs. Pepperdine Research Inst., 1966-69. Served with AUS, 1950-52; mem. Rep. Bd. Govs., 1962-63. Decorated Bronze medal; recipient Excellence award Am. Security Council, 1969, John W. Campbell award 1973. Fellow AAAS; mem. Inst. Strategic Studies, AIAA, Ops. Research Soc. Am., Univ. Prof. for Acad. Order (bd. dirs. 1971), Sci. Fiction Writers Am. (pres. 1973-74). Episcopalian. Home and Office: 3960 Laurel Canyon Ste 372 Studio City CA 91604

POVHE, THOMAS JEROME, school librarian, investment advisor; b. Grand Forks, N.D., Oct. 19, 1950; s. Frank Fred and Mollie Anne (Zgonc) P. BS in Edn., Bemidji (Minn.) State U., 1972; MEd in Library Sci., Ariz. State U., 1988. Educator St. Leo's Cath. Sch., Hibbing, Minn., 1973-77; realtor Ryan Real Estate, Glendale, Ariz., 1978-81; investment advisor Investwave, Glendale, Ariz., 1985-88; sch. library media specialist Unified Sch. Dist. 21, Coolidge, Ariz., 1987-89, dist. media coordinator, planner, 1989—; mem. Lit. Essential Skills Ariz. Bd. Edn., 1988—, Ariz. dept. edn. Library Guidelines Steering Com., 1988—, chmn. sub.-com.Devel. Info. Skills, 1989—. With USN, 1981-85. Mem. ALA (Young Adult Svcs. div.), Am. Assn. Sch. Librarians (Reference and Svcs. div.), Assn. Supervision Curriculum Devel. Democrat. Roman Catholic. Home: 4443 West Solano Dr N Glendale AZ 85301

POVLICK, THOMAS PAUL, electrical engineer; b. Washington, Pa., May 28, 1953; s. Peter Charles and Hene Grace (Homa) P. BSEE, U. Pitts., 1975; MSEE, Union Coll., 1982. Registered profl. engr. Field engr. Gen. Electric Co., Pitts., 1975-78; instr. Gen. Electric Co., Schenectady, N.Y., 1978-80, research engr., 1980-87; sr. specialist Northrop Corp., Pico Rivera, Calif., 1987—. Patentee in field. Mem. IEEE, Assn. Computing Machinery. Avocations: weight lifting, biking, swimming, photography, scuba. Office: Northrop Corp M127/3M 8900 E Washington Blvd Pico Rivera CA 90660

POWELL, AMARYLLIS LILLES, music educator; b. Portland, Oreg., Nov. 12, 1931; d. Thomas Peter and Mary Jean (Manos) Lilles; m. George Chris Drougas, Jan. 1, 1956; m. 2d, Richard Lee Powell, June 7, 1962; children: Leslie, Christian, Donald, David, Mary. BME, Willamette U., 1953, MME, 1966. Mem. Honolulu Symphony, 1954-55; tchr. vocal/band Iolani Episc. Sch. for Boys, Honolulu, 1954-55; tchr. vocal music Beaverton (Oreg.) Schs., 1962-63, 63-64; tchr. elem./jr. high band, dist. music coord. Tigard (Oreg.) Schs., 1976-88, dist. dir. fine arts, 1989—; mem. talented and gifted com., 1977—; mem. music textbook com. State Oreg. Dept. Edn., 1980—; trustee Sunriver Music Festival, 1989—; com. mem. Nat. Invention Conv. Conf., 1989. Mem. alumni bd. Willamette U.; mem. troop com. Century Club, Boy Scouts Am.; mem. ednl. com. Oreg. Symphony Orch.; active Oreg. Episc. Schs. Rodney Soc., also alumni bd.; active Portland Rose Festival, Interlochen Nat. Music Camp. Mem. Music Educator's Nat. Conf., Oreg. Music Educators Assn. (bd. dirs.), NEA, Assn. Supervision and Curriculum Devel., Assn. Sch. Suprs., N.W. Women in Ednl. Adminstrn., Oreg. Advocates for the Arts, Oreg. Assn. Sch. Suprs. (chmn. art and music 1986-89, pres. 1989—), Metro Area Music Educators (co-founder, 1986), Oreg. Edn.

Assn. (pres. 1989—), Conf. Oreg. Sch. Adminstrs., Oreg. Alliance for the Arts (edn. bd.), Mid-Willamette Valley Music Suprs. (chmn.), 13th Coast Guard Dist. Retiree Coun., West HIlls Raquet Club, Pi Beta Phi, Mu Phi Epsilon. Republican. Episcopalian. Home: 7455 SW Newton Pl Portland OR 97225 Office: Twality Jr High Sch 14650 SW 97th St Tigard OR 97223

POWELL, EARL ALEXANDER, III, art museum director; b. Spartanburg, S.C., Oct. 24, 1943; s. Earl Alexander and Elizabeth (Duckworth) P.; m. Nancy Landry Powell, July 17, 1971; children—Cortney, Channing, Sumner. AB with honors, William Coll., 1966; AM, Harvard U., 1970, PhD, 1974. Teaching fellow in fine arts Harvard U., 1970-74; curator, Michener Collection U. Tex., Austin, 1974-76, asst. prof. art history, 1974-76; mus. curator, sr. staff asst. to asst. dir. and chief curator Nat. Gallery Art, Washington, 1976-78, exec. curator, 1979-80; dir. Los Angeles County Mus. Art, 1980—; cons. Nat. Endowment for the Arts; mem. So. Calif. Adv. Council Archives of Am. Art, 1980—; career advisor Harvard U. Author: American Art at Harvard, 1973, Selections from the James Michener Collection, 1975, Abstract Expressionists and Imagists: A Retrospective View, 1976, Milton Avery, 1976. Trustee Pitzer Coll. Served with U.S. Navy, 1966-69, comdr. Res., 1976-80. Harvard U. traveling fellow, 1973-74; recipient King Olav medal, 1979; decorated chevalier Arts and Letters. Mem. Walpole Soc., Am. Assn. Museums, Am. Assn. Mus. Dirs., Am. Fedn. Arts (trustee). Office: L A County Mus Art 5905 Wilshire Blvd Los Angeles CA 90036

POWELL, HELEN DOWELL, medical manufacturing company executive; b. Council Grove, Kans., Apr. 19, 1932; d. Morris Seth and Alice Elizabeth (Holm) Dowell; m. C. Richard Powell, Aug. 28, 1955; children: John Dowell, Ann Elizabeth, Richard Cortland. AA, Cottey Coll., Nevada, Mo., 1952; student, Sorbonne, U. Paris, 1952-53; BA in French, U. Kans., 1954. Dir. admissions, pub. relations Cottey Coll., Nevada, Mo., 1954-55; editor-in-chief Sertoman mag. Sertoma Internat., Kansas City, Mo., 1955-58; adminstr. internat. dept. Codman & Shurtleff, Inc., Evergreen, Colo., 1984—. Sect. editor: Ameica's Best, 1983. Trustee Cottey Coll., Nevada, Mo., 1969-77, Kent Dever Country Day Sch., Englewood, Colo., 1983-84; bd. dirs. Forest Heights Lodge, Evergreen, 1966-70; pres. Evergreen Scholarship Assn., 1973-78. Mem. Cottey Coll. Alumnae Assn. (pres. 1961-62), Pi Beta Phi, Phi Theta Kappa, Pi Delta Phi. Republican. Presbyterian. Office: Codman & Shurtleff Inc 6851 Highway 73 Evergreen CO 80439

POWELL, JAMES LAWRENCE, college president; b. Berea, Ky., July 17, 1936; s. Robert Lain and Lizena (Davis) P.; m. Joan Hartmann; children: Marla, Dirk, Joanna. AB, Berea Coll., 1958; PhD, MIT, 1962; DSc (hon.), Oberlin Coll., 1983; LHD (hon.), Tohoku Gakuin U., 1986. Mem. faculty Oberlin Coll., Ohio, 1962-83, also prof. geology, asso. dean, 1973-75, v.p., provost, 1976-83; pres. Franklin and Marshall Coll., Lancaster, Pa., 1983-88, Reed Coll., Portland, Oreg., 1988—; mem. Nat. Sci. Bd., 1986—. Author: Strontium Isotope Geology, 1972. Fellow Geol. Soc. Am. Home: 6230 SE 36th Ave Portland OR 97202 Office: Reed Coll Office of Pres Portland OR 97202

POWELL, JULIA GERTRUDE, volunteer; b. Fenton, Mich., Jan. 25, 1907; d. Thomas James and Leila May (Bishop) Selman; m. Ronald Douglas Powell, June 25, 1924 (div. May 4, 1961); 1 child, Delva Dorothea (dec.). BA in Edn., Colo. Coll., 1949, MA in Edn., 1949; M in Adminstrn., UCLA, 1950; postgrad., Chapman Coll. Tchr. kindergarten Garden Grove (Calif.) Elem. Sch., Garden Grove Unified Sch. Dist., 1950-71. Pres. Garden Grove Tchrs. Assn., Calif., 1961, Ebell of Laguna Hills, Leisure World, 1983, Beethoven chpt. Guild, Orange County, 1984; Worthy Matron Hermosa chpt. Eastern Star, Santa Ana, Calif., 1972; Worthy High Priestess White Shrine of Jerusalem, 1976; Queen Merret Temple Daus. of Nile, Anaheim, Calif., 1988—. Mem. Calif. Retired tchrs. Assn., NEA-Am. Assn. Retired Persons, Am. Assn. Univ. Women. Republican. Presbyterian.

POWELL, LANE ALAN, editor; b. Alamogordo, N.Mex., Mar. 8, 1955; s. Cecil Lane Holmes and Janet Marie (LeRoux) Powell; m. Mari Catherine Priemesberger, July 15, 1989. BS in Journalism, U. Fla., 1984. Info. specialist Engring. Coll. U. Fla., Gainesville, 1983-85; editor Windsor Publs., L.A., 1985-89; coord. publs. East Bay Regional Park Dist., Oakland, Calif., 1989—. Editor: Jacksonville and Florida's First Coast, 1989; contbr. articles to profl. jours. Named an Outstanding Hard Cover Pub. of Yr. Am. Chambers of Commerce Execs., 1989. Home: 3810 Maybelle Ave #7 Oakland CA 94619 also: 1146 McKinley Ave #8 Oakland CA 94619 Office: East Bay Regional Park Dist 11500 Skyline Blvd Oakland CA 94619

POWELL, LORRAINE, food company executive; b. Woodbury, N.J., Sept. 27, 1956; d. John and Betty Eleanor (Grafton) P. BS in Food Sci, Rutgers U., 1983. Quality control lab. coord. Durling Farms, Whitehouse, N.J., 1983-84; quality control lab. technician Haagen-Dazs, Woodbridge, N.J., 1984-85; plant chemist DeSoto, Inc., Union City, Calif., 1985-87; product devel. scientist Shaklee Corp., Hayward, Calif., 1987—. Mem. Inst. of Food Technologists. Home: 219 Entrada Plaza Union City CA 94587 Office: Shaklee Corp 1992 Alpine Way Hayward CA 94545

POWELL, PEGGY JEAN, public relations executive; b. La Grande, Oreg., June 29, 1933; d. Kenneth Gladstone and Clara Gertrude (Hercher) LaViolette; m. Donald Allan Powell, Sept. 14, 1957; children: Anthony Forrest, Alison Carol. BA, U. Calif., Berkeley, 1956; postgrad, Wayne State U., 1967. Writer Mademoiselle Mag., N.Y.C., 1955-56; reporter Berkeley Daily Gazette, 1956-57, Vancouver (B.C., Can.) Sun, 1957-59; freelance writer Calif., 1960-75; pvt. practice pub. rels. cons. Irvine, 1975-85; ptnr. Investor Communication Systems, Irvine, 1985-88; exec. editor The Investment Reporter, 1989—; bd. dirs. Shareholder Communication Systems. Contbr. numerous articles to profl. and entertainment jours. Mem., docent, patron Newport Harbor Art Mus., Newport Beach, Calif., 1972-84; bd. dirs. Campus View Homeowners Assn., Irvine, 1976. Recipient Golden Orange award Orange County (Calif.) Advt. Fedn., 1981. Mem. Pub. Rels. Soc. Am., Orange County Chpt. Pub. Rels. Soc. Am. (3 Excellence awards 1984, 2 Excellence awards 1985), Publicity Club Am., U. Calif. Berkeley Alumni Assn., Prytanean Alumni Assn., Alpha Gamma Delta. Democrat. Unitarian. Office: Shareholder Communication Systems 1 Corporate Park Irvine CA 92714

POWELL, TED FERRELL, micrographics specialist; b. Rexburg, Idaho, Feb. 2, 1935; s. Edward Lewis and Thelma Mae (Arnold) P.; m. Nedra Scoresby, Jan. 15, 1954; children: Janeal, Julia, Greg F., Megan, Kara, N. Elizabeth. BS in Acctg., U. Utah, 1962; MBA, U. Phoenix, 1987. Supr. geneal. library Ch. Jesus Christ Latter-day Saints, Salt Lake City, 1967-70, supr. granite mountain records vault, 1970-71, dir. microfilming field ops., 1971-85, ops. analyst geneal. dept., 1985—; chmn. East Canyon Resort, Inc., 1988—; mem. com. preservation hist. records Nat. Research Council, Washington, 1984—. Co-author: A Guide to Micrographics, 1984; also articles. Mem. Assn. Info. and Image Mgmt. (chpt. pres. 1976-77, bd. dirs. 1977-80, Disting. award 1978), Inst. Internal Auditors (cert.), Internat. Council Archives (com. reprography 1976—). Republican. Home: 3144 S 160 W Bountiful UT 84010 Office: Ch Jesus Christ Latter-day Saints 50 East North Temple Salt Lake City UT 84150

POWELL, THOMAS WERNER, construction engineer; b. Union City, Tenn., Sept. 30, 1961; s. Robert Coffee and Irmentraud (Sorge) P.; m. Jill Jolene Cowden, Aug. 22, 1981 (div. June 1983); 1 child, Taryn Jaclyn. Student, U. Tenn., 1979-81. Constrn. supr. J.R. Hatmaker Constrn. Co., Knoxville, Tenn., 1982-83; constrn. engr. GTE Sprint-US Sprint, Burlingame, Calif., 1983-89, GTE Mobilnet, Hayward, Calif., 1989—. Vol. Greenpeace, San Francisco, 1987. Mem. Am. Mensa Ltd., Nat. Audubon Soc. Baptist. Office: GTE Mobilnet 3857 Breadwater Ave Hayward CA 94545

POWER, DENNIS MICHAEL, museum director; b. Pasadena, Calif., Feb. 18, 1941; s. John Dennis Power and Ruth Augusta (Mott) Zwicky; m. Kristine Moneva Fisher, Feb. 14, 1965 (div. Aug. 1984); children: Michael Lawrence, Matthew David; m. Leslie Gabrielle Baldwin, July 6, 1985; 1 stepchild, Katherine G. Petrosky. B.A., Occidental Coll., 1962, M.A., 1964; Ph.D. (NSF fellow), U. Kans., 1967. Asst. curator ornithology Royal Ont. Mus.; also asst. prof. zoology U. Toronto, 1967-71; asso. curator Royal Ont. Mus., Toronto, 1971-72; dir. Santa Barbara (Calif.) Mus. Natural History, 1972—; biol. researcher; cons. ecology. Editor: The California Islands: Proceedings of a Multidisciplinary Symposium, 1980, Current Ornithology, 1989; contbr. articles to sci. jours. Grantee NRC Can., 1968-72; Grantee NSF, 1974-78. Mem. Cooper Ornithol. Soc. (dir. 1976-79, pres. 1979-81), Am. Ornithologists Union (life sec. 1981-83, v.p. 1988-89), Am. Assn. Mus. (council 1980-83, hon fellow 1981—), Calif. Assn. Mus. (dir. 1980—, chmn. 1987-89), Western Mus. Conf. (dir. 1977-83, pres. 1981-83), AAAS, Am. Soc. Naturalists, Assn. Sci. Mus. Dirs., Ecol. Soc. Am., Soc. Study of Evolution, Soc. Systematic Zoology, Sigma Xi. Office: Santa Barbara Mus Natural History 2559 Puesta del Sol Rd Santa Barbara CA 93105

POWER, JAMES PATRICK, marketing executive; b. Yarmouth, N.S., Can., Oct. 25, 1935; came to U.S., 1981; s. James Edward and Elsie Mary (Saulnier) P.; m. Renee Marie Mailhot, Oct. 24, 1964; children: Patrick James Jr., Stephanie Anne. BCE, U. New Brunswick, 1957. Registered profl. engr. Pres. Johns-Manville Can. Inc., Montreal, Quebec, 1979-81; v.p., gen. mgr. Johns-Manville Corp., Denver, 1981-83; pres. Power Mktg. Group Inc., Denver, 1983—. Lt. Can. Army Engrs., 1953-60. Home: 5991 S Akron Way Englewood CO 80111 Office: Power Mktg Group 6416 S Quebec St Ste 41 Englewood CO 80111

POWERS, CHRISTOPHER MARK, electronic technician; b. Okinawa, Japan, Mar. 12, 1962; (parents Am. citizens); s. Roland Leroy and Karen Ruth (Christopherson) P. AAS in Electronics, Pima Community Coll., 1986; BSBA, U. Phoenix, 1988; postgrad., U. Ariz., 1989—. Asst. mgr. J.B.'s Restaurants, Inc., Tucson, 1982-86; gen mgr. J.B.'s Restaurants, Inc., 1986-87; electronic technician Burr-Brown Corp., Tucson, 1987--. Republican. Lutheran. Home: 6710 E Golf Links Rd Apt 1009 Tucson AZ 85730 Office: Burr-Brown Corp 6730 S Tucson Blvd Tucson AZ 85734

POWERS, DAVID VINCENT, physical therapist; b. Des Moines, Sept. 9, 1954; s. Edward Vincent and Minerva Adelia (Mowery) P.; m. Sharon Kay Jenkins, Dec. 19, 1986. BS, Loma Linda U., 1978; MA, U. Redlands, 1985; cert. in mgmt. and adminstrn. health care facilities, UCLA, 1987, cert. in exec. bus., 1988; MBA, U. Redlands, 1989. Lic. phys. therapist, Calif. Sr. phys. therapist San Antonio Community Hosp., Upland, Calif., 1978-83; sr. therapist Loma Linda (Calif.) Community Hosp., 1978-83; dir. rehab. svcs. Hollywood Presbyn. Hosp., L.A., 1983-84; phys. therapist Casa Colina Rehab. Hosp., Pomona, Calif., 1984-87; dir. rehab. svcs. UCLA Med. Ctr., 1984—. v.p. Michael Lane Homeowners Assn., Pacific Palisades, Calif., 1987, pres. 1989. Recipient UCLA Mgmt. and Profl. award, 1987, 88. Mem. Am. Phys. Therapy Assn. (assembly rep. 1986-87), Nat. Mgmt. Assn., L.A. Rehab. Dirs. Forum (chmn. 1986—), Med. Group Mgmt. Assn., Calif. Adminstrs. Spl. Interest Group (treas. 1988—), UCLA Adminstrs. Assn., Wooden Ctr. (Westwood, Calif.). Home: 1553 Palisades Dr Pacific Palisades CA 90272 Office: UCLA Med Ctr 1000 Veteran Ave Rm A7-62 Los Angeles CA 90024

POWERS, EDWIN MALVIN, consulting engineer; b. Denver, July 20, 1915; s. Emmett and Bertha Malvina (Guido) P.; m. Dorothy Lavane Debler, Jan. 18, 1941; children: Dennis M., Kenneth E., James M., Steven R. BS in Chem. Engring., U. Denver, 1939, MS, 1940. Registered profl. engr., N.J., Colo., Fall Out Analysts Engr., U.S. Fed. Emergency Mgmt. Agency, 1975-87. Prodn. supr. Nat. Aniline Div., Buffalo, 1940-45; engr., project supr. Merck & Co., Rahway, N.J., 1945-67, chief project coordinator, 1967-72, purchasing engr., 1972-82; ret., 1982; cons. engr., Conifer, Colo., 1982—. Capt. Air Raid Wardens, River dist., Buffalo, 1942-45. Mem., del. Conifer Home Owners Assns. Protect Our Single Homes, 1984-86, Regional Environ. Assn. Concerned Home Owners, 1985-86, task force area devel. Hwy. 285/Conifer Area County Planning Bd. Community, 1986-88. Mem. NSPE, Am. Chem. Soc. (emeritus), Am. Inst. Chem. Engrs. (treas. N.J. 1960, exec. com. 1961-63). Home and Office: 26106 Amy Circle Dr Conifer CO 80433

POWERS, PHILIP DENNIS, physical therapist; b. Los Angeles, Dec. 13, 1948; s. Albert Oliver and Afton (Murphy) P.; m. Kathleen Reese, Aug. 14, 1971; children: Christopher Glenn, Elizabeth Reese. BA, U. Nev., Reno, 1972; MS in Health Care Adminstrn., U. LaVerne, Calif., 1984. Staff therapist Therapeutic Assocs., Inc., Van Nuys, Calif., 1974-82, v.p., co-owner, 1982—; assoc. dir. ops. St. Joseph Med. Ctr., Burbank, Calif., 1986—. Author tape-slide presentation Exercise and the Elderly, 1986. Served to staff sgt. USAFR, 1969-74. Mem. Am. Phys. Therapy Assn. (chief rep. Greater Los Angeles dist. 1987—, treas. sect. on geriatrics 1984—, chmn. nominating com. Greater Los Angeles dist. 1986, chmn. fin. com. geriatrics sect. 1988). Episcopalian. Lodge: Kiwanis. Office: Therapeutic Assocs Inc 15216 Vanowen Ste 2-D Van Nuys CA 91405

POWERS, SHARON ANN, accountant; b. Pitts., May 28, 1955; d. Raymond Gerald and Florence Rosella (Kelly) Coffman; m. William Thomas Powers, May 21, 1983. BBA, Nat. U., Las Vegas, 1988—. Br. auditor Union Nat. Bank, Pitts., 1974-78; office mgr. Hawaii-Nev. Investment Co., Las Vegas, 1978-81; full chg. bookkeeper Stewart, Archibald & Barney, Las Vegas, 1981-84; ops. mgr. BRS, Inc./LeMaron Corp., Las Vegas, 1984-87; acctg. mgr. Las Vegas C. of C., Las Vegas, 1987—; com. mem. pension planning Las Vegas C. of C., 1988—. Exec. bd. Muscular Dystrophy Assn., So. Nev. chpt., 1989, adv. com., 1988; bd. dirs. Nev. Animal Soc., Las Vegas, 1985-87. Mem. Nat. Assn. Female Execs. Religious Sci. Office: Las Vegas C of C 2301 E Sahara Ave Las Vegas NV 89104

POWERS, STEPHEN, educational researcher, consultant; b. Bakersfield, Calif., June 10, 1936; s. Robert Boyd and Mildred (Irwin) P.; m. Gail Marguerite Allen, Dec. 28, 1968; children—Rick, Joseph, Rebecca. B.S in Edn., No. Ariz. U., 1959; M.A., U. Ariz., Tucson, 1970, M.Ed., 1972, Ph.D., 1978. Cert. tchr., Calif.; cert. tchr., adminstr., jr. coll. tchr., Ariz. Policeman, City of Bakersfield, 1967-69; tchr. Marana (Ariz.) Pub. Schs., 1969-72; dir. Am. Sch. Belo Horizonte, Brazil, 1972-73; tchr. Nogales (Ariz.) Pub. Schs., 1973-75; research specialist Tucson Unified Sch. Dist., 1975—; adj. prof. ednl. psychology, U. Ariz.; assoc. faculty mem. in computer sci. Pima Coll. Nat. Inst. Edn. grantee, 1980; Ariz. State Reading Council, 1982. Mem. Am. Ednl. Research Assn., Psychometric Soc., Am. Psychol. Assn., Am. Sociol. Assn., Am. Statis. Assn. Bahai. Contbr. articles to profl. jours. Office: 1010 E 10th St Tucson AZ 85719

POWERS, WILLIAM ALAN, real estate executive; b. Tucson, Nov. 27, 1952; s. Hugh Reid Pelphrey and Marjorie June (Johnson) P.; m. Karen Elizabeth DeWitt, May 12, 1984; children: Nicholas William, Cassandra Amy. Student, Mesa (Ariz.) Community Coll., 1970-72. Assoc., agt. Red Carpet Realtors, Phoenix, 1974-78; assoc., owner Homebrokers, Phoenix, 1978-81; assoc. Realty Execs., Phoenix, 1981-87, dir. nat. mktg., 1987—. Mem. Ariz. Assn. Realtors (bd. dirs. 1984—), Ariz. Realtors Credit Union (Incorporator 1978), Phoenix Bd. Realtors (v.p. 1987-88, pres. 1988-89, bd. dirs. 1981, 84-87), Rotary (pres. 1986-88). Republican. Office: Realty Execs 4427 N 36th St Phoenix AZ 85018

POZO, SANTIAGO, marketing executive; b. Logrono, Rioja, Spain, Nov. 4, 1957; came to U.S., 1983; s. Santiago Pozo and Asuncion Arenas. MFA, U. So. Calif., 1986; PhD, Univ. Complutense, Madrid, 1982. Mgr. spl. mkts. Universal Pictures, MCA, L.A., 1985-88; pres., founder The Arenas Group, L.A., 1988—. Author: The Spanish Film Industry, 1983 (Best Cinema Book of Yr. 1983); dir., writer The First Meters, 1977; producer: Argos, 1984 (1st prize Internat. Film Festival Huesca, 1984); responsible for U.S. Hispanic mktg. campaigns for An. American Tail, Born in East L.A., Milagro Beanfield War, Colors, My Stepmother is an Alien. Mem. Hispanic Acad. Arts, Publicists Guild. Office: The Arenas Group 8833 Sunset Blvd Suite 408 West Hollywood CA 90069

PRASAD, RAM CHANDRA, manufacturing executive; b. Patna, Bihar, India, Jan. 5, 1939; s. Lala and Laxami (Singh) P.; m. Dixie K. Davidson, Aug. 8, 1969; children: Seema, Jai Komar. BA honors, U. Patna, India, 1958; MA, U. Patna, 1960, postgrad., 1959-60; postgrad., U. Washington, 1961-65. Systems analyst Boeing Co., Seattle, 1966-75, project leader, 1976-78; cons. automation Paccar Inc., Renton, Wash., 1979-86; supr. automation Boeing Co., Seattle, 1986—; chmn. Automation Seminar, 1986 (recipient Pres. award 1986). V.p. Lake Washington Soccer Assn., Redmond, Wash., 1986; pres. Redmond Soccer Club, 1987. Mem. Computer and Automated System Assn. (vice chair 1987-88, chair 1988—), Soc. Mfg. Engrs. Home: 14532 190th Ave NE Woodinville WA 98072

PRATER, WALTER LLOYD, mechanical engineer; b. Tulsa, Apr. 11, 1955; s. Samuel Lewis and Patricia (Gaylor) P.; m. Shari Lynn Loeffler, July 28, 1985. BSME, U. Kans., 1978; MSME, San Jose State U., 1985. Registered mechanical engr., registered mfg. engr. Mfg. engr. IBM, San Jose, Calif., 1978-80, test engr., 1980-83; adv. prodn. devel. engr. IBM, San Jose, 1983—. Contbr. five articles to profl. jours. Scholar Amoco, 1977-78; recipient First Pl. award in Zoology Long's Peak Sci. Fair, 1973. Mem. ASME, Soc. Mfg. Engrs., Tau. Beta Pi, Pi Tau Sigma. Democrat. Home: 325 El Portal Way San Jose CA 95119-1416 Office: IBM H28/70B 5600 Cottle Rd San Jose CA 95193

PRATKANIS, ANTHONY RICHARD, psychologist, educator; b. Portsmouth, Va., Apr. 2, 1957; s. Tony R. and Rosemarie (Gray) P. B.S. summa cum laude, Eastern Mennonite Coll., 1979; M.A., Ohio State U., 1981, Ph.D., 1984. Research assoc. Ohio State U., Columbus, 1981-83; postdoctoral fellow Carnegie-Mellon U., Pitts., 1983-84; asst. prof. indsl. adminstrn. and psychology, U. Calif., Santa Cruz, 1984-87, asst. prof. psychology, 1987—; reviewer acad. jours. Author profl. papers, book chpts. J.B. Smith scholar Eastern Mennonite Coll., Harristonburg, Va., 1975-79; editor (with A. Greenwald and S. Breckler): Attitude Structure and Function. Mem. Am. Psychol. Assn., Midwestern Psychol. Assn., Soc. for Personality and Social Psychology. Democrat. Avocations: reading; personal computers. Research includes attitudes, persuasion, the self, consumer behavior. Home: 218 Dickens Way Santa Cruz CA 95064 Office: U Calif Bd Psychology Santa Cruz CA 95064

PRATT, CHARLES DUDLEY, JR., utility company executive; b. Honolulu, Sept. 30, 1927; s. Charles Dudley and Dora (Broadbent) P.; divorced; children by previous marriage: Charles Dudley, Timothy G., Sarah E., Melinda L. BCE with honors, Yale U., 1950, M in Structural Engring., 1951; MBA, U. Hawaii, 1971. Registered profl. engr., Hawaii. With Hawaiian Electric Co., Inc., Honolulu, 1953—, v.p. planning, 1971, exec. v.p., 1980-81, pres., from 1981, now chmn., chief exec. officer; pres., dir. Hawaiian Elec. Industries, Inc. (parent co.), Honolulu, 1983—, now also chief exec. officer; chmn. bd. Hawaiian Electric Renewable Systems Inc., HEI Investment Corp., Malama Pacific Corp., Hawaiian Tug & Barge Corp., Young Bros. Ltd., Hawaiian Ins. Group, Am. Savs. Bank. Chmn. bd. Hawaii Bus. Roundtable and Hist. Hawaii Found.; bd. dirs. Econ. Devel. Corp. Honolulu, Friends Iolani Palace, Hawaii Maritime Ctr., Aloha United Way; bd. dirs., v.p. Aloha Council Boy Scouts Am. Served with AUS, 1946-48, 51-53. Mem. ASCE (past pres. Hawaii sect.), Pacific Coast Electrical Assn. (pres. 1988-89), Edison Electric Inst., Hawaii Soc. Corp. Planners, Hawaii C. of C. (bd. dirs.), U. Hawaii MBA Alumni Group, USCG Aux., Beta Gamma Sigma, Tau Beta Pi. Clubs: Pacific, Kaneohe Yacht. Home: 276 N Kalaheo Ave Kailua HI 96734 Office: Hawaiian Elec Co Inc 900 Richards St Honolulu HI 96813 *

PRATT, GEORGE JANES, JR., psychologist, author; b. Mpls., May 3, 1948; s. George Janes and Sally Elvina (Hanson) P.; BA cum laude, U. Minn., 1970, MA, 1973; PhD with spl. commendation for overall excellence, Calif. Sch. Profl. Psychology, San Diego, 1976; 1 dau., Whitney Beth. Psychology trainee Ctr. for Behavior Modification, Mpls., 1971-72, U. Minn. Student Counseling Bur., 1972-73; predoctoral clin. psychology intern San Bernardino County (Calif.) Mental Health Services, 1973-74, San Diego County Mental Health Services, 1974-76; affiliate staff San Luis Rey Hosp., 1977-78; postdoctoral clin. psychology intern Mesa Vista Hosp., San Diego, Calif., 1976; clin. psychologist, dir. Psychology and Cons. Assocs. of San Diego, 1976—; chmn. Psychology and Cons. Assocs. Press, 1977—; bd. dirs. Optimax, Inc., 1985—; pres. George Pratt Ph.D., Psychol. Corp., 1979—; chmn. Pratt, Korn & Assocs., Inc., 1984—; founder La Jolla Profl. Workshops, 1977; clin. psychologist El Camino Psychology Ctr., San Clemente, Calif., 1977-78; grad. teaching asst. U. Minn. Psychology and Family Studies div., 1971; teaching assoc. U. Minn. Psychology and Family Studies div., Mpls., 1972-73; instr. U. Minn. Extension div., Mpls., 1971-73; faculty Calif. Sch. Profl. Psychology, 1974-83, San Diego Evening Coll., 1975-77, Nat. U., 1978-79, Chapman Coll., 1978, San Diego State U., 1979-80; vis. prof. Pepperdine U., Los Angeles, 1976-80; cons. U. Calif. at San Diego Med. Sch., 1976—, also instr. univ., 1978—, Facial Pain Clinic at U. Calif. San Diego Med. Ctr., 1983—; psychology chmn. Workshops in Clin. Hypnosis, 1980-84; cons. Calif. Health Dept., 1974, Naval Regional Med. Ctr., 1978-82, ABC-TV; also speaker. Mem. South Bay Youth Services Com., San Diego, 1976-80. Served with USAR, 1970-76. Licensed and cert. psychologist, Calif. Fellow Am. Soc. Clin. Hypnosis; mem. Am. Psychol. Assn., Calif. Psychol. Assn., Internat. Soc. Hypnosis, San Diego Psychology Law Soc. (exec. com.), Am. Assn. Sex Educators, Counselors and Therapists (cert.), San Diego Soc. Sex Therapy and Edn. (past pres.), San Diego Soc. Clin. Hypnosis (past pres.), Acad. San Diego Psychologists, Soc. Clin. and Exptl. Hypnosis., U. Minn. Alumni Assn., Nat. Speakers Assn., Beta Theta Pi. Author: HyperPerformance, 1987; A Clinical Hypnosis Primer, 1984, 88; Release Your Business Potential, 1988; Sensory/Progressive Relaxation, 1979; Effective Stress Management, 1979; Clinical Hypnosis: Techniques and Applications, 1985; contbr. chpts. to various books. Office: Scripps Hosp Med Bldg 9834 Genesee Ave Suite 321 La Jolla CA 92037

PRATT, MARTHA LOUISE, information officer; b. Buffalo, July 18, 1942; d. John and Mary Edna (Peer) McGowan; m. Donald S. Pratt, Mar. 27, 1967 (div. Dec. 1980); children: Joel, Steven. BA, U. Western Ont., London, Can., 1964; MLS, Syracuse U., 1966. Info. mgr. Sci. Applications Internat. Corp., San Diego, 1984—. Mem. Spl. Libr. Assn., Calif. Libr. Assn. Roman Catholic. Home: 5850 Honors Dr San Diego CA 92122 Office: Sci Applications Internat 10260 Campus Point Dr San Diego CA 92122

PRATT, ROSALIE REBOLLO, harpist, educator; b. N.Y.C., Dec. 4, 1933; d. Antonio Ernesto and Eleanor Gertrude (Gibney) Rebollo; Mus.B., Manhattanville Coll., 1954; Mus.M., Pius XII Inst. Fine Arts, Florence, Italy, 1955; Ed.D., Columbia U., 1976; m. George H. Mortimer, Esquire, Apr. 22, 1987; children—Francesca Christina Pratt Ferguson, Alessandra Maria Pratt Jones. Prin. harpist N.J. Symphony Orch., 1963-65; soloist Mozart Haydn Festival, Avery Fisher Hall, N.Y.C., 1968; tchr. music public schs., Bloomfield and Montclair, N.J., 1962-73; mem. faculty Montclair State Coll., 1973-79; prof. Brigham Young U., Provo, Utah, 1984—, coordinator grad. studies dept. music, 1985-87. Fulbright grantee, 1979; Myron Taylor scholar, 1954. Mem. Am. Harp Soc. (Outstanding Service award 1973), AAUP (co-chmn. legis. relations com. N.J. 1978-79), Internat. Assn. of Music for the Handicapped (co-founder, exec. dir., jour. editor), Coll. Music Soc., Music Educators Nat. Conf., Brigham Young U. Grad. Coun., Phi Kappa Phi, Sigma Alpha Iota. Co-author: Elementary Music for All Learners, 1980; contbr. articles to Music Educators Jour., Am. Harp Jour., others. Editor procs. 2d, 3d and 4th Internat. Symposia Music Edn. for Handicapped, 1981, 83, 85. Office: Brigham Young U Harris Fine Arts Ctr Provo UT 84602

PRATT, VAUGHAN RONALD, computer engineering educator; b. Melbourne, Australia, Apr. 12, 1944; s. Ronald Victor and Marjorie (Mirams) P.; m. Margot Frances Koster, Feb. 2, 1969; children: Jennifer Katherine, Jacqueline Andrea. BSc with honors, Sydney U., Australia, 1967, MSc, 1970; PhD, Stanford U., 1972. From asst. to assoc. prof. MIT, Cambridge, 1972-82; head of research Sun Microsystems Inc., Mountain View, Calif., 1983-85; prof. Stanford (Calif.) U., 1981—; pres. Triangle Concepts Inc., Palo Alto, Calif., 1988—. Author: Shellsort and Sorting Networks, 1979. Mem. Assn. for Computing Machinery, Assn. for Symbolic Logic. Office: Stanford U Dept Computer Sci Stanford CA 94305

PRAUSNITZ, JOHN MICHAEL, chemical engineer, educator; b. Berlin, Germany, Jan. 7, 1928; came to U.S., 1937, naturalized, 1944; s. Paul Georg and Susi Prausnitz; m. Susan Frieda Prausnitz, June 10, 1956; children: Stephanie, Mark Robert. B. in Chem. Engring., Cornell U., 1950; MS, U. Rochester, 1951; Ph.D., Princeton, 1955; DEng, U. L'Aquila, 1983; Dr. Ing., Tech. U. Berlin, 1989. Mem. faculty U. Calif., Berkeley, 1955—, prof. chem. engring., 1963—; cons. to cryogenic, polymer, petroleum and petrochem. industries. Author: (with others) Computer Calculations for Multicomponent Vapor-Liquid Equilibria, 1967, (with P.L. Chueh) Computer Calculations for High-Pressure Vapor-Liquid Equilibria, 1968, Molecular Thermodynamics of Fluid-Phase Equilibria, 1969, 2d edit., 1986, (with others) Regular and Related Solutions, 1970, Properties of Gases and Liquids, 3d edit., 1977, 4th edit., 1987, Computer Calculations for Multicomponent Vapor-Liquid and Liquid-Liquid Equilibria, 1980; contbr. to profl. jours. Guggenheim fellow, 1962, 73; Miller research prof., 1966, 78; recipient Alexander V. Humboldt Sr. Scientist award, 1976, Carl von Linde Gold Meml. medal German Inst. for Cryogenics, 1987; fellow Inst. Advanced Study, Berlin, 1985. Mem. Am. Inst. Chem. Engrs. (Colburn award 1962, Walker award 1967), Am. Chem. Soc. (E.V. Murphree award 1979), Nat. Acad. Engring., Nat. Acad. Scis., Am. Acad. Arts and Scis. Office: U Calif 308 Gilman Hall Berkeley CA 94720

PRAY, RALPH EMERSON, metallurgical engineer; b. Troy, N.Y., May 12, 1926; s. George Emerson and Jansje Cornelius (Owejan) P.; student N.Mex. Inst. of Mining and Tech., 1953-56, U. N.Mex., 1956; BSMetE, U. Alaska, 1961; DScMetE. (Ideal Cement fellowship, Rsch. grant), Colo. Sch. of Mines, 1966; m. Beverley Margaret Ramsey, May 10, 1959; children: Maxwell, Ross, Leslie, Marlene. Engr.-in-charge Dept. Mines and Minerals, Ketchikan, Alaska, 1957-61; asst. mgr. mfg. rsch. Universal Atlas Cement div. U.S. Steel Corp., Gary, Ind., 1965-66; rsch. metallurgist Inland Steel Co., Hammond, Ind., 1966-67; owner, dir. Mineral Rsch. Lab., Monrovia, Calif., 1968—; pres., Keystone Canyon Mining Co., Inc., Pasadena, Calif., 1972-79, U.S. Western Mines, 1973—, Silveroil Research Inc., 1980-85; v.p. Mineral Drill Inc., 1981—; owner Precision Plastics, 1973-82; ptnr. Mineral R&D Co., 1981-86; lectr., Purdue U., Hammond, Ind., 1966-67, Nat. Mining Seminar, Barstow (Calif.) Coll., 1969-70; guest lectr. Calif. State Poly U., 1977-81, Western Placer Mining Conf., Reno, Nev., 1983, Dredging and Placer Mining Conf., Reno, 1985, others; v.p., dir. Wilbur Foote Plastics, Pasadena, 1968-72; strategic minerals del. People to People, Republic of S. Africa, 1983. With U.S. Army, 1950-52. Fellow Geol. Mining and Metall. Soc. India (life), Am. Inst. Chemists, South African Inst. Mining and Metallurgy; mem. Soc. Mining Engrs., Am. Chem. Soc., Am. Inst. Mining, Metall. and Petroleum Engrs., NSPE, Can. Inst. Mining and Metallurgy, Geol. Soc. South Africa, Sigma Xi, Sigma Mu. Contbr. articles to sci. jours.; guest editor Calif. Mining Jour., 1978—; patentee chem. processing and steel manufacture. Office: 805 S Shamrock Ave Monrovia CA 91016

PREECE, MCCOY D., travel corporation executive, high school official; b. Moab, Utah, May 5, 1954; s. Charles Merlin and Jacqulyn (Swain) P.; m. Karen Lucille Gividen, Aug. 20, 1976; children: Justin Coy, Joshua Charles, Nicolas Bert, Nikita Karen. Student, Utah State U., 1972-73, 76; completion cert., Branif Airlines, 1975. Cert. Travel Agent, 1988, Weather Observer, 1979, Weight Balance Instr., 1979-81. Ramp agent Frontier Airlines, Rock Springs, Wyo., 1978-79; ticket and ramp agent Frontier Airlines, Vernal, Utah, 1979-80, ops. instr., 1980-81; gen. mgr. Frontier Travel and Tours, Vernal, Utah, 1981-82; ticket and ramp agent Frontier Airlines, Seattle, 1982-84; asst. mgr. system aircraft appearance Frontier Airlines, Denver, 1984-85; mgr. Nomad Travel, Inc., Salt Lake City, 1985-86, pres., gen. mgr., 1986—; group coord. Inst. of Cert. Travel Agents, Salt Lake City, 1985-88; bd. dirs. Nomad Travel Inc.; v.p. Fiesta Internat. Festivals, Salt Lake City, 1986—. Mem. Ind. Travel Agents Alliance (com. mem. 1988—). Republican. Ch. of Jesus Christ of Latter Day Saints. Home: 3536 W Piera Circle West Jordan UT 84084 Office: Nomad Travel 2600 S State ST Salt Lake City UT 84115

PREGNALL, WILLIAM STUART, seminary dean; b. Charleston, S.C., Mar. 26, 1931; s. Alexander Howard and Marion Lockwood (Lewis) P.; m. Gabrielle Joye Uzzell, Dec. 20, 1952; children: William Stuart, A. Marshall, Garielle Joye Ford. BA, U. N.C., 1952; MDiv., Va. Theol. Sem., 1958, DD (hon.), 1987; DMin., U. of the South, 1975. Ordained priest Episcopal Ch., 1959. Vicar Holy Trinity Episcopal Ch., Grahamville, S.C., 1958-59; dir. christian edn. Diocese of S.C., Charleston, 1960; asst. rector St. John's Ch., Charleston, W.Va., 1961-62, rector, 1962-65; episcopal chaplain La. State U. St. Albans Chapel, Baton Rouge, 1965-70; rector St. Augustine's Ch., Washington, 1970-73; prof. field edn. Va. Theol. Sem., Alexandria, 1973-81; dean, pres. Ch. Div. Sch. of the Pacific, Berkeley, Calif., 1981-89; rector St. Mary's Parish, Washington, 1989—; vicar Ch. of the Cross, Bluffton, S.C., 1958-59, St. Luke's Ch., Hilton Head Island, S.C., 1958-59. Author (books) Laity and Liturgy, 1975, The Episcopal Seminary System During the Decline of the American Empire, 1988. Chair Citizens Com. Against Police Violence, Baton Rouge, 1972. Lt. USN, 1952-60. Named to Order of Holy Grail U. N.C.-Chapel Hill, 1951, Order of Golden Fleece, 1952. Mem. Associated Parishes Inc., Episcopal Peace Fellowship, Phi Eta Sigma, Phi Beta Kappa. Democrat. Home: 1730 Arch St Berkeley CA 94709 Office: Ch Div Sch of the Pacific Office of the Pres 2451 Ridge Rd Berkeley CA 94709

PREOVOLOS, JAMES PETER, lawyer; b. San Francisco, July 27, 1919; s. Peter John and Kalliope (Barbari) P.; divorced; 1 child, Penelope Athene. BS, U. San Francisco, 1941, JD, 1947. Bar: Calif., 1947. Commd. ensign USNR, 1941, advanced through grades to comdr., 1961, ret., 1979; pvt. practice in family law San Francisco, 1948—; judge Marital Settlement Conf. Superior Ct., San Francisco; lectr. Continuing Edn. of the Bar, Calif.; bd. dirs. U. Calif. Research Expedition Program. Author: Discovery in Family Law, 1986. Mem. State Bar Calif., San Francisco Bar Assn., Am. Acad. Matrimonial Lawyers, Hellenic Law Soc., Lowell High Alumni Assn. (bd. dirs.). Democrat. Greek Orthodox. Club: San Francisco Lawyers. Office: 220 Montgomery St Suite 300 San Francisco CA 94104

PRESCOTT, LAWRENCE MALCOLM, medical and health writer; b. Boston, July 31, 1934; s. Benjamin and Lillian (Stein) P.; BA, Harvard U., 1957; MSc, George Washington U., 1959, PhD, 1966; m. Ellen Gay Kober, Feb. 19, 1961 (dec. Sept. 1981); children: Jennifer Maya, Adam Barrett; m. Sharon Lynn Kirshen, May 16, 1982; children: Gary Leon Kirshen, Marc Paul Kirshen. Nat. Acad. Scis. postdoctoral fellow U.S. Army Research, Ft. Detrick, Md., 1965-66; microbiologist/scientist WHO, India, 1967-70, Indonesia, 1970-72, Thailand, 1972-78; with pub. rels. Ted Klein & Co., Van Vechten, Smith, Kline, Beekman, others, 1984—; cons. health to internat. orgns., San Diego, 1978—; author mans. and contbr. articles in diarrheal diseases and lab. scis. to profl. jours., 1965-81; contbr. numerous articles, stories, poems to mags., newspapers, including Living in Thailand, Jack and Jill, Strawberry, Bangkok Times, Sprint, 1977-81; mng. editor Caduceus, 1981-82; pub., editor Teenage Scene, 1982-83; pres. Prescott Pub. Co., 1982-83; med. writer numerous jours. including Modern Medicine, Dermatology Times, Cope, ACP Observer, Medical Tribune, American Family Physician, Ophthalmology Times, Group Practice News, Cardiovascualr News, Genetic Engineering News, Medical Week, Medical World News, Urology Times, Gastroenterology and Endoscopy News; author Curry Every Sunday, 1984. Home and Office: 11307 Florindo Rd San Diego CA 92127

PRESLEY, ROBERT BUEL, state senator; b. Tahlequah, Okla., Dec. 4, 1924; s. Doyle and Annie (Townsend) P.; grad. FBI Nat. Acad., Washington, 1962; student Riverside City Coll., 1960; A.A., UCLA, m. Ahni Ratliff, Aug. 20, 1944; children—Donna Thurber, Marilyn Raphael, Robert Buel. Various positions Riverside County Sheriff's Dept. (Calif.), 1950-62, undersheriff, 1962-74; mem. Calif. Senate, 36th Dist., 1974—; lectr. ethics. Served with U.S. Army, 1943-46. Decorated Bronze Star. Mem. FBI Nat. Acad. Assn. (pres. Calif. chpt. 1974). Baptist. Clubs: Lions, Elks, Am. Legion, V.F.W., Moose, Riverside County Democratic Century (pres. 1972-73). Home: 5508 Grassy Trail Dr Riverside CA 92504 Office: Office of the State Senate State Capitol Sacramento CA 95814

PRESSLEY, JAMES RAY, electrical engineer; b. Ft. Worth, July 14, 1946; s. Loy Dale and Dorothy Helen (Foust) P.; m. Barbara Kay McMillin, Oct. 9, 1968 (div. 1981); children: James Foust Pressley, Kreg Milam Pressley; m. Susan Marie Straw, Apr. 27, 1985 (div.); children: Shaye Eugene Straw, Rebecca Alycen Straw, Rachel Leilani Straw. BSEE, U. Tex., Arlington, 1970. Registered profl. engr., Alaska, Hawaii, Oreg., Wash. Designer/draftsman Romine & Slaughter, Ft. Worth, 1967-71; engr. Crews MacInnes & Hoffman, Anchorage, 1971-73, O'Kelly & Schoenlank, Anchorage, 1973-75, Theodore G. Creedon, Anchorage, 1975-77; v.p. Fryer, Pressley Elliott, Anchorage, 1977-80, Fryer/Pressley Engring., 1980—; mem. elec. constrn. and maintenance industry evaluation panel, 1982—. Mem. Illuminating Engring. Soc., Internat. Assn. Elec. Inspectors, Alaska Profl. Design Council. Office: 560 E 34th St Ste 300 Anchorage AK 99503

PRESTON, DAVID JOSEPH, financial planner; b. Cleve., July 31, 1945; s. Freeman J. and Veronica (Pantlikas) P.; m. Marilyn T. Preston, Mar. 21, 1970; children: Scott D., Jennifer R., Rebecca L. BEd, Kent (Ohio) State U., 1969, MA, 1972. Cert. fin. planner, registered investment adviser. Ind. life and health ins. agt. Lakewood and Westlake, Ohio, 1969-78; fin. planner Preston Assocs., Inc., Westlake, 1979—, Kingman, Ariz., 1988—. Mem. Internat. Assn. for Fin. Planners, Inst. Cert. Fin. Planners, Internat. Bd. Standards for Cert. Fin. Planning, Kingman C. of C. Republican. Roman Catholic. Lodge: Rotary. Home and Office: 661 Shadow Mountain Dr Kingman AZ 86401

PRESTON, EDGAR HARLAN, real estate broker; b. Emporia, Kans., July 11, 1931; s. Cecil Alvin and Grace Marie (Benedict) P.; m. Jean Ann Walker, Dec. 23, 1951 (div. June 1981); children: Blair W., Melissa A., Christy A.; m. Kate Kramer, Aug. 21, 1981. Student, Southwestern Coll., Winfield, Kans., 1949-50; BS in Polit. Sci., USN Post Grad. Sch., Monterey, Calif., 1967. Enlisted USN, 1950-51, commd. ensign, 1951, advanced to cmmdr., 1967, naval aviator various shipboard/land-based billets, 1951-73; commanding officer RECONRON 3, Agana, Guam, 1967-69; project mgr. SPECOMM U.S. Naval Air System Command, Washington, 1969-73; with flight test U.S. Naval Electronic System Command, Dallas, 1969-73; ret. USN, 1973; mng. dir. Collin Radio Ltd., Hong Kong, 1973-75; mgr., broker DBWF Andy Hughes Realty (GOH), Sedona, 1976-85; broker, owner Ed Preston Realty, Sedona, 1985—; pres. Sedona-Verde Valley Bd. Realtors, 1983. Treas., bd. dirs. Sedona C. of C., 1986-87; life. mem. Realtors Polit. Action Com., Washington, 1981—; pres. Keep Sedona Beautiful, 1986-87. Decorated Navy Commendation medal, Air medal; named Realtor of Yr. Sedona-Verde Valley Bd. Realtors, 1982. Mem. Ariz. Assn. Realtors (regional v.p., v.p. 1987-88, bd. dirs. subs. corp. 1987—, pres.-elect 1989, honor soc. 1988-89), Realtors Nat. Mktg. Inst. (CRB award, CRS award 1984-89), Real Estate Securities & Syndication, Am. Legion, Kiwanis, Elks (local treas. 1978-83). Republican. Home: Box 281 Sedona AZ 86336 Office: Profl Realty Organization 45 Sunset Dr Ste 195 Sedona AZ 86336

PRESTON, JAMES BARTON, editor, publisher; b. Seattle, Wash., Sept. 23, 1946; s. Chester Howard and Yvonne (Burton) P.; m. Sheila Ann Bruseth, May 15, 1982; 1 child, Kayla Joy. BA, U. Calif., Santa Barbara, 1968; MA in English, U. Calif., 1976. Editor Academic Therapy Publs., Novato, Calif., 1973-79; editor, pub., owner Spl. Child Publs., Seattle, 1980—; propr. Scriptus Document Svc., Mountlake Terrace, Wash., 1987—. Del., Wash. Dem. Conv., Tacoma, 1983; chmn. bd. dirs. Stop Abuse, Everett, Wash., 1988—. Mem. NRA, Cathedral Sch. San Francisco Alumni Coun. (chmn. 1978-79), Thacher Sch. Alumni Assn. (class rep. 1988—). Episcopalian. Office: Spl Child Publs PO Box 33548 Seattle WA 98133

PRESTON (PRICE), LISA LYNN, design and drafting specialist, educator; b. Denver, Aug. 8, 1961; d. Garnet Zane and Elizabeth Ann (Wehe) P. BS in Environ. Design, U. Colo., 1983; MArch, U. Nebr., 1986. Cert. vocat. edn., drafting, computers instr., Colo. Drafter Centennial Engr., Arvada, Colo., 1979-80, Atkinson Noland and Assocs. Inc., Boulder, Colo., 1980-83; computer aided design drafting research in Coll. Arch. U. Nebr., Lincoln, 1984-86; instr. computer aided design U. Hannover (West Germany) Inst. Arch. & Planning Theory, 1986-87; drafting, computer instr. Pikens Vocat. Sch., Aurora, Colo., 1987; computer aided design, drafting specialist SDG, Inc., Lakewood, Colo., 1987—. Co-contbr. articles to profl. jours. Elder Westminster Presbyn. Ch., Colo., 1987—. Mem. AIA (assoc.). Clubs: Nebr. State Grange, Colo. State Grange.

PRESTWOOD, RONALD MARTIN, lumberman, manager; b. San Mateo, Calif., May 21, 1941; s. Leon Cullen and Vivian Stella (Stout) P.; m. Lisa A., Oct. 6, 1972 (div. May 1988); 1 child, Amanda Kay. Grad., Hartwell Jr. Coll., 1961; BE, Humboldt State U., 1970; postgrad., Coll. of Redwoods, 1978. With Arcata (Calif.) Redwood Co., 1963—, sawmill supt., 1972-78, sawmill mgr., 1978-80, sawmill and poser plant mgr., 1980-88; plant engr. U.C. Operating Svcs. div. Ultrapower Constellation, Blue Lake, Calif., 1988—; speaker U. Calif. Richmond. Active Eureka (Calif.) Fire Dept., sec./treas., named Firefighter Yr., 1987. Mem. Forest Products Research Soc. (workshop coordinator 1984, 86, program chmn. 1984-85, sect. chmn. 1986-87, bd. dirs. 1987-88, numerous publs.), Calif. Forest Protective Assn. (co. rep. environ. affairs com.). Home: 2428 S St Eureka CA 95501

PREVIN, ANDRE, composer, conductor; b. Berlin, Germany, Apr. 6, 1929; came to U.S., 1938, naturalized, 1943; s. Jack and Charlotte (Epstein) P.; m. Mia Farrow, Sept. 10, 1970 (div. 1979); children: Matthew and Sascha (twins), Fletcher, Lark, Daisy, Soon-Yi.; m. Heather Hales, Jan. 1982; 1 son, Lukas. Student, Berlin Conservatory, Paris Conservatory; privately with, Pierre Monteux, Mario Castelnuovo-Tedesco. mem. faculty Guildhall Sch., London, Royal Acad. Music., Berkshire Music Ctr. Rec. artist classical music, for RCA, EMI, Phillips, Telarc, 1946—; composer chamber music, Cello Concerto, Guitar Concerto, piano music, serenades for violin, brass quintet, song cycle on poems by Philip Larkin Every Good Boy Deserves Favour, Principals, Reflections, Piano Concerto, 2d Cello Concerto, Triplet for Brass Ensemble, film scores, 1950-59; condr.-in-chief Houston Symphony, 1967-69; prin. condr. London Symphony Orch., 1968-79, Royal Philharmonic Orch., Eng., 1985—; guest condr. maj. symphony orchs. and festivals in U.S. and Europe including: Covent Garden Opera, festivals in Salzburg, Edinburgh, Flanders, Vienna, Osaka, Prague, Berlin, Bergen; music dir. South Bank Music Festival, London, 1972-74, Pitts. Symphony, 1976-84, Los Angeles Philharmonic, 1984-89; author: Music Face to Face, 1971, Orchestra, 1979. Served with AUS, 1950-51. awards Nat. Grammophone Soc. Mem. Acad. Motion Picture Arts and Scis., Dramatists Guild, Brit. Composers Guild, Nat. Composers and Condrs. League. Club: Garrick. Office: care Los Angeles Philharm 135 N Grand Los Angeles CA 90012 also: care Harrison/Parrott Ltd, 12 Penzance Pl, London W11 4PA, England also: London Symphony Orch, 1 Mortage St, London WC1 England *

PREY, STEPHEN CARL, engineer; b. Balt., Mar. 28, 1950; s. Charles William and Dorothy MayBelle (Taylor) P.; m. Judith Aviva. BS in Engr. & Training, U. Calif., Berkeley, 1968-72. Cert. state energy conservation auditor & program trainer, Calif. Tech. rep. Honeywell, Inc., San Francisco, 1966-70; asst. engr. T. F. Jackson, Long Island, N.Y., 1970-72; control system engr. Honeywell, Inc., San Francisco, 1972-76; owner/cons. Energy Control Systems, San Francisco, 1976-77; energy systems specialist Calif. State Energy Commn., Sacramento, 1977-81; energy prooogram mgr. State Dept. Parks & Recreation, Sacramento, 1981-83; resource engr. State Dept. Transp., Sacramento, 1983—; computer cons., rehab. program coord. Author: Carpenter Shop: SFSHP, 1984;. Actor Living History Soc. Mem. Sutter's Fort Docent Assn. (program mgr. 1983), Apple's User Group (adv. coun.), U.C. Octett Alumni Assn. (bd. dirs.). Republican. Episcopalian. Office: Caltrans 1120 N Street RM 4320 Sacramento CA 95814

PRICE, ARTHUR R., petroleum company executive; b. Calgary, Alta., Oct. 22, 1951; married; 3 children. BSc, U. Alta., 1973. With NOVA an Alta. Corp., 1973-79; v.p. Husky Oil Ltd., 1979-84; pres. Husky Oil Ltd., Calgary, Alta.; exec. v.p. Husky Oil Ops. Ltd., 1979-84, pres., 1984—. Office: Husky Oil Ltd, 707 8th Ave SW, Calgary, AB Canada T2P 3G7 *

PRICE, CLIFFORD WARREN, metallurgist, researcher; b. Denver, Apr. 22, 1935; s. Warren Wilson and Vivian Fredrika (Cady) P.; m. Carole Joyce Waterman, June 14, 1969; children: Carla Beth, Krista Lynn. MetE, Colo. Sch. Mines, 1957, PhD, 1975; MS, Ohio State U., 1970. Design engr. Sundstrand Aviation-Denver, 1957-60; materials specialist Denver Rsch. Inst., 1960-63; sr. metallurgist Rocky Flats div. Dow Chem. Co., Golden, Colo., 1963-66; staff metallurgist Battelle Columbus (Ohio) Labs., 1966-75; sr. scientist Owens-Corning Fiberglas, Granville, Ohio, 1975-80; metallurgist Lawrence Livermore (Calif.) Nat. Lab., 1980—. Contbr. articles to profl. jours. Battelle Columbus Labs. fellow, 1974-75. Mem. Metall. Soc. of AIME, Electron Microscopy Soc. Am. (treas. Denver 1961-62), Am. Soc. for Metals, Livermore Valley Tennis Club. Republican. Office: Lawrence Livermore Nat Lab PO Box 808 L-482 Livermore CA 94550

PRICE, CYNTHIA ANN, electrical engineer; b. Tucson, Aug. 29, 1957; d. Gene Price and Peggy Ann (Purcell) Eid. BSEE, San Diego State U., 1986. Office mgr. VA, San Diego, 1983-84; elec. engr. intern, tech. Alexander Systems, San Diego, 1984-86; jr. engr. intern Naval Ocean Systems Ctr., San Diego, 1985-86; elec. engr. Arinc Res. Corp., San Diego, 1987—. With U.S. Navy, 1975-81. Mem. IEEE, Am. Soc. Quality Control, Surface Mount Tech. Assn., Toastmasters (sec. 1987—). Republican. Mem. Christian Ch. Office: Arinc Res Corp 4055 Hancock St San Diego CA 92110

PRICE, D. SCOTT, publisher; b. Hamilton, Ont., Can., Apr. 22, 1955; s. Clifford C. and M. June (Fredin) P. BA, BM, Mich. State U., 1977. Pub. San Francisco Weekly, 1981—. Home: San Francisco Weekly 230 Ritch St San Francisco CA 94107

PRICE, EUGENE ELONA, management consultant; b. Columbus, Ga., Jan. 23, 1958; s. Roy Clarence and Althea Cecelia (Kala) P.; m. Brenda Jean Dow, Sept. 4, 1982; children: Evan E., Erik E. BBA, U. Hawaii, 1981, MBA, 1984. Acctg. mgr. McInerny Ltd., Honolulu, 1983-85; treas., controller Creative Strategies Inc., Honolulu, 1985-87, leasing dir., 1987—, also bd. dirs., chmn. bd., 1986-87; fin. cons., Honolulu, 1982—. Mem. Nat. Retail Merchants Assn., U. Hawaii MBA Alumni Assn. Home: 2069 California Ave #18G Wahiawa HI 96786 Office: Creative Strategies Inc 735 Sheraton St #209 Honolulu HI 96814

PRICE, FREDERICK KENNETH CERCIE, minister; b. Santa Monica, Calif., Jan. 3, 1932; s. Fred Cercie and Winifred Bernice (Ammons) P.; m. Betty Ruth Scott, Mar. 29, 1953; children: Angela Marie Price Evans, Cheryl Ann Price Crabbe, Stephanie Pauline, Frederick Kenneth. Diploma (hon.), Rhema Bible Tng. Ctr., Tulsa, 1976; DD (hon.), Oral Roberts U., 1982. Ordained to ministry Bapt. Ch., 1955, African Meth. Episcopal Ch., 1957, Kenneth Hagin Ministries, 1975. Asst. pastor Mt. Sinai Bapt. Ch., Los Angeles, 1955-57; pastor African Meth. Episcopal Ch., Val Verde, Calif., 1957-59; pastor, Christian Missionary Alliance W. Washington Community Ch., Los Angeles, 1965-73; pastor Crenshaw Christian Ctr., Los Angeles, 1973—; founding mem. bd. trustees Internat. Conv. Faith Ministers, Inc., Tulsa, 1979—. Author numerous books including How Faith Works, 1976, Explanation to Receiving Your Healing by the Laying on of Hands, 1980, High Finance, God's Financial Plan, Tithes and Offerings, 1984, How to Believe God for a Mate, 1987, Marriage and the Family, Practical Insight for Family Living, 1988, The Origin of Satan, 1988. Democrat. Office: Crenshaw Christian Ctr Attention Angela Evans Mailing PO Box 90000 Los Angeles CA 90009

PRICE, GINGER L., dentist; b. L.A., Apr. 23, 1956; d. Halford R. and Virginia E. (Baker) P. Student, Loma Linda (Calif.) U., La Sierra, 1974-75, DDS, 1983; student, Ariz. State U., 1975-76, Pacific Union Coll., 1976-78. Gen. practice dentistry G.L. Price, DDS, Phoenix, 1984—. Mem. ADA, Am. Assn. Women Dentists, Acad. Gen. Dentistry, Cen. Ariz. Dental Soc., Women's Exec. Assn. Met. Phoenix. Office: 2201 E Camelback Rd Ste 224B Phoenix AZ 85016

PRICE, GUY ROBERT, lawyer; b. Pocatello, Idaho, Oct. 13, 1954; s. Horace L. and Clarice (Thomas) P.; m. Julie Ann Henry, Sept. 1, 1978; children: Emily, Casey, Morgan, Abigail. BS magna cum laude, Brigham Young U., 1980; JD, U. Utah, 1983. Bar: Idaho 1983, U.S. Dist. Ct. Idaho 1983, U.S. Ct. Appeals (9th cir.) 1983. Ptnr. Green, Service, Gasser & Kerl, Pocatello, 1983—. Mem. planning and zoning commn. Bannock County; hearing chmn. Med. Malpractice Screening Panels Idaho Bd. Medicine. William Leary scholar U. Utah Law Sch., 1983-85. Mem. ABA (tort and ins. practice sect., vice chmn. alternate dispute resolution com.), Am. Trial Lawyers Assn., Idaho Trial Lawyers Assn., Idaho State Bar (chmn. alternative dispute resolution com. 1989—). Office: Green Svc Gasser & Kerl PO Box 4883 Ste C-1 Center Pl Pocatello ID 83205

PRICE, HOWARD WILLIAM, management consultant; b. Trenton, N.J., Aug. 4, 1930; s. Martin and Sadye (Singer) P.; m. Vita Eve Price, Jan. 20, 1958; children: Cole Jeffrey, Lori Melissa, Lisa Marla. BA, Norwich U., 1951; postgrad., Harvard U., 1951-52, Johns Hopkins U., 1954-55. Rsch. mgr. air pollution engring. program USPHS, Washington, 1955-57; rsch. program mgr. Western Precipitation Corp., L.A., 1957-60; div. mgr. contracts F-14 program div. Hughes Aircraft Co., El Segundo, Calif., 1961-83, asst. program mgr. F-14 program div., 1983-85; dir. engring. adminstrn. Cubic Corp., San Diego, 1985-87; pres. Integrated Mgmt. Cons., San Diego, 1988—; contract advisor Naval Air System Command, Washington, 1969-85; bd. dirs. contracts Endevco San Juan Capistrano. Inventor in field. 1st lt. U.S. Army, 1952-54. Mem. Nat. Contract Mgmt. Assn., Inst. Cost Analysis, Program Mgmt. Inst. Jewish. Home and Office: 7515 Solano St La Costa CA 92009

PRICE, HUMPHREY WALLACE, aerospace engineer; b. San Antonio, Sept. 25, 1954; s. Humphrey Rodes and Ruth (Wallace) P. BS in Engring., U. Tex., 1976, MS in Engring., 1978. Rsch. asst. Nuclear Reactor Lab., U. Tex., Austin, 1976; nuclear engr. EDS Nuclear, Inc., San Francisco, 1977-78; engr. Jet Propulsion Lab., Pasadena, Calif., 1978-82, tech. group leader, 1984—; rsch. engr. SW Rsch. Inst., San Antonio, 1982-84; cons. Am. Rocket Co., Camarillo, Calif., 1986-87; tech. staff World Space Found., Pasadena, 1980—. Patentee in field. Mem. Brit. Interplanetary Soc. Office: HW Price Cons PO Box 454 La Canada-Flintridge CA 91012

PRICE, JACK STANLEY, school district administrator, consultant; b. Hamilton, Ont., Can., Feb. 28, 1931; came to U.S., 1935; s. Jasper and Edythe Marie (McCourt) P.; m. Barbara Ann Mangum, Jan. 8. 1981; children by previous marriage: Michael, Robert; adopted children: Sally Price, Susan Strehlow, Sherry, Stephanie Hickethier. BA, Ea. Mich. U., Ypsilanti, 1952; MEd, Wayne State U., 1957; postgrad. Yale U., 1959-60; EdD, Wayne State U., 1965. Tchr. math., sci. Detroit Pub. Schs., 1953-65; mathematics and sci. cons. San Diego County Office Edn., 1965-68, dir. curriculum, 1968-71; asst. supt. programs San Diego City Schs., 1971-76; supt. schs. Vista Unified Sch. Dist., Calif., 1976-83, Palos Verdes Peninsula Sch. Dist., Palos Verdes Estates, Calif., 1983—. Author 7 textbooks in field of sci., math. Editor: Changing School Mathematics, 1982. Named Disting. Alumnus, Wayne State U. Coll. Edn., 1976. Fellow AAAS; mem. Nat. Council Tchrs. Math. (bd. dirs. 1972-74, math. sci. edn. bd., 1985-88), Am. Assn. Sch. Adminstrs. Democrat. Lodge: Rotary. Home: 1405 Via Zumaya Estates CA 90274 Office: Palos Verdes Peninsula Unified Sch Dist 3801 Via La Selva Palos Verdes Estates CA 90274

PRICE, JAMES NEWTON, engineer; b. Dinuba, Calif., Nov. 2, 1947; s. W.N. and Jean (Asquith) P.; m. Joan C. Sieber, Feb. 18, 1978. BSEE, U. Calif., Santa Barbara, 1969, MSEE, 1971. Electronics engr. Naval Ocean Systems Ctr., San Diego, 1971-82, engring. supr. and head, system devel. br., 1982—. Editor jour.; contbr. articles to prof. jours. Recipient Superior Performance award Naval Ocean Systems Ctr., 1978, Performance Exceeding Expectations awards Naval Ocean Systems Ctr., 1981-88. Mem. Soc. for Info. Display (mem. various coms., bd. dirs., editor jour., symposium chmn. 1985, 88), Packards Internat. (pres. San Diego chpt. 1976-78), Mission Trail Network (pres. Calif. chpt. 1973-75), Classic Chevys of San Diego (editor). Democrat. Office: Naval Ocean Systems Ctr Code 713 San Diego CA 92152

PRICE, JAY BERRY, city official; b. Los Angeles, Mar. 9, 1915; s. John Berry and Nancy Alice (Gipson) P.; A.A., Compton Coll., 1957; m. Gertrude Margaret Lydon, Apr. 19, 1941; children—William Berry, John Jay, Nancy Alice. Insp., U.S. Internal Revenue Service, Los Angeles, 1939-76. Mayor, councilman, Bell, Calif., 1958—; dist. dir. So. Calif. Rapid Transit Dist., Los Angeles, 1971—. Dir. Los Angeles County Sanitation Dists. 1 and 2; mem. revenue and taxation com. Los Angeles County div., also mem. state revenue and taxation com. League Calif. Cities; trustee, pres. S.E. Mosquito-Abatement Dist., South Gate; alt. trustee rep. So. Calif. to trustee corporate bd. Calif. Mosquito Control Assn.; mem. adv. council 4th West County region Los Angeles County Library; City of Bell rep. of gen. assembly So. Calif. Assn. Govts. Mem. Christian Ch. (deacon, trustee, treas.). Home: 6900 Crafton Ave Bell CA 90201 Office: 6330 Pine Ave Bell CA 90201

PRICE, JEANNINE ALLEENICA, clinical psychologist; b. Cleve., Oct. 29, 1949; d. Q. Q. and Lisa Denise (Wilson) Ewing; m. T. R. Price, Sept. 2, 1976. BS, Western Res. U., 1969; MS, Vanderbilt U., 1974; MBA, Stanford U., 1985. Cert. alcoholism counselor, Calif. Health Service coordinator Am. Profile, Nashville, 1970-72; exec. dir. Awareness Concept, San Jose, Calif., 1977-80; mgr. employee assistance program Nat. Semiconductor, Santa

Clara, Calif., 1980-81; mgmt. cons. employee assistant programs. Mem. Gov.'s Adv. Council Child Devel. Programs. Mem. Am. Bus. Women's Assn., Nat. Assn. Female Execs., AAUW, Coalition Labor Women, Calif. Assn. Alcohol counselors, Almaca. Author: Smile a Little, Cry a Lot, Gifts of Love, Reflection in the Mirror, The Light at the Top of the Mountain.

PRICE, JOE, artist, educator; b. Ferriday, La., Feb. 6, 1935; s. Edward Neill and Margaret (Hester) P. B.S., Northwestern U., 1957; postgrad. Art Ctr. Coll., Los Angeles, 1967-68; M.A., Stanford U., 1970. Free-lance actor, artist, N.Y.C., 1957-60; free-lance illustrator, actor, Los Angeles, 1960-68; free-lance comml. artist, San Carlos, Calif., 1968-69; package designer Container Corp. Am., Santa Clara, Calif., 1969; prof. studio art Coll. San Mateo, Calif., 1970—. One man shows include Richard Sumner Gallery, Palo Alto, Calif., 1975, San Mateo County Cultural Ctr., 1976, 82, Tahir Galleries, New Orleans, 1977, 82, Kerwin Galleries, Burlingame, Calif., 1977, Edits. Gallery, Melbourne, Australia, 1977, Ankrum Gallery, Los Angeles, 1978, 84, Edits. Ltd. West Gallery, San Francisco, 1981, Miriam Perlman Gallery, Chgo., 1982, San Mateo County Arts Council Gallery, 1982, Candy Stick Gallery, Ferndale, Calif., 1984, Assoc. Am. Artists, N.Y.C. and Phila., 1984, Gallery 30, San Mateo, 1984, Triton Mus. Art, Santa Clara, Calif., 1986, Huntsville (Ala.) Mus. Art, 1987, Gallery 30, San Mateo, 1988; exhibited in groups shows at Berkeley Art Ctr., Calif., 1976, Burlingame Civic Art Gallery, 1976, Syntex Gallery, Palo Alto, Calif., 1977, Gump's Gallery, San Francisco, 1976, 77, Nat. Gallery of Australia, 1978, Sonoma County Gallery, 1979, Gov. Dummer Acad. Art, Byfield, Mass., 1979, Miss. Mus. Art, 1982, C.A.A. Galleries, Chautauqua, N.Y., 1982, Huntsville Mus. Art, 1983, Tahir Gallery, New Orleans, 1983, Hunterdon Art Ctr., N.J., 1984, Editions Galleries, Melbourne, Australia, 1988, Van Stratten Gallery, Chgo., 1988, 6th Internat. Exhibition, Carnegie-Mellon U., Pa., 1988, Forum Gallery, Jamestown, N.Y., 1988; represented in permanent collections San Francisco Mus. Modern Art, Achenbach Found. Graphic Arts, San Francisco, Phila. Mus. Art, New Orleans Mus. Art, Portland Mus. Art, Maine, The Library of Congress, Washington. Huntsville Mus. Art, Midwest Mus. Am. Art, Ind., Cracow Nat. Mus., Poland, Cabo Frio Mus., Brazil, Nat. Mus. Am. Art, Smithsonian Inst., Washington. Recipient Kempshall Clark award Peoria Art Guild, 1981; Paul Lindsay Sample Meml. award 25th Chautauqua Nat. Exhbn. of Am. Art, 1982. Mem. Am. Color Print Soc., Audubon Artists (assoc. mem., Louis Lozowick Meml. award 1978), Boston Printmakers (Ture Bengtz Meml. award 1987), Calif. Soc. Printmakers (mem. council 1979-81), Los Angeles Printmaking Soc., Phila. Print Club (Lessing J. Rosenwald prize 1979), Arts Council of San Mateo County. Democrat. Home: 2031 Belle Monti Belmont CA 94002 Office: Coll San Mateo 1700 W Hillside Blvd San Mateo CA 94402

PRICE, KATHLEEN MCCORMICK, book editor; b. Topeka, Kans., Dec. 25, 1932; d. Raymond Chesley and Kathleen (Shoffner) McCormick; m. William Faulkner Black, Aug. 25, 1956 (div. 1961); 1 child, Kathleen Serena; m. William Hilliard Price, Aug. 13, 1976. BA, U. Colo., Denver, 1971. Book reviewer Denver Post, 1971-78; book editor San Diego Mag., 1978—; cons. editor St. John's Cathedral, Denver, 1985—. Author: There's a Dactyl Under My Foot, 1986. Historian, Altar Guild, St. John's Cathedral, Denver. Mem. Nat. Book Critics Cir., Denver Woman's Press Club, Denver Country Club, La Garita Club, Sigma Delta Chi. Episcopalian. Home: 27 Crestmoor Dr Denver CO 80220 Office: San Diego Mag 4206 W Point Loma Blvd San Diego CA 92110

PRICE, KEITH GLENN, accountant; b. Ft. Morgan, Colo., Nov. 24, 1941; s. George Felt and Irene Lois (Gibbs) P.; m. Norma Helen Witt, Feb. 28, 1970; children: Diana, Michael, Troy, Aaron, Christopher. BS, BA, Colo. State U., 1968. CPA. Auditor IRS, Casper, Wyo., 1968-75; ptnr. Hines, Price and Co., Cheyenne, Wyo., 1975-76, Fisher, Hines and Price, Cheyenne, Wyo., 1976-80; sole practice Cheyenne, Wyo., 1980—; chmn. bd. dirs. Goodwill Industries of Wyo., 1980-87. Treas. North Christian Ch., 1986, 87, 88, Salesman with a Purpose, 1980; mem. Heels, 1975—. Served to sgt. USMCR, 1963-71. Mem. Am. Inst. CPAs, Wyo. Soc. CPAs, Nat. Soc. Pub. Accts., Nat. Fedn. Ind. Businesses. Republican. Mem. Ind. Ch. of Christ. Lodges: Kiwanis, Masons. Home: 5533 Frederick Dr Cheyenne WY 82009 Office: 721 East 16th St Cheyenne WY 82001

PRICE, MARGARET RUTH, financial services company executive; b. Phoenix, Sept. 12, 1956; d. James John and Mavis Marie (Anderson) Knopp; m. Michael Reid Price, Sept. 15, 1979. BS in Instl. Food Svc. and Mgmt., Mont. State U., 1978. CFP; registered dietitian. Dir. nutrition programs Human Resource Devel. Coun., Bozeman, Mont., 1979-82; investment cons. Shearson Lehman Bros., Anchorage, 1982-85; v.p., investment cons. Boettcher & Co.-Kemper Fin. Svcs., Anchorage, 1985-88, Bateman Eichler, Hill Richards-Kemper Fin. Svcs., Anchorage, 1988—; nutrition cons., Bozeman, 1979-82; presenter radio talk show Sta. KENI, Anchorage, 1987. Mem. Alaska Pub. Interest Rsch. Group, 1986—; bd. dirs. Alaska Bot. Garden, 1987—; vol. Anchorage Community Schs.; mem. exec. com. Anchorage Employee Retirement Income Security Act, 1987—. Mem. Internat. Assn. Fin. Planners, Amnesty Internat., Anchorage Nordic Ski Club. Home: 831 Harbor Circle Anchorage AK 99515 Office: Bateman Eichler Hill Richards 550 W 7th St Ste 1980 Anchorage AK 99501

PRICE, MARTIN LLOYD, architect; b. San Mateo, Calif., July 12, 1958; s. Lloyd Ewart and Virginia Nancy (Schneider) P.; m. Brenda Carol Trayer, Oct. 24, 1987. AA, Santa Rosa (Calif.) Jr. Coll., 1978; BS in Architecture, U. Mich., 1981; BA in Mgmt., Sonoma State U., 1983. Lic. architect Calif., Colo. Architect Della & Hansen, Santa Rosa, 1978, 79, 83-84, Roland, Miller & Assocs., Santa Rosa, 1981, Keith, Hall & Bartley, Santa Rosa, 1982, 84-85; civil engr. Campbell & Pestell, Santa Rosa, 1985-86; architect Flewelling & Logsdon & Assoc., Santa Rosa, 1986-88; structural engr. Dennis Fagent Assoc., Santa Rosa, 1988—. Recipient Frank Doyle scholar Santa Rosa Jr. Coll., 1976-77, James B. Angell scholar U. Mich. 1981. Mem. U. Mich. Alumni Soc., Sonoma State U. Alumni Soc. Republican. Office: Dennis Fagent Assocs & Engrs 604-1/2 Seventh St Santa Rosa CA 95404

PRICE, PAUL BUFORD, physicist, educator; b. Memphis, Nov. 8, 1932; s. Paul Buford and Eva (Dupuy) P.; m. JoAnn Margaret Baum, June 28, 1958; children—Paul Buford III, Heather Alynn, Pamela Margaret, Alison Gaynor. B.S. summa cum laude, Davidson Coll., 1954, D.Sc., 1973; M.S., U. Va., 1956, Ph.D., 1958. Fulbright scholar U. (Eng.) Bristol, 1958-59; NSF postdoctoral fellow Cambridge (Eng.) U., 1959-60; physicist Gen. Elec. Research & Devel. Center, Schenectady, 1960-69; vis. prof. Tata Inst. Fundamental Research, Bombay, India, 1965-66; adj. prof. physics Rensselaer Poly. Inst., 1967-68; prof. physics U. Calif. at Berkeley, 1969—, chmn. dept. physics, 1987—; dir. U. Calif. at Berkeley (Space Scis. Lab.), 1979-85; dir. Terradex Corp., Walnut Creek, Calif., 1978-86; cons. for NASA (on Lunar Sample Analysis Planning Team); mem. space sci. bd. Nat. Acad. Scis.; vis. prof. U. Rome, 1983; sci. assoc. CERN, 1984; Miller research prof. U. Calif.-Berkeley, 1972-73; researcher on space and astrophysics, nuclear physics, particularly devel. solid state track detectors and their applications to geophysics, space and nuclear physics problems. Author: (with others) Nuclear Tracks in Solids; Contbr. (with others) articles to profl. jours. Recipient Distinguished Service award Am. Nuclear Soc., 1964, Indsl. Research awards, 1964, 65, E.O. Lawrence Meml. award AEC, 1971, medal exceptional sci. achievement NASA, 1973; John Simon Guggenheim fellow, 1976-77. Fellow Am. Phys. Soc., Am. Geophys. Union; mem. Nat. Acad. Scis. (chmn. geophysics sect. 1981-84, sec. phys.-math. scis. 1985-88, chmn. 1988—).

PRICE, ROBERT EDWARD, sales executive; b. Laan AFB, Asine, France, Feb. 25, 1956; s. Bobby Jess and Donna Jean (Hottle) P.; m. Dorinda Kay Massey (div. 1981); 1 child, Staci Gayle; m. JoAnn Olson Miller, Dec. 18, 1988. Student, Blinn Coll., 1974-75, U. Md., 1979-82, Dale Carnegie Course in Effective Speaking and Human Rels., 1988. Electronics tech. USAF, 1976-82, Lane Telecommunications, Houston, 1982-84; communications cons. Textel Communications, Houston, 1984-85; high tech. sales RCA, San Francisco, 1985-88; regional sales mgr. Master Systems, Pinole, Calif., 1989—. Unit comdr. Civil Air Patrol, N. Mex. and Eng., 1976-82, Houston, 1982-85, lt. col., Calif. wing ops., spl. projects mgr., 1988—; sr. arbitrator Better Bus. Bur., 1984—. Recipient Exceptional Svc. award Civil Air Patrol, 1982. Republican. Home: 487 Camelback Rd Pleasant Hill CA 94523 Office: Master Systems 1249 Pinole Valley Rd Pinole CA 94564

PRICE, SUSAN ELLEN, writer; b. New Brunswick, N.J., Aug. 17, 1943; d. John E. and Sabina L. P.; m. Clayton Dyer Root III (div. 1973). BA, Rutgers U., 1965. Columnist Chgo. Daily News, 1969-73; v.p. devel. David Susskind Co. MGM/United Artists, 1982-84; decorating editor House Beautiful, 1974-76; independent writer 1984-88; editor L.A. Style Mag., 1984—; cons. Wood Knapp Video, L.A., 1988. Contbr. articles to Mirabella, Harpers Bazaar, Town and Country, House and Garden, Elle, McCalls, Ladies Home Journal, and others. Recipient Best Mag. Reporting award nomination, Delta Sigma Chi, 1981. Mem. Independent Writers of So. Calif., Women in Film, So. Calif. Skeptics.

PRICE, TIMOTHY RICHARD, sales executive; b. Rapid City, S.D., Apr. 30, 1962; s. Earl Richard Price and Nadine Louise (Carpenter) Zeller; m. Leonna Dee Carter, Sept. 27, 1986. Floor mgr. Freed's Fine Furnishing, Rapid City, 1979-83; sales rep. McMahan's Furniture, Torrance, Calif., 1983-85, Monroe Bus. Systems, Garden Grove, Calif., 1985-86; regional sales mgr. Johdan Imports, Los Alimitos, Calif., 1986-88; v.p. sales Tremont Furniture, Santa Fe Springs, Calif., 1988—. Mem. U.S. Golf Assn. Republican. Home: 16630 Chicago Ave Bellflower CA 90706

PRICE, VIRGIL, investor, real estate associate; b. Boggy Depot, Okla., July 30, 1908; s. Stephen C. and Minnie M. (Rumelhart) Hieronymus; m. Viola Thomas, Aug. 26, 1933 (div. 1949); children: Dorothy Jean, Myrna Mae, Mary Ann; (widower Dec. 1979); 1 child, Stephen V. Grad. high sch. Free-lance investor. Commr. San Juan County, Utah. Home and Office: 216 E Mountain View Rd Phoenix AZ 85020

PRICE, WARREN, III, state attorney general; b. Washington, June 19, 1943; s. Warren II and Frances (Davis) P.; m. Johna Kanoho, Mar. 21, 1967 (div. Mar. 1987); children: Warren Price IV, Brandon Phillip Price. BA in Econs., U. N.C., 1965; JD, U. Calif., San Francisco, 1972. Ptnr. Goodsill, Anderson, Quinn and Stifel, Honolulu, 1972-87; atty. gen. State of Hawaii, Honolulu, 1987—; mem. Jud. Selection Commn., Honolulu, 1985-87. Served to lt. USNR, 1965-69. Mem. Nat. Inst. of Trial Advocacy (faculty 1984-87), Pacific Law Inst. (bd. dirs., faculty 1985—), Order of the Coif, Am. Inns of Ct. Democrat. Episcopalian. Office: Atty Gen's Office 415 S Beretania St Rm 405 Honolulu HI 96813

PRICE BODAY, MARY KATHRYN, choreographer, small business owner; b. Fort Bragg, N.C., May 20, 1945; d. Max Edward and Katharine (Jordan) P.; m. Les Boday (div. 1982); children: Shawn Leon Boday, Irmali Ferecho Boday; m. Richard A. Weil, May 1, 1986. BFA, U. Okla., 1968, MFA, 1970. Soloist dancer Mary Anthony Dance Co., N.Y.C., 1971-74, Larry Richardson Dance Co., N.Y.C., 1971-73; dancer Pearl Lang Dance Co., N.Y.C., 1971-73, Gaku Dance Theater, N.Y.C., 1972-74; ballet mistress and dancer St. Gallen Ballet, Switzerland, 1974-75; dancer, tchr. Zurich Ballet, Switzerland, 1975-76; asst. prof. U. Ill., Champaign-Urbana, 1976-79; artist-in-residence Cornish Inst., Seattle, 1979-80; pres. The Dance Work, Inc., Seattle, 1981—; tchr. Harkness Ballet of N.Y., Mary Anthony Dance Sch., Zurich Ballet, Nat. Acad. Arts Ill., Jefferson High Sch. of Performing Arts of Portland, choreographer; tchr. Summer Dance Lab; choreographer Mary K. Price Dance Co., U. Ill., Nat. Acad. Arts, Cornish Inst., Seahurst Ballet. Choreographer 3 ballets for Ballet Co. of St. Gallen, 1988. Outstanding Dancer award U. Okla., 1968; named one of Outstanding Young Women of Am., 1977.

PRICHARD, ROBERT ALEXANDER, JR., telecommunicatins engineer; b. Paris, Tex., Feb. 23, 1953; s. Robert Alexander and Reba Marie (Fields) P.; m. Debra Ruth Holbrooks, Apr. 9, 1977; children: Robert Ross, Christopher Dean. BS, Trinity U., San Antonio, Tex., 1975; cert. communications engring., Capitol Radio Engring. Inst., Washington, 1978; MS in Telecommunications, Denver U., 1989. Owner Stamford (Tex.) Communications, 1979-85; sr. telecommunications engr. Martin-Marietta Data Systems, Denver, 1985-86, mgr. plans and analysis, 1986-87; supr. telecommunications engring. Pub. Svc. Co. Colo., Denver, 1987—; cons. broadcast engr. Sta. KDWT Radio, Stamford, 1980-86; chief sound engr. Univ. Hills Bapt. Ch., Denver, 1987. Adjunct tchr. Denver Jr. Achievement, 1986. 1st lt. U.S. Army, 1975-79. Named One of Outstanding Young Men Am., 1985. Mem. Nat. Assn. Radio and Telecommunications Engrs. (cert.), Alpha Chi. Republican. Baptist. Office: Pub Svc Co Colo 969 Broadway Denver CO 80203

PRICKETT, DAVID CLINTON, physician; b. Fairmont, W.Va., Nov. 26, 1918; s. Clinton Evert and Mary Anna (Gottschalk) P.; m. Mary Ellen Holt, June 29, 1940; children: David C., Rebecca Ellen, William Radcliffe, Mary Anne, James Thomas, Sara Elizabeth. AB, W.Va. U., 1944; MD, U. Louisville, 1946; MPH, U. Pitts., 1955. Intern, Louisville Gen. Hosp., 1947; surg. resident St. Joseph's Hosp., Parkersburg, W.Va., 1948-49; gen. practice, 1949-50, 55-61; physician USAF, N.Mex., 1961-62, U.S. Army, Calif., 1963-64, San Luis Obispo County Hosp., 1965-66, So. Calif. Edison Co., 1981-84; assoc. physician indsl. and gen. practice Los Angeles County, Calif., 1967—; med. dir. S. Gate plant GM, 1969-71; physician staff City of L.A., 1971-76. Med. Officer USPHS, 1953-55, surgeon, res. officer, 1957-59; pres. W.Va. Pub. Health Assn., 1951-52, health officer, 1951-53, sec. indsl. and pub. health sect. W.Va. Med. Assn., 1956. Author: Public Health, A Science Resolvable by Mathematics. Served to 2d lt. AUS, 1943-46. Named to Hon. Order Ky. Cols. Mem. Am., Western occupational med. assns., Am., Calif., L.A. County med. Assns., Am. Acad. Family Physicians, Phi Chi. Address: PO Box 4032 Whittier CA 90607

PRIDE, KENNETH RODNEY, lawyer, consultant; b. L.A., Dec. 31, 1953; s. James Allen and Mable Louise (Jones) P.; divorced; children: Kenneth Rodney II, Jason Alexander. AA, Los Angeles Harbor Coll., 1975; BA, U. So. Calif., 1977; JD, Loyola U., Los Angeles, 1982; MBA, Pepperdine U., 1988. House counsel Mark Industries, Long Beach, Calif., 1982—; chmn. Am. Equipment Ins. Ltd., Cayman Islands; bd. dirs. Mark Credit Corp, Powered Mobile Platforms Corp, Mark Comml. Fin. Corp, Mark Industries Corp.; cons. Golden West Risk Mgmt. Inc., Los Angeles, 1986—. Author: The Cook Book for Men, 1986. Active Los Angeles County Cen. Com., 1974-79, State Cen. Com., Calif., 1975-78; asst. scout master Boy Scouts Am. Served with USAF, 1971-73. Recipient Outstanding Community Service Resolution Calif. State Legis., 1975. Mem. Farm and Indsl. Equipment Inst. (legal and legis. com. 1983—). Roman Catholic. Home: 6520 Selma Ave Hollywood CA 90028 Office: 4204 Palos Verdes Dr Rancho Palos Verdes CA 90274

PRIDGEON, JAMES STEPHEN, artist, research administrator; b. Nashville, Feb. 26, 1948; s. James McCoy and Angilee Frankie (Power) P.; m. Nancy Daryl Farher Pridgeon, June 13, 1970 (div. May 1975); children: Elinor Daryl, Benjamin Shand; m. Carol Edith Fahrenbruch Pridgeon, Dec. 17, 1977. BA, Stanford U., 1970. Adminstrv. asst. Stanford Hosp., Calif., 1970-72; intern, office of the sec. HEW, Washington, 1972-73; adminstrv. resident Univ. Hosp. U. Wash., Seattle, 1973-74; adminstrv. staff Univ. Hosp. U. Wash., 1974-75, adminstr. Regional Epilepsy Ctr., 1975-81, dir. of devel. Neurosurgery Epilesy Ctr., 1981—; cons. artist space sta. task force NASA, Goddard, Md., 1983-84. Contbr. articles to profl. jours. Mem. Centennial Arts Com., Wash., 1986-88, Seattle Artists '88, Seattle Arts Commn., 1988; design team artist Wash. State Arts Commn., 1986—; bd. dirs. Western Wash. Epilepsy Assn., Seattle, 1977-79, Wash. State Citizens for Space, 1987—, King County Bd. for Devel. Disabilities, Seattle, 1977-80. Fellow Art Matters, Inc., 1985; recipient Nat. Endowment for Arts Visual Arts Fellow/NEA, 1984. Mem. Soc. Research Adminstrn. (pres. 1988—, Seattle chpt.), Am. Assn. for Advancement of Sci. Office: Neurosurgery Epilesy Ctr 325 9th Ave Seattle WA 98104

PRIEST, LETA DENISE, marketing executive; b. Columbus, Ohio, July 13, 1959; d. Donald Raymond and Daphne Josephine (Dietrich) P. Student, Ohio U., 1981. Mktg. analyst Shasta Beverages, Columbus, 1982-84; asst. product mgr. Shasta Beverages, Hayward, Calif., 1984-85; asst. product mgr. Dole Packaged Foods, San Francisco, 1986, product mgr., 1986-87, sr. product mgr., 1987, bus. dir., 1988-. Republican. Roman Catholic. Home: 1901 Shoreline Dr #102 Alameda CA 94501

PRIESTLEY, CAROL LYNN, image consultant company executive; b. Salt Lake City, Sept. 8, 1943; d. John Cope and Bernice (Haigh) Sudbury; m. Byron Priestley, June 1, 1963 (dec. 1983); children: Byron, Leslie, Michael, Eric. BA, U. Utah, 1965; MA, Henneger Bus. Coll., 1966. Cert. make-up artist. Dir., trainer John Robert Powers Co., Salt Lake City, 1967-74; dir., v.p. Acad. of Fashion Arts, Salt Lake City, 1974-76; nat. sales mgr. Chambre Cosmetic Corp., Austin, Tex., 1976-81; co-owner Personal Mktg./The Elitist, El Toro, Calif., 1981-86; pres. Personal Image Mktg. Corp., El Toro, 1986—; fashion cons. Pulling-It-All-Together Seminars, 1976-86, Century 21, Anaheim, Calif., 1986—; image cons. Miss Universe Beauty Pageant, Salt Lake City, 1973. Fund raiser, Rep. Party, Newport Beach, Calif., 1984. Mem. NAFE (dir. 1979), El Toro C. of C., Fullerton C. of C., Cosmopolitan Club (co-chairwoman 1982). Republican. Mormon. Office: Personal Image Mktg Corp 23532 El Toro Rd #8 El Toro CA 92630

PRIESTLEY, MITCHELL BLAINE, computer training company executive; b. Portland, Oreg., Jan. 10, 1963; s. Chester Carroll and Darlene Blanche (Jeske) P. Student, Multnomah Sch. Bible, Portland, 1988. Computer instr. Oreg. Mus. Sci. and Ind., Portland, 1979-81; ptnr., mgr. Portland Computer Svcs., 1981-83; computer instr. Portland Community Coll., 1984-85; pres., br. mgr. Computer Edn. Internat., Inc., L.A., 1984-87; pres., chief exec. officer Computer Edn. Internat., Inc., Beaverton, Oreg., 1980—; cons. First Interstate Bank Calif., L.A., 1984-87; trainer/cons. Grossmont Bank, San Diego, 1985-87; trainer San Diego Trust & Savs. Bank, 1986-87. Missionary/discipler Reign Ministries/Royal Servants, Europe, 1987; evangelism trainer Calvary Bible Ch., Burbank, Calif., 1986-87; missionary Reign Ministries/Royal Servants, Middle East, Asia, 1988. Mem. Beaverton C. of C., Portland C. of C., Van Nuys C. of C., Rotary. Republican. Mem. Evangelical Ch. Home: 11624 SW Iron Horse Ln Beaverton OR 97005 Office: Computer Edn Internat Inc 8285 SW Nimbus Ave Ste 102 Beaverton OR 97005

PRIETO, VICENTE, chiropractor; b. Moline, Ill., May 19, 1947; s. John Mariano and Dolores (Hernandez) P. AA in Psychology, Black Hawk Coll., 1967; student, Mac Murray Coll., Jacksonville, Ill., 1967-69; Doctor of Chiropractic, Palmer Coll. of Chiropractic, Davenport, Iowa, 1978. Cert. chiropractic sports physician. Pvt. practice Phoenix, 1980—; bd. eligible chiropractic orthopedist, L.A. Coll. Chiropractic grad. sch., 1986—. Foster parent World Vision, Peru, S.Am., 1984—. With USN, 1970-71. Recipient MacMurray Coll. athletic scholarship, MacMurray Coll., Jacksonville, Ill., 1967, 68. Mem. Am. Chiropractic Assn., Chiropractic Assn. Ariz. (del. Phoenix dist. 14 1982-85), Am. Coll. Chiropractic Orthopedists, Coun. on Nutrition, Coun. on Sports Injuries and Physical Fitness. Roman Catholic. Office: Prieto Chiropractic Office 549 W Southern Ave Phoenix AZ 85041

PRIETTO, CAROLE ANNE, library assistant; b. L.A., Jan. 11, 1962; d. William Albert Jr. and Charlotte Marilyn (Mercurio) P. BA, U. Calif., Santa Barbara, 1984; MA, U. Calif., L.A., 1987. Libr. asst. UCLA Archives, 1986—. Mem. Am. Classical League. Democrat. Roman Catholic. Office: UCLA Archives 134 Powell Libr Los Angeles CA 90024

PRILIKA, ROBERT ANTHONY, electrical engineer; b. Denver, July 13, 1961; s. Anthony Michael and Kathy (Palan) P.; m. Lynda Susan Prilika, May 17, 1986. BA, U. Colo., 1984. Registered profl. engr. Elec. apprentice Blair Electric Co., Broomfield, Colo., 1972-76; dir., v.p. Reliable Electric Co., Inc., Denver, 1976—; sr. project mgr., estimator Run-Nel Electric Co., Denver, 1987—; cons. A&K Investments, Denver, 1984—, Reliable Electric Co., Inc., Denver, 1987—. Mem. Associated Builders and Contractors, Associated Gen. Contractors, Apt. Assn. of Metro Denver, U. Colo. Alumni Assn. Methodist. Home: 13712 W Warren Dr Lakewood CO 80228 Office: Reliable Electric Co Inc 1740 S Broadway Denver CO 80210

PRIMES, GARY LOUIS, service merchandising company executive; b. L.A., Mar. 17, 1959; s. James Howard and Stephanie Kay (Miller) P. BArch with honors, Calif. Poly. State U., 1981. Data processing mgr. Merchandising Unltd., San Diego, 1981-85, head buyer, 1982-85, v.p. ops., 1985—; v.p. ops. Merchandising Unltd. Ariz., Phoenix, 1985—; mem. adv. bd. Nat. Back to Sch. Mdse. Show, 1987-90. Mem. Nat. Coun. Archtl. Registration Bds. Jewish. Office: Tash Inc MU Div 5502 W Hadley Phoenix AZ 85043

PRIMM, RICHARD KIRBY, physician; b. Thomasville, N.C., May 23, 1944; s. Richard Wesley and Gertrude (Berrier) P.; m. Sharon Kay Lucas, Dec. 28, 1968; children: Heather, Lucas. BA, Duke U., 1966; postgrad., Baylor U., 1966-67; MD, U. N.C., 1970. Intern internal medicine Vanderbilt U. Hosp., Nashville, 1970-71, resident in internal medicine, 1973-75, chief resident, 1975-76; fellow cardiovascular diseases U. Ala., Birmingham, 1976-78, chief fellow, instr. medicine, 1978-79; asst. prof. medicine Vanderbilt U. Sch. Medicine, Nashville, 1979-84; staff cardiologist Wenatchee (Wash.) Valley Clinic, 1984--; clin. asst. prof. medicine U. Wash., Seattle, 1985--; dir. dept. cardiology Wenatchee Valley Clinic, 1987--. Contbr. articles to profl. jours. Med. dir. Wenatchee Cardiac Rehab. Program, 1985--. Capt. U.S. Army, 1971-73. Recipient Heusner Pupil award U. N.C., 1969, Hillman Teaching Excellence award Vanderbilt U., 1976. Fellow Am. Coll. Cardiology; mem. Am. Heart Assn., AMA, U. N.C. Alumni Coun., Wash. Heart Assn., Alpha Omega Alpha. Democrat. Home: 141 Heather Ln Wenatchee WA 98801 Office: Wenatchee Valley Clinic 820 N Chelan Ave Wenatchee WA 98801

PRINCE, BETTY JEAN, realtor; b. Richmond, Kans., Feb. 1, 1935; d. Paul Emet Keithley and Mildred Leota (Gifford) Heffley; m. Melvin J. Wynia, Oct. 24, 1950 (div. Mar. 1977); children: Gregg A., Michelle L.; m. Homer C. Prince, Sept. 22, 1977. Student, Colo. Real Estate Inst., Casper, Wyo., 1977, N.Mex. Real Estate Coll., 1978. Realtor Miracle Realty, Casper, 1977-78, 80-82, Albuquerque, 1978-79; realtor Arrow Realty, CAsper, 1982-83, Wright Properties, Bakersfield, Calif., 1983-87, Century 21 Crosstown Realty, Bakersfield, 1987-88, Stroope Realtors, Bakersfield, 1988—; v.p. Century-21 Nat., 1988. Bd. dirs. St. Lukes Fellowship, Bakersfield, 1982—; registrar Pat Robertson Presdl. Campaign, Bakersfield, 1988. Mem. Bd. Realtors, PTA (v.p. 1975-76). Republican. Office: Stroope Realtors 8200 Stockdale Hwy Bakersfield CA 93304

PRINDLE, ROBERT WILLIAM, geotechnical engineer; b. Los Angeles, Nov. 19, 1950; s. Robert Edward and Margaret Elizabeth (Johnson) P.; m. Nancy K. Hayden, Apr. 5, 1986. Student St. John's Coll., Camarillo, Calif., 1968-70; BSCE summa cum laude, Loyola U., Los Angeles, 1974; MS, Calif. Inst. Tech., 1975. Lic. geotechnical engr., Calif.; registered profl. civil engr., Calif. Engring. aide Los Angeles County Sanitation Dists., 1973-74; student engr. Los Angeles Dept. Water and Power, 1974, 75; staff engr. Fugro, Inc., Long Beach, Calif., 1976-78; sr. staff engr. Woodward-Clyde Consultants, Orange, Calif., 1978-79; mem. tech. staff Sandia Nat. Labs., Albuquerque, 1980-89, v.p. engring. Deuel & ASsocs, Inc., Albuquerque, 1989—. Mem. N. Mex. Symphony Orch. Chorus, 1981-84. Calif. State Grad. fellow, 1974-75, Calif. Inst. Tech. Inst. fellow, 1974-75. Mem. ASCE, NSPE, Internat. Soc. for Soil Mechanics and Found. Engring., Tau Beta Pi. Republican. Roman Catholic. Contbr. articles to profl. jours. Office: Deuel & Assocs Inc 7208 Jefferson St NE Albuquerque NM 87109

PRINTZ, THOMAS LEE, construction executive; b. Pueblo, Colo., Mar. 28, 1953; s. Charles Alf Printz and Shirley Ann (Murphy) Ratliff; m. Aug. 12, 1981 (div. Jan. 1987); children: Thomas Anthony, Jodi Marie. Student, So. Colo. U., 1971-72. Carpenter John Stavast, Pueblo, 1972-73, Bassett Constr. Co., Pueblo, 1973-76; v.p. Landmark Constrn. Co., Pueblo, 1976-79; pres. T.L. Printz Constr. Co., Pueblo, 1979—; bd. dirs. Pueblo Assn. Home Builders, Pueblo. Commn., mem. Pueblo Regional Bldg. Commn., Pueblo, 1988—; mem. Pueblo Econ. Devel. Mem. Associated Gen. Contractors Am., Pueblo Gen. Contractors, Colo. Contractors Assn., Pueblo C. of C., Pueblo Country Club. Democrat. Roman Catholic. Home: 63 MacAlester Rd Pueblo CO 81001 Office: T L Printz Contsrn Co 1114 N Erie Ave Pueblo CO 81001

PRITCHARD, JOEL, lieutenant governor; b. Seattle, May 5, 1925; m. Damaris Pritchard; children: Peggy, Frank, Anne, Jeanie. Student, Marietta Coll.; PhD (Hon.), Seattle U. Pres. Griffin Envelope Co., Seattle; mem. Wash. Ho. of Reps., Olympia, 1958-66 Wash. State Senate, 1966-70, U.S. Ho. of Reps., Washington, 1972-84; dir. govt. rels. Bogle & Gates, 1985-88; lt. gov. State of Wash., Olympia, 1989—; mem. Merchant Marine and

Fisheries Com. U.S. Ho. of Reps., subcom. on Asia and the Pacific Fgn. Rels. Com., Panama Canal Consultative Commn., 1987-88; U.S. del. to UN Gen. Assembly, 1983. With U.S. Army, PTO, WWII. Office: Lt Gov's Office 304 Legislature Bldg AS-31 Olympia WA 98504-0431

PRITCHARD, YVONNE TUDOR, administrator analyst; b. San Bernardino, Calif., Aug. 28, 1953; d. Martin and Barbara Tudor; m. John T. Pritchard, Apr. 17, 1982. BA, Calif. State Polytech. U., 1976; MPA, U. So. Calif., 1979. Personnel analyst County of San Bernardino, San Bernardino, 1976-79; sr. compensation analyst U. Calif., L.A., 1979; personnel analyst City of San Bernardino, 1980-84; staff analyst mun. ct. County of San Bernardino, 1984-86; sr. adminstrv. analyst County of Riverside, Riverside, Calif., 1986—. Chairperson San Bernardino County Commn. on the Status of Women, 1986. Mem. Am. Soc. Pub. Adminstrn., Inland Area Personnel Mgmt. Assn. (treas. 1982-84, pres. 1984-85), Bus. and Profl. Women (treas. 1986). Republican. Episcopalian. Office: County of Riverside Health Adminstrn Bldg 4065 County Circle Dr 4th Fl Riverside CA 92503

PRITZ, MICHAEL BURTON, neurological surgeon; b. New Brunswick, N.J., Oct. 8, 1947; s. John Ernest and Helen Violet (Rockoff) P.; m. Edmay Marie Gregorcy, Feb. 18, 1973; children: Edmond Louis, Benjamin David. BS, U. Ill., 1969; PhD, Case Western Res. U., 1973, MD, 1975. Diplomate Am. Bd. Neurol. Surgery. Asst. prof. neurol. surgery U. Calif. Irvine Med. Ctr., Orange, 1981-85, assoc. prof., 1985—. Contbr. articles to profl. jours. Recipient Herbert S. Steuer award Case Western Res. U., Cleve., 1975; NSF fellow, 1968; Edmund J. James scholar U. Ill., Champaign, 1968-69. Mem. Soc. Neurosci., Am. Assn. Anatomists, Am. Assn. Neurol. Surgeons, Congress Neurol. Surgeons, Soc. Neurol. Surgeons of Orange County (pres. 1985-86, sec.-treas. 1984-85). Office: U Calif Irvine Med Ctr 101 City Dr S Orange CA 92668

PRITZKER, STEVEN, television and film writer and producer; b. Chgo., Nov. 7, 1939; s. Max Richard and Marion (Jaffe) P.; m. Blythe Egan, July 6, 1974; 1 child, Sonya. BSBA, Northwestern U., 1962; MS in Edn., U. So. Calif., 1982. Writer-producer for TV and films various studios, 1967-74, Steven Pritzker & Assocs. Ltd., Santa Monica, Calif., 1974—; guest lectr. various univs. including Stanford U., UCLA, 1974—. Exec. editor, TV show Room 222; writer TV show Mary Tyler Moore Show, 1970-72; writer, producer TV shows Silver Spoons, 1982-85, Valerie, 1986. Vol. Big Bros. Am., L.A., 1964-76; counselor Pasadena (Calif.) Clinic, 1982-83; bd. dirs. Parents Anonymous Calif., 1984-87, pres., 1985-86. Recipient Commendation Parents Anonymous Calif., 1987. Mem. ASCAP, Writers Guild Am. West (nominee award, 1970), Acad. TV Arts and Scis. Jewish. Office: Freedman Kinzelberg & Broder 2121 Avenue of Stars 9th Fl Los Angeles CA 90067-5003

PROBER, ALEXANDRA JAWORSKI, educator; b. Nadryb, Poland, Dec. 11, 1907; came to U.S., 1912; d. Leon and Wladyslawa (Bojkowska) Jaworski; widowed; children: Walter, Martha, Thomas. AA, Pasadena (Calif.) City Coll., 1954, BA, 1957; MA, L.A. State U., 1965. Cert. tchr., Calif. Treas., mgr. AR-EX Cosmetics, Chgo., 1937-43; legal sec. Warner Bros. Studio, Burbank, Calif., 1943; tchr. Sierra Madre (Calif.) Schs., 1960-61, Pasadena Unified Sch. Dist., 1962-73, L.A. City Coll., 1980-81; reader Nat. Edn. Assn., 1988—. Contbr. articles and poems to profl. jours. Vol. UCLA Hosp., 1981-84; lectr. for various civic groups, 1980; active Friends of Huntington Library. Recipient 4th prize Nat. Writers Club Article Contest, 1983, 5th prize poetry 1988, 1st prize for poetry Vega mag., 1983, Golden Poet award World of Poetry, 1985, 87, 88. Mem. AAUW, Nat. League Am. Pen Women, Sherlock Holmes Club, Pi Lambda Theta, Calif. State U. Alumni Assn., UCLA Alumni Assn., Calif. Tchrs. Assn. (life, TEPS com. 1938-43, hiring com, 1942), Variety Club Charities (pub. chmn. 1982). Home: 1274 Sonoma Dr Altadena CA 91001

PROBERT, GEOFFREY, electrical engineer; b. St. Louis, Apr. 17, 1950; s. Geoffrey and Opal Beatrice (Myers) P.; m. Vi Marie Newcomb, Feb. 6, 1987. BSEE, U. Mo., 1972; MSEE, U. Colo., 1975. Mem. tech. staff Bell Telephone Labs., Denver, 1972-78; staff engr. STC Communications, Louisville, Colo., 1978-83; mgr. hardware Telwatch, Boulder, Colo., 1983—. Patentee in field. Computer software and electronics designer Faith Bible Chapel, Arvada, Colo., 1980—. Republican. Pentecostal Ch. Home: 1435 E Abilene Dr Broomfield CO 80020 Office: Telwatch 2905 Wilderness Pl Boulder CO 80301

PROBSTFELD, DOUGLAS LANE, infosystems specialist; b. Tacoma, Wash., Mar. 21, 1946; s. Howard Herbert Probstfeld and Naomi June (Hazelton) Cole; children: Eric Scott, Ryan Thomas. BSEE, Wash. State U., 1972. Project engr. Underwriters Labs., Inc., Santa Clara, Calif., 1972-76; component/product safety engr. Intel Corp., Sunnyvale, Calif., 1976-80; mgr. corp. product regulations Intel Corp., Hillsboro, Oreg., 1980—; cons. various cos., 1982—. Bd. dirs. Solo Ctr., Portland, Oreg., 1986—. Sgt. USAF, 1964-68. Named Trainer of Yr., Intel Systems Engring., Hillsboro, Oreg., 1984. Mem. Product Safety Soc., Computer and Bus. Equipment Mfrs. Assn., Industry Adv. Conf. Underwriters Labs., Bergfruende Club, After Hours Club (Beaverton, Oreg.). Republican. Home: 10550 SW Barnes Rd Apt 2 Portland OR 97225-5238 Intel Corp: 5200 NE Elam Young Pkwy Hillsboro OR 97124-6497

PROCHASKA, EDWARD JOHN, JR., investment company executive; b. Braham, Minn., June 12, 1928; s. Edward John and Hazel (Ahearn) P.; m. Nancy E. Kelley, June 28, 1955; children: Daniel A., Kay E., Edward John III. Student, U. Minn., 1946-48, U. Ariz., 1948-50; cert. in pharmacy, Brooke Army Med. Sch., San Antonio, 1952; BA, Minn. Coll. Bus., 1956. Salesman Western Bio Chem. Co., Phoenix, 1958-60; sales mgr. Western Serum Co., Tempe, Ariz., 1960-70, v.p., 1970-82; pres. Wall-Ed Fin., Phoenix, 1982—; chmn. bd. dirs. Mobile Garden, Phoenix; bd. dirs. Ariz. Automated Equipment, Phoenix, Chemalytics, Tempe. Sgt. U.S. Army, 1951-54, Korea. Democrat.

PROCHASKA, JAMES JOSEPH, communications executive; b. Cleve., Sept. 1, 1943; s. James Charles and Helen Josephine (Skala) P.; m. Susan Howard, June 24, 1968 (div. Sept. 1975); children: Mark, Megan. BS in Constrn. Mgmt., Iowa State U., 1966. Registered profl. engr., Colo. Mgr. US West Communications, Denver, 1969—; pres. PLatte Valley Builders. Mem. Inst. for Internat. Edn., Denver, 1981—; leader Jr. Great Books Program, Archdiocese of Denver, 1985—. Lt. U.S. Army, 1966-69. Mem. Profl. Engrs. Colo., Nat. Soc. Profl. Engrs., Rocky Mountain Roadrunners (v.p. pub. rels., 1983) Denver. Republican. Roman Catholic. Home: 4303 S Zenobia St Denver CO 80236

PROCTOR, LARRY LEE, training company executive, software consultant; b. Santa Monica, Calif., Nov. 5, 1946; s. Austin and Roberta (Sperry) P.; m. Judy Ann Nowak, Mar. 10, 1972; 1 child, Jennifer. AA, Orange Coast Coll., 1967; BA, Humboldt State U., 1970. Sales rep. Burroughs Inc., Long Beach, Calif., 1970-71; MIS dir. Sambo's Restaurant, Santa Barbara, Calif., 1971-74; project mgr. So. Calif. Edison Co., Rosemead, Calif., 1974-83; pres. Proctor & Assocs., Long Beach, 1983-87, cons., 1984—; sr. v.p. prodn. and rsch. Emtech Edn. Corp., Santa Monica, 1987—; bd. dirs. Structural Devel. Formon, L.A. Fellow IEEE; mem. Data Processing Mgmt. Assn., SDF (bd. dirs.). Home: 11672 Kensington Rd Los Alamitos CA 90720 Office: Emtech Edn Corp 2401 Colorado Ave Santa Monica CA 90404

PROCTOR, RICHARD MACFARLANE, art educator, artist, writer, gallery owner; b. Detroit, Feb. 27, 1936; s. Edgar Elmer and Kathryn Isobel (Macfarlane) P. Student, Henry Ford Community Coll., 1954-55; BS in Art Edn., Mich. State U., 1959, MA in Painting, 1962. Teaching credential K-12. Art tchr. Dearborn (Mich.) Pub. Schs., 1959-60; teaching asst. Mich. State U., East Lansing, 1960-61, acting instr., 1961-62; instr. U. Wash., Seattle, 1962-64, asst. prof., 1964-69, assoc. prof., 1970—; co-owner, gallery dir., design cons. Childers/Proctor Gallery, Langley, Wash., 1983—. Author: Principles of Pattern for Craftsmen and Designers, 1969; (with others) Surface Design for Fabric, 1984 (Merit prize for tech. writing 1986). Exhibited in group shows at Mus. of Contemporary Crafts, N.Y.C., Seattle Art Mus., Detroit Art Inst., Henry Art Mus., Kresge Art Ctr., East Lansing, Kerns Gallery, Eugene, Oreg., Contemporary Crafts Gallery, Portland, Seattle U., Northwest Craft Ctr. and Gallery, Wichita (Kansas) Art Assn., Kittredge Gallery, Tacoma, Cornell U., Ithaca, N.Y., Alberta Coll. of Art, Cranbrook Acad. of Art, Wash. State Capitol Mus., Yaw Gallery, Birmingham, Mich., Greenville County Art Mus., S.C., Cerulean Blue Gallery, Seattle, Cheney Cowles Meml. Mus., Spokane, Bellevue Art Mus., Richard White Gallery, Seattle, Childers/Proctor Gallery, Smithsonian Instn. (travelling exhibition); represented in collections Seattle/Tacoma Internat. Airport, Unigard Ins. Group Hdqrs., Rainier Bank, Seattle, Peoples Bank, Bellevue, Safeco Ins. Hdqrs., Seattle Waterfront Banners, 1979. Bd. dirs., founding mem. Island Arts Council, Langley, 1979—; chmn. Design Review Bd. City of Langley, 1985—. Mem. N.W. Designer Craftsmen (pres. 1968-70), Surface Design Assn. (N.W. reg. rep. 1984-87), AAUP, NW Orchid Soc. (v.p. 1987—). Democrat. Episcopalian. Club: Useless Bay Golf and Country (Langley). Home: 118 Goodell Ln PO Box 458 Langley WA 98260 Office: U Wash Sch of Art DM-10 Seattle WA 98195

PROCTOR, RONALD CHARLES, investment firm executive; b. Key West, Fla., June 28, 1946; s. Russell Bynum and Rose Anna (Tomavic) P.; 1 son, Michael John. Cert. investment mgmt. analyst. Br. mgr. United Mortgage Co., Denver, 1975-79; mktg. staff ReMax of Am., Englewood, Colo., 1979; mktg. dir. ReMax of So. Calif., Tustin, 1979; pres. Proctor Real Estate, Inc., Littleton, Colo., 1980; stock broker OTC Net, Inc., Denver, 1981-82; sr. fin. planner Dominick & Dominick, Inc., Denver, 1982-83; assoc. v.p. Prudential-Bache Securities, Denver, 1983-88; pres. Prudent Man Investment Mgmt., Inc., Denver, 1988—. Served with Army Nat. Guard, 1966-71. Named Man of Yr. Ency. Americana, Denver, 1970. Mem. Investment Mgmt. Cons. Assn., Denver Bicycle Touring Club, League Am. Wheelman. Office: Prudent Man Investment Mgmt 3003 E 3d Ave Ste 302 Denver CO 80206

PROESCHER, WARD HORNBLOWER, entrepreneur, writer, public speaker; b. Cary, N.C., Aug. 31, 1935; s. Andrew Jay and Gladys (Jones) P.; m. Susan Dittmar, May 1, 1971; children; Tobin Dittmar, Morgan Boehm. BS in Indsl. Relations, U. N.C., 1958. Personnel supr. Campbell Soup Co., Modesto, Calif., 1960-62; sales mgr. U.S. Audio & Copy Corp., San Francisco, 1962-65; stockbroker Hornblower & Weeks-Hemphill, Noyes, San Francisco, 1966-73; founder, pres. Hornblower Yachts, Inc., Berkeley, Calif., 1973-80; prin., chmn. Hornblower, Upson, Monfils & Proeschcer, Pleasant Hill, Calif., 1985; pres. Sea Ventures, Inc., Fla., 1975—; founder Commodore Cruises, Oakland, Calif., 1986—; founder, pres. Data Tab Inc., Castro Valley, Calif., 1982. Author: Secrets of Success-Techniques for Building Greater Personal Effectiveness; founder, host (TV show) How Now Mr. Dow?, The Ward Proescher Forum, 1968-72; pub. Montgomery Street Opinion, 1968-70; founder seminars Secrets of Success. Bd. dirs. Andrew and Gladys Proescher Ednl./Vocat. Loan Fund, 1975—. Served with USN, 1958-60. Mem. Internat. Platform Assn., Nat. Speakers Assn., Bay Area Speakers Service (v.p. 1986—). Clubs: Little Venice Yacht (Stockton, Calif.) (fleet capt. 1984); Campbell Soup Mgmt. (Modesto) (pres. 1961-62). Home: 3266 Elvia St Lafayette CA 94549 Office: 91 Gregory Ln Ste 7 Pleasant Hill CA 94523

PROHOSKY, DONALD E., social worker; b. Omaha, Feb. 25, 1930; s. Joseph Prohosky and Anna Mae (Drost) Taylor; m. Holly Idelle Ringsby, Aug. 28, 1964 (dec. May 1973); 1 child, Kathleen Kay Feeken. BS, Regis Coll., 1952; MSW, Ariz. State U., 1985. Chem. dependency therapist Camelback Hosp. Inc., Phoenix, 1983—; social worker VA Med. Ctr., Phoenix, 1984—; counselor, educator City of Phoenix DWI Ctr., 1984-85; mem. Research Soc. Process-Oriented Psychology, Zurich. Mem. Nat. Assn. Social Workers, Ariz. Bd. Cert. Alcoholism Counselors, Nat. Assn. Alcoholism and Drug Abuse Counselors, Phoenix Friends Carl Jung. Democrat. Roman Catholic. Home: PO Box 15072 Phoenix AZ 85060 Office: VA Med Ctr 7th St and Indian Sch Rd Phoenix AZ 85012

PROKOP-ROBERTS, JOAN DIANE, nurse, dance educator; b. Berwyn, Ill., June 24, 1946; d. Otto James and Pauline Anne (Smith) Prokop; m. Ronald Roberts, Aug. 1972 (div. Aug. 1976). BS in Nursing, U. Md., 1968; M in Nursing, UCLA, 1976. RN, Calif. Staff nurse surg. unit, relief nurse supr. Victor Valley Hosp., Victorville, Calif., 1971-72; surg. asst. Dr. Richard Dauphine, Monterey, Calif., 1972-87; nursing supr. Sherman Oaks (Calif.) Community Hosp., 1975, Eskaton Monterey Hosp., Monterey, Calif., 1976-84, Natividad Med. Ctr., Salinas, Calif., 1984-85; sr. instr. Natividad Med. Ctr., Salinas, 1985—; coord., instr. Pro-Ed Svcs., Marina, Calif. Contbr. articles to Orthopedic Nursing Jour. Maj. U.S. Army Nurse Corps, 1968-71, with USAR, 1972-87. Mem. Nat. Assn. Orthopedic Nurses, Bay Area Nursing Diagnosis Assn., Sigma Theta Tau. Home: 119 Redondo Ct Marina CA 93933 Office: Natividad Med Ctr 1330 Natividad Rd Salinas CA 93912

PROPHET, MATTHEW WALLER, JR., school superintendent; b. Okolona, Miss., Apr. 4, 1930; s. Matthew Waller and Elzira Elise (Walker) P.; m. Freddye Maxine Adams, Jan. 17, 1954; children—Michael, Matthew, Tony Michelle. B.Gen. Edn., U. Omaha, 1960; M.A. in Ednl. Supervision and Adminstrn., Roosevelt U., 1970; Ph.D., Northwestern U., 1972. Enlisted U.S. Army, 1951; commd. 2d lt., 1952; advanced through grades to comdr.; various assignments in Germany, Korea, other countries; advisor to Ohio N.G., 1964-65; personnel mgmt. advisor, Vietnam, 1965-66; chief ind. tng. 5th U.S. Army, Fort Sheridan, Ill., 1967-71; dep. supt. Lansing Sch. Dist., Mich., 1972-1978, supt., 1978-82; supt. Portland Pub. Schs., Oreg., 1982—; adj. prof. Coll. Edn. Mich. State U., East Lansing, Mich., 1974-82; coordinator Edn. Policy Fellowship Program, Mich., 1975-82; dir. Inst. Ednl. Leadership, Inc., Washington. Active United Way, Jr. Achievement, Mich. Soc. to Prevent Blindness, others. Decorated Bronze Star, Air medal, Legion of Merit, others. Mem. Mich. Assn. Sch. Adminstrs. (former nat. del.), Am. Assn. Sch. Adminstrs., Nat. Program for Ednl. Leadership, Mich. Middle Cities Edn. Assn., Area Educators Committed to Cooperation (former chmn.), Roundtable (Ingham County), Edn. Policy Fellowship Program, Adv. Council for Equal Ednl. Opportunity, Ret. Officers Assn. (U.S. Army), Alpha Chi, Phi Delta Kappa. Office: Portland Pub Schs 501 N Dixon Portland OR 97227 *

PROPST, MICHAEL TRUMAN, pathologist; b. Lebanon, Oreg., July 3, 1940; s. Lynn Edward and Vera Ruth (Forbes) P.; m. Susan Jean Joesting, Dec. 26, 1974; children: Christopher M., Andrew J., Matthew A., Michael Jonathan, Edwin Cam. BS, Oreg. State U., 1962; MD, U. Oreg., 1966. Diplomate Am. Bd. Pathology. Pathologist Humana Hosp., Anchorage, 1974-84; med. examiner State of Alaska, Anchorage, 1975—; med. dir. Physicians Med. Lab., Anchorage, 1984—. Served to maj. USAF, 1971-74. Fellow Coll. Am. Pathologists, Am. Soc. Clin. Pathologists, Am. Acad. Forensic Scientists; mem. Nat. Assn. Med. Examiners, Alaska State Med. Assn. Episcopalian. Office: Physicians Med Lab 4335 Laurel Anchorage AK 99508

PROSSER, JOHN MARTIN, architect, educator, university dean, urban design consultant; b. Wichita, Kans., Dec. 28, 1932; s. Francis Ware and Harriet Corinne (Osborne) P.; m. Judith Adams, Aug. 28, 1954 (dec. 1982); children—Thomas, Anne, Edward; m. Karen Ann Cleary, Dec. 30, 1983; children—Timothy, Jennifer. B.Arch., U. Kans., 1955; M.Arch., Carnegie Mellon U., 1961. Registered architect, Kans., Colo. Architect, Robinson and Hissem, Wichita, 1954-56, Guirey, Srnka, and Arnold, Phoenix, 1961-62, James Sudler Assocs., Denver, 1962-68; ptnr., architect Nuzum, Prosser and Vetter, Boulder, 1969-73; from asst. prof. to prof. U. Colo., Boulder, U. Colo.-Denver, 1968—, acting dean, 1980-84, dean, 1984; dir. urban design U. Colo.-Denver, 1972-85; cons. John M. Prosser Assoc., Boulder and Denver, 1974—; vis. prof. urban design Oxford Poly. U., Eng., 1979; vis. Critic Carnegie Mellon U., U. N.Mex., U. Ariz., Wright Ingraham Inst., Colo. Coll., Ft. Lewis Coll. Author, narrator PBS TV documentary Cities Are For Kids Too, 1984. Prin. works include (with others) hist. redesign Mus. Western Art, Denver (design honor 1984), Villa Italia, Lakewood, Colo., Mt. Carbon Community Ctr., Lakewood, Republic Bldg. parking facility, Denver, Auraria Higher Edn. Ctr., Colo., Auto World, Fiarfield, Calif., Motor World, Colorado Springs Colo., Pueblo C. of C. campus plan and new classroom facilities, Ft. Lewis Coll., county comprehensive campus plan. Bd. dirs. Balarat Outdoor Edn. Assn., Denver, 1978-86, Cranmer Park Hilltop Assn., Denver, 1974—, Cherry Creek Found., Denver, 1981—; chmn. design rev. bd. Univs. Colo., Boulder, Denver and Colorado Springs, 1980—; mem. archtl. control com. Denver Tech. Ctr., 1984—, Meridian Internat. Bus. Ctr.; planning cons. Denver Trans Global Airport Environs Expansion Project. Served to capt., as pilot USAF, 1956-59. Co-recipient 2d place nat. award Am. Soc. Interior Designers, 1984, honor award Colo. Soc. Architects, 1984. Mem. AIA (v.p. Denver chpt. 1979-80, pres. 1983, v.p. Colo. chpt. 1972-73, treas. 1974-75, sec. Western Mountain region 1984-86, treas. Colo. Central chpt. 1977-78). Republican. Club: Denver Country (bd. dirs. 1984-88, pres. 1986-87). Lodge: Rotary. Home: 324 Ash St Denver CO 80220 Office: U Colo 1200 Larimer St Denver CO 80204

PROTIC, EMIL GEORGE, marketing executive; b. Novi Becej, Serbia, Yugoslavia, Feb. 23, 1948; came to U.S., 1980; s. George and Zorka (Boberic) P.; m. Jovanka Balac, Dec. 28, 1973; children: Milica, Zorica. BS in Econs., Sch. Econs., Belgrade, Yugoslavia, 1976; BS in Mktg., Barry U., Miami, Fla., 1982; MBA, Embry-Riddle Aero. U., Daytona Beach, Fla., 1983. With Yugoslav Airlines; mktg./sales mgr. Pan Am. Airlines, Ea. Europe, 1977-81; internat. cons. Miami, 1981-84; sales/mktg. mgr. co. Yugoslav Airlines, L.A., 1984; mktg. cons. Alto Loma, Calif., 1985—; conductor seminars, lectr. in field. Contbr. articles to profl. jours. Mem. Am. Mktg. Assn., Internat. Assn. Fin. Planners, Rotary. Republican. Serbian-Orthodox. Home and Office: 10959 San Mateo Pl Alta Loma CA 91701

PROUDFIT, DONNA MAE, marketing executive; b. Washington, Iowa, Nov. 28, 1951; d. Donald Eugene and Virginia Ruth (Warden) P. BS in Journalism, Iowa State U., 1974. Asst. dir. pub. relations St. Luke's Hosp., Cedar Rapids, Iowa, 1974-78; from adminstrv. asst. to v.p. LaCrosse (Wis.) Luth. Hosp., 1978-85; v.p. mktg. Franciscan Health Svcs. of Wash., Tacoma, 1985—. Mem. allocations com. United Way, Tacoma, 1986—; bd. dirs. Pierce Co. Diabetes Assn., Tacoma, 1985—; mem. Tacoma Art Museum, 1986—, Jr. League. Named one of Outstanding Young Women in Am., 1984. Mem. Am. Mktg. Assn. (Distbn. award 1986), Internat. Assn. Bus. Communicators, Am. Soc. for Bus. Communications, Iowa State U. Alumni Assn. (bd. dirs. 1984—). Republican. Methodist. Office: Franciscan Health Svcs Wash PO Box 2197 Tacoma WA 98401

PROUT, CARL WESLEY, history educator; b. Bakersfield, Calif., Apr. 19, 1941; s. George Hecla and Ruth (King) P. BA, U. Calif., Santa Barbara, 1964, MA, 1965; postgrad., U. Tenn., Knoxville, 1968-71, Am. U., Cairo, 1974, U. So. Calif., 1981, Ain Shams U., Cairo, 1981. Instr. history Santa Barbara Coll., 1965-66, U. Tenn., Knoxville, 1968-71; instr. Orange Coast Coll., Costa Mesa, 1966-68, asst. prof., 1971-73, assoc. prof., 1973-75, prof., 1975—; treas. Willmore Corp., 1980-81, sec., 1984-85, v.p., 1985-86, pres., chmn., 1988-89, also bd. dirs.; group facilitator Coastview Meml. Hosp., Long Beach, 1986-89. Research and publs. in field. Pres., chmn. bd. Alamitos Heights Improvement Assn., 1979-80, bd. dirs., 1980-82; mem. East Long Beach Joint Council, 1979-80, Local Coastal Planning Adv. Com., 1979-80. Recipient Salgo Outstanding Tchr. award, 1974-76. Mem. Am. Hist. Assn., Meml. West Alumni Club, Sigma Nu. Office: Orange Coast Coll 2701 Fairview Rd Costa Mesa CA 92626

PROUT, RALPH EUGENE, physician; b. Los Angeles, Feb. 27, 1933; s. Ralph Byron and Fern (Taylor) P.; m. Joanne Morris, Sept. 17, 1980; children: Michael, Michelle. BA, La Sierra Coll., 1953; MD, Loma Linda U., 1957; D of Nutri-Medicine (hon.), John F. Kennedy Coll., 1987. Diplomate: Nat. Bd. Med. Examiners. Intern Los Angeles County Hosp., 1957-58; resident internal medicine White Meml. Hosp., Los Angeles, 1958-60; resident psychiatry Harding Hosp., Worthington, Ohio, 1960-61; practice medicine specializing in internal medicine Napa, Calif., 1961-63; staff internist Calif. Med. Facility, Vacaville, 1963-68, chief med. officer, 1968-84; chief med. cons. Calif. Dept. Corrections, 1977-86, chief med. services, 1983; med. cons. Wellness Cons., Placerville, Calif., 1986—; pres. Total Living Inc., 1984—; instr. Sch. Medicine, Loma Linda U., 1965-66; clin. asso. U. Calif. at Davis Sch. Medicine, 1978-84; med. cons. Substance Abuse Pine Grove Camp, 1985—. Treas. Vacaville Republican Assembly, 1972-75; del. Republican Central Com. Solano County, 1975-78; Bd. dirs. Napa-Solano County United Crusade, Vallejo, Calif., 1969-71, v.p., 1970-71; bd. dirs. Project Clinic, Vacaville, 1974-77, Home Health Com. Inter-Community Hosp., Fairfield, 1978-80; pres. MotherLode Citizens for Drug-Free Youth, Amador County, 1985—. Named One of Outstanding Young Men of Am., 1968. Mem. Am. Nutrimed. Assn., Internat. Acad. Nutrition and Preventive Medicine, Inst. for Advancement Health, Calif. Soc. Treatment of Alcoholism and other Drug Dependencies, Nat. Fedn. Parents Drug-Free Youth, Mother Lode Citizens for Drug-Free Youth, Amador C. of C., Native Sons of Golden West, Alpha Omega Alpha. Republican. Home and Office: 24405 Shake Ridge Volcano CA 95689

PRUETT, RUTH ANN, realtor; b. Pampa, Tex., May 4, 1942; d. R.V. and Vivian (Hale) Plato; m. J. Tom Pruett, Oct. 21, 1960; children: Sundelei Kay, J. Tom II, Cortne Ann. Grad., Century Sch. Real Estate. Lic. realtor. Art gallery dir. Hobbs, N.Mex., 1974-78; realtor First Equity Realtors, Hobbs, 1978—; v.p. Option, Inc., Hobbs, 1988—. Mem. Nat. Assn. Realtors, N.Mex. Assn. Realtors, Hobbs Bd. Realtors (hospitality chmn. 1988-89), Grad. Realtors Inst. (cert.). Republican. Home: 1004 W Gold Hobbs NM 88240 Office: First Equity Realtors 1819 N Turner Hobbs NM 88240

PRUGH, VINCENT HAROLD, municipal goverment official; b. Omaha, Apr. 12, 1945; s. Harold Homer and Janice Belle (Fryer) P.; m. Lisa Rose Sohr, July 10, 1982; children: Jocelyn Belle, Justin Vincent. BA, UCLA, 1968; JD, U. Calif., San Francisco, 1972. Investigator Office of Dist. Atty., San Francisco, 1977-80, sr. investigator, 1980-82, sr. investigator in charge, 1982—. With USAR, 1963-71. Mem. Nat. Assn. Consumer Protection Investigators, Calif. Dist. Atty. Investigators Assn., No. Calif. Fraud Investigators Assn., San Francisco Dist. Atty. Investigator Assn. Democrat. Office: San Francisco Dist Atty 732 Brannan St San Francisco CA 94103

PRUITT, J. DOUG, construction executive; b. Duncan, Okla., June 22, 1945; s. Mike E. and D. Ruth (Kaiser) P.; m. Rebecca L. Black, July 6, 1968; children: Joey Lynn, Jeffrey Michael. AS in Civil Tech., Okla. State U., 1965; BSBA, U. Phoenix, 1983; postgrad., Stanford U., 1987. Estimator, project coord. M.M. Sundt Constrn. Co., Phoenix, 1966-71, chief estimator, 1971-75, mgr. constrn. mgmt. svcs., 1975-80, Phoenix area mgr., 1980-82, group v.p., 1982-84; sr. v.p. Sundt Corp., Phoenix, 1984—, also bd. dirs.; bd. dirs. Lincoln Health Resources Corp., Phoenix, John C. Lincoln Hosp. amd Health Ctr., Phoenix. Contbr. articles to profl. publs. Mem. Com. to Re-elect Sen. DeConcini, Phoenix, 1987—; mem. constrn. program adv. coun. Ariz. State U., 1988; bd. dirs. Phoenix Community Alliance, 1987—. With USAR, 1965-71. Mem. Associated Gen. Contractors Am. (mem. legis. com. Ariz. bldg. chpt. 1980—, spl. contracts com. 1987—), Ariz. Assn. Indsl. Devel., Ariz. C. of C. (bd. dirs. 1987—), Phoenix Country Club, La Camarilla Club. Office: Sundt Corp 2630 S 20th Pl Phoenix AZ 85034

PRUITT, KELLY BERNICE, early childhood educator; b. Vallejo, Calif., Aug. 1, 1956; d. Jack Joshua and B. Phyllis (Willoughby) Whittiker; m. Jerry Wayne Pruitt, Aug. 7, 1976; 1 child, Jeremy Wayne. AA in Social Sci., York Coll., 1976; BS in Social Work, Abilene Christian U., 1980; MA in Theology, Pepperdine U., 1983; MA in Edn. Adminstrn., U. San Francisco, 1985. Cert. elem. tchr., elem. sch. adminstr., Calif. Tchr. Young Children's World, Abilene, Tex., 1976-79; dir. Campbell (Calif.) Christian DayCare, 1980-81, tchr., curriculum dir., 1981-86; head tchr., prin., dir. Madison Sch., Redwood City, Calif., 1986-87; dir. HeadsUp! Child Devel. Ctr., San Jose, Calif., 1987-88; dir., prin. Mulberry Sch., San Jose, Calif., 1988—; lectr. seminars, classes Confs. on Early Childhood Edn., State Clif., 1987-88, lectures, classes Women's Church Retreats, Calif., 1985-88. Mem. Cupertino Hist. Mus., 1985-88, Women in Bus., San Jose, 1987-88; tchr., leader Ch. Christ activities, classes, Campbell, 1980-88. Recipient acad. scholarship Pepperdine U., 1982-83. Mem. Nat. Assn. Edn. Young Children, Edn. Young Children, Assn. For Childhood Edn. Internat., South Bay Coalition Employer-Supported Child Care, Peninsula Child Care Dirs. Assn., Assn. Christian Schs. Internat., San Jose C. of C., AAUW, Profl. Assn. Childhood Edn., Assn. Supervision and Curriculum Devel. Democrat. Home: 10962 Northseal Sq Cupertino CA 95134 Office: Mulberry Sch 1980 Hamilton Ave San Jose CA 95125

PRUSSIA, LELAND SPENCER, banker; b. San Jose, Calif., 1929; s. Leland Spencer and Doris E. (Fowler) P.; m. Vivian Blom; children: Leslie, Alan L., Gregory. BA in Econs., Stanford U., 1951, MA in Econs., 1956; grad. Advanced Mgmt. Program, Harvard U., 1970; D in Econ. (hon.), U. San Francisco, 1984. Research economist Bank of Am. Nat. Trust & Savs. Assn., San Francisco, 1956-62, with bank investments securities div., 1962-65, v.p. investment portfolio activities, 1965-71, sr. v.p. investment securities div., 1971-74; exec. v.p., chief fin. officer Bank of Am. Nat. Trust & Savs. Assn., BankAm. Corp., San Francisco, 1974-78, 84-86, exec. officer World Banking div., 1979-81; chmn. bd. BankAm. Corp., San Francisco, 1981-87, ret., 1987; adv. dir. Gen. Motors-Hughes Electronics Corp.; bd. dirs. Calif. Econ. Devel. Corp., chmn. Pacific Rim Task Force; bd. dirs. Dimensional Corp. Fin., Inc.; prin. Diversified Corp. Loans, Inc.; mem. Calif. Senate Commn. on Corp. Governance, Shareholders Rights, Securities Transactions; lectr. in econs., U. San Francsico, 1957-65. Author: The Changing World of Banking: Bank Investment Portfolio Management. Trustee U. San Diego, Neighborhood Housing Services Am.; bd. dirs. Council for Basic Edn., U. San Francisco, U. Calif. Santa Barbara Found., Com. For Responsible Fed. Budget, St. Francis Found. of St. Francis Meml. Hosp.; adv. council J.L. Kellogg Grad. Sch. Mgmt. Northwestern U., San Francisco State U. Sch. Bus.; chmn. bd. Calif. Nature Conservancy, gov. nat. orgn.; mem. San Francisco Bay Area Leadership Task Force, Bus. Com. for Arts; adv. bd. Holy Family Day Home. Mem. Am. Econ. Assn., Western Econ. Assn., Am. Fin. Assn., Securities Industry Assn. (former Calif. region chmn., former dir. gov. bd.), Security Analysts of San Francisco, Stanford Assocs., Am. Polit. Found. (bd. dirs.). Clubs: Commonwealth of Calif., San Francisco Bond, Bankers San Francisco, Merchants Exchange, Pacific-Union, Bohemian. Office: Bank of Am Ctr 9996 Unit 5th Fl PO Box 37000 San Francisco CA 94137 *

PRY, GEORGE LAWRENCE, art institute administrator; b. Denver, Mar. 23, 1952; s. James Russell and Flavia Elizabeth (Bridge) P.; m. Barbara Irene Bodnar, Oct. 20, 1979; children: Jessica Lee, Gregory Richard. BA with honors, St. Fidelis Coll., Herman, Pa., 1975; MA in Clin. Psychology, Indiana U. Pa., 1977. Registered counselor, Wash. Assoc. prof. psychology St. Fidelis Coll., 1977-80; dir. counselling svcs. Art Inst. Pitts., 1977-80, dir. student svcs., 1980-81; pres. Art Inst. Houston, 1981-84, Art Inst. Seattle, 1984—; sr. v.p. Edn. Mgmt. Corp.; v.p. Edn. Mgmt. Corp., Pitts., 1985-88, sr. v.p., 1988—. Mem. Nat. Assn. Trade and Tech. Schs. (condr. student svcs. workshops 1987, mem. appeals bd., teamleader accrediting commn. 1988—), Wash. Fedn. Pvt. Vocat. Schs. (bd. dirs.-at-large 1984-88, pres. 1987-88), Pa. Psychol. Assn. Roman Catholic. Home: 10917 154th Ave NE Redmond WA 98052 Office: Art Inst Seattle 2323 Elliott Ave Seattle WA 98121

PRYOR, PETER PATRICK, newspaper editor; b. N.Y.C., Mar. 5, 1946; s. Thomas Mathew and Marie (Schmidt) P. Student, Pierce Jr. Coll., Woodland Hills, Calif., 1964-65. With editorial dept. L.A. Times, 1968-71; news editor Daily Variety Ltd., Hollywood, Calif., 1971-73, mng. editor, 1973-88, editor, 1988—. With USN, 1965-68, including Vietnam. Office: Daily Variety Ltd 5700 Wilshire Blvd Los Angeles CA 90036

PRZASNYSKI, ZBIGNIEW HENRYK, quantitive management educator; b. London, Apr. 28, 1952; came to U.S., 1985; s. Zygmunt and Halina (Blaszczak) P.; m. Gigi Maria Berardi, July 1985. BSc, U. Sussex, Eng., 1972; PhD, U. Sussex, 1976; MSc, U. Essex, Eng., 1973. Lectr. Brighton (Eng.) Poly. U., 1976-77, North London Poly. U., 1978-85; assoc. prof. quantitive mgmt. Loyola Marymount U., L.A., 1985--. Mem. Inst. Mgmt. Sci., Decision Scis. Inst., Operational Rsch. Soc. Gt. Britain. Office: Loyola Marymount U 7107 W 80th St Los Angeles CA 90045

PUCCI, ROBERT FRANK, banker; b. Cleve., June 14, 1947; s. June Blossom (Urquhart) P.; m. Cynthia Rose Pleasant, June 8, 1968 (div. 1981); children: Robert, Christopher; m. Gail Ann Johnson, Sept. 20, 1982; 1 child, Anthony. BS, So. Oregon State U., Ashland, 1969; MBA, Portland State U., 1982. Loan adjustor U.S. Nat. Bank Oreg., Medford, 1973-74; loan officer U.S. Nat. Bank Oreg., Bend, 1974-77; br. mgr. U.S. Nat. Bank Oreg., Gladstone, 1977-81; asst. v.p. U.S. Nat. Bank Oreg., Portland, 1981-82, v.p., 1982-83; comptroller Kellum Motor Group Inc., Gladstone, 1983-84; area sales mgr. Citicorp Savs., Concord, Calif., 1984-86, area v.p., 1986-87; v.p. Citicorp Acceptance Co., Concord, 1987-89, Citicorp N.Am., Walnut Creek, Calif., 1989—; instr., trainer Citicorp Exec. Devel. Ctr., St. Louis, 1986—. Chmn. Clackamas County Community Action Agy., Gladstone, 1979-83; vol. Packwood Re-Election Campaign, Bend, 1974. Served with U.S. Army, 1970-73. Mem. Super Dealers' Round Table. Republican. Presbyterian. Club: Toastmasters. Lodge: Kiwanis (Disting. Lt. Gov. Portland 1981). Home: 2132 Ward Dr Walnut Creek CA 94596

PUCCINELLI, LEONARD, firearms designer; b. San Francisco, Jan. 13, 1933; s. Louis August and Lola (Giorgi) P. BS, U. San Francisco, 1954. Rep. P. Beretta, S.p.A. Italy, 1961; exclusive world rep. Armi Fabbri Italy, 1966-77; rep. Fratelli Rizzini Italy, 1973-84; rep. I.A.B. S.p.A. Italy 1978-84; dealer V. Bernardelli S.p.A. Italy, 1984-87; rep. Beretta U.S.A. Corp., Accokeek, Md., 1986-87; dealer Beretta U.S.A. Corp., Accokeek, 1987—; dir. The Saloon, Vail, Colo., 1976-86; owner, Puccinelli Galleries, San Francisco, 1979; weapons cons. Cagney-Lacy Prodns., Hollywood, Calif., 1987-88. Editor, designer: The Giorgi Sisters Cookbook, 1986; editor: Castellana mag., 1963-64. Contbr. Republican Party, Washington. 1st Lt. U.S. Army, 1955-57. Recipient Nat. Intercollegiate Individual Rifle Champion, U. Calif., 1955, German Nat. Shooting Championship, Dusseldorf, Germany, 1956; winner of more than 100 internat. shooting championships. Mem. NRA, Amateur Trapshooting Assn., Royal Soc. Shooting (Madrid). Republican. Roman Catholic. Home and Office: PO Box 2222 San Anselmo CA 94960

PUCCIO, BERNARDO ROBERT, interior designer; b. Birmingham, Ala., Feb. 24, 1944; s. Michael Joseph and Maggie (Lorino) P. BA, U. Ala., 1968. Interior designer Robinson Beverly Hills, Calif., 1968-70, Cannell & Chaffin, L.A., 1978-80; chief exec. officer Puccio Designs Inc., L.A., 1980—. Design projects included in L.A. Times, Designers West, L.A. mag., Town and Country mag., Archtl. Digest. Design chmn. AIDS Project Benefit. Mem. Am. Soc. Interior Designers. Home and Office: 935 N Westbourne Dr Los Angeles CA 90069

PUCK, THEODORE THOMAS, geneticist, biophysicist, educator; b. Chgo., Sept. 24, 1916; s. Joseph and Bessie (Shapiro) Puckowitz; m. Mary Hill, Apr. 17, 1946; children: Stirling, Jennifer, Laurel. B.S., U. Chgo., 1937, Ph.D., 1940. Mem. commn. airborne infections Office Surgeon Gen., Army Epidemiol. Bd., 1944-46; asst. prof. depts. medicine and biochemistry U. Chgo., 1945-47; sr. fellow Am. Cancer Soc., Calif. Inst. Tech., Pasadena, 1947-48; prof. biophysics U. Colo. Med. Sch., 1948—, chmn. dept., 1948-67, disting. prof., 1986—; dir. Eleanor Roosevelt Inst. Cancer Research, 1962—; Disting. research prof. Am. Cancer Soc., 1966—; nat. lectr. Sigma Xi, 1975-76. Author: The Mammalian Cell as a Microorganism: Genetic and Biochemical Studies in Vitro, 1972. Mem. Commn. on Physicians for the Future. Recipient Albert Lasker award, 1958; Borden award med. research, 1959; Louisa Gross Horwitz prize, 1973; Gordon Wilson medal Am. Clin. and Climatol. Assn., 1977; award Environ. Mutagen Soc., 1981; Heritage Found. scholar, 1983; E.B. Wilson medal Am. Soc. Cell Biology, 1984; Bonfils-Stanton award in sci., 1984; Phi Beta Kappa scholar, 1985. Fellow Am. Acad. Arts and Scis.; mem. Am. Chem. Soc., Soc. Exptl. Biology and Medicine, AAAS (Phi Beta Kappa award and lectr. 1983), Am. Assn. Immunologists, Radiation Research Soc., Biophys. Soc., Genetics Soc. Am., Nat. Acad. Sci., Tissue Culture Assn. (Hon. award 1987), Paideia Group, Santa Fe Inst. Sci. Bd., Phi Beta Kappa, Sigma Xi. Recipient U. Colo. Disting. Prof. award, 1987; ARCS Man of Sci. award, 1987. Office: Eleanor Roosevelt Inst for Cancer Rsch 1899 Gaylord St Denver CO 80206

PUCKETT, ALLEN EMERSON, aeronautical engineer; b. Springfield, Ohio, July 25, 1919; s. Roswell C. and Catherine C. (Morrill) P.; m. Betty J. Howlett; children—Allen W., Nancy L., Susan E.; m. Marilyn I. McFarland; children—Margaret A., James R. B.S., Harvard, 1939, M.S., 1941; Ph.D., Calif. Inst. Tech., 1949. Lectr. aeronautics, chief wind tunnel sect. Jet Propulsion Lab., Calif. Inst. Tech., 1945-49; tech. cons. U.S. Army Ordnance, Aberdeen Proving Ground, Md., 1945-60; mem. sci. adv. com. Ballistic Rsch. Labs., 1958-65; with Hughes Aircraft Co., Culver City, Calif., 1949—, exec. v.p., 1965-77, pres., 1977-78, chmn. bd., chief exec. officer, 1978-87; chmn. emeritus Hughes Aircraft Co., Culver City, 1987—; dir. Gen. Dynamics, Fluor, Logicon Investment Co. of Am., Am. Mut. Fund, Lone Star Industries; mem. steering group OASD adv. panel on aeros.; cons. Pres.'s Sci. Adv. Com.; chmn. rsch. adv. com. control, guidance and navigation NASA, 1959-64; vice-chmn. Def. Sci. Bd., 1962-66; mem. Army Sci. Adv. Panel, 1965-69, NASA tech. and rsch. adv. com., 1968-72, space program adv. coun. 1974-78; Wilbur and Orville Meml. lectr. Royal Aero. Soc., London, 1981. Author: (with Hans W. Liepmann) Introduction to Aerodynamics of a Compressible Fluid, 1947; editor: (with Simon Ramo) Guided Missile Engineering, 1959; contbr. tech. papers on high-speed aerodynamics. Trustee U. So. Calif. Recipient Lawrence Sperry award Inst. Aero. Scis., 1949, Lloyd V. Berkner award Am. Astronautical Soc., 1974; named Calif. Mfr. of Yr., 1980. Fellow AIAA (pres. 1972); mem. Aerospace Industries Assn. (chmn. 1979), Los Angeles World Affairs Coun. (pres.), Nat. Acad. Scis., Nat. Acad. Engring., AAAS, Sigma Xi, Phi Beta Kappa. Office: Hughes Aircraft Co PO Box 45066 Los Angeles CA 90045

PUCKETT, RICHARD EDWARD, artist, retired recreation executive; b. Klamath Falls, Oreg., Sept. 9, 1932; s. Vernon Elijah and Leona Belle (Clevenger) P.; m. Velma Faye Hamrick, Apr. 14, 1957 (dec. 1985); children—Katherine Michelle Briggs, Deborah Alison Bolinger, Susan Lin Rowland, Gregory Richard. Student So. Oreg. Coll. Edn., 1951-56, Lake Forest Coll., 1957-58; Hartnell Jr. Coll., 1960-70; B.A., U. San Francisco, 1978. Asst. arts and crafts dir., Fort Leonard Wood, Mo., 1956-57; arts and crafts dir., asst. spl. services officer, mus. dir., Fort Sheridan, Ill., 1957-59; arts and crafts dir., Fort Irwin, Calif., 1959-60, Fort Ord, Calif., 1960-86; dir. arts and crafts br. Art Gallery, Arts and Crafts Center Materials Sales Store, 1960. Recipient First Place, Dept. Army and U.S. Army Forces Command awards for programming and publicity, 1979, 80, 81, 83, 84, 85, 1st and 3d place awards Monterey County Fair Fine Arts Exhibit, 1979, Comdrs. Award for Civilian Svcs., 1986, numerous other awards. Mem. Am. Park and Recreation Soc., Am. Craftsman Assn., Glass Arts Soc., Monterey Peninsula Art Assn., Salinas Fine Arts Assn. One-man shows: Seaside City Hall, 1975, Fort Ord Arts and Crafts Center Gallery, 1967, 73, 79, 81, 84, 86, Presidio of Monterey Art Gallery, 1979; Glass on Holiday, 1981; also pvt. collections. Home: 1152 Jean Ave Salinas CA 93905 Office: Arts and Crafts Ctr Community Recreation Div 2250 2d Ave Fort Ord CA 92941

PUDNEY, GARY LAURENCE, television executive; b. Mpls., July 20, 1934; s. Lawrence D. and Agnes (Hansen) P. B.A., UCLA, 1956. V.p. ABC, Inc., N.Y.C., 1968—; v.p., sr. exec. in charge of spls. and talent ABC Entertainment, 1979-89; pres. The Gary L. Pudney Co., Beverly Hills, Calif., 1988—. Exec. producer for United Cerebral Palsy Aspen and Lake Tahoe Pro-Celebrity Tennis Festivals, 4 yrs., AIDS Project Los Angeles Dinner, 1985. Bd. dirs. Nat. Cerebral Palsy Found., Ctr. Theater Group Ahmanson Theater, Los Angeles. Served to capt. USAF, 1957-60. Recipient Helena T. Deveraux Meml. award, 1985, Humanitarian award Nat. Jewish Ctr. for Immunology and Respiratory Medicine, 1986, Gift of Love award Nat. Ctr. Hyperactive Children, 1988. Mem. Hollywood Radio and TV Soc. (bd. dirs.), Acad. TV Arts and Scis. (exec. com.), Met. Mus. Art, Mus. Modern Art. Democrat. Lutheran.

PUENTE, JOSE GARZA, safety engineer; b. Cuero, Tex., Mar. 19, 1949; s. Roque Leos and Juanita Vela (Garza) P.; m. Francisca Rodriguez Estrada, Sept. 7, 1969; 1 son, Anthony Burk. B.A., W. Tex. State U., Canyon, 1972; postgrad. U. Ariz.-Tucson, 1980; grad. U.S. Army transp. courses, 1972, 78. Cert. U.S. Council Accreditation in Occupational Hearing; cert. Audiometric Technicians of Am. Indsl. Hygiene Assn. Asst. gen. mgr. Am. Transit Corp., Tucson, 1972-75; pub. transp. supt. City of Tucson, 1975-77; asst. safety coordinator, Tucson, 1977-81; safety coordinator Mesa, Ariz., 1981-88; corp. safety dir. Am. Fence Corp., Phoenix, 1988—; owner La Paz Gospel Supplies & Gift shop, Tucson, 1979-80. Mem. Tucson Child Care Assn., 1973-74; mem. Citizen Task Force, Sunnyside sch. bd., 1977; co-founder Ray Morales Aid Fund, 1980. Serving as maj. USAR, 1971—. Fellow Advanced Mgmt. Seminar Urban Mass Transp. Adminstrn., Northeastern U., Boston, 1976-77; recipient Excellence award Ariz-Safety Assn., 1984. Mem. Am. Soc. Safety Engrs. (profl., Safety Profl. of Yr. 1984), Mexican-Am. Govtl. Employees (charter Tucson chpt.), Res. Officers Assn., Ariz. Safety Engrs., Ariz. Mcpl. Safety Assn. (Profl. of Yr. 1986), Internat. Platform Assn. Democrat. Baptist. Clubs: Internat. Order DeMolay (charter), Lions, Mesa Bowling League, Toastmasters. Home: 2253 S Estrella Mesa AZ 85202 Office: 2525 N 27th Ave Phoenix AZ 85009

PUGAR, ELOISE ANN, research chemist; b. Pitts.; d. Mark Louis and Olga Rose P. Student, Carnegie-Mellon U., 1974-76; BS summa cum laude, U. Pitts., 1978; PhD in Chemistry, U. Calif., Santa Barbara, 1988. Inorganic chemist Rockwell Internat., Thousand Oaks, Calif., 1982—. Contbr. articles to profl. jours. Patentee in field. Mem. AAAS, Am. Chem. Soc., Am. Inst. Chemists, Internat. Union of Pure and Applied Chemistry, Am. Ceramic Soc. (1st Place Ceramographic award 1984), N.Y. Acad. Arts and Scis. Republican. Office: Rockwell Internat Sci Ctr 1049 Camino Dos Rios Thousand Oaks CA 91360

PUGAY, JEFFREY IBANEZ, mechanical engineer; b. San Francisco, June 26, 1958; s. Herminio Salazar and Petronila (Ibanez) P. BSME, U. Calif., Berkeley, 1981, MSME, 1982; MBA, Pepperdine U., 1986. Registered profl. engr., Calif. Engring. asst. Lawrence Berkeley Nat. Lab., 1978-80; assoc. tech. staff Aerospace Corp., Los Angeles, 1981; technical head Hughes Aircraft Co., Los Angeles, 1982—. Mem. SME, Pi Tau Sigma. Republican. Roman Catholic. Home: 8180 Manitoba St 120 Playa del Rey CA 90293 Office: Hughes Aircraft Co. PO Box 92919 MS S21/E300 Los Angeles CA 90009

PUGH, HELEN PEDERSEN, realtor; b. San Francisco, Feb. 17, 1934; d. Christian Edward and Gladys Phoebe Zumwalt Pedersen; m. Howard Brooks Pugh, Sr., Oct. 11, 1974; children: Catherine Collier, Stephen Leach, Matthew Leach, Virginia Schmitt. AA, U. Calif., Berkeley, 1953. Pvt. sec. to exec. dir. Rep. party, Phoenix, 1972, Henderson Realty, Phoenix, 1973; sta. mgr. Mobil Oil Co., Phoenix, 1973-74; realtor, Russ Lyon Realty, Scottsdale, Ariz., 1978—. Vol. coordinator William Baker for Congress, Phoenix, 1972; vol. Phoenix Meml. Hosp., Scottsdale Hosp. North Devel. Com.; master tchr. Presbyn. Ch., youth leader; troop leader Cactus-Pine council Girl Scouts U.S.A., 1960-74; asst. den leader Roosevelt Council Boy Scouts Am.; instr. Jr. Achievement; v.p. Planned Parenthood Aux., Family Svc. Agy. Aux.; bd. dirs. Phoenix Symphony Aux., Phoenix Art Mus.; deacon Presbyn. Ch. Mem. Scottsdale Bd. Realtors, Scottsdale Comml. Bd., Phoenix Comml. Bd. (Multiple Listing Service Forms Com. award 1981), Internat. Real Estate Fedn. (Ariz. chpt. bd. dirs.), Farm and Land Inst., Valley of Sun Real Estate Exchangers, LWV, Scottsdale C. of C. (ambassador), U. Calif. Alumni Assn. (Ariz. chpt. pres.), Scottsdale Rep. Forum, Cactus Wren Rep. Women, Palo Verde Rep. Women, Delta Zeta, Toastmasters (past pres., youth leader, gov. area 7, disting. toastmaster), Soroptimists. Home: 7463 E Raintree Ct Scottsdale AZ 85258 Office: 7150 E Lincoln Dr Scottsdale AZ 85253

PUGH, JEFFREY MITCHELL, lawyer; b. Pasadena, Calif., Aug. 21, 1961; s. Harry Whisner and Camilla (Karger) P. BA, U. Southern Calif., L.A., 1983; JD, U. Calif., San Francisco, 1987. Bar: Calif. 1987. Assoc. Shea & Gould, L.A., 1987—. Panel atty. Calif. Lawyers for the Arts, 1988—; adv. dir. Words Project for Aids, 1988—. Mem. ABA, Calif. Bar Assn., L.A. County Bar Assn., Beverly Hills Bar Assn., Santa Monica Rugby Club. Office: Shea & Gould 1800 Ave of the Stars 500 Los Angeles CA 90067

PUGH, KYLE MITCHELL, JR., musician, music educator; b. Spokane, Wash., Jan. 6, 1937; s. Kyle Mitchel, Sr. and Lenore Fae (Johnson) P.; m. Susan Deane Waite, July 16, 1961; children: Jeffray, Kari. BA in Edu., East Wash. U., 1975. Cert. tchr., Wash. Tuba player Spokane Symphony Orch., 1958-63; rec. assoc. Century Records, Spokane, 1965-73; tuba player World's Fair Expo '74, Spokane, 1974; bass player Russ Carlyle Orch., Las Vegas, 1976, Many Sounds of Nine Orch., northwest area, 1969-81; band tchr. Garry Jr. High School, Spokane, 1976-79, Elementary Band Program, Spokane, 1979—; bass player Doug Scott Cabaret Band, Spokane, 1982—; dept. head Elementary Band Dept., Spokane, 1984—. Editor (newsletter) The Repeater, 1987 (Amateur Radio News Service award 1987). Active in communications Lilac Bloomsday Assn., Spokane, 1977. Served to E-5 USNR, 1955-63. Recipient Disting. Service award Wash. State Commn., 1974, Nev. Hollerin' Champ Carl Hayden Scribe, 1979. Mem. Am. Fedn. Musicians (life), Spokane Edn. Assn. (rec. sec. 1987), Music Educator's Nat. Conf., Am. Radio Relay League (asst. dir. 1987), Ea. Wash. Music Educator's Assn. (pres. 1978-79). Democrat. Clubs: Dial Twisters (pres. 1979-80), VHF Radio Amateurs (dir. 1980-83). Lodges: Elks, Moose. Home: W 5006 Houston Ave Spokane WA 99208 Office: Elem Mus Office W 503 4th Ave Spokane WA 99204

PUGH, MARY JOHANNA, archivist; b. Polson, Mont., June 16, 1944; d. David Ray and Johanna M. (Kray) P.; m. Thomas Michael McCort; children: Catherine Johanna, Christopher David. AB, U. Chgo., 1966; AM, U. Mich., 1968, MLS, 1969. Archivist Mich. Hist. Collections, Ann Arbor, 1969-84; cons. in hist. documentation Concord, Calif., 1985—; lectr. U. Mich., Ann Arbor, 1980-84, U. Calif., Berkeley, 1986—. Author: A Pictorial History of Ann Arbor, 1974; editor: Achievements of Michigan, 1987. Mem. Mich. Archival Assn., Soc. Am. Archivists (council 1988—), Soc. Calif. Archivists, Maroon Key, Beta Phi Mu. Democrat. Home and Office: 1730 Argonne Dr Concord CA 94518

PUGH, WARREN EDWARD, engine company executive; b. Salt Lake City, Dec. 21, 1909; s. William Edward and Eva May (Murphy) P.; m. Leta Vivian Curtis, Sept. 1, 1933; children: Carol Matheson, Lorin K., Donald E. Student, Latter-day Sts. Bus. Coll., Stevens Hennager Coll.; LLD (hon.), U. Utah, 1986. Mgr. Cummins Intermountain Diesel Sales Co., Salt Lake City, 1943-75, chmn. exec. com., 1975—; also chmn. bd. dirs. Cummins Intermountain Idaho Inc., Boise; pres. Indsl. Devel. and Sales Co., Salt Lake City, 1945—. Chmn. transp. and pub. safety standing com., 1967-72, edn. subcom. Joint Appropriations Com., 1971-72, senate appropriations com. 1973—, Utah Hwy. Users Conf.; chmn., trustee Latter-day St. Hosp., Utah Found.; mem. Utah Ho. of Reps., 1959-60, Utah State Senate, 1967—, U. Utah Nat. Adv. Coun., Latter-day St. Ch. Gen. Ch. Audit Com.; majority leader Utah Senate, 1969-70, pres. 1973-74; co-chmn. Senate and Ho. Exec. Appropriation Com., 1973—; trustee U. Utah Rsch. Inst.; pres. Salt Lake Area C. of C. 1972-73; past mem. Latter-day St. Ch. Gen. Sunday Sch. Bd., High Coun. Salt Lake Holladay South Stake Latter-day St. Ch.; past bishop Halladay 8th Ward Latter-day St. Ch.; past pres. No. Calif. Latter-day St. Ch. Mission; patriarch Salt Lake Holladay South Stake Latter-day St. Ch. Clubs: Ft. Douglas Hidden Valley Country, Alta (Salt Lake City). Home: 5124 Cottonwood Ln Salt Lake City UT 84117 Office: Cummins Intermountain Diesel Sales Co 1030 Gale St Salt Lake City UT 84125

PUGSLEY, ROBERT ADRIAN, legal eductor; b. Mineola, N.Y., Dec. 27, 1946; s. Irvin Harold and Mary Catherine (Brusselars) P. B.A., SUNY-Stony Brook, 1968; J.D., NYU, 1975, LL.M. in Criminal Justice, 1977. Instr. sociology The New Sch. Social Research, N.Y.C., 1969-71; coordinator Peace Edn. programs The Christophers, N.Y.C., 1971-78; assoc. prof. law Southwestern U., Los Angeles, 1978-81, prof., 1981—; adj. asst. prof. criminology and criminal justice Southampton Coll.-Long Island U., 1975-76; acting dep. dir. Criminal Law Edn. and Research Ctr., NYU, 1983-86; bd. advisors Ctr. Legal Edn. CCNY-CUNY, 1978, Sta. KPFK-FM, 1985-86; founder, coordinator The Wednesday Eveing Soc., Los Angeles, 1979—. Mem. exec. com. non-govtl. orgns. UN Office of Pub. Info., 1977; mem. issues task force Los Angeles Conservancy, 1980-81, seminar for law tchrs. Nat. Endowment for the Humanities UCLA, 1979; co-convener So. Calif. Coalition Against Death Penalty, 1981-83, convener, 1983-84; mem. death penalty com. Lawyer's Support Group, Amnesty Internat. U.S.A.; founding mem. Ch.-State Council, Los Angeles, 1984—. Robert Marshall fellow Criminal Law Edn. and Research Ctr., NYU Sch. Law, 1976-78; bd. dirs. Equal Rights Sentencing Found., 1983-85, Earth Alert Inc., 1984-87. Mem. Am. Legal Studies Assn., Am. Soc. Polit. and Legal Philosophy, Assn. Am. Law Schs., Inst. Soc. Ethics and Life Scis., Soc. Am. Law Tchrs. Democrat. Roman Catholic. Creative advisor Christopher Closeup (nationally syndicated pub. service TV program), 1975-83; host Earth Alert, Cable TV, 1983-87; producer, moderator: Indside L.A., pub. affairs discussion program Sta. KPFK-FM, 1979-86; contbr. articles to legal jours. Office: Southwestern U Sch Law 675 S Westmoreland Ave Rm 410 Los Angeles CA 90005

PUK, RICHARD FRANK, computer graphics company executive; b. Smyrna, Tenn., Jan. 19, 1945; s. Frank J. and Valliere Anne (Kelly) P.; m. Donna Gwyn Jensen, Oct. 28, 1972. BS, U. Ariz., 1967; MS, Purdue U., 1969, PhD, 1976. Mem. tech. staff Sandia Nat. Labs., Albuquerque, 1976-79; dir. software devel. Megatek Corp., San Diego, 1979-81; dir. research Megatek Corp., 1981-82; pres. Puk Cons. Svcs. Carlsbad, Calif., 1982—; mem. ANSI accredited stds. com. X3H3, Washington, 1979—, chmn. task group 1, 1979-82; U.S. del. on computer graphics Internat. Stds. Orgn., 1981—. Designer, developer Graphics Compatibility Systems software. Capt. U.S. Army, 1967-73, Vietnam. Mem. ACM (spl. interest group in graphics 1973—, graphics stds. planning com. 1973-79), Nat. Computer Graphics Assn. Republican. Methodist. Address: 7644 Cortina Ct Carlsbad CA 92009

PULITZER, MICHAEL EDGAR, newspaper editor; b. St. Louis, Feb. 23, 1930; s. Joseph and Elizabeth (Edgar) P.; m. Cecille Stell Eisenbeis, Apr. 28, 1970; children: Michael Edgar, Elizabeth E., Robert S., Frederick D., Catherine D. Hanson, Christina H. Eisenbeis, Mark C. Eisenbeis, William H. Eisenbeis. Grad., St. Mark's Sch., Southborough, Mass., 1947; AB, Harvard U., 1951, LLB, 1954. Bar: Mass. 1954. Assoc. Warner, Stackpole, Stetson & Bradlee, Boston, 1954-56; reporter Louisville Courier Jour., 1956-60; reporter, news editor, asst. mng. editor St. Louis Post-Dispatch, 1960-71, assoc. editor, 1978-79; editor, pub. Ariz. Daily Star, Tucson, 1971—; pres. chief operating officer Pulitzer Pub. Co. (and subs.), 1979-84, vice chmn., 1984-86, pres., 1986—, also bd. dirs. Clubs: St. Louis Country; Mountain Oyster (Tucson). Office: Pulitzer Pub Co St Louis Post-Dispatch 900 N Tucker Blvd Saint Louis MO 63101 also: Arizona Daily Star PO Box 26807 Tucson AZ 85726 *

PULLEN, KENT EDWARD, state legislator, chemist; b. El Paso, Tex., May 4, 1942; s. Eugene Hoyt and Maris Morie (Glover) P.; m. Fay Lynnette Endres, June 13, 1964; children: Katherine Ann, Walter David. BS, U. N.Mex., 1963; PhD, U. Wash., 1967. Asst. prof. chemistry U. Idaho, Moscow, 1967-68; engr. Boeing Co., Seattle, 1968—; mem. Wash. Ho. Reps., Olympia, 1973-75, Wash. Senate, 1975—; chmn. Senate Law and Justice com., 1988—. Bd. dirs. Citizen Taxpayers Assn., Kent, Wash., 1979-85; chmn. Citizens Against Crime, 1975; co-chmn. Com. for Honest Elections, Kent, 1977. Mem. Seattle Profl. Engring. Employees Assn. (council), Mountaineers Club. Wash. State Chess Champion, 1985. Office: Wash State Senate Legislature Bldg Olympia WA 98504

PULLENZA-ORTIZ, PATRICIA, English teacher, writer; b. Phoenix, July 23, 1950; d. George Anthony and Miyuki (Sase) Pullenza; m. Anthony Ortiz, Mar. 31, 1975; children: Alexandra P., Max. BA, Ariz. State U., 1972, MA, 1976. Equal edn. opportunity specialist Dept. of Edn. State of Ariz., Phoenix, 1975; dir. ESL program, mining div. ARCO, Inguaran, Michoacan, Mexico, 1975-76; dir. Instituto Americano, Cananea, Sonora, Mexico, 1977-78; faculty assoc. Ariz. State U., Tempe, 1978—; designer, owner Patrice Pullenza Collection, Mesa, Ariz., 1987—; Organizer plenary session USIA English as a Fgn. Lang. Inst., Tempe, 1984. Contbr. articles to profl. jours. Mem. Good Samaritan Med. Ctr. Auxiliary, Phoenix, 1985—, Ariz. State U. Asian Am. Faculty/Staff Assn., 1986, Entrepreneurial Mothers Assn., Mesa, 1987—. Mem. Ariz. State U. Faculty Women's Assn., Ariz. State U. Faculty Assn. (bd. dirs. 1985-87, bd. trustees 1988). Democrat. Roman Catholic. Home: 1931 S Brooks Ln Mesa AZ 85202 Office: Ariz State U Am Lang & Culture Program Tempe AZ 85287

PULLIAM, EUGENE SMITH, newspaper publisher; b. Atchison, Kans., Sept. 7, 1914; s. Eugene Collins and Myrta (Smith) P.; m. Jane Bleecker, May 29, 1943; children—Myrta, Russell, Deborah. A.B., DePauw U., 1935, LL.D., 1973. Reporter, UP, Chgo., Detroit, Buffalo, 1935-36; news editor Radio Sta. WIRE, Indpls., 1936-41; city editor Indpls. Star, 1947-48; mng. editor Indpls. News, 1948-62; asst. publisher Indpls. Star and News, 1962-76; pub., pres. Phoenix Newspapers, 1979—; exec. v.p. Central Newspapers, Indpls., 1979—. Mem. Am. Soc. Newspaper Editors, Am. Newspaper Pubs. Assn. Found. (past pres.), Hoosier State Press Assn. (treas.), Soc. Profl. Journalists, Delta Kappa Epsilon. Club: Paradise Valley Country. Office: The Indpls Star Indpls Newspapers Inc 307 N Pennsylvania St Indianapolis IN 46204 also: Phoenix Newspapers Inc 120 E Van Buren St Phoenix AZ 85004

PULLIAM, FRANCINE S., real estate broker and developer; b. San Francisco, Sept. 14, 1937; d. Ralph C. Stevens and Frances I. (Wilson) Sarno; m. John Donald Pulliam, Aug. 14, 1957 (div. Mar. 1965); 1 child, Wendy; m. Terry Kent Graves, Dec. 14, 1974. Student, U. Ariz., 1955-56, U. Nev., Las Vegas, 1957-59. Airline stewardess Bonanza Airlines, Las Vegas, 1957; real estate agt. The Pulliam Co., Las Vegas, 1958-68, Levy

Realty, Las Vegas, 1976-79; real estate broker, owner Prestige Properties, Las Vegas, 1976—; importer, exporter Exports Internat., Las Vegas, 1984—. Bd. dirs. Las Vegas Bd. Realtors, Fedn. Internation Realtors, Las Vegas Taxi Cab Authority, Citicorp Bank, Nat. Kidney Found., Citizens for Pvt. Enterprises, Assistance League, Sen. Chic Hecht Adv. Bd., Better Bus. Bur., Cancer Soc., Easter Seals, Economic Research Bd., Children's Discovery Museum, New Horizons Ctr. for Children with Learning Disabilities, Girl Scouts, Home of the Good Shepard, St. Jude's Ranch for Homeless Children. Mem. Las Vegas C. of C. Republican. Roman Catholic. Office: Prestige Properties 601 S Ranch Rd Ste A5 Las Vegas NV 89106

PULLIAM, PAUL EDISON, electrical engineer; b. Nickerson, Kans., June 6, 1912; s. George Washington and Hattie Lucy (Vandeventer) P.; BSEE, U. Mo., 1951; m. Ila M. Catrett, Feb. 3, 1945; children—Carol Ann Pulliam Rolls, Paula Ann Pulliam Bermingham. Elec. engr. Ozark Dam Constructors, Powerhouse, Bull Shoals Dam, Baxter County, Ark., 1951-52; commd. 2d lt. U.S. Army Res., 1937, advanced through grades to maj., 1961; field engr. RCA, Fighter Wing Tactical Air Command, 1952-53; elec. engr. Goodyear Atomic Corp., 1957-60; missiles engr. Chrysler Corp., Redstone Arsenal, Ala., 1957-60; ret., 1972 constrn. insp. Sacramento County Dept. Pub. Works, Sacramento, Calif., 1977-80. Registered profl. engr., Mo., Nev., Calif. Concept creator Pershing Weapon System, boiling water in nuclear reactors and submarines. Mem. Soc. Am. Mil. Engrs., IEEE (life), Res. Officers Assn. (life), SAR (past pres. Sacramento chpt.), VFW (life). Democrat. Baptist. Club: Toastmasters. Initiated VHF Radio Balun antenna assemblies devel. by USAF personnel, 1986, provided concept for electric-drive torpedoes for USN, USCG, initiated devel. of four barrel four caliber rifles. Home: 7916 Grandstaff Dr Sacramento CA 95823

PULMAN, MICHAEL BARRACLOUGH, educator; b. Liverpool, United Kingdom, Apr. 20, 1933; s. Maurice and Beatrice Sara (Roberts) P. AB, Princeton U., 1960; MA, U. Calif., Berkeley, 1961, PhD, 1964. Instr., asst. prof. Fla. State U., Tallahassee, 1964-71; assoc. prof. U. Denver, 1971—; co-dir. Liberal Studies Univ. Coll., Univ. Denver, 1985—. Author: The Elizabethan Privy Council in the Fifteen Seventies, 1971; contbr. numerous articles to profl. jours. Capt. British Army, 1952-57, United Kingdom. Fellow Royal Hist. Soc. Democrat. Home: 2620 S Fillmore Denver CO 80210-6213 Office: History Dept Univ Denver Denver CO 80208

PULS, NORMAN M., electro-mechanical engineer, consultant; b. Phila., Aug. 20, 1936; s. Bernard and Ethel (Cooperson) P.; m. Eleanor Beck, Sept. 28, 1958; children: David, Lorie. BSME, Drexel U., 1959; MS in Mech. Engring., U. So. Calif., L.A., 1962. Design engr. computer div. NCR, 1959-63; sr. project engr. Atomics, Internat., 1963-64; sr. mem. engring. staff computer div. RCA Corp., 1964-66; mgr. advanced rsch. and devel. Compute Measurement Corp., 1966-68; mgr. mech. engring. and magnetic recording depts. Computer Products div. Ampex Corp., 1968-70; dir. engring. div. Houston Fearless Corp., 1970-73; tech. dir. Nore Industries, Inc., 1973-78; dir. engring. Micro Peripherals, Inc., 1978-80; founder, engring. mgr. Tandon Corp., 1980-82; pvt. practice cons. Woodland Hills, Calif., 1982—. Patentor flying characteristics and mechanisms for magnetic recording heads. Recipient Achievement award Fore-Fathers of Phila., 1954. Mem. Aircraft Owners and Pilots Assn., ASME. Home and Office: 1705 Sherington Pl #205 Newport Beach CA 92663

PURDY, JOSEPH DONALD, small business owner; b. Oklahoma City, May 28, 1942; s. Allen B. and Ruth (Sanders) P.; m. Annelie S. Purdy, Sept. 7, 1969; 1 child, Kimberly. BA, Calif. State U., Long Beach, 1960; MA, Chapman Coll., Orange, Calif., 1965; PhD, U. Okla., 1968. Asst. prof. U. Miss., Oxford, 1969-71; asst. prof., head dept. Southwestern Okla. State U., Weatherford, 1971-75; adminstr. spl. edn. Santa Barbara County (Calif.) Schs., 1975-81; chief exec. officer, owner Purdy Enterprises, Santa Maria, Calif., 1981—. Contbr. articles to profl. jours. Pres. bd. dirs. Santa Maria Symphony Orch., 1986-87. With U.S. Army, 1955-57. Mem. Internat. Reading Assn., Santa Maria Valley Developers (chmn. membership com. 1987—), Lake Maria Valley Club (pres. 1984-86). Office: PO Box 2802 Santa Maria CA 93455

PURE, MELINDA ALICE, business manager; b. San Bernardino, Calif., Sept. 17, 1960; d. Kenneth Walter and Marian Lucille (Bown) P. BA in Mgmt., cert. computers and programming, Calif. State U., San Bernadino, 1983. Bus. mgr. Bruggeman, Smith & Peckham, Attys. (now Smith & Peckham), San Bernadino and Rancho Cucamonga, Calif., 1983—. Mem. Employer's Adv. Council, San Bernadino, 1984—. Mem. ABA (assoc.), Assn. Legal Administrators, Alumni Assn. Calif. State U. San Bernadino (life), Nat. Assn. Female Execs. Republican. Presbyterian. Office: Smith & Peckham 524 N Mountain View Ave San Bernardino CA 92401-1295

PURISCH, ELLEN CAROL, clinical social worker; b. Washington, June 29, 1953; d. Albert Phillip and Adelaide Sylvia (Yarus) Maslow; m. Arnold David Purisch, Aug, 10, 1975; 1 child, Daniel Zachary. Lic. clin. social worker, marriage, family and child counselor. Psychiat. social worker United Family and Children's Soc., Plainfield, N.J., 1979-83; clin. social worker Child Guidance of Orange County, Huntington Beach, Calif., 1983-85; dir. Health Directions, Fountain Valley, Calif., 1985—; cons. Johnson & Johson, New Brunswick, N.J., 1981-83; mem. extended faculty UCLA, 1985. Mem. Nat. Assn. Social Workers, Acad. Cert. Social Workers, Phi Kappa Phi. Office: Health Directions 8840 Warner Ave Suite 301 Fountain Valley CA 92708

PURNELL, WILLARD DALE, engineering geologist; b. Seattle, Dec. 27, 1931; s. Harry Francis and Eleanor Dagmar (Olson) P.; m. Helen Georgina Coates, Aug. 24, 1957; children: Angela Gail, Marcus Girard. AAS, Everett Community Coll., 1956; BS in Geology and Engring., U. Wash., 1959. Registered geologist, Calif., Idaho; cert. engring. geologist, Calif. Staff geologist Dames & Moore, Seattle, 1958-69; chief soils engr., engring. geologist The Sanwick Corp., Seattle, 1969-72; prin. W.D. Purnell & Assocs., Seattle and Bellingham, Wash., 1972—; v.p. Sun Mark Property Devel., Bellevue, Wash., 1972-73; gen. ptnr. The Glen Co., Bellingham, 1973—. Chmn. bd. dirs. Lower Snoqualmie Valley Sch. Dist., Carnation, Wash., 1964-69. Served with USN, 1952-53. Mem. Wash. State Assn. Engring. Geologists (chmn. 1970-71), N.W. Wash. Engrs. Club (vice chmn. 1989), Am. Legion, Bellingham Yacht Club. Republican. Home: 1392 Chuckanut Dr Bellingham WA 98226 Office: W D Purnell & Assocs 4202 Meridian Ste 200 Bellingham WA 98226

PURSEL, HAROLD MAX, SR., mining engineer, civil engineer, architectural engineer.; b. Fruita, Colo., Sept. 15, 1921; s. Harold Maurice and Viola Pearl (Wagner) P.; B.S. in Civil Engring., U. Wyo., 1950; m. Virginia Anna Brady, May 6, 1950; children—Harold Max, Leo William, Dawn Allen, Helen Virginia, Viola Ruth. Asst. univ. architect U. Wyo., 1948-50; with Sharrock & Pursel, Contractors, 1951-55; owner Max Pursel, Earthwork Constrn., 1955-59; project engr. Farson (Wyo.) Irrigation Project, 1960-61; owner Wyo. Builders Service, Casper, 1962-66; head dept. home improvement Gamble Stores, Rawlins, Wyo., 1967; resident work instr. Casper (Wyo.) Job Corps Conservation Center, 1968; P.M. coordinator Lucky Mc Uranium Mine, Riverton, Wyo., 1969-80; constrn. insp. U.S. Bur. Reclamation, 1983—; cons. freelance heavy and light constrn., 1984—. Served with U.S. Army, 1942-45. Mem. Nat. Rifle Assn., Internat. Platform Assn., Mensa. Lodges: Eagles, Masons, Shriners. Exptl. research with log, timber and frame constrn. in conjunction with residential applications. Home: PO Box 572 Riverton WY 82501

PURSLEY, CHARLES ROBERT, lawyer; b. Safford, Ariz., Feb. 24, 1936; s. Joseph Robert and Josephine (Alger) P.; m. Carole J. Preston, Sept. 9, 1960; children: Rob, Thomas, Carolyn, Linda, Jennifer, David. BA, Brigham Young U., 1961; JD, U. Ariz., 1973. Bar: Ariz. Spl. agt. FBI, San Antonio, 1966-67; assoc. May, Dees and Barassi, Tucson, Ariz., 1973-78; prof. justice adminstrn. Ea. Ariz. Coll., Thatcher, 1978-79; pvt. practice Safford, 1979-87; chief dep. county atty. County of Graham, Safford, 1987—. Contbr. articles to profl. jours. Pres. Graham County Assn. Retarded Citizens, Safford, 1980-87, Spl. Svcs. for Spl. People, Safford, 1987-88; bd. dirs. Graham County Hist. Soc., Safford, 1987—. Comdr. USNR, 1961-71. Recipient George Washington medal Freedoms Found., Valley Forge, Pa., 1967, 68. Mem. Ariz. Bar Assn., Graham-Greenlee Bar Assn. (treas. 1987—). Mormon. Home: 143 3d Ave Thatcher AZ 85552 Office: Graham County Atty 800 N Main St Safford AZ 85548

PURVES, WILLIAM KIRKWOOD, biologist, educator; b. Sacramento, Oct. 28, 1934; s. William Kirkwood and Dorothy (Brandenburger) P.; m. Jean McCauley, June 9, 1959; 1 son, David William. B.S., Calif. Inst. Tech., 1956; M.S., Yale U., 1957, Ph.D., 1959. NSF postdoctoral fellow U. Tubingen, Fed. Republic Germany, 1959-60; Nat. Cancer Inst. postdoctoral fellow UCLA, 1960-61; asst. prof. botany U. Calif., Santa Barbara, 1961-65; assoc. prof. biochemistry U. Calif., 1965-70, prof. biology, 1970-73, chmn. dept. biol. scis., 1972-73; prof. biology, head biol. sci. group U. Conn., Storrs, 1973-77; Stuart Mudd prof. biology Harvey Mudd Coll., Claremont, Calif., 1977—, chmn. depts. biol. and computer sci., 1985—; adj. prof. plant physiology U. Calif., Riverside, 1979-85; vis. fellow computer sci. Yale U., 1983-84. Author: Life, the Science of Biology, 1983, 2d ed., 1987. NSF sr. postdoctoral fellow U. London, 1967; NSF sr. postdoctoral fellow Harvard U., 1968; NSF research grantee, 1962—. Fellow AAAS; mem. Am. Soc. Plant Physiologists, Am. Inst. Biol. Scis., Am. Assn. Artificial Intelligence, Cognitive Sci. Soc., Sigma Xi. Democrat. Home: 2817 N Mountain Ave Claremont CA 91711 Office: Harvey Mudd Coll Claremont CA 91711

PURVIANCE, DANIEL JOE, automotive company official, consultant; b. Venice, Calif., Jan. 7, 1956; s. Donald Leroy Purviance and Diane Gail (Arnold) Harrington. AA, AS, Northrup U., 1976. Ptnr. owner Don's Automotive and Machine Shop, Sepulveda, Calif., 1971—; flight line technician Am. Jet Inc., Van Nuys, Calif., 1976-78; flight line tech., leadman Lockheed Co., Burbank, Calif., 1978-83; line tech. Canoga AMC-Jeep-Renault, Canoga Park, Calif., 1983-84, Rueff AMC Buick, San Fernando, Calif., 1984-86; fuel system checkout technician Rockwell Internat., Palmdale, Calif., 1986-87, Gen. Dynamics Co., Edwards AFB, Calif., 1987—, McDonnell Douglas Corp., Edwards AFB, Calif., 1988—; pres. Corvette Internat., Lancaster, Calif., 1983—; cons. NASA, Edwards AFB, 1986—, Jet Propulsion Lab., Edwards AFB, 1987—. Contbr. articles to fishing mags. Oeganizer Kids' Fishing Derby, Apollo !ark, Calif., 1983—. With U.S. Army, 1973-75. Mem. Antelope Valley Flyrodders (pres. 1988—), Antelope Valley Vettes, Fedn. of Flyfishers, John Birch Soc., Audubon Soc., Nat. Geol. Soc., Trout Unltd. Republican. Home: 44561 Lostwood Ave Lancaster CA 93534 Office: 10241 Woodley Ave Sepulveda CA 91343

PURVIS, JOHN ANDERSON, lawyer; b. Greeley, Colo., Aug. 31, 1942; s. Virgil J. and Emma Lou (Anderson) P.; m. Charlotte Johnson, Apr. 3, 1976; 1 child, Whitney; children by previous marriage—Jennifer, Matt. B.A. cum laude, Harvard U., 1965; J.D., U. Colo., 1968. Bar: Colo. 1968, U.S. Dist. Ct. Colo. 1968, U.S. Ct. Appeals (10th cir.) 1978, U.S. Ct. Claims, 1980. Dep. dist. atty. Boulder, Colo., 1968-69; asst. dir. and dir. legal aid U. Colo. Sch. Law, 1969; assoc. Williams, Taussig & Trine, Boulder, 1969; head Boulder office Colo. Pub. Defender System, 1970-72; assoc. and ptnr. Hutchinson, Black, Hill, Buchanan & Cook, Boulder, 1972-85; ptnr. Buchanan, Gray, Purvis and Schuetze, 1985—; acting Colo. State Pub. Defender, 1978; adj. prof. law U. Colo., 1981, 84-88 , others; lectr. in field. Chmn., Colo. Pub. Defender Commn., 1979—; mem. nominating commn. Colo. Supreme Ct., 1984—; chmn. Boulder County Criminal Justice Com., 1975-81, Boulder County Manpower Council, 1977-78. Recipient Ames award Harvard U., 1964; Outstanding Young Lawyer award Colo. Bar Assn., 1978. Mem. Internat. Soc. Barristers, Colo. Bar Assn., Boulder County Bar Assn., Colo. Trial Lawyers Assn., Am. Trial Lawyers Assn., Trial Lawyers for Pub. Justice. Democrat. Address: 1050 Walnut St Ste 501 Boulder CO 80302

PURYEAR, JENNIFER ANNE, dentist; b. Fountainebleau, France, Aug. 6, 1960; came to U.S., 1963; d. Robert Eric and Anna (Ray) Moss; m. Robert Wayne Puryear, Feb. 14, 1981. BS in Zoology, Tex. A&M U., 1983; DDS, U. Tex., 1987. Sr. asst. dental surgeon, edn. officer, prevention officer USPHS, Kotzebue, Alaska, 1987—. Author: tchr. manual: Dental Curriculum Guide for Alaska Native Schs., 1988. Leader Girl Scouts U.S., Kotzebue, 1988—. Lt. USPHS, 1987—. Mem. Am. Dental Assn., Acad. Gen. Dentistry, Commd. Officers Assn., Am. Assn. Pub. Health Dentistry, Lioness. Home and Office: USPHS Hosp Kotzebue AK 99752

PUTHUFF, STEVEN HENRY, computer company executive; b. Placervile, Calif., Nov. 20, 1940; s. Romey Lee and Sula Ester (Dentist) P.; m. Judith Eleanor Puthuff; children: Wendy Sue, Jennifer Kay. AA, Sacramento City Coll., 1960; BSEE, Ariz. State U., 1963. Assoc. engr. IBM, San Jose, Calif., 1963; engring. project mgr., founder Aerometrics Aerojet Gen., San Ramone, Calif., 1964-69; engring. mgr. Wavetek Data Comm., San Diego, 1969-73; dir. engring. Digital Devel. Corp., San Diego, 1973-77; v.p. engring. Memorex Corp., Santa Clara, Calif., 1977-81; v.p. engring, founder Britton Lee Corp., Los Gatos, Calif., 1981-82; v.p. engring., founder Fortune Systems Corp., San Carlos, Calif., 1982-84; pres., chief exec. officer Sequence, Inc., San Jose, 1984-85; chmn., chief exec. officer Integrated Fin. Systems Internat., Troy, N.Y., 1987—; bd. dirs. Sequence, Inc., San Jose; bd. dirs., chmn. Integrated Fin. Systems Internat. Inventor frequency detector. Chmn. U.S. Tech. Adv. Com. (PTAC) DOC, Washington, 1979-82; bd. dirs. Jr. Achievement of Santa Clara, 1978-85. Mem. AIEE (pres. Ariz. State U. chpt. 1962-63), Eta Kappa Nu (pres. Ariz. State U. chpt. 1962-63). Republican. Home: 13001 Saratoga Sunnyvale Rd Saratoga CA 95070

PUTMAN, CAROL JEAN, photographer; b. San Francisco, Jan. 1, 1943; d. Joe Alfred and Jessie Jane (Harris) P. BA, Calif. State U., Hayward, 1968. Freelance photographer Clayton, Calif., 1975—; exec. sec. Bank of Am., San Francisco, 1980; group sec. physics dept. U. Calif., Berkeley, 1974-75, sec. civil engring. dept., 1981-84, faculty sec. journalism dept., 1984-85, adminstrv. asst. math. dept., 1985-86, 87-88; photographer Walnut Creek, Calif., 1986—.

PYE, DAVID THOMAS, life sciences company executive; b. Darby, Pa., June 12, 1942; s. David and Grace Marie (Dale) P. B.S., Widener U., 1964. C.P.A., Pa., Calif. Tax cons. Price Waterhouse & Co., Phila., 1964-70; dir. taxes AID, Inc., Phila., 1970-75; dir. tax adminstrn. Syntex Corp., Palo Alto, Calif., 1975—. Mem. Am. Inst. C.P.A.s, Calif. C.P.A. Soc., Pa. Inst. C.P.A.s, Tax Execs. Inst. Home: 9 Crags Ct San Francisco CA 94131 Office: Syntex Corp 3401 Hillview Ave Palo Alto CA 94304

PYE, DORI, association executive; b. Atlanta; d. Irving Joseph and Grayce Edna (Dobbins) Nowak; div.; children: Joshua, Kenneth. M.A., Columbia U. Sch. Journalism, 1948; postgrad. advanced acad. program mgmt. U. Notre Dame, 1978, exec. mgmt. UCLA, 1981. Cert. C. of C. exec., Calif.; pres., chief exec. officer Los Angeles Bus. Coun., 1969—; apptd. mem. Calif. Conf. Small Bus., 1980; mem. adv. com. bus. ins. Calif. State Senate, 1984—; founder-organizer, Westwood Thrift & Loan Assn., 1982—; mem. Nat. Women's Forum, 1986. Bd. dirs. Century City Hosp.; vice chmn. Los Angeles City Housing Commn., 1984—. Recipient nat., state and city awards. Club: Regency (Los Angeles). Office: 10880 Wilshire Blvd Ste 1103 Los Angeles CA 90024

PYKE, RONALD, mathematics educator; b. Hamilton, Ont., Can., Nov. 24, 1931; s. Harold and Grace Carter (Digby) P.; m. Gladys Mary Davey, Dec. 19, 1953; children: Darlene, Brian, Ronald, Gordon. BA (hon.), McMaster U., 1953; MS, U. Wash., 1955, PhD, 1956. Asst. prof. Stanford U., Calif., 1956-58; prof. Columbia U., N.Y.C., 1958-60; prof. math. U. Wash., Seattle, 1960—; vis. prof. U. Cambridge, Eng., 1964-65, Imperial Coll., London, 1970-71, Colo. State U., Ft. Collins, 1979, Technion, Israel, 1988; pres. Inst. Math. Stats., 1986-87; mem. bd. math. scis. NRC/NAS, 1984-88, chmn. com. applications and theoretical stats., 1985-88; cons. Boeing Co. Editor Ann. Prob., 1972-75; contbr. articles to profl. jours. NSF grantee, 1961—. Fellow Internat. Statis. Inst. (v.p. 1989—), Am. Statis. Assn., Inst. Math. Stats. (pres. 1986-87); mem. Am. Math. Soc., Math. Assn. Am. Office: U Wash Dept Math Seattle WA 98195

PYLE, JON D(UDLEY), hotel executive; b. Santa Monica, Calif., Aug. 2, 1955; s. Jack and Dolores (Bruns) P.; m. Catherine Yeakle, Feb. 26, 1989. BA in Journalism, San Diego State U., 1978. Sales rep. Am. Tobacco Co., San Carlos, Calif., 1981-83, Avis Rent-A-Car System, Inc., San Mateo, Calif., 1983-84; sr. sales rep. Hertz Corp., Denver, 1984-85; regional sales mgr. Hertz Corp., Chgo., 1985-86; staff v.p. travel industry sales Hertz Corp., L.A., 1986-87; dir. sales and mktg. Jetset Tours, N.Am., L.A., 1987-89; v.p. sales the Americas Mandarin Oriental Hotel Group, L.A., 1989—. Office: Mandarin Oriental Hotel Group 6151 W Century Blvd Los Angeles CA 90045

PYLES, JAMES DAVID, JR., accountant, financial advisor; b. Springfield, Mass., Jan. 31, 1953; s. James David Sr. and Ernestine Alma (Brereton) P. BS, Western New Eng. Coll., 1977. Recreation supr. Parks and Recreation Dept., Springfield, 1974-77; fin. analyst Prudential Ins. Co., Boston, 1977-80; budget analyst City Auditors, Springfield, 1980-81; acct. W. Kurt Wood Assocs., Long Beach, Calif., 1981-82; advisor The Colleto Group, Harbor City, Calif., 1987—; tax acct. Miramar Income Tax Service, Long Beach, Calif., 1987—; pres. The Jay Pyles Co., Long Beach, 1983—. Democrat. Episcopalian.

PYPER, JAMES WILLIAM, chemist; b. Wells, Nev., Sept. 5, 1934; s. William Jones and Wilma (Bjelke) P.; m. Phyllis Diane Henry, Aug. 30, 1957; children: Scott, Mark, Gregory, Heather, Melanie, Tara, Tammy, Wendy, Michael, Tanya, David. BS, Brigham Young U., 1958, MS, 1960; PhD, Cornell U., 1964. Ordained bishop Ch. Jesus Christ of Latter-day Saints, 1973. Research chemist Lawrence Livermore (Calif.) Nat. Lab., 1963-84, mass spectrometry group leader, 1973-75, tritium tech. group leader, 1977-78, applied phys. chemistry group leader, 1979-80, sect. leader for analytical chemistry, 1980-83, dep. sect. leader for analytical chemistry, 1983-87, assoc. div. leader condensed matter and analytical scis. div., 1987—. Contbr. articles to sci. jours. Presided over local congregations, 1973-75, 87—; mem. stake high council, 1976-87. Republican. Office: U Calif Lawrence Livermore Nat Lab Livermore CA 94550

QUADROS, JOHN DAVID, meteorologist; b. Boston, Mar. 23, 1946; s. Ernest Cameron and Nora (Mulligan) Q.; m. Karma Brown, Dec. 23, 1980 (div. 1984). BS, Pa. State U., 1967. Meteorologist Nat. Weather Svc., Washington, 1970-77, San Francisco, 1977—; pres. Nat. Weather Svc. Employees Orgn., Washington, 1984—. With U.S. Army, 1967-70. Mem. Nat. Weather Assn. (councillor 1983-85). Democrat. Office: 400 N Capitol St Ste 326 Washington DC 20001

QUAN, STUART FUN, internist, educator; b. San Francisco, May 16, 1949; s. Stuart Fun and Mabel (Wing) Q.; m. Diana Lee, Dec. 18, 1971; children: Jason Stuart, Jeremy Ryan-Stuart. AB, U. Calif., Berkeley, 1970; MD, U. Calif., San Francisco, 1974. Diplomate Am. Bd. Internal Medicine, Am. Bd. Pulmonary Diseases; accredited clin. polysomnographer. Intern in internal medicine U. Wis., Madison, 1974-75, resident, 1975-77; fellow in critical care and emergency medicine U. Calif., San Francisco, 1977-79; fellow in pulmonary medicine U. Ariz., Tucson, 1979-80, from instr. to asst. prof. medicine, 1980-86, assoc. prof., 1986—, med. dir. respiratory care, 1980—; med. dir. ICU Univ. Med. Ctr., Tucson, 1980-87; dir. Sleep Disorders Ctr. U. Ariz., Tucson, 1984—, chief pulmonary and crit. care medicine sect., 1987—; chmn. adv. panel on anesthesia and respiratory devices FDA, 1987—. Co-author: Respiratory Diseases--A Pathophysiological Approach, 1984; contbd. chpts. to various books; contbr. numerous articles to med. jours. Pres. Gymnastics Support Orgn., Tucson, 1985-87. Fellow Am. Coll. Chest Physicians, Clin. Sleep Soc.; mem. Am. Thoracic Soc., Am. Fedn. Clin. Research, Soc. for Critical Care Medicine, Phi Beta Kappa, Alpha Omega Alpha. Office: U Ariz Div Respiratory Scis 1501 N Campbell Tucson AZ 85724

QUATRINI, JOHN, sales, marketing executive; b. Chicago Heights, Ill., May 22, 1959; s. Tommaso and Luisa(Nirchi) Q.; m. Sherri Lynn Johnson, Dec. 29, 1984. BS, So. Ill. U., 1977-81. Asst. mgr., mgr. Stouffers Corp., Chgo., 1980-82; mgr. dining svc. Canteen Co. div. T.W. Services Inc., Chgo., 1982-84; dist. mgr. Canteen Co. div. T.W. Services Inc., L.A., 1984-85; region account exec., mgr. mktg. and sales Canteen Co. div. T.W. Services Inc., Phoenix and Tucson, 1985—. Mem. Nat. Restaurant Assn., Pres.'s Roundtable Canteen Co., Phoenix C. of C. (mem. spl. activities council 1985-87). Republican. Roman Catholic. Home: 18214 N 18th Pl Phoenix AZ 85022 Office: Canteen Co 2902 W Virginia Ave Phoenix AZ 85009

QUATTROCCHI, OSCAR LUIS, custom mirror design company executive; b. Buenos Aires, Mar. 9, 1947; came to U.S., 1971; s. Remo Julio and Abelina (Resumil) Q. Lic. in pub. rels., U. Asuncion, 1969; BS in Hotel & Restaurant, Calif. Poly. U., Pomona, 1976. Waiter Queen Mary-Castaway, Long Beach, Calif., 1972-74; asst. mgr. Blackbear's Restaurant, Newport Beach, Calif., 1974-77; supr. Eppaminondas Restaurant, Sacramento, 1977-79; restaurant svc. cons. Champ's, Phoenix, 1979-80, Soledad Franco, San Diego, 1979-80, Mizpah Hotel and Casino, Nev., 1979-80; owner, designer Unique Plant Design, Huntington Beach, Calif., 1980-87; pres., designer Oscar's Custom Mirror Design, Huntington Beach, 1987-. Mem. U.S. C. of C., Orange County Market Pl. Sellers Assn. (v.p. 1988-89). Republican. Roman Catholic. Home: 16421 Silver Ln Huntington Beach CA 92647 Office: 16392 Gothard St Huntington Beach CA 92647

QUENSE, ERIC LAWRENCE, architect; b. Annapolis, Md., Aug. 31, 1943; s. John Adolph and Helen Henrietta (Howe) Q. BArch., U. Wash., 1973, MArch., cert. Urban Design, 1980. Participant Arcosanti IV, Scottsdale, Ariz., 1971; draftsman Nat. Architectural and Engring. Record U.S. Dept. Interior, 1981; designer William Wrede Assocs., Seattle, 1981-83, 86-87; instr. Seattle Coll. Design, 1983; assoc. Jeffrey Bellows Architects, Seattle, 1983-85; designer Gregory Dixon, Landscape Architect, Seattle, 1988—. Vol. U.S. Peace Corps, Palau, Micronesia, 1967-69; active Statue of Liberty, Ellis Island Found., 1984—. Served with USAF, 1969-70. Recipient award of Merit Nat. Endowment for the Arts Design Arts Competition, 1988. Mem. Disabled Am. Vets., Tau Sigma Delta. Office: 1611 Belmont Ave Seattle WA 98122

QUIAT, GERALD M., lawyer; b. Denver, Jan. 9, 1924; s. Ira L. and Esther (Greenblatt) Q.; m. Roberta M. Nicholson, Sept. 26, 1962; children: James M., Audrey L., Melinda, Daniel P., Ilana L., Leonard E. A.A., U. Calif., Berkeley, 1942; A.B. and LL.B., U. Denver, 1948, changed to J.D., 1972. Bar: Colo. 1948, Fed. Ct. 1948. Dep. dist. atty. County of Denver, Colo., 1949-52; partner firm Quiat, Seeman & Quiat, Denver, 1952-68, Quiat & Quiat (later changed to Quiat, Bucholtz & Bull, P.C.), 1968; pres. firm Quiat Bucholtz Bull & Laff, P.C. (and predecessors), Denver, 1968-85; sole practice Denver, 1985—. Colo. post comdr. Am. Legion, 1955-56; past judge adv. Colo. dept.; dir., chmn. audit com. Guaranty Bank & Trust Co., Denver.; trustee Rose Health Care Systems, Rose Med. Ctr., Denver, 1967—, pres., chmn. bd. 1976-79; mem. Colo. Civil Rights Com., 1963-71, chmn., 1966-67, 1969-70, chief hearing officer, 1963-71; bd. dirs. AMC Cancer Research Ctr., Denver; mem. nat. civil rights com., nat. exec. com. and nat. commr. Anti-Defamation League of B'nai B'rith, bd. dirs. Mountain States Region of Anti-Defamation League of B'nai B'rith, also exec. com. mem., chmn. bd. dirs. 1980-82. Served with U.S. Army Inf., 1942-45. Decorated Bronze Star. Mem. Denver Bar Assn., Colo. Bar Assn., ABA, Am. Trial Lawyers Assn. Home: 8130 Lt Wm Clark Rd Parker CO 80134 Office: 1720 S Bellaire Penthouse Ste Denver CO 80202

QUIGLEY, DAVID ROBIN, research chemist; b. Muskegon, Mich., July 2, 1953; s. Robert David and Bette (Howard) Q.; m. Jennifer Jan Ferrell, May 27, 1978. BS in Chemistry, Fla. Atlantic U., 1976; MS in Chemistry, U. Mo., Rolla, 1979, PhD in Chemistry, 1982. Research assoc., instr. U. Colo. Health Scis. Ctr., Denver, 1982-86; assoc. EG&G Idaho Inc./Idaho Nat. Engring. Lab., Idaho Falls, 1986-87, scientist, 1987-88, sr. scientist, 1988—; cons. J.K. Rsch., Bozeman, Mont., 1989—; faculty Bacteriology and Biochemistry Dept. U. Idaho, Moscow, 1988—. Contbr. articles to profl. jours. Wouter Bosch scholar U. Mo., Rolla, 1981, 82. Mem. AAAS, Am. Chem. Soc., Am. Soc. Microbiology. Office: EG&G Idaho Inc PO Box 1625 Idaho Falls ID 83415-2203

QUIGLEY, JEROME HAROLD, management consultant; b. Green Bay, Wis., Apr. 19, 1925; s. Harold D. and Mabel (Hansen) Q.; BS, St. Norbert Coll., 1951; m. Lorraine A. Rocheleau, May 3, 1947; children: Kathy, Ross, Michael, Daniel, Mary Beth, Andrew, Maureen. Personnel adminstr. Gen. Motors Corp., 1959-64; dir. indsl. rels. Raytheon Co., Santa Barbara, Calif., 1964-67; dir. personnel U. Calif., Santa Barbara, 1967-72; corp. dir. indsl. rels. Gen. Rsch. Corp., 1972-73; dir. indsl. rels. ISS Sperry Univac, 1973-75; corp. dir. indsl. rels. Four-Phase Systems, Inc., Cupertino, Calif., 1975; sr.

v.p. human resources UNC, Annapolis, Md., 1975-86; pres. Profl. Guidance Assocs. Inc., 1986—. Aviator with U.S. Navy, 1943-47. Mem. Am. Electronics Assn., Assn. Former Intelligence Officers, Machinery and Allied Products Inst., Assn. Naval Aviation, Tailhook Assn., Navy Aviation Mus. Found., Navy League, Am. Soc. Personnel Adminstrs., Scottsdale Racquet Club. Republican. Roman Catholic. Home: 7789 E Joshua Tree Ln Scottsdale AZ 85253 Office: Profl Guidance Assocs Inc 7031 E Camelback Rd Ste 571 Scottsdale AZ 85251

QUIGLEY, JOHN MICHAEL, economist, educator; b. N.Y.C., Feb. 12, 1942. B.S. with distinction, U.S. Air Force Acad., 1964; M.Sc. with honors, U. Stockholm, Sweden, 1965; A.M., Harvard U., 1971, Ph.D., 1972. Commd. 2d lt. U.S. Air Force, 1964, advanced through grades to capt., 1968; asst. prof. econs. Yale U., 1972-74, assoc. prof., 1974-81; prof. pub. policy U. Calif., Berkeley, 1979—, prof. econs., 1981—; vis. prof. econs. and stats. U. Gothenberg, 1978; cons. numerous govt. agys. and pvt. firms; econometrician Hdqrs. U.S. Air Force, Pentagon, 1965-68; research assoc. Nat. Bur. Econ. Research, N.Y.C., 1968-78; mem. com. on nat. urban policy Nat. Acad. Sci., 1985—. Author, editor, contbr. articles to profl. jours.; editor in chief Reg. Sci. and Urban Econs., 1987—; mem. editorial bd. Land Econs., 1974-81, Jour. Urban Econs., 1978—, Council on Pub. Policy and Mgmt., 1979—, AREUEA Jour., 1985—. Fulbright scholar, 1964-65; fellow NSF, 1968-69, Woodrow Wilson, 1968-71, Harvard IBM, 1969-71, NDEA, 1969-71, Thord-Gray Am. Scandinavian Found. 1971-72, Social Sci. Research Council, 1971-72. Mem. Am. Econ. Assn., Econometric Soc., Regional Sci. Assn. (bd. dirs. 1986—), Nat. Tax Assn., Assn. for Pub. Policy and Mgmt. (bd. dirs. 1986—, v.p. 1987—). Home: 875 Hilldale Ave Berkeley CA 94708 Office: U Calif 2607 Hearst Ave Berkeley CA 94720

QUINLAN, CLAIRE, educational administrator; b. Westerly, R.I., Oct. 3, 1929; d. William James and Mary Cecilia (Murray) Q. BA, U. R.I., 1951; MA, U. No. Colo., 1961, PhD, 1964; MBA, Calif. State U., Sacramento, 1986. English tchr. Jeffersonville (Vt.) High Sch., 1952-53, Rangely (Colo.) High Sch., 1953-58; social studies, English tchr. Babcock Jr. High Sch., Westerly, 1958-59; English tchr. Westminster (Colo.) High Sch., 1959-60; psychometrist U. No. Colo., Greeley, Colo., 1960-61; asst. prof. U. No. Colo., Greeley, 1961-64, assoc. dean, psych. svcs., 1964-69; v.p. for student affairs Jamestown (N.D.) Coll., 1969-75; administr. program evaluation and rsch. Dept. of Edn., Sacramento, Calif., 1975—. Recipient Fulbright scholarship, USA Office of Edn., India, 1977. Mem. Am. Edn. Rsch. Assn., Am. Assn. for Counseling & Devel., Assn. for Measurement and Evaluation in Counseling & Devel., Nat. Coun. on Measurement in Edn., Pi Lambda Theta. Roman Catholic. Office: Dept of Education 721 Capitol Mall Sacramento CA 95814

QUINN, DAVID PHILLIP, electrical engineer, consultant; b. Pennsville, N.J., Dec. 26, 1956; s. Gorman Leonard and Helen (Stone) Q. SBEE, MIT, 1979; MBA, Ariz. State U., 1986. Circuit designer H.G. Fischer, Chgo., 1979; engr. Litton Inc., Woodland Hills, Calif., 1980-81, Martin Marietta Corp., Orlando, Fla., 1981-84; sr. software engr. Motorola Inc., Scottsdale, Ariz., 1984-88; ind. cons. Mesa, 1988—; cons. in field. Mem. IEEE, MIT Enterprise Network (charter), Leadership Tng. and Devel., Beta Gamma Sigma, Sigma Iota Epsilon. Club: Toastmasters (Orlando sgt. at arms 1982-83). Home and Office: 1031 S Stewart St Apt 1053 Mesa AZ 85202

QUINN, DIANA SEANNE, systems engineer; b. Binghamton, N.Y., Feb. 14, 1954; d. Terrance John and Phyllis Elizabeth (Mulderig) Q. BS, U. No. Colo., 1977, MS, 1980. Programmer OAO, Lakewood, Colo., 1980-81, Lockheed, Houston, 1981-83; programmer/analyst Ford Aero Space, Houston, 1983-86; software engr. Intermetrics, Houston, 1986-87; systems engr. IBM/System Integration div., Colorado Springs, Colo., 1987—. Mem. ACM, Nat. Space Soc. Office: IBM NTB Div MS N8950 Falcon AFB CO 80912

QUINN, FRANCIS A., bishop; b. Los Angeles, Sept. 11, 1921. Ed., St. Joseph's Coll., Mountain View, Calif., St. Patrick's Sem., Menlo Park, Calif., Cath. U., Washington, U. Calif., Berkeley. Ordained priest Roman Cath. Ch., 1946; ordained titular bishop of Numana and aux. bishop of San Francisco 1978, apptd. bishop of Sacramento, 1979. Office: 1119 K St PO Box 1706 Sacramento CA 95812-1706

QUINN, JOHN BRIAN PATRICK (PAT QUINN), professional sports team manager; b. Hamilton, Ont., Can., Jan. 29, 1943; came to U.S., 1960; s. John Ernest and Jean (Ireland) Q.; m. Sandra Georgia Baker, May 1, 1963; children: Valerie, Kathleen. BA in Econs., York U., 1972; JD, Del. Law Sch., 1987. Player Toronto Maple Leafs, Ont., 1968-70, Vancouver Canucks, B.C., Can., 1970-72, Atlanta Flames, 1972-77; coach Phila. Flyers, 1977-82, L.A. Kings, 1984-86; pres., gen. mgr. Vancouver Canucks, 1987—; player rep. NHL, Atlanta, 1973-77, bd. govs., 1987—. Named Def. Man of Yr., Vancouver Canucks, 1971; named Coach of Yr. NHL, 1979-80; Coach of Yr., Sporting News, 1980, Hockey News, 1980. Mem. Players Assn. Roman Catholic. Office: care Vancouver Canucks, Pacific Coliseum, 100 N Renfrew St, Vancouver, BC Canada V5K 3N7

QUINN, JOHN R., archbishop; b. Riverside, Calif., Mar. 28, 1929; s. Ralph J. and Elizabeth (Carroll) Q. Ph.B., Gregorian U., Rome, 1950, S.T.B., 1952, S.T.L., 1954. Ordained priest Roman Catholic Ch., 1953; asst. priest St. George Ch., Ontario, Calif., 1954-55; prof. theology Immaculate Heart Sem., San Diego, 1955-62, vice rector, 1960-62; rector St. Francis Coll. Sem., El Cajon, Calif., 1962-64, Immaculate Heart Sem., 1964-68; aux. bishop, vicar gen. San Diego, 1967-72; bishop Oklahoma City, 1972-73, archbishop, 1973-77; archbishop San Francisco, 1977—; provost U. San Diego, 1968-72; pres. Nat. Conf. Cath. Bishops, 1977-80; apptd. pontifical del. for religious in U.S., 1983. Mem. Cath. Theol. Soc. Am., Canon Law Soc. Am., Am. Cath. Hist. Soc., Calif. Cath. Conf. (pres. 1985—). Address: 445 Church St San Francisco CA 94114

QUINN, JOHN ROBERT, conservationist, retired advertising executive; b. L.A., July 4, 1927; s. James Robert Lawrence and Enid Ruth (Skootsky) Q.; m. Jeanne Leanora Miller, Oct. 15, 1949 (div. 1960). BA, Stanford U., 1947; postgrad., UCLA, 1947, U. Edinburgh (Scotland), 1949. Designer, publisher Quinn-Quinn Greeting Cards, L.A., 1953-59; designer, printer L.A. County Mus. History, Sci. and Art, 1959-62; art dir. UCLA, 1963-65; creative dir. Modernage Photography, Art & Printing, L.A., 1966-68; owner Quinn & Assocs., L.A., 1968-70; pres., creative dir. Mktg. Plus (a Calif. Corp.), L.A., 1971-86; co-founder Pioneertown (Calif.) Mountains Conservancy, 1985, conservationist, 1986—. Cpl. U.S. Army, 1945-46. Mem. The Nature Conservancy, The Cousteau Soc., Greenpeace, The Wilderness Soc., Sierra Club. Democrat. Home and Office: 56356 Cobalt Rd Yucca Valley CA 92284

QUINN, JOSEPH R., state supreme court judge; b. Elizabeth, N.J., Nov. 18, 1932; s. Patrick F. and Claire E. Quinn; m. Olga B. Taylor, July 28, 1962; children: Theresa, Lisa, Rita, James, Maria. A.B., St. Peter's Coll., 1957; LL.B., Rutgers U., 1961. Apptd. judge Colo. Dist. Ct., Dist. 2, 1973-80; justice Supreme Ct. of Colo., Denver, 1980—, now chief justice. Office: Colo Supreme Ct 2 E 14th Ave Denver CO 80203 *

QUINN, MAUREEN T., nurse; b. Pitts., Dec. 28, 1959; d. Edmund Joseph and Isabell Rosemarie (Stott) Q. BS in Nursing, Edinboro U. Pa., 1981; MS in Nursing Edn., Calif. State U., Dominguez Hills, 1988. RN, Calif. Nurse Presbyn. U. Hosp., Pitts., 1981-82, Allegheny Gen. Hosp., Pitts., 1982-85, Desert Hosp., Palm Springs, Calif., 1985-88; nurse supr. Palm Desert (Calif.) br. Profl. Nurses Bur., 1988—; asst. instr. nursing Coll. of Desert, Palm Desert, 1987; cons. in nursing edn. El Centro (Calif.) Regional Med. Ctr., summer 1988. Mem. Am. Nurses Assn., VFW Ladies Aux. Democrat. Roman Catholic. Home: 603 S Calle Amigos Palm Springs CA 92262 Office: Profl Nurses Bur 72-261 Hwy 111 Ste 206 Palm Desert CA 92260

QUINN, PHYLLIS, association executive; b. Chgo.; m. James Quinn; children: Bobby, Debby, Diane, Teddy. Graduated high sch., Chgo. Agt. Hollywood, Calif.; pres. Motion Picture Mothers, Hollywood. Co-Author: Cookbook of the Stars, Star Mothers. Pres. Screen Smart Set aux. of Motion Picture and TV Fund; active Variety Club Telethon; lectr. for Am. Heart Assn. Art Inst. Chgo. scholar. Home: 11755 Addison St North Hollywood CA 91607

QUINN, VELMA DEAN, real estate professional; b. Slaton, Tex., Apr. 1, 1938; d. John Orville Jenkins and Opal Erma (Henson) Hahn; m. Walter Gregory Quinn Jr., June 21, 1957; children: Bryan David, Gregory Allen, John Eric, Linda Kay. Grad. high sch., Wheatridge, Colo. Sales rep. Stanley Home Products, Colo.,Tex., 1959-62; lectr. Weight Watchers, Ill., Colo., 1970-73; pub. rels. hostess Safeway Stores, Inc., Denver, 1975-79; sales assoc. Charlie Brown Realtors, Lakewood, Colo., 1978-79, Mitchell Real Estate, Lakewood, 1979-80; broker assoc. Poole Calvert Realtors, Lakewood, 1980-84; broker owner Century 21 Quinn & Assocs., Lakewood, 1984—; tchr. property mgmt. programs. Mem. Colo. Assn. Realtors (facilitator, arbitrator), Jefferson County Bd. Realtors (bd. dirs. 1984-85, arbitrator 1982-84), Nat. Assn. Realtors, Grad. Realtors Inst. (cert. residential specialist, cert. real estate brokerage mgr.). Democrat. Baptist. Home: 14133 W Alaska Dr Lakewood CO 80228 Office: Century 21 Quinn Assocs Ste 200 198 Union St Lakewood CO 80228

QUINONES-D'BRASSIS, R. RAFAEL, civil engineer; b. San German, P.R., Aug. 16, 1937; s. Rafael Angel and Teresa (D'Brassis) Q.; m. Miriam Esther Rivera, Oct. 12, 1960 (div. 1982); children: Maria C., Rafael I., Lourdes M., Jose R.; m. Martha Otilia Neris, Oct. 22, 1982. BSCE, U. P.R., 1961; cert., Caribbean Acad. Mgmt., 1968. Cert. engr., U.S. Army, 1988; registered profl. engr. Ariz., Fla., P.R. Field engr. Maxon Constrn. Corp., Rincon, P.R., 1960-64, Austin Co., Barceloneta, P.R., 1967-68; project engr. Rexach Constrn. Co., Inc., San Juan, 1965-67; project mgr. Fuentes Concrete Pile Co., Bayamon, P.R., 1968-70, IBEC Constrn. Corp., Dorado, P.R., 1970-74; prin. R.R. Quinones-D'Brassis & Assoc., Mayaguez, P.R., 1974-80; liaison engr. Howard, Needles, Tammen & Bergendoff, Tampa, Fla., 1980-81; sr. civil engr., project mgr. Howard, Needles, Tammen & Bergendoff, Phoenix, 1981—; lectr. in field. Contbr. articles to profl. jours; inventor in field. Mem. ASCE, Lions, Rotary, KC. Home: 820 E Fremont Rd Phoenix AZ 85040 Office: Howard Needles Tammen & Bergendoff 2207 E Camelback Rd Ste 400 Phoenix AZ 85016

QUIRK, RUTH MARIE, library systems manager; b. West Newton, Mass., June 12, 1955; d. Edward Joseph and Ruth Mary (Mouquin) Q.; m. Gene Stowell, June 22, 1986; 1 child, Shane Paul. BA, U. Calif. at San Diego, 1979; MLS, U. Hawaii, 1981. Sch. librarian Am. Schs., Tegucigalpa, Honduras, 1979-80; library systems intern U. Hawaii Libraries, Honolulu, 1980-81, library systems librarian, 1981-87, head library systems, 1987—; cons. Advanced Libraries Info. Inc., Honolulu, 1983—. Mem. Hawaii Library Assn., Am. Soc. Info. Sci., Spl. Library Assn., Beta Phi Mu. Democrat. Roman Catholic. Club: Paniolo Kickers (sec. 1987—). Office: U Hawaii 2550 The Mall HL-111E Honolulu HI 96822

QUISENBERRY, ROBERT MAX, architect, researcher; b. Eugene, Oreg., Nov. 18, 1956; s. Clifford Hale and Annemaria Gertrude (Frank) Q.; m. Dawnese Elaine Tarr, Sept. 18, 1982. BArch, U. Oreg., 1982. Registered architect, Wash. Intern R. Merriman Assocs., Tacoma, 1978-81; owner Solar Design Assocs., Tacoma, 1981-83; job capt. Robert Jones, AIA, Tacoma, 1983; project architect Merritt & Pardini, Tacoma, 1984-87; project mgr. Lorimer-Case, San Diego, 1987—. Recipient Washington State Passive Solar Design and Building award Western Solar Utilization Network, 1981. Mem. AIA, Am. Sect. of Internat. Solar Energy Soc., Earthquake Engring. Research Inst. Republican. Home: 644 Hartford St Chula Vista CA 92013 Office: Architects Lorimer-Case 1747 Hancock St San Diego CA 92101

QUIST, DAVID, real estate developer, photographer; b. San Mateo, Calif., Mar. 12, 1955; s. Elmer B. and Florence (Prince) Q. Student, U. Calif., Berkeley, 1975-80, U. Utah, 1981-83. Assoc. dir. photography Salt Lake Art Ctr., 1983; owner David Quist Photography, Salt Lake City, DQE Group, Salt Lake City. One-man photography shows Utah Arts Festival, 1985, U. Utah, 1986, Hands Observed: Photographic Study, Cuisine Mktg. Group, Salt Lake City, 1989. Mem. Art Dirs. Salt Lake City, Urban Design Coalition, Advertising Photographers of Am. Office: 1 Broadway Salt Lake City UT 84101

QUITEVIS, MINDA ALTEA, sales executive; b. Bacolod, Philippines, Apr. 25, 1937; came to U.S., 1967; d. Lazaro Onang and Estelita (Villar) Altea; m. Hilario P. Quitevis, Aug. 14, 1968; 1 child, Richard Joseph. BS in Pharmacy, Uno Recoletos, Bacolod City, Philippines, 1960; BS in Edn., Notre Dame, Jolo, Philippines, 1966. Pharmacist Farmacia San Benito, Zamboanga, Philippines, 1960-61, New Life Drug Store, Zamboanga, 1961-62, Universal Pharmacy, Zamboanga, 1962-64, San Antonio Drugstore, Jolo, Philippines, 1964-67; sci. tchr. Notre Dame, Jolo, 1964-67; pharmacy clk. Get Pharmacy, San Francisco, 1967-68; rep. Avon, San Francisco, 1968-81; med. claims examiner Blue Shield Calif., San Francisco, 1971-81; sales dir., Cadillac dir. Mary Kay Cosmetics, San Francisco, 1983—; jeweler Minda's Jewelry, San Francisco, 1981—. Editor, pub. Minda's Goldmines, 1983-89. Recipient Mink Coats, Diamond Bee pins Mary Kay., 1984, 85, 86, 87, 88. Mem. Fayco. Roman Catholic. Home: 397 Moscow St San Francisco CA 94112 Office: Mindas Goldmines 163 El Camino Real South San Francisco CA 94080

QUOCK, JOAN MARIE, financial executive; b. N.Y.C., Mar. 29, 1941; d. Shau Hong and Daisy (Chau) Chin; m. Stephen Quock, Aug. 7, 1966; children: Monica Troy, Dean Barry. BA with honors, U. Calif., Berkeley, 1963; cert., Calif. State U., Hayward, 1966; postgrad., Ariz. State U., 1967-68, Chabot Coll., 1981, Butte Coll. Cert. tchr. (life). Legal sec. Miller, Williams & Brown, San Francisco, 1960-63; asst. to sr. editor Archtl. Record, N.Y.C., 1963-64; reporter Burlingame (Calif.) Advance, 1964; elem. tchr. Tempe (Ariz.) Unified Sch. Dist., 1966-69; assoc. realtor Century 21 Goodman Realty, Paradise, Calif., 1980; rep. Tchrs. Mgmt. & Investments Inc., Newport Beach, Calif., 1981-87, Titan Capital Corp., Tustin, Calif., 1988—; referral assoc. Fox & Carskadon Inc., San Carlos, Calif., 1986—; speaker in field. Mem. adv. com. gifted and talented edn. program Hayward Unified Sch. Dist., 1983-84. Mem. AAUW (chmn. money talks Hayward-Castro Valley chpt. 1982-83), Nat. Assn. Securities Dealers (registered rep.), Internat. Tng. in Communications Assn. (accredited, v.p. Eden chpt. 1987-88), Internat. Assn. Fin. Planning (v.p. programs Alameda County chpt. 1988), Commonwealth Club Calif., Oakland-Dalian Friendship City Soc., U. Calif.-Berkeley Alumni Assn., U.S. Law Tennis Assn. (cert. 1976), East Bay Chinese Tennis Assn., Tennis H.A.R.D. Women's League. Office: Titan Capital Corp 3000 Arden Way Ste 2 Citrus Heights CA 95825

QUON, DENNIS KIM, architect; b. Nurnberg, Fed. Republic Germany, Nov. 2, 1956; s. Henry and Esperanza (Ramirez) Q.; m. Gwen Cecilia Quon, Dec. 17, 1977; children: Jonathan Henry, David Matthew. BS, Calif. Poly. State U., 1978. Registered profl. engr. Calif.; lic. architect Calif. Engr. Anderson, Bjornstad, Kane, Jacobs, Seattle, 1978-79, Culp and Tanner, Dana Point, Calif., 1979-81; architect in tng. Meyer, Lasley, Wilkinson, Irvine, Calif., 1981-82, Timothy Wilkes A.I.A., Laguna Beach, Calif., 1982-83; with Danielson Design Group, San Juan Capistrano Beach, Calif., 1983-84, project architect, 1985-89; pvt. practice architect Capistrano Beach, Calif., 1984-85, Elsinore, Calif., 1989—. Mem. Design Rev. Bd., San Clemente, Calif., 1982-83; bd. chmn. Dana Point Christian Sch., 1983-86. Republican. Home: 3524 Lake Crest Dr Lake Elsinore CA 92330

QUONG, TERRENCE O., engineering manager; b. Camp Wheeler, Ga., June 25, 1943; s. James Lee and Jennie Lou (Grey) Q. AS, Utah Tech. Coll., 1987; BS, SUNY, Albany, 1987. Program dir. Radio Sta. KIBE-KDFC, San Francisco, 1968-69; MPE mechanic U.S. Postal Svc., San Francisco, 1970-73; engring. technician Signetics GmbH, Noerdlingen, Fed. Republic Germany, 1973-76; reliability engr. Signetics Co., Sunnyvale, Calif., 1976-81; instrument technician Western Geophysical Co., United Arab Emirates, 1981-83; QRA engr. Signetics Co., Sunnyvale, 1983-84; QRA sect. head Signetics Co., Orem, Utah, 1984—. SCAT team mem. Utah County Sheriff' Communications Aux. Team, Provo, Utah, 1984-85. With USMC, 1961. Mem. IEEE, Am. Soc. for Quality Control, Overseas Craftsman's Assn. Democrat. Episcopalian. Home: PO Box 51 American Fork UT 84003 Office: Signetics Co 1275 S 800 E Orem UT 84058

QURESHI, AZAM SAJJAD, manufacturing company executive; b. Hyderabad, India, Oct. 18, 1942; came to U.S., 1965; naturalized; s. Khadim Hussain and Rafath Q.; m. Asima Qureshi, Jan. 4, 1969; children: Huma, Huda, Ali. BE in Mech. Engring., Osmania U., India, 1965; MS in Mech. Engring., Okla. State U., 1967; MBA, U. Santa Clara, 1974. Lic. profl. engr., Ont. Engr. rsch. and devel. div. Allis-Chalmers Corp., West Allis, Wis., 1967-69; sr. analytical engr. mobile div. Sperry-Vickers, Troy, Mich., 1969-72; design specialist ground vehicle systems group Lockheed Missiles & Space Co., Sunnyvale, Calif., 1972-75; mgr. engring. Tomco, Inc., Racine, Wis., 1975-77; v.p. engring. and product safety Calavar Corp., Santa Fe Springs, 1977—. Contbr. articles to profl. jours. Patentee in field (Queen's Silver Medal 1983). Mem. Soc. Automotive Engrs., Am. Soc. Safety Engrs., Am. Nat. Standards Inst., Mfr. Elevating Work Platform Council, Mfr. Aerial Devices and Digger Derricks Council. Republican. Islamic. Home: 1661 Camden Pl Fullerton CA 92633 Office: Calavar Corp 9200 Sorensen Santa Fe Springs CA 90670

QURESHI, MOHAMMED JAMIL, college official, consultant; b. Jagadhri, Panjab, India, Mar. 29, 1939; came to U.S., 1971; s. Mohammad Ibrahim and Fatima (Bibi) Q.; m. Saeeda Farhat, Apr. 13, 1975; children—Khalid Jamil, Naz Jamil. B.S. U. Panjab, 1962, D.L.S., 1964; M.A., U. Karachi, Pakistan, 1966; M.L.S., U. Toronto, Ont., Can., 1968; Ed.D., U. No. Colo., 1978. Audit clerk, fin. advisor, chief accounts officer Pakistan Western Rys., Lahore, 1960-63; lectr. Forward Coll., Lahore, 1963-65; librarian Panjab U. Library, 1964-65; bookmobile librarian Cape Breton Regional Library, Sydney, N.S., Can., 1966-67; adult services librarian North York Pub. Libraries, Toronto, 1968-69; asst. librarian, asst. dir. learning resources ctr. Red River Community Coll., Winnipeg., Man., Can., 1969-72; dir. learning resources ctr. State Community Coll., East St. Louis, Ill., 1971-72, dean learning resource services, 1972-73; dir. learning resources ctr. Pikes Peak Community Coll., Colorado Springs, Colo., 1974-80, assoc. dean, 1980-83, v.p. student services, 1981-86, v.p. adminstrv. services, 1987—; mem. library formula com. State of Colo., 1976-82; mem. instrn./instructional support/student services subcom., centralization/decentralization com. Colo. Bd. Community Colls. and Occupational Edn., 1982-83, chmn. instructional support com., mem. student services com., mem. credential rev. com. for vocat. guidance specialist and job devel. specialist, 1982-84, chmn. state adv. com. for student personnel services, 1983-85; vice chmn. ednl. accountability com., chmn. vocat. edn. sub-com. Sch. Dist. 11, Colorado Springs, 1982—. Author: Book Selection Aids for the Community College Staff, 1970; Cataloging and Classification Use and Trends in Canadian Community College Libraries (survey), 1971; compiler (with Master Rasheeduddin) bibliography on 1st prime minister of Pakistan, Nawabzada Liaqat Ali Khan, 1966; mem. Urban League Colorado Springs, 1974—; mem. planning com. Plains and Peaks Regional Library System, Colorado Springs, 1975-76, pres. governing bd., 1977-78; chmn. edn. com. Colorado Springs br. NAACP, 1979-83, bd. dirs., 1979-85. Grad. library fellow U. Toronto, 1967-68; grad. acad. scholar U. No. Colo., 1971-72. Mem. ALA, Assn. Ednl. Communications and Tech., Community Coll. Assn. Instrn. and Tech., Colo. Library Assn. (chmn. coll. and univ. action subcom. 1976-77, mem. legis. com. 1977-78, budget com. 1978-79), Nat. Assn. Coll. and Univ. Bus. Officers, Western Assn. Coll. and Univ. Bus. Officers, Assn. Colo. Community Coll. Learning Resources Ctrs. (v.p. 1977-78, pres. 1978-79), Colo. Ednl. Media Assn., Nat. Assn. Student Personnel Adminstrs., Kappa Delta Pi. Home: 2855 Villa Loma Dr Colorado Springs CO 80917 Office: Pikes Peak Community Coll 5675 S Academy Blvd Colorado Springs CO 80906

RABE, BRADFORD L., dentist; b. Portland, Oreg., May 1, 1958; s. Ronald Cleone and Valerie Beatrice (Strahl) R.; m. Susan K. Shultz, Sept. 3, 1988. BS, Portland State U., 1980; DMD, Oreg. Health Scis. U., 1984. Winemaking asst. Oak Knoll Winery, Hillsboro, Oreg., 1971-82; pvt. practice dentistry Hillsboro, 1984—. Mem. Am. Dental Assn., Oreg. Dental Assn., Washington County Dental Soc. (editor jour. 1986-88), Hillsboro Jaycees (bd. dirs. 1986). Republican. Office: 246 SE 2d St Hillsboro OR 97123

RABINOWITZ, JAY ANDREW, state supreme court justice; b. Phila., Feb. 25, 1927; s. Milton and Rose (Rittenberg) R.; m. Anne Marie Nesbit, June 14, 1957; children: Judith, Mara, Max, Sara. B.A., Syracuse U., 1949; LL.B., Harvard, 1952. Bar: N.Y. 1952, Alaska 1958. Practiced in N.Y.C., 1952-57; law clk. U.S. Dist. Ct. judge, Fairbanks, Alaska, 1957-58; asst. U.S. atty. Fairbanks, 1958-59; dep. atty. gen., chief civil div. State of Alaska, 1959-60; judge Superior Ct. Alaska, 1960-65; justice Alaska Supreme Ct., Juneau, 1965—, chief justice, 1972-75, 78-81, from 1984; lectr. U. Alaska. Served with AUS, 1945-46. Mem. N.Y. Bar Assn., Alaska Bar Assn. Club: Harvard (N.Y.C.). Office: Alaska Supreme Ct 303 K St Anchorage AK 99501 *

RACCA, ERNEST LEE, government official, real estate broker; b. San Antonio, July 6, 1925; s. Anastas Ernest and Theresa (Benoit) R.; m. Margaret Apalategui, Apr. 17, 1948; children: Kathleen T. Racca Albertson, Timothy J., John F., Jane M. Racca Hirsch. BABA, Whittier Coll., 1951; postgrad. in Labor and Indsl. Rels., U. So. Calif., 1951-52; postgrad. in Law, Western State U., 1978-79. Lic. real estate broker, Calif. With State Fund, 1952-64; dist. mgr. State Compensation Ins. Fund, Ventura, Calif., 1961-64; revenue officer IRS, U.S. Treasury Dept., Santa Ana, Calif., 1966—. With USNR, 1943-45, PTO. Democrat. Roman Catholic. Home: 536 N Wilson Ave Fullerton CA 92631

RACHINSKI, HOWARD DALE, church copyright licensing company executive; b. Vancouver, B.C., Can., Apr. 26, 1951; s. Ernest and Ida (Wirch) R.; m. Donna Gem Kirkpatrick, Feb. 10, 1973; children: Dyane Gem, Deryk James. Diploma, Glad Tidings Bible Coll., 1976. Purchasing agt. Placer Devel. Ltd., Vancouver, 1970-77; sales mgr. Praise Industries Ltd., Vancouver, 1977-78; assoc. pastor Glad Tidings Ch., Bellingham, Wash., 1978-82; ins. agt. Interwest Agy., Bellingham, 1982-84; music minister Bible Temple, Portland, Oreg., 1984-88; pres., chief exec. officer Christian Copyright Licensing, Inc., Portland, 1988—; elder Bible Temple, Portland, 1988—; bd. dirs. Christian Copyright Licensing, Inc., Portland. Contbr. articles to Resources, 1988, Progressions, 1989, Psalmist, 1989. Founder Noncommercial Copyright Licensing/Ch. Copyright License, 1985. Office: Christian Copyright Licensing Inc 7031 NE Halsey St Portland OR 97213

RACICOT, MARC, attorney general; b. Thompson Falls, Mont., July 24, 1948; s. William E. and Patricia E. (Bentley) R.; m. Theresa J. Barber, July 25, 1970; children: Ann, Timothy, Mary Catherine, Theresa, Joseph. BA, Carroll Coll., Helena, Mont., 1970; JD, U. Mont., 1973; postgrad., U. Va., 1973, Cornell U., 1977. Bar: Mont. Commd. officer U.S. Army, 1973; advanced through grades to capt. 1976; legal assistance officer U.S. Army, Ft. Lewis, Wash., 1973; chief trial counsel U.S. Army, Kaiserslautern, Fed. Republic of Germany, 1975-76; resigned 1976; dep. county atty. Missoula (Mont.) County, 1976-77; bur. chief County Prosecutor Svcs. Bur., Helena, Mont., 1977-89; asst. atty. gen. State of Mont., Helena, 1989—; spl. prosecutor for the Atty. Gen.'s Office State of Mont., atty. gen. Founder Missoula Drug Treatment Program, 1977; bd. mem. Carroll Coll. Pres.'s Coun.; cabinet mem. United Way, Helena; bd. visitors U. Mont. Sch. Law. Inducted into Basketball Hall of Fame Carroll Coll., 1982. Mem. Mont. Bar Assn., Nat. Assn. Attys. Gen, Carroll Coll. Century Club (bd. dirs.). Republican. Roman Catholic. Office: Mont Dept Justice Justice Bldg 215 N Sanders Helena MT 59620

RACINA, THOM (THOMAS FRANK RAUCINA), writer, editor; b. Kenosha, Wis., June 4, 1946; s. Frank G. and Esther May (Benko) Raucina. B.F.A., Goodman Sch. Drama, Art Inst. Chgo., 1970, M.F.A. in Theatre Arts and Directing with honors, 1971. TV writer Hanna-Barbera Co., Hollywood, Calif., 1973-74, MTM Enterprises, Inc., Hollywood, 1974-76; head writer General Hospital ABC-TV, Hollywood, 1981-84; head writer Days of Our Lives NBC-TV, 1984-86, head writer Another World, 1986-88, co-head writer Generations daytime series, 1988—. Author: Lifeguard, 1976, The Great Los Angeles Blizzard, 1977, Quincy, M.E., 2 vols., 1977, Kodak in San Francisco, 1977, F.M., 1978, Sweet Revenge, 1978, The Gannon Girls, 1979, Nine to Five, 1980, Tomcat, 1981, Secret Sex: Male Erotic Fantasies (as Tom Anicar), 1976, Magda (as Lisa Wells), 1981; ghost writer: non-fiction The Happy Hustler (Grant Tracy Saxon), 1976, Marilyn Chambers: My Story (Marilyn Chambers), 1976, Xaviera Meets Marilyn (Xaviera Hollander and Marilyn Chambers), 1977; musical plays A Midsummer Night's Dream, music and lyrics, 1968, Allison Wonderland, music and lyrics, 1970, The Marvelous Misadventure of Sherlock Holmes, book, music and lyrics, 1971; TV scripts Sleeping Over segment of Family, ABC, 1978, Russian Pianist segment, ABC, 1979, 1 Child of the Owl, NBC After-Sch. Spl., 1979; contbr. articles to Playboy, Cosmopolitan, Penhouse, Oui, Los Angeles, Gentleman's Quar., Westways; West Coast editor: Grosset & Dunlap, Inc., N.Y.C., 1978—; theatre dir., pianist, organist, composer. Recipient Emmy award nomination 1982, 83, 84, 85, 87; U.S. Nat. Student Assn. grantee, 1965. Mem. Authors Guild Am., Writers Guild Am. West. Democrat. Roman Catholic. Home: 3449 Waverly Dr Los Angeles CA 90027

RADA, ALEXANDER, university official; b. Kvasy, Czechoslovakia, Mar. 28, 1923; s. Frantisek and Anna (Tonnkova) R.; came to U.S., 1954, naturalized, 1959; M.S., U. Tech. Coll. of Prague, 1948; postgrad. Va. Poly. Inst., 1956-59, St. Clara U., 1966-67; Ed.D., U. Pacific, 1975; m. Ingeborg Solveig Blakstad, Aug. 8, 1953; children: Alexander Sverre, Frank Thore, David Harald. Head prodn. planning dept. Mine & Iron Corp., Kolin, Czechoslovakia, 1941-42; mgr. experimenting and testing dept. Avia Aircraft, Prague, 1943-45; sec.-gen. Central Bldg. Office, Prague, 1948; head metal courses dept. Internat. Tech. Sch. of UN, Grafenaschau, W.Ger., 1949-50; works mgr. Igref A/S, Oslo, 1950-51; cons. engr., chief sect. machines Steel Products Ltd., Oslo, 1951-54; chief engr., plant supr. Nelson J. Pepin & Co., Lowell, Mass., 1954-55; sr. project engr., mfg. supt. Celanese Corp. Am., Narrows, Va., 1955-60; mgr. mfg., facilities and maint. FMC Corp., San Jose, Calif., 1960-62; mgr. adminstrn. Sylvania Electronic Systems, Santa Cruz, Calif., 1962-72; asst. to pres., devel. officer Napa (Calif.) Coll., 1972-88; chief exec. officer NAVCO Pacific Devel. Corp., Napa, 1984—; prof. indsl. mgmt. Cabrillo Coll., Aptos, Calif., 1963-72; mgmt. and engring. cons., 1972—. Pres. ARC, Santa Cruz, 1965-72, bd. dirs., pres., Napa, 1977-88; mem. Nat. Def. Exec. Res., U.S. Dept. Commerce, Washington, 1966—, chmn. No. Calif. region 9, 1981-88; mem. President's Export Council-DEC, San Francisco, 1982—. Recipient Meritorious Service citation ARC, 1972, Etoile Civique l'Ordre de l'Etoile Civique, French Acad., 1985; registered profl. engr., Calif. Mem. Nat., Calif. socs. profl. engrs., Am. Def. Preparedness Assn., Assn. Calif. Community Coll. Adminstrs., World Affairs Council No. Calif., Phi Delta Kappa. Editor-in-chief Our Youth, 1945-48; co-editor (with P. Boulden) Innovative Management Concepts, 1967. Home: 1019 Ross Circle Napa CA 94558 Office: 5 Financial Pla Ste 120 Napa CA 94558

RADAKOVITZ, WILLIAM MICHAEL, small business owner; b. Portland, Oreg., Nov. 26, 1942; s. Herman Andrew and Jean May (McComie) R.; m. Nancie Lynne Freeman, Apr. 21, 1962; children: William Michael Jr., Michael John. AA, American River Coll., 1966; BA in Psych., Sacramento State U., 1970. Claims Calif. State Auto Assn., Auburn, Calif., 1966-78; owner Nancie's Records, Auburn, 1972—, Placeville, 1978—. Councilman, City of Rocklin, Calif., 1972-76, mayor pro-tem, 1974-76; pres. Sierra Coll. Found., Rocklin, 1985-88; bd. dirs. Golden Sierra, Auburn, 1974—. With USAF, 1961-65. Mem. Rotary (bd. dirs. Auburn chpt. 1988—). Republican. Home: 5165 Topaz Ave Rocklin CA 95677 Office: Nancies Records 875 Lincoln Way Auburn CA 95603

RADCLIFFE, COURTNEY LANE, hypnotherapist; b. Aug. 4, 1962. Student, U. Wash., 1981-85. Therapist, psychic cons. to pvt. and law enforcement agys. 1974--; pres, chief exec. officer Alternatives Unlimited, Inc., Bellingham, Wash., 1987—; co-owner Transpersonal Hypnotherapy Assocs., Bellingham, Wash., 1987—; herbalist, 1974—; mem. faculty Transpersonal Coll., Bellevue, Wash. Contbr. numerous articles to various publs. Bd. dirs. Pacific Women's Resources, Seattle, 1985; co-dir. Change Project, 1989—; active numerous environ. groups. Mem. NAFE, Mensa, Women's Mysteries Project, Bus. Women's Inst. Office: Alternatives Unltd Inc 119 N Commercial St Ste 810 Bellingham WA 98225

RADCLIFFE, STEPHANIE ANNE, educator; b. McPherson, Kans., Apr. 10, 1937; d. Lawrence Russell and Mildred Mae (Head) Schoenhals; m. Robert James Radcliffe, July 10, 1964; children: Richard James, Robyn Suzanne. BA, Seattle Pacific U., 1959; MA, Biola U., 1984. Cert. tchr., Calif. Tchr. elem. schs. Norwalk (Calif.) La Mirada Unified Sch. Dist., 1984--. Mem. NEA, Calif. Tchrs. Assn., Tchrs. Assn. Norwalk/La Mirada, Falconettes. Office: John H Nuffer Sch 14821 Jersey Ave Norwalk CA 90650

RADDER, BRUCE MILTON, business owner; b. Bloomington, Ind., Dec. 7, 1925; s. Norman John and Elsie (Fjelstad) R.; m. Shirley Ann Abeles, Nov. 25, 1948; children: Susan Beecher, Bruce Jr., Brian, Scott, Robin Matthews. BA, Lake Forest (Ill.) Coll., 1949. Account exec. Sta. WOBT, Rhinelander, Wis., 1953-55, Sta. WBBM, Chgo., 1956-57, Sta. WOTV-TV, Grand Rapids, Mich., 1953-58; pres. Indoor Mktg., Inc., Grand Rapids, Mich., 1961-63, Silver Jack Wanigan, Inc., Grand Rapids, Mich., 1963-65, Radder Advt., Inc., Grand Rapids, Mich., 1958-74, Main St., Inc., Grand Rapids, Mich., 1974-78; owner, mgr. Print Pros, Escondido, Calif., 1978—. Served as ensign USMC, 1943-46. Recipient ADDY awards Advt. Fedn. Am., 1960, 61, 62. Mem. Agy. Group (founding dir., pres. 1969), Soc. for Preservation and Encouragement of Barber Shop Quartet Singing in Am. (pres. Palomar Pacific chpt. 1980-81). Republican. Congregationalist. Clubs: Advt. North County (Escondido) (chmn. bd. dirs. 1986-87); Advt. (Grand Rapids) (pres. 1960). Home: 1401 82 El Norte Pkwy San Marcos CA 92069 Office: Print Pros 217 E Grand Ave Escondido CA 92025

RADER, DOUGLAS LEE, professional baseball manager; b. Chgo., July 30, 1944; m. Jeanette Rader; children: Matthew, Christine, Elizabeth. Student, Ill. Wesleyan U. Third baseman Houston Astros, Nat. League, 1967-75, San Diego Padres, Nat. League, 1976, Toronto Blue Jays, Am. League, 1977; coach San Diego Padres, Nat. League, 1977-78; mgr. Hawaii, Pacific Coast League, 1980-82, Texas Rangers, Am. League, 1983-85; coach Chgo. White Sox, 1986-87; mgr. California Angels, Anaheim, 1988—. Recipient Gold Glove award Nat. League, 1970-72. Office: care Calif Angels Anaheim Stadium 2000 State College Blvd Anaheim CA 92806 *

RADER, PHILIP DOUGLAS, management and marketing consultant; b. Washington, Ind., Oct. 10, 1955; s. Owen Richard and Kathleen Virginia (Eads) R.; m. Debra Jovetta Broxton, June 16, 1973 (div. Mar. 1983); 1 stepchild, Stephanie Lea. Cert. Acctg., Ind. U., 1976, BS, 1976; MBA, Ariz. State U., 1989. Cert. Mgmt. Acct. Fin. acct. Blue Cross & Blue Shield of Ind., Indpls., 1976-79, systems specialist, 1979-80, fin. analyst, 1980-82, corp. planning specialist sr., 1982-84, sales rep., 1984; mgr. fin. planning Ind. Health Plan, Southfield, Mich., 1984-86; dir. mktg. svcs. Ind. Health Plan, Southfield, 1986-87; mktg. cons., grad. asst. Ariz. State U., Tempe, 1987—. Fundraiser Indpls. Humane Soc., 1984. Mem. Nat. Assn. Accts., Am. Mktg. Assn., Beta Gamma Sigma. Home: 510 N Alma School Rd #288 Mesa AZ 85201

RADER, RALPH WILSON, humanities educator; b. Muskegon, Mich., May 18, 1930; s. Ralph McCoy and Nelle Emily (Fargo) R.; m. June Willadean Warring, Sept. 3, 1950; children—Lois Jean, Eric Conrad, Michael William, Nancy Anne, Emily Rose. B.S., Purdue U., 1952; Ph.D., Ind. U., 1958. Instr. dept. English U. Calif., Berkeley, 1956-58; asst. prof. U. Calif., 1958-63, assoc. prof., 1963-67, prof., 1967—, chmn. dept., 1976-80; F.I. Carpenter vis. prof. English, U. Chgo., 1970; dir. seminar Nat. Endowment for Humanities, summer 1975, 83, 85; editorial com. U. Calif. Press, 1963-72, co-chmn., 1968-72; mem. exec. com. Assn. Depts. English, 1978-80. Author: Tennyson's Maud: The Biographical Genesis, 1963, reprinted, 1978. Co-author: Essays in Eighteenth Century Biography, 1968; New Approaches to Eighteenth Century Literature, 1974. Editor: (with Sheldon Sacks) Essays: An Analytic Reader, 1964; adv. bd. Yale edit. Private Papers of James Boswell; editorial bd. Critical Inquiry; The 18th Century: Theory and Interpretation; Prose Studies. Am. Council Learned Socs. grantee, 1959; Guggenheim fellow, 1972-73; recipient Disting. Teaching award U. Calif.-Berkeley, 1975-76. Mem. MLA, Phi Beta Kappa. Democrat. Home: 465 Vassar Ave Berkeley CA 94708

RADFORD, JOHN JOSEPH, state agency administrator, accounting educator; b. Mpls., Nov. 27, 1949; s. Edwin Phillip and Elizabeth Ann (Aulwes) R.; m. Leah Eileen Briedall, July 10, 1971; children: Christopher, Kathryn. BA of Gen. Studies, U. Nebr., 1974, MA in Pub. Adminstrn., 1979. Cert. internal auditor, cert. cost analyst. Acct. mgmt. svcs. City of Omaha, 1972-83; instr. Coll. St. Mary's, Omaha, 1982-83, Metro Community Coll., Omaha, 1982-83; dir. mgmt. svcs. div. Oreg. Jud. Dept., Salem, Oreg., 1983—; instr. City U., Portland, Oreg., 1988. Pres. Big Bros./Big Sisters, Omaha, 1980-82; cons. Keep Omaha Beautiful com., 1979-83. Served to sgt. USAF, 1968-72. Mem. Govt. Fin. Officers Assn., Am. Assn. Pub. Adminstrs., Oreg. Soc. CPAs. Republican. Roman Catholic. Club: Investments (Portland) (treas.). Home: 7296 S Tenino Ln Tualatin OR 97062 Office: Oreg Jud Dept Supreme Ct Bldg Salem OR 97310

RADLOFF, WILLIAM HAMILTON, editor, writer; b. Milw., Mar. 5, 1914; s. Alfred Carl and Florence (Hamilton) R.; m. Mary Ellen Borgman, Nov. 9, 1940; children: Thomas M., Susan M. BA, Ripon Coll., 1936. Reporter, writer Milw. Sentinel, 1937-42; reporter, writer Milw. Jour., 1946-49, asst. city editor, 1949-60, asst. feature editor, 1960-61, feature editor, 1961-69; asst. story editor 20th Century Fox Film Corp., L.A., 1969-72; freelance writer L.A., 1972—. Author and editor numerous news and feature articles; asst. editor of film and TV scripts. Lt. U.S. Army (M.I. Corps), 1942-46, PTO. Home: 313 S Anita Ave Los Angeles CA 90049

RADOSEVICH, CAROL DEATON, utility official, venture capitalist; b. Albuquerque, Sept. 1, 1949; d. William R. and Patricia Ann (Baxter) Erdman; m. Raymond Radosevich, July 25, 1985. BS in Mktg., Ariz. State U., 197l; M Mgmt., U. N.Mex., 198l. Asst. rsch. mgr. Phoenix Newspapers, 197l-73; market analyst Greyhound, Armour, Dial, Phoenix, 1973; asst. br. mgr. lst Nat. Bank in Albuquerque, 1973-75; installment loan officer Sunuest Bak, Albuquerque, 1975-76; installment loan officer Pub. Svc. Co. N.Mex., Albuquerque, 1976-78, budget analyst, 1976-78, econ. analyst, 1978-80, sr. strategic planner PNM & Meadows Resources subs., 1980-85, venture capital mgr., 1985-88, investment mgr., 1988-89, indsl. devel. svc. dir., 1989—; bd. dirs. Community Devel. Corp., Albuquerque. Bd. dirs. Big Bros.-Big Sisters, Albuquerque, 1984-85; bd. dirs., v.p. Women's Econ. Self-Sufficiency Team, Albuquerque, 1988--. Recipient award N.Mex. Gov.'s Econ. Devel. Planning Commn., 1988. Mem. Nat. Venture Capital Assn., Am. Mktg. Assn. (bd. dirs. Albuquerque 1983-84), N.Mex. Entrepreneurs Assn., Assn. Commerce and Industry (bd. dirs., exec. com. 1987--), Chi Omega. Office: Pub Svc Co NMex 1650 University NE Ste 500 Albuquerque NM 87102

RADUCHEL, WILLIAM JAMES, information technology executive; b. Hancock, Mich., May 25, 1946; s. William Reece and Olive Helen (Fricke) R.; B.A., Mich. State U., 1966; A.M., Harvard U., 1968, Ph.D. (Grad. Prize fellow), 1972. Asst. prof. econs. Harvard U., 1971-74; asst. dean admissions Harvard and Radcliffe colls., 1973-77; mem. research staff Inst. Def. Analyses, Arlington, Va., 1977-78; dir. tech. services Data Resources, Inc. subs. McGraw-Hill, Inc., Washington, 1978-79, sr. v.p., Lexington, Mass., 1979-83; corp. v.p. McGraw-Hill, Inc., N.Y.C., 1983-84, corp. sr. v.p., 1984-85; corp. strategy prin. Xerox Corp., Stamford, Conn., 1985-87, v.p. strategic bus. office/document systems, 1987-88; v.p. corp. planning and devel. Sun Microsystems Inc., Mountain View, Calif., 1988—. Mem. Assn. Computing Machinery, IEEE, Am. Econs. Assn., Econometric Soc., Am. Statis. Assn., Beta Gamma Sigma, Phi Eta Sigma. Office: Sun Microsystems Inc 2550 Garcia Ave Mountain View CA 94043

RADYS, ARVIN ANTHONY, sales executive; b. Regensburg, Germany, June 20, 1942; came to U.S., 1949; s. Valerian Felix and Ella Lydia (Heinrich) R.; m. Karen Pauline Horn, Dec. 24, 1960; children: Eric Valerian, Konrad Marshall. Student, Bethany Coll., Mankato, Minn., 1959, Sch. of Art Inst. Chgo., 1961. Sales engr. Autogas Co., Bellwood, Ill., 1960-65, Porter County Plumbing and Heating, Valparaiso, Ind., 1965-69, Temperature Equipment Co., Melrose Park, Ill., 1969-75, Lennox Industries, Portland, Oreg., 1975-78, Enviro-Air Systems, Portland, 1978-84; pres. Ratec Corp., Portland, 1984—; v.p. sales Tri-M, Inc., Portland, 1988—. Pres., Portland Mountain Rescue, 1984-88. Mem. Oreg. Judo Club (pres.), Toastmasters, Optimists, Mazamas Club. Republican. Office: Ratec Corp PO Box 2845 Portland OR 97208

RADZIEMSKI, LEON JOSEPH, physicist; b. Worcester, Mass., June 18, 1937; s. Leon Joseph and Josephine Elizabeth (Janczukowicz) R.; married; children: Michael Leon, Timothy Joseph. BA, Coll. Holy Cross, 1958; MS, Purdue U., 1961, PhD, 1964. Staff physicist Los Alamos (N.Mex.) Nat. Lab., 1967-83; head dept. physics N.Mex. State U., Las Cruces, 1983-88, assoc. dean, dir. arts and scis. rsch. ctr. Coll. of Arts & Scis., 1988—; vis. scientist Laboratoire Aime Cotton, Orsay, France, 1974-75; vis. assoc. prof. dept. nuclear engring. U. Fla., Gainesville, 1978-79. Editor Marcel Dekker Series: Laser Advances; contbr. articles to profl. jours.; patentee in field. 1st lt. USAF, 1964-67. Hughes Aricraft Co. fellow, 1958-59. Mem. Am. Phys. Soc., Optical Soc. Am., Soc. Applied Spectroscopy, Laser Inst. Am. (bd. dirs. 1986—). Home: 4709 Falcon Dr Las Cruces NM 88001 Office: NMex State U Box RC Las Cruces NM 88003

RAE, MATTHEW SANDERSON, JR., lawyer; b. Pitts., Sept. 12, 1922; s. Matthew Sanderson and Olive (Waite) R.; m. Janet Hettman, May 2, 1953; children: Mary-Anna, Margaret, Janet, Rae-Dupree. AB, Duke, 1946, LLB, 1947; postgrad., Stanford U., 1951. Bar: Md. 1948, Calif. 1951. Asst. to dean Duke Sch. Law, Durham, N.C., 1947-48; assoc. Karl F. Steinmann, Balt., 1948-49, Guthrie, Darling & Shattuck, Los Angeles, 1953-54; nat. field rep. Phi Alpha Delta Frat., Los Angeles, 1949-51; research atty. Calif. Supreme Ct., San Francisco, 1951-52; ptnr. Darling, Hall & Rae and predecessor firms, Los Angeles, 1955—; mem. Calif. Commn. Uniform State Laws, 1985—. V.p. Los Angeles County Rep. Assembly, 1959-64; mem. Los Angeles County Rep. Cen. Com., 1960-64, 77—, exec. com., 1977—; vice chmn. 17th Congl. Dist., 1960-62, 28th Congl. Dist., 1962-64; chmn. 46th Assembly Dist., 1962-64, 27th Senatorial Dist., 1977-85, 29th Senatorial Dist,m 1985—; mem. Calif. Rep. State Cen. Com., 1966—, exec. com., 1966-67; pres. Calif. Rep. League, 1966-67; trustee Rep. Assocs., 1979—, pres., 1983-85, chmn. bd. dirs., 1985-87. Served to 2d lt. USAAF, World War II. Fellow Am. Coll. Probate Counsel; academician Internat. Acad. Estate and Trust Law (exec. council 1974-78); mem. ABA, Los Angeles County Bar Assn. (chmn. probate and trust law com. 1964-66, chmn. legislation com. 1980-86, chmn. program com. 1981-82, chmn. membership retention com. 1982-83, trustee 1983-85, dir. Bar Found. 1987—), South Bay Bar Assn., State Bar Calif. (chmn. state bar jour. com. 1970-71, chmn. probate com. 1974-75, exec. com. estate planning trust and probate law sect. 1977-83, chmn. legislation com. 1977—, probate law cons. group Calif. Bd. Legal Specialization 1977-88, chmn. conf. dels. resolutions com. 1987, exec. com. conf. dels. 1987—), Lawyers Club of Los Angeles (bd. govs. 1981-87, 1st v.p. 1982-83), Am. Legion (comdr. Allied post 1969-70), Legion Lex (dir. 1964—, pres. 1969-71), Air Force Assn., Aircraft Owners and Pilots Assn., Town Hall (gov. 1970-78, pres. 1975), World Affairs Council, Internat. Platform Assn., Los Angeles Com. on Fgn. Relations, Phi Beta Kappa (councilor Alpha Assn. 1983—, v.p. 1984-86), Omicron Delta Kappa, Phi Alpha Delta (supreme justice 1972-74, elected to Disting. Service chpt. 1978), Sigma Nu. Presbyterian. Clubs: Breakfast (law, pres. 1989—), Commonwealth (San Francisco); Chancery, Petroleum (L.A.). Lodge: Rotary. Home: 600 John St Manhattan Beach CA 90266 Office: Darling Hall & Rae 550 S Flower St 6th Fl Los Angeles CA 90071

RAEBURN, SANDRA BIRD, accountant; b. Englewood, N.J., Sept. 10, 1937; d. Victor Thorne and Gertrude Emma (Bird) R. BA, Duke U., 1959; postgrad. in bus., acctg., Santa Monica Coll., 1980. Asst. to mgr. Hoechst Fibers Co., L.A., 1973-76; exec. asst. Lee Mar of Calif., L.A., 1976-78, Mitsui Bank, L.A., 1978-79; adminstrv. asst. Santa Monica (Calif.) Bank, 1979-82; acctg. asst. Buckeye Realty, L.A., 1983-84; acct., computer operator Bernstein, Fox, Goldberg, CPAs, West Los Angeles, Calif., 1984-85; ind. acct. L.A., 1985-87; with accounts receivable dept. Casual Lamps Co., Gardena, Calif., 1987—. Mem. Am. Soc. Bus. and Preofl. Women, NOW, Sierra Club. Republican. Presbyterian. Home: 3311 W 3d St Apt 217 Los Angeles CA 90020

RAEDEKE, LINDA DISMORE, geologist; b. Great Falls, Mont., Aug. 20, 1950; d. Albert Browning and Madge (Hogan) Dismore; m. Kenneth John Raedeke, Dec. 26, 1971 (div. 1982). BA in History, U. Wash., 1971, MS in Geology, 1979, PhD, 1982. Geomorphologist, park planner Corporacion Nacional Forestal and U.S. Peace Corps, Punta Arenas, Chile, 1972-74; glacial geologist Empresa Nacional del Petroleo, Punta Arenas, 1972-75; geologist FAO, UN, Punta Arenas, 1974; geologist Lamont-Doherty Geol. Obs., Columbia U., Tierra del Fuego, Chile, 1974-75; Wetlands evaluation project coordinator Wash. Dept. Agr., U. Wash., Seattle, 1975-76; geomorphol. cons. Okanogan County Planning, Oceanographic Inst. Wash., Seattle, 1976; curator Remote Sensing Applications Lab., U. Wash., 1976-77; geol. cons. Amoco, Denver, 1978; petrologist Lamont-Doherty Geol. Obs., 1979; geol. cons. Empresa Minera de Mantos Blancos, Tierra del Fuego, 1980; geol. rsch. asst. U. Wash., Seattle, 1977-81; exploration geologist Chevron Resources Co., Denver, 1981-84; rsch. geologist Chevron Oil Field Rsch. Co., La Habra, Calif., 1984-89; sr. compensation analyst Chevron Corp., San Francisco, 1989—. Contbr. articles to profl. jours. Recipient Cert. of Achievement YWCA, 1988. Mem. Am. Geophys. Union, Geol. Soc. Am., Am. Assn. Petroleum Geologists (poster chmn. 1987). Office: Chevron Corp Orgn Devel and Compensation PO Box 7643 San Francisco CA 94120-7643

RAEL, HENRY SYLVESTER, health administrator; b. Pueblo, Colo., Oct. 2, 1928; s. Daniel and Grace (Abyeta) R.; m. Helen Warner Loring Brace, June 30, 1956 (dec. Aug. 1980); children: Henry Sylvester, Loring Victoria Bush. AB, U. So. Colo., 1955; BA in Bus Adminstrn., U. Denver, 1957, MBA, 1958. Sr. boys counselor Denver Juvenile Hall, 1955-58; adminstrv. asst. to pres. Stanley Aviation Corp., Denver, 1958-61; Titan III budget and fin. control supr. Martin Marietta Corp., Denver, 1961-65; mgmt. adv. services officer U. Colo. Med. Center, Denver, 1965-72; v.p. fin., treas. Loretto Heights Coll., Denver, 1972-73; dir. fin. and adminstrn. Colo. Found. for Med. Care, 1973-86, Tri-County Health Dept., Denver, 1986—; instr. fin. mgmt., mem. fin. com. Am. Assn. Profl. Standards Rev. Orgn., 1980-85 ; speaker systems devel., design assns., univs., 1967-71. Mem. budget lay adv. com. Park Hill Elem. Sch., Denver, 1967-68, chmn., 1968-69; vol. worker Boy and Girl Scouts, 1967-73; bd. dirs. Community Arts Symphony, 1981-83, 85-87; controller St. John's Episcopal Cathedral, 1982-83; charter mem. Pueblo (Colo.) Coll. Young Democrats, 1954-55; block worker Republican party, Denver, 1965-68, precinct committeeman, 1978-84 ; trustee Van Nattan Scholarship Fund, 1974—; bd. dirs. Vis. Nurse Assn., 1977-84, treas., 1982-84. Served with USAF, 1947-53; res. 1954-61. Recipient Disting. Service award Denver Astron. Soc., 1968, Citation Chamberlin Obs., 1985; Stanley Aviation masters scholar, 1957; Ballard scholar, 1956. Mem. Assn. Systems Mgmt. (pres. 1971-72), Hosp. Systems Mgmt. Soc., Budget Execs Inst. (v.p. chpt. 1964-65, sec. 1963-64), Denver Astron. Soc. (pres. 1965-66), Am. Assn. Founds. for Med. Care (fin. com. 1981-82), Nat. Astronomers Assn. (exec. bd. 1965—). Epsilon Xi, Delta Psi Omega. Episcopalian. Home: 70 S Albion Denver CO 80222

RAE-VENTER, BARBARA, lawyer; b. Auckland, New Zealand, July 17, 1948; d. John Donald and Veronique (Grant) Rae; m. J. Craig Venter, Nov. 7, 1968 (div. Oct. 1980); 1 child, Christopher; m. Joseph Elmer Huff III, Sept. 21, 1981 (div. Apr. 1983). BS, Coll. San Mateo, 1970; BA, U. Calif., San Diego, 1972, PhD, 1976; JD, U. Tex., 1985. Bar: Tex. 1986, Calif. 1987. Cancer rsch. scientist Roswell Park Meml. Inst., Buffalo, 1978-79; asst. prof. U. Tex. Med. Br., Galveston, 1977-83; rsch. asst. U. Tex. Law Sch., Austin, 1984; law clk. Davis & Davis, Austin, 1984-85; assoc. atty. Richards, Harris, Medlock & Andrews, Dallas, 1985-86, Leydig, Voit & Mayer, Palo Alto, Calif., 1986—; cons. U. Tex. Med. Br., Galveston, 1983-84; vis. asst. prof. Stanford U., 1988—. Contbr. articles to profl. jours. Dir. Am. Cancer Soc., Galveston, 1979-83; vol. Bar Assn. San Francisco, 1988. Am. Cancer Soc. grantee, 1978, 79-81, NIH grantee, 1983. Mem. ABA, Peninsula Intellectual Property Law Assn. Office: Leydig Voit & Mayer 350 Cambridge Ave Ste 200 Palo Alto CA 94306

RAFAEL, RUTH KELSON, archivist, librarian, consultant; b. Wilmington, N.C., Oct. 28, 1929; d. Benjamin and Jeanette (Spicer) Kelson; m. Richard Vernon Rafael, Aug. 26, 1951; children—Barbara Jeanette Rafael Martinez, Brenda Elaine. B.A., San Francisco State U., 1953, M.A., 1954; M.L.S., U. Calif.-Berkeley, 1968. Tchr. San Francisco Unified Sch. Dist., 1956-57; life credential librarian Congregation Beth Sholom, San Francisco, 1965-83; archivist Western Jewish History Ctr. of Judah L. Magnes Mus., Berkeley, Calif., 1968, head archivist, librarian, 1969—; cons. NEH, Washington, Congregation Sherith Israel, San Francisco, Mount Zion Hosp., San Francisco, Benjamin Swig archives project, San Francisco, Camp Swig, Saratoga, Calif.; project dir. Ethnicity in Calif. Agriculture, 1989. Author: Continuum, San Francisco Jews of Eastern European Origin, 1880-1940, 1976, rev. edit., 1977; (with Davies and Woogmaster) (poems) Relatively Speaking, 1981; Western Jewish History Ctr.: Archival and Oral History Collections, Judah L. Magnes Meml. Mus., 1987, Second Hand, Maybe, Ghetto, No, The Californians, 1986; contbg. editor Western States Jewish Hist., 1979—. Mem. exec. bd. Bay Area Library Info. Network, 1986-88. Bur. Jewish Edn. scholar, San Francisco, 1983; NEH grantee, 1985. Mem. Soc. Am. Archivists, ALA, Soc. Calif. Archivists, Calif. Library Assn., No. Calif. Assn. Jewish Librarians (pres. 1975-76), Jewish Arts Council of the Bay (bd. dirs. 1981-83), Spl. Libraries Assn. Office: Western Jewish History Ctr Judah L Magnes Mus 2911 Russell St Berkeley CA 94705

RAFEEDIE, EDWARD, federal judge; b. Orange, N.J., Jan. 6, 1929; s. Fred and Nabeeha (Hishmeh) R.; m. Ruth Ann Horton, Oct. 8, 1961; children: Fredrick Alexander, Jennifer Ann. BS in Law, U. So. Calif., 1957, JD, 1959; LLD (hon.), Pepperdine U., 1978. Bar: Calif. 1960. Sole practice law Santa Monica, Calif., 1960-69; mcpl. ct. judge Santa Monica Jud. Dist., Santa Monica, 1969-71; judge Superior Ct. State of Calif., Los Angeles, 1971-82; dist. judge U.S. Dist. Court for Central Dist. Calif., Los Angeles, 1982—. Trustee Santa Monica Hosp. Med. Ctr., 1979—; bd. dirs. Luth. Hosp. Soc. Corp., Los Angeles, 1985; mem. adv. bd. Greater Western council Boy Scouts Am., Los Angeles, 1980—. Served with U.S. Army, 1950-52, Korea. Office: US Dist Ct 312 N Spring St Los Angeles CA 90012

RAFFETY, MICHAEL EDWARD, newspaper editor, photography instructor; b. Berlin, Oct. 23, 1946; came to U.S., 1948; s. Charles Alva and Lois Fae (Nordean) R.; m. Cherie Lynn Albusche, Oct. 18, 1980; children: Natasha Jane, Michael Wolfgang. BA in Classics, San Francisco State U., 1977; postgrad., Calif. State U., Sacramento, 1988—. Co-editor San Francisco News, 1975; photographer Daily Democrat, Woodland, Calif., 1977; news editor Amador Progress-News and Amador Ledger, Jackson, Calif., 1977-78; city editor Mountain Democrat, Placerville, Calif., 1978-86, editor, 1986—; advisor, Cosumnes River Coll.-Placerville Ctr., 1981-85, photography instr., 1980—. With USN, 1965-69. Recipient 6 1st Place awards Calif. Newspaper Pubs. Assn., 1979, 81, 84, 87, 88 7 2d Place awards, 1981, 82, 83, 86, 87, 1st Place writing award Sigma Delta Chi, Sacramento, 1985. Mem. Soc. Profl. Journalists (2 first place awards, 1983, 2d place award, 1983), Nat. Press Photographers Assn., Am. Soc. Newspaper Editors, Lions (v.p. Diamond Springs, Calif. club 1987-89). Office: Mountain Democrat PO Box 1088 Placerville CA 95667

RAFFIN, THOMAS A., physician; b. San Francisco, Jan. 25, 1947; s. Bennett L. and Carolyn M. R.; m. Michele, June 19, 1987; children: Elizabeth S., Ross Daniel. AB in Biol. Sci., Stanford Med. Sch., 1968, MD, 1973. Diplomate Am. Bd. Respiratory Medicine, Am. Bd. Internal Medicine (also in Critical Care Medicine). Intern Peter Brent Brigham Hosp., 1973-75; fellow in respiratory medicine sch. medicine Stanford U., Stanford, Calif., 1975-78, med. fiberoptic bronchoscopy service dir. med. ctr., 1978—, acting asst. prof. sch. medicine, 1978-80, assoc. dir. med. ctr. intensive care units, med. dir. dept. respiratory therapy hosp., 1978—, assoc. prof. medicine sch. medicine, 1986—, acting chief div. respiratory medicine, 1988—; chmn. Section on Lung Cancer, Am. coll. Chest Physicians, 1986, Ethics Com., Stanford U. Hosp., 1987—, Calif. Med. Assn. Section Chest Diseases, 1984-85; rep. Council Subspecialty Socs. Am. Coll. Physicians, 1986. Author: Intensive Care: Facing the Critical Choices, 1988; contbr. articles to profl. jours. V.p. Lung Cancer Com., No. Calif. Oncology Group, 1983-85; chmn. Calif. Med. Assn. Section on Chest Diseases, 1984-85; com. mem. NIH Workshop, 1984; program com. mem. Am. Coll. Chest Physicians, 1985—. Recipient Henry J. Kaiser Found. award, 1981, 84, 88, Arthur L. Bloomfield award, 1981. Fellow Am. Coll. Chest Physicians; mem. Am. Assn. for the Advancement of Sci., Am. Fedn. for Clin. Research, Am. Thoracic Soc., Santa Clara County Lung Assn.and Med. Soc., Calif. Med. Assn., Soc. for Critical Care Med., Calif. Thoracic Soc.. Jewish. Home: 13468 Three Forks Ln Los Altos Hills CA 94022 Office: Stanford U Med Ctr Dept Medicine Div Respiratory Medicine C-356 Stanford CA 94305

RAFIE, SEYED, hyperthermia research associate; b. Qazvin, Iran, Oct. 30, 1955; arrived in U.S., 1975; s. Tahere and Zia Rafie. AA, Marymount Coll.,

Palos Verdes, Calif., 1977; BS, Loyola Marymount U., 1979; MS, Calif. State U., Carson, 1982. Instr. Calif. State U., Carson, 1982-84; researcher Allergy Med. Group, Los Angeles, 1983; hyperthermia physics coordinator Long Beach (Calif.) Meml. Med. Ctr., 1983—; research cons. Long Beach Arthritis Ctr., 1983—; clin. cons. UCI Med. Ctr., Orange, Calif., 1983—, Hoag Meml. Med. Ctr., Newport Beach, Calif., 1987, Pacific Radiation Oncology Group, Orange, 1988. Computer Cons. Endocurietherapy/Hyperthermia Jour., 1984—, editor, 1985—; contbr. articles to profl. jours. Vol. med. lab. technician Manhattan Beach (Calif.) Free Clinic, 1977-81. Mem. Am. Endocurietherapy Soc., Internat. Clin. Hyperthermia Group. Home: 306 Miraleste Dr San Pedro CA 90703 Office: Long Beach Meml Med Ctr 2801 Atlantic Ave Long Beach CA 90801

RAFT, STEVEN HOWARD, accountant; b. Montreal, Que., Oct. 29, 1960; s. Martin Albert and Marlene (Dale) R.; m. Sherri Lynn Berman, Oct. 11, 1987. BS in BA, Calif. State U., 1984. CPA, Calif. Asst. controller Chauvin Internat., Ltd., L.A., 1985; acct. Entous & Entous, Inc., Encino, Calif., 1985—; cons./dir. S.S.A.M. Ltd., L.A., 1988. Mem. AICPA's, Calif. Soc. CPA's. Republican. Jewish.

RAGAB, MOHAMED MAHMOUD, aerospace engineer; b. Cairo, Dec. 7, 1952; came to U.S., 1982; s. Mahmoud Mostafa Ragab and Gazbeya Mohamed El-Alayli; m. Iman Abdel-Rahim, July 17, 1986; children: Cindy Mohamed, Sami Mohamed. BS in Aero. Engring., Cairo U., 1975; Diplome d'Ingenieur, Ecole Nat. Superieure de l'Aeronaut. et de l'Espace, Toulouse, France, 1980, Docteur Ingenieur, 1982. Rsch. and devel. engr. Arab Orgn. Industrialization, Cairo, 1977-78; grad. rsch. asst. French Space Agy., Toulouse, 1980-82; teaching asst. Ecole Nat. Superieure de l'Aeronaut. et de l'Espace, 1981-82; sr. engr. Beech Aircraft Corp., Wichita, Kans., 1983-88; engr. specialist space systems div. Gen. Dynamics, San Diego, 1988—, flight instr., 1986—. Author numerous tech. papers. With Egyptian Army, 1975-76. Diplome des Etudes Approfondies grantee, 1980. Mem. AIAA, Aircraft Owners and Pilots Assn. Republican. Home: 14123 Capewood Ln San Diego CA 92128 Office: Gen Dynamics Space Systems Div MZ C4-8841 PO Box 85990 San Diego CA 92138

RAGGIO, NORA GENEVIEVE, marketing executive; b. Madison, Wis., June 24, 1958; d. Miguel Mario and Nora Elba (Moro) R. BA in Chemistry, U. Calif., Berkeley, 1981, MBA, 1984. Customer svc. rep. Nixdorf Computer Co., Paderborn, Fed. Republic of Germany, 1982; mktg. rep. IBM, Brussels, 1983, Spectra-Physics, San Jose, Calif., 1985-88; mktg. project mgr. Hewlett-Packard, Palo Alto, Calif., 1988—; pub. relations intern Access Los Altos Cable TV, Calif. 1985-87; mem. spl. events com. Mill Valley Film Festival, Calif., 1987—. Edward Frank scholar U. Calif., Berkeley, 1977; Haas fellow U. Calif., 1982, Robert Bosch Found. fellow, Stuttgart, 1984-85, Walter Kaitz fellow, Piedmont, Calif., 1988. Mem. Phi Beta Kappa. Home: 999 Green St Apt 2802 San Francisco CA 94133 Office: Hewlett Packard Co 3200 Hillview Ave Palo Alto CA 94304

RAGGIO, WILLIAM JOHN, state senator; b. Reno, Oct. 30, 1926; s. William John and Clara M. (Cardelli) R.; student La. Poly. Inst., 1944-45, U. Okla., 1945-46; BA, U. Nev., 1948; JD, U. Cal. at Hastings, 1951; m. Dorothy Brigman, August 15, 1948; children: Leslie Ann, Tracy Lynn, Mark William. Admitted to Nev. bar, 1951, U.S. Supreme Ct. bar, 1959; since practiced in Reno and Las Vegas; asst. dist. atty. Washoe County, Nev., 1952-58, dist. atty., 1958-71; ptnr. firm Wiener, Goldwater, Galatz & Raggio, Ltd., 1971-72, Raggio, Walker & Wooster Reno and Las Vegas, 1974-78, Raggio, Wooster & Lindell, 1978—; mem. Nev. Senate, 1973—, minority floor leader, 1977-81, 82-87, majority fl. leader, 1987— ; mem. legis. commn., vice chmn. criminal law and adminstrn. com. Council State Govts., 1972-75. Bd. dirs. Am. Savs. & Loan Assn., 1967-70. Adv. bd. Salvation Army, Reno; mem. Nev. Am. Revolutionary Bicentennial Commn., 1975-81; mem. Republican State Cen. Com. Bd. dirs. YMCA, Reno chpt. NCCJ, Salvation Army, Am. Legislative Exchange Council, bd. dir., v.p. Sahara Resorts, Casino Properties, Inc., Sahara Las Vegas, Inc.; trustee Nat. Dist. Attys. Found. (vice chmn. 1962-65); trustee Community Action Program Washoe County. Republican candidate for U.S. Senate, 1970. Served with USNR, 1944-46; to 2d lt. USMCR, 1946-47. Named Young Man of Yr., Reno-Sparks Jr. C. of C., 1959; recipient Disting. Nevadan award, 1968. Fellow Am. Bd. Criminal Lawyers (v.p. 1978—); mem. ABA (state chmn. jr. bar conf. 1957-60, ho. dels.) Am. Judicature Soc., Navy League, Air Force Assn., Nat. (nat. pres. 1967-68; named Outstanding Prosecutor 1965), Nev. State (sec. 1959, pres. 1960-63) Dist. Attys. Assn., NCCJ (Brotherhood award 1965), Nev. Peace Officers Assn., Internat. Assn. Chiefs Police, Am. Legion, Elks, Lion Club, Prospectors Club, Alpha Tau Omega, Phi Alpha Delta. Republican. Roman Catholic. Office: Box 3137 Reno NV 89505

RAGLAND, SAMUEL CONNELLY, industrial engineer; b. Nashville, July 12, 1946; s. Julian Potter and Stella (Thompson) R.; m. Marilyn Margaret Oppelt, July 15, 1967; children: Sherry Anne, David Michael. BSBA, Ariz. State U., 1974. Indsl. engr. First Interstate Bank, Phoenix, 1966-76, Beckman Instruments, Scottsdale, Ariz., 1976-78; mgmt. analyst Ariz. Legislative Budget Com., Phoenix, 1978; indsl. engr. mgmt. systems ITT Courier Terminal Systems, Tempe, Ariz., 1978-81; project control adminstr. Gen. Host Corp., Phoenix, 1981; sr. cons. Arthur Young & Co., Phoenix, 1981-82; ops. analyst City of Phoenix, 1982-84; project leader engine div. Allied-Signal Corp. (formerly Garrett Turbine Engine Co.), Phoenix, 1984—; dir. Mary Moppets of Highland Inc., 1977-81. Mem. Inst. Indsl. Engrs. (sr. mem., v.p. cen. Ariz. chpt. 1986—, dir. community relations 1983-85, dir. chpt. devel. 1985-86, pres.-elect 1986-87, pres. 1987-88, past pres. 1988-89), Inst. Indsl. Engrs. (nat. chpt. devel. com.), Assn. Systems Mgmt., Phoenix Philatelic Assn. Contbr. articles to profl. publs. Address: 11319 E Jenan Dr Scottsdale AZ 85259

RAHAM, RICHARD GARY, graphic artist; b. Ann Arbor, Mich., Nov. 12, 1946; s. Waldron Roy Thompson and Hilda (Euston) R.; m. Sharon Sue Waufle, Apr. 8, 1971; children: Deanna Celeste, Lindsay Marie. BS in Biology, U. Mich., 1968, MS in Biology, 1969. Cert. secondary tchr., Colo. Tchr. Akron (Colo.) Sch. Dist. R-1, 1969-71; graphic artist Citizen Printing Co., Ft. Collins, Colo., 1971—. Author: Dinosaurs in the Garden, 1988; contbr. various articles to profl. jours.; editor: Guild of Nat. Sci. Illustration Newsletter, 1983-84; art dir. jour. Rivers, 1988—. Pres., Eyestone Elem. PTA Bd., Wellington, Colo., 1985; co chmn. Wellington Jr. High PTA Bd., 1988. Regents alumni scholar, U. Mich., 1964; Rackham grantee, 1968. Mem. Guild Natural Sci. Illustrators, Soc. Children's Book Writers, Nat. Writer's Club. Democrat. Home: Box 399 3714 Grant Ave Wellington CO 80549 Office: Citizens Printing Co 1309 Webster Ave Fort Collins CO 80524

RAHEB, GEORGE E., industrial engineer; b. El Fayoum, Egypt, May 20, 1940; s. Selim Girgis and Bahia (El Shoura) El Raheb; m. Samia M. Raheb, Jan. 9, 1975; children: Monica Mary, Julie Marriette. BSME/BSIE, Ain Shams U., Cairo, Egypt, 1963; MSME, U. Alexandria, Egypt, 1968; MSIE, Northeastern U., Boston, 1977. Registered profl. engr., Calif. Indsl. engring. mgr. El Naqsr Auto. Mfg. Co., Cairo, 1968-73; indsl. engr. Hersey Products, Inc., Dedham, Mass., 1973-75; sr. indsl. engr. G.T.E. Internat., Burlington, Mass., 1975-80; sr. staff engr. Avco Systems div., Wilmington, Mass., 1980-81; sr. indsl. engr. Hughes Aircraft Co., Fullerton, Calif., 1981-84; sr. staff engr. Hughes Aircraft Co., El Segundo, Calif., 1985—; mgr. spl. projects MTM Assn., Newport Beach, Calif., 1983-84; pres. G. Raheb & Assocs., Indsl. Engring. Cons., Yorba Linda, Calif., 1984—. Maj. Egyptian Navy, 1963-68. Fellow Method Time Measurement Assn. for Research & Devel.; mem. Soc. Mfg. Engrs., Inst. Indsl. Engrs. Democrat. Coptic Orthodox Ch. Home: 4644 Via La Primavera Yorba Linda CA 92686 Office: Hughes Aircraft Co PO Box 902 El Segundo CA 90245

RAI, GULSHAN, physicist; b. Rurka Kalan, India, May 28, 1959; s. Harbans and Neelan R. BS in Physics, U. Birmingham, Eng., 1980, PhD in Nuclear Physics, 1985. Cons. dept. Physics. U. Birmingham, Eng., 1985; research fellow Lawrence Berkeley Lab. Dept. Nuclear Sci. U. Calif., Berkeley, 1986-87, staff scientist Lawrence Berkeley Lab. Dept. Nuclear Sci., 1988—. Contbr. articles to profl. jours. Mem. IEEE, Inst. Physics. (assoc.), Am. Physical Soc. Office: Lawrence Berkeley Lab MS70A 3307 Cyclotron Rd Berkeley CA 94720

RAIBLE, PETER SPILMAN, minister; b. Peterborough, N.H., Nov. 22, 1929; s. Robert Jules and Mildred (Galt) R.; m. Dee Dee Rainbow, June 18, 1950 (div. 1968); children: Stephen M., Robin S., Robert R., Deborah R.; m. Marcia McClellan Barton, June 7, 1987. PhB, U. Chgo., 1949; BA, U. Calif., Berkeley, 1952; MDiv, Starr King Sch. Ministry, 1953, D in Sacred Theology (hon.), 1974. Ordained to ministry Unitarian Ch. Asst. minister First Unitarian Ch., Providence, 1953-55; minister Unitarian Ch., Lincoln, Nebr., 1955-61, Univ. Unitarian Ch., Seattle, 1961—; bd. pres. Starr King Sch., Berkeley, 1967-68; mem. exec. com. Council Chs., Seattle, 1982-88; adj. prof. Meadville Lombard, 1987-88, Northwest Theol. Union, 1989. Author: How to Case a Church, 1982; book editor Jour. Liberal Ministry, 1965-71. Bd. dirs. Council Planning Affiliates, Seattle, 1969-73, Wash. State chpt. ACLU, Seattle, 1963-67; chmn. ministerial adv. com. Planned Parenthood Ctr., Seattle, 1963-68; pres. United Nations Assn., Lincoln, 1959-61. Served as cpl. USAF, 1948-49. Merrill fellow Harvard U., Cambridge, Mass., 1972. Mem. Unitarian Universalist Ministers Assn. (pres. 1973-75, Pacific N.W. dist. exec. 1962-64, pres. 1985-87, mem. commn. on appraisal 1977-81). Office: U Unitarian Ch 6556 35th Ave NE Seattle WA 98115

RAIKES, ROBERT WALTER, II, sculptor, designer; b. Van Nuys, Calif., Oct. 13, 1947; s. Robert Walter and Catherine (Ciccimarro) R.; m. Carol Lynette Morris, Aug. 15, 1970; children: Jason, Jennifer, Emily. With USN, 1968-70.

RAILEY, BETTY GRIFFITH, educator; b. Birmingham, Ala., Mar. 2, 1931; d. Francis Muriel and Dora (Naylor) Nabors; m. Albert V. Griffith, June 14, 1952 (June 1981); 1 child, Alan Brian; m. Jimmy Howard Railey, Mar. 26, 1988; four stepchildren. BA, East Carolina Coll., 1963, MA, 1965; PhD, U. So. Calif., 1975. Asst. prof. Mass. State Coll., Boston, 1965-68; asst. prof. to full prof. Calif. State U., Long Beach, Calif., 1968-88; prof. emeritus Calif. State U., Long Beach, 1988—. Contbr. articles to profl. jours.; Author: Dance for Fitness, 1980, 82; choreographer numerous jazz, ballet, and modern dances. Dir., Dance for Heart, Am. Heart Assn., Long Beach, 1984-87. Recipient 1st Pl. award Dance Methods Video, Inst. Creative Research and Sports Art Acad., Reston, Va., 1988, 89; nominated Am. Video Conf. award, Am. Film Inst., L.A., 1988. Mem. Internat. Dance Exercise Assn. (adv. bd. 1983—), Nat. Dance Assn. (v.p. edn. 1978-82, pres. 1983-86, Plaudit award, 1980), Am. Alliance for Health, Physical Edn., Recreation and Dance, Calif. Assn. for Health, Physical Edn., Recreation and Dance. Democrat. Home: 429 Jaycee Dr San Luis Obispo CA 93401

RAINER, FLETCHER YOUNG, III, music educator; b. Pueblo, Colo., Oct. 30, 1943; s. Fletcher Young Jr. and Mabel Marie (Titus) R.; m. Patricia Curran, Feb. 2, 1969 (div. 1979); m. Shei-Li Cheng, July 29, 1984. Student, We. State Coll., Gunnison, Colo., 1961-63, 67; BA, Morehead (Ky.) State U., 1969; postgrad. in Music, U.S. Naval Acad., 1964; postgrad., We. State Coll., 1972-74, UCLA, 1970-74, U. Hawaii, 1982-83. Cert. tchr., Calif., Hawaii. Chmn. dept. music Pasadena (Calif.) High Sch., 1969-70; chmn. dept. performing arts Sunny Hills High Sch., Fullerton, Calif., 1970-84; dir. student activities Hana (Hawaii) High Sch., 1984-85; dir. instrumental music Iao Sch., Wailuku, Hawaii, 1985-86; dir. elem. music Lynwood (Calif.) Unified Sch. Dist., 1986—; guest conductor N. Orange County City Honor Band, 1974, 77, 81, 83. Contbr. articles to profl. jours. Mem. Selective Service Bd., Orange County, Calif., 1983-84, Goldengate Sq. Homeowners Assn., v.p., 1987—. Served with U.S. Army, 1964-67. Recipient scholarship We. State Coll., 1961, Morehead State Coll., 1967; grantee East Asian Inst., U. Hawaii., 1982. Mem. Fullerton Secondary Tchrs. Orgn. (pres. 1982-84), Hawaii State Tchrs. Assn. (v.p. Maui chpt. 1985-86), Calif. Tchrs. Assn., So. Calif. Sch. Band and Orch. Assn., So. Calif. Judges Assn. (dir. qualification 1971-88), All-Am. Judges Assn. (dir. qualification 1972-79, music judge 1972-88), Calif. Music Edn. Assn. (conf. participant 1969—), NEA, Lynwood Tchrs. Assn. (rep. 1986—, chmn. polit. action com. 1988—). Methodist. Home: 730 W 4th St #401 Long Beach CA 90802 Office: Lynwood Unified Sch Dist 11331 Plaza Lynwood CA 90262

RAINER, WILLIAM GERALD, cardiac surgeon; b. Gordo, Ala., Nov. 13, 1927; s. Jamie Fluornoy and Lula (Davis) R.; m. Lois Sayre, Oct. 7, 1950; children: Vickie, Bill, Julia, Leslie. Student, Emory U., Atlanta, Ga., 1943-44, U. Ala., 1944-45; MD, U. Tenn., Memphis, 1948; MS in Surgery, U. Colo., Denver, 1958. Diplomate Am. Bd. Surgery, Am. Bd. Thoracic Surgery. Intern Wesley Hosp., Chgo., 1949; gen. practice medicine Blue Island, Ill., 1950-52; resident Denver VA Hosp., 1954-59; practice medicine specializing in cardiac surgery Denver, 1960—; bd. dirs. St. Joseph Hosp. Found., Denver. Contbr. articles to profl. jours. Mem. Nightingale Award com. U. Colo. Sch. Nursing, 1985—; mem. vis. bd. Ctr. for Human Caring, Denver, 1986—. Mem. Soc. Thoracic Surgeons (sec. 1980-85, pres. 1989), Colo. Med. Soc. (pres. 1984-85), Denver Med. Soc. (pres. 1984), Am. Coll. Chest Physicians (pres. 1984), Am. Bd. Thoracic Surgeons (bd. dirs. 1982-88), Denver Athletic Club. Office: 2005 Franklin Ste 700 Denver CO 80205

RAINS, CATHERINE BURKE, mortgage company executive; b. Richmond, Va., Oct. 31, 1959; d. Michael Evan and Marthann (Coleman) Burke; m. Cal Rains II, Jan. 24, 1981. Student Polit. Sci., U. Tenn., Knoxville, 1977-81; BA in Polit. Sci., U. West Fla., 1982. Sr. loan servicer First Mutual Savings & Loan, Pensacola, Fla., 1983-84; escrow officer First Am. Title Co., Yuma, Ariz., 1984-85; asst. v.p., branch mgr. The Hammond Co., Honolulu, Hi, Newport Beach, Calif., 1985—. Swimming instr. ARC, Knoxville, Tenn., 1979; bible sch. tchr., Naval Air Station, Pensacola, Fla., 1984; runner in March of Dimes Walkathon, 1985, Am. Cancer Soc. Marathon, 1985. Recipient scholarship, U. Tenn. , 1980. Mem. Golden Key, Gamma Beta Pi, Phi Kappa Phi, Pi Sigma Alpha, Alpha Delta Pi (exec. v.p. 1979-80, named Outstanding Young Women 1986). Republican. Episcopalian. Home: 31590 Jewel St South Laguna CA 92677 Office: The Hammond Co 4910 Campus Dr Newport Beach CA 92660

RAINS, DOLORES VELIA, educator; b. Gary, Ind., Dec. 17, 1932; d. Ladislao and Rosario (Fernandez) Rodriguez; m. Roger Theodore Rains, May 27, 1956; children: Angela Rains Light, Andrea, Pamela. BA, Ind. U., 1953; MA, 1958. Cert. secondary tchr., Calif. Tchr. Atascadero (Calif.) Union High Sch., 1957-59; Morro Bay Jr. and Sr. High Sch., 1959-60; Oxnard Adult Edn. 1963-78; from asst. to assoc. prof. St. John's Seminary Coll., Camarillo, 1975—; chair Spanish program St. John's Seminary Coll., 1981—; instr. Oxnard Coll., 1978-81. Trustee Pleasant Valley Elem., Ventura County Sch. Bd. Assoc. pres., 1986-88, Moorpark Coll. Found. 1980-82; bd. dirs. Hospice, 1986-89. Recipient Cert. of Award, City of Camarillo, 1969; named Woman of Yr. Woman's Day, Oxnard Coll. 1984, Camarillo C. of C. 1988. Mem. AAUW (charter, pres. 1969-71,74-75, grantee 1973), Nat. Charity League, Pleasant Valley Hist. Soc. Home: 363 Calle Larios Camarillo CA 93010 Office: St John's Seminary Coll 5118 E Seminary Rd Camarillo CA 93010

RAINSON, BRENDA THOMPSON, educator; b. Glendale, Calif., Aug. 19, 1945; d. Lacy Irvin and Katherine Teresa (Grady) Thompson. AA, Bakersfield Jr. Coll., 1965; BA in Art, San Jose Statee U., 1968; postgrad., John F. Kennedy U., 1986--. Tchr. art, chmn. dept. San Marin High Sch., Novato, Calif., 1970--; instr. art Orme Sch., Mayer, Ariz., summers 1968, 69; instr. Marin County Winter Arts Festival, Novato, 1978; artist, instr. Telluride Nat. Basketry Symposium, 1986. Exhibited in group shows Holy Names Coll., 1983, Textile Expressions-Fiberworks, 1985, 87, Telluride Nat. Basketry Symposium, 1986, Marin Soc. Artists, 1986, New Basket mag., 1988. Home: l05 Upham St Petaluma CA 94952

RAISCH, ANN TRUMBLE, lawyer; b. Denver, Feb. 28, 1947; d. Charles Paul and Roberta Mae (Kimball) Trumble; m. Jerry William Raisch, Nov. 27, 1970; children: Robert, Michael. BA, Creighton U., 1969; JD, U. Colo., 1971. Bar: Colo. 1972. Law clk. to justice 20th Jud. Dist., Boulder, Colo., 1972-74; asst. county atty. County of Boulder, 1974-78, county atty., 1978-86. Pres. Shining Mountain Waldorf Sch., 1987-88. Mem. Boulder Bar Assn. (treas. 1985-86), Colo. Bar Assn., (bd. govs.1986—, exec. council 1988—), Colo. County Attys. Assn. (pres. 1979-81). Democrat. Home: 2967 Middlefork Rd Boulder CO 80302

RAKOCHEVICH, WOOLAY, public mediator, behavioral scientist; b. Belgrade, Yugoslavia, Jan. 10, 1939; came to U.S., 1969; s. Milinko and Zivana (Zujovic) R.; married; 1 child, Beck. PhD in Behavioral Sci., Ljubljana U., Yugaslavia, 1964; postgrad., Columbia U., 1976; PhD, NYU, 1980. Pvt. practice psychology Paradise Valley, Ariz., 1977-85; founder Pub. Mediator Office, Inc., Scottsdale, Ariz., 1981—. Author: How to Become a Public Mediator, 1985; contbr. articles on marriage to profl. jours.; inventor method of mind control without drugs, 1987. Republican. Serbian Orthodox.

RAKOWER, STEPHEN RALPH, surgeon; b. N.Y.C., Sept. 1, 1943; s. Joseph George and Blanche (Baumgold) R.; children; DAvid Ira Stephen, Michael Charles. BSChemE, Princeton, 1965; MD, U. Pa., 1969. Mem. staff gen. and vascular surgery Fountain Valley, Calif., 1987. Contbr. articles to profl. jours. Mem. Am. Assn. Surgery Trauma, Soc. Critical Care Medicine, ACS, Soc. Acad. Surgery. Office: 11180 Warner #363 Fountain Valley CA 92708

RALEY, CHERI ELAINE, sales, market executive; b. Jacksonville, Fla., Mar. 30, 1951; d. Harvey and Helen (Bowen) Lottman; m. Donald Keith Raley, Jan. 16, 1970 (div. Oct. 1980); 1 child, Brian. Grad. high sch., Pasadena, Tex.; cert., ITT Middle Mgmt. Program, 1988. Fashion coordinator Montgomery Ward, Houston, 1970-76; freelance model Ben Shaw Studios, Houston, 1970-76; leasing cons. R&B Enterprises, Houston, 1976-84; sales, tng., mktg. and advert. mgr. ITT Employer Svcs., Encino, Calif., 1984-89; dist. mgr. Remedy Personnel Svcs., San Diego, 1989—. Recipient of Personal Progress award and Outstanding Performance award, Dale Carnegie Inst., 1987. Mem. Saddleback C. of C., Personnel Indsl. Relations Assn. Calif. Assn. of Temporary Svcs., San Diego C. of C., Am. Soc. Tng. and Devel. Home: 7099 Park Mesa Way San Diego CA 92111 Office: Remedy Personnel Svcs 5430 Clairmont Mesa Blvd San Diego CA 92117

RALSTIN, RICHARD LOWELL, academic administrator; b. Rushville, Ind., Aug. 29, 1947; s. Loval Lowell and Emily Rose (Nighbert) R.; m. Linda Ralstin, Dec. 10, 1983; 1 child, Brian Andrew. AA, ITT Tech. Internat., Indpls., 1967; BA, St. Louis Christian Coll., 1972. Chief instr. ITT Tech. Inst., San Diego, 1984-85, placement dir., 1985-87; dir. placement Muir Tech. Coll., San Diego, 1988—; campus dir. Muir Tech. Coll., Tuscon, 1988; asst. campus dir. Muir Tech. Coll., Tucson and San Diego, 1988—. Home: 2045 W Georgia Ave Phoenix AZ 85015

RALSTON, GILBERT ALEXANDER, author, educator; b. Los Angeles, Jan. 5, 1912; s. Alexander Gilbert and Jeanette (Johnston) R.; grad. Pasadena Coll., 1929-32; grad. Am. Acad. Dramatic Arts, 1935; B.C.A., Sierra Nev. Coll., 1972; M.A., Fielding Inst., 1983, D in Psychology, 1987; PhD, Columbia Pacific U., 1986; m. Mary K. Hart, Dec. 20, 1938; children—Michael, David. Actor, stage mgr. theatre prodns. N.Y.C., 1931-35; writer, dir. radio shows NBC, N.Y.C., 1936-38; prodn. supr. Compton Advt., Inc., N.Y.C., West Coast, 1939-42; organizer, mgr. radio dept. Proctor & Gamble, Cin., 1943-47, exec. producer inc. TV div., 1947-50; free lance producer TV films, 1950-55; exec. producer in charge TV drama CBS, 1955, dir. network programs originating in N.Y.C., 1956; producer High Adventure documentaries with Lowell Thomas, 1957; chmn. sch. communication arts Tahoe (Cal.) Paradise Coll., 1968; dean sch. communicative arts Sierra Nevada Coll., Incline Village, Nev., 1960-73, pres., 1973-83, pres. emeritus, 1983—; pres. Ralston Sch. Communicative Arts, Genoa, Nev., 1971—; v.p. Rule of Three Prodns., Los Angeles, 1973—; lectr. Fordham U., City Coll. City U. N.Y., Loyola U. of Los Angeles, St. Mary's Coll. of Calif. Mem. Authors Guild, ASCAP, Western Writers Am., Writers Guild Am., Am. Massage and Therapy Assn. Author: Ben, 1972; (with Richard Newhafer) The Frightful Sin of Cisco Newman, 1972; Dakota Warpath, 1973; Dakota: Red Revenge, 1973; Dakota Cat Trap, 1974; Dakota Murder's Money, 1974; Dakota: Chain Reaction, The Deadly Art, 1975, The Third Circle, 1976, The Tao of Touch, 1983, others. Author screenplays: No Strings Attached, 1962; A Gallery of Six, 1963; A Feast of Jackals, 1963; Cockatrice, 1965; Kona Coast, 1967; Night of the Locust, 1969; Ben, 1971, Third Circle, 1975, Sure, 1975. Author screen adaptations: Willard (by Stephen Gilbert), 1970; Bluebonnet (by Boris Sobelman and Jack H. Robinson), 1971; Dakota Red, 1987. Author scripts for TV under sometime pseudonym Gil Alexander: High Adventure, Naked City, Route 66, Follow the Sun, Bus Stop, The Untouchables, Alcoa Theatre, Ben Casey, Richard Boone Show, 12 O'Clock High, The Name of the Game, Daktari, Laredo, Combat, Big Valley, Gunsmoke, Amos Burke, Slattery's People, Alfred Hitchcock, Star Trek, It Takes a Thief, O'Hara, Cannon, numerous others. Address: PO Box 350 Genoa NV 89411

RALSTON, HERSCHEL ROBERT, physicist; b. L.A., Oct. 31, 1926; s. Leo Ralston and Evelyn (Atkin) Farber; m. Natalene Ruth Miller, June 27, 1948 (dec. 1974); children: Deborah Ann, David Bernard; m. Carolyn Kay Armour, Aug. 6, 1976. AB in Physics, U. Calif., Berkeley, 1950; MS in Counseling Psychology, Calif. State U., Hayward, 1971. Physicist Lawrence Livermore (Calif.) Nat. Lab., 1950-80; pvt. practice counseling, Port Orford, Oreg., 1980-84; data analyst Assoc. Resources, Sacramento, 1987—. Contbr. articles to profl. jours. V.p. Port Orford Arts Council, 1983; bd. dirs. Family Service East Bay, San Leandro, Calif., 1969-71. With USNR, 1944-46. Mem. Sigma Xi (assoc.). Democrat. Home: 2418 Seventh Ave Sacramento CA 95818 Office: Assoc Resources 1421 16th St Sacramento CA 95814

RALSTON, JOANNE SMOOT, public relations counseling firm executive; b. Phoenix, May 13, 1939; d. A. Glen and Virginia Lee (Smoot); m. Joseph P. Ralston, May 13, 1972 (dec. June 1982). B.A. in Journalism, Ariz. State U., 1960. Reporter, The Ariz. Republic, Phoenix, 1960-62; co-owner, pub. relations dir. The Patton Agy., Phoenix, 1962-71; founder, pres., owner Joanne Ralston & Assocs., Inc., Phoenix, 1971-87; pres. Nelson Ralston Robb Communications, Phoenix, 1987—. Contbr. articles to profl. jours. Bd. dirs. Ariz. Parklands Found., 1984-86, Gov.'s Council on Health, Phys. Fitness and Sports, 1984-86; task force mem. Water and Natural Resources Council, Phoenix, 1984-86; mem. Ariz. Republican Caucus, 1984—, others. Recipient Lulu' awards Los Angeles Advt. Women, 1964—, Gold Quill (2) Internat. Assn. Bus. Communicators, 1985, Excellence awards Fin. World mag., 1982-88, others; named to Walter Chronkite Sch. Journalism Coll. Pub. Programs Ariz. State U., 1987. Mem. Pub. Relations Soc. Am. (counselor sect.), Internat. Assn. Bus. Communicators, Phoenix Press Club (pres. bd.), Investor Relations Inst., Phoenix Met. C. of C. (bd. dirs. 1977-84, 85—). Republican. Clubs: Phoenix Country, Phoenix City. Avocations: horses. Office: Nelson Ralston Robb Communications 3003 N Central Ave Ste 1800 Phoenix AZ 85012

RALSTON, RACHEL WALTERS, health association administrator; b. Max, N.D., June 13, 1915; d. Lewis David and Wilhelmina May Bertha (Freitag) W.; m. William Clifton Hollowell, May 22, 1944 (div. May 1962); m. John Elvin Ralston, June 24, 1964. AA, Foothill Jr. Coll., 1964; BA, San Francisco State U., 1969; postgrad., Can. Coll., 1975-81. Chair North Fair Oaks Adv. Coun., Redwood City, Calif., 1975-77; initiator Community Concern for Sr. Citizens, Menlo Park and San Mateo County, Calif., 1975-80; organizer, pres. Concerned Srs., Inc., San Mateo County, 1980-86; chair exec. bd. Concerned Srs., Inc., Redwood City, 1987-88; peer counselor for the elderly Mental Health div. Health Dept., San Mateo County, 1986—; bd. dirs. Ret. Sr. Vol. Program, San Mateo, 1978—, Older Adults Com., Mental Health Adv. Bd., 1985—; mem. emeritus inst. adv. bd. Coll. of San Mateo, 1987—. Mem. com. on aging San Mateo County, 1979—; del. State House Conf. on Aging, Sacramento, 1980. Recipient Commendation Pvt. Sector Initiative, Washington, D. C., 1986; named Citizen of The Day Sta. KABL, San Francisco, 1985. Mem. AAUW, Am. Soc. on Aging, Menninger Found., Am. Assn. Ret. Persons. Republican. Home: 610 17th Ave Menlo Park CA 94025

RAM, TRACY SCHAEFER, ballet company manager; b. San Francisco, June 4, 1960; d. Donald Worth and Leslie Lorraine Wells Schaefer; m. Michael Francis Ram, May 29, 1987. BA in Polit. Sci. and Mass Communications, U. Calif., Berkeley, 1982. Legal asst. Morrison & Foerster, San Francisco, 1982-84; asst. to gen. mgr. San Francisco Ballet, 1984-86, mgr. co., 1986—. Democrat. Home: 761 Noe St San Francisco CA 94114 Office: San Francisco Ballet 455 Franklin St San Francisco CA 94102

RAMASWAMY, PADMANABHAN, materials scientist; b. Ambattur, India, Mar. 5, 1953; came to U.S., 1977; s. Ramaswamy Iyer and Bhagavathy (Narayanan) Padmanabhan; m. Nongluck Pankurddee, Jan. 8, 1986. BSc in Physics, Loyola Coll., Madras, India, 1972; B of Engring. in

Metallurgy, Indian Inst. Sci., Bangalore, 1975; PhD in Materials Sci., Oreg. Grad. Ctr., 1982. Research and devel. engr. Bharat Electronics, Ltd., Bangalore, 1975-77; research scientist Oreg. Grad. Ctr., Beaverton, 1982-83; sr. staff engr. Motorola, Inc., Phoenix, 1984-86, prin. staff scientist, 1987—. Contbr. articles to profl. jours. Mem. Am. Vacuum Soc., Am. Inst. Mining, Metall. and Petroleum Engrs., Materials Research Soc., Electrochem. Soc. Home: 1325 E Grandview St Mesa AZ 85203 Office: Motorola Inc B-136 5005 E McDowell Phoenix AZ 85026

RAMER, BRUCE, lawyer; b. Teaneck, N.J., Aug. 2, 1933; s. Sidney and Anne S. (Strassman) R.; m. Ann G. Ramer, Feb. 15, 1965; children—Gregg B., Marc K., Neal I. AB, Princeton U., 1955; JD, Harvard U., 1958. Bar: Calif. 1963, N.J. 1958. Assoc., Morrison, Lloyd & Griggs, Hackensack, N.J., 1959-60; ptnr. Gang, Tyre, Ramer & Brown, Inc., L.A., 1963—. Exec. dir. Entertainment Law Inst.; bd. of councilors Law Ctr. U. So. Calif.; past pres. Los Angeles chpt., bd. govs.; chmn. Nat. Affairs Commn. Am. Jewish Com.; trustee Loyola Marymount U.; mem. corp. bd., chmn. discretionary fund distribution com. United Way; bd. of trustees Los Angeles Children's Mus.; v.p. Fraternity of Friends of Los Angeles Music Ctr.; bd. dirs. L.A. Urban League, 1987—; bd. govs. Calif. Community Found.; mem. Fellows of Am. Bar Found. Served to pvt. U.S. Army, 1958-59, 2d lt., 1961-62. Mem. L.A. County Bar Assn., ABA, Calif. Bar Assn., Beverly Hills Bar Assn., L.A.Copyright Soc. (pres. 1974-75), Calif. Copyright Conf. (pres. 1973-74), Princeton Club (pres. 1975-78). Office: Gang Tyre Ramer & Brown Inc 6400 Sunset Blvd Los Angeles CA 90028

RAMER, WILLIAM LEE, nuclear physics program manager; b. Washington, Apr. 5, 1924; s. William Alexander and Evelyn Ann (Nutwell) R.; m. Elena Quaglieri, Feb. 2, 1952; children: Linda D., Shelley W. BS Mech. Engring., Tufts U., 1945. Registered profl. engr., Colo. Comml. engr. Poltomac Elec. Power Co., Washington, 1947-51; area rep. Hotpoint Co., Denver, 1954-55; project engr. Vulcan Hart Mfg. Co., Balt., 1955-59, Star Mfg. Co., St. Louis, 1959-61; chief engr. Speedster, Inc., Denver, 1961-62; sr. project engr. Dow Chem. Co., Golden, Colo., 1963-75; program mgr. Rockwell Internat., Golden, 1975—. Developer, patentee electric heat transfer. Lt. USN, 1943-54, USNR, 1954-66. Mem. ASME, Retired Officers Assn., 21st Century Energy Found., Citizens for Energy & Freedom (exec. v.p.). Republican.

RAMEY, CHERI DOLORES, advertising agency executive; b. Montreal, Que., Can., Apr. 17, 1944; d. Harold Edward and Bette Evlyn (Cameron) R.; came to U.S., 1951, naturalized, 1961; grad. Sch. Visual Arts, N.Y.C., 1961-64. Asst. art dir./designer Composing Room, N.Y.C., 1964-65, Katz Jacobs & Zlotnick, N.Y.C., 1965-66; art dir. Young & Rubicam, N.Y.C., 1966-69, sr. art dir., Los Angeles, 1969-71; creative dir. Ramey Communications Co., Los Angeles, 1971-88, exec. v.p., exec. creative dir. Ramey Ruud & Ptnrs., 1989—; judge numerous advt. awards shows; instr. Ad Ctr., L.A.; co-chair Belding Awards, 1985, 86. Adv. bd. Los Angeles Trade Tech. Recipient awards Cannes Film Festival, 1969, N.Y. Art Dirs. Club, 1966, 68, 73, 76; Best in West award, 1980, others. Mem. Western States Advt. Agys. Assn. (dir., co-founder, instr. Carson & Roberts Creative Course, co-chair Summer Conf.), Los Angeles Creative Club (dir.), Am. Assn. Advt. Agys. Democrat. Office: Ramey Ruud & Ptnrs 701 Santa Monica Blvd Ste 200 Santa Monica CA 90401

RAMIREZ, RICARDO, bishop; b. Bay City, Tex., Sept. 12, 1936; s. Natividad and Maria (Espinosa) R. B.A., U. St. Thomas, Houston, 1959; M.A., U. Detroit, 1968; Diploma in Pastoral Studies, East Asian Pastoral Inst., Manila, 1973-74. Ordained priest Roman Catholic Ch., 1966; missionary Basilian Fathers, Mex., 1968-76; exec. v.p. Mexican Am. Cultural Ctr., San Antonio, 1976-81; aux. bishop Archdiocese of San Antonio, 1981-82; bishop Diocese of Las Cruces, N.M., 1982—; cons. U.S. Bishop's Com. on Liturgy, from 1981; advisor U.S. Bishop's Com. on Hispanic Affairs, from 1981. Author: Fiesta, Worship and Family, 1981. Mem. N.Am. Acad. on Liturgy, Hispanic Liturgical Inst., Padres Asociada Derechos Religiosos Educativos y Sociales. Lodges: K.C; Holy Order Knights of Holy Sepulcher. Office: Diocese of Las Cruces 1280 Med Park Las Cruces NM 88004

RAMIREZ, RICHARD GONZALO, computer science educator; b. Guadalajara, Mexico, May 13, 1952; came to U.S., 1983; s. Gonzalo and Estela (Ruiz) Ramirez Ponce de Leon; m. Eva Rodriguez, Oct. 28, 1972 (div. 1987); children: Susan, Lety. BS, U. Guadalajara, 1980; MS, Postgrad. Coll., Chapingo, Mex., 1982; PhD, Tex. A&M U., 1987. Supr. computer ops. Inst. Computing, Guadalajara, 1972-74; data processing mgr. Bank of Rural Credit, Mexico City, 1974-78; instr. Postgrad. Coll., Chapingo, 1981-83, chmn. admissions and records, 1981-83; asst. prof. Ariz. State U., Tempe, 1987—; cons. to many orgns., 1975—. Contbr. articles to profl. jours. Mem. Assn. for Computing Machinery, IEEE Computer Soc., Delta Sigma Pi. Office: Ariz State U Decision Info Systems Tempe AZ 85287-4206

RAMIREZ, WILLIAM EARL, clothing company executive; b. Dalhart, Tex., July 15, 1951; s. Manuel and Isabella Mary (Lindsay) R.; BBA in Acctg., Tex. Tech U., 1973; JD, U. Iowa, 1976; LLM in Taxation, DePaul U., 1980. Bar: Iowa 1976, Ill. 1976. Tax. acct. Price Waterhouse & Co., Chgo., 1976-77; tax rsch. analyst Sunbeam Corp., Chgo., 1977-80; tax atty. Hughes Tool Co., Houston, 1980-85; Levi Strauss & Co., San Francisco, 1985—; speaker Internat. Joint Ventures, 1984. Bd. dirs., treas. Bellerive Homeowners, Houston, 1984-85; vol. Big Bros.-Big Sisters, Houston, 1983-85. Named an Outstanding Young Man U.S. Jaycees, 1984. Mem. ABA, Internat. Bar Assn., Internat. Fiscal Assn. Am. C. of C., Mensa. Democrat. Methodist. Avocations: travel, reading, spectator sports. Office: Levi Strauss & Co, 489 Ave Louise, 1050 Brussels Belgium also: Levi Strauss Fin Svcs, Ave Louise 489, Brussels 1050, Belgium

RAMO, ROBERTA COOPER, lawyer; b. Denver, Aug. 8, 1942; d. David D. and Martha L. (Rosenblum) Cooper; m. Barry W. Ramo, June 17, 1964. BA magna cum laude, U. Colo., 1964; JD, U. Chgo., 1967. Bar: N.Mex., 1967, Tex. 1971. With N.C. Fund, Durham, N.C., 1967-68; nat.teaching fellow Shaw U., Raleigh, N.C., 1968-70; mem. Sawtelle, Goode, Davidson & Troilo, San Antonio, 1970-72, Rodey, Dickason, Sloan, Akin & Robb, Albuquerque, 1972-74; sole practice law, Albuquerque, 1974-77; mng. dir. Poole, Tinnin & Martin, Albuquerque, 1977-87; bd. dirs. United N.Mex. Bank of Albuquerque, 1983-88. Bd. dirs., past pres. N.Mex. Symphony Orch., 1977-86; bd. dirs. Albuquerque Community Found., N.Mex. First; trustee Manzano Day Sch., 1975-77; bd. regents U. N.Mex. Mem. Albuquerque Bar Assn. (dir., pres. 1980-81), N.Mex. Bar Assn. (chmn. bus., banking sect. 1979-80, Outstanding Contbn. award 1981, 84), ABA (vice chmn. 1981-82, chmn. law practice sect. 1984), Albuquerque C. of C. (bd. dirs.), Greater Albuquerque C. of C. (exec. com.). Contbr. articles to profl. jours. Address: PO Box 1769 Albuquerque NM 87103

RAMO, SIMON, engineering executive; b. Salt Lake City, May 7, 1913; s. Benjamin and Clara (Trestman) R.; m. Virginia Smith, July 25, 1937; children: James Brian, Alan Martin. B.S., U. Utah, 1933, D.Sc. (hon.), 1961; Ph.D., Calif. Inst. Tech., 1936; D.Eng. (hon.), Case Inst. Tech., 1960, U. Mich., 1966, Poly. Inst. N.Y., 1971; D.Sc. (hon.), Union Coll., 1963, Worcester Poly. Inst., 1968, U. Akron, 1969, Cleve. State U., 1976; LL.D. (hon.), Carnegie-Mellon U., 1970, U. So. Calif., 1972, Gonzaga U., 1983, Occidental Coll., 1984, Gonzaga U., 1983, Occidental Coll., 1984. With Gen. Electric Co., 1936-46; v.p. ops. Hughes Aircraft Co., 1946-53; with Ramo-Woolridge Corp., 1953-58; sci. dir. U.S. intercontinental guided missile program 1954-58; dir. TRW Inc., 1954—, vice chmn. bd., 1961-78, chmn. exec. com., 1969-78; chmn. bd. TRW-Fujitsu Co., 1980-83; pres. The Bunker-Ramo Corp., 1964-66; vis. prof. mgmt. sci. Calif. Inst. Tech., 1978—; Regents lectr. UCLA, 1981-82, U. Calif. at Santa Cruz, 1978-79; chmn. Center for Study Am. Experience, U. So. Calif., 1978-80; Faculty fellow John F. Kennedy Sch. Govt., Harvard U., 1980—; dir. Union Bank, 1965—, Atlantic Richfield Co., 1984-86; past dir. Times Mirror Co., 1968-83; Mem. White House Energy Research and Devel. Adv. Council, 1973-75; mem. adv. com. on sci. and fgn. affairs U.S. State Dept., 1973-75; chmn. Pres.'s Com. on Sci. and Tech., 1976-77; mem. adv. council to Sec. Commerce, 1976-77; co-chmn. Transitition Task Force on Sci. and Tech. for Pres.-elect Reagan; mem. roster consultants to adminstr. ERDA, 1976-77; bd. advisors for sci. and tech. Republic of China, 1981—. Author: The Business of Science, 1988, other sci., engring. and mgmt. books. Bd. dirs. Los Angeles World Affairs Council; bd. dirs. Music Center Found., Los Angeles, Los Angeles Philharm. Assn.; trustee Calif. Inst. Tech., Nat. Symphony Orch. Assn., 1973-83; trustee emeritus Calif. State Univs.; bd. visitors UCLA Sch. Medicine, 1980—; bd. dirs. W. M. Keck Found., 1983—; bd. govs. Performing Arts Council of Music Ctr. Los Angeles, pres., 1976-77. Recipient award IAS, 1956; award Am. Inst. Elec. Engrs., 1959; award Arnold Air Soc., 1960; Am. Acad. Achievement award, 1964; award Am. Iron and Steel Inst., 1968; Distinguished Service medal Armed Forces Communication and Electronics Assn., 1970; medal of achievement WEMA, 1970; awards U. So. Calif., 1971, 79; Kayan medal Columbia U., 1972; award Am. Cons. Engrs. Council, 1974; medal Franklin Inst., 1978; award Harvard Bus. Sch. Assn., 1979; award Nat. Medal Sci., 1979; Disting. Alumnus award U. Utah, 1981; UCLA medal, 1982; Presdl. Medal of Freedom, 1983; Jr. Achievement Bus. Hall of Fame award, 1984; others. Fellow IEEE (Electronic Achievement award 1953, Golden Omega award 1975, Founders medal 1980), Am. Acad. Arts and Scis.; mem. Nat. Acad. Engring. (founder, council mem. Bueche award), Nat. Acad. Scis., Am. Phys. Soc., Am. Philos. Soc., Inst. Advancement Engring., Internat. Acad. Astronautics, Eta Kappa Nu (eminent mem. award 1966). Office: TRW 1 Space Pk Redondo Beach CA 90278 *

RAMO, VIRGINIA M. SMITH, civic worker; b. Yonkers, N.Y.; d. Abraham Harold and Freda (Kasnetz) Smith; B.S. in Edn., U. So. Calif., D.H.L. (hon.), 1978; m. Simon Ramo; children—James Brian, Alan Martin. Nat. co-chmn. ann. giving U. So. Calif., 1968-70, vice chmn., trustee, 1971—, co-chmn. bd. councilors Sch. Performing Arts, 1975-76, co-chmn. bd. councillors Schs. Med. and Engring.; vice-chmn. bd. overseers Hebrew Union Coll., 1972-75; bd. dirs. The Muses of Calif. Mus. Sci. and industry, UCLA Affiliates, Estelle Doheny Eye Found., U. So. Calif. Sch. Medicine; adv. council Los Angeles County Heart Assn., chmn. com. to endow Chair in cardiology at U. So. Calif.; vice-chmn., bd. dirs. Friends of Library U. So. Calif.; bd. dirs., nat. pres. Achievement Rewards for Coll. Scientists Found., 1975-77; bd. dirs. Les Dames Los Angeles, Community TV So. Calif.; bd. dirs., v.p. Founders Los Angeles Music Center; v.p. Los Angeles Music Center Opera Assn.; v.p. corp. bd. United Way; v.p. Blue Ribbon-400 Performing Arts Council; chmn. com. to endow chair in gerontology U. So. Calif.; vice chmn. campaign Doheny Eye Inst., 1986. Recipient Service award Friends of Libraries, 1974; Nat. Community Service award Alpha Epsilon Phi, 1975; Disting. Service award Am. Heart Assn. 1978; Service award U. So. Calif.; Spl. award U. So. Calif. Music Alumni Assn., 1979; Life Achievement award Mannequins of Los Angeles Assistance League, 1979; Woman of Yr. award PanHellenic Assn., 1981; Disting. Service award U. So. Calif. Sch. Medicine, 1981; U. So. Calif. Town and Gown Recognition award, 1986; Asa V. Call Achievement award U. So. Calif., 1986; Phi Kappa Phi scholarship award U. So. Calif., 1986. Mem. UCLA Med. Aux., U. So. Calif. Pres.'s Circle, Commerce Assos. U. So. Calif., Cedars of Lebanon Hosp. Women's Guild (dir. 1967-68), Blue Key, Skull and Dagger.

RAMOS, ALBERT A., electrical engineer; b. Los Angeles, Feb. 28, 1927; s. Jesus D. and Carmen F. (Fontes) R.; B.S. in Elec. Engring., U. So. Calif., 1950, M.S. in Systems Mgmt., 1972; Ph.D., U.S. Internat. U., 1975; m. Joan C. Pailing, Sept. 23, 1950; children—Albert A., Richard R., James J., Katherine. With guided missile test group Hughes Aircraft Co., 1950-60; with TRW DSG, 1960—, sr. staff engr. Norton AFB, San Bernardino, Calif., 1969—. Served with USNR, 1945-46. Registered profl. engr., Calif. Mem. IEEE, Nat. Soc. Profl. Engrs., Air Force Assn., Mexican-Am. Engring. Soc., Mexican Am. Profl. Mgmt. Assn. (mem. adminstering commn. dept. community services), Sigma Phi Delta, Eta Kappa Nu, Tau Beta Pi.Beta Pi. Home: 1457 W Cypress Ave Redlands CA 92373 Office: PO Box 1310 San Bernardino CA 92402

RAMOS, JACK MARKUS, dentist; b. Fresno, Cal., June 15, 1925; s. Joseph Markus and Gladys (Leonardo) R.; AB, Fresno State U., 1950; DDS, U. Pacific, 1954; postgrad. in Edn., U. Calif.-San Francisco, 1958; m. Marie J. Rojas, June 11, 1950; children: Loretta Marie, Laura Ann. Gen practice dentistry, Fresno, 1954—. Mem. planning com. Adult Activity Ctr. for Mentally Retarded, 1969-71; mem. mental retardation com. Fresno Community Coun., 1965-67; mem. exec. com. Cen. Calif. Regional Ctr. for Retarded, 1971-72; mem. nominating com. Calif. Assn. for Retarded, 1972-73, v.p., 1973-76, chmn. fiscal affairs com., 1976-79, pres., 1977-79; mem. Atty. Gen.'s Vol. Adv. Coun., 1972-78; chmn. adv. bd. Porterville State Hosp., also Fresno County Mental Health Adv. Bd., 1973—; active PTA; pres. Fresno Assn. Mentally Retarded, recipient Ann. Golden Circle award, 1975, 82; mem. Parents of Gifted, Fresno County Coordinating Coun. Developmentally Disabled; mem. long-range planning com. Valley Med. Center, 1980-83; pres. Valley Dental Care 1980-83. Found., 1980-83. Bd. dirs. Fresno Found. Mental Retardation; mem. Cen. Valley citizen adv. coun. U. Calif. Served with USNR, 1943-46; PTO. Fellow Acad. Gen. Dentistry, Acad. Dentistry Internat.; mem. Am. Dental Assn., Federation Dentaire Internationale, AAAS, V.F.W. (life), Fresno-Madera Dental Soc. (treas. 1976-77, sec., 1977-78, pres. 1980-82, chmn. legis. com., chmn. ins. com., chmn. peer rev. com. 1984—), Acad. Dentistry for Handicapped, Calif. Dental Assn. (by-laws reference com. 1980-81), Am. Soc. Preventative Dentistry, Pub. Health League, Calif. State Sheriff's Assn., Xi Psi Phi. Democrat. Roman Catholic. Clubs: Cabrillo, Rotary (vocat. services chmn., dir., Paul Harris fellow). Home: 1163 W Morris Ave Fresno CA 93705 Office: 946 N Van Ness Ave Fresno CA 93728

RAMOS, LINDA MARIE, endoscopy technician; b. San Jose, Calif., July 8, 1961; d. Albert Sequeira and Catherine Marie (Souza) Vieira; m. John Bettencourt Ramos, June 12, 1982. AA, De Anza Coll., 1986; BA, St. Mary's Coll. Calif., Moraga, Calif., 1988. Endoscopy technician O'Connor Hosp., San Jose, 1979—; instr. aerobic 1st Lady Spas, Mountain View, Calif., O'Connor Hosp., San Jose, Calif. Contbr. articles to profl. jours. Vol. O'Connor Hosp., 1975-79; active campaign Santa Clara City Council, 1980-81. Fellow Irmandade Da Festa Do Espirito Santo (sec. 1974-82, queen 1975-76), Soc. Gastrointestinal Assts., No. Soc. Gastrointestinal Assts., Soc. Espirito Santo of Santa Clara, Luso Am. Fraternal Fedn. (state youth pres. 1979-80, youth leader local coun. Santa Clara Mountain View 1979-87, scholar, 1979, founder, organizer Mountain View-Santa Clara chpt. 1980, pres. local region 1980-84, state 20-30 pres. 1984-85, state dir. youth programs 1988—). Republican. Roman Catholic. Home: 1101 Civic Center Dr 10 Santa Clara CA 95050 Office: O'Connor Hosp 2105 Forest Ave San Jose CA 95126

RAMOS, VIVIAN ELEANOR, realtor; b. St. Louis, Oct. 19, 1946; d. John Dominic and Aurea Genevieve (Schottel) Baron; m. John Paul Hargis, Aug. 21, 1964 (div. Mar. 1968); m. Filomeno Mariano Ramos, June 30, 1973 (dec.); children: William S., Kiersten E., Leilani A. Student, St. Louis U., 1968-69, U. Hawaii, 1986-87. Real estate broker Coldwell Banker, Chesterfield, Mo., 1988—; cons. Hawaii Govtl. Affairs Com., Honolulu, 1975-76, Brokers Adv. Com., Honolulu, 1984-85. Assoc. Pres.'s Youth Opportunity Program, St. Louis, 1968. Mem. Nat. Assn. Realtors (mem. com. pub. relations 1987), St. Louis Real Estate Bd., Mililani Merchants Assn. (pres. 1985). Democrat. Roman Catholic. Home: 70 Willow Dr PO Box 474 Eureka MO 63025

RAMSAY, JOHN BARADA, research chemist, educator; b. Phoenix, Dec. 28, 1929; s. John A. and Helen G. Ramsay; m. Barbara Ann Hilsenhoff, Apr. 18, 1953; children—Bryan J., Kathleen L., Carol A., David A. B.S. in Chemistry, Tex. Western U., 1950; Ph.D. in Analytical Chemistry, U. Wis., 1954. Mem. staff Los Alamos Nat. Lab., 1954-70, 73—; assoc. prof. Coll. Petroleum and Minerals, Dhahran, Saudi Arabia, 1970-73; cons. U.S. Navy, USAF, 1980—; adj. prof. U. N.Mex., Los Alamos, 1980-85. Author sci. articles. Recipient award of excellence U.S. Dept. Energy, 1984. Mem. AAAS, N.Mex. Acad. Sci. (pres. 1988), Am. Archeol. Soc. (chpt. pres. 1979), Westerners Internat. (chpt. pres. 1988-89), Sigma Xi. Democrat. Home: 6 Erie Ln Los Alamos NM 87544 Office: PO Box 1663 Los Alamos NM 87545

RAMSBY, MARK DELIVAN, lighting designer and consultant; b. Portland, Oreg., Nov. 20, 1947; s. Marshall Delivan and Verna Pansy (Culver) R.; divorced; children: Aaron Delivan, Venessa Mercedes. Student, Portland (Oreg.) State U., 1966-67. With C.E.D., Portland, 1970-75; minority ptnr. The Light Source, Portland, 1975-78, pres., 1978-87; prin. Illume Lighting Design, Portland, 1987—; pvt. practice cons. Portland, 1979—. Recipient Top Ten Outstanding Achievement award Metalux Corp., 1981-85, 100% award, Gardco Lighting, 1985. Mem. Illuminating Engring. Soc. Am. (sec.-treas. Oreg. sect. 1978-79, Oreg. Section and Regional award 1989, Lighting Design awards), Internat. Assn. Lighting Designers. Republican. Lutheran. Office: Illume Lighting Design 205 SE Grand Ave Portland OR 97214

RAMSDELL, JAMES VANNER, JR., atmospheric scientist; b. Tacoma, Wash., Aug. 19, 1939; s. James Vanner Sr. and Martha Jane (Williams) R.; m. Carol Ellen Berglund, June 8, 1962; children: James Vanner III, Charles Michael. BS in Gen. Sci., Oreg. State U., 1961, MS in Meteorology, 1962. Aviator U.S. Navy, 1962-67; research scientist Battelle, Pacific NW Lab., Richland, Wash., 1967—. Contbr. articles to profl. jours. Leader Boy Scouts Am., Richland, 1972-80; judge Sci. Fairs, Richland, 1977-82. Served as lt. USN. 1962-67. Mem. Am. Meteorol. Soc., Columbia Basin Racquet Club. Episcopalian. Home: 4312 Laurel Dr West Richland WA 99352 Office: Battelle Pacific NW Lab PO Box 999 Richland WA 99352

RAMSDELL, LAWRENCE D., real estate executive; b. Phila., June 26, 1947; s. Samuel Carter and Edna May (Ungerer) R.; 1 child, Jeffrey Miller. BSBA, Drexel U., 1970. Mgr. Blue Cross/Blue Shield, Denver, 1972-76; dir. Am. TV & Communications, Denver, 1976-82; v.p. Mile Hi Cablevision, Denver, 1982-85; asst. v.p. First Interstate Bank Denver, 1985-86; v.p. First Interstate Structures, Denver, 1986-87; pres. The Properties Group, Inc., Denver, 1987—; bd. dirs. Denver Moving & Storage. Chmn. Peoples' Fair, Capitol Hill Unite Neighborhood, Denver, 1982. With U.S. Army, 1970-72. Mem. Denver Building owners and Mgrs. Assn. (com. chmn. 1988-89). Home: 5595 E Iliff Ave Denver CO 80222 Office: Properties Group Inc 17th St Ste 915 Denver CO 80293

RAMSDEN, NORMA LA VONNE HUBER, nurse; b. Lewiston, Idaho, Aug. 1, 1921; d. Lawrence Henry and Gertrude Melissa (Ryder) Huber; m. John Burton Wormell, Nov. 18, 1942 (div. 1950); m. Everett Glenn Ramsden, Dec. 25, 1957; 1 child, Valerie Ann Ramsden Brooks. Diploma in nursing, St. Joseph's Hosp., Lewiston, 1952. Psychiatric nurse Oreg. State Hosp., Salem, 1952-57; nurse to pvt. psychiatrist Pullman, Wash., 1957; clin. instr. Idaho State Hosp., Orofino, Idaho, 1957-58; night nurse ICU Tri State Hosp., Clarkston, Wash., 1969-88; adv. bd. The Rogers Counseling Ctr., Clarkston, 1971-88. Leader Camp Fire Girls Am., 1958-61, 69-71. Recipient Woman Achievement award Altrusa Club, 1985. Mem. Am. Nurses Assn., Anatone Grange, Pollyette (pres., sec., treas.). Episcopalian. Home: Main St PO Box 98 Anatone WA 99401 Office: Tri State Hosp 1221 Highland St Clarkston WA 99403

RAMSDEN, WILLIAM JAMES, finance consultant; b. Seattle, Oct. 3, 1955; s. Robert Richard and Rosemary Laura (Dennis) R. AA, Seattle Cen. Community Coll., 1976; BS cum laude, Seattle U., 1978. Acad. cons. Seattle U., 1977-78, sr. cons., 1980-83, mgr., 1983-86; sr. mgr. Price Waterhouse, Seattle, 1986—. Mem. Data Processing Mgmt. Assn. Republican. Roman Catholic. Office: Price Waterhouse 1001 4th Ave Pl Seattle WA 98154

RAMSEY, ANNE CATHERINE, nurse; b. Mpls., Oct. 21, 1959; d. William Andres and Rosemary Elizabeth (Kotilinek) Mossberg; m. Thomas Edmond Ramsey, Feb. 12, 1988. AS in Nursing, Lakewood Community Coll., St. Paul, Minn., 1984; BS in Biology, Calif. State U., San Bernadino, 1988. Registered nurse, Minn., Calif. Nurse ICU Saint Bernardine Med. Ctr., San Bernadino, 1984-86, Loma Linda (Calif.) U. Med. Ctr., 1986—; staff edn. asst., instr. Loma Linda U. Med. Ctr., 1987—. Mem. Am. Assn. Critical Care Nurses (cert.), Smithsonian Inst. Republican. Club: Sierra (Calif.). Office: Loma Linda U Med Ctr 11234 Anderson St Loma Linda CA 92354

RAMSEY, CLAUDE, foundation executive; b. Ramsey, W.Va., May 25, 1918; s. Melvin G. and Maude (Hawkins) R.; m. Lilien Ernst, June 9, 1945; children: Patrick (dec.), Terry, Perry. BS, Morris Harvey Coll., 1938; BJ, U. MO., 1939. Writer, United Press, Kansas City and Denver, 1940-42, bur. chief Houston and Lower Rio Grande Valley, 1945-52; pub. relations counsellor Kostka & Assocs., Denver, 1953-55; founder, pres. Pub. Relations Inc., Denver, 1956-64; exec. dir. Morris Animal Found., Denver, 1964-88; exec. dir. Digit Fund, 1988—; guest lectr. pub. relations Colo. State U., 1972-79. Mem. City Council, City of Greenwood Village (Colo.), 1973-75; mem. Arapahoe County Republican Exec. Com., 1976-80, 84-85; chmn. Rep. 6th Congl. Dist., 1982—; chmn. Colo. div. Am. Cancer Soc., 1979-81. Served to capt. Signal Corps, U.S. Army, 1941-45. Decorated Bronze Star; recipient award of Excellence, Colo. div. Am. Cancer Soc., 1976; Award of Merit, Am. Animal Hosp. Assn. Mem. Pub. Relations Soc. Am. (past pres. Colo. chpt., mem. nat. bd. 1962-63, Silver Anvil award 1959), Council on Founds., Sigma Delta Chi. Lutheran. Home: 9293 E Arbor Circle Apt C Englewood CO 80111 Office: 45 Inverness Dr E Englewood CO 80112

RAMSEY, ELIZABETH A., information systems executive; b. Woodland, Calif., June 21, 1955; d. James Emil and Antoinette (Rodriquez) Felix; m. Lance Hillery Ramsey, Apr. 2, 1983; children: David Lane, Brandon James. BS in Home Econs., U. Calif., 1977. Food engr. trainee Contadina Foods, Woodland, 1975-76; quality control lab. technician Gen. Mills, Lodi, Calif., 1978-84, quality control hold order, computer technician, 1984-88, quality control info. systems coordinator, 1988—. Mem. Cal Aggie Alumni Assn., Alpha Zeta Fraternity. Democrat. Methodist. Office: General Mills Inc PO Box 3002 Lodi CA 95241

RAMSTEIN, WILLIAM LOUIS, manufacturing company executive; b. L.A., July 9, 1950; s. Robert James and Norma Elaine (Knapp) R.; m. Sue Ann Cooper, Oct. 9, 1983 (div. 1985). BSBA magna cum laude, Calif. State U., Northridge, 1975; MBA, U. So. Calif., 1984. CPA, Calif. Sr. internal auditor County of Los Angeles, L.A., 1975-78; mgmt. cons. Alexander Grant & Co., Van Nuys, Calif., 1978-80; head of acctg. sect. Hughes Aircraft Co., Missile Systems Group, Canoga Park, Calif., 1980—; fin. cons. Mem. Calif. Soc. CPAs, Beta Gamma Sigma. Republican. Home: 4310 Torreon Dr Woodland Hills CA 91364 Office: Hughes Aircraft Missile Sys 8433 Fallbrook Ave Canoga Park CA 91304

RANCE, QUENTIN E., interior designer; b. St. Albans, Eng., Mar. 22, 1935; came to U.S., 1981; s. Herbert Leonard and Irene Ann (Haynes) R.; m. India Perlin, May 17, 1974. Grad., Eastbourne (Eng.) Sch. Art, 1960. Soft furnishings buyer Dickeson & French Ltd., Eastbourne, 1960-61, outside sales mgr., 1961-62; design dir. Laszlo Hoenig, Ltd., London, 1962-73; mng. dir. Quentin Rance Interiors Ltd., London, 1973-81; pres. Quentin Rance Enterprises, Inc., Encino, Calif., 1981—. Works featured in Designers West, 1983, Design House Rev., 1983, Profiles mag., 1987, Nat. Assn. Mirror Mfrs. Jour., 1988. Mem. Founders for Diabetic Research/City of Hope. Served with RAF, 1953-55. Fellow Chartered Soc. Designers of Eng.; mem. Am. Soc. Interior Designers (chpt. dir. 1983-87, 89—, chmn. Avanti 1983-85, admissions chmn. 1985—, Presdl. Citations 1984-87), Knights of the Vine. Home and Office: 18005 Rancho St Encino CA 91316

RANCER, SUSAN PAULA, music therapist; b. Phila., Feb. 19, 1953; d. Saul Joseph and Rhoda Libby (Stein) Shapiro; m. Jack Paul Nunley, Oct. 17, 1973 (div. Apr. 1977); m. Michael Dennis Rancer, Sept. 20, 1981; 1 child, Emily Rebecca. BA, Eastern N.Mex. U., 1975. Registered music therapist. Music therapist Killgore Children's Hosp., Amarillo, Tex., 1975-77; pvt. practice music therapist Amarillo, 1977-80, San Jose, Calif., 1980—. Mem. Women's Am. Orgn. Rehab. & Tng., San Jose, 1980—. Mem. Nat. Assn. Music Therapy, Music Tchrs. Nat. Assn., Calif. Assn. Profl. Music Tchrs. Democrat. Jewish. Home: 5229 Rafton Dr San Jose CA 95124

RANCK, JOHN STEVENS, human resources executive; b. Warren, Ohio, Sept. 14, 1945; s. Charles Thomas and Helen Marie (Weir) R.; m. Bibbie-Ann Rose Robertson, Dec. 25, 1975; children: James L., Edward L. BS, USAF Acad., 1971; MS in Human Resources, Gonzaga U., 1979, MBA, 1984. Cert. adminstrv. mgr. Salesman Neal's Family Shoes, Warren, 1964-65; prodn. staff Packard Elec. div. GMC, Warren, 1965-66; personnel mgr. United Paint Mfg., Inc., Greenacres, Wash., 1981-82; personnel dir. Sheraton-Spokane Hotel, 1982-83; personnel mgr. Students Book Corp., Pullman, Wash., 1984-87; personnel analyst Spokane Co., 1988--. Active Repub. Cen. Com., Spokane. Capt. USAF, 1966-80. Mem. Adminstrv. Mgmt. Soc. (chpt. dir. 1982-84, sec. 1983), Am. Soc. Tng. and Devel., Am. Compensation Assn., Internat. Personnel Mgmt. Assn., Pacific NorthwestPersonnel. Mgmt. Assn. (exec. bd. 1989--), Am. Soc. Personnel Adminstrn., Masons(knight york cross of honor, knight comdr. ct. of honor), K.T. (grand comdr. 1987-88), Red Cross of Constantine, Royal Order of Scotland Shrine, Grotto, Order Eastern Star. Lutheran. Home: E 16004 Rich Ave Spokane WA 99216-1525 Office: Spokane County Personnel W 1116 Broadway Spokane WA 99260

RANDALL, BEATRICE JANET, educator; b. Everett, Wash., Sept. 4, 1944; d. Bert Kermit and Una Mamie (Cushman) Wangerin; m. Charles Vern Randall, Sept. 12, 1964; children: William Eugene, Vern Leon, Aaron Charles. AA, Everett Community Coll., 1962-64; BA in Edn., Western Wash. U., 1966, MA, 1972. Cert. tchr., counselor. Tchr. Sedro Woolley (Wash.) Sch. Dist., 1966-67, Arlington (Wash.) Sch. Dist., 1967-68, 84—, Mukilteo (Wash.) Sch. Dist., 1968-70; coach various sports Post Middle Sch. and Arlington High Sch., Wash., 1984—. Airport commr. City of Arlington, 1978-82; commr. Snohomish County Mental Health Bd., 1980-82; city council mem. City of Arlington, 1982—; mem. Snohomish County Solid Waste Adv. Com., 1988—. Named Pacific N.W. Discus Champion Record Holder, 1986—, Pacific N.W. Master's Shot-Put Champion, 1986-88, Master's discus champion, 1986-87, javelin, 1988—, triple jump record holder, 1988. Mem. Wash. Edn. Assn., NEA, Assn. of Wash. Cities, Wash. Coaches Assn., Am. Athletic Unio, Wash. Sci. Tchrs Assn, AAUW (sec. 1976-78, v.p. 1978-80, pres. 1980-82). Democrat. Methodist. Home: 427 S French Arlington WA 98223

RANDALL, CHANDLER CORYDON, church rector; b. Ann Arbor, Mich., Jan. 22, 1935; s. Frederick Stewart and Madeline Leta (Snow) R.; m. Marian Archias Montgomery, July 2, 1960; children: Sarah Archais, Elizabeth Leggett, Rebekah Stewart. AB in History, U. Mich., 1957; S.T.B. in Theology, Yale U., 1960; PhD in Hebraic Studies, Hebrew Union Coll., 1969; D.D. (honoris causa), Yale U., 1985. Rector St. Paul's Episcopal Ch., Richmond, Ind., 1967-71; rector Trinity Episcopal Ch., Ft. Wayne, Ind., 1971-88, St. Peter's Episcopal Ch., Del Mar, Calif., 1988—; bd. dirs. Living Ch. Found., Milw.; bibl. theologian Episcopal Ch. Stewardship, N.Y.C., 1985; alumni coun. Berkeley Divinity at Yale, New Haven, Conn., 1981-87; bishop's cabinet Diocese of No. Ind., South Bend, 1983-87. Author: Satire in the Bible, 1969; contbr. articles to profl. jours. Founder Canterbury Sch., Ft. Wayne, 1977; commr. Ind. Jud. Qualifications Commn., Indpls., 1981-87; pres. Ft. Wayne Plan Commn., 1977; bd. dirs. Ft. Wayne Park Found., 1983-88; platform com. Ind. Republican Party, Indpls., 1974. Recipient Disting. Svc. medal U. Mich., 1981, Scheuer scholar Hebrew Union Coll., 1963-66, Liberty Bell award Ft. Wayne Bar Assn., 1988; named Sagamore of the Wabash, Gov. Ind., 1987. Mem. Am. Schs. Oriental Research, Yale U. Alumni Club (pres. 1982-88), Quest Club (pres.), Chi Psi (nat. chaplain 1982). Republican. Office: St Peters Episcopal Church PO Box 336 Del Mar CA 92014

RANDAZZO, JOSEPH ALBERT, small business owner; b. Bklyn., Mar. 27, 1942; s. Liborio Albert and Josephine (Caruso) R.; m. Irene Grigioni, June 6, 1964; children: Rosemarie, Renee, Michael, Amy. Cert. in ins. mgmt., Northwest Mo. State U., 1975. Mgr. Alpha Beta Markets, Calif., 1966-73; sales mgr. Prudential Ins. Co., Pomona, Calif., 1973-78; v.p. Randazzo Sales Co., El Cajon, Calif., 1978-82; owner, v.p. Spray Art Finishers, Inc., Escondido, Calif., 1982—; sec., Ejana Optics, Inc., Poway, Calif.; presenter lectures on ins. mgmt. and sales, 1973-78. Mem. Explorers Club, Elks. Home: 243 Vista Del Escuela El Cajon CA 92019

RANDISI, ELAINE MARIE, apparel manufacturing executive; b. Racine, Wis., Dec 19, 1926; d. John Dewey and Alveta Irene (Raffety) Fehd; A.A., Pasadena Jr. Coll., 1946; B.S. cum laude (Giannini scholar), Golden Gate U., 1978; m. John Paul Randisi, Oct. 12, 1946 (div. July 1972); children—Jeanine Randisi Manson, Martha Randisi Chaney, Joseph, Paula, Catherine Randisi Tateo, George, Anthony (dec.). With Raymond Kaiser Engrs., Inc., Oakland, Calif., 1969-75, 77-86, corp. acct., 1978-79, sr. corp. acct., 1979-82, sr. payroll acct., 1983-86, acctg. mgr., Lilli Ann Corp., San Francisco, 1986—; corp. buyer Kaiser Industries Corp., Oakland, 1975-77; lectr. on astrology Theosophical Soc., San Francisco, 1979—; mem. faculty Am. Fedn. Astrologers Internat. Conv., Chgo., 1982, 84. Mem. Speakers Bur., Calif. Assn. for Neurologically Handicapped Children, 1964-70, v.p. 1969; bd. dirs. Ravenwood Homeowners Assn., 1979-82, v.p., 1979-80, sec., 1980-81; mem. organizing com. Minority Bus. Fair, San Francisco, 1976; pres., bd. dirs. Lakewood Condominium Assn., 1984-87. Mem. Am. Fedn. Astrologers, Nat. Assn. Female Execs., Calif. Scholarship Fedn. (life), Alpha Gamma Sigma (life). Mem. Ch. of Religious Science (lic. practioner). Initiated Minority Vendor Purchasing Program for Kaiser Engrs., Inc., 1975-76. Home: 742 Wesley Way Apt 1-C Oakland CA 94610 Office: Lilli Ann Corp 2701 16th St San Francisco CA 94103

RANDKLEV, GERALD THEODORE, fast food company executive; b. Rupert, Idaho, Dec. 31, 1946; s. Maurice Theodore and Hilda (Kerbs) R.; m. Martha Sue Honaker, Aug. 30, 1974; children: Shannon Lee, Erica Dawn. BA, Idaho State U., 1969, MEd, 1971; postgrad., Willamette U., 1970. Employment counselor State of Idaho, Burley, 1975-81; supr., mgr., staff dir. potato quality assurance McDonald's Corp., Burley, 1981—; cons., J.R. Simplot Co., Lamb-Weston, Inc., Carnation Foods. Instr. Pomerelle Ski Resort. Capt. U.S. Army, 1971-75; lt. col. Idaho N.G., 1975—. Mem. Lions. Democrat. Presbyterian. Home: PO Box 755 Burley ID 83318

RANDLE, ELLEN EUGENIA FOSTER, opera, classical singer, educator; b. New Haven, Conn., Oct. 2, 1948; d. Richard A.G. and Thelma Lousie (Brooks) Foster; m. Ira James William, Mar. 7, 1947 (div. 1972); m. John Willis Randle. Student, Calif. State Coll., Sonoma, 1970; studied with Boris Goldovsky, 1970; student, Grad. Sch. Fine Arts, Florence, Italy, 1974; studied with Tito Gobbi, Florence, 1974; student, U. Calif., Berkeley, 1977; BA in World History, Lone Mountain Coll., 1976, MA in Performing Arts, 1978; studied with Madam Eleanor Steber, Graz, Austria, 1979; studied with Patricia Goehl, Munich, Fed. Republic Germany, 1979; postgrad., U. San Francisco, 1989—. instr. East Bay Performing Art Ctr., Richmond, Calif., 1986, Chapman Coll., 1986. Singer opera prodns. Porgy & Bess, Oakland, Calif., 1980-81, LaTraviata, Oakland, 1981-82, Aida, Oakland, 1981-82, Madame Butterfly, Oakland, 1982-83, The Magic Flute, Oakland, 1984, numerous others; performances include TV specials, religious concerts, musicals; music dir. Natural Man, Berkeley, 1986. Art commr. City of Richmond, Calif. Recipient Bk. Am. Achievement award. Mem. Music Tchrs. Assn., Nat. Council Negro Women, Nat. Assn. Negro Musicians, Calif. Arts Fedn., Calif. Assn. for Counseling and Devel. (mem. black caucus), The Calif.-Nebraskan Orgn., Inc., San Francisco Commonwealth Club, Gamma Phi Delta. Democrat. Mem. A.M.E. Zion Ch. Home: 5314 Boyd Ave Oakland CA 94618

RANDLE, MICHAEL CHARLES, computer scientist; b. Clarksdale, Miss., Apr. 28, 1952; s. Jesse Frank Sr. and Eleanor Marjana (Mothershed) R.; m. Jan Ceile Parry, Jan. 27, 1973. BS in Biology, Rhodes Coll., 1973; MS in Natural Sci., Memphis State U., 1976. Sr. systems programmer Planning Rsch. Corp., Honolulu, 1982-85, test and evaluation chief, 1985-88, system integrator intelligence work sta., 1988—; designer, programmer computer software. Active Citizens Against Noise, Honolulu, 1986-88. Capt. USAF, 1976-82. Mem. Assn. for Computing Machinery. Republican. Home: 46-362 Nahewai St Kaneohe HI 96744 Office: Planning Rsch Corp 98-211 Pali Momi St Ste 401 Aiea HI 96701

RANDLES, KEVIN LEE, mortgage company executive; b. Sacramento, Oct. 29, 1963; s. Keith Borland and Marlene Ann (Bowman) R. BS in Fin., Calif. State U., Fresno, 1987, Cert. in Mgmt., 1989; Cert. in Mgmt., Am. Mgmt. Assn. Extension Inst., 1989. Lic. real estate salesperson. Loan adminstr. Weyerhaeuser Mortgage Co., Fresno, 1987—. Mem. Fin. Mgmt. Assn., Fresno C. of C., Diplomat Club, Lambda Chi Alpha (chmn. recruitment com. 1986-87). Republican.

RANDOLPH, CARL LOWELL, chemical company executive; b. Pasadena, Calif., May 30, 1922; s. Carl L. and Lulu (McBride) R.; m. Jane Taber, June 25, 1943; children—Margaret, Stephen. B.A., Whittier Coll., 1943; M.S., U. So. Calif., 1947, Ph.D., 1949; LL.D. (hon.), Whittier Coll., 1982; D. Pub. Service (hon.), U. Alaska, 1983. Licensed shipmaster. Prin. chemist Aerojet-Gen. Corp., 1949-57; v.p. U.S. Borax Research Corp., Anaheim, Calif., 1957-63; asst. to pres. U.S. Borax & Chem. Corp., Los Angeles, 1963-66; v.p. U.S. Borax & Chem. Corp., 1966-68, exec. v.p., 1968-69, pres., 1969-86, vice chmn., 1983-87, also dir. Trustee, chmn. bd. Whittier Coll.; trustee Hollywood Presbyn. Hosp.; bd. dirs. Orange County Philharm. Soc., Ind. Colls. So. Calif. Served from ensign to lt. (j.g.) USNR, 1944-46. Mem. Am. Chem. Soc., Phi Beta Kappa, Sigma Xi. Home: 16812 Baruna Ln Huntington Beach CA 92649

RANFTL, ROBERT MATTHEW, management consulting company executive; b. Milw., May 31, 1925; s. Joseph Sebastian and Leona Elaine (Goetz) R.; m. Marion Smith Goodman, Oct. 12, 1946. BSEE, U. Mich., 1946; postgrad. UCLA, 1953-55. Product engr. Russell Electric Co., Chgo., 1946-47; head engring. dept. Radio Inst. Chgo., 1947-50; sr. project engr. Webster Chgo. Corp., 1950-51, product design engr., 1951-53, head equipment design group, 1953-54, head electronic equipment sect., 1954-55, mgr. product engring. dept., 1955-58, mgr. reliability and quality control, 1958-59, mgr. adminstrn. 1959-61, mgr. product effectiveness lab., 1961-74; corp. dir. engring./design mgmt., 1974-84, corp. dir. managerial productivity Hughes Aircraft Co., Los Angeles, 1984-86; pres. Ranftl Enterprises Inc., Mgmt. Cons., Los Angeles, 1981—; guest lectr. Calif. Inst. Tech., Cornell U., U. Calif.; mem. White House Conf. on Productivity, 1983; mem. human resources productivity task force Dept. of Def., 1985-86. Author: R&D Productivity, 1974, 78; (with others) Productivity: Prospects for Growth, 1981; contbr. articles to profl. jours. Mem. AAAS, AIAA, Am. Soc. Engring. Edn., Am. Soc. Tng. and Devel., IEEE, Inst. Mgmt. Scis., Acad. Mgmt., N.Y. Acad. Scis., U. Mich. Alumni Assn., UCLA Alumni Assn. Office: Ranftl Enterprises Inc PO Box 49892 Los Angeles CA 90049

RANGILA, NANCY ARNEVNA, savings and loan executive, investment consultant; b. Petrozavodsk, Russia, Mar. 23, 1936; d. Henry Hjalmar and Myrtle Marie (Jacobson) R. B.A. in Am. History, U. S.C., 1958, M.A. in Am. History, 1964; M.B.A. in Fin., U. So. Calif., 1973. Chartered fin. analyst; cert. employee benefit specialist, cert. fin. planner. Fin. analyst Capital Rsch. Co., L.A., 1964-73; v.p., portfolio mgr., fin. analyst Capital Cons., Inc., Portland, Oreg., 1973-82; sr. v.p., Franklin Fin. Svcs. (subs. Benj. Franklin Fed. Savs. & Loan Assn.), Portland, 1982—; lectr. investments, retirement plans. Chmn. City of Portland Hosp. Facilities Authority. Mem. Portland Soc. Fin. Analysts, Fin. Analysts Fedn., L.A. Soc. Fin. Analysts, Western Pension Conf. (Portland chpt.), Oreg. Women's Forum, City Club, Multnomah Athletic Club (Portland). Republican. Home: 2221 SW 1st Ave Apt 1625 Portland OR 97201 Office: Benjamin Franklin Fin Svcs 1 SW Columbia St Ste 900 Portland OR 97258

RANIERI, JOSEPH PASQUALE, building materials company executive; b. Celano, Italy, Nov. 6, 1933; came to U.S., 1954; s. Agostino and Luigetta (Stornelli) R.; m. May 6, 1957; children: Gino, Luisa, Joseph Pasquale Jr. Student, Celano. Former mason, title sette; owner, mgr. Mortarless Bldg. Supply Co., L.A., 1977--. Fellow Garibaldina Soc.; mme. UNICO. Republican. Roman Catholic. Office: Mortarless Bldg Supply Co 2707 Fletcher Dr Los Angeles CA 91206

RANISH, DONALD ROSEMAN, political science educator, political consultant; b. Newburgh, N.Y., Nov. 19, 1943; s. Harry and Sylvia (Roseman) R.; m. Leslee Ann Guttman, Aug. 29, 1970. BA, Calif. State U., Fullerton, 1970; MA, U. Calif., Santa Barbara, 1972, PhD, 1975. Prof. polit. sci. Alma (Mich.) U., 1975-76, Calif. State U., San Bernardino, 1976-77; prof. polit. sci. and law Antelope Valley Coll., Lancaster, Calif., 1977—, Kyung Hee U., Seoul, 1987—; Fulbright lectr., Republic of Korea, 1987. Author: American Political Process, 1982, 4th edit., 1989, Rhetoric of a Rebel, 1975. Bd. dirs. United Way Antelope Valley, Lancaster, 1986-88. U.S. Sea grantee, 1974-75; U.Calif. Regents grantee, 1975. Mem. Am. Polit. Sci. Assn., Acad. Criminal Justice Scis., Fulbright Alumni Assn., Phi Kappa Phi, Pi Sigma Alpha. Democrat. Home: 42953 Cherbourg Ln Lancaster CA 93536

RANKAITIS, SUSAN, artist; b. Cambridge, Mass., Sept. 10, 1949; d. Alfred Edward and Isabel (Shimkus) Rankaitis; m. Robbert Flick, June 5, 1976. B.F.A. in Painting, U. Ill., 1971; M.F.A. in Visual Arts, U. So. Calif., 1977. Represented by Meyers/Bloom Gallery, Santa Monica, Calif., Gallery Min, Tokyo; assoc. prof. art, chair Chapman Coll.; overview panelist visual arts Nat. Endowment for Arts, 1983, 84. One-man shows include L.A. County Mus. Art, 1983, Internat. Mus. Photography, George Eastman House, 1983, Gallery Min of Tokyo, 1988, Meyers/Bloom Gallery, Santa Monica, 1989; represented in permanent collections U. Ill., Santa Monica Coll., Ctr. for Creative Photography, UCLA, Mus. Modern ARt, Santa Barbara Mus. Art, L.A. County Mus. Art, Mpls. Inst. Arts, San Francisco Mus. Modern Art, Security Pacific Bank, Mus. Modern Art, Lodz, Poland, Nat. Mus. Am. Art. Active Friends of Photography, 1985-88, mem. adv. bd. trustees. Nat. Endowment for Arts fellow, 1980, 88, Chapman rsch. fellow 1984-87, U.S./France fellow, 1989; Djerassi resident, 1989; recipient Graves award in the humanities, 1985. Mem. Coll. Art Assn., Los Angeles Inst. Contemporary Art, Los Angeles County Mus. Art, Friends of Photography, Center Creative Photography, Calif. Council Fine Arts Deans. Office: Myers/Bloom Gallery 2112 Broadway Santa Monica CA 90404-2912

RANKIN, HELEN CROSS, cattle rancher, guest ranch executive; b. Mojave, Calif; d. John Whisman and Cleo Rebecca (Tilley) Cross; m. Leroy Rankin, Jan. 4, 1936 (dec. 1954); children—Julia Jane King Sharr, Patricia Helen Denvir, William John. A.B., Calif. State U.-Fresno, 1935. Owner, operator Rankin Cattle Ranch, Caliente, Calif., 1954—; founder, pres. Rank Ranch, Inc., Guest Ranch, 1965—; mem. sect. 15, U.S. Bur. Land Mgmt.; mem. U.S. Food and Agrl. Leaders Tour China, 1983, Australia and N.Z., 1985; dir. U.S. Bur. Land Mgmt. sect. 15. Pres., Children's Home Soc. Calif., 1945. Recipient award Calif. Hist. Soc., 1983, Kern River Valley Hist. Soc., 1983. Mem. Am. Nat. Cattlemen's Assn., Calif. Cattlemen's Assn., Kern County Cattlemen's Assn., Kern County Cowbelles (pres. 1949, Cattlewoman of Yr. 1988), Calif. Cowbelles, Nat. Cowbelles, Bakersfield Country Club, Bakersfield Raquet Club. Republican. Methodist. Office: Rankin Ranch Caliente CA 93518

RANKIN, WILLIAM PARKMAN, educator, former publishing company executive; b. Boston, Feb. 6, 1917; s. George William and Bertha W. (Clowe) R.; m. Ruth E. Gerard, Sept. 12, 1942; children: Douglas W., Joan W. BS, Syracuse U., 1941; MBA, NYU, 1949, PhD, 1979. Sales exec. Redbook mag., N.Y.C., 1945-49; sales exec. This Week mag., N.Y.C., 1949-55, adminstrv. exec., 1955-60, v.p., 1957-60, v.p., dir. advt. sales, sales devel. dir., 1960-63, exec. v.p., 1963-69; gen. exec. newspaper div. Time Inc., N.Y.C., 1969-70; gen. mgr. feature svc. Newsweek, Inc., N.Y.C., 1970-74, fin. and ins. advt. mgr., 1974-81; prof., asst. to the dir. Walter Cronkite Sch. Journalism and Telecommunication, Ariz. State U., Tempe, 1981—; lectr. Syracuse U., NYU, Berkeley Sch.; mem. adv. coun. Sch. Journalism, N.Y. Dutch Treat CLub, Met. Adv. Golf Assn., Mesa Country Club, Syracuse U. Mem. Soc. Profl. Journalists/Sigma Delta Chi, Alpha Delta Sigma. Author: Selling Retail Advertising, 1944; The Technique of Selling Magazine Advertising, 1949; Business Management of Consumer Magazines, 1980, 2 ed. 1984, The Practice of Newspaper Mgmt., 1986. Home: 1220 E Krista Way Tempe AZ 85284 Home: Bridge Rd Bomoseen VT 05732 Office: Ariz State U Walter Cronkite Sch Journalism/ Telecommunication Tempe AZ 85287

RANKINE, BAXTER JAMES, aerospace company executive; b. Moncks Corner, S.C., June 30, 1936; s. Baxter Grey and Mary DeLellis (Bradley) R.; m. Joyce Marie Lemery, July 24, 1965; children: David James, Julie Dee. BS in Engring., UCLA, 1959. Indsl. engr. GE, 1960-65; material control mgr. Collins Radio Co., Newport Beach, Calif., 1965-67; v.p., mktg. Paco Pumps, Oakland, Calif., 1967-75; dir. corp. devel. Mark Controls Corp., Evanston, Ill., 1975-77; pres. Ctr. Line, Tulsa, Okla., 1977-78, Pacific Valves, Long Beach, Calif., 1978-87, All-Power Mfg Co., Santa Fe Springs, Calif., 1987—; bd. dirs. Bus. Network, Torrance, Calif. Mem. Kappa Sigma. Republican. Roman Catholic. Home: 30330 Cartier Dr Palos Verdes CA 90274 Office: All-Power Mfg Co 13141 Molette St Santa Fe Springs CA 90670

RANNEY, HELEN MARGARET, physician, educator; b. Summer Hill, N.Y., Apr. 12, 1920; d. Arthur C. and Alesia (Toolan) R. A.B., Barnard Coll., 1941; M.D., Columbia, 1947; Sc.D., U. S.C., 1979. Diplomate: Am. Bd. Internal Medicine. Intern Presbyn. Hosp., N.Y.C., 1947-48; resident Presbyn. Hosp., 1948-50; practice medicine specializing in internal medicine, hematology N.Y.C., 1954-70; asst. physician Presbyn. Hosp., 1954-60; instr. Coll. Phys. and Surg. Columbia, 1954-60; asso. prof. medicine Albert Einstein Coll. Medicine, 1960-64, prof. medicine, 1965-70; prof. medicine SUNY-Buffalo, 1970-73; prof. medicine U. Calif.-San Diego, 1973—, chmn. dept. medicine, 1973-86, disting. physician vet. adminstr., 1986—. Fellow AAAS, A.C.P.; mem. Am. Soc. for Clin. Investigation, Am. Soc. Hematology, Harvey Soc., Am. Assn. Physicians, Nat. Acad. Sci., Inst. Medicine, Am. Acad. Arts and Scis., Phi Beta Kappa, Sigma Xi, Alpha Omega Alpha. Home: Vet Adminstrn Med Ctr 6229 La Jolla Mesa Dr La Jolla CA 92037

RANOLA, NELSON LIM, electronics executive, systems engineer; b. Guinodatan, Albay, Philippines, Feb. 7, 1951; came to U.S., 1982; s. Nicolas Tincan and Severina (Lim) R.; m. Rosalie Te, May 8, 1982; children: James Abe So, Neil. BSME, Cebu Inst. Tech., Philippines, 1974; MBA, Southwestern U., 1982. Registered profl. engr., Philippines. Sales mgr. Ranola Motor Ctr., Philippines, 1974-82; office mgr. Audio Video Shoppe, Culver City, Calif., 1982-84; with Quotron Systems, L.A., 1979-84, supr. media prodn. div., 1986-88, project planning mgr. product quality dept., 1989—; pres. RMT Corp., Culver City, 1987—. Mem. Lions (bd. dirs. Philippines chpt. 1979-82), Quotron Systems, Inc. Golf Club, NRA. Republican. Methodist. Home: 11531 Braddock Dr Culver City CA 90230 Office: Quotron Systems Inc 5454 Beethoven St Los Angeles CA 90066

RANSOM, GARY ELLIOTT, judge, lawyer; b. New Brunswick, N.J., Dec. 23, 1941; s. Edward A. Sr. and Rose Ransom. BA in Econs., Rutgers U., 1965; JD, U. of the Pacific, 1974. Bar: Calif. 1974, U.S. Dist. Ct. (ea. dist.) Calif. 1974, U.S. Supreme Ct. 1979. Field rep. N.J. Dept. Pub. Safety, Trenton, 1965-66; sr. trial atty. Sacramento County, 1974-81; judge Mcpl. Ct., Sacramento County, 1981-88, Sacramento County Superior Ct., 1988—. Mem. bd. Family Svcs. Agy., Sacramento, 1980-88; pres. Easter Seals Soc. of Sacramento, 1988—. Recipient Earnest E. Robinson award U. of the Pacific, 1985. Mem. Nat. Bar Assn., Calif. Assn. Black Lawyers (chair Oakland, Calif. sect. 1978—, Bernard S. Jefferson award for Jud. Excellence 1989), NAACP, Calif. Judges Assn., Wiley Manuel Bar Assn. (pres. Sacramento chpt. 1980-81), Rutgers U. Alumni Assn., U. of the Pacific Alumni Assn. (past v.p.), Exemplar Consistory, Masons, Phi Delta Phi (pres. Sacramento chpt. 1973-74), Kappa Alpha Psi, Sigma Pi Phi. Democrat. Episcopalian. Home: 1406 Commons Dr Sacramento CA 95825 Office: Superior Ct County Courthouse Sacramento CA 95814

RAO, KAMESWARA KOLLA, physicist, electrical engineer; b. Kasimkota, Andhra, India, July 28, 1944; came to U.S., 1970; d. Subbarao and Ammaji (Paluri) Kolla; m. Vasavi Namburi, Nov. 17, 1972; children: Swathi, Sandhya, Preethi, Srinivas. BS in Physics with honors, Andhra U., 1963, MSc in Physics, 1964; MS in Physics, U. Wis., 1972, PhD, 1975. Asst. prof. physics Western Mich. U., Kalamazoo, 1975-79; staff engr. Nat. Semicondr. Co., Santa Clara, Calif., 1979-81; sect. head engr. Signetics, Sunnyvale, Calif., 1981-83; project mgr. Intel., Santa Clara, Calif., 1983-86; design engring. mgr. Catalyst Semicondr. Inc., Santa Clara, 1986--. Co-inventor software programs. Mem. IEEE. Home: 1172 Arlington Ln San Jose CA 95129-3740

RAPAGE, LOUIS, broadcasting executive; b. Geneva, N.Y., Aug. 26, 1954; s. Louis Jay and Ann (Monacelli) Ripich. BS in Psychology and Religion, Syracuse U., 1977. Dir. mktg. spl. projects Lorimar-Colepicture co., L.A., 1986-87; dir. programming and promotion Sta. KERO-TV, McGraw Hill Broadcast, Inc., Bakersfield, Calif., 1987—. Mem. Nat. Assn. Video Arts and Scis. Home: 1541 Ocean Ave Santa Monica CA 90401 Office: McGraw Hill Broadcast Inc KERO TV 321 21st St Bakersfield CA 93301

RAPHAEL, DAMON S., gynecologist/obstetrician; b. Tucson, Sept. 2, 1934; s. Henry Holiday and Sylvia Gertrude (Moskowitz) R.; m. Joan Frances Sobel, Apr. 1, 1958; children: Patricia Dawn Moseley, Marjorie Ann, Lisa Lynn Rodriguez. AB, Columbia Coll., N.Y.C., 1956; MD, N.Y. U., 1960. Diplomate Am. Bd. Obstetrics and Gynecology. Intern N.Y.U. Bellevue Med. Ctr., N.Y.C., 1960-61, resident, 1961-62,1964-67; pvt. practice Tucson, 1967—; mem. staff Tucson Clinic, P.C., 1967-71; pres Damon S. Raphael, M.D., Ltd., 1976--; chief of gynecology El Dorado Hosp., 1970-72. Mem. AMA, Pima County Med. Soc., Ariz. Med. Assn., Tucson Computer Soc., Alpha Omega Alpha. Republican. Jewish.

RAPHAEL, MARTIN GEORGE, research wildlife biologist; b. Denver, Oct. 5, 1946; s. Jerome Maurice and Alys (Salmonson) R.; m. Susan Williams, August 4, 1967; 1 child, Samantha Marie. BA, Sacramento State U., 1968; BS, U. Calif., Berkeley, 1972, MS, 1976, PhD, 1980. Staff research assoc. U. Calif., Berkeley, 1974-80, assoc. specialist, 1980-84; project leader USDA Forest Service, Laramie, 1984—; adj. prof. U. Wyo., Laramie, 1986—; cons. ecologist Pacific Gas and Electric Co., San Ramon, Calif., 1981-84. Contbr. articles to sci. jours. Mem. AAAS, Am. Soc. Mammalogists (recipient Best Poster award 1984), Am. Ornithologists' Union, Cooper Ornithol. Soc. (chmn. membership com. 1985—, asst. sec. 1986—, bd. dirs. 1989—), The Wildlife Soc. (local pres. publs. com. 1983-84, assoc. editor Wildlife Soc. Bull. 1987—), Phi Beta Kappa, Sigma Xi, Xi Sigma Pi. Home: 2205 Skyview Ln Laramie WY 82070 Office: Rocky Mountain Forest and Range Experiment Sta 222 S 22nd St Laramie WY 82070

RAPHAEL, MARYANNE JEANNE D'ARC, author; b. Waverly, Ohio, Mar. 18, 1938; d. Vincent Ignatius and Doris Louise (Brown) Patterson; m. Lennox Alison Raphael, Sept. 17, 1939 (div. July 1972); 1 child, Raphael Azariah. BA with honors, Ohio U., 1959; postgrad., The Sorbonne, Paris, France, 1960, U. Brazil, 1961, NYU, 1963-64. Social dir. US Air Force Svc. Club, Hahn, Germany, 1960-61; tchr. Latin American Inst., N.Y.C., 1962-63; editor Prentice Hall, Inc., N.Y.C., 1963-64; editorial asst. Women's Day Mag., N.Y.C., 1979—; tchr. Alternative U., N.Y.C., 1965-66, Frederick Douglas High Sch., N.Y., 1965-66, U. of the streets, N.Y.C., 1968-73; women's studies tchr. New Sch. for Social Research, N.Y.C., 1971-72; activities dir. Pike Manor Nursing Home, Piketon, Ohio, 1982; editor, publisher Writer's World Press, Encinitas, Calif., 1984—; book reviewer Writer's Lifeline, Ontario, Canada, 1978—, tchr. interpretor St. James Mission Circle, 1988—, language tchr. CoWorkers of Mother Teresa, Tijuana, Mex., 1989—. Author: How To Survive As A Freelance Writer, 1974, An Interview With Anais Nin, 1980, biographical book, Une Annee a Paris, 1960, How to Survie as a Age Writer, 1988, Akita A Dog for All Seasons, 1980, Run Runaways, America's Lost Youth, 1974, Your Psychic Powers, the Key to Success, 1974. Bd. dirs. YMCA Women's Ctr., Family Crisis Shelter, Hilo, Hawaii, 1978-79, Pike County Community Action, coordinator St. Mary's Ctr., Waverly, Ohio, 1982-84. Mem. Nat. Assn. for Female Execs., Nat. Writer's Club, Shawnee U. Poets Cir., Catholic Women, San Luiz Rey Prayer Group. Democrat. Home and Office: 488 La Veta Encinitas CA 92024

RAPIER, PASCAL MORAN, chemical engineer; b. Atlanta, Jan. 11, 1914; s. Paul Edward and Mary Claire (Moran) R.; m. Martha Elizabeth Doyle, May 19, 1945; children: Caroline Elizabeth, Paul Doyle, Mollie Claire, John Lawrence, James Andrew. BSChemE, Ga. Inst. Tech., 1939; MS in Theoretical Physics, U. Nev., 1959; postgrad., U. Calif., Berkeley, 1961. Registered profl. engr., Calif., N.J. Plant engr. Archer-Daniels-Midland, Pensacola, Fla., 1940-42; group supr. Dicalite div. Grefco, Los Angeles, 1943-54; process engr. Celatom div. Eagle Picher, Reno, Nev., 1955-57; project mgr., assoc. research engr. U. Calif. Field Sta., Richmond, 1959-62; project mgr. sea water conversion Bechtel Corp., San Francisco, 1962-66; sr. supervising chem. engr. Burns & Roe, Oradell, N.J., 1966-74; cons. engr. Kenite Corp., Scarsdale, N.Y., Rees Blowpipe, Berkeley, 1960-66; sr. cons. engr. Sanderson & Porter, N.Y.C., 1975-77; staff scientist III Lawrence Berkeley Lab., 1977-84; bd. dirs. Newtonian Sci. Found.; v.p. Calif. Rep. Assembly, 1964-65; discoverer phenomena faster than light, origin of cosmic rays and galactic red shifts. Contbr. articles to profl jours.; patentee agts. to render non-polar solvents electrically conductive, direct-contact geothermal energy recovery devices. Mem. Am. Inst. Chem. Engrs., Gideons Internat. Presbyterian. Home: 3154 Deseret Dr Richmond CA 94803

RAPPAPORT, DANIEL CHARLES, sales executive; b. Bklyn., Oct. 10, 1943; s. Simon and Mildred (Bork) R.; m. Michele C. Green, July 11, 1965; children: Sandra, Jason. BSEE, Columbia U., N.Y.C., 1964; MBA, Rutgers U., 1969. Mktg. engr. Westinghouse Corp., Newark, 1964-66; sales engr. Tex. Instruments, Springfield, N.J., 1966-69, Nat. Semiconductor, Ft. Lee, N.J., 1969-70; product mgr. Arrow Electronics, Farmingdale, N.Y., 1970-71; dist. sales mgr. Fairchild Semiconductor, Melville, N.Y., 1971-78; area sales dir. Harris Semiconductor, Woodland Hills, Calif., C, 1978--. Mem. IEEE. Home: 5120 Orrville Ave Woodland Hills CA 91367 Office: Harris Semiconductor 6400 Canoga Ave Ste 205 Woodland Hills CA 91367

RASE, WILLIAM, communications executive; b. Sacramento, Oct. 25, 1926; s. William Antone and Della (Romig) R.; m. Shirley Bishop, Aug. 24, 1952; children: Susan, Lori. AA, Sacramento City Coll., 1952, postgrad., 1952-54. Disk jockey, radio announcer Sta. KCRA Radio, Sacramento, 1952-64; TV personality Bill Rase Show Sta. KCRA-TV, Sacramento, 1954-64; pres., owner Bill Rase Prodns., Inc., Sacramento, 1965—; as leader of Bill Rase Orch., performed with Bob Hope Show, Cab Calloway Show, over 5,500 others, 1948—. Chmn. City of Sacramento Mayor's Com. To Hire The Handicapped, 1968; pub. relations dir. 52d Agrl. Dist. Fair, 1967-86; spl. events dir. Placer County Fair, Sacramento County Fair, Dixon May Fair. Recipient Disting. Service award San Francisco Chpt. TV Arts and Scis., 1964; various other awards for radio, TV commls., video prodns. Mem. Sacramento Musicians Union, Advt. Club Sacramento (pres. 1972-73). Republican. Office: 955 Venture Ct Sacramento CA 95825

RASK, MICHAEL RAYMOND, orthopaedist; b. Butte, Mont., Oct. 24, 1930; s. Barth John and Marguerite Sadie (Joseph) R.; m. Elizabeth Anne Shannon, Mar. 21, 1984; children: Dagny Marguerite Rask-Regan, Badih John, Patrick Henry, Molly Michelle. BS, Oreg. State U., 1951; MD, Oreg. Health Scis. U., 1955; PhD, 1978, U. Humanistic Studies, 1986. Diplomate Am. Bd. Orthopaedic Surgery, Am. Bd. Neurological Orthopaedic Surgery, Am. Bd. Bloodless Surgery, Am. Bd. Medical-Legal Analysts, Am. Bd. Hand Surgery, Am. Bd. Sportsmedicine Surgery, Am. Bd. Spinal Surgery. Intern Kings County Hosp., Bklyn., 1955-56; orthopaedic resident U. Oreg. Med. Sch., Portland, 1959-63; with neurological orthopaedic surgery preceptorships Oreg. Emmanuel Hosp., Portland, 1962-76; pvt. practice in neurol. orthopaedic surgery Las Vegas, 1976—; clin. instr. orthopaedics U. Oreg., 1964-71; prof. Am. Acad. Neurological and Orthopaedic Surgery, 1985—; editorial reviewer Clin. Orthopaedics & Related Rsch., 1978—, Am. Med. Reports, 1985—, Muscle & Nerve, 1987—, Am. Jour. Cranio-Mandibular Practice. Author: Seminoma, 1970, Orthopod, 1972; editor in-chief: Jour. Neurological Orthopedic Medicine & Surgery, 1976—, Jour. Bloodless Medicine & Surgery, 1980—; editorial rev. bd. Jour. Cranio-mandibular Practice; numerous lectures in field. Lectr. Arthritis Found., Las Vegas, 1976-78, cons. orthopaedist Easter Seal Ctr. for Crippled Children & Adults, Las Vegas, 1978-81, med. advisor so. Nev. chpt. Nat. Multiple Sclerosis Soc.; bd. dirs. Gov's. Com. on the Employment of the Handicapped, Nev., 1980-82. Capt. USAF, 1956-63. Fellow Cuban Soc. Orthopaedics Traumatology; mem. Am. Acad. Neurological Orthopaedic Surgeons (hon. 1979, course chmn. 1977-79, pres. 1978, chmn. bd. dirs. 1976—), Nev. State Pharmacy Assn., Am. Back Soc. (bd. dirs. 1983-88), Semmelweiss Sci. Soc. (pres. Nev. chpt. 1980—), Am. Fedn. Med. Accreditation (chmn. 1979—), Neurol. Orthopaedic Inst. (chmn. 1979—), Bd. Neurol. Orthopaedic Surgeons (chmn. 1977—), Sundry Primary Certifying Bds. (chmn. bd. dirs. 1976—), Silkworm Club, Caterpillar Club. Republican. Office: Am Acad Neurol & Orthopaedic Med Surgeons 2320 Rancho Dr Ste 108 Las Vegas NV 89102-4592

RASKOB, ANTHONY WILLIAM, JR., mechanical engineer; b. Colorado Springs, Colo., May 5, 1960; s. Anthony William and Marilyn Ann (Claypoole) R.; m. Jorji Marie Griffin, Aug. 2, 1986. BS in Mech. Engring., U. Colo., 1982. Patent examiner U.S. Patent and Trademark Office, Washington, 1982-84; staff engr. Sci. Applications Intnat. Corp., Colorado Springs, 1984-86; program mgr. Aptek, Inc., Colorado Springs, 1986—. Mem. St. Mary's High Sch. Endowment Bd. Mem. Am. Soc. Mech. Engrs. Republican. Roman Catholic.

RASMUS, ALFRED ANDERS, insurance executive; b. Astoria, Oreg., Jan. 7, 1947; s. Runar Emil and Martha (Niemi) R.; m. Anne Marie Lemke, Dec. 6, 1969. BS in Maths., Oreg. State U., 1969. With Transamerica Title Ins. Co., 1976-84; county mgr. Transamerica Title Ins. Co., Albany, Oreg., 1978-82; cen. svcs. mgr. Transamerica Title Ins. Co., Salem, Oreg., 1982-84; owner, mgr. Am. Pacific Title & Escrow, Salem, 1984—. Mem., contbr. Com. to Build A Better Oreg., Salem, 1980—. Mem. Oreg. Land Title Assn., Oreg. Escrow Coun. (legis. chmn. Portland chpt. 1987—), Am. Land Title Assn., Am. Escrow Assn., Oreg. State Home Builders Assn. (past assoc. v.p. Salem chpt., bd. dirs. 1980—), Mid Valley Execs. Republican. Lutheran. Home: 2138 Chicago St SE Albany OR 97321

RASMUSON, ELMER EDWIN, banker, former mayor Anchorage; b. Yakutat, Alaska, Feb. 15, 1909; s. Edward Anton and Jenny (Olson) R.; m. Lile Vivian Bernard, Oct. 27, 1939 (dec. 1960); children: Edward Bernard, Lile Muchmore (Mrs. John Gibbons, Jr.), Judy Ann; m. Col. Mary Louise Milligan, Nov. 4, 1961. B.S. magna cum laude, Harvard U., 1930, A.M., 1935; student, U. Grenoble, 1930; LL.D., U. Alaska, 1970. C.P.A., N.Y., Tex., Alaska. Chief accountant Nat. Investors Corp., N.Y.C., 1933-35; prin. Arthur Andersen & Co., N.Y.C., 1935-43; pres. Nat. Bank of Alaska, 1943-65, chmn. bd., 1966-74, chmn. exec. com., 1975-82, now chmn. emeritus; mayor City of Anchorage, 1964-67, dir., emeritus and cons., 1989; civilian aide from Alaska to sec. army 1959-67; Swedish consul Alaska, 1955-77; Chmn. Rasmuson Found.; Rep. nominee U.S. Senate from Alaska, 1968; U.S. commr. Internat. N. Pacific Fisheries Commn., 1969-84; mem. Nat. Marine Fisheries Adv. Com., 1974-77, North Pacific Fishery Mgmt. Council, 1976-77, U.S. Arctic Research Commn., 1984—. Mem. City Council Anchorage, 1945, chmn. city planning commn., 1950-53; pres. Alaska council Boy Scouts Am., 1953; sec.-treas. Loussac Found.; regent U. Alaska, 1950-69; trustee King's Lake Camp, Inc., 1944—, Alaska Permanent Fund Corp., 1980-82; bd. dirs. Coast Guard Acad. Found. Decorated knight first class Order of Vasa, comdr. Sweden; recipient silver Antelope award Boy Scouts Am., Japanese citation Order of the Sacred Treasure, Gold and Silver Star, 1988; outstanding civilian service medal U.S. Army; Alaskan of Year award, 1976. Mem. Pioneers Alaska, Alaska Bankers Assn. (past pres.), Defense Orientation Conf. Assn., NAACP, Alaska Native Brotherhood, Explorers Club, Phi Beta Kappa. Republican. Presbyn. Clubs: Masons, Elks, Anchorage Rotary (past pres.); Harvard (N.Y.C.; Boston); Wash. Athletic (Seattle), Seattle Yacht (Seattle), Rainier (Seattle); Thunderbird Country (Palm Desert, Calif.); Bohemian (San Francisco); Eldorado Country (Indian Wells, Calif.); Boone & Crockett. Home: PO Box 600 Anchorage AK 99510

RASMUSSEN, A. THOMAS, optometrist, state legislator; b. Plentywood, Mont., Nov. 20, 1940; s. Arnie Alfred R.; m. Karen L. Murphy, Aug. 1, 1964; children: Lisa, Lori, Erin. Student, Mont. State U., 1958-61; OD, Pacific U., Forest Grove, Oreg., 1964. Mem. Ho. of Reps., Mont., 1975-76, Mont. Senate, 1977-80, 1987—. Mem. Am. Optometric Assn., Mont. Optometric Assn. (pres. 1971, Optometrist of Yr., 1973, 77), Better Vision Inst. Republican. Mem. Assembly God Ch. Home: 1353 Rimini Helena MT 59601 Office: Office State Senate State Capitol Helena MT 69620 also: 550 N Montana Helena MT 59601

RASMUSSEN, CAROL MILLER, research center official, writer, editor; b. Mpls., Dec. 13, 1950; d. Stanley Wheeler Rasmussen and Theona R. Anderson; m. Martin Charles Noecker, Nov. 1, 1987. BMus, U. Colo., 1973; MLS, U. Ill., 1977. Book rev. editor Library Jour., N.Y.C., 1978-81; free-lance writer, editor N.Y.C., 1980-83, Boulder, 1983--; writer, editor Nat. Ctr. for Atmospheric Rsch., Boulder, 1983--; editor Univ. Corp. for Atmospheric Rsch. Corp. Report, 1988--. Editor Staff Notes, 1987--. Mem. Soc. for Tech. Communications (Disting. Tech. Communication award Rocky Mountain region 1988), Ars Nova Chamber Singers (bd. dirs. 1986-87). Democrat. Episcopalian. Home: 602 University Ave Boulder CO 80302 Office: Nat Ctr for Atmospheric Rsh PO Box 3000 Boulder CO 80302

RASMUSSEN, JOHN OSCAR, JR., chemistry educator, scientist; b. St. Petersburg, Fla., Aug. 8, 1926; s. John Oscar and Hazel (Ormsby) R.; m. Louise Brooks, Aug. 27, 1950; children—Nancy, Jane, David, Stephen. B.S., Calif. Inst. Tech., 1948; Ph.D., U. Calif. at Berkeley, 1952; M.A. (hon.), Yale U., 1969. Mem. chemistry faculty U. Calif. at Berkeley, 1952-68, 73—, prof. chemistry, 1973—; mem. research staff Radiation Lab., 1952-68; sr. research asso. Lawrence Berkeley Lab., 1972—; prof. chemistry Yale U. 1969-73; asso. dir. Yale Heavy Ion Accelerator Lab., 1970-73; vis. research prof. Nobel Inst. Physics, Stockholm, 1953; vis. prof. Inst. Nuclear Sci. U. Tokyo, 1974, Fudan U., Shanghai, 1979, hon. prof., 1984. Contbr. articles on radiochemistry, nuclear models, heavy ion reactions. Served with USN, 1944-46. NSF sr. post-doctoral fellow Niels Bohr Inst., Copenhagen, Denmark, 1961-62; NORDITA fellow, 1979; recipient E.O. Lawrence Meml. award AEC, 1967; J.S. Guggenheim Meml. fellow, 1973. Fellow Am. Phys. Soc., AAAS; mem. Am. Chem. Soc. (Nuclear Applications in Chemistry award 1976), Fedn. Am. Scientists (chmn. 1969), IBM-U. Calif. Berkeley Conf. on Acad. Computing (chmn. 1987). Office: U Calif Dept Chemistry Berkeley CA 94720

RASMUSSEN, KIMBERLY JANE, interior designer, educator; b. Volga, S.D., Nov. 10, 1957; d. George W. and Jane Ann (Vernon) Korver; m. Scott L. Rasmussen, Aug. 19, 1978; 1 child, Thomas. BS in Interior Design, U. Ariz., 1982. Cert. Nat. Council for Interior Design Qualification, 1987. Head interior designer Contents, Tucson, 1982-86; owner In A Nutshell, Tucson, 1986—; tchr. Pina Community Coll., Tucson. Mem. Homeowners Assn., 1987—. Mem. Am. Soc. Interior Designers. Office: In A Nutshell 6737 E Camino Principal St E Tucson AZ 85715

RASMUSSEN, NANCY LEE, personnel analyst; b. Denver, Sept. 15, 1953; d. George Edward and Laura Kathryn (Schwemmer) R.; m. Duane Scott Thompson, May 25, 1975. BA, U. Colo., Colorado Springs, 1975; MBA, Calif. State U., Fresno, 1987. Accredited human resources profl. Pers. analyst Tulare County Personnel, Visalia, Calif., 1977—. Bd. dirs. Family Svcs. Tulare County, 1988—. Mem. Am. Soc. Pers. Adminstrs., Western Regional Ingovtl. Pers. Assessment Coun., Networking for Women. Democrat. Office: Tulare County Pers 2900 W Burrel Visalia CA 93277

RASMUSSEN, STUART RICARD, newspaper librarian; b. San Francisco, Nov. 7, 1906; s. Emil Jorgen and Christine (Johnsen) R.; student U. Calif. Extension; m. Nairn Margaret Abbott, June 1, 1940; children—Nairn Christine, Mark Abbott. In library San Francisco Examiner, 1929-37; head librarian San Francisco Call Bull., 1937-59, San Francisco News Call Bulletin, 1959-66; library staff San Francisco Examiner, 1966—, asst. head librarian, 1966-75, acting head librarian, 1975-78; engaged in spl. research for Metro-Goldwyn-Mayer movies, San Francisco Bay area, 1935—; actor Maxwell Burke Stock Co., Oakland and Berkeley, Calif., 1927-28, Blake, Turner Stock Co., San Francisco area, 1928; dir. children and adult plays San Geronimo Valley Community Centers; sometimes dir. Ross Valley Players Barn Theatre. Pres. Lagunitas Dist. Sch. Bd., 1955-58, San Geronimo Valley Little League, 1961. Mem. Spl. Libraries Assn., Am. Newspaper Guild (charter mem. San Francisco/Oakland chpt.). Democrat. Club: San Francisco Press (life mem.). Author drama revs. for The Peninsulan, 1936; several plays for children, 1955-60. Home: Alta Rd Lagunitas CA 94938 Office: 110 5th St San Francisco CA 94118

RASMUSSEN, THOMAS VAL, JR., lawyer, small business owner; b. Salt Lake City, Aug. 11, 1954; s. Thomas Val and Georgia (Smedley) R.; m. Donita Gubler, Aug. 15, 1978; children: James, Katherine, Kristin. BA magna cum laude, U. Utah, 1978, JD, 1981. Bar: Utah 1981, U.S. Dist. Ct. Utah 1981, U.S. Supreme Ct. 1985. Atty. Salt Lake Legal Defender Assn., Salt Lake City, 1981-83, Utah Power and Light Co., Salt Lake City, 1983-89, Hatch, Morton & Skeen, Salt Lake City, 1989—; co-owner, developer Handi Self-Storage, Kaysville, Utah, 1984—; instr. bus. law Brigham Young U., Salt Lake City, 1988—. Adminstrv. editor Jour. Contemporary Law, 1980-81, Jour. Energy Law and Policy, 1980-81. Missionary Ch. of Jesus Christ of Latter-Day Sts., Brazil, 1973-75. Mem. ABA, Utah Bar Assn., Salt Lake County Bar Assn., Intermountain Miniature Horse Club (pres. 1989—), Phi Eta Sigma, Phi Kappa Phi, Beta Gamma Sigma. Home: 7079 Pine Cone Circle Salt Lake City UT 84121 Office: Utah Power and Light Co 1407 W North Temple Ste 340 Salt Lake City UT 84140

RATHFON, CONSTANCE WAISANEN, product quality and development specialist; b. Moose Lake, Minn., July 30, 1952; d. Lauri Raymond and Walma Helene (Penttinen) Waisanen; m. Robert Kent Rathfon, Oct. 1, 1979; children: Michael Paul, Jesse Gibson. BS in Chem. Engring., U. Calif.-Davis, 1978. Process engr. Crown Zellerbach Co., Clatskanie, Oreg., 1979-82, supr. testers and technicians, 1981-84, Kraft mill foreman, 1984-86; mgr. product quality and devel. James River Co., Clatskanie, Oreg., 1986--. Lutheran. Home: Rt 4 Box 578 Astoria OR 97103 Office: James River Co Wauna Div Clatskanie OR 97016

RATICAN, PETER S., health maintenance organization executive. Now chmn., pres., chief exec. officer Maxicare Health Plans Inc., 1988—, also bd. dirs. Office: Maxicare Health Plans Inc 5200 W Century Blvd Los Angeles CA 90045 *

RATLIFF, JACK ROBERT (BOB), cattle rancher, investor; b. San Angelo, Tex., Sept. 27, 1938; s. Jack L. and Roberta E. (Milligan) R.; m. Nancy Louise Johnston, Jan. 25, 1965; children: Katherine Ann, Lee Robert. BA, U. Tex., El Paso, 1965. Field engr. Schlumberger Well Svc., Kermit, Tex., 1965-67; sr. field engr. Schlumberger Well Svc., Hobbs, N.Mex., 1967-69; staff field engr. Schlumberger Well Svc., Houston, 1969-71; dist. mgr. Schlumberger Well Svc., Farmington, N.Mex., 1971-73; pres. San Juan Stationers, Inc., Farmington, 1973-84, Ratliff Ranch, Ft. Sumner, N.Mex., 1984—; owner Ratliff Well Logs, Farmington, 1973-84, Ft. Sumner, 1984—. Chmn. De Baca Soil and Water Conservation Dist., Ft. Sumner, 1987-88. Mem. Nat. Cattleman's Assn., N.Mex. Cattle Growers Assn., Kiwanis (v.p. Farmington club 1976). Republican. Presbyterian. Home: Drawer 670 Fort Sumner NM 88119 Office: Ratliff Ranch Drawer 670 Fort Sumner NM 88119

RATLIFF, JAMES CONWAY, hotel executive; b. Evanston, Ill., Mar. 28, 1940; s. Harold Sugart and Marjorie (Elmore) R. BA, Mich. State U., 1967. Dir. food & beverage ops. Detroit Hilton, 1970-71; dir. food & beverage purchasing Hilton Hotels Corp., N.Y.C., 1972-77; corp. dir. procurement Hilton Hotels Corp., Beverly Hills, Calif., 1977—; Bd. dirs. Am. Inst. Food Distbn., Fair Lawn, N.J., 1984—, treas., 1989—; instr. Calif. State Poly. U., Pomona, 1987—. With U.S. Army, 1963-65. Mem. Food Svc. Purchasing Assn. Canada (hon. mem.), Produce Mktg. Assn. (bd. dirs. 1986-88, v.p. 1989—), Produce Mktg. Assn. (chmn. foodservice div. 1989—, bd. dirs. foodservice div. 1985-88), Nat. Restaurant Assn. Foodservice Purchasing Mgrs. (bd. dirs. 1977-81, chmn. 1981-83), Pacific Corinthian Yacht Club. Republican. Methodist. Office: Hilton Hotels Corp 9336 Civic Ctr Dr Beverly Hills CA 90209

RATLIFF, JAMES LEE, management, industrial engineer; b. Oakland, Calif., Nov. 18, 1953; s. Jack Wesley and Gloria Josephine (Bracker) R.; m. Millet Diedre, Oct. 4, 1980 (div. 1981); m. Irma Blech, May 19, 1984; children: Kevin A., Erica J. AS in Constrn. Tech., Cabrillo Coll., Aptos, Calif., 1973; BS in Indust. Tech., CSUF, Fresno, Calif., 1975. Lic. A Calif. State Contrctors Gen. Engring. Foreman Underwood Pipeline, Clovis, Calif., 1975-78; estimator Underwood Pipeline, Clovis, 1978-79; v.p. Aqua Underground, Clovis, 1979-81; div. engr. W.M. Lyles Co., Stockton, Calif., 1981-83; sls. mgr. Astro-Aire Enterprises, Oakland, Calif., 1983-84; v.p. sls. mktg. Astro-Aire Enterprises, Oakland, 1984-85, pres. and chief exec. officer, 1985—; chmn. Oakland Airport Tenants Avd. Com. 1988—. Mem. U.S. Navy League. Protestant. Office: Astro-Aire Enterprises PO Box 2335 Airport Station Oakland CA 94614

RATLIFF, LEIGH ANN, pharmacist; b. Long Beach, Calif., May 20, 1961; d. Harry Warren and Verna Lee (Zwink) R. D in Pharmacy, U. Pacific, 1984. Registered pharmacist, Calif., Nev. Pharmacist intern Green Bros. Inc., Stockton, Calif., 1982-84, staff pharmacist Thrifty Corp., Long Beach, Calif., 1984-85, head pharmacist, 1986-87, pharm. buyer, 1987—. Mem. Nat. Assn. Female Execs., Am. Pharm. Assn., Am. Inst. History Pharmacy, Calif. Pharmacist Assn., Lambda Kappa Sigma. Republican. Methodist. Avocations: creative writing, horseback riding, fishing, house plants, painting. Home: 3913 Virginia Rd #301 Long Beach CA 90807 Office: Thrifty Corp 3424 Wilshire Blvd Los Angeles CA 90010

RATNER, DAVID LOUIS, legal educator; b. London, Sept. 2, 1931. AB magna cum laude, Harvard U., 1952, LLB magna cum laude, 1955. Bar: N.Y. 1955. Assoc. Sullivan & Cromwell, N.Y.C., 1955-64; assoc. prof. Cornell Law Sch., Ithaca, N.Y., 1964-68, prof., 1968-82; dean, prof. law U. San Francisco Law Sch., 1982—; exec. asst. to chmn. SEC, Washington, 1966-68; chief counsel Securities Industry Study, Senate Banking Com., Washington, 1971-73; vis. prof. Stanford (Calif.) U., 1974, Ariz. State U., Tempe, 1974, U. San Francisco, 1980; Fulbright scholar Monash U., Australia, 1981. Author: Securities Regulation; Materials for a Basic Course, 3d edit., 1986; Securities Regulation in a Nutshell, 3d edit., 1988; Institutional Investors: Teaching Materials, 1978. Home: 84 Polhemus Way Larkspur CA 94939 Office: U San Francisco Law Sch Kendrick Hall 2130 Fulton St San Francisco CA 94117

RATTLE, SIMON, symphony conductor; b. Liverpool, Eng., 1954. Studied conducting and piano, Royal Acad. Music; PhD (hon.), Birmingham U., 1985. At age 15 occasional percussion player Royal Liverpool Philharmonic Orch.; prin. condr., artistic adv. City of Birmingham Symphony Orch., 1980—; prin. guest condr. L.A. Philharm. Orch., 1981—, Rotterdam Philharm. Orch., 1981-84; prin. condr. London Choral Soc., 1979-84; assoc. condr. Royal Liverpool Philharmonic Orch., 1977-80, BBC Scottish Symphony Orch., 1977-80; artistic dir. South Bank Summer Music, 1981-83; asst. condr. Bournemouth Symphony Orch. and Bournemouth Sinfonietta, 1974-76; debut at Glyndebourne Festival Opera, 1977, appeared regularly since. Recipient 1st prize John Player Internat. Condrs. Competition, 1974, Comdr. of the British Empire, 1987. Office: care Harold Holt Ltd, 31 Sinclair Rd, London W14 ONS, England also: Capitol Records Inc care Pub Rels Office 1370 Avenue of the Americas New York NY 10019

RATTY, TESS MCBRIDE, media executive; b. Billings, Mont., July 20, 1944; d. Murray Wallace and Patricia Jean (Franzen) McBride; m. Raymond W. Nunn, Apr. 24, 1964 (div. 1969); children: Shannon McBride Waibel, Amy McBride Nunn; m. Brian Dudley Ratty, Dec. 4, 1971. Student, Calif. Coll. Arts and Crafts, Oakland, 1962-65; BS, Portland (Oreg.) State U., 1988. Mgr. advt. prodn. Meier & Frank, Portland, 1967-69; asst. mgr. advt. Pendleton Woolen Mills, Portland, 1969-74; corp. v.p. Media West, Inc., Beaverton, Oreg., 1974—. Exec. producer spl. interest videos, 1986, 87 (Double 5-Star award Video Choice Mag. 1988). Bd. dirs. Northwest Pilot Project, Portland, 1984-86; pres. bd. dirs. Beaverton Arts Commn., 1988-89; chmn. Art in the Marketplace, Beaverton, 1987; trustee Parry Ctr. for Children, Portland, 1987—; judge Oreg. Jr. Miss Scholarship, Eugene, 1986; adv. Metro Pub. Art Adv. Panel, 1987—; active in Edn. Svc. Dist. County of Washington, Oreg., 1987—. Recipient Vol. award Beaverton Arts Commn., 1987, 88. Mem. NAFE, Oreg. Media Producers Assn., Portland Advt. Fedn. (Nat. Addy award nat. fedn. 1972), Portland State Alumni Assn., Portland C. of C. Republican. Office: Media West Inc 10255 SW Arctic Dr Beaverton OR 97005

RATZLAFF, VERNON PAUL, educator, consultant; b. Mt. Lake, Minn., May 16, 1925; s. Peter Benjamin and Helen (Dick) R.; m. Bonnie Lou Sommers, Dec. 17, 1955; children: Paul, Gwen, Jay, Peter. BA in Elem. Edn., German, Goshen Coll., 1954; MA, U. N.D., 1971; student, U. Minn., 1956-57, U. Oreg., 1965, U. No. Ariz., 1968. Cert. tchr. Elem. tchr. Richfield (Minn.) Pub. Schs., 1954-74; tchr. Tuba City (Ariz.) Pub. Sch., 1975—; resource person to tchrs., Grand Forks, N.C., 1970-72, resource person to upper elem. tchrs. and children, Richfield, 1967-70; adminstr. of Christian Sch. Hopi Mission, Oraibi, Ariz., 1971-75; math tchr. Nortland Pioneer Coll.; established "Look Folks-No Fail" classrooms. Author: Look Folks-No Fail (Where Students Take Responsibility for Learning); contbr. articles to numerous jours. Mem. NEA, Ariz. Edn. Assn., Am. Assn. Retired People. Republican. Home: Grandview # 17 Tuba City AZ 86045

RAU, DAVID EDWARD, real estate company executive; b. Lincoln, Nebr., Sept. 27, 1956; s. Leo George and Anne Marie (Pavel) R.; m. Kathy Georgette Wilcox, May 17, 1980; children: Andrew David, Peter Nicholas, Victoria Anne. BBA, U. Ariz., 1978. CPA, Ariz., N.Mex. Sr. Peat Marwick Main, Albuquerque, 1978-82; supervising sr. Peat Marwick Main, Phoenix, 1982-83; asst. treas. Kroy Inc., Scottsdale, Ariz., 1983-85; acct. Zolondek & Blumenthal, Phoenix, 1985; v.p. taxes Del Webb Corp., Phoenix, 1985—. Advisor Phoenix Sky Harbor Ctr. Tech. Adv. panel, 1987. Mem. Assn. for Corp. Growth, Ariz. Soc. CPA's, Greater Phoenix C. of C. (downtown redevel. task force 1986), Albuquerque Jaycees (treas. 1981-82), Beta Alpha Psi. Republican. Roman Catholic. Office: Del E Webb Corp 2231 E Camel Back Rd Phoenix AZ 85038

RAU, NORMAN D., broadcast executive; b. Sandusky, Ohio, Apr. 8, 1951. BA, Miami U., Oxford U., 1973. Pres. Sandusky Radio, Santa Monica. Republican. Office: Sandusky Radio 401 Wilshire Blvd Ste 1010 Santa Monica CA 90401

RAUCH, HERBERT EMIL, electrical engineer; b. St. Louis, Oct. 6, 1935; s. Herbert Leopold and Vera Hilda (Sieloff) R.; m. Marjorie Ann Beyer, June 18, 1961; children: Marta, Erik, Evan, Loren. BSEE, Calif. Inst. Tech., 1957; MSEE, Stanford U., 1958, PhDEE, 1962. Mem. tech. staff Hughes Space Systems Div., Los Angeles, 1957-62, Lockheed Palo Alto Research Lab., Calif., 1962—; gen. co-chmn. Astrodynamics Conf., 1975; gen. chmn. Asilomar Conf. Circuits, Systems and Computers, 1983, Am. Control Conf., 1984; organizing chmn. Internat. Symposium on Control of Distributed Parameter Systems, 1986; part time tchr. San Jose (Calif.) State U., 1968-70. Editor and co-editor 4 books; editor-in-chief Jour. Astron. Scis., 1980-86; contbr. articles to profl. jours. Mem. Peninsula Sch. Bd., Menlo Park, Calif., 1973-82, Selective Service Bd., Santa Clara County, 1972-75; trustee Los Altos Sch. Dist., 1974-75; chmn. People for Los Altos Now (PLAN), 1974-75. Fellow Am. Astronautical Soc. (v.p. publs. 1980-82, v.p. tech. 1982-84); mem. IEEE (sr. mem., chmn. San Francisco chpt. Control Systems Soc. 1976-77, 1980-82, editor Control Systems mag. 1985—; community service award region 6, 1977, centennial award 1984), AIAA (mem. publs. com. 1980—, Space Shuttle award 1984), Soc. Indsl. & Applied Mechanics, Internat. Fedn. Automatic Control (chmn. math. control com. 1984-87, organizing chmn. working group control applications nonlinear programming 1978-84, mem. publs. com. 1987—). Office: Lockheed 92-20/254E 3251 Hanover St Palo Alto CA 94304

RAUCH, ROBERT ANDREW, service executive; b. Flushing, N.Y., Dec. 4, 1953; s. Richard Allen and Joan (Resnick) R. BA in Hotel Mgmt., Western Internat. U., 1983; MS in Tourism, Ariz. State U., 1986. Cert. hotel adminstr. Gen. mgr. Ramada Inns Inc., Phoenix, 1976-79; restaurant mgr. Hyatt Hotel Corp., Phoenix, 1980; gen. mgr. Camelhead Granada Royale, Phoenix, 1981-83; mgr. tng. and devel. Best Western Internat., Phoenix, 1984-85; v.p., gen. mgr. Hilton Pavilion, Mesa, Ariz., 1985-88; sr. mgr. Touche Ross and Co., Phoenix, 1988—; chmn. Mesa Conv. Bur., 1985—. Founder, chmn. 10 kilometer run Phoenix Children's Hosp., 1982—; bd. dirs. Arts in Mesa, 1986—. Mem. Am. Hotel and Motel Assn. (chmn. nat. rsch. com. 1984—), Ariz. Hotel and Motel Assn. (bd. dirs. 1987—), Valley Innkeepers Assn. (chmn. 1983—). Home: 1316 E Broadmor Dr Tempe AZ 85282 Office: Touche Ross and Co 2901 N Central Ste 1200 Phoenix AZ 85012

RAUCINA, THOMAS FRANK See RACINA, THOM

RAUE, JORG EMIL, electrical engineer; b. Stettin, Federal Republic of Germany, June 13, 1936; came to U.S., 1952; s. Ludwig and Liselotte (Barth) R.; m. Anke Volkmann, June 29, 1957; children: Monika Kay, Jennifer Faye. BSEE, Milw. Sch. Engring., 1961; MSEE, Marquette U., 1965, PhDEE, 1968. Mem. faculty Milw. Sch. Engring., 1961-68, chmn. dept., 1968-69; research engr. TRW Systems, Redondo Beach, Calif., 1969-76; mgr. dept. TRW Systems, Redondo Beach, 1976-79; sr. research scientist TRW Electronic Systems, Rendondo Beach, Calif., advanced systems mgr., 1980—; chmn. dept. elec. engring. Calif. Polytech State U., San Luis Opispo, 1979-80; mem. faculty Marquette U., Milw., 1968-69, Loyola U., Los Angeles, 1970-72, U. So. Calif., Los Angeles, 1983—. Contbr. articles to profl. jours. Served with U.S. Army, 1955-58. Recipient Disting. Tchr. award Milw. Sch. Engring., 1968; named Outstanding Alumnus Milw. Sch. Engring., 1985. Fellow IEEE; mem. Microwave Soc. of IEEE (sec. adminstrn. com. 1985—), Sigma Xi. Home: 28813 Rothrock Dr Rancho Palos Verdes CA 90274

RAUGHTON, JIMMIE LEONARD, urban planner, educational administrator; b. Knoxville, Tenn., Oct. 9, 1943; s. George L. and Ann (Simotes) R.; B.A. in Urban and Regional Planning, U. No. Colo., 1974, M.A., 1976, postgrad. U. Colo., 1986. Mgr., Flexitran div. Gathers, De Vilbiss Architects and Planners, Denver, 1966-68; asst. dir. planning City of Aurora, Colo., 1970-71, asst. dir., operational planner, 1973-74; planner City of Lakewood, Colo., 1971-73; planner City of Boulder, Colo., 1973-74; instr. urban planning Community Coll. of Denver, 1974-76, div. dir. human resources and svcs., 1976-81, div. dir. sci. and tech., 1981-85; dir. program ops. State of Colo. Community Colls., 1985—; coordinator community coll. devel. Rocky Mountain Energy and Environ. Tech. Center, 1980. cons. Denver Regional Council of Govts. for Model Sign Code, 1973, City of Boulder Transp. Dept., 1975—; chmn. profl. advisory com. to Colo. Gov.'s Land Use Adviser, 1973; also public speaker. Mem. exec. bd. Civic Center Assn., Denver, 1973-75; supervisory com. Colo. State Employees Credit Union, 1986—;mem. bd. Support Systems Consol., 1984, Bridge Industry, 1984-85; Democratic candidate for Denver City Council, 1975; bd. dirs. Plan Metro Denver, 1975-76, Four Corner Art Collection, 1973—. Recipient Citizen Award of Honor, Assn. of Beautiful Colo. Roads, 1972. Mem. Am. Inst. of Planners (mem. exec. bd. Colo. 1970-75, treas. 1972-73), Colo. City Mgrs. Assn., Am. Soc. Planning Ofcls., Am. Vocat. Assn., Am. Soc. for Tng. and Devel. Methodist. Contbr. articles to local newspapers. Home: 2501 High St Denver CO 80205 Office: State of Colo Community Colls 1391 North Speer Denver CO 80204

RAUTENBERG, ROBERT FRANK, management consultant; b. Milw., Sept. 14, 1943; s. Raymond Clarence and Anna Josephine (Winter) R.; m. Meredith Taylor, June 2, 1965 (div. Feb. 1975); 1 child, Matthew Carl. PhD in Bus. Adminstrn., Pacific Western U., 1983. Pvt. practice acctg. Kansas City, Mo., 1975-76; pres. Seven Diamond Enterprises, San Francisco, 1976-78; chief exec. officer Assurance Systems, San Francisco, 1984—. Author: The Analytical Management Handbook, 1985. Rep. organizer, San Francisco, 1988. Mem. Am. Statis. Assn., Inst Mgmt. Cons. (cert.). Episcopalian. also: 225 Broadway 9th Fl San Diego CA 92101 Office: Assurance Systems 220 Montgomery St Ste 929 San Francisco CA 94104

RAVELING, DENNIS GRAFF, biology educator; b. Devil's Lake, N.D., Feb. 28, 1939; s. Ralph Gordon and Martha Irene (Graff); R. m. Olga Catherine Masnyk, Mar. 3, 1962. BA, So. Ill. U., 1960, PhD, 1967; MA, U. Minn., 1963. Research scientist Can. Wildlife Service, Winnipeg, Man., Can., 1967-71; asst. prof. dept. wildlife-fisheries biology U. Calif., Davis, 1971-74, assoc. prof., 1974-80, prof., 1980—. Contbr. articles to profl. jours. Trustee Calif. Wetlands Found. NSF grantee, 1963, 73, 75, 77, 78. Fellow AAAS; mem. Am. Ornithologists Union (elective mem.), Am. Soc. Naturalists, Cooper Ornithol. Soc., Wildlife Soc., Wilson Ornithol. Soc., Sigma Xi. Home: 504 Del Oro Davis CA 95616 Office: U Calif Dept Wildlife & Fisheries Biology Davis CA 95616

RAWAL, SURAJ PRAKASH, materials engineer; b. Multan, Punjab, India, Apr. 12, 1945; came to U.S., 1969; s. Sham Dass and Kesar Bai (Gandhi) R.; m. Eileen R. Roche, Apr. 3, 1976 (dec. 1977); m. Brenda L. Warner, June 21, 1980; children: Timothy, Evan, Alex. BS, Indian Inst. Tech., Kanpur, India, 1967, MS, 1969; PhD, Brown U., 1975. Sr. rsch. asst. coun. sci. and indsl. rsch. Indian Inst. Tech., 1968-69; rsch. asst. Brown U., Providence, 1969-73, tchng. asst., 1973-75; quality control mgr. New Metal Industries, Manville, R.I., 1974-82; tech. dir. A.J. Oster Co. div. Cookson Industries, Providence, 1982-84; staff engr. Martin Marietta Astronautics, Denver, 1984-86, sr. staff engineer, 1986-; tchr. Jewelry Inst. R.I., Providence, 1981-84. Author tech. reports, papers, also poems. Mem. Am. Soc. Metals, Am. Ceramic Soc., Brown Alumni Assn., Sigma Xi. Home: 6266 S Gray Ct Littleton CO 80123 Office: Martin Marietta Astronautic PO Box 179 Denver CO 80201

RAWLINGS, ROBERT HOAG, newspaper publisher; b. Pueblo, Colo., Aug. 3, 1924; s. John W. and Dorothy (Hoag) R.; student Colo. U., 1944-45; B.A., Colo. Coll., 1947; m. Mary Alexandra Graham, Oct. 18, 1947; children—Jane Louise, John Graham, Carolyn Anne, Robert Hoag II. Reporter Pueblo Chieftain and Pueblo Star-Jour., 1947-51, advt. rep. 1951-62, gen. mgr., 1962-79, pub. and editor, 1980—; sec. Star-Jour. Pub. Corp., 1962-84, pres., 1984—; dir. Colo. Nat. Bank-Pueblo. Served with USNR, 1942-46. Mem. Colo. Press Assn., (dir. 1963-66, 76-78, v.p. and pres.-elect 1984, pres. 1985, chmn. bd. dirs. 1986), Rocky Mountain Ad Mgrs. (past pres.), Colo. AP (past pres.), Elks, Rotary. Presbyn. Office: 825 W 6th St Pueblo CO 81003

RAWLINSON, STUART ELBERT, geologist; b. Oakland, Calif., Dec. 2, 1950; s. Bradford Stevon and Margaret Edna (Lisman) R.; m. Carol Ann Baran, Jan. 6, 1979; children: Karen Lynn, Kathryn Marie. AA, Los Angeles Harbor Coll., 1972; BS, Calif. State U., Long Beach, 1974; MS, U. Alaska, 1979, postgrad., 1979—. Field asst. Holmes and Narver, Inc., McMurdo Sta., Antarctica, 1970-71; supply and logistics coordinator Holmes and Narver, Inc., South Pole Sta., Antarctica, 1974-75; instr. geology Tanana Valley Community Coll., Fairbanks, Alaska, 1977; diver, technician U. Alaska, Fairbanks, 1978-79, research asst., 1977-80; geologist State Alaska Dept. Natural Resources, Fairbanks, 1980-88; sr. project engr. Holmes & Narver, Inc., Las Vegas, 1988—; liaison mem. Permafrost com. NRC, Washington, 1984-88, U.S. Permafrost delegate to People's Republic of China, 1984; leader field trip to Prudhoe Bay Oilfield 4th Internat. Conf. on Permafrost, 1983. Contbr. articles to profl. jours. Recipient U.S. Antarctic Service medal NSF, 1975. Mem. Am. Assn. Petroleum Geologists, Soc. Econ. Paleontologists and Mineralogists, Am. Inst. Profl. Geologists, Phi Kappa Phi. Republican. Methodist. Office: Holmes & Narver Inc Energy Support Div 1050 E Flamingo Rd Ste 230N Las Vegas NV 89119

RAWSON, RAYMOND D., dentist; b. Sandy, Utah, Nov. 2, 1940; s. James D. and Mable (Beckstead) R.; B.S., U. Nev. at Las Vegas, 1964; D.D.S., Loma Linda U., 1968; M.A., U. Nev., 1978; m. Linda Downey, July 23, 1959; children—Raymond Blaine, Mark Daniel, Pamela Ann, David James, Kristi Lynn, Kenneth Glenn, Richard Allen. Gen. practice dentistry, Las Vegas, 1968—; instr. dental hygiene, dental dir. Clark County Community Coll., 1977—, dep. coroner, chief dental examiner, 1977—; adj. prof. U. Nev., 1977—, adj. assoc. prof. oral diagnosis and forensic dentistry Northwestern U., Chgo., 1985—. Contbr. articles to profl. jours. Active Boy Scouts Am., 1968—; bishop Ch. Jesus Christ Latter-day Saints, 1978-84; asst. majority leader Nev. State senator. Diplomate Am. Bd. Forensic Odontology (sec. 1984). Fellow Am. Acad. Forensic Scis. (pres., chmn.), ADA (editorial rev. bd. jour.), Federation Dentaire International, Omicron Kappa Upsilon. Republican. Office: 4121 Sahara Ave W Las Vegas NV 89102

RAY, BENJAMIN LOUIS, corporate executive; b. Sedalia, Mo., Mar. 12, 1949; s. Benjamin Jacob and Mary Ruth (Booth) R.; m. Penny Lee Peterson; 1 child, Rachael Lynne. BA in History, U. Colo., 1978; MBA, U. Phoenix, 1989. Enlisted USN, 1969, resigned, 1973; systems analyst Dun & Bradstreet, Boulder, Colo., 1974—. Home: 584 Juniper Ct Louisville CO 80027 Office: Neo Data Svcs 633 SW Boulder Rd Louisville CO 80027

RAY, BRIAN DANIEL, education and science educator; b. Vancouver, Wash., Oct. 30, 1954; s. Eugene Lamont and Nora G. (Kelleher) R.; m. Betsy Anne Briggs, Sept. 2, 1978; children: Hallie B., Rachel M., Hannah K., Daniel B. BS, U. Puget Sound, 1976; MS, Ohio U., 1979; PhD, Oreg. State U., 1988. Tchr. sci. Sacred Heart Acad., Salem, Oreg., 1980-83; grad. teaching asst. gen. sci. dept. Oreg. State U., Corvallis, Oreg., 1983-88; instr. We. Oreg. State Coll., Monmouth, Oreg., 1985; supr. edn. students Oreg. State U., Corvallis, 1987-88, grad. research asst. coll. liberal arts, 1986-88; asst. prof. edn. Seattle Pacific U., 1988—; instr. anatomy and physiology Chemeketa Community Coll., Salem, summer 1983, biology Oreg. State Penitentiary, Salem, summers 1982, 83, 84, Upward Bound, Oreg. State U., Corvallis, summers 1987, 88. Editor, Home Sch. Researcher, Seattle, 1985—; contbr. articles to Edn. and Urban Soc., 1988, Christianity Today, 1988. Bowerman Grad. scholar Bowerman Found., 1986-88. Mem. Nat. Assn. for Research in Sci. Teaching, Am. Ednl. Research Assn., Oreg. Acad. Sci., Phi Delta Theta. Republican. Office: Seattle Pacific Univ School of Education Seattle WA 98119

RAY, BRUCE DAVID, lawyer; b. Denver, Dec. 19, 1955; s. John Denver Ray and Jane (Guiney) Mitchell; m. Faith Theofanus, Aug. 20, 1978; 1 child, Elena. BA magna cum laude, U. Colo., 1978; JD, Union U., Albany, N.Y., 1981. Bar: Colo. 1981. Spl. environ. counsel URS-Berger, San Bernardino, Calif., 1982-84; asst. regional counsel EPA, Denver, 1984--; spl. asst. U.S. atty. U.S. Dept. Justice, Denver, 1987--; seminar lectr. Nat. Resources Ctr., U. Colo. Law Sch., Boulder, 1985--. Contbr. articles to legal jours. Recipient bronze medal EPA, 1986, Environ. Excellence award, 1987, Best Article award, 1988, Roach prize, 1981. Mem. ABA (water quality com. 1984--), Colo. Bar Assn. (environ. law council 1987--), Denver Bar Assn., Environ. Law Inst., Phi Beta Kappa. Office: EPA 999 18th St Ste 500 Denver CO 80202

RAY, DAVID CHRISTIAN, aerospace engineer; b. Northridge, Calif., July 31, 1961; s. Don Brandon and Laurel Irene (Epstein) R. BA in Phys. Sic., U. Calif., Berkeley, 1984. Aerospace engr. Space Astrophysics Group U. Calif., Berkeley, 1984—, cons. contamination control, high voltage, high vacuum systems Space Astrophysics Group, 1987—. Contbr. articles to profl. jours. Mem. AIAA, Am. Vacuem Soc., Internat. Soc. fo rOptical Engring. Home: 422 48th St Oakland CA 94609 Office: U Calif Space Sci Lab Centennial at Grizzly Peak Blvd Berkeley CA 94720

RAY, ELEANOR HOUGHTON ANDERSON, manufacturing executive; b. N.Y.C., Sept. 10, 1928; m. William McKinley Ray, June 22, 1985; children: Libby, Mark, Melody, Brian. Student, London Conservatory of Music. Ptnr. Corning (N.Y.) Glass Works. Trustee Lewis and Clark Coll.; co-chmn. Polio-Plus campaign, Rotary Internat., Paul Harris fellow; bd. dirs. Sellwood Harbor, Portland Opera Assn.; active Pacific Ballet Theater, Garthwick Symphony Aux., Oreg. Advocates for Arts, Met. Arts Commn., West Coast Chamber Orch., Ballet Oreg., Met. Opera Nat. Patron Council at Lincoln Ctr. Avocations: ballet, music.

RAY, GEORGE LEWIS, real estate associate; b. Potosi, Mo., June 26, 1938; s. Giles M.W. and Emma Jane (Karns) R.; m. Dorothy Virginia Holmes, May 23, 1963; children: Holly Jane Ray Romanov, Goerge L. Jr. BA, Calif. Bapt. Coll., 1962; MDiv, Golden Gate Sem., 1965. Agt. Lincoln Nat. Life, San Bernardino, Calif., 1973-75, Horace Mann, San Bernardino, 1976-77; real estate assoc. Capitol Realty, Riverside, Calif., 1978-79, Connelly Realty, Riverside, 1979-80, Heyming & Johnson Realty, Riverside, 1980—. Mem. Nat. Assn. Realtors, Calif. Assn. Realtors, Riverside Area Bd. Realtors. Republican. Baptist. Office: Heyming & Johnson Realty 7130 Magnolia Ste N Riverside CA 91504

RAY, GEORGE THOMAS, financial executive; b. Kankakee, Ill., Mar. 24, 1958; s. George A. and Adlorene V. (Studer) R.; m. Maria C. Martinez, Oct. 11, 1986. A in Applied Sci., Kankakee Community Coll., 1979. Cert. fin. planner. Registered rep. First Colo. Investments and Securities, Denver, 1979-83, B. J. Leonard & Co., Englewood, Colo., 1983-84; v.p. Genesis Capital Corp., Denver, 1984-85; registered rep. Pittock Fin. Corp., Englewood, 1985-86; fin. planner Woodward Fin. Group Inc., Denver, 1986—. Mem. Internat. Assn. for Fin. Planning, Inst. Cert. Fin. Planners, Colo. Soc. Cert. Fin. Planners (charter). Republican. Roman Catholic. Home: 2370 Cherry St Denver CO 80207 Office: Woodward Fin Group Inc 300 S Jackson St Ste 500 Denver CO 80209

RAY, GREG ALLAN, aerospace engineer; b. Canton, Ohio, Aug. 11, 1948; s. Clarence G. and Margaret May (Kopf) R.; m. Mary Lou Bowdlear, June 26, 1971; children: David Andrew, Mary Catherine. BS in Aerospace Engring., Calif. State Poly. U., 1971. Aerospace engr. aircraft div. Rockwell Internat., L.A., 1971-79; aerospace engr. space div. Rockwell Internat., Downey, Calif., 1979-85, engring. supr., 1985-87, project mgr., 1987-89, chief project engr., 1989—. Mem. Nat. Mgmt. Assn. Republican. Methodist. Home: 11320 Lorene St Whittier CA 90601 Office: Rockwell Internat Space Div 12214 Lakewood Blvd Downey CA 90241

RAY, JEREMIAH BLAND, manufacturing executive; b. Nashville, Aug. 24, 1940; s. Joseph Ben and Helen Estell (Williams) R.; m. Bonnie E. Hammond; children: Drew Justice, Corey Elizabeth. BS, Clark U., 1967; Diploma in Nursing, Olympic Coll., 1976. Tchr. Seattle Pub. Schs., 1969-70; nurse Harborview Hosp., Seattle, 1976-80, Fred Hutchinson Cancer Ctr., Seattle, 1980-81; owner, pres. ECM Corp., Seattle, 1981--. Producer, dir. Religious TV, 1985--; patentee in field. Served with USN, 1958-61. Home and Office: 6111 Cultus Bay Rd Whidbey Island Clinton WA 98236

RAY, JUANITA LORAINE, small business owner; b. Maryville, Mo., Dec. 28, 1950; d. Marion Oren and Versie Jerraldine (Saffell) Riley; m. Bobby Dee Francis, Nov. 15, 1969 (div. Sept. 1984); 1 child, Mary Ann; m. Kevin Scott Ray, May 11, 1985. Grad. high sch., Council Bluffs, Iowa. Saleswoman, asst. mgr. Look In/Women's Dept. Richmond Gordman, Council Bluffs, 1973; bus driver Oakland Community Sch. Dist., Iowa, 1976-78; sales clk. Earl May Garden Ctr., Maryville, 1979, 38th St. Fish & Pet Store, Tacoma, 1986; with molding rm. dept. Union Carbide Corp., Maryville, 1979-85; mgr. S. Tacoma Fish & Pet Store, Tacoma, 1986-87; owner, mgr. Southgate Fish & Pet Store, Tacoma, 1987—. Democrat. Methodist. office: Southgate Fish & Pet Store 10310 S Tacoma Way Ste 1 Tacoma WA 98499

RAY, LEO ELDON, fish breeding and marketing company executive; b. Logan County, Okla., Dec. 9, 1937; s. Wilbur Houston and Florence Ivy (Doggett) R.; B.S. in Zoology, U. Okla., 1963; m. Judith Kay Croddy, Aug. 29, 1959; children—Tana Kim, Tod Kent, Kacy Kay. Research asst. U. Okla., 1961-63; tchr. public schs., Dumas, Tex., 1963-64, Grants, N.Mex., 1964-65, Anaheim, Calif., 1965-69; co-owner Fish Breeders, Niland, Calif., 1969-87; owner, pres. Fish Breeders of Idaho, Inc., Buhl, 1971—; pres. Big Bend Trout, Inc., 1977-88. Served with U.S. Army, 1957-60. Mem. Calif. Catfish Farmers Am. (past pres.), Catfish Farmers Am. (past pres., dir.), U.S. Trout Farmers Assn. (past pres., dir.). Address: Rte 3 Box 234 Buhl ID 83316

RAY, LEOPOLD AUGUSTUS, architect; b. Port Antonio, Jamaica, Oct. 30, 1951; came to U.S., 1959, naturalized, 1961; s. Robert, Jr. and Doris Beatrice (Byrd) R.; B.Arch. (AIA scholar Ariz. chpt. 1971, Sun Angel Found. archtl. scholar 1974, Dubois Found. scholar 1975, Dougherty scholar 1975), Ariz. State U., 1976; M.A. in Urban Planning (grad. fellow 1979), UCLA, 1980. Architect-in-tng. firms in Las Vegas, Nev., 1976-78; asst. economist L.A. Office Econ. Devel., 1980; assoc. A.K. Ngai & Assocs., architects/planners, Los Angeles, 1980-82; urban design cons. Vitalize Van Nuys, Inc., 1980; coord. Sat. scholar program UCLA, 1979-80; architect/rehab. specialist Mark Briggs & Assocs., 1982; ptnr. The AEP Partnership, Architects and Engrs., 1986, Alexander Haagen Co., 1987—. prin. works include Baldwin Hills Mall, DeMille Dr. Residence, Spreading Oak Residence (both L.A.), others. Mem. AIA, Am. Inst. Cert. Planners. Democrat. Roman Catholic. Co-author: Earth-Integrated Architecture, 1975. Office: 3500 Sepulveda Blvd Manhattan Beach CA 90266

RAY, MALA MARIE, accountant; b. Hays, Kans., Apr. 20, 1958; d. Paul Lawrence and Nadeen (Robben) Kaiser; m. Randul Lee Ray, May 6, 1978. AS, Westminster (Colo.) Community Coll., 1979; BBA, Regis Coll., Denver, 1984. CPA, Colo. Acct., office mgr. Primec, Inc., Denver, 1978-84; mfg. systems supr. Enmark Corp., Denver, 1985-86; div. acct., office mgr. Duo-Fast Corp., Denver, 1986-87; cost acct. McData Corp., Broomfield, Colo., 1988—; tax preparer Peter Mahr, CPA, Arvada, Colo., 1988. Home: 2522 W 99th Pl Denver CO 80221

RAY, MARIANNE YURASKO, social services administrator; b. Mpls., Sept. 25, 1934; d. Andrew George and Ann (Rusinko) Yurasko; m. Raymond Robert Ray, Nov. 22, 1962 (div. July 1980); children: Joel Christopher, Angela Christine. BA, U. Utah, 1956; student, U. Wash., 1975; MA, Pacific Lutheran U., 1978. Case worker, vol. agy. liaison State of Wash. Dept. Social and Health Services, Tacoma, Wash., 1963-65, 1971-79, 1983; child placement project dir. State of Wash. Dept. Social and Health Services, Olympia, Wash., 1979-80; casework supr. Child Protective Service State of Wash. Dept. Social and Health Services, Tacoma, Wash., 1980-81, foster home recruiter and licenser, 1981-83; owner, cons. Myray Focuses, Seattle, 1983—; pres. Delta Dynamics Inc., Seattle, 1984-86; mental health therapist Children's Indsl. Home, Tacoma, 1985-86, Good Samaritan Mental Health, Puyallup, Wash., 1986-87; part-time faculty Cen. Wash. U., Ellensburg, 1985—, Highline Community Coll., Midway, Wash., 1985-87, Renton (Wash.) Vocational Tech. Inst., 1985—, Lake Washington Vocational Tech. Inst., Kirkland, Wash., 1985—; dir. child abuse treatment Cath. Community Services, Seattle, 1987—; cons. Tacoma Sch. Dist., 1985-86; presenter nat. conferences and workshops. Creator workshops: Humor Techniques for Stress Management in the Classroom, 1985, Humor in Stress Management: Applications in Helping Professions, 1987, Kicking the Holiday Blues, 1986, Humor for the Health of It, 1987, Laughing Matters--It Really Does!, 1984—, Relocation: What it means for the Employee and Family, 1984—, Humor in the Workplace for Higher Productivity and Team Building, 1984—, Laughter and Liberation in the Classroom to Promote Learning, 1987—, Creative Imagery in Relaxation Techniques, 1987—. Mem. Am. Psychol. Assn. (assoc.), Pacific Northwest Orgn. Devel. Network, Pacific Northwest Speakers Assn. Office: Myray Focuses Counseling/Consulting PO Box 98570 Seattle WA 98198 also: Cath Community Svcs 100 23d Ave S Seattle WA 98144

RAY, MICHAEL FRANKLYN, chemical company executive; b. Corona, Calif., Mar. 9, 1953; s. Franklin Alfred and Eva Catheran (Ryan) R. BS in Indsl. Mgmt., Western Wash. U., 1977. Furnace operator Intalco Aluminum Corp., Ferndale, Wash., 1973-77; gen. contractor Callahan/Ray Contracting, Bellingham, Wash., 1977-79; mgr. trainee Liquid Carbonic Corp., Ferndale, 1979-80; plant mgr. Liquid Carbonic Corp., Ft. Dodge, Iowa, 1980-81; reg. ops. mgr. Liquid Carbonic Corp., Chgo., 1981-85; v.p. mktg. Wycon Chem. Corp., Cheyenne, Wyo., 1985-86; v.p. corp. devel. & adminstrn. Wycon Chem. Corp., 1986--. Mem. Frontier Mus. (Cheyenne, Wyo.), Soc. Chem. Engrs. (speaker 1985), C. of C Cheyenne. Republican. Lutheran. Home: 205 Longs Peak Dr Cheyenne WY 82009 Office: Wycon Chem Co PO Box 1287 Cheyenne WY 82003

RAY, RICHARD STANLEY, accountant; b. Miami, Ariz., June 12, 1937; s. Milton Sevier and Anne Elizabeth (Mickelson) R.; m. Laura Ann Young, Apr. 11, 1963; children: Denise, Mark, Melanie, Laura, Jordon. AA, Ea. Ariz. Jr. Coll., 1957; BS in Acctg., Ariz. State U., 1962, MS in Acctg., 1964. CPA, Ariz. Staff acct. Deloitte, Haskins & Sells, Phoenix, 1963-65; controller AMECO, Phoenix, 1965-70, U-Haul Co., Phoenix, 1970-76; dir., acctg. svcs. Ariz. Pub. Service Co., Phoenix, 1976—; advisor to bd. Credit Data of Ariz., Phoenix, 1981—, chmn. bd., 1980-81; dir. Arcoa Internat., Phoenix, 1973-76. Treas., bd. mem. Big Sisters of Ariz., Phoenix, 1972-78; dist. coun. Boy Scouts Am., Phoenix, 1982-84; stake pres. Mormon Ch., Tempe, Ariz. 1987—. Grad. rsch. fellowship, Ariz. Bankers Assn., Phoenix, 1962. Mem. Am. Inst. CPA's, Ariz. Soc. CPA's (Acctg. Achievement award 1962), Ariz. State Bd. Accountancy (continuing profl. edn. com. 1986—), Edison Electric Inst. (com. mem. 1976—), Rotary. Republican. Mormon.

RAY, WILLIAM MCKINLEY, health and economic development specialist; b. Chiloquin, Oreg., Apr. 27, 1943; s. Ernest August and Isabel (English) Duus; m. Eleanor Houghton Anderson, June 22, 1985; stepchildren: libby, Mark, Melody, Brian. BS, U. Oreg., 1974; postgrad., Oreg. State U., 1974-76. Cert. in Secondary Art Edn. Tchr. Chemawa Indian Sch., Salem, Oreg., 1973-74; counselor Oreg. State U., Corvallis, Oreg., 1974-76; tchr. Portland (Oreg.) Pub. Schs. #1, 1976-77; evaluator NW Regional Edn. Lab., Portland, 1978-80; counselor Urban Indian Council, Portland, 1981; cons. Oreg. Hist. Soc., Portland, 1982; mem. floor staff 62d Legis. Assembly, Salem, 1983; career counselor NW Portland Indian Health, 1983-84; econ. devel. cons. The Klamath Tribe, Chiloquin, Oreg., 1986—; bd. dirs. Oreg. Sch. Arts and Crafts, Oreg. Art Inst.; mem. restoration com. The Klamath Tribe, Chiloquin, 1984-86; mem. 1992 Christopher Columbus Quincentenary Jubilee Commn., native Am. adv. com. Photographer The Pow Wow An American Celebration, 1976 (1st Place award The Oregonian newspaper, Portland, 1976). Mem. adv. bd. Portland State U.. 1987—; bd. dirs. Oreg. Peace Inst., Portland, 1987—, indian ministries com. Ecumenical Ministries of Oreg., Portland, 1987—. With U.S. Army, 1967-70. Recipient E.C. Allworth award Oreg. State U. Meml. Union, 1966, Indian World award KBOO FM Radio, Portland, 1987; Newberry fellow, Chgo., 1981. Mem. Assn. Am. Indian Affairs (bd. dirs. 1988—), Nat. Congress Am. Indians (life), University Club (Portland), City Club (Portland), Garfield Grange, Rotary (sec. 1987—). Republican. Methodist. Home: 288 SE Spokane St Portland OR 97202 Office: Commn on Indian Svcs 454 State Capitol Bldg Salem OR 97624

RAYBURN, PAUL BECK, entrepreneur; b. Phoenix, Nov. 23, 1942; s. Paul Beck and Edith (Rolfs) R.; m. Nadine Neil, June 17, 1967; 1 child, Julie Ann. Sales rep. Nat. Microfilm Co. Inc., Kansas City, Mo., 1964-67, 3M Corp., St. Paul, 1967-70; owner, mgr. Tiki Lodge Inc., Spokane, Wash., 1970—; pres., owner Northwest Microfilm Inc., Spokane, 1970—; v.p., owner FarWest Micrographix Inc, Sacramento, 1982—; pres., owner Bus. Equipment Ctr. Inc., Springfield, Oreg., 1982—. Served as cpl. USMC. Republican. Mem. Plymouth Congregational Ch. Lodge: Rotary. Home: W 416 High Dr Spokane WA 99203 Office: NW Microfilm PO Box 2199 Spokane WA 99210

RAYDON, STEPHEN MITCHELL, television computer editor; b. Chgo., Oct. 13, 1948; s. Donald and Velma (Norman) R.; m. Kathryn Phillips, Apr. 1, 1974. Student, U. Denver, 1966-67; BA in Mass Communications, U. Colo., 1972. TV technician Sta. KWGN-TV, Denver, 1968-72; freelance musician, musical instr. Chgo., Denver, 1964-72; TV tech. dir. Sta. KWGN-TV, Denver, 1972-85; pres., founder Video/Audio Artistry Corp., Boulder, Colo., 1973-89; TV editor Sta. KWGN-TV, Denver, 1982-85; musician, composer Mirror, Boulder, 1980-85; freelance tech. dir., composer and musician Boulder, L.A., 1985—; TV editor Video Transitions Inc., Hollywood, Calif., 1986—. Inventor, patentee audio pan generator. Office: Video Transitions Inc 910 N Citrus Hollywood CA 90038

RAYMOND, DAVID, business executive; b. Pittsfield, Mass., Mar. 26, 1955; s. Richard Raymond and Virginia (Robinson) R. BSBA, Ariz. State U., 1978. Pres., sec., treas. Playtronics S.A., Las Palmas, Spain, 1978-82; pres., treas. Elsafe Nevada, Inc., Las Vegas, 1982—, v.p. ops., contr., 1987—; pres. Elsafe Inc., Irvine, Calif., 1987—; pres., sec., treas. Guest Terminal Systems, Inc., Las Vegas, 1987—. Republican. Mem. Christian Ch. Office: Guest Terminal Systems Inc 3389 Del Marino Las Vegas NV 89121

RAYMOND, EUGENE THOMAS, technical writer, retired aircraft engineer; b. Seattle, Apr. 17, 1923; s. Evan James and Katheryn Dorothy (Kranick) R.; m. Bette Mae Bergeson, Mar. 1, 1948; children: Joan Kay Hibbs, Patricia Lynn, Robin Louise Flashman. BSME, U. Wash., 1944; postgrad., 1953-55; registered profl. engr., Tex. Rsch. engr. The Boeing Co., Seattle, 1946-59, sr. group engr., 1959-63, 66-71, sr. specialist engr., 1971-81, prin. engr. flight control tech., 1982-88; project design engr. Gen. Dynamics, Ft. Worth, 1963-66. Lt., USNR, 1943-46, 49-52; PTO. Recipient prize Hydraulics and Pneumatics mag., 1958. Mem. Soc. Automotive Engrs. (cert. of appreciation, chmn. adv. bd.com. A-6 nat. com. for aerospace fluid power and control tech. 1983-88, vice-chmn. com. 1986-88), Fluid Power Soc., Puget Sound Fluid Power Assn., AIAA, Beta Theta Pi, Meridian Valley Country Club, Masons, Shriners. Lutheran. Aircraft editorial adv. bd. Hydraulics and Pneumatics mag., 1960-70; contbr. articles profl. jours. Patentee in field. Home and Office: 25301 144 Ave SE Kent WA 98042

RAYMOND, GENE, actor, producer; b. N.Y.C., Aug. 13, 1908; s. LeRoy D. and Mary (Smith) Guion; m. Jeanette MacDonald, June 16, 1937 (dec. Jan. 14, 1965); m. former Mrs. Nel Bentley Hees, Sept. 8, 1974. Student, Profl. Children's Sch., N.Y.C. Broadway debut in: The Piper, 1920; other Broadway appearances include Eyvind of the Hills, 1921, Why Not?, 1922, The Potters, 1923, Cradle Snatchers, 1925, Take My Advice, 1927, Mirrors, 1928, Sherlock Holmes, 1928, Say When, 1928, The War Song, 1928, Jonesy, 1929, Young Sinners, 1929, A Shadow of My Enemy, 1957; other theater appearances include The Man in Possession, Dennis, Mass., 1946; appeared in The Guardsman, 1951, The Voice of the Turtle, 1952, Angel Street, Richmond, Va., 1952, Petrified Forest, 1952, Call Me Madam, 1952, Private Lives, 1953, The Moon is Blue, 1953, Be Quiet, My Love, 1953, Detective Story, 1954, The Devil's Disciple, 1954, The Fifth Season, 1955, Will Success Spoil Rock Hunter, Los Angeles, San Francisco, 1956, Los Angeles, San Francisco, 1956, Romeo and Juliet, 1956, The Seven Year Itch, 1958, Holiday for Lovers, Chgo., 1959; appeared as Joseph Cantwell in nat. touring co.: The Best Man, 1960; other theater appearances include Majority of One, 1962, Write Me A Murder, 1962, Mr. Roberts, 1962, Kiss Me Kate, 1962; other roles include Candida, 1961, The Moon is Blue, 1963, Madly in Love, 1963; film appearances include Personal Maid, 1931, Stolen Heaven, 1931, Ladies of the Big House, 1932, The Night of June 13th, 1932, Forgotten Commandments, 1932, If I Had a Million, 1932, Red Dust, 1932, Ex-Lady, 1933, The House on 56th Street, 1933, Zoo in Budapest, 1933, Brief Moment, 1933, Ann Carver's Profession, 1933, Flying Down to Rio, 1933, Sadie McKee, 1934, I Am Suzanne, 1934, Coming Out Party, 1934,

Transatlantic Merry-Go-Round, 1934, Behold My Wife, 1935, The Woman in Red, 1935, Seven Keys to Baldpate, 1935, Hooray for Love, 1935, Love on a Bet, 1936, Walking on Air, 1936, The Bride Walks Out, 1936, The Smartest Girl in Town, Transient Lady, 1936, There Goes My Girl, 1937, Life of the Party, 1937, That Girl From Paris, 1939, Mr. and Mrs. Smith, 1939; film appearances include: Cross-Country Romance, 1940, Smilin' Thru', 1941; film appearances include The Locket, 1946, Assigned to Danger, 1948, Million-Dollar Weekend, 1948, Sofia, 1948, Hit the Deck, 1955, Plunder Road, 1957, The Best Man, 1964, I'd Rather Be Rich, 1964; TV appearances include: U.S. Steel Hour, The Defenders, Playhouse 90, Ironside, Name of the Game, Judd for the Defense, Bold Ones, Mannix, others; author: teleplay Prima Donna; composer: songs Release, Will You?, Let Me Always Sing. Past v.p. Arthritis Found. So. Calif.; pres. Motion Picture and TV Fund, 1980; trustee Falcon Found., USAF Acad. Served with USAAF, 1942-45, ETO; served to col. USAFR, 1945-68. Decorated Legion of Merit and others.; Recipient Disting. Service award Arthritis Found.; Humanitarian award Air Force Assn.; Better World award VFW; Bronze Halo award So. Calif. Motion Picture Council. Mem. Screen Actors Guild (dir.), Acad. TV Arts and Scis. (bd. dirs.), Air Force Assn. (pres. Los Angeles chpt.). Clubs: Players (N.Y.C.); N.Y. Athletic; Bel Air Country (Los Angeles); Army and Navy (Washington); Order of Daedalians. Address: 9570 Wilshire Blvd Beverly Hills CA 90212

RAYMOND, GREGORY ALAN, political science educator; b. Irvington, N.J., Jan. 5, 1947; s. Andrew and Irene (Skalicky) R.; m. Christine Lawton, June 12, 1971. BA, Park Coll., 1968; MA, U. S.C., 1973, PhD, 1975. Asst. prof. Boise (Idaho) State U., 1975-79, assoc. prof., 1979-83, prof. polit. sci., 1983—; cons. State Exec. Inst., Idaho, 1985, Human Rights Commn., Idaho, 1988, Office of the Gov., Idaho, 1988; bd. dirs. Univ. Survey Rsch. Ctr., Boise. Author: Conflict Resolution and the Structures of the State System, 1980, The Other Western Europe, 1983. Mem. State Higher Edn. Resource Coun., Idaho, 1988—. With U.S. Army, 1969-71. Recipient Outstanding Teaching award Boise State U. Alumni Assn., 1985. Mem. Internat. Studies Assn., Internat. Polit. Sci. Assn. Office: Boise State U 1910 University Dr Boise ID 83725

RAYMOND, JAN WAYNE, materials scientist; b. Sault St. Marie, Mich., Oct. 23, 1931; s. Fred John and Mildred Victoria (Blixt) R.; m. Roberta Kay Knudson, June 17, 1955 (div. 1964); 1 child, Kurt Jon. BSc. in Metallurgy, U. Wis., 1957, MSc., 1959. Rsch. asst. U. Wis., Madison, 1957-59; metallurgist North Am. Aviation, Canoga Park, Calif., 1960-70; chief metallurgist Cryomagnetics Corp., Denver, 1970-75; staff metallurgist Litton Systems, Canoga Park, Calif., 1975-79; failure analyst Northup Aircraft Corp., Hawthorne, Calif., 1979-80; rsch. scientist Lockheed Materials Lab., Valencia, Calif., 1980—; cons. materials scientist various companies, 1975-77; chief metallurgist Hi-Rel Labs., Monrovia, Calif., 1978-79. Inventor: (6 patents) metallic materials and processing rsch. processes, 1955-75; contbr. articles to profl. jours. Mem. Am. Soc. Metals (exec. com. 1983-87, chmn. 1986-87, 5 star chpt. award, San Fernando Valley chpt. chmn. 1987), Litton 4-wallers (pres. 1976-79). Home: 23619 Via Delfina Valencia CA 91355 Office: Lockheed Corp Rye Canyon Materials Lab 23619 Via Delfina Valencia CA 91355

RAYMOND, JENETTE LEE, graphic designer, artist; b. Oskaloosa, Iowa, May 23, 1945; d. Harry Paul and Helen Louise (White) Biller; m. William Joseph Butcher, Aug. 7, 1965 (div. Oct. 1979); 1 child, Johanna Lynn; m. Robert Michael Raymond, May 9, 1981; 1 child, Stephanie Louise. Student, U. Ill., 1963-65, Coll. Marin, 1967-73, Napa Valley Coll., 1977—. Dental asst. Richard Lammermeyer, DDS, Kenilworth, Ill., 1965-67; customer service rep. Scott Foresman Co., Glenview, Ill., 1967-68; sec. to controller Milton Meyer & Co., San Francisco, 1968-70; asst. adminstr. William J. Butcher, Napa, Calif., 1969-79; freelance photographer Jenette Butcher Photography, Napa, 1978-81; graphic designer Raymond Graphic Design, Napa, 1981—. Graphic designer Napa Valley Symphony Orch., 1986—, Kiwanis, Napa, 1985—. Republican. Home and Office: 1855 Fuller Way Napa CA 94559

RAYMOND, MICHAEL DENNIS, insurance executive; b. San Diego, Dec. 10, 1945; s. Francis Xavier and Jessie Lenore (Hoffman) R.; m. Christine Marie Terry, Oct. 30, 1971; children: Paul Eric, Emily Terry, Brian Andrew. BA, U. New Orleans, 1967, MA, 1971. CPCU. Tchr., dept. head Mt. Carmel Acad., New Orleans, 1967-73; underwriter Aetna Life and Casualty, San Francisco, 1973-75; ins. broker Westly Ins. Agy., Los Altos, Calif., 1975-84, R.B. Suhr & Co., Santa Clara, Calif., 1984—; instr. Ins. Edn. Assn., San Francisco, 1988—. Mem. Santa Clara Valley CPCU Soc. Republican. Roman Catholic. Home: 3551 Shafer Dr Santa Clara CA 95051 Office: Robert B Suhr and Co 976 Poplar St Santa Clara CA 95050

RAYMOND, SUSAN GRANT, sculptor; b. Denver, May 23, 1943; d. Edwin Hendrie and Marybelle (McIntyre) G; m. Macpherson Raymond Jr., Aug. 18, 1967 (div. Mar. 1987); children: Lance Ramsay, Mariah McIntyre. BA in English, Cornell U., 1965; MA in Anthropology, U. Colo., 1968. Curator of anthropology Denver Mus. of Nat. History, 1968-71, contract artist, 1976-77, 79, 81, 83; instr. in anthropology U.S. Internat. U., Steamboat Springs, Colo., 1971-73. Sculpted monumental bronze sculpture for Littleton Colo., 1987, Vail, Colo., 1986, inspirational sculpture Childrens Hosp., 1977, diorama figures for Denver Mus. of Nat. History, 1971, 76, 77, 79, 81, 83; other prin: works include sculptures Routt Meml. Hosp, 1977, U. Denver, 1982, Craig Hosp. 1984, Lakewood Westernaires, 1984. Mem. Nat. Ski Patrol, 1965-75; bd. dirs. Tread of Pioneers Mus., Steamboat Springs, 1971-87. Recipient Maurice Hexter award Nat. Sculpture Soc., 1984, Art Castings award N. Am. Sculpture Exhibition, 1982, Summerart award Steamboat Springs Arts and Humanities, 1984.

RAYNAUD, LORETTA ROSE, nurse; b. Modesto, Calif., June 25, 1950; d. Charles Leroy and Maxine Margaret (Ritter) Peterson; m. Michael Anthony Raynaud, July 17, 1971; children: Michelle Lynn, Maureen Kristen, Matthew Charles. Diploma in nursing, St. Joseph's Sch. Nursing, 1971. RN. Staff nurse Mills Meml. Hosp., San Mateo, Calif., 1971-73, Med. Pers. Pool, San Mateo, 1974, Children's Hosp. Stanford, Palo Alto, Calif., 1975-80, San Jose Med. Clinic, 1982, Valley Community Hosp., Santa Maria, Calif., 1982-85; oncology program coord. Valley Community Hosp., Santa Maria, 1985-87, UpJohn Healthcare Svcs., San Luis Obispo, Calif., 1987—. Pub. edn. chairperson Am. Cancer Soc., 1985—, bd. dirs., 1987—, Santa Maria br. chmn., 1988—. Mem. Oncology Nursing Soc., Oncology Nursing Interest Group Club. Republican. Roman Catholic. Office: UpJohn Healthcare Svcs 265 South St Ste A San Luis Obispo CA 93401

RAYNER, ANTHONY GEORGE, bakery manager; b. Caterham, Surrey, Eng., July 11, 1944; came to U.S., 1974; s. George Victor and Nora Helen (Braker) R.; m. Ann Marie Louis Brush, Apr. 2, 1966 (div. Apr. 1983); children: Michelle Christine, Nicola Anne; m. Margaret Jean Davidson, June 29, 1985. City and guilds baking degrees, Croydon Tech. Coll., London, 1963. Mgr. bakery Sun Valley (Idaho) Co., 1974-76; v.p., gen. mgr. Anthony's Continental Bakery, Boise, Idaho, 1976-78; asst. gen. mgr. Mammas Restaurant and Old World Catering, Boise, 1978-83; bakery mgr. Smiths Mgmt. Corp., Boise, 1983-84; v.p. mfg.. Le Chatel Corp., Seattle, 1984—. Fellow City and Guilds Baking Inst.; mem. Idaho State Chef's Assn. (v.p. 1977-80), Royal Scottish Dance Soc. Presbyterian. Office: Le Chatel Corp 12735 28th Ave NE Ste A Seattle WA 98025

RAZRAN, GILBERT BRUCE, research company executive, industrial engineer; b. Walsenburg, Colo., Sept. 25, 1926; s. Bernard A. and Carolina I. (De Mallieu) R.; AB, U. Miami (Fla.), 1949, MS, 1950; PhD in Indsl. Bioengring., Purdue U., 1953; m. Charlotte D. Bellant, Nov. 8, 1969; children: Rita Lynn, Steven Barry. Project engr. Gen. Electric Co., Ithaca, N.Y., 1953-55, The George Washington U., research specialization in electrophysiology, 1955-59, systems analyst Burroughs Corp. Research Center, Paoli, Pa., 1959-63; dir. ops. research office Command & Control Systems, Washington, 1963-65; pres. Sci. Operational Systems, San Diego, 1965—; chmn., chief exec. officer Kingrexx, Inc., 1983—; prof. Grad. Sch., U.S. Internat. U., Calif., 1969-73; mem. U.S. Sci. Study Rev. Group, UN, Geneva, 1971. Mem. Library Bd., Upper Merion Twp., Pa., 1960-63. Bd. dirs. SOS-Disc, Inc., Las Vegas, Nev., chmn., 1972-75. Served with USNR, 1944-46; PTO; to capt. USAF, 1950-52. Recipient Inventor of Yr. award Patent Law Assn., 1980; registered profl. engr., N.Y., Pa., Calif. Mem. Nat. Security Indsl. Assn., Assn. for Advancement Med. Instrumentation, Mil. Ops. Research Soc., Am. Psychol. Assn., IEEE, Psi Chi, Sigma Xi. Author: Programmed Instruction Book in Electronics, 1966; CAI in Vocational Training, 1967. Contbr. articles to sci. jours. Inventor of oculometer.

RAZY, MICKEY, data processing executive, volunteer; b. Las Vegas, Nev., Feb. 16, 1947; s. Robert H. and Helen Joy (Malner) R.; m. Mary A. McCulloch, Oct. 14, 1968; children: Paulette E., Tiffany A. AAS in Bus. Mgmt., U. Nev., Las Vegas, 1977. Computer operator First Nat. Bank Nev., Las Vegas, 1965-67; asst. cashier First Nat. Bank Nev., Reno, 1967-71; asst. mgr. data processing First Nat. Bank Nev., Las Vegas, 1971-75, Western Bancorp Data Processing Co., Las Vegas, 1975-81, First Interstate Services Co., Las Vegas, 1981-83; asst. v.p., media processing mgr. First Interstate Bancard Co., Simi Valley, Calif., 1983—. vol. treas. Royal Band Booster, Simi Valley, 1986—; Boy Scouts Am., Las Vegas, 1958—; bd. dirs. Girl Scouts U.S., Simi Valley, 1986—. Recipient Eagle Scout award Boulder Dam Area CouncilBoy Scouts Am., Las Vegas, 1963, Silver Beaver award Boulder Dam Area Council Boy Scouts Am., 1982, Medilian award Girl Scout U.S., Las Vegas, 1982. Mem. Assn. Info. and Image Mgmt. Democrat. Roman Catholic. Lodge: Sertoma. Office: First Interstate Bancard Co N Am 1700 Surveyor Ave Simi Valley CA 93097-0072

RAZZAGHI, PAUL PARVIZ, artist; b. Shemiran, Iran, Apr. 22, 1948; came to U.S., 1972; s. Gholamreza and Ashraf (Meshkati) R.; m. Connie Marie Hoyle, May 17, 1980. BS in Math., Campbell U., Buies Creek, N.C., 1980. Purchasing mgr. SNAM Project Co., Rome, 1975-77; div. mgr. Hudson-Belk Inc., Cary, N.C., 1981-85; estate disposition mgr. Ghaffari Estates, Bethesda, Md., 1985-87; naturalistic artist Beverly Hills, Calif., 1965—. Works exhibited in pvt. clubs and art festivals in L.A. met. area. Home: 143 D South Canon Dr Beverly Hills CA 90212

REA, DONALD GEORGE, space research and exploration executive; b. Portage la Prairie, Man., Can., Sept. 21, 1929; came to U.S., 1951, naturalized, 1962; s. Hugh Charles and Jessie Mae (Miners) R.; m. Therese Hillman, Nov. 11, 1967; children: Michael Hugh, Steven Martin. BS, U. Man., Winnipeg, Can., 1950, MS, 1952, DSc, 1980; PhD, MIT, 1954. Postdoctoral research fellow Oxford (Eng.) U., 1954-55; dep. dir. planetary program office NASA, Washington, 1968-70; asst. lab. dir. for sci. Jet Propulsion Lab., Pasadena, Calif., 1970-76, dep. asst. lab. dir. for tech. and space program devel., 1979-80, asst lab dir. for tech. and space program devel., 1980-87, spl. asst. to dir., mgr. Mars Rover Sample Return Devel. Flight Project, 1987—; research fellow J.F. Kennedy Sch. Govt. Harvard U., Cambridge, Mass., 1979-80. Assoc. editor ICARUS, 1968-76, Jour. of Geophys. Research, 1968-70; tech. editor IEEE Trans. Geosci. Electronics, 1976—; contbr. articles to profl. jours. Recipient Exceptional Sci. Achievement medal NASA, 1969, Exceptional Service medal NASA, 1985. Mem. AIAA, AAAS, Am. Astron. Soc., Am. Chem. Soc., Am. Inst. Physics, Am. Geophys. Union, Linda Vista Annandale Assn. (pres. bd. dirs. 1981-82). Democrat. Home: 1605 Pegfair Estates Dr Pasadena CA 91103 Office: Jet Propulsion Lab MS 264-726 4800 Oak Grove Dr Pasadena CA 91109

REA, GEARY FREDERIC, general contracting company executive, developer; b. Oakland, Calif., May 4, 1951; s. Frederic M. and Nancy H. Rea; m. Leslie Barbieri, Aug. 31, 1978; children: Riley, Nathan. BA, U. Calif., Santa Barbara, 1975. Pres. Geary F. Rea & Assocs., Inc., Santa Rosa, Calif., 1975--; bd. dirs. Hawley Terminal, Inc., San Francisco. Active Big Bros. Am., San Francisco, 1976-85. Mem. No. Calif. Solar Energy Assn., South of Market Bus. Assn., North Coast Builders Exchange, Historic R.R. Square Assn. (bd. dirs., past pres.), Nat. Trust for Historic Preservation, Santa Rosa (Calif.) C. of C., Commonwealth Club Calif., Olympic Club, Parkpoint Club. Home and Office: PO Box 3306 Santa Rosa CA 95402

REA, JAMES THOMAS, investment management executive; b. Glendale, Calif., Mar. 31, 1945; s. Hosea Devoe and Margarette Elizabeth (Polly) R.; m. Marsha McDivitt, Aug. 4, 1984; 1 child, Suzanne Elizabeth. BSBA cum laude, Menlo Coll., 1967; investment mgmt. program, Stanford U., 1981. Controller Container Corp. of Am., Santa Clara, Calif., 1967-69; exec. v.p. Fields, Grant & Co., Menlo Park, Calif., 1969-74; prin. Rea, Nelson & Staight, Inc., Palo Alto, Calif., 1974-83; pres. James T. Rea & Assoc. Inc., Portola Valley, Calif., 1983-86; mng. dir., West Coast regional mgr. BIL, Trainer Worthan, Inc., Menlo Park, 1986—; dir. BIL, Trainer Wortham, Inc., N.Y.C., 1986; dir. BIL, Trainer Wortham, Inc. Trust Co., N.Y.C., 1986—. Treas. Town of Portola Valley, 1979-80, chmn. fin. com., 1986. Recipient Wall Street Jour. award, Wall Street Jour., N.Y., 1967. Mem. We. Pension Conf., Mcpl. Fin. Officers Assn., St. Francis Yacht Club (San Francisco), Univ. Club (San Francisco). Office: BIL Trainer Wortham Inc 3000 Sand Hill Rd Menlo Park CA 94025

REA, KATHRYN POLLYANNA, management consultant, data processing consultant; b. Los Angeles, Aug. 23, 1957; d. Virginia (Robinson) Rea. BS, SUNY, Albany, 1981; Cert. in Data Processing, U. Calif., 1983. Real estate agt. Beverly Hills, Calif., 1977-80; real estate broker Beverly Hills, 1980—; pres., chmn. bd. The Consulting Edge, Inc., Beverly Hills, 1983—; project mgr. and advisor banking automation, 1984—; instr. of data communications, systems analysis and design seminars, 1984—, devel. of fin. models related to automation, assessment of automation for commercial and banking, 1985—. Author: Data Communications For Business, 1987; contbr. articles to profl. jours. Mem. IEEE, Nat. Computer Graphics Assn., Assn. for Computing Machinery. Office: The Cons Edge Inc 9107 Wilshire Blvd Ste 320 Beverly Hills CA 90210

REA, KENNETH HAROLD, terrestrial ecologist, environmental restoration; b. Red Oak, Iowa, Aug. 20, 1946; s. Morris Richard and Mary Lucille (Atherton) R.; m. Cherri Eileen Wenslay,. BS in Wildlife Sci., N. Mex. State U., 1969, MS in Range Sci., 1972; PhD in Ecology, Utah State U., 1976. Staff mem. Los Alamos Nat. Lab., 1976-87, assoc. group leader, 1987-88, project leader, 1988--. Mem. Masons. Home: PO Box 62 Los Alamos NM 87544 Office: Los Alamos Nat Lab Environ Restoration Prog Tech Support Office PO Box 1663 MS 485 Los Alamos NM 87545

REA, SHARON WALLIS, business executive; b. Tacoma, Dec. 19, 1945; d. Donald William Porter and Beth Marie Barton. Degree in secretarial sci., Kinman Bus. U., Spokane, Wash., 1965; postgrad., U. Nev., 1974, 77, 82. Adminstrv. sec. to dir. Desert Research Inst., Reno, 1973-83, exec. asst. to pres., 1983-84; contracts mgr. Sierra Nev. Corp., Reno, 1984—. Editor: (sci. publ.) Third International Cloud Condensation Nuclei Workshop, 1981, Complex Aerosol Nucleation Experiment, 1983. Active Com. to Aid Abused Women, Reno, 1983-84, Juvenile Diabetes Assn., Reno, 1987-88. Mem. Nat. Assn. Female Execs. Democrat. Roman Catholic. Home: 1955 Railway Ct Sparks NV 89431 Office: Sierra Nev Corp PO Box 6900 Reno NV 89503

REA, WILLIAM J., federal judge. Judge U.S. Dist. Ct. (cen. dist.) Calif., Los Angeles. Office: US Dist Ct 312 N Spring St Los Angeles CA 90012

READ, ELEANOR MAY, financial analyst; b. Arcadia, N.Y., July 4, 1942; d. Henry and Lena May (Fagner) Van Koevering; 1 child, Robin Jo. Typist, clk., sec., credit corr. Sarah Coventry, Inc., Newark, N.Y., 1957-61; exec. sec. Mobil Chem. Co., Macedon, N.Y., 1961-68; bus. mgr. Henry's Hardware, Newark, 1968-72; with Xerox Corp., Fremont, Calif., 1973—, internat. clk. analyst, personnel adminstrv. asst., employment coordinator, exec. sec., cycle count analyst., tax preparer H&R Block, 1985—. Mem. Xerox/Diablo Mgmt. Assn., Am. Mgmt. Assn., Profl. Businesswomen's Assn., NAFE. Office: H&R Block 910 Page Ave FM-261 Fremont CA 94538

READ, P. DANIEL, architect; b. Seymour, Ind., July 23, 1927; s. Basil Bernard and Elsie Waneta (Albrich) R.; m. Lorraine Smith, Nov. 30, 1957; children: D. Kent, Kathi A., Daniel D., Doran L. BArch, U. Cin., 1953. Registered architect, Oreg. Pvt. practice Corvallis, Oreg., 1962-86; asst. prof. Oreg. State U., Corvallis, 1969—, university architect, 1986—. City councilor Corvallis City Council, 1981-82. Republican. Baptist. Home: 2650 NW Princess St Corvallis OR 97330-3219 Office: Oreg State U Adams Hall Corvallis OR 97331-2001

READ, PETER ROSS, mechanical engineer, geological engineer; b. San Francisco, Nov. 21, 1948; s. John Marion and Margaret Elizabeth (Peters) R.; m. Ellen Pauline Paillasou, June 26, 1976 (div. Nov. 1979); m. Ellen Eugenia Youngblut, Oct. 17, 1981; 1 child, Halley Eugenia. BS in Mech. Engring., U. Colo., 1971; BS in Geol. Engring., U. Nev., 1975. Foreman trainee, foreman Magma Copper Co., San Manuel, Ariz., 1976-77, engr., 1977-80, constrn. foreman, 1980-81, gen. contrn. foreman, 1981-88, div. safety dir., 1989—; pres. Rancho Linda Vista, Inc., 1987-89. Chair water com. Oracle (Ariz.) Town Hall, 1987-88. Mem. ASSE, AIME. Episcopalian. Home: HCL Box 2360 Oracle AZ 85623 Office: Magma Copper Co PO Box M San Manuel AZ 85631

READ, ROBERT LOGAN, realtor; b. Portland, Oreg., Sept. 27, 1938; s. Logan Acton Read and Florence May (Brosnan) Neuheisel. Cadet, U.S. Mil. Acad., West Point, N.Y., 1960-63; BA, U. Oreg., 1963-64, postgrad., 1968-70. Instr. math. Peace Corps, Indore, India, 1965-67; officer pub. affairs Peace Corps, San Francisco, 1967-68; anchorman, reporter, news dir. various NBC, CBS affiliates, Portland, Medford, Oreg., Reno, Nev., Santa Maria, Calif., 1970-77; realtor various cos., Portland, 1978-83; realtor Profls. 100, Portland, 1983—, dir. corp. bus., assoc. broker. Producer, author, anchorman TV documentaries. Served with AUS, 1959-62. Ford Found. fellow U. Oreg., 1969; recipient John Swett award Calif. Pub. Schs., 1976. Mem. Nat. Assn. Realtors, Oreg. Assn. Realtors, Wash. County Bd. Realtors. Democrat. Club: Bergfreunde Ski (Beaverton, Oreg.). Office: Profls 100 Realtors 10260 SW Greenburg Rd Lincoln Tower 250 Portland OR 97223

READE, BEN BRUCE, fleet operations administrator; b. Los Angeles, Apr. 9, 1939. Pres., chief exec. officer B.R.T. Mgmt. Inc., Los Angeles, 1979-83; fleet operations dir. Walt Disney Pictures, Burbank, Calif., 1985—. Mem. Rotary. Republican. Office: Walt Disney Pictures 500 S Buena Vista Burbank CA 91521

READE, ROBERT MELLOR, convenience store executive; b. Elmhurst, Ill., Jan. 9, 1940; s. M.G. and Virginia A. (Mellor) R.; m. Carol Jean Coon, May 26, 1962; children—Christopher, Gregory. B.A. in Liberal Arts, U. Ariz., 1962. Charting mgr. Eller Outdoor Advt., Phoenix, 1964-69; sales mgr. Mullins Neon, Denver, 1969-70; pres. Gannett Outdoor Co. Ariz., Phoenix, 1970-84; sr. v.p. Gannett Outdoor Group, N.Y.C., 1984-85; sr. v.p. real estate and devel. Circle K Corp., Phoenix, 1985-86; pres., chief operating officer Circle K Internat., Phoenix, 1986—; bd. dirs. Western Savs. and Loan. Chmn. Phoenix chpt. Am. Humanics, 1983, Valley Youth Coalition, 1981, Phoenix City Bond Election, 1984; active Thunderbirds, 1978-83, Theodore council Boy Scouts Am., Community Council, Phoenix United Way, Camelback Mental Health Found. Served with USAR, 1963-69. Recipient U. Ariz. Alumni Appreciation award, 1975, 77, Slouaker award, 1977; Anti Defamation League Torch of Liberty award, 1981. Mem. Ariz. Safety Assn. (pres. 1981), Young Pres. Orgn., Outdoor Assn. Am., Inst. Outdoor Advt., Phoenix Advt. Club (pres. 1974). Club: Rotary (pres. 1982). Office: The Circle K Corp 1601 N 7th St PO Box 52084 Phoenix AZ 85006

READER, SCOT ANTHONY, aerospace engineer; b. Huntington Park, Calif., Nov. 13, 1967; s. Don Ange and Linda Kay (Moore) R. Student, U. So. Calif., L.A., 1986—. Bank teller Security Pacific Nat. Bank, Upland, Calif., 1987; rsch. asst. dept. aerospace engring. U. So. Calif., L.A., 1986-88; engring. intern Gen. Dynamics Co., Pomona, Calif., 1988—. Mem. Golden Key, Tau Beta Pi. Republican. Home: 1909 Eloise Way Upland CA 91786

REAGAN, GARY DON, lawyer; b. Amarillo, Tex., Aug. 23, 1941; s. Hester and Lois Irene (Marcum) R.; m. Nedra Ann Nash, Sept. 12, 1964; children—Marc, Kristi, Kari, Brent. A.B., Stanford U., 1963, J.D., 1965. Bar: N.Mex. 1965, U.S. Dist. Ct. N.Mex., 1965, U.S. Supreme Ct. 1986. Assoc. Smith & Ransom, Albuquerque, 1965-67; ptnr. Smith, Ransom, Deaton & Reagan, Albuquerque, 1967-68, Williams, Johnson, Houston, Reagan & Porter, Hobbs, N.Mex., 1968-77, Williams, Johnson, Reagan, Porter & Love, Hobbs, 1977-82; sole practice, Hobbs, 1982—; city atty. City of Hobbs, 1978-80; City of Eunice, N.M., 1980—; instr. N.Mex. Jr. Coll. and Coll. of S.W., Hobbs, 1978-84. Mayor, City of Hobbs, 1972-73, 76-77, city commr., 1970-78; pres., dir. Jr. Achievement of Hobbs, 1974-85; pres., trustee Landsun Homes, Inc., Carlsbad, N.Mex., 1972-84; trustee Lydia Patterson Inst., El Paso, Tex., 1972-84, N.Mex. Conf. United Meth. Ch., 1988—, Meth. Home, Waco, Tex., 1988—, Coll. of S.W., Hobbs, 1989—; chmn. County Democratic Com., 1983-85. Mem. ABA, State Bar N.Mex. (coms.), Lea County Bar Assn. (pres. 1976-77), Hobbs C. of C. (v.p. 1986-87, pres. 1989—), Rotary (pres. Hobbs 1985-86), Hobbs Tennis (pres. 1974-75). Home: 200 Eagle Dr Hobbs NM 88240 Office: 501 N Linam Hobbs NM 88240

REAGAN, JANET THOMPSON, psychologist, educator; b. Monticello, Ken., Sept. 15, 1945; d. Virgil Joe and Carrie Mae (Alexander) Thompson; m. Robert Barry Reagan, Jr., Aug. 7, 1977; children—Natalia Alexandria, Robert Barry. B.A. in Psychology, Berea Coll., 1967; Ph.D. in Psychology, Vanderbilt U., 1972. Mgr. research and eval. Nashville Mental Health Center, 1971-72; mgr. eval. Family Health Found., New Orleans, 1973-74; asst. prof. dept. health systems mgmt. Tulane U., New Orleans, 1974-77; dir. eval. Project Heavy West, Los Angeles, 1977-78; asst. prof. health adminstrn. Calif. State U.-Northridge, 1978-83, assoc. prof., director health adminstrn., 1983-87, prof., dir. health adminstrn., 1987—; cons. in field. Mem. Am. Pub. Health Assn., Assn. Health Services Research, Western Psychol. Assn., Eval. Research Soc., Am. Coll. Health Care Execs., Assn. Univ. Programs in Health Adminstrn. (task force on undergrad. edn. 1985—, chmn. 1988-89), Am. Coll. Health Care Execs. (com. on higher edn.), Am. Coll. Health Care Adminstrn, Psi Chi, Phi Kappa Phi. Mem. editorial adv. bd. Jour. of Long Term Care Adminstrn.; contbr. articles to profl. jours., papers to profl. assns. Home: 9354 Encino Ave Northridge CA 91325 Office: Calif State U Dept Health Sci Northridge CA 91330

REAGAN, JOSEPH BERNARD, aerospace executive; b. Somerville, Mass., Nov. 26, 1934; s. Joseph B. and Helen Lowry R.; m. Dorothy Hughes; children: Patrick, Michael, Kevin, Kathleen, Brian, John, Maureen. BS in Physics, Boston Coll., 1956, MS in Physics, 1959; PhD in Space Sci., Stanford U., 1975; postgrad. exec. mgmt., Pa. State U., State College, 1981. Staff scientist, rsch. scientist, sr. scientist, scientist Lockheed Rsch. & Devel. Div., Palo Alto, Calif., 1959-75, mgr., 1975-84, dir., 1984-86, dep. gen. mgr., 1986-88, v.p., asst. gen. mgr., 1988—; bd. dirs. Southwall Technologies Inc., Palo Alto. Contbr. articles to profl. jours. Capt. U.S. Army, 1956-64. Assoc. fellow AIAA (outstanding engr. San Francisco chpt. 1988); mem. Am. Geophys. Union. Republican. Roman Catholic. Home: 13554 Mandarin Way Saratoga CA 95070 Office: Lockheed Rsch & Devel 0/90-01 B/201 3251 Hanover Palo Alto CA 94304

REAGAN, NANCY DAVIS (ANNE FRANCIS ROBBINS), wife of former President of United States; b. N.Y.C., July 6, 1923; d. Kenneth and Edith (Luckett) Robbins; step dau. Loyal Davis; m. Ronald Reagan, Mar. 4, 1952; children: Patricia Ann, Ronald Prescott; stepchildren: Maureen, Michael. BA, Smith Coll.; LLD (hon.), Pepperdine U., 1983; LHD (hon.), Georgetown U., 1987. Contract actress, MGM, 1949-56; films include The Next Voice You Hear, 1950, Donovan's Brain, 1953, Hellcats of the Navy, 1957; Author: Nancy, 1980; formerly author syndicated column on prisoner-of-war and missing-in-action soldiers and their families; author: (with Jane Wilkie) To Love a Child. Civic worker, visited wounded Viet Nam vets., sr. citizens, hosps. and schs. for physically and emotionally handicapped children, active in furthering foster grandparents for handicapped children program; hon. nat. chmn. Aid to Adoption of Spl. Kids, 1977; spl. interest in fighting alcohol and drug abuse among youth: hosted first ladies from around the world for 2d Internat. Drug Conf., 1985; hon. chmn. Just Say No Found., Nat. Fedn. of Parents for Drug-Free Youth, Nat. Child Watch Campaign, President's Com. on the Arts and Humanities, Wolf Trap Found. bd. of trustees, Nat. Trust for Historic Preservation, Cystic Fibrosis Found., Nat. Republican Women's Club; hon. pres. Girl Scouts of Am. Named one of Ten Most Admired Am. Women, Good Housekeeping mag., ranking #1 in poll, 1984, 85, 86; Woman of Yr. Los Angeles Times, 1977; permanent mem. Hall of Fame of Ten Best Dressed Women in U.S.; recipient humanitarian awards from Am. Camping Assn., Nat. Council on Alcoholism, United Cerebral Palsy Assn., Internat. Ctr. for Disabled; Boys Town Father Flanagan award; 1986 Kiwanis World Service medal; Variety Clubs

Internat. Lifeline award; numerous awards for her role in fight against drug abuse. Address: 11000 Wilshire Blvd Los Angeles CA 90024 *

REAGAN, RONALD WILSON, former President of United States; b. Tampico, Ill., Feb. 6, 1911; s. John Edward and Nelle (Wilson) R.; m. Jane Wyman, Jan. 25, 1940 (div. 1948); children: Maureen E., Michael E.; m. Nancy Davis, Mar. 4, 1952; children: Patricia, Ronald. AB, Eureka Coll., 1932. Gov. State of Calif., 1967-74; businessman, rancher, commentator on public policy 1975-80, Pres. of U.S., 1981-89. Sports announcer, motion picture and TV actor, 1932-66. Served as capt. USAAF, 1942-45. Mem. Screen Actors Guild (pres. 1947-52, 59), Tau Kappa Epsilon. Republican. Address: 11000 Wilshire Blvd Los Angeles CA 90024 *

REAL, JACK GARRET, helicopter company executive; b. Baraga, Mich., May 31, 1916; s. Edward Ignatius and Elizabeth Irene (Leary) R.; m. Janeth May Paden, Nov. 20, 1941; children: Daniel, Patricia. BSME, Mich. Tech. U., 1937, D in Engring. (hon.), 1968; D in Engring. (hon.), Selma Coll., 1984, Northrop U., 1985. Registered profl. engr., Calif. Jr. engr. to chief devel. engr. Lockheed Aircraft, Burbank, Calif., 1939-65, v.p. rotary wing, 1965-71; v.p. aviation Hughes Tool Co., Encino, Calif., 1971-76; sr. v.p. aviation Summa Corp., Las Vegas, 1977-79; pres. Hughes Helicopter Co., Culver City, Calif., 1979-84; pres., dir. McDonnell Douglas Helicopter Co., Culver City, Calif., 1984—; bd. dirs. Midway Airline, Chgo., Evergreen Internat., McMinnville, Oreg., Davey Industries, Cin. Contbr. articles to profl. jours. Bd. dirs. Great Western council Boy Scouts Am., Los Angeles, 1965—; bd. overseers U. Pa. Sch. Engring. and Applied Sci., Phila., 1975-81. Served to 1st lt. C.E., U.S. Army, 1937-42. Recipient Americanism award Boy Scouts Am., 1983. Fellow AIAA; mem. Am. Helicopter Soc., Am. Assn. Army Aviation, Aero Club So. Calif. (bd. dirs.). Democrat. Roman Catholic. Office: McDonnell Douglas Helicopter Co Centinela & Teale Sts Culver City CA 90230

REAL, MANUEL LAWRENCE, U.S. district judge; b. San Pedro, Calif., Jan. 27, 1924; s. Francisco Jose and Maria (Mansano) R.; m. Stella Emilia Michalik, Oct. 15, 1955; children: Michael, Melanie Marie, Timothy, John Robert. B.S., U. So. Calif., 1944, student fgn. trade, 1946-48; LL.B., Loyola Sch. Law, Los Angeles, 1951. Bar: Calif. 1952. Asst. U.S. Atty.'s Office, Los Angeles, 1952-55; pvt. practice law San Pedro, Calif., 1955-64; U.S. atty. So. Dist. Calif., 1964-66; U.S. dist. judge 1966—, now chief judge. Served to ensign USNR, 1943-46. Mem. Am., Fed., Los Angeles County bar assns., State Bar Calif., Am. Judicature Soc., Chief Spl. Agts. Assn., Phi Delta Phi, Sigma Chi. Roman Catholic. Club: Anchor (Los Angeles). Office: US Dist Ct 312 N Spring St Los Angeles CA 90012

REAMS, LEE THOMAS, business executive, tax accountant, mechanical engineer; b. El Centro, Calif., Sept. 11, 1934; s. Lee B. and Sarah E. R.; m. Anne M. Morton, Sept. 18, 1965; children—Cheryll, Susan, Lee, Robert. B.S. in Mech. Engring., Calif. State U.-San Luis Obispo, 1957. Enrolled agt. IRS. Mech. engr. Rocketdyne div. Rockwell Internat., Canoga Park, Calif., 1957-75; pvt. practice tax acctg., Woodland Hills, Calif., 1972—; founder, pres. Ind. Preparer Services, Inc., Glendale, Calif., 1977—; gen. ptnr. Realty Investment Fund, Los Angeles, 1981—; lectr. tax law. Served with USN, 1952-60. Republican. Presbyterian. Author: Tax Implications of Divorce, 1981; Tax Implications of Real Estate Transactions, 1980, Tax Implications of Rental Property, 1981; Building A Successful Tax Practice, 1980. Office: Ind Preparer Svcs Inc 5115 Douglas Fir Ste H Calabasas CA 91302

REARDEN, CAROLE ANN, clinical pathologist, educator; b. Belleville, Ont., Can., June 11, 1946; d. Joseph Brady and Honora Patricia (O'Halloran) R. BSc, McGill U., 1969, MSc, MDCM, 1971. Diplomate Am. Bd. Pathology, Am. Bd. Immunohematology and Blood Banking. Resident and fellow Children's Meml. Hosp., Chgo., 1971-73; resident in pediatrics U. Calif., San Diego, 1974, resident then fellow, 1975-79, dir. histocompatability and immunogenetics lab., asst. prof. pathology, 1979-86, assoc. prof., 1986—, head div. lab. medicine, 1989—; prin. investigator devel. monoclonal antibodies to erythroid antigens. Contbr. articles to profl. jours. Mem. Mayor's Task Force on AIDS, San Diego, 1983. Recipient Young Investigator Rsch. award NIH, 1979; grantee U. Calif. Cancer Rsch. Coordinating Com., 1982, NIH, 1983. Mem. Am. Assn. Pathologists, Am. Fed. Clin. Rsch., Am. Soc. Hematology, Am. Assn. Blood Banks (com. organ transplantation and tissue typing 1982-87), Am. Soc. Histocompatibility and Immunogenetics, Am. Soc. Transplant Physicians. Office: U Calif Med Ctr Dept Pathology H-720 225 Dickinson St San Diego CA 92103

REARDON, CRAIG, film special effects designer/make-up artist; b. Los Angeles, Apr. 10, 1953; s. Richard F. and Barbara L. (Brown) R.; m. Nancy M. Nee, Oct. 12, 1986; 1 child, Dana. Make-up artist, spl. effects designer for films, TV Los Angeles, 1978—. designer, make-up artist for films: Big Business, 1988, The Seventh Sign, 1988, A Time of Destiny, 1988, The Gate, 1987, Weird Science, 1985, The Goonies, 1985, The Mean Season, 1985, Dreamscape, 1984, Twilight Zone-The Movie, 1983, Dance of the Dwarves, 1983, E.T., 1982, Poltergeist, 1982, Strange Behavior, 1981, The Beast Within, 1981, An American Werewolf in London, 1982, The Fun House, 1981, The Unseen, 1981, Altered States, 1981, The Incredible Shrinking Woman, 1981, Prophecy, 1978, The Incredible Melting Man, 1977, Dick Tracy, 1989, The Gate II, 1988, Night Life, 1988; for TV films: Living Proof: The Hank Williams Jr. Story, 1983, Roots II: The Next Generations, 1978, Battlestar Galactica, 1978; for TV Series episodes: Solomon's Universe, 1985, The Hitchhiker, 1985; for TV commercials: Miller Lite Beer commercials and others; contbr. articles toprofl.jours. Democrat. Home: 5622 N Fairview Pl Agoura Hills CA 91301 Office: Craig Reardon Inc 850 Calle Plano Unit A Camarillo CA 93010

REAVILL, DAVID WILLIAM, financial investment company executive; b. Los Angeles, Sept. 18, 1948; s. William Arthur and Marian Elizabeth (Stocks) R.; m. Rachel Mary Valcho, Apr. 12, 1985 (div. 1983). BA, Westmont Coll., 1971; MA, U. Calif., Santa Barbara, 1978, Calif. State U., Los Angeles, 1988. Registered fin. & ops. prin., gen. securities prin., mcpl. securities prin. Assoc. prof. U. Calif., Santa Barbara, 1975-78; pres. First Los Angeles Securities, 1979-86; cons. Wedbush Securities, Los Angeles, 1986-87; regional dir. Fidelity Investments, Los Angeles, 1988—; bd. dirs. Internat. Bus. Securities, Los Angeles; cons. Spear Securities, Los Angeles, 1986-87. TV broadcaster KWHY-TV, 1980-85, KSCI-TV, 1981-83; commentator Am. Radio Network, 1985-86; editor-in-chief Univ. Times newspaper, 1987. Mem. County Art Mus., Los Angeles, 1979-88. Mem. Nat. Assn. Securities Dealers, Securities Industry Assn., Fin. Mgrs. Assn., Greater Los Angeles Zoo Assn., Wood Ranch (Calif.) Golf Club. Office: Fidelity Investments 1800 Avenue of the Stars Ste 130 Los Angeles CA 90067

REAVIS, THEODORE EDWARD, training and organization development consultant; b. Valhalla, N.Y., Nov. 2, 1937; s. Lawrence Edward and Theodosia Cordelia (Madison) R.; m. Geraldine Rita Le Boeuf, July 3, 1964. BA, Va. State U., 1962; MA, San Francisco State U., 1970. Orgn. devel. specialist Kaiser Aluminum & Chem., Oakland, Calif., 1969-72; assoc. dir. orgn. research & devel. Kaiser Permanente, Oakland, 1972-79; mgr. coll. relations Kaiser Aluminum & Chem., Oakland, 1979-81; cons. training and orgn. devel. Berkeley, Calif., 1981-82; mgr. training and orgn. devel. Kaiser Permanente Med. Ctr., Oakland, 1982—; cons. in field. Mem. Bay Area Black Consortium for Quality Health Care Inc., Oakland, 1986-88; mem. Mayor's Task Force on Employment and TRaining, Oakland, 1983; adv. bd. mem. A Better Chance, Inc., Oakland, 1987. Recipient Cert. of Appreciation Nat. Urban League, N.Y., 1971-72, Mayor's Council on Youth Opportunity, Oakland, 1970. Democrat.

REAY, JED ALLEN, cariological technician; b. Eugene, Oreg., Jan. 22, 1957; s. George Robert and Ann (Stockman) R. BS, U. Oreg., 1987. Cert. Emergency Med. Technician. Laborer Standard Utilities Co., Salem, Oreg., 1975-79, Fleetwood Industries, Pendleton, Oreg., 1979-81; direct care staff Nova Enterprise, Pendleton, 1982-84; asst. mgr. Eastern Oreg. Alcohol Found., Pendleton, 1980-81; detoxification technician Umatilla County Detixification, Pendleton, 1980; research asst. U. Oreg. Child Lab., Eugene, 1984-86; cardiol. technician Oreg. Cardiology Cons., Eugene, 1987—; research asst. Child Research Lab., U. Oreg., Eugene, 1984-86, U. Oreg. Counseling Psychology Dept., Eugene, 1987; para-profl. Acad. Advising Student Services, U. Oreg., Eugene, 1986-87. Firefighter, emergency med. technician, Coburg (Oreg.) Rural Fire Dist., 1986—. Mem. Internat. Soc. Conflict Mgmt., Internat. Communication Assn., Speech Communication Assn., Am. Psychol. Assn., Soc. Profls. in Dispute Resolution. Democrat. Home: 91297 Stallings Ln Eugene OR 97401

REBENSTORF, THOMAS ANDREW, mining company executive; b. Danville, Ill., July 25, 1961; s. John Christian III and Dorothy Jean (Wodetzki) R. Student, San Bernardino Valley Coll., 1979-8l, U. Redlands, 198l-83, Riverside City Coll., 1983-84. Metal trader Gold Field Deep Mines Co., San Bernardino, Calif., 1981-83; metal trader Superior Gold-N-Silver, Inc., San Bernardino, 1983-84, v.p., 1984—; pres. R-Star Metals Inc., San Bernardino, 1985—; v.p. Precious Metals Mining Cons., San Bernardino, 1987—, Diamond Solid State Electronic, Inc., San Bernardino, 1988—. Mem. Soc. Mining Engrs. Office: Precious Metals Mining Cons 2990 Del Rosa Ave Ste D San Bernardino CA 92404

REBER, JAMES PATRICK, theatrical producer, writer; b. Butte, Mont., Mar. 17, 1952; s. Leonard James and Lorraine Helen (Sullivan) R.; m. Debra Anne Webster, July 18, 1981. BA in Sociology, U. Calif., Berkeley, 1977. Gen. mgr. Berkeley (Calif.) Shakespeare Festival, 1977-79; founder, exec. producer San Jose (Calif.) Repertory Co., 1980--. Author: (plays) A Night in Illyria, 1988, Arouet: Young Voltaire, 1988. Founder, pres. San Jose Arts Round Table, 1987--; treas., bd. dirs. San Jose Conv. and Visitors Bur., 1987--. With USN, 1972-75. Recipient Disting. Citizen award San Jose City Council-Exchange Club, 1984, Arts Achievement award San Jose State U., 1987, also numerous awards for theatre prodns., 1979--. Democrat. Home: 5689 Keymar Dr San Jose CA 95123

RECALDE, VINCENT ENRIQUE, banker; b. Guayauil, Guayas, Ecuador, Mar. 11, 1934; came to U. S., 1960; s. Enrique Celio and Luzmila (Trivino) R.; m. Patricia Edna Young, Aug. 27, 1971; children: Vinicia, Carol, John, Daniel. BS, Brigham Young U., 1970; MBA, Golden State U., 1977. Cert. air traffic controller, Mexico City. Station mgr. ASA Internat. Airlines, Guayauil, Ecuador, 1956-60; credit officer Union Bank, San Francisco, 1972-75; asst. mgr. Crocker Bank, L.A., 1975-78; loan mgr. Calif. Overseas Bank, L.A., 1978-80; br. mgr. Sanwa Bank, L.A., 1980-82; asst. v.p. Calif. Fed. Savs., L.A., 1983—. Bd. dirs., treas., Wilshire Ctr. Community Involvement Assn., 1985-87. With USAF, 1961-65. Named Internat. Civil Aviation Orgn. scholar, 1954. Mem. Hollywood C. of C., (com. mem.), Deseret Businessmen's Assn. (treas. 1986—), Rotary (com. mem.). Mormon. Home: 6852 Van Noord Ave North Hollywood CA 91605 Office: Calif Fed Savs 270 N Vermont Ave Los Angeles CA 90004

RECHTIN, EBERHARDT, aerospace educator; b. East Orange, N.J., Jan. 16, 1926; s. Eberhardt Carl and Ida H. (Pfarrer) R.; m. Dorothy Diane Denebrink, June 10, 1951; children: Andrea C., Nina, Julie Anne, Erica, Mark. B.S., Calif. Inst. Tech., 1946, Ph.D. cum laude, 1950. Dir. Deep Space Network, Calif. Inst. Tech. Jet Propulsion Lab., 1949-67; dir. Advanced Research Projects Agy., Dept. Def., 1967-70, prin. dep. dir. def. research and engring., 1970-71, asst. sec. def. for telecommunications, 1972-73; chief engr. Hewlett-Packard Co., Palo Alto, Calif., 1973-77; pres., chief exec. officer Aerospace Corp., El Segundo, Calif., 1977-87; prof. U. So. Calif., 1988—. Served to lt. USNR, 1943-56. Recipient major awards NASA, Dept. Def. Fellow AIAA (major awards), IEEE (major awards); mem. Nat. Acad. Engring., Tau Beta Pi. Home: 1665 Catalina Pl Palos Verdes Estates CA 90274 Office: U So Calif University Park Los Angeles CA 90089-1454

RECK, DONALD HARRY, public affairs specialist; b. Chgo., Aug. 12, 1936; s. Harry August and Emma Marie (Rauch) R.; m. Joan Ann Lernert, Aug. 11, 1962 (div. Nov. 1975); children: Laurance Russell, Valarie Cheryl, Diana Claire; m. Marie Pearl Nadeau, Nov. 28, 1981. Student, U. Ill., Chgo., 1954-56; BJ, U. Mo., 1958. Reporter Ill. State Jour., Springfield, 1958-60; columnist Chgo. Daily News, 1960-63; info. rep. data processingdiv. IBM, White Plains, N.Y., 1963-65; mgr. internal communications corp. hdqrs. IBM, Armonk, N.Y., 1965-69; bur. chief div. data processing IBM, Mpls., 1970-73; mgr. area communications IBM, N.Y.C., 1973-77; div. info. mgr. office products IBM, Franklin Lakes, N.J., 1977-80; mgr. communications/community rels. div. gen. products IBM, Tucson, 1980-85, state mgr. external program for Ariz., 1985-88, mgr. policy programs for Ariz., 1988—. Bd. dirs., v.p. Arizonans for Cultural Devel., 1988—, Goodwill Industries, 1989; mem. Mayor's Task Force for Econ. Devel., 1988—; bd. dirs. Tuscon Mus. of Art; pres., 1987; Tucson Pima Arts Council; pres., 1986; founder Tucson Bus. Com. for the Arts, 1986—; bd. dirs. Ariz. Coun. on Econ. Edn., 1986—, Ariz. Sonora Desert Mus. Found. Recipient Best Corp. Mag. award Internat. Assn. Bus. Communicators, 1967, Best Corp. Communications award United Way, 1985. Mem. Am. Electronics Assn. (bd. dirs. 1985—), Ariz. C. of C. (vice chmn. 1985—), Tucson C. of C. (bd. dirs. 1981-88), Ariz. Club (Phoenix), Sigma Delta Chi (bd. dirs. N.Y. Deadline Club 1974-80). Republican. Lutheran. Office: IBM 2850 E Camelback Rd Phoenix AZ 85016

RECKER, ROBERT IGNATIUS, JR., finance company executive; b. Appleton, Wis., Dec. 14, 1941; s. Robert Ignatius and Winifred Vondilla (Dunkel) R.; m. Mary Virginia Lussier, Dec. 19, 1982; children: Michael Bernard, Robert Ignatius III, Richard Anthony. MusB, Lawrence U., 1964; MS in Systems Mgmt., USC, 1976. Commd. 2d lt. USAF, 1964, advanced through grades to capt., 1968, resigned, 1976; stockbroker Dean Witter & Co., Monterey, Calif., 1976-80; trader, floorbroker Pacific Stock Exchange, San Francisco, 1980-85; mng. gen. ptnr. Aequus Assocs., Orinda, Calif., 1985—; v.p. Inst. Personal Econs., Berkeley, Calif., 1987—. Dist. chmn. Boy Scouts of Am., Monterey, 1977-79, dist. commr., San Francisco, 1980-85. Served to col. USAFR 1976-88. Mem. USAF Assn., Nat. Assn. Securities Dealers (arbitrator 1985—), Galbraith Golf Club (Oakland, Calif., pres. 1987—), Kiwanis (bd. dirs. 1986—, pres. elect. 1988—). Office: Aequus Assoc PO Box 480 Orinda CA 94563

RECTOR, JOEL KIRK, lawyer; b. Moberly, Mo., Nov. 6, 1948; s. Hartman Jr. and Constance (Daniel) R.; m. Jannifer Nielsen, Apr. 3, 1972; children: Molly, Constance, Donna. BA, Brigham Young U., 1974, MBA, 1977, JD, 1978; M in Pub. Adminstrn., Harvard U., 1985. Bar: Utah 1978, U.S. Dist. Ct. Utah 1978, Hawaii 1989, U.S. Dist. Ct. Hawaii 1989. Assoc. Beaslin, Nygaard, Coke & Vincent, Salt Lake City, 1978-79, Walker & Hintze, Salt Lake City, 1979-80; pvt. practice Salt Lake City, 1980-87, Kailua-Kona, Hawaii, 1987—. State legislator, Utah Ho. Reps., Salt Lake City, 1981-84, chmn. judiciary com. and speaker of 3d House, 1983-84; co-chmn. Utah Rep. Platform Com., 1983; chmn. Utah Rep. Rules Com., 1984; del. to Rep. Nat. Conv., New Orleans, 1988. Serves as capt. USAR, 1974—. Mem. Utah Gov.'s Club (bd. govs. 1985—). Mormon. Office: 78-6610 Alii Dr Kailua-Kona HI 96740

REDD, MARY LOUISE, marketing executive; b. Mt. Vernon, Wash., Nov. 28, 1961; d. Barry Bruce and Frances Marie (Minerich) D.; m. Leslie Harrison Redd III, June 25, 1988. BBA, Wash. State U., 1985. Mktg. svc. dir. Heart Interface, Kent, Wash., 1986-88; rsch. dir. Hebert Rsch., Bellevue, Wash., 1988—. Democrat. Episcopalian. Home: 2040 Kirkland Pl NE Renton WA 98056

REDDERSEN, BRAD RAWSON, marketing professional; b. Chgo., Aug. 5, 1952; s. John Kernachan and Margaret (Sampson) R. BS in Physics, Harvey Mudd Coll., 1973; MS in Optical Engring., U. Rochester, 1974. Sr. engr. Harris Govt. Systems Group, Palm Bay, Fla., 1974-76, lead engr., 1976-79, group leader, 1979-80; sr. devel. engr. Storage Tech. Corp., Louisville, Colo., 1980-81, sr. sect. mgr., 1981-85; sr. engring. mgr. Spectra-Physics Corp., Eugene, Oreg., 1985-87, product mktg. mgr., 1987--. Patentee optical recording system; contbr. tech. articles to various publs. Recipient Tech. award for optical recording concept NASA, 1980. Mem. Soc. Photo-Optical Instrument Engrs., Am. Mgmt. Assn., Am. Mktg. Assn. Home: 610 Startouch Dr Eugene OR 97405 Office: Spectra Physics Retail Sys 959 Terry St Eugene OR 97405

REDDIEN, CHARLES HENRY, JR., lawyer, business executive, securities financial consultant; b. San Diego, Aug. 27, 1944; s. Charles Henry and Betty Jane (McCormick) R.; m. Paula Gayle, June 16, 1974; 1 child, Tyler Charles. BSEE, U. Colo., Boulder, 1966; MSEE, U. So. Calif., 1968; JD, Loyola U., L.A., 1972. Bar: Calif. 1972, Colo. 1981, U.S. Dist. Ct. 1981. Mgr., Hughes Aircraft Co., 1966-81; pvt. practice, 1972—; owner, broker, real estate brokerage firm, 1978—; mem. spl. staff, co-dir. tax advantage group OTC Net Inc., 1981-82; pres., chmn. Heritage Group Inc., investment banking holding co., 1982-84, Plans and Assistance Inc., mgmt. cons., 1982-83, Orchard Group Ltd., investment banking holding co., 1982-84, J.W. Gant & Assocs., Inc., investment bankers, 1983-84; mng. ptnr., chief exec. officer J.W. Gant & Assocs., Ltd., 1984-85; chmn. bd. Kalamath Group Ltd., 1985-87, Heritage group Ltd. Investment Bankers, 1985-87; dir. Virtusonics Corp., 1985—; v.p., dir. Heritage Fin. Planners Inc., 1982-83; pres., chmn. PDN Inc., 1987-89; pub., exec. v.p., dir. World News Digest Inc., 1987—, Leisurenet Internat'l, Inc., 1988—; chief exec. officer, Somerset Group Ltd., 1988—. Recipient Teaching Internship award, 1964. Mem. Calif. Bar Assn., Nat. Assn. Securities Dealers, IEEE (chmn. U. Colo. chpt. 1965), Am. Inst. Aero. and Astronautical Engrs., Phi Alpha Delta, Tau Beta Pi, Eta Kappa Nu. Contbr. articles to profl. jours. Office: Denver Pl Ste 2760 999 Eighteenth Denver CO 80202

REDDITT, RICHARD WHITSON, transportation executive; b. Santa Barbara, Calif., Nov. 11, 1944; s. Richard Cleveland and Grace Joann (Beavers) R.; m. Patricia Joan Evans, July 7, 1973; children: Michael James, Amy Elizabeth. BS in Indsl. Engring., Ga. Inst. Tech., 1968. Commd. ensign USN, 1968; advanced through grades to commdr. UNSR, 1983, instr. Top Gun Squadron, 1975-78, resigned active duty, 1978; dir. flight ops.-tech. Flying Tigers, Los Angeles, 1987%; capt. USNR, 1989. Author aviation publ.: Many Versus Many, 1977. Advisor Boy Scouts Am., Encinitas, calif., 1986; soccer coach La Costa Youth Orgn., 1987. Mem. Air Superiority Assocs. (sr. v.p., bd. dirs. 1982—), Tailhook Assn., Naval Inst., Airline Pilots Assn. Republican. Home: 2051 Encenico Terr Rancho La Costa CA 92009 Office: Flying Tigers T-200 7401 World Way W Los Angeles CA 90009

REDDY, NAGENDRANATH K., biochemist, researcher; b. Bangalore, India, Nov. 18, 1937; came to U.S., 1968; s. K. Rami and K. (Gnanamma) R.; m. Saraswati K., May 11, 1967; children: Kalpana, Sandip. BS, SRI Venkateswara U., Andhra, India, 1957; MS, U. Saugor, Madhya Pradesh, India, 1959; PhD, Indian Inst. Sci., Bangalore, 1971. Jr. research asst. Nat. Dairy Research Inst., Bangalore, 1959-60; sr. research asst. Indian Inst. Sci., Bangalore, 1965-68; research assoc. Roswell Park Meml. Inst., Buffalo, 1968-73; asst. prof. U. Cin., 1975-80; asst. prof. research biochemistry U. So. Calif., Los Angeles, 1980—. Editor: Fibrinolysis, 1980; contbr. articles to profl. jours. Recipient Research Career Devel. award NIH, 1978. Mem. AAAS, Am. Chem. Soc., Am. Soc. Biol. Chemists, N.Y. Acad. Scis., Internat. Soc. Thrombosis and Haemostasis. Home: 3402 Punta Del Este Hacienda Heights CA 91745 Office: U So Calif 1303 N Mission Rd Los Angeles CA 90033

REDEMANN, ERIC JOHN, systems engineer, consultant; b. Calif., 1952; s. Carl T. and Phyllis S. Redemann. BA in Math., Revelle Coll., U. Calif., San Diego, 1975. With Scripps Inst. Oceanography, La Jolla, Calif., 1972-75, Los Alamos Nat. Lab., 1975-77; project engr. Identronix Inc., Santa Cruz, Calif., 1977-78, Calif. R&D, Culver City, 1979-80; cons., Marina del Rey, Calif., 1980-84; mgr. mfg. engring. Cyberdisk Inc., Anaheim, Calif., 1984-87; cons. Caphren Corp., Laguna Niguel, Calif., 1988—. Mem. IEEE, NSPE, Internat. Platform Assn., Audio Engring. Soc., Assn. Computing Machinery, Soc. Info. Display. Avocations: hiking, swimming, camping. Office: Caphren Corp PO Box 7684 Laguna Niguel CA 92677

REDER, STUART ALLEN, dentist; b. Bklyn., June 22, 1949; s. Max M. and Thelma Dianne (Zelkind) R.; m. Sherri Yvette Stein, June 10, 1984;children: Samuel, Annette, Max. BA in cultural anthrop., U. Calif., San Diego, 1971; DDS, Emory U., 1976. Dentist USPHS, Anchorage, 1977-79; gen. practice dentistry Anchorage, 1979-87; surveillance and utilization review specialist Va. Computer Co., Anchorage, 1988—; forensic cons., Anchorage, 1982-88; chmn. Alaskan Dental Emergency Response Team, 1986-87. Chmn. Rep. Cen. Com., Anchorage, 1982; advt. mgr. Gruenberg for Ho. of Reps., Campaign, 1983. Mem. Southcen. Dental Soc., Alaskan Dental Soc., Am. Acad. Forensic Sci., Am. Acad. Forensic Odontology (cert.). Jewish. Home: 7081 Chad St Anchorage AK 99518

REDMON, BOB GLEN, insurance company executive; b. Snyder, Okla., July 30, 1931; s. Ed Ray and Gertrude (Lett) R.; m. Harriet Ann Nicholas, Mar. 12, 1953; children: Patricia, Pamela, Susanne. Student, Phoenix Coll., 1949-51. Ins. adjuster various ins. cos. L.A., 1953-63; ins. adjuster various ins. cos. Phoenix, 1953-63; branch claims mgr. Western Ins. Cos., Phoenix, 1963-71; pres. B.G. Redmon & Assocs., Inc., Phoenix, 1971—; risk mgmt. cons. Bashas' Markets, Chandler, Ariz., 1976—. Sgt. USAF, 1951-52. Recipient Robert Charles Meml. award Ariz. Pond Blue Goose Internat., 1072. Mem. Inst. Noetic Scis., Ariz. Ins. Claims Assn. (pres. 1961), Self-Insurers Inst. Am., Internat. Found. Employee Benefit Plans, Blue Goose Assn., Early V8 Ford Club Am., Inst. Noetic Scis., Ariz. Club. Home: 8655 N Farview Dr Scottsdale AZ 85258 Office: B G Redmon & Assocs Inc 4041 N Central Ave Ste 533 Phoenix AZ 85012

REDMON, EDWARD JOHN, aerospace company executive; b. Freeport, Ill., Sept. 25, 1914; s. Alexander E. and Mary Mabel (Hines) R.; A.B., UCLA, 1937; M.A., U. So. Calif., 1939; m. Helen Louise Brown, June 1, 1944. Sr. job analyst Lockheed Aircraft, Burbank, Calif., 1940-51, wage and salary adminstr., Marietta, Calif., 1951-53, with Missile Systems Div., 1953-57, mgr. wage and salary adminstrn., head mgmt. compensation, Sunnyvale, Calif., 1957-80; dir. spl. compensation projects Lockheed Corp., 1982-86, cons. in exec. compensation, Burbank, Calif., 1986-87; chmn. fin. policy devel. bd. Fairbanks and Haas Inc., oil, gas and mineral brokers, Ventura, Calif., 1988—. Mem. Western Mgmt. Assn., Calif. Personnel Assn., Electronics Salary and Wage Assn., Electronics Industries Assn., Calif. Salary Adminstrs. Assn., Am. Mgmt. Assn. Republican. Methodist. Contbr. articles in field to profl. jours. Home: 1471 Fallen Leaf Ln Los Altos CA 94022

REDMOND, PAUL ANTHONY, utility executive; b. Lakeview, Oreg., 1937. BSEE, Gonzaga U., 1965. Asst. elec. engr. Wash. Water Power Co., Spokane, 1965-67, maintenance engr., 1967-69, supt. contract constrn., 1969-73, constrn. and maintenance supt., 1973-75, mgr. constrn. and maintenance, 1975-77, asst. to pres., 1977-78, v.p., asst. to pres., 1978-79, sr. v.p. ops., 1979-80, exec. v.p., pres., 1982—, chief operating officer, pres., 1984—, chmn. bd., pres., chief exec. officer, 1985, also bd. dirs.; former pres. Wash. Irrigation & Devel. subs. Wash. Water Power Co., Spokane, now chmn., pres., chief exec. officer, 1985—; bd. dirs. Security Pacific Bank Washington, Spokane Indsl. Park Inc., Limestone Co. Inc., Devel. Assocs. Inc., Pentzer Corp., Water Power Improvement Co., Wash. Irrigation and Devel. Co., Itron Inc. Lt. col. USNG. Office: Wash Water Power Co PO Box 3727 Spokane WA 99220

REDMOND, SCOTT DOUGLAS, corporate consultant, producer; b. Fresno, Calif., Apr. 11, 1954; s. Donald Claire and Jackie (Salisbury) R. BA, San Francisco State U., 1978. Registered profl. optics engr., Calif.; lic. civil investigator. Pres. Redmond Prodns., Inc., San Francisco, 1970—; journalist Baldwinsville Messenger, Syracuse, N.Y., 1972-73; chief exec. officer Events Am. Found., Inc., San Francisco, 1977-79; producer The Lights Sky Shows, San Francisco, 1979, San Francisco Examiner, 1983—; investigator SDR, San Francisco, 1979—; producer, creator world's largest balloon sculpture, San Francisco, 1979, world's largest ribbon and bow bldg. wrap promotion, San Francisco, 1984, world's largest indoor snowstorm, San Francisco, 1986-88, 25 sq. mile light show promotion, 1978, 30 foot valentine 3-dimensional card; producer, designer Royal Fireworks Display Her Majesty Queen Elizabeth II, 1983; producer Footstock, San Francisco's largest single site festival, 1982-89; prodn. mgr. San Francisco Blues Festival, 1986-89; producer, creator The Human Billboard Promotion, San Francisco, 1980; designer, creator Earthstar, L.A., 1983. Author: screenplay Glitter City, 1980. dir. spl. project March of Dimes, Oakland, Calif., 1977; mgr. Ctr. Policy and Responsibility, San Francisco, 1986-88; mayoral undercover investigator City and County of San Francisco, 1987; bd. dirs. Election Equalization, 1986-87. Named in proclamation by mayor of San Francisco, 1979. Mem. Pyrotechnics Guild Internat. (cert.), Nat. Assn. Exposition Mgrs., Am. Film Inst., Internat. Assn. Fairs and Expositions, Am. Inst. Physics, Internat. Coun. Pub. Events (pres. 1987-88), Am. Soc. Indsl. Security, Am. Fedn. Police, Narcotic Enforcement Officers Assn., Illuminating Engrs., Calif. Assn. Lic. Investigators, Optical Soc. Am. Office: Redmond Prodns Inc PO Box 14607 San Francisco CA 94114

REDPATH, JAMES DOUGLAS RANDALL, lawyer; b. Fayetteville, Ark., Feb. 13, 1962; s. James Robert Redpath and Neva (Sutherlan) Pschier; m. Loretha Faye Combs, May 15, 1984. BA in Mgmt. with honors, U. Ark., 1984, JD, 1987. Bar: Ark. 1987, Ariz. 1988. Law clk. Jeff C. Harper, Springdale, Ark., 1986-87, Superior Ct., Phoenix, 1987-88, Maricpoa County Atty.s Office, 1988—. Speaker Superior Ct's. and Maricopa County, Phoenix, 1987—. Freshman Acad. scholar U. Ark., 1980, Waterman Hall Scholar, U. Ark., 1984, E.B. Meriweather scholar U. Ark., 1987, C.R. Warner scholar Ark. Bar Found., 1987. Mem. Ark. Bar Assn., U.S. Tennis Assn., Lions Club. Republican. Baptist. Home: 5202 E Marilyn Scottsdale AZ 85253

REED, ANITA COMTOIS, college official; b. Putnam, Conn., Nov. 2, 1946; d. Lucien Arthur and Flora Anita (Comtois) Comtois; m. Arden Reed (div. 1988); 1 child, Jonathan. BA, Goucher Coll., 1973. Asst. buyer Abraham & Straus, N.Y.C., 1967-68; prodn. dir. Geneal. Pub. Co., Balt., 1971-77; asst. dir. internat. edn. Pomona Coll., Claremont, 1979-81, dir. found. and corp. relations, 1981--. Vol., mem. allocations com. Mt. Baldy Region United Way, Ontario, Calif., 1987--. Mem. Council for Advancement and Support Edn. (treas., bd. dirs. dist. VII 1987--). Democrat. Office: Pomona Coll Sumner Hall Claremont CA 91711

REED, DIANE MARIE, psychologist; b. Joplin, Mo., Jan. 11, 1934; d. William Marion and Olive Francis (Smith) Kinney; married; children: Wendy Robison, Douglas Funkhouser. Student, Art Ctr. Col., Pasadena, Calif., 1951-54; BS, U. Oreg., 1976, MS, 1977, PhD, 1981. Lic. psychologist. Illustrator J.L. Hudson Co., Detroit, 1954-56; designer, stylist N.Y.C., 1960-70; designer, owner Decor To You, Inc., Stamford, Conn., 1970-76; founder, exec. dir. Alcohol Counseling and Edn. Svcs., Inc., Eugene, Oreg., 1981-86, clin. supr., 1986; clin. supr. Christian Family Svcs., Eugene, 1986-87; pvt. practice Eugene, 1985—. Evaluator Vocat. Rehab. Div., Eugene, 1982—; alcohol and drug evaluator and commitment examiner Oreg. Mental Health Div., 1981-86. Mem. Am. Psychol. Assn., Oreg. Psychol. Assn., Lane County Psychol. Assn. (pres. 1989—), Alcohol and Drug Profls. Assn., C2 Investors (treas. 1987-88), Altair Ski and Sport, Oreg. Track. Republican. Office: 630 E 13th Ave Ste 200 Eugene OR 97401

REED, EDWARD CORNELIUS, JR., federal judge; b. Mason, Nev., July 8, 1924; s. Edward Cornelius Sr. and Evelyn (Walker) R.; m. Sally Torrance, July 14, 1952; children: Edward T., William W., John A., Mary E. BA, U. Nev.; JD, Harvard U. Atty. Arthur Andersen & Co., 1952-53; spl. dep. atty. gen. State of Nev., 1967-69; judge U.S. Dist. Ct. Nev., Reno, 1979—, now chief judge. Former vol. atty. Girl Scouts Am., Sierra Nevada Council, U. Nev., Nev. Agrl. Found., Nev. State Sch. Adminstrs. Assn., Nev. Congress of Parents and Teachers; mem. Washoe County Sch. Bd., 1956-72, pres. 1959, 63, 69; chmn. Gov.'s Sch. Survey Com., 1958-61; mem. Washoe County Bd. Tax Equalization, 1957-58, Washoe County Annexation Commn., 1968-72, Washoe County Personnel Com., 1973-77, chmn. 1973; mem. citizens adv. com. Washoe County Sch. Bond Issue, 1977-78, Sun Valley, Nev., Swimming Pool Com., 1978, Washoe County Blue Ribbon Task Force Com. on Growth, Nev. PTA (life); chmn. profl. div. United Way, 1978; bd. dirs. Reno Siver Sox, 1962-65. Served as staff sgt. U.S. Army, 1943-46, ETO, PTO. Mem. ABA (jud. adminstrn. sect.), Nev. State Bar Assn. (adminstrv. com. dist. 5, 1967-79, lien law com. 1965-78, chmn. 1965-72, probate law com. 1963-66, tax law com. 1962-65), Am. Judicature Soc. Democrat. Baptist. Office: US Dist Ct 5147 US Courthouse 300 Booth St Reno NV 89509 *

REED, FRANK FREMONT, II, lawyer; b. Chgo., June 15, 1928; s. Allen Martin and Frances (Faurot) R.; student Chgo. Latin Sch.; grad. St. Paul's Sch., 1946; A.B., U. Mich., 1952, J.D., 1957; m. Jaquelin Silverthorne Cox, April 27, 1963; children—Elizabeth Matthiessen Mason, Laurie Matthiessen Stern, Mark Matthiessen, Jeffrey, Nancy, Sarah. Admitted to Ill. bar, 1958; asso. Byron, Hume, Groen & Clement, 1958-61, Marks & Clerk, 1961-63; individual practice, Chgo., 1963-78; dir. Western Acadia (Western Felt Works), 1960-75, chmn. exec. com., 1969-71. Republican precinct capt. 1972-78; candidate for 43d ward alderman, 1975; bd. dirs., sec. Chgo. Found. Theater Arts, 1959-64; vestryman St. Chrysostom's Ch., 1975-79, mem. ushers guild, 1964-79, chmn., 1976-78; bd. dirs. North State, Astor, Lake Shore Dr. Assn., 1975-78, pres. 1977-78; bd. dirs. Community Arts Music Assn. of Santa Barbara, 1984—, treas. 1988—; bd. dirs. Santa Barbara Arts Coun., 1987—. Served to cpl. AUS, 1952-54. Mem. ABA, Ill. Bar Assn., Phi Alpha Delta, Racquet Club, Wausaukee Club (sec., dir. 1968-71) (Chgo.); Birnam Wood Golf Club (Santa Barbara, Calif.). Episcopalian. Author: History of the Silverthorn Family, 4 vols., 1982, Allen Family of Allen's Grove, 1983, Goddard and Ware Ancestors, 1987, Faurot Family, 1988. Contbr. articles to The Am. Genealogist, 1972-73, 76-77. Home: 1944 E Valley Rd Santa Barbara CA 93108

REED, FRANK METCALF, banker; b. Seattle, Dec. 22, 1912; s. Frank Ivan and Pauline B. (Hovey) R.; student U. Alaska, 1931-32; B.A., U. Wash., 1937; m. Maxine Vivian McGary, June 11, 1937; children—Pauline Reed Mackay), Frank Metcalf. Vice pres. Anchorage Light & Power Co., 1937-42; pres. Alaska Electric & Equipment Co., Anchorage, 1946-50; sec., mgr. Turnagain, Inc., Anchorage, 1950-56; mgr. Gen. Credit Corp., Anchorage, 1957; br. mgr. Alaska SBA, Anchorage, 1958-60; sr. v.p. First Interstate Bank of Alaska, Anchorage, 1960-87, also dir., corp. sec.; dir. First Interstate Corp. of Alaska, pres., dir. Anchorage Broadcasters, Inc.; past pres., chmn. Microfast Software Corp.; ptnr. R.M.R. Co.; dir. Anchorage Light & Power Co., Turnagain, Inc., Alaska Fish and Farm, Inc., Life Ins. Co. Alaska, Alaska Hotel Properties, Spa Inc. Pres., Anchorage Federated Charities, Inc., 1953-54; mem. advisory bd. Salvation Army, 1948-58; mem. Alaska adv. bd. Hugh O'Brian Youth Found., 1987—; trustee Anchor Age Endowment Fund, 1988—; mem. City of Anchorage Planning Commn., 1956; mem. City of Anchorage Council, 1956-57; police commr. Ter. of Alaska, 1957-58; chmn. City Charter Commn., 1958; mem. exec. com. Greater Anchorage, Inc., 1955-65; pres. Sch. Bd., 1961-64; mem. Gov.'s Investment adv. com., 1970-72; mem. Alaska State Bd. Edn.; mem. citizens adv. com. Alaska Meth. U.; chmn. Anchorage Charter Commn., 1975; chmn. bldg. fund dr. Community YMCA, 1976—; bd. dirs., mem. exec. com. Arts Alaska, 1976-78; sec.-treas. Breakthrough, 1976-78; bd. dirs. Anchorage Civic Opera, 1978, Rural Venture Alaska, Inc.; bd. dirs Alaska Treatment Ctr., 1980-87, pres. 1985-86; trustee Marston Found., Inc., 1978, exec. dir. 1988. Served as lt. USNR, 1942-46. Elected to Hall Fame, Alaska Press Club, 1969; named Outstanding Alaskan of Year Alaska C. of C., 1976; recipient Community Service award YMCA, 1975-78. Mem. Am. Inst. Banking, Am. (exec. council 1971-72) Alaska (pres. 1970-71) bankers assns., Nat. Assn. State Bds. Edn. (sec.-treas. 1969-70), C. of C. U.S. (Western region legislative com.), Anchorage C. of C. (pres. 1966-67, dir.), Pioneers of Alaska, Navy League (pres. Anchorage council 1961-62). Clubs: Tower (life), San Francisco Tennis. Lodges: Lions (sec. Anchorage, 1953-54, dir. 1988, pres., 1962-63), Elks. Home: 1361 W 12th Ave Anchorage AK 99501

REED, FREDRIC DARELL, lawyer; b. Seattle, Sept. 24, 1947; s. Erling Reed; m. Tana West, Jan. 20, 1985. BA in Bus. Adminstn., U. Wash., 1969, JD, 1972. Bar: Wash. 1972, U.S. Dist. Ct. (we. dist.) Wash. 1972, U.S. Ct. appeals (9th cir.) 1982. Ptnr. Maltman, Weber, Reed, North & Ahrens, Seattle, 1972—. Mem. Wash. State Bar Assn., Wash. State Trial Lawyers Assn., Club Chivas (pres. 1988-89). Office: Maltman Reed North et al 1415 Norton Bldg Seattle WA 98104

REED, GEORGE FORD, JR., investment executive; b. Hollywood, Calif., Dec. 26, 1946; s. George Ford and Mary Anita Reed; B.A. in Econs. with honors, U. So. Calif., 1969, M.A., 1971; m. Kathryn Nixon, 1981. Analyst planning and research Larwin Group, Beverly Hills, Calif., 1971-72; with Automobile Club So. Calif., Los Angeles, 1972—, supr. mgmt. info., research and devel., 1973-74, mgr. fin. and market analysis, 1975-81, group mgr. fin. analysis and forecasting, 1981-86; pres. Reed Asset Mgmt. Co., Inc., Los Angeles, 1986—; instr. bus. and econs. Los Angeles Community Coll. Mem. population task force Los Angeles C. of C., 1974—; mem. Gov. Calif. Statewide Econ. Summit Conf., 1974. Served with U.S. Army, 1969. Mem. Assn. Corp. Real Estate Execs., Nat. Assn. Bus. Economists, Western Regional Sci. Assn., Am. Mgmt. Assn., Am. Fin. Assn., So. Calif. Planners Assn., Rotary Internat., Omicron Delta Epsilon. Home: 1001 S Westgate Ave Los Angeles CA 90049 Office: 10960 Wilshire Blvd Ste 2200 Los Angeles CA 90024

REED, GREGORY WILLIAM, broadcasting executive; b. Oakland, Calif., Mar. 6, 1943; s. William Andker and Guinevere Kathleen (Klint) R.; children: Stephen Gregory, Christian Andker; m. Leann Chambers. B.S., U. Oreg., 1966, M.S., 1969. Asst. dean men U. Oreg., 1966-69; trainee Procter & Gamble Co., 1969-70; rep. Radio 1, Pacific & So. Broadcasting Co., Los Angeles, 1970-71; account exec. Sta. KABC, Los Angeles, 1971-72; with Golden West Broadcasting, 1974—; gen. sales mgr. Sta. KSFO, San Francisco, 1978-79; corp. v.p., gen. mgr. Sta. KEX-AM, Portland, Oreg., 1979-82, Sta. KSFC, San Francisco, 1982-83; pres., chief exec. officer Media Sports Inc., San Francisco, 1983—; exec. v.p. Focus Mgmt. Co., San Francisco, 1982-83, Henry Broadcasting Co., San Francisco, 1986—. Bd. dirs. Portland Goodwill Industries, Portland Jr. Achievement, Portland Urban League. Recipient various public service awards. Mem. Nat. Assn. Broadcasters, Oreg. Assn. Broadcasters, Greater Portland Radio Broadcasters Assn. (v.p. 1981-82), No. Calif. Broadcast Assn. (bd. dirs. 1982-83), Portland Advt. Fedn., Sigma Alpha Epsilon, Kappa Tau Alpha. Methodist. Office: KYTE 2040 SW 1st St Portland OR 97201

REED, HARRY WENDEL, real estate executive; b. Kansas City, Mo., Nov. 24, 1933; s. Fred W. and Alma Rosa (Mewius) R.; m. Margie Hoffman, Aug. 4, 1954; children: Terri Lee, Ida Sue, Harry W. II, John Carl, Ronald Wayne. AA in Elec. Engring., San Bernardino Coll., 1967; cert. in para legal, Chapman Coll., 1984; student, Coll. Appraisal, 1988. Gen. supt. Scheidts Elec., San Jose, Calif., 1968-79; installer cen. office equipment Gen. Telephone, Palm Springs, Calif., 1979—. With USN, 1952-58, Korea. Mem. Am. Soc. Profl. Appraisers, Am. Legion, DAV Club, Palm Springs Club, Desert Hot Springs Club,Elks. Republican. Home: PO Box 776 Desert Hot Springs CA 92240 Office: Gen Telephone 15 Redlands Pla Redlands CA 92373

REED, HENRY EDWARD, geologist; b. Maplewood, N.J., Sept. 21, 1927; s. Henry E. and Hazel Holland (Hogan) R.; m. Mary French Hischier, Jan. 11, 1952; children: Thomas E., John F., Polly A., James N. BS, Williams Coll., 1950. With Century Geophys. Corp., various locations, 1951; geologist Amerada Petroleum Corp., Williston, N.D., 1951-52, Gt. No. Ry., Williston, 1952-65; asst. dir., mgr. Gt. No. Ry., Seattle, 1965-73; dir. indsl. minerals Burlington No., Billings, Mont., 1973-78, asst. v.p., 1980-81; dir. BurWest, Billings, 1978-80; asst. v.p. Meridian Minerals Co., Billings, 1981-85; ind. cons. geologist Billings, 1986—; mem. adv. com., Mont. Bur. Mines and Geology, Butte, 1981-85; bd. dirs. Mont. Coal Coun., Helena, 1980-86. Contbr. articles to profl. publs. Elder 1st Presbyn. Ch., Williston, N.D. and Bellevue, Wash., 1960-69. With U.S. Army, 1946-47, Korea. Mem. AIME (past chmn. Pacific sect.), Northwest Mining Assn. (past trustee), Mont. Coal Coun., Mont. Geol. Soc., Williston C. of C., Seattle C. of C., Yellowstone Country Club, Billings YMCA. Republican. Home: 3121 McBride St Billings MT 59102 Office: 3203 3d Ave N Room 306 Billings MT 59101

REED, JAMES ANTHONY, travel industry consultant; b. Marion, Ohio, June 12, 1939; s. James E. and Sue (McCurdy) R.; m. Ann M. O'Carroll, July 30, 1988. Student, Fla. State U., U. N.H. Food and beverage mgr. Caneel Bay Plantation, St. John, Virgin Islands, 1960-64; mgr. Mauna Kea Beach Hotel, Kamuela, Hawaii, 1964-72; v.p. C. Brewer & Co., Ltd., Honolulu, 1972-77, Dunfey Hotel Corp., Hampton, N.H., 1977-80, Marriott Hotels & Resorts, Costa Mesa, Calif., 1980-89; pres., dir. The Reed Group, Irvine, Calif., 1989—; pres. Kilauea Volcano House, Inc., MacKensie Hawaii, Ltd. Named Outstanding Young Men of Am., 1969. Mem. Calif. Thoroughbred Breeders Assn., Calif. Hotel Assn., Appaloosa Horse Club. Home: 78 Havenwood Irvine CA 92714 Office: The Reed Group 78 Havenwood Irvine CA 92714

REED, JOHN CHARLES, physician; b. San Francisco, Nov. 23, 1944; s. Charles Palmer and Martha Jane (Rice) R.; m. Carla Oswald, June 20, 1970; children: Rachel, Alexa, Shawna, Matthew. AB, Bucknell U., 1966; MD, U. Pa., 1970. Diplomate Am. Bd. Family Practice. Med. officer, dir. field health unit USPHS Sells (Ariz.) Svc., 1970-74; physician, dept. chief, health maintenance assocs. CIGNA Health Plan, Phoenix, 1980-81; med. dir. Habilation Assoc. P.C., Phoenix, 1982—; cons. Nat. Com. for Quality Assurance, Washington, 1980-83; pres. Ariz. Bd. Homeopathic Med. Examiners, Phoenix, 1987—. Facilitator Inst. of Cultural Affairs, Town Meeting Ariz., N.Mex., Wash., Ga., 1975-77. Mem. Am. Acad. Med. Dirs., Am. Inst. Homepathy, Am. Holistic Med. Assn. (founder), Am. Assn. Orthopedic Med. (charter), Am. Acad. Med. Acupuncture (v.p., founder), Phi Beta Kappa. Office: Pain & Stress Recovery Ctr 4538 N 40th St Phoenix AZ 85018

REED, JOHN THEODORE, publisher, writer; b. Camden, N.J., July 5, 1946; s. Theodore and Marion Theresa (Simonsick) R.; m. Margaret Ogden Tunnell, May 31, 1975; children: Daniel Tunnell, Steven Tunnell, Michael Tunnell. BS in Mil. Sci., U.S. Mil. Acad., West Point, N.Y., 1968; MBA, Harvard U., 1977. Salesman Pritchett & Co., Pine Hill and Collingswood, N.J., 1972-74; property mgr. Fox & Lazo Inc., Cherry Hill, N.J., 1974-75; writer Harcourt Brace Jovanovich, Boston, 1976-86; bank exec. Crocker Nat. Bank, San Francisco, 1977-78; writer, pub. Danville, Calif., 1977—. Author, pub.: Apartment Investing Check Lists, 1978, Aggressive Tax Avoidance for Real Estate Investors, 1981, 8th edit. 1988, How to Manage Residential Property for Maximum Cash Flow and Resale Value, 1985, How to Use Leverage to Maximize Your Real Estate Investment Return, 1984, 86, How to Increase the Value of Real Estate, 1986, Office Building Acquisition Handbook, 1982, 85, 87, John T. Reed's Real Estate Investor's Monthly Newsletter, 1986—. Served to 1st lt. U.S. Army, 1968-72, Vietnam. Mem. Author's Guild, Nat. Assn. Real Estate Editors, Nat. Apt. Assn. Club: Round Hill Country, Alamo, Calif. Home: 342 Bryan Dr Danville CA 94526 Office: Reed Pub Co 342 Bryan Dr Danville CA 94526

REED, NANCY JEAN, nurse; b. La Jolla, Calif., Nov. 5, 1954; d. Albert Frank Bossert and Dian Arlene (Simmons) Carlson; m. Mark William Reed, Aug. 23, 1980 (div. 1982); m. Gerald Anthony Ferrera, Mar. 27, 1983. AA, Palomar Community Coll., 1978. RN, Calif.; cert. critical care nurse, Calif. Staff nurse Palomar Community Coll., Escondido, Calif., 1978-79, Pioneers Hosp., Brawley, Calif., 1979-80, Scripps Meml. Hosp., Encinitas, Calif., 1981-84, Staff Builders, San Diego, 1980-81, 86--; med. litigation support specialist Gray, Cary, Ames & Frye, San Diego, 1984-87; pvt. practice, Leucadia, Calif., 1987--. Creator, co-chmn. Friends of Leucadia, 1984--; candidate for Encinitas City Coun., 1986; active Leucadia Community Adv. Bd., 1987--, Encinitas Planning Commn., 1987--. Named Mover, Shaker and Doer, Citizen newspaper, Solana Beach, Calif., 1986. Mem. Am. Assn. Critical Care Nurses, San Diego Assn. Med. and Legal Nurse Cons. (v.p. 1987--). Democrat. Home: 1653 Hygeia Ave Leucadia CA 92024 Office: Harris & Barry 101 W Broadway Ste 1420 San Diego CA 92101

REED, NORMAN BRUCE, real estate developer; b. Long Beach, Calif., Jan. 15, 1949; s. Eugene Cameron and Lorine Vivian (Gross) R. BS, U. So. Calif., 1971, postgrad., 1974-76. Chpt. mgmt. cons. Sigma Nu Fraternity, Lexington, Va., 1971-73; redevel. project mgr. City of Long Beach, 1973-78; project mgr. and cons. various cos., Long Beach, 1978-84; sales and mktg. dir. Island Resorts Catalina, Inc., Long Beach, 1984-87; loan and investment agt. Calif. Western Fin. Corp., Los Alalmitos, Calif., 1987-88; asst. v.p. comml. and indsl. div. Chicago Title, Pasadena, Calif., 1988—; lectr. redevel. Calif. State U., Long Beach, 1977-79, Long Beach City Coll., 1977-79. Bd. dirs. Grand Prix Com of 300, Long Beach, 1975—, Pub. Corp. for the Arts, Long Beach, 1982-88, Cedar House Child Abuse Prevention Ctr., Long Beach, 1982-83; chmn. Long Beach Centennial Internat. Festival, 1988. Named Nat. Man of Yr., 1971. Mem. Long Beach Jr. C. of C. (recipient Disting. Service award), Long Beach Area C. of C. (bd. dirs. 1980-81), Long Beach Dist. Bd. of Realtors, Long Beach Conv. and Visitors Council (mktg. com. mem. 1984-86), Long Beach Jaycees (officer 1973-83), Sigma Nu. (officer 1968-71). Democrat. Presbyterian. Home: 9314 N Marina Pacifica Dr Long Beach CA 90803 Office: Chicago Title 3280 E Foothill Blvd Pasadena CA 91107

REED, ROBERT GEORGE, III, petroleum company executive; b. Cambridge, Mass., Aug. 9, 1927; s. Robert George and Marjorie B. Reed; m. Maggie L. Fisher, Mar. 22, 1974; children: Sandra McNickle, Valerie Sloan, Jonathan J., John-Paul. BA in Econs., Dartmouth Coll., 1949; AMP, Harvard U., 1970. Mktg. mgr. Tidewater Oil subs. Getty Oil Co., Los Angeles, 1957-64; v.p. mktg. Cities Service Oil Co., Tulsa, 1964-72; exec. v.p. Tesoro Petroleum Corp., San Antonio, 1972-79; chmn. bd., chief exec. officer Clark Oil & Refining Corp., Milw., 1979-81, pres., chief exec. officer div. Apex Oil Co., St. Louis, 1981-85; chmn. bd., chief exec. officer Energy Sources Exchange, Inc., Houston, 1981—; chmn., pres., chief exec. officer Pacific Resources, Inc., Honolulu, 1985—; bd. dirs. Alexander and Baldwin, Inc., Honolulu, First Hawaiian Bank, Hawaiian Telephone Co. Active Aloha United Way. Served with USN, 1945-46. Mem. Am. Petroleum Inst., Nat. Petroleum Refiners Assn., Nat. Petroleum Council, Hawaii C. of C. Clubs: Pacific, Plaza, Waialae Country, Plaza. Office: Pacific Resources Inc 733 Bishop St PO Box 3379 Honolulu HI 96842

REED, RONALD DEAN, environmental, safety and health manager; b. Palo Alto, Calif., Mar. 8, 1950; s. Verlin Dean and Anita May (Wilson) R.; m. Sophie Judy Wells, Mar. 22, 1979. AA in Chemistry, Foothill Coll., Los Altos Hills, Calif., 1971; BS in Chem. Engring., U. Calif., Berkeley, 1973. Process engr. Pfizer, Inc., Emeryville, Calif., 1974-75; chem. engr. Firestone Tire and Rubber Co., Salinas, Calif., 1975-76, Calif. Cir. Engring., Sunnyvale, Calif., 1976; staff cons. Statewide Tech. and Cutter Labs., San Francisco, San Jose and Berkeley, Calif., 1976-77; pub. health engr. Accident Prevention div. State of Oreg., Portland, 1977-80; safety engr. Tenn. Valley Authority, Chatanooga, 1980-82; chem. engr. Tenn. Valley Authority, Knoxville, Tenn., 1982-83; safety engr. Savannah River ops. office U.S. Dept. of Energy, Aiken, S.C., 1983-86; chief safety and environ. br. Rocky Flats area office U.S. Dept. of Energy, Golden, Colo., 1986—; mem. accident investigators team TVA Crane Accident, Paducah, Ky., 1981, Savannah River Trucker Fatality, Aiken, 1984-85, Savannah River Helicopter Accident, Aiken, 1985, team mem. tech. safety appraisal Dept. of Energy, Fernald, Ohio, 1986. Rep. State of Oreg. Employees Assn., Portland, 1979. Mem. Am. Conf. of Govtl. Indsl. Hygienists, Nat. Fire Protection Assn., Mensa. Republican. Office: US Dept Energy Rocky Flats Area Office PO box 928 Golden CO 80402-0928

REEDER, F. ROBERT, lawyer; b. Brigham City, Utah, Jan. 23, 1943; s. Frank O. and Helen H. (Heninger) R.; m. Joannie Anderson, May 4, 1974; children—David, Kristina, Adam. J.D., U. Utah, 1967. Bar: Utah 1967, U.S. Ct. Appeals (10th cir.) 1967, U.S. Ct. Mil. Appeals 1968, U.S. Supreme Ct. 1972, U.S. Ct. Appeals (D.C. and 5th cirs.) 1979. Shareholder, officer Parsons, Behle & Latimer, Salt Lake City, 1968—, bd. dirs., 1974—. Bd. dirs., chmn. Holy Cross Hosp. Found, 1979—, treas., 1986-87, chmn., 1987—. Served with U.S. Army, 1967-68. Mem. ABA, Utah State Bar, Salt Lake County Bar, Cottonwood Country Club (pres. local chpt. 1981-82, bd. dirs. 1979-82, 83-86). Office: Parsons Behle & Latimer PO Box 11898 Salt Lake City UT 84147

REEDER, MICHAEL DAVID, engineer; b. Houston, Sept. 3, 1949; s. Joseph Russell and Mary Marguerite (Kettrick) R.; m. Anna Lillian Duffy Patterson, Sept. 1976 (div. 1980); m. Linda Gale Moore, Nov. 29, 1985; children: Austin Glen Jordan, Judith Lauren. BS, U.S. Mil. Acad., 1972; MA in Econs., Fin., U. Tex., El Paso, 1986. Commd. 2d lt. U.S. Army, 1972, advanced through grades to capt., resigned, 1977; pres., owner El Paso Auto Photo, 1977-80; sr. quantitative bus. analyst Northrop Aircraft, El Segundo, Calif., 1981-82; mgr. mktg. Gen. Dynamics, San Diego, 1985-87; system engr., mgr. program devel. Rockwell Internat., Downey, Calif., 1982-85; chief project engr., mgr. program devel. Rockwell Internat., Downey, 1987—. Fellow Inst. Advancement Engring.; mem. Nat. Space Soc., AIAA, Life Extension Found. Republican. Jewish. Home: 2133 Citron St La Habra Heights CA 90631 Office: Rockwell Internat 12214 Lakewood St Downey CA 90241

REEDER, VIRGINIA LEE (VIRGINIA LEE FOSTER), educator; b. Tuskahoma, Okla., Jan. 25, 1929; d. Clarence William and Alice (King) Foster; m. Walter Lee Reeder, July 24, 1950; children: Ralph Wesley, Alice Jean. BA, U. Redlands, 1974; MS, Pepperdine U., 1976. Elem. tchr. Harbor City Pub. Schs., 1960-61, First Bapt. Sch., Compton, Calif., 1961-64, Compton Unified Sch., 1980—; head start tchr. Compton Community Youth Ctr., Compton, 1964-76, Charles R. Drew Sch., Compton, 1976-80; tchr. early childhood edn. Compton Coll., 1974-80; tchr. 3d grade gifted program Compton Unified Schs., 1980—. Democrat. Baptist. Home: 11919 E 161st St Norwalk CA 90650

REENAN, DEBORAH ELLEN, stockbroker; b. Cin., Apr. 8, 1951; d. Joseph John and LaVerne Roberta (Kroeger) R.; m. Michael Joseph Norris, Dec. 9, 1983. BBA, U. Cin., 1974, MBA, 1978. Sales rep. Ralston Purina, Cin., 1974-78; dist. mgr. Bell & Howell, Boston, 1979-81; account exec. IFG Leasing, Denver, 1981-82; regional mktg. mgr. Uniwest Leasing, Denver, 1983-84; stockbroker Paine Webber Inc., Denver, 1984-85; regional mktg. mgr. AEI, Inc., Denver, 1986-87; stockbroker Hanifen Imhoff Inc., Denver, 1987—. Roman Catholic. Office: Hanifen Imhoff 1125 17th St #1700 Denver CO 80202

REES, GROVER JOSEPH, III, judge; b. New Orleans, Oct. 11, 1951; s. Grover Joseph and Patricia (Byrne) R.; 1 child, Grover Joseph. B.A., Yale U., New Haven, 1975; J.D., La. State U., Baton Rouge, 1978. Bar: La. 1978, U.S. Supreme Ct. 1982. Asst. prof. law U. Tex., Austin, 1979-86; spl. asst. to Atty. Gen. U.S. Dept. Justice, Washington, 1985, spl. counsel judicial selection, 1985-86; chief justice High Ct. Am. Samoa, Pago Pago, 1986-88, assoc. justice, 1988—. Editor-in-Chief: La. Law Rev., 1977-78. Justice of Peace, New Haven, 1973-75. Mem. Order of Coif. Republican. Roman Catholic. Home: Tafuna Tutuila Island AS 96799 Office: High Ct Am Samoa Pago Pago AS 96799

REES, LANE CHARLES, industrial relations consultant; b. Longview, Tex., June 23, 1951; s. Holly Elias and Charlene Elizabeth (Quin) R.; m. Brenda Faye Anderson, July 1, 1978; children: Brian Andrew, Lauren Catherine. BBA in Mgmt. magna cum laude, Tex. A&M U., 1973, MEd in Ednl. Adminstrn., 1978. Personnel rep. Tex. A&M U., College Sta., 1973-77; v.p. Brazos Gen. Svcs., Bryan, Tex., 1977-78; successively personnel office supr., wage and salary administrator, employee relations rep., sr. employee relations rep. ARCO, various cities, Tex., 1979-83; from sr. employee relations rep. to employee relations dir. ARCO, Anchorage and Kuparuk, Alaska, 1983-87; dir. employee relations ARCO, Prudhoe Bay, Alaska, 1987—; ptnr. Rees and Assocs., Anchorage and Tex., 1978—. Mem. editorial staff (jour.) Conference Leadership, 1978. Precinct committeeman Rep. Party of Alaska, Anchorage, 1988—; mem., com. sec. United Meth. Communication Commn., Nashville, 1988—; evangelism chmn., mem. adv. council St. John United Meth. Ch., Anchorage, 1986—; trustee Nat. Found. Evangelism, Lake Junaluska, N.C., 1988—. Mem. Acad. Mgmt., Tex. A&M U. Assn. of Former Students (nat. councilman 1987—), Am. Numismatic Assn., Phi Eta Sigma, Phi Kappa Phi, Sigma Iota Epsilon (pres. 1972-73), Ala. Soc. of SAR (pres. 1989—, alt. trustee Nat. Soc., Silver Good Citizenship award 1989), So Beta Gamma Sigma. Home: 2430 Nancy Circle Anchorage AK 99516 Office: ARCO Alaska Inc PO Box 100360 Anchorage AK 99510-0360

REES, RICHARD DEE, psychologist, educator; b. Ogden, Utah, Aug. 3, 1939; s. Dee L. and Bertha May (Burnett) R.; m. Teresa Lee Taylor; children: David Richard, Carol Lee, Kenneth Dee, Donna Marie. BS, Utah State U., 1961; MS, Brigham Young U., 1963, EdD, 1968. Cert. psychologist Ariz. Tchr. English Ogden High Sch., 1961-62; instr. psychology Northeastern Jr. Coll., Sterling, Colo., 1963-64, Brigham Young U., Provo, 1964-65; counselor, asst. prof. psychology Utah State U., 1968-69; instr. psychology Glendale (Ariz.) Community Coll., 1965-67, prof. psychology, 1969—, chmn. dept., 1969-77, 81-85; vis. prof. ednl. psychology Brigham Young U., 1974, 75, 85-88. Contbr. articles to profl. jours. Grad. fellow Brigham Young U., 1967-68. Mem. Am. Psychol. Assn. Office: 6000 W Olive Ave Glendale AZ 85302

REES, WILLIAM SMITH, JR., chemistry educator; b. Quanah, Tex., Nov. 2, 1959; s. William Smith Sr. and Gertrude (Lunsford) R.; m. Phyllis Ann Waite, June 14, 1986. BS, Tex. Tech U., 1980; student, Palais Kinsky, Vienna, Austria, 1980; PhD, UCLA, 1986. Research chemist Cosden Chem. Co., Big Spring, Tex., 1981; grad. fellow UCLA, 1981-86; cons. 1984—;

postdoctoral fellow MIT, Cambridge, 1986—; vis. instr. UCLA, 1983; teaching asst. cons. office instructional devel., UCLA, 1982-83; instr. UCLA Extension, 1982-83. Co-author: Synthetic Methods in Inorganic Chemistry, 1988; contbr. articles to profl. jours.; patentee in field. Vol. Big Bros. Greater Los Angeles, 1981-86. Grantee NRC, 1985, UCLA Grad. div., 1984; Univ. scholar, 1977. Mem. AAAS, Am. Chem. Soc., N.Y. Acad. Scis., Am. Inst. Chemists, Internat. Union Pure and Applied Chemistry, Internat. Platform Assn., Future Farmers Am., Am. Ceramic Soc., Grad. Students Assn., Materials Research Soc., Nat. Geographic Soc., Smithsonian Soc., Sigma Xi, Phi Eta Sigma. Republican.

REESE, LOWELL D., association executive; b. Pikeville, Ky., Mar. 12, 1940; s. Palmer R. and Ollie (Rose) R.; m. Carol Rowe, Dec. 26, 1970; 1 stepson, Tracy Lee Huffman. B.A., Berea Coll., 1963. Mktg. rep. Mobil Oil Corp., East Orange, N.J., 1967-68; chief Ky. Bur. Child Devel., Frankfort, 1969-70; exec. dir. Our Common Heritage, Lexington, Ky., 1970-71; v.p. govtl. affair Ky. C. of C., Frankfort, 1972-79; exec. v.p. S.C. C. of C., Columbia, 1979-86; pres. Ariz. C. of C., Phoenix, 1987—. Exec. dir. Pres. Ford election campaign, 1976. Served to 1st lt. U.S. Army, 1963-67, Vietnam. Decorated Purple Heart, Bronze Star, Air medal, others. Mem. Ariz. C. of C. (exec. assns.), Ariz. Econ. Forum, Cen. Ariz. Water Project Assn. Home: 5975 E Orange Blossom Ln Phoenix AZ 85018 Office: Ariz C of C 1366 E Thomas Rd Ste 202 Phoenix AZ 85014

REESE, ROBERT JENKINS, senator, lawyer; b. Green River, Wyo., June 2, 1947; s. William David and Elsa Edith (Bluhm) R.; m. Karen Lee Thompson, Nov. 27, 1971 (div. Dec. 1984); 1 child, William Derek; m. Mary Lynn Cockriel, Dec. 24, 1986, 1 child, Tyler Eric; stepchildren: Kelley Aldra Cockriel, Meagan Mary Cockriel. BA, Harvard U., 1969; JD, U. Wyo., 1978. Bar: Wyo. 1978, U.S. Dist. Ct. Wyo. 1978, U.S. Ct. Appeals (10th cir.) 1984. Tchr. Stratford Jr. High Sch., Arlington, Va., 1971-75; dep. county atty. Sweetwater County, Green River, Wyo., 1978-82; pvt. practice Green River, 1983-86; ptnr. Reese, Mathey & Schofield, Green River, 1986—. Dem. chmn. Sweetwater County, Green River, 1983-85; senator Wyo. State, Cheyenne, Wyo., 1985—; mem. Nat. Conf. State Legislators, law and justice com., internat. trade com. Mem. Wyo. Trial Lawyers Assn. (health and edn. com., edn., health and welfare com., minerals, bus. and econ. devel. com., rules and procedures com., bd. dirs. 1985-86), Green River C. of C. (bd. dirs. 1984-86), Sweetwater County Bar Assn. (pres. 1985-86). Democrat. Office: Reese Mathey & Schofield PO Box 1060 Green River WY 82935

REESE, WILLIAM GRIFFITH, III, transportation executive, consultant; b. Palo Alto, Calif., Sept. 18, 1947; s. William G. Reese Jr. and Virginia (Bolt) R.; m. Barbara E. Neal, May 7, 1970 (div. 1977); m. Nancy Jenkins; 1 child, William Griffith IV. BA in History, Parsons Coll. Asst. mgr. Roadway Express, Greenville, S.C., 1970-75; team mgr. sales Watkins Motor Lines, Charlotte, S.C., 1975-80; founder, chief exec. officer Am. Way Transport, Los Angeles, 1980—. Served to 1st lt. U.S. Army, 1967-70. Republican. Presbyterian. Lodge: Rotary.

REESMAN, ROBERT EUGENE, real estate associate, retired teacher; b. Harper County, Okla., Mar. 21, 1928; s. Kenneth Earl and Myrtle (Foster) R.; m. Betty Jane Preston, Dec. 22, 1950; children: Marvin Eugene, Kathryn Elizabeth. BEd, Cen. Wash. U., 1951. Cert. elem. and jr. high tchr., Wash., Calif. Tchr. various dists. Washington, 1951-59; owner Reesman's Dairies, Toppenish, Wash., 1959-64; tchr. Desert Ctr. (Calif.) Unif. Sch. Dist., 1964-84; ptnr. Sandstone Assocs., Las Vegas, Nev., 1986—. Coordinator com. Yakima (Wash.) County Rep. Party to elect Dan Evans, 1964. Served with USN, 1946-48. Mem. Internat. Real Estate Appraisers, Desert Ctr. Unit Tchr. Assn. Lutheran. Clubs: Toastmasters, Exchange (Las Vegas). Home: 5801 Gordon Las Vegas NV 89108

REESMAN, WILLIAM RICHARD, insurance marketing executive, financial planner; b. Wooster, Ohio, Dec. 21, 1940; s. John Kingsley and Esther Mae (Tanner) R.; m. Patricia Louise Greenawald, June 11, 1960; children: Jacqwyn, Suzanne. BSBA, Ohio State U., 1963; MBA, Pacific Western U., 1987. Airline pilot Northwest Orient, Mpls., 1969-70; sales dir. No. Nat. Life Ins. Co., Mpls., 1970-76; chief pilot Air N.G., Sioux City, Iowa, 1976-79; instr. pilot United Airlines, Denver, 1979-80; pres. Brokers Mktg. Group, Inc., Denver, 1980—, Fin. Profiles Group, Inc., Denver, 1987—. Author: How to Earn $360,000 a Year by Mass-Marketing Insurance, 1984. Served to capt. USAF, 1963-69, lt. col. N.G., 1984—. Decorated D.F.C., Air medals (11). Republican. Home: 11803 E Yale Way Aurora CO 80014 Office: Brokers Mktg Group 2600 S Parker Rd #3-233 Aurora CO 80014

REEVERTS, DONALD JOHN, foundation adminstrator; b. Mpls., Aug. 25, 1937; s. Edward John and Margaret (Muyskens) R.; m. Diane Kay Dunsmoor, Apr. 4, 1965; children: Diedre, Ashley. BS in Edn., U. Tenn., 1959; MDiv., Fuller Theol. Sem., Pasadena, Calif., 1963. Western div. dir. Young Life, Denver, 1963-79; pres. Denver Leadership Found., 1979—; bd. dirs. Vickers Found., Lewis Found., Denver Leadership Found. Mem. Gov.'s Drug Prevention Council, 1987—; dir. Denver Broncos Youth Found., 1985—; trustee Colo. Women's Coll., 1979-81. Mem. Cherry Hills Country Club, Phi Delta Kappa. Office: Denver Leadership Found 1780 S Bellaire St Ste 808 Denver CO 80222

REEVES, ARTHUR B., finance executive, business executive; b. Flagstaff, Ariz., Aug. 12, 1938; s. Albert and Melinda (Johnson) Reaves; m. Ernie Mae Flemons, Oct. 11, 1958; children: Roxana Ranae, Arthur B. Jr. BSBA, No. Ariz. U., 1966; MBA, Ariz. State U., 1983. Sr. acct. Motorola, Inc., Phoenix, 1966-69; exec. dir. Progress Assn. Econ. Develop., Phoenix, 1969-78; pres. Progress Investment Assn. Econ. Devel., Phoenix, 1971-73; property mgr. Coldwell Banker, Phoenix, 1972-74; dir. labor affairs Phoenix Urban League, Phoenix, 1979-82; fin. cons. State of Ariz., Phoenix, 1982-84; fin. dir. Maricopa County Health Plan, Phoenix, 1984—; instr. Maricopa Community Coll., 1979-81. Contbr. to textbook. Active Maricopa Assn. of Govt., Phoenix, 1976-77, bond com. City of Phoenix, 1971, 78, adv. com. Phoenix Sts., 1971-78. Mem. Healthcare Fin. Mgmt. Assn., Phoenix Met. C. of C. (bd. dirs. 1972-74, govt. fin. com. 1976-81), Small Bus. Assn. (active corps of execs. 1972—). Home: 1849 E Ellis Dr Tempe AZ 85282 Office: Maricopa County Health Plan 400 N 7th St Phoenix AZ 85006

REEVES, DANIEL EDWARD, professional football coach; b. Rome, Ga., Jan. 19, 1944; m. Pam Reeves; children: Dana, Laura, Lee. Grad., U. S.C. Running back Dallas Cowboys, NFL, 1965-72, player-coach, 1970-71, asst. coach, 1972, 74-80; head coach Denver Broncos, NFL, 1981—, also v.p. Player NFL Championship Game, 1966, 67, 70, 71. Mem. S.C. Hall of Fame. Office: care Denver Broncos 5700 Logan St Denver CO 80216 *

REEVES, JOAN HUTCHINS, painter; b. Seattle, June 22, 1932; d. John Marvin and Bess Irene (Sowler) Hutchins; m. George Catherwood Reeves, Sept. 5, 1953; children: David Alan, John Michael. Mem. Art Stall Gallery Cooperative (chmn. 1986-89), Northwest Watercolor Soc. (signature mem., exhibition chmn. 1984, NWWS Purchase award 1988), Women Painters of Wash. (membership chmn. 1986-88, Transparent Watercolor award 1985-86). Democrat. Home: 4028 NE 196 Seattle WA 98155

REEVES, MARIANNE R., accountant; b. St. Louis, Feb. 7, 1949; d. Roger Louis and Marguerite M. (Hegarty) Rice; m. Stephen J. Reeves, Oct. 17, 1969 (div. June 1986); children: Anne, Jeffrey. AA in Bus., Everett Community Coll., Wash., 1975; BBA, U. Nev., 1978. Staff acct. Fox & Co., Las Vegas, Dallas, Nev., 1978-79, Tuggle Burton & Co., Dallas, 1979-82; tax acct. John Mobbs, PC, Alamogordo, N.Mex., 1982-84, Deloitte Haskins & Sells, Las Vegas, 1984-86; dir acctg. and tax services Cashman Equipment Co., Las Vegas, 1986--. Mem. allocation com. United Way, Las Vegas, 1988—, team capt., 1989. Mem. Exec. Women Internat. (sgt.-at-arms 1989, chmn. ways and means com. 1988). Republican. Roman Catholic. Office: Cashman Equipment Co PO Box 2080 Las Vegas NV 89125

REEVES, MARTIN WYLIE, lawyer; b. Denver, July 17, 1953; s. Melvin Heid and Mary Louise (Zimmerman) R.; m. Darcia Rorie, 1972 (div. 1974); m. Beth Ellen Marks, Aug. 21, 1982; 1 child, Justin Randall. BA with honors, Fairhaven Coll., 1978; JD, U. Oreg., 1981. Bar: Oreg. 1981. Pvt. practice Portland, Oreg., 1981-83, 84-87; assoc. Niehaus, Hanna, Murphy et al, Portland, 1983-84; ptnr. Reeves & Kahn, Portland, 1987—. Vice pres. Spinal Cord Assn., Portland, 1987-89. Mem. Oreg. Bar Assn., City Club, Multnomah Athletic Club (com. chmn. Portland chpt. 1987-88). Democrat. Office: Reeves & Kahn 610 SW Alder St Portland OR 97205

REEVES, MICHAEL STUART, lawyer; b. Salt Lake City, Jan. 23, 1956; s. Dale Stuart and Mary Faye (Nichols) R.; m. Fredda Jolayne Kenney, June 5, 1980; children: Daniel Stuart, Laura Nichol, Benjamin Kenney. BA, Brigham Young U., 1980; JD, U. Utah, 1983. Bar: Queen's Bench Calgary Can. 1983, Supreme Ct. of Can. 1985, Ariz. 1986, U.S. Dist. Ct. Ariz. 1986. Missionary Ch. of Jesus Christ of the Latter Day Saints, Concepcion, Chile, 1975-77; intern Salt Lake City Prosecutor's Office;, 1979-80; barrister Kenney and Kaleva, Calgary, Alta., Can., 1983-85; assoc. Levenbaum, Cohen & Jeckel, Phoenix, 1985--; dir. Vitol Internat., Phoenix, 1987--, Ariz. Ins. Tng., Phoenix, 1987--, JBC Industries, Inc., Phoenix, 1986--. Author: Super Salesman, 1988. Atty. Vol. Lawyers Assn., Phoenix, 1985--; asst. dist. commr. Boy Scouts Am., Mesa, Ariz., 1987--. Mem. ABA, The Law Soc. Alberta, State Bar Ariz., Maricopa County Bar Assn. Mormon. Home: 1434 W Pampa Mesa AZ 85202

REEVES, RONALD EUGENE, insurance company executive; b. Orange, Calif., Dec. 13, 1961; s. Isaac and Irma June (Liggans) R. BA, San Jose State U., 1984. Youth employment dir. Campbell (Calif.) C. of C., 1982-84; asst. dir. Willard Straight Hall Cornell U., Ithaca, N.Y., 1984-86; customer relations mgr. Allstate Insur., Orange, Calif., 1986—. Corp. advisor Calif. State U. Black Bus. Students' Assn., Fullerton, 1986—; bd. dirs. Orange County Urban League, Santa Ana, 1986-87, sec., 1988, chmn. 1988—. Democrat. Baptist. Home: 1764 Illinois Ave Riverside CA 92707 Office: Allstate Insur Co 725 W Town & Country Rd Ste 400 Orange CA 92668

REFSLAND, GARY ARLAN, health facility administrator, educator; b. Big Timber, Mont., May 5, 1944; s. William Anton and Agnes Eline (Freeberg) R.; m. Judith Estelle Hall, Aug. 20, 1969 (div. Aug. 1974). BS in Sociology, Mont. State U., 1970, MS in Sociology, 1971; postgrad., Internat. Grad. Sch., Stockholm, 1970; AA in funeral directing, Calif. Coll. Mortuary Sci., 1973. Cert. funeral dir., mortician. Instr. sociology Mont. State U., Bozeman, 1971-72, lectr., 1976—, coordinator of aging services Coll. Letters and Sci., 1976-77, acting dir. Ctr. Gerontology, 1977-79, dir. Mont. Ctr. Gerontology, 1979—; mortician Dokken Nelson Funeral Service, Bozeman, 1974-76; cons. State Agy. Aging, 1979—, Legacy Legis., 1987—; program coordinator Mont. Area Health Edn. Ctr./Office Rural Health, 1987—; mem. adv. bd. Sr. Community Services Employment program, Mont., 1983—, Regional Edn. and Tng. program Fed. Region VIII, 1980-82, Mont. State U., 1986—, Mont. Area Health Edn. Ctr., 1987; mem. planning com. Gov's. Adv. Council, Mont. Aging Policy Perspectives: 1990, 1987—; mem. Gov's. Third Priorities for People, 1988; state coordinator White Ho. Conf. on Aging, 1981-82. Writer, producer (TV show) Mont.'s Priorities for Aging, 1981; producer The Mental Health Problems of Older Adults, 1988; writer, exec. producer (videotape) Senior Centers.: Opportunities for Older Montanans; contbr. articles to profl. jours. Pres. Gallatin County Housing Authority Bd., Bozeman, 1981-82, sec. 1978-81; pres. Sourdough Ridge Property Owners Assn., Bozeman, 1982-84, Gallatin County Council on Aging, 1978-80. Served with USN, 1962-66. Recipient Armed Forces Community award San Diego C. of C., 1966; Cert. Appreciation U.S. Dept. Health and Human Services, Denver, 1982; named one of Outstanding Young Men Am., U.S. Jaycees, 1981. Mem. Am. Soc. Aging, Mont. Gerontology Soc. (charter officer 1982-83), Nat. Council on Aging (del. council 1982-83), Am. Legion, Alpha Kappa Delta. Home: 212 Ridge Trail Rd Bozeman MT 59715 Office: Mont State U Ctr Gerontology Bozeman MT 59717

REGALADO, RAUL L., airport executive; b. L.A., Jan. 31, 1945; s. Raul and Antonia (Estavillo) R.; m. Christa Kohler, Mar. 16, 1971; children: Horst, Stephanie, Jennifer. BS, Embry-Riddle Aero. U., 1972. Mgr. airport City of Klamath Falls, Oreg., 1972-74, City of Fresno, Calif., 1974-79, Orange County, Santa Ana, Calif., 1979-80; dir. aviation San Jose (Calif.) Airport, 1980—. Capt. U.S. Army, 1966-71, lt. col. res. Decorated Bronze Star, D.F.C., Air medal with 49 oak leaf clusters. Mem. Am. Assn. Airport Execs., Calif. Assn. Airport Execs. (pres. 1980-81), Res. Officers Assn., Assn. U.S. Army, Calif., Airport Operators Council Internat. (bd. dirs. 1986-88), Aero Club No. Calif. (bd. dirs. 1982—, pres. 1987-88), Quiet Birdmen. Lodge: Rotary. Office: San Jose Internat Airport 1661 Airport Blvd Ste C205 San Jose CA 95110-1285

REGALIA, ANDREW MARIO, JR., real estate developer; b. San Francisco, Jan. 12, 1950; s. Andrew Mario and Eleanor Marie (Sheehan) R.; 1 child Amy Marie. BS in Bus. Admin., U. San Francisco, 1976. Certified Review Appraiser. Asst. v.p. Bank of Am., San Francisco, 1971-80; v.p. Bank of Calif., San Francisco, 1980-83; ptnr. Pacific Heights Devel. Co, Inc., San Francisco, 1983-88; owner R & R Investments, San Francisco, 1989--. Mem. Cercle De L' Union.

REGAN, CAROLE ANN BENNETT, business executive, psychologist; b. Fayettville, Ark., Nov. 10, 1936; d. Dante Wayland and Mary Agnes (Hughes) Bennett; m. Robert Regan, July 23, 1960 (div. 1988); children: Christopher, Alison, Amelia. BA, Pomona Coll., 1958; MEd, U. Va., 1966; PhD, U. Pa., 1972, postgrad., 1980. Lic. psychologist, Pa. Counseling psychologist U. Pa., Phila., 1970-72; asst. prof. St. Joseph's U., Phila., 1972-80; sr. assoc. Drake Beam Morin, Inc., N.Y.C., 1981, v.p., 1981-82; sr. v.p. Drake Beam Morin, Inc., Phila., 1982-87, San Francisco, 1987—. Contbr. articles to profl. jours. Fellow, U. Pa., 1969-72; recipient scholarship, Pomona Coll., 1956-58. Mem. Am. Psychol. Assn., Calif. Psychol. Assn., No. Calif. Human Resources Council, Phila. Soc. Clinical Psychologists, Aircraft Owners and Pilots Assn., Cosmopolitan Club (Phila.). Democrat. Episcopalian. Home: 57 Sereno Circle Oakland CA 94619 Office: Drake Beam Morin Inc 4 Embarcadero San Francisco CA 94111

REGAN, JOHN DENNISS, insurance company executive; b. Bklyn., Oct. 29, 1943; s. Cornelius and Margarite Regan; m. Lynda Louise Heider, May 5, 1968; children: Alysia, Melissa. CLU, Chartered Fin. Cons. Agt. Washington Nat. Ins. Co., San Francisco, 1968-73; pres. Regan Co., Sausalito, Calif., 1973-84, Regan Group Ins. Mktg., Sausalito, 1979-86; pres. & chief exec. officer Gen. Services Life Holding Co. and Gen. Services Life Ins. Co., Novato, Calif., 1986—; chmn. bd. Regan Reassurance Co., Phoenix, The Regan Group Ins. Mktg., Novato; frequent speaker various groups. Author: Complete Book of Retired Lives Reserves, 1979; contbr. numerous articles to profl. jours. Founder, bd. dirs. Nat. Ins. Polit. Action Com., Washington, 1984—. Mem. Ins. Coalition Am. (founding), Assn. for Advanced Life Underwriting, Nat. Assn. Life Underwriters, Internat. Assn. Fin. Planners, Million Dollar Round Table, Internat. Forum, Top of Table (charter mem.). Republican. Roman Catholic. Office: Gen Svcs Life Holding Co 201 Alameda del Prado Novato CA 94949

REGAN, JOHN RANDALL, construction company executive; b. Knoxville, Tenn., Apr. 19, 1945; s. Robert W. and LaVonne Ruth (Fox) R.; m. Linda Diane Allen, Nov. 23, 1968; children: Mark, Heather, Allissa, Britta, Hadley. AA, Orange Coast Coll., Costa Mesa, Calif., 1965; BSCE, Calif. State U., Long Beach, 1968. Registered profl. engr., Calif., Tex. Civil engr. The Bechtel Group, San Francisco, 1968-73, project engr., 1973-76, 76-77, project engr. mgr., 1977—; ptnr. Ronald Regan Constrn. Co., Jackson, Calif., 1976-77. Author: (short stories) Luck Comes to Blackie, 1977, (essay) Working On It, 1974; contbr. articles to profl. jours. Mem. Telluride Inst., Mensa. Lodge: Elks. Home: 4212 Player Ct Bakersfield CA 93306 Office: Bechtel Constrn Co PO Box 80607 Bakersfield CA 93380

REGAN, RAYMOND JOHN, small business owner; b. Chgo., Mar. 18, 1934; s. Ray John and Gladys Rose (Garner) R.; m. Patricia Burkholder, 1959 (div. 1975); children: Debra, Patricia, Lisa; m. Linda Jean Memmler, Aug. 30, 1975. AA, Wright Coll., 1954. Lic. driving sch. instr. Driving instr. N. Shore Driving Sch., Chgo., 1955-59; prin., pres. Universal Driving Sch., Chgo., 1959-75, World Wide Driving Schs., Chgo., 1962-75, Universal Driving Sch. of Indpls., 1971-75; sales mgr. Calif. Driving Sch., Monterey Park, Calif., 1978-80; prin., pres. W. Coast Driving Sch., San Gabriel, Calif., 1980—, Lettuce Amuse U Comedy Schs., San Gabriel, 1980—, Comedians Plus Traffic Sch., Glendale, Calif., 1986—; sec., acting pres. Driving Sch. Assocs. of Ill., Chgo., 1969-70; sec., charter mem. Driving Sch. Assocs. of Am., 1971; sec., mem. Exec. Assn. Am., 1972, sec., comptroller Calif. Assoc. Alcohol & Traffic Schs., Los Angeles, 1981-82; sec. Driving Sch. Assoc. of Calif., 1980. Created with spouse concept of comedy traffic sch. Recipient Achievement of Excellence in Edn. award Calif. Safety Council, 1987. Mem. Kiwanis. Office: Lettuce Amuse U Comedy Schs 1740 1740 S New Ave Suite 105 San Gabriel CA 91776

REGAN, ROBERT DANA, hotel executive; b. Quincy, Mass., Jan. 30, 1951; s. Arthur Thomas and Cynthia (Sylvester) R.; m. Christine Rollins; m. Pamela J. Adams, Aug. 1, 1981; 1 child, Ashley Dana. AA, Palomar Coll., San Marcos, Calif., 1977; BA, U.S. Internat. U., 1978. Cert. hotel adminstr. Engring. supr. La Costa Resort Hotel and Spa, Carlsbad, Calif., 1973-76; co. mgr. Lyceum Theatre, San Diego, 1980; advt. and pub. rels. dir. Harlequin Dinner Playhouse, Costa Mesa, Calif., 1980-82; mktg. dir. Lyric Dinner Theatre, La Mesa, Calif., 1982-84; gen. mgr. Shelter Island Marina Inn, San Diego, 1984—; trustee Hotel and Restaurant Ins. and Pension Trusts, San Diego, 1987—. With U.S. Army, 1969-72, Vietnam. Decorated Bronze Star. Mem. Am. Hotel and Motel Assn., San Diego Hotel and Motel Assn. (bd. dirs. 1988—). Democrat. Mem. Ch. of Religious Sci. Office: Shelter Island Marine Inn 2051 Shelter Island Dr San Diego CA 92106

REGENIE, VICTORIA ANN, infosystems engineer; b. Rockville Ctr., N.Y., July 4, 1952; d. Thomas Richard and Dorethea Ann (Culleton) R. BS in Systems Engring. with honors, U. Ariz., 1974; MBA, Golden Gate U., 1982; postgrad., Simmons Coll., 1987. With mfg. mgmt. program Gen. Electric, Milw. and Clearwater Fla., 1974-76; engr. Honeywell Avionics, Mpls., 1977-80; systems engr. Systems Control Tech., Edwards, Calif., 1980-83; aerospace engr., Ames research ctr. Dryden Flight research facility NASA, Edwards, 1983—. Office: NASA Ames-Dryden Flight Rsch Facility PO Box 273 Edwards CA 93523-5000

REGENSBURG, ANTHONY SHEPARD, wholesale distribution company executive; b. N.Y.C., July 31, 1928; s. Edward J. and Josephine (Copeland) R.; m. Patricia Hentz, Sept. 6, 1949; children: Victoria Regensburg Kahn, Paul Patric. B.S., Yale U., 1948; postgrad., Harvard U., 1966. Leaf tobacco trainee Gen. Cigar Co., N.Y.C., 1948-49; tobacco buyer, asst. factory supt., v.p. sales Admiration Cigar Co., N.Y.C., 1949-57, exec. v.p., 1958-64; with Bayuk Cigars Inc., Phila., 1964-78, sr. v.p., 1970-73, exec. v.p., 1973-78; sr. v.p. mktg. Gen. Cigar & Tobacco div. Culbro Corp., N.Y.C., 1978-79; pres. Glaser Bros., Los Angeles, 1979-82, also dir.; pres. Core Mark Distbrs., Inc., Bel Air, Calif., 1983-87; pres., chief exec. officer Core Mark Internat., Bel Air, 1987, exec. v.p., dir., 1987—. Served to capt. arty. U.S. Army, 1952-54. Named Man of Yr. N.Y. Tobacco Table, 1970, Anti-Defamation League Man of Yr., 1982; recipient Brotherhood award NCCJ, 1985. Dir. Cigar Assn. Am., Nat. Assn. Tobacco Distbrs. (Young Exec. Achievement award 1968). Republican. Office: Core-Mark Distbrs Inc 2934 1/2 Beverly Glen Circle #420 Bel Air CA 90077

REGINATO, ROBERT JOSEPH, soil scientist; b. Palo Alto, Calif., Apr. 13, 1935; s. Giuseppe Primo and Carolina Theresa (Boccignone) R.; m. Donna Marie LeStum, Aug. 26, 1956; children—Richard Lynn, David Lewis, Christopher Michael, Michael Jeffrey. B.S., U. Calif.-Davis, 1957; M.S., U. Ill., 1959; Ph.D., U. Calif.-Riverside, 1973. Research asst. U. Calif., Davis, 1956-57, U. Ill., Urbana, 1957-59; soil scientist U.S. Water Conservation Lab., U.S. Dept. Agr.-Agrl. Research Service, Phoenix, 1959-89 , research leader, 1980-89; assoc. area dir. Pacific W. Area U.S. Dept. Agr. Agrl. Rsch. Svc., Albany, Calif., 1989—; vis. scientist U. Calif.-Davis, 1977-78; U.S. Dept. Agr. collaborator U. Ariz., Tucson, 1959—. Contbr. over 160 articles to tech. jours. Active Roosevelt council Boy Scouts Am., 1960-76. Fellow Am. Soc. Agronomy, Soil Sci. Soc. Am.; mem. Internat. Soil Sci. Soc., Western Soil Sci. Soc., Am. Geophys. Union, Sigma Xi, Alpha Zeta, Kappa Sigma. Roman Catholic. Home: Bayside Commons 535 Pierce St #474 Albany CA 94700 Office: Pacific West Area 800 Buchanan Ave Albany CA 94710

REGIS, MARIO ENRIQUE, management executive, management consultant; b. San Eduardo, Santa Fe, Argentina, Nov. 8, 1946; came to U.S., 1979; s. Mario Victor Regis and Martina Cuello; m. Lidia Gamulin de Regis, March 10, 1972; 1 child, Maximiliano. BA in Social Work, Nat. U., Rosario, Argentina, 1971; degree internat. cons. of pub. rels., U. Rome, 1974; BA in Econs., Cen. U. of Venezuela, 1980. Comml. attache Argentina embassy, Mexico City, 1970-71, Caracas, Venezuela, 1971-75; op. gen. mgr. Sears Roebuk, Caracas, Venezuela, 1975-82; dir. pprr C.M.L.A. Med. Ctr., Los Angeles, 1984-87; v.p., owner Am. Mgmt. and Filing Corp., Los Angeles, 1985—; pres., owner Shamanta Mgmt. Corp., Los Angeles, 1986—; sales mgr. Calif. Network Cons. Group, Torrance, Calif., 1987—; ptnr. Multiple Enterprise Corp., Torrance, Calif., 1987—; pres., owner Med. Arts Imaging, Inc., Los Angeles, 1988—. Mem. Tongan Com. (Waianae Dist., 1983-88), Rep. Party, 1985-88. Republican. Roman Catholic. Club: Yacht (Marina del Rey). Office: Medical Arts Imaging Inc 3175 S Hoover St Ste 563 Los Angeles CA 90007 also: Shamanta Mgmt Corp 1625 W Olympic Blvd Ste M105 Los Angeles CA 90015

REGO, PAUL JOSEPH, computer company executive; b. Brockton, Mass., Oct. 26, 1954; s. Joseph and Mary (Rampino) R.; m. Sylvia Irene Leverich, Aug. 1, 1987; 1 child, Lalina Marie. Student, Fla. Jr. Coll., 1972-74, Jacksonville U., 1973. Programmer, office mgr. Sunspot, Albuquerque, 1982-84; mem. mktg. staff Kelly Svcs., Albuquerque, 1984-86; chief exec. officer, programmer Insight Data, Albuquerque, 1985--; Author: Computer Encounters...of the First Kind, 1988, Computer Encounters ...of the Second Kind, 1988, Albuquerque Computer Resource Guide, 1988; author, editor: Computer Encounters...of the Third Kind, 1988, Computer Encounters...of the Fourth Kind, 1988; inventor in field, developer programs. Mem. Apple User Group (cert. developer), Applequerque Computer Club (pres. 1987, ambassador 1986--). Office: Insight Data PO Box 3972 Albuquerque NM 87190

REGUERO, MELODIE HUBER, financial services professional; b. Montebello, Calif., May 10, 1956; d. Adam W. and Helen Carolyn (Antrim) Huber; m. Edward Anthony Reguero, Oct. 3, 1987. BA in Econs. magna cum laude, UCLA, 1978; M in Bus. Taxation, U. So. Calif., 1983. CPA, Calif. Mem. tax audit staff Arthur Young & Co., Los Angeles, 1978-80; sr. mem. Singer, Lewak, Greenbaum & Goldstein, Los Angeles, 1980-82; tax supr. Coldwell Banker & Co., Los Angeles, 1983-84; fin. analyst, acquisitions specialist Coldwell Banker Residential Group, Newport Beach, Calif., 1984-86; fin. svcs. profl. The Acacia Fin. Group, Newport Beach, Calif., 1986-88; chief fin. officer Fin. Engring. Concepts, Inc., Santa Ana, Calif., 1988—; treas. Champions Choice, Inc., Anaheim, Calif., 1980—. Active Censer Club, Costa Mesa, 1989—, Ctr. 500 Performing Arts, Costa Meas, 1989—. Mem. AICPA, Calif. Soc. CPAs (pres. 1980—), Newport Harbor C. of C., Irvine C. of C., Orange County Triathlon Club. Republican. Office: Fin Engring Concepts Inc 1221 E Dyer Rd Ste 220 Santa Ana CA 92705

REHAK, THOMAS FRANK, social services administrator; b. Rhinelander, Wis., June 29, 1952; s. Frank and Violet (Wurst) F.; m. Delee Rose Banwarth, June 20, 1975; 1 child, Cherish Ann. BS in Criminal Justice, U. Wis., Platteville, 1974; MA in Counseling, Loras Coll., 1978. Police officer City of Dubuque, Iowa, 1974-79; group home mgr. Lake Havasu Assn. Retarded and Handicapped, Lake Havasu City, Ariz., 1980-81, asst. exec. dir., 1981-82, exec. dir., 1982-86; assoc. dir. programs Community Psychology and Edn. Svcs., Tucson, 1986—; bd. dirs., chmn. Pima County Bd. #3; mem. foster care rev. bd. Ariz. Supreme Ct., Tucson, 1987—, chmn. bd. dirs., 1989; mem. program and rsch. rev. com. devel. disabilities div. Ariz. Dept. Econ. Security, 1988. Mem. counsel Grand Canyon Synod Evang. Luth. Ch. in Am., Phoenix, 1987; troop leader Girl Scouts U.S., Tucson, 1987—; host family Up With People, 1987—. Recipient Mayor's Proclamation award City of Lake Havasu, 1985, Olive Leaf award Mount Olive Luth. Ch., 1985. Mem. Assn. Retarded Citizens, Clowns of Am., Internat. Brotherhood Magicians. Republican. Home: 3865 W Orangewood Dr Tucson AZ 85741 Office: Community Psychology and Edn Svcs 211 S Fourth St Tucson AZ 85701

REHFELDT, DAVID JOHN, savings and loan executive; b. Appleton, Wis., May 21, 1955; s. Ewald and Lorraine E. (Schmidt) R.; m. Katherine Ann Kleinhuizen, May 24, 1975; children: Norah, Brittany, Charles. BBA in Acctg., U. Alaska, Anchorage, 1979. CPA, Alaska. Sr. acct. Touche Ross and Co., Anchorage, 1979-83; sr. v.p., chief fin. officer Home Savs. Bank, Anchorage, 1983—; bd. dirs. ARS Inc., Anchorage, Western Ins. Svcs. Inc., Anchorage. Mem. AICPA, Alaska Soc. CPA's, Fin. Mgrs. Soc., Anchorage Rebounders Boosters (pres. 1984—), Anchorage Seawolf Boosters (v.p. 1987—). Republican. Office: Home Savs Bank 1001 E Benson Blvd Anchorage AK 99510

REHORST, ERIC DWIGHT, dentist; b. Waterloo, Iowa, Mar. 20, 1945; s. Charles Henry and Susie Catherine (Rush) R.; m. Linda Susan Brauhn, May 1, 1971; children: John Christopher, Johanna Rachael, Katherine Elizabeth. BS, U. Iowa, 1967, DDS, 1972. Resident paedodontic surgery U. Man., Winnipeg, 1973; sr. dental officer Indian Health Service, Cass Lake, Minn., 1973-75, Warm Springs, Oreg., 1975-78; sr. dental officer USCG Air Sta., Traverse City, Mich., 1978-82; dep. dental officer USCG Group Kodiak, Alaska, 1982-84; sr. dental officer USCG Group Astoria, Warrenton, Oreg., 1984-88, Big Spring (Tex.) Fed. Prison Camp, 1988. Unit commr. Boy Scouts Am., Astoria, Oreg., 1986--, asst. troop leader, 1986--, asst. pack leader, 1984--; Sunday sch. tchr. First Luth. Ch., 1986--. Mem. ADA, Acad. Gen. Dentistry, Acad. Dentistry for Children, Oreg. Dental Assn. (del. 1986-88), Clatsop County Dental Soc. (pres. 1986-88), Columbia River Warrent Officers Assn. (Astoria, pres. 1987-88), Luth. Brotherhood. Republican. Home: RR 2 Box 436G Warrenton OR 97146 Office: USCG Group Astoria 2185 SE Airport Rd Warrenton OR 97146

REICH, CHARLES WILLIAM, nuclear physicist; b. Oklahoma City, Sept. 12, 1930; s. Fred William And Gertrude Evelyn (Veal) R.; m. Juana Sue Woods, June 8, 1952; children: Paul William, Jane Kristen, Donna Karen. BS in Physics, U. Okla., 1952; MA in Physics, Rice U., 1954, PhD in Physics, 1956. Physicist, group leader Atomic Energy Div. Phillips Petroleum Co., Idaho Falls, Idaho, 1956-66; group leader, sect. chief Idaho Nuclear Corp., Idaho Falls, 1966-71; sect. chief Aerojet Nuclear Corp., Idaho Falls, 1971-76; prin. scientist, sect. chief EG&G Idaho, Inc., Idaho Falls, 1976—, sci., engring. fellow, 1982—; guest scientist Niels Bohr Inst., Copenhagen, 1964-65; U.S. rep., coordinator Internat. Atomic Energy Agy. coordinated research program, 1977-86; com. mem. U.S. Dept. Energy Transplutonium Program com., 1978—; chmn. Decay Data subcom. Cross Sects. Evaluation Working Group, 1974—. Contbr. articles to profl. jours. NSF Predoctoral fellow, 1954-55; recipient H.A. Wilson research award Rice Inst., Houston, 1956. Fellow Am. Phys. Soc. (editorial bd. Phys. Rev. 1978, 1982-84); mem. AAAS, N.Y. Acad. Scis., Sigma Xi, Phi Beta Kappa. Mem. Ch. Nazarene. Office: EG&G Idaho Inc Idaho Nat Engring Lab PO Box 1625 Idaho Falls ID 83415

REICHARDT, CARL E., banker; b. 1931. AB, U. So. Calif., 1956; student, Stanford U., 1965; student in mortgage banking, Northwestern U., 1965. Program mgr. ops. and lending Citizens Nat. Bank, 1955-59; sr. statistics analyst North Am. Aircraft, 1959-60; area exec. v.p. Union Bank, 1960-70; with Wells Fargo Realty Advisors, 1970—; exec. v.p. real estate industries group Wells Fargo Bank, N.A., San Francisco, 1975-78, corp. pres., from 1981, now chmn., chief exec. officer, also bd. dirs.; with parent co. Wells Fargo & Co., San Francisco, 1973—, exec. v.p. real estate industries group, 1875-79, pres., 1979-84, chief operating officer, 1979-82, chmn., chief exec. officer, 1982—, also bd. dirs. Served with USN, 1951-54. Office: Wells Fargo & Co 420 Montgomery St 12th Fl San Francisco CA 94163 *

REICHARTZ, DAN, hotel executive. Pres. Caesar's Palace Hotel, Las Vegas. Office: Caesar's Palace Hotel 3570 Las Vegas Blvd S Las Vegas NV 89109 *

REICHBACH, NAOMI ESTELLE, social service administrator; b. N.Y.C., Apr. 19, 1934; d. Nathaniel S. and Sara (Hirsch) R. BS in Edn., SUNY, New Paltz, 1955; MS in Spl. Edn., CCNY, 1969. Tchr. Shield Inst. for the Retarded, Bronx, N.Y., 1956-58; tchr., parent educator Shield Inst. for the Retarded, 1961-63; head tchr., program developer Oakland (Calif.) Unified Sch. Dist., 1959-60; head tchr., program developer N.Y.C. Assn. Retarded Children, 1963-67, edn. dir., 1967-69; co-founder, exec. dir. Burt Children Ctr., Psychiatric Residential Treatment Ctr. and Sch., San Francisco, 1969—. Fellow Am. Orthopsychiat. Assn., Royal Soc. Health; mem. Calif. Svcs. for Children. Home: 3086 Washington St San Francisco CA 94115 Office: Burt Ctr 940 Grove St San Francisco CA 94117

REICHE, MARVIN GARY, restaurant executive; b. Sacramento, Sept. 2, 1949; s. Robert A. and Kate Kathleen (Groo) R.; m. Kathleen Louise Price, Feb. 10, 1968; children—Bradford, Renee, Darren, Michelle, Ryan, Brandon. With Harman Mgmt. Corp., 1967-79, cook and pie shell operator, Lodi, Calif., 1967, cook, Carmichael, Calif., 1967-68, store mgr., Sacramento, 1968-72, Fair Oaks, Calif., 1972-77, dist. mgr. Central Sacramento, 1977-79; owner, investor Kentucky Fried Chicken, Covina, West Covina, Long Beach, Lakewood, Bellflower, Los Angeles County, Garden Grove and Anaheim, Calif., 1979—; sole owner Kasmar Enterprises; dir. So. Calif. Kentucky Fried Chicken Advt. Assn. Judge Bank Am. Achievement Awards Program, 1983. Mem. Assn. Kentucky Fried Chicken Franchisee (nat. dir., pres. So. Calif. chpt. 1989—), Republican. Mormon.

REICHEK, JESSE, artist; b. Bklyn., Aug. 16, 1916; s. Morris and Celia (Bernstein) R.; m. Laure Guyot, May 16, 1950; children—Jonathan, Joshua. Student, Inst. Design, Chgo., 1941-42; diploma, Academie Julian, Paris, 1951. instr. dept. architecture U. Mich., 1946-47; prof. Inst. Design Ill. Inst. Tech., 1951-53; prof. dept. architecture U. Calif. at Berkeley, 1953—; Cons. Nat. Design Inst. Ford Found. project, Ahmedabad, India, 1963, San Francisco Redevel. Agy. Embarcadero Center, 1966—; lectr. Nat. Inst. Architects, Rome, 1960, U. Florence, 1960, U. Naples, 1960, Israel Inst. Tech., 1960, Greek Architects Soc., Athens, 1960, U. Belgrade, 1960, MIT, 1965, U. N.Mex., 1964, Am. Cultural Center, Paris, 1960, 64, Gujarat Inst. Engrs. and Architects, 1963, U. Colo., 1961, Harvard, 1962, U. Minn., 1962, U. Coll. London, 1967, Inst. Contemporary Arts, London, 1967, Ecole Nationale des Beaux-Ats, 1967; artist in residence Tamarind Lithography Workshop, 1966, Am. Acad. in Rome, 1971-72; research prof. Creative Arts Inst. U. Calif., 1966-67; artist in residence IBM Los Angeles Sci. Center, 1970-71. Exhibited one man shows at, Galerie Cahiers d'Art Paris, 1951, 59, 68, U. Calif. at Berkeley, 1954, Betty Parsons Gallery, N.Y.C., 1958, 59, 63, 65, 67, 69, 70, Molton Gallery, London, 1962, Am. Culture Center, Florence, Italy, 1962, Bennington Coll., 1963, U. N.Mex., 1966, U. So. Calif., 1967, Axiom Gallery, London, 1968, Yoseido Gallery, Tokyo, 1968, Los Angeles County Mus. Art, 1971; exhibited in group shows, Bklyn. Mus., 1959, Mus. Modern Art, N.Y.C., 1962, 65, 69, Knox-Albright Art Gallery, 1962, Art Inst. Chgo., 1963, Cin. Art Mus., 1966, Balt. Art Mus., 1966, Yale Art Gallery, 1967, Grand Palais, Paris, 1970, Nat. Mus. Art, Santiago, Chile, 1970, art and tech. exhibit, Los Angeles County Mus. Art, 1971, Maeght Found., St. Paul de Vence, France, 1971, Mus. Modern Art, Paris, 1971; represented in permanent collections, Mus. Modern Art, Art Inst. Chgo., Bibliotheque Nationale, Paris, Victoria & Albert Mus., London, Los Angeles County Art Mus., Grunwald Graphic Arts Found., U. Calif. at Los Angeles, San Diego Mus. Art, Amon Carter Mus., Fort Worth; Author: Jesse Reichek-Dessins, 1960, La Monte de la Nuit, 1961, Fontis, 1961, Etcetera, 1965, Le Bulletin Des Baux, 1972; e.g., 1976. Served to capt. C.E. AUS, 1942-46. Home: 5925 Red Hill Rd Petaluma CA 94953

REICHENBACH, THOMAS, veterinarian; b. N.Y.C., Jan. 6, 1947; s. Henry J. and Helen M. (Kelly) R.; m. Cleda L. Houmes, Nov. 23, 1984. BS in Chemistry, U. Notre Dame du Lac, 1968; MS in Chemistry, U. Calif., Davis, Calif., 1973; AA, Shasta Coll., 1975; DVM, U. Calif., Davis, Calif., 1981. Doctor of Veterinary Medicine. Sentry dog handler U.S. Army, 1970-71; indsl. chemist Syntex, Palo Alto, Calif., 1973-75; gestation herd mgr. Llano Seco Rancho, Chico, Calif., 1976-80; pres. Veterinary Mgmt. Svcs., Salinas, Calif., 1981—; lectr. in field; adv. bd. Veterinary Post Grad. Inst., Santa Cruz, Calif., 1988. Contbr. articles to profl. jours.; author computer software Personal Wedding Planner, 1985, Veterinary Clinical Simulation, 1988. With U.S. Army, 1969-71. Mem. Am. Vet. Med. Assn., Calif. Vet. Med. Assn., Nat. Notre Dame Monogram Club. Republican. Roman Catholic. Office: Vet Mgmt Svcs 1887 #1 Cherokee Dr Salinas CA 93906

REICHERT, ROGER LEE, small business owner; b. Houston, Feb. 11, 1951; s. Edward Lee and Elizabeth O. (Black) R.; m. Susan Lipp, May 8, 1971 (div. Jan. 1974); 1 child, Paul Zachary; m. Regina Catherine Saylor, July 28, 1980. Grad. high sch., Houston, 1969. Cert. master mechanic, Porsche and Audi technician. Mechanic, machinist, salesman parts Pete Auto Supply, Houston, 1969-72; mechanic Norman Scott Porsche-Audi Dealer, Houston, 1972-73, Four Day Tire Store, L.A., 1972; technician Bob Hagestad Porsche-Audi Dealer, Denver, 1973-85, Allan Johnson Porsche-Audi Dealer, San Diego, 1985; foreman, asst. service mgr. Pioneer Porsche-Audi Dealer, San Diego, 1985-86; prin. Reichert Porsche Repair, Arvada, Colo., 1986—. Home and Office: 6316 W 66th Ave Arvada CO 80003

REID, BELMONT MERVYN, brokerage house executive; b. San Jose, Calif., May 17, 1927; s. C. Belmont and Mary Irene (Kilfoyl) R.; B.S. in Engring., San Jose State U., 1950, postgrad.; m. Evangeline Joan Rogers, June 1, 1952. Pres., Lifetime Realty Corp., San Jose, 1969-77, Lifetime Fin. Planning Corp., San Jose, 1967-77; founder, chmn. bd. Belmont Reid & Co., Inc., San Jose, 1960-77; pres., registered investment adv. JOBEL Fin. Inc., Carson City, Nev., 1980—; pres., chmn. bd. Data-West Systems, Inc., 1984-85 . County chmn. 1982-85, Carson City Rep. Cen. Com., treas., 1979-81; mem. Brewery Arts Ctr., chmn. Carson City Gen. Obligation Bond Commn., 1986—; rural county chmn., 1984-88. Nev. Rep. Cen. Com., 1984—; vice chmn. Carson City Charter Rev. Com., 1986—. Served with USN, 1945-46, 51-55. Decorated Air medals. Mem. Nat. Assn. Securities Dealers, Mcpl. Securities Rulemaking Bd., Nat. Futures Assn., Carson City C. of C. (pres. 1986-87, dir. 1982-88). Clubs: Capital of Carson City. Lodge: Rotary (chpt. sec. 1983-84, 86-87, pres.1988—). Home: 610 Bonanza Dr Carson City NV 89706 Office: 711 E Washington St Carson City NV 89701

REID, BILL (WILLIAM EARL REID), Canadian provincial official; b. Nelson, B.C., Can., Aug. 13, 1934; s. William Earl and Dolly (Renwick) R.; m. Marion Joan Meehan, June 21, 1957; children: Cathy Darlene, Laurie Joan, Gail Patricia, Sheila Marie. Alderman Delta, B.C., 1973-78; charter mem. Urban Transit Authority, 1978-79; chmn. bd. Metro Transit Authority, 1980-85; mem. B.C. Legis., from 1983, chief govt. whip, 1985-86, min. tourism, recreation and culture, 1986-88, minister tourism, provincial sec., 1988—. Candidate Progressive Conservative election, 1972. Anglican. Club: Kinsmen. Lodge Rotary. Office: BC Legislature, Parliament Bldg, Victoria, BC Canada V8V 1X4

REID, CHRISTOPHER JOHN, manufacturing executive; b. Newark, Nov. 25, 1947; s. Edwin John Reid and Isabelle (Murray) Fitzwilliam; m. Paula J. Holmes, Jan. 3, 1970; children: Tracy E., Courtney A. BA, Baldwin Wallace Coll., 1969; MBA, Ohio State U., 1980. CPA, N.J. Sr. acct. Price Waterhouse and Co., N.Y.C., 1969-74; sr. auditor Cooper Industries, Cleve., 1974-76; mgr. internal audit Midland Ross Corp., Cleve., 1976-77; div. controller Midland Ross Corp., Urbana, Ohio, 1977-85; mgr. planning Midland Ross Corp., Cleve., 1985-86; corp. controller Leach Corp., Buena Park, Calif., 1987—. Treas. various civic and ednl. orgns., Cleve., 1975, Urbana, 1982. Mem. Fin. Execs. Inst., Price Waterhouse Alumni Assn., Ohio State Alumni Assn. Republican. Methodist. Home: 13032 Eton Pl Santa Ana CA 92705 Office: Leach Corp 6900 Orangethorpe Ave Buena Park CA 90620

REID, DONALD ROLF, SR., sales consultant; b. Pittsburg, Calif., Mar. 14, 1932; s. Donald Bruce and Sylvia Elizabeth (Eyre) R.; m. Marlene Joyce Hartman, Sept. 20, 1958; 1 child, Donald Rolf Jr. Student, Calif. State U., Fresno, Fresno Community Coll. Cert. mgmt. cons. Account exec. KVVG-TV, Tulare, Calif., 1956, McClatchy, Fresno, 1956-62; owner Don Reid & Assocs., Fresno, 1962-68; sales rep. Prince Gardner Leather, 1968-71; pres. Donald R. Reid Assocs., Fresno, 1971—; instr. Clovis Unified Sch. Dist., Calif., 1971-82. Pubr. mgmt. newsletter: The Reid Report, 1984—; contbr. articles to profl. jours. With USMC 1953-57. Mem. Inst. Mgmt. Cons., Rotary, 20-30's Club, Elks. Republican. Mem. Ch. of Jesus Christ of Latter Day Saints. Office: Donald R Reid Assocs 1925 W Fedora Fresno CA 93705

REID, HARRY, senator; b. Searchlight, Nev., Dec. 2, 1939; s. Harry and Inez Reid; m. Landra Joy Gould; children—Lana, Rory, Leif, Josh, Key. AA in Sci., U. So. Utah, 1959, LLD (hon.), 1984; BS, Utah State U., 1961; JD, George Washington U., 1964. Bar: Nev. 1963, U.S. Supreme Ct. City atty. Henderson, Nev., 1964-66; trustee So. Nev. Meml. Hosp. Bd., 1967-69, chmn. bd. trustees, 1968-69; mem. Nev. Assembly, 1969-70; lt. gov. Nev., 1970-74; chmn. Nev. Gaming Commn., 1977-81; mem. 98th-99th Congresses, 1983-87; U.S. senator from Nev. 1987—, mem. appropriations, environ. and pub. works, aging coms., 1987—; sec., Indian Affairs com. Calif. Dem. Congl. Del., 1983-86. Mem. Helsinki Commn. Named Nev. Jaycees Outstanding Young Man of Yr., 1970, Man of Yr., City of Hope, 1970; recipient Nat. Jewish Hosp.-Asthma Ctr. Humanitarian award, 1984, Honor award Am. Lung Assn., 1987. Mem. Nev. Bar Assn., Am. Bd. Trial Advocates, Phi Kappa Phi. Office: US Senate 702 Hart Senate Bldg Washington DC 20510

REID, JOSEPH LEE, physical oceanographer, educator; b. Franklin, Tex., Feb. 7, 1923; s. Joseph Lee and Ruby (Cranford) R.; m. Freda Mary Hunt, Apr. 7, 1953; children: Ian Joseph, Julian Richard. BA in Math., U. Tex., 1942; MS, Scripps Instn. Oceanography, 1950. Rsch. staff Scripps Instn. Oceanography, La Jolla, Calif., 1957-74; prof. oceanography Scripps Instn. Oceanography, La Jolla, 1974—; dir. Marine Life Rsch. Group, 1974-87; assoc. dir. Inst. Marine Resources, 1975-82; cons. Sandia Nat. Labs., Albuquerque, 1980-86. Author: On the Total Geostrophic Circulation of the South Pacific Ocean: Flow Patterns, Tracers and Transports, 1986; contbr. articles to profl. jours. Lt. USNR, 1942-46, ETO, PTO. Recipient award Nat. Oceanographic Data Ctr., Washington, 1984, Albatross award Am. Miscellaneous Soc., 1988. Fellow AAAS, Am. Geophys. Union (pres. Ocean Scis. sec. 1972-74, 1984-86); mem. Am. Soc. Limnology and Oceanography, Am. Meteorol. Soc. Home: 1105 Cuchara Dr Del Mar CA 92014 Office: Scripps Instn Oceanography Marine Life Rsch Group A-030 La Jolla CA 92093

REID, MICHAEL EDWARD, wholesale distribution executive; b. Casper, Wyo., Apr. 6, 1950; s. James Edward and Genevieve Sylvia (Maxon) R.; m. Pamla Kay Bretey, Dec. 14, 1968 (div. 1987); 1 child, Kelly Lynn. Student, Casper Coll., 1968-70. From city delivery driver to v.p., sales mgr. N.O. Nelson Co., Casper, 1970-77; pres. Plumdustrial Inc., Casper, 1977-84, Am. Pipe and Supply, Casper, 1984ú. Councilman Casper City Council, 1988—; mem. Bd. Pub. Utilities, Casper, 1988. Served as tech. sgt. USAFNG, 1970-78. Mem. Am. Supply Assn. Republican. Methodist. Lodge: Elks. Home: 1190 Cheshire Casper WY 82609 Office: Am Pipe & Supply 435 W 1st St Casper WY 82601

REID, PAMELA, dietitian, caterer; b. Enid, Okla., Mar. 17, 1951; d. James Richard and Betty Jane (Bradley) R.; m. Gordon J. Shamblin, May 12, 1974 (div. Nov. 1987); 1 child, Kelly Kathleen. BS in Food and Nutrition, U. Okla., 1974; MS in Food and Nutrition, San Diego State U., 1977. Registered dietitian. Food svc. dir. Clairemont Community Hosp., Am. Med. Internat., San Diego, 1978-80; adminstrv. dietitian Scripps Meml. Hosp., La Jolla, Calif., 1980-82; food and nutrition dir. Coronado (Calif.) Hosp., 1982—; pres. Catering Good Taste, Coronado, 1987—. Mem. Am. Soc. for Hosp. Food Svcs. Adminstrs. of the Am. Hosp. Assn. (San Diego chpt. founder and pres.), Am. Dietetic Assn. Members with Mgmt. Responsibilities in Health Care Delivery Systems (area coord. 1987—). Office: Coronado Hosp 250 Prospect Pl Coronado CA 92118

REID, PAUL, mortgage company executive; b. San Pedro, Calif., June 14, 1947; s. George Patrick and Helen Louise (Dilworth) R.; m. Marci Searles, Apr. 21, 1979; children: Andrew Paul, Whitney Beth. BA, Loyola U., 1969. Cert. secondary tchr., Calif. Fireman Snowmass (Colo.) Wildcat Fire Dist., 1972-77; driver Statewide Trucking Co., Englewood, Colo., 1977-79; sales mgr. B.F. Walker, inc., Denver, 1979-85; loan officer Universal Lending Corp., Denver, 1985—. Mem. Citizen Adv. Budget kCom., Aurora, Colo., 1982-87, Transp. Task Force, 1984-86; commr. Aurora Housing kAuthority, 1987—; coun. mem. Aurora City Coun., 1988—. Mem. Aurora Realto Bd., Aurora C. of C. (bd. dirs. 1987—), Aurora Rep. Forum (bd. dirs. 1985-86). Roman Catholic. Office: Universal Lending Corp 6775 E Evans Ave Denver CO 80224

REID, RALPH RALSTON, JR., engineer, electronics executive; b. Topeka, Nov. 19, 1934; s. Ralph Ralston Sr. and Else May (Whitebread) R.; m. Gloria Ann Cook, Feb. 3, 1957; children: Terri L., Jeffrey S. BS in Physics, Washburn U., 1956. V.p. engring. div. Loral Def. Systems Ariz., Litchfield, Ariz., 1963-89, sr. v.p., 1989—. Served to capt. USAF, 1957-60. Mem. Am. Electronics Assn., Am. Def. Preparedness Assn., Assn. U.S. Army. Republican. Home: 3853 W Port Royale Phoenix AZ 85023 Office: Loral Def Systems Ariz Litchfield AZ 85340

REID, SHARON JASEK, county official; b. San Diego, Aug. 13, 1944; d. Stanley John and Agnes Mercedes (Allen) J.; m. Douglas David Reid, Jan. 27, 1968. BA in English, San Diego State U., 1967, MA in Edn., 1971, postgrad. Cert. tchr. Tchr., chmn. curriculum Sweetwater Union High Sch. Dist., Chula Vista, Calif., 1968-73; exec. asst. Bd. of Suprs. County of San Diego, 1973-77, with waste resources office, 1977-80, solid waste program mgr., 1980-86, dep. dir. Dept. Pub. Works, 1986--. Mem. Calif. Commn. on Aging, 1978-81, Human Relations Commn., Chula Vista, 1968-74, Charter Rev. Commn., 1986--; cons. polit. campaigns, 1966--; bd. dirs. ASPA, San Diego, 1977-80, Girls and Boys Clubs of Chula Vista, 1980--. Named Tchr. of Yr., Chula Vista Jaycees, 1972; recipient awards Calif. Women in Govt., San Diego, 1987, United Way, San Diego, 1986. Mem. Am. Pub. Works Assn., Exec. Assn. San Diego, Bd. Registered Profl. Engrs. and Land Surveyores (bd. dirs. 1983--). Democrat. Roman Catholic. Home: 719 Melrose Ave Chula Vista CA 92010 Office: County of San Diego 5555 Overland Ave San Diego CA 92123

REID, SHARON MARIE, manufacturing executive; b. Syracuse, N.Y., Jan. 12, 1947; d. James Leroy and Gertrude Veronica (Kelly) La Montagne; m. Robert John Reid, Apr. 20, 1968 (div. Dec. 1979); children: Matthew Robert, Amy Lynn. BABA, Western Ill. U., 1968. With accounts payable dept. Am. Hosp. Supply Co., Edison, N.J., 1968-70; personnel asst. Am. Hosp. Supply Co., Edison, 1970-72; substitute tchr. nursery sch. Metuchen, N.J., 1977-78; office sec., mgr. Exec. ERA Real Estate, Phoenix, 1979-80; escrow sec. Minn. Title Ins. Co., 1980-82, br. mgr., escrow officer, 1984-86; escrow sec., asst. escrow officer Western Title, 1982-84; br. mgr., escrow officer 1st Southwestern Title Co., Phoenix, 1986; pres., chief fin. officer Duraplex, Orange, Calif., 1987—. Sec. Villa de Fildeles, 1986-88. Office: Duraplex 1005 W Hoover Abe Orange CA 92667

REID-BILLS, MAE, editor, historian; b. Shreveport, La.; d. Dayton Taylor and Bessie Oline (Boles) Reid; m. Frederick Gurdon Bills (div.); children—Marjorie Reid, Nancy Hawkins, Frederick Taylor, Virginia Thomas, Elizabeth Sharples. A.B., Stanford U., 1942, M.A., 1965; Ph.D., U. Denver, 1977. Mng. editor Am. West mag., Tucson, Ariz., 1979—. Gen. Electric fellow, 1963, William Robertson Coe fellow, 1964. Mem. Orgn. Am. Historians, Am. Hist. Assn., Phi Beta Kappa, Phi Alpha Theta. Office: Am West 7000 E Tanque Verde Tucson AZ 85715

REIDELL, MICHAEL CHARLES, telecommunications executive; b. Buffalo, Feb. 20, 1957; s. Edward Charles and Carol Ann (Dunning) R. Diver New Orleans, 1977-79; with Exxon, Anchorage, 1984-85, Standard Oil, Anchorage, 1986—; freelance cons., Anchorage, 1985—. Sgt. USAF, 1979-83. Home: 3014 Kerry Circle Anchorage AK 99504

REIDY, RICHARD ROBERT, publishing company executive; b. Patchogue, N.Y., May 9, 1947; s. Joseph Robert and Irene (Jennings) R.; m. Carolyn Alyce Armstrong, Mar. 21, 1970; children: Dawn Patricia, Shawn Patrick, Christopher Keith. Student, Suffolk County Community Coll., 1966-68, L.I. Tech. Sch., 1969-70, Scottsdale Community Coll., 1983-84, 85-86. Lic. real estate agt., Ariz. Restaurant owner Reidy's, Patchogue, 1973-77; design draftsman Sverdrop & Parcel, Tempe, Ariz., 1978-79, Sullivan & Masson, Phoenix, 1979-81; pres. Success Pub. Co., Scottsdale, Ariz., 1983—, Am. Real Estate and Devel. Co., Scottsdale, 1986—; with U.S. Postal Dept., 1980—. Editor, owner, pub.: Who's Who's in Ariz., 1984-85, 89—. Chief Scottsdale YMCA, 1983-84; eucharistic minister St. Daniel the Prophet Cath. Ch., Scottsdale, 1985—; World Wide Marriage Encounter, 1986—; pres. Coronado High Sch. Band Boosters, 1988—. Mem. Scottsdale C. of C., Phoenix Better Bus. Bur. Home: 7801 E CypressSt Scottsdale AZ 85257

REIF, JOSEPH ROLAND, airport management executive, security consultant; b. Sheboygan, Wis., May 15, 1924; s. Gerhart and Amelia Elizabeth (Lubach) R.; m. Margaret Elizabeth Walker, May 15, 1976. AA, Antelope Valley Coll., Lancaster, Calif., 1979. Enlisted USAF, 1941, advanced through grades to sr. master sgt., ret., 1962; mgr. airfield USAF Flight Test Ctr., Edwards AFB, Calif., 1963-79, Ravalli County Airport, Hamilton, Mont., 1980-86; capt. security Burns Internat. Airport, Reno, 1986—. Precinct sec. Rep. caucus, Reno, 1988; sustaining mem. Rep. Nat. Com., Washington, 1984—; mem. NSC, 1980—. Recipient Silver Snoopy award NASA Shuttle Astronauts, 1977, Spl. Recognition award NASA, 1978, 17 awards for excellence in airfield mgmt. U.S. Dept. Defense. Mem. Am. Assn. Airport Execs., Washington (safety, security com. 1983-85), Aircraft Owners and Pilots Assn., Experimental Aircraft Assn., Air Force Sergeants Assn., The Ret. Enlisted Assn. Lutheran. Lodges: Masons (30 degree, master), Shriners (32 degree). Home: 8355 Cub Ct Reno NV 89506 Office: Burns Internat 11111 Stead Blvd Reno NV 89506

REIFF, THEODORE CURTIS, investment banker; b. Cleve., Aug. 6, 1942; s. William Fred and Dorothy Louise (Knauer) R.; m. Janis Lynn Brunk, May 6, 1966 (div. Aug. 1980); m. Theresa Dolores Baranello, Oct. 30, 1982. BS, Ohio State U., 1969. Lic. real estate broker. Dir. adminstrv. svcs. Mgmt. Horizons, Inc., Columbus, Ohio, 1969-73; v.p. Danco Mgmt. Co., Lancaster, Ohio, 1973-74; sr. v.p. Anchor Lighting Corp., Columbus, 1974-75; ptnr. Curtis-Lee & Assocs., Delaware, Ohio, 1974-77; pres. Cartunes Corp., San Diego, Calif., 1977—; also bd. dirs. Cartunes Corp., San Diego; facilities coord. Raytheon Co., Burlington, Mass., 1979-82; ptnr. Greenstone & Reiff, San Diego, 1982-86; ptnr. Creative Bus. Strategies, Inc., San Diego, 1986—, pres., bd. dirs.; pres. Bus. Pubs. Inc., San Diego, 1989—, also bd. dirs.; bd. dirs. Integrated Ceramic Tech., San Marcos, Calif., Pacific Rim Interface Mems. Entreprises Inc.; instr. Miramar Coll., San Diego, 1984—. Mem. Friends of San Diego Zoo, 1980—; chmn. bus. adv. com. San Diego State U. Coll. of Bus., 1979-82. Served with Ohio N.G., 1966-72. Named Outstanding Businessman City of Columbus, Ohio, 1974; recipient Recognition award San Diego State U. Coll. of Bus., 1983, Appreciation award Am. Mktg. Assn., 1984, IEEE, 1986. Mem. Am. Electronics Assn., Computer Electronic Mfrs. Assn., Connector Study Group, Assn. for Corp. Growth, San Diego World Trade Assn. Home: 2805 Camino del Mar Del Mar CA 92014 Office: Creative Bus Strategies 10055 Barnes Canyon Rd Ste A San Diego CA 92121

REIL, KRIN MARIE, computer systems analyst; b. Lakeview, Mich., June 7, 1962; d. Frederick Laurie and Phyllis Jean (Edison) R. AS, DeVry Inst. Tech., Phoenix, 1984; BS, DeVry Inst. Tech., 1985. Programmer Internat. Fitness Ctrs., Scottsdale, Ariz., 1985-86; lead programmer Internat. Fitness Ctrs., 1986-87, database adminstr., 1987-88; systems analyst Cir. K. Corp., Phoenix, 1988—. Author profl. manuals. Active Big Sister/Big Bros., Big Rapids, Mich., 1981. Republican. Club: Scottsdale Bicycle. Home: 9259 E Raintree Scottsdale AZ 85260 Office: Cir K Corp 4500 S 40th St Phoenix AZ 85040

REILLY, ESTHER HUNTINGTON, interior designer; b. Portland, Maine, Aug. 19, 1917; d. Charles Huntington and Rachel Jones (Foster) Whitman; m. James Herbert Reilly, May 18, 1943; children: Diane English, Rachel Van Dessel, Allison. BA in English, Douglass Coll., 1939; cert. in interior architecture and decorating, Parsons Sch. Design, N.Y.C., 1943. Asst. interior designer Lucille B. Chisholm, Charlottesville, Va., 1950-58; interior designer Richardson's Contract Furniture Co., Menlo Park, Calif., 1963-68; prin. Esther H. Reilly Interiors, Palo Alto, 1958-63, 70—; instr. De Anza Coll., Cupertino, Calif., 1970-78, Coll. of San Mateo, Calif., 1977-78, Canada Coll., Redwood City, Calif., 1979—. Author: At Home with Decorating, 1970; contbr. articles to newspapers and mags. Mem. Am. Soc. Interior Designers (pres. Peninsula chpt. 1980, 3d prize 1984), Nat. Home Fashions League (v.p. no. Calif. chpt. 1977-78, catalyst of yr. 1978), Nat. Council for Interior Design Qualification (cert.), AAUW, Kappa Pi. Republican. Home: 401 Marlowe St Palo Alto CA 94301

REILLY, LAURA J., lawyer; b. Ames, Iowa; d. Lawrence J. and Dorothy J. (Waller) R.; m. James L. Abrams, 1975; children: Reilly Katherine, Merrill Elizabeth, Jacqueline Lee. BS, U. Iowa, 1969; MS, U. Calif., San Francisco, 1970; JD, Rutgers U., 1975; LLM, U. Denver, 1983. Bar: Colo. 1975, Tex. 1978. Rsch. asst. Baker, Baker & Wilson, Oklahoma City, 1975-77; atty. Office of Gen. Counsel, U. Tex., Austin, 1977-79; asst. to Atty. Gen. Colo., Denver, 1979-81; atty. U.S. West Communications, Denver, 1981—; bd. dirs. Vis. Nurses Support Svcs., Inc., 1985—, chmn., 1987—. Mem. ABA, Colo. Bar Assn., Colo. Women's Bar Assn. Roman Catholic. Office: U S West Communications 1801 California Ste 5100 Denver CO 80202

REILLY, MICHAEL GEORGE, sales professional; b. Tucson, Mar. 9, 1949; s. Christopher A. and Bess (Callaway) R.; m. Sara Spencer, June 9, 1973 (div. 1986); children: Michael Patrick, Stephen McCord. BSBA, U. Ariz., 1971. Sales rep. Carnation Co., Phoenix, 1971-74, M&M/Mars Co., Tucson, 1974-77; unit mgr. M&M/Mars Co., Buffalo, 1977-81; brands mgr. M&M/Mars Co., Hackettstown, N.J., 1981; mem. nat. sales planning staff M&M/Mars Co., Hackettstown, 1981-82; dist. mgr. M&M/Mars Co., San Francisco, 1982-85, region dir., 1985—. Mem. Sales Mgrs. Club San Francisco, Illuminators of Calif. Republican. Episcopalian. Office: M&M Mars Ste 220 1111 Bay Hill Dr San Bruno CA 94066

REILLY, PATRICK JOHN, engineering-construction company executive; b. Nutley, N.J., Oct. 10, 1925; s. Philip and Anna (Cox) O'Reilly; m. Marcia Garcia Vazquez, July 27, 1957; children: Anne Maria, Patrick John, Thomas J., Frank P. BSCE, NYU, 1950; cert. practical constrn. law, U. Santa Clara, 1977. Registered gen. engring. contractor, Calif. Shaft engr. Lincoln Tunnel third tube Walsh Constrn. Co., N.Y.C., 1950-54; asst. equipment mgr. Brown-Raymond-Walsh, Madrid, 1954-55, project engr., 1955-57; v.p., project mgr. wastewater treatment plants Shanley Constrn. Co., San Francisco, 1957-65; constrn. mgr. W.W. Kimmins and Sons, Buffalo, 1965-70, gen. supt. hwy., utilities and underground constrn., 1970; dir. mcpl. waste projects, constrn. mgr. Monsanto Environ. Chem. Co., Chgo., 1970-74; v.p., project mgr., dir. constrn. and regional constrn. mgr. solid waste facilities BSP div. Envirotech Corp., Menlo Park, Calif., 1974-84, v.p. project mgmt., 1984-88; ptnr., v.p. Legal/Tech Strategies, Inc., Menlo Park, 1988—; bd. dirs. Bank of Montreal, Laidlaw Transp. Ltd. With USAAF, 1943-45. Decorated D.F.C., Air medal with 5 oak leaf clusters. Mem. ASCE, Am. Arbitration Assn. (panel arbitrators), NSPE (Nat. Soc. Profl. Engrs.). Roman Catholic. Home: 20719 Woodward Ct Saratoga CA 95070 Office: Legal/Tech Strategies Inc 1720 S Amphlett Blvd San Mateo CA 94402

REILLY, ROBERT E., JR., transportation company executive; b. Paterson, N.J., July 7, 1948; s. Robert and Ruth (Veronelli) R.; m. Dolce B. Mosco Reilly (div. 1986); children: David, Amy; m. Marcia Elizabeth Otis Reilly, Feb. 14, 1987. BS in Mktg., Seton Hall U., 1970. Sales rep. A.R. Mecken Co., Springfield, N.J., 1970-73, Harris-Sybold Co., Cleve., 1973-74; sales rep., sales planning mgr., br. mgr. AB Dick Co., Niles, Ill., 1974-83; v.p. DHL Airways Inc., Redwood City, Calif., 1983—. Office: DHL Airways Inc Twin Dolphin Dr Redwood City CA

REIM, KENNETH MAURICE, mining executive; b. Ashland, Nebr., July 7, 1926; s. Herman August and Gertrude Bessie (Hennig) R.; m. Ann Aronitz, Nov. 10, 1973. BS, N.Mex. Sch. Mines, 1950; MS, U. Wash., 1951. Registered profl. engr., N.Mex. Exploration geologist United Geophys. Corp., Tucson and western U.S., 1953-57; dist. geologist Kern County Land Co., various locations, 1957-67; chief mining engr. Kern County Land Co., Bakersfield & S.Francisco, Calif., 1967-68, Tenneco Oil Co., Houston, 1968-69; minerals staff geologist Getty Oil Co., L.A., 1969-75; v.p., bd. dirs. Getty Mines, Ltd., L.A., 1970-73; mgr. mining devel. U.S. Borax, L.A., 1975-81, 85—, dep. project mgr. engring. Quartz Hill project., 1981-85. Contbr. papers to profl. publs. Corp. Chem. Corps., U.S. Army, 1951-53. Rsch. fellow U.S. Bur. Mines, 1950. Mem. AIME, Soc. Mining Engrs., Can. Inst. Mining Engrs., Soc. Econ. Geologists (fin. com. 1988—), Masons. Home: 12245 Sunset Park Way Los Angeles CA 90064 Office: US Borax & Chem Corp 3075 Wilshire Blvd Los Angeles CA 90010

REIMER, CHRIS RUSSEL, manufacturing company executive; b. Milw., Nov. 1, 1949; s. Russel Frank and Audrey Carol (Filbrandt) R.; m. Cindi Lou Stuessy, Dec. 27, 1969; children: Keri Alicia, Lisa Kristen, Jill Diana. BA, U. Wis., 1971; postgrad., San Diego State U., 1983. Div. mgr. Hoffman Fire Equip. Co., Inc., Madison, Wis., 1971-79, Interstate Welding & Supply, Marinette, Wis., 1979-83; sales engr. Devcon Systems Corp., San Diego, 1983-84; reg. mgr. Chemetron Fire Systems, San Diego, 1984-85, Fike Fire Suppression Systems, San Diego, 1985—; fire sci. instr. Madison ARea Tech. Coll., 1975-77; lectr. in field. Coordinator Christian Svc. Brigade, Madison, 1977-79; mem. gov.'s task force on product liability State of Wis., 1977-79. Named Mgr. of the Yr., Fike Fire Suppression, 1986. Republican. Baptist. Home: 11825 Caminito Ronaldo #118 San Diego CA 92128 Office: Fike Fire Suppression 11825 Caminito Ronaldo #118 San Diego CA 92128

REINBOLD, GEORGE WILMER, microbiologist, consultant; b. Williamsport, Pa., Apr. 10, 1919; s. George Wilmer and Emma Pearl (Schramm) R.; m. Hazel Strope; children: George W. III, Hope A. Posegate, Robert S. BS in Dairy Mfg., Pa. State U., 1942; MS in Dairy Mfg., U. Ill., 1947, PhD in Dairy Sci., 1949. Group leader rsch. and devel. Kraft Foods, Glenview, Ill., 1949-53; product technician Kraft Foods, Glenview, 1953-58; product mgr. Tolibia Cheese Mfg. Co., Fond Du Lac, Wis., 1958-59; prof. food technology, bacteriology Iowa State U., Ames, 1959-74; v.p. rsch. and devel. Leprino Foods, Denver, 1974-83; cons. Reinbold & Assocs. Inc., Wheat Ridge, Colo., 1983—; cons. numerous cheese mfg. cos., worldwide, 1983—. Author: Italian Cheese Varieties, 1963, American Cheese Varieties, 1965, Swiss Cheese Varieties, 1972; co-author various books; contbr. more than 200 articles to profl. jours.; patentee in field. Maj. U.S. Army, 1942-46, Guam. Recipient Pfizer award, Am. Dairy Sci. Assn., 1970, D.R.I.N.C. award, Am. Dairy Sci. Assn., 1977, Disting. Svc. award, Am. Dairy Sci. Assn., 11981. Republican. Methodist. Home and Office: 4180 Dudley St Wheat Ridge CO 80033

REINER, ERROL GENE, data processing executive; b. Billings, Mont., Dec. 12, 1941; s. Eugene Theodore and Edna Mary (Halverson) R.; m. Patricia Joy Shehee, Dec. 19, 1965 (div. July 1972); children: Eric Maxwell, Lorre Leigh; m. Donna Jane Cole, Oct. 20, 1973; children: Errol Maxwell, Corey Christopher. BS, USAF Acad., 1965; MPA, Golden Gate U., 1979. Commd. 2d lt. USAF, 1965, advanced through grades to lt. col., 1981, fighter pilot, 1965-76; ops. officer 480th Tactical Fighter Squadron, Spangdahlem Air Base, Fed. Republic Germany, 1976-77; staff officer U.S. Readiness Command, Tampa, Fla., 1978-80; chief ops. plan 8th Tactical Fighter Wing, Kunsan AFB, Republic of Korea, 1981; officer space plans Aerospace Command, Colorado Springs, Colo., 1982-84; ret. 1984; dir. ops. Xebec Corp., Colorado Springs, 1984-85; dir. C3I program devel. Planning Research Group, Colorado Springs, 1985—. Chmn. parish council Ch. at Woodmoor, Monument, Colo., 1986. Decorated DFC with oak leqaf cluster, Disting Svc. Meritoriuous medal, Meritorious Svc. medal, Air medal with 10 oak cleaf clusters. Mem. Air Force Assn. (Def. Meritorious Service award), Armed Forces Communications and Electronics Assn., Nat. Security Indsl. Assn. (bd. dirs. 1987—), Daedalians. Republican. Lutheran. Office: Planning Rsch Corp/EIS 1250 Academy Park Loop Ste 102 Colorado Springs CO 80910

REINES, FREDERICK, physicist, educator; b. Paterson, N.J., Mar. 16, 1918; s. Israel and Gussie (Cohen) R.; m. Sylvia Samuels, Aug. 30, 1940; children: Robert G., Alisa K. M.E., Stevens Inst. Tech., 1939, M.S., 1941; Ph.D., NYU, 1944; D.Sc. (hon.), U. Witwatersrand, 1966, D. Engring. (hon.), 1984. Mem. staff Los Alamos Sci. Lab., 1944-59; group leader Los Alamos Sci. Lab. (Theoretical div.), 1945-59; dir. (AEC expts. on Eniwetok Atoll), 1951; prof. physics, head dept. Case Inst. Tech., 1959-66; prof. physics U. Calif.-Irvine, 1966—, dean phys. scis., 1966-74, disting. prof. physics, 1987—; co-discoverer elementary nuclear particles, free antineutrino, 1956. Contbr. numerous articles to profl. jours.; contbg. author: Effects of Atomic Weapons, 1950. Mem. Cleve. Symphony Chorus, 1959-62. Recipient J. Robert Oppenheimer meml. prize, 1981, Nat. medal of Sci., 1983, U. Calif. Irvine medal, 1987; Guggenheim fellow, 1958-59; Sloan fellow, 1959-63. Fellow Am. Phys. Soc., AAAS; mem. Am. Assn. Physics Tchrs., Argonne U. Assn. (trustee 1965-66), Am. Acad. Arts and Scis., Nat. Acad. Sci., Phi Beta Kappa, Sigma Xi, Tau Beta Pi. Office: U Calif at Irvine Irvine CA 92717

REINHARD, JEAN BERYL, trombonist, violinist; b. Bishop, Calif., Sept. 9, 1915; d. Harry and Florence (Arnold) Shaw; m. Joel J. Reinhard, Jan. 22, 1938; children: Sandra Jean Reinhard Jackson, Joel William. AA, Shasta Coll., 1953; BEd, Chico State Coll, 1959. Elem. tchr. Shasta County Pub. Schs., Anderson, Calif., 1953-74; tchr. Spanish Anderson Elem. Sch., 1968; substitute tchr. Spanish Spanish Anderson Elem. Sch., 1974-88; pvt. tchr. piano Redding, Calif., 1980--; tchr. trombone Shasta County Youth Summer Camp, 1984. Trombonist, violinist Shasta Symphony, also pres.; pres. Cottonwood (Calif.) PTA, 1950, Internat. Community Concert Assn., Redding, Calif., 1982; telephone chmn. Redding Rep. Women, 1985. Mem. AAUW (historian Redding 1969--), Redding Women's Club (chmn. fine arts and scholarship awards 1985-88), Emblem Club (Americanism chmn. 1981-82), Shasta Coll. Alumni Assn. (life), Alpha Delta Kappa (del. Calif. conv., past pres.). Home: 3841 Alma Ave Redding CA 96002

REINHARDT, STEPHEN ROY, judge; b. N.Y.C., Mar. 27, 1931; s. Gottfried and Silvia (Hanlon) R.; children: Mark, Justin, Dana. B.A. cum laude, Pomona Coll., 1951; LL.B., Yale, 1954. Bar: Calif. 1958. Law clk. to U.S. Dist. Judge Luther W. Youngdahl, Washington, 1956-57; atty. O'Melveny & Myers, L.A., 1957-59; partner Fogel Julber Reinhardt Rothschild & Feldman (L.C.), L.A., 1959-80; judge U.S. Ct. Appeals for 9th Cir., L.A., 1980—; Mem. exec. com. Dem. Nat. Com., 1969-72, nat. Dem. committeeman for Calif., 1976-80; pres. L.A. Recreation and Parks Commn., 1974-75; mem. Coliseum Commn., 1974-75, L.A. Police Commn., 1975-78, pres., 1978-80; sec., mem. exec. com. L.A. Olympic Organizing Com., 1980—; bd. dirs. Amateur Athletic Found. of L.A., 1984—; adj. prof. Loyola Law Sch., L.A., 1988—. Served to 1st lt. USAF, 1954-56. Mem. ABA (labor law coun. 1975-77).

REINHART, ARTHUR SULLIVAN, consultant; b. Sabinal, Tex., Dec. 1, 1919; s. A.F. and Pocahontas E. (Sullivan) R.; B.S., Tex. Tech. U., 1941; postgrad., Air War Coll., 1961, Air Force Inst. Tech., 1962; M. Internat. Affairs, George Washington U., 1966; B.B.A., Boise State U., 1977; m. Hilma H. Ruuttila, Feb. 22, 1947; children—Arthur K., LauriAnne, Robin M., Brian M. Engr., U.S. Bur. Reclamation, Denver, 1946-51; commd. 2 lt. C.E., 1941, transferred to U.S. Air Force, advanced through grades to col., 1969; engaged in personnel, planning, ops.; dir. plans, comptroller Air Res. Personnel Center, Denver, 1969-74; ret., 1974; pvt. practice cons., Boise, Idaho, 1974—. Community adv. Downtown Boise Urban Renewal; chmn. Boise City Transit Com.; vice chmn., treas. Ada County Air Quality Bd. Served with USAAF, 1941-46; Decorated Legion of Merit. Mem. Ret. Officers Assn., Air Force Assn., Acad. Polit. Sci., Boise Com. on Fgn. Relations, Tex. Tech U. Dad's Assn. (trustee). Episcopalian. Clubs: Masons, Kiwanis. Home and office: 4933 Sunderland Dr Boise ID 83704

REINING, BETH LAVERNE (BETTY REINING), public relations consultant, journalist; b. Fargo, N.D.; d. George and Grace (Twiford) Reimche; student N.D. State Coll., U. Minn., Glendale Community Coll., Calif. State Coll., Carson; 1 dau., Carolyn Ray Toohey Hiett; m. Jack Warren Reining, Oct. 3, 1976 (div. 1984). Originated self-worth seminars in Phoenix, 1970-76; owner Janzik Pub. Relations, 1971-76; talk show reporter-hostess What's Happening in Ariz., Sta. KPAZ-TV, 1970-73; writer syndicated column People Want to Know, Today newspaper, Phoenix, 1973; owner JB Communications, Phoenix, 1976-84; owner, pres. Media Communications, 1984—; freelance writer; tchr. How to Weigh Your Self-Worth courses Phoenix Coll., Rio Solado Community Coll., Phoenix, 1976-84; instr. pub. rels. Scottsdale (Ariz.) Community Coll., 1987; muralist, works include 25 figures in med. office. Founder Ariz. Call-A-Teen Youth Resources, Inc., pres., 1975-76, v.p., 1976-77, now bd. dirs. Recipient awards including 1st pl. in TV writing Nat. Fedn. Press Women, 1971-88, numerous state awards in journalism Ariz. Press Women, 1971-76, Good Citizen award Builders of Greater Ariz., 1961. Mem. Ariz. Press Women (1st place award 1988), No. Ariz. Press Women (pres. 1983), Nat. Fedn. Am. Press Women, Pub. Relations Soc. Am., Phoenix Pub. Relations Soc., Nat. Acad. TV Arts and Scis., Phoenix Valley of Sun Convention Bur., Verde Valley C. of C. (bd. dirs., tourism chmn. 1986-87, Best Chair of Yr. award 1986), Phoenix Metro C. of C. Cottonwood C. of C. (chmn. of Yr. award, 1986). Inventor stocking-tension twist footlet, 1962. Club: Phoenix Press. Office: PO Box 10509 Phoenix AZ 85064

REINISCH, NANCY RAE, social worker, consultant; b. Chgo., Mar. 31, 1953; d. Charles Richard and Marianne (Gross) R.; m. Paul A. Salmen, June 14, 1980; children: Chas, Marcus. BA in Sociology cum laude, Colo. Coll., 1975; cert. drug and alcohol counseling, U. Minn., 1980; MSW, U. Denver, 1982. Counselor Rampart Boys' Home, Colorado Springs, Colo., 1975; advocate bilinqual community Migrants in Action, St. Paul, 1976; therapist Chrysalis Ctr. for Women, Mpls., 1979; team leader and prevention specialist Project Charlie, Edina, Minn., 1977-80, also trainer, cons., 1985—; mental health worker Bethesda Mental Health Ctr. and Hosp., Denver, 1980-83; therapist Gateway Alcohol Recovery Ctr., Aurora, Colo., 1983-84; pvt. practice therapy, also dir. Family Practice Counseling Service, Glenwood Springs, Colo., 1984—; bd. dirs. Garfield Youth Services Teen Assistance Program, Glenwood Springs, Adv./Safehouse Project, Glenwood Springs; mem. Valley View Hosp. Ethics com., Glenwood Springs, 1986—. Mem. Nat. Assn. Social Workers, NOW, Nat. Abortion Rights Action League, Common Cause, Colo. Pub. Interest Research Group. Democrat. Jewish. Office: Family Practice Counseling Svc 1905 Blake St Glenwood Springs CO 81601

REINSTEIN, HENRY ALLEN, real estate management and franchising consultant, mail order executive; b. Bklyn., July 8, 1922; s. Harry M. and Jennie (Blam) R.; m. Claire Steckman, Nov. 9, 1947; children: Jon Eric (Rick), Lisa. BA, Bklyn. Coll., 1949; MBA, Wichita U., 1954; postgrad., UCLA; grill master cert. (hon.), McDonald's Hamburger U., Los Angeles, 1975. Gen. mgr. Hurley Distbg., Jamaica, N.Y., 1946-50; ptnr. Geneva Electronics, Elmhurst, N.Y., 1950-55; regional sales mgr. Philco-Bendix Laundercenters, Woodside, N.Y., 1955-68; real estate and franchise dir. Internat. House of Pancakes, Los Angeles, 1969-76; real estate dir. West Winchell's Donuts, La Mirada, Calif., 1976-80; pres. Henry Allen Co., Northridge, Calif., 1980—; cons. Papallini Hair Inst., Los Angeles, 1965-67, Permac Dry Cleaner, Los Angeles, 1968-69, Gibraltar Transmission, San Diego, 1980-84, Auto Oil Changers, Long Beach, Calif., 1985—. Served with U.S. Army Air Corps, 1942-46, ETO. Mem. City of Hope (Northridge, Calif. chpt.), Assn. Corp. Real Estate Execs., Am. Entrepreneurs Assn., Kitco Internat. Inc. Import-Export Assn. Democrat. Jewish. Home and Office: Henry Allen Co 11641 Viking Ave Northridge CA 91326

REISBERG, LEON ELTON, education educator; b. Dallas, Sept. 1, 1949; s. Morris Abraham and Gertrude (Turner) R.; m. Iris Fudel, July 3, 1973 (div. 1986); children: Joshua Fudell, Leah Fudell. BS in Edn., U. Tex., Austin, 1971; MEd, U. Ark., Fayetteville, 1972; EdD, U. Kans., Lawrence, 1981. Cert. tchr., Wash. Tchr. Oklahoma City Sch. Dist., 1972-75, Putnam City Sch. Dist., Oklahoma City, 1975-78, U. Kans. Med. Ctr., Kansas City, 1978-79; asst. prof. Pacific Luth. U., Tacoma, 1981-88; assoc. prof. edn. Pacific Luth. U., 1988—, chmn. dept. spl. edn., 1986—; project dir., Consulting Spl. Edn. Personnel Tng. Project, Tacoma, 1983-86. Consulting editor, Learning Disability Quar., 1981—, Acad. Therapy, 1988—; contbr. articles to profl. publs. Mem. Coun. Exceptional Children, Coun. Learning Disabilities, Assn. Trainer Spl. Edn. Personnel, Phi Kappa Phi. Democrat. Jewish. Office: Pacific Luth U Sch Edn Tacoma WA 98447

REISINGER, GEORGE LAMBERT, management consultant; b. Pitts., Aug. 28, 1930; s. Eugene Merle and Pauline Jane (Lambert) R.; m. Judith Ann Brush, Nov. 24, 1967; children—Douglas Lambert, Christine Elizabeth. B.S. in Bus. Adminstrn., Central Coll., 1953; postgrad., Cleveland-Marshall Law Sch., 1962-67. Asst. personnel mgr. Continental Can Co., Houston, 1958-60; mgr. labor relations The Glidden Co., Cleve., 1960-67; dir. employee relations Mobil Oil Corp., N.Y.C., Caracas, Dallas, Denver, 1967-78; sr. v.p. Minton & Assocs., Denver, 1978-82; v.p., ptnr. Korn-Ferry Internat., Denver, 1982-86; pres., mng. ptnr. The Sigma Group, Inc., Denver, 1986—. Bd. dirs. Ponderosa Hills Civic Assn., 1977-80, Arapahoe County Youth League; Republican campaign dir. for county commr., 1978; pres. Douglas County Youth League. Served with USAF, 1953-58. Mem. Am. Soc. Personnel Adminstrs., N.Y. Personnel Mgmt. Soc., Colo. Soc. Personnel Adminstrn., Am. Soc. Profl. Cons., Rocky Mountain Inst. Fgn. Trade and Fin., Employment Mgmt. Assn., Lions Internat. Republican. Methodist. Clubs: Denver Petroleum, Pinery Country, Republican 1200. Lodge: Lions. Home: 7924 Deertrail Dr Parker CO 80134 Office: The Sigma Group Inc 717 17th St Ste 1440 Denver CO 80202-3314

REISMAN, ANNE ELIZABETH, social worker; b. Inglewood, Calif., Sept. 19, 1957; d. Karl and Hedy (Davis) R.; m. Brian Mittman, Nov. 20, 1988. BA in Psychology, UCLA, 1980, MSW, 1985. Research assoc. York Clinic, Guy's Hosp., London, 1980-81; intern W.I.S.E, Santa Monica, Calif., 1983-84, Los Angeles County Dept. Mental Health, L.A., 1984-85; dir. shared housing program Westside Ind. Services to Elderly, Santa Monica, Calif., 1985--; mem. Community Housing Resources Bd., 1985--; mem. adv. council Ret. Sr. Vol. Program, 1985--. Vol. Jewish Family Service, Van Nuys, Calif., 1986--. Mem. Nat. Assn. Social Workers, Am. Soc. on Aging, Nat. Council on Aging, UCLA Sch. Social Welfare Alumni Assn., Jr. League L.A. Democrat. Office: Westside Ind Svcs 1320 Santa Monica Mall Santa Monica CA 90401

REISTETTER, DAVID PETER, mechanical engineer; b. Binghamton, N.Y., Nov. 13, 1950; s. Andrew Charles and Stephanie Agnes (Vlasak) R.; m. Janet Louise Stewart, Aug. 17, 1974; children: Matthew David, Christine Michelle, Steven David. BSME, Purdue U., 1972; med. cert. in prosthetics and orthotics, UCLA, 1978; MBA with distinction, Nat. U., 1987. Registered profl. engr., Calif. Practitioner in prosthetics and orthotics Orthomedics, San Diego, 1978-79; gas design engr. San Diego Gas and Electric Co., 1979-81, sr. engr. gas standards, 1981--. Sponsored exec., Combined Arts and Edn. coun., San Diego, 1983; scout leader Boy Scouts Am., San Diego, 1988. Lt. (j.g.) USN, 1972-77, Vietnam. Mem. Pacific Coast Gas Assn., ASME (mem. gas piping tech. com.), Model A Ford Club San Diego. Home: 2721 S Barcelona St Spring Valley CA 92077 Office: San Diego Gas and Electric 101 Ash St San Diego CA 92101

REITAN, HAROLD THEODORE, management consultant; b. Max, N.D., Nov. 3, 1928; s. Walter Rudolph and Anna Helga (Glesne) R.; m. Margaret Lucille Bonsac, Dec. 29, 1954; children—Eric, Karen, Chris, Jon. B.A., St. Olaf Coll., 1950; M.A. in Social Psychology, U. Fla., 1962, Ph.D., 1967. Commd. officer U.S. Air Force, 1951, advanced through grades to col.; comdr., U.S. Air Force Spl. Treatment Ctr., Lackland, Tex., 1971-74, U.S. Air Force Corrections and Rehab. Group, Lowry, Colo., 1974-76, Tech. Tng. Wing, 1976-78, ret., 1978; mgr. health services Coors Industries, Golden, Colo., 1978-84, mgr. tng. and organizational devel., 1984—. Decorated Legion of Merit with oak leaf cluster, D.F.C. with oak leaf cluster, Bronze Star, Meritorious Service medal, Air medal with four oak leaf clusters. Mem. Am. Psychol. Assn., Phi Kappa Phi. Republican. Lutheran. Contbr. articles to profl. jours. Home: 12098 E Colorado Pl Aurora CO 80012 Office: Coors Industr Golden CO 80401

REITEMEIER, (TIMOTHY) GEORGE, chamber of commerce executive; b. Pueblo, Colo., Jan. 17, 1931; s. Paul John and Ethel Regina (McCarthy) R.; m. JoAnn Lillian Perkins, May 19, 1952 (dec. July 1977); children: Michael Douglas, Ann Ellen Loutzenhiser; m. Joy Arlene Little Duvall, Nov. 16, 1985. A of Arts and Scis., U. So. Colo., 1951. Cert. chamber exec. Mgr. C. of C., Florence, Colo., 1952-53; asst. mgr. C. of C., Cheyenne, Wyo., 1953; mgr. C. of C., Longmont, Colo., 1953-55; dist. mgr. southwest div. C. of C., Washington, 1955-57; mgr. C. of C., Canon City, Colo., 1957-59, Casper, Wyo., 1959-64; v.p. C. of C., Niagara Falls, N.Y., 1965-70; pres., gen. mgr. C. of C., Spokane, Wash., 1970—; bd. dirs. Spokane Unltd. Bd. dirs. Expo '74 Worlds Fair, Spokane, SEACAB. Served with USAF, 1949-50. Mem. Assn. of Wash. Bus. (bd. dirs.), U.S. C.of C. (local chamber com.), Wash. C. of C. Execs. (past v.p., pres.), Colo. C. of C. Execs. (v.p.), Oreg.-Wash. Idaho Chamber Officers/Mgrs. Assn. (pres. 1973-74). Republican. Roman Catholic. Home: 4717 Pittsburg Spokane WA 99223 Office: Spokane Area C of C PO Box 2147 Spokane WA 99210

REITER, ELIZABETH A., dentist; b. Canton, Ohio, Sept. 30, 1960; d. Richard Dudley and Elinor Elizabeth (Wilson) L.; m. Holger Otto Reiter, Feb. 13, 1988. AB, Occidental Coll., 1982; DDS, U. So. Calif., 1986. Pvt. practice Phoenix, 1986-87, San Francisco, 1987--. Mem. ADA, Calif. Dental Assn., Am. Assn. Women Dentists, Omicron Kappa Upsilon. Presbyterian.

REITHEL, ROBERT JAMES, physics and mathematics educator; b. Rosiclare, Ill., Oct. 15, 1917; s. Fred Arthur and Ruth Jane R.; BS, Western Ky. U., 1939; MS, U. Ky., 1953; m. Ada Louise Emmick, July 15, 1939; children: Mary Elaine, Theresa Louise, Robert Julian, Catherine June, James Fredrick, Brian Joseph. Grad. asst. dept. physics U. Ky., 1939-40; tchr. math. and sci., Henderson County, Ky., 1947-51; instr. dept. physics U. Ky., Lexington, 1951-53; physicist, staff mem. U. Calif., Los Alamos Sci. Lab., 1953-69; tchr. math. Clovis (N.Mex.) Mcpl. Schs., 1969-81; dir. SW Capital Corp., Albuquerque. Democratic chmn., Precinct 31, Curry County, N.Mex.; Scoutmaster Boy Scouts Am., 1958-61, 74-77, 80-82, dist. commr. Los Alamos dist., 1961-65, v.p. Kit Carson council, 1965; chmn. Los Alamos United Fund, 1966-67; chmn. Los Alamos City-wide PTA, 1962. With U.S. Army, 1940-47, lt. col. Res. ret. Decorated Bronze Star medal with V, Purple Heart. Mem. AAAS, Am. Assn. Physics Tchrs., Am. Phys. Soc., NEA, Ret. Officers Assn., Air Force Assn., Clovis Edn. Assn., Sigma Xi, Kiwanis (pres. El Desayuno, lt. gov. Div. 13, SW Dist.). Democrat. Methodist. Home: 1004 W Christopher Dr Clovis NM 88101

REITZ, JEANNE GEIGER, mathematics educator; b. New Orleans, Feb. 2, 1941; d. George Thomas and Leonora Agnes (Ziifle) Geiger; m. Ronald Charles Reitz, Jan. 23, 1965; children: Erica Anne, Pieter Brett. BS, La. State U., 1963. Research asst. Tulane Med. Sch., New Orleans, 1963-64; tchr. Jefferson Parish Sch. Dist., Gretna, La., 1965-66; sales rep. Jacobson's, Ann Arbor, Mich., 1966-67; tchr. Novi (Mich.) Schs., 1967-68, Washoe County Sch. Dist., Reno, 1982—; mem. testing com. Washoe County Schs., 1987—; mem. equity in math. adv. bd. U. Nev., Reno, 1987-88; with publicity Chapel Hill Sch. Art Guild, 1971-74. Bd. dirs. Nev. Opera Assn., Reno, 1987—, Young Audiences No. Nev., Reno, 1981-83; dist. dir. Met. Opera Nat. Council, Reno, 1985-86. Mem. NEA, AAUW (sec. 1981-83, 86-88), Washoe County Tchrs. Assn. (Disting. Performance award 1987), Washoe County Math. Assn. (newsletter editor 1987-88), Faculty Wives U. Nev. Club (sec., 2nd v.p.). Republican. Roman Catholic. Home: 3237 Susileen Dr Reno NV 89509 Office: Swope Mid Sch 901 Keele Dr Reno NV 89509

REITZ, RICHARD ELMER, physician; b. Buffalo, Sept. 18, 1938; s. Elmer Valentine and Edna Anna (Guenther) R.; m. Gail Ida Pounds, Aug. 20, 1960; children: Richard Allen, Mark David. BS, Heidelberg Coll., 1960; MD, SUNY-Buffalo, 1964. Intern Hartford (Conn.) Hosp., 1964-65, resident in medicine, 1966-67; asst. resident in medicine Yale U., 1965-66; vis. research assoc. NIH, Bethesda, Md., 1967-68; research fellow in medicine Harvard Med. Sch., Mass. Gen. Hosp., Boston, 1967-69; asst. dir. clin. investigation ctr. Naval Regional Med. Ctr., 1969-71; dir. Endocrine Metabolic Center, Oakland, Calif., 1973—; asst. prof. medicine U. Calif.-San Francisco, 1971-76; assoc. clin. prof. medicine U. Calif.-Davis, 1976-86 ; clin. prof. med. 1986—; chief endocrinology Providence Hosp., Oakland, Calif., 1972—. Contbr. articles to profl. jours., chpt. to book. Mem. scholarship com., Bank of Am., San Francisco, 1983. Served to lt. comdr. USNR, 1969-71. Mem. Endocrine Soc., Am. Soc. Bone and Mineral Research, Am. Fedn. Clin. Research, Am. Fertility Soc., Am. Soc. Internal Medicine, AAAS. Democrat. Lodge: Rotary. Home: 867 Stonehaven Dr Walnut Creek CA 94598 Office: Endocrine Metabolic Ctr 3100 Summit St Oakland CA 94623

RELYEA, ROBERT GORDON, management consultant; b. Bloomington, N.Y., Nov. 10, 1917; s. Aaron Dewitt and Margaret (Smedes) R.; m. Eleanor Florence Caminiti, June 2, 1938 (dec. Feb. 1984); children: Robert Paul, Peter Douglas, Paula Florence Relyea Holsinger; m. Ann P. Delmonico, June 23, 1985. BGS, Rollins Coll., 1966; MS, Fla. State U., 1969; PhD, Clayton U., 1987. Mgr. UTC div. United Aircraft, Inc., Cape Canaveral, Fla., 1969-71, Sun Lakes, Ariz., 1973—; mgr. quality and svc. United Mobile Homes, Inc., Chandler, Ariz., 1971-73; instr. Maricopa Community Colls., PHoenix, 1974—; quality mgr. IMC Magnetics, Inc., Tempe, Ariz., 1979-80; asst. to pres. Ecotronics Labs., Inc., Scottsdale, Ariz., 1980-81; quality mgr. Parker-Hannifin Co., Goodyear, Ariz., 1981-83; sr. quality auditor Govt. Electronics

Group/Radar Systems Div. Motorola, Inc., Tempe, 1983-88; bd. dirs. SanTan Adobe, Inc., Sun Lakes. Contbr. articles to profl. publs. Scoutmaster Boy Scouts Am., Ridgewood, N.J., 1946-57; bd. dirs. Sun lakes Home Owners Assn., 1974-78, Adult Action, Inc., Mesa, 1975-85, Cactus-Pine Coun. Girl Scouts U.S.A., Phoenix, 1980-83. Mem. Nat. Contract Mgmt. Assn., Am. Soc. for Quality Control (del. to USSR, Bulgaria and Hungary 1988), Missile, Space and Range Pioneers (life), Order of Arrow, Masons, Shriners, Pi Lambda Theta. Home and Office: Better Mgmt Assocs Inc 9003 N Citrus Ln Sun Lakes AZ 85248

REMBIS, MICHAEL ANTHONY, hospital administrator; b. San Pedro, Calif., Dec. 21, 1953; s. Anthony Frank and Irene Marie (Matthews) R.; m. Kristine Ann Stark, June 21, 1981; children: Grant, Kathryn. BA in Polit. Sci., UCLA, 1976; MPA, U. So. Calif., 1980. Adminstrv. asst. Eisenhower Med. Ctr., Rancho Mirage, Calif., 1978-79; assoc. adminstr. Eisenhower Med. Ctr., 1979-85, adminstr./v.p., 1985—. Mng. editor Healthscope Newsletter, 1977-78. Bd. dirs. Rancho Mirage Magnesia Falls HoA, 1986. Mem. Am. Coll. Hosp. Adminstrs., Healthcare Execs. of So. Calif. (exec. com.). Office: Eisenhower Meml Hosp 39000 Bob Hope Dr Rancho Mirage CA 92270

REMILLONG, DONALD FRANK, insurance salesman; b. Fargo, N.D., Nov. 7, 1936; s. George and Matilda R.; m. Janet Remillong (div. 1983); children: Brock, Elizabeth, Barbara, Kathleen; m. Sharon Elaine Walls, Aug. 16, 1984. BS, N.D. State U., 1962. Ins. salesman Northwestern Mutual Life, Fargo, N.D. and Ariz., 1960-70; owner Desert Dweller, Scottsdale, Ariz., 1970-77; ins. salesman New York Life Ins. Co., Phoenix, 1977--. Mem. Nat. Assn. of Life Underwriters (Nat. Quality award 1966--, Nat. Sales Achievement award 1967--). Republican. Lutheran. Office: N Y Life Ins Co 100 W Clarendon Ste 1500 Phoenix AZ 85013

REMINGTON, JACK SAMUEL, physician; b. Chgo., Jan. 19, 1931; s. Nathan and Sylvia R.; children—David Nathan, Lynne Denise. B.S., U. Ill., Chgo., 1954, M.D., 1956. Diplomate Am. Bd. Internal Medicine. Intern U. Calif. Service, San Francisco County Hosp., 1956; research assoc. NIH, Bethesda, Md., 1957-59; resident in medicine U. Calif. Med. Center, San Francisco, 1959-60; sr. postdoctoral fellow Harvard U. Sch. Medicine, Thorndike Meml. Lab., Boston City Hosp., 1960-62; mem. faculty dept. medicine, div. infectious diseases Stanford (Calif.) U. Sch. Medicine, 1962—, prof., 1974—; chmn. dept. Immunology and Infectious Diseases, Research Inst. Palo Alto (Calif.) Med. Found., 1962—, Marcus A. Krupp Research Chair, 1987—; chief cons. in infectious diseases Palo Alto Med. Clinic, 1962—; cons. VA Hosp., Palo Alto, 1962—; cons. in infectious diseases WHO, 1967—, Pan Am. Health Orgn., 1967—, Dept. Army, 1971—; cons. Letterman Gen. Hosp., 1975—; sci. cons. Merit Rev. Bd. in Infectious Diseases VA, 1972-76; mem. adv. sci. bd. Gorgas Meml. Inst. of Tropical and Preventive Medicine, 1972—; mem. com. on infectious diseases Am. Bd. Internal Medicine, 1973-78; mem. adv. panel Am. Bd. Med. Lab. Immunology, 1978—, Sci. Adv. Com. Am. Found. for AIDS Research, 1985—. Editor: (with J.O. Klein) Infectious Diseases of the Fetus and Newborn Infant, 1976-89, (with M.N. Swartz) Current Clinical Topics in Infectious Diseases, 1980-89; Mem editorial bd.: Antimicrobial Agts. and Chemotherapy, 1973-76, Jour. Clin. Investigation, 1975—, Am. Rev. Respiratory Disease, 1978—, Jour. Immunopharmacology, 1978—, European Jour. Clin. Microbiology, 1981. Served with USPHS, 1957-59. Recipient Maxwell Finland award. Fellow A.C.P.; mem. Infectious Diseases Soc. Am. (bd. dirs. 1974-77, pres. 1988), Western Soc. Clin. Research (pres. 1975, mem. council 1975-77), Immunocompromised Host Soc. (pres. 1988—), Western Assn. Physicians (councillor 1980), AAAS, Am. Assn. Immunologists, Am. Fedn. Clin. Research, AMA, Am. Soc. Clin. Investigation, Am. Soc. Microbiology, Am. Soc. Parasitologists, Am. Soc. Tropical Medicine and Hygiene, Assn. Am. Physicians, Internat. Coll. Tropical Medicine, Soc. Protozoologists, Reticuloendothelial Soc., Assn. Am. Physicians, Alpha Omega Alpha. Office: 860 Bryant St Palo Alto CA 94301 also: Stanford U Sch Medicine Stanford CA 94305

REMINGTON, RICHARD AUSTIN, personnel executive; b. Lincoln, Nebr., Sept. 5, 1935; s. Calvin B. and Agnes Remington; m. Marlene Morrow; children: Todd Richard, Kristen Louise, Brooke Elizabeth. BS, U. Nebr., 1958; cert., Harvard U., 1976. From personnel mgr. to v.p. fin., compt. Mountain Bell, 1974-87; v.p. human resources U S West, Inc., Denver, 1988—. Trustee Carroll Coll. Served to lt. USN, 1958-61. Mem. Leadership Denver Assn. Presbyterian. Office: U S West Inc 7800 E Orchard Rd Ste 200 Englewood CO 80111

REMPP, PATRICIA YVONNE, nurse; b. Salt Lake City, Mar. 2, 1935; d. Daniel Edwin Price and Mary Beth (Gentry) Lahmann; m. Theodore Roosevelt Rempp Jr., Oct. 13, 1957; children: Theodore Roosevelt III, Gregory Herman, Norman Edwin, Arthur David. Diploma in nursing, Holy Cross Hosp., 1956. RN, Nev. Staff nurse Lyon Health Ctr., Yerington, Nev., 1956-71, surg. nurse, 1968-75; nurse Lyon County Sch. Dist., Yerington, Nev., 1971—; chairperson Rural Clinic Yerington, 1979-82; coord. sci fair Yerington Sch., 1981-88; instr. sign language. Contbr. articles to profl. jours. Pianist, state missionary L.D.S. Ch., Fallon, Nev. Home: 16 S Mountain View St Yerington NV 89447 Office: Lyon County Sch Dist 25 E Goldfield St Yerington NV 89447

REMY, IRMA MARJORIE, educational administrator; b. Maywood, Calif., Oct. 16, 1925; d. Charles Henry and Irma (Page) Bowers; m. Edward Earl Remy, Oct. 3, 1946; children—Christine Ann, Shelly Katherine. Student U. Redlands, 1943, Long Beach City Coll., 1959-60, Pepperdine U., 1974; B.A., Calif. State U.-Long Beach, 1963; M.A., 1966. Cert. secondary tchr., adminstr. Calif. Tchr. home econs. Westminster High Sch., Huntington Beach (Calif.) Union High Sch. Dist., 1963-72, dept. chmn., 1967-72, dist. dept. chmn., 1970-72; coordinator home econs., women's occupations Orange County Dept. Edn., Santa Ana, Calif., 1972-73; regional supr. home econs. vocat. cons. Specialist Regional Occupational Ctrs./Programs, State of Calif. Dept. Edn., Los Angeles, 1973-82, regional coordinator (so. region) vocat. edn., 1982-84; asst. supt. So. Calif. Regional Occupational Ctr., Torrance, 1984—.Mem. Am. Vocat. Assn., Calif. Assn. Vocat. Adminstrs., Calif. Assn. Regional Occupational Programs/Ctrs., So. Calif. Council Vocat. Edn. Adminstrs., Calif. Assn. Vocat. Educators. Democrat. Mem. Ch. Jesus Christ of Latter-day Saints. Office: So Calif Regional Occupational Ctr 2300 Crenshaw Blvd Torrance CA 90501

REMY, RAY, chamber of commerce executive; b. San Francisco. B in Polit. Sci., Claremont Men's Coll. (now Claremont McKenna Coll.); M in Pub. Adminstrn., U. Calif., Berkeley. Adminstrv. intern City of Berkeley, 1962-63; with So. Office League of Calif. Cities, 1963, then asst. to exec. dir. and mgr., to 1969; exec. dir. So. Calif. Assn. Govt., 1969-76; appointed dep. mayor City of Los Angeles, 1976-84; pres. Los Angeles Area C. of C., 1984—, also prin. spokesman. Mem. exec. com. Mus. Sci. and Industry; past chmn. bd. councilors Sch. Pub. Adminstrn. U. So. Calif., Los Angeles; vice chmn. bd. dirs. Rose Inst. for state and local govt.; mem. state adv. com. Revision of Master Plan for Higher Edn.; trustee, Claremont McKenna Coll., Calif. Trust for the Environ. Recipient numerous awards including Fletcher Bowron award, Donald Stone award, Mus. of Sci. and Industry Fellowship award, others. Mem. Nat. Acad. Pub. Adminstrn., Jr. Statesmen Found. (trustee, vice chmn. So. Calif. region), Am. Soc. Pub. Adminstrn. (past pres.), exec. com. Mus. Sci. and Industry, L.A. County Transp. Com. Office: L A Area C of C 404 S Bixel St PO Box 3696 Los Angeles CA 90017

RENARD, KENNETH GEORGE, civil engineer; b. Sturgeon Bay, Wis., May 5, 1934; s. Harry Henry and Margaret (Buechner) R.; m. Virginia Rae Heibel, Sept 8, 1956; children: Kenlynn T., Craig G., Andrew T. BCE, U. Wis., 1957, MCE, 1959; PhD in Civil Engring., U. Ariz., 1972. Registered profl. civil engr., Ariz. Hydraulic engr. Agrl. Research Service, USDA, Madison, Wis., 1957-59; resident engr. Agrl. Research Service, USDA, Tombstone, Ariz., 1959-64; resident hydraulic engr. Agrl. Research Service, USDA, Tucson, 1964-72, research leader, 1972—. Contbr. articles to profl. jours. Recipient Superior Service award USDA, 1984. Fellow Soil Conservation Soc. Am. (pres. Ariz. sect. 1975, Conservationist of Yr. 1983), ASCE (pres. Ariz. sect. 1981, mem. exec. com. irrigation and drainage div., 1987—, editor Jour. of Irrigation and Drainage Engrs. 1983-85, John C. Park award 1987); mem. Am. Soc. Agrl. Engrs. (pres. Ariz. sect. 1976), Am. Geophys. Union. Roman Catholic. Lodge: Lions (pres. Tombstone chpt. 1963). Home: 4822 E Paseo Del Bac Tucson AZ 85718 Office: USDA Agrl Rsch Svc 200 E Allen Rd Tucson AZ 85719

RENAUD, JULES LEE, health science facility administrator; b. Cedar City, Utah, July 5, 1940; s. Jules Sinton and Mary (Lee) R.; m. Nancy Ann Whitaker, June 25, 1962 (div. 1983); children: Jason Emile, Francoise Juliette; m. Mary Margaret Donnelly, Aug. 16, 1984. Student, Antioch Coll., 1958-62, Roosevelt U., 1964-66; MPA, Portland State U., 1988. Dir. spl. services Community Fund Chgo., 1962-68; dir. pub. relations Bachman/Ferris Assoc., Portland, Oreg., 1968-70; pvt. practice cons. Portland, 1970-75; counselor Alcohol Counseling and Recovery Program, Portland, 1975-77; dir. treatment MPY Council of Alcoholism, Salem, Oreg., 1977-80; exec. dir. Clark Council on Alcoholism, Vancouver, Wash., 1980-83; dir. community relations New Day Ctr., Portland, 1984—; editorial bd. Nat. Assn. Alcoholism and Drug Addiction Counselors, 1986—; cons. Oreg. Council on Alcoholism, 1978-87. Author: Diagnostic Instrument Treatment Planning, 1978; editor profl. jour. The NAAC Quarterly, 1976-78. Bd. dirs. Assn. Alcoholism Programs State Wash., 1978-81. Mem. Assn. Labor/Mgmt. Cons. Alcoholism, Nat. Assn. Alcoholism Counselors (exec. bd., editor 1976-78, Achievement award 1978), City Club. Home: 7402 NE 58th St Vancouver WA 98662 Office: New Day Ctr 6012 SE Yamhill Portland OR 97215

RENAUD, MARY MARGARET, nurse; b. Santa Fe, N.Mex., Jan. 11, 1943; d. John Howard Donnelly and Donna Maxine (Perschbacher) Mecum; m. John Burt Wilcox (div. Feb. 1977); children: Michael Scott, Douglas Aaron, Kathi Lynn; m. Jules Lee Renaud, Aug. 16, 1984. Student, Oreg. State U., 1961-62, U. Oreg., 1962-63; AS, Clark Coll., Vancouver, Wash., 1975; BS in Nursing cum laude, U. Portland, 1977. Staff nurse Vancouver Meml. Hosp., 1977-78; pub. health nurse Southwest Wash. Health Dist., Vancouver, 1978—; cons. Wash. State Dept. Social and Health Services, 1979-80; mem., trainer Nursing Child Assessment Sattelite Tnm. U. Wash. Sch. Nursing. Mem. steering com. Teen-Parent Program Vancouver Health and Welfare Planning Council, 1981-83, child protection team Wash. Dept. Social and Health Services, Vancouver, 1987—; bd. dirs. Vancouver YWCA, 1982. Mem. Wash. Pub. Health Assn. Democrat. Home: 7402 NE 58th St Vancouver WA 98662 Office: SW Wash Health Dist 2000 Fort Vancouver Way Vancouver WA 98663

RENCEHAUSEN, LINDA MARY, industrial hygienist; b. Springfield, Mass., Feb. 1, 1950; d. Victor Frank and Lorraine Ruth (Perusse) Antienowicz; m. Walter William Rencehausen, Apr. 16, 1970; 1 child, Will. BS in Microbiology, Ariz. State U., 1977. Microbiology technician Armour-Dial, Phoenix, 1976; histology technician Phoenix Meml. Hosp., 1977-78; soils technician U.S. Forest Service, Flagstaff, Ariz., 1979; secondary sch. tchr. Logan (N.Mex.) Schs., 1980-81, Ft. Sumner (N.Mex.) Schs., 1981-83; industrial hygienist Westinghouse Electric Co., Carlsbad, N.Mex., 1984—. Assoc. safety profl. Served with USMC, 1968-70. Mem. Am. Soc. Safety Engrs., Am. Indsl. Hygiene Assn., Am. Chem. Soc. (div. chem. health and safety). Republican. Roman Catholic. Home: 2835 Western Way Carlsbad NM 88220 Office: Westinghouse Electric PO Box 2078 Carlsbad NM 88221

RENDE, KAREN ANN, development director; b. San Francisco, Jan. 9, 1947; d. Charles Franklin and Sylvia Solveig (Rogenes) Cottrill; m. Frank Joseph Rende, June 6, 1970; children: Christopher, Nicole, Kari. BA, U. San Francisco, 1969. Cert. tchr. Cons. ESTE Assocs., San Carlos, Calif., 1979-83; asst. to chancellor Coll. of Notre Dame, Belmont, Calif., 1983-84; dir. Notre Dame High Sch., Belmont, 1985—; dir., organizer San Mateo County Ct. Hist. Rev., Belmont, 1988—. Dir. San Mateo County div. March of Dimes, Brisbane, CAlif., 1985; organizing com. San Mateo County Women's Adv. Council, 1980; pres. San Mateo County Parent Tchr. Group, 1981-83; docent Ralston Hall Hist. Site. Mem. AAUW Profl. Women's network (founder San Mateo County chpt. 1981, pres. San Carlos chpt. 1980-81, dist. dir. Calif. State div. 1982-84) U. San Francisco Alumni Assn. (founder San Mateo County chpt. 1986). Republican. Roman Catholic. Home: 1951 Elizabeth St San Carlos CA 94070 Office: Notre DAme High Sch 1540 Ralston Ave Belmont CA 94002

RENETZKY, ALVIN, publisher; b. Bklyn., Aug. 2, 1940; s. Sam and Anna (Presiser) R.; m. Phyllis (div.); 1 child, Davida; m. Cheryl Linden. PhD, U. Southern Calif., 1966. Publisher Academic Media, Los Angeles, 1967-70, Ready Reference Press, Santa Monica, Calif., 1974—. Editor: Directory of Career Resources for Women, 1980, Directory of Career Resources for Minorities, 1981, Career Employment Opportunities Directory, 1985, Directory of Internships. Mem. Am. Soc. Tng. and Devel. Office: Ready Reference Press PO Box 5879 Santa Monica CA 90405

RENFRO, DONALD WILLIAM, architect; b. Bakersfield, Calif., Nov. 13, 1931; s. Donald Francis and Lennie Lorraine (Despain) R.; student Bakersfield Coll., 1949-51; cert. energy auditor, Calif.; registered, cert. Nat. Council Archtl. Registration Bds.; m. Nancy M. Henry, Aug. 6, 1982; children—Dayna, Trisha, Donna. Staff designer Whitney Biggar, Architect, 1955-61; asso. Eddy & Paynter Assos., Bakersfield, Calif., 1961-70; prin. Eddy Paynter Renfro & Assos., Bakersfield, 1970-78; pres. Donald Renfro & Assocs., Bakersfield, 1978-84; pres. Renfro-Russell & Assocs., Inc., 1984—; pres., dir. Design Research Assos., Inc. Mem. Bakersfield Coll. Archtl. Adv. Com.; mem. Bakersfield Design Rev. Bd. Served with U.S. Army, 1952-54. Mem. AIA (past pres. Golden Empire chpt.) past dir. So. Calif. chpt.). Republican. Lodge: Kiwanis (past dir.). Office: 4800 Stockdale Hwy Ste 304 Bakersfield CA 93309

RENGARAJAN, SEMBIAM RAJAGOPAL, electrical engineering educator, researcher, consultant; b. Mannargudi, Tamil Nadu, India, Dec. 12, 1948; came to U.S., 1980; s. Srinivasan and Rajalakshmi (Renganathan) Rajagopalan; m. Kalyani Srinivasan, June 24, 1982; children: Michelle, Sophie. BE with honors, U. Madras, India, 1971; MTech, Indian Inst. Tech., Kharagpur, 1974; PhD in Elec. Engring., U. N.B., Fredericton, Can., 1980. Mem. tech. staff Jet Propulsion Lab., Pasadena, Calif., 1983-84; asst. prof. elec. engring. Calif. State U., Northridge, 1980-83, assoc. prof., 1984-87, prof., 1987—; cons. Hughes Aircraft Co., Canoga Park, Calif., 1982-87, NASA/Jet Propulsion Lab., Pasadena, 1987—; vis. researcher UCLA, 1984—, vis. prof., 1987-88. Contbr. sci. papers to profl. publs. Recipient Outstanding Faculty award Calif. State U., Northridge, 1985, Meritorious Performance and Profl. Promise award, 1986, 88; Nat. Merit scholar Govt. India, 1965-71, Merit award San Fernando Valley Engrs. Coun., 1989. Fellow Inst. Advancement Engrs.; mem. IEEE (sr., Los Angeles chpt. sec., treas. Antennas and propagation Soc. 1981-82, vice chmn. 1982-83, chmn. 1983-84), Calif. Faculty Assn., Am. Soc. Engring. Edn., Internat. Union of Radio Sci. (U.S. Nat. Com.), Sigma Xi. Office: Calif State U 18111 Nordhoff St Northridge CA 91330

RENICK, MARIE ALICE, molecular biologist, immunologist; b. Jamaica, N.Y., Oct. 1, 1959; d. Dewey Paul and Elizabeth Mary (Fleming) Cecchini; m. Robert E. Renick Jr., Oct. 18, 1987. BS, U. Colo., 1981. Research assoc. Amgen, Boulder, Colo., 1982—. Instr. Winter Park (Colo.) Handicap Ski Program, 1980—. Mem. Assn. Soc. for Quality Control, Women in Science (Boulder), Rallysport Club (Boulder). Republican. Congregationalist.

RENNE, JANICE LYNN, interior designer; b. Los Angeles, July 16, 1952; d. George Joseph and Dolly Minni (Neubauer) R.; m. William Lee Kile, Dec. 6, 1975 (div. Sept. 1983). BA, Sweet Briar Coll., 1974; AA, Interior Designers Inst., 1985. Exec. trainee Bullock's, Santa Ana, Calif., 1974, Pub. Fin., Inc., Huntington Beach, Calif., 1975; bookkeeper William L. Kile DDS, Inc., Santa Barbara, Calif., 1979-81, Nelson & Hamilton, Inc., Santa Barbara, 1981-82; interior designer Ultimate Designs, Irvine, Calif., 1984-85, sr. designer, 1985-86; draftsperson JBI Inc., Long Beach, Calif., 1984-85; prin. designer Janice Renne Interior Designs, Newport Beach, Calif., 1986—; space planner Design Pak II, Newport Beach, 1987-88. Created utility room design for Easter Seals Design House, 1985; weekly radio show host on restaurant design, 1986; work published in Orange County mag. and L.A. Times., 1988. Recipient scholarship Calif. Inst. Applied Design, Newport Beach, 1984. Mem. Internat. Soc. Interior Designers (grad. assoc. designer butler's pantry, assoc. designer Design House powder room, 1988 Orange County chpt. 1988, 89, asst. editor Orange County chpt. Quar. Newsletter), Color Assn. of U.S., Constrn. Specifier Inst., Nat. Exec. Women in Hospitality, Orange County and Newport Harbor, Letip Internat. (sec. 1987, 89). Republican. Lutheran. Office: 2240 Newport Blvd Newport Beach CA 92663

RENNER, GEORGE R., mayor; b. Glendale, Ariz.; m. Pamela Petty; children: Molly, David. BS in Bus., U. Ariz., 1967. With mktg. dept. Union Oil Co.; owner Renner's Realty and Ins.; mayor City of Glendale, 1982—; v.p. Glendale Bd. Realtors. Mem. Salvation Army Adv. Bd.; v.p. Valley of the Sun United Way Bd.; treas. Regional Pub. Transit Authority. Mem. Nat. Conf. Rep. Mayors, Ariz. League Cities and Towns, Ariz. Mcpl. Water Users Assn., Maricopa Assn. Govts., Glendale C. of C., Rotary, Am. Legion. Office: Office of the Mayor 7022 N 57th Dr Glendale AZ 85301 *

RENO, JOSEPH HARRY, orthopaedic surgeon; b. Allentown, Pa., Mar. 5, 1915; s. Harvey Luther and Olive May (Wilson) R.; m. Maude Olivia Mutchler, June 27, 1942; children: Joseph David, Diana Jane, Deborah Marion. Student, Temple U., 1934-37, MD, 1941. Intern. Chester (Pa.) Hosp., 1941-42; residency Tex. Scottish Rite Hosp. for Crippled Children, Dallas, 1942-43, 44-45, Robert Packer Hosp., Sayre, Pa., 1943-44; assoc. Homer Stryker, M.D., Kalamazoo, 1945-46; pvt. practice Bethlehem, Pa., 1946-71, Flaggstaff, Ariz., 1971-77; team physician No. Ariz. U., Flaggstaff, 1971-77, Ariz. State U., Tempe, 1977-84; chief surgical staff, Flaggstaff Hosp., 1975. Contbr. articles to profl. jours.; producer surgical films for Am. Acad. Ortho. Surgeons and others, 1952—. Pres. Coconino County Easter Seal Soc., 1973; bd. dirs., med. advisor Ariz. Easter Seal Soc., 1974-84. Recipient Pioneer award Ariz. Med. Assn., 1981, Cert. of Appreciation, Pa. Dept. Health Crippled Children's Div., 1971; Dr. Joseph Reno Sports Medicine award named in honor, No. Ariz. State U. and Blue Cross Blue Shield, 1986. Fellow Am. Acad. Ortho. Surgeons, Am. Assn. for the Surgery of Trauma, Am. Coll. Sports Med., Am. Cell Surgeons (chmn. Lehigh Valley subcom. on trauma 1954-66, Ea. Pa. chpt. pres. 1969); mem. Am. Bd. Ortho. Surgery (cert., diplomate 1948), Cocino County Med. Soc. (pres. 1976), We. Ortho. Assn., Babcock Surgical Soc., NRA, Phi Chi, Alpha Tau Omega. Home and Office: 621 Beal Rd Flagstaff AZ 86001

RENSCH, JOSEPH ROMAINE, public utility holding company executive; b. San Bernardino, Calif., Jan. 1, 1923; s. Joseph R. and Lucille (Ham) R.; m. June Elizabeth Burley, Mar. 25, 1946; children: Steven R., Jeffrey P. BS, Stanford U., 1947; JD, Golden Gate U., 1955. Bar: Calif.; registered profl. engr., Calif. Successively sales engr., regional gas engr., asst. regional gas supt., asst. mgr. gas supply and control Coast Counties Gas & Electric Co., San Francisco, 1947-54; sr. pipeline operations engr. Pacific Gas & Electric Co., 1954-56; prodn. control supt. Western div. Dow Chem. Co., Pittsburg, Calif., 1956; asst. counsel So. Counties Gas Co. of Calif., Los Angeles, 1957-58; asst. v.p., spl. counsel Pacific Lighting Gas Supply Co., Los Angeles, 1958- 61, v.p., bd. dirs., 1962-65; sr. v.p. Pacific Lighting Service Co., 1965-67, exec. v.p., 1967-69, pres., 1969-71, chmn. bd., 1971-73; exec. v.p., dir. Pacific Lighting Corp., Los Angeles, 1968-72, pres., 1972-86, vice chmn., 1986-88; bd. dirs. McKesson Corp. Served with USNR, 1942-46. Mem. Pacific Coast Gas Assn. (pres. 1966-67), Am. Gas Assn., Tau Beta Pi, Alpha Tau Omega. Office: Pacific Enterprises 810 S Flower St Los Angeles CA 90017

RENTFROW, JOHNNY HAYDEN, manufacturing executive; b. Sapulpa, Okla., July 19, 1934; s. John Franklin Rentfrow and Pearl Belle (Stanberry) Beasley; m. Beatrice Joan Fairbanks, Sept. 4, 1954; children: Johnny Franklin, William Jay, Donald Ray, William and Donald (twins). Student, Billings Bus. Coll., 1953-54, Ea. Mont. Coll., 1960-62. Sr. statistician N.Am. Aviation Co., Luke AFB, Ariz., 1964-69; loan officer Ist Interstate Bank, Phoenix, 1969-71, mgr. Scottsdale (Ariz.) Office, 1971-76; pres., chief exec. officer Rentfrow, Inc., Phoenix, 1976—, Hydro Mite Corp., Phoenix, 1976—. Home: 3919 E Andorra Dr Phoenix AZ 85032 Office: 5050 N 19th Ave Ste 409 Phoenix AZ 85015

REPH, GLENN ALLEN, JR, financial executive; b. Waco, Tex., May 21, 1953; s. Glenn Allen and Mary Ann (Schier) R.; m. Sharon Colleen Wilcox, June 15, 1974; children: Timothy, Wendy, Rachel, Michel. Student, Bapt. Bible Coll. of Pa., 1971-72; BA, Faith Bapt. Bible Coll., Ankeny, Iowa, 1975; MA, Denver Bapt. Theol. Sem, 1980. With Walgreens Drugs, Ankeny, Iowa, 1972, Jacobsons Warehouse, Des Moines, 1974-75; youth and mus. dir. First Bapt. Ch., Eldora, Iowa, 1975-76; with Colo. Nat. Bank, Denver, 1976-77; pres./chief exec. officer Reph Ent., Inc., Denver, 1977-82, First Nat. Fin. Network, Inc., Denver, 1982-85; v.p. dir. devel. Credit Card Sys. of Am. Inc., Denver, 1985-86; pres./ chief exec. officer Nat. Bankcard Assn., Inc., San Diego, 1986--. Editor NBA World 1987; contbr. articles to profl. jours.;. Deacon, Vista Grande Ch., Tierrasanta, Calif., 1986-87. Mem. Am. Bankcard Assn. Republican. Baptist. Home: 11478 Via Promesa San Diego CA 92124 Office: Nat Bankcard Assn 9089 Clairemont Mesa Blvd San Diego CA 92123

RESCH, GERALD WILLIAM, data processing executive; b. Independence, Mo., July 10, 1938; s. Gerald Elmer and Esther Elizabeth (Van Tuyl) R.; m. Mamie Boling Go, Nov. 18, 1978; children: Nicole Michelle, Derek Alexander, Shannon Lynn. AA in Engring., Graceland Coll., 1959; BEE, Iowa State U., 1963. Field and systems engr. Hughes Aircraft Co., Fullerton, Calif., 1963-70; electronic designer Actron Industries Inc., Monrovia, Calif., 1971-73; asst. chief engr. Bergmaster Houdaille Inc., L.A., 1973; head elec. engr. Compucorp., L.A., 1973-75; dir. ops. Ednl. Data Systems, Irvine, Calif., 1975-76; cons. electronic mfg. Irvine, 1976-77; head Elec. Div. ITT Jabsco, Costa Mesa, Calif., 1977-79; dir. ops. and personnel Convergence Corp., Irvine, 1979-81; pres. Vango Enterprises, Anaheim, Calif., 1980—; v.p., owner Omni Technics, Los Alamitos, Calif., 1983—; chmn. bd. dirs. Omni Technics, Los Alamitos; pres., owner Microcomputer Tng. Specialist, Anaheim, 1984—; computer cons. Dun & Bradstreet Bus. Edn. Svc., 1987—; instr. Chapman Coll., Yorba Linda Continuing Edn., 1981—, Orange Coast Coll., Coastline Coll., Golden West Coll., 1987—, USMA Missile Electronic Sch., 1968-69; cons. U.S. Missile Bases; head New Eng. Air Def. Missile Mentor System, 1967-68; asst. in design and mfg. Can. Vegreville Pysanka Monument, 1975. Chmn. So. Anaheim Neighborhood Council, 1986—; mem. Anaheim Ambassador, 1986—. Mem. Am. Prodn. and Inventory Control Soc., Orange County Prodn. and Inventory Control Soc., L.A. Prodn. and Inventory Control Soc., Far West Ski Assn., U.S. Ski Assn. (bd. dirs. 1978-81), Orange County Council Ski Clubs (pres. 1978-81, treas. 1981-82), North Orange County Computer Club/Apple Users Group (pres. 1982—), NOCCC (bd. dirs. 1984—), Computer Wave Apple Users Group (pres. 1982-85), Orange Apple Users Group (bd. dirs. 1982-84), Anaheim C. of C. Home: 1452 Westmont Dr Anaheim CA 92801 Office: 3321 Cerritos Ave Bldg #5 Los Alamitos CA 90720

RESKE, FREDERICK MICHAEL, logistics engineer; b. Detroit, Nov. 12, 1941; s. John Frederick and Anna Catherine (Becker) R.; m. Patricia Louis Gould, June 23, 1962; children: Michael Blaine, Judith Marie. BS, Ohio State U., 1971, Weber State Coll., 1985. Advanced profl. designation in Logistics Mgmt., 1985. Licensed secondary edn. tchr., Alaska, 1975, Utah, 1976. Maintenance technician USAF, 1959-71, maintenance officer, 1971-81; systems analyst 16 Acquisition Div., Hill AFB, Utah, 1982-85; systems engr. Hercules Aerospace, Magna, Utah, 1985; reliability engr. Eyring Research Inst., Ogden, Utah, 1985-87; logistics engr. TRW, Ogden, 1987—. Recipient The Logistics Mgmt. Achievement Award In Operation Research and Systems Analysis Soc. of Logistics Engrs., 1987. Mem. Soc. Logistics Engrs. (chmn. operations, 1987-88, tech. chmn. 1987—), Air Force Assn. Republican. Roman Catholic. Home: 5451 S 200 E Ogden UT 84405 Office: TRW Ogden Engring Ops 1104 Country Hills Dr Ogden UT 84403

RESTER, GEORGE G., architect, painter, sculptor; b. Ponchatoula, La., Oct. 5, 1923; s. Kelly Caldwell Rester and Myra Vira (Adams) Smith; m. Virginia Wilhelmena, June 25, 1955; children: Gina Louise, Taira Elizabeth, Licia Therese. Student, U.S. Army Engring. Sch., Ft. Belvoir, Va., 1943, Soulé Coll., 1945-48, Delgado Tech. Inst., 1949-50, Art Ctr. Coll. Design, 1961-62. Registered architect, La., Calif., Fla., Colo., N.Y., Ariz., Tex., N.J., Mich., Minn., Wash., N.Mex. Architect, designer, draftsman various firms, New Orleans, 1953-60; pvt. practice architecture Culver City, Calif., 1960-61; project architect Welton Beckett Architect, Beverly Hills, Calif., 1961-64; chief architect, dir. archtl. design and prodn. Walt Disney Imagineers, Glendale, Calif., 1965-71, 76-87; sr. prin. engr. Ralph M. Parsons Engring. Co., Pasadena, Calif., 1973-76; prin. George G. Rester Architect & Assocs.,

Rolling Hills Estates, Calif., 1987—; founder, pres., chief exec. officer New Visions Resorts Inc., Rolling Hills Estates, 1987—. Prin. works include Theme Park, New Orleans Sq., Disneyland, 1965, Destination Resort and Theme Park (internat. accolades 1987), Walt Disney World, Fla., 1967, Resort Community (internat. accolades 1987), E.P.C.O.T. at World Disney World, 1982, Theme Park (Calif. and nat. accolades, 1983), Disneyland, 1983, Theme Park , Tokyo Disneyland, Japan, 1983. Served as pfc. C.E., U.S. Army Engrs., 1943-45, ETO, Africa, Mid. East. Mem. AIA, Internat. Platform Assn., Smithsonian Instn., New Orleans Amateur Artists Soc. (founding pres. 1940-42). Republican. Roman Catholic. Home and Office: 26337 Dunwood Rd Rolling Hills Estates CA 90274

RESTIVO, RICHARD RENE, service company executive; b. Winnipeg, Man., Can., May 30, 1944; s. Sam and Teresa (Berube) R. BA, Calif. State U., Fullerton, 1968. Pres. Relocation Systems (N.Am. Van Lines Moving Co.), City of Industry, Calif., 1976—. Sgt. U.S. Army, 1968-70, Vietnam. Decorated Silver Star, Bronze Star, Purple Heart. Republican. Roman Catholic.

RETTER, TERRIL ALAN, infosystems and telecommunications executive; b. Maywood, Calif., Jan. 17, 1940; s. Clyde A. and Wilda Grace (Kellams) R.; m. Sandra Marie Enos, Oct. 3, 1945; 1 child, Alyson Paige. BS in Civil Engrng., Stanford U., 1962, MS in Structural Engrng., 1964; MBA, UCLA, 1968. Dir. McDonnell Douglas Aircraft, Long Beach, Calif., 1965-75; mgr. Continental Airlines, Culver City, Calif., 1975-77; asst. dir. Petrolane, Long Beach, 1977-79; dir. Hughes Aircraft Co., Culver City, 1979-81; owner, pres. TR& Assoc. (dba Hdqrs. Co.), L.A., 1980-83; v.p. Hdqrs. Cos., San Francisco, 1983-85, Grubb & Ellis, San Francisco, 1985-87, HEALS Health Svcs., Emeryville, Calif., 1987-88; sr. product mgr. DHL Global MIS, San Mateo, Calif., 1989—; sec., bd. dirs. Syntellisys Network, Inc., Newport Beach, Calif. Fund raiser Stanford Keystone Program, San Mateo, 1985—; vol. AYSO, San Mateo, 1988—. Recipient scholarships McDonnell Douglas Aircraft, Long Beach, 1977, 78, Gen. Electric, San Jose 1964, 65. Mem. Stanford U. Alumni Assn. Republican. Office: DHL Global MIS 1700 S Amphlett #116 San Mateo CA 94402

RETTIG, PENN WARREN, II, financial planner, consultant; b. Santa Monica, Calif., Aug. 25, 1953; s. Eugene and Elizabeth (D'aigle) R.; m. Debra D. Albertson, Aug. 15, 1981; 1 child, Rachel Elizabeth. Student, Dominican Coll., San Rafael, Calif., 1973-75; BS in Forest Mgmt., Humboldt State U., 1978; MBA in Fin., U. Oreg., 1982. Cert. fin. planner Internat. Bd. Cert. Fin. Planning. Asst. v.p. Empire Fin. Svcs., Eugene, Oreg., 1982-83; sr. account rep. Bank N.W., Eugene, 1983-84; fin. planner IDS-Am. Express, Mpls., 1984-88; account exec. Integrated Resources Inc., Eugene, 1988—; cons. Genesis II Corp., Eugene, 1985—. Editor Timber Svc. and Mktg. Jour., 1981. Bd. dirs. Community Substance Abuse Consortium, Eugene, 1986-88, Gt. Oreg. Duck Race, Eugene, 1988. Mem. Internat. Assn. Fin. Planning, Mensa, Rotary (bd. dirs. Eugene 1986-87), Kiwanis (fin. chmn. Eugene 1987). Republican. Home: 5180 Miramar Eugene OR 97405 Office: Integrated Resources Inc 1400 Executive Pkwy Ste 360 Eugene OR 97401

RETZLER, KATHRYN, entrepreneur, management consultant; b. Denison, Ohio, Jan. 7, 1948; children: Jason Russell, Cheryl Russell. BA, U. Miami, Fla., 1970. Buyer Higbee Co., Cleve., 1970-71; v.p., gen. mgr. pvt. oil co., Phila., 1971-79; owner, pres. Russell-Meade Gallery, Del Mar, Calif., 1980-81, Russell, Inc. Constrn., San Diego, 1980-84, Greentree Cons. Group, San Diego, 1983—; owner Jiovana Design, Inc., La Jolla, Calif., 1989—; adj. faculty Nat. U., San Diego, 1985—; leader seminars in field. Author: How to Start a Service Business and Make It a Success, 1987, Direct Marketing: The Proven Path to Successful Sales, 1988; contbr. articles to profl. pubs. Mem. Nat. Mgmt. Assn. (bd. dirs. pub. relations 1987-88), Nat. Assn. Female Execs., Writers Guild, Book Publicists' San Diego. Office: Giovana Design Inc PO box 12294 La Jolla CA 92037

REUBENS, JOHN B., writer, editorial consultant; b. New York City, July 11, 1917; s. Raymond and Henrietta (Stern) R.; m. Joyce T. Bloomfield, June 6, 1947 (div. 1957); children: Jean Reubens Lorrey, Vivian Reubens Spiro; m. Madonna Curran, Oct. 17, 1959. Student, Horace Mann, N.Y.C., 1929-35; BA cum laude, Yale U., 1939; JD, Columbia U., 1952. Bar: N.Y. 1942, U.S. Dist. Ct. (so. dist.) N.Y., 1947. Ptnr. Sterns & Reubens, N.Y.C., 1946-51; newspaperman Colorado Springs (Colo.) Free Press, 1951-57; info. officer Nat. Bur. Standards, Boulder, Colo., 1958-63; proposal editor Ball Bros., Boulder, 1964-66; mng. editor Cen. States Constrn., Topeka, 1966-68; pvt. practice editor, cons. Boulder, 1964-78; outdoor columinst Town & Country Mag., Boulder, 1970-76; free-lance writer Livingston, Mont., 1978—; cons. Glencoe Press, L.A., 1968-70, Colo. Sch. of Mines, Golden, 1971-77. Author: And A Cat Named Sorpresa, 1981; contbr. articles to FlyFishing, Fly Fisherman, Rod & Reel. With U.S. Army, 1942-46, ETO. Decorate Silver Star, Bronze Star. Home and Office: P O Box 682 Livingston MT 59047

REUBENSTEIN, STANLEY, manufacturers representative; b. L.A., Apr. 20, 1946; s. Robert and Esther (Kapshut) R.; student Calif. State U., L.A., 1963-65, BA, Northridge, 1967; m. Loretta Gayle Masucci, Mar. 1, 1977; children: Benjamin Daniel, Alexander King, Robert Drake. With, Photovoltaics Engring. Lab., Jet Propulsion Lab., Calif. Inst. Tech., Pasadena, 1967-68; nat. sales mgr. Standard Communications Corp., L.A., 1970-73, mktg. mgr., 1975-77; nat. sales mgr. TPL Communications, Gardena, Calif., 1973-75; founder, owner Aurora Mktg. Co., Denver, 1977—. Served with M.C., U.S. Army, 1968-70. Mem. Assn. Pub. Safety Communications Officers (nat. committeeman), Communications Mktg. Assn. (pres. 1979-81, dir. 1981-83), Radio Club Am., Nat. Eagle Scout Assn. (life), Quarter Century Wireless Assn. (life), Alpha Phi Omega. Jewish. Home: 220 Ivanhoe Denver CO 80220-5840 Office: Aurora Mktg 2018 S Pontiac Way Denver CO 80224

REUSCHEL, RICK EUGENE, professional baseball player; b. Quincy, Ill., May 16, 1949; m. Barbara Thompson, June 12, 1988; children by previous marriage: Darryl, Elizabeth. Student, Western Ill. U. Pitcher Chgo. Cubs (Nat. League), 1972-81, 83-84, N.Y. Yankees (Am. League), 1981-83, Pitts. Pirates (Nat. League), 1985-87, San Francisco Giants (Nat. League), 1987—. Mem. Nat. League All-Star Team, 1977, 87, 88, 89; recipient Golden Glove award, 1977, 87. Office: San Francisco Giants Candlestick Pk San Francisco CA 94124 *

REVEAL, ARLENE HADFIELD, librarian, consultant; b. Riverside, Utah, May 21, 1916; d. Job Oliver and Mabel Olive (Smith) Hadfield; children—James L., Jon A. B.S. with hons., Utah State U., 1938; grad. in librarianship San Diego State U., 1968; M.L.S., Brigham Young U., 1976. librarian, Calif. Social case worker Boxelder County Welfare, Brigham City, Utah, 1938-40; office mgr. Strawberry Inn, Strawberry, Calif., 1950-65, Dodge Ridge Ski Corp., Long Barn, Calif., 1948-65; adminstrv. asst. Mono County Office of Edn., Bridgeport, Calif., 1961-67; catalog librarian La Mesa-Spring Valley Sch. Dist., La Mesa, Calif., 1968-71; librarian Mono County Library, Bridgeport, Calif., 1971—; chmn. Mountain Valley Library System, 1987—. Author: Mono County Courthouse, 1980. Recipient John Cotton Dana award H.W. Wilson Co., 1974. Mem. Delta Kappa Gamma (pres. Epsilon Alpha chpt. 1984-88), Beta Sigma Phi (treas. Xi Omicron Epsilon chpt. 1981, 83-85, pres. 1982, 85, 89), Beta Phi Mu. Lodge: Rebekah (treas. 1973—). Home: PO Box 532 Bridgeport CA 93517 Office: Mono County Free Libr PO Box 398 Bridgeport CA 93517

REVELL, JOHN HAROLD, dentist; b. Lead, S.D., Dec. 12, 1906; s. Aris LeRoy and Margaret (O'Donnell) R.; AB in Engring., Stanford, 1930; postgrad. McGill Med. Sch., 1930; DDS summa cum laude, U. So. Calif., 1941; postgrad. in Maxillo Facial and Plastic Surgery, Mayo Found., U. Minn., 1944; m. Catherine Cecelia Gerrard, Sept. 14, 1936; children: Mary Margaret, Kathleen Dianne Revell, Timothy John, Maureen Frances Brown, Dennis Cormac. Engaged as instr. U. So. Calif. Dental Coll., L.A., 1941-42; practice oral surgery, maxillo facial-plastic surgery, Shafter, Calif., 1946—; mem. staff Mercy Hosp., Bakersfield, Calif., 1948—, chmn. dental sect., 1955-60, 70-71; mem. surg. staff San Joaquin Hosp., Bakersfield; lectr. on applied nutrition; internat. pioneer lectr. surg. orthodontics. Served with AUS, 1932-37, 42-46; now maj. ret. Recipient of Special Clinic award Am. Soc. Dentistry for Children, 1964; Rotary Internat. Presdl. citation, 1982. Diplomate Internat. Bd. Applied Nutrition. Fellow Internat. Coll. Applied Nutrition; mem. ADA (life), Calif. Dental Assn. (life), Ventura Dental Soc. (life), So. Calif., Kern County (dir.), Los Angeles County (award 1941), Santa Barbara-Ventura County dental assns., Am. Acad. Dental Medicine, Am. Acad. Applied Nutrition, Am. Soc. Dentistry for Children (life), Pierre Fauchard Acad., Shafter C. of C. (dir. 1948-50), Alpha Tau Epsilon, Omicron Kappa Upsilon, Phi Kappa Phi, Theta Xi. Republican. Roman Catholic. Rotarian (pres. Shafter 1950-51, dir. 1951-52). Patentee precisioner. Research on maxillary dental papilloma, rotation unerupted impacted teeth, channeling for extensive movement of teeth; also clin. research in cleft palate surgery; inventor rapid fabrication device for infant feeding; pioneer in prefab. bldgs. and homes while constrn. officer U.S. Army, 1932-37; developer prototype WW-2 Jeep machine gun mount. Author publs. in field; all research data presented to and housed at La. State U. Dental Coll., New Orleans. Home: 81 620 Ave 49 Indio CA 92201

REVIS, GEORGE JOSEPH, dentist; b. Denver, Sept. 19, 1921; s. Edward and Sarah (Rosenberg) R.; m. Feb. 6, 1955 (div. 1980); children: Daniel, Amy. Student, U. Denver, 1939-41; BSc, DDS, U. Nebr., 1944. Pvt. practice dentistry Denver, 1947--; research assoc. div. immunology Webb Waring Inst. for Med. Research, 1965-83; researcher U. Colo. Health Sci. Ctr., Denver, 1966-83, fellow dept. neurology, 1973-85, vis. asst. prof. dept. oral biology Sch. Dentistry, 1973-83, research assoc. dept. microbiology and immunology, 1976-83, now clin. asst. dept. surgery, 1966--. Contbr. articles dental jours. NIH research grantee, 1977-83. Mem. ADA (council on dental therapeutics 1980-86), Am. Assn. Endodontics, Am. Acad. Periodontology. Home: 10268 E Jewell Ave #40 Denver CO 80231

REVKIN, JAMES HAROLD, physician, educator; b. Providence, R.I., Oct. 26, 1954; s. William and Amelia Carol (Stern) R.; m. Carrie Ann Redlich, May 31, 1982; 1 child, Mara. Diplôme d'études françaises, U. Paris, 1975; BA, Williams Coll., 1976; MD, Brown U., 1981. Diplomate Am. Bd. Internal Medicine. Resident in internal medicine Columbia-Presbyn. Med. Ctr., N.Y.C., 1981-84; postdoctoral cardiology fellow Yale U. Sch. Medicine, New Haven, Conn., 1984-87; sr. fellow Ctr. Bioengring. U. Wash., Seattle, 1987-88, asst. prof. medicine div. cardiology, dir. transplant cardiology, 1988—. Contbr. articles to profl. jours. Fellow Am. Coll. Cardiology; mem. ACP, Internat. Soc. for Heart Transplantation, Am. Fedn. for Clin. Residents, Internat. Star Class Yacht Racing Assn., Corinthian Yacht Club, Phi Beta Kappa, Sigma Xi. Office: U Wash Div Cardiology RG-22 Seattle WA 98195

REX, DOUGLAS LELAND, accountant; b. Logan, Utah, May 22, 1945; s. Robert Raymond and Pearl (Bullock) R.; m. Earlene Satterthwaite, Aug. 6, 1963; children: Wendy, Teresa, Marcie, Angela. BS, U. Utah, 1968. CPA, Calif. Staff acct. Seidman and Seidman, Beverly Hills, Calif., 1968-72; mgr. Tebbs, Smith and Assocs., Salt Lake City, 1972-76, officer, stockholder, 1976-87; pres. Tebbs and Smith, P.C., Salt Lake City, 1988—. Mem. Nat. League Families of Missing in Action in Vietnam, Utah, 1978—, Rep. Mem. Utah Assn. CPAs (chmn. mgmt. acctg. practice com. 1986-87), AICPAs (tax div.), Mtn. States Pension Conf., Cottonwood Country Club (fin. advisor to bd. dirs. Salt Lake City chpt. 1978-84). Ch. of Jesus Christ Latter-day Saints. Office: Tebbs and Smith PC 4885 S 900 E Ste 208 Salt Lake City UT 84117

REX, TOM R., infosystems specialist, researcher; b. Toledo, Oct. 29, 1954; s. Donald H. and Rhea E. (Heiptman) R. BBA, U. Toledo, 1975; MBA, Ariz. State U., 1976. Cons. Arthur Young & Co., Phoenix, 1977-78; planning analyst 1st Fed. Savs., Phoenix, 1978-80; rsch. mgr. Ariz. State U. Ctr. for Bus. Rsch., Tempe, 1980--. Contbr. articles to profl. jours. Vol. Nat. Forest Svc., Payson, Ariz., 1983--. Office: Ariz State U Ctr for Bus Rsch Tempe AZ 85287-4406

REYES, CANDACE MULCAHY, business administrator; b. Chgo., Feb. 16, 1946; d. Robert Emmet and Rita Helen (Schultz) Mulcahy; m. Phillip John Manzella, Aug. 18, 1964 (div. May 1967); 1 child, Janet Manzella; m. James Theodore Shell, Aug. 13, 1971 (div. May 1976); 1 child, Julia; m. Jaime Magbual Reyes, Aug. 12, 1978 (July 1987). Commodity broker Earl K. Riley, Chgo., 1968-72; acct. R.J. O'Brien, Chgo., 1974-75; commodity broker E.F. Hutton, Chgo., 1975-77; make-up artist Elizabeth Arden, Chgo., 1977-78; acct. Crocker Nat. Bank, San Francisco, 1978-80; bus. adminstr. Jaime Reyes, Casa Grande, Ariz., 1980—; exec. sec. Martin & Marbry Realty, Skokie, Ill. Fund raiser Pinal County Med. Soc. Aux., Casa Grande, Ariz., 1983—. Fellow AMA Aux. (del. 1984), Nat. Assn. Female Execs., Pinal County Med. Soc. Aux. (pres. 1984-85), Assn. Phillippine Practicing Physicians Ariz. Aux. (sec. 1983, treas. 1982), Internat. Platform Assn. Roman Catholic. Home: 5265 W Devon Ave Chicago IL 60646 Office: 1131 Avenida Fresca Casa Grande AZ 85222

REYES, CHRISTOPHER MICHAEL, city official; b. Tokyo, July 3, 1956; (parents Am. citizens); s. Peter and Irene (von Lenski) R. AB in History and Econs., U. Calif., 1978. Planner Dept. Econ. Devel. City of Oakland, Calif., 1979-84; mgr. Econ. Devel. Program Los Angeles Area C. of C., 1984-85; dir. community devel. County of Monterey, Calif., 1985-89; asst. dir. project mgmt. Hollister Redevel. Agy., 1989—. Vol. United Way, Salinas, Calif., 1987—. Mem. Internat. City Mgrs. Assn., Am. Planning Assn., U. Calif. Alumni Assn. Home: 155 Montecresta Ave Oakland CA 94611 Office: City of Hollister 375 5th St Hollister CA 95023

REYES, DAVID ALFRED, consulting firm executive; b. Torrance, Calif., Apr. 5, 1951; s. Adelberto Reyes and Ruth M. (Armendariz) Brown; m. Constance Ann Hawkins, Oct. 14, 1969 (div. April 1981); children: Jennifer Marie, Yolanda Christina. Student, Am. River Coll., Citrus Heights, Calif., 1981-85. Personnel asst. I dept. gen. services State of Calif., Sacramento, 1977-79, mgmt. services, 1980, field rep., office of local asst., 1980-85; pres., cons. Sch. Facility Cons., Sacramento, 1985—; cons. Murdoch, Mockler & Assocs., Sacramento, 1985—. Author, editor: (newletter) Blueprint, 1986—. Active Calif. Sch. Bond Campaign, Sacramento, 1988—; Served to sgt. USAF, 1970-76. Mem. Coalition for Adequate Sch. Housing, Council Edn. Facility Planners, Small Sch. Dists. Assn., Nat. Audobon Soc. Republican. Home: 4032 Renick Way North Highlands CA 95660 Office: Sch Facility Cons 1130 K St Ste LL 10 Sacramento CA 95814

REYES, ROBERTO TIANGCO, planner, architect, food service executive; b. Manila, Mar. 18, 1952; came to U.S., 1984; s. Crispin Tulod Reyes and Remedios (De Leon) Tiangco. BS in Architecture, U. Santo Tomas, Manila, 1974. Project asst. Devel. Acad. Philippines, Quezon City, 1974-76; project officer Human Settlements Commn., Quezon City, 1976-78; exec. asst. Human Settlements Commn., Manila, 1978-79; svc. chief Metro Manila Commn., Quezon City, 1979-85; v.p. Landhaus Mgmt. & Mktg. Corp., Manila, 1984—; clk. Balboa Life & Casualty, Phoenix, 1986-87; v.p., sec. Kowloon Chinese Restaurant, Inc., Phoenix, 1988—; pres. Alliance Mgmt. Corp., Quezon City, 1975-80; cons. City Realty Devel. Corp., Makati, Philippines, 1980-81. Agt. Civil Rels. Svc., Armed Forces of the Philippines, Quezon City, 1983-85. Roman Catholic. Home: 9222-6 N 35th Ave Phoenix AZ 85051 Office: Kowloon Chinese Restaurant 3501 N Central Ave Phoenix AZ 85012

REYNOLDS, BYRON LEE, aviation engineering executive; b. Frankfort, Ohio, Aug. 30, 1930; s. Robert and Elsie (Wallace) L.; m. Margaret Anspach, June 30, 1956; children: Kathleen, Russell, Michael, Robert. BS in Aeronautical Engrng., U. Cin., 1953. Registered profl. engr., Ohio, Wash. Chief engr. Aeronca, Middletown, Ohio, 1953-74; with Boeing Comml. Airplane, Seattle, 1974—, dir. automation, 1986-87, with payloads mgmt., 1987—. Chmn. Sch. Levy, Issaquah, Wash. Recipient Welding award Soc. Aeronautical Engrs., 1971. Mem. AIAA, Mirrormont Country Club (pres.), MF Tennis Club. Republican. Presbyterian. Home: 3200 162nd Pl SE Bellevue WA 89008 Office: Boeing Comml Airplanes PO Box 3707 Seattle WA 98124-2207

REYNOLDS, CATHERINE LOUISE, retail company executive, fashion consultant; b. Maywood, Calif., July 6, 1954; d. Roy Thagard and Ann Lucille (Churchwell) R. BS, U. So. Calif., 1979, MS, 1980. Cert. elem. tchr., Calif. Mgr. sales Cacilles, Monterey Park, Calif., 1980-83; ptnr. Morey's Fashions, Long Beach, Calif., 1983-87; pres. C & L Ltd., Inc., 1987—; cons. fashion Gov. and Mrs. Deukmejian, 1984—, So. Calif. Ins. Women, Long Beach, 1986—. Writer newspaper Fashion Forecast, 1988—. Active in Jonathan Jaques Cancer Found., Long Beach, Grand Prix Benevolent Assn., Long Beach, Republican Women Orgn. Mem. Com. of 300 (cons. fashion 1986—). Methodist. Office: C & L Ltd Inc 6527 E Pacific Coast Hwy Long Beach CA 90803

REYNOLDS, DONALD WORTHINGTON, publisher; b. Ft. Worth, Sept. 23, 1906; s. Gaines Worlie and Anna Louise (Elfers) R. B.J., U. Mo., 1927. Pub. Southwest Times Record, Ft. Smith, Ark., Okmulgee (Okla.) Times, 1940—, Moberly (Mo.) Monitor-Index, Las Vegas (Nev.) Rev. Jour., 1949—, Ely (Nev.) Times and Carson City (Nev.) Appeal, 1950—, Blackwell (Okla.) Jour. Tribune, 1955—, Chickasha (Okla.) Express, 1956—, Guthrie (Okla.) Leader, 1958—, Hawaii Tribune-Herald of Hilo, 1961—, Pawhuska (Okla.) Daily Jour.-Capital, 1964—, Guymon (Okla.) Daily Herald, 1966—, Aberdeen (Wash.) Daily World, 1968, The Daily Report, Ontario, Calif., Northwest Arkansas Morning News, Rogers, Pomona (Calif.) Progress-Bull., Frederick (Okla.) Daily Leader, Borger (Tex.) News Herald, 1977, Pauls Valley (Okla.) Daily Democrat, Wewoka (Okla.) Daily Times, 1967—, Jacksonville (Tex.) Progress, 1978, Cleburne (Tex.) Times Rev., 1976, Red Bluff (Calif.) Daily News, 1968—, Booneville (Ark.) Democrat, 1968—, Holdenville (Okla.) News, 1969—, Weatherford (Tex.) Democrat, 1967, Washington (Ind.) Times Herald, 1972—, Sherman (Tex.) Democrat, 1977, Springdale (Ark.) News, Kailua-Kona (Hawaii) West Hawaii Today, 1968—, Henryetta (Okla.) Freelance, Lompoc (Calif.) Record, Picayune (Miss.) Item, Bartlesville (Okla.) Examiner-Enterprise, Kilgore (Tex.) News Herald, Gainesville (Tex.) Daily Register, Chico (Calif.) Enterprise-Record, Auburn (Wash.) Daily Globe News, Sweetwater (Tex.) Reporter, Glasgow (Ky.) Daily Times, Oskaloosa (Iowa) Herald, Redlands (Calif.) Daily Facts, Vallejo (Calif.) Times-Herald, Poplarville (Miss.) Democrat, Durant (Okla.) Daily Democrat; pres., chief exec. officer Donrey Cablevision, Guymon, Bartlesville, and Blackwell, Okla., Vallejo, Calif.; Pub. Donrey Cablevision, Rogers, Ark.; pres., chief exec. officer Donrey Outdoor, Inc., Las Vegas, Reno, Albuquerque, Spokane, Tulsa, Oklahoma City and Ft. Smith, Donrey Outdoor Advertising, Little Rock, Columbus, Ohio, Amarillo, Tex.; owner, pres. and chief exec. officer radio stas. KEXO, Grand Junction, Colo., radio stas. KBRS, Springdale, Ark., radio stas. KOCM-FM, Newport Beach, Calif., KOLO, Reno, 1955—, KOLO-TV, Reno, 1954—, Wichita (Kans.) Donrey Outdoor Co., 1973—. Hon. disch., maj. M.I. 1945. Awarded Legion of Merit, Bronze Star, Purple Heart, 5 combat stars; Broadcaster of Year award Nev. Broadcasting Assn., 1978. Mem. Nat. Assn. Radio-TV Broadcasters, Am. Soc. Newspaper Editors, So. Newspaper Pubs. Assn., Am. Legion, Sigma Delta Chi, Pi Kappa Alpha. Clubs: Overseas Press (San Francisco); Hillcrest Country (Bartlesville); Tulsa, Dallas Athletic; Hardscrabble Country (Ft. Smith); Prospector's (Reno); Pacific (Honolulu).

REYNOLDS, JEFFREY HANN, molecular biologist; b. Ft. Pierre, Fla., Oct. 23, 1961; s. Woodrow Wilson and Victoria Kathran (Hann) R. AA, Monterey Peninsula Coll., 1981; BS, U. Calif., Davis, 1983; PhD in Molecular Biology, U. Calif., Berkeley, 1989. Exhibit researcher/designer Monterey (Calif.) Bay Aquarium, 1978-83; rsch. asst. in molecular biology U. Calif., Berkeley, 1983—. Regents fellow U. Calif., 1982-86; Bank Am. scholar, 1981; NIH trainee U. Calif., 1984-88. Mem. Alpha Gamma Sigma (treas. Monterey chpt. 1979, Kathleen Lolly award 1981), Phi Kappa Phi. Home: 2208 Grove St #1 Berkeley CA 94704 Office: U Calif Dept Molecular Biology Stanley Hall Berkeley CA 94720

REYNOLDS, JERRY OWEN, professional basketball coach; b. French Lick, Ind., Jan. 29, 1944. Student, Vincennes U., Oakland City Coll., Ind. U., Ind. State U. Coach Rockhurst Coll., Kansas City, Mo., 1975-84, Pittsburg (Kans.) State U., 1984-85; asst. coach Sacramento Kings, 1985-86, 86-87, 87-88, head coach, 1988—. Office: Sacramento Kings 1 Sports Pkwy Sacramento CA 95834 *

REYNOLDS, JOHN CURBY, sales representative; b. San Jose, Calif., Aug. 15, 1948; s. Ivan Randolph and Lillie Murrel (McBrown) R.; m. Sharon Taylor, June 12, 1982; children: Brian James, Chris John. AA, Cabrillo Jr. Coll., Aptos, Calif., 1969. Sales rep. Equitable of Iowa Ins. Co., Sacramento, 1973-79, Grand Auto Inc., Sacramento, 1979-82, Princess House, Sacramento, 1982-84; sales telemktg. Montgomery Ward, Sacramento, 1984-85; sales rep. Sanitary Supply Co., Tucson, 1986—; mem. SVEA Bus. Group, Sierra Vista, Ariz., 1986—. Deacon of bd., moderator of ch. bd., sec. Evang. Free Ch. Mem. Sierra Vista C. of C. (mil. affairs com.). Democrat. Office: Sanitary Supply Co Inc 360 S 7th St Sierra Vista AZ 85635

REYNOLDS, JOHN DOUGLAS, Canadian government official; b. Toronto, Ont., Can., Jan. 19, 1942; s. Thomas Douglas Reynolds and Helen Alberta (Martindale) Ragen; m. Yvonne Patricia, Dec. 4, 1984; children: Paul, Michael, Robert, Neil, Kelly, Katie, Christopher. Grad. high sch., Montreal, Can. Host, moderator radio open-line program 1978-82; M.P. Progressive Conservative Party Govt. of Can., Burnaby-Richmond-Delta, 1972-78; Social Credit Mem. Legis. Assembly, W. Vancouver-Howe Sound, 1983, 86—; speaker Can. Legis.; chmn. agrl. legis. com.; mem. pub. accounts com.; parliamentary sec. Minister of Health. Office: BC Legislature, Parliament Bldgs, Victoria, BC Canada V8V 1X4

REYNOLDS, JOHN HAMILTON, physicist, educator; b. Cambridge, Mass., Apr. 3, 1923; s. Horace Mason and Catharine (Coffeen) R.; m. Ann Burchard Arnold, July 19, 1975; children from previous marriages: Amy, Horace Marshall, Brian Marshall, Karen Leigh, Petra Catharine. AB, Harvard U., 1943; MS, U. Chgo., 1948, PhD, 1950; D. honoris causa, U. Coimbra, Portugal, 1987. Rsch. asst. Electroacoustic Lab., Harvard U., 1941-43; assoc. physicist Argonne Nat. Lab., 1950; physicist U. Calif. at Berkeley, 1950—, prof. physics, 1961-88; chmn. dept. physics U. Calif., Berkeley, 1984-86, faculty rsch. lectr., 1974; emeritus prof., recalled rsch. physicist U. Calif. at Berkeley, 1989—. Contbr. articles to profl. jours. Lt. USNR, 1943-46. Recipient Wetherill medal Franklin Inst., 1965, Golden Plate award Am. Acad. Achievement, 1968, Exceptional Sci. Achievement award NASA, 1973; Guggenheim fellow U. Bristol, Eng., 1956-57, Los Alamos Nat. Lab., 1987, NSF fellow U. São Paulo, Brazil, 1963-64; Fulbright-Hays rsch. grantee U. Coimbra, Portugal, 1971-72; U.S.-Australia Coop. Sci. Program awardee U. Western Australia, 1978-79, Berkeley citation, 1988. Fellow AAAS, Am. Acad. Srts and Scis., Am. Phys. Soc., Am. Geophys. Union, Geochem Soc., Meteoritical Soc. (Leonard medal 1973); mem. Nat. Acad. Scis. (J. Lawrence Smith medal 1967), AAUP, Phi Beta Kappa. Democrat. Club: Faculty (Berkeley). Office: U Calif Dept Physics Berkeley CA 94720

REYNOLDS, KATHLEEN ANN, laser printing and electronic typesetting company executive; b. Mt. Kisco, N.Y., Oct. 12, 1947; d. Paul Victor and Elizabeth May (Sanders) McNutt; m. Thomas Eugene Reynolds, Feb. 3, 1968; children: Roseanne, Trueman. Grad. high sch., San Diego. Exec. sec. North Island, San Diego, 1967-71; mail carrier U.S. Post Office, Santee, Calif., 1973-75; saleswoman Garris Realtors, San Diego, 1972-78, Allstate Realtors, San Diego, 1978-80; ops. mgr. Computer Output Performance Specialists, San Diego, 1980-84, pres., 1984—; cons. in field, 1986—. Mem. Direct Mktg. Assn., Data Processing Mgmt. Assn., XPLOR, Escondido C. of C. Office: Computer Output Performance Specialists 9919 Hibert St Ste F San Diego CA 92131

REYNOLDS, RICHARD HENRY, art educator; b. N.Y.C., May 16, 1913; s. Raymond R. and Sarah Alice (Weeks) R.; m. Marjorie Merrihew Sharrer, Aug. 10, 1939; 1 dau., Barbara Gwynne Nagata. A.B., U. Calif., 1936; student U. Calif., Los Angeles, 1939, Mills Coll., 1940; M.A., Coll. Pacific, 1942; postgrad. Oreg. State U., 1962; D.F.A., Morningside Coll., Sioux City, Iowa, 1976. Window display artist Emporium, San Francisco, 1936-37. Foreman-Clark, 1937, Hastings Clothing Co., 1937-38; asst. chmn. div. arts and letters Stockton Jr. Coll., 1939-43; prof. art, chmn. dept. U. of the Pacific, 1948-73, sr. prof., 1973-80, prof. emeritus, 1980, faculty research lectr., 1960, chairman academic council (senate), 1967-68, chmn. president's task force on acad. programs, 1980; mem. Stockton Arts Commn., 1980-81; guest lectr. Alaska Meth. U., Liberal Arts Inst., Anchorage, 1962; lectr. in field; judge numerous competitive art exhbns.; judge art sect. Ariz. State Fair, 1971; one-man show (sculpture) John Muir Gallery, Modesto, Calif., 1956, (painting) Lanai Gallery, Sacramento, 1956, (polychromed wood-reliefs) Stockton Fine Arts Gallery, 1972, 74, U. Pacific Alumni House Gallery, 1972; mem. show, Five Artists, invited E. B. Crocker Gallery, Sacramento, 1956; sculpture accepted for national exhbn. 10th Ann. New Eng. Exhbn., New Canaan, Conn., 1958; invited exhibit sculpture Eric Locke Gallery, San Francisco, 3d Ann. West Coast Sculptors, 1960; exhibited painting Purdue U., 1966; 2-man show (with wife) Stockton Savs. Loan Bank Invitational, 1968; exhibited paintings at No. Calif. Arts Exhbn., Sacramento, 1970; exhibited selected paintings Mother Lode Art Assn. Annual Show, Sonora, Calif., 1968; commd. sculptures buildings and campus U. of the Pacific, 1958, 60, 62, 63, bronze relief Swenson Golf Course, Stockton, 1968, metal falcon sculpture Atwater (Calif.) High Sch., 4 foot bronze relief for Stockton Record Bldg., bronze plaque Quemado (N.Mex.) Library, 1973; TV and radio lectr., 1955—; pvt. architectural sculpture commns., 1956—; exhibited Da Vinci Internat. Exhbn., N.Y.C., 1970, U. Pacific, 1973, Modesto Jr. Coll., 1973, Unitarian Arts Festival, Stockton, 1976-80, Ann. Delta Art Assn. show, Pittsburgh, Calif., 1976, Stockton Art League Show, annually, 1976-85; judge Merced Art Assn., 1976. Bd. dirs. Stockton Art League, 1978-79 hon. bd. dirs. Stockton Symphony Ballet Assn., 1978-84, San Joaquin Concert Ballet Assn. Served as lt. (j.g.), U.S. Naval Res., active duty, 1943-46. Awarded prize in oils Spring Art Festival, Stockton Art League, 1951; Bronze medal sculpture, Oakland Art Gallery's Oil Painting-Sculpture Ann. Exhbn., 1952; Kingsley award for sculpture Crocker Art Gallery, Sacramento, 1952, 53, 79; San Joaquin Pioneer Museum, 1953; 2d prize, Nat. Mag. Cover Contest, 1957; sculpture prizes Unitarian Arts Festival, Stockton, 1959, 61; jurors mention Nat. Exhbn. Small Paintings, Tour Gallery Assos., N.Mex., 1962; hon. mention Stockton Art League, 1964, 68; Best of Show award, 2d prize (painting), honorable mentions in Calif. exhibitions, 1966; Transparent Painting award No. Calif. Spring Art Festival Haggin Mus., Stockton, Calif., 1968; Acrylic Painting award Unitarian Arts Festival, Stockton, 1968; purchase prize, painting Lodi Art Ann., Acampo, 1971, 79; 2d prize, painting San Joaquin County Fair and Expn., 1972, drawing and painting awards, 1974, 3d award, mixed media, 1981; 3 painting awards Stockton Art League Ann., 1974, purchase award, 1975; 1st prize sculpture San Joaquin County Fair and Expn. Art Show, 1976, 82; spl. award sculpture Crocker Kingsley Exhbn., 1982. 2d prize and hon. mention Bank of Stockton, 1976; 2d prize, other media San Joaquin County Fair, 1978; 2d award Lodi Spring Wine Show, 1982, 3d award, 1983; hon. mention Lodi Grape Festival and Nat. Wine Show, 1982; 2d award Unitarian Arts Festival, Stockton, 1982; hon. mention No. Calif. Arts, Inc. Exhbn., Sacramento, 1982; 2d award San Joaquin County Fair, also hon. mention, 1983, 3rd prize Joaquin County Fair, 1988; 1st prize junk sculpture Alan Short Gallery, Stockton, Calif., 1983; 3d award Lodi Spring Wine Show Art Exhbn., 1983, 2 Exhibitor awards No.Calif. Arts Exhbn., Sacramento, 1983, 3d award San Joaquin County Fair Art Exhbn., 1984, Bronze Relief plaque for San Joaquin County Hosp., 1984, Columnist Stockton Art League's newsletter, The Collagraph, 1984-86, 3 2d Place awards, Hon. Mention for sculpture, 1985; 1st prize Stockton Symphony program cover competition, 1984; Order of Pacific award U. of Pacific, 1980; honorable mention Spring Wine Show Art Exhibition, Lodi, Calif., 1986; honorable mention No. Calif. Arts, Inc. Open Exhbn., 1986; judge's choice 16th annual Nat. Small Painting Show, Albuquerque, N.Mex., 1987, 18th annual, 1989, hon. mention 4th Nat. N.C. Miniature Painting Show, 1988; purchase prize for sculpture 37th Ann. Art Exhibition, 1988; Haggin Mus., 1988. Shell grantee, 1960. Life fellow International Inst. Arts and Letters, 1960. Mem. Coll. Art Assn. of Am., Pacific Arts Assn. (editor Journalette 1951-52; pres. No. Cal. sect. 1951-52), Stockton Art League (pres. 1952-53, 80-82), Nat. Art Edn. Assn. (nat. chmn. membership com. 1952-53), AAUP (v.p. local chpt. 1958-59), Navy League U.S. (dir. Stockton br. 1981-83), Phi Kappa Phi (pres.-elect 1980-81, emeritus), Delta Epsilon, Phi Sigma Kappa, Phi Delta Kappa (emeritus). Episcopalian. Richard H. Reynolds Gallery named in his honor U. Pacif, Stockton, 1986. Contbr. articles to art publs. Exhibitor paintings, sculptures. Home: 1656 W Longview Ave Stockton CA 95207

REYNOLDS, RICHARD PAULSEN, computer scientist; b. Berkeley, Calif., Nov. 16, 1946; s. Theodore Robert and Mary Louise (Green) R.; m. Barbara Jean Trent, Jan 21, 1967; 1 child, Debra Jean. AA, Chabot Coll., 1972; BA, Calif. State U., Hayward, 1973. Computer scientist AT&T, Sunnyvale, Calif., 1973—. With U.S. Army, 1967-69, Vietnam. Mem. Engring. Achievement Soc. (Outstanding Achievement award 1988), Nat. Trust for Hist. Preservation. Republican. Home: 5504 Jasmine Ct Castro Valley CA 94552 Office: AT&T 1090 E Duane Ave Sunnyvale CA 94552

REYNOLDS, ROBERT HARRISON, export company executive; b. Mpls., Sept. 6, 1913; s. Clarence H. and Helen (Doyle) R.; student pub. schs., Vinton, Iowa; m. Gladys Marie Gaster, Apr. 7, 1934; 1 dau., Shirley Anne (Mrs. Frank S. Potestio); m. 2d, Viola E. Shimel, June 26, 1982. Export sales mgr., rolled products sales mgr. Colo. Fuel & Iron Corp., Denver, 1938-46; pres. Rocky Mountain Export Co., Inc., Denver, 1941—; dir. Electromedics, Inc. Club: Denver. Home: 580 S Clinton St Denver CO 80231 Office: Rocky Mountain Export 11111 Mississippi Ave Aurora CO 80012

REYNOLDS, STEPHEN PHILIP, utility company executive; b. Berkeley, Calif., Jan. 5, 1948; s. Philip Elmore and Annette (Medefind) R.; m. Sharon Ann Rudd, Sept. 6, 1969; 1 child, Matthew. BA in Econs., U. Calif., Berkeley, 1970; MBA in Prodn. Mgmt., U. Oreg., 1972. Various mktg./rate positions Pacific Gas and Electric Co., San Francisco, 1967-75, sr. rate engr., 1975-77, supervising rate engr., 1977-80, mgr. rate dept., 1980-84, v.p. rates, 1984—; pres., chief exec. officer Pacific Gas Transmission Co. (subs. Pacific Gas and Electric), 1988—; mem. adv. com. Mich. State U. Inst. Pub. Utilities. Contbr. numerous articles to trade publs. and profl. symposiums on rate issues. Served with Calif. Army N.G., 1970-76. Fellow Council on Econ. Regulation; mem. Internat. Assn. Energy Economists, Pacific Coast Gas Assn./Pacific Coast Electric Assn., San Francisco World Affairs Council. Clubs: San Francisco Engrs., Commonwealth. *

REYNOLDS, WAYNE MCFALL, restaurant owner; b. Richmond, Va., Nov. 21, 1947; s. Jesse Anthony and Muriel (Clarke) R.; m. Judy Anne Derr, Dec. 22, 1974; children: Stephanie Danielle, Amber Christine, Michael Jesse. Student, Pfeiffer Coll., 1965-67; BA, Humboldt State Coll., 1969; MA, Humboldt State U., 1976. Tech. dir., designer Old Brewery Theatre, Helena, Mont., 1968-69; stage technician Humboldt State U., Arcata, Calif., 1968-69, 75-76; owner Two Traveler's Restaurant, Valier, Mont., 1976—; lectr. drama Coll. Great Falls, Mont., 1984—. Appointed to mont. State Foster Care Review Bd., 1986; sec., chmn. bd. Valier Area Devel. Corp., 1980-82; founder Valier Community Theatre, 1980, artistic dir., 1980—; chmn. bd., 1980-82, pres. Luth. Ch. council, Valier, 1981-85; trainer and speaker for Spl. Needs Adoption Workshops, Mont. State Dept. Social Services, 1983—. Served with USCG, 1969-73. Recipient Five Star Thespian award Nat. Thespian Soc., 1965, Founders award Valier Community Theatre, 1982. Mem. Am. Legion, Alpha Phi Omega. Club; Valier Community (v.p. 1980-81). Home: 307 Teton Ave Valier MT 59486

REYNOLDS, W(YNETKA) ANN, university system administrator, educator; b. Coffeyville, Kans., Nov. 3, 1937; d. John Ethelbert and Glennie (Beanland) King; m. Thomas H. Kirschbaum; children—Rachel Rebecca, Rex King. BS in Biology-Chemistry, Kans. State Tchrs. Coll., Emporia, 1958; MS in Zoology, U. Iowa, Iowa City, 1960, PhD, 1962; DSc (hon.), Ind. State U., Evansville, 1980; LHD (hon.), McKendree Coll., 1984, U. N.C., Charlotte, 1988; DSc (hon.), Ball State U., Muncie, Ind., 1985, Emporia (Kans.) State U., 1987; PhD (hon.), Fu Jen Cath. U., Republic of China, 1987. Asst. prof. biology Ball State U., Muncie, Ind., 1962-65; asst. prof. anatomy U. Ill. Coll. Medicine, Chgo., 1965-68, assoc. prof. anatomy, 1968-73, research prof. ob-gyn, from 1973, prof. anatomy, from 1973, acting assoc. dean acad. affairs Coll. Medicine, 1977, assoc. vice chancellor, dean grad. coll., 1977-79; prof. ob-gyn Ohio State U., Columbus, 1979-82, prof. anatomy, 1979-82, provost, 1979-82; chancellor Calif. State Univ. system, Long Beach, 1982—, prof. biology, 1982—; cons. and lectr. in field; prof. biology Calif. State U., Dominguez Hills, 1982—; prof. biol. scis. (hon.) San Francisco State U., 1982—; clin. prof. ob/gyn. U. Calif., Los Angeles, 1985—; co-chair Fed. Task Force on Women, Minorities and Handicapped in Sci. and Tech., 1987—; bd. dirs. GTE Calif., Maytag Corp., Abbott Labs., Am. Electric Power Co. Contbr. chpts. to books, articles to profl. jours. Active numerous civic activities involving edn.; chair Econ. Literacy Coun. Calif., 1983-89; pres. Nat. Assn. System Heads, 1987-88; bd. dirs. Am. Council for the Arts, 1986—; trustee Internat. Life Scis. Inst.-Nutrition Found., 1987—, Southwest Mus., L.A., 1986—, L.A. County High Sch. For Arts Found., 1985—. Recipient Disting. Alumni award Kans. State Tchrs. Coll., 1972. Fellow Calif. Acad. Scis.; mem. AAAS, Am. Assn. Anatomists, Am. Diabetes Assn., Am. Soc. Zoologists, Am. Assn. for Higher Edn. (bd. dirs. 1984—), Endocrine Soc., Perinatal Research Soc., Soc. Exptl. Biology and Medicine, Soc. Gynecologic Investigation, Sigma Xi. Office: Calif State U System Office 400 Golden Shore Long Beach CA 90802-4275

REZAC, STEPHAN ROBERT, trade association executive; b. Sioux Falls, S.D., Dec. 4, 1953; s. Gerald Robert and Nila Jean (Kunkel) R.; m. Donna Gail Blumenfeld, May 24, 1986. Student, S.D. State U., 1972-74, U. Wyo., 1984, Casper Coll., 1984. Dir. promotion, edn. S.D. Credit Union League, Sioux Falls, 1975-76; mktg. dir. Chanute Credit Union, Rantoul, Ill., 1976-80; dir. edn., mktg. Wyo. Credit Union League, Casper, 1980-86; pres., chief exec. officer N.Mex. Credit Union League, Albuquerque, 1986—, N.Mex. Credit Union League Services Corp., Albuquerque, 1986—; nat. dir. Credit Union Nat. Assn., Madison, Wis., 1986—, lobbyist N.Mex. Credit Union League, 1987—. Mem. AMA, Assn. Credit Union League Execs., N.Mex. Soc. Assn. Execs., Albuquerque C. of C. (govtl. affairs policy com. 1988—). Republican. Baptist. Home: 1237 Monte Verde Dr NE Albuquerque NM 87123 Office: NMex Credit Union League 9426 Indian School Rd NE Albuquerque NM 87112

RHAME, DAVID POPE, land development company executive; b. Mpls., Mar. 22, 1920; s. Paul William and Edith (Pope) R.; m. Jean Ann Coe, Sept. 1, 1950; children: Ann Rochelle, William David. Student, U. Mich., 1937-39; BSBA with honors, UCLA, 1947. Owner, mgr. bldg. contracting co. Calif., 1950-65; pres. Prestwick, Inc., Tantallon, Md., 1966-71, Maurice River Co., Millville, N.J., 1971-76; pres. Rhames Assocs., Inc., Arlington, Tex., 1977-87, Del Mar, Calif., 1987—; adj. prof. real estate dept. Coll. Bus. Adminstrn., U. Tex., Arlington, 1986-87. Lt. col. USAAF, 1942-46, ETO. Mem. Nat. Assn. Home Builders (life bd. dirs.), Urban Land Inst. (coun. exec. group), Community Assns. Inst. (founder, chmn. 1973-75). Home and Office: 12861 Caminito De Las Olas Del Mar CA 92014

RHEA, ANN CRAWFORD, interior designer; b. Somerville, Tenn., Oct. 30, 1940; d. James Samuel and Annie Marie (Crawford) R. BA in Art Edn., U. Miss., 1962; BFA, Memphis Coll. Arts, 1967; postgrad., Scottsdale Community Coll., 1975-85. Cert. Nat. Council Interior Design. Interior designer Dottie Sanders Interiors, Memphis, 1968-70; designer Holiday Inns Inc., Memphis, 1970-72, Ramada Inns Inc., Phoenix, 1972-78; assoc. Continental Design, Scottsdale, Ariz., 1978-80, Hauser Designs, Scottsdale, 1980-82; prin. Design Criteria Group, Scottsdale, 1983—; cons. Embassy Suites Hotels Inc., 1985, 87. Active Heard Mus., Phoenix, Smithsonian Assn., Nat. Trust Hist. Preservation. Mem. Nat. Arts and Crafts Assn., Ariz. Hotel Motel Assn. (com. for hospitality show 1987-89, com. for allied membership 1987-88), Nat. Mus. Women in the Arts. Democrat. Methodist. Home and Office: 6801 E Camelback S-305 Scottsdale AZ 95251

RHOADES, EDWARD WILLIAM, mechanical engineer; b. Iola, Kans., Sept. 22, 1933; s. Willie William and Minnie Grace (Erbe) R.; m. Donna Dee Gerstel, Jan. 2, 1945 (div. May 1988); 1 child, Rebecca. AA, Independence Jr. Coll., 1953; BS, Kans. State Coll., 1956. Design engr. N.Am. Aviation, Downey, Calif., 1956-57; mech. engr. Naval Civil Engring. Lab., Port Hueneme, Calif., 1959-61; program mgr., gen. engr. Pacific Missile Range, Point Mugu, Calif., 1961-73; supr. plans coordination office Pacific Missile Test Ctr., Point Mugu, Calif., 1973-75, head fin. planning comptroller office, 1975-79, program mgr., 1979-83, head plans, 1983—; liaison officer USN, Washington, 1978-79. Served with U.S. Army, 1957-59. Mem. Am. Soc. Mil. Comptrollers, El Conejo Sports Car Club (pres. 1965-66). Republican. Home: 2465 Grand Ave #247 Ventura CA 93003 Office: Pacific Missile Test Ctr Point Mugu CA 93042

RHOADES, JOHN S., SR., federal judge; b. 1925; m. Carmel Rhoades; children: Mark, John, Matthew, Peter, Christopher. AB, Stanford U., 1948; JD, U. Calif., San Francisco, 1951. Prosecuting atty. City of San Diego, 1955-56, dep. city atty., 1956-57; pvt. practice San Diego, 1957-60; ptnr. Rhoades, Hollywood & Neil, San Diego, 1960-85; judge U.S. Dist. Ct. (so. dist.) Calif., San Diego, 1985—. Served with USN, 1943-46. Office: US Dist Ct 940 Front St San Diego CA 92189

RHOADS, DEAN A., state senator, cattle rancher; b. Tonasket, Wash., Oct. 5, 1935; s. Clyde Chester and Mamie Katerine (Kennedy) R.; m. Sharon Lois Packer, Jan. 8, 1964; children: Slamaria, Chandra. BS in Agrl. Bus. Mgmt., Calif. State Poly. Coll., San Luis Obispo, 1963. Mgr. Calif. Livestock Mktg. Assn., Visalia, 1963-66; cow-calf operator Tuscarora, Nev., 1966—; assemblyman Nev. State Legislature, Carson City, 1976-82, senator, 1984-88. Past pres., bd. dirs. Pub. Lands Council, Washington, 1970-88. Mem. Nev. Tax Payers Assn. (bd. dirs. 1982-88), Nev. Cattlemen's Assn. (bd. dirs. 1968-88, Cattleman of Yr. 1980), Rotary. Republican. Presbyterian. Home: Tuscarora NV 89834

RHOADS, DEBORAH LOUISE, futurist; b. New Braunfels, Tex., Sept. 9, 1950; d. Ellsworth Earl and Pauline Marie (Hoffman) R. BS, Tex. A&M U., 1975; MA, Ariz. State U., 1978, PhD, 1982. Teaching asst. Ariz. State U., Tempe, 1975-76; legis. asst. Ariz. Ho. Reps., Phoenix, 1976-77; rsch. intern Codama Svcs., Phoenix, 1977-78, rsch. coordinator, 1978-79, rsch. dir., 1979-82; adj. asst. prof. Ariz. State U., 1982—; pres. Future Directions, Cave Creek, 1982—; speaker in field. Publisher newsletter Future Directions Bulletin, 1988—; contbr. articles to profl. jours. Judge pub. svc. awards Nat. Acad. TV Arts and Scis., Phoenix, 1982; mem. panel Scottsdale (Ariz.) Town Enrichment Program, 1982; judge environ excellence awards Valley Forward, Phoenix, 1985; mem. planning com. Phoenix Futures Forum, 1989. Mem. World Future Soc., Southwest Profl. Geographic Assn., Coun. Urban Econ. Devel., Tech. Transfer Soc., Valley Citizens League. Office: Future Directions PO Box J Cave Creek AZ 85331

RHOADS, SHEILA LUBIN, French educator; b. L.A., June 11, 1946; d. David and Martha (Prochnik) Lubin; m. Donald Perry Rhoads, Jan. 5, 1969; children: Emma, Perry, John, Anna. Diploma, U. Dijon, France, 1966, U. Grenoble, France, 1967; BA in French and German, UCLA, 1968, MA in French, 1970. Tchr. French Westridge Sch. for Girls, Pasadena, Calif., 1970-73; supr. teaching program French and German Mt. St. Mary's Coll. and Hamilton High Sch., L.A., 1974; tchr. French L.A. City Sch. Dist., 1975-81; instr. French San Bernardino (Calif.) Valley Coll., 1984-87, instr. French evening div., 1984—; tchr. French World High Sch., Lake Arrowhead, Calif., 1988-89; tchr. English as a second lang. Belmont Community Adult Sch., 1975-81. Bd. dirs. Arrowhead Lake Assn., Calif., 1984-87, mem. lake ops. com., 1984-88; asst. dir. instr. Lake Arrowhead Elem. Sch. Ski Club, 1982-86; co-founder, asst. dir., ski team coach Mary Putnam Henk Intermediate Sch. Ski Club, 1987-88, 89—. . Mem. Alliance Francaise, San Bernardino-Riverside (acad. rep. 1985, leader book club div. 1985—), AAUW, Am. Assn. Tchrs. French. Home: 675 Grass Valley Rd Lake Arrowhead CA 92352 Address: PO Box 8094 San Bernardino CA 92412-8094

RHODE, EDWARD ALBERT, veterinary medicine educator, university administrator; b. Amsterdam, N.Y., July 25, 1926; s. Edward A. and Katherine (Webb) R.; m. Dolores Bangert, 1955; children: David E., Peter R., Paul W., Robert M., Catherine E. DVM, Cornell U., 1947. Diplomate Am. Coll. Veterinary Internal Medicine. Prof. vet. medicine U. Calif., Davis, 1964—, chmn. dept. vet. medicine, 1968-71, assoc. dean instrn. Sch. Vet. Medicine, 1971-77, 78-81, dean sch. Vet. Medicine, 1982—. Mem. Am. Vet. Medicine Assn., Calif. Vet. Medicine Assn., Am. Acad. Vet. Cardiology, Am. Physiol. Soc., Calif. Biomed. Research Assn. Office: U Calif Sch Vet Medicine Davis CA 95616

RHODES, ANNE LOU, retired social service administrator; b. Richmond, Ind., Oct. 9, 1935; d. George E. and Margaret (Jones) R. BA, Whittier Coll., 1957; MSW, Fresno State Coll., 1968. Social worker San Bernardino (Calif.) County Welfare Dept., 1959-62, social work supr. I, 1962-63, social work supr. II, 1963-68, social service supr. III, 1968-89; instr. social welfare U. Calif., Riverside, 1969; cons. Headstart program Riverside County Econ. Opportunity Bd., 1970, Delman Heights Welfare Rights Orgn., 1968-71.; participant German profl. minority exchange program, 1979, Statehouse Cong. on Children and Youth, 1979; mem. Calif. Com. on Credentials, 1980; bd. dirs. Inland Area Adolescent Clinic, 1970—. Mem. task force YWCA, 1976; bd. dirs. Inland Area Urban League, 1970-71, v.p. leadership devel., 1970-71, Arrowhead United Way, 1980. Mem. NAACP (pres. 1960-61), Acad. Certified Social Workers, LWV (pres. San Bernardino chpt. 1981-82, friends welfare rights), Nat. Urban League (mem. com. 1970-71), Friends Welfare Rights Orgn., Nat. Council Negro Women, Zonta Internat., Alpha Tau Chi (dir. 1979-80). Home: 5710 Belvedere Ave Highland CA 92346 Office: St Bernardine Hosp 2101 N Waterman Ave San Bernardino CA 92404

RHODES, JAMES LAMAR, JR., educator, research historian; b. Montgomery, Ala., May 3, 1948; s. James Lamar Rhodes and Mae Ellen (Childers) Holley; divorced; 1 child, Sharon Michelle Rhodes Carswell; m. Saturnina Alvarado Avina, Feb. 14, 1977; children: James Lamar III, Aaron Abraham, David Isaiah. AA in English Lit., Coll. of Marin, 1972; BS in Criminal Justice Adminstrn., Calif. State U., San Jose, 1977; AA in Law Enforcement, Canada Coll., Redwood City, Calif., 1978; MA in Bus. Mgmt., Webster U., St. Louis, 1988. Cert. peace officer, Calif.; cert. detention and corrections officer, Ariz. Communications technician Pacific Telephone Co., Calif., 1970-83; detention officer Yuma County, Yuma, Ariz., 1984-86; correctional svc. officer State of Ariz., Yuma, 1986-88; tchr. Immaculate Conception Sch., Yuma, 1988—. Author detention and correctional handbooks. Mem. Milpitas (Calif.) San. Dist. Bd., 1978-80; bd. dirs. Ctr. for Employment and Tng., Yuma, 1986—; founder no-fee counseling svcs. for Vietnam vets., Yuma; mem. Agt. Orange Adv. Com.; union organizer Communication Workers Am., Calif., 1972-80. Sgt. USAF, 1967-69, Vietnam. Recipient Citizen of Honor award Vietnamese Community, Santa Clara County, Calif., 1983, appreciation award Cath. Social Svc., Santa Clara County, 1983, Luth. Soc. Svc., Santa Clara County, 1983, Am. Legion, Indpls., 1983, AMVETS, Yuma, 1986. Mem. Vietnam Combat Vets. (nat. chmn. 1981—), Justice for Vet. Victims of VA (v.p. 1988—), DAV, U.S. Chess Fedn., AFSCME, World Federalist Assn., Vietnam Helicopter Crew Mems. Assn., Ariz. Indian Vietnam Vets. Assn., Am. Legion (post comdr. San Jose, Calif. chpt.), AMVETS (chaplain Yuma chpt. 1985, state judge advocate Ariz. chpt. 1986). Mem. Baha'i Faith. Home: 1740 W 24th Ln Yuma AZ 85364 Office: Immaculate Conception Sch 501 Ave B Yuma AZ 85364

RHODES, JAMES M., JR., sales executive; b. Santa Monica, Calif., June 21, 1937; s. James M. Rhodes and Sybil Wescott; m. Catherine H. Rhodes, June 4, 1959 (div . Oct. 1971); m. Sylvia E. Dunlevy, Dec. 7, 1977; children: James Mavran IV, Joam Rhodes Goetze, Jeffrey Michael. BS in Mil. Sci., USAF Acad., Colo., 1959; MS in System Mgmt., U. So. Calif., L.A., 1970, cert. in info. systems, 1988. Commd. 2nd lt. USAF, 1959, advanced through grades to brig. gen., pilot, 1960-65; student USAF Aerospace Rsch., Edwards AFB, Calif., 1966; flying, acad. & space simulation inst. USAF Aerospace Rsch., Edwards AFB, 1967-70; flight cmdr. 8th Spec Ops Sqdn, Bien Hoa AB, Republic of South Vietnam, 1970-71; staff planning officer HQ USAF, Washington, 1972-76; cmdr. 10th Tac Recon Wing, RAF Alconbury, UK, 1982-84; command dir. HQ Norad, Colorado Springs, Colo., 1985-86; cmdr. 23rd Air Div/Norad Region SE Air Def Sector, Tyndall AFB, Fla., 1986-88; ret. USAF; dir. Clearbrook Co., San Diego, 1989, Rhodes Distbn., San Diego, 1989—. Author: Aircraft Dynamics (USAF Aeospace research pilot sch. text) 1969. Mem. Order of Daedalians, Red River Valley Fighter Pilots Assn. (v.p. 1975-77). Republican. Home: 10922 Riesling Dr San Diego CA 92131 Office: Rhodes Distbn 5333 Mission Center Rd Ste 109 San Diego CA 92108

RHODES, JOHN J., III, congressman, lawyer; b. Mesa, Ariz., Sept. 8, 1943; s. John J. II and Betty (Harvey) R.; m. Peggy Withers (div.); children: John, Taylor, Jeremy; m. Ann Chase, May 27, 1978; 1 child, Arthur. BA in History, Yale U., 1965; JD, U. Ariz., 1968. Bar: Ariz. 1968, U.S. Dist. Ct. Ariz. 1968, U.S. Supreme Ct. 1973. Ptnr. Killian and Legg, Mesa, 1970-77; v.p., gen counsel Health Maintenance Assocs., Phoenix, 1977-80; ptnr. Rhodes and Golston, Mesa, 1980-86; mem. 100th, 101st Congresses from Ariz. dist. 1, 1987—; mem. gov.'s exec. com. for Plan 6 and CAP financing, Phoenix, 1985-86. V.p. Cen. Ariz. Water Conservation Dist., Phoenix, 1982-87; pres. Mesa Bd. Edn., 1972-76; chmn. Dist. 29, 1973-75; pres. Mesa C. of C., 1973-77. Served to capt. U.S. Army, 1968-70, Vietnam. Republican. Club: HoHoKams. Lodge: Rotary. Office: 412 Cannon House Office Bldg Washington DC 20515

RHOY, NICHOLAS ALAN, publisher; b. Oakland, Calif., Oct. 9, 1938; s. Thomas Frederick and Mary Jane (Armstrong) R. BBA, Armstrong Coll., Berkeley, Calif., 1964; student, The Graham Sch., Walnut Creek, Calif., 1968; Student, City Coll., Santa Barbara, Calif., 1976, The Am. Sch., Anaheim, Calif., 1984. Sales mgr. R.H. Macy & Co., San Francisco, 1960-68; real estate sales Red Carpet Realty Co., Orinda, Calif., 1968-72; ptnr. Rancho Notsogrande, Santa Barbara, 1972--; pres. The Silver Bear, Santa Barbara, 1982—; ptnr. Huckleberry Farms, Hamilton, Mont., 1984—; pub. Travelhost mag., Ventura, Calif., 1988—; v.p. El Montecito Oaks Press, Inc, Santa Barbara, 1988—; founding dir. Internat. Lalita Kalas Found., Santa Barbara 1984-; contbr. U. Calif. Archives, Berkeley, 1986. Author: A Glossary of Silver- A Compendium of Terms, 1989. Mem. Cabrillo Arts Ctr., Santa Barbara, 1985-88; founder Plaque Preservation com., Santa Barbara, 1986. With U.S. Army, 1956-59. Recipient cert. merit Am. Mgmt. Assn., San Francisco, 1966, Eastman Kodak Co., San Francisco, 1968. Mem. Travelhost Press Assn., Ojai (Calif.) C. of C., Oxnard C. of C., Ventura C. of C., Calif. Restaurant Assn., Calif. Travel Industry Assn. Republican. Home: 135 Santa Isabel Ln Montecito CA 93108 Office: Travelhost Mag PO Box 50641 Santa Barbara CA 93150

RHYNE, WILLIAM JAMES, surgical equipment company official, musician; b. Russell, Kans., Aug. 10, 1954; s. Francis Lewis and Elizabeth Jane (Little) T.; m. Callie Sanae Konno, Jan. 18, 1986. Student electronics, Butler County Community Coll., El Dorado, Kans., 1972-74; BA in Music, U. Hawaii, Honolulu, 1977. Musician Honolulu, 1977-78; retail clk. Harry's Music Store, Honolulu, 1978-80; musician, entertainer Honolulu, 1980-82; salesman Med. Supplies Co. Hawaii, Honolulu, 1982-84; salesman, trainer Profl. Music Products, Greenwood, S.C., 1984-88; salesman ALM Surg. Equipment, Inc., Santa Ana, Calif., 1988—. Composer, musician (music cassettes) A Different Madness, 1982, Chicken Fried Brerrhyne, 1986. Mem. No. Calif. Songwriters Assn., San Francisco Conservatory Music. Democrat. Roman Catholic.

RIACH, DOUGLAS ALEXANDER, marketing and sales executive; b. Victoria, B.C., Can., Oct. 8, 1919; s. Alex and Gladys (Provis) R.; came to U.S., 1925, naturalized, 1942; student U. Calif. at Los Angeles, 1937-38, Fenn Coll., 1959, Grad. Sch. Sales Mgmt. and Mktg., 1960, U.S. Army Command and Gen. Staff Coll., 1966, Armed Forces Staff Coll., 1968, Indsl. Coll. of the Armed Forces, 1970-71; m. Eleanor Montague, Mar. 28, 1942; 1 dau., Sandra Jean. Field rep. Gen. Motors Acceptance Corp., 1940-41, 46-47; with Ridings Motors, 1947-48; with Gen. Foods Corp., 1948-80, terr. sales mgr., San Francisco, 1962-80; with Mel-Williams Co., Elgaaen-Booth Co., 1980-86, Summit Mktg., 1986-87, Thunderbird Mktg., 1987—; exec. v.p. Visual Market Plans Inc., Novato, Calif., 1984-87. Asst. scoutmaster Boy Scouts Am., Los Angeles, 1936-39, asst. dist. commr., 1940-41; co-chmn. Long Beach Tournament Roses, 1947. Served to capt. AUS, 1941-46; to col. inf. USAR, 1946-79, ret. comdr. 2d inf. brigade Calif. State mil. res., 1984-87. Decorated Bronze Star with V and cluster, Legion of Merit, Purple Heart, Combat Infantryman's badge; Medaille de la France Liberee (France); Cross of Freedom (Polish); Grand Cross of Homage (Ardennes); Commemorative War Cross (Yugoslavia); Medialle de la Reconnaissance, Commemorative War medal (Belgium), Medaille Commemorative Francais (France); knight Order of the Compassionate Heart (internat.); knight Sovereign Mil. Order, Temple of Jerusalem (knight templar); named to U.S. Army Inf. Hall of Fame, 1982; recipient Calif. Medal of Merit with cluster, Commendation medal. Mem. Long Beach Food Sales Assn. (pres. 1950), Asso. Grocers Mfrs. Reps. (dir. 1955), Am. Security Council (nat. adv. bd. 1975—), Res. Officers Assn. (San Francisco Presidio pres. 1974-76, v.p. 1977-82, v.p. Calif. 1979, exec. v.p. 1980, pres. 1981, nat. councilman 1981-82), Assn. U.S. Army (gov. East Bay chpt. 1974-82, San Francisco chpt. 1982—). Republican. Presbyterian. Clubs: Exchange (v.p. Long Beach 1955); Merchandising Execs. (dir. 1970-75, sec. 1976-77, v.p. 1978-79, pres. 1980, bd. dirs. 1981) (San Francisco), Commonwealth of Calif. (nat. def. sect. vice chmn. 1964-66, chmn. 1967-72). Lodge: Elks. Home: 2609 Trousdale Dr Burlingame CA 94010

RIBBE, KRISTIN KAY, clinical nurse; b. Belleview, Nebr., May 12, 1964; d. Allen Leonard and LaVonne Kathleen (Fischer) R. BSN, St. Olaf Coll., 1986. Registered nurse, Minn., Wis., Ariz. Store mgr. The Cat House Inc.,

Minnetonka, Minn., 1980-83; clerical worker Cargill Inc., Riverside, N.D., 1983; field worker Cargill Inc., Fargo, N.D., 1984; tchr.'s asst. St. David's Sch. for Exceptional Children, Minnetonka, Minn., 1985; staff nurse Children's Hosp. of Wis., Milw., 1986-87; nurse neonatal intensive care Good Samaritan Med. Ctr., Phoenix, 1987—. Mem. Nat. Assn. Neonatal Nurses, Cen. Ariz. Assn. Neonatal Nurses. Lutheran. Home: 3632 S George Dr Tempe AZ 85292 Office: Good Samaritan Med Ctr 1111 E McDonnell Rd Phoenix AZ 85006

RIBNIK, THELMA NAOMA, art and antique appraiser, small business owner; b. Denver, Dec. 25, 1934; d. Hyman and Mollie (Goodman) Rosenberg; m. Harold Philip Ribnik (dec. 1982); children: Harlan, Linda, Susan. BA in Arts and Antiques, Colo. Women's Coll., 1976. Writer, columnist Univ. Park News, Denver, 1961-65; office mgr. Clermont Med. Assn., Denver, 1965-69; tchr., librarian Congregation Emanuel, Denver, 1965-72; owner, operator Thelma's, Denver, 1970-82, Thelma's of Santa Fe, 1982—; instr. continuing edn. Colo. Women's Coll., 1976-77; lectr. as appraiser various orgns., Santa Fe, 1983—. Painter, artist Cheyenne Art Show (2d pl. 1979), Colo. Art Fair (3d pl. 1978); actress Bonfils Theatre, Denver (named best supporting actress 1980-81), Santa Fe Community Theatre, 1984. Vol. Los Compadres for United Way, Santa Fe, 1984—; docent Scottsdale Ctr. for Performing Arts, 1989. Named Very Important Woman Intermountain Jewish News, Denver, 1982. Mem. AAUW, Bus. and Profl. Women Capitol City, Appraisers Assn. Am., Nat. Appraisers Assn., Santa Fe C. of C. Office: PO Box 6298 Santa Fe NM 87502

RICARDI, LEON JOSEPH, electrical engineer; b. Brockton, Mass., Mar. 21, 1924; s. Philip Julius and Eva Isabel (DuBois) R.; m. Angelena Marie Giorgio, Jan. 19, 1947; children: Eva Marie, John Philip, Richard Christopher. B.S. in Elec. Engring, Northeastern U., 1949, M.S., 1952, Ph.D., 1969. Engr. Andrew Alford Cons. Engrs., Boston, 1950-51; project engr. Gabriel Labs., Needham, Mass., 1951-54; group leader, head Tech. Adv. Office, MIT-Lincoln Lab., Lexington, Mass., 1954-84; pres. L.J. Ricardi, Inc., Torrance, Calif., 1984—; part-time tchr. Northeastern U., Boston, 1969-80; cons. U.S. Air Force. Served with USAF, 1943-45. Fellow IEEE. Roman Catholic. Office: L J Ricardi Inc 3051 Fujita St Torrance CA 90505

RICARDO-CAMPBELL, RITA, economist, educator; b. Boston, Mar. 16, 1920; d. David and Elizabeth (Jones) Ricardo; m. Wesley Glenn Campbell, Sept. 15, 1946; children—Barbara Lee, Diane Rita, Nancy Elizabeth. B.S., Simmons Coll., 1941; M.A., Radcliffe Coll., 1945, Ph.D., 1946. Instr. Harvard U., Cambridge, Mass., 1946-48; asst. prof. Tufts U., Medford, Mass., 1948-51; labor economist U.S. Wage Stabilization Bd., 1951-53; economist ways and means com. U.S. Ho. of Reps., 1953; cons. economist 1957-60; vis. prof. San Jose State Coll., 1960-61; sr. fellow Hoover Instn. on War Revolution and Peace, Stanford, Calif., 1968—; lectr. Health Service Adminstrn., Stanford Med. Sch., 1973-78; dir. Watkins-Johnson Co., Palo Alto, Calif., Gillette Co., Boston. Author: Voluntary Health Insurance in the U.S., 1960, Economics of Health and Public Policy, 1971, Food Safety Regulation: Use and Limitations of Cost-Benefit Analysis, 1974, Drug Lag: Federal Government Decision Making, 1976, Social Security: Promise and Reality, 1977, The Economics and Politics of Health, 1982, 2d edit., 1985; co-editor: Below-Replacement Fertility in Industrial Societies, 1987, Issues in Contemporary Retirement, 1988; contbr. articles to profl. jours. Commr. Western Interstate Commn. for Higher Edn. Calif., 1967-75, chmn., 1970-71; mem. Pres. Nixon's Adv. Council on Status Women, 1969-76; mem. task force on taxation Pres.'s Council on Environ. Quality, 1970-72; mem. Pres.'s Com. Health Services Industry, 1971-73, FDA Nat. Adv. Drug Com., 1972-75; mem. Pres. Reagan's Econ. Policy Adv. Bd., 1981-89, Pres. Reagan's Nat. Council on Humanities, 1982-89, Pres. Reagan's Nat. Medal of Sci. com., 1988—, Pes. Reagan's Nat. Coun. on Humanities, 1982-89; bd. dirs. Ind. Colls. No. Calif., 1971-87; mem. com. assessment of safety, benefits, risks Citizens Commn. Sci., Law and Food Supply, Rockefeller U., 1973-75; mem. adv. com. Ctr. Health Policy Research, Am. Enterprise Inst. Pub. Policy Research, Washington, 1974-80; mem. adv. council on social security Social Security Adminstrn., 1974-75; bd. dirs. Simmons Coll. Corp., Boston, 1975-80; mem. adv. council bd. assocs. Stanford Libraries, 1975-78; mem. council SRI Internat., Menlo Park, Calif., 1977—. Mem. Am. Econ. Assn., Mont Pelerin Soc. (bd. dirs. 1988—), Phi Beta Kappa. Home: 26915 Alejandro Dr Los Altos Hills CA 94022 Office: Stanford U Hoover Instn Stanford CA 94305

RICCIUTI, PAUL RALPH, mechanical engineer; b. N.Y.C., Apr. 10, 1939; s. Ralph R. and Evelyn Irene (Mottola) R.; m. Jacqueline Lillian Basilotta, June 6, 1965; children: Christine, Paul II. AS, SUNY, Farmingdale, 1970; BS, U. Phoenix, 1985, MBA, 1987. Mfg. methods engr. Grumman Aerospace Corp., Bethpage, N.Y., 1963-79; sr. mfg. cost engr. Garrett Turbine Engine Div. Allied Signal Corp., Phoenix, 1979—. With U.S. Army, 1959-62. Mem. Soc. Mfg. Engrs. (cert.), Am. Inst. Estimating Soc., Computer and Automated Systems Assn. (cert.). Republican. Roman Catholic. Home: 4424 E Kelton Ln Phoenix AZ 85032 Office: Garrett Turbine Engine Div lll S 34th St PO Box 5217 Phoenix AZ 85010

RICE, BARBARA POLLAK, advertising and marketing executive; b. Ft. Scott, Kans., Nov. 11, 1937; d. Olin N. and Jeanette E. (Essen) Brigman; student N. Central Coll., 1955, Elmhurst Coll., 1956; B.A. in Communications, Calif. State U., Fullerton, 1982; m. Stanley Rice, Apr. 28, 1978; 1 dau., Beverly Johnson. Art dir. Gonterman & Assos., St. Louis, 1968-71; advt. mgr. Passpoint Corp., St. Louis, 1971-73; advt., pub. relations mgr. Permaneer Corp., St. Louis, 1973-74; advt. cons., advt. mgr. Hydro-Air Engring., Inc., St. Louis, 1974-76; mgr. mktg. services Hollytex Carpet Mills subs. U.S. Gypsum Co., City of Industry, Calif., 1976-79; pres. B.P. Rice & Co., Inc., Cerittos, Calif., 1979—; press affiliate Inst. Bus. Designers. Recipient Designer Best Exhibit award Nat. Farm Builders Trade Show. Mem. Am. Advt. Fedn. (dist. officer), Los Angeles Advt. Women (pres., dir.), Bus. Profl. Advt. Assn., Calif. State U.-Fullerton Sch. Communications Alumni Assn. (bd. dirs.), Beta Sigma Phi (past pres., outstanding mem.). Author: Truss Construction Manual, 1975. Home: 8178 Havasu Circle Buena Park CA 90621 Office: 13079 Artesia Blvd Ste 228 Cerritos CA 90701

RICE, DAVID GORDON, archaeologist, consultant; b. Seattle, Nov. 30, 1942; s. Gordon Alfred and Marion Anna (McGonigle) R.; m. Signe Lynn Johnson, Apr. 25, 1970 (div. Feb. 1975). BA in Anthropology, U. Wash., 1965; MA in Anthropology, Wash. State U., 1967, PhD in Anthropology, 1972. Instr. anthropology Wash. State U., Pullman, 1968; asst. prof. U. Idaho, Moscow, 1969-74, assoc. prof., 1974-79; archaeol. cons. Troy (Idaho) and Seattle, 1979-81; archaeologist U.S. Army Corps of Engrs., Seattle, 1981—, chief river basin studies, 1988—; archeol. cons. Rockwell Hanford Ops., Richland, Wash., 1981-87, Westinghouse Hanford Co., 1987, Wash. Pub. Power Supply System, Richland, 1975-82, Richland Ops. U.S. Dept. Energy, 1974-77; exec. com. mem. Wash. Archeol. Research Ctr., Pullman, 1983-86. Author: Cultural Resources at Hanford, 1982, Windust Phase in Lower Snake River Region Prehistory, 1972; contbr. articles to profl. jours. Del. Idaho State Dem. Conv., Sun Valley, 1972, chmn. Human Rights subcom. of platform com. Named one of Outstanding Young Men Am., Jaycees, 1979. Fellow Am. Anthrop. Assn.; mem. Soc. Am. Archaeology, Soc. Hist. Archaeology, Mid-Columbia Archeol. Soc. (tech. adv. 1967-81), Assn. Humanities in Idaho (chmn. 1980), Sigma Xi, Alpha Kappa Delta. Home: 1114 17th Ave 201 Seattle WA 98122 Office: US Army Corps Engrs 4735 E Marginal Way South Seattle WA 98134

RICE, DEVEREUX DUNLAP, marketing executive; b. Johnson City, Tenn., Jan. 28, 1952; s. Charles Bailey and Hazel Hunt (Donaldson) R.; m. Marcia Diane Fish, Mar. 20, 1980; 1 child, Melissa Susanne. BEE, Ga. Inst. Tech., 1974; MBA, U. Santa Clara, 1979. Engr. Motorola Semicondr., Phoenix, 1974-75, McDonnell Douglas Co., St. Louis, 1975-76; mktg. mgr. Fairchild Semicondr., Mountain View, Calif., 1976-80; pres. N.W. Mktg., Bellevue, Wash., 1980—. Contbr. articles to mags. Office: NW Mktg Assocs Inc 12835 Bel-Red Ste 330N Bellevue WA 98005

RICE, DONALD BLESSING, research institute executive; b. Frederick, Md., June 4, 1939; s. Donald Blessing and Mary Celia (Santangelo) R.; m. Susan Fitzgerald, Aug. 25, 1962; children: Donald Blessing III, Joseph John, Matthew Fitzgerald. BSChemE, U. Notre Dame, 1961, DEng (hon.), 1975; MS in Indsl. Adminstrn., Purdue U., 1962, PhD in Mgmt. and Econs., 1965, D. Mgmt. (hon.), 1985. Dir. cost analysis Office Sec. Def., Washington, 1967-69, dep. asst. sec. def. resource analysis, 1969-70; asst. dir. Office Mgmt. and Budget, Exec. Office Pres., 1970-72; pres., chief exec. officer The RAND Corp., Santa Monica, Calif., 1972—; bd. dirs. Vulcan Materials Co., Pacific Enterprises, Wells Fargo Bank, Wells Fargo & Co.; mem. Nat. Sci. Bd., 1974-86; chmn. Nat. Commn. Supplies and Shortages, 1975-77; mem. Nat. Commn. on U.S.-China Relations; mem. nat. adv. com. oceans and atmosphere Dept. Commerce, 1972-75; mem. adv. panel Office Tech. Assessment, 1976-79; adv. council Coll. Engring., U. Notre Dame, 1974-88; mem. Def. Sci. Bd., 1977-83, sr. cons., 1984-88; U.S. mem. Trilateral Commn.; dir. for sec. def. and Pres. Def. Resource Mgmt. Study, 1977-79. Author articles. Served to capt. AUS, 1965-67. Recipient Sec. Def. Meritorious Civilian Service medal, 1970; Ford Found. fellow, 1962-65. Fellow AAAS; mem. Am. Econ. Assn., Council Fgn. Relations, Inst. Mgmt. Scis. (past pres.), Los Angeles Area C. of C. (dir.), Los Angeles World Affairs Council (dir.), Tau Beta Pi. Office: The RAND Corp 1700 Main St Santa Monica CA 90406

RICE, DOROTHY PECHMAN (MRS. JOHN DONALD RICE), medical economist; b. Bklyn., June 11, 1922; d. Gershon and Lena (Schiff) Pechman; m. John Donald Rice, Apr. 3, 1943; children: Kenneth D., Donald B., Thomas H. Student, Bklyn. Coll., 1938-39; B.A., U. Wis., 1941; D.Sc. (hon.), Coll. Medicine and Dentistry N.J., 1979. With hosp., and med. facilities USPHS, Washington, 1960-61; med. econs. studies Social Security Adminstrn., 1962-63; health econs. br. Community Health Service, USPHS, 1964-65; chief health ins. research br. Social Security Adminstrn., 1966-72, dep. asst. commr. for research and statistics, 1972-75; dir. Nat. Center for Health Stats., Rockville, Md., 1976-82; prof. Inst. Health & Aging, U. Calif.-San Francisco, 1982—; developer, mgr. nationwide health info. svcs. Contbr. articles to profl. jours. Recipient Social Security Adminstrn. citation, 1968, Disting. Service medal HEW, 1974, Jack C. Massey Found. award, 1978. Fellow Am. Public Health Assn. (domestic award for excellence 1978, Sedgwick Meml. medal, 1988), Am. Statis. Assn.; mem. Inst. Medicine, Assn. Health Scvs. Rsch. (President's award 1988), Am. Econ. Assn., Population Assn. Am., LWV. Home: 1055 Amito Ave Berkeley CA 94705 Office: U Calif Sch Nursing N631 San Francisco CA 94143

RICE, FRANK BERTRAN, JR., English educator; b. Houston, July 28, 1927; s. Frank Bertran and Zelma Lee (Thomas) R.; m. Rita Ernestine Mhoon, Apr. 22, 1936. BS, Ark. State Tchrs. Coll., 1951; MA, Memphis State U., 1962; PhD, Wash. State U., 1973. Pastor various chs., Ark., 1951-56; tchr. Southwestern Bible Inst., Waxahachie, Tex., 1956-59; asst. pastor First Assembly of God, West Memphis, Ark., 1959-62; English instr. Northwest Coll., Kirkland, Wash., 1962-67; academic dean Northwest Coll., Kirkland, 1967-84, prof. English, 1985—. Author: poem On Death of President Kennedy, 1965. Mem. Nat. Council Tchrs. of English, Alpha Chi.

RICE, GENE EDWARD, savings and loan association executive; b. Greenleaf, Kans., June 26, 1930; s. Edward E. and Myrtle (Hogan) R.; m. Lola Margaret Long, Apr. 23, 1951; children—Mary Pat, Nancy Jo, Michael, Paul, Ann, Mathias, Barry, Regina. B.S. in Bus. Administrn., Ariz. State U., 1957; grad., Grad. Sch. Savs. and Loan, Ind. U., 1961. With First Fed. Savs. & Loan Assn. (now Merabank), Phoenix, 1954—, v.p., 1962-63, exec. v.p., sr. v.p., pres., now chmn. bd., chief exec. officer, dir.; formerly public interest dir. Frontier Fidelity Savs. & Loan Assn., Las Vegas, from 1967; dir. Mountain Bell., Fed. Home Loan Bank of San Francisco, Phoenix. Treas., dir. Casa Grande (Ariz.) Jaycees, 1957; pres. Casa Grande C. of C., 1960-61; treas. Phoenix Thunderbirds, 1966-67; Mem. Casa Grande City Council, 1960-62; Bd. dirs. Phoenix Catholic Social Service, 1967-71, Phoenix Jr. Achievement, 1963-64; mem. advisory bd. Bishops Fund, United Fund; chmn. Ariz. dr. Negro Coll. Fund; bd. dirs. Maricopa County Sheriffs Posse, Ariz. Jr. Rodeo Assn.; trustee Pro Rodeo Hall of Champions. Served with USN, 1949-53. Mem. Am. Savs. and Loan Inst. (nat. pres. 1969), Savs. and Loan League Ariz. (pres. 1967-68, dir.), Phoenix Jaycees (life), Profl. Rodeo Cowboys Assn., Delta Sigma Pi. Clubs: Elk (Phoenix), Kiwanian (Phoenix) (pres. Aurora club 1964), Phoenix Country (Phoenix), Paradise Valley (Phoenix), Kiva (Phoenix). Office: MeraBank 3003 N Central Ave #1700 Phoenix AZ 85012 *

RICE, JACQUELINE ANN, nurse; b. St. Joseph, Mo., Apr. 13, 1952; d. Jack Clifford and Shirley Ann (Fails) Root; m. Edward A. Rice, May 6, 1972 (div. 1984); 1 child, Daniel Edward. AA, Coll. San Mateo, Calif., 1976. Lic. vocat. nurse, Calif. Nurse Kaiser Permanente, South San Francisco, Calif., 1976--. Health educator AIDS Found., 1987.

RICE, JERRY LEE, professional football player; b. Starkville, Miss., Oct. 13, 1962; m. Jackie Rice; 1 child, Jaqui. Student, Miss. State Valley U. Football player San Francisco 49ers, 1985—; mem. NFL Championship Team, 1988; player NFL Pro Bowl team, 1987-89. Named Most Valuable Player, Super Bowl XXIII, 1989. Office: care San Francisco 49ers 711 Nevada St Redwood City CA 94061 *

RICE, JULIAN CASAVANT, lawyer; b. Miami, Fla., Jan. 1, 1924; s. Sylvan J. and Maybelle (Casavant) R.; m. Dorothy Mae Haynes, Feb. 14, 1958; children—Scott B., Craig M. (dec.), Julianne C., Linda D., Janette M. Student, U. San Francisco, 1941-43; JD cum laude, Gonzaga U., 1950. Bar: Wash. 1950, Alaska 1959, U.S. Tax Ct. 1988. Pvt. practice law Spokane, 1950-56, Fairbanks, Alaska, 1959—; mem. firm Rice & Ringstad and predecessor firms, Fairbanks, 1959; bd. dirs., mem. exec. com. Key Bank of Alaska, Anchorage; founder, gen. counsel Mt. McKinley Mut. Savs. Bank, Fairbanks, 1965—, chmn. bd., 1979-80; v.p., bd. dirs., gen. counsel Skimmers, Inc., Anchorage, 1966-67; gen. counsel Alaska Carriers Assn., Anchorage, 1960-71, Alaska Transp. Conf., 1960-67; bd. dirs. Alaska Pacific Trust Co., Anchorage. Mayor City of Fairbanks, 1970-72. 1st lt. AUS, 1943-46. Decorated Bronze Star. Fellow Am. Bar Found.; mem. ABA, Wash. Bar Assn., Alaska Bar Assn., Am. Judicature Soc., Assn. Transp. Practitioners, Transp. Lawyers Assn. Office: Rice Bldg 330 Wendell St Fairbanks AK 99701

RICE, KRIS EUGENE, dentist; b. Spokane, Wash., Apr. 17, 1955; s. Harry Bernard and Donna Jean (Stephens) R.; m. Diane Patrice Wong, Feb. 23, 1985. BA in Biology, Portland State U., 1977; DMD, U. Oreg., 1981. Assoc. dentist Dr. George J. Collings, Portland, Oreg., 1981-85; pvt. practice Portland, 1985—; dental cons. Porthaven Rest Home, Portland, 1981-85; vol. dentist Creston Dental Ctr., Portland, 1985--. Mem. ADA, Am. Soc. Dentistry for Children. Office: 10340 SE Division Ste 3 Portland OR 97266

RICE, LARRY ANTHONY, data processing executive; b. San Bernardino, Calif., Oct. 16, 1950; s. Arthur Erwin and Rita (Muckenheide) R.; m. Ruth Marie Fowler, June 17, 1972; children: Heather Renee, Erin Michelle. AA, San Bernardino Valley Coll., 1970; BA, Calif. State U., San Bernardino, 1975; MBA, Calif. State U., 1978. Area mgr. Fotomat Corp., La Jolla, Calif., 1976-80; with Kaman Bearing & Supply, Ontario, Calif., 1980—; MIS coord. Kaman Bearing & Supply, to date. Office: Kaman Bearing & Supply 910 Wanamaker Ave PO Box 50 Ontario CA 91761

RICE, ROSS RICHARD, political science educator; b. Shenandoah, Iowa, Jan. 13, 1922; s. Bird Oshea and Della (Goodner) R.; m. Marie Puzach, Apr. 20, 1948; children: Marilyn, Roxanne, Valerie, Laurie. Student, Creighton U., 1939-41, U. No. Iowa, 1941-42; MA, U. Chgo., 1949, PhD, 1956. Instr. Ariz. State U., Tempe, 1950-53; asst. prof. Ariz. State U., 1953-57, assoc. prof., 1957-60, prof. polit. sci., 1960—. Author: Extremist Politics, 1964, An Annotated Bibliography of Arizona Politics and Government, 1976; contbr. numerous articles to scholarly pubs. Mem. council, mayor City of Tempe, 1958-62. With U.S. Army, 1942-45. NEH grantee, 1972. Mem. Tempe Hist. Soc. (pres. 1971-73), Am. Polit. Assn., Western Polit. Sci. Assn. Democrat. Home: 108 W Palmcroft Dr Tempe AZ 85282 Office: Ariz State U Tempe AZ 85287

RICE, STEPHEN MANFRED, insurance executive; b. San Francisco, Oct. 3, 1959; s. Manfred and Claire Ruth (Lincoln) R.; m. Karen Ann Sprague, Dec. 19, 1981. BA in Fin., San Jose State U., 1981. CLU, Pa.; chartered fin. cons., Pa. Field rep. and career devel. supr. The Guardian Life Ins. Co. Am., San Jose, Calif., 1982—. Res. police officer; bd. dirs., v.p. Calif. Res. Peace Officers Assn., 1982—, v.p. North coast chpt., 1981-82; active in Santa Clara County (Calif.) Young Republicans, 1986—. Mem. Santa Clara County Estate Planning Coun., Am. Soc. CLU and Chartered Fin. Cons., Nat. Assn. Life Underwriters, Internat. Assn. for Fin. Planning, Million Dollar Round Table, Calif. Peace Officer's Assn., Gen. Agts. and Mgrs. Conf; Aircraft Owners and Pilots Assn., Commonwealth Club of Calif., Soc. Calif. Pioneers. Republican. Club: San Jose Country, Rotary Club Los Gatos, Live Oak Gun (sec., treas. 1986—). Office: Guardian Life 1602 The Alameda Ste 204 San Jose CA 95126

RICE, SUSAN KARYL, health care executive; b. N.Y.C., June 21, 1954; d. Herbert Lewis and Ann Judith (Katz) Niebloom; m. Eugene Joseph Rice, Nov. 5, 1978; 1 child, Adam Matthew. Student, Boston U., 1971-74; BSN, Calif. State U., Long Beach, 1979. Research asst. Children's Hosp., Boston, 1975-77; staff nurse pediatric ICU Children's Hosp., L.A., 1977-79; staff nurse neonatal intensive care Cedars-Sinai Med. Ctr., L.A., 1979-81; staff nurse Hollywood Presbyn. Med. Ctr., L.A., 1980-84, neonatal and perinatal cons., 1981-84; perinatal supr. Downey (Calif.) Community Hosp., 1984-85; dept. adminstr. perinatal and neonatal svcs. Kaiser Permanente Med. Ctr., Woodland Hills, Calif., 1985-87; clin. specialist, supr. svc. ctr. Healthdyne Perinatal Svc., Woodland Hills, Calif., 1987—; neonatal-perinatal cons., 1982-84; cons. in field. Mem. Perinatal Adv. Coun. L.A. Communities. Mem. Nurses Assn. Am. Coll. Ob-Gyn., Calif. Nurses Assn., Perinatal Adv. Coun. L.A. Communities. Home: 6190 Locust Ave Agoura CA 91301

RICE, VIRGINIA RUTH, nurse; b. Baton Rouge, July 8, 1953; d. Luther Allen and Mable (Rosenbaum) Broomfield; m. Riley Warren Rice, Mar. 4, 1988; 1 child, Aaron Kent. AA, U. Cen. Ark., 1975. Critical care RN. Charge nurse Conway (Ark.) Meml. Hosp., 1973-76, St. Vincent Infirmary, Little Rock, 1976-77, St. Luke's Hosp. Med. Ctr., Phoenix, 1977-85; pvt. scrub nurse Dwight Lundell, MD, Phoenix, 1980-84; med. ICU nurse VA Med. Ctr., Phoenix, 1984-85; staff nurse Garrett Turbine Engine Co., Phoenix, 1985-86; surgery charge nurse Humana Hosp., Phoenix, 1986; mem. ICU relief staff Janamar Nurses, Phoenix, 1985—; gen. surgery nurse, educator St. Joseph's Hosp. Med. Ctr., Phoenix, 1986-89; pvt. scurb nurse Arnold Serota, MD., Phoenix, 1989—. instr. CPR, Ariz. affiliate Am. Heart Assn., Phoenix, 1978—. Named Outstanding Young Women Am., 1983. Mem. Am. Assn. Critical Care Nurses (Greater Phoenix area chpt. corr. sec. 1980-82, edn. com., point com.), Gamma Beta Phi. Republican. Mem. Soc. Friends. Home: 4354 W Villa Theresa Dr Glendale AZ 85308

RICER, N. DEAN, park superintendent; b. Stewartsville, Ohio, Nov. 1, 1936; s. Newell D. and Cleo (Dean) R.; m. Will Anne Moeller, Oct. 29, 1956; children: Karen, Wendy. BS in Floriculture, Tex. A&M U., 1965. Supt. grounds C.W. Murchison Jr., Dallas, 1965-68, U. Mont., Missoula, 1968-72; park supt. Living Desert Zool. and Bot. State Park, Carlsbad, N.Mex., 1972—. Mem. Riverfront Devel. Com., Carlsbad, 1987; field coordinator N.Mex. State Police Search and Rescue Plan, Carlsbad, 1980—. Mem. Am. Assn. of Bot. Gardens and Arboreta, Carlsbad Caverns Nat. History Assn. (bd. dirs. 1975-86, Service award 1986), Carlsbad C. of C. (hon. bd. dirs. 1978—), Masons. Home: 1506 Monroe Carlsbad NM 88220 Office: Living Desert State Park Skyline Dr Carlsbad NM 88220

RICH, ADRIENNE, writer; b. Balt., May 16, 1929; d. Arnold Rice and Helen Elizabeth (Jones) R.; m. Alfred H. Conrad (dec. 1970); children: David, Paul, Jacob. A.B., Radcliffe Coll., 1951; Litt.D. (hon.), Wheaton Coll., 1967, Smith Coll., 1979, Brandeis U., 1987, Coll. Wooster (Ohio), 1988. Tchr. workshop YM-WHA Poetry Center, N.Y.C., 1966-67; vis. lectr. Swarthmore Coll., 1967-69; adj. prof. writing div. Columbia U., 1967-69; lectr. CCNY, 1968-70, instr., 1970-71, asst. prof. English, 1971-72, 74-75; Fannie Hurst vis. prof. creative lit. Brandeis U., 1972-73; prof. English Douglass Coll., Rutgers U., 1976-79; Clark lectr. and Disting. vis. prof. Scripps Coll., 1983-84; A.D. White prof.-at-large Cornell U., 1981-87; Disting. vis. prof. San Jose State U., 1984-85; prof. English and feminist studies Stanford U., 1986—; Marjorie Kovler vis. lectr. U. Chgo., 1989. Author: A Change of World, 1951, The Diamond Cutters and Other Poems, 1955, Snapshots of a Daughter-in-Law, 1963, Necessities of Life: Poems, 1962-65, 1966, Leaflets, Poems, 1965-68, Necessities of Life: Poems, 1965-68, 1969, The Will to Change, 1971, Diving into the Wreck, 1973, Poems Selected and New, 1950-74, 1975, Of Woman Born: Motherhood as Experience and Institution, 1976, 10th anniversary ed., 1986, The Dream of a Common Language: Poems, 1974-1977, 1978, On Lies, Secrets and Silence: Selected Prose, 1966-1978, 1979, A Wild Patience Has Taken Me This Far: Poems, 1978-81, 1981, The Fact of a Doorframe: Poems 1978-81, 1979; Your Native Land, Your Life: Poems, 1986, Blood, Bread and Poetry: Selected Prose, 1986, Time's Power: Poems 1985-88, 1989; co-editor: Sinister Wisdom, 1980-84; contbr. to numerous anthologies; contbr. numerous articles, revs. to jours. and mags. Mem. nat. adv. bd. New Jewish Agenda, Boston Women's Fund, Sisterhood in Support of Sisters in South Africa. Recipient Yale Series of Younger Poets award, 1951; Ridgely Torrence Meml. award Poetry Soc. Am., 1955; Nat. Inst. Arts and Letters award poetry, 1961; Bess Hokin prize Poetry mag., 1963; Eunice Tietjens Meml. prize, 1968; Shelley Meml. award, 1971; Nat. Book award, 1974; Fund for Human Dignity award Nat. Gay Task Force, 1981, Ruth Lilly Poetry prize, 1986, Brandeis U. Creative Arts medal for Poetry, 1987; Guggenheim fellow, 1952, 61; Amy Lowell traveling fellow, 1962; Bollingen Found. translation grantee, 1962; Nat. Translation Center grantee, 1968; Nat. Endowment for Arts grantee, 1970; Ingram Merrill Found. grantee, 1973-74; Lucy Martin Donnelly fellow Bryn Mawr Coll., 1975; hon. fellow MLA. Office: care W W Norton Co 500 5th Ave New York NY 10110

RICH, BEN ARTHUR, lawyer, university official; b. Springfield, Ill., Mar. 27, 1947; s. Ben Morris and Betty Lorraine (Ingalls) R.; m. Caroline Rose Castle, Oct. 4, 1984 (div. Nov. 1988). Student, U. St. Andrews, Scotland, 1967-68; BA, DePauw U., 1969; JD, Washington U., 1973. Bar: Ill. 1973, N.C. 1975, Colo. 1984. Rsch. assoc. U. Ill. Coll. Law, Urbana, 1973-74; staff atty. Nat. Assn. Attys. Gen., Raleigh, N.C., 1974-76; prin. Hollowell, Silverstein, Rich & Brady, Raleigh, 1976-80; dep. commr. N.C. Indsl. Commn., Raleigh, 1980-81; counsel N.C. Meml. Hosp., Chapel Hill, 1981-84; assoc. univ. counsel U. Colo. Health Scis. Ctr., Denver, 1984-86; gen. counsel U. Colo., Boulder, 1986—; asst. prof. attendant U. Colo. Sch. Med., 1986—, adj. instr. Sch. Law, 1988—; lectr. U. Denver Coll. Law. Contbr. articles to jours., chpt. to book. Mem. Nat. Health Lawyers Assn., Nat. Assn. Coll. and Univ. Attys. (sect. co-chair 1986—), Am. Coll. Legal Medicine (assoc.-in-law 1987—), Am. Soc. Law and Medicine (house counsel sect. 1986—), Toastmasters Internat. (pres. 1978). Unitarian. Home: 71 Ridge Dr Boulder CO 80302 Office: U Colo 203 Regent Administrv Ctr Campus Box 13 Boulder CO 80309-0013

RICH, BEN ROBERT, aerospace executive, aero-thermodynamicist; b. Manila, Philippines, June 18, 1925; came to U.S., 1941; s. Isadore and Annie (Kupfermann) R.; m. Faye Mayer, June 25, 1950 (dec. Aug. 1980); m. Hilda Herman, July 1, 1982; children: Michael D., Karen Rich Erbeck. B.S., U. Calif.-Berkeley, 1949; M.S., UCLA, 1950; Advanced Mgmt. Program, Harvard U., 1968. Program mgr. advanced devel. projects Lockheed Calif. Co., Burbank, 1965-69, chief engr. advanced design, 1969, chief preliminary design, 1969-71, v.p. advanced design, 1972-75, v.p., gen. mgr. advanced devel. projects, 1975-84; pres. Lockheed Advanced Aeros. Co., Burbank, 1984—. Recipient nat. award for aircraft design AIAA, 1972; named Engr. of Yr. San Francisco Engring. Soc., 1981, Alumnus of Yr. UCLA, 1982. Fellow Nat. Acad. Engring., Inst. Aero. Scis. Office: Lockheed Calif Co PO Box 551 Burbank CA 91520 also: Lockheed Corp 4500 Park Granada Blvd Calabasas CA 91399

RICH, DAVID BARRY, city official, auditor, accountant; b. Bronx, N.Y., July 3, 1952; s. Steven and Gizella (Kornfeld) R.; m. Mindy Hope, Aug. 3, 1983; 1 child, Suzanne Stephanie. BS in Health Adminstrn., Ithaca Coll., 1976; postgrad. in acctg., Bryant and Stratton Coll., Buffalo, 1977. Office mgr. Rubin Gorewitz, CPA, N.Y.C., 1977-78; auditor State of Ariz., Phoenix, 1979-83; internal auditor City of Phoenix, 1983-84; sales use tax auditor City of Mesa (Ariz.), 1984—; pres. Clovis Acctg. Inc., Mesa, 1980—; rep. H.D. Vest Investment Inc., Irving, Tex., 1985—. Treas., bd. dirs. Missing Mutts Inc., Tempe, Ariz., 1986-88. With USAF, 1971-76. Fellow Nat. Soc. Pub. Accts., Ariz. Soc. Practicing Accts.; mem. Toastmasters (treas. Mesa 1986-87), Phi Beta Kappa.

RICH, GARETH EDWARD, certified financial planner; b. Gainesville, Fla., Feb. 28, 1961. Assoc. in Bus. Adminstrn., Gainesville Coll., 1981; BBA, U.

Ga., 1983; postgrad., Coll. for Fin. Planning, Denver, 1986-88. Acct. exec. Gallo Wine Co., L.A., 1983-84; ins. and investment counselor Fin. Design Group, Inc., Calabasas, Calif., 1984—. Vol. City of Hope, L.A.; referee Am. Youth Soccer Orgn., Conejo Valley, Calif.; umpire Little League Baseball, Conejo Valley. Mem. San Fernando Valley Underwriters Assn., Summit Orgn., Warner Ctr. Tennis Club. Republican. Home: 5626 Fairview Pl Agoura CA 91301 Office: Fin Design Group Inc 24011 Ventura Blvd PO Box 8573 Calabasas CA 91302

RICH, JONATHAN DAVID, psychologist; b. Mt. Vernon, N.Y., Jan. 17, 1957; s. David Arnold and Veronica Edith (Paganuzzi) R.; m. Nancy Colleen Halsey, Aug. 2, 1986. BA in Psychology, U. Calif., San Diego, 1978; MA in Psychology, San Diego State U., 1981; PhD, Calif. Sch. Profl. Psychology, 1985. Lic. psychologist, Calif. Postdoctoral fellow Alvarado Pkwy Inst., San Diego, 1985-86; clin. psychologist Tex. Dept. Corrections, Huntsville, 1986-87, Orange County Health Care Agy., Santa Ana, Calif., 1987—; dir. rsch. instr. Profl. Sch. Psychology Studies, Tustin, Calif., 1988. Mem. Am. Psychol. Assn., Mensa. Home: 23212-6 Orange Ave El Toro CA 92630 Office: Orange County Health Care Agy 1725 17th St Santa Ana CA 92706

RICH, JULIE MARGARET, real estate developer; b. Big Bear Lake, Calif., Mar. 28, 1950; d. Robert Stuart and Lillian (Samstad) R.; m. Keith N. Tasker, Nov. 15, 1981; children: Sarah Rose, John Robert. BA magna cum laude, U. Calif., Riverside, 1975. V.p., auditor Riverside Nat. Bank, 1975-78; v.p. Jones Co., Cerritos, Calif., 1979-82; v.p. purchasing Long Beach Constrn. Co., Cerritos, 1979-82; v.p., treas. Creative Products Enterprises, Highland, Calif., 1982—; owner, mgr. Rich Devel., Yucaipa, Calif., 1984—; cons. Gene Dixon Constrn. Co., Riverside, 1985—, Yucaipa Sch. Dist., 1987—; ptnr. Tasker Constrn. Co., Yucaipa, 1988—. Chmn. Calimesa (Calif.) Elem. Site Coun., 1987—, Select Com. for Acad. Excellence, Yucaipa, 1988—. Mem. Phi Beta Kappa. Republican. Lutheran.

RICH, ROBERT STEPHEN, lawyer; b. N.Y.C., Apr. 30, 1938; s. Maurice H. and Natalie (Priess) R.; m. Myra N. Lakoff, May 31, 1964; children: David, Rebecca, Sarah. AB, Cornell U., 1959; JD, Yale U., 1963. Bar: N.Y. 1964, Colo. 1973, U.S. Tax Ct. 1966, U.S. Sup. Ct. 1967, U.S. Ct. Clms. 1968, U.S. Dist. Ct. (so. dist.) N.Y. 1965, U.S. Dist. Ct. (ea. dist.) N.Y. 1965, U.S. Dist. Ct. Colo. 1980, U.S. Ct. Apls. (2d cir.) 1964, U.S. Ct. Appeals (10th cir.) 1978; conseil juridique, Paris, 1968. Assoc. Shearman & Sterling, N.Y.C., Paris, London, 1963-72; ptnr. Davis, Graham & Stubbs, Denver, 1973—; Am. Coll of Tax counsel, 1987—; adj. faculty U. Denver Law Sch., 1977—; bd. dirs. Clos du Val Wine Co. Ltd., Danskin Cattle Co., Areti Wines , Ltd., Taltarni Vineyards, Rocky Mountain Internat. Bus. Service Ctr., several other corps.; mem. Colo. Internat. Trade Adv. Council, 1985—. Author treatises on internat. taxation; contbr. articles to profl. jours. Bd. dirs. Denver Internat. Film Festival, 1978-79, Alliance Française, 1977—; actor, musician N.Y. Shakespeare Festival, 1960; trustee, sec. Denver Art Mus., 1982—. Served to capt., AUS, 1959-60. Fellow Am. Coll. of Tax Counsel; mem. ABA, Union Internationale des Avocats, Internat. Fiscal Assn., Internat. Bar Assn., Colo. Bar Assn., N.Y. State Bar Assn., Assn. of Bar City of N.Y., Confrerie des Chevaliers du Tastevin, Meadowood Club (Napa Valley), Denver Club, Yale Club (N.Y.C.). Office: Davis Graham & Stubbs PO Box 185 370 17th St Denver CO 80201

RICH, SUSAN WARREN, artist; b. Boston, Jan. 28, 1937; d. Harry Allen and Edith (Stone) Warren; m. Richard Starks Rich, Aug. 4, 1957; children: Robin, Robert. BA, Stanford U., 1959. Cert. tchr. Research technician Stanford Electronics Research Lab., Stanford, Calif., 1956-58; tchr. Mendocino County Schs., Mendocino, Calif., 1958-61; tchr.-lead Menlo Park Presbyterian Ch. Pre-Sch., Menlo Park, Calif., 1971-88; artist Sunshine Gallery, Friday Harbor, Wash., 1988—; staff artist Sunshine Gallery, Friday Harbor, 1988—. Mem. Med. Ctr. Guild, Friday Harbor, 1988—, Jr. League Palo Alto, 1964-74. Mem. AAUW (v.p. mem. 1989—), Nat. Assn. Edn. Young Children, San Mateo County Assn. Edn. Young Children, DAR (regent 1989—), San Joan Island Garden Club (sec.), Afternoon Guild (v.p. 1989—). Republican. Presbyterian.

RICHARD, ANITA LOUISE, entrepreneur, management consultant; b. Willard, N.Y., June 22, 1951; d. Marvin Gerald and Illene (Rosenberg) Isaacson; m. J.E. Richard, May 16, 1981: stepchildren: Christine, Chad. Student, U. Fla., 1969-70, CUNY, Bklyn., 1972-74, Barnard Baruch U., 1974-76; BA magna cum laude, Golden Gate U., 1981. Mktg. mgr. Exxon Office Systems, N.Y.C., 1976-77; program mgr. Exxon Office Systems, Dallas, 1977-78; br. mgr. Exxon Office Systems, Pasadena, Calif., 1978-79; br. sales mgr. Exxon Office Systems, Century City, Calif., 1979; mgr. regional sales program Exxon Office Systems, Marina Del Rey, Calif., 1979-81; mktg. mgr. Exxon Office Systems, San Francisco, 1981-82; product mgr. Wells Fargo Bank, San Francisco, 1984; mgmt. cons. J. Richard and Co., Montara, Calif., 1984—. Mem. Am. Mgmt. Assn., Am. Soc. for Personnel Adminstrn., Calif. Assn. for HMO's (chairperson career placement com.), Am. Compensation Assn., Group Health Assn. Am., No. Calif. Human Resource Council, No. Calif. Health Care Mktg. Assn., Practicing Law Inst. Republican. Jewish. Clubs: Los Angeles Athletic. Office: 1301 Main St PO Box 779 Montara CA 94037

RICHARD, DAVID HUNT, architect; b. Columbus, Ohio, Oct. 25, 1949; s. David O. and Elizabeth N. (Lindenberger) R. BA, Yale U., 1972. Registered architect, Calif. Detailer Warren Meyerhoff, L.A., 1974-75; job capt. Kyra Design, L.A., 1976-78, Fields & Silverman, L.A., 1978-83; project architect Fields & Silverman (name now Fields, Silverman & Devereaux), L.A., 1983-85, projects mgr., 1985-87, assoc., 1988—. Bd. dirs. Hollywoodland Homeowners Assn., L.A., 1987-89. Mem. AIA, Yale Club. Home: 3185 Durand Dr Los Angeles CA 90068-1613 Office: Fields Silverman & Devereaux 116 N Robertson Blvd 802 Los Angeles CA 90048

RICHARD, DONALD (DICK RICHARD), service executive, marketing professional; b. Lebanon, Mo., Oct. 16, 1933; s. Lance Richard and Sue Elizabeth (Shumate) Lane; m. Norma Jean Lewis, July 26, 1953; children: Steven Lynn, Todd L. BBA, Wichita U., 1960. Credit mgr. State Fin., Wichita, 1955-57; firefighter Boeing Airplane Co., Wichita, 1957-59; acct. Frontier Chem. Co., Wichita, 1959-63; credit mgr. GMC, Phoenix, 1963; mktg. adminstr., mtg. planner Motorola, Inc., Phoenix, 1964-80; owner, mktg. mgr. Sun County Tours, Inc., Scottsdale, Ariz., 1979--. With USAF 1951-55. Mem. Scotsdale C. of C., Phoenix Conv. Bur., Mtg. Planners Internat. (assoc., bd. dirs. 1985-86), Hotel Sales and Mktg. Assn. (bd. dirs. 1984-85). Republican. office: Sun Country Destination 4120 N 70th St now Goldwater Blvd #211 Scottsdale AZ 85251

RICHARD, ROBERT CARTER, psychologist; b. Waterloo, Iowa, Apr. 4, 1938; s. Quentin Leroy and Adeline Pauline (Halverson) R.; student Pomona Coll., 1956-57, Westmont Coll., 1957; BA, Wheaton (Ill.) Coll., 1960; BD, Fuller Theol. Sem., 1963, PhD, 1973; STM, Andover Newton Theol. Sch., 1964; m. Shirley Ruth Jones, Aug. 25, 1962; children: David, John. Ordained to ministry Am. Bapt. Conv., 1963; pastor Peninsula Bapt. Ch., Gig Harbor, Wash., 1965-68; marriage and family counselor Glendale (Calif.) Family Service, 1970-71; psychol. asst., Oakland and Pleasant Hill, Calif., 1972-74; clin. psychologist Rafa Counseling Assos., Pleasant Hill, 1974—; mem. faculty John F. Kennedy U., Orinda, Calif., 1975-78; adj. faculty mem. New Coll., Berkeley, Calif., 1986. Co-founder, bd. dirs. New Directions Counseling Center, 1974-81. Recipient Integration of Psychology and Theology award, 1973; lic. psychologist, marriage, family and child counselor, Calif. Mem. Am., Calif., Contra Costa County (past pres.) psychol. assns., Christian Assn. Psychol. Studies. Republican. Presbyterian. Contbr. articles to profl. pubs. Researcher assertiveness tng., stress mgmt., lay counselor tng., psychotherapy and religious experience. Office: Counseling Assocs 101 Gregory Ln Ste 33 Pleasant Hill CA 94523

RICHARD, ROBERT JOHN, librarian; b. Oakland, Calif., Sept. 20, 1947; s. John Argyle and Vern Elizabeth (Bauer) R.; m. Anne Elizabeth Terrell, June 8, 1968 (div. 1982); children: Jennifer Lynn, Laura Ellen, Constance Anne, Andrea Lee. Student, Fullerton Coll., 1965-67; B.A. in Biology, Chapman Coll., Orange (Calif.), 1972; M.S.L.S., Calif. State U.-Fullerton, 1973. Cert. county librarian, Calif. Audiovisual specialist Fullerton Pub. Library, 1969-72, asst. to city librarian, 1972-73, librarian, 1973-76; br. librarian Orange County Pub. Library, Orange, 1976-78; regional adminstr. Orange County Pub. Library, 1979-80; assoc. dir. Long Beach Pub. Library, Calif., 1980-81; dir. Sacramento Pub. Library, 1981-86, Santa Ana (Calif.) Pub. Library, 1986—; chmn. Santiago (Calif.) Library System. Mem. ALA, Pub. Library Execs. Assn So. Calif., Calif. Library Assn., Library Adminstrn. and Mgmt. Assn., Library Info. and Tech. Assn., Pub. Library Assn. Office: Santa Ana Pub Libr 26 Civic Ctr PO Box 1988 Santa Ana CA 92702-1988

RICHARDS, CAROLYN LOUISE, lawyer; b. Ventura, Calif., July 8, 1933; d. Clark Croll and Mattie Eleanor (Gibbens) Richard; m. Ellsworth Eugene Tulberg, Feb. 8, 1953; children: Robbi Tulberg Winkler, Amy Tulberg Gurrola, Terri Tulberg Marzec, Ellsworth Eugene Jr., Patty Tulberg Arguelles, Clark, Mary Tulberg Dean, Mattie Tulberg Oehmke, Carl, Christine. AS, Ventura Coll., 1977, AA, 1978; JD, Ventura Coll. Law, 1982. Bar: Calif. 1982. Rsch. atty. Calif. Ct. Appeals (2d dist.), L.A., 1984—. Mem. Calif. Bar Assn. Roman Catholic. Home: 931 Greenwood Dr Santa Paula CA 93060 Office: 3580 Wilshire Blvd Los Angeles CA 90010

RICHARDS, CHRISTOS, management consultant; b. Athens, Greece, Aug. 13, 1957; came to U.S., 1960; s. Arthur Terry Richards and Katrina (Nikita) Winsor; m. Pia Erismann, Sept. 23, 1977. B Guest Svc. Mgmt., Swiss Wirtschule, 1979. Mgr. Hotel Europe Express Restaurant, Davos, Switzerland, 1978-80; mng. dir. Jakobshorn Club, Davos, 1980-82; exec. v.p. Winsor-Richards & Assocs., Westlake Village, Calif., 1982-86; pres. Richards Cons., Thousand Oaks, Calif., 1986—; bd. dirs. Scherr Entertainment, Thousand Oaks. Charter mem. Rep. Presdl. Task Force, Washington, 1982. Mem. L.A. World Affairs Coun., So. Calif. Golf Assn. Office: 468 Pennsfield Pl Ste 105 Thousand Oaks CA 91360

RICHARDS, DAVID H., architect; b. Columbus, Ohio, Oct. 25, 1949; s. David O. and Elizabeth N. (Lindenberger) R. BA, Yale U., 1972. Registered architect, Calif. Detailer Warren Meyerhoff, L.A., 1978-83; job capt. Kyra Design, L.A., 1976-78; job capt. Fields & Silverman (name now Fields, Silverman & Devereaux), L.A., 1978-83, project architect, 1983-85, projects mgr., 1985-87, assoc., 1988--. Bd. dirs. Hollywoodland Homeowners Assn., L.A., 1987--. Mem. AIA, Yale Club. Home: 3185 Durand Dr Los Angeles CA 90068 Office: Fields Silverman & Devereaux 116 N Robertson Blvd 802 Los Angeles CA 90048

RICHARDS, DICK AUGUSTUS, insurance executive, financial planner; b. Las Vegas, Nev., Feb. 13, 1936; s. Albert and MAbel Elvina (Lundgren) R.; m. Fern Fontenot, Oct. 21, 1954; children: Jill Ann Richards Down, Judi Rene, Rick B. Grad. high sch., Galveston, Tex. Salesperson Prin. Fin. Group, Las Vegas, 1969-72, unit mgr., 1976-83, rep., 1987—; mgr. Payment & Sears Ins. Agy., Las Vegas, 1972-74, Pa Porta Ins. Agy., Las Vegas, 1974-76; pres. Silver State Ins. Brokers Inc., Las Vegas, 1983-87. Mem. Rep. Cen. Com., Clark County, Nev., 1987-88. Mem. Nev. Assn. Health Underwriters (v.p. 1987-88), So. Nev. Assn. Health Underwriters (pres. 1980-81, 82-83), Nev. Assn. Life Underwriters (pres. 1981-82), Nat. Assn. Health Underwriters (chartered), Life Underwriters Tng. Council (life). Republican. Lodges: Lions (bd. dirs. Las Vegas chpt. 1985-86), Kiwanis (v.p. Las Vegas chpt. 1987-88, Kiwanian of Yr. 1986). Home: 2612 Cabot Las Vegas NV 89102 Office: Prin Fin Group 3360 W Sahara Ste 200 Las Vegas NV 89102

RICHARDS, GERALD THOMAS, lawyer, consultant; b. Monrovia, Calif., Mar. 17, 1933; s. Louis Jacquelyn Richards and Inez Vivian (Richardson) Hall; children: Patricia M. Richards Grauf, Laura J., Dag Hammarskjold; m. Mary Lou Richards, Dec. 27, 1986. BS magna cum laude, Lafayette Coll., 1957; MS, Purdue U., 1963; JD, Golden Gate U., 1976. Bar: Calif. 1976, U.S. Dist. Ct. (no. dist.) Calif. 1977, U.S. Patent Office 1981, U.S. Ct. Appeals (9th cir.) 1984, U.S. Supreme Ct. 1984. Computational physicist Lawrence Livermore (Calif.) Nat. Lab., 1967-73, planning staff lawyer, 1979, mgr. tech. transfer office, 1980-83, asst. lab. counsel, 1984—; sole practice, Livermore, 1976-78; mem. exec. com., policy advisor Fed. Lab. Consortium for Tech. Transfer, 1980—; panelist, del. White House Conf. on Productivity, Washington, 1983; del. Nat. Conf. on Tech. and Aging, Wingspread, Wis., 1981. Commr. Housing Authority, City of Livermore, 1977, vice chairperson, 1978, chairperson, 1979; pres. Housing Choices, Inc., Livermore, 1980-84; bd. dirs. Valley Vol. Ctr., Pleasanton, Calif., 1983, pres., 1984-86. Recipient Engring. award Gen. Electric Co., 1956. Maj. U.S. Army, 1959-67. Mem. ABA, San Francisco Bar Assn., Alameda County Bar Assn., Livermore-Amador Valley Bar Assn. (sec. 1978), Phi Beta Kappa, Tau Beta Pi, Sigma Pi Sigma. Home: 1070 Shady Creek Pl Danville CA 94526 Office: Lawrence Livermore Nat Lab PO Box 808 L-701 Livermore CA 94550

RICHARDS, JAMES CORNELIUS, III, chemical company executive; b. Akron, Ohio, May 23, 1941; m. James Cornelius and Erma Jean (Miller) R.; m. Barbara Boicourt Richards, June 11, 1963; children: Wynne E., John M. BSChemE, Cornell U., 1964; MBA, Stanford U., 1966. Sr. tech. rep. Hercules, Inc., San Francisco, 1966-68; assoc. venture planning Hercules, Inc., Wilmington, Del., 1968-71, sales mgr. AWT Systems div., 1971-73; devel. mgr. Hercules, Inc., Tokyo, 1973-75; product mgr. Hercules, Inc., Wilmington, 1975-78, bus. ctr. dir., 1978-82, regional dir., 1982-84; v.p. semiconductor chem. div. Jones-Hamilton Co., Newark, Calif., 1984-88; v.p. and gen. mgr. Ablestik Labs subs. Nat. Starch and Chem., Gardena, Calif., 1988—. Active Campaign to Elect Ed Szchau, Calif., 1986. Republican. Episcopalian. Home: 295 Argonne Ave Long Beach CA 90803 Office: Ablestik Labs 833 W 182d St Gardena CA 90248

RICHARDS, JAMES WILLIAM, electromechanical engineer; b. Portland, Oreg., Oct. 24, 1921; s. Jarvis William and Thelma Helen (Eoff) R.; m. Violet Victor Ray, Oct. 9, 1946; children: Betty, Sandra, Diane, William. Student, Nat. Tech. Sch., 1942, Nat. Radio Inst., 1948, Internat. Corr. Sch., 1955; AA, Pierce Coll., 1968. Mgr. Western Design, Santa Barbara, Calif., 1948-55; sr. engr. Bendix Corp., North Hollywood, Calif., 1955-66; v.p. Talley Corp., Newbury Park, Calif., 1966-75, dir. engring., 1982-87; pvt. practice electromech. engr., Eugene, Oreg., 1975-82, 87—. Mem. Mason, Ancient Mystical Order Rosae Crucis. Republican. Baptist. Home: PO Box 5498 Eugene OR 97405 Office: JRE 28983 Fox Hollow Rd PO Box 5549 Eugene OR 97405

RICHARDS, JOHN ABBOTT, architectural firm executive; b. Rapid City, S.D., Aug. 6, 1955; s. John A. and Pauline A. Richards; m. Madelyn L. Ferro, Dec. 1, 1984; children: Nicholas, David. Grad. high sch., Tucson. Mason 86th Civil Engrs., Ramstein, Fed. Republic Germany, 1974-75; cons. to v.p. Petroleos Mexicanos (PEMEX), Mexico City, 1979-80; v.p. mktg. and design Metal Masters Co., Tucson, 1980-82; v.p. ops. R/MIS Corps., Tucson, 1982-85, pres. Design and Presentation Assocs., 1985—; mem. exec. com. Sta. KXCI, Tucson, 1986—; operator GPI Gallery 3l; bd. dirs. N. Coalition of Greater Tucson. Bd. dirs. Found. for Creative Broadcasting, Tucson, 1985--; mem. Tucson Bus. Com. for Arts, 1988--, Tucson Arts Coalition, 1988--, Tucson Downtown Adv. Commn., 1986--; chmn. Tucson Streets and Transp. Com., 1987. Mem. AIA (assoc.), Bldg. Owners and Mgrs. Assn., Downtown Bus. Assn. (pres. 1987), So. Ariz. Home Bldrs. Assn., Met. C. of C., Nat. Trust for Historic Preservation. Office: Design & Presentation Assocs 3l N 6th Ave PO Box 2l89 Tucson AZ 85702

RICHARDS, LILLIAN LAIRD, clinical social worker; b. Worcester, Mass., June 28, 1925; d. James and Beatrice Maude (Gill) Laird; m. Rauel Armand Richards, July 9, 1954 (dec. Jan. 1969). AB, Syracuse (N.Y.) U., 1952; MSW, Cath. U. Am., 1971. Lic. clin. social worker, Calif. Social worker L.A. County Dept. Social Svcs., 1963, supervisory social worker, 1963-69, program analyst, 1971-72; med. social worker L.A. County Dept. Health Svcs., 1974-84; pvt. practice Westminster, Calif., 1984—; mem. Westminster Commn. on Aging, 1984—, Orange County Sr. Citizens Adv. Coun., 1984—, Adv. Com. for Handicapped, Westminster, 1987—. Pres. Westminster Coordinating Coun., 1987-88. Recipient Cert. of Recognition Long Beach City Coll. Adv. Com., 1985, Westminster C. of C., 1986—; Calif. Dept. Social Welfare grantee, 1969-70. Mem. Am. Soc. on Aging, Nat. Coun. on Aging, Am. Assn. Ret. Persons (editor 1986-87), Westminster Hist. Soc. (sec., editor 1987-88), Am. Bus. Women's Assn. (vocat. chmn. Westminster chpt. 1985—, pres. 1986—), Friends Westminster Libr. (v.p., editor 1987), Shakespeare Soc., Women's C. of C., Amb., Soroptimist. Home and Office: 14352 Beach Blvd #90 Westminster CA 92683

RICHARDS, MORRIS DICK, social work administrator; b. Los Angeles, Aug. 20, 1939; s. Morris Dick Richards and Annette (Fox) Briggs; m. Leslie Sondra Lefkowitz, Mar. 22, 1975. BA cum laude, Claremont Men's Coll., 1962; MA, U. Chgo., 1964; M in Pub. Adminstrn., U. So. Calif., 1965; LLB, La Salle Ext. U., 1971; MS in Hygiene, PhD in Social Work, U. Pitts., 1973; MBA, Chapman Coll., 1987. Diplomate Acad. Cert. Social Workers. Asst. dep. dir. children and youth services Orange County (Calif.) Dept. Mental Health, 1973-77; gen. mgr., indsl. therapist Paragon West, Anaheim, Calif., 1977-83; acting dir. alcohol and drug program Horizon Health Corp., Newport Beach, Calif., 1983; editor, pub. relations rep., sr. social worker Orange County Social Services Agy., 1983-85; staff analyst Environ. Mgmt. Agy., Orange County, 1985—; adj. clin. prof. Chapman Coll., Orange, Calif., 1974-85; instr. Calif. Grad. Inst., 1988—; program analyst, head child welfare worker Los Angeles County Pub. Social Services, 1967-71; psychiat. clin. specialist Jewish Big Bros., Los Angeles County, 1964-67; med. social work cons. Whittier (Calif.) Presbyn. Hosp., 1973-76; pvt. practice psychotherapy, Tustin, Calif., 1975-77; instr. CAlif. Grad. Inst. Editor newsletter Orange County Adv., 1984-85; contbr. articles to profl. jours. Bd. dirs. Orange County chpt. Am. Jewish Com., 1982-88, Broadmore Community Assn., Anaheim Hills, Calif., 1981-83; mem. Orange County Mental Health Adv. Bd., 1981-88, sec., bd. dirs.; mem. Juvenile Diversion Task Force of Orange County, 1977. Served with U.S. Army, 1958-64. Fellow U. Chgo., 1962, NIMH, 1962, 72; Haynes scholar U. So. Calif. Sch. Pub. Adminstrn., 1964; grantee Faulk Program in Urban Mental Health, U. Pitts., 1973. Mem. ACLU (Orange County chpt.), Nat. Assn. Social Workers (mental health liaison, v.p. local chpt. 1975-88, Social Worker of Yr. award Orange County chpt. 1987), Acad. Cert. Social Workers (lic. clin. social worker and marriage, family, child counselor), Registry Clin. Social Workers (diplomate in clin. social work), Orange County Mental Health Assn. (sec.), Orange County Chpt. Alliance for Mentally Ill. Home: 6506 E Via Estrada Anaheim CA 92807 Office: Environ Mgmt Agy 12 Civic Ctr Plaza Santa Ana CA 92702-4048

RICHARDS, NATALIE VIRGINIA, art director, design consultant; b. Piedmont, Calif., Oct. 20, 1953; d. Franklin Sells Richards and Natalie Virginia (Van Order) Harmon; m. Charles John Michael Hebden, Apr. 7, 1987. Student, U. Calif., Santa Barbara, 1971-73; BA in Biolocy, U. Calif., Santa Cruz, 1975; MArch, UCLA, 1982. Designer L.A., 1982—; design cons. L.A. and San Francisco, 1987—; freelance art director L.A., 1988—. Mem. Sierra Club, The Cousteau Soc. Democrat.

RICHARDS, PAUL A., lawyer; b. Oakland, Calif., May 27, 1927; s. Donnell C. and Theresa (Pasquale) R.; m. Ann Morgans, May 20, 1948 (dec. 1984); 1 child, Paul M. BA, U. Pacific, 1950; JD, U. San Francisco, 1953. Bar: Nev. 1953, U.S. Dist. Ct. Nev. 1953, U.S. Supreme Ct. 1964, U.S. Ct. Claims 1976, U.S. Ct. Appeals (9th cir.) 1982. Pvt. practice, Reno, 1953—, prin. Paul A. Richards, Ltd.; prof. environ. law Sierra Nevada Coll., 1970-80. Mem. Washoe Dem. Central Com., 1959-74, chmn., 1964-66, vice chmn., 1966-68; trustee Sierra Nevada Coll., 1970-82, Ducks Unltd., 1964-72; trustee emeritus, 1974—; mem. Fed. Land Law Commn., Nev., 1973-80; bd. dirs. Reno Rodeo Assn., 1963, pres., 1979. Served with U.S. Navy, 1945-46. Recipient Pres.'s Buckle and award Reno Rodeo Assn., 1979. Mem. Nev. Bar Assn., Washoe County Bar Assn. Democrat. Roman Catholic. Club: Press. Lodge: Elks. Office: 248 S Sierra St Richards Bldg Ste 1 Reno NV 89501

RICHARDS, RICHARD DALE, marketing executive; b. Chgo., Ill., Aug. 11, 1931; s. Carroll Ogden and Cecile Gail (Mohrfeld) R.; m. Sandra Elaine Richards. BSBA, Millikin U., 1953. Asst. treas. Weiman Furniture Co., Rockford, Ill., 1956-60; v.p. T&T Metal Products, Inc., Rockford, 1960-66; sr. systems analyst Ingersoll Milling Machine Co., Rockford, 1966-69; dist. mgr. Sanitary Dist. of Rockford, Rockford, 1969-73; bus. devel. mmgr. Warren & Van Praag, Inc., Chgo., 1973-80; bus. devel. mgr. Donohue & Assoc., Inc., Chgo., 1980-86; regional mktg. mgr. Donohue & Assoc., Inc., Phoenix, 1986—; trustee, Sanitary Dist. of Rockford, Ill., 1967-69; instr. Rockford Coll., 1968-72. Precinct Committeeman, Winnebago County Republican Party, Rockford,. Recipient Achievement award Assn. for Systems Mgmt., 1973. Mem., Am. Pub. Works Assn. (meritorious award 1982, pres. south suburban br. 1979), Cen. States Water Pollution Control Assn. (pres. 1981-82). Republican. Lutheran. Home: 4142 W Kent Dr Chandler AZ 85226 Office: Donohue & Assoc Inc 3055 W Indian School Rd Phoenix AZ 85017

RICHARDS, RICHARD EARL, biologist; b. New Haven, Conn., Feb. 14, 1934; s. Oscar W. and Cecilia (Rosser) R.; m. Erna C. Sharrer, 1960 (div. 1980); children: Kenneth E., Cecilia R.; m. Sarah J. Cole, Apr. 30, 1980. BA, Colo. Coll., 1956; MA, U. N. Mex., 1958; DA, U. No. Colo., 1976. Exec. dir. Rocky Mountain Biol. Lab., Crested Butte, Colo., 1978-80; prof. biology Western State Coll., Gunnison, Colo., 1965-82; assoc. dir. rsch. and edn. Wildlife Safari, Winston, Oreg., 1982-89; pvt. practice cons. Colorado Springs, 1989—; cons. in field. Comdr. Gunnison (Colo.) Composite Squad, 1974-79; chmn. Colo. Nongame Adv. Coun., Denver, 1973-75; treas. Rocky Mountain Biol. Lab., Crested Butte, Colo., 1972-80; pres. Gunnison Community Choir, 1980-82; co-founder Roseburg (Oreg.) Unitarian Ch., 1985. Mem. Am. Assn. Mammalogists, Rocky Mountain Biol. Lab. Corp., Southwestern Naturalistic Assn. Democrat. Unitarian. Home and Office: 1227 N Corona Colorado Springs CO 80903

RICHARDS, STEPHEN FREDERICK, zoning administrator, planner; b. Oakland, Calif., Oct. 5, 1948. BA in Architecture, U. Calif., Berkeley, 1972; MA in Urban Planning, San Jose U., 1986. Engring. aid Pacific Gas & Electric Co., Belden, Calif.; planning aid to planner III Alameda County Planning Dept., Hayward, Calif., 1970-86, zoning adminstr., 1986—. With USAFR.

RICHARDS, VINCENT PHILIP HASLEWOOD, librarian; b. Sutton Bonington, Nottinghamshire, Eng., Aug. 1, 1933; emigrated to Can., 1956, naturalized, 1961; s. Philip Haslewood and Alice Hilda (Moore) R.; m. Ann Beardshall, Apr. 3, 1961; children: Mark, Christopher, Erika. A.L.A., Ealing Coll., London, 1954; B.L.S. with distinction, U. Okla., 1966. Cert. profl. librarian, B.C. Joined Third Order Mt. Carmel, Roman Catholic Ch., 1976; with Brentford and Chiswick Pub. Libraries, London, 1949-56; asst. librarian B.C. (Can.) Pub. Library Commn., Dawson Creek, 1956-57; asst. dir. Fraser Valley Regional Library, Abbotsford, B.C., 1957-67; chief librarian Red Deer (Alta., Can.) Coll., 1967-77; dir. libraries Edmonton (Alta.) Pub. Library, 1977—; pres. Faculty Assn. Red Deer Coll., 1971-72, bd. govs., 1972-73. Contbr. articles to profl. jours., 1954—. Vice pres. Jeunesses Musicales, Red Deer, 1969-70; bd. dirs. Red Deer TV Authority, 1975-76, Alta. Found. Lit. Arts, 1984-86. Served with Royal Army Ednl. Corps, 1951-53. Mem. Can. Library Assn., Library Assn. Alta. (pres. 1984-85), Pacific N.W. Library Assn., Council Adminstrs. Large Urban Public Libraries. Club: Rotary. Office: Edmonton Pub Libr, 7 Sir Winston Churchill Sq, Edmonton, AB Canada T5J 2V4

RICHARDSON, A(RTHUR) LESLIE, medical group consultant; b. Ramsgate, Kent, Eng., Feb. 21, 1910; s. John William and Emily Lilian (Wilkins) R.; came to U.S., 1930, naturalized, 1937; student spl. courses U. So. Calif., 1933-35; m. B. Kathleen Sargent, Oct. 15, 1937. Mgr., Tower Theater, Los Angeles, 1931-33; accountant Felix-Krueper Co., Los Angeles, 1933-35; indsl. engr. Pettengill, Inc., Los Angeles, 1935-37; purchasing agt. Gen. Petroleum Corp. Los Angeles, 1937-46; adminstr. Beaver Med. Clinic, Redlands, Calif., 1946-72, exec. cons. 1972-75; sec.-treas. Fern Properties, Inc., Redlands, 1955-75, Redelco, Inc., Redlands, 1960-67; pres. Buinco, Inc., Redlands, 1956-65; vice chmn. Redlands adv. bd. Bank of Am., 1973-80; exec. cons. Med. Adminstrs. Calif., 1975-83. Pres., Redlands Area Community Chest, 1953; volunteer exec. Internat. Exec. Service Corps; mem. San Bernardino County (Calif.) Grand Jury, 1952-53. Bd. dirs. Beaver Med. Clinic Found., Redlands, 1961—, sec.-treas., 1961-74, pres., 1974-75. Served to lt. Med. Adminstrv. Corps., AUS, 1942-45. Recipient Redlands Civic award Elks, 1953. Fellow Am. Coll. Med Group Adminstrs. (life, disting. fellow 1980, pres. 1965-66, dir.); mem. Med. Group Mgmt. Assn. (hon. life; mem. nat. long range planning com. 1963-68, pres. western sect. 1960). Episcopalian. Mason, Kiwanian (pres. 1951). Home: 1 Verlie Dr Redlands CA 92373

RICHARDSON, BRUCE LEVOYLE, dentist; b. Corvallis, Oreg., Jan. 28, 1950; s. Richard LeVoyle Richardson and Bonney Willard (Blair) Williams; m. Rhonda Kay Stratton, Sept. 11, 1976; children: Zachary LeVoyle, Nicklis Emery Christopher, Jessica Christine. BS, U. Oreg., 1972; DDS, U. Oreg., Portland, 1977. Pvt. practice Newport, Oreg., 1982--. Chmn. Lincoln County Extension Citizens Adv. Com., 1980-82; bd. dirs. Lincoln County YMCA, 1983--, chmn. advance gifts campaign, 1984, current support campaign 1985, bldg. com., 1985--. Fellow Nat. Acad. Gen. Dentistry (long-range planning coun. 1986-88, Mastership award 1987); mem. ADA, Oreg. Dental Assn. (ho. of dels. 1983-87, trustee 1984-87, v.p. 1987-88, pres.-elect 1988—, pres. 1989—), So. Willamette Dental Soc. (pres. 1985), Oreg. Soc. Dentistry for Children, Oreg. Acad. Gen. Dentistry (pres. 1984-85, long-range planning com. 1986-87), Avcanced Periodontic Study Club, Lincoln County Study Club, Newport C. of C. Republican. Methodist. Home: 333 N Beaver Valley Dr Seal Rock OR 97376 Office: 123 SE Douglas St Newport OR 97365

RICHARDSON, BRYAN JESSE, electrical engineer; b. Columbus, Nebr., June 26, 1962; s. Marvin Jesse and Sharon Lois (Torell) R. BSEE, U. Nebr., 1984. Electrical engineer Motorola, Inc., Scottsdale, Ariz., 1985—. Mem. Tau Beta Pi, Eta Kappa Nu. Home: 5847 E Ellis St Mesa AZ 85205 Office: Motorola Inc 8220 E Roosevelt St Scottsdale AZ 85252

RICHARDSON, DIANE, cosmetics company executive; b. Athens, Tex., Apr. 12, 1951; d. Bruce Wallace Richardson and Loma Rae (Graham) Chandler. Student, North Fla. Jr. Coll., 1970; BS Elem Edn. with honors, North Tex. State U., 1972; MEd with honors, U. Houston, 1974, postgrad., 1975-76. Tchr. Deer Park (Tex.) Elem Sch., 1972-76; child abuse counselor Houston Family Svc., 1975-76; family counselor Houston Epilepsy Assn., 1975-76; supr. Casual Corner, San Jose, Calif., 1976-77; creator, owner, mgr., exec. v.p. Bare Escentuals, Los Gatos, Calif., 1977--; cons. Panache, Santa Cruz, Calif., 1981-82. Vol. family counselor Deer Park Sch. Dist., 1975-76; chmn. Taste of Los Gatos, 1985; cons. Music in Park, Los Gatos, 1988. Mem. Assn. Women in Natural Foods, Vallco Mchts. Assn., Los Gatos Downtown Mchts. Assn. (founding, v.p. 1982-84, sec. 1984), Los Gatos C. of C. Office: Bare Escentuals Inc 104 Cooper Ct Los Gatos CA 95030

RICHARDSON, DONALD JAMES, English language educator; b. Correctionville, Iowa, July 22, 1942; s. Floyd Spencer and Bertha Leone (DesJarlais) R.; m. Yvonne Kay Misegadis, July 24, 1963 (div. 1982); children: Anne Darlene, Douglas Edward; m. LaDonna Denise Douglass, Aug. 8, 1987. BA in English and Speech, Ft. Hays State U., 1967, MA in English, 1971; PhD, Ariz. State U., 1985. Cert. tchr., community coll. tchr. Radio lab. asst. Phoenix Coll., 1971-72, instr. mass communications, 1972-78, instr. English composition, 1978—; guest prof. U. Heidelberg, Fed. Republic Germany, 1987-88. Contbr. revs. and articles to profl. publs. and newsletters. Mem. Soc. Preservation and Encouragement of Barbershop Quartet Singing in Am. (pres. 1977, 85, show chmn. 1973-75), Phi Kappa Phi. Democrat. Methodist. Home: 3006 N 15th Ave Phoenix AZ 85015-6133 Office: Phoenix Coll 1202 W Thomas Rd Phoenix AZ 85015-7366

RICHARDSON, EVERETT VERN, hydraulic engineer, educator, administrator; b. Scottsbluff, Nebr., Jan. 5, 1924; s. Thomas Otis and Jean Marie (Everett) R.; m. Billie Ann Kleckner, June 23, 1948; children—Gail Lee, Thomas Everett, Jerry Ray. B.S., Colo. State U., 1949, M.S., 1960, Ph.D., 1965. Registered profl. engr., Colo. Hydraulic engr. U.S. Geol. Survey, Wyo., 1949-52; hydraulic engr. U.S. Geol. Survey, Iowa, 1953-66; rsch. hydraulic engr. U.S. Geol. Survey, Ft. Collins, Colo., 1956-63, project chief, 1963-68; prof. civil engring., adminstr. engring. rsch. ctr. Colo. State U., Ft. Collins, 1968-82, prof. in charge of hydraulic progress and dir. hydraulic lab. engring rsch. ctr., 1982-88, dir. Egypt water use project, 1977-84, dir. Egypt irrigation improvement project, 1985-88, dir. Egypt water rsch. ctr., 1988—; Dir. Consortium for Internat. Devel., Tucson, Ariz., 1972-87; cons. in field. Editor: Highways in the River Environment, U.S. Bur. Pub. Rds., 1975, 88. Contbr. articles to profl. jours., chpts. to books. Mem. Ft. Collins Water Bd., 1969-84. With AUS, 1943-45. Decorated Bronze Star, Purple Heart; U.S. Govt. fellow MIT, 1962-63. Fellow ASCE (J.D. Stevens award 1961); mem. Internat. Congress for Irrigation and Drainage (bd. dirs.), AAAS, Sigma Xi, Chi Epsilon, Sigma Tau. Home: 824 Gregory Rd Fort Collins CO 80524 Office: Colo State U Engring Rsch Ctr Fort Collins CO 80523

RICHARDSON, H. L., state senator; b. Terre Haute, Ind., 1927; m. Barbara Budrow; children—Laurie R. Paredes, Carrie R. Herbertson, Doug. Student Olympic Coll.; advt. degree, Cornish Conservatory, Seattle. Former owner graphic arts and advt. bus.; mem. Calif. State Senate, 1967-88, bd. dirs. minority caucus; mem. elections, judiciary coms.; vice chmn. natural resources and wildlife com. chmn. bd. Computer Caging Corp.; pres. Red Barn Video Prodns. Mem. Republican State Central Com. Served with U.S. Navy, 1946. Recipient Outstanding Legislator award Calif. Rep. Assembly, annually 1968-76, Calif. Dist. Attys. Assn., Calif. Correctional Officers Assn., Calif. So. Council of Conservation Clubs, George Washington award Freedom Found., Valley Forge. Mem. Nat. Rifle Assn., Gun Owners Am. (founder, chmn.), Gun Owners Calif., Free Market PAC, Law and Order Campaign Com. (founder), NRA (bd. dirs.), Future Freedom Found. (chief exec. officer), Safari. Office: Office State Senate State Capitol Sacramento CA 95814

RICHARDSON, JAMES T., sociology educator; b. Charleston, S.C., Aug. 25, 1941; s. Lysle K. and Vera V. (King) R.; m. Cynthia M. Brown, Sept. 2, 1966; 1 child, Tamatha Lea. BA in Sociology, Tex. Tech U., 1964, MA in Sociology, 1965; PhD in Sociology, Wash. State U., 1968; JD, Nev. Sch. Law, 1986. Bar: Nev. 1986. Prof. sociology U. Nev., Reno, 1968—, prof. jud. studies, 1987—; v.p. Market Systems Rsch., Inc., Reno, 1981—; pres. Litigation Techs., Inc., Reno, 1986—. Author: Basic Programmed Learning Aid, 1974, Organized Miracles, 1979, Conversion Careers, 1978, The Brainwashing/Deprogramming Controvery, 1983, Money and Power in the New Religions, 1989; contbr. numerous articles to profl. jours. Chmn. Nev. Group Ins. Com., 1984—. Fulbright fellow The Netherlands, 1981. Mem. Assn. for Sociology Religion (pres. 1986-87), Law and Soc. Assn., Soc. for Sci. Study Religion (coun. 1982-85), Am. Sociol. Assn., ABA, Nev. Bar. Democrat. Home: 2075 Marlette Ave Reno NV 89503 Office: U Nev Dept Sociology Reno NV 89557

RICHARDSON, JOHN DAY, trust bank executive; b. Memphis, June 3, 1950; s. Harry Morton and Blanche Naomi (Day) R.; m. Carol Ann Mocella, Nov. 28, 1975. BS, Ariz. State U., 1972; MBA, Miami U., Oxford, Ohio, 1975. Chartered fin. analyst. Account exec. Reynolds Securities, Chgo., 1975-76; asst. v.p. 1st Chgo. Corp., 1976-85; v.p. Harris Trust Bank Ariz., Scottsdale, 1985—. Trustee Barrows Neurol. Found., Phoenix, 1987—, Edgar and Ellen Higgins Scholarship Found., Scottsdale, 1987—; mem. President's Club, Ariz. State U., Tempe, 1988—. Fellow Fin. Analysts Fedn.; mem. Inst. Chartered Fin. Analysts (grader 1986—, mem. Rsch. Found. 1988—), Phoenix Soc. Fin. Analysts, Prodesse Soc., John Gardiner's Tennis Ranch, Paradise Valley Country Club, Delta Sigma Pi (golden coun. 1982—). Home: 7251 Clearwater Pkwy Paradise Valley AZ 85253 Office: Harris Trust Bank Ariz 6710 E Camelback Rd Scottsdale AZ 85251

RICHARDSON, JOHN EDMON, management educator; b. Whittier, Calif., Oct. 22, 1942; s. John Edmon and Mildred Alice (Miller) R.; m. Dianne Elaine Ewald, July 15, 1967; 1 child, Sara Beth. BS, Calif. State U., Long Beach, 1964; MBA, U. So. Calif., 1966; MDiv, Fuller Theol. Sem., 1969, D of Ministry, 1981. Assoc. prof. mktg. Pepperdine U. Sch. Bus. and Mgmt., Malibu, Calif., 1969—. Author: (leader's guides) Caring Enough to Confront, 1984, The Measure of a Man, 1985; editor: Ann. Editions: Marketing 1987/88, 87, 88/89, 88, 89/90, 89, Ann. Edits.: Business Ethics 89/90, 88. Lay counselor La Canada (Calif.) Presbyn. Ch., 1978-84, mem. lay counseling task force, 1982-84. Mem. Am. Mgmt. Assn., Soc. Bus. Ethics, Christian Writers Guild, Fuller Sem. Alumni Cabinet (pres. 1982-85), Am. Mktg. Assn., Beta Gamma Sigma. Office: Pepperdine U Sch Bus and Mgmt 400 Corporate Pointe Culver City CA 90230

RICHARDSON, KEITH EDWARD, design engineer; b. Havre, Mont., Jan. 10, 1947; s. Gerald and Caroline Julian (Labing) R. Grad. high sch., Havre, 1965; student, No. Mont. Coll., Havre, 1967. Auto mechanic G&B Motors, Havre, 1964, Beck & Akerlund, Havre, 1965-70; motorcycle mechanic Havre Cycle, 1970-74; aircraft mechanic Burgess Aircraft, Havre, 1974-75; diesel mechanic No. Mfg., Havre, 1975-76, design engr., 1976-81; custom farmer Goodian Custom Farming, Box Elder, Mont., 1981-83; design engr. Big Bud Mfg., Havre, 1983-88. Designer Largest Tractor, 1978, 2 Point Oscillation, 1986. Elected to Mont. Inventors Hall Fame, 1988. Republican. Home: PO Box 387 Havre MT 59501 Office: Big Bud Mfg Hi Way #2 W Havre MT 59501

RICHARDSON, LINFORD LAWSON, protective services official; b. Glendale, Calif., Dec. 31, 1941; s. Linford Lawson and Phillis Anette (German) R.; m. Nancy Jane White, Apr. 9, 1961; 1 child, Robin Anette. AA, Riverside Community Coll., 1972; BA, Calif. Bapt. Coll., 1976. Fireman Riverside (Calif.) Fire Dept., 1964-67; police officer Riverside Police Dept., 1967-82, police chief, 1982—; chmn. adv. bd. POST Basic Acad., Riverside County, 1985; chmn. Law Enforcement Adminstrn., Riverside County, 1985. Mem. adv. com. Calif. Bapt. Coll., Riverside, 1985—; advisor Riverside County Coalition for Alternatives to Domestic Violence, 1983—; chmn. Salvation Army, Riverside, 1985; bd. dirs. Riverside Employee Credit Union, 1984—. Served with U.S. Army, 1960-63. Republican. Baptist. Lodge: Rotary (bd. dirs. Riverside club 1985). Office: City of Riverside Police Dept 4102 Orange St Riverside CA 92501 *

RICHARDSON, MELVIN RODELL, JR., aircraft manufacturing company official; b. Conway, S.C., Nov. 27, 1941; s. Melvin Rodell and Edith Irene (Williams) R.; m. Susan Carol Brown, June 1, 1963; children: Robert Martin, Jeffrey Wayne. Grad. high sch., Florence, S.C. Aerial cameraman USAF, Edwards AFB, 1960-66; photographic specialist Gen. Dynamics, Ft. Worth, 1966-72; cinematographer McDonnell Douglas, Long Beach, Calif., 1972-85, br. mgr., 1985—. Scoutmaster, com. mem. Boy Scouts Am., Garden Grove, Calif., 1972-82. Baptist. Home: 11402 Bowes Ave Garden Grove CA 92641 Office: McDonnell Douglas Aircraft 3855 Lakewood Blvd Long Beach CA 90846

RICHARDSON, RICHARD COLBY, JR., higher education educator, researcher; b. Burlington, Vt., Sept. 10, 1933; s. Richard Colby and Florence May (Barlow) R.; m. Patricia Ann Barnhart, Dec. 21, 1954; children—Richard Colby III, Michael Donald, Christopher Robin. B.S., Castleton State Coll., 1954; M.A., Mich. State U., 1958; Ph.D., U. Tex., 1963; Litt.D. (hon.), Lafayette Coll., 1973. Instr., counselor Vt. Coll., Montpelier, 1958-61; dean instrn. Forest Park Community Coll., St. Louis, 1963-67; pres. Northampton County Area Community Coll., Bethelehem, Pa., 1967-77; chmn. dept. higher edn. and adult edn. Ariz. State U., Tempe, 1977-84, prof. higher edn., 1984—; assoc. dir. Nat. Ctr. Postsecondary Governancy and Fin., 1985—. Jr. author: The Two Year College: A Social Synthesis, 1965; sr. author: Governance for the Two-Year College, 1972, Functional Literacy in the College Setting, 1981, Literacy in the Open Access College, 1983, Fostering Minority Acess and Achievement in Higher Education, 1987. Bd. dirs. Easton Hosp., 1973-77, v.p., 1975-77; exec. council Minsi Trails council Boy Scouts Am., Bethelehem, 1973-77. Named Disting. Grad., Coll. Edn., U. Tex., Austin, 1982; recipient Outstanding Research Publ. award Council Univ. and Colls.-Am. Assn. Community and Jr. Colls., 1983, Disting. Service award, 1984. Mem. Am. Assn. Higher Edn. (charter life, dir. 1970-73), AAUP, Assn. for Study of Higher Edn. (bd. dirs. 1984), Am. Assn. Community and Jr. Colls. (dir. 1980-83). Democrat. Home: 5654 E Wilshire Scottsdale AZ 85257 Office: Ariz State U Tempe AZ 85287

RICHARDSON, ROBERT KURT, electrical engineer; b. El Paso, Tex., July 11, 1961; s. R.L. and Jannette E. (Robbins) R. BSEE, N.Mex. State U., 1985. Sales clk. Grand Central, Albuquerque, 1979-80; drafting trainee Sandia Nat. Labs., Albuquerque, 1980; draftsman Engring. Research Ctr., Las Cruces, N.Mex., 1982-83; computer programmer Opti Metrics, Inc., Las Cruces, 1983-85; elec. engr. OptiMetrics, Inc., 1985—. Republican.

RICHARDSON, THOMAS STURGIS, JR., construction executive; b. Detroit, Sept. 23, 1952; s. Thomas Sturgis and Linnie Belle (Jackson) R.; m. Gina Rosa, Oct. 3, 1987 (div. 1989). Student, Temple U., 1970-71, Howard U., 1971-73, Pepperdine U., 1989—; grad., Am. Acad. Dramatic Art, Pasadena, Calif., 1982. Lic. contractor, Calif. Gen. contractor Johnson Bldg. and Improvement Co., Detroit, 1967-75; profl. actor L.A., 1975—; pres. Nightstriper, Studio City, Calif., 1986—; writer, producer Sta. WXYZ-TV, Detroit, 1973-75; mgr. Nat. Mktg. Service, Carson, Calif., 1986—; guest lectr. Wayne County Community Coll. Detroit, 1974. Produced TV documentary on mastectomy, 1974 (Emmy finalist 1974). Speaker Jimmy Carter for Pres. campaign, L.A., 1975; fundraiser Jesse Jackson for Pres. Campaign, Culver City, Calif., 1988; little league coach L.A. City Tri League, North Hollywood, Calif., 1986—. Mem. Screen Actors Guild, Contractors State Lic. Bd., Alpha Phi Alpha (v.p. Beta chpt. 1972). Democrat. Episcopalian. Office: Nightstriper 3960 Laurel Canyon #306 Studio City CA 91604

RICHARDSON, WILLIAM BLAINE, congressman; b. Pasadena, Calif., Nov. 15, 1947; m. Barbara Flavin, 1972. BA, Tufts U., Medford, Mass., 1970; MA, Fletcher Sch. Law and Diplomacy, 1971. Mem. staff U.S. Ho. of Reps., 1971-72, Dept. State, 1973-75; mem. staff fgn. relations com. U.S. Senate, 1975-78; exec. dir. N. Mex. State Democratic Com., 1978, Bernalillo County Democratic Com., 1978; businessman Santa Fe, N. Mex., 1978-82; mem. 98th-101st Congresses, 1982—. Co-chmn. Dem. Nat. Platform Com., Dukakis-Bentsen Campaign; sr. advisor for hispanic affairs for Dukakis-Bentsen; active Big. Bros.-Big Sisters, Santa Fe. Mem. Santa Fe Hispanic C. of C., Santa Fe C. of C., Council Fgn. Relations, NATO 2000 Bd., Congl. Hispanic Caucus, Am. G.I. Forum. Office: 332 Cannon House Office Bldg Washington DC 20515

RICHER, STEPHEN BRUCE, municipal official; b. Newark, Aug. 18, 1946; s. Seymour Albert Richer and Rosalind (Greenberg) Anderson; m. Kathleen Shagner, Jan. 10, 1981; children—Sean Edmund, Jack Albert. AB in Politics, Princeton U., 1968. Acctg. mgr. N.J. Bell. Tel., Teaneck, 1969-70; rep. Tailored Tours, Trenton, N.J., 1970-74, dep. dir. N.J. Bicentennial Commn., Trenton, 1974-77; spl. asst. to gov. N.J., Trenton, 1977-79; dir. N.J. Div. of Tourism, Trenton, 1979-82; pres. Travel & Recreation Info. Products, Springfield, N.J., 1982-83; exec. dir. Nev. Commn. on Tourism, Carson City, 1983-89; pres. Atlantic City Conv. and Visitors Bur., 1989—; chmn. Visit US West, Sacramento, 1987-89; mem. fed. agy. Nev. dist. Export Council, Reno, 1984-89. Mayor, councilman Randolph Twp., Randolph, N.J., 1974-80; mem. N.J. County and Mcpl. Govt. Study Commn., Trenton, 1979-82; chmn. Pine Nut (Nev.) dist. advancement commn. Eagle Scout, 1986-89. Recipient Tourism award N.J. Hotel and Motel Assn., 1980. Mem. Nat. Govs. Assn. (staff adv. com. on internat. trade and fgn. relations 1984-89), Nat. Council State Travel Dirs. (bd. dirs. 1980-82, 86-89), Nev. Hotel-Motel Assn. (ex. officio bd. dirs. 1984-89), Am. Bus. Assn., Nat. Tour Assn. (Outstanding Destination Mktg. award 1988), Am. Soc. Travel Agts. Travel Industry Assn. Am. (Outstanding Mkgt. award 1980), Japan Assn. of Travel Agts. Democrat. Jewish. Club: Princeton Assn.(chmn. schs. com. Northwestern, N.J. 1972-81, Nev. 1985-89). Club: Skal of No. Nev. Lodge: Kiwanis (pres. Dover, N.J. 1974). Avocations: stamp collecting, travel.

RICHES, KENNETH WILLIAM, electrical engineer; b. Long Beach, Calif., Oct. 23, 1962; s. William Murray Riches and Carlene Katherine (Simmons) Anderson. BSEE, U. Ill., 1984; MS in Engring. Mgmt., Santa Clara U., 1989. Registered profl. engr., Calif. Engr. Pacific Gas & Electric Co., San Francisco, 1984-88, elec. engr., 1988—. Mem. Rep. Nat. Com., 1986—; active Corp. Action in Pub. Schs., San Francisco, 1987, 88, San Francisco Music Conservatory World Wildlife Fund. Univs. Rsch. Assn. scholar, 1980. Mem. IEEE (chpt. chmn. 1986-87, sect. dir. 1988—), Pacific Coast Engring. Assn., Nature Conservancy, Zool. Soc. San Francisco, San Francisco Young Reps., Order of DeMolay (master counselor Paul Revere chpt. 1979). Methodist. Home: 1890 Clay St Apt 508 San Francisco CA 94109 Office: Pacific Gas & Electric 333 Market St Rm 1194 San Francisco CA 94106

RICHIE, WILBUR BENJAMIN, dentist, municipal official; b. Danville, Ill., Feb. 19, 1927; s. Wilson Leaverton and Emma (Keenan) R.; m. Jane Louise Brooks, Mar. 3, 1949; children: Cavin, Jeffrey, Brian. BS in Agronomy, Colo. State U., 1952; DDS, U. Mo., 1959. Diplomate Am. Bd. Forensic Odontology. Agronomist Adolph Coors Co., Golden, Colo., 1949-55; gen. practice dentistry Lakewood, Colo., 1959—; practice dentistry specializing in forensic odontology Lakewood, 1976—; bd. dirs. Internat. Assn. for Identification, Colo, Wyo. Coroner Jefferson County, Golden, 1982—. Served to sgt. AAF, 1945-47. Fellow Am. Acad. Forensic Sci.; mem. Am. Soc. Forensic Odontology (bd. govs. 1985—, pres. 1988—), Am. Bd. Forensic Odontology (sec. 1988—); mem. Motorcycle Doctors Assn. (pres. 1986-88), Am. Soc. Forensic Odontology (pres. 1987-88), IAI (chmn. body Identification team, Colo., Wyo.). Republican. Club: Mt. Vernon Country (v.p. 1968-69). Lodge: Shriners (pres. motorcycle unit 1970-72). Home: 25001 Ridgeway Golden CO 80401 Office: 2500 Youngfield Lakewood CO 80215

RICHMAN, ANTHONY E., textile rental company executive; b. Los Angeles, Dec. 13, 1941; s. Irving M. and Helen V. (Muchnic) R.; m. Judy Harriet Richman, Dec. 19, 1964; children: Lisa Michele, Jennifer Beth. BS, U. So. Calif., 1964. With Reliable Textile Rental Services, Los Angeles, 1964—, service mgr., 1969, sales and service mgr., 1970-73, plant mgr., 1973-75, gen. mgr., bd. dirs., 1975-78, chief exec. officer, 1978-82, v.p., sec.-treas., 1975-82, exec. v.p., chief exec. officer, 1982-84, pres., chief exec. officer, 1984—. Bd. dirs. Guild for Children, 1979—, Valley Guild for Cystic Fibrosis, 1974—; Cystic Fibrosis Found., 1985—; founding mem. Patrons for Cystic Fibrosis, 1983—. Recipient cert. of Achievement Linen Supply Assn. Am., 1979. Mem. Textile Rental Services Assn. Am. (past bd. dirs.). Office: Reliable Textile Rental Svcs 3200 N Figueroa St Los Angeles CA 90065

RICHMAN, MARVIN JORDAN, real estate developer; b. N.Y.C., July 13, 1939; s. Morris and Minnie (Graubart) R.; m. Amy Paula Rubin, July 31, 1966; children—Mark Jason, Keith Hayden, Susanne Elizabeth, Jessica Paige. BArch, MIT, 1962; M Urban Planning, N.Y. U., 1966, postgrad., 1967-69; MBA, U. Chgo., 1977; U.S. Dept. State fellow U. Chile, 1960. Architect, planner Skidmore, Owings & Merrill, N.Y.C., 1964, Conklin & Rossant, N.Y.C., 1965-67; ptnr. Vizbaras & Ptnrs., N.Y.C., 1968-69; v.p. Urban Investment & Devel. Co., Chgo., 1969-79, sr. v.p., 1979; pres. First City Devels. Corp., Beverly Hills, Calif., 1979-80, Olympia & York (U.S.) Devel. (West), 1987—, Olympia & York Calif. Equities Corp., L.A., 1981-87, Olympia & York Calif. Devel. Corp., 1981-87, Olympia & York Hope St. Mgmt. Corp., 1982-87, Olympia & York Homes Corp., 1983—, Olympia & York Calif. Constrn. Corp., 1986—; lectr. NYU, 1967-69, Nat. Humanities Inst., other univs. Adv. Nat. Endowment for Arts. Mem. UCLA Ctr. Fin. and Real Estate Bd. Advisors. With USAF, 1963-64. Registered architect; lic. real estate broker. Mem. AIA, Am Planning Assn.,Internat. Coun. Shopping Ctrs., L.A. World Affairs Coun., Urban Land Inst., Nat. Assn. Office and Indsl. Parks, Chief Exec.'s Round Table, Air Force Assn., Lambda Alpha. Home: 3238 Fond Dr Encino CA 91436 Office: Olympia & York 11601 Wilshire Blvd Los Angeles CA 90025

RICHMOND, CLAUDE HARRY, provincial government official; b. Blue, River, B.C., Can., Aug. 3, 1935; s. Francis Joseph and Olive Evelyn (Sloan) R.; m. Dorothy Patricia Simpson, Feb. 28, 1958; children: Bradley Craig, Valerie Dianne, Jeffrey Scott. With 'NL Broadcasting, 1970-78, gen. mgr., 1978-82; mem. Legis. Assembly, Province of B.C., 1981—, minister of tourism, 1982-86, minister responsible for Expo 86, minister social services and housing, 1986—. Alderman, City of Kamloops, 1975-78. Served with RCAF, 1952-55. Mem. Social Credit Party. Club: Kamloops Flying, Rivershore. Lodges: Masons, Shriners. Home: 1051 Ollek St, Kamloops, BC Canada V2B 5B1 Office: BC Legislature, 113 Parliament Bldgs, Victoria, BC Canada V8V 1X4

RICHMOND, DAN LAWRENCE, data processing executive; b. L.A., May 6, 1961; s. Bryant Sage and Jill Linda (Jasper) R.; m. Karen White, Aug. 2, 1987. BS in Computer Sci., UCLA, 1984. Supr. tech. staff Emory & Assoc., L.A., 1985-87; ptnr. Computer Age Software, L.A., 1987—. Home: 1318 S Beverly Glen #1 Los Angeles CA 90024

RICHMOND, HAROLD WAYNE, physician; b. Oakdale, La., July 11, 1925; s. Harold Easborn and Essie (Seals) R.; m. Frances Alexa Womack, Sept. 30, 1950; children—Mark Kimbrough. BS, U. Southwestern La., 1946; MD, La. State U., 1948. Diplomate Am. Bd. Family Practice, Am. Bd. Preventive Medicine. Intern Confederate Meml. Med. Ctr., Shreveport, La., 1948-49, resident in surgery and orthopedics, 1949-50; practice gen. medicine and surgery Oakdale, La., 1953-60; staff physician exec. health program St. Luke's Hosp, Med. Ctr., Phoenix, 1987—; med. dir. Cummins Engine Co., Inc., Columbus, Ind., 1960-74, corp. med. dir., 1974—, chief corp. cons. Ariz. Pub. Svc. Corp., Phoenix, 1987—; med. dir. Valley Nat. Bank, 1988—, First Interstate Bank Ariz., 1989. Co-founder, med. dir. Columbus Occupational Health Ctr., 1970-85. Lt. (j.g.) M.C., USNR, 1951-53. Recipient Ind. Good Samaritan award, 1979. Fellow Am. Coll. Occupatioanl Preventive Medicine, Am. Acad. Family Practice, Columbia Club (Indpls.). Home: 102 W Echo Ln Phoenix AZ 85021 Office: St Lukes Med Ctr Exec Health 1800 E Van Buren Phoenix AZ 85006

RICHMOND, LOUIS BARRY, public relations executive; b. Phila., Sept. 16, 1942; s. Samuel and Edith (Klebanoff) R.; m. Betty Ann Goldstein, Nov. 22, 1964; 1 child, Lorne Scott. Student, U. Rochester, 1960-61; MusB, Temple U., 1964, MusM, 1967. Cellist Nat. Symphony Orch., Washington, 1964-66; prof. U. Nev., Reno, 1968-70, U. of Puget Sound, Tacoma, 1970-72; adminstrv. dir. Suzuki Sch. of Music, Seattle, 1978-79; conductor N.W. Chamber Orch., Seattle, 1973-80; sr. music specialist City of Seattle, 1980-82; found. cons. Peace Train Arts Orgn., Hartford, Conn., 1982; dir. mktg. Alexis Hotel, Seattle, 1982-84; dir. of communications and pub. rels. Seattle Sheraton Hotel and Towers, 1984—. Mem. Ind. Colls. of Washington, 1987—, Puget Sound Pub. Rels. Round Table, 1986; bd. dirs. The Bob Hope Internat. Heart Research Inst., 1987—, Am. Cancer Soc., 1982-84, Danceworks N.W., 1979-80, Vol. Lawyers for the Arts, 1977-80, Allied Arts of Seattle, 1974-76, N.W. Chamber Orch., 1973-76. Mem. Internat. Hotel Mktg. Assn. (bd. dirs. Pacific N.W. Chpt.), Soc. of Am. Travel Writers, Public Relations Soc. of Am., Club N.W. Democrat. Jewish. Home: 2045 Boyer Ave E Seattle WA 98112 Office: Seattle Sheraton Hotel and Towers 1400 6th Ave Seattle WA 98101

RICHMOND, ROCSAN, television producer; b. Chgo., Jan. 30, 1945; d. Alphonso and Annie Lou (Combest) R.; divorced; 1 child, Tina S. Student, Wilson Jr. Coll., 1963, 2d City Theatre, Chgo., 1969, Alice Liddel Theatre, Chgo., 1970. Lic. 3d class radio/telephone operator FCC. Vegetarian editor Aware mag., Chgo., 1977-78; investigative reporter, film critic Chgo. Metro News, 1975-81; producer, talk show host Sta. WSSD Radio, Chgo., 1980-81; dir. pub. rels. IRMCO Corp., Chgo., 1981-82; newsletter editor Hollywood (Calif.) Reporter newspaper, 1985-86; exec. producer Donald Descendent's Prodns., Hollywood, 1985—, (TV show) Future News, 1985—. Jehovah's Witness. Office: 1762 N Orchid Ave Ste 109 Hollywood CA 90028

RICHTER, BURTON, physicist, educator; b. N.Y.C., Mar. 22, 1931; s. Abraham and Fanny (Pollack) R.; m. Laurose Becker, July 1, 1960; children: Elizabeth, Matthew. B.S., MIT, 1952, Ph.D., 1956. Research assoc. Stanford U., 1956-60, asst. prof. physics, 1960-63, assoc. prof., 1963-67, prof., 1967—, Paul Pigott prof. phys. sci., 1980—, tech. dir. Linear Accelerator Ctr., 1982-84, dir. Linear Accelerator Ctr., 1984—; cons. NSF, Dept. Energy; dir. Middlefield Capital Corp. Contbr. over 200 articles to profl. publs. Recipient E.O. Lawrence medal Dept. Energy, 1975; Nobel prize in physics, 1976. Fellow Am. Phys. Soc., AAAS; mem. Nat. Acad. Sci. Research elementary particle physics, Am. Acad. Arts and Scis. Office: Stanford U PO Box 4349 Stanford CA 94305

RICHTER, HANK CHARLES, JR., artist; b. Cleve., Oct. 10, 1928; s. Henry Charles and Alvina (Cross) R.; m. Beverly Ann Loomis, June 2, 1956; children: Lélia Louise, Karin Sue, Julie Ann. Student, Phila. Sch. Art, 1949-53. Art dir. Paul Lefton, Phila., 1953-55; creative dir., art dir. Fuller Smith & Ross Inc., Cleve., 1955-56; v.p. Ptak & Richter Advt., Phoenix, 1957-60; v.p., creative dir. Phillips Ramsey, San Diego, 1960-62; v.p. Bozell-Jacobs, Phoenix, 1963-65; pres. Henry C. Richter Advt., Phoenix, 1965-70; v.p., mgr. Harwood Advt., Phoenix, 1970-72; pres. Henry C. Richter Advt., Phoenix, 1972-75; pres. Westlund Sound Inc., 1975—; tchr., sculpture Principia Coll., Elsha, Ill.; ptnr. Forever Glass Masterpieces; bd. dirs. C.R.E.A.T.E. Illustrator: Gift of an Elephant, 1973. Pres. Goodwill of Cen. Ariz. Served as cpl. U.S. Army, 1946-48, Korea. Recipient Best of Festival, Gold medal Atlanta and Washington Film Festivals, 1969. Mem. Am. Indian and Cowboy Artists (pres. 1987-89), Art Group 12. Republican. Christian Scientist. Home and Office: 219 W Montebello Phoenix AZ 85013

RICHTER, MAURICE R., radiologist, retired; b. Effingham, Kans., July 1, 1903; s. Dominic and Pearl (Woolfolk) R.; m. Dorothy Allison, Mar. 18, 1948 (dec. BS, Ottowa (Kans.) U., 1924; DMS, U. Kans., 1935. Diplomate Am. Bd. Radiology. Chief of radiology Milw. County Hosp., 1941-42, St. Joseph's Hosp., Phoenix, 1946-48; pvt. practice Phoenix, 1948-68; team physician Ariz. State U., Tempe, Ariz., 1947-70. Maj. U.S. Army, 1943-46, PTO. Mem. Ariz. Med. Assn., Radiol. Soc. No. Am., AMA, Ariz. Club (Phoenix). Home: 337 El Parque Tempe AZ 85282

RICHTER, THOMAS ANTHONY, optical engineer, marketing and sales executive, aerospace consultant; b. Chgo., Feb. 25, 1938; s. Theodore John and Agnes (O Shonney) R.; m. Eugenia O'Connell, May 27, 1961 (div. Sept. 1980); 1 child, Steven Anthony; m. Janet Kathleen Munce, Nov. 26, 1982. BS, U. Wis., 1961, B Naval Sci., 1961, MS, 1964; MBA, U. Chgo., 1969. Research engr. Griffin Wheel Co., Chgo., 1964-67; chief metallurgist Chgo. Rawhide Mfg. Co., 1968; sales mgr. Optical Coating Lab. Inc., Santa Rosa, Calif., 1969-75; dir. mktg. Optical Radiation Corp., Azusa, Calif., 1976-79; v.p. Exotic Materials Inc., Costa Mesa, Calif., 1980; v.p., gen. mgr. Magnum Technologies, Inc., Hermosa Beach, Calif., 1981-83; pres. Richter Enterprises, Manhattan Beach, Calif., 1984—; cons. OAC, Inc., Irvine, Calif., 1985—, NASA, Pasadena, Calif., 1987—. Patentee optical and lamp systems; contbr. articles to profl. jours. Mem. com. Boy Scouts Am., Manhattan Beach, Calif., 1981-86. Served to Lt. (j.g.) USN, 1961-62, capt. USNR. Mem. Am. Am. Astronomical Soc., Soc. Photo-Optical Instrumentation Engrs. (Industrial rels. com. 1987—), Optical Soc. So. Calif. (pres. 1983-84), Internat. Soc. Hybrid Microelectronics. Republican. Home: 640 19th St Manhattan Beach CA 90266 Office: Richter Enterprises 1140 Manhattan Ave Ste 18 Manhattan Beach CA 90266

RICKER, GERALD WILLIAM, real estate executive, management consultant; b. Ancon, Panama C.Z., May 17, 1947; s. Merle Leslie and Rosa Benilda (Velarde) R.; m. Kathleen Sullivan, Aug. 10, 1974; children: Erin, Mollie. BS, U.S. Mil. Acad., 1969; MBA, U. Denver, 1981. Registered profl. engr., Colo.; lic. real estate broker, securities broker, Colo. Salesman, sales mgr. Baca Grande Corp., Crestone, Colo., 1972-76, v.p., gen. mgr., 1976-80; pres., chief exec. officer Schuck Corp., Colorado Springs, Colo., 1980—. Bd. dirs. Jr. Achievement, Colorado Springs, 1980—, Penrose-St. Francis Healthcare System, Colorado Springs, 1984—; mem. fin. coun. Cath. Diocese Colorado Springs, 1984—; precinct committeeman Colorado Springs Rep. Com., 1984—; mem. steering com. Colorado Springs Econ. Devel. Coun., 1986—. Capt. U.S. Army, 1969-74, Vietnam. Decorated Bronze Star with oak leaf cluster, Purple Heart. Mem. Young President's Orgn., El Paso Club. Home: 1326 N Cascade Ave Colorado Springs CO 80903 Office: Schuck Corp 25 N Cascade Ave Colorado Springs CO 80903

RICKEY, JUNE EVELYN MILLION, retired teacher; b. Joliet, Ill., Oct. 15, 1923; d. Lawrence Ernest and Ethel Alden (Ringler) Million; m. Paul Rickey, June 29, 1944; children: William, Mary Ann, John, James. BS in Edn., Ill. State U., 1946; MA in Journalism, Adams State Coll., 1970. Cert. tchr., Colo. Tchr. English Ottawa (Ill.) Twp. High Sch., 1946-47, Alamosa (Colo.) High Sch., 1953-55, 59-77, Evans Jr. High Sch., Alamosa, 1956-59; tchr. drama McAllen (Tex.) High Sch., 1955-56. Publicity chmn. Women's Citizenship Club, Alamosa, 1978—, Am. Cancer Soc., bd. dirs. 1986—; editorial staff San Luis Valley Hist. Soc., Alamosa, 1985—, Ethnic Heritage Project, 1977-78; trustee Creede (Colo.) Repertory Theatre, 1987—. Wall St. Jour. grantee, 1964. Mem. AAUW (sec. 1983-87), Adams State Coll. Alumni Assn., PEO Sisterhood. Democrat. Presbyterian. Home: 16365 County Rd BB Alamosa CO 81101

RICKS, MARK G., state senator; b. Rexburg, Idaho, July 4, 1924; s. Peter J. and Emily E. (Arnold) R.; m. Evelyn Tonks, July 9, 1944; children: Michael T., Gary M., Alan D., Adele Ricks Nielsen, Glen L., Kathie Ricks Tensmeyer, Grant H., Merle K., Douglas T. AS in Agr., Ricks Coll. Mem. Idaho Senate, majority leader, 1979—, vice chmn. taxation, trade, econ. devel., chmn. reapportionment com., 1982, chmn. senate commerce and labor commn., state fin. com., state affairs com., chmn., 1988-89, chmn. revenue and projection com., 1988-89, Mem. exec. council Boy Scouts Am. Named to Eastern Idaho Agrl. Hall of Fame, 1989, named One of Ten Outstanding Legislators Nat. Rep. Legislators Assn., 1987; recipient Community Svc. Prodn. and Example award Rexburg C. of C., 1976, Outstanding Svc. award Madison Sch. Dist., 1987, Distinguished Alumni award Ricks Coll., 1988. Mem. Nat. Conf. State Govts. (exec. com., chmn. nominating com. 1988, mem. rsch. and grants com., vice chmn. ted. taxation com., vice chmn. trade and econ. devel. com., mem. budget and rules com., vice chmn. reapportionment com. 1989), Conf. State Govts. (chmn. budget com. 1989, chmn. western legislative conf. 1988-89), Idaho Wheat Growers, Nat. Fedn. Ind. Bus. Republican. Mormon. Home: 3348 S 1400 West Rexburg ID 83440 Office: Idaho State Legislature Senate Capitol Bldg Boise ID 83720

RICO, LAURA CLARK, mathematics educator; b. Asheville, N.C., Jan. 5, 1933; d. Henry Hamblin and Susan Evans (Smith) Chapman; m. Walter Groch, Aug. 21, 1966 (div. 1970); m. Raul Rico, Mar. 7, 1970; 1 child, May Maria. AB, Middlebury Coll., 1953; MA, St. Margaret's House, Berkeley, Calif., 1958. Tchr. Craig (Alaska) Sch., 1953-54, Ketchikan (Alaska) Sch. Dist., 1954-56; dir. Christian edn. St. Peter's by-the-Sea, Sitka, Alaska, 1958-60; tchr. Plonk Sch., Asheville, N.C., 1962-63; social worker Henderson County Dept. Pub. Welfare, Hendersonville, N.C., 1964-66; tchr., tutor Merced Coll., Los Banos, Calif., 1979—. Mem. AAUW. Episcopalian. Home: PO Box 907 Los Banos CA 93635 Office: Merced Coll Westside Ctr 16570 S Mercey Springs Rd Los Banos CA 93635

RICUCCI, ROBERT JOHN, JR., security company executive; b. Detroit, Feb. 23, 1962; s. Robert John Ricucci Sr. and Angela Maria (Rossetti) Brauer. BSBA, U. Pacific, 1984. Gen. mgr. Romex Security Co., Stockton, Calif., 1983-86; owner, dir. Vid-Alert Security, Stockton, 1986—; co-owner Pictoball, Internat.,, Cupertino, Calif., 1986—; actor, writer. Cons. San Joaquin Employers' Coun., Stockton, 1984-86; guest instr. Rape Crisis Ctr., Stockton, 1985-86; assoc. mem. United Cerbral Palsy Assn., Stockton, 1984—. Recipient Legion of Honor award Am. Police Hall of Fame, 1987. Mem. AFTRA, SAG, AGVA, Nat. Assn. Chiefs of Police, Phi Kappa Phi. Republican. Roman Catholic. Office: Vid-Alert Security 540 E Market Stockton CA 95202

RIDDER, DANIEL HICKEY, newspaper publisher; b. N.Y.C., May 3, 1922; s. Bernard Herman and Nell (Hickey) R.; m. Frani Cooper Ackerman, Oct. 13, 1971; children by previous marriage—Daniel Hickey, Randy Helen, Richard J. A.B., Princeton U., 1943. Reporter N.Y. Jour. Commerce, Grand Forks (N.D.) Herald; pub. St. Paul Dispatch and Pioneer-Press, 1952-58; co-pub. Long Beach (Calif.) Ind. Press-Telegram, 1958-69, pub., 1969-88, chmn., 1988—; v.p. Knight-Ridder, Inc.; pres. Twin Coast Newspapers, Inc.; bd. dirs. AP, 1975-84. Chmn. bd. St. Mary Med. Ctr.; dir. sta. KCET; bd. dirs. Los Angeles United Way ; past bd. dirs. Newspaper Advt. Bur., Los Angeles County Mus. Art, Calif., 1974-84; former chmn. bd. trustees Calif. State U. and Colls.; trustee Long Beach Mus. Art; vice chmn. bd. govs. Calif. Community Found. Lt. (j.g.) USN, 1942-46, ETO, PTO. Clubs: Virginia Country (Long Beach, Calif.); El Dorado Country (Palm Springs, Calif.); Los Angeles Country; Cypress Point (Pebble Beach, Calif.). Home: 5531 Bryant Dr Long Beach CA 90815 Office: 604 Pine Ave Long Beach CA 90844

RIDDER, VICTOR FRANK (RICK RIDDER), political consultant; b. Washington, Jan. 27, 1953; s. Walter Thompson and Marie (Wasserman) R.; m. Jeannie Braden, Oct. 17, 1981; children: Alexander, Nathaniel, Jennifer. BA, Middlebury Coll., 1977; MS, Boston U., 1980. Exec. producer Backstage Ltd., Cambridge, Mass., 1978-80; field dir. Nat. Citizens Commn. Broadcasting, Washington, 1981, Lamm for Gov. campaign, Denver, 1982; nat. field dir. Ams. with Hart, Washington, 1983-84; pres. Ridder/Braden Inc., Denver, 1985—. Democrat. Office: Ridder Braden Inc Union Sta 239 Denver CO 80202

RIDER, LARRY V., real estate broker; b. Kansas City, Mo., Feb. 22, 1942; s. Vernon R. and Betty Jane (Nichols) R.; m. Diane Lynn Knaub, Dec. 6, 1972 (div. June 1982); m. Lynn Ann Chisman, June 11, 1982; 1 child, Justin Paul. BS, Ball State U., 1964; student, U. No. Colo., 1970-76; MS, Troy State U., 1978. Cert. real estate broker, Calif. Figher pilot 431st/555th Tactical Fighter Squadron, George AFB, Calif., 1965-67; instr. pilot 3500th Pilot Tng. Wing, Reese AFB, Tex., 1967-70; faculty mem., chief soaring branch USAF Acad., Colo., 1970-76; staff officer, mgmt. cons. HQ Air U., Maxwell AFB, Calif., 1976-80; ops. officer 14th Mil. Airlift Squadron, Norton AFB, Calif., 1980-84; owner, broker Chisman Real Estate, Laguna Beach, Calif., 1984—; bd. dirs. South Coast Med. Ctr., Winners Cir., Laguna Beach, Calif., 1988—. Author: Modern Tactical Warfare, 1972, Airmanship 101, 1973, Appraisal Assistance Reports, 1988. Pres. Calif. Riviera Assn., Inc., Dana Point, Calif., 1987-88; chmn. Winners Cir. Com., Laguna Beach, Calif., 1985-88. Lt. col. USAF, 1964-81. Decorated Meritorious Service medal, Disting. Flying Cross, Air medal, Purple Heart. Mem. Nat. Assn. Realtors, Calif. Assn. Realtors, Rotary (dir. South Laguna 1986-87). Republican. Presbyterian. Office: Chisman Real Estate 32351 Pacific Coast Hwy South Laguna Beach CA 92677

RIDGLEY, ROBERT LOUIS, gas company executive, lawyer; b. Ft. Wayne, Ind., Mar. 4, 1934; s. Charles Herbert and Margaret (Sparling) R.; m. Marilyn A. Hester, Aug. 24, 1957; children: Gregory C., Derek W. A.B., Cornell U., 1956; J.D., Harvard, 1959. Bar: Oreg. bar 1959. Practice in Portland, 1960-84; assoc. Stoel, Rives, Boley, Fraser and Wyse (and predecessors), 1960-66, ptnr., 1966; exec. v.p. N.W. Natural Gas Co., 1984, pres., chief exec. officer, 1985—. Co-editor: Pleading and Practice Handbook, 1964. Mem. Nat. Adv. Council for Edn. Disadvantaged Children, 1969-70; mem. Nat. Commn. on Reform of Secondary Edn.; Mem. Multnomah County Republican Exec. Com., 1962-66; alt. del. Nat. Conv., 1964; Chmn. bd. dirs. Portland Sch. Dist.; bd. dirs. Cornell U. Council, Nat. Pub. Affairs Center for TV; trustee Cornell U., 1970-76; trustee Lewis and Clark Coll., 1975-88, chmn. bd. dirs., 1985-88; chmn. bd. visitors Northwestern Sch. Law, 1975-76; bd. dirs. Oreg. Symphony Assn., 1981-84; mem. Exposition-Recreation Commn., 1980-85; chmn. gov. com. on sch. funding reform. Served to 1st lt., arty. AUS, 1959-60. Named Jr. First Citizen Portland, 1968, First Citizen Portland, 1987. Mem. Nat. Sch. Bds. Assn. (dir.), Oreg. Sch. Bds. Assn. (pres.), Portland C. of C. (dir. 1981— vice chmn. 1986-88, chmn. 1989). Lodge: Portland Rotary (dir. 1983-85, v.p. 1986-87, pres. 1987-88). Home: 4927 SW Downsview Ct Portland OR 97221 Office: NW Natural Gas Co 220 NW 2d Ave Portland OR 97209

RIDGWAY, DAVID WENZEL, educational film producer, director; b. Los Angeles, Dec. 12, 1904; s. David Nelson and Marie (Wenzel) R.; AB UCLA, 1926; MBA, Harvard U., 1928; m. Rochelle Devine, June 22, 1955. With RKO Studios, Hollywood, Calif., 1930-42; motion picture specialist WPB, Washington, 1942-43; prodn. mgr., producer Ency. Brit. Films, Wilmette, Ill., 1946-60; dir. film activities, exec. dir. Chem. Edn. Material Study, U. Calif. at Berkeley, 1960—; producer, on-screen interviewer Am. Chem. Soc. TV series Eminent Chemists, 1981; advisor TV project Mech. Universe, Calif. Inst. Tech., 1985 also Am. Inst. Biol. Scis.; introduced CHEM study films to People's Republic of China, 1983. Lt. comdr. USNR, 1943-46. Recipient Chris award for prodn. CHEM Study Ednl. Films in Chemistry, Film Coun. Greater Columbus, 1962-63; Bronze medal, Padua, Italy, 1963; CINE Golden Eagle awards, 1962-64, 73; Gold Camera award for film Wondering About Things, U.S. Indsl. Film Festival, 1971; diploma of honour Internat. Sci. Film Assn. Festival, Cairo, 1st prize Am. Biol. Photog. Assn. for film MARS: Chemistry Looks for Life, 1978. Mem. Soc. Motion Pictures and TV Engrs. (chmn. San Francisco sect. 1970-72), Am. Sci. Film Assn. (trustee 1974-81), Delta Upsilon, Alpha Kappa Psi. Clubs: Faculty (U. Calif.), Bohemian (San Francisco). Author: (with Richard J. Merrill) The CHEM Study Story, 1969; also articles in ednl. jours. Home: 1735 Highland Pl Berkeley CA 94709 Office: U Calif Lawrence Hall of Sci Berkeley CA 94720

RIDGWAY, MARY JO, small business owner; b. Kansas City, Mo., Dec. 16, 1955; d. Floyd Robert and Mary Gertrude (Kornbrust) Lambert; m. Jeffrey Brian Ridgway, Nov. 29, 1975 (div. 1983); children: Samantha Michelle, Matthew Brian. Assoc. in Acctg., N.E. Mo. State U., 1976. Acctg. clk., engring coordinator Sta. KCTV 5-Meredith Corp., Fairway, Kans., 1981-84; out-of-state tax specialist H&R Block Co., Mission, Kans., 1983-84; tax preparer, supr., instr., out-of-state tax specialist The Tax Doctor, Clovis, Calif., 1985-88, prin., 1988—. Mem. Nat. Soc. Enrolled Agts., Fresno Women's Network, Fresno Friends. Democrat. Roman Catholic. Home and Office: 1200 Scott Ave #156 Clovis CA 93612

RIDINGER, CHRISTOPHER DAVID, entrepreneur, franchise owner; b. Grass Valley, Calif., Aug. 4, 1965; s. David Warren Ridinger and Christy Ann Musser. Profl. racer All Terrain Vehicle Assn., Westerville, Ohio, 1984-86; mgr. Carcos Auto Painting & Body Works, Canoga Park, Calif., 1986; owner Rebuilder-R-Us, Sacramento, 1985--; mgr. MAACO Auto Painting & Body Works, Sacramento, 1986-88, franchise owner, 1988--. Fund raiser Am. Diabetes Assn., 1977-79; active Folsom (Calif.) Police Dept. Explorer Post, 1980-84. Named top individual fund raiser Am. Diabetes Assn., 1978, 79, state champion Am. Motorcycle Assn. Continental Motor Sports, Calif., 1984. Republican. Presbyterian. Office: Rebuilders-R-Us 3317 Julliard Dr Ste 261 Sacramento CA 95826

RIDLEY-TREE, PAUL HERBERT, aircraft parts distributing company executive; b. N.Y.C., Dec. 29, 1916; s. Herbert Beerbohm-Tree and Anne Ridley; m. Leslie layne Aronade-Furnival, Feb. 14, 1988. Student, Puget Sound Coll., 1933-36. Mgr. parts sales Douglas Aircraft Co., Santa Monica, Calif., 1941-50; v.p. GMH Air Parts Co., Santa Monica, 1950-59; pres. Pacific Air Industries, Santa Monica, 1959-76, chmn. bd. dirs., chief exec. officer, 1976—; chief exec. officer Air Cert., Inc., Santa Monica, 1955—; bd. dirs. Hydraulic and Landing Gear Inc., Santa Monica. Mem. Santa Barbara Polo Club. Republican. Episcopalian. Home: 204 Hot Springs Rd Montecito CA 93108

RIDLON, STEPHEN ALLAN, computer scientist; b. Boston, Oct. 31, 1943; s. Richard E. and Eleanor Marie (Dold) R.; m. Karen Ann Winzen, June 22, 1972; children: Christopher, Susanne, Daniel. BSCE, Northeastern U., Boston, 1966; MSCE, Northeastern U., 1970. Registered profl. engr., Calif. Instr. Wentworth Inst., Boston, 1966-68; engr. Jackson & Moreland, Boston, 1968-72; sr. engr. Bechtel Corp., San Francisco, 1972-85; application specialist Boeing Computer Svcs., Seattle, 1985—. Co-author: Finite Element Idealization, 1987; contbr. articles to profl. jours. Active PTA, Soccer League, Issaquah, 1986—; prin. ch. sch. St. Joseph Ch., Issaquah, 1986—. With U.S. Army, 1964-66. Mem. ASCE, ASME, Tau Beta Pi, Chi Epsilon. Home: 18713 SE 43rd St Issaquah WA 98027

RIEBE, CYNTHIA MORRIS, interior designer; b. Mpls., Mar. 20, 1946; d. Arthur Marvin and Virginia (Swanke) Morris; m. Frederick Charles Riebe, Jan. 22, 1972; children: Uli Youn-Ho, Ilse Ae-Yoon. BA, U. Minn., 1969. Cert. Nat. Coun. for Interior Design Qualification. Staff interior designer Gabberts, Inc., Mpls., 1970-72; chief interior designer HGA, Architects Inc., Mpls., 1974-75; prin. Cynthia Riebe Interior Design, Mpls., Tokyo and Carmel, Calif., 1975--; cons. interior designer for Minn. gov.'s residence, St. Paul, 1983. Mem. Leadership Monterey Peninsula, 1986-87; docent Monterey History and Art Assn., 1986--. Recipient cert. of honor Design Internat., 1981, winner Halo Lighting Design Competition, 1981; Scalamandre grantee, 1982. Mem. Am. Soc. Interior Designers (dir. significant interiors 1982-84, chmn. historic preservation 1984, bd. dirs. Minn. chpt. 1984, President's citation 1982, 83), Nat. Trust for Historic Preservation. Republican. Episcopalian. Office: Lincoln at Ocean Box 4724 Carmel CA 93921

RIEDELL, EDWIN HENRY, obstetrician; b. Anamoose, N.D., Mar. 4, 1912; s. Henry Thayer and Christine (Kreiser) R.; widowed; children: Louise, Christine, Nancy, Edwin Jr. D Osteopathy, Coll. Osteopathic Physicians and Surgeons, Los Angeles, 1939; MD, Calif. Coll. Medicine, Los Angeles, 1962. Intern Monte Sano Hosp., Los Angeles, 1939-40, resident physician, 1940-41; resident obstetrician Los Angeles County Maternity Service, 1941; attending surgeon Los Angeles County Hosp. Unit II, 1946-66, chief obstetrical surgeon, 1960-66; active and cons. surgeon various hosps., 1946-80. Contbr. articles to profl. jours. Fellow Am. Coll. Osteopathic Surgeons. Republican. Lodge: Rotary (pres. 1962-63). Home: 147 E Cascade Ct Brea CA 92621

RIEGEL, BYRON WILLIAM, ophthalmologist, educator; b. Evanston, Ill., Jan. 19, 1938; s. Byron and Belle Mae (Huot) R.; B.S., Stanford U., 1960; M.D., Cornell U., 1964; m. Marilyn Hills, May 18, 1968; children—Marc William, Ryan Marie, Andrea Elizabeth. Intern, King County Hosp., Seattle, 1964-65; asst. resident in surgery U. Wash., Seattle, 1965; resident in ophthalmology U. Fla., 1968-71; pvt. practice medicine specializing in ophthalmology, Sierra Eye Med. Group, Inc., Visalia, Calif., 1972—; mem. staff Kaweah Delta Dist. Hosp., chief of staff, 1978-79; mem. staff Visalia Community Hosp.; med. staff ophthalmology Valley Med. Center-Univ. Calif. Fresno Med. Edn. Program, 1972—; asst. clin. prof. ophthalmology U. Calif., San Francisco, 1981—. Bd. dirs., asst. sec. Kaweah Delta Dist. Hosp., 1983—. Served as flight surgeon USN, 1966-68. Co-recipient Fight-for-Sight citation for research in retinal dystrophy, 1970. Diplomate Am. Bd. Ophthalmology, Nat. Bd. Med. Examiners. Fellow A.C.S., Am. Acad. Ophthalmology; mem. AMA, Calif. (del. 1978-79), Med. Assn., Tulare County Med. Assns., Calif. Assn. Ophthalmology,Am. Soc. Cataract and Refractive Surgery, Internat. Phacoemulsification and Cataract Methodology Soc. Roman Catholic. Club: Rotary (Visalia). Home: 1101 W Whitendale St Visalia CA 93277 Office: 2830 W Main St Visalia CA 93291

RIEGER, ELAINE JUNE, nurse; b. Lebanon, Pa., June 7, 1937; d. Frank and Florence (Hitz) Plasterer; m. Jere LeFever Longenecker, Sept. 13, 1958 (div. 1968); children: Julie Lynn Porto, Jere Lee Longenecker; m. Bernhard Rieger, Oct. 12, 1971. Nursing diploma, Coatesville (Pa.) Hosp. Sch. of Nursing, 1958; BA, U. Redlands, 1976; MS in Healthcare Mgmt., Calif. State U., L.A., 1984. Cert. nursing adminstr. From staff nurse to clin. supr. to dir. of nurses St. Johns Regional Med. Ctr., Oxnard, Calif., 1968-86; dir. of nurses Motion Picture and TV Hosp., Woodland Hills, Calif., 1987—. Mem. Nurses Adminstrn. Council (sec. 1988—), Calif. League of Nurses, Nat. League of Nurses, Calif. Soc. Nursing Svc. Adminstrn. (Mem. by laws com.), Am. Orgn. Nurse Execs. Home: 1817 Shady Brook Dr Thousand Oaks CA 91362 Office: Motion Picture and TV Hosp 23388 Malholland Dr Woodland Hills CA 91364

RIEGLER, ALAN M., data processing consultant; b. Cleve., Aug. 30, 1946; s. Martin and Caroline (Bartsche) R. BS, Case Western Res. U., 1968; MBA, Xavier U., 1970; JD, No. Ky. U., 1978. Bar: Ohio, Tenn. Sr. systems analyst Proctor & Gamble, Cin., 1968-72; systems and processing mgr. Automatic Data Processing, Cin., 1972-78; v.p. MIS Leader Fed. Savs. & Loan, Memphis, 1978-81; v.p. sys. First Tenn. Bank, Memphis, 1982-85; sr. mgr., fin. svcs. specialty Price Waterhouse, L.A., 1985—; editorial advisor Sml. Sys. World, Chgo., 1981-83. Contbr. articles to profl. jours. Mem. The Computer Soc. Home: 1213 Cordova #4 Pasadena CA 91106 Office: Price Waterhouse 400 S Hope St Los Angeles CA 90071

RIEMAN, RONALD RODNEY, transportation executive; b. Monroe, Wash., Sept. 28, 1955; s. Ronald Rodney and Doreen Caroline (Grimley) R.; m. Ronda Ruth Langham, June 24, 1985. AS, Lane Community Coll., Eugene, Oreg., 1978; BS in Physics, U. Oreg., 1981. Pilot Am. Airlines, Dallas and Ft. Worth, Tex., 1987—; owner, operator Rieman Aircraft Sales, Canby, Oreg., 1989—. Capt. USMC, 1981-87, USMCR, 1987—. Mem. Aircraft Owners and Pilots Assn., Allied Pilots Assn., CAP. Republican. Home: 9764 S Gribble Rd Canby OR 97013

RIEMENSCHNEIDER, PAUL ARTHUR, physician, radiologist; b. Cleve., Apr. 17, 1920; s. Albert and Selma (Marting) R.; m. Mildred McCarthy, May 12, 1945; children: Barbara Anne, Nancy Emelia, David Andrew, Paul Albert, Mary Elizabeth, Sarah Bache. BS magna cum laude, Baldwin-Wallace Coll., 1941; MD, Harvard U., 1944. Diplomate Am. Bd. Radiology (trustee 1973-85), Nat. Bd. Med. Examiners. Prof., chmn. dept. radiology SUNY, Syracuse, 1945-64; chief diagnostic radiology Santa Barbara (Calif.) Cottage Hosp., 1964—, also bd. dirs.; vis. prof. in residence SUNY, Syracuse, 1983—. Co-editor: N.Y. State Jour. Medicine, 1960-64; mem. editorial adv. bd. Yearbook of Cancer, 1960-64; contbr. articles to profl. jours. Mem. appropriations com. Santa Barbara Found., 1984—; vestryman All STs. Episcopal Ch., 1970-76, sr. warden, 1973; bd. dirs. ARC, Santa Barbara, 1968-72, Am. Cancer Soc., Santa Barbara, 1967-70, Casa Dorinda Retirement Residence, 1975-76, 89—, Wood Glen Hall Retirement Residence, 1980—, Cancer Found. Santa Barbara, 1966-82, 89—, chmn. equipment com., 1973-82. Served to lt. comdr. USNR, 1945-47, 54-56. Recipient Alumni Merit award Baldwin-Wallace Coll., 1985. Fellow Am. Coll. Radiology (cancer com. 1952-54, council 1956-64, bd. chancellors 1967-73, chmn. commn. standards in radiologic practice 1968-71, v.p. 1972, pres. 1974, chmn. com. manpower 1972-86, chmn. com. manpower in armed servies 1975-86, Gold medal 1982); mem. AMA, Calif. Med. Assn., Santa Barbara County Med. Soc. (chmn. med. sch. com. 1967-71), Am. Roentgen Ray Soc. (mem. publs. com. 1965-75, chmn. 1970-75, exec. council 1970-75, 77-82, chmn. program com. 1977-79, pres.-elect 1977-79, pres. 1979, Disting. Service award 1986), South Coast Radiol. Soc. (pres. 1967), Assn. Univ. Radiologists (sec. 1960, pres. 1961, com. resident tng. 1984—), Radiol. Soc. N.Am., Am. Soc. Neuroradiology, Soc. Pediatric Radiology, Eastern Radiol. Soc. (pres.-elect 1987, pres. 1988—), Calif. Radiol. Soc., So. Calif. Radiol. Soc., Detroit Roentgen Soc. (hon.), Bluegrass Radiol. Soc. (hon.), Pacific N.W. Radiol. Soc. (hon.), Alpha Omega Alpha. Republican. Clubs: Birnamwood Golf (Santa Barbara); Skaneateles Country (N.Y.). Home: 112 Olive Mill Rd Santa Barbara CA 93108

RIETZ, KENNETH CHARLES, advertising executive; b. Appleton, Wis., May 3, 1941; s. Howard K. and Catherine (Abbey) R.; 1 child, Kenneth Charles. Grad. George Washington U., 1973. Dep. chmn. Rep. Nat. Com., 1973; v.p. MGM Records, L.A., 1974, Mike Curb Prodns., 1974-76; pres. Ken Rietz & Co., L.A., 1976—. Chmn. 70001 Tng. & Employment Inst., bd. trustees Fund for Am. Studies; bd. dirs. VOA Found. Producer: (TV spls.) Fifth International Tchalkovsky Competition, 1974, An Olde Fashioned Christmas, 1985, Silver Dollar Jubilee, 1985. Mem. Am. Assn. Polit. Cons., Am. Coun. Young Polit. Leaders, Rep. Eagles. Presbyterian. Office: PO Box 10418 Marina Del Rey CA 90295

RIFE, JERRY LEE, television and film production executive; b. New Albany, Ind., Apr. 21, 1945; s. Morris Andrew and Gladys Nadine (Taylor) R. BS, U. Tulsa, 1967, JD, 1969. Bar: Okla. Co-mgr., acct. Disney on Parade, Burbank, Calif., 1973-76; contract adminstr. Cinexport-Interfilm, Hollywood, Calif., 1976-78; dir. TV prodn. fin. Paramount Pictures, Hollywood, 1978-86; dir. prodn. fin. Taft Entertainment, Hollywood, 1986-88; v.p. prodn. fin. Imagine Films Entertainment, Hollywood, 1988—; exec. dir. Miss Los Angeles county Pageant, 1976-78; prodn. cons. Miss Calif. Pageant, 1980-85. Sponsor, Aids Project L.A., 1986—. Mem. Smithsonian Assocs., Los Angeles County Mus. Art, Partnership for Improved Air Travel, Fin./Mgmt. Execs. In Entertainment, TV Acad. Arts and Sci., Am. Film Inst., Lambda Chi Alpha. Democrat. Religious Sci.

RIGGEN, JOHN WILLIAM, electronics executive, electrical engineer; b. Walden, Colo., Jan. 16, 1938; s. John William and Virginia (Mitchell) R.; m. Janet Gail Snell, Aug. 25, 1957 (div. 1975); children: John Randall, Jeffrey Dean, Joel Scott; m. Rosemart Pearl Pfander, Nov. 19, 1977; 1 child, Shawn Renee. BSEE, Colo. State U., 1960; MSEE, Stanford U., 1964, postgrad. exec. program, 1978. Research and devel. engr. Hewlett-Packard Co., Palo Alto, Calif., 1960-64, Colo. Springs, Colo., 1964-70; mgr. research and devel. sec. Hewlett-Packard Co., Colo. Springs, 1970-74, mgr. CRT mfg., 1974-77; gen. mgr. Colo. Springs div. Hewlett-Packard Co., 1977-83; mgr. Colo. pub. affairs Hewlett-Packard Co., Colo. Springs, 1983--. Patentee in electronic circuits field. Chmn. energy com. Colo. Gov.'s Front Range Futures, 1980; pres., campaign chmn. Pikes Peak United Way, 1982-85; co-chmn. Pikes Peak Clean Air Consortium, 1986--. Recipient Silver award Nat. Jr. Achievement, Colo. Springs, 1987. Mem. Am. Electronics Assn. (exec. com. Denver 1984--), IEEE (chmn. Ft. Collins, Colo. 1954-56), Colo. Assn. Commerce and Industry (v.p. southeast region 1983-88), Garden of Gods. Republican. Presbyterian. Home: 240 Tam O'Shanter Monument CO 80132 Office: Hewlett Packard Co PO Box 617 Colorado Springs CO 80901

RIGGS, DENNIS ROY, accountant; b. Stratton, Nebr., Sept. 20, 1945; s. Robert Leroy and Ophal J. (Breitling) R.; m. Marvalynn Nutt, Mar. 23, 1968; children: Sherri Lynn, Cimberly Michelle. BSBA, Valparaiso U., Ind., 1966; MBA, U. Colo., Colorado Springs, 1976. CPA, Colo. Staff acct. various cos., Colorado Springs, 1971-73; pvt. practice tax acctg. Colorado Springs, 1974-78; ptnr. Tillman & Long, CPA's, Colorado Springs, 1979-80, Tillman, Giblin & Riggs, CPA's, Colorado Springs, 1981, Giblin & Riggs, CPA's, Colorado Springs, 1982-86; pvt. practice acctg. Colorado Springs, 1987--. Capt. USAF, 1966-71, Vietnam. Decorated Bronze Star medal. Mem. AICPA, Colo. Soc. CPA's. Republican. Lutheran. office: 212 N Wahsatch St #102 Colorado Springs CO 80903

RIGGS, DONALD EUGENE, librarian, university dean; b. Middlebourne, W.Va., May 11, 1942; m. Jane Vasbinder, Sept. 25, 1964; children: Janna Jennifer, Krista Dyonis. BA, Glenville State Coll., 1964; MA, W.Va. U., 1966; MLS, U. Pitts., 1968; EdD, Va. Poly. Inst. and State U., 1975. Head librarian, tchr. sci. Warwood (W.Va.) High Sch., 1964-65; head librarian, audiovisual dir. Wheeling (W.Va.) High Sch., 1965-67; sci. and econs. librarian California State Coll. of Pa., 1968-70; dir. library and learning center Bluefield State Coll., 1970-72; dir. libraries and media services Bluefield State Coll., Concord Coll., Greenbrier Community Coll., and So. campus W.Va. Coll. of Grad. Studies, 1972-76; dir. libraries U. Colo., Denver, Met. State Coll., and Community Col. of Denver—Auraria Campus, 1976-79; univ. librarian Ariz. State U., 1979-88, dean univ. libraries, 1988—; adj. prof. Calif. State Coll., 1968-70, W.Va. U., 1970-72, U. Colo., 1977-79, U. Ariz., 1985; fed. relations coordinator Am. and W.Va. library assns., 1970-75; chmn. bd. dirs. Cen. Colo. Library System, 1976-79; chmn. Colo. Council Acad. Libraries, 1977-78; exec. bd. Colo. Alliance Research Libraries, 1978-79; cons. to libraries; del. Users Coun. Online Computer Library Ctr., 1987—, chair artificial intelligence and expert systems nat. group, 1987-88. Editor W.Va. Libraries, 1973-75; assoc. editor: Southeastern Librarian, 1973-75; contbg. author: Libraries in the Political Process, 1980, Options for the 80's, 1982, Library and Information Technology: At the Crossroads, 1984; contbg. author, editor: Library Leadership: Visualizing the Future, 1982; author: Strategic Planning for Library Managers, 1984, (with Rao Aluri) Expert Systems in Libraries, 1989, (with Gordon Sabine) Libraries in the '90s: What Leaders Expect, 1988, Communication: The Language of Library Leadership, 1989, Creativity, Innovation and Entrepreneurship in Libraries, 1989, History of the Arizona State University Libraries, 1989; editorial bd. Jour. Library Adminstrn., 1987—, Am. Libraries, 1987—, editor Library Adminstrn. and Mgmt., 1987-89; contbr. articles to profl. publs. Trustee Mesa (Ariz.) Pub. Library, 1980-86, chmn., 1985-86; mem. Ariz. State Library Adv. Council, 1981-84; bd. dirs. Documentation Abstracts, Inc., 1986—. Named Outstanding Young Educator Ohio County Schs., 1966; Council on Library Resources grantee, 1985; sr. fellow UCLA, 1989. Mem. ALA (councilor-at-large 1982-86, chmn. council's resolutions com. 1985-86, pub. com. 1988—), Ariz. Library Assn. (pres. coll. and univ. div. 1981-82, pres. 1983-84, Spl. Service award 1986), Colo. Library Assn. (pres. 1978-79), W.Va. Library Assn. (pres. 1975-76), Assn. Coll. and Research Libraries (pres. Tri-State chpt. 1972-74, pres. Ariz. chpt. 1981-82), So. Library Assn. (chmn. coll. and univ. sect. 1982-83), Assn. Research Libraries (mem. 100th meeting planning com. 1982), AMIGOS Bibliograph. Council, Inc. (trustee 1986—, chmn. bd. trustees, 1988-89), Library Adminstrn. and Mgmt. Assn. (bd. dirs. 1987-89), Library Info. and Tech. Assn., Mountain Plains Library Assn. (bd. dirs. 1987—), Beta Phi Mu, Chi Beta Phi, Phi Delta Kappa, Phi Kappa Phi. Home: 2120 E Knoll Circle Mesa AZ 85213 Office: Ariz State U Tempe AZ 85287

RIGGS, DONALD EUGENE, principal; b. Bloomington, Ind., Sept. 10, 1931; s. Elmer Donald and Josephine Mariene (Denbo) R.; m. Iris Jean Evans, Sept. 5, 1952; children: Karla Riggs Norton, Kathy Riggs Sorenson. AB, Greenville (Ill.) Coll., 1953; postgrad., Greenville (Ill.) Coll., Glendale, 1977; MA, Calif. Grad. Sch. Theology, Glendale, 1978, PhD, 1979. With Free Meth. Ch., 1952-79; sr. pastor Free Meth. Ch., Indpls., 1965-77, 85-88, L.A., 1977-79; gen. dir. communications F. Meth Hdqrs., Winona Lake, Ind., 1979-82; sr. pastor Free Meth. Ch., Newberg, Oreg., 1982-85; adminstr., prin. Pacific Christina High Sch., L.A., 1988—. Author: Make it Happen, 1981. Mem. Jr. C. of C., Exch. Club, Kiwanis, Civitan. Republican. Home: 130 Monterey Rd #203 South Pasadena CA 91030 Office: Pacific Christian High Sch 625 Coleman Ave Los Angeles CA 90042

RIGGS, HENRY EARLE, engineering management educator, academic administrator; b. Chgo., Feb. 25, 1935; s. Joseph Agnew and Gretchen (Walser) R.; m. Gayle Carson, May 17, 1958; children: Elizabeth, Peter, Catharine. BS, Stanford U., 1957; MBA, Harvard U., 1960. Indsl. economist SRI Internat., Menlo Park, Calif., 1960-63; v.p. Icore Industries, Sunnyvale, Calif., 1963-67, pres., 1967-70; v.p. fin. Measurex Corp., Cupertino, Calif., 1970-74; prof. engring. mgmt. Stanford U., Calif., 1974-88, Ford prof., 1986-88, v.p. for devel., 1983-88; pres. Harvey Mudd Coll., Claremont, Calif., 1988—; bd. dirs. Finnigan Corp., San Jose, Sera Solar Corp., Santa Clara. Author: Accounting: A Survey, 1981, Managing High-Tech Companies, 1983; contbr. articles to Harvard Bus. Rev. Bd. dirs. Stanford Area council Boy Scouts Am., 1986-88, Palo Alto YMCA, 1977-79. Baker scholar Harvard Bus. Sch., Boston, 1959; recipient Gores Teaching award Stanford U., 1980. Mem. Phi Beta Kappa, Tau Beta Pi. Congregationalist. Club: Palo Alto. Office: Harvey Mudd Coll Kingston Hall 201 Claremont CA 91711

RIGHTER, GROVER PRESCOTT, computer systems engineer; b. Hampton, Va., May 29, 1956; s. Hall Twinning Righter and Josephine (Grover) Kidder; m. Sandra Jo Isle, Nov. 28, 1975; children: Courtney, Sean, Shannon. BS in Computer Sci., Brigham Young U., 1981. Pres. RMS, Inc., Salt Lake City, 1983-87; standards liaison Unisys, Salt Lake City, 1987-88; dir. hybrid systems Novell, Inc., Provo, Utah, 1988—. cons. Motorola Inc., Wasatch. With USCG, 1975-80. Mem. IEEE Computer Soc. Office: Novell Inc 122 East 1700 South Provo UT 84606

RIGNEY, JOHN SHANNON, retail executive; b. Jacksonville, Fla., Apr. 3, 1945; s. Thomas James Jr. and Catherine Adeline (Shannon) R.; m. Melinda Evans Mattis, June 24, 1967; children: Peter Dungan, Rebecca Catherine. BS in Psychology, Spring Hill Coll., Mobile, Ala., 1966; MS in Journalism, Northwestern U., 1970. Mgr. consumer rsch. CNA Ins., Chgo., 1970-76; mgr. mktg. rsch. Kraft Foods, Glenview, Ill., 1976-79; dir. mktg. rsch. Red Lobster Restaurants, Orlando, Fla., 1979-86; dir. mktg. svcs. Safeway Stores Inc., Oakland, Calif., 1986—. Mem. Am. Mktg. Assn. (pres. cen. Fla. chpt. 1982-83, v.p. Chgo. chpt. 1973-75). Home: 200 Lakeside Dr Oakland CA 94612 Office: Safeway Stores Inc Oakland CA 94660

RIGNEY, ROBERT BUFORD, county official; b. Long Beach, Calif., May 1, 1926; s. Harold Nevins and Nelly Amanda (Buford) R.; A.B., Stanford U., 1950; postgrad. Mexico City Coll., 1951, U. Redlands, Claremont, 1956, U. So. Calif., 1972; m. Lowenda May Morris, Dec. 21, 1952; children—Michael Owen, Jeffrey Owen. Sr. adminstrv. analyst, coordinator spl. dist. County of San Bernardino (Calif.), 1960-66, asst. county adminstrv. officer, 1966-73, 80, county adminstrv. officer, 1980—, adminstr., exec. officer Environ. Improvement Agy., 1973—; chmn. Nat. Acad. Scis. NRC Panel on Earthquake Estimation exec, officer San Bernardino County Redevel. Agy.; mem. Calif. Seismic Safety Com., chmn., 1977-78; mem. Governor's Earthquake Preparedness Task Force Steering Com., 1981-83, chmn. Long-Range Reconstruction and Recovery Com.; del. Governor's Commn. of Californians, 1980—, chmn. environ. com. 1985—; mem. Energy Resources Com., 1983; mem. County Relations with Cities Com., 1984; chmn. Infrastructure Fin. Com., 1984; chmn. Housing Land Use and Transp. Com., 1984; chmn. Peoples Republic of China/U.S. Construction Specialists Exchange Tour, 1978; chmn. Peoples Republic of China Local Govt. Exchange Tour, 1980; cons. U.S. Office of Sci. and Tech. Policy; bd. dirs. City-County Joint Powers Authority for a Greater San Bernardino, 1983—; chmn. program adv. bd. on public adminstr. Calif. State U., San Bernardino, 1983—; bd. dirs. Kimberly-Shirk Found.. Bd. dirs. Calif. Inland Empire council Boy Scouts Am. 1974-79, pres., 1983—; bd. dirs. Inland Empire Cultural Found., 1982—, Kimberly Shirk Found. Recipient 16 Achievement awards Nat. Assn. Counties, Silver Beaver award Boy Scouts Am., 1977, Community award Lighthouse for Blind, 1977. Teachers Hall of Fame, 1983; Community award Public Relations Soc. Am., 1979; govt. medal Shizuoka Prefecture, Japan, 1984; mem. County Supervisors Assn. of Calif., 1980—, League of Calif. Cities, Earthquake Engring. Research Inst., Nat. Assn. of Counties, Nat. Assn. County Adminstrs., Phi Alpha Theta, Phi Delta Kappa. Author publs. in field. Clubs: Native Sons of the Golden West, Rotary, Redlands Dance (pres.), Redlands Roundtable (pres. 1959—). Home: 1101 Cajon St Redlands CA 92373

RIGSBY, LARRY WAYNE, business owner; b. Moses Lake, Wash., Nov. 13, 1950; s. Floyd William and Frances Elizabeth (Womack) R.; m. Katie Reneé Copenhaver, Dec. 19, 1970; 1 child, Claudia Kay. Student, Wash. State U., 1969-70, Big Bend Community Coll., Moses Lake, Wash., 1970-71; BS in Bus. Mgmt., Ea. Wash. State U., 1974. Svc. technician Westlake Shell Svc., Moses Lake, 1967-69; salesperson Wendle Ford, Spokane, Wash., 1972; with Moses Lake Ford Sales, Inc., 1974—, gen. mgr., 1985-86, owner, 1987—; bd. dirs., co-owner Katie-Lynn, Ltd., Grand Turk Islands, 1988—. Mem. Together for Drug Free Communities, Moses Lake, 1989—. Mem. Lions (pres. Moses Lake chpt. 1983), Elks. Republican. Office: Moses Lake Ford Sales Inc 323 S Pioneer Way Moses Lake WA 98837

RILES, SUSANA KAY BARBER, educator, consultant; b. Berkeley, Calif., Nov. 16, 1947; d. Walter Carlisle and Katherine Marie (Bregler) B.; divorced; children: Ishmael Riles, Poyom Riles. BA in Speech, Drama, Stanford U., 1969. Cert. in early childhood edn. and adult edn., Calif. Tchr. Phoebe Hearst Pre-Sch., San Francisco, 1969-71; tchr. pre. sch. Sacramento Pub. Schs., 1971-73; tchr. trainer Compañeros del Barrio Pre-Sch., San Francisco, 1977-79; tchr. ESL Sequoia Adult Sch., Redwood City, Calif., 1980—; devel, tng. staff Dept. Edn., State Calif., San Francisco, 1984—, ESL Inst., Burlingame, Calif., 1985—. Bd. dirs. Compañeros del Barrio Family Ctr., San Francisco, 1980-84. Democrat. Home: 13290 Lenox Way Los Altos Hills CA 94022 Office: Sequoia Adult Sch Broadway/Brewster Redwood City CA 94062

RILES, WILSON CAMANZA, educational consultant; b. Alexandria, La., June 27, 1917; m. Mary Louise Phillips, Nov. 13, 1941; children: Michael, Narvia Riles Bostick, Wilson, Phillip. B.A., No. Ariz. U., 1940; M.A., 1947, LL.D., 1976; LL.D., Pepperdine Coll., 1965, Claremont Grad. Sch., 1972, U. So. Calif., 1975, U. Akron, 1976, Golden Gate U., 1981; L.H.D., St. Mary's Coll., 1971, U. Pacific, 1971, U. Judaism, 1972. Tchr. elem. schs., adminstr. pub. schs. Ariz., 1940-54; exec. sec. Pacific Coast region Fellowship of Reconciliation, Los Angeles, 1954-58; with Calif. Dept. Edn., 1958-83, dep. supt. pub. instrn., 1965-70, supt. pub. instruction, 1971-83; pres. Wilson Riles & Assocs., Inc.; dir. emeritus Wells Fargo Bank, Wells Fargo Co.; dir. Pacific Gas and Electric Co. Mem. editorial adv. bd.: Early Years mag. Ex-officio mem. bd. regents U. Calif., 1971-82; ex-officio trustee Calif. State Univs. and Colls., 1971-82; nat. adv. council Nat. Schs. Vol. Program; former mem. council Stanford Research Inst.; former mem. adv. council Stanford U. Sch. Bus.; former mem. adv. bd. Calif. Congress Parents and Tchrs.; former trustee Am. Coll. Testing Program; former mem. Edn. Commn. of States; past 2d v.p. Nat. PTA.; former trustee Found. Teaching Econs.; former mem. Joint Council Econ. Edn.; former mem. Nat. Council for Children and TV. With USAF, 1943-46. Recipient Spingarn medal NAACP, 1973. Mem. Assn. Calif. Sch. Adminstrs., Cleve. Conf., NAACP (Spingarn medal 1973), Nat. Acad. Pub. Adminstrn., Phi Beta Kappa. Office: Wilson Riles & Assocs Inc 555 Capitol Mall Ste 740 Sacramento CA 95814

RILEY, B. GRESHAM, college president; b. Jackson, Miss., June 27, 1938; married; 2 children. B.A., Baylor U., 1960; M.A., Yale U., 1963, Ph.D., 1965. Asst. instr. philosophy Yale U., 1963-64; from asst. prof. to assoc. prof. New Coll., 1965-75, acting provost, 1972-73, provost, 1973-75; prof. philosophy, dean faculty arts and sci. U. Richmond, 1975-81; pres. Colo. Coll., Colorado Springs, 1981—; younger scholar fellow Nat. Found. Arts and Humanities, 1968-69; vis. fellow Ctr. Advanced Studies Behavior Sci Stanford U., 1968-69; cons. Nat. Endowment for Humanities, 1971—; mem. adv. bd. Project Gen. Edn. Models, 1978-81. Contbr. articles to profl. jours. Bd. dirs. Ind. Coll. Fund of Colo., 1981—, Ind. Higher Edn. Colo., 1989—; chmn. selection com. Colo. Rhodes Scholarship, 1981-85; pres. bd. trustees, campaign chmn. Pikes Peak United Way, 1988. Mem. Nat. Assn. Ind. Colls. and Univs. (chair task force on nat. and community svc. 1988-89, mem. commn. on financing higher edn. 1988-89), Am. Philos. Assn., CS Peirce Soc., Soc. Values Higher Edn., Assn. Am. Colls. (oversight com., project on redefining the meaning and purpose of Baccalaureate degrees 1981-85), Commn. on Women in Higher Edn., Am. Council on Edn., North Cen. Assn. Assn. (cons., evaluator 1984—), Associated Colls. of the Midwest (bd. dirs. 1981—). Office: Colo Coll Office Pres Colorado Springs CO 80903

RILEY, DERRELL WAYNE, coal company executive; b. East St. Louis, Ill., Nov. 5, 1951; s. Elmo Martin and Wilma Irene (Hale) R.; m. Barbara Ann Milton, Apr. 15, 1972 (div. May 1985); children: Jonathan, Lauren; m. Dianne Carol Arp Stricker, June 22, 1985; stepchildren: Jeremy Stricker, Nathan Stricker. BSBA, So. Ill. U., Edwardsville, 1979. Constrn. clerk Peabody Coal Co., St. Louis, 1979-80, constrn. auditor, 1980-82, office mgr., 1982-83; acctg. mgr. N. Antelope Coal subs. Peabody Holding Co., Gillette, Wyo., 1983-85; materials mgr. Powder River Coal subs. Peabody Holding Co., Gillette, Wyo., 1985—; advisor and instr. materials mgmt. assocs. art program Sheridan Coll., Gillette. Served with U.S. Army, 1970-73. Mem. Purchasing Mgmt. Assn. Wyo. (bd. dirs., dir. at large 1986-87, pres. 1987-88, dir. nat. affairs, 1988—). Office: Powder River Coal PO Box 3034 Gillette WY 82717

RILEY, JACQUELINE ANN, real estate broker; b. Shamokin, Pa., June 16, 1935; d. Michael and Helen V. (Kurtz) B.; m. Vincent Joseph Riley, Aug. 17, 1957; children: Mark V., Kevin M., Thomas P., Joann M. Student, U. Buffalo, 1954-55, Bryant and Stratton Bus. Sch., 1956. Cert. residential specialist, real estate appraiser. Realtor Carl Erickson & Assoc., Phoenix, 1971-73; realtor/broker Realty Execs., Phoenix, 1973—. Mem. Ariz. Assn. Realtors, Phoenix Bd. Realtors (pres. roundtable 1975, 76), Realtors Nat. Mktg. Inst. of Nat. Assn. Realtors. Republican. Roman Catholic. Clubs: St. Paul's Women's (Phoenix), Moon Valley Country, Moon Valley Country Women's Golf Assn., Moon Valley Women's.

RILEY, KENNETH GENE, oil company executive; b. Rolla, Mo., Nov. 20, 1935; s. Lee Elmer and Marietta (Eddy) R.; m. Erika Anne Borchers, June 5, 1965; children: Cynthia E., Donna M. BS ChemE, U. Mo., Rolla, 1956. V.p. Sinclair Venezuelan Oil Co., Caracas, 1968-70; mgr. crude supply Atlantic Richfield Co., Los Angeles, 1972-76; v.p. ARCO Products Co., Los Angeles, 1977—. Mem. San Marino (Calif.) City Club, 1972—. Republican. Presbyterian. Club: Jonathan (Los Angeles). Home: 3390 Monterey Rd San Marino CA 91108 Office: ARCO Products Co 515 S Flower St Los Angeles CA 90071

RILEY, PATRICK JAMES, professional basketball coach; b. Rome, N.Y., Mar. 20, 1945; s. Leon R.; m. Chris Riley. Grad., U. Ky., 1967. Guard San Diego Rockets, 1967-70; guard Los Angeles Lakers, 1970-75, asst. coach, 1979-81, head coach, 1981—; guard Phoenix Suns, 1975-76; broadcaster Los Angeles Lakers games Sta. KLAC and Sta. KHJ-TV, Los Angeles, 1977-79; player NBA Championship Team, 1972, coach, 1982, 85, 87, 88. Office: care Los Angeles Lakers PO Box 10 Inglewood CA 90306 *

RILLING, FLORA JEANE, software engineer; b. OshKosh, Wis., July 31, 1944; d. Walter Miles and Dorothy May (Eggelston) R.; m. Patrick William Daugherty, June 21, 1964 (div.). AA in Computer Programming, Pierce Coll., 1983. Trainee micro welder Litton Guidance & Control Co., Woodland Hills, Calif., 1963-69, software programmer, 1978-84, software quality engr., 1984-. Mem. NAFE.

RIMOIN, DAVID LAWRENCE, physician, geneticist; b. Montreal, Que., Can., Nov. 9, 1936; s. Michael and Fay (Lecker) R.; m. Mary Ann Singleton, Sept. 9, 1962 (div. 1979); 1 dau., Anne; m. Ann Piilani Garber, July 27, 1980; children: Michael, Lauren. BSc, McGill U., Montreal, 1957, MSc, MD, CM, 1961; PhD, Johns Hopkins U., 1967. Asst. prof. medicine, pediatrics Washington U., St. Louis, 1967-70; assoc. prof. medicine, pediatrics UCLA, 1970-73, prof., 1973—, chief med. genetics, Harbor-UCLA Med. Ctr., 1970-86; dir. dept. pediatrics, dir. Med. Genetics and Birth Defects Ctr., Cedars Sinai Med. Ctr., 1986—. Co-author: Principles and Practice of Medical Genetics, 1983; contbr. articles to profl. jours., chpts. to books. Recipient Ross Outstanding Young Investigator award Western Soc. Pediatric Research, 1976, E. Mead Johnson award Am. Acad. Pediatrics, 1976. Fellow ACP; mem. Am. Fedn. Clin. Research (sec./treas. 1972-75), Western Soc. Clin. Research (pres. 1978), Am. Bd. Med. Genetics (pres. 1979-83), Am. Soc. Human Genetics (pres. 1984), Am. Pediatric Soc., Soc. Pediatric Research, Am. Soc. Clin. Investigator, Assn. Am. Physicians. Home: 512 N Palm Dr Beverly Hills CA 90210 Office: Cedars-Sinai Med Ctr 8700 Beverly Blvd Box 48750 Los Angeles CA 90048

RINALDO, JEFFREY ALLEN, communications company executive; b. Sterling, Colo., June 24, 1955; s. Marion and Elizabeth Jane (Collins) R. AS cum laude, Casper Coll., 1975. Instr. credential, Calif. Communications technician Two Way Radio Svc., Inc., Casper, Wyo., 1975-78, 84, portable products specialist, 1980-81; systems technician Custom Radio, Inc., Casper, 1979-80, svc. mgr., 1984-86; field tech. rep. Automation & Electronics, Casper, 1981-83; supr. test dept. TPL Communications, Inc., L.A., 1987; instr. communications L.A. Trade-Tech. Coll., 1987-88; communications mgr. V.C. Telecommunication Systems, Big Bear Lake, Calif., 1988—; communications cons. Haymaker & Assocs.-Larry Brown, Casper, 1984-86, 4 JV Enterprises, Big Bear Lake, 1988—. Spl. dep. Natrona County Sheriff's Dept., Casper, 1979-82. Mem. Police Marksman Assn. (life), NRA (life), Rotary (treas. Casper 1973), Phi Theta Kappa. Home: 658 Elm St Box 6057 Big Bear Lake CA 92315 Office: VC Telecommunications 41947 Big Bear Blvd 16ll Big Bear Lake CA 92315

RINCON, DALE TIMOTHY, title insurance company executive; b. Pasadena, Calif., Apr. 6, 1971; s. Joe and Margaret (Escobedo) R.; m. Ann M. Grochalskis, Oct. 30, 1971; children: April, Yvonne. Student, UCLA, 1972-73. Salesman Calif. land Title Co., Universal City, Calif., 1975-78; owner Pasadena Escrow Co., 1978-82; salesman Ticor Title Ins., Newport Beach, Calif., 1982-87; pres. Stewart Title Co., Santa Ana, Calif., 1987—. Coach Ayso Soccer, Newport Beach, 1985, Bobby Sox Softball, Irvine, Calif., 1984. Republican. Roman Catholic. Home: 2301 Aralia St Newport Beach CA 92660 Office: Stewart Title Co 900 N Broadway Santa Ana CA 92701

RINEARSON, PETER MARK, journalist, author; b. Seattle, Aug. 4, 1954; s. Peter Morley and Jeannette Irene (Love) R. Student, U. Wash., 1972-78. Editor Sammamish Valley News, Redmond, Wash., 1975-76; reporter Seattle Times, 1976-78, govt. and polit. reporter, 1979-81, aerospace reporter, 1982-84, Asian corr., 1985-86. Author: Word Processing Power with Microsoft Word, 2d edit., 1986, 3d edit., 1989, Microsoft Word Style Sheets, 1987, Quick Reference Guide to Microscoft Word, 1988, 2d edit., 1989, Microsoft Word Companion Disk, 1989, 2nd edit., Microsoft Word Companion Disk, 1988-89. Recipient Spl. Paul Myhre award-series Penney-Mo. Newspaper awards, 1983, Disting. Writing award Am. Soc. Newspaper Editors, 1984, Pulitzer prize for feature writing, 1984, Lowell Thomas Travel Writing award, 1984, John Hancock award,1985, semi-finalist NASA Journalist-in-Space Project, 1986; U.S.-Japan Leadership Program fellow Japan Soc., 1988. Office: 219 1st Ave N #410 Seattle WA 98109

RINEHART, CAROLYN COKER, writer, editor; b. Athens, Tex., Dec. 7, 1942; d. Garland and Willie Belle (Blythe) Coker; m. Robert P. Rinehart, July 4, 1964; 1 child, Roberta. BJ, U. Tex., 1964. State co-editor The Missoulian, Missoula, Mont., 1974-77; reporter Anchorage (Alaska) Times, 1977-80; edn. writer Am. Statesman, Austin, Tex., 1980-82; writer, editor U.S. Army Corps of Engrs., Anchorage, 1984—. Mem. Alaska Press Women (pres. 1985-87). Democrat. Methodist. Office: US Army Corps of Engrs PO Box 898 Anchorage AK 99506-0898

RINEHART, CHARLES R., finance company executive; b. San Francisco, Jan. 31, 1947; s. Robert Eugene and Rita Mary Rinehart; married; children: Joseph B., Kimberly D., Michael P., Scott. BS, U. San Francisco, 1968. Exec. v.p. Fireman's Fund Ins. Cos., Novato, Calif., 1969-83; pres., chief exec. officer Avco Fin. Services, Irvine, Calif., 1983—, also bd. dirs. Served to 2d lt. U.S. Army, 1968-69. Fellow Casualty Actuarial Soc.; mem. Am. Mgmt. Assn., Am. Acad. Actuaries, Young Pres. Orgn. (Calif. Coast chpt.). Repubican. Roman Catholic. Office: Avco Fin Svcs Inc 3349 Michelson Dr Irvine CA 92715-1606

RINEHART, LARRY, electronics engineer; b. Columbus, Ohio, Sept. 7, 1954; s. Charles Edward and Angeline (Santuomo) R.; m. Suzanne Marie Unangst, Apr. 28, 1984; 1 child, Gabrielle Maleen. BEE, U. Calif., Berkeley, 1976, postgrad., 1976-78. Design engr. Serata Geomechanics, Berkeley, 1976-78; with res. and devel. labs. Hewlett Packard, Santa Rosa, Calif., 1978-82; sr. engr. Compumotor Corp., Petaluma, Calif., 1982-85; cons. Intelligence in Motion, Oakland, Calif., 1985-86; program mgr. IXYS Corp., San Jose, Calif., 1986—; cons. in field, 1985—. Contbr. articles to profl. jours. Office: IXYS Corp 2355 Zanker Rd San Jose CA 95131

RING, JAMIE CHILDS, library assistant; b. Bismarck, N.D., July 30, 1939; d. James Lucian and Madeline Elizabeth (Cordner) Childs; m. Thomas Allen Ring, July 24, 1965; children: David Allen, Susan Elizabeth. BS in Edn., Mont. State U., 1961, postgrad., 1962; postgrad., U. Mont., 1963, U. Wyo., 1979, 82. Instr. Helena (Mont.) Pub. Schs., 1961-64, Billings (Mont.) Pub. Schs., 1964-65; payroll clk. U. Mont. Food Services, Missoula, 1965-66; instr. Missoula Pub. Schs., 1966-67; substitute tchr. Casper (Wyo.) Pub. Schs., 1970-80; catalogue asst. Casper Coll. Libr., 1980-86, history specialist, 1986—. Author: (pamphlets) Women and Credit, 1982, Child Care, 1988. Chairwoman State Adv. Commn. to U.S. Commn. on Civil Rights,m 1979-83; youth coord. First United Meth. Ch., 1988—. Mem. Wyo. Libr. Assn. (bd. dirs.), Mountain Plains Libr. Assn., Calif. Soc. Archivists, LWV, AAUW (sec. 1973, v.p. 1974), Wyo. Commn. for Women (chmn. 1981-83, chmn. for child care com. 1985—), Natrona County Hist. Soc., Natrona County Historis Preservation Commn., Oreg.-Calif. Trail Assn. Republican. Home: 520 Parkview Dr Casper WY 82609 Office: Goodstein Found Libr 125 College Dr Casper WY 82601

RING, RAYMOND HENRY, freelance novelist; b. Glendale, Calif., Oct. 2, 1949; s. Raymond Henry Sr. and Kathryn Moore R.; m. Linda Ellen Platts, Apr. 28, 1984: 1 child, Molly Dutcher. Student, Pa. State U., 1966-68, So. Ill. U., 1968-69, U. Ill., 1969-70, Gov.'s State U., 1973-74; BS in Journalism, U. Colo., 1979. Reporter Denver Post, 1979; news editor Tucson Weekly News, 1979-80; reporter, columnist Ariz. Daily Star, Tucson, 1980-85; freelance writer Tucson, 1985—. Author: (novel) Telluride Smile, 1988; columnist Boondocks News, 1986-88; contbr. articles to jours., mags. Recipient Disting. Investigative Reporting Scroll Investigative Reporters & Editors Assn., Columbia, Mo., 1982, ABA Gavel Awards, Chgo., 1982. Mem. Ariz. Press Club (Journalist of Yr. 1984, v.p. 1985). Home and Office: 2855 W Tippecanoe Trail Tucson AZ 85745

RINGE, ROBERT ALAN, theatrical manager; b. Bklyn., Aug. 25, 1946; s. William and Honey (Friedman) R. Grad. high sch., Oceanside, N.Y. Agent C.M.A., N.Y.C., 1968-70; co-head A&R, RCA Records, N.Y.C., 1970-72; agent William Morris Agy., London, 1972-81; v.p. Upstart Mgmt., L.A., 1982-84; agent Agy. for the Performing Arts, L.A., 1984-86; co-founder Rissky Bus. Agy., L.A., 1986-87; agt. Variety Artist Inc., L.A., 1988—; owner Vault Mgmt., Inc., Hollywood, Calif., 1989—; speaker U. S. Calif., Los Angeles, 1989—. With USN, 1963-67. Recipient Outstanding Service Citation Police Athletic League, 1968, Gold Record Producer award RCA Records, 1975, Gold Record Mgr. CBS Records, 1977. Mem. Big Brother Am. Home: 5516 Matilija Ave Van Nuys CA 91401

RINGERT, WILLIAM FREDERICK, lawyer, state senator; b. Castleford, Idaho, June 1, 1932; s. Frederick William and Elizabeth (Knypstra) R.; m. Lynne Bing Kutchback, Mar. 20, 1959; children—John Franklin, Beth Anne. BS in Agronomy, U. Idaho, 1953; postgrad. San Angelo (Tex.) Coll., 1955; LLB, So. Meth. U., Dallas, 1962. Bar: Idaho 1962, U.S. Dist. Ct. Idaho, 1962, U.S. Ct. Appeals (9th cir.) 1978, U.S. Supreme Ct. 1979. Flight engr. Braniff Internat. Airways, Dallas, 1956-62; ptnr. Ringert, Clark, Harrington, Reid, Christenson & Kaufman, Ctd., Boise, 1962—; sec., dir. Farm Devel. Corp., Boise, 1964—, Grindstone Butte Mut. Canal Co., Boise, 1972—; pres., dir. B & B Farms, Inc., Boise, 1973—; mem. Idaho Senate, 1982-88; commr. Idaho State Building Authority, 1985-88, water policy com. Western Legis. Conf, 1986-88. 1st lt. USAF, 1953-56. Mem. ABA (vice chmn. agrl. law com. gen. practice sect. 1979—), Idaho Bar Assn. (governing coun. water law sect. 1988—, Delta Theta Phi, Crane Creek Country Club, Elks. Republican. Methodist. Office: 599 W Bannock St Boise ID 83702

RINNERT, HENRY JOSEPH, civil engineer; b. Columbus, Ohio, May 11, 1937; s. Henry Lewis and Gertrude Erminie (Hoagland) R.; m. Sharon Lee Flesher, Sept. 14, 1960 (div. 1978); children: Stacey Ann, Robin Leeann; m. Ann Eiko Kirihara, June 20, 1981; children: Lance Doiguchi, Lee Ann Doiguchi. BS, U.S. Naval Acad., 1960; BCE, U. Colo., 1965, MCE, 1966. Registered profl. engr., Hawaii; lic. realtor, Calif. Commn. ensign U.S. Navy, 1960, advanced through grades to capt., 1967; officer-in-charge contrn. Republic of Vietnam, 1966-67; officer Naval Support Activity, Republic of Vietnam, 1971-72; comdr.-in-chief U.S. Pacific Fleet, Pearl Harbor, Hawaii, 1972-74; commanding officer Chief of Staff Base Support and Logisitics, Comdr. U.S. Navy, Marianas, Guam, USA, 1978-84; ret. U.S. Navy, 1986; resident engr. R.M. Towill Corp., Honolulu, 1986-88; pres. Keahole Assoc. Inc., Honolulu, 1988—; lectr., civil engr., constrn. mgmt. U. Hawaii, 1986—. Scout master Boy Scouts Am., Honolulu, 1978-81; chmn. golf adv. bd. of Navy/Marine Golf Courses, Honolulu, 1985-86. Decorated Navy Meritorious Svc. medal (3), Navy Legion of Merit medal, Navy Commednation award with Combat V. Mem. Soc. Am. Mil. Engrs., Nat. Soc. Profl. Engrs. (chmn. state Math Counts 1987-88, treas. 1987-88, sec. 1988-89), Water Pollution Control Fedn. (sec.), Rotary. Home: 98-1023 Kupukupu Pl Aiea HI 96701 Office: Keahole Assocs Inc 420 Waiakamico Rd Ste 411B Honolulu HI 96817-4941

RINSCH, MARYANN ELIZABETH, occupational therapist; b. L.A., Aug. 8, 1939; d. Harry William and Thora Analine (Langlie) Hitchcock; m. Charles Emil Rinsch, June 18, 1964; children: Christopher, Daniel, Carl. BS, U. Minn., 1961. Registered occupational therapist, Calif. Staff occupational therapist Hastings (Minn.) State Hosp., 1961-62, Neuropsychiat. Inst., L.A., 1962-64; staff and sr. occupational therapist Calif. Children's Svcs., L.A., 1964-66, head occupational therapist, 1966-68; researcher A. Jean Ayres, U. So. Calif., L.A., 1968-69; pvt. practice neurodevel. and sensory integraton Tarzana, Calif., 1969-74; pvt. practice occupational therapy Tarzana, 1989—. Mem. alliance bd. Natural History Mus., L.A. County, 1983-86; cub scouts den mother Boy Scouts Am., Sherman Oaks, Calif., 1986-88; project chmn. Vol. League San Fernando Valley, Van Nuys, Calif., 1986—; trustee Viewpoint Sch., Calabasas, Calif., 1961—. Mem. Nat. Occupational Therapy Assn., Calif. Occupational Therapy Assn. Home: 19849 Greenbriar Dr Tarzana CA 91356

RIORDAN, CAROL CAMPBELL, producer; b. Fresno, Calif., May 15, 1946; d. Alexander Boyle and Jeanne Carol (Yarnell) Campbell; m. Samuel Gresham Riordan, May 27, 1966; children; Loren Jeremy, Rachel Elisabeth. AA, San Diego City Coll., 1976; BA, Union for Experimenting Colls. and Univs., 1986; postgrad., San Diego State U. Instr., dir. San Diego Jr. Theatre, 1966-68, Actor's Lab., San Francisco, 1963-66; costume designer Playhouse Interplayers Theatres, San Francisco, 1966-68, Stage 7 Dance Theater, San Diego, 1981-83; producer TV edn. County Edn. Office, San Diego, 1974-76; producer, dir. Community Video Ctr., San Diego, 1976-78, program mgr., 1978-79; designer-in-residence Three's Co. and Dancers, San Diego, 1976-89, also bd. dirs., 1981; media producer TV San Diego State U., 1982—; cons. in field;. Producer, dir. TV, Poems of Wonder and Magic, 1986 (Emmy award 1987, Best of Western Ednl. Soc. Telecommunicaitons 1986 ITVA Excellence award 1986), The Fearless Vampire Dressers, 1984 (Best of Western Ednl. Soc. Telecommunications 1985); author (with others) Framework & Instructional Units for Teaching CCTV, 1980. Calif. Coun. Humanities grantee, 1988, N. County Community TV Found. grantee, 1985. Mem. Women in Film, Nat. Acad. TV Arts and Scis. (bd. govs. San Diego chpt. 1989—, Internat. TV Assn. (San Diego chpt. Merit award 1986), Sierra (com. mem. 1982), Environ. Def. Fund., Greenpeace Internat. Zen Buddhist. Office: San Diego State U Media Tech Svcs San Diego CA 92182-0524

RIORDAN, MARY MARGUERITE, department chairperson; b. Bakersfield, Calif., Sept. 13, 1931; d. John J. and Genevieve (McNulty) R. AA, San Francisco Coll. for Women, 1951, AB, 1953; MA, San Francisco State U., 1961; postgrad., U. Calif., Berkeley, Yale U., Columbia U. Cert. tchr. Tchr. English and history Presentation High Sch., San Francisco, 1953-56; tchr. English George Washington Hig Sch., San Francisco, 1956-62; chmn., prof. City Coll. San Francisco, 1963—; adj. prof. Emmanuel Coll., Boston, 1977-82; cons. in field, 1972-88. Author: Lillian Hellman, A Biblography: 1926-78; author, editor numerous poetry collections. Bd. dirs. Presentation High Sch., San Francisco, 1982-84, mem. adv. com., 1984-85; founding mem. Cath. Inter-racial Council, San Francisco, 1956. Recipient Coro Found. award, 1951, Yale Summer Shakespeare award, 1960; John Hay Green Found. fellow, 1959, NEH fellow, 1974. Mem. Modern Lang. Assn., Calif. Assn. Tchrs. of English, AAUW, U. Calif. Alumni Assn., The Hopkins Soc., The Wharton Soc. Democrat. Roman Catholic. Home: 215 Corbett San Francisco CA 94114 Office: City Coll San Francisco 50 Phelan San Francisco CA 94112

RIORDAN, PATRICK MICHAEL, retail food executive; b. Watsonville, Calif., Nov. 8, 1949; s. John Michael and Mary Jane (Farrell) R. Grad. high sch., Watsonville. Owner, sec. Moncs Consol. Products, Inc., Watsonville, 1970-75; owner, pres. The Riordan Co., Inc., Watsonville, 1975—; owner, v.p. New West Fruit Corp., Watsonville, 1985—, New West Cooling Co., Watsonville, 1987—; owner Western Plastic Container, Corona, Calif., 1987—. With USNG, 1969-75. Home: 51 Carol Way Aptoj CA 95003 Office: New West Fruit Corp 330 Industrial Ave Watsonville CA 95076

RIPINSKY-NAXON, MICHAEL, archaeologist, art historian; b. Kutaisi, USSR, Mar. 23, 1944; s. Pinkus and Maria (Kokielov) R.; div.; 1 son, Tariel. A.B. in Anthropology with honors, U. Calif.-Berkeley, 1966, Ph.D. in Archeology and Art History, 1979. Research asst. Am. Mus. Natural History, N.Y.C., 1964, U. Calif.-Berkeley, 1964-66; mem. faculty dept. anthropology and geography of Near East, Calif. State U.-Hayward, 1966-67; asst. prof. Calif. State U.-Northridge, 1974-75; researcher, assoc. UCLA, 1974-75, sr. research anthropologist Hebrew U., Hadassah Med. Sch., Jerusalem, 1970-71; curator Anthropos Gallery of Ancient Art, Beverly Hills, Calif., 1976-78; chief research scientist Archaeometric Data Labs., Beverly Hills, 1976-78; dir. Ancient Artworld Corp., Beverly Hills, 1979-82; conducted excavations Israel, Egypt, Jordan, Mesopotamia, Mexico, Cen. Am; specialist in the development of early religions, phenomenon of origins of domestication and camel ancestry; expert on art works from French Impressionists to ancient Egypt and classical world. Contbr. articles to sci. and scholarly jours. Recipient Cert. of Merit for Sci. Endeavour, Dictionary of Internat. Biography, 1974. Mem. Archaeol. Inst. Am. (life), Soc. for Am. Archaeology, Israel Exploration Soc., Am. Anthropol. Assn., Royal Anthropol. Inst., Am. Oriental Soc., Am. Geog. Soc., Am. Ethnol. Soc., History of Sci. Soc., Am. Chem. Soc., Soc. Archeol. Scis. (life), New England Appraisers Assns. Home: PO Box 2088 Cathedral City CA 92234

RIPLEY, ETHEL IRENE JACKSON, educator; b. Appleton, Wash.; d. Leonard Dean and Edna Irene (Robinson) Jackson; m. Robert Clayton Ripley, Jan. 1, 1960; children: Edward Duane, Suzan Irene Ripley Wright. AA, Mt. San Antonio Coll., 1973; BA, La Verne U., 1974; MS, Calif. State U., 1979. Cert. adult adn. tchr., secondary, elem., vocat. and bus. edn. tchr., computer resource and tchr. specialist, community coll. counselor, chief adminstr. inst., student personnel supr., Calif. Sec. Bonita Unified Sch. Dist., San Dimas, Calif., 1963-75; tchr. Bonita Unified Sch. Dist., San Dimas, 1975—, mentor tchr., 1984-86; tchr. Mt. San Antonio Coll., Walnut, Calif., 1982--. Officer Presbyn. Mariners, 1963-83; advisor at San Dimas High Sch. for Student Against Drunking Driving, Future Bus. Leader Am. Mem. Am. Vocat. Assn., NEA, Internat. Bus. Edn. Assn., Nat. Bus. Edn. Assn., Western Bus. Edn. Assn., Calif. Bus. Edn. Assn., Calif. Assn. Vocat. Edn., Calif. Tchrs. Assn., Bonita Unified Tchrs. Assn., Computer Users Educators, San Gabriel Valley Computer Users Educators, Mt. San Antonio Coll. Assocs., La Verne Coll. Accelerated Program for Adults Assocs. (charter), Safe Ride and Computer Club. Home: 3252 Robin Way Pomona CA 91767 Office: Bonia Unified Sch Dist 115 W Allen Ave San Dimas CA 91773

RIPLEY, STUART MCKINNON, real estate consultant; b. St. Louis, July 28, 1930; s. Rob Roy and Nina Pearl (Young) R.; B.A., U. Redlands, 1952; M.B.A., U. Calif., Berkeley, 1959; m. Marilyn Haerr MacDiarmid, Dec. 28, 1964; children—Jill, Bruce, Kent. Vice pres., dir. J.H. Hedrick & Co., Santa Barbara and San Diego, 1958-63; v.p. mktg. Cavanaugh Devel. Co., San Gabriel, Calif., 1963-65; v.p. mktg. dir. Calabasas Park, Bechtel Corp., Calabasas, Calif., 1967-69; v.p. mktg. Avco Community Developers, Inc., La Jolla, Calif., 1969-74; mktg. dir. U.S. Home Corp., Fla. Div., Clearwater, 1974-75; pres., dir. Howard's Camper Country, Inc., National City, Calif., 1975-77; v.p., mktg. dir. Valcas Internat. Corp., San Diego, 1976-77, pres., 1977-79; pres. Stuart M. Ripley, Inc., 1977—, Sunview Realty, Inc., a Watt Industries Co., Santa Monica, Calif., 1979-80; owner Everett Stunz Co., Ltd., La Jolla, 1981—; exec. v.p. Harriman-Ripley Co., Fallbrook, Calif.; avocado rancher, Fallbrook, 1978—; lectr. UCLA, 1961. Served with USN, 1952-55. U. Redlands fellow, 1960—. Mem. Nat. Assn. Homebuilders, Sales and Mktg. Council, Sales and Mktg. Execs., Pi Chi. Republican. Episcopalian. Club: Elks. Home: 13180 Portofino Dr Del Mar CA 92014 Office: 7644 Girard Ave La Jolla CA 92037

RIPPER, RITA JO (JODY RIPPER), financial executive; b. Goldfield, Iowa, May 8, 1950; d. Carl Phillip and Lucille Mae (Stewart) Ripper; B.A., U. Iowa, 1972; M.B.A., N.Y.U., 1978. Contracts and fin. staff Control Data Corp., Mpls., 1974-78; regional mgr. Raytheon Corp., Irvine, Calif., 1978-83; v.p. Caljo Corp., Des Moines, Iowa, 1983-84; asst. v.p. Bank of America, San Francisco, 1984—. Vol. and alt. del. Republican Party, Edina, Minn., N.Y.C., 1975—; vol. Cancer, Heart, Lung Assns., Edina, N.Y.C., Calif., 1974-78, 84—; Lita, 1986—. Mem. Internat. Mktg. Assn., World Trade Ctr. Assn., Acctg. Soc. (pres. 1975-76), Engring. Club of San Francisco, Mensa, Beta Alpha Psi (chmn. 1977-78), Phi Gamma Nu (v.p. 1971-72) Presbyterian. Clubs: Corinthian Yacht, Mt. Tamalpai Racquet. Home: 22 Marinero Circle #46 Tiburon CA 94920 Office: Bank of Am 2 Embarcadero Ctr San Francisco CA 94111

RIRIE, CRAIG MARTIN, periodontist; b. Lewiston, Utah, Apr. 17, 1943; s. Martin Clarence and VaLera (Dixon) R.; m. Becky Ann Ririe, Sept. 17, 1982; children: Paige, Seth, Theron, Kendall, Nathan, Derek, Brian, Amber, Kristen. AA, San Bernadino Valley Coll., 1966; DDS, Creighton U., 1972; MSD, Loma Linda U., 1978. Staff mem. Flagstaff (Ariz.) Med. Ctr., 1974—; pvt. practice dentistry specializing in periodontics Flagstaff, 1974—; assoc. prof. periodontics No. Ariz. U., Flagstaff, 1979—, chmn. dept. dental hygiene, 1980-81; med. research cons. W.L. Gore, Flagstaff, 1983—. Contbr. articles to profl. jours. Health professions scholarship Creighton U., Omaha, 1969-71; recipient Mosby award Mosby Pub. Co., 1972; research fellowship U. Bergen, Norway, 1978-79. Mem. ADA, Am. Acad. Periodontology (cert.), Western Soc. Periodontology (chmn. com. on research 1982—, bd. dirs. 1983—), No. Ariz. Dental Soc., Am. Acad. Oral Implantologists, Internat. Congress Oral Implantologists, Ariz. Dental Assn. Republican. Mormon. Lodge: Rotary. Home: 1320 N Aztec Flagstaff AZ 86001 Office: 1421 N Beaver Flagstaff AZ 86001

RISCH, JAMES E., lawyer; b. Milw., May 3, 1943; s. Elroy A. and Helen B. (Levi) R.; m. Vicki L. Choborda, June 8, 1968; children—James E., Jason S., Jordan D. B.S. in Forestry, U. Idaho, 1965, J.D., 1968. Dep. pros. atty. Ada County, Idaho, 1968-69, chief dep. pros. atty., 1969-70, pros. atty., 1971-75; mem. Idaho Senate, 1974-88, majority leader, 1977-82, pres. pro tem, 1983-88; ptnr. Risch Goss, Insinger & Salladay, Boise, Idaho, 1975—; prof. law Boise State U., 1972-75. Mem. ABA, Idaho Bar Assn., Boise Bar Assn., Am. Judicature Soc., Nat. Dist. Attys. Assn. (bd. dirs. 1977), Idaho Pros. Attys. Assn. (pres. 1976), Phi Delta Theta, Xi Sigma Pi. Republican. Roman Catholic. Home: 5400 S Cole Rd Boise ID 83709 Office: Risch Goss Insinger & Salladay 407 W Jefferson Boise ID 83702

RISDON, DAVID LYON, banker; b. Des Moines, Aug. 14, 1951; s. James Waldo and Evelyn Louise (Lyon) R.; m. Karen Ann Cree, Aug. 12, 1972. BA, Drake U., 1974, MBA, 1976. Acct. officer United Bank of Ariz., Phoenix, 1976-81; various mgmt. positions Security Pacific Mcht. Bank, L.A. and N.Y.C., 1981-88; mng. dir. mergers and acquisitions Security Pacific Merchant Bank, L.A., 1988—. Home: 337 St Joseph Long Beach CA 90814 Office: Security Pacif Mcht Bank 333 S Hope St H13-56 Los Angeles CA 90071

RISHER, PAUL D., travel industry executive; b. Huntington, W.Va., Oct. 21, 1935; s. Paul R. and Katherine E. (Estep) R.; m. Patricia Munro, Mar. 13, 1965; children: Nancy, Cameron. BSME, Duke U., 1957. Engr. Procter and Gamble, Cin., 1957-58; market mgr. Olin Corp., N.Y.C., 1958-65; cons. McKinsey and Co. Inc., N.Y.C., 1965-69; pres. Newburger, Loeb and Co. Inc., N.Y.C., 1971-75; pvt. practice in mgmt. Stamford, Conn., 1975—; pres. Panorama Air Tours, Honolulu, 1983—, also bd. dirs. Contbr. chpt. to book. Mem. Duke U. Gen. Alumni Assn., Ensign Class Assn. (commodore 1981-82, pres. 1987-88), Greenwich Cove Racing Assn. (commodore 1977-78), Indian Harbor Yacht Club, Waikiki Yacht Club. Home: 22 Pheasant Ln Stamford CT 06903 Office: Panorama Air 100 Kaulele Pl Honolulu HI 96819

RISKAS, HARRY JAMES, construction company executive; b. Shelton, Wis., Mar. 27, 1920; s. James and Anna (Pappeoanou) R.; student St. Mary's Naval Coll., 1941-43; m. Joan Evelyn Clark, Aug. 1, 1964; children—Lawrence, Douglas, Kimberly. Pres., Pacific Western Contractors, Inc., Millbrae, Cal., from 1951; pres., dir. Riskas Baker Riskas Devel. Corp., San Luis Properties, Inc.; pres., chmn. bd. Pacific Western Contractors, Inc., Sanfo-Bay Corp., H.J.R. Developers, Inc., Windrock Corp. Dir., Am. Properties, & Investment Fund, 1970. Lt. comdr. USNR, 1942-46. Mem. Young Pres.'s Orgn., Bankers Club, K.C. (San Francisco). Home: 237 Thatcher Ln Foster City CA 94404 Office: 1103 Juanita Ste B Burlingame CA 94010

RISSER, JAMES VAULX, JR., journalist, educator; b. Lincoln, Nebr., May 8, 1938; s. James Vaulx and Ella Caroline (Schacht) R.; m. Sandra Elizabeth Laaker, June 10, 1961; children: David James, John Daniel. B.A., U. Nebr., 1959, cert. in journalism, 1964; J.D., U. San Francisco, 1962. Bar: Nebr. bar 1962. Sole practice Lincoln, 1962-64; reporter Des Moines Register and Tribune, 1964-85, Washington corr., 1969-85, bur. chief, 1976-85; dir. John S. Knight fellowships for profl. journalists, prof. communication Stanford U., 1985—; lectr. Wells Coll., 1981; mem. com. on agrl. edn. in secondary schs. Nat. Acad. Scis., 1985-88. Profl. Journalism fellow Stanford U., 1973-74; recipient award for disting. reporting public affairs Am. Polit. Sci. Assn., 1969; Thomas L. Stokes award for environ. reporting Washington Journalism Center, 1971, 79; Pulitzer prize for nat. reporting, 1976, 79; Worth Bingham Found. prize for investigative reporting, 1976; Raymond Clapper Meml. Assn. award for Washington reporting, 1976, 78; Edward J. Meeman award for Conservation Reporting, 1985. Mem. Nebr. Bar Assn., Soc. Profl. Journalists (Disting. Service award 1976), Investigative Reporters and Editors Assn. Club: Gridiron. Home: 725 Evergreen St Menlo Park CA 94025 Office: Stanford U Communication Dept Stanford CA 94305

RISSO, JAY STUART, teacher; b. San Mateo, Calif., Apr. 7, 1940; s. Roland Joseph and Bernice C. (Senner) R.; m. Judith M. Ristrem, Dec. 16, 1961; children: Michael John, David James, Robin Sue. BA, San Jose State Coll., 1967. Cert. gen. secondary, life standard tchr., Calif.; cert. personnel cons. Secondary tchr., coach Amador Valley High Sch., Pleasanton, Calif., 1964—, athletic dir., 1987-88; salesman ROA Films, Milw., 1976-81; owner, personnel cons. Amador Valley Agy., Pleasanton, 1981-85. Mem. NEA, Calif. Tchrs. Assn., Valley Tchrs. Assn. (treas. 1987-89), Student Calif. Tchrs. Assn. (pres. 1961-62), Sunol Valley Men's Golf Club (Calif.). Republican. Roman Catholic. Home: 5577 Corte Sonora Pleasanton CA 94566 Office: Amador Valley High Sch 1155 Santa Rita Rd Pleasanton CA 94566

RISTOW, BRUNO VON BUETTNER, plastic surgeon; b. Brusque, Brazil, Oct. 18, 1940; came to U.S., 1967, naturalized, 1981; s. Arno and Ally Odette (von Buettner) R.; student Coll. Sinodal, Brazil, 1956-57, Coll. Julio de Castilhos, Brazil, 1957-58; M.D. magna cum laude, U. Brazil, 1966; m. Urania Carrasquilla Gutierrez, Nov. 10, 1979; children by previous marriage: Christian Kilian, Trevor Roland. Intern in surgery Hosp. dos Estrangeiros, Rio de Janeiro, Brazil, 1965, Hospital Estadual Miguel Couto, Brazil, 1965-66, Instituto Aposentadoria Pensão Comerciarios Hosp. for Gen. Surgery, 1966; resident in plastic and reconstructive surgery, Dr. Ivo Pitanguy Hosp. Santa Casa de Misericordia, Rio de Janeiro, 1967; fellow Inst. of Reconstructive Plastic Surgery, N.Y. U. Med. Center, N.Y.C., 1967-68, jr. resident, 1971-72, sr. and chief resident, 1972-73; practice medicine specializing in plastic surgery, Rio de Janeiro, 1967, N.Y.C., 1968-73, San Francisco, 1973—; asst. surgeon N.Y. Hosp., Cornell Med. Center, N.Y.C., 1968-71; clin. instr. surgery N.Y. U. Sch. of Medicine, 1972-73; chmn. plastic and reconstructive surgery div. Presbyn. Hosp., Pacific Med. Center, San Francisco, 1974—. Served with M.C., Brazilian Army Res., 1959-60. Decorated knight Venerable Order of St. Hubertus; Knight Order St. John of Jerusalem; fellow in surgery Cornell Med. Sch., 1968-71; diplomate Am. Bd. Plastic and Reconstructive Surgery. Fellow A.C.S., Internat. Coll. Surgeons; mem. Am. Soc. Aesthetic Plastic Surgery, Am. Soc. Plastic and Reconstructive Surgeons, Internat. Soc. Aesthetic Plastic Surgeons, Calif. Soc. Plastic Surgeons, AMA (Physician's Recognition award 1971-83), Calif. Med. Assn., San Francisco Med. Assn. Republican. Mem. Evang. Lutheran Ch. Club: San Francisco Olympic. Contbg. author: Cancer of the Hand, 1975; contbr. articles on plastic surgery to profl. publs. Office: Pacific Presbyn Med Bldg 2100 Webster St Ste 502 San Francisco CA 94115

RISTREM, FREDERICK JONATHAN, printing company executive; b. Oakland, Calif., Nov. 25, 1954; s. George Jr. and Mary Ann (Lantz) R. Student, Calif. Inst. tech., 1968-69, UCLA, 1971; MA, Kingman Coll., 1976. Owner, mgr. Victorian Restoration, Oakland, 1974-77; owner, mgr. drafting svc., San Francisco, 1974, Oakland, 1975-76; owner, mgr. Rustprints Ltd., Oakland, 1980—; salesman Tiffany's Lubricant Products, Dayton, Ohio, 1985--. Republican. Episcopalian. Home and Office: 1501 Alice St Oakland CA 94612

RITCHEY, SAMUEL DONLEY, JR., retired retail store executive; b. Derry Twp., Pa., July 16, 1933; s. Samuel Donley and Florence Catherine (Litsch) R.; m. Sharon Marie Anderson, Apr. 6, 1956; children: Michael Donley, Tamara Louise, Shawn Christopher. B.S., San Diego State U., 1955, M.S., 1963; postgrad., Stanford U., 1964. Store mgr. supermarkets Lucky Stores Inc., San Diego and Phoenix, 1957-61; store supr. Gemco div. Lucky Stores Inc., 1965-66, dist. mgr., 1966-68, nonfood mdse. mgr. parent co., 1968-69, div. mgr., v.p. parent co., 1969-72; sr. v.p. Lucky Stores Inc., Dublin, Calif., 1972-75; exec. v.p. Lucky Stores Inc., 1975-78, pres., chief operating officer, 1978-80, pres., chief exec. officer, 1980-81, chmn., chief exec. officer, 1981-85, chmn. bd., 1981-86; bd. dirs. Pacific Telesis, McClatchey Newspapers, De La Salle Inst., Mont LaSalle Vineyards, Calif. Tomorrow, Rosenberg, FDT, MALDEF; grad. mgr. San Diego State U., 1961-63; lectr. in field. Bd. dirs. Calif. Roundtable, Sloan Alumni Adv. Bd.; adv. coun. Grad. Sch. Bus. Stanford U. Sloan Found. fellow. Mem. Western Assn. Food Chains (dir., pres.), Food Mktg. Inst. (dir., vice chmn.). Office: 383 Diablo Rd Ste 100 Danville CA 94526

RITCHIE, CINDY LOU, health facility administrator; b. Big Spring, Tex., Nov. 22, 1955; d. Bob Lee and Peggy Jane (Stringfellow) Craig; m. Barry Ritchie, Dec. 27, 1980 (div. May 1985); 1 child, Jennifer Lyn Adams. AA in Media Tech., Pima Community Coll., 1981. Mktg. rep. Brochure Co., Tucson, Ariz., 1980-82; pres. Conglomeration Advt. and Pub. Rels., Tucson, 1982-85; community rels. coordinator Life Care Ctrs. Am., Scottsdale, Ariz., 1987-88; account exec. Haltom Recognition, Scottsdale, 1988—; publicity chmn. Scottsdale Health Coun., 1987—; account exec. Klute Communications, Scottsdale, 1989; pub. speaker. Contbr. articles to profl. jours. Mem. Area Coun. Aging, Phoenix, 1986-87. Recipient Contbn. to Fundraising award YWCA, Tucson, 1985. Mem. North Scottsdale Kiwanis Coub (del, bd. mem., mktg. dir. 1987-89), Soroptimist Club. Methodist.

RITCHIE, ERNEST LEROY, computer specialist, researcher; b. Vancouver, Wash., Sept. 14, 1953; s. LeRoy Eugene Ritchie and Phyllis Jean (Storm) Smith; m. Gloria Esther Rivera, May 9, 1974 (div. Sept. 1979); 1 child, Nathaniel Eric; m. Joyce Anne Guest, June 23, 1980; children: Mary Viola Bunce, Micheal Lynn Dower. BA in Psychology, Portland (Oreg.) State U., 1978; postgrad., Sheridan Coll., 1986—. Lic. psychologist. Strike coord. The Wakenhut Corp., various locations, 1976-80; gen. mgr. Sousa's Lock & Key, Gillette, Wyo., 1980-82; pres., chief exec. officer Tek Security Svcs., Gillette, 1982-87, cons., 1987—. Organizer Young Reps., Miami, Fla., 1974; leader Boy Scouts Am., 1977-79. With USCG, 1972-76; 2d lt. U.S. Army N.G., 1986. Mem. Security Cons. (bd. dirs. 1982-86), Wyo. Locksmiths Assn. (cons. 1980-87), Associated Locksmiths Am., Gillette C. of C., K.C., Elks. Roman Catholic. Home: 822 Aspen Ln Gillette WY 82716 Office: Tek Security Svc 822 Aspen Ln Gillette WY 82716

RITCHIE, JO ANN, city official; b. Miami, Fla., Aug. 6, 1946; d. Miller A.F. and Josephine (Barnett) R. BA, U. Redlands, 1968; MEd, U. Wash., 1973; postgrad., Seattle U., 1987. Mgr. student activities U. Wash., Seattle, 1968-76; asst. dean student affairs U. Calif., San Diego, 1976-77; budget analyst City of Seattle, 1978, dep. dir. policy planning, 1979; dir. adminstrv. svcs. Dept. Human Resources, 1980-82; dep. budget dir. King County, Seattle, 1982-84, mgr. housing and community devel., 1984-86; capital project coord. Metro Transit, Seattle, 1986—. Vice chmn. health svcs. allocation panel Seattle United Way; mem. Seattle Art Mus. Mem. AAUW. Democrat. Office: Metro Transit 821 2d Ave Seattle WA 98104

RITCHIE, JOHN BENNETT, real estate executive; b. West Point, N.Y., Sept. 23, 1924; s. Isaac and Charlotte (Bennett) R.; B.A., Yale, 1946; postgrad. student George Washington U., 1946-47, U. Wash. Law Sch., 1948-50; m. Suzanne Raisin, Dec. 27, 1952; children—Randolph, Charlotte, Mark, Victoria. Pres. Ritchie & Ritchie Corp., indsl. and comml. realtors, San Francisco, Oakland, San Jose, Calif., Ritchie & Ritchie Ins. Brokers, Inc.; v.p. Cotton-Ritchie Corp., San Diego, Ritchie MacFarland Corp., Portland, Oreg.; owner, trustee Ritchie-Chancery Bldg., Barrett-Ritchie Block, Ritchie & Ritchie Devel. Co., Ritchie Western Mortgage Corp., Ritchie Western Equities Co.; past mem. San Francisco Planning Commn.; past mem. San Francisco Landmarks Bd.; hon. counsul Uruguay. Served with AUS. Mem. Soc. Indsl. Realtors, Calif. Assn. of Realtors (v.p. 1967), San Francisco (pres. 1966), Oakland, San Jose real estate bds., San Francisco C. of C., Calif. Hist. Soc. (pres. 1973), Japan Soc. San Francisco (pres. 1976). Republican. Mem. Ch. of Jesus Christ of Latter-day Saints (elder). Clubs: Concordia Argonaut, Presidio Golf (San Francisco); Tahoe Yacht (Lake Tahoe); Athenian-Nile (Oakland, Calif.); Alta (Salt Lake City); Brook (N.Y.); Caledonian (London); Outrigger Canoe (Honolulu). Home: 2 Presidio Terr San Francisco CA 94118 also: 209 S Meadow Rd Glenbrook NV 89413 also: 989 Rutherford Cross Rd Rutherford CA 94573 Office: 41 Sutter St 200 Ritchie Chancery Bldg San Francisco CA 94612 also: 363 15th St Oakland CA 94612 also: 34 W Santa Clara St San Jose CA 95112 also: 233 A St Ste 1400 San Diego CA 92101 also: 133 SW 2d Ave Portland OR 97205

RITNER, RONALD JOSEPH, architectural designer; b. Belleville, N.J., May 8, 1958; s. Paul C. and Maureen (Murphy) R.; m. Barbara Lee Radtke, Aug. 15, 1987. Draftsman Don Edwards Architect, Newport Beach, Calif., 1978-79, L.W. Rylee Architect, Newport Beach, 1980-82, N.P.S. Design, Orange, Calif., 1982; job capt. S.B.E. Devel., Huntington Beach, Calif., 1982-83; project mgr. Robert Earl Architect, Irvine, Calif., 1983-86, Kober, Cedargreen, Rippon, Santa Ana, Calif., 1986-87, Thomas Maurer Assoc., Tustin, Calif., 1987—. Mem. AIA (assoc.). Republican. Lutheran. Home: 5051 Alton Pkwy 176 Irvine CA 92714

RITTENHOUSE, CARL HARRIS, psychologist; b. Garden City, S.D., Feb. 17, 1922; s. Carl Harris and Helen Alice (Doxrude) R.; m. Marilyn Jeanne Hawkins, Sept. 24, 1947; children—Eric Carl, Christine Amanda. B.A., Stanford U., 1947, M.A., 1949, Ph.D., 1951. Lic. psychologist, Calif. Research psychologist U.S. Air Force, Lowry AFB Colo., 1951-53; research scientist Human Resources, Monterey, Calif., 1953-58; head tng. group Philco Western Devel. Labs., Palo Alto, Calif., 1958-59; research psychologist Stanford Research Inst., 1959-66; asst. dir. edn. dept. SRI Internat. Menlo Park, Calif., 1966-78; cons. Oreg. Shakespeare Festival Assn., 1978-79; Rockwell-Patterson, Palo Alto, 1978-79; mng. ptnr. Roth-Kolker-Rittenhouse Assocs., 1979-82. Contbr. articles to profl. jours. Mem. Am Psychol. Assn., Phi Beta Kappa, Sigma Xi. Democrat. Lutheran.

RITTER, DALE WILLIAM, obstetrician, gynecologist; b. Jersey Shore, Pa., June 17, 1919; s. Lyman W. and Weltha (Packard) R.; m. Winnie Mae Bryant, Nov. 13, 1976; children—Eric, Lyman, Michael, Gwendolyn, Daniel. A.B., UCLA, 1942; M.D., U. So. Calif., 1946. Diplomate Am. Bd. Obstetrics and Gynecology. Intern, Los Angeles County Hosp., Los Angeles, 1945-46, resident, 1949-52, admitting room resident, 1948-52; practice medicine specializing in obstetrics and gynecology, Chico, Calif., 1953—; founder, mem. staff, past chmn. bd. dirs. Chico Community Meml. Hosp.; guest lectr. Chico State Coll., 1956—; mem. staffs Enole Hosp., Chico, 1952—, Glenn Gen. Hosp., Willows, Calif., 1953—, Gridley Meml. Hosp., Calif., 1953-80; spl. cons. obstetrics Calif. Dept. Pub. Health, No. Calif., 1958-70. Contbr. articles to med. and archeol. jours. Bd. dirs. No. dist. Children's Home Soc., Chico, 1954-70. Served with AUS, 1943-45, with M.C., AUS, 1946-48. Fellow ACS, Am. Coll. Obstetrics and Gynecology; mem. AMA, Calif. Med. Assn., Internat. Soc. Hypnosis, Am. Soc. Clin. Hypnosis, Am. Fertility Soc., Pacific Coast Fertility Soc., Soc. for Sci Study of Sex, Assn. Am. Physicians and Surgeons, Pvt. Doctors of Am., Butte-Glenn County Med. Soc. (past pres.), Am. Cancer Soc. (former bd. dirs. Butte County), AAAS, Christian Med. Soc., Am. Assn. Pro-Life Obstetricians and Gynecologists, Butte-Glenn County Tumor Bd., Anthrop. Assn. Am., Archaeol. Inst. Am., Soc. Calif.

Archaeology, Oreg. Archaeology Soc., Archeol. Survey Assn., Southwestern Anthrop. Soc., Oreg. Archaeol. Soc., Internat. Assn. for Study of Prehistoric and Ethnologic Religions, Fretted Instrument Guild Am. (dir. Banjo Kats 'n Jammers), North Valley Banjo Band, Am. Philatelic Soc., Am. Horse Council, Am. Horse Shows Assn., Internat. Peruvian Horse Assn., Assn. Owners Breeders Peruvian Paso Horses, Phi Chi, Lambda Sigma, Zeta Beta Sigma. Republican. Lodge: Rotary. Office: 572 Rio Lindo Chico CA 95926

RITTER, FRANCIS DUDLEY, private investigator; b. San Fernando, Calif., Oct. 13, 1943; s. John Joseph and Grace Dudley (Kirby) R.; m. Mary Eileen Fennell, Apr. 4,1964 (div. 1973); children: Michael Francis, Stephen James. BA, St. Edwards U., 1968. Ops. officer First Western Bank, L.A., 1965-68; dir. personnel and ops. Walston & Co., L.A., 1969-72; syndicate coord. Mitchum, Jones & Templeton, L.A., 1972-73; owner, mgr. Backtrack Unlimited Co., Huntington Beach, Calif., 1975—; prs. Backtrack Unlimited Tng. & Weapons Ctr., Huntington Beach, 1982—; instr., Regional Occupational Program, Orange County, Calif., 1976—, Calif. Community Colls., Orange County, 1986-87; asst. trainer women's anti-rape self def. program, Garden Grove (Calif.) Unified Sch. Dist. Adult Edn., 1980-83. Capt., squadron comdr., CAP, Long Beach, Calif., 1964-70. Recipient City of Hope award, Newport Beach, Calif., 1982. Mem. Nat. Assn. Legal Investigators, Nat. Trust Historic Preservation, Glen Eden Club, Mensa. Republican. Roman Catholic. Office: Backtrack Unlimited Co 18311 Patterson Ln Ste 3 Huntington Beach CA 92646

RITTER, RUSSELL JOSEPH, mayor, college official; b. Helena, Mont., July 22, 1932; s. Walter A. and Sally C. (Mellen) R.; m. Linaire Wells, Aug. 4, 1956; children—Michael, Leslie, Teresa, Gregory, Daniel. Student Carroll Coll., Helena, 1950-53; A.B. in History, U. Mont.-Missoula, 1957, M.A. in History and Polit. Sci., 1962, postgrad. in History, 1963. Salesman, Capital Ford, 1953-54, 56-57; tchr., coach Billings (Mont.) Central High Sch., 1957-58, Loyola High Sch., Missoula, 1958-62, Flathead High Sch., Kalispell, Mont., 1962-69; dir. devel. and community relations Carroll Coll., Helena, 1969-76, v.p. for coll. relations, 1976—; commr. City of Helena, 1977-80, mayor pro-tem, 1980, mayor, 1981—; exec. sec.-treas. Carroll Coll. Found., Inc.; owner Danny's Drive In, Kalispell, 1965-69; ptnr. R-B Enterprises, Inc., Kalispell, 1967-71; bd. dirs. Brubaker & Assos., Inc., Kalispell, 1971-74; v.p. Capital Investment, Inc. (KMTX Radio), Helena, 1973-80; pres. Swinging Door Art Gallery, Inc., Helena, 1973—. Bd. dirs. All Am. Indian Hall of Fame, 1972-78, Jr. Achievement, 1975-79, Mont. Physicians Service, 1984-86, Blue Cross/Blue Shield Mont., 1986—, Mont. C. of C., chmn., Mont. Community Fin. Corp., 1986; bd. govs. Montt. Spl. Olympics, 1984-86; mem. Citizen's Adv. Council, 1975-76; chmn. City-County Bldg., Inc., 1978; mem. Mont. Friendship Force; co-chmn. Mont. Centenial Celebration. Served with USMC, 1953-56. Mem. Helena C. of C. (dir. 1972-75, v.p. 1973, pres. 1974, Ambassador's Club 1976—, chmn. 1978), Mont. Ofcls. Assn., Mont. Ambassadors (Ambassador of Yr. 1986, bd. dirs. 1989, 2d v.p. 1989). Club: Montana. Lodge: K.C. (4th degree). Office: Carroll Coll Rm 258 Helena MT 59601

RITTMEISTER, RUTH, travel executive; b. Norway, Mar. 1, 1924; came to U.S., 1951; Asst. AEC, Oslo, Norway, 1945-49; assoc. Bob Burbank Travel, L.A., 1951-54; v.p., gen. mgr. Internat. Travel Svc., Honolulu, 1955-83; owner, pres. A Touch of Class Travel, Inc., Honolulu, 1984—; coord. internat. exhibits Kaliala Hilton, Honolulu, 1967-74. Contbr. articles on travel to various mags. Commr. Mayor's Commn. on Culture and Art, Honolulu, 1977-82; hon. consul of Norway for Hawaii, 1989—. Mem. Am. Soc. Travel Agts. (chmn. pub. rels. com. 1968-75), Inst. Cert. Travel Agts. (charter mem.), Pacific Asia Travel Assn., Friends of the East-West Ctr. Club: Century (charter mem.). Home: 1650 Ala Moana Blvd Honolulu HI 96815 Office: A Touch of Class Travel Inc 1585 Kapiolani Blvd Honolulu HI 96814

RITZA, BARBARA FOLLETTE, visual information specialist; b. Martinez, Calif., Apr. 28, 1928; d. Marley Vernon and Mazie Follette (Black) Greene; m. Kenneth Marcel, Dec. 16, 1976; children: Follette, Deron. AA, Ventura (Calif.) Coll., 1953; student, U. Calif., Santa Barbara, 1971-82. Dir. of exhibits and art dept. Ventura (Calif.) Library Systems, 1961-68; dir. graphic dept. Officers Sch., Civil Engr. Corps, Port Hueneme, Calif., 1970-76; dir. publs. and graphics Civil Engrs Support Office, Port Hueneme, Calif., 1976—; cons., evaluator Civil Svc. Artists Register, L.A., 1973-78; owner Barbara's Graphics World, Ventura, 1984-87. Mem. Interlab. Com. on Editing and Publ. Republican. Roman Catholic. Home: 225 Westminster Ave San Buenaventura CA 93003 Office: Civil Engr Support Office Naval Constrn Battalion Ctr Port Hueneme CA 93043

RIVERA, VICTOR MANUEL, retired bishop; b. Penuelas, P.R., Oct. 30, 1916; s. Victor and Filomena (Toro) R.; m. Barbara Ross Starbuck, Dec. 1944; 3 children. Student, Modern Bus. Coll. P.R., 1937, DuBose Meml. Ch. Tng. Sch., 1938; B.D., Ch. Div. Sch. Pacific, 1944, D.D., 1965; postgrad., St. Augustine Coll., Eng., 1957. Ordained deacon Episcopal Ch., 1943, priest, 1944; curate St. John's Cathedral, Santurce, P.R., 1944-45; rector St. Paul's Ch., Visalia, Calif., 1945-68; consecrated bishop San Joaquin, Fresno, Calif., 1968-88.

RIVERA, WILLIAM XAVIER, architect; b. L.A., Nov. 14, 1959; s. Guillermo and Lolita (Ormaza) R. AA, Santa Barbara (Calif.) Community Coll., 1983; BArch, Calif. Polytech., 1987; postgrad., Ecoles D'Art Americaines-Beau Arts, Fontainbleau, France, 1986. Archtl. draftsman Lenvik & Minor, Architects, Santa Barbara, Calif., 1977-78, Ketzel & Goodman, Architects, Santa Barbara, 1978-79, Designworks Architects, Santa Barbara, 1980-83, James J. Zimmerman, Architect, Santa Barbara, 1984; drafter, designer Mahan & Lenny, Architects; tchr. U. Calif., Santa Barbara, 1987--; with design devel. and custom residential div. Barry A. Berkus, Architects, 1988--. Recipient 3d Place award Indsl. Edn. Expn. Calif. State Fair, 1978. Mem. AIA (assoc.), Design Village. Republican. Home: 510 Meigs Rd Santa Barbara CA 93109

RIVERMAN, RYLLA CLAIRE, health association administrator; b. Brewster, Wash., Apr. 16, 1955; d. Francis William and Helen Edna (Caldwell) Hicks; m. Brian Matthew Riverman, Nov. 2, 1985. BS in Nursing, Walla Walla Coll., 1978. RN. Nurse Portland (Oreg.) Adventist Med. Ctr., 1978-80; dir. pub. affairs Seaside (Oreg.) Gen. Hosp., 1980-82; pub. affairs assoc. Providence Child Ctr., Portland, 1982-83; utilization rev. coordinator St. Vincent Hosp., Portland, 1983-88; dir. internal ops. Metrocare Adminstrv. Svcs., 1988—; lectr. Portland Community Coll., 1983—, Walla Walla Coll., 1983-85, 87, Portland Bus. Group on Health, 1987. Contbr. articles to profl. jours. Mem. Pacific St. Neighbor Watch, Portland, 1986—, Mansfield (Wash.) Grange # 883, 1976—, World Forestry Ctr., Portland, 1986—; chairperson employee fundraising United Way, 1986-87. Recipient Merit award St. Vincent Med. Found., Portland, 1986, U.S. flag for community service, U.S. Senate, Washington, 1982. Mem. NW Healthcare Roundtable (v.p. 1984-85, pres. 1985-87, bd. dirs. 1987—, Merit award 1983), Arch Cape (Oreg.) Country. Republican. Home: 6335 NE Pacific Portland OR 97213 Office: St Vincent Hosp & Med Ctr 9205 SW Barnes Rd Portland OR 97225

RIVERS, HELENE, freelance writer; b. San Francisco, July 14, 1916; d. Walter Allen and Eva (Graff) R. BA, U. Calif., Berkeley, 1938. Copy girl San Francisco Chronicle, 1942-43, reporter women's pages, 1943-53, editor, 1953-1956; writer, editor — This World, 1956-82; freelance writer book sect. 1982—. Recipient Black Cat trophy San Francisco Press Club, 1976. Mem. San Francisco-Oakland Newspaper Guild, Media Alliance, Mechanics Libr. (life), AAUW. Marin Soc. Artists, Calif. Tennis Club (past editor). Democrat. Home: 368 Via Hidalgo Greenbrae CA 94904

RIVIECCIO, NICHOLAS JERRY, military officer; b. N.Y.C., July 15, 1964; s. Ciro Jerry and Rafaela (Ramirez) R. B in Engring., Manhattan Coll., 1986. Registered profl. engr. Calif. Commd. 2d lt. USAF, 1986, advanced through grades to 1st lt., 1988; rsch. asst. Langley Rsch. Ctr. NASA USAF, Hampton, Va., 1986; engring. project officer Ballistic Systems div. USAF, Norton AFB, Calif., 1987—. Creator model rockets, radio-controlled glider, nat. champion, 1981, free-flight glider, U.S. record, 1981; contbr. articles to Model Rocketeer. Mem. ASME, Nat. Assn. Rocketry, Tau Beta Pi, Pi Tau Sigma, Epsilon Sigma Pi. Roman Catholic. Home: 1400 Barton Rd #1116 Redlands CA 92373

RIVIERA, DANIEL JOHN, lawyer; b. N.Y.C., May 28, 1927; s. Charles Adrian and Ruth Blanche (Sinclair) R.; B.A. cum laude, Syracuse U., 1950; LL.B., Georgetown U., 1953; children—Daniel C., Sara J., Jeffrey, Gloria, Spencer. Bar: Wash. 1953, Idaho 1981. Practiced in Seattle, 1953—; mem. firm Foster, Pepper & Riviera, Seattle, 1953—, ptnr., 1968—. Instr. bus. law U. Wash., 1957-59, Journalism law Seattle U., 1965-67, 75-77; mem. Statute Law Com., 1963-72; mem. Bench, Bar, Press Com., 1964-72. Mem. Mercer Island City Council, 1961-68; bd. visitors J. Reuben Clark Law Sch., Brigham Young U., Provo, Utah, 1978-80. Served with AUS, 1946-47. Mem. ABA (vice-chmn. projects com. jr. bar conf. 1959-60), Wash. State Bar Assn. (mem. subcom. of local adminstrv. com. 1967-70), Seattle-King County Bar Assn. (labor law com. 1967—). Clubs: Bellevue (Wash.) Athletic; Harbor (Seattle). Home: 4818 102nd Ln NE Kirkland WA 98101 Office: 1111 Third Ave Bldg Seattle WA 98101

RIZVI, TANZEEM RAFIQ, electrical engineer; b. Lahore, Pakistan, July 9, 1949; came to U.S., 1975; s. Syed Rafiq Hassan and Haseena Rizvi; m. Hiza Sardar, Feb. 9, 1982; 1 child, Shan. BSEE, U. Peshawar, Pakistan, 1970; MSEE, U. So. Calif., 1977. Registered profl. engr., Calif., Alaska. Asst. exec. engr. Karachi (Pakistan) Electric Supply Corp., 1971-75; field designer Fischback and Moore Inc., L.A., 1975-77; project engr. Crews MacInnes and Hoffman/Vitro Inc., Anchorage, 1977-80; contract employee, project group, project mgr., lead engr., facilities engr. Standard Oil Co. Inc., Anchorage, 1980-85; project mgr. Alaska Power Authority, Anchorage, 1985-88, Donald Dickerson Assocs., Panorama City, Calif., 1988—. Mem. IEEE (chmn. Alaska sect. 1980-81, mem. nat. engrs. week edn. com. 1986), Alaska Profl. Design Council (bd. dirs. 1979-81), Nat. Soc. Profl. Engrs., Power Engrs. Soc., Communication Soc., Nordic Ski Club, Bridge Club. Home and Office: PO Box 4112 West Hills CA 91308

RIZZUTO, CARMELA RITA, nursing administrator; b. Waterbury, Conn., Aug. 26, 1942; d. Joseph Anthony and Carmella Rose R.; m. Thomas Lee Chernesky, Aug. 28, 1982. BS, St. Joseph Coll., 1965; MS, Boston Coll., 1971; EdD, Sch. Edn., UCLA, 1983. RN, Calif. Nursing instr. Samaritan Hosp. Sch. Nursing, Troy, N.Y., 1969; med. nursing coord., clin. specialist Harvard Community Health Plan, Boston, 1971-72; instr. inservice edn. Tufts-New Eng. Med. Ctr., Boston, 1972-73; instr. inservice edn. St. John's Hosp. and Health Ctr., Santa Monica, Calif., 1974-76; asst. clin. prof. Sch. Nursing, UCLA, 1976-79; educator, continuing edn. for nurses, Calif. State U., L.A., 1979-80, U. Calif., Santa Barbara, 1981-83; assoc. dir. nursing edn. St. Francis Hosp. of Santa Barbara, 1981-83; asst. dir. nursing edn. and rsch. Stanford U. Hosp., 1983—; USPHS coronary care nurse trainee, 1968; USPHS nurse trainee, 1969-71; recipient Chancellor's Patent Fund, UCLA, 1972-73. Mem. Am. Assn. Critical Care Nurses. Contbr. articles to profl. publs. Office: Stanford U Hosp Dept Nursing Rsch Stanford CA 94304

ROACH, THOMAS BANKSON, defense industry executive; b. N.Y.C., Sept. 17, 1938; s. Thomas Bankson and Katherine Walter (Hunter) R. AA in Human Resource Adminstrn., St. Leo's Coll., 1976. Pres. Shrike Software, Cupertino, Calif., 1982-85; dir. microcomputer systems Lockheed Missile and Space Co., Sunnyvale, Calif., 1984-88; pres. Sovsig Rsch., San Jose, Calif., 1988—. Club: Merlin (Cupertino) (pres. 1980-82), Piwacket. Home: 1330 Copper Peak Ln San Jose CA 95120-4271

ROACH, WILLIAM LESTER, JR., psychologist; b. Brookhaven, Miss., Sept. 4, 1948; s. W. Lester and Ethie Doris (Young) R.; m. Debra Cheryl Clements, May 29, 1971; children—William Lester III, Brian Lamar. B.A. in Edn., U. Miss., 1970, M.Ed., 1971; Ph.D., 1976. Cert. counselor Nat. Bd. Counselors, cert. sch. psychologist. Tchr. math. W.P. Daniel High Sch., New Albany, Miss., 1970, Oxford Jr. High Sch., Miss., 1970-71; grad. asst. U. Miss., University, 1971-72; dir. guidance Lafayette County Schs., Oxford, 1972-87; sch. psychologist Sierra Vista (Ariz.) Pub. Schs., 1987-89, dir. personnel svcs., 1989—; mem. adj. faculty counseling and edn. psychology dept. U. Miss., 1977—; mem. adj. faculty dept. psychology N.W. Jr. Coll., Senatobia, Miss., 1982—; psychologist North Cen. Regional Screeing Team, Oxford, 1980-86; adj. faculty Cochise Coll., Sierra Vista, 1986—. Author: Registration Guide for Students and Parents, 1980—. Named Outstanding Counselor, U. So. Miss., 1980. Mem. Am. Psychol. Assn., Nat. Assn. Sch. Psychologists, Miss. Counseling Assn., Miss. Sch. Counselor Assn. (pres.-elect 1981-82, pres. 1982-83). Avocations: hunting; fishing; golf; working with summer baseball program. Home: 1964 Baywood Ln Sierra Vista AZ 85635 Office: Sierra Vista Pub Schs 3555 Fry Blvd Sierra Vista AZ 85635

ROALDSON, R. STEPHEN, restaurant owner; b. Seattle, June 4, 1947; s. Ralph Sievert and Anne Jennie (Kline) R.; m. Maureen J. McHenry, Aug. 4, 1972 (div. 1987); children: R. Sven, Kjersta Anne. BBA, Seattle U., 1970. With sales mgmt. staff Coats and Clark Sales Corp., Stamford, Conn., 1971-76; pres. South Shore Enterprises, Chelan, Wash., 1977-84; exec. dir. Cascade Loop Assn., Wenachee, Wash., 1983-84; restaurant mgr. Sand and Surf, Chelan, Wash., 1984-87; cons., pres. Tourism Cons., Inc., Kirkland, Wash., 1979—; restaurant mgr. ARG/Black Angus, Lynwood, Wash., 1987—; v.p., dir. Cascade Loop Assn., 1980-84, Wash. State Visitor Assn., 1983-86. Mem. Legis. Budget com., Olympia, Wash., 1983; mem. task force Wash. State Convention Ctr., Seattle, 1982-84; mem. transition team on tourism for Gov. Gardner, Olympia, 1984. Mem. Chelan C. of C. (pres. 1982, named Mem. of Year 1983).

ROARK, TERRY PAUL, university president; b. Okeene, Okla., June 11, 1938; s. Paul J. and Erma K. (Morrison) R.; m. Beverly Brown, Sept. 17, 1963; 1 child, David C. BA in Physics, Oklahoma City U., 1960; MS in Astronomy, Rensselaer Poly. Inst., 1963, PhD in Astronomy, 1966. Asst. provost for curricula Ohio State U., Columbus, 1977-79, assoc. provost for instrn., 1979-83; prof. physics Kent (Ohio) State U., 1983-87, v.p. acad. and student affairs, 1983-87, provost, 1985-87; pres. U. Wyo., Laramie, 1987—; commr. Western Interstate Commn. for Higher Edn., 1987—; mem. adv. bd. Wyo. Geol. Survey, 1987—; mem. Warren AFB Civilian Adv. Council, 1987—; mem. Council on Competitiveness, 1988—. Mem., treas. Ctr. for Pub. Edn., Columbus, 1980-83; mem. fin. adv. com. LWV, Kent, 1986; mem. long range planning com. Cleve. Urban League, 1985-86; mem. adv. com. Battelle youth sci. program Columbus and Ohio Pub. Schs., 1982; bd. dirs. Ivinson Hosp. Found., 1987—. Mem. Am. Astron. Soc., Astron. Soc. Pacific, Internat. Astron. Union, AAUP, Am. Assn. for Higher Edn., Sigma Xi, Phi Kappa Phi, Omicron Delta Kappa. Home: 1306 Ivinson Ave Laramie WY 82071 Office: U Wyo Office of Pres Box 3434 Univ Sta Laramie WY 82071

ROBART, NINA RAE, non-profit organization administrator, lawyer; b. Lakeview, Oreg., Aug. 13, 1941; d. Jack Edward and Carolyn Louise (Grubbs) Anderson; children: Shauna Elise Azizian Keller, Deanna Kay Lewis. B in Music Edn., U. Idaho, 1970; JD, Lewis & Clark Coll., 1977. Legal intern Metro Pub. Defender, Portland, Oreg., 1974-76; dep. dist. atty. Multnomah County, Portland, 1976-80; pvt. practice Hillsboro, Oreg., 1980-85; loss prevention atty. Profl. Liability Fund of Oreg. State Bar, Portland, 1978-87; exec. dir. Oreg. Council on Alcoholism and Drug Addiction, Portland, 1987—. Chair Multnomah Council on Chem. Dependency, Portland, 1986—, Task Force on Women's Alcoholism and Drug Issues, State of Oreg., 1987-88; pres. Assn. Labor and Mgmt. Adminstrn. Cons. on Alcoholism, 1985—; choir dir., organist Pioneer United Meth. Ch. Mem. ABA, Oreg. State Bar (chair detention and corrections com., 1984-87), Am. Trial Lawyers Assn., Oreg. Trial Lawyers Assn., Washington County Bar Assn., Multnomah County Bar Assn., Profl. Assn. Council Execs., City Club of Portland. Democrat. Office: Oreg Council on Alcoholism and Drug Addiction 4506 SE Belmont Suite 220 Portland OR 97215

ROBB, JOHN DONALD, JR., lawyer; b. N.Y.C., Jan. 11, 1924; s. John D. and Harriett (Block) R.; m. Peggy Hight, Feb. 8, 1946; children—John D., Celeste Robb Nicholson, Ellen, Bradford, George G., David. Student Yale U., N.Mex.; B.S.L., U. Minn., 1948, LL.B., 1949. Bar: N.Mex. 1950, U.S. Dist. Ct. N.Mex. 1950, U.S. Ct. Appeals (10th cir.) 1955, U.S. Supreme Ct. 1961. Sole practice, Albuquerque, 1950-51; assoc. Rodey, Dickason, Sloan, Akin & Robb, P.A., Albuquerque, 1951-56; ptnr., 1956-65, sr. dir., 1965—; mem. nat. adv. com. legal services program OEO, 1966-73. Pres. Albuquerque Legal Aid Soc., 1957, bd. dirs., 1960-74; bd. dirs. Navajo Legal Services, 1967-68; chmn. Albuquerque Christian Legal Aid and Referral Service, 1982; pres. Albuquerque Community Council, 1958-60; pres. Family Consultation Service of Albuquerque, 1955-57; bd. dirs. United Community Fund, 1962-64; chmn. bd. Drug Addicts Recovery Enterprises, 1974-79. Recipient Outstanding Man of Yr. award Albuquerque Jr. C. of C., 1956; Disting. Service award Albuquerque United Community Fund, 1960; Hatton W. Sumners award Southwestern Legal Found., 1971. Fellow Am. Bar Found.; mem. ABA (nat. chmn. standing com. on legal aid and indigent defendants 1966-73), Nat. Legal Aid and Defendants Assn. (v.p. 1966-72), Albuquerque Bar Assn. (chmn. legal aid com. 1962-65), N.Mex. Bar Assn. (chmn. legal aid com.), Internat. Legal Aid Assn., Christian Legal Soc. (bd. dirs. 1982), Albuquerque Christian Lawyers Assn. (chmn. 1979—), Am. Judicature Soc., Am. Bd. Trial Advs. Contbr. articles to profl. jours. Home: 7200 Rio Grande Blvd NW Albuquerque NM 87107 Office: PO Box 1888 Albuquerque NM 87103

ROBBINS, ALAN, state senator; b. Phila., Feb. 5, 1943; s. Martin and Gladys (Kessler) R.; B.A., UCLA, 1963, J.D., 1966; m. Miriam Elbaum, Sept. 27, 1967 (div. 1980); children—Jacob Harold, Leah Susan. Bar: Calif. 1966. Practice law, San Fernando Valley, Calif., 1966—; mem. Calif. Senate from 20th Dist., 1973—, chmn. com. on ins., claims and corps. Democrat. Office: Office State Senate State Capitol Sacramento CA 95814

ROBBINS, ANNE FRANCIS See REAGAN, NANCY DAVIS

ROBBINS, CHARLES DUDLEY, III, manufacturing executive; b. Montclair, N.J., Sept. 21, 1943; s. Charles Dudley Robbins Jr. and Elaine (Siebert) Stark; m. Johanna Evans, Oct. 13, 1963 (div.); m. Barbara Ruth Psiaki, Feb. 15, 1969 (div. Sept. 1977); m. Rebecca Lucille Bender, Feb. 8, 1980; children: Seta A., Evan F., Gwendolyn M., Catherine E., Christopher W. BS in Bus. Adminstrn., U. Phoenix, Irvine, Calif., 1982; MBA, U. Phoenix, Salt Lake City, 1986. Cert. mfg. engr., robitics. Project engr. Mead Paper Corp., Atlanta, 1969-73; engr. McGaw Labs., Glendale, Calif., 1973-75; mgr. tool engring. Weiser Lock Co., South Gate, Calif., 1975-77; chief engr. Bivans Corp., L.A., 1977-79; sr. project engr. Charls Wyle Engring. Corp., Torrance, Calif., 1979-80; automation specialist Mattel Toys Inc., Hawthorne, Calif., 1980-83; dir. automation engring. Deseret Med., Warner Lambert, Sandy, Utah, 1983-88; dir. mfg. Deseret Med., Becton Dickinson, Sandy, 1988—; dir. bus. devel. and strategic planning Deseret Med., Becton Dickinson Co., Franklin Lakes, N.J., 1988. Patentee in field. Dist. chmn. Utah Dem. party, Sandy, 1987-88. With U.S. Army, 1961-64. Mem. U. Phoenix Alumni Assn., L.A. Aquarium Soc. (prs. 1980-82, dir. 1982-83). Democrat. Episcopalian. Home: 9915 Falcon View Dr Sandy UT 84092 Office: Deseret Med 9450 State St Sandy UT 84070

ROBBINS, ELEANOR CLARK, real estate associate; b. Indpls., Dec. 11, 1936; d. Melvin Edward and Mary Virginia (Clark) R.; m. Paul David Shein, July 13, 1958 (div. Feb. 1970); children: David Edward, Mary Abigail. BA, Hood Coll., 1958. Adminstrv. sec. State Ct. Ariz., Tucson, 1970-76; adminstrv. asst. U.S. Dist. Ct. Ariz., Tucson, 1976-84; adminstr. Mesch, Clark & Rothschild, P.C., Tucson, 1984-87; real estate assoc. Tucson Realty & Trust Co., Tucson, 1987—. Co-chair Speakers Bur. Steering Com.; vol. Crime Prevention League, Tucson, 1988—, Michael Landon Tennis Classic, Tucson, 1988—. Mem. NAFE, Assn. Legal Adminstrs., Tucson Personnel Assn., Resources for Women, Pla. Club (soc. com.). Office: Tucson Realty & Trust Co 1890 E River Rd Tucson AZ 85718

ROBBINS, GARY SAMUEL, airport manager; b. Ellensburg, Wash., July 10, 1937; s. Harold William and Catherine May (Randall) R.; m. Patricia Ann Morrison, July 14, 1957; children: Teresa Ann, Becky Jo, Michael Guy. BA in Edn., Cen. Wash. U., 1960; MA in Psychology, U. No. Colo., 1980. Commd. U.S. Air Force, 1960, advanced through grades to lt. col., 1977, ret., 1980; mgr. Yakima (Wash.) Air Terminal, 1980—. Mem. Wash. Airport Mgmt. Assn. (v.p.). Republican. Methodist. Office: Yakima Air Terminal 2300 W Washington Ave Yakima WA 98903

ROBBINS, JAMES EDWARD, electrical engineer; b. Renovo, Pa., May 11, 1931; s. James Edward and Marguerite Neva (Cleary) R.; m. Elizabeth Anne Caton, 1959 (div. July 1971); children: James, Katherine, Ellen; m. Dorothy Raye Bell, July 23, 1971; stepchildren: Mark, Lori. BEE, Pa. State U., 1958; MS in Math., San Diego State U., 1961. Registered profl. engr., Calif., Ariz. Rsch. engr. Astronautics div. Gen. Dynamics Co., San Diego, 1961-62; mgr. tech. ops. Electronics div. Gen. Dynamics Co., Yuma, Ariz., 1976-82; sr. engr. Kearfott div. Gen. Precision Co., San Marcos, Calif., 1962-65; systems engring. specialist Teledyne Ryan Aerospace Co., San Diego, 1965-76; v.p. Cibola Info. Systems, Yuma, 1982-84; cons. engr. Robbins Engring. Co., Yuma, 1984-85; sr. engring. specialist Gen. Dynamics Svcs. Co., Yuma, Ariz., 1985—. Contbr. articles to profl. jours. With USN, 1951-55, Korea. Mem. Inst. Navigation, Nat. Soc. Profl. Engrs., Ariz. Soc. Profl. Engrs. (pres. western div. 1986), Am. Legion, VFW (post comdr. 1963-65), Tau Beta Pi. Home: 2765 Julie Ln Yuma AZ 85365 Office: Gen Dynamics Svcs Co PO Box 1488 Yuma AZ 85364

ROBELOTTO, JOSEPH VINCENT, human resource generalist; b. Albany, N.Y., June 25, 1941; s. Joseph Anthony and Emma Rose (Botteghi) R.; m. Judith Ann Hatch, Nov. 29, 1964 (div. Nov. 1975); children: Christian, Lara; m. Susan Elizabeth Arndt, Sept. 26, 1985; stepchildren: Donald Hocking, Dennis Hocking. A Applied Sci., Hudson Valley Community Coll., 1963; BS, Calif. State U., Northridge, 1972. Quality control supr. Gen. Electric, Schenectady, N.Y., 1968-69; quality control mgr. Electron Beam Welding, Los Angeles, 1969-70; personnel asst. Cal Mat, Los Angeles, 1972-76; personnel adminstr. Am. Honda, Gardena, Calif., 1976-78; equal employment opportunity coordinator Baker Internat., Orange, Calif., 1978-81; mgr. employee benefits Kerr Glass Mfg., Los Angeles, 1981-84, Golden Nugget, Las Vegas, 1984-85; mgr. indsl. relations Associated Spring, Gardena, 1986—. Loaned exec. United Way, 1984-85; coach, referee Am. Youth Soccer Orgn., Nat. Intercollegiate Soccer Officials Assn., SCSOA. Mem. Am. Soc. Personnel Adminstrs., Personnel and Indsl. Relations Assn. (vice chmn. 1982-83), So. Bay Referees Assn. (sec./treas. 1986—). Republican. Home: 21618 Ellinwood Dr Torrance CA 90503 Office: Associated Spring 15001 S Broadway Gardena CA 90248

ROBENSON, JAMES MELFORD, protective services official; b. Brookhaven, Miss., Oct. 28, 1941; m. Susan Burt. BA in Sociology, Calif. State U., Los Angeles, 1972; M in Pub. Adminstrn., U. So. Calif., 1976; postgrad., Pub. Exec. Inst., Lyndon B. Johnson Sch. Pub. Affairs, 1986. Police officer Pasadena (Calif.) Police Dept., 1964, police agt., 1969, police sgt., 1971, police lt., 1974, police commdr., 1979, police chief, 1985. Contbr. articles to profl. jours. Mem. Pasadena Hispanic Scholarship Com., Pasadena Edn. Found.; mem. exec. bd. San Grand Valley council Boy Scouts Am.; bd. dirs. United Way. Recipient Law Enforcement award Crown City Optimist Club, 1975, Community Svc. award Pasadena Alliance of Substance Abuse Agys., 1982, Respect for Law commendation Altadena Optimist Club, 1986, Outstanding Svc. award Just Say No Found. Mem. Nat. Orgn. Black Law Enforcement Execs., San Gabriel Valley Police Chiefs, Internat. Assn. Chief's of Police, Calif. Police Chiefs' Assn., San Gabriel Valley Mental Health Edn. Found., Alpha Kappa Delta. Club: University (Pasadena). Office: Pasadena Police Dept 142 N Arroyo Pkwy Pasadena CA 91103

ROBERSON, GINGER CALHOUN, horse trainer, sculptor; b. Columbia, S.C., June 20, 1947; d. George Clifton Salvo and Eugenia Calhoun (Gerald) Landon; m. Forrest Jon Roberson, Apr. 22, 1967; 1 child, Tiffany Ann. Student, Rollins Coll., 1965. Horse trainer Mountain Home, Idaho, 1965—; designer Mountain Home, 1975—; instr. Wyo. Barrel Racing Club, Jackson, 1980, Idaho High Sch. Rodeo Assn., 1985. Leader 4-H Club, Mountain Home, 1975; founder, pres. Idaho High Sch. Rodeo Club, Mountain Home High Sch. Recipient several awards for sculptures Nat. Cowgirl Hall of Fame, numerous championships Idaho Cowboys Assn., Idaho Barrel Racing Futurity Assn., Am. Quarter Horse Assn., Utah Barrel Racing Futurity, Eastern Idaho Barrel Racing Futurity, Golden Spike Barrel Racing Futurity, Sweetwater Barrel Futurity, Idaho Quarter Horse Breeders Assn. Mem. NW Barrel Futurities Assn., Idaho Barrel Racing Futurity Assn. (bd. dirs. 1981-83, champion 1979, 83), Idaho Cowboys Assn. (bd. dirs. 1974-75, res. champion 1984), Ea. Idaho Rodeo Assn. Home and Office: RFD 1 Box 756-A Mountain Home ID 83647

ROBERSON, KIM ELIZABETH, real estate broker; b. Seattle, Sept. 20, 1955; d. Frank Tracey and Zetta Elizabeth (Jacobson) R. BS in Nursing, Seattle U., 1977. Commd. 2d lt., U.S. Army, 1977, advanced through grades to maj., 1980; asst. head nurse, Frankfurt-W.Ger., 1980-81, chief nurse Health Clinic, 1981-83, clin. staff nurse, San Francisco, 1983-85,; house supr. Seattle VA Med. Ctr., 1985-87; occupational health nurse, Boeing Aerospace Co., Seattle, 1987-89 sales assoc. Kamas Realty, Inc, 1988—; co-chairperson dept. nursing quality assurance com., 1980-81; mem. affiliate faculty Am. Heart Assn., San Francisco, 1984-85. Maj. USAR, 1989—. Avocations: kayaking, study of wines, music, reading, travel. Home: 8730 Wabash Ave S Seattle WA 98118

ROBERT, LEON EMILE, III, test pilot; b. Alexandria, La., Sept. 23, 1947; s. Leon Emile Jr. and Marjorie (Berry) R.; m. Charlene Ann Fontenot, Sept. 12, 1970 (div. Mar. 1986); children: Anne Renee, Nicole Leigh, Marie Aline. BSME, La. Tech. U., 1970; postgrad., U. West Fla., 1971-72. lic. FAA airline transport pilot. Flight test engr. Boeing Comml. Airplane Co., Seattle, 1978-81, flight test pilot, 1981—. Lt. USN, 1971-78. Mem. Naval Res. Assn., Mountaineers Club. Republican. Roman Catholic. Home: 13631 E Lake Kathleen Dr Renton WA 98056

ROBERTIN, HECTOR, clinical psychologist; b. N.Y.C., June 18, 1932; s. Vincent and Maria (Jimenez) R.; m. Linda Green, June 29, 1952 (div. June 1972); 1 child, Hector; m. Thida Kuugun, Aug. 23, 1972. B of Gen. Studies, Chaminade U., 1975; MA, U. No. Colo., 1977; PhD, Union Grad. Sch., Cin., 1979. Lic. psychologist. Enlisted U.S. Army, 1951-71, advanced through grades to sgt., 1967; researcher Inst. Behavioral Sci., Honolulu, 1979-80; instr. Chaminade U., Honolulu, 1980-82; clin. psychologist Hawaii State Dept. Health, Honolulu, 1982—; corp. exec. officer JHC Cons., Inc., Honolulu, 1985—, bd. dirs. Mem. Hawaii Psychol. Assn., Am. MENSA. Democrat. Buddhist. Office: JHC Cons Inc 4614 Kilanea Ave #484 Honolulu HI 96816

ROBERTO, EDWARD PANGELINAN, software company executive; b. Agana, Guam, Jan. 27, 1960; s. Antonio Q. and Annie (Pangelinan) R.; m. Leslie L. Landers, July 2, 1988. Student mech. engring., U. Colo., Denver, 1979-82. Log analyst Schlumberger Well Svcs., Houston, 1978-83; chmn. bd. Roberto & Assocs., Denver, 1983-86; ops. mgr. Sci. Calculations, San Jose, Calif., 1985-86; pres., founder PARSEC Group, Denver, 1986—; cons. equipment Milliken Rsch. Corp., Spartanburg, S.C., 1985—; cons. Dept. of the Interior, Bur. of Reclamation, Washington, 1983-84, Hewlett-Packard Co., Sunnyvale, Calif., 1985-86, Digital Equipment Corp., Mayyard, Mass., 1986-88, Nat. Semicondr. Corp., Santa Clara, Calif., 1986-87; prime contractor Calif. Senate, Sacramento, 1987—. Author: VAX/VMS Utilities and Commands, 1985, Introduction to Networking, 1985. Mem. Digital Equipment Users Soc. (speaker 1986-88). Republican. Roman Catholic. Office: PARSEC Group 9101 Harlan St Ste 230 Westminster CO 80030

ROBERTS, ALAN SILVERMAN, orthopedic surgeon; b. N.Y.C., Apr. 20, 1939; s. Joseph William and Fannie (Margolies) S.; BA, Conn. Wesleyan U., 1960; MD, Jefferson Med. Coll., 1966; children: Michael Eric, Daniel Ian. Rotating intern, Lankenau Hosp., Phila., 1966-67; resident orthopaedics Tulane U. Med. Coll., 1967-71; pvt. practice medicine, specializing in orthopedics and hand surgery, Los Angeles, 1971—; mem. clin. faculty UCLA Med. Coll., 1971-76; mem. staff Brotman Meml. Hosp., Culver City, Calif. Served with AUS, 1961. Recipient Riordan Hand fellowship, 1969; Boyes Hand fellowship, 1971. Mem. Riordan Hand Soc., Western Orthopaedic Assn., A.C.S., AMA, Calif., Los Angeles County Med. Assns., Am. Acad. Orthopaedic Surgeons. Republican. Jewish. Contbr. articles to profl. jours.

ROBERTS, ARCHIBALD EDWARD, retired army officer, author; b. Cheboygan, Mich., Mar. 21, 1915; s. Archibald Lancaster and Madeline Ruth (Smith) R.; grad. Command and Gen. Staff Coll., 1952; student U.S. Armed Forces Inst., 1953, U. Md., 1958; m. Florence Snure, Sept. 25, 1940 (div. Feb. 1950); children—Michael James, John Douglas; m. 2d, Doris Elfriede White, June 23, 1951; children—Guy Archer, Charles Lancaster, Christopher Corwin. Enlisted U.S. Army, 1939, advanced through grades to lt. col., 1960; served in Far East Command, 1942, 1953-55, ETO, 1943-45, 57-60; tech. info. officer Office Surgeon Gen., Dept. Army, Washington, 1950, Ft. Campbell, Ky., 1952-53, info. officer, Camp Chicamauga, Japan, Ft. Bragg, N.C., Ft. Campbell, Ky., 1953-56, Ft. Campbell, 1956-57, Ft. Benning, Ga., Wurzburg, Germany, 1957-58, spl. projects officer Augsburg, Germany, 1959-60, U.S. Army Info. Office, N.Y.C., 1960-61; writer program precipitating Senate Armed Services Hearings, 1962; ret., 1965; mgr., salesman Nu-Enamel Stores, Ashville, N.C., 1937-38; co-owner, dir. Roberts & Roberts Advt. Agy., Denver, 1946-49; pres. Found. for Edn., Scholarship, Patriotism and Americanism, Inc.; founder, nat. bd. dirs. Com. to Restore Constn., Inc., 1965—; Recipient award of merit Am. Acad. Pub. Affairs, 1967; Good Citizenship medal SAR, 1968; Liberty award Congress of Freedom, 1969; Man of Yr. awards Women for Constl. Govt., 1970, Wis. Legislative and Research Com., 1971; medal of merit Am. Legion, 1972; Speaker of Year award We, The People, 1973; Col. Arch Roberts Week named for him City of Danville, Ill., 1974; recipient Spl. Tribute State of Mich., 1979. Mem. Res. Officers Assn., Airborne Assn., SAR, Sons Am. Colonists. Author: Rakkasan, 1955; Screaming Eagles, 1956; The Marne Division, 1957; Victory Denied, 1966; The Anatomy of a Revolution, 1968; Peace: By the Wonderful People Who Brought You Korea and Viet Nam, 1972; The Republic: Decline and Future Promise, 1975; The Crisis of Federal Regionalism: A Solution, 1976; Emerging Struggle for State Sovereignty, 1979; How to Organize for Survival, 1982; The Most Secret Science, 1984; also numerous pamphlets and articles. Home: 2218 W Prospect PO Box 986 Fort Collins CO 80522

ROBERTS, BARBARA, state official; b. Corvallis, Oreg., Dec. 21, 1936; m. Frank Roberts, 1974; children—Mark, Michael. Mem. Multnomah County Bd. Commrs., Oreg., 1978; mem. Oreg. Ho. of Reps., 1981-85; sec. of state State of Oreg., 1985—. Mem. Parkrose Sch. Bd., 1973-83. Office: Office of Sec State 136 State Capitol Salem OR 97310 *

ROBERTS, DENNIS WILLIAM, association executive; b. Chgo., Jan. 7, 1943; s. William Owen and Florence Harriet (Denman) R.; BA, U. N.Mex., 1968; MA, Antioch U., 1982, St. John's Coll., 1984. Cert. assn. exec. Gen. assignment reporter Albuquerque Pub. Co., 1964, sports writer, 1960-64, advt. and display salesman, 1967-68; dir. info. N.Mex. bldg. br. Asso. Gen. Contractors Am., Albuquerque, 1968-79, asst. exec. dir., 1979-82, dir., 1982—. Active United Way, Albuquerque, 1969-78; chmn. Albuquerque Crime Prevention Council, 1982. Recipient Pub. Relations Achievement award Assoc. Gen. Contractors Am., 1975, 78. Mem. N.Mex. Pub. Relations Conf. (chmn. 1975, 82-83), Pub. Relations Soc. Am. (accredited, pres. N.Mex. chpt. 1981, chmn. S.W. dist. 1984, chmn. sect. 1988), Am. Soc. Assn. Execs. (cert.), Contrn. Specifications Inst. (Outstanding Industry Mem. 1974, Outstanding Com. Chmn. 1978), Sigma Delta Chi (pres. N.Mex. chpt. 1969). Republican. Lutheran. Clubs: Toastmasters (dist. gov. 1977-78, Disting. Dist. award 1978, Toastmaster of Year 1979-80), Masons, Shriners, Elks. Home: 1709 Hiawatha NE Albuquerque NM 87112 Office: Assn Gen Contractors 1615 University Blvd NE Albuquerque NM 87102

ROBERTS, DONALD JOHN, economics and business educator, consultant; b. Winnipeg, Man., Can., Feb. 11, 1945; came to U.S., 1967; s. Donald Victor and Margaret Mabel (Riddell) R.; m. Kathleen Eleanor Taylor, Aug. 26, 1967. B.A. (honours), U. Man., 1967; Ph.D., U. Minn., 1972. Instr. dept. managerial econs. and decision scis. J.L. Kellogg Grad. Sch. Mgmt., Northwestern U., Evanston, Ill., 1971-72, asst. prof., 1972-74; assoc. prof. J. L. Kellogg Grad. Sch. Mgmt., Northwestern U., Evanston, Ill., 1974-77; prof. J.L. Kellogg Grad. Sch. Mgmt., Northwestern U., Evanston, Ill., 1977-80, Grad. Sch. Bus., Stanford U., Calif., 1980; Jonathan B. Lovelace prof. grad. sch. bus. Stanford U., 1980-87, assoc. dean grad. sch. of bus., 1987—; vis. research faculty U. Catholique de Louvain, (Belgium), 1974-75; cons. econs. and antitrust, 1976—; spl. econs. cons. U.S. Dept. Transp., Washington, 1978-79. Assoc. editor: Jour. Econ. Theory, 1977—, Econometrica, 1985-87, Games and Economic Decisions, 1988—; contbr. articles to profl. jours. NSF grantee, 1973—; Ctr. Ops. Research and Econometrics research fellow Heverlee, Belgium, 1974. Fellow Econometric Soc.; mem. Am. Econ. Assn., Beta Gamma Sigma. Home: 835 Santa Fe Ave Stanford CA 94305 Office: Stanford U Grad Sch Bus Stanford CA 94305-5015

ROBERTS, DWIGHT LOREN, management executive, novelist; b. San Diego, June 3, 1949; s. James Albert and Cleva Lorraine (Conn) R.; B.A., U. San Diego, 1976, M.A., 1979; m. Phyllis Ann Adair, Mar. 29, 1969; children—Aimee Renee, Michael Loren, Daniel Alexandr. Engring. aide Benton Engring. Inc., San Diego, 1968-73; pres. Robert's Tech. Research Co., also subs. Marine Technique Ltd., San Diego, 1973-76; pres. Research Technique Internat., 1978—; freelance writer, 1979—; owner Agrl. Analysis, 1985-88; constrn. mgr. Homestead Land Devel. Corp., 1988—. Served with U.S. Army, 1969-71. Mem. ASTM, AAAS, Nat. Inst. Sci., N.Y. Acad. Scis., Nat. Inst. Cert. in Engring. Techs., Soil and Found. Engr. Assn., Phi Alpha Theta. Baptist. Author: Geological Exploration of Alaska, 1898-1924, Alfred Hulse Brooks, Alaskan Trailblazer; contbr. articles to profl. jours. Office: 3111 Victoria Dr Alpine CA 92001

ROBERTS, ELIZABETH PORCHER, library director; b. St. Louis, Jan. 17, 1928; d. Francis Davis and Mary (Callaway) Porcher; m. Lorin W. Roberts, June 11, 1949 (div. 1965). AA, William Woods Coll., Fulton, Mo., 1947; BA, U. Mo., 1949; MLS, Emory U., 1956. Reference librarian Emory U. A.W. Calhoun Med. Library, Atlanta, 1954-56; with classified staff sci. library Wash. State U., Pullman, 1957, reference librarian, 1958-62, head serial record sec., 1963-72, acting head sci. library, 1965-66, 69-70, head interlibrary loan, 1970, head sci. library, 1972-76, head Owen Sci. and Engring. Library, 1977—. Contbr. articles to profl. jours. USDA Northwest and Intermountain Regional Document Delivery System grantee, Fred Meyer Chairtable Trust, 1977—. Mem. ALA (sci. tech. sect. com. on comparison of sci. libraries, task for on preconf.), Wash. Library Assn. (com. state interlibrary loan code 1972, com. women's rights 1972), Am. Soc. Engring. Edn. (PNW chmn. engring. sch. libraries div. 1966-68, v.p., program chmn. 1969-70, pres. 1970-71), Am. Soc. Info. Sci. (chmn. mentoring catalyst program 1983-84), Assn. for Faculty Women (chmn. com. on temporary appointments 1984—, faculty status com. 1985—), Assn. Acad. and Rsch. Libraries (sec./treas. 1973, nominating com. 1980), Pacific Northwest Library Assn. Home: Box 2114 CS Pullman WA 99165 Office: Wash State U Owen Sci and Engring Libr Pullman WA 99164-3200

ROBERTS, GEORGE ADAM, metallurgist; b. Uniontown, Pa., Feb. 18, 1919; s. Jacob Earle and Mary M. (Bower) R.; m. Betty E. Matthewson, May 31, 1941; children: George Thomas, William John, Mary Ellen; m. Jeanne Marie Polk. Student, U.S. Naval Acad., 1935-37; B.Sc., Carnegie Tech., 1939, M.Sc., 1941, D.Sc., 1942. Technician Bell Telephone Labs., N.Y.C., 1938; research dir. Vasco Metals Corp. (formerly Vanadium Alloys Steel Co.), Latrobe, Pa., 1940-45; chief metallurgist Vasco Metals Corp. (formerly Vanadium Alloys Steel Co.), 1945-53, v.p., 1953-61, pres., 1961-66; pres., dir. Teledyne, Inc. (merger with Vasco Metals Corp.), Los Angeles, 1966—, chief exec. officer, 1986—; hon. lectr. Societe Francaise de Metallurgie, 1960. Author: Tool Steels, 1944, 62; contbr. articles to trade jours. Recipient silver medal from Paris, 1955. Fellow Metall. Soc. Am. Inst. Mining, Metall. and Petroleum Engrs., Am. Soc. for Metals (chmn. Pitts. chpt. 1949-50, internat. pres. 1954-55, trustee Found. Edn. and Research 1954-59, 63-64, pres. Found. 1955-56, Gold medal 1977); mem. Nat. Acad. Engring., Metal Powder Industries Fedn. (dir. 1952-55, pres. 1957-61), Am. Soc. Metals, Am. Iron and Steel Inst., Soc. Mfg. Engrs., Tau Beta Pi; hon. life mem. several fgn. socs. Methodist. Office: Teledyne Inc 1901 Ave of the Stars Ste 1800 Los Angeles CA 90067 *

ROBERTS, GEORGE CHRISTOPHER, manufacturing executive; b. Ridley Park, Pa., May 27, 1936; s. George H. and Marion C. (Smullen) R.; m. Adriana Toribio, July 19, 1966; children: Tupac A., Capac Y. Sr. engr. ITT, Paramus, N.J., 1960-65; program mgr. Arde Research, Mawah, N.J., 1965-67; Space-Life Sci. program mgr., research div. GATX, 1967-69; dir. research and devel. Monogram Industries, Los Angeles, 1969-71; chmn. Inca Mfg. Corp, 1970-72; pres. Inca-One Corp., Hawthorne, Calif., 1972—; pres. Environ. Protection Center, Inc., L.A.s, 1970-76. Bd. dirs., trustee Fairborn Obs.; founder Culver Nat. Bank, 1983; trustee Calif. Mus. Sci. and Industry, 1988—; trustee Internat. Am. Profl. Photoelectric Photometrists, 1983—, Buckley Sch., 1984—; chmn. solar and stellar physics Mt. Wilson Research Corp., 1984-87; bd. dirs. Peruvian Found. 1981, pres. 1986—, appt. rep. govt. of Peru in L.A., 1988—. Mem. Am. Astron. Soc., Astron. Soc. Pacific. Patentee advanced waste treatment systems, automotive safety systems. Office: 13030 S La Cienega Blvd Hawthorne CA 90250

ROBERTS, HARRY FREDERICK, marketing consultant; b. Kingston, N.Y., June 27, 1942; s. Theresa Grace (Salanitro) Roberts; m. Lynda M. Hamilton; children: Christina, Robin, Becky, Melissa, Serra. New products mgr. J.C. Penney Co., N.Y.C., 1965-71; pres. Everfast Inc., N.Y.C., 1971-75; founder, pres. Kitchen Kaboodle, Portland, Oreg., 1975-82, The Roberts Group, Portland, 1982—; cons. Support Techs. Inc., Portland, 1985—; bd. dirs. Inter-Lock Inc., Ramagon Toys, Inc. Inventor workshop tools. Active March of Dimes Gourmet Gala, Portland, 1984, chmn., 1980. Named one of Top Ten Retail Execs. in U.S., entree mag., N.Y.C., 1981. Club: Portland Yacht. Home: 4702 NE Alameda Portland OR 97213 Office: The Roberts Group 618 NW Glisan Portland OR 97209

ROBERTS, HELEN MARIE, nurse; b. Bakersfield, Calif., July 12, 1951; d. Charles Ross and Joyce Marie (Bolles) Lindsey; m. Richard James Roberts, Aug. 3, 1974; children: Micah James, Luke Charles. AA in Nursing, Bakersfield Jr. Coll., 1971; BS in Nursing, Calif. State U., Bakersfield, 1974; MS, U. Calif., Davis, 1979. Cert. physicisn'a asst., family nurse practitioner. RN Meml Hosp., Bakersfield, 1971-73, Kern Med.Ctr., Bakersfield, 1973-75; supr. Biomedical Hemodialysis Unit, Bakersfield, 1975; head nurse intensive care unit San Joaquin Community Hosp., Bakersfield, 1975-77; instr. nursing Calif. State U., Bakersfield, 1975, Bakersfield Jr. Coll., 1973-75; family nurse practitioner Bakersfield Cardiopulmonary Med. Group, 1977—. Tchr. Stine Rd. Bapt. Ch., Bakersfield, 1979—; coach Am. Youth Service Orgn., Bakersfield, 1986—; den leader Cub Scouts Am., Bakersfield, 1987—. Mem. Calif. Nurses Assn., Am. Nurses Assn., Kern Nurse Practitioner and Physcians' Asst. Assn. (pres. 1982-83), Calif. Acad Physicians' Assts. Republican. Office: Bakersfield Cardiopulmonary Med Group 1524 27th St Ste 150 Bakersfield CA 93312

ROBERTS, JACK EARLE, lawyer, ski resort operator, wood products company executive, real estate developer; b. L.A., Nov. 5, 1928; s. James Earle and Illa Ann (Morgan) R.; m. Marilyn Humphreys, Sept. 13, 1954; children: Ronda, Cyndi, Scott, Robynne, Craig. B.S. in Accounting and Bus. Adminstrn, Brigham Young U., 1952; J.D., George Washington U., 1955, LL.M. in Taxation (Teaching fellow), 1956. Bar: Calif. bar 1957; C.P.A., Ariz. Pvt. practice L.A.; atty. Office Chief Counsel, IRS, L.A., 1956-60; mem. firm Roberts, Carmack, Johnson, Poulson & Harmer, L.A., 1961-78; pres. Park West Ski Resort, Park City, Utah, 1975—; pres., dir. Accudyne Corp., Los Angeles, 1972—, Richmark Corp., Los Angeles, 1972-77; chmn., dir. Comml. Wood Products Co., Los Angeles, 1968—; pres., dir. Snyderville Devel. Co., Inc., Utah, 1978—. Contbr. articles on legal subjects to tech. jours. Pres. Westwood Republican Club, 1968; mem. Calif. State, Los Angeles County Rep. central coms., 1974-77, Utah State Cen. and Exec. coms., 1981—, Summit County Rep. central and exec. coms.; state sec. Utah Rep. party, 1985-88, chmn., 1989—; mem. Rep. Nat. Com., 1988—; chmn. Summit County Rep. party, 1981-83; bd. dirs. Ettie Lee Homes for Boys, sec., 1971-78. Mem. Calif. Bar Assn., D.C. Bar Assn. Office: Roberts Mgmt Corp 150 N Virginia St Salt Lake City UT 84103

ROBERTS, JAMES MCGREGOR, professional association executive; b. Moncton, N.B., Can., Nov. 24, 1923; came to U.S., 1949, naturalized, 1956; s. Roland M. and Edith M. (Shields) R.; m. Thelma E. Williams, May 6, 1944; 1 dau., Jana M. B.Commerce, U. Toronto, Ont., Can., 1949. Auditor Citizens Bank, Los Angeles, 1949-54; auditor Acad. Motion Picture Arts and Scis., Hollywood, Calif., 1954—; controller Acad. Motion Picture Arts and Scis., 1956-71, exec. dir., 1971—, exec. sec. acad. found., 1971—. Served as pilot Royal Can. Air Force, World War II. Mem. Beverly Hills (Calif.) C. of C. Home: 450 S Maple Dr Beverly Hills CA 90212 Office: Acad Motion Pictures Arts Scis 8949 Wilshire Blvd Beverly Hills CA 90211

ROBERTS, JAN, financial executive; b. Santa Monica, Calif., Feb. 20, 1950; d. John Andrew and June Norma (Billings) Anderson; m. John Jay Roberts, Apr. 14, 1970 (div. 1976); children: Julie Ann, Jayme Lee, Justin Anderson. Diploma, Pima Coll., 1975; BS, Calif. Poly. U., 1982. Lic. vocat. nurse Tucson Med. Ctr., 1975-77, Parkview Hosp., Riverside, Calif., 1977-79; sales mgr. Apollo Wine Distbrs., Corono, Calif., 1979-85, Youngs Market Co., Anaheim, Calif., 1985-86; agy. supr. Travelers Express Co. Inc., Pacific region, 1986—; part-time lectr. Calif. Poly. U., Pomona, 1986—. Mem. Calif. Faculty Assn., Assn. of U. Profs. Club: Toastmasters, Corona (sec. 1987-88, pres. 1988—). Home: 1676 Sumac Pl Corona CA 91720 Office: Travelers Express Co 1970 W Corporate Way Anaheim CA 92801

ROBERTS, JOHN D., chemist, educator; b. Los Angeles, June 8, 1918; s. Allen Andrew and Flora (Dombrowski) R.; m. Edith Mary Johnson, July 11, 1942; children: Anne Christine, Donald William, John Paul, Allen Walter. A.B., UCLA, 1941, Ph.D., 1944; Dr. rer. nat. h.c., U. Munich, 1962; D.Sc., Temple U., 1964. Instr. chemistry U. Calif. at Los Angeles, 1944-45; NRC fellow chemistry Harvard, 1945-46, instr. chemistry, 1946; instr. chemistry Mass. Inst. Tech., 1946, asst. prof., 1947-50, asso. prof., 1950-52; vis. prof. Ohio State U., 1952, Stanford U., 1973-74; prof. organic chemistry Calif. Inst. Tech., 1953-72, Inst. prof. chemistry, 1972—, dean of faculty, v.p., provost, 1980-83, chmn. div. chemistry and chem. engring., 1963-68, acting chmn., 1972-73; Foster lectr. U. Buffalo, 1956; Mack Meml. lectr. Ohio State U., 1957; Falk-Plaut lectr. Columbia U., 1957; Reynaud Found. lectr. Mich. State U., 1958; Bachmann Meml. lectr. U. Mich., 1958; vis. prof. Harvard, 1958-59, M. Tishler lectr., 1965; Reilly lectr. Notre Dame U., 1960; Am.-Swiss Found. lectr., 1960; O.M. Smith lectr. Okla. State U., 1962; M.S. Kharasch Meml. lectr. U. Chgo., 1962; K. Folkers lectr. U. Ill., 1962; Phillips lectr. Haverford Coll., 1963; vis. prof. U. Munich, 1962; Sloan lectr. U. Alaska, 1967; Disting. vis. prof. U. Iowa, 1967; Sprague lectr. U. Wis., 1967; Kilpatrick lectr. Ill. Inst. Tech., 1969; Pacific Northwest lectr., 1969; E.F. Smith lectr. U. Pa., 1970; vis. prof. chemistry Stanford U., 1973-74; S.C. Lind lectr. U. Tenn.; Arapahoe lectr. U. Colo., 1976; Mary E. Kapp lectr. Va. Commonwealth U., 1976; R.T. Major lectr. U. Conn., 1977; Nebr. lectr. Am. Chem. Soc., 1977; Leermakers lectr. Wesleyan U., 1980; Iddles Meml. lectr. U. N.H., 1981; Arapahoe lectr. Colo. State U., 1981; Winstein lectr. UCLA, 1981; Gilman lectr. Iowa State U., 1982; Marvel lectr. U. Ill., 1982; vis. lectr. Inst. Photog. Chemistry, Beijing, People's Republic of China, 1983, King lectr. Kans. State U., 1984, Lanzhou U., People's Republic of China, 1985, Davis lectr. U. New Orleans, 1986, Du Pont lectr. Harvey Mudd Coll., 1987, 3M vis. lectr. St. Olaf Coll., 1987, Swift lectr. Calif. Inst. Tech., 1987, Berliner lectr. Bryn Mawr Coll., 1988; dir., cons. editor W.A. Benjamin, Inc., 1961-67; cons. E.I. du Pont Co., 1950—; mem. adv. panel chemistry NSF, 1958-60, chmn., 1959-60, chmn. divisional com. math., phys. engring. scis., 1962-64, mem. math. and phys. sci. div. com., 1964-66; chemistry adv. panel Air Force Office Sci. Research, 1959-61; chmn. chemistry sect. Nat. Acad. Scis., 1968-71; chmn. Nat. Acad. Scis. (Class I), 1976-78, councillor, 1980-83; dir. Organic Syntheses, Inc. Author: Basic Organic Chemistry, Part I, 1955, Nuclear Magnetic Resonance, 1958, Spin-Spin Splitting in High-Resolution Nuclear Magnetic Resonance Spectra, 1961, Molecular Orbital Calculations, 1961, (with M.C. Caserio) Basic Principles of Organic Chemistry, 1964, 2d edit., 1977, Modern Organic Chemistry, 1967, (with R. Stewart and M.C. Caserio) Organic Chemistry-Methane To Macromolecules, 1971; cons. editor: McGraw-Hill Series in Advanced Chemistry, 1957-60; editor-in-chief: Organic Syntheses, vol. 41; editorial bd.: Tetrahedron, Nouveau Chimie, Spectroscopy, Organic Magnetic Resonance. Trustee L.S.B. Leakey Found.; bd. dirs., treas. Huntington Med. Research Insts., Organic Syntheses Inc. Recipient Alumni Profl. Achievement award UCLA, 1967; Guggenheim fellow, 1952-53, 55-56; recipient Am. Chem. Soc. award pure chemistry, 1954; Harrison Howe award, 1957, Roger Adams award in organic chemistry, 1967, Alumni Achievement award UCLA, 1967, Nichols medal, 1972, Tolman medal, 1975, Michelson-Morley award, 1976, Norris award, 1978, Pauling award, 1980, Theodore Wm. Richards medal, 1982, Willard Gibbs Gold medal, 1983, Golden Plate award Am. Acad. Achievement, 1983, Priestley medal, 1987, Madison Marshall award, 1989. Mem. Am. Chem. Soc. (chmn. organic chemistry div. 1956-57, exec. com. organic div. 1953-57), Nat. Acad. Scis. (com. sci. and engring. pub. policy 1983-87), Am. Philos. Soc. (council 1983-86), Am. Acad. Arts and Scis., Sigma Xi, Phi Lambda Upsilon, Alpha Chi Sigma. Office: Calif Inst Tech Div of Chem 164-30CR Pasadena CA 91125

ROBERTS, KAREN VERNA, software engineer; b. Covina, Calif., Dec. 25, 1952; d. Ernest R. and Verna Jo (Sellers) R.; m. James Mamoru Sagawa, Sept. 6, 1981. BS, Calif. Inst. Tech., 1974. Trainee IBM, San Jose, Calif., 1974-75, assoc.-staff programmer, 1982-85, software devel. mgr., 1985-88, adv. programmer, 1988—. Mem. Assn. for Computing Machinery, Am. Mgmt. Assn. Office: IBM 5600 Cottle Rd San Jose CA 95193

ROBERTS, LAMONT KARLTON, real estate executive; b. Jacksonville, Fla., Dec. 2, 1954. BSBA, U. Fla., 1976, MA, 1978. Asst. trust officer United Calif. Bank, L.A., 1978-81; syndication administr. Am. Devel. Corp., L.A., 1981-82; asst. v.p. Shearson/Am. Express Real Estate corp., L.A., 1982-84; sr. real estate devel. agt. Community Redevel. Agy., L.A., 1984—. Mem. Mus. Contemporary Art. Mem. Assn. Corp. Real Estate Execs. Republican. Methodist. Home: 14010 Captains Row 321 Marina Del Rey CA 90292

ROBERTS, LARRY PAUL, broadcasting executive; b. Marengo, Iowa, June 17, 1950; s. Paul V. and Marcheta Jean (Moore) R.; m. Sheryl Irene Delamarter, Aug. 18, 1973; children: Jason, Stacey, Adam. Student, Northwestern U., 1968-69; BS, U. Minn., 1972. Ops. mgr. Sta. WPEO Radio, Peoria, Ill., 1969-70, Sta. WAYL Radio, Mpls., 1970-76; program dir. Sta. KXL and KXL-FM, Portland, Oreg., 1976-82; pres. Sunbrook Broadcasting, Inc. and Sunbrook Communications Corp., licensee of Stas. KDXT and KGRZ, Missoula, Mont., Stas. KQUY and KXTL, Butte, Mont., Sta. KBLG, Billings, Mont., and Stas. KAAK and KXGF, Great Falls, Mont., 1982—; owner Mont. Radio Network. Past pres. Salvation Army Bd., Pueblo; v.p. United Way, Pueblo; bd. dirs. Rocky Mountain council Boy Scouts Am., Wayside Cross Rescue Mission, Pueblo; Christian edn. dir. Rocky Mountain Conf., Free Meth. Ch., mem. ofcl. bd., lay minister. Recipient Outstanding Radio Broadcaster award So. Colo. Press Club, 1986; named Radio Copywriter of Yr., Mont. Broadcasters Assn., 1983, Editorial Writer of Yr., Sigma Delta Chi, 1979, one of Outstanding Young Men in Am., Jaycees, 1980, 85. Republican. Lodges: Lions (v.p. Portland club 1982), Rotary (v.p. Pueblo club). Home: E 7922 Woodview Dr Spokane WA 99212 Office: 1212 Washington Ste 124 Spokane WA 99201

ROBERTS, MICHAEL DENNIS, air force officer; b. Knoxville, Tenn., July 13, 1949; s. James Edward and Lorah Ruth (Shipley) R.; m. Lois Jean Sprenger, Aug. 1, 1970; children: Lora Marie, Lisa Michelle, Marsha Lynn. AB in Math., San Diego State U., 1972; MS in Systems Mgmt., U. So. Calif., 1981. Commd. 2nd lt. USAF, 1972, advanced through grades to capt., 1976; navigator USAF, Grand Forks, N.D., 1973-78; instr. navigation USAF, Sacramento, 1978-82; instr. navigation USAF, Rapid City, S.D., 1982-83, scheduling officer, 1983-84, ops. planner, 1984-85; command and control officer USAF, Misawa, Japan, 1985-87; emergency actions officer March AFB, Riverside, Calif., 1987—. Mem. Alpha Mu Gamma. Republican. Mem. Assembly of God Ch. Home: 12982 Velvetleaf St Moreno Valley CA 92388 Office: 22 AREFW/DOC March AFB CA 92518

ROBERTS, MICHAEL JOSEPH, retail executive; b. San Francisco, Mar. 2, 1942; s. Clifford Joseph and Helen Berniece (Foyen) R.; m. Patricia Jean Porth, Sept. 23, 1967; 1 child, Phillip James. BA, U. Calif., Berkeley, 1967. Archeologist State of Calif., Sacramento, 1967; tchr. County of Monterey, Pacific Grove, Calif., 1967-68; mgmt. trainee Thrifty Corp., Monterey, Calif., 1968; 2d asst. mgr. Thrifty Corp., Monterey, 1968-69; 1st asst. mgr. Thrifty Corp., Salinas, Calif., 1969-70, mgr., 1971; mgr. Thrifty Corp., Los Gatos, Calif., 1972-77, Pacifica, Calif., 1977-80; buyer Thrifty Corp., Los Angeles, 1980—. Fundraiser capt. Torrance-South Bay (Calif.) YMCA, 1988; active Y's Mens Internat., Torrance, 1988; mgr., coach No. Torrance West Little League, 1984-86; coach Am. Youth Soccer Orgn., Torrance, 1983-84. Democrat. Club: Pacific Golf (mem. sec. 1983—) (Redondo Beach, Calif.). Office: Thrifty Corp 3424 Wilshire Blvd Los Angeles CA 90010

ROBERTS, MICHAEL LAWRENCE, aerospace company executive; b. Enid, Okla., Oct. 10, 1939; s. H.S. Roberts and Ruth Caroline (Koehn) Watts; m. Judy Paulette White, Aug. 21, 1974; children: Sherie Ann, Jay

R. Enlisted USN, 1957; aircraft div. chief Alameda, Calif., 1957-79; store supr. World Airways, Inc., L.A., 1980-86, Jet Am., Inc., Long Beach, Calif., 1987; coord. engring., flight test McDonnell Douglas Corp., Long Beach, 1987—. Mem. Fleet Res. Assn., USN Meml. Found. Democrat. Home: 3138 Stevely Ave Long Beach CA 90808

ROBERTS, NORMAN FRANK, English composition educator; b. Guilford, Maine, Aug. 18, 1931; s. John Francis and Pearl Estelle (Crozier) R.; m. Shoko Kawasaki, Sept. 18, 1959; children: Norman F. Jr., Kenneth K., Kathryn M. BA, U. Hawaii, 1960, MA, 1963, cert. in linguistics, 1972. Instr. ESL, U. Hawaii, Honolulu, 1962-68; instr. of English, Linguistics Leeward Community Coll., Pearl City, Hawaii, 1968—, chmn. language arts, 1975-81; cons. Nat. Council Tchrs. of English, 1972—. Co-author: Community College Library Instruction, 1979. Contbr. articles to profl. jours. V.p. Pacific Palisades Community Assn., Pearl City, pres., 1973-74; Aloha council Boy Scouts of Am., Honolulu, 1972—, dir. wood badge course, 1985. Served with U.S. Army, 1951-55. Recipient Dist. award of Merit Boy Scouts Am., 1986. Mem. Nat. Council Tchrs. of English, Hawaii Council Tchrs. of English (program chmn. 1974), Am. Dialect Soc. (program chmn. Honolulu conf. 1977), Linguistic Soc. Am., Phi Kappa Phi. Office: Leeward Community Coll Lang Arts Div 96 045 ALA IKE Pearl City HI 96782

ROBERTS, PAUL T., public relations executive; b. Mpls., Jan. 9, 1956; s. Eugene J. and Kathryn M. (Keating) R.; m. Janet M. Nealon, Sept. 1, 1988. BA magna cum laude, U. Mich., 1978. Account exec., v.p. Tom Masters Co., Beverly Hills, Calif., 1980-82, Rosenfeld, Goldman Pub. Relations, L.A., 1982-84; ptnr. Reflections, Inc., L.A., 1984-86; prin. Roberts & Co., L.A., 1986-89; promoter Peter Vitale Invitational (Billiards) Tournament, L.A., 1987, McDermottMasters World Open, Detroit, 1988; nat. media dir. Billiard Congress of Am., 1988-89. Press sec. Maureen Reagan Senate Campaign, 1984. Mem. Prof. Billiards Assoc., Billiard Congress of Am., So. Calif. Billiard Dealers. Roman Catholic. Office: Roberts & Co 8961 Sunset Ste B Los Angeles CA 90069

ROBERTS, STEVEN E., service aide; b. Oakland, Calif., Apr. 19, 1954; s. Elmore and Ann (Thompson) R.; m. Lois Elaine Roberts; children: Steven I., Sterlen. AA, Chabot Coll., 1974; student, Sonoma State U., 1974. Patient care orderly Mills Hosp., San Mateo, Calif., 1973—; Musician, pianist 2d Bapt. Ch., Vallejo, Calif., 1975-77, dir. music, 1977-86, Elisabeth Bapt. Ch., VAllejo, 1986—; contract writer Bloomfield Music, Southfield, Mich., 1984—; co-chairperson Gospel Music Workshop of Am. Mass Choir, Detroit, 1987—. Contbr. numerous articles to profl. jours. Winner 1st Pl. award Am. Song Festival, 1982, 1st Pl. award Internat. Song Festival, 1983, 1st Pl. award Music City Song Festival, 1984. Mem. Nat. Acad. Recording Arts and Scis., No. Calif. Gospel Acad. Democrat. Pentecoastal. Home: 22740 Lorand Way Hayward CA 94541

ROBERTS, THOMAS CLARK, JR., range conservationist; b. Buffalo, Aug. 1, 1946; s. Thomas Clark and Hortense Roberts; m. Barbara J. Witter, Sept. 6, 1975. AAS, SUNY, 1973; BS in Range Sci., Utah State U., 1975, MS in Range Sci., 1978. Range conservationist Bur. of Land Mgmt., Salt Lake City, 1978—. Contbr. articles to profl. jours. With USN, 1966-72. Mem. Soc. Range Mgmt. (pres. Utah sect. 1987-88), Internat. Soc. Range Mgmt., Am. Assn. Agrl. Economistr, Western Assn. Agrl. Economists. Office: Bur of Land Mgmt 2370 So 2300 West Salt Lake City UT 84120

ROBERTS, WAYNE ARTHUR, JR., business educator; b. Grand Junction, Colo., Feb. 23, 1949; s. Wayne Arthur and LaVerne Annette (Mathews) R.; m. Frances Mary Krueger, Jan. 18, 1953; children: Wayne Arthur III, Julia Frances. BS in Geology, U. Wash., 1972, MBA in Fin., 1975; ABD in Mktg., Ariz. State U., 1986. Land use planner King County Dept. of Planning, Seattle, 1972-73; owner, mgr. Naja Co., Seattle, 1973-76; instr. U. Alaska S.E., Juneau, 1975-79, asst. prof., 1979—. Livingston Wernecke Meml. scholar U. Wash., 1969. Mem. Am. Mktg. Assn. Home: 9452-B La Perouse Juneau AK 99801 Office: U Alaska SE 1108 F St Juneau AK 99801

ROBERTSON, CRAIG MICHAEL, science educator; b. Seattle, Nov. 1, 1943; s. Charles M. and Lillian Mae (Passehls) R.; m. Linda Rose Sacco, Dec. 26, 1971; children: Christian Maurice, Monique Marie. BS in Biology, San Diego State Coll., 1966, MS in Biology, 1969. Cert. elem., secondary and community coll. tchr. 5th grade tchr. Sierra Sands Unified Sch. Dist., Ridgecrest, Calif., 1969-71; sci. tchr. Sierra Sands Unified Sch. Dist., Ridgecrest, 1971—, mentor tchr., 1986; coord., field biologist Mojave Rattlesnake Antivenin Project, Ridgecrest, 1969—; reptile docent tng. dir. Maturango Mus., China Lake, Calif., 1983-89. Author: Ecological Behavior of Chukar Partridge, 1969. Mem. AAAS, The Wildlife Soc., Nat. Sci. Tchrs. Assn. Republican. Home: 480 E Laura Ridgecrest CA 93555

ROBERTSON, DANIEL CARLTON, museum director; b. Portland, Oreg., Sept. 17, 1951; s. Jerold Dean and Elsie Mae (Keck) R.; m. Emily A. Dana, June 17, 1979 (div. Apr. 1985); 1 child, Katherine Elizabeth; m. Shannon Lee Applegate, Aug. 17, 1985; children: Jessica, Colin, Ione, Max, Edane. BA, Portland State U., 1975. Intern curator Clatsop County Hist. Soc., Astoria, Oreg., 1979-80; dir. hist. services Benton County Hist. Soc., Corvallis, Oreg., 1980-83; dir. Douglas County Mus. of History and Nat. History, Roseburg, Oreg., 1983—. Mem. Roseburg City Council, 1987—; vice chmn. Roseburg Visitors and Conv. Bur., 1986—. With USN, 1969-71. Mem. Oreg. Mus. Assn. (pres. 1982-84, editor Dispatch 1980-82), Am. Assn. for State and Local History (chmn. region 11 1987—), Clatsop County Hist. Soc. (life mem.), Rotary (chmn. programs com. Roseburg club 1987—). Democrat. Unitarian. Home: 848 SE Blakeley Roseburg OR 97470 Office: Douglas County Mus History & Natural History PO Box 1550 Roseburg OR 97470

ROBERTSON, DAWNA L., advertising executive; b. Oklahoma City, Apr. 22, 1956; d. J.C. and Joyce (Neal) R. BA in Advt., U. Okla., 1978. Copywriter Oklahoma Jour., Oklahoma City, 1977-78, GKD Advt., Oklahoma City, 1978-80, Margo Wood Advt., Honolulu, 1980-82; advt. mgr. Blackfield Hawaii Corp., Honolulu, 1982-85; copywriter Gib Black Advt., Honolulu, 1985-86; copy dir. Beals Advt., Oklahoma City, 1986-87; dir. advt. Hawaiiana Resorts, Honolulu, 1987—. Recipient Honor award Honolulu Pele Awards, 1980, 81, 82, 86. Mme. Honolulu Ad Club II (copywriter pub. svcs. 1980-82), Oklahoma City Ad Fedn. (Addy Awards coms. 1978-79). Republican. Office: Hawaiiana Resorts 1270 Ala Moana Blvd Honolulu HI 96814

ROBERTSON, FRANCIS E., JR. (ROBIN ROBERTSON), data processing specialist; b. Bryan, Tex., May 9, 1944; s. Francis Elmer and Virginia M. (Dunman) R.; m. Katherine Esmela Mitchell, May 28, 1971. BS in Math., BA in English, U. Md., 1967; MA in Psychology, Internat. Coll., 1981, PhD in Psychology with distinction, 1985. Asst. v.p. Occidental LIfe Ins. Co., Los Angeles, 1969-81; cons. actuary, data processing specialist McGinn Assocs., Anaheim, Calif., 1982-86, Mercer-Meidinger-Hansen, Los Angeles, 1986—; cons. Western Conf. Teamster's Supplemental Pension Plan, Seattle, 1983—, Calif. Frozen Food Industry Pension Plan, Dublin, 1986—. Author: Handle with Care, 1964, Card Modes, 1983, C.G. Jung and the Archtypes of the Collective Unconscious, 1987; editor Psychol. Perspectives; contbr. articles to hobby and psychology jours. Mem. Soc. Actuaries, Western Pension Conf., Internat. Brotherhood of Magicians. Democrat. Office: Mercer-Medinger-Hansen 3303 Wilshire Blvd Los Angeles CA 90010

ROBERTSON, H. RICHARD, federal agency administrator; b. Roanoke Rapids, N.C., Jan. 29, 1950; s. Ben Nicholson and Lila Alice (Chichester) R. BA, East Carolina U., 1972, MA in Edn., 1974; postgrad. cert., U. Tenn., 1974; communicology cert., Gallaudet U., 1976. Cert. rehab. counselor. Counselor, Reinhardt Psychiat. Assn. Va. Dept. Rehab., Alexandria, 1974-76; spl. asst. Pres.'s Commn. EEO for Handicapped, Washington, 1976-78; team leader office civil rights HHS, San Francisco, 1978-86; AIDS coordinator HHS, 1986—; cons. various fed. agys. and depts., 1986—, Indian Health Svcs., Gallup, N.Mex., 1988—. Vol. Stop AIDS Project, San Francisco,1985-86; com. mem. AIDS Awareness Month, L.A., 1986-88; mem. adv. bd. Calif. Coun. Partnerships, 1987-88. Recipient cert. appreciation Office Civil Rights, San Francisco, 1986, 87, 88, Sec.'s Spl. Service award HHS, 1988. Home: 18 Vicksburg St San Francisco CA 94114 Office: HHS 50 United Nations Pl Rm 322 San Francisco CA 94102

ROBERTSON, JAMES ALLEN, risk management consultant, author, lecturer; b. Burlington, Iowa, Jan. 24, 1948; s. George Allen and Betty Irene (Beck) R.; student Knox Coll., 1965-66; BA, U. Iowa, 1969; postgrad. San Francisco Theol. Sem./Grad. Theol. Union, 1969-70; MSA, Pepperdine U., 1976; m. Stephanie Peacock. Casualty underwriter Hartford Ins. Group, San Francisco, 1970-72, supervising underwriter, 1972-73, L.A., 1973-74; asst. v.p. Tausch Ins. Brokers, Santa Ana, Calif., 1974-75; cons. Warren, McVeigh, Griffin & Huntington, 1975-76; sr. v.p. Reed Risk Mgmt., San Francisco, 1976-78; pres. James A. Robertson & Assoc., Inc., 1978-87; prin. cons. Warren, McVeigh & Griffin, Newport Beach, Calif., 1979-83; pres. Ins. Litigation Cons., 1984-87; nat. dir. ins. litigation svcs. Coopers & Lybrand, Newport Beach, 1987—; assoc. in risk mgmt. CPCU. Mem. Soc. Chartered Property Casualty Underwriters (pres. Orange Empire chpt. 1985-86, nat. publs. com. 1984-87, chmn. 1987-88, nat. dir. 1988—), Soc. Risk Mgmt. Cons. (chmn. profl. practices com. 1986-87), Omicron Delta Kappa. Republican. Author: The Umbrella Book, 1976, 2d edit., editor, 1979-83, Key Financial Ratios, 1978; ISO Commercial Liability Forms, 1984, 4th edit., 1986, It's Time to Take the Mystery Out of Umbrellas, 1984; editor Risk Mgmt. Letter, 1981-83, Risk Management and Insurance in The Handbook of Cash Flow and Treasury Management, 1988, Going for a Broker in Business Strategy International, 1989; contbr. over 40 articles to profl. jours. Office: Coopers & Lybrand One Newport Pl 1301 Dove St Newport Beach CA 92660

ROBERTSON, KAREN LEE, county official, acoustical consultant; b. Whittier, Calif., Mar. 21, 1955; d. Lethal Greenhaw Robertson and Lloydine Ann (Pierce) Robertson-Reese; 1 child, Kimberlee Ann Kubski. Student Calif. State U. Acoustical technician Hilliard & Bricken, Santa Ana, Calif., 1977-79, John J. Van Houten, Anaheim, Calif., 1979; prin. Robertson & Assocs., Boulder, Colo., 1980; acoustical technician David Adams & Assocs., Denver, 1980; v.p. engring. John Hilliard & Assocs., Tustin, Calif., 1985—; acoustical specialist County of Orange, Santa Ana, 1980-87; airline access, noise officer John Wayne Airport Adminstrn. of Orange County, 1987—; chair Noise Abatement Com., 1987—. Co-author Land Use/Noise Compatibility Manual, 1984; editor Noise Element of General Plan, 1984. Speaker in field. Mem. acoustical adv. bd. Orange County, 1985—; mem. Calif. Noise Officers Forum, 1987—. Recipient Achievement award Nat. Assn. Counties, 1986. Mem. Acoustical Soc. Am. (bd. dirs. 1985-86), Transp. Research Bd. (tech. mem. 1985—), Nat. Assn. Noise Control Ofcls., Community/Indsl. Noise Control Assn., Inst. Noise Control Engring. (affiliate), Calif. Assn. Window Mfrs. (STC Task Group 1985). Republican. Home: 2409 S Towner St Santa Ana CA 92807 Office: John Wayne Airport Adminstrn County of Orange 3151 Airway Ave Bldg K #101 Costa Mesa CA 92626

ROBERTSON, LAWRENCE MARSHALL, JR., neurosurgeon; b. Denver, Feb. 4, 1932; s. Lawrence M. and Mildred Eleanor (Blackwood) R.; m. Joan T. White, May 13, 1958 (div. Oct. 1973); children: Colette M., Michele E., Laurienne J., Lawrence M. III; m. Lee Ann Crawford, Sept. 24, 1982; one child, William M. BA, U. Colo., 1954; MD, U. Colo., Denver, 1957; postgrad., U. Denver, 1981-85. Intern Kings County Hosp., Bklyn., 1957-58; resident in gen. surgery St. Joseph Hosp., Denver, 1958-59; resident in neurology U. Colo., Denver, 1959-60; resident in neurosurgery Boston City Hosp., 1960-64; fellow in neurosurgery Lahey Clinic, Boston, 1963; practice medicine specializing in neurosurgery Denver, 1964—; arbitrator Am. Arbitration Assn., 1983—. Contbr. articles on malpractice to legal jours. Capt. USNR, 1979-83, 85. Recipient Continuing Edn. Cert., Am. Assn. Neurol. Surgeons and Cong. Neurol. Surgeons, 1976, 1980-83, Physicians Recognition award AMA 1976-79, 80-83, 84-87. Mem. Colo. Neurosurg. Soc., Interurban Neurosurg. Soc., Rocky Mountain Traumatologic Soc., Colo. Bar Assn., Denver Bar Assn., N.Y. Acad. Scis., Assn. Trial Lawyers Am., Nat. Railway Hist. Soc., Assn. Mil. Surgeons of U.S., Naval Res. Assn., Res. Officers Assn., U.S. Naval Inst., AAAS, Phi Alpha Delta. Office: Colo Neurosurgery PC 1635 Gilpin St Denver CO 80218

ROBERTSON, MARIAN ELLA (MARIAN ELLA HALL), handwriting analyst; b. Edmonton, Alta., Can., Mar. 3, 1920; d. Orville Arthur and Lucy Hon (Osborn) Hall; m. Howard Chester Robertson, Feb. 7, 1942; children: Elaine, Richard. Student, Willamette U., 1937-39; BS, Western Oreg. State U., 1955. Cert. elem., jr. high. tchr., supt. (life) Oreg.; cert. graphoanalyst. Tchr. pub. schs. Mill City, Albany, Scio and Hillsboro, Oreg., 1940-72; cons. Zaner-Bloser Inc., Columbus, Ohio, 1972-85, assoc. cons., 1985-89; pres. Write-Keys, Scio, 1980—; tchr. Internat. Graphoanalysis Soc., Chgo., 1979; instr. Linn-Benton Community Coll., 1985-86. sr. intern 5th Congl. Dist. Oreg., Washington, 1984, mem. sr. adv. council; precinct committeemem. Rep. Cen. Com., Linn County, 1986, alt. vice-chair, 1986, parlimentarian, 1988—; candidate Oreg. State Legis., Salem, 1986. Mem. Altrusa Internat. (internat. chmn. 1985-86, chmn. pub. rels. 1989—), Internat. Platform Assn. Republican. Mem. Soc. of Friends. Home: 37929 Kelly Rd Scio OR 97374 Office: Write-Keys PO Box 54 Jefferson OR 97352

ROBERTSON, MATTHEW ROGER, systems software consultant, entrepreneur; b. Tacoma, Dec. 23, 1957; s. Roger Raymond and Karolina (Högel) R. AA in Computer Sci., U. Puget Sound, 1979, BS in Math., 1979, BS in Chem. Physics, 1979. Programmer, system mgr. Boeing Computer Services, Seattle, 1979-82; software instr. Boeing Aerospace Co., Seattle, 1982-85; systems analyst CADDEX Corp, Woodinville, Wash., 1985-86; founder Robertson Enterprises, Redmond, Wash., 1986—. Musician Tacoma Concert Band, 1982-85; pres. Homeowner's Assn., 1986-87, 87-88. Mem. Boeing Mgmt. Assn., Digital Equipment Corp. Users Soc., Boeing Employees VAX User Group. Republican. Presbyterian. Home and Office: 15922 NE 42d Ct Redmond WA 98052

ROBERTSON, ORAN B., retail company executive; b. Turner, Ore., 1917; married; student, U. Wash. With Boeing Aircraft Co. until 1946, Fred Meyer, Inc., Portland, Oreg., v.p., dir. engring., formerly chmn., chief exec. officer, now chmn. exec. com., also dir. Office: Fred Meyer Inc 3800 SE 22nd St Portland OR 97202 *

ROBERTSON, ROBERT T., freight transportation company executive. Pres. CF Land Svcs. Inc., Palo Alto, Calif. Office: CF Land Svcs Inc 5 Palo Alto Sq Ste 600 Palo Alto CA 94306 *

ROBERTSON, SAMUEL HARRY, III, transportation safety research engineer, educator; b. Phoenix, Oct. 2, 1934; s. Samuel Harry and Doris Byrle (Duffield) R.; m. Nancy Jean Bradford, Aug. 20, 1954; children: David Lyle, Pamela Louise. BS, Ariz. State U., 1956; D in Aviation Tech. (hon.), Embry-Riddle Aero. U., 1972. Registered profl. engr. Chief hazards div. Aviation Safety Engring. and Research, Phoenix, 1960-70; pres. Robertson Research Engrs., 1960-70; research prof., dir. Safety Ctr. Coll. Engring. and Applied Scis., Ariz State U., Tempe, 1970-79; pres. Robertson Research Inc., 1970—, Robertson Aviation Inc., 1977—, Internat. Ctr. for Safety Edn., 1982—; pres., chief exec. officer Robertson Research Group, Inc., Tempe, 1987—; cons. design and accident investigation of airplanes, 1961—; instr. Inst. Aerospace Safety, U. So. Calif., 1962-70, Armed Forces Inst. Pathology, 1970—, Dept. Transp. Safety Inst., 1970—; pres. Flying R Land & Cattle Co., 1976—; mem. adv. bd. Rio Salado Bank, Tempe, 1985—. Contbr. 60 articles to profl. jours. and pubs.; patentee applying plastic to paper, fuel system safety check valves, crash resitant fuel system, safety aircraft seats; holder FAA STC's various fuel systems, fuel system components; designer, developer, mfr. crash resistant fuel systems for airplanes, helicopters, championship racing cars. Served as pilot USAF, 1956-60, Ariz. Army NG 1960-61, 70-74, Ariz. Air NG, 1961-69. Recipient Contbns. Automotive Racing Safety award CNA, 1957, Adm. Luis DeFlorez Internat. Flying Safety award, 1969, Cert. Commendation Nat. Safety Council, 1969, Gen. W. Spruance award for safety edn., SAFE Soc., 1982; holder Nat. Speed Record for one class of drag racing car, 1955-67, 5 nat. records for flying model aircraft, 1950-56. Mem. Internat. Soc. Air Safety Investigators (Jerome Lederer internat. award 1981), Aerospace Med. Assn., AIAA, AMA, Soc. Automotive Engrs., Am. Helicopter Soc., Nat. Fire Protection Assn., Aircraft Owners and Pilots Assn., U.S. Automobile Club (mem. tech. com.). Office: 1024 E Vista del Cerro Tempe AZ 85281

ROBINS, MIRIAM CLAIR, former insurance company executive, former interior design consultant; b. Denver, Sept. 19, 1935; d. H. Rupard and Mildred L. (Opie) R. BA, Colo. Coll., 1957; MA, U. Denver, 1959. Instr. piano and organ, Denver, 1957-62; v.p. Olinger Life Ins. Co., Denver, 1961-63, exec. v.p., 1963-73, pres., 1973-78, vice chmn. bd., 1978-85; v.p. Robins Agy., Inc., Denver, 1963-85; cons. Cherry Creek Interiors, Denver, 1984. Tchr., music arranger for talent competition Miss America, 1958. V.p. Colo. Life Conv., Denver, 1966-67; mem. Pres.'s Council Colo. Coll. Mem. AAUW, Denver Art Mus., Chancellor's Soc. U. Denver, Kappa Delta Pi, Mu Phi Epsilon, Kappa Alpha Theta. Republican. Clubs: Denver, Denver Athletic, Cherry Hills Country; Garden of the Gods (Colorado Springs, Colo.); Metropolitan. Home: Polo Club North 2552 E Alameda Ave # 61 Denver CO 80209

ROBINSON, AMBER MARY, food service manager; b. Glendora, Calif., Nov. 1, 1961; d. Jack Butler and Janet Ann (Double) R. Student, Long Beach (Calif.) City Coll., 1982-83. Mgr. Merry Go Round Enterprises, San Diego, 1983; quality control mgr. Merry Go Round Enterprises, Houston, 1985; dist. mgr. Merry Go Round Enterprises, San Francisco, 1987—. Democrat. Office: 1220 E Joppa Rd Towson MD 21204

ROBINSON, ANNETTMARIE, entrepreneur; b. Fayetteville, Ark., Jan. 31, 1940; d. Christopher Jacy and Edith Lucille (Cook) Simmons; m. Roy Robinson, June 17, 1966; children: Steven, Sammy, Doug, Pamela, Olen. BA, Edison Tech. U., 1958; BA in Bus., Seattle Community Coll., 1959. Dir. personnel Country Kitchen Restaurants, Inc., Anchorage, 1966-71; investor Anchorage, 1971—; cons. Pioneer Investments, Anchorage, 1983—, M'RAL, Inc. Retail Dry Goods, Anchorage, 1985. Mem. Rep. Presdl. Task Force, Washington, 1984—, Reps. of Alaska, Anchorage, 1987; mem. chmn. round table YMCA, Anchorage, 1986—. Mem. NAFE.

ROBINSON, BARBARA JANE, retired educator; b. Portland, Oreg., Mar. 26, 1925; d. Ralph and Ethelyn Jane (Hatheway) Ellis; m. William G. Robinson, June 9, 1955 (dec. 1978); children: Margorie, Linda. BSEd, Southern Oreg. State Coll., 1957, MS in Edn., 1972. Cert. tchr., Oreg. Elem. tchr. Jackson County Schs., Jacksonville, Oreg., 1957-59; Elem. tchr. Medford Sch. Dist. 549C, Jacksonville, 1959-83, adminstrv. asst. to prin., 1979-83. Mem. Oreg. Ret. Educators Assn., Am. Assn. Ret. Persons, AAUW, Sojourners Club. Republican.

ROBINSON, BARBARA L., accountant; b. Framingham, Mass., Dec. 11, 1962; d. Joseph P. and Rosalie L. (Caporuscio) R. BA in Acctg., Western State Coll. Colo., 1986. Staff acct. Campbell, DeVasto and Assocs., Scituate, Mass., 1986-87; auditor Def. Contact Audit Agy., Needham, Mass., 1987; jr. acct. Colo. Interstate Gas Co., Colorado Springs, 1988—. Home: 1615 W Cheyenne Rd 6 Colorado Springs CO 80906

ROBINSON, BARRY WESLEY, physicist, aerospace company executive; b. Eugene, Oreg., Oct. 24, 1948; s. Richard D. and Jean V. (Chase) R.; m. Rebecca L. Tooman, Sept. 18, 1970 (div. 1986); 1 child, Sean C. BS, U. Wash., 1970; PhD, Rutgers U., 1974. Teaching asst. Rutgers U., New Brunswick, N.J., 1970-72, rsch. asst., 1972-74; rsch. assoc. Physics dept. U. Wash., Seattle, 1974-76; rsch. investigator Physics dept. U. Pa., Phila., 1976-78, rsch. asst. prof. Physics dept., 1978-80, asst. prof., 1980-84; prin. engr. FEL program Boeing Aerospace, Seattle, 1984—. Contbr. articles to profl. jours. Mem. Am. Phys. Soc. Office: Boeing Aerospace M/S 2R-00 PO Box 3999 Seattle WA 98124

ROBINSON, BERNARD LEO, lawyer; b. Kalamazoo, Feb. 13, 1924; s. Louis Harvey and Sue Mary (Starr) R.; BS, U. Ill., 1947, MS, 1958, postgrad. in structural dynamics, 1959; JD, U. N.Mex., 1973; m. Betsy Nadell, May 30, 1947; children: Robert Bruce, Patricia Anne, Jean Carol. Rsch. engr. Assn. Am. Railroads, 1947-49; instr. architecture Rensselaer Poly. Inst., 1949-51; commd. 2d lt. Corps Engrs., U.S. Army, 1945, advanced through grades to lt. col., 1965, ret., 1968; engr. Nuclear Def. Rsch. Corp., Albuquerque, 1968-71; admitted to N.Mex. bar, 1973, U.S. Supreme Ct. bar, 1976; practiced in Albuquerque, 1973-85, Silver City, N.Mex., 1985-89; sec., treas. Rento Inc., 1987—. Dist. commr. Boy Scouts Am., 1960-62. Vice chmn. Rep. Dist. Com., 1968-70. Decorated Air medal. Mem. ASCE, ABA, N.Mex. Bar Assn., Grant County Bar Assn., Ret. Officers Assn., DAV, Assn. U.S. Army, Am. Legion, VFW. Home: 1785 W Cumino Urbano Green Valley AZ 85614 Office: PO Box 753 Green Valley AZ 85622

ROBINSON, CALVIN STANFORD, lawyer; b. Kalispell, Mont., Mar. 31, 1920; s. Calvin Alton and Berta Ella (Green) R.; m. Nancy Hanna, Dec. 13, 1945; children—Terrill S., Calvin D., Robert B., Barbara E. B.A., U. Mont., 1944; postgrad. U. Wash., U. Calif.; J.D., U. Mich., 1949. Bar: Ill. 1949, Mont. 1949. Assoc. Rooks & Freeman, Chgo., 1949-50; ptnr. Murphy, Robinson, Heckathorn & Phillips and predecessors, Kalispell, Mont., 1950—; dir. Semitool Inc., Kalispell, 1979—, Winter Sports Inc., Whitefish, Mont., 1984—; mem. Mont. Gov.'s Com. Bus. Corp. Laws, Gov's. Revenue Estimating Coun., 1986—. Mem. Mont. Environ. Quality Council; past vice chmn. Mont. Bd. Housing; past mem. Mont. Bd. Edn., Mont. U. Bd. Regents. Served to lt. USNR, 1942-46. Fellow Am. Coll. Probate Counsel; mem. Mont. Bar Assn., N.W. Mont. Bar Assn., Ill. Bar Assn., ABA. Episcopalian. Home: 315 Crestview Dr Kalispell MT 59901 Office: One Main Bldg PO Box 759 Kalispell MT 59901

ROBINSON, CHARLES WESLEY, energy company executive; b. Long Beach, Calif., Sept. 7, 1919; s. Franklin Willard and Anna Hope (Gould) R.; m. Tamara Lindovna, Mar. 8, 1957; children: Heather Lynne, Lisa Anne, Wendy Paige. AB cum laude in Econs., U. Calif., Berkeley, 1941; MBA, Stanford U., 1947. Asst. mgr. mfg. Golden State Dairy Products Co., San Francisco, 1947-49; v.p., then pres. Marcona Corp., San Francisco, 1952-74; undersec. of state for econ. affairs Dept. State, Washington, 1974-75, dep. sec. of state, 1976-77; sr. mng. partner Kuhn Loeb & Co., N.Y.C., 1977-78; vice chmn. Blyth Eastman Dillon & Co., N.Y.C., 1978-79; chmn. Energy Transition Corp., Santa Fe and Washington, 1979—; bd. dirs. Arthur D. Little, The Allen Group, Northrop Corp., NIKE, Inc.; internat. adv. bd. Pan Am. World Airways. Patentee slurry transport. Trustee Trilateral Commn., N.Y.C., 1972-74, 77—, Brookings Instn., Washington, 1977—. Served to lt. USN, 1941-46. Recipient Disting. Honor award Dept. State, 1977. Mem. Council on Fgn. Relations N.Y.C. Republican. Methodist. Club: Pacific Union (San Francisco). Office: Energy Transition Corp PO Box 2224 Santa Fe NM 87504

ROBINSON, DANIEL ARLEY, retail executive; b. Perkins, Okla., Nov. 20, 1928; s. Elmer Edward and Pauline Grace R.; m. Julia Marie Koslov, Feb. 19, 1950 (div. 1969); children: Daniel, Paulette, Henry, Michael, Jeanette, Annette; m. Judy Arlene Kleve, Feb. 28, 1970. Student, Pierce Coll., 1961-63; grad. gemologist, Gemological Inst. Am., 1982. Cert. mfg. engr. Technician Exline Engring., Tulsa, 1952-58; prodn. foreman Summers Gyroscope, Santa Monica, Calif., 1958-60; methods engr. RCA, Van Nuys, Calif., 1960-65; mech. engr. Raytheon Co., Lexington, Mass., 1965-69; engring. mgr. I.T.T., Milan, Tenn. and Van Nuys, 1969-74; dir. mfg. Flow Research Inc., Kent, Calif., 1974-77; pres. Robinson Jewelry Inc., Cut Bank, Mont., 1977—. Inventor automated assembly work sta. Served with USN, 1948-52, Korea. Mem. Am. Gem Soc., Mont.-Wyo. Jewelers Assn. (bd. dirs. 1978-82, pres. 1982-83), Havre C. of C. (bd. dirs. 1981-83), Cut Bank C. of C. Republican. Home: 138 First Ave SW Cut Bank MT 59427 Office: Robinson Jewelry Northern Village Shopping Ctr Cut Bank MT 59427

ROBINSON, DAVID DORMAN, psychologist; b. Pontiac, Mich., Feb. 11, 1938; s. Alfred Henry and Emma (Lockwood) R.; m. Sheila Black, Dec. 27, 1976; children: Joshua, Alex, Anthony. BA, Mich. State U., 1959, MA, 1963; PhD, Ohio State U., 1969. Diplomate Am. Bd. Indsl. and Organizational Psychology. Rsch. assoc. Human Resources Internat., Cleve., 1963-66; rsch. psychologist Battelle Meml. Inst., Clumbus, Ohio, 1966-68; mgmt. cons. supr. Ernst & Whinney, Boise, Idaho, 1969-72; pvt. practice Boise, Idaho, 1972-87; psychol. contractor Meml. Hosp., Boulder, Colo., 1987—. Author: (manual) Worker Rehabilitation Questionnaire; contbg. author in field. Bd. dirs. United Way, Boise. 1lt., U.S. Army, 1959-61. Mem. Am. Psychol. Assn., Colo. Psychol. Assn., Idaho Psychol. Assn., Soc. Indsl., Organizational Psychology, Boise Exec. Assn. (pres. 1980). Democrat. Roman Catholic. Home: 4265 Corriente Pl Boulder CO 80301

ROBINSON, DAVID ROGER, infosystems specialist; b. Coshocton, Ohio, Aug. 10, 1951; s. Roger Linzey and Hazel Lucille (Snedeker) R.; m. Kathleen Margaret Carpenter, Aug. 12, 1972; children: Kristina Rose,

Kimberley Gayle. BS in Math., BS in Physics, Ohio U., 1973; MS Indsl. Engring., U. Wis., Madison, 1975. Cert. systems profl. Systems analyst Burroughs Corp., Detroit, 1975-77, project leader, 1977-83, mgr. data networks, 1980-83, mgr. tech. services, 1983-85; mgr. data communications Joseph & Cogan, Woodland Hills, Calif., 1985-86; project mgr. network integration Burroughs and Sperry Corp., Woodland Hills, 1986-87; mgr. tech. svcs. Joseph & Cogan, Westlake Village, Calif., 1987-88, mgr. software devel., 1989—; adjunct lectr. U. Mich., Ann Arbor, 1985; guest lectr. U. Detroit, 1985. Author: (software) Bitnet, 1979. Mem. GTE Telenet Users Group (pres. 1982-84, 84-86, sec. 1981-82). Republican. Baptist.

ROBINSON, EDWARD N., investment banker; b. Savannah, Ga., Nov. 22, 1945; s. Aaron A. Robinson and Beatrice (Biberman) Nava; m. Carol Scott Robinson, Nov. 12, 1977; children: Jacob Scott, Jennifer Scott. BA, U. Mich., 1967; JD, NYU, 1974. Law clk. U.S Dist. Ct., Los Angeles, 1974-75; atty. Tuttle & Taylor, Los Angeles, 1975-77; mortgage officer Ctr. Fin. Group, Los Angeles, 1978-79; co-owner Robinson, Ross & Gallagher, Los Angeles, 1979-83; v.p. The First Boston Corp., Los Angeles, 1983-87, dir., mergers and acquisitions, 1988—; trustee Sundance Inst., Sundance, Utah, 1987—; exec. com. The Lexington Group, Los Angeles, 1984—. Trustee Greater Los Angeles Zoo Assn., 1988—. Mem. Wilshire C. of C. Office: The First Boston Corp 333 S Grand Ave Los Angeles CA 90071

ROBINSON, FRANK ROBERT, radio station executive; b. Hollywood, Calif., Sept. 17, 1938; s. Frank Robert and Helen Macdonnel (James) R.; m. Ann Katherine Carman, Apr. 24, 1965 (div. 1984); children: Geoffrey Scott, Hilary Ann. BS, Westminster Coll., 1967. Account exec. Sta. KLUB, Sta. KISN, Salt Lake City, 1965-69, ops. mgr., 1970-73, gen. mgr., 1974-85; sta. mgr. Sta. KUER U. Utah, 1986—. Bd. dirs. Salt Lake City chpt. ARC, 1975, Salt Lake City YMCA, 1976, Jr. Achievement, Salt Lake City, 1984; mem. pub. utilities adv. com. Salt Lake City, 1986—. Mem. Utah Broadcasters Assn. (bd. dirs. 1982-83, pres. 1983—), Salt Lake Radio Broadcasters Assn. (sec. 1981-82). Republican. Roman Catholic. Lodge: Kiwanis (Salt Lake City chpt. bd. dirs. 1976-77, pres. 1982-83).

ROBINSON, GERALDINE MARLENE HELWING, psychologist, psychoanalyst; b. Milw., Apr. 5, 1947; d. William Frederick and Olga Wilhelmina (Syring) Helwig; m. Ian Robinson, June 23, 1969; children: Rya (dec.), Chelsea Siobhàn Antoinette, Krystal Georgiana Victoria, Lisa Ralet. BA in Psychology, U. Wis.-Stout, 1970, MSE in Sch. Psychology, 1975. Lic. psychologist, Minn. Research assoc., psychotherapist N.W. Psychiat. Clinic, Eau Claire, Wis., 1974-77; pvt. practice psychology and psychotherapy Eau Claire, 1977-79; ptnr. Inst. Psychol. Therapies, Mpls., 1980-84; owner psychol. practice Robinson and Assoc., Mpls., 1984-88; pvt. practice cons., writer Seattle, 1988—; adj. asst. prof. counseling and psychol. services St. Mary's Coll. Grad. Ctr., Mpls., 1987-88; psychoanalytic preceptorship Interpersonal/Sullivanian Analysis with J.M. Tobin, M.D., Eau Claire, 1970-77; cons.; expert witness; pub. speaker, guest on TV and radio shows; allied profl. staff mem. St. Joseph's Hosp., Chippewa Falls, Wis., 1978-80; mem. med. research staff Sacred Heart Hosp., Eau Claire, 1974-77; co-owner, v.p. computer software mfg. co. Interactive Analytic Node, 1985-87. Contbr. articles to profl. jours.; author research papers presented to various profl. orgns. Co-founder, official spokesperson, chmn. tng. com., vol. Disaster Stress Team, Twin Cities ARC and Minn. Network for Disaster Stress Intervention MNDSI, 1985-88; vol. instr. and moderator ARC North Star Disaster Tng. Inst., 1987-88; organizer Minn. Assn. Mental Health Infants; organizer, v.p. pregnancy and drug prevention, intervention and edn. Concerned, Inc., Menomonie, Wis., 1971-73; bd. dirs. Geriatric Day Care Ctr., Luth. Hosp., Eau Claire, 1975-77. Mem. Group-Without-A-Name (GWAN) Internat. Psychiat. Research Soc., Internat. Soc. Human Ethology, Internat. Assn. Infant Mental Health (bd. dir. 1988—), Minn. Psychol. Assn. (social action com. 1984-85, author official policy statement on sexual exploitation children and teenagers, co-chair entertainment com. 50th anniversary 1986), Wis. Assn. Infant Devel. (steering com. 1977-79), Minn. Women Psychologists, Minn. Assn. Mental Health of Infants, Midwest Assn. Comatose Care (v.p. 1984-85, pres. 1985-88), Minn. Geneal. Soc., Clan Gunn Soc. N.Am. Lodge: Zonta (corp., gallery fund-raising coms. 1983-84; chair service com. 1984-85, co-chair 1985-86; co-chair corp. collection com. 1985-86, status of women com. 1987—, initiated orgn. with high sch. women, mentoring program for local chpt.). Home and Office: 4727 148th Ave NE CC103 Bellevue WA 98007

ROBINSON, HERBERT FISK, newspaper executive; b. Seattle, Nov. 22, 1924; s. Wallace Craig and Gladys (Lillie) R.; m. Mary Mulligan, Aug. 25, 1949 (div. 1984); children—Michael, Mark, Susan. B.A., U. Wash., 1949; M.S., Columbia U., 1950. Reporter The Times, Seattle, 1941-53, assoc. editor, 1965-77, editorial page editor, 1977—; news dir. Sta. KOMO-TV, Seattle, 1953-65; Served to capt. U.S. Army, 1943-46, CBI. Recipient Spot TV News Reporting award Sigma Delta Chi, 1956, Top Local TV News award Sylvania Corp., 1960, Outstanding Govt. Reporting award Mcpl. League, 1983; Pulitzer scholar, 1950. Mem. Am. Soc. Newspaper Editors, Nat. Conf. Editorial Writers. Clubs: Rainier, Wash. Athletic (Seattle). Office: Seattle Times PO Box 70 Seattle WA 98111 *

ROBINSON, JENS JOSEPH, college dean; b. Portland, Oreg., Jan. 5, 1937; s. James J. and Gladys E. (Masten) R.; m. Kathryn P. Robinson, June 10, 1961; children: Jodi, Jaymi, Jini, Jared, Josie. BS, Pacific U., 1958; MS, Oreg. State U., 1960; PhD, U. Oreg., 1970. Supt. Woodburn (Oreg.) Sch. Dist., 1971-86, McMinnville (Oreg.) Sch. Dist., 1982-86; dean Sch. Edn. Ea. Oreg. State Coll., La Grande, 1986—; cons. Oreg. Sch. Bds. Assn., Salem, 1982—, Idaho Sch. Bds. Assn., Boise, 1984-86; bd. dirs. Oreg. Total Info. Systems, Eugene. Bd. dirs. McMinnville Community Hosp., 1986—. Mem. Confedn. Oreg. Sch. Adminstrs., Oreg. Assn. Sch. Execs. (mem. exec. com.). Republican. Roman Catholic. Office: Ea Oreg State Coll Sch Edn 8th & K La Grande OR 97850

ROBINSON, JOHN ALEXANDER, professional football coach; b. Chgo., July 25, 1935; s. Matthew and Ethlyn (Alexander) R.; m. Barbara Lee Amirkhan, July 31, 1960; children: Teresa, Lynn, David, Christopher. B.S., U. Oreg., 1958. Asst. football coach U. Oreg., Eugene, 1960-71, U. So. Calif., Los Angeles, 1971-74, Oakland (Calif.) Raiders, 1975; head fooball coach U. So. Calif., 1976-82, v.p., 1982-83; head coach Los Angeles Rams Football Team, 1983—; coached winning Rose Bowl teams, 1977, 79, 80. Served with U.S. Army, 1958-59. Named Nat. Football Conf. Coach of Yr., UPI, 1983-84 season. Roman Catholic. Office: care L A Rams 2327 W Lincoln Ave Anaheim CA 92801

ROBINSON, JOHN DENNIS, data processing and infosystems executive; b. Niigata, Japan, Feb. 2, 1953; came to U.S., 1959; s. Allison and Eiko (Kikuchi) R.; m. Catherine Ellen Hielen, Feb. 13, 1971; 1 child, Joseph. Constrn. sales rep. Overland Lumber, Boise, Idaho, 1971-75; program analyst County of Ada, Boise, 1975-78; dist. mgr. RGIS, Salt Lake City and Boise, 1978-79; data processing ops. mgr. Waremart Inc., Boise, 1979-85; cen. services mgr. County of Walla Walla, Wash., 1985—; chmn. credit com. Mountain States Wholesale Credit Union, Boise, 1983-85; cons. Meridian (Idaho) Data Service, 1983-84. Mem. editorial bd. Computer World Info. Mgrs., 1986—. Vol. Expanded Food and Nutrition Edn. Program, Boise, 1985. Mem. Assn. County Info. Svcs. (sec.-treas. 1989—), Common Cause. Home: 1809 Plaza Way 10 PO Box 492 Walla Walla WA 99362 Office: County of Walla Walla 315 W Main Rm 103 Walla Walla WA 99362

ROBINSON, KIRK MCCAULEY, civil engineer; b. Portland, Oreg., May 19, 1942; s. Vernon Gelino and Marian Frances (Bronson) R.; m. Sheryl Ann Vaughn, Oct. 17, 1975; children: David Mark, Jerald McCauley. AS in Math., Clackamas Community Coll., 1979, AS in Engring., 1980; BS in Civil Engring., U. Portland, 1982. Civil engr. Bonneville Power Adminstrn., Portland, 1982, civil engr. transmission engring., 1982-87, civil engr. facilities engring., 1987—. Mem. Am. Soc. Civil Engrs. (assoc dir. 1986-87), Portland Adv. Com. for Engring. Edn. (conf. chmn. 1988). Republican. Lutheran. Club: Portland Roller Ball Hockey. Office: Bonneville Power Adminstrn PO Box 3621 Portland OR 97208

ROBINSON, MARK LEIGHTON, oil company executive, petroleum geologist, horse farm owner; b. San Bernadino, Calif., Aug. 4, 1927; s. Ernest Guy and Florence Iola (Lemmon) R.; m. Jean Marie Ries, Feb. 8, 1954; children: Francis Willis, Mark Ries, Paul Leighton. AB cum laude in Geology, Princeton U., 1950; postgrad. Stanford U., 1950-51. Geologist Shell Oil Co., Billings, Mont., Rapid City, S.D., Denver, Midland, Tex., 1951-56, dist. geologist, Roswell, N.Mex., 1957-60, div. mgr., Roswell, N.Mex., 1961-63, Jackson, Miss., 1964-65, Bakersfield, Calif., 1967-68, mgr. exploration econs., N.Y.C., 1969; mgmt. advisor BIPM (Royal Dutch Shell Oil Co.), The Hague, The Netherlands, 1966; pres., chmn. bd. dirs. Robinson Resource Devel. Co., Inc., Roswell, 1970—. Campaign chmn. Chaves County Republican Com., Roswell, 1962; mem. alumni schs. com. Princeton U., 1980—. Served with USNR, 1945-46. Mem. Roswell Geol. Soc. (trustee 1972), Am. Assn. Petroleum Geologists, Stanford U. Earth Scientists Assn., Yellowstone Bighorn Research Assn., Am. Horse Shows Assn., SAR, Sigma Xi. Episcopalian. Discovered Lake Como oil field, Miss., 1971, McNeal oil field, Miss., 1973, North Deer Creek Gas Field, Mont., 1983, Bloomfield East Oil Field, Mont., 1986. Home: Rt 1 Box 31D Roswell NM 88201 Office: Robinson Resource Devel Co Inc PO Box 1227 Roswell NM 88201

ROBINSON, MICHAEL G., service executive; b. Stillwater, Okla., Oct. 1, 1948; s. William G. and Ava Lee (Ray) R.; m. Treva M. Brown, Sept. 6, 1969 (div. June 1982); children: Eric G., Carrie M.; m. Janie M. Storm, March 26, 1983; children: Timothy M., Katherine E. BE, U. Mo., 1970. Resident mgr. Stouffer's Riverfront Inn, St. Louis, 1972-74; gen. mgr. Hilton Inn McAllen, Tex., 1974-76, Park Plaza Hotel, Cleve., 1976-78, Hilton at Merrimack, N.H., 1978-80, Wichita (Kans.) Airport Hilton Inn, 1980-82; resident mgr. Marriott's Mark Resort, Vail, Colo., 1982-83, Tulsa Marriott Hotel, 1983-84, Santa Clara (Calif.) Marriott Hotel, 1985-86; gen. mgr. Marriott's Mark Resort, Vail, 1986—. Mem. Jaycees, McAllen, 1974-76. Mem. Vail Resort Assn. (dir. 1988), Santa Clara County Hospitality Assn. (dir. 1985-86), So. N.H. Assn. Commerce and Industry (dir. 1988), Vail C. of C. (vice-chmn. 1988). Lodge: Rotary. Home: PO Box 1802 Avon CO 81620 Office: Marriott's Mark Resort 715 W Lionsaend Circle Vail CO 81657

ROBINSON, RICHARD ALLEN, JR., consultant, human resources development trainer; b. Ellensburg, Wash., Aug. 21, 1936; s. Richard Allen and Rosa Adele (Oswalt) R.; m. R. Elaine Whitham, Sept. 8, 1956; children—Sharon E. Robinson Losey, Richard Allen, René L. B.A., U. Wash., 1958; postgrad. U.S. Army Command and Gen. Staff Coll., 1969-70; M.A., U. Mo., 1971. Commd. 2d lt. U.S. Army, 1958, advanced through grades to lt. col., 1972, various infantry assignments including command, 1958-72, research and devel. assignments including dep. dir. test of behavioral sci., dep. commandant U.S.A. Organizational Effectiveness, 1975-77, ret., 1979; chief office orgn. and employee devel. Wash. Dept. Social and Health Services, Olympia, 1979—; pvt. practice orgn. and mgmt. devel. cons./trainer, 1979—. Decorated Legion of Merit with oak leaf cluster, Bronze Star. Mem. Am. Soc. Tng. and Devel., Organizational Devel. Network, Internat. Platform Assn., Mass. Hort. Soc. Contbg. author: Games Trainers Play, vol. II, 1983. Office: DSHS Mail 8315 W 27th St Tacoma WA 98466

ROBINSON, RICHARD EDMUND, company executive; b. York, Nebr., Jan. 25, 1936; s. Ernest Edmund and Dorothy (Bowen) R. Student, Art Ctr. Sch., L.A., 1954-56; BFA, Calif. Coll. Arts of Crafts, 1958. Display regional dir. J. Magnin, San Francisco, 1958-63; sales promotion dir. Howells Stores, Denver, 1963-65; advtg. dir. May D&F Stores, Denver, 1965-67; sales promotion dir. Fashion Bar Stores, Denver, 1967-73; visual mdseg. dir. May D&F Stores, Denver, 1973-75, sales promotion dir., 1975-76; sales promotion dir. Powers Stores, Mpls., 1976-77; visual dir. Roos-Atkins Stores, San Francisco, 1978-79; v.p., sales promotion dir. Roos-Atkins, San Francisco, 1979-80; v.p. Roth Display, San Ysidro, Calif., 1980—. Founder, dir. AMITZVAH. Recipient: NRMA Advtg. Grand award, Nat. Retail Merchants Assn., N.Y.,. mem. Western Assn. Visual Merchandiser. Republican. Home and Office: 5798 Balmoral Dr Oakland CA 94619

ROBINSON, RICHARD HUTCHINSON, real estate executive, investor; b. N.Y.C., Aug. 11, 1949; s. Richard Henry and Elizabeth (Hutchinson) R.; m. Kate Oliver Barry, Sept. 3, 1981; 1 child, States Wylie. AB, U. N.C., 1971. With Norris Beggs & Simpson, San Francisco, 1977-81; v.p. Cushman & Wakefield, San Francisco, 1981—; lectr. in field; tour leader. Chmn. San Francisco Mayor's Task Force. Mem. Urban Land Inst., St. Francis Yacht Club, Point O Woods Club. Home: 2033 Jefferson St San Francisco CA 94123 Office: Cushman & Wakefield 555 California St San Francisco CA 94104

ROBINSON, RICHARD OWEN, V, marketing professional; b. Sacramento, Nov. 10, 1962; s. Richard Owen Robinson IV and Dorotea Theresa (Chiodo) Sarti. AA, Stockton (Calif.) Jr. Coll., 1984; student, San Francisco State U., 1985—. Sr. operator Sumiden Wire, Stockton, 1980-85; account exec. Tiffany & Co., San Francisco, 1986-87; mktg. mgr. Ackerley Communications, San Francisco, 1987-88; account exec. Am. Media Network, Inc., San Francisco, 1989—. Mem. San Francisco Ad Club. Republican. Roman Catholic. Home: 3206 Hollis St Oakland CA 94608 Office: Am Media Network 120 Howard St #450 San Francisco CA 94105

ROBINSON, ROBERT BLACQUE, association executive; b. Long Beach, Calif., Apr. 24, 1927; s. Joseph LeRoi and Frances Hansel R.; m. Susan Amelia Thomas, Jan. 21, 1960; children: Victoria, Shelly, Blake, Sarah. Student, Oreg. State Coll., 1946; BA, UCLA, 1950; student, U. Hawaii. Partner, Pritchard Assocs. (Mgmt. Cons.), Honolulu, 1956-58; asst. dir. Econ. Planning and Coordination Authority, Hawaii, 1959; dep. dir. dept. econ. devel. State of Hawaii, 1960-63; asst. mgr. Pacific Concrete and Rock Co., Ltd., Honolulu, 1963-66, exec. v.p. and gen. mgr., 1966-68, pres. and gen. mgr., 1968-75; chmn. Pacific Concrete and Rock Co., Ltd., 1976-77; pres. C. of C. of Hawaii, Honolulu, 1977—. Bd. govs. Hawaii Employers Council, 1969-74, mem. exec. com., 1969-74, vice chmn., 1973-74; bd. dirs. Pacific Aerospace Mus., 1982-86; mem. Hawaii Tourism Conf., 1977—, chmn., 1981-82; bd. dirs. Aloha United Fund, 1970-76, sec., 1972, v.p., 1973-76; bd. dirs. Oahu Devel. Conf., 1970-75; treas., bd. dirs. Crime Stoppers Hawaii, 1981—; mem. Hawaii Joint Council on Econ. Edn., 1985—; bd. dirs. Jr. Achievement Hawaii, 1967-73, pres., 1969; bd. dirs. Hawaii Ednl. Council, 1974-75, Health and Community Services Council Hawaii, 1982-84; mem. exec. com. Hawaii Conv. Ctr. Council, 1984—, Interagency Energy Conservation Council, State of Hawaii, 1978—; trustee Cen. Union Ch., 1983-86; bd. dirs. Waikiki Improvement Assn. Inc., 1986—; mem. Ctr. for Tropical and Subtropical Aquacultute industry Adv. Coun., 1987—; chmn. Mayor's Adv. Com. on Pacific Nations Ctr., 1988—. Lt. comdr. USNR, 1945-46, ret. Mem. Japan-Am. Conf. of Mayors and C. of C. Pres. (mem. Am. exec. com. 1974—), Am. Soc. Assn. Execs. (past dir. Hawaii chpt.), Hawaii Execs. Council (found. , Young Pres. Assn. (past mem.), Aloha Soc. Assn. Execs., C. of C. Hawaii (dir. 1972-75, chmn. 1975), Council of Profit Sharing Industries (past dir. Hawaii sect.), Cement and Concrete Products Industry of Hawaii (pres. 1968), Hawaii Mfrs. Assn. (past dir.), Navy League of U.S. (Hawaii council), Engring. Assn. Hawaii, Pacific Club, Rotary, Sigma Chi. Home: 1437 Kalaepohaku St Honolulu HI 96816 Office: C of C Hawaii 735 Bishop St Honolulu HI 96813

ROBINSON, ROBERT WILLIAM, writer; b. Gloversville, N.Y., Apr. 12, 1925; s. George William and Isador (Kelly) R. Student, Syracuse U., 1946-48. Teletype operator CBS, N.Y.C., 1952-53; book pub. Vantage Publs., N.Y.C.; ret. Vantage Publs., 1985. Author: The Execution of Adolf Hitler, 1969. With U.S. Army, 1943-45, ETO.

ROBINSON, STACEY HOWARD, entrepreneur; b. Chgo., Mar. 7, 1953; d. Bailey Knieriam and Frankie Louise (Canady) Howard; m. Gary Edward Robinson, July 4, 1973 (div. May 1987); children: Barrie Kay, Noah Howard. BS in Nursing, Rush U., 1975; diplomate in skin care sci., Internat. Dermal Inst., 1983. RN.; cert. childbirth educator ACCE. RN labor and delivery Rush-Presbyn. St. Luke's Hosp., Chgo., 1975-76; childbirth educator Am. Soc. Psychoprophylaxis Obstetrics, Chgo., 1976-82; cosmetic broker/ skin care cons., owner Nobar Ltd., Palm Springs, Calif., 1980-86; investor Palm Springs, 1975—; cons. Allied Chgo., Wheeling, Ill., 1983—; cons./skin care dir. Heartland Spa and Retreat, Chgo., 1983—. Bd. dirs. Chgo. Maternity Ctr., 1980, Nat. Charity League, Coachella Valley chpt., Calif., 1988. mem. Am. Soc. Psychoprophylaxis Obstetrics (bd. dirs. 1975, pres. 1979-81, Outstanding Vol. 1981), Latin Sch. Chgo. Alumni Assn. (bd. dirs. 1980), Nurse's Assn. Am. Coll. Oby.-Gyn., Am. Nurses Assn. Democrat. Home: 1700 Via Norte Palm Springs CA 92262-2947 Office: Nobar Ltd 1700 Via Norte Palm Springs CA 92262-2947

ROBLEDO, ARMANDO RAMOS, cavalry scout; b. Palo Alto, Calif., Oct. 25, 1957; s. Edward Garcia and Mary Virginia Robledo. AS in Gen. Sci., Foothill Coll., 1977; BA in Geography, U. Calif., Santa Barbara, 1980. Math. tchr. U.S. Peace Corps, Cen. African Republic, 1980-81; math. tchr. U.S. Peace Corps, Swaziland, 1981-84, meteorologist, 1984-85; pvt. practice geography Mountain View, 1985-87; cav. scout U.S. Army, 1987—; lectr. U. Swaziland, 1984-85. Mem. Assn. Am. Geographers. Democrat. Roman Catholic.

ROBLES, ROSALIE MIRANDA, teacher; b. L.A., Oct. 30, 1942; d. Richard and Carmen (Garcia) Miranda; m. Ralph Rex Robles, July 12, 1986; children: Gregory, Eric, Karen. BA, Calif. State Coll., L.A., 1964; postgrad., Northridge State Coll. Playground supr. L.A. City Schs., 1961-64; elem. tchr. Montebello (Calif.) Unified Schs., 1964—; rep. Montebello Credit Union, 1973-75; chmn. Sch. Site Coun., 1980-83, bi-lingual rep. Bilingual Com., 1983-88. Chmn. Monterey Park Christmas Food Baskets, 1973-88; mem. Am. Youth Soccer; chmn. Boy Scouts Am., 1980-85; mem. exec. bd. PTA, 1978, 80, 85, 87, pres. 1978—. Recipient Hon. Svc. award PTA, 1979, Hon. Svc. Continuing award PTA, 1982. Roman Catholic.

ROBRAHN, TERRY JAY, banker; b. Colorado Springs, Colo., Dec. 5, 1950; s. John Charles and Enid Marie (Luke) R.; m. Corinne Judith Cannone, June 20, 1970 (div. Oct., 1978); m. Patricia Marie Barbieri, June 27, 1981; children: Brita Jean, Kristen Jenell. Student, So. Colo. State Coll., 1969-70, Nat. Coll., 1982-83. Mgr. Western Fin. Resources, Colorado Springs, 1979-83; account exec. Granite Mortgage Corp., Colorado Springs, 1983-84, Lion Funding Corp., Colorado Springs, 1984-88, ICA Mortgage Corp., Colorado Springs, 1988—. Mem. Home Builders Assn., Colorado Springs Bd. Realtors, Colo. Mortgage Bankers Assn. Republican. Lodge: Elks. Office: ICA Mortgage Corp 6145 Lehman Dr #200 Colorado Springs CO 80918

ROBROCK, JAMES LAWRENCE, plastic surgeon; b. Cleve., Aug. 21, 1956; s. Richard Barker and Joan Louise (Peers) R. BA, Kenyon Coll., Gambier, Ohio, 1978; MD, Ohio State U., 1981. Cert. in liposuction surgery Ea. Va. Med. Sch., 1985. Intern in gen. surgery Northwestern U., Chgo., 1981-82, resident in gen. surgery, 1981-84; resident in plastic surgery Rush-Presby. St. Luke's Med. Ctr., Chgo., 1984-86; fellow in plastic surgery Maricopa Med. Ctr., Phoenix, 1986-87; pvt. practice Chandler, Ariz., 1987—; instr., attending surgeon Maricopa Med. Ctr., Phoenix, 1988—. Named All-Am. in Swimming NCAA, 1976, 77, 78, Humanitarian of Yr. Chgo Hosp. Council, 1983. Mem. AMA, Maricopa County Plastic Surgery Soc., Maricopa County Med. Soc., Am. Coll. Surgeons (candidate), Am. Soc. Plastic and Reconstructive Surgeons (candidate), Delta Tau Delta. Office: 485 S Dobson #205 Chandler AZ 85224

ROBSON, SYBIL ANN, film producer; b. Tulsa, Dec. 8, 1956; d. John Nicholas and Alma (White) R. BFA, So. Meth. U., 1979. Anchor, reporter Sta. WRR-AM Radio, Dallas, 1976-78; researcher Sta. WFAA-TV, Dallas, 1977-78; polit. researcher ABC News, Paris, 1978-79; anchor, reporter Sta. KOLR-TV, Springfield, Mo., 1979-80, Sta. WFMY-TV, Greensboro, N.C., 1980-83, Paramount Pictures, L.A., 1983-86; investor Robson Investments, L.A., 1982—; film producer Robson Entertainment, L.A., 1987—, Bernhard/Robson Entertainment, L.A., 1988—. Mem. Am. Film Inst., Ind. Feature Project, Women in Film, Sigma Delta Chi. Universal Ch.

ROCHE, DAVID ALAN, certified public accountant; b. Inglewood, Calif., Feb. 6, 1946; s. Francis John and Christine Cora (Coolidge) R.; m. Theo Lucia Kuys, June 29, 1974; 1 child, Kevin. BA in Bus., U. Wash., 1972. CPA. Staff person Touche Ross & Co., Seattle, 1972-77, supr., 1977-79, mgr., 1979-83, ptnr., 1983-86; ptnr. in charge audit service Touche Ross & Co., Portland, Oreg., 1986—; treas. bd. trustees Oreg. Sch. Arts and Crafts, Portland, 1988—; bus. advisory council Oreg. State U., Corvallis, Internat. Trade Inst., Portland, 1988—. Mem. Leadership Tomorrow C. of C., Seattle, 1985. With USN, 1967-72. Mem. Japan Am. Soc.(Oreg. chpt.), Downtown Rotary. Republican. Roman Catholic. Office: Touche Ross & Co One SW Columbia Suite 1500 Portland OR 97258

ROCHE, LISA RILEY, reporter; b. Las Vegas, Nev., Aug. 16, 1958; d. Joseph Thomas and Shirley Arlene (Schulz) Riley; m. Vaughn Stewart Roche, Jan. 1, 1986. BA with honors, U. Nev., 1980. Editor coll. newspaper U. Nev., Las Vegas, 1980-81; newspaper reporter Las Vegas Sun, 1981-84, Las Vegas Rev. Jour., 1984-86, Desert News, Salt Lake City, 1987—. Winner 1st Pl., Nev. State Press Assn., 1984; recipient Spl. merit Desert News, 1989.

ROCHETTE, EDWARD CHARLES, retired association executive; b. Worcester, Mass., Feb. 17, 1927; s. Edward Charles and Lilia (Viau) R.; m. Mary Ann Ruland, July 29, 1978; children by previous marriage—Edward Charles, Paul, Philip. Student, Washington U., St. Louis, Clark U. Exec. editor Krause Publs., Iola, Wis., 1960-66; acting exec. dir. Am. Numismatic Assn., Colorado Springs, Colo., 1967-68, exec. v.p., 1972-87, ret., 1987; editor jour. The Numismatist, Colorado Springs, Colo., 1968-72. Bd. overseers Inst. Philatelic and Numismatic Studies, Adelphi U., Garden City, N.Y., 1979-81; chmn. medals com. Colo. Centennial Bicentennial Commn., 1976; mem. adv. panel Carson City Silver Dollar program Gen. Services Adminstrn., 1979-80; mem. U.S. Assay Commn., 1965. Served with USN, 1944-46. Recipient Gold medal for syndicated column Numismatic Lit. Guild, 1980, 86-88. Mem. Am. Numis. Assn. (life, medal of merit 1972), Am. Soc. Assn. Execs., Colo. Soc. Assn. Execs. (pres. 1988-89). Democrat. Roman Catholic. Lodge: Pikes Peak Kiwanis (pres. 1987-88). Office: Am Numis Assn PO Box 7083 Colorado Springs CO 80933

ROCKE, DAVID MORTON, statistician, educator; b. Chgo., June 4, 1946; s. Sol J. and Verva (Coleman) R.; m. Carrie Clausen, Dec. 30, 1971; children: Emily Carolyn, Miriam Ruth. AB, Shimer Coll., 1966; PhD, U. Ill., Chgo., 1972, postdoctoral, 1977-79. Vis. lectr. math. dept. U. Ill., Chgo., 1972-74; prof. Govs. State U., Park Forest South, Ill., 1974-80; assoc. prof. grad. sch. mgmt. U. Calif., Davis, 1980-86, prof., 1986—; cons. Calif. State Water Bd., Sacramento, 1987, U.S. Bur. Reclamation, Sacramento, 1986, Sherwin-Williams Rsch. Ctr., Chgo., 1980. Contbr. articles to profl. jours. Recipient Youden prize for articles Technometrics, 1983. Mem. Am. Statis. Assn. (Interlab. Testing award 1985), Inst. Math. Stats., Royal Statis. Soc., Am. Soc. for Quality Control (Shewell award 1987), Biometric Soc., Bernoulli Soc., Am. Math. Soc., Soc. for Indsl. and Applied Math., Math. Assn. Am., AAAS. Office: U Calif Sch Mgmt Davis CA 95616

ROCKEY, TRAVIS O., television executive; b. Detroit, July 11, 1950; s. Harry J. and Marjorie (Lethemon) R.; m. Gail Dianne Drake, Nov. 30, 1974; 1 child, J. Remington Matthew. BS, U. Fla., 1973; MS in Personnel and Indsl. Relations, Winthrop Coll., Rock Hill, S.C., 1979; MS in Mass Communications, Ind. U., 1987. Circulation mgr. Broward Times, Tamarac, Fla., 1974-76, classified advt. mgr., 1976-77; classified advt. dir. Evening Herald, Rock Hill, 1977-79; dir. classified advt. Caller Times, Corpus Christi, 1979-81; dir. sales Independent-Mail, Anderson, S.C., 1981-83; publisher Banner Corp., Cambridge, Md., 1983-86; pres. Cordillera Communications, Billings, Mont., 1986—. Pres. Dorchester County, Md. United Way, 1984; vice chmn. adv. com Salvation Army, Cambridge, 1985. Mem. Nat. Assn. of Broadcasters, Internat. Advt. and Mktg. Exec. Assn. (state v.p. 1981-85). Lodge: Rotary (chmn. environ. com. 1983-85) (Cambridge). Home: 2520 Emerson Pl Billings MT 59102 Office: Cordillera Communications Ste 116 490 N 31st St Billings MT 59101

ROCKOWER, JO ANNE, service executive; b. Patterson, Calif., Aug. 23, 1943; d. Joseph Louis and Wilma Mae (English) Manetti; m. Fred L. Kurlander, Oct. 4, 1964 (div. 1981); children: Peter Litman, Oliver Louis; m. Edward B. Rockower, June 17, 1982. BBA, Golden Gate U., 1964. Jr. exec. Emporium Capwell, San Francisco, 1964-66; travel advisor Farroads Travel, San Francisco, 1975-78; travel instr. Kaleidoscope Travel, San Francisco, 1978-81, Crow Canyon Travel, San Ramon, Calif., 1981-82; travel advisor Baja Safari, Monterey, Calif., 1985-88, Uniglobe/Ambassador Travel, Monterey, 1988—; travel instr. Monterey Pen. Coll., 1989—. Mem. Hadassah (pres. 1988-89), Staff Wives (v.p. 1986-87). Jewish. Home: 49 Alta Mesa Circle Monterey CA 93940 Office: Hadassah Monterey Pen Chpt 49 Alta Mesa Circle Monterey CA 93940

ROCKSTAD, HOWARD KENT, physicist; b. Ada, Minn., Aug. 5, 1935; s. Gust A. and Petra C. (Ramstad) R. BA in Physics and Math., St. Olaf Coll., 1957; MS in Physics and Math., U. Ill., 1959, PhD in Physics, 1964. Research physicist Corning (N.Y.) Glass Works, 1963-70, Energy Conversion Devices, Troy, Mich., 1970-74; project engr. Micro-Bit Corp., Lexington, Mass., 1974-79; sr. project engr. Control Data Corp.-Micro Bit, Lexington, 1979-81; sr. research scientist ARCO Solar Industries, Calabasas, Calif., 1981-82, Atlantic Richfield Co., Chatsworth, Calif., 1982-86, Jet Propulsion Lab. Calif. Inst. Tech., Pasadena, 1987—; math. lectr. Elmira (N.Y.) Coll. 1967. Contbr. articles to profl. jours.; patentee in field. Mem. World Hunger Appeal com. Luth. Ch. Am., 1985-87, Evang. Luth. Ch. Am., 1988—; treas. CWS/CROP, Thousand Oaks, Calif., 1985-86, 88—; bd. dirs. Ventura County Hunger Coalition, Calif., 1984—. Mem. Am. Phys. Soc., Microbeam Analysis Soc. So. Calif. (treas. 1984-85, 88—), IEEE, Alfa Romeo Owners Club (nat. pres. 1980-83), Sigma Pi Sigma (pres. St. Olaf Coll. chpt. 1956-57).

ROCKSTROM, ALBERT RAYMOND, retired grocer; b. Spokane, Aug. 10, 1917; s. Claes Albert and Ruth Elizabeth (Jonsson) R.; B.S. in Chemistry and Biol. Scis., U. Oreg., 1947; m. Emma Alice Doran, Mar. 14, 1942; children—Thomas Albert, Ronald Charles, David Keith. Self-employed in grocery bus., 1948-75; maj. stockholder Sta. KARY-AM, Prosser, Wash., 1953-59, pres., 1957-58; engaged in real estate investing, 1950-75. Pres. Grandview (Wash.) Jr. C. of C., 1951-52, Grandview C. of C., 1977; mem. Grandview Kiwanis Club, 1971-78, pres., 1975-76; treas. Yakima (Wash.) chpt. S.P.E.B.S.Q.S.A., 1978-79, 83, pres., 1981-82, sec. 1982-83, sec.-treas., 1983-86, adminstrv. v.p. Grandview chpt., 1978-79, Barbershopper of Yr., 1980, area counselor, 1982—; mem. Grandview Sch. Bd., 1956-69, chmn., 1968-69; mem. Citizens Adv. Com. Sch. Dist. Grandview, 1976-77; mem. KYVE-TV Bd., 1962-69. Named Distinguished Club Pres. in Kiw. is Pacific NW Dist., 1976, recipient new club bldg. award, 1977. Mem. Delta Tau Delta. Republican. Methodist. Club: Toastmasters (adminstrv. v.p. Grandview 1978). Lodge: Yakima Kamiakin Kiwanis (pres. 1987-88, lt. gov. Pacific N.W. dist. 1982-83, 2d v.p. 1985-86, 1st v.p. 1986-87, lt. gov.'s honor award 1982-83, disting. club mem. award 1986). Address: 120 Terrace Park Dr Yakima WA 98901

ROCKWELL, DON ARTHUR, psychiatrist; b. Wheatland, Wyo., Apr. 24, 1938; s. Orson Arthur and Kathleen Emily (Richards) R.; m. Frances Pepitone-Arreola, Dec. 23, 1965; children: Grant, Chad. BA, Wash. U., 1959; MD, U. Okla., 1963; MA in Sociology, U. Calif., Berkeley, 1967. Diplomate Am. Bd. Psychiatry and Neurology. Intern in surgery San Francisco Gen. Hosp., 1963-64; resident in psychiatry Langley-Porter Neuropsychiatric Inst. U. Calif. Med. Ctr., San Francisco, 1964-67; instr. dept. psychiatry U. Calif. Sch. Medicine, Davis, 1969-70, asst. prof., 1970-74, assoc. prof., 1974-80, acting. assoc. dir., dean curricular affiars, 1979-80, acting assoc. dean student affairs, 1980, assoc. dean student affairs, 1980-82, prof., 1980-84; career tchr. NIMH, 1970-72; assoc. psychiatrist Sacramento Med. Ctr.; med. dir. U. Calif. Med. Ctr., Davis, 1982-84; prof., vice chmn. dept. psychiatry and biobehavioral scis. UCLA, 1984—; dir. UCLA Neuropsychiat. Hosp., 1984—; exec. assoc. dir. UCAL Neuropsychiat. Inst., 1984—, chief of profl. staff, 1984-85; chmn. U. Calif. Hosp. Dirs. Council, 1988-89; cons. Nat. Commn. on Marijuana, Washington, 1971-73. Co-author: Psychiatric Disorders, 1982; contbr. chpts. to books; articles to profl. jours. Bd. dirs. Bereavement Outreach, Sacramento, 1974-84, Suicide Prevention, Yolo County, 1969-84; bd. visitors U. Okla. Sch. Medicine; chmn. bd. dirs. coun. Univ. Calif. Hosp. Capt. USAF, 1967-69. Fellow Am. Psychiat. Assn., Am. Coll. Psychiatrists; mem. AMA, Am. Coll. Psychiatrists, Soc. Biol. Psychiatry, Soc. Health and Human Values, Am. Sociologic Assn., Cen. Calif. Psychiatric Assn. (sec.-pres. 1977-78), U. Okla. Alumni Assn. (trustee 1981—), Alpha Omega Alpha. Home: 1061 Palisair Pl Pacific Palisades CA 90272

ROCKWELL, LLEWELLYN HARRISON, JR., economics educator; b. Boston, July 1, 1944; 1 child, Alexandra. Founder, pres. The Ludwig von Mises Inst., Burlingame, Calif., 1982—. Office: Ludwig von Mises Inst 851 Burlway Rd Burlingame CA 94010

RODDICK, DAVID BRUCE, construction executive; b. Oakland, Calif., Oct. 31, 1948; s. Bruce Ergo and Hortensia Cabo (Castedo) R.; m. Sharon Ann Belan, May 25, 1975; children: Heather Marie, Christina Deeann. BSCE, U. Calif., Davis, 1971. Engr. Bechtel Corp., San Francisco, 1971-77, contract specialist, 1977-78; subcontract adminstr. Boecon Corp., Richland, Wash., 1978-79; constrn. mgr. BE&C Engrs., Inc., Vancouver, Wash., 1979-81; contracts mgr. BE&C Engrs., Inc., Tukwila, Wash., 1981-83; sr. constrn. mgr. BE&C Engrs., Inc., Wichita, Kans., 1983-84; v.p. ops. Carl Holvick Co., Sunnyvale, Calif., 1984-88; v.p., gen. mgr. The Brookman Co., Inc., Burlingame, Calif., 1988—. Pres. unified coun. San Jose County PTA, 1988—. With USAR, 1969—, maj. C.E. Mem. ASCE, Res. Officers Assn., Am. Arbitration Assn. (panel arbitrators), Elks. Republican. Baptist.

RODDICK, ELLEN HAWLEY, writer, consultant; b. Bronxville, N.Y., Feb. 13, 1936; d. Harrison Arnold and Mary Elizabeth (Henrici) R.; m. Karl W. Haffenreffer, Mar. 11, 1961 (div. July 1965); m. Walter W. Meade, Nov. 2, 1967; 1 child, Luke Harrison. BA, Wellesley Coll., 1958. Freelance writer 1966—; columnist Cosmopolitan mag., N.Y.C., 1975-81; owner Write/Action, Yorktown Heights, N.Y., 1983-86; pres. Ellen Roddick Inc., Bodega Bay, Calif., 1986—. Author: (fiction) Together, 1979, Holding Patterns, 1981; (nonfiction) Young Filmmakers, 1969 (N.Y. Pub. Library prize 1969), Writing That Means Business, 1984, Everyone Can Write: Thinking Skills for Writing (Activities Kit for grades 4-8), 1987; contbr. articles to mags., profl. jours. Vol. various pro-environ. and anti-nuclear activities. Mem. Am. Soc. Tng. and Devel., Women in Communications, Authors Guild. Club: Wellesley (No. Calif.). Office: Ellen Roddick Inc PO Box 548 Bodega Bay CA 94923

RODDY, JOSEPH HODGES MCKENZIE, investment banker; b. Clinton, IA, Nov. 3, 1960; s. James Patrick and Dorothy (Hodges) R.; m. Carol Lynn Roberts, Nov. 22, 1986; 1 child, Michael McKenzie. BS in Commerce, U. Va., 1982. CPA, Colo. Asst. acct. Peat, Marwick, Mitchell & Co., Denver, 1982-83, staff acct., 1983-84, sr. acct., 1984-85, supervising sr. acct., 1985-87, mgr., 1987; controller Cen. Bancorporation, Inc., Denver, 1987-89; v.p. Cen. Bank Denver, 1989—. Mem. Colo. Soc. CPA's, Am. Inst. CPA's, Fin. Execs. Inst. Home: 3037 S Cook St Denver CO 80210

RODE, EDWARD J., chemical engineering educator; b. Louisville, Feb. 6, 1958; s. Clarence J. and Mary Frances (Kennedy) R. BS, U. Ky., 1981; PhD, Va. Poly. Inst. and State U., 1985. Rsch. asst. Brown & Williamson Tobacco Co., Louisville, 1978-79; environ. engr. Rohm & Haas Co., Louisville, 1980, process engr., 1981; instr. Va. Poly. Inst. and State U., Blacksburg, 1985; assoc. prof. chem. engring. San Jose (Calif.) State U., 1985—. Contbr. articles to profl. jours. Tenn. Eastman fellow, 1981-82, Dow Chem. Co. fellow, 1983-85. Mem. AAAS, Am. Chem. Soc., Am. Inst. Chem. Engrs., Materials Rsch. Soc., Sigma Xi. Home: 2571 Derby Dr San Ramon CA 94583 Office: San Jose State U Dept Chem Engring One Washington Sq San Jose CA 95192

RODENGEN, JEFFREY LEE, nationally syndicated columnist, author, motion picture producer and director; b. Mpls., June 5, 1949; s. Marvin Albany and Geraldine Maude (Wooley) R.; m. Karine N. Chapus, Nov. 3, 1985; student Moorhead (Minn.) State U., 1967-68, Universidad de las Americas, 1968-69, Riverside City Coll., 1969-70; B.A., U. Calif., Riverside, 1972; M.S., Ph.D. in Systems and Design Engring., U. Beverly Hills, 1982. Pres., Pythagoras Instruments, 1972, D.C. Recording Studios, Riverside, Calif., 1972, AVIII, Inc., 1973-78, AV Am., 1979-80; exec. producer, dir. mktg. Lights & Sounds Images, Tustin, Calif., 1979-81; pres. Grand Illusions Unltd., Las Vegas, 1981-83; Write Stuff Syndicate, 1986—; maj. prodns. include: Libra Colony, 1977, Latin Lasers, 1978, Galactic Laser Experience, 1978, Beyond Magic, 1981; Knowledge, 1978; Achieving Excellence, 1979; Celebrate, 1978; Fiesta Fantastico, 1979. Mem. Riverside Adminstrv. Bd. Appeals, 1973-77. Named Best Actor, Riverside Community Players, 1974; recipient Silver Cindy award, 1977; Honor award Soc. Tech. Communicators, 1984; holder Black Belt in Karate; lic. single and multi-engine pilot, instrument rating. Mem. Internat. Film Producers Am., Assn. Multi-Image, Aircraft Owners and Pilots Assn., Soc. Tech. Writers, Boating Writers Internat. Democrat. Presbyterian. Author: The Legend of Chris-Craft, 1988, Iron Fist: The Authorized Biography of Carl Kiekhaefer, 1989; inventor photo-optical laser and holographic devices, electronic ruler, space-docking game for Am.-Soviet space flight; patentee in field. Home and Office: 1108 Citrus Isle Fort Lauderdale FL 33315

RODERICK, SUE SCHOCK, health sciences executive; b. Muskogee, Okla., Oct. 28, 1937; d. Willie Orville and Dona Leona (Gordon) Perry; m. Kenneth Robert Schock, Nov. 22, 1955 (div. 1971); m. John Kenneth Roderick, Aug. 9, 1981. BS with distinction, San Jose (Calif.) State U., 1970; MS, San Jose State U., 1973; M in Pub. Adminstrn., U. So. Calif., 1982, D in Pub. Adminstrn., cert. in gerontology, 1984. cert. tchr., Calif. Sr. citizens dir. City of San Jose, 1968-72; chief gerontology Kings View Mental Health, Visalia, Calif., 1972-74; cons. on aging State of Calif., Sacramento, 1974-76; dir. edn. Calif. Assn. Health Facilities, Sacramento, 1976-77; exec. dir. Hilhaven Found., Tacoma, Wash., 1977-83; pres. Med. Ednl. Services Devel., Alameda, Calif., 1979—; asst. v.p. planning and research Am. Bapt. Homes of the West, Oakland, Calif., 1984—; cons. St. Mary's Hosp., San Francisco, 1973-74, Hillsdale Manor, Inc., San Mateo, Calif., 1973—; bd. dirs. St. Peter's Adult Day Care Ctr., San Leandro, Alameda County Long Term Care Planning Coun.; co-founder Shades of Gray: Perspective in Aging, Alameda, 1987. Contbr. articles to profl. jours. Chi Kappa Rho scholar San Jose State U., 1970, U. So. Calif.-Gerontology Ctr. scholar, 1971-74. Mem. Am. Soc. on Aging, Gerontol. Soc. Am., Intercare, Am. Assn. of Homes for Aging, Am. Coll. Health Care Adminstrs., Calif. Specialists on Aging, Calif. Assn. Homes for Aging. Democrat. Home: 3406 Redhook Ln Alameda CA 94501 Office: Am Bapt Homes of the West 400 Roland Way Oakland CA 94621

RODGERS, AUSSIE, food service executive; b. Columbus, Ga., Aug. 24, 1947; s. Joseph and Lena Bell (Scott) R.; divorced; children: Stacey Yvette, Aussie Kevin. BSBA, Ind. U., 1971. Supr. personnel Standard Oil Co. (Ind.), Chgo., 1968-74; personnel mgr. Chgo. Faucet Co., 1974-77; employment mgr. G.D.Searle, 1977-79; personnel mgr. Pillsbury Co., Mpls., 1979-83; dir. human resources Burger King Corp., Fountain Valley, Calif., 1983—. Named Black Achiever Family Christian Soc., Miami, Fla., 1985. Mem. Am. Soc. Personnel Adminstrs. Democrat. Baptist. Office: Burger King Corp 17330 Brookhurst # 250 Fountain Valley CA 92728

RODGERS, BARRY, aerospace company executive; b. Blackpool, Eng., Nov. 9, 1938; came to U.S., 1965; s. Henry and Edith Helen (Sandford) R.; m. Una Horan McLaughlin, July 24, 1965 (div. Dec. 1972); 1 child, Genevieve Susanna; m. Phyllis Marlyn Lewin, Dec. 20, 1973; 1 child, Samantha Michelle. Cert., Blackpool Tech. Coll., 1957; HNC, Harris Coll., Preston, Eng., 1960; DCAE, Cranfield (Eng.) Inst. Tech., 1962; ME, UCLA, 1972. Aerodynamacist Brit. Aircraft Co., Warton, Lancashire, Eng., 1955-65; engring. scientist McDonnell Douglas Aircraft Co., Long Beach, 1965-66; sect. head engring. Astronautics div. Lear Siegler, Inc., Santa Monica, Calif., 1966-68, div. pres., 1969-85, corp. v.p., 1985-87; ptnr. Raebarn Corp., Sherman Oaks, Calif., 1987-88; chief exec. officer BFM Aerospace Corp., Santa Ana, Calif., 1987—. Republican. Home: 10213 Overhill Dr Santa Ana CA 92705-1561 Office: BFM Aerospace Corp 1 Corporate Park Dr Ste 150 Irvine CA 92714

RODGERS, FREDERIC BARKER, judge, lawyer; b. Albany, N.Y., Sept. 29, 1940; s. Prentice Johnson and Jane (Weed) R.; m. Valerie McNaughton, Oct. 8, 1988. AB, Amherst Coll., 1963; JD, Union U., 1966. Bar: N.Y. 1966, U.S. Ct. Mil. Appeals 1968, Colo. 1972, U.S. Supreme Ct. 1974, U.S. Ct. Appeals (10th cir.) 1981. Chief dep. dist. atty., Denver, 1972-73; commr. Denver Juvenile Ct., 1973-79; mem. Mulligan Reeves Teasley & Joyce, P.C., Denver, 1979-80; pres. Frederic B. Rodgers, P.C., Breckenridge, Colo., 1980—; county judge County of Gilpin, 1987—; presiding mcpl. judge cities of Breckenridge, Blue River, Black Hawk, Central City, Edgewater, Empire, Idaho Springs and Westminster, Colo., 1979—; chmn. com. on mcpl. ct. rules of procedure Colo. Supreme Ct., 1984—. Mem. Colo. Commn. on Children, 1982-85. Served with JAGC, U.S. Army, 1967-72; to maj. USAR, 1972—. Decorated Bronze Star with oak leaf cluster, Air medal. Recipient Spl. Community Service award Colo. Am. Legion, 1979. Mem. ABA, Colo. Bar Assn. (bd. govs. 1986-88), Denver Bar Assn. (bd. trustees 1979-82), Continental Divide Bar Assn., First Jud. Dist. Bar Assn., Nat. Conf. Spl. Ct. Judges (chmn. 1988-89), Colo. Mcpl. Judges Assn. (pres. 1986-87), Denver Law Club (pres. 1981-82), Am. Judicature Soc., Marines Meml. Club (San Francisco), Univ. Club (Denver). Episcopalian. Contbr. articles to profl. jours.. Home: 108 Casey St Central City CO 80427 Office: 130 Ski Hill Rd Ste 135 PO Box 567 Breckenridge CO 80424-0567

RODGERS, JAMES LOWELL, electronics engineer; b. Altadena, Calif., Jan. 13, 1940; s. William Lowell Rodgers and Helen Ruth (Lester) Selzer; m. Merry Beth Malin, Aug. 8, 1964; children: Kent Matthew, James Garret. BSEE, Calif. State Poly. U., 1961; MBA, UCLA, 1964. Project engr. Motorola, Scottsdale, Ariz., 1964-69; dir. engring. D.S.E. Corp., Tempe, Ariz., 1969-71; v.p. engring. Calcomp (formerly Talos System Corp.), Scottsdale, 1971-79; v.p. rsch., devel. and engring. Kurta Corp., Phoenix, 1979—, also bd. dirs. Patentee in field; pioneer computer graphic tablets and digitizers. Mem. AZ Electronics Assn. Republican. Home: 2440 S Playa Mesa AZ 85202 Office: Kurta Corp 3007 E Chambers Phoenix AZ 85040

RODGERS, NED, television producer; b. Chambersberg, Pa., Dec. 10, 1937; s. Horace Edgar and Lois Celie (Cox) R.; m. Jean Amanda Wilson, Aug. 25, 1967 (div. 1982); children: Jean Love, John Edgar, Ned Alan, Steven David, Laura Joanne; m. Robin Leslie McCaul, June 11, 1988. BA, Calif. State U., Northridge, 1972, MA, 1978. Program dir. Sta. KVEN-KHAY Radio, Ventura, Calif., 1969-78; instr. Moorpark (Calif.) Community Coll., 1976-79; media adminstr. GTE Calif., Thousand Oaks, 1978-87; producer Janco Prodns., Thousand Oaks, 1987-88, Internat. Television Prodns., Woodland Hills, Calif., 1988—. Recipient Higby award, L.A. Lung Assn., 1975, Internat. TV Assn., L.A., 1984. Mem. Assn. Audio-Visual Communicators (chair awards com. 1988). Democrat. Home: 21550 Burbank Blvd Woodland Hills CA 91367

RODGERS, RAYMOND GENE, data processing executive; b. Detroit, July 14, 1936; s. Eugene and Evelyn Virginia (Little) R.; m. Alice Jeannette Butts, July 21, 1956 (div. 1975); children: Catherine Virginia, Connie Marie, Lawrence Eugene, Timothy Ray, Cynthia Lee; m. Joy Patti Spies, Dec. 4, 1981. AA, AS, Aims Community Coll., Greeley, Colo., 1978; BA, U. No. Colo., 1980. Cert. tchr., Colo. Enlisted USAF, San Antonio, 1954, advanced through grades to master sgt., mgr. data processing, 1954-68; chief of systems Hdqrs. Command Spl. Activities USAF, Stuttgart, Germany, 1968-70; chief of systems 1st Combat Support-Macdill USAF, Tampa, Fla., 1970-72; chief mgmt. info. systems USAF Acad., Colorado Springs, Colo., 1972-74; ret. USAF, 1974; tchr. Poude High Sch., Ft. Collins, Colo., 1978-79; project dir. Bur. Reclamations, Lakewood, Colo., 1981-82; exec. v.p. Northland Assocs., Inc., Wheat Ridge, Colo., 1982—; also bd. dirs. Northland Assocs., Inc., Wheat Ridge; exec. officer Automobile Warranty Corp., Wheat Ridge, 1982-88, Ins. Specialists, Inc., Wheat Ridge, 1982-88. Recipient Meritorious Service medal, 1974, Air Force Commendation medals, 1969, 72. Mem. User's Group, Data Processing Mgmt. Assn., Assn. Retired Noncommd. Officers. Republican. Club: Toastmasters (pres. 1955-56). Lodge: Elks. Home: 13131 W Mont Ave Lakewood CO 80228 Office: Northland Assocs Inc 3885 Upham St Wheat Ridge CO 80033

RODMAN, ALLISON ELIZABETH, chef; b. Bend, Oreg., May 12, 1952; d. Merlin Dallas and Frances Elenore (Mitchell) R. Student, U. Oreg., 1970-73. Formerly with numerous restaurants and caterer; owner Food Talk Prodns., Inc., San Francisco, 1988-. Mem. San Francisco Profl. Food Soc., Bay Area Caterers Assn., Bay Area Women's Culinary Assn. (founder, pres. 1984-87), Food Runners San Francisco (founder, community organizer), San Francisco League Urban Gardeners. Home: 238 Banks St San Francisco CA 94210 Office: Food Talk Prodns Inc 3998 Army St San Francisco CA 94131

RODMAN, ALPINE CLARENCE, small business owner; b. Roswell, N.Mex., June 23, 1952; s. Robert Elsworth and Verna Mae (Means) R.; m. Sue Arlene Lawson, Dec. 13, 1970; 1 child, Connie Lynn. Student Colo. State U., 1970-71, U. No. Colo. Ptnr. Pinel Silver Shop, Loveland, Colo., 1965-68, salesman, 1968-71; real estate salesman, Loveland, 1971-73; mgr. Traveling Traders, Phoenix, 1974-75; owner Deer Track Traders, Loveland, 1975-85, pres. Deer Track Traders, Ltd., 1985—. Author: The Vanishing Indian: Fact or Fiction?, 1985. Mem. Civil Air Patrol, 1965-72, 87—, dep. comdr. cadets, 1988—; cadet comdr. Ft. Collins, Colo., 1968, 70, Colo. rep. to youth tng. program, 1969, U.S. youth rep. to Japan, 1970. Mem. Bur. Wholesale Sales Reps., Mountain States Men's, Boy's and Western Apparel Club, Eastern States Western Salesman's Assn., Internat. Platform Assn., Indian Arts and Crafts Assn. (bd. dirs. 1988—, exec. com. 1989), Crazy Horse Grass Roots Club. Republican. Baptist. Office: Deer Track Traders Ltd PO Box 448 Loveland CO 80539

RODMAN, SUE ARLENE, wholesale Indian crafts company executive, artist; b. Fort Collins, Colo., Oct. 1, 1951; d. Marvin F. and Barbara I. (Miller) Lawson; m. Alpine C. Rodman, Dec. 13, 1970; 1 child, Connie Lynn. Student Colo. State U., 1970-73. Silversmith Pinel Silver Shop, Loveland, Colo., 1970-71; asst. mgr. Traveling Traders, Phoenix, 1974-75; co-owner, co-mgr. Deer Track Traders, Ltd., Loveland, 1975-85, exec. v.p., 1985—. Author: The Book of Contemporary Indian Arts and Crafts, 1985. Mem. Rep. Presdl. Task Force, 1982-87; mem. U.S. Senatorial Club, 1982-87, Civil Air Patrol, 1969-73, 87—, personnel officer, 1988—. Mem. Internat. Platform Assn., Nat. Assn. Female Execs., Indian Arts and Crafts Assn., Native Am. Art Studies Assn., Inc. Baptist. Club: Crazy Horse Grass Roots (S.D.). Avocations: museums, recreation research, fashion design, reading, flying. Office: Deer Track Traders Ltd PO Box 448 Loveland CO 80539

RODRIGUE, CHRISTINE M., geography educator, business consultant; b. Los Angeles, Oct. 27, 1952; d. John-Paul and Josephine Genevieve (Gorsky) R. AA in French, German, Los Angeles Pierce Coll., 1972; BA in Geography summa cum laude, Calif. State U., Northridge, 1973, MA in Geography, 1976; PhD in Geography, Clark U., 1987. Computer analyst Jet Propulsion Labs., Pasadena, Calif., 1977; teaching asst. Clark U., Worcester, Mass., 1976-79, research asst., 1977-78; instr. geography Los Angeles Pierce Coll., Woodland Hills, Calif., 1981—; cons. Area Location Systems, Northridge, 1984—; asst. prof. urban studies and geography Calif. State U., Northridge, 1980-89; asst. prof. geography Calif. State U., Chico, 1989—. Recipient Meritorious Performance and Profl. Promise award Calif. State U., 1987, 88. Mem. NOW, AAAS, Assn. Am. Geographers (chmn. specialty group 1983-84), Los Angeles Geog. Soc. (v.p. 1987, pres. 1988, editor 1981-84), Union Concerned Scientists, The Planetary Soc., Sierra Club, Internat. Arabian Horse Assn., Arabian Horse Registry. Democrat. Office: Calif State U Dept Geography Chico CA 95929

RODRIGUE, LISA MAURIN, nurse; b. New Orleans, Dec. 1, 1961; d. Joseph LeBrun and Marilyn Rose (Torres) Maurin; m. Rene Charles Rodrigue, May 25, 1984. BS in Nursing, Southeastern La. U., 1983. R.N., La., Colo. Staff nurse East Jefferson Gen. Hosp., Metairie, La., 1983-84, Westpark Community Hosp., Hammond, La., 1984-85; staff nurse Doctors Hosp. Jefferson, Metairie, 1985-86, charge nurse, 1986-87, acting head nurse, 1987, head nurse, 1987-88; charge nurse Penrose Hosp., Colorado Springs, Colo., 1988—. Mem. Oncology Nursing Soc. Republican. Roman Catholic. Home: 2629 Hatch Circle Colorado Springs CO 80918 Office: Penrose Hosp 2215 N Cascade Ave Colorado Springs CO 80907

RODRIGUES, ALFRED BENJAMIN KAMEEIAMOKU, advertising company executive; b. Honolulu, Jan. 23, 1947; s. Alfred Benjamin Kameeiamoku and Ruth Shiegeko (Kameda) R. BA, U. San Francisco, 1969; postgrad. U. Wis., 1977. Pub. info. mgr. Hawaiian Tel.-GTE, Honolulu, 1979-80, pub. affairs program mgr., 1980-84, dir. pub. affairs, 1984-85, dir. mktg. communications, 1986-87, dir. mktg. communications and svcs., 1987-89 sr. v.p., Milici, Valenti, Park and Gabriel Advt., Inc., 1989—. Bd. dirs., pub. rels. chmn. Am. Lung Assn., 1981—; trustee, v.p. Hawaii Army Mus. Soc., 1982—; bd. dirs. ARC Hawaii, 1983-85; budget com. Aloha United Way. Capt. U.S. Army, 1969-79. Decorated Bronze Star with three oak leaf clusters, Meritorious Svc. medal with oak leaf cluster, Army Commendation medal with oak leaf cluster, Purple Heart with oak leaf cluster, Air medal with oak leaf cluster. Mem. Am. Mktg. Assn., Am. Advt. Fedn., Hawaii Advt. Fedn. (bd. dirs., pres.), Pub. Rels. Soc. Am. (pres. Hawaii), Res. Officers Assn., Hawaii C. of C., Rotary. Republican. Roman Catholic.

RODRIGUES, CYNTHIA LOUISE, business executive, computer consultant; b. Tacoma, Jan. 12, 1958; d. John Neto and Velvet (Ferriera) R. Degree in Acctg., Knapp Coll., Tacoma, 1981, degree in computer mgmt., 1984. System operator H & R Block, Tacoma, 1983—; data systems mgr. Pentadent, Tacoma, 1984-86; pres. Aacres Community Assn., Tacoma, 1987—; owner Start Now, Tacoma, 1987—. Served with USAF, 1977-79. Mem. Washperg, NOW. Democrat. Roman Catholic.

RODRIGUES, RAYMOND JOSEPH, academic administrator; b. Somerville, N.J., May 2, 1938; s. Joseph Batiste and Vera (Fedechena) R.; m. Dawn Droskinis; 1 child, Brad. AB, Rutgers U., 1960, MEd, 1965; PhD, U. N.Mex., 1974. Cert. secondary tchr. From asst. prof. to assoc. prof. English and Edn. U. Utah, Salt Lake City, 1974-78, head dept. secondary education, 1978-79; head dept. Curriculum and Instruction N.Mex. State U., Las Cruces, 1982-86; dir., tchr. edn. U. Colo., Colorado Springs, 1979-82; assoc. acad. v.p. Colo. State U., Ft. Collins, 1986—. Author: Teaching Writing with a Word Processor, 1986, A Guide Book for Teaching Literature, 1978. Served to 1st lt. U.S. Army, 1960-62. Mem. Nat. Council Tchrs. English (exec. bd. conf. English edn. 1984-88, editorial bd. 1987—). Office: Colo State U Office of VP Acad Affairs Fort Collins CO 80523

RODRIGUEZ, ELOY, toxicology educator; b. Edinburg, Tex., Jan. 7, 1947; s. Everardo and Hilaria (Calvillo) R.; m. Helena Viramontes, June 5, 1982; children: Pilar, Eloy Francisco. BA in Zoology, U. Tex., 1969, PhD in Phytochemistry and Plant Biology, 1975. Asst. prof. phytochemical lab., devel. and cell biology U. Calif., Irvine, 1975-76, assoc. prof. phytochem. lab., dpets. ecology, evolutionary biology and devel. and cell biology, 1979-83, prof. phytochemical lab., devel. and cell biology and cell. Medicine, 1983—, dir. internat. Chicano studies program, 1985—; lectr. Indo-Am. and Fulbright Sr. Scholarship, 1983; vis. prof. and research scientist dept. botany Univ. B.C., 1984, dept. pharm. chemistry sch. of pharmacy, 1985; faculty asst. internat. affairs U. Calif., Irvine, 1988—; dir. Nat. Chicano Council Higher Edn. Sci. Fellowship Program for Hispanics, 1986—. Author: Biology and Chemistry of Plant Trichomes, 1984; contbr. over 100 articles to profl. jours.; editor (newsletters) Parthenium, 1976-79, Ciencias, 1986—; Internat. Soc. Chem. Ecology Jour., 1984-87; reviewer profl. jours. Recipient Sr. Scholar Lectureship award Fulbright-Hayes, 1978, Letter of Recognition for US-Mex. Symposium on Renewable Phytochem. Resources U. of Calif., 1983, Research Career Devel. award Nat. Inst. of Allergy and Infectious Diseases NIH, 1982-87, First Ann. Hispanic Educator award League of United Latin Am. Citizens, 1984; grantee Am. Cancer Soc., 1977, NIH, 1978-80, 1982-85, 1985-1990, 1987-1990; Ford Found. Mexican-Am. Grad. fellow, 1972-74; Can. Med. fellow, depts. Botany and Dermatology, U.B.C., Vancouver, 1975-76. Mem. Phytochem. Soc. N.Am., Phytochem. Sect. of the Am. Bot. Soc., Calif. Native Plant Soc., Mexican Bot. Soc., Soc. for the Advancement of Chicanos and Native Ams. in Sci., Am. Chem. Soc., AAAS, Internat. Soc. of Chem. Ecology editor newsletter 1984-86), Am. Pharmacognosy Soc., Biol. Scis. (coun.), Fulbright Alumni Assn. Office: U Calif Sch Biol Scis Phytochem Lab Depts Developmental and Cell Biology Irvine CA 92717

RODRIGUEZ, LEONARD, public relations executive; b. Phoenix, Jan. 27, 1944; s. Jesus H. and Manuela (Razo) R.; m. Jo Ann Gama, Jan. 16, 1965; 1 child, Lena Teresa. BS in Mktg., Ariz. State U., 1981. Cert. tchr., Ariz. Adminstrv. svcs. officer Title XX Adminstrn., Phoenix, 1979-81, Block Grants Adminstrn., Phoenix, 1981-84; property mgmt. mgr. State of Ariz., Phoenix, 1984-86; pres. LTR Mgmt. Svcs., Phoenix, 1986—; adj. clin. instr., faculty assoc. Ariz. State U., 1979—; cons. Applied Econs. Curriculum, Jr. Achievement of Cen. Ariz., Inc., 1987. Chmn. community rels. Ariz. State U. Minority Recruitment Program, Tempe, 1985-86; cons. Jr. Achievement Cen. Ariz., 1987; bd. dirs. Friendly House Inc., Phoenix, 1985—, vice chmn., 1986, pres., 1987; mem. community problem solving coordinating com. Valley of the Sun United Way, 1988—. Mem. Ariz. Adminstrs. Assn., Counterparts (founder 1986), Hispanic C. of C., Vesta Club (chmn. scholarship com. 1983), Rotary (pres. 1987-88, voting del. internat. conv. 1987). Home: 7650 S 14th St Phoenix AZ 85040

RODRIGUEZ, RODRI J., entertainment executive, film producer; b. Havana, Cuba, Jan. 2, 1955; came to U.S., 1962; d. Leoncio Alejo and Luz

Marina (Castaneda) R. Grad., Immaculate Heart High Sch., Hollywood, Calif., 1973. Prin. The Rodri Group, Los Angeles, 1976—. Commr., v.p. Cultural Affairs Commn., City of L.A., 1984—; commr. Legal Svcs. Trust Fund Commn., State Bar Calif., 1986-87; pres., Vicki Carrr Scholarship Found., 1989—. Mem. The Vikki Carr Scholarship Found. (bd. dirs. 1983—), The Nat. Network Hispanic Women (bd. dirs. 1986—, named outstanding entrepreneur 1985). Republican. Office: The Rodri Group 8721 W Sunset Blvd Penthouse Ste Los Angeles CA 90069

RODRIGUEZ, ROMAN, child psychiatrist, educator; b. N.Y.C., Jan. 21, 1951; s. Roman Rodriguez and Margarita (Castillo) Torres. BS in Biology, St. Mary's Coll. of Calif., 1972; MD, U. Calif.-San Francisco, 1976. Diplomate Nat. Bd. Med. Examiners. Resident in gen. psychiatry Menninger Found., Topeka, 1976-79, fellow in child psychiatry, 1978-80; resident physician Topeka VA Med. Ctr., 1976-79; dir. psychiat. services Youth Ctr. Topeka, 1979-80; assoc. med. dir. mission SE Adolescent Day Treatment Ctr., San Francisco, 1980-81; staff psychiatrist, med. advisor Youth Guidance Ctr., San Francisco, 1980-82; clin. dir. Growing Mind Corp., San Rafael, Calif., 1980-85; pvt. practice child psychiatry, San Francisco and San Rafael, Calif., 1980-85; child team leader dept. psychiatry Kaiser Permanente Med. Ctr., South San Francisco, 1985—, med. staff Children's Hosp., San Francisco, 1980-85; St. Luke's Hosp., San Francisco, 1981-85; Marin Gen. Hosp., Greenbrae, Calif., 1983-87; asst. clin. prof. U. Calif., San Francisco, 1981—; mem. admissions com. Sch. Medicine, 1980-85. Bd. dirs. Canal Community Alliance, San Rafael, 1985-86, Community Health Ctr. Marin, Fairfax, Calif., 1985-86, Bahia de Rafael Fourplex, San Rafael, 1986. Mem. AMA, Am. Psychiat. Assn., Am. Acad. Child Psychiatry, No. Calif. Psychiat. Soc. Republican. Roman Catholic. Home: 116 City View Dr Daly City CA 94014-3446 Office: Kaiser Permanente Med Ctr Dept Psychiatry 1200 El Camino Real South San Francisco CA 94080-3299

RODRIQUEZ, LISA PARTICE, violinist; b. Winchester, Mass., Nov. 17, 1960; d. Felix Alfred and Mary Ann Malinverni V.; m. Luis Eduardo Rodriguez,. Student, Harvard U., Cambridge, 1978, U. Nevada, Las Vegas, 1979-81. Musician Las Vegas (Nev.) Symphony, Las Vegas, 1979-81; stolling violinist Sasha Semenoff's Romantic Strings MGM Grand Hotel, Las Vegas, 1979-86; freelance violinist A Touch of Romance, Las Vegas, 1986; violinist Golden Nugget Orchetra, Las Vegas, 1988, Caesars Place Orch., Caesars Pl. Strings, Las Vegas, 1988—; violinist, Tanglewood B.U. Young Artist Orch., Lenox, Mass., 1975-78, Greater Boston Youth Symphony Orch., 1975-78. Major Bass Meml. scholar Major Bass Meml. Fund. Mem. Musicians Local 369. Democrat. Roman Catholic. Home: 5287 Stampa Ave Las Vegas NV 89102

ROE, BENSON BERTHEAU, surgeon, educator; b. Los Angeles, July 7, 1918; s. Hall and Helene Louise (Bertheau) R.; m. Jane Faulkner St. John, Jan. 20, 1945; children: David B., Virginia St. John. A.B., U. Calif.-Berkeley, 1939; M.D. cum laude, Harvard U., 1943. Diplomate Am. Bd. Surgery, Am. Bd. Thoracic Surgery. Intern Mass. Gen. Hosp., Boston, 1943-44; resident Mass. Gen. Hosp., 1946-50; nat. research fellow dept. physiology Harvard U. Med. Sch., 1947; Moseley traveling fellow (Harvard U.) U. Edinburgh, Scotland, 1951; instr. surgery Harvard Med. Sch., 1950; asst. clin. prof. surgery U. Calif., San Francisco, 1951-58; chief cardiothoracic surgery U. Calif., 1958-76, prof. surgery, 1966—; pvt. practice medicine specializing in cardiothoracic surgery San Francisco, 1952—; cons. thoracic surgery VA Hosp., San Francisco Gen. Hosp., Letterman Army Hosp., St. Lukes Hosp., Blue Shield of Calif., Baxter Labs., Ethicon, Inc.; bd. dirs. Control Laser Corp.; vis. prof. U. Utah, U. Ky., U. Gdansk, Poland, Nat. Heart Hosp., London, U. Ibadan, Nigeria, Sanger Clinic, Charlotte, Rush-Presbyn. Hosp., Chgo., Penrose Hosp., Colorado Springs. Mem. editorial bd. Annals of Thoracic Surgery, 1969-82, Pharos; editor 2 med. texts; author 18 textbook chpts.; contbr. chpts. 152 articles to profl. jours. Bd. dirs. United Bay Area Crusade, 1958-70, mem. exec. com., 1964-65; bd. dirs. chmn. exec. com. San Francisco chpt. Am. Cancer Soc., 1955-57; bd. dirs. San Francisco Heart Assn., 1964-72, pres., 1964-65, chmn. research com., 1966-71; mem. various coms. Am. Heart Assn., 1967-70; pres. Miranda Lux Found.; trustee Avery Fuller Found. Served with Med. Service Corps, USNR, 1944-46. Fellow Am. Coll. Cardiology, ACS (chmn. adv. council thoracic surgery, program chmn. thoracic surgery, mem. cardiovascular com.), Polish Surg. Assn. (hon.); mem. Am. Assn. Thoracic Surgery (chmn. membership com. 1974-75, chmn. program com. 1977, chmn. exam. com. 1978, chmn. long-range planning com., chmn. bd. 1981—, bd. dirs. 1971-83), AMA (residency rev. com. for thoracic surgery), Am., Pacific Coast surg. assns., Calif. Acad. Medicine (pres. 1974), Calif. Med. Assn., Howard C. Naffziger Surg. Soc., Internat. Cardiovascular Soc., Mid Century Surgeons Club, Samson Thoracic Surg. Soc., San Francisco County Med. Soc., Thoracic Surgery Dirs. Assn. (pres. 1979-80), San Francisco Surg. Soc., Soc. Thoracic Surgeons (council 1971—, pres. 1972), Soc. Univ. Surgeons, Soc. Vascular Surgery (past v.p.), Western Soc. Clin. Research, Chilean Soc. Cardiology, Am. Soc. Artificial Internal Organs, Harvard U. Med. Alumni Assn. (councillor at large, pres. No. Calif. chpt. 1974). Clubs: Cruising of Am, Pacific Union, St. Francis Yacht, Calif. Tennis. Office: U Calif Dept Surgery M896 San Francisco CA 94143

ROE, ELLEN JANE, civic worker; b. Seattle, Mar. 20, 1928; d. George Albert and Gladys Florence (Jenkins) Tallman; m. Harold Kirby Roe, Feb. 25, 1948; children: Janet, William, Rebecca, Robert, Mark, James. Student, U. Wash., 1946-48. Dir., Seattle Sch. Bd., 1975—; mem. exec. com. Coun. Great City Schs., Washington, 1987—; com. chmn. KCTS Bd., Seattle, 1976-86; mem. Seattle King County Youth Commn., 1972-75. Recipient Outstanding Citizen award, Seattle Mcpl. League, 1978, Outstanding Svc. award, Wash. Parent Tchr. Student Assn., 1975. Fellow Wash. State Sch. Dirs., Nat. Sch. Bds. Assn., Lake City C. of C. Home: 3562 NE 96th St Seattle WA 98115

ROEHM, ROBERT EMIL, credit union executive; b. Bloomington, Nebr., Jan. 6, 1932; s. William Jesse and Ola Irene (Bell) R.; m. Arleta Mae Boles, Nov. 3, 1953; children: Veronica Louise Wheeler, Randy Ray, Robert Sean. Student, Metro State Coll., Denver, 1972; student, Regis Coll., Denver, 1975, U. Calif., Berkeley, 1978, Syracuse U., 1981. Supply commondity mgr. Fitzsimons Army Med. Ctr., Aurora, Colo., 1954-56; mgmt.analyst Fitzsimons Army Med. Ctr., 1956-62, chief program and budget div., 1962-68, dep. dir. resources mgmt., compt., 1968-88; v.p. Jeffco Schs. Credit Union, Lakewood, Colo., 1988—. Bd. dirs., treas. Lakewood Ch. Nazarene, Lakewood, Colo., 1971—. With USN, 1950-54, Korea. Recipient Disting. Svc. award Lakewood Ch. Nazarene, 1982, Edward A. Filene award Colo. Credit Union League, 1985, Friedrich W. Raiffeisen award Colo. Credit Union League, 1987. Mem. Am. Soc. Mil. Compt., Phi Theta Pi (pres. Denver chpt. 1980-81). Republican. Home: 8083 Routt St Arvada CO 80005

ROEHNERT, JOY ESHBACH, nurse; b. Atlantic City, Apr. 30, 1955; d. Walter Russell and Alyce (Van Sant) Eshbach; m. Henrick Anton Roehnert, Dec. 30, 1978; 1 child, Nickolas. AS in Nursing, Atlantic Community Coll., 1976; BS in Nursing, Stockton State Coll., 1978; MS in Nursing, U. Pa., 1987. R.N., N.J., Pa., N.Mex. Staff nurse Atlantic City Med. Ctr., 1976-77; clinic supr. Madison House Presbyterian Homes N.J., Atlantic City, 1977-78; commd. 2d lt. U.S. Air Force, 1978, advanced through grades to capt., 1979; staff nurse U.S. Air Force, various locations, 1978-82; resigned U.S. Air Force, 1982; nurse coord. oncology clinic Children's Hosp. Phila., 1987-88; pediatric oncology nurse practitioner U. N.Mex. Hosp. Trauma Ctr., Albuquerque, 1988—; speaker at profl. confs.; childbirth educator, ARC, Ramstein Air Base, Fed. Republic Germany, 1984; car seat safety cons., 1983-84. Mem. Pediatric Nursing Network, Nat. Assn. Pediatric Nurse Assoc and Practitoners, Sigma Theta Tau. Republican. Episcopalian. Office: U NMex Hosp Pediatric Onc Lomas St NE Albuquerque NM 87111

ROEHRS, ROBERT CHRISTIAN, exploration company executive, geologist; b. Graniteville, Mo., May 6, 1931; s. Paul Martin and Margaret Marie (Dinger) R.; m. Shirley Lucille McHenry, Mar. 30, 1956; children: Lizabeth Anne, Robert Christian Jr., Louis Fulton. BA, U. Mo., 1957, MA, 1958. Geologist Shell Oil Co., Casper, Wyo. and Denver, 1958-65; exploration geologist Davis Oil Co., Denver, 1965-68; ptnr. Lotus Petroleum Co., Denver, 1968-69; v.p., dir. Westgate Oil Co., Inc., Denver, 1969-71; pvt. practice in geology Denver, 1971-79; pres. ROMAC Exploration Co., Inc., Denver, 1979—, also bd. dirs. Bd. trustees Leukemia Soc. Am., Rocky Mountain, Colo. With USAF, 1948-52. Recipient Betty McWhorter Meml. award Desk and Derrick Club, 1980. Mem. Am. Assn. Petroleum Geologists, Rocky Mountain Assn. Geologists, Wyo. Geol. Assn., Ind. Petroleum Assn. Am. (bd. dirs. 1982—, v.p. Mountain States chpt. 1978, pres. 1979, bd. dirs. 1979—), Petroleum Pioneers Club. Republican. Lutheran. Home: 4 Waring Ln Greenwood Village Littleton CO 80121 Office: ROMAC Exploration Co Inc 621 17th St Denver CO 80293

ROELKE, ADA E(LLEN), social services administrator; b. Cumberland, Md., Aug. 24, 1928; d. George William Knock and Mary Emma (Roelke) Eichelberger; children: Karen Bahnsen, Steven Leveen. BA, Syracuse U., 1950; MSW, San Diego State U., 1967; PhD, Profl. Sch. of Psychol. Studies, 1986. Lic. clin. social worker, Calif. Tchr. pub. schs., Syracuse, N.Y., 1960-61; social worker Dept. Pub. Welfare, San Diego, 1964-66; psychiat. social worker State of Calif., Bakersfield, 1967-68; child protection worker Dept. Social Service, San Diego, 1968-77; coordinator, psychotherapist, Chronic Program Grantville Day Treatment Ctr., San Diego, 1977-81; chief social services Edgemoor Geriatric Hosp., Santee, Calif., 1981-88; clin. dir. Calif. Halfway Houses, Inc., San Diego, 1989—; pvt. practice psychotherapy, La Mesa, Calif., 1969—. Fellow Nat. Assn. Social Workers; mem. Marriage Family and Child Counselors Assn., Lic. Clin. Social Workers Assn. Unitarian. Home: 4015 King St La Mesa CA 92041 Office: Calif Halfway House Inc 1516 Ft Stockton Dr San Diego CA 92103

ROEMER, ELIZABETH, astronomer, educator; b. Oakland, Calif., Sept. 4, 1929; d. Richard Quirin and Elsie (Barlow) R. B.A. with Honors (Bertha Dolbeer scholar), U. Calif. at Berkeley, 1950, Ph.D. (Lick Obs. fellow), 1955. Tchr. adult class Oakland pub. schs., 1950-52; lab technician U. Calif. at Mt. Hamilton, 1954-55; grad. research astronomer U. Calif. at Berkeley, 1955-56; research asso. Yerkes Obs. U. Chgo., 1956; astronomer U.S. Naval Obs., Flagstaff, Ariz., 1957-66; asso. prof. dept. astronomy, also in lunar and planetary lab. U. Ariz., Tucson, 1966-69; prof. U. Ariz., 1969—; astronomer Steward Obs., 1980—; Chmn. working group on orbits and ephemerides of comets commn. 20 Internat. Astron. Union, 1964-79, 85-88, v.p. comm. 20, 1979-82, pres., 1982-85, v.p. commn. 6, 1973-76, 85-88, pres., 1976-79, 88—; mem. adv. panels Office Naval Research, Nat. Acad. Scis.-NRC, NASA; researcher and author numerous publs. on astrometry and astrophysics of comets and minor planets including 79 recoveries of returning periodic comets, visual and spectroscopic binary stars, computation of orbits of comets and minor planets. Recipient Dorothea Klumpke Roberts prize U. Calif. at Berkeley, 1950, Mademoiselle Merit award, 1959; asteroid (1657) named Roemera, 1965; Benjamin Apthorp Gould prize Nat. Acad. Scis., 1971; NASA Spl. award, 1986. Fellow AAAS (council 1966-69, 72-73), Royal Astron. Soc. (London); mem. Am. Astron. Soc. (program vis. profs. astronomy 1960-75, council 1967-70, chmn. div. dynamical astronomy 1974), Astron. Soc. Pacific (publs. com. 1962-73, Comet medal com. 1968-74, Donohoe lectr. 1962), Internat. Astron. Union, Am. Geophys. Union, Brit. Astron. Assn., Phi Beta Kappa, Sigma Xi. Office: U Ariz Lunar and Planetary Lab Tucson AZ 85721

ROEMER, WILLIAM FRANCIS, JR., investigative consultant, writer; b. South Bend, Ind., June 16, 1926; s. William Francis Sr. and Carmelita (Luther) R.; m. Jeanne Uphaus, June 12, 1948; children: William Francis III, Robert Walter. JD, U. Notre Dame, 1950. Spl. agt. FBI, Washington, 1950-80; pres. Roemer Enterprises, Inc., Tucson, 1980—; cons. Chgo. Crime Commn., 1983-88. With USMC, 1945-46, ETO.

ROESCH, RAYMOND AUGUST, former university president, clergyman; b. Jenkintown, Pa., Sept. 16, 1914; s. Aloysius Adam and Anna Estelle (Fleck) R. B.A., U. Dayton, 1936; M.A., Cath. U. Am., 1945; postgrad., Columbia U., 1949; Ph.D., Fordham U., 1954; D. Pedagogy (hon.), Coll. of Steubenville, 1976; H.H.D. (hon.), Wright State U., 1979; P.H.L. (hon.), U. Dayton, 1982—. High sch. tchr. Cathedral Latin Sch., Cleve., 1936-41; ordained priest Roman Cath. Ch., 1944; guidance dir. Chaminade High Sch., Mineola, N.Y., 1945-49; parish priest St. Mary's Ch., Mt.Vernon, N.Y., 1949-51; prof. psychology, chmn. dept. U. Dayton, 1951-59, pres., 1959-79, pres. emeritus, 1979—; pres. Chaminade U. of Honolulu, 1982-89; dir. Kokoi Gardens Corp., 1985—; pres. Dayton-Miami Valley Consortium, 1968-78. Sec. bd. trustees Ohio Higher Edn. Assistance Commn.; mem. Ednl. Commn. of States, 1969-79; mem. adv. council ROTC Affairs, 1963-66; mem. Ohio Higher Edn. Facilities Commn., 1968-78, 79—; bd. dirs. Serenity Found., Dayton, Dayton Met. YMCA, 1975, Dayton APC, 1979; chmn. bd. Ohio Found. Independent Colls., 1976-78; trustee Good Samaritan Hosp., Dayton, Mary Manse Coll., Toledo; mem. gov.'s bd. Ohio Scholarship Fund; mem. Dayton Area Progress Council, 1979; bd. dirs. Dayton chpt. NCCJ, 1980—, Dayton chpt. ARC, 1980—; mem. Hawaii Ednl. Loan Program Council, 1984—. Recipient Disting. Civilian Service award, 1969, Outstanding Service to Civic Affairs award Am. Soc. for Pub. Adminstrn., 1972, Disting. Alumnus award, 1973, named to U. Dayton Hall of Fame, 1979, award Nat. Council Christians and Jews, 1982. Mem. AAAS, Am., Am. Cath. psychol. assns., N.E.A., Ohio Coll. Assn. (pres. 1967-68), Assn. Am. Colls. (mem. commn. faculty and students 1965), Ind. Colls. and Univs. Ohio (v.p. 1968), Assn. Urban Univs. (v.p. 1976—), Hawaii Assn. Ind. Colls. and Univs. (chmn. 1984), Phi Delta Kappa, Tau Alpha Pi. Rotarian. Home: 300 College Park Ave Dayton OH 45409 Office: 3140 Waialae Ave Honolulu HI 96816

ROESCH, WARREN DALE, retail company executive; b. Oakland, Calif., Aug. 8, 1945; s. George Oscar and Dorothy Wenifred (Smith) R.; AA, Coll. of San Mateo, 1966; BA, Calif. State U., 1968; m. Marguerite Mary Whitman, Aug. 1, 1970; 1 son, Warren Whitman. Programmer, operator Western Title Ins. Co., San Francisco, 1973-74, mgr. data processing, 1974; mgr. data processing E. Bay Regional Park Dist., Oakland, 1974-78, Jacuzzi Whirlpool Bath, Walnut Creek, Calif., 1978-82; sr. bus. programmer Bechtel Corp., San Francisco, 1978; cons. systems analyst Packaging div. Crown Zellerbach, San Francisco, 1979, project mgr. MIS installations, 1980; founder, chief exec. officer Total Resource Group, Inc., San Mateo, Calif., 1982—; project mgr. Point-of-Sale and Service Systems, Businessland, Inc., 1984-86, mgr. service MIS, 1986-89, sr. mgr. customer support svcs., 1989—. Home: 646 Alhambra Rd San Mateo CA 94402 Office: Businessland Inc 1001 Ridder Park Dr San Jose CA 95131

ROESSER, MARY CAROL, resort company executive; b. L.A., Aug. 22, 1959; d. J.A. and S.M.R. R. BA, U. So. Calif., 1981. Sales rep. Moore Bus. Forms, 1981-82, U.S. Home, Chgo., 1984; dir. customer relations Am. Resorts Internat., Oak Brook, Ill., 1985-86; pres. Resort Svcs. Internat., San Clemente, Calif., 1986—. Mem. Am. Resort and Residential Devel. Assn., Cruise Line Internat. Assn., Nat. Assn. Female Execs., Nat. Fedn. Ind. Bus., U. So. Calif. Alumni Assn., San Clemente C. of C., Kappa Kappa Gamma Alumni Assn. Republican. Roman Catholic. Office: Resort Svcs Internat 910 S El Camino Real San Clemente CA 92672

ROGALLA, CAROLYN JANETTE, nurse, consultant; b. San Francisco, Feb. 3, 1945; d. William Henry and Janette Malene (Nelson) Bohn; m. Marion Leonard Rogalla, Sept. 8, 1973. Grad., St. Luke's Sch. Nursing, San Francisco, 1967; BA in Mgmt., Redlands U., 1986. RN, Calif. Staff nurse ICU Stanford U. Hosp., Palo Alto, Calif., 1967-69; mgr. cardiovascular rsch. Stanford U. Hosp., 1969-71; cardiovascular researcher, Stanford U. grantee Ames Rsch. Lab., 1971-73; ICU nurse VA Hosp., Mpls., 1973; operating room nurse VA Hosp., 1974-76, Western Med. Ctr., Santa Ana, Calif., 1977-80, 81-86; oper. rm. nurse Mt. Vernon Hosp., Alexandria, Va., 1980-81; cons. med. rels. Xanar/Coherent Laser, Colo., 1987; regional nurse cons. Candela Laser Corp., Yorba Linda, Calif., 1987—. Mem. Assn. Oper. Rm. Nurses, Am. Urol. Assn. Allied, Far West Ski Assn. (conv. chmn. 1972). Republican. Home: 6052 Grandview Ave Yorba Linda CA 92686 Office: Candela Laser Corp 530 Boston Post Rd Wayland MA 01778

ROGAN, GERALD NEAL, family physician; b. Miami, Aug. 21, 1946; s. Albert F. and Elaine N. (Newman) R.; m. Patricia C., Nov. 4, 1984. Diploma with honors, Interlochen Arts Acad., Mich., 1964; BA with honors, U. Mich., 1968, MD, 1972. Diplomate Am. Bd. Emergency Medicine. Intern San Joaquin Gen. Hosp., Stockton, Calif., 1972-73; with Calif. Emergency Physicians, Oakland, Calif., 1974-80; physician Family & Urgent Care, Walnut Creek, Calif., 1980—; cons. Medico-Legal Matters, 1975—, Cardiac Resuscitation, Calif., 1976-80; chmn. Dept. of Family Practice John Muir Meml. Hosp., Walnut Creek, Calif., 1989—. Mem. Mich. Marching Band, 1964. Mem. Calif. Med. Assn., Alameda Contra Costa Med. Assn., Rotary Club. Office: Family & Urgent Care 112 La Casa Via #A130 Walnut Creek CA 94598

ROGERS, AILEEN S., public accountant; b. Stamford, Conn., Sept. 1, 1912; d. Clarence T. and Alice (Dawson) Smith; m. James L. Rogers, July 4, 1942; children: Bronson, Judith, Carolen. Student, Chgo. Tng. Sch., 1934; BA in Music, Detroit Inst. Mus. Art, 1937, MA in Music, 1938, PhD, 1939; postgrad., U. So. Calif., 1941. Lic. pub. acct., Calif., 1946. Instr. Detroit Inst. of Musical Art; pvt. practice music tchr. Alhambra, Calif., 1940-41; prin. A.S. Rogers Acctg. Firm, Alhambra, 1942—; owner Rogers Sch. of Income Tax. Author: Hymnology Through the Ages; Composer: Lift of Christ, Cruxifiction for full orchestra, 1939. Mem. Nat. Soc. Pub. Accts., Alhambra C. of C., Eastern Star. Home: 1763 Windsor Rd San Marino CA 91108 Office: A S Rogers 511 W Main St Alhambra CA 91801

ROGERS, ALEXANDER KEIR, physicist; b. San Diego, Feb. 27, 1942; s. Fred Terry and Marguerite (Moilliet) R.; m. Frances Ann Guice, Jan. 24, 1965; children: Eliot Keir, Philip Norman, James Alexander. AB, Pomona Coll., 1963; MS, N.C. State U., 1965. Staff physicist Naval Weapons Ctr., China Lake, Calif., 1965-71; tech. project mgr. Naval Weapons Ctr., China Lake, 1977-78; staff asst. Office of Chief of Naval Ops., Washington, 1978-79; tech. project mgr. Applied Physics Lab./John Hopkins U., Laurel, Md., 1979-84; assoc. head, weapons dept. Naval Weapons Ctr., China Lake, 1984—. Co-inventor in field (Michelson Lab award, Naval Weapons Ctr., 1988). Vestry mem. St. Michael's Episcopal Ch., Ridgecrest, Calif., 1985—. Mem. Optical Soc. of Am., (assoc. mem.) Sigma Xi, Sigma Pi Sigma, Phi Kappa Phi. Republican. Home: 833 Lynn Way Ridgecrest CA 93555 Office: Code 3901 Naval Weapons Ctr China Lake CA 93555

ROGERS, BARBARA ANN, educator; b. Frackville, Pa., Aug. 25, 1941; d. John R. and Clara M. (Chudzwick) R. BA in Edn., Millersville State Coll., 1963; MA in Chemistry, Bowling Green State U., 1968. Cert. tchr. Scis. tchr. N. Penn High Sch., Lansdale, Pa., 1963-68; sci. tchr. McKinley High Sch., Honolulu, 1968—; mem. adv. com. Hawaii State Sci. and Engring Fair, 1983-85, chmn. sci. tour com., 1979-87; coordinator Dreyfus Chemistry Workshop, State of Hawaii, 1985, ECIA Chpt. 2 Devel. Grant, 1988—; mem. staff Ann. Student Symposium on Marine Affairs, 1983—; advanced placement chemistry workshop leader Hawaii Bd. Edn., Coll. Bd., 1979, 85; mem. Presdl. Award Selection Com., 1986—. Mem. Ellison Onizuka Scholarship Com., State of Hawaii, 1986-88. Named Sci. Tchr. of Yr., Hawaii Acad. Sci., 1980; recipient NW Regional award High Sch. Chem. Teaching, Am. Chem. Soc., 1987, Presdl. Excellence in Sci. and Math. Teaching award Pres. of U.S., 1985, Dedication to Teaching Sci.and Encouragement of Research award Sigma Xi, 1983, Teaching Excellence award Nat. Marine Educators Assn., 1984, 85, 86; grantee NSF, Dreyfus Found. Mem. Am. Chem. Soc. (sec. Hawaii sect. 1982-84, chmn. 1984-86, numerous subcoms., grants, awards), Acad. Alliance in Chemistry (dir. Hawaii chpt.), Nat. Sci. Tchrs. Assn., Hawaii State Sci. Tchrs. Assn., NEA, Hawaii State Tchrs. Assn., Smithsonian, Honolulu Acad. Arts. Democrat. Home: 425 Ena Rd #607-C Honolulu HI 96815 Office: McKinley High Sch Sci Dept 1039 S King St Honolulu HI 96814

ROGERS, BOB, producer; b. L.A., Feb. 3, 1950; s. Howard N. and Trudi Rogers; m. Karen P. Rogers, May 18, 1974. Student, Stanford U., 1968-70; BA, Calif. Inst. of Arts, 1972. Magician Disneyland, Anaheim, Calif., 1968-72; writer Walt Disney Prodns., Burbank, Calif., 1972—; cons. Walt Disney Imagineering, Glendale, Calif., 1979-81; pres. Bob Rogers and Co., Inc., Burbank, 1981—. Producer of numerous shows at EPCOT/Disney World, 1982, 89, Vancouver World Fair, 1986; two patents. Active U'mista Cult. Ctr. Recipient numerous awards for creative excellence, including Acad. Award nominations. Mem. Acad. Motion Picture Arts and Scis., Am. Film Inst., U'mista Cultiral Ctr. Office: Bob Rogers & Co Inc 824 N Victory Blvd Burbank CA 91502

ROGERS, CELESTE ANN, systems analyst; b. Cleve., Oct. 9, 1953; d. Joseph Eugene and Clara Dorothy Vasas; m. Clinton Warner First, Feb. 17, 1973 (div. 1974); m. Thomas Edward Rogers, June 6, 1981. AAB, North Cen. Tech. Coll., Mansfield, Ohio, 1972. Cert. data processor. Data processing mgr. Newark (Calif.) Unified Sch. Dist., 1976-77; mem. tech. staff Bus. Programmer Svcs., San Jose, 1978; programmer/analyst County of Santa Cruz, Calif., 1979; sr. programmer/analyst William Wrigley Jr. Co., 1976-77; sr. programmer, analyst Plantronics, Inc., 1981-84; systems analyst, data processing svcs. br. dept. edn. State of Hawaii, 1984-85; with Electronic Data Systems, Hawaii, 1985; cons. Pacific Resources, Inc., 1985-86; with Planning Rsch. Corp., Hawaii, 1986-87; systems analyst Sterling Software, Intelligence & Mil. div., Honolulu, Hawaii, 1987—; prin. Celeste A. Rogers, CDP, Waipahu, 1986—; personal trainer to Kathy Conway (bodybuilding championship), Honolulu, 1988. Mem. Data Processing Mgmt. Assn. (dir. 1988—), Honolulu Bus. and Profl. Women's Club (editor 1987—), Armed Forces Communications and Electronics Assn., NAFE, Powerful Women of Hawaii, Mensa (treas. Hawaii group 1988—, editor Mensaloha 1988—), Harley Owners Group, Sierra. Home: PO Box 720 Waipahu HI 96797

ROGERS, CHARLES THEODORE GRAHAM (TED ROGERS), metapsychologist; b. N.Y.C., Oct. 8, 1907; s. Charles T. and May (Church) G-R.; B.S., Wagner Coll., 1933; M.S., San Diego State U., 1962; certificate in counseling U. So. Calif., 1965; D.Sc., Miss. State Christian Coll., 1969; C.H., Dominion Coll., 1975; Ph.D., Newport U., 1977; Ph.D. in Metapsychology, U. Humanistics Studies, 1978; M.S.D., Inst. Metapsychology, 1980; m. Consuelo Yvonne d'Aguilar, March 11, 1933 (dec. July 1975); 1 dau., Patricia Suzanne. Dir. delinquency prevention N.Y.C. schs., 1934-39; assistant dir. personnel tng. Pub. Works Adminstrn., N.Y.C., 1940-41; mem. N.Y. State Div. Parole, 1941-46; chief probation officer San Diego County, San Diego, 1947-67; cons., researcher parapsychology, psychic phenomena, survival, metaphys. healing, 1967—; dir. Ctr. for Edn. and Research, 1965-78; chmn. metapsychology U. Humanistic Studies, 1977-78, mem. psychology faculty, 1977-83, dean Inst. Metapsychology, 1981—; dir. Voyage of Discovery Internat. Inst. Metapsychology, 1982—, Project Exploration, 1988—; guest lectr. San Diego State Coll., 1948; lectr. Calif. Western U., 1958-61; lectr., hon. fellow Lynwood Fellowship, Eng., 1984—; cons. Nat. Probation and Parole Assn., Ariz. Correctional Study, 1958; cons. Deliquency Control Inst., Ariz. State U., 1959-64; cons. Youth Studies Ctr. U. So. Calif., 1963-65, youth problems Bishopric of Fiji, 1966; mem. County Parole Bd., 1961-67; mem. com. Probation Study, Dependent Child Study, State of Calif., 1963-67; mem. profl. advisory com. social work curriculum San Diego State Coll., 1959-61; probation adv. com. Calif. Youth Authority, 1958-67; v.p., chmn. research com. Parapsychology Found., lectr., 1962-67. Served to capt. USAAF, 1942-46; PTO. Recipient Legion of Honor, Order of DeMolay. Fellow World Assn. Soc. Psychiatry, Royal Soc. Health, Inst. Parapsychol. Research, Coll. Psychic Studies; mem. Am. Soc. Psychical Research, Internat., Am. assns. social psychiatry, Acad. Parapsychology and Medicine, Am. Orthopsychiatric Assn., Assn. for Humanistic Psychology, Soc. for Sci. Study of Religion, Acad. Religion and Psychical Research, Nat. Assn. Social Workers (charter), Acad. Religion and Mental Health, Internat. Assn. Metapsychology (pres. 1980—), So. Calif. Soc. Psychical Research, Cosmosophy Soc. (pres.), Am. Assn. Study Mental Imagery, Assn. Transpersonal Psychology, Spiritual Frontiers Fellowship, Calif. Probation, Parole and Correctional Assn. (pres. 1961-62), Acad. Certified Social Workers, Church's Fellowship for Psychic Studies, Theosophical Soc., Pi Sigma Alpha. Contbr. articles to various publs. Address: 962 Greenlake Ct PO Box 609 Cardiff by the Sea CA 92007

ROGERS, DENNIS LEE, architect; b. Athens, Tenn., Jan. 26, 1953; s. Franklin O'Dean and Mary Nell (Benson) R.; m. Hada Luz Chavarria, Dec. 17, 1977; children—O'Dina Maria, Angela Emperatriz. B.Arch., U. Tenn., 1980. Archtl. design draftsman U.S. Air Force, Luke AFB, Ariz., 1980-81; engring. design draftsman Marathon Steel Co., Tempe, Ariz., 1981-82; facilities design engr. Hughes Helicopter, Inc., Mesa, Ariz., 1982-83; facilities engr./planner Four-Phase/ISO, Inc., Tempe, 1983-84; architect Motorola, Inc., Mesa, 1984-85, cons., 1987-88, Ariz. Architects and Planners, Inc., Phoenix, 1985-86; project architect Greyhound Lines, Inc., Phoenix, 1986-87; cons. Motorola, Inc., Mesa, 1987-88, Sun-Mos Tech., Tempe, 1988—. Prin. works include passive solar home, Lake Tahoe, Nev., 1982. Recipient Outstanding Performance award Hughes Helicopter, Inc., 1983. Mem. AIA (assoc.), Toastmasters, Mesa Jaycees (treas. 1984-85). Office: Sun-Mos Tech 1430 W Broadway Tempe AZ 85281

ROGERS, DENNIS SCOTT, process engineer, educator; b. Ft. Thomas, Ky., Nov. 22, 1957; s. Lloyd Kenneth and Blanche Lucille (Foy) R.; m. Lauren Ann Gavin, Aug. 7, 1982. BS, No. Ky. U., 1979; MA, San Diego State U., 1983; PhD, U. Calif., San Diego, 1985. Sr. engr. Cin. Milacron, 1986-87, Unisys Corp., San Diego, 1987—; Pres. Ellipse Tech. Search, Escondido, Calif., 1987-89. Contbr. articles to profl. jours. Mem. Am. Chem. Soc. Republican.

ROGERS, DONALD ROBERT, pathologist; b. Tacoma, Apr. 7, 1932; s. John Robert and Thelma Ethel (Neely) R.; m. Georgia Lee Miller, June 9, 1956; children: Steven, Julie. BS, U. Puget Sound, 1954; MD, U. Wash., 1958. Diplomate Am. Bd. Pathology. Intern Mpls. Gen. Hosp., 1958-59; resident U. Wash., Seattle, 1963-66; pathologist Humana Hosp., Anchorage, 1967—; med. examiner State of Alaska, 1967—. Contbr. articles to profl. jours. Bd. dirs. Am. Cancer Soc., Alaska, 1967—, nat. del. dir., 1983-84. Served to Lt. comfr. U.S. Navy, 1959-62. Fellow Coll. Am. PAthologists; mem. Am. Soc. Clin. Pathologists, Alaska State Med. Assn., Anchorage Med. Soc. (pres. 1972), Nat. Assn. Med. Examiners. Republican. Club: Rotary (Anchorage). Home: 921 W Klatt Rd Anchorage AK 99515 Office: Humana Hosp Alaska 2801 DeBarr Rd Anchorage AK 99508

ROGERS, D(ONALD) TERRY, lawyer; b. Lovell, Wyo., Aug. 20, 1940; s. Donald Grant and Elma (Shumway) R.; m. Gloria Ann Bailey, Mar. 25, 1978; children: Ryan Terry, Gary Matthew, Jennifer Lynn, Dana Leigh. BS, U.S. Naval Acad., 1963; JD, U. Wyo., 1970. Bar: Wyo. 1970, U.S. Dist. Ct. Wyo. 1970. Joined U.S. Navy, 1959, commd. ensign, 1963, advanced through grades to lt., resigned, 1967; sole practice, Jackson, Wyo., 1970-83; atty. Town of Jackson (Wyo.), 1971-75; pros. atty. County of Teton, Wyo., 1975-89; dist. judge 9th Jud. Dist., Jackson, 1989—; mem. Jail Standards Adv. Com., City of Cheyenne, Wyo., 1977; mem. Wyo. Gov's Adv. Com. on Criminal Investigation, Crime Victims Compensation Commn., 1989—. Bd. dirs. Wyo. Little League Baseball, 1974, del. Wyo. Republican State Conv. Lt. USN, 1959-67. Mem. Wyo. Pros. Attys. Assn. (pres. 1984), Teton County Bar Assn. (pres. 1983), ABA, Assn. Trial Lawyers Am., Nat. Dist. Attys. Assn. Mormon. Office: 9th Jud Dist PO Box 606 181 S King St Jackson WY 83001

ROGERS, DWANE LESLIE, management consultant; b. Maywood, Calif., Oct. 6, 1943; s. Lloyd Donald and Della (McAlister) R.; B.S., Ariz. State U., 1967; M.S., Bucknell U., 1968; m. Doris L. Fantel, Aug. 22, 1970; 1 dau., Valerie Lynn. Successively mktg. research coordinator, customer service analyst, merchandising mgr., product planning mgr., order processing mgr. Samsonite Corp., Denver, 1968-74; dir. adminstrn. WISCO Equipment Co., Inc., Phoenix, 1974-75; dir. discontinued ops. Bowmar Instrument Corp., Phoenix, 1975-77; mgmt. cons., dir. Ariz. ops. Mariscal & Co., Phoenix, 1977-80; mgmt. cons. Ariz. Small Bus. Devel. Center, 1980-81; dir. accounts payable, accounts receivable, crude and finished product acctg. Giant Industries, Phoenix, 1981—; instr. Maricopa County Community Coll., 1979-83. Mem. Am. Mktg. Assn., Mass Retailing Inst. Republican. Episcopalian. Home: 2844 E Acoma Dr Phoenix AZ 85032

ROGERS, GARDNER SPENCER, railroad company executive, retired, consultant; b. Bryn Mawr, Pa., Sept. 16, 1926; s. Gardner Spencer and Frances (Lloyd) R.; m. Margaret Elizabeth Windsor, July 18, 1954; children: Ann Rogers Wilbanks, Barbara Lloyd. Student Episcopal Acad., 1940-44, MIT, 1944-45; BS, U. Colo., 1951. Registered profl. engr., Calif. With Western Pacific R.R. Co., San Francisco, 1947-70, engr. costs, valuation and stats., 1964-69, asst. to gen. mgr. planning and control, 1969, asst. gen. mgr., 1970; gen. mgr. Civil & Mech. Maintenance Pty. Ltd., 1970-77; mgr. Western Australian ops. Fluor Australia Pty. Ltd., 1971-73, gen. mgr. ry. div., 1973-77; gen. mgr. Pilbara Industries, 1971-73; dir. budgets and control Consol. Rail Corp., 1978-79, sr. dir. budgets, planning and control, 1980, dir. corp. planning, 1981-87; cons., 1987—; mem. spl. adv. team R.R. ofcls. to U.S. Govt., 1962; adv. com. on R.R. property ICC, 1966-70. Mng. trustee Daniel B. Gardner Trust, Chgo.; alt. trustee Cathedral Sq. Found., Perth; vestryman Ch. of Eng., 1971-77, mem. synod and provincial synod, 1973-77, mem. diocesan coun., 1974-77, bd. dirs. sch.'s trust, 1975-77. Mem. Instn. Engrs. Australia, Am. C. of C. in Australia (bd. dirs., v.p., chmn. Western Australian exec. com. 1976-77), Swanleigh (chmn. exec. com. 1974-77, coun.), Am. Mgmt. Assn., Am. Ry. Engr. Assn. (sec. com. 11 1983-87), Ry. and Locomotive Hist. Soc., Soc. of Cin., Mil. Order Loyal Legion (vice comdr.), Colo. Alumni Assn. No. Calif. (pres. 1951-52), Alpha Tau Omega (high coun. 1964-68, 82—). Republican. Clubs: Berkeley Tennis, Pacific Railway (San Francisco); Commonwealth (Calif.); Australian-Am. (Perth). Home and Office: 9 Mal Paso Rd Rte 1 Carmel CA 93923

ROGERS, HELEN EVELYN WAHRGREN, newspaperwoman; b. Tacoma, Jan. 24, 1924; d. John Sigurd and Emma Elina (Carlson) Wahrgren; B.A., U. Wash., Seattle, 1946; m. Charles Dana Rogers, July 24, 1948. Mem. editorial staff Holiday mag., Phila., 1946; civilian public relations writer, Ft. Lewis, Wash., 1946-47; asst. society editor Tacoma News Tribune-Sunday Ledger, 1947-51, 1957-61, radio-TV editor-columnist, 1951-86. Author: What's Your Line? vol. I: Delila Sprague Sherburne Harrington: Her Ancestors and Descendants. Mem. Newspaper Guild, Wis. Geneal. Soc., Tacoma-Pierce County Geneal. Soc., U. Wash. Alumni Assn. Democrat. Lutheran. Home: 2906 N 24th St Tacoma WA 98406 Office: 2906 N 24th St Tacoma WA 98406

ROGERS, JACK DAVID, plant pathologist; b. Point Pleasant, W.Va., Sept. 3, 1937; s. Jack and Thelma Grace (Coon) R.; m. Belle C. Spener, June 7, 1958. BS in Biology, Davis and Elkins Coll., 1960; MF, Duke U., 1960; PhD, U. Wis., 1963. Asst. prof. then assoc. prof. Wash. State U., Pullman, 1963-86, prof., chmn. dept. plant pathology, 1986—. Contbr. articles to profl. jours. mem. Mycological Soc. of Am. (pres., 1977-78), Am. Phytopathol. Soc., Botanical Soc. Am., British Mycological Soc.

ROGERS, LELAND KAY, insurance executive; b. Salt Lake City, Sept. 8, 1958; s. Glenn H. and Vadis Clark Rogers; m. Jana Jolene Carroll, Jan. 12, 1985; children; Jaren Lee, Kaylene Juna. BS, U. Utah, 1982; MBA, Ariz. State U., 1983. Account rep. Met. Life Ins. Co., Tempe, Ariz., 1983-85; agy. mgr. Chandler, Ariz., 1985—. Mem. Nat. Assn. Life Underwriters (cert., Nat. Quality award 1987), Gen. Agy. Mgr. Assn. (cert.), Chandler C. of C. Republican. Mormon. Office: Met Life Ins Co 1351 N Alma School Rd #205 Chandler AZ 85224

ROGERS, MARC FRANCIS, financial consultant; b. San Jose, Calif., Oct. 27, 1957; s. Lloyd Vernon Rogers and Susan Agatha (Nerney) Rogers Schumann. BS, Coll. Notre Dame, 1981. Account exec. DRB Fin., Inc., Redwood City, Calif., 1981-83; fin. cons. Merrill, Lynch, Pierce, Fenner & Smith, Colorado Springs, Colo., 1983-85; fin. cons. Paine Webber, Inc., Colorado Springs, 1985-88, Palo Alto, Calif., 1988—; instr. Colo. Coll., 1984—. Mem. Econ. Devel. Coun., 1987—; planning comr. City of Colorado Springs, 1987—. Mem. Colorado Springs C. of C. (mem. city affairs coun. 1984—), San Francisco Jr. C. of C. (past v.p.), Colorado Springs Symphony Club, Winter Nights Club, Plaza Club. Home: 1042 Oakland Ave Menlo Park CA 94025 Office: Paine Webber Inc 755 Page Mill Rd A#100 Palo Alto CA 94304

ROGERS, MARK ALLAN, dentist; b. Salem, Oreg., Feb. 28, 1955; s. Barnes Deering and Virginia Dale (Currier) R.; m. Kristina Schetky; children: Kristin, Ashley, Mikayla. BS in Biology and BA in German, Oreg. State U., 1979; DMD, Oreg. Health Scis. U., 1986. Pvt. practice Salem, 1986—. Team capt. Salem YMCA, bd. dirs. 1989—, youth donar cpt., 1987—. Mem. ADA (student clinician), Oreg. Dental Assn., Marion-Polk-Yamhill Dental Soc. (sec.-treas. 1989—), Acad. Gen. Dentistry, Salem C. of C. (chmn. program com. 1987—. bd. dirs. 1988—).

ROGERS, MICHAEL ALAN, writer; b. Santa Monica, Calif., Nov. 29, 1950; s. Don Easterday and Mary Othilda (Gilbertson) R.; m. Janet Louise Hopson, Oct. 23, 1976. BA in Creative Writing, Stanford U., 1972. Assoc. editor Rolling Stone Mag., San Francisco, 1972-76; editor-at-large Outside mag., San Francisco, 1976-78; sr. writer Newsweek mag., San Francisco, 1983—; vis. lectr. fiction U. Calif., Davis, 1980. Author: Mindfogger, 1973, Biohazard, 1977, Do Not Worry About The Bear, 1979, Silicon Valley, 1982, Forbidden Sequence, 1988; contbr. articles to mags., newspapers. Recipient Disting. Sci. Writing award AAAS, 1976, Best Feature Articles award Computer Press Assn., 1987. Mem. Authors Guild. Office: Newsweek 505 Sansome St Ste 1501 San Francisco CA 94111

ROGERS, MICHAEL HOLMES, corporate planner, naval pilot; b. Natick, Mass., Nov. 1, 1949; s. Harrison Holmes and Amelia Mary (Remidies) R.; m. Carole Rose Anderson, Mar. 27, 1976 (div. Dec. 1981); m. Melanie Marie Carl, July 28, 1984; 1 child. BS in Indsl. Tech., Calif. State Poly. U., 1972; MBA Fin. San Francisco State U., 1988. Lic. helicopter pilot. Food service clk. United Airlines, San Francisco, 1972-73; configuration analyst Kaiser Electronics, San Jose, Calif., 1980-81; corp. sr. planner U.S. Sprint, Burlingame, Calif., 1981-87; stockbroker Baraban Securities, San Bruno, Calif., 1988—; workload planner United Airlines, San Francisco, 1988—. Served to comdr. USN, 1973-79, USNR, 1980—. Mem. Res. Officers Assn., Naval Reserve Assn., Naval Helicopter Assn., Am. Legion. Democrat. Office: United Airlines San Francisco Internat Airport San Francisco CA 94128

ROGERS, NATHAN, oral and maxillofacial surgeon; b. San Francisco, Aug. 22, 1912; s. Dr. Nathan and Maria (de la Luz Urtuzuastegui) R.; A.B., Stanford U., 1937; B.S., U. Calif., 1943, D.D.S., 1943, postgrad., 1949, 55; postgrad. U.S. Nat. Naval Med. Center, 1944; m. Eleanor Marie Ludes, July 5, 1941; children—Ann Lenore, James William, Craig Edward, Glenn Joseph, Wayne Phillip. Grad. in oral and maxillofacial surgery Columbia-Presbyn. Med. Center, N.Y.C., 1947-48; resident oral and maxillofacial surgery Presbyn. Hosp., N.Y.C., 1948-49; pvt. practice oral and maxillofacial surgery, San Francisco, 1950-60; mem. exec. med. staff French Hosp., 1950-59, vis. oral and maxillofacial surgeon, 1950-60, lectr. in oral and maxillofacial surgery, 1955-60; vis. oral and maxillofacial surgeon St. Francis Meml. Hosp., 1951-61, cons. oral and maxillofacial surgery Cleft Palate Guidance Group Clinic, 1951-60; vis. oral and maxillofacial surgeon St. Mary's Hosp., 1951-60; oral and maxillofacial surgeon to Disaster Council and Corps, City and County of San Francisco, 1950— (all in San Francisco). Contributor U.S. Dept. Interior, Fish and Wildlife Service, 1961—. Instnl. rep. San Francisco council Boy Scouts Am., 1957-63, merit badge counselor, 1972—. Served as surgeon Dental Corps, USN, 1943-47. Mem. ADA, Calif. State, San Francisco dental assns., Internat. Assn. Anesthesiologists (charter mem.), Am. Dental Soc. Anesthesia, Pacific Marine Research Soc., No. Calif. Soc. Oral and Maxillofacial Surgeons (emeritus), Stanford (life), U. Calif. (life), Columbia Dental (life), Presbyn. Hosp. N.Y.C. alumni assns., San Francisco Opera Assn. (contbg.), San Francisco Symphony Assn. (contbg.), VFW (life), Ducks Unltd. (contbg.), Nat. Rifle Assn. Am. (life), Nat. Bench Rest Shooters' Assn., Original Pa. 1000 Yard Bench Rest Club, Alpha Sigma Phi (life, pres. San Francisco grad. chpt. 1953), Delta Sigma Delta (life mem., pres. San Francisco grad. council 1954). Republican. Episcopalian. Clubs: Chabot Gun; Associated Sportsmen of California; Refuge Gun 2 (pres. 1976-82). Home: 22 Lopez Ave San Francisco CA 94116

ROGERS, PATRICIA LOUISE, nurse; b. Ellensburg, Wash., June 17, 1926; d. Benjamin Bab and Ethel Mae (Cheney) Colwell; m. Clifford J. Rogers, Jr., Mar. 20, 1949. Diploma in nursing Swedish Hosp., Seattle, 1948; BSc in Nursing, U. Wash., 1962. Staff nurse Swedish Hosp., Seattle, 1948-49, White Pass Hosp., Skagway, Alaska, 1949-51; physician's office nurse, Whitehorse, Y.T., Can., 1954-57; staff nurse, acting head nurse Doctor's Hosp., Seattle, 1960-61, pub. health nurse Seattle-King County Health Dept., 1962-64; staff and head nurse Fairbanks Clinic (Alaska), 1965-67; pub. health nurse Fairbanks Health Ctr., 1967-69, regional pub. health nursing supr. II, 1970-75, nursing mgr., 1975-81, regional nursing mgr., 1981—. adv. com. Salvation Army Drug Abuse Treatment Program. Served with Cadet Nursing Corps, 1945-48. Mem. Am. Pub. Health Assn., Alaska Pub. Health Assn., Am. Nurses Assn., Alaska Nurses Assn., Fairbanks Rehab. Assn. Episcopalian. Office: State Alaska Dept Health Social Services Div Pub Health Office Regional Nursing 1001 Noble St Ste 450 Fairbanks AK 99701

ROGERS, ROBERT REED, manufacturing company executive; b. Oak Park, Ill., Feb. 22, 1929; s. Glen Charles and Lucile (Reed) R.; m. Barbara June Fain, Feb. 22, 1951 (div.); children—Robin, Janeen, Kevin. B.S. in Chemistry, Berea Coll., 1951; M.B.A., Ill. Inst. Tech., 1958, postgrad., 1959-62. Asst. mgr. metallurgy research dept. Armour Research Found., Ill. Inst. Tech., 1955-56, mem. faculty, econs. dept., 1956-62; cons. McKinsey & Co., Inc., 1962-64; mgr. devel. planning, profl. group Litton Industries, Inc., 1964-67; pres. N.Am. subs. Muirhead & Co., Ltd., 1967-68; group v.p. Am. Electric Inc. subs. City Investing Co., 1968-70; pres. Cleartight Corp., 1971-73; pres. Newport Internat. Metals Corp., 1973-76; pres. Kensington Assocs., Inc., Newport Beach, Calif., 1976-83; pres., chmn. bd. Proteus Group, Inc., Newport Beach, 1981-83, pres., chmn. bd. Comparator Systems Corp., Irvine, Calif., 1983—. Served as officer USN, 1951-55. Decorated Knight of Grace Sovereign Order St. John; Machinery and Allied Products Inst. fellow, 1956-62; Berea Coll. grantee, 1947-51. Mem. Navy League, Mensa, Intertel, Ferrari Owners Club, Lido Isle Yacht Club. Republican. Mem. Ch. of Religious Sci. Home: 2800 Broad St Newport Beach CA 92663 Office: Comparator Systems Corp 18552 MacArthur Blvd Ste 400 Irvine CA 92715

ROGERS, WILLIAM CORDELL, financial executive; b. Louisville, Apr. 16, 1943; s. Delbert Clifton and Nelle Frances (Grimsley) R.; m. Elaine Elizabeth Nicolay, Apr. 10, 1966; children: William C. II, Erin D., Nicole M., Shannon D. AA, Lincoln Coll., 1969; BS, Ill. State U., 1971; MBA, U. Phoenix, 1989. With Ill. Dept. Revenue, Springfield, 1971-72; exec. v.p., treas. Life Ins. Co., Lincoln, Ill., 1972-77; controller DEN, Inc. CPAs, Tempe, Ariz., 1977-83; corp. fin. cons. Dahlberg Industries, Scottsdale, Ariz., 1983—; instr. econ. Lincoln Coll., 1972-77, real estate taxation, 1978-80. With U.S. Army, 1964-67, Vietnam. Recipient Dow Jones award Dow Jones-Wall St. Jour., 1969. Mem. Nat. Assn. Pub. Accts., Ariz. Soc. Pub. Accts. Republican. Lodge: Rotary (bd. dirs. Scottsdale club 1986—, pres. elect, Paul Harris fellow 1985—). Home: 8549 E Turney Ave Scottsdale AZ 85251 Office: Dahlberg Industires 6535 E Osborn Rd Scottsdale AZ 85251

ROGERS, WILLIAM SHIELDS, JR., architect; b. Evanston, Ill., Aug. 1, 1943; s. William Shields Sr. and Eleanor (Males) R.; m. Sally Kay Buckmaster, June 3, 1967; children: Therease Lynell, James Larson, Jayna Marie. BArch, U. Nebr., 1968. Registered architect, Nebr., Ill., Colo., Iowa, Mont., Ohio, Mo. Architect ARE, Omaha, 1971-73, Hastings and Chivette, Denver, 1973-74; architect, dir. constrn. CM Corp., Souix City, Iowa, 1974-76; architect, office mgr. Eugene Wright and Assocs., Lincoln, Nebr., 1976-77; architect Woodworth Assocs., Lakewood, Colo., 1977-81, Lee & Associated, Lakewood, 1981-84, 84-85; pvt. bus. Will Rogers Architect, Denver, 1985-88; architect, v.p. Am. Healthcare Designers, Ltd., Denver, 1988—. Sec., Holy Shepard Lutheran Ch., Denver, 1981-83, pres., 1984. Mem. Kiwanis (Bear Valley chpt., sec. 1981, 85). Republican. Office: Am Healthcare Designers Ltd 1873 S Bellaire Ste 300 Denver CO 80222

ROGERS-LEIMBACH, JULIE ANN, speech and language pathologist, educator; b. Lynwood, Calif., June 20, 1960; d. Robert Irvin and Joyce Felicia (Berta) R. AA in Psychology, Calif. State U., Fullerton, 1982, BA in Communicative Disorders, 1982; MA in Speech Pathology, Calif. State U., Long Beach, 1985. Cert. in clin. rehab. svcs., Calif. Speech and lang. specialist ABC Unified Sch. Dist., Norwalk, Calif., 1985; tchr. aphasia Norwalk-La Mirada Unified Sch. Dist., 1985—. Mem. Am. Speech and Hearing Assn.

ROGERSON, LINDA GAIL, small business owner; b. Seattle, Sept. 20, 1952; d. James M. Myers and June Ione (Hart) Fritts; m. Kern Alan Rogerson, Jan. 22, 1972; children: Kern Aron, Jarrett James. Grad. high sch., Seattle. Pub. br. exchange operator Kelley's Telephone Answering Svc., Seattle, 1970-72; owner Areis Restaurant, Seattle, 1972-73; gen. office mgr. Environ. Properties, Lynwood, Wash., 1973-74; prodn. asst. Putney Prodns., L.A., 1976-78; realtor assoc. Island Style, Kailua, Hawaii, 1984-85, Kailua Realty, 1985-88; owner Someplace Else, Kailua, 1986—. Mem. Exchange Club. Office: Someplace Else 33 Aulike St Kailua HI 96734

ROGGE, RICHARD DANIEL, former government executive, security consultant, investigator; b. N.Y.C., July 5, 1926; s. Daniel Richard and Bertha (Sarner) R.; m. Josephine Mary Kowalewska, June 6, 1948; children—Veronica Leigh Rogge Erbeznik, Richard Daniel, Christopher Ames, Meredith Ann. BS in Bus. Adminstrn., NYU, 1952. Cert. profl. investigator. Clerical worker FBI, N.Y.C., 1947-52, spl. agt., Phila., 1952-54, Washington, 1954-58, supr., 1958-65, asst. spl. agt. in charge, Richmond, Va., 1965-66, Phila., 1966-67, L.A., 1967-69, inspector, 1969, spl. agt. in charge, Honolulu, 1969-72, Richmond, 1972-74, Buffalo, 1974-77, now security cons., investigator, Calif.; police tng. instr.; writer, lectr. in field. With USMC, 1944-46; PTO. Recipient Order of Arrow award Boy Scouts Am., 1943, Svc. to Law Enforcement awards Va. Assn. Chiefs Police, 1975, N.Y. State Assn. Chiefs Police, 1977, others. Mem. Am. Soc. Indsl. Security, Calif. Assn. Lic. Investigators, Calif. Peace Officers Assn., Soc. Former Agts. FBI, Inc., Am. Legion. Republican. Roman Catholic. Lodge: K.C. Home and Office: 32010 Watergate Ct Westlake Village CA 91361-4022

ROGNESS, RICHARD RUSSELL, mortgage company executive; b. St. Louis Park, Minn., June 7, 1956; s. Darwin Lowell and Joyce C. (Pederson) R.; m. Jennifer M. Hartman, Oct. 22, 1983; 1 child, Kelsey Joyce. BS cum laude, Mankato State U., 1978. Title examiner Transam. Title, Phoenix, 1979; loan originator S.W. Savs., Phoenix, 1980, Ralph C. Sutro Co., Mesa, Ariz., 1980; mktg. rep. Stewart Title Co., Tempe, Ariz., 1980-82; loan originator Valentine Mortgage, Scottsdale, Ariz., 1982-83, The Gill Co., Mesa, Ariz., 1983-84; asst. v.p., br. mgr. D&N Mortgage Corp., Mesa, 1984—. Precinct committeeman Ariz. Rep. party, Mesa, 1988. Mem. Ariz. Mortgage Bankers Assn., Assn. Profl. Mortgage Women, Young Mortgage Bankers (pres. 1989—), Mesa-Chandler-Tempe Bd. Realtors. Office: D&N Mortgage Corp 1745 S Alma Sch Rd Ste 115 Mesa AZ 85210

ROGSTAD, MARK ROLAND, teacher; b. Belvidere, Ill., Mar. 1, 1957; s. Ronald Glenn and Mary Ellen (Kugath) R. BS, Ea. Ill. U., 1979, MS, 1981; EdD, U. Wyo., 1988. Grad. asst. Ea. Ill. U., Charleston, 1980-81; electronics instr. Proviso West High Sch., Hillside, Ill., 1981-85; tech. educator U. Wyo., Laramie, 1985-88, Mont. State U., Bozeman, 1988—; cons. Wyo. State Dept. Edn., Cheyenne, 1986—. Recipient Faculty Growth award U. Wyo., Laramie, 1987, Prin. Tech. award Wyo. State Dept. Edn., Cheyenne, 1986-87. Mem. Internat. Tech. Edn. Assn., Am. Vocational Assn., Council on Tech. Tchr. Edn., Nat. Assn. Indsl. Tech., Mont. Vocational Assn., Epsilon Pi Tau, Phi Delta Kappa, EIU Alumni Assn. Lutheran. Club: Panther (Charleston). Office: Mont State U 115 Cheever Hall Bozeman MT 59717

ROHDE, JAMES VINCENT, software systems company executive; b. O'Neill, Nebr., Jan. 25, 1939; s. Ambrose Vincent and Loretta Cecilia R.; m. Deborah L. Todd, June 6, 1966; children: Maria, Sonja, Daniele. BCS, Seattle U., 1962. Chmn. bd. dirs., pres., Applied Telephone Tech., Oakland, 1974; v.p. sales and mktg. Automation Electornics Corp., Oakland, 1975-82; pres., chmn. bd. dirs. Am. Telecorp, Inc., 1982—. Pres. Council Regents Heritage Coll., Toppenish, Wash., 1985-88; chmn. emeritus exec. com. Council Regents Heritage Coll. Republican. Roman Catholic. Office: Am Telecorp Inc 10 Twin Dolphin Dr Redwood City CA 94065

ROHRABACHER, DANA, congressman; b. June 21, 1947; s. Donald and Dorothy Rohrabacher. Student, L.A. Harbor Coll., 1965-67; BA in History, Long Beach State Coll., 1969; MA in Am. Studies, U. So. Calif. Reporter City News Svc./Radio West, L.A., 4 yrs.; editorial writer Orange County Register; asst. press sec. Reagan for Pres. Campaign, 1976, 80; speechwriter, spl. asst. to Pres. Reagan White House, Washington, 1981-88; mem. 101st Cong. from 42d Calif. dist., 1989—; U.S. del. Young Polit. Leaders Conf., USSR; disting. lectr. Internat. Terrorism Conf., Paris, 1985. Recipient Disting. Alumnus award L.A. Harbor Coll., 1988. Office: US Ho of Reps Longworth Bldg Rm 1017 Washington DC 20515

ROHRBERG, RODERICK GEORGE, consultant; b. Minneola, Iowa, Sept. 26, 1925; s. Charles H. and Emma (Minsen) R.; BS in Naval Sci., Marquette U., 1946; BSCE, Iowa State U., 1949; m. Genevieve Mary Sogard, June 19, 1949; children—Karla (Mrs. George H. Witz, Jr.), Roderick K., Cheries, Timothy, Christopher. Bridge design engr. Alaska Rd. Commn., U.S. Dept. Interior, 1949-51; sr. tech. specialist North Am. Rockwell, research, Los Angeles, 1951-69; pres. Creative Pathways, Inc., advanced welding services, Torrance, Calif., 1969—; pvt. practice as cons. advanced welding process, equipment design and devel., Torrance, Calif., 1972—. Served with USNR, 1944-46. Recipient 1st nat. Airco Welding award, 1966, commendation NASA, 1965, Engring. Profl. Achievement citation Iowa State U., 1973, 3d pl. Von Karman Meml. Grand award, 1974. Registered profl. engr., Calif. Mem. Am. Welding Soc. Lutheran. Patentee in field. Home: 2742 W 234th St Torrance CA 90505 Office: Creative Pathways Inc 3121 Fujita St Torrance CA 90505

ROHRING, JOHN GARY, landman; b. L.A., Dec. 31, 1939; s. Frank John R. and Muriel Howard-Head; m. Claudia M. Brown, Sept. 7, 1962; children: Jeffrey Claude, Brett Frank. Student, Santa Monica (Calif.) Coll., 1957-59, UCLA, 1960-61; cert. real estate, UCLA, 1964; AA, Ventura (Calif.) Coll., 1969. Lic. real estate broker, Calif. Right of way agt. So. Calif. Edison, Rosemead; property adminstr. Mission Land Co., Garden Grove, Calif., 1976-83; mktg. and devel. adminstr. Mission Land Co., Garden Grove, 1983-86; mgr. property devel. Mission Land Co., Brea, Calif., 1986—; pres. John G. Rohring Assocs., Inc., Huntington Beach, Calif., 1983—. Active Olympic Yachting Com., Long Beach, Calif., 1984; charter chmn. Fountain Valley (Calif.) Sch. Community Council, 1976. Mem. Nat. Assn. Indsl. and Office Parks, Soc. Indsl. Realtors, Orange County C. of C., Balboa Power Squadron (comdr. 1979), Shriners, Masons, Lambda Alpha (pres. 1987, bd. dirs. 1988—). Republican. Episcopalian. Office: Mission Land Co 1150 W Central D Brea CA 92621

ROHSE, MITCHEL HOMER, land-use planner; b. Las Cruces, N.Mex., Apr. 6, 1943; s. Homer Frederick and Elaine (Dahl) R.; m. Louann D. Boehmer, July 28, 1979. BA, U. Oreg., 1972, M in Urban Planning, 1973. Cert. planner. Planner 2 Lane County Planning Dept., Eugene, 1973-75; grad. teaching asst. U. Hawaii, Honolulu, 1975-76; planner 3 Polk County Planning Dept., Dallas, Oreg., 1977; deputy dir. Polk County Planning Dept., Dallas, 1978, dir., 1978-79; plan reviewer Oreg. State Dept. of Land Conservation and Devel., Salem, 1980-84, info. officer, 1984—. Author: Land-Use Planning in Oregon, 1987; contbr. numerous papers and articles for profl. jours. Vol. U.S. Peace Corps, Sarawak, Malaysia, 1965-67. Staff sgt. USAF, 1967-70. Mem. Am. Planning Assn. (bd. dirs. Oreg. chpt. 1986—, spl. achievement award 1988), Am. Inst. Cert. Planners. Home: 3246 Caribou Ct NW Salem OR 97304 Office: Dept Land Conservation 1175 Court St NE Salem OR 97310

ROIZ, MYRIAM, foreign trade firm executive; b. Managua, Nicaragua, Jan. 21, 1938; came to U.S., 1949; d. Francisco Octavio and Maria Herminia (Briones) R.; m. Nicholas M. Orphanopoulos, Jan. 21, 1957 (div.); children—Jacqueline Doggwiler, Gene E. Orphanopoulos, George A. Orphanopoulos. BA cum laude in Interdisciplinary Social Sci., San Francisco State U., 1980. Lic. ins. agt. Sales rep. Met. Life Ins. Co., San Francisco, 1977-79; mktg. dir. Europe/Latin Am., Allied Canners & Packers, San Francisco, 1979-83; mktg. dir. Europe/Latin Am., M-C Internat., San Francisco, 1983-88; v.p. mktg. Atlantic Brokers, Inc., Kinard Foods, Inc., Bayamon, P.R., 1988—. Mem. Common Cause; coordinator Robert F. Kennedy Presdl. campaign, Millbrae, San Mateo County, local mayoral campaign, Millbrae, 1975; dir., organizer fund-raising campaign for earthquake-devastated Nicaragua; active Brown U. World Hunger Program, Covenant House. Named Outstanding Employee of Yr. Hillsborough City Sch. Dist., 1973; recipient Sales award Met. Life Ins. Co., 1977. Mem. Am. Soc. Profl. and Exec. Women, AAUW, Altrusas Internat. Democrat. Roman Catholic. Office: Atlantic Brokers Inc Edif Borden Lote 10 Hato Tejas Ind Park Bayamon PR 00619

ROKEACH, BARRIE, photographer; b. Mansfield, Ohio, Feb. 26, 1947. BA, U. Calif., Berkeley, 1970, MA, 1974. Prin. Aerial Terrestrial, Berkeley, 1980—; instr. U. Calif. at Berkeley, 1977, 84, U. Calif. at Davis, 1977. Contbr. articles to profl. jours.; photographer for numerous feature articles; editor ASMP, San Francisco, 1987—; feature book of images Timescapes: California From The Air, 1989. Recipient Calif. design award Am. Inst. Graphic Artists, 1980-82, Epcot/Kodak award, 1982, Art Direction award, N.Y.C., 1983, Graphics Mag. award, Switzerland, 1983. Mem.

Am. Soc. of Mag. Photographers. Office: Rokeach Aerial Photograph 499 Vermont Ave Berkeley CA 94707

ROKOVITZ, THOMAS WILLIAM, medical company executive; b. Cleve., Aug. 21, 1952; s. John Anthony and Salvatora Teresa (Terese) R.; m. Lorraine Roehl, Nov. 10, 1985. BA, Miami U., Oxford, Ohio, 1974; postgrad., Cen. Mich. U., 1974-76. Gen. contractor Mich., and Calif., 1976-81; office mgr. Santa Barbara (Calif.) Cash Register Co., 1981-84; sales mgr. Rayne Water Conditioning Co., Ventura and San Jose, Calif., 1984-87; gen. mgr. western region Micro-Bio-Medics, Inc., South San Francisco, Calif., 1987—. Activity coord. youth and adult athletic programs, Mich., Calif., 1976-86. Miami U. grantee, 1970-74. Mem. Nat. Athletic Trainers Assn. Republican. Roman Catholic. Office: Micro Bio-Medics Inc 2ll Harbor Way South San Francisco CA 94080

ROLAND, WILLIAM STUART, electronics executive; b. Galveston, Tex., July 5, 1944; s. John Clarence and Mary Louise (Brown) R.; m. Judith Diane Hughes, June 25, 1983; children: Christina, Gregory, Duane, Jana. Grad. high sch., Auburn, Wash. Mgr. mktg. product Victor Comptometer Corp., Chgo., 1972-74, dir. product mgmt. and planning, 1975-77; mgr. worldwide mktg. Rockwell Internat., Anaheim, Calif., 1974-75; area sales mgr. Zilog Inc., Dallas, 1977-80; v.p. mktg. and sales Sci-Pro Inc., Denver, 1980-82; v.p. mktg. Eagle Computer, Los Gatos, Calif., 1982-84; v.p., gen. mgr. Microsoft, Redmond, Wash., 1984-86; pres., chmn., chief exec. officer Renaissance GRX Inc., Bellevue, Wash., 1986—. Served with USN, 1962-66, Vietnam. Mem. The Lakes Club (co-chmn. 1988), Bellevue Athletic Club. Republican. Episcopalian. Home: 1015 Pike St NE Auburn WA 98002 Office: Renaissance GRX Inc 2265 116th Ave NE Bellevue WA 98004 *Died Feb. 6, 1989.*

ROLLER, DAVID ISAAC, financial services company executive; b. Bklyn., Jan. 13, 1949; s. Morton and Helen (Deligtisch) R.; m. Susan Firtle, June 3, 1973; children: Aviva Natanya, Yael Elisheba. BA, L.I. U., 1971; MA, NYU, 1980; rabbi, Tifereth Israel Rabbinic Acad., Bklyn., 1980; postgrad., NYU, 1980-83. Ordained rabbi. Rabbi N. Rockland Jewish Community Ctr., Pomona, N.Y., 1980-81; asst. rabbi, educator Old Westbury Hebrew Congregation, Westbury, N.Y., 1982-83; rabbi Beth Emek, Livermore, Calif., 1983-85; founder, pres. Roller Fin. Assocs., Livermore, 1983—. Mem. Internat. Assn. Fin. Planners, Am. Council Ind. Life Underwriters, Am. Assn. Rabbis, East Bay Bd. Rabbis, Mensa, Rotary. Republican. Lodges: Mecca AAONMS (N.Y.C.), Aahmes AAONMS (Oakland, Calif.), Mosaic 218 (chaplain 1985-86). Home: 1031 Bluebell Dr #1 Livermore CA 94550 Office: Roller Fin Assocs 1031 Bluebell Dr Livermore CA 94550

ROLLER, ROBERT DOUGLAS, III, psychiatrist; b. Charleston, W.Va., Nov. 17, 1928; s. Francis Oliver and Mary Elizabeth (Rice) R.; m. Anthonia Ijsselstein, Mar. 7, 1970; children: Robert Douglass IV, Katherine Willis, David Nelson, Anthonia Elizabeth, Alexander Robert, John Richard. BA, U. Va., 1950, MD, 1960; postgrad. in philosophy, U. Pa., 1953-56. Tchr. Chestnut Hill Acad., Phila., 1953-56; intern U. N.C. Hosp., Chapel Hill, 1960-61, resident, 1961-62; resident Med. Coll. of Va., Richmond, 1963; NIMH research and teaching fellow U. Calif. Med. Ctr., San Francisco, 1963-66; pvt. practice Berkeley, 1966—; assoc. psychiatrist, research psychiatrist U. Calif. Berkeley, 1965-71; clin. asst. prof. U. Calif. Med. Sch., San Francisco, 1970—, Stanford U. Med. Sch., Palo Alto, Calif., 1969—; mem. staff Alta Bates Hosp., Berkeley, Herrick Hosp., Berkeley, Walnut Creek (Calif.) Hosp., Lodi (Calif.) Meml. Hosp., Lodi Community Hosp., 1965-72; chief psychiatrist Clear Water Ranch for Children, Santa Rosa, Calif., 1964-71. Served with USNR, 1950-51. Mem. Farmington Country Club, U. Calif. Faculty Club, St. Anthony Club of N.Y., St. Elmo Club, Sleepy Hollow Tennis Club. Home: 757 San Diego Rd Berkeley CA 94707 Office: 2999 Regent St Ste 422 Berkeley CA 94705

ROLLER, SUSAN LORRAYNE, industrial communications specialist, consultant; b. Portsmouth, Va., Sept. 13, 1954; d. Gilbert John Roller and Lois Carolyn (Moore) Logan. BS in Med. Scis., U. Wash., 1976, BA, 1980. Dir. med. programming Omnia Corp., Mpls., 1980-82; program developer Golle & Holmes, Mpls., 1982-83; dir. mktg. Santal Corp., St. Louis, 1983; pres. Fine Line, Ltd., St. Louis, 1984—. Fundraiser Jerry Lewis Telethon, Seattle and Tacoma, 1974-76. Mem. NAEB, Variety Club (activities com. 1984-86), St. Paul C. of C., Reno C. of C., Kappa Kappa Gamma. Republican. Episcopalian. Office: 6052 D Plumas Ave Reno NV 89509

ROLLIN, BERNARD ELLIOT, philosophy educator, consultant on animal ethics; b. N.Y.C., Feb. 18, 1943; s. Phillip and Yetta Ethel (Bookchin) R.; m. Linda Mae Schieber, Aug. 31, 1964; 1 child, Michael David Hume. BA, CCNY, 1964; PhD, Columbia U., 1972. Lectr. Columbia U., N.Y.C., 1968-69; asst. prof. philosophy Colo. State U., Ft. Collins, 1969-73, assoc. prof., 1973-78, prof., 1978—, prof. physiology and biophysics, 1980—, dir. bioethical planning, 1981—; cons. Can., Australian, U.S. govts., various univs. including U. Calif.-Berkeley, Wash. State U., U. Fla., 1980-, United Airlines, Denver, 1985--; lectr. on animal ethics, 1987--. Author: Natural and Convention Meaning, 1976, Animal Rights and Human Morality, (Outstanding Acad. Book award Choice mag. Am. Assn. U. Libraries 1982), 1981, The Unheeded Cry, 1989, The Experimental Animal in Biomedical Research, 1989; mem. editorial bd. Jour. AVMA, Between the Species, Agroethics, Acta Semiotica et Liguistica, Studies in Animal Welfare Sic., numerous others; contbr. articles to profl. jours. Recipient Harris T. Guard award Colo. State U., 1981, Honors prof., 1983, Waco F. Childers award Am. Humane Assn., 1982, service award Colo. Vet. Med. Assn., 1983; Fulbright fellow U. Edinburgh, 1964-65. Jewish. Office: Colo State U Dept Philosophy Fort Collins CO 80523

ROLLOFF, PAUL DOUGLAS, healthcare company executive; b. New Ulm, Minn., Nov. 23, 1957; s. Elmer Henry Jr. and Marlene Helen (Wille) R.; m. Cheryl Ann Lawrence, July 12, 1986; 1 child, Stephanie Joy. BEE, U. Minn., 1980. Engr. Ampex Inc., Redwood City, Calif., 1980-83; design engr. Aracor, Sunnyvale, Calif., 1983-84; sr. design engr. Giltronix Inc., Palo Alto, Calif., 1984-85; engring. cons. Amfit Inc., Sunnyvale, 1985-86, v.p. engring., 1986—; electronics cons. Giltronix Inc., 1985—, Lamb Labs., Belmont, Calif., 1982-86. Treas. Hope Evang. Luth. Ch., Fremont, Calif., 1987—. Mem. IEEE, Eta Kappa Nu. Home: 33776 Shallow Ct Fremont CA 94555 Office: Amfit Inc 384 San Aleso Ave Sunnyvale CA 94086

ROLSTON, HOLMES, III, philosopher, educator; b. Staunton, Va., Nov. 19, 1932; s. Holmes and Mary Winifred (Long) R.; m. Jane Irving Wilson, June 1, 1956; children: Shonny Hunter, Giles Campbell. BS, Davidson Coll., 1953; BD, Union Theol. Sem., 1956; MA in Philosophy of Sci., U. Pitts., 1968; PhD in Theology, U. Edinburgh, Scotland, 1958. Ordained to ministry Presbyn. Ch., 1956. Pastor Walnut Grove Presbyn. Ch., Bristol, Va., 1959-67; prof. philosophy Colo. State U., Ft. Collins, 1968—; vis. scholar Ctr. Study of World Religions, Harvard U., 1974-75. Author: The Cosmic Christ, 1966, John Calvin versus the Westminster Confession, 1972, Religious Inquiry--Participation and Detachment, 1985, Philosophy Gone Wild, 1986, Science and Religion: A Critical Survey, 1987, Environmental Ethics, 1988; assoc. editor Environ. Ethics, 1979—; mem. editorial bd. Oxford Series in Environ. Philosophy and Pub. Policy, Zygon: Jour. of Religion and Sci.; contbr. chpts. to books, articles to profl. jours. Recipient Pennock award Disting. Scholarship Colo. State U., 1984; NSF and NEH grantee. Mem. Am. Acad. Religion/Soc. Bibl. Lit. (pres. Rocky Mountain-Gt. Plains region), AAAS, Am. Philos. Assn. Home: 1712 Concord Dr Fort Collins CO 80526 Office: Colo State U Dept Philosophy Fort Collins CO 80523

ROMAN, ROBERT J., electrical engineer; b. N.Y.C., Sept. 24, 1923; s. John A. and Lucy N. (Christiano) R.; m. Hilda Bolton, 1948 (dec. 1979); children: Kenneth J., Richard B., William R., James P.; m. Betty Taylor, May 23, 1980. BSEE, Columbia U., 1944; MBA, U. Rochester, 1969. Prog. mgr. Eastman Kodak Co., Rochester, N.Y., 1946-83; sr. ptnr. AEREA Assocs., Salt Lake City, 1983—; cons. Eastman Kodak Co., Rochester, 1984-86; instr. U.S. Naval Acad., 1945. Patentee in field. Chmn. Greater Rochester Internat. Airport Users Com., 1984-88. With USN, 1943-46; PTO. Mem. IEEE, Indsl. Electronics Soc. (treas.), Hunt Hollow Ski Club, Rochester Pilots Assn. (pres. 1984-87), Tau Beta Pi, Beta Theta Pi, Beta Gamma Sigma. Republican. Presbyterian. Home: 3685 Oak Rim Way Salt Lake City UT 84109

ROMANELLI, PETER NICHOLAS, real estate developer; b. Bklyn., May 28, 1948; s, Otto Charles and Dorothy (Hicks) R.; m. Deborah Nuse, May 13, 1978 (div. 1984); m. Barbara Lee Roberts, Dec. 20, 1986 (div. 1987). BA in Cinema, SUNY, Binghamton, 1978; MA in Geography, Columbia U., 1984. Assoc. prod. MRC Films McLaughlin Enterprises, Ltd., N.Y.C., 1978-83; v.p. Minturn (Colo.) Realty subchpt. McLaughlin Ptnrs., 1984—; freelance photographer, cinematographer. Home and Office: PO Box 130 Minturn CO 81645

ROMANO, ENNIO, oncologist, researcher; b. Assoro, Italy, Jan. 1, 1925; came to U.S., 1981; s. Marcello and Giuseppina (Fasanaro) R.; m. Giuseppina Digrazia, Oct. 25, 1952; children: Marcello, Anita, Maria. MD, U. Rome, 1951; specialist in gen. surgery, U. Catania, Italy, 1967; specialist in oncology, U. Rome, 1969, specialist in gen. pathology, 1978. Gen. surgeon U. Catania, Italy, 1952-54, head gen. surgeon, 1963-81; gen. surgeon U. Rome, 1954-63; cancer researcher UCLA, 1981-86; head surgery cons. Italian Navy, Rome, 1964-81; dir. clin. pathol. St. Louis Hosp., Catania, 1965-81; chmn. art dept., prof. Galilei U. Calif.; pres. Calif. Acad. Art, L.A.; pres. Theatine Acad. Anatomy, Calif. Author: Tumors of the Thoracic Skeleton, 1981, Intestinal Obstructions, 1982, Gastrointestinal Tumors, 1984. Mcpl. dep. Partito Repubblicano Italiano, Catania, 1975-81; pres. Italian Nat. Assn. Friends of the U.S.A., Rome, 1978—; mem. Nat. Rep. Congr. Com., U.S., 1984—, Nat. Com. to Preserve Social Security, 1984; chmn. art dept., prof. Galilei U., Calif.; pres. The Calif. Acad. of Art, L.A., Theatine Acad., Calif. Recipient commendatore Ordine Repubblica Italiana, 1981. Mem. Am. Cancer Soc., The N.Y. Acad. Sci., AAAS, Internat. Burckhardt Acad. (Switzerland), Italian Am. Med. Assn., Italian Soc. Surgery, Lions. Roman Catholic. Office: 1886 Rosemount Ave Claremont CA 91711

ROMANO, GEORGE CARMINE, surgeon, naval officer; b. Providence, Dec. 21, 1939; s. Randolph Slavatore and Alice Louise (Holmes) R.; m. Ginny Lee Joyner, Feb. 15,1975; children: Dominic Salvatore, Carmen Elena, Vincent Joseph; children by previous marriage: Christopher Mark, Karen Michelle, Shannon Elizabeth. BS, U. Ala., 1979; MD, Cen. State U. Xochicalo, Ensenada, Baja, 1981; MPH, Tulane U., 1985. Enlisted USMC, 1959; jet fighter pilot USMC, Vietnam; resigned USMC, 1970; pres., owner Romano Constron & Devel. Co. and G&G Constrn. Co., West Palm Beach, Fla., 1971-77; resident in surgery Chgo. Med. Sch., North Chicago, Ill., 1981-83; commd. ensign USN, 1983, sr. med. officer USS Independence, 1983-85; resident Naval Aerospace Med. Inst. USN, Pensacola, Fla., 1986-88; sr. med. officer USS Nimitz USN, 1988—. Chmn. fund raiser, Bahrain Burn Ctr. Hosp., USS Nimitz, 1988. Decorated Navy Cross, Purple Heart medal. Mem. AMA, Aerospace Med. Assn., Assn. Mil. Surgeons, Am. Assn. Flight Surgeons, Nat. Assn. Residents and Interns. Republican. Roman Catholic. Home: 16255 Virginia Point Rd NE Poulsbo WA 98370

ROMANOWSKI, CHRISTOPHER ANDREW, sales executive; b. London, July 23, 1953; came to U.S., 1979; s. Zbigniew Marian and Janina Walentyna (Kuklinska) Romanowski. BS with honors, U. Surrey, 1975, PhD, 1978. European chartered engr. Research asst. U. Surrey, Guildford, Eng., 1978-79; research assoc. Drexel U., Phila., 1979-82, asst. prof., 1982-83; tech. devel. engr. Pechiney-Howmet, Lancaster, Pa., 1983-84; tech. mgr. Alumax-Howmet, Hawesville, Ky., 1984; tech. dir. Hunter Engring., Riverside, Calif., 1984-87; sales mgr. Hunter Engring., Riverside, 1987—; cons. Alcoa Tech. Ctr., Alcoa Ctr., Pa., 1979-82. patentee in field. Mem. Inst. Metals, Am. Soc. Metals, Metall. Soc. Office: Hunter Engring 1455 Columbia Ave Riverside CA 92507

ROMBERG, JACQUELYN RAE, accountant, financial planner; b. San Diego, July 18, 1944; d. John And LaRayne Marjorie (Halverson) Stevenson; m. Gary Paul Romberg, Sept. 3, 1966; children: Paul Martin, Megan Kara. BA, U. Wyo., 1967; MBA, U. Colo., Colo. Springs, 1983. CPA, Colo., Wyo. Prin. Jacquelyn Romberg, CPA, Sheridan, Wyo., 1985—. Fellow Soc. CPA Fin. Planners; mem. Am. Soc. Women Accts., Am. Woman's Soc. CPA's, Calif. Soc. CPA's. Republican. Home: PO Box 1000 Sheridan WY 82801-1000

ROMBOUGH, BARTLETT B., oil company executive; b. Winnipeg, Man., Can., Dec. 6, 1924; s. Earl B. and Muriel M. (Wallace) R.; m. Mary J. Hamilton, 1953; children—Bruce, Robert. With Home Oil Co., Ltd., Calgary, Alta., Can., 1952-76, v.p. finance, 1973-76; exec. v.p. PanCan. Petroleum, Ltd., Calgary, 1976-80, pres., 1980—, chief exec. officer, 1982—, also dir.; bd. dirs. Fording Coal, Ltd., Marathon Realty Co. Ltd., Econ. Council Can. Served with RCAF, 1943-46. Mem. Inst. Chartered Accts. Man., Inst. Chartered Accts. Alta., Can. Petroleum Assn. (bd. govs., vice-chmn.). Clubs: Calgary Petroleum, Calgary Golf & Country, Glencoe. Office: PanCan Petroleum Ltd, 150-9th Ave SW PO Box 2850, Calgary, AB Canada T2P 2S5

ROMER, ROY R., governor of Colorado; b. Garden City, Kans., Oct. 31, 1928; s. Irving Rudolph and Margaret Elizabeth (Snyder) R.; m. Beatrice Miller, June 10, 1952; children: Paul, Mark, Mary, Christopher, Timothy, Thomas, Elizabeth. B.S. in Agrl. Econs., Colo. State U., 1950; LL.B., U. Colo., 1952; postgrad., Yale U. Bar: Colo. 1952. Engaged in farming in Colo. 1942-52; ind. practice law Denver, 1955-66; mem. Colo. Ho. of Reps., 1958-62, Colo. Senate, 1962-66; owner, operator Arapahoe Aviation Co., Colo. Flying Acad., Geneva Basin Ski Area; engaged in home site devel; owner chain farm implement and indsl. equipment stores Colo.; commr. agr. State of Colo., 1975, chief staff, exec. asst. to gov., 1975-77, 83-84, state treas., 1977-86, gov., 1987—; chmn. Gov. Colo. Blue Ribbon Panel, Gov. Colo. Small Bus. Council; mem. agrl. adv. com. Colo. Bd. Agr. Bd. editors Colo. U. Law Rev., 1960-62. Past trustee Iliff Sch. Theology, Denver. Served with USAF, 1952-54. Mem. Colo. Bar Assn. (gov.), Order of Coif1. Democrat. Presbyterian. Office: Office of Gov Capitol Bldg Rm 136 Denver CO 80203 *

ROMERO, FREDERICK, educator; b. Kobe, Japan, Oct. 3, 1947; came to U.S., 1950; s. Raoul Pete and Yoshiko (Matayoshi) R.; m. Pamela Nortan Heinrich, June 18, 1972; children: Tom H., Adrian F., Arthur E. AA in Mental Health, Marcopa Tech. Community Coll., 1972; BA in Psychology, Ottawa U., 1979; MA in Guidance and Counseling, No. Ariz. U., 1981. Cert. trainer. Mental health counselor Ariz. State Hosp., Phoenix, 1970-75; tng. coordinator behavioral health div. City of Phoenix, 1975-81, program dir. Dept. Health, 1981-83; lobbyist Ariz. Pub. Employee Assn., Am. Fedn. State, County and Municipal Employees, AFL-CIO, Phoenix, 1983-88; adj. faculty Ottawa U., Phoenix, 1981-88, asst. prof., 1988—; pvt. practice counseling, Phoenix, 1980-84. Author: Training the Chronic Mentally Ill, 1980; editor (newsletter) Community Support Project, 1981, Legislative Line-Up, 1988—; contbr. articles to profl. jours. Mem. steering com. Ottawa U. Labor Studies; Dem. precinct committeeman, Phoenix, 1988—; mem. minority adv. bd. Sta. KPNX-TV, Phoenix, 1986. Decorated Bronze Star, Air medal. Mem. Labor Council Latin Am. Advancement. Roman Catholic. Office: Ottawa U 2340 W Mission Ln Phoenix AZ 85021

ROMERO, RAFAEL DURAZO, III, state official; b. Douglas, Ariz., Aug. 8, 1949; s. Rafael Hoyos and Maria (Durazo) R.; m. Gemma Samaniego, Nov. 13, 1973; children: Gemma Odette, Jeanette Claudine, Rafael IV, Yvette Marie. AA in Fgn. Rels., Cochise Coll., Douglas, 1972; BA in Polit. Sci., Ariz. State U., 1974, cert. pub. mgr., 1986. Mgmt. analyst Ariz. Dept. Econ. Security, Phoenix, 1974-78, exec. staff asst., 1978-82, dep. asst. dir., 1982—; regional dir. United Coun. on Welfare Fraud, Phoenix, 1984—; v.p. Social Svcs. Indemnity Pool, Phoenix, 1988. Mem. Maryvale Concerned Citizens Com., Phoenix, 1987-89, Arizonans Concerned for Edn., 1988; bd. dirs. Brown Sacred Heart Ctr., Phoenix, 1987; Ariz. state dir. League United Latin Am. Citizens, 1988. Named Man of Yr., League United Latin Am. Citizens, 1988, 89. Mem. Ariz. Soc. Cert. Pub. Mgrs. (charter, treas. 1987-88), Ariz. Adminstrs. Assn., Lions (2d v.p. Phoenix 1988-89). Democrat. Roman Catholic. Home: 3421 N 61st Dr Phoenix AZ 85033 Office: Ariz Dept Econ Security 1140 E Washington Phoenix AZ 85034

ROMIG, ALTON DALE, JR., metallurgist, educator; b. Bethlehem, Pa., Oct. 6, 1953; s. Alton Dale and Christine (Groh) R.; B.S., Lehigh U., 1975, M.S., 1977, Ph.D., 1979; m. Julie H. Romig. Metallurgist, supr. physical metallurgy Sandia Nat. Labs., Albuquerque, 1979—; adj. assoc. prof. N.Mex. Inst. Mining and Tech., Socorro, 1981—. Mem. Am. Soc. for Metals (various chpt. offices), AIME, Microbeam Analysis Soc. (nat. officer), Materials Reseach Soc., Sigma Xi, Tau Beta Pi. Republican. Mem. United Ch. of Christ. Mem. bd. rev. Metallurg. Transactions; contbr. articles to sci. jours. Home: 4923 Calle de Luna NE Albuquerque NM 87111 Office: Sandia Nat Labs Div 1832 Albuquerque NM 87185

ROMIG, PHILLIP RICHARDSON, geophysics educator; b. Dennison, Ohio, July 24, 1938; s. Phillip R. and Beatrice W. (Medley) R.; m. Jane Ellen Curfman, Aug. 11, 1962; children: Phillip III, Timothy. BSEE, U. Notre Dame, 1960; MS in Geophysics, Colo. Sch. Mines, 1967, PhD in Geophysics, 1969. Registered geophysicist, Calif. System analyst AC Electronics div. Gen. Motors Corp., Milw., 1963-64; with Colo. Sch. Mines, Golden, 1969—, successively research assoc., assoc. prof., prof. and head dept. geophysics; trustee Geophysics Fund Inc., Golden, 1983—; mem. assoc. panel NRC, Washington, 1984—; cons. U.S. Bur. Reclamation, Sandia Labs., Denver and Albuquerque, 1980-83; mem. Gov.'s Sci. and Tech. adv. council, Denver, 1984-87. Conbtg. editor, author Geophysics, 1985, 86. Mem. coms. on communications and supercomputing Colo. Adv. Tech. Inst., Denver, 1985-86. Served to lt. USN, 1960-63. Mem. Am. Geophys. Union (bd. dirs. Front Range br. 1986—), Soc. Exploration Geophysicists (chmn. engring. and groundwater geophysics com. 1981-83), IEEE, Seismological Soc. Am., Sigma Xi. Republican. Methodist. Office: Colo Sch Mines Dept Geophysics Golden CO 80401

RONALD, ANN, English literature educator; b. Seattle, Oct. 9, 1939; d. James Quintin and Cleo Elizabeth (Keller) R. BA, Whitman Coll., 1961; MA, U. Colo., 1966; PhD, Northwestern U., 1970. Prof. English lit. U. Nev., Reno, 1970—, acting dean grad. sch., 1988-89, dean Coll. of Arts and Scis., 1989—. Author: The New West of Edward Abbey, 1982, revised edit., 1988, Functions of Setting in the Novel, 1980; editor: Words for the Wild, 1987; mem. editorial bd. Western Am. Lit., 1982—, U. Nev. Press, 1985—, Studies in Short Fiction, 1988—. Office: U Nev Reno Coll Arts and Scis Reno NV 89557

RONDEAU, DORIS JEAN, entrepreneur, consultant; b. Winston-Salem, N.C., Nov. 25, 1941; d. John Delbert and Eldora Virginia (Klutz) Robinson; m. Robert Breen Corrente, Sept. 4, 1965 (div. 1970); m. Wilfrid Dolor Rondeau, June 3, 1972. Student Syracuse U., 1959-62, Fullerton Jr. Coll., 1974-75; BA in Philosophy, Calif. State U.-Fullerton, 1976, postgrad., 1976-80. Ordained to ministry The Spirit of Divine Love, 1974. Trust real estate clk. Security First Nat. Bank, Riverside, Calif., 1965-68; entertainer Talent, Inc., Hollywood, Calif., 1969-72; co-founder, dir. Spirit of Divine Love, Capistrano Beach, Calif., 1974—; pub., co-founder Passing Through, Inc., Capistrano Beach, 1983—; instr. Learning Activity, Anaheim, Calif., 1984—; chmn. bd., prin. D.J. Rondeau, Entrepreneur, Inc., Capistrano Beach, 1984—; co-founder, dir. Spiritual Positive Attitude, Inc., Moon In Pisces, Inc., Vibrations By Rondeau, Inc., Divine Consciousness, Expressed, Inc., Capistrano Beach. Author, editor: A Short Introduction To The Spirit of Divine Love, 1984; writer, producer, dir. performer spiritual vignettes for NBS Radio Network, KWVE-FM, 1982-84; author: Spiritual Meditations to Uplift the Soul, 1988. Served with USAF, 1963-65. Recipient Pop Vocalist First Place award USAF Talent Show, 1964, Sigma chpt. Epsilon Delta Chi, 1985, others. Mem. Hamel Bus. Grads., Smithsonian Assocs., Am. Mgmt. Assn., Nat. Assn. Female Execs. Avocations: long-distance running, body fitness, arts and crafts, snorkeling, musical composition.

RONÉR, KENT HARRY, accountant; b. Stockholm, Aug. 17, 1948; came to U.S., 1956; s. Harry and May (Johansson) R.; m. Janice Larsen, June 6, 1972; children: Lisa, Rachel, Janette, Michael, Allison, Angela. BA, U. Utah, 1973; M Pub. Adminstrn., Brigham Young U., 1987. Lic. health facility adminstr.; CPA. Internal auditor Zions Utah Bancorp., Salt Lake City, 1973-75; mgr. claims payment Dept. Social Services, Salt Lake City, 1975-79; dir. med. asst. Dept. Health, Salt Lake City, 1979—; pvt. practice acctg. Centerville, Utah, 1983—. Rep. del. Davis County, Utah, 1984-86. Recipient Incentive award Dept. Health, 1981. Mem. Utah Pub. Health Assn., Am. Inst. CPA's, Utah Assn. CPA's, Jaycees (sec., treas. 1985-86). Home: 239 W 1125 N Centerville UT 84014 Office: Dept Health UMAP 288 N 1460 W Salt Lake City UT 84116-0700

RONEY, KIRK VINCENT, cosmetics company executive; b. San Bernardino, Calif., Apr. 26, 1954; s. Arden E. and Jeane (Fronk) R.; m. Melanie Kuuipo Aldous, Aug. 8, 1985: children: Ty Kekauoha, Lea Kaluapalaoa, Kara Nalia. BA, Brigham Young U., 1978; MA, Cen. Mich. U.; MBA, Am. Grad. Sch. Internat. Mgmt., Glendale, Ariz., 1984. Devel. intelligence analyst A. Copeland Ent. (Popeyes), New Orleans, 1984-85; v.p. Nu Skin Internat., Provo, Utah, 1985—. Bd. dirs. Kids on the Move, Provo, 1988—. Recipient Presidential scholarship, Brigham Young U., Provo, 1977-78; Eagle Scout award, Boy Scouts Am., Lake Arrowhead, Calif., 1970. Republican. Mormon. Office: Nu Skin Internat 145 E Center St Provo UT 84604

RONISH, ROBERT RAY, retired civil service administrator; b. Cheyenne, Wyo., Sept. 10, 1934; s. Theodore Roosevelt and Beulah Irene (Logan) R.; m. Lois Irene Dallas, Sept. 5, 1954; children: Renee Ellen, Shane Theodore, Clayton Robert. BA, U. Wyo., 1957; MA, U. No. Colo., 1974. Hdqr. commdt., co. comdr. USASTRATCOM, Ft. Huachuca, Ariz., 1967-69; subsystems mgr. SAFCA, Ft. Huachuca, 1969-73; chief morale and welfare, mgmt. analyst USACC, Ft. Huachuca, 1973-82; resource mgmt. chief USACOMISA, Ft. Huachuca, 1982-84; support div. chief USAISCA, Ft. Huachuca, 1984-86; records mgmt. chief USAISCA, 1986-89. Contbr. articles to profl. jours. Pres. Mountain Ranch Estates Home Owners Assn., Bisbee, Ariz.,1984-86. Capt. U. S. Army, 1958-68, col. Res. ret. Recipient Grand Cross of Color Internat. Order of Rainbow for Girls, Tucson, 1975. Mem. Res. Officers Assn. (pres. 1985-87), Masons. Republican. Baptist. Home: 816 Calledel Norte Sierra Vista AZ 85635

RONSMAN, WAYNE JOHN, insurance company executive; b. Milw., Jan. 21, 1938; s. Harry Martin and Martha Elizabeth (Popp) R.; student Marquette U., 1955-58, U. San Francisco, 1960-66; m. Joan P. Murphy-Mays, Nov. 30, 1974; children: Allison, Alanna; children by previous marriage: Rosemary, Harry, Martha. Accountant, Otis McAllister & Co., 1960-62; accountant, salesman of data processing Statis. Tabulation Corp., San Francisco, 1962-66; chief accountant, gen. mgr. Dillingham Bros. Ltd., Honolulu, 1966-67; ins. salesman Mut. Benefit Life Ins. Co., 1968—; v.p. Brenno Assos., Honolulu, 1972—; prin. Ronsman-Brenno, Anchorage, Alaska, 1980—; bd. dirs. Aloha Nat. Bank, Kihei, Maui. Mem. Gov's Task Force to Program Correctional Facilities Land, 1970-72; mem. State Bd. Paroles and Pardons, 1972-75; treas. Spl. Edn. Center of Oahu, 1969-78; pres. Ballet Alaska, 1986-87. Served with USMCR, 1958-60. Mem. Nat. Assn. Accts. (pres. Anchorage chpt. 1989—), Am. Soc. CLUs, Internat. Assn. Registered Fin. Planning, Inst. Cert. Fin. Planners, Anchorage Estate Planning Council, Honolulu Assn. Life Underwriters (million dollar round table 1973—), Hawaii (state editor 1970-71, nat. dir. 1972-73), Kailua (pres. 1968-69) Jaycees, Honolulu Bd. Realtors, Anchorage C. of C., Small Bus. Mgmt. Assn., Nat. Assn. Securities Dealers, Kailua C. of C. (pres. 1977-78). Roman Catholic. Home: 3251 Eastwind Ct Anchorage AK 99516 Office: Ronsman-Brenno Alaska Anchorage AK 99516

RONSTADT, PETER, city official; b. Tucson, Feb. 1, 1942; s. Gilbert and Ruthmary (Copeman) R.; m. Jacqueline A. Castle, Nov. 26, 1946; children—Philip Charles, Melinda Marie. B.A., U. Ariz., 1969. Cert. peace officer, Ariz. Police officer including var. positions of patrolman, detective, sgt., lt., capt., maj. Tucson Police Dept., 1963-81, chief of police, 1981—. Bd. dirs. Salvation Army, Tucson. Mem. Ariz Acad., Police Exec. Research Forum, Nat. Exec. Inst., FBI Nat. Acad. Assocs., Police Mgmt. Assn., Ariz. Chiefs of Police Assn., Internat. Assn. Chiefs Police, Sigma Alpha Epsilon. Club: Centurions (Tucson). Lodge: Rotary. Office: Tucson Police Dept 270 S Stone PO Box 1071 Tucson AZ 85702 *

ROOKS, GEORGE MALCOLM, writer, educator; b. Anderson, S.C., Mar. 5, 1951; s. George and Miriam (Bailey) R.; divorced, 1983; children: George, Brendan; m. Hila Zizov, Feb. 1, 1983; children; Kanon, Maayan. BA in English, U. Ga., 1973; MA in English, U. Calif., Davis, 1975. Lectr. ESL U. Calif., Davis., 1976—. Author: The Book of Losers, 1980, The Nonstop Discussion Workbook!, 1980, Can't Stop Talking, 1981, Share Your Paragraph, 1988, Paragraph Power, 1988; (with others) Conversar Sin Parar, 1981, Conversations San Fin, 1982, Was Sagen Sie Dazu?, 1983; contbr.

articles to profl. jours. Mem. Calif. Tchrs. ESL, Zionist Orgn. Am. Jewish. Home: 2128-9 Bueno Ave Davis CA 95616 Office: U Calif Bus Surge 4 UNEX Davis CA 95616

ROONEY, JOHN LOSSIN, telecommunication educator; b. Oak Park, Ill., Oct. 10, 1940; s. James J. and Dorothy W. (Lossin) R.; children: James Scott, Jenny Louise Rooney Shotts, Jeffrey Christian. BS, U. So. Calif., 1965, MBA, 1966, MS, 1974; D in Bus. Adminstrn., 1988. Mgr. Ralphs, Los Angeles, 1961-78; dir. FedMart, San Diego, 1978-83; asst. prof. tech. Nat. U., San Diego, 1983-85, chmn., prof. telecommunications, 1985. Home: 1844 Chickasaw Los Angeles CA 90041 Office: Nat U 6672 University Ave San Diego CA 92115

ROOP, JOSEPH MCLEOD, economist; b. Montgomery, Ala., Sept. 29, 1941; s. Joseph Ezra and Mae Elizabeth (McLeod) R.; B.S., Central Mo. State U., Warrensburg, 1963; Ph.D., Wash. State U., Pullman, 1973; m. Betty Jane Reed, Sept. 4, 1965; 1 dau., Elizabeth Rachael. Economist, Econ. Research Service, U.S. Dept. Agr., Washington, 1975-79; sr. economist Evans Econs., Inc., Washington, 1979-81; sr. research economist Battelle Pacific N.W. Labs., Richland, Wash., 1981—; instr. dept. econs. Wash. State U., 1969-71. Contbr. tech. articles to profl. jours. Served with U.S. Army, 1966-68. Dept. Agr. Coop. State Research Service research grantee, 1971-73. Mem. Am. Econ. Assn., Am. Agrl. Econs. Assn., Econometric Soc., Nat. Assn. Bus. Economists, Internat. Assn. Energy Economists. Home: 715 S Taft St Kennewick WA 99336 Office: PO Box 999 Richland WA 99352

ROOS, NESTOR ROBERT, publisher; b. St. Louis, Aug. 19, 1925; s. Maurice and Fannie (Friedman) R.; m. Fay Weil, July 9, 1951; children: Marilyn Roos Hall, Eileen Roos Ruddell, Robert F. BBA, Washington U., St. Louis, 1948; MSBA, Washington U., 1949; D of Bus. Adminstrn., Ind. U., 1959. Instr. bus. La. State U., Baton Rouge, 1949-51; teaching fellow Ind. U., Bloomington, 1951-53; asst. prof. Ga. State U., Atlanta, 1953-55; prof. U. Ariz., Tucson, 1955-86, prof. emeritus, 1986; pres. Risk Mgmt. Pub. Co., Tucson, 1976—; cons., expert witness in field; bd. dirs. Blue Cross-Blue Shield Ariz.; mem. Ins. Dirs.' Adv. Com., Phoenix, 1987—, Reverse Mortgage Adv. Com., Tucson, 1988—. Author: (with others) Multiple Line Insurers, 1970, Governmental Risk Management, 1976, Industrial Accident Prevention, 1980. Bd. dirs. Handmaker Geriatric Ctr., Tucson, 1987—; pres. Temple Emanu-El, Tucson, 1981-83. With U.S. Army, 1943-45, ETO. Grantee Nat. Inst. Occupational Safety and Health, 1975. Mem. Risk and Ins. Mgmt. Soc., Western Risk and Ins. Assn. (pres. 1972-73), Public Risk and Ins. Mgmt. Assn. (dir. edn. and tng. 1982—). Democrat. Jewish. Home: 7311 Camino de Cima Tucson AZ 85715 Office: Risk Mgmt Pub Co 2030 E Broadway Ste 106 Tucson AZ 85719

ROOT, CHARLES JOSEPH, JR., finance executive, consultant; b. Pierre, S.D., July 26, 1940; s. Charles Joseph and Hazel Ann (Messenger) R.; 1 child, Roseann Marie Root. Student, San Francisco Jr. Coll., Coll. of Marin, La Salle Extension U., Am. Coll. Life Underwriters. Registered investment advisor; charter fin. cons. Estate planner Bankers Life Co., San Francisco, 1966-78; fin. planner Planned Estates Assocs., Corte Madera, Calif., 1978-81; mng. dir. Double Eagle Fin. Corp., Santa Rosa, Calif., 1981—, investment advisor, 1983—. V.p. Big Bros. of Am., San Rafael, Calif., 1976-80; treas. com. to elect William Filante, San Rafael, 1978, Community Health Ctrs. of Marin, Fairfax, Calif., 1982-83, Wellspring Found., Philo, Calif., 1981-85; treas., bd. dirs. Ctr. for Attitudinal Healing, Tiburon, Calif.; bd. dirs. Pickle Family Circus, San Francisco, 1988; mem. Redwood Estate Planning Assn., Santa Rosa, Calif., 1988. With USN, 1959-63. Mem. Internat. Assn. Fin. Planners, Coll. Fin. Planning (cert. fin. planner 1988), Registry of Fin. Planning, Redwood Empire Estate Planning Assn., Nat. Assn. Life Underwriters, Marin County Assn. Life Underwriters (v.p. 1971-76, editor newsletter 1976-80), Rotary (Paul Harris fellow 1980). Republican. Office: Double Eagle Fin Corp 2050 W Steele Ln PO Box 6265 Ste D1 Santa Rosa CA 95406

ROOT, DAVID EMERSON, preventive medicine physician; b. Salt Lake City, Mar. 25, 1936; s. Frank K. and Sarah H. R.; m. Mary Virginia Forbis, Jan. 2, 1959; children:. BS in Psychology, U. Utah, 1958; MD, Wake Forest U., 1968; MPH, Johns Hopkins U., 1970. Diplomate Am. Bd. Preventative Medicine. Commd. 2d lt. USAF, 1960, advanced through grades to col., 1976; intern Wright-Patterson AFB, Dayton, Ohio, 1962-63; chief of aviation medicine, chief aerospace medicine Beale AFB, Marysville, Calif., 1962-65, 73-76; class commdr. pilot tng. Moody AFB, Valdosta, Ga., 1965-66; resident in aerospace medicine Johns Hopkins Sch. Hygiene and Pub. Health, Balt., 1969-70, USAF Sch. Aerospace Medicine, San Antonio, 1970-72; commdr. USAF Hosp., Takhli, Thailand, 1972-73; adviser (ret.) USAF Life Support System Program Officer, Wright-Patterson AFB, 1978-80; pvt. practice in occupational and aerospace medicine Sacramento, 1981--; mem. staff Doctors Med. Ctr., Sharonville, Ohio, 1980-81; sr. assoc. cin. Author numerous sci. papers and presentations. Decorated Bronze Star, Legion of Merit, Queen's Commendation (RAF), numerous. Fellow Am. Coll. Preventative Medicine, Royal Aero. Soc., Aerospace Medicine. Republican. Presbyterian. Office: 1 Scipps Dr Ste 205 Sacramento CA 95825

ROOT, JAMES MYRON, food processing executive; b. Medford, Oreg., Feb. 4, 1947; s. Donald Goffe and Doris (Southwick) R.; m. Valerie Kay Grobe, Dec.18, 1971; 1 child, Chrysten Anne. BS, Oreg. State U., 1969; MBA, U. Oreg., 1971. Pres. Sabroso Co., Medford, 1971—, also bd. dirs. Mem. Oreg. Internat. Trade Com., 1980; vice chmn. Oreg. Fin. Com., 1985, Oreg. Econ. Devel., 1982-86; founder, chmn. Southern Oreg. Internat. Trade Council, 1988; bd. dirs. Rogue Valley Health Found., 1985—. Recipient Oreg. Internat. Marketer Yr. award, Econ. Devel Dept., 1982; named Outstanding Econ. Devel., Jackson County, 1986. Mem. Inst. Food Technologists, Medford C. of C. (bd. dirs. 1982—, pres., 1987, Glen Jackson award, 1986), Rotary, Beta Gamma Sigma. Republican. Home: 216 Mariposa Terr Medford OR 97504

ROOT, WILLIAM DIXON, construction company executive; b. Medford, Oreg., July 27, 1951; s. Earl Merrit and Helen Edith (Dixon) R.; m. Catherine Jeanine Smiraglia, June 10, 1981; children: Stacie Marie, Shawn Dixon. BSBA, U. Nev., Reno, 1978. Contr., sec.-treas. Jensen Elec., Inc., Reno, 1977-82; v.p., sec.-treas. Clark & Sullivan, Inc., Reno, 1982—; v.p., asst. sec. G & S Gen. Inc., Reno, 1986—; v.p., sec., treas. Westech Devel., Reno, 1986—, also bd. dirs.; cons. Micro-Tech., Reno, 1984—. Recipient Centurian award, 1986. Mem. Assn. Sys. Mgrs., Constrn. Fin. Mgrs. Assn. (v.p. 1986-88, pres. 1988—, nat. bd. dirs.), Assoc. Gen. Contractors, Sierra Nev. IBM Users, Sertoma Club (treas. 1983-88). Republican. Home: 2505 Homeland Dr Reno NV 89511 Office: Clark & Sullivan Inc 905 Industrial Sparks Reno NV 89431

ROPCHAN, JIM R., research chemist, administrator; b. Leamington, Ont., Can., Apr. 14, 1950; s. William George and Katie (Rudyka) R. Degree in chem. tech., St. Clair Coll. Applied Arts and Tech., Ont., Can., 1971; BS with honors, Detroit Inst. Tech., 1972; PhD, U. Detroit, 1981. Quality control chemist Ford Motor Co., Windsor, Ont., 1973-76; postdoctoral scholar UCLA, 1981-85, assoc. investigator div. nuclear medicine and biophysics, 1983-85; dir., chief chemist chemistry sect., positron emission tomography facility VA Med. Ctr., Los Angeles, 1986—, sec. radioactive drug rsch. com., 1987—, instr. radiopharmacy, 1987—; part-time tchr. high sch. math. and sci., Windsor, Ont., 1977; part-time instr. organic chemistry Detroit Inst. Tech., 1977. Contbr. articles to profl. jours.; inventor lab. accessories. Recipient Outstanding Scholar award Detroit Inst. Tech., 1972; grantee UCLA, 1983. Fellow Am. Inst. Chemists; mem. AAAS, N.Y. Acad. Scis., Am. Chem. Soc. (divs. Carbohydrate, Organic, Medicinal Chemistry), Am. Heart Assn., The Cousteau Soc., The Planetary Soc. Office: VA Med Ctr-Wadsworth Bldg 500 Room 0091 Div Nuclear Medicine UltraSound Sawtelle and Wilshire Blvds Los Angeles CA 90073

ROPER, DALE ALLEN, civil engineer, land surveyor; b. Eureka, Calif., July 7, 1955; s. John David and Miriam Esther (Stone) R.; m. Carla Grace Baldassari, Feb. 14, 1987. BS, Humboldt State U., 1978; MS, San Jose State U., 1983. Registered profl. engr., Calif.; lic. land surveyor, Calif. Jr. engr. Baird and McBride, Fortuna, Calif., 1979-80; jr. engr. WTW, Inc., San Jose, Calif., 1980-82; project mgr. Mid-State Engrs., Inc., San Luis Obispo, Calif., 1982; sr. engr., surveyor George S. Nolte & Assocs., Walnut Creek, Calif., 1983-86; sr. engr. John Wright & Assocs., Cloverdale, Calif., 1986-88; engr. Carlile Assocs., Santa Rosa, Calif., 1988--. Mem. ASCE, Calif. Land Surveyors Assn., Tau Beta Pi. Home: 14783 Grove St Healdsburg CA 95448

ROPER, WALTER WILLIAM, grain cooperative executive; b. American Falls, Idaho, Mar. 31, 1945; s. Allen Dwight and Evelyn Ruth (Schneider) R.; B.A. in Journalism, U. Idaho, 1968; m. Patrica Jo Morgan, June 20, 1970; children—Valorie Jo, Jason William, Alison Evon. Part time elevator operator, Power County Grain Growers, American Falls, summers 1963-68, bookkeeper, 1970, asst. mgr., 1971-76, mgr., sec., treas., 1976—; city, county news reporter, Moscow (Idaho) Daily Idahonian, 1968, Rexburg (Idaho) Standard and Jour., 1969, part time Power County Press, American Falls, 1970-71. Co-chmn. Concerned Citizens for Clean Growth, 1977; trustee Am Falls Sch. Dist. #381, 1987—. Mem. Grain Elevator and Processors Soc. (v.p. Intermountain chpt. 1982-83, pres. 1983-84), Idaho Feed and Grain Assn. (bd. dirs. Eastern dist. 1982—, bull. editor 1986—, exec. bd. 1987—), Farmers Grain Coop. Mgrs. Orgn. (sec., treas. 1976-85, pres. 1985-87). Democrat. Methodist. Clubs: American Falls Toastmasters (sec., treas. 1976-77), Tuesday Nighters Bowling League (pres. 1975-76, 76-77, sec., treas. 1977-78, 78-79). Home: 3054 Sunbeam Rd American Falls ID 83211 Office: 138 Elevator Ave American Falls ID 83211

RORRISON, PATRICIA ANN, business owner; b. Forest Hills, N.Y., July 21, 1960; d. John George and Frances May (Hauenstein) Kelsch; m. Lawrence Dale Rorrison Jr., Aug. 17, 1980; 1 child, David Adam. Student, U. Alaska, 1978-80; AA, Kenai Peninsula Community Coll, Soldotna, Alaska, 1985. Sr. acctg. clk. Kenai Peninsula Borough Fin. Dept., Soldotna, 1980-88; bd. dirs. Patror, Inc., Soldotna, 1982—; owner Salamatoff Plumbing & Heating, Kenai, 1985—; owner, jeweler Rorrison Jewelry Mfg., Kenai, 1987—. Mem. Amnesty Internat. USA, United Fishermen of Alaska, Mfg. Jeweler's and Silversmith's Am., Inc., Kenai Peninsula Fisherman's Assn., Peninsula MacIntosh Users Group (sec., treas. Soldotna chpt. 1987—). Lutheran. Office: Patror Inc PO Box 2246 Soldotna AK 99669

ROSA, FREDRIC DAVID, insurance company executive; b. Monroe, Wis., Oct. 31, 1946; s. Fredric Carl and Irene (Sommers) R.; m. Melanie A. Downs, May 31, 1986; 1 child, Mark. BBA in Mktg., U. Wis., 1968. Dir. mktg. Swiss Colony Stores, Inc., Monroe, 1968-80; pres. Videotape Indsl. Prodns., Inc., Madison, Wis., 1980-82; agt. VR Bus. Brokers, Colorado Springs, Colo., 1982-83; sales rep. NCR Corp., Denver, 1983-85; prin. F. D. Rosa & Assocs., Denver and Eagle, Colo., 1985-89; pres. Peak Benefit Cons., Colorado Springs, 1989—; cons. Kolb-Lena Cheese Co., Lena, Ill., 1983-85. Trustee Eagle Community United Meth. Ch.; pres. United Meth. Men. Mem. Am. Soc. CLU and Chartered Fin. Consultants, Mensa, Intertel Eagle Valley C. of C., Internat. Frat. Delta Sigma Pi (life). Club: Ducks Unltd. (dir. Monroe, Wis. chpt. 1977-78, mem. Eagle, Colo. chpt. 1987-88). Home: 901 Crown Ridge Dr Colorado Springs CO 80904 Office: Peak Benefits Cons PO Box 6070 Colorado Springs CO 80934-6070

ROSANDER, ARLYN CUSTER, mathematical statistician, management consultant; b. Mason County, Mich., Oct. 7, 1903; s. John Carl and Nellie May (Palmer) R.; m. Beatrice White, Aug. 26, 1933 (div.); children—Nancy Rosander Peck, Robert Richard Roger (dec.); m. 2d, Margaret Ruth Guest, Aug. 15, 1964. B.S., U. Mich. 1925; M.A., U. Wis., 1928; Ph.D., U. Chgo., 1933; postgrad. Dept. Agr., 1937-39. Research asst. U. Chgo., 1933-34; research fellow Gen. Edn. Bd. Tech. dir. Am. Youth Commn., Balt. and Washington, 1935-37; chief statistician urban study U.S. Bur. Labor Stats., Washington, 1937-39; sect. and br. chief War Prodn. Bd., Washington, 1940-45; chief statistician IRS, Washington, 1945-61; chief math. and stats. sect. ICC, Washington, 1961-69; cons. Pres.'s Commn. on Fed. Stats., Washington, 1970-71; cons., Loveland, Colo.; lectr. stats. George Washington U., 1946-52. Recipient Civilian War Service award War Prodn. Bd., 1945; Spl. Performance award Dept. Treasury, 1961. Fellow AAAS, Am. Soc. Quality Control (25 yr. honor award 1980, Howard Jones Meml. award 1984); mem. Am. Statis. Assn. Author: Elementary Principles of Statistics, 1951; Statistical Quality Control in Tax Operations, IRS, 1958; Case Studies in Sample Design, 1977; Application of Quality Control to Service Industries, 1985, Washington Story 1985, The Quest for Quality in Services, 1989. Home and Office: 4330 N Franklin Ave Loveland CO 80538

ROSBOROUGH, DONALD MARK, financial analyst; b. Chgo., Apr. 30, 1957; s. Paul Armour Rosborough and. Student, U. Arz., 1980. CLU. Aft. Prudential Ins. Co., Tucson, 1981—; Moderator, Life Underwriter Training Council, Tucson, 1986-87. Fellow Life Underwriter Tng. Coun.; mem. Nat. Assn. Life Underwriters. Democrat. Office: Prudential Ins Co 310 S William 250 Tucson AZ 85711

ROSCH, STANLEY, retired port official; b. N.Y.C., June 8, 1918; s. Meyer and Mollie (Silver) R.; m. Lila Kendall Joralemon, 1979; children—Edward Arthur, Brenda Huelani. B.B.A., CCNY, 1938; postgrad., Columbia, 1938-40, George Washington U., 1946-48. C.P.A., D.C., Hawaii, N.Y., Calif., La. Accountant John Berg (C.P.A.), Washington, 1945-48; with Young, Lamberton & Pearson (C.P.A.'s), Honolulu, 1948-56; partner Young, Lamberton & Pearson (C.P.A.'s), 1953-56; partner Haskins & Sells (C.P.A.'s), Honolulu, 1956-63, Los Angeles, 1963-65; controller Castle & Cooke, Inc., Honolulu, 1965-72; v.p. Castle & Cooke, Inc., 1966-69, sr. v.p., 1970-72; sr. v.p. finance, controller World Airways, Inc., Oakland, Calif., 1972-74; dir. fiscal affairs Port of Oakland, 1974-88; past pres. Hawaii Soc. C.P.A.s. Served with USNR, 1942-45. Mem. Am. Inst. C.P.A.s, Nat. Assn. Accountants, Financial Execs. Inst., Govt. Fin. Officers Assn., Assn. Water Transp. Acctg. Officers (v.p. No. Calif. 1980-82). Club: Kiwanis. Home: 1201 Monument Blvd #31 Concord CA 94520

ROSCOE, ROBERT STANLEY, civil engineer; b. Eureka, Calif., Jan. 23, 1956; s. Charles Milton and Mary Patricia (Gross) R.; m. Deborah Joan Lynch, May 5, 1979; children: Sara Patricia, Lauren Kathleen. BS, U. Calif., Davis, 1978; MS, Calif. State U., Sacramento, 1986. Registered civil engr., Calif. Jr. environ. engr. East Bay Mcpl. Utility Dist., Oakland, Calif., 1978-80; project engr. Storm Engrng., Davis, 1980-82; project mgr. Oscar Larsen & Assocs., Eureka, Calif., 1982-87, dir. water and wastewater engrng., 1987—. Active Humboldt Hist. Soc., Eureka, 1985—. Mem. ASCE (Young Engr. of Yr. 1985, bd. dirs. 1987-89, pres. north cent. br., 1986-87), Am. Waterworks Assn., Assn. Environ. Profls., Calif. Water Pollution Control Assn. (vice chair north cent. br., 1986-88). Democrat. Lodge: Rotary. Home: 2805 H St Eureka CA 95501 Office: Oscar Larson & Assocs 317 Third St Eureka CA 95501

ROSE, GREGORY MANCEL, neurobiologist; b. Eugene, Oreg., Feb. 3, 1953; s. Mancel Lee and Ilione (Schenk) R.; m. Kathleen Ann Frye, June 30, 1979; 1 child, Julian Mancel. BS cum laude, U. Calif., Irvine, 1975, PhD, 1980. Research fellow M.P.I. for Psychiatry, Munich, 1976; research assoc. Miescher Labor, M.P.I., Tuebingen, Republic of Germany, 1980-81; regular fellow dept. pharmacology U. Colo. Health Sci. Ctr., Denver, 1981-84, asst. prof., 1984-89, assoc. prof., 1989—; research biologist VA Med. Ctr., Denver, 1981—, co-dir. neurosci. tng. program, 1986—. Contbr. articles to sci. jours. Bd. dirs. Greater Park Hill Community. VA Rsch. Svc. grantee, 1984, 86, 89, NSF grantee, 1988, NIMH grantee, 1989. Mem. AAAS, Am. Aging Assn., Soc. Neurosci. Democrat. Episcopalian. Office: VA Med Ctr Rsch Svc 1055 Clermont St Box 151 Denver CO 80220

ROSE, JACK WARREN, educator; b. Grand Rapids, Mich., Nov. 16, 1929; s. Forrest James and Gladys (Goodwin) R.; m. Susan Jacobsen, June 19, 1955; children: Mike, Mark, Scott. BS, U. Mich., 1952, MA, 1955; PhD, U. So. Calif., 1962. Grad. asst. U. Mich., Ann Arbor, 1954-55, U. So. Calif., L.A., 1955-56; prof. Calif. State U., Long Beach, 1956—; dir. Nat. Track and Field Hall of Fame, Indpls., 1974-88; nat. meet dir. Hershey's Track and Field Youth Program. Presentator numerous articles, U.S. Olympic Acad., 1977-88. Record, sec. Nat. Hall of Fame Rsch. Library, Indpls., 1988; ceremonies mgr. L.A. Olympics Games, 1984, official, 1984. Lt. USAF, 1952-54. Recipient Centennial Honors award, Centennial Com., Long Beach, Calif., 1988. Mem. Calif. Assn. Health, Physical Edn. and Recreation (adv. 1978-88). Republican. Home: 390 Peralto Ave Long Beach CA 90803 Office: Calif State U 1250 Bellflower Blvd Long Beach CA 90814

ROSE, JOHN MICHAEL, electronics technician; b. Madera, Calif., July 15, 1955; s. John Mitchell and Virginia Mae (Bradford) R.; m. Patricia Ann Hogue, June 28, 1977 (div. 1983); children: Shaun Michael, Patrick; m. Kathleen Mary Chandler, Aug. 30, 1986. Student, Calif. State U.-Fresno, 1974-76, Mesa Community Coll., 1986; diploma, DeVry Inst., Phoenix, 1981. Carpenter, electrician Brown Constrn. Co., Madera, 1974-77; residential electrician Dana Electric Co., Madera, 1977; electronics technician ITT Courier Terminal Systems, Tempe, Ariz., 1978-85; avionics supr. Sundstrand ATG, Phoenix, 1985-88; avionics technician Sperry Comml. div. Honeywell, Inc., Glendale, Ariz., 1988—; rsch. adviser Aviation Week mag., 1988—. Republican. Home: 406 W Wahalla Ln Phoenix AZ 85027

ROSE, RANDALL JOSEPH, master locksmith; b. Denver, Nov. 8, 1951; s. Joseph Richard and Sylvia Della (Shaner) R. Master locksmith cert., Locksmithing Inst., N.J., 1976; pres., Locksmith Assocs. Enterprises Ltd., Denver, 1974—. Pres. Locksmith Assocs. Enterprises. Ltd., Denver, 1974—, Archtl. Hardware Assocs. Ltd., Denver, 1983—. Mem. Am. Soc. for Indsl. Security. Democrat. Reformed Jew. Office: Locksmith Assocs Enterprises Ltd PO Box 22476 Denver CO 80222-0476

ROSE, RICHARD SCOTT, financial services executive; b. Bklyn., July 7, 1959; s. Edward and Rose (Turetsky) R. BS in Bus. Adminstrn., Bryant Coll., 1981. CPA, Ariz. Staff acct. Toback & Co. CPAs, Phoenix, 1981-83; sr. acct. Freeman & Lewis CPAs, Phoenix, 1983-85; chief fin. officer Mitchell Sweet and Assocs., Inc., Tempe, Ariz., 1985—. Republican. Jewish. Home: 4901 E Kelton Ln #1261 Scottsdale AZ 85254 Office: Mitchell Sweet & Assocs Inc 1626 S Edward Dr Tempe AZ 85281

ROSE, ROBERT E., state supreme court justice. B.A., Juniata Coll., Huntingdon, Pa.; LL.B., N.Y.U., N.Y.C. Bar: 1965. Formerly judge, Nev. Dist. Ct., 8th Jud. Dist., Las Vega; justice Nev. Supreme Ct., Carson City, 1989—. Office: Nev Supreme Ct 100 N Carson St Carson City NV 89710 *

ROSE, ROBERT R., JR., lawyer; b. Evanston, Ill., Nov. 1, 1915; s. Robert R. and Eleanor B. R.; m. Kathryn Lorraine Warner, June 14, 1948; children: Robert R. III, Cynthia Ann. LL.B., U. Wyo., 1941. Bar: Wyo. bar 1941. Atty. Dept. Justice, 1941; with UNRRA, China; asst. sec. Dept. Interior, 1951-52; sr. partner firm Rose, Spence, Dobos and Duncan, Casper, Wyo., 1968-75; justice Wyo. Supreme Ct., 1975-85, chief justice, 1981-82; assoc. Spence, Moriarity and Schuster, Cheyenne, Wyo., 1985—; organizer, past pres., chmn. bd. Title Guaranty Co. Wyo.; faculty Nat. Coll. Criminal Def., 1977-83, Western Trial Advocacy Inst., 1977-88; vis. prof. trial practice U. Wyo. Coll. Law, 1985-86; Milward Simpson chmn. in polit. sci. U. Wyo., 1985-86. Author legal articles. Past chmn. fund drive Casper Community Chest, Am. Cancer Soc.; mem. Wyo. Ho. of Reps., 1949-51; mayor of, Casper, 1950-51; past trustee Casper Coll. Served with USAAF, World War II. Recipient Jud. Achievement award Nat. Assn. Criminal Def. Lawyers, 1983. Mem. Am. Law Inst. Episcopalian. Address: PO Box 1006 Cheyenne WY 82003

ROSE, SHIELA ANNE, technical products consultant; b. Missoula, Mont., Feb. 27, 1954; d. Robert Sayre and Coralie Mae (Segraves) R. Student, U. Mont., 1972-73; BA Spl. Studies in Counseling and Nutrition, Graceland Coll., Iowa, 1976; postgrad. in counseling, Mont. State U., 1978-79. Records specialist Gallatin County, Mont., 1978-79; prodn. supr. High Country News, Bozeman, Mont., 1979-81; prodn. specialist Insty-Prints, Bozeman, 1981-82; press supr. Star Printing, Gillette, Wyo., 1982-83; owner Rose Enterprises, Wright, Wyo., 1983—; tech. writing/publs. cons. space div. Morton Thiokol Inc. Wasatch Ops., Brigham City, Utah, 1987—; tech. writing cons. printer products div. Eaton Corp., Riverton, Wyo., 1986—; bus. plan cons. Diamond "L" Industries Inc., Gillette, 1986—, Allstar Video Inc., Gillette, 1985; subcontractor Amax Coal Co., Gillete, 1986—; tech. svcs./drafting cons. Thunder Basin Coal Co., Wright, Wyo., 1983-86. Active Nat. Coalition Against Sexual Assault. Mem. Am. Inst. Design and Drafting (state sec. 1984-85, asst. editor D&D News 1983-84, co-chair nat. editorial and pub. relations com.), Soc. for Tech. Communications, NOW, AAUW, Women in Bus. (v.p. 1987), NAFE, Associated Photographer's Internat., Wright Area C. of C., Douglas Area C. of C. Avocation: graphic arts/photography. Office: Rose Enterprises 2551 Whititar Antelope Valley Gillette WY 82716

ROSEHNAL, MARY ANN, educational administrator; b. Bklyn., July 25, 1943; d. Frank Joseph and Mary Anna (Corso) R.; 1 child, Scott Stoddart. BA in Sociology, San Francisco State U., 1968; M in Sch. Bus. Adminstrn., No. Ariz. U., 1985. Lic. substitute tchr., Ariz.; lic. vocat. nurse, Calif.; cert. sch. bus. mgr., Ariz. Deliquency counselor, Calif., 1969-73; office mgr. Nurses Central Registry, Sun City, Ariz., 1973-75; bus. mgr. Nadaburg sch. dist., Wittmann, Ariz., 1975-78, Morristown (Ariz.) sch. dist., 1978—; served on 1st Assessment Handbook editing task force, Fair Employment Practices Handbook task force, 1979-80. Columnist Wickenburg Sun, 1975—. Clk. Morristown sch. bd., 1974-76; pres. Morristown PTA, 1977-78; sec. Wickenburg area bd., 1979; bd. dirs. Future Frontiers, 1979-81; rep. HUD block grant adv. com., 1979-85; active Wickenburg Friends of Music, 1984—; sec. of bd. dirs., 1986—; trustee Wickenburg Community Hosp. Found. Named to Ariz. Sch. Bd. Assn. Honor Roll, 1976; named Morristown Area Vol. of Yr., 1988. Mem. Ariz. Assn. Sch. Bus. Ofcls. (fin. dir., bd. dirs., Gold award 1986, 87, 88), Assn. Sch. Bus. Ofcls. U.S. and Can., Assn. Govt. Accts., Morristown Federated Women's Club, Ariz. Theatre Guild. Roman Catholic. Office: PO Box 98 Morristown AZ 85342

ROSELL, SHARON LYNN, physics and chemistry educator, researcher; b. Wichita, Kans., Jan. 6, 1948; d. John E. and Mildred C. (Binder) R. BA, Loretto Heights Coll., 1970; postgrad., Marshall U., 1973; MS in Edn., Ind. U., 1977; MS, U. Wash., 1988. Cert. profl. educator, Wash. Assoc. instr. Ind. U., Bloomington, 1973-74; instr. Pierce Coll. (name formerly Ft. Steilacoom (Wash.) Community Coll.), 1976-79, 82, Olympic Coll., Bremerton, Wash., 1977-78; instr. physics, math. and chemistry Tacoma (Wash.) Community Coll., 1979—; instr. physics and chemistry Green River Community Coll., Auburn, Wash., 1983-86; researcher Nuclear Physics Lab., U. Wash., Seattle, 1985-88. Mem. Math. Assn. Am., Am. Assn. Physics Tchrs. (rep. com. on physics for 2 yr. coll. 1986-87, v.p. 1987-88, pres. 1988—, Wash. chpt.), Am. Chem. Soc., Internat. Union Pure and Applied Chemistry (affiliate). Democrat. Roman Catholic. Home: 1204 N 7th Apt A Tacoma WA 98403 Office: Tacoma Community Coll 5900 S 12th Tacoma WA 98465

ROSEN, ALBERT LEONARD, professional baseball team executive; b. Spartanburg, S.C., Feb. 29, 1924; s. Louis and Rose (Levine) R.; m. Rita Kallman, July 24, 1971; children: Robert, Andrew, James, Gail, David. B.B.A., U. Miami, 1947. Profl. baseball player Cleve. Indians Baseball Team, 1947-56; with Bache & Co., Cleve., 1955-73, 1st Continental Investment Corp., Cleve., 1973-75; br. office mgr. Caesars Palace, Las Vegas, Nev., 1975-77; pres. N.Y. Yankees, N.Y.C., 1977-79; with Bally's Park Pl., Atlantic City, N.J., 1979-80; pres., gen. mgr. Houston Astros Baseball, 1980-85, San Francisco Giants Baseball Club, 1985—. Served to lt. (j.g.) USNR, 1943-46, PTO. Named Most Valuable Player Am. League, 1953. Jewish. Club: Westwood Country. Office: care San Francisco Giants Candlestick Park San Francisco CA 94124 *

ROSEN, CHARLES HENRY, film production designer; b. N.Y.C., Nov. 10, 1930; s. Ferdinand Shack and Sara (Levinson) R.; m. Marygrace Kirkpatrick, July 28, 1959; children: Amy, John, Robert. BFA, U. Okla., 1952; MFA, Yale U., 1955. Designer NBC TV, N.Y.C., 1956-61; freelance art dir. N.Y.C., 1961-67; freelance prodn. designer N.Y.C., Los Angeles, 1967—. Mem. United Scenic Artists, Soc. Motion Picture and TV Art Dirs., Acad. Motion Picture Arts and Scis. Jewish. Home and Office: 2705 Outpost Dr Los Angeles CA 90068-2008

ROSEN, LOUIS, physicist; b. N.Y.C., June 10, 1918; s. Jacob and Rose (Lipionski) R.; m. Mary Terry, Sept. 4, 1941; 1 son, Terry Leon. BA, U. Ala., 1939, MS, 1941; PhD, Pa. State U., 1944; DSc (hon.), U. N.Mex., 1979, U. Colo., 1987. Instr. physics U. Ala., 1941-44, Pa. State U., 1943-44; mem. staff Los Alamos Sci. Lab., 1944—, group leader nuclear plate lab., 1949-65, alt. div. leader exptl. physics div., 1962-65, dir. meson physics facility, 1965-85, div. leader medium energy physics div., 1965-86, sr. lab. fellow, 1985—; Sesquicentennial hon. prof. U. Ala., 1981. Author papers in nuclear sci. and applications of particle accelerators.; bd. editors: Applications of Nuclear Physics. Mem. Los Alamos Town Planning Bd., 1962-64; mem. Gov.'s

Com. on Tech. Excellence in N.Mex.; mem. Nat. Acad. Panel on Nuclear Sci., chmn. sub-panel on accelerators; mem. N.Mex. Cancer Control Bd., 1976-80 , v.p., 1979-81; mem. panel on future of nuclear sci. Nat. Research Council of Nat. Acad. Scis., 1976; mem. panel on instl. arrangements for orbiting space telescope NRC-Nat. Acad. Scis., 1976; mem. U.S.A.-USSR Joint Coordinating Com. on Fundamental Properties of Matter, 1976—; Co-chmn. Los Alamos Vols. for Stevenson, 1956; Democratic candidate for county commr., 1962; bd. dirs. Los Alamos Med. Center, 1977-83, chmn., 1983; bd. gov's. Tel Aviv U., 1986. Recipient E.O. Lawrence award AEC, 1963; Golden Plate award Am. Acad. Achievement, 1964; N.Mex. Disting. Public Service award, 1978; named Citizen of Year, N.Mex. Realtors Assn., 1973; Guggenheim fellow, 1959-60; alumni fellow Pa. State U., 1978; Louis Rosen prize established in his honor by bd. dirs. Meson Facility Users Group, 1984. Fellow Am. Phys. Soc. (mem. council 1975-78, chmn. panel on public affairs 1980, chmn. div. nuclear physics 1985, mem. subcom. internat. sci. affairs 1988—), AAAS (mem. council 1989). Home: 1170 41st St Los Alamos NM 87544 Office: Los Alamos Sci Lab PO Box 1663 Los Alamos NM 87545

ROSEN, MARTIN JACK, lawyer; b. Los Angeles, Sept. 9, 1931; s. Irving and Sylvia (Savad) R.; B.A., UCLA, 1953; J.D., U. Calif.-Berkeley, 1956; m. Joan D. Meyersieck, Oct. 22, 1954; children—Dirk Rosen, Marika. Bar: Calif. 1957. Pvt. practice, Merced, Calif., 1960-62, San Francisco, 1962-82; mem. Silver, Rosen, Fischer & Stecher, P.C., San Francisco, 1964—. Pres. Trust for Pub. Land, 1979—. Served with USAF, 1958-60. Fellow internat. legal studies U. Calif. Law Sch./Inst. Social Studies, The Hague, 1956-57.

ROSEN, MOISHE, religious organization administrator; b. Kansas City, Mo., Apr. 12, 1932; s. Ben and Rose (Baker) R.; m. Ceil Starr, Aug. 18, 1950; children: Lyn Rosen Bond, Ruth. Diploma, Northeastern Bible Coll., 1957; DD, Western Conservative Bapt. Sem., 1986. Ordained to ministry Bapt. Ch., 1957. Missionary Am. Bd. Missions to the Jews, N.Y.C., 1956; minister in charge Beth Sar Shalom Am. Bd. Missions to the Jews, Los Angeles, 1957-67; dir. recruiting and tng. Am. Bd. Missions to the Jews, N.Y.C., 1967-70; founder, chmn. Jews for Jesus Movement, San Francisco, 1970-73, 78—, San Rafael, Calif., 1973-78; speaker in field. Author: Sayings of Chairman Moishe, 1972, Jews for Jesus, 1974, Share the New Life with a Jew, 1976, Christ in the Passover, 1977, Y'shua, The Jewish Way to Say Jesus, 1982. Trustee Western Conservative Bapt. Sem., Portland, Oreg., 1979-85, 86—, Bibl. Internat. Council on Bibl. Inerrancy, Oakland, Calif., 1980-87. Office: Jews for Jesus 60 Haight St San Francisco CA 94102

ROSEN, RICHARD LEWIS, company executive; b. Chgo., Feb. 14, 1948; m. Nancy Elizabeth Warner, Sept. 2, 1984; 1 child, Bonnie Ellen. Student, L.A. Valley Jr. Coll., 1967-70, UCLA, 1970-71. Asst. to gov. State of Ill., Springfield, 1972-77; asst. to sec. HHS, Washington, 1978-81; cons. RLR & Co., Washington, 1981-85; pres. RLR & Co., Woodland Hills, Calif., 1988—; cons. recruiting Search Assocs., Metacor Corp., Sherman Oaks, Calif., 1985-88. Recipient numerous letters of commendation from civic groups, charities, polit. orgns. 1970—. Mem. Internat. Assn. Bus. Communicators. Democrat. Jewish. Office: RLR & Co 23800 Oxnard St Woodland Hills CA 91387

ROSEN, STANLEY GILBERT, military officer; b. Corsicana, Tex., June 6, 1947; s. Maurice R. and Roslyn (Daiches) R.; m. Lisa Marie Neufeld (div. Oct. 1986); children: Matthew, Benjamin. BS, USAF Acad., 1969; MS, MIT, 1970, U. So. Calif., 1973; Dr Ing, U. Stuttgart, Germany, 1981. Commd. 2d lt. USAF, 1969, advanced through grades to lt. col., 1986; project engr. USAF Rocket Propulsion Lab., Edwards AFB, Calif., 1970-73; staff mem. U.S. House Reps., Washington, 1973-74; visiting scientist German Aerospace Rsch. Est., Heilbronn, Fed. Republic Germany, 1974-76; spacecraft mgr. USAF Space Div., L.A., 1976-80; chief space policy Spl. Projects Sec. Air Force, L.A., 1980-84; chief space plans USAF Space Command, Colo. Springs, Colo., 1984-87; dir. long range planning USAF Space Div., L.A., 1987—. Contbr. numerous articles to profl. jours. Named White House Fellow Finalist, 1984. Mem. AIAA (dir. at-large).

ROSENAU, JAMES NATHAN, political scientist, author; b. Philadelphia, Nov. 25, 1924; s. Walter Nathan and Fanny Fox (Baum) R.; m. Norah McCarthy, Aug. 5, 1955 (dec. July 5, 1974); 1 child, Heidi Margaret; m. Pauline Vaillancourt, June 14, 1987. A.B., Bard Coll., 1948; A.M., Johns Hopkins U., 1949; Ph.D., Princeton U., 1957. Instr. Rutgers U., New Brunswick, N.J., 1949-54; asst. prof. Rutgers U., New Brunswick, 1954-60, assoc. prof., 1960-62, prof., 1962-70; prof. Ohio State U., Columbus, 1970-73; prof. polit. sci. U. So. Calif., Los Angeles, 1973—; research asst. Inst. Advanced Study, Princeton, N.J., 1953-54; research assoc. Princeton U., N.J., 1960-70; dir. Sch. Internat. Relations U. So. Calif., Los Angeles, 1976-79; dir. Inst. for Transnat. Studies, U. Southern Calif., Los Angeles, 1973—. Author: Public Opinion and Foreign Policy, 1961, National Leadership and Foreign Policy, 1963, The Dramas of Politics, 1973, Citizenship Between Elections, 1974, The Scientific Study of Foreign Policy, 1980; co-author: American Leaders in World Affairs, 1984; co-editor: Journeys Through World Politics, 1989, Global Changes and Theoretical Challenges, 1989. Trustee Bard Coll., Annandale-on-Hudson, 1968-70, Odyssey Theater Ensemble, Los Angeles, 1987-88. Served with U.S. Army, 1942-46. Ford Found. fellow, 1958-59; research grantee NSF, 1970, 73, 78, 79, 83, 88; Guggenheim fellow, 1987-88; recipient stipend NEH, 1976. Mem. Internat. Studies Assn. (pres. 1984-85), Am. Polit. Sci. Assn. (mem. exec. council 1975-77). Democrat. Home: 1700 San Remo Dr Pacific Palisades CA 90272 Office: U So Calif Inst Transnat Studies University Park Los Angeles CA 90089

ROSENAUER, ADOLF ALOIS, neurosurgeon; b. Linz, Austria, Sept. 20, 1922; came to U.S., 1951; s. Alois and Rosa (Fiorioli) R.; m. Eva Moore, Nov. 25, 1954; children: Patricia, Kathleen, Michael. MD, U. Innsbruck, Austria, 1947; MS in Surgery, U. Cin., 1952. Diplomate Am. Bd. Neurol. Surgery. Instr. anatomy U. Innsbruck, 1943-47, asst. prof., 1947-50; intern Barmh. Brueder Hosp., Linz, 1950-51; fellow Rockefeller Found. Good Samaritan Hosp., Cin., 1951-52; resident in neurol. surgery U. Cin., 1951-53; resident Barmherzige Brueder Hosp., Linz, Austria, 1954-55; instr. neurosurgery U. Chgo., 1955-57; assoc. prof. Sch. Medicine U. Nev., Reno, 1957—. Contbr. articles to profl. jours. With Austrian Army, 1940-45. Decorated Iron Cross. Fellow Olympic Physicians; mem. Am. Assn. Neurol. Surgeons, Congress Neurol. Surgeons, Western Neurosurgey Soc., Order of Quiet Birdmen, Internat. Order St. Hubert (knight commdr.), Sigma Xi. Roman Catholic. Home: 2150 Willow Tree Ln Reno NV 89509 Office: 890 Mill St Reno NV 89502

ROSENBAUM, ELIKA SOSNICK, accountant; b. Princeton, N.J., June 16, 1957; d. Stephen H. and Galya Natalie (Chernow) Sosnick; m. Michael Francis Rosenbaum, March 8, 1986. BA in Econs., U. Calif., Los Angeles, 1980. CPA. Sr. acct. Arthur Andersen & Co., L.A., 1980-84, instr., 1983-84; sr. acct. Price Waterhouse, San Francisco, 1984-85; with Appel Venture, Inc., Mill Valley, Calif., 1985-87; pvt. practice Ross, Calif., 1987—. Mem. The Jr. League, San Francisco, 1985—, Nat. Ski Patrol, 1988—; bd. mem. Ross (Calif.) Recreation, 1988—. Mem. Am. Inst. CPA's, Calif. Soc. CPA's, Magic Castle Club. Democrat. Jewish. Office: E Rosenbaum Co PO Box 1035 Ross CA 94957

ROSENBAUM, HAROLD D., pediatric dentist; b. Montreal, Que., Canada, Nov. 3, 1921; came to U.S., 1946; s. David and Sophie (Darabaner) R.; m. Mildred R. Hardin, Dec. 25, 1945; 1 child, Betsy Davida Schneier. BS, McGill U., Montreal, 1942, DDS, 1946; cert. in clin. pedodontia, Guggenheim Clinic, N.Y.C., 1947. Pvt. practice specializing in pediatrics Seattle, 1947—; clin. asst. Dental Sch. U. Wash., Seattle, 1974-78, clin. assoc., 1980—; staff Children's Hosp., Seattle, 1954—. Served to capt. USAF, 1953-55. Mem. ADA (life), Seattle-King County Dental Soc. (life), Wash State Dental Assn. (life, editor jour. 1961-63), Am. Acad. Pediatric Dentistry (life), Evergreen Pediatric Dental Study and Research Group (pres. 1980-81), Alpha Omega (pres. 1975-76). Democrat. Jewish.

ROSENBERG, DAN YALE, retired plant pathologist; b. Stockton, Calif., Jan. 8, 1922; s. Meyer and Bertha (Naliboff) R.; A.A., Stockton Jr. Coll., 1942; A.B., Coll. Pacific, 1949; M.S., U. Calif. at Davis, 1952; m. Marilyn Kohn, Dec. 5, 1954; 1 son, Morton Karl. Jr. plant pathologist Calif. Dept. Agr., Riverside, 1952-55, asst. plant pathologist, 1955-59, assoc. plant pathologist, 1959-60, pathologist IV, 1960-63, program supr., 1963-71, chief exclusion and detection, div. plant industry, 1971-76, chief nursery and seed services div. plant industry, 1976-82, spl. asst. div. plant industry, 1982-87; pres. Health, Inc., 1972-73; agrl. cons.; mem. Gov.'s Interagy. Task Force on Biotech., 1986—; bd. dirs. Health Inc., Sacramento, 1967, pres., 1971-72, 79-81, 81-83. Served with AUS, 1942-46; ETO. Mem. Am. Phytopath. Soc. (fgn. and regulatory com. 1975—, grape diseases sect. 1977-79, grape pests sect. 1979-84), Calif. State Employees Assn. (pres. 1967-69). Contbr. articles to profl. jours. Home and Office: 2328 Swarthmore Dr Sacramento CA 95825

ROSENBERG, HOWARD ALAN, manufacturing executive; b. N.Y.C., Nov. 2, 1927; s. Nathan and Anna (Bernstein) R.; m. Carol Hirsch, Feb. 21, 1951; children: Ellen Sue, Robin Jill, Ira Scott. BS, L.I. U., 1949; MA, NYU, 1951. Registered profl. engr. Jr. engr. Wright Aeronaut. Corp., Woodridge, N.J., 1950-52; quality engr. Fairchild Engine Div., Farmingdale, N.Y., 1952-55; quality control mgr. Burndy Corp., Norwalk, Conn., 1955-60; reliability mgr. LFE Corp., Boston, 1960-64; reliability dir. AIL-Cutler Hammer, Comack, N.Y., 1964-69; pres. Western Tech. Assocs., Anaheim, Calif., 1969-80, chief exec. officer, 1980—; cons. in field; instr. at various colls. Contbr. articles to profl. jours. Chmn. Anti-Defamation League, Santa Ana, Calif., 1984-86, nat. commr.; pres. Orange County Jewish Community Ctr., 1989. 1st lt. USNG, 1949-54. Mem. Am. Soc. Quality Control, Calif. Circuits Assn. (dir. 1970-75), Am. Electroplaters Soc., Am. Legion, Jewish War Vets, B'nai B'rith, Masons. Home: 13592 Carroll Way Tustin CA 92680 Office: Western Tech Assocs 2897 E LaCresta Ave Anaheim CA 92806

ROSENBERG, HOWARD ANTHONY, journalist; b. Kansas City, Mo., June 10, 1942; s. Sherman Rosenberg and Claire (Kanchuk) Rosenberg Magady; m. Carol Finkel; 1 child, Kirsten. Journalist Los Angeles Times, now TV critic, columnist. Recipient Editorial award Los Angeles Times, 1981; Headliner award Atlantic City Press Club, 1984; Pulitzer prize Columbia U., 1985. Office: Los Angeles Times Times Mirror Sq Los Angeles CA 90053 *

ROSENBERG, LISA JEANNE, screenwriter, journalist; b. Washington, Dec. 29, 1951; d. Herbert Harris Rosenberg and Mae Stephen; m. Lennis Jay Carlson, July 30, 1988. BA, San Francisco State U., 1977; Cert. Screenwriting, Am. Film Inst., Beverly Hills, Calif., 1981. Contbr. articles to mags.; scripts include Another Word for Monster, 1983, Adagio, 1983, Heroes and Fools, 1983, Alcoholism and the Family, 1984, The Sean Marsee Story (for Walt Disney Productions), 1985-86, U.S. Constitution Series (with Bill Moyers), 1986-87 (Gold Medal "Federalism" segment N.Y. Film Festival 1987), (edn1. TV series) Your Choice/Our Chance, 1988-89. Proposal writer pub. T.V., 1985—. Recipient Action Children's TV award, 1988, Recognition award AECT, 1987. Mem. Women in Film. Democrat. Home and Office: 249 Dimmick Ave Venice CA 90291

ROSENBERG, MORTON KARL, dentist; b. Sacramento, Aug. 25, 1960; s. Dan Yale and Marilyn Carol (Kohn) R.; m. Diane Lois Gibson, Sept. 25, 1983; 1 child, Rebekah Leigh. BS, U. Pacific, 1982, DDS, 1985. Pvt. practice Sacramento, 1986-87, Yuba City, Calif., 1987—; vol. dentist Am. Dental Vols. for Israel, Kibbutz Yahel, 1985. Mem. ADA, Butte-Sierra Dist. Dental Soc. (membership chmn. 1988—), Acad. Gen. Dentistry, Calif. Dental Assn., Butte-Sierra Dental Soc. (membership chmn. 1988, treas. 1989-80), Rotary, Alpha Omega, Alpha Chi Sigma. Democrat. Jewish. Home: 859 Jones Rd Apt 37 Yuba City CA 95991

ROSENBERG, RICHARD MORRIS, banker; b. Fall River, Mass., Apr. 21, 1930; s. Charles and Betty (Peck) R.; m. Barbara K. Cohen, Oct. 21, 1956; children: Michael, Peter. B.S., Suffolk U., 1952; M.B.A., Golden Gate Coll., 1962, LL.B., 1966. Publicity asst. Crocker-Anglo Bank, San Francisco, 1959-62; banking services officer Wells Fargo Bank, N.A., San Francisco, 1962-65; asst. v.p. Wells Fargo Bank, N.A., 1965-68, v.p. mktg. dept., 1968, v.p., dir. mktg., 1969, sr. v.p. mktg. and advt. div., 1970-75, exec. v.p., from 1975, vice chmn., 1980-83; vice chmn. Crocker Nat. Corp., 1983-85; pres., chief operating officer Seafirst Corp., 1986-87, also dir.; pres., chief operating officer Seattle First Nat. Bank, 1985-87; vice chmn. bd. BankAmerica Corp., San Francisco, 1987—; dir. Airborne Express, Visa, Am. Magnetics Corp.; chmn. Mastercard Internat. Bd. dirs. Marin Ecumenical Housing Assn.; bd. regents Sch. Bank Mktg., U. Colo. Served from ensign to lt. USNR, 1953-59. Mem. Am. Bankers Assn. (exec. com. mktg./savs. div.), Bank Mktg. Assn. (dir.), State Bar Calif. Jewish. Clubs: Ranier, Hillcrest. Office: BankAm Corp Bank America Ctr San Francisco CA 94104 also: Seafirst Corp PO Box 3586 Seattle WA 98124 *

ROSENBERG, STEVEN LOREN, microbiologist; b. Oakland, Calif., Sept. 27, 1941; s. Benjamin and Elaine Rosenberg; m. Emiko A. Yamamoto, Nov. 6, 1968. AB, U. Calif., Berkeley, 1963, PhD, 1970. Research microbiologist Gen. Electric Co., Schenectady, N.Y., 1972-76, Lawrence Berkeley Lab., Berkeley, 1976-81; lectr. in biochem. engring. U. Calif., Berkeley, 1976-81; sr. scientist, project leader SRI Internat., Menlo Park, Calif., 1981-86; sr. scientist Biosys, Inc., Palo Alto, Calif., 1987-88; cons., investor S.L. Rosenberg and Assocs., Castro Valley, Calif., 1988—. Contbr. articles to profl. and scientific publs. Cons. Vols. in Tech. Assistance, Arlington, Va., 1988—. NIH fellow, 1968. Mem. Am. Chem. Soc., Am. Soc. for Microbiology, Soc. for Indsl. Microbiology. Home and Office: 5555 Greenridge Rd Castro Valley CA 94552

ROSENBERG, SYDNEY J., corporate executive; b. San Francisco, Sept. 3, 1914; s. Morris and Gussie (Kaufman) R.; m. Joyce Wexler, Nov. 15, 1939 (div. Mar. 1968); children: Brad, Jill Rosenberg Hughes, Todd; m. 2d Jaclyn Barde, Mar. 22, 1968; stepchildren: Gregg Cobarr, Glenn Cobarr. B.A., Stanford U., 1936; M.B.A., Harvard U., 1938. Pres., chief exec. officer Am. Bldg. Maintenance Industries, Los Angeles, from 1938; now chmn. bd. Am. Bldg. Maintenance Industries, San Francisco; dir. Craig Corp.; pres. OPTIC Fund. Bd. govs. Performing Arts Council; bd. govs. Los Angeles Music Ctr.; trustee Jewish Big Bros.; mem. dirs. council Children's Orthopaedic Hosp. Mem. Chief Execs. Orgn., Urban Land Inst., World Bus. Council. Republican. Jewish. Clubs: Hillcrest (Los Angeles); Big Canyon (Newport, Calif.). Office: Am Bldg Maintenance Industries 333 Fell St San Francisco CA 94102 *

ROSENBERGER, RALPH WILLIAM, accountant, small business owner; b. Orofino, Idaho, Nov. 29, 1939; s. Manford James Rosenberger and Rosie Lee (Brown) Dominique; m. Arnette Post, Sept. 17, 1964 (div. 1973); children: Richard J., Mary, Bruce, Todd; m. Sadako Hirrhi, May 20, 1974 (dec. 1977); one child, Juko; m. Lauramy Davis, Sept. 16, 1977; children: Richard L., Joseph E., Daniel J., Jessica J. Assoc. spec. bus in acctg, Ctr. for degree studies ICS, Scranton, Pa., 1985. Leadman elect. tech. Rockwell Internat., Golden, Colo., 1980-85; owner Blue Rose Tax and Acctng., Aurora, Colo., 1984--. Dist. delegate Rep. Party, Longmont, Colo., 1982; asst. scout master Boy Scouts of Am., 1984--, chmn. 1968-71, scoutmaster 1971-72, cub master 1972-84. With USAF, 1958-71; with U.S. Army, 1971-79. Republican. Roman Catholic. Office: Blue Rose Tax and Acctg 10165 E Colfax Ave Aurora CO 80010

ROSENBLATT, GERALD FREDERIC, lawyer; b. N.Y.C., Feb. 25, 1937; s. Irving and Grace (Willen) R. BA cum laude, Bklyn. Coll., 1958; JD, U. Mich., 1961. Bar: N.Y. 1962, U.S. Dist. Ct. (so. dist.) N.Y., 1964, Calif. 1974. Of counsel FTC, N.Y.C., 1962-66, Columbia Pictures, N.Y.C., 1966-69, CBS Records, N.Y.C., 1969-72; asst. gen. counsel Capitol Records, Hollywood, Calif., 1973-74; head bus. affairs Twentieth Century Fox Records, Hollywood, Calif., 1974-76; sr. atty. Motown Record Corp., Hollywood, Calif., 1976-79; assoc. Mason and Sloane, Los Angeles, 1979-84; sole practice Santa Monica, Calif., 1984—; of counsel Mason, Sloane, Gilbert; v.p. Calif. Copyright Conf., 1985-86, pres., 1986-87. Mem. ABA (entertainment law forum com.), Nat. Acad. Recording Arts and Scis., Zeta Beta Tau (exec. trustee 1965). Office: Mason & Gilbert 1299 Ocean Ave PH Santa Monica CA 90401

ROSENBLATT, GERD MATTHEW, chemist; b. Leipzig, Fed. Republic Germany, July 6, 1933; came to U.S., 1935, naturalized, 1940; s. Edgar Fritz and Herta (Fisher) R.; m. Nancy Ann Kaltreider, June 29, 1957 (dec. Jan. 1982); children: Rachel, Paul. BA, Swarthmore Coll., 1955; PhD, Princeton U., 1960; Doctorate in Physics (hon.), Vrijie Universiteit Brusssel, 1989. Chemist Lawrence Radiation Lab., Univ. Calif., 1960-63, cons., guest scientist, 1968-84; from asst. to assoc. prof. chemistry Pa. State U., University Park, 1963-70, prof., 1970-81; assoc. div. leader Los Alamos (N.Mex.) Nat. Lab., 1981-82, chemistry div. leader, 1982-85; dep. dir. Lawrence Berkeley (Calif.) Lab., 1985—; lectr. U. Calif., Berkeley, 1962-63; vis. prof. Vrije U. Brussels, 1973; vis. fellow Southampton U., 1980, King's Coll., Cambridge, 1980; adj. prof. chemistry U. N.Mex., 1981-85; cons. Aerospace Corp., 1979-85, Solar Energy Rsch. Inst., 1980-81, Xerox Corp., 1977-78, Hooker Chem. Co., 1976-78, Los Alamos Nat. Lab, 1978, mem. external adv. com. Ctr. for Materials Sci., 1985—, mem. rev. com. chemistry div., 1985—; mem. rev. com. for chem. engring. div. Argonne Univ. Assn. , 1974-80, chmn. 1977-78; mem. rev. com. for chem. sci. Lawrence Berkeley Lab. , 1984; chmn. rev. com. for chem. and material sci. Lawrence Livermore Nat. Lab. , 1984—; mem. bd. advs. Combustion Rsch. Facility, Sandia Nat. Lab., 1985—; mem. bd. advs. rsch. and devel. div. Lockheed Missiles & Space Co., 1985—; mem. U.S. Nat. Com., Com. on Data for Sci. and Tech., 1986—, Internat. Union of Pure and Applied Chemistry, 1986—. Editor: (jour.) Progress in Solid State Chemistry, 1977—; mem. editorial bd. High Temperature Sci., 1979—; contbr. articles to profl. jours. Du Pont grad. fellow, Princeton U., 1957-58; fellow Solvay Inst., 1973, U.S. Research Council, 1980. Fellow AAAS; mem. Am. Chem. Soc., Am. Physical Soc., Nat. Rsch. Coun. (chmn. high temperature sci. and tech. com. 1977-79, 84-85, mem. panel on exploration of materials sci. and tech. for nat. welfare, 1986—, mem. commn. on materials sci. and engring., 1986-87), Numerical Data Adv. Bd. (chmn. 1986—, solid state scis. com. 1988—). Home: 1177 Miller Ave Berkeley CA 94708 Office: Lawrence Berkeley Lab Cyclotron Rd Berkeley CA 94720

ROSENBLATT, MURRAY, mathematics educator; b. N.Y.C., Sept. 7, 1926; s. Hyman and Esther R.; m. Adylin Lipson, 1949; children—Karin, Daniel. B.S., CCNY, 1946; M.S., Cornell U., 1947, Ph.D. in Math., 1949. Asst. prof. statistics U. Chgo., 1950-55; assoc. prof. math. Ind. U., 1956-59; prof. probability and statistics Brown U., 1959-64; prof. math. U. Calif., San Diego, 1964—; vis. fellow U. Stockholm, 1953; vis. asst. prof. Columbia U., 1955; guest scientist Brookhaven Nat. Lab., 1959; vis. fellow U. Coll., London, 1965-66, Imperial Coll. and Univ. Coll., London, 1972-73, Australian Nat. U., 1976, 79; overseas fellow Churchill Coll., Cambridge U., Eng., 1979; Wald lectr., 1970; vis. scholar Stanford U., 1982. Author: (with U. Grenander) Statistical Analysis of Stationary Time Series, 1957, Random Processes, 1962, (2d edit), 1974, Markov Processes, Structure and Asymptotic Behavior, 1971, Studies in Probability Theory, 1978, Stationary Sequences and Random Fields, 1985; editor: The North Holland Series in Probability and Statistics, 1980; mem. editorial bd. Jour. Theoretical Probability. Recipient Bronze medal U. Helsinki, 1978; Guggenheim fellow, 1965-66, 71-72. Fellow Inst. Math Statistics, AAAS; mem. Internat. Statis. Inst., Nat. Acad. Scis. Office: U Calif Dept Math La Jolla CA 92093

ROSENBLATT, PAUL G., federal judge. AB, U. Ariz., 1958, JD, 1963. Asst. atty. gen. State of Ariz., 1963-66; adminstrv. asst. to U.S. Rep., 1967-72; sole practice, Prescott, 1971-73; judge Yavapai County Superior Ct., Prescott, 1973-84; judge, U.S. Dist. Ct. Ariz., Phoenix, 1984—. Office: US Dist Ct US Courthouse & Fed Bldg 230 N 1st Ave Rm 7012 Phoenix AZ 85025

ROSENBLATT, ROGER ALAN, physician, educator; b. Denver, Aug. 8, 1945; s. Alfred Dreyfus and Judith Ann (Ginsburg) R.; m. Fernne Schnitzer, Sept. 23, 1942; children: Eli Samuel, Benjamin. BA magna cum laude, Harvard U., 1967, MD cum laude, M in Pub. Health, 1971. Diplomate Am. Bd. Family Practice, Nat. Bd. Med. Examiners. Intern internal medicine U. Wash., Seattle, 1971-72, resident in family medicine, 1974; regional med. cons. region X Pub. Health Service, Seattle, 1974-76, dir. Nat. Health Services Corps., 1976-77; asst. prof. dept. family medicine U. Wash., Seattle, 1977-81, assoc. prof. dept. family medicine, 1981-85, prof., vice chmn. dept. family medicine, 1985—; cons. U.S. Agy. for Internat. Devel., 1978, Western Interstate Commn. Higher Edn., 1981-82; vis. prof. medicine U. Auckland, New Zealand, 1983-84, Royal Australia Coll. Gen. Practitioners, Victoria, 1984. Author: Rural Health Care, 1982; contbr. numerous articles on healthcare to profl. jours. Mem. Beyond War, Physicians for Social Responsiblity. Served with USPHS, 1974-77. Mem. Am. Acad. Family Physicians, Am. Pub. Health Assn., Soc. Tchrs. Family Medicine, Nat. Rural Health Assn., Nat. Council Internat. Health, Nat. Acad. Sci. (elected inst. medicine 1987), Am. Rural Health Assn. (Research award 1985), Phi Beta Kappa. Office: U Wash Dept Family Medicine HQ-30 Seattle WA 98195

ROSENBLUM, CARLA NADINE, travel agent, retirement community executive; b. Seattle, Apr. 25, 1937; d. Carl August and Nadine Chaffa (Schwartz) Mahne; m. A. Leon Rosenblum, Feb. 28, 1965; 1 child, Sara Lynnette. BS, Mills Coll., Oakland, Calif., 1959. Buyer, stationery City of Paris Dept. Store, San Francisco, 1959-63, Diamond's Dept. Store, Phoenix, 1963-65; corp. buyer Arkwright Corp., L.A., 1965-66; mgr. various travel agys. San Jose, Calif., 1977-84; supr. Incentive Journeys, San Jose, Calif., 1984-86, Internat. Passages, Santa Clara, Calif., 1986—; ptnr. Willow Glen Villa, San Jose. Mem. San Jose Pacific Area Travel Assn., Travelarians San Jose, Assn. Retail Travel Agts. Democrat. Jewish. Home: 15999 Bohlman Rd Saratoga CA 95070 Office: Willow Glen Villa 1660 Gaton Dr San Jose CA 95125

ROSENBLUM, RICHARD MARK, utility executive; b. N.Y.C., Apr. 28, 1950; s. Victor Sigmund and Julia (Kessler) R.; BS, MS, Rensselaer Poly. Inst., Troy, N.Y., 1973; m. Michele E. Cartier, Aug. 30, 1979; children: Gialisa, Jeremy Scott. Startup engr. Combustion Engring. Inc., Windsor, Conn., 1973-76; engr. So. Calif. Edison Co., Rosemead, 1976-82, project mgr. San Onofre Nuclear Generating Sta., 1982-83, tech. mgr., 1983-84, nuclear safety mgr., 1984-86, mgr. quality assurance, 1986-89, mgr. nuclear regulatory affairs, 1989—. N.Y. State Regents scholar, 1968-73; registered profl. engr., Calif. Mem. Am. Nuclear Soc. (STD com.), Electric Power Research Inst. (nuclear safety analysis com.). Office: 2244 Walnut Grove Rosemead CA 91770

ROSENBLUM, WILLIAM MARC, numismatist; b. Orange, N.J., Apr. 10, 1945; s. Carl and Laura (Root) R.; m. Rita Iris Berkowitz, Aug. 20, 1967; children: Brian, Sarah. BA in History, U. Bridgeport, 1971; cert. in Counterfeit Detection, Colo. Coll., 1973. Owner Wm. Rosenblum/Rare Coins, Evergreen, Colo., 1971—. Mem. editorial bd. Modern World Coins, 13th edit., 1984; editor Judaic Numismatic Newsletter, 1979—; contbr., cons. numerous edits. Standard Catalog of World Coins, Standard Catalog of World Paper Money; contbr. various mags. including Coin World, The Shekel. Mem. steering com., editor newsletter Beth Evergreen (Colo.) Congregation, 1987—; membership chmn. Colo. Libertarian Party, Denver, 1977; founder, active P.A.N.D.A., 1976—. Recipient numerous Customer Service awards Krause Publs., 1974-88. Mem. Am. Numis. Assn. (numerous Edn. awards 1974—), Am. Numis. Soc., Internat. Numis. Soc., Internat. Bank Note Soc., Am. Israel Numis. Assn. (bd. dirs. 1988—), Colo.-Wyo. Numis. Assn. (past v.p.), Israel Numis. Soc. of Colo. (founding pres. 1985—), Classical Numis. Bourse, Numis. Lit. Guild, Judaic Syngraphic Collectors Assn. Jewish. Clubs: Denver Postcard; Evergreen Yacht. Office: PO Box 355 Evergreen CO 80439

ROSENER, BETH, realtor; b. Palo Alto, Calif., Apr. 19, 1940; d. Leland Sylvan and Eleanor R. BA, San Jose State U., 1963. Teller, mgmt. trainee Wells Fargo Bank, San Francisco, 1965-66, asst. mgr. master charge, 1966-69, with personal banking ctr., 1969-71, with mktg., 1971-75, asst. v.p., 1975-77; realtor TRI Realtors, Mill Valley, Calif., 1977—. Bd. dirs. Big Bros./Big Sisters of Marin Inc., San Rafael, Calif., 1976—, pres., 1988-89; bd. dirs. Jr. League San Francisco Inc., 1968-69. Office: TRI Realtors 104 Tiburon Blvd Mill Valley CA 94941

ROSENFIELD, JAMES STEVEN, real estate developer; b. L.A., June 22, 1962; s. Robert Allan and Elyse Harriet (Bernstein) R. BA in Polit. Sci., U. Calif., Berkeley, 1984. Polit. cons. Senator John Tunney, L.A., 1985—; assoc. Cloverleaf Group, Inc., L.A., 1985-87; ptnr. J.S. Rosenfield & Co., L.A., 1987—; developer Sears Roebuck & Co. store, Fresno, Calif. Bd. dirs. L.A. Arts Coun., 1988—. Coro Found. fellow, 1985. Mem. Internat. Coun. Shopping Ctrs. Democrat. Jewish. Office: 1801 Avenue of the Stars Ste 1201 Los Angeles CA 90067

ROSENFIELD, WILLIAM BERNARD, electromechanical engineer, designer; b. Mpls., Aug. 1, 1922; s. Arnold and Bertha (Stern) R.; m. Edith Marion Brown, Sept. 26, 1954; children: Gary Charles, Robert Alan. B of Profl. Arts, Art Ctr. Coll., Pasadena, Calif., 1952; postgrad., U. Minn., 1941-42, 46; student, Walker Art Ctr., Mpls., 1946-47. Indsl. designer Pereira & Luckman, AIA, Los Angeles, 1952-56; product design engr., indsl. engr. Sunbeam Lighting Co. div. Keene Corp., Los Angeles, 1956-60; sr. project engr. space and info. systems div. Radio Corp. Am., Moorestown, N.J., 1960-62; sr. research engr. N.Am. space and info. systems div. Rockwell Internat., Downey, Calif., 1962-65; sr. crew and mission engr. Northrop Space Labs. div. Northrop Corp., Hawthorne, Calif., 1965-66; human factors specialist Lockheed Calif. Co. div. Lockheed Corp., Burbank, Calif., 1966-70; contract design engr., staff engr. splty. lighting and Teledyne Brown engring., Rockwell Marine Systems, Anaheim, Calif., 1970-84; crew systems engr. space sta. systems div. Rockwell Internat., Downey, 1984-88; lighting engr. N.Am. aircraft ops. Rockwell Internat., Lakewood, Calif., 1988—; sr. engr., scientist MD-11 program Douglas Aircraft Co., Long Beach, Calif., 1988—; mem. cons. Illuminating Engring. Soc., Los Angeles, 1963-70. Patentee lighting assemblies and fixtures; contbr. tech. papers to profl. jours. Served to sgt. U.S. Army, 1943-46. Mem. Internat. Soc. Optical Engring., Art Ctr. Coll. Alumni Assn. (life), Mason (lectr. 1946-49), Scottish Rite. Democrat. Jewish. Home: 1345 Cameo Ln Fullerton CA 92631 Office: Douglas Aircraft Co 3855 Lakewood Blvd Long Beach CA 92631

ROSENGARD, RICHARD JAY, psychiatrist; b. Boston, June 30, 1956; s. Jacob Maurice and Beverly (Levine) R.; m. Jane Goldberger, Sept. 5, 1982. BA, Yeshiva U., N.Y.C., 1978; DO, U. New Eng., Biddeford, Mass., 1983. Intern Hillside Hosp., San Diego, 1983-84; resident in psychiatry Good Samaritan Med. Ctr., Phoenix, 1984—, chief resident, 1987; pvt. practice psychiatry Glendale/Phoenix, Ariz., 1988—. Pres. Phoenix Mikv Soc., 1986—. Mem. Am. Psychiat. Assn., AMA, Am. Osteo. Assn., Am. Psychiat. Assn. Office: Thunderbird Behavioral Health Inst 5620 W Thunderbird Rd Ste D-6 Glendale AZ 85306

ROSENKRANZ, ROBERTO PEDRO, pharmacologist; b. Mexico City, Mar. 30, 1950; s. George and Edith R.; m. Heather Blum, Aug. 21, 1983; 1 child, Tamara Ann. AB in Psychology, Stanford U., 1971; PhD in Comparative Pharmacology/Toxicology, U. Calif.-Davis, 1980; MBA U. Santa Clara, 1989. Neurobiologic researcher Instituto Nacional de Neruologia, Mex., 1971-72; Mexican del. Internat. Group on Drug Legis. and Programs, Geneva, 1971-73; dir. rsch. Centro Mexicano de Estudios en Farmacodependencia, 1972-73; rsch. fellow dept. medicine Stanford U., Calif., 1980-82; head inst. ops. and renovascular pharmacology Inst. Pharmacology Syntex Rsch., Palo Alto, Calif., 1982—; cons.; pres. Lic. Luis Echeverria Alvarez. Contbr. articles on pharmacology to profl. jours. Mex. del. Joint U.S.-Mex. Exec. Conf. on Drug Abuse Planning, 1972; Mexican del. UN Social Def. Rsch. Inst., Rome, 1971-72. Mem. AAAS, N.Y. Acad. Scis., Soc. Neurosci., Am. Soc. Pharmacology and Exptl. Therapeutics, Western Pharmacology Soc. (sec. 1988—), Internat. Soc. Study of Xenobiotics, Internat. Soc. Cardiovascular Pharmacology. Office: Syntex Rsch 3401 Hillview Palo Alto CA 94304

ROSENSTEIN, ALLEN BERTRAM, electrical engineering educator; b. Balt., Aug. 25, 1920; s. Morton and Mary (Epstein) R.; m. Betty Lebell; children: Jerry Tyler, Lisa Nan, Adam Mark. B.S. with high distinction, U. Ariz., 1940; M.S., UCLA, 1950, Ph.D., 1958. Elec. engr. Consol. Vultee Aircraft, San Diego, 1940-41; sr. elec. engr. Lockheed Aircraft Corp., Burbank, Calif., 1941-42; chief plant engr. Utility Fan Corp., Los Angeles, 1942-44; prof. engring. UCLA, 1946—; founder, chmn. bd. Inet, Inc., 1947-53, cons. engr., 1954—; founder, chmn. bd. dirs. Pioneer Magnetics, Inc., Pioneer Research Inc., Anadex Instruments Inc.; dir. Internat. Transformer Co., Inc., Fgn. Resource Services; cons. ednl. planning UNESCO, Venezuela, 1974-76. Author: (with others) Engineering Communications, 1965, A Study of a Profession and Professional Education, 1968; contbr. articles to profl. jours.; patentee in field. Bd. dirs. Vista Hill Psychiat. Found. Served with USNR, 1944-46. Fellow IEEE; mem., Am. Soc. Engring. Edn., N.Y. Acad. Scis., AAAS, Sigma Xi, Phi Kappa Phi, Delta Phi Sigma, Tau Beta Pi. Home: 314 S Rockingham St Los Angeles CA 90049

ROSENTHAL, JACK, broadcasting executive; b. Chgo., Aug. 7, 1930; s. Samuel J. and Celia (Weinberg) R.; m. Elaine Lois Brill, May 2, 1954; children: Michael Bruce, Robert Joseph, Richard Scott. BA in History, U. Wyo., 1952. Sec., treas. Buffalo Theatre Corp., 1952-57, No. Wyo. Broadcasting Corp., 1957-64; v.p., gen. mgr. Sta. KTWO Radio and TV, Casper, Wyo., 1964-69; exec. v.p. Harriscope Broadcasting Corp., 1969-77; pres. broadcast div. Harriscope Broadcasting Corp., Los Angeles, 1977-87; pres. Clear Channel Radio, Inc., 1988—; chmn. Wyo. industry adv. com. FCC; dir. Wyo. Nat. Bank, Affiliated Bank Corp. of Wyo.; dir. TV Info. Office, 1984; pres. Clear Channel Radio, Inc., 1988—. Producer (TV film) Conrad Schwiering-Mountain Painter (Western Heritage award 1974). Mem. Wyo. Travel Commn., 1969-71, Wyo. Land and Water Commn., 1965-66, Yellowstone Nat. Park Centennial Commn., 1972, Wyo. Council Arts, 1969, City of Casper Art Fund, 1979-80; bd. dirs. Milward Simpson Endowment, U. Wyo. Found., 1970— ; adv. Nat. Park Service, Dept. Interior, 1974-76; mem. jud. planning com. Wyo. Supreme Ct., 1976-77; mem. citizens stamp adv. com. U.S. Postal Service, 1985—; trustee The Philatelic Found. Served to 1st. lt. U.S. Army, 1952-54, Korea. Recipient Alfred I. DuPont Found. award broadcast journalism, 1965, U.S. Conf. Mayors award for outstanding community service, 1966, Disting. Alumnus award U. Wyo., 1982, Commendation Casper C. of C., 1984; named hon. mem. Shoshoni and Arapahoe Indian Tribes, 1965. Mem. Nat. Assn. Broadcasters (nat. chmn. TV and radio polit. action com. 1977-79, Grover C. Cobb meml. award 1983), Wyo. Assn. Broadcasters (pres. 1963), Fedn. Rocky Mountain States Ednl. TV Com. Office: Sta KTWO 150 N Nichols Ave Casper WY 82601

ROSENTHAL, JOHN DAVID, dentist; b. Portland, Oreg., Feb. 26, 1950; s. Lawrence A. and H. Bertha (Klein) R.; m. Barbara J. Loomis, Apr. 1, 1977; children: Kristin, Benjamin. BS, U. Oreg., 1973; DMD, U. Oreg. Health Sci. U., 1976. Dentist Rosenthal & Rosenthal, DMD, Portland, 1976-79; pvt. practice Portland, 1979—. Dental chmn. United Way of Oreg., Portland, 1985; mem. membership com. Temple Beth Israel, Portland, 1984-87; mem. adv. com. Robison Retirement Home, Portland, 1986—. Fellow Acad. Gen. Dentistry, Acad. Dentistry Internat.; mem. Oreg. Soc. Dentistry for Children, Western Soc. Peridontology, Multnomah Dental Soc. (bd. dirs. 1979-81, pres. 1986), Oreg. Dental Assn. (membership chmn. 1984-88, chmn. mem. svcs. coun. 1988—), Oreg. Acad. Gen. Dentistry (dir. 1986—), Oreg. Health Sci. U. Sch. Dentistry Alumni Assn. (dir. 1987—), Theta Chi. Home: 6565 SW 88th Pl Portland OR 97223 Office: 1110 SW Salmon St Portland OR 97205

ROSENZWEIG, LANCE EVAN, investment banker. BS, Northwestern U., 1984, MS in Mgmt., 1985. Internal cons. Eastman Kodak Co., Rochester, N.Y., 1982-84; mgr. corp. planning Jefferson Smurfit Corp., St. Louis, 1985-87; sr. v.p. Capel Ct. Pacific Inc., L.A., 1987—, also bd. dirs.; pres. Far West Media Corp., L.A., 1987—; bd. dirs. Gen. Investments Am. Inc., L.A. Mem. Assn. Corp. Growth, Australian Am. C. of C., Internat. Bankers Assn. Calif., Tau Beta Pi, Alpha Lambda Delta. Office: Capel Ct Pacific Inc 2049 Century Pk E Ste 840 Los Angeles CA 90067

ROSICH, RAYNER KARL, physicist; b. Joliet, Ill., Aug. 28, 1940; s. Joseph F. and Gretchen (Cox) R.; BS in Physics cum laude with honors, U. Mich., 1962, MS in Physics, 1963; PhD, U. Colo., 1977; MBA, U. Denver, 1982; m. Judy Louise Jackson, Aug. 20, 1966; children: Heidi Ann, Kimberly Ann, Dawn Ann. Teaching fellow and research asst. U. Mich., Ann Arbor, 1962-67; staff, Argonne (Ill.) Nat. Lab. Applied Math. Div., summers 1961-63; physicist, project leader Inst. for Telecommunication Sci., U.S. Dept. Commerce, Boulder, Colo., 1967-80; sr. scientist and program mgr. Electro Magnetic Applications, Inc., Denver, 1980-82; applications mgr. Energy Systems Tech., Inc., Denver, 1982-83, mgr. R&D, 1983; prin. scientist, program mgr. Contel Info. Systems, Inc., Denver, 1983-84, dir. tech. audits, 1985, dir. basic and applied research and devel., 1986; lab. scientist for systems engring. lab. Hughes Aircraft Co., Denver, 1986, lab scientist data systems, 1986—. Vol. judo instr., county recreation dist., 1976-77. Recipient Spl. Achievement award U.S. Dept. Commerce, 1974, Outstanding Performance award, 1978, Sustained Superior Performance award, 1979; Libbey-Owens-Ford Glass Co./U. Mich Phoenix Meml. fellow, 1964-66; NSF Summer fellow, 1965. Mem. Am. Phys. Soc., AAAS, IEEE, Assn. Computing Machinery, Am. Assn. Artificial Intelligence, Sigma Xi, Phi Kappa Phi. Home: 7932 W Nichols Ave Littleton CO 80123 Office: Hughes Aircraft Co Space and Communications Group 16800 E Centre Tech Pkwy Aurora CO 80011

ROSKELLEY, CONRAD ARTHUR, financial planner; b. Preston, Idaho, Feb. 7, 1941; s. Arthur Franklin and Wanda (Peterson) R.; m. Valory Richards, Aug. 15, 1969; children: Alyson, Jared, Corynn. Cert., Coll. Fin. Planning, Denver, 1982. Cert. fin. planner. Ins. agt. Ability Ins. Agy., Logan, Utah, 1967-68, Farmers Ins. Group, Logan, 1968-72, Alpha Ins. Ctr., Tempe, Ariz., 1972-80; fin. planner Omega Fin. Planning, Tempe, 1980-82, Cornerstone Fin. Planning, Mesa, Ariz., 1982—. Contbr. articles to profl. jours. Pres. Pres.'s Com. of Handicapped, Phoenix, 1978; chmn. Cub Scout com. Tempe council Boy Scouts Am., 1984-87. Mem. Internat. Assn. Fin. Planning, Inst. Cert. Fin. Planners, Internat. Assn. Fin. Planning (chmn. coms. 1983-86). Republican. Mem. LDS Church. Home: 1506 E Laguna Dr Tempe AZ 85282 Office: Cornerstone Fin Planning 1930 S Alma Sch Ste C-109 Mesa AZ 85210

ROSKY, BURTON SEYMOUR, lawyer; b. Chgo., May 28, 1927; s. David T. and Mary W. (Zelkin) R.; m. Leatrice J. Darrow, June 16, 1951; children: David Scott, Bruce Alan. Student, Ill. Inst. Tech., 1944-45; B.S., UCLA, 1948; J.D., Loyola U., Los Angeles, 1953. Bar: Calif. 1954, U.S. Supreme Ct 1964, U.S. Tax Ct 1964; C.P.A., Calif. Auditor City Los Angeles, 1948- 51; with Beidner, Temkin & Ziskin (C.P.A.s), Los Angeles, 1951-52; supervising auditor Army Audit Agy., 1952-53; practiced law Los Angeles, Beverly Hills, 1954—; partner Duskin & Rosky, 1972-82, Rosky, Landau & Fox, 1982—; lectr. on tax and bus. problems. Judge pro tem Beverly Hills Mcpl. Ct.; mem. Los Angeles Mayor's Community Adv. Council. Contbr. profl. publs. Charter supporting mem. Los Angeles County Mus. Arts; contbg. mem. Assocs. of Smithsonian Instn.; charter mem. Air and Space Mus; mem. Am. Mus. Natural History, Los Angeles Zoo; supporting mem. Los Angeles Mus. Natural History; mem. exec. bd. So. Calif. council Nat. Fedn. Temple Brotherhoods, mem. nat. exec. bd. Served with USNR, 1945-46. Walter Henry Cook fellow Loyola Law Sch. Fellow Jewish Chautauqua Soc. (life mem.); mem. Am. Arbitration Assn. (nat. panel arbitrators), Am. Assn. Attys.-C.P.A.s (charter mem. pres. 1968), Calif. Assn. Attys.-C.P.A.s (charter mem., pres. 1963), Calif. Soc. C.P.A.s, Calif., Beverly Hills, Century City, Los Angeles County bar assns., Am. Judicature Soc., Chancellors Assocs. UCLA, Tau Delta Phi, Phi Alpha Delta.; mem. B'nai B'rith. Jewish (mem. exec. bd., pres. temple, pres. brotherhood). Club: Mason. Office: 8383 Wilshire Blvd Beverly Hills CA 90211

ROSMINI, GARY DAVID, financial marketing executive, consultant; b. Sewickley, Pa., Dec. 20, 1952; s. Silvio and Evelyn (Casciola) R.; m. Vivian Hooks, Jan. 7, 1978 (div. July 1984). BA, Pa. State U., 1975. Acct. mgr. Atwood-Vandell Assocs., Inc., N.Y.C., 1976-80, Clayton Brokerage, N.Y.C., 1980-81; assoc. v.p. Whitehall Investors Internat., Inc., N.Y.C., 1981-82; v.p. Monetary Futures Inc., N.Y.C., 1982-84; regional mktg. dir. Barrick Group, New Haven, Conn., 1984-86; pres. Rosmini Assocs., San Raphael, Calif., 1986-88; regional mgr. Chilmark Commodities, Emeryville, Calif., 1987-88; exec. v.p. Calif. Custom Constrn., Ignacio, Calif., 1988—; mem. bd. advisors Pacific Investment Banking Group, Portland, Oreg., 1986—; bd. dirs. Superior Robotics Am., Petaluma, Calif., 1983-84; cons. in field. Creative dir. corp. brochure, 1986; copy writer bus. publ., 1983-84. Foster parent Save the Children, Ind., 1983-86, 88—, Found. for Inner Peace, N.Y.C., 1976-78; choir dir. Saint Frances Cabrini Ch., Monaca, Pa., 1970-72; mem. Sewickley (Pa.) Civic Symphony, 1970-72, N.Y.C. Choral Soc., 1979-81. Recipient Billy Mitchell award CAP, 1970. Mem. Internat. Assn. Fin. Planning. (bd. dirs. 1981-84), Pa. State Alumni Assn. Home: 125 Wild Horse Valley Dr Novato CA 94947

ROSS, ALVIN, manufacturing executive; b. Minot, N.D., Apr. 4, 1922; s. Samuel and Goldie (Perlin) R.; m. Barbara Wechsler, Apr. 14, 1946; children: Talby W., Gelb, Elyse M. Pazak, Mark W. Ross. BA, U. Wash., 1946, Master degree, 1958. Sales mgr. midwest H.D. Lee Co., Mission, Kans., 1963-72; v.p. Wrangler Boys div., regional mgr. midwest Blue Bell Corp. (Wrangler Co.), Greensboro, N.C., 1972-85; V.P. Cheerful Internat. Corp., Lavon Sportswear, City of Industry, Calif., 1985—. Office: Lavon Sportswear 19433 E San Jose Ave City of Industry CA 91748

ROSS, CLARENCE SELLERS, III, financial executive; b. Phila., May 29, 1955; s. Clarence S. Jr. and Bessie Louise R.; m. Carolyn Evans, Nov. 28, 1980; children: Tajuana, Victoria, Evan. BA in Econs., Dickinson Coll., 1976; MBA, Harvard U., 1980. CPA, Pa. Acct. in charge Coopers & Lybrand, Phila., 1976-78; sr. fin. analyst Corning (N.Y.) Glass Works, 1980-81; supr. fin. control Corning, Surabaya, Indonesia, 1981-82; bus. contr. Corning, 1982-83; mgr. fin. analysis Pepsi-Cola Internat., Purchase, N.Y., 1983-87; area chief fin. officer Pepsi-Cola Co., San Francisco, 1987—. Mem. Nat. Assn. Black Accts., Nat. Assn. Accts., Planning Forum. Presbyterian. Home: 1056 C Larch St Moraga CA 94556 Office: Pepsi Cola Co 30 Van Ness Ave San Francisco CA 94108

ROSS, DEBORAH LYNN (DEBBIE ROSS), reporter, photographer; b. Pitts., Mar. 29, 1961; d. David William and Joan Muriel (Reinhardt) R. BS in Journalism, Ball State U., 1984. Reporter, photographer High Country Ind. Press, Belgrade, Mont., 1986-87, Dillon (Mont.) Tribune-Examiner, 1987—. Recipient first prizes for best sports photo and best editorial page Mont. Newspaper Assn., 1987, third place award Nat. Newspaper Assn., 1988. Mem. Nat. Press Photographer's Assn. (best photo 1983, 1984), Mont. Press Assn. Democrat. Presbyterian. Home: PO Box 749 Dillon MT 59725 Office: Dillon Tribune-Examiner Dillon MT 59725

ROSS, DENNIS HAMILTON, civil engineer; b. Lancaster, Calif., Oct. 15, 1949; s. Donald Hensel and Elizabeth E. Ross; divorced; children: Scott, Stephen; m. Susan Lynne Spencer, May 7, 1983. AS, Mt. Hood Community Coll., 1972; BS, Portland (Oreg.) State U., 1976; MA in Mgmt., U. Redlands, 1988, MBA, 1989. Registered profl. engr., Calif., Oreg., Wash. Civil engr. City of Portland, 1972-78; city engr. City of Silverton, Oreg., 1979-80; mgr. engring. Mitchell & Nelson Assocs., Inc., Portland, 1980-81; asst. dir. pub. works City of Vancouver, Wash., 1981-85; engr. City of La Mesa, Calif., 1985-89; v.p., engr. Mgmt. Svcs. Inst., Inc., La Mirada, Calif., 1989—. Recipient Merit award Am. Soc. Landscape Architects, 1981. Mem. ASCE, Am. Pub. Works Assn. (faculty edn. found. 1984—, bd. dirs. San Diego/Imperial chpt. 1987-89, sec. 1989—), Water Pollution Control Fedn. Office: Mgmt Svcs Inst Inc Firestone Blvd La Mirada CA 90638

ROSS, ERNEST, poultry nutritionist; b. N.Y.C., Dec. 23, 1920; s. George and Mary (Mendelson) R.; m. Mary Elizabeth Krausnick, Jan. 9, 1949; children: Stephanie Ann, Walter Patrick, Jonathan McDonough, Sean Nuuan. BS, U. Ariz., 1946; MS, Ohio State U., 1951, PhD, 1955. Asst. prof. U. Hawaii, Honolulu, 1957-60, assoc. prof., 1960-65, prof. poulty nutrition, 1965—. Contbr. articles to sci. jours. Served to sgt. USAF, 1946-47. Fulbright scholar U. Queensland, Brisbane, Australia, 1962-63. Mem. Poultry Sci. Assn., Worlds's Poultry Sci. Assn. Democrat. Mem. Unitarian Ch. Home: 1909 Kakela Dr Honolulu HI 96822 Office: U Hawaii at Manoa Dept of Animal Sci 1800 E West Rd Honolulu HI 96822

ROSS, GARY MCCABE, dentist; b. San Diego, Apr. 18, 1952; s. John Stillman and Patricia Ann (Toomey) R. BS, U. New Mex., 1976; DDS, U. Mo., 1980. Pvt. practice, Albuquerque; cons. Children's Psychiat. Ctr., Albuquerque, 1980-88, Albuquerque Christian Children's Ctr., 1989. Mem. Acad. Gen. Dentistry, ADA. Republican. Office: 3500 Constitution NE Albuquerque NM 87106

ROSS, GLYNN, opera administrator; b. Omaha, Dec. 15, 1914; s. Herman and Ida (Carlson) R.; m. Angelamaria Solimene, Nov. 15, 1946; children: Stephanie, Claudia, Melanie, Anthony. Student, Leland Powers Sch. Theater, Boston, 1937-39. bd. dirs. O.P.E.R.A. Am., Nat. Opera Inst., Soc. for Germanic Music Culture; founder, dir, Pacific N.W. Festival, 1975—. Opera stage dir., U.S., Can., 1939-63, debut, San Francisco Opera, 1948, gen. dir., Seattle Opera Assn., Inc., 1963-83, dir., Ariz. Opera, 1983—. Served to 1st lt. AUS, 1942-47. Office: Ariz Opera Assn 3501 N Mountain Ave Tucson AZ 85719

ROSS, HARVEY MYRON, physician; b. Denver, June 10, 1929; s. Marion B. and Beatrice L.R. PhB, U. Chgo., 1949; MD, Emory U., 1954. Diplomate Am. Bd. Psychiatry. Staff psychiatrist Grace Sq. Hosp., N.Y.C., 1960-65, clin. dir., 1965-68; pvt. practice N.Y.C., 1968-72, L.A., 1972—; dir. The Huxley Inst. for Biosocial Research, 1979-88. Author: Fighting Depression, 1975; co-author: Hypoglycemia: The Disease Your Dr. Won't Treat, 1978, The Executive Success Diet, 1987. Lt. USN, 1955-57. Fellow Acad. Orthomolecular Psychiatry (pres. 1980-85); mem. Am. Psychiatric Assn., Internat. Coll. Applied Nutrition (pres. 1981-83). Office: 7080 Hollywood Blvd #1015 Los Angeles CA 90028

ROSS, HUGH COURTNEY, electrical engineer; b. Dec. 31, 1923; s. Clare W. and Jeanne F. Ross; m. Sarah A. Gordon (dec.); m. Patricia A. Malloy; children: John C., James G., Robert W. Student, Calif. Inst. Tech., 1942, San Jose State U., 1946-47; BSEE, Stanford U., 1950, postgrad., 1954. Registered profl. elec. engr., Calif. Instr. San Benito (Calif.) High Sch. and Jr. Coll., 1950-51; chief engr. vacuum power switches Jennings Radio Mfg. Corp., San Jose, Calif., 1951-62; chief engr. ITT Jennings, San Jose, Calif., 1962-64; pres. Ross Engring. Corp., Campbell, Calif., 1964—. Contbr. articles to tech. jours.; patentee in field. Fellow IEEE (chmn. Santa Clara Valley subsect. 1960-61), mem. Am. Vacuum Soc., Am. Soc. Metals, Pacific Coast Electronics Assn. Home: 11915 Shadybrook Ct Saratoga CA 95070 Office: 540 Westchester Dr Campbell CA 95008

ROSS, JANET, retired English educator; b. Duluth, Minn., Apr. 19, 1914; d. Guy Whittier Chadbourn and Helen (Mason) Ross. Student, Carleton Coll., 1931-32; BA, U. Minn., 1935, MA, 1941; PhD, U. Iowa, 1960. Asst. prof. English Fla. State U., Tallahassee, 1949-52, Macalester Coll., St. Paul, 1957-60; instr. English U. Iowa, Iowa City, 1952-54, 55-57, U. B.C. (Can.), Vancouvaer, 1960-62; prof. English, coord. MA teaching English as fgn. lang. Ball State U., Muncie, Ind., 1961-80; emeritus prof. Ball State U., Muncie, 1980—; vis. prof. U. Colo., Boulder, summers 1956-58, 60, 71-72, 83-85, Pontificia U. Rio Grande do Sol, Porto Alegre, Brazil, 1973; guest lectr. Montgomery (Md.) Community Coll., 1977, U. Saga (Japan), 1980, U. Panama, Panama City, 1981. Co-author: Language and Life in the U.S.A., 1961, 4th edit., 1982, To Write English, 1965, 3rd edit., 1984; author: Understanding English, 1982. Fulbright fellow, Netherlands, 1954-55; Danforth Found. grantee U. Mich., 1964; Nat. Assn. Fgn. Student Affairs travel study grantee Yale U., 1962, travel grantee, France, 1966. Mem. Tchrs. English to Speakers Other Langs. (regional sec. 1976-80), Colo. Authors League (sec. 1987—). Home: 500 Mohawk Dr Apt 606 Boulder CO 80303

ROSS, JOHN, physical chemist; b. Vienna, Austria, Oct. 2, 1926; came to U.S., 1940; s. Mark and Anna (Krecmar) R.; m. Virginia Franklin (div.); children: Elizabeth A., Robert K.; m. Eva Miller Madarasz. BS, Queens Coll., 1948; PhD, MIT, 1951; D (hon.), Weizmann Inst. Sci., Rehovot, Israel, 1984, Queens Coll., SUNY, 1987, U. Bordeaux, France, 1987. Prof. chemistry Brown U., Providence, 1953-66; prof. chemistry MIT, Cambridge, 1966-80, chmn. dept., 1966-71; prof. Stanford (Calif.) U., 1980—, chmn. dept., 1983-89; cons. to industries, 1979—; mem. bd. govs. Weizmann Inst., 1971—. Author: Physical Chemistry, 1980; editor Molecular Beams, 1966; contbr. articles to profl. jours. Served as 2d lt. U.S. Army, 1944-46. Fellow AAAS, Am. Phys. Soc.; mem. Nat. Acad. Scis., Am. Chem. Soc. Home: 738 Mayfield Ave Stanford CA 94305 Office: Stanford U Dept Chemistry Stanford CA 94305

ROSS, JOSEPH JAY, lawyer, advertising executive; b. N.Y.C., Dec. 4, 1937; s. Martin and Frances (Gelb) R. BA, U. Miami, Coral Gables, Fla., 1959; JD, Northrup U., 1976. Bar: Calif. 1977. TV dir. Bendix Field Engring., Pasadena, Calif., 1970-71; regional mgr., lawyer Marvin Advt. Co., Chgo., 1971—; pvt. practice law L.A., 1977—; sec. W. J. Asher and Co. Inc., Calabasas, Calif., 1978—. Active Beverly Hills Mens Charities, L.A., 1986, 87, 88, The Guardians, L.A., 1987. Capt. U.S. Army, 1959-69. Mem. State Bar Calif. Republican. Jewish. Home and Office: 3435 Violet Trail Calabasas CA 91302

ROSS, JUDITH PARIS, life insurance executive; b. Boston, Dec. 23, 1939; d. Max and Ruth Paris; ed. Boston U., 1961, UCLA, 1978; grad. Life Underwriting Tng. Council, 1978; 1 son, Adam Stuart. Producer, co-host Checkpoint TV show, Washington, 1967-71; hostess Judi Says TV show, Washington, 1969; brokerage supr., specialist impaired risk underwriting Beneficial Nat. Life Ins. Co. (now Nat. Benefit Life), Beverly Hills, Calif., 1973-82, dir. Salary Savs. program for West Coast, 1982-87; ins. and benefits specialist, cons. Alliance Assocs., 1987—; mktg. dir. Brougher Ins. Group, 1982-87; ins. and benefits specialist Alliance Assocs., Beverly Hills, 1987—; featured speaker ins. industry seminars. Active local PTA, Boy Scouts Am., Beverly Hills local politics; mem. early childhood edn. adv. com. Beverly Hills Unified Sch. Dist., 1977. Mem. Nat. Assn. Life Underwriters, Calif. Assn. Life Underwriters (dir. W. Los Angeles 1980—, v.p. chpt. 1982—, chmn. pub. relations), West Los Angeles Life Underwriters Assn. (v.p. fin. 1983-84). Office: Alliance Assocs 449 S Beverly Dr #206 Beverly Hills CA 90212

ROSS, KATHLEEN ANNE, college president; b. Palo Alto, Calif., July 1, 1941; d. William Andrew and Mary Alberta (Wilburn) R. B.A., Ft. Wright Coll., 1964; M.A., Georgetown U., 1971; Ph.D., Claremont Grad. Sch., 1979. Cert. tchr., Wash. Secondary tchr. Holy Names Acad., Spokane, Wash., 1964-70; dir. research and planning Province Holy Names, Wash. State, 1972-73; v.p. acads. Ft. Wright Coll., Spokane, 1973-81; research asst. to dean Claremont Grad. Sch., Calif., 1977-78; assoc. faculty mem. Harvard U., Cambridge, Mass., 1981; pres. Heritage Coll., Toppenish, Wash., 1981—; cons. Wash. State Holy Names Schs., 1971-73; coll. accrediting assn. evaluator N.W. Assn. Schs. and Colls., Seattle, 1975—; dir. Holy Names Coll., Oakland, Calif., 1979—; cons. Yakima Indian Nation, Toppenish, 1975—; speaker, cons. in field. Author: (with others) Multicultural Pre-School Curriculum, 1977, A Crucial Agenda: Improving Minority Student Success, 1989; Cultural Factors in Success of American Indian Students in Higher Education, 1978. Chmn. Internat. 5-Yr. Convocation of Sisters of Holy Names, Montreal, Que., Can., 1981; TV Talk show host Spokane Council of Chs., 1974-76. Recipient E.K. and Lillian F. Bishop Founds. Youth Leader of Yr. award, 1986; Holy Names medal Ft. Wright Coll., 1981; Disting. Citizenship Alumna award Claremont Grad. Sch., 1986; named Yakima Herald Rep. Person of Yr. 1987; numerous grants for projects in multicultural higher edn., 1974—. Mem. Nat. Assn. Ind. Colls. and Univs. (bd. dirs.), Nat. Cath. Edn. Assn. (N.W. regional assoc. 1974-82), Am. Assn. Higher Edn., Soc. Intercultural Edn., Tng. and Research, Sisters of Holy Names of Jesus and Mary. Roman Catholic. Office: Heritage Coll Rte 3 Box 3540 Toppenish WA 98948

ROSS, LANSON CLIFFORD, JR., broadcaster, author, consultant; b. Killdeer, N.D., June 23, 1936; s. Lanson Charles and Mabel (Smith) R.; children—David F., Lanson III. BA in Biblical Studies, Seattle Pacific U., 1960; M. Sacred Theology, Internat. Coll., 1984; D of Ministries, 1986. Pres. Evangelistic Enterprises, Inc., Seattle, 1960—; v.p. Christa Ministries, Seattle, 1972-75; founder Planned Living Seminars, Seattle, 1978—. Club: Seattle Yacht. Author: Total Life Prosperity, 1983; Give Your Children a Target, 1985, Take Charge of Your Life, 1986, The Bubble Burst, 1987; producer 5 vol. video seminar A Planned Life Style, 1986, and film A Time to Grow (J.C. Mc Pheeters award 1988). Home: 4555 S Mission Rd #347 Tucson AZ 95714 Office: 3105 E Oasis De Palmeras Tucson AZ 85716

ROSS, MARY ANN L., librarian; b. Abington, Pa., Apr. 3, 1943; d. George Ora and Mary Begbie (Lockhart) Ladner; m. Arthur H.M. Ross, Feb. 20, 1971 (div. July 1981); children: Andrew L.M., Mary Kathryn. BA in Internat. Rels., U. So. Calif., 1965; MS in LS, Simmons Coll., 1967; MBA, U. San Diego, 1980. Social worker Los Angeles County, Pasadena, Calif., 1965-66; librarian Lincoln Lab., MIT, Lexington, 1967-71, M/A-Com Govt. Systems, San Diego, 1980--; head reader svcs. Framingham (Mass.) State Coll., 1971-75. Troop leader Girl Scouts Am., San Diego, 1986-87; troop com. mem. Boy Scouts Am., San Diego, 1988--. U. San Diego fellow, 1978-80. Mem. Spl. Libraries Assn. (treas. 1986-88). Republican. Roman Catholic. Home: 12064 Medoc Ln San Diego CA 92131 Office: M/A-Com Govt Systems 3033 Science Park Rd San Diego CA 92121

ROSS, PAMELA JANE, computer scientist; b. Phoenix, Apr. 29, 1958; d. William Albert and Marian Jean (Morgan) R.; m. Gregory Martin Eitzman,

May 23, 1981 (div. 1984). BS in Math., Ariz. State U., 1981. Software engr. Digital Equipment Corp., Colorado Springs, Colo., 1981-86; head electronic warfare simulation sect. Naval Weapons Ctr., China Lake, Calif., 1986—. Mem. IEEE (mem. Computer Soc.). Lutheran. Office: Naval Weapons Ctr Commander Code 31332 China Lake CA 93555

ROSS, ROBERT DONALD, banker; b. Great Falls, Mont., June 23, 1948; s. Donald Robert and Jesslyn Edith (Tipton) R.; m. Amy Baxter Colburn, Sept. 21, 1985; 1 child, Caitlin Baxter. BA in Bus., U. Mont., 1971. Lic. in real estate and ins., Utah. Asst. mgr. Edgewater Inn, Missoula, Mont., 1972-73; adv. coordinator Ambassador Film Releasing, Salt Lake City, 1974; real estate assoc. Landmark Realtors, Salt Lake City, 1975-78; loan officer Comml. Security Bank, Salt Lake City, 1978-83; coordinator real estate Am. 1st Mortgage, Salt Lake City, 1983-84; v.p., mgr. real estate Capital City Bank, Salt Lake City, 1984—. Vol., East Seals, United Way, Utah Heart Assn., Salt Lake City. Mem. Home Builders Utah, Sports Mall, U. Mont. Alumni Assn. Republican. Presbyterian. Home: 4098 S 1400 E Salt Lake City UT 84124 Office: Capital City Bank 515 S 700 E Salt Lake City UT 84102

ROSS, RUSSELL, pathologist, educator; b. St. Augustine, Fla., May 25, 1929; s. Samuel and Minnie (DuBoff) R.; m. Jean Long Teller, Feb. 22, 1956; children: Valerie Regina, Douglas Teller. A.B., Cornell U., 1951; D.D.S., Columbia U., 1955; Ph.D., U. Wash., 1962; DSc (hon.P, Med. Coll. of Pa., 1987. Intern Columbia-Presbyn. Med. Ctr., 1955-56, USPHS Hosp., Seattle, 1956-58; spl. research fellow pathology sch. medicine U. Wash., 1958-62, asst. prof. pathology and oral biology sch. medicine and denistry, 1962-65, asso. prof. pathology sch. medicine and dentistry, 1965-69, prof. sch. medicine and dentistry, 1969—, adj. prof. biochemistry sch. medicine and dentistry, 1978—, assoc. dean for sci. affairs sch. medicine, 1971-78, chmn. dept. pathology sch. medicine, 1982—; vis. scientist Strangeways Research Lab., Cambridge, Eng.; mem. research com. Am. Heart Assn.; mem. adv. bd. Found. Cardiologique Princess Liliane, Brussels, Belgium; life fellow Clare Hall, Cambridge U.; mem. adv. council Nat. Heart, Lung and Blood Inst., NIH, 1978-81; vis. prof. Royal Soc. Medicine, U.K., 1987. Mem. editorial bd. Proceedings Exptl. Biology and Medicine, 1971-86, Jour. Cell Biology, 1972-74, Exptl. Cell Research, Jour. Exptl. Medicine, Growth Factors, Am. Jour. Pathology, Internat. Cell Biology jour.; assoc. editor: Arteriosclerosis, Jour. Cellular Physiology, Jour. Cellular Biochemistry; reviewing editorial bd. Science mag.; contbr. articles to profl. jours. Trustee Seattle Symphony Orch. Recipient Birnberg Research award Columbia U., 1975, Gordon Wilson medal Am. Clin. and Climatol. Assn., 1981; named to Inst. Medicine, Nat. Acad. Scis.; Japan Soc. Promotion of Sci. fellow, 1985, Guggenheim fellow, 1966-67. Fellow AAAS; mem. Am. Soc. Cell Biology, Tissue Culture Assn., Gerontol. Soc., Am. Assn. Pathologists, Internat. Soc. Cell Biology, Electron Microscope Soc. Am., Am. Heart Assn. (fellow Council on Arteriosclerosis), Royal Micros. Soc., Harvey Soc. (hon.), Am. Soc. Biol. Chemists, Belgian Acad. Medicine (fgn. corr. mem.), Sigma Xi. Home: 4811 NE 42d St Seattle WA 98105 Office: U Wash Sch Medicine Seattle WA 98195

ROSS, SIDNEY, past company president; b. Saskatoon, Sask., Can., Apr. 15, 1914; came to U.S. 1924; s. Nathan and Bertha (Singer) Rosenbaltt; m. Ruth Douglas Ross, Dec. 25, 1943; children: Ronnee, Heidi. BS, U. Calif., Berkeley, 1936. Plant mgr. Stanislaus Food, Modesto, Calif., 1946-50; pres. Martinez, Canners, Calif., 1950-55, NCC Foods, San Jose, Calif., 1955-70, Glorietta Foods, San Jose, Calif., 1970-75. Bd. dirs. John Muir Hosp. Found., Walnut Creek, Calif., 1980-87; chmn. planning commn. Walnut Creek, 1961. Calif. Food Processors, Sacramento. Republican. Jewish. Home: 3711 Terra Granada 3A Walnut Creek CA 94595 Office: Sidney Ross Assocs 33 Quail Ct Ste 104 Walnut Creek CA 94596

ROSS, STANLEY RALPH, writer, publisher; b. N.Y.C., July 22, 1940; s. Morris Harvey and Blanche (Turer) R.; m. Neila Hyman, Dec. 14, 1957; children: Andrew Steven, Lisa Michelle Turer, Nancy Ellen. Student, Pratt Inst.; DD, Universal Life Ch., Modesto, Calif., 1973, PhD, 1976. Self-employed photographer N.Y.C., 1956; copywriter Fuller, Smith & Ross, Los Angeles, 1956-60, Universal Pictures, Los Angeles, 1960-61; advt. exec. Universal Studios, Universal City, Calif., 1960-62; program exec. ABC-TV, Los Angeles, 1961-63; creative dir. Cole, Fischer & Rogow, Beverly Hills, Calif., 1963-65, Becker Advt., Long Beach, Calif., 1964-65; pres., freelance film and TV writer Neila, Inc., Los Angeles, 1965—; guest lectr. U. So. Calif., Calif. Luth. Coll., Los Angeles Coll., Sherwood Oaks U., others; tchr. writing UCLA; cons. in field; exec. v.p., bd. dirs. Cine Books, Inc., Evanston, Ill., 1983—; bd. dirs. The Writers Group, Los Angeles, 1985—, Laurelwood Prodns., Hollywood, Calif., 1986—. Author: Games For Planes, 1974, Speak When You Hear The Beep, 1975, Swan Song, Any Port in a Storm; writer: (TV programs) All In The Family, The Monkees, Batman, The Man From UNCLE; developer programs Wonder Woman, The Kallikaks, The Electric Co. The Monster Squad, The Challenge of the Sexes; Scriptwriter Banacek, Colombo, Kids, Inc., (TV films) Coffee, Tea or Me?, Gold of the Amazon Women, Murder at the Mardi Gras, The Town That Went on a Diet, (films) The Answer, It Happened Tomorrow, Jojo, Rodeo Drive, Follow Me; editor, author: (with Jay Robert Nash) The Motion Picture Guide, feature film ency., 12 vols; actor appeared in (TV) Punky Brewster, The Facts of Life, Falcoln Crest, Ellery Queen, Hart to Hart, Superior Court, Family Medical Center, Bill Cosby Show, Double Life of Henry Phyfe, Divorce Court, (films) Sleeper, Romantic Comedy, John Goldfarb Please Come Home, Tony Rome, numerous commls.; voice over cartoons, commls.; columnist Restaurant Row mag., Master Chef mag. Vol. The Thalians, Beverly Hills, 1972—, Nosotros, Los Angeles, 1985—. Recipient UNICEF award, 1974, West Los Angeles Coll. Presdl. citation, 1974, Carson (Calif.) citation, 1973, Cert. Appreciation Personal Freedom Alliance, 1974, Inkpot award San Diego Comicon, 1977, Emmy award nomination Nat. Acad. TV Arts and Scis., 1970, 71, 72, Golden Eagle awards, Nat. Assn. Theater Owners awards,3 Emmy nominations Nat. Acad. TV Arts and Scis. Mem. Writers Guild Am. West (award 1971, 72, 74), Producers Guild, Dirs. Guild, Dramatists Guild, Screen Actors Guild, AFTRA, ASCAP, Hon. Order Ky. Cols, TV Acad. Republican. Mem. Universal Life Ch. Club: Saints and Sinners (Los Angeles). Home: 451 Beverwil Dr Beverly Hills CA 90212 Office: Neila Inc 7865 Willoughbye Ave Los Angeles CA 90046

ROSS, SUE BARBARA, interior designer; b. Phila., May 27, 1940; d. Martin Peter and Lillian (Jaffee) Blumberg; (div. 1983); 1 child, Jennifer Lynn. Student, UCLA, 1983. Owner, designer Sue Ross Designs, Los Angeles, 1971-73; ptnr. R&R Interiors, Beverly Hills, Calif., 1973-81; prin., creative dir. SRD, Inc., Los Angeles, 1981—; instr. UCLA, 1988—. Author, artist: (with others) Four Seasons, 1983; prins. works include Bigelow-Chgo., Bigelow Huega, Chgo (AIA award 1986), Heitman Fin., Birtcher Properties, Pacific Crest Carpet Mills, Designweave Carpet Mills. Founder, pres. Legal Study Soc., Los Angeles, 1981. Mem. Internat. Bus. Designers, Color Mktg. Group, Network Exec. Women, Am. Women in Architecture, Women in Design. Office: SRD Inc 2710 Claray Dr Los Angeles CA 90077

ROSS, SUSAN JULIA, lawyer; b. Phila., July 24, 1943; d. Herbert Joseph and Susan Eshleman (Reese) R.; BA, magna cum laude, U. Pa., 1965, JD magna cum laude, 1969; postgrad. N.Y. U. Law Sch., 1972-75. Bar: N.Y., 1971, N.Mex., 1976, U.S. Dist. Ct. (so. and ea. dists.) N.Y., U.S. Dist. Ct. N.Mex., U.S. Ct. Appeals (2d cir.), U.S. Tax Ct.; assoc. Dewey, Ballantine, Bushby, Palmer & Wood, N.Y.C., 1969-76; ptnr. Natelson & Ross, Taos, N.Mex., 1976—; vis. assoc. prof. law U. Oreg., 1978; dir. Beneficial Corp., Wilmington, Del., 1979—. Trustee Millicent Rogers Mus., Taos, 1979—. Thouron-U. Pa. fellow, Oxford U., 1969-70; Am. Scandinavian Assn. fellow, Stockholm U., 1970. Mem. Phi Beta Kappa, Order Coif. Editor U. Pa. Law Rev., 1967-69; contbr. in field articles to jours. Democrat. Avocations: skiing, tennis, scuba diving, windsurfing, horseback riding.

ROSS, TERENCE WILLIAM, architect; b. Saginaw, Mich., Sept. 27, 1935; s. Oran Lewis and Drucilla (Chadman) R.; BArch, U. Mich., 1958; m. Patricia Ann Marshall, Sept. 27, 1974; children by previous marriage: Deborah, David. Designer, Roger W. Peters Constrn. Co., Fond du Lac, Wis., 1958-62; draftsman Kenneth Clark, Architect, Santa Fe, N.Mex., 1962-63, Holien & Buckley, Architects, Santa Fe, 1963-64; office mgr. Philippe Register, Architect, Santa Fe, 1964-68; v.p. Register, Ross, & Brunet architects, engrs., Santa Fe, 1968-71; v.p. Luna-Ross & Asso., 1971-77; staff CNWC Architects, Tucson, to 1981, ADP Architects, 1981-89; sr. architect med. ctr. campus, U. Calif., Davis, 1989—. Vice chmn. N.Mex. R.R. Authority, 1969-74, sec., 1970-72. Bd. dirs. Colo., N.Mex. Soc. Preservation of Narrow Gauge. Recipient award for hist. preservation N.Mex. Arts Commn., 1971, award for outstanding svcs.to community Santa Fe Press Club, 1972; named col. aide-de-camp State of N.Mex., 1968, hon. mem. staff atty. gen. Mem. AIA (chpt. pres. 1970, dir.), Constrn. Specifications Inst., N.Mex. Soc. Architects (dir. 1972), Ariz. Soc. Architects, N.Mex. R.R. Authorities (chmn. joint exec. com. 1970-74), San Gabriel Hist. Soc. (hon.), Alpha Rho Chi, Sashay Rounders Sq. Dance Club (pres. 1974), Diamond Squares Sq. Dance Club, Railroad Club (pres. N.Mex. 1969, 70, dir.). Author: Track of the Cats. Home and Office: 5050 N Avenida de La Colina Tucson AZ 85749

ROSS, VICTOR JULIUS, school superintendent; b. Salina, Kans., Mar. 2, 1935; s. Victor J. and Lola Ruth (Sloop) R.; m. Anna Marie Berger, June 15, 1957; children: Victor III, Diane E., Linda M. BA, U. Denver, 1958, MA, 1964; EdD, U. Colo., 1978. Tchr. English Littleton (Colo.) Schs., 1958-65; prin. Littleton Jr. High Sch., 1965-69, Moline (Ill.) High Sch., 1969-72, Lakewood (Colo.) High Sch., 1972-76; asst. supt. Bettendorf (Iowa) Community Sch. Dist., 1976-81; supt. Aurora (Colo.) Pub. Sch., 1981—. Author: The Forbidden Apple, 1985, Bite the Wall, 1986; contbr. articles to profl. jours. City councilman City of Littleton, 1964-68. Named Pub. Servant of Yr., Littleton Ind., 1965. Mem. Nat. Sch. Bds. Assn. (jour. conf. faculty 1982—, named one of 100 Top Exec. Educators, 1984), Collegial Assn. Devel. and Renewal Educators (jour. editor 1982—), Phi Delta Kappa. Episcopalian. Lodge: Rotary. Home: 15890 E 8th Circle Aurora CO 80011 Office: Aurora Pub Schs 1085 Peoria St Aurora CO 80011 *

ROSSER, EDWIN MICHAEL, mortgage company executive; b. Denver, Oct. 11, 1940; s. Edwin Michael and Anne (Ratliff) R.; m. Keren Call, July 17, 1969; children: Kevin, William. BS, Colo. State U., 1964; MA, U. No. Colo., 1974. Cert. mortgage banker. Mktg. officer United Bank Mortgage, Denver, 1968-74; dir. nat. accounts PMI Mortgage Ins. Co., Denver, 1974-85; v.p. Moore Mortgage Co., Denver, 1985-87, Pacific First Mortgage Corp., Englewood, Colo., 1987—. Photographer represented in Denver Art Mus., The Buffalo in Winter, (1st place award 1981). Steering com. Blueprint for Colo., Govs. Unified Housing Task Force; mem. Colo. Housing Coun. (chmn. 1986-87); bd. dirs. Colo. State Found. Mem. Mortgage Bankers Assn. Am. (bd. govs. 1986-88, state and local achievement award 1986, Ernest P. Schumacher award 1988), Colo. Mortgage Bankers Assn. (bd. dirs. 1979-88, pres. 1986, E.C. Spelman award 1978), Colo. Assn. Commerce and Industry, Denver Mus. Natural History, Denver C. of C., Colo. State U. Alumni Assn. (nat. pres. 1987, bd. dirs. 1969-87, Honor Alumnus 1984). Republican. Roman Catholic. Home: 12478 E Amherst Circle Aurora CO 80014 Office: Pacific First Mortgage Corp 7430 E Caley Ave Englewood CO 80111

ROSSER, JAMES MILTON, university president; b. East St. Louis, Ill., Apr. 16, 1939; s. William M. and Mary E. (Bass) R.; m. Carmen Rosita Colby, Dec. 27, 1962; 1 son, Terrence. B.A., So. Ill. U., 1962, M.A., 1963, Ph.D., 1969. Diagnostic bacteriologist Holden Hosp., Carbondale, Ill., 1961-63; research bacteriologist Eli Lilly & Co., Indpls., 1963-66; coordinator Black Am. studies, instr. health edn. So. Ill. U., Carbondale, 1968-69; asst. prof. Black Am. studies dir. So. Ill. U., 1969-70, asst. to chancellor, 1970; asso. vice chancellor for acad. affairs U. Kans., Lawrence, 1970-74; asso. prof. edn., toxicology and pharmacology U. Kans., 1971-74; vice chancellor dept. higher edn. State of N.J., Trenton, 1974-79; acting chancellor State of N.J., 1977; pres., prof. health care mgmt. Calif. State U., Los Angeles, 1979—; mem. tech. resource panel Ctr. for Research and Devel. in Higher Edn., U. Calif., Berkeley, 1974—; mem. health maintenance orgn. com. Health Planning Council, State of N.J., 1975-79; mem. standing com. on research and devel. bd. trustees Ednl. Testing Service, 1976-77; mem. steering com. and task force on retention of minorities in engring. Assembly of Engring. NRC, 1975-78; mem. Bd. Med. Examiners, State of N.J., 1978-79; vis. faculty mem. Inst. Mgmt. of Lifelong Edn., Grad. Sch. Edn., Harvard U., 1979; mem. Calif. State U. Trustees Spl. Long Range Fin. Planning Com., 1982—, mem. Am. Council on Edn., 1979—, AFL/CIO Labor Higher Edn. Council, 1983, Nat. Commn. Higher Edn. Issues, 1981-82; mem. The Achievement Council, 1983—, strategic adv. council Coll. and Univs. Systems Exchange, 1988—; bd. dirs. Am. Humanities Council, So. Calif. Edison, Fedco, Inc., Maga Link Inc. Author: An Analysis of Health Care Delivery, 1977. Mem. exec. bd., chmn. varsity scouting program Los Angeles Area council Boy Scouts Am., 1980-84, local council rep. Nat. Council Boy Scouts Am., 1980—; bd. dirs. Hispanic Urban Ctr., Los Angeles, 1979—, Los Angeles Urban League, 1982—, Community TV of So. Calif., Sta. KCET, 1980—, United Way, Los Angeles, 1980—, Orthopaedic Hosp., 1983-86; mem. Citizen's Adv. Council Congl. Caucus Sci. and Tech., 1983—; bd. dirs. Los Angeles Philharm. Assn., 1986—; mem. performing arts council/edn. council Music Ctr., 1984—; mem. minority bus. task force Pacific Bell, 1985-86; mem. bd. of govs Nat. ARC, 1986—, Mayor's Blue Ribbon Task Force on Drugs City of L.A., 1988—; Nat. Adv. Council on Aging, 1989—. NSF fellow, 1961; NDEA fellow, 1967-68; recipient award of recognition in Edn. Involvement for Young Achievers, 1981, Pioneer of Black Hist. Achievement award Brotherhood Crusade, 1981, Alumni Achievement award So. Ill. U., 1982, Friend to Youth award Am. Humanics, Inc., 1985. Mem. Alhambra C. of C. (bd. dirs. 1979—), Los Angeles C. of C. (bd. dirs. 1984—), Am. Assn. State Colls. and Univs., Am. Public Health Assn., Kappa Delta Pi, Phi Delta Kappa, Phi Kappa Phi. Roman Catholic. Home: PO Box 1846 Rosemead CA 91770 Office: Calif State U Office of the Pres 5151 State University Dr Los Angeles CA 90032

ROSSI, AMADEO JOSEPH, chemist; b. Seattle, Sept. 23, 1954; s. Amadeo Joseph and Maria Asilia (Chinella) R.; m. Frances Marie Stotts, Sept. 19, 1981; 1 child, Anthony Joseph. BS in Wood and Fiber Sci., U. Wash., 1979, MS in wood chemistry, 1987. Research aide U. Wash., Seattle, 1978-79; environ. engr. Georgia-Pacific Corp., Eugene, Oreg., 1980; engr., dir. hazardous waste remediation projects Envirosphere Co. subs. EBASCO Services, Inc., Seattle, 1981—. Contbr. articles to profl. jours. Mem. Am. Chem. Soc., Air Pollution Control Assn., Forest Products Research Soc., Xi Sigma Pi. Office: EBASCO Svcs Inc 10900 NE 8th St Bellevue WA 98004

ROSSI, JOHN LOREN, real property administrator; b. Rockford, Ill., Aug. 18, 1951; s. Geno A. and Marie A. (Moscarelli) R. BS, Loyola U., Chgo., 1973; cert. real property adminstrn., Bldg. Owners & Mgrs. Inst., Phoenix, 1987. Lic. realtor, Ariz. Ops. mgr. Oxford Properties, Phoenix, 1980-83; mgr. property mgmt. Western Savs., Phoenix, 1984-85; dist. mgr. RREEF Funds, Phoenix, 1985—. Mem. Bldg. Owners and Mgrs. Assn., Soc. Real Property Adminstrs., Phoenix C., of C., Electric. League Ariz., Blue Key. Democrat. Roman Catholic. Office: RREEF Funds 2813 E Camelback St Ste 430 Phoenix AZ 85016

ROSSI, LYNN ELLEN, furniture manufacturing company executive; b. Kenosha, Wis., Apr. 14, 1954; d. Richard George and Julia Ruth (Bayer) R. BBA, U. Minn., 1977. Paralegal asst. Poletti, Freiden, Prashker & Feldman, N.Y.C., 1977-79; account rep. N.Y. Daily News, 1979-85; account exec. Xerox Corp., N.Y.C. and Denver, 1984-85; maj. account sales rep. Pandick Techs., Denver, 1985-86; sales rep. Desks, Inc., Denver, 1986-88; ter. mgr. Sunar Hauserman, Phoenix, 1988; acct. mgr. Knoll Internat., Denver, 1988—. Mem. Leag Profl. Women Denver. Office: Knoll Internat 1660 Wynkoop Ste 100 Denver CO 80202

ROSSI, WALTER T., department store executive. Formerly pres., chief exec. officer Mervyns, Hayward, Calif.; now chmn., chief exec. officer Mervyns, Hayward. Office: Mervyns 25001 Industrial Blvd Hayward CA 94545 *

ROSSI, WILLIAM JOSEPH, oil company executive; b. Deadwood, S.D., Mar. 7, 1926; s. Samuel and Catherine (Gadler) R.; m. Honora Katherine Ellis, Dec. 20, 1958. B in ChemE, Cornell U., 1947; MBA, Stanford U., 1959. Lic. chem. engr., Calif. Design engr. Chevron Rsch. Co., Richmond, Calif., 1947-60; lic. exec. Chevron Rsch. Co., San Francisco, 1960-79; mgr. catalytic ops. Chevron Rsch. Co., Richmond, Calif., 1979-86, mgr. lic. and catalytic, 1986—. Contbr. articles to profl. jours.; patentee in field. Mem. Am. Inst. Chem. Engrs., World Trade Club, World Affairs Coun. No. Calif., Commonwealth Club. Republican. Roman Catholic. Home: 1333 Jones St San Francisco CA 94109 Office: Chervon Rsch Co 576 Standard Ave Richmond CA 94802

ROSSNER, JOHN THEODORE, farmer; b. McMinnville, Oreg., Jan. 24, 1944; s. Theodore Bertram and Frances Eleanor (Duerst) R.; m. Astutiningsih Rahagu Rossner, Mar. 9, 1974; children: Madae Frances, Christina Astuti. BS, Oreg. State U., 1966, MS, 1968. Devel. officer Ch. World Svc., Sunabaya, E. Java, Indonesia, 1969-74; farmer Rossner Farms, McMinnville, Oreg., 1974—; v.p. then pres., bd. dirs. Sheridan Grain Co., Oreg., 1981-88. Elder, Presbyn. Ch., McMinnville, 1976-81, deacon, 1986-89; mem. Rep. Central Com., 1986-88. Named Outstanding Young Farmer, Jaycees, 1979. Mem. West Valley Farmers (v.p., bd. dirs. 1988—), Oreg. Seed Growers League (v.p. then pres. 1979-81), Oreg. Farm Bur. (2nd v.p. 1987—), Yamhill County Farm Bur. (pres. 1982-87), Oreg. Wheat Growers League, Nat. Railway Hist. Soc. Home and Office: 18930 SW Bellevue Hwy McMinnville OR 97128-9515

ROSSO, LOUIS T., scientific instrument manufacturing company executive; b. San Francisco, 1933; married. A.B., San Francisco State Coll., 1955; M.B.A., U. Santa Clara, 1967. Product specialist Spinco div. Beckman Instruments, Inc., Fullerton, Calif., 1959-63; mktg. mgr. Beckman Instruments, Inc., 1963-69, mgr. Spinco div., 1969-70, mgr. clin. instruments div., 1970-74, corp. v.p., mgr. analytical instruments group, 1974-80, corp. sr. v.p., 1980-83, pres., 1983—, also bd. dirs.; v.p. SmithKline Beckman Corp., Phila. Office: Beckman Instruments Inc 2500 Harbor Blvd Fullerton CA 92634 *

ROSTRON, JAMES THOMAS, civil engineer; b. Troy, Ohio, June 3, 1918; s. Charles E. and Edith (Prugh) R.; m. Fredda Norton, Nov. 14, 1942; children: Geraldine J. Rostron Afshari, Lorraine E. Rostron Schwarm. AA, Pasadena Jr. Coll., 1939; BS, U.Calif.-Berkeley, 1941; MS, Calif. Inst. Tech., 1948. Registered profl. engr., Calif. Rsch. hydraulic engr. Soil Conservation Svc. USDA, Pasadena, Calif., 1941-47; civil engr. C.F. Braun Engrs., Alhambra, Calif., 1947-49; civil engr. Dept. Engring. Los Angeles County, 1949-79, acting county engr., 1976; staff cons. civil engr. Engring. Sci. Consultancy, Pasadena, 1979—; mem. archtl. rev. bd., Arcadia, Calif., 1960—. Lt. (j.g.) USN, 1944-46, PTO, to lt., 1951-52. Mem. Am. Water Works Assn., ASCE, Am. Assn. Environ. Engrs., Am. Pub. Works Assn., Masons. Republican. Home: 422 Monte Vista Rd Arcadia CA 91006 Office: Engring Sci Inc 75 N Fair Oaks St Pasadena CA 91009

ROSUL, LOUISE C(LARA), real estate broker; b. Rockville Centre, N.Y., Aug. 5, 1942; d. Henry and Rosanna (Musgnug) Dietershagen; m. Ronald C. Rosul, Apr. 8, 1962 (div. 1985); children: Ronald C., Linda, Sean. Student Nassau Hosp. Sch. Radiology, 1962; grad. N.Mex. Real Estate Inst., 1980, Dale Carnegie Courses, 1984, 86. Lic. real estate broker, N.Mex. Real estate sales Kennedy Realty, Los Lunas, N.Mex., 1978-79, Valencia Valley Real Estate, 1979-82, Camco Realty, 1982-83; founder Real Estate Assocs., 1983; broker Realty World, Inc., Los Lunas, 1983-88; mem. Realty World-Land of Enchantment Broker's Council, pres. 1986-87; founder Gifts for You, 1983-84; mem. Homeowners Mktg. Service. Sec., Los Alamos Republican Central Com., 1973; mem. Planning and Zoning Commn. Valencia County, 1982-85; bd. dirs. Greater Los Lunas Bus. Assn., 1980-82; chmn. Valencia Crimestopper Program, 1980-86, 88—; founder Bed and Breakfast of El Cerro, 1988. Recipient sales awards Valencia County Bd. Realtors, 1981. Mem. Nat. Assn. Realtors, Realtors Assn. N.Mex. (state bd. dirs. 1985), Albuquerque Bd. Realtors , Valencia County Bd. Realtors, Profl. Salespersons Am., U.S. C. of C. Roman Catholic. Address: PO Box 1045 Los Lunas NM 87031

ROSVALL, CHARLES RICHARD, auctioneer, liquidator, appraiser; b. Denver, Nov. 7, 1948; s. Charles William and Opal Mae (Jackson) R.; m. Rolinda Louise Strickland, Jan. 2, 1972; children: Heidi Nicole, Stephanie, Brittanie. Student, SW Union Coll., Keene, Tex., 1967. Pres. Rosvall Auction Co., Denver, 1973—. Mem. Internat. Soc. Appraisers (assoc.). Republican. Seventh Day Adventist. Office: Rosvall Auction Co 1238 S Broadway Denver CO 80210

ROTALO, SUSANE KAY, teacher; b. Sacramento, Sept. 24, 1948; d. Alfred Joseph and Mary Virginia (Salsi) R. BA, Calif. State U., 1971; postgrad., Sonoma State, 1974. Cert. secondary sch. tchr. English tchr. Madera (Calif.) Unified Sch. Dist., 1972-73; English and art tchr. San Luis Coastal Unified Sch. Dist., San Luis Obispo, Calif., 1974—; freelance writer Calif., 1975—; adj. prof. Calif. Polytech. State U., San Luis Obispo, 1986, extn. tchr., 1988; fine arts mentor tchr. San Luis Coastal Unified Sch. Dist., 1987—; curriculum cons. Western Assn. of Schs. and Colls., 1987—; advanced tchr. trainer Visual and Performing Arts Staff Devel. Unit, Marin, Calif., 1985—; coordinator Writer's Workshop, San Luis Obispo High Sch., 1980—, Arts Are Core, San Luis Obispo, 1988. Author: Right Brain Lesson Plans for a Left-Brain World, 1982, Waiting for the Real Thing, 1988; contbr. various articles to newspapers and jours.; editor Anonymous, 1971-72. Bd. dirs. San Luis Obispo Edn. Found., 1988. Mem. Calif. Assn. Educators of Art (secondary rep. 1987-88), Calif. Tchrs. Assn., Women's Nat. Mus. of Art, San Luis Obispo Arts Council, Calif. PolyArts for Youth (dist. rep. 1986—). Roman Catholic. Office: San Luis Coastal Unified Sch Dist PO Box 8125 San Luis Obispo CA 93406

ROTENBERG, MANUEL, physics educator; b. Toronto, Ont., Can., Mar. 12, 1930; came to U.S., 1946; s. Peter and Rose (Plonzker) R.; m. Paula Weissbrod, June 23, 1952; children: Joel, Victor. BS, MIT, 1952, PhD, 1956. Mem. staff Los Alamos (N.Mex.) Nat. Lab., 1955-58; instr. physics Princeton (N.J.) U., 1958-59; asst. prof. U. Chgo., 1959-61; prof. applied physics U. Calif., San Diego, 1961—, dean grad. studies and research, 1975-84, chair dept. elect. engring. and computer engring., 1988—. Author: The 3-j and 6-j Symbols, 1959; founding editor: Methods of Computational Physics, 1963, Jour. of Computational Physics, 1962; editor: Biomathematics and Cell Kinetics, 1981. Fellow Am. Phys. Soc.; mem. AAAS, Sigma Xi. Office: U Calif R-007 La Jolla CA 92093

ROTH, JEFFREY HAROLD, lawyer; b. Seward, Alaska, Apr. 21, 1947; s. Jacque Elmer and Genevieve Louise (Walch) R.; m. Gayle Colleen Petersen, Aug. 22, 1970; children: Kory David, Ryan Casey. BA, U. Idaho, 1970, JD, 1972. Assoc. Jensen & Harris, Anchorage, 1973-75; ptnr. Jensen, Harris & Roth, Anchorage, 1975—. Mem. ABA, Alaska Bar Assn., Anchorage Bar Assn., Assn. Trial Lawyers Am., Alaska Trial Lawyers Assn. Home: 4321 Sunstone Circle Anchorage AK 99516 Office: Jensen Harris & Roth 1029 W 3d Ave Ste 600 Anchorage AK 99501

ROTH, LELAND MARTIN, art and architecture educator; b. Harbor Beach, Mich., Mar. 22, 1943; s. Leland Monroe and Margaret Hannah (Martin) R.; m. Carol Lynn Mangold, June 25, 1965; 1 child, Amanda Catherine. BArch, U. Ill., 1966; M in Philosophy, Yale U., 1971, PhD, 1973. Instr. U. Ill., Urbana, 1966-67, Ohio State U., Columbus, 1971-73; asst. prof. Northwestern U., Evanston, Ill., 1973-78; assoc. prof. archtl. history, art history U. Oreg., Eugene, 1978-82, assoc. prof., 1982—; cons. historian Boston Pub. Libr., 1985—, The N.Y. Hosp., N.Y.C., 1985-86. Author: Architecture of McKim, Mead & White, 1978, Concise History of American Architecture, 1979, McKim, Mead & White, Architects, 1983; editor: Monograph of McKim, Mead & White, 1974, America Builds, 1983. NEH fellow, 1982-83; Kamphoefner Found. grantee, Raleigh, N.C., 1985. Mem. Coll. Art Assn., Soc. Archtl. Historians (bd. dirs. 1977-80, founder's award 1979). Office: U Oreg Dept Art History Eugene OR 97403

ROTH, ROBERT A., university administrator; b. Cleve., Jan. 26, 1943; s. August Joseph and Carmel Maria (Narducci) R.; m. Doris Elaine Mullen, Mar. 9, 1970 (div. 1984); children: Rub Eugene, Todd Jason, Tracy Lynn. BA, Hiram Coll., 1964; MEd, Pa. State U., 1967; PhD, Kent State U., 1970; postgrad., Rutgers U., 1972-73. Cert. tchr., Calif. Tchr., coach Cuyahoga Heights High Sch., Cleve., 1965-67, Kirkland (Ohio) Schs., 1968-69; mem. edn. faculty Rutgers U., New Brunswick, N.J., 1971-73; state supr. State of Mich. Dept. Edn. Certification, Lansing, 1974-79, state dir., 1979-83; dir. Ctr. for Rsch. on Teaching and Human Resources Devel. U. So. Fla., Tampa, 1985-86; dir., chmn., edn. tchr. Calif. State U., Long Beach, 1987—; dir. performance project State of N.J., Trenton, 1971-73; cons. Grand Valley (Mich.) State U., 1985-87, Saginaw (Mich.) State U., 1987—. Contbr. over 150 articles to profl. jours., mags. and newsletters. Recipient Resolution of Tribute Mich. Legislature, 1983, Resolution of Recognition of Leadership Mich. State Bd. Edn., 1982, 84. Mem. Assn. Tchr. Educators of Mich. (Leadership award 1979, past pres.), Nat. Assn. State Dirs. of Edn. (past nat.

pres., Distingushed Leadership award 1984), Assn. Tchr. Educators (past nat. pres., Leadership award 1985, Distingushed mem. 1988), Phi Delta Kappa. Officer: Calif State U 1250 Bellflower Long Beach CA 98040

ROTH, SANFORD HAROLD, rheumatologist, health care administrator, educator; b. Akron, Ohio, June 12, 1934; s. Charles and Rose Marie (Zelman) R.; m. Marcia Ann, June 9, 1957; children—Shana Beth, Sari Luanne. B.Sc., Ohio State U., 1955, M.D., 1959. Intern Mt. Carmel, Columbus, Ohio, 1959-60; fellow Mayo Grad. Sch. Medicine, 1962-65; pvt. practice medicine specializing in rheumatology Phoenix, 1965—; med. dir. Arthritis Ctr., Ltd., Phoenix, 1983-89; dir. Arthritis Program Humana Hosp., Phoenix, 1987-89, med. dir. Arthritis/Orthopedic Ctr. for Excellence, 1989—; dir. arthritis rehab. program St. Luke's Hosp., Phoenix, 1978-87; med. research dir. Harrington Arthritis Research Ctr., Phoenix, 1984-88; prof., dir. aging and arthritis program Coll. Pub. Programs, Ariz. State U., Tempe, 1984—; dir. medicine Ariz. Insts., Phoenix, 1985—; past state chmn. Gov.'s Conf. on Arthritis in Ariz., 1967; cons., rep. arthritis adv. com. FDA, 1982—, chmn. anti-rheumatic new drug guidelines, 1984—; cons. Ciba-Geigy, 1983—, Upjohn, 1985-87, Pennwalt, 1985-88, Arthritis Found. Clinics, 3M-Riker Labs, Inc., 1981—, VA, 1970—, FTC, 1980—, Boots Pharm. Co., 1980-87, Greenwich Pharm., 1986-87, Hoffman-LaRoche, 1986—, FDA Office Compliance, 1987—, G.D. Searle, 1987—; prin. investigator Coop. Systematic Studies of Rheumatic Diseases; vis. scholar in rheumatology Beijing Med. Coll., People's Republic China, 1982; proctor, vis. scholar program U.S.-China Edn. Inst., 1982—; med. research dir., exec. bd., trustee Harrington Arthritis Research Ctr., 1983-88. Author: New Directions in Arthritis Therapy, 1980; Handbook of Drug Therapy in Rheumatoloy, 1985; med. contbg. editor RISS, Hosp. Physician, 1960-68, Current Prescribing, 1976-80; hon. internat. cons. editor Drugs, 1977—; editor-in-chief Arthron, 1982-85; editor, contbg. author: Rheumatic Therapeutics, 1985; med. cons. editor Update: Rheumatism, 1985, AMA Drug Evaluations, 6th edit., 1986; mem. editorial bd. VA Practitioner, 1985—, Comprehensive Therapy, 1987; mem. internat. editorial bd. Jour. Drug Devel., 1988—; contbr. numerous articles to profl. jours., chpts. to books. Fellow Am. Rheumatism Assn. (founding, liaison com. to regional med. program 1974-76, co-dir. med. info. system ARAMIS, computer com., chmn. antiinflammatory drug study club 1974—, com. on clubs and councils 1977-80, western regional co-chmn. 1977—, therapeutic and drug com. 1979—, glossary com. 1981-83, ad hoc com. on future meeting sites 1983); mem. AMA, ACP (regional program com., ann. Philip S. Hench lectureship chmn. 1978-79), Arthritis Found. (dir. central Ariz. chpt. 1982-83, past chmn. med. and sci. com. 1967-72), Lupus Found. Am. (bd. 1981—), Internat. Soc. Rheumatic Therapy (sec.-gen., bd. dirs. 1987—), Maricopa County Med. Soc. (rehab. com.), Am. Soc. Clin. Rheumatology (past pres. exec. council), Am. Coll. Clin. Pharmacology, Soc. Internal Medicine, Mayo Clinic Alumni Assn., Mayo Clinic Fellows Assn. (sec. 1964-65), Argentine Rheumatology Soc. (hon.), Mayo Clinic Fellows Rheumatology Soc. (pres. 1964-65), Mayo Clinic Film Soc. (bd. dirs. 1964-65), Pan Am. League Against Rheumatism (chmn. clin. trials com. 1987—). Office: Arthritis Ctr Ltd 3330 N 2d St #601 Phoenix AZ 85012

ROTHENBERG, ALAN I., lawyer, basketball executive; b. Detroit, Apr. 10, 1939; m. Georgina Rothenberg; 3 children. B.A., U. Mich., 1960, J.D., 1963. Bar: Calif. 1964. Instr. sports law U. So. Calif., 1969, 76, 84; instr. sports law Whittier Coll. Law, 1980, 84; ptnr. Manatt Phelps Rothenberg & Phillips, Los Angeles; pres. Los Angeles Clippers Basketball Team, 1982—. Mem. soccer commn. 1984 Olympic Games, Equal Edn. Opportunities Commn. State Calif. Bd. Edn., 1972-75. Mem. Nat. Basketball Assn. (bd. govs. 1971-79, 82—, N.Am. Soccer League (bd. govs. 1977-80), Constitutional Rights Found. (dir., pres. 1987—), ABA, local and county bar assns. Office: Los Angeles Clippers 3939 S Figueroa Los Angeles CA 90037 *

ROTHENBERG, HARVEY DAVID, educational administrator; b. Fort Madison, Iowa, May 31, 1937; s. Max and Cecelia Rothenberg; A.A., Wentworth Mil. Acad., 1957; B.B.A., State U. Iowa, 1960; M.A., U. No. Colo., 1961; postgrad. Harris Tchrs. Coll., 1962-63, St. Louis U., 1962-63; Ph.D., Colo. State U., 1972; m. Audrey Darlynne Roseman, July 5, 1964; children—David Michael, Mark Daniel. Distributive edn. tchr. Roosevelt High Sch., St. Louis, 1961-63, Proviso West High Sch., Hillside, Ill., 1963-64, Longmont (Colo.) Sr. High Sch., 1964-69, 70-71; supr. research and spl. programs St. Vrain Valley Sch. Dist., Longmont, Colo., 1971-72; chmn. bus. div. Arapahoe Community Coll., Littleton, Colo., 1972-75; dir. vocat., career and adult edn. Arapahoe County Sch. Dist. 6, Littleton, 1975—; instr. Met. State Coll., Denver, part-time, 1975—, Arapahoe Community Coll., Littleton, 1975—, Regis Coll., 1979—; vis. prof. U. Ala., Tuscaloosa, summer 1972; dir. Chatfield Bank, Littleton, 1974-83, Yaak River Mines Ltd., Amusement Personified Inc.; pres. Kuytia Inc., Littleton, 1975—; co-owner Albuquerque Lasers, profl. volleyball team. Mem. City of Longmont Long-Range Planning Commn., 1971-72, pres. Homeowners Bd., 1978—. Recipient Outstanding Young Educator award St. Vrain Valley Sch. Dist., 1967. Mem. Am., Colo. (mem. exec. com. 1966-68, treas. 1972-73) vocat. assns., Littleton C. of C., Delta Sigma Pi, Delta Pi Epsilon, Nat. Assn. Local Sch. Adminstrs., Colo. Council Local Sch. Adminstrs. Clubs: Elks, Masons, Shriners. Home: 7461 S Sheridan Ct Littleton CO 80123 Office: Arapahoe County Sch Dist 6 5776 S Crocker St Littleton CO 80120

ROTHENBERG, PAMELA JEAN, marketing executive, consultant; b. North Hampton, Eng., Aug. 10, 1943; came to U.S., 1956; d. Larry Louis and Rae (Lubart) Fieldman; children: Paul-Henry, Paul Jason. Student, UCLA, 1968-69. Therapist Julie Ann Singer Presch. Psychiat. Ctr., Los Angeles, 1970-72; adminstrv. asst. A.C. Nielsen Co., Los Angeles, 1972-75; co-pres. Calif. Creative Arts, Los Angeles, 1975-78; v.p. Lilly Lipton Internat., Los Angeles, 1978-83; pres., chief exec. officer P.J. Roth & Assocs. Inc., Los Angeles, 1983—; cons. SPC Ctr., Culver City, Calif., 1983—; instr. creative writing Carthay Elem. Sch., Los Angeles, 1975. Playwright, producer: Game of Time, 1976 (bicentennial endorsement); contbr. articles to mags. Co-producer theatrical prodns. Los Angeles Sch. Dist. under Title I fed. funds, play for Hollywood Bowl Summer Program, 1976. Mem. Nat. Assn. Female Execs. Office: PJ Roth & Assoc 310 N Vista Los Angeles CA 90036

ROTHENBERG, RUSSELL ALLEN, small business owner; b. Boulder, Colo., June 17, 1958; s. Marvin Leon Rothenberg and Karlin Lee (Reich) Blake. BS, Colo. U., 1981. V.p. Whitehall-Denver Ltd., 1981-84; nat. sports show dir. Orthopedic Tech., San Leandro, Calif., 1985-87; v.p. One Step Brace Stop, Westwood, Calif., 1987—; cons. U.S. Water and Snow Ski Teams. Mem. U.S. Water Ski Team. Republican. Office: One Stop Brace Shop 10921 Wilshire Blvd Ste U-8 Westwood Med Pla Los Angeles CA 90024

ROTHENBERG, SHELDON ISRAELI, communications company executive; b. Roanoke, Va., Aug. 7, 1948; s. Tobias and Ethel (Barbanel) R.; m. Wendy Kupsaw, Dec. 27, 198l. BA, Franklin Pierce Coll., 1976; EdM, Harvard U., 1979. Mental health worker McLean Hosp., Belmont, Mass., 1974-78; health counselor Harvard U. Sch. Pub. Health, Boston, 1978-80; programmer, analyst lab. data ctr. Alta Bates Hosp., Berkeley, Calif., 1980-85; methods analyst Pacific Bell, Oakland, Calif., 1985-87; knowledge engr. Pacific Bell, San Ramon, Calif., 1988—. Mem. Assn. for Computing Machinery, Computer Soc., Internat. Assn. Electronic and Elec. Engring. Office: Pacific Bell 2600 Camino Ramon Rm 2E8505 San Ramon CA 94583

ROTHERMICH, EUGENE WAYNE, electrical engineer, consultant; b. St. Louis, Sept. 19, 1951; s. Eugene Victor and Mary Alice (Struckmann) R.; m. Mary Suzanne Geist, May 18, 1974 (div. May 1977). BEE, U. Mo., Rolla, 1973, MEE, 1981. Mem. tech. staff BunkerRamo Corp., Westlake Village, Calif., 1975-83; mgr. engring. Amplica, Inc., Newbury Park, Calif., 1983-87, program mgr., 1988; cons. Bendix Corp., Sylmar, Calif., 1983-84, Rogow & Bernstein, Hollywood Calif., 1988. Patentee in field. Advisor Consortium for Advanced Tech. Edn., Thousand Oaks, Calif., 1984—. Mem. IEEE, Audio Engring. Soc., Acoustical Soc. Am.

ROTHGEB, WALLACE MILTON, JR., sportswear company executive; b. Seattle, Nov. 8, 1946; s. Wallace Milton Sr. and Elizabeth Jean (Hobson) R.; m. Mary Katherine Kilkenny, June 25, 1983; 1 child, Taylor Scott. BA, U. Nev., Reno, 1970. Nat. sales mgr. Dura Fiber, Inc., Carson City, Nev., 1970-75; v.p. Sports Mont., Inc., Helena, 1975-78; tournament dir. World Pro Skiing, Aspen, Colo., 1979-80; pres. Sawtooth Mktg. Co., Sun Valley, Idaho, 1980—; v.p. Peregrine, Ltd., Sun Valley, 1984-86, pres., 1986—; pres. E.I.R. Sports, Sun Valley, 1989—. Bd. dirs., chmn. Dirs. Invitational Ski Classic, Sun Valley, 1980—; bd. dirs. Spider Sabich Meml. Found., Aspen, 1986—. Office: Peregrine Ltd PO Box 4689 Ketchum ID 83340

ROTHHAMMER, CRAIG ROBERT, social worker, consultant; b. San Francisco, May 17, 1954; s. Robert Charles and Gloria Lee (Molloy) R.; m. Dawn Alicia Alvarez, 1988. BA, U. Calif., Santa Barbara, 1976; MSW, San Diego State U., 1979. Lic. clin. social worker, Calif. Social work asst. Mercy Hosp., San Diego, 1977; psychiat. social worker Lanterman State Hosp., Pomona, Calif., 1979-83, Sonoma State Hosp., Eldridge, Calif., 1983-84; children's social worker County Adoption Service, San Bernardino, Calif., 1984-86; psychiatric social worker Patton State Hosp., 1987-88; psychiat. soc. worker II Crisis Outpatient Services Riverside (Calif.) County Mental Health, 1988—; expert examiner Behavioral Sci. Examiners, Calif.; pvt. practice (part time) social work Redlands, Calif., 1986—. Vol. Social Advs. for Youth, Santa Barbara, Calif., 1974-76, Am. Diabetes Assn., San Diego, 1978-79, San Diego Assn. For Retarded, 1978-80; liason Adoptive Family Assn., San Bernardino, 1986. Mem. Nat. Assn. Social Workers, Acad. Cert. Social Workers. Democrat. Office: Crisis Outpatient Svcs 9707 Magnolia Dr Riverside CA 92503

ROTHMAN, JULIUS LAWRENCE, English educator; b. N.Y.C., Sept. 22, 1920; s. Samuel and Bessie (Kantor) R.; m. Stella Lambert, June 23, 1948. BSS, CCNY, 1941; MA, Columbia U., 1947, PhD, 1954. Lectr. Hunter Coll., N.Y.C., 1947-50, Rutgers U., New Brunswick, N.J., 1950-53; tech. writer Olympic Radio & TV, L.I. City, N.Y., 1951-61; prof. English Nassau Community Coll., Garden City, N.Y., 1962-86; prof. emeritus Nassau Community Coll., Garden City, 1986—; broadcaster, talk show host weekly program Sta. WHPC, 1974-82. Editor, contbg. author The Cabellian, 1968-72; contbr. sects. to books on folklore and legend; contbr. articles to profl. jours. Active Nat. Com. to Preserve Social Security and Medicare; mem. adv. bd. 9th Senatorial Dist. N.Y., 1984-88. With USAF, 1943-45. Mem. Cabell Soc. (founder 1967, exec. v.p. 1968-72), Ariz. State U. Alumni Assn., Am. Assn. Retired Persons, Arthritis Found., Retired Pub. Employees Assn., Nat. Wildlife Fedn., Nat. Retired Tchrs. Assn., Columbia U. Alumni Assn. Jewish.

ROTHMAN, N. PAUL, hospitality executive; b. Chico, Calif., June 16, 1936; s. Hiram and Bess (Bulasky) R.; m. Dona Rothman, Aug. 8, 1959 (div.); m. Toby Marantz, Dec. 27, 1987. BS, U. Calif., Berkeley, 1958. With Associated Hosts, Beverly Hills, Calif., 1958—, v.p., 1964-69, v.p. ops., 1969-75, exec. v.p., 1975-78, pres., 1978—. Bd. dirs. Freeman Hosp., Inglewood, Calif., 1987—; Friends of Hebrew U. Mem. Nat. Restaurant Assn., Calif. State Restaurant Assn. (bd. dirs.). Jewish. Office: Associated Hosts S 200 Beverly Hills CA 90211

ROTHMAN, NATHAN FRANK, manufacturing and trading executive; b. N.Y.C., Mar. 26, 1945; s. Morris and Sylvia (Frank) R.; student Bradley U., 1962-64, Ill. Inst. of Tech., 1964-65, Northwestern U., 1965-67, Roosevelt U., 1967-69; m. Ruthann Shigeko Kurose; 1 child, Mika Leah Fannie. Salesman, Valspar Paint Co., Chgo., 1967; v.p., Count Down, Inc., Chgo., 1968; v.p., treas. The Garment Dist., Inc., Chgo., 1969; pres., Paralines, Chgo., 1969-71; sec.-treas., gen. mgr. Jay R. Benford & Assocs., Inc. and assoc. cos. (Bedford Boat Bldg., Bedford Pub.), Seattle, Wash., 1972-73, chief. exec. and sole proprieter Sea Life, Seattle, 1972-74; pres. Valiant Yacht Corp., Seattle, 1974-80, Trade Interface Corp., 1982—; dir. world sales Valiant Yachts div. Uniflite, Inc., 1981-82. Recipient Offshore Cruiser of Decade award Sail mag. Mem. Wash. State China Rels. Coun. (bd. dirs., editor Insiders newsletter), Wash. State Athletic Club. Home: 3711 58th Ave SW Seattle WA 98116 Office: 1932 1st Ave Seattle WA 98101

ROTHMAN, STEWART NEIL, photographer; b. Rochester, N.Y., Dec. 27, 1930; s. Morris Zeus and Rose Mary (Cotler) R.; student Wayne State U., 1952-54; m. Shirley Mae Derry, Sept. 12, 1957; children—Leslie Paula, Karen Pat. Free-lance photographer, Detroit, 1952-57; photographer NASA, Gilmore Creek, Alaska, 1965-68; writer, photographer Jessen's Daily, Fairbanks, Alaska, 1968-69; propr. The Lens Unlimited, Fairbanks, 1959—; staff photographer Gen. Mac Arthur's Hdqrs., Tokyo, 1948-50; pres., chmn. bd. Arctic Publs., 1968-72; pres. Public Relations Specialists Co., 1973—; editor Arctic Oil Jour., 1968-72, This Month in Fairbanks, 1974--85; pub. The Fairbanks Mag., 1985—. Publicity adviser to mayor of Fairbanks; pres. Tanana-Yukon Hist. Soc. Served with U.S. Army, 1948-52, Korea, then USAF, 1957-65. Decorated Purple Heart with oak leaf cluster. Fellow Master Photographers Assn. Gt. Britain; mem. European Council Photographers, Fairbanks C. of C. Club: Farthest North Press. Lodges: Lions (pres.), Elks. Author: Nudes of Sixteen Lands, 1971; Hobo and Dangerous Dan McGrew, 1975; The Lens is My Brush, 1977; China, The Opening Door, 1980; Pope John Paul II's First Visit to Alaska, 1981; Window on Life, 1982; The Pope and the President, 1984. Home and Office: 921 Woodway St Fairbanks AK 99709

ROTHMILLER, MICHAEL JOHN, television producer and host, consultant; b. Lynwood, Calif., Oct. 12, 1950; s. John Michael and Elizabeth (Kovach) R.; m. Nancy Marie O'Connor, May 10, 1975. AA, East Los Angeles Jr. Coll., 1971; BA, U. Redlands, 1978; cert. in teaching, UCLA, 1976. Patrol officer, patrol sergeant, intelligence officer Los Angeles Police Dept., 1972-83; pres. MJR Cons., Huntington Beach, Calif., 1983-84; pres. West Coast ops. Klassic Security Service, Beverly Hills, Calif., 1984-86, cons. concert security, 1986—; pres. M.J. Rothmiller Prodns., Hollywood, Calif., 1986—; TV host, producer of adventure/outdoor programming on ESPN and PBA Stas. Author: D.C. Connection, 1987, Sandlions, 1988; (with others) Policemen's Guide to Street Crime Survival, 1988. Sgt. Calif. N.G., 1969-75. Mem. Nat. Rifle Assn., Calif. Explorers Club (founder, chmn. 1985—). Republican. Roman Catholic.

ROTHSCHILD, JOHN DAVID, lawyer; b. San Francisco, Dec. 8, 1945; s. August Barnet and Kathryn (Wolf) R.; m. Toni Friedman, May 28, 1978; children: Hilary, Elizabeth, David. AB, U. Calif., Berkeley, 1967; JD, U. Calif., San Francisco, 1971. Bar: Calif. 1972. Assoc. Dal Poggetto & Jess, Sonoma, Calif., 1972-74; ptnr. Dal Poggetto & Rothschild, Sonoma, 1974-76; pvt. practice law Sonoma, 1976—; lectr. Calif. Continuing Edn. Bar, 1987. Fellow Am. Acad. Matrimonial Lawyers; mem. ABA (family law sect.), Assn. Cert. Family Law Specialists (pres. 1987, pres. 1987), State Bar Assn. Calif., Bar Assn. Sonoma County (pres. 1983-84, lectr. family law 1980-85, exec. com. of family law sect. 1989—), Calif. Bd. Legal Speciality (cert. specialist family law). Office: 165 E Spain St Sonoma CA 95476

ROTHSTEIN, BARBARA JACOBS, federal judge; b. Bklyn., Feb. 3, 1939; d. Solomon and Pauline Jacobs; m. Ted L. Rothstein, Dec. 28, 1968; 1 child, Daniel. B.A., Cornell U., 1960; LL.B., Harvard U., 1966. Bar: Mass. 1966, Wash. 1969, U.S. Supreme Ct. Pvt. practice law Boston, 1966-68; asst. atty. gen. State of Wash., 1968-77; judge Superior Ct., Seattle, 1977-80; judge Fed. Dist. Ct. Western Wash., Seattle, 1980-87, chief judge, 1987—; faculty Law Sch. U. Wash., 1975-77, Hastings Inst. Trial Advocacy, 1977, N.W. Inst. Trial Advocacy, 1979—. Recipient Matrix Table Woman of Yr. award, 1980. Mem. ABA (jud. sect.), Am. Judicature Soc., Nat. Assn. Women Judges, Felloes of the Am. Bar, Wash. State Bar Assn., Phi Beta Kappa, Phi Kappa Phi. Office: US Dist Ct 411 US Courthouse 1010 5th Ave Rm 410 Seattle WA 98104-1187

ROTI, KAREN MARIE, marketing and communications executive; b. Port Angeles, Wash., Aug. 4, 1946; d. Lloyd Donald and Virginia Ruth (Larsen) R. BS, Seattle Pacific U., 1968; BA, Art Ctr., L.A., 1978. Owner, mgr. Roti & Co., Seattle, 1979-84; account exec. Manus Dir. Mktg. Co., Seattle, 1984-85; dir. mktg., community relations Ballard Community Hosp., Seattle, 1985-. Mem. founding bd. Women's Bus. Exchange, Seattle, 1980-82. Recipient Merit award Nat. Healthcare Advt. Awards, 1988. Mem. Am. Mktg. Assn., Wash. State Health Planning Soc., Seattle Dir. Mktg. Assn., Seattle Hosp. Assn. (mktg. bd. 1988). Episcopalian. Office: Ballard Community Hosp Box C-70707 Seattle WA 98107

ROTOLO, ELIO RICHARD, management consultant; b. N.Y.C., Jan. 2, 1924; s. Rosario and Antoinette Carbonaro; children: Claudia Ann, Debra Carla. Student Bklyn. Coll., 1942; BS, Lehigh U., 1949; postgrad. Rutgers U., 1953-55, Stevens Inst., 1963-66. Registered profl. engr., Calif. Mgr. indsl. engring. Dollin Corp., Irvington, N.J., 1952-60; prin. Arthur Young & Co., N.Y.C., 1960-70; dir. mfg. engring. ITT, N.Y.C., 1970-75; v.p. Security Pacific Nat. Bank, L.A., 1975-82; pres. Rotolo & Whitney, Inc., Pasadena, Calif., 1982—; sr. v.p. Fin. Corp. Am., 1984-88; mem. faculty Sch. Bank Adminstrn., Madison, Wis. Chmn., L.A. County Productivity Adv. Com.; Rep. county committeeman, Union, N.J., 1955-60; chmn. bd. dirs. Productivity Ctr. S.W.; bd. dirs. Opera Guild So. Calif. 1st lt. AUS, 1942-45. Fellow Am. Inst. Indsl. Engrs. (nat. pres. 1967-68); mem. Engrs. Joint Council (dir.), Office Automation Council (dir.), Nat. Soc. Profl. Engrs., Newcomen Soc., Lions. Contbr. articles to profl. jours.; editorial adv. bd. Office Adminstrn. and Automation mag.; editor-in-chief: Handbook of Office and Information Automation. Home and Office: 21875 Parvin Dr Santa Clarita CA 91350

ROTTAS, RAY, state official; b. Cleve., Oct. 20, 1927; s. Nicholas and Jessie Mabel (Herpst) T.; m. Barbara Lucas, Sept. 1, 1956; children—Steven, Donna, Paul, Diane. B.B.A., Case Western Res. U., 1951. Owner, operator Auto Warehousing Inc., Phoenix, 1956-83; mem. Ariz. Senate, 1971-74, 77-82; treas. State of Ariz., Phoenix, 1983—. Bd. dirs. YMCA, Phoenix, 1971—; pres. Jr. Achievement, Phoenix, 1979-80, bd. dirs., 1972—; pres. Ariz. Econ. Forum, 1983—. Served to col. USAF, 1951-55, Korea. Republican. Methodist. Lodges: Rotary (pres. Phoenix 1982-83, treas. 1984-85), Masons, Elks. Home: 3500 E Lincoln Dr Phoenix AZ 85018 Office: Ariz State Treas 1700 W Washington St Phoenix AZ 85007

ROTTSOLK, JAMES ERIC, computer company executive; b. Annapolis, Md., Dec. 24, 1944; s. James Eugene and Katherine Marie (Syrdal) R. B.A. cum laude, St. Olaf Coll., 1966; student (dean's list) Cuttington Coll., Liberia, 1965-66; A.M. (Ford Found. Fellow), U. Chgo., 1968, J.D., 1971. Admitted to Wash. bar, 1971; assoc. firm Jones, Grey & Bayley, P.S., Seattle, 1971-76, partner, 1976-78; v.p. finance, gen. counsel Mannesmann Tally Corp., Kent, Wash., 1977-80; v.p. fin. and corp. devel. Denelcor, Inc., Aurora, Colo., 1981-84; v.p. fin. and adminstrn. Star Techs., Inc., Portland, Oreg., 1984—. Mem. ABA, Wash. State Bar Assn. Club: Aurora Athletic. Home: 156 N Hayden Bay Dr Portland OR 97217

ROUBAL, GERALD GREGORY, construction executive; b. Barron County, Wis., Sept. 5, 1936; s. Joseph Phillip and Irene Sarah (Zastoupil) R.; m. Eula Grayce Kuykendall ; children: Deanna Ruth Kuykendall VanZant, Kyle Miles. BS, U. Wis., 1960; M of City Planning, U. Calif., Berkeley, 1966. Lic. gen. contractor, real estate broker, N.Mex. Asst. planner City of Corpus Christi, Tex., 1960-64; assoc. planner San Diego County, 1966-68; regional planner Mid Rio Grande Council of Govts., Albuquerque, 1968-72; mgr. planning McIntire & Quiros, Albuquerque, 1972—; owner, operator Roubal & Assocs., Albuquerque, 1975—; cons. project mgr. Mountain Run Shopping Ctr., Albuquerque, 1983-85; past pres. RIW, Inc., Albuquerque. Past bd. dirs. Christian Profl. Counseling Service, Mid-Rio Grande Health Planning Council, Vis. nursing service, Albuquerque. Democrat. Baptist. Home and Office: 3612 Chelwood Blvd NE Albuquerque NM 87111

ROUCH, LARRY EVAN, designer; b. Lawrence, Kans., Sept. 22, 1946; s. Edward Herbert Jr. and Inez Leah (Van Dyne) R. Student in Architecture, Okla. State U., 1964-68; BA in Environ. Design, U. Wash., 1971, MArch, 1979. Designer Arne Bystrom Architects, Seattle, 1973-74; project mgr. G. Cichanski Architects, Seattle, 1976-78, Charles Kober Architects, Seattle, 1978, Clayton Joyce Architects, Seattle, 1979-81; pvt. practice interior and archtl. design Seattle, 1981—; panelist KCTS Weekly Report, Seattle, 1980; symposium dir. Henry Art Gallery, Seattle, 1980; juror Design Awards, Portland chpt. AIA, 1985, juror artist selection Met. Transit Authority, 1985; juror design awards, founding mem. Blueprint: For Architecture, 1985; mem. steering com. U. Wash. Architecture Dept., 1986; panelist AIA/U. Wash. Dept. Architecture, 1986; lectr. U. Wash. Coll. Arch. Urban Planning, 1975, 78-79, 86, 1988, So. Calif. Inst. Architecture, Santa Monica, 1989. Contbr. profl. papers and studies; group shows include Ranier Sq. Atrium, 1985, Boise Gallery Art, Missoula Mus. Art, Cheney Cowles Meml. Mus., 1985. Mem. downtown planning study Seattle Arts Commn., 1984. With USNG, 1965-68. Recipient Bronze award Inst. Bus. Designers and Contract Mag. Product Design, 1987. Office: 210 Third S Seattle WA 98104

ROULEAU, BEVERLY JO, retail executive; b. Denver, Apr. 25, 1948; d. Abraham and Roslyn Theresa (Slack) Shur; m. Morris Rouleau, Jan. 10, 1970; children: Debra, Michelle, Kimberly. Grad. high sch., Denver. Cert. tchr., Colo. Co-owner, sec.-treas. BevRo Optics, Denver, 1976-80, Den Internat. Eyewear, Denver, 1980—. Mem. B'nai B'rith Women (life mem., nat. bd. dirs. Women Metro Denver chpt. 1986-88, mem.-at-large 1986-88, pres. 1978-80, bd. dirs. community vol. svc. internat. chpt. 1986-88, chmn. Anti Defamation League Women's Dist. 2 1976-78, Life Membership award 1979), B'nai B'rith (community vol. svc. com. 1986-88). Democrat. Home: 1536 S Vaughn Creek Aurora CO 80012 Office: 1642 S Parker Rd #201 Denver CO 80231

ROUNTREE, DOUGLAS BRIAN, stockbroker; b. Savannah, Ga., Oct. 30, 1956; s. Edward Donald and Dorothy Ann (Small) R. BS, Calif. Inst. Tech., 1978; MBA, UCLA, 1982. Engr. Kennedy Co., Monrovia, Calif., 1978-80; mktg. products specialist Micom Systems, Chatsworth, Calif., 1981-83; product mgr. Rockwell Internat., Newport Beach, Calif., 1983-85; owner D.B. Rountree and Co., San Francisco, 1984—; del. U.S. State Dept. team to UN, 1984-85; mem. N.Y. Stock Exch., 1986—, listings com. Pacific Stock Exch., San Francisco, 1986—; ptnr. Hanson Enterprises, San Francisco, 1987—. Mem. UCLA Mgmt. Alumni Assn., Caltech. Alumni Assn., Options Mem. Assn. Democrat. Office: D B Rountree and Co 220 Montgomery St Ste 900 San Francisco CA 94104

ROUSH, WILLIAM, placement director; b. Portland, Oreg., Mar. 25, 1925; s. John Houston and Josephine Barbara (Schuster) R.; m. Mary Jane Hunter, Apr. 15, 1945 (div. 1972); children: Laura Ann, Pegi, Beverly, William Jr., Ronald, Robert; m. Margaret Louise Sandblom, June 29, 1972. Student, Wash. State U., 1943-44; AA, USAF Inst., 1948. Advanced through grades to maj. USAF, 1943; gen. mgr. United Auto Lease, Phoenix, 1966-69; regional sales mgr. Prescott Valley Corp., Phoenix, 1970-72; sr. enrollment dir. Ariz. Automotive Inst., Glendale, 1972-77; placement dir. Nat. Edn. Ctr., Glendale, 1977—. Author: Where Do We Go From Here?, 1978. Campaign coord. Steiger for Congress, 1966. Mem. Am. Soc. Tng. and Devel., Nat. Assn. Student Employment Administrs., Automotive Svc. Assn., Plaza Club. Republican. Methodist. Home: 10245 N 105th Dr Sun City AZ 85351 Office: Nat Edn Ctrs 6829 N 46th Ave Glendale AZ 85301

ROUTT, RUEL GERALD, controller; b. Louisville, June 19, 1949; s. Wilbur Thomas Routt and Anna Marion (Estes) Ray; m. Susan Leslie Hardesty, Oct. 4, 1980; 1 child, Joseph Addison. BS, Western Ky. U., 1971. Sr. auditor Coopers & Lybrand, Louisville, 1971-75; corp. auditor Honeywell Inc., Mpls., 1975-80, supr. fin. planning residential div., 1980-82, supr. cost acctg. residential div., 1982; controller advanced indsl. sr. unit Honeywell Inc., Denver, 1982—. Named to Hon. Order Ky. Cols., 1967. Mem. Am. Inst. CPA's, Ky. Soc. CPA's, Alpha Kappa Psi (alumni). Republican. Baptist. Home: 7976 S Gaylord Way Littleton CO 80122 Office: Honeywell Inc 4800 E Drycreek Rd Littleton CO 80122

ROVIRA, LUIS DARIO, state justice; b. San Juan, P.R., Sept. 8, 1923; s. Peter S. and Mae (Morris) R.; m. Lois Ann Thau, June 25, 1966; children—Douglas, Merilyn. B.A., U. Colo., 1948, LL.B., 1950. Bar: Colo. bar 1950. Now justice Colo. Supreme Ct., Denver.; Mem. Pres.'s Com. on Mental Retardation, 1970-71; chmn. State Health Facilities Council, 1967-76. Bd. dirs. YMCA, 1969-78; pres. Lowe Found. Served with AUS, 1943-46. Mem. Colo. Assn. Retarded Children (pres. 1968-70), ABA, Colo. Bar Assn., Denver Bar Assn. (pres. 1970-71), Alpha Tau Omega, Phi Alpha Delta. Republican. Clubs: Athletic (Denver), Country (Denver). Home: 4810 E 6th Ave Denver CO 80220 Office: Colo Supreme Ct 2 E 14th Ave Denver CO 80203

ROWE, CARL OSBORN, management consultant; b. ColoradoSprings, Colo., Feb. 3, 1944; s. Prentiss Eldon and Jo Ann (Osborn) R.; m. Dale Robin Oren, Apr. 12, 1984; 1 child, Stefanie Osborn. BA in Govt. cum laude, George Mason U., 1972; M Urban Affairs, Va. Poly. Inst. and State U., 1976. Spl. clk. FBI, Washington, 1968-71; mgmt. analyst ICC, Washington, 1972-75; dir. policy and mgmt. U.S. Bur. Reclamation, Washington, 1975-82; pres. Rowe Bus. Consulting, Las Vegas, Nev., 1982—; bd. dirs., Sportstech, Inc., Scottsdale, Ariz., Flowtronics, Inc., Phoenix, MSP Systems Inc., Scottsdale. Columnist Las Vegas Business Press, 1989—. Vol. cons. to various non-profit orgns. Sgt. USAF, 1963-66. Mem. Phi Theta Kappa. Office: Rowe Bus Cons 2250 E Tropicana Ave Ste 19-277 Las Vegas NV 89119

ROWE, JOHN BOCKLER, lawyer; b. Hibbing, Minn., June 10, 1933; s. Nathaniel Hawthorne and Edna (Bockler) R. BS in Archtl. Engring., Tex. A&M U., 1956; LLD, Emory U., 1970. Bar: Ga., Ariz., U.S. Dist. Ct. Ariz., U.S. Dist. Ct. (no, mid., and so. dists.) Ga., U.S. Ct. Appeals (5th, 9th and 11th cirs.), U.S. Tax Ct., U.S. Supreme Ct. Ariz., U.S. Supreme Ct. Ga. Constr. engr. Phillips Pet Co., Bartlesville, Okla., 1956-67; pvt. pratice atty. Phoenix, 1970—. Mem., co-chmn. Trunk and Tusk Rep. Party, Phoenix, 1973-75, Early Birds Rep. Party. Served to capt. USAF, 1956-60. Mem. ABA, Fed. Bar Assn., Tex. Aggie Bar Assn., Ga. State Bar Assn., Ariz. State Bar Assn. (treas. bankruptcy sect. 1975, mem. 1972—), Valley of the Sun A&M Club (pres. 1985, dir. 1982-87), University Club. Presbyterian. Home: 8014 N 8th Ave Phoenix AZ 85021

ROWE, MARY, nurse; b. Drogheda, Ireland, Nov. 11, 1955; came to U.S., 1980; d. John Cormac and Monica Mary (O'Brien) R. Diploma in Nursing, St. Vincents, Dublin, Ireland, 1977; diploma in Midwifery, Lourdes Hosp., Ireland, 1979. RN, Alaska. Staff nurse Brit. Hosp., Paris, 1977-78, Victoria Hosp., Miami, Fla., 1980-81; insvc. coord. Petersburg Hosp., Alaska, 1982-85; emergency med. svcs. coord. Southeast Region Emergency Med. Svcs. Council, Sitka, Alaska, 1985-87; staff nurse Providence Hosp., Seattle, 1988—. Author tng. manual. Commn. Post-Secondary Edn. grantee, 1984. Mem. Wash. State Nurses Assn., Emergency Nurses Assn. Home and Office: 1928 43d Ave E Apt 1 Seattle WA 98112

ROWE, MARY SUE, accounting professional; b. Melrose, Kans., Aug. 31, 1940; d. Gene and Carmen (Glidewell) Woffard; m. Edward Rowe, Nov. 27, 1985; children from previous marriage: Denise, Dynell, Dalene, Denette. Student, MTI Bus. Coll., 1968, Calif. State U., Fullerton, 1969; cert. Sch. Bus. Mgmt., Calif. State U., San Bernardino, 1986. Variou bookkeeping and secretarial 1968-76; asst. mgr., acct. RM Dean Contracting, Chenango Forks, N.Y., 1976-80; acctg. asst. Hemet (Calif.) Unified Sch. Dist., 1981-86; dir. acctg. Desert Sands Unified Sch. Dist., Indio, Calif., 1986—. Bd. dirs. Family Svcs. Assn., Hemet, 1982-83. Mem. NAFE, Riverside Assn. Chief Accts. (co-chmn. 1986-88), Calif. Assn. Sch. Bus. Ofcls. (acctg., rsch. and devel. com., vice chairperson 1988—, Desert Schs. Mgmt. Assn. Republican. Home: 78670 Sagvaro Rd La Quinta CA 92253 Office: Desert Sand Unified Sch Dist 82-879 Hwy 111 Indio CA 92201

ROWE, TEMPLE SCOTT, optics engineer; b. Oakland, Calif., June 24, 1956; s. Temple Charles and Adeline (Diede) R.; m. Minerva Lucia Cordova, Dec. 5, 1981; children: Evan Scott, Elliott Steven. BSME, U. Calif., Irvine, 1978; postgrad., UCLA, 1980. Registered profl. engr., Calif. Assoc. engr. Ford Aerospace Corp., Newport Beach, Calif., 1978-79, electo-optics engr., 1979-84; optical engr. Excellon Photonics, Inc., Costa Mesa, Calif., 1984-87; sr. engr., optics Alcon Surg., Inc., Irvine, Calif., 1987—; cons. T. Scott Rowe, Irvine, 1986—. Author of articles in field; patentee pending in field. Mem. Soc. Photo-Instrumentation Engrs., Optical Soc. Am., Am. Phys. Soc., U. Calif Engr. Alumni Soc. (pres. elect 1988), U. Calif. Alumni Assn. (bd. dirs. 1988-89). Republican. Home: 25231 Campina Dr Mission Viejo CA 92691 Office: Alcon Surg Inc 17701 Cowan Dr Irvine CA 92714

ROWEKAMP, BARRY LEWIS, osteopathic physician; b. Cin., Feb. 4, 1955. BS, U. Ala., 1977; DO, U. Health Scis., 1985. Diplomate Nat. Bd. Examiners for Osteo. Physicians and Surgeons. Intern U. Ind. Med. Ctr. Westview Hosp., 1985-86; assoc. med. dir. SW Health Inst., Phoenix, 1986—. Capt. USAF. Mem. Am. Osteo. Assn., Ariz. Osteo. Med. Assn., Assn. Mil. Surgeons U.S. Republican. Office: SW Health Inst 4602 N 16th St #200 Phoenix AZ 85016

ROWELL, RONALD MICHAEL, health agency executive; b. Corpus Christi, Tex., Feb. 22, 1949. AB, U. Calif., Berkeley, 1976, MPH, 1978. Health planner West Bay Health Systems Agy., San Francisco, 1978-81; dir. San Francisco Refugee Health Agy., 1981-83; assoc. dir. Catholic Social Svc. Archdiocese of San Francisco, 1983-85; pres., prin. cons. Achukma, Inc., Oakland, Calif., 1985-87; coord. HIV Antibody Testing Program San Francisco Dept. Pub. Health, 1987-88; exec. dir. Nat. Native Am. AIDS Prevention Ctr. Oakland, 1988—; planning cons. Ministry of Health Kingdom of Jordan, Amman, 1982. Mem. subcommittee Minority Affairs Calif. AIDS Leadership Com., Sacaramento, 1988—; bd. dirs. Nat. Minority AIDS Coun., Washington, 1988—, Calif. Native Am. AIDS Adv. Bd., Sacramento, 1987—; chairperson bd. dirs. Friendship House Assn. Am. Indians, San Francisco, 1985—; citizen Choctaw Nation of Okla. Mem. Internat. AIDS Assn., Nat. AIDS Network, Am. Pub. Health Assn., Nat. Coun. Internat. Health. Democrat. Office: Nat Native Am AIDS Ctr 6239 College Ave Ste 201 Oakland CA 94618

ROWE-MAAS, BETTY LOU, real estate investor; b. San Jose, Calif., Apr. 2, 1925; d. Horace DeWitt and Lucy Belle (Spiker) Rowe; children: Terry Lee, Clifford Lindsay, Craig Harrison, Joan Louise. Real estate investor, Saratoga, Calif., 1968—. Mem. Nat. Trust Hist. Preservation, Smithsonian Instn., San Jose Mus., Saratoga Mus., San Francisco Mus., Los Gatos Mus., San Jose Symphony, Moltalvo; bd. dirs. Valley Inst. Theatre Arts; San Francisco Ballet, City Ctr. Ballet of San Jose and Cleve., Music and Arts Found.; mem. Route 85 Task Force, 1978—, treas., 1984-89; mem. Saratoga Good Govt., 1970—; treas. Traffic Relief for Saratoga. Mem. LWV. Republican. Clubs: Commonwealth of Calif. (life), Saratoga Country. Home: 4563 Carriage Hill Dr Santa Barbara CA 93110

ROWEN, HENRY STANISLAUS, public management educator; b. Boston, Oct. 11, 1925; s. Henry S. and Margaret Isabelle (Maher) R.; m. Beverly Camille Griffiths, Apr. 18, 1951; children: Hilary, Michael, Christopher, Sheila Jennifer, Diana Louise, Nicholas. BS, MIT, 1949; M in Philosophy, Oxford (Eng.) U., 1955. Economist Rand Corp., Santa Monica, Calif., 1950-61, pres., 1967-72; dep. asst. sec. nat security affairs Dept. Def., Washington, 1961-64; asst. dir. Bur. Budget, Washington, 1965-66; prof. pub. policy Stanford (Calif.) U., 1972—, dir. pub. policy program, 1972-75; sr. fellow Hoover Inst., Stanford, Calif., 1983—; Edwin B. Rust prof. pub. policy Stanford (Calif.) U., 1986—; chmn. nat. intelligence council CIA, Washington, 1981-83; mem. organizers group European Am. Workshop, Marina del Rey, Calif., 1974—, Security Council on Asia and the Pacific, Marina del Rey, 1974—; co-founder PanHeuristic div. RDA, Marina del Rey, 1974—. Author: (with R. Imai) Nuclear Energy and Nuclear Proliferation, 1980; editor: Options for U.S. Energy Policy, 1977; contbr. numerous articles to profl. jours. Chmn. chief naval ops. exec. panel USN, Washington, 1972-81, mem., 1983—; mem. def. sci. bd. Dept. Def., Washington, 1983—, World Resources Inst. Served with USN, 1943-46, PTO. Mem. Internat. Inst. Strategic Studies. Republican. Roman Catholic. Office: Stanford U Hoover Inst War Revolution & Peace 10th Floor Stanford CA 94305-6011 *

ROWEN, MARSHALL, radiologist; b. Chgo.; s. Harry and Dorothy (Kasnow) R.; m. Helen Lee Friedman, Apr. 5, 1952; children: Eric, Scott, Mark. AB in Chemistry with highest honors, U. Ill., Urbana, 1951; MD with honors, U. Ill., Chgo., 1954, MS in Internal Medicine, 1954. Diplomate Am. Bd. Radiology. Intern Long Beach (Calif.) VA Hosp., 1955; resident in radiology Los Angeles VA Hosp., 1955-58; practice medicine specializing in radiology Orange, Calif., 1960—; chmn. bd. dirs. Moran, Rowen and Dorsey, Inc., Radiologists, 1969—; asst. radiologist Los Angeles Children's Hosp., 1958; assoc. radiologist Valley Presbyn. Hosp., Van Nuys, Calif., 1960; dir. dept. radiology St. Joseph Hosp., Orange, 1961—, v.p. staff, 1972; dir. dept. radiology Children's Hosp., Orange County, 1964—, chief of staff 1977-78, v.p. 1978-83; asst. clin prof. radiology U. Calif., Irvine, 1967-70, assoc. clin. prof., 1970-72, clin. prof. radiology and pediatrics, 1976, pres. clin. faculty assn., 1980-81; trustee Children's Hosp. Orange County, Choc. Padrinos; sec. Choco Health Services, 1987-89; trustee Found. Med. Care Orange County, 1972-76, Calif. Commn. Adminstrn. Services Hosp., 1975-79; v.p. Found. Med. Care Children's Hosp., 1988-89. Mem. editorial bd. Western Jour. Medicine; contbr. articles to med. jours. Founder Orange County Performing Arts Ctr., mem. Laguna Art Mus., Laguna Festival of Arts, Opera Pacific, S. Coast Reportory, Am. Ballet Theater, World Affairs Council. Served to capt. M.C., U.S. Army, 1958-60. Recipient Rea sr. med. prize U. Ill, 1953; William Cook scholar U. Ill., 1951. Fellow Am. Coll. Radiology; mem. AMA, Am. Heart Assn., Soc. Nuclear Medicine (trustee 1961-62), Orange County Radiol. Soc. (pres. 1968-69), Calif. Radiol. Soc. (pres. 1978-79), Radiol. Soc. So. Calif. (pres. 1976), Pacific Coast Pediatric Radiologists Assn. (pres. 1971), Soc. Pediatric Radiology, Calif. Med. Assn. (chmn. sect. on radiology 1978-79), Orange County Med. Assn. (chmn. VCI liason com. 1976-78), Cardioradiology Soc. So. Calif., Radiol. Soc. N.Am., Am. Roentgen Ray Soc., Phi Beta Kappa, Phi Eta Sigma, Omega Beta Phi, Alpha Omega Alpha. Clubs: Rams Booster, Center (Orange County). Office: 1201 W La Veta Orange CA 92668

ROWLAND, JAMES NORMAN, architect; b. Loraine, Tex., Feb. 20, 1934; s. Clarence and Annie (Norman) Rowland; m. Elizabeth Nix, Aug. 15, 1956 (div. Oct. 1970); children: Mark Stephen, Tawnya Leigh; m. Glenda Victor, Dec. 1, 1972. BA, Tex. Tech U., 1958. Registered architect, N.Mex., Ariz., Tex., Colo., Oreg., Fla. Architect McHugh, Hooker, Kidder, Santa Fe, 1959-62, Kenneth S. Clark, Santa Fe, 1962-64, Stevens, Mallory & Pearl, Albuquerque, 1964-66; pvt. practice architecture Albuquerque, 1966—. Recipient Design Excellence award Featherlite Corp., Dallas, 1953. Mem. AIA (v.p., Execellence in Architectural Design award 1981, 87, 88), Constrn. Spsecification Inst. (v.p.). Democrat. Club: Tanoan Country. Lodge: Elks. Office: 925 Luna Circle NW Albuquerque NM 87102

ROWLAND, RUTH GAILEY, hospital official; b. Salt Lake City, Dec. 7, 1922; d. Frederick George and Lucy Jane (Hill) N.; m. Joseph David Gailey, Apr. 9, 1942 (dec. July 1984); children: Sherylynne Harris-Roth, Joseph David Jr., Robert Nelson; m. Joseph Brigham Rowland, Oct. 14, 1986. Student, Felt-Tarrant Community Coll., Salt Lake City, 1941-42, U. Utah. Dir. vol. svcs. Lakeview Hosp., Bountiful, Utah, 1961—. Mem. com. Women's State Legis. Coun., Salt Lake City, 1970—; mem. legis. com. Utah Comprehensive Planning Agy., Salt Lake City; mem. Farmington (Utah) Bd. Health, 1979-85; mem. Davis County Adv. Bd. Volunteerism; mem. social svcs. com. LDS Ch. Mem. Assn. Dirs. Vol. Svcs. of Am. Hosp. Assn., Utah Assn. Vol. Auxs. (pres.), Utah Dirs. Vol. Svcs. (pres.), Utah Dental Assn. Aux. (pres.), Bountiful C. of C. (bd. dirs. 1975-80), Soroptimists. Republican. Home: 871 South 750 East Bountiful UT 84010 Office: Lakeview Hosp 630 E Med Dr Bountiful UT 84010

ROWLES, CHARLES SCOTT, nurse; b. Phoenix, Mar. 6, 1953; s. Wilbur Lee and Maude Ella (Allison) R.; m. Patricia Ann Anderson, Oct. 22, 1972. Degree in nursing, Lower Columbia Sch. Nursing, Longview, Wash., 1984. RN, Wash. Nurse Monticello Med. Ctr., Longview, 1984-87, Self Employed Staff Agy., Wash., and Oreg., 1985-86, St. Johns Med. Ctr., Longview, 1988-89; clin. dir. Quick Care Inc., Longview, 1989—. Developer computer software. Mem. AIDS Task Force. With USN, 1971-73. Mem. Wash. Nurses Assn. (vice chmn. 1985-86), Am. Nurses Assn., Lower Columbia Nurses Assn., Audubon Soc., Trout Unltd. Republican. Home: 245 Holcomb Spur Rd Kelso WA 98626 Office: Quick Care Inc 1952 9th Ave Longview WA 98632

ROWLES, JAMES GEORGE, musician, composer; b. Spokane, Wash., Aug. 19, 1918; s. James Polk Hunter and Eileen Cicely (McCarthy) Hunter-Rowles-Byrd; m. Dorothy Jewel Paden, Aug. 12, 1941; children: Gary Leonard, Stacy Amanda, Stephanie Heather. Student, Gonzaga U., 1937-38. Pianist, rec. artist numerous band leaders, performers including Lester Young, Benny Goodman, Woody Herman, Les Brown. Tommy Dorsey, Billie Holiday, Vic Damone, Peggy Lee, Carmen McRae, Sarah Vaughan, Ella Fitzgerald, Henry Mancini, Hollywood and Los Angeles, Calif., 1940—. Composer: The Peacocks (rec. Bill Evans, Branford Marsalis), 1973 (Grammy nomination 1978, featured in film 'Round Midnight 1986), various songs with Johnny Mercer. Active wildlife and marine life conservation. Served as sgt. U.S. Army, 1943-46. Recipient 5 Grammy nominations, 1978-82, Peabody award, 1986; honored by Los Angeles Jazz Soc., 1986. Mem. Am. Fedn. Musicians, ASCAP, Songwriters Guild Am., Am. Guild Authors and Composers. Democrat. Roman Catholic. Club: Giraffe (Washington). Home and Office: 520 N Bel Aire Dr Burbank CA 91501

ROWLES, MICHAEL GRIDLEY, military officer; b. Arco, Idaho, Oct. 6, 1946; s. Donald Gridley and Betty Jane (Bean) R.; m. Marti L. Dewey, Aug. 30, 1969; children: Eric, Ryan, Brandon. BS, U. Idaho, 1969; MS, SUNY, 1979. Cert. communications-computer systems officer, USAF. Commd. USAF, 1969, advanced through grades to lt. col.; with communications and field ops. 20th air div. USAF, Ft. Lee, Va., 1970-72; maintenance supr. 14th Communications squadron USAF, Yokota AFB, Japan, 1972-74; chief of maintenance 1998 communications squadron USAF, Korat RTAFB, Thailand, 1974-75; div. chief communications ops. no. communications area USAF, Griffiss AFB, N.Y., 1975-79; comdr. detachment 6, 1989 communications group USAF, Zaragoza AFB, Spain, 1979-82; br. chief corp. hdqrs. ops. AF communications command USAF, Scott AFB, Ill., 1982-85; comdr. 2019 communications squadron USAF, Griffiss AFB, 1985-88; chief mgmt. cons. team communications-computers. Air Force insp. and safety Ctr. USAF, Norton AFB, Calif., 1988—; chief mil. affil. radio system, USAF, Scott AFB, 1984-85; chief AF reps. joint communications comdrs., Scott AFB, 1982-83. Creator various music arrangements, 1977-79. Com. mem. Boy Scouts Am., Redlands, Calif., 1988—, scoutmaster, Shiloh, Ill.,m 1983-85; bd. dir. Rome (N.Y.) Choral Soc., 1986-88, Zaragoza AFB Chapel Choir, 1979-82. Recipient Mayor's Svc. award City of Rome, 1988. Mem. Air Force Assn., Armed Forces Communications and Electronics Assn. (chpt. v.p., 1987-88), Aircraft Owners and Pilots Assn., Community Band (Rome), Masons. Office: Hdqrs AF Insp & Safety Ctr/IGSI Norton AFB CA 92409

ROWLEY, DANIEL JAMES, business administration educator; b. Denver, Mar. 16, 1946; s. James Mitchell and Nellie Elizabeth (Carlson) R.; m. Barbara Jean Starland, June 11, 1970; 1 child, Rebecca Jean. BA, U. Colo., 1969, MPA, 1979, PhD, 1987. Dist. exec. Boy Scouts Am., Glencoe, Ill., 1969-72; comml. notes mgr. 1st Nat. Bank Highland Park, Ill., 1972-73; bus. mgr. Woden Woods, Denver, 1973-75; bus. mgr., ptnr. Earthly Woods, Boulder, Colo., 1975-76; bus. mgr., hosp. adminstr. Raleigh Hills Hosp., Denver, 1976-79; contracts mgr. Motorola Regional Offices, Englewood, Colo., 1980; instr. U. Colo., Boulder, 1981-83, Met. State Coll., Denver, 1982-83; asst. prof. dept. bus. adminstrn. U. No. Colo., Greeley, 1983—; researcher, Selura, Inc., Boulder, 1981-85; bus. cons., Daniel James Ltd., Greeley, 1983—. Author mgmt. textbook: Managing Complex Organizations, 1989. Mem. Acad. Mgmt., Assn. HRMOB (bd. dirs. 1988—, nat. dir. organizational behavior directorate 1988—). Democrat. Episcopalian. Office: Coll Bus Adminstrn U No Colo Greeley CO 80639

ROWLEY, WILLIAM DEAN, history educator; b. Chariton, Iowa, Aug. 4, 1939; s. Ernest W. and Rachel (Davis) R. B.A., U. Puget Sound., 1961; M.A., U. Nebr., 1963, Ph.D., 1966. Asst. prof. U. Nebr., 1966-67; asst. prof. U. Nev.-Reno, 1967-71, assoc. prof. Am. history, 1971-85, prof., 1986— ; cultural resource contractor U.S. Forest Service. Mem. Orgn. Am. Historians, Forest History Soc., Western History Assn. (exec. sec. 1974—). Author: M.L. Wilson and the Campaign for the Domestic Allotment, 1970; Reno: Hub of the Washoe Country, 1983, U.S. Forest Service Grazing and Rangelands: A History, 1985. Office: U Nev Dept History Reno NV 89557

ROWLEY, WILLIAM ROBERT, surgeon; b. Omaha, June 7, 1943; s. Robert Kuhlmeyer and Dorothy Eleanor (Larson) R.; m. Eileen Ruth Murray, Aug. 11, 1968; children: Bill II, Jeff, Jill. BA in Psychology, U. Minn., 1966, MD, 1970. Diplomate Am. Bd. Surgery. Commd. lt. USN, 1972, advanced through grades to capt., 1985; intern U. Calif., San Diego, 1970-71, gen. surgery resident, 1971-72; gen. surgery resident Naval Regional Med. Ctr., Phila., 1973-76; peripheral vascular surgery fellow Naval Regional Med. Ctr., San Diego, 1977-78; staff surgeon Naval Regional Med. Ctr., Phila., 1977; staff vascular surgeon Naval Regional Med. Ctr., San Diego, 1978-85, chmn. dept. surgery, 1985-88, dir. surg. svcs., 1987-88; asst. chief of staff for plans and ops. Naval Med. Command S.W. Region, San Diego, 1988—; program dir. Vascular Surgery Fellowship Naval Hosp., San Diego, 1980-85, Gen. Surgery Residency, 1985-89; assoc. prof. surgery uniformed svcs. U. for the Health Scis., Bethesda, Md., 1985-89. High adventure leader Boy Scouts Am. Fellow ACS; mem. AMA, Am. Coll. Physician Execs., Internat. Soc. Cardiovascular Surgery, Peripheral Vascular Surgery Soc. Home: 14340 Aedan Ct Poway CA 92064 Office: Naval Med Comman SW Region San Diego CA 92134-7000

ROY, CATHERINE ELIZABETH, physical therapist; b. Tucson, Jan. 16, 1948; d. Francis Albert and Dorothy Orme (Thomas) R.; m. Richard M. Johnson, Aug. 31, 1968 (div. 1978); children: Kimberly Anne, Troy Michael. BA in Social Sci. magna cum laude, San Diego State U., 1980; MS in Phys. Therapy, U. So. Calif., 1984. Staff therapist Sharp Meml. Hosp., San Diego, 1984-89, chairperson patient and family edn. com., 1986-87, chairperson sex edn. and counselling com., 1987-89, chairperson adv. bd. for phys. therapy, asst. for edn. program, 1987—; supr. rehab. phys. therapy San Diego Rehab. Inst., 1989—; lectr. patient edn., family edn., peer edn.; mem. curriculum rev. com. U. So. Calif. Phys. Therapy Dept., 1982; bd. dirs. Ctr. for Edn. in Health; writer, reviewer licensure examination items for phys. therapy Profl. Examination Services.. Tennis coach at clinics Rancho Penasquitos Swim and Tennis Club, San Diego, 1980-81; active Polit. Activities Network, 1985. Mem. Am. Phys. Therapy Assn. (research presenter nat. conf. 1985, del. nat. conf. 1986-89, rep. state conf. 1987-89, Mary McMillan student award 1984, mem. exec. bd. San Diego dist. 1985—), AAUW, NAFE, Am. Coll. Sports Medicine, Am. Congress Rehab. Medicine, Phi Beta Kappa, Phi Kappa Phi, Chi Omega. Home: 13133 Via del Valedor San Diego CA 92129 Office: San Diego Rehab Inst Alvarado Hosp San Diego CA 92120

ROY, HAROLD EDWARD, research chemist; b. Stratford, Conn., June 2, 1921; s. Ludger Homer and Meta (Jepsen) R.; B.A., Duke U., 1950; m. Joyce E. Enslin, Oct. 9, 1946 (div. 1975); children—Glenn E., Barbara Anne, Suzanne Elizabeth; m. Gail LaVer Jensen, Feb. 11, 1983. Chemist research div. Lockheed Propulsion Co., Redlands, Calif., 1957-61; sec., treas. The Halgene Corp., Riverside, Calif., 1961-63; self-employed chemist, Glendora, Calif., 1963-64; chief engr. propellant devel. Rocket Power, Inc., Mesa, Ariz., 1964-65; cons., Glendora, 1965-66; engring. specialist Northrop Corp., Anaheim, Calif., 1966-69; pres. Argus Tech., Beverly Hills, 1969-70, dir. Harold E. Roy & Assos., Glendora, 1969—. Served to lt. (j.g.) USNR, 1943-46. Mem. Exptl. Aircraft Assn., Am. Ordnance Assn., Am. Inst. Aeros. and Astronautics, Internat. Platform Assn., Acad. Parapsychology and Medicine, Calif. Profl. Hypnotists Assn., World Future Soc. Republican. Home: 143 Warren Rd PO Box 414 Selma OR 97538

ROY, RAYMOND, bishop; b. Man., Can., May 3, 1919; s. Charles-Borromée and Zephirina (Milette) R. B.A. in Philosophy and Theology, U. Man., 1942; student, Philos. Sem., Montreal, 1942-43, Major Sem., Montreal, 1943-46, Major Sem. St. Boniface, 1946-47. Ordained priest Roman Catholic Ch. 1947. Asst. pastor, then pastor chs. in Man., 1947-50, 53-66; chaplain St. Boniface (Man.) Hosp., 1950-53; superior Minor Sem., St. Boniface, 1966-69; pastor Cathedral Parish, St. Boniface, 1969-72; ordained bishop 1972; bishop of St. Paul, Alta., Can., 1972—. Club: K.C. Address: 4410 51st Ave, Box 339, Saint Paul, AB Canada T0A 3A0 *

ROY, STANLEY ARTHUR, farmer; b. Yakima, Wash., Oct. 23, 1944; s. William Arthur and Edithe (Wood) R.; m. Susan Rickert, Feb. 12, 1947; children: Christopher E., Brenton A. AA, Big Bend Community Coll., 1965; BA, Gonzaga U., 1967; MA, Bowling Green U., 1969. Speech pathologist, asst. prog. dir. Umatilla County Ednl. Service Dist., Pendleton, Oreg., 1970-74; pres., owner Oasis Farms, Inc., Prosser, 1974—; bd. dirs. Meadowood Speech Camp, Pendleton, 1972-74. Mem. Prosser Sch. Dist. No. 116 Sch. Bd., 1983—, chmn. bd., 1988—. NSF grantee, 1968. Mem. Wash. Hort. Assn., Farm Bur. Wash. Republican. Roman Catholic. Home and Office: Rt 2 Box 2495 Prosser WA 99350

ROYALL, CYNTHIA RUTH, real estate company executive; b. Los Angeles, July 17, 1952; d. Charles Lee and Mildred K. Royall. Account coordinator Ayer, Jorgensen, MacDonald, L.A., 1974-75; exec. asst. N. Richard Lewis & Assocs., L.A., 1975-76; real estate saleswoman Day Realty, Woodland Hills, Calif., 1976-78, James R. Gary & Co. Ltd., Woodland Hills, 1978—. Active Big Sisters; com. chmn. North Canoga Park (Calif.) Residents Assn.,1 987—. Mem. Execs. Assn. San Fernando Valley (com. mem. 1988—). Republican. Presbyterian. Office: James R Gary & Co Ltd 21747 Erwin St Woodland Hills CA 91367

ROYBAL, EDWARD R., congressman; b. Albuquerque, Feb. 10, 1916; m. Lucille Beserra, Sept. 27, 1940; children: Lucille (Olivarez), Lillian (Rose), Edward R. Student, U. Calif. at Los Angeles, Southwestern U., Kaiser Coll., Los Angeles; LL.D. (hon.), Pacific States U., Claremont Grad. Sch. With Civilian Conservation Corps, 1934-35; social worker, pub. health educator Calif. Tb Assn.; then dir. health edn. Los Angeles County Tb and Health Assn., 1942-49; mem. 88th-101st Congresses from 25th Dist. Calif.; mem. appropriations com., select com. on aging, chmn. Congl. Hispanic Caucus; Mem. L.A. City Council, 1949-62, pres. pro tem, 1961-62. Served with AUS, 1944-45. Recipient Excellence in Pub. Service award Am. Acad. Pediatrics, 1976; Chubb fellow Yale U. Mem. Nat. Assn. Latino Elected Ofcls. (chmn.), Am. Mem. Am. Legion. Democrat. Roman Catholic. Club: K.C. Office: 2211 Rayburn House Office Bldg Washington DC 20515 *

ROYER, CHARLES THEODORE, mayor; b. Medford, Oreg., Aug. 22, 1939; s. Russell Theodore and Mildred Mae (Hampson) R.; m. Rosanne Gostovich, Oct. 19, 1968; children—Jordan, Suzanne. B.S., U. Oreg., 1967; postgrad., Harvard U., Mass. Inst. Tech., 1969-70. Polit. reporter KOIN-TV, Portland, Oreg., 1966-68; news analyst KING-TV, Seattle, 1970-77; mayor City of Seattle, 1978—. Mem. Dem. Nat. Com.; bd. dirs. Ctr. Nat. Policy, Nat. Council for Fgn. Langs. and Internat. Studies. Served with U.S. Army, 1961-63. Recipient Am. Polit. Sci. Assn. fellowship, 1969-70; Washington Journalism Center fellow, 1968; Sigma Delta Chi award, 1976; Edward R. Murrow award, 1976. Democrat. Office: Office Mayor 1200 Municipal Bldg Seattle WA 98104

ROYER, DONALD E., corporate lawyer; b. 1949. Grad., Ariz. State U.; JD, Western State U., 1976. V.p. Am. Savs. and Loan Assn., Irvine, Calif., 1983-85, exec. v.p., acting gen. counsel, 1985, sr. exec. v.p., gen. counsel, 1985—; v.p., asst. gen. counsel Fin. Corp. of Am. (parent), Irvine, Calif., 1983-84, sr. v.p., acting gen. counsel, 1984-85; exec. v.p., gen. counsel Fin. Corp. of Am. (parent), Irvine, 1985-88, Am. Savs. Bank, Irvine, 1988—. Office: Am Savs Bank 18401 Von Karman Ave Irvine CA 92715

ROYER, DOYLE L., company executive; b. Des Moines, Dec. 20, 1937; s. David L. and Anna Mae (Emmert) R.; m. June 28, 1958; children: Kim, Steve, Jeff. BS, McPherson Coll., 1960. With Hessler Co., Denver, 1960-63; sales mgr. Hessler Co., 1963-65; with Mastercraft, Denver, 1965-66; sales mgr., v.p. Mastercraft of Ariz., Phoenix, 1966-67; pres. Mastercraft of Ariz., 1967-77, Avant Garde, Tempe, Ariz., 1977—, Royer Ent., Las Vegas, Nev., 1986—. Mem. Sch. Bd. Kyrene, Tempe; merit bd. City of Tempe. Mem. Nat. Home Bldrs. Assn., Nat. Kitchen Cabinet Assn., Nat. Plastic Fabricators Assn., Cultured Marble Assn., Tempe Diablos (pres.), Fiesta Bowl. Home: 1339 Calle de Caballos Tempe AZ 85284 Office: Avant Garde Ltd 8980 S McKemy Tempe AZ 85284

ROYER, JOHN JAMES, marketing professional; b. Marinette, Wis., Oct. 15, 1931; s. Arthur William and Freida Emma (Wuhrman) R.; m. Teresa Marie Greenwood, Aug. 22, 1953; children: Donald Richard, Thomas Dale, James William, Robert Fredrick. BSEE, U. Wis., 1955. Engr. North Am. Aviation, Downey, Calif., 1955-57; sales engr. Jewett Co., North Hollywood, Calif., 1957-66; sales mgr. Pulse Engring., Santa Clara, Calif., 1966-68, Gulton Industries, Visalia, Calif., 1968-71; pres. JJ Component Sales, Escondido, Calif., 1971-76; sales mgr. DeAngelo Rothman, San Diego, 1976-81, Wabash, Inc., Huntington, Ind., 1982-84; owner TJ Mktg., Lake Havasu, Ariz., 1984—; cons. Calif. Indsl. Components, Fullerton, Calif., 1983—. Served with U.S. Army, 1949-51, Europe. Republican. Home: 615 Sand Dab Dr Lake Havasu City AZ 86403 Office: TJ Mktg PO Box 1233 Lake Havasu City AZ 86403

ROYSUM, HAROLD KING, sales professional; b. Thief River Falls, Minn., Mar. 14, 1916; s. Henry G. and Lissa Margaret (Knudsen) R.; m. Virginia N. Emmrich, July 23, 1947; children: Richard Charles, Lynne Margaret. BA, U. Oreg., 1938. Mktg. dir. Alexander Smith Carpet Co.,

Yonkers, N.Y., 1937; pres. Western Carpet Sales Internat., San Francisco, 1937—. Bd. dirs. U.S. Def. Com., Washington, 1980—. Named to Aviation Hall of Fame, Dayton, Ohio, 1978. Mem. Nat. Cong. Floor Covering Assns. (bd. dirs. 1976—). Republican. Lutheran. Office: Western Carpet Sales Internat 1355 Market St San Francisco CA 94103

ROZIER, SYLVIA GLADYS, business official; b. Menominee, Mich., Nov. 28, 1932; d. Carl Oscar and Elvira Irene Marie (Christianson) Vedin; m. George W. Rozier, Oct. 26, 1962 (dec. 1985). BA, No. Mich. U., 1956. Secondary teaching cert., Mich. Tchr. social studies Ironwood (Mich.) High Sch., 1956; sec. to field supr. Beneficial Mgmt. Corp., San Francisco, 1956-59; sec. Buckheim & Philip, CPA's, San Francisco, 1959-62; legal sec., asst. supr. secs. Pillsbury, Madison & Sutro, San Francisco, 1962-72, legal sec. to sr. ptnr., 1981-82; exec. sec. to judge U.S. Dist. Ct., San Francisco, 1972-80; confidential asst. to dep. atty. gen. U.S. Dept. Justice, Washington, 1980-81; exec. sec. to v.p. law Chevron Corp., San Francisco, 1983-88, exec. asst. to chmn. bd., 1988—. Mem. LWV, Mus. Soc., San Francisco Zool. Soc., Desk and Derrick Club. Republican. Office: Chevron Corp 225 Bush St San Francisco CA 94104

RUBACH, PEGGY, mayor; b. N.Y.C., July 7, 1947; m. Jon Rubach; children: Kristin, Jon, Matthew. BA in Psychology, SUNY, Buffalo; postgrad., Ariz. State U.; Diploma, Harvard U. Cost analyst, med. claims adminstr. Aetna Life and Casualty; project coordinator Mesa (Ariz.) community Coll.; dist. asst. Congressman John McCain; mayor City of Mesa, 1988—; mcpl. rep. Ariz. Consortium on Edn.; cons. Luth. Healthcare Network. Adv. bd. U. Ariz. Cancer Ctr.; treas. Ariz. Women Mcpl. Govt.; gov's. task force Cactus League Baseball; chmn. math. basic goals com. Ariz. Bd. Edn.; mem. Sister City Assn. of Mesa, East Valley Partnership, policy com. Nat. league of Cities' and Econ. Devel.; bd. dirs. Regional Pub. Transp. Authority; assoc. mem. Urban Land Inst. Home: 2145 E Glencove Mesa AZ 85030 Office: City of Mesa 55 N Center St PO Box 1466 Mesa AZ 85211-1466 *

RUBAYI, SALAH, surgeon, educator; b. Baghdad, Iraq, Oct. 1, 1942; came to U.S., 1981; s. Abdulla Mossa Rubayi and Fatma (Ibriham) Al-Jarah; m. Cecile-Rose, June 23, 1985. MD, U. Baghdad, Iraq, 1966; LRCP and LRCS, Royal Coll. Surgeons and Physicians, Scotland, 1974. Lic. physician and surgeon, Calif. Surgeon burn and reconstructive surgery Birmingham Accident Hosp., Eng., 1978-81; fellow burn unit Los Angeles County/U. So. Calif. Med. Ctr., 1981-82; fellow plastic surgery Rancho Los Amigos Med. Ctr, Downey, Calif., 1982-85; staff physician and chief pressure ulcer mgmt. service Rancho Los Amigos Med. Ctr, Downey, 1985—; chmn. Laser Safety Com. Rancho Los Amigos Med. Ctr., 1985—; asst. prof. surgery U. So. Calif. Contbr. articles to profl. jours. Fellow Internat. Coll. Surgeons, Am. Soc. Laser Medicine and Surgery; mem. Internat. Soc. Burn Injury, Am. Burn Assn., Internat. Soc. Paraplegia. Office: Rancho Los Amigos Med Ctr HB121 7601 E Imperial Hwy Downey CA 90242

RUBENSTEIN, LEONARD SAMUEL, communications executive, ceramist, painter, sculptor, photographer; b. Rochester, N.Y., Sept. 22, 1918; s. Jacob S. and Zelda H. (Gordon) R.; widowed May 28, 1983; children—Carolinda, Eric, Harley. B.F.A. cum laude, Alfred U., 1939; student Western Reserve, 1938; postgrad. U. Rochester, 1940-41. Creative dir. Henry Hempstead Advt. Agy., Chgo., 1949-55; v.p., exec. art dir. Clinton E. Frank Advt. Agy., Chgo., 1955-63; v.p., nat. creative dir. Foster & Kleiser div. Metromedia, Inc., Los Angeles, 1967-73, v.p. corp. creative cons., Metromedia, Inc., Los Angeles, 1973-88; guest lectr. U. Chgo.; instr. Columbia Coll., Chgo.; past. pres. Art Dirs. Club Chgo. (spl. citation); instr. Fashion Inst., Los Angeles; lectr. in field. Mem. Soc. Typog. Arts (past dir.), Am. Ceramic Soc. (design chpt.), Am. Craft Coun., Inst. Outdoor Advt. (past plans bd.), Los Angeles County Mus. Art, Mus. Contemporary Art of L.A. (charter), Palos Verdes (Calif.) Art Ctr., Phi Epsilon Pi. Lodge: B'nai B'rith. Author: (with Charles Hardison) Outdoor Advertising; contbr. articles in field to profl. publs. One-man show: Calif. Mus. Sci. and Industry, 1970; two-person exhibition of porcelains, Palos Verdes Art Ctr., 1987; numerous juried nat. and regional group shows; creator concept for Smithsonian exhibition Images of China: East and West, 1982; writer-producer (ednl. video) Paul Soldner, Thoughts on Creativity, 1989. Home and Office: 30616 Ganado Dr Rancho Palos Verdes CA 90274

RUBENSTEIN, MICHAEL ALAN, architect; b. St. Louis, July 18, 1944; s. Melvin Paul and Miriam (Schwartz) R. BArch, Wash. U., 1966, MArch, 1968. Registered architect, Calif. Designer Skidmore, Owings, Merrill, N.Y.C., 1967-68, Helmuth, Obata, Kassabaum, St. Louis, 1968-69, Peckham/Guyton Assocs., St. Louis, 1969-70, B.A. Berkus, L.A., 1970-71, Gruen Assocs., L.A., 1971-72; design cons. Gruen Assocs., N.Y.C., 1971, Studio Works, N.Y.C., 1972; design cons., mem. staff Experiments in Art and Tech., N.Y.C., 1972-73; pvt. practice architecture Healdsburg, 1975-86; ptnr. Anderson & Rubenstein, Santa Rosa, 1986-87; prin. Rubenstein Architects, AIA, Santa Rosa, 1987—. Exhibited Eugenia Butler Gallery, Los Angeles, 1970, Calif. 101, Monterey Design Conf., 1980, Cultural Arts Council Sonoma County, 1986. Mem. Design Rev. Com., Healdsburg, Calif., 1978-80, chmn. 1980-83; mem. Steering Com., Healdsburg, 1981-83; coordinator Regional Urban Design Assistance Team, Healdsburg, 1982; chmn. Cultural Resource Survey Rev. Com., Healdsburg, 1982-83. Recipient Key to City Wine Honorarium, Healdsburg, 1982, Cert. Outstanding Design Lawrence Galleries City of Santa Rosa, 1984, Calif. Solar Council Energy Saving Builder awards 3 houses, 1982, Design and Planning award for pvt. house, Builder Mag., 1982, 83. Mem. AIA (bd. dirs. Redwood Empire chpt., v.p., pres. elect Redwood Empire chpt. 1986, pres. 1987, past pres., bd. dirs. 1988, Honor award 1984, Design awards, Plaza St. Cafe Merit award 1984, 86), Metal Constrn. Assn. (Honor award 1988), Quivira Winery.

RUBIN, LAWRENCE IRA, podiatrist; b. Buffalo, Dec. 19, 1945; s. Harold Philip and Rose (Kaiser) R.; m. Janis Bernstein, Sept. 12, 1970 (div. Apr. 1986); children: Alison Meredith, Stacy Heather; m. Linda Sleeth, Apr. 30, 1989. Student, Am. U., 1963-65; D of Podiatric Medicine, N.Y. Coll. of Podiatric Medicine, 1969. Diplomate Am. Bd. Podiatric Surgery. Resident in podiatry Kensington Hosp., Phila., 1970; practice medicine specializing in podiatry Clarence, N.Y., 1970-76; chief podiatric surgery and medicine Meml. Hosp. of Gardena, Calif., 1977—; cons. South Bay Free Clinic, Gardena, 1979—. Fellow Am. Coll. Foot Surgeons; mem. Calif. Podiatric Med. Assn. (peer review com.), L.A. County Podiatric Med. Soc. (pres. 1983-84, parliamentarian 1985-88, chmn. seminar com. 1980-82, 87-88, Pres.'s award 1984), Am. Acad. Podiatric Sports Medicine (assoc.). Democrat. Jewish. Lodge: Masons (master mason 1974—). Office: Gardena Podiatrist's Group 1141 W Redondo Beach Blvd Gardena CA 90247

RUBINO, PETER JAMES, civil engineer; b. Torrington, Conn., Aug. 24, 1952; s. Bernard Paul and Katherine Emile (Bzullak) R.; m. Mahvash Sedigheh Tahtolkassaie, Aug. 20, 1978; children—Jasper Antoni, Jason Cyrus. B.S. in Civil Engring., U. Conn., 1974; M.B.A., U. Okla., 1985. Registered profl. engr., Conn., Tex. Acting mng. dir. I.H.L., Baghdad, Iraq, 1976, asst. project mgr., Bandar Abbas, Iran, 1976-77, office/field engr., Tehran, Iran, 1977-78; office engr. IRATEX, Houston, 1978-80; project engr. ARAMCO, Dhahran, Saudi Arabia, 1980-86; sr. facility engr., team leader leased facilities projects Intel Corp., Chandler, Ariz., 1987— . Designer Jordan Army Dining Hall, 1977. Mem. ASCE, Nat. Soc. Profl. Engrs. Republican. Avocations: photography; home computers; investment; swimming; biking; woodworking. Home and Office: 5000 W Chandler Blvd Chandler AZ 85224

RUBINSTEIN, ELAINE PERLE, technical writer; b. L.A., Dec. 22, 1953; d. William Crandall and Charlotte Rhoda (Streifer) R.; m. Theodore Perle, June 19, 1983. BA cum laude, Yale U., 1976. Editorial asst. Fawcett Publs., N.Y.C., 1973-74; adminstrv. asst. Japan Calif. Bank, L.A., 1977-78; word processing specialist U. Calif., Irvine, 1979-82; jr. tech. writer Burroughs Corp. (name now Unisys), Mission Viejo, Calif., 1982-85; intermediate tech. writer AST Research, Inc., Irvine, 1985-87; sr. tech. writer Emulex Corp., Costa Mesa, Calif., 1987—; founder cons. firm P.C. Spectrum Services, Irvine, 1987—. Author computer user and tech. reference manuals, AST Enhanced Graphics Diagnostics Manual, 1986 (Achievement award), others; rsch. asst. history for Women Artists, 1984 (ALA award 1982). Mem. Soc. Tech. Communication (Orange County chpt., sec. 1983-84, coeditor newsletter 1984-85, writer 1985—, Disting. Tech. Communication Newsletter award 1985), NOW, AAUW. Democrat. Jewish. Home: 3 Bellflower Irvine CA 92714 Office: Emulex Corp 3545 Harbor Blvd Costa Mesa CA 92626

RUBLE, ANN, clergywoman; b. Seattle, Oct. 26, 1953; d. Monte Rahe and Stella (Terefinko) Ruble; m. Francis Michael Trotter, Aug. 29, 1984. Cert. sec., Met. Bus. Coll., Seattle, 1972. Ordained to ministry Ch. of Scientology, 1980. Minister Ch. of Scientology, Seattle, 1980—, dir. pub. affairs, 1983; pres. Ch. of Scientology of Wash. State, Seattle, 1984-88, dir., 1989—. Bur. chief Jour. Freedom News, 1984-88. Mem. Citizen's Commn. Human Rights, Seattle, 1984—, Com. on Religious Liberties, Seattle, 1985—. Mem. Internat. Platform Assn., Washington Environ. Coun. Office: Ch of Scientology of Washington State 2004 Westlake Ave Seattle WA 98121

RUBNER, BETSY DAY, infosystems executive; b. Cleve., June 4, 1948; d. Henry and Mary Hannah (Day) R. BA in Math., U. Mich., 1970; MBA, U. Phoenix, 1989. Systems mgr. DTSS Inc., Hanover, N.H., 1978-79, dir. ops., 1980-81, systems dir., 1981-84; field mktg. dir. Denver, 1984-87; acct. mgr. CLARIS, Denver, 1988—. Office: CLARIS 1200 17th St Ste 1950 Denver CO 80202

RUBOTTOM, CAROLE MARIE, music educator; b. Seattle, July 28, 1944; d. Virgil Earl and Jessie Margaret (Cress) Cutler; m. Lawrence Lemar Rubottom, july 31, 1965. BA in Music, U. Calif., Santa Barbara, 1966. Cert. tchr., Calif. Music tchr. Pleasant Valley Sch. Dist., Camarillo, Calif., 1967-69; founder, dir., owner Jr. Music Acad., Ventura, Calif., 1967—. Author music instrn. manuals, 1976, 88. Mem. Ventura Arts Council. Mem. Music Tchrs. Assn. Calif., Nat. Assn. Female Execs. Democrat. Home: 697 Via Cielito Ventura CA 93003 Office: Jr Music Acad 2351 E Main St Ventura CA 93003

RUBY, CHARLES LEROY, educator, lawyer, civic leader; b. Carthage, Ind., Dec. 28, 1900; s. Edgar Valentine and Mary Emma (Butler) R.; certificate Ball State U., 1921-22; AB, Cen. Normal Coll., 1924, LLB, 1926, BS, 1931, BPE, 1932; MA, Stanford, 1929; JD, Pacific Coll. of Law, 1931; PhD, Olympic U., 1933; m. Rachael Elizabeth Martindale, Aug. 30, 1925; children: Phyllis Arline (Mrs. Norman Braskat), Charles L., Martin Dale. Prin., Pine Village (Ind.) High Sch., 1923-25; Glenwood (Ind.) Pub. Schs., 1925-26; tchr. El Centro (Calif.) Pub. Sch., 1926-27, Central (Calif.) Union High Sch., 1927-29; prof. law Fullerton Coll., 1929-66; prof. edn. Armstrong Coll., summer 1935, Cen. Normal Coll., summers 1929-33; admitted to Ind. bar, 1926, U.S. Supreme Ct. bar, 1970; pres. Ret. Service Vol. Program, North Orange County, Calif., 1973-76, 83-84; dir. North Orange County Vol. Bur., Fullerton Sr. Citizens Task Force. Life trustee, Continuing Learning Experiences program Calif. State U., Fullerton, hon. chmn. fund com. Gerontology Bldg; founder, dir. Fullerton Pub. Forum, 1929-39; founder Elks Nat. Found.; co-founder, benefactor Gerontology Ctr. Calif. State U., Fullerton; pres. Fullerton Rotary, 1939-40, hon. mem., 1983—; mem. U.S. Assay Commn., 1968—; mem. Orange County Dem. Cen. Com., 1962-78; bd. dirs. Fullerton Sr. Multi-purpose Ctr., 1981—; bd. dirs. Orange County Sr. Citizens Adv. Council; mem. pres.'s com. Calif. State U., Fullerton. Recipient Medal of Merit, Am. Numis. Assn., 1954, Spl. Commendation, Calif. State Assembly, 1966, 88, Calif. State Senate, 1978, 86, Commendation, Ind. Sec. of State, 1984, Commendation, Bd. Suprs. Orange County, 1985, Commendation, Fullerton City Council, 1986, 88, Commendation, Orange County Bd. Supervisors, 1986, Commendation, Calif. State Senate, 1986, Commendation, Exec. Com. Pres. Calif. State U., Fullerton, 1986; Charles L. and Rachael E. Ruby Gerontology Ctr. named in his and late wife's honor, Calif. State U., Fullerton. Fellow Ind. Bar Found.; mem. Pres. Assocs. Calif. State U. Fullerton, Fullerton Coll. Assocs. (named Spl. Retiree of Yr. 1986, Commendation, 1986), Calif. (life, pres. So. sect. 1962-63, treas. 1964-65, pres. 1960-61, dir. 1956-65), Orange County Tchrs. Assn. (pres. 1953-55), Fullerton Coll. (pres. 1958-60) Tchrs. Assn., NEA (life), Ind. Bar Assn., Stanford U. Law Soc., Calif. State Council Edn., Am. Numismatic Assn. (gov. 1951-53, life adv. bd.), Ind. Bar Assn. (hon. life), Calif. Bus. Educators Assn. (hon. life), Calif. Assn. Univ. Profs., Pacific S.W. Bus. Law Assn. (pres. 1969-70, life), Numismatic Assn. So. Calif. (life, pres. 1961), Calif. Numis. Assn., Indpls. Coin Club (hon. life), Los Angeles Coin Club (hon. life), U.S. Supreme Ct. Hist. Soc., Calif. Town Hall, North Orange County Mus. Assn. (life, benefactor dir.), Stanford U. Alumni Assn., Old Timers Assay Commn. Methodist. Clubs: Elks, Fullerton Jr. Coll. Vets. (hon. life). Contbr. articles in field to profl. jours. Home: 308 N Marwood Ave Fullerton CA 92632

RUCKER, HAYNE JERNIGAN, data processing executive; b. Durham, N.C., May 10, 1948; s. Driftwood Hayne and Bernice (Jernigan) R. BS in Systems Sci., U. West Fla., 1971. V.p. Basic Systems, Denver, 1971-77; mgr. data processing Internat. Med. Corp., Englewood, Colo., 1977-80; mgr. mgmt. info. systems Carefree of Colo., Inc., Broomfield, 1980-81; sr. systems analyst Adams County Adminstrn., Brighton, Colo., 1981—; pres. AmStar Group, Thornton, Colo.; speaker in field. Active Big Bros., Denver, 1974-75; coordinator Jr. Achievement, Denver, 1975; program specialist Community Living Alternatives, Denver, 1979—. Mem. Urban and Regional Info. Systems Assn., Delta Sigma Pi. Office: Adams County Adminstrn 450 S 4th Ave Brighton CO 80601

RUCKER, THOMAS DOUGLAS, purchasing executive; b. Ottumwa, Iowa, Aug. 30, 1926; s. Everett Henry and Harriett Mary (Evans) R.; A.B., Loyola U., 1951; postgrad. St. Patrick's Coll., 1950-52; m. Rita Mary Rommelfanger, Apr. 18, 1953; children—David, Theresa, Martin, Paul. Asst. purchasing agt. Radio TV Supply, Los Angeles, 1952-53; buyer Consol. Western Steel div. U.S. Steel, Commerce, Calif., 1953-64, S.W. Welding & Mfg. Co., Alhambra, Calif., 1964-70; dir. purchasing Southwestern Engring., Commerce, Calif., 1970-87, ret. Served with USAAF, 1945-46. Home: 10642 Abisko Dr Whittier CA 90604 Office: Southwestern Engring 5701 S Eastern Ave Ste 300 Commerce CA 90040

RUDD, ELDON, lawyer, former congressman; b. Camp Verde, Ariz.; m. Ann Merritt. B.A., Ariz. State U., 1947; J.D., U. Ariz., 1950. Bar: Ariz. 1949, U.S. Supreme Ct. 1953. Spl. agt.-diplomatic assignment principally Latin Am. FBI, 1950-70; pvt. practice Tucson, 1970—; mem. Maricopa County (Ariz.) Bd. Suprs., 1972-76; bd. dirs. Ariz.-Mex. Commn., 1972-76, 87—; mem. Gov. Ariz. Adv. Commn. Intergovtl. Affairs, 1975-76, 95th-99th Congresses from 4th Dist. Ariz., 1976-87; of counsel Shimmel, Hill, Bishop & Gruender, P.C., Phoenix, 1987—; bd. dirs. So. Pacific Transp. Co., 1987-88, Salt River Project, 1988—. Author: World Communism-Threat to Freedom, 1987. Mem. numerous pub. service orgns. including energy and water, mil. affairs, internat. affairs. Served as aviator USMCR, 1942-46. Mem. Fed. Bar Assn. (chpt. pres. 1976), Ariz. Bar Assn., Maricopa County Bar Assn., Scottsdale Bar Assn., Phi Delta Phi, Blue Key. Republican. Roman Catholic. Address: PO Box 873 Scottsdale AZ 85252 Office: 3700 N 24th St Phoenix AZ 85016

RUDDICK, STEPHEN RICHARD, state representative, lawyer, political consultant; b. Denver, Nov. 6, 1954; s. Paul Richard and Myra Jane (Brooks) R.; m. Ana Maria Peters, June 16, 1984. B.A., Met. State U., Denver, 1977; J.D., U. Denver, 1980. Bar: Colo. 1980, U.S. Dist. Ct. Colo. 1980, U.S. Ct. Appeals (10th cir.) 1980. Steward, I.B. of Teamsters, Denver, 1979; law clk., later assoc. law firm Anderson, Calder & Lembke, P.C., Aurora, Colo., 1979-80; sole practice law, Aurora, Colo., 1980-81; asst. city atty. City Atty.'s Office, Aurora, Colo., 1981—; state rep. Colo. Gen. Assembly, 1987—. Chmn., 18th Jud. Dist. Dem. Cen. Com., 1983—; vice-chmn. Arapahoe County Dem. Com., 1983-85; mem. Colo. Common Cause, Arapahoe-Denver NOW. Mem. Aurora Bar Assn. (sec.-treas. 1983-84, v.p. 1984-85, pres. 1985-86), Colo. Bar Assn. Democrat. Roman Catholic. Club: Aurora East Lions. Lodge: Masons (master 1983—). Home: 1031 Sable Blvd Aurora CO 80011 Office: City Atty Office 15001 E Alameda Dr Aurora CO 80012

RUDDY, IRIS MITTENDORF, non-profit organization administrator; b. Cleve., May 14, 1924; d. Francis H. and Edna H. (Webber) Mittendorf; m. Edward Michael Ruddy, Feb. 21, 1946; children: Michael, Sara, Barbara. BS, N.E. Mo. State U., 1945; MA, St. Louis U., 1969, PhD, 1975. Dept. chairwoman Webster Groves (Mo.) High Sch., 1952-59; organizer high sch. program Shriner's Hosp., St. Louis, 1970-74; prof. history St. Louis Community Coll., 1975-79; realtor Ira E. Berry, Real Estate, St. Louis, 1979-85; health coord. Am. Assn. Retired Persons, Las Cruces, N.Mex., 1987—. Vol. Casa de Peregrino Emergency Food Pantry, Las Cruces, 1985—. Ford fellow Yale U., 1955, Hamline U. fellow, 1976. Mem. AAUW, LWV, Women's Improvement Assn.-Nat. Fedn. Women's Clubs, Alpha Sigma Alpha. Democrat. Congregationalist. Home: 2105 Sagecrest Ave Las Cruces NM 88001

RUDIN, ANNE NOTO, mayor; b. Passaic, N.J., Jan. 27, 1924; m. Edward Rudin, June 6, 1948; 4 children. BS in Edn., Temple U., 1945, RN, 1946; MPA, U. So. Calif., 1983. R.N., Calif. Mem. faculty Temple U. Sch. Nursing, Phila., 1946-48; mem. nursing faculty Mt. Zion Hosp., San Francisco, 1948-49; mem. Sacramento City Council, 1971-83; mayor City of Sacramento, 1983—; mem. World Conf. of Mayors for Peace. Pres., LWV, Riverside, Sacramento, 1957, 61, Calif. Elected Women's Assn., 1973-89; mem. Dem. State Cen. Com., Calif., 1984-87; bd. dirs. Sacramento Commerce and Trade Orgn., 1984-89; bd. dirs. League of Calif. Cities; mem. U.S. Conf. of Mayors. Recipient Woman of Yr. award Soroptimist Club, 1976; Women in Govt. award U.S. Jaycee Women, 1984; Woman of Distinction award Sacramento Area Soroptimist Clubs, 1985; Woman of Courage award Sacramento History Ctr., 1989; named Girl Scouts Am. Role Model, 1989. Office: City of Sacramento 915 I St Rm 205 Sacramento CA 95814

RUDIN, JENNY, violinist, educator; b. Baranowicze, Poland, Apr. 1, 1928; came to U.S., 1954; d. David and Ita (Zelikowicz) Sadowsky; m. Benjamin Rudin, Mar. 18, 1956; children: Norah, Dana. Student, Moscow Conservatory, 1944-45, Adademie der Kunst, Munich, 1946-47, Manhattan Sch. Music, 1955-56; MusB, Tel-Aviv Conservatory, 1954. Violin soloist, chamber music performer Israel and U.S., 1950—; pvt. violin instr. Palo Alto, Calif., 1960—; concertmistress, soloist Master Sinfonia Chamber Orch. Foothill Coll., Los Altos, 1966-75; head of Yehudi Menuhin program Nueva Learning Ctr., Hillsborough, Calif., 1975-83; guest lectr. Yehudi Menuhin Sch. Music., Surrey, Eng., 1978; mem. faculty San Jose (Calif.) State U., 1979-80; Coll. Notre Dame, Belmont, Calif., 1977—, Sequoia Chamber Music Workshop, Humboldt (Calif.) State U., 1976-81; master classes Palo Alto Chamber Orchestra, Calif. Youth Symphony, 1971—; founder, dir. summer string workshop, Coll. Notre Dame, 1983—, Baroque Sinfonietta Youth Chamber Ensemble, Palo Alto, 1986—. Contbr. articles to profl. publs. Mem. Am. String Tchrs. Assn., Music Tchrs. Assn. Calif. Home: 744 Holly Oak Dr Palo Alto CA 94303 Office: Coll Notre Dame Belmont CA 94002

RUDOLPH, KAREN MARGARET, space designer, property manager; b. San Jose, Calif., Mar. 30, 1953; d. Onslow Hamilton and Betty Jo (Fry) R.; m. James Marvin Simmons, Sept. 19, 1987. BA, U. Wash., 1979; MA, Antioch Coll., 1984. Instr. U. Wash., Seattle, 1976-83; exec. dir. Multi-Svc. Ctr., Seattle, 1980-81; fl. mgr. Downtown Emergency Svc. Ctr., Seattle, 1982-83, Bear Valley Svc. Ctr., Seattle, 1983-84; property mgr. Rudolph & Sletten, Inc., Foster City, Calif., 1984—. Author: (with others) Changing Our Power, 1987. Founding mem. Women Against Thirteen, Seattle, 1978; bd. dirs. Women Studies Student Union U. Wash., 1975-78, Native Am. Prisoner Support Group, Seattle, 1979-83. Mem. Nat. Women Studies Assn. (exec. bd. dirs. 1986—), Internat. of Cupertino, Quota. Office: Rudolph & Sletten Inc 989 E Hillsdale Blvd Foster City CA 94404

RUDOLPH, MARK EDWARD, lawyer; b. Milw., July 23, 1960. BA, Coll. William & Mary, 1982; JD, U. Va., 1985. Assoc. Whyte & Hirschboeck, S.C., Milw., 1985-87, Thelen, Marrin, Johnson, & Bridges, San Francisco, 1987—. Mem. Am. Judiciary Soc., ABA (litigation sec.), Wis. Bar Assn., Ariz. Bar Assn., Calif. Bar Assn., Bay Club, Barristers' Club. Office: Thelen Marrin Johnson & Bridges Two Embarcadero Ctr Ste 2100 San Francisco CA 94111

RUDOLPH, THOMAS KEITH, engineer; b. Jamestown, N.D., Oct. 4, 1961; s. Arthur John and Melinda Magdelina (Nehlich) R. BS in Aerospace Engring., Iowa State U., 1983. Registered profl. engr., Wash. Engr. Boeing Advanced Systems, Seattle, 1984-88, sr. engr., 1988—; chmn. Weight Improvement Program B-2 Program, Seattle, 1986—. Named one of Outstanding Young Men in Am., 1985, Employee of the Quarter B-2 Tech. Staff, 1986. Mem. Soc. Allied Weight Engrs. (sr. mem., chmn. activities com. 1985-86, treas. 1986-87, facilities chmn. internat. conf. 1987, v.p. 1987-88), Am. Inst. Aeronautics and Astronautics, Iowa State Alimni Assn. Republican. Methodist. Home: 4615 South 170th St Seattle WA 98188 Office: Boeing Advanced Systems PO BoX 3707 M/S 4A-06 Seattle WA 98124

RUDOLPH, WALTER PAUL, engineering research company executive; b. Binghamton, N.Y., Aug. 17, 1937; s. Walter Paul and Frieda Lena (Hennemann) R.; m. Leila Ortencia Romero, Dec. 18, 1960; children: Jonathan, Jana, Catherine. BEE, Rensselaer Poly. Inst., 1959; MSBA, San Diego State U., 1964. Elec. engr. Gen. Dynamics/Astronautics, San Diego, 1959-62; ops. research analyst Navy Electronics Lab., San Diego, 1962-64; mem. profl. staff Gen. Electric Tempo, Honolulu, 1964-70, Ctr. for Naval Analysis, Arlington, Va., 1970-77; pres. La Jolla (Calif.) Research Corp., 1977—. Served to capt. USNR, 1959—. Republican. Presbyterian. Home: 1559 El Paso Real La Jolla CA 92037 Office: La Jolla Rsch Corp PO Box 1207 La Jolla CA 92038

RUDY, ANNEMARIE, charitable association executive; b. N.Y.C., July 17, 1957; d. John and Anna (Fill) R. BS magna cum laude, Oral Roberts U., 1978; postgrad., U.N.Mex., 1982—. Sec., receptionist Rosner and Estrada, Albuquerque, 1975-77; asst. bookkeeper Med. Collection Svc., Houston, 1978-79; customer svc. rep. Allied Sch. and Office Products, Albuquerque, 1979-85; exec. dir. dist. II Am. Cancer Soc., Albuquerque, 1986—. Sec. William H. Tucker Found., Albuquerque, 1988; mem. Women Concerned with Smoking, Santa Fe, 1987-88; mem. coms. United Way, Albuquerque, 1987-88. Mem. NAFE, Rio Grande Zoo Parents. Home: 1800 Father Sky NE Albuquerque NM 87112 Office: Am Cancer Soc 5800 Lomas Blvd NE Albuquerque NM 87110

RUE, BILLY MACK, company president; b. Bonham, Tex., Feb. 12, 1944; s. Arvill Franklin and Enla Virginia (Mac Rae) R.; m. Jo Gail Phillips, 1964 (div. 1973); children: Michael Phillip, Christine Diane; m. Michelle Trujeque, 1973 (div. 1977); 1 child, Billy Mack Jr.; m. Melynda Sue Harmon, Jan. 8, 1979; children: Tammera Marie, Mack Robert. Pipefitter apprenticeship local 469. Apprentice Local Union 469, Phoenix, 1967-72; svc. mechanic various orgns., Phoenix, 1972-78; svc. mgr. Climate Control Inc., Phoenix, 1978-82, Metro Plumbing & Mech., Phoenix, 1982-84; pres. Metro Mechanic Inc., Phoenix, 1984—; joint apprenticeship com. mem. Phoenix Air Conditioning Contractors, 1988—. With U.S. Army, 1962-65. Democrat. Office: Metro Mech Inc 1714 W Lincoln Phoenix AZ 85007

RUE, ROBERT WESLEY, real estate executive; b. Chester, Pa., June 10, 1950; s. Robert Wesley and Alice Irene (Pusey) R.; m. Jeanne Marie DeCecco, June 9, 1973 (div. 1977); m. Jennifer Ann Jennings, Dec. 3,1978; 1 stepdau., Christa Noel Abel. BSBA, Widener U., 1983. . Sr. acct. Sun Oil Cod., Marcus Hook, Pa., 1968-83; sales rep. Strawbridge & Clothier, Wilmington, Del., 1982-84, Erico Fastening Systems, Phoenix, 1985-87; real estate broker Russ Lyon Realty, Scottsdale, Ariz., 1987--. Republican. Presbyterian. Home: 5539 E Marilyn Rd Scottsdale AZ 85254

RUEBE, BAMBI LYNN, interior/environmental designer; b. Huntington Park, Calif., Nov. 13, 1957; d. Leonard John Ruebe and Vaudis Marie Powell. BS, UCLA, 1988. Millwright asst. Kaiser Steel Corp., Fontana, Calif., 1976-79; electrician Fleetwood Enterprises, Riverside, Calif., 1977; fashion model internat., 1977-85; freelance draftsman 1982-83; project coordinator Philip J. Sicola Inc., Culver City, Calif., 1982-83; prin. designer Ruebe Inclusive Design, Highland, Calif., 1983—; cons. mfg. design Burlington Homes New Eng. Inc., Oxford, Maine, 1987—, DeRose Industries, Chambersburg, Pa., 1984, Skyline Corp., Redlands, Calif., 1982-84; cons. lighting Lightways Corp., Los Angeles, 1984—; mem. design rev. bd. San Bernadino (Calif.) Downtown Main St. Redevel. Co., 1987—. Mem. World Affairs Coun., Inland So. Calif., 1986—, citizens adv. com. Highland (Calif.) Gen. Plan, 1988—; co-chmn. civil rights com. AFL-CIO, Fontana, 1978-79. Recipient Cert. Merit Scholastic Art award Scholastic Mags. Inc., Southeastern Calif., 1974. Mem. Nat. Trust for Hist. Preservation.

Democrat. Office: Ruebe Inclusive Design 27000 Meines St Highland CA 92346

RUFF, FRED T., banker; b. Scottsbluff, Neb., Jan. 11, 1958; s. Fred W. and Shirly (Green) R.; m. Judith A. Bauer, June 17, 1979; 1 child, Chase. AA in Bus., Neb. Western Coll., 1978; BBA, Chadron State Coll., 1982. V.p. Ft. Morgan (Colo.) Bank, 1983—. Mem. N.E. Colo. Bankers Adminstrn. Inst. (pres.), Kiwanis (pres. Ft. Morgan chpt. 1986-87), Elks. Office: Fort Morgan State Bank 520 Sherman St Fort Morgan CO 80701

RUGE, EUGENE ARNO, electrical engineer, aerospace engineer; b. Sheboygan, Wis., Oct. 1, 1933; s. Fred William and Hertha Marie (Stubenrauch) R.; m. Patricia Mae Farner, Nov. 23 1960 (div. May 1981); children: Richard, Rodney, Robert. BSEE, U. Wis., 1959; MSEE, Purdue U., 1961; postgrad., U. So. Calif., 1964-65, UCLA, 1965-70. Registered profl. engr., Calif. Mem. tech. staff Bell Tel. Labs., Indpls., 1959-61; sr. rsch. engr. Gen. Dynamics Corp., Pomona, Calif., 1962-65; rsch. engr. GM Rsch. Labs., Warren, Mich., 1971; design analyst TRW Systems Group, San Bernardino, Calif., 1971-72; staff engr. Burroughs Corp., Westlake Village, Calif., 1972-73; electronics engr. Hughes Helicopters, Culver City, Calif., 1973-74, Hughes Aircraft Co., L.A., 1974-78; engrng. specialist Northrop Corp., Hawthorne, Calif., 1978-79; project engr. The Aerospace Corp., El Segundo, Calif., 1979—. With U.S. Army, 1953-55. Bell Tel. Labs. fellow, 1959-61, Gen. Dynamics Corp. fellow, 1964-67. Republican. Lutheran. Home: 9510 Lucerne Ave Culver City CA 90232 Office: The Aerospace Corp 2350 E El Segundo Blvd El Segundo CA 90009-2957

RUGGE, HENRY FERDINAND, corporate executive; b. South San Francisco, Oct. 28, 1936; s. Hugo Heinrich and Marie Mathilde (Breiholz) R.; m. Sue Callow, Dec. 29, 1967. BS in Physics, U. Calif., Berkeley, 1958, PhD in Physics, 1963. Sr. physicist Physics Internat. Co., San Leandro, 1963-68; dir. adminstrn. and fin. Arkon Sci. Labs., Berkeley, Calif., 1969-71; v.p. Norse Systems, Inc., Hayward, Calif., 1972-74; v.p. Rasor Assocs., Inc., Sunnyvale, Calif., 1974-81, v.p., gen. mgr., 1983-87, exec. v.p. fin., 1988—; pres. Berliscan, Inc., Sunnyvale, 1981-82; cons. The Rugge Group, Berkeley, 1987-; bd. dirs. Rasor Assocs., Inc. Patentee in area med. devices. U. Calif. scholar, 1954-58. Mem. Am. Heart Assn., Berkeley Bicycle (treas. 1983-84), Phi Beta Kappa. Home: 44 Hiller Dr Oakland CA 94618 Office: Rasor Assocs Inc 253 Humboldt Ct Sunnyvale CA 94089

RUGGERI, ZAVERIO MARCELLO, medical researcher; b. Bergamo, Italy, Jan. 7, 1945; came to U.S., 1978; s. Giovanni and Anna (Dolci) R.; m. Rosamaria Carrara, June 12, 1971. MD magna cum laude, U. Milan, 1970; degree in Clin. and Exptl. Hematology magna cum laude, U. Pavia, Italy, 1973, degree in Internal Medicine magna cum laude, 1981. Asst. clin. prof. hematology U. Milan, 1972-80; assoc. dir. hemophilia ctr. Policlinico Hosp., Milan, 1980-82; vis. investigator Scripps Clinic and Research Found., La Jolla, Calif., 1978-80, asst. mem., 1982-85; assoc. mem. Scripps Clinic and Rsch. Found., La Jolla, Calif., 1985—; dir. Roon Ctr. for Arteriosclerosis and Thrombosis, 1989—; head div. Exptl. Hemostasis, 1989—; vis. investigator St. Thomas/St. Bartholomews Hosps., London, 1974-76. Editor: Clinics in Haematology, 1985; mem. editorial bds. Blood, 1988—, Peptide Research, 1988—; contbr. articles to profl. jours., chpts. to books. Research scholar Italian Ministry of Edn., 1970, Italian Hemophilia Found., 1970-72. Mem. AAAS, Italian Hemophilia Found., Am. Soc. Clin. Investigation, Italian Soc. Thrombosis and Hemostasis, Internat. Soc. Thrombosis and Hemostasis, Am. Heart Assn. (council on thrombosis), World Fedn. Hemophilia, Am. Fedn. Clin. Research, N.Y. Acad. Scis., Am. Soc. Hematology. Office: Scripps Clinic Rsch Found 10666 N Torrey Pines Rd La Jolla CA 92037

RUGGIERI, DOMINIC JULES, electronics executive; b. Ravenna, Ohio, June 27, 1936; s. Ralph Leonard and Mary Jacquelyn (Camtelmo) R.; m. Shirley Kay Haze, May 26, 1956; children: Ralph Leonard, Denise Linda, Scott Leonard. BEE, Santa Clara U., 1958, MSEE, 1982. Sr. engr. Kaiser Aerospace & Electronics, Mountain View, Calif., 1958-61; group leader Optics Technology, Palo Alto, Calif., 1961-67; ops. mgr. Varian Assocs., Palo Alto, 1967-76, product/program mgr., 1976-82, mgr. mktg. div., 1982-84; v.p. mktg., sales Star Microwave, Palo Alto, 1986-88; mgr. product line electronic devices div. Litton Industries, San Carlos, Calif., 1988—. Patentee in field. Bd dirs., treas. Children's Cancer Research Inst., San Francisco, 1978—; bd. dirs. Santa Clara (Calif.) U. Republican. Roman Catholic.

RUGGILL, SOLOMON P., psychologist; b. N.Y.C., Sept. 29, 1906; s. Abraham and Sarah (Silverberg) R.; m. Sophie Stock, June 8, 1938; children: Robert Zachary, Peter Alan. BS, CCNY, 1927; MA in Edn., Columbia U., 1930, PhD in Psychology, 1934. Lic. psychologist, N.Y. Tchr. elem. and jr. high sch. Bd. of Edn. of N.Y.C., 1929-59, psychologist, Bur. of Child Guidance, 1959-62; psychologist Baro Civic Ctr. Clinic, Bklyn., 1961-62; assoc. prof. L.I. U., Bklyn., 1962-69, prof., 1969-79, prof. emeritus, 1979—, acting chmn. dept. guidance and counseling, 1972-73; dir. Flatback Progressive Sch., Bklyn., 1943-45, Camp Kinderwelt, Fraternal Order Farband, N.Y.C., 1959-60; lectr. in gerontology to various orgns., Tucson, 1980—. Pres. Chancy Meml. Found., N.Y.C., 1961-63; mem. adv. council Pima Council on Aging, Tucson, 1987—. Mem. N.Y. Acad. Pub. Edn., N.Y. State Guidance Assn., Jewish Tchrs. Assn. (life). Jewish. Home: 425 W Paseo Redondo Apt 7E Tucson AZ 85701

RUGGLES, KENNETH WARREN, meteorologist; b. San Francisco, May 18, 1932; s. Charles Francis and Helen Elizabeth (Anderson) R.; m. Gilda Ruggles, June 26, 1958; children: Anne Catherine, Kenneth William. BS, U.S. Naval Acad., 1954; MS, Naval PG Sch., Monterey, Calif., 1960; PhD, MIT, 1969. Commd. ensign USN, 1954, advanced through grades to capt., 1972, retired, 1978; v.p. Ocean Data Systems, Inc., Monterey, 1978-80; pres. Global Weather Dynamics, Inc., Monterey, 1980-86, Systems West, Inc., Carmel, Calif., 1986—; mem. com. Nat. Acad. Engring., Washington, 1987; cons. Dept. Commerce, Washington, 1987. Mem. Am. Meteorol. Soc. Office: Systems West Inc 27880 Dorris Dr Carmel CA 93923

RUIS, STEPHEN PAUL, chemistry educator; b. Palo Alto, Calif., Oct. 23, 1946; s. Roy James and Catherine Clara (Long) R.; m. Nancy Myrtle Ray, Aug. 29, 1969 (div. July 1985); 1 child, Andrew Ray; m. Elisabeth Mann, Sept. 7, 1985. BS, San Francisco State Coll., 1969; MS, San Diego State Coll., 1971. Lectr. San Diego State Coll., 1971-72; instr. Skyline Coll., San Bruno, Calif., 1972—. Pres. acad. senate Skyline Coll., San Bruno, 1980-81. Mem. Calif. Assn. Chem. Tchrs., Acad. Senate for Calif. Community Colls. (mem. exec. com. 1982-84, v.p. 1984-85), Am. Fedn. Tchrs. (pres. Local 1493 1988-89). Home: 388 Edgewood Ave Mill Valley CA 94941 Office: Skyline Coll 3300 College Dr San Bruno CA 94066

RUIZ, JOSE GARCIA, public administrator; b. Ferriday, La., Mar. 18, 1947; s. Carlos and Maria Pascuala (Garcia) R.; m. Susan Marie Mortensen, Oct. 25, 1986. AA, Big Bend Coll., 1969; BA, Evergreen State Coll., 1973. Employment interviewer Wash. State Employment Security, Moses Lake, 1969-71; labor market analyst Wash. State Employment Security, Olympia, 1971-72, employment program coordinator, 1972-74; employment office mgr. Wash. State Employment Security, Yakima, 1974-77, Mt. Vernon, 1977—. Active Valley Mus. of Northwest Art; trustee United Way, Mt. Vernon, 1979-82, Skagit Valley Coll., Mt. Vernon, 1987—; bd. dirs. Self Help Housing, Mt. Vernon, 1985-87, Community Action Agy., 1981—. Mem. Econ. Devel. Assn., Mt. Vernon C. of C. (bd. dirs. 1978-82). Roman Catholic. Office: Wash Employment Security 320 Pacific Pl Mount Vernon WA 98273

RULEY, STANLEY EUGENE, cost analyst; b. Akron, Ohio, Jan. 24, 1934; s. Royal Lovell and Opal Lenora (McDougall) R.; m. Annie Adam Patterson, Dec. 15, 1962; children: Cheryl Ann, Janice Lynn. Student, Kent State U., 1951-53; BSBA, Ohio State U., 1955. Registered profl. engr., Calif. Indsl. engr. Gaffers & Satler Inc., Hawthorne, Calif., 1961-62; mfg. engr. data systems div. Litton Industries Inc., Van Nuys, Calif., 1962-65; contract price analyst Naval Plant Rep. Office Lockheed, Burbank, Calif., 1966-72; contract negotiator Naval Regional Procurement, Long Beach, Calif., 1972-75; cost/price analyst Def. Contract Adminstrn. Services, Van Nuys, 1975-82; chief of contract pricing, dir. contracting Air Force Flight Test Ctr., Edwards AFB, Calif., 1982—; cons. engr., Northridge, Calif., 1971—. Served as sgt. U.S. Army, 1956-59. Recipient Sustained Superior Performance award Air Force Flight Test Ctr., 1984, Excellent Performance award Air Force Flight Test Ctr., 1982-83, Outstanding Performance award NAVPRO Lockheed, 1970. Mem. Am. Inst. Indsl. Engrs., IBM Computer User Group (Madison, Wis., Conn., San Fernando Valley), Air Force Assn. (life), Nat. Contract Mgmt. Assn. Republican. Presbyterian. Clubs: Lockheed Employee Recreation (treas. Gem and Mineral 1976, pres. 1976), Camper (Burbank) (pres. 1974). Lodge: Masons. Home: 18751 Vintage St Northridge CA 91324 Office: Air Force Flight Test Ctr Directorate of Contracting Stop 130 Edwards AFB CA 93523

RUMBLE, EDMUND TAYLOR, III, engineering manager, consultant; b. Phila., Oct. 26, 1942; s. Edmund Taylor and Dorothy (Brookes) R.; m. Katja Maria Kost, Aug. 14, 1976; children—Natalie Michelle, Nadine Vanessa. B.S., U.S. Naval Acad., 1965; M.S., UCLA, 1971, Ph.D., 1974. Registered profl. engr., Calif. Ensign, USN, 1965, advanced through grades to lt., 1970, resigned; corp. v.p. Sci. Applications Internat. Corp., Palo Alto, Calif., 1974—. Author numerous technical publs. Mem. Am. Nuclear Soc. Club: Foothills Tennis and Swimming. Office: Sci Applications Internat Corp 5150 El Camino Real Ste C-31 Los Altos CA 94022

RUMBOLZ, MICHAEL DAVID, gaming control board chairman, lawyer; b. Biloxi, Miss., Mar. 20, 1954; s. Richard Henry Rumbolz and Nikki (Sirginson) Brown; m. Carol Rumbolz, June 4, 1983. BA in Polit. Sci., U. Nev., Las Vegas, 1976; JD, U. So. Calif., 1980. Bar: Nev., U.S. Dist. Ct. Nev., U.S. Ct. Appeals (9th cir.), U.S. Tax Ct. Assoc. Jones, Jones, Bell, Close & Brown Cht., Las Vegas, 1980-83; chief, dep. atty. gen. State of Nev., Las Vegas, 1983-84, chief, dep. atty. gen. gaming div., 1984-85; mem. Nev. Gaming Control Bd., Las Vegas, 1985-87; chmn., Carson City, Nev., 1987—. Mem. Internat. Assn. Gaming Attys. (com. chmn. 1986—), ABA (gen. practice sect., mem. gaming law com.), Nev. Bar Assn. (mem. exec. com.). Democrat. Home: 4498 Farmcrest Dr Las Vegas NV 89121 Office: Nev Gaming Control Bd 1150 E William St Carson City NV 89710

RUMMEL, JACK THOMAS, dentist; b. Tacoma, Aug. 17, 1939; s. Bartlett and Augusta Bogert (Place) R.; m. Lynne Hartshorn, Aug. 26, 1962; children: Gretchen, Thomas. BS, U. Puget Sound, Tacoma, 1961; DMD, U. Oregon, 1965. Cert. Doctor of Dental Medicine. Pvt. practice Boulder, Colo., 1968—. Contbr. numerous articles to musical mag. "Rag Times" on ragtime piano; composer of numerous piano ragtime tunes; albums include Back to Ragtime, 1985, Contemporary Ragtime, 1989. Bd. dirs. Boulder Phil. Orch., 1982-85. Served to capt. U.S. Army, 1965-68. Mem. ADA, Colo. Dental Assn., Boulder County Dental Assn. (sec. 1984-86). Democrat. Unitarian. Lodge: Rotary (pres. Boulder chpt. 1979-80). Office: 3400 Penrose Pl Boulder CO 80301

RUMMEL, ROBERT WILAND, aeronautical engineer; b. Dakota, Ill., Aug. 4, 1915; s. William Howard and Dora (Ely) R.; m. Marjorie B. Cox, Sept. 30, 1939; children—Linda Kay, Sharon Lee, Marjorie Susan, Robert Wiland, Diana Beth. Diploma aeronautical engring., Curtiss Wright Tech. Inst. Aeros., 1935. Stress analyst Hughes Aircraft Co., Burbank, Calif., 1935-36, Lockheed Aircraft Corp., Burbank, 1936; draftsman Aero Engring. Corp., Long Beach, Calif., 1936, Nat. Aircraft Co., Alhambra, Calif., 1936-37; chief engr. Rearwin A/C & Engines, Inc., Kansas City, Kans., 1937-42; chief design engr. Commonwealth A/C, Inc., Kansas City, Kans., 1942-43; v.p. engring. Trans World Airlines, Inc., Kansas City, Mo., 1943-59; v.p. planning and research Trans World Airlines, Inc., 1959-69, v.p. tech. devel., 1969-78; pres. Robert W. Rummel Assos., Inc., Mesa, Ariz., 1978-87; aerospace cons. 1987—; commnr. Presdl. Commn. Space Shuttle Challenger Accident, 1986; chmn. nat. rsch. coun. Aero Space Engring. Bd. Fellow Inst. Aero. Scis., Soc. Automotive Engrs.; mem. Nat. Acad. Engring. Clubs: N.Y. Yacht (N.Y.C.); Saugatuck Harbor Yacht (Westport, Conn.); Masons (32 deg.), Shriners. Home: PO Box 7330 Mesa AZ 85206 Office: PO Box 7330 Mesa AZ 85216

RUMMEL, WILLIAM DAVID, ophthalmologist; b. Johnstown, Pa., Feb. 12, 1925; s. William D. and Cora G. (Gashaw) R.; m. J. Wanda McCart, Dec. 5, 1950; children: Martha, David, Mark, John, Mary. MD, Hahnemann U., 1948. Diplomate Am. Bd. Opthalmology. Intern Huron Rd. Hosp., East Cleveland, 1949; resident in opthalmalogy Ohio State U. Hosp., 1954; practice medicine specializing in opthalmalogy and aviation medicine Cen. Ariz. Eye Clinic, Prescott, 1982—. Lt. (j.g.) USNR, 1949-51. Fellow Am. Acad. Opthalmology. Office: Cen Ariz Eye Clinic 1022 Willow Creek Rd #200 Prescott AZ 86301

RUMMELSBURG, RODNEY ALAN, software engineering executive; b. San Francisco, Oct. 10, 1952; s. Charles Wallace and Merilyn Rummelsburg; m. Rosalie Odell, Dec. 18, 1984. BA in Fine Arts, UCLA, 1976; MS in Computer Sci., Loyola Marymount U., L.A., 1981. Software engr. Hughes Aircraft, El Segundo, Calif., 1979-84, TRW, Redonda Beach, Calif., 1984-85; pres. White Star Data Systems, Inc., Saugus, Calif., 1985—. Mem. Ind. Computer Cons. Assn., Software Cons. Bus. Assn., Inst. Electrical and Electronic Engrs. Office: White Star Data Systems Inc 25655 Springbrook Ave Ste 8 Saugus CA 91350

RUMPELTES, SHERRIE JAN, educator; b. Weiser, Ida., Jan. 23, 1952; d. Louis Kinji and Hide (Sako) Ishino; m. Craig Robert Rumpeltes, Aug. 21, 1976; stepchildren: Justin James, Brittan. BA, Boise State U., 1974. Std. teaching cert., Idaho. Tchr. Sch. Dist. #393, Wallace, Idaho, 1974-75, Zion Luth. Presch., Corvallis, Oreg., 1984—. Mem. Luthn. Edn. Assn., Luth. Early Childhood Edn. Assn. Lutheran. Home: 1810 NE Conifer Blvd Corvallis OR 97330 Office: Zion Luth Sch 2800 NW Tyler St Corvallis OR 97330

RUNDELL, THERESA RAE DEL, nurse; b. Anchorage, June 3, 1954; d. Royce William and Caroline Kathryn (Metz) Yeager Arnold; m. Craig Evan Rundell, Aug. 10, 1974; children: Jesse Evan, Seth Martin. AA, Columbia Basin Coll., 1977; Adv.RN Practitioner, Planned Parenthood Wis., 1983. Clin. nurse Planned Parenthood, Madison, Ind., 1983-84; nurse practitioner ob-gyn. Bloomington, Ind., 1984-85; pub. health nurse/clinic supr. S.W. Wash. Health Dist., White Salmon, 1985—; cons. in field. Sec. Underwood Community Council, 1986-87, v.p., 1988; mem. Teen Pregnancy Prevention Task Force, 1988; curriculum advisor for AIDS edn. in pu. schs., Kirkland County; med. advisor Headstart, Goldendale. Recipient Young Careerist award Bus. Profl. Women's Assn., 1989. Mem. Am. Nurses Assn., NACCOG. Home: Rundell Rd Underwood WA 98651 Office: SW Wash Health Dist PO Box 159 White Salmon WA 98672

RUNDLE, MELANIE KAY, architect; b. Mpls., Nov. 2, 1960; d. Don Phillip and Ardys Lorraine (Hazard) R. BArch, U. Ariz., 1985. Intern architect Douglas Childs Architect, San Diego, 1988—. Mem. AIA (exec. bd. dirs., assoc. dir. 1988, programs dir. 1989). Home: 4452 North Ave San Diego CA 92116 Office: Douglas Childs Architect 964 Fifth Ave #509 San Diego CA 92101

RUNICE, ROBERT E., corporate executive; b. Fargo, N.D., Aug. 20, 1929; s. E.M. and Ruth (Soule) R.; m. Geraldine Kharas, June 26, 1954; children: Michael, Christopher, Paul, Karen. B.S., N.D. State U., 1951. Sr. v.p. Northwestern Bell Telephone Co., Omaha, Nebr., 1945-81; v.p. Am. Tel. & Tel. Co.-Info. Systems, Morristown, N.J., 1981-83; v.p., pres. comml. devel. div. US West, Inc., Englewood, Colo., 1983—, also bd. dirs.; bd. dirs. Tandy Brands, Inc., Ft. Worth, Flow Mole Corp., Kent, Wash., New Vector Group, Bellevue, Wash.; trustee Denver Symphony Orch., Met. Club. Republican. Episcopalian. Home: 7665 S Yampa St Aurora CO 80016 Office: 7800 E Orchard Rd Ste 200 Englewood CO 80111

RUNKLE, E. MONA, artist; b. Davenport, Iowa, Dec. 4, 1921; d. Louis and Agnes (Jungjohann) Behrens; m. Karl Ehresman Runkle, Jan. 25, 1947; children: Carol Ann, Richard Louis. Grad., Shimer Coll., Mt. Carroll, Ill., 1942; student, St. Ambrose Coll., Davenport, Iowa, 1943, Chgo. Art Inst., 1945, N.Y. Sch. Interior Design, 1955. Cert. Nat. Watercolor Soc. Illustrator Rock Island (Ill.) Arsenal, 1942-44; stewardess United Air Lines, Chgo., 1944-46; craft dir. Westbury (N.Y.) Country Club, 1967; owner, operator Polynesian Fashions, Huntington, N.Y., 1967-71, The Woodshed, Escondido, Calif., 1975-77; art dir. Holland-Am. Lines, Seattle, 1986-87; artist San Diego, 1983—; operator Hawaii Condo Rentals, San Diego, 1964—; art demonstrator San Marcos Art Assn., Calif., 1987, Escondido Art Assn., Calif., 1987, La Jolla Art Assn., La Jolla, Calif., 1986. illustration San Diego, 1987; executed mural, 1987; represented in pvt. collections; exhibited in group show of Nat. Watercolor Soc., Los Angeles, 1987. Historian Clipped Wings, San Diego, 1985-86, Lloyd Harbor Hist. Assn., N.Y., 1966-71, Huntington Hist. Soc., N.Y., 1963-71, Soc. Preservation L.I. Antiquities, N.Y., 1967-70. Recipient Pres.'s Citation of Merit, Nat. Soc. Paint Casein & Acrylic, N.Y., 1988, second place award Escondido Art Assn., 1987. Mem. Am. Soc. Marine Artists, Internat. Soc. Women Marine Artists, Nat. Watercolor Soc. (rep. Alaska and Hawaii, 1987-88), U.S. Coast Guard Art Program, Clairmont Art Guild, San Diego Watercolor Soc. (pres. 1987-88, third place award 1988), La Jolla Art Assn. Republican. Lutheran. Home: 17772 Via Gracia San Diego CA 92128

RUNO, STEVEN CHARLES, aeronautical systems engineer; b. Everett, Wash., Jan. 22, 1956; s. Chris Jr. and Doretta Faye (Fleming) R.; m. Diane Thomas, June 21, 1980; children: Stephanie Renae, William Christopher. BS in Engring., Harvey Mudd Coll., 1978; MBA, Seattle U., 1984, MS in Software Engring., 1986. Assoc. engr. Rohr Marine, Inc., Chula Vista, Calif., 1977; from assoc. to sr. engr. Boeing Comml. Airplane Co., 1978-86; prin. engr. Sperry Avionics, Glendale, Ariz., 1986-87; head engring. sect. Honeywell, Inc. Bus. & Commuter Aviation Systems div., Glendale, 1987—. Mem. AIAA. Home: 7849 W Wethersfield Rd Peoria AZ 85345 Office: Honeywell Inc Bus & Commuter Aviation Systems div. Sperry Comml Flight Systems Group PO Box 29000/AV5710 Phoenix AZ 85038

RUNYON, STEVEN CROWELL, university administrator, communications educator; b. San Rafael, Calif., June 20, 1946; s. Charles A. and Katherine C. (Pease) R.; m. Lynna Lim, Mar. 9, 1974; 1 child, Wendy Victoria. BA in Econs., U. San Francisco, 1971, postgrad., 1978—; MA in Radio and TV, San Francisco State U., 1976. Radio producer Sta. KGO, San Francisco, 1965-68; engr., announcer Stas. KSFR, KSAN, San Francisco, 1966-68; publicist Kolmar Assocs./Chuck Barris Prodns., San Francisco, 1970; instructional media technician U. San Francisco, 1968-72; technician, archivist, mgr. Wurster, Bernardi & Emmons, San Francisco, 1972-73; projectionist So. Pacific R.R., San Francisco, 1974; broadcast ops. engr. Stas. KPEN, KIOI, KIQI, San Francisco, 1968-74, public and community affairs program producer, 1971-74, AM transmitter engr., 1974; lectr. communication arts, U. San Francisco, 1974—, gen. mgr. Sta. KUSF-FM, 1974—, dir. mass media studies program, 1975—, acting chmn. communication arts dept., 1976; TV historian; producer, engr., cons. radio and TV programs; communications and audiovisual cons. Author: A Study of the Don Lee Broadcasting Systems' Television Activities, 1930-41, 1976; Educational Broadcast Management Bibliography, 1974. Contbr. articles to profl. jours. Grantee Calif. Council Humanities in Public Policy, Rockefeller Found., Father Spieler Meml. Trust, NSF; recipient cert. of merit for documentary radio series Peninsula Press Club, 1979, Diploma of Honor, Internat. Robert Stolz Soc., 1981, Fr. Dunne award U. San Francisco, 1986, Coll. Svc. award Coll. Arts and Scis. U. San Francisco, 1988; lic. gen. class radiotelephone operator FCC. Mem. Soc. Broadcast Engrs., Broadcast Edn. Assn., Assn. Communication Adminstrs., Assn. for Edn. in Journalism and Mass Communication, AAUP, Assn. Recorded Sound Collections, Pres.'s Ambassadors of U. San Francisco, Internat. Communication Assn., Com. Ethics in Pub. Affairs Broadcasting. Club: Press of San Francisco. Office: U San Francisco 2130 Fulton St San Francisco CA 94117-1080

RUOTSALA, JAMES ALFRED, historian, writer; b. Juneau, Alaska, Feb. 17, 1934; s. Bert Alfred and Eva (Karppi) E.; m. Janet Ann Whelan, July 31, 1987; stepchildren: Theresa Cowden, Douglas Whelan, Peggy MacInnis, Michael Whelan, Bruce Whelan. Student, U. Md., 1960-61, Basic Officers Sch., Maxwell AFB, 1964, Air U., Maxwell AFB, 1984, U. Alaska, Kenai, 1987. Asst. div. mgr. Macmillan Pub. Co., 1964-80; mgr. Denny's Restaurants, 1980-82; dir. mktg. and sales Air Alaska, 1982—; archival dir. Alaska Aviation Heritage Mus., 1987—. Author: Lockheed Vegas in Southeast Alaska, 1980, We Stand Ready, 1986, Eielson, Father of Alaskan Aviation, 1986; Alaska's Aviation Heritage Air Alaska newspaper. Journalist 1st cl. USN, 1951-56; sgt. U.S. Army, 1958-64; lt. col. USAR, 1983—. Decorated Meritorious Svc. medal, Army Commendation medal, Army Achievement medal; recipient USAF Brewer Aerospace award, Grover Loening award, Paul E. Garber award, 1984-85, State of Alaska Gov.'s Cert. Appreciation, 1983, Mayor's Pub. Service award, Anchorage, Alaska, 1985. Mem. VFW, Res. Officers Assn. (pub. affairs officer 1985—), U.S. Naval Inst., Aviation and Space Writers Assn., U.S. Submarine League Am., Anchorage Philatelic Soc., Am. Aviation Hist. Soc., Am. Legion, Pioneers of Alaska (sec. 1988, v.p. 1989— Igloo 33, Cert. Appreciation 1988), Rotary. Methodist. Home: 36976 Chinulna Ct Kenai AK 99611 Office: 900 W 5th Ave Ste 410 Anchorage AK 99501

RUPAAL, AJIT SINGH, physics educator; b. Mangwal, India, June 25, 1933; came to U.S., 1964; s. Puran Singh and Panmaisary Kaur (Panesar) R.; m. Evelyn O. Dzugalo, June 1, 1963; children: Amrit Kaur, Rajin Singh. BS, Panjab U., Hoshiarpur, India, 1954, MS, 1955; PhD, U. B.C., Vancouver, Can., 1963. Postdoctoral fellow Atomic Energy Can., Chalk River, Ont., 1963-64; prof. physics Western Wash. U., Bellingham, 1964—, chmn. physics/astronomy dept., 1980—; sr. research scientist Battelle Meml. Inst., Richland, Wash., 1976, 77. Contbr. articles to sci. jours. Mem. Am. Assn. Physics Tchrs., Can. Assn. Physicists. Democrat. Mem. Sikh Ch. Office: Western Wash U Dept Physics & Astronomy 516 High St Bellingham WA 98225

RUPEL, DANIEL PATRICK, retailing excutive; b. Long Beach, Calif., July 19, 1955; s. Edgar Lee and Bobetta (Quantrell) R.; m. Karen Marie Connair, Sept. 26, 1973; 1 child, Danielle Patricia. Grad., Goldenwest Coll., 1978. Cert. tchr., Calif. Ops. mgr. Treasury Stores, Orange, Calif., 1976-78; mdse. mgr. Sav-On Drugs, Anaheim, Calif., 1978-81; divisional mgr. HRT Corp., L.A., 1981-83; gen. mgr. Ross Stores, Norwalk, Calif., 1983-88; exec. v.p. New China Emporia, Huntington Beach, Calif., 1988—; educator Woodbury U., Los Angeles, 1986—, Fashion Inst. Design and Mdse., 1987—, Brooks Coll., 1988—; pres., chief exec. officer Kujawa Entertainment Corp., Huntington Beach, 1977—. Author: A Song for You, 1979; columnist: Fashion Facts mag., 1987—; songwriter musical scores. Mem. adv. bd., Woodbury U., 1986—, chmn. 1987—; vol. Am. Diabetes Assn., Orange, 1984, Ocean View Little League, Huntington Beach, 1986—, Girl Scouts of U.S., Huntington Beach, 1984. With U.S. Army, 1973-76. Mem. Am. Songwriters Assn. (hon. mention 1977), Am. Poetry Writers Assn. (hon. mention 1988, Golden Poet award 1988), Norwalk C. of C., Norwalk Mchts. Assn. (pres. 1988), Meadowlark Country Club. Democrat. Roman Catholic. Home: 6841 Sowell Ave Westminster CA 92683 Office: New China Emporium 322 S Date Ave Alhambra CA 91801

RUPERT, CAROLA G., museum director; b. Washington, Jan. 2, 1954; d. Jack Burns and Shirley Ann (Orcutt) Rupert. BA in history cum laude, Bryn Mawr Coll., 1976; MA, U. Del., 1978, cert. in mus. studies, 1978. Personnel mgmt. trainee Naval Material Command, Arlington, Va., 1972-76; teaching asst. dept. history, U. Del., Newark, 1976-77; asst. curator/exhibit specialist Hist. Soc. Del., Wilmington, 1977-78; dir. Macon County Mus. Complex, Decatur, Ill., 1978-81; dir. Kern County Mus., Bakersfield, Calif., 1981—; tchr. mus. studies course U. Calif.-Santa Barbara Extension, 1982; advisor Kern County Heritage Commn.; chmn. Historic Records Commn., 1988; sec.-treas. Arts Council of Kern, 1984-86, pres. 1986—; county cochmn. United Way, 1981, 82; chmn. steering com. Calif. State Bakersfield Co-op Program, 1982-83; mem. Community Adv. Bd. Calif. State Bakersfield, Anthro; Soc. 1986—; bd. dirs. Mgmt. Council, 1983-86, v.p., 1987, pres. 1988; bd. dirs. Calif. Council for Promotion of History, 1984-86, v.p., 1987-88. pres., 1988—; Community Adv. Bd. mem. Calif. State U.-Bakersfield Sociology Dept., 1986-88. Hagley fellow Eleutherian Mills-Hagley Found., 1977-78; Bryn Mawr alumnae regional scholar, 1972-76. Mem. Nat. Trust for Hist. Preservation, Am. Assn. Mus., Am. Assn. for State and Local History. Unitarian Universalist. Office: Kern County Mus 3801 Chester Ave Bakersfield CA 93301

RUPKALVIS, JOHN ARTHUR, stereoscopic consultant; b. Mpls., Oct. 23, 1937; 1 child, John Thomas. BA, U. Minn., 1966. Technologist photo engring. Pako Corp., Mpls., 1960-64; sr. photographer & technologist James Ford Bell Tech. Ctr., Mpls., 1964-72; photo engr. Photo Bus. Machines

Corp., Mpls., 1972-74; stereoscopic cons. StereoScope Internat., Burbank, Calif., 1972—; v.p. StereoMed, Inc., Mpls., 1978—; stereoscopic cons. StereoScope Internat., Mpls. Conbtr. articles to profl. jours.; inventor stereoscopic TV system, Stereoscopic motion picture system, StereoScope 3-D imaging system. Mem. Soc. Motion Picture & TV Engring. (standards com.), Stereoscopic Soc. So. Calif., Internat. Stereoscopic Union.

RUPNIK, JOHN KENYON, physician; b. Tulsa, Feb. 21, 1947; s. John Joseph and Dorothy Beryl (Baugher) R.; m. Lauren Achor, Sept. 12, 1971; children: Brian Kenyon, Carolyn Lauren. BA cum laude, Stanford U., 1969; MD, U. Calif., San Francisco, 1973. Diplomate Am. Bd. Internal Medicine, Am. Bd. Infectious Diseases. Extern occupational medicine USPHS, Cin., 1972; intern U. Calif., Irvine, 1973-74; resident in internal medicine U. Calif., 1974-75; staff physician internal medicine and infectious diseases So. Calif. Permanent Med. Group, Bellflower, 1977-80; cons. med. staff. Vallejo (Calif.) Gen. Hosp., 1980-84, Sonoma Valley (Calif.) Hosp., 1980-84, St. Helena Med. Ctr., 1980—; staff physician Queen of the Valley Hosp., Napa, Calif., 1980—; practice internal medicine Napa, 1980—; asst. clin. prof. U. Calif.-Irvine, 1977-79, assoc. clin. prof., 1979-80; cons., lectr. in field; chmn. infection control com. Kaiser-Permanente Hosp., Bellflower, 1979-80; treas. Napa Valley Physician's Plan, Inc., 1986-88; mem. utilization rev. com. Napa Nursing Ctr., 1985—; mem. ad hoc com. on AIDS policy Napa City Bd. Edn., 1987; med. dir. Silverado Nursing Ctr., Napa, 1985-86. Mem. AMA, AAAS, Am. Coll. Physicians, Am. Soc. Microbiology, Napa County Med. Soc. (community health liaison com. 1985—), Calif. Med. Assn., Am. Soc. Internal Medicine, Calif. Soc. Internal Medicine, Stanford Alumnus Club. Democrat. Presbyterian. Office: 3443 Villa Ln Ste 9 Napa CA 94558

RUPP, GERALD EARL, realtor; b. Slayton, Minn., June 26, 1940; s. Earl Spencer Rupp and Helen Barbara (Thuringer) Kirkland; m. Barbara Lynn Davis, June 25, 1965; children: Mariss Michele, David Earl. BSBA, Ariz. State U., 1962; postgrad., U. the Philippines, Quezon City, 1962-64; BFT, Am. Grad. Sch. Internat. Mgmt., 1966; MBA, Ariz. State U., 1966. Mgr. indsl. relations Goodyear Tire and Rubber Co., Akron, Ohio, 1966-78, Armstrong Tire Co., Des Moines, 1978-79, Northrop, Hawthore, Calif., 1980-84; realtor J.J. Graves & Assocs., Phoenix, 1984-86, John Hall & Assocs., Phoenix, 1986—. Mem. Thunderbird Alumni Assn. (pres. 1985), Delta Sigma Pi (pres. 1988), Phi Delta Theta. Lodge: Elks. Home: 2549 E Sahuaro Dr Phoenix AZ 85028 Office: John Hall & Assocs 11209 N Tatum Blvd Phoenix AZ 85028

RUPPEL, EDWARD THOMPSON, geologist; b. Ft. Morgan, Colo., Oct. 26, 1925; s. Henry George and Gladys Myrtle (Thompson) R.; m. Phyllis Beale Tanner, June 17, 1956; children: Lisa, David, Douglas, Kristin. BA, U. Mont., 1948; MA, U. Wyo., 1950; PhD, Yale U., 1958. Cert. profl. geologist. Geologist U.S. Geol. Survey, Washington and Denver, 1948-86; chief cen. regional br. U.S. Geol. Survey, Denver, 1971-75, geologist, 1975-86; dir., state geologist Mont. Bur. Mines and Geology, Butte, 1986—. Contbr. about 40 articles to profl. jours. With USNR, 1943-46. Fellow Geol. Soc. Am.; mem. Soc. Econ. Geologists, Mont. Geol. Soc.; Assn. Am. State Geologists, Tobacco Root Geol. Soc., Rotary. Office: Mont Bur of Mines and Geology West Park St Butte MT 59701

RUSCO, GENE EARL, radio broadcasting executive; b. Stockton, Calif., Mar. 4, 1949; s. Forrest Albert and Mildred Lea (Overholser) R.,; m. Linda S. Collins, Mar. 4, 1989. News dir. KDON AM-FM, Salinas, Calif., 1971, KIDD Radio, Monteray, Calif., 1971-76, KMFO Radio, Aptos Capitola, Calif., 1976-81; reporter, anchor KGO/ABC Radio, San Francisco, 1981-83, bur. chief South Bay, 1983—. Writer, anchor documentary Dying for a Drink, 1986 (St. Francis Media award 1986), writer anchor news series Alcoholism, 1986 (Best Series award 1986); reporter spot news Crash of Airlines, 1987 (Best Coverage award 1987). Mem. Radio and TV News Dirs., Alpha Epsilon Rho, Alpha Omega (pres.), Cen. Mo. State U. Office: KGO Radio 900 Front St San Francisco CA 94111

RUSCONI, ROBERT DENNIS, research company executive; b. Redwood City, Calif., Feb. 11, 1957; s. Bruno Bernard and Sylvia Jean (Firpo) R. AS, Coll. San Mateo, 1977; BS, Calif. Poly U., 1981. Engr. dept. engring. rsch. Pacific Gas and Elect. co-founder Power Fluid and Metals Co., Redwood City, 1983-84; researcher Pyromet, Inc., San Carlos, Calif., 1984-85; founder, mgr., chief rsch. analyst Ind. (Oreg.) Rsch. Co., 1987--; cons. Nutone, Hayward, Calif., 1985. Mem. Independence Firefighters Assn. (chmn. fin. com. 1988—, pres.).

RUSH, CARL HARRISON, III, management consultant; b. Detroit, Nov. 17, 1947; s. Carl Harrison and Ruth Louise (Roller) R.; m. Bonnie K. Allison Gould, May 28, 1975 (div. Jan. 9, 1979); m. Bunny Blair Gunyou, June 11, 1983. BS, Cornell U., 1969, M of Regional Planning, 1976. Project dir. Pub. Technology, Washington, 1972-74; instr. Cornell U., Ithaca, N.Y., 1974-76; sr. assoc. Ecosometrics, Inc., Bethesda, Md., 1976-78; mgr. Levi Strauss & Co., San Francisco, 1979-81; dir. nat. and regional programs Levi Struass Found., San Francisco, 1981-84; pres. Dole Found., Washington, 1984-86; chief fin. officer United Seniors Health Cooperative, Washington, 1987; prin. Carl Rush & Assocs., San Rafael, Calif., 1988—; trustee Cooperative Assistance Fund, Washington, 1982—; bd. visitors Inst. for Pub. Policy & Adminstrn., Washington, 1985—. Chmn. Mayor's Task Force on Protective Services, San Francisco, 1982; mem. Mayor's Task Force on Refugee Employment, San Francisco. With U.S. Army, 1970-72. Mem. Am. Soc. on Aging, Nat. Council on Aging, San Rafael C. of C. Democrat. Home: 357 Hibiscus Way San Rafael CA 94903

RUSH, DOMENICA MARIE, health facilities administrator; b. Gallup, N.Mex., Apr. 10, 1937; d. Bernardo G. and Guadalupe (Milan) Iorio; m. W. E. Rush, Jan. 5, 1967. Diploma, Regina Sch. Nursing, Albuquerque, 1958. RN N.Mex.; lic. nursing home adminstr. Charge nurse, house supr. St. Joseph Hosp., Albuquerque, 1958-63; dir. nursing Cibola Hosp., Grants, 1960-64; supr. operating room, dir. med. seminars Carrie Tingley Crippled Children's Hosp., Truth or Consequences, N.Mex., 1964-73; adminstr. Sierra Vista Hosp., Truth or Consequences, 1974-88, pres., 1980—; bd. dirs. N.Mex. Blue Cross/Blue Shield, 1977-88, chmn. hosp. relations com., 1983-85, exec. com. 1983—; bd. dirs. Region II Emergency Med. Svcs. Originating bd. SW Mental Health Ctr., Sierra County, N.Mex., 1975; chmn. Sierra County Personnel Bd., 1983—. Mem. Am. Coll. Health Care Adminstrs., Sierra County C. of C. (bd. dirs. 1972, 75-76, svc. award 1973, Businesswoman of the Yr. 1973-74), N.Mex. Hosp. Assn. (bd. dirs., sec.-treas., pres.-elect, com. chmn., 1977-88, pres. 1980-81, exec. com., 1980-83, 84-85, recipient meritorius svc. award 1988), N.Mex. So. Hosp. Coun. (sec. 1980-81, pres. 1981-82), Am. Hosp. Assn. (N.Mex. del. 1984-88, regional adv. bd. 1984-88). Republican. Roman Catholic. Home: PO Box 1030 Truth or Consequences NM 87901

RUSH, STEVEN MATTHEW, dentist; b. Wichita Falls, Tex., Jan. 19, 1959; s. Francis Eugene Rush and Kathleen Evelyn (Hoch) Jarrett; m. Laura Jean Mosczynski, June 25, 1988. BA in Chemistry, U. Colo., 1982, BA in Molecular Biology, 1982; DDS, Emory U., 1987. Assoc. dentist Donald F. Almeida & Assocs., P.C., Littleton, Colo., 1987--. Home: 9658 C W Chatfield Ave Littleton CO 80123 Office: 9025 E Mineral Cir 200 Englewood CO 80112

RUSHFORTH, RANDY GLEN, construction company executive; b. Tacoma, Aug. 27, 1946; s. William S. and Nita L. (Jeffords) R.; m. Linnea D. Swanstrom, May 5, 1967 (div. Apr. 1977); children: Bryan Todd, Troy Matthew; m. Teri Katrina Dickason, Sept. 24, 1978; children: Kirsten Louise, William Scott. BS, U. Wash., 1971. Estimator, project mgr. Careage Corp., Bellevue, Wash., 1971-76; v.p. Rushforth Constrn. Co. Inc., Tacoma, 1976-80, pres., 1980—. Bd. dirs. Puget Sound Grand Prix Assn. Mem. Tacoma/Pierce County C. of C. (bd. dirs.). Club: President's (Seattle). Lodge: Rotary (Tacoma). Office: Rushforth Constrn Co Inc 1308 Alexander Ave E Tacoma WA 98424

RUSHTON, TERRY WESLEY, financial planner, accountant; b. Salt Lake City, Aug. 22, 1947; s. Samuel Wesley and L. Florence (Meadow) R.; m. Sylvia Jean Evans, Nov. 17, 1973; children: Brian Scott, Robyn Anne, Kevin N. BS, U. Utah, 1972, MBA, 1974. CPA, Wash. Installment loans officer Walker Bank & Trust Co., Salt Lake City, 1970-72; auditor Ernst & Whinney, Seattle, Vancouver, B.C., Can., 1976-78; analyst R.W. Beck & Assocs., Seattle, 1979; contr. Assoicated Sand & Gravel Co., Seattle, 1980-82; contr., treas. Environ. Systems, Seattle, 1983-86; assoc. The Prin. Fin. Group, Bellevue, Wash., 1986—. Bd. dirs. Everett (Wash.) family YMCA, 1982. With USAR, 1969. Mem. Cascade Assn. Life Underwriters. Republican. Mormon. Home: 17828 30th Dr SE Bothell WA 98012 Office: The Prin Fin Group 925 Denny Bldg Seattle WA 98121

RUSSELL, BILL, professional basketball team executive; b. Monroe, La., Feb. 12, 1934. Grad., San Francisco State Coll., 1956. Player, NBA Boston Celtics Profl. Basketball Club, 1956-69, coach, 1966-69; sportscaster ABC-TV, 1969-80, CBS-TV, 1980-83; coach NBA Seattle Supersonics, 1973-77; coach NBA Sacramento Kings, 1987-88, v.p. basketball ops, 1988—; mem. U.S. Olympic Basketball Team (Gold medal), 1956. Appeared in: TV series Cowboy in Africa; also commls.; co-host: The Superstars, ABC-TV, 1978-79; Author: Second Wind: Memoirs of an Opinionated Man, 1979. Inducted into Basketball Hall of Fame, 1974; mem. 11 NBA championship teams. Office: Sacramento Kings 1 Sports Pkwy Sacramento CA 95834 *

RUSSELL, CHRISTOPHER THOMAS, geophysics educator; b. St. Albans, Eng., May 9, 1943; came to U.S., 1964; s. Thomas Daniel and Teresa Ada Susan (Mary) R.; m. Arlene Ann Thompson, June 25, 1966; children: Jennifer Ann, Danielle Suzanne. BS in Physics, U. Toronto, Ont., Can., 1964; PhD in Space Physics, UCLA, 1968. Research geophysicist Inst. Geophysics UCLA, 1969-81, prof. geophysics dept. earth and space sci., Inst. Geophysics, 1982—; chmn. com. on data mgmt. and computation Nat. Acad. Scis. Space Sci. Bd., 1985-88, commn. D. Com. on Space Research., 1982-86; Harold Jeffreys lectr. Royal Astron. Soc., 1987. Editor: Solar Wind Three, 1974, Auroral Processes, 1979, The IMS Source Book, 1982, Solar Wind Interactions, 1986. Fellow AAAS, Am. Geophys. Union (pres. solar planetary relations sect. 1988-90, Macelwane award 1977); mem. Planetary Scis. div. Am. Astron. Soc., European Geophys. Soc. Office: UCLA Inst Geophysics & Planetary Physics Los Angeles CA 90024

RUSSELL, DONALD EUGENE, internist; b. Lincoln, Nebr., Sept. 26, 1956; s. Charles Arlington and Marjorie Marie (Holm) R. BA in Biology, Union Coll., 1978; MS in Anatomy, U. Nebr., 1981; MD, Loma Linda U., 1985. Intern Loma Linda (Calif.) Med. Ctr., 1985-86, resident in internal medicine, 1986-88; emergency physician Lloyd Emergency Med. Group, Loma Linda, 1988—. Mem. ACP, San Bernardino County Med. Soc. Office: Lloyd Emergency Med Group 11165 Mountain View Ave Ste 137 Loma Linda CA 92354

RUSSELL, DOUGLAS HENRY, business college instructor; b. Austin, Tex., Apr. 30, 1948; s. William Acie and Avis Jean (Strong) R. BA, West Tex. State U., 1971. Cert. secondary sch. tchr., Tex. Tchr. Thomas Jefferson High Sch., San Antonio, 1978, Greenwood High Sch., Midland, Tex., 1980-82; owner Odyssey Book Store, Parker, Colo., 1985-86; interviewer Heakin Research, Inc., Houston, 1986; instr. Cen. Tex. Coll., Ft. Carson, 1987, with, 1989—; instr. Holbrook Bus. Coll. (formerly Adelphi Bus. Coll.), Colo. Springs, 1986—; instr. Pueblo (Colo.) Coll. Bus. and Tech., 1988; sponsor expository writing team, Greenwood High Sch., Midland, 1981. Vol. tutor Neighborhood Reading Project, Colorado Springs, 1986-87, Chess Club, Eagleview Mid. Sch., 1988. U.S. Chess Fedn., Wilson Ctr. Assocs. (charter mem.), Alpha Chi. Home: 735 Rock Creek Mesa Rd Colorado Springs CO 80926 Office: Holbrook Bus Coll 824 S Union Blvd Colorado Springs CO 80910 Other: Cen Tex Coll Fort Carson Colorado Colorado Springs CO 80913

RUSSELL, FRANCIA, ballet director, educator; b. Los Angeles, Jan. 10, 1938; d. W. Frank and Marion (Whitney) R.; m. Kent Stowell, Nov. 19, 1965; children: Christopher, Darren, Ethan. Studies with, George Balanchine, Vera Volkova, Felia Doubrouska, Antonina Tumkovsky, Benjamin Harkarvy; student, NYU, Columbia U. Dancer, soloist N.Y.C. Ballet, 1956-62, ballet mistress, 1965-70; dancer Ballets USA/Jerome Robbins, N.Y.C., 1962; tchr. ballet Sch. Am. Ballet, N.Y.C., 1963-64; dir. staging over 90 George Ballanchine ballet prodns. including Soviet Union and Peoples Republic of China for the first time., throughout N.Am., Europe and Asia, 1964—; co-dir. Frankfurt (Fed. Republic Germany) Opera Ballet, 1976-77; artistic, sch. dir. Pacific N.W. Ballet, Seattle, 1977—; affiliate prof. of dance U. Wash. Named Woman of Achievement Matrix Table Women in Communications, Seattle, 1987. Mem. Dance/USA, Ballet Am. (v.p.). Home: 2833 Broadway E Seattle WA 98102 Office: Pacific NW Ballet 4649 Sunnyside Ave N Seattle WA 98103

RUSSELL, GAY MARTIN, television and film educator; b. Alpine, Tex., June 3, 1933; d. St. John and Ada (Harris) Martin; m. Harley E. Russell (div. 1981); children: Melodie Gay Russell McAren, Howard Wesley Russell. AS, Arlington (Tex.) State U., 1952; BA, San Diego State U., 1967, MA, 1969. Cert. lifetime community coll. instr., Calif. Grad. asst. San Diego State U., 1967-69; prof. TV and film Grossmont Coll., El Cajon, Calif., 1969—, chmn. dept. TV and film, 1984—, chair of council of chairs, 1985-87. Writer, producer, dir., editor, advisor several videos and film: Who? Me, In College, 1969, Expressions of Love-James Hubbell, 1982, Half of Heaven-The New China, 1983-84, Empowering Children Against Molestation-No, It's My Body, 1985, A Montage of Preschool Days, 1985, Cooking With Preschoolers, 1985, A Directed Movement, 1985, Registration, 1987, Our Goal Is Your Success, 1988. Pres. Murray Hill Homeowners Assn., La Mesa, Calif., 1985-87. Mem. Calif. Tchrs. Assn. (exec. bd. 1979—, communication liasion, caucus chmn. region IV, treas. 1987—, state council 1986—), Broadcast Edn. Assn., Western Edn. Soc. Telecommunications, Am. Film Inst., NEA., Community Coll. Assn. Democrat. Home: 7200 Melody Ln #76 La Mesa CA 92041 Office: Grossmont Coll 8800 Grossmont Coll Dr El Cajon CA 92020

RUSSELL, GERALD VINCENT, principal; b. Nettleton, Mo., Dec. 12, 1946; s. Gene Vincent and Bette Mae (Johnson) R.; m. Judy Lurree Baker; children: Brian Vincent, Garrett Joseph. BA, Colo. State U., 1968; MA, U. No. Colo., 1974; JD, U. Denver, 1989. Cert. tchr. Spanish, social studies, 1970. Asst. prin. Jefferson County Sch., Wheat Ridge, Colo., 1973—; legis. liaison Jefferson County Schs., Lakewood, Colo., 1987-88. Team capt. Denver Corp. Games, Spl. Olympics, 1983-88; del. Congl. Dist., alt. del. Jefferson County Assembly, Denver, 1988; legis. aide to Rep. Jerke, Colo. Ho. Reps., 1989. Served with USN, 1969-70. Recipient Am. Jurisprudence award 1988. Republican. Methodist. Clubs: Lakewood Tennis (pres., v.p. 1976-80); Catalina 22 Fleet (Denver) (vice commodore 1987-88). Home: 7945 W Geddes Pl Littleton CO 80123 Office: Everitt Jr High 3900 Kipling Wheat Ridge CO 80033

RUSSELL, GLENDA MARIE, psychologist; b. Leonardtown, Md., July 21, 1949; d. Leonard Cecil and Mary Agnes (Hayden) R.; m. Jay Dorrance Burch, Sept. 16, 1968 (div. 1972); 1 child, Shana Elysse. BA, U. Colo., 1979, MA, 1983, PhD, 1984. Lic. clin. psychologist, Colo. Grant writer, cons. Boulder (Colo.) County Hospice, Inc., 1976-80; profl. rsch. assoc. grad. com. on arts and humanities U. Colo., Boulder, 1980-81, psychology intern counseling svcs., 1981-83, instr. dept. psychology, 1984—; pvt. practice Boulder, 1984—; psychology intern neuropsychiat. inst. UCLA, 1983-84, researcher in field; instr. Community Coll. Denver, 1982, U. Colo., 1982. Commr. Boulder Human Rels. Commn., 1987—; mem. Boulder County Women's Polit. Caucus. U. Colo. fellow, 1980. Mem. Am. Psychol. Assn., Am. Orthopsychiat. Assn., Colo. Psychol. Assn., Colo. Soc. for Study Multiple Personality and Disassn. Office: 1919 14th St Ste 405 Boulder CO 80302

RUSSELL, LAURA WIMBERLY, artist; b. Rapid City, S.D., Aug. 17, 1949; d. Charles Leslie Wimberly and Peggy (Whitehead) Minier; m. Michael L. Russell, Aug. 21, 1971 (dec. Feb. 1986). BA in Creative Studies, U. Calif., Santa Barbara, 1970; MA, San Jose State U., 1974. One-woman shows William Sawyer Gallery, San Francisco, 1976, Art Mus. South Tex., Corpus Christi, 1980, Watson de Nagy Gallery, Houston, 1988, Watson/Willour Gallery, Houston, 1981, U. Redlands, Calif., 1982, Contemporary Arts Mus., Houston, 1983, Hadler/Rodriguez Gallery, Houston, 1983, 84, Caranchua Gallery, Corpus Christi, 1985, Southwest Tex. U., San Marcos, 1985, Fuller Goldeen Gallery, San Francisco, 1985, Sheffield Gallery, Houston, 1987, 88, Berman Gallery, Palo Alto Calif., 1988, Fuller Gross Gallery, San Francisco, 1989, Cabrillo Coll., Santa Cruz, Calif., 1989, Butler Gallery, Santa Monica, Calif., 1989. Nat. Endowment for Arts fellow, 1981. Home: 110 Delacosta Santa Cruz CA 95060 Studio: 2537B Mission Dr Santa Cruz CA 95060 also: 66 1/2 Windward Ave Venice CA 90291

RUSSELL, LOUISE, educator, folklorist; b. Stratford, Okla., Aug. 9, 1931; d. Virgel Wylie and Louise J. (Hayden) R. BA magna cum laude, Oklahoma City U., 1953; MA, Northwestern U., 1955; PhD, Ind. U., 1977. Tchr., Sterling, Colo., 1958-59, Washington-Lee High Sch., Arlington, Va., 1959-62, John Handley High Sch., Winchester, Va., 1962-63, Weld Sch. Dist. No. 6, Greeley, Colo., 1963-68, 72-87; faculty assoc. Northland Pioneer Coll., Holbrook, Ariz., 1987—, chmn. staff devel. team English basic skills Colegio Internacional, Valencia, Venezuela, 1968-69, Holmdel Schs., N.J., 1971-72; folklorist. Author: Understanding Folklore, 1975; Understanding Folk Music, 1977; also articles. Mem. mus. bd. Apache County Hist. Soc. Active Named Tchr. of Yr. Masons. Mem. Am. Anthrop. Assn., Am. Folklore Soc., NEA, Greeley Tchrs. Assn., Colo. Edn. Assn., Blue Key, Phi Delta Kappa. Office: Northland Pioneer Coll Saint Johns AZ 85936

RUSSELL, MARK EDWARD, recreation specialist; b. Angola, Ind., Apr. 8, 1965; s. Robert Eugene and Wilma Lee (Kovich) R.; m. Donna Lynn Corless, Sept. 20, 1987. BS in Recreationa and Pks. Adminstrn. Counselor Camp Tecumseh, Brookston, Ind., 1985; program supr. parks and recreation Bloomington (Ind.) Pks. Dept., 1985; supr. Recreational Sports Div. Ind. U., Bloomington, 1986; lifeguard Bloomington Pks. Dept., 1986; intramural dir. dept. recreation svcs. USN, St. Davids, Bermuda, 1987; dir. youth activites MWR U.S. Navy, Mare Island, Calif., 1988—. CPR instr. ARC, Travis Air Force Base, 1988, also mem. Super Sitter Inst., 1988. Mem. DeMolay (master counselor 1983). Republican. Home: RR 2 Box 347 Angola IN 46703

RUSSELL, NEWTON REQUA, state senator; b. Los Angeles, June 25, 1927; s. John Henry and Amy (Requa) R.; m. Diane Henderson, Feb. 12, 1953; children—Stephen, Sharon, Julia. BS, U. So. Calif., 1951; postgrad. UCLA, Georgetown U., Webb Prep. Sch. Spl. agt. Northwestern Mut. Life Ins. Co., Calif., 1954-64; mem. Calif. State Assembly, 1964-74, Calif. Senate, 1974—; vice-chmn. com. on energy and pub. utilities, mem. com. on local govt., vice chmn. com. on banking and commerce, mem. com. on transp., joint com. on rules, joint com. on state's economy, task force on legis. efficiency. Mem. Republican State Central Com., former precinct chmn.; former chmn. residential campaign Tujunga United Way; past bus. solicitor Community Chest . Served with USN, 1945-46. Recipient Outstanding Legislator award Calif. Rep. Assembly, 1968, 76, 81, Mayor's commendation City of Burbank, 1978, Disting. Service award County Suprs. Assn. Calif., 1980, Nat. Rep. Legislator of Yr., 1981, Legislator of Yr. award Los Angeles County Fedn. Rep. Women, 1982, Legislator of Yr. award Calif. Credit Union League, 1983, numerous honors from community orgns. and instns. Mem. Delta Tau Delta, Alpha Kappa Phi. Mem. Church on the Way. Office: Office State Senate State Capitol Sacramento CA 95814

RUSSELL, PATRICK ROY, internal revenue agent; b. Cheyenne, Wyo., Mar. 17, 1954; s. Harold Allen and May Lois (Newman) R.; m. Anna Maria Lopez, Dec. 1, 1973; 1 child, Jennifer Marie. BS in Acctg., U. Wyo., 1986. Asst. mgr. Sherwin-Williams Co., Laramie, Wyo., 1977; revenue agt. IRS, Rock Springs, Wyo., 1986—, dist. support technician, 1988—. Coordinator Vol. Income Tax Assistance, Rock Springs, 1988. Home: 3930 Cribbon Ave Cheyenne WY 82001

RUSSELL, PAUL EDGAR, electrical engineering educator; b. Roswell, N.Mex., Oct. 10, 1924; s. Rueben Matthias and Mary (Parsons) R.; m. Lorna Margaret Clayshulte, Aug. 29, 1943; children: Carol Potter, Janice Russell Gregory, Gregory. BSEE, N.Mex. State U., 1946, BSME, 1947; MSEE, U. Wis., 1950, PhDEE, 1951. Registered elec. engr., Ariz. From instr. to asst. prof. elec. engring. U. Wis., Madison, 1947-52; sr. engr., design specialist Gen. Dynamics Corp., San Diego, 1952-54; from prof. to chmn. elec. engring. dept. U. Ariz., Tucson, 1954-63; dean engring. Kans. State U., Manhattan, 1963-67; prof. Ariz. State U., Tempe, 1967-85; dir. engring. Ariz. State U. West, Phoenix, 1985-88; dir. Sch. Constrn. and Tech. Ariz. State U., Tempe, 1988—; cons. in field, 1954—; programs evaluator, mem. engring. commn. Accreditation Bd. for Engring. and Tech., N.Y.C., 1968—. Contbr. articles to jours. and chpts. to books. Served as sgt. U.S. Army, 1944-46. Recipient Disting. Service award N.Mex. State U., 1965. Mem. IEEE (chmn. Ariz. sect. 1960), Am. Soc. Engring. Educators. Home: 5902 E Caballo Ln Scottsdale AZ 85253

RUSSELL, RAY L., veterinarian, management consultant; b. Mesa, Ariz., Mar. 14, 1932; s. Ernest Edward and Ethel H. (Stewart) R.; m. Evangeline Davis, June 28, 1951; children: Stanford, Sheree, Evan, Renee, Joan, Melanie, Marcy. BS, Kans. State U., 1956, DVM, 1956; MA in Mgmt., U. Phoenix, 1983. Pres. Mesa Vet. Hosp., Ltd., 1956-77, Can.-Toronto (Ont.) Mission, 1977-80, Execu-Trends, Mesa, 1980-84; exec. dir. Am. Animal Hosp. Assn., Denver and South Bend, Ind., 1984-86; spl. asst. to gov. State of Ariz., Phoenix, 1986—; cons. in field. Author: Hospital Management, 1983; contbr. articles to profl. jours. Mem. exec. com., former pres. Theodore Roosevelt Coun., Boy Scouts Am., Phoenix, 1966—; active various charitable orgns. Capt. USAF, 1956-72. Named Mesa's Citizen of the Yr., 1969, others. Mem. Am. Animal Hosp. Assn. (pres. 1973-74), Ariz. Vet. Med. Assn. (pres. 1962-63, Named Ariz. Vet. of the Yr. 1965), Nat. Speakers Assn., Nat. Acad. Practice, Am. Vet. Med. Assn., Mesa C. of C., Rotary. Republican. Mem. Ch. of Jesus Christ of Latter-day-Saints. Home and Office: 758 E 7th Pl Mesa AZ 85203

RUSSELL, ROBERT R., leasing company executive; b. Grand Island, Ill., June 11, 1932; s. William H. and Hanna (Ramsey) R.; m. Mary Lou Rosenquist, Apr. 30, 1960; children: Jacqueline Lee Russell Stranz, Craig William. BS, U. Nebr., 1954. Mktg. rep. IBM, Phoenix, 1957-67; v.p. Greyhound Computer Corp., Chgo., 1967-68, Boothe Computer corp., L.A., 1968-71; chief exec. officer Systems Mktg., Inc., Phoenix, 1971-88; chief exec. officer Russcor Fin., Inc., Phoenix, 1988—, also bd. dirs.; bd. dirs. Abbys Holding Co., Roseburg, Oreg., Neoka, Inc., Phoenix, Nehawka Energy Ltd., Phoenix. Pres. bd. dirs., Phoenix Goodwill Industries, 1978-84; bd. regents, Brophy High Sch., Phoenix, 1985—; bd. dirs. St. Vincent DePaul, Phoenix, 1985—. 1st lt. U.S. Army, 1954-56. Mem. Computer Dealer and Lessors Assn. (bd. dirs. 1980), Rep. Senatorial Trust, Forest Highlands C. of C., White Mountain C. of C., Phoenix Country Club, Desert Mountain Country Club. Presbyterian. Office: Russcor Fin Inc 4647 N 32d St Phoenix AZ 85018

RUSSELL, THOMAS ARTHUR, lawyer; b. Corona, Calif., Aug. 2, 1953; s. Larry Arthur Russell and Patricia Helena (Collins) Heath. BS, U. Calif., Berkeley, 1976; JD, U. So. Calif., 1982. Bar: Calif. 1983, U.S. Dist. Ct. (cen. dist.) Calif. 1983, U.S. Ct. Appeals (9th cir.) 1986, U.S. Supreme Ct. 1988. Law clk. Calif. Ct. Appeal, Los Angeles, 1981; assoc. Graham & James, Long Beach, Calif., 1982-88; ptnr. Williams Woolley Cogswell Nakazawa & Russell, Long Beach, 1988—; speaker, panelist Nat. Marine Bankers Assn., Chgo., 1987—; mem. U. So. Calif. Environ. Law Adv. Bd., Los Angeles, 1985—. Co-Founder U. So. Calif. Jour. Law and Environment. Mem. ABA (Bronze Key award, 1982), Maritime Law Assn. U.S. (proctor, mem. legislation and fin. coms.), Calif. Bar Assn. (legis. com.), Los Angeles County Bar Assn., Long Beach Bar Assn., Legion Lex Am. Inn Ct. (barrister). Republican. Roman Catholic. Home: 5928 Bixby Village Dr #152 Long Beach CA 90803 Office: Williams Woolley Cogswell Nakazawa & Russell 200 Oceangate Ste 700 Long Beach CA 90802

RUSSELL, WILLIAM CHARLES, aerospace engineer; b. St. Louis, Nov. 11, 1956; s. William Eugene and Virginia Blanche (McMurtrey) R.; m. Connie Sue Childers; children: Felicia Marie Caroline, William Joshua Anthony. BS, Ohio State U., 1983; MS, George Washington U., 1985. Rsch. asst. Langley Rsch. Ctr. NASA, Hampton, Va., 1983-85; sr. engr. Boeing Aerospace, Seattle, 1985—. With USMC, 1975-79. Joint Inst. Acoustics and Flight Scis. scholar, 1983. Office: Boeing Aerospace PO Box 3999 Seattle WA 98124

RUSSELL, WILLIAM JOHN, health service administrator; b. Chgo., Feb. 8, 1933; s. Arthur James Russell and Jarie Susan (Pease) Russell Losinger; m. Frances JoAnn Hunter, June 24, 1958; children: James Patrick, John

William, Joseph Folsom, Arthur Justin. BA in Psychology, St. Martin's coll., 1982. Drafted U.S. Army, 1954-56, enlisted, 1958, advanced through grades to sgt. 1st class, 1975; neuropsychiat. Letterman Army Med. Ctr., San Francisco, 1959-63; orthopaedic specialist Camp Zama, Japan, 1965-68; combat medic 5th Bn., 46th Inf., Socialist Republic of Vietnam, 1969-70; medic, tchr. Ft. Lewis and Madigan Army Hosp., Tacoma, 1970-80; ret. 1980; nurse, counselor Comprehensive Mental Health, Tacoma, 1981-86; prin. Mendocino County Mental Health, Ukiah, Calif., 1986—; tchr. Knapp Bus. Coll., Tacoma, 1983-86, Mendocino Coll., 1986-87. Author poetry. Coord. Tacoma council Boy Scouts Am., 1983. Decorated Bronze Star; recipient Golden Poet award World of Poetry, 1987, 88. Lodge: Odd Fellows (inside guardian Willits, Calif. chpt.). Home: 149 E Valley St Willits CA 95490 Office: Mendocino County Mental Health 564 S Dora St Ukiah CA 95482

RUSSO, LAURA, gallery director; b. Waterbury, Conn., Mar. 7, 1943; d. Lawrence and Lillian A. (Russo) Kaplan; m. John I. Lawrence, May 6, 1962 (div. 1974); children: Maia Giosi, Dylan Russo. Cert., Pacific N.W. Coll. Art, 1975. Art instr. Tucker Maxon Oral Sch., Portland, Oreg., 1970-74, Pacific N.W. Coll. of Art, Portland, 1977-78; assoc. dir. Fountain Fine Arts, Seattle, 1981-82; asst. dir. The Fountain Gallery of Art, Portland, 1975-86; owner, dir. The Laura Russo Gallery, Portland, 1986—; lectr. Seattle Art Mus., 1987; juror Oreg. Sch. of Design, Portland, 1988; com. mem. Oreg. Com. for the Nat. Mus. Women in the Arts, 1988. Mem. com. award and grants Metro. Arts Commn., Portland, 1988, 89; active Friends of Oreg. Pub. Broadcasting, P.N.C.A. Mem. Contemporary Arts Council, Friends Print Soc., Oreg. Art Inst., L.A. Mus. Contemporary Art (program chmn. 1989-90), Seattle Art Mus. Democrat. Office: Laura Russo Gallery 805 NW 21st Ave Portland OR 97209

RUSSO, VINCENT JOSEPH, orthopedic surgeon; b. Amsterdam, N.Y., Oct. 23, 1950; s. Vincent Peter and Vera (Ippolito) R.; m. Janie Lee Cavanaugh, June 22, 1974; children: Gregory, Matthew, Timothy. BA with honors, Holy Cross Coll., Worcester, Mass., 1972; MD, Albany Med. Coll., 1976. Intern/surg. resident Grady Meml. Hosp., Atlanta, 1976-78; resident in orthopedics U. Pitts., 1978-81; practice medicine specializing in orthopedic surgery Scottsdale, Ariz., 1981—; attending physician Crippled Children Svcs., Phoenix, 1985—; pres. med. staff Scottsdale Meml. Hosp. North, 1987—. Contbr. articles to profl. jours. Fellow ACS, Am. Acad. Orthopedic Surgeons; mem. Scottsdale C. of C., Cen. Ariz. orthopedic Soc., Western Orthopedic Assn. (chpt. sec.-treas.), AMA, Ariz. Med. Assn., Maricopa County Med. Assn., Alpha Omega Alpha. Republican. Roman Catholic. Home: 8611 N 66th Pl Paradise Valley AZ 85253 Office: 3501 N Scottsdale Rd Ste 134 Scottsdale AZ 85251

RUSSUM, SUSAN LEE, nurse; b. Erwin, N.C., Nov. 5, 1952; d. Jack Lee Stewart and Virginia Catherine (Camp) Nelson. Assoc. diploma in nursing, Coll. Desert, 1976. RN, Nev. Charge nurse Creighton U. Hosp., Omaha, 1976-78, Desert Springs Hosp., Las Vegas, 1977-83, U. Med. Ctr., Las Vegas, 1983-88; nurse, legal asst. Beckley, Singleton, DeLanoy, Jemison and List Charted Law Firm, Las Vegas, 1988—; expert nurse witness Las Vegas, 1984—; paramedic preceptor Paramedic Program U. Med. Ctr., 1987—; paramedic evaluator fire dept. City of Las Vegas. Mem. Am. Assn. Critical Care Nurses, Nat. Assn. Female Execs., Nev. Bar Assn. (assoc.). Republican. Baptist. Home: 5256 Blossom Ave Las Vegas NV 89122 Office: Beckley Singleton DeLanoy Jemison & List 411 E Bonnieville Las Vegas NV 89101

RUSTEBAKKE, ALVIN SYVER, miller, farmer; b. Scobey, Mont., Aug. 25, 1919; s. Martin and Annie Catherine (Christensen) R.; m. Dorothy Mae Cochran, Oct. 16, 1946; children: Carolyn, David, Paul, John, Kathryn. G-rad. high sch., Scobey. Farmer Scobey, 1945—; owner,mgr. Great Grains Milling Co., Scobey, 1979—. Bd. dirs., v.p. Daniels County Farm Bur., Scobey; past bd. dirs., Four Buttes (Mont.) Sch., Scobey Schs.; past sec., Daniels County Fair Assn. Sgt. inf., U.S. Army, 1940-45, ETO. Home: PO Box 427 Scobey MT 59263 Office: Great Grains Milling Co PO Box 427 Scobey MT 59263

RUST-PHILLIPS, PATRICIA, writer, producer; b. L.A., Sept. 24, 1958; d. William Evans and Jacquelyn (Knox) Rust; m. Victor Frederic Phillips III, Mar. 29, 1986. BA magna cum laude, UCLA, 1978, postgrad. in film, 1978-80. Fashion model Internat. Cos., various, 1972-78; contbg. writer, freelance various magazines, 1972-78; writer, producer PBS, L.A., 1978-79; correspondent ABC TV, L.A., 1979-82; pres. Patricia Rust Prodns., L.A. and Honolulu, 1982-87, writer, producer TV comedy spls. and episodes, 1987—; mem. Emmy Awards Com., Acad. of Television Arts and Scis., Hollywood, Calif., 1988-89; cons. in communications. U. Hawaii, Honolulu, 1982-83. Host/creator/writer: (television show) The Rust Report, 1984 (several awards 1986), On Cue, 1984 (Golden Mike award 1985), On Location, 1983 (Kiwanis award 1984); producer/host/writer (magazine) The Entertainment Report, 1986; syndicated TV columnist: The Rust Report, 1988-89; writer TV movie Maybe Baby, 1988, NBC primetime comedy spl., 1989; host TV spl. California Girl, 1976. Pres. of Provisionals, Fashionettes, Hollywood Presbyn. Hosp., 1988; pub. chmn. Venice Bible Tabernacle, Venice, Calif., 1987; host, moderator local TV debates, Santa Monica, 1985—. Named Miss American Health and Beauty, KCOP Television, Hollywood, 1976; winner sketch comedy writing competition Am. Film Inst., 1989. Mem. Radio and Television News Assn. (Golden Mike award 1984), Acad. of Television Arts and Scis., Newsletter Assn. for Women in Entertainment (contbg. editor, 1988—), Women in Film, Television Acad. Film Soc., Hollywood Radio and Television Soc. (mem. com. 1986-89), Malibu/Pacific Club, Masters Swim Team (Palisades), Assn. Producers and Assoc. Producers, Women in Communications, Nat. Cable TV Acad. Republican. Presbyterian. Office: Patricia Rust Prodns 616 San Vicente Blvd Ste A Santa Monica CA 90402

RUTAN, RICHARD GLENN (DICK RUTAN), aircraft company executive; b. Loma Linda, Calif., Jan. 1, 1938; s. George and Irene Rutan. BS, Am. Technol. U., 1974; D in Sci. and Tech. (hon.), Cen. New Eng. Coll., 1987. Commd. 2d lt. USAF, 1959, advanced through grades to lt. col., 1975, ret., 1978; prodn. mgr., chief test pilot Rutan Aircraft Factory, 1978-81; cofounder Voyager Aircraft Co., Mojave, Calif., 1981—. Decorated Silver Star, D.F.C. with silver oak leaf cluster, Purple Heart, Air medal (16). Recipient Louis Bleroit medal Fedn. Aeronautique Internationale, 1982, Collier trophy Nat. Aviation Club, 1986, Presdl. Citizen's Medal of Honor, 1986, Godfrey L. Cabot award Aero Club New Eng., 1987, Patriot of Yr. award, 1987, Newsmaker of Yr. award Aviation Writers Am., 1987, Deedalian Dist, Achievement award, 1987, Lindbergh Eagle award San Diego Aerospace Mus., 1987, Ivan P. Kinslow award Soc. Expl. Test Pilots, 1987, Gold medal Royal Aero Club, Grande Medallion, Medalle de Ville Paris Paris Aero Club, Richard Glenn (Dick) World Record for 1st closed circuit, great circle distance around-the-world, non-stop, non-refueld flight, numerous others. Office: Voyager Aircraft Inc Hangar 77 2833 Del Mar Mojave CA 93501

RUTH, CRAIG, business executive; b. July 18, 1930; s. Clarence Miller and Kathryn Dorothy (Buch) R.; m. Marion Nelson, Apr. 19, 1958; children: Robert Nelson, Lee Kathryn, William Water, Ann Alva. BA, Muskingum Coll., 1952; postgrad., Northwestern U., 1956. Dir. mktg. Great Lakes Carbon Co., Los Angeles, 1966-68; exec. v.p. Ketchum, Peck & Tooley, Los Angeles, 1968-75; pres. Tooley & Co., Los Angeles, 1975—; bd. dirs. Los Angeles Internat. Bus. Ctr.; council mem. Urban Land Inst., 1982—. Bd. dirs. Bldg. Owner & Mgrs. Assn.; chmn. Elgin Baylor & Jerry West Nights Los Angeles Lakers, Ed Sherman Night, Muskingum Coll., Los Angeles. Named one of Outstanding Men of Am. C. of C., 1965; recipient Humanitarian award Nat. Conf. Christians and Jews, 1988. Mem. Internat. Assn. Corp. Real Estate Execs. Republican. Presbyterian. Home: 4045 Miraleste Dr Rancho Palos Verdes CA 92074 Office: Tooley & Co 3303 Wilshire Blvd Los Angeles CA 90010

RUTHERFORD, EDWARD ARNOLD, clergyman; b. Fresno, Calif., Feb. 20, 1945; s. Edgar Lee and Lena (Dabbs) R.; m. Mary Helen Blackburn, July 22, 1967; children: Roben Renee, Michele Lenise. BS in Acctg., Calif. State U., Bakersfield, 1973, MS in Bus., 1976; postgrad. in religion, Berean Coll., Springfield, Mo., 1977; DD (hon.), So. Calif. Theol. Sem., 1985. Ordained to ministry Assemblies of God Ch., 1980. Various mgmt. positions Pacific Telephone Co., Bakersfield, 1966-77; sr. pastor Wofford Heights (Calif.) Assembly, 1977-8l, Cerritos (Calif.) Assembly, 1982-87; pastor Calvary Christian Ch., Buena Park, Calif., 1987—; bd. dirs. World Wide Missions, Bellflower, Calif., 1985-86; ministerial rep. Forest Lawn, Long Beach, Calif., 1987-88; sec., bd. dirs. Tri Care Plus, Bell Gardens, Calif., 1987—; sec.-treas., bd. dirs. Missions Internat., Sacramento, 1988—; adj. prof. So. Calif. Coll., Costa Mesa, 1980-85, So. Calif. Theol. Sem., Stanton, 1985-87. Author: Church Business Administration, 1983; contbr. articles to religious mags. and newspaper. Mem. Bell Gardens Homeless Coalition, 1988; bd. dirs. Tri Care Ctrs., Bell Gardens, 1988. With USN, 1962-66. Fellow Nat. Assn. Ch. Bus. Adminstrs.; mem. Performex (assoc.). Democrat. Office: Calvary Christian Ch PO Box 5457 Buena Park CA 90626

RUTHERFORD, REID, finance company executive; b. Morristown, N.J., Dec. 30, 1952; s. Clinton Homer and Bonnie Beth (Bergner) R.; m. Beth Ann Husak, Apr. 3, 1977; children: Ian Michael, Laurel Bryce, Corinne Leigh, Alyse Allyne. BA, Pepperdine U., 1975; MBA, Stanford U., 1981. Exec. v.p. Analytics, Inc., N.Y.C., 1976-79; pres. Softlink Corp., Santa Clara, Calif., 1981-83, Research Applications for Mgmt., Menlo Park, Calif., 1984-85, Concord Growth Corp., Palo Alto, Calif., 1985—. Contbr. articles to profl. jours. Office: Concord Growth Corp 1086 E Meadow Cir Palo Alto CA 94303

RUTHERFORD, THOMAS TRUXTUN, II, state senator, lawyer; b. Columbus, Ohio, Mar. 3, 1947; s. James William and Elizabeth Whiting (Colby) R.; m. Linda Sue Rogers, Aug. 28, 1965 (div.); 1 child, Jeremy Todd. BBA, U. N.Mex., 1970, JD, 1982. Page, reading clk. N.Mex. State Legislature, 1960-65; mem. N.Mex. Atty. Gen. Environ. Adv. Commn., 1972; radio broadcaster Sta. KOB Radio and TV, 1963-72; mem. N.Mex. Senate, Albuquerque, 1972—, majority whip, 1978—, chmn. econ. devel. and new tech. interim com., mem. sci. and new tech. oversight com.; pres. Rutherford & Assocs., Albuquerque, 1978-83; pvt. practice, Albuquerque, 1983—; bd. dirs. Union Savs. Bank, Albuquerque; past chmn. Albuquerque Cable TV adv. bd.; mem. Southwest Regional Energy Council, N.Mex. Gov.'s Commn. on Public Broadcasting; bd. dirs., v.p. Rocky Mountain Corp. for Pub. Broadcasting; mem. Am. Council Young Polit. Leaders, del. mission to Hungary, Austria, Greece, 1983; mem. Fgn. Trade Adv. Com. Bd. Econ. Devel. and Tourism; trade del. to People's Republic of China, 1985—. N.Mex. Broadcasting Assn. scholar, 1970. Home: 426A Quincy NE Albuquerque NM 87108 Office: PO Box 1610 Albuquerque NM 87103

RUTLAND, GEORGE ADAMS, electronics executive; b. Demopolis, Ala., July 30, 1944; s. Robert Horton Rutland and Mary Louise (Torbert) Sherrill; m. Patricia Helen Trawick, July 2, 1965; children: Adam, Will, Caroline Elizabeth. BS in Applied Physics, Auburn U., 1966. Mng. dir. Nat. Semiconductor (UK), Ltd., Greenock, Scotland, 1973-75; gen. mgr. Asia/Pacific div. Nat. Semiconductor Corp., Singapore, 1975-77; group dir. Nat. Semiconductor Corp., Santa Clara, Calif., 1977-80; v.p. Synertek, Inc., Santa Clara, 1980-81; pres. Solid State Sci., Inc., Willow Grove, Pa., 1981-84; pres., chief exec. officer Ultratech Stepper, Inc., Santa Clara, 1984—; bd. dirs. Bipolar Integrated Tech., Beaverton, Oreg., 1984-88; semiconductor tech. adv. com. Dept. of Commerce, 1986—. Mem. Semiconductor Equipment and Materials Inst. (govt. rels. com. 1986), Young Presidents Orgn. Club: Toastmasters (Campbell, Calif.) (pres. 1980-81). Office: Ultratech Stepper Inc 3230 Scott Blvd Santa Clara CA 95054

RUTSTEIN, HARRY SIDNEY, business and foundation executive, explorer; b. Balt., Dec. 2, 1929; s. Joseph Edward Israel and Reba Zelda (Singer) R.; m. Eleanor Marx, Jan. 23, 1953 (div. Feb. 1977); children: Richard L., Sonia D., Cynthia R.; m. Nancy A. Susman, Feb. 14, 1980; children: Jessica Jane, Sarah E. Student, Johns Hopkins U., 1948-78. Rsch. engr. Radiation Lab., Johns Hopkins U., Balt., 1948-55; sales engr. H.L. Hoffman & Co., Balt., 1955-57; pres., v.p. Ea. Instrumentation, Inc., Balt., 1957-75; expdn. leader Marco Polo Expdn., Europe and Asia, 1975-85; dir. mtkg. Nurad, Inc., Balt., 1976-78; exec. dir. Marco Polo Found., Inc., Balt., 1979—; pres. Dorado Co., Seattle, 1979—; exec. producer (film) On the Roof of the World, Pakistan, 198l. Author: In the Footsteps of Marco Polo, 1980. Co-chmn. Polit. Action Com. for Oregon Ridge, Towson, Md., 1978. Sgt. U.S. Army, 195l-54. Named hon. lord propr. Baltimore County, 1976. Mem. Assn. Old Crows (founder, chpt. pres. 1970-7l), Wash. State-China Rels. Coun. Office: Dorado Co-Marco Polo Found 4l9 Lake Washington Blvd Seattle WA 98122

RUTTER, DEBORAH FRANCES, orchestra adminstrator; b. Pottstown, Pa., Sept. 30, 1956; d. Marshall Anthony and Winifred (Hitz) R. BA, Stanford U., 1978; MBA, U. So. Calif., 1985. Orch. mgr. Los Angeles Philharm., 1978-86; exec. dir. Los Angeles Chamber Orch., 1986—. Bd. dirs. AIDS project Los Angeles, 1985—, Assn. Calif. Symphony Orch., 1987—, pres. 1988—; active Jr. League Los Angeles, 1982—. Mem. Am. Symphony Orch. League, Assn. Calif. Symphony Orchs., Chamber Music Soc. L.A. (bd. dirs. 1987—, pres.'s council Ojai Festival). Democrat. Episcopalian. Office: LA Chamber Orch 315 W 9th St Ste 300 Los Angeles CA 90015

RUTTER, MARSHALL ANTHONY, lawyer; b. Pottstown, Pa., Oct. 18, 1931; s. Carroll Lennoxx and Dorothy (Tagert) R.; m. Winifred Hitz, June 6, 1953 (div. 1970); m. Virginia Ann Hardy, Jan. 30, 1971; children: Deborah Frances, Gregory Russell, Theodore Thomas. BA, Amherst (Mass.) Coll., 1954; JD, U. Pa., 1959. Bar: Calif 1960. Assoc. O'Melveny & Meyers, Los Angeles, 1959-65; assoc. Flint & MacKay, Los Angeles, 1965-67, ptnr., 1967-72; ptnr. Rutter, O'Sullivan, Greene & Hobbs, Los Angeles, 1973—. Gov. Los Angeles Performing Arts Council, 1978-86; dir. Chorus Am., Phila., 1987—; bd. dirs., pres. Los Angeles Master Chorale Assn., 1963—; vestryman All Saints Ch., Beverly Hills, Calif., 1983-86, 88—. Served with U.S. Army, 1954-56. Mem. ABA, Assn. Bus. Trial Lawyers (bd.dirs. 1980-82), Los Angeles County Bar Assn., The English-Speaking Union (various offices Los Angeles chpt. 1963—), Los Angeles Jr. C. of C. (bd. dirs. 1964-67). Democrat. Episcopalian. Home: 149 N Van Ness Ave Los Angeles CA 90004 Office: Rutter O'Sullivan Greene & Hobbs 1900 Ave of the Stars #2200 Los Angeles CA 90067

RUYBALID, LOUIS ARTHUR, social worker, community development consultant; b. Allison, Colo., Apr. 6, 1925; s. Mike Joseph and Helen Mary (Rodriguez) R.; m. Seraphima Alexander, June 12, 1949; children: Mariana, John. BA, U. Denver, 1946-49, MSW, 1951; PhD, U. Calif., Berkeley, 1970; Professor Ad-Honorem (hon.), Nat. U., Caracas, Venezuela, 1964. Social worker Ariz., Calif., Colo., 1951-62; advisor community devel. Unitarian Service Com., Caracas, 1962-64, U.S. Agy. for Internat. Devel., Rio de Janeiro, Brazil, 1964-66; area coordinator U.S. Office Econ. Opportunity, San Francisco, 1966-68; prof., dept. head U. So. Colo., Pueblo, 1974-80; licensing analyst State of Calif., Campbell, 1984—; prof. sch. of social work Highlands U., Las Vegas, N.Mex., 1988-89; cons. UN, Caracas, 1978, Brazilian Govt., Brazilia, 1964-66, Venezuelan Govt., Caracas, 1962-64. Author: (books) Favela, 1970, Glossary for Hominology, 1978, (research instrument) The Conglomerate Hom., 1976. Mem. exec. com. Pueblo (Colo.) Regional Planning Com., 1974-79, Nat. Advisory com. The Program Agy. United Presbyn. Ch., 1978-79. Served with USN, 1944-46. Recipient Pro Mundo Beneficio medal Brazilian Acad. Human Sci., Sao Paulo, 1976; United Def. Fund fellow U. Calif., Berkeley, 1961-62, Cert. World Leadership Internat. Leaders of Achievement, 1988-89. Mem. Nat. Assn. Social Workers (cert.), Ethnic Minority Commn., IMAGE (nat. edn. chair), Am. Hominol. Assn. (nat. pres. 1975-79), U. Calif. Alumni Assn., Phi Beta Kappa, Phi Sigma Iota. Democrat. Home: 129 Calle Don Jose Santa Fe NM 87501 Office: NMex Highlands U Sch Social Work Las Vegas NM 87701

RUYS, FRANK CONSTANTYN, orthopedic surgeon; b. Maassluis, Netherlands, Aug. 31, 1920; s. Jan Daniel and Johanna Woutrina (Lambrechksen) R.; m. Jyce Elaine West, Feb. 14, 1947 (div. 1976); children: Elaine C., Patricia L., W. Timothy, Jennifer L., Renee M.; m. Patricia Antoinette Rafael, Dec. 31, 1978; 1 child, Cassandra Marie. MD, Tulane U., 1944. Diplomate Am. Bd. Orthopedic Surgery, 1957. Practice medicine specializing in orthopedic surgery Redwood City, Calif., 1952-53, 1955--. Mem. Woodside (Calif.) Sch. Dist. Sch. Bd., 1956-58. Served to lt. commdr. M.C., USNR, 1953-55, Korea. Fellow ACS, Am. Acad. Orthopedic Surgeons, Internat. Coll. Surgeons. Republican. Office: 260 A Main St Redwood City CA 94063

RYAN, ARTHUR NORMAN, movie company executive; b. Gloucester, Mass., Dec. 22, 1938; s. Arthur Stanley and Mary (Ross) R.; children: Maya, Mark. B.S. in Polit. Sci, Suffolk U., Boston, 1962. Sr. acct. Price Waterhouse & Co., N.Y.C., 1962-66; asst. treas. Paramount Pictures, N.Y.C., 1966-67; dir. adminstrn. and bus. affairs Paramount Pictures, Los Angeles, 1967-70; v.p. prodn. adminstrn. Paramount Pictures, 1970-75, sr. v.p. prodn. ops., 1975-76; pres., chief operating officer Technicolor, Inc., Los Angeles, 1976-83, vice chmn., chief exec. officer, 1983-84; chmn., chief exec. officer Technicolor, Inc., 1985—; chmn. bd., chief exec. officer Compact Video Services, Inc., 1984—; chmn. exec. com. Four Star Internat. Inc., 1984—; dir. MacAndrews & Forbes Holdings Inc. Bd. dirs. Hollywood Canteen Found., trustee Calif. Inst. Arts, vice chmn., 1985—. Served with inf. U.S. Army, 1963. Mem. Acad. Motion Picture Arts and Scis., Acad. TV Arts and Scis. Office: Technicolor Inc 4050 Lankershim Blvd North Hollywood CA 91608 *

RYAN, BRADLEY EARLE, electrical engineer; b. Grundy Center, Iowa, Jan. 5, 1961; s. Archie Earle and Madonna Kay (Wright) R.; m. Catherine Ann Sealock, Aug. 6, 1983. BSEE, Iowa State U., 1984. Engr. Ariz. Pub. Svc. Co., Phoenix, 1984—, sr. customer svc. engr., 1988—. Loaned exec., Phoenix United Way, 1988. Mem. IEEE, Iowa State Alumni Club. Republican. Lutheran. Home: 19021 N 8th Ave Phoenix AZ 85027

RYAN, CATHERINE L., college administrator; b. Goshen, Ind., Jan. 22, 1964; d. Howard Russell and Evelyn (Earlean) Fought; m. Gary W. Ryan, Feb. 5, 1983. AA, Phoenix Coll., 1979; BA, Ottawa U., 1988. Dental asst. Bloomington, 1974-77; svc. rep. Ind. U., Bloomington, 1977-78; grad. evaluator Rio Salado Community Coll., Phoenix, 1979-81, program adviser, 1981-83; supr. Phoenix Coll., 1984—, mem. pres. mgr.'s group, 1988—. Tutor Literacy Plus program; mem. Valley of Sun Sweet Adeline. Mem. Assoc. Records Mgrs. Adminstrn., Phoenix Coll. Mgmt., Adminstrn. Home: 7026 S 42d St Phoenix AZ 85013 Office: Phoenix Coll 1202 W Thomas Rd Phoenix AZ 85013

RYAN, CATHRINE SMITH, publisher; b. Calif., May 9, 1930; d. Owen W. and Margarette D. (Grimsley) Griffin; A.A., Bellevue Jr. Coll., Denver, 1948; grad. Barnes Sch. Commerce, Denver, 1950; student N.Y. Ballet Acad., 1954; m. Patrick J. Ryan, Apr. 28, 1972. Dir. Ballet Workshop, Enumclaw, Wash., 1958-64; dir. confs. and seminars San Francisco Theol. Sem., 1977-80; pres., dir. Cathi, Ltd., pub. and cons. office orgn. and mgmt., San Francisco, 1980—; freelance travel photographer, 1968-80; guest instr. in field. Active local PTA, March of Dimes, ARC. Recipient various certs. of recognition. Republican. Mormon. Author: Face Lifting Exercises, 1980, Sullivan's Chain, 1986; procedure and policy manuals. Avocations: geneol. research, family histories, translating old German script.

RYAN, D(UDLEY) JAY, lawyer; b. N.Y.C., May 19, 1943; s. Dudley F. and Maud D. (Delaney) R.; m. Janeen L. Bausch, Aug. 12, 1979; 1 child, Erin. AB in Am. Govt., Georgetown U., 1965; JD, U. Ariz., 1968. Bar: Ariz. 1968, U.S. Dist. Ct. Ariz. 1968, U.S. Ct. Appeals (9th cir.), U.S. Supreme Ct. 1972. Pvt. practice Phoenix, 1968-69, 72—; asst. atty. gen. State of Ariz., Phoenix, 1970-72; lay mem. Ariz. State Bd. Accountancy, 1974-79, pres. 1979. Contbr. articles to porfl. jours. V.p., bd. dirs. Ariz. Recreational Ctr. for Handicapped, 1981—; pres., bd. dirs. Cen. Ariz. Regional Epilepsy Soc., 1973-78. Mem. Ariz. Bar Assn. (adminstrv. law com.), Maricopa County Bar Assn. (pub. relations), Jaguar Club. Republican. Roman Catholic. Home: 1602 W Vernon Phoenix AZ 85007 Office: 2627 N 3d St Phoenix AZ 85004

RYAN, EDWARD J., JR., manufacturing executive; b. Cleve., Aug. 8, 1953; s. Edward J and Dorothy A. (Wasilewsky) R.; m. Cynthia R. Carlson, Apr. 7, 1972; 1 child, Emily Ryan. Heat treater Garrett Corp., Phoenix, 1975-76, metall. tech., 1977-78, mfg. supr., 1979-80, indsl. engr., 1981-82, mfg. engring. supr., 1983-84, quality assurance mgr., 1985-86; gen. mgr. Sonee Heat Treating, Inc., Phoenix, 1987—; quality freelance cons., Phoenix, 1986—. Speaker in field. Mem. Am. Soc. for Metals, Am. Soc. Quality Control, Metal Treating Inst., Ariz. Assn. of Industries. Republican. Club: Moon Valley Country (Phoenix). Office: Sonee Heat Treating Inc 3900 N 31st Ave Phoenix AZ 85017

RYAN, JAMES HARRY, retail executive; b. Somerset, Pa., Apr. 30, 1943; s. James H. and Ethel M. Walker) R.; m. Diana R. Hollenshead, Sept. 2, 1962; children: Richard, Dana, kara. Grad. high sch., Somerset. Store mgr. Kamps Shoe Stores, Inc., Somerset, Pa., 1961-69, Stride Rite Retail Corp., Salt Lake City, 1970-71; dist. mgr. Stride Rite Retail Corp., Chgo., 1972-73; sr. dist. mgr. Stride Rite Retail Corp., L.A., 1974-76; regional dir. Stride Rite Retail Corp., Phoenix, 1977-85; pres. Ryan's Shoe Things, Inc., Phoenix, 1985—; bd. dirs. Colonnade Mall, Phoenix, Valley West Mall, Glendale, Ariz. Bd. dirs. Somerset County Easter Seals, Somerset. Mem. 2/10 Shoe Assn., Colonnade Mchts. Assn. (VIP award 1986). Home: 4926 W Kaler Dr Glendale AZ 85301 Office: Ryans Shoes Things 1859A Camelback Rd Phoenix AZ 85016

RYAN, JOHN EDWARD, federal judge; b. Boston, Jan. 22, 1941; s. Howard Frederick and Mary (Burke) R.; m. Terri Reynolds; children: Valerie, Jennifer, Keely. BSEE, U.S. Naval Acad., 1963; LLB, Georgetown U., 1972; MS, Pacific Christian U., 1979. Assoc. Hale and Dorr, Boston, 1972-76, C.F. Braun, Alhambra, Calif., 1976-77; gen. counsel Altec Corp., Anaheim, Calif., 1977-79; v.p., sr. atty. Oak Industries, San Diego, 1979-82; sr. v.p. Oak Media, San Diego, 1982-84; ptnr. Dale and Lloyd, La Jolla, Calif., 1984-85, Jennings, Engstrand and Henrikson, San Diego, 1985-86; bankruptcy judge U.S. Bankruptcy Ct., Santa Ana, Calif., 1986—; dir. Orange County Bankruptcy Forum. Editor Calif. Bankruptcy Jour. With USN, 1963-69. Mem. Mass. Bar Assn., Calif. Bar Assn., Orange County Bar Assn., Bankruptcy Judges Assn. Republican. Roman Catholic. Home: 3155 Summit Dr Escondido CA 92025 Office: US Bankruptcy Ct PO Box 12600 Santa Ana CA 92712

RYAN, LYNN BANKER, professional speaker; b. Holtville, Calif., Oct. 8, 1935; d. Fredrick William and Mary (Setz) Waterman; m. Edward Everett Banker, Sept. 18, 1954 (div. Sept. 1987); children: Bret Howard, Bruce Edward, Bradley Allen; m. Vernon Joseph Ryan, Sept. 19, 1987. Office mgr. Design Scis., Inc., El Centro, Calif., 1967-74; office mgr. U. Calif., Irvine, 1979-81, fin. bus. mgr., 1981-85; pres. Lynn Banker & Assoc., Costa Mesa, Calif., 1984—; mem. classification com. U. Calif., 1980-84; pres., v.p. Internat. Tng. in Communications, Huntington Beach, Calif., 1982-84. Author audio tape album and single tapes; contbr. articles to profl. jours. Mem. by laws task force, 1st v.p., bd. dirs. congregation St. Matthews Old Cath. Mission, Huntington Beach, 1988. Mem. Nat. Speakers Assn. (bd. dirs. 1986-87, membership chair 1985-87, 2d v.p. 1987-88, 1st. v.p., program chmn. 1988-89, pres. 1989-90, Bronze Mike 1986, Silver Mike 1987, Gold Mike 1988), Women's Bus. Assn., Connections Club (Cerritos, ethics com. 1986-88), Ind. Cons. Club (L.A.). Republican. Home: 1953 Flamingo Dr Costa Mesa CA 92626 Office: Lynn Baker & Assoc PO Box 2397 Costa Mesa CA 92628

RYAN, MARY GENE, military officer; b. Corona, Calif., Sept. 11, 1953; d. Robert James and Genevieve Louise (Kubilis) Guzinski; m. Robert Eldon Ryan III, June 9, 1979; children: Michael Warren, Jessica Gene. BSN, So. Conn. State Coll., 1975; MPH, U. Tenn., 1980. Commd. 2d lt. USAF, 1976, advanced throught grades to maj., 1987; staff nurse obstetrics U. Conn. Med. Ctr., Farmington, 1975-76; med.-surgical staff nurse Williams AFB (Ariz.) Hosp., 1976-77; flight nurse instr. 2d Aeromed. Evacuation Squadron, RheemMaen, Fed. Republic of Germany, 1977-79; officer in charge environ. health Wolford Hall Med. Ctr., Lackland AFB, Tex., 1980-84; chief environ. health AFSC Hosp., Edwards AFB, Calif., 1984-88; dir. occupational health Peterson Med. Clinic, Oxnard, Calif., 1988-89; health and safety officer County of Ventura (Calif.)/Gen. Svcs. Agy., 1989—; cons. environ. health L.A. AFB, 1984-88. Contbr. articles to profl. jours. Mem. choir, soloist, lay eucharestic minister Edwards AFB Cath. Chapel, 1984--, mem. religious edn. com., 1984-85, lectr., commentator, 1986-87; AIDS educator, Edwards AFB, 1986-88. Mem. Aerospace Med. Assn., Soc. Environ. Health Profls., Am. Pub. Health Assn. (flight nurse sect.), Am. Assn. Occupational Health Nurses, Calif. Assn. Occupational Health Nurses, Calif. Gen. Coast Assn., Occupational Health Nurses, Officers Wives, Med. Wives. Home: 5415 Topa Topa Dr Ventura CA 93523-5300

RYAN, MAUREEN, psychotherapist; b. Jersey City, N.J., Nov. 14, 1952; d. Michael J. and Margaret E. (Keeley) R.; m. Robert Joe Stout, Apr. 14, 1988. BS, St. Peter's Coll., 1974; MA, Calif. State U., Chico, 1979. Counseling intern Family Services Assn., Chico, 1977-79; crisis counselor Butte County Crisis Service, Chico, 1976-79, coordinator youth services, 1979-80; social worker in nephrology New West Dialysis Clinic, Chico, 1982-84; cons. Catalyst: Women's Advocates Inc., Chico, 1981-84, exec. dir., 1984-86; psychotherapist, owner Butte Counseling Clinic, Chico, 1981—; cons. Communication Workers Am., Chico, 1981-82. Mem. Am. Council Nephrology Social Workers, Am. Assn. Counseling and Devel., Calif. Assn. Marriage and Family Therapists, Calif. Marriage and Family Therapists. Democrat. Office: Butte Counseling Clinic 344 Flume St Chico CA 95928

RYAN, PHILIP DAVID, small business owner; b. Rantoul, Ill., Nov. 30, 1955; s. Edward John and Julie Louise (Rossi) R. Lic. blue seal engr., N.J.; operators lic., NRC. Electronics technician Digital Devel. Corp., San Diego, 1980-81; health physics instr. Gen. Atomic Co., San Diego, 1981-82; nuclear control operator Jersey Cen. Power & Light, Forked River, N.J., 1982-86; nuclear operator Ariz. Nuclear Power Project, Wintersburg, 1986—; owner Desert Air, Buckeye, Ariz., 1987—. Served with USN, 1973-79. Mem. NRA, Aircraft Owners and Pilots Assn. Republican.

RYAN, RANDEL EDWARD, JR., airline pilot; b. N.Y.C., Jan. 11, 1940; s. Randel Edward and Ann Augusta (Horwath) R.; m. Pamela Michael Wiley, May 12, 1962; children—Katherine, Gregory. B.S. in Sci., Trinity Coll., 1961. Quality control supr. Ideal Toy Corp., Jamaica, N.Y., 1961-62; airline pilot United Airlines, San Francisco, 1967—, chmn. speakers panel, 1983—. Editor: The Bayliner, 1984-86, The Lowdown, 1980-83. Pres., Highlands Community Assn., San Mateo, Calif., 1975; chmn. Com. to Re-elect County Supr., San Mateo, 1976; rep. Highlands Community Assn., San Mateo, 1970-86; coach Little League and Babe Ruth Baseball, San Mateo, 1979-83. Served to capt. USAF, 1962-68. Recipient Vandor award San Mateo PTA, 1976, awards of merit United Airlines, San Francisco, 1975, 79. Mem. Air Line Pilots Assn. (editor newspaper 1984-86, chmn. community relations com. 1983—, mem. contract study com. 1984—, chmn. grievance com. 1982-86, council vice chmn. 1986—).Democrat. Club: Highland Tennis (San Mateo). Home: 1768 Lexington Ave San Mateo CA 94402 Office: United Airlines San Francisco Internat Airport San Francisco CA 94128

RYAN, STEPHEN JOSEPH, JR., ophthalmologist, educator; b. Honolulu, Mar. 20, 1940; s. S.J. and Mildred Elizabeth (Farrer) F.; m. Anne Christine Mullady, Sept. 25, 1965; 1 dau., Patricia Anne. A.B., Providence Coll., 1961; M.D., Johns Hopkins U., 1965. Intern Bellevue Hosp., N.Y.C., 1965-66; resident Wilmer Inst. Ophthalmology, Johns Hopkins Hosp., Balt., 1966-69, chief resident, 1969-70; fellow Armed Force Inst. Pathology, Washington, 1970-71; instr. ophthalmology Johns Hopkins U., Balt., 1970-71, asst. prof., 1971-72, assoc. prof., 1972-74; prof., chmn. dept. ophthalmology LAC-USC Med. Ctr., Los Angeles, 1974—; acting head ophthalmology div., dept. surgery Children's Hosp., Los Angeles, 1975-77; med. dir. Doheny Eye Inst. (formerly Estelle Doheny Eye Found.), Los Angeles, 1977—; chief of staff Doheny Eye Hosp., Los Angeles, 1985-88; mem. advisory panel Calif. Med. Assn., 1974—. Editor: (with M.D. Andrews) A Survey of Ophthalmology—Manual for Medical Students, 1970, (with R.E. Smith) Selected Topics in the Eye in Systemic Disease, 1974, (with Dawson and Little) Retinal Diseases, 1985; assoc. editor: Ophthalmol. Surgery, 1974—; mem. editorial bd.: Am. Jour. Ophthalmology, 1981—, EYESAT, 1981—, Internat. Ophthalmology, 1982—, Retina, 1983—, Graefes Archives, 1984—; contbr. articles to med. jours. Recipient cert. of merit AMA, 1971; Louis B. Mayer Scholar award Research to Prevent Blindness, 1973; Rear Adm. William Campbell Chambliss USN award, 1982. Mem. Wilmer Ophthal. Inst. Residents Assn., Am. Acad. Ophthalmology and Otolaryngology (award of Merit 1975), Am. Ophthal. Soc., Pan-Am. Assn. Ophthalmology, Assn. Univ. Profs. of Ophthalmology, Los Angeles Soc. Ophthalmology, AMA, Calif. Med. Soc., Los Angeles County Med. Assn., Pacific Coast Oto-Ophthal. Soc., Los Angeles County Acad. Medicine, Pan Am. Assn. Microsurgery, Macula Soc., Retina Soc., Nat. Eye Care Project, Research Study Club, Jules Gonin Club, Soc. of Scholars of Johns Hopkins U. (life). Office: USC Sch Med Doheny Eye Inst Dept Ophthalmology 1355 San Pablo St Los Angeles CA 90033

RYAN, STEPHEN VINCENT, automotive services executive; b. Oakland, Calif., Mar. 15, 1950; s. John E. and Gloria K. (Gaasch) R.; m. Nancy L. Young (div. June 1978); children: Heather M.K., Sean V., John R.; m. Pamela S. Conrow. Student, Colo. State U., 1972-73. Pres., gen. mgr. Ryan Automotive, Inc., Ft. Collins, Colo., 1972--, Quick Inspect & Lube, Inc., Ft. Collins, 1986--, Midtown Rent-A-Car, Ft. Collins, 1988--. Sec., treas. Larimer County Petroleum Retailers, Ft. Collins, 1975. With USN, 1968-72, Vietnam. Mem. Colo. Jaycees (regional v.p. 1978), Ft. Colllins Jaycees (pres. 1976), Elks. Republican. Office: Midtown Rent A Car 602 S College Ave Fort Collins CO 80524

RYCHETSKY, STEVE, civil engineer, consultant; b. Phoenix, Oct. 9, 1951; s. Edward and Maria (Zabroni) R.; m. Dawna Marie Strunk, June 10, 1972 (div. Oct. 1985); children: Brian, Melissa; m. Michaele Ann Turner, Dec. 28, 1986; stepchildren: Mike, Kristi, Jaye, Karly Reeves. AA in Engring., Oreg. Inst. Tech., 1972, BTech, 1976. Registered profl. civil engr., Oreg., Calif. Mgr. sales engring. Varcopruden, Turlock, Calif., 1976-79, AMCA Internat., Winston-Salem, N.C., 1979-82; civil engr. USDA Soil Conservation Service, Klamath Falls, Oreg., 1983-85, tech. advisor, 1983-88; civil engr., tech. advisor USDA Soil Conservation Service, Tillamook, Oreg., 1985—; private cons. engr. Tillamook, Oreg., 1985—. Democrat. Roman Catholic. Home: PO Box 338 Tillamook OR 97141 Office: USDA Soil Conservation Svc 2204 4th St Ste B Tillamook OR 97141

RYDBOM, KARI ANN FRANTZ, small business owner; b. Denver, Aug. 8, 1961; d. Frederick Harold and Leslie Ann (Higgins) F.; m. Kevin Alan Rydbom, Feb. 21, 1987. AAS, Northeastern Jr. Coll., Sterling, Colo., 1981. Asst. mgr. Motel 6, Greeley, Colo., 1983-84; acct. exec. Greeley (Colo.) Tribune, 1984-87; prin. Budget Movie Rental, Windsor, Colo., 1987—. Mem. Windsor C. of C. (bd. dirs.). Republican. Presbyterian. Home: 2 Rochester Dr Windsor CO 80550 Office: Budget Movie Rental 201 4th St Windsor CO 80550

RYDDER, NIELS LEEGAARD, manufacturing company executive, accountant; b. Roskilde, Denmark, Nov. 28, 1952; came to U.S., 1984; s. Henning and Rita (Leegaard) R.; m. Sonja Moller Madsen, May 8, 1978; children: Carina, Martin. Handelshojskolens Diplomprøe in Acctg., Copenhagen Sch. Bus. Adminstn., Denmark, 1977, MBA in Tax, Audit Test, 1979; MBA Test for state, Authority Pub. Accts., Denmark, 1981. State authorized pub. acct., Denmark. Jr. auditor, acct. Revisions Firmaet C. Jespersen, Sta. KPMG, Copenhagen, 1973-76; auditor, state authorized pub. acct. Revisions Firmaet Askeaard Olesen Horwath & Horwath, Roskilde, Denmark, 1976-82; pres., chief executive officer Danish Decision Support Systems, Roskilde, 1982-84; chief fin. officer, dir. The Micon Group, Randers, Denmark, 1983-84; pres., chief executive officer Micon Wind Turbines, Inc., San Diego, 1984—; dir. Micon Wind Turbines, Inc., San Diego, 1983—, MWT Enterprises, Inc., San Diego, 1985—. With The Royal Danish Life Guard, 1972-73, Copenhagen. Mem. Am. Mgmt. Assn., Assn. State Authorized Pub. Accts. (Denmark). Office: Micon Wind Turbines Inc 1455 Frazee Rd #305 San Diego CA 92108-1336

RYDELL, THEODORE NELSON, engineer; b. St. Cloud, Minn., Nov. 23, 1961; s. Warren Lerone and Margaret Louise (Johnson) R. BS, U. Minn., Mpls., 1984. Engr. Boeing Commercial Airplanes, Seattle, 1985-89, McDonnell Douglas Helicopter Co., Mesa, Ariz., 1989—. Mem. Soc. of Allied Weight Engrs. Republican. United Methodist. Home: 1313 S Val Vista # 154 Mesa AZ 85204

RYDER, GARY ALAN, lawyer, investor; b. Souix City, Iowa, Aug. 23, 1955; s. Bernard Joseph and Alanna Louis (Johnstone) R. BS in Polit. Sci., So. Oreg. State Coll., 1978; JD, U. Mont., 1984. Bar: Mont. Law clk. to presiding justice 7th Jud. Dist., Glendive, Mont., 1984; Treasure County atty. Hysham, Mont., 1984-87; dep. Rosebud County atty. Forsyth, Mont., 1987—. Mem. Council for Mid-Yellowstone Electric Coop., Incx., Hysham, 1985—. Mem. ABA (young lawyers' sect.), Lions, Elks. Democrat. Roman Catholic. Home: 15 S Strevell Miles City MT 59327 Office: Rosebud County Rosebud County Courthouse Forsyth MT 59327

RYDER, HAL, theatre educator, director; b. Evanston, Ill., Aug. 21, 1950; s. Lee Sigmund and Katherine (Philipsborn) Rosenblatt; m. Caroline Margaret Ogden, Nov. 17, 1976. Student, U. Ariz., 1968-72, U. Miami, summer 1971; cert. in drama, Drama Studio London, 1973; BA in Drama, U. Wash., 1987. Drama specialist Rough Rock (Ariz.) Demonstration Sch., 1971-72; artistic dir. Mercury Theatre, London, 1973-75, Fringe Theatre, Orlando, Fla., 1976-79; dir. Drama Studio London, 1980-82, interim adminstrv. dir., 1985; artistic dir. Alaska Arts Fine Arts Camp, Sitka, 1987, Shakespeare Plus, Seattle, 1983—; instr. Cornish Coll. Arts, Seattle, 1982—, producer theatre, 1987—; creative cons. Sea World Fla., Orlando, 1979; lit. mgr. Pioneer Square Theatre, Seattle, 1983; space mgr. Seattle Mime Theatre, 1986-87. Author: Carmilla, 1976, (with others) Marvelous Christmas Mystery, 1978; editor: Will Noble Blood Die, 1987, The New Emperor's New Cloths, 1988; dir. over 100 stage plays; appeared in over 40 prodns. Recipient Faculty Excellence award Seafirst Bank, Seattle, 1988. Mem. SAG, AFTRA, Am. Fedn. Tchrs. (Cornish chpt.). Democrat. Jewish. Home: 1012 NE 62d St Seattle WA 98115 Office: Cornish Coll Arts 710 E Roy Seattle WA 98102

RYDER, LOIS JUANITA, loan officer; b. Fairoaks, Ind., Jan. 18, 1931; d. Lyle Everett Handley and Louise Elizabeth (Leech) Clausen; m. Freeman Charlie Ryder, Aug. 27, 1950; children: Steven Joseph, Raymond Dean. AA in Banking and Fin., Portland Community Coll., 1978; BS in Mgmt., Marylhurst Coll., 1984. Switchboard operator Pacific Telephone Co., Monte Rio, Calif., 1954-57; bus. officer, teller Pacific Northwest Bell Telephone, Vancouver, Wash., 1957-59; bookkeeper Pennco Auto Supply, Vancouver, 1959-69; bank teller First Indep. Bank, Vancouver, 1970-73; banking officer, loan officer First Interstate Bank of Oreg., Portland, 1973—; owner Scipios Goble Landing, Rainier, Oreg., 1984—. Mem. North Portland Sapporo com., 1979—; mem. St. Johns' Boosters, North Portland, 1979-87; bd. dirs. YMCA North/Inner NE chpt., 1985. Mem. Am. Bus. Women Pacific (Wonderland chpt. treas. 1986—, Woman of the Year 1984-85). Republican. Seventh Day Adventist. Home: 70360 Columbia River Way Rainier OR 97048 Office: First Interstate Bank of Oreg 1300 SW 5th Ave Portland OR 97201

RYDER, SANDRA SMITH, communications specialist, publicist; b. Great Lakes, Ill., July 6, 1949; d. Dennis Murrey and Olga (Grosheff) Smith. BS, Northwestern U., 1971; MA, Annenberg Sch. Communications at U. So. Calif., 1986. Columnist Camarillo Daily News (Calif.), 1971-76; editor Fillmore Herald (Calif.), 1976-78; pub. info. officer Oxnard Union High Sch. Dist. (Calif.), 1980-82; pub. info. officer Ventura County Community Coll. Dist., 1982-83; pub. relations dir. Murphy Orgn., Oxnard, Calif., 1983-84; pub. affairs rep. Gen. Telephone Calif., Thousand Oaks, 1984-88; adminstr. internat. communications, Gen. Telephone Ops., Irving, Tex., 1988—. Co-chmn. Ventura County Commn. for Women, 1981—. Mem. Women in Communications, Soc. Profl. Journalists, Pub. Info. and Communications Assn. (life).

RYDER, STEPHANIE M., nurse educator; b. Atlanta, Sept. 19, 1947; d. George Bernard and Mary Louise (Bininger) Tremmel. RN, Good Samaritan Sch. Nursing, Phoenix, 1969; BS in Health Edn., Ariz. State U., 1975. Cert. Health Edn. Specialist. Obstetrical nurse Phoenix Indian Med. Ctr., 1970-75; flight nurse/edn. nurse air evacuation Samaritan Health Svc., Phoenix, 1976-78; emergency dept. nurse St. Luke's Hosp., Phoenix, 1978-85; prog. dir./health educator Am. Diabetes Assn., Phoenix, 1978-80; diabetes educator Maricopa Med. Ctr., Phoenix, 1982-83; diabetes nurse specialist Scottsdale (Ariz.) Meml. Hosp., 1984-86; with Good Control Newsletter, Phoenix, 1981-84; pvt. diabetes educator/cons. Phoenix, 1978-86; reg. diabetes edn. specialist Boehringer Mannheim Diagnostics, Scottsdale, 1986—; cons. in field. editor, pub. Good Control Newsletter, Phoenix, 1981-84. Mem. Am. Assn. Diabetes Educators (bd. dirs. 1984-86), Internat. Diabetic Athletes Assn. (bd. dirs. 1987—), Appaloosa Horse Club. Republican. Roman Catholic. Office: Boehringer Mannheim Diag PO Box 2112 Scottsdale AZ 85252-8586

RYDER, STEVEN LEROY, manufacturing executive; b. Redding, Calif., May 2, 1949; s. Lawrence Ryder and Bonnie Zelda (Hess) Patterson; m. Joyce Jean Jeffredo, Mar. 5, 1977; children: Christopher Lee, Jeremiah Sean, Jonathan Brent. BS, cert. physician asst., Loma Linda U., 1980. Cert. respiratory practitioner, physician asst. Respiratory practitioner Loma Linda (Calif.) Community Hosp., 1978-79; physician asst. Jerry Pettis VA Hosp., Loma Linda, 1979-81; program dir. Inst. Med. Studies, Garden Grove, Calif., 1981-82; dir. clin. edn. Allied Health, La Puente, Calif., 1982-85; prin. Biometrix Med. Labs., Fullerton, Calif., 1985-87; pres. Theotek Corp., Fullerton, 1988—. Inventor positional insensitive aspirator. Mem. Nat. Commn. on Cert. Physician Assts., Nat. Bd. Respiratory Care, Calif. Entrepreneur Assn., Inventors Workshop Internat., Am. Assn. for Respiratory Care. Republican. Mem. Christian Ch. Home: 1334 W Woodcrest Ave Fullerton CA 92633 Office: Theotek Corp PO Box 6547 Fullerton CA 92634

RYE, DAVID EDWARD, publishing company executive; b. Casper, Wyo., Dec. 15, 1942; s. Edward F. and Reta (France) R.; m. Cheri A. Dengel, Jan. 13, 1968; children: Kristi, Kori. BA, Wash. State U., 1966; MBA, Seattle U., 1970. Dir. Computech Corp., Seattle, 1966-84; mgr. IBM, Boulder, Colo., 1985—; pres. Western Publs. Co., Boulder, 1986—. Author: Corporate Game, 1985, Two for the Money, 1986, Colorado's Guide To Fishing, 1988, Colorado's Guide To Hunting, 1989. Home: 2 Silver Cloud Ln Boulder CO 80302 Office: Western Publs 2525 Arapahoe Ave E4-194 Boulder CO 80302

RYERSON, FAIRY ELECTA, real estate agent, actress; b. Kans. City, Mo., June 17, 1914; d. Edwin Nelson and Alice Marancy (Hunter) Cunningham; m. El Joseph Sunyogh, May 20, 1951 (div. Nov. 1951); m. Robert Charles Ryerson, June 1, 1953. Student, Mo. U., 1933; cert. real estate, Edn. Dynamics, Las Vegas, Nev., 1972; degree in Russian Ballet, Kelly-Mack, Kansas City, Mo., 1935. Ballet dancer Ballet Russe De Monte Carlo, Kansas City, 1929; dance tchr. Kelley-Mack Sch., 1929-36; profl. dancer theaters, Kansas City, Mpls., Chgo.; actress Booth Theater, N.Y.C., 1937-38; ballerenia state fairs, Can. Provices, Toronto,Calgary, Can., N.J., Pa., 1938-46; night club dancer Chgo., Milw., Los Angeles, Las Vegas, Nev., 1946-66; sch. tchr. Las Vegas Pub. Schs., 1966-73; owner Ryerson Research, Las Vegas, 1969-74; real estate agt. Norman Kaye Real Estate Co., Las Vegas, 1975—; motion picture actress Paramount Pictures, Hollywood, Calif., 1943-53; dancer Sta. KTLA-TV, Hollywood, 1950-52. Hostess weekly show exptl. TV; 1st dancer to appear on TV, 1931. Candidate city commr. sch. bd., Las Vegas, 1971-72; sponsor Piute Indian Crafts Sch., Las Vegas, 1974; mem. Rep. Cen. Com., Las Vegas. Named most humorous female Senator Cannon, Las Vegas, 1972. Mem. DAR (regent Valley Fire chpt. 1972-74), Toastmistresses (pres. 1974-80), Col. Dames XVII Century (pres. 1976-78), Screen Actors Guild (sec., 1980-82). Republican. Home: 4217 El Jardin Las Vegas NV 89102 Office: Norman Kaye Real Estate Co 1019 S Decatur Las Vegas NV 89102

RYGEL, MARY AVERKAMP, accountant; b. Dubuque, Iowa, Feb. 27, 1953; d. Aloysius Paul and Shirley Marie (Meyer) Averkamp; m. Daniel Lee Rygel, Jan. 7, 1975; children: Justin Carissa, Megan. Student, Macalester Coll., 1970-72; BA, U. Calif., Davis, 1876; postgrad., So. Oreg. State Coll., 1982-85, Boise State U., 1985-88. CPA, Idaho. Staff acct. Ripley, Doorn and Co., Boise, 1987-88; chief acct. Fabeo, Inc., Eagle, Idaho, 1988; owner, mgr. Big O Tires, Auburn, Wash., 1988—. Asst. treas. Amity United Meth. Ch., Boise, 1987; treas. Amity Sch. PTA, Boise, 1987-88; leader Silver Sage Coun. Girl Scouts USA, 1987-88. Nat. Merit scholar, 1970-72. Mem. AICPA (Elijah Watt Sells Cert. with high distinction 1986), Nat. Assn. Accts., Beta Alpha Psi. Home: 21610 124th Ave SE Kent WA 98031 Office: Big O Tires 1901 Auburn Way N Ste A Auburn WA 98002

RYGIEWICZ, PAUL THADDEUS, plant ecologist; b. Chgo., Feb. 19, 1952; s. Sigismund Thaddeus and Regina (Korpalski) R. BS in Forestry, U. Ill., 1974; MS in Wood Sci., U. Calif., Berkeley, 1976; PhD in Forest Resources, U. Wash., 1983. Research wood technologist ITT Rayonier, Inc., Shelton, Wash., 1977; research assoc. Centre National de Recherches Forestières, Nancy, France, 1983-84; research soil microbiologist U. Calif., Berkeley, 1984-85; research ecologist EPA, Corvallis, Oreg., 1985—; asst. prof. dept. forest sci. Oreg. State U., 1987—. Contbr. articles to profl. jours. Vol. Big Bros. of Am., Urbana, Ill., 1972-74. Fellow Regents U. Calif., Berkeley, 1973-74, Weyerhaeuser U. Calif., Berkeley, 1978-79, Inst. Nat. de la Recherche Agronomique, France, 1983-84, French Ministry of Fgn. Affairs, 1983-84. Mem. AAAS, Ecol. Soc. Am., Am. Soc. Plant Physiologists, Sigma Xi, Gamma Sigma Delta, Xi Sigma Pi (officer 1973-74). Clubs: Portland Wheelmen Touring; Forestry (Urbana and Berkeley). Office: EPA 200 SW 35th St Corvallis OR 97330

RYLAND, STEVEN BYRD, engineer; b. Long Beach, Calif., Apr. 16, 1949; s. Byrd Worthington and Betty Eileen (White) R.; m. Roseanne Mary Ryland. Student, Embry Riddle Aero. U., Daytona Beach, Fla., 1988, Nat. Technical Sch., L.A., 1983-84. V.p. sr. instr. scuba com. Calif. Scuba Ltd., Newport Beach, 1972-74; air traffic control specialist FAA Monterey Airport, Calif., 1974-75, FAA San Jose Airport, Calif., 1975-78, FAA-L.A. Airport, 1978-81; mgr. airport ops. Hughes Helicopters, Culver City, Calif., 1981-82; sr. systems analyst Unisys Corp., Camarillo, Calif., 1982—. Inventor: Invention, Aquacisor 1978; Author: Book, Racquetball, Rules,. Speaker D.O.T. Accident Prevention Specialist, San Jose Calif., 1978; com. mem. Facility Air Traffic Adv. Com., L.A., 1980, Profl. Air Traffic Control Orgn. Safety L.A., 1981. Mem. Nat. Assn. Underwaters Instrs., Profl. Air Traffic Control Orgn. Office: Unisys Corp 747 Calle Plano Camarillo CA 93010

RYLANDER, ROBERT ALLAN, financial service executive; b. Bremerton, Wash., Apr. 8, 1947; s. Richard Algot and Marian Ethelyn (Peterson) R.; m. Donna Jean Marks, June 28, 1984; children: Kate, Josh, Erik, Meagan. BA in Fin., U. Wash., 1969; postgrad., U. Alaska, 1972-74. Controller Alaska USA Fed. Credit Union, Anchorage, 1974-77, mgr. ops., 1977-80, asst. gen. mgr., 1980-83, exec. v.p., chief operating officer, 1983—; pres., chief exec. officer, treas. Alaska Option Services Corp., Anchorage, 1983—; bd. dirs. Alaska USA Ins., Inc., Anchorage. Served to capt. USAF, 1969-74. Mem. Credit Union Execs. Soc., Shared Networks Exec. Assn. Home: 6514 Lakeway Dr Anchorage AK 99502 Office: Alaska USA Fed Credit Union PO Box 196613 Anchorage AK 99519-6613

RYMER, PAMELA ANN, federal judge; b. Knoxville, Tenn., Jan. 6, 1941. A.B., Vassar Coll., 1961; LL.B., Stanford U., 1964. Bar: Calif. 1966, U.S. Ct. Appeals (9th cir.) 1966, U.S. Ct. Appeals (10th cir.), U.S. Supreme Ct. Assoc. Lillick McHose & Charles, Los Angeles, 1966-72, ptnr., 1973-75; ptnr. Toy and Rymer, Los Angeles, 1975-83; judge U.S. Dist. Ct. (cen. dist.) Calif., Los Angeles, 1983—; faculty The Nat. Jud. Coll., 1986. Mem. Calif. Postsecondary Edn. Commn., 1974—, chmn., 1980-84; mem. Los Angeles Olympic Citizens Adv. Commn.; bd. visitors Stanford U. Law Sch., 1986—, Pepperdine U. Law Sch., 1987; mem. Edn. Commn. of States Task Force on State Policy and Ind. Higher Edn., 1987; bd. dirs. Constl. Rights Found., 1985—. Mem. ABA, Los Angeles County Bar Assn. (chmn. antitrust sect. 1981-82), Assn. of Bus. Trial Lawyers. Office: US Dist Ct 312 N Spring St Los Angeles CA 90012

RYNIKER, BRUCE WALTER DURLAND, industrial designer, manufacturing executive; b. Billings, Mont., Mar. 23, 1940; s. Walter Henry and Alice Margaret (Durland) R.; B. Profl. Arts in Transp. Design (Ford scholar), Art Ctr. Coll. Design, Los Angeles, 1963; grad. specialized tech. engring. program Gen. Motors Inst., 1964; m. Marilee Ann Vincent, July 8, 1961; children—Kevin Walter, Steven Durland. Automotive designer Gen. Motors Corp., Warren, Mich., 1963-66; mgmt. staff automotive designer Chrysler Corp., Highland Park, Mich., 1966-72; pres., dir. design Transform Corp., Birmingham, Mich., 1969-72; indsl. designer, art dir. James R. Powers and Assocs., Los Angeles, 1972-75; sr. design products mgr. Mattel Inc., Hawthorne, Calif., 1975—; dir. design and devel. Microword Industries, Inc., Los Angeles, 1977-80, also dir.; exec. mem. Modern Plastics Adv. Council, 1976-80; elegance judge LeCercle Concours D'Elegance, 1976-77; mem. nat. adv. bd. Am. Security Council, 1980; cons. automotive design, 1972—. Served with USMC, 1957-60. Mem. Soc. Art Ctr. Alumni (life), Mattel Mgmt. Assn., Second Amendment Found., Am. Def. Preparedness Assn., Nat. Rifle Assn. Designer numerous exptl. automobiles, electric powered vehicles, sports and racing cars, also med. equipment, electronic teaching machines, ride-on toys. Home: 21329 Marjorie Ave Torrance CA 90503 Office: 5150 Rosecrans Ave Mail Stop 11-337 Hawthorne CA 90250

RYPKA, EUGENE WESTON, microbiologist; b. Owatonna, Minn., May 6, 1925; s. Charles Frederick and Ethel Marie (Ellerman) R.; m. Rosemary Speeker, June 1, 1967. Student, Carleton Coll., 1946-47; BA, Stanford U., 1950, PhD, 1958. Prof. microbiology, systems, cybernetics U. N.Mex., Albuquerque, 1957-62; bacteriologist Leonard Wood Meml. Lab. Johns Hopkins U., Balt., 1962-63; sr. scientist Lovelace Med. Ctr., Albuquerque, 1963-71, chief microbiologist, 1971—; adj. prof. U. N.Mex., 1973—; cons. Hoffmann-LaRoche Inc., Nutley, N.J., 1974—, Airline Pilots Assn., Washington, 1976, Pasco Lab., Denver, 1983—; advisor Nat. Com. Clinic Lab. Standards, Pa., 1980-84. Contbr. articles to profl. jours. Served with USNR, USMC 1943-46. Fellow AAAS; mem. IEEE, Internat. Soc. Gen. Systems Research. Republican. Presbyterian. Home: 8345 Highland Sta Albuquerque NM 87198

SAAD, JOSEPH KANAN, lawyer; b. Clarksdale, Miss., Oct. 28, 1948; s. Joseph Saad and Jeanette (Farris) Chilli. BBA, U. Miss., 1970, JD, 1973. Bar: Miss. 1973, U.S. Dist. Ct. (no. dist.) Miss. Account exec. Dean Witter & Co., Memphis, 1973-75, Reynolds Securities, Houston, 1974, Lincoln Nat. Life Ins. Co., Houston, 1974-75; claims atty. Fidelity & Deposit Co. Md., Balt., New Orleans, Cleve. and Miami, 1975-80; bond claims atty. Transam Ins. Co., L.A., 1980-83, mgr. surety claims, 1983-84, asst. v.p. bonds, 1984-86, v.p. splty. claims, 1986—, claims counsel, 1988—; asst. v.p. Trans. Premier Ins. Co., L.A., 1987—, Fairmont Ins. Co., L.A., 1987—, Childton Ins. Co., Dallas, 1987—. Mem. ABA (fidelity and Surety com. 1976—), Miss. Bar Assn., Fedn. Ins. and Corp. Counsel, Internat. Assn. Def. Counsel, Def. Rsch. Inst., So. Calif. Surety Assn. Office: Transam Ins Co 6300 Canoga Blvd Woodland Hills CA 91367

SAAR, FREDERICK ARTHUR, data processing executive; b. Scranton, Pa., Aug. 30, 1946; s. Frederick Arthur and Mary (Gray) S.; m. Linda Keziah, Feb. 27, 1968; children: Frances Alisa, Jennifer Elizabeth. Sr. programmer Fed. Reserve Bank, Charlotte, 1967-74; EDP auditor First Commerce Corp., New Orleans, 1974-76; audit dir. First Interstate Bancorp, Phoenix, 1976-84; mgr. info. resource mgmt. First Interstate Bank div. First Interstate Bancorp, Phoenix, 1984—; pres. Hogan Users Group, Dallas, 1983-84. Served with U.S. Army, 1964-67, Vietnam. Named Auditor of Yr. Inst. Internal Auditors, Phoenix chpt., 1981-82. Mem. EDP Auditors Assn. (pres. Phoenix chpt. 1985, cert. info. systems auditor), Am. Assn. Artificial Intelligence, Inst. Cert. Computer Profls. (cert. systems profl.). Republican. Episcopalian. Office: First Interstate Bank 1336 W Alameda Tempe AZ 85282

SABA, MARK DAVID, retail executive; b. Phoenix, Aug. 3, 1952; s. Norman and Glennys (Paul) S.; m. Terri Marie Wood, Nov. 20, 1982; children: Sara, Mark, Andrew. BSBA, U. Ariz., 1975. CPA, Ariz. Staff acct. Wayne Brown & Co., Mesa, Ariz., 1975-79; ptnr. Saba & Mulkey CPA's, Chandler, Ariz., 1979-83; controller, owner Saba's Western Wear, Mesa, 1983—. Chmn. bd. dirs. St Lukes East Valley Behavioral Health Ctr., 1988—; bd. dirs. Chandler Housing Authority, 1984, Chandler Regional Hospital, 1988; candidate city council, Chandler, 1984. Mem. Am. Inst. CPA's, Ariz. Soc. CPA's, Chandler C. of C. Republican. Lutheran. Club: Chandler Compadres (treas. 1984, pres. 1988). Lodge: Rotary (bd. dirs. 1988).

SABAH, JOSEPH, writer; b. Logan, W.Va., May 31, 1931; s. Moses and Anna B. (Bussab) S.; m. Evelyn R. Sabah, May 21, 1956 (div. 1972); m. Judy Pfeifer, Dec. 26, 1981; children: Jo-Ellen, Joseph Samuel, David John. Asst. supt. agys. Western and Southern Life Ins., San Francisco, 1968-72; regional v.p. Am. Motivational Assn., Denver, 1972-75; mgr., recruiter Aurora (Colo.) Beauty Coll., 1975-79; freelance writer, speaker Denver, 1979—. Author: How to Get the Job You Really Want, 1986, How to Get on Radio Talk Shows, 1988. Precinct committeeman Denver Reps., 1976. Mem. Nat. Speakers Assn. (founding pres. Colo. chpt. 1981), Salesmen With a Purpose (pres. 1976-77). Office: Pacesetter Pubs PO Box 24147 Denver CO 80224

SABATINI, LAWRENCE, bishop; b. Chgo., May 15, 1930; s. Dominic and Ada (Piloi) S. Ph.L., Gregorian U., Rome, 1953, S.T.L., 1957, J.C.D., 1960; M.S. in Edn., Iona Coll., 1968. Ordained priest, Roman Catholic Ch., 1957, bishop, 1978. Prof. canon law St. Charles Sem., S.I., N.Y., 1960-71; pastor St. Stephen's Parish, North Vancouver, B.C., Canada, 1970-78; provincial superior Missionaries of St. Charles, Oak Park, Ill., 1978; aux. bishop Archdiocese Vancouver, B.C., Can., 1978-82; bishop Diocese Kamloops, B.C., Can., 1982—; procurator, adviser Matrimonial Tribunal, N.Y.C., 1964-71; founder, dir. RAP Youth Counseling Service, S.I., N.Y., 1969-71; vice ofcl. Regional Matrimonial tribunal of Diocese Kamloops, 1978-82; chmn. Kamloops Cath. Pub. Schs., 1982—. Named Man of Yr. Confratellanza Italo-Canadese, 1979. Mem. Can. Canon Law Soc., Canon Law Soc. Am., Can. Conf. Cath. Bishops. Home: 635A Tranquille Rd, Kamloops, BC Canada V2B 3H5 *

SABEL, ROBERT WALTER, security company executive; b. Chgo., Oct. 22, 1920; s. Walter Reuben and Ella Elizabeth (Andersson) S.; student Coe Coll., 1939-40, U. Md., 1948-49, El Camino Coll., 1980; m. Faith Carol Hammarlund, Dec. 9, 1950; children—Karen L., Ingrid M., James R., John G., Paul F., Kristin E. Mgr. nuclear research and devel. Cook Electric Co., Chgo., 1952-55; mem. tech. staff Ramo-Wooldridge Corp., Los Angeles, 1955-57; western regional mgr. Control Data Corp., Los Angeles, 1957-62; v.p. Electro Vision Industries, Los Angeles, 1962-65; owner Sabel Assos., Los Angeles, 1965-79; owner Sabel Investigation and Security Svc., Redondo Beach, Calif., 1988—; lectr. Internat. Police Acad., 1969-72, U. So. Calif. Pres., chmn. Liaison League Rehab. Group, Inc. Served to lt. col. USAF, 1941-50. Decorated D.F.C. with 1 oak leaf cluster, Air medal with 3 oak leaf clusters; Croix de Guerre with Palm (France). Mem. Internat. Assn. Identification, Calif. Peace Officers Assn., Internat. Acad. Criminology, Calif. Assn. Lic. Investigators, Res. Officers Assn. U.S., Am. Law Enforcement Officers & Assn., VFW. Republican. Baptist. Clubs: Army-Navy (Washington); Elks, Masons. Home: 341 Paseo de Gracia Redondo Beach CA 90277

SABHARWAL, RANJIT SINGH, mathematician; b. Dhudial, India, Dec. 11, 1925; came to U.S., 1958, naturalized, 1981; s. Krishan Ch and Devti (An) S.; m. Pritam Kaur Chadha, Mar. 5, 1948; children—Rajinderpal, Amarjit, Jasbir. B.A. with honors, Punjab U., 1944, M.A., 1948; M.A. U. Calif, Berkeley, 1962; Ph.D., Wash. State U., 1966. Lectr. math. Khalsa Coll., Bombay, India, 1951-58; teaching asst. U. Calif., Berkeley, 1958-62; instr. math. Portland (Oreg.) State U., 1962-63, Wash. State U., 1963-66; asst. prof. Kans. State U., 1966-68; mem. faculty Calif. State Hayward, 1968—, prof. math., 1974—. Author papers on non-Desarguesian planes. Mem. Am. Math. Soc., Math. Assn. Am., Sigma Xi. Address: 27892 Adobe Ct Hayward CA 94542

SABIN, JACK CHARLES, engineering and construction firm executive; b. Phoenix, June 29, 1921; s. Jack Byron and Rena (Lewis) S.; B.S., U. Ariz., 1943; B.Chem.Engring., U. Minn., 1947; m. Frances Jane McIntyre, Mar. 27, 1950; children—Karen Lee, Robert William, Dorothy Ann, Tracy Ellen. With Standard Oil Co. of Calif., 1947-66, sr. engr., 1966—; pres., dir. Indsl. Control & Engring., Inc., Redondo Beach, Calif., 1966—; owner/mgr. Jack C. Sabin, Engr.-Contractor, Redondo Beach, 1968—; staff engr. Pacific Molasses Co., San Francisco, 1975-77; project mgr. E & L Assos., Long Beach, Calif., 1977-79; dir. Alaska Pacific Petroleum, Inc., 1968—, Marlex Petroleum, Inc., 1970, 71—, Served with U.S. Army, 1942-46; capt. Chem. Corps, Res., 1949-56. Registered profl. engr., Calif., Alaska; lic. gen. engring. contractor, Ariz., Calif. Mem. Nat. Soc. Profl. Engrs., Ind. Liquid Terminals Assn., Conservative Caucus, Calif. Tax Reduction Com., Tau Beta Pi, Phi Lambda Upsilon, Phi Sigma Kappa. Republican. Clubs: Elks; Town Hall of Calif. Address: 151 Camino de las Colinas Redondo Beach CA 90277

SABLOSKY, WARREN FRIEDLAND, health products distribution company executive; b. Phila., Feb. 5, 1953; s. Mark J. and Rosalyn (Friedland) S.; m. Paula Margaret Hennelly, Oct. 13, 1985; 1 child, Mitchell Allan. BA, U. Oreg., 1979. Prin. Earth Evolution Products, Eugene, Oreg., 1979-83; nat. sales dir. Quantum, Inc., Eugene, 1983-86, pres., 1986—; also bd. dirs. Quantum, Inc. Author: Home Baked Pizza Cookbook, 1983; pub. Earth Evolution Publs., 1983—. Home: PO Box 644 Eugene OR 97440 Office: Quantum Inc 754 Washington Eugene OR 97401

SABO, JOSEPH RANDY, minerals consultant; b. Port Huron, Mich., Dec. 9, 1952; s. Joseph E. and Jeanne E. (Hubley) S. BS, Mich. Tech. U., 1976. Dir. Vietnamese negotiations VFW, Detroit, 1976-77; asst. to exec. v.p. Phelps Dodge Industries Inc., N.Y.C., 1977-79; asst. to the pres. Western Nuclear Inc. subs. Phelps Dodge Corp., Lakewood, Colo., 1979-85; cons. to the pres. Energy Fuels Corp., Denver, 1986-88, Umetco Minerals Corp. subs. Union Carbide Corp., Denver, 1989—. Recipient Presdl. Medal of Am., 1976, Americanism award VFW, 1976. Mem. Nat. Dem. Club. Democrat. Roman Catholic. Home: 10555 W Jewell Ave Lakewood CO 80226 Office: Umetco Minerals Corp 920 Trinity Pl 1801 Broadway Denver CO 80202

SABSAY, DAVID, library administrator; b. Waltham, Mass., Sept. 12, 1931; s. Wiegard Isaac and Ruth (Weinstein) S.; m. Helen Glenna Tolliver, Sept. 24,1 966. AB, Harvard U., 1953; BLS, U. Calif., Berkeley, 1955. Circulation dept. supr. Richmond (Calif.) Pub. Library, 1955-56; librarian Santa Rosa (Calif.) Pub. Library, 1956-65; dir. Sonoma County Library, Santa Rosa, 1965—; coordinator North Bay Coop. Library System, Santa Rosa, 1960-64; cons. in field, Sebastopol, Calif., 1968—. Contbr. articles to profl. jours. Commendation, Calif. Assn. Library Trustees and Commrs., 1984. Mem. Calif. Library Assn. (pres. 1971, cert. appreciation 1971, 80), ALA. Club: Harvard (San Francisco). Home: 667 Montgomery Rd Sebastopol CA 95472 Office: Sonoma County Libr 3rd & E Sts Santa Rosa CA 95404

SACHS, ALVA JUNE, psychologist; b. Detroit, June 11, 1933; d. I. Ernest and Ann Rae (Fogelson) S.; m. Robert Chilton Calfee, June 1960 (div. 1974); children: Robert William Calfee, Elise Rael. BS, U. Mich., 1953; MS, UCLA, 1962, PhD, 1965. Lic. psychologist, Calif., Hawaii, Mich.; cert. elem. tchr., community coll. instr., community coll. counselor. Asst. tchr. art U. Mich., Ann Arbor, 1953-54; tchr. Loring AFB (Maine) Sub-Primary Sch., 1954-55, Alameda Sch. Dist., Downey, Calif., 1955-56, Redondo Beach (Calif.) Unified Sch. Dist., 1956-57, Inglewood (Calif.) Sch. Dist., 1957-58; clin. intern dept. psychology UCLA, 1959-60; regional supr. marketing research firm, 1960-61; psychology trainee VA Hosp., Palo Alto, Calif., 1963-64; psychologist U. Wis. Med. Sch., 1965-69; supr. sch. psychologists Ramat Gan, Israel, 1969-70; pvt. practice psychology 1971—; tchr. Coll. San Mateo, Calif., 1973-78; psychologist Ten Southfield (Mich.) Clinic, 1978-80, West Hawaii Mental Health Service, Kealakekua, 1980—; founding mem. Nat. Register Health Service Providers in Psychology; lectr. in field. Mem. exec. bd. Hawaii Family Support Council. Mem. Am. Psychol. Assn. (div. 35), Western Assn. Women in Psychology, Hawaii Psychol. Assn., Assn. for Women in Psychology, Am. Assn. Women in Community and Jr. Colls., Women's Studies Assn., NOW, Older Women's League, LWV. Jewish. Office: West Hawaii Mental Health Svc PO Box 228 Kealakekua HI 96750

SACIA, JOHN FREDERICK, insurance brokerage executive; b. Galesville, Wis., Feb. 28, 1946; s. Robert H. and Joyce (Spittler) S.; m. Jane Elizabeth Andersen; 1 child, Kent John. BS, U. Wis., Stevens Point, 1969. Ins. claims adjuster Employers of Wausau, San Francisco, 1969-70, Missoula, Mont., 1970-71; ins. sales rep. Employers of Wausau, Missoula, 1971-74; ins. broker Rollins, Burdick, Hunter of Mont., Missoula, 1974-81; pres. Rollins, Burdick, Hunter of Mont., Billings, 1981-84, Seattle, 1984—; mem. mgmt. adv. group Rollins Burdick Hunter Corp., Chgo., 1986, 87, mem. compensation com., 1987—; producer adv. council Home Ins. Co., N.Y.C., 1987—. Mem. Ranier Club, Columbia Tower Club, Kiwanis. Republican. Presbyterian. Home: 8776 Paisley Dr NE Seattle WA 98115

SACKTON, FRANK JOSEPH, university official, lecturer, retired army officer; b. Chgo., Aug. 11, 1912; m. June Dorothy Raymond, Sept. 21, 1940. Student, Northwestern U., 1936, Yale, 1946, U. Md., 1951-52; B.S., U. Md., 1970; grad., Army Inf. Sch., 1941, Command and Gen. Staff Coll., 1942, Armed Forces Staff Coll., 1949, Nat. War Coll., 1954; M.Pub. Adminstrn., Ariz. State U., 1976. Mem. 131st Inf. Regt., Ill. N.G., 1929-40; commd. 2d lt. U.S. Army, 1934, advanced through grades to lt. gen., 1967; brigade plans and ops. officer (33d Inf. Div.), 1941, PTO, 1943-45; div. signal officer 1942-43, div. intelligence officer, 1944, div. plans and ops. officer, 1945; sec. to gen. staff for Gen. MacArthur Tokyo, 1947-48; bn. comdr. 30th Inf. Regt., 1949-50; mem. spl. staff Dept. Army, 1951; plans and ops. officer Joint Task Force 132, PTO, 1952; comdr. Joint Task Force 7, Marshall Islands, 1953; mem. gen. staff Dept. Army, 1954-55; with Office Sec. Def., 1956; comdr. 18th Inf. Regt., 1957-58; chief staff 1st Inf. Div., 1959; chief army Mil. Mission to Turkey, 1960-62; comdr. XIV Army Corps, 1963; dep. dir. plans Joint Chiefs Staff, 1964-66; army general staff mil. ops. 1966-67, comptroller of the army, 1967-70, ret., 1970; spl. asst. for fed./state relations Gov. Ariz., 1971-75; chmn. Ariz. Programming and Coordinating Com. for Fed. Programs, 1971-75; lectr. Am. Grad. Sch. Internat. Mgmt., 1973-77; vis. asst. prof., lectr. public affairs Ariz. State U., Tempe, 1976-78; dean Ariz. State U. Coll. Public Programs, 1979-80; prof. public affairs Ariz. State U., 1980—, v.p. bus. affairs, 1981-83, dep. dir. intercollegiate athletics, 1984-85. Contbr. articles to public affairs and mil. jours. Mem. Ariz. Steering Com. for Restoration of the State Capitol, 1974-75, Ariz. State Personnel Bd., 1978-83, Ariz. Regulatory Council, 1981—. Decorated D.S.M., Silver Star, also Legion of Merit with 4 oak leaf clusters, Bronze Star with 2 oak leaf clusters, Air medal, Army Commendation medal with 1 oak leaf cluster, Combat Inf. badge. Mem. Ariz. Acad. Public Adminstrn., Pi Alpha Alpha (pres. chpt. 1976-82). Clubs: Army-Navy (Washington); Arizona (Phoenix). Home: 12000 N 90th St Apt 2071 Scottsdale AZ 85260 Office: Ariz State U Coll Pub Programs Tempe AZ 85287

SACULLES, VICTORIA OBEDENCIO, chemist; b. Manila, Philippines, Dec. 23, 1936; d. Casimiro Tangowan Obedencio and Victorina (Marzo) Obedencio; m. Teopilo Saculles, Feb. 27, 1965; children: Faith Ann, Jason Marc. BS in Chemistry, U. Philippines, 1957. Cert. tchr., Calif. Tchr. math. several colls., Philippines, 1957-65; chemist Santee Water Reclamation, Calif., 1969-71; World Environ. Systems, Santee, 1971-73, Teledyn-Ryan Aero, San Diego, 1974-83; sr. chemist 1983-87, group engr., 1988—; chemist, cons. Padre Dam Mcpl. Water Dist., Santee, 1972—. Recipient Wastewater Cert., Am. Water and Wastewater Assn., 1970. Mem. Nat. Assn. Female Execs., Am. Water and Wasstwater Assn. Roman Catholic. Home: 10009 Via Rita Santee CA 92071 Office: Teledyne-Ryan Aero Co 2701 N Harbor Dr San Diego CA 92138

SADAVA, DAVID ERIC, biology educator; b. Ottawa, Ont., Can., Mar. 14, 1946; came to U.S., 1967; s. Samuel and Ruth (Bloom) S.; m. Angeline Douvas, June 15, 1972; 1 child, Dana Louise. BS, Carleton U., Ottawa, 1967; PhD, U. Calif. San Diego, La Jolla, 1971. Prof. biology Scripps Coll., Claremont, Calif., 1972—, chmn. Joint Sci. Program, 1980—; vis. prof. dept. pediatrics U. Colo., Denver, 1979—, dept. molecular biology, 1981—. Coauthor: Plants, Food, People, 1977; contbr. articles to profl. jours. Woodrow Wilson Found. fellow, 1968. Office: Claremont Colls Joint Sci Dept Claremont CA 91711

SADEGHI, ALI, architectural planner; b. Tehran, Iran, May 10, 1955; came to U.S., 1973; s. Mohammad Sadeghi and Homay Sadeghi-Nejad; m. Mitra Afsaneh Farokhpay, Apr. 18, 1980; children: Sanam Elika, Arya Farokh. BS in Architecture, Ohio State U., 1978, MArch, M in City and Regional Planning, 1981. Registered profl. architect, Ohio. Phys. planner Karlsberger Cos., Columbus, Ohio, 1981-83; med. planner Rochlin & Baran Assocs., L.A., 1983-84; facility planner Am. Med. Internat., L.A., 1984-86; dir. planning URS Corp, L.A., 1986—. Mem. AIA, Calif. Council Architects, L.A. Inst. Architects. Office: URS Corp 401 E Ocean Blvd Long Beach CA 90802

SADEGHI, FIROOZ, anesthesiologist; b. Maraghe, Iran, Jan. 25, 1941; came to U.S., 1970; s. Ahamad Sadeghi and Zarintaj (Sadeghi) Alavi; m. Amy Mcginnis, Apr. 1973 (div.); m. Maryam Razin, 1982; 1 child, Yassman. MD with honors, U. Tehran, Iran, 1967. Intern Mt. Sinai Hosp. & Med. Ctr., Chgo., 1970-71; resident in surgery Mercy Hosp. & Med. Ctr., Chgo., 1971-73; resident in anesthesiology N.Y. Med. Coll., N.Y.C., 1973-77; anesthesiologist Chgo., 1977-88, L.A. County Hosp., 1988—, U. So. Calif., L.A., 1988—. Med. doctor, Iranian Health Corps. Mem. AMA, Am. Soc. Anesthesiologists, Calif. Soc. Anesthesiologists, Calif. Med. Soc. Home: 360 W Pioneer 212 Glendale CA 91203 Office: LA County Hosp & Med Ctr Dept of Anesthesiology 1200 N State St Los Angeles CA 90033

SADEGHI, NASSER, architect; b. Tehran, Iran, Apr. 21, 1934; came to U.S., 1957; s. Mort and Roughie (Medikhan) S.; m. Apr. 19, 1976 (div. July 1982); 1 child, Sabrina Darya. BArch, U. Colo., 1963; M in Urban Design, Archtl. Assn. Sch. of Archt., London, England, 1971. Registered profl. architect Ariz., La., Colo. Architect Associated Design Forum, Aspen, Colo., 1969-74; vis. lectr. U. Colo. Sch. Environ. Design, Boulder, Colo., 1971-72; asst. prof. U. Colo. Sch. Environ. Design, Boulder, 1972-73; architect, interior designer Sadeghi Assocs., Aspen, 1973—; Trustee Internat. Wine & Food Soc., Aspen, 1978—; sec., treas. Plaza Devel. Corp., Salt Lake City, 1985—. Mem. Am. Inst. Architects, Colo. West Chpt. Am. Inst. Architects, Am. Soc. Interior Designers. Home: PO Box 1411 470 Red Mountain Rd Aspen CO 81612 Office: Sadeghi Assocs Architects 415 E Hyman Ave Ste 303 Aspen CO 81611

SADEGHI, SHAHEEN, clothing company executive; b. Tehran, Iran, May 10, 1954; came to U.S., 1965; s. Ali and Dee (Hamidi) S.; m. Linda Harvey, Aug. 10, 1980. AA in Bus., Mich. State U., 1974; BA in Design, Pratt Inst., 1977. Designer Charles James Co., N.Y.C., 1976, Mary McFadden Co., N.Y.C., 1977, John Anthony Co., N.Y.C., 1978, Catalina, Inc., L.A., 1979-80; merchandising mgr. Jantzen, Inc., L.A., 1980-88; v.p. merchandising Gotcha Co., Costa Mesa, Calif., 1988—; guest lectr. ednl. instns.; cons. Far East trade, 1980—. Recipient Costume Design Award, MGM Studios, 1975, Critic Award, Rose Puleo-Szule, N.Y.C., 1977. Home: 630 Diamond St Laguna Beach CA 92651 Office: Gotcha Co 3030 Airway St Costa Mesa CA 92626

SADILEK, VLADIMIR, architect; b. Czechoslovakia, June 27, 1933; came to U.S., 1967, naturalized, 1973; s. Oldrich and Antoine (Zlamal) S.; Ph.D. summa cum laude in City Planning and Architecture, Tech. U. Prague, 1957; m. Jana Kadlec, Mar. 25, 1960; 1 son, Vladimir, Jr. Chief architect State Office for City Planning, Prague, 1958-67; architect, designer Bank Bldg. Corp., St. Louis, 1967-70, asso. architect, San Francisco, 1970-74; owner, chief exec. officer Bank Design Cons., San Mateo, Calif., 1974-81, West Coast Development Co., San Mateo, 1975—; pres., chief exec. officer Orbis Devel. Corp., San Mateo, 1981—. Served with Inf. of Czechoslovakia, 1958. Recipient awards of excellence from Bank Building Corp. and AIA for planning and design of fin. instns. in Hawaii, Calif. (1971), Ariz., N.Mex., Tex. (1972), Colo., Wyo. (1973), Idaho, Oreg., Washington (1974); lic. architect, 28 states. Republican. Roman Catholic. Home: 80 Orange Ct Hillsborough CA 94010 Office: 1777 Borel Pl San Mateo CA 94402

SADLER, CAROL MARIE, advertising executive; b. Boulder, Colo., Sept. 27, 1946; d. Edward Joseph and Elvia Arabella (Manzanares) Abeyta; m. Jay Aston Sadler, Dec. 16, 1967; children: Kimberlee, Jennifer, Colby. Grad. high sch., Lafayette, Colo. Sec. IBM, Boulder, 1966-68, U. Colo., Boulder, 1972-73; dir. recreation City of Lafayette, 1978-82; pres. Sadler's Flyer Delivery Service, Lafayette, 1982—. Mem. planning commn. City of Lafayette, 1975; mem. adv. com. Boulder Valley Sch. Dist. 2, 1977; vol. Am. Cancer Soc., 1988. Mem. Lafayette C. of C. (bd. dirs. 1985—, Chamber Person of Yr. 1987). Republican. Roman Catholic. Club: Leads (Louisville, Colo.) (recorder 1988—).

SADLER, THEODORE R., JR., thoracic and cardiovascular surgeon; b. St. Louis, Mar. 26, 1930; s. Theodore R. and Nellie R. (Guffey) S.; m. Roberta Cary Moody, Nov. 26, 1953; children: Michael, Patrick, Susan, Daniel, Shelley. AB, U. Mo., 1951, BS in Medicine, 1954; MD, Washington U., 1956. Diplomate Am. Bd. Thoracic and Cardiovascular Surgery. Commd. U.S. Army, 1956, advanced through grades to col.; chief of surgery Noble Army Hosp., Ft. McClellans, Ala., 1964-66; comdr. 3d Surgery Hosp., Vietnam, 1966-67; chief thoracic surgery Fitzsimmons Army Hosp., Denver, 1968-71; resigned U.S. Army, 1971, with Res., 1971-82; comdr. 181st Thoracic Detachment, 1971-73, 5502d U.S. Army Hosp. Augmentation Fitzsimmons Army Hosp., Denver, 1974-77; brig. gen. 2d Hosp. Ctr., Hamilton AFB, Calif., 1977-81; ret. Res. U.S. Army, 1982; rotating intern Walter Reed Hosp., Washington, 1956-57; resident in gen. surgery Brooke Gen. Hosp., San Antonio, 1958-61, resident thoracic and cardiovascular surgery, 1964-66; practice medicine specializing in thoracic and cardiovascular surgery St. Joseph's Hosp. and Presbyn. Hosp., Denver, 1971—; comdr. 147th U.S. Army Hosp. Colo. N.G., 1987—; cons to surgeon gen. Fitzsimmons Army Hosp., 1983—; past pres. bd. dirs. St. Joseph's Hosp. Contbr. articles to profl. jours. Vice chmn. Bd. of Health and Hosps., 1982-88; mem. Commn. Mental Health, Denver, 1985-88. Fellow ACS, Am. Coll. Chest Physicians; mem. Soc. Thoracic Surgeons, Western Thoracic Assn., AMA, Colo. Med. Soc. (pres.-elect 1986, bd. dirs., house speaker, pres. 1987-88), Denver Med. Soc. (bd. dirs., past pres.). Republican. Presbyterian. Clubs: Denver Athletic, Bookcliff Country, Metropolitan. Home: 2680 Kimberly Grand Junction CO 81506 Office: 2525 N 8th St #102 Grand Junction CO 81501

SADOWY, HAROLD STEPHEN, health care executive; b. Laufen, Bavaria, West Germany, Sept. 27, 1947; came to U.S., 1950; s. Stephen J. and Anna A. (Frank) S.; m. Bonnie Drena Leeds, June 14, 1969; children: Jennifer Rebecca, Jesse Leeds. BS, So. Conn. State U., 1969, MS, 1975; MS, So. Conn. State U., 1976; PhD, U. Conn., 1984. Sen. research assoc. Conn. Med. Soc., New Haven, 1972-75; systems analyst, lectr. Yale U., New Haven, 1975-77; dir. data research N.W. Conn. Health Systems, Waterbury, Conn., 1977-80; dir. planning Cen. Ariz. Health Systems Agy., Phoenix, 1980-81; sr. v.p. planning and mktg. PMH Health Resources, Phoenix, 1981—; cons. in field; adj. prof. Ariz. State U. Contbr. numerous articles to profl. jours. Pub. speaker in field; vol. coach; mem. Greater Phoenix Affordable Healthcare Coalition. With U.S. Army, 1970-72. Recipient Disting. Speaker award Yale U., 1978, U. So. Calif., 1985, Phoenix Valley Leadership award Phoenix C. of C., 1986. Mem. Am. Coll. Healthcare Execs., Am. Hosp. Assn., Am. Mktg. Assn., Ariz.-Mexico Border Health Found. (treas. 1975—), Coun. on Community Rels. Ariz. Hosp. Assn., Ariz.-Mexico Commn., UCONN Alumni Assn., Phoenix Valley Leadership Alumni. Home: 12831 N 39th Way Phoenix AZ 85032 Office: PMH Health Resources Inc PO Box 21207 Phoenix AZ 85036

SADOYAMA, NANCY ARTIS, administrative operations analyst; b. Oakland, Calif., June 12, 1947; d. Robert Lee and Norma Lee (Dyches) Artis; m. Edward T. Sadoyama, June 18, 1978. BA in Psychology, Calif. State U., Hayward, 1974, MPA with highest deptl. honors, 1987. Personnel rep. Mack Western, Hayward, 1970-73; with Calif. State U., Hayward, 1974-87, adminstrv. ops. analyst, 1987—; microcomputer cons. Meiklejohn Hall, Calif. State U., Hayward, 1984—. Recipient Vivian Cunniffe Outstanding Staff award Calif. State U., Hayward, 1986. Mem. Pub. Alumni Assn. Calif. State U., Women's Coun. of the State Univ., Faculty Club. Club: Commonwealth of San Francisco. Office: Calif State U Liberal Studies Hayward CA 94542

SADR, RAMIN, electrical engineer; b. Tehran, Iran, Mar. 9, 1958; came to U.S., 1974; s. Abolhassan and Zohreh Sadr. BSEE, Calif. State U., Long Beach, 1978; MSEE, UCLA, 1980, PhD in Elec. Engring., 1983. Engr. Macrodata Corp., Woodland Hills, Calif., 1978-80; faculty system scis. dept. UCLA, 1980-83; with speech recognition dept. IBM, Yorktown Heights, N.Y., 1983-84; elec. engr. UCLA, 1984-86; communications rsch. sect. staff NASA/JPL, Pasadena, Calif., 1986—; instr. UCLA, 1988—; cons. Cylink Corp., Sunnyvale, Calif., 1984-85, Satellite Tech. Mgmt., Torrance, Calif., 1984-86. Author: Generalized MSK Modulation, 1983; contbr. articles to profl. jours.; patentee in field. Mem. IEEE, Westlake Swim and Tennis (Calif.), Eta Kappa Nu. Office: NASA/Jet Propulsion Lab 4800 Oak Grove Dr Pasadena CA 91109

SADRUDDIN, MOE, oil company executive, consultant; b. Hyderabad, India, Mar. 3, 1943; came to U.S., 1964; m. Azmath Oureshi, 1964; 3 children. BSME, Osmania U., Hyderabad, 1964; MS in Indsl. Engring., NYU, 1966; MBA, Columbia U., 1970. Cons. project engr. Ford, Bacon & Davis, N.Y.C., 1966; staff indsl. engr. J.C. Penney, N.Y.C., 1966-68; sr. cons. Drake, Sheahan, Stewart & Dougall, N.Y.C., 1968-70, Beech-Nut Inc. subs. Squibb Corp., N.Y.C., 1970-72; founder, pres. Azmath Constrn. Co., Englewood, N.J., 1972-77; crude oil cons., fgn. govt. rep. 1977—; pres. A-One Petroleum Co., Fullerton, Calif., 1985—; govt. advisor Puerto Rico, 1980-82, Dominica, 1983-84, St. Vincent, 1981-82, Kenya, 1983-84, Belize 1984-85, Costa Rica 1983-86, Paraguay 1984-87. Mem. Los Angeles World Affairs Council. Mem. Internat. Platform Assn. Address: A-One Petroleum Co 2656 Camino Del Sol Fullerton CA 92633

SADUN, ALFREDO ARRIGO, neuro-ophthalmologist; b. New Orleans, Oct. 23, 1950; s. Elvio H. and Lina (Ottoleghi) S.; m. Debra Leigh Rice, Mar. 18, 1978; children: Rebecca Eli, Elvio Aaron, Benjamin Maxwell. BS, MIT, 1972; PhD, Albert Einstein Med. Sch., Bronx, N.Y., 1976, MD, 1978. Intern Huntington Meml. Hosp. U. So. Calif., Pasadena, 1978-79; resident Harvard U. Med. Sch., Boston, 1979-82, HEED Found. fellow in neuro-ophthalmology Mass. Eye and Ear Inst.,, 1982-83, instr. ophthalmology, 1983, asst. prof. ophthalmology, 1984; dir. residential tng. U. So. Calif. Dept. Ophthalmology, L.A., 1984-85; asst. prof. ophthalmology and neurosurgery U. So. Calif., L.A., 1984-87, assoc. prof., 1987—; prin. investigator Howe Lab. Harvard U., Boston, 1981-84, E. Doheny Eye Inst., L.A., 1984—. Author: Optics for Opthalmologists, 1988, New Methods of Sensory Visual Testing; contbr. articles to profl. jours. and chpts. to books. Fellow Am. Acad. Ophthalmology; mem. NIH (Med. Scientist Tng. award, 1972-78), Soc. to Prevent Blindness, Nat. Eye Inst. (New Investigator Rsch. award 1983-86), Soc. Neurosciss., Assn. Rsch. in Vision and Ophthalmology, Am. Assn. Anatomists, N.Am. Neuro-Ophthal. Soc. Home: 2478 Adair St San Marino CA 91108 Office: U So Calif E Doheny Eye Inst 1355 San Pablo Los Angeles CA 90033

SADWICK, DAVID BRIAN, lawyer; b. St. Paul, Apr. 15, 1961. BA, U. Calif., San Diego, 1983; JD, Stanford U., 1986. Bar: Calif. 1986, U.S. Ct. Appeals (9th cir.) 1987, U.S. Dist. Ct. (cent. dist.) Calif. 1988. Jud. law clk. U.S. Ct. Appeals, 9th Cir., San Francisco, 1986-87; assoc. O'Melveny & Myers, L.A., 1987—. Liaison San Diego Com. on Constl. Bicentennial, 1987. Mem. ABA, Calif. Bar Assn., L.A. County Bar Assn.

SADWITH, JOHN ALAN, lawyer; b. New Brunswick, N.J., Nov. 28, 1950; s. Howard Marvin and Elizabeth (Glasser) S.; m. Karen Marie Grote, June 15, 1985. BA, Ithaca Coll., 1972; JD, U. Denver, 1978. Bar: Colo. 1979. Asst. to dean Ithaca (N.Y.) Coll., 1972-75; owner restaurant, Dillon, Colo., 1975-76; staff atty. Colo. State Pub. Defenders, Denver, 1979-85, coordinator state tng., 1983-85, office head, 1984-85; exec. dir. Colo. Trial Lawyers Assn., Denver, 1985—. V.p. Congress Pk. Neighbors, Denver, 1988—, also bd. dirs. 1986—; chmn. Colo. Senate Dist. 34, Denver, 1983-85. Mem. Assn. Trial Lawyers Am., Colo. Bar Assn., Colo. Criminal Defense Bar, Am. Soc. Assn. Execs., Colo. Soc. Assn. Execs., Colo. Trial Lawyers Assn., Nat. Assn. Trial Lawyer Execs. (treas. 1987—), Colo. Lawyers Arts (bd. dirs. 1986—). Democrat. Office: Colo Trial Lawyers Assn 1888 Sherman St #370 Denver CO 80203

SAEKS, RICHARD EPHRAIM, electrical engineer; b. Chgo., Nov. 30, 1941; s. Morris G. and Elsie E. S. B.S., Northwestern U., 1964; M.S., Colo. State U., 1965; Ph.D., Cornell U., 1967. Elec. engr. Warwick Mfg. Co., Niles, Ill., 1961-63; asst. prof. dept. elec. engring. U. Notre Dame, 1967-71, asso. prof., 1971-73; asso. prof. dept. elec. engring., math. Tex. Tech U., Lubbock, 1973-77; prof. Tex. Tech U., 1977-79, Paul Whitfield Horn prof. elec. engring., math., computer sci., 1979-82; prof., chmn. elec. engring. Ariz. State U., 1983-88; dean Armour Coll. Engring., Ill. Inst. Tech., 1988—; cons. Research Triangle Inst., 1978-80, Marcel Dekker Inc., 1978—. Author: Generalized Networks, 1972, Resolution Space Operators and Systems, 1973, Interconnected Dynamical Systems, 1981, System Theory: A Hilbert Space Approach, 1982; contbr. articles to profl. jours.; Editor: Large-Scale Dynamical Systems, 1976, Rational Fault Analysis, 1977, The World of Large Scale Systems, 1982. Recipient Disting. Faculty Research award Tex. Tech U., 1978. Fellow IEEE; mem. Soc. for Indsl. and Applied Math., Am.

Math. Soc., Am. Assn. for Engring. Edn., Sigma Xi. Home: 111 E Chestnut Apt 40K Chicago IL 60611

SAELMAN, BENJAMIN, aerospace engineer; b. Los Angeles, Nov. 15, 1917; s. Samuel Henry and Ray (Kashtan) S.; m. Phyllis Markman, July 28, 1964; children: David, Raymond. BA with honors, UCLA, 1939. Registered profl. engr., Calif. With Lockheed Aircraft Corp., Burbank, Calif., 1940-85, group engr., 1969—; cons. aerospace engring., 1985—; lectr. strength of materials. Contbg. editor Design News, 1953-74; reviewer Prentice-Hall Pubs., 1971; contbr. numerous articles to profl. jours. Recipient numerous awards. Mem. AIAA (tech. papers com. 1959-60), Soc. Allied Weight Engrs. (book preparation com. 1970—, lectr.,), Sierra Club, Pi Mu Epsilon. Democrat. Jewish. Home: 7762 Melita St North Hollywood CA 91605

SAFFAFIAN, ALLISON HARRISON, aerospace engineer; b. Beirut, Oct. 5, 1938; came to U.S., 1939; s. George and Katharine (Harrison) S. Student, MIT, 1956-58; BS, So. Meth. U., 1961; postgrad., San Jose State Coll., 1965-66; MDiv, Talbot Theol. Sem., La Mirada, Calif., 1979. Engr. Lockheed Missiles and Space Co., Sunnyvale, Calif., 1963-67; mem. tech. staff ITT Aerospace Co., San Fernando, Calif., 1967-70; cons. optical engring. ITT Gilfillan Co., San Fernando, 1971-72; cons. Hughes Aircraft Co., El Segundo, Calif., 1977-80; sr. engr. Aerojet Gen. Corp., El Monte, Calif., 1972-74, Organon Diagnostics, El Monte, 1974-76; mem. tech. staff Aerospace Corp., El Segundo, 1980—. Mem. AEA Video Club (pres. 1986-88), AEA Audiophile Club (pres. 1983-84), Kappa Tau Epsilon. Mem. Grace Community Ch. Home: 12508 Daryl Ave Granada Hills CA 91344 Office: Aerospace Corp 2350 E El Segundo Blvd El Segundo CA 90245

SAFRAN, WILLIAM, political science educator; b. Dresden, Germany, July 8, 1930; s. Abraham Joshua and Golda (Chajes) S.; m. Marian Celia (Folk) S.; Mar. 25, 1961; children: Gabriella Sarah, Joshua Abraham. BA, CUNY, 1953, MA, 1955; PhD, Columbia U., 1964. Lectr., instr. Bklyn. Coll., CUNY, 1960-65, Hunter Coll., 1962; asst. prof. U. Colo., Boulder, 1965-68, assoc. prof., 1968-73, prof. polit. sci., 1973, assoc. chmn. polit. sci. dept., 1974-76, dir. internat. rels. program, 1971-73, 79, 81, 86, 87-88; vis. prof., Jerusalem, Paris, Nice. With U.S. Army, 1955-57. Social Sci. Found. fellow, 1966; U. Colo. faculty rsch. grantee, 1966, 69-70; grantee NEH, 1980-81, Am. Coun. Learned Socs., 1989; recipient history honors award CUNY, 1953. Mem. Am. Polit. Sci. Assn., Internat. Studies Assn., Am. Acad. Polit. Sci., Western Polit. Sci. Assn., Assn. Française de Sci. Politique, Conf. Group French Politics and Soc. (program coord.), Conf. Group German Politics, Tocqueville Soc., Internat. Polit. Sci. Assn. (v.p. resch. com. on politics and ethnicity). Democrat. Jewish. Author: Veto-Group Politics, 1967, The French Polity, 1977, 79, 2d edit., 1985, Ideology and Politics: The Socialist Party of France, 1979, Comparative Politics, 1982; co-author: The Political Economy of Collectivized Agriculture, 1979, Global Human Rights, 1981, The Fifth Republic at Twenty, 1981, Constitutional Democracy: Essays in Comparative Politics, 1983, Europe and the Superpowers, 1985, Political Economy in Western Democracies, 1985, Antisemitism in the Contemporary World, 1986, Ethnoterritorial Politics, 1989, American Constitutionalism and the World, 1989. Office: U Colo Dept Polit Sci Boulder CO 80309

SAGATELIAN, ALEXANDER ANDREEVICH, marketing professional; b. San Francisco, Oct. 8, 1959; s. Andranik Ovannes and Anne Nikitishna (Avetisoff) S. BS in Mktg., San Jose State U., 1984. Purchasing mgr. Biggam Enterprises Inc., San Jose, Calif., 1979-83; product mktg. mgr. Hamilton Avnet, Sunnyvale, Calif., 1983-87; mktg. and sales mgr. Arrow Electronics, Sunnyvale, 1987—; with semi-conductor mktg. dept. Cypress Electronics, Santa Clara, Calif., 1987-89; field sales rep. Bradas Micro Tech. (subs. Cypress Electronics), Santa Clara, 1989—. Russian Orthodox. Home: 1395 Koch Ln San Jose CA 95125 Office: Bradas Micro Tech 3263 Scott Blvd Santa Clara CA 95050

SAGAWA, YONEO, horticulturist; b. Olaa, Hawaii, Oct. 11, 1926; s. Chikatada and Mume (Kuno) S.; m. Masayo Yamamoto, May 24, 1962 (dec. Apr. 1988); children: Penelope Toshiko, Irene Teruko. A.B., Washington U., St. Louis, 1950, M.S., 1952; Ph.D., U. Conn., 1956. Postdoctoral research asso. biology Brookhaven Nat. Lab., Upton, N.Y., 1955-57; guest in biology Brookhaven Nat. Lab., summer 1958; asst. prof., then asso. prof. U. Fla., 1957-64; dir. undergrad. sci. ednl. research participation program NSF, summer 1964; cons. biosatellite project NASA, 1966-67; prof. horticulture U. Hawaii, 1964—; dir. Lyon Arboretum, 1967—; asso. dir. Hawaiian Sci. Fair, 1966-67, dir., 1967-68; research asso. in biology U. Calif., Berkeley, 1970-71; mem. Internat. Orchid Commn. on Classification, Nomenclature and Registration; sci. adv. bd. Pacific Tropical Garden, 1975—; councillor Las Cruces Bot. Garden, Costa Rica; cons. UN/FAO, Singapore, 1971; dir. Hawaii Tropical Botanical Garden. Editor: Hawaii Orchid Jour, 1972—, Pacific Orchid Soc. Bull, 1966-71; editorial bd.: Allertonia, 1976; contbr. numerous articles to profl. jours. Hon. trustee Friends of Foster Garden, 1973—. Served with AUS, 1945-47. Recipient Disting. Service award South Fla. Orchid Soc., 1968; grantee Am. Orchid Soc., AEC, NIH, HEW, Stanley Smith Hort. Trust, Honolulu Orchid Soc., 1958—. Hon. life mem. Am. Anthurium Soc., Am. Orchid Soc., Kaimuki Orchid Soc., Honolulu Orchid Soc., Garden Club Honolulu; mem. Bot. Soc. Am., Am. Soc. Hort. Sci., Internat. Assn. Hort. Sci., AAAS, Am. Assn. Bot. Gardens and Arboreta, Hawaiian Bot. Soc., Internat. Assn. Plant Tissue Culture, Palm Soc., Lyon Arboretum Assn. (trustee 1974—), Phi Kappa Phi (past chpt. pres.). Democrat. Club: Aloha Bonsai (Honolulu). Office: Harold L Lyon Arboretum 3860 Manoa Rd Honolulu HI 96822

SAGE, JOSEPH ROBERT, advertising agency executive; b. N.Y.C., Sept. 12, 1949; s. Joseph and Letitia (Lyon) S. BA in Architecture, Washington U., St. Louis, 1971. Designer Lathrop Constrn. Co., Steamboat Springs, Colo., 1972-73; owner, mgr. Sage Design and Advt., Steamboat Springs, Colo., 1973—; cons. Steamboat Ski Corp., 1983—. Creative chmn., chmn. subcom. Steamboat Mktg. Com., 1984—, Steamboat Vintage Auto Race, 1986—; cons. Steamboat Springs Chamber Resort Assn., 1984—. Mem. Hobie Fleet 106 Club, Spl. Interst Car Klub of Steamboat. Home: PO Box 1590 150 Santa Fe Trail Steamboat Springs CO 80477 Office: Sage Design and Advt PO Box 3930 1475 Pine Grove Rd Steamboat Springs CO 80477

SAGE, WILLIAM HAMPDEN, IV, advertising agency executive; b. Charlottesville, Va., Dec. 10, 1946; s. William Hampden III and Evelyn Cathelle (Updike) S.; m. Julie Theresa Percell, Sept. 20, 1976 (div. Dec. 1980); m. Jan Patricia Sax, Apr. 10, 1981. BS in English and Biology, Lewis and Clark Coll., 1959; postgrad. Environ. Scis. in Humanities, U. Mont., 1972-73. Announcer, newscaster Sta. WXLE Space and Missile Test Ctr., Canton Island, 1971-72, Sta. KGMY, Missoula, Mont., 1973-74, Sta. KGU, Honolulu, 1975; announcer, producer Sta. KGVO, Missoula, 1974-75; producer, writer Sta. KORL, Honolulu, 1976-80, Sta. KSSK-AM and Sta. KULA-FM, Honolulu, 1980-83, Sta. KKUA-AM and Sta. KQMQ-FM, Honolulu, 1983-86; pres. Sage Corp., Honolulu, 1987—; ptnr. Armstrong-Sage "The Odd Agy.", Honolulu, 1987-88; comedy writer, character voice Sta. KSSK, Honolulu, 1980-83; conf. standup comedian, Hawaii, 1984—; comedy cons., character voices Sta. KPOI-FM, Honolulu, 1987—; voice-overs, writer radio and TV commls., producer, 1977—. Creator (comedy album) Honk if you Love George, 1982. Moderator pub. affairs program Sta. KTUH, U. Hawaii, 1976—; active Amnesty Internat., Ctr. for Def. Info., Cousteau Soc., Common Cause, Nature Conservancy. Recipient Pele Best Radio award Honolulu Advt. Fedn., 1981, 83, 85, Pele award excellence, 1981—, Pele award merit, 1981—. Episcopalian. Home and Office: Sage Corp 1760 S Beretania St Apt 12-D Honolulu HI 96826-1134

SAGERS, ROBERT EDWARD, infosystems specialist; b. Rochester, N.Y., Mar. 28, 1937; s. Louis Peter and Amelia Louise (Keller) S.; m. Aileen Stoel Armstrong, July 1, 1967; 1 child, Alexander Todd. BS, Calif. State U., Chico, 1975. Systems rep. Burroughs Corp., San Jose, Calif., 1975-76; systems programmer SRI Internat., Menlo Park, Calif., 1976-81; systems analyst ITT Fed. Electric, Edwards AFB, Calif., 1981-84, systems mgr., 1984—. Republican. Home: PO Box 1279 Tehachapi CA 93581

SAGINIAN, ARMEN ASHLY, mechanical engineer; b. Tabriz, Iran, Feb. 2, 1933; came to U.S., 1955, naturalized, 1966; s. Hovsep and Varditer (Melik-Djhanian) S.; m. Assik Stella Saginian, Sept. 13, 1959; children: Arthru George, Alan Patrick. BSME, U. Tenn., 1961; cert., UCLA, 1979. Registered profl. engr., Calif. Engr. Boeing Co., Seattle, 1961-63, Gen. Dynamics, San Diego, 1963-64, North Am. Aviation, Van Nuys, Calif., 1964-65; engr., mgr. Garrett Corp., Los Angeles, 1965-85; gen. mgr. TTL Turbo-Supply, Los Angeles, 1985—; bd. dirs. Paysage Devels., Telex Terminals, Ltd.; chmn. bd. dirs. Pak-Chem Corp. Pres. Iran Armenian Soc., Los Angeles, 1970; sec. Iran Nat. Affairs Council, Los Angeles, 1984. Mem. ASME. Republican. Lodges: Mason, Arabic. Home and Office: 9841 Tunney Ave Northridge CA 91324 Address: Turbo-Supply 4523-C San Fernando Rd Glendale CA 91204

SAGUM, ROLAND DIAZ, former state official, investment company executive; b. Batangas, Phillippines, Jan. 1, 1912; s. Macario A. and Dionicia (Diaz) S.; came to U.S., 1912, naturalized, 1946; certificate Pub. Adminstrn., U. Hawaii, 1935; certificate Delinquency Control, U. So. Calif., 1958; m. Genevieve Anguay, Aug. 27, 1932; children—Roland Diaz, Ginger Vea, Marvin I., Nelson A., Catherine A. Hudson. With Honolulu Police, 1934-70, capt. of police, 1960-67, community relations coordinator, 1967-68, maj. in charge night ops., 1968-69, police commr., 1969, v.p., dir. pub. relations, 1969-75; chmn. bd. United Hawaiian Investment Corp.; pres. Ambassador Travel Agy., Inc.; dir. United Hawaiian Acceptance, Inc., Paterrin Co., Nuuanu Meml. Park, Financial Security Ins. Co. Chmn. state bd. lay activities Meth. Ch., 1963-65, del. 1st world conf. Human Relations, 1958, del. 1st nat. conf. Christian Social Concerns, Washington, 1960, del. Jurisdictional Conf., World Meth. Conf. and World Meth. Conf. on Family Life, 1964. Mem. Gov.'s Com. on Sex Deviations, 1960-61, Com. on Alcholism, 1960-69, State Com. on Correction, 1968-69; commr. State Criminal Injuries Compensation, 1971-79; mem. Mayor's Com. on Children and Youth to study Drug Abuse, 1962-70, Citizens Com. on Municipal Auditorium, 1964-66; pres. Nat. Polio Found. Hawaii, Police Relief Assn.; pres. United Filipino Council, 1959-61, Haoula Club, 1950, pres. Honolulu Council Chs., Police Activities League; youth dir. Internat. Assn. Y's Men's Clubs; pres. Mental Health Assn. Hawaii, 1972-73, Palama Inter-Church Council, Filipino C. of C., 1979-82; treas. Internat. Christian Leadership, Hawaii Council on Crime and Delinquency, 1980; pres. Palama Settlement, 1970-72, Philippine Meml. Found., 1950; mem. Hawaii CD Adv. Council, 1979-85; bd. dirs. Oahu Tb and Health Council, Nat. Assn. Mental Health, Liliuokalani Adv. Council, Child and Family Service, Pacific and Asian Affairs Council, Hawaiian Govt. Assn., Hawaii Cancer Soc., John Howard Assn., Nat. Soc. for Crippled Children and Adults, Honolulu Community Chest, Honolulu Met. YMCA, Nuuanu br. YMCA, Goodwill Industries; adv. bd. Salvation Army, Hawaii Commn. Criminal Justice. Recipient award U.S. Bur. Prisons, 1962; Nat. Lane Bryant award for civic achievements, 1967; Outstanding Service to Youth award Pacific S.W. Area YMCA. 1964; certificate of appreciation Nat. Bd. YMCA, 1963; named Father of Year, Hawaii chpt. World Brotherhood, 1960; Am. of Week, Honolulu C. of C., 1950, Man of Week, 1952; Outstanding Citizen of Year, Hawaii Govt. Assn., 1964, Outstanding Community Worker, 1973; recipient Hawaii Pioneer award, 1986. Mem. Internat. Assn. Chiefs of Police, Nat. Police Officers Assn., Am. Soc. Tng. Dirs., Am. Soc. Pub. Adminstrn. (dir.). Internat. Juvenile Officers Assn. (award merit 1966), Acad. Sci. Interrogation. Hawaii Assn. Parliamentarians, Am. Inst. Parliamentarians (cert.), Am. Correctional Assn. Methodist (del. numerous world confs.). Clubs: Masons, Knights of Rizal (comdr.). Home: 3008 Makini St Honolulu HI 96815 Office: 33 S King St Ste 407 Honolulu HI 96813

SAHARA, ROBERT FUMIO, veterinarian; b. Ogden, Utah, Mar. 13, 1942; s. William Hiroshi and Chiyo (Shimada) S.; m. Joyce Michiko Sanwo, July 23, 1967; 1 child, Jennifer Yuki. AA in Zoology, Santa Monica City Coll., 1962; AB in Zoology, U. Calif., Davis, 1965, MS in Animal Physiology, 1967, DVM, 1972. Staff veterinarian, Romie Lane Vet. Hosp., Salinas, Calif., 1972-73, Bay Pet Hosp., Monterey, Calif., 1972-73, Midtown Animal Hosp., Sacramento, 1973-74; chief of staff Sacramento Emergency Vet. Clinic, 1974-76; co-owner, veterinarian Greenhaven Vet. Hosp., Sacramento, 1976—, reserve warden Calif. Dept. Fish and Game, 1985—. Bd. dirs. Jan Ken Po Gakko, Sacramento, 1981-84. Mem. AVMA, Calif. Vet. Med. Assn. (gov. dist V, 1983—, pres.-elect 1988), Sacramento Valley Vet. Med. Assn. (exec. bd. 1978-82, pres. 1981). Republican. Buddhist. Home: 841 E El Macero Dr El Macero CA 95618 Office: Greenhaven Veterinary Hosp 1 Valine Ct Sacramento CA 95831

SAIDMAN, SANDER BARRY, radiologist; b. Washington, Feb. 26, 1952; s. Aaron Gilbert and Ruth Gladys (Berman) S.; m. Judy Jill Meyer, June 20, 1978. BA, Washington U., St. Louis, 1974; MD, George Washington U., 1978. Diplomate Am. Bd. Radiology. Intern in surgery George Washington U. Hosp., Washington, 1978-79, resident in radiology, 1979-82; staff radiologist Montrose (Colo.) Meml. Hosp., 1982-84; clin. instr. U. Colo. Health Scis. Ctr., Denver, 1985; staff radiologist St. Mary's Hosp., Tucson, 1985-86, Espanola (N.Mex.) Hosp., 1986—; chief of staff Espanola Hosp., 1989—. Mem. Am. Coll. Radiology, Radiology Soc. N.Am., Am. Inst. Ultrasound in Medicine. Home: Rte 4 Box 57J Santa Fe NM 87501 Office: Espanola Hosp 1010 Spruce St Espanola NM 87532

SAIKI, PATRICIA (MRS. STANLEY MITSUO SAIKI), congresswoman; b. Hilo, Hawaii, May 28, 1930; d. Kazuo and Shizue (Inoue) Fukuda; m. Stanley Mitsuo Saiki, June 19, 1954; children: Stanley Mitsuo, Sandra Saiki Williams, Margaret C., Stuart K., Laura H. BA, U. Hawaii, 1952. Tchr. U.S. history Punahou Sch., Kaimuki Internat. Sch., Kalani High Sch., Honolulu, 1952-64; sec. Rep. Party Hawaii, Honolulu, 1964-66, vice chmn., 1966-68, 82-83, chmn., 1983-85; research asst. Hawaii State Senate, 1966-68; mem. Hawaii Ho. of Reps., 1968-74, Hawaii State Senate, 1974-82, 100th, 101st Congresses from 1st Hawaii dist., Washington, 1987—; mem. Pres.'s Adv. Council on Status of Women, 1969-76; mem. Nat. Commn. Internat. Women's Yr., 1969-70; commr. Western Interstate Commn. on Higher Edn.; fellow Eagleton Inst., Rutgers U., 1970. Mem. Kapiolani Hosp. Aux.; sec. Hawaii Rep. Com., 1964-66, vice chmn., 1966-68, chmn., 1983-85; del. Hawaii Constl. Conv., 1968; alt. del. Rep. Nat. Conv., 1968, del., 1984; Rep. nominee for lt. gov. Hawaii, 1982; mem. Fedn. Rep. Women.; trustee Hawaii Pacific Coll.; past bd. govs. Boys and Girls Clubs Hawaii; mem. adv. council Am. Nat. Red Cross; bd. dirs. Nat. Fund for Improvement of Post-Secondary Edn., 1982-85 ; past bd. dirs. Straub Med. Research Found., Honolulu, Hawaii's Visitors Bur., Honolulu, Edn. Commn. of States, Honolulu, Hawaii Visitors Bur., 1983-85; trustee U. Hawaii Found., 1984-86, Hawaii Pacific Coll., Honolulu. Episcopalian. Home: 784 Elepaio St Honolulu HI 96816 Office: US Ho of Reps 1609 Longworth Bldg Washington DC 20515 *

SAINER, ELLIOT ARNOLD, health care executive; b. Bayshore, N.Y., Mar. 10, 1946; s. Herman L. and Janet (Salpeter) S.; m. Marcia Lisa Heim, Sept. 12, 1976; children: Todd, Diana. BA, U. Pitts., 1968; MBA, George Washington U., 1971; PhD, City U. Los Angeles, 1981. Assoc. adminstr. dept. psychiatry Albert Einstein Coll. Medicine, Bronx, N.Y., 1971-74; adminstr. dept. pediatrics Albert Einstein Coll. Medicine, Bronx, 1974-78; assoc. adminstr. Peachford Hosp., Atlanta, 1978-79; project dir. Charter Med. Corp., Honolulu, 1979-81; adminstr. Charter Oak Hosp., Calif., 1981-84, Charter Suburban Hosp., Paramount, Calif., 1984-86; regional dir. Charter Med. Corp., El Monte, Calif., 1986-88; pres., chief exec. officer Life Plus Found., North Hollywood, Calif., 1988-89; chief. oper. officer Coll. Health Enterprises, Huntington Beach, Calif., 1989—; bd. govs. Fedn. Am. Health Systems, Washington, 1984-; bd. dirs. Hosp. Council So. Calif., Los Angeles. Mem. Am. Coll. Health Care Execs. Home: 2000 Edgewood Dr South Pasadena CA 91030 Office: Coll Health Enterprises 7711 Center Ave #300 Huntington Beach CA 92647

ST. JOHN, CAITLIN, musician, library assistant; b. Boston, Jan. 9, 1951; d. Roland Phlippe Lussier and Sarah (Vosper) Williams; m. Paul Marion St. John, Mar. 13, 1982; 1 child, Susan Mary. Student, Northwestern U., 1969-70, Cleve. Inst. Music, 1970-72; BA with highest honors, U. Calif., Riverside, 1988. Gen. ptnr. Cathedral Hill Photo, San Francisco, 1980-85; accompanist U. Calif. Choral Soc., Riverside, 1988—, library asst., 1988—. Mem. Cleve. Orch. Chorus, 1972-73, San Francisco Symphony Chorus, 1977-82, St. George's Episcopal Ch., Riverside, 1986—; music dept. rep. grad. student assn. U. Calif., Riverside, 1988—. Pres.'s fellow U. Calif., 1987-88, U. Calif. fellow 1988—. Mem. Am. Musicological Soc., U. Calif.-Riverside Madrigal Singers, U. Calif.-Riverside Collegium Musicum. Democrat. Home: PO Box 1375 San Bernardino CA 92402 Office: U Calif Music Dept Riverside CA 92507

ST. JOHN, DAVID RUSSELL, state government executive; b. L.A., July 8, 1947; s. James Neil and Audrey (Johnson) St. J.; m. Kyle L. Kammer, Dec. 26, 1968; children: Kimberly H., Richard B.. BS, Ariz. State U., 1981, MBA, 1984. Asst. dir. Ariz. Dept. of Public Safety, Phoenix, 1970--; bd. dirs. Ariz. Emergency Med. Services, Phoenix, 1980-82. Mem. Ariz. Supreme Ct. Drug Com., Phoenix , 1987-88. Sgt. U.S. Army, 1971-74. Mem. Fraternal Order of Police (treas. 1978-79), Ariz. Hwy. Patrol Assn., Sigma Iota Epsilon, Masons. Republican. Office: Ariz Dept Pub Safety 2102 Encanto Blvd Phoenix AZ 85009

ST. JOHN, DIANE ELIZABETH, educator; b. Palo Alto, Calif., Oct. 15, 1944; d. Clares Herman and Elsie Elizabeth (Moran) Thompson; m. John Otto St. John, Aug. 17, 1963; 1 child, Courtney Elizabeth. BA, Calif. Polytechnic State U., 1970, MA, 1972. Cert. elem. and secondary tchr., Calif. Travel agt. Dale Johnson Travel, San Jose, Calif., 1963-67; 6th grade tchr. Orcutt Sch. Dist., Santa Maria, Calif., 1971-80; jr. high sch. tchr. Orcutt Sch. Dist., Santa Maria, 1980-88, lit. mentor, 1986—; dir. North County Lit. Task Force, Santa Maria, 1988-89. Edn. dir. San Luis Obispo United Meth. Ch., 1986—. Mem. Am. Coun. Tchrs. English, Calif. Assn. Tchrs. English, San Luis Bay Club. Democrat. Home: 6798 Avila Valley Dr San Luis Obispo CA 93401 Office: Orcutt Sch Dist Soares & Dyer Sts Santa Maria CA 93455

SAINT-PIERRE, JANN MADDALENA, language educator; b. Montreal, Que., Can., Nov. 23, 1950; d. Leopold Andrew and Maddalena (Silvano) S.; m. Jay Alan Muehlhausen, Aug. 8, 1983; 1 child, Jennifer Maddalena. BA, McGill U., Montreal, 1972; cert., Calif. State U., Northridge, 1985; postgrad., U. So. Calif., 1987. Cert. tchr., Calif. Dist. mgr. Jhirmack Enterprises, Inc., Redding, Calif., 1979-80, dir. sch. programs, 1980-83; nat. sales mgr. Nicole Rsch. Inc., Redding, 1983-85; bilingual tchr. L.A. Unified Sch. Dist., 1985-87; tchr. Redding Sch. Dist., 1987-88; tchr. English as second lang. and French, cons., co-dir. bilingual program Enterprise Sch. Dist., Redding, 1988—. Author: Anatomy of a Permanent Wave, 1981. State of Calif. grantee, 1986. Mem. Assn. for Supervison and Curriculum Devel., CATESOL. Roman Catholic. Office: Parsons Jr High Sch 750 Hartnell Ave Redding CA 96002

ST. PIERRE, PAUL, writer; b. Chgo., Oct. 14, 1923; immigrated to Can., 1924; s. Napoleon and Pearl Clayton (Stanford) St. P.; m. Carol Mildred Roycroft, Dec. 12, 1950 (dec. 1972); children—Paul Robert, Michelle Anne, Suzanne Ellen; m. Melanie Anne McCarthy, Nov. 17, 1978. Newspaperman, mostly Vancouver Sun, B.C., 1948-79; M.P. from Coast Chilcotin riding, 1968-72; parliamentary sec. external affairs, Ottawa, Can., 1971-72; del. UN Spl. Com., 1971-72; rapporteur Sci. and Cultural Com. NATO Parliamentary Group, 1972; chmn. B.C. Govt. Caucus, 1970-72; Can. observer Orgn. Am. States, 1972; police commr. Province of B.C., 1979-83. Author: Smith and Other Events, 1983; Breaking Smith's Quarter Horse, 1967; Chilcotin Holiday, 1970; Sister Balonika, 1971; British Columbia Our Land, 1973; Boss of the Namko Drive, 1966; others; playwright over 25 plays including Cariboo (CQ) Country; contbr. articles to mags. Recipient Spur Award (Western Writers of Am.) for best short fiction of 1984 for story Sale of One Small Ranch. Served with RCAF, 1941-42. Club: University (Vancouver). *

ST. PIERRE, RICHARD W., mining company executive; b. Adams, Mass., Mar. 8, 1940; s. George Raymond and Viola Marie (Tremblay) S.; m. Margaret Mary Nealon, June 17, 1961; children: Michelle M., Deborah J., Jeanine M., Sheryl L. BS, North Adams State Coll., 1961; MS, Union Coll., Schenectady, N.Y., 1966; MA, St. Joseph's Coll., West Hartford, Conn., 1967; EdD, Nova U., 1976. Tchr. high schs., Conn. and Mass., 1961-64; elem. science coordinator elem. sch., Pittsfield, Mass., 1964-66; prof. geology and biology Berkshire Community Coll., Pittsfield, 1966-69, dir. of admissions, 1969-71; dean of acad. affairs Bristol Community Coll., Fall River, Mass., 1971-79; acting pres. Quinsigamond Community Coll., Worcester, Mass., 1979-80; pres. Cent. Wyo. Coll., Riverton, 1980-83, Riverton Resources Corp., 1983—; gubernatorial appointee State of Mass., 1969-76, State of Wyo., 1980-83. Built first pub. TV sta. in Wyo., 1982-3; built Arts and Conv. Ctr., Riverton, 1983. Recipient three NSF scholarships. Mem. Prospectors and Developers Assn. of Can. Republican. Lodge: Elks. Home and Office: Riverton Resources Corp 125 Fairway Dr Riverton WY 82501

SAITO, FRANK KIYOJI, import/export firm executive; b. Tokyo, Feb. 28, 1945; s. Kaoru and Chiyoko S.; LL.B., Kokugakuin U., 1967; m. Elaine Tamami Karasawa, Feb. 22, 1975; children—Roderic Kouki, Lorine Erika. With import dept. Trois Co. Ltd., Tokyo, Japan, 1967-68; founder import/export dept. Three Bond Co., Ltd., Tokyo, 1968-71; sales mgr. Kobe Mercantile, Inc., San Diego, 1971-76; pres. K & S Internat. Corp., San Diego, 1976—. Office: K & S Internat Corp 7626 Miramar Rd Ste 3600 San Diego CA 92126

SAITO, KATHLEEN KEIKO, architect, interior design; b. Honolulu, May 4, 1955; d. Raymond Mitsuyoshi and Midlred Tomiko (Kuromoto) Kawano; m. Sanford Sadamu Saito, July 31, 1982. BArch, U. Hawaii. Registered architect, Hawaii. Intern architect Group 70, Honolulu, 1979-81, assoc. architect, interior design, 1982-87; interior designer, draftsperson Paul Kamada and Assocs., Honolulu, 1981-82; self-employed Honolulu, 1987—; archtl. draftsperson Zephyr Archtl. Ptnrship, Honolulu, 1981-82. Recipient Lishman award for Interior Design, Bldg. Industry Assn. and Am. Soc. Interior Designers, 1984. Mem. AIA.

SAITO, SANFORD S., dentist; b. Honolulu, June 1, 1954; s. Richard K. and Agnes T. (Kakuda) S.; m. Kathleen Kawano Saito, July 31, 1982; 1 child, Holly K. BA, U. Hawaii, 1976; DDS, Ind. U., 1981. advisor U. Hawaii Predental Soc., Honolulu, 1981-86. Mem. Am. Dental Assn., Hawaii Dental Assn., Honolulu County Dental Assn., Honolulu Execs. Assn. Office: 1580 Makaloa St Ste 844 Honolulu HI 96814

SAKALAUSKAS, MICHAEL L., registered nurse, substance abuse counselor, fire arms dealer; b. N.Y.C., Dec. 17, 1951; s. Clifford and Roselyn S.; m. Colleen M. Brady, July 18, 1982 (div. 1989); children: Sean Christophner Louis. ADS, U. Hawaii; BGS, Chaminade U. Federally lic. firearms dealer. Emt Honolulu City and County, 1978-81; EMT/firefighter Dynalectron Corp., Barking Sands, Hawaii, 1981-83; poison info. specialist Hawaii Poison Ctr., Honolulu, 1986—; crisis response sys. specialist Suicide & Crisis Ctr., Honolulu, 1986—; pediatric intensive care nurse Kapiolani Womans and Childrens Med. Ctr., Honolulu, 1988; substance abuse nurse Castle Med. Ctr., Kailua, 1988—; cons. Buckmaster Assocs., Honolulu, 1988—; pres. Substance Abuse Svcs., Kailua, 1988—; prog. dir. RTR Assocs., Kailua, 1988—. Active Mothers Against Drunk Driving, 1984. Recipient Community Svc. award Karunya Ednl. Assn., 1988. Mem. Hawaii Nurses Assn., Hawaii Assn. for Deaf, Nat. Rifle Assn., Nat. Assn. Drug and Alcohol Abuse Counselors, Delta Epsilon Sigma. Republican. Office: Substance Abuse Svcs 1020 Aloha Pl #208B Kailua HI 96734

SAKKAL, MAMOUN, interior designer; b. Damascus, Syria, Dec. 31, 1950; came to U.S., 1978; s. Lutfi Sakkal and Dourieh Khatib; m. Seta K. Sakkal, Mar. 13, 1980; children: Aida, Kindah. BArch with honors, U. Aleppo, Syria, 1974; MArch, U. Wash., 1982, cert. urban design, 1982. Registered architect, Syria; lic. interior designer, U.S. Archtl. designer MCE, Damascus, 1974-75; dir. design MCE, Aleppo, 1975-76; prin. Sakkal & Assocs., Aleppo, 1976-78; archtl. designer Arch. Assocs., Seattle, 1978-82; sr. designer RD&S, Bellevue, Wash., 1982-84; prin. Restaurant/Hotel Design, Seattle, 1984—; lectr. U. Aleppo, 1974-75, Applied Arts Inst., 1977-78. Author: Geometry of Muqarnas in Islamic Architecture, 1981; designer Oct. Mus., Damascus, Syria, 1977 (1st prize award Syrian Ministry Def.); one man shows include: Nat. Mus. Aleppo, Syria, 1969, U. Aleppo, 1974, U. Wash., 1979, 80; contbr. articles to profl. jours. Recipient Best Logo Design award Arab Union Sports, 1976, Best Project Design award Aleppo Ministry of Culture, 1975, Best Modernization Project award Hilton Inns. System, 1986, Best Lounge Renovation award Bowlers Jour. Annual Design Contest,

1987. Mem. Am. Soc. Interior Designers. Office: Restaurant/Hotel Design 852 NE 91 St Seattle WA 98115

SAKOMOTO, KAREN KEIKO, university administrator; b. Honolulu, Feb. 26, 1952; d. Creighton Naoyuki and Ruth Kaoru (Kozuma) Kusunoki; m. Ronald Rikio Sakamoto, May 25, 1986; 1 child, Aaron Naoyuki. BEd, U. Hawaii, 1974; MS, U. Calif., Long Beach, 1978. Coord. learning assistance ctr. U. Hawaii, Honolulu, Manoa, 1979—. Contbr. articles to profl. jours. Bd. dirs. Hawaii Lupus Found., 1974—; chmn. scholarship com. Te Chih Sheh Sorority Alumnae, 1983-88. Recipient Merit award U. Hawaii, 1981, 86, 1st Lady's Outstanding Vol. award State of Hawaii, 1985. Mem. Am. Bus. Women's Assn., NEA, Am. Assn. Counseling and Devel., Nat. Assn. Devel. Edn., Coll. Reading and Learning Assn., Internat. Reading Assn., Phi Kappa Phi. Home: 3055 Polohinano Pl Honolulu HI 96817

SAKOVER, RAYMOND PAUL, radiologist; b. Chgo., Oct. 8, 1944; s. Max and Lena (Berardi) S.; BS (James scholar), U. Ill., 1965, MD, 1969; m. Patricia Ellyn Taylor, June 7, 1969; children: Shelley Lynn, Michael Paul, David Evan, Raymond Taylor. Intern, St. Francis Hosp., Evanston, Ill., 1969-70, resident, 1970-73; practice medicine specializing in radiology, Riverside, Calif., 1975—; staff radiologist Riverside Community Hosp., 1975-86, pres. Computerized Diagnostic Imaging, 1986—; clin. instr. Loma Linda (Calif.) U. Med. Ctr., 1976—. Bd. dirs. Lung Assn. Riverside, 1978-83, Riverside Humane Soc., 1980—. Served with USNR, 1973-75. Diplomate Am. Bd. Radiology. Mem. Am. Coll. Radiology, Soc. Nuclear Medicine, AMA, Calif. Med. Soc., N.Am., Calif. radiol. socs. Roman Catholic. Lodge: Rotary. Contbr. articles in field to profl. jours. Office: Riverside Radiology 6941 Brockton Ave Riverside CA 92506

SALAMON, MIKLOS DEZSO GYORGY, mining educator; b. Balkany, Hungary, May 20, 1933; came to U.S., 1986; s. Miklos and Sarolta (Obetko) S.; m. Agota Maria Meszaros, July 11, 1953; children: Miklos, Gabor. Diploma in Engring., Polytech U., Sopron, Hungary, 1956; PhD, U. Durham, Newcastle, England, 1962. Research asst. dept. mining engring. U. Durham, 1959-63; dir. research Coal Mining Research Controlling Council, Johannesburg, South Africa, 1963-66; dir. collieries research lab Chamber of Mines of South Africa, Johannesburg, 1966-74, dir. gen. research org., 1974-86; disting. prof., head dept. mining engring., dir. ctr. advanced mining systems Colo. Sch. Mines, Golden, 1986—; hon. prof. U. Witwatersrand, Johannesburg, 1979-86; vis. prof. U. Minn., Mpls., 1981, U. Tex., Austin, 1982. Co-author: Rock Mechanics Applied to the Study of Rockbursts, 1966, Rock Mechanics in Coal Mining, 1976; contbr. articles to profl. jours. Mem. Pres.'s Sci. Adv. Council, Cape Town, South Africa, 1984-86, Nat. Sci. Priorities Com., Pretoria, South Africa, 1984-86. Recipient Nat. award Assn. Scis. and Tech. Socs., South Africa, 1971. Fellow South African Inst. Mining and Metallurgy (v.p. 1974-76, pres. 1976-77, Stokes award 1986); Am. Inst. Mining, Metallurgical and Pertoleum Engrs., Internat. Soc. Rock Mechanics. Roman Catholic. Office: Colo Sch of Mines Dept of Mining Engring Golden CO 80401

SALAND, JOEL, physician; b. N.Y.C., Dec. 21, 1941; s. Emanuel and Bertha (Ryshpan) S.; m. Linda, Aug. 16, 1964; children:. BS in Biochemistry, 1962; MD, Albert Einstein Coll., 1966. Diplomate Am. Bd. Pediatrics. Asst. chief of pediatrics Indian Health Service, Tuba City, Ariz., 1969-71; pvt. practice in pediatrics Albuquerque, 1971—; clin. assoc. prof. pediatrics U. N.Mex., chief med. Lt. comdr. USPHS, 1969-71. Mem. Greater Albuquerque Med. Soc., Multiple Health Plans. Office: 8012 Constitution Pl NE Albuquerque NM 87110

SALAS, MARILYN SUE, academic director; b. Sabetha, Kans., June 4, 1943; d. Lee R. and Agnes M. (McPeak) Cashman; m. Henry C. Salas, Aug. 1, 1970. Student, Kans. State U., 1961-62, Kans. U., 1962-64; BA in Bus. Adminstrn., Emporia State U., 1965. Cert. secondary bus. edn. and psychology tchr., Kans., Calif. High sch. tchr. Pacifica High Sch., Garden Grove, Calif., 1966-68; word processor Orange County, Calif., 1968-72; ednl. service rep. IBM, Anaheim, Calif., 1969-70; coll. instr. Cerritos Coll., Norwalk, Calif., 1970-74; adult edn. instr. Lincoln Edn. Tng., Garden Grove, 1972-78; coll. instr. Golden West Coll., Huntington Beach, Calif., 1973-80, Orange Coast Coll., Costa Mesa, Calif., 1976-79, Cypress (Calif.) Coll., 1977-79; freelance word processor Burlington Northern, Newport Beach, Calif., 1978-79; cons. in field, Orange County, 1979; coll. instr. Saddleback Coll., Mission Viejo, Calif., 1979; dir. The Word Processing and Computer Sch., Anaheim, 1980-87. Mem. Assn. Info. Systems Profls. (mem. ednl. task force), Am. Soc. Tng. and Devel., Calif. Bus. Educators Assn., Anaheim C. of C., Nat. Assn. Trade and Tech. Schs. Accrediting Agy. (accredited). Democrat. Methodist. Home: 41105 Valle Vista Murrieta CA 92362

SALAZAR, ANITA TERESA, educator; b. Greeley, Colo., Apr. 2, 1947; d. Fermin and Helen (De La Torre) S. BA, U. No. Colo., 1968, MA, 1969; PhD, Ohio State U., 1981. Instr., coordinator Centennial High Sch., San Luis, Colo., 1969-72; evaluation specialist State Bd. Community Colls. and Occupational Edn., Denver, 1972-74; instr., coordinator Red Rocks Community Coll., Golden, Colo., 1973-77; adminstrv. asst., grad. research asst. Nat. Ctr. Research in Vocat. Edn. Ohio State U., Columbus, 1978-81; asst. prof. U. No. Colo., Greeley, 1982-87, dir. bus. affairs, coord. staff devel., 1987—. Contbr. articles to profl. jours. Named Rookie Tchr. Yr. Colo. State Bd. Community Colls. and Occupational Edn., 1971. Mem. Greeley C. of C. (mem. leadership class 1986). Democrat. Roman Catholic. Home: 1015 Trapper Dr Fort Lupton CO 80621 Office: Fort Lupton Sch Dist Fort Lupton CO 80621

SALAZAR, DANIEL REYNOLDS, fire fighter, grocery clerk; b. Miami, Ariz., May 7, 1942; s. Daniel Reynolds and Alice Lena (Martinez) S.; m. Patricia Ann Doyle, Mar. 23, 1963 (div. 1973); children: Corrine Marie, Kevin Daniel; m. Gail Lester, Mar. 6, 1977; children: Ryan Daniel, Bret Tristan. Student, U. Calif., Berkeley, 1959-62, UCLA, 1960. Clk. City Main Libr., L.A., 1958; groundskeeper U. Calif., Berkeley, 1959-62; insp. Continental Can Co., L.A., 1962; truck driver Foremost Dairies, San Francisco, 1966-67; grocery clk. Safeway Stores, San Francisco, 1963-66, Concord, Calif., 1968-73, 74—; fire fighter San Francisco Fire Dept., 1967—. Named L.A. City Baseball Player of Yr., 1959, Fireman of Yr. Firehouse Mag., 1984, Lions Club, San Francisco, 1984; recipient Sullivan medal City San Francisco, 1984, medal of valor San Francisco Fire Dept., 1984, commendation Calif. State Senate, 1984, two commendations Nat. Sojourners, 1984; D. Salazar Day proclaimed by City of San Francisco mayor, 1984. Mem. St. Francis Hook and Ladder Soc., Lawrence Hall of Sci., U. Calif. Alumni Assn., Big C. Soc., Bear Backers. Republican. Roman Catholic. Home: 74 Nottingham Pl Clayton CA 94517 Office: San Francisco Fire Dept 1067 Post St San Francisco CA 94109

SALAZAR, LUIS ADOLFO, architect; b. New Orleans, Sept. 17, 1944; s. Gustavo Adolfo and Luz Maria (Florez) S.; m. Sandra Kay Bucklew, May 30, 1969 (div. Jan. 1984); 1 child, Staci Dahnal. AA, Harbor Coll., 1966; BArch, Ariz. State U., 1971. Registered architect, Ariz., Calif., N.Mex. Area architect Peace Corps, Sierra Leone, 1971-73; project architect Van Sittert Assocs., Phoenix, 1973-77; pres., owner Salazar Assoc. Architects, Ltd., Phoenixand Design Team, Inc., 1977—; Prin. works include bldg. design Kenema Cathedral, Kenema, Sierra Leone, West Africa, 1980. Bd. dirs. Community Behavioral Services, Phoenix, 1983-85; Phoenix Meml. Hosp., 1984—, Terraco Properties. mem. Subcom. on Bond Election, Phoenix, 1984; mem. Visual Improvement Awards Com., City of Phoenix, 1985-88. Mem. AIA (chmn. program com., honor award Ariz. chpt. 1984, visual improvement awards coms. 1985, 86), Soc. Am. Value Engrs., Inst. Architects. Roman Catholic. Office: Salazar Assocs Architects Ltd 4518 N 12th St Ste 100 Phoenix AZ 85014

SALAZAR, MICHAEL JOSEPH, engineering company executive; b. Santa Fe, Sept. 27, 1931; s. Michael and Anna (Baca) S.; m. Marilyn Lucille Lobato, Dec. 29, 1956; children: Michael L. (dec.), Sherry, Gregory, Renee. BS, Coll. Santa Fe, 1959; MPH, Tulane U., 1962; postgrad., U. N.Mex., 1969-74. Registered profl. engr., Colo., Wis. Chief environ. health Ill. Health Dept., Springfield, 1962-65; regional environ. supr. N.Mex. EPA, Albuquerque, 1969-71; assoc. prof. N.Mex. Highlands U., Las Vegas, 1971-74; chief engr. EPA, Denver, 1974-83; pres. Salazar Assocs., Westminster, Colo., 1983—. Patentee in field. Served to lt. comdr. USPHS, 1965-69. Mem. NSPE, Colo. Soc. Profl. Engrs., Profl. Engrs. in Pvt. Practice. Democrat. Roman Catholic. Home: 4650 W 99th Ave Westminster CO 80030 Office: Salazar Assocs Internat 8791 Wolf Ct Bldg 15 Westminster CO 80030

SALE, GEORGE EDGAR, pathologist; b. Missoula, Mont., Apr. 18, 1941; s. George Goble and Ruth Edna (Polleys) S.; m. Nancy Current, 1978 (div. 1987); children: George Gregory, Teo Marie. AB, Harvard U., 1963; MD, Stanford U., 1968. Intern U. Oreg., Portland, 1968-69; sr. asst. surgeon USPHS, Albuquerque, 1969-71; resident in pathology U. Wash., Seattle, 1971-75, instr. pathology, 1975-78, asst. prof., 1978-81, assoc. prof., 1981-88, prof., 1988—; mem. faculty dept. oncology Hutchinson Cancer Ctr., Seattle, 1975—. Author, editor: Pathology of Bone Marrow Transplantation, 1984, Pathology of Transplantation, 1989. Mem. AAAS, Internat. Acad. Pathology, Coll. Am. Pathologists, Am. Assn. Pathologists, Physicians for Social Responsibility. Home: 12146 Sunrise Dr NE Bainbridge WA 98110 Office: Fred Hutchinson Cancer Rsh Ctr 1124 Columbia Pathology Seattle WA 98104

SALEM, G(EORGE) MELVIN, retired aeronautical engineer, small business owner; b. Ypsilanti, Mich., Aug. 22, 1927; s. George and Pearl Helen (Newton) S.; divorced, 1970; children: Linda Sue, Michael George, Robert Melvin; m. Patricia Wagener Jones, May 29, 1971; stepchildren: Janice Louise, Jeffrey William (dec.), Jon Michael. BS in Aeronautics, St. Louis U., 1952. Engr., flight test div. Lockheed Co., Burbank, Calif., 1952-56; engr., Chrysler missile div. Lockheed Co., Detroit, 1956-57; engr., mgr. Jet Propulsion Lab., Pasadena, Calif., 1957-86, ret., 1986; owner, mgr. Knob Hill Mercantile Grocery and Delicatessen, Alturas, Calif., 1987—. Active Boy Scouts Am., La Crescenta, Calif., 1972-78; founder St. George Episcopal Mission, Northridge. Sgt. U.S. Army, 1946-49, Korea. Mem. Am. Inst. Plant Engrs. (sec., v.p. 1969-73), U.S. Power Squadron (editor Pasadena Rose mag. 1980-85). Republican. Episcopalian. Home and Office: Knob Hill Mercantile Calif Pines Unit III PO Box 274 Alturas CA 96101

SALERNO, JOSEPH MICHAEL, air cargo company executive; b. Port Washington, N.Y., Jan. 12, 1917; s. Angelo and Anna Marie (Fasano) S.; m. Edith Evangeline Fields, Apr. 2, 1949; children: Linda Marie, Bruce Charles, Paul Michael, David Brian. BS, Tri-State Coll., 1943. Flight engr. Pan Am. World Airways, Inc., San Francisco, 1943-77; owner, pres. Salair, Inc., Seattle, 1980—, also bd. dirs. Pres. Horizon View Community, Bellevue, Wash., 1958-63; mem. Bellevue Citizens Sch. Adv. Coun., 1964; pres. Eastgate Elem. Sch. PTA, Bellevue, 1963. Republican. Roman Catholic. Home: 14560 SE 51st St Bellevue WA 98006 Office: Salair Inc Spokane Internat Airport Hanger 745 Spokane WA 99204

SALISBURY, DAVID FRANCIS, newspaper, television science writer; b. Seattle, Feb. 24, 1947; s. Vernon H. and Lurabelle (Kline) S. BS, U. Wash., 1969. Sci. editor Christian Sci. Monitor, Boston, 1972-76; correspondent Christian Sci. Monitor, Los Angeles, Boulder (Colo.) and San Francisco, 1976-85; sci. and tech. writer U. Calif., Santa Barbara, 1985—; mem. research adv. com. Pub. Service Electric and Gas Co., Newark, N.J., 1979-83. Author: Money Matters, 1982. contbr. many articles to popular mags. and tech. jours. Recipient Sci. Writing awards AAAS, 1976, NSPE, 1978, Aviation Space Writers Assn., 1981. Mem. Nat. Assn. Sci. Writers (Sci.-in-Soc. award 1974), No. Calif. Sci. Writers Assn., Computer Press Assn. Christian Scientist. Office: U Calif Pub Info Office Santa Barbara CA 93106

SALISBURY, FRANK BOYER, plant physiologist, educator; b. Provo, Utah, Aug. 3, 1926; s. Frank M. and Catherine (Boyer) S.; m. Lois Marilyn Olson, Sept. 1, 1949; children: Frank Clark, Steven Scott, Michael James, Cynthia Kay, Phillip Boyer (dec.), Rebecca Lynn, Blake Charles. BS, U. Utah, 1951, MA, 1952; PhD, Calif. Inst. Tech., 1955. Asst. prof. botany Pomona Coll., Claremont, Calif., 1954-55; faculty Colo. State U., Ft. Collins, 1955-66; prof. plant physiology Colo. State U., 1961-66; plant physiologist Expt. Sta., 1961-66; prof. plant physiology Utah State U., Logan, 1966—, disting. prof. Agr., 1987—, head dept. plant sci., 1966-70; tech. rep. plant physiology AEC, Germantown, Md., 1973-74; vis. prof. U. Innsbruck, Austria; Lady Davis fellow Hebrew U. Jerusalem, 1983; mem. aerospace medicine adv. com., NASA, 1988—, life scis. adv. com., 1986-88, now chmn. Controlled Ecol. Life Support System Discipline Working Group. Author: The Flowering Process, 1963, (with R.V. Parke) Vascular Plants, Form and Function, 2d edit, 1970, Truth by Reason and by Revelation, 1965, (with C. Ross) Plant Physiology, 1969, 3d edit., 1985, The Biology of Flowering, 1971, (with W. Jensen) Botany: An Ecological Approach, 1972, Botany, 2d edit., 1984, The Utah UFO Display, 1974, The Creation, 1976, (with E. Kormondy, T. Sherman, N. Spratt, and G. McCain) Biology, 1977; editor: Jour. of Plant Physiology, North America and the Pacific Rim. Trustee Colo. State U. Rsch. Found., 1959-62; leader People to People bot. del. to Republic South Africa, 1984, to Peoples Republic China, 1988. Served with USAAF, 1945. NSF sr. postdoctoral fellow Germany and Austria, 1962-63. Fellow AAAS; mem. Am. Soc. for Gravitational and Space Biology, Am. Soc. Plant Physiologists (editorial bd.), Ecol. Soc. Am., Utah Acad. Sci., Arts and Letters, Am. Inst. Biol. Scis. (governing bd. 1976-79), Bot. Soc. Am. (Merit award), Sigma Xi, Phi Kappa Phi. Mormon. Home: 2020 North 1250 E North Logan UT 84321 Office: Utah State U Dept Plant Sci Logan UT 84322-4820

SALISBURY, FRANK PRESSLEY, writer; b. Ft. Worth, Mar. 2, 1930; s. Frank Albert and Burmah Elizabeth (Pressley) S.; m. Manuela Jones. Student, L.A. City Coll., 1950-51. Author numerous plays. Sgt. U.S. Army, 1951-52. Recipient Emmy award, Emmy Nomination TV Acad., 1981-82. Mem. Dramatists Guild, Writers Guild West, Acad. TV Arts and Scis. Democrat.

SALK, JONAS EDWARD, physician, scientist; b. N.Y.C., Oct. 28, 1914; s. Daniel B. and Dora (Press) S.; m. Donna Lindsay, June 8, 1939; children: Peter Lindsay, Darrell John, Jonathan Daniel; m. Francoise Gilot, June 29, 1970. BS, CCNY, 1934, LLD (hon.), 1955; MD, NYU, 1939, ScD (hon.), 1955; LLD (hon.), U. Pitts., 1955; PhD (hon.), Hebrew U., 1959; LLD (hon.), Roosevelt U., 1955; ScD (hon.), Turin U., 1957, U. Leeds, 1959, Hahnemann Med. Coll., 1959, Franklin and Marshall U., 1960; DHL (hon.), Yeshiva U., 1959; LLD (hon.), Tuskegee Inst., 1964. Fellow in chemistry NYU, 1935-37, fellow in exptl. surgery, 1937-38, fellow in bacteriology, 1939-40; Intern Mt. Sinai Hosp., N.Y.C., 1940-42; NRC fellow Sch. Pub. Health, U. Mich., 1942-43, research fellow epidemiology, 1943-44, research asso., 1944-46, asst. prof. epidemiology, 1946-47; asso. research prof. bacteriology Sch. Medicine, U. Pitts., 1947-49, dir. virus research lab., 1947-63, research prof. bacteriology, 1949-55, Commonwealth prof. preventive medicine, 1955-57, Commonwealth prof. exptl. medicine, 1957-63; dir. Salk Inst. Biol. Studies, 1963-75, resident fellow, 1963-84, founding dir., 1976—, disting. prof. internat. health scis., 1984—; developed vaccine, preventive of poliomyelitis, 1955, cons. epidemic diseases sec. war, 1944-47, sec. army, 1947-54; mem. commn. on influenza Army Epidemiol. Bd., 1944-54, acting dir. commn. on influenza, 1944; mem. expert adv. panel on virus diseases WHO; adj. prof. health scis., depts. psychiatry, community medicine and medicine U. Calif., San Diego, 1970—. Author: Man Unfolding, 1972, The Survival of the Wisest, 1973, (with Jonathan Salk) World Population and Human Values: A New Reality, 1981, Anatomy of Reality, 1983; Contbr. sci. articles to jours. Decorated chevalier Legion of Honor France, 1955, officer, 1976; recipient Criss award, 1955, Lasker award, 1956, Gold medal of Congress and presdl. citation, 1955, Howard Ricketts award, 1957, Robert Koch medal, 1963, Mellon Inst. award, 1969; Presdl. medal of Freedom, 1977; Jawaharlal Nehru award for internat. understanding, 1976. Fellow AAAS, Am. Pub. Health Assn., Am. Acad. Pediatrics (hon., assoc.); mem. Am. Coll. Preventive Medicine, Am. Acad. Neurology, Assn. Am. Physicians., Soc. Exptl. Biology and Medicine, Inst. Medicine (sr.), Phi Beta Kappa, Alpha Omega Alpha, Delta Omega. Office: Salk Inst Biol Studies PO Box 85800 San Diego CA 92138 *

SALKIN, GERALDINE FAUBION (JERI SALKIN), dancer, dance therapist, educator; b. Denver, Mar. 18, 1916; d. George Everett and Hanna Viola (Harvey) Faubion; m. Leo Salkin, June 29, 1936; 1 child, Lynn Salkin Sbiroli. Student Lester Horton Dance Theater, Carmelita Maracci, Trudi Schoop, Los Angeles, 1937-47, Doris Humphrey, N.Y.C., 1952-53, Rudolf Von Laban, London, 1956-57, Hanna Fenichel, PhD,Westwood, Calif., 1965-70, UCLA, 1959-60; PhD, 1978. Concert dancer Lester Horton Dance Group, Los Angeles, 1937-47, tchr. creative modern dance, 1939-47; tchr. creative modern dance Dance Assos., Hollywood, Calif., 1949-53, Am. Sch. of London (Eng.), 1956-57, Jeri Salkin Studio and Ctr. for Child Study, Hollywood, 1968-73; developer body ego technique Camarillo (Calif.) State Hosp., 1957-64; movement specialist Nat. Endowment Arts grantee, 1973—; dir., body ego technique dept. Cedars-Sinai Thalians Community Mental Health Ctr., Los Angeles, 1965—; dance cons., tchr. Nat. Head Start Program, Calif., 1964; conductor yearly workshops for tchrs., dancers, psychologists, psychiatrists, therapists, Rome, 1979—, mem. aux. faculty Goddard Coll., Antioch Coll., various hosps. and univs. Calif. Dept. Mental Hygiene grantee, 1960-63. Mem. Am. Dance Therapy Assn., AAHPER, Calif. Dance Educators Assn., Calif. Assn. Health, Phys. Edn. Dance and Recreation, Nat. Assn. Edn. Young Children, Assn. Child Devel. Specialists, Com. Research in Dance. Democrat. Author: Body Ego Technique, an Educational and Therapeutic Approach to Body Image and Self-Identity, 1973; author, choreographer film (with Leo Salkin and Trudi Schoop) Body Ego Technique, 1962 (U.S. Golden Eagle Council on Internat. Nontheatrical Events award 1963).

SALKIND, MILTON, conservatory president; b. Wilmington, Del., Feb. 21, 1916; s. Nathan and Rose (Dektor) S.; m. Peggy Rippé Snyder, Aug. 9, 1948; children: Karen, Mark. B.S. in Econs, George Washington U., 1942; B.S. in Music, Juilliard Sch. Music, 1949. Faculty Lone Mountain Coll., 1962-66; pres. San Francisco Conservatory Music, 1966—; Mem. performing arts panel Calif. Arts Commn.; chmn. arts San Francisco Symphony; mem. music adv. council Young Musicians Found.; mem. music advisory panel Nat. Endowment for the Arts. Performances of four-hand piano with Peggy Salkind in U.S., Europe, Can. and Mexico; guest artist: Bell Telephone Hour, NBC's Recital Hall; appeared on French television; pvt. instr. piano; commd. works for numerous composers. Served with AUS, 1942-46. Recipient Disting. Univ. medal U. Calif.-Berkeley, 1982. Mem. Assn. Independent Conservatories Music (chmn.), Coll. Music Soc. (council), San Francisco Chamber Music Soc. (adv. bd.). Club: Bohemian. Office: 1201 Ortega St San Francisco CA 94122 *

SALLEE, ALVIN LLOYD, social worker, educator; b. Albuquerque, Jan. 19, 1950; s. Lloyd Alvin and Carol (Williams) S.; m. Kathleen Estelle Bickerstaff, Jan. 1, 1971; children: Charles, Shawn, Joan. BA, Phillips U., Enid, Okla., 1972; MSW, Ariz. State U., 1974. Adminstrv. asst. Ariz. Tng. Program at Tucson, 1972-73; rsch. asst. Community Council, Phoenix, 1973-74; instr. S.W. Tex. State U., San Marcos, 1974-76; assoc. prof., head dept. social work N.Mex. State U., Las Cruces, 1976-88, prof., head dept., 1988—; cons. Ctr. for Social Work Rsch., U. Tex., Austin, 1975-79, City of Lubbock, Tex., 1982, Santa Fe Community Found., N.Mex., 1983-84, Social Svcs. div. N.Mex. Human Svcs. Dept., Santa Fe, 1983-84, Northeastern Ill. U., 1988, No. Ariz. U., 1988. Author: (with Elaine LeVine) Listen to Our Children: Clinical Theory and Practice, 1986; editor Jour. of Alliance of Info. and Referral Systems, 1978-80. Southwest coordinator Dem. presdl. and congl. campaigns, Las Cruces, 1980; mem. Task Force on Adoptions, 1983-84, Nat. Task Force Future of Social Work Edn., 1988—; mem. nomination com. house of dels. Council of Social Work Edn., 1985—; chmn. Gov.'s Family Impact Com., Gov.'s Office on Youth, Santa Fe, 1983—, N.Mex. Family Policy Task Force, Santa Fe, 1980-83, United Way of Orange County, Calif., 1985; bd. dirs. Colo. Christian Home, Denver, 1983—. Grantee N.Mex. Human Svcs. Dept., 1977-89, N.Mex. State Agy. on Aging, 1983. Mem. Alliance of Info. and Referral Systems (bd. dirs. 1978-89, sec. 1981-85), Assn. Baccalaurate Social Work Program Dirs. (pres. 1987-89, exec. dir. Program Dirs.' Conf. 1986-89, conf. chmn. 1986-89), Nat. Assn. Social Workers (bd. dirs. 1972-74, cert. competence bd. 1988—, mem. long range planning com., mem. nominations com. N.Mex. State chpt. 1988—), Council Social Work Edn., N.Mex. Council Social Work Edn., Internat. Schs. of Social Work, Am. Orthopsychiatry Assn. Home: 2700 Crestview Dr Las Cruces NM 88001 Office: NMex State U Dept Social Work Box 35 W Las Cruces NM 88003

SALLEE, JOAN SELKE, educational administrator; b. Lansdowne, Pa., Nov. 16, 1940; d. Hans Emil and Mary Dorothy (Pasternack) Selke; m. G. Thomas Sallee, June 18, 1966; children: Kathleen Brooke (dec.), Kristin Paige, Claire Courtney, Margaret Whitney. AB, Trinity Coll., Washington, 1962; MA, Mills Coll., 1964; postgrad., U. Calif., Berkeley, 1981. Asst. head resident Mills Coll., Oakland, Calif., 1962-64; personnel asst. AEC, Berkeley, Calif., 1964-66; career advisor U. Calif., Davis, 1966-69, asst. dean women, 1969-70, extension instr., 1970-75, ednl. placement officer, 1972-79; postsecondary ednl. specialist Calif. Postsecondary Edn. Commn., Sacramento, 1980-83, sr. policy analyst, 1983—; cons. Far West Lab., San Francisco, 1985-88. Contbr. articles to profl. jours. Pres. Davis Parent Nursery Sch., 1972-73, PTA, Davis, 1974-75, 79-80, 82-83, 87-88, Univ. Farm Circle, Davis, 1980-81; chmn. Sacramento City Coll. Outreach, 1979-81, Davis, Davis Sch. Site Coun., 1985-86; pres., bd. dirs. Davis Sch. Arts Found., 1986-89; also active Mental Health Assn. Yolo County, Valley Oak Parent Adv. Com., United Way, Sacramento Symphony Assn., Davis Art Ctr., March of Dimes, various others. Fund for Improvement Postsecondary Edn. grantee, 1984-86. Mem. Am. Ednl. Rsch. Assn., Am. Evaluation Assn., Calif. Assn. for Instnl. Rsch. (exec. bd. 1988-89), Mills Coll. Alumnae Assn. (bd. govs.). Democrat. Roman Catholic. Home: 913 Plum Ln Davis CA 95616 Office: Postsecondary Edn Commn 1020 12th St 3d Fl Sacramento CA 95814

SALLEE, WESLEY W(ILLIAM), nuclear chemist; b. Perry, Okla., June 5, 1951; s. Jimmie Richard and Nadine A. (Barnes) S.; m. Exine Mamie Clark, Mar. 21, 1979; children: Rachel Nadine, Daniel Mason. BS in Chemistry, Okla. State U., 1974; PhD in Chemistry, U. Ark., 1983. Commd. 1st lt. USAF, 1976, advanced through grades to capt., 1978, resigned, 1979; nuclear physicist U.S. Army White Sands Missile Range, 1983—. Author technical reports and symposium papers; contbr. articles to profl. jours. Mem. ASTM, Am. Nuclear Soc., Am. Chem. Soc. Republican. Mem. Ch. of Christ. Home: 1515 Dorothy Circle Las Cruces NM 88001-1625 Office: Nuclear Effects Lab PO Box 333 White Sands Missile Range NM 88002

SALMON, CHARLES RAY, manufacturing company executive, professional engineer; b. Stockton, Mo., Oct. 18, 1927; s. John Ray and Eunice May (Jones) S.; m. Billie Jean Finnell, Sept. 5, 1950; children: Jon Wheaton, Steven Clay, Christopher Craig. B.A., Pomona Coll., 1950; postgrad. U. Wis., 1950-51, UCLA, 1951-52. Registered profl. engr., Calif. Pres. Evans Industries West, Los Angeles, 1975—, Le Clos de Salmon, Inc., Lafayette, Calif., 1979—; vice chmn. Ball Brass & Aluminum, Auburn, Ind., 1979—; dir. Evans Industries, Inc., Detroit; cons., dir. various corps. Mem. Am. Inst. Indsl. Engrs. (sr.), Phi Beta Kappa. Republican. Calvinist. Author: The Book of Purpose, 1974; Introduction to the Fourth Dimension, 1974, Les Croyances Normandes, 1984.

SALMON, MERLYN LEIGH, laboratory executive; b. Macksville, Kans., June 24, 1924; s. Kenneth Elbert and Inez Melba (Prose) S.; student U. Kans., 1943-44; BS, U. Denver, 1951, MS, 1952; m. Flora Charlotte Sievers, Mar. 20, 1948; children: Charla Lee, Merlyn Leigh. Rsch. engr. Denver Rsch. Inst., U. Denver, 1951-56; owner-operator Fluo-X-Spec Lab., Denver, 1956—; cons. in field. With AUS, 1943-45, 45-47. Mem. Am. Chem. Soc., Soc. for Applied Spectroscopy (Outstanding Svc. award 1970), Am. Soc. Metals, Sigma Xi, Tau Beta Pi, Phi Lambda Upsilon. Omicron Delta Kappa. Democrat. Contbr. articles to profl. jours; editor column Applied Spectroscopy. Address: 718 Sherman St Denver CO 80203

SALMON, RAYMOND MERLE, cartoonist, creative arts educator; b. Akron, Colo., Sept. 6, 1931; m. Donna E. Hartness; children: Lynne A., Stephen L., Jennifer L. MFA, U. No. Colo., 1965. Artist Salmon Studios, Vallejo, Calif., 1960—; chmn. dept. fine arts John F. Kennedy U., Orinda, Calif., 1966-74; dean Sch. Creative Arts Solano Community Coll., Suisun City, Calif., 1977—. Author: The Little Man, 1979, rev. edit., 1988. Mem. Nat. Cartoonist Soc., Soc. Profl. Journalists. Office: PO Box 712 Vallejo CA 94590

SALMON, STEPHEN RUSH, computer company executive; b. Brownsville, Tenn., Jan. 28, 1933; s. Stuart Hansell and Gladys Dorothy (Dornblaser) S.; m. Susan Humphrey, July 13, 1955 (div. July 1973); children: Charles Stuart, Dorothy Elizabeth, Catherine Gwynne, Margaret Anne, Thomas Andrew, Carolyn Emily; m. Christina Olton, Sept. 24, 1973; 1 child, Holly Carina. Student, Austin Coll., Sherman, Tex., 1951-53, UCLA, 1955; AB with honors, U. Calif., Berkeley, 1957, MLS, 1958. Librarian George

Mason U., Fairfax, Va., 1959-6l; asst. chief photoduplication Library of Congress, Washington, 1962-64, asst. dir. processing, 1966-69; assoc. dir. libraries Washington U., St. Louis, 1964-66; pres. Xerox Bibliographics, Cheverly, Md., 1969-7l; dir. libraries U. Houston, 197l-75; asst. v.p. U. Calif., Berkeley, 1976-83; chmn. Carlyle Systems, Inc., Emeryville, Calif., 1983—. Author: Library of Congress Microfilming, 1964, Library Automation Systems, 1975, University of California Libraries: A Plan, 1977; compiler, editor: Library Automation, 1969. Recipient Superior Svc. award Library of Congress, 1968. Mem. ALA (coun. 1965-67, 74-78), Library and Info. Tech. Assn. (pres. 1966-67, bd. dirs. 1967-68), Am. Radio Relay League, Seven Seas Cruising Assn., Berkeley Yacht Club (commodore. 1988). Home: 2915 Shasta Rd Berkeley CA 94708 Office: 5750 Hollis St Emeryville CA 94608

SALMON, VINCENT, acoustical consultant; b. Kingston, Jamaica, Jan. 21, 1912; came to U.S., 1914; s. Albert James and Ethlin (Baruch) S.; m. Madeline L. Giuffra, June 11, 1937 (dec. 1977); children—Margaret Elizabeth, Jean Louise. B.A., Temple U., 1934, M.A., 1936; Ph.D., MIT, 1938. Registered profl. engr., Calif., Ill. Physicist research and devel. Jensen Mfg. Co., Chgo., 1939-49; mgr. sonics sect. Stanford Research Inst., Menlo Park, Calif., 1949-65; staff scientist SRI Internat., Menlo Park, Calif., 1965—; acoustical cons., Chgo., 1946-49, Menlo Park, 1949-71, 76—; dir. Acoustical Services, v.p., sec. Indsl. Health, Inc., 1971-76; cons. prof. dept. aeronautics and astronautics Stanford U., Calif., 1977—. Contbr. articles to profl. jours.; inventor new family of horns, 1942, 46. Pres. Palo Alto Sr. Housing Project, Calif., 1966; v.p. Stebbins Found. for Community Facilities, San Francisco, 1966; pres. Planned Parenthood Assn. of Santa Clara County, 1967, Sr. Coordinating Council of Palo Alto, 1971. Recipient Disting. Alumnus award Temple U., Phila., 1964. Fellow Acoustical Soc. Am. (pres. 1970-71, Biennial award 1946, Silver Medal in engring. acoustics 84), Audio Engring. Soc. (life charter, western v.p. 1958-59); mem. Chgo. Audio and Acoustical Group (founder, pres. 1948), Inst. Noise Control Engring. (pres. 1974-75), Nat. Council of Acoustical Cons. (pres. 1969-71). Democrat. Unitarian. Club: Stanford Faculty. Home: 765 Hobart St Menlo Park CA 94025

SALOIS, KATHY LOUISE, nurse; b. Lexington, Va., Nov. 11, 1946; d. Donald Jones and Margaret Elizabeth (Secor) Skerritt; m. Chane Weymer Salois, Mar. 18, 1968; children: Charles Vincent, Jason Drew. BS in Nursing, Mont. State U., 1969. RN. Office nurse Dr. John Heetderks, Bozeman, Mont., 1969-70; staff nurse Fergus County Hosp., Lewistown, Mont., 1970; office nurse St. John's Luth. Hosp., Lander, Wyo., 1971; nurse Indian Health Svc., various locations, 1972-77; sch. nurse Troy (Mont.) Pub. Schs., 1975-76; community health nurse Indian Health Svc., Nespelem, Wash., 1978-83; home health nurse Lake County Home Health, Polson, Mont., 1984-87; clinic nurse Kicking Horse Job Corp., Ronan, Mont., 1985-86; instr. Salish-Kootenai Coll., Pablo, Mont., 1984-87; pub. health nurse Confederated Salish & Kootenai Tribes, Ronan, 1987—; preceptor Pacific Luth. U., Tacoma, Wash., 1978-83; bd. mem. ad hoc com. Grand Coulee Dam (Wash.) Schs., 1983. Den mother Cub Scouts Am., Lame Deer, Mont., 1977-78, Coulee Dam, 1978-82. Mem. Panther Booster Club, Polson Booster Club. Lutheran. Home: PO Box 591 Polson MT 59860

SALSBURY, BARBARA GRACE, consumer specialist, consultant, author, lecturer, enterprises executive; b. Toledo, Dec. 27, 1937; d. Vincent Joseph and Dorothy Minerva (Ramm) Thayer; m. Larry Philip Salsbury, Sept. 24, 1959; children—Erin Scott, Sandi Grace Salsbury Simmons. Student El Camino Coll., 1954-56; student in Resource Mgmt. and Home Econs., Brigham Young U., 1975—. Spl. faculty mem. Brigham Young U., Provo, Utah, 1972—; consumer specialist Channel 20 TV Salt Lake City; shopping expert Gt. Am. Homemaker Show, U.S.A. Cable TV; guest lectr., condr. workshops and seminars on consumerism, emergency homepreparedness, practical home mgmt., supermarket survival, self improvement, various groups U.S., Can., 1961—. Leader, tchr. Women's Relief Soc. Orgn. Calif.-Wash., 1960—. Author: Just Add Water, 1972; Tasty Imitations, 1973; Just in Case, 1975; If You Must Work, 1976; Cut Your Grocery Bills in Half, 1982; booklets: The Lowly Little Lentil, 1971, Basic Home Drying of Fruits and Vegetables, 1975, Plan or Panic, 1983, The Best Time to Buy, 1985, Supermarket Survival, 1985, Emergency Evacuation!, 1986. Mem. Utah Authors League. Mormon. Office: PO Box 1305 Orem UT 84057

SALTA, STEVEN ANTHONY, infosystems executive; b. Portland, Oreg., Oct. 10, 1955; s. Joseph L. and Juanita M. (Sharp) S. BA, Portland State U., 1978. Systems specialist Multnomah County Edn. Service Dist., Portland, 1978-79; team leader Tektronix, Inc., Beaverton, Oreg., 1979-81, project mgr., 1981-83, systems devel. mgr., 1983-85, infosystems mgr., 1985-89; mgr. automation sales Sequent Computer Systems, Inc., Beaverton, 1989—; cons. Custom Software Systems, San Francisco, 1980-85; bd. dirs. The Excellence Found., Mindnet, Inc., 1988—; founder, pres. Salta Assocs., Portland, 1988. Contbr. articles to profl. jours. Mem. adv. bd. Boy Scouts Am., 1974, presently active; mem. computer sci. adv. bd. Portland Pub. Schs., 1980; mem. steering com. Oregon Mus. of Sci. and Industry, 1988; bd. dirs. The Excellence Found., Portland, 1987—. Recipient Eagle Scout award Boy Scouts Am., 1969, William T. Hornaday award Boy Scouts Am., 1973. Mem. Data Processing Mgmt. Assn., Assn. Systems Mgmt. (Spl. Achievement award 1984), Assn. Computing Machinery, Computer Soc. of IEEE, Computer Profls. for Social Responsibility. Club: Hampton Court (Portland). Office: Sequent Computer Systems Inc 15450 SW Koll Pkwy Beaverton OR 97006

SALTER, JAMES H., lawyer; b. Stockton, Calif., Jan. 20, 1955; s. Robert K. and Jean L. (Kolb) S.; m. Pamela J. Polk, Aug. 13, 1983;. BS in Computer Sci., U. So. Calif., 1978; JD, U. Puget Sound Law Sch., Tacoma, 1988. Bar: Wash. 1988; lic. pvt. pilot; cert. scuba diver. Software engr. Gen. Dynamics Inc., Pomona, Calif., 1978-80; v.p., co-owner Micro Projects Co., Culver City, Calif., 1979-82; computer cons. Intercon Systems Corp., Cerritos, Calif., 1980-82, Seattle, 1982-89; pvt. practice Seattle, 1988-89; assoc. Blakely, Sokoloff, Taylor & Zafman, Sunnyvale, Calif., 1989—. Mem. ABA, Wash. State Bar Assn., Am. Intell. Prop. Law Assn., Computer Law Assn., Wash. Software Assn. Republican. Home: 480 Westlake Dr San Jose CA 95117

SALTMAN, SHELDON ARTHUR, television sports promoter and producer; b. Boston, Aug. 17, 1933; s. Nathan Herbert and Rose (Governman) S.; m. Mollie Heifetz, Aug. 26, 1956; children: Steven Gary, Lisa Faye. BA, U. Mass., 1953; postgrad., Boston Coll., 1956-58; MS, Boston U., 1984. Pres., chief exec. officer sports div. 20th Century Fox; exec. v.p., gen. mgr. 20th Century Fox-Telecommunications; exec. v.p. Calif. Sports (Lakers, Kings, Forum); v.p. advt., promotion, mktg. and pub. rels. MCA-TV; pres. Saltman Assocs; v.p. spl. projects Lorimar Telepictures; pres. Cinetex '88, Encino, Calif.; bd. dirs. Prism Entertainment, Phila., Hollywood Home Theatre, N.Y.C., Fanfare Pay TV, Houston, Choice Channel, L.A.; mktg. cons. World Cup Soccer, 1985; guest lectr., instr. mktg., promotion mgmt. and TV prodn. U. Mass., U. Ariz., Calif. State U., Northridge, 1970-; keynote speaker Internat. Sports Summit, Monte Carlo, 1977, Nat. High Sch. Fedn., Cambridge, Mass. Author: Evel Knievel on Tour, 1977;creator, exec. producer final event Olympic Salute Week, 1980. Event-TV cons. adv. bd. Nat. Fitness Inst. of President's Coun. on Phys. Fitness, 1980-; vol. TV coord., asst. commr. for boxing, 1984 Olympics. Recipient Outstanding Trade Promotion-Mktg. award Broadcast Promotion Assn., 1964, Broadcast Promotion Man of Yr. award, 1965; named one of 5 men who did most for women in sports in 1970's, Women's Sports mag., 1979. Mem. NATAS (blue ribbon panel 1966), AFTRA, SAG, Am. Film Inst. Jewish.

SALVAGNO, WILLIAM ROBERT, JR., stockbroker; b. Corning, Calif., Aug. 28, 1947; s. William Robert and Annie Sue (Hopkins) S.; m. Ann Maria Salinas, July 5, 1975; children: Robert William, Lita Diana, Alexa Sue. BA, Chico State Coll., 1969; MS, U. Tex., San Antonio, 1975. Registered rep., N.Y. Environ. sanitarian L.A. County Health Dept., Inglewood, Calif., 1969-71; rsch. assoc. Tex. Transp. Inst., College Station, 1974-75; systems mgr. Alamo Area Coun. Govts., San Antonio, 1975-77; pres. Allied Energy Systems Inc., Chico, Calif., 1977-81; v.p. investments Paine Webber, Chico, 1981—; pacesetter Paine Webber, Chico, 1982-88, mem. direct investment adv. bd., 1982-87. Producer, writer TV film Stream Surveys, 1973; co-producer TV film Bacteriological Analysis of Water, 1972. Bd. dirs. Chico Youth Football, 1988. With U.S. Army, 1971-74. Recipient Mgmt. Devel. award Paine Webber, N.Y.C., 1987. Mem. Rotary, Elks. Republican. Episcopalian. Home: 580 Grand Smokey Ct Chico CA 95926 Office: Paine Webber 1051 Mangrove Ave Chico CA 95926

SALVERSON, CAROL ANN, library administrator, clergywoman; b. Buffalo, June 30, 1944; d. Howard F. and Estella G. (Zelie) Heavener; B.A. in Philosophy, SUNY, Buffalo, 1966; M.S. in Library Sci., Syracuse U., 1968; grad. Sacred Coll. Jamilian Theology and Div. Sch., 1976. Library trainee and research asst. SUNY, Med. Center, Syracuse, 1966-67; asst. editor SUNY Union List of Serials, Syracuse, 1967-68; readers services librarian, asst. prof. Jefferson Community Coll., Watertown, N.Y., 1968-75; ordained to ministry Internat. Community of Christ Ch., 1974; adminstr. public services dept. Internat. Community of Christ, Chancellery, Reno, 1975-84, dir. Jamilian Theol. Research Library, 1975—; mem. faculty Sacred Coll. Jamilian U. of the Ordained, Reno, 1979—, Jamilian Parochial Sch., Internat. Community of Christ, 1978—. Chmn. religious edn. com. All Souls Unitarian-Universalist Ch., Watertown, N.Y., 1970-71, treas., 1974-75; trustee North Country Reference and Research Resources Council, Canton, N.Y., 1974-75; dir. Gene Savoy Heritage Museum and Library, 1984—; violist Symphonietta, Reno, 1983—. Mem. ALA, Nev. Library Assn., Friends of Library Washoe County, Friends of Library U. Nev. Club: Coll. Women's. Contbr. articles on library sci. to profl. jours. Home: 2025 La Fond Dr Reno NV 89509 Office: Internat Community of Christ Chancellory 643 Ralston St Reno NV 89503

SALVESON, MELVIN ERWIN, business executive, educator; b. Brea, Calif., Jan. 16, 1919; s. John T. and Elizabeth (Green) S.; m. Joan Y. Stipek, Aug. 22, 1944; children: Eric C., Kent Erwin. B.S., U. Calif. at Berkeley, 1941; M.S., Mass. Inst. Tech., 1947; Ph.D., U. Chgo., 1952. Cons. McKinsey & Co., N.Y.C., 1948-49; asst. prof., dir. mgmt. sci. research U. Calif. at Los Angeles, 1949-54; mgr. advanced data systems Gen. Electric Co., Louisville and N.Y.C., 1954-57; pres. Mgmt. Scis. Corp., Los Angeles, 1957-67; group v.p. Control Data/CEIR, Inc., 1967-68; pres. Electronic Currency Corp., 1968—; chmn. OneCard Internat., Inc., 1983—; bd. dirs. OneCard Internat. Inc., Diversified Earth Scis., Inc., Algeran, Inc., Electronic Currency Corp.; founder Master Card System, Los Angeles, 1966; chmn. Corporate Strategies Internat.; prof. bus. Pepperdine U. 1972-85; adj. prof. U. So. Calif.; adviser data processing City of Los Angeles, 1962-64; futures forecasting IBM, 1957-61; adviser strategic systems planning USAF, 1961-67; info. systems Calif. Dept. Human Resources, 1972-73, City Los Angeles Automated Urban Data Base, 1962-67; tech. transfer NASA, 1965-70, others; mem. bd. trustees, Long Beach City Coll. Contbr. articles to profl. jours. Served to lt. comdr. USNR, 1941-46. Named to Long Beach City Coll. Hall of Fame. Fellow AAAS; mem. Inst. Mgmt. Sci. (founder, past pres.). Republican. Club: Founders (Los Angeles Philharmonic Orch.), Calif. Yacht. Home: 1577 N Bundy Dr Los Angeles CA 90049

SALYER, JON DAVID, systems and management consultant; b. Chillicothe, Ohio, Mar. 8, 1939; s. Herbert Salyer and Nora Catherine (Jenks) Preis; m. Joan Elizabeth Vernier, Dec. 19, 1975; children: Michael David, Michele Lynne, Frederick Lawrence Huston. BS in Bus. cum laude, Wright State U., 1971; MA in Mgmt., Cen. Mich. U., 1974. Hdqrs. supr. logistics command USAF, Wright-Patterson AFB, Ohio, 1966-76; MIS dir. U.S. Dept. Energy, Oakland, Calif., 1976-84; prin. S.I.S. Cons., Penn Valley, Calif., 1984—; instr. Golden Gate U., San Francisco, 1984. With USN, 1957-60. Mem. Fedn. Govt. Info. Processing Councils, Intergovtl. Council for Telecommunications and Info. Processing. Home and Office: 11334 Buckeye Cir Penn Valley CA 95946

SALZMAN, MARILYN B. WOLFSON, service company executive; b. Chgo., Dec. 25, 1943; d. Joseph and Sera (Krol) Wolfson; 1 son, Lawrence Todd. Student, U. Ill., Barat Coll., Lake Forest, Ill., 1961-64. Adminstrv. project asst. Sci. Research Assocs., Chgo., 1964-70; reporter Suburban Trib of Chgo. Tribune, 1979-80; pres. MWS Assocs., Los Angeles and Fullerton, Calif., 1980—; exec. adminstrv. dir. Crystal Tips of No. Ill., Inc., 1980-83; dir. adminstrn. Ice Dispensers, Inc., 1981-83, Sani-Serv of Ill., Inc., 1981-83; adminstrv. and organizational cons. 1140 Corp., 1980-83; adminstrv. dir. Iceman's Ico Co., Inc., 1980-83; founder, moderator DWC Workshops, 1984; mgr. support svcs., data processing Florence Crittenton Svcs. Orange County 1984—; panelist computers in residential treatment Child Welfare League Am. Biennial Conf. Workshop, 1986. Active Friends of Fullerton Library, Boy Scouts Am.; panelist Child Welfare League Am., Bienniel Conf. Workshop. Mem. Mgmt. Forum, Women's Am. ORT. Contbr. articles to newspapers and indsl. jours. Home: 1112 N Ferndale Dr Fullerton CA 92631

SAM, DAVID, judge; b. Hobart, Ind., Aug. 12, 1933; s. Andrew and Flora (Toma) S.; m. Betty Jean Brennan, Feb. 1, 1957; children: Betty Jean, David Dwight, Daniel Scott, Tamara Lynn, Pamela Rae, Daryl Paul, Angie, Sheyla. BS, Brigham Young U., 1957; JD, Utah U., 1960. Bar: Utah 1960, U.S. Dist. Ct. Utah 1966. Sole practice Duchesne, Utah, 1963-76; dist. judge State of Utah, 1976-85; judge U.S. Dist. Ct. Utah, Salt Lake City, 1985—; atty. City of Duchesne, 1963-72, Duchesne County, 1966-72; commr. Duchesne County, 1972-74; mem. adv. com. on Codes of Conduct of the Jud. Conf. U.S., 1987—. Chmn. Jud. Nomination Com. for Cir. Ct. Judge, Provo, Utah, 1983; bd. dirs. Water Resources, Salt Lake City, 1973-76. Served to capt. JAGC, USAF, 1961-63. Mem. ABA, Utah Bar Assn., Am. Judicature Soc., Am. Inns of Ct. VII (counseler 1986—), Utah Jud. Conf. (chmn. 1982—), Utah Dist. Judges Assn. (pres. 1982-83). Mormon. Home: 1171 E 300 North Springville UT 84663 Office: US Dist Ct 148 US Courthouse 350 S Main St Salt Lake City UT 84101

SAMANIEGO, PAMELA SUSAN, advertising agency director; b. San Mateo, Calif., Nov. 29, 1952; d. Armando C. and Harriott Susan (Croot) S. Student, UCLA, 1972, Los Angeles Valley Coll., 1970-72. Asst. new accts. supr. Beverly Hills Fed. Savings, 1970-72; asst. controller Bio-Science Enterprises, Van Nuys, Calif., 1972-74; adminstr. asst. Avery/Tirce Prodns., Hollywood, Calif., 1974-78; sr. estimator N. Lee Lacy and Assocs., Hollywood, 1978-81; head of prodn. Film Consortium, Hollywood, 1981-82; exec. producer EUE/Screen Gems Ltd., Burbank, Calif., 1982-88; advt. agency dir. Barrett & Assocs., Las Vegas, Nev., 1988—. Author: Millimeter & Backstage, 1982-88. Emergency room vol. San Mateo (Calif.) County Hosp., 1968-70; Sunday sch. tchr. Hillsdale Meth. Ch., San Mateo, 1968-70; vol. worker Hillsdale Meth. Ch. Outreach, San Francisco, 1967-70. Recipient CLIO award CLIO Awards, Inc., 1985, ADDY award Las Vegas Advt. Fedn., 1988. Mem. Dirs. Guild Am. (2nd asst. dir. 1987-88), Assn. Ind. Comml. Producers, Am. Horse Show Assn., Internat. Arabian Horse Assn., AHASFV (sec. 1978-79), AHASC (sec. 1978-88). Democrat. Methodist. Home: 3285 W Martin Circle Las Vegas NV 89118 Office: Barrett and Assocs 2000 E Flamingo Rd Ste A Las Vegas NV 89119

SAMBORSKI, ROBERT MICHAEL, association executive; b. Fayetteville, N.C., Oct. 12, 1950; s. Henry John and Rose Helen (Vahila) S.; m. Sheila Miller Wylie, Sept. 1, 1978; children: Andrew Wylie, Catriona Anne. BA in Psychology, U. Colo., 1972; M Pub., Internat. Affairs, Tex. Christian U., 1976. Project mgr. Roy Jorgenson Assocs., Inc., Gaithersburg, Md., 1977-79; dir. mem. svcs. Am. Pub. Works Assn., Chgo., 1979-84; v.p. Burke & Assocs., Inc., Aurora, Colo., 1984-88; exec. dir. AM/FM Internat., Englewood, Colo., 1988—. Co-author textbook: Public Works Organizations, 1983; contbr. articles to various jours., newsletters. Mem. Citizens Com. on Village Water Supply, Park Forest, Ill., 1983; mem. Smoky Hill Homeowners' Assn., Aurora, 1987. 2d lt. U.S. Army, 1972-75. Mem. Urban and Regional Info. Systems Assn., Am. Pub. Works Assn. (edn. chmn. 1986-88), Am. Gas Assn., Am. Soc. Assn. Execs., Grad. Students of Pub. and Internat. Affairs Tex. Christian U. Roman Catholic. Office: AM FM Internat Ste 820 8775 E Orchard Rd Englewood CO 80111

SAMEYAH, RAMIN DAVID, textile executive; b. Santa Monica, Calif., June 1, 1965; s. Imanouel and Zari (Khazaie) S. BS in Internat. Mktg., Pepperdine U., 1986. Textile broker Imantex Textile Enterprises, L.A., 1986—; sales and motivation trainer Cioffi and Kane Seminars & Recruting Specialist, Encino, Calif., 1987—. Fellow Textile Assn. L.A., Inc.; mem. Beverly Hills Health & Fitness. Republican. Jewish. Home: 262 N Crescent Dr Beverly Hills CA 90210-4852 Office: Imantex Textile Enterprises 117 W 9th St Ste 1220 Los Angeles CA 90015

SAMLOFF, I. MICHAEL, gastroenterology educator; b. Rochester, N.Y., Jan. 24, 1932; s. Max and Bluma (Rabinovitz) S.; divorced; children: Ann, David. Student, Cornell U., 1949-52; MD cum laude, SUNY, Syracuse, 1956. From asst. to assoc. prof. gastroenterology U. Rochester (N.Y.) Sch. Med., 1965-68, asst. prof. psychiatry, 1965-68; assoc. prof. U. So. Calif. Sch. Med., Los Angeles, 1968-72; prof. UCLA, 1972—; assoc. chief of staff research VA Med. Ctr., Sepulveda, Calif., 1980—; chief div. gastroenterology Harbor-UCLA Med. Ctr., 1968-80; investigator Ctr. for Ulcer Research and Edn., Los Angeles, 1974—. Editor: The Genetics and Heterogeneity of Common Gastrointestinal Disorders, 1980, Pepsinogens in Man: Clinial and Genetic Advances, 1985. Served to capt. USAF, 1959-61. Fellow ACP; mem. Am. Gastroenterol. Assn., Am. Soc. Clin. Investigation, Western Assn. of Physicians, Western Soc. for Clin. Research. Home: 3611 Sapphire Dr Encino CA 91436 Office: VA Med Ctr Rsch 151 16111 Plummer St Sepulveda CA 91343

SAMOJLA, SCOTT ANTHONY, accountant; b. Chgo., Dec. 29, 1955; s. Richard John and Jane Louise (Novesel) S. BS in Acctg., So. Ill. U., 1978; postgrad., U. So. Calif., 1987—. Staff acct. Price Waterhouse & Co., Chgo., 1979-81; sr. ops. acct. McGraw-Edison Co., Rolling Meadows, Ill., 1982-83; sr. internal auditor McGraw-Edison Co., Rolling Meadows, 1983-85; asst. controller Dresser Industries Masoneilan N.Am. ops., Montebello, Calif., 1985, controller, 1985—. Mem. Am. Inst. CPA's, Ill. Soc. CPA's (younger mem. com. 1982-83). Republican. Home: 7165 Leota Canoga Park CA 91304 Office: Dresser Industries Masoneilan NA Ops 1040 S Vail Ave Montebello CA 90814

SAMOY, GREGORIO DALUZ, JR., pediatrician; b. Manila, Mar. 21, 1929; Came to U.S, 1973; s. Gregorio T. Sr. and Marcela (Daluz) S.; m. Laura Navarrete, 1956; children: Deborah May, Vernon Joey, Sarah Liz. AA, U. Philippines, 1950; MD, Manila Cen. U., 1955. Resident in pediatrics Mary Johnson Hosp., Manila, 1957-60; house physician Am. Hosp. Manila, 1960-61; resident in pediatrics Beth Israel Med. Ctr., N.Y.C., 1961-64; sr. resident in pediatrics Meml.-Sloan Kettering Ctr., N.Y.C., 1964-65; research assoc. in pediatrics and oncology St. Jude Children's Research Hosp., Memphis, 1965-66; sr. research assoc.in pediatrics and oncology Exxon Indonesia, S. Gerong, 1967-71; med. officer Mobil Oil Indonesia, Sumatra, 1971-73; ambulatory med. officer U. Chgo. Hosp., 1973-74; pvt. practice in pediatrics Clinton, Mass., 1974-78; staff pediatrician El Rio Santa Cruz Health Ctr., Tucson, 1978—; sr. lectr. dept. pediatrics Univ. Med. Ctr., Tucson, 1978—. Fellow Am. Acad. Pediatrics. Home: 4461 N Avenida Cazador Tucson AZ 85718 Office: El Rio Santa Cruz Health Ctr 839 W Congress Tucson AZ 85745

SAMPLE, CORLIS HARU, graphic designer; b. Long Beach, Calif., Aug. 18, 1955; d. Donald Reid and Kiyoko (Hasegawa) S. BFA, U. Tex., Arlington, 1979. Prodn. artist Typeset, Inc., Dallas, 1979-80, Nichols Advt., Dallas, 1980-81; asst. advt. dir. Jas. K. Wilson, Dallas, 1981-82; layout designer Frederick & Nelson, Seattle, 1983-84; asst. art dir. Leni, Inc., Marina del Rey, Calif., 1984; sr. layout designer, asst. art dir. The Broadway, L.A., 1984—; art. dir. Vera White/Ware Assocs., L.A., 1988. Grantee U. Tex., 1978-79. Mem. Amnesty Internat. (freedom writer 1986—). Democrat. Roman Catholic. Home: 433 N Jackson St Apt 311 Glendale CA 91206

SAMPLE, MARVIN EDWARD, insurance executive; b. Etowah, Tenn., Aug. 10, 1928; s. Sara (Waits) S.; m. Colleen Dakan, Feb. 18, 1950 (dec. 1961); children: Marvin E. Jr., Robert J., Richard J., Martin W.; m. Jacqueline Mae Grant, Apr. 1, 1985. Student, U. Ala., 1947-49. Gen. agt. Mass. Mut. Life Ins. Co., El Paso, Tex., 1952-70; v.p. Life of Calif., Los Angeles, 1970-76; pres. Sample Fin. Ins. Mktg. Corp., Los Angeles and Palm Desert, Calif., 1976—. V.p. El Paso Heart Assn., 1961, El Paso Cancer Soc., 1961-62; active Lincoln Reps., Palos Verdes, Calif., 1970-80; mem. Rep. Pres. Task Force, 1985—. Served as capt. U.S. Army, 1949-52. Baptist. Club: Chaparral Country (Palm Desert). Home: 25 Camino Arroyo N Palm Desert CA 92260 Office: Sample Fin Ins Mktg Corp 74-075 El Paseo A-6 Palm Desert CA 92260

SAMPLEY, FRANKLIN D., JR., foundation administrator; b. Lebanon, Ind., Dec. 30, 1958; s. Franklin D. and Dorothy Jane (Flanagan) S. Student, Cameron U., 1979-80, Christian Life Coll., 1980-81; AA, San Joaquin Delta Coll., 1984; BS in Orgnl. Behavior, U. San Francisco, 1989. Lic. cosmetology instr., cert. tchr., Calif. Svc. asst. Social Security Adminstrn., Duncan, Okla., 1977-79; tchr. Jonet Dee, Inc., Lodi, Calif., 1982-84; owner/operator Best Little Hairhouse in Lodi, 1984; supr. instr. Jonet Dee, Inc., Stockton, Calif., 1984-86; fin. aid administr., asst. gen. mgr. Jonet Dee, Inc., Lodi, 1986-88; exec. dir. San Joaquin Aids Founds., Stockton, 1988—. Tchr. Duncan (Okla.) Apostolic Christian Sch., 1978-79; facilitator Gays and Friends, U. of Pacific, Stockton, 1983-86; chief fiscal officer, San Joaquin Aids Found., Stockton, 1986-88. Mem. Calif. Assn. Student Fin. Aid Administrs. Democrat. Office: San Joaquin Aids Found 4410 N Pershing Ste C-5 Stockton CA 95207

SAMPLINER, DONALD WALLACE, record producer; b. Cleve., May 4, 1928; s. Jerome Mortimer and Charlotte J. Sampliner; B.A., UCLA, 1941, M.A., 1949; postgrad. Calif. State U.-Los Angeles, 1952-53; DSc City U. L.A., 1988. Tchr., Los Angeles City Schs., 1948-75; lectr. psychology Los Angeles City Coll., 1952-84; host radio program Sta. KPFK, 1971-74, Sta. KMAX-FM, 1973-78; prod., annotator phonograph records, 1982—. Coordinator, CanServ program Good Samaritan Hosp., 1975; pres. Canyon Dr. Hollywood Hills Improvement Assn., 1977-80. Mem. Am. Psychol. Assn., Am. Fedn. Tchrs. Coll. Guild, Theatre Hist. Soc., Am. Theatre Organ Soc. (chmn. Los Angeles chpt. 1961-62). Home: 5823 Green Oak Dr Hollywood CA 90068

SAMPSON, ARTHUR LEE, engineering executive; b. Davenport, Iowa, May 9, 1944; s. William Henry and Margaret (Cundiff) S.; m. Dorcas Eglentine, Apr. 5, 1969; 1 child, Bridget René. ASEE, Eastern Iowa Community Coll., Davenport, 1968; BSEE, Iowa State U., 1976. Product area mgr. Hach Co., Loveland, Colo., 1968—. With U.S. Army, 1962-65. Mem. ASTM, Instrument Soc. Am., Am. Legion, Elks. Home: 3210 Logan Loveland CO 80538 Office: Hach Co 5600 Lindbergh Dr Loveland CO 80538

SAMPSON, CAROL ANN, interior design firm executive, writer; b. Wabash, Ind., Dec. 5, 1942; d. John Roland Bennett and Virginia Ann (Garthwait) Mulholland; student Bradley U., 1961-62; AA, Riverside City Coll., 1971; BS cum laude, Woodbury U., 1975; children: Tracy Lee, John Russell IV (Arrison). Interior designer Imperial Co., Riverside, Calif., 1971-72; asso. interior designer Booth & Assos., Riverside, 1972-74; owner, prin., project designer Carol Sampson's Interior Designs, Riverside, 1974—; tchr. interior design bus. procedures San Bernardino Valley Coll., 1978-80; house and home editor Inland Empire mag., 1978—; interior design staff writer Inland Empire Bus. Quar., 1978-81; home interiors editor for Inland News on cable TV for Falcon, Liberty and Group P-W stas.; interior design cons. radio program Sta. KPRO, Riverside, 1978-81. Recipient Gold Key award (2), Nat. Home Fashions League, 1975, Proclamation award City of Riverside Mayor's Office, 1983. Mem. Internat. Soc. Interior Designers (profl.). Episcopalian. Office: Carol Sampson Interior Designs 2441 E Granite View Dr Phoenix AZ 85044

SAMPSON, RICHARD ARNIM, security professional; b. New Haven, June 9, 1927; s. Richard Arnim Sampson and Ora Viola (Reese) Jackson; m. Marilyn Jo Gardner, Jun. 10, 1950 (div. 1962); children: Gary, Susan; m. Janet Margaret Battaglia, Jan. 26, 1963 (div. 1987); children: Cynthia, David; m. Alice Annette Whitfield, July 23, 1988. BS, Mich. State U., 1951; MPA, Auburn U., 1972; grad., Air War Coll., 1972. Adminstrv. officer CIA, Washington, 1951-76; mgr. spl. projects Hughes Aircraft Co., El Segundo, Calif., 1976-80; mgr. security Advanced Systems div. Northrop Aircraft Co., Pico Rivera, Calif., 1980-83, Electronics div. Gen. Dynamics Corp., San Diego, 1983—; instr., Southwest L.A. Coll., 1979-80, Nat.Mgmt. Assn., San Diego, 1983. Author: Excessive Bureaucracy-Causes and Cures, 1972. Active, Boy Scouts Am., McLean, Va., 1974, Palos Verdes, Calif., 1978. Mem. Am. Soc. Indsl. Security (chmn. 1958-59), Signa Soc., CIA Retirees Assn. (treas. 1986-87), Assn. Former Intelligence Officers, Nat. Mgmt. Assn., Indsl. Security Working Group (bd. dirs. 1987-88), Contractor SAR/SAP Working Group, Secutiy Affairs Support Assn. Republican. Home: 1408 Westwood Pl Escondido CA 92026

SAMSON, ANTHONY DONALD, lawyer; b. Huntington Park, Calif., Nov. 27, 1933; s. Nick and Alice Marguerite (Livingston) Hulbert S.; m. Betty White, May 1, 1957 (div. June 1964); 1 child, Nickie Michelle; m. Gloria Perez, Jan. 30, 1965; children: Ixchel Alyssa, Kyra Marina. AA, Riverside City Coll., 1958; AB, U. Calif., Riverside, 1963; JD, UCLA, 1968. Bar: Calif. 1969, U.S. Dist. Ct. (so. dist.) Calif. 1969. Asst. credit mgr. Sears Roebuck & Co., Riverside, Calif., 1957-65; pvt. practice, Riverside, 1968-70; chief fraud div. San Diego Dist. Atty.'s Office, 1983—; lectr. Fla. Gov.'s Conf., Orlando, 1975, Nat. Coll. Dist. Attys., Houston, 1978; lectr., cons. Tng. Ctr., Dept. Justice, Sacramento, 1978—; instr. real estate U. San Diego. Treas. Dem. Profl. Club, San Diego, 1978—; del. State Dem. Conv., Sacramento, 1983, Conf. Dels. to State Bar, 1985-86; bd. dirs. Utility Consumer Action Network, San Diego, 1983; mem. consumer edn. trust disbursement com. Pub. Utilities Commn., 1988—; treas. disbursement com., Telecommunications Edn. Trust of Calif. Pub. Utilities Commn. With U.S. Army, 1953-55, Korea, Japan. Recipient Cert. of Appreciation, So. Calif. Fraud Investigators, Ventura, 1982, 83, Disting. Service award Calif. Dist. Atty. Investigators Santa Barbara, 1983. Mem. Consumer Protection Council (sec. 1980-83), State Bar Calif. (exec. com. real property sect. 1985-88, consumer fin. subcom. bus. law sect. 1986-89, del. conf. of dels. 1984-86), Calif. Dist. Attys. Assn., San Diego County Bar Assn., San Diego Lawyer's Club. Democrat. Episcopalian. Office: San Diego Dist Atty 220 W Broadway San Diego CA 92103

SAMUELSON, MITCHELL, lawyer; b. Boston, Nov. 28, 1936; s. Edward Joseph and Claire Laura Samuelson; m. Joan Oppenheimer, July 30, 1967; children: Lawrence James, Jennifer Sue. BA cum laude, Boston U., 1958, JD cum laude, 1960. Clk. to mem. NLRB, Washington, 1960-62; trial atty: tax div. U.S. Dept. Justice, Washington, 1962-67; assoc. Hurwitz & Hurwitz, Orange, Calif., 1968-71; pvt. practice Santa Ana, Calif., 1971-76; ptnr. Cohen, Stokke & Davis, Santa Ana, 1976-86, Davis, Samuelson, Blakely & Goldberg, Santa Ana, 1986—; judge pro tem Superior & Mcpl. Cts., Orange County, Calif., 1980—; designated arbitrator Superior Ct., Orange County, 1980—. Bd. dirs. Alzheimer's Assn. of Orange County, 1989. Mem. ABA (del. state bar conv. 1989), Orange County Bar Assn. (bd. dirs. 1988—, client relations com., chmn. mandatory fee arbitration 1986-88), Fed. Bar Assn. (bd. dirs. 1989—), Lincoln Club. Republican. Jewish. Office: Davis Samuelson et al 540 N Golden Circle Dr 300 Santa Ana CA 92705

SAN AGUSTIN, JOE TAITANO, Guam senator, financial institution executive, management researcher; b. Agana, Guam, Oct. 15, 1930; s. Candido S. and Maria P. (Taitano) San A.; m. Carmen Santos Shimizu, June 18, 1955; children—Mary, Ann, Joe, John. B.A., George Washington U., 1954, M.A., 1965. Chief budget and mgmt. Office of Govt. Guam, Agana, 1966-68; dir. dept. administrn. Govt. Guam, Agana, 1968-74; senator Guam Legislature, Agana, 1976—, minority leader 16th Guam Legislature, 1981-82, vice-speaker 17th Guam Legislature, 1983—, chmn. com. on ways and means 17th and 18th Guam Legislatures, 1983-86; chmn. Com. on Ways and Means 17th and 18th, 1983-86; chmn. com. on health, edn. and welfare 19th Guam Legislature, 1987; chmn. bd. dirs. Guam Greyhound, Inc., Agana, 1975-86; dir. Bank of Guam, Agana. Democrat. Roman Catholic. Office: 163 Chalan Santo Papa Agana GU 96910

SANBORN, DOROTHY CHAPPELL, librarian; b. Nashville, Apr. 26, 1920; d. William S. and Sammie Maude (Drake) Chappell; BA, U. Tex., 1941; MA, George Peabody Coll., 1947; MPA, Golden Gate U., 1982; m. Richard Donald Sanborn, Dec. 1, 1943; children: Richard Donald, William Chappell. Asst. cataloger El Paso (Tex.) Pub. Library, 1947-52, Library of Hawaii, Honolulu, 1953; cataloger Redwood (Calif.) City Pub. Library, 1954-55, 57-59, Stanford Research Inst., Menlo Park, Calif., 1955-57; librarian Auburn (Calif.) Pub. Library, 1959-62; cataloger Sierra Coll., Rocklin, Calif., 1962-64; reference librarian Sacramento City Library, 1964-66; county librarian Placer County (Calif.), Auburn, 1966-89; chmn. Mountain Valley Library System, 1970-71, 75-76, 1984-85; cons. county librarian Alpine County Library, Markleeville, Calif., 1973-80. Served with WAVES, 1944-46. Mem. AAUW (pres. chpt. 1982-84), ALA, Calif. Library Assn. Democrat. Mem. United Ch. Christ. Club: Soroptimists. Home: 135 Midway St Auburn CA 95603 Office: Auburn Placer County Libr 350 Nevada St Auburn CA 95603

SANBORN, FRANK GEORGE, physiotherapist, acupuncturist; b. Ft. Wayne, Ind., Oct. 23, 1943; s. Frank and Violet (Waring) S.; student No. Coll. Phys. Therapies Life Scis. Inst., 1976; cert. Nat. Acad. Acupuncture, 1978; children: Michael, Tabitha. Physiotherapist Vienna Clinics, until 1978; owner Stillpoint Clinics, Calgary, Alta., 1977-82; accupuncturist Royal Acupuncture Accupressure Assocs., 1980-81; nutritional cons. Can. Mt. Everest Expdn., 1982, Calgary rowing team, Can. full contact karate team; rep. Can. div. No. Coll. Phys. Therapies, Blackpool, Eng., 1976-79; dir. Northwestern Sch. Massage, Calgary, 1980—; bd. dirs. Calgary Currie Progressive Conservative Assn. Alta., 1979-84, Provincial United Found. Masseurs and Physars, 1980-81. Lic. physiotherapist. With USAF, 1962-66. Home: 1415 Quebec Ave SW, Calgary, AB Canada T2T 5R8 Office: Stillpoint Clinics Ltd, 10-519 17th Ave SW, Calgary, AB Canada T2S 0A9

SANBORN, KATHLEEN YVONNE, therapist; b. Grangeville, Idaho, Apr. 14, 1952; d. Harry James and Beatrice (Young) David; m. David F. Potter, Apr. 23, 1973 (div. Sept. 1982); children: Benjamin, Gabriel, Ona, Joshua, Matthew; m. Grant Peter Sanborn, July 21, 1983. Student, Spokane Community Coll., 1983-85, Washington State U., 1986-88, E. Washington U. Sr. youth advisor Unity Ch. Spokane, Wash., 1985—; instr. first aid ARC, Spokane, 1983—; v.p. G&R Enterprises, Spokane, 1984—. Chmn. health room unit Shaw Jr. High Sch., Spokane, 1982-84; pres. Logan Parent Assn., 1983-84; sec. Shaw Jr. High Sch., 1983-84; mem. Youth Edn., Spokane, 1986. Home: W454 23rd Ave Spokane WA 99203

SANCHEZ, ERWIN ARTURO, hair salon owner; b. Guatemala, Guatemala, Mar. 21, 1949; came to U.S., 1962; d. Manuel Francisco and Magdalena S.; m. Cynthia Ann McCarthy, June 20, 1969 (div. 1975); 1 child, Stephanie Ann; m. Kristina Nadia Shelebian, Nov. 20, 1982. Student, El Camino Coll., Torrance, Calif., 1980. Aircraft mechanic Hughes Tool Co., Culver City, Calif., 1967-71; cosmetologist Hair Dresser's Guild, L.A., 1972-84; camp supr. L.A. County Probation Dept., 1984-85; salon owner Scandal Hair Salon, L.A., 1985—; instr. Wilfred Acad., L.A., 1985-88. Editor: Skin Care International, 1979; hair cons., stylist, Your Friends and Mine, 1979, 87. With U.S. Army, 1969-71, Vietnam. Decorated Bronze medal. Mem. Masons. Republican. Roman Catholic. Home: 22040 Gault St #2 Canoga Park CA 91303

SANCHEZ, GERARD ANTHONY, engineering assistant; b. Habana, Cuba, Feb. 2, 1931; came to U.S., 1964; s. Gerardo de las Mercedes Sanchez-Fernandez and Maria Teresa Estopinan-Ramirez; m. Haydee Navarro-Gonzalez, Dec. 10, 1953 (div. 1962); 1 child, Haydee; m. Zenia Jacqueline Martinez-Hernandez, July 7, 1963 (div. Jan. 1983); children: Gerard Anthony, Raymond Manuel. Grad., Comm. Nat. Physical Edn., Habana, 1948; engine lathe operator II, Pierce Coll., Woodland Hills, Calif., 1967. Prof. physical edn. Sec. Edn., Habana, 1948-49; clk. Mcpl. Ct. 3rd Dist., Habana, 1950-61; sales distributor Robert's Tobacco Co., Habana, 1956-61; dep. adminstr. Sec. Commerce, Habana, 1961-62; asst. mgr. Reader's Digest of Mexico, Mexico, 1963-64; machinist various aircraft cos., L.A., 1964-68; craftsman Gen. Telephone Co. Calif., L.A., 1968-78, engring. asst., 1978—. Mem. Independent Telephone Pioneer Assn., Communication Workers of Am. Home: 5460 White Oak Ave E203 Encino CA 91316

SANCHEZ, GILBERT, university president, microbiologist, researcher; b. Belen, N.Mex., May 7, 1938; s. Macedonio C. and Josephine H. Sanchez; m. Lorena T. Tabet, Aug. 26, 1961; children—Elizabeth, Phillip, Katherine. B.S. in Biology, N.Mex. State U., 1961; Ph.D. in Microbiology, U. Kans., 1967. Research asst. U. Kans., Lawrence, 1963-67; research assoc., postdoctoral fellow Rice U., Houston, 1967-68; prof. N.Mex. Inst. Tech., Socorro, 1968-79; dean grad. studies Eastern N.Mex. U., Portales, 1979-83; v.p. acad. affairs U. So. Colo., Pueblo, 1983-85; pres. N.Mex. Highlands U., Las Vegas, 1985—; cons. NIH, NSF, Solvex Corp., Albuquerque, 1979-83; bd. dirs. Fed. Res. Bank, Denver. Contbr. numerous articles to profl. jours. Patentee in field. Pres. Socorro Sch. Bd., 1974-79, Presbyn. Hosp. Bd., Socorro, 1977-79. Research grantee Dept. Army, 1976-79, N.Mex. Dept. Energy, 1979-83, NSF, 1979. Mem. Am. Soc. Microbiology, Am. Soc. Indsl. Microbiology, AAAS, Am. Assn. Univs. and Colls. (bd. dirs. 1988—), Hispanic Assn. Univs. and Colls. (pres. 1986—). Roman Catholic. Lodge: Rotary. Office: NMex Highlands U Las Vegas NM 87701

SANCHEZ, LEONEDES WORTHINGTON, fashion designer; b. Flagstaff, Ariz., Mar. 15, 1951; s. Rafael Leonedes and margaret (Monarrize) S. BS, No. Ariz. U., 1974; studied, Fashion Inst. Tech., N.Y.C., 1974-75; AA, Fashion Inst. D&M, L.A., 1975. Dress designer-in-residence Flagstaff, 1978—; mem. faculty No. Ariz. U., Flagstaff, 1978-80; designer Ambiance, Inc., L.A., 1985—. Bd. dirs. Roman Cath. Social Svcs., 1985-86, Northland Crisis Nursery, 1985—, Pine Country Transit, 1986-88, also chmn.; pres. Chicanos for Edn. Recipient Comilion Design award 1988, Atlanta. Fellow Phi Alpha Theta, Pi Kappa Delta; mem. Lehesion Dela Mode Parisian. Republican.

SANCHEZ, RAYMOND G., state legislator; b. Albuquerque, Sept. 22, 1941; s. Gillie and Priscilla S.; 1 child, Raymond Michael. B.A., U. N. Mex., 1964, J.D., 1967. Bar: N. Mex. 1967. Mem. N. Mex. Ho. of Reps., 1977—, speaker, 1983-84, 87-88, 89—. Bd. dirs. Alburquerque Assn. Retarded Citizens, Gov.'s Council Criminal Justice Planning, Community Council, Albuquerque, exec. bd.; bd. dirs. NCCJ; mem. standards and goals com., Criminal Justice Dept., juvenile justice com.; mem. Alburquerque Leadership Devel. Program Steering Com., YMCA Youth and Govt. State Com., adv. com. social svcs.; bd. advisors Nat. Health Council Consumers and Providers. Mem. N. Mex. Bar Assn. (mem. con. on jud. selection and reform, law study com.), U. N. Mex. Alumni Assn. (dir.), Constrn. Industry (mem. law study com), Elks, KC, Sigma Chi. Democrat. Office: State Capitol Office of Speaker Santa Fe NM 87501 also: PO Box 1966 Albuquerque NM 87103

SANCHEZ, ROBERT FORTUNE, archbishop; b. Socorro, N.Mex., Mar. 20, 1934; s. Julius C. and Priscilla (Fortune) S. Student, Immaculate Heart Sem., Santa Fe, 1954, N.Am. Coll., Gregorian U., Rome, 1960. Ordained priest Roman Cath. Ch., 1959; prof. St. Piux X High Sch., Albuquerque, 1960-68; dir. extension lay vols. Archdiocese Santa Fe, 1965-68, chmn. priest personnel bd., 1968-72, vicar gen., 1974, archbishop, 1974—; rep. instl. ministry pastoral care N.Mex. Council Chs., 1968; pres. Archdiocesan Priests Senate, 1973-74; rep. region X Nat. Fedn. Priests Councils, 1972-73; bd. dirs. Mexican Am. Cultural Center; mem. regional com. Nat. Conf. Catholic Bishops, N.Am. Coll., Rome; pres. N.Mex. Conf. Chs. Mem. U.S. Cath. Conf. (chmn. ad hoc com. Spanish speaking). Office: The Cath Ctr Archdiocese of Santa Fe St Joseph's Pl NW Albuquerque NM 87120 *

SANCHEZ-OWENS, YVETTE ANITA, city official; b. L.A., Oct. 7, 1960; d. Ismael Gilbert and Joyce Lucille (Martinez) Sanchez; m. Stephen Brian Owens, July 14, 1984; 1 child, Stephen Brian II. BS in Pub. Affairs, U. So. Calif., 1983. Jr. adminstrv. asst. City of L.A., 1984-85, adminstrv. asst. I, 1985-86, adminstrv. asst. II, 1986-88, mgmt. analyst II, 1988–; v.p. adv. affirmative action com., City of L.A., 1987-88, pres., 1988--. Democrat. Lutheran. Home: 2746 Fyler Pl Los Angeles CA 90065 Office: City of LA Dept Gen Svcs 200 N Main St Rm 800 Los Angeles CA 90012

SAND, DONALD WAYNE, physician; b. Rugby, N.D., Feb. 1, 1943; s. Stranford A. and Lucille A. (Hartvickson) S.; married, 1966; children: Laura, Sara. BS, Jamestown Coll., 1965, U. N.D., 1967; MD, U. Wash., 1969. Diplomate Am. Bd. Internal Medicine. Practice medicine specializing in internal medicine Grants Pass, Oreg., 1975—. Served to maj. U.S. Army, 1969-75. Mem. Am. Soc. Internal Medicine, Oreg. Med. Assn., Josephine County Med. Soc. (pres. 1987). Office: 124M NW Midland Grants Pass OR 97526

SANDBACK, PATRICIA RAE, dancer, choreographer, educator; b. West St. Paul, Minn., June 14, 1937; d. Raymond and Teresa (Lepsche) Pedersen; m. William Walter Sandback, Sept. 6, 1959 (div. 1988); children: Daven William, Steven Raymond. BS in Phys. Edn., U. Minn., 1959; MA in Phys. Edn., San Diego State U., 1976; MFA in Dance, U. Calif., Irvine, 1984. Dance instr. San Diego City Coll., 1959, San Diego YWCA, 1960-63, San Diego Ballet, 1978-79, Mesa Coll., San Diego, 1981-82; dir. children's dance workshop San Diego State U., 1978-81, assoc. prof., 1972—; assoc. choreographer San Diego Dance Theatre, 1983—; co-dir. Big Ladies Small Dance Co., San Diego, 1986—; dance instr. Calif. State U. Summer Arts 86, 87, San Luis Obispo, 88, coordinator, 1988, Arcata; dir. Patricia Sandback and Dancers, San Diego, 1988—; dance instr Nat. Summer Dance Workshop, San Diego, 1978. Contbr. articles to profl. jours.; choreographer numerous dances, 1967—. Recipient Choreography award Lawrence S. Epstein, 1986; dance fellow Nat. Endowment for Arts, San Diego, 1987, dance project, 1988; Individual Artist Grant Pub. Arts Adv. Coun., San Diego, 1987, Affirmative Action Faculty Devel. Grant San Diego State U., 1986, Rsch., Scholarship and Creative Activity award San Diego State U., 1989. Mem. San Diego Area Dance Alliance (bd. dirs. 1982-85, 1987-88), Am. Dance Guild, Nat. Dance Assn. Am., Assn. Health, Phys. Edn., Recreation and Dance. Home: 5938 Alta Mesa Way San Diego CA 92115 Office: San Diego State U Womens Gym San Diego CA 92182

SANDBERG, DAVID DUANE, psychotherapist; b. Galesburg, Ill., Mar. 24, 1949; s. Duane Walter and Helen Maxine (Hasselbacher) S.; m. Patricia Ruth Elving, Aug. 29, 1970; 1 child, Karin Lindsy. BA, North Park (Ill.) Coll., 1971; MS in Counselling Psychology, U. Alaska, 1974; postgrad., Fielding Inst., Santa Barbara, Calif. Lic. psychological assoc., Alaska. Live-in counselor Alaska Children's Svcs., Anchorage, 1971-72, group home house parent, 1973-74; psychotherapist Ohlson Psychological Svcs., Anchorage, 1974-85; pvt. practice Anchorage, 1985—; clin. dir. Couples Inst., Anchorage, 1989—; instr. Mat-Su Community Coll., Palmer, Alaska, 1980, Alasak Pacific U., Anchorage, 1987, U. Alaska, 1988; mem. regional faculty Midlife Devel. Inst., Santa Barbara, 1986—; psychotherapy trainer U. LaVerne, Anchorage, 1983-84; trustee Wilson Family Trust, Anchorage, 1987—. Student missionary Evangel. Covenent Ch. of Am., Unakleet, Alaska, 1969; vol. student clinic, Alaska Native Med. Ctr., Anchorage, 1971-74; profl. sponsor Parents Anonymous, Anchorage, 1975-78; mem. child ad hoc com. on child abuse Alaska DHOC, 1975-78. Mem. Alaska Psychol. Assn. (assoc.), Am. Psychol. Assn. (assoc.), Internat. Transactional Analysis Assn. Democrat. Home and Office: PO Box 141731 Anchorage AK 99514

SANDE, BARBARA, interior decorating consultant; b. Twin Falls, Idaho, May 5, 1939; d. Einar and Pearl M. (Olson) Sande; m. Ernest Reinhardt Hohener, Sept. 3, 1961 (div. Sept. 1971); children: Heidi Catherine, Eric Christian. BA, U. Idaho, 1961. Asst. mgr., buyer Home Yardage Inc., Oakland, Calif., 1972-76; cons. in antiques and antique valuation, Lafayette, Calif., 1977-78; interior designer Neighborhood Antiques and Interiors, Oakland, Calif., 1978-86; owner, Claremont Antiques and Interiors, Berkeley, Calif., 1987—; cons., participant antique and art fair exhibits, Orinda and Piedmont, Calif., 1977—. Decorator Piedmont Christmas House Tour, 1983, 88, Oakland Mus. Table Setting, 1984, 85, 86, Piedmont Showcase Family Room, 1986, Piedmont Showcase Music Room, 1986, Piedmont Kitchen House Tour, 1985, Santa Rosa Symphony Holiday Walk Benefit, 1986, Piedmont Benefit Guild Showcase Young Persons Room, 1987, Piedmont Showcase Library, 1988, Piedmont Showcase Solarium, 1989, Jr. League Table Setting, Oakland-East Bay, 1989. Bd. dirs. San Leandro Coop. Nursery Sch., 1967; health coord. parent-faculty bd., Miramonte High Sch., Orinda, 1978, Acalanes Sch. Dist., Lafayette, Calif., 1978; bd. dirs. Orinda Community Ctr. Vols., 1979; originator Concerts in the Park, Orinda, 1979. Assoc. Am. Soc. Interior Design, Am. Soc. Appraisers; mem. Am. Decorative Arts Forum, De Young Mus., Nat. Trust Historic Preservation, San Francisco Opera Guild, San Francisco Symphony Guild. Democrat. Avocations: travel; hiking.

SANDER, SUSAN BERRY, environmental planning engineering corporation executive; b. Walla Walla, Wash., Aug. 26, 1953; d. Alan Robert and Elizabeth Ann (Davenport) Berry; m. Dean Edward Sander, June 3, 1978. BS in Biology with honors, Western Wash. U., 1975; MBA with honors, U. Puget Sound, 1984. Biologist, graphic artist Shapiro & Assocs., Inc., Seattle, 1975-77, office mgr., 1977-79, v.p., 1979-84, pres., owner 1984—, also bd. dirs. Merit scholar Overlake Service League, Bellevue, Wash., 1971, Western Wash. U. scholar, Bellingham, 1974-75, U. Puget Sound scholar, 1984. Mem. Soc. Mktg. Profl. Services (treas., bd. dirs., Employer of Yr. 1987, Small bus. of Yr. City of Seattle), Seattle C. of C. Club: Wash. Athletic (Seattle). Avocations: swimming, hiking, traveling, painting. Office: Shapiro & Assocs Inc 1400 Smith Tower Seattle WA 98104

SANDERLIN, OWENITA HARRAH, author, educator; b. L.A., June 2, 1916; d. Owen Melville and Marigold (Whitford) H.; BA summa cum laude, Am. U., 1937; postgrad. U. Maine, U. Calif., San Diego State U.; m. George William Sanderlin, May 30, 1936; children: Frea Elizabeth, Sheila Mary, David George, John Owen. Freelance writer, speaker, 1940—; tchr. English, U. Maine, 1942, 46; head dept. speech and drama Acad. of Our Lady of Peace, San Diego, 1961-68; cons. gifted programs San Diego City Schs., 1971-73, 80-85; pvt. practice real estate mgr., El Cajon, 1970—. Author: Jeanie O'Brien, 1965; Johnny, 1968; Creative Teaching, 1971; Teaching Gifted Children, 1973; Tennis Rebel, 1978; Match Point, 1979; co-author: Gifted Children: How to Identify and Teach Them, 1979. Recipient Poetry award Alpha Chi Omega, 1936; Double Ruby award Nat. Forensic League, 1965. Mem. San Diego Natural History Museum, AAUW, Scripps Clinic and Rsch. Found., Mortar Bd., San Diego State U. Women's Club, Singing Hills Tennis Club. Avocations: tennis, bridge. Home: 997 Vista Grande Rd El Cajon CA 92019

SANDERS, AUGUSTA SWANN, nurse; b. Alexandria, La., July 22, 1932; d. James and Elizabeth (Thompson) Swann; m. James Robert Sanders, Jan. 12, 1962 (div. 1969). Student, Morgan State U., 1956. Pub. health nurse USPHS, Washington, 1963-64; mental health counselor Los Angeles County Sheriff's Dept., 1972-79; program coordinator Los Angeles County Dept. Mental Health, 1979—. Mem. Assemblyman Mike Roo's Commn. on Women's Issues, 1981—, Senator Diane Watson's Commn. on Health Issues, 1979—; chmn. Commn. Sex. Equity Los Angeles Unified Sch. Dist., 1984—. Mem. Los Angeles County Employees Assn. (v.p. 1971-72), So. Calif. Black Nurses Assn. (founding mem.), Nat. Assn. Female Execs., Internat. Fedn. Bus. and Profl. Women (pres. Los Angeles Sunset dist. 1988—, dist. officer 1982—), Chi Eta Phi. Democrat. Methodist. Office: Augustus F Hawkins Mental Health Ctr 1720 E 120th St Los Angeles CA 90805

SANDERS, DAVID CLYDE, management consultant; b. Lubbock, Tex., Oct. 8, 1946; s. Jasper Clyde and Mary Jo (Baber) S.; m. Barbara Ann Huck 1976 (div. July 1983); m. Marcia Lynn Fik, Nov. 20, 1983; children: Ashton Harrison, Geoffrey Davidson. Student, U. Tex., 1964; BA, Tex. Tech. U., 1969; postgrad., So. Meth. U., 1969-70, U. Tex., 1970-71. Exec., auditor Ch. Scientology Tex., Austin, 1971-75; exec., cons. Expansion Consultants, L.A., 1975-77; cons. pub. relations Exec. Mgmt. Specialists, L.A., 1977-80; exec. dir. Inst. for Fin. Independence, Glendale, Calif., 1980-83; mktg. dir. Michael Baybak & Co., Beverly Hills, Calif., 1983-85; sr. cons., ptnr. Mgmt. Tech. Consultants, L.A., 1985-86; sr. v.p., sr. cons. Sterling Mgmt. Systems, Glendale, 1986—; exec. coun. mem., exec. establishment officer Sterling Mgmt. Systems, Glendale, 1988—; speaker, ptnr. JPR & Assocs., L.A., 1985-88. Author, Sanders Newsletter, 1983-88. Co-founder, pres. Bus. Adv. Bur. So. Calif., Huntington Beach, 1977-79; mem., contbr. Citizen's Commn. on Human Rights, L.A., 1976—; co-founder Vol. Ministers L.A., 1977-78. Mem. World Inst. Scientology Enterprises (charter mem.), Internat. Hubbard Ecclesiastical League of Pastors, Alpha Phi Omega (sec. Tex. Tech U. chpt.1965-69). Libertarian. Home: 610 S Van Ness Ave Los Angeles CA 90005 Office: Sterling Mgmt Systems 520 N Central Ave Glendale CA 91203

SANDERS, DAVID SCOTT, JR., humanities professor, writer; b. Kellogg, Idaho, June 14, 1926; s. David Scott and Marjorie Elizabeth (Wheat) S.; m. Mary-Frances Finch, Feb. 28, 1948; children: Scott, Bonnie, Peter. BA in English, UCLA, 1949, MA in English, 1953, PhD, 1956. Tchr. Nordhoff Union High Sch., Ojai, Calif., 1950-52; teaching asst. UCLA, 1953-56; instr. U. Md., College Park, 1956-59; assoc. prof., asst. prof. Harvey Mudd Coll., Claremont, Calif., 1959-69, prof., 1969-70, prof., chmn., 1973-85, Miller prof. Humanities, 1985—; prof., chmn. Clarkson Coll., Potsdam, N.Y., 1970-73; Fulbright lectr. U. Salamanca, Spain, 1966-67. Author: John Hersey, 1967, Studies in U.S.A., 1972, John Dos Passos: A Bibliography, 1987. With USN, 1944-46, PTO. Mem. Modern Lang. Assn., Popular Culture Assn., Wednesday Group. Democrat. Home: 1630 Rutgers Ct Claremont CA 91711 Office: Harvey Mudd Coll Claremont CA 91711

SANDERS, DEBORAH LEE, insurance company official; b. Norfolk, Va., Mar. 29, 1953; d. William Dale and Mariella C. (Ahearn) Patterson; m. Eugene H. Sanders, June 26, 1976; children: Seneca Christine, Regan Jean. BA in Edn., Northeastern Ill. U., 1975. Advt. exec. Sierra Vista (Ariz.) Herald, 1978-82; agt. State Farm Ins. Co., Sierra Vista, 1982—; owner, mgr. Debi Sanders Ins., Sierra Vista, 1982—. Bd. dirs. United Way, Sierra Vista, 1984—; sec. U. Ariz. Found., Sierra Vista, 1988—. Fellow Life Underwriters Tng. Coun. (moderator 1988), Southeastern Assn. Life Underwriters (pres. Sierra Vista chpt. 1988—), Sierra Vista C. of C. (bd. dirs. 1984—, Ken Ferguson award 1985), Kiwanis (pres. Sierra Vista chpt. 1987-88). Democrat. Roman Catholic. Home: 601 Essex Dr Sierra Vista AZ 85635 Office: 108 El Camino Real Sierra Vista AZ 85635

SANDERS, EUGENE H., assistant city manager; b. Chgo., Oct. 27, 1950; s. Harvey E. and Pauline W. Sanders; m. Deborah L. Patterson, June 27, 1976; children: Seneca C., Regan J. BA, Northeastern U., 1975. Custodian Chgo. Bd. Edn., 1972-75; tchr. phys. edn. Proviso West High Sch., Hillside, Ill., 1975-78; recreation coordinator City of Sierra Vista, Ariz., 1979-81; personnel mgr. City of Sierra Vista, Sierra Vista, 1981-83, asst. city mgr., 1983—. Vol. coach Gymnix Gymnastic Ctr., Sierra Vista, Ariz., 1987—; bd. dirs. Am. Heart Assn., Sierra Vista, 1988—. Mem. Internat. City Mgrs. Assn., Ariz. City Mgrs. Assn., Ariz. Asst. City Mgrs. Assn., Internat. Personnel Mgrs. Assn. Clubs: Cochise Health (Sierra Vista); Am. Turners (Chgo.). Office: City of Sierra Vista 2400 Tacoma Sierra Vista AZ 85635

SANDERS, JAMES DAVID, art dealer; b. Indpls., Jan. 16, 1946; s. Roscoe and Miriam Elizabeth (Higgins) S.; m. Antoinette Louise Malizia, Aug. 10, 1968; children: James David Jr., Michael Vincent, Christopher John. BS in Econs., Xavier U., Cin., 1968. Lic. art appraiser. Tchr. parochial schs. Indpls., 1968-69; v.p. Ind. Veneers, Inc., Indpls., 1969-71; registered rep. Hornblower Weeks, N.Y.C., 1971-73; founder, chief exec. officer Bowman Sanders, Inc., Tucson, 1973-74, Sanders Galleries, Tucson, 1974—. Mem. Tucson Conv. Bur., 1983—; bd. dirs. Friends of Western Art, Tucson, 1982—. Served with m.c. USAR, 1968-69. Mem. Tucson C. of C. Democrat. Roman Catholic. Lodge: Cursillo. Office: 6420 N Campbell Ave Tucson AZ 85718

SANDERS, JOAN, novelist; b. Three Forks, Mont., Aug. 28, 1924; d. M. Thatcher and Pearl (Oberhansley) Allred; m. Raymond T. Sanders, 1947 (div. 1969); 1 child, Raymond Craig; m. Gail T. Kubik, Sept. 5, 1970 (div. 1971). AA, Weber Jr. Coll., 1944; BA cum laude, U. Utah, 1947. Instr. English and creative writing U. Utah, 1950-52, Utah State U., 1956-69, Claremont Colls., 1970, Calif. Polytech. U., 1971-73; tech. editor SRI, 1973-74; writer Fairfax, Calif., 1978—. Author: La Petite: Louise de la Valliere, 1959, The Marquis, 1963, The Nature of Witches, 1964, Baneful Sorceries or the Countess Bewitched, 1969, Other Lips and Other Hearts, 1982, Catalyst, 1989, The Breath of the Panther, 1989; (with Geoffrey F. Hall): D'Artagnan The Ultimate Musketeer, 1964; contbr. articles to profl. jours. Newell scholar Leland Stanford Jr. U., 1946; recipient 1st prize short story Cabrillo Mystery and Suspense Writers' Conf., 1986; grantee Marin Arts Council, 1987. Mem. PEN. Home and Office: 152 Dominga Fairfax CA 94930

SANDERS, MARGO CATHLEEN, writer; b. Kansas City, Mo., June 2, 1954; d. Leonard and Janis Rae (McBride) Law; m. Darrell Lewis Sanders, Apr. 4, 1976; children: Nicholas Galen, Christopher Lewis. BA in Anthropology, Wash. State U., 1976. Freelance writer Vancouver, Wash., 1980—; clk. B. Dalton Bookseller, Vancouver, Wash., 1987—. Author: Child Abuse: Empowering Victims to Become Survivors, 1987; contbr. articles to various publs. Community rep. region 6 div. child and family svcs., Dept. of Soc. and Health Svcs., 1987—. Southwest Wash. Ind. community grantee, 1986-87. Mem. AAUW (editor quar. jour. Wash. div. B, 1985-87, br. treas., chmn. div. nominating com., grantee, 1986-87), Wash. Women United, Clark County Coalition Sex Edn., Am. Rose Soc. Democrat. Mem. Christian Ch. Office: PO Box 3909 Vancouver WA 98662

SANDERS, WALTER JEREMIAH, III, electronics company executive; b. Chgo., Sept. 12, 1936; s. Walter J. and Kathleen (Finn) S.; m. Linda Lee

Drobman, Nov. 13, 1965 (div. 1982); children: Tracy Ellen, Lara Whitney, Alison Ashley. BEE, U. Ill., 1958. Design engr. Douglas Aircraft Co., Santa Monica, Calif., 1958-59; applications engr. Motorola, Inc., Phoenix, 1959-60; sales engr. Motorola, Inc., 1960-61; with Fairchild Camera & Instrument Co., 1961-69; dir. mktg. Fairchild Camera & Instrument Co., Mountain View, Calif., 1961-68, group dir. mktg. worldwide, 1968-69; pres. Advanced Micro Devices Inc., Sunnyvale, Calif., until 1987, chmn. bd., chief exec. officer, 1969—; dir. Donaldson, Lufkin & Jenrette. Mem. Semicondr. Industry Assn. (co-founder, dir.), Santa Clara County Mfg. Group (co-founder, dir.). Office: Advanced Micro Devices Inc 901 Thompson Pl Sunnyvale CA 94086 *

SANDERSON, CHERYL ANNE, utility company manager; b. Seattle, July 9, 1948; d. Charles F. and Anna Mae (Jones) Bradford; m. Lanny V. DeMoss, Aug. 15, 1968 (div.); 1 child, Sean; m. Von R. Sanderson, Oct. 28, 1977; stepchildren: Gavin, Craig, Todd. Student in Telecommunications, City U., 1988—. With Pacific N.W. Bell, Seattle, 1967—, supr. art graphics and typesetting, 1974-75, mgr. word processing ctrs., 1975-77, mgr. staff, advanced office systems, 1977-85, mgr. mechanization, 1985—; tech. advisor N.W. Ctr. Industries, Seattle, 1983-85; advisor Seattle Opportunities Industrialization Ctr., 1982-83; chmn. adv. council South Seattle Community Coll., 1987—. Chmn. Telephone Pioneers, Seattle, 1985—; donor platelets Pheresis program Seattle Blood Ctr. Mem. Soc. Info. Mgmt., Data Processing Mgmt. Assn. Republican. Home: 4905 133d St SW Edmonds WA 98020 Office: US West Communications 1600 Bell Pla Rm 1905 Seattle WA 98191

SANDERSON, DEBORAH JOY, data processing educator; b. Brockport, N.Y., Dec. 23, 1953; d. Harold Francis and Winifred Helen (Bateman) Redinger: m. Bruce Scott Sanderson, Dec. 2, 1978; foster children. BBA, U. Phoenix, 1987. Mem. data entry staff Am. Express Internat., Phoenix, 1979-80; internat. ops. coord., reservationist Best Western, Phoenix, 1982-84; sec. Garrett Corp./Allied Signal, Tempe, Ariz., 1984-86; tchr. data processing Ariz. Bus. and Tech., Mesa, 1987—; pvt. practice music instruction, Phoenix, 1987—. Music dir. Friendship Baptist Ch., Phoenix, 1987—, cons., 1987—. Mem. Am. Soc. Tng. and Devel. Republican. Home: 5044 E Oneida St Phoenix AZ 85044 Office: Ariz Inst Bus and Tech 1660 Alma Sch Rd Mesa AZ 85202

SANDERSON, RICHARD ALEXANDER, health facility administrator; b. L.A., Sept. 30, 1943; s. Bruce Andrew MD and Dorothy Marie (McIntyre) Sanderson; m. Hilary Joy Walton, Aug. 26, 1968. BA, Loma Linda U., 1967, MPH, 1974. Adminstr. trainee Calif. Dept. of Mental Health, Sacramento, 1969-70; community health planner Community Health Plan Assn., San Diego, 1970-71; exec. dir. San Diego Biomedical Research Inst., 1971-73; caridac monitor tech. Loma Linda U. Med. Ctr., 1973-74; admin. residency Riverside Gen. Hosp., Riverside, Calif., 1974-75; adminstr. and chief exec. officer Burbank Community Hosp., Burbank, Calif., 1975-83, W. Covina Hosp., W. Covina, Calif., 1983-86, Woodland Park Hosp., Portland, Oreg., 1987—; dir. Hosp. Council of S. Calif., Los Angeles, 1981-83; pres. Verdago Hills VNA, Glendale, Calif., 1982-84; treas. at Home Health Services, La Canada, Calif., 1985-87; v.p. Consortium Hosps. Orgn. in Cooperative Efforts, Burbank, 1982-83. Mem. Am. Coll. of Healthcare Adminstrs., Founders Club. Home: 11878 SW Riverwood Rd Portland OR 97219 Office: Woodland Park Hosp 10300 NE Hancock Portland OR 97220

SANDLER, HERBERT M., savings and loan association executive; b. N.Y.C., Nov. 16, 1931; s. William B. and Hilda (Schattan) S.; m. Marion Osher, Mar. 26, 1961. B.S.S., CCNY, 1951; J.S.D., Columbia U., 1954. Bar: N.Y. 1956. Asst. counsel Waterfront Commn. N.Y. Harbor, 1956-59; partner firm Sandler & Sandler, N.Y.C., 1960-62; pres., dir., mem. exec. com. Golden West Savs. & Loan Assn. and Golden West Fin. Corp., Oakland, Calif., 1963-75; chmn. bd., chief exec. officer, dir., mem. exec. com. World Savs. & Loan Assn. and Golden West Fin. Corp., Oakland, 1975—; charter mem. Thrift Instns. Adv. Council to Fed. Res. Bd., Oakland, 1963-75; mem. com. on industry restructuring U.S. League of Savs. Instns.; bd. dirs. Fed. Home Loan Bank, San Francisco; bd. dirs. adv. com. Fed. Home Loan Mortgage Corp.; m. task force U.S. League of Savs. Inst.; former chmn. legis. and regulation com. Calif. Savs. Loan League. Pres., trustee Calif. Neighborhood Services Found.; chmn. Urban Housing Inst.; mem. policy adv. bd. Ctr. for Real Estate and Urban Econs. U. Calif., Berkeley. Served with U.S. Army, 1954-56. Office: Golden W Fin Corp 1901 Harrison St Oakland CA 94612 *

SANDLER, HOWARD EUGENE, manufacturing company executive; b. Pitts., Dec. 19, 1941; s. Harry and Selma (Goldsmith) S.; m. Marlene Phylis Pertcheck, June 16, 1964; children: Jaye, Damon. BCE, U. Toledo, 1964; JD, Duquesne U., 1969. Bar: Pa. 1970, U.S. Supreme Ct. 1973; registered profl. engr., Pa., Ohio. Project engr. Am. Bridge div. U.S. Steel Co., Pitts., 1964-68, PB&I Industries, Pitts., 1968-69; sr. licensing counsel Joy Mfg. Co., Pitts., 1969-76; pvt. practice law Pitts., 1976-82; exec. v.p. adminstrn. Wahlco, Inc., Santa Ana, Calif., 1982—; also bd. dirs. Wahlco, Inc. Contbr. articles to topical publs. Mem. ABA, Am. Patent Law Assn., Licensing Execs. Soc. Republican. Jewish. Home: 25901 Rich Springs Circle Laguna Hills CA 92653 Office: Wahlco Inc 3600 W Segerstrom Ave Santa Ana CA 92704

SANDLER, MARION OSHER, savings and loan association executive; b. Biddeford, Maine, Oct. 17, 1930; d. Samuel and Leah (Lowe) Osher; m. Herbert M. Sandler, Mar. 26, 1961. BA, Wellesley Coll., 1952; postgrad., Harvard U.-Radcliffe Coll., 1953; MBA, NYU, 1958; LLD (hon.), Golden Gate U., 1987. Asst. buyer Bloomingdale's (dept. store), N.Y.C., 1953-55; security analyst Dominick & Dominick, N.Y.C., 1955-61; sr. fin. analyst Oppenheimer & Co., N.Y.C., 1961-63; sr. v.p., dir. Golden West Fin. Corp. and World Savs. & Loan Assn., Oakland, Calif., 1963-75, vice chmn. bd., co-mng. officer, dir., mem. exec. com., 1975-80, pres., co- chief exec. officer, dir., mem. exec. com., 1980—. Vice-chmn. industry adv. com. Fed. Savs. and Loan Ins. Corp., 1987-88; controller's office idea audit task force State of Calif., 1987; bd. overseers NYU Schs. Bus., 1987-89; mem. capital formation task force White House Conf. on Small Bus., 1979; mem. Pres. Carter's Housing Task Force, 1980, Pres.'s Mgmt. Improvement Council, 1980; mem. exec. com., policy adv. bd. Ctr. for Real Estate and Urban Econs. U. Calif., Berkeley, 1981—; mem. ad hoc com. to rev. Schs. Bus. Adminstrn. U. Calif., Berkeley, 1984-85; past mem. adv. council Fed. Nat. Mortgage Assn.; mem. Thrift Insts. Adv. Coun. to Fed. Res. Bd., 1989—. Mem. Phi Beta Kappa, Beta Gamma Sigma. Office: Golden W Fin Corp 1901 Harrison St Oakland CA 94612

SANDLIN, SAMUEL LEWIS, engineer; b. Sandersville, Ga., Sept. 11, 1961; s. Jack Lewis Jr. and Barbet Ann (McCearey) S. Diploma in Weapons Systems, Lowary Tech. Sch., 1980; postgrad., Orange Coast Coll., 1983—. Staff weapons control USAF, Minot, N.D., 1979-81; system test technician N.L. Shaffer, Fullerton, Calif., 1981-86; sr. engring. technician Medstone Internat., Costa Mesa, Calif., 1987—. Republican. Methodist. Home: 1884 Monrovia Ave Costa Mesa CA 92627 Office: Medstone Internat 1607 Monrovia Ave Costa Mesa CA 92627

SANDOVAL, BARBARA COLLEEN, nurse; b. Orange, Calif., Nov. 14, 1955; d. Rodolfo Martinez and Rosalie (Bagley) S. AA in Liberal Arts, Fullerton Coll., 1978; nursing diploma, Lawton Inst. Med. Studies, 1979. Lic. vocat. nurse, Calif. Nursery coord. First So. Baptist Ch., La Habra, Calif., 1973-80; tchr.'s asst. Las Lomas Elem. Sch., Las Lomas, Calif., 1977-78; charge nurse Whittier Care Ctr., Whittier, Calif., 1980-83, Care West, Sonoma, Calif., 1983-88; dir. staff devel. Care West, Sonoma, 1988—. Democrat. Baptist. Home: 500 W Spain St Sonoma CA 95476 Office: Care West Sonoma CA 95476

SANDOVAL, CECIL C., dentist, rancher; b. Santa Fe, Apr. 30, 1949; s. Cilio and Adella (Valdez) S.; m. Alberta Marie Gallegos, Aug. 15, 1975; children: April, Susanne, Anthony. BS in Biology, Chemistry, N. Mex. State U., 1978; DDS, U. Mo., Kansas City, 1982. Med. adv. student com. Belen (N.Mex.) Schs., 1982. With U.S. Army, 1979-82. Mem. ADA, Acad. Gen. Dentistry. Republican. Roman Catholic. Office: 601 Dalies Ave Belen NM 87002

SANDOVAL, RIK (CHARLES), broadcasting executive; b. Chgo., May 20, 1952; s. Placido Jr. and Ophelia (Lugo) S.; m. Theresa Maria Ruiz, May 7, 1988. BA in Communications, Columbia Coll., 1974. With prodn. dept. Sta. WSNS-TV, Chgo., 1971-72; dir., producer Sta. WCAE-TV, St. John, Ind., 1972-73; producer Sta. WBBM-FM, Chgo., 1973-74; prodn. mgr. Sta. WLS-TV, Chgo., 1972-76, on-air mgr., 1976-77; sr. publicist, producer Sta. KABC-TV, Hollywood, Calif., 1977-79; dir. creative svcs. Sullivan & Assocs, L.A., 1979-81; producer ABC, Hollywood, 1981-82; pres. Sandoval Prodns., Studio City, Calif., 1982-87; sr. v.p. The Agy., Studio City, 1987-88; pres. Tri-Mark Group, Inc., Studio City, 1988—; Judge The Clio Awards. Producer, writer: (broadcast promotions) A.K.A. Pablo, 1984 (Silver award), Entertainment Tonight, 1984 (Silver award), Hunter, 1985, People, 1985 (Telly award, 1985, Gold Statuette award). Mem. NOSOTROS, L.A., 1987. Recipient 8 Clio nominations, 1977, 79-81, 2 Gold medals Internat. Radio Festival N.Y., 1985, 4 Bronze Telly awards, 1983-88, Silver Telly award, 1988, 2 ITVA awards, 1988. Mem. Broadcast Promotion Mktg. Execs. (Gold medal, Silver medal 1985), Nat. Assn. Broadcasters (cert. merit 1974), The Publicist Guild, Acad. TV Arts and Scis. Roman Catholic. Home: 17516 Raymer St Northridge CA 91325

SANDS, RUSSELL BERTRAM, insurance broker; b. Santa Cruz, Calif., Feb. 14, 1940; s. Clarence Russell and Betty Ellyn (Weeks) S.; m. Jacquelyn Marie Hall, Sept. 9, 1960; children: Douglas Clarence, Gwendolyn Marie. Student, Wheaton Coll., 1957-59, U. Calif., Berkeley, 1960-61; BA, Western Ill. U., 1984; postgrad., Stanford U., 1988-89. Mgr. CIGNA Corp., San Francisco, 1961-69; v.p. Bayly, Martin & Fay, San Francisco, 1969-76; exec. v.p. Frank B. Hall & Co., San Francisco, 1976—; mng. gen. ptnr. Wendy Petroleum, San Carlos, Calif., 1980—; ptnr. Sanbro Properties, 1987—; bd. dirs. Hammerwell Inc., Los Gatos, Calif.; prin. Sands Properties, San Carlos, Calif., 1972—; gen. ptnr. Sanbro Holdings I, 1987—. Bd. dirs. Fellowship Acad., San Francisco, 1985—, Young Life of San Francisco, 1981—, Fellowship Urban Outreach, 1987—; mem. adv. council Mount Hermon Assn., Felton, Calif., 1984—; moderator First. Bapt. Ch., San Carlos, 1979-80. Mem. Ind. Ins. Brokers Assn. Republican. Presbyterian. Clubs: World Trade (San Francisco); Churchill (Palo Alto, Calif.). Office: Frank B Hall & Co One Market Pl #2100 San Francisco CA 94105

SANDS, WILLIAM ARTHUR, physiology educator; b. Madison, Wis., Feb. 8, 1953; s. Arthur Mathew and Joan Marie (Ehredt) S. BS in Phys. Edn. magna cum laude, U. Wis., Oshkosh, 1975; MS in Exercise Physiology, U. Utah, 1985, PhD in Exercise Physiology. Asst. coach Am. Acad. Gymnastics, Des Plaines, Ill., 1975-78; dir., founder Mid-America Twisters, Northbrook, Ill., 1978-83; dir. edn. and research U.S. Gymnastics Fedn., Ft. Worth, 1980-81; asst. gymnastics coach U. Utah, Salt Lake City, 1983—; Cons. biomechanics Chgo. Sports Medicine, 1983—, mem. exercise physiology com., biomechanics com. U.S. Gymnastics Fedn., Indpls., 1984—; asst. nat. coach U.S. Gymnastics Fedn. World Championships, 1979, coached U.S. team in various internat. tournaments, 1978-81; dir. sport scis. U.S. Women's Gymnastics Team. Author: Coaching Women's Gymnastics, 1984, Everybody's Gymnastic Book, 1984, Modern Women's Gymnastics, 1982, Beginning Gymnastics, 1981. Recipient Nat. Assn. Intercollegiate Athletics All-Am. Gymnastics award, 1974, 75; nominee U. Wis. Oshkosh Athletic Hall of Fame, 1985. Mem. Am. Coll. Sports Med., AAAS, Phi Kappa Phi. Home: PO Box 8798 Salt Lake City UT 84108 Office: U Utah Coll Health Exercise and Sport Sci Salt Lake City UT 80158-4728

SANDSTROM, ROBERT EDWARD, physician, pathologist; b. Hull, Yorkshire, Eng., Apr. 4, 1946; came to U.S., 1946; s. Edward Joseph and Ena Joyce (Rilatt) S.; m. Regina Lois Charlebois (dec. May 1987); children: Karin, Ingrid, Erica. BSc, McGill U., Montreal, 1968; MD, U. Wash., 1971. Diplomate Am. Bd. Pathology, Am. Bd. Dermatopathology. Internship Toronto (Can.) Gen. Hosp., 1971-72; resident pathologist Mass. Gen. Hosp., Boston, 1974-78; clin. fellow Harvard U. Med. Sch., Boston, 1976-78; cons. King Faisel Hosp., Riyadh, Saudi Arabia, 1978; pathologist, dir. labs. St. John's Med. Ctr., Longview, Wash., 1978—; chmn. bd. Cowlitz Med. Svc., Longview, 1988; participant congl. sponsored seminar on AIDS, Wash., 1987. Script writer movie Blood Donation in Saudi Arabia, 1978; contbr. articles to profl. jours. Surgeon USPHS, 1972-74. Fellow Coll. Am. Pathologists; mem. Cowlitz-Wahkiakum County Med. Soc. (pres. elect 1988). Roman Catholic. Home: 2135 Mt Pleasant Rd Kelso WA 98626 Office: Lower Columbia Pathologists 1606 E Kessler Blvd Ste 100 Longview WA 98632

SANDUL, DUANE G., public relations executive; b. Brawley, Calif., Oct. 3, 1950; s. Gaylord Arthur and Anna May (Gates) S.; m. Diana L. Holmes, Dec. 20, 1970 (div. Apr. 1986); children: Glenn, Paul. Student, Coll. San Mateo, 1968-70. Staff writer Redwood City (Calif.) Tribune, 1968-73; staff writer San Mateo (Calif.) Times, 1973-85; pres. Sandul Co., Redwood City, 1985—; cons. San Mateo Parks Bond Issue, 1987. Author: When Faith Steals Home, 1980. Mem. San Mateo County Bus. Commn., Redwood City, 1988—; bd. dirs. Masterworks Chorale, San Mateo. Recipient award for best series of articles Calif. Newspaper Pubs. Assn., award for disting. reporting on adminstrn. of justice State Bar Calif., 1977, cert. of appreciation Govtl. Refuse Collection and Disposal Assn., 1986. Mem. Peninsula Mktg. Assn., San Mateo County-Redwood City C. of C. (communications dir. 1987—), Peninsula Press Club. Episcopalian. Home: 216 Sheffield Ln Redwood City CA 94061 Office: 2000 Broadway Redwood City CA 94063

SANELLO, FRANK ANTHONY, journalist, columnist; b. Joliet, Ill., May 17, 1952; s. Frank Anthony and Evelyn Justine (Stiglic) S. BA with honors, U. Chgo., 1974; MA, UCLA, 1976. Mng. editor Eastside Sun, L.A., 1977; tech. writer Litton Data Systems, Van Nuys, Calif., 1977-79; columnist Cashbox mag., Hollywood, Calif., 1979, United Features Syndicate, L.A., 1986—; film crtic Daily News, Van Nuys, 1982-84; reporter UPI, L.A., 1984, People mag., L.A., 1984—. Mng. editor Real Estate Illustrated, Van Nuys, 1980. Democrat. Home: 1155 N La Cienega Blvd Apt 107 Los Angeles CA 90069

SANETO, RUSSELL PATRICK, neurobiologist; b. Burbank, Calif., Oct. 10, 1950; s. Arthur and Mitzi (Seddon) S. BS with honors, San Diego State U., 1972, MS, 1975; PhD, U. Tex. Med. Br., 1981. Teaching asst. San Diego State U. 1969-75; substitute tchr. Salt Lake City Sch. Dist., 1975; teaching and research asst. U. Tex. Med. Br., 1976-77, NIH predoctoral fellow, 1977-81, postdoctoral fellow, 1981; Jeanne B. Kempner postdoctoral fellow UCLA, 1981-82, NIH postdoctoral fellow, 1982-87; asst. prof. Oreg. Regional Primate Rsch. Ctr. div. Neurosci., Beaverton, 1987-89; asst. prof. dept. cell biology and anatomy Oreg. Health Scis. U., Portland, 1988—; lectr. rsch. methods Grad. Sch., 1982; vis. scholar in ethics So. Baptist Theol. Sem., Louisville, 1981. Contbr. articles to profl. jours. Recipient Merit award Nat. March of Dimes, 1978; named one of Outstanding Young Men in Am., 1979, 81, Man of Significance, 1985. Mem. Bread for World, Save the Whales, Sierra Club, Am. Soc. Human Genetics, AAAS, Winter Confs. Brain Research, Neuroscis. Study Program, N.Y. Acad. Scis., Am. Soc. Neurochem., Soc. Neurosci., Am. Soc. Neurochemistry, Soc. Neurosci. Democrat. Mem. Evangelical Free Ch. Club: World Runners. Office: Oreg Regional Primate Rsh Ctr Div Neurosci 505 NW 185th Ave Beaverton OR 97006

SANFILIPPO, ROBERT, financial planner; b. Jamestown, N.Y., Sept. 16, 1950; s. Joseph and Eva Margaret (Benenati) S.; m. Linda Jean Downey, June 16, 1984; children: Brian, Ian. BA in English, U. Calif., Irvine, 1972. Auditor, employment tax specialist IRS, Los Angeles, 1973-77; prin. Robert Sanfilippo Acctg. Services, Tustin, Calif., 1977-80; ptnr. Gutkin-Sanfilippo Co., Orange, Calif., 1980-84; prin. Robert Sanfilippo and Assocs., Fountain Valley, Calif., 1984—; bd. dirs. Cambria English Inst., Los Angeles. Treas., bd. dirs. Huntington Beach (Calif.) Ch. Religious Sci., 1986—. Mem. Internat. Assn. Fin. Planning, Nat. Assn. Enrolled Agts. (cert.), Calif. Soc. Enrolled Agts. Office: Robert Sanfilippo and Assocs 8840 Warner Ave Ste 202 Fountain Valley CA 92708

SANFORD, LOUIS WILLIAM, hospitality finance executive; b. Chgo., Dec. 8, 1954; s. Harold Lester and Shirley Eileen (Litcherman) S.; m. Charlene Replogle, Dec. 11, 1977; children: Felisha Ann, Heather Eileen. BS in Hotel, Restaurant Mgmt., Okla. State U., 1975; postgrad., Loyola U., Chgo., 1976. CPA, Ill. Fin. analyst Westin Hotel, Seattle, 1975-80; comptroller Regent Hotel, Chgo., 1980-81; assoc. vending systems coordinator Canteen Corp., Chgo., 1981-83; treas. Sanford Mgmt. Services, Inc., Glenview, Ill., 1983-85; regional contr. Doubletree Inc., Phoenix, 1985-88; contr. Methotels, Inc. (parent co. of Doubletree), Phoenix, 1988—. Mem. Am. Inst. CPA's, Ill. Soc. CPA's (mem. com. pub. relations). Home: 15811 N 38th Pl Phoenix AZ 85032 Office: Methotels Inc 410 N 44th St Ste 700 Phoenix AZ 85008

SANFORD, WAYNE UNSWORTH, corporate executive; b. Salt Lake City, Jan. 20, 1926; s. Fred Charles and Mary Alice (Unsworth) S.; m. Nadine Todd, Apr. 2, 1946; children: LaRene, Darryl, Gayle, Jolane, Kerry, Ryan. Student, LDS Bus. Coll., Salt Lake City, 1948-49. Salesman Utah Paper Box Co., Salt Lake City, 1948-69, sales mgr., 1970-75, v.p. sales and credit, 1975-84, exec. v.p., 1984—, also bd. dirs., 1970—. Pres. Utah State Umpires Assn., Salt Lake City, 1955-75, NACM Intermountain, Salt Lake City, 1965; bishop Latter-day Saint Mormon Ch., Bountiful, Utah, 1964-69. With USN, 1944-46. Mem. Nat. Assn. Credit Mgmt. Intermountain (dir. 1965-88, Credit Mgr. of Yr. 1988). Mormon. Home: 688 E 200 South Bountiful UT 84010

SANGUINETTI, EUGENE FRANK, art museum administrator, educator; b. Yuma, Ariz., May 12, 1917; s. Eugene F. and Lilah (Balsz) S.; children: Leslie, Gregory. BA, U. Santa Clara, 1939; postgrad., U. Ariz., 1960-62. Instr. art history U. Ariz., Phoenix, 1960-64; dir. Tucson Mus. and Art Ctr., 1964-67, Utah Mus. Fine Arts, Salt Lake City, 1967—; adj. prof. art history U. Utah, Salt Lake City, 1967—. Contbr. articles to profl. jours. Served with USAAF, 1942-44, to capt. M.I., U.S. Army, 1944-46. Mem. Am. Assn. Museums, Am. Assn. Mus. Dirs., Am. Fedn. of Arts, Coll. Art Assn., Western Assn. Art Museums, Salt Lake City C. of C. Home: 30 S St Salt Lake City UT 84103

SANNWALD, WILLIAM WALTER, librarian; b. Chgo., Sept. 12, 1940; s. William Frederick and Irene Virginia (Stanish) S.; divorced; children: Sara Ann, William Howard. B.A., Beloit Coll., 1963; M.A.L.S., Rosary Coll., River Forest, Ill., 1966; M.B.A., Loyola U., Chgo., 1974. Mktg. mgr. Xerox Univ. Microfilms, 1972-75; assoc. dir. Detroit Public Library, 1975-77; dir. Ventura (Calif.) County Library, 1977-79; city libr. San Diego Public Library, 1979—; vis. instr. mktg. San Diego State U. Editor: Checklist of Library Building Design Considerations. Recipient Outstanding Prof. award and Outstanding Mktg. Prof. award, 1985; Award of Merit AIA San Diego chpt., 1988. Mem. ALA, Calif. Library Authority for Systems and Services (pres. congress of mems. 1980), Calif. Library Assn. Roman Catholic. Home: 3538 Paseo Salamoner La Mesa CA 92041 Office: San Diego Pub Libr 820 E St San Diego CA 92101

SANO, ROY, bishop. Ordained to ministry United Meth. Ch., later consecrated bishop; appointed Bishop Rocky Mountain Conf., United Meth. Ch., Denver. Office: Rocky Mt Conf United Meth Ch 2200 S University Blvd Denver CO 80210 *

SANSWEET, STEPHEN JAY, journalist, author; b. Phila., June 14, 1945; s. Jack Morris and Fannie (Axelrod) S. BS, Temple U., 1966. Reporter Phila. Inquirer, 1966-69; reporter Wall Street Jour., Phila., 1969-71, Montreal, Que, Can., 1971-73; reporter Wall Street Jour., L.A., 1973-84, dep. bur. chief, 1984-87, bur. chief, 1987—; lectr. bus. journalism U. So. Calif., L.A., 1984-87. Author: The Punishment Cure, 1976, Science Fiction Toys and Models, 1981. Recipient award for best fire story Phila. Fire Dept., 1968, Pub. Svc. award Sigma Delta Chi, 1977. Mem. Soc. Profl. Journalists. Office: Wall Street Jour 6500 Wilshire Blvd Ste 1500 Los Angeles CA 90048

SANTILLAN, ANTONIO, banker, motion picture finance executive; b. Buenos Aires, May 8, 1936; naturalized, 1966; s. Guillermo Spika and Raphaella C. (Abaladejo) S.; children: Andrea, Miguel, Marcos. Grad., Morgan Park Mil. Acad., Chgo., 1954; student, Coll. of William and Mary, 1958. Cert. real estate broker. Asst. in charge of prodn. Wilding Studios, Chgo., 1964; pres. Adams Fin. Services, Los Angeles, 1965-88. Writer, producer, dir. (motion pictures) The Glass Cage, co-writer Dirty Mary/ Crazy Harry, Viva Knievel; contbg. writer Once Upon a Time in America; TV panelist Window on Wall Street; contbr. articles to profl. fin. and real estate jours. Served with USNR, 1959. Recipient Am. Rep. award San Francisco Film Festival, Cork Ireland Film Fest, 1961. Mem. Writer's Guild Am., Los Angeles Bd. Realtors, Beverly Hills Bd. Realtors (income/investment div. steering com.), Westside Realty Bd. (bd. dirs.), Los Angeles Ventures Assn. (bd. dirs.). Lodge: Rotary. Office: Adams Fin Svcs Inc 425 N Alfred St Los Angeles CA 90048

SANTO PIETRO, VINCENT ALBERT, museum education administrator; b. Phila., Apr. 5, 1957; s. Albert Robert and Doris Mae (Sperber) S.P. BA in chemistry, Temple U., 1981; MS in chemistry, U. Pa., 1983. Part-time instr. Franklin Inst. Sci. Museum, Phila., 1972-83, mgr. floor program, 1983-85; supr. visitor edn. Pacific Sci. Ctr., Seattle, 1985—; cons. Ctr. Sci. and Industry, Columbus, 1983-84, Sci. Mus. Minn., St. Paul, 1987-88. Presented papers in field. Commr. Phila. council Boy Scouts AM., 1975-81. Recipient Service award Temple U. dept. chemistry, Phila., 1981, Outstanding Dramatics award Lincoln Drama Club, Phila., 1976. Mem. Am. Chem. Soc., Am. Assn. Mus., Nat. Sci. Tchrs. Assn., Wash. Sci. Tchrs. Assn., Montlake Karate Club, Order of Arrow. Office: Pacific Sci Ctr 200 2d Ave N Seattle WA 98109

SANTOR, KEN, state treasurer. Real estate developer, gen. contractor, treas. state of Nev., 1987—. Served with USMC, Korea. Office: Office of State Treas Capitol Bldg Carson City NV 89710 *

SANTOS, JOAO MIGUEL, aircraft manufacturing company executive; b. Lisbon, Portugal, Nov. 28, 1953; came to U.S., 1974; s. Jaime Jose d'Almeida and Maria Isabel Santos; m. Debra Lynn Brennan, June 17, 1978. BS in Aeronaut. and Astronautical Engring., Geol. Scis., U. Wash., 1978; MBA, Pepperdine U., 1983; postgrad., Naval War Coll. Airport-aircraft compatibility engr., scientist McDonnell Douglas Corp., Douglas Aircraft Co., Long Beach, Calif., 1979; resident sales rep. McDonnell Douglas Corp., Douglas Aircraft Co., Portugal, 1979-80; sales engr. McDonnell Douglas Corp., Douglas Aircraft Co., Africa, 1980-82, sr. sales engr., 1982-83, mktg. mgr., 1983-84; area mgr. airline analysis Boeing Comml. Airplanes Boeing Co., Seattle, 1984-85; account mgr. sales Boeing Comml. Airplanes Boeing Co., Africa, 1985-87, mgr. sales programs, 1987—; Plant rep. Boeing Employees Good Neighbor Fund, Seattle, 1986, 87, 88. Lt., USNR, 1984—. Mem. AIAA (assoc.), Boeing Mgmt. Assn., U. Wash. Alumni Assn., Pepperdine U. Alumni Assn., U.S. Naval Inst., USN League. Republican. Roman Catholic. Home: 25329 215th Pl SE Maple Valley WA 98038 Office: Boeing Co BCA PO Box 3707 M/S 76-73 Seattle WA 98124

SANTOS, PAULO MEIRELLES, banker; b. Rio De Janeiro, Brazil, Nov. 25, 1957; s. Vespasiano Oliveira and Hebe (Meirelles) S.; m. Marta Musso Meirelles Santos, July 19, 1987. BSCE, Instituto Militar De Engenharia, 1981. Analyst Esso Brasileira De Petroleo, Rio De Janeiro, 1981-83; credit trainee Chase Manhattan Brazil, Sao Paulo, Brazil, 1983-84; credit analyst Chase Manhattan Brazil, Rio De Janeiro, 1984-85, account officer, 1985-86; asst. v.p. Chase Bank Ariz., Phoenix, 1987—. Mem. Robert Morris Assn., Am. Grad. Sch. Internat. Mgmt. Alumni Assn. Roman Catholic. Home: 26 W Oraibi Ave Phoenix AZ 85027 Office: Chase Bank Ariz 4000 N Central Ave Phoenix AZ 85012

SAPERSTEIN, JEFFREY STANLEY, marketing executive; b. N.Y.C., Dec. 4, 1949; s. Harry and Ruth (Dworsky) S.; m. Chantal Marie El-Bez, Apr. 24, 1974; children: David, Michael. BA in Communications cum laude, Queens Coll., 1971; MA in Communications, U. Denver, 1972. Media planner Rosenfield, Sirowitz & Lawson, N.Y.C., 1973-75; account exec. Marschalk, N.Y.C., 1975-76, Ted Bates, N.Y.C., 1976-77; account supr. Foote, Cone & Belding, San Francisco, 1978-83; dir. mktg. Jewish Community Fed., San Francisco, 1983-85; prin. Jeff Saperstein & Asocs., Mill Valley, Calif., 1985—; instr. U. Calif. Berkeley Ext., San Francisco, 1983-88; cons. Sosnick Cos., Santa Clara, Calif., 1985-88. Author: Practical Applications of Impromptu Speaking, 1988; contbr. articles to profl. jours. Fund raiser Jewish Community Fed., San Francisco, 1981-88; bd. dirs. Mgmt. Ctr., San Francisco, 1988. Democrat. Home and Office: 18 Azalea Dr Mill Valley CA 94941

SAPICO, FRANCISCO LEJANO, internist, educator; b. Manila, July 18, 1940; came to U.S., 1967; s. Urbano Loyola and Asuncion Limon (Lejano) S.; m. Margaret Mary Armstrong, Nov. 7, 1969; children: Erica Anne, Derek Armstrong. AA, U. Philippines, 1960, MD, 1965. Diplomate Am. Bd. Internal Medicine, Am. Bd. Infectious Diseases. Rotating intern, resident in internal medicine Philippine Gen. Hosp.-U. Philippines, Manila, 1964-67; resident in internal medicine SUNY Upstate Med. Ctr., Syracuse, 1967-69; fellow in infectious diseases UCLA Ctr. for Health Scis., 1969-71; fellow in infectious diseases Wadsworth VA Hosp., L.A., 1971-72, staff physician dept. medicine, 1972-77; physician specialist dept. medicine Rancho Los Amigos Med. Ctr., Downey, Calif., 1977—; adj. asst. prof. medicine UCLA Sch. Medicine, 1972-77; asst. prof. medicine U. So. Calif. Sch. Medicine, L.A., 1977-82, assoc. prof., 1982—. Contbr. articles to med. jours., chpts. to books. Judge Fullerton (Calif.) Youth Sci. Fair, 1982-86, Orange County Sci. and Engring. Fair, Fullerton, 1984; coach, asst. coach Fullerton Rangers Youth Soccer Club, 1982-89. Fellow ACP, Infectious Diseases Soc. Am.; mem. Am. Soc. for Microbiology, Am. Fedn. for Clin. Rsch. Republican. Office: Rancho Los Amigos Med Ctr 7601 S Imperial Hwy Downey CA 90242

SAPOCH, JOHN CRIM, JR., management consultant; b. Allentown, Pa., Feb. 1, 1937; s. John Crim and Dorothy Salome (Rems) S.; m. Betty Katherine Wingert, Aug. 9, 1958 (div.); children: John Crim III, William Martin. AB, Princeton U., 1958; MBA, U. Pa., 1964. Tchr., coach, dean students Kent (Conn.) Sch., 1958-61; asst. to dean admissions U. Pa., Phila., 1961-62; sec. for alumni assns. Princeton (N.J.) U., 1962-65, dir. Princeton U. Conf., 1965-66; adminstrv. dir., treas., gen. mgr., exec. v.p. J.P. Cleavar Co. Inc., Princeton, 1966-78, also pres. subs., bd. dirs., 1966-78; chmn., pres., treas., bd. dirs. SINC, Princeton, 1978—, Princeton Pacific Inc., Manhattan Beach, Calif., 1980—. Author tng. manuals. Vice pres., pres. class of 1958, Princeton U., 1958-68; bd. dirs., treas. Princeton Youth Ctr., 1966-70; founder, trustee Princeton Youth Fund, 1967-68; founder, bd. dirs. Princeton Midget Football League, 1968-73; chmn. Friends Princeton U. Football, 1974-78; founder, chmn. Friends Princeton High Sch. Athletics, 1978-80. Named hon. mem. Princeton High Sch. Class of 1980. Mem. Princeton U. Alumni Assn., Wharton Grad. Sch. Alumni Assn., Princeton Alumni Club (founder, treas. 1965), Princeton Area Alumni Assn., Princeton Club (N.Y.C.), Ivy Club (Princeton), 200 Club (Trenton, N.J.). Home: 4003 The Strand Manhattan Beach CA 90266 Office: Princeton Pacific Inc PO Box 279 Manhattan Beach CA 90266

SAPP, DONALD GENE, minister; b. Phoenix, Feb. 27, 1927; s. Guerry Byron and Lydia Elmeda (Snyder) S.; m. Anna Maydean Nevitt, July 10, 1952 (dec.); m. Joann Herrin Mountz, May 1, 1976; children: Gregory, Paula, Jeffrey. AB in Edn., Ariz. State U., 1949; M Sacred Theology, Boston U., 1952, M of Div., 1960; D in Ministry, Calif. Grad. Sch. Theology, 1975. Ordained deacon, 1950, ordained elder, 1952. Dir. youth activities Hyde Park (Mass.) Meth. Ch., 1950-52; minister 1st Meth. Ch., Peabody, Mass., 1952-54, Balboa Island (Calif.) Community Meth. Ch., 1954-57, Ch. of the Foothills Meth., Duarte, Calif., 1957-63; sr. minister Aldersgate United Meth. Ch., Tustin, Calif., 1963-70, Paradise Valley (Ariz.) United Meth. Ch., 1970-83; dist. supt. Cen. West Dist. of Desert S.W. Conf. United Meth. Ctr., Phoenix, 1983—. Editor Wide Horizons, 1983—; contbr. articles to profl. jours. Chaplain City of Hope Med. Ctr., Duarte, 1957-63; trustee Plaza Community Ctr., Los Angeles, 1967-70; corp. mem. Sch. Theology at Claremont, Calif., 1972-80; pres. Met. Phoenix Commn., 1983-85; del. western jurisdictional conf. United Meth. Ch., 1982, 88, World Meth. Conf., Nairobi, Kenya, 1986, 88; bd. dirs. So. Calif. Council Chs., Los Angeles, 1963-67, Wesley Community Ctr., Phoenix, 1983—, Orange County (Calif.) Human Relations Council, 1967-70, Interfaith Counseling Service Found., 1982—. Served with USN, 1945-46. Mem. Ariz. Ecumenical Council, Kappa Delta Pi, Tau Kappa Epsilon, Blue Key. Democrat. Lodge: Rotary (pres.). Home: 5225 E Road Runner Rd Paradise Valley AZ 85253 Office: United Meth Ctr 1807 N Central Ave Ste 100 Phoenix AZ 84004-1508

SAPSOWITZ, SIDNEY H., entertainment and media company executive; b. N.Y.C., June 29, 1936; s. Max and Annette (Rothstein) Sapsowitz; m. Phyllis Skopp, Nov. 27, 1957; children—Donna Dawn Chazen, Gloria Lynn Aaron, Marsha Helene Gleit. BBA summa cum laude, Paterson (N.J.) State Coll., 1980. Various fin. and systems positions Metro Goldwyn Mayer, N.Y.C., 1957-68; exec. v.p., chief fin. officer Metro Goldwyn Mayer, Los Angeles, 1980-86, also bd. dirs.; exec. v.p. Penta Computer Assoc. Inc., N.Y.C., 1968-70, Cons. Actuaries Inc., Clifton, N.J., 1970-73, Am. Film Theatre, N.Y.C., 1974-76; exec. v.p., chief fin. officer Cinema Shares Internat. Distributors, N.Y.C., 1976-79; sr. cons. Solomon, Finger & Newman, N.Y.C., 1979-80; various positions leading to exec. v.p.fin. and adminstrn., chief fin. officer MGM/UA Entertainment Co., Culver City, Calif., 1985-86; sr. exec. v.p., bd. dirs. exec. com. Beverly Hills, Calif., 1986—; chmn. bd., chief exec. officer MGA/UA Telecommunications Corp., Beverly Hills, 1986—; dir. Penta Computer Assoc., N.Y.C., 1968-70, Metro Goldwyn Mayer, N.Y.C., 1985-86; MGM/UA Communications Co., Beverly Hills, 1986—. Pres., Wayne Conservative Congregation, N.J., 1970-77. Mem. Am. Mgmt. Assn. (cons., lectr. 1967), Am. Film Inst., Acad. Motion Picture Arts & Scis., Fin. Exec. Inst. Lodge: Knights of Pythias (chancellor 1970).

SARAF, DILIP GOVIND, electronics executive; b. Belgaum, India, Nov. 10, 1942; s. Govind Vithal and Indira Laxman (Divekar) S.; m. Mary Lou Arnold, July 25, 1970; 1 son, Rajesh Dilip. B. Tech with honors, Indian Inst. Tech., Bombay, 1965; M.S.E.E., Stanford U., 1969. Sr. mgmt. trainee Delhi Cloth and Gen. Mills Co. (India), 1965-68; sr. research engr. SRI Internat., Menlo Park, Calif., 1969-78; project dir. Kaiser Electronics, San Jose, Calif., 1978-87; sr. engring. mgr. Varian Assocs., Santa Clara, Calif., 1987— ; cons. teaching U. Santa Clara, 1972, 73. Vice-chmn. bd. Peninsula Childrens' Ctr., Palo Alto, Calif. Mem. IEEE, Soc. Am. Inventors, Speakers' Bur. Contbr. articles to profl jours. Patentee in field. Club: Toastmasters. Home: 28050 Horse Shoe Ct Los Altos Hills CA 94022 Office: 3200 Patrick Henry Dr Santa Clara CA 95054

SARAFIAN, ARMEN, university president emeritus; b. Van Nuys, Calif., Mar. 5, 1920; s. Kevork and Lucy (Gazarian) S.; m. Doris Manoogian, 1941; children: Winston, Norman, Joy. A.B. magna cum laude, La Verne Coll., 1940, LL.D. (hon.), 1967; M.A., Claremont Grad. U., 1947; Ph.D., U. So. Calif., Los Angeles, 1964. Tchr. public elem. and secondary schs. Calif., 1940-47; tchr. English and Am. history and polit. sci. Pasadena (Calif.) Jr. Coll. Dist., 1947-51; mem. part-time faculty various colls. and univs. in Calif., 1947-68; coordinator secondary and jr. coll. edn. Pasadena City Schs., 1951-59; adminstrv. dean for instruction Pasadena City Coll., 1959-65, pres., 1965-76, pres. emeritus, 1976-85; also supt. Pasadena Area Community Coll. Dist., 1966-76; adj. prof. community coll. adminstrn. U. So. Calif., Los Angeles, 1968-78; pres. La Verne (Calif.) Coll. (name changed to La Verne U. 1978), 1976-85, pres. emeritus, 1985—; founder Am. Armenian Internat. Coll., 1976; interim pres. Colo. Mountain Coll., Glenwood Springs, 1986-87; pres. emeritus Colo. Mountain Coll., 1987—; interim chancellor Peralta Community Coll. Dist., Oakland, Calif., 1987—; cons. to industry, govt. and bus., 1952—; dir. mgmt. reorgn. of Conn. System of Regional Community Colls., 1974-75; mem. adult and continuing edn. com. for Calif. Community Colls., 1974-75; Delta Epsilon disting. lectr. U. So. Calif., 1973; project dir., cons. joint legis. com. on higher edn. State of Alaska, 1973-77; mem. mgmt. team U. Alaska System, 1977; acad. planning specialist Mary Hardin-Baylor Coll., Belton, Tex., 1974; mem. western regional adv. bd. Coll. Entrance Examination Bd., 1971-75; mgmt. adv. to City of Pasadena Mcpl. Govt., 1972-73; founder Am. Armenian Internat. Coll., 1976; mem. Calif. State Bd. Edn., 1986—; mem. Calif. Ednl. Tech. Com., 1986—; chmn. Joint Vocat. Edn. Com., 1986—; mem. Gov.'s Commn. on Ednl. Quality, 1987-88;. Mem. policy bd. Gt. Plains Nat. Instructional TV Library, 1975-79; founder and mem. exec. com. Pasadena Hall of Sci. Project, 1965-76; founder, adult adv. Pasadena Area Youth Council, 1953-66; mem. St. Luke Hosp. Adv. Bd., 1969-71, Mayor's Com. on Children and Youth, Pasadena, 1960-62; pres. Calif. Conservation Council, 1966-68; mem. nat. adv. council for nurse tng. USPHS, 1967-71; judge Los Angeles Times Scholarship Award Contest, 1974; bd. dirs. Pasadena Urban Coalition, 1973-76; trustee La Verne Coll., 1969-76. Recipient Disting. Community Service award Pasadena Edn. Assn., 1956, Conservation Merit award Calif. Conservation Council, 1960, Meritorious Service award Pasadena City Coll. Faculty Senate, 1960, Ralph Story award Pasadena City Coll. Faculty Assn., 1974, U. So. Calif. Service award, 1974, Recognition award USPHS, 1972, Others award Salvation Army, 1975, Recognition award Pasadena Arts Council, 1976; named Citizen of the Day Sierra Madre City Council, 1972, Arthur Noble disting. citizen City of Pasadena, 1976. Mem. Calif. Scholarship Fedn., Calif. Jr. Coll. Assn. (mem. legis. com. 1973-76), Pasadena Area Sch. Trustees Assn. (founder 1966), Pasadena Arts Council, Pasadena Hist. Soc., La Verne C. of C. (pres. 1978-79), Native Sons of the Golden West, Pasadena Council of Parents and Tchrs. (hon. life), Assoc. Student Body of Pasadena City Coll., Pasadena C. of C. (v.p. 1972), La Verne C. of C. (pres. 1978-79), Calif. State Bd. Edn., Calif. State Ednl. Tech. Com., Phi Delta Kappa (Spl. Recognition award 1970). Office: Colo Mountain Coll PO Box 10001 Glenwood Springs CO 81602 also: Peralta Comm Coll 333 E 8th St Oakland CA 94606

SARAZEN, ROBERT ELDON, computer engineer; b. Pasadena, Calif., Nov. 3, 1957; s. Eugene Peter and Theresa Marie (O'Callahan) S. BS in Bus., Computer Sci., Calif. State U., Long Beach, 1982; postgrad., Northrop U., 1985—. Database configuration specialist ATV Systems Inc., Santa Ana, Calif., 1983; systems analyst Rockwell Internat. Corp., El Segundo, Calif., 1984-87; software engr. Unisys Corp., Santa Monica, Calif., 198-89; systems analyst, cons. AIL Eaton, Edwards AFB, Calif., 1989—; sr. analyst, prin. Dove Micro-Systems, El Segundo, 1988—. With USN, 1976-82. Republican. Mem. Four Square Gospel Ch.

SARAZIN, RONALD JAMES, utilities executive, consultant; b. Nyssa, Oreg., May 10, 1953; s. Norbert James and Dorothy (Schwartz) S.; m. Vicki Beth Humphreys, June 12, 1976; children: Andrea (Annie) Nicole, Trevor James, Brittany Beth. BS in Indsl. Engring., Oreg. State U., 1976. Indsl. engring. supr. Aluminum Co. Am., Davenport, Iowa, 1976-78; facilities/indsl. engr. parts div. Paccar, Renton, Wash., 1978-79; v.p., gen. mgr. Cook-Newhouse and Assocs., Portland, Oreg., 1979-83; mgr. customer service Portland Gen. Electric, 1983—; cons. OECO, Portland, 1984-87, Kaiser-Permanante, Portland, 1986-87. Author: (computer program) Fixed Asset Depreciation, 1984, M105-D, 1986. Mem. Tualatin City Coun., 1989—. Mem. Inst. Indsl. Engrs., Alpha Pi Mu, Tau Beta Pi. Republican. Home: 5769 SW Joshua St Tualatin OR 97062 Office: Portland Gen Electric 121 SW Salmon St Portland OR 97204

SARDINAS, JOSE RAMON, pharmacist; b. Cuba, Apr. 13, 1934; came to U.S., 1967; s. Pablo and Julia (Marin) S.; m. Latife Marina Thomas, Dec. 15, 1962; 1 child, Adis. BS, La Progresiva Coll., Cardenas, Cuba, 1952; PharmD, Havana U., 1957, U. So. Calif., L.A., 1970. Registered pharmacist. Pharmacist, owner Sardinas Pharmacy, Ciego de Avila, Cuba, 1959-63; prof. of fisic and chemistry Ciego de Avila Inst., Ciego de Avila, 1958-63; prof. fisic Instituto de Superacion Educacional, Camagüey, Cuba, 1963-65; pharmacist internist U. So. Calif. Med. Ctr., L.A., 1970-71; pharmacist, mgr. N.E. Clinic Pharmacy, L.A., 1971-76; pharmacist, owner Mission Pharmacy, Long Beach, Calif., 1976—, Plaza Pharmacy, Hawthorne, Calif., 1978—; pres. Tropical Builders, Hawthorne, 1988—; tutor in fisic, Ciego de Avila, 1965-67. Mem. Logia Acacia, Ciego de Avila, 1958-67. Mem. Am. Soc. Hosp. Pharmacists, Am. Pharmacist Assn., Calif. Pharmacist Assn., Long Beach Pharmacist Assn., Sociedad Jose Marti (Inglewood, Calif.), Manhattan Country Club (Manhattan Beach, Calif.), Lions. Republican. Roman Catholic. Office: Plaza Pharmacy 11930 Hawthorne Blvd Hawthorne CA 90250

SARGEANT, VICTOR WOODROW, geophysicist, consultant; b. St. Philip, Barbados, W.I., Oct. 14, 1946; came to U.S., 1959; s. James N. and Lois F. (Clark) S. BA in Psychology, U. Ariz., 1976, BS in Geophysics, 1979. Geophysicist Seismograph Svc. Corp., Tulsa, 1980-84, 87-88, Arabian Am. Oil Co., Dhahran, Saudi Arabia, 1984-86; cons. Tucson, 1988—. Mem. Soc. Exploration Geophysicist. Home and Office: 6733 B Calle La Paz Tucson AZ 85715

SARGENT, DIANA RHEA, corporate executive; b. Cheyenne, Wyo., Feb. 20, 1939; d. Clarence and Edith (de Castro) Hayes; grad. high sch.; m. Charles Sargent, Apr. 17, 1975; children: Rene A. Coburn, Rochelle A. Rollins, Clayton R. Weldy, Christopher J.; stepchildren: Laurie Branch, Leslie E. Sargent. IBM proof operator Bank Am., Stockton, Calif., 1956-58, gen. ledger bookkeeper, Modesto, Calif., 1963-66; office mgr., head bookkeeper Cen. Drug Store, Modesto, 1966-76; pres. Sargent & Sargent Inc., Modesto, 1976—; ptnr. R.C.D. Farms (almond ranch), Just a Little Something (antique dolls and miniatures). Mem. Stanislaus Women's Center, Mem. NOW, San Francisco Mus. Soc., Nat. Soc. Public Accts. Office: 915 14th St Modesto CA 95353

SARGENT, MARTHA SHIRLEY, educator; b. Livermore, Calif., Jan. 15, 1954; d. Joseph E. and Shirley J. (Gildersleeve) Regan; m. Dennis J. Sargent, Aug. 25, 1979. BS in Bus., Calif. Poly State U., San Luis Obispo, 1976; MBA, Oreg. State U., 1984. CPA, Oreg., cert. mgmt. acct., Oreg. Sr. acct. Arthur Andersen & Co., Portland, Oreg., 1976-79; instr. Portland State U., 1979-81; dir. communications Gregory Affiliates, Beaverton, Oreg., 1981-83; asst. prof. Linfield Coll., McMinnville, Oreg., 1984-86, Western Oreg. State Coll., 1986—; cons. Stover and Sinclair, CPA's, Corvallis, Oreg., 1983—. Recipient Robert Beyer Gold medal Inst. Cert. Mgmt. Accts., 1988. Mem. Oreg. Soc. CPA's, Nat. Assn. Accts., Oreg. Internat. Council, Ptnrs. of the Am.'s, Friendship Force, Crossroads Internat. Home: 575 NW Merrie Dr Corvallis OR 97330 Office: Western Oreg State Coll Monmouth OR 97361

SARGIS, JOY CATHERINE, research scientist; b. Oakland, Calif., Sept. 16, 1960; d. David Albert and Marguerite Mary (Drexler) S. BA in Engring. and Math., UCLA, 1982; MA in Math, U. Calif.-San Diego, 1988, postgrad. studies, 1988—. Engr. TRW, Redondo Beach, Calif., 1982-84; scientist Jaycor, La Jolla, Calif., 1984—. Author: (publ.) Threat Vehicle Performance in Dust Environments, 1983, Role of Secondary Electrons in Box Iemp Coupling, 1984. Mem. AIAA, IEEE, Soc. Women Engrs., ACM, Am. Math. Soc., UCLA Alumni Assn., San Diego Track Club, San Diego Porsche Club. Office: Jaycor 11011 Torreyana Rd San Diego CA 92138

SARLO, GEORGE STEPHEN, venture capitalist; b. Budapest, Hungary, Jan. 31, 1938; came to U.S., 1956; s. Frank and Cecilia S.; children: Gabriella, Susannah. BSEE, U. Ariz., 1959; MBA, Harvard U., 1963. Mem. tech. staff Hughes Aircraft Co., Newport Beach, Calif., 1959-61; sr. analyst Capital Rsch. Co., L.A., 1962-66; 1st v.p., bd. dirs. William D. Witter, Inc., N.Y.C., 1966-70; chmn., pres. Ashfield & Co., Inc., San Francisco, 1973—; gen. ptnr. Walden, San Francisco, 1974—; bd. dirs., Rugged Digital Systems, Inc., Sunnyvale, Calif., Elantec,Inc., Milpitas, Calif., Raster-Ops, Inc., Cupertino, Calif., Dataware Devel. Co., San Diego, Calif. Trustee, San Francisco Conservatory of Music, 1988—; bd. dirs. KQED, San Francisco, 1988—. Office: 750 Battery St San Francisco CA 94111

SARSFIELD, GEORGE P., lawyer; b. Vancouver, B.C., Can., Jan. 14, 1913 (parents Am. citizens); s. John M. and Margaret (LaValle) S.; B.A., J.D., U. Mont., 1950; m. Margeret Davis, May 23, 1942. Blk., laborer, miner, 1930-41; admitted to Mont. bar, 1950, since practiced in Butte. Past pres. Butte YMCA. Republican nominee Congress, 1st dist. Mont., 1960. Chmn. exec. bd. Mont. Coll. Mineral Sci. and Tech., 1968-71; chmn. bd. trustees U. Mont. Devel. Fund, 1967-70; adv. bd. Salvation Army, 1952—. Served from pvt. to capt. U.S. Army, 1941-46. Recipient Disting. Service award U. Mont., 1971, Pantzer award, 1975. Mem. Am., Mont. (past v.p.) bar assns., Am. Trial Lawyers Assn., U. Mont. Alumni Assn. (pres. 1964, chmn. bd. 1964-66), Mont. State Golf Assn. (past pres.), U.S. Golf Assn. (mem. sectional affairs com. 1968—), Phi Delta Phi, Alpha Kappa Psi, Phi Delta Theta. Clubs: Rotary (past local pres.; dist. gov. 1963-64, chmn. internat. constn. and by-laws com. 1969-70, internat. dir. 1973-75, internat. 1st v.p. 1974-75, chmn. exec. com. internat. bd. dirs. 1974-75). Club: Butte Country (past pres.). Former Mont. open golf champion; Mont. amateur golf champion, 4 years. Home: 2700 Floral Blvd Butte MT 59701 Office: Mayer Bldg Butte MT 59701

SARVER, SHARON MARIE, accountant; b. Wapato, Wash., May 17, 1942; d. Roy Clifton and Mila Ann (Logan) S.; children: Jeffrey Dale Taylor, Rebecca Anne Johnston, Donald Gene Taylor, Jerry Dean Sims. Student Edison Tech. Sch., 1960-63, Data Control Systems, 1964-65, Ventura Coll., 1966-67, Bellevue Community Coll., 1969-71, U. Wash., 1975; Emergency Med. Technician cert., 1974; Acct., Rochester Electronics, Redmond, Wash., 1972, Adby Industries, Seattle, 1973, Koenigsberg, Brown, Sin-Seimer, Stone & Meltzer, Seattle, 1975; bus. mgr. Community Psychiat. Centers, Kirkland, Wash., 1976; acct., owner Gen. Office Services, Woodinville, Wash., 1977—; preliminary rsch. initiation and start up class for pub. kindergarten into Spokane Pub. Sch. System, 1963. Bd. dirs. Lower Snoqualmie Valley Sch. Bd., 1974-78, Redmond Miss Pageant, 1977-78, The Devel. and Initiation of New Math. into Wash. Pub. Schs., 1962; dir. citizen's adv. com. Bellevue Wash. Sch. Dist., bd. legis. com. for state tchrs. arbitration rights, 1961. Recipient Cert. for improved devel. Bellevue Community Coll. Mem. Nat. Assn. Accountants, Redmond C. of C. (dir.), U.S. C. of C., Nat. Fedn. Ind. Businesses, Assn. Wash. Bus. Office: GOS Taxes and Acctg 16810 NE 185th Woodinville WA 98072

SASAKI, Y. TITO, business services company executive; b. Tokyo, Feb. 6, 1938; came to U.S., 1967, naturalized, 1983; s. Yoshinaga and Chiyoko (Imada) S.; m. Janet Louise Cline, June 27, 1963; 1 child, Heather N. BS, Chiba U., 1959; postgrad. Royal Coll. Art, London, 1961, U. Oslo, 1962; MS, Athens Tech. Inst., Greece, 1964; postgrad. U. Calif., Berkeley, 1969. Chief designer Aires Camera Industries Co., Tokyo, 1958-59; tech. officer London County Council, 1961-62; researcher Athens Ctr. Ekistics, 1964-66; sr. researcher Battelle Inst., Geneva, 1966-68; project engr. Marin County Transit Dist., San Rafael, Calif., 1968-69; chief planning, research Golden Gate Bridge Dist., San Francisco, 1969-74; pres. Visio Internat. Inc., Somona, Calif., 1973—; chmn. steering com. Kawada Industries Inc., Tokyo, 1974-82; chief exec. officer Quantum Mechanics Corp., Somona, 1981—; bd. dirs., v.p. Sonoma Skypark, Inc., 1986—. Mem. Rep. Nat. Com. Mem. ASME, Am. Welding Soc., Helicopter Assn. Internat., AIAA, Am. Inst. Cert. Planners, World Soc. Ekistics, Brit. Soc. Long-Range Planning, Am. Vacuum Soc., Aircraft Owners and Pilots Assn. Roman Catholic. Office: Visio Internat Inc PO Box 1888 Sonoma CA 95476

SASMOR, HELENA ANNE, manufacturing company executive; b. Niagara Falls, N.Y., Mar. 31, 1959; d. Daniel Joseph and Bette (Pianin) S. BBA, U. N.Mex., 1984; MA, Webster U., 1989. Purchasing agt. Sky Chefs, Albuquerque, 1984-86; v.p. purchasing Gen. Energy Techs., Albuquerque, 1986-88; nat. accts mgr. Main Line Equipment Co., Gardena, Calif., 1988—. Named to Outstanding Young Women Am., 1983, 86. Office: Main Line Equipment Co 1650 W 180th St Gardena CA 90248

SASSENRATH, JULIUS MARLIN, psychology educator; b. Eldridge, Calif., Nov. 11, 1923; s. Juliuis Joseph and Mabel Irene (Barrick) S.; m. Ethelda Norberg, June 12, 1951 (div. 1985); children: Paul N., Joseph N.; m. Doris Ellen Winter, July 21, 1985. BA, U. Calif., Berkeley, 1950, MA, 1954, PhD, 1957, postgrad., 1957-58. Postdoctoral researcher dept. psychology U. Calif., Berkeley, 1957-58; instr. San Francisco State U., 1957-58; from asst. prof. to assoc. prof. dept. ednl. psychology Ind. U., Bloomington, 1958-64; assoc. prof. U. Calif., Davis, 1964-67, prof., chmn. dept. edn., 1967—. Staff sgt. USAF, 1943-46, CBI. Fellow Am. Psychol. Assn., Am. Ednl. Research Assn. Democrat. Home: 1020 Vassar Davis CA 95616 Office: U Calif Dept Edn Davis CA 95616

SASSOON, VIDAL, hair stylist; b. London, Eng., Jan. 17, 1928; s. Nathan and Betty (Bellin) S.; divorced 1980; children—Catya, Elan, Eden, David. Student, NYU. Founder, former chmn. bd. Vidal Sassoon, Inc. (beauty treatment products, appliances), Europe and Am.; Pres. Vidal Sassoon Found.; lectr. in field. Author: autobiography A Year of Beauty and Health, 1976. Served with Palmach Israeli Army. Recipient award French Ministry of Culture, award for services rendered Harvard Bus. Sch.; Intercoiffure award Cartier, London, 1978; Hair Artists Internat. fellow. Clubs: Anabelle (London, Eng.), Ambassadeurs (London, Eng.), Claremont (London, Eng.); Le Club (N.Y.C.). Office: Vidal Sassoon Inc 2029 Century Park E Los Angeles CA 90067 *

SATHER, GLEN CAMERON, professional hockey team coach and executive; b. High River, Alta., Canada, Sept. 2, 1943. Former professional hockey playe; pres., gen. mgr. Edmonton Oilers, Nat. Hockey League, Alta., Can.; coach Edmonton Oilers, Nat. Hockey League, 1977-89; coach winning team in Stanley Cup competition, 1987. Recipient Jack Adams Award for NHL Coach of the Yr., 1986. Office: care Edmonton Oilers, Northlands Coliseum, Edmonton, AB Canada T5B 4M9 *

SATHYADEV, ALLAN, aerospace engineer; b. Madras, India, Jan. 24, 1950; came to U.S., 1980; s. Gnanamuthu John Arnold and Chandrakanthi Iris (Lamech) Duraisingh; m. Rachael Kalpana Thambuswamy, June 6, 1987; 1 child, Malini Elizabeth. BTech, Indian Inst. Tech., Madras, 1973; MS, Cranfield Inst. Tech., Bedford, Eng., 1975, U. London, 1979. Sr. engring. cons. Lloyds Register Shipping, London, 1978-80; sr. engr. Martin Marietta Aerospace Co., New Orleans, 1980-86, Rohr Industries Inc., Chula Vista, Calif., 1986-87; sr. engring. cons. Space Systems div. Gen. Dynamics, San Diego, 1987—. Mem. New Orleans Symphony Chorus, 1982-86, San Diego Master Chorale, 1986—. Mem. Royal Aero. Soc. (assoc.). Republican. Episcopalian. Home: 2545 San Clemente Terr San Diego CA 92122

SATIN, JOSEPH, university administrator; b. Phila., Dec. 16, 1920; s. Reuben Philip and Harriet (Price) S.; m. Selma Rosen (dec. 1978); children: Mark, Diane; m. Barbara Jeanne Dodson (dec. 1987). BA, Temple U., 1946; AM, Columbia U., 1948, PhD, 1952. Instr. integrated studies W.Va. U., Morgantown, 1952-54; prof. English and Comparative Lit. Moorhead (Minn.) State U., 1954-63; chmn. dept. English and Journalism Midwestern U., Wichita Falls, Tex., 1963-73; dean Sch. Arts and Humanities Calif. State U., Fresno, 1973—; mgr. concert series Moorhead State U., 1956-61; mem. nat. bd. cons. NEH, Washington, 1979—; dir. London semester Calif. State U., Fresno, 1982—. Author: Ideas in Context, 1958, The 1950's: America's "Placid" Decade, 1960, Reading Non-Fiction Prose, 1964, Reading Prose Fiction, 1964, Reading Drama, 1964, Reading Poetry, 1964, Shakespeare and His Sources, 1966, Reading Literature, 1968, The Humanities Handbook (2 Vols.), 1969; editor: Frank Lloyd Wright-Letters to Apprentices, 1982, Letters to Architects, 1984, Letters to Clients, 1986, Treasures of Taliesin, 1985, The Guggenheim Correspondence, 1986, Frank Lloyd Wright: His Living Voice, 1987, Frank Lloyd Wright, The Crowning Decade, 1989; translator: Federico Fellini, Comments on Film, 1987; contbr. to Ency. Internat. Edn., 1978; dir., editor-in-chief Univ. Press, Calif. State U., 1982—. Served with U.S. Army, 1943-46, ETO. Jewish. Home: 1428 W Calimyrna Fresno CA 93711 Office: Calif State U Sch of Arts & Humanities Shaw & Maple Aves Fresno CA 93740

SATO, HIDEMARU, computer engineer; b. Osaka, Japan, Nov. 27, 1953; came to the U.S., 1979; s. Hisami and Mitsuko (Oda) S.; m. Manami Koyama, June 20, 1983; 1 child, Mai. BS, Waseda U., Tokyo, 1978; MS, Stanford U., 1980. Mgr. Nippon Unisys, Ltd., Tokyo, 1980-87, Citizen Watch Co., Ltd., Tokyo, 1987—. Author: (with others) Pioneer of Computer Graphics, 1984, Presentation Graphics, 1986; dir. computer graphics film Antman, 1983 (3d prize 1983). Mem. IEEE Computer Soc., Soc. Info. Display, ACM. Home: 10980 Wellworth Ave #413 Los Angeles CA 90024 Office: Citizen Systems Inc 2401 Colorado Ave Ste 190A Santa Monica CA 90404

SATOH, YOSHIHARU, banker; b. Tokyo, Nov. 18, 1928; came to U.S., 1967; s. Sotoji and Miyuki (Odake) S.; m. Ikuko Nakatsuka, May 6, 1955; children: Kaoru, Keiichi. Law degree, Tokyo U., 1952. Sr. v.p., dir. Sumitomo Bank of Calif., San Francisco, 1967-72; sr. v.p. Central Pacific Bank, Honolulu, 1972-73; exec. v.p., dir. Central Pacific Bank, 1973-78, pres., chief exec. officer, 1978-88, chmn., pres., chief exec. officer, 1988-89, chmn., chief exec. officer, 1989—; trustee Kuakini Health Systems, Honolulu, 1983—. Trustee, U. Hawaii Found.; bd. regents Chaminade U. of Honolulu, 1984-87. Mem. Hawaii Bankers Assn. (pres. 1978-79), C. of C. of Hawaii (dir. 1980-83, 88—), Honolulu Japanese C. of C. (dir.), Japan-Am. Soc. of Honolulu, United Japanese Soc. of Hawaii, Hawaii Joint Council on Econ. Edn. Clubs: Waialae Country, Honolulu Internat. Country, Pacific. Office: Cen Pacific Bank 220 S King St Honolulu HI 96813

SATRE, PHILIP GLEN, business executive, lawyer; b. Palo Alto, Calif., Apr. 30, 1949; s. Selmer Kenneth and Georgia June (Sterling) S.; m. Jennifer Patricia Arnold, June 30, 1973; children—Malena Anne, Allison Neal, Jessica Lilly, Peter Sterling. B.A., Stanford U., 1971; J.D., U. Calif.-Davis,

1975; postgrad sr. exec. program MIT, 1982. Bar: Nev., Calif. Assoc. Vargas & Bartlett, Reno, 1975-79; v.p., gen. counsel, sec. Harrah's, Reno, 1980-83, sr. v.p., 1983-84, pres. Harrah's East, Atlantic City, 1984; pres., chief exec. officer Harrah's Hotels and Casinos, Reno, 1984—. Mem. ABA, Nev. Bar Assn., Calif. Bar Assn., Order of Coif, Phi Kappa Phi, Stanford Alumni Assn. (pres. Reno chpt. 1976-77), Young Pres. Orgn. Office: Harrah's 300 E 2d St PO Box 10 Reno NV 89504

SAUER, HENRY JACK, educator; b. Portland, Oreg., Oct. 23, 1946; s. Henry Jack and Pauline Catherine (Rahn) S.; B.A., Wash. State U., 1970, M.Ed., 1981; m. Nancy Lee Lauber, July 25, 1970. Tchr., coach schs. in Wash., 1970—; learning mgr. experienced based career edn. Kennewick Sch. Dist., 1979-80, project mgr. CETA employer-edn. demonstration project, 1980-81, project dir. CETA employer-edn. project, 1981-82; asst. prin. Desert Hills Middle Sch., 1982—; cons. social studies. Active local United Way, Boy Scouts Am. Mem. Wash. Assn. Sch. Adminstrs., Assn. Supervision and Curriculum Devel., Phi Delta Kappa. Lutheran. Club: Kiwanis. Home: 2306 S Anderson Pl Kennewick WA 99337 Office: Desert Hills Mid Sch 6011 W 10th Pl Kennewick WA 99337

SAUER, JAMES EDWARD, JR., hospital administrator; b. Sanborn, N.D., Feb. 14, 1934; s. James Edward and Rose Marie (Grafton) S.; m. Sharon Ann Groom, Aug. 18, 1962; children—Scott Michael, Jeffrey William, Steven Douglas. B.S. in Bus. Adminstrn., U. N.D., 1956; M.H.A., U. Minn., 1964. Administrv. asst. Meth. Hosp., Madison, Wis., 1961-62; adminstrv. resident San Jose Hosp. and Health Ctr., Calif., 1963-64; asst. adminstr. Providence Hosp., Portland, Oreg., 1967-69, assoc. adminstr., 1969-73; pres., exec. dir. Calif. Hosp. Med. Ctr., Los Angeles, 1973-79; adminstr. St. Joseph Med. Ctr., Burbank, Calif., 1979—; mem. hosp. adv. com. Blue Cross So. Calif., 1976-79. Trustee, Sisters of Providence in Calif., 1979—; mem. exec. com. retirement bd. Sisters of Providence, 1983—. Contbr. articles to profl. jours. Served to capt. USAF, 1956-62. Fellow Am. Coll. Hosp. Adminstrs.; mem. Am. Hosp. Assn. (chmn. 1982-84), Oreg. Conf. Cath. Hosps. Assn. (pres. 1973-74), Hosp. Council So. Calif. (bd. dirs. 1975-81, exec. com. 1977-81, chmn. 1979-80), Calif. Hosp. Assn. (trustee 1979-84, chmn. 1983, Walker Fellow 1983), Calif. Assn. Cath. Hosps. (trustee 1981-82), Am. Arbitration Assn. (Los Angeles adv. council), Hollywood Acad. Medicine, Central Area Teaching Hosps. (bd. dirs. 1976-79). Lodge: Rotary. Office: St Joseph Med Ctr Buena Vista and Alameda Sts Burbank CA 91505

SAUER, JAMES PHILIP, engineer; b. Valley City, N.D., June 12, 1961; s. DuWayne Maurice and Phylis Jeanine (Jansen) S. BS in Mech. Engring. cum laude, U. N.D., Grand Forks, 1983; postgrad., Ariz. State U., 1983-87. Mfg. engr. Sperry Flight Systems, Phoenix, 1983-85, mfg. project engr., 1985-86; advanced mfg. tech. engr. Honeywell, Sperry Comml. Flight Systems Group, Phoenix, 1986—; tech. speaker MG Exposition Group, St. Paul, 1987. Recipient Crouch scholarship, U. N.D., 1980, 81. Mem. ASME (sec. 1982-83), Surface Mount Tech. Assn. Republican. Club: Internat. Fitness (Phoenix). Home: 243 W Sequoia Dr Phoenix AZ 85027 Office: Honeywell Sperry Comml Flight Systems 21111 N 19th Ave Phoenix AZ 85027

SAUL, DONNA FRANCES, corporate professional; b. St. Paul, Aug. 31, 1960; d. Herman James and Nellie Frances (Williams) S. BA cum laude, U. Pitts., 1984; MFA, Calif. Inst. of Arts, 1986. Prodn. stage mgr. Calif. Inst. of Arts, Valencia, 1984-86; logistics coord. L.A. Festival, 1986-88; div. planner Walt Disney Imagineering, Glendale, Calif., 1988—; stage mgr. CBN-TV spl., Los Angeles, 1988; cons. Sussman/Prejza, Santa Monica, Calif., 1988. Active 1st AME Polit. Action Com. Mem. NAACP, NAFE. Democrat. Home: 1516 E 2d St #10 Long Beach CA 90802 Office: Walt Disney Imagineering 1401 Flower St Glendale CA 91221

SAUL, WILLIAM EDWARD, academic administrator, civil engineering educator; b. N.Y.C., May 15, 1934; s. George James and Fanny Ruth (Murokh) S.; m. J. Muriel Held Eagleburger, May 11, 1976. BSCE, Mich. Tech. U., 1955, MSCE, 1961; PhD in Civil Engring., Northwestern U., 1964. Registered profl. engr., Wis., Idaho, Mich. Mech. engr. Shell Oil Co., New Orleans, 1955-59; instr. engring. mechanics Mich. Tech. U., Houghton, 1960-62; asst. prof. civil engring. U. Wis., Madison, 1964-67, assoc. prof., 1967-72, prof., 1972-84; dean Coll. Engring., prof. civil engring. U. Idaho, Moscow, 1984—; cons. engr., Madison, 1961—; bd. dirs. Idaho Research Found.; vis. prof. U. Stuttgart, Fed. Republic Germany, 1970-71. Co-editor Conf. of Methods of Structural Analysis, 1976. Fulbright fellow 1970-71; von Humboldt scholar, 1970-71. Mem. ASCE (pres. Wis. sect. 1983-84), NSPE, Idaho Soc. Profl. Engrs., Internat. Assn. Am. Concrete Inst., Bridge and Structures Engrs., Am. Soc. Engring Edn., Sigma Xi, Phi Kappa Phi, Tau Beta Pi, Chi Epsilon. Home: 1221 Ponderosa Dr Moscow ID 83843 Office: U Idaho Coll Engring Moscow ID 83843

SAULS, FREDERICK INABINETTE, artist; b. Seattle, Mar. 22, 1934; s. Frederick Inabinette and Borghild Caroline (Zakarison) S.; div.; children: Karoline, Fritz. Student, Stanford U., 1951-57, San Francisco Acad. Art, Calif. Coll. Arts and Crafts; A. in Art U. Calif., Berkeley, 1965; vis. artist U. Ky., 1966-68; asst. prof. U. Minn., 1969-70; prof. U. Calif., Santa Cruz, 1972-73. One-man shows include R.J. Reynolds Gallery, U. Ky., 1966, Tortue Gallery, Santa Monica, Calif., 1972, Gille Mansillon Gallery, Santa Monica, 1984; group shows: travelling exhibit internat. art UNESCO; works represented in permanent collections include Skopje (Yugoslavia) Mus. Modern Art, Cornell U., Berkeley Mus., Mus. Modern Art, N.Y., Woodrow Wilson Sculpture Garden, N.Y., Oakland (Calif.) Art Mus., Calif. With U.S. Army, 1952-54. Recipient Harry Lord Ford prize U. Calif., Berkeley, 1962, grand prize for sculpture Paris Biennale, 1965. Mem. Dramatists Guild. Address: PO Box 726 Lone Pine CA 93545

SAUNDERS, ALAN KEITH, professional football coach; b. London, Feb. 1, 1947; m. Karen Saunders: children: Korrin Elizabeth, William Joseph, Robert Charles. Grad., San Jose State U., 1969; MA, Stanford U., 1970; postgrad., U. So. Calif., 1983-85. Football coach U. Mo., 1972, Utah State U., 1973-75; asst. head coach U. Calif., 1976-81; offensive coordinator, quarterback coach U. Tenn., 1982; coach San Diego Chargers, NFL, 1983—, asst. head coach, 1985-86, head coach, 1986-88. Mem. ad-hoc com. state lic. and designated sports Calif. State Legis.; hon. chmn. S.D. chpt. Arthritis Found.; bd. dirs. Easter Seal Soc., San Diego; bd. govs. Athletes for a Stronger America; mem. S.D. Chem. Dependency Adv. Bd. Office: San Diego Chargers San Diego Stadium PO Box 20666 San Diego CA 92120

SAUNDERS, FRANK HENRY, investigator, police court witness; b. Rochester, N.Y., Dec. 6, 1934; s. William H. and Frances (Lovejoy) S.; m. Michele-Anne LaMar, July 18, 1981. Student, U. Ariz., 1954-56, 58-59; grad., L.A. Police Acad., 1965. Cert. police expert witness, Calif., Fed. Ct., 1983; lic. pvt. investigator, Calif. Investigator Continental Casualty Ins. Co., L.A., 1964-65; agt., police officer Santa Monica (Calif.) Police Dept., 1965-80; pvt. investigator Forensic Svcs., Inc., Huntington Beach, Calif., 1980-81, Frank Saunders Investigations, Capitola, Calif., 1981—; cons., expert witness Frank Saunders & Assocs., Capitola, 1981—. Recipient award for bravery Santa Monica Police Dept., 1967, 78, medal of valor, 1978; citation of bravery Calif. Senate, 1967. Mem. Nat. Forensic Ctr., Nat. Assn. Chiefs of Police, Peace Officers Rsch. Assn. Calif., Santa Monica Police Officers Assn. (editor Soundoff 1970-79), Internat. Platform Assn., Seascape Tennis Club (Aptos, Calif.). Republican. Office: PO Box 1730 Capitola CA 95010

SAUNDERS, GENE, banker, administrator; b. El Paso, Tex., May 15, 1937; s. Eugene Caldwell and Ruth (Powelson) S.; m. Joann Crabb, May 18, 1963; children: Mark, Amy, Richard, Debra. BBA, U. Tulsa, 1959. Cert. data processor. Bank clk. Carlsbad (N.Mex.) Nat. Bank, 1955-64; cashier 1st Nat. Bank, Roswell, N.Mex., 1964-68; data processing systems project mgr. Valley Nat. Bank, Phoenix, 1969-78, advanced systems mgr., 1978-80, project adminstr., 1980-88, compliance adminstr., 1988—; advisor Fed. Res. Bank Return Items Task Force, Washington, 1984-88, Fed. Res. Bank Future Electronic Funds Transfer Group, Washington, 1987—; mem. X-9 banking group Am. Nat. Standards Inst., Washington, 1980—. Republican. Mormon. Office: Valley Nat Bank PO Box 71 A-LAW Phoenix AZ 85001

SAUNDERS, JAMES, economic development consultant, councilman; b. Chgo., Sept. 22, 1924; s. James Windam and Carrie Evelyn (Cox) S.; m. Gwendolyn Haithcox, Oct. 21, 1945 (dec. May 1971); children: Patricia Ann, Kathryn Lynn; m. Anita Joanne Laster, Sept. 16, 1972 (div. Oct. 1977); m. Bettye Jean Ricks, Apr. 18, 1981. BS in Math., Roosevelt U., 1953. Quality assurance rep. Dept. Army and Signal Corps., Chgo., 1945-70; dep. dir. quality assurance U.S. Naval Ordnance Plant, Forest Park, Ill., 1963-70; quality systems mgr. Gen. Foods Corp., Chgo., 1970-82; pres. Saunders and Assocs., Peoria, Ariz., 1982—; councilman City of Peoria, 1985—. Bd. dirs., sec. Araiz. Retirement Ctrs., Peoria, 1984-85; mem. Peoria Personnel Bd., 1984-85; mem. Maricopa County Pvt. Industry Coun., 1984—, chmn., 1988; founding chmn. Project VOICE, consumer adv. panel, Phoenix, 1987-88; pres., chmn. bd. dirs., founder Peoria Econ. Devel. Group, 1987—; mem. exec. com. Westside Transport Com., Peoria, 1988—. Recipient Black Achiever of Industry award Chgo. YMCA, 1977, NAACP Image govt. award., 1989; also various other awards. Mem. Peoria C. of C. (v.p. 1985), Westside Coalition Chambers Commerce, Lions (sec., v.p., bd. dirs. Peoria 1983-86), Masons, Alpha Phi Alpha. Democrat. Home: 10430 W Royal Palm Rd Peoria AZ 85345 Office: Peoria Econ Devel Group 8815 W Peoria Ave Peoria AZ 85345

SAUNDERS, JAMES HARWOOD, accountant; b. Carlsbad, N.Mex., Apr. 2, 1948; s. Eugene C. and Ruth (Powelson)S.; m. Kathleen Sue Matson, Jan. 26, 1974 (div. Apr. 1982); m. Bette Kim McCutcheon, Sept. 4, 1982; children: James C., Carl J., William K. AA in Adminstrn. Justice, Glendale Coll., Glendale, Ariz., 1975; BSBA, Ariz. State U., 1978. CPA, N.M., Ariz.; lic. funeral dir. and embalmer, N.M., Ariz. Funeral dir., embalmer Denton Funeral Home, Carlsbad, 1964-69; clk., trainee Sears & Roebuck Co., Dallas, Phoenix, 1969-73, Albuquerque, 1969-73; police sgt. spl. ops. Phoenix Police Dept., 1973-80; staff acct. various CPA firms, Carlsbad, 1980-83; owner James H. Saunders Acctg., Carlsbad, 1983-86; pvt. practice acctg. Carlsbad, 1986-87, Eagar, Ariz., 1988—; auditor, mgmt. advisor to several Ariz. municipalities, 1987—. Vol. fireman Carlsbad Fire Dept., 1965-68; reserve dep. Bermallio County Sheriff Dept., Albuquerque, 1969-70. Mem. AICPA, Ariz. Soc. CPAs, N.Mex. Soc. CPAs, N.Mex. Assn. Funeral Dirs., Lions (sec. Carlsbad chpt. 1985-87, pres. Springerville, Ariz. chpt. 1987—). Office: PO Box 1270 28 N Main Eagar AZ 85925

SAUNDERS, LAUREL BARNES, librarian; b. Ainsworth, Nebr., Aug. 17, 1926; d. Howard Enos and Flossie Agnes (Marr) Barnes; married; 1 child, Kelvin Edwin Saunders. BA, U. S.D., 1948; MA, U. Mich., 1950. Librarian pub. schs. Howell, Mich., 1950-51; asst. librarian, U.S. Army post Ft. Bliss, Tex., 1951-53; librarian, USAF base Biggs AFB, Tex., 1953-62; supervisory librarian U.S. Air Def. Sch., Ft. Bliss, 1962-64; chief cataloguing and acquistions U.S. Army Tech. Library, White Sands Missile Range, N.Mex., 1964-74, chief librarian, 1975—. Pres. Quaestors Sunday Sch. class, Trinity First Meth. Ch., 1985-88, adminstrv. bd., 1986-87. Mem. Fed. Mgrs. Assn. (2d v.p. 1982-83, 1st v.p. 1989, pres. 1984-87, bd. dirs., Mgr. of Yr. award 1985, pres. Quaestors 1985—, sec. 1988), N.Mex. Library Assn. (vice-chmn. Documents Roundtable 1984-85, chmn. 1985-86), Border Regional Library Assn., U.S. Army Library Inst. (active procurement working group 1980-84). Republican. Club: Past Matrons (Anthony, N.Mex.). Lodge: Order of Eastern Star (Worthy Matron 1970, treas. 1982—).

SAUNDERS, PETER PAUL, finance executive; b. Budapest, Hungary, July 21, 1928; emigrated to Can., 1941, naturalized, 1946; s. Peter Paul and Elizabeth (Halom) Szende; m. Nancy Louise McDonald, Feb. 11, 1956; children: Christine Elizabeth, Paula Marie. Student, Vancouver Coll., 1941-44; B.Com., U. B.C., 1948. Acct. Canadian Pacific Ry. Co., 1948-50; founder, pres. Laurentide Fin. Corp., Ltd., 1950-66, vice chmn., 1966-67; pres. Coronation Credit Corp. Ltd., Vancouver, B.C., Can., 1968-78; chmn., pres. Cornat Industries Ltd., Vancouver, B.C., Can., 1969-78, Versatile Corp. (formerly Coronation Credit Corp. and Cornat Industries Ltd.), Vancouver, B.C., Can., 1978-87; prin. Saunders Investment Ltd., Vancouver, 1987—; bd. dirs. China Bus. Machines, Inc., B.C. Broadcasting Co. Ltd., Wajax Ltd., N.W. Sports Enterprises Ltd., WIC Western Internat. Communications Ltd., Laurentian Gen. Ins. Co., Inc., Jannock Ltd.; mem. Vancouver adv. bd. Nat. Trust Co. Ltd. Adv. com. inmate employment Correctional Svc. Can.; gov. Vancouver Opera Assn.; pres. Vancouver Symphony Soc., 1968-70, Can. Cancer Soc., B.C. and Yukon region, 1975-77, Vancouver Art Gallery Assn., 1981-83; pres., chmn. Vancouver Soc. for Bus. and Arts; bd. dirs. Coun. for Bus. and the Arts in Can., Coun. for Can. Unity. Clubs: Vancouver Lawn Tennis and Badminton, Shaughnessy Golf and Country, Royal Vancouver Yacht, Vancouver; Thunderbird Country (Rancho Mirage, Calif.). Home: 2186 SW Marine Dr, Vancouver, BC Canada V6P 6B5 Office: Saunders Investment Ltd, PO Box 49352 Bentall Centre, Vancouver, BC Canada V7X 1L4

SAUNDERS, RANDAL SCOTT, architect; b. Bakersfield, Calif., Jan. 13, 1957; s. Thomas Lee and Carol Ann (Moore) S. BArch, U. Oreg., 1980. Registered architect, Oreg., Wash. Staff draftsman Coxwell Miller Levine Wyttenbach Architects, P.C., Billings, Mont., 1980-81, David L. Trapp & Assocs., Woodburn, Oreg., 1982-83, Petersen-Kolberg & Assocs., Wilsonville, Oreg., 1983-84; staff architect Samuels & Clay Architects, Coos Bay, Oreg., 1984-86; owner, architect RSS Architecture, North Bend, Oreg., 1986-87, Woodburn, 1987—; adviser North Bend Waterfront Devel. Advocates, 1986-87. Mem. assoc. pastor nominating com. 1st Presbyterian Ch., North Bend, 1987; mem. feasibility com. Coos County Conv. Ctr., 1985; mem. North Bend Planning Commn., 1987, North Bend Downtown Assn., 1986. Mem. Nat. Trust Hist. Preservation, Coos Bay Yacht Club, Rotary. Home: 1824 Liberty St NE Salem OR 97303

SAUNDERS, ROBERT MALLOUGH, engineering educator, college administrator; b. Winnipeg, Man., Can., Sept. 12, 1915; s. Robert and Mabel Grace (Mallough) S.; m. Elizabeth Lenander, June 24, 1943. BEE, U. Minn., 1938, MS, 1942; D.Eng., Tokyo Inst. Tech., 1971. Design engr. Electric Machinery Co., Mpls., part-time 1938-42; teaching asst. elec. engring. U. Minn., 1938-42, instr., 1942-44; faculty U. Calif.-Berkeley, 1946-65, prof. elec. engring., 1957-65, chmn. dept., 1959-63; asst. to chancellor for engring. U. Calif.-Irvine, 1964-65, prof. elec. engring., 1965—, dean Sch. Engring., 1965-73; vis. assoc. prof. MIT, 1954-55; cons. Gen. Motors Research Lab., Apollo Support Dept., Gen. Electric Co., Aerospace Corp., Rohr Corp.; sec. Nat. Commn. for Elec. Engring. films, 1962-71; mem. ECPD Engring. Edn. and Accreditation Com., 1965-71, chmn., 1969-70, bd. dirs., 1971-75; mem. engring. adv. com. NSF, 1968-71; mem. Sec. Navy's Bd. Edn. and Tng., 1972-78. Co-author: Analysis of Feedback Control Systems, 1956; contbr.: Ency. Brit.; tech. jours. Bd. visitors U.S. Army Transp. Sch., 1970-73. Served to lt. (j.g.) USNR, 1944-46. Simon fellow engring. Manchester U., Eng., 1960. Fellow AAAS, IEEE (chmn. ednl. activities bd. 1973-74, mem. exec. com., dir. 1973-79, v.p. regional activities 1975-76, pres. 1977, Centennial medal 1984), mem. Am. Soc. Engring. Edn. (chmn. elec. div. 1965-66), Am. Assn. Engring. Socs. (organizing com. 1977-80, exec. com. 1982-84, chmn. bd. govs. 1983, chmn. awards com. 1984-85, nominating com. 1984-85), Nat. Research Council (mem. com. on edn. and utilization of engr., 1983-84), Sigma Xi, Tau Beta Pi, Eta Kappa Nu. Lodge: Rotary. Office: U Calif Sch Engring Irvine CA 92717

SAUNDERS, SANDRA JEAN, lawyer; b. Cleve., Jan. 1, 1944; d. Alexander V. and Rosemary (Sunyog) Toth. BA, Brown U., 1964; MA, Fordham U., 1965; JD, Lewis and Clark U., 1978. Bar: Oreg. 1979, U.S. Dist. Ct. Oreg. 1979. Securities analyst various cos., N.Y.C., Boston, Chgo., 1964-73; econ. cons., Portland, 1973-76; pvt. practice law, Portland, 1979—. V.p. bd. dirs. Pittock Mansion Soc., Portland, 1981—; legal cons. Oreg. Apt. Assn., Multi Family Housing Coun., Homebuilders Assn.; trustee Leukemia Assn. Oreg., 1984—; area rep. Nat. Alumni Schs. Program, Brown U., 1981—; mem. Portland Met. Citizens Cable TV Com., 1973-74; pres. Oreg. Mus. Sci. and Industry, Portland, 1974, mem. coun., 1984—, mem. auction bd., 1987—; mem. women's council Portland Art Assn., 1973—; bd. dirs. Vol. Braille Svcs., Inc., Portland, 1985—. Law rev. staff Environ. Law, 1977. Recipient Am. Jurisprudence award, 1978. Mem. ABA, Oreg. State Bar, Multnomah County Bar Assn., Oreg. Trial Lawyers Assn., Oreg. Young Attys. Assn. (dir. 1981-83), Portland City Club, Multnomah Athletic Club, Women's Assn. (pres.) Internat. Club, Phi Alpha Delta. Office: 700 Morgan Bldg 720 SW Washington St Portland OR 97205

SAUSEDO, ANN ELIZABETH, newspaper librarian; b. Douglas, Ariz., Nov. 19, 1929; d. Eugene Ephraim and Bertha Florence (Kimpton) Bertram; m. Richard Edward Sausedo, July 22, 1952 (div. 1966); 1 dau., Robin Marie. Student Calif. schs. Asst. librarian Stockton Record (Calif.), 1948-51, head librarian, 1955-67; stewardess Calif. Central Airlines, 1951; library dir. Washington Star, 1967-76; free-lance organizer file systems, Palo Alto, Calif., 1976-78; library dir. Los Angeles Herald Examiner, 1978—. Contbr. chpt. to book in field. Mem. Spl. Libraries Assn., Nat. Assn. Female Execs., Calif. Bus. Women's Network. Office: LA Herald Examiner 1111 S Broadway Los Angeles CA 90015

SAUSEN, JOHN HIGDON, consulting mechanical engineer; b. Great Falls, Mont., May 1, 1919; s. Alfred Leo and Estelle E. (Higdon) S; m. Jane Mary Mathews, Jan. 3, 1942; children: David, Janet, Mark, Kevin, Karen, Nancy, Gretchen. BS in Petroleum Engring., U. Minn., 1941. Staff engr. Reserve Mining Co., Minn., 1952-65; mgr. Brobeck Engrs., Berkeley, Calif., 1965-71; dir. Ladco Engrs., Hong Kong, 1971-75; pres. JHS Cons. Engrs., Las Vegas, Nev., 1975-82; project mgr. Sverdrup Corp., San Francisco, 1983—. Mem. Nat. Soc. Profl. Engrs., Soc. Energy Engrs., Nat. Soc. Heating Ventilation Air Conditioning Engrs. Republican. Home: 312 Indian Way Novato CA 94947 Office: Sverdrup Corp 417 Montgomery San Francisco CA 94104

SAUVAGE, MICHAEL, food and beverage executive, researcher, consultant; b. Paris, Feb. 9, 1948; came to U.S., 1981; s. Roger Alfred and Genevieve (Ferre) S.; m. Marie-Dominique Douheret, Oct. 6, 1973; children: Arnaud, Celine. Grad., Law U., Paris, 1969. Asst. atty. Versailles, France, 1971-72; fin. asst. Groupe Palvel Marmont, Paris, 1972-74; pres., chief exec. officer Warm Internat., Paris, 1974-76; pvt. practice cons. Paris and London, 1976-77; chief exec. officer Frucoop Internat., Avigvon, France, 1977-81; wine cons. Biltmore Hotel, L.A., 1981-82; food and beverage exec. WCO Disney Magic, Long Beach, Calif., 1986—; owner, pres. Mktg. Wine Rsch., South Pasadena, Calif., 1985—. Contbr. articles to profl. jours. Recipient Spl. award Comite Nat. des Vins de France, 1984. Fellow Chevalier du Tastevin Bougogne; mem. Les Toques Blanches (com. dir. L.A. chpt. 1985—), Confrerie de Saint Etienne, Confrerie des Compagnons Beaujolais, Academie du Vin de Bordeaux. Roman Catholic. Home: 830 Monterey Rd South Pasadena CA 91030 Office: Mktg Wine Rsch PO Box 3263 South Pasadena CA 91030

SAVAGE, JOHN LAWRENCE, agriculturist, provincial government official; b. Qualicum Beach, B.C., Can., Feb. 23, 1936; s. Harold Roland and Veronica Mary (Wolfe) S.; m. Margaret Johnson; children: Kim, Pamela, Lori. Alderman Dist. of Delta, 1985-88; mem. B.C. Legis. Assembly, Victoria, 1986—, minister of agr. and fisheries, 1986—. Pres., dir. Delta C. of C., 1981-82; pres. B.C. Fedn. Agr., 1983-85, dir. 1976-86; chmn. Delta Parks and Recreation Com., 1985; exec. dir. Can. Fed. Agr., Ottawa, 1981-85. Office: Ministry of Agr & Fisheries, Parliament Bldgs, Victoria, BC Canada V8V 1X4

SAVAGE, WAYNE, biology educator; b. Sudan, Tex., Oct. 31, 1931; s. Raymond Lee and Mellie (Long) S.; m. Sandra Joanne Stallings, Sept. 14, 1957; children: Scott Matthew, Alison Diana, Stephen Andrew. AB, San Francisco State U., 1958; PhD, U. Calif., Berkeley, 1967. Biology tchr. Capuchino High Sch., San Bruno, Calif., 1959-62; asst. prof. biology San Jose (Calif.) State U., 1966-70, assoc. prof., 1970-76, prof., 1976—, chmn. dept. biol. scis., 1985—; sr. cons. Harvey and Stanley Assocs., Alviso, Calif., 1970—; sr. scientist Wellspring Corp., Cupertino, Calif., 1983-85. Pres. Youth Sci. Inst., San Jose, 1979-81. Grantee NSF, 1972, NASA, 1983—. Mem. AAAS, Am. Inst. Biol. Scis., Assn. Biologists Computing (pres. 1982-85), Bot. Soc. Am., Calif. Bot. Soc. (pres. 1980), Internat. Assn. Plant Taxonomy, Soc. Archimedes (bd. dirs. 1985—). Office: San Jose State U Dept Biology San Jose CA 95192-0100

SAVARESE, THERESA MARIE, academic administrator; b. Bklyn., Nov. 9, 1950; d. Francis Anthony and Frances Mary (Calabro) S. AA with distinction, Phoenix Community Coll., 1971; BEd with distinction, Ariz. State U., Tempe, 1973, MEd, 1975. Cert. bus. edn. tchr., Ariz. Data entry operator Sears, Roebuck & Co., Phoenix, 1969-73, supr. computer dept., 1973-74; tchr. bus. Alhambra High Sch., Phoenix, 1976 summer; chmn. bus. dept., dir. activities Gerard Cath. High Sch., Phoenix, 1974-81; instr. Rio Salado Community Coll., Phoenix, 1983-84; coordinator coop. edn. office Deer Valley High Sch., Glendale, Ariz., 1981-86; chmn. bus. dept. Barry Goldwater High Sch., Phoenix, 1986—; mem. high tech. equipment selection com. Barry Goldwater High Sch., Phoenix, 1986-87, chmn., 1987-88. Tchr. religion St. Gregory's Roman Cath. Ch., Phoenix, 1969-81, minister communion, 1978—. Mem. Internat. Bus. Edn. Assn., Nat. Bus. Edn. Assn., Western Bus. Edn. Assn., Ariz. Bus. Edn. Assn., Am. Vocat. Assn., Ariz. Vocat. Assn. (sec., editor newsletter 1985-87), NEA, Ariz. Edn. Assn., Deer Valley Edn. Assn., Delta Pi Epsilon, Pi Omega Pi, Nat. Orgn. Italian Am. Women. Home: 935 W Avalon Dr Phoenix AZ 85013 Office: Barry Goldwater High Sch 2820 W Rose Garden Ln Phoenix AZ 85027

SAVASTANO, PAOLA ANNE, nurse; b. Waltham, Mass., Jan. 11, 1961; d. Charles Leo and Margaret Ellen (McLean) Tirone; m. Donald Matthew Savastano, June 28, 1986; 1 child, Aaron Matthew. Diploma in nursing, New Eng. Deaconess Sch. Nursing, Boston, 1983. Nurse CCU Brigham & Women's Hosp., Boston, 1983-85, nurse coronary, 1986-87; nurse Petaluma Valley (Calif.) Hosp. Home Health Care, 1987; nurse, liason Jewish Meml. Hosp., Roxbury, Mass., 1988—; nurse Favorite Nurses, Boston, 1988—. Democrat. Roman Catholic. Home: 4 Knoll Crest Circle Attleboro MA 02703

SAVILLE, ANTHONY, educational administration educator; b. Montreal, Que., Can., June 16, 1930; came to U.S., 1931; m. Joy Lee Randolph, May 22, 1955. BS in Edn., Ill. State U., 1951; MEd, U. Mo., 1957, EdD, 1961. Tchr., coach Centerville (Mo.) High Sch., 1951, Bland (Mo.) High Sch., 1951-55; prin. Wentzville (Mo.) High Sch., 1955-57; adminstr. Pkwy. High Sch., Creve Coeur, Mo., 1957-60; asst. to dean Coll. Edn. U. Mo., Columbia, 1960-61; asst. prof. edn. Fresno (Calif.) State coll., 1961-64; dept. chair Coll. Edn. Bowling Green (Ohio) U., 1964-67; dean Coll. Edn. U. Nev., Las Vegas, 1967-78, prof. edn. adminstrn. and higher edn., 1978—, dist. prof. Coll. Edn., 1988; cons. various sch. dists., 1961—. Author: Instructional Programming, 1973, Will of the People: Education in Nevada, 1977; contbr. articles to profl. jours. Mem. citizens com. Clark County Sch. Dist., Las Vegas, 1984-85. Mem. Am. Assn. Sch. Adminstrs., Nat. Assn. Secondary Sch. Prins., Am. Assn. Supervision and Curriculum Devel., Phi Delta Kappa (pres. 1983-86). Democrat. Methodist. Home: 1517 Kirkland Ave Las Vegas NV 89102 Office: U Nev 4505 Maryland Pkwy Las Vegas NV 89154

SAVONA, MICHAEL RICHARD, physician; b. N.Y.C., Oct. 21, 1947; s. Salvatore Joseph and Diana Grace (Menditto) S.; B.S. summa cum laude, Siena Coll., 1969; M.D., SUNY, Buffalo, 1973; m. Dorothy O'Neill, Oct. 18, 1975. Intern in internal medicine, Presbyn. Hosp., Columbia U., N.Y.C., 1973-74, resident in internal medicine, 1974-76, vis. fellow internal medicine Delafield Hosp./Columbia U. Coll. Physicians and Surgeons, 1974-76; practice medicine specializing in internal medicine, Maui Med. Group, Wailuku, Hawaii, 1976-87; gen. practice medicine, 1987—; dir. ICU, Maui Meml. Hosp., also dir. respiratory therapy, CCU., chmn. dept. medicine, 1980—; clin. faculty John A. Burns Sch. Medicine, U. Hawaii. Bd. dirs. Maui Heart Assn.; dir. profl. edn. Maui chpt. Am. Cancer Soc.; mem. Maui County Hosp. Adv. Commn.; mem. council Community Cancer Program of Hawaii. Recipient James A. Gibson Wayne J. Atwell award, 1970, physiology award, 1970, Ernest Whitebsky award, 1971, Roche Lab. award, 1972, Pfiser Lab. award, 1973, Phillip Sang award, 1973, Hans Lowenstein M.D. Meml. award, 1973. Diplomate Am. Bd. Internal Medicine. Mem. AMA, Am. Thoracic Soc., Hawaii Thoracic Soc., Maui County Med. Assn. (past pres.), Hawaii Med. Assn., Hawaii Oncology Group, A.C.P., SW Oncology Coop. Group, Alpha Omega Alpha, Delta Epsilon Sigma. Office: 1830 Wells St Wailuku HI 96793

SAVONEN, GENE LEONARD, wholesale distribution company executive; b. Chgo., Dec. 4, 1926; s. Leonard L. and Louise A. (Krueger) S.; children: Carol Ann, Lynn Ellen. BSME, U. Colo., 1950. Br. mgr. Cherry Burrell Corp., St. Paul, 1960-69; v.p. Cherry Burrell Corp., Claremont, Calif., 1969-73, WPM Systems Inc., Denver, 1973-77; pres. Seaview Electronics Inc., San Diego, 1977-85, Southview Corp., San Diego, 1985—. Office: Southview Corp 11526 Sorrento Valley Rd Ste A San Diego CA 92121

SAVOY, JAMES CUNNINGHAM, zoo administrator; b. Cin., Mar. 18, 1930; s. Albert E. and Lillian (Cunningham) S.; m. Nancy Lefebure, May 14, 1953; children—Scott, Susan. D.V.M., Ohio State U., 1960. Veterinarian Columbus Zoo, Ohio, 1960-64, dir., 1964-74; dir. Detroit Zoo, Mich., 1974-78, Phoenix Zoo, Ariz., 1978—. Fellow Am. Vet. Med. Assn., Am. Assn. Zoo Veterinarians, Ariz. Vet. Med. Assn.; mem. Am. Assn. Zool. Parks and Aquariums (bd. dirs. 1983-85, 2 Outstanding Service awards). Republican. Presbyterian. Home: 2410 E Cairo St Tempe AZ 85282 Office: The Phoenix Zoo Office of Dir PO Box 5155 Phoenix AZ 85010

SAWICKI, EDWARD JAMES, corporate consulting service executive; b. Phila., Aug. 24, 1946; s. Edward Joseph and Catherine (Rita) S.; m. Anita Gale Sottler, July 15, 1972. AS in Sci. and Math., West Valley Coll., 1972; student, San Jose State U., 1973-76, U. San Francisco, 1977-78. Watch comdr. Ampex Corp., Redwood City, Calif., 1973-74; watch comdr., safety engr. Signetics, Sunnyvale, Calif., 1974-76; corp. safety dir. Intel Corp., Santa Clara, Calif., 1976-82; pres. Microsafe, Inc., Santa Clara, 1982—. Served as staff sgt. U.S. Army, 1966-70, Vietnam. Decorated Bronze Star with V device; recipient Plaque City of Santa Clara, 1980, Award of Merit City of Sunnyvale, 1981. Mem. World Safety Orgn. (cert.), Am. Soc. Safety Engrs. (pres. San Jose chpt. 1985-86), Am. Indsl. Hygiene Assn., Health Physics Assn., Nat. Safety Council (research and devel. com.), Nat. Fire Protection Assn., Semiconductor Safety Assn. (bd. dirs. Cen. Counties Nat. Safety Council), Bay Area Electronics Safety Group (founder 1978). Home: 854 Hilmar St Santa Clara CA 95050 Office: Microsafe Inc 1500 Wyatt Dr Ste #5 Santa Clara CA 95051

SAWICKI, WALTER JOSEPH JR., interior designer; b. Wolbach, Nebr., July 7, 1917; s. Walter Joseph Sr. and Emma Josephine (Lowe) S.; m. Mary Katherine Christensen, Oct. 11, 1941; children: John Gerald, Walter J. III, Lawrence Mitchell, Audna Marie, David Alan. BFA, U. Colo., 1938. Various interior design positions various orgns., Colo., 1945-64; mgr. various cos., Calif., Ariz., 1964-69; coordinator, dir. Bullock's of So. Calif., L.A., 1969-74; entrepreneur Calif. Design Assoc., Irving, 1974-76; salesperson James Davis Showroom, 1976-78; design services dir. J.H. Biggar Furniture & Interior Design, Pasadena, Calif., 1978-80; mgr. James Davis & Assoc., 1980-84; owner Walter Sawicki Designs, Inc., 1984-88. Capt. USAF, 1942—. Mem. Am. Soc. Interior Designers (pres. 1954-56; bd. dirs. 1954-58), Rotary, Lions. Democrat. Roman Catholic. Home and Office: 2820 Jasmine Circle Hemet CA 92343

SAWYER, RAYMOND ETON, bishop; b. Woonsocket, R.I., Nov. 7, 1946; s. Edgar Bertrand Decelles and Juliette Laurence (Breault) Robbins. BA, St. Thomas Aquinas U., Houston, 1976; STL, Faculte Libre Theology, Paris, 1978; STM, STD, Sorbonne, 1980. Ordained priest Old Cath. Ch. (Utrecht) and Brazilian Cath. Apostolic Succession, 1974. Priest Old Cath. Ch. (Utrecht) and Brazilian Cath. Apostolic Succession, Fla., N.Y. and Tex., 1974-88; bishop Old Cath. Ch. (Utrecht) and Brazilian Cath. Apostolic Succession, Salt Lake City, 1988—; mem. Nat. U.S. Synod of Bishops, Highlandville, Mo., 1988—. Decorated Chevaliers Hospitalier de Pomerol, France, 1982. Mem. Phi Alpha Theta. Home: St Luke's Old Cath Rectory 1924 East 3900 S Salt Lake City UT 84124 Office: St Lukes Old Cath Cathedral 1910 East 3900 S Salt Lake City UT 84124

SAWYER, THOMAS ARTHUR, corporation executive; b. Pocatello, Idaho, Apr. 26, 1946; s. Fred Ellis and Bertha Elizabeth (Adkins) S.; m. Cora Ada Davis, Sept. 4, 1969; children—Gaylan Thomas, Rebecca Lynn, Bradley Arthur, Mark Twain, Joseph Edward, James Ellis. Student Idaho State U., 1966-69, Boise State U., 1970-77; cert. data processing mgmt., 1971 cert. in prodn. and inventory mgmt., 1979, cert. system devel. profl., 1984. Programmer, FMC Corp., Pocatello, 1967-70; mgr. systems and programming Ore Ida Foods, Inc., Boise, Idaho, 1970-77; mgr. systems devel. Tektronix, Inc., Beaverton, Oreg., 1977-83; dir. mgmt. info. systems and adminstrn. Sidereal Corp., Portland, Oreg., 1983-86; pres. Advanced Bus. Solutions, Inc., 1986—; cons., instr. mfg. system principles. Served in USAF, 1966-73. Mem. Assn. Systems Mgmt. Data Processing Mgmt. Assn., Am. Prodn. and Inventory Control Soc. Republican. Mormon. Home: 12295 SW Tippitt Pl Tigard OR 97223 Office: Sidereal Corp 9600 SW Barnes Rd Portland OR 97225

SAWYER, THOMAS EDGAR, management consultant; b. Homer, La., July 7, 1932; s. Sidney Edgar and Ruth (Bickham) S.; B.S., UCLA, 1959; M.A., Occidental Coll., 1969; m. Joyce Mezzanatto, Aug. 22, 1954; children—Jeffrey T., Scott A., Robert J., Julie Anne. Project engr. Garrett Corp., Los Angeles, 1954-60; mgr. devel. ops. TRW Systems, Redondo Beach, Calif., 1960-66; spl. asst. to gov. State of Calif., Sacramento, 1967-69; prin., gen. mgr. Planning Research Corp., McLean, Va., 1969-72; dep. dir. OEO, Washington, 1972-74; asso. prof. bus. mgmt. Brigham Young U., 1974-78; pres. Mesa Corp., Provo, 1978-82, chmn. bd., 1978-82; pres. and dir. Sage Inst. Internat., Inc., Provo, Utah, 1982-88; pres., chmn. bd. Pvt. Telecom Networks, Inc., Orem, Utah, 1988—; dir. Intechna Corp., HighTech Corp., Nat. Applied Computer Tech. Inc. (chmn.), Indian Affiliates, Inc. Chmn. Nat. Adv. Council Indian Affairs; chmn. Utah State Bd. Indian Affairs; mem. Utah Dist. Export Council; mem. Utah dist. SBA Council; chmn. So. Paiute Restoration Com.; mem. adv. council Nat. Bus. Assn.; mem. Utah Job Tng. Coordinating Council. Served with USMC, 1950-53. Mem. Am. Mgmt. Assn., Am. Soc. Public Adminstrn., Utah Council Small Bus. (dir.). Republican. Mormon. Club: Masons. Author: Assimilation Versus Self-Indentity: A Modern Native American Perspective, 1976; Computer Assisted Instruction: An Inevitable Breakthrough. Home: 548 W 630 S Orem UT 84058 Office: Pvt Telecom Networks Inc 744 South 400 E Orem UT 84058

SAX, JOSEPH LAWRENCE, lawyer, educator; b. Chgo., Feb. 3, 1936; s. Benjamin Harry and Mary (Silverman) S.; m. Eleanor Charlotte Gettes, June 17, 1958; children—Katherine Elaine, Valerie Beth, Anne-Marie. A.B., Harvard, 1957; J.D., U. Chgo., 1959. Bar: D.C. 1960, U.S. Supreme Ct. 1966. Atty. Dept. Justice, Washington, 1959-60; pvt. practice Washington, 1960-62; prof. U. Colo. Law Sch., 1962-65, U. Mich. Law Sch., Ann Arbor, 1966-86, U. Calif., Berkeley, 1987—; vis. prof. U. Calif. Law Sch., Berkeley, 1965-66, 86, U. Paris I, 1981, 82, Stanford Law Sch., 1985; fellow Ctr. Advanced Study in Behavioral Scis., 1977-78; cons. U.S. Senate Com. on Pub. Works, 1970-71; mem. cons. council Conservation Found., 1969-73; mem. legal adv. com. Pres.'s Council on Environ. Quality, 1970-72; mem. environ. studies bd. Nat. Acad. Sci., 1970-73; mem. Mich. Environ. Rev. Bd., 1973-74. Author: Waters and Water Rights, 1967, Water Law, Planning and Policy, 1968, Defending the Environment, 1971, Mountains Without Handrails, 1980, Legal Control of Water Resources, 1986. Bd. dirs. Environ. Law Inst., Washington, 1970-75; trustee Center for Law and Social Policy, 1970-76; regional gov. Internat. Council Environmental Law; gov.'s rep. Gt. Lakes Task Force, 1984-85. Served with USAF, 1960. Home: 850 Powell St #106 San Francisco CA 94108

SAXENA, NARENDRA K., marine research educator; b. Agra, India, Oct. 15, 1936; came to U.S., 1969; s. Brijbasi Lal and Sarbati Saxena; m. Cecilia H. Hsi, Mar. 21, 1970; Sarah Vasanti, Lorelle Sarita. Diploma Geodetic Engring., Tech. U., Hanover, Fed. Republic Germany, 1966; D in Tech Scis., Tech. U., Graz, Austria, 1972. Research assoc. geodetic sci. Ohio State U., Columbus, 1969-74; asst. prof. U. Ill., Urbana, 1974-78; asst. prof. U. Hawaii, Honolulu, 1978-81, assoc. prof., 1981-86, prof., 1986—; adj. research prof. Naval Postgrad. Sch., Monterey, Calif., 1984—; co-chmn. Pacific Congresses on Marine Tech., Honolulu, 1984, 86, 88; pres. Pacon Internat. Inc., 1987—. Editor Jour. Marine Geodesy, 1976—. Mem. Neighborhood Bd., Honolulu, 1984. Fellow Marine Tech. Soc. (various offices 1974—); mem. ASCE, Am. Geophys. Union, The Tsunami Soc. (sec. 1985—). Office: U Hawaii Dept Civil Engring Honolulu HI 96822

SAXON-ANDREEN, LINDA LEE, contract administrator, writer; b. Chgo., Oct. 28, 1948; d. George William and Shirlee Joan (Francioni) Simpson; m. David John Andreen; children: Susan Lynn, Jeffrey Scott. Roosevelt U. Purchasing agt. Valley Nat. Bank, Phoenix, 1989—; contract adminstr. Ariz. Bank (Security Pacific Corp.), Phoenix, 1989—; editor, Purchasing Mgmt. Assn. of Ariz. Phoenix, 1984-87, pub. relations chmn.; public relations chmn. Arix. Minority Supplier Devel. Council, Phoenix, 1986-89, exec. com. 1986-89, Planning com chmn. 1986-89, rep. Contributing author: Pacific Purchaser; Purchasing Exec. Bulletin. Republican. Home: 5122 E Shea Blvd 2084 Scottsdale AZ 85254 Office: Ariz Bank PO Box 2511 Phoenix AZ 85002

SAXTON, DENNIS MICHEAL, engineer; b. Cleve., May 31, 1947; s. LeRoy and Ann Cecilia (Jennyo) S.; m. Deborah Ellen Bryan, June 34, 1973; children: Micheal Joseph, Andrew James, Stephen Patrick, Peter Samuel. Student, Tri-State U., 1972. Draftsman Magnavox, Ft. Wayne, Ind., 1972-73; sr. designer Admiral Corp., Chgo., 1973-76; sr. designer FXC Corp., Santa Ana, Calif., 1976-77, chief engr., 1977-82, adv. design engr., 1982-83, 85—, program mgr., 1984-85; engr., owner, machine shop Proto Engring., Long Beach, Calif., 1982; design engr. Hi-Tek Corp., Garden Grove, Calif., 1983-84. Inventor in field. Served with U.S. Army, 1967-69, Vietnam. Mem. Nat. Soc. Profl. Engrs. Republican. Roman Catholic. Club: Chess. Home: 37950 E Benton Rd Temecula CA 92390 Office: FXC Corp 3410 S Susan St Santa Ana CA 92704

SAXTON, HARRY JAMES, laboratory executive; b. Bell, Calif., July 2, 1939; s. James Alfred and Suzanne Esther (Williams) S.; m. Vicki Lee Franklin, June 17, 1961 (div. May 1983); children: Michael James, Susan Lee; m. Elizabeth Gwyn, Aug. 20, 1983. MS in Materials Sci. and Engring., Stanford U., 1962, PhD in Materials Sci. and Engring., 1969. Mil. rsch. assoc. USN at the Lawrence Livermore (Calif.) Nat. Lab., 1964-66; systems analyst Ctr. for Naval Analyses, Rosslyn, Va., 1969-71; staff mem. metallurgy Sandia Nat. Labs., Livermore, 1971-74, div. supr. materials characterization div., 1974-76; mgr. composites, ceramics and thermophys. properties dept. Sandia Nat. Labs., Albuquerque, 1976-79, mgr. power sources dept., 1979-83, dir. components, 1983-87, mng. dir. microelectronics, 1987—. Contbr. articles to profl. jours. With USN, 1962-66. NSF trainee; Alfred P. Sloan fellow; recipient Naval Inst. award, 2 Gold medals Am. Inst. Mil. Engrs. Mem. Am. Soc. for Metals, Phi Beta Kappa, Tau Beta Pi, Sigma Xi. Republican. Episcopalian. Office: Sandia Nat Labs Org 2100 Albuquerque NM 87185

SAYANO, REIZO RAY, electrochemical engineer; b. Los Angeles, Dec. 15, 1937; s. George Keiichiro and Miyo (Nakao) S.; m. Tamiko Shintani, May 28, 1967; children—Kiyomi Coleen, Naomi Jennifer. A.A., Los Angeles Community Coll., 1958; B.S., UCLA, 1960, M.S., 1962, Ph.D., 1967. Research asst. electrochem. and shock tube research dept. engring. UCLA, 1961-66; mem. staff TRW Systems, corrosion and advanced battery research and devel. Redondo Beach, Calif., 1966-78; dir. engring. Intermedics Intraocular Inc., Pasadena, Calif., 1978-80, dir. research and devel., 1980-82, v.p. engring. devel. and research, 1982-84; v.p. research and devel. Interpore Internat. Inc., 1984-85; dir. research and devel., product process devel. IOLAB Corp. subs. Johnson & Johnson Co., Claremont, Calif., 1985-87, dir. new tech., research and devel., 1987-88; v.p., gen. mgr. Nidek Techs., Inc., Pasadena, Calif., 1988—. NASA predoctoral trainee, 1964-65. Mem. Electrochem. Soc., Nat. Assn. Corrosion Engrs., AAAS, Am. Mgmt. Assn., Sigma Xi. Office: 675 S Arroyo Pkwy Ste 330 Pasadena CA 91106

SAYKA, ANTHONY, process engineer; b. Merced, Calif., May 1, 1957; s. Harry Michael and Monica (Smith) S. AS, Pikes Peak Community Coll., 1982; BS in Chemistry, U. Colo., 1985. Air conditioning and heating contractor Callaway heating & Cooling Co., Panama City, Fla., 1977-80; process engr. NCR Corp., Colorado Springs, 1984-88; rsch. scientist Microtech Rsch. Co., Colorado Springs, 1986-87; sr. process engr. Micron Tech., Boise, Idaho, 1988—; broker assoc. Preferral, Inc., Colorado Springs, 1986—. Election asst. El Paso County Rep. Party, Colorado Springs, 1984. Mem. Am. Vacuum Soc., Electrochem. Soc., Am. Chem. Soc., Laser Inst. Am., IEEE (assoc. mem.). Roman Catholic. Home: 5735 Marvin Ln Boise ID 83705

SAYKALLY, RICHARD JAMES, chemistry educator; b. Rhinelander, Wis., Sept. 10, 1947; s. Edwin L. and Helen M. (Janda) S. BS, U. Wis., Eau Claire, 1970; PhD, U. Wis., Madison, 1977. Postdoctoral Nat. Bur. Standards, Boulder, Colo., 1977-79; assoc. prof. U. Calif., Berkeley, 1979—; Merck-Frost lectr. U. B.C., 1988; prin. investigator Lawrence Berkeley Lab., 1981—. Contbr. articles to profl. jours. Dreyfuss Found. fellow, 1977; presdl. investigator NSF, 1983; recipient Bomem Michelson prize for Spectroscopy, 1988, E.K. Plyler prize for Molecular Spectroscopy, 1989. Mem. Am. Chem. Soc., Am. Phys. Soc., Optical Soc. Am., AAAS. Office: U Calif Dept Chemistry Berkeley CA 94720

SAYRE, EDWARD CHARLES, librarian; b. Longview, Wash., Aug. 15, 1923; s. Kenneth C. Sayre and Clare (Davis) Clingan; m. Virginia A. Hoy, June 9, 1951; children: Steven Anthony, Sabrina Karen. BA, Coll. of Gt. Falls, 1955; MA, U. Idaho, 1961; MLS, U. Md., 1968. Coordinator library services Thomas Nelson Community Coll., Hampton, Va., 1968-69; dir. Roswell Pub. Library, N.Mex., 1969-70; cons. N.Mex. State Library, Santa Fe, 1970-72; dir. Central Colo. Library System, Denver, 1972-78, Serra Coop. Library System, San Diego, 1978-79, Los Alamos County (N.Mex.) Library System, 1979-88; county adminstr. Los Alamos County, 1988—; cons., 1976—. Contbr. articles to profl. jours. Served to maj. USAF, 1951-67. HEA Title II fellow, 1968. Mem. ALA, N.Mex. Library Assn. (pres.-elect 1972), Beta Phi Mu (dir. 1973-74). Democrat. Unitarian. Home: 3 Timber Ridge Los Alamos NM 87544 Office: Mesa Pub Libr 1742 Central Ave Los Alamos NM 87544

SAYRE, JOHN MARSHALL, lawyer; b. Boulder, Colo., Nov. 9, 1921; s. Henry Marshall and Lulu M. (Cooper) S.; m. Jean Miller, Aug. 22, 1943; children—Henry M., Charles Franklin, John Marshall, Ann Elizabeth Sayre Taggart (dec.). B.A., U. Colo., 1943, J.D., 1948. Bar: Colo. 1948, U.S. Dist. Ct. Colo. 1952, U.S. Ct. Appeals (10th cir.) 1964. Law clk. trust dept. Denver Nat. Bank, 1948-49; asst. cashier, trust officer Nat. State Bank of Boulder, 1949-50; ptnr. Ryan, Sayre, Martin, Brotzman, Boulder, 1950-66, Davis, Graham & Stubbs, Denver, 1966—. Bd. dirs. Boulder Sch. Dist. 3, 1951-57; city atty. City of Boulder, 1952-55; gen. counsel Colo. Mcpl. League, 1956-63; counsel No. Colo. Water Conservancy Dist. and mcpl. subdist., 1964-87, spl. counsel, 1987, bd. dirs. dist., 1960-64; legal counsel Colo. Assn. Commerce and Industry. Lt. (j.g.) USNR, 1943-46. Decorated Purple Heart. Fellow Am. Bar. Found.; mem. ABA, Colo. Bar Assn., Boulder County Bar Assn., Denver Bar Assn., Nat. Water Resources Assn. (Colo. dir. 1980—, pres. 1984-86), Denver Country Club, Denver Club, Phi Beta Kappa. Republican. Episcopalian. Office: Davis Graham & Stubbs 370 17th St Ste 4700 PO Box 185 Denver CO 80201

SAZAMA, PATRIC ANTHONY, electronics executive; b. Redwood City, Calif., Jan. 16, 1952; s. Frank James and Susan Patricia (Schiedeck) S.; m. Jeanette Louise Preston, June 11, 1977; children: Heather Danielle, Sarah Lisette. BA in Mgmt. Tech., Lewis and Clark Coll., 1983; MBA, U. Idaho, 1987. Machine operator Bacharach Instruments, Mountain View, Calif., 1971-76; mgr. prodn. control Varian Assocs., Palo Alto, Calif., 1976-79; buyer Reytronic Corp., Spokane, Wash., 1979-81; mgr. Hewlett-Packard, Spokane, 1981--. Vol. firefighter Kootenai County Fire Dist., Coeur D'Alene, Idaho. Mem. Vol. Firefighter Assn. (pres.). Home: 6952 Colfax St Coeur D'Alene ID 83814 Office: Hewlett Packard 1620 Signal Dr Liberty Lake WA 99019

SBRAGIA, GARY W., communications company executive; b. Chgo., Aug. 25, 1941; s. Gertrude Harriet (Legge) S.; m. Sharyn Lee Simpson, Aug. 26, 1961; children: Marci Lee, Melissa Ann. Student, Waldorf Jr. Coll., 1959-60, 61-62, Colo. State U., 1962-65. V.p. Lift Trucks, Inc., Denver, 1972-74; mgr. Levenworth (Kans.) Cable TV, 1974-75; gen. mgr., then div. mgr. Athena Cablevision of Corpus Christi (Tex.), Inc., 1976-81; regional mgr., then asst. dir. ops. Telecommunications, Inc., Corpus Christi and Denver, 1981-84; v.p. Telecrafter Corp., Denver, 1984—; pres. Telecrafter Services Corp., Denver, 1987—. Home: 11425 Last Dollar Pass Littleton CO 80127 Office: Telecrafter Svcs Corp 12596 W Bayaud St Ste 300 Denver CO 80228

SCAFE, LINCOLN ROBERT, JR., sales executive; b. Cleve., July 28, 1922; s. Lincoln Robert and Charlotte (Hawkins) S.; student Cornell U., 1940-41; m. Mary Anne Wilkinson, Nov. 14, 1945; children—Amanda Katharine, Lincoln Robert III. Service mgr. Avery Engring. Co., Cleve., 1946-51; nat. service mgr. Trane Co., LaCrosse, Wis., 1951-57; service and installation mgr. Mech. Equipment Supply Co., Honolulu, 1957-58; chief engr. Sam P. Wallace of Pacific, Honolulu, 1958-62; pres. Air Conditioning Service Co., Inc., Honolulu, 1962-84; sales engr. G.J. Campbell & Assocs., Seattle, 1984—. Served with USNR, 1942-45; PTO. Mem. ASHRAE, Alpha Delta Phi. Clubs: Cornell Hawaii (past pres.); Outrigger Canoe. Republican. Author tech. service lit. and parts manuals; contbr. articles to trade publs. Home: Rte 1 Box 444 Vashon WA 98070 Office: GJ Campbell and Assocs 11613 Rainier Ave S Seattle WA 98178

SCAGLIONE, CECIL FRANK, marketing executive; b. North Bay, Ont., Can., Dec. 2, 1934; came to U.S., 1967, naturalized, 1982; s. Frank and Rose (Aubin) S.; m. Mary Margaret Stewart, Nov. 11, 1954 (div. 1982); children: Cris Ann, Michael Andrew, Patrick Andrew; m. Beverly Louise Rahn, Mar. 25, 1983; student North Bay Coll., 1947-52, Ryerson Tech. Inst., Toronto, Ont., 1955-56, San Diego State U. Inst. World Affairs, 1979. Fin. writer Toronto Telegram, 1955; reporter Sarnia (Ont.) Observer, 1956-57; reporter, editor Kitchener-Waterloo (Ont.) Record, 1957-61; reporter, editor, analyst Windsor (Ont.) Star, 1961-67; writer, editor, photo editor Detroit News, 1967-71; reporter, assoc. bus. editor San Diego Union, 1971-80; mgr. corp. communications Pacific Southwest Airlines, San Diego, 1981-83; sr. v.p. media rels. Berkman & Daniels, Inc., San Diego, 1984-87, prin. Scaglione Mktg. Communications, 1987—; chmn., chief exec. officer Spl. Info. Svcs., Inc. Mem. adv. coun. SBA, Accredited Pub. Rels. Soc. Am. Recipient award B.F. Goodrich Can., Ltd., 1962, 66, Spl. Achievement award Nat. Assn. Recycling Industries, 1978, award SBA, 1980; Herbert J. Davenport fellow, 1977; Can. Centennial grantee, 1966. Mem. San Diego Press Club (hon. life, past pres., awards 1978, 80, 84), Airline Editors Forum awards 1982, 83), Pub. Rels. Soc. Am., Sigma Delta Chi. Roman Catholic. Founding editor-in-chief Aeromexico mag., 1973; contbr. articles, columns and photographs to various publs. Home and Office: 3911 Kendall St San Diego CA 92109

SCALAPINO, ROBERT ANTHONY, political science educator; b. Leavenworth, Kans., Oct. 19, 1919; s. Anthony and Beulah (Stephenson) S.; m. Ida Mae Jessen, Aug. 23, 1941; children: Diane Jablon, Sharon Leslie, Lynne Ann Thompson. AB, Santa Barbara Coll., 1940; MA, Harvard U., 1943, PhD, 1948; LLD (hon.), China Acad., Republic of China, 1976; D in Polit. Sci. (hon.), Hankuk U. Fgn. Studies, Seoul, Republic of Korea, 1983. Instr. Harvard U., Cambridge, Mass., 1948-49; asst. prof. U. Calif., Berkeley, 1949-51, assoc. prof., 1951-56, prof., 1956-77, chmn. dept. polit. sci., 1962-65, Robson research prof. govt., 1977—; dir. Inst. East Asian Studies, 1978—; cons. govtl. and edni. studies; Bernard Moses lectr. U. Calif., 1983, Reischauer lectr. Harvard U., 1988. Co-author: Modern China and Its Revolutionary Process, 1985, Communism in Korea, 1972 (Woodrow Wilson Found. Book award 1974); author: Asia and the Road Ahead, 1975, Major Power Relations in Northeast Asia, 1987; editor: The Foreign Policy of Modern Japan, 1977, (jour.) Asian Survey, 1962—. Founder, chmn., bd. dirs. Nat. Com. U.S.-China Relations, 1966—; bd. dirs. Council on Fgn. Relations, N.Y., 1982—; trustee The Asia Found., San Francisco, 1983—; chmn. Com. Internat. Relations Studies with Peoples Republic of China, 1984—; head N.E. Asia Study Mission, Asia Soc., 1982—, trustee, 1988—. Served to lt. (j.g.) USN, 1943-46. Guggenheim fellow, 1965-66, Social Sci. Research Council fellow, 1952-53. Mem. Am. Acad. Arts Scis., Am. Polit. Sci. Assn., Assn. Asian Studies, Pacific Forum (bd. dirs.). Democrat. Office: U Calif Inst East Asian Studies 2223 Fulton St Berkeley CA 94720

SCALES, NICHOLAS STRYKER, realtor; b. San Francisco, July 30, 1946; s. Percival McGalliard and Katharine Stryker (Plant) S.; m. Ann Pomeroy, Feb. 20, 1971; children: Nathaniel Walker, Laura Ann. BA in Econs., U. Calif., Santa Barbara, 1968. Sales cons. Coldwell Banker, Seattle, 1970-80; dir. mktg. Evergreen Mgmt., Bellevue, Wash., 1980-83; v.p. office and indsl. Northwest Bldg. Corp., Seattle, 1983-85; owner Scales Co., 1985--. Bd. dirs. Bellevue Boy and Girl Club, 1986--, Bellevue Art Mus., 1986. 1st lt. USAR, 1968-70, Vietnam. Mem. Bellevue C. of C. (v. chmn. 1986--), Bellevue Athletic Club, Overlake Country Club, Rotary. Republican. Roman Catholic. Office: Scales Co 405 114th Ave SE #324 Bellevue WA 98004

SCALIA, DEAN THOMAS, accountant; b. L.A., Apr. 27, 1958; s. Lawrence Francis and Donna Mae (Mangiagli) S. BA in Econs., UCLA, 1980; MBA, U. So. Calif., 1982. CPA, Calif. Audit mgr. Peat Marwick Main & Co., San Jose, Calif., 1982-86; asst. treas. Guess? Inc., L.A., 1986—. Mem. AICPA, Calif. Soc. CPA's. Republican. Roman Catholic. Office: Guess? Inc 123 E 35th St Los Angeles CA 90011

SCANLON, CYNTHIA MARY, librarian, humor consultant; b. Las Vegas, Nev., Apr. 30, 1960; d. Ronald J. and Crystal J., S. BA in Journalism, Ariz. State U., 1982. Tech. editor Spec., Inc., Scottsdale, Ariz., 1982; reference librarian Phoenix Pub. Library, 1984—; staff writer Phoenix Mag., 1985-86; freelance writer, pub. speaker, Phoenix, 1983—; cons. Ariz. State U., Tempe, 1983-86. Contbr. articles to numerous gen. interest publs. Mem. Am. Soc. Tng. & Devel., Toastmasters Internat. Office: PO Box 5565 Mesa AZ 85201

SCANNELL, EDWARD EARL, university adminstrator; b. Fond du Lac, Wis., Jan. 26, 1934; children: Mary, Karen, Michael, Catherine. BA, U. No. Colo., 1959, MA, 1960; postgrad., U. Wis., U. Iowa. Instr. U. No. Iowa, Cedar Falls, 1960-64; asst. prof. mktg. Ariz. State U., Tempe, 1964-68, coord. continuing edn., 1969-74, dir. univ. conf. bur., 1974—; rsch. assoc. U. Iowa, Iowa City, 1968-69. Author: (books) Supervisory Communication, 1982, Human Resource Development, 1981, 2d edition, 1987, Games Trainers Play, 1981, More Games Trainers Play, 1983. Capt. U.S. Army, 1954-57. Mem. Meeting Planners Internat. (pres. 1988—), Nat. Speakers Assn. (pres. Ariz. chpt. 1987-88, bd. dirs. 1984—, Pres.'s award 1985), Am. Soc. Tng. Devel. (bd. dirs. 1981-84, pres. 1982), Internat. Coun. for Small Bus. (sec.-treas. 1965-68, Outstanding Svc. award 1969), Tempe C. of C. (bd. dirs. 1982-87), Internat. Redn. Tng. and Devel. Orgns. (exec. chmn. 1983-86). Republican. Roman Catholic. Office: Ariz State U Univ Conf Bur Tempe AZ 85287

SCANNELL, WILLIAM EDWARD, aerospace company executive; b. Muscatine, Iowa, Nov. 11, 1934; s. Mark Edward and Catharine Pearson (Fowler) S.; m. Barbara Ann Hoemann, Nov. 23, 1957; children: Cynthia Kay, Mark Edward, David Jerome, Terri Lynn, Stephen Patrick. BA in Gen. Edn., U. Nebr., 1961; BS in Indsl. Engring., Ariz. State U., 1966; MS in Systems Engring., So. Meth. U., 1969; postgrad., U.S. Internat. U., 1983—. Commd. 2d lt. USAF, 1956, advanced through grades to lt. col., 1972; forward air contr. 20th Tactical Air Support Squadron USAF, Danang, Vietnam, 1970-71; program mgr. USAF, Washington, 1971-74, staff asst. Office of Sec. Def., 1974-75, ret., 1975; account exec. Merrill Lynch, San Diego, 1975-77; program engring. chief Gen. Dynamics, San Diego, 1977-79, engring. chief, 1979-80, program mgr., 1980-83; mgr. integrated logistics support Northrop Corp., Hawthorne, Calif., 1984-88; mgr. integrated B-2 program planning and scheduling Northrop Corp., Pico Rivera, Calif., 1988—. Decorated DFC with three oak leaf clusters, Air medal with 11 oak leaf clusters. Mem. Inst. Indsl. Engrs., Coronado Cays Yacht Club, Psi Chi. Republican. Roman Catholic. Home: 7 Laguna Ct Manhattan Beach CA 90266 Office: Northrop Corp 8900 E Washington Blvd Pico Rivera CA 90660

SCAPPATICCI, BRIAN ANTHONY, sales executive; b. Worcester, Mass., May 7, 1957; s. Benjamin Anthony and Nancy Lou (Cofske) S. BS in Plastics, U. Lowell, 1979; MBA, Nat. U., San Diego, 1986. Plastics engr. Welch Allyn, Inc., Skaneateles Falls, N.Y., 1979-80; project engr. IVAC Corp., San Diego, 1980-85; engring. mgr. Nimbus Water Systems, Escondido, Calif., 1985-86; from product devel. engr. to dist. sales mgr. IMED Corp., San Diego, 1986—. Mem. Soc. Plastics Engrs. (chmn. 1982—). Home: 151 Masonic Ave San Francisco CA 94118 Office: IMED Corp 9775 Businesspark Ave San Diego CA 92131

SCARANO, ELIZABETH JANE, construction executive; b. Omaha, Nov. 3, 1961; d. Robert Michael and Kathryn (Hargelroad) Jacobson; m. Charles Joseph Scarano, Aug. 13, 1983; children: Ryann Alyse, Andrew Michael. Student, U. Nebr., 1980, Pepperdine U., 1980; BA, Ariz. State U., 1981-83. Mktg. asst. Bank of Scottsdale, Ariz., 1982; bus. mgr. Caruso Turley Scott Inc., Phoenix, 1986—. Mem. Profl. Women in Architecture and Engring. (treas. 1987—), Sales & Mktg. of Profl. Svcs. (ednl. com. 1987—). Republican. Roman Catholic. Home: 945 N Pasadena #12 Mesa AZ 85201 Office: Caruso Turley Scott Inc 2500 N 24th St Ste 300 Phoenix AZ 85008

SCARBOROUGH, TONY, state supreme court justice. Former presiding judge 1st Jud. Dist., N.Mex. Dist. Ct.; judge N.Mex. Supreme Ct., Santa Fe, 1987—, chief justice, 1987-88. Office: NMex Supreme Ct PO Box 848 Santa Fe NM 87504

SCARFF, EDWARD L., diversified company executive; b. 1930. BS, Mich. Tech. U., 1954. With Ansul Chem. Co., 1953-56, Stanford Research Inst., 1956-60; dir. investment research Investors Diversified Services, Inc., 1960-63; pres., chief exec. officer N. Am. Securities Co., 1963-65; v.p., then pres. Transam. Corp., 1965-71; pres. Edward L. Scarff and Assocs., San Francisco, 1971—; with Arcata Corp., San Francisco, 1971—, now chmn. bd. dirs., also bd. dirs. Office: Arcata Corp 601 California St San Francisco CA 94108 *

SCARNE, PAUL THOMAS, magician, real estate consultant, author; b. N.Y.C., Dec. 21, 1947; s. Robert and Elizabeth (Zick) S.; m. Beth Marie Gardner,Sept. 11, 1967; children: Marie, Kenneth, Alice, Angelo, Madelena. BBA, U. Calif., Berkeley, 1969. Ind. profl. magician 1963--; dir., chief handicapper Scarne on Sports, Las Vegas, Nev., 1980--; dir. pub. rels. Krause-Anderson Devel. Co., Mpls., 1980--; cons., regional mgr. So. Calif. Maui Horizons, Inc. subs. Kraus-Anderson Devel. Co., 1980--; bd. dirs. Dana Niguel Bank, Dana Point, Calif., Dallas Line, Las Vegas. Author: Scarne on Cards, 1964, Scarne on Card Tricks, 1965, Scarne on Magic Tricks, 1968, Scarne on Baseball Wagering, 1976, Scarne's Guide to Football Handicapping, 1978; columnist Boardwalker mag., 1981--. Named Football Handicapper of Yr. Nat. Invitational Pro Football Handicap Contest, 1981, NFL Experts Bowl Press Sports Syndication, 1982. Mem. Internat. Brotherhood of Magicians, Soc. Am. Magicians (Close-Up Magician of Yr. 1969). Democrat. Roman Catholic. Home: 23704-5 El Toro Rd Apt 385 El Toro CA 92630 Office: 400 N Tustin Ave Ste 112 Santa Ana CA 92705

SCARR, MARSHAL A., lawyer; b. Bayshore, N.Y., Feb. 6, 1956; s. Marshall A. and Edna Scarr; m. Dina Feldman, Aug. 5, 1979. BA in Polit. Sci., San Diego State U., 1978; JD, U. Santa Clara, 1983. Bar: Calif. 1983, U.S. Dist. Ct. (so. dist.) Calif. 1983. Pvt. practice San Diego, 1983-85; assoc. Peterson, Thelan & Price, San Diego, 1985—. Mem. ABA, Calif. Bar Assn., San Diego County Bar Assn. (chmn. environ. law-land use sect. 1986-88). Democrat. Office: Peterson Thelan & Price 530 B St Ste 2300 San Diego CA 92101

SCARUFFI, BETTY MAY, realtor, artist; b. Medford, Oreg., May 17; d. Ocie Sylvanis and Edith Nannett (DuPray) Newman; children: Perry Joseph, Caroline Marie, Louis Fred. AA, Napa Valley Coll., 1978, Cert. in Real Estate, 1985. Jeweler Whitman & Bailey Jewelers, Napa, Calif., 1958-73, ptnr., owner, 1975-77; realtor Lowell Black Realtors, Inc., Napa, 1973-75, 80—; mgr. Kerns Fine Jewelers, San Mateo, Calif., 1978-80. Editor: Napanee, 1954. Commr. hist. records Napa County, 1987—; multiple listing com. Napa County Bd. Realtors, 1989—, profl. standards com., 1989—; bd. dirs. Napa County Hist. Soc., 1989—. Mem. Napa County Bd. Realtors (mem. grievance com. 1984—), Calif. Assn. Realtors, Nat. Assn. Realtors, Calif. Lawyers for Arts, Napa County Hist. Soc., Napa County Geneal. and Biog. Soc., DAR, Young Ladies Inst., Mayflower Descendants Soc., Napa County Hist. Soc. (scribe for bd. dirs. 1987-89). Office: Lowell Black Realtors Inc 1721 First St Napa CA 94559

SCATENA, LORRAINE BORBA, rancher; b. San Rafael, Calif., Feb. 18, 1924; d. Joseph and Eugenia (Simas) de Borba; m. Louis Giovanni, Feb. 14, 1960; children: Louis Vincent, Eugenia Gayle. BA, Dominican Coll., San Rafael, 1945; postgrad., Calif. Sch. Fine Arts, 1948, U. Calif., Berkeley, 1956-57. Cert. elem. tchr., Calif. Tchr. Dominican Coll., 1946; tchr. San Anselmo (Calif.) Sch. Dist., 1946, Fairfax (Calif.) Pub. Elem. Sch., 1946-53; asst. to mayor Fairfax City Recreation, 1948-53; tchr., librarian U.S. Dependent Schs., Mainz am Rhine, Fed. Republic Germany, 1953-56; translator Portugal Travel Tours, Lisbon, 1954; bonding sec. Am. Fore Ins. Group, San Francisco, 1956-60; rancher, farmer Yerington, Nev., 1960—; hostess com. Caldecott and Newbury Authors' Awards, San Francisco, 1959; adv. com. Fleischmann Coll. Agr. U. Nev., 1977-80, 81-84. Active Lyon County Friends of Library, Yerington, 1971—, Lyon County Mus. Soc., 1978, Lyon County Rep. Cen. Com., 1973-74, Nev. State Legis. Commn., 1975; trustee Wassuk Coll., Hawthorne, Nev. 1984-87; sec., pub. info. chmn. Lyon County Rep. Women, 1968-73, v.p. programs, 1973-75; coordinator Nevadans for ERA, 1975-78, rural areas rep., 1976-78; lobbyist for Equal Rights Amendment, 1975; Nev. rep. to 1st White House Conf. for Rural Am. Women, Washington, 1980. Recipient Soroptimist Internat. Women Helping Women award 1983, invitation to first all-women delegation to U.S.A. from People's Republic China, U.S. House Reps., 1979. Mem. Lyon County Ret. Tchrs. Assn. (unit pres. 1979-80, 84-86, v.p. 1986-88, Nev. div. Outstanding Service award 1981), Rural Am. Women Inc., AAUW (br. pres. 1972-74, 74-76, state convention gen. chmn. 1976, 87, state div. sec. 1970-72, legis. program chmn. 1976-77, div. pres. 1981-83, Humanities award 1975, Future Fund award 1983), Mason Valley Country Club, Italian Cath. Fedn. Club (pres. 1986-88), Uniao Portuguesa Estado da Calif. Roman Catholic. Home: 1275 Hwy 208 Yerington NV 89447

SCATES, JOHN CHARLES TIMOTHY, lawyer, business executive; b. Montrose, Colo., Aug. 2, 1943; s. Erskine Edward and Faith Marie (Shield Phillips) S.; m. Charlotte Lynne Hull, Aug. 21, 1965; children: Julie Ann, Jill Megan. Student, Mesa Coll., 1961-63; AB in History, U. Northern Colo., 1966; JD, Washington Coll. Law, 1972. Bar: Colo. 1972, U.S. Dist. Ct. Colo. 1972. Legis. aide to Wayne Aspinall U.S. Ho. Reps., Washington, 1966-68, 70-72; prin., atty. Hindry & Meyer, P.C., Denver, 1972-78; co-founder, atty., prin. Wegher & Fulton P.C., Denver, 1978-81; founder, atty., prin. Scates & Assocs., P.C., Aurora, Ill., 1981-86; of counsel Scates & Bergner, P.C., Aurora, 1986-89; chief exec. officer, pres. The Master Works Fin. Co., Denver, 1988—, The Master Works Mgmt. Corp., Denver, 1988—; spl. counsel Gorsuch, Kirgis, Campbell, Walker & Grover, Denver, 1989—; exec. v.p., gen. counsel The Christian Ch. Extension Found., Lakewood, Colo., 1977-88. Pres., chmn. bd., Missions Impossible, Inc., Denver, 1982—; bd. dirs. Denver Area Youth for Christ, 1988—. With U.S. Army, 1968-70, Vietnam. Mem. ABA, Colo. Bar Assn., Denver Bar Assn., Christian Ministries Mgmt. Assn., Am. Corp. Counsel Assn. Democrat. Home: The Master Works Fin Co 4101 S Quebec St Denver CO 80237 Office: 1401 17th St Ste 1100 Denver CO 80217-0180

SCEPER, DUANE HAROLD, lawyer; b. Norfolk, Va., Nov. 16, 1946; s. Robert George and Marion Eudora (Hynes) S.; m. Sharon Diane Cramer, July 4, 1981; stepchildren: Karin Stevenson, Diane Stevenson. BS in Law, Western State U., 1979, JD, 1980. Bar: Calif. 1982, U.S. Dist. Ct. (so. dist.) Calif. 1982. Field engr. Memorex/Tex. Instruments, San Diego, 1968-70; computer programmer San Diego, 1970-81; atty. Allied Ins. Group, San Diego, 1981-85; sole practice San Diego, 1985-87; ptnr. Zybelman, Paluso, Alter, Graham and Sceper, San Diego, 1987—; cons. computers 1980—; lectr. estate planning various orgns. Patentee in field. Active Com. to Elect King Golden to Congress, San Diego, 1978. Served with USAF, 1965-68. Recipient Am. Jurisprudence award, 1979. Mem. ABA, San Diego County Bar Assn., Assn. Trial Lawyers of Am., Calif. Trial Lawyers Assn., San Diego Trial Lawyers Assn., So. Calif. Defense Counsel, Delta Theta Phi. Democrat. Home: 2641 Massachusetts Ave Lemon Grove CA 92045 Office: 707 Broadway Suite 1100 San Diego CA 92101

SCHAAB, WILLIAM COLSON, lawyer; b. Wildwood, N.J., Dec. 28, 1927; s. William Louis and Lillian (Colson) S.; divorced; children: William Colson, Sarah, Susan; m. Judith C. Schaab. BA, Conn. Wesleyan U., 1949, MA, 1951; JD, Yale U., 1952. Bar: N.Y. 1954, N.Mex. 1956. Assoc., Cravath, Swaine & Moore, N.Y.C., 1952-56; assoc. Rodey, Dickason, Sloan, Akin & Robb P.A., Albuquerque, 1956-59, mem. firm, 1959-72, v.p., dir., 1972—. Editorial bd. Yale Law Jour. Mem. ABA, Albuquerque Bar Assn., Phi Beta Kappa. Democrat. Episcopalian. Contbr. articles to profl. jours. Home: 1401 Sigma Chi NE Albuquerque NM 87106 Office: First Pla Albuquerque NM 87103

SCHAAR, JACQUELINE KAY COUCH (MRS. ROBERT L. SCHAAR), public relations executive; b. San Diego, Apr. 2, 1933; d. Edwin Newton and Nina Mae (Sweetwood) Couch; grad. pub. schs., 1951; m. Robert L. Schaar, May 11, 1962; children: Robert, Denise. Exec. sec. various firms, 1951-57; asst. to community relations dir. Convair-Astronautics, San Diego, 1957-59; advt., pub. relations exec. Frederick C. Whitney & Assos., San Diego, 1959-62, J. Jessop & Sons, 1962-64; regional dir. pub. relations United Way, Los Angeles, Calif., 1964-73; dir. pub. relations Orange County United Way, 1973-77; asso. exec. dir. Orange County chpt. Bldg. Industry Assn. Calif., 1977-80; founder, pres., chief exec. officer Jacqueline Schaar Assos., 1980—. V.p. bd. dirs. Orange County council Girl Scouts U.S.A.; mem. adv. council Orange County Performing Arts Center, mem. public relations council U. Calif., Irvine; mem. pub. relation curriculum adv. bd. Calif. State U. at Fullerton; founding pres. Friends of KOCE-TV, mem. found. bd. Recipient Thanks Badge Girl Scouts U.S. Mem. Pub. Relations Soc. Am. (accredited, past pres. Orange County chpt., nat. dir., Disting. Service award), Orange County Press Club. Home: 23282 Morobe Circle Laguna Niguel CA 92677 Office: 484 N Coast Hwy Laguna Beach CA 92651

SCHABER, GORDON DUANE, lawyer, academic dean; b. Ashley, N.D., Nov. 22, 1927; s. Ronald and Esther (Schatz) S. A.B. with distinction, Sacramento State Coll., 1949; J.D. with honors, U. Calif. at San Francisco, 1952; LL.D., McGeorge Sch. Law, 1961, John Marshall Law Sch., 1983, Widener U., Del. Law Sch., 1984. Bar: Calif. 1953. Practice in Sacramento, 1953—; ptnr. firm Schaber & Cecchettini, Sacramento, 1953-65; lectr. McGeorge Coll. of Law (now McGeorge Sch. Law of U. Pacific), Sacramento, 1953-56, prof., 1956—; asst. dean McGeorge Coll. of Law (now McGeorge Sch. Law of U. Pacific), 1956, dean, 1957—; presiding judge Superior Ct. Sacramento County, 1964-70; dir. Air Calif., 1974-81, Westgate Corp., 1979-82, Sacramento Cablevision, 1980-82, Capitol Bank of Commerce, vice chmn., 1987—; chmn. bd. dirs. River City Cablevision Inc.; mem. Calif. Bd. Control, 1962-64; chmn. Greater Sacramento Plan Com., 1970; cons. on establishment Sch. Law at U. Puget Sound, 1970-71; cons. study on jud. workload Jud. Council Calif., 1971-72; mem. Adv. Com. to Chief Justice Calif. on Superior Ct. Mgmt., 1971; cons. vehicle theft study Calif. Hwy. Patrol, 1972; panelist Sacramento Bee Secret Witness Program, 1971—; mem. adv. com. to Calif. Office Econ. Opportunity, Calif. Legal Services Expt., 1972; vice chmn. Calif. Ednl. Facilities Authority, 1978—; bd. dirs. Nat. Center Adminstrv. Justice, 1978; mem. President's Adminstrn. Justice Task Force, 1980. Author: Contracts in a Nutshell, 1975, rev. 2d edit., 1984; contbr. articles to profl. jours. Mem. Sacramento-San Joaguin chpt. Muscular Dystrophy Assn. Telethon Gift com. 1980; trustee Stanford Homes Found., 1980-87; bd. dirs. Sacramento Regional Foundation, 1982—, Sutter Hosps. of Sacramento, 1978; mem. bd. advisors Coll. Public Interest Law, Pacific Legal Found., 1974—; vice chmn. Calif. Edn. Facilities Authority, 1978;chmn. Sacramento County Democratic Central Com., 1960-64; mem. Dem. State Central Com., 1960-64, 74—; trustee Sierra Found. for Health, 1987—, Hon. Lorenzo Patino Scholarship trust, 1984; active numerous other civic coms. Named Sacramento County Young Man of Year, 1962, Trial Judge of Year Calif. Trial Lawyers Assn., 1969; recipient Legal Edn. and Jud. award Am. Trial Lawyers Assn., 1965, award Orderof Hornet, Calif. State U., Sacramento, 1972; grantee Law Enforcement Assistance Adminstrn. and Office Calif. Criminal Justice Planning, 1974. Fellow Am. Bar Found.; mem. ABA (council sect. legal edn. and admissions to bar 1975, chmn. 1981, sec. 1982—, adv. com. pres.-elect on competence of lawyers continuing edn. 1978, numerous other coms.), Sacramento Bar Assn. (v.p. 1970), State Bar Calif. (mem. com. legislation 1969—, spl. com. appellate cts. 1970-72, long range adv. planning com. 1972—, vice chmn. com. law sch. edn. 1973, chmn. 1974, mem. commn. to study bar examination processes 1976-80, others), Am. Judicature Soc., Order of Coif, Phi Delta Phi. Lutheran. Clubs: Commonwealth, Comstock, Sutter, Univ., Harry S. Truman. Home: 937 Piedmont Dr Sacramento CA 95822 Office: U of Pacific McGeorge Sch of Law Sacramento CA 95817

SCHABOW, JOHN WILLIAM, accountant; b. Chgo., Mar. 30, 1937; s. William John and Mary V. (Brink) S.; m. Gail P. Ekren, Oct. 17, 1959; children: Robin, John R. Student, Davis Elkins Coll., 1955-58, Ariz. State U., 1972-74. Cost clk. G.D. Searle, Skokie, Ill., 1958-60; acct. Sugarcreek Foods, Chgo., 1960-63, Arlington Park Rack Track, Chgo., 1963-65, G. Heiss & Assocs., Chgo., 1965-69, Murray & Murray CPA's, Phoenix, 1969-70, Wm. R. Schulz & Assocs., Phoenix, 1970-73; pres., owner John W. Schabow, Ltd., Phoenix, 1973—; registered rep. H.D. Vest Investment Securities, Inc., Phoenix, 1985—, adv. bd. dirs. Bd. dirs. Inst. for Partially Sighted, Phoenix, 1986-87. Served with U.S. Army, 1961-62. Mem. Ariz. soc. Practicing Accts. (pres. 1987-88, co-founder), Nat. Soc. Pub. Accts. (state dir. 1983-87, bd. govs. 1988—), Nat. Assn. Tax Preparers, Internat. Assn. Fin. Planners. Republican. Lutheran. Home: 4440 W Bluefield Glendale AZ 85308 Office: 11725 N 19th Ave Phoenix AZ 85029

SCHACHT, LINDA JOAN, broadcast journalist; b. Berkeley, Calif., Sept. 11, 1944; d. Henry Mevis and Mary (Turnbull) S.; m. John Burdette Gage, May 1, 1976; children: Peter Turnbull, Katharine Burdette. BA, U. Calif., Berkeley, 1966, MJ, 1978. Reporter Sta. KQED-TV, San Francisco, 1974-76, Sta. KPIX-TV, San Francisco, 1976—. Reporter Dem. conv., 1980 (Emmy award 1981), investigative article on second mortgage brokers, 1977 (Emmy award), on children as witnesses, 1984 (Calif. State Bar award 1985, ABA award 1986. Mem. Nat. Acad. TV Arts and Scis.

SCHACHT, WILLIAM EUGENE, manufacturing company executive, accountant; b. Kokomo, Ind., Nov. 6, 1941; s. Francis Albert and Estella Lillian (Brockman) S.; m. Lucia Fatima Camara, Nov. 21, 1985; children: Julie Ann, Susan Ruth, Randolph Lee, Sabrina Carla. BS in Acctg., Ball State U., 1970. CPA, Calif. Acct. Davidson, Dreyer and Hopkins, CPA's, 1973-74, mgr., 1974-77; pvt. practice acctg. San Francisco, 1977-88; chmn., chief exec. officer BX-100 Internat. Inc., Pinole, Calif., 1988—; chief fin. officer Unique Adventures, Inc.; bd. dirs. Rio-Cal, Inc., Tigs of San Francisco, Inc. Served with U.S. Army, 1959-62. Recipient Scholastic award Price-Waterhouse, 1968. Mem. AICPA. Republican. Office: 2550 Appian Way Ste 211 Pinole CA 94564

SCHADER, HARRY W., III, real estate developer, financial consultant; b. Alameda, Calif., Oct. 21, 1956; s. Harry W. Jr. and Evelyn A. (Smith) S.; m. Lynnette Hazelrigg, Jan. 9, 1975 (div. Feb. 1986); children: Harry W. IV, Shari V. Owner Beverly Hills (Calif.) Devel. Co., 1980—, Beverly Hills Constrn. Services, 1980—; chief fin. officer Beverly Hills 1st Capital Corp., 1983-85; bd. dirs. Market Street, Newport Beach, Calif. Office: Beverly Hills Devel Co PO Box 1833 Beverly Hills CA 90213

SCHAEFER, DAN L., congressman; b. Gutenberg, Iowa, Jan. 25, 1936; s. Alvin L. and Evelyn (Everson) S.; m. Mary Margaret Lenney, 1959; children: Danny, Darren, Joel, Jennifer. B.A., Niagara U., 1961, LLD (hon.), 1986; postgrad., Potsdam State U., 1961-64. Pub. relations cons. 1967-83; mem. Colo. Gen. Assembly, 1977-78; mem. Colo. Senate, 1979-83, pres. pro tem, 1981-82, majority whip, 1983; mem. 98th-101st Congresses from 6th dist. Colo., Washington, 1983—; mem. house small bus. com., 1983, govt. ops com., 1983, energy and commerce com. 1984-86 (subcoms. on fossil and synthetic fuels; commerce, transp. and tourism; oversight/investigations), environ. and energy study com., Rep. study com.; mem. house sci. and high tech. task force, mil. reform caucus, congl. grace caucus; mem. adv. com. of concern for Soviet jewry. Pres. Foothills Recreation Bd., 1973-76; sec. Jefferson County Republican Party, Colo., 1975-76. Served with USMCR, 1955-57. Recipient Colo. Park and Recreation citation, 1976; named Elected Ofcl. of Yr., Lakewood/South Jeffco C. of C., 1986, Leadership award U.S. Congl. Adv. Bd., Am. Security Council Found.; Taxpayers Best Friend award Nat. Taxpayer's Union, 1985-86; Golden Bulldog award Watchdog of Treasury, 1985-86; Best of Colo. award Aspen Assocs., 1986. Mem. C. of C., Beta Theta Pi. Roman Catholic. Lodge: Rotary. Office: 1317 Longworth House Office Bldg Washington DC 20515 *

SCHAEFER, DAVID HAROLD, marketing executive; b. San Francisco, Oct. 17, 1951; s. Klaus H. and Ann (Schuster) S.; m. Ellen Audrey Van Vliet, May 17, 1981; children: Kristen, Alison. BA, U. Calif., Santa Cruz, 1973; MBA, Harvard U., 1975. Product mgr. Gen. Foods Corp., White Plains, N.Y., 1975-78, Crown Zellerbach, San Francisco, 1978; v.p. Foote, Cone & Belding Advt., San Francisco, 1978-84; acting pres., v.p. Mt. Zion Med. Ctr., San Francisco, 1984-87; cons. San Francisco, 1987-88; pres. Optiquick, Inc., San Francisco, 1988-89, cons., 1989—. Mem. Harvard Bus. Sch. Assn. (v.p. San Francisco chpt. 1982-88). Office: Optiquick Inc 262 24th Ave San Francisco CA 94121

SCHAEFER, DENNIS MICHAEL, military officer; b. Belleville, Ill., May 11, 1955; s. Clarence Joseph and Vera Margaret (Smereck) S.; m. Darlene Sue Kmiecik, July 10, 1982; 1 child, Neil Edward. AA, Belleville Area Coll., 1979; BA in Fine Arts, Photography and Gen. Studio Art, So. Ill. U., 1981. Enlisted USCG, 1985, advanced through grades to petty officer 2d class; editor Compass Point NW 13th dist. USCG, Seattle, 1985-86; pub. affairs specialist USCG, Kodiak, Alaska, 1986—. Decorated Meritorious medal. Office: USCG PO Box 687 Kodiak AK 99619-5000

SCHAEFER, ROBERT JOHN, real estate developer, banker; b. St. Cloud, Minn., Mar. 18, 1930; s. Vincent S. and Jacqueline (Van der Hagen) S.; m. Irene T. Kost, Sept. 26, 1953; children: Eileen, Susan, Robert, Thomas, Karen, Mary. BS, U. Minn., 1951. Pres. Ariz. Bldg. Systems, Inc., Phoenix, 1972-85; owner South 40 Devel. Co., Phoenix, 1973—; chmn. bd. Scottscom BanCorp. Inc., Scottsdale, Ariz. Bd. dirs. Scottsdale Boys Club, 1972-89. With U.S. Army, 1952-54, Korea. Mem. Metal Bldg. Dealer Assn. (pres. 1978). Republican. Roman Catholic. Home: 4525 N 66th St Scottsdale AZ 85251 Office: South 40 Devel Co 5002 S 40th St R Phoenix AZ 85040

SCHAEFER, ROBERT TAYLOR, manufacturing company executive; b. Cin., July 17, 1937; s. Richard Joseph and Ruth Mae (Stoecklin) S.; m. Nanci Brock, June 9, 1963 (div. 1969); children: Robert Taylor Jr., Richard M.; m. Sandra Jane Loomer, Aug. 11, 1969. BBA, U. Cin., 1960, MBA, 1962, postgrad., 1966. Asst. prof. mktg. U. Cin., 1962-66; sales and mktg. mgr. Gen. Electric Co., Detroit, 1966-81; pres. Tulon, Inc., Gardena, Calif., 1981-86; v.p., gen. mgr. Megatool, Inc., Buena Park, Calif., 1986--; pres. Schaefer Mktg. Assocs., Buena Park, 1983-85; cons. Mitsubishi Co., 1983-85. Author: Principles of Selection/Application, 1975; contbr. articles to profl. trade publs. Mem. Am. Electronic Assn., Internat. Printed Cir. Assn., Soc. Mfg. Engrs., Industry Hills Golf Club. Republican. Presbyterian.

SCHAEFER, THOMAS ARTHUR, mechanical engineering consultant; b. Milw., July 20, 1935; s. Arthur Albert Otto and Lilly (Grosklags) S.; m. Jeanette Lenore Philleo, July 13, 1957; children: Paul, Mark, Thomas, Jenny Lynn. BSME, U. Wis., 1959. Sr. process engr. West Bend (Wis.) Co., 1959-73; chief engr. West Bend (Wis.) Co., Ogden, Utah, 1973-78; gen. mgr. Skyline Assocs., Ogden, 1978-85; cons. mech. engr. Ogden, 1985—; evaluator Falcon Energy Co., Irvine, Calif., 1986—. Mem. Elks. Presbyterian. Home and Office: 355 East 3350 North Ogden UT 84414

SCHAFER, JERRY SANFORD, film company executive, producer, writer, director; b. Los Angeles, July 4, 1934; s. Sidney Sanford and Belle (Bass) S.; children : Mark, Morgan, Martin, Aaron, Erik; m. Marianne Marks, Oct. 1, 1979. Masters, UCLA, 1956. Writer, producer, dir. The Legend of Billy the Kid Repuplic Studios, 1958; writer, producer, dir. worlds fair presentation The Quick Draw Theatre, Seattle, N.Y.C., 1962, 66; writer, producer, dir. mus. shows Speaking of Girls, Las Vegas, Nev., 1963, That Certain Girl, Las Vegas, 1967, Belle Starr, London, 1968, The Piece-Full Palace, Las Vegas, 1969; writer, producer, dir. western stunt show Cowboys, Cowgirls & Kata, Osaka, Japan, 1970; pres. Sanford Internat. Entertainment, Inc., Las Vegas, 1978—; freelance writer, producer, dir. 1981—; entertainment dir. Del E. Webb Corp., Las Vegas, 1961-69; lectr., vis. prof. U. Nev., Las Vegas, 1985—. Writer, producer, dir.: (feature films) Tonight For Sure, 1959, The Little People, 1960, Along Came Jasper, 1961, The Blackhawk Gunfighters, 1963, Like it Is, 1972, Not My Daughter, 1972, The Low Price of Fame, 1973, Shortcut to Terror, 1975, Horace & Fred, 1976, Go for Your Gun, Fists of Steel, 1988, (mus. prodns.) On Stage with Judy Garland, An Evening with Pat Boone, Presenting Mr. Jack Benny!, Betty Grable/A Musical Musical!, Robert Goulet The Camelot Prince, The Polly Bergen Show, Brenda Lee on Stage!, Girls a la Carte, C'est la Femme; producer, dir., 1962-69, Soul Follies, Flower Drum Song, Under the Yum Yum Tree, The Ziegfeld Follies, numerous TV spls., 1983-87. Named Producer of Yr. Am. Guild Variety Artists, 1964, 66; recipient PAVCA award Profl. Audio-Visual Communications Assn., 1985; holder world record for fastest draw. Mem. Nat. Constables Assn. (comd. 1985—), Nat. Counter Intelligence Assn. (invited), Ky. Cols. Assn. (invited), Nat. Orch. Leaders Assn., ASCAP, Nev. Motion Picture and TV Bd. (appointed to adv. com. by Gov. Richard Bryan 1987), Dirs. Guild Am. Office: Sanford Entertainment PO Box 15101 Las Vegas NV 89114-5101

SCHAFF, ANTHONY EDWARD, aeronautical engineer; b. Santa Monica, Calif., Mar. 23, 1937; s. Carl Edward Schaff and Kathryn Paralta (Blanchard) Loughead; m. Christine Ruth Svendsen, June 19, 1959 (div. 1972); children: Karen Adele Schaff Parker, Barbara Ann; m. Phyllis Maxine Hodges, June 8, 1979. BS in Aero. Engring., U. Wash., 1962. Aero. engr. Boeing Corp., Seattle. Served with USAF, 1954-58. Republican. Home: 13410 249th Ave SE Issaquah WA 98027

SCHAFF, WILLIAM EARL, electronics engineer, lecturer; b. Holdenville, Okla., Nov. 28, 1950; s. Hartzell and Ruth Natali Vernon. BSEE, U. Okla., 1973; MSEE, Purdue U., 1975. Staff scientist Mark Resources, L.A., 1976-79; sr. engr. Math. Systems Design, L.A., 1979—, also sec., 1987—; sr. instr. ICS, L.A., 1977—. Home: 1920 S Sawtelle Los Angeles CA 90025 Office: Math Systems Design 11835 W Olympic Blvd Ste 745 Los Angeles CA 90064

SCHAFFER, DEBORAH BETH, English language educator; b. Syracuse, N.Y., May 12, 1955; d. Elliott Jacob and Bernice Esther (Samuels) S. BA, U. Rochester, 1976; MA, Ohio State U., 1978, PhD, 1982. Teaching and research assoc. linguistics Ohio State U., Columbus, 1977-82, lectr. ESL, 1983; asst. prof. English Eastern Mont. Coll., Billings, 1983-87, assoc. prof., 1987—. Co-editor: Language Files, 1979; contbr. articles to profl. jours. Named Outstanding Young Woman Am., 1984-86. Mem. Linguistic Soc. Am., Am. Assn. Applied Linguistics, Nat. Council Tchrs. English, Internat. Soc. Phonetic Scis., Mont. Assn. Tchrs. English and Lang. Arts., Eastern Mont. Coll. Faculty Women's Club (rep. 1985—), Phi Beta Kappa, Phi Kappa Phi. Democrat. Jewish. Office: Ea Mont Coll Dept English 1500 N 30th St Billings MT 59101-0298

SCHAFFER, JOEL LANCE, dentist; b. Bklyn., Oct. 18, 1945; s. Martin Alter and Irene Natalie (Shore) S.; m. Susan Anne Swearingen, Feb. 14, 1980 (div.); 1 child, Jericho Katherine. BS, L.I. U., 1967; DDS, Howard U., 1971. Dental intern Eastman Dental Ctr., Rochester, N.Y., 1971-72; gen. practice dentistry, Boulder, Colo., 1973—; evaluator Clin. Research Assocs.; lectr. in field, 1972—. Contbr. articles to dental jours. Mem. Boulder County Com. for Persons with Disabilities. Named outstanding clinician Boulder County Dental Forum, 1979. Mem. ADA, Am. Acad. Oral Implantology, Boulder County Dental Soc., Am. Soc. Dental Aesthetics. Jewish. Home: 3874 Campo Ct Boulder CO 80301 Office: 2880 Folsom St Boulder CO 80302

SCHAFFER, ROBERT WARREN, state senator; b. Cin., July 24, 1962; s. Robert James and Florence Ann (Bednar) S.; m. Maureen Elizabeth Menke, Feb. 8, 1986; children: Jennifer, Emily, Justin. BA in Polit. Sci., U. Dayton, 1984. Legis. asst. State of Ohio, Columbus, 1985; majority adminstrv. asst. Colo. Senate, Denver, 1985-87; Colo. senator representing Dist. 14 Ft. Collins, 1987—; mem. (ex-officio) Colo. Advanced Tech. Inst., 1988—. Mem. Mental Health Bd. Larimer County, 1986-87, Colo. Senate Com. Fin., Nat. Conf. State Legislatures Com. on Econ Devel. Commerce; campaign co-chair Arnold for Lt. Gov., Larimer and Weld Counties, 1986; communications dir. Johnson for City Council, Ft. Collins, 1986; head coach Ft. Collins Youth Baseball, 1986—; vice-chmn. Colo. Senate Judiciary Com.,. Mem. Colo. Press Assn., Colo. Press Club, Jaycees (Jaycee of the Month Ft. Collins chpt. 1987). Republican. Roman Catholic. Home: 3273 Gunnison Dr Fort Collins CO 80526 Office: The State Senate State Capitol Denver CO 80203

SCHAFFER, WALTER SYLVESTER, electrical engineer, consultant; b. Warren, Ohio, June 2, 1924; s. Harry Leo and Mabel (Bickel) S.; m. Ruth Bores, Apr. 30, 1949; children: Susan, Arden, Renelle. BEE, Fenn Coll., Cleve., 1950; postgrad., Clev. Marshall Law Sch., 1952-53; MEE, Syracuse (N.Y.) U., 1956. Field engr. IBM Corp., Cleve., 1950-54; design engr. IBM Corp., Poughkeepsie, N.Y., 1954-58; corp. power supply mgr. IBM Corp., Endicott, N.Y., 1958-59; tech. advisor IBM Corp., Endicott, 1960-68; system engring. mgr., advanced devel. mgr. IBM Corp., Rochester, Minn., 1968-85; div. liaison IBM Corp., Tucson, 1985-87; pvt. practice cons. Tucson, 1987-89; pres. Ryandax Ltd., Tucson, 1989—. Patentee in field. Bd. dirs. Rochester Redevel., 1983-84; fundraiser Rochester Arts Ctr., 1982-85, Paws & Claws, Rochester, 1970-85, Salvation Army, Rochester, 1980-85. Served with Air Corp, 1943-46. Recipient Minority Engring. award Case Western Res. U., 1987. Mem. Kiwanis (pres. Rochester chpt. 1980-81, bd. dirs. Tucson chpt. 1986--, Local Kiwanian of Yr. 1987), Odd Fellows (nobel grand 1983-85). Home and Office: 6631 Calle de San Alberto Tucson AZ 85710

SCHAFFLER, RUTH LAURINE, nurse, educator; b. Iowa City, Apr. 3, 1942; d. Chester Blaine and Audrey Serene Gunderson; m. Albert Benjamin Schaffler, Dec. 7, 1963; children: Lauri Elizabeth, Gregory Thomas, Kristina Lynn. BSN, Pacific Luth. U., 1963; MA, Ball State U., 1984. R.N., Wash. Staff and charge nurse Mary Bridge Children's Hosp., Tacoma, 1963-65; staff nurse Williamsburg (Va.) Community Hosp., 1965-66, Hawley Army Hosp., Ft. Harrison, Ind., 1981-85, Madigan Army Med. Ctr., Ft. Lewis, Wash., 1985; instr. ARC, worldwide, 1969-79; instr., trainer Fed. Republic Germany, 1974-75; asst. nurse mgr. Tacoma Gen. Hosp., 1985--; instr. Ind. Emergency Med. Services, Indpls., 1982-85, Am. Heart Assn., Ind., Wash., 1969—. Emergency med. technician State of Ind., 1981-88, State of Wash., 1987--; vol. Steilacoom (Wash.) Fire Dept., 1986--. Mem. Emergency Nurses Assn. (instr. trauma nursing core course, 1987—, Wash. state trauma com., 1988—). Republican. Lutheran. Home: 70 Silver Beach Dr Steilacoom WA 98388

SCHAIBLE, GRACE BERG, state attorney general. BA in History and Polit. Sci., U. Alaska; MA in History, George Washington U.; LLB, Yale U., 1959. Mem. staff Alaska Legis. Council, 1953-56, acting dir., 1956; assoc. McNealy and Merdes, 1959-66; ptnr. Schaible, Staley, DeLisio and Cook (formerly Merdes, Schaible, Staley and DeLisio), from 1966; also past gen. counsel U. Alaska; past city atty. Cities of Fairbanks, Barrow, Kotzebue and North Pole; past gen. corp. counsel Arctic Slope Regional Corp.; atty. gen. State of Alaska, 1987-89, ret., 1989. Mem. Fairbanks Estate Planning Council; bd. dirs. United Way of Tanana Valley; past bd. dirs., treas. Fairbanks Devel. Authority; mem. bd. regents U. Alaska, 1985-87; trustee Alaska Permanent Fund Corp., 1982—. Mem. U. Alaska Found. (trustee), ABA, Alaska Bar Assn., Juneau Bar Assn., Fairbanks C. of C. (past bd. dirs.), U. Alaska Alumni Assn., (past bd. dirs., officer). Office: Office of Atty Gen State Capitol PO Box K Juneau AK 99811 *

SCHAIRER, GEORGE SWIFT, aeronautical engineer; b. Pitts., May 19, 1913; s. Otto Sorg and Elizabeth Blanche (Swift) S.; m. Mary Pauline Tarbox, June 20, 1935; children: Mary Elizabeth, George Edward, Sally Helen, John Otto. With Bendix Aviation Corp., South Bend, Ind., 1935-37, Consol. Vultee Aircraft Corp., San Diego, 1937-39; joined Boeing Airplane Co., Seattle, 1939, successively chief aerodynamist, staff engr. aerodynamics and powerplant, 1948-51, chief tech. staff, 1951-56, asst. chief engr., 1956-57, dir. research, 1957-59, v.p. research and devel., 1959-73, v.p. research, 1973-78, cons., 1978-88; mem. sci. adv. group USAAF, 1945-46; mem. com. on aerodynamics NACA; mem. tech. adv. panel on aeros. Dept. Def., 1954-61; sci. adv. bd. USAF, 1955-60; cons. ops. evaluation group USN, 1961; panel sci. and tech. manpower Pres.'s Sci. Adv. Com., 1962-64; sci. adv. com. Def. Intelligence Agy., 1966-70; mem. aeros. and space engring. bd. NRC, 1977-79. Contbr. articles to profl. jours. Trustee A Contemporary Theatre, Cornish Coll. Recipient Spirit of St. Louis award ASME, 1959, Guggenheim medal, 1967. Fellow Am. Inst. Aeros. and Astronautics (hon. fellow, Sylvanus Albert Reed award 1950, Wright Bros. lectr. 1964); mem. Nat. Acad. Engring., Nat. Acad. Scis., Internat. Acad. Astronautics, Am. Helicopter Soc., Soc. Naval Architects and Marine Engrs., Sigma Xi, Sigma Tau. Address: 4242 Hunts Pt Rd Bellevue WA 98004

SCHALLIG, HANS HENDRIK, general manager; b. Tjirebon, Indonesia, Jan. 2, 1939; came to U.S., 1955; s. Willem Hendrik Christiaan and Elizabeth Blanche (PluimMentz) S.; m. Alice Ann Mayhugh, Sept. 19, 1959; children: Hans Hendrik, Analise D., Alice M., Lesa G. BS, Oreg. State U., 1969. Librarian CH2M/Hill, Corvallis, Oreg., 1962-69; mgr. tech. ref. Battelle-N.W. Labs, Richland, Wash., 1969-71; research scientist soil/algae relationship QEI-Gen. Matis, Richland, 1971-75, Walla Walla, Wash., 1975-83, Albany, Oreg., 1983-85; gen. mgr. B-J Scientific, Inc., Albany, 1985—; dir. Terra Scis. Corp., Scio, Oreg. Author: Motion , Time & Time Stopped, 1962, (with others) Environmental and Nutritional Requirements of Worms, 1987. Vol., Am. Legion Club, 1987—. Mem. Toastmasters (pres. 1988—, central div. lt. gov. 1988—). Republican. Home: 1242 NW Skyline Dr Albany OR 97321

SCHAMBACH, BRUCE JOSEPH, dentist; b. Covington, Ky., Oct. 7, 1951; s. William Anthony and Lois Janette (Huber) S.; m. Angela Marie Kelly, June 22, 1973 (div. Mar. 1978); m. Yuvarin Sensamee, July 4, 1984; 1 child, Malee. BS, U. Ky., Lexington, 1971; DMD, U. Ky., 1975. Gen. practice dentistry Walsenburg, Colo., 1978-88; chief dentistry Muerfano Meml. Hosp., Walsenburg, 1987—. Served as capt. USAF, 1975-78. Mem. ADA, Colo. Dental Assn., SE Colo. Dental Soc., Short St. Dental Study Club (pres. 1983), Muerfano County C. of C. (bd. dirs. 1985—). Roman Catholic. Clubs: Walsenburg (bd. dirs. 1980—); Cuchap-A (Colo.) Ski (v.p. 1987-88); Grandote Golf (La Jeta, Colo.). Office: 104 E 6th St Walsenburg CO 81089

SCHAMP, CRAIG HARRISON, software engineer; b. Piqua, Ohio, Dec. 21, 1956; s. James Addison and Margaret Ann (Fronda) S. Student, Sinclair Community Coll., 1976-77, U. Calif., San Diego, 1980-84; BA in Computer Sci., U. Calif., San Diego, 1984; student, Navy Personnel R & D Ctr., 1981-82. Insp. Bell Optical Lab., Dayton, Ohio, 19841977-78; clk. Custom Craft Optical Labs., San Diego, 1978-79; data processing monitor NCR Corp., San Diego, 1979-80; sr. software engr. MassPar, Inc., Santa Clara, Calif., 1988—. Treas. San Diego Young Reps., 1985; assoc. San Diego County Rep. Com., 1985; vol. Mus. Photog. Arts, San Diego, 1988--. Mem. Assn. for Computing Machinery, Usenix Assn., User Group. Office: MassPar Inc 2840 San Tomas Expwy Ste 140 Santa Clara CA 95051

SCHANDER, EDWIN, law librarian; b. Harbin, Peoples Republic of China, Mar. 9, 1942; came to U.S., 1957; s. Robert and Olga (Linder) S.; m. Mary Lea, July 3, 1971. BA, Calif. State U., Northridge, 1969; postgrad., UCLA, 1969-72, MLS, 1973. Reference librarian Los Angeles County Law Library, 1973-79, sr. reference librarian, 1979-86, head reference services, 1986—; library commr. City of Pasadena, 1987—; cons. Rand Corp., Santa Monica, Calif., 1975. Contbr. articles on law to profl. jours. Freelance TV producer Community Access Channel, City of Pasadena. Served with U.S. Army, 1964-66. Mem. Am. Assn. Law Libraries, Humane Soc. U.S., LWV. Club: Los Angeles Athletic. Home: 430 C Orange Grove Circle Pasadena CA 91105 Office: LA County Law Libr 301 W First St Los Angeles CA 90012

SCHANDER, MARY LEA, police official; b. Bakersfield, Calif., June 11, 1947; d. Gerald John Lea and Marian Lea Coffman; B.A. (Augustana fellow) Calif. Luth. Coll., 1969; M.A., U. Calif., Los Angeles, 1970; m. Edwin Schander, July 3, 1971. Staff aide City of Anaheim (Calif.) Police Dept., 1970-72, staff asst., 1972-78, sr. staff asst., 1978-80; with Resource Mgmt. Dept., City of Anaheim, 1980-82; asst. to dir. Pub. Safety Agy., City of Pasadena Police Dept., 1982-85, spl. asst. to police chief, 1985-88, adminstrv. comdr., 1988—; freelance musician, publisher Australian Traditional Songs, 1985; lectr. Calif. Luth. Coll. Bd. dirs. Community Dispute Resolution Ctr. Pasadena. Producer (cable TV program) Traditional Music Showcase. Contbr. articles in field to profl. jours. Recipient Women at Work Medal of Excellence, 1988. Mem. Am. Mgmt. Assn., LWV. Club: Los Angeles Athletic. Home: 430-C Orange Grove Circle Pasadena CA 91105 Office: Pasadena Police Dept 142 N Arroyo Pkwy Pasadena CA 91103

SCHANKMAN, ALAN ROBERT, ophthalmologist; b. Bklyn., Jan. 1, 1947; s. Barnet and Sylvia (Barken) S.; m. Vicky Barbara Gellman, Dec. 10, 1973; children—Dana, Lauren, Alison, Michael. B.S., Bklyn. Coll., 1968; M.D., Downstate Med. Sch., SUNY-Bklyn., 1972. Diplomate Am. Bd. Ophthalmology. Intern Beth Israel Med. Ctr., N.Y.C., 1973; resident in ophthalmology E.J. Meyer Meml. Hosp., Buffalo, 1973-76; pvt. practice, N.Y.C., 1976-78, Los Angeles, 1978—; co-founder, v.p. and sec. S & S Med. Office Systems, Inc.; clin. instr. Jules Stein Eye Inst., UCLA Med. Sch., 1980—; co-founder, v.p. S&S Med. Office Systems, Inc.; cons. Braille Inst. Developer refractive eye surgery, myopia, 1980; investigator Yag laser surgery, 1982. Fellow Am. Acad. Ophthalmology; mem. Internat. Assn. Ocular Surgeons, Calif. Assn. Ophthalmology, Los Angeles County Ophthal. Soc., Calif. Med. Soc., Los Angeles County Med. Assn., Internat. Glaucoma Congress, Am. Soc. Contemporary Ophthalmology, Am. Assn. Ophthalmology, Keratorefractive Soc., N.Y. Acad. Scis. Office: 12840 Riverside Dr North Hollywood CA 91607

SCHAPIRA, MOREY RAEL, electronics sales executive; b. Chgo., Jan. 4, 1949; s. Julius and Rose (Schwartz) S.; BS with honors in Physics (Ill. State Scholar 1966, Case scholar 1966-70), Case Western Res. U., 1970; MBA, Harvard U., 1977; m. Barbara Stein, May 29, 1977; children: Rachel, Deborah, Michael. Research scientist research div. Raytheon Co., Waltham, Mass., 1970-75; cons. scientist M.I.T. Lincoln Labs., Lexington, summer 1976; product mktg. engr. microwave semicondr. div. Hewlett Packard Co., San Jose, Calif., 1977-80, domestic sales mgr. optoelectronics div., Palo Alto, Calif., 1980-81, distbr. mktg. mgr. optoelectronics div., 1981-83; corp. distbn. mgr. Hewlett Packard Components, San Jose, Calif., 1983-85; nat. distbr., sales mgr. Micro Power Systems, Santa Clara, Calif., 1985-87; nat. sales mgr. Network Gen. Corp., Mountain View, Calif., 1987—. Div. chmn. United Way Campaign., 1978; nat. v.p. Union of Councils for Soviet Jews, 1979-84, nat. pres., 1984-86; pres. Bay Area Council on Soviet Jewry, San Francisco, 1980-84. Mem. Am. Mgmt. Assn., Tech. Mktg. Soc. Am., Am. Enterprise Inst. Assos., Am. Phys. Soc., Assn. Old Crows, World Affairs Council, Bus./Profl. Advt. Assn. Democrat. Editor-in-chief, then pub. A Guide to Jewish Boston, 1974-77; pub., editor-in-chief HarBus News, 1976-77. Home: 1154 Crespi Dr Sunnyvale CA 94086 Office: Network Gen Corp 1945 A Charleston Rd Mountain View CA 94043

SCHARF, GUY T., computer consultant; b. Chgo., Jan. 4, 1943; s. Guy J. and Gladys Ann (McCracken) S.; m. Christine Dickson, Mar. 21, 1982. BS, U. Ill., 1966. Cert. office automation profl. Rsch. programmer U. Ill., Urbana, 1963-68; programming mgr. Stanford (Calif.) U., 1968-81; sr. developer Tandem Computers, Inc., Cupertino, Calif., 1981-82; pres. Software Architects, Inc., Mountain View, Calif., 1982—. Contbr. articles to computer publs. Mem. Ind. Computer Cons. Assn. (pres. No. Calif. chpt. 1985, chmn. nat. govt. rels. com. 1986-87), Software Entrepreneurs Forum, Mountain View C. of C. Office: Software Architects Inc 2163 Jardin Dr Mountain View CA 94040

SCHARFY, G. CHARLES, lawyer, bank executive; b. Cleve., Nov. 26, 1916; s. Gottlieb Charles and Teresa (Klemm) S.; m. April Mildred Stemple, Sept. 27, 1942; children: Philip, Madelon, Ralph. PhB magna cum laude, U. Toledo, 1938, LLB cum laude, 1940, JD, 1968. Bar: Ohio 1940. Acct. The Barrett Co., Toledo, 1936-40; assoc. Shumaker, Loop & Kendrick, Toledo, 1940-51, ptnr., 1951-82, of counsel, 1982—; bd. dirs. Bank of Fountain Hills, Ariz. Trustee Fountain Hills Spl. Rd. Dists., 1984-88, joint powers chmn., 1986-87; mem. Com. for Incorporation Fountain Hills; former trustee Toledo Area C. fo C. Served to lt. col. USMCR. Mem. ABA, Ohio State Bar Assn., Toledo Bar Assn. (past exec. com.). Republican. Episcopalian. Club: Kiwanis (Scottsdale, Ariz.). Home: 15232 E Palomino Blvd Fountain Hills AZ 85268

SCHATZ, JOHN FRANK, geoscience consultant; b. N.Y.C., July 27, 1942; s. Rudolph and Marie (Weinhofer) S.; m. Mary Spencer, Sept. 6, 1969; children: Katherine, Andrew. BS, MIT, 1964, PhD, 1971. Staff physicist Lawrence Livermore Nat. Lab., Livermore, Calif., 1971-79; v.p. Terra Tek, Inc., Salt Lake City, 1979-84, Sci. Applications Internat. Corp., San Diego, 1984-89; pvt. practice, cons. Del Mar, Calif., 1989—. Contbr. numerous articles profl. jours. Named Outstanding Student U.S. Nat. Com. on Rock Mechanics, 1973. Mem. Soc. Petroleum Engrs., Soc. of Core Analysts, Internat. Soc. for Rock Mechanics. Home and Office: 4636 S Ln Del Mar CA 92014

SCHATZ, MONA CLAIRE STRUHSAKER, social worker, educator; b. Phila., Jan. 4, 1950; d. Milton and Josephine (Kivo) S.; m. James Fredrick Struhsaker, Dec. 31, 1979; 1 child, Thain Mackenzie. BA, Metro State Coll., 1976; postgrad., U. Minn., 1976; MSW, U. Denver, 1979; D in Social Work/Social Welfare, U. Pa., 1986. Teaching fellow U. Pa., Phila., 1981-82; asst. prof. S.W. Mo. State U., Springfield, 1982-85; researcher family & children policy, foster care & children svcs., generlaist and advanced generalist practice Colo. State U., Ft. Collins, 1979—, asst. prof., 1985—, field coord., 1986-88, project dir. Colo. foster care tng. program, 1987—, dir. youth agy. adminstrn. program Am. Humanics, 1988—; cons. Mgmt. and Behavioral Sci. Ctr., The Wharton Sch. U. Pa., 1981-82; resource specialist So. N.J. Health Systems Agy., 1982; adj. faculty mem. U. Mo., Springfield, 1984; med. social worker Rehab. and Vis. Nurse Assn., 1985—. Contbr. articles to profl. jours. Cons., field rep. Big Bros./Big Sisters of Am., Phila., 1979-83; acting dir., asst. dir. Big Sisters of Colo., 1971-78; owner Polit. Cons. in Colo., Denver, 1978-79; active Food Co-op, Ft. Collins, Foster Parent, Denver, Capital Hill United Neighbors, Adams County (Denver) Social Planning Coun., Co., Colo. Justice Coun., Denver, Regional Girls Shelter, Springfield; bd. dirs. Crisis Helpline and Info. Svc. Scholar Lilly Endowment, Inc., 1976, Piton Found., 1978; recipient Spl. Recognition award Big Bros./Big Sisters of Am., 1983. Mem. Counsel Social Work Edn., Group for Study of Generalist Social Work, Social Welfare History Group, Nat. Assn. Social Workers (nominating chmn. Springfield chpt.), Student Social Work Assn. of Colo. State U. (adv. 1986—), Permanency Planning Coun. for Children and Youth, NOW (treas. Springfield chpt. 1984-85), Student Nuclear Awareness Group (advisor), Student Social Work Assn. (advisor), Alpha Delta Mu. Democrat. Jewish. Office: Colo State U Social Work Dept Eddy Bldg Fort Collins CO 80523

SCHATZ, ROBERT KEITH, former police chief; b. Pocatello, Idaho, May 23, 1927; s. John and Irene B. (Blackborn) S.; m. Vivian Marie Spears; children: John, Suzanne, Matthew, Michael. BA, San Jose State U., 1955; postgrad. FBI Nat. Acad., 1966. Police officer, Mountain View Police Dept., Calif., 1950-53, police sgt., 1953-56, police lt., 1956-61, asst. chief of police, 1961-73, chief of police, 1973-84; instr. San Jose State U., 1974. Mem. Mountain View city council, 1988—; vice mayor, 1986, mayor, 1987—. Served to lt. U.S. Army, 1951-53. Mem. Internat. Assn. Chiefs Police, Calif. Police Chiefs' Assn., FBI Nat. Acad. Grads., Calif. Peace Officers' Assn. Republican. Lodge: Kiwanis. Home: 314 Wildflower Park Ln Mountain View CA 94043

SCHATZKA, RICHARD LEE, electrical engineer; b. Great Falls, Mont., July 13, 1945; s. Walter Richard and June Louise (Beckett) S.; m. Delane C. Taylor, July 1, 1967 (div. 1975); 1 child, David Richard; m. Martha Jane Smith, June 20, 1981. ASEE, No. Mont. Coll., 1967. Sr. electronics technician Mont. Power Co., Butte, 1973-80; hardware engr. Tetragenics Co., Butte, 1980-84, project mgr., 1984—. Patentee in field. Active Amateur Radio League, Newington, Conn., 1967—. Served with USN, 1967-73, Vietnam. Lutheran. Club: Butte Amateur Radio Club (pres. 1985-86). Home: 100 Milky Way Butte MT 59701 Office: Tetragenics Co 55 E Granite Butte MT 59701

SCHAUB, JOHN STEPHEN, physician; b. Portland, Oreg., Nov. 27, 1936; s. Walter Herman and Kathryn Louise (Wightman) S.; m. Diane Porter, June 20, 1960; children: Doris K., Douglas P., Heidi L. BA in Chemistry, Lewis and Clark Coll., 1959; MD, Oreg. U., 1964. Intern/resident San Bernardino (Calif.) County Hosp., 1964-66; physician NW Permanente, PC, Portland, 1971—, gen. internist, 1971-84, orthopedic physician, 1984—; comdr. 45th Sta. Hosp., Vancouver Barracks, Wash., 1981-85. Maj. U.S. Army 1966-71; col. USAR, 1971—. Decorated Meritorious Service medal, U.S. Army, 1986. Fellow Am. Back Soc.; mem. Clackamas County Med. Soc., Oreg. Med. Assn., AMA, N. Am. Acad. Musculoskeletal Medicine, Mason, Shriners. Office: NW Permanente PC 10180 SE Sunnyside Rd Clackamas OR 97015

SCHAWLOW, ARTHUR LEONARD, physicist, educator; b. Mt. Vernon, N.Y., May 5, 1921; s. Arthur and Helen (Mason) S.; m. Aurelia Keith Townes, May 19, 1951; children: Arthur Keith, Helen Aurelia, Edith Ellen. B.A., U. Toronto, 1941, M.A., 1942, Ph.D., 1949, LL.D. (hon.), 1970; D.Sc. (hon.), U. Ghent, Belgium, 1968, U. Bradford, Eng., 1970, U. Ala., 1984, Trinity Coll., Dublin, Ireland, 1986; D.Tech. (hon.), U. Lund, Sweden, 1987. Postdoctoral fellow, research asso. Columbia, 1949-51; vis. assoc. prof. Columbia U., 1960; research physicist Bell Telephone Labs., 1951-61, cons., 1961-62; prof. physics Stanford U., 1961—, now J.G. Jackson-C.J. Wood prof. physics, exec. head dept., 1966-70, acting chmn. dept., 1973-74. Author: (with C.H. Townes) Microwave Spectroscopy, 1955; Co-inventor (with C.H. Townes), optical maser or laser, 1958. Recipient Ballantine medal Franklin Inst., 1962, Thomas Young medal and prize Inst. Physics and Phys. Soc., London, 1963, Schawlow medal Laser Inst. Am., 1982; Nobel prize in physics, 1981; named Calif. Scientist of Year, 1973, Marconi Internat. fellow, 1977. Fellow Am. Acad. Arts and Scis., Am. Phys. Soc. (council 1966-70, chmn. div. electron and atomic physics 1974, pres. 1981), Optical Soc. Am. (hon. mem. 1983, dir.-at-large 1966-68, pres. 1975, Frederick Ives medal 1976); mem. Nat. Acad. Scis., IEEE (Liebmann prize 1964), AAAS (chmn. physics sect. 1979), Am. Philos. Soc. Office: Stanford U Dept Physics Stanford CA 94305-4060

SCHECK, DENNIS RANDALL, religious educator; b. Chgo., Apr. 30, 1951; s. Wilbur B. and Lucille H. (Weber) S.; m. Margaret M. Zoebl, Nov. 18, 1972; children: Jennifer, Timothy, Aleisha. BA in Edn., Concordia Coll., River Forest, Ill., 1972; MRE, Loyola U., Chgo., 1975; postgrad., Calif. Coast U. Cert. tchr., Ill. Dir. Christian edn. various Luth. churches, Chgo., 1972-75, U.S. Army, Ft. Carson, Colo., 1975—; mem. U.S. Army Religious Edn. Planning and Strategy Group, Washington, 1980—; mem. Coop. Curriculum Selection group, Washington, 1989; tng. assoc. Ktisma Ctr., Inc., Colorado Springs, Colo., 1988—. Co-author handbook on vol. mgmt., 1983; producer local weekly radio program, 1984-85; contbr. articles to various publs. Mem. Assn. Vol. Adminstrn., Luth. Edn. Assn. Office: Office of Staff Chaplain US Army Fort Carson CO 80913-5006

SCHEEL, RANDALL LAWRENCE, utilities executive; b. St. Helens, Oreg., June 26, 1952; s. John D. and Edith T. S.; m. Vicki J., Dec. 4, 1984. BA in Polit. Sci., U. Wash., 1974; MA Studies of the Future, U. Houston, 1978. Cert. secondary tchr. Tchr. high sch. Opheim (Mont.) Pub. Schs., 1975-77; prin. Strategic Corp., Portland, Oreg., 1979-86; mgr. strategic planning So. Calif. Gas Co., L.A., 1986—. Author: Introduction to the Future, 1988. Recipient Spl. Merit award Western Ednl. Soc. Telecommunications, 1983. Mem. The Issue Exchange (dir. 1987—), World Future Soc., Planning Forum, So. Calif. Issues Network (chmn. 1987). Office: So Calif Gas Co 810 S Flower St Los Angeles CA 90017

SCHEERER, ERNEST WILLIAM, dentist; b. Wabash, Ind., May 18, 1932; s. Ernest William and Anna Lucille (Bahler) S.; m. Ingrid Elvy Yvonne, Sept. 28, 1973. BS, Purdue U., 1954; DDS, Ind. U., 1961. Intern The Queen's Hosp., Honolulu, 1961-62; assoc. Pvt. Dental Practice, Honolulu, 1963-65; owner Pvt. Solo Dental Practice, Honolulu, 1965-75; ptnr. Dental Adminstrn., Honolulu, 1975-78; pres. Scheerer & West Dental Corp., Honolulu, 1978—; chief Dept. Dentistry Queen's Hosp., Honolulu. Contbr. various clin. articles to profl. jours. Mem. Big Bros., Hawaii, 1968-74. Fellow Acad. Gen. Dentistry, Hawaii Acad. Gen. Dentistry (pres.), Am. Coll. Dentists; mem. Am. Dental Assn., Hawaii Dental Assn. (treas.), Internat. Acad. of Gnathology, Pierre Fauchard Soc., Fedn. Dental Internat., Am. Equilibration Soc., Am. Assn. Osseuintegration, Hawaii Med. Library (sec.). Mem. United Ch. of Christ. Club: Honolulu, Pacific. Lodge: Elks. Office: Scheerer & West Inc 735 Bishop St #211 Honolulu HI 16812

SCHEFFY, HUBERT, JR., real estate company executive; b. Rochester, N.Y., Aug. 13, 1940; s. Hubert and June Clark (Brackett) S.; m. Elgonde Marleen Van Assen, Sept. 9, 1967; children: Clark Willem, Marieke Sarah. AB in Econs., Harvard U., 1962, MBA, 1965. Audit mgr. Arthur Andersen & Co., Boston, 1965-70; mgr. mgmt. info. USM Corp., Boston, 1970-72; controller Midland-Ross Corp., Somerset, N.J., 1972-74; asst. v.p. City Investing Co., N.Y.C., 1974-76; sr. v.p. fin. Wood Bros. Homes, Inc., Denver, 1976-81; v.p. fin. Miller-Klutznick-Davis-Gray Co., Denver, 1982-83; gen. ptnr. Crestone Investment Co., Denver, 1983-85; sr. v.p., chief fin. officer Pacific Scene Inc., San Diego, 1985; v.p., controller Lewis Homes Co., Upland, Calif., 1985—. Mem. Am. Inst. CPA's, Mass. Soc. CPA's. Episcopalian.

SCHEFSKY, RICHARD JOSEPH, chemical engineer; b. Sheboygan, Wis., Oct. 27, 1931; s. Milton F. Schefsky and Marie (Gangelbauer) Barchacky; m. Darlene Jennie Wendt, Sept. 11, 1954; children: Catherine, Mary Jean, Richard J. II. BS in Chem. Engring., U. Wis., 1958; MBA, U. Louisville, 1964. Project engr. Pillsbury Co., New Albany, Ind., 1958-65; asst. plant mgr. Am. Potato Co., Moses Lake, Wash., 1965-67; plant mgr. Rogers Bros. Co., Rexburg, Idaho, 1967-70; owner R. J. Schefsky Co., Seattle, 1970-75; pres. Northwest Labs., Seattle, 1975—. Mem. ASTM (standards cons. 1986—), Am. Coun. Ind. Labs. (div. bd. dirs. 1982-84). Republican. Roman Catholic. Office: NW Labs 1530 1st Ave S Seattle WA 98134

SCHEI, KENNETH GEORGE, civil engineer; b. Iron Mountain, Mich., Dec. 3, 1940; s. Kasper Goldbrand and Mary Ann (Serena) S.; m. E. Suzanne Hart, July 11, 1970; children: Elliot G., Kelley S. BSCE, Mich. Tech. U., 1966. Registered profl. engr. Jr. engr. Colo. State Hwy. Dept., Denver, 1967-68; structural engr. Stearns-Roger, Inc., Denver, 1968-72, structural supr., 1972-79, project engr., 1979-83; sr. project engr. Holmes & Narver, Inc., Las Vegas, Nev., 1983-87; project mgr. Holmes & Narver, Inc., Albuquerque, 1987—. Author (procedure manuals) IDS Site Survey Guidelines, 1988, Project Management Standards & Procedures, 1987-88, Quality Assurance Standards & Procedures, 1984-85; designer 4-span, 6-lane hwy. bridge on I-70, 1967. Soccer coach Vegas West Youth Soccer League, Las Vegas, 1983-87, soccer referee Cherry Creek Soccer League, Denver, 1979-82. Served with USN, 1964-66, Vietnam. Mem. ASCE, NSPE, Am. Soc. Indsl. Security. Republican. Methodist. Club: Albuquerque Road Runners. Home: 14329 Marquette Dr NE Albuquerque NM 87123 Office: Holmes & Narver Inc 6501 Americas Pkwy NE Albuquerque NM 87110

SCHEIBE, JOHN MICHAEL, information technology, financial management consultant; b. Tacoma, Apr. 11, 1963; s. Raymond Kenneth and Emily Agnes (Toth) S. BBA in Acctg. magna cum laude, Pacific Luth. U., 1985, BA in Computer Sci. magna cum laude, 1985. CPA, Wash.; Cert. Data Processor, Wash. Cons. Peat, Marwick, Main & Co., Seattle, 1985—. Mem. IEEE, Am. Inst. CPA's, Beta Gamma Sigma, Beta Alpha Psi. Office: Peat Marwick Main & Co 2600 Security Pacific 1301 Fifth Ave Seattle WA 98101

SCHEIBEL, ARNOLD BERNARD, psychiatrist, educator, researcher; b. N.Y.C., Jan. 18, 1923; s. William and Ethel (Greenberg) S.; m. Madge Mila Ragland, Mar. 3, 1950 (dec. Jan. 1977); m. Marian Diamond, Sept. 1982. B.A., Columbia U., 1944, M.D., 1946; M.S., U. Ill., 1952. Intern Mt. Sinai Hosp., N.Y.C., 1946-47; resident psychiatry Barnes and McMillan Hosp., St. Louis, 1947-48, Ill. Neuropsychiat. Inst., Chgo., 1950-52; asst. prof. psychiatry and anatomy U. Tenn. Med. Sch., 1952-53, asso. prof., 1953-55; asso. prof. UCLA Med. Center, 1955-67, prof. psychiatry and anatomy, 1967—; mem. Brain Research Inst., 1960—, acting dir., 1987—; cons. VA hosps., Los Angeles, 1956—. Contbr. numerous articles to tech. jours, chpts. to books.; editorial bd.: Brain Research, 1967-77, Developmental Psychobiology, 1968—, Internat. Jour. Neurosci., 1969—, Jour. Biol. Psychiatry, 1968—, Jour. Theoretical Biology, 1980—. Mem. Pres.'s Commn. on Aging, Nat. Inst. Aging, 1980—. Served with AUS, 1943-46; from lt. to capt. M.C. AUS, 1948-50. Guggenheim fellow (with wife), 1953-54, 59. Fellow Am. Acad. Arts and Scis., Norwegian Acad. Scis.; mem. AAAS, Am. Psychiat. Assn. (lifetime fellow), Am. Neurol. Assn., Soc. Neurosci., Psychiat. Research Assn., Am. EEG Assn., Am. Assn. Anatomists, Soc. Biol. Psychiatry, Am. Acad. Neurology, So. Calif. Psychiat. Assn. Home: 16231 Morrison St Encino CA 91316 Office: UCLA Los Angeles CA 90024

SCHEIDT, NICHOLAS LEE, mortgage banking executive; b. Denver, Sept. 22, 1959; s. Paul Anthony and Mary Jane (Belton) S. Sec.-treas. A.D.L., Inc., Westminster, Colo., 1980-83; pres., chmn. bd. Apex Fin. Svcs. Corp., Westminster, 1983—, Apex Realty Investments, Inc., Westminster, 1985—, Cain Travel of Westminster, Inc., 1986—; cons. U.S. Dept. Labor, Washington, 1987—; ofcl. Apex. Fin. Svcs. Corp., Apex Realty Investments; bd. dirs. Douglas County Nat. Bank., Bergen Park Nat. Bank. Mem. Colo. Mortgage Bankers Assn., Met. N. C. of C., Mortgage Bankers Assn. Democrat. Roman Catholic. Office: Apex Fin Svcs Corp 8753 Yates Dr Ste 230 Westminster CO 80030

SCHEINBAUM, DAVID, photography educator; b. Bklyn., Apr. 14, 1951; s. Louis and Rhoda (Feerman) S.; m. Vicki Golden, May 30, 1973 (div. 1975); m. Janet Ann Goldberg-Russek, Mar. 21, 1982; stepchildren: Jonathan Russek, Andra Russek; 1 child, Zachary. BA, CUNY, 1973. Instr. photography Pace U., N.Y.C., 1974-75, LaGuardia (N.Y.) Community Coll., 1975-78; instr. Coll. Santa Fe, 1979-81, asst. prof. photography, 1981—; printer, asst. to Beaumont Newhall, Santa Fe, 1980—; printer to Eliot Porter, Santa Fe, 1983—; co-dir. Scheinbaum & Russek, Santa Fe, 1979—. Photography exhibitions include Pace U., 1974, Midtown Y Gallery, N.Y., 1977, Santa Fe Gallery for Photography, 1979, 81, The Armory for the Arts, Santa Fe, 1980, 1981, Sea Breeze Gallery, Block Island, R.I., 1982, Highlands U., Las Vegas, N.Mex., 1982, Gov's. Gallery, Santa Fe, 1982, Santa Fe Festival for the Arts, 1982, Coll. Santa Fe, 1983, Dem. Conv., San Francisco, 1984, Mus. Natural History, Albuquerque, 1987, Photo Gallery Internat., Tokyo, 1987; permanent collections include Norton Gallery Mus., West Palm Beach, Fla, Amon Carter Mus., Ft. Worth, N.Mex. State U., Las Cruces, Ctr. Creative Photography, Tucson, Ariz., Mus. Fine Arts, Santa Fe, Bklyn. Mus., U. Okla., Norman, Bibliothque Nationale France, Paris, Gernsheim Collection. U. Tex., Austin, Albuquerque Mus. Mem. N.Mex. Council on Photography (v.p.), Santa Fe Ctr. Photography (bd. dirs. 1978-85). Jewish. Home: 328 Guadalupe St Ste M Santa Fe NM 87501 Office: Coll Santa Fe Saint Michaels Dr Santa Fe NM 87501

SCHELESKI, JOHN EDWARD, controller; b. Chgo., Feb. 5, 1953; s. John R. and Virginia M. (Zonsius) S.; m. Gail Su Ling Chang, Aug. 10, 1980; children: Linda, Helen. Assoc. of Bus., Triton Coll., 1973; BBA, U. Hawaii, 1983, M in Acctg., 1985; MBA, Chaminade U., 1986. CPA. Regional sales rep. Kennametal, Inc., Bedford, Pa., 1976-81; lectr., instructor U. Hawaii (Manoa), Honolulu, 1983-85; acct. Wikoff/Kodani CPAs, Honolulu, 1985-86; controller E.E. Black Constrn., Honolulu, 1986-87, Frito-Lay of Hawaii, Honolulu, 1987—; lectr., Am. Inst. of Banking, Honolulu, 1984-87. Co-authored and developed computer competency course and examination which has become the entrance requirement for both grad. and undergrad. admission into the Coll. of Bus. Adminstrn. and Sch. of Accountancy, U. Hawaii. Chmn. planning and zoning, Manoa Neighborhood Bd., Honolulu, 1983—. Mem. Am. Mgmt. Assn. (hon. degrees, 1977, 79), Elks, Beta Gamma Sigma, Beta Alpha Psi. Home: 94-591 Palai St Waipahu HI 96797 Office: 99-1260 Iwaena St Aiea HI 96701

SCHELLER, SANFORD GREGORY, printing company executive; b. Newark, July 7, 1931; s. John Arthur Scheller and Harriet (Gregory) Tate; m. Marjory Meyer, Dec. 31, 1950; children: Sanford Gregory Jr., Douglas Meyer, Bradford John, Frances Scheller Lavin, Eric Bruce. BBA, Westminster Coll., New Wilmington, Pa., 1953. V.p., gen. mgr. St. Regis Corp., N.Y.C., 1978-84, Champion Internat., Stamford, Conn., 1984-85; pres., chief exec. officer Treasure Chest Advt., Glendora, Calif., 1986—. Republican. Office: Treasure Chest Advt Co Inc 511 W Citrus Edge Glendora CA 91740

SCHENDEL, WINFRIED GEORGE, insurance company executive; b. Harpstedt, Germany, June 19, 1931; s. Willi Rudolf Max and Anna Margarete (Sassen) S.; came to U.S., 1952, naturalized, 1956; B.S. in Elect. and Indsl. Engring., Hannover-Stadthagen U., Hannover, W. Germany, 1952; m. Joanne Wiiest, Aug. 24, 1953; children—Victor Winfried, Bruce Lawrence, Rachelle Laureen. Elec. draftsman Houston Lighting & Power Co., 1954-57; elec. draftsman, corrosion technician Transcontinental Gas Pipeline Co., Houston, 1957-59; elec. engr. Ken R. White Cons. Engrs., Denver, 1959-61; sales engr. Weco div. Food Machinery & Chem. Corp., various locations, 1961-64; ins. field underwriter N.Y. Life Ins. Co., Denver, 1964-66, asst. mgr., 1966-70, mgmt. asst., 1970-71, gen. mgr., 1971-77, mgr., 1979-85, field underwriter, 1985—; ind. gen. agt., Denver, 1978-79. Instl. rep., advancement chmn. Denver Area council Boy Scouts Am., Lakewood, Colo., 1968-72; precinct chmn. Republican Party, Jefferson County, Colo., 1976, 78; founder, mem. (life) Sister City Program, Lakewood, Colo.; chmn. adv. bd. ARC, Jefferson County, Colo., 1987-89. Recipient Centurion award, 1966; Northwestern Region Leader Manpower Devel. award N.Y. Life Ins. Co., 1968, Salesman of Yr. award Jefferson County Salesman with a Purpose Club, 1983. Mem. Nat. Assn. Life Underwriters, Gen. Agents and Mgrs. Assn. (recipient Conf. Nat. Mgmt. award, 1975), Colo. Life Underwriters Assn. (v.p. 1989—), Mile High Assn. Life Underwriters (pres. 1986-87, nat. com. 1988—), Lakewood C. of C. (pres. people-to-people, Trailblazer of Yr. award 1982, 83, Trail Boss of Yr. 1983). Presbyterian (elder). Clubs: Lions, Edelweiss, Internat. Order Rocky Mountain Goats, N.Y. Life Star (leading asst. mgr. Continental region 1980), Masons, Shriners. Home: 13802 W 20th Pl Golden CO 80401 Office: NY Life Ins Co 10403 W Colfax Ave Ste 540 Lakewood CO 80215

SCHENK, RAY M(ERLIN), electronics company executive; b. Logan, Utah, Dec. 18, 1946; s. Merlin F. and Thelma E. (Birch) S.; B.S. in Acctg. magna cum laude, Utah State U., 1969. C.P.A., Utah. Staff acct. Haskins and Sells, Phoenix, 1969, Salt Lake City, 1969-71; controller Kimball Electronics, Salt Lake City, 1971—. Recipient Scholastic Achievement cert. Phi Kappa Phi, 1967, 68; 1st Security Found. scholar, 1968; Alpha Kappa Psi scholarship award, 1969; C.P.A. medallion, 1970. Mem. Nat. Assn. Accts., Am. Acctg. Assn., Utah Assn. C.P.A.s, Am. Inst. C.P.A.s. Home: 5044 S Boabab Dr Salt Lake City UT 84117 Office: Kimball Electronics 350 Pierpont Ave Salt Lake City UT 84101

SCHER, LAURA SUSAN, financial company executive; b. Passiac, .NJ., Jan. 18, 1959; d. Alan E. and Frances Scher; m. Ian H. Altman, May 28, 1984. BA in Econs., Yale U., 1980; MBA, Harvard U., 1985. Assoc. Cons. Bain & Co., Boston, 1981-83; chief exec. officer Working Assets Funding Service, San Francisco, 1985—. Named Baker Scholar, Harvard U., 1985. Office: Working Assets 230 California St San Francisco CA 94111

SCHERBA, STEPHEN, JR., financial executive, analyst, consultant; b. Milw., Mar. 14, 1948; s. Stephen and Emma Hirtes (Ross) S.; m. Elaine Louise Podolske, June 19, 1971. BS, Carroll Coll., 1970; MS, U. Wash., 1975, MBA, 1981. Fin. analyst Puget Power, Bellevue, Wash., 1981-86; mgr. profit planning and fin. analysis Nalley's Fine Foods, Tacoma, 1986-89; cons. Northwest Fin. Adv. Svcs., Inc., Seattle, 1989—; cons. Scherba and Assocs., Seattle, 1981—. Bd. dirs. Jr. Achievement Greater Puget Sound, Seattle, 1982. Mem. Sigma Xi, Beta Beta Beta. Clubs: Wash. Athletic, Rainier (Seattle). Home: 509 Crockett St Seattle WA 98109

SCHERER, ELIZABETH KING, data processing executive; b. Henderson, Ky., June 19, 1960; d. Leo Jr. and Gail (Lansden) King; m. Randall Steven Scherer, May 25, 1986. BS, Vanderbilt U., 1982. Systems analyst On-Line Computing, Nashville, 1982-84; pres., owner Profl. Computer Cons., Los Angeles, 1984—.

SCHERER, MILO WINSTON, psychologist (clinical); b. Yakima, Wash., Aug. 10, 1936; s. Byron Hanes and Elizabeth Warren (Lovell) S.; m. Mary Ellen Worrell,. BA, Pacific Lutheran U., 1958; MA, San Francisco State U., 1964; PhD, U.C.L.A., 1969. Asst. prof. McGill Univ., Montreal, 1969-72; intership dir. Patton State Hosp., San Bernardino, Calif., 1973--; chief psychologist Patton State Hosp., San Bernardino, 1986-. Mem. Am. Psychol. Assn., Soc. Sigma Xi. Democrat. Office: Patton State Hosp 3202 E Highland Ave Patton CA 92369

SCHERICH, ERWIN THOMAS, civil engineer, consultant; b. Inland, Nebr., Dec. 6, 1918; s. Harry Erwin and Ella (Peterson) S.; student Hastings Coll., 1937-39, N.C. State Coll., 1943-44; B.S., U. Nebr., 1946-48; M.S., U. Colo., 1948-51; m. Jessie Mae Funk, Jan. 1, 1947; children—Janna Rae Scherich Thornton, Jerilyn Mae Scherich Dobson, Mark Thomas. Civil and design engr. U.S. Bur. Reclamation, Denver, 1948-84, chief spillways and outlets sect., 1974-75, chief dams br., div. design, 1975-78, chief tech. rev. staff, 1978-79, chief div. tech. rev. Office of Asst. Commr. Engring. and Research Ctr., 1980-84; cons. civil engr., 1984—. Mem. U.S. Com. Internat. Commn. on Large Dams. Served with AUS, 1941-45. Registered profl. engr., Colo. Fellow ASCE; mem. Nat. Soc. Profl. Engrs. (nat. dir. 1981-87), Profl. Engrs. Colo. (pres. 1977-78), Wheat Ridge C. of C. Republican. Methodist. Home and Office: 3915 Balsam St Wheat Ridge CO 80033

SCHEURER, CHERYL ANN, accountant; b. Redwood City, Calif., Nov. 10, 1954; d. Jack L. and Thelma M. (Jaton) S. Student, Peterson Sch. Bus., 1971-72, Golden Gate U., 1980-83. Acctg. clk. Seattle First Nat. Bank, 1973-74, Simpson Timber Co., Kirkland, Wash., 1974-76; controller, office mgr. Maida Constrn. Co., Walnut Creek, Calif., 1978-80; acct. Castle, CPA, Oakland, Calif., 1981-82; pvt. practice acctg., tax planning Alameda, Calif., 1980—; guest speaker ESL Adult Sch., Alameda, 1988. Active Big Bros./Big Sisters Am., Oakland, 1986-87. Office: 2254 Encinal Ave Ste A Alameda CA 94501

SCHICK, SUSAN JORDIS, architect; b. Salem, Oreg., Aug. 17, 1956; d. Harold Ralph Jr. and Jordis Adele (Benke) S. BArch, U. Oreg., 1981. Registered architect, Idaho. Intern architect Willamette Commn. Design Ctr., Eugene, Oreg., 1976; dir. art dept. Four Winds Westward Ho, Deer Harbour, Wash., 1980; intern architect Environment West, Ketchum, Idaho, 1982-85; project architect McLaughlin Architects, Chartered, Sun Valley, Idaho, 1985-88; architect, prin. Susan J. Schick, AIA, Sun Valley, 1988—. Mem. AIA, Nat. Council Archtl. Registration Bds., Nat. Coun. Hist. Preservation, Idaho Conservation League. Democrat. Office: PO Box 2716 Sun Valley ID 83353

SCHIELE, PAUL ELLSWORTH, JR., educator; b. Phila., Nov. 20, 1924; s. Paul Ellsworth Sr. and Maud (Barclay) S.; m. Sarah Irene Knauss, Aug. 20, 1946; children: Patricia Schiele Tiemann, Sandra Schiele Kicklighter, Deborah Schiele Hartigan. AT, Temple U., 1949; BA, LaVerne U., 1955; MA, Claremont Coll., 1961; PhD, U.S. Internat. U., San Diego, 1970. Cert. sec. tchr., Calif. 1961. Tchr. sci. and math. Lincoln High Sch., Phila., 1956-57, Ontario, Calif., 1957-65; math. and sci. cons. Hacienda La Puente U. Sch. Dist., Calif., 1965-75; asst. prof. Calif. State U., Fullerton, 1975-83; pres., owner Creative Lng. Environments and Resources, Glendora, Calif., 1983—; cons. in field. Author: Primary Science, 1972, 2d edit., 1976; editor: A Living World, 1974, 2d edit., 1986; co-dir. TV show Marine Biology Series, 1970-71; designer in field. Appt. adv. com. Sci. and Humanities Symposium Calif. Mus. Sci. and Industry, 1974. Mem. Calif. Music Theatre, Calif. Elem. Edn. Assn. (hon.), Nat. PTA (hon.), Calif. Inter-Sci. Coun. (pres., chmn. 1971), Elem. Sch. Scis. Assn., Phi Delta Kappa (chartered). Republican. Lutheran. Home: 231 N Catherine Park Dr Glendora CA 91740

SCHIELL, CHARLES RANDALL, leasing company executive; b. Aurora, Colo., Nov. 15, 1952; s. Charles and Audrey Margaret (Parsons) S.; m. Janelle Marie Norris, Dec. 28, 1974; children: Charles Christopher, Angela Janelle. BA, U. Colo., 1975; MBA, Colo. State U., 1985. Br. mgr. Gen. Fin. Corp., Ft. Collins, Colo., 1977-78; collection mgr. 1st Nat. Bank, Ft. Collins, 1978-79; mgr. ops. Tri Continental Leasing Corp., Englewood, Colo., 1979-82; credit mgr. Colo. Nat. Leasing Corp., Golden, 1982-83, v.p. credit and ops., 1983-84; v.p. ops, treas. 1st Centennial Leasing Corp., Denver, 1984—. Precinct committeeman Denver County Dem. Com., 1976, 77, Arapahoe County Dem. Com., 1984-86, dist. capt., 1986-88. Mem. Am. Assn. Equipment Lessors, Western Assn. Equipment Lessors. Presbyterian. Home: 12172 W 84th Pl Arvada CO 80005 Office: First Centennial Leasing Corp 2480 W 26th Ave Ste 140B Denver CO 80211

SCHIER, ROBERT MORTON, sales executive, consultant; b. Bronx, N.Y., July 19, 1937; s. Alex and Gertrude (Feinberg) S.; m. Marybelle Rosenberg, Sept. 20, 1976 (div.); m. Donnita Hope DeGoede, June 21, 1986; children: Robin Tidwell, Laura. Assocs. in Bus. Adminstrn., NYU, 1958. Account exec. William, Warren Advt., N.Y.C., 1958-68; sales mgr. Walton Rug Co., Chgo., 1968-74; with exec. sales Phoenix Mut. Life, 1974-76; gen. mgr. King Carpet Co., Phoenix, 1976-80; proprietor Carpet Fashions, Youngstown, Ariz., 1980-87; sales mgr. Carpetime, Phoenix, 1987—. Served to U.S. Army, 1954-56. Democrat. Jewish. Lodges: B'nai Brith (sec. local chpt. 1968, pres. 1969), Elks (pub., editor Glendale, Ariz. chpt.). Home: 10815 W Northern #128 Glendale AZ 85307

SCHIESS, ULRICH JOHN, mortgage company executive, accountant; b. Dodgeville, Wis., June 10, 1949; s. Ulrich Schiess and Florence Helen (Walstad) Lenaway; m. Christin Catherine Lewis, June 5, 1971 (div. Aug. 1983); m. Judy Dee Euliss, Nov. 28, 1987; children: Jason, Travis, Tyler, Betsy, Jessica and Danielle. BBA, U. Wis., 1974. CPA, Ariz., Wis. Supr. Alexander Grant & Co, CPAs, LaCrosse, Wis., 1974-78, Greer DeFoor & Hawley, CPAs, Tucson, 1979; ptnr. DeFoor Grady & Schiess, CPAs, Tucson, 1979-83; pres. 1st City Fed., Inc., Tucson, 1983—. Mem. AICPAs, Ariz. Soc. CPAs, Nat. Assn. Mortgage Brokers, Ariz. Mortgage Brokers Assn. Republican. Lutheran. Office: 1st City Fed Inc 6149 E Broadway Ste 226 Tucson AZ 85711

SCHIFF, DAVID GEORGE, furniture company executive; b. Opelousas, La., Dec. 17, 1949; s. Vernon A. and Jean (Kohn) S.; children: Christopher, Stephen. Mgr. sales Allen Furniture, Omaha, 1972-74; v.p. Schiff Furniture, Opelousas, 1974-84; mgr. Universal Furniture, New Orleans, 1984-87; mgr. gen. Ikard's Furniture, Las Cruces, N.Mex., 1987—. Mem. Nat. Home Furnishing Assn., S.W. Furnishing Assn. Office: Ikard's Furniture 101 E Lohman Las Cruces NM 88001

SCHIFF, MARTIN, physician, surgeon; b. Phila., July 16, 1922; s. Isidore and Cecelia (Miller) S.; m. Mildred Tepley, Jan. 5, 1946; children: Denise Schiff Simon, Michael, David. BS, Pa. State U., 1943; MD, U. Calif.-Irvine, 1951. Intern L.A. County Gen. Hosp., 1950-51; gen. practice medicine specializing in bariatrics L.A., 1951—; mem. staff Brotmam Meml. Hosp.; lectr. L.A. area community colls. Author: Eat & Stay Slim, 1972, Miracle Weight-Loss Guide, 1976, One-Day-At-A-Time Weight Loss Plan, 1980, (tape) Weight Loss Plan for Health, Happiness & A Longer Life Span, 1982, The Thin Connection, 1986. Lt. USN, 1943-45, PTO. Mem. AMA, Calif. Med. Assn., L.A. Med. Assn., Am. Soc. Weight Control Specialists. Home: 1220 Corsica Dr Pacific Palisades CA 90272 Office: 12900 Venice Blvd Los Angeles CA 90066

SCHIFF, STEVEN HARVEY, congressman, lawyer; b. Chgo., Mar. 18, 1947; s. Alan Jerome and Helen M. (Ripper) S.; m. Marcia Lewis, Nov. 8, 1968; children: Jaimi, Daniel. BA, U. Ill., Chgo., 1968; JD, U. N.Mex., 1972. Bar: N.Mex. 1972, U.S. Dist. Ct. N.Mex. 1972, U.S. Ct. Appeals (10th cir.) 1980. Asst. dist. atty. Dist. Atty.'s Office, Albuquerque, 1972-77, sole practice, 1977-79; asst. city atty. City of Albuquerque, 1979-81; dist. atty. State of N.Mex., Albuquerque, 1981-88; mem. 101st Congress from 1st Dist. N.Mex., 1989—; lectr. U. N.Mex., Albuquerque, 1981—. Chmn. Bernalillo County Rep. Party Conv., Albuquerque, 1984, 87. Served to lt. col. and staff judge adv. N.Mex. Air N.G. Recipient Law Enforcement Commendation medal SR, 1984. Mem. Albuquerque Bar Assn., N.Mex. Bar Assn., ABA, N.Mex. Dist. Atty.'s Assn., Nat. Dist. Atty.'s Assn. Republican. Jewish. Club: Civitan. Lodge: B'nai Brith (pres. 1976-78). Home: 804 Summit NE Albuquerque NM 87106 Office: US Ho of Reps 1520 Longworth Bldg Washington DC 20515 also: 500 Gold SW Albuquerque NM 87102

SCHIFFNER, CHARLES ROBERT, architect; b. Reno, Sept. 2, 1948; s. Robert Charles and Evelyn (Keck) S.; m. Iovanna Lloyd Wright, Nov. 1971 (div. Sept. 1981); m. Adrienne Anita McAndrews, Jan. 20, 1983. Student, Sacramento Jr. Coll., 1967-68, Frank Lloyd Wright Sch. Architecture, 1968-77. Registered architect, Ariz., Wis. Architect Taliesin Associated Architects, Scottsdale, Ariz., 1977-83; pvt. practice architecture Phoenix, 1983—; instr. Ariz. State U., Tempe, 1983-87. Prin. works include Ahwatukee House of the Future (cert. distinction Am. Architecture 1985), addition to Richard Black Residence, Encanto Park, Ariz. (1st place J. Brock 1986), The Pottery House, Paradise Valley, Ariz., Seventh Day Adventist Exec. Hdqrs., Scottsdale, Condominium Project, Phoenix; author (poem) Yellowstone Stream (2d prize Winter Wheat contest 1986). Named one of 35 Most Promising Young Americans Under 35, US mag., 1979. Democrat. Roman Catholic. Home: 4540 N 44th St #1 Phoenix AZ 85018 Office: Camelhead Office Ctr 2600 N 44th St #208 Phoenix AZ 85018

SCHILBRACK, KAREN GAIL, system analyst; b. Tomahawk, Wis., Sept. 28; d. Edward Richard and Irene Angeline (Ligman) S. Student U. Calif.-Santa Barbara, 1967-69; B.A. in Anthropology, U. Calif.-Davis, 1971; postgrad. in Edn. and Archeology, Calif. State Poly. U., San Luis Obispo, 1971-72. Cert. computer specialist; cert. data processing; lic. cosmetologist. Computer specialist Facilities Systems Office, Port Hueneme, Calif., 1975-78, sr. computer specialist, 1978-80, project mgr. U.S. Naval Constrn. Bn. Ctr., 1980—, tng. cons. FACSO, 1981, 82; curriculum cons. Ventura Community Coll., Calif., 1981—; instr. U.S. Navy, Port Hueneme, 1983, Civil Service Commn., Port Hueneme, 1978-80. Author: AMALGAMAN Run Procedures, 1976; Cobol Programming Efficiencies, 1978; co-author, editor: Training Manual for Direct Data Entry System, 1983. Vol. Vols. for Camarillo State Hosp., Camarillo, 1978-88, coordinator Ventura County, 1981; chmn. scholarship fund drive Ventura, Santa Barbara, Los Angeles, Counties, 1980. Named Young Career Woman of Yr., Calif. Bus. and Profl. Women, 1979. Mem. Young Ladies Inst. (pres. Santa Paula, dist. dep. Ventura/Santa Barbara Counties), Am. Biog. Inst. Research Assn. (lifetime dep. gov.). Lodge: Toastmistress. Home: 6993 Wheeler Canyon Santa Paula CA 93060 Office: FACSO Code 18211 USNCBC Port Hueneme CA 93042

SCHILD, PETER, lawyer; b. Berkeley, Calif., Dec. 13, 1949; s. Manfred and Hannah Schild; m. Sherrill Amendt, Mar. 20, 1982; children: Ryan, Rebecca, Alexa. BA, U. Calif., Berkeley, 1971; JD, U. Colo., 1975. Bar: Colo. 1975, U.S. Dist. Ct. Colo. 1976, Calif. 1977, U.S. Ct. Appeals (10th cir.) 1986. Staff atty. pub. defender's office State of Colo., La Junta, 1976-77, Golden, 1976-79; office head pub. defender's office State of Colo., Boulder, 1979-84; pvt. practice Boulder, 1984-87; sr. ptnr. Eisner & Schild, Boulder, 1987—; chmn. Criminal Law Com., Boulder, 1986-88. Mem. com. Criminal Justice Adv. Commn., Boulder, 1979-84. Mem. Colo. Bar Assn., Colo. Criminal Def. Bar Assn., Colo. Trial Lawyers Assn. Democrat. Office: Eisner & Schild 1881 9th St #315 Boulder CO 80302

SCHILL, ROBERT JAMES, architect, business owner; b. Chgo., Aug. 30, 1939; s. Edward John and Mabel Edna (Harroun) S.; m. Janice Elaine Dahlstrom, Dec. 23, 1963; children: Carla Grace, Craig Robert, Kelvin Edward. BA in Architecture, U. Ill., Urbana, 1962, MA in Architecture, 1963. Registered architect; N.C.A.R.B. cert. Assoc. ptnr. Richarson, Severns, Scheeler & Assocs., Inc., Champaign, Ill., 1964-72; prin. Metz Train & Youngren, Inc., Chgo., 1972-81; pres. Metz Train & Youngren, Inc., Phoenix, 1981-86; prin., pres. Robert J. Schill Architects, Inc., Phoenix, 1986—. Prin. works include SW Forest Industries Corp. Hdqrs. Phoenix, 1981, Engring. Research Ctr. Ariz. State U., Tempe, 1983, Gold-Simpson Sci. Bldg., U. Ariz., Tucson, 1985, Windmill Inn, Sun City West, 1988. Mem. Missionary Tech. Team. Mem. AIA, Constrn. Specifications Inst., Nat. Trust for Hist. Preservation, Ariz. Profl. Svcs. Mgrs. Assn. (bd. dirs.), Ariz. State U. Archtl. Guild. Home: 5345 E Orchard Ln Paradise Valley AZ 85253 Office: Robert J Schill Architects Inc 2214 N Central Ave Phoenix AZ 85004

SCHILLER, PAUL OMAR, pianist, technical consultant; b. Grinnell, Iowa, Apr. 13, 1950; s. Johannes August and Aleen Barbara (Linhardt) S.; m. Debra Patrice Casperson, June 3, 1972. MusB, Pacific Luth. U., 1972; postgrad., U. Iowa, 1973, Western Iowa Tech. Coll., 1974; grad. study piano, Steinway & Sons, N.Y.C., 1984. Piano technician Aspen (Colo.) Music Sch., 1974; piano technician, piano technician instr. Shenandoah Cons. Music, Winchester, Va., 1974-75; tech. cons. Dunkley Music, Inc., Boise, Idaho, 1975—; prin. pianist, celeste player Boise Philharm. Orch., 1978—. Mem. Piano Technicians Guild, Am. Keyboard Artists, Idaho Hist. Soc. (hon. curator antique mus. instruments). Office: Dunkley Music Inc 410 S Capitol Blvd Boise ID 83706

SCHILLER, THOMAS BENNETT, motion picture writer, director; b. Los Angeles, Apr. 12, 1949; s. Robert Achille and Joyce Gloria (Harris) S. Documentary film maker Los Angeles; writer "Saturday Night Live", N.Y.C., 1975-80; writer, dir. MGM, N.Y.C., 1982; writer Paramount Pictures, Hollywood, Calif., 1984; writer, dir. Home Box Office, Los Angeles, 1986; free-lance writer, dir. Los Angeles, 1986—. Producer: (documentary films) Buckminster Fuller on Spaceship Earth, 1968, A Glimpse of De Kooning, 1969, Anais Nin Observed, 1971, The Henry Miller Odyssey, 1974, Henry Miller Asleep and Awake, 1974; writer, dir. (Saturday Night Live segments) Schiller's Reel, 1977-80, (feature film) Nothing Lasts Forever, 1982, (TV film) From Here to Maternity, 1986, Flapjack Floozie, 1988, (TV show) Baby Boom. Recipient 2 Emmy awards for Saturday Night Live, 1976, 77. Mem. ASCAP, Am. Fedn. TV and Radio Actors, Writers Guild of Am. (annual award 1976, 79), Dirs. Guild of Am. Lodge: Masons.

SCHILLING, DEAN WILLIAM, manufacturing executive; b. Waverly, Iowa, Apr. 25, 1944; s. Alvin Louis and Etta Christine (Poppe) S.; m. Betty Ann (Homeister), Aug. 5, 1962; children: Angela Marie, Christine Ann. AS, Iowa State U., 1964, BS, 1969. Engr. Systems Genetics, Clarksville, Iowa, 1970-81; cons. Systems Genetics, Clarksville, 1985—; sr. tech. support Hewlett Packard, Sunnyvale, Calif., 1983-85; pres. Cryo Genetic Technology, Soquel, Calif., 1985—. Inventor biol. devices and methods to remedy human infertility. Mem. Am. Fertility Soc., Soc. Cryobiology, Iowa State Alumni. Lutheran. Lodge: Order of Knoll (founders club 1988). Office: CryoGenentic Tech Inc 400 Hoover Rd Soquel CA 95073

SCHILT, ALEXANDER FRANK, academic administrator; b. Cheyenne, Wyo., Mar. 4, 1941; s. Louis Ford and Mary Alice (Linton) S.; m. Charlotte Frances Snyder, May 25, 1967 (div.); children: Paige Eileen, Kristen Rose. BA, U. Wyo., 1964; MA, Ariz. State U., 1966, PhD, 1969. Dir. residence Ariz. State U., Tempe, 1964-70; dean of students, assoc. prof. edn. Ind. U., New Albany, 1970-76; chancellor Ind. U., Richmond, 1976-80, U. Houston-Downtown, 1980-87; pres. Eastern Washington U., 1987—; bd. dirs. Cen. Houston, Inc.; lectr. on urban univs. to profl. confs. Bd. dirs. Whitewater Opera Co., Greater Houston Area ARC, Spokane Symphony Orch., Spokane Unltd., Washington Centennial Summer Games. Mem. AAUP, Am. Council Edn., Am. Assn. State Colls. and Univs. (chmn. urban affairs com. 1982-86), Am. Assn. Counseling and Devel., Houston C. of C. (downtown com. 1982-83), Nat. Assn. State Univs. and Land-Grant Colls. (exec. com. for urban affairs 1983-86), Spokane Area C. of C. (bd. dirs.). Roman Catholic. Clubs: Houston, Petroleum, Spokane. Office: Eastern Washington U Office of Pres 214 Showalter Hall MS #130 Cheney WA 99004

SCHINDLER, MARY JEAN, nurse; b. Hastings, Nebr., Aug. 6, 1925; d. Harold Henry and Freda Louise (Schmitt) Binions; m. Wallace Andrew Achindler, Jan. 21, 1947 (div. 1972); children: Sandra Kay, John Alfred, Carol Jean, Kurt Andrew. Diploma in nursing, U. Nebr., 1946; BS, Westminster Coll., 1973; MA in Nursing, U. Wash., Seattle, 1975; DEd, Portland (Oreg.) State U., 1987. RN, Oreg., Wash., Nebr., Utah. Wash. mem. crisis outreach team Highline-West Seattle Mental Health, 1975; instr. Lower Columbia Coll., Longview, Wash., 1975-77; supr. Oreg. State Hosp., Salem, 1977-78; specialist mental health div. Ea. Oreg. Hosp., Pendleton and Salem, 1978-81; nurse mgr. Dammasch Hosp., Wilsonville, Oreg., 1981-83, psychiat. clin. nursing specialist, 1986—; cons., tchr. Dammasch Hosp., Portland, 1986—. Del. People to People Citizen Ambassador, Spokane, Wash., 1988—. Mem. Nurse Practitoners Spl. Interest Group, Oreg. Nurses Assn., Am. Nurses Assn., Coun. Psychiat. Mental Health Nursing. Republican. Presbyterian.

SCHINNERER, ALAN JOHN, entrepreneur; b. Long Beach, Calif., June 8, 1925; s. Walter John and Esther Schinnerer; m. Barbara Elaine Daniger, Aug. 17, 1951 (div. Aug. 1971); children: Gregory, Scott, Brett, Vicky. AA, Long Beach City Coll., 1948; B of Elec. Engring., U. So. Calif., 1952, postgrad. law, 1956-57, postgrad. bus., 1958-59. Purchasing agt. McCulloch Corp., Los Angeles, 1952-56; systems engr. Hughes Aircraft Co., Culver City, Calif., 1956-59; sales engr. Gilfillan Corp., Los Angeles, 1959-61; mktg. specialist N.Am. Rockwell Corp., Downey, Calif., 1961-68; sr. project engr. Hughes Aircraft Co., El Segundo, Calif., 1968-74, dir. satellite tests, 1974-76, assoc. program mgr., 1976-84; pres., gen. ptnr., founder Calif. Classic Boats, Huntington Beach, 1979—. Author: (catalog) Parts for Antique and Classic Chris-Craft, Dodge, Gar Wood and Hacker Runabouts, 1979-89. Bd. dirs. Antique Powercraft Hist. Soc., 1984-85. Served with USN, 1943-46, PTO. Mem. Antique and Classic Boat Soc. (founding pres. So. Calif. chpt. 1983-86), Delta Tau Delta. Republican. Clubs: Porsche of Am., Tahoe Yacht (Tahoe City, Calif.). Home: 5581 Ridgebury Dr Huntington Beach CA 92649 Office: Calif Classic Boats 15632B Product Ln Huntington Beach CA 92649

SCHIPPER, MERLE, art historian; b. Toronto, Ont., Can.; came to U.S., 1943; d. Leon J. and Libby (Genesove) Solway; m. Bernard Schipper, May 22, 1943 (div. June 1980); children: Lee, Amy Schipper Howe. BA, U. Toronto, 1943; MA, UCLA, 1970, PhD, 1974. Instr. extension UCLA, 1974-78, 83-84, lectr. summer session, 1977-79, 84; vis. artist grad. sch. Claremont (Calif.) U., 1979; lectr. U. So. Calif., L.A., 1985; corr. L.A.

ARTNews, N.Y.C., 1985-87; columnist ARTScene, L.A., 1987—; project dir. Santa Monica (Calif.) Arts Commn., 1987—. Panelist, mem. grants com. Art Orgn. Dept. Cultural Affairs, L.A., 1984-85; mem. selection com. of sculpture installation Calif. Med. Ctr., L.A., 1986; mem. Rev. Com. Hist. Resources Survey Project, L.A., 1978-85, So. Calif. Com. for Contemporary Art Documentation, L.A., 1985—. Rsch. fellow Indo-U.S. Subcommn. N.Y. State, 1988. Mem. Coll. Art Assn., Internat. Assn. Art Critics, Art Table, Assn. Ind. Art Historians. Home and Office: 1439 18th St Apt 1 Santa Monica CA 90404

SCHIRMER, TAD WILLIAM, oil company exploration geologist; b. Greenwich, Conn., Sept. 10, 1956; s. Howard William and Beatrice (Cody) S.; m. Virginia Picone, Aug. 6, 1983; children: Jennifer Lynn, Edward Fredrick. BS, Weber State Coll., 1982; MS, Utah State U., 1985. Seismic technician United Geophys. Corp., Douglas, Wyo., 1981; field geologist U.S. Geol. Survey, Menlo Park, Calif., 1982; mining geologist Tinglefoot Mining Co., Idaho City, 1982-83; geologist Utah Bur. Hazardous Waste, Salt Lake City, 1985; exploration geologist Chevron U.S.A., Inc., Denver, 1986-88; exploration geophysicist Chevron U.S.A., Inc., San Ramon, Calif., 1988—; tchg. asst. Weber State Coll., Ogden, Utah, 1981-82; grad. tchg. asst. Utah State U., Logan, 1983-84. Conn. State scholar Coll. Testing Bd., 1974; grad. fellow Utah State U., 1984. Mem. Am. Assn. Petroleum Geologists (research grantee 1984), Sigma Xi Scientific Research Soc.(research grantee 1984). Republican. Presbyterian. Office: Chevron USA Inc Chevron Park San Ramon CA 94583

SCHIRRIPA, ROBERT ROCCO, chemical engineer; b. Bklyn., Apr. 13, 1948; s. Dominico Ralph and Carmela Francis (Curro) S.; divorced; m. Virginia Mae Hildebrandt, July 31, 1977; children: Kenneth, Kevin, Jennifer. BChemE, Pratt Inst., 1970; MChemE, U. Conn., 1973. Engr. Exxon Research and Engring. Co., Florham Park, N.J., 1972-73; process engr. Exxon Chem. Co., Linden, N.J., 1973-78; sr. engr. Exxon Chem. Am., Bayway, N.J., 1978-81, Santa Fe Braun, Alhambra, Calif., 1981-86, IT Corp., Irvine, Calif., 1986-87, Thortee Internat., San Bernardino, Calif., 1987-88, SOS On-Site Treatment Corp., Claremont, Calif., 1988, C F Braun, Alhambra, 1988—. Cubmaster Cub Scout Pack 124, Madison, N.J., 1977-79; chmn. Parent Faculty Assn. Carnival, Madison, 1977-79; coach Madison Little League, 1978; pres. Spina Bifida Assn., Los Angeles, 1986-88. Mem. Am. Inst. Chem. Engrs., Am. Chem. Soc., ASTM. Roman Catholic. Home: 1914 Wheaton Ave Claremont CA 91711

SCHLAICH, CARL JOHN, aeronautical engineer; b. Visalia, Calif., Mar. 23, 1943; s. Senes John Carl and Beatrice Marie (Cote) S.; m. Barbara Jean Alverson, June 25, 1966 (div. Feb. 1972); 1 child, Carleen; m. Lani Lund, Aug. 29, 1972; children: Christine, Paul, Teresa, Andrew. BS in Aero. Engring., Calif. State Poly. U., San Luis Obispo, 1971. Design engr. Morton Thiokol Inc., Brigham City, Utah, 1972-77, sr. project engr., 1984—; project engr. USAF Air Force Systems Command, West Palm Beach, Fla., 1977-84. Com. chmn. Boy Scouts Am., Jupiter, Fla., 1982-84. With USAF, 1964-68. Mem. Brigham City Golf and Country Club, Elks. Republican. Mormon. Home: 629 Beecher Ave Brigham City UT 84302 Office: Morton Thiokol Inc PO Box 689 Brigham City UT 84302

SCHLEGEL, ROBERT PHILIP, healthcare executive; b. Columbus, Ohio, May 23, 1929; s. Edward Paul and Sylvia Elizabeth (Kahler) S.; m. Marylou Peters, June 15, 1952; children: Debra Lynn, Edward Paul, Dana Sue. BS, Capital U., Bexley, Ohio, 1951; postgrad., Harvard U., 1972. V.p., gen. mgr. Ames Co. of Can., Toronto, Ont., 1960-63; worldwide mktg. dir. Ames Co, Elkhart, Ind., 1963-66; exec. v.p. Ames Co. of Japan, Tokyo, 1967-69; pres. Miles Labs.-Japan, Tokyo, 1969-70, Ames Co., Elkhart, 1970-76; sr. v.p. Miles Labs., Inc., Elkhart, 1976-83; pres. Intelligent Images, Inc., San Diego, 1984-86; gen. mgr. Syntro Diagnostics, Inc., San Diego, 1987-88; group v.p. Intermark, Inc., San Diego, 1989—; dir. Mast Immuno Systems, Inc., Mt. View, Calif., SCI Diagnostics, Inc., Digene Diagnostics, Inc., College Park, Md., Yellowstone Diagnostics, Inc., Palo Alto, Calif., Western Sizzlin Inc., Dallas. Mem. Am. Assn. Clin. Chemists, Biomed. Mktg. Assn., Clin. Lab. Mgmt. Assn. Home and Office: 1020 Prospect La Jolla CA 92038-1149

SCHLEI, NORBERT ANTHONY, lawyer; b. Dayton, Ohio, June 14, 1929; s. William Frank and Norma (Lindsley) S.; m. Jane Moore, Aug. 26, 1950 (div. 1963); children: Anne C. Buczynski, William K., Andrew M.; m. Barbara Lindemann, Mar. 7, 1965 (div. 1981); children: Bradford L., Graham L., Norbert L., Norma Blake. BA, Ohio State U., 1950; LLB magna cum laude, Yale U., 1956. Bar: Ohio 1956, Calif. 1958, D.C. 1963, U.S. Supreme Ct. 1963. Law clk. to Justice Harlan U.S. Supreme Ct., 1956-57; assoc. atty. O'Melveny & Myers, Los Angeles, 1957-59; ptnr. Greenberg, Shafton & Schlei, Los Angeles, 1959-62; asst. atty. gen. U.S. Dept. Justice, Washington, 1962-66; ptnr. Munger, Tolles, Hills & Rickershauser, 1966-70, Kane, Shulman & Schlei, Washington, 1968-70; ptnr.-in-charge Los Angeles office Hughes Hubbard & Reed, 1972-89; now chmn., chief exec. officer Kahala Capital Corp., Santa Monica, Calif., Brea Devel. Corp.; bd. dirs. Wedbush Corp., Wedbush Securities, Inc., Los Angeles; pres. Kahala Homes, Inc., 1984—. Author: (with M.S. McDougal and others) Studies in World Public Order, 1961 (Am. Soc. Internat. Law ann. book award); State Regulation of Corporate Financial Practices, 1962; editor-in-chief Yale Law Jour., 1955-56. Democratic nominee for Calif. Assembly, 1962, for sec. of state Calif., 1966. Served to lt. (j.g.) USNR, 1950-53. Mem. ABA, Fed. Bar Assn., Los Angeles County Bar Assn., State Bar Calif., Am. Judicature Soc., Am. Soc. Internat. Law, Ctr. for Pub. Resources, Japan-Am. Found., Inc. (bd. dirs.). Clubs: Yale (So. Calif.); Calif. Yacht (Marina Del Rey), Plaza (Honolulu). Office: Kahala Capital Corp 2800 28th St Ste 321 Santa Monica CA 90405

SCHLESINGER, DEBORAH LEE, librarian; b. Cambridge, Mass., Sept. 13, 1937; d. Edward M. and Edith D. (Schneider) Hershoff; divorced; children: Suzanne, Richard. BA, U. Mass., 1961; MS, Simmons Coll., 1974; postgrad., U. Pitts., 1983. Reference librarian Bently Coll., Waltham, Mass., 1964-65; dir. Carnegie Library, Swissvale, Pa., 1973-77, South Park Twp. Library, Library, Pa., 1977-81, Monessen (Pa.) Library, 1981-82, Lewis & Clark Library, Helena, Mont., 1983-88, 89—; state librarian Mont. State Library, Helena, Mont., 1988-89; vis. scholar Pitts. Regional Library Ctr., 1982-83. Editor Pa. Union List, 1982-83. Mem. exec. bd. Mont. Cultural Advocacy, 1983—. Mem. Mont. Library Assn. (chmn. legis. com. 1984—), Mont. Assn. Female Execs. (fin. com. 1986—), AAUW (exec. com. 1985-86). Democrat. Club: Montana (Helena). Home: 507 5th Ave Helena MT 59601 Office: Lewis and Clark Libr 120 S Last Chance Mall Helena MT 59601

SCHLESINGER, LEBER, court reporter; b. Tuscumbia, Mo., Nov. 23, 1929; s. Frank Samuel and Mary Jane (Burks) S.; m. Nadine Bommer, July 3, 1954; children: Aaron, Sabina. Student Ct. Reporter Sch., Mound City Coll., 1954. Ct. reporter Bouley, Schlesinger, Di Curti and Schippers, Tucson, 1961—. With USN, 1946-51. Mem. Nat. Shortland Reporters Assn. (cert. of merit), Ariz. Shorthand Reporters Assn. (pres. 1970), Am. Shortland Reporters, Soc. for Preservation and Encouragement Barbershop Quartet Singing in Am., Oldtime Fiddlers Club (pres. 1983-84). Republican. Home: 7751 E Elida St Tucson AZ 85715 Office: Bouley Schlesinger DiCurti and Schippers 601 Pioneer Pla 100 N Stone St Tucson AZ 85701

SCHLIEWEN, RICHARD DOUGLAS, former educator, chorale director; b. L.A., Nov. 8, 1937; s. Edgar Erich and Beulah May (Offutt) S.; m. Mizue Tonogi, July 18, 1962; children: Hiroko, Douglas, Joanne. AB, UCLA, 1962. Cert. gen. elem. tchr., Calif. Tchr. L.A. Unified Sch. Dist., 1962-88; dir. Asian Am. Chorale, L.A., 1983—. Producer motion pictures Rodeo Girl, 1952, Vacation for Janet, 1954, Christmas for Chris, 1958. With U.S. Army, 1959. Mem. NEA, Calif. Tchrs. Assn. Democrat. Home and Office: PO Box 8439 Van Nuys CA 91409-8439

SCHLOESSLIN, MARK EDWARD, system safety engineer; b. Pitts., Apr. 2, 1955; s. Milton E. and Helen J. (Dugan) S. BS in Computer Sci., U. Pitts., 1978. Programmer/analyst NCR Corp., Dayton, Ohio, 1979-84; system safety engineer Martin Marietta, Denver, 1984—. Republican. Roman Catholic.

SCHLOSE, WILLIAM TIMOTHY, health care executive; b. West Lafayette, Ind., May 16, 1948; s. William Fredrick and Dora Irene (Chitwood) S.; m. Linda Lee Fletcher, June 29, 1968 (div. 1978); children: Vanessa Janine Schlose Hubert, Stephanie Lynn; m. Kelly Marie Martin, June 6, 1987. Student, Bowling Green State U., 1966-68, Long Beach City Coll., 1972-75; teaching credential, UCLA, 1975. Staff respiratory therapist St. Vincent's Med. Ctr., L.A., 1972-75; cardio-pulmonary chief Temple Community Hosp., L.A., 1975-76; adminstrv. dir. spl. svcs. Santa Fe Meml. Hosp., L.A., 1976-79; mem. mktg. and pub. rels. staff Nat. Med. Homecare Corp., Orange, Calif., 1979-81, Medtech of Calif., Inc., Burbank, Calif., 1981-84; regional mgr. Mediq Health Care Group Svcs., Inc., Chatsworth, Calif., 1984-88; pres. Baby Watch Homecare, Whittier, Calif., 1988—; staff instr., Montebello (Calif.) Adult Schs. Author: Fundamental Respiratory Therapy Equipment, 1977. With USN, 1968-72. Mem. Am. Assn. Respiratory Care, Calif. Soc. Respiratory Care (past officer), Nat. Bd. Respiratory Care, Am. Assn. Respiratory Care, Nat. Assn. Apnea Profls., Am. Assn. Physicians Assts., L.A. Pediatric Soc., Calif. Perinatal Assn., Porsche Owners Club L.A., Porsche Club Am. Republican. Methodist. Office: Baby Watch Homecare 13006 Philadelphia St Whittier CA 90601

SCHLOSSER, JOHN ROLLAND, JR., management consultant; b. Palo Alto, Calif., May 1, 1949; s. John Rolland Sr. and LaVonne Elizabeth (Halverson) S.; m. Carissa Marie Comstock, Mar. 13, 1971; children: Elke Marie, Gretchen Elizabeth. BA, U.S. Internat. U., 1971; MPH, UCLA, 1974. Asst. exec. dir. Long Beach (Calif.) Community Hosp., 1974-77; mgr., cons. Coopers & Lybrand, L.A., 1977-79; v.p. then sr. v.p. Northridge (Calif.) Hosp. Med. Ctr., 1979-85; chief exec. officer Clinishare, Chatsworth, Calif., 1985-88; v.p., ptnr. Korn/Ferry Internat., L.A., 1988—. Contbr. articles to profl. jours. Mem. Presdl. Task Force, 1976. Fellow Am. Coll. Healthcare Execs.; mem. UCLA Hosp. Adminstr. Alumni Assn. (pres. 1979), Healthcare Forum, Healthcare Execs. So. Calif. Republican. Home: 11215 W Cashmere St Los Angeles CA 90049 Office: Korn/Ferry Internat 1800 Century Park E Ste 900 Los Angeles CA 90067

SCHLOSSER, MARK STEVEN, design engineer; b. Buffalo, Aug. 18, 1953; s. George Aloys and Rose Florence (Montagino) S.; m. Maria Emilia Eisenreich, Sept. 25, 1982; 1 child, Stephanie Marisa. BS in Indsl. Engring., U. Wash., 1977. Scientist Weyerhaeuser Rsch., Seattle, 1977-78; pres. Mark Schlosser Engring., Seattle, 1978-79; sr. design engr. Korry Electronics, Seattle, 1979-83; sr. devel. engr. illuminated displays div. Bell Industries, Redmond, Wash., 1983-86; R & D engr. Ariel Electronics Inc., Sunnyvale, Calif., 1986-89; sr. staff engr. Space Labs., Inc., Redmond, Wash., 1989—. Patentee flip-action guard and position indicator, low profile lamp assembly, push button electric switch, polymer thick film extrusion system. Recipient award Boeing Comml. Airplane Co., 1982. Mem. IEEE, ASME, Soc. Plastic Engrs. Home: 3036 47th SW Seattle WA 98116 Office: Space Labs Inc 4200 150th Ave NE Redmond WA 98073

SCHLOTTER, WALLY, chamber of commerce executive, television director; b. San Diego. AA in Bus., Grossmont Jr. Coll., 1972; BS in Telecommunications and Film, San Diego State U., 1975; student, Nat. Acad. TV Arts and Scis., 1974. With KPBS-TV, San Diego, 1973-75; asst. to exec. producer Police Story NBC Columbia Pictures TV, San Diego, 1975-76; production coord. nat. TV commls. San Diego, writer, production assistant, production coord., location scout, location mgr., assoc. producer/dir.; assoc. dir., dir. Motion Picture and TV Bur., San Diego; v.p. Greater San Diego C. of C. Creator, producer many fundraisers including San Diego EMMY Awards broadcast to benefit Nat. Acad. TV Arts and Scis. scholarship fund, 1978, 79, Kids Day at the Movies for orphaned children, Oscar Nite Variety Club fundraiser for children. Bd. govs. Muscular Dystrophy Assn.; trustee San Diego Festival of Arts; bd. dirs. Young Friends of the Symphony; active Multiple Sclerosis Soc., Socail Advocates for Youth, others. Recipient Nat. Best of West Producer award, 1975, San Diego Emmy citation for assoc. dir., 1976, Green Derby award Simon and Simon campaign, 1982, Appreciation award SAG, 1985, numerous others. Mem. Nat. Acad. TV Arts and Scis. (bd. govs., past v.p., co-founder/chmn. scholarship fund), Am. Film Inst., Variety Club (bd. govs., past chmn. spl. events, past. v.p.), Ad Club. Home: 5135 67th St San Diego CA 92115 Office: 110 C St W Ste 1600 San Diego CA 92101

SCHMALENBERGER, JERRY L., pastor, seminary administrator; b. Greenville, Ohio, Jan. 23, 1934; s. Harry Henry and Lima Marie (Hormel) S.; m. Carol Ann Walthall, June 8, 1956; children: Stephen, Bethany Allison, Sarah Layton. BA, Wittenberg U., 1956, DDiv (hon.), 1984; MDiv, Hamma Sch. Theology, Springfield, Ohio, 1959, D of Ministry, 1976. Ordained to ministry Luth. Ch., 1959. Dir. Camp Mowana, Mansfield, Ohio, 1958-59; pastor 3d Luth. Ch., Springfield, 1959-61, 1st Luth. Ch., Bellefontaine, Ohio, 1961-66; sr. pastor 1st Luth. Ch., Tiffin, Ohio, 1966-70, Mansfield, 1970-79; sr. pastor St. John's Luth. Ch., Des Moines, 1979-88; pres. Pacific Luth. Theol. Sem., Berkeley, Calif., 1988—; co-dir. Iowa Luth. Hosp. Minister of Health Program, Des Moines, 1986-88; Roland Payne lectr. Gbarnga (Liberia) Sch. Theology, 1987. Author: Lutheran Christians' Beliefs Book One, 1984, Book Two, 1987, Iowa Parables and Iowa Psalms, 1984, Saints Who Shaped The Church, 1986, Caretakers of Creation, 1987, Nights Worth Remembering, 1989; columnist "Rite Ideas", 1987-88. Bd. dirs. Grand View Coll., Des Moines, 1980—, Wittenberg U., Springfield, Ohio, 1974-87, Luth. Social Services of Iowa, 1980-87, chmn. pre fund drive, 1988; bd. dirs. Planned Parenthood of Mid-Iowa, Des Moines, 1987-88; dir. Evang. Outreach/Luth. Ch. Am., 1983-85; mem. Iowa Luth. Hosp. Charitable Trust, 1986-88; chair Com. for Homeless Fund, Des Moines, 1986. Named Outstanding Alumni Wittenberg U., 1965, Young Man of Yr. Tiffin Jaycees, 1965, Man of Yr. Bellefontaine Jaycees, Disting. Alumni award Trinity Sem., Columbus, 1989. Mem. NAACP, Acad. Preachers, Acad. Evangelists (organizer 1986—), Kiwanis, Rotary. Home and Office: 2770 Marin Ave Berkeley CA 94708

SCHMALTZ, ROY EDGAR, JR., artist, art educator; b. Belfield, N.D., Feb. 23, 1937; s. Roy and Mercedes (Martin) S.; m. Julia Mabel Swan, Feb. 1, 1958; children—Liese Marlene, Jennifer Lynn, Gregory Jason. Student Otis Art Inst., Los Angeles, 1959-60, U. Wash., 1960-61, Akademie der Bildenden Kunste, Munich, W. Ger., 1965-66; B.F.A., San Francisco Art Inst., 1963, M.F.A., 1965. Lectr. art Coll. of Notre Dame, Belmont, Calif., 1968-70, M. H. De Young Meml. Art Mus., San Francisco, 1968-70; prof. art St. Mary's Coll. of Calif., Moraga, 1969—, chmn. dept. art; exhbns. include: Seattle Art Mus., 1959, M. H. De Young Meml. Art Mus., 1969, Frye Art Mus., Seattle, 1957, San Francisco Mus. Modern Art, 1971, U. Calif.-Santa Cruz, 1977, Fine Arts Mus. of San Francisco, 1978, Oakland Art Mus., 1979, Rutgers U., Camden, N.J., 1979, Springfield (Mo.) Art Mus., 1980, Butler Inst. Am. Art, Youngstown, Ohio, 1981, Huntsville (Ala.) Mus. Art, 1982, Haggin Mus., Stockton, Calif., 1982, U. Hawaii-Hilo, 1983, Alaska State Mus., Juneau, 1981, Tex. State U., San Marcos, 1980, Crocker Art Mus., Sacramento, 1982, Hearst Art Gallery, 1986; represented in permanent collections: Richmond Art Ctr. (Calif.), U. Hawaii-Hilo, Las Vegas Art Mus. (Nev.), Hoyt Mus. and Inst. Fine Arts, New Castle, Pa., Frye Art Mus., San Francisco Art Inst., M. H. De Young Meml. Art Mus., Mills Coll., Oakland, Amerika-Haus, Munich, Contra Costa County Art Collection, Walnut Creek, Calif., Western Wash. U., Bellingham, Clemson U., S.C.; dir. Hearst Art Gallery, St. Mary's Coll.; vis. artist lectr. Academie Art Coll., San Francisco, 1971, grad. program Lone Mountain Coll., San Francisco, 1973-74. Coach Little League Baseball Team, Concord, Calif., 1982. Fulbright fellow, 1965-66; Frye Art Mus. traveling fellow, 1957; recipient Painting award All Calif. Ann., 1965; Nat. Watercolor award Chautauqua Inst., 1980; Seattle Art Assn. Painting award, 1957; San Francisco Art Inst. award, 1961; Otis Art Inst. award, 1959; Walnut Creek Civic Art Ctr. award, 1982, San Francisco Art Commn. award, 1985, Calif. State Fair Art award, 1985. Mem. Coll. Art Assn., Fine Arts Mus. of San Francisco, AAUP, San Francisco Art Inst. Alumni Assn. Home: 1020 Whistler Dr Suison City CA 94585 Office: Saint Marys Coll Dept Art Moraga CA 94575

SCHMALZ, ANGELA LUCILLE, nurse; b. Regina, Sask., Can., May 17, 1962; d. John and Helen Cecelia (Frey) S. Diploma in Nursing, Wascana Inst. Applied Health, Regina, 1982; student, U. Regina, 1984-85. RN, Can. Staff nurse ICU Regina Gen. Hosp., 1982-86, St. Agnes Med. Ctr., Fresno, Calif., 1987-88; staff nurse, cardiac catheterization specialist St. Agnes Med. Ctr., Fresno, 1988—. Mem. Sask. Registered Nurse Assn., Bd. Registered Nurse Can. Roman Catholic.

SCHMECHEL, WARREN P., utilities executive; b. 1927; married. BS, Mont. State U., 1953; student, Harvard U., 1965. With Mont. Power Co., Butte, 1953—, various mgmt. positions, 1953-73, v.p., 1973-79, from pres. to pres., chief exec. officer, 1979-84, chmn. bd., chief exec. officer, 1984—. Office: Mont Power Co 40 E Broadway Butte MT 59701 *

SCHMELING, HELEN MARGARET, clinical social worker; b. Denver, Jan. 31, 1951; d. Herbert Henry and Lillian Anna (Meyer) Thimm; m. William Allan Schmeling, Jr., July 24, 1982; children: Dustin William, Alexander Thimm. BA in Psychology, U. Colo., 1973; MSW, U. Denver, 1982. Lic. profl. social worker, Wyo. Peer counselor Met. Community Coll., Omaha, 1975-76; outreach worker South Omaha Crisis Ctr., 1976-77; child care worker Mt. St. Vincent's Youth Home, Denver, 1978-81; social work intern health scis. ctr. U. Colo., Denver, 1981-82; coord. crisis line Vol. Info. Referral Service, Rock Springs, Wyo., 1983-85; clin. social worker, coord. elderly program S.W. Counseling Service, Rock Springs, 1985—; med. social worker Wyo. Home Health Care, Rock Springs, 1986—; facilitator Alzheimer's Family Support Group, Rock Springs, 1983—. Democrat. Home: 2721 Westridge Dr Rock Springs WY 82901 Office: SW Counseling Svc 1124 College Rd Rock Springs WY 82901

SCHMID, HORST A., Canadian provincial administrator; b. Munich, Fed. Republic Germany; came to Can., 1952. Educated pub. schs., Europe; LLD (hon.) U. Alta., 1986. Gold miner Yellowknife, 1952-56; Alta. agt. for Canola dealer in Europe; chief exec. officer Internat. Export Corp., 1956-71; active in civic provincial and fed. polit. campaigns, 1960—; advisor preservation of ethnocultural heritage of Alta. to leader Progressive Conservative Assn. Alta., 1965-71; mem. Alta. Legis. Assembly from Edmonton-Avonmore, 1971-86, minister of culture, youth and recreation, 1971, minister govt. services and minister responsible for culture, 1975, minister of state for econ. devel. and internat. trade, 1979, minister internat. trade, 1982-86; commr. gen. trade and tourism Govt. Alta., 1986—; Alta. commr. for Spokane World's Fair. Recipient numerous awards from provincial, nat. and internat. cultural orgns., including Silver Ribbon award City of Edmonton, Spl. award Nat. Music Council for Encouragement to Music in Alta. and Can., Disting. Service award Alta. Motion Picture Industries Assn.; named Hon. Indian Chief Flying Eagle, Man of Yr., Commonwealth Games Found. Address: Commr Gen Trade and Tourism, 1800 Royal Trust Tower, Edmonton Centre, Edmonton, AB Canada T5J 2Z2

SCHMID, RUDOLF, botanist, educator; b. Springfield, Mass., Aug. 8, 1942; s. Fritz K. and Ruth (Wertz) S.; m. Marvin J. Taylor, Aug. 19, 1967 (div. 1976);1 child, Acmena Maria. BS, U. Calif., Davis, 1964, MA, 1965; MS, U. Mich., 1967, PhD, 1971. Smithsonian Fellow Smithsonian Inst., Washington, 1971-72; asst. prof. U. Calif., Berkeley, 1972-79, assoc. prof., 1979—; assoc. curator U. Herbarium, U. Calif., Berkeley, 1983—. Contbr. numerous articles to profl. jours. Chmn. Blake Estate Architectural Com., Kensington, Calif., 1988—. Fellow Botanical Soc., Linnean Soc.; m. Botanical Soc. Am. (officer 1977-80), Internat. Assn. for Plant Taxonomy (editor, reviews and notices of publs., Utrecht, Holland, 1986—), Internat. Assn. of Wood Anatomists, Calif. Botanical Soc. (officer 1976-79). Office: Dept of Integrative Biology U of Calif Berkeley CA 94720

SCHMIDT, BALDWIN STEPHEN, manufacturing company executive; b. Cin., Aug. 3, 1942; s. William Christian and Edna Marie (Baldwin) S.; m. Barbara Diana Naisby, Feb. 16, 1979. BS, U.S. Naval Acad., 1964; MA, Calif. State U., San Francisco, 1974. Lic. contractor, Calif. Commd. ensign USN, 1964; advanced through grades to lt. USN, Vietnam; resigned USN, 1969; mental health worker Ross (Calif.) Gen. Hosp., 1974-76; pres. Marin Energy Planning, San Rafael, Calif., 1976-81; sales mgr. Le Fiell Co., San Francisco, 1981-83; pres. LeFiell Co., San Francisco, 1984—, LeFiell, Ltd., Calgary, Atla., 1987—; trustee local AFL-CIO Welfare Plan, Oakland, Calif. Marin County dir. Calif. for Nuclear Safety, San Francisco, 1974-76; mem. Dem. cen. com. Marin County, 1977-81; bd. dirs. Acad. World Studies, San Francisco, 1978-81, Golden Gate Energy Ctr., San Francisco, 1979-81, Marin Community Video, San Rafael, Calif., 1976-78. Mem. Calif. Metal Trades Assn. (bd. dirs. 1983—). Home: 375 Texas St San Francisco CA 94107 Office: Le Fiell Co 1469 Fairfax Ave San Francisco CA 94124

SCHMIDT, CONNIE LU, small business owner, consultant; b. Mason City, Iowa, Apr. 8, 1949; d. Conrad Eugene and Lucie Dorathea (Apel) S.; m. Don Allen Walford, May 24, 1975 (div. Mar. 1978). AA, North Iowa Area Community Coll., 1971; BA, Ariz. State U., 1984. Teller, proof encoder, bookkeeper Am. State Bank, Mson City, 1970-72; vault teller Ariz. Bank, Tempe, 1973; utility clk. 1st Nat. Bank, Lincoln, Nebr., 1974-75, supr. account info., 1977-81; teller, bookkeeper, sec. Farmers Nat. Bank, Central City, Nebr., 1975-77; teller II Thunderbird Bank, Tempe, 1981-82; mktg. sec. Tri-Continental Leasing, Phoenix, 1982-83; saleswoman, dept. head Dillard's Dept. Stores, Mesa, Ariz., 1984-86; teller 1st Interstate Bank Ariz., Mesa, 1986-87; beauty cons., team leader Mary Kay Cosmetics, Inc., Mesa, 1979—; owner, mgr. dressmaking and alterations svc., Mesa, 1981—; ptnr. WISH Promotions, Mesa, 1986—. Mem. Ariz. State U. Alumni Assn., Nora Springs-Rocks Falls Alumni Assn., Am. Inst. Banking (basic cert.). Republican. Presbyterian. Home and Office: 5948 E Casper Rd Mesa AZ 85205

SCHMIDT, DEBORAH SUE, aerospace executive; b. Oceanside, Calif., Nov. 14, 1953; d. Melvin Cecil and Doris Jean (Townsend) Halbert; m. Dana Charles Schmidt (div. Feb. 1987); 1 child, Kevin Charles. BA, La. State U., 1976. Soc. wkr. State of La., Baton Rouge, 1978-79; claims rep. U.S. Social Security Adminstrn., County of Los Angeles, 1980-83; systems analyst McDonnell Douglas Corp., Long Beach, Calif., 1983-87; sect. mgr. McDonnell Douglas Corp., Long Beach, 1988—. Author, instr. mgmt. tng. seminar for Shanghai A/C Indsl. Corp., People's Republic of China, 1988. Active in PROUD, Irvine, CAlif., 1986-88, Assn. Retarded Citizens, Long Beach, 1985—, Spl. Olympics, Santa Monica, Calif., 1987—, Nat. Downs Syndrome Congress. Mem. NAFE, Am. Mgmt. Assn., Nat. Air and Space Mus., Nat. Mus. for Women in Arts (charter mem.), Smithsonian (nat. assoc.). Lutheran. Office: Douglas Aircraft Co 3855 Lakewood Blvd Long Beach CA 90846

SCHMIDT, DIANE GAFFNEY, real estate developer; b. Laramie, Wyo., July 12, 1952; d. Harold Max and Margaret Adella (Vincent) Gaffney; A.A., Pasadena (Calif.) City Coll., 1972; B.S. in Mgmt., San Diego State U., 1977. Fin. asst. Cabrillo Med. Center, San Diego, 1974-76, personnel mgr., 1976-78, personnel services adminstr., 1978-80; asst. adminstr., profl. services, 1980-81; owner, pres. Health Care Profls., 1981-82; employee benefits cons. Johnson & Higgins of Calif., 1983-84, ptnr., 1985—; v.p. adminstrn. Sandpiper Homes Ltd., Palm Desert, Calif., 1984—. Pres. Sharing Vol. Tutoring Program, Inc., Jr. League San Diego; bd. dirs. Pres.'s Council San Diego. Active Nat. Kidney Found. Mem. Bldg. Industry Assn. Office: Sandpiper Homed Ltd 41-995 Boardwalk Ste L-3 Ste 1950 Palm Desert CA 92260

SCHMIDT, GRANT JACOB, Canadian government official; b. Balcarres, Sask., Can., July 28, 1948; s. George and Helen (Banerd) S.; m. Sheron L. Schmidt, Aug. 28, 1971; children: Kurt, Luke. LLB, U. Sask., 1972. Bar: Sask. 1973. Ptnr. Schmidt & Graff, Melville, Sask., 1973-88; mem. Sask. Legis. Assembly, 1982—; dep. chmn. house fin. com. Govt. of Sask., 1985—, minister human resources, labor and employment, 1986—, minister of social svcs., 1986—, chmn. legis. rev. com. Mem. Commonwealth Parliamentary Assn., Can. Bar Assn., Law Soc. Sask. Conservative. Lutheran. Lodge: Lions. Home: 16 Vanier Dr, Melville Can S0A 2P0 Office: Sask Legis Assembly, Legislative Bldg, Regina, SK Canada S4S 0B3

SCHMIDT, JOHN ALLAN, accountant; b. Waterloo, Iowa, Nov. 4, 1946; s. Lloyd Glenn and Oma Fay (Ratliff) S.; m. Patricia Stout, Aug., 1967 (div. 1976); 1 child, Laurinda; m. Carol Ann, Dec. 31, 1987. BA, U. No Iowa, 1973. CPA, Iowa, Ill., Ariz. Staff acct. Carney, Alexander & Marold, Waterloo, Iowa, 1970-73; ptnr. Lindgren, Callihan & Van Osdol, Ltd., Freeport, Ill., 1973-82; owner, pres. Schmidt, Hopkins & Co., P.C., Phoenix, 1982—; tchr. Highland Community Coll., Freeport, Ill., 1973-74. With USAF, 1964-68, Vietnam. Named Jaycee of Yr., Freeport Jaycees, 1975.

Mem. AICPA, Ariz. Soc. CPAs, Ill. CPA Soc., Praying Monk Kiwanis (pres. 1987, Kiwanis of Yr. 1986), Elks, Masons. Republican. Episcopalian. Office: Schmidt Hopkins & Co PC 1730 E Northern St Ste 124 Phoenix AZ 85020

SCHMIDT, KLAUS DIETER, university administrator, marketing and management educator; b. Eisenach, Germany, May 8, 1930; came to U.S., 1949, naturalized, 1952; s. Kurt Heinrich and Luise (Kruger) S.; B.A. in Econs., U. Calif., Berkeley, 1951; M.B.A., Stanford U., 1953; Ph.D. in Bus. Adminstrn., Golden Gate U., 1978; m. Lynda Hollister Wheelwright, June 29, 1950; children: Karen, Claudia. Buyer, jr. mdse. mgr. Broadway Hale, 1952-54; sales mgr. Ames Harris Neville Co., 1954-56, ops. mgr., 1956-57; gen. mgr. Boise Cascade Corp., 1957-60; pres., chmn. bd. Kimball-Schmidt Inc., San Rafael, Calif., 1960-73, chmn. subs. Kalwall Pacific, 1962-67, chmn. subs. AFGOA Corp., 1966-69; asst. prof. mgmt. and mktg. San Francisco State U., 1970-75, assoc. prof. mgmt., 1975-80, prof. mgmt. and mktg., 1980-85, chmn. dept. mgmt. and mktg., 1979-85, prof. emeritus, 1989—, assoc. dean sch. bus. emeritus, 1985-88; chmn. Schmidt Cons. Group, 1989—; dir. Ctr. for World Bus., 1976-88, dir. U.S.-Japan Inst., 1981-88, editor-in-chief Sch. Bus. Jours., 1980-88; U.S. negotiator on Afghanistan issue, 1980-88; mem. Dept. Commerce Dist. Export Council, 1982-88; research cons. SRI Internat. Republican. Club: University (San Francisco). Author 20-booklet series Doing Business In ..., 1978-80. Office: Rte 175 North Brooklyn ME 04661

SCHMIDT, ROBERT MILTON, physician, scientist; b. Milw., May 7, 1944; s. Milton W. and Edith J. (Martinek) S.; children Eric Whitney, Edward Huntington. A.B., Northwestern U., 1966; M.D., Columbia U., 1970; M.P.H., Harvard U., 1975; Ph.D., Emory U., 1982. Diplomate: Am. Bd. Preventive Medicine. Intern Univ. Hosp. U. Calif.-San Diego, 1970-71; resident in preventive medicine Ctrs. Disease Control, Atlanta, 1971-74; commd. med. officer USPHS, 1971; advanced through grades to comdr. 1973; dir. hematology div. Nat. Ctr. for Disease Control, Atlanta, 1971-78, spl. asst. to dir., 1978-79, inactive res., 1979—; clin. asst. prof. pediatrics Tufts U. Med. Sch., 1976-87; clin. asst. prof. medicine Emory U. Med. Sch., 1976-81, clin. asst. prof. community health, 1976—; clin. assoc. prof. humanities in medicine Morehouse Med. Sch., 1977-79; pres., med. dir. Internat. Health Resource Ctr. of Hawaii, Lihue, Kauai, 1979-82; cons. physician dept. medicine Pacific Presbyn. Med. Ctr., San Francisco, 1983—; dir. Ctr. Preventive Medicine and Health Research, 1983—, dir. Health Watch, 1983—; sr. scientist Inst. Epidemiology and Behavioral Medicine, Inst. Cancer Research, Pacific Presbyn. Med. Ctr., San Francisco, 1983—; prof. hematology and gerontology, dir. health professions program San Francisco State U., 1983—; cons. WHO, FDA, NIH, Govt. of China, Mayo Clinic; Mem. numerous sci. and profl. adv. bds., panels, coms. Mem. editorial bd.: Am. Jour. Clin. Pathology, 1976-82; author: 15 books and manuals including Hematology Laboratory Series, 4 vols., 1979-86, CRC Handbook Series in Clinical Laboratory Science, 1976—; contbr. over 100 articles to sci. jours. Alumni regent Columbia U. Coll. Physicians and Surgeons, 1980—. Northwestern U. scholar, 1964-66; NSF fellow, 1964-66; Health Professions scholar, 1966-70; USPHS fellow, 1967-70; Microbiology, Urology, Upjohn Achievement, Borden Research and Virginia Kneeland Frantz scholar awards Columbia U. Coll. Physicians and Surgeons, 1970; recipient Am. Soc. Pharmacol. & Exptl. Therapy award in pharmacology, 1970, Commendation medal USPHS, 1973, Leadership Recognition awards San Francisco State U., 1984-88. Fellow ACP, Am. Coll. Preventive Medicine, Am. Soc. Clin. Pathology, Internat. Soc. Hematology; mem. AAAS, Am. Pub. Health Assn., Internat. Commn. for Standardization in Hematology, Am. Soc. Hematology, Internat. Soc. on Thrombosis and Hemostasis, Acad. Clin. Lab. Physicians and Scientists, Assn. Tchrs. Preventive Medicine, AMA, ASM, Am. Soc. Microbiology, Gerontol. Soc. Am., Am. Soc. Aging, Am. Geriatrics Soc., N.Y. Acad. Scis., Sigma Xi. Club: Army and Navy (Washington). Home: 25 Hinckley Walk San Francisco CA 94111 Office: Pacific Presbyn Med Ctr PO Box 7999 San Francisco CA 94120 also: San Francisco State U Sch Sci 1600 Holloway Ave San Francisco CA 94132

SCHMIDT, RUDOLPH DAVID, design engineer; b. Deshler, Nebr., Dec. 11, 1928; s. Rudolf and Myrtle (Imhoff) S.; m. Mary Elizabeth Seidlemann, Sept. 16, 1950; children: Karen Lee Schmidt Henry, Alan David. BS in Physics, San Diego State U., 1973; MS in Mgmt., U. LaVern (Calif.), 1982. Registered profl. engr., Calif.; cert. tchr., Calif. Electronic technician RCA Svc. Co., San Diego, 1955-65; broadcast engr. San Diego State U., 1965-70; elec. engring. mgr. Naval Aviation Depot, San Diego, 1973—; instr. San Diego Community Coll. Dist., 1970-84. Sgt. USMC, 1946-48, 50-51, Korea. Mem. North Island Profl. Engrs. Assn., North Island Assn. (dept. rep. 1984-86), E. Clampus Vitus Hist. Soc. Republican. Lutheran. Home: 4236 Lomo Del Sur La Mesa CA 92041 Office: Naval Aviation Depot NAS North Island San Diego CA 92135

SCHMIDT, SUSAN COOPER, marketing executive; b. Anchorage, Feb. 7, 1950; d. Joseph Earl and Bess Lucille (Tilford) Cooper; m. Paul Martin Schmidt, Sept. 1, 1969; children: Saska Ann, Jarud Paul. Student, U. Puget Sound, 1968-70, Alaska Meth. U., 1970-71; BA in Edn., U. Alaska, 1972. Tchr. Anchorage Borough Sch. Dist., 1972-75, Mat Su Borough Sch. Dist., Palmer, Alaska, 1974-75, Alaska State Operated Schs., Wasilla, 1975-77; reservations agt. Columbia Glacier Cruises, Anchorage, 1979; substitute tchr. Anchorage Borough Sch. Dist., 1979-80, 80-81; with Alaska Yukon Motorcoaches, Anchorage, 1980; visitor's ctr. coord. Anchorage Conv. and Visitor's Bur., 1981-82, dir. tourism, 1983-84; interim exec. dir. Spokane (Wash.) Area Conv. and Visitor's Bur., 1985; mktg. coord. Spokane Community Coll., 1987—. Chmn. Deer Park Winter Festival, Wash., 1986, co-chmn., 1987; v.p. Deer Park Festival Assn., 1987-88; active membership com. Action Women's Exch., Spokane. Mem. Spokane C. of C. Home: Rt 2 Box 433 Deer Park WA 99006 Office: Spokane Community Coll N1810 Greene st MS2063 Spokane WA 99207

SCHMIDT, THEODORE ANDREW, librarian; b. Hammond, Ind., Feb. 6, 1949; s. Harry Theodore and Mildred Martha (Farbak) S.; m. Martha Jane Schuldt, July 14, 1973; 1 child, Rachel Elizabeth. B.A., Purdue U., 1971; M.A., U. Denver, 1974. English instr. Addison Trail High Sch. (Ill.), 1971-73; media ctr. dir. Park R-3 Sch. Dist., Estes Park, Colo., 1974-77; asst. library dir. Loveland Pub. Library (Colo.), 1977-80; library dir. Estes Park Library, 1980-85, Missoula (Mont.) County Library, 1985—; bd. dirs. Tamarack Fedn. Libraries. Photographer, producer: slide-audio tape Yesterday Was Not Today, 1979 (CEMA award 1980), LSCA VI Literacy Program grantee, others. Pub. edn. chmn. Am. Cancer Soc., Estes Park, 1980-82; v.p. Missoula Community Access TV, Inc., Literacy Vols. Am., Missoula. Colo. Humanities Program grantee, 1982, 83. Mem. ALA, Colo. Library Assn. (chmn. pub. library div. 1983-84), Mont. Library Assn., Mountain Plains Library Assn. (exec. bd. dirs.). Office: Missoula County Libr 301 E Main St Missoula MT 59802

SCHMIDT, THOMAS FRANK, real estate developer; b. Cleve., July 30, 1944; s. Frank Joseph and Dolores Mae (Urmetz) S.; m. Carol Ann Sernka, June 1, 1968, (div. Aug. 1976); 1 child, Kristen Alexis; m. Diane Lee Gaffney, Nov. 15, 1985; 1 child, Maryn Mae. BBA, Kent State U., 1967; MBA, Nat. U., 1974. CPA, Calif. Sr. acct. Ernst & Whinney CPAs, San Diego, 1971-74; sr. v.p. Cabrillo Med. Ctr., San Diego, 1974-81; exec. v.p. Daniels Cable Vision, San Diego, 1981-83; pres. Sandpiper Homes Ltd., San Diego, 1983—; adv. bd. Kent State Sch. Bus., Kent, Ohio, 1986—. Lt. USN, 1967-71, Far East. Mem. Bldg. Industry Assn., Nat. Assn. Homebuilders, Am. Inst. CPAs, San Diego Active 20-30 Club (pres. 1981). Home: 39680 St Michael Pl Palm Desert CA 92260 Office: Sandpiper Homes Ltd 41-995 Boardwalk C-3 Palm Desert CA 92260

SCHMIEDER, CARL, jeweler; b. Phoenix, Apr. 27, 1938; s. Otto and Ruby Mable (Harkey) S.; m. Carole Ann Roberts, June 13, 1959; children: Gail, Susan, Nancy, Amy. Student Bradley Horological Sch., Peoria, Ill., 1959-61; B.A., Pomona Coll., 1961; Owner timepiece repair service, Peoria, 1959-61; clock repairman Otto Schmieder & Son, Phoenix, 1961-65, v.p., 1965-70, pres., 1970—, chief exec. officer, 1970—. Mem. subcom. Leap Commn., 1966; area rep. Pomona Coll., 1972-76. Cert. jeweler; cert. gemologist, gemologist appraiser; recipient Design award Diamonds Internat., 1965, Cultured Pearl Design award, 1967, 68, Diamonds for Christmas award, 1970; winner Am. Diamond Jewelry Competition, 1973; bd. dirs. Lincoln Hosp., 1983—, Ariz. Mus., 1984-88; delegate White House Conf. on Small Bus., 1986; chmn. Gov.'s Conf. on Small Bus., 1988—; col. Confederate Air Force. Mem. Am. Gem. Soc. (dir. 1973-86, nat. chmn. nomenclature com. 1975-77, chmn. membership com. 1977-81, officer 1981-86), Ariz. Jewelers Assn. (Man of Yr. 1974), Jewelers Security Alliance (dir. 1974-78), Jewelers Vigilance Com. (dir. 1981-87), Jewelry Industry Council (dir. 1982-88), 24 Karat Club So. Calif., Exptl. Aircraft Assn., Deer Valley (Ariz.) Airport Tenants Assn. (dir. 1980—, pres. 1983—), Ariz. C. of C. (bd. dirs. 1985—), Small Bus. Council (bd. dirs. 1985—, chmn. 1988, del. to White House Conf., 1986, chmn. Govs. Conf. on small bus. 1988-89). Republican. Methodist. Lodges: Kiwanis (pres. Valley of the Sun chpt. 1975-76), Friends of Iberia. Home: 537 W Kaler St Phoenix AZ 85021 Office: Park Central Phoenix AZ 85013

SCHMITT, CARVETH JOSEPH RODNEY, office supplies manufacturing official; b. Manitowoc, Wis., Sept. 10, 1934; s. Clarence C. and Thelma J. (White) S.; m. Carolyn Sue Jarrett, May 14, 1965. diploma in bus. adminstrn. and acctg. Skadron Coll. Bus., 1959; A.A. in Bus. Mgmt., San Bernardino Valley Coll., 1962; B.S. in Bus. Adminstrn., U. Riverside-Calif., 1970; M.A. in Edn.-Manpower Adminstrn., U. Redlands, 1975; B.S. in Liberal Studies, SUNY-Albany, 1977; B.A. in Social Sci., Edison State Coll., Trenton, 1978; cert. in Human Services, U. Calif. Extension, Riverside, 1977, postgrad., 1977-80. Registered rep. Ernest F. Boruski, Jr., N.Y.C., 1956-61; acct. Barnum & Flagg Co., San Bernardino, Calif., 1959-70; registered rep., ins. agt. (part-time) Inland Am. Securities, Inc., San Bernardino, 1966-70; registered rep. (part-time) Parker-Jackson & Co., San Bernardino, 1970-73, LeBarron Securities, Inc., 1973-74. credit mgr. Stationers Corp., San Bernardino, 1970-77, office mgr., credit mgr., 1977-83; internal auditor Stockwell & Binney Office Products Ctrs., San Bernardino, 1983-85, corp. credit mgr., 1985—. Served with USAF, 1954-58. cert. tchr., community coll. counselor and personnel worker, Calif. Mem. Nat. Geog. Soc., Nat. Rifle Assn. (life), Nevada Mining Assn., Colo. Mining Assn., N.W. Mining Assn., Modern Woodmen Am., Am. Philatelic Soc., Nat. Travel Club, Edison State Coll. Alumni Assn., U. Redlands Fellows, Friends of Library Assn. U. Redlands, Valley Prospectors (life), SUNY Regents Alumni Assn., U. Redlands Alumni Assn., Am. Legion, Am. Assn. Ret. Persons, Gold Prospectors Assn. Am. (life mem.). Republican. Rosicrucian. Clubs: Fontana Tour, Hiking, Badminton, Bowling, Arrowhead Stamp, M & M Tour, Rosicrucian (San Jose). Lodge: Masons. Home: 538 N Pampas Ave Rialto CA 92376 Office: 420 South E St PO Box 5129 San Bernardino CA 92412

SCHMITT, LISA MARIE, sales representative; b. Neptune, N.J., Oct. 31, 1963; d. James Alfred and Charlene Mary (Marty) S. BSChemE, U. Ariz., 1986. Prodn. supr. Pepsi-Cola West, Phoenix, 1986-87; prodn. supr. Pepsi-Cola West, Torrance, Calif., 1987-88, warehouse supr., 1988; tech. sales rep. Union Carbide Indsl. Svc. Co., Huntington Beach, Calif., 1988—. Mem. Am. Inst. Chem. Engrs., Soc. Women Engrs., Pacific Energy Assn., NAFE. Republican. Roman Catholic. Office: Union Carbide Indsl Svcs Co 15573 Commerce Ln Huntington Beach CA 92649

SCHMITT, PETER OYHUS, retired newspaper publishing company executive; b. Mt. Vernon, N.Y., June 29, 1938; s. Henry John and Viola Dorisclare (Oyhus) S.; m. Linda Joyce Hren, May 9, 1964; children: Laura, Paul. Student U. Mich., 1956-58; BA in Econ., U. S.D., 1960. Mgmt. trainee Ridder Publs., San Jose, Calif., 1963-65; with circulation dept. Grand Forks Herald, N.D., 1965-66; gen. mgr. Am. News subs. Knight-Ridder Newspapers Inc., 1968-75, pub., 1976-85 , pres., 1978-85 . Bd. regents Presentation Coll., Aberdeen. Served with USAF, 1961-67. Mem. Elks, Sigma Delta Chi. Republican. Home: 3914 Antone Rd Santa Barbara CA 93110 Office: PO Box 6844 Santa Barbara CA 93160

SCHMITT, RICHARD GEORGE, industrial engineer; b. St. Cloud, Minn., June 18, 1948; s. George William and Viola Theresa (Mechenich) S.; m. Ligia Marie Pereira, Aug. 29, 1970; children: Christopher Michael, Scott Andrew. B in Indsl. Engring. with honors, Gen. Motors Inst., 1971. Indsl. engr. Gen. Motors, Fremont, Calif., 1966-78; sr. indsl. engr. Gen. Motors, Oklahoma City, 1978-80; indsl. engring. mgr. Shugart Assocs., Sunnyvale, Calif., 1980-81; mfg. tech. mgr. Magnex Corp., San Jose, Calif., 1981-82, prodn. mgr., 1982-83; facilities mgr. Apple Computer, Fremont, 1983, indsl. engring. mgr., 1984-85, robotics mgr., 1985-86, new product ops. mgr., 1987, Pacific logistics ops. mgr., 1988—. Transp. chmn. Mt. Diablo council Boy Scouts Am., 1984; chief YMCA Indian Guides, San Jose, 1977-83; asst. scout master Boy Scouts Am., Mt. Hamilton Dist., 1986-88. Mem. Am. Assn. Indsl. Engrs. (sr.), Soc. Mfg. Engrs. (sr.), Am. Prodn. Inventory Control Soc., Lions (scholar 1966). Democrat. Roman Catholic. Home: 1963 Wave Pl San Jose CA 95133 Office: Apple Computer Worldwide Materials Group 10201 N DeAnza Blvd Cupertino CA 95014

SCHMITT-NOBLE, CYNTHIA LYNN, science educator; b. Redwood, Calif., Feb. 13, 1956; d. John Powers Schmitt and Donavee Bowen; m. Joseph A. Noble, Apr. 21, 1979; children: Erik Ulysses, Rex Ulysses. BS, Niagara U., 1977; MEd in Computer Sci., Calif. Luth. U., 1989. Instr., elem., computer task force, sci. curriculum Elsinore Unified Schs., Lake Elsinore, Calif., 1981-83; adult edn., computers St. Margaret's Sch. and various businesses, So. Calif. area, 1982-85; dir. computer sci., instr. St. Margaret's Sch., San Juan Capistrano, Calif., 1983-84; instr., biology, chemistry, sci., co-chair. Villanova Prep. Sch., Ojai, Calif., 1986-87; sci. instr., fellow, cons. Ojai (Calif.) Unified Sch. Dist., NSF, 1987—; curriculum cons. Calif. Luth. U., Thousands Oaks, 1988—. Choir dir. Luth. Ch. of the Holy Cross, Ojai, 1985-89; mem. Ojai Community Chorus, 1986-89; asst. choir, Peace Child Internat., Ojai, 1988; coach, Pony Club Internat., Ojai, 1986-89; vol. Mounted State Park Ranger Calif. State Park System. Mem. NSF, Am. Chem. Soc., Search for Extra-Terrestrial Intelligence, Greater San Diego Math. Coun., Equestrian Trails Internat. (v.p., mem. 1980-88), Ojai Arabian Horse Club, Calif. Dressage Soc., Christian Women's Club. Republican. Lutheran. Home: 4440 Grand Ave Ojai CA 93023

SCHMUHL, VINCENT EDMUND, food products executive; b. Denver, Dec. 1, 1956; s. James Walter and Wilma Darlene (Shy) S.; m. Christine Ann Miller, Aug. 4, 1984. BSBA, U. N.C., 1981. Pres. chief exec. officer Blackjack Pizza Inc., Denver, 1983—, also chmn. bd. dirs. Republican. Office: Blackjack Pizza Inc 494 Sheridan #106-B Denver CO 80226

SCHNACK, HAROLD CLIFFORD, lawyer; b. Honolulu, Sept. 27, 1918; s. Ferdinand J. H. and Mary (Pearson) S.; m. Gayle Hemingway Jepson, Mar. 22, 1947; children: Jerrald Jay, Georgina Schnack Hankinson, Roberta Schnack Poulin, Michael Clifford. BA, Stanford, 1940, LLB, 1947. Bar: Hawaii, 1947. Dep. prosecutor City and County Honolulu, 1947-48; gen. practice with father F. Schnack, 1948-60; pvt. practice, Honolulu, 1960-86; pres. Harcliff Corp., 1961—, Schnack Indsl. Corp., 1969-73, Instant Printers, Inc., 1971-81, Koa Corp., 1964—, Nutmeg Corp., 1963-89, Global Answer System, Inc., 1972-78. Pres. Goodwill Industries of Honolulu, 1971-72. Mem. ABA, Hawaii Bar Assn., Internat. Platform Soc., Nat. Fedn. Ind. Bus. Coun. of 100, Outrigger Canoe Club, Pacific Club, Phi Alpha Delta, Alpha Sigma Phi. Office: 817 A Cedar St PO Box 3077 Honolulu HI 96802

SCHNACK, LORI RAE, speech and language pathologist, educator; b. Newton, Kans., May 28, 1953; d. Loren Rex and Phyllis Helen (Krehbiel) Schmidt; m. Theodore Sherman Schnack, Jr., July 14, 1984; 1 child, Alexandria. Lic. speech-lang. pathologist, Calif.; clin. rehab. svcs. credential with spl. class authorization, Calif. Clin. fellow in speech pathology VA Med. Ctr., Long Beach, Calif., 1985; tchr. communicatively disordered Orange (Calif.) Unified Sch. Dist., 1985; speech-lang. specialist Anaheim (Calif.) Union High Sch. Dist., 1986—. Mem. Am. Speech-Lang. Hearing Assn., Calif. Speech-Hearing Assn. Democrat. Office: Anaheim Union High Sch Dist 501 Crescent Way Anaheim CA 92803

SCHNACKE, ROBERT HOWARD, judge; b. San Francisco, Oct. 8, 1913; s. Carl H. and Elfriede A. (Hanschen) S.; m. June Doris Borina, Sept. 7, 1956. Student, U. Calif. at Berkeley, 1930-32; J.D., Hastings Coll. of Law, 1938. Bar: Calif. 1938. Practiced in San Francisco, 1938-42, 51-53, 59-68; dep. commr. div. corps. San Francisco, State of Calif., 1947-51; chief criminal div. Office U.S. Atty., San Francisco, 1953-58; U.S. atty. No. Dist. Calif., San Francisco, 1958-59; judge Superior Ct., San Francisco, 1968-70, U.S. Dist. Ct., No. Dist. Calif., San Francisco, 1970—; Chmn. uniform rules of evidence com. 9th Circuit Jud. Conf., 1963-76. Pres. Guide Dogs for Blind, 1959-62; Bd. dirs. Fed. Jud. Center, 1975-79; mem. Jud. Panel on Multidist. Litigation, 1979—. Served with AUS, 1942-46. Mem. Fed. Bar Assn., San Francisco Bar Assn., Am. Judicature Soc., Masons, Burlingame Country Club. Home: Hillsborough CA 94010 Office: US Dist Ct 450 Golden Gate Ave PO Box 36060 San Francisco CA 94102

SCHNAPP, ROGER HERBERT, lawyer; b. N.Y.C., Mar. 17, 1946; s. Michael Jay and Beatrice Joan (Becker) S.; m. Candice Jacqueline Larson, Sept. 15, 1979. BS, Cornell U., 1966; JD, Harvard U., 1969; grad. Pub. Utility Mgmt. Program, U. Mich., 1978. Bar: N.Y. 1970, Calif. 1982, U.S. Dist. Ct. (so. dist.) N.Y. 1975, U.S. Dist. Ct. (no. dist.) Calif. 1980, U.S. Dist. Ct. (cen. dist.) Calif. 1982, U.S. Dist. Ct. (ea. dist.) Calif. 1984), U.S. Ct. Appeals (2d cir.) 1970, U.S. Ct. Appeals (4th and 6th cirs.) 1976, U.S. Ct. Appeals (7th cir.) 1977, U.S. Ct. Appeals (8th cir.) 1980, U.S. Supreme Ct. 1974. Atty. CAB, Washington, 1969-70; labor atty. Western Electric Co., N.Y.C., 1970-71; mgr. employee relations Am. Airlines, N.Y.C., 1971-74; labor counsel Am. Electric Power Service Corp., N.Y.C., 1974-78, sr. labor counsel, 1978-80; indsl. relations counsel Trans World Airlines, N.Y.C., 1980-81; sr. assoc. Parker, Milliken, Clark & O'Hara, Los Angeles, 1981-82; ptnr. Rutan & Tucker, Costa Mesa, Calif., 1983-84; ptnr. Memel, Jacobs, Pierno, Gersh & Ellsworth, Newport Beach, Calif., 1985-86; ptnr. Memel, Jacobs & Ellsworth, Newport Beach, 1986-87; sole practice, Newport Beach, 1987—; commentator labor rels. Fin. News Network; lectr. Calif. Western Law Sch., Calif. State U.-Fullerton, Calif. State Conf. Small Bus.; lectr. collective bargaining Pace U., N.Y.C. N.E. regional coordinator Pressler for Pres., 1979-80. Mem. ABA (R.R. and airline labor law com., internat. labor law com.), Calif. Bar Assn., Am. Arbitration Assn. (adv. com. Orange County area, cons. collective bargaining com.), Conf. R.R. and Airline Labor Lawyers, Newport Harbor Area C. of C. Republican. Jewish. Clubs: Balboa Bay, Lincoln of Orange County, Center, Back Bay, Madison's Eagles Ctr. Lodge: Masons. Author: Arbitration Issues for the 1980s, 1981; A Look at Three Companies, 1982; editor-in-chief Industrial and Labor Relations Forum, 1964-66; contbr. articles to profl. publs. Office: PO Box 9049 Newport Beach CA 92658

SCHNEBLY, F(RANCIS) DAVID, aerospace company executive; b. San Francisco, May 1, 1926; s. Frederick Daniel and Mary Florence (Blake) S.; m. Miriam Louise Ford, Aug. 27, 1949; children: Mary Diane, Linda Marie, Anne Louise, David Albert, Kathleen Marie. BE in Areo. Engring., U. So. Calif., 1950; postgrad., U. Hawaii, 1970. Project engr. Hiller Aircraft Corp., Palo Alto, Calif., 1950-55, mgr. ops. rsch., 1955-58; mgr. ops. analysis Lockheed Missiles & Space Co., Sunnyvale, Calif., 1958-63, mgr. mil. programs, 1963-65, asst. dir. advanced programs, 1965-67, project mgr. advanced aircraft, 1967-70, dir. airborne systems, 1970-76, dir. remotely piloted vehicles, 1976-83; pres. F. David Assocs., Inc., Santa Rosa, Calif., 1983—; bd. dirs. Command Systems Group, Inc., Torrance, Calif.; mem. panel U.S. Army Sci. Adv. Bd., Washington, 1965-66; presenter seminars in field.. Author: Helicopter Performance Analysis Method, 1955. Pres. Hiller Mgmt. Club, Palo Alto, 1957; capt. Mounted Patrol San Mateo County, Woodside, Calif., 1976. Mem. Am. Unmanned Systems Orgn., Am. Assn. Profl. Mgrs., Shack Riders (bd. dirs. Woodside chpt. 1983-87). Republican. Roman Catholic. Home and Office: 453 Cahill Ln Santa Rosa CA 95401

SCHNEIDER, CALVIN, physician; b. N.Y.C., Oct. 23, 1924; s. Harry and Bertha (Green) S.; A.B., U. So. Calif., 1951, M.D., 1955; J.D., LaVerne (Calif.) Coll., 1973; m. Elizabeth Gayle Thomas, Dec. 27, 1967. Intern Los Angeles County Gen. Hosp., 1955-56, staff physician, 1956-57; practice medicine West Covina, Calif., 1957—; staff intern Community Hosp., Covina, Calif. Cons. physician Charter Oak Found., Covina, 1960—. Served with USNR, 1943-47. Mem. AMA, Calif., Los Angeles County med. assns. Republican. Lutheran. Office: 224 W College Covina CA 91723

SCHNEIDER, LAWRENCE PAUL, mayor; b. Regina, Sask., Can., Mar. 23, 1938; s. Paul Martin and Helen Caroline (Exner) S.; cert. in bus. adminstrn. U. Regina; m. Shirley Anne Wolfe, July 20, 1960; children—Janet, Joanne, Jon. Engring. technician Can. Dept. Agr., 1957-69; mgmt. cons., 1970-79; now mayor City of Regina. Mem. Royal Lifesaving Soc. (award of Merit). Roman Catholic. Clubs: Optimist (pres. 1970), Rotary, Toastmasters (pres. 1972), Regina Flying (Regina). *

SCHNEIDER, LYNN CLAIRE, lawyer, historian; b. San Francisco, May 15, 1959; d. Richard John and Jacqueline (Cowie) S. BA in Econs. magna cum laude with distinction, with honors in Philosophy, Wells Coll., 1981; JD, U. Calif., Berkeley, 1984. Bar: Calif. 1984, U.S. Dist. Ct. (no. dist.) Calif. 1984, U.S. Dist. Ct. (ea. dist.) Calif. 1986, U.S. Ct. Appeals (9th cir.) 1986. Rsch. asst. to Prof. Edward C. Halback U. Calif., Berkeley, 1983-84; law clk. to justice N.Mex. Supreme Ct., Santa Fe, 1984-85; assoc. Wilson, Elser, Moskowitz, Edelman & Dicker, San Francisco, 1985-87, Brobeck, Phleger & Harrison, San Francisco, 1987-89, Law Offices of David Jay Morgan, San Mateo, Calif., 1989—. Mem. Masterworks Chorale; organizer Mondale for Pres. Com., Santa Fe, 1984; campaign mgr. Lepore for Mayor Com., Millbrae, 1981-82; mem. Millbrae City Coun. Beautification Com., 1982-84. Mem. ABA, San Francisco Bar Assn., Ninth Jud. Cir. Hist. Soc., Sierra Club, Commonwealth Club, San Mateo Marlins, Phi Beta Kappa. Office: David Jay Morgan Inc 520 S El Camino Real San Mateo CA 94402

SCHNEIDER, MARK LYLE, cable television company executive, lawyer; b. Casper, Wyo., July 7, 1955; s. Gene Walter and Phyllis Gertrude (Stelter) S. BSBA cum laude, U. Denver, 1977, JD, 1980. Staff atty. Denver, 1978-79; spl. asst. to gov. State of Alaska, Anchorage and Washington, 1979-80; staff counsel, chief legis. staff to Senator Ted Stevens, U.S. Senate, Washington, 1980-84; dir. fed. govt. rels. Standard Oil Co.-Brit. Petroleum Co., Washington, 1984-87; v.p. acquisitions and corp. devel. United Cable TV, Denver, 1987-89; sr. v.p. United Internat. Holdings, Inc., Denver, 1989—; bd. dir. CIC-United Artists Theatres U.K. Joint Venture, London, Republic Pictures-United Artists Joint Venture, L.A., Think Entertainment, L.A., Interactive Owners Co., San Francisco. Bd. dirs. Young Ams. Bank, Denver, 1987; mem. adv. bd. U. Denver Sch. Media, 1988. Mem. Colo. Bar Assn., Alaska Bar Assn., Cherry Hills Country Club, Beta Gamma Sigma. Republican. Roman Catholic. Home: 1001 E Bayaud St Denver CO 80209 Office: United Internat Holdings Inc 7800 E Union Ave Ste 400 Denver CO 80237

SCHNEIDER, ROBERT DOUGLAS, systems analyst, consultant; b. Queens, N.Y., Jan. 30, 1962; s. Jerome Philip and Florence Ray (Berson) S.; m. Lynn Sue Zlotnick, Sept. 7, 1986. BA magna cum laude, SUNY, Albany, 1983. Computer mktg. analyst Ziff-Davis Pub. Co., N.Y.C., 1983-84; software analyst The Montran Corp., N.Y., 1984-87; systems analyst The Circle K Corp., Phoenix, 1987—; ptnr. Spectrum Assocs., N.Y., 1983-87; mng. ptnr. The Saratoga Group, Phoenix, 1987—. Author: Personal Inventory, 1986. N.Y. State Regents scholar Bd. of Regents, Albany, 1979. Mem. Assn. for Systems Mgmt. (sec. 1987-88, v.p. 1988—), Digital Equipment Users Soc. Home: 1425 E Manhattan Dr Tempe AZ 85282

SCHNEIDERMAN, BARRY ALAN, lawyer; b. Seattle, June 28, 1933; s. Harry and Margaret S.; m. Judith Arron, July 1, 1968; children: Paul L., Leah. BA, U. Wash., 1955, JD, 1957. Bar: Wash. 1957. Dep. King County Pros. Atty.'s Office, Seattle, 1959-61; ptnr. Burns & Schneiderman, Seattle, 1961-67, pres., 1968-77; pres. Burns Schneiderman & Finkle, Seattle, 1977—; asst. to gen. counsel U.S. Army (IMA), 1979-84; commdr. 6th JAG Mil. Law Ctr., 1974-78. Trustee Temple DeHirsch Sinai, Seattle, 1976-84; pres. bd. dirs. Caroline Kline Galland Home Aged, Seattle, 1980-83. Served as officer AUS, 1957-59; col. JAGC res., ret. Grantee Nat. Endowment for the Arts, 1988. Mem. ABA, Fed. Bar Assn., Wash. Bar Assn., Seattle-King County Bar Assn., B'Nai B'Rith (pres. 1967-68). Clubs: Wash. Athletic, College (Seattle), Rainier (Seattle), Seattle Tennis. Lodge: Shriners, Seattle. Home: 5135 NE Latimer Pl Seattle WA 98105 Office: 2200 4th Ave Seattle WA 98121

SCHNEIDMILLER, WALTER ERIC, air force officer, electrical engineer; b. Arlington, Tex., Mar. 30, 1959; s. Kenneth Alexander and Loraine Faye (Rich) S.; m. Tami Dawn Berberick, May 25, 1985. BSEE, N.C. State U., 1982. Commd. 2nd lt. USAF, 1982, advanced through grades to capt., 1987; orbiter flight controls engr. 6595th Shuttle Test Group, Vandenberg AFB, Calif., 1983-86; chief Titan elec. engring. sect. 6595th Aerospace Test Group, Vandenberg AFB, 1986—. Mem. Air ForceAssn., Apollo Soc. Republican.

Methodist. Office: Dept Def 6595th Aerospace Test Group Vandenberg AFB CA 93437

SCHNEITER, GEORGE MALAN, golfer, development company executive; b. Ogden, Utah, Aug. 12, 1931; s. George Henery and Bernice Slade (Malan) S.; B.Banking and Fin., U. Utah, 1955; m. JoAnn Deakin, Jan. 19, 1954; children—George, Gary, Dan, Steve, Elizabeth Ann, Michael. With 5th Army Championship Golf Team U.S. Army, 1955-56; assoc. golf pro Hidden Valley Golf Club, Salt Lake City, 1957; golf pro Lake Hills Golf Club, Billings, Mont., 1957-61, sec., 1957-61, pres., 1964—; pres. Schneiter Enterprises, Sandy, Utah, 1964—; developer Schneiter's golf course and subdiv., 1975; player PGA tour 1961-75; sr. player PGA tour, 1981—. With U.S. Army, 1956. Winner Salt Lake City Parks Tournament, Vernal Brigham Payson Open, Yuma Open, Ariz.; named U.S. Army Ft. Carson Post Golf Champ, 1955-56. Mem. Profl. Golfers Assn. Am. Mormon. Office: 8968 S 1300 E Sandy UT 84070

SCHNELDER, LAWRENCE FRANK, industrial engineer; b. Seattle, Sept. 19, 1949; s. Howard Frank and Bonnie Jean (Hungerford) S.; m. Pamala Lorrie Lamphear, Feb. 21, 1976; children: Melissa, Matthew. AA, Highline Community Coll., Seattle, 1972. Storkeeper, 2d cook Szabo Food Industries, Kent, Wash., 1967; salesman Chevron Oil, Kent, 1967; storekeeper Boeing Comml. Airplanes, Seattle, 1968-70; bartender, asst. mgr. Shakey's Pizza Parlor, Burien, Wash., 1971-73; storekeeper, expeditor, investigator Boeing Aerospace, Seattle, 1973-78; schedule planner Boeing Mil. Airplanes, Seattle, 1978-82, lead indsl. engr., 1982-87; lead indsl. engr. Boeing Adv. Systems, Seattle, 1987—. Office: Boeing Advanced Systems Seattle WA

SCHNELL, ROGER THOMAS, military officer; b. Wabasha, Minn., Dec. 11, 1936; s. Donald William and Eva Louise (Barton) S.; m. Barbara Ann McDonald, Dec. 18, 1959 (div. Mar. 1968); children: Thomas Allen, Scott Douglas; m. Young H. Kim, Sept. 25, 1987; children: Eunice, Candice. A in Mil. Sci., Command and Gen. Staff Coll., 1975; A in Bus. Administn., Wayland Bapt. U., 1987. Commd. 2d lt. Alaska N.G., 1959, advanced through grades to col., 1975; shop supt. Alaska N.G., Anchorage, 1965-71, personnel mgr., 1972-74, chief of staff, 1974-87; electrician Alaska R.R., Anchorage, 1955-61, elec. foreman, 1962-64; dir. support personnel mgmt. Joint Staff Alaska N.G., 1988—. Mem. Fed. Profl. Labor Relations Execs. (sec. 1974-75), Alaska N.G. Officers Assn. (bd. dirs. 1988—), Am. Legion, Amvets. Republican. Methodist. Lodge: Elks. Home: 2751 Pelican Ct Anchorage AK 99515 Office: Hdqrs Alaska NG 3601 C St Anchorage AK 99503

SCHNIDRIG, HERMAN EDWARD, maufacturing executive; b. Trail, British Columbia, Can., Oct. 13, 1930; s. J. Herman and Olga (Watzlawik) S.; m. Winefride J Bourchier, Feb. 6, 1954. BS, Wash. State U., Pullman, 1954. Cert. profl. engr. Design engr. Hyster Co., Portland, 1955-62; sales engr. Hydreco div. N.Y. Air Brake, Kalamazoo, 1962-68; v.p. mfg. Wagner Mining Equipment, Portland, 1968-75; dist. sales mgr. N.L. Rucker, Portland, 1965-80; v.p. mfg. Columbia Machine Inc., Vancouver, Wash., 1980—; pres. Selkirk Ent. Inc., Portland, 1986—, sec. treas. D&S Hydraulics, Bend, Oreg., 1978—; dir. C.C.B.M., Australia, 1988—. With Can. Army, 1948-50. Mem. Profl. Engrs. of Oreg., Irvington Club.

SCHNIEDERS, EDMUND FRANCIS, JR., real estate corporation officer; b. Los Angeles, Mar. 12, 1935; s. Edmund F. and Mildred (O'Neill) S.; m. Martha Sweeney, Nov. 30, 1963; children: Edmund F. III, Ann E. BA in Econs., Stanford U., 1956. Cert. real estate broker, Calif.; cert. gen. contractor, Calif. With bus. tng. dept. Gen. Electric Co., Schenectady, N.Y., 1956-57; v.p. 20th Century Underwiters, Los Angeles, 1958-61; v.p. John D. Lusk & Son, Inc., Whittier, Calif., 1962-65, also bd. dirs.; pres., chmn. bd. dirs., founder Am. Nat. Co., Beverly Hills, Calif., 1965-86; chmn. bd. dirs. First Pacific Group, Carlsbad, Calif., 1987—. Regent Loyola Marymount U., Los Angeles, 1978—. Seved to capt. U.S. Army, 1956-62. Mem. World Bus. Council, Chief Execs. Orgn. Republican. Roman Catholic. Club: Stanford (San Diego). Home: 3473 Topeka St Carlsbad CA 92008 Office: First Pacific Group 2225 Faraday Rd Ste E Carlsbad CA 92008

SCHNITZER, ARLENE DIRECTOR, art dealer; b. Salem, Oreg., Jan. 10, 1929; d. Simon M. and Helen (Holtzman) Director; m. Harold J. Schnitzer, Sept. 11, 1949; 1 son, Jordan. Student U. Wash., 1947-48; BFA (hon.) Pacific NW Coll. Art., 1988. Founder, pres. Fountain Gallery of Art, Portland, Oreg., 1951-86; sr. v.p. Harsch Investment Corp., 1951—. Appointed to Oreg. State Bd. Higher Edn., 1987; former bd. dirs. Oreg. Symphony Assn., v.p. Oreg. Symphony; bd. dirs., exec. com. U.S. Dist. Ct. Hist. Soc.; bd. dirs. Boys & Girls Club, 1988—; mem. Gov.'s Expo '86 Commn., Oreg.; mem. exec. com., former bd. dirs. Artquake; mem. adv. bd. New Beginnings; Recipient Aubrey Watzek award Lewis and Clark Coll., 1981; Pioneer award U. Oreg., 1985; Met. Arts Commn. award, 1985; White Rose award March of Dimes, 1987, disting. service award Western Oreg. Coll. 1988, Oreg. Urban League Equal Opportunity award 1988; Gov's. award for Arts, 1987; honored by Portland Art Assn., 1979; Woman of Achievment award YWCA, 1987. Clubs: University, Multnomah Athletic (Portland), Portland Golf. Office: Harsh Investment Corp 1121 SW Salmon St Portland OR 97205

SCHNORR, JANET KAY, psychology educator, researcher; b. Clintonville, Wis., Dec. 16, 1944; d. Arthur Albert and Louise Martha (Kreuger) S. BS, U. Wis., Oshkosh, 1967; MS, Iowa State U., 1969, PhD, 1971. Asst. prof. No. Ariz. U., Flagstaff, 1971-74, assoc. prof., 1975-85, 86—; researcher assoc. office of med. edn. U. Ariz., Tucson, 1985-86. Contbr. articles to profl. jours. Bd. dirs. Environ. Rsch. and Devel., Tucson, 1985—, Ariz. Solar Energy Commn., Phoenix, 1981-87; bd. dirs., v.p. Child Abuse Ctr., Flagstaff, 1982—; del. Ariz. Dem. Caucus, Phoenix, 1984. Mem. Am. Psychol. Assn., Western Psychol. Assn., Rocky Mountain Psychol. Assn., AAUP, Women in Higher Edn. (bd. dirs. 1987—), Sigma Xi. Office: No Ariz U Dept Psychology Flagstaff AZ 86011

SCHNUR, JOEL ALAN, information systems specialist, consultant; b. Newark, Dec. 27, 1935; s. Morris and Lena Schnur; m. Janice Lee, Aug. 24, 1971. BSME, N.J. Inst. Tech., 1957; MS in Systems Mgmt., U. Southern Calif., 1970, MS in Mgmt. Sci., 1971. Commd. 2nd lt. USAF, 1957, advanced through grades to lt. col., 1974, navigator, 1958-60; launch vehicle engr. USAF, El Segundo, Calif., 1960-66; combat navigator USAF, Vietnam, 1966-67; with manned space program USAF, El Segundo, 1967-72; satellite ops. officer USAF, 1972-78, ret., 1978; from head computer ops. to program mgr. Hughes Aircraft Co., El Segundo, 1978--; guest lectr. mfg. subjects, 1983--. Editor: Computer Integrated Manufacturing Review, 1985; contbr. articles to profl. publs. Decorated D.F.C. Mem. Am. Prodn. and Inventory Control Soc., Soc. Mfg. Engrs. (steering council 1986--), Computer Aided Mfg. Internat. (bd. dirs. 1987--). Home: 3641 Dellvale Pl Encino CA 91436

SCHNYDER, LINDSAY ANNE, broadcasting company executive; b. Bloomington, Ill., July 2, 1952; d. Robert John Schnyder and Constance (Sherbert) Chaplin. Grad. high sch., Huntington Beach, Calif. Gen. mgr. KZZX Radio, Albuquerque, 1978-80; account exec. KRDO TV, Colorado Springs, Colo., 1980-81, KVOR Radio, Colorado Springs, 1981; mktg. dir. Columbus (Ohio) Zoo, 1981-83; pres., gen. mgr. KOTE-KKZZ Radio, Lancaster, Calif.; v.p., gen. mgr. Programming Consultants, Inc., Albuquerque, 1987-88; v.p. Drake Chenault Enterprises, Albuquerque, 1987—; bd. dirs. Antelope Valley Health Found., Lancaster. Bd. dirs. C. of C., Lancaster. Named Exec. of Yr., Sunbelt Communications, 1979, Wagontrain Communications, 1984. Office: Drake Chenault Enterprises 2000 Randolph Rd SE Albuquerque NM 87106

SCHOBER, SUSAN CULLEN, educator; b. Dubuque, Iowa, Mar. 25, 1952; d. John R. Cullen and Ruth (Sippel) Louden; m. Charles Thomas Schober, May 5, 1979. BA in English and Fgn. Langs., Cen. U. Iowa, 1975; MA in Theoretical Linguistics, U. So. Calif., 1979; grad. Spanish lang., U. Madrid, 1978. Instr. Spanish and English U. So. Calif., Los Angeles, 1976-79; Spanish instr. Los Angeles Unified Dist., 1977-79; English instr. U. Calif., Irvine, 1980—; owner/dir. Translation and Editing Services, Irvine, Calif., 1986—. Translator U.S. Olympics, Los Angeles, 1984; mem. Scholarship Fundraising com. for U. So. Calif., 1985—. Mem. Nat. Orgn. for Bus. and Profl. Women, Western Coll. Learning Assn., Irvine C. of C. Lutheran. Home: 5031 Paseo De Vega Irvine CA 92715 Office: U Calif Student Svcs II Bldg Irvine CA 92717

SCHOCKLEY, ELIZABETH VIRGINIA, food service administrator; b. Youngstown, Ohio, Nov. 11, 1947; d. Floyd D. and Elizabeth V. (Linge) Perry; children: Sean, Dustin. AS, U. Wyo., 1987. With day care ctr. Jackson (Wyo.) Pub. Schs. System, 1972-79; concessions mgr. Jackson Hole Rodeo Assn., 1979-80; food svc. dir. Residential Sch. for Handicapped, Jackson, 1980—; coord. food svc. program for handicapped, Wilson, Wyo., 1983—. Author: mag. Am. Sch. Food Svc., 1987. Coord. Muscular Dystrophy Assn., Jackson, 1986-88; sec. Babe Ruth Assn., Jackson, 1986-88. Named Woman of the Yr., Bus. & Profl. Women, 1979. Mem. Am. Sch. Food Svc. Assn., Wyo. Sch. Food Svc. Assn. (regional rep. 1978—, Louise Sublette award 1988). Democrat. Episcopalian. Office: Residential Sch Handicapped Box 240 Wilson WY 82041

SCHOENEMANN, PAUL THOMAS, educator; b. Bklyn., Feb. 3, 1936; s. Oscar Paul and Helen Martha (Hornbostel) S.; m. Nancy Denny Poole, June 20, 1959 (div. Aug., 1977); children: Paul Thomas, Amanda Wiehl; m. Joan Lamona Honsberger, Aug. 24, 1979. BE, Yale U., 1958, ME, 1959; PhD, U. Calif., Berkeley, 1965. Registered profl. engr., Mass. Staff engr. Sandia Corp., Livermore, Calif., 1961-65; cons. Arthur D. Little, Inc., Cambridge, Mass., 1965-68; sr. cons. Arthur D. Little, Inc., London, 1968-70, San Francisco, 1970-80; cons. Hay Mgmt. Cons., San Francisco, 1980-85; assoc. prof. San Francisco State U., 1985—; lectr. San Francisco State U., 1983-85; pvt. practice cons., 1985—. Commr. Lafayette Traffic Commn., 1978-82; chmn. Tri-City Traffic Com. 1982. Study grant Pacific Bell, 1988. Mem. ops. Research Soc. Am., No. Calif. Human Resource Council, IEEE, Oakland Hills Tennis Club, Univ. Club (pres. San Francisco State U. chpt. 1988), Lafayette Club, Tennis Club. Office: San Francisco State U 1600 Holloway Ave San Francisco CA 94132

SCHOENFELD, LAWRENCE JON, jewelry manufacturing company executive, travel industry consultant; b. Los Angeles, Nov. 30, 1945; s. Donald and Trudy (Libizer) S.; Carol Sue Gard, Aug. 24, 1969. AA, Los Angeles Valley Coll., Van Nuys, Calif., 1963; BBA, Wichita State U., 1969, MSBA, 1970. Cert. tchr. (life), Calif. Asst. treas. Advance Mortgage, Los Angeles, 1970-72; v.p. ops. Unigem Internat., Los Angeles, 1972—; bd. dirs. Schoenfeld Constrn. Co., The Telcom Group, Uniorr Corp., Execucentre-West, Schoenfeld & Co., Schoenfeld Constrn. Co., Customer Ground Handling Service Corp.; co-developer Bay-Osos Mini Storage Co., San Luis Obispo, Calif., El Mercadeo World Trade Show, Guatemala, 1986, Santiago, 1987, Bahai, 1988, Paraguay, 1989. Mem. Improvement Commn., Hermosa Beach., Calif. 1976-78. Served to maj. US Army Med. Service Corps, 1970-72, lt. col. with res. 1972—. Mem. South Am. Travel Assn., World Trade Assn. (assoc.), Town Hall, Wichita State U. Alumni Assn. (Nat. dist. rep.), Res. Officer Assn. Jewish. Office: Unigem Internat 448 S Hill 12th Floor Los Angeles CA 90266

SCHOETTLER, GAIL SINTON, state treasurer; b. Los Angeles, Oct. 21, 1943; d. James and Norma (McLellan) Sinton; m. John H. Schoettler, Sept. 11, 1965; children: Lee, Thomas, James. BA in Econs., Stanford U., 1965; MA in History, U. Calif., Santa Barbara, 1969, PhD in History, 1975. Businesswoman Denver, 1975-83; exec. dir. Colo. Dept. of Personnel, Denver, 1983-86; treas. State of Colo., Denver, 1987—; bd. dirs. Pub. Employees Retirement Assn., Denver; past bd. dirs. Women's Bank, Denver; Littleton, Colo., Equitable Bankshares of Colo., Denver. Mem. Douglas County Bd. Edn., Colo., 1979-87, pres., 1983-87; trustee U. No. Colo., Greeley, 1981-87; pres. Denver Children's Mus., 1975-85. Mem. Nat. Women's Forum (bd. dirs., pres. 1983-85), Women Execs. in State Govt. (bd. dirs. 1981-87, chmn. 1988), Leadership Denver Assn. (bd. dirs. 1987, named Outstanding Alumna 1985), Nat. Assn. State Treas., Stanford Alumni Assn. Democrat. *

SCHOFIELD, NORMAN JAMES, educator; b. Rothesay, Bute, Scotland, Jan. 30, 1944; s. James Schofield and Muriel (MacIlravey) McDermott; m. Elizabeth Mary Moore, July 29, 1967; children: Thomas, Isobel, Camilla. BSc in Physics, Liverpool U., 1965, BSc in Math., 1966; PhD in Govt., Essex U., 1976, PhD in Econs., 1985. Assoc. prof. U. Tex., Austin, 1976-79; reader in econs. U. Essex, Colchester, Eng., 1979-86; Hallsworth fellow U. Manchester, Eng., 1982-83; Sherman Fairchild fellow Calif. Inst. Tech., Pasadena, 1983-84, visiting prof., 1984-85; fellow Ctr. for Advanced Study, Stanford U., Stanford, Calif., 1988—; prof. econs. Wash. U., St. Louis, 1986—; lectr. govt. U. Essex, 1970; lectr. polit. sci. Yale U., New Haven, Conn., 1973; cons. Productive Employment Program, L.A., 1984; rsch. polit. scientist U. Irvine, Irvine, Calif., 1984-85. Author: Social Choice & Democracy, 1985; co-author: Statistical Methods in Social Sciences, 1986; editor: Economic Relations between North and South, 1984. Grantee British Coun., Brussels, Belgium, 1973, Social Sci. Rsch. Coun., London, 1972-73, British Acad., London, 1980, Nuffield Found., London, 1975; Wolfson fellowship, British Acad., Berlin, 1976, Leverhulme fellowship, Brussels, 1977. Mem. Soc. for Promotion of Economic Theory, Am. Economic Assn., Pub. Choice Soc.

SCHOLES, VON ALVIN, engineering specialist; b. Rigby, Idaho, Jan. 3, 1945; s. Alvin Adam and LaVon (Hunter) S.; m. Rosemary Stephens, Aug. 25, 1966; children: Von Alan, Robert, William, Ryan, Michael, Stephanie. BA in Bus. Adminstrn., Calif. State U., Fulerton, 1977. Ordained bishop, Mormon Ch., 1985. Programmer FMC, Pocatello, Idaho, 1967-69, 73-74, programmer, analyst, 1974-76; computer specialist Hughes Aircraft Co., Fullerton, 1976-78; project leader EG&G, Idaho Falls, Idaho, 1978—; spl. interest chmn. INTEREX, Sunyvale, Calif., 1985-87. Dist. scout chmn. Boy Scouts Am., Shelley, Idaho, 1982; v.p. Bonneville Assn. Retarded Citizens, Idaho Falls, 1983. Served with USN, 1969-72. Home: 633 E 800 N Firth ID 83236 Office: EG&G Idaho 1955 Fremont Ave Idaho Falls ID 83236

SCHOLFIELD, DIANE SLEZAK, public relations executive; b. Bay City, Mich., Nov. 22, 1955; d. James M. and Ann F. Slezak; m. Steven J. Scholfield, July 14, 1979. BA in Journalism, U. So. Calif., 1977. Sports editor Coast Dispatch, Encinitas, Calif., 1977-78; newswriter, sports info. dir. MiraCosta Coll., Oceanside, Calif., 1978-81; pub. info. mgr. MiraCosta Coll., Oceanside, 1981-84; asst. media rels. mgr. Del Mar (Calif.) Fair, 1985, media rels. mgr., 1986—. Contbr. many articles to newspapers and mags. Mem. Choir (soloist) Carlsbad (Calif.) Union Ch. Recipient several pub. rels., writing awards in San Diego County. Mem. U.S. Ski Writers Assn., North County Press Club. Home: 3533 Sea Ridge Rd Oceanside CA 92054 Office: Del Mar Fair 2260 Jimmy Durante Blvd Del Mar CA 92014

SCHOLL, ALLAN HENRY, school system administrator; b. Bklyn., May 6, 1935; s. Joseph Arnold and Edith (Epstein) S.; m. Marina Alexandra Mihailovich, July 3, 1960. BA, UCLA, 1957; MA, U. So. Calif., 1959, PhD, 1973. Lic. gen. secondary tchr. (life), administrv. svcs. (life), jr. coll. tchr. (life) Calif. Instr. history U. So. Calif., L.A., 1972-73, Community Colls., L.A., Cerritos, Whittier, Calif., 1963-72; tchr. social studies L.A. Unified Sch. Dist., 1960-82, advisor social studies, 1982-84, secondary specialist social studies, 1984—; cons. in field. Cons. High School Government textbook, 1987; contbr. articles to profl. jours. Bd. dirs. Pasadena Chamber Orch., 1977-78, Pasadena Symphony Orch., 1984-85, Pasadena Centennial Com., 1985. Served with U.S. Army, 1958-59. Fellow U. So. Calif., 1968-69; NDEA Fellow, 1962; scholar Chouinard Art Inst., 1952. Mem. Am. Hist. Assn., Nat. Council Social Studies, Calif. Council Social Studies, So. Calif. Social Studies Assn. (bd. dirs. 1982-84), Assoc. Adminstrs. L.A. (legis. council 1984—), Nat. Found. Ileitis and Colitis, Phi Alpha Theta. Office: LA Unified Sch Dist Office Instruction 450 N Grand Ave Rm A-327 Los Angeles CA 90012

SCHOLL, SARAH RODERICK, teacher; b. Detroit, Feb. 19, 1938; d. Howard Franklin and Emily (Olmsted) Roderick; m. Robert Allan, Aug. 17, 1963; children: Jennifer Legate, Andrew Minter. BS, U. Mich., 1960; MA, Calif. State U., Hayward, 1981. Calif. Tchrs. Life Credential. Tchr. Springfield Twp. Sch. Dist., Springfield, Pa., 1960-62, Mpls. Sch. Dist., 1962-63, Fargo (N.D.) Unified Sch. Dist., 1963-64, San Ramon Valley Unified Sch. Dist., Danville, Calif., 1974—; mentor tchr. San Ramon Valley Unified Sch. Dist., Danville, 1984-86; tchr. Children and Youth in Am. History, Berkeley, Calif., 1986-88. Campaign co-mgr. San Ramon City Council, 1983, 87; vol. U. Rsch. Expedition Program, Berkeley, 1988. Named Woman of Distinction San Ramon Sorptimists, 1988; recipient Reading Incentive/Authors Program award San Ramon Valley Edn. Found., 1986, Author's Program to Sch. Tri Valley Community Fund award, 1985. Mem. Oakland Mus. Assn. (docent 1976-88), Calif. Reading Assn., Red Barn Assn. (pres. 1985-88), San Ramon Arts Council (v.p. 1988—), San Ramon Valley Community Concerts Assn. (sec. 1985-88), AAUW. Home: 30 Broadmoor Ct San Ramon CA 94583 Office: Walt Disney Sch 3250 Pine Valley Rd San Ramon CA 94583

SCHOMAKER, MICHAEL EDWARD, forest pathologist; b. Lincoln, Nebr., Sept. 25, 1947; s. Carl Eldon and Ferne Marguerite (Lynch) S.;m. Nancy Elaine Spinner, Apr. 14, 1968 (div. Oct. 1974); 1 child, Sheryl Stacy; m. Judith Ann Lemon, Nov. 20, 1982; 1 child, Damon Peter Thomas. BS in Phys. Sci., Colo. State U., 1969, MS in Mycology, 1972. Forest pathologist Colo. State Forest Svc., Fort Collins, 1972—. Co-author: Dutch Elm Disease - A Bibliography, 1976; contbr. articles to profl. jours. Rep. United Way campaign, Colo. State U., Ft. Collins, 1983-84; host home Larimer County Youth Svcs., Ft. Collins, 1987—, Nacel Fgn. Exchange Program, Denver, 1987-88. Mem. Colo. Urban Foresters Coun. (pest com. 1984—), Western Internat. Forest Disease Work Conf. Group, Colo. Mycological Soc. (pres. 1986), Great Plains Agr. Coun. (pest com. forestry), Nat. Arbor Day Found., Toastmasters Club (area gov. 1984-85), Norco Jrs. Volleyball Club (pres. 1988-89), Arsenal Soccer Club (coach 1984-86). Republican. Methodist. Home: 1530 Rolf Ct Fort Collins CO 80525 Office: Colo State Forest Svc Forestry Bldg Fort Collins CO 80523

SCHONBERGER, RICHARD JOHN, manufacturing consultant; b. Devils Lake, N.D., July 7, 1937; s. Robert Theodore and Dorothy (Young) S.; m. Nancy Louise Sell, Sept. 10, 1960; children: Steven John, Clayton James. BS, U.N.D., 1961; MA, U. Iowa, 1969; PhD, U. Nebr., 1971. Indsl. engr. U.S. Naval Repair Facility, San Diego, 1961-62, McClellan AFB, Sacramento, 1964-66, U.S. Army Mgmt. Engrng. Tng. Agy., Rock Island, Ill., 1966-69; mng. analyst U.S. Naval Supply Depot, Guantanamo Bay, Cuba, 1962-64; tchng. asst. dept. mgmt. U. Nebr., 1969-71, prof., 1971-86, George Cook Disting. Prof., 1986; pres. Schonberger & Assocs., Inc., Lincoln, Nebr., 1983-86, Seattle, 1986--. Author: Japanese Manufacturing Techniques, 1982, World Class Manufacturing, 1986, World Class Manufacturing Casebook, 1987, Operations Management, 1988. Mem. Inst. Indsl. Engrs. (Prodn. and Inventory Control award 1987), Am. Prodn. and Inventory Control Soc. (bd. advisors book series 1988--), Am. Soc. for Quality Control, Soc. Mfg. Engrng. Office: PO Box 66948 Seattle WA 98166

SCHONBRUN, MICHAEL KEITH, hospital executive; b. N.Y.C., Jan. 26, 1948; s. Arnold Laurence and Madeline (Courland) S.; m. Michelle Fredson, June 6, 1971; 1 child, Ethan F. BA, Yale U., 1969; JD, U. Pa., 1973. Bar: Ohio 1973, Colo. 1976. Gen. counsel Gov.'s Commn. Health Care, Columbus, Ohio, 1973-74; research atty. Spectrum Research Inc., Denver, 1974-75; asst. health affairs Gov.'s Office, State of Colo., Denver, 1975-76; asst. dir. med. care regulation Colo. Dept. Health, Denver, 1976-79; exec. v.p. Nat. Jewish Ctr. for Immunology and Respiratory Medicine, Denver, 1979-82, pres., 1982—; bd. dirs. United Bank of Denver; mem. editorial bd. Healthspan Inc., Washington, 1984—; com. chmn. Nat. Gov.'s Assn., Washington, 1977-78; ad hoc group mem. Govt. Research Corp., Washington, 1976-77. Contbr. articles to profl. jours. Chmn. Met. Air Quality Council, Denver, 1985—, Gov.'s Search Com. for Exec. Dir. of State Health Dept., Denver, 1986. Mem. Nat. Health Lawyers Assn., Young Pres.'s Orgn. Democrat. Jewish. Club: Yale (N.Y.C.); Meadows (Boulder, Colo.). Office: Nat Jewish Ctr Immunology & Respiratory Medicine 1400 Jackson St Denver CO 80206

SCHONEMAN, SCOTT ROBERT, aerospace engineer; b. Upland, Calif., Sept. 21, 1961; s. Earl George and Carole Jean (Anderson) S. BS in Aerospace Engring., Calif. State Polytech. U., Pomona, 1983; postgrad., Calif. State Polytech. U., 1983—. Assoc. engr. Gen. Dynamics, Pomona, Calif., 1983-84, aerodynamics engr., 1984-86; aerodynamics engr. Valley Systems div. Gen. Dynamics, Rancho Cucamango, Calif., 1986-87, sr. aerodynamics engr. Valley Systems div., 1987—; lectr. Calif. State Polytech. U., Pomona, 1984—. Co-inventor Telescoping Airfram submunition. Active Friends of Ontario (Calif.) Internat. Airport, 1987. Mem. AAIA (student cof. coordinator 1986-88, dep. dir. student activities 1988—), Nat. Mgmt. Assn. Republican. Methodist. Home: 1926A E Yale St Ontario CA 91764 Office: Gen Dynamics Valley Systems div PO Box 50-800 Ontario CA 91761

SCHONFELD, WILLIAM ROST, political science educator, researcher; b. N.Y.C., Aug. 28, 1942; s. William A. and Louise R. (Rost) S.; m. Elena Beortegui, Jan. 23, 1964; children: Natalie Beortegui, Elizabeth Lynn Beortegui. Student, Cornell U., 1960-61; B.A. cum laude with honors, NYU, 1964; M.A., Princeton U., 1968, Ph.D., 1970. Research asst. Princeton U., 1966-69, research assoc., 1969-70, vis. lectr., 1970; asst. prof. polit. sci. U. Calif.-Irvine, 1970-75, assoc. prof., 1975-81, prof., 1981—, dean Sch. Social Scis., 1982—; sr. lectr. Fond. Nat. de Sci. Politique, Paris, 1973-74; researcher Centre de Sociologie des Organisations, Paris, 1976-78. Author: Youth and Authority in France, 1971, Obedience and Revolt, 1976, Ethnographie du PS et du RPR, 1985. Recipient Disting. Teaching award U. Calif.-Irvine, 1984; Fulbright fellow Bordeaux, France, 1964-65; Danforth grad. fellow, 1964-69; Fulbright sr. lectr. Paris, 1973-74; NSF-CNRS Exchange of Scientists fellow Paris, 1976-78; Ford Found. grantee France, Spain, 1978-79; finalist Prof. Yr. Council for Advancement and Support of Edn., 1984. Mem. Am. Polit. Sci. Assn., Assoc. France de Sci. Pol., Phi Beta Kappa. Office: U Calif Sch Social Scis Irvine CA 92717

SCHONLAND, ADDISON MICHAEL, oil executive, researcher; b. Worcester, South Africa, Sept. 1, 1957; came to U.S., 1987; s. Michael Addison and Peggy (Schell) S.; m. Stephanie Widan, Jan. 27, 1985; 1 child, Robin. B. Com. with honors, U. Cape Town, South Africa, 1987, BA in Econ. with honors, 1981, B. in Soc. Sci., 1980. Orgn. & Methods Analyst Shell South Africa (Pty) Ltd., Cape town, South Africa, 1984-87; research analyst Interprsca, Inc., La Jolla, Calif., 1987-88; mgr. new bus. devel. CIC Research, Inc., San Diego, Calif., 1988—. Mem. South African Fin. Analysts Soc., The Fin. Analyst. Fedn. Office: CIC Rsch Inc 1215 Cushman Ave San Diego CA 92110

SCHOON, STEVEN WARREN, mechanical engineer; b. Luverne, Minn., Sept. 23, 1944; s. Warren Eugene and Doris Elizabeth (Johnson) S.; m. Natalie Ann Keller, Apr. 23, 1971 (div. 1972); 1 child, Laura Jean; m. Donna Lee Merrill, Dec. 29, 1973; 1 child, James Warren. BS in Mech. Engring., U. Mo., 1969. Cognizant engr. Westinghouse Hanford Co., Richland, Wash., 1973-81; contract administr. Martin Marietta Aerospace, Denver, 1981-85, dep. mgr. Titan IV vehicle engring., 1986—. Committeeman Oliver for Congress, Richland, 1979-80, Forrest for Congress, Colo. Springs, 1983-84; dist. leader Dole for Pres., Colo. Springs, 1987-88; group leader Young Astronauts, Colo. Springs, 1986—. Cpt. USAF, 1966-73. Decorated Nat. Def. Svc. medal; Recipient Bronze cert. Am. Soc. Actuaries, 1961. Mem. Mensa, Lindbergh Assn. Republican. Presbyterian. Home: 5270 Bunkhouse Ln Colorado Springs CO 80917 Office: Martin Marietta Astronautics GP PO Box 179 Denver CO 80201

SCHOPFER, STEPHEN WILLIAM, data processing executive; b. Austin, Tex., Aug. 11, 1951; s. William Eugene and Nina Lou (Lindsay) S.; m. Patricia Cowperthwait, Jan. 14, 1972 (div. 1977): 1 child, Daniel Franklin; m. LaJane Hutchins, Mar. 13, 1982; children: Charles Lindsay, Laura Jane. BS in Computer Science, East Tex. State U., 1980; MBA, Houston Baptist U., 1986. Ops. mgr. Digicon, Top Ticket, Applied Theory Assn., Houston and Dallas, 1978-81; systems analyst Intercomp, Houston, 1981-82; data processing cons. Diamond Software Systems, Houston, 1982-83, 86; systems analyst Hudson Products, Houston, 1983-86; data processing mgr. City of Lacey, Wash., 1987--; data processing cons. Delphi Systems, Olympia, Wash., 1987--. With U.S. Navy, 1970-74. Mem. Data Processing Mgrs. Assn. Democrat. Mormon. Home: 4813 Forest Glen Ct SE Olympia WA 98503 Office: City of Lacey 420 College St SE Lacey WA 98503

SCHOPPA, ELROY, accountant, financial planner; b. Vernon, Tex., Aug. 25, 1922; s. Eddie A. and Ida (Foerster) S.; m. Juanita C. Young, Aug. 11, 1956 (div.); children: Karen Marie, Vickie Sue; m. Gail O. Martin, May 12, 1984; stepchildren: Veronica, Vanessa. BBA, Tex. Tech U., 1943; postgrad.

Law Sch., U. Tex., 1946-47; MA, Mich. State U., 1950. CPA, Tex., Calif.; cert. real estate broker; cert. ins. agt. Mem. faculty Tex. Tech U., Lubbock, 1943, U. Tex., Austin, 1946-47, Mich. State U., East Lansing, 1947-50; auditor Gen. Motors Corp., 1950-56; dir. systems and procedures Fansteel Metall. Corp., 1956-59; gen. auditor Consol. Electro Dynamics Corp., 1959-60; auditor, sr. tax acct. Beckman Inst. Inc., Fullerton, Calif., 1960-70; pres. Elroy Schoppa Acctg. Corp., La Habra, Calif., 1960—; cons. to bus. Treas. La Habra Devel. Corp.; organizer, pres. 4-H Club, Vernon; adviser Jr. Achievement, Waukegan, Ill.; bd. dirs. Klein Ctr. for Prevention of Domestic Violence; asst. football and basketball coach, Manzanola, Colo.; coach Am. Girls Sport Assn., La Habra. Served with USN, 1942-46. Mem. Calif. Soc. CPA's, Alpha Phi Omega, Theta Xi. Republican. Lutheran. Club: Phoenix (Anaheim, Calif.). Avocations: hunting, fishing, camping. Office: 801 E La Habra Blvd La Habra CA 90631

SCHOR, EDWARD LEWIS, physician; b. Denver, Aug. 14, 1944; s. Manny and Marjorie (Lewis) S.; m. Nicole Nystrom, May 30, 1970 (div. May 1972); m. Delynn Irene Harrison, Oct. 21, 1988. AB, Washington U., St. Louis, 1966; MD, Chgo. Med. Sch., 1970; postgrad., Johns Hopkins U., 1981-83. Intern, resident Baylor Coll. of Medicine, Houston, 1970-72; pediatric resident Johns Hopkins Hosp., Balt., 1972-73; faculty Johns Hopkins U., Balt., 1973-81; med. dir. Chesapeake Health Plan, Balt., 1976-81; faculty U. N.Mex., Albuquerque, 1983-87; program officer Kaiser Family Found., Menlo Park, Calif., 1987—; clin. faculty Stanford U., 1988—. Author: The Health Care of Children in Out-of-Home Care, 1988; editorial rev. bd. Child Welfare, Washington, 1984—. Fellow Am. Acad. Pediatrics (com. on early childhood, adoption and dependent care 1984—); mem. Ambulatory Pediatric Assn. (bd. dirs. 1985-88, Mead-John Vis. Prof. 1981). Home: 403 O'Keefe St Menlo Park CA 94025 Office: Kaiser Family Found 2400 Sand Hill Rd Menlo Park CA 94025

SCHORR, ALAN EDWARD, librarian, publisher; b. N.Y.C., Jan. 7, 1945; s. Herbert and Regina (Fingerman) S.; m. Debra Genner, June 11, 1967; 1 son, Zebediah. B.A., CUNY, 1966; M.A., Syracuse U., 1967; postgrad., U. Iowa, 1967-71; M.L.S., U. Tex., 1973. Tchr., rsch. asst. dept. history U. Iowa, 1967-70; govt. publs. and map libr., asst. prof. Elmer E. Rasmuson Library, U. Alaska, Fairbanks, 1973-78; assoc. prof., dir. library U. Alaska, Juneau, 1978-84; prof., univ. library dean Calif. State U., Fullerton, 1984-86; pres. The Denali Press, Juneau, Alaska, 1986—; free lance indexer and bibliographer; vis. lectr. Birmingham (Eng.) Poly., 1981; mem. Alaska Ednl. Del. to People's Republic China, 1975. Author: Alaska Place Names, 1974, 3d edit., 1986, Directory of Special Libraries in Alaska, 1975, Government Reference Books, 1974-75, 76, 1976-77, 78, Government Documents in the Library Literature, 1909-1974, 1976, ALA RSBRC Manual, 1979, Federal Documents Librarianship 1879-1987, 1988; editor: The Sourdough, 1974-75, Directory of Services for Refugees and Immigrants, 1987, edit., 1989, Guide to Smithsonian serial publs., 1987, Hispanic Resource Directory, 1988; book reviewer, columnist: Southeast Alaska Empire, 1979—, Los Angeles Times; contbr. articles to profl. jours. Mem. Auke Bay (Alaska) Vol. Fire Dept.; mem. Juneau Borough Cemetery Adv. Com., 1980-81, Am. Book Awards Com., 1980, Juneau Borough Library Adv. Com., 1981-82. Mem. ALA (reference and subscription books rev. com. 1975-86, reference and adult services div. publs. com. 1975-77, Mudge citation commn. 1977-79, 84-86, Dartmouth Coll. Medal Commn., Governing Council 1977-84, Dewey medal com. 1984-85), Alaska Library Assn. (exec. bd. 1974-75, nominating com. 1977-79), Pacific N.W. Library Assn. (rep. publs. com. 1973-75), Assn. Coll. and Research Libraries (publ. com. 1976-80), Spl. Libraries Assn. (assoc. editor geography and map div. bull. 1975-76), Soc. for Scholarly Pub., Internat. Assn. Small Presses, Pubs. Mktg. Assn., Alaska Assn. Small Presses. Clubs: Explorers N.Y, Book of Calif. (sustaining). Home: PO Box 1535 Juneau AK 99802

SCHORR, MARK SCOTT, writer, journalism educator; b. N.Y.C., Sept. 6, 1953; s. Bernard and Vera Emma (Zernik) S.; m. Sima Epstein. Freelance writer N.Y.C., 1973-80; investigative reporter Los Angeles Herald Examiner, 1980-82; field producer Sta. KNXT (now KCBS), Los Angeles, 1982, NBC, Los Angeles, 1983; freelance writer Los Angeles, 1983—; instr. journalism UCLA, 1984-88. Novelist: Red Diamond, Private Eye, 1983 (Edgar award nomination Mystery Writers Am.), Ace of Diamonds, 1984, Diamond Rock, 1985, Bully!, 1985, The Borzoi Control, 1986, Overkill, 1988, Seize the Dragon, 1989, An Eye for an Eye, 1989; screenwriter; contbr. numerous articles to mags. and newspapers. Recipient AP award, Hearst Orgn. award, Valley Press Club award. Mem. Writers Guild Am. West, Mystery Writers Am. (regional bd. dirs. 1986-88), Calif. Writers Club.

SCHORR, MARTIN MARK, psychologist, educator, writer; b. N.Y.C., Sept. 16, 1923; m. Dolores Gene Tyson, June 14, 1952; 1 child, Jeanne Ann. Student, Balliol Coll., Eng., 1945-46; AB cum laude, Adelphi U., 1949; postgrad., U. Tex., 1949-50; MS, Purdue U., 1953; PhD, U. Denver, 1960; postgrad., Balliol Coll., U. Tex. Lic. clin. psychologist. Project dir. human services San Diego County, 1959-60; clin. psychologist Dept. Corrections, San Diego, 1961-63; chief clin. psychol. svcs. San Diego County Mental Hosp., 1963-67; pvt. practice, forensic specialist San Diego, 1962—; forensic examiner superior, fed. and mil. cts., San Diego, 1962—; guest prof. abnormal psychology, San Diego State U., 1965-68; chief dept. psychology Ctr. City (Calif.) Hosp., 1976-79; mem. staff Dept. Corrections State of Calif., Minnewawa, 1970-73, Disability Evaluation Dept. Health, 1972-75, State Indsl. Accident Commn., Calif., 1972-78, Calif. Criminal Justice Adminstrn., 1975-77; cons. Vista Hill Found., Mercy Hosp. Mental Health, Foodmaker Corp., Convent Sacred Heart, El Cajon, FAA Examiner. Author: (screenplay) Prescription for Murder, 1988. Recipient award for aid in developing Whistle Blower Law Calif. Assembly, 1986. Fellow Internat. Assn. Soc. Psychiatry; mem. AAAS, PEN, Am. Psychology Assn., Am. Acad. Forensic Scis., Internat. Platform Assn., World Mental Health Assn., Mystery Writers Am., Nat. Writers' Club, Mensa. Home and Office: 2970 Arnoldson Ave San Diego CA 92122

SCHORZMAN, MARK HEWIT, industrial hygienist; b. Spokane, Wash., Sept. 6, 1937; s. Lester Richard and Esther Ann (Cowen) S.; m. Judy Kennett Lavender, Aug. 22, 1959; children: Mark Hewit, Douglas Wheeler. BS, U. Wash., 1961, MS in Pub. Health, 1975; grad. with honors, Army Command and Gen. Staff Coll., 1976; registered sanitarian, Wash.; diplomate Am. Acad. Sanitarians, Am. Acad. Indsl. Hygiene. Sanitarian, Thurston-Mason Health Dist., Wash., 1961-62; commd. 2d lt., U.S. Army, 1962, advanced through grades to maj., 1967, ret., 1982, chief environ. sanitation, N. Baveria Med. Dist., W. Germany, 1968-69, chief preventive medicine Madigan Gen. Hosp., Tacoma, 1970-74, preventive medicine cons. Comdr. U.S. Army Health Svcs. Command, Ft. Sam Houston, Tex., 1975-77, chief environ. sci. Fitzsimons Army Med. Center, Denver, 1977-82; risk mgmt. officer Adams County, Colo., 1982-84; cons. in indsl. hygiene Mark H. Schorzman and Assocs., Denver, 1984—; instr. Nat. Inst. for Food Svc. Industry, 1980-83. Scouting chmn. Centennial dist. Boy Scouts Am., 1977-79, mem. tng. com., 1977-82. U.S. Army Med. Dept. scholar, 1974. Mem. Am. Indsl. Hygiene Assn., Nat. Environ. Health Assn., Automatic Merchandising Assn., Am. Conf. Govtl. Indsl. Hygienists, Royal Soc. Health U.K., Sigma Chi. Anglican Catholic. Contbr. articles to profl. jours. Home: 3419 S Nucla Way Aurora CO 80013

SCHOUWEILER, STEVEN HARVEY, insurance company executive; b. St. Paul, Nov. 28, 1946; s. Thomas John and Bette Lou (Hanson) S.; m. Helen Gilbert, Sept. 9, 1967 (div. 1975); m. Jeannette Ann DeLafe, Dec. 22, 1979; children: Christine Marlyn, Christian Paul. BA, U. Minn., 1971. Sr. v.p. John Alden Life Ins. Co., Boise, Idaho, 1973-86; group dir. Coll. Life Ins. Co., Indpls., 1986-87; v.p. Universe Life Ins. Co., Lewiston, Idaho, 1987-88; with Health Brokerage Agy., Lewiston, 1989—. Author: Alfred Thayer Mahan III, 1979. Served with U.S. Army, 1965-71. Mem. Boise Corvette Club (pres. 1985-86). Republican. Lutheran. Home: 3425 Syringa Dr Lewiston ID 83501

SCHOW, TERRY D., state investigator; b. Ogden, Utah, Dec. 14, 1948; s. Hugh Stuart Sloan and Minnie Aurelia (Ellis) Mohler; m. June Hansen, Feb. 14, 1973; children: Amy, Jason. Associates, Honolulu Community Coll., 1975; Bachelors, Chaminade U., 1975. Mgmr. cert. Utah. Spl. and criminal investigator State of Utah, Ogden, 1976-83, lead investigator, 1984—; investigator Fed. Govt., Salt Lake City, Denver, 1983-84; with United Coun. on Welfare Fraud, Harrisburg, Pa., 1984—. Chmn. 1st Congressional Dist. Utah Rep. Party, 1982-83, mem. state exec. com., 1982-83; chmn. legis. dist. Weber County Rep. Party, Ogden, 1987—; bd. trustees Utah's Vietnam Meml., Salt Lake City, 1988—; leader Boy Scouts Am., Ogden, 1985—. Sgt. U.S. Army, 1967-70, 72-76; Vietnam. Decorated Bronze Star U.S. Army, 1970, Combat Inf. Badge, 1970; recipient Championship Team Trophy Pistol U.S. ARmy, 1975. Mem. Utah Peace Officers Assn., Utah N. Mission 2000 (natural resource task force 1987—), Utah Pub. Employees Assn. (bd. dirs. 1988-89, chmn. Ogden Valley dist., vice-chmn. Citizen Action for Pub. Employees 1989-90), NRA (life), VFW, Disabled Am. Vets. (life, jr. vice-comdr. Weber chpt. 4 1989-90), Kiwanis (bd. dirs. Ogden chpt. 1988—, pres. Layton chpt. 1985-86, named Kiwanian of Yr. 1982-83). Republican. Mormon. Home: 1540 Sunview Dr Ogden UT 84404 Office: State of Utah Office Recoveries 2650 Washington Blvd 4th Fl Ogden UT 84401

SCHOWENGERDT, FRANKLIN DEAN, physics educator; b. Bellflower, Mo., Mar. 8, 1936; s. John Hermann and Muriel Juanita (Taylor) S.; m. Ellen Jeanette Johnson, Feb. 10, 1941; children: Anna Kristine, John Stephen. BS in Physics, U. Mo., Rolla, 1966, MS in Physics, 1967, PhD in Physics, 1969. Vis. asst. prof. U. Neb., Lincoln, 1969-73; asst. prof. Colo. Sch. Mines, Golden, 1973-76, assoc. prof., 1976-79, head dept. physics, 1977—, prof., 1980—; chmn. bd. dirs. Advanced Materials Inst., Golden, 1983—; disting. vis. scientist Jet Propulsion Lab. Calif. Inst. Tech., Pasadena, 1987-88. Contbr. articles to profl. jours; patentee in field. Mem. Am. Vacuum Soc. (chmn. Rocky Mountain chpt.), Am. Phys. Soc., Materials Research Soc., Sigma Xi. Democrat. Presbyterian. Home: 2819 Sunset Dr Golden CO 80401 Office: Colo Sch of Mines Physics Dept Golden CO 80401

SCHOWENGERDT, LOUIS W., bishop. Ordained to ministry United Meth. Ch., later consecrated bishop. Bishop N. Mex. Conf., United Meth. Ch., Albuquerque, also, N.W. Tex. Conf., Lubbock. Office: United Meth Ch 8100 Mountain Rd NE #114 Albuquerque NM 87110 other: 1415 Ave M Lubbock TX 79401 *

SCHOWENGERDT, ROBERT ALAN, electrical and computer engineering educator; b. St. Charles, Mo., Oct. 10, 1946. BS in Physics, U. Mo., Rolla, 1968; PhD in Optical Scis., U. Ariz., 1975. Rsch. assoc. U. Ariz., Tucson, 1972-77, asst. prof. elec. and computer engring., 1977-84, assoc. prof., 1984--, dir. Digital Image Analysis Lab., 1984--; rsch. phys. scientist U.S. Geol. Survey, Reston, Va., 1975-80. Author: Techniques for Image Processing and Classification in Remote Sensing, 1983; contbr. articles to profl. jours. Recipient H.J.E. Reid award NASA Langley Rsch. Ctr., 1983; Am. Soc. for Engring. Edn. summer faculty fellow, 1983; Fulbright Sr. scholar U. New South Wales, 1989. Mem. Optical Soc. Am., Am. Soc. Photogrammetry and Remote Sensing. Office: U Ariz Elec-Computer Engring Dept Tucson AZ 85721

SCHRADY, DAVID ALAN, operations research educator; b. Akron, Ohio, Nov. 11, 1939; s. Marvin G. and Sheila A. (O'Neill) S.; m. Mary E. Hilt, Sept. 1, 1962; children: Peter, Patrick, Matthew. BS, Case Inst. Tech., 1961, MS, 1963, PhD, 1965. Prof., chmn. Naval Postgrad. Sch., Monterey, Calif., 1974-76, dean acad. planning, 1976-80, provost and acad. dean, 1980-87, prof. ops. research, 1988—; vis. prof. Cranfield Inst. Tech./Royal Mil. Coll. of Sci., Shrivenham, Eng., fall 1987-spring 88. Contbr. articles to profl. jours. Mem. Ops. Research Soc. Am. (pres. 1983-84), Mil. Ops. Research Soc. (pres. 1978-79, Internat. Fedn. Ops. Research Socs. (hon. treas. 1988-92), Wanner Meml. award 1984), Inst. Mgmt. Scis., Navy League (bd. dirs. Monterey Peninsula council). Office: Naval Postgrad Sch Dept Ops Rsch Monterey CA 93943-5000

SCHRAER, ROSEMARY S. J., university chancellor; b. Ilion, N.Y., Aug. 1, 1924; d. Ulysses Sidney and Rose Katherine (Ortner) Schmidt; m. Allan Gramlick Jenkins, May 3, 1946 (dec. Aug. 13, 1947); 1 child, David; m. Harald Schraer, June 12, 1952. AB, Syracuse U., 1946, MS, 1949, PhD, 1953. Vis. research assoc. Harvard Med. Sch., Boston, Mass., 1967-68; vis. scientist Radcliffe Inst. Ind. Study, Cambridge, Mass., 1967-68; acting head dept. computer sci. Pa. State U., Univ. Park, 1973-74, assoc. dean for research, 1973-78, prof. biochemistry, 1975-86, assoc. provost, 1981-85; exec. vice chancellor U. Calif., Riverside, 1985-87, chancellor, 1987—; vis. fellow Cavendish Coll., Cambridge U., Eng., 1984-85; bd. dirs. Am. Council on Pharm. Edn., Chgo., 1988—, Accrediting Commn. for Sr. Colls. & Univs., Oakland, Calif., 1988—, Presley Inst. of Corrections Research & Tng., Sacramento, Calif., 1988; bd. visitors Southwestern U. Sch. Law, Los Angeles, 1988. Mem. Monday Morning Group, Riverside, 1987—; bd. dirs. Community Health Corp., Riverside. 1988—, Riverside Land Conservancy, 1988—. University fellow Syracuse U., 1951-52. Mem. AAUP, AAAS, Am. Chem. Soc., Am. Inst. Chemists, Am. Soc. for Cell Biology, Phi Beta Kappa. Office: U Calif-Riverside 900 University Ave Riverside CA 92521-4009 *

SCHRECK, JACQUELYN, teacher; b. San Francisco, Sept. 24, 1946; d. Alfred Jackson and Lily (Caffodio) Malnick; m. Carl B. Schreck, Sept. 10, 1966; children: Steven Paul, Carlyn Marie. Student, U. Calif., Berkeley, 1964-66, Humboldt State U., Arcata, Calif., 1966-67; BS in Sociology, Anthropology, Colo. State U., 1968. Adult services caseworker State Colo., Ft. Collins, 1969-70; instr. Linn-Benton Community Coll., Corvallis, Oreg., 1986; sub. instl. asst. for learning disabled 509-J Sch. Dist., Corvallis, 1984—. Pres. Friends of Library, 1979-80; pres. Hoover Elem. Sch. Parents Group, 1980-81, Cheldelin Parents Group, 1985-86; mem. Intermediate Sch. Study Com., 1985-86; trustee Benton-Corvallis Pub. Library, 1983—; councilor City of Corvallis, 1981-82, budget commr., 1981—; bd. dirs. Raider Athletic Booster Club, 1986-87; mem. steering com. Raider Parent Club, 1987—. Home: 3060 NW Seneca Pl Corvallis OR 97330

SCHREIBEIS, RONALD G., revegetation and reclamation executive, environmental consultant; b. Torrington, Wyo.; s. Gene and Bonnie S.; m. Valerie Lenz, June 26, 1976; children: Sabrina, Veronica, Ryan. BS, U. Wyo., 1975, MS, 1977. Rancher Home Ranch, Worland, Wyo., 1962-72; cons. Mine Reclamation Cons., Laramie, Wyo., 1972-78; owner, mgr. Range Inventory & Analysis Co., Laramie, 1978—, Wyo. Tool & Equipment Co., Laramie, 1978—, Rocky Mountain Reclamation, Laramie, 1985—; threatened and endangered plant specialist, cons. mining State of Wyo., 1973—, revegetation specialist, cons., 1985—; erosion control specialist, cons. engring. and mining, 1978—. Author: Reclamation Procedures, 1978; contbr. articles to profl. publs.; inventor reclamation equipment. Mem. Nat. Fedn. Ind. Bus., Luth. Laymen's League. Office: Rocky Mountain Reclamation 1114 Shield St Laramie WY 82070

SCHREIBER, EDWARD, computer scientist; b. Zagreb, Yugoslavia, Mar. 17, 1943; came to U.S., 1956, naturalized, 1960; s. Hinko and Helen (Iskra) S.; m. Barbara Nelson, 1967 (div. 1969); m. Lea Lusia Hausler, Nov. 7, 1983. BSEE, U. Colo., Denver, 1970. Registered profl. engr. Colo.; cert. data processor. Sr. software scientist Autotrol, Denver, 1972-78; software engr. Sigma Design, Englewood, Colo, 1979-82; founder, v.p. Graphics, Info., Denver, 1982-86; pres. Schrieber Instruments, 1987—; instr. computer sci. U. Colo., Denver, 1971-72, Colo. Women's Coll., Denver, 1972-73, U. Denver, 1983. Contbr. articles on computer graphics to profl. jours. Trustee 1st Universalist Ch., Denver, 1972-78; Dem. candidate for U.S. Ho. of Reps., 1980. Served with U.S. Army, 1960-66. Mem. IEEE, Assn. for Computing Machinery, Nat. Computer Graphics Assn., Mensa. Home and Office: 7250 Eastmoor Dr #226 Denver CO 80237

SCHREIBER, JOHN EDWARD, chemical engineer; b. Toledo, Feb. 28, 1949; s. Edward Gordon and Doris Emily (Baldwin) S.; m. Pamela Jean Bender, Mar. 20, 1970; children: Heidi, Holly. BSChemE, U. Toledo, 1971. Applications engr. Liquid Carbonic Co., Chgo., 1971-72; plant mgr. Liquid Carbonic Co., Oregon, Ohio, 1972-73; mktg. engr. Liquid Carbonic Co., Chgo., 1974-76, prodn. engr., 1976-78, prodn. mgr., 1978-80, prodn. and engring. mgr., 1980-84; owner, mgr. Carbonic Enterprises, Toledo, 1973-74; v.p. prodn. Cardox div. Liquid Air Co., San Ramon, Calif., 1984-86; v.p. ops. Liquid Air Co., Walnut Creek, Calif., 1986—. Mem. Am. Inst. Chem. Engrs., Internat. Inst. Ammonia Refrigeration. Republican. Lutheran. Home: 1009 Overlook Dr San Ramon CA 94583 Office: Cardox Div Liquid Air Co 2121 California Ave Walnut Creek CA 94596

SCHREIBER, OTTO WILLIAM, manufacturing company executive; b. Greenwood, Wis., July 4, 1922; s. Otto Waldemar and Meta Wilhelmina (Suemnicht) S. BSEE, U. Wis., Madison, 1944. Electroacoustic scientist Navy Electronics Lab., San Diego, 1946-56; electronics engr. then mgr. electronic engring. dept., ordnance div. Librascope, Sunnyvale, Calif., 1956-65; chief engr. Teledyne Indsl. Electronics Co., San Jose, Calif., 1965-68; exec. v.p. Marcom Corp., San Francisco, 1969; test mgr. MB Assocs., San Ramon, Calif., 1970-71; ops. mgr. Am. Svc. Products, Inc., Newhall, Calif., 1972-75; mfg. mgr. UTI, Inc., Sunnyvale, Calif., 1975-80; dir. mfg. Hi-Shear Ordnance/Electronics, Torrance, Calif., 1980-82; tech. writing supr. Marine div. Westinghouse, Sunnyvale, 1980—. Lt. comdr. USNR, 1944-59. Mem. IEEE (life), Soc. Tech. Communication, Eta Kappa Nu, Kappa Eta Kappa. Republican. Lutheran. Home and Office: 1623 New Brunswick Ave Sunnyvale CA 94087

SCHRIBER, JACQUELYN BUSHNER, business research executive; b. Milw.; d. John and Jennie Bushner; m. William T. Schriber, Sept. 9, 1972 (div. Feb. 1983). BA Lawrence U., 1970; MA Northwestern U., 1978; MA Claremont Grad. Sch., 1981, PhD, 1986. Placement asst. Globe-Union Inc., Milw., 1970-72; supr. compensation analysis Container Corp. Am., Chgo., 1972-76; lectr. Calif. State U.-Fullerton, 1981; various positions Claremont Colls., Calif., 1980-83; owner, cons. Schriber & Assocs., Pomona Calif. , 1983-85; sr. cons. The Orgn. Devel. Ctr., Los Angeles, 1986—; assoc. prof. Calif. Sch. Profl. Psychology, Los Angeles, 1986—; sr. cons. Touche Ross, 1987-88; dir. research Coldwell Banker Residential Group, Newport Beach, 1988—. Author in field. Claremont Grad. Sch. fellow, 1979-81. Mem. Am. Psychol. Assn., Acad. Mgmt., Am. Soc. Tng. and Devel., Am. Assn. Counseling and Devel., Am. Mtkg. Assn., Soc. for Indsl. and Organizatioal Psychology, Sigma Xi (assoc.). Avocations: sports, travel. Office: Coldwell Banker Residential Group 4000 MacArthur Blvd Newport Beach CA 92660

SCHRIEFFER, JOHN ROBERT, research institute administrator; b. Oak Park, Ill., May 31, 1931; s. John Henry and Louise (Anderson) S.; m. Anne Grete Thomsen, Dec. 30, 1960; children: Anne Bolette, Paul Karsten, Anne Regina. B.S., Mass. Inst. Tech., 1953; M.S., U. Ill., 1954, Ph.D., 1957, Sc.D., 1974; Sc.D. (hon.), Tech. U., Munich, Germany, 1968, U. Geneva, 1968, U. Pa., 1973, U. Cin., 1977, U. Tel Aviv, 1987. NSF postdoctoral fellow U. Birmingham, Eng., also; Niels Bohr Inst., Copenhagen, 1957-58; asst. prof. U. Chgo., 1958-59; asst. prof., then assoc. prof. U. Ill., 1959-62; prof. U. Pa., Phila., 1962-79; Mary Amanda Wood prof. physics U. Pa., 1964-79; Andrew D. White prof. at large Cornell U., 1969-75; prof. U. Calif., Santa Barbara, 1980—, Chancellor's prof., 1984—, dir. Inst. for Theoretical Physics, 1984-89; vis. prof. Niels Bohr Inst., summer 1960, 67, U. Geneva, fall 1963, 67; vis. prof. Stanford U., 1978. Author: Theory of Superconductivity, 1964. Guggenheim fellow Copenhagen, 1967; Recipient Comstock prize Nat. Acad. Sci.; Nobel Prize for Physics, 1972; John Ericsson medal Am. Soc. Swedish Engrs., 1976; Alumni Achievement award U. Ill., 1979; recipient Nat. Medal of Sci., 1984; Exxon faculty fellow, 1979-89. Fellow Am. Phys. Soc. (Oliver E. Buckley solid state physics prize 1968), Los Alamos Nat. Lab. (dir. Advanced Studies Program in High Temperature Superconductivity); mem. NAS, Am. Acad. Arts and Scis., Am. Philos. Soc. (Nat. Medal Sci. 1985), Royal Danish Acad. Scis. and Letters, Acad. Sci. USSR. Office: U Calif Inst Theoretical Physics Santa Barbara CA 93106

SCHRIFT, SANDRA JUNE, speakers bureau executive, consultant; b. N.Y.C., Jan. 21, 1937; d. George and Lila (Marcus) Wolff; m. Alan Robert Schrift, Dec. 23, 1956; children: Steven, Laurence, Barbara, Amy, Francine. BA in Social Sci., Hunter Coll., 1957, postgrad., 1957-59. Cert. secondary and adult sch. tchr., N.Y., Calif. Tchr. Morris High Sch., N.Y.C., 1957-59, Eastern High Sch., Balt., 1959-60; tchr. adult sch. Syracuse, N.Y., 1960-62, Grossmont Sch. Dist., San Diego, 1978-82; speaker, trainer San Assocs., San Diego, 1982--; pres., chief exec. officer The Podium, Inc., San Diego, 1983--; mem. Spring Valley (Calif.) Dist. Adv. Council, 1975; mem. competency requirements for social sci. com. Grossmont Union High Sch., El Cajon, Calif., 1978-79. Chmn. parent-tutor vol. program Murdock Elem. Sch., La Mesa, Calif., 1973-77; leader Grow Network, La Mesa, 1983-85. Recipient hon. service award Murdock Elem. Sch., 1975. Mem. Nat. Speakers Assn. (chmn. bur. 1976--), Meeting Planners Internat., Am. Soc. Assn. Execs., Conv. and Visitors Bur. San Diego, LWV (Woman of Vision award San Diego 1988), Network (San Diego) (pres. 1984--). Republican. Jewish. Office: The Podium Inc 6136 Mission Gorge Rd Ste 220 San Diego CA 92120

SCHRODER, DIETER KARL, electrical engineering educator; b. Lübeck, Germany, June 18, 1935; came to U.S., 1964; s. Wilhelm and Martha (Werner) S.; m. Beverley Claire Parchment, Aug. 4, 1961; children: Mark, Derek. BSc, McGill U., Montreal, Que., Can., 1962, MSc, 1964; PhD, U. Ill., 1968. Sr. engr. research and devel. sect. Westinghouse Electric Corp., Pitts., 1968-73, fellow engr., 1973-77, adv. engr., 1977-79, mgr., 1979-81; prof. elec. engring. Ariz. State U., Tempe, 1981—; researcher Inst. Solid-State Physics, Freiburg, Fed. Republic Germany, 1978-79. Author: Advanced MOS Devices, 1987; patentee in field; contbr. articles to profl. jours. Fellow IEEE; mem. Electrochem. Soc., Sigma Xi. Baha'i. Home: 1927 E Bendix Dr Tempe AZ 85283 Office: Ariz State U Dept Elec Engring Tempe AZ 85287

SCHROEDER, ARNOLD LEON, mathematics educator; b. Honolulu, May 27, 1935; s. Arnold Leon and Wynelle (Russell) S.; BS in Math., Oreg. State U., 1960, MS in Stats., 1962; NSF Insts. at UCLA, 1964, U. So. Calif., 1965; m. Maybelle Ruth Walker, Nov. 9, 1956; children: Steven, Michael, Wendy. Computer engr. Autonetics div. N.Am. Aviation Co., 1960-61; NSF fellow, research asst. State of Oreg., Corvallis, 1961; assoc. prof. math. Long Beach (Calif.) Community Coll., 1962—; computer cons. McDonnell-Douglas Corp., 1966-74, statis. researcher in med. and social sci., 1976-80; cons. statis. software including SPSS, BMDP, and Fortran, 1980—; dir. Schroeder's Statis. Svcs. and CHOC Statis. Cons., Long Beach, 1985—. Chmn. bd. elders Grace Bible Ch., South Gate, Calif., 1985—. Served with USAF, 1953-57. Mem. Faculty Assn. Calif. Community Colls., Calif. Teaching Assn., Am. Bowlers Tour (life). Home: 5481 E Hill St Long Beach CA 90815 Office: 4901 E Carson St Long Beach CA 90808

SCHROEDER, FLORENCE JEANNE, lawyer, consultant; b. San Mateo, Calif., Aug. 19, 1927; d. Edward Ignatius and Florence (Marie) McAuliffe; m. Alan Latham Schroeder (dec. 1982); children: Jeanne Toal, Carole, Judith Schott. BS, U. Nev., 1967, MA, 1971, JD, 1985. Bar: Nev. 1985. Tchr. Washoe County Sch. Dist., Reno, 1967-85; legal asst. Lionel, Sawyer & Collins, Reno, 1985-86; assoc. Conner & Steinheimer, Reno, 1987—; adj. faculty U. Nev., Reno; cons. on edn. of at-risk gifted children. Chmn., Task Force for At-Risk Gifted, Reno, 1987-88. Mem. Women Lawyers Assn., Sierra Nev. Mus. Art, Phi Kappa Phi, Delta Theta Phi. Republican. Roman Catholic. Home: 25 Avelina Circle Reno NV 89511

SCHROEDER, JOHN GERARD, lawyer; b. Madison, Wis., Jan. 15, 1950; s. John Peter and Jean (Brucken) S.; m. Silvia Maria Rodriguez, Aug. 11, 1974; 1 child, Michael Albert. BS, Santa Clara U., 1972; JD, Ariz. State U., 1974. Bar: Ariz. 1975, U.S. Dist. Ct. Ariz. 1975, U.S. Supreme Ct. 1981. Assoc. Flaherty & Bennett, San Jose, Calif., 1975-77, Alan L. Nobler, Inc., San Jose, 1977-85; ptnr. Nguyen & Schroeder, San Jose, 1985—; instr. law West Valley Coll., Saratoga, Calif., 1983—; judge pro tem Santa Clara Superior Ct., San Jose, 1985—. Assoc. editor Ariz. State U. Law Jour., 1974. Mem. San Jose Parking Commn., 1983--; v.p. Lions Eye Found., San Francisco, 1986--; pres. Santa Clara Valley Blind Ctr., San Jose, 1987-88. Recipient Doer award San Jose Mercury News, 1985; Helen Keller fellow, Lions Eye Found., 1987. Mem. Santa Clara County Bar Assn. (del. 1985—), Santa Clara Trial Lawyers Assn., Santa Clara Valley Blind Ctr. (life), Lions (Lion of Yr. dist. 4C6 1984, 85). Republican. Roman Catholic. Office: Nguyen & Schroeder 15 N Market St San Jose CA 95113

SCHROEDER, LON MICHAEL, instrument engineer; b. Missoula, Mont., Jan. 21, 1949; s. Cleo Henry and Esther Nadean (Kircheis) S.; m. Laura Lee Willing, Aug. 28, 1971; children: Christopher, Patrick. Student, U. Mont., 1967-70, Bates Tech. Inst., Tacoma, 1972-74, Portland Community Coll., 1977-78. Instrument technologist Boise Cascade Corp., St. Helens, Oreg., 1974-78, instrument supr., 1978-80; instrument engr. Champion Internat. Co., Missoula, 1980-85, asst. supt. power, 1985-88; power and recovery supt. Stone Container Corp., Missoula, 1988—; cons. engr. Western Control Systems,

Missoula, 1983-85. Sgt. USAF, 1971-74. Mem. Instrument Soc. Am. (sr.), TAPPI, Black Liquor Boiler Assn. (adv. instrument chmn. 1987—), Sigma Nu. Office: Stone Container Corp PO Drawer D Missoula MT 59806

SCHROEDER, MARY ESTHER, wood products executive; b. Dayton, Ohio, July 29, 1947; d. James Walter and Mary Agnes (Danzig) McIver; m. Reinhard Schroeder, Sept. 10, 1966 (div. Mar. 1989). BS in Forest Industries Mgmt., Ohio State U., 1978. Fiber supply supr. Crown Zellerbach, Inc., Port Townsend, Wash., 1978-83; fiber supply and transp. mgr. Port Townsend Paper Corp., Bainbridge Island, Wash., 1983-87; dir. Pacific Wood Fuels, Redding, Calif., 1987—; bd. dirs. Peninsula Devel. Assn., Port Angeles, Wash., 1985—. Screenwriter: As the Chips Fall, 1988. Precinct committeeman Kitsap County Reps., Poulsbo, Wash., 1984-86; active Rep. Presdl. Task Force. Mem. Soc. Am. Forestors, Shasta Alliance for Resources and Environment, Am. Pulpwood Assn., Western Timber Assn. Calif., Writers' Forum, Am. Film Inst. Home: 320 Hilltop Dr #216 Redding CA 96003 Office: Pacific Wood Fuel 2659 Balls Ferry Rd Anderson CA 96007

SCHROEDER, MARY MURPHY, judge; b. Boulder, Colo., Dec. 4, 1940; d. Richard and Theresa (Kahn) Murphy; m. Milton R. Schroeder, Oct. 15, 1965; children: Caroline Theresa, Katherine Emily. B.A., Swarthmore Coll., 1962; J.D., U. Chgo., 1965. Bar: Ill. 1966, D.C. 1966, Ariz. 1970. Trial atty. Dept. Justice, Washington, 1965-69; law clk. Hon. Jesse Udall, Ariz. Supreme Ct., 1970; mem. firm Lewis and Roca, Phoenix, 1971-75; judge Ariz. Ct. Appeals, Phoenix, 1975-79, U.S. Ct. Appeals (9th Cir.), Phoenix, 1979—; vis. instr. Ariz. State U. Coll. Law, 1976, 77, 78. Contbr. articles to profl. jours. Mem. Am. Bar Assn., Ariz. Bar Assn., Fed. Bar Assn., Am. Law Inst., Am. Judicature Soc. Democrat. Club: Soroptimists. Office: US Ct Appeals 6421 US Courthouse & Fed Bldg 230 N 1st Ave Phoenix AZ 85025

SCHROEDER, PATRICIA SCOTT (MRS. JAMES WHITE SCHROEDER), congresswoman; b. Portland, Oreg., July 30, 1940; d. Lee Combs and Bernice (Lemoin) Scott; m. James White Schroeder, Aug. 18, 1962; children: Scott William, Jamie Christine. B.A. magna cum laude, U. Minn., 1961; J.D., Harvard U., 1964. Bar: Colo. 1964. Field atty. NLRB, Denver, 1964-66; practiced in Denver, 1966-72; hearing officer Colo. Dept. Personnel, 1971-72; mem. faculty U. Colo., 1969-72, Community Coll., Denver, 1969-70, Regis Coll., Denver, 1970-72; mem. 93d-101st congresses from 1st Colo. dist., 1973—; co-chmn. Congl. Caucus for Women's Issues, 1976—; mem. Ho. of Reps. armed services com., chair subcom. mil. installations and facilities, judiciary com., post office and civil service com.; mem. select com. on children, youth and families. Congregationalist. Office: 2208 Rayburn House Office Bldg Washington DC 20515

SCHROEDER, RITA MOLTHEN, chiropractor; b. Savanna, Ill., Oct. 25, 1922; d. Frank J. and Ruth J. (McKenzie) Molthen; m. Richard H. Schroeder, Apr. 23, 1948 (div.); children—Richard, Andrew, Barbara, Thomas, Paul, Madeline. Student, Chem. Engring., Immaculate Heart Coll., 1940-41, UCLA, 1941, Palmer Sch. of Chiropractic, 1947-49; D. Chiropractic, Cleve. Coll. of Chiropractic, 1961. Engring.-tooling design data coordinator Douglas Aircraft Co., El Segundo, Santa Monica and Long Beach, Calif., 1941-47; pres. Schroeder Chiropractic, Inc., 1982—; dir. Pacific States Chiropractic Coll., 1978-80, pres. 1980-81. Recipient Palmer Coll. Ambassador award, 1973. Parker Chiropractic Research Found. Ambassador award, 1976, Coll. Ambassador award Life West Chiropractic Coll. Mem. Internat. Chiropractic Assn., Calif. Chiropractic Assn., Internat. Chiropractic Assn. Calif., Assn. Am. Chiropractic Coll. Presidents, Council Chiropractic Edn. (Pacific State Coll. rep.). Home: 9870 N Millbrook Ave Fresno CA 93710 Office: Schroeder Chiropractic Inc 2535 N Fresno Ave Fresno CA 93703

SCHROEDER, THEODORE L., software design engineer; b. Dayton, Ohio, Apr. 21, 1958; s. Karl S. Schroeder and Christine C. (Johnson) Dull; m. Dana J. Crowder, Aug. 25, 1981; children: Timothy E., Allison L. BS in Math., Case Western Res. U., 1980, MS in Computer Engring., 1983. Mgr. diagnostics Amdahl Corp., Sunnyvale, Calif., 1980-84; mgr. network architecture Cohesive Network Corp., Los Gatos, Calif., 1984-88; mem. tech. staff Ultra Network Techs., San Jose, Calif., 1988—. Sustaining mem. Calif. Reps., Burbank, Calif., 1986—, sustaining mem. Rep. Nat. Com., 1986—. Smith scholar Case Inst. Tech. Alumni Assn., Cleve., 1976, R.S. Oelman scholar NCR Corp., Dayton, 1976. Republican. Home: 6961 Lenwood Way San Jose CA 95120 Office: Ultra Network Techs 101 Daggett Dr San Jose CA 95134

SCHROEDER, WILLIAM ROBERT, actor, entrepreneur; b. Los Angeles, July 9, 1941; s. Robert Manville and Miriam Ruth (Sloop) S.; m. Marie Paule Fautrel, Sept. 7, 1963. BA, UCLA, 1964; BFA, Art Ctr. Coll. Design, Pasadena, Calif., 1971. Mailman U.S. Post Office, Santa Monica, Calif., 1967-71; art dir., producer N.W. Ayer/West, Los Angeles, 1971-75; pres., gen. mgr. Advt. Ctr., Los Angeles, 1976-77, Alouette Internat., Santa Monica, Calif., 1972—; free-lance woodcarver, Santa Monica, 1981—; free-lance actor, Hollywood, Calif., 1983—; appeared in feature films King of the Streets, 1983, The Forbidden Tome, 1984, The End of Innocense, 1985, Poltergeist II, 1986. Producer TV commercials, 1972-75; author, creator computerized lang. courses Mattel Intellivision, 1980-82. Publicity mgr. Concerned Homeowners of Santa Monica, 1981-82. Recipient 1st Pl. award Belding award for Excellence in Advt., Los Angeles, 1974, Cert. of Merit, Art Dirs. Club Los Angeles, 1972. Mem. Am. Fedn. Radio and TV Artists, Santa Monica C. of C., Mensa (Los Angeles), Combat Pilots Assn., Orange County Squadron, Internat. Plastic Modelers Soc., The Found. Brain Research. Libertarian. Office: Alouette Internat 1626 Montana Ave Santa Monica CA 90403

SCHRUMPF, ROBYN LYNN, dentist; b. San Francisco, July 15, 1959; d. Walter Fred and Donna De Ella (Rogelstad) S. BS, U. Calif., Davis, 1981; DDS, Creighton U., 1985; cert. gen. practice residency, VA Med. Ctr., Palo Alto, Calif., 1986. With dental staff VA Med. Ctr., Palo Alto, 1985-86; with dental staff VA Med. Ctr., Menlo Park, Calif., 1985-86, respite team cons. dentist, 1986; assoc. Milpitas (Calif.) Dental Ctr., 1987—, Sunnyvale (Calif.) Dental Group, 1987—; dentist Macy (Nebr.) Indian Reservation, 1984, Spinal Cord Injury Ctr., Palo Alto, 1985-86, Blind Rehab. Ctr., Palo Alto, 1985-86; instr. preventive dental care Girl Scouts U.S., Sunnyvale, 1987. Regents scholar U. Calif., Davis, 1977-78, Albert Bijou Meml. scholar U. Calif., Davis, 1978-79; Lonney White scholar Creighton U., 1984. Mem. ADA, Am. Soc. Dentistry for Children (pres. Creighton U. chpt. 1982-85, merit award 1985), Calif. Dental Assn., Calif. Soc. Dentistry for Children, Calif. Scholarship Fedn. (pres. 1977), U.S. Gymnastics Fedn., Omicron Kappa Upsilon. Lutheran.

SCHRYVER, BRUCE JOHN, safety engineer; b. Newark, Aug. 14, 1944; s. Francis Henry and Ann Laura (Hart) S.; m. Lorraine Patricia Simodis, Oct. 8, 1966; children: Holly Lynn, Wendy Marie. BA in Occupational Safety and Health, Western States U., 1984. Cert. safety profl.; cert. products safety mgr.; cert. hazard control mgr.; cert. hazardous materials mgr.; cert. healthcare safety profl. Inspector Lansing B. Warner Inc., Chgo., 1968-69; engring. rep. Glens Falls Ins. Co., Newark, 1969; safety dir. Hillside Metal Products, Newark, 1969-70; loss prevention specialist Warner Ins. Group, Chgo., 1970-79, regional loss control mgr., 1979-82, nat. loss control coordinator, 1982-85; mgr., asst. v.p. loss control svcs. Ins. Co. of the West, San Diego, 1985—. Inventor Emergency Light Mount, 1971. Mem. Town of Clay (N.Y.) Pub. Safety Com., 1976-78, Beacon Woods East Homeowners Assn., Hudson, Fla., 1979-85, Meadowridge Homeowners Assn., La Costa, Calif., 1986—; cons. Town of Clay Police Dept., 1975-78. With USCG, 1964-68. Recipient Letter of Appreciation Town of Clay, 1977, Cert. of Appreciation Disabled Am. Vets., 1968. Mem. Am. Soc. Safety Engrs., Soc. Fire Protection Engrs., Nat. Safety Mgmt. Soc., Veterans Safety, Nat. Fire Protection Assn., San Diego Safety Coun. Republican. Roman Catholic. Home: 3047 Camino Limero Carlsbad CA 92009 Office: Ins Co of the West 10140 Campus Point Dr San Diego CA 92121

SCHUBERT, RONALD HAYWARD, aerospace engineer; b. Bklyn., Aug. 25, 1932; s. John and Joan Sarah (Hayward) S.; m. Dorothy May Smith, Mar. 5, 1953 (div. 1961); children: Marcus H., Malcolm F., Ronald J. (dec.), Ann E.; m. Linda Jane van der Ploeg, Mar. 6, 1961 (div. 1988). BA cum laude, Ohio State U., 1956. Assoc. engr. Hughes Aircraft Co., Fullerton, Calif., 1957-61; physicist Nat. Cash Register Co., Dayton, Ohio, 1962-63; sr. research engr. Lockheed Missiles and Space Co., Sunnyvale, Calif., 1963—. Served as sgt. USMC, 1951-54. Recipient Hon. mention Woodrow Wilson Fellowship Com. Mem. Phi Beta Kappa. Democrat. Roman Catholic. Home: 1220-361 Tasman Dr Sunnyvale CA 94089 Office: Lockheed Missiles and Space Co 1111 Lockheed Way Sunnyvale CA 94088

SCHUCKER, LYNN ANN, nurse; b. Mesa, Ariz., Apr. 22, 1958; d. Paul and Barbara Lucille (Galeucia) Pavlovich; m. Douglas William Schucker, June 22, 1985. AA, Mesa Community Coll., 1978; BSN, Ariz. State U., 1980. RN, Ariz. Lab. aide Dowell Labs., Mesa, 1976-78; nursing asst. Scottsdale (Ariz.) Nursing Ctr., 1978; unit sec. Mesa Luth. Hosp., 1978-81, RN-critical care, 1981-82; RN supr. Casa Blanca Westwood Family Practice Clinic, Mesa, 1982—, diabetes educator, 1983—. Mem. Phi Beta Kappa. Republican. Lutheran. Office: Cas Blanca Westwood 443 N Alma School Rd Mesa AZ 85201

SCHUELER, JAMES ROBERT, small business owner, real estate broker; b. Stoughton, Wis., Jan. 21, 1947; s. Robert and Eleanor (Jacobsen) S.; m. Nancy Jay; children: Jessica Cody, Luke. BSBA, U. Wis., Eau Claire, 1970. Lic. real estate broker, Mont. Loan officer Littleton 1st Indsl. Bank, Denver, 1971-73; owner Steamboat Liquor Co., Steamboat Springs, Colo., 1973-74; owner, pres. Rocky Mountain Log Homes, Hamilton, Mont., 1974—; real estate broker, owner Ranch & Land Co., Hamilton, 1976—. Mem. Mont. C. of C., Hamilton C. of C., Nat. Assn. Home Builders (best brochure award 1986), Log Home Council (pres. 1986-87), Ducks Unltd., Elks, Phi Sigma Epsilon. Republican. Lutheran. Office: Rocky Mountain Log Homes 3353 Hwy 93 South Hamilton MT 59840

SCHUESSLER, MARY ANN, executive recruiter; b. Portland, Oreg., June 1, 1936; d. Walter Henry and Ida May (Harzell) Bauer; children: Melinda, Lorri. Degree in mgmt., Harvard U., 1977. With Selma Pressure Treating Co., Calif., 1965—; sec./treas. Selma Leasing Co., 1971-77; pres. Selma Leasing Co., Calif., 1978-85; recruiter exec. ITT Employer Services, West Los Angeles, 1985-86; pres. Drake & Assocs., Beverly Hills, Calif., 1986—; cons. SBA; mem. adv. council to chancellor forest products dept. U. Calif.; mem. adv. council Sch. Bus., Calif. State U., Fresno; del. White House Conf. Small Bus.,; del 1980 White House Conf. om Small Bus. Mem. Town Hall, Los Angeles, 1986, Friends Hollywood Bowl, Los Angeles, 1988. Mem. Am. Wood Preservers Assn., Harvard Bus. Sch. Assn., Better Bus. Bur. (dir.), Fresno County Hist. Soc., DAR, Fresno Geaneal. Soc., Am. His. Soc. Germans from Russia, New Eng. Geaneal. Soc. Methodist. Club: Harvard-Radcliff So. Calif. Office: Drake & Assocs 9454 Wilshire Blvd Ste 650 Beverly Hills CA 90212

SCHUETZ, JOHN MICHAEL, sales executive; b. Chgo., Apr. 16, 1947; s. Henry Allen and Ann Delores (Kunst) S.; m. Jacqueline Claire Furneaux, Apr. 22, 1972; children: Michael Richard, Sean David. BS in Advt., Marquette U., Milw., 1969. Gen. field mgr. Ford Motor Co., San Jose, 1972-85; v.p. we. region IVECO Trucks of N.Am., Huntington Beach, Calif., 1985—; bd. dirs. Forsyte Research Group, Santa Rosa, Calif., 1988—. Ldr. Boy Scouts Am., El Toro, Calif., 1988-89; coach Am. Youth Soccer Orgn., Saddleback Valley, 1988. Lt. USN, 1969-72. Mem. Sun and Sail Club, Phi Theta Psi. Republican. Roman Catholic. Home: 21821 Ticonderoga Ln El Toro CA 92630 Office: IVECO Trucks of N Am 5500 Bolsa Ave #125 Huntington Beach CA 92649

SCHUHMANN, BARBARA LUCILLE, lawyer; b. Louisville, Jan. 26, 1949; d. Joseph Bosler and Dolores (Moellman) S.; m. Robert B. Groseclose, May 26, 1974; 1 child, Jane S. Groseclose. BA, Am. U., 1971; JD, Georgetown U., 1974. Bar: Alaska 1974, D.C. 1975. Staff asst. to Senator Marlow W. Cook U.S. Senate, Washington, 1969-74; researcher Pub. Def. Svc., Washington, 1974; atty., govt. rels. specialist Republic Steel Corp., Washington, 1975; assoc. Staley, DeLisio, Cook & Sherry, Inc., Fairbanks, Alaska, 1976-78, ptnr., 1978—; lectr. U. Alaska, Fairbanks, 1980-82. Mem. Alaska Jud. Coun., 1982-88; chairperson Alaska Women's Commn., Anchorage, 1978-83; alt. del. Rep. Nat. Conv., 1984; bd. dirs. Fairbanks United Way, 1987—. Mem. ABA, LWV, Alaska Bar Assn., Tanana Valley Bar Assn., Washington D.C. Bar Assn., Am. Judicature Soc. (sec.-treas 1988-89, bd. dirs. 1987-88), Fairbanks C. of C. (bd. dirs. 1987—), Am. Trial Lawyers Assn. Home: 520 Marshall Dr Fairbanks AK 99712 Office: Staley DeLisio Cook et al 714 4th Ave Ste 200 Fairbanks AK 99701

SCHULER, MICHAEL HAROLD, professional basketball coach; b. Portsmouth, Ohio, Sept. 22, 1940; s. Boyd and Dorothy (Seagraves) S.; m. Gloria Sissea, July 20, 1963; children: Kimberly Suzanne, Kristin Ann. BS in Edn., Ohio U., 1962. Asst. basketball coach U.S. Mil. Acad., West Point, N.Y., 1965-66, Ohio U., Athens, 1966-69, U. Va., Charlottesville, 1972-77, NBA N.J. Nets, East Rutherford, 1981-83, NBA Milw. Bucks, 1983-86; head basketball coach Va. Mil. Inst., Lexington, 1969-72, Rice U., Houston, 1977-81, NBA Portland (Oreg.) Trail Blazers, 1986-89; asst. coach Golden State Warriors, Oakland, Calif., 1989—. Named NBA Coach of the Year, 1987, Basketball Weekly, 1987, Hoop mag., 1987. Mem. Nat. Basketball Coaches Assn. Office: Golden State Warriors Oakland Coliseum Arena Oakland CA 94621

SCHULHOFER, ERNA KOMPA, art association administrator; b. Essen, Federal Republic of Germany; d. Auguste and Hermine Louisa (Leonhardt) Kompa; m. Sanford Billings Schulhofer, Sept. 21, 1962 (dec. July 1988); 1 child from previous marriage, Margot Spence. Student, Columbia U. Sec. hospitality Friends of U. So. Calif. Sch. of Music; pres. Internat. Com. for L.A. Philharmonic, 1964-66, Valley Com. for L.A. Philharmonic, 1968-71, Palm springs Friends of L.A. Philharmonic, 1972-74, Community Concerts, Palm Springs, Calif., 1981-83, Women's Com. Desert Mus., 1986-88; exec. chmn. Women for the Music Ctr., L.A., 1972-74; chmn. Ernst Krenek Festival Coll. of the Desert, Palm Desert, Calif., 1975; founder, pres. The Muses 100, McCallum Theatre, Palm Desert, 1988, The Patroness Circle of the Muses 100; active fundraising Young Musicians, Music Ctr. Opera Co. and Chorale.

SCHULLER, EDDIE, engineering executive; b. Cluj, Romania, Feb. 11, 1956; came to U.S., 1974; s. Francisco B. and Yolanda B. (Kohn) S. BS in Elec. Engring., U. Ill., Chgo., 1981; MBA, So. Ill. U., 1985; MS in Elec. Engring., Calif. State U., 1989. Engr. Gen. Dynamics, San Diego, 1981-84; v.p. mktg. Hytech Micronics Corp., Encinitas, Calif., 1983-86; mem. tech. staff Interstate Electronics Corp., Anaheim, Calif., 1984-86; sr. engr. Norden Systems, Santa Ana, Calif., 1986-88; pres. Schuller Investment Corp., Anaheim, 1986—. Recipient Service award Evanston (Ill.) Police Dept., 1980. Mem. IEEE, Am. Soc. Mil. Engrs. Jewish. Office: Schuller Investment Co PO Box 9260 Anaheim CA 92812-7260

SCHULLER, GUNTHER ALEXANDER, composer; b. N.Y.C., Nov. 22, 1925; s. Arthur E. and Elsie (Bernartz) S.; m. Marjorie Black, June 8, 1948; children—Edwin Gunther, George Alexander. Student, St. Thomas Choir Sch., N.Y.C.; MusD (hon.), Manhattan Sch. Music, 1987, Northeastern U., 1967, U. Ill., 1968, Colby Coll., 1969, Williams Coll., 1975, Cleve. Inst. Music, 1977, New Eng. Conservatory Music, 1978, Rutgers U., 1980, Manhattan Sch. Music, 1987, Oberlin Coll., 1989. tchr. Manhattan Sch. Music, 1950-63; head composition dept. Tanglewood, 1963-84; pres. New Eng. Conservatory of Music, 1967-77; artistic dir. Berkshire Music Center, Tanglewood, 1969-84, Festival at Sandpoint, 1985—; founder, pres. Margun Music Inc., 1975, GM Recs., 1980. French horn player, Ballet Theatre, then prin. horn player, Cin. Symphony Orch., prin. French horn, Met. Opera Orch., 1945-59, Concerto #1 for Horn, 1945; composer: Quartet for Four Double Basses, 1947, Fantasy for Unaccompanied Cello, 1951, Recitative and Rondo for Violin and Piano, 1953, Music for Violin, Piano and Percussion, 1957, Contours, 1958, Woodwind Quintet, 1958, Seven Studies on Themes of Paul Klee, 1959, Spectra, 1960, Six Renaissance Lyrics, 1962, String Quartet No. 2, 1965, Symphony, 1965, opera The Visitation 1966, opera Fisherman and His Wife, 1970, Capriccio Stravagante, 1972, The Power Within Us, 1972, Tre Invenzioni, 1972, Three Nocturnes, 1973, Four Soundscapes, 1974, Concerto No. 2 for Orch., 1975, Triplum II, 1975, Horn Concerto No. 2, 1976, Violin Concerto, 1976, Diptych for organ, 1976, Sonata Serenata, 1978, Contrabassoon Concerto, 1978, Deaï for 3 orchs., 1978, Trumpet Concerto, 1979, Octet, 1979, Eine Kleine Posaunenmusik, 1980, In Praise of Winds (Symphony for Large Wind Orch.), 1981, Symphony for Organ, 1982, Concerto Quaternio, 1983, Concerto for Bassoon and Orch., 1984, Farbenspiel (Concerto No. 3 for Orch.), 1985, On Light Wings (piano quartet), 1984; author: Horn Technique, 1962, Early Jazz: Its Roots and Development, 1968, Musings: The Musical Worlds of Gunther Schuller, 1985, The Swing Era, 1989; premiere of Symphony for Brass and Percussion, Cin., 1950, Salzburg Festival, 1957, Dramatic Overture, N.Y. Philharm., 1956, String Quartet, Number 1 Contemporary Arts Festival, U. Ill., 1957, String Quartet Number 3, 1986, Concertino for Jazz Quartet and Orch, Balt. Symphony Orch., 1959, Seven Studies on Themes of Paul Klee, Ford Found., commn., Minn. Symphony, 1959, Spectra, N.Y. Philharm. 1960, Music for Brass Quintet, Coolidge Found., Library of Congress, 1961, Concerto No. 1 for Orch, Chgo. Symphony Orch., 1966, Triplum, N.Y. Philharm. commd. Lincoln Center, 1967, Aphorisms for Flute and String Trio commd, Carlton Coll. Centennial, 1967, Eine Kleine Posaunenmusik, 1980, In Praise of Winds, 1983, Concerto Quaternio, 1983, Duologue for Violin and Piano, Library of Congress, 1984, Farbenspiel, 1985, Concerto for Viola and Orch., 1985, String Quartet No. 3, 1986, Chimeric Images, 1988, Concerto for String Quartet and Orchestra, 1988, Concerto for Flute and Orchestra, 1988, On Winged Flight: A Divertimento for Band, 1989, Chamber Concerto, 1989. Recipient Creative Arts award Brandeis U., 1960, Deems Taylor award ASCAP, 1970, Alice M. Ditson Conducting award, 1970, Rodgers and Hammerstein award, 1971, Friedheim award, 1988, William Schuman award Columbia U., 1989; Guggenheim grantee, 1962, 63. Mem. Nat. Inst. Arts and Letters, Am. Acad. Arts and Scis. Address: care Margun Music 167 Dudley Rd Newton Center MA 02159 also: care Festival at Sandpoint Box 695 Sandpoint ID 83864

SCHULLER, ROBERT HAROLD, clergyman, author; b. Alton, Iowa, Sept. 16, 1926; s. Anthony and Jennie (Beltman) S.; m. Arvella DeHaan, June 15, 1950; children: Sheila, Robert, Jeanne, Carol, Gretchen. B.A., Hope Coll., 1947, D.D., 1973; B.D., Western Theol. Sem., 1950; LL.D., Azusa Pacific Coll., 1970, Pepperdine U., 1976; Litt.D., Barrington Coll., 1977. Ordained to ministry Reformed Ch. in Am., 1950; pastor Ivanhoe Ref. Ch., Chgo., 1950-55; founder, sr. pastor Garden Grove (Calif.) Community Ch., 1955—; founder, pres. Hour of Power TV Ministry, Garden Grove, 1970—; founder, dir. Robert H. Schuller Inst. for Successful Ch. Leadership, Garden Grove, 1970—; chmn. nat. religious sponsor program Religion in Am. Life, N.Y.C., 1975—; bd. dirs. Freedom Found. Author: God's Way to the Good Life, 1963, Your Future Is Your Friend, 1964, Move Ahead with Possibility Thinking, 1967, Self Love, the Dynamic Force of Success, 1969, Power Ideas for a Happy Family, 1972, The Greatest Possibility Thinker That Ever Lived, 1973, Turn Your Scars into Stars, 1973, You Can Become the Person You Want To Be, 1973, Your Church Has Real Possibilities, 1974, Love or Loneliness— You Decide, 1974, Positive Prayers for Power-Filled Living, 1976, Keep on Believing, 1976, Reach Out for New Life, 1977, Peace of Mind Through Possibility Thinking, 1977, Turning Your Stress Into Strength, 1978, Daily Power Thoughts, 1978, The Peak to Peek Principle, 1981, Living Positively One Day at a Time, 1981, Self Esteem: The New Reformation, 1982, Tough Times Never Last, But, Tough People Do!, 1983, Tough Minded Faith for Tender hearted People, 1984, The Be-Happy Attitudes, 1985, Be Happy You Are Loved, 1986, Success is Never Ending, Failure is Never Final, 1988; co-author: The Courage of Carol, 1978. Bd. dirs. Religion in Am. Life; pres. bd. dirs. Christian Counseling Service; founder Robert H. Schuller Corr. Center for Possibility Thinkers, 1976. Recipient Disting. Alumnus award Hope Coll., 1970, Prin. award Freedoms Found., 1974; named Headliner of Year in Religion, Orange County, 1977, Clergyman of Year, Religious Heritage Am., 1977. Mem. Religious Guild Architects (hon.), AIA (bd. dirs. 1986—). Club: Rotary. Office: Religion in Am Life 12141 Lewis St Garden Grove CA 92640 *

SCHULTE, HENRY GUSTAVE, college administrator; b. Seattle, Oct. 14, 1920; s. John Henry and Alma (Winter) S.; m. Joan Noel Burton, Aug. 20, 1949; children—Steven Craig, Scott John, Jane Martha. B.A. in Econs. and Bus., U. Wash., 1948. With D.K. MacDonald & Co., Seattle, 1952-67, asst. treas., 1957-60, treas., 1960-67; bus. mgr. legal firm Bogle, Gates, Dobrin, Wakefield & Long, Seattle, 1967; adminstr. Child Devel. and Mental Retardation Ctr. U. Wash., Seattle, 1968-86; mem. steering com. mental retardation research ctrs. group Nat. Inst. Child Health and Human Devel., 1971-85. Mem. exec. bd., treas. Assn. Univ. Affiliated Facilities, 1974-77. Served with AUS, 1940-45. Mem. Soc. Research Adminstrs. (mem. exec. com. 1971-72), Am. Assn. Mental Deficiency. Office: U Wash WJ-10 Seattle WA 98195

SCHULTE, WILLIAM HOBART, III, restaurateur; b. Phoenix, Oct. 4, 1962; s. William Hobart and Carolyn (Dunkin) D. BS in Advt., Ariz. State U., 1984. Pres. Left Field Inc., Pinetop, Ariz., 1984—. Mem. Show Low C. of C. (dir. 1987—), Sports Village. Democrat. Home: PO Box 3372 Show Low AZ 85901 Office: Left Field Inc PO Box 1111 Pinetop AZ 85935

SCHULTZ, DONALD FRANK, insurance agent; b. Dayton, Ohio, Mar. 10, 1932; s. Frank and Gladys Marie (Harnish) S.; m. Ellen Marie Spath, Jan. 10, 1953 (div. May 1982); children: Cynthia A. Schultz Nelson, Donald B., Bryan P., Darrel B. Grad. high sch., Dayton; CLU, Am. Coll., Bryn Mawr, Pa., 1962. Chartered fin. cons., 1983. Agt. State Mut. Cos., Denver, 1953—. Precinct committeeman Rep. Orgn. Denver, 1968, scout leader, 1959-62; pres. PTA, 1964-65; campaign mgr. Nat. Found. March of Dimes. Specialist U.S. Army, 1954-56. Elected to Hall of Ambassadors, State Mut. Cos., 1973. Mem. Denver Assn. Life Underwriters (pres. 1970-71), Colo. Assn. Life Underwriters (pres. 1980-81), Nat. Assn. Life Underwriters, Am. Soc. CLUs and Chartered Fin. Cons., Denver Estate Planning Coun., Million Dollar Round Table, Rocky Mountain Assn. CLUs, Colo. Consistory; Los Verdes Gold, Colo. Golf Club, Masons. Office: State Mut Cos 44 Cook St Denver CO 80206-5898

SCHULTZ, FREYA JEAN, county government official; b. Honolulu, Mar. 18, 1945; d. Robert Martin and Muriel (Swift) S.; m. Joe Compton Luker, March 18, 1974 (div. 1984); 1 child, Jonathan Charles. AB in Anthropology, Stanford U., 1966; postgrad., U. Calif., Berkeley, 1967. Mgmt. analyst USN, San Francisco, 1967-70; personnel analyst USN, Alameda, Calif., 1970-74, Social Security Adminstrn., N.Y.C., 1974-75; coord. for victim/witness services Dist. Atty. Santa Barbara (Calif.) County, 1983-85; affirmative action officer, advisor affirmative action commn. Affirmative Action Commn. County of Santa Barbara, 1985—; advisor Commn. for Women, Santa Barbara, 1985—, Sr. Citizens Adv. Commn., Santa Barbara, 1985-86. Community chmn. and vol. Ark. Bar Auxiliary, Little Rock, 1976-80; vol. community based child care program, Goleta, Calif. and Santa Barbara, 1987—; founding mem. San Francisco bay area chpt. Federally Employed Women, 1973; pluralism com. mem. Tres Condados council Girl Scouts U.S., 1986—; active Victim/Witness Coordinating Council, 1983-85, Ark. Advocates for Children and Families, 1977-78. Scholar Stanford U., 1962-66; NIMH fellow U. Calif., 1966-67. Mem. Calif. Assn. Affirmative Action Officers. Democrat. Home: 5717 Encina Rd #102 Goleta CA 93117 Office: County of Santa Barbara 105 E Anapauiu Santa Barbara CA 93101

SCHULTZ, GARY DAVID, lawyer; b. Long Beach, Calif., May 25, 1953; s. S.L. and Lorraine (Donohue) S.; m. Yvonne Y. Boyer, Sept. 17, 1982; 1 child, Raymond A. BA, Claremont McKenna Coll., 1975, MA, 1977; JD, Am. Coll. Law, 1982. Bar: Mont. 1986. Mgr. corp. real estate STW, Long Beach, 1977-81, asst. v.p. real estate, 1982-85; mng. ptnr. S&K Properties, Long Beach, 1981-82, Schultz-Boyer Properties, Long Beach, 1980—; mgr. real estate aquisitions and leasing UCLA, 1985—. Pres. United Coun. Claremont (Calif.) Colls., 1972-73; legis. intern Calif. State Assembly, Sacramento, 1975; dep. registrar of voters County of L.A., 1971-76; v.p. Town Sq. Homeowners Assn., Santa Ana, Calif., 1986-87. Recipient Voter Registration award, L.A., 1976, Am. Jurisprudence award, 1982. Mem. ABA, Assn. Trial Lawyers Am., Am. Mgmt. Assn.

SCHULTZ, GARY DEAN, health care executive, consultant; b. Bellingham, Wash., July 15, 1945; s. Herbert Phillip and Hazel Mary (Anthony) S.; m. Alice Vineyard, Feb. 1, 1977. BS, Pacific Christian Coll., 1979; MBA, Century U., 1988, PhD, 1989. Chief pulmonary function Meml. Hosp., Redding, Calif., 1971-80; adminstr. Beverly Enterprises, Inc., Tillamook, Oreg., 1980-82; pres. Health Systems Mgmt. & Devel., Inc., San Dimas, Calif., 1982-85; regional dir. ops. Adventist Living Ctrs., Warrenville, Fla., 1985-87; dir.

Schultz Mgmt. & Devel., Cathedral City, Calif., 1987—; cons. in field. Mem. Nat. Coun. on Aging, Calif. Health Care Assn. (v.p. San Gabriel, Calif. chpt. 1985), Oreg. Health Care Assn. (chmn. West region 1980). Republican. Adventist. Home and Office: 67645 Ovante Rd Cathedral City CA 92234

SCHULTZ, GUSTAV HOBART, religious organization administrator; b. Foley, Ala., Sept. 23, 1935; s. Gustav H. and Anna H. (Coaker) Schultz; m. Flora Redd, June 16, 1958; children: Gustav Hobart III, Timothy Martin, Locke Elizabeth, Bettina Pauley. BD, Concordia Sem., 1961; MST, Luth. Sch. Theology, 1977. Pastor Holy Trinity Luth. Ch., Rome, Ga., 1961-65; asst. pastor Ascension Luth. Ch., Riverside, Ill., 1965-69; pastor U. Luth. Chapel, Berkeley, Calif., 1969—; dean of chapel Pacific Luth. Sem., Berkeley, 1977-78; aux. bishop Southwest Province Assn. Evang. Luth. Chs., 1979-87; chmn. Nat. Sanctuary Def. Fund, San Francisco, 1985—, SHARE Found., Washington, 1984—. Commr. City Planning, Berkeley, 1981-83; bd. dirs. Berkeley Emergency Food Project, 1983—, No. Calif. Ecumenical Council, San Francisco, 1984-87. Recipient Annual Berkeley Peace Prize, Warwick and Assocs. and Mayor of Berkeley, 1985. Office: U Luth Chapel 2425 College Ave Berkeley CA 94704

SCHULTZ, HARRIET BAUMGARTEN, landscape company executive; b. N.Y.C., Feb. 11, 1947; d. William and Sonia (Eizenman) Baumgarten; m. Edward J. Schultz, Nov. 30, 1974; children: Jonathan and Johanna. BS, Buffalo State U., 1968. Editorial asst. Harper's Mag., N.Y.C., 1968-70; reporter Time Mag., N.Y.C., 1970-73; pub. info. officer Reg. Med. progs., Oakland, Calif., 1973-75; writer/editor Stanford U. Med. Ctr. News Bur., 1975-77; gen. ptnr. The Silk Peddlers, San Rafael, Calif., 1981—; copy editor Overseas Press Club Awards Pub., N.Y.C., 1970. Editor mag. The Healing Arts, 1975-77. Recipient Award of Merit, Council for Advancement and Support of Edn., 1975, First Place award, Acad. Hosp. Pub. Relations, 1976. Mem. Northbridge Club. Home: 54 Edward Ave San Rafael CA 94903

SCHULTZ, KENNETH A., mayor of Albuquerque; b. Chgo., Oct. 27, 1937; s. William Edward and Marie (Scmitt) Strang S.; m. Diane Jean Capodice, Nov. 11, 1962; children—Kenneth G., Steve H. Student, Gen. Motors Sales Sch., Gen. Motors Fin. and Budget Sch., Gen. Motors Mgmt. Sch.; student, Loyola Acad. Pres., owner Ken Schultz Buick Inc., Kenosha, Wis., 1970-74; pres., owner Ken. Schultz Buick GMC Inc., Albuquerque, 1974-84; mem. city council City of Albuquerque, 1981-85; owner, pres. KSI, 1984—; mayor City of Albuquerque, 1985—. Legis. chmn. N.Mex. Mcpl. League, 1984-85. Served with USMCR, 1960-66. Named Crimestopper of Yr., Albuquerque, 1983. Mem. Nat. League Cities, U.S. Conf. Mayors, Marine Corps League, Navy League, Am. G.I. Forum, Am. Legion. Democrat. Roman Catholic. Lodge: Lions. Office: City of Albuquerque Mayor's Office PO Box 1293 Albuquerque NM 87103

SCHULTZ, LESLIE BROWN, bookkeeper; b. Fresno, Calif., Dec. 9, 1936; d. Albert Brown and Marion Jean (Riese) Brown-Propp; m. Howard R. Schultz, Jan. 20, 1957 (div. 1972); children: Susan, Steven, David, Thomas. BS, U. So. Calif., 1958. Office mgr. pvt. practice physician, Long Beach, Calif., 1971-73; cost acct. Panavision, Inc., Tarzana, Calif., 1974-76; exec. sec. Hartman Galleries, Beverly Hills, Calif., 1976-78; adminstrv. asst. Galanos Originals, L.A., 1978—. Mem. Alpha Epsilon Phi (nat. pres.). Republican. Jewish. Home: 1745 Bentley Ave Los Angeles CA 90025 Office: Galanos Originals 2254 Sepulveda Blvd Los Angeles CA 90064

SCHULTZ, STEVEN MICHAEL, restaurant executive; b. Denver, Feb. 22, 1954; s. Harlen John and Helen Marie (Molinaro) S.; m. Dorothea Boettcher; 1 child, Erika. BSBA, Regis Coll., Denver, 1986. Quality control technician, then quality engr. Sundstrand ATG, Denver, 1972-86; product rep. Proactive Technologies, Inc., Denver, 1986—; importer, exporter Schultz & Assocs., Loveland, Colo., 1984—; restaurant owner Schultz & Assocs., Loveland, 1987—. Illustrator, Job/Task Analysis, 1987, OJT Training Manual, 1987, Audit Manual, 1987. Mem. Loveland C. of C., Better Bus Bur., TEV Edelweis Club. Home: 207 W 4th St Loveland CO 80537 Office: Schultz & Assocs 205 W 4th St Loveland CO 80537

SCHULTZ, VICKI PAULA, financial advisor; b. Phila., Nov. 5, 1944; d. Nathan and Etta (Strongin) Blank; m. Harvey E. Levitt, Dec. 10, 1966 (div. 1985); children: Ilyse Stacey, Lori Michelle; m. Russell Corey Schultz, Dec. 29, 1985; 1 child, Nicole Stephanie. BS summa cum laude, Temple U., 1966; MBA, Calif. State U., Long Beach, 1983. Cert. fin. planner. Elem. tchr. Pennsauken (N.J.) Sch. Dist., 1966-67, Keystone Oaks Sch. Dist., Pitts., 1967-68, Bensalem Twp. Sch. Dist., Cornwells Heights, Pa., 1968-72; fin. advisor Schultz & Schultz, Inc., Laguna Niguel, Calif., 1983—. Mem. Nat. Assn. Personal Fin. Advisors, Beta Gamma Sigma. Office: Schultz & Schultz Inc 23942 Ibis Ct Laguna Niguel CA 92677

SCHULTZE, ERNST EUGENE, marketing communications executive; b. Columbia, Mo., Jan. 20, 1944; s. Andrew Byron and Jeanne V. (Homsley) S.; m. Marlene Diane Finke, June 7, 1964 (div. 1981); 1 child: Nicole Joanna Dove. BA, Nebr. Wesleyan U., 1968; MBA, San Diego State U., 1975. Mktg. coord. Ektelon Corp., San Diego, 1976-79, ops. project mgr., 1979-80; exec. v.p. Mktg. Group, San Diego, 1980-83; v.p. Jack Lewis Agy., San Diego, 1983-84; mktg. strategist Gable Agy., San Diego, 1984-85; pres. Schultze & Wilson, San Diego, 1985—; pres. Nat. Mgmt. Assn., 1979; mktg. com. Gaslamp Quarter Coun., San Diego, 1988-89. Contbr. articles to profl. jours. Counsel Schulze City Coun. campaign, San Diego, 1975, Killea City Coun. campaign, San Diego, 1981. Named Big Hitter in Bus. City San Diego. Mem. Am. Mktg. Assn., Nat. Mktg. Assn. (pres. 1979). Republican. Office: Schultze & Wilson 1446 Front St San Diego CA 92101

SCHULZ, CAROL ANNE, college administrator; b. San Jose, Calif., Sept. 25, 1960; d. John Peter and Alice Anne (Sutton) Giammona; m. Kenneth P. Schulz, June 17, 1984. BA magna cum laude, Santa Clara U., 1982; student, Santa Clara U. Grad. Sch. Bus., 1987—. Devel. asst. Santa Clara U., Calif., 1983, dir. devel. research, 1983-85; dir. devel. info. services Menlo Sch. & Coll., Atherton, Calif., 1985—. Com. mem. Beacon Shores Homeowners Assn., Redwood Shores, Calif., 1987. Mem. Council for Advancement and Support of Edn., Phi Beta Kappa, Phi Sigma Iota. Republican. Home: 723 Newport Circle Redwood Shores CA 94065 Office: Menlo Sch & Coll 1000 El Camino Real Atherton CA 94025

SCHULZ, JOHN CHRISTIAN, aerospace company executive; b. Bklyn., July 12, 1936; s. John Valentin and Betty (Dauelsberg) S.; m. Patricia Joan Hurlburt, Feb. 26, 1961 (div. 1973); children: Alison Melinda, Christian Eric; m. Kathleen Margaret Brower, Aug. 16, 1986; 1 child, Amanda Karla. ME, Rensselaer Poly. Inst., 1958. Registered profl. engr., Calif. Dir. quality control Bourns, Inc., Riverside, Calif., 1962-68; mgr. purchasing quality, quality engring. and control Gen. Dynamics Co., Pomona, Calif., 1969-80; mgr. quality assurance services Ford Aerospace Co., Newport Beach, Calif., 1981--. Contbr. articles to profl. publs. Lt. USN, 1958-62. Mem. ASME, Am. Soc. Quality Control (sr. sect. chmn.), Measurement Sci. Conf. (chmn. bd. dirs. 1988--), Nat. Mgmt. Assn. (cert. mgr.). Republican. Home: 4492 11th St Riverside CA 92501 Office: Ford Aerospace Co 1000 Ford Rd Newport Beach CA 92660

SCHULZ, RAINER WALTER, computer company executive; b. Berlin, Jan. 29, 1942; s. Horst and Marta S.; came to U.S., 1959, naturalized, 1964; B.A. summa cum laude in Math., San Jose State U., 1964; children—Heidi, Kenneth, Kirsten. System devel. asso. IBM, San Jose, Calif., 1964-65, SDS, Santa Monica, Calif., 1965-67, U. Calif., Berkeley, 1967-70; system mgmt. asso. Stanford (Calif.) U., 1970-77; v.p. Computer Curriculum Corp., Palo Alto, Calif., 1973-81, dir., sec., 1978-81; mgr. Tandem Computers Inc., Cupertino, Calif., 1981-83; v.p. computing and info. systems Teknowledge, Palo Alto, 1983-88; pres. Modernsoft Inc., Palo Alto, Calif., 1989—; cons. NSF., 1974-77. Mem. Am. Electronics Assn., Conf. Bd. Republican. Lutheran. Home: PO Box 50243 Palo Alto CA 94303 Office: Modernsoft Inc 260 Sheridan Ave #210 Palo Alto CA 94306

SCHUMACHER, WELDON DAVID, physician; b. Tacoma, Wash., Jan. 4, 1936; s. Alden B. and Marie Kathryn (Harm) S.; m. Bonnie Joan Skinner, Aug. 15, 1957; 1 child, Cindy Lou. A in Liberal Arts, Loma Linda U., 1958, D in Medicine, 1962. Diplomate Am. Bd. Family Practice. Gen. rotating intern Glendale (Calif.) Adventist Hosp., 19962-63, resident in gen. surgery, 1963-64; chmn. bd. Lodi (Calif.) Community Hosp., 1978-79, chief of staff, 1980-87; bd. dirs. Dr.'s Hosp. Lodi, 1988—; bd. dirs. Bank of Lodi, chmn. audit com. Mosby scholar, 1960. Mem. Lodi C. of C., San Joaquin County Med. Soc., Calif. Med. Soc., Am. Med. Soc., Loma Linda U. Sch. Medicine Alumni Assn. (bd. dirs. 1989), Alpha Omega Alpha, Exec. Club (pres. 1980). Republican. Home: 1303 Rivergate Dr Lodi CA 95240 Office: 1240 W Vine St Lodi CA 95240

SCHUMANN, JOHN WILLIAM, engineering consultant; b. Plainfield, N.J., July 20, 1942; s. William Henry and Frances Kaley (Durham) S.; m. June Junko Arima, Aug. 20, 1966. BA in Bus. Adminstrn., Ottawa (Kans.) U., 1964; MS in Civil Engring., Drexel U., 1972. With Humble Oil & Refining Co., Bala Cynwyd, Pa., 1965-70; project engr. Louis T. Klauder & Assocs., Phila., 1971-79; sr. planner Sacramento (Calif.) Regional Transit Dist., 1979-81; exec. dir. Sacramento Transit Devel. Agy., 1981-84; sr. engr. LTK Engring. Svcs., Portland, Oreg., 1985—; mem. Transp. Rsch. Bd., Washington, 1980—; cons. in field. Contbr. articles to profl. jours. With USAR, 1965-72. Mem. Am. Soc. Civil Engrs., Inst. Transp. Engrs. Democrat. Home: 3025 NE 34th Ave Portland OR 97212 Office: LTK Engring Svcs Norton House 33 NW 1st Ave Portland OR 97209

SCHURLE, ROBERT RAY, small business owner; b. Manhattan, Kans., Nov. 25, 1936; s. George Ervin and Fannie Mille (Schwab) S.; m. Shirley Ann Regier, Feb. 24, 1957 (div. May, 1980); children: Steven, Ruth, Mark, Timothy, Rebecca, Deborah, Matthew. Grad. high sch., Keats, Kans. Certified plumber. Laborer, helper Beck & Hahn Plumbing, Van Nuys, Calif., 1957-59; counterman, estimator West Valley Plumbers of Woodland Hills, Calif., 1959-66; owner, pres. Pipe Plumbing Contractors of the Valley, Inc., Canoga Park, Calif., 1966—. Republican. Baptist. Home: 22201 Roscoe Blvd West Hills CA 91304 Office: Pipe Plumbing Contractors 8757 Canoga Ave Canoga Park CA 91304

SCHUSTER, ANN SHEARER, insurance executive; b. Spokane, Wash., Nov. 4, 1940; d. Earl Phillip and Lallie Virginia (Newsom) Shearer; m. Paul Hubert Watt, 1960 (div. 1963); children: Cindy Ann, Tamera Paulene; m. Theodore Douglas Schuster, Jan. 16, 1969; 1 child, Suzanne Renae'. BS, Whitworth Coll., Spokane, 1971. With Safeway, Spokane, 1961-69; loss adjuster and trainer Fed. Govt., Spokane, 1979-85; crop ins. agt. LongView Crop Ins. Agy., Greeley, Colo., 1986—. Address: The Crop Insurance Center Route 2 Box 47 Saint John WA 99171

SCHUSTER, PHILIP FREDERICK, II, lawyer; b. Denver, Aug. 26, 1945; s. Philip Frederick and Ruth Elizabeth (Robar) S.; m. Barbara Lynn Nordquist, June 7, 1975; children: Philip Christian, Matthew Dale. BA, U. Wash., 1967; JD, Willamette U., 1972. Bar: Oreg. 1972, U.S. Dist. Ct. Oreg. 1974, U.S. Ct. Appeals (9th cir.) 1986, U.S. Supreme Ct. 1986. Dep. dist. atty. Multnomah County, Portland, Oreg., 1972; title examiner Pioneer Nat. Title Co., Portland, 1973-74; assoc. Buss, Leichner et al, Portland, 1975-76; from assoc. to ptnr. Kitson & Bond, Portland, 1976-77; pvt. practice Portland, 1977—; arbitrator Multnomah County Arbitration Program, 1985—. Contbr. articles to profl. jours. Organizer Legal Aid Svcs. for Community Clinics, Salem, Oreg. and Seattle, 1969-73; Dem. committeeman, Seattle, 1965-70. Mem. ABA, NAACP (exec. bd. 1979—), ACLU, Sertoma. Office: 1500 NE Irving Ste 540 Portland OR 97232

SCHUSTER, ROBERT CONRAD, state official; b. St. John, Wash., July 17, 1935; s. Robert Charles and Alma Lydia (Schierman) S.; m. Marcia Sue Delaplain, Oct. 1, 1960; children: Robert Calvin, Douglas Westfield, Scott Alan. BSCE, Wash. State U., 1957. Registered profl. engr., Wash. Various positions Wash. State Dept. Transp., Seattle, 1958-67; dist. reconaissance engr. Wash. State Dept. Transp., Yakima, 1967-70, dist. location engr., 1970-75, dist. adminstr., 1975-85; asst. sec. hwys. Wash. State Dept. Transp., Olympia, 1985—; Mem. Wash. Road Jurisdiction Com., 1985—, Wash. Transp. Improvement Bd., 1988—. Recipient Silver Beaver award Boy Scouts Am., 1984. Fellow ASCE. Methodist. Office: Wash State Dept Transp Transp Bldg KF-01 Olympia WA 98504

SCHUSTER, ROBERT PARKS, lawyer; b. St. Louis, Oct. 25, 1945; s. William Thomas Schuster and Carolyn Cornforth (Daugherty) Hathaway; 1 child, Susan Michele. A.B., Yale U., 1967; J.D. with honors, U. of Wyo., 1970; LL.M., Harvard U., 1971. Bar: Wyo. 1971, U.S. Ct. Appeals (10th cir.) 1979, U.S. Supreme Ct. 1984. Dep. county atty. County of Natrona, Casper, Wyo., 1971-73; sole practice, Casper, 1973-76; assoc. Spence & Moriarity, Casper, 1976-78; ptnr. Spence, Moriarity & Schuster, Jackson, Wyo., 1978—. Trustee U. Wyo., 1985-89; polit. columnist Casper Star Tribune, 1987—. Ford Found. Urban Law fellow, 1970-71; pres. United Way of Natrona County, 1974; bd. dirs. Dancers Workshop, 1981-83. Mem. ABA, Assn. Trial Lawyers Am., Nat. Assn. of Criminal Defense Lawyers. Wyo. Trial Lawyers Assn. Home: PO Box 548 Jackson WY 83001 Office: Spence Moriarity & Schuster 265 W Pearl Jackson WY 83001

SCHUTZ, ARTHUR HENRY, JR., dentist; b. Fullerton, Calif., May 19, 1958; s. Arthur Henry and Marian Louise (Ament) S.; m. Valerie Jeanne Stedman, Aug. 20, 1983. BS, U. Calif., Davis, 1980; DDS, U. Calif., San Francisco, 1985. Resident in gen. practice VA Hosp., Long Beach, Calif., 1985-86; gen. practice dentistry Fullerton, 1986—. Mem. ADA, Calif. Dental Assn., Orange County Dental Soc., Acad. Gen. Dentistry, Fullerton C. of C. Republican. Lutheran. Office: 1723 N Euclid St Fullerton CA 92635

SCHUTZ, JOHN ADOLPH, university dean, historian; b. Los Angeles, Apr. 10, 1919; s. Adolph J. and Augusta K. (Glueker) S. A.A., Bakersfield Coll., 1940; B.A., UCLA, 1942, M.A., 1943, Ph.D., 1945. Asst. prof. history Calif. Inst. Tech., Pasadena, 1945-53; assoc. prof. history Whittier (Calif.) Coll., 1953-56, prof., 1956-65; prof. Am. history U. So. Calif., Los Angeles, 1965—; chmn. dept. history U. So. Calif., 1974-76, dean social scis. and communication, 1976-82. Author: William Shirley: King's Governor of Massachusetts, 1961, Peter Oliver's Origin and Progress of the American Rebellion, 1967, The Promise of America, 1970, The American Republic, 1978, Dawning of America, 1981, Spur of Fame: Dialogues of John Adams and Benjamin Rush, 1980; editor: Boston's First City Directory 1789, 1989; joint editor: Golden State Series; contbg. author: Spain's Colonial Outpost, 1985, Generations and Change: Genealogical Perspectives in Social History, 1986, Making of America: Society and Culture of the United States, 1987. Trustee Citizens Research Found., 1985—. NEH grantee, 1971; Sr. Faculty grantee, 1971-74. Mem. Am. Hist. Assn. (pres. Pacific Coast br. 1972-73), Am. Studies Assn. (pres. 1974-75), Mass. Hist. Soc. (corr.), New. Eng. Hist. Geneal. Soc. (trustee 1988—, editor, author intro. book Boston Merchant Census of 1789, 1989), Colonial Soc. Mass. (corr.). Home: 1100 White Knoll Los Angeles CA 90012 Office: U So Calif Los Angeles CA 90089-0034

SCHWAB, ALICE MAE GWILLIAM, nursing educator; b. Park City, Utah, Feb. 10, 1938; d. James Llewellyn and Alice (Lefler) Gwilliam; diploma L.A. County (Calif. Gen. Hosp. Sch. Nursing, 1959; BA, U. Redlands, 1975, MA, 1978; m. Harry Loren Holbrook, Aug. 19, 1960 (dec.); children: Jimmy Edward, William Loren, Mary Alice, Daniel Raymond; m. Donald E. Schwab, June 1988. Nurse, VA Hosp., Long Beach, Calif., 1959-61; supervising nurse U. Calif., Irvine Med. Ctr., 1964-74; patient care coord. Fountain Valley (Calif.) Community Hosp., 1975-78; supervising nurse Hoag Meml. Hosp., Newport Beach, Calif., 1978-79; dir. nursing svc. Los Banos (Calif.) Community Hosp., 1979-81, ; dir. nursing Sonoma Valley Dist. Hosp., 1981-83; nursing edn. Rancho Arroyo Vocat. Tech. Inst., Sacramento, 1985-88; instr. North Orange County Community Coll. Dist., 1976-79, Merced Community Coll.; cons. human resources devel. and personal growth, 1988—. Mem. Dirs. Nursing Council, AAUW. Mormon. Home: 620 Jones Way Sacramento CA 95818

SCHWAB, CHARLES R., discount broker. m. Helen O'Neill; 5 children from previous marriage. Grad., Stanford Bus. Sch., Stanford U. Formerly mut. fund mgr. Marin County, Calif.; founder brokerage San Francisco, 1971; now chmn. Charles Schwab & Co., Inc. Author: How to be Your Own Stockbroker, 1984. Republican. Office: Charles Schwab & Co Inc 101 Montgomery St 28th Floor San Francisco CA 94104 *

SCHWABAUER, MARIAN DRAKE, graphics director; b. Lewiston, Maine, July 14, 1956; d. Francis William and Doris Constance (Cloutier) Drake; m. Kurt Frederick Schwabauer, May 8, 1982. Student, U. Idaho, Moscow, 1976, U. Mont., Missoula, 1977; BS, U. So. Maine, 1979; MBA, U. Phoenix, 1987. Sec. gym U. So. Maine, Gorham, 1974-79; instr. fitness Elaine Powers, South Portland, Maine, 1979; sales cons. Packaging Corp. Am., Denver, 1979, graphic artist, 1980-84, dir. art, 1985—. Vol. naturalist Jefferson County Open Space, Golden, 1987-88. Mem. Mountain Area Women's Forum (pres. 1988—). Republican. Roman Catholic. Office: Packaging Corp Am 1377 S Jason Denver CO 80223

SCHWABE, CALVIN WALTER, educator, veterinarian, medical historian; b. Newark, Mar. 15, 1927; s. Calvin Walter and Marie Catherine (Hassfeld) S.; m. Gwendolyn Joyce Thompson, June 7, 1951; children: Catherine Marie, Christopher Lawrence. B.S., Va. Poly. Inst., 1948; M.S., U. Hawaii, 1950; D.V.M., Auburn U., 1954; M.P.H., Harvard U., 1955, Sc.D., 1956. From assoc. prof. to prof. parasitology and epidemiology, chmn. dept. tropical health, and asst. dir. Sch. Pub. Health, Am. U. Beirut, 1956-66; mem. Secretariat of WHO, Geneva, 1964-66; prof. epidemiology Sch. Vet. Medicine, also Sch. Medicine, U. Calif., 1966—, chmn. dept. epidemiology and preventive medicine, 1966-70; assoc. dean Sch. Vet. Medicine, U. Calif. at Davis, 1970-71, adj. prof. Agrl. History Ctr., 1984—; cons. WHO, UN Environ. Program, FAO, NIH, Pan Am. Health Orgn., Nat. Rsch. Coun.; univ. lectr. U. Sask.; Fulbright fellow Univ. Coll. E. Africa, Cambridge (Eng.) U., U. Khartoum; Srinivasan Meml. lectr. U. Madras; Spink lectr. comparative medicine U. Minn.; Franklin lectr. scis. and humanities Auburn U.; Entwhistle lectr. Cambridge U.; Schofield lectr. U. Guelph. Author: Veterinary Medicine and Human Health, 1969, 84, What Should a Veterinarian Do?, 1972, Epidemiology in Veterinary Practice, 1977, Cattle, Priests and Progress in Medicine, 1978, Unmentionable Cuisine, 1980; also articles. Fellow Am. Pub. Health Assn.; mem. AVMA, Am. Soc. Tropical Medicine and Hygiene. Democrat. Mem. Soc. of Friends. Home: 849 A St Davis CA 95616

SCHWABE, PETER ALEXANDER, JR., judge; b. Portland, Oreg., July 23, 1935; s. Peter Alexander and Evelyn (Zingleman) S.; A.B., Stanford, 1958; J.D., Willamette U., 1960; m. Bonnie Jean LeBaron, June 21, 1958; children—Mark, Karen, Diane, Patricia, Kurt. Admitted to Oreg. bar, 1960; pvt. practice, Portland, 1960-76; fed. adminstrv. law judge, 1976—. Del. nat. policy council Office of Hearings and Appeals, Social Security Adminstrn., Dept. Health and Human Services, 1980—. Mem. ABA, Oreg. State Bar Assn., Beta Theta Pi, Phi Delta Phi. Home: 4366 Dorking Ct Sacramento CA 95864 Office: 2031 Howe Ave Sacramento CA 95825

SCHWANINGER, THOMAS TYLER, infosystems specialist; b. Easton, Md., July 8, 1957; s. Eugene Spedden and Anna May (Jones) S. BS in Computer Sci., Purdue U., Lafayette, Ind., 1979; MBA, Stanford U., 1983. Systems engr. IBM, Kalamazoo, 1979-83; cons. infosystems The Index Group, Los Angeles, 1983-84; asst. v.p. First Interstate Services Co., Los Angeles, 1984-87; dir. infosystems The Bekins co., Glendale, Calif., 1987--; cons. infosystems The Chesapeake Group, Los Angeles, 1986--. Mem. Internat. Assn. Fin. Planners, Assn. Computing Machinery, Omicron Delta. Home: 7520 Lolina Ln Los Angeles CA 90046

SCHWARTZ, DAVID WAYNE, physician; b. Chgo., Oct. 17, 1944; s. Joseph Robert and Marta Henrietta (Somlo) S.; m. Elizabeth Marion Dinielli, Nov. 30, 1980; children: Liz, Carie, Debbie. BS in Engring., Calif. Tech., 1966; MD, UCLA, 1970. Diplomate Am. Bd. Emergency Medicine, Am. Bd. Family Practice. Intern Cedars-Sinai Med. Ctr., L.A., 1970-71, resident, 1971-72; family practice specialist 1972-82, emergency medicine specialist, 1982—. Capt. USAR, 1970-77. Fellow Am. Acad. Family Physicians; mem. Am. Coll. Emergency Physicians. Republican. Jewish. Home: 50300 Highway 245 Badger CA 93603 Office: Fischer Mangold Med Group 24 Happy Valley Rd PO Box 788 Pleasanton CA 94566

SCHWARTZ, FRANK EDWIN, ophthalmologist; b. Beaver, Pa., Mar. 26, 1919; s. Frank Rambo and Ella Leona (Mackall) S.; m. Betty Jean Carney, July 28, 1944 (div. 1957): children: Michael and Laurie; m. Betty Margaret Melvin, May 20, 1957; children: Jo-Hanna, Heidi Lyn. BS, U. Pitts., 1943, MD, 1943. Diplomate Am. Bd. Ophthalmologist. Ophthalmologist, Millbrae, Calif., 1954-57, Lancaster, Calif., 1958-77, Newport, Oreg., 1978—. Maj. U.S. Army, 1950-53, Korea. Decorated Purple Heart, Bronze Star. Fellow Am. Coll. Surgery, Am. Acad. Ophthalmology; mem. AMA, Oreg. Med. Assn. Republican. Presbyterian. Home: 3187 Yasek Loop Toledo OR 97391 Office: 775 SW 9th St Ste F Newport OR 97365

SCHWARTZ, JOHN CHARLES, chemical engineer; b. Seattle, Apr. 30, 1939; s. Charles and Elizabeth Mercy (Dougherty) S.; m. Sandra Helene Waroff, Aug. 20, 1960 (div. Sept. 1982); children: Barry, Allan, Craig. BS in Chemistry, U. Okla., 1960; MS in Chemistry, Rutgers U., 1968. Research chemist FMC Corp., Carteret and Princeton, N.J., 1962-74; sr. process engr. FMC Corp., Green River, Wyo., 1974—; lab. stockroom operator U. Okla., Norman, 1956-60. Contbr. articles to prof. jours.; patentee in field. Founder Cong. Beth Israel of Sweetwater County, Wyo; active New Jewish Agenda; sec. Wyo. chpt. Nat. Alliance for Mentally Ill, pres. Sweetwater County, Wyo. chpt. Capt. Chem. Corps., U.S. Army, 1960-66. Mem. VFW, Am. Legion, Am. Chem. Soc. (pres. U. Okla. chpt. 1957), Nat. Mental Health Consumer's Assn., Alpha Epsilon Pi, Alpha Chi Sigma, Phi Lambda Upsilon, Phi Eta Sigma. Democrat. Jewish. Lodge: Eagles. Home: PO Box 648 Green River WY 82935 Office: FMC Wyo Corp PO Box 872 Green River WY 82935

SCHWARTZ, MARK BRUCE, construction executive; b. Forest Hills, N.Y., May 1, 1945; s. Stanley and Lenore (Cooper) S. V.p. mktg. Selection Imports, N.Y.C., 1970-73; v.p. mfg. So. Am. Mktg. Exchange, N.Y.C., 1974-77; carpenter T.B.C. Constrn., 1977-81; pres. Skyline Constrn. Mgmt., Inc. and D.B.A. Ezra Constrn., Franktown, Colo., 1982—. Counselor N.Y.C. Drug Rehab. Clinic, 1979. Sgt. USAF, 1966-70. Mem. Nat. Assn. Home Builders, Home Builders Assn. Met. Denver. Office: Ezra Constrn PO Box 384 Franktown CO 80116

SCHWARTZ, MARSHALL ZANE, pediatric surgeon; b. Mpls., Sept. 1, 1945; s. Sidney Shay and Peggy Belle (Lieberman) S.; m. Michele Carroll Walker, Oct. 16, 1971; children: Lisa, Jeffrey. BS, U. Minn., 1968, MD, 1970. Diplomate Am. Bd. Surgery, Am. Bd. Pediatric Surgery,. Instr. Med. Sch. Harvard U., Boston, 1978-79; asst. in surgery Childrens Hosp. Med. Ctr., Boston, 1978-79; asst. prof. Med. Br. U. Tex., Galveston, 1979-81, assoc. prof. Med. Br., 1981-83, chief. pediatric surgery Med. Br., 1980-83; assoc. prof. U. Calif., Davis, 1983-86, prof., 1986—, chief pediatric surgery, 1983—, chmn. helicopter svcs., programmatic subcom., 1984-86. Editor Pediatric Surgery, 1985. Recipient Basil O'Connor Rsch. award March of Dimes Found., 1981, Young Investigator award NIH, 1982, Found. for Children Rsch. award, 1982, James W. McLaughlin award U. Tex., 1983. Fellow ACS; mem. Soc. Univ. Surgeon, Am. Pediatric Surg. Assn., Soc. Surgery of the Alimentary Tract, Sigma Xi. Jewish. Office: U Calif Davis Med Ctr Dept Surgery 4301 X St Rm 2310 Sacramento CA 95817

SCHWARTZ, MILTON LEWIS, federal judge; b. Oakland, Calif., Jan. 20, 1920; s. Colman and Selma (Lavenson) S.; m. Barbara Ann Moore, May 15, 1942; children: Dirk L., Tracy Ann, Damon M., Brooke. A.B., U. Calif. at Berkeley, 1941, J.D., 1948. Bar: Calif. bar 1949. Research asst. 3d Dist. Ct. Appeal, Sacramento, 1948; dep. dist. atty. 1949-51; practice in Sacramento, 1951-79; partner McDonough, Holland, Schwartz & Allen, 1953-79; U.S. dist. judge Eastern Dist. Calif., 1979—; prof. law McGeorge Coll. Law, Sacramento, 1952-55; Mem. Com. Bar Examiners Calif., 1971-75. Pres. Bd. Edn. Sacramento City Sch. Dist., 1961; v.p. Calif. Bd. Edn., 1967-68; Trustee Sutterville Heights Sch. Dist. Served to maj. 40th Inf. Div. AUS, 1942-46, PTO. Fellow Am. Coll. Trial Lawyers; mem. State Bar Calif., Am. Bar Assn., Am. Bd. Trial Advocates. Office: US Dist Ct 2504 US Courthouse 650 Capitol Mall Sacramento CA 95814

SCHWARTZ, RICHARD ALAN, franchise owner, lawyer; b. Bklyn., Dec. 8, 1943; s. Maurice B. and Joan Rose (Chasen) S.; children: Amy Leigh, Julie Marie. BS, U. Fla., 1965; JD, U. Miami, 1971. Bar: Fla. 1971, Oreg. 1984. Pvt. practice Cutler Ridge, Fla., 1971-77; county ct. judge State of Fla.,

Miami, 1977-82; Burger King franchise owner R&S Mgmt., Inc., Hillsboro, Oreg., 1982—; pres. Northwest Burger King Franchise Assn., Hillsboro, Oreg., 1987-89. Author: Florida D.U.I. and Traffic Manual, 1980. With USN, 1965-67. Named Cornelius Man of Yr., Cornelius C. of C., Oreg., 1985. Mem. Oreg. Bar Assn., Fla. Bar Assn., South Dade Bar Assn. (pres. 1975), South Dade C. of C. (dir. 1974-76), Civitan Club (pres. 1975). Office: R&S Mgmt Inc 410 SE Baseline Hillsboro OR 97123

SCHWARY, RICHARD JOSEPH, investment company executive; b. L.A., Dec. 7, 1944; s. Joseph Louis and Mary (Koury) S.; m. Rose Ann Martin, June 10, 1978; children: Kristen Rose, Brandon Richard. BS, Calif. State U., Long Beach, 1973. With. Hughes Aircraft, El Segundo, Calif., 1973-76; v.p. JCI Inc., Ingelwood, Calif., 1976-80; pres. Calif. Numis. Investments, Inc., Redondo Beach, Calif., 1980—; chmn. bd. Am. Numis. Exch., Newport Beach, Calif., 1988—; expert witness FTC, FBI, L.A., 1988—. Contbg. author United States Pattern: Experimental and Trial Pieces, 7th edit., 1982; contbr. articles to trade publs. With USAF, 1965-69. Mem. Profl. Numismatists Guild, Calif. Coin and Precious Metals Assn. (v.p. 1987—). Republican. Roman Catholic. Office: Calif Numis Investments Inc 1712 S Pacific Coast Hwy Redondo Beach CA 90277

SCHWARZ, GERARD RALPH, conductor, musician; b. Weehawken, N.J., Aug. 19, 1947; s. John and Gerta (Weiss) S.; B.S., Juilliard Sch., 1972; D.M.A. (hon.) m. Jody Greitzer, June 23, 1984; children—Alysandra, Daniel. Trumpet player Am. Symphony Orch., 1965-72, Am. Brass Quintet, 1965-73, N.Y. Philharm., 1973-77; trumpet player, guest condr. Aspen Music Festival, 1969-75, bd. dirs., 1973-75; music dir. Erick Hawkins Dance Co., 1967-72, SoHo Ensemble, 1969-75, Eliot Feld Ballet Co.; music dir., condr. N.Y. Chamber Symphony, 1977—, Los Angeles Chamber Orch., 1978-86, White Mountains (N.H.) Music Festival, 1978-80, Music Today, 1981—, Mostly Mozart Festival, Lincoln Ctr., 1982—; music dir., prin. condr. Waterloo Festival, 1975—, Music Sch. Princeton U.; music dir. Seattle Symphony, 1983—; mem. faculty Juilliard Sch., 1975-83, Mannes Coll. Music, 1973-79, Montclair State Coll., 1975-80; rec. artist Columbia, Nonesuch, Vox, MMO, Desto, Angel, Delos records; guest condr. various orchs. including St. Louis, Buffalo, Detroit, San Francisco, Atlanta, Houston, Pitts., Minn. Sommerfest, Indpls., Kansas City, Syracuse, N.Y., Louisville, Cin. Great Woods Festival, Vancouver, St. Paul Chamber Orch., Nat. Arts Centre Orch., Ottawa, Hong Kong Philharm., Jerusalem Symphony, Israel Chamber Orch., Helsinki Philharm., Ensemble InterContemporain, Monte Carlo Philharm., Nat. Orch. Spain, English Chamber Orch., London Symphony, Scottish Chamber Orch., City of Birmingham Symphony, Orchestre National Paris, Nouvel Orchestre Philharmonique, Sydney Symphony, Melbourne Symphony, Orchestre National de Lyon, France, Orchestre Philharm. de Montpellier, Wash. Opera, Da Capo Chamber Players, 20th Century Chamber Orch., Montclair State Coll., Chamber Music Soc. Lincoln Ctr., Seattle Opera, Orchestre Nationale de France. Bd. dirs. Naumburg Found., 1975—. Recipient award for concert artists Ford Found., 1973; Record of Year award for cornet favorites Stereo Rev., 1975, Recording of Distinction award Ovation; Grammy award nominee; Asso. Music Publishers, 1975—. *

SCHWARZ, JIM WOLFRAM, irrigation executive, consultant; b. Schramberg, West Germany, May 25, 1942; came to U.S., 1965; s. Ludwig M. and Anna (Mueller) S.; m. Jackie L. Dial, Jan. 18, 1977 (div. 1982); m. Bonita Kay Baker, June 18, 1989. Cert. retail mgmt., Handelsschule Coll., 1959. Office mgr. Kellermann Waelzlager, Munich, 1963-65, FAG Bearings Co., Stamford, Conn., 1967-72; with sales dept. Thompson Pipe & Steel, Denver, 1973-75; sales cons. I.B.T.C., Tehran, Iran, 1975-76; with sales dept. Denver Brass & Copper Co., 1976-81; pres. Summer Creations, Inc., Aurora, Colo., 1981-83; with sales dept. Hills Sprinkler Co., Denver, 1983-86, A.J.I. Landscape & Design, Denver, 1986-87; v.p. A.J.I. Irrigation Co., Denver, 1987-89; with BH&L Turf Irrigation, Lincoln, Nebr., 1989—; mem. Water Conservation Task Force, Denver, 1981—; sr. arbitrator Better Bus. Bur., Denver, 1984—. Vol. probation counselor Adams County, Brighten, Colo., 1971-75; tour dir. Denver Bicycle and Touring Club, 1986-87. Mem. Colo. Mountain Club (bd. dirs. Denver chpt. 1970-75, chmn. 1972-73). Roman Catholic. Home: 1420 Rosemary St Denver CO 80220 Office: BH&L Turf Irrigation 5040 Rentworth Ct Lincoln NE 68506

SCHWARZ, JOHN HENRY, theoretical physicist, educator; b. North Adams, Mass., Nov. 22, 1941; s. George and Madeleine (Haberfeld) S.; m. Patricia Margaret Moyle, July 11, 1986. AB, Harvard U., 1962; PhD, U. Calif., Berkeley, 1966. Instr. physics Princeton (N.J.) U., 1966-69, asst. prof., 1969-72; research assoc. Calif. Inst. Tech., Pasadena, 1972-85, prof. theoretical physics, 1985—. Co-author: Superstring Theory, 1987. Trustee Aspen (Colo.) Ctr. for Physics, 1982—. MacArthur Found. fellow, 1987. Fellow Am. Phys. Soc. Office: Calif Inst Tech Dept Theoretical Physics Pasadena CA 91125

SCHWARZ, JOSEPH RICHARD, gallery owner; b. Pomona, Calif., Dec. 7, 1954; s. Robert Joseph and Edith M. (Varian) S.; m. Pamela Anne Galligan, Apr. 8, 1978 (div. June 1983). BSEE, Calif. State Polytech. U., Pomona, 1977. Digital systems engr. Metron Corp., Upland, Calif., 1977-78; installation mgr. Hughes Aircraft, Denmark, Hawaii and Fed. Republic Germany, 1978-88; co-owner Penrose Gallery, Big Bear Lake, Calif., 1988—. Telephone counselor Garden Grove (Calif.) Community Ch., 1984—. Mem. Eta Kappa Nu, Tau Beta Pi. Republican. Home: 611 Opal Ct Upland CA 91786

SCHWARZ, MICHAEL HOWARD, lawyer; b. Brookline, Mass., Oct. 19, 1952; s. Jules Lewis and Estelle (Kosberg) S.; BA magna cum laude, U. No. Colo., 1975; postgrad. U. N.Mex., 1977, JD, 1980. Rsch. reader in Negligence Law, Oxford U., 1978; diploma in Legal Studies, Cambridge U., 1981. VISTA vol., Albuquerque, 1975-77; rsch. fellow N.Mex. Legal Support Project, Albuquerque, 1978-79. Bar: N.Mex. 1980, U.S. Dist. Ct. N.Mex. 1980, U.S. Ct. Appeals (10th, D.C., and Fed. cirs.) 1982, U.S. Ct. Internat. Trade, 1982, U.S. Tax Ct. 1982, U.S. Supreme Ct. 1983, N.Y. 1987. Supr. law Cambridge (Eng.) U., 1980-81; law clk. to chief justice Supreme Ct. N.Mex., Santa Fe, 1981-82; pvt. practice law, Santa Fe, 1982—; spl. prosecutor City of Santa Fe, 1985; spl. asst. atty. gen., 1986-88. Vice dir. Colo. Pub. Interest Research Group, 1974; scoutmaster Great S.W. Area coun. Boy Scouts Am., 1977-79; mem. N.Mex. Acupuncture Licensing Bd., 1983. Recipient Cert. of Appreciation Cambridge U., 1981, Nathan Burkan Meml. award, 1980. Mem. ABA, Fed. Bar Assn. (coun. on adminstrv. law 1983), N.Y. Trial Lawyers Assn., Assn. Trial Lawyers Am., N.Y. Trial Lawyers Assn., State Bar N.Y., State Bar N.Mex., N.Y. Bar Assn., First Jud. Dist. Bar Assn. (sec. 1988—, treas. 1987-88, sec. 1988-89, v.p. 1989—, local rules com. mem.). Editorial adv. com. Social Security Reporting Svc.; author: New Mexico Appellate Manual, 1989; contbr. articles to profl. jours. Home and Office: PO Box 1656 Santa Fe NM 87504

SCHWARZBERG, HENRY, investment banker, consultant; b. Munich, Oct. 27, 1947; came to U.S., 1949; s. Berek and Agnes (Löwinger) S.; m. Sheila Doyschen, Aug. 30, 1969; 1 child, Jonathan David. BA in Polit. Sci., CCNY, 1969; JD, Bklyn. Law Sch., 1973. Bar: N.Y. 1984. Gen. counsel Feldman Bros., Great Neck, N.J., 1975-77; v.p., counsel Ind. Fin. Planners Corp., Parsippany, N.J., 1978-80; asst. gen. counsel Bankers Nat. Life Ins. Co., Parsippany, 1978-80; pres. Phoenix Fin. Corp., Atlanta, 1980-81; v.p. FSC Securities Corp., Atlanta, 1981-82; pres. MAI Securities Corp., Phoenix, 1982-87, MAI Capital Corp., Phoenix, 1986-87. Co-devel.: (software) "Brass", 1985. Sustaining mem. Phoenix Zoo, 1985—; del. Wildest Club in Town (zoo aux.). Served with USAR, 1970-75. Mem. Internat. Assn. Fin. Planning, N.Y. State Bar Assn., N.Y. County Lawyers Assn. Republican. Jewish. Home: 19214 N 31st Ln Phoenix AZ 85027 Office: 19214 N 31st Ln Phoenix AZ 85027

SCHWARZER, WILLIAM W., federal judge; b. Berlin, Apr. 30, 1925; came to U.S., 1938, naturalized, 1944; s. John F. and Edith M. (Daniel) S.; m. Anne Halbersleben, Feb. 2, 1951; children: Jane Elizabeth, Andrew William. A.B. cum laude, U. So. Calif., 1948; LL.B. cum laude, Harvard U., 1951. Bar: Calif. 1953, U.S. Supreme Ct. 1967. Teaching fellow Harvard U. Law Sch., 1951-52; asso. firm McCutchen, Doyle, Brown & Enersen, San Francisco, 1952-60; ptnr. McCutchen, Doyle, Brown & Enersen, 1960-76; judge U.S. Dist. Ct (no. dist.) Calif., San Francisco, 1976—; sr. counsel Pres.'s Commn. on CIA Activities Within the U.S., 1975; chmn. U.S. Jud. Conf. Com. Fed.-State Jurisdiction com., 1988—; mem. faculty Nat. Inst. Trial Advocacy, Fed. Jud. Center, U.S.-Can. Legal Exchange, 1987. Author: Managing Antitrust and Other Complex Litigation, 1982, Effective Discovery, 1988; contbr. articles to legal publs., aviation jours. Trustee World Affairs Council No. Calif., 1961-88; chmn. bd. trustees Marin Country Day Sch., 1963-66; chmn. Marin County Aviation Commn., 1969-76; mem. vis. com. Harvard Law Sch., 1981-86. Served with Intelligence U.S. Army, 1943-46. Fellow Am. Coll. Trial Lawyers; mem. ABA (jud. rep. council antitrust sect.) Am. Law Inst., San Francisco Bar Assn., State Bar Assn. Calif. Office: US Dist Ct 450 Golden Gate Ave PO Box 36060 San Francisco CA 94102

SCHWEIGER, SEYMOUR MORTON, real estate and business consultant, trust manager; b. Newark, Oct. 11, 1920; s. Joseph and Anna Toby (Bernstein) S.; m. Sahm Sahmantha, June 10, 1945; children: Edward, Dona. Lic. real estate broker, Ariz. Vice-pres. Morris Schwartz Assocs. Inc., N.Y.C., 1945-59; pres. Normandie Constrn. Co., Inc., Phoenix, 1959-60; v.p. Guardian Mortgage & Trust Co. Inc., Phoenix, 1960-61; pres. Atlas Mortgage & Trust Co. Inc., Phoenix, 1960-87; v.p. Ariz. Ranch House Realty, Inc., Phoenix, 1960-87; pres. SMS Realty & Cons. Svcs., Inc., Phoenix, 1987—; adv. bd. mem. First Central Bank, Phoenix, 1985-88; bd. dirs. We. Econ. Devel. Corp., Phoenix. Mem. use of force/disciplinary rev. bd. City of Phoenix Police, 1985—; pres. Midtown Phoenix Lion's Club, 1969-70; mem. adjustment bd. City of Phoenix, 1970-75, chmn., 1974; chmn. environ. quality commn. City of Phoenix, 1975-76, mem. sign ordinance rev. com., 1975, mem. Sky Harbor Airport ground transp. adv. com.; mem. Ariz. State Treasurers Adv. Com., 1973-75; chmn. bd. office edn. adv. Maricopa Skill Ctr., Phoenix, 1971-72, bd. dirs. adminstrv. adv., 1983—; pres. J.A. Paxton Midtown Phoenix Lions Found., 1983-85; chmn. Republican Trunk & Tusk, Phoenix, 1981-82. Recipient Nat. Performance award Nat. Assn. Life Underwriters, 1964, Cert. appreciation Phoenix Police Dept./FBI, 1976, Bus. Man award Retherford Broadcasting Co., Phoenix, 1965. Mem. Valley Commerce Assn. (pres. 1982-83), USN League (bd. dirs. Phoenix coun. 1988—), Lions, Ancient Arabic Order Nobles of Mystic Shrine for N.Am. (Phoenix chpt.). Republican. Jewish. Office: SMS Realty & Cons Svcs Inc 301 W Indian School Rd C143 Phoenix AZ 85013

SCHWEIGERT, LYNETTE AILEEN, interior designer, consultant; b. Sacramento, July 6, 1949; d. Marvin Gerhardt and Aileen Helen (Velcoff) S.; m. Alan H. Randolph, May 1, 1976; 1 child, Tyler Mason Randolph. BS in Design, U. Calif., Davis, 1971. Display designer Weinstock's, Sacramento, 1971-72, Roos-Atkins, Sacramento, 1972-73; prin., project designer Randolph-Schweigert & Co., Reno, 1975—; prin. Design Ctr. Cons., Reno, 1982—, ptnr., project designer Hospitality Design Group, Reno, 1985—; cons. interior design Dan Carne AIA, Reno, 1980—, Paul Huss AIA, Reno, 1985—, U.S. West Investments, Reno, 1984—; cons. space planning Family Counseling Service of No. Nev., Reno, 1986—. Named one of Top 60 Restaurant Designers, Contract Mag., 1985; recipient Finalist prize Sierra Arts Found., Reno, 1980, Cert. Recognition for Participation in Preprofessional Internship Program U. Nev., 1987. Mem. Inst. Bus. Designers (affiliate).

SCHWEIKHER, PAUL, architect; b. Denver, July 28, 1903; s. Frederick and Elisabeth Ann (Williams) S.; m. Dorothy Miller, Dec. 17, 1923; 1 child, Paul. Student, U. Colo., 1921-22; B.F.A. (fellow), Yale U., 1929, M.A. (hon.), 1953. Registered Nat. Council Archtl. Registration Bds., also in 14 states. Practicing architect 1933—; partner Schweikher & Elting, 1945-53; co-founder Chgo. Workshops, 1933-35; vis. critic architecture Yale, 1947, 50-53, chmn. architecture, 1953-56; head dept. architecture Carnegie-Mellon U., 1956-68; now prof. emeritus architecture; vis. prof. Princeton U., 1960-61; vis. critic architecture U. Kans., 1950; lectr. Syracuse U., 1951; Mem. U. Ill. Conf. Archtl. Edn., 1949; mem. panel Sch. Planning Conf., Nat. Art Edn. Assn., N.Y.C., 1951; mem. Conf. on Edn. in Architecture and the Fine Arts, Carnegie Inst. tech., 1953; mem. jury architecture Fulbright awards Inst. Internat. Edn., 1953-54; fellowships Am. Acad. Rome, 1955; mem. Pitts. Planning Commn., 1961-64; Mem. adv. council Sch. Architecture, Princeton, 1961-69. Contbr. articles to profl. publs.; prin. works include Paul Schweikher House and Studio (hist. site), Schaumburg, Ill.; exhibited Mus. Modern Art, N.Y.C., Renaissance Soc., U. Chgo., Carnegie Inst. Tech., Akron (Ohio) Art Inst., galleries U. Minn., U. Ill., U. Kans., Yale, Princeton, Ariz. State U., Carnegie Inst. Mus. Fine Arts; 2 one-man exhbns., Harvard U., 1968, Yale, 1968; represented in permanent collection Art Inst. Chgo. Served to lt. comdr. USNR, 1942-45. Recipient Ford Found. research grant in theater design, 1960-61. Mem. Art Inst. Chgo. (life), Chi Psi. Club: Arts (Chgo.). Address: 50 Tonto Rd Sedona AZ 86336

SCHWEITZER, JOSH DAWSON, architect; b. Cin., May 22, 1953; s. Paul Franklin and Barbara Ann (Dawson) S. BA in Econs., Pitzer Coll., 1976; MArch, U. Kans., Lawrence, 1980. Designer, draftsman Spence & Webster Architects, London, 1980-81; owner Josh Schweitzer Designer, Neddesha, Kans., 1981-82; job capt. PBNA Architects, Kansas City, Mo., 1983-84; project architect Frank O. Gehry & Assocs., L.A., 1984; owner Schweitzer - Kellen, L.A., 1984-88, Schweitzer BIM,, L.A., 1988--. Contbr. articles in field to profl. jours. Office: Schweitzer BIM 7424 Beverly Blvd Los Angeles CA 90036

SCHWENKER, ROBERT OTTO, physicist; b. New Haven, Mar. 19, 1942; s. Robert August and Alma Sophia (Soell) S.; m. Jane Martha Levin, Mar. 26, 1966; children: Lisa Ann, Adam Philip, Alison Beth. BS, U. Mo., Rolla, 1963; MS, U. Ill., 1964, PhD, 1969. Jr. engr. IBM Corp., Rochester, Minn., 1963; staff engr. IBM Corp., East Fishkill, N.Y., 1968-71; adv. engr. IBM Corp., East Fishkill, 1971-73, devel. engr., 1973-78; rsch. staff mem. IBM Corp., San Jose, Calif., 1978-82; sr. engr. mgr. IBM Corp., San Jose, 1982—. Author: (with others) Magnetic Storage Technology and Concepts, 1981; inventor: has 15 U.S. Patents; contbr. articles to profl. jours. Mem. Am. Physical Soc., The Electrochem. Soc., Sigma Xi, Pioneer Boosters (pres. 1986-89). Democrat. Office: IBM Corp 5600 Cottle Rd San Jose CA 95193

SCHWERIN, KARL HENRY, anthropology educator, researcher; b. Bertha, Minn., Feb. 21, 1936; s. Henry William and Audrey Merle (Jahn) S.; m. Judith Drewanne Altermatt, Sept. 1, 1958 (div. May 1975); children: Karl Frederic, Marguerite DelValle; m. Partha Louise Hake Buell, Jan. 23, 1979; stepchildren: Tamara, Brent, Taryn. BA, U. Calif., Berkeley, 1958; PhD, UCLA, 1965. Instr. Los Angeles State Coll., 1963; asst. prof. anthropology U. N.Mex., Albuquerque, 1963-68, assoc. prof., 1968-72, prof., 1972—, asst. chmn. dept. anthropology, 1983-85, chmn. dept. anthropology, 1987—; prof. invitado Inst. Venezolano de Investigaciones Cientificas, Caracas, 1979. Author: Oil and Steel Processes of Karinya Culture Change, 1966, Antropologia Social, 1969, Winds Across the Atlantic, 1970; editor: Food Energy in Tropical Ecosystems, 1985; contbr. articles to profl. jours. V.p. Parents without Ptnr., Albuquerque, 1976-77. Grantee Cordell Hull Found., Venezuela, 1961-62, N.Y. Zool. Soc., Honduras, 1981; Fulbright scholar Cañar, Ecuador, 1969-70, Paris, 1986. Fellow Am. Anthropol. Assn.; mem. Am. Ethnol. Soc., Am. Soc. Ethnohistory (pres. 1975), Southwestern Anthropol. Assn. (co-editor Southwestern Jour. Anthropology 1972-75), N.Mex. Cactus and Succulent Society (v.p. 1970-71), Maxwell Mus. Assn. (bd. dirs. 1984-85), Internat. Congress of Americanists (35th-40th, 43d, 46th), Sigma Xi (chpt. pres. 1980-81). Office: U NMex Dept Anthropology Albuquerque NM 87131

SCHWICHTENBERG, DARYL ROBERT, drilling engineer; b. nr. Tulare, S.D., Nov. 8, 1929; s. Robert Carl and Lillian Rose (Hardie) S.; m. Helen M. Spencer, 1955 (div. Jan. 1971); children: Helayne, Randall, Hyalyn, Halcyon, Rustan; m. Helen Elizabeth Doehring, Nov. 11, 1971 (div. May 1982); 1 child, Suzanne. BS in Mech. Engring., U. Wyo., 1955; postgrad., S.D. Sch. Mines and Tech., 1955-57, Alexander Hamilton Inst., N.Y.C., 1962—. Office engr. Ingersoll-Rand Co., Mpls., 1957-58; sub br. mgr. Ingersoll-Rand Co., Duluth, Minn., 1959-60; product engr. Ingersoll-Rand Co., N.Y.C., 1960-63, devel. engr., 1964; sales mgr. Ingersoll-Rand Co., Phillipsburg, N.J., 1965; pres., founder Daryl Drilling Co., Inc., Flagstaff, Ariz., 1965-82; pres. Silent Rose Mining Co., Fallon, Nev., 1982-85; sr. design engr. Nev. test site Fenix & Scisson, Inc., Mercury, 1985—; co-owner, mgr. Dead Shot Ranch, Bondurant, Wyo., 1977-82. Inventor electronic subtitling for opera patrons. 1st lt. U.S. Army, 1950-54, Korea. Decorated Bronze Star. Mem. ASME, Inst. Shaft Drilling Tech. (speaker, instr. 1986—), Mensa. Republican. Office: Fenix & Scisson Inc PO Box 498 Mercury NV 89023

SCHWICKRATH, BRUCE ROBERT, engineer; b. Yonkers, N.Y., July 7, 1953; s. Louis and Jacquelyn (Wherry) S.; m. Crystal Ann Taggart, May 7, 1977; children: Kevin Daniel, Brian Michael. Student, Metro State Coll., SUNY Maritime Coll., 1971; AAS with highest honors, Westchester Community Coll., 1975. Field engr. Xerox Corp., Tarrytown, N.Y., 1974-75; advanced mfg. engr. Union Carbide Corp., Pleasantville, N.Y., 1975-78; mech. engr. Cobe Labs, Inc., Lakewood, Colo., 1978-80; mgr., mfg. engr. Data Electronics, Inc., San Diego, 1984-85; adv. engr. Storage Tech., Louisville, Colo., 1980-84, Intellistor Inc., Longmont, Colo., 1985—. Patentee in field. Republican. Roman Catholic. Home: 4303 E 127 Pl Thornton CO 80241 Office: Intellistor Inc 2120 Miller Dr Longmont CO 80501

SCHWINDEN, TED, former governor of Montana; b. Wolf Point, Mont., Aug. 31, 1925; s. Michael James and Mary (Preble) S.; m. B. Jean Christianson, Dec. 21, 1946; children: Mike, Chrys, Dore. Student, Mont. Sch. Mines, 1946-47; B.A., U. Mont., 1949, M.A., 1950; postgrad., U. Minn., 1950-54. Owner-operator grain farm Roosevelt County, Mont., 1954—; land commr. State of Mont., 1969-76, lt. gov., 1977-80, gov., 1981-89; mem. U.S. Wheat Trade Mission to Asia, 1968. Chmn. Mont. Bicentennial Adv. Council, 1973-76; mem. Mont. Ho. of Reps., 1959, 61, Legis. Council, 1959-61, Wolf Point Sch. Bd., 1966-69, Pub. Employees Retirement System Bd., 1969-74. Served with inf. AUS, 1943-46. Decorated Combat Inf. badge. Mem. Mont. Grain Growers (pres. 1965-67), Western Wheat Assos. (dir.). Democrat. Lutheran. Clubs: Masons, Elks. Office: State Capitol Office of Gov Helena MT 59620

SCHWINGER, JULIAN, physicist, educator; b. N.Y.C., Feb. 12, 1918; s. Benjamin and Belle (Rosenfeld) S.; m. Clarice Carrol, 1947. A.B., Columbia U., 1936, Ph.D., 1939, D.Sc., 1966; D.Sc. (hon.), Purdue U., 1961, Harvard U., 1962, Brandeis U., 1973, Gustavus Adolphus Coll., 1975; LL.D., CCNY, 1972. NRC fellow 1939-40; research asso. U. Calif.-Berkeley, 1940-41; instr., then asst. prof. Purdue U., 1941-43; staff mem. Radiation Lab., MIT, 1943-46; staff Metall. Lab., U. Chgo., 1943; asso. prof. Harvard U., 1945-47, prof., 1947-72, Higgins prof. physics, 1966-72; prof. physics UCLA, 1972-80, Univ. prof., 1980—; mem. bd. sponsors Bull. Atomic Sci.; sponsor Fedn. Am. Scientists; J.W. Gibbs hon. lectr. Am. Math. Soc., 1960. Author: Particles and Sources, 1969, (with D. Saxon) Discontinuities in Wave Guides, 1968, Particles, Sources and Fields, 1970, Vol. II, 1973, Vol. III, 1989, Quantum Kinematics and Dynamics, 1970, Einstein's Legacy, 1985; editor: Quantum Electrodynamics, 1958. Recipient C. L. Mayer nature of light award, 1949, univ. medal Columbia U., 1951, 1st Einstein prize award, 1951; Nat. Medal of Sci. award for physics, 1964; co-recipient Nobel prize in Physics, 1965; recipient Humboldt award, 1981, Monie A. Fest Sigma Xi award, 1986, Castiglione di Sicilia award, 1986, Am. Acad. of Achievement award, 1987; Guggenheim fellow, 1970. Mem. AAAS, ACLU, Nat. Acad. Scis., Am. Acad. Arts and Scis., Am. Phys. Soc., N.Y. Acad. Scis. Office: U Calif Dept Physics Los Angeles CA 90024

SCHWITALLA, STEPHEN EDWARD, food service executive; b. Tacoma, Nov. 16, 1953; s. Alfred M. and Joan E. (Howard) S.; m. Susan Eileen Schwitalla, Mar. 10, 1973; children: Michael Howard, Diane Kelly. Region mgr. Servomation, Fremont, Calif., 1971-73; distbn. supr. Fleming Foods Co., Fremont, 1973-77; warehouse and transp. mgr. Fleming Foods Co., Oakland, Calif., 1977-79; warehouse and purchasing mgr. Distron/Burger King, San Jose, Calif., 1979-80; div. mgr. Nat. Convenience Stores, Los Angeles, 1980-82; v.p. distbn. and foodservice Circle K Corp., Phoenix, 1982-85, corp. sr. v.p. foodservice, 1985-89; pres. Sparkle Ice Co., Polar Beverage Corp., Deli Pride Fodds, Inc., Phoenix, 1985-89, Mclane Convenience Foods, Inc., Phoenix, 1989—; bd. dirs. IICA Corp., Phoenix. Recipient Clio award for Advt. Excellence, 1985. Mem. Am. Mgmt. Assn., Nat. Assn. Convenience Stores, Ariz. Retail Grocers Assn., Internat. Food Mfg. Assn., Internat. Deli/Bakery Assn. Republican.

SCHWYN, CHARLES EDWARD, accountant; b. Muncie, Ind., Oct. 12, 1932; s. John and Lela Mae (Oliver) S.; m. Mary Helen Nickey, May 25, 1952; children: Douglas, Craig, Beth. BS, Ball State U., 1957. CPA, Calif. With staff Haskins & Sells, Chgo., 1958-60; sr. acct. R.F. Stonerock & Co., Orlando, Fla., 1960-62, Deloitte, Haskings & Sells, Orlando, 1962-67; mgr. Deloitte, Haskings & Sells, Milan, 1967-70, San Francisco, 1970-72; ptnr.-in-charge small bus. svcs. Deloitte, Haskings & Sells, Oakland, Calif., 1980—, mem. operating com., 1980—. Bd. dirs. Jr. Ctr. of Art and Sci., 1982—, pres., 1987-88; bd. dirs., trustees Oakland Symphony, 1982-86; bd. dirs. Oakland Met. YMCA, 1984—, fin. com., 1986—; bd. dirs. Oakland Police Activities League, 1981—, Joe Morgan Youth Found., 1982—, Marcus A. Foster Ednl. Inst., 1986—, chmn. ann. awards dinner, 1987, 88; adv. bd. Festival of the Lake, 1984—. Served with USN, 1952-56. Recipient Cert. Recognition Calif. Legis. Assembly, 1988. Mem. Oakland C. of C. (chmn. bd. dirs. 1987-88, exec. com. 1982—), AICPA (coun. mem. 1987—), Calif. Soc. CPA's (bd. dirs. 1979-81, 83-84, 85-87), Nat. Assn. Accts. (pres. Fla. chpt. 1967), Round Hill Golf and Country Club, Claremont Country Club, Lakeview Club (bd. govs. 1987-88), Rotary (bd. dirs. local club 1986-88, treas. 1984-86). Office: Deloitte Haskins & Sells 300 Lakeside Dr Ste 2700 Oakland CA 94612

SCIAME, DONALD RICHARD, computer systems analyst, dentist; b. Bklyn., Sept. 10, 1945; s. Mario and Ruth Marie (Kozell) S.; m. Kathy Ann Thamann, Mar. 17, 1987. AB, Rutgers U., 1967; DMD, N.J. Coll. Medicine & Dentistry, 1971; MAPA, U. N.Mex., 1984. Dep. chief svc. unit dental program USPHS Indian Hosp., Whiteriver, Ariz., 1971-73; chief svc. unit dental program USPHS Indian Hosp., Sacazon, Ariz., 1973-76, Santa Fe, 1976-88; systems analyst USPHS Indian Hosp., Albuquerque, 1988—. Contbr. articles to profl. jours. Mem. IHS Dental Profl. Speciality Group, IHS Dental Computer Users Group, ADA, Acad. Gen. Dentistry (editor component newsletter), Am. Assn. Pub. Health Dentistry (dist. membership chmn.), Fedn. Dentaire Internat., Internat. Coll. Dentists, N.Mex. Dental Assn., Santa Fe Dist. Dental Soc., Psi Omega Dental Fraternity, N.J. Dental Sch. Alumni Assn., USPHS Commn. Officers Assn., Albuquerque Area Dental Soc. Indian Health Services, Mumps User's Group. Home: 1914 Conejo Dr Santa Fe NM 87501 Office: IHS Area Office 505 Marquette NW Ste 1506 Albuquerque NM 87102

SCIBA, DARWIN ROY, container and packaging company executive; b. San Antonio, Aug. 24, 1943; s. Edwin D. Sciba and Margaret P. (Bradfute) Kenslow; m. Rebecca L. Crowe, June 6, 1966; children: Bret A., Ryan E., Derek T. BSE, Abilene Christian U., 1966. Cert. tchr., Tex. Pres., owner Crowe Splty. Foods div. Alleys, Denver, 1968-77; co-owner Tri County Ford, Mountain Grove, Mo., 1977-86; v.p., gen. mgr. Tharco Northwest, Seattle, 1977—, trustee Tharco Retirement Fund, 1984—. Pres. Circle C Camp, Denver, 1982-83; bd. dirs. Auburn (Wash.) 400, 1987—; chmn. citizens adv. com. King County Planning Commn., 1988—; mem. citizens adv. group Soos Creek, 1988—. Mem. Soc. Packaging Profls., Auburn Area C. of C. (bd. dirs. 1988—). Republican. Mem. Ch. of Christ. Office: Tharco NW PO Box 1876 Auburn WA 98071

'SCIBOR-MARCHOCKI, ROMUALD IRENEUS, mathematician, consultant; b. Highland Park, Mich., Dec. 29, 1926; s. Sigismond August and Sophy L. 'Scibor-Mar. BS, Wayne State U., 1947, MS, 1948; postgrad. Calif. Inst. Tech., U. So. Calif. Asst. physics Wayne State U., 1943-47, spl. instr., 1947-48; sr. engr. labs. div. Hoffman Radio Corp., 1949-59; design specialist Aerojet Gen. Corp. div. Gen. Tire & Rubber Co., 1959-62; sr. scientist Nortonics div. Northrop Corp., 1962-68; mem. tech. staff Jet Propulsion Lab., Pasadena, 1968-72, staff scientist, 1970-72; owner Mädchental Kennels, Baldwin Park, 1955—; with Wells Fargo Security Guard Svcs. div. Baker Protective Svcs., 1973-81; tutor Mt. San Antonio Coll., 1978— , staff math. dept., 1979—; cons. in math. and computer sci., 1980—. Mem.AAAS, Calavo Growers Assn., Acoustical Soc., Math. Assn., Am. Def. Preparedness Assn., Assn. Physics Tchrs., N.Y. Acad. Sci., Nat. Rifle Assn., Free for All, Mensa, Naturist Soc., Nat. Free Lance Photographers Assn., Sigma Xi. Contbr. articles to profl. jours. Home: 15250 E Arrow Hwy Baldwin Park CA 91706

SCITOVSKY, ANNE AICKELIN, economist; b. Ludwigshafen, Germany, Apr. 17, 1915; came to U.S., 1931, naturalized, 1938; d. Hans W. and Gertrude Margarete Aickelin; 1 dau., Catherine Margaret. Student, Smith Coll., 1933-35; B.A., Barnard Coll., 1937; postgrad., London Sch. Econs., 1937-39; M.A. in Econs., Columbia U., 1941. Mem. staff legis. reference service Library of Congress, 1941-44; mem. staff Social Security Bd., 1944-46; with Palo Alto (Calif.) Med. Research Found., 1963—, chief health econs. div., 1973—; Lectr. Inst. Health Policy Studies, U. Calif., San Francisco, 1975—; mem. Inst. Medicine, Nat. Acad. Scis., Pres.'s Commn. for Study of Ethical Problems in Medicine and Biomed. and Behavioral Research, U.S. Nat. Com. on Vital and Health Stats., 1975-78; cons. U.S. Dept. Health and Human Services, Inst. Medicine Council on Health Care Tech. Assessment. Mem. Am. Econ. Assn., Am. Public Health Assn. Home: 161 Erica Way Menlo Park CA 94025 Office: Palo Alto Med Found Rsch Inst 860 Bryant St Palo Alto CA 94301

SCOGGIN, VAN ROGERS, retired real estate executive; b. Las Cruces, N.Mex., Nov. 8, 1912; s. William Turner Scoggin and Merle Rogers; m. Shirley Marie Decker, Dec. 27, 1941; children: Sara Scoggin Seward, James Patrick. BA, N. Mex. State U. (formerly N.Mex. A&M U.), 1934. Tchr. Las Cruces (N.Mex.) High Sch., 1934-37; farmer Las Cruces, 1937-42; co-owner, mgr. SARSA, Torreon Coah, Mex., 1949-57; owner, operator Van R. Scoggin Motel Broker, Las Cruces, 1959-70; co-owner Scoggin-Blue Motel Broker, Las Cruces, 1970-83; owner, developer Picaho Hills Country Club, Las Cruces, 1978-86, ret., 1986. Lt. (j.g.) USN, 1942-45. Mem. Motel Brokers Assn. (pres. 1967, 71, Motel Broker of Yr. 1967), Las Cruces Country Club (pres. 1976), Torreon Country Club (bd. dirs. 1955), Monterrey Country Club (bd. dirs. 1949). Republican. Home: 6648 Vista Hermosa Las Cruces NM 88004 Office: PO Box 334 Las Cruces NM 88004

SCOPATZ, MARY PORPIGLIA, educational administrator; b. Albany, N.Y., July 1, 1934; d. Paul Vincent and Antoinette Mary (Cambareri) Porpiglia; B.S., SUNY, Albany, 1956; M.S., Syracuse U., 1967; Ed.D., Nova U., 1980; m. John Anthony Scopatz, Apr. 1, 1956 (dec. 1973); children—Stephen David, Robert. Tchr. bus. Liverpool (N.Y.) High Sch., 1965-67; tchr. Los Angeles City Schs., 1967-69; tchr. Santa Barbara (Calif.) High Sch., 1970-78, chairperson bus. edn. dept., 1971-78, dir. project for disadvantaged students Santa Barbara County Schs., 1978-79, dir. career and youth employment programs, 1979—; bd. dirs. Santa Barbara Industry Edn. Council. Mem. Am. Vocat. Assn., Calif. Assn. Vocat. Edn. (pres. 1979-80), Calif. Bus. Edn. Assn. (pres. So. sect. 1976), So. Calif. Consortium of Industry Edn. Councils (pres. 1985-86). Home: 26-3 Barranca Santa Barbara CA 93109 Office: Santa Barbara County Schs 4400 Cathedral Oaks Rd Santa Barbara CA 93160

SCOPINICH, JILL LORIE, editor, writer; b. Seattle, Dec. 7, 1945; d. Oscar John and Marcella Jane (Hearing) Younce; 1 child, Lori Jill. AA in Gen. Edn., Am. River Coll., 1969; BA in Journalism with honors, Sacramento State U., 1973. Reporter Carmichael (Calif.) Courier, 1968-70; mng. editor Quarter Horse of the Pacific Coast, Sacramento, 1970-75, editor, 1975-84; editor Golden State Program Jour., 1978, Nat. Reined Cow Horse Assn. News, Sacramento, 1983-88, Pacific Coast Jour., Sacramento, 1984-88, Nat. Snaffle Bit Assn. News, Sacramento, 1988; pres., chief exec. officer Communications Plus, Bellevue, Wash., 1988—; mag. cons., 1975—. Interviewer Pres. Ronald Reagan, Washington, 1983; assoc. editor Wash. Thoroughbred, 1989—. Mem. 1st profl. communicators mission to the U.S.S.R., 1988; bd. dirs. Carmichael, Winding Way, Pasadena Homeowners Assn., Carmichael, 1985-87. Recipient 1st pl. feature award, 1970, 1st pl. editorial award Jour. Assn. Jr. Colls., 1971, 1st pl. design award WCHB Yuba-Sutter Counties, Marysville, Calif., 1985. Mem. Am. River Jaycees (recipient speaking award 1982), Am. Horse Publs. (recipient 1st pl. editorial award 1983, 88), Mensa (bd. dirs., asst. local sec., activities dir. 1987-88, membership chair 1988—). Republican. Roman Catholic. Club: 5th Wheel Touring Soc. (Sacramento) (v.p. 1970). Home: 440 Adelma Beach Rd Port Townsend WA 98368

SCORSINE, JOHN MAGNUS, lawyer; b. Rochester, N.Y., Dec. 3, 1957; s. Frank and Karin (Frennby) S.; m. Susan Nauss, May 31, 1980 (div.); m. Theresa A. Burke, Dec. 17, 1988. BS, Rochester Inst. Tech., 1980; JD, U. Wyo., 1984. Bar: Wyo., 1984, U.S. Dist. Ct. Wyo., 1984. Police officer Casper (Wyo.) Police Dept., 1980-81; intern U.S. Atty. Office, Cheyenne, Wyo., 1983-84; sole practice Rock Springs, Wyo., 1984-85; ptnr. Scorsine and Flynn, Rock Springs, 1986; owner Scorsine Law Office, Rock Springs, 1986—; v.p. Emoni, Inc., 1988—; ptnr. Sunset Advt., 1987—; chmn. bd. Youth Home, Inc., Rock Springs, 1987-88. Leader Medicine Bow Ski Patrol, Laramie, Wyo., 1983; legal advisor Rocky Mountain div. Nat. Ski Patrol, 1984; asst. patrol leader White Pine Ski Area, Pinedale, Wyo., 1986; avalanche advisor Jackson Hole Snow King Ski Patrol, 1987—; mem. 1989 Am. North Peary Land Expdn. Mem. Wyo. State Bar, ABA, Wyo. Trial Lawyers Assn., Assn. Am. Trial Lawyers, Rock Springs C. of C. Democrat. Lutheran. Lodge: Rotary. Home: 519 Wasatch Circle Rock Springs WY 82901 Office: Scorsine Law Office 1400 Dewar Dr Rock Springs WY 82902-1152

SCOTT, BRIAN DOUGLAS, association executive; b. Portland, Oreg., Apr. 5, 1958; s. William Craven and Louise (Krengel) S.; m. Debra Suzanne Clem, June 21, 1980 (div. 1986); m. Ruth Elizabeth Pritchard, Aug. 30, 1986. BS, Oreg. State U., 1980; M Landscape Arch., N.C. State U., 1982. Downtown planner City of Raleigh (N.C), 1982-84; dir. design svcs. Oreg. Downtown Devel. Assn., Salem, 1984, program coordinator, 1984-85, pres., exec. dir., 1985—. Editor Oregon's Downtowns: The Next Five Years, 1988 (award 1988); contbr. articles to profl. publs. Mem. Nat. Main St. Network, Am. Soc. Landscape Architects (sec. Oreg. chpt. 1986, Honor award N.C. chpt. 1983, Cert. of Honor 1982), Internat. Downtown Assn. (citation 1988). Democrat. Office: Oreg Downtown Devel Assn 921 SW Morrison #508 Portland OR 97205

SCOTT, C. RONALD, pediatrics educator; b. San Diego, Calif., Jan. 25, 1935; s. Clifford Walter and Hattie Mary (Quintrell) S.; m. Susan J. Berg, May 6, 1984; children: Lauren, John, Joseph. MD, U. Wash., 1959. Diplomate Am. Bd. Pediatrics, Am. Bd. Med. Genetics. Resident in pediatrics U. Minn., Mnpls., 1959-61; postdoctoral fellow in genetics Calif. Inst. Tech., Pasadena, Calif., 1961-62; postdoctoral fellow in genetics U.Wash., Seattle, 1964-65, asst. prof., assoc. prof. pediatrics, 1966-76, prof., 1976--, head div. pediatric genetics, 1976--. Contr. numerous articles to med. jours., chpts. to books. Capt. M.C., USAF, 1962-64. Numerous research grants. Mem. Soc. Pediatric Research, Am. Pediatric Soc., Am. Soc. Human Genetics (program chmn. 1984), Soc. Inherited Metabolic Disease (bd. dirs. 1985--, pres. 1988), Western Soc. Pediatric Research (council 1974-77). Office: U Wash Dept Pediatrics RD-20 Seattle WA 98195

SCOTT, CHARLES R., diversified company executive; b. 1928. With Dallas Morning News, 1949-51, Branham Co., 1951-55, Southwestern Investment, Inc., 1955-56, Parker Ford and Co., 1957-62; with Intermark, Inc., 1970—, now pres., also bd. dirs.; chmn. Pier One Imports Inc., Fort Worth, until 1988, vice chmn., 1988—; also chmn., pres., chief exec. officer Triton Grp. Ltd., La Jolla, Calif., 1987—. Office: Intermark Inc 1020 Prospect St La Jolla CA 92037 *

SCOTT, CLIFFORD RAY, broadcast executive, minister; b. Wilmington, N.C., June 15, 1930; s. DeWitt Talmadge and Ruth Elvera (Hufham) S.; student Reedley (Calif.) Coll., 1963-64, Internat. Coll., Honolulu, 1977-80; m. Billie Jean Gibson, Jan. 3, 1956; children—Clifford, Lisa, David, Rebecca. Ordained minister Bapt. Gen. Conf. Announcer, Sta. WGBR, Goldsboro, N.C., 1956, Sta. WMFD, Wilmington, N.C., 1956-58, Sta. KBIS, Bakersfield, Calif., 1958; announcer, account exec. Sta. KRDU, Dinuba, Calif., 1958-67; asst. mgr. Sta. WFGW, Black Mountain, N.C., 1967-71; gen. mgr. Sta. KAIM, Honolulu, 1971-88; interim pastor Wahiawa (Hawaii) Christian Ch., 1988-89; min. of devel. Waikiki Bapt. Ch., 1989—. Served with U.S. Army, 1949-52. Mem. Nat. Religious Broadcasters, Nat. Assn. Broadcasters. Republican. Baptist. Club: Kiwanis (past pres.). Home: 4300 Waialae Ave Apt 803B Honolulu HI 96816 Office: Waikiki Bapt Ch 428 Kuamoo St Honolulu HI 96815

SCOTT, CONSTANCE MARY, computer company executive; b. Prescott, Ariz., July 5, 1952; d. Robert LeeRoy and Carol Jean (Markel) Carothers; m. David Edward Scott, June 10, 1972; children: Rosemary, Jody. LPN, Prescott Sch. of Nursing, 1971. From gen. adminstrv. asst. to project mgr. Mus. No. Ariz., 1975-79; product mgr. diskette div. Flagstaff (Ariz.) Engring., 1983-87, gen. mgr., 1987-88; owner Internat. Micro Solutions, Flagstaff, 1988—. Leader, Girl Scouts of U.S., Flagstaff, 1981-84, CASA, 1989—, DPMA, 1988—. Republican. Roman Catholic. Home and Office: 1737 N Navajo Dr Flagstaff AZ 86001

SCOTT, DAVID IRVIN, resident manager; b. Yakima, Wash., Dec. 5, 1947; s. Jack Phillip and Betty Lucille (Paronto) S.; m. Jill Louise Baker, June 23, 1982. AA, Monterey Peninsula Coll., Calif., 1975. Accredited resident mgr., Inst. Real Estate Mgmt., 1987. Courier Gallery Hawaii, Inc., Honolulu, 1981; acting resident mgr. Fairway Gardens, Honolulu, 1981; resident mgr. Waimalu Park, Honolulu, 1981-83, Waikiki Skyliner, Honolulu, 1983-84, Bishop Gardens, Honolulu, 1985-86, Plaza Landmark, Honolulu, 1986-88, Westlake Apts., Honolulu, 1988, Fairway Gardens, Honolulu, 1988—; condo mgmt. cons. Mem. Honolulu Bd. Realtors, Inst. Real Estate Mgmt., Alpha Gamma Sigma. Libertarian. Office: Success Internat 1290D Maunakea St #345 Honolulu HI 96817

SCOTT, DONALD MICHAEL, educational association administrator; b. Los Angeles, Sept. 26, 1943; s. Bernard Hendry and Barbara (Lannin) S.; m. Patricia Ilene Pancoast, Oct. 24, 1964 (div. June 1971); children: William Bernard, Kenneth George. BA, San Francisco State U., 1965, MA, 1986. Cert. tchr. Calif. Tchr. Mercy High Sch., San Francisco, 1968-71; park ranger Calif. State Park System, Half Moon Bay, 1968-77; tchr. adult div. Jefferson Union High Sch. Dist., Daly City, Calif., 1973-87; dir. NASA-NPS Project Wider Focus, Daly City, 1983—, also bd. dirs.; nat. park ranger Grant-Kohrs Ranch Nat. Hist. Site, Deer Lodge, Mont., 1987-88; nat. park ranger pub. affairs fire team Yellowstone Nat. Park, 1988; nat. park ranger Golden Gate Recreation Area, 1988—; lectr. photography Skyline Coll., 1989—; research subject NASA, Mountain View, Calif., 1986; guest artist Yosemite (Calif.) Nat. Park, 1986; nat. park ranger Golden Gate Nat. Recreation Area, Nat. Park Svc., San Francisco, 1986. Photographs pub. in Americana mag., 1989. Pres. Youth for Kennedy, Lafayette, Calif., 1960; panelist Community Bds. of San Francisco, 1978-87; city chair Yes on A Com., So. San Francisco, San Mateo City, Calif., 1986; mem. Friends of George R. Stewart. Mem. Nat. Assn. of Interpretation (state coordinator Mont. 1988), Nat. Parks and Conservation Assn., Planetary Soc. Democrat. Home: c/o 608 Myrtle South San Francisco CA 94080 Office: Wider Focus c/o Irene Sterling PO Box 771 Pacifica CA 94044

SCOTT, GENE, engineer, marketing professional; b. N.Y.C., Apr. 23, 1939; s. Frank and Catherine Anna (McNally) Schlossman; m. Linda DeSoucey, Feb. 1, 1969; children: Denise, Eve. BSEE, CCNY, 1969; MS in Indsl. Adminstrn., Union Coll., 1975. Ops. mgr. Gen. Electric Co., Hudson Falls, N.Y., 1969-75; mktg. mgr. Leybold Heraeus, Monroeville, Pa., 1975-77, Material Research, Orangeberg, N.Y., 1977-79; v.p. mktg. Xinix, Santa Clara, Calif., 1982-84; mem. tech. staff Rockwell Internat., Anaheim, Calif., 1979-82, 84—; pres. bd. dirs. Scott Assocs., El Toro Calif., 1980—; mktg. dir. Window Tinting Assocs., Le Habre, Calif., 1985-86; pres., mktg. dir. Macro-Search Info. Services, El Toro, 1985—. Inventor high vacuum thin film. Mktg. supporter City of Santa Ana (Calif.) Community Ctrs., 1985, 86, vol. work with poor, 1985, 86; mem. internat. music outreach com. Lake Hills Community Ch., Laguna Hills, Calif., 1985—, mem. choir, 1984-87; big brother Big Bros. Big Sisters Orange County, Tustin, Calif., 1984-85; pres. Inventors Workshop Internat. Edn. Found., Orange County, 1988—. Served with USNG, 1964-69. Ednl. Fin. grantee State of N.Y., 1964-68. Mem. Am. Vacuum Soc. (exec. com. 1985-88), Assn. Indsl. Metallizers Coaters Laminators (film quality com. 1975-76). Republican. Home: 25061 Castlewood St El Toro CA 92630 Office: Rockwell Internat 3370 Miraloma Anaheim CA 92803

SCOTT, GEORGE EDMOND, psychiatrist; b. LaJunta, Colo., Nov. 9, 1924; s. John Ferdinand and Ida Harriet (Spurlock) S.; m. Leila Ruth Hafer, June 24, 1950; children: George E. Jr., John C., James L., Elizabeth A. BA cum laude, U. Colo., 1946; MD, U. Colo., Denver, 1948; postgrad. in history, U. Iowa, 1948-50; student, Denver Sem., 1976-79. Intern, resident U. Iowa Hosp., Iowa City, 1948-50; practice medicine specializing in psychiatry Colo., 1950—; resident in psychiatry and neurology U. Colo. Med. Ctr., Denver, 1951-52, 56-59; assoc. psychiatrist Emory John Brady Hosp., Colorado Springs, Colo., 1950-56; chief neurology Colo. State Hosp., Pueblo, 1961-63; psychiatrist Denver Gen. Hosp., 1964-80, electroencephalographer, 1964-68, dir. hosp. psychiat. services, 1965-68, fellow in community psychiatry, 1968-69, head outpatient consultation unit, 1976-78; clin. dir. N.W. Denver Counseling Ctr., 1969-75, dir. emergency psychiat. services, 1975-76; med. dir. alcohol rehab. unit VA Med. Ctr., Ft. Lyon, Colo., 1980-83; med. dir. S.E. Colo. Family Guidance and Mental Health Ctr., Inc., La Junta, 1983—; adj. clin. prof. psychiatry Okla. State U. of Osteopathic Physicians and Surgeons, 1980-83; electroencephalographer VA Med. Ctr., Ft. Lynn, Colo., 1980-82, Mount Airy Psych. Ctr., 1968-78, mem. med. staff, 1964-83; cons. Prowers Meml. Hosp., Lamar, Colo, 1984—, Prowers Adolescent Ctr., Lamar, 1984-86, Colo. Dept. Rehab., 1959-61, St. Joseph's Sch. for Boys, Denver, 1969-71. Contbr. articles to profl. jours. Served to lt. col. USAR, 1942-44, 48-62, 76-85. NIH grantee, 1967. Mem. Am. Assn. Community Psychiatrists, Otero County Med. Soc., S.E. Colo. Med. Soc., Colo. Assn. Community Psychiatrists (exec. com. 1987—). Democrat. Lutheran. Home: 504 East C St Box 3-286 Fort Lyon CO 81038 Office: SE Colo Family Guidance and Mental Health Ctr Inc 711 Barnes Ave La Junta CO 81050

SCOTT, GERALD RUSSELL, information scientist; b. San Francisco, Sept. 11, 1959; s. David Russell and Barbara Ann (Nystrom) S.; m. Marie Gabriel Kotos, Apr. 22, 1989. BA in History, U. Santa Clara, 1981. Software systems engr. Jones Futura Found., Fair Oaks, Calif., 1982-87; product mgr. Jones Futurex, Rancho Cordova, Calif., 1987—. Mem. Info. Systems Security Assn. (v.p.), IEEE (local area network security com. 1989), Am. Nat. Standards Inst. (retail banking security com. 1986—, electronic data interchange com. 1987—), Phi Alpha Theta. Republican. Roman Catholic. Home: 3111 60th St Sacramento CA 95820 Office: Jones Futurex 10933 Trade Center Dr Rancho Cordova CA 95670

SCOTT, ILEY STANLEY, public policy researcher, writer; b. Plainview, Tex., Nov. 1, 1921; s. Iley Stanley and Myrtle Ruth (Westbrook) S.; m. Ana Melendez, July 24, 1954; children: James Wesley, Philip, Laila. BS, Tex. Tech. U., 1942; MA, U. Chgo., 1947. Adminstrv. asst. Pub. Adminstrn. Clearing House, Chgo., summer 1947; research analyst Civic Fedn. Chgo., summer 1947, Inst. Govtl. Studies, U. Calif., Berkeley, 1947-58; then research polit. scientist, asst. dir. Inst. Govtl. Studies, U. Calif., 1958—. Co-author: California Government, 1951-82; author: Governing California's Coast, 1975, Policies for Seismic Safety, 1979; contbr. articles on coastal governance and seismic safety to profl. jours. Mem. Calif. Seismic Safety Commn., 1975—, chmn., 1981-84; mem. bd. Bay Area Reg. Earthquake Preparedness Project, Oakland, Calif., 1984—. Recipient Most Disting. Research award, Govtl. Research Assn., 1969, 76, commendation Calif. Legislature, 1973, Berkeley citation U. Calif., Berkeley, 1982. Mem. Earthquake Engring. Research Inst., Western Govt. Research Assn. (exec. sec. 1950-82). Democrat. Home: 1141 Vallecito Ct Lafayette CA 94549 Office: U Calif Inst Govtl Studies 109 Moses Hall Berkeley CA 94720

SCOTT, JACK, corporate executive; b. Scranton, Pa., Mar. 3, 1942; s. John Joseph and Lydia Louise (Brennan) S.; m. Micki McGee; children: Jonah Gregory, Lydia Brennan, Emma Lou. AB, Syracuse U., 1966; PhD, U. Calif., Berkeley, 1971. Sports editor Ramparts Mag., Berkeley, Calif., 1968-70; founder, dir. Inst. for Study of Sports & Soc., Oakland, Calif., 1970-72; athletic dir., chmn. phys. edn. dept. Oberlin Coll., Ohio, 1972-74; writer/cons. Portland, Oreg., 1975-80; therapist, cons. Berkeley, Calif., 1980-85; pres. Electro-Med. Instruments, Inc., Berkeley, Calif., 1985—; med. staff Olympic Games, L.A., 1984, Seoul, Korea, 1988, World Track & Field Championship, Rome, 1987. Author: Athletics for Athletes, 1970, The Athletic Revolution, 1971; co-author: Out of Their League, 1971; contbr. articles to profl. jours. Founder, mem. bd. dirs. Athletes United for Peace, San Francisco, 1985—. Democrat. Office: EMI Inc 1683 Shattuck Ave Berkeley CA 94709

SCOTT, JOHN NOEL, JR., oil company executive; b. Panhandle, Tex., Mar. 28, 1930; s. John Noel and Eura (Waldren) S.; m. Freddie Lewis, May 24, 1952; children: John Noel III, Carolyn, Kay. BA in Chemistry & Math., Howard Payne U., 1952; postgrad., Stanford U., 1975. Rsch. chemist Phillips Petroleum Co., Bartlesville, Okla., 1952-56; supr. plastics, tech. svcs. & devel. Phillips Petroleum Co., Bartlesville, 1956-66; mng. dir. Phillips Internat. Belgium, Overjise, 1966-71; product mgr. polyethylene Phillips Petroleum Co., Houston, 1971-73; gen. mgr. Phillips Driscopipe, Dallas, 1973-76; v.p. rubber chemicals Phillips Chem. Co., Bartlesville, 1976-78; v.p. plastics Phillips Chem. Co., Houston, 1978-83; v.p. fed. rels. Phillips Petroleum Co., Washington, 1983-87; pres., chief exec. officer Incinatrol Inc., Denver, 1987—. Patentee in field. Presbyterian. Office: Incinatrol Inc 8055 E Tufts Ave Pkwy Denver CO 80237

SCOTT, LARRY, electronics engineer; b. Des Moines, May 18, 1935; s. Glenn Filmore and Helen Marie (Mann) S.; m. Ursula Deiss, June 21, 1959 (div. June 1971); children: Ulrike, Barbara; m. Caroline Patricia Driver, Dec. 21, 1972; adopted children: Robert, Michael, Dhyana, Leah, Ananda. AA, Los Angeles City Coll., 1955; BS in Engring with honors, U. Calif., Berkeley, 1957, MS in Elec. Engring., 1959; Dr sc techn, Swiss Fed. Inst. Tech., 1966. Instrumentation engr. Lawrence Radiation Lab., Berkeley, 1959-62; teaching asst. Swiss Fed. Inst. Tech., Zurich, 1962-66; design engr. Hewlett Packard Co., Bobelingen, Fed. Republic Germany, 1966-67; program mgr. TRW Systems, Redondo Beach, Calif., 1967-69; scientist Systems Sci. and Software Co., San Diego, 1969-71; ind. cons. Del Mar, Calif., 1971-72; sr. scientist Sci. Applications Internat. Corp., La Jolla, Calif., 1972-77; chief scientist Def. Tech. Group, La Jolla, Calif., 1980—; sr. scientist JAYCOR, Del Mar, Calif., 1977-80; instrumentation advisor Def. Nuclear Agy., Washington, 1976--; speaker in field. Contbr. articles to tech. pubis; Patentee Pulse Stretching Network, Planar MOS Transistor with Dielectric Isolation. Mem. IEEE (sr.), Sigma Xi, Tau Beta Pi, Eta Kappa Nu. Republican. Buddhist. Club: Southwestern Yacht (San Diego) (fin. com. 1987--). Home: 7325 Paseo Verde Carlsbad CA 92009

SCOTT, LARRY MARCUS, aerospace engineer, mathematician; b. Bingham Cnyn., Utah, June 14, 1945; s. Wright Marcus Scott and Margaret Ruth (Jackson) Sturzenegger; m. Paula Inger Elisabeth Kjellman, Aug. 21, 1972; children: Paul Marcus, Laura Elizabeth. BS, Brigham Young U., 1971; MS, Boston U., 1983. Engr. lifting body re-entry mechs. Douglas Missile and Space Systems, Sant Monica, Calif., 1965-66; missionary and dist. leader Ch. of Jesus Christ of Latterday Saints, Finland, 1966-69; researcher Math. Dept. Brigham Young U. for Air Force, Provo, Utah, 1969-71; researcher Russian Translation Linguistics Brigham Young U. for Nat. Security Agy., Provo, 1971-72; internship in Plasma Physics, Physics Dept. Brigham Young U., Provo, 1972-73; sci. programmer Lockheed Elect. Co., Edwards AFB, Calif., 1973-75; mathematician 6521 Range Squadron, 6520 Test, Edwards AFB, 1976-80 1982-85; exchange sci. Inst. for Flight Dynamics, DFVLR, Federal Republic Germany, 1980-82; mathematician A.F. Logistics Command, Hill AFB, Utah, 1985-87; software engineer Ball Systems Engring. Div., Edwards AFB, 1987-89. Co-author: Invention disclosure 1976; author: report for laser nozzle DFVLR in Germany 1982, USAF Disclosure 1984. Quorum Pres. Ch. of Latter Day Saints, Palmdale, Calif. 1973-74, Lancaster, Calif. 1984-85, Quorum Counselor, Lancaster 1988—; asst. varsity scout, Bountiful, Utah 1985-86. Recipient Bank of Am. Language Award, Hawthorne, Calif. 1963, Scholarship to Brigham Young U. 1963, Hon. Cert.(99%) Defense Language Inst., Monterey, Calif. 1980. Republican.

SCOTT, LARY R., freight transportation company executive; b. 1936; married. BS, Bowling Green U., 1961. With Roadway Express, 1961-67; with Consolidated Freightways Motor Freight, 1967—, staff asst., 1967-68, asst. to pres., 1968-69, div. mgr., 1969-70, area v.p., 1970-76, exec. v.p. ops., 1976-80, pres., chief exec. officer, 1980—; with Consolidated Freightways, Inc., Palo Alto, Calif., 1967—, exec. v.p., from 1983, pres., chief operating officer, 1986—, chief exec. officer, 1988—, dir.; v.p. Am. Trucking Assn. Served with USMC, 1954-57. Office: Consol Freightways Inc 3240 Hillview Ave Palo Alto CA 94303 *

SCOTT, LAURIE (ARLENE GOODMAN), foundation director, producer; b. St. Louis, May 21, 1940; d. Louis Ben and Rose (Oberman) Goodman; m. Lawrence Kubik, Nov. 14, 1965 (div. May 1968); m. Jim Clark, Oct. 21, 1972 (div. Nov. 1974); m. Michael Jon Humfrey, Jan. 6, 1975 (separated); children: Shannon, Jonathan, Erin; m. J. Student high sch., University City, Mo. Freelance actress N.Y.C. and Hollywood, Calif., 1957-70, 78-82; various positions including newspaper editor, producer Big Sur, Calif., 1970-78; pres., exec. dir. World Concerts for Humanity, Burbank, Calif., 1983—; producer Laurie Scott and Assocs., Burbank, 1986—; coord. Visible Horizons, Kansas City, Mo., 1987—; cons. Chumash Nation/Indian Nation, Santa Ynez, Calif., 1987—. Democrat. Universalist.

SCOTT, MERILLA MCCURRY, psychologist; b. Tacoma, Oct. 29, 1957; d. Spencer Leroy and Millison Margaret (McKnight) McCurry; m. Wallace Lee Scott, Aug. 11, 1984; 1 child, Jasmin Cortney. BS, UCLA, 1978, MA, 1981, PhD, 1988. Cons. Fernald Sch. UCLA, 1981-82, teaching asst., 1982-83, supr. student clinic, 1984-86, cons. psychology clinic, 1986-87; child interviewer Children's Inst. Internat., L.A., 1983-84; coord. child abuse treatment program Didi Hirsch Community Mental Health Ctr., Culver City, Calif., 1988—; child therapist Didi Hirsch Community Mental Health Ctr., Culver City, 1983-87, cons., 1984-88; psychology clinic assoc. UCLA, 1985-86, tchr. tng. workshops UCLA, 1984-86. Mem. Am. Psychol. Assn., L.A. Soc. Clin. Psychologists (bd. dirs. 1987—). Democrat. Office: Didi Hirsch Community Mental Health Ctr 4760 S Sepulveda Blvd Culver City CA 90230

SCOTT, MORRIS DOUGLAS, ecologist; b. Mason City, Iowa, Sept. 8, 1945; s. Morris William and Maxine Imogene (Eppard) S.; m. Suvi Annikki Lehtinen, Aug. 12, 1983. BS, Iowa State U., 1967; PhD, Auburn U., 1971. Instr. zoology Auburn U., Ala., 1971-72; asst. prof. So. Ill. U., Carbondale, 1972-74; sr. ecologist Amax Coal Co., Indpls., 1974-75, environ. mgr., Billings, Mont., 1975-77; rsch. assoc. Mont. State U., Bozeman, 1977-80, dir. Inst. Natural Resources, 1980-86; biologist, rsch. div. Yellowstone Nat. Park, Wyo., 1986—; cons. mining industry. Author: Heritage from the Wild, Familiar Land and Sea Mammals of the Northwest. Editor Conf. Proceedings Plains Aquatic Research, 1983. Contbr. articles to profl. jours. Bd. dirs. Bridger Canyon Property Owners Assn., Bozeman, 1984—. Auburn U. fellow, 1970. Mem. Ecol. Soc. Am., Wildlife Soc., Animal Behavior Soc., Gamma Sigma Delta. Current work: Land use planning systems for microcomputers; wildlife mgmt. on reclaimed surface mines; behavioral ecology of feral dogs; ecology of waterfowl and grouse; biology of pronghorn antelope. Subspecialties: Behavioral ecology; Resource management; Conservation Biology. Home: 16257 Bridger Canyon Bozeman MT 59715 Office: Yellowstone Nat Park Rsch Div Yellowstone National Park WY 82190

SCOTT, PATRICIA IRENE, biochemist, researcher; b. San Francisco, June 28, 1960; d. Frank Louis and Patricia Ann (Couher) Mighetto; m. Michael Harrell Scott, June 1, 1985. BA in Biochemistry, U. Calif., Berkeley, 1983. Lab. technician Heart Rsch. Inst. at Med. Rsch. Insts., San Francisco, 1983; lab technician microbiology and immunology lab. U. Calif., Berkeley, 1983-84; rsch. assoc. BioResponse, Inc., Hayward, Calif., 1984-87; rsch. assoc. IV Chiron Corp., Emeryville, Calif., 1987—. Contbr. articles to profl. jours. Mem. Scholarship Rsch. Awards for Coll. Scientists. Home: 121 Begonia St Marintez CA 94553 Office: Chiron Corp 4560 Horton St Emeryville CA 94608

SCOTT, PETER BRYAN, lawyer; b. St. Louis, Nov. 11, 1947; s. Gilbert Franklin and Besse Jean (Fudge) S.; m. Suzanne Rosalee Wallace, Oct. 19, 1974; children: Lindsay W., Sarah W., Peter B. Jr. A.B., Drury Coll., 1969; J.D., Washington U., St. Louis, 1972, LL.M., 1980. Bar: Mo. 1972, Colo. 1980; diplomate Ct. Practice Inst. Sole practice, St. Louis, 1972-80; assoc. firm McKie and Assocs., Denver, 1980-81; ptnr. firm Scott and Chesteen, P.C., Denver, 1981-84, Veto & Scott, Denver, 1984—; tchr. Denver Paralegal Inst. Served to capt. USAR, 1971-79. Mem. ABA, Mo. Bar Assn., Colo. Bar Assn., Denver Bar Assn. Republican. Mem. United Church of Christ. Home: 26262 Wolverine Trail Evergreen CO 80439 Office: Veto & Scott 6595 W 14th Ave Ste 200 Lakewood CO 80214

SCOTT, PETER DALE, English educator; b. Montreal, Quebec, Can., Jan. 11, 1929; s. Francis Reginald and Marian Mildred (Dale) S.; m. Mary Elizabeth Marshall, June 16, 1956; children: Catherine Dale, Thomas, John Daniel. BA, McGill U., Montreal, Que., Can., 1949, PhD, 1955; postgrad, Inst. d'Etudes Politiques, Paris, 1950, U. Coll., Oxford/London, 1950-52. Fgn. service officer Canadian Dept. External Affairs, Ottawa, Ont., 1957-61; asst. prof. speech U. Calif., Berkeley, 1961-66, from asst. prof. to assoc. prof.

English, 1966-80, prof., 1980—. Author: The War Conspiracy, 1972, Crime and Cover-Up, 1977, Coming to Jakarta, 1988; co-author: The Assassinations, 1976, The Iran-Contra Connection, 1987. Fellow Internat. Ctr. Devel. Policy (Freedom award 1987). Mem. Assn. for Responsible Dissent (bd. dirs. 1988). Office: U Calif Dept English Berkeley CA 94720

SCOTT, PETER FRANCIS, food products company executive; b. Honolulu, 1927; married. B.S., U. Calif., 1952. Staff acct. Touche Ross Bailey & Smart, 1952-58; with Tay-Holbrook, Inc., 1958-63; asst. treas. Di Giorgio Corp., San Francisco, 1963-64, treas., 1964-69, v.p., treas., 1969-74, v.p., chief fin. officer, mem. exec. com., 1974-80, pres., chief operating officer, dir., 1980-84; chmn., pres., chief exec. officer Di Giorgio Corp., 1984—; dir. Hale Tech. Corp./Scott Corp. Calif. Served to capt. U.S. Army, 1946-49. Office: Di Giorgio Corp 1 Maritime Pla San Francisco CA 94111 *

SCOTT, PETER JAMES, data processing executive; b. Great Wakering, Essex, Eng., July 7, 1961; s. Frederick James and Grace Elizabeth (White) S. BA, St. John's Coll., Cambridge, Eng., 1983, MA, 1987. Vice pres. software Micrographic Images, Woodland Hills, Calif., 1982-86; systems analyst Jet Propulsion Lab. div. NASA, Pasadena, Calif., 1983—. Mem. Space Studies Inst., Nat. Space Soc., Planetary Soc.

SCOTT, RICHARD THOMAS, electronics company administrator; b. Ogden, Utah, Oct. 17, 1939; s. Thomas Bradshaw and Reah (Child) S.; m. Connie Greenwood, May 15, 1959; children: Richard T. Jr., Paul S., Stephen B., Aaron D. Student, U. Utah, 1958-59, Weber State Coll., Ogden, Utah, 1959-60. Customer engr. data processing div. IBM, Salt Lake City, 1960-64; instr. field engrng. div. IBM, Kingston, N.Y., 1964-71; systems engr. data processing div. IBM, St. Louis, 1971-73, staff instr., 1973-77; staff instr. IBM, San Jose, Calif., 1977-78; adv. instr. headqrs. function IBM, Los Angeles, 1978-86, sr. instr., 1986—. Served with USAFR, 1957-65. Mem. Am. Soc. Tng. and Devel., Trainer's Assn. So. Calif. (bd. dirs. 1988-). Republican. Mormon. Home: 79 E Avenida de los Arboles Thousand Oaks CA 91360 Office: IBM Corp Dept 332 355 S Grand Ave Los Angeles CA 90071

SCOTT, STEPHEN THOMAS, hospital administrator; b. Lincoln, Nebr., Dec. 19, 1931; s. Thomas Charles and Ada Myrll (Graham) S.; m. Ann Elizabeth Enstrom, July 5, 1965; children: Chet, Lee, John. BS, Midland Luth. Coll., 1957; MA, U. Iowa, 1959. Resident Nebr. Meth. Hosp., Omaha, 1959-60, staff asst., 1960; hosp. adminstr. Southwest Meml. Hosp., Cortez, Colo., 1960-70, Montrose Meml. Hosp., Montrose, Colo., 1970—. Chmn. Rep. Cen. Com., Cortez, Colo., 1967-70. Served in USN, 1951-55. Fellow, Am. Coll. Healthcare Execs., Am. Coll. Hosp. Adminstrs.; mem. Voluntary Hosps. of Am. (Mountain States, founding ptnr., sec., treas. 1982—), Colo. Hosp. Assn. Republican. Methodist. Office: Montrose Meml Hosp 800 S 3d Montrose CO 81401

SCOTT, TERRI RENAE, corporate professional; b. Denver, May 11, 1959; d. James Alvin Sumey and Maxine May (Meyer) Inman. Student, Colo. State U., 1977-78; BEd in Music, U. No. Colo., 1982; postgrad., Colo. U., 1985—. Electronic test technician Inex Inc., Denver, 1981-83; electronic test technician Fischer Imaging Corp., Thornton, Colo., 1983-84, prodn. supr., 1984-86, electronic engrng. technician, 1986-88, corp. quality facilitator, product acct. mgr., 1988—. Mem. NAFE, Am. Soc. Quality Control, IEEE (student chpt.), Denver Musician's Assn., Network Colo., Internat. Trumpet Guild (sec. Colo. chpt. 1980-81). Office: Fischer Imaging Corp 12300 N Grant St Thornton CO 80241

SCOTT, TIM, electronics engineer; b. Encino, Calif., Feb. 23, 1959; s. William Edward and Rena (Cicci) S. AS, Pierce Coll., Woodland Hills, Calif., 1980; BSEE, Calif. Poly. State U., 1984. Project engr. Volumetrics, Paso Robles, Calif, 1985-88, ITT Fed. Elec., Vandenberg AFB, Calif., 1980—. Home: 957 Johnson Ave San Luis Obispo CA 93401 Office: ITT Fed Elec Corp IS 420 PO Box 5728 Vandenberg AFB CA 93437

SCOTT, VIVIAN SUE, vocational counseling supervisor; b. Martin's Ferry, Ohio, Mar. 23, 1953; d. James Robert Bosley and Jane (Kirby) Knutzen; m. Stephen Jacobs, Jan. 28, 1984. BA magna cum laude, Humboldt State U., 1977, postgrad., 1989. Ltd. svcs. teaching credential. Piano tchr. Eureka, Calif., 1974-78; Job counselor Women's Resourses, Eureka, 1979-81; church organist Eureka, 1980—; trainer Employment Tng. Dept., Eureka, 1981, Pvt. Indsl. Coun., Eureka, 1986—. Advisor Coll. Redwoods, Eureka, 1989; bd. dirs. YWCA, Eureka, 1983-89, pres., 1986-89; choral mem. Humboldt Light Opera Co., 1988. Home: 2207 Fairfield Eureka CA 95501 Office: Pvt Indsl Council 930 6th St Eureka CA 95501

SCOTT, WALTER, JR., business consultant; b. Balt., July 24, 1925; s. Walter and Margaret Catherine (Pfeiffer) S.; m. Barbara Main, July 6, 1946 (dec. 1964); children: Stephen Walter, Susan Marjorie, Cynthia Margaret, Christopher Main; m. Mary Joan Braun, Aug. 5, 1966 (dec. 1986); m. Helene Lyda Burke, May 1, 1987. AB, Duke U., 1945; MBA with distinction, Harvard U., 1949. Advtg. mgr. The Quaker Oats Co., Chgo., 1950-57; v.p. mktg. J.H. Filbert, Inc., Balt., 1957-67, pres., 1968-77; div. gen. mgr. Cen. Soya Co., Ft. Wayne, Ind., 1972-77; exec. v.p. Fairmont Foods Co., Des Plaines, Ill., 1978-81; pres. McKeon, Scott, Woolf & Assocs., Palo Alto, Calif., 1982-84; chmn. bd. Integral Cons. Group, Mill Valley, Calif., 1986-87, Scott, Woolf & Assocs., Palo Alto, 1984—, Mulford Moreland & Assocs., San Jose, Calif., 1986—; chmn., speaker pres. courses, Am. Mgmt. Assn., N.Y.C., 1970—; dir. Mulford Moreland & Assocs., San Jose, 1986—; trustee Calif. Inst. Integral Studies, San Francisco, 1983—. With USNR, 1943-46, PTO. Mem. Phi Beta Kappa. Home: 564 Santa Rita Palo Alto CA 94301 Office: Scott Woolf & Assocs 701 Welch Rd Ste 1119 Palo Alto CA 94304

SCOTT, WANDA LEE, interior designer; b. Portland, Maine, July 8, 1950; d. Harold B. and Ursula E. Hammond. AA, Laney Coll., 1979. Dir. design Soulie Assocs., San Francisco, 1975-80; project cost acct. TERA/Teknekron Industries, Berkeley, Calif., 1980-83; owner, designer Wanda Lee Interiors, Oakland, Calif., 1983-87, Focal Point Design, Grass Valley, Calif., 1987--. Bd. dirs. Nevada County Hist. Soc., 1988—. Mem. Nevada County Arts Coun., Am. Soc. Interior Designers, Smithsonian Assocs., NRA. Democrat. Roman Catholic. Home: 137 Rockwood Dr Grass Valley CA 95945 Office: Focal Point Design 137 Rockwood Dr Grass Valley CA 95945

SCOTT, WILLIAM CORYELL, medical director; b. Sterling, Colo., Nov. 22, 1920; s. James Franklin and Edna Ann (Schillig) S.; m. Jean Marie English, Dec. 23, 1944 (div. 1975); children: Kathryn, James, Margaret; m. Carolyn Florence Hill, June 21, 1975; children: Scott, Amy Jo, Robert. AB, Dartmouth Coll., 1942; MD, U. Colo., 1944, MS in OB/GYN, 1951. Cert. Am. Bd. Ob-Gyn, 1956, 1979. Intern USN Hosp., Great Lakes, Ill., 1945-46, Denver Gen. Hosp., 1946-47; resident Ob-Gyn St. Joseph's Hosp., Colo. Gen. Hosp., Denver, 1946-51; practice medicine specializing in Ob-Gyn Tucson, 1951-71; assoc. prof. Ob-Gyn U. Ariz. Med. Sch., Tucson, 1971—; med. dir. U. Med. Ctr., Tucson, 1984—. Contbr. articles to med. jours. and chpt. to book. Pres. United Way, Tucson, 1979-80, HSA of Southeastern Ariz., Tucson, 1985-87; chmn. Ariz. Health Facilities Authority, Phoenix, 1974-83. Served to capt. USNR, 1956-58. Recipient Man of Yr. award, Tucson, 1975. Fellow Am. Coll. Ob-Gyn, Am. Coll. Surgeons, Pacific Coast Ob-Gyn Soc., Cen. Assn of Ob-Gyn; mem. AMA (Council on Sci. Affairs, 1984—), Ariz. Med. Assn.; nominee Am. Coll. of Healthcare Execs. Republican. Episcopal. Club: Old Pueblo (Tucson). Home: 335 Country Club Rd Tucson AZ 87516 Office: University Med Ctr 1501 N Campbell Ave Tucson AZ 85724

SCOTT, WILLIAM DENNES, metallurgical engineer; b. Louisville, Dec. 10, 1949; s.Charles Bartle and Jane Kendrick (Wolf) S.; m. Jeanne P. Bargeron, Sept. 2, 1981. BS, Purdue U., 1971, MS, 1972; Continued Degree in Environ. Engrng., U. Ala., 1982. Assoc. metallurgist So. Rsch. Inst., Birmingham, Ala., 1972-78; rsch. dir. Atlas Foundry & Machine, Tacoma, 1978-83; cons. pvt. practice Mt. Brook, Ala., 1983-85; process control engr. ESCO Corp., Portland, Oreg., 1985—. Contbr. articles to profl. jours. Served with USN, 1968-71. INCO scholar 1970. Mem. Am. Foundry Soc. (sci. merit award 1987), Am. Soc. for Metals, Am. Inst. Metallurgic Engr., Nat. Soc. Profl. Engrs. Libertarian. Presbyterian. Home: PO Box 10923 Portland OR 97210 Office: ESCO Corp PO Box 10123 Portland OR 97210

SCOTT-BOYD, SARA MARIE, software engineer; b. Ft. Worth, June 12, 1955; d. Will E. and Jennie Jean (Breckenridge) Scott; m. William Lynn Boyd, Oct. 2, 1975; children: Christian L., Michael Alexander, Lisa Noelle. Student, Colo. Coll., 1973-74; BA, U. Colo., 1979; MSBA, U. No. Colo., 1983. Mgr. office systems United Techs. Microelectronics Ctr., Colorado Springs, Colo., 1981-85; sr. adminstr. computer-aided design software United Techs. Microelectronics Ctr., Colorado Springs, 1985—. Publicity chmn. Colorado Springs chpt. Nat. Kidney Found., 1982-84; publicist Boy Scouts Am., Colorado Springs, 1984-86; edn. chmn. First United Meth. Ch., Fountain, Colo., 1983-86. Republican. Home: 770 Allegheny Dr Colorado Springs CO 80919 Office: United Techs Micro Ctr 1575 Garden of Gods Rd Colorado Springs CO 80907

SCOTT-DEROSIER, LINDA PRESTON, psychology educator; b. Boones Camp, Ky., Feb. 20, 1941; d. E. Jay and Grayce (Mollette) Preston; m. Brett D. Scott, Aug. 7, 1960 (div.); 1 child, Brett Preston; m. Arthur H. DeRosier, Jr.; children: Deborah, Marsha, Melissa. BA, Pikeville Coll., 1962; MA, Eastern Ky. U., 1968; PhD, U. Ky., 1972. Teaching asst. Eastern Ky. U., Richmond, 1967-68; instr. U. Ky., Lexington, 1968-72; assoc. prof. psychology Ky. State U., Frankfort, 1972-78, dir. Edn./Psychology Rsch. Ctr., 1973-78; dir. Inst. for Appalachian Affairs E. Tenn. State U., Johnson City, 1978-80, assoc. prof. psychology, 1978-80; prof. psychology The Coll. of Idaho, Caldwell, 1980-88, Rocky Mountain Coll., Billings, Mont., 1988—; claims rep. Social Security Adminstrn., Louisville, Corbin, Pikeville, Ky., 1962-67. Contbr. articles to profl. jours. Dir. Inst. for Appalachian Affairs, 1978-80; researcher Am. Assn. for Colls. and Tchr. Edn., 1972, Harvard U. Ctr. for Moral Edn., 1976; researcher tng. Leadership Tng. Seminars, 1973-84; bd. dirs. West Valley Med. Ctr., 1980-88. Danforth fellow U. Ky., 1980—. Mem. AAUP (acad. freedom and tenure com. 1972-78), Plaget Soc., Tenn. Com. for Humanities (bd. mem. 1978-80),Assn. for Humanistic Psychologists. Baptist. Home: 1809 Mulberry Dr Billings MT 59102 Office: Rocky Mountain Coll Poly Dr Billings MT 59102

SCOUGHTON, TROY EUGENE, electrical engineer; b. Orlando, Fla., Feb. 15, 1956; s. Bert E. Scoughton and Nancy J. (Lyles) Staples; m. Sylvia Torres, June 6, 1975; children: Troy Desmond, Tiffany Ann. AA, St. Leo Coll., 1978; BS in Physics, Park Coll., 1984; MEE, N.Mex. State U., 1988. Instr. N.Mex. State U., Las Cruces, 1980-81; sr. field engr. Raytheon, El Paso, Tex., 1981-85; RF/digital engr. Phys. Sci. Lab. N.Mex. State U., Las Cruces, 1985-87, antenna range engr. Phys. Sci. Lab., 1987—. Served with U.S. Army, 1974-80, Korea. Mem. IEEE, Assn. of Old Crows, Antenna Measurement Assn. Republican. Roman Catholic. Home: 5487 La Paloma Las Cruces NM 88005 Office: Phys Sci Lab Box 30002 Las Cruces NM 88003-0002

SCRITSMIER, JEROME LORENZO, lighting fixture manufacturing company executive; b. Eau Claire, Wis., July 1, 1925; s. Fredrick Lorenzo and Alvera Mary (Schwab) S.; B.S., Northwestern U., 1950; m. Mildred Joan Lloyd, June 27, 1947; children—Dawn, Lloyd, Janet. Salesman, Sylvania Elec. Products, Los Angeles, 1951-69; chmn. Cameron Properties Inc.; chief fin. officer Environ. Lighting for Architecture Co., Los Angeles, 1973—. Served with USAAF, 1943-46. Mem. Apt. Assn. (pres., dir. Los Angeles County). Republican. Club: Jonathan (Los Angeles). Home: 2454 N Cameron Ave Covina CA 91724 Office: 17891 Arenth St City of Industry CA 91748

SCROGGIN, MARTIN MONROE, electrical engineer; b. Little Rock, Feb. 22, 1930; s. Martin Monroe and Inez Americus (Sudduth) S.; m. Wayna Bird, June 7, 1952, (div. Apr.1969); children: Daniel Dean, David Alan; m. Cathrine Murphy Mahr, Jan. 1, 1980. BSEE, U. Ark., 1952; postgrad., UCLA, 1956. Profl. engr. Test engr. GE, Sarycoge, N.Y., 1952; tech. staff Hughes Aircraft Co., Culver City, Calif., 1955-68; cons. M. Scroggin Assocs., L.A., 1968-69; system engr. Hughes Aircraft Co., Culver City, 1969-75; sr. system engr. Hughes Aircraft Co., El Segundo, Calif., 1975-80; dept. mgr. Hughes Aircraft Co., El Segundo, 1980-86, asst. lab. mgr., 1986-88, asst. program mgr., 1988—. 1st lt. U.S. Army, 1952-54. Republican. Methodist. Office: Hughes Aircraft Co Dept 75-32-00/Bldg E55/MS G225 PO Box 902 El Segundo CA 90245

SCRUGGS, LARRY GLEN, college administrator; b. White City, Oreg., Oct. 24, 1943; s. William Freeman and Claudia Rae (Constable) S.; m. Patricia Shafer, Sept. 16, 1967; children—Larry Glen, Laura Rae, William Price, Kerry Wright, Berry Monroe. B.S., So. Oreg. Coll., 1971, M.S., 1972; postgrad. Portland State U.; grad. Wacubo Bus. Mgrs. Inst., Stanford U., 1986. Conf. dir. U. Portland, 1975-83, dir. aux. services, 1983—; founder Larry G. Scruggs & Assocs., 1981—, 53 MPG Scruggs Mktg. Mng. Meeting Planning Group, 1985—; cons. on conf. ops. Portland Rose Festival Assn., also grand floral parade chmn.; Bd. dirs. Greater Portland Conv. and Visitors Assn., Columbia-Williamette council Boy Scouts Am.; chmn. Big Thunder dist. Boy Scouts Am. Served with USAF, 1961-65. Recipient Charles A. Miltner award U. Portland, 1986. Mem. Portland C. of C., Western Assn. Coll. Aux. Services, Nat. Assn. Coll. Aux. Services, Oreg. Soc. Assn. Execs., Meeting Planners Internat., Meeting Planning Alert (adv. bd.), Portland Sales and Mktg. Execs. (bd. dirs., Pres.'s Rose award 1986), Portland Rose Festival Assn. (exec. com., bd. dirs.). Roman Catholic. Author: Conferences on Campus: Marketing and Managing, 1982, rev. 3d edit., 1986; contbr. articles to profl. jours. Home: 6942 N Villard St Portland OR 97217 Office: U Portland Columbia 107 Portland OR 97203

SCUDDER, THAYER, anthropologist, educator; b. New Haven, Aug. 4, 1930; s. Townsend III and Virginia (Boody) S.; m. Mary Eliza Drinker, Aug. 26, 1950; children: Mary Eliza, Alice Thayer. Grad., Phillips Exeter Acad., 1948; A.B., Harvard U., 1952, Ph.D., 1960; postgrad., Yale U., 1953-54, London Sch. Econs., 1960-61. Research officer Rhodes-Livingstone Inst., No. Rhodesia, 1956-57; sr. research officer Rhodes-Livingstone Inst., 1962-63; asst. prof. Am. U., Cairo, 1961-62; research fellow Center Middle East Studies, Harvard U., 1963-64; asst. prof. Calif. Inst. Tech., Pasadena, 1964-66; assoc. prof. Calif. Inst. Tech., 1966-69, prof. anthropology, 1969—; dir. Inst. for Devel. Anthropology, Binghamton, N.Y., 1976—; cons. UN Devel. Program, FAO, IBRD, WHO, Ford Found., Navajo Tribal Council, AID. Author: The Ecology of the Gwembe Tonga, 1962; co-author: Long-Term Field Research in Social Anthropology, 1979, Secondary Education and the Formation of an Elite: The Impact of Education on Gwembe District, Zambia, 1980, No Place to Go: The Impacts of Forced Relocation on Navajos, 1982, For Prayer and Profit: The Ritual Economic and Social Importance of Beer in Gwembe District, Zambia, 1950-1982, 1988. John Simon Guggenheim Meml. fellow, 1975. Mem. Am. Anthrop. Assn. (1st recipient Solon T. Kimball award for pub. and applied anthropology 1984), Soc. Applied Anthropology, Am. Alpine Club. Office: Calif Inst Tech #228-77 Pasadena CA 91125

SCULLEY, JOHN, computer company executive; b. N.Y.C., Apr. 6, 1939; s. John and Margaret (Blackburn) S.; m. Carol Lee Adams, Mar. 7, 1978; children: Margaret Ann, John Balckburn, Laura Lee. Student, R.I. Sch. Design, 1960; BArch, Brown U., 1961; MBA, U. Pa., 1963. Asst. account exec. Marschalk Co., N.Y.C., 1963-64, account exec., 1964-65, account supr., 1965-67; dir. mktg. Pepsi-Cola Co., Purchase, N.Y., 1967-69, v.p. mktg., 1970-71, sr. v.p. mktg., 1971-74, pres., chief exec. officer, 1977-83; pres. PepsiCo Foods, Purchase, 1974-77; pres., chief exec. officer Apple Computer Inc., Cupertino, Calif., 1983—; also chmn. Apple Computer Inc., Cupertino, Calif, 1986—; bd. dirs. Comsat Corp. Chmn. Wharton Grad. Exec. Bd., 1980; mem. art adv. com. Brown U., 1980; bd. dirs. Keep Am. Beautiful; mem. bd. overseers Wharton Sch., U. Pa. Mem. U. S. C. of C. Clubs: Indian Harbor, N.Y. Athletic; Coral Beach (Bermuda); Wharton Bus. Sch. of N.Y. (bd. dirs.); Camden (Maine) Yacht. Office: Apple Computer Inc 20525 Mariana Ave Cupertino CA 95014 *

SCULLON, DEBORAH IRENE, nurse anesthetist; b. Fairless Hills, Pa., Feb. 22, 1955; d. Harry Alexander and Irene Elizabeth (Smith) Scullon. BS in Nursing, U. Mich., 1977, cert. in anesthesia, 1985. R.N., Mich., Calif. Staff nurse St. Joseph Mercy Hosp., Ann Arbor, Mich., 1977-78, Biomed. Applications, Ann Arbor, 1978-79; asst. nursing supr. med.-surg. unit Dearborn (Mich.) Med. Ctr. Hosp., 1979-81; nurse ICU-CCU U. Mich. Hosp., Ann Arbor, 1981-83; nurse anesthetist, preceptor U. Mich. Hosp., 1985-86; nurse anesthetist Kaiser Permanente HMO, San Francisco, 1986-87, Daly City Med. Anesthesia Group, San Francisco, 1988—; speaker at seminars, symposia. Contbr. articles to nursing jours. Mem. Am. Assn. Nurse Anesthetists (U.S. rep. to China 1988), Calif. Nurses Assn., Mich. Nurses Assn. Republican. Presbyterian. Home: 595 John Muir Dr Apt 711C San Francisco CA 94132 Office: Daly City Med Anesthesia Ste 302 203 Willow St San Francisco CA 94102

SCULLY, STEPHEN CHAVEL, transportation executive; b. Toronto, Ont., Can., Oct. 30, 1948; came to U.S., 1948; s. Harold Edward S. and Stephanie Chavel. Student, Glendale Coll., 1972. Recording artist All-Am. Music, 1972-73, Turquoise Records, Bakersfield, Calif., 1973-74; import mgr. Trans-Air, Inglewood, Calif., 1975-77; v.p. Milgard Trucking, Inglewood, 1982-83; pres. World of Music Records, Hollywood, Calif., 1981-83, Scully & Co., Inc., El Segundo, Calif., 1977—. Songwriter numerous pub. songs. Mem. Broadcast Music, Inc. Office: 149 Sheldon St El Segundo CA 90245

SEABORG, GLENN THEODORE, chemistry educator; b. Ishpeming, Mich., Apr. 19, 1912; s. H. Theodore and Selma (Erickson) S.; m. Helen Griggs, June 6, 1942; children: Peter, Lynne Seaborg Cobb, David, Stephen, John Eric, Dianne. AB, UCLA, 1934; PhD, U. Calif.-Berkeley, 1937; numerous hon. degrees; LLD, U. Mich., 1958, Rutgers U., 1970; DSc, Northwestern U., 1954, U. Notre Dame, 1961, John Carroll U., Duquesne U., 1968, Ind. State U., 1969, U. Utah, 1970, Rockford Coll., 1975, Kent State U., 1975; LHD, No. Mich. Coll., 1962; DPS, George Washington U., 1962; DPA, U. Puget Sound, 1963; LittD, Lafayette Coll., 1966; DEng, Mich. Technol. U., 1970; ScD, U. Bucharest, 1971, Manhattan Coll., 1976; PhD, U. Pa., 1983. Research chemist U. Calif.-Berkeley, 1937-39, instr. dept. chemistry, 1939-41, asst. prof., 1941-45, prof., 1945-71, univ. prof., 1971, leave of absence, 1942-46, 61-71, dir. nuclear chem. research, 1946-58, 72-75, asso. dir. Lawrence Berkeley Lab., 1954-61, 71—; chancellor Univ. (U. Calif.-Berkeley), 1958-61, dir. Lawrence Hall of Sci., 1982—; sect. chief metall. lab. U. Chgo., 1942-46; chmn. AEC, 1961-71, gen. adv. com., 1946-50; research nuclear chemistry and physics, transuranium elements.; chmn. bd. Kevex Corp., Burlingame, Calif., 1972—; mem. Pres.'s Sci. Adv. Com., 1959-61; mem. nat. sci. bd. NSF, 1960-61; mem. Pres.'s Com. on Equal Employment Opportunity, 1961-65, Fed. Radiation Council, 1961-69, Nat. Aeros. and Space Council, 1961-71, Fed. Council Sci. and Tech., 1961-71, Nat. Com. Am.'s Goals and Resources, 1962-64, Pres.'s Com. Manpower, 1964-69, Nat. Council Marine Resources and Engring. Devel., 1966-71; chmn. Chem. Edn. Material Study, 1959-74, Nat. Programming Council for Pub. TV, 1970-72; dir. Ednl. TV and Radio Center, Ann Arbor, Mich., 1958-64, 67-70; pres. 4th UN Internat. Conf. Peaceful Uses Atomic Energy, Geneva, 1971, also chmn. U.S. del., 1964, 71; U.S. rep. 5th-15th gen. confs. IAEA, chmn., 1961-71; chmn. U.S. del. to USSR for signing Memorandum Cooperation Field Utilization Atomic Energy Peaceful Purposes, 1963; mem. U.S. del. for signing Limited Test Ban Treaty, 1963; mem. commn. on humanities Am. Council Learned Socs., 1962-65; mem. sci. adv. bd. Robert A. Welch Found., 1957—; mem. Internat. Orgn. for Chem. Scis. in Devel., UNESCO, 1980—, chmn., 1981; mem. Nat. Commn. on Excellence in Edn., Dept. Edn., 1981—; co-discoverer elements 94-102 and 106: plutonium, 1940, americum, 1944-45, curium, 1944, berkelium, 1949, californium, 1950, einsteinium, 1952, fermium, 1953, mendelevium, 1955, nobelium, 1958, element 106, 1974; co-discoverer nuclear energy isotopes Pu-233, U-233, Np-237, other isotopes including I-131, Fe-59, Te-99m, Co-60; originator actinide concept for placing heaviest elements in periodic system. Author: (with Joseph J. Katz) Chemical Actinide Elements, 1954, 2d ed. (with Joseph J. Katz and Lester R. Morss) Vols. I & II, 1986, The Chemistry of the Actinide Elements, 1957, The Transuranium Elements, 1958, (with E.G. Valens) Elements of the Universe, 1958 (winner Thomas Alva Edison Found. award), Man-Made Transuranium Elements, 1963, (with D.M. Wilkes) Education and the Atom, 1964, (with E.K. Hyde, I. Perlman) Nuclear Properties of the Heavy Elements, 1964, (with others) Oppenheimer, 1969, (with W.R. Corliss) Man and Atom, 1971, Nuclear Milestones, 1972, (with Ben Loeb) Kennedy, Khruschev and the Test Ban, 1981; editor: Transuranium Elements: Products of Modern Alchemy, 1978; asso. editor: Jour. Chem. Physics, 1948-50; editorial adv. bd.: Jour. Inorganic and Nuclear Chemistry, 1954-82, Indsl. Research, Inc, 1967-75; adv. bd.: Chem. and Engring. News, 1957-59; editorial bd.: Jour. Am. Chem. Soc, 1950-59, Ency. Chem. Tech., 1975—, Revs. in Inorganic Chemistry, 1977—; mem. hon. editorial adv. bd.: Internat. Ency. Phys. Chemistry and Chem. Physics, 1957—; mem. panel: Golden Picture Ency. for Children, 1957-61; mem. cons. and adv. bd.: Funk and Wagnells Universal Standard Ency, 1957-61; mem.: Am. Heritage Dictionary Panel Usage Cons, 1964—; contbr. articles to profl. jours. Trustee Pacific Sci. Center Found., 1962-77; trustee Sci. Service, 1965—, pres., 1966—; trustee Am.-Scandinavian Found., 1968—, Ednl. Broadcasting Corp., 1970-72; bd. dirs. Swedish Council Am., 1976—, chmn. bd. dirs., 1978-82; bd. dirs. World Future Soc., 1969—, Calif. Council for Environ. and Econ. Balance, 1974—; bd. govs. Am. Swedish Hist. Found., 1972—. Recipient John Ericsson Gold medal Am. Soc. Swedish Engrs., 1948; Nobel prize for Chemistry (with E.M. McMillan), 1951; John Scott award and medal City of Phila., 1953; Perkin medal Am. sect. Soc. Chem. Industry, 1957; U.S. AEC Enrico Fermi award, 1959; Joseph Priestley Meml. award Dickinson Coll., 1960; Sci. and Engring. award Fedn. Engring. Socs., Drexel Inst. Tech., Phila., 1962; named Swedish Am. of Year, Vasa Order of Am., 1962; Franklin medal Franklin Inst., 1963; 1st Spirit of St. Louis award, 1964; Leif Erikson Found. award, 1964; Washington award Western Soc. Engrs., 1965; Arches of Sci. award Pacific Sci. Center, 1968; Internat. Platform Assn. award, 1969; Prometheus award Nat. Elec. Mfrs. Assn., 1969; Nuclear Pioneer award Soc. Nuclear Medicine, 1971; Oliver Townsend award Atomic Indsl. Forum, 1971; Disting. Honor award U.S. Dept. State, 1971; Golden Plate award Am. Acad. Achievement, 1972; John R. Kuebler award Alpha Chi Sigma, 1978; Founders medal Hebrew U. Jerusalem, 1981; Henry DeWolf-Smyth award Am. Nuclear Soc., 1982, Great Swedish Heritage award, 1984, Ellis Island Medal of Honor, 1986, Vannevar Bush Award, Nat. Sci. Bd., 1988; decorated officier Legion of Honor France; Daniel Webster medal, 1976. Fellow Am. Phys. Soc., Am. Inst. Chemists (Pioneer award 1968, Gold medal award 1973), Chem. Soc. London (hon.), Royal Soc. Edinburgh (hon.), Am. Nuclear Soc., Calif., N.Y., Washington acads. scis., AAAS (pres. 1972, chmn. bd. 1973), Royal Soc. Arts (Eng.); mem. Am. Chem. Soc. (award in pure chemistry 1947, William H. Nichols medal N.Y. sect. 1948, Charles L. Parsons award 1964, Gibbs medal chgo. sect. 1966, Madison Marshall award No. Ala. sect. 1972, Priestley medal 1979, pres. 1976), Am. Philos. Soc., Royal Swedish Acad. Engring. Scis. (adv. council 1980), Am. Nat., Argentine Nat., Bavarian, Polish, Royal Swedish, USSR acads. scis., Royal Acad. Exact, Phys. and Natural Scis. Spain (acad. fgn. corr.), Soc. Nuclear Medicine (hon.), World Assn. World Federalists (v.p. 1980), Fedn. Am. Scientists (bd. sponsors 1980), Deutsche Akademie der Naturforscher Leopoldina (East Germany), Nat. Acad. Pub. Adminstrn., Internat. Platform Assn. (pres. 1981—), Am. Hiking Soc. (dir. 1979—, v.p. 1980), Phi Beta Kappa, Sigma Xi, Pi Mu Epsilon, Alpha Chi Sigma (John R. Kuebler award 1978), Phi Lambda Upsilon (hon.); fgn. mem. Royal Soc. London, Chem. Soc. Japan, Serbian Acad. Sci. and Arts. Clubs: Bohemian (San Francisco); Chemists (N.Y.C.); Cosmos (Washington), University (Washington); Faculty (Berkeley). Office: U Calif Lawrence Berkeley Lab Berkeley CA 94720 *

SEAL, LAWTON ANTHONY, microbiologist, virology researcher, army officer; b. Houma, La., Feb. 23, 1950; s. Max Kenneth and Marie Yvette (Baldwin) S.; m. Janet Hemperley, Feb. 12, 1977; children: Ronald, Ryan, Lawton Anthony II. BS, La. State U., Baton Rouge, 1972; MS, La. State U., New Orleans, 1977; PhD, La. State U., Shreveport, 1985. Med. rsch. technologist La. State U. Med. Ctr., Shreveport, 1972-77; commd. 1st lt. U.S. Army, 1977, advanced through grades to maj., 1987; microbiologist Brooke Army Med. Ctr., San Antonio, 1977-83; chief microbiology Tripler Army Med. Ctr., Honolulu, 1985—; clin. instr. John A. Burns Sch. Medicine, U. Hawaii, Honolulu, 1986—. Contbr. articles to profl. jours. Mem. NRA, Am. Soc. for Microbiology (v.p. Hawaii br. 1987-88, pres. 1988-89), Am. Assn. for Advance of Sci. Democrat. Home: 448-B Halawa View Honolulu HI 96818 Office: Tripler Army Med Ctr Dept Pathology Honolulu HI 96859-5000

SEALE, MARK ALAN, real estate broker; b. Abeline, Tex., Sept. 7, 1962; s. Dan Moody and Billie Jo (McCarty) S.; m. Jacqui Lynn Judd, Dec. 30, 1988. BS, Ariz. State U., 1984. Sales agt. Coldwell Banker, Tempe, Ariz., 1984-85, CBS Property Svcs., Phoenix, 1985—. Republican. Baptist. Home: 502 W Palm Ln Phoenix AZ 85003 Office: CBS Property Svcs Inc 100 W Clarendon #2300 Phoenix AZ 85013

SEALE, ROBERT MCMILLAN, office services company executive; b. Birmingham, Ala., Feb. 1, 1938; s. Robert McMillan and Margaret Sutherland (Miller) S.; B.A., Emory U., 1959. With N.Y. Life Ins. Co., San Francisco, 1960-67; with Dictaphone Office Services div. Dictaphone Corp., San Francisco, 1967-69; pres. Am. Profl. Service, Inc., Dictation West, Miss Jones' Word Processing, San Francisco, Pleasant Hill, South San Francisco, Calif., Los Angeles, Beverly Hills, Riverside, Portland, Phoenix, Las Vegas., Orange County, Calif. and Denver, 1969—, Environments West, 1980—, Los Arcos Properties, 1980—; bd. dirs. The Rose Resnic Ctr. for Blind and Handicapped; med. word processing cons. to hosps., health care insts., office equipment mfrs.; lectr. in field. Chmn. San Francisco Mayor's Com. for Employment of Handicapped, 1971-73; mem. Calif. Gov.'s Planning and Adv. Com. for Vocat. Rehab. Planning, 1968-69; pres. Calif. League for Handicapped, 1968-70, bd. dirs., 1966-73, 84—, adv. council, 1973-77; v.p. Stebbins Found., 1980—; pres Stebbins Housing Corp., 1980—. Recipient Spoke and Spark award U.S. Jr. C. of C., 1967; KABL Outstanding Citizen's award, 1965, 71. Mem. Am. Med. Records Assn., Adminstrv. Mgmt. Soc., Sales and Mktg. Execs. Assn., Am. Assn. Med. Transcription (Disting. Service award 1985), Emory U. Alumni Assn., Emory Lamplighters Soc., Internat. Word Processing Inst., U.S. C. of C., Delta Tau Delta. Republican. Club: Olympic Athletic. Contbr. articles in field to profl. jours. Office: 1177 Mission Rd S San Francisco CA 94080

SEALS, BUFORD VALENTINE, JR., retail executive; b. Braley, Calif., May 17, 1919; s. Buford Valentine and Cathryn (Jeans) S.; m. Zola Attaberry, June 15, 1939 (dec. Sept. 1947). Attended high sch. Owner, prin. grocery and restaurant, Seattle, 1937-39, Three G.I.s, Seattle, 1946-48, gas stas., Seattle, 1951-54, convalescent hosps., Portland, Oreg., 1956-60, supermarkets, Seattle, 1951-54, auto bus., Seattle, 1951-54, Buford's Candy Circus, San Diego, 1978-. Served as chief petty officer USN, 1942-45, PTO. Featured in newspapers, nat. mags., TV, radio programs. Home: 3710 Pio Pico San Diego CA 92106 Office: 1959 Abbott St San Diego CA 92107

SEAMAN, DARYL KENNETH, oil company executive; b. Rouleau, Sask., Can., Apr. 28, 1922; s. Byron Luther and Letha Mae (Patton) S.; m. Lois Maureen deLong (dec.); children: Diane Maureen Lefroy, Robert Byron, Kenneth Alan, Gary Ross Seaman. B.S. in Mech. Engring., U. Sask., 1948, LLD (hon.), 1982. Cert. mech. engr. Chmn., chief exec. officer Bow Valley Industries Ltd., Calgary, Alta., Can., 1962-70, 1970-82, chmn., pres., chief exec. officer, 1985-87, chmn., chief exec. officer, 1988—; bd. dirs. Pan-Alta. Gas Ltd., Calgary, NOVA, Calgary, Vencap Equities Alta. Ltd., Edmonton, BioTechnica Internat. of Can., Calgary, Bow Valley Resource Services Ltd.; co-owner, dir. Calgary Flames Hockey Club. Mem. Royal Commn. Econ. Union and Devel. Prospects for Can., 1982-85; active numerous coms. for fundraising U. Sask. Served with RCAF, 1941-45, Eng., North Africa, Italy. Mem. Assn. Profl. Engrs., Geologists and Geophysicists (hon. life) (Frank Spragins award, 1985, McGill Mgmt. Achievement award, 1979), Ranchmen's Club, RAF Club, Earl Grey Golf Club, Calgary Petroleum Club, Calgary Golf and Country Club, U. Calgary Chancellor's Club. Progressive Conservative. Mem. United Ch. Can. Home: Rural Rt #8, Calgary, AB Canada T2J 2T9 Office: Bow Valley Industries Ltd, 321 6th Ave SW Ste 1800, Calgary, AB Canada T2P 3R2

SEAMON, ROBERT EDWARD, physicist; b. Worcester, Mass., May 18, 1939; s. H. Burton and Mildred Bernice (Bamford) S. BS with distinction, Worcester Poly. Inst., 1961; MS, Yale U., 1963, PhD, 1968. Rsch. staff physicist SUNY, Buffalo, 1968; mem. staff Los Alamos (N.Mex.) Nat. Lab., 1969—; mem. staff, Nuclear Data sect., Internat. Atomic Energy Agy., Vienna, Austria, 1978-79. Mem. Am. Phys. Soc., Am. Nuclear Soc., Am. Guild of Organists. Republican. Episcopalian. Home: Box 421 Los Alamos NM 87544 Office: Group X6 MS B226 Los Alamos Nat Lab Los Alamos NM 87545

SEARCY, JOHNNY DUANE, insurance executive; b. Porterville, Calif., Mar. 12, 1960; s. Marshall Ross and Shirley Jean (Howard) S.; m. Penny Diane Bost, Aug. 18, 1979; children: John David, Jessica Diane. BS, Golden Gate U., 1984. Comml. lines support Hartford Ins. Group, San Francisco, 1977-84; prin. Searcy Ins. Ctr., Porterville, 1984—. Mem. Profl. Ins. Agts., Ind. Ins. Agts. and Brokers, Porterville C. of C. (ambassador 1986-87). Republican. Home: 1641 W Mulberry Ave Porterville CA 93257 Office: Searcy Ins Ctr 308 N 2nd Porterville CA 93257

SEARIGHT, PATRICIA ADELAIDE, retired radio and television executive; b. Rochester, N.Y.; d. William Hammond and Irma (Winters) S. BA, Ohio State U. Program dir. Radio Sta. WTOP, Washington, 1952-63, gen. mgr. info., 1964; radio and TV cons., 1964-84; ret., 1984; producer, dir. many radio and TV programs; spl. fgn. news corr. French Govt., 1956; v.p. Micro Beads, Inc., 1955-59; sec., dir. Dennis-Inches, Corp., 1955-59; exec. dir. Am. Women in Radio and TV, 1969-74; fgn. service officer U.S. Dept. State, AEC, ret. Mem. pres.'s coun. Toledo Mus. Art. Recipient Kappa Kappa Gamma Alumna achievement award. Mem. Am. Women in Radio and TV (program chmn.; corrs. sec.; dir. Washington chpt.; pres. 1958-60, nat. membership chmn. 1962-63, nat. chmn. Industry Info. Digest 1963-64, Mid-Eastern v.p. 1964-66), Soc. Am. Travel Writers (treas. 1957-58, v.p. 1958-59), Nat. Acad. TV Arts and Scis., Women's Advt. Club (Washington, pres. 1959-60), Nat. Press Club, Soroptimist, Kappa Kappa Gamma. Episcopalian. Home: 10549 E Desert Cove Ave Scottsdale AZ 85259

SEARLE, LEROY FRANK, literature educator; b. American Fork, Utah, Sept. 21, 1942; s. Charles L. and Verda (Woffinden) S.; m. Yvonne C. Holz, 1962 (div. 1966); children: Cassandra Searle Ewer, Sabrina Searle Porter; m. Margaret Ann Sowers, Feb. 15, 1969; 1 child, James Harrison Sowers. BS, Utah State U., 1965; MA, U. Iowa, 1968, PhD, 1970. Teaching asst. in English U. Iowa, Iowa City, 1968-70; asst. prof. lit. U. Rochester, N.Y., 1970-77; assoc. prof. lit. U. Wash., Seattle, 1977—, assoc. chmn. English dept., 1982-85; dir. Humanities and Arts Computer Ctr., 1985-87; vis. fellow Princeton (N.J.) U., 1975; v.p. Delphi Devel., Inc., Seattle, 1983—. Author: (poetry) The Book of Lambspring, 1975; editor: (with H. Adams) Critical Theory Since 1985, 86; contbr. articles on photography and lit. criticism to profl. jours. Mem. Metro-Act, Rochester, 1971-76. Woodrow Wilson Found. fellow, 1965, NDEA Title IV fellow, 1967-69. Mem. MLA, Soc. for Critical Exchange (founding bd. dirs. 1975-80), Soc. for Photog. Edn. Democrat. Home: 6273 19th Ave NE Seattle WA 98115 Office: U Wash English Dept GN 30 Seattle WA 98195

SEARLE-KUBBY, JAN L., sculptor; b. Ellensburg, Wash., Aug. 27, 1938; d. Kenneth Gifford and Lillian (Storey) B.; m. Sheldon Walter Searle, Dec. 5, 1969 (div. Nov. 1982); m. Dan Kubby July 24, 1983; children: Scott William, LoyAnne. Student in art and edn., Cen. Wash. State U., 1957-59, U. Colo., 1962-63. Supr., art dir. Yakima (Wash.) Herald, 1963-69; owner, art dir. Ad Mauk, Denver, 1970-72, Nat. Western Mktg., Ft. Worth, 1972-74, Jan Dihel & Assoc., Denver, 1975-81; sculptor Denver, 1976—. Works include permanent exhibits at State Capitol, Bismark, N.D., 1981, Buffalo Bill Cody Mus., 1978-82, Cowboy Hall of Fame, 1978-80, Profl. Rodeo Cowboys Mus., 1978-84, Tex. Tech. U. Western Heritage Art Mus., 1983-84 (1st and 2d in sculpture 1979-80, 82), Omni Banks one man show, Denver, 1982 and encore, 1983, life size statue founder Nat. Jewish Hosp., Colo., 1987, commn. Colo. Ballet, 1987; sculpture shown on 6 month European tour sponsored by TWA, 1986-87, 6 month exhibit World's Fair, 1982; contbr. articles to profl. jours. Recipient Florence Nightengale award Colo. Nurses Assn. Mem. Internat. Sculptor Soc., Woman Artists Am. West (v.p., Best of Show and 1st in sculpture 1979-83), Nat. Western Artists (1st in sculpture Nat. Western Art Show 1980, 82), Profl. Artists of Colo., Am. Artists Profl. League. Home: 8 Cherrymoor Dr Englewood CO 80110

SEARNS, ROBERT MICHAEL, urban planner, consultant; b. Toronto, Ont., Can., May 14, 1946; s. James Milton and Bernice (Frankel) S.; m. Sally Preston, June 6, 1982; children: Bryn, Noah. BS, SUNY, Binghamton, 1968; MArch, SUNY, Buffalo, 1971, SUNY, Buffalo. Research assoc. BOSTI, Inc., Buffalo, 1969-71; assoc. planner Erie/Niagara Co. Regional Planning, Buffalo, 1971-74; sect. head Denver Planning Office, 1974-76; cons. to mayor City of Denver, 1976-78; prin. Urban Edges, Inc., Denver, 1978—; appointed mem. Gov.'s Open Space & Agrl. Group, Denver, 1981; devel. cons. South Suburban Found., Denver, 1982—. Author (booklet) The Other Colorado, 1981, Pierre, S.D. Waterfront Masterplan, 1987, Silverthorn County Blue River Master Plan, 1988, Colorado Springs County Midland Corridor Plan, 1989; contbr. articles to profl. jours. Trustee Vols. for Outdoor Colo., 1987—; mem. Colo. Outdoor Recreation Resource steering com. Recipient Friend of The River award Denver Greenway Found., 1982, Boettcher Innovations award Denver Council of Govts., 1986. Mem. Am. Planning Assn. (Nat. Current Topic award 1986), Urban Land Inst. (assoc.), Nat. Recreation and Parks Assn., Colo. Urban Design Forum, Denver Urban Design Forum (trustee 1988—), Am. Inst. Cert. Planners. Office: Urban Edges Inc 1624 Humboldt St Denver CO 80218

SEARS, ROBERT EUGENE, retired aerospace company executive; b. Los Angeles, Nov. 22, 1921; s. Albert Eugene and Edythe (Lund) S.; m. Marjorie Welch, Dec. 24, 1946; children: Marjorie Camusi, Elizabeth Edythe, Robert E. Jr. BSME, Princeton U., 1947. Registered profl. engr., Calif. From sect. head to div. mgr. Hughes Aircraft Co., El Segundo, Calif., 1949-84, group v.p., 1984-86. Active L.A. World Affairs Council. Mem. Phi Beta Kappa, Tau Beta Pi. Clubs: Los Angeles Country; Salt Air; Princeton (N.Y.C.). Home: 204 S Plymouth Blvd Los Angeles CA 90004

SEARS, STEVEN LEE, screenwriter, consultant; b. Ft. Gordon, Ga., Dec. 23, 1957; s. Richard Bruce Sr. and Marian (Dean) S.; m. Winnie McCarron, July 2, 1987. AA, U. Fla., 1976; BA in Theater cum laude, Fla. State U., 1980. Writer TV shows Riptide Stephen J. Cannell Prodns., Hollywood, Calif., 1984-86, writer TV shows A-Team, 1986-87, writer TV shows Stingray, 1987, story editor TV show J.J. Starbuck, 1987-88; story editor TV show The Father Dowling Mysteries VIACOM/Hardgrove/Silverman Prodns., 1988—; exec. story cons. Highwayman Glen Larson/New West Prodns., Universal City, Calif., 1988—. Writer: (TV show) Hardcastle and McCormick, 1985, Jesse Hawkes, 1989, Superboy, 1989. Mem. Writers Guild Am., Screen Actors Guild, AFTRA. Democrat.

SEATON, CHARLES HERBERT, engineering and marketing consultant; b. Uniontown, Pa., Sept. 13, 1928; s. Charles Swan Seaton and Mary Elizabeth Kelley; m. Jean Louise Harte, Dec. 1950 (div. 1983); children: Charles Brete, Gary Bruce, Carl Evan, Scott Montgomery, Lauren Louise. BS in Aeronautical Engring., Pa. State U., 1949, postgrad., 1949-51. Aerodynamics engr. to design specialist Gen. Dynamics, 1951-59; prin. engr. aeronutronic div. Ford Motor Co., 1959-62; asst. dir. Nuclear Flight Systems NASA Hdqrs., 1962-63; mgr. applications engring., Spl. Purpose Nuclear Systems Op. Gen. Electric Co., 1963-66; cons. 1966—; mgr. computer application engring. Universal Data Systems, 1968-70; tech. mgr. software svcs. dept. Northrop Corp., Anaheim, Calif., 1970-71; founder, dir. Wastemate Corp., 1975-80, 86—; guest lectr. Nat. U.; cons. Nat. Sci. Found., 1971-75. Troopleader Boy Scouts Am., 1975-76, scoutmaster, 1976—. Recipient Silver Beaver award Boy Scouts Am. Mem. Rotary (bd. dirs. Kearny Mesa chpt.). Republican. Home and Office: PO Box 283 Cardiff by the Sea CA 92007

SEATON, W. B. (BRUCE SEATON), container transport and distribution executive; b. Phila., Apr. 1, 1925; married. B.S., UCLA, 1949. With J.F. Forbes & Co., 1950-53; treas., controller Douglas Oil Co., 1953-66; asst. treas. Occidental Petroleum Co., 1966-70; v.p., sec., treas. Natomas Co., 1970-72, v.p. fin., treas., 1972-74, sr. v.p., 1974-78, exec. v.p. mktg. and transp., 1978-79, exec. v.p., dir., 1979-83, pres., 1983; pres., chief oper. officer Am. Pres. Lines Ltd., Oakland, Calif., 1977-83, chief exec. officer, 1983—; chmn., pres., chief exec. officer, bd. dirs. Am. Pres. Cos., Oakland, 1983—. Bd. trustees UCLA Found. Recipient Excellence in Tech. award Gartner Group, 1988, Internat. Achievement award World Trade Club of San Francisco, 1988; named Maritime Man of Yr. U.S. Propeller Club, 1987. Office: Am Pres Cos Ltd 1800 Harrison St Oakland CA 94612

SEAWELL, DONALD RAY, lawyer, publisher, arts center executive, producer; b. Jonesboro, N.C., Aug. 1, 1912; s. A.A.F. and Bertha (Smith) S.; m. Eugenia Rawls, Apr. 5, 1941; children: Brook Ashley, Donald Brockman. A.B., U. N.C., 1933, J.D., 1936, D.Litt., 1980; L.H.D., U. No. Colo., 1978. Bar: N.C. 1936, N.Y. 1947. With SEC, 1939-41, 45-47, Dept. Justice, 1942-43; chmn. bd., dir., pub., pres. Denver Post, 1966-81; chmn. bd., dir. Gravure West, L.A., 1966-81; dir. Swan Prodns., London; of counsel firm Bernstein, Seawell, Kove & Maltin, N.Y.C., 1979—; chmn. bd., chief exec. officer Denver Ctr. for Performing Arts, 19723—; ptnr. Bonfils-Seawell Enterprises, N.Y.C. Chmn. bd. ANTA, 1965—; mem. theatre panel Nat. Council Arts, 1970-74; bd. govs. Royal Shakespeare Theatre, Eng.; trustee Am. Acad. Dramatic Arts, 1967—, Hofstra U., 1968-69, Central City Opera Assn., Denver Symphony; bd. dirs., chmn. exec. com. Air Force Acad. Found., Nat. Ints. Outdoor Drama, Walter Hampden Meml. Library, Hammond Mus.; pres. Helen G. Bonfils Found., Denver Opera Found.; past chmn., mem. founding bd. Civilian/Mil. Inst. Served with AUS, World War II. Recipient Am. Acad. Achievement award, 1980, Tony award for producing On Your Toes, 1983, Voice Research and Awareness award Voice Found., 1983. Clubs: Bucks (London); Players, Dutch Treat (N.Y.C.); Denver Country, Denver, Cherry Hills Country, Mile High (Denver); Garden of Gods (Colorado Springs, Colo.). Office: Denver Ctr for Performing Arts 1050 13th St Denver CO 80204

SEBALD, CHARLES WILLIAM, JR., electrical company executive; b. Danville, Ill., Feb. 3, 1947; s. Charles William and Harriet (Hecker) S.; m. Jane Marie Mitchell, Feb. 25, 1967; children: Charles Dale, Delora Marie. BA in Bus., Ball State U., 1969, MA in Mgmt., 1970. Mgmt. trainee Ind. Nat. Bank, Indpls., 1970-71; sr. materials planner Western Electric div. AT&T, Westminster, Colo., 1971-74; sr. buyer Storage Tech., Louisville, Colo., 1974-78, mgr. procurement, 1978-80; gen. mgr. Ren Electronics Corp., Canon City, Colo., 1980—; chmn. Mfg. Round Table, Fremont County, Colo., 1983—; lectr. bus. colls., Colo., 1976—. Chmn. bd. dirs. Jr. Achievement, Fremont County, Colo., 1984—, United Way, 1987—. Mem. Colorado Springs Exec. Assn. Lodges: Rotary, Elks. Home: 1006 Beech Canon City CO 81212 Office: Ren Electronics Corp PO Box 1410 Canon City CO 81212

SEBASTIAN, ROBERT FRANK, international financial executive; b. Chgo., July 11, 1941; s. Nicholas Michael and Marion Ann (Kerber) S.; m. Margaret Marie Alexander, May 30, 1944; children: Robert, Brian, Gregory. BA, U. Ill., Urbana, 1963; MBA, De Paul U., 1969. Comml. officer Can. Consulate Gen., Chgo., 1965-69; asst. treas. Continental Ill. Nat. Bank, Chgo., 1969-74; asst. mgr. Continental Ill. Nat. Bank, Tokyo, 1974-76; asst. v.p. Mercantile Bank, St. Louis, 1976-79; v.p. Bank of Tokyo, Chgo., 1979-82; systems cons. Internet Systems, Chgo., 1982-84; pres. Export Assistance Ctr., Seattle, 1984—; lectr. No. Ill. U., De Kalb, Ill., 1983; visiting scholar U. Wash., Seattle, 1984; cons. Coll. So. Idaho, Twin Falls, 1988; lectr. Pacific Luth. U., Tacoma, Wash., 1989. Contbr. articles to profl. jours. Mem. U.S. Dept. of Commerce, Dist. Export Coun., Seattle Community Coll., Export Program adv. com. Mem. Wash. Coun. Internat. Trade, Mensa. Presbyterian. Home: 2606 170th SE Bellevue WA 98008 Office: Export Assistance Ctr 2001 6th Ave Ste 1700 Seattle WA 98121

SEBASTIANI, DONALD AUGUST, winery executive. Former Calif. state assemblyman; chmn., chief exec. officer Sebastiani Vineyards, Sonoma, Calif. Office: Sebastiani Vineyards PO Box AA Sonoma CA 95476 *

SECRIST, DOLLY ALVAREZ, translator; b. Bucaramanga, Colombia, June 24; d. Justo Jose and Elvira Maria (Rodriguez) Alvarez; grad. John Robert Powers, 1966; A.A., El Camino Coll., 1971; student UCLA, 1971-73; grad. Dale Carnegie Sch., 1976; B.S., U. Beverly Hills, 1982; postgrad. Golden Gate U., 1983; m. Harold B. Secrist, Aug. 30, 1975, Varitypist Biddle Publ. Co., Los Angeles, 1963-67; exec. sec. Alfred M. Lewis Co., Riverside, Calif., 1967-69; multilingual exec. sec. Gen. Electric TEMPO, Santa Barbara, Calif., 1969-71; multilingual exec. sec. UCLA, Westwood, Calif, 1971-73; adminstrv. asst., translator, expediter Bechtel Power Corp., Los Angeles, 1973-83; exec. staff asst. Denny's Internat., 1984—. Mem. Nat. Assn. Female Execs., Calif. Bus. Women's Network, Success Motivation Inst. Roman Catholic. Club: Toastmasters (officer). Office: Dennys Internat 16700 Valley View La Mirada CA 90657

SEDA, PETER EUGENE, cardiologist; b. North Platte, Nebr., Nov. 5, 1946; s. Edward Robert and Irene Germain (Damstrom) S.; m. Carole Celeste Ogoshi, Oct. 25, 1974; children: Erin Aislinn, Jeremy Peter. BS, U. Nebr., 1969, MD, 1973. Diplomate Am. Bd. Internal Medicine, Intern U. Oreg. Med. Sch. Hosp. Clinic, Portland, 1973-74; resident in internal medicine U. Oreg. Health Sci. Ctr., Portland, 1974-76, fellow in cardiovascular medicine 1976-78; dir., cardiologist Mid-Columbia Heart and Lung Inst., Richland, Wash., 1978—, Kadlec Hosp., Richland, 1980—; tchr. for physicians, cons. Kennewick Gen. Hosp., Wash., 1984—; dir. Doppler Echocardiography Lab., Our Lady of Lourdes Hosp., Pasco, Wash. Contbr. articles and reports to profl. jours. Regents scholarship U. Nebr., 1971. Fellow Am. Coll. Cardiology, Am. Coll Chest Physicians, Am. Heart Assn., Council Clinical Cardiology; mem. Benton Franklin Med. Soc. (sec. 1988—), Wash. State Heart Assn. Republican. Methodist. Home: 1301 S Quay St Kennewick WA 99337 Office: Mid-Columbia Heart & Lung Inst 969 Stevens Ste 2A Richland WA 99352

SEDARES, LORNA WOOD, music educator, musician; b. Albion, Mich., Jan. 7, 1956; d. E. Alan and Lois (Sakaguchi) W.; m. James Louis Sedares, July 28, 1984. BMus., St. Louis Conservatory of Music, 1977. Violist San Antonio (Tex.) Symphony, 1978-83; mus. dir. Sta. KPAC Radio, San Antonio, 1982-84; strings instr. Northeast Ind. Sch. Dist., San Antonio, 1984-86; violin/viola tchr. Mandel Music Studio, Phoenix, Ariz., 1986-88; violin/viola instr. Glendale Community Coll., 1987-89, Phoenix Sch. Ballet, 1988—. Recipient Stamper scholarship St. Louis Conservatory of Music, 1975-77, scholarship Ladies Friday Musical Club, 1975. Mem. Phoenix Symphony Aux., Phoenix Symphony Guild, San Antonio Symphony League, Mid-Tex. Symphony Assn.

SEDEÑO, EUGENE RAYMOND, electronics engineer, consultant; b. Honolulu, Aug. 31, 1952; s. Josephine Marie Sedeño Rosa; m. Theresa Ann Contreras, Dec. 28, 1980; children: Roxanne Guadelupe, Raymond Contreras. ASET, Heald Engring. Coll., 1974; BSEE, Coll. Allied Sci., 1980. Field svc. engr. Bausch & Lomb, San Leandro, Calif., 1974-81; project mgr. Tylan Corp., Carson, Calif., 1981-85; field svc. supr. Sci. Atlanta, Santa Fe Springs, Calif., 1985-86; facilities and systems engr. Refractory Composities, Inc., Whittier, Calif., 1986—; cons. Refractory Composites, Whittier, Calif., 1985—. Served with U.S. Army, 1970-72. Mem. Am. Mgmt. Assn., Mensa. Democrat. Roman Catholic. Home: 16137 Minnitonka St Victorville CA 92392 Office: Refractory Composites Inc 12220 A Rivera Rd Whittier CA 90606

SEDLOCK, JOY, psychiatric social worker; b. Memphis, Jan. 23, 1958; d. George Rudolph Sedlock and Mary Robson; m. Thomas Robert Jones, Aug. 8, 1983. AA, Ventura (Calif.) Jr. Coll., 1978; BS in Psychology, Calif. Luth. U., 1980; MS in Counseling and Psychology, U. LaVerne, 1983; MSW, Calif. State U., Sacramento, 1986. Research asst. Camarillo (Calif.) State Hosp., 1981, tchr.'s aide, 1982; sub. tchr. asst. Ventura County Sch. Dist., 1981; teaching asst. Ventura Jr. Coll., 1980-82, tchr. adult edn., 1980-84; psychiatric social worker Yolo County Day Treatment Ctr., Broderick, Calif., 1986, Napa (Calif.) State Hosp., 1986—. Mem. NOW. Mem. Humanist Orgn. Ch. Home: PO Box 1095 Yountville CA 94599 Office: Napa State Hosp Napa/Vallejo Hgwy Napa CA 49558

SEEGALL, MANFRED ISMAR LUDWIG, physicist, educator; b. Berlin, Germany, Dec. 23, 1929; s. Leonhard and Vera Antonie (Vodackova) S.; came to U.S., 1952, naturalized, 1957; m. Alma R. Sterner Clarke; 2 stepchildren: James, Mark. BS magna cum laude, Loyola Coll., 1957; MS, Brown U., 1960; PhD, Stuttgart (Germany) Tech. U., 1965. Research engr. Autonetics Corp. div. N.Am. Aviation, Downey, Calif., 1959-61; physicist Astronautics div. Gen. Dynamics, Inc., San Diego, 1961-62; research scientist Max Planck Inst., Stuttgart, 1962-65; instr. stats. and algebra San Diego City Coll., 1966; sr. research engr. Solar div. Internat. Harvester Co., San Diego, 1967-73; research cons. in energy and pollution, San Diego, 1974-83; part-time evening instr. Mesa Coll., San Diego, 1980-81; instr. Grossmont Coll., El Cajon, Calif., 1981; sr. scientist Evaluation Research Corp., San Diego, 1981-82, RCS analyst Teledyne Micronetics, San Diego, 1983-84, sr. design specialist Alcoa Defense Systems, San Diego, 1984-87, cons. phys scis., 1987— . Mem. IEEE (sr.), Internat. Platform Assn., Calif. Parapsychology Found. (sec. research com.), Cottage of Czechoslovakia of House of Pacific Relations, Rosicrucian Order, Loyola Coll., Brown U. alumni assns. Republican. Club: San Diego Lodge AMORC. Contbr. articles on acoustics, pollution and temp. measurement methods to tech. jours.; patentee in field. Address: 8735 Blue Lake Dr San Diego CA 92119

SEELENFREUND, ALAN, distribution company executive; b. N.Y.C., Oct. 22, 1936; s. Max and Gertrude (Roth) S.; m. Ellyn Bolt; 1 child, Eric. BME, Cornell U., 1959, M. in Indsl. Engring., 1960; PhD in Mgmt. Sci., Stanford U., 1967. Asst. prof. bus. adminstrn. Grad. Sch. Bus. Stanford U., Palo Alto, Calif., 1966-71; mgmt. cons. Strong, Wishart and Assocs., San Francisco, 1971-75; various mgmt. positions McKesson Corp., San Francisco, 1975-84, v.p., chief fin. officer, 1984-86, exec. v.p., chief fin. officer, 1986—, also bd. dirs.; bd. dirs. Armor All Products Corp., PCS, Inc. Mem. Fin. Execs. Inst., Fin. Officers No. Calif., Washington Pvt. Sector Coun., World Affairs Coun. No. Calif., San Francisco C. of C. (bd. dirs.), Bankers CLub, St. Francis Yacht Club, San Francisco Yacht Club, Villa Taverna Club. Office: McKesson Corp One Post St San Francisco CA 94104

SEELEY, DAVID ODOM, lawyer; b. Battle Creek, Mich., Sept. 22, 1949; s. Howard L. and E. Mildred (Odom) S.; m. Charlene F. Stoutsenberger, Sept. 12, 1969; children: Jason, Jeremy, Allison, Jonathan, Annalynne, Jeffrey. BS, U. Calif., Riverside, 1971; postgrad., Brigham Young U., 1971-73, JD, 1980. Bar: Utah 1980, U.S. Dist. Ct. Utah 1980, U.S. Patent and Trademark Office 1981, U.S. Ct. Appeals (fed. cir.) 1986, (10th cir.) 1989. Assoc. Mallinckrodt & Mallinckrodt, Salt Lake City, 1980-81, Fox, Edwards & Gardiner, Salt Lake City, 1981-84; ptnr. Workman, Nydegger & Jensen, Salt Lake City, 1984—. Maj. USAF, 1974-77. Mem. ABA, Am. Intellectual Property Law Assn., Utah State Bar Assn. (litigation sect.). Home: 1292 E Canyon Creek Dr Bountiful UT 84010 Office: Workman Nydegger & Jensen 60 E South Temple Salt Lake City UT 84111

SEELEY, MILES PARDEE, health care foundation executive; b. Evanston, Ill., Sept. 21, 1929; s. Miles Gay and Jane (Pardee) S.; m. Marilyn Halley (div. 1986); children: Dana Morgan, Laura MacDonell. BA, Stanford U., 1951. Ops. officer CIA, Washington, 1952-71; pres. Jackson (Wyo.) Sporting Goods Co., 1971-88; founder, ptnr. Curran-Seeley Found., Jackson, 1988—; trustee, The Seeley Found., Chgo., 1951—, The Menninger Found., Topeka, 1978—. Chmn. continuing edn. com., St. John's Hosp., Jackson, 1978—; bd. dirs. Western Wyo. Mental Health, 1983-85, Southwestern Wyo. Alcohol Rehab. Assn., 1986. Capt. USAF, 1952-55, Korea. Mem. Biofeedback Soc. Am. Republican. Home: PO Box 732 Wilson WY 83014 Office: Curran Seeley Found PO Box 468 Jackson WY 83001

SEELY, BEN KETROW, research chemist; b. Springfield, Ohio, Apr. 21, 1914; s. David William and Zola Delite (Ketrow) S.; m. Beverly Bodell, Jan. 5, 1937 (dec. 1969); children: Sandra, Cynthia, Tomacia, David; m. Louisa C. Hillis, Sept. 7, 1977. BS, Wittenberg U., 1936. Chief chemist Crowell-Collier, Springfield, 1938-45; research chemist N.Mex. Inst. Mining and Tech., Socorro, 1946-55, assoc. prof. chemistry, 1976—, sr. research chemist, 1986—; supr. chemistry Sandia Nat. Labs., Albuquerque, 1956-74; investigator atmospheric studies Commonwealth Sci. Indsl. Research Orgn. U. Grounds, Sydney, Australia, 1953, Pineapple and Sugarcane Research Inst. U. Hawaii, Honolulu, 1954, project shower Internat. Research Project, Hawaii, 1955; mem. hurricane com. Nat. Weather Bur., Washington, 1955. Contbr. articles to profl. jours.; developed microchem. procedures for identification of sub-micron particles in the atmosphere. Comdr. CAP, Socorro, 1952-55; pres. PTA, Socorro, 1953-54. Mem. AAAS, Am. Chem. Soc., N.Mex. Acad. Sci. Republican. Presbyterian. Lodge: Lions. Home: 4923 Alberta Ln NW Albuquerque NM 87120 Office: NMex Inst Mining & Tech Socorro NM 87801

SEELY, LINDA LEE, bank executive; b. Sacramento, July 5, 1955; d. Gordon Lee Christensen and Jenny Marie (Yerkovich) Harris. Student, Am. River Coll., 1973-74, Southwestern Oreg. Coll., 1982-88. Mgmt. trainee Western Bank, Redmond, Oreg., 1978-79; ops. officer Western Bank, Prineville, 1979-80, Medford, Oreg., 1980-82; employee relations officer, affirmative action coordinator Western Bank, Coos Bay, Oreg., 1982-84; asst. v.p., employee relations officer, affirmative action coordinator Western Bank, Coos Bay, 1984-88, asst. v.p., asst. dir. human resources, affirmative action officer, 1988—; TV hostess Wells Nat. Services Inc., Sacramento, 1971-74;

asst. mgr. Pub. Fin., Sacramento, 1974-76; relief mgr. Pub. Fin., Portland, Oreg., 1976-77; part-time instr. Southwestern Oreg. Community Coll., Coos Bay, 1983, 87—. Chair United Good Neighbor, Medford, 1982; vol. speaker various orgns., 1982—; supr. adv. curriculum com. Southwestern Oreg. Community Coll., Coos Bay, 1984. Mem. Nat. Assn. Bank Women (charter, past pres., various offices), Tri-County Affirmative Action Assn., Coos Bay C. of C., Toastmasters (chmn., past pres., various offices). Office: Western Bank 212 S Fifth St Coos Bay OR 97420

SEELYE, MARVIN VERN, educational administrator; b. Bellingham, Wash., May 10, 1937; s. Clarence and Mable (Hogan) S.; m. Elizabeth Lind, July 8, 1961; children: Eric Martin, Mark Steffen. BA in Edn., Western Wash. U., 1962, adminstrv. credential, 1970; MA in Edn., Ariz. State U., 1968. Cert. tchr., sch. adminstr., Wash. Tchr. Oak Harbor (Wash.) Sch. Dist., 1962-74, asst. prin., 1974-83, coord. staff devel., 1983-86, instrnl. support adminstr., 1986—; cons. in ednl. leadership, 1984—; adj. prof. Seattle Pacific U., 1985—. Contbn. coord., March of Dimes, Island County, 1982. Mem. Assn. for Supervision and Curriculum Devel., Wash. Assn. Supervision and Curriculum Devel., Wash. Assn. Sch. Adminstrs., Whidbey Golf and Country Club (bd. dirs. 1986—). Home: 3625 375 West Oak Harbor WA 98277 Office: Oak Harbor Sch Dist 1250 Midway Blvd Oak Harbor WA 98277

SEEMAN, JAMES LESTER, property management executive; b. Ravenna, Ohio, Apr. 15, 1940; s. Ralph Lester and Frances Mae (Bayley) S. BA in Edn., Ariz. State U., 1962. Theater educator Arcadia High Sch., Phoenix, 1965-72; theater mgr. Phoenix Little Theater, 1972-73; facilities mgr. music dept. Ariz. State U., Tempe, 1973-75; co. mgr. New Christy Minstrels, L.A., 1975-82; asst. to v.p. 1st Interstate Bank, Ltd., L.A., 1982-86; v.p. Condominium Concepts, Playa del Rey, Calif., 1986—. Home: 5930-F Seville Ave Huntington Park CA 90255 Office: Condominium Concepts 8055 Manchester Ave Apt 625 Playa Del Rey CA 90293

SEETHALER, WILLIAM CHARLES, international business executive, consultant; b. N.Y.C., Dec. 4, 1937; s. William Charles and Catherine Frances (Flaherty) S.; student Quinnipiac Coll., Conn., 1955-56, Ohio State U., 1956-58; BS in Bus. Adminstrn., U. San Francisco, 1977; MBA, Pepperdine U., 1982. Asst. to v.p. sales T. Sendzimir, Inc., Waterbury, Conn. and Paris, 1960-66; mgr. internat. ops. Dempsey Indsl. Furnace Co., E. Longmeadow, Mass., 1966-67; mgr. internat. sales Yoder Co., Cleve., 1967-74; mng. dir., owner Seethaler & Assocs.; owner, chief exec. officer Seethaler Internat. Ltd., Palo Alto, Calif., 1974—; ptnr. DFS Computer Assocs., San Jose, Calif., 1976-87. Bd. dirs. Palo Alto Fund, 1979—, chmn., 1986—; mem. community adv. panel Stanford U., 1986—. Mem. Menlo Park C. of C., Palo Alto C. of C. (v.p. orgn. affairs 1976-77, pres. 1977-78, dir. 1975-79), Assn. Iron and Steel Engrs., Inst. Indsl. Engrs. (sr. mem., v.p. profl. relations Peninsula chpt. 1988—), U. San Francisco Alumni Assn., Stanford U. Alumni Assn., Pepperdine U. Alumni Assn., Assn. MBA Execs., Am. Mgmt. Assn. Clubs: Stanford Buck, Stanford Cardinal Cage, Stanford Diamond. Office: 701 Welch Rd Ste 1119 Palo Alto CA 94304

SEFERIAN, EDWARD, symphony conductor; b. Cleve., Mar. 23, 1931; s. Loutfeg and Berjhewie (Kouzouian) S.; m. Jan Barbara Spears, June 11, 1955; children: Susan, Linda, Marc. BS in Violin, Juilliard Sch. Music, N.Y.C., 1957; MS, Juilliard Sch. Music, 1958. Prof. music U. Louisville, 1958-59, U. Puget Sound, Tacoma, Wash., 1959—; asst. concert master Seattle Symphony, 1960-66; conductor and musical dir. Tacoma Symphony, 1959—; bd. dir. Winterim program U. Puget Sound, 1973-74. Violinist U. Puget Sound Faculty Trio, Tacoma Symphony String Quartet; first performance of William Bergsma's Concerto for Violin and Orchestra, 1966, Leroy Ostransky's Concerto for Violin and Orchestra, 1980. Sgt. USMC, 1951-54. Honored with invitation by Pablo Casals to Casals Festival, P.R., 1959-69; recipient Nat. Award for Cultural Achievement Steinway Piano Co., 1967, Faculty Recognition award U. Puget Sound Alumni Assn., 1972, Tacoma Arts Commn. Achievement in the Arts award, 1983, James H. Binns Disting. Svc. award Friends of Tacoma Community Coll. Libr., 1988. Mem. Music Educators Nat. Conf. Home: 4131 Madrona Tacoma WA 98407 Office: U Puget Sound 1500 N Warner Tacoma WA 98416

SEGALL, HERVEY D., neuroradiologist, educator; b. Moose Jaw, Sask, Can., Aug. 11, 1937; s. Ben and Anna Helen (Belovich) S.; m. Doris Muriel Zwirn, July 14, 1962; children: Julie Lynne, Aviva Esther, Penina Louise. BA, U. B.C., 1957, MD, 1961. Dir. neuroradiology U. So. Calif. Med. Sch., L.A., 1976—, prof. radiology, 1979—. Assoc. editor: Radiology, 1982—; mem. editorial bd. Jour. of Computer Assisted Tomography, 1983—, Jour. Child Neurology, 1987—; contbr. numerous articles to profl. jours. Lt. comdr. USNR, 1966-68. Mem. Western Neuroradiological Soc. (pres. 1978), RSNA, ASNR, LARS CRS. Home: San Marino CA 91108 Office: U So Calif Med Sch 1200 N State St Los Angeles CA 91108

SEGE, THOMAS DAVIS, electronics company executive; b. Novi Sad, Yugoslavia, May 17, 1926; came to U.S., 1941; m. Dorothea Zimmer; children—Kathy, Ron. B.S. in Elec. Engring., Columbia U., 1946, M.S. in Elec. Engring., 1948. With Sperry Gyroscope Co., N.Y.C., 1948-63, chief engr. Electron Tube div., until 1963; mgr. Power Grid Tube div. EIMAC, San Carlos, Calif., 1963-65, v.p. ops., 1965; v.p., gen. mgr. EIMAC div. Varian Assocs., Palo Alto, Calif., 1965-68, v.p. equipment group, 1968-71, pres. electron device group, 1971-81, pres., chief exec. officer, 1981-84, chmn. bd. dirs., chief exec. officer, 1984—; mem. adv. council SRI Internat., Menlo Park, Calif.; dir. Calif. Microwave. Patentee microwave output window, 1957, electron beam forming device, 1959. Campaign chmn. United Way Santa Clara County, 1983, chmn. policy com., 1984. Mem. IEEE (sr.), Santa Clara County Mfg. Group (bd. dirs. 1981-86). Office: Varian Assocs Inc 611 Hansen Way Palo Alto CA 94303

SEGGER, MARTIN JOSEPH, museum director, art history educator; b. Felixtowe, Eng., Nov. 22, 1946; s. Gerald Joseph and Lillian Joan (Barker-Emery) S.; m. Angele Cordonier, Oct. 4, 1968; children: Cara Michelle, Marie-Claire, Margaret Ellen. B.A., U. Victoria, 1969, Diploma in Edn., 1970; M. in Philosophy, U. London, 1973. Prof. art history U. Victoria, 1970-74, dir. Maltwood Art Mus., prof. art history, 1977—; museologist B.C. Provincial Mus., Victoria, 1974-77; cons. Nat. Mus. Corp., Ottawa, 1977, UNESCO, O.E.A., Cairo, 1983; bd. dirs. Canaap Press, Can., 1980—. Author: exhbn. catalogue House Beautiful, 1975, Arts of the Forgotten Pioneers, 1971, Victoria: An Architectural History, 1979, (commendation Am. Assn. State and Local History 1980), This Old House, 1975, This Old Town, 1979, British Columbia Parliament Buildings, 1979, The Heritage of Canada, 1981, Samuel Maclure: In Search of Appropriate Form, 1986 (Hallmark award 1987). Bd. govs. Heritage Can. Found., 1979-83; chmn. City of Victoria Heritage Adv. Com., 1975-79; bd. dirs. B.C. Heritage Trust, 1977-86; mem. B.C. Heritage Adv. Bd., 1977-83; alderman City of Victoria, 1987—; bd. dirs. B.C. Govt. House Found., 1987—. Recipient Heritage Can. Communications award, 1976. Fellow Royal Soc. Arts; mem. Can. Museums Assn. (counsellor 1975-77), Internat. Council Museums (exec.), Internat. Council Monuments and Sites (bd. dirs. 1980—),Soc. Study Architecture Can. (bd. dirs. 1979-81). Roman Catholic. Home: 1035 Sutlej St, Victoria, BC Canada V8V 2V9 Office: U Victoria, PO Box 1700, Victoria, BC Canada V8W 2Y2

SEGHINI, JOANN BAGLEY, school system administrator; b. Salt Lake City, Aug. 4, 1937; d. Ben G. and Marie (Pehrson) Bagley; m. William G. Calkins, Sept. 17, 1956 (div. 1962); m. Robert L. Seghini (div.); children: Stephen John, Edward Wayne. BS, U. Utah, 1958, MEd, 1972, PhD, 1979. Cert. tchr. N.Y., Utah. Tchr. Jordan Sch. Dist., Sandy, Utah, 1958-62, 66-73, Utah Network Instrnl. TV, Sandy, 1968-69; cons., workshop trainer Creativity Workshop U. Utah, Sandy, 1970-72, Brigham Young U., Honolulu, 1973-74; curriculum dir. State Office of Edn. and Egyptian Study Project, Salt Lake City, 1976; with Jordan Sch. Dist., Sandy, 1977—; dir. curriculum and staff devel., coordinator programs Jordan Sch. Dist., 1984—; adj. dept. spl. edn. U. Utah, 1984—; cons. in field. Co-author guide books. Pres., Citizen's Animal Mgmt. and Protection Soc., Salt Lake City, 1984-87; bd. dirs.Human Soc. Utah, 1985-91; coun. mem. Midvale City, Utah, 1985-89; co-chmn. Brigham Young U. Pub. Sch. Task Force, 1986—. Named Humanatarian of Yr., Human Soc. Utah, 1986; Ford Found. scholar, 1954. Mem. Utah Assn. Supervision and Curriculum Devel. (past pres.), Utah Coun. Social Studies, Utah Heritage Found. (Svc. award 1979), Nat. Assn. of Gifted and Talented, Utah Assn. of Gifted and Talented, Order Eastern Star, Daughters of Nile, Delta Kappa Gamma (pres. 1980-81), Phi Delta Kappa. Home: 170 Pioneer St Midvale UT 84047 Office: Jordan Sch Dist 9361 S 300 E Sandy UT 84070

SEGINSKI, WILLIAM ENOCH, sales company executive; b. Englewood, Colo., July 9, 1933; s. Ignatius Albert and Helen Veronica (Mescier) S.; BS in Metall. Engring., U. Ariz., 1960; m. Cora Creswell, July 12, 1957; children: Cynthia, Catherine, Joseph. Mechanic, Am. Airlines, 1956-57; nuclear design engr. GE, Richland, Wash., 1960-61; sales engr. Worthington Air Conditioning Corp., L.A., 1962; pres., owner J & B Sales Co., Phoenix, 1963—; vice chmn. Ariz. State Boiler Adv. Bd., 1977-82; lectr. solar energy. Mem. adv. bd. T-Roosevelt Coun. Boy Scout of Am., 1987-89. With USN, 1950-55. Mem. U. Ariz. Alumni Assn. (bd. dirs. 1972-73, pres. Phoenix chpt. 1971-72), Ariz. Elec. League (pres. solar div.), Ariz. Solar Energy Industries Assn. (bd. dirs., founding officer), NSPE (sr.), ASHRAE (bd. dirs. 1985-86), Am. Soc. Plumbing Engrs. (affiliate), Ariz. Plumbing Mfrs. Rep. Assn. (pres. 1982), Internat. Solar Energy Soc., U. Ariz. Alumni Assn. (pres. Dean's Assocs. 1981), Roosevelt Rough Riders (bd. dirs. 1986, pres.-elect 1986, pres. 1987), Sigma Gamma Epsilon (pres., founding mem.), Sigma Alpha Epsilon. Episcopalian. Clubs: Moon Valley Country, Arizona, Masons. Home: 7050 N 11th Ave Phoenix AZ 85021 Office: J & B Sales 3441 N 29th Ave Phoenix AZ 85017

SEGUNDO, LESLIE PAUL, environmental health specialist; b. Honolulu, Apr. 17, 1953; s. Miles Melecio and Florence Palisin (Balasbas) S. AA, Leeward Coll., 1974; BA in Chemistry, U. Hawaii, 1983. Environ. health specialist Hawaii Dept. Health, Honolulu, 1983-85; environ. health specialist assigned to EPA Region 9 Hawaii Dept. Health, San Francisco, 1985—. Mem. AAAS, Am. Chem. Soc. Roman Catholic.

SEIBEL, ERWIN, oceanographer, educator; b. Schwientochlowitz, Germany, Apr. 29, 1942; came to U.S., 1952. BS, CCNY, 1965; MS, U. Mich., 1966, PhD, 1972. Asst. research oceanographer U. Mich., Ann Arbor, 1972-75, assoc. research oceanographer, 1975-78, asst. dir. sea grant, 1975-78; environ. lab dir. San Francisco State U., 1978-81, chmn. dept. geoscis., 1981-88, dean undergraduate studies, 1988—; sr. scientist cruises U. Mich., 1971-78; mem. sea grant site rev. teams Nat. Sea Grant Program, Washington, 1978—; bd. govs. Moss Landing Marine Labs., Calif., 1981—; mem. adv. com. Ctr. Advancement Mercantile Spacefaring; coordinator Biology Forum Calif. Acad. Scis., 1988—; exec. sec. Oceans 83 Marine Tech. Soc., IEEE, San Francisco, 1982-83; co-ordinator Symposium for Pacific AAAS El Nino Effect, 1983-84; dir. environ. monitoring nuclear power plant, 1972-78. Contbr. articles to profl. jours.; developer photogrammetric technique for continuous shoreline monitoring. Advisor MESA program for Minority Students, San Francisco area, 1981-88; vol. San Francisco Bay Area council Girl Scouts U.S., 1982-86. Served to capt. U.S. Army, 1967-71, Vietnam. Grantee Am. Electric Power Co., 1972-78, Gt. Lakes Basin Commn., 1975-76, Calif. Div. Mines and Geology, 1986-88. Recipient Exceptional Merit Service award San Francisco State U., 1984. Fellow AAAS, Calif. Acad. Scis., Geol. Soc. Am.; mem. N.Y. Acad. Scis., Am. Geophys. Union, Marine Tech. Soc. (pres. San Francisco Bay chpt. 1982-83), U. Mich. Alumni Assn., Gold Key (hon.), Sigma XI (pres. San Francisco State U. chpt. 1982-84). Office: San Francisco State U Office of Dean Undergrad Studies 1600 Holloway Ave San Francisco CA 94132

SEIBOLD, ROBERT WILLIAM, aerospace engineer; b. Washington, Apr. 2, 1940; s. Herman Rudolph and Clara Bond (Taylor) S.; m. Louana Marie Workman, Sept. 27, 1969 (div. 1983); children: Heidi Starlyn, Whitney Stephen. BS in Chem. Engring., Auburn (Ala.) U., 1960. Registered profl. engr., Calif. Engr. Douglas Aircraft Co, Santa Monica, Calif., 1961-65; tech. specialist McDonnell Douglas Astronautics Co., Huntington Beach, Calif., 1966-78; project mgr. Hughes Aikrcraft Co., El Segundo, Calif., 1979—. Contbr. articles to profl. jours.; patentee in field. Singer L.A. Master Chorale, 1963-88. Mem. Soc. Advancement of Matl. and Process Engring., Adhesion Soc., Sigma Xi. Democrat. Home: PO Box 7 El Segundo CA 90245 Office: Hughes Aircraft Co PO Box 902 El Segundo CA 90245

SEIDEL, ANGELA, nurse; b. Bisbee, Ariz., Jan. 29, 1939; d. Eli Phillip and Zorka Davcevich; divorced; children: Dawn Marie, Lisa Diane. Diploma, Good Samaritan Hosp., Phoenix, 1960; BA in Health Edn., Ariz. State U., 1974, BSN, 1988; postgrad., No. Ariz. U., 1982. R.N., Ariz.; nat. cert. in psychiat. mental health nursing. Staff nurse Bisbee Hosp., 1960-61; head nurse Providence Hosp., Waco, Tex., 1961-62, Bay Meml. Hosp., Panama City, Fla., 1963-64; asst. head nurse Good Samaritan Hosp., Phoenix, 1974-77; coordinator primary care VA Hosp., Phoenix, 1977—. Mem. Ariz. Nurses Assn. (bd. dirs. 1987—), Sigma Theta Tau., Am. Slavic Club (Phoenix, bd. dirs. 1980-87). Democrat. Serbian Orthodox. Home: 3911 E Earll Dr Phoenix AZ 85018

SEIDEL, EUGENE MAURICE, entrepreneur; b. Ft. Wayne, Ind., Mar. 18; s. Emil Richard and Tona Therese (Aden) S.; m. Nancy Ward Biddle, Sept. 2, 1950; children: Amy Aden Seidel Marks, Betsy Roberts Seidel Martin. BS in Chemistry, Bus. Adminstrn., Ind. U., 1944. Tech. service chemist Eberbach & Son Co., Ann Arbor, Mich., 1945-46; with tech. purchasing dept. W.A. Sheaffer Pen Co., Ft. Madison, Iowa, 1946-48; dir. chem. labs. Ind. U., Bloomington, 1948-53; mktg. and comml. developer Comml. Solvents Corp., Terre Haute, Ind., 1953-57; mgr. bus. exploration Crown Zellerbach Co., Camas, Wash., 1957-82; pres. Eugene M. Seidel Assocs., Inc. (including EMSA, Inc.), Gleneden Beach, Oreg., 1982-88, 1988—. Elder First Presbyn. Ch., Vancouver; mem. Clark County (Wash.) Comprehensive Health Planning Com., 1984 Ad Hoc com.; bd. dirs. Columbia Bus. Community for the Arts, Vancouver, 1980-86, pres. 1984-86, v.p., 1987—; bd. dirs. Clark Coll. Found., Vancouver, 1983-88, Clark County Arts Council; trustee Neskowin (Oreg.) Valley Sch.; bd. dirs. Clark Coll. Found., 1983-88; appointed by gov. to 4 yr. term Health Coordination Council; past pres. Southwest Wash. Health Systems Agy., Shorewood West Condominium Owners Assn. Mem. AAAS, Am. Econ. Assn., Am. Mktg. Assn. (past bd. dirs.), Am. Chem. Soc. (past bd. dirs.), Chem. Mktg. Research Assn. (life), Tech. Assn. Pulp and Paper Industry, Salishan Leaseholders, Inc. (asst. chmn. bd. dirs., mem. archtl. com.). Lodge: Rotary. Home: 142 Salishan Dr PO Box 709 Gleneden Beach OR 97388 Office: The Marketplace at Salishan Ste A-11 PO Box 495 Gleneden Beach OR 97388

SEIDEL, GEORGE ELIAS, JR., animal scientist, educator; b. Reading, Pa., July 13, 1943; s. George E. Sr. and Grace Esther (Heinly) S.; m. Sarah Beth Moore, May 28, 1970; 1 child, Andrew. BS, Pa. State U., 1965; MS, Cornell U., 1968, PhD, 1970; postgrad., Harvard U. Med. Sch., Boston, 1970-71. Asst. prof. physiology Colo. State U., Ft. Collins, 1971-75, assoc. prof., 1975-83, prof., 1983—; vis. scientist Yale U., 1978-79, M.I.T., 1986-87. Co-editor: New Technologies in Animal Breeding, 1981; contbr. articles to profl. jours. Recipient Alexander Von Humboldt award, N.Y.C., 1983, Animal Breeding Research award Nat. Assn. Animal Breeders, Columbia, Mo., 1983, Clark award Colo. State U., 1982, Upjohn Physiology award, 1986; Gov's. award for Sci. and Tech., Colo., 1986. Mem. Am. Dairy Sci. Assn., Am. Soc. Animal Sci. (Young Animal Scientist award 1983), AAAS, Soc. for Study of Reprodn., Internat. Embryo Transfer Soc. (pres. 1979). Home: 3101 Arrowhead Rd Laporte CO 80535 Office: Colo State U Animal Reprodn Lab Fort Collins CO 80523

SEIDEL, NEIL DOUGLAS, professional guitarist; b. N.Y.C., Oct. 7, 1946; s. Benjamin Boris and Margaret (Altshuler) S.; children: Carla Marie, Reva Michelle. BA, Calif. State U., L.A., 1973. Profl. freelance guitarist 1952—; lead guitarist Gary Lewis & the Playboys, 1968-70, Shanti Atlantic Records, 1970-72; college instr. L.A. Community Coll., L.A., 1972-80, Ambassador Coll., L.A., 1972-80, Loyola Marymount, L.A., 1972-80, Calif. State U., Dominguez Hills, 1972-80. Composer (musical soundtrack documentary) Dera, 1972 (Info. Film Festival Silver award); producer (record albums). Mem. Calif. Republican Golden Circle, L.A., 1988. Mem. Meeting Planners Internat., Internat. Soc. Spl. Events, L.A. Conv. & Visitors Bur., Nat. Assn. Catering Execs., Beverly Hills C. of C., Hollywood C. of C., St. James's Club. Republican. Jewish. Office: Seidel Event Prodns 720 N Spaulding Ave Los Angeles CA 90046

SEIDEL, ROBERT WAYNE, museum administrator; b. Kansas City, Mo., June 9, 1945; s. Wayne Herman and Harriet Anita (Day) S.; m. Judy Irene Sharp, Dec. 28, 1966 (div. 1969); m. Alison Publicover, Aug. 26, 1972 (div. 1989); 1 child, Mary Ruth. BA, Westmar Coll., 1967; MA, U. Calif., Berkeley, 1968, PhD, 1978. Exhibit designer Lawrence Hall Sci., Berkeley, 1970-72; specialist Poland 4-city tour USIA, Warsaw, 1971-72; grad. rsch. and teaching asst. U. Calif., 1972-78; asst. prof. Tex. Tech U., Lubbock, 1978-83, dir. rsch., 1979-83; rsch. historian U. Calif., Berkeley, 1980-82, Laser History Project, Albany, Calif., 1983-88; adminstr. Bradbury Sci. Mus., Los Alamos, N.Mex., 1985—; cons. Office Naval Rsch., Washington, 1984—. Author: Lawrence and HIs Laboratory: A Hisotry of the Lawrence Berkeley Laboratory, 1989. Mem. Lubbock Heritage Soc., 1983, N.Mex. Sci. Ctr. Commn., 1989; mem. adv. com. County Cultural Ctr., Los Alamos, 1986—. Woodrow Wilson fellow, 1967, U. Calif. Regent's fellow, 1968, German Marshall Fund fellow, Grenoble, France, 1975. Mem. History Sci. Soc., Soc. for History Tech., Am. Hist. Assn., Soc. for Philosophy Tech., N.Mex. Acad. Scis. Democrat. Home: 314 Mimbres Dr Los Alamos NM 87544 Office: Bradbury Sci Mus Mail Stop M897 Los Alamos NM 87545

SEIDENBAUM, ART, newspaper editor, writer; b. N.Y.C., Apr. 4, 1930; s. William George and Lida (Aretsky) S.; m. Judith Weiner, June 14 (div. May 1974); children: Kyle Scott, Kerry Kai; m. Patricia Houser, June 20, 1974. BS, Northwestern U., 1951. Reporter Life mag., N.Y.C., 1955-59; corr. Los Angeles, 1960-61; West Coast Bureau chief Saturday Evening Post, Los Angeles, 1961-62; columnist Los Angeles Times, 1962-78, book editor, 1978-85, opinion editor, 1985-; host; Sta. KCET-TV, Los Angeles, 1965-76; disting. vis. prof. Calif. State U., Dominguez Hills, 1980. Author: Confrontation on Campus, 1970, This is California, 1975, Los Angeles 200, 1980. Mem. Calif. Council for Humanities, 1977-81. Lt. USN, 1952-55. Recipient award for conbn. to architecture Calif. council AIA, 1965, award for contbn. to lit. Loyola-Marymount U., Los Angeles, 1979. Mem. Soc. Profl. Journalists. Home: 1260 Linda Flora Dr Los Angeles CA 90049 Office: LA Times Times Mirror Sq Los Angeles CA 90053

SEIDENVERG, NORMAN FRANKLIN, surgeon; b. Portland, Oreg., July 23, 1937; s. Sanford and Nettie (Mondschein) S.; m. Diane M. Schlitz, Jan. 21, 1967; children: Scott, Tracy. BA, U. Oreg., 1958, MD, 1961. Diplomate Am. Bd. Surgery. Intern U.S. Naval Hosp., Oakland, Calif., 1961-62; resident Presbyn. Med. Ctr., San Francisco, 1964-68; pvt. practice in gen. surgery Vallejo, Calif., 1968—; chief of surgery Vallejo Gen. Hosp., 1970-72; bd. dirs. Surety Fed. Savs. Bank; instr. Solano Community Coll., 1972-73; instr. Nursing extension schs. U. Calif., Davis, 1977-79; continuing edn. provider Calif. State Bd. Registered Nursing, 1980—. Bd. dirs. Solano County unit Am. Cancer Soc., 1970—, pres. 1984-87. Lt. USN, 1961-64. Fellow ACS, Pan Pacific Surgical Assn.; mem. Solano County Med. Soc., Calif. Med. Assn., Commonwealth Club. Republican. Jewish. Home: 1844 Vervais St Vallejo CA 94571 Office: 1460 N Camino Alto #209 Vallejo CA 94589

SEIDLER, JERRY HUGH, lawyer; b. N.Y.C., July 14, 1958; s. Hans H. and Liselotte V. (Dyczek) S.; m. Kathy L. Bress, Aug. 19, 1984. BA, U. Pa., 1980; JD, Vanderbilt U., 1983. Bar: Ga. 1983, U.S. Ct. Mil. Appeals 1985, Pa. 1986, N.J. 1986, U.S. Dist. Ct. (ea. dist.) Pa. 1987. Assoc. Driker Biddle & Reath, Phila., 1987—. Capt. U.S. Army, 1983-87. Mem. ABA, Pa. Bar Assn., Ga. Bar Assn., Phila. Bar Assn. Democrat. Jewish. Office: Drinker Biddle & Reath 1100 PNB Bldg Philadelphia PA 19107

SEIFERT, CHARLES ROBERT, business owner; b. Rio de Janeiro, Sept. 14, 1935; s. Charles Esseleur and Margaret (Andrews) S.;m. Mary Jim Shannon, May 19, 1958 (div. 1979); children: Nina Michele, Charles Robert II, Erika Ann; m. Rosemarie Cislaghi, Apr. 17, 1979. Student, Am. Sch Rio de Janeiro, 1952, Tex. Tech. U., 1952-53, U. Ariz., 1959-60, Pima Coll., 1982-83. Sales agt. Am. Nat. Ins. Co., Galveston, Tex., 1956-70; owner, sales exec. Littso Sports, Littleton, Colo., 1970-78; tchr. tennis Clube Juvenil, Cakias Do Sol, Brazil, 1978-79; owner, sales exec. Soccerr & Tennis El-Tenista, Tucson, 1979—. Various positions Colo. State Jr. and Soccer Assn., 1970-78. Mem. Optimists, Civitans. Republican. Office: Soccer & Tennis El Tenista 3455 E Speedway Tucson AZ 85716

SEIFERT, GEORGE, professional football coach; b. San Francisco, Jan. 22, 1940; m. Linda Seifert; children: Eve, Jason. Grad., U. Utah, 1963. Asst. football coach U. Utah, 1964; head coach Westminster Coll., 1965; asst. coach U. Iowa, 1966, U. Oreg., 1966-71; secondary coach Stanford U., 1972-74; head coach Cornell U., 1975-76; from secondary coach to defensive coord. San Francisco 49ers, 1980-89, head coach, 1989—. With AUS, 1963. Office: San Francisco 49ers 711 Nevada St Redwood City CA 94061 *

SEIFERT-COHEN, SALLY ANN, educational association administrator; b. Zanesville, Ohio, Mar. 20, 1942; d. Walter W. and Jean (Bateman) Seifert; m. Donald B. Cohen, Sept. 16, 1967. BS, Miami U., Oxford, Ohio, 1964; MA with honors, Loyola Marymount U., Los Angeles, 1976. Teacher secondary schs. Columbus, Ohio and Beverly Hills, Calif., 1965-74; adminstrv. officer Hollywood Community Hosp., L.A., 1974-76; exec. officer Coll. Letters and Sci. UCLA, 1976-86, fund mgr. Office Gift Policy Admnisnrtn., 1986-88; career trainer, UCLA, 1976-78; mem. univ. policies commn., 1985-86. Mem. Nat. Assn. Female Execs. Republican. Unitarian. Home: 804 Hillcrest St El Segundo CA 90245 Office: UCLA Gift Policy Adminstrn 405 Hilgard Ave Los Angeles CA 90024

SEIFTER, HARVEY, theater director, consultant; b. Cleve., Jan. 20, 1954; s. Benjamin and Betty (Levinsky) S. BA with high honors, Brandeis U., 1976. Exec. dir. Theater for the New City, N.Y.C., 1981-87; mng. dir. Magic Theatre, San Francisco, 1988—; panelist Nat. Endowment for the Arts, 1982-83; cons. Nat. Inst. for Archtl. Edn., N.Y.C., 1987-88, N.Y. State Council on the Arts, 1987-88; guest lectures on theatre include Harvard U., NYU, Ecole Nat., Paris. Translator play Scrapers in the Sky, 1985. Recipient 11 Obie awards, 1981-87. Democrat. Jewish. Office: Magic Theatre Fort Mason Ctr Bldg D San Francisco CA 94123

SEIL, FREDRICK JOHN, neuroscientist, neurologist; b. Nova Sova, Yugoslavia, Nov. 9, 1933; s. Joseph and Theresa (Krieger) S.; m. Daryle Faith Wolfers, July 2, 1955; children: Jonathan Fredrick, Joel Philip Timothy. BA, Oberlin Coll., 1956; MD, Stanford U., 1960. Intern Kaiser Found. Hosp., San Francisco, 1960-61; resident in neurology Stanford (Calif.) U., 1961-64, fellow in neurology, 1964-66; staff neurologist VA Med. Ctr., Palo Alto, Calif., 1969; clin. investigator VA Med. Ctr., Portland, Oreg., 1976-79, staff neurologist, 1979-81, dir. VA office regeneration research programs, 1981—; asst. prof. neurology Stanford U., 1969-75, assoc. prof. neurology Oreg. Health Sci. U., Portland, 1976-78, prof. neurology, 1978—. Editor: Nerve, Organ and Tissue Regeneration: Research Perspectives, 1983, Neural Regeneration, 1987, Current Issues in Neural Regeneration Research, 1988, Neural Regeneration and Transplantation, 1989; contbr. articles to profl. jours. Served to capt. U.S. Army, 1966-68. Grantee VA, 1970—. Mem. AAAS, Am. Neurol. Assn., Internat. Brain Research Orgn., Am. Assn. Neuropathologists, Soc. Neurosci. Democrat. Home: 10306 SW Radcliffe Rd Portland OR 97219 Office: VA Med Ctr Office Regeneration Rsch Portland OR 97201

SEILING, ALFRED WILLIAM, semiconductor processing executive, consultant; b. Watseka, Ill., May 28, 1936; s. Alfred William and Edith Mae (Miller) S.; m. Patricia Ann Whalen, Sept. 7, 1957; children: David, Sheryl, Brad, Bryan. BA in Chemistry, Blackburn Coll., 1957; PhD in Chemistry, Ind. U., 1962; postgrad. exec. program, Stanford U., 1979. Rsch. chemist Morton Chem. Co. div. Morton Internat., Woodstock, Ill., 1961-64; tech. svc. supr. Morton Chem. Co. div. Morton Internat., 1964-67, tech. mgr. electronics, 1967-74; group mgr. electronics Morton Chem. Co. div. Morton Internat., Chgo., 1974-77; gen. mgr. electronics Morton Chem. Co. div. Morton Thiokol, Chgo., 1977-83; v.p. Morton Chem. Co. div. Morton Thiokol, 1979-83; v.p. mktg. Dynachem div. Morton Chem. Co. div. Morton Thiokol, Tustin, Calif., 1983-84; owner, mgr., cons. Seiling & Assocs., Monterey, Calif., 1984--. Contbr. numerous articles to tech. publs.; patentee in field. Pres. Lake Region YMCA, Crystal Lake, Ill., 1968-70; lay leader, chmn. bd. United Meth. Ch., Crystal Lake, 1976-78, Laguna Hills, Calif., 1985-87. Mem. Semiconductor Equipment & Materials Inst., Sigma Xi, Phi Lambda Upsilon. Republican. Home and Office: 2 Windsor Rise Monterey CA 93940

SEITZMAN, JERRY MICHAEL, research scientist, software executive; b. Albuquerque, Apr. 30, 1960; s. Leonard Harold and Gloria (Stein) S. BS, U. Tex., 1982; MS, Stanford U., 1983. Field engr. Amoco Prodn. Co., Levelland, Tex., 1980; engring. intern, govtl. relations ASME, Washington, 1981; rsch. asst. Stanford (Calif.) U., 1983—; software engr., exec. Cogent Software, Menlo Park, Calif., 1988—. Contbr. articles to profl. jours., chpts. to books. Vol. Jewish Community Ctr., San Antonio, 1978-85. IMB Grad. fellow, 1986, 87. Mem. ASME, Optical Soc. Am., Soc. Photo-Optical Instrumentation Engrs., Pi Tau Sigma, Tau Beta Pi, Sigma Xi. Office: Stanford U Mech Engring Bldg 520 Stanford CA 94305

SEKICH, KAREN S., collection agent; b. Longmont, Colo., June 12, 1944; d. Clarence Herbert and Pauline (Leinweber) Newman; m. Nicholas John Sekich Jr., July 7, 1962; children: Nicholas John III, Dominick Donald, Veronica June Herren. AA in Liberal Arts, Aims Jr. Coll., 1986; BBA, Regis Coll., 1988. Writer Phillips Mktg., Longmont, 1974-77; ptnr. Sekich Bus. Park, Longmont, 1974—; accounts receivable specialist Sekich Equipment Co., Longmont, 1977-82; mgr. Furrow Restaurant, Longmont, 1980-86; pres. mgr. Quest R&I Ltd., Longmont, 1981—; seminar leader, regional mgr. Sklar Fin. Control Corp., San Mateo, Calif., 1987-88; chmn. S.W. Weld Devel. Group, Longmont, 1988. Campaign coordinator Weld County Reps., Greeley, Colo., 1982; bd. dirs. St. Vrain Valley Sch. Dist., Boulder and Weld Counties, Colo., 1977-80, Olde Columbine Sch., Longmont, 1985—; candidate House Seat 49, Longmont, 1980. Mem. NFIB, Associated Collection Agys., Inc. (bd. dirs. Colo. and Wyo. chpts.), Platteville C. of C., Longmont C. of C. (bd. dirs.), Greeley C. of C., Carbon Valley C. of C., Ft. Lupton C. of C., Phi Beta Lamda (named bus. person of yr. 1984). Roman Catholic. Office: Quest R&I Ltd 4311 Hwy 66 Longmont CO 80501

SELBY, JEROME M., mayor; b. Wheatland, Wyo., Sept. 4, 1948; s. John Franklin and Claudia Meredith (Hudson) S.; m. Gloria Jean Nelson, June 14, 1969; children: Tyan, Cameronn, Kalen. BS in Math., Coll. Idaho, 1969, MA in Ednl. Adminstrn., 1974; MPA, Boise State U., 1978. Assoc. engr. Boeing Co., Seattle, 1969-71; dir. evaluation WICHE Mountain States Regional Med. Program, Boise, 1971-74; dir. rsch., evaluation Mountain States Health Corp., Boise, 1974-76, with health policy analysis and accountability, 1976-78; dir. health Kodiak (Alaska) Area Native Assn., 1978-83; mgr. Kodiak Island Borough, 1984-85, mayor, 1985—; proprietor Kodiak Tax Svc., 1978—, Registered Guide, Kodiak, 1987—; cons. Nat. Cancer Inst., Washington, 1973-78, others. Contbr. articles to profl. jours. Treas. ARC, Kodiak, 1978—, bd. dirs. 1978—, mem. western ops. hdqrs. adv. bd. 1986—, mem. group IV and V nat. adv. com., 1986—; pres. S.W. Alaska Mcpl. Conf., Anchorage, 1988—; v.p. Alaska Mcpl. League, 1988-89, pres. 1989—; active Alaska Resource Devel. Coun. Mem. Alaska Conf. Mayors, Nat. Soc. Tax Profls., Acad. Polit. Sci., Alaska Mcpl. Mgrs. Assn., Kodiak C. of C. (dir. 1983—), Rotary. Office: Kodiak Island Borough 710 Mill Bay Rd Kodiak AK 99615

SELBY, MICHAEL JOHN, air force officer, tactical instructor; b. Webster City, Iowa, Dec. 31, 1942; s. E. George and Maryjane (Cassady) S.; m. Vo Thu Nhi Thi, Aug. 20, 1971; children: Adrian A., Domenique K. BA in English Lit., UCLA, 1964; MBA, Nat. U., 1988. Tchr. U.S. Peace Corps, Thailand, 1965-67; commd. 2d lt. USAF, Ft. Walton Beach, Fla., 1968; advanced through grades to maj. USAF; instr. spl. ops. sch. USAF, Ft. Walton Beach, 1968-70; civic action officer USAF, Phan Rang, Vietnam, 1970-72; intelligence officer USAF, Cannon AFB, N.Mex., 1972-74, Clark AB, The Philippines, 1975-77; minuteman ICBM officer USAF, Minot AFB, N.D., 1977-81; intelligence staff officer USAF, Offutt AFB, Nebr., 1981-84; tactics instr. USAF, Nellis AFB, Nev., 1984-88; ret. USAF, 1988; ins. agt. Las Vegas, Nev., 1988—. Decorated Bronze Star. Mem. Old Crows Assn., Ret. Officer's Assn., U.S. Tennis Assn. Republican. Congregationalist. Home and Office: 505 Westridge Las Vegas NV 89107

SELEZNOV, ANDREW IAN, management executive; b. Phila., Mar. 10, 1952; s. Samuel and Pearl Seleznov. BS, Ariz. State U., 1975. Prodn. mgr. Lisa Frank, Inc., Tucson, 1983-84; gen. mgr. Munday Motors, Benson, Ariz., 1984-86; pres NOB Industries, Tucson, 1986—; cons. Eglin Cohen Assoc., Tucson, 1983—. Inventor in field. Arbitrator Better Bus. Bur., Tucson, 1988. Mem. Speciality Equipment Mfg. Assn. Office: NOB Industries 3542 N Geronimo Tucson AZ 85705

SELF, BARBARA ANN, nurse; b. L.A., Oct. 9, 1939; d. Paul Cline and Clara (Shapiro) Lutz; div.; 2 children. AA, L.A. City Coll., 1964; BS in Nursing, Calif. State U., L.A., 1977. R.N., Calif. Staff nurse Moore-White Med. Group, L.A., 1957-77, head nurse, 1977-78; sr. kidney transplant coord. St. Vincent Med. Ctr., L.A., 1978—. Mem. N.Am. Transplant Coord. Orgn., So. Calif. Transplant Soc., So. Calif. Transplant Coords., Anatomical Transplant Assn. Calif. (bd. dirs.). Democrat. Office: St Vincent Med Ctr 2131 W 3d St Los Angeles CA 90057

SELF, CHARLES EDWIN, fin. cons., retail company executive; b. Roanoke, Va., June 6, 1934; s. Loy Evry and Louzelle (Childers) S.; m. Phyllis Ann Stevens, Sept. 2, 1961; children: Tim, Randy, Betsy. BA, Randolph Macon Coll., 1956. Budget specialist Gen. Electric Co., Schenectady, N.Y., 1960-64; merchandise controller Montgomery Ward & Co., N.Y.C., 1964-67; controller The Hecht Co., Washington, 1967-70; v.p., asst. controller Zayre Corp., Framingham, Mass., 1970-79; v.p. fin. Wal-Mart Stores, Inc., Bentonville, Ark., 1979-87; pvt. practice fin. cons. Bellingham, Wash., 1987—; mem. fin. steering com. Nat. Mass Retail Inst., N.Y.C., 1980-86; chmn. Nat. Cap Group of Controllers, Washington, 1969. Commr. Conservation Commn., Mass., 1976-79; dir. Am. Field Service, Ark., 1984. Lt, USNR, 1956-60. Mem. B'Ham (Wash.) Yacht Club. Republican. Episcopalian. Home: 324 Bayside Rd Bellingham WA 98225

SELF, MARY OLDERSHAW, data processing executive; b. Ancon, CZ, Republic of Panama, Oct. 19, 1950; came to U.S., 1952; d. Arthur Salvin and Darlene Rosetta (Henning) Oldershaw; m. Edward Ronald Self, May 26, 1979 (div. Dec. 1984); 1 child, Darlene. Student, High Point Coll., 1968-70; BS in Mgmt. Info. Sci., Christopher Newport Coll., 1974; MS, George Washington U., 1978. Applications programmer George Washington U., Hampton, Va., 1975-80; analyst/designer OAO Corp., Hampton, 1980-82; scientist Systems and Applied Scis. Techs. Corp., Hampton, 1982-85; project program analyst Systems Devel. Corp., Newport News, Va., 1985-86; sr. systems analyst Bell Tech. Ops. Corp., Sierra Vista, Ariz., 1986-88; bus. devel. coord. Combustion-Engring. Ops. and Mgmt. Svcs., Tucson, Ariz., 1988—. Contbr. articles to profl. jours. Instr. computer post Explorer's Boy Scouts Am., Hampton, 1982-86. Mem. Am. Bus. Women's Assn. (chmn. 1977-85), Assn. for Computing Machinery, Nat. Rifle Assn. (life), U.S. Practical Shooters Assn. (life), Peninsula Indoor Pistol League (statistician 1982-86), Lafayette Gun Club (range officer 1978—), Combat Pistol Team (treas. 1981-85). Baptist. Office: Combustion Engring Ops and Mgmt Svcs 1050 E Valencia Rd Tucson AZ 85706

SELFRIDGE, MICHAEL LOUIS, manufacturing executive; b. Long Beach, Calif., Nov. 16, 1957; s. Gerald Edward and Diane Lenore (Wolenski) S.; m. Paula Gayle Cooke, June 20, 1987; children: Heather Debelak, Hillary Debelak. Student, Grove City Coll., 1975-76. Supr. Hughes Helicopter, Culver City, Calif., 1977-79; engring. analyst Arco Solar, Chatsworth, Calif., 1980-83; prodn. specialist Rockwell Internat., El Segundo, Calif., 1983—. Mem. Speakers Bur., Chatsworth, 1980-83. Mem. Inst. Cost. Analysis. Republican. Roman Catholic. Office: Rockwell Internat 827 N Douglas St El Segundo CA 90245

SELL, PATRICIA KING, educator; b. Annapolis, Md., Aug. 2, 1936; d. George Edward and Grace Georgina (Damon) King; m. Stewart Sell, June 21, 1958 (div. Jan. 1986); children: Sherri, Stacy, Sean, Stephanie. BS, Coll. of William and Mary, 1958; cert. teaching, Carnegie-Mellon U., 1960; MEd, U. San Diego, 1988. Cert. math. and sci. tchr., Calif., Pa., Mass., Md. Substitute tchr. Pitts. City Schs., 1967-68; tchr. math. and sci. San Diego Unified Sch. Dist., 1984—; pres. PTA Torrey Pines Elem. Sch., La Jolla, Calif., 1975-76, site coun., co-chair, 1979-81; v.p. edn., parent edn. 9th Dist. PTA, 1979-83,; mem. parent edn. commn. Calif. State PTA, L.A., 1982-83. Nat. co-chair ann. fundraising drive Coll. of William and Mary, Williamsburg, Va., 1981-82; candidate Bd. Edn., San Diego, 1983; pres. med. ctr. aux. U. Calif.-San Diego, 1982-83; chmn. bd. Torrey Pines Christian Ch., 1982-84. U. San Diego fellow, 1986. Mem. NEA, San Diego Sci. Educators Assn., Coll. of William and Mary Alumni Assn. (bd. dirs., sec., treas. 1976-82), Coll. of William and Mary Endowment Assn. (bd. dirs. 1983—), Pi Beta Phi, P.E.O. (pres. La Jolla chpt. 1980-82). Republican. Home: 8440 Clif-fridge Ln La Jolla CA 92037 Office: San Diego Unified Sch Dist 4100 Normal St San Diego CA 92103

SELL, ROBERT EMERSON, electrical engineer.; b. Freeport, Ill., Apr. 23, 1929; s. Cecil Leroy and Ona Arletta (Stevens) S.; B.S., U. Nebr., 1962; m. Ora Lucile Colton, Nov. 7, 1970. Chief draftsman Dempster Mill Mfg. Co., Beatrice, Nebr., 1949-53; designer-engr. U. Neb., Lincoln, 1955-65; elec. design engr. Kirkham, Michael & Assos., Omaha, 1965-67; elec. design engr. Leo A. Daly Co., Omaha, St. Louis, 1967-69; mech. design engr. Hellmuth, Obata, Kassabaum, St. Louis, 1969-70; chief elec. engr. Biagi-Hannan & Assos., Inc., Evansville, Ind., 1971-74; elec. project engr. H.L. Yoh Co., under contract to Monsanto Co., Creve Coeur, Mo., 1974-77; elec. project engr. Dhillon Engrs., Inc., Portland, Oreg., 1978-85; project coordinator Brown-Zammit-Enyeart Engring., Inc., San Diego, 1985-88; elec. engr. Morgen Design, Inc., San Diego, 1988; lead elec. engr. Popov Engrs., Inc., San Diego, 1988—; instr. Basic Inst. Tech., St. Louis, 1971. Registered profl. engr., Nebr., Mo., Ill., Ind. Ohio, W.Va., Ky., Ark., Tex., Oreg., Wash. Mem. ASHRAE, IEEE. Home: PO Box 261578 San Diego CA 92126 Office: Brown-Zammit-Enyeart Engring Inc 7950 Dunbrook Rd San Diego CA 92126

SELLERS, CHAD D., electronic design engineer; b. Idaho Falls, Idaho, Apr. 30, 1954; s. H. Allen and Lula W. (Frandsen) S.; m. Marchelle Dunkley, May 4, 1977. Student, Ricks Coll., Rexburg, Idaho, 1976; BS in Electronic Engring. Tech., Weber State Coll., 1986. Engr. apprentice Sharex, Salt Lake City, 1976-79; project engr. Texscan/MSI, Salt Lake City, 1979-83; software engr. Quanta Co., Salt Lake City, 1983-85; design engr. Am. Microsystems Inc., Pocatello, Idaho, 1985—; electronic design cons. Hi-Tek Systems, San Bernadino, Calif., 1980—. Mormon. Office: Am Microsystems Inc 2300 Buckskin Rd Pocatello ID 83201

SELLERS, JOEL SCOTT, sports medicine physician; b. Tulsa, Oct. 8, 1957; s. Jimmy Lloyd and Nita (Long) S.; m. Lori Kaye Irwin, Apr. 29, 1988. BA, U. Okla., 1980; DO, Okla. State U., 1985. Intern Phoenix Gen. Hosp., 1985-86; fellow in sports medicine Ctr. Sports Medicine and Orthopedics, Phoenix, 1986-87, staff physician, 1987—; team physician, USA Wrestling Fedn., Stillwater, Okla., 1986—, Ironwood High Sch., Glendale, Ariz., 1986—; consulting physician, Phoenix Suns basketball team, 1986—, area community colls., Phoenix; lectr. intern tng. program, Phoenix Gen., Hosp., 1986; speaker in field; U.S. physician, U.S. vs. USSR Wrestling Dual Meet, Phoenix, 1988. Contbr. articles on wrestling to various pubs. Mem. Am. Osteo. Acad. Sports Medicine, Am. Osteo. Assn. Ariz. Osteo. Assn., Okla. Alumni Assn., Sigma Chi. Democrat. Roman Catholic. Home: 2254 Mandalay Ln Phoenix AZ 85023

SELLERS, MICHAEL DONALD, marketing professional; b. Denver, Apr. 7, 1956; s. Donald Ralph and Mary (Magdalene) S.; m. Marianne Ledder, Aug. 23, 1977; children: Brian Michael, John Patrick. BBA, U. Colo., 1978. Sales rep. Univair Aircraft Corp., Aurora, Colo., 1978-81; mktg. mgr. Univair Aircraft Corp., Aurora, 1981-85, sales/mktg. mgr., 1985—. Contbr. articles to profl. jours. Tchr. Peace With Christ Luth. Ch., Aurora, 1988. Mem. Colo. Hist. Soc. Republican. Lutheran. Home: 1570 S Bahama St Aurora CO 80017 Office: Univair Aircraft Corp 2500 Himalaya Rd Aurora CO 80011

SELLERS, ROBERT SCOT, real estate developer; b. L.A., Jan. 26, 1957; s. Walter DeWitt and Diolenda Teresa (Bernardes) S.; m. Gretchen Alice Geddes, June 6, 1987. BS, Lewis & Clark Coll., 1978; MBA, Stanford U., 1981. Lic. real estate broker, Calif., Colo. Loan officer The Oreg. Bank, Portland, 1978-79; controller CFI Mgmt. Svcs., Portland, 1979; cons. Boston Consulting Group, Palo Alto, Calif., 1980; asst. project mgr. Lincoln Property Co., Denver, 1981-82, v.p., 1982-83, ptnr., Colo., 1983-87; ptnr., So. Calif. Lincoln Property Co., San Diego, 1987—; real estate cons. to Apt. and Hotels, Denver, San Diego, 1985—. Chmn. bd. Christian Internat. Scholars Found., Seattle, 1988—; bd. dirs. Youth for Christ, San Diego, 1988—; founding mem., bd. advs. High Ground Assocs., San Diego, 1988—. Mem. Bldg. Industry Assn. (president's coun. 1987—, speakers bur., 1988—), Apt. Assn. of Metro Denver (membership dir. 1987), Construction Industry Fedn., Christian Exec. Officers (San Diego). Republican. Office: Lincoln Property Co 4330 La Jolla Vill Dr #240 San Diego CA 92122

SELLS, PATRICIA LYNN, nurse; b. Streator, Ill., Nov. 27, 1956; d. Charles William and M. Jane (Murray) Mackley; m. Lloyd DeWayne Hill, Oct. 14, 1975 (div. 1980); m. Fred Sells III, Nov. 21, 1942. A in Nursing, Coolidge Acad. Coll., Ariz., 1977. RN, Ariz. Nurse Casa Grande (Ariz.) Regional Med. Ctr., 1978—; cons. in field.l. Chmn. Health Care Task Force, 1984. Roland Wilpits scholar. Mem. Bur. Bus. Practices Assn., NAFE, State Emergency Svcs. Assn. Democrat. Office: Casa Grande Regional Med Ctr 1800 E Florence Blvd Casa Grande AZ 95222

SELNA, MICHAEL WILLIAM, civil engineer; b. Oakland, Calif., Dec. 18, 1948; s. Leland Robert and Georgie (Earnshaw) S.; m. Maria Dawn Hoffman, Mar. 18, 1972; children: Blake, Kevin, Andrew. BSCE, U. Calif., Berkeley, 1970; MSCE, U. Calif., Davis, 1973. Registered prof. engr., Calif. Project engr., rsch. L.A. County Sanitation Dists., Whittier, Calif., 1973-78, supr. engr. solid waste, 1978-81, div. engr. solid waste, 1981-86, dept. head engring. dept., 1986—; project mgr. Commerce (Calif.) Refuse to Energy Facility, 1981—. Contbr. tech. papers to profl. publs. Chmn. Huntington Beach (Calif.) Environ. Bd., 1981-86. Mem. Water Pollution Control Fedn. (disinfection com. 1977), Calif. Water Pollution Control Assn. Democrat. Office: LA County Sanitation Dists PO Box 4998 Whittier CA 90607

SELTMAN, KENT DANIELS, health science facility administrator; b. Great Bend, Kans., Dec. 29, 1941; s. Albert August and Alice Jean (Daniels) S.; m. Kristine Lee Swanson, Aug. 10, 1965; children: Lee Robyn, Ann Kristine. BA, Union Coll., Lincoln, Nebr., 1964; MA, U. Nebr., 1967, PhD, 1974; MBA, Rollins Coll., 1987. Instr. English Columbia Union Coll., Takoma Park, Md., 1965-70; prof. English Pacific Union Coll., Angwin, Calif., 1970-84, chmn. English dept., 1976-84; asst. v.p. for pub. rels. Fla. Hosp., Orlando, 1984-87; adminstrv. dir. internat. heart inst. Loma Linda (Calif.) U. Med. Ctr., 1987—. Sec. Calif. State English. Liaison Com., 1976-82; mem. Orlando Opera Bd., 1986-87, promotion com. Redlands (Calif.) Symphony Orch., 1987—. Mem. Am. Mktg. Assn., Fla. Hosp. Assn. (Merit award 1986), Orlando Advt. Club (Merit-Addy award 1986). Democrat. Adventist. Home: 1615 Elizabeth St Redlands CA 92373 Office: Loma Linda U Med Ctr PO Box 2000 Loma Linda CA 92354

SELTSAM, JAMES DONALD, JR., sales and marketing professional; b. Kansas City, Mo., May 6, 1961; s. James D. and Janice I. (Langford) S. BSBA, Emporia (Kans.) State U., 1984. With sales and mktg. dept. Seltsam-Hanni, Inc., Topeka, 1980-84; asst. mgr. Westin Hotels & Resorts, Denver and Vail, Colo., 1985-88; with sales and mktg. dept. Resort Data Prcoessing, Inc., Vail, 1988—; cons. Resort Data Processing, Inc., 1988—. Mem. Kans. Real Estate Commn., Colo. Real Estate Commn., Sigma Phi Epsilon. Republican. Methodist. Office: Resort Data Processing Inc 1650 E Vail Valley Dr #C1 Vail CO 81657

SELTZER, RONALD ANTHONY, radiologist, educator; b. Washington, Mar. 7, 1935; s. Lawrence H. and Sarah (Levin)S.; m. Adele Wishnow, June 25, 1961; children: Jeffrey David, Lauren Jill. AB with distinction, U. Mich., 1956; MD with high distinction, Wayne State U., 1960. Diplomate Am. Bd. Radiology. Resident in radiology Mass. Gen. Hosp., Boston, 1961-62, 64-66; asst. prof. radiology Stanford (Calif.) U. Med. Sch., 1966-67, asst. clin. prof., 1967-73, assoc. clin. prof., 1974--; pvt. practice San Mateo, Redwood City,, Calif., 1967; mem. med. staff Mills Meml. Hosp., San Mateo, Calif., 1967-69; mem. med. staff Sequoia Hosp., Redwood City, 1969--, pres., 1986--; cons. on radiation exposure div. radiol. health USPHS, 1964-67; cons. on nuclear medicine Palo Alto VA Hosp., 1967-75; cons. on computerized reeporting in radiology Gen. Electric Co., 1975-78; cons. advanced imaging div. Xerox Corp., 1978-82; cons. on electronic imaging Stanford Research Internat., 1980-84; bd. dirs. Hosp. Consortium San Mateo County, 1986--. Contbr. articles on biol. behavior and radiation dosimaty of radioactive materials, diagnostic radiology and uses of computers in medicine to med. jours. Sr. asst. surgeon USPHS, 1962-64. Fellow Inst. Cardiology Gt. Britain; mem. AMA, Calif. Med. Assn., Radiol. Soc. N. Am., Am. Roentgen Ray Soc., Western Angiography Soc. (pres. 1976-78), San Mateo County Ind. Practice Assn. (bd. dirs. Bay Pacific health plan 1979-84), Alpha Omega Alpha. Home: 1422 Edgewood Dr Palo Alto CA 94301 Office: Sequoia Hosp Redwood City CA 94062

SELWOOD, ALEXIS FUERBRINGER, psychotherapist; b. N.Y.C., Jan. 9, 1943; d. Otto and Winona (Gunn) Fuerbringer; m. Pierce Taylor Selwood, June 8, 1964; children: Allison Taylor, Jonathan Gunn. BA, Smith Coll., 1964; MSW, U. So. Calif., 1980, PhD, 1987. Journalist Calif. Apparel News, Los Angeles, 1964-68; dir. vol. services Family Services of Los Angeles, 1977; caseworker, dir. student programs Catholic Social Svc., Long Beach, Calif., 1980-83; pvt. practice psychotherapy L.A., 1982—; faculty Calif. Inst. Clin. Social Work, 1988—; lectr. U. So. Calif. and UCLA, 1984-85. Fellow Soc. Clin. Social Work; mem. Nat. Assn. Social Workers (cert.), Nat. Registry Health Care Providers in Clin. Social Work. Office: 420 1/2 N Larchmont Blvd Los Angeles CA 90004

SELWYN, DAVID CAMERON, electronics company executive; b. Bklyn., Jan. 1, 1953; s. Louis and Lillian (Diamond) S.; m. Maria Elena Pavva, Dec. 1, 1979; children: Vanessa, Sarah. Student, N.Mex. State U., 1979. Owner, chief exec. officer Selco Electronics Inc., Las Cruces, N.M. Author software DB use, spread sheet use, minerals, Comal-Spanish. Clubs: SWMCUG (pres. 1983—) ACE (v.p. 1985—) Las Cruces. Office: Selco Electronics Inc 1455 Plains St Las Cruces NM 88001

SEMEL, GEORGE HERBERT, plastic surgeon; b. N.Y.C., Apr. 20, 1938; s. Louis Bennett and Sara Sonja (Eutis) S.; children: Alexis Christy, Daniel Louis Bennett. AB, Columbia U., 1959; MD, Boston U., 1963. Diplomate Am. Bd. Plastic Surgery. Intern L.A. County Gen. Hosp., 1963-64; resident gen. surgery Long Beach (Calif.) VA Hosp., 1964-67; residency in plastic surgery Mayo Clinic, Rochester, Minn., 1967-69; chief resident plastic surgery Med. U. S.C., Charleston, 1969-70; pvt. practice L.A., 1970—. Founder L.A. Music Ctr., 1978, Mus. Contemporary Art, 1980; mem. Fraternity of Friends of Music Ctr., 1978—. With Calif. NG, 1964-69, USNG, 1969-73. Mem. AMA, Am. Soc. Plastic Surgery, Am. Lipoplasty Soc., L.A. Soc. Plastic Surgeons, L.A. County Med. Soc., Flaming Colossus, Phi Gamma Delta. Office: 9201 Sunset Blvd #609 Los Angeles CA 90069

SEMEL, MITCHELL ROSS, television executive; b. Highland Park, Ill., Apr. 3, 1959; s. Charles Eugene and Arlene Varda (Freed) S.; m. Colleen Catherine Carroll, Oct. 15, 1988. BA, Princeton U., 1981. Pres., chief exec. officer Focus on Youth, Inc., Princeton, N.J., 1979-81; with NBC Entertainment, Burbank, Calif., 1981-85, dir. current comedy programs, 1985; v.p. UBU Prodns., L.A., 1985-89, exec. in charge of prodn., 1985—, pres. TV, 1989—. Trustee, Focus on Youth, Inc., 1981—. Mem. Acad. TV Arts and Scis. Jewish. Office: UBU Prodns Paramount Pictures Corp 5555 Melrose Ave Los Angeles CA 90038

SEMEL, TERRY, motion picture company executive; b. N.Y.C., Feb. 24, 1943; s. Ben and Mildred (Wenig) S.; m. Jane Bovingdon, Aug. 24, 1977; 1 child, Eric Scott. BS in Acctg., L.I.U., 1964; postgrad. in market research, CCNY, 1966-67. Domestic sales mgr. C.B.S. Cinema Center Films, Studio City, Calif., 1970-72; v.p., gen. mgr. Walt Disney's Buena Vista, Burbank, Calif., 1972-75; pres. W.B. Distbn. Corp., Burbank, 1975-78; exec. v.p., chief operating officer Warner Bros., Inc., Burbank, 1979-80, now pres., chief operating officer, 1980—; bd. dirs. Revlon. Office: Warner Bros Inc 4000 Warner Blvd Burbank CA 91522 *

SEMENSE, JOSEPH, corporate executive; b. Long Beach, Calif., Aug. 26, 1967; s. Emerito Ramos and Calinica (Ouano) S. Student, Calif. State U., Long Beach, 1985—. Culinary host Disneyland, Walt Disney Prodns., Anaheim, Calif., 1985-89; video editor Video Affairs Prodns., Huntington Beach, Calif., 1988—; pres., chief exec. officer, Indulgence Products, Long Beach, 1986—. Writer, dir.: (video film) They're Cops!, 1988, Who Dogged Rocky Rabbit, 1989. Roman Catholic. Home: 101 East Pepper Dr Long Beach CA 90807

SEMMENS, JOHN HOWARD, economist; b. Oswego, N.Y., Oct. 28, 1945; s. Charles Alfred Semmens and Mildred Catherine (Schnably) Giordano; m. Angela White, Apr. 17, 1982 (div.); children: Harold Alfred, Ayn Lucile. BA, Montclair State Coll., 1967; cert. bus. mgmt., U. Calif., Riverside, 1975; MBA, Ariz. State U., 1980. Teaching asst. Ariz. State U., Tempe, 1967-69; asst. mgr. Circle K, Tempe, 1971-72; mgmt. analyst Ariz. Bank, Phoenix, 1972-75; research analyst Ariz. Dept. Transp., Phoenix, 1976-77, economist, 1977-82, sr. policy analyst, 1982-88, sr. mktg. analyst, 1988—; instr. econs. Phoenix Coll., 1983—; research assoc. Heartland Inst., Chgo., 1987—; economist Laissez Faire Inst., 1987—. Author numerous Ariz. Dept. Transp. publs. and conbtr. articles to profl. jours. and newspapers. Served to ensign USNR, 1969-71. Research fellow Goldwater Inst., Flagstaff, Ariz., 1988—. Libertarian. Home: 121 W Erie Tempe AZ 85282 Office: Ariz Dept Transp 206 S 17th Ave Rm 147A Phoenix AZ 85007

SEMONES, ELIZABETH ANN, nurse, educator; b. Deadwood, S.D., Nov. 10, 1952; d. Arthur M. and Irene (Fredericks) S.; children: Kathryn M., Shannon E. BA, U. Denver, 1974; BS, U. Colo., 1976, MS, 1980. RN, Colo. Charge nurse Bethesda Hosp., Denver, 1976-79; psychiat. clin. specialist St. Luke's Hosp., Denver, 1980-85, Depression Treatment Ctr., Denver, 1985-86; coord. Rocky Mountain Heart Rsch. Inst., Denver, 1986-87; dir. mental health Denver Indian Health and Family Svcs., 1988—; chmn. planning com. Psychiat. Nursing Inst., Denver, 1982; mem. clin. faculty Met. State Coll., Denver, 1981—; clin. preceptor grad. program U. Colo., Denver, 1981-85. Contbr. chpt. to Contemporary Nursing Management, 1982. bd. dirs., chmn. ednl. programs Aurora-Adams County chpt. Am. Heart Assn., 1981-85. NIMH grantee, 1978-80. Mem. Am. Nurses Assn. (cert. psychiat. clin. nurse specialist, med. coord. 9 health fair site 1989), Colo. Soc. for Clin. Specialists in Psychiat. Nursing, P.E.O., Sigma Theta Tau. Roman Catholic. Office: Denver Indian Health 1739 Vine St Denver CO 80206

SENDROY, PETER GYULA, orthodontist; b. Chgo., Oct. 17, 1938; s. Julius Jr. and Jeanette (Candee) S.; children: Suzanne C., Christopher M., Melissa M. DDS, Georgetown U., 1964; MS in Dentistry, U. Wash., 1968. Pvt. practice, Denver, 1968—; acting head dept. orthdontics U. Colo., Denver, 1978-79; pres. Three R Automotive Inc., Englewood, Colo., 1984—; bd. dirs. Rocky Mountain Beverage Co., Denver. Bd. dirs. Denver Dumb Fiends League. 1988—. Capt. USAF, 1964-66. Mem. ADA, Colo. Dental Assn., Am. Assn. Orthodontists. Home: 2139 E Floyd Pl Englewood CO 80110 Office: 7150 E Hampden Ave Denver CO 80224

SENG, VIRGINIA ROSE, computer analyst; b. Pitts., Sept. 2, 1940; d. Frank Wilbert and Katherine Leigh (Gray) Grosick; m. Richard E. Seng, July 11, 1959 (div. June 1967); 1 child, Lisa Leigh. BA, Chaminade U., 1978; MBA, U. Hawaii, 1985; cert. in data processing, Inst. for Certification of Computer Profls., 1987. Computer programmer Hickam AFB, Honolulu, 1977-81, computer programmer analyst, 1981-83, computer programmer analyst USAF Command Control and Intelligence Support Squadron, 1983-88; mgr. data base USAF command Control and Intelligence Support Squadron, Honolulu, 1988—. Vol. Am. Cancer Soc. Mem. Armed Forces Communications and Electronics Assn., IEEE Computer Soc., Assn. Computing Machinery, Hawaii Intergovtl. Info. Processing Council, Federally Employed Women (Aloha chpt.), Diamond Head Gardens Owner's Assn. (v.p., bd. dirs.). Home: 3055 Pualei Circle #202 Honolulu HI 96815 Office: HQ PACAF/SCC Hickam AFB HI 96853

SENGA, ROBERT MAUNDU, environmental scientist, microbiologist; b. Machakos, Kenya, East Africa, Oct. 16, 1947; s. Gedion M. Senga; m. Dorcas M. Mutungi, July 7, 1979; children—Grace Wanza, Esther Nzilani, William K. Mutuku. B.S., Calif. Poly. U., Pomona, 1975; M.S., U. LaVerne, 1978; M.S., Calif. State U.-Fullerton, 1984. Tech. dir., mgr. Electronic Reclamation Service, Anaheim, Calif., 1979; v.p. Reliable Recovery, Inc., Anaheim, 1980; environ. specialist Donald Bright & Assocs., Inc., Anaheim, 1981; prodn. chemist Armstrong Rubber, Inc., South Gate, Calif., 1982—; sr. hazardous materials specialist Calif. Dept. Health Services, Los Angeles,

1984—; cons. environ. problems. Mem. AAAS, Am. Soc. for Indsl. Microbiology. Developer chem. method for precious metal refining, also non-chrominated aluminium cleaning compound.

SENGER, LINDA RAYE KELLEY, educator; b. Tacoma, Wash., Mar. 29, 1940; d. E.L. and Alma M. (Wollesen) Kelley; m. Don E. Senger, July 31, 1965; children: David A., Drew A. BA in Edn., We. Wash. U., 1962; MA in Child and Family Studies, Wash. State U., 1978. Tchr. Sumner (Wash.) Sch. Dist., 1962-67, Rush-Hentietta Sch. Dist., Rochester, N.Y., 1967-68, Puyallup (Wash.) Sch. Dist., 1975—; coord., tchr. home and family life class Puyallup Sch. Dist., 1987—. Mem. Wash. Vocat. Assn., NEA, Wash. Edn. Assn., Puyallup Edn. Assn., AAUW (co-pres. 1974-75). Office: Puyallup High Sch 105 7th St SW Puyallup WA 98371

SEN GUPTA, RATAN, utility company executive; b. Calcutta, West Bengal, India, May 22, 1947; s. Ranendra Lal and Anjali (Dutta Choudhury) Sen G.; m. Shikha Choudhury, Feb. 19, 1976; 1 child, Indranil. BTech with honors, Indian Inst. Tech., Kharagpur, West Bengal, 1969; MS, U. Cin., 1971; MBA, Syracuse U., 1973. Sr. project estimator The Ralph M. Parson Co., Pasadena, Calif., 1980-81; supr., project cost engr., estimator Bechtel Petroleum Inc., San Francisco, 1981-83; supr. cost estimating sect. Pacific Gas & Electric Co., San Francisco, 1983—. Mem. Expt. in Internat. Living, Putney, Vt., 1969-76; treas. Bay Area Prabasi, San Francisco, 1985-86, mem. bd. 1987-89. Mem. ASCE, Am. Assn. Cost Engrs. (treas. 1986-88, v.p. 1988-89, pres. 1989— San Francisco Bay chpt.). Hindu. Home: 45216 Elk Ct Fremont CA 94539 Office: Pacific Gas & Electric Co 77 Beale St Rm 2248F San Francisco CA 94106

SENNE, STEPHEN MICHAEL, manufacturing executive, consultant; b. Pasadena, Calif., July 5, 1944; s. Delmar Vincent and Penelope Ann (Hahn) S.; m. Karen Jean Tertocha, Dec. 4, 1964 (div. Aug., 1979); m. Ingrid Joy Larsen, Nov. 22, 1980. Student, Gendale Coll., 1969-71; AA, Riverside City Coll., 1972; student, U. So. Calif., 1972-73, U. Redlands, 1975-79; PhD in Physiology (hon.). Asst. supr. nondestructive testing Stainless Steel Products, Inc., Burbank, Calif., 1962-65; supr. nondestructive testing Stainless Steel Products, Inc., Burbank, 1984-87; pvt. practice fin. planning Hesperia, Calif., 1970-86; lab. supr. Gamma-Rays Inc., San Dimas, Calif., 1983-84; mgr. nondestructive engring. The Marquardt Co., Van Nuys, Calif., 1987—; karate instr. Leopard Karate Sch., Burbank, Calif. 1955—; instr. nondestructive testing Don Bosco Tech. Inst., Rosemead, Calif., 1969-87. Author: The Jungle Detective, 1979, Your Financial Report Card, 1979; editor: The Titan mgmt. news 1969, '69 (NMA award 1969). Mem. Am. Soc. for Non-Destructive Testing. Republican. Lutheran. Office: The Marquardt Co 16555 Saticoy St Van Nuys CA 91409

SENNSTROM, JOHN HAROLD, manufacturing company executive; b. Schenectady, N.Y., Mar. 15, 1941. B.S. in Indsl. Mgmt., Purdue U., 1965; M.B.A., U. Wash., 1982. Prodn. supr. Haller Inc., Northville, Mich., 1965-69; plant mgr. IPM Corp., Columbus, Ohio, 1969-76; mfg. mgr. Fentron Industries, Seattle, 1976-79; pres. Fentron Bldg. Products Co., Seattle, 1984-87, Hytek Finishes Co., Kent, Wash., 1979-84, Demcron, Redmond, Wash., 1987—. Home and Office: 2310 187th Ave NE Redmond WA 98052

SENUNGETUK, VIVIAN RUTH, lawyer; b. Syracuse, N.Y., Sept. 27, 1948; d. George Albert and Ethel Margaret (Hearl) Bender; children: Adam George Moore, William Guugzhuk Senungetuk. BA, SUNY, Binghamton, 1968; MAT, U. Alaska, 1972; JD, Boston U., 1984. Bar: Alaska 1985, Mass. 1985, U.S. Dist. Ct. Alaska 1985. Adminstr. Indian Edn., Sitka, Alaska, 1974-76, Cook Inlet Native Assn., Anchorage, 1977-80; assoc. Erwin, Smith & Garnett, Anchorage, 1984-86; sole practice Anchorage, 1986—; adj. prof. constitutional law U. Alaska, Anchorage, 1986—. Author: A Place for Winter, 1987. Mem. ABA, Assn. Trial Lawyers Am., Nat. Assn. Women Lawyers. Democrat. Methodist. Office: 400 D St Ste 310 Anchorage AK 99501

SEPPEN, JUDITH, infosystems specialist; b. Rochester, N.Y., Dec. 21, 1959; d. Alfred Marvin Seppen and Constance Marguerite (Hospers) Neenan. BBA in Fin., U. Miami, Coral Gables, Fla., 1980. Customer svc. rep. Dataccount Corp., L.A., 1981-83; supr. field svc. Travelers/EBS, Orlando, Fla., 1983-86; supr. customer support dept. Network Data Systems, Flint, Mich., 1987-88; supr. tech. support group Delphi Info. Systems, Westlake Village, Calif., 1988—. Jewish. Home: 300 Rolling Oaks Dr #296 Thousand Oaks CA 91361

SEPPI, EDWARD JOSEPH, physicist; b. Price, Utah, Dec. 16, 1930; s. Joseph and Fortunata S.; m. Betty Stowell, Aug. 25, 1953; children: Duane Joseph, Kevin Darrell, Cynthia Rae. BS, Brigham Young U., 1952; MS, U. Idaho, 1956; PhD, Calif. Inst. Tech., 1962. Staff physicist Gen. Electric Co., Richland, Wash., 1952-58; rsch. fellow Calif. Inst. Tech., Richland, Wash., 1962; staff physicist Inst. for Def. Analysis, Washington, 1962-64; rsch. area dept. head SLAC, Stanford, Calif., 1966-68, head exptl. facility dept., 1968-74; mgr. med. diagnosis Varian Assocs., Palo Alto, Calif., 1974-76, sr. scientist, 1980-. Author (with others) The Stanford Two-Mile Accelerator, 1968; contbr. articles to popular mags.; patentee med. instrumentation. Asst. scoutmaster Boy Scouts Am., Menlo Park, Calif., 1969-75; bd. dirs. Ladera Community Assn., 1988—. Mem. Am. Phys. Soc. Home: 320 Dedalera Dr Menlo Park CA 94025

SERAFINI, VICTOR RENATO, aerospace engineer; b. Chgo., June 9, 1934; s. Renato Victor and Stella (Koch) S. BS in Aero. Engring., U. Ill., 1957, postgrad., 1957-65; postgrad., UCLA, 1957-65. Research and project engr. Rocketdyne Div. N.Am. Aviation, Canoga Park, Calif., 1957-67; program/project mgr. TRW Inc., Redondo Beach, Calif., 1967-78; dir. spacecraft programs Communications Satellite Corp., El Segundo, Calif., 1978—; bd. dirs. Autobahn West, Westlake Village, Calif.; mgmt. cons. Westoaks Realty, Westlake Village, 1975—; pres. STD Assocs., Rancho Palos Verdes, Calif., 1965—. Recipient award of Recognition, TRW Inc., 1965, Recognition of Outstanding Effort award NASA and TRW, 1963-64. Mem. AIAA (liquid rocket tech. com. 1985-86). Mem. Christian Ch. Home: PO Box 2665 Rancho Palos Verdes CA 90274 Office: Communications Satellite Corp 2250 E Imperial Hwy Suite 720 El Segundo CA 90245

SERBEIN, OSCAR NICHOLAS, business educator, consultant; b. Collins, Iowa, Mar. 31, 1919; s. Oscar Nicholas and Clara Matilda (Shearer) S.; m. Alice Marie Bigger, Sept. 16, 1952; children: Mary Llewellyn Serbein Parker, John Gregory. BA with highest distinction, U. Iowa, 1940, MS, 1941; PhD, Columbia U., 1951. Grad. asst. math. U. Iowa, Iowa City, 1940-41; clk. Met. Life Ins. Co., N.Y.C., 1941-42; lectr. U. Calif., Berkeley, summer 1948, 50; lectr., asst. prof., assoc. prof. Columbia U., N.Y.C., 1947-59; prof. ins. Stanford (Calif.) U., 1959—; cons. Ins. Info. Inst., N.Y.C., 1971-78, N.Am. Re-Assurance Life Service Co., Palo Alto, 1973, SRI Internat., Menlo Park, Calif., 1980-81, other bus.; cons., expert witness various law firms. Author: Paying for Medical Care in the U.S., 1953, Educational Activities of Business, 1961; co-author: Property and Liability Insurance, 4 ed., 1967, Risk Management: Text and Cases, 2 ed., 1983; also articles. Bd. dirs. Sr. Citizens Coordinating Council, Palo Alto, 1986. Served to maj. USAF, WWII. Decorated Bronze star 1944. Mem. Am. Risk and Ins. Assn., Western Risk and Ins. Assn., Phi Beta Kappa, Sigma Xi, Beta Gamma Sigma. Democrat. Methodist. Club: Stanford Faculty. Home: 734 San Rafael Pl Stanford CA 94305 Office: Stanford U Grad Sch Bus Stanford CA 94305

SERBIN, MARK DWIGHT, safety director; b. Takoma Park, Md., June 20, 1953; s. Alfred James and Edith (Ginsberg) S. BA, Oglethorpe U., 1975. Balance cl. First Ga. Bank, Atlanta, 1976-77; sr. auditor Mut. of Omaha, Rockville, Md., 1977-79; adjuster III Crawford & Co., Las Vegas, 1979-80, 84-85; dir. safety Las Vegas Hilton Hotel, 1985—. Author: Population & Housing Projection for Cobb County, Georgia. For year 1983, 1974. Compensation officer State of Nev. Aid to Certain Victims of Crime Program, Las Vegas, 1984-85. Mem. So. Nev. Claims Assn., Am. Soc. Safety Engrs., Las Vegas Jaycees. Democrat. Jewish. Home: 713 E Sahara Ave #418 Las Vegas NV 89104 Office: Las Vegas Hilton Hotel 3000 Paradise Rd Las Vegas NV 89109

SEROKA, ANNA M., nursing administrator; b. Apr. 24, 1947; d. William and Stella Violet (Kozlosky) M.; m. Leonard Lynn Seroka, Feb. 28, 1976. Nursing diploma, Allentown Hosp. Sch. Nursing, Allentown, Pa., 1968; student, Boston U., 1969-71; BS, Cedar Crest Coll., 1973; MEd, Lehigh U., 1978. Staff nurse Mass. Gen. Hosp., Boston, 1969-71; staff nurse CCU St. Joseph Hosp., Hazleton, Pa., 1971-72; school nurse Cedar Crest Coll., Allentown, 1972-73; instr. critical care Allentown Hosp. Sch. Nursing, 1973-75; adminstrv. instr. Lehigh Valley Hosp. Ctr., Allentown, 1975-82; instr. continuing edn. dept. Allentown Coll., 1976-82; editor clin. Intermed Communications, Inc., Springhouse, Pa., 1982; staff devel. instr. U. Colo. Health Sciences Ctr., Denver, 1983-84; unit adminstr. U. Colo. Health Sciences Ctr., 1984-85, asst. dir. nursing/medicine, 1985—; critical care cons., Emmaus, Pa., 1976-83; legis. intern Nat. Fedn. for Specialty Nursing Orgns., Washington, 1989. Author: Basic Arrhythmia Workbook, 1987, contbg. author: Ethics of Care & Cure, 1988, Cardiovascular Nursing, 1988. Bd. dirs., chairperson Columbing Family Health Ctrs., Boulder County, Gilpin County, Colo., 1983-88; mem. adv. bd. Hale Nui Edn., Inc., Denver, 1986-87; adminstrv. liaison Hosp. Ethics Com., 1984—; reviewer Aspen Publs., 1986—. Recipient Critical Care cert. Critical Care Nurses Assn., 1982-85, Nursing Adminstrn. award Met. State Coll., Denver, 1985. Mem. Colo. Nurses Assn., Colo. Assn. Nurse Execs., Pa. Nurses Assn. (state continuing edn. task force), Am. Heart Assn. (task force in continuing edn. for nurses). Democrat. Ukranian Catholic. Home: PO Box 46 Black Hawk CO 80422 Office: Univ Colo Health Sciences Ctr 4200 E 9th Ave Box A021 Denver CO 80262

SERRE, KENNETH LEE, social services administrator; b. Murray, Utah, Oct. 2, 1947; s. Joseph and Lillian (Leoncicni) S.; m. Linda Prothero, Aug. 24, 1968 (div. Jan. 1984); children: Shannon, Chara Soo, Joseph. BS, Utah State U., 1970; MS in Bus., U. Utah, 1976, MSW, 1981. Cert. social worker. Teaching asst. Utah State U., Logan, 1970-71; counselor Job Svc., Salt Lake City, 1971-76; dist. coord. Office of Community Ops., Vernal, Utah, 1976-78; coord. mgmt. svcs. Office of Community Ops., Vernal, 1978-86; state specialist Div. of Family Svcs., Salt Lake City, 1986-88; asst. dir. Dept. Social Svcs. 2K, Salt Lake City, 1988—. Pres. Vernal (Utah) Boys Baseball, 1978; dir. Western Assn. Govt. Employees, 1988. Named Male Employee of the Yr. Uintah Basin Employees, Vernal, 1984. Mem. Utah Pub. Employees Assn. (v.p. 1985-86, pres. 1985-88). Home: 420-A Creekside Circle Murray UT 84107 Office: Office of Community Ops 55 N Redwood Rd Salt Lake City UT 84106

SERTNER, ROBERT MARK, producer; b. Phila., Oct. 7, 1955; s. Morton I. Sertner and Laurie (Hymes) Blicker. BBA, U. Tex., 1977. Ptnr. von Zerneck/Sertner Films, Los Angeles, 1985—. Producer numerous works including (tv movies) Hostage Flight, Combat High, To Heal A Nation, 1987, Trouble in the City of Angeles, Celebration Family, Proud Men, Gore Vidal's Billy The Kid, Man Against The Mob, Maybe Baby; co-producer (mini series) Queenie. Mem. Acad. TV Arts and Scis., Hollywood Radio and TV Soc. Office: von Zerneck/Sertner Films 12001 Ventura Pl #400 Studio City CA 91604

SERVAAS, MARGARET ANN, realtor; b. Clearfield, Pa., Sept. 11, 1952; d. Robert Leonard and Dorothy Ann (Harter) Smeal; m. Thomas Michael SerVaas, Mar. 10, 1978 (div. July 1981). BA in Polit. Sci., Juniata Coll., Huntingdon, Pa., 1974; MS in Mgmt., Purdue U., 1976. Mktg. rep. IBM, Idpls., 1977-78, Lanier Bus. Products, Denver, 1978-80; real estate sales Realty World, Castle Rock, Colo., 1980-85, Re/Max Town and Country, Castle Rock, 1985—; guest lectr. Arapahoe Community Coll., Littleton, Colo., 1986—. Patron, mem. Douglas County (Colo.) Econ. Devel. Council, 1986—; planning commr., Town of Castle Rock, 1984—; mem. LWV, 1984—, Douglas County Arts and Humanities Council, 1984—. Mem. Colo. Assn. Realtors, Nat. Assn. Realtors, Douglas/Elbert Bd. Realtors (Community Svc. award 1984), AAUW (exec. bd. dirs. 1981—, past pres., state bd. dirs. 1987—, named honoree for ednl. found. program 1987). Republican. Methodist. Home: 1280 South St Castle Rock CO 80104 Office: Re/Max Town and Country 719 Wilcox St Castle Rock CO 80104

SERWETZ, MICHAEL LEE, marketing executive; b. Bklyn., May 29, 1949; s. Robert George and Rose (Balan) S; m. Lucy Anne Von, July 22, 1978; children: Justin, Ross. BA, Bklyn. Coll., 1972; MBA, NYU, 1978; MA, Dominican Coll., San Rafael, Calif., 1989. Buyer Abraham & Straus, Bklyn., 1968-78; mdse mgr. Levi Strauss & Co., San Francisco, 1979-80, gen. mdse. mgr., 1980-84; dir. merchandising and design Koret of Calif., San Francisco, 1984-86; v.p. merchandising Eber Internat., San Francisco, 1987-88; pres., prin. Worldwide Apparel Svcs., San Francisco, 1988—. Sgt. U.S. Army, 1970-78. Mem. Am. Mgmt. Assn., Inst. Mgmt. Cons., Tampala Runners, Am. Motorcyclist Assn. Home: 33 Calumet Ave San Anselmo CA 94960 Office: Worldwide Apparel Svcs 33 Calumet Ave San Anselmo CA 94960

SESHIKI, CAROLE SUE, nurse; b. Chgo., Feb. 18, 1938; d. Lawrence Richard and Suzanne Marguerite (Wagner) Brady; m. Richard Seshiki; children: Clayton, Regina, Laurie, Lisa. AA, Kauai Community Coll, Lihue, Hawaii, 1975. R.N., Hawaii. Staff nurse G.N. Wilcox Meml. Hosp., Lihue, Hawaii, 1975—. Mem. Hawaii Nurses Assn., Am. Urol. Assn. Allied.

SESSLER, ANDREW MARIENHOFF, physicist; b. Bklyn., Dec. 11, 1928; s. David and Mary (Baron) S.; m. Gladys Lerner, Sept. 23, 1951; children: Danial Ira, Jonathan Lawrence, Ruth. BA in Math. cum laude, Harvard U., 1949; MA in Theoretical Physics, Columbia U., 1951, PhD in Theoretical Physics, 1953. NSF fellow Cornell U., N.Y., 1953-54; asst. prof. Ohio State U., Columbus, 1954, assoc. prof., 1960; on leave Midwestern Univs. Research, 1955-56; vis. physicist Lawrence Rediation Lab., 1959-60, Niels Bohr Inst., Copenhagen, summer 1961; researcher theoretical physics U. Calif. Lawrence Berkeley Lab., Berkeley, 1961-73, researcher energy and environment, 1971-73, dir., 1973-80, sr. scientist plasma physics, 1980—; U.S. advisor Panjab U. Physics Inst., Chandigarh, India; mem. U.S.-India Coop. Program for Improvement Sci. Edn. in India, 1966, high energy physics adv. panel to U.S. Atomic Energy Commn., 1969-72, adv. com. Lawrence Hall Sci., 1974-78; chmn. Stanford Synchrotron Radiation Project Sci. Policy Bd., 1974-77, EPRI Advanced Fuels Adv. Com., 1978-81, BNL External Adv. Com. on Isabelle, 1980-82. Mem. editorial bd. Nuclear Instruments and Methods, 1969—; correspondent Comments on Modern Physics, 1969-71; contbr. articles in field to profl. jours. Recipient E.O. Lawrence award U.S. Atomic Energy Commn., 1970; fellow Japan Soc. for Promotion Sci. at KEK, 1985. Fellow Am. Phys. Soc. (chmn. com. internat. freedom scientists 1982, mem. study of directed energy weapons panel 1985-87, vice chmn. panel pub. affairs 1987), AAAS (nominating com. 1984-87); mem. Fedn. Am. Scientists Council (vice chmn. 1987-88, chmn. 1988—), N.Y. Acad. Sci., Sigma Xi. Home: 225 Clifton St Apt 201 Oakland CA 94618 Office: U Calif Lawrence Berkeley Lab 1 Cyclotron Rd Berkeley CA 94720

SESTINI, VIRGIL ANDREW, biology teacher; b. Las Vegas, Nov. 24, 1936; s. Santi and Merceda Francesca (Borla) S. BEd, U. Nev., 1959; postgrad., Oreg. State U., 1963-64; MNS, U. Idaho, 1965; postgrad., Ariz. State U., 1967, No. Ariz. U., 1969; cert. tchr., Nev. Tchr. biology Rancho High Sch., 1960-76; sci. chmn., tchr. biology Bonanza High Sch., Las Vegas, 1976—; part time tchr. Meadows Sch., 1987—. Served with USAR, 1959-65. Recipient Rotary Internat. Honor Tchr. award, 1965, Region VIII Outstanding Biology Tchr. award, 1970, Nev. Outstanding Biology Tchr. award Nat. Assn. Biology Tchrs., 1970, Nat. Assn. Sci. Tchrs., Am. Gas Assn. Sci. Teaching Achievement Recognition award, 1976, 1980, Gustov Ohaus award, 1980, Presdl. Honor Sci. Tchr. award, 1983; Excellence in Edn. award Nev. Dept. Edn., 1983; Presdl. award excellence in math. and sci. teaching, 1984, Celebration of Excellence award Nev. Com. on Excellence in Edn., 1986, Hall of Fame award Clark County Sch. Dist., 1988, Excellence in Edn. award, Clark County Sch. Dist., 1987, 88, Spl. Edn. award Clark County Sch. Dist., 1988; grantee Nev. State Bd. Edn., 1988, 89, Nev. State Edn. Assn., 1988-89. Mem. NEA, Nat. Sci. Tchrs. Assn., Nat. Assn. Biology Tchrs., Am. Soc. Microbiology, Nat. Audobon Assn., Nat. Sci. Suprs. Assn., Am. Inst. Biol. Scis. Roman Catholic. Office: Bonanza High Sch 6665 W Del Rey Ave Las Vegas NV 89102

SETCHKO, EDWARD STEPHEN, minister, theological educator; b. Yonkers, N.Y., Apr. 27, 1926; s. Stephen John and Mary Elizabeth (Dulak) S.; m. Penelope Sayre, Nov. 18, 1950; children—Marc Edward, Kip Sherman, Robin Elizabeth, Jan Sayre, Dirk Stephen. B.S., Union Coll., 1948; M.Div. cum laude, Andover Newton Theol. Sch., 1953, S.T.M., 1954; Th.D., Pacific Sch. Religion, 1962. Ordained to ministry United Ch. of Christ, 1954; cert. profl. hosp. chaplain. Psychometrician, Union Coll. Character Research Project, Schenectady, N.Y., 1947-50; asst. pastor Eliot Ch., Newton, Mass., 1950-54; clin. tng. supr. Boston City Hosp., 1951-54; intern, chaplain Boston State Mental Hosp., 1953-54; univ. campus minister U. Wash., Seattle, 1954-58; Danforth grantee, 1958-59; grad. fellow in psychotherapy Pacific Sch. Religion, Berkeley, Calif., 1959-60, instr. dept. pastoral psychology, 1960-61, grad. fellow, lectr. theology and psychology, 1961-62, asst. prof. psychology and counseling, 1962-63, dir. continuing theol. edn., 1962-63; field research sec. laity div. United Ch. Christ, Berkeley, Calif. and N.Y.C., 1963-68; vis. prof. psychology Starr King Ctr. for Religious Leadership, Berkeley, 1967-69; assoc. prof. religion and soc. Starr King Ctr., Grad. Theol. Union, Berkeley, Calif., 1969-71, prof., 1971-83; career counselor The Ctr. for Ministry, Oakland, Calif., 1986—; mem. faculty, chmn. curriculum and faculty com. Layman's Sch. Religion, Berkeley, 1960-67; cons. and lectr. in field. Mem. Peace Del., Mid-East, 1983; lectr. Internat. Conf. on the Holocaust and Genocide, Tel Aviv, 1982, Nuclear Disarmament Conf., W.Ger., 1980, 81, 82, Internat. Ctr. for Peace in the Middle East, Resource Ctr. for Non-Violence, Clergy & Laity Concerned, Ecumenical Peace Inst., Internat. Peace Acad.; World Policy Inst., Inst. Peace and World Order, Am. Friends Service Com. (bd. dirs.), Ristad Found.; dir. The Project for Peace and Reconciliation in the Middle East (non-profit Calif. Found. 1983-89). Lt. (j.g.) USNR, 1944-46, WW II. Mem. Am. Psychol. Assn. (cert.), Calif. State Psychol. Assn., Assn. Clin. Pastoral Edn., World Future Soc., Soc. Sci. Study of Religion, Inst. Noetic Scis., Com. for Protection Human Subjects (U. Calif.-Berkeley). Democrat. Contbr. articles to profl. jours.; condr. seminars: Futurology; Intricacies of Being Human, Images of Women and Men; Changing Values in Roles Between the Sexes in a Technological Society; developer curriculum: Peace and Conflict Studies (U. Calif., Berkeley).

SETELIK, JAMES JOSEPH, JR., priest; b. Balt., Oct. 16, 1952; s. James Joseph and Jacqueline (Reisinger) S. BA in Criminology, Fla. State U., 1974; M. Div., Cath. Theol. Union, Chgo., 1981. Ordained priest Roman Cath. Ch., 1984. Pastor Diocese Reno and Las Vegas, Nev. Co-author: (booklet/workbook) Before...The Death Experience, 1988. So. Research and Scholarship Found. scholar, 1973-74. Mem. K.C. Democrat. Address: St John Bosco Cath Ch 384 S Reese St PO Box 428 Battle Mountain NV 89820

SETEROFF, SVIATOSLAV STEVE, computer systems consultant; b. Shanghai, People's Republic of China, Oct. 6, 1937; came to U.S., 1949; s. Leo G. and Olga D. (Pankova) S.; m. Deanna Catherine Rogers (div. 1964); children: Steven James, Richard Aubrey; m. Joyce Eileen Schieldge, Feb. 22, 1965; children: Barbara Lynn Seteroff Anderson, Leanne Marie. AA, Chapman Coll., 1974, BA cum laude, 1975; MBA, U. Puget Sound, 1983. Enlisted USN, 1955-75, commd. warrant officer, 1976-85; sr. analyst McDonnell Douglas Astronautics Co., Rockville, Md., 1985-87; program mgr. Anadac, Inc., Arlington, Va., 1987; v.p., bd. dirs. Systems Mgmt. Am. Corp., San Diego, 1987-89; computer systems cons. MERIT Systems, Inc., Bremerton, Wash., 1989—; instr. Residence Edn. Ctr., Chapman Coll., Bangor, Wash., 1985. Mem. Am. Soc. Naval Engrs., Assoc. MBA Execs., The Ret. Officers Assn., Masons. Home: 12890 Old Military Rd NE Poulsbo WA 98370

SETHI, HARINDAR SINGH, dentist; b. Armitsar, Punjab, India, Dec. 5, 1933; came to U.S., 1981; s. Narain Singh and Narain (Kaur) S.; m. Surrinder Cindy, Feb. 19, 1963; children: Ritu Chug, Vineet Mona, Jaineet Ricky. BDS, PB Govt. Dental Coll., Punjab, India, 1956; MDS, Armed Forces Med. Coll., Poona, India, 1969. Dental demonstrator Madras (India) Med. Coll. Hosp., 1956-57; enlisted Army Dental Corps, India, 1957, advanced through grades to lt. col., dental surgeon, 1957-63, oral surgeon, 1963-69, prosthodontist, 1969-79, ret., 1979; pvt. practice New Delhi, India, 1979-81, Los Angeles, 1981—; sr. specialist Army Dental Corps, India, 1977-79. Contbr. articles to profl. jours. Mem. Amrical Endodontic Soc. Sikh. Home: 308 N Stoneman Ave #E Alhambra CA 91801 Office: Dr Sethi's Family Dental Ctr 8236 E Garvey Ave Rosemead CA 91770

SETTER, JOHN GEORGE, JR., military officer; b. Washington, Oct. 10, 1959; s. John George and Margaret Gail (Sloan) S.; m. Sheryl Anne Kearns, June 5, 1982. BA in History, U. Notre Dame, 1981. Commd. USAF, 1981, advanced through grades to capt., 1988; student navigator 323d Flying Tng. Wing USAF, Mather AFB, Calif., 1981-82; B-52 navigator 93d Bombardment Wing USAF, Castle AFB, Calif., 1982-83; B-52 standardization evaluation navigator 5th Bombardment Wing USAF, Minot AFB, N.D., 1983-85; student pilot Euro-NATO Joint Jet Pilot Tng-80th Flying Tng. Wing USAF, Sheppard AFB, Tex., 1984-86; F-4 pilot 563d Tactical Fighter Squadron USAF, George AFB, Calif., 1986—. Mem. Air Force Assn., Air Force Hist. Found. Roman Catholic. Home: 13212 Pocono Rd Apple Valley CA 92308 Office: USAF 563 Tactical Fighter Squadron/DO George AFB CA 92394

SETTLER, EUGENE BRIAN, record company executive; b. Balt., Apr. 24, 1936; s. Myer Martin and Esther (Levinson) S.; m. Phyllis Goldfinger, June 10, 1956 (div. Oct. 1975); m. Sharon O'Brasky, May 27, 1976 (div. July 1988); children: Richard Dean, Michael Scott, Robert Marc. BS in Bus., Loyola Coll., Balt., 1957. V.p. Edge Ltd., Washington, 1954-65; dir. mktg. Epic Records, N.Y.C., 1965-71; exec. v.p. Music West/Music 2, N.Y.C., 1971-73; exec. v.p. mktg. RCA Records, N.Y.C., 1971-73; pres. Rimiro Corp., N.Y.C., 1971-73; exec. v.p. Transcontinental Music Corp., Los Angeles, 1973-76; pres. Request Records, Hollywood, Fla., 1976-82; exec. v.p. Kid Stuff div. IJE, Inc., Plantation, Fla., 1982-87; pres. Internat. Mgmt. and Mktg. Sales Co., 1987-88; pres., chief exec. officer The Singing Machine Co., Inc., Los Angeles, 1988—; cons. in field; bd. dirs. LCS Entertainment, Inc., Music West/Music 2. Music arranger: (film) Raiders of the Lost Ark, 1981, (album) Hooked on Exercise, 1983. Dir., treas. Ft. Lauderdale Film Festival, 1986—. Mem. Nat. Assn. Rec. Arts and Scis., Friars Club. Lodges: Masons, B'nai Brith. Home: 14004 Palawan Way PH-6 Marina Del Rey CA 90292 Office: 5521 Grosvenor Blvd Los Angeles CA 90066

SETTLES, F. STAN, JR., manufacturing executive; b. Denver, Oct. 3, 1938; s. Frank S. and Dorothy Marie (Johnson) S.; m. Evelyn Brown, June 10, 1961; children: Frank S. III, Richard, Charles, Michael. BS in Prodn. Tech., Indsl. Engring., LeTourneau Coll., Longview, Tex., 1962; MS in Indsl. Engring., Ariz. State U., 1967, PhD in Indsl. Engring., 1969. Sr. systems analyst AiResearch Mfg. Co., Phoenix, 1968-70, project mgr., 1970-74, mgr. operational planning, 1974-80; mgr. indsl. engrs. Garrett Pneumatic Systems, Phoenix, 1980-83; mgr. indsl. mfg. engring. Garrett Turbine Engring. Co., Phoenix, 1983-85; v.p. mfg. ops. AiResearch Mfg. Co., Torrance, Calif., 1985-87; dir. indusl. mfg. engring. The Garrett Corp., Phoenix, 1987-88; dir. planning Garrett Engine Div., Phoenix, 1988—; faculty assoc. Ariz. State U., Tempe, 1974-85. Mem. sch. bd. Tempe Elem. Sch. Dist., 1976-80; mem. YMCA Indian Guides, nat. chief, 1978-79. Fellow Inst. Indsl. Engrs. (pres. 1987-88, Ops. Research award 1980); mem. Soc. Mfg. Engrs. (sr.), Inst. Mgmt. Sci. (sr.). Republican. Presbyterian. Home: 1627 E La Jolla Tempe AZ 85282 Office: The Garrett Corp PO Box 5217 Dept 76 Bldg 301-2A Phoenix AZ 85010

SEUBERT, RONALD C., electronics executive; b. Cottonwood, Idaho, Apr. 17, 1950; s. John L. and Valeria P. (Jentges) S.; m. Sara Ann Zastrow, Nov. 28, 1986. BSEE, Gonzaga U., 1972. Registered profl. engr., Wash. Engr. Boeing Co., Seattle, 1972-75; pres. Envision, Inc., Seattle, 1975-77; electronics design cons. Seattle, 1977-81; pres. Microtask Corp., Seattle, 1981—; v.p. Applied Precicion, Inc., Mercer Island, Wash., 1985—. Patentee, designer and product mgr. presicion motion control product (named one of top 25 products of yr. Photonics mag., 1988). Democrat. Roman Catholic. Office: Applied Precision Inc 8505 SE 68th St Mercer Island WA 98040

SEVERAID, RONALD HAROLD, lawyer; b. Berkeley, Calif., July 13, 1951; s. J. Harold and Irene Ann (Clark) s.; m. Peggy R. Chappus. B.A., U. Calif.-Davis, 1973; J.D., Georgetown U., 1977. Bar: Calif. 1977, D.C. 1979, U.S. Dist. Ct. (ea. and cen. dists.) Calif. 1977. Assoc. Kindel & Anderson, Los Angeles, 1977-79; exec. v.p., gen. counsel Pacific Mktg. Devel., Sacramento, 1979-80, pres., 1980-81; sec. Aaron-Ross Corp., Glendora, Calif., 1983-84; sole practice, Sacramento, 1979-84; sr. atty. Severaid & Seegmiller, Sacramento, 1984—. Co-editor Internat. Cts. of Justice Opinion Briefs, 1978; sr. topics editor Law and Policy in Internat. Bus., 1975-76; contbr. articles to profl. jours. Pres. Sacramento Valley chpt. Community Assns. Inst., 1988-89; pres. Pacifica Villas Homeowners Assn., 1978-79. Mem. ABA, Calif. State Bar Assn., Sacramento County Bar Assn., Community Assns. Inst., Calif. Trustees Assn. Republican. Roman Catholic. Office: Severaid & Seegmiller 1780 Creekside Oaks Dr Ste 125 Sacramento CA 95833

SEVERSON, DON R., small business owner; b. Eugene, Oreg., Apr. 4, 1934; s. Roy Vernon and Bertie (Scott) S.; m. Betty Lou Prigge, Dec. 28, 1966; 1 child, Brandon Scott Hokulani. BS in Civil Engring., Oreg. State U., 1958. Civil engr. Kaiser Ind. Hawaii Kai, Honolulu, 1959-62; founder, owner Severson Enterprise, Ltd. (Tahiti Imports), Honolulu, 1963—; navigator yacht Koae, South Pacific, 1962-63; founder Hawaiian Atiquities, 1973—; pres. Severson Surfing Enterprise, Honolulu, 1967—. Author: Specimens of Hawaiian Kapa, 1978, Cave Specimens of Hawaiian Kapa, 1980, Cave Specimens of Polynesian Tapa, 1983. Pres. pub. com. Hawaiian Furniture Project, Honolulu, 1980-83; v.p. Hawaiian Antique Dealers Assn., 1987. With U.S. Army, 1953-55. Mem. Acad. Art, Bishop Mus. Assn., Honolulu Athletic Club, Elks. Home: 4303 Papu Circle Honolulu HI 96816 Office: Severson Surfing Enterprise Ltd 1174 Waimanu St Honolulu HI 96814

SEVERSON, JANET MAE, accountant; b. Yakima, Wash., Mar. 17, 1935; d. Ernest Henry Albert and Mary (Manda) Luepke; m. Robert Edward Severson, Feb. 14, 1953; children: Mark Lance, Roberta Jan Severson Sarvey, Joanthan Eric. Grad., Yakima Sr. High Sch., 1952. Lic. tax cons., Oreg. With various county and fed. agys. 1952-61; adminstrv. asst. dist. office Social Security Adminstrn., Washington, 1961-66; taxpayer svc. rep. IRS, Yakima and Pasco, Wash., 1969-74; pres., owner Acctg. & Tax Svcs., Inc., Hermiston, Oreg., 1974—; chmn. Oreg. State Bd. Tax Svc. Examiners, Salem, 1984—. Active numerous civic orgns. Mem. Hermiston C. of C., Oreg. Soc. Tax Cons. (pres. 1980-88), Nat. Assn. Enrolled Agts., Altrusa (Hermiston) (pres. 1984-85). Home: 945 W Ridgeway Hermiston OR 97838 Office: Acctg and Tax Svcs 205 NE 4th St Hermiston OR 97838

SEVERSON, JERRY LEE, insurance underwriting manager; b. Portland, Oreg., Apr. 29, 1941; s. Clarence Harold and Theresea May (Henderson) S.; m. Louise Marie Ramme, Jan. 25, 1964; children: Todd L., Nicole Ann. BSBA, Portland State U., 1963. Loan officer Commerce Mortgage Co., Portland, Oreg., 1964-68; ins. broker Durham and Bates Agency, Portland, Oreg., 1968-76; marine mgr. Marsh and McLennan & Co., Portland, Oreg., 1976-79, Aetna Ins. Co., Portland, Oreg., 1979-81; ins. agent Yaquina Ins. Agency, Newport, Oreg., 1981-82; underwriting mgr. GRE Am. (formerly GRE Talbot, Bird and Co., Lake Oswego, Oreg., 1982—; instr. at various schs. of ins.; owner Oreg. Coast Boat Sales Co. Author: (with others) U.S. Power Squadrons Boat Ins., 1986. Mem. Alpha Kappa Psi Bus. Fraternity, Propeller Club, Shipping Club, Elks. Republican. Office: GRE Am 5285 SW Meadows Rd Ste 170 Lake Oswego OR 97035

SEVEY, ROBERT WARREN, broadcast journalist; b. Mpls., Dec. 6, 1927; s. Benjamin Warren and Helen Margaret (Benham) S.; m. Rosalie Fergueson Thomas, Jan. 28, 1950; children: Michael Warren, David Ellis. BA, U. Calif., Santa Barbara, 1951. Announcer, newscaster WOI and KASI, Ames, Iowa, 1947-49; sports dir. KIST, Santa Barbara, 1949-51; prodn. asst. CBS-TV, Hollywood, Calif., 1951-52; producer, announcer KPHO-TV, Phoenix, 1952-54; prodn. mgr. KULA-TV, Honolulu, 1954-57; prodn. mgr. radio-TV Holst & Male Inc., Honolulu, 1957-59; sta. mgr. KGMB-TV, Honolulu, 1959-61, news dir., 1961-65; news dir. KHVH-TV, Honolulu, 1960-65, KGMB-TV, Honolulu, 1966-86; v.p. news/corporate affairs Heftel Broadcasting Co., Honolulu, 1987—. Bd. dirs. Aloha Week Hawaii, Inc., Honolulu, 1988—. S/Sgt. U.S. Army, 1945-47. Mem. Radio-TV News Dirs. Assn., Honolulu Press Club (pres. 1969-70, mem. Hall of Fame 1987—).

SEVIN, DOUGLAS JAY, social worker; b. Limestone, Maine, Aug. 20, 1955; s. Daniel Joseph and Laura Mae (Boyce) S.; m. Karen Marie Hirchert, Feb. 14, 1981; 1 child, Rebecca Lynn. Assoc. in Arts and Scis., Fort Steilacoom Community Coll., 1975; B of Psychology, Western Wash. State Coll., 1977. Drug outreach worker Puyallup (Wash.) Valley Youth Svcs., 1977-78; mental health technician Puget Sound Hosp., Tacoma, 1978-80; fin. svcs. technician Wash. State Dept. Social and Health Svcs., Ballard, 1980-83, social worker, 1983-89; program mgr. div. income assistance OB-31C Wash. State Dept. Social and Health Svcs., Olympia, 1989—. Treas. People's Ctr. Park Adv. Bd., Tacoma, 1988. Office: Dept Social & Health Svcs 1949 S State St N67-1 Tacoma WA 98405

SEWARD, JAMES PICKETT, internist; b. N.Y.C., Oct. 14, 1949; s. George C. and Carroll Frances (McKay) S. AB, Harvard U., 1971; M of Pub. Policy, U. Calif., Berkeley, 1977; MD, U. Calif., San Francisco, 1977. Diplomate Am. Bd. Internal Medicine, Am. Bd. Occupational Medicine. Resident U. Calif. Hosps., San Francisco, 1977-80; Robert Woods Johnson postdoctoral fellow U. Calif., San Francisco, 1980-82; med. dir. Occupational Health Service U. Calif., Berkeley, 1982—; asst. clin. prof. U. Calif., San Francisco, 1983—; lectr. Sch. Pub. Health, U. Calif., Berkeley, 1986—. Fulbright scholar, 1972-73. Mem. Am. Pub. Health Assn. Office: Cowell Hosp Occupational Health Svc Berkeley CA 94720

SEWELL, CHARLES ROBERTSON, geologist, exploration company executive; b. Malvern, Ark., Feb. 7, 1927; s. Charles Louis and Elizabeth (Robertson) S.; m. Margaret Helen Wilson, Dec. 26, 1953 (dec. July 1985); children—Michael Stuart, Charles Wilson, Marion Elizabeth; m. Louise T. Worthington, Nov. 29, 1985; 1 child, Ginger B. B.S., U. Ark.-Fayetteville, 1950; M.A., U. Tex.-Austin, 1955, postgrad., 1961-64. Registered geologist, Calif., Ariz. Well logging engr. Baroid, Houston, 1950; asst. metallurgist Magcobar, Malvern, Ark., 1951; geologist Socony-Mobil Petroleum Co., Roswell, N.Mex., 1955; sr. geologist Dow Chem. Co., Freeport, Tex., 1956-61; spl. instr. U. Tex., Austin, 1962-65; pvt. practice cons. geologist, Austin, 1962-65; dist. geologist, mgr. Callahan Mining Corp., Tucson, 1965-68; owner, cons. geologist Sewell Mineral Exploration, worldwide, 1968—. Contbr. articles to profl. jours. Elder, Presbyn. Ch., Tucson, 1973—. Served with USN, 1944-46, 51-53. NSF grantee, 1962-64, 63. Mem. AIME, Ariz. Geol. Soc., Mining Club Southwest (bd. govs. 1982-86, pres. 1984), Colo. Mining Assn., Sigma Xi. Republican. Lodge: Masons. Discoverer/co-discoverer numerouis metallic and non-metallic ore deposits. Home and Office: 260 S Sewell Pl Tucson AZ 85748

SEWELL, ROBERT DALTON, pediatrician; b. Newman, Calif., Apr. 28, 1950; s. James Dalton and Mary Louise (Hartwell) S.; m. Esther Madiedo, Oct. 26, 1975; children: Kevin, David. BA magna cum laude, Pacific Union Coll., 1972; MD, Loma Linda U., 1975. Diplomate Am. Bd. Pediatrics. Pediatric intern and resident White Meml. Med. Ctr., L.A., 1975-77; pediatric resident, chief resident Milton S. Hershey Med. Ctr., Pa. State U., Hershey, 1977-80; pediatrician Children's Med. Ctr. Asheville, N.C., 1980-81, Lincoln City Med. Ctr. P.C., Lincoln City, Oreg., 1982—; examining physician C.A.R.E.S. Ctr. Emanuel Hosp. & Health Ctr., Portland, Oreg., 1988—; chmn. child protection team North Lincoln Hosp., Lincoln City, 1983—; mem., chmn. perinatology com. North Lincoln Hosp., Lincoln City, 1982—; mem. Citizens' Rev. Bd. Lincoln County, Newport, Oreg., 1986—, Early Intervention Adv. Com., Newport, 1986—. Mem. North Lincoln Local Sch. Com., Lincoln City, 1983—, chmn., 1986-88; mem. bd. dirs. Lincoln Shelter & Svcs., Inc., Lincoln City, 1983—, chmn., 1987-89; mem. North Lincoln div. Am. Heart Assn., Lincoln City, 1986—, v.p., 1987-89; mem. Drug & Alcohol Task Force, Lincoln City, 1988—; mem., 2nd vice-chmn. yr. 2000 plan housing com. Lincoln City Planning Commn., 1987-88; mem. AIDS taskforce Lincoln County Sch. Dist., 1987-88; mem. Lincoln County Children's Agenda Taskforce, 1988. Named Citizen of Yr. child protection com. Lincoln County, 1984, Man of Yr. Lincoln City C. of C., 1988. Mem. Am. Acad. Pediatrics (sect. on child abuse), Oreg. Pediatric Soc., Oreg. Med. Assn., Lincoln County Med. Soc., Am. Profl. Soc. on the Abuse of Children (charter mem.), Nat. Assn. Counsel for Children, Internat. Soc. for the Prevention Child Abuse and Neglect, N. Am. Soc. for Pediatric and Adolescent Gynecology. Democrat. Seventh-day Adventist. Office: Lincoln City Med Ctr PC 2870 NE W Devils Lake Rd Lincoln City OR 97367

SEXTON, JOYCE FORRESTER, audiologist; b. Dillon, Mont., May 20, 1957; d. Roy William and Dorothy Anne (Davis) Forrester; m. Shaun Edward Sexton, Aug. 20, 1983. AA, Cottey Coll., 1977; BS, Purdue U., 1979; MA, U. Mont., 1981. Cert. clin. competence audiologist, speech pathologist. Tchr. infant learning Tanana Chiefs Native Corp., Fairbanks, Alaska, 1981-82, coord. infant program, 1982-83; audiologist Anchorage Sch. Dist., 1983—; pvt. practice audiology Anchorage, 1988—; mem. health bd. Chugiak (Alaska) Children's Svcs., 1985—. Vol. audiologist Chevron Alaska Health Fairs, Anchorage, 1986—. Mem. Am. Speech Lang. and Hearing Assn. (cert.), Alaska Speech and Hearing Assn. (treas. 1985-86, chairperson continuing edn. 1986-89), Ednl. Audiologists Assn., Presbyn. Women's Assn. (pres. Eagle River chpt. 1986-87), Quota Internat. Club. (pres. cook-inlet 1988—). Office: No Hearing Svcs 3820 Lake Otis Pkwy Anchorage AK 99508

SEXTON-ISAAC, MARGARET, nurse educator; b. N.Y.C., June 10, 1943; d. Cornelius J. and Mary Elizabeth (Martin) Sexton; children: Meaghan Laura, Heather Katherine. BSN, Georgetown U., 1965; MA, Columbia U., 1970; EdD, No. Ariz. U., 1988. Staff nurse, instr. Holy Name Hosp., Teaneck, N.J., 1965-66; counterpart nurse Project Hope, Cuenca, Ecuador, 1966-67; staff nurse VA Hosp., Newark, 1967-69, St. Joseph Hosp., Tucson, 1972; instr. Pima Community Coll., Tucson, 1972-76, Navajo Community Coll., Tsaile, Ariz., 1970-71, 76-77; nurse mgr. King Community Hosp., Tucson, 1977-79; instr. Cochise Coll., Douglas, Ariz., 1979-86; curriculum dir., assoc. prof. nursing Lewis & Clark State Coll., Lewiston, Idaho, 1986—; site visitor Nat. League for Nursing Coun. Assoc. Degree Programs, N.Y.C., 1987—; item writer State BD. Test Pool Exam., 1976-77. Pres. bd. dirs. Lewis & Clark Vol. Bur., 1987-88; driver Meals on Wheels, Lewiston, 1987—; mem. parish coun. St. James Ch., 1988—. Rural Health Edn. Consortium grantee 1987-88. Mem. Nat. League Nursing (chmn. resolutions com. coun. of assoc. degree nursing 1987—, exec. com. 1989—), Orgn. for Advancement Assoc. Degree Nursing (treas. 1985-88), NAFE. Roman Catholic. Office: Lewis and Clark State Coll 8th Ave and 6th St Lewiston ID 83501

SEYER, PHILIP CHARLES, author, consultant; b. Concord, Calif., Oct. 13, 1941; s. Herman Daniel and Emeline (Seeger) S.; m. Louise Ann Craft, June 13, 1964 (div. 1979); children: Kristina Louise, Daniel Philip; m. Kumiko Goto, June 21, 1985. AA, Calif. Concordia Coll., Oakland, 1959; BMus. Edn., Valparaiso U., 1964; VA, San Fransicso State U., 1969. Instructional technologist U. Calif. Med. Ctr., San Francisco, 1970-73, Berkeley, 1973-78; sr. assoc. Seyer Assocs., San Francisco, 1978-81, Walnut Creek, Calif., 1983-85, Concord, Calif., 1988—; writer, programmer Fireman's Fund, San Francisco, 1981-83; programmer, analyst Planning Rsch. Corp., Vallejo, Calif., 1985-88; cons. PMT Mortgage Ins. Co., San Francisco, 1977, Control Data Corp., Mpls., 1980, Whitney Edn. Labs., San Mateo, Calif., 1983, Apple Computer, Inc., Cupertino, Calif., 1988, The Tng. Co., San Francisco, 1988. Author: Choosing Success, 1978, What Makes Music Work, 1982, Atari Player-missle Graphics, 1984, Turbo Prolog Advanced Programming Techniques, 1988, Hypertext Concepts and Applications, 1989; designer-editor: SideKick Plus Made Easy, 1989, Mastering Sprint Macro Programming, 1989; developer computer software. Recipient award for Most Innovative, Outstanding Ind. Study Course, Nat. U. Extension Assn., 1974. Mem. Nat. Soc. Performance and Instrn. (pres. chpt. 1979-80). Democrat. Mem. Unity Ch. Office: Seyer Assocs 1079 Mohr Ln D14 Concord CA 94518

SEYFERT, HOWARD BENTLEY, JR., podiatrist; b. Clifton Heights, Pa., July 10, 1918; s. Howard Bentley and Mabel (Ashenbach) S.; m. Anna Mary van Roden, June 26, 1942; 1 child, Joanna Mary Irwin. D of Podiatric Medicine, Temple U., 1940. Cert. Nat. Bd. Podiatry Examiners (past pres.), Ariz. State Bd. Podiatry Examiners (past pres.). Pvt. practice podiatry Phoenix, 1950-82, Sedona, Ariz., 1982—; mem. med. staff Marcus J. Lawrence Meml. Hosp., Cottonwood, Ariz. Served to capt. USAAF, 1942-46, ETO, lt. col. Res. ret. Decorated Bronze Star. Fellow Acad. Ambulatory Foot Surgery, Am. Coll. Foot Surgeons; mem. Ariz. Podiatric Med. Assn. (past pres.), Am. Podiatric Med. Assn. Republican. Presbyterian. Clubs: OakCreek Country (Sedona); Fairfield Flagstaff Country (Flagstaff, Ariz.). Home: 370 Oakcreek Dr Sedona AZ 86336 Office: Roadrunner Profl Pla 105 Roadrunner Dr Sedona AZ 86336

SEYFERTH, HAROLD HOMER, real estate appraising company executive, educator; b. Stockton, Calif., Jan. 22, 1922; s. Lester L. and Bernice (Perkins) S.; m. Betty Jean Stanley, Apr. 12, 1943; children: Mary B., Laurence P. BA, San Jose State U., 1948; MBA, Ph.D., Pacific Western U., 1981. Locomotive engr. Western Pacific R.R., 1939-50; asst. planner City of San Jose, 1950-54; mgr. City of Hollister (Calif.), 1959-63; property mgr. City of Salinas (Calif.), 1963-68; redevel. chief land officer City of Seaside (Calif.), 1968-69; pres. H. Seyferth Assocs., Monterey, Calif., 1969—; lectr. in field. Chmn., bd. dirs. Carmel Riviera Mut. Water Co.; bd. dirs. Boy's City Boy's Club, San Jose, Am. Cancer Soc., San Jose; trustee Enterprise Sch. Dist., Hollister, Calif. With USN, 1942-45. Coro fellow, 1950. Mem. Am. Assn. Cert. Appraisers (cert.), Am. Planning Assn., Calif. Assn. Real Estate Tchrs., Internat. Coll. Real Estate Cons. Profls., Internat. Inst. Valuers, Internat. Orgn. Real Estate Appraisers, Internat. Right of Way Assn., Nat. Assn. Cert. Real Property Appraisers, Nat. Assn. Rev. Appraisers, Real Estate Educators Assn., Urban Land Inst. Office: 734 Lighthouse Ave Pacific Grove CA 93950

SEYMOUR, ANN BERNADETTE, insurance executive; b. Newark, May 17, 1950; d. George F. and Ava B. (Simon) S. Student, San Diego State U., 1969-74. Ins. agt. Am. Gen. Life & Accident, San Diego, 1983-85; ins. sales State Mutual, San Diego, 1985-86; ins. broker San Diego, 1985-87; owner Seymour Ins. Agy., San Diego, 1987—. Mem. Rebeccas, Qyamaca Riding Club. Office: Seymour Ins Agy 1081 Camino Del Rio S #220 San Diego CA 92108

SEYMOUR, HERBERT E., company executive; b. N.Y.C., May 16, 1936; s. Sidney and Pearl (Dix) Sadolsky; m. Roberta L. Morgenstern, Jan. 14, 1967 (div. 1980); children: Pier Dionne, Anissa Danielle; m. Earlene Marilyn Cunningham. BEE, Rensselaer Poly. Inst., Troy, N.Y., 1957; MBA, U. Pa., 1959. Adminstr. Gen. Precision Labs., Pleasantville, N.Y., 1959; sales mgr. Polarad Electronics, L.I.C., 1959-64; asst. to pres. James B. Lansing Sound, L.A., 1964-68; sales mgr. United Control div. Sunstrand, So. El Monte, Calif., 1968-70; chmn. bd., chief exec. officer Xantech Corp., Sylmar, Calif., 1970—. Patentee in field. Office: Xantech Corp 12950 Bradley Ave Sylmar CA 91347

SEYMOUR, JEFFREY ALAN, governmental relations consultant; b. Los Angeles, Aug. 31, 1950; s. Daniel and Evelyn (Schwartz) S.; m. Valerie Joan Parker, Dec. 2, 1973; 1 child, Jessica Lynne. AA in Social Sci., Santa Monica Coll., 1971; BA in Polit. Sci., UCLA, 1973, M Pub Adminstrn., 1977. Councilmanic aide Los Angeles City Council, 1972-74; county supervisor's sr. dep. Los Angeles Bd. Suprs., 1974-82; v.p. Bank of Los Angeles, 1982-83; prin. Jeffrey Seymour & Assocs., Los Angeles, 1983-84; mem. comml. panel Am. Arbitration Assn., 1984—; Chmn. West Hollywood Parking Adv. Com., Los Angeles, 1983-84, chmn. social action com. Temple Emanuel of Beverly Hills., 1986, bd. dirs. 1988—; mem. Pan Pacific Park Citizens Adv. Com., Los Angeles, 1982—; bd. dirs. William O'Douglas Outdoor Classroom, Los Angeles, 1981—; exec. sec. Calif. Fedn. Young Democrats, 1971; mem. Calif. Dem. Cen. Com., 1979-82; pres. Beverlywood-Cheviot Hills Dem. Club, Los Angeles, 1978-81; co-chmn. Westside Chancellor's Assocs. UCLA, 1986-88; mem. Los Angeles Olympic Citizens Adv. Com.; mem. liaison adv. commn. with city and county govt. for 1984 Olympics, 1984; v.p. community relations metro region, Jewish Fedn. Council of Los Angeles, 1985-87, co-chmn. urban affairs commn., 1987—; mem. platform on world peace and internat. relations Calif. Dem. Party, 1983; pres. 43d Assembly Dist. Dem. Council, 1975-79; arbitrator Better Bus. Bur., 1984—. Recipient Plaques for services rendered Beverlywood Cheviot Hills Dem. Club, Los Angeles, 1981, Jewish Fedn. Council Greater Los Angeles, 1983; Certs. of Appreciation, Los Angeles Olympic Organizing Com., 1984, County of Los Angeles, 1984, City of Los Angeles, 1987; commendatory resolutions, rules com. Calif. State Senate, 1987, Calif. State Assembly, 1987, County of Los Angeles, 1987, City of Los Angeles, 1987. Mem. Am. Soc. Pub. Adminstrn., Am. Acad. Polit. and Social Scis., Town Hall of Calif., So. Calif. Planning Congress, Bldg. Industry Assn. So. Calif., Greater Los Angeles C. of C., UCLA Alumni Assn. (govtl. affairs steering com. 1983—). Office: Morey/Seymour and Assocs 12424 Wilshire Blvd Ste 1050 Los Angeles CA 90025-1044

SFERRAZZA, PETER JOSEPH, lawyer, mayor of Reno; b. N.Y.C., Apr. 30, 1945; s. Peter Joseph and Jane S. (Terry) S.; m. Vivian Ann Canty, 1968 (div.); children—Jessica, Joey. BA, Mich. State U., 1967; JD, U. Wis., 1972. Bar: Wis. 1972, Nev. 1977. Legal intern Wis. Judicare, Madison, 1971-72; staff atty. Wis. Judicare, Wausau, 1972-75, Dane County Legal Services, Wausau, 1972; sole practice Wausau, 1975-76; dir. Nev. Indian Legal Service, Carson City, 1976-79; ptnr. Howard, Cavallera & Sferrazza, Reno, 1979-81; sole practice Reno, 1981—; mayor City of Reno, 1983—; tribal judge Washoe Tribe, Carson City, 1979-80. Alderman city of Wausau, 1976; councilman City of Reno, 1981-83; del. Nat. Democratic conv., 1984; chmn. Nev. Dem. Conv., 1984. Roman Catholic. Office: City of Reno PO Box 1900 Reno NV 89505

SHABEN, LAWRENCE, Canadian provincial official; b. Hanna, Alta., Can., Mar. 20, 1935; s. Albert Mohammed and Lila (Kazeil) S.; m. Alma Amina Saddy, July 8, 1960; children—Linda, Carol, Larry, James, Joan. student U. Alta., 1954-55. Real estate agent Lawrence Agys., Alta., 1962-66; dept. mgr. Sears Can. Ltd., Alta., 1966-67; retail mcht., Alta., 1967-78; mem. legis. assembly from Lesser Slave Lake dist. Govt. of Alta., Edmonton, 1975-89, min. of utilities, 1979-82, min. of housing, 1982-89; pvt. cons. Shaben World Enterprise Inc., 1989—; pres. Lawrence Devels. Ltd., High Prairie, Alta., 1967—, Shaben Stores Ltd., High Prairie, 1967—; min. Econ. Devel. and Trade, Alta., 1986—. Pres. High Prairie Housing Assn., 1967—; mem. High Prairie Town Coun., 1969-74, High Prairie Recreation Bd., 1969-74; pres. Lesser Slave Lake Progressive Conservative Assn., 1969-74, High Prairie Minor Hockey Assn., 1973-74; v.p., bd. dirs. Peace Tourist Assn., 1970-72. Moslem. Lodges: Kiwanis (Northgate, Alta.) (bd. dirs. 1965-66), Lions, Elks, Optimists (sec. local club 1967-71). Office: Shaben World Enterprises Inc, 14735-124 Ave, Edmonton, AB Canada T5L 3B2

SHACKELFORD, GORDON LEE, JR., educator; b. South Bend, Ind., Apr. 7, 1948; s. Gordon Lee and Leatha Mae (Andrews) S.; BS in Physics, San Diego State U., 1970, MS in Radiol. Physics, 1974; m. Janis Elizabeth Mead, Apr. 6, 1974. Electronic designer for physics dept. San Diego State U., 1969-70; electronic engr. Naval Electronics Lab., Point Loma, Calif., 1970; electronic engr. product design Info. Machine Corps., Santee, Calif., 1970-71; lectr. physics San Diego State U., 1971—, asst. dir. alumni and devel. Coll. of Scis., 1980-81, assoc. dean scis., external relations, 1981— , project mgr. Biomass Power Plant, 1984—; cons. power supply design, 1970—. Mem. quality life bd. City of San Diego; vice chmn. Lakeside Community Planning Group. Mem. Health Physics Soc. Author lab. manuals. Home: 9716 Red Pony Ln El Cajon CA 92021 Office: San Diego State U Physics Dept San Diego CA 92182

SHACTER, DAVID MERVYN, lawyer; b. Toronto, Ont., Can., Jan. 17, 1941; s. Nathan and Tillie Anne (Schwartz) S. BA, U. Toronto, 1963; JD, Southwestern U., 1967. Bar: Calif. 1968, U.S. Supreme Ct. 1982. Law clk., staff atty. Legal Aid Found., Long Beach, Calif., 1967-70; asst. city atty. City of Beverly Hills, Calif., 1970; ptnr. Shacter & Berg, Beverly Hills, 1971-83, Capalbo, Lowenthal & Shacter Profl. Law Corp., 1984—; del. State Bar Conf. Dels., 1976—; lectr. Calif. Continuing Edn. of Bar, 1977, 82, 83, 86; judge pro tem Los Angeles and Beverly Hills mcpl. cts., also Los Angeles Superior Ct.; disciplinary examiner Calif. State Bar, 1986. Bd. dirs. and pres. Los Angeles Soc. Prevention Cruelty to Animals, 1978—. Mem. Beverly Hills Bar Assn. (bd. govs. 1985—, editor-in-chief jour., bd. govs. award 1986, sec. 1987-88, treas. 1988-89), Los Angeles County Bar Assn., Am. Arbitration Assn. (nat. panel arbitrators), City of Hope Med. Ctr. Aux., Wilshire C. of C. (bd. dirs., gen. counsel 1985-87). Office: 3580 Wilshire Blvd Ste 1510 Los Angeles CA 90010

SHAFAAT, SYED TARIQ, mechanical engineer; b. Karachi, Pakistan, Oct. 28, 1953; came to U.S., 1975; s. Syed Shafaat Ali and Azra (Sufi) Shafaat; m. Melanie Alison Malchman, July 10, 1976; children: Hannah Syeda, Oliver Syed. Student, Middle East Tech. U., Ankara, Turkey, 1973-75; BSME, Mich. Tech. U., 1977; grad., U. Ariz., 1986. Jr. engr. CPU products IBM Corp., Endicott, N.Y., 1977-79; assoc. engr. IBM Corp., Tucson, 1979-81, sr. assoc. engr. Servowriter Test Engring., 1981-83, staff engr., scientist Tape Drive Devel. Engring., 1983-86, staff engr., scientist Optics/Actuator Technology, 1987-88, adv. engr., optical head devel., 1988—. Advisor Explorers Tucson council Boy Scouts Am., 1982; coach Pantano Soccer League, Tucson, 1980; mem. Tucson YMCA, 1986—. Recipient Cert. Merit Bd. Edn., Sargodha, Pakistan, 1972, Cert. Recognition IBM Corp., Tucson, 1985; Merit scholar Regional Cooperation for Devel., Ankara, Turkey, 1973, 74, 75, Merit scholar Mich. Tech. U., 1976-77. Mem. Robotics Internat., Soc. Mfg. Engrs. (activity coord. 1982-83), IBM Ski Club. Republican. Moslem. Home: 10016 E Leila Dr Tucson AZ 85730 Office: IBM Corp 78G/021-2 9000 S Rita Rd Tucson AZ 85744

SHAFER, ANN DURNO, social worker; b. Grand Rapids, Mich., Oct. 11, 1939. AB, Brown U., 1961; MEd, Boston U., 1965; MSW, George Williams Coll., 1980. Tchr. Concord (Mass.) Pub. Schs., 1961-66; editor Houghton Mifflin Co., Boston, 1966-69; tchr. Glen Ellyn (Ill.) Pub. Schs., 1969-78; social worker Valley View Pub. Schs., Romeoville, Ill., 1980-86, Los Alamos (N.Mex.) Family Council, 1986—. Editor Sch. Social Work Jour., 1982-86. Named Woman of the Yr., Glen Ellyn League Women Voters, 1975. Mem. Nat. Assn. Social Workers (bd. dirs. N.Mex. chpt.), Acad. Cert. Social Workers. Mem. Unitarian Ch. Club: Las Tejedoras Weaving Guild (Los Alamos/Santa Fe) (current pres.). Home: 1322 Big Rock Loop Los Alamos NM 87544 Office: Los Alamos Family Coun 1505 15th St Los Alamos NM 87544

SHAFER, GEORGE R., civil servant, design engineer; b. Granite City, Ill., Oct. 30, 1931; s. George Roe and Viola Allison (Smith) S.; m. June Burrow, Oct. 10, 1935; 1 child, George Roe. BSME, La. State U., 1958. Registered profl. engr., La. Design engr. Babcock & Wilcox, Ltd., Barberton, Ohio, 1958-60, A.M. Lockett & Co., New Orleans, 1960-62; contract insp. New Orleans Dist. Army C.E., 1962-65; project engr. Mediterranean div. Army C.E., Livorno, Italy, 1965-67; dir. maintenance control and engring. div. Naval Tng. Command, Kenitra, Morocco, 1967-69; head logistics and ops. dept. Mobile Utilities Support Equipment Naval Constrn. Bn. Ctr., Port Hueneme, Calif., 1969-71; head engring. and design criteria dept. Civil Engrs. Support Office, Port Hueneme, 1971--. Served with USN, 1949-53. Mem. ASTM. Home: 34 Vientos Rd Camarillo CA 93010 Office: Commanding Officer Attn Code 156 Naval Constrn Bn Port Hueneme CA 93043-5000

SHAFER, JAMES ALBERT, health care administrator; b. Chgo., Aug. 26, 1924; s. James Earl and Kathleen (Sutterland) S.; m. Irene Jeanne Yurcega, June 20, 1948; children: Kathleen Mary Shafer-Petras, Patricia Ann. Technician Zenith Radio Corp., Chgo., 1946-47; owner, operator Eastgate Electronics, Chgo., 1947-61; applications engr. Perfection Mica Co., Bensenville, Ill., 1961-71; pres. Electronics Unltd., Northbrook, Ill., 1972-73, Ariz. Geriatric Enterprises Inc., Safford, 1974—; bd. dirs. Mt. Graham Community Hosp., Safford. Mem. Ariz. Nursing Home Assn. (pres. 1985-86), Am. Coll. Health Care Aminstrs. (cert. 1985). Republican. Roman Catholic. Home: Skyline Ranch Pima AZ 85543-0630 Office: Ariz Geriatric Enterprises Inc 1706 20th Ave Safford AZ 85546

SHAFF, BEVERLY GERARD, educational administrator; b. Oak Park, Ill., Aug. 16, 1925; d. Carl Tanner and Mary Frances (Gerard) Wilson; m. Maurice A. Shaff, Jr., Dec. 20, 1951 (dec. July 1967); children: Carol Maureen, David Gerard, Mark Albert. MA, U. Ill., 1951. Tchr. Haley Sch., Berwyn, Ill., 1948-51; assoc. prof. English, Huntingdon Coll., Montgomery, Ala., 1961-62; tchr. English, William Palmer High Sch., Colorado Springs, Colo., 1964-67, 72-76, dir., 1967-72; tchr. English, Burns (Oreg.) High Sch., 1976-78; tchr. ESL, Multnomah County Ednl. Svc. Dist., Portland, Oreg., 1979-85; coord. gen. studies Portland Jewish Acad., 1984—. Del. Colorado Springs Dem. Com., 1968, 72; active Rainbow Coalition, Portland. Mem. Nat. Assn. Adminstrs., Nat. Assn. Schs. and Colls., Nat. Counc. Tchrs. of Math., Nat. Coun. Tchrs. of English. Home: 4676 SW Comus Pl Portland OR 97219 Office: Portland Jewish Acad 6651 SW Capitol Hwy Portland OR 97219

SHAFF, ROBERT LELAND, marketing executive; b. Phoenix, Sept. 11, 1943; s. Leland Howard and Elizabeth (Kelly) S.; m. Lynda Kay Nelson, Apr. 8, 1967; children: Steven, Scott, John. BSEE, U. Ariz., 1966. Mktg. rep. IBM Corp., Phoenix, 1966-71; program adminstr. IBM Corp., Princeton, N.J., 1971-73; mktg. mgr. IBM Corp., Los Angeles, 1973-77; nat.

mktg. mgr. IBM Corp., Princeton, N.J., 1977-81; location mgr. IBM Corp., Norfolk, VA., 1981-83; nat. mktg. mgr. IBM Corp., Tucson, 1983-87, branch mgr., 1987—. Chmn. Dropout Adv. Council, Tucson, 1986-88. Republican. Roman Catholic. Home: 8231 E Ridgewood Dr Tucson AZ 85715 Office: IBM Corp 5255 E Williams Circle Tucson AZ 85711

SHAFFER, LINDA JEAN, publishing executive; b. Pasadena, Calif., Oct. 28, 1950; d. John Anthony and Barbara Ann (Brown) S.; m. John William Dahlberg, Mar. 4, 1964 (div. 1973); children: Deborah M., David J.; m. Timothy Bruce Lyons, July 29, 1979; 1 child, Aundrea Ann. Grad. high sch., Upland, Calif. Owner, mgr. Fish Barrow Restaurant, Dana Point, Calif., 1975-77; designer J.W. Jewelers, Dana Point, 1977-78; asst. mgr. Weisfield's Jewelers, Seattle, 1978-79; mktg. mgr. State Credit, Seattle, 1979-81; N.W. dir. mgr. Penthouse, Seattle, 1981-82; mgr. Washington Schs., Seattle, 1982-83; RDA dir. Flynt Distributing, Beverly Hills, Calif., 1983—. Republican. Mem. Office: Larry Flynt Publs 9171 Wilshire Blvd Beverly Hills CA 90210

SHAFFER, MARY LOUISE, art educator; b. Blufton, Ind., Nov. 23, 1927; d. Gail H. and Mary J. (Graves) S. AB, Northwest Nazerene Coll., 1950; MA, Ball State Tchrs. Coll., 1955; EdD, MS, Ind. U., 1964. Art and music tchr. Kuna (Ind.) High Sch., 1950-55; asst. prof. art Northwest Nazerene Coll., Nampa, Idaho, 1955-56, head art dept., 1971—; asst. prof. art Pasadena (Calif.) Coll., 1956-61; prof. art Olivet Nazerene Coll., Kankakee, Ill., 1964-71; dir. music Kankakee Congl. Ch., 1964-71, Nampa Christian Ch., 1971-76, Nampa Meth. Ch., 1976-81; speaker various civic clubs and confs., 1965-81. E.I. Lilly grantee, 1961-62; women's singles tennis champion Boise (Idaho) Racquet and Swim Club, 1973; Idaho Sr. Tennis champion Sun Valley, 1984. Mem. Nat. Art Edn. Assn., Idaho Arts Edn. Assn. Home: 4755 E Victory Rd Meridian ID 83642 Office: NW Nazerene Coll Holley at Dewey Nampa ID 83651

SHAFTO, MICHAEL GAIL, federal agency administrator; b. Clinton, Mo., Feb. 22, 1948; s. Gene Alvin and Frances Alice (Kepferle) S.; m. Sylvia Alice Smoker, June 10, 1970; children: Jay Willis, Meredith Allaire. BA, Carleton Coll., 1970; MA, Princeton U., 1972, PhD, 1974. Lic. cons. psychologist, Minn. Asst. prof. psychology Gustavus Adolphus Coll., St. Peter, Minn., 1974-81, assoc. prof. psychology, 1981-85; rsch. assoc. U. Mich., Ann Arbor, 1981-82; sci. officer U.S. Office Naval Rsch., Arlington, Va., 1984-87; asst. div. chief rsch. Aerospace Human Factors Rsch. Div., NASA-Ames Rsch. Ctr., Moffett Field, Calif., 1987—; mem. regional adv. com. Danforth Found., 1977-80; mem. adv. com. Symposium on Empirical Founds. of Info. and Software Scis., 1988. Editor: How We Know, 1986, Diagnostic Monitoring of Knowledge and Skill Acquisition, 1989; contbr. articles to profl. jours. Recipient Disting. Svc. award N.J. Psychol. Assn., 1975, James McKeen Cattell award N.Y. Acad. Scis., 1975; Woodrow Wilson grantee, 1982. Mem. Assn. Computing Machinery, IEEE, Cognitive Sci. Soc. Office: NASA Ames Rsch Ctr Mail Stop 239-1 Moffett Field CA 94035

SHAGAM, MARVIN HÜCKEL-BERRI, teacher; b. Monongalia, W.Va.; s. Lewis and Clara (Shagam) S. AB magna cum laude, Washington and Jefferson Coll., 1947; postgrad., Harvard U., 1947-48, Oxford (Eng.) U., 1948-51. Tchr. Mount House Sch., Tavistock, Eng., 1951-53, Williston Jr. Sch., Easthampton, Mass., 1953-55, Westtown (Pa.) Sch., 1955-58, The Thacher Sch., Ojai, Calif., 1958—; dept. head Kurasimi Internat. Edn. Centre, Dar-es-Saluam, Tanzania, 1966-67, Nkumbi Internat. Coll., Kabwe, Zambia, 1967-68; vol. visitor Prisions in Calif., 1980—, Calif. Youth Authority, 1983—; sr. youth crisis counsellor InterFace, 1984—. 1st lt. M.I. res., U.S. Army, 1943-46. Danforth Found. fellow, 1942; Coun. for the Humanities fellow, Tufts U., 1983. Mem. Western Assn. Schs. and Colls. (accreditation com.), Phi Beta Kappa, Delta Sigma Rho. Republican.

SHAH, GIRISH POPATLAL, data processing services company executive; b. Junagadh, India, Apr. 11, 1942; came to U.S., 1963; s. Popatlal Gulabchand and Lalitaben Popatlas (Kamdar) S.; m. Devmani Manilal Jhaveri, June 18, 1968; children: Nivisha, Munjal, Bhavin. B in Tech., Indian Inst. Tech., Bombay, 1963; MS, U. Calif., Berkeley, 1965. Project analyst IBM Corp., Palo Alto, Calif., 1965-67; v.p. Optimun Systems, Inc., Palo Alto, 1967-72; pres. Banking Systems Internat. Corp., Jakarta, Indonesia and Campbell, Calif., 1972-76; dir. software services Tymshare Transactions Services, San Francisco, 1980-83; sr. scientist McDonnell Douglas Corp., Fremont, Calif., 1984-86; dir. corp. devel. Sysorex Internat., Inc., Cupertino, Calif., 1986-87; sr. v.p. Sysorex Info. Systems Inc., Mountain View, Calif., 1987—. Mem. adv. bd. Goodwill Industries, San Francisco; bd. dirs. Gujarate Cultural Assn., 1982; pres. Jain Ctr. of No. Calif., 1983-84. J.N. Tata Trust nat. scholar, 1963. Mem. Ops. Research Soc. Am., Assn. Indians in Am. (v.p. 1980). Democrat. Home: 4048 Twyla Ln Campbell CA 95008 Office: Sysorex Info Systems Inc 335 E Middlefield Rd Mountain View CA 94043

SHAHAN, GARY BERNARD, educator, travel consultant; b. Denver, May 19, 1946; s. Bernard and Marion (Allen) S. BA in Edn., Ariz. State U., 1969, MA in Edn., 1972. Tchr. social studies Tempe (Ariz.) Union High Sch., 1970—; travel cons. Diversified Travel Co., Tempe, 1972—. Recipient award of excellence Tempe Diablos, 1985, Tchr. of Yr. award Tempe Union High Sch., 1987. Republican. Home: 433 E Marigold Ln Tempe AZ 85281-1414 Office: Tempe High Sch 1730 Mill Ave Tempe AZ 85281

SHAINSKY, MICHAEL KURTIS, marketing and sales consultant; b. Santa Rosa, Calif., Apr. 5, 1956; s. Allen B. and Marcia R.; m. Janice Lynn Wapnick, Mar. 7, 1987. BA in History with honors, Sonoma State U., 1981, postgrad., 1981-83. Gen. ptnr. Got the Hang of It, Sherman Oaks, Calif., 1982-85; owner Classic Hang Ups, Cotati, Calif., 1985-88; with real estate marketing and sales The Fountaingrove Group, Inc., Santa Rosa, Calif., 1988--. Mem. Guild Profl. Paperhangers, Bd. Realtors Sonoma County, Sonoma County Hist. Soc. (exec. bd. dirs. 1987--), Sonoma Valley Hist. Soc. Democrat. Home: 8721 Gravenstein Way Cotati CA 94928

SHAKELY, JOHN BOWER (JACK SHAKELY), foundation executive; b. Hays, Kans., Jan. 9, 1940; s. John B. and Martha Jean (Gaston) S.; 1 son, Benton. B.A., U. Okla., 1962. Vol. Peace Corps., Costa Rica, 1963-64; editor publs. Dept. Def., 1967-68; dir. devel. U. Okla., 1968-70, Resthaven Mental Health Ctr., L.A., 1970-74; pres. Jack Shakely Assocs., L.A., 1974-75; sr. adv. Grantsmanship Ctr., L.A., 1975-79, Coun. on Founds., Washington, 1979; pres. Calif. Community Found., L.A., 1980—; lectr. in field. Bd. dirs. Coro Found., L.A., 1982-85; bd. dirs. So. Calif. Assn. Philanthropy, 1980—, Calif. Hist. Soc., 1985-88. 1st lt. U.S. Army, 1965-68. Decorated Army Commendation medal. Democrat. Office: Calif Community Found 3580 Wilshire Blvd Ste 1660 Los Angeles CA 90010

SHAKLEY, LARRY EUGENE, oil company executive; b. Butler, Pa., Feb. 10, 1949; s. Daniel Edgar and Virginia Ruth (Say) S.; m. Susan Jane Smith, Sept. 2, 1972; children: Catherine, Amanda, Angela. BSME, Clarkson U., 1971. Test engr. Pa. Power & LIght Co., Allentown, 1971-75; maint. engr. Arabian Am. Oil Co., Dhahran, Saudi Arabia, 1975-77; plant engr. USI Chems. Co., Tuscola, Ill., 1977-79, maint. supr., 1979-80; facility engr. Prudhoe Bay region Arco Alaska, Inc., Anchorage, 1980-81, maint. supr., 1982-84; supt. ops. Arco Alaska, Inc., 1982-84, mgr. maint., 1984-88, regional engr., 1988—. Mem. ASME, Lions (pres. Arthur III chpt. 1979-80). Baptist. Home: 3750 Amber Bay LP Anchorage AK 99515 Office: Arco Alaska Inc 7th and G Sts PO Box 100360 Anchorage AK 99510

SHALLCROSS, HELEN CLANAHAN, volunteer worker; b. Springfield, Ill., Apr. 21, 1913; d. Robert H. and Helen (Lax) Clanahan; m. Lawrence Butler, June 20, 1942; 1 child, Lawrence Butler Jr. AB, Ill. Coll., 1934; MA, Columbia U., 1940; postgrad., Georgetown U., 1959, S.D. State Coll., 1969. Tchr. elem. health, hygiene and phys. edn. Effingham, Ill., 1934-35, New Berlin, Ill., 1935-37; supr. dining rooms Home for Incurables, N.Y.C., 1938-39; mem. staff ARC, Ft. Riley, Kans., 1940-42; instr. health and phys. edn. Hebrew Acad., Washington, 1959-60; youth advisor, cons., counselor Commrs. Youth Coun. Exec. Br. Govt. D.C., Washington, 1960-64; instr. health scis. and phys. edn. Catonsville (Md.) Community Coll., 1964-68; vol. svcs. coord. McFarland Zone Ctr., Springfield, Ill., 1968-69; lectr. George Washington U., Washington, 1966; tutor Enhancement of Reading for Illiterates, Belen, N.Mex.; bd. dirs. U. N.Mex. Valencia Literacy Coun., Los Lunas, N.Mex., 1987—. Author: Herbs: Garden to Market Place, 1986. Mem. U.S.A. Women in Arts, AARP (pres. 1980-82), Alkali Belden Garden Club (pres. 1977-79). Republican. Episcopalian. Home: 305 Gorman Belen NM 87002

SHAMAS, JAMES E., oil pipeline company executive; b. 1934. BSME, Okla. State U.; JD, U. Tulsa. With Conoco Oil Co. Denver, 1957-65; with Texaco Inc., 1965—, now pres., chief exec. officer, also bd. dirs. Texaco Trading & Transp. Co., Denver. Office: Texaco Trading & Transp Co 1670 Broadway Denver CO 80202 *

SHAMBAUGH, STEPHEN WARD, lawyer; b. South Bend, Ind., Aug. 4, 1920; s. Marion Clyde and Anna Violet (Stephens) S.; m. Marilyn Louise Pyle; children—Susan Wynne Shambaugh Hinkle, Kathleen Louise Shambaugh Thompson. Student San Jose State Tchrs. Coll., 1938-40, U. Ark., 1951; LL.B., U. Tulsa, 1954. Bar: Okla. 1954, Colo. 1964. Mem. staff Reading & Bates, Inc., Tulsa, 1951-54; v.p., gen. mgr., legal counsel Reading & Bates Drilling Co. Ltd., Calgary, Alta., Can., 1954-61; sr. ptnr. Bowman, Shambaugh, Geissinger & Wright, Denver, 1964-81; sole practice, Denver, 1981—; dir., fin. counsel various corps. Served to col. USAF ret. Mem. ABA, Fed. Bar Assn., Colo. Bar Assn., Okla. Bar Assn., Denver Bar Assn., P-51 Mustang Pilots Assn., Phi Alpha Delta. Clubs: Spokane; Petroleum of Bakersfield (Calif.); Masons, Shriners, Elks.

SHAMLEY, RICHARD THOMAS, mayor; b. Miles City, Mont., Sept. 16, 1940; m. Wilma Shamley; children: Kirk, Debora, Mark. BSBA, Black Hills State Coll., Spearfish, S.D., 1962. CPA, Wyo. Acct. Texaco Inc., Craig, Colo. and LaBarge, Wyo., 1962-67, Chapin, McNamara & Macy, 1967-77; pvt. practice acctg. Casper, Wyo., 1977—; pres. Shamley & Killmer Inc., Casper. Mayor City of Casper, 1989—, councilman, 1984—. Mem. AICPA, Wyo. Soc. CPAs, Casper Country Club, Lions, Rotary, Elks. Office: Office of Mayor 200 N David St Casper WY 82601

SHAMS, KAMRUDDIN, infosystems executive; b. Chittagong, Bangladesh, July 4, 1953; came to U.S., 1972; s. Shamsuddin and Sherbano Shams; m. Mahin Hashemian, Oct. 29, 1983. BS in Quantitative Methods and Info. Systems, St. Cloud State U., 1978; M Healthcare Adminstrn., Webster U., 1983. Analyst Fed. Res. Bank, Mpls., 1973-77; contract system cons. Mpls., 1978-81; dir. info. systems Alexian Bros., Schaumburg, Ill., 1981-83; v.p. info. systems Meml. Hosps. Assn., Modesto, Calif., 1984—. Chmn. Internat. Friendship com. Modesto City Council, 1986. Mem. Am. Mgmt. Assn., Am. Coll. Healthcare Execs., Am. Assn. Systems Info., Healthcare Fin. Mgmt. Assn., Med. User's Software Exchange (pres.). Home: 3748 Terneuzen Ave Modesto CA 95356 Office: Meml Hosps Assn 1700 Coffee Rd Modesto CA 95355

SHAMS, RAHM, project engineer, consultant; b. Isfahan, Iran, Mar. 5, 1944; came to U.S., 1969; s. Hasam Shams; m. Hannelore Kohn; children: Susanne, Leila, Julia. MSEE, IIT, 1970; postgrad., San Francisco State U., 1976. Registered profl. engr., Calif. Elec. engr. various engring. cos. and contractors, 1971-76; sr. elec. engr. Ralph M. Parsons, Pasadena, Calif., 1976-78; supervising elec. engr. Western Precipitation/Sog Tech., Los Angeles, 1980-82; chief engr. Everest Engring. Co., El Monte, Calif., 1982-87; pres. Associated Cons. Engrs. Corp., Anaheim, Calif., 1987—. Mem. IEEE. Home: 9457 Cormorant Circle Fountain Valley CA 92708 Office: Associated Cons Engrs Corp 2141 W La Palma Ave Unit 0 Anaheim CA 92801

SHANAFELT, FRED (GEORGE FREDERICK SHANAFELT), accountant; b. Seattle, Sept. 12, 1946; s. Eugene Maxwell and Jane (Trockmorton) S.; m. Susan Lee Collins, Apr. 18, 1971; Margaret Anne, Callie Elizabeth, Andrew Frederick. BA in Acctg., U. Wash., 1969. CPA, Wash. Mem. staff Price Waterhouse, Seattle, 1969-72, sr. acct., 1972-75, mgr., 1975-78, sr. mgr., 1978-82; ptnr. Sweeney Conrad, Bellevue, Wash., 1982—; Mem. steering com. Bd. Accountancy, State of Wash., 1987—. Mem. tech. adv. com. Wash. State Hosp. Commn., 1986—, coms. United Way; treas. Bellevue Art Mus., 1980-85, bd. dirs., 1980—; treas. 1st Congl. Ch., Bellevue, 1988. Mem. Wash. Soc. CPAs (chmn. various coms.), Am. Inst. CPAs, Redmond C. of C. (treas.). Republican. Clubs: Glendale Golf and Country, Lakes (Bellevue). Office: Sweeney Conrad 1416 112th Ave NE Bellevue WA 98004

SHANAFELT, NANCY SUE, federal agency administrator; b. Northampton, Mass., Nov. 21, 1947; m. John D. Shanafelt; children: Amy, Nicholas. BS, U. Mass., 1969. Tchr. Southwick (Mass.) Pub. Schs., 1969-70; acctg. asst. Maricopa County Schs., Phoenix, Ariz., 1973-74; tax auditor to br. chief IRS, San Jose, 1974—; enrolled agt. IRS, Phoenix, 1984-85; creator IRS Women's Network, San Francisco, 1981—. Leader Girl Scouts U.S., Santa Clara, 1980-81, cons., 1981-82, svc. mgr., 1982-84, trainer, 1982-84. Mem. Bus. and Profl. Women, AAUW (sec. 1983-84), NAFE, Commonwealth Club, Am. Soc. Tng. and Devel. (sec. 1983-84). Office: IRS 55 South Market St Ste 900 San Jose CA 95113

SHANAHAN, MICHAEL GEORGE, police officer; b. Seattle, Oct. 14, 1940; s. Raymond Roderick and Carletta (Anderson) S.; m. Jo-Anne Genevieve David, Sept. 16, 1961; children: Patrick, Matthew, Raymond. BA in Psychology, Stanford U., 1962. Asst. police chief U. Wash., Seattle, 1970-71, police chief, 1971—; mem. law enforcement task force interim mcpl. com. Wash. State Legis., 1970-71, campus law enforcement task force-higher edn. com., 1970-71; co-chmn. Wash. Law Enforcement Standards Task Force; founding chmn. Washington Law Enforcement Exec. Forum, 1981; others. Author: Private Enterprise and the Public Police: The Professionalizing Effects of a New Partnership, 1985; contbr. articles to profl. jours. Mem. nat. exploring com. Boy Scouts Am., 1977, exec. bd., chief Seattle council; mem. Blanchet High Sch. Bd., Seattle, 1978-79. Decorated Bronze Star; recipient Award for Pub. Service, U.S. Dept. Transp., 1984, Humanitarian award Seattle chpt. NCCJ, 1985, Silver Beaver award Boy Scouts Am., 1986; recipient St. Matthew's award Northwest Harvest, 1987. Mem. Wash. Assn. Sheriffs and Police Chiefs (exec. bd. 1976-79, pres. 1980-81), Internat. Assn. Chief of Police (exec. com. 1986-87), FBI Nat. Acad. Assocs. Roman Catholic. Lodge: Rotary (pres. Univ. club. Seattle 1985-86). Office: U Wash Police Dept 1117 NE Boat St Seattle WA 98105

SHANAHAN, MIKE, professional football coach. M. in Phys. Edn., Ea. Ill. U., Charleston, Ill., 1974. Student coach, Ea. Ill. U; asst. coach U. Okla., 1975-76; offensive coord., No. Ariz. U., 1976-77, Ea. Ill. U., 1977-78, U. Minn., 1979-8, offensive coord., U. Fla., 1980-84, asst. head coach, 1983-84, offensive coord., Denver Broncos, NFL, 1984-88, head coach, Los Angeles Raiders, NFL, 1988—. Office: LA Raiders 332 Center St El Segundo CA 90245 *

SHANAHAN, TERESA ANN, therapist; b. Scotia, Calif., Nov. 23, 1955; d. Laurence and Katherine (Nansel) S. BA, San Diego State U., 1981, MS in Counseling, 1983. Cert. fitness instr., health mgmt. Therapeutic recreation specialist Grossmont Hosp., La Mesa, Calif., 1980-85, Sharp Cabrillo Hosp., San Diego, 1984--; owner, founder, operator Lifeline Healthcare, San Diego, 1986--; cons. to skilled nursing facilities, San Diego, 1982--; fitness instr. San Diego Community Coll., 1984-86; lectr., educator in field. Columnist Calendar Mag., 1986--. Chmn. San Diego Stroke Club Facilitators, Am. Heart Assn., 1987—, mem. spl. events com.; parade announcer La Jolla (Calif.) Town Council, 1987. Mem. Am. Therapeutic Recreation Assn., Toastmasters (pres. LaJolla chpt. 1985-86, Best Serious Speaker award (1987). Home: 4914 Lamont San Diego CA 92109

SHANAHAN, THOMAS PATRICK, computer software executive; b. L.A., Aug. 13, 1946; s. Emmett Jackson and Bonnie Jean (Havard) S.; m. Robyn Lynn Wood, Dec. 26, 1981; children: Thomas Alan, Kelly Jean. BA, Stanford U., 1968; MBA, Harvard U., 1972. V.p. Donaldson, Lufkin and Jenrette, N.Y.C., 1972-77; v.p. 1st Boston Corp., N.Y.C., 1977-79, San Francisco, 1979-86; chief fin. officer Quintus Computer Systems Corp., Mountain View, Calif., 1986-87, SBT Corp., Sausalito, Calif., 1987—. Capt. U.S. Army, 1968-70. Decorated Bronze Star with V device; Baker scholar Harvard U., 1972. Mem. Univ. Club, Phi Beta Kappa. Office: SBT Corp One Harbor Dr Sausalito CA 94965

SHANE, CINDY LEE, physical fitness educator; b. Monte Vista, Colo., Sept. 16, 1959; d. Harold Stroup and Ellen Nora Howard.; m. Jerry Patrick Shane, Oct. 5, 1985. BS, Colo. State U., 1985. Cert. tchr., Colo. Women's gymnastic coach Rocky Mountain High Sch., Ft. Collins, Colo., 1979-82; co-owner, dir. Gymnastics U.S.A., Cheyenne, Wyo., 1982-85; asst. mgr. Fashion Bar Stores, Inc., Colorado Springs, 1985-87; computer aide, substitute tchr., head women's gymnastics coach Liberty High Sch., Colorado Springs, 1987—; co-owner, dir. Gymnastics Sportsch. Inc., Colorado Springs, 1987—. Mem. Colo. Assn. Phys. Edn. and Recreation, U.S. Gymnastics Fedn. (Wyo. rhythmic state dir. 1983-85). Republican.

SHANE, LEONARD, savings and loan executive; b. Chgo., May 28, 1922; s. Jacob and Selma (Shayne) S.; m. Marjorie Cynthia Konecky, Jan. 14, 1941; children: Judith Shane Shenkman, Marsha Kay Shane Palmer, William Alan, Shelley Rose Shane Asidon. Student, U. Chgo., 1939-41, Ill. Inst. Tech., 1941-42. Writer-editor UPI, 1942-44; cons. indsl. areas 1944-46; writer-rancher Tucson, 1946-48; writer-producer ABC, Los Angeles, 1948-49; owner cons. agency Los Angeles, 1949-64; chmn. bd., dir., chief exec. officer Mercury Savs. and Loan Assn., Huntington Beach, Calif., 1964—. Chmn. United Jewish Welfare Fund of Orange County, 1972-73; pres. Western region, mem. internat. bd. govs. Am. Assos. Ben Gurion U., Israel; pres. Los Angeles Recreation and Park Commn., 1960-63, Jewish Fedn. Council of Orange County, 1973-74; trustee Ocean View Sch. Dist., 1970-72, City of Hope, 1968—. Mem. U.S. League Savs. Instns. (vice chmn. 1981-82, chmn. 1982-83, legis. chmn. 1987-89—), Calif. Savs. and Loan League (dir. 1969-73, v.p. 1979-80, pres. 1980-81), Phi Sigma Delta. Clubs: Big Canyon Country, Masons, Shriners. Office: Mercury Savs & Loan Assn 7812 Edinger Ave Huntington Beach CA 92647

SHANK, DAVID ARNOLD, management consultant; b. Seattle, Aug. 10, 1927; s. Corwing Phillip and Esther (Arnold) S.; m. Doris Mae McCormick, Aug. 25, 1950 (div. Oct. 1963); children: Karen Baker, David McCallum, Mary Kelly; m. Karen Anne Skold, Mar. 31, 1989. BS in Bus. Adminstrn., U. Wash., 1950; MBA, Harvard U., 1956. Pres. Shank Ins., Inc., Mercer Island, Wash., 1950-54, Shank & Assocs., Inc., Seattle, 1956—; bd. dirs. Shank & Assocs., Inc., Portland, Oreg., Centro de Tranquilidad, Portland. Author: The Financial Revolution, 1969. Bd. dirs. DePaul Alcohol Treatment Ctr., Portland, 1984. With USN, 1944-46, PTO. Mem. Portland Alano Club (dir. 1986). Republican. Office: Shank & Assocs Inc 3919 SE 32d Ave Portland OR 97202

SHANK, RUSSELL, librarian, educator; b. Spokane, Wash., Sept. 2, 1925; s. Harry and Sadie S.; m. Doris Louise Hempfer, Nov. 9, 1951 (div.); children: Susan Marie, Peter Michael, Judith Louise. B.S., U. Wash., 1946, B.A., 1949; M.B.A., U. Wis., 1952; Dr.L.S., Columbia U., 1966. Reference librarian U. Wash., Seattle, 1949; asst. engring. librarian U. Wis.-Madison, 1949-52; chief personnel Milw. Pub. Library, 1952; engring.-phys. scis. librarian Columbia U., N.Y.C., 1953-59; sr. lectr. Columbia U., 1964-66, assoc. prof., 1966-67; asst. univ. librarian U. Calif.-Berkeley, 1959-64; dir. sci. library project N.Y. Met. Reference and Research Agy., 1966-68; dir. libraries Smithsonian Instn., Washington, 1967-77; univ. librarian, prof. UCLA, 1977—, asst. vice chancellor for library & info. planning, 1989—; cons. Indonesian Inst. Sci., 1970; bd. cons. Pahlavi Nat. Library, Iran, 1975-76; pres. U.S. Book Exchange, 1975. Trustee OCLC, Inc., 1978-84, 87, chmn., 1984; mem. library del. People's Republic of China, 1979; bd. dirs. Am. Council on Edn., 1980-81. Served with USNR, 1943-46. Recipient Disting. Alumnus award U. Wash. Sch. Librarianship, 1968; fellow Council on Library Resources, 1973-74. Fellow AAAS; mem. ALA (pres. 1978-79, council 1961-65, 74-82, exec. bd. 1975-80, chmn. internat. relations com. 1980-83, pres. info. sci. and automation div. 1968-69), Assn. Coll. and Research Libraries (pres. 1972-73), Assn. Research Libraries (dir. 1974-77), Spl. Libraries Assn., Am. Soc. Info. Sci. Home: 4754B La Villa Marina Marina del Rey CA 90292 Office: UCLA Rsch Libr 405 Hilgard Ave Los Angeles CA 90024-1575 *

SHANKS, ROLAND EUGENE, state official; b. San Jose, Calif., Nov. 1, 1949; s. Robert Sanford and Chloris Dorethea (Bilyeu) S.; m. Robin Joy Burt, Dec. 4, 1983. BS in Natural Resources Mgmt. with honors, Calif. Poly. State U., 1973. Realty specialist Bur. Land Mgmt., Fairbanks, Alaska, 1976-78; realty officer Tanana Chief. Conf., Fairbanks, 1978-81; lobbyist various environ. groups Fairbanks and Juneau, Alaska, 1981-82; mgr. land adminstrn. Cook Inlet Region, Inc., Anchorage, 1982-83; dir. div. rsch. and devel. Alaska Dept. Natural Resources, Anchorage, 1983; land. mgr. Eklutna, Inc., Anchorage, 1983-85; spl. asst. to commr. Alaska Dept. Fish and Game, Juneau, 1985-89; with Human Dimensions Unit Dept. Natural Resources Cornell U., Ithaca, N.Y., 1989—. Mem. editorial bd. Alaska Fish and Game. Bd. dirs. Fairbanks Environ. Ctr., 1977-81, Alaska Health Project, 1984-85, Gasteneau Humane Soc., Juneau, 1988; mem. Dem. State Cen. Com., 1981-85, Gov's Transition Team, 1982-83; founder, mem. Alaska Environ. Assembly, 1981, Alaska Environ. Polit. Action Com., 1981; founder, exec. dir. Alaska Environ. Lobby, 1981; mem. Campbell Tract Task Force, Anchorage, 1982-83; mem. adv. com. Alaska Land Use Coun., 1985. Mem. Interior Land Mgrs. Assn. (pres. 1981), Nat. Assn. Rev. Appraisers (cert.), Internat. Right of Way Assn., Internat. Assn. Fish and Wildlife Agys., Western Fish and Wildlife Agys., Urban and Regional Info. System Assn., Alaska Land Mgrs. Assn. (founder, exec. com. 1978-85), Sierra Club (founder, chmn. Delai group 1977-81, chmn. Alaska chpt. 1984-85). Home: 1309 3d St Douglas AK 99824 Office: Cornell U Dept Natural Resources Human Dimensions Unit Ithaca NY 14853

SHANKS, STEVEN BRUCE, engineering supervisor; b. Denver, Apr. 4, 1955; s. Gerald R. and Virginia R. (Hovey) S. BSME, U. Colo., 1977. Mech. engr. Pub. Svc. Co. Colo., Denver, 1977-83, engring. supr., 1983—. Mem. Project Mgmt. Inst., U.S. Cycling Fedn., Columbine Cycle Club. Home: 3211 S Glencoe St Denver CO 80222

SHANNON, AUBREY JACK, aerospace engineer; b. Brenham, Tex., July 19, 1938. BS in Aerospace Engring., U. Tex., 1961. Registered profl. engr., Wash. Mem. aerodynamics staff Boeing Co., Seattle, 1961-74; pres. Shannon Engring, Inc., Seattle, 1974—. Patentee in field. Bd. dirs. Seattle Opera; stellar mem. Mus. Flight, Seattle. Mem. AIAA, Seattle C. of C., Soc. Automotive Engrs. Office: Shannon Engring Inc 7675 Perimeter Rd S 200 Seattle WA 98108

SHANNON, DEBRA CATHERINE, sales executive; b. Camden, N.J., July 10, 1951; d. Henry Frederick and Julia (Skibo) Steffens; m. Francis Joseph Shannon, May 22, 1972 (div. 1977); m. Dennis Clay Beaver, June 25, 1983; 1 child, Jamison Travis Beaver. BA in Edn., Villanova U., 1973. Asst. dept. mgr. Sears Roebuck and Co., St. Davids, Pa., 1969-73; store mgr. Capezio & Things, Plymouth Meeting, Pa., 1973-74, The Gap Stores, San Bruno, Calif., 1974-76; operational auditor The Gap Stores, San Bruno, 1976-77, dist. mgr., 1977-80; store mgr. Casual Corners Stores, Enfield, Conn., 1980-82; dist. mgr. Casual Corners Stores, Enfield, 1982-84; regional sales mgr. Recycled Paper Products, Chgo., 1984-87, v.p. chain account sales, 1987—. Republican. Roman Catholic. Home and Office: 1705 Easton Dr Burlingame CA 94010

SHANNON, DONALD THOMAS, electrical engineer; b. Bay Shore, N.Y., Oct. 27, 1951; s. John Joseph and Lauretta Anita (Florio) S.; m. Dora Virginia Baracaldo, Jan. 31, 1987; 1 child, John Ernest. BS in Elec. Engring., Northern Ariz. U., 1985. Shift supr. Southwest Presto Log, Flagstaff, Ariz., 1979-80; mfg. engr. W.L. Gore & Assocs., Flagstaff, 1980—; owner Control Technologies, Flagstaff, 1983—. Life mem. Nat. Rifle Assn. With USMC, 1969-73. Mem. IEEE, Am. Soc. for Quality Control. Republican. Roman Catholic. Office: W L Gore & Assocs PO Box 1300 Flagstaff AZ 86002

SHANNON, EDFRED L., JR., transportation company executive; b. 1926; (married). B.S., U. Calif., Berkeley, 1951. Petroleum engr. Union Oil Co. of Calif., 1951-53; with Santa Fe Internat. Corp., Alhambra, 1953—, v.p., 1960-63, chmn., from 1963, chief exec. officer, 1963—, pres., 1986—, also dir. Office: Santa Fe Internat Corp 100 S Fremont Ave Box 4000 Alhambra CA 91802 *

SHANNON, GARY WAYNE, electronics engineer, educator; b. Athens, Ala., Oct. 24, 1947; s. James Wesley and Ruth Helen (Bauer) S.; m. Barbara Jean Wood, July 3, 1969; children: Scott Bauer, Craig Wood, Sara Diane. AS, Calhoun Community Coll., Decatur, Ala., 1968; BSEE, Auburn U., 1971, MSEE, 1973. Instr. engring. Auburn (Ala.) U., 1971-73; satellite engr. Sandia Nat. Lab., Albuquerque, 1980-84, spacecraft engr., 1984—; assoc. prof. Chapman Coll., Albuquerque, 1977—; engring. cons. Air Force Weapons Lab., Albuquerque, 1980—. Contbr. articles to profl. publs. Youth dir. Pennsylvania Street Ch. of Christ, Albuquerque, 1977-84; coach Am. Youth Soccer Orgn., Albuquerque, 1983-85. Capt. USAF, 1973-80, maj. Res. Mem. IEEE, Instrumentation Soc. Am. (session chmn. 1979, cert. 1980), Air Force Assn., Auburn U. Alumni Assn., Bighorn Club, Eta Kappa Nu. Republican. Office: Sandia Nat Labs PO Box 5800 Albuquerque NM 87185

SHANNON, KEVIN PAUL, chemical company executive; b. Billings, Mont., July 3, 1958; s. Paul Hugh and Helen Francis (Riley) S. BBA, U. Tex., Austin, 1980. Product movement coordinator Dow Chem. U.S.A., Freeport, Tex., 1980-81; field svc. rep. Dow Chem. U.S.A., Detroit, 1982-84; regional distbn. mgr. DowBrands (Dow Consumer Products, Inc.), L.A., 1984—. Office: Dow Consumer Products Inc 17870 Castleton St Box 881 City of Industry CA 91749

SHANNON, RICHARD ELLIOTT, office products company executive; b. Portland, Oreg., July 23, 1944; s. Richard Elliott and Maxine Louise (Steignewald) S.; m. Patricia Elaine Herndon, May 2, 1969; children: Richard Elliott III, Zachary, Julie. BS, Portland State U., 1967. Salesman Saxon Bus. Products, Portland, Oreg., 1968-70; br. mgr. Saxon Bus. Products, Denver, 1970-76; regional mgr. Savin Bus. Products, Denver, 1976-77; v.p. copier sales Lewan & Assocs., Inc., Denver, 1977—; advisor Hansens Guidelines, Setauket, N.Y., 1984—; speaker, motivator, sales trainer various dealerships in western U.S., 1983—. Dir. COMDA, Colo., 1988; coordinator Christmas for the Needy, Colorado Springs, 1983-88; v.p. Salesman with A. Purpose, Colo., 1985-86. Named to Pres. Club Lewan & Assocs., 1977-85. Mem. Nat. Office Machine Dealers Assn., Colo. Office Machine Dealers Assn. (bd. dirs. 1988—). Republican. Club: Mercedes. Home: 19415 Old Fort Ln Monument CO 80132

SHANNON, RICHARD STOLL, III, financial executive; b. N.Y.C., Mar. 22, 1943; s. Richard Stoll Jr. and Margaret (Cather) S.; m. Ann Wright Schmidt, June 14, 1965; children: Clea Cather, Kathryne Baltzelle, Arianna Wright. BA, Stanford U., 1966, MA, 1969; PhD, Harvard U., 1973. Asst. prof. U. Mich., Ann Arbor, 1973-78; mgr., trustee, gen. ptnr. various family trusts, partnerships and corps. Englewood, Colo., 1978-84; pres. Shannon Mgmt. Corp., Englewood, 1985—; bd. dirs. Escalante Internat. Corp., Denver. Author: The Arms of Achilles, 1975; editor (with others) Oral Literature and The Formula, 1976. Bd. dirs. Cherryvale Sanitation Dist., Englewood, 1984—, pres., 1986—; regional chmn. Stanford Ann. Fund/Keystone Project, Colo., N.Mex., Nebr., 1985—. Teaching fellow Harvard U., 1970-73. Mem. Am. Philol. Assn., Denver C. of C., Cherry Creek Commerce Assn., Cherry Hills Country Club, Denver Petroleum Club, Phi Beta Kappa. Office: Shannon Mgmt Corp 3098 S Pennsylvania St Englewood CO 80110

SHANNON, ROBERT RENNIE, optical sciences center administrator, educator; b. Mt. Vernon, N.Y., Oct. 3, 1932; s. Howard A. and Harriebell (Rennie) S.; m. Helen Lang, Feb. 13, 1954; children—Elizabeth, Barbara, Jennifer, Amy, John, Robert. B.S., U. Rochester, 1954, M.A., 1957. Dir. Optics Lab., ITEK Corp., Lexington, Mass., 1959-69; prof. Optical Scis. Ctr., U. Ariz., 1969—, dir., 1983—, prof., 1969—; cons. Lawrence Livermore Lab., 1980—; trustee Aerospace Corp., 1985—; mem. Air Force Sci. Adv. Bd., 1986—. Editor: Applied Optics and Optical Engineering, Vol. 7, 1980, Vol. 8, 1981, Vol. 9, 1983, Vol. 10, 1987. Fellow Optical Soc. Am. (pres. 1985), Soc. Photo-Optical Instrumentation Engrs. (pres. 1979-80, recipient Goddard award 1982), Sigma Xi. Club: Tucson Soaring (past pres.). Home: 7040 E Taos Pl Tucson AZ 85715 Office: U Ariz Optical Scis Ctr Tucson AZ 85721

SHANNON, SHAD, flight attendant, model; b. Orlando, Fla., May 7, 1955; d. Edward Hoyt and Ozella (Shannon) Murray. AA, Valencia Community Coll., 1976; BA, Xavier U., New Orleans, 1978. File clk., computer operator Am. 1st Fed., Orlando, 1973; substitue tchr. Orange County Sch. Bd., Orlando, 1974-75; dancer Walt Disney World, Orlando, 1975; peer advisor Valencia Community Coll., Orlando, 1975-76; instr. drama Audobon Arts Ctr., New Orleans, 1976-77; flight attendant Pan Am. World Airways, L.A., 1979—; substitute tchr. Compton (Calif.) Unified Sch. Dist., 1981-83; cosmetic cons. Isabel Sanford Cosmetics, Inglewood, Calif., 1987. Actor: The Pasadena Playhouse Alumni & Assocs., 1985—. Campaign aide Ernest "Dutch" Morial mayoral campaign, New Orleans, 1977. Named D'Elegance Top Model of Yr. Emily Walker Sch. Charm 1985; recipient Trio Achievers award U. Miami, 1984, Community Svc. award Brookins A.M.E. Ch., L.A., 1987. Mem. Alpha Phi Alpha. Home: 411 Lincoln Ave #30 Glendale CA 91205

SHANOR, CLARENCE RICHARD, clergyman; b. Butler, Pa., Dec. 26, 1924; s. Paul L. and Marion (McCandless) S.; B.A., Allegheny Coll., 1948; S.T.B., Boston U., 1951, Ph.D., 1958; m. Anna Lou Watts, June 23, 1948; 1 son, Richard Watts. Ordained to ministry Methodist Ch., 1950; pastor Meth. Ch., South Hamilton, Mass., 1951-54; research asso. Union Coll., Schenectady, 1954-55; prof. Christian edn. Nat. Coll., Kansas City, Mo., 1956-58; asso. minister First United Meth. Ch., St. Petersburg, Fla., 1958-61, First United Meth. Ch., Fullerton, Calif., 1961-66; coord. metro dept. San Diego dist. United Meth. Union, San Diego, 1966-87, ret., 1987; pres. Human Svcs. Corp., 1972-77. Treas. San Diego County Ecumenical Conf., 1970-71, pres., 1975-77; chmn. Coalition Urban Ministries, 1970-71, Cultural and Religious Task Force Rancho San Diego, 1970-74; chmn. western jurisdiction Urban Network United Meth. Ch., 1978. Chmn. San Diego Citizens Com. Against Hunger, 1969-72; bd. dirs. Interfaith Housing Found., chmn., 1979, pres. 1988—; v.p. North County Interfaith Coun., 1987—; mem. Gaslamp Quarter Project Area Com., San Diego, 1978, mem. coun., 1980-84; chmn. bd. Horton House Corp., 1978; mem. Mayor's Task Force on the Homeless, 1983-84; chmn. Downtown Coordinating Coun., 1983-84; mem. regional Task Force on Homeless, 1986-87; vice-chmn. Community Congress, 1987. Recipient San Diego Inst. for Creativity award, 1969, Boss of Yr. award Am. Bus. Women's Assn., 1972, Christian Unity award Diocesan Ecumenical Commn., 1984, Congl. Disting. Svc. award, 1984, Helen Beardsley Human Rights award, 1986, Mayor O'Connor's Seahorse award 1989. Mem. Lions. Author: (with Anna Lou Shanor) Kindergartner Meet Your World, 1966. Home: 1636 Desert Glen Escondido CA 92026-1849

SHANSBY, JOHN GARY, investment banker; b. Seattle, Aug. 25, 1937; s. John Jay and Jule E. (Boyer) S.; m. Joyce Ann Dunsmore, June 21, 1959 (div.); children: Sheri Lee, Kimberly Ann, Jay Thomas.; m. Barbara Anderson De Meo, Jan. 1, 1983 (div.). B.A., U. Wash., 1959. Sales exec. Colgate-Palmolive Co., N.Y.C., 1959-67; subs. pres. Am. Home Products Corp., N.Y.C., 1968-71; v.p. Clorox Co., Oakland, Calif., 1972-73; ptnr. Booz, Allen & Hamilton, San Francisco, 1974-75; chmn. bd., chief exec. officer, dir. Shaklee Corp., San Francisco, 1975-86; mng. gen. ptnr. The Shansby Group, San Francisco, 1986—. Bd. dirs. San Francisco Symphony, Calif. Econ. Devel. Corp.; chmn. Calif. State Commn. for Rev. of Master Plan Higher Edn.; founded J. Gary Shansby chair Mktg. Strategy, U. Calif., Berkeley; trustee Calif. State U. Mem. San Francisco C. of C. (past pres.), Sigma Nu. Republican. Clubs: Villa Traverna, Olympic (San Francisco); Silverado (Calif.) Country; Lincoln of No. Calif; Pennask Lake Fishing (B.C.); St. Francis Yacht; Sky Club (N.Y.). Office: The Shansby Group 250 Montgomery St San Francisco CA 94104

SHAO-CHI, KAREN, research biologist; b. Amoy, Fukien, Republic of China, July 4, 1947; came to U.S., 1969; d. Lieh and Shih-Chu (Yin) Lin; m. Peter Young-Tai Lin, May 26, 1979; 1 child, Yi Ning. BA in Zoology, Nat. Taiwan U., 1969; MA in Biology, Wake Forest U., 1971. Rsch. scientist Xoma Corp., Berkeley, Calif., 1985—. Fellow Am. Soc. Clin. Pathologists. Democrat. Presbyterian.

SHAPELL, NATHAN, financial and real estate executive; b. Poland, Mar. 6, 1922; s. Benjamin and Hela S.; m. Lilly Szenes, July 17, 1948; children: Vera Shapell Guerin, Benjamin (dec.). Co-founder Shapell Industries, Inc., Beverly Hills, Calif., 1955; now chmn. bd. Shapell Industries, Inc.; mem. adv. bd. Union Bank, Beverly Hills; mem. residential bldgs. adv. com. Calif. Energy Resources Conservation and Devel. Commn.; speaker in field. Mem. Calif. Commn. Govt. Reform, 1978; Atty. Gen. Calif. Adv. Council, Dist. Atty. Los Angeles County Adv. Council; chmn. Calif. Govt. Commn. Orgn. and Economy, 1975—, Gov.'s Task Force on Affordable Housing, 1980—; mem. adv. council Pres.'s Commn. on the Holocaust, 1979; pres. Am. Acad. Achievement, 1975—; mem. deans council UCLA Sch. Architecture and Urban Planning, 1976—. Author: Witness to the Truth, 1974. Trustee U. Santa Clara, Calif., 1976—; bd. councillors U. So. Calif. Med. Sch., 1973—. Recipient Golden Plate award Am. Acad. Achievement, 1974, Fin. World award, 1977. Jewish. Club: Hillcrest Country (Los Angeles). Address: Shapell Industries Inc 8383 Wilshire Blvd Suite 700 Beverly Hills CA 90211 *

SHAPERO, HARRIS JOEL, pediatrician; b. Winona, Minn., Nov. 22, 1930; s. Charles and Minnie Sara (Ehrlichman) S.; m. Byong Soon Yu, Nov. 6, 1983; children by previous marriage: Laura, Bradley, James, Charles. A.A., UCLA, 1953; B.S., Northwestern U., 1954, M.D., 1957. Diplomate and cert. specialist occupational medicine Am. Bd. Preventive Medicine; cert. aviation medicine FAA. Intern, Los Angeles County Harbor Gen. Hosp., 1957-58, resident in pediatrics, 1958-60, staff physician, 1960-64; attending physician Perceptually Handicapped Children's Clinic, 1960-63; disease control officer for tuberculosis, Los Angeles County Health Dept., 1962-64; practice medicine specializing in pediatrics and occupational medicine, Cypress, Calif., 1965-85; pediatric cons. Los Angeles Health Dept., 1963-85, disease control officer sexually transmitted diseases, 1984-85; pediatric cons. Bellflower Clinic, 1962-85; emergency room dir. AMI, Anaheim, Calif., 1968-78; mem. med. staff Anaheim Gen. Hosp., Beach Community Hosp., Norwalk Community Hosp.; courtesy staff Palm Harbor Gen. Hosp., Bellflower City Hosp.; pediatric staff Hosp. de General, Ensenada, Mex., 1978—; primary care clinician Sacramento County Health, 1987-88; pvt. practice medico-legal evaluation, 1987-88; founder Calif. Legal Evaluation Med. Group; health care provider, advisor City of Anaheim, City of Buena Park, City of Cypress, City of Garden Grove, Cypress Sch. Dist., Magnolia Sch. Dist., Savanna Sch. Dist., Anaheim Unified Sch. Dist., Orange County Dept. Edn.; pediatric and tuberculosis cons. numerous other orgns.; FAA med. examiner, founder Pan Am. Childrens Mission. Author: The Silent Epidemic, 1979. Named Headliner in Medicine Orange County Press Club, 1978. Fellow Am. Coll. Preventive Medicine; mem. Los Angeles County Med. Assn., Los Angeles County Indsl. Med. Assn., Acad. Neuromuscular Thermography, Los Angeles County Pediatric Soc., Orange County Pediatric Soc., Am. Pub. Health Assn., Mex.-Am. Border Health Assn. Republican. Jewish. Avocations: antique books and manuscripts, photography, graphics, beekeeper. Home: PO Box 10874 Beverly Hills CA 90213-3874

SHAPIRO, BARRY, toy company executive; b. Bklyn., Apr. 18, 1942; s. Sidney and Anne (Sokol) S.; m. Frances Rosenfeld, Apr. 5, 1970; children: David Scott, Sean Jonathan. BA in English, Rutgers U., 1963. Asst. buyer J.C. Penney Co., N.Y.C., 1966-69; dir. product planning and internat. ops. Gabriel Industries, Inc., N.Y.C., 1969-78; exec. v.p. Lakeside Games div. Leisure Dynamics, Inc., Mpls., 1978-79, pres., 1979-80; exec. v.p. Toy Game & Hobby Group div. Leisure Dynamics, Inc., Mpls., 1980-81; exec. v.p., gen. mgr., chief exec. officer Wham-O, San Gabriel, Calif., 1981-83; exec. v.p., gen. mgr. Imagineering, Inc., Phoenix, 1984—; cons. to various toy cos. Vol. mem. Jewish Big Brothers, 1964-78, vice chmn. Big Brothers of N.Y., 1976-78; coach Little League, Mpls., Arcadia, Calif., 1979—; v.p. Temple Shaarei Tikvah, Arcadia, 1982-84; bd. dirs. Har Zion Synagogue, 1988—, v.p. 1989—. 1st lt. U.S. Army, 1963-66. Recipient Army Commendation medal. Mem. Assn. Toy Mfg. Am. Jewish. Home: 5421 E Via Buena Vista Paradise Valley AZ 85253

SHAPIRO, BURT JAY, personal manager; b. N.Y.C., June 18, 1947; s. Gustav Samuel and Helen (Futerman) S. BA, SUNY, Stonybrook, 1969; JD, U. Houston, 1972. Bar: Tex., 1972, U.S. Dist. Ct. (so. dist.) Tex., 1972, U.S. Ct. Appeals (5th cir.), 1972, U.S. Supreme Ct., 1977. Atty. Law Offices of W.D. Luther, Houston, 1972-75, Lo-Vaca Gathering Co., Houston, 1975-77; ptnr. Jerry Levias Mgmt. Enterprises, Houston, 1977-80; v.p. Wallach Enterprises, Beverly Hills, Calif., 1980-87; pres. Burt Shapiro Mgmt., L.A., 1987—. Mem. Phi Delta Phi. Democrat. Jewish. Home: 2147 N Beachwood Dr Los Angeles CA 90068 Office: PO Box 69813 Los Angeles CA 90069

SHAPIRO, GARY ALAN, real estate broker; b. Rochester, N.Y., Feb. 21, 1949; s. Arthur Richard and Irene (Gluskin) S. Student, Ariz. State U., 1971. Sales assoc. Tom Fannin Realtors, Scottsdale, Ariz., 1971-76; sales mgr. Tom Fannin Realtors, Scottsdale, 1974-76; owner Price/Shapiro Realtors, Scottsdale, 1976-80, Shapiro Realtors, Scottsdale, 1980—; profl. standards chmn. Scottsdale Bd. Realtors, 1988—. Chmn. Scottsdale Leadership, 1988—. Republican. Jewish. Office: Shapiro Realtors Inc 8989 E Via Linda #112 Scottsdale AZ 85258

SHAPIRO, ISADORE, material scientist, consultant; b. Mpls., Apr. 25, 1916; s. Jacob and Bessie (Goldman) S.; B. in Chem. Engring. summa cum laude, U. Minn., 1938, PhD, 1944; m. Mae Hirsch. Sept. 4, 1938; children: Stanley Harris, Jerald Steven. Asst. instr. chemistry U. Minn., 1938-41, rsch. fellow, 1944-45; rsch. chemist E. I. duPont de Nemours and Co., Phila., 1946; head chem. lab. U.S. Naval Ordnance Test Sta., Pasadena, Calif., 1947-52; dir. rsch. lab. Olin-Mathieson Chem. Corp., 1952-59; head chemistry Hughes Tool Co., Aircraft div., Culver City, Calif., 1959-62; pres. Universal Chem. Systems Inc. 1962—, Aerospace Chem. Systems, Inc., 1964-66; dir. contract rsch. HITCO, Gardena, Calif., 1966-67; prin. scientist Douglas Aircraft Co. of McDonnell Douglas Corp., Santa Monica, Calif., 1967; prin. scientist McDonnell Douglas Astronautics Co., 1967-70; head materials and processes AiResearch Mfg. Co., Torrance, Calif., 1971-82, cons., 1982—; inaugurated dep. gov. Am. Biographical Inst. Rsch. Assn., 1988; dep. gov. gen. Internat. Biographical Ctr., Eng. Rater U.S. Civil Svc. Bd. Exam., 1948-52. Served 1st lt. AUS, 1941-44. Registered profl. engr., Calif. Fellow Am. Inst. Chemists, Am. Inst. Aeros and Astronautics (assoc.); mem. AAAS, Am. Ordnance Assn., Am. Chem. Soc., Soc. Rheology, Soc. Advancement Materials and Process Engring., Am. Inst. Physics, AIM, Am. Phys. Soc., N.Y. Acad. Sci., Am. Assn. Contamination Control, Am. Ceramic Soc., Nat. Inst. Ceramic Engrs., Internat. Plansee Soc. for Powder Metallurgy, Sigma Xi, Tau Beta Pi, Phi Lambda Upsilon. Author articles in tech. publs. Patentee, discoverer series of carborane compounds; creater term carborane. Home: 5624 W 62d St Los Angeles CA 90056

SHAPIRO, RICHARD STANLEY, physician; b. Moline, Ill., June 11, 1925; s. Herbert and Esther Dian (Grant) S.; B.S., St. Ambrose Coll., 1947; B.S. in Pharmacy, U. Iowa, 1951, M.S. in Preventive Medicine and Environ. Health, 1951, M.D., 1957; m. Arlene Blum, June 12, 1949; children—Michele Pamela, Bruce Grant, Gary Lawrence; m. 2d, Merry Lou Cook, Oct. 11, 1971. Pharmacist, Rock Island, Ill., 1951-53; research asst. U. Iowa Coll. Medicine, Iowa City, 1950-51, 53-57; practice medicine specializing in allergy, Beverly Hills, Calif., 1958-62, Lynwood, Calif., 1962—; attending physician Good Hope Found. Allergy Clinic, Los Angeles, 1958-62, Cedars of Lebanon Hosp., Hollywood, Calif., 1959-68, U. So. Calif.-Los Angeles County Med. Center, 1962—; physician St. Francis Hosp., Lynwood, 1962—; assoc. clin. prof. medicine U. So. Calif., 1978-84, emeritus, 1984—. Bd. dirs. Westside Jewish Community Center, 1961-65, Camp JCA, 1964-65. Served with USNR, 1943-45; PTO. Diplomate Am. Bd. Allergy and Immunology. Fellow Am. Geriatric Soc., Am. Coll. Allergy, Am. Assn. Clin. Immunology and Allergy; mem. Am. Soc. Tropical Medicine and Hygiene, Am. Acad. Allergy, Los Angeles Allergy Soc., AMA, Calif., Los Angeles County med. assns., West Coast Allergy Soc., AAAS, Am., Calif. socs. internal medicine, Calif. Soc. Allergy, Am. Heart Assn., Sierra Club, Sigma Xi. Jewish. Mason; mem. B'nai B'rith. Contbr. articles to profl. jours. Office: 11411 Brookshire Ave Downey CA 90241

SHARECK, HELEN MARIE, educator; b. Avalon, Calif., May 29, 1930; d. William Joseph and Muriel Jane (Pearring) Kokott; m. Adan Shareck (div. 1988); children: Richard William, Carol Ann. BA, Calif. State U., Los Angeles, 1962, MA, 1968; EdD, U. LaVerne, 1980. Elem., jr. tchr. Glendale (Calif.) Unified, 1962-72, gifted coordinator, 1972-80, elem. prin., 1977-79; math. tchr. Immaculate Heart Coll., Los Angeles, 1966-67; elem. prin. Scotts Valley (Calif.) Schs., 1980-85; elem., jr. tchr. Inglewood (Calif.) Unified, 1986—; cons. State Dept. Calif., Fremont Unified, 1977, 80, 83, San Diego Unified, Santa Clara County, Pomona Unified, 1977-82; speaker Shasta County Assn., 1983, Gifted Assn., various locations, 1980-84. Contbr. articles to profl. jours. Home: 9209 S Crenshaw Inglewood CA 90305

SHARIAT, HORMOZ, research scientist; b. Teheran, Iran, Sept. 9, 1955; came to U.S., 1979; s. Javad and Shamsi (Rastegar) S.; m. Donnell Jean Roper, Oct. 23, 1977; children: Hanniel Mina, Jonathan Navid. BSEE, Arya Mehr U., Tehran, Iran, 1978; MSEE, U. So. Calif., 1981, PhD, 1986. Mem. technical staff Rockwell Internat., Seal Beach, Calif., 1981-87; rsch. scientist Lockheed Artificial Intelligence Ctr., Menlo Park, Calif., 1987—. Author: (with others) Motion Understanding: Robot and Human Vision 1988; contbr. articles profl. jours. Sec. to bd. dirs. Radio Voice of Christ, Portland, Oreg., 1983-88; lectr. Fellowship of Iranian Christians, L.A., 1983—; assoc. pastor Iranian Christian Ch., San Jose, Calif., 1988—. Mem. IEEE, Internat. Soc. for Optical Engring. Republican. Home: 1026 Whitebick Dr San Jose CA 95129 Office: Lockheed AI Ctr 3251 Hanover St Palo Alto CA 94304

SHARKEY, CHRISTINE ANN, nurse; b. Oakland, Calif., Oct. 3, 1951; d. Robert Jack and Lois Veronica S.; 1 child, Robert Jack. Diploma R.N., Tex. Eastern Sch. Nursing, 1984. RN, Tex., Calif. Staff nurse Mother Frances Hosp., Tyler, Tex., 1984-86; clinical nurse II U. Calif. Davis Med. Ctr., Sacramento, 1986-88, clinical nurse III, 1988—; chair emergency room task force com., Sacramento, 1987—. Mem. Calif. Nurses Assn., Emergency Nurses Assn., Tex. Student Nurses Assn. (v.p. 1983-84). Republican. Office: U Calif Davis Med Ctr 2315 Stockton Blvd Sacramento CA 95817

SHARKEY, RICHARD DAVID, product designer; b. Columbus, Ohio, May 8, 1957; s. John David and Beatrice Diane (Ziesler) S.; m. Melissa Duke Smith, Dec. 21, 1980; 1 child, Flax Allistair Linden. Student, U. No. Colo., 1975-77, Emporia State U., 1977-78, U. Denver, 1978-81. Music tchr., pvt. studio, piano, cello, composition theory Evergreen, Colo., 1978-82; pvt. bus., period residential restoration Sharkey and Assocs., Evergreen and Denver, 1978-86; stair apprentice Denver Stair Co., 1985-86; stair master Heidelberg Stair Co., Evergreen, 1986; pvt. bus., designer period staircases, millwork O'Searcaigh, Ltd., Evergreen and Denver, 1986—; cons. stair design, Heidelberg Stair, Evergreen, Frank's Woodworking, Lyons, Colo., numerous contractors, architecture, design firms, 1987—. Composer/music: numerous piano compositions, 1972—; designer: numerous architecture, millwork and interior designs; inventor: woodworking tools and accessories, 1986—. Recipient scholarship Outward Bound Colo., Optimist Club of Evergreen, 1973, music grant, U. No. Colo., Greeley, 1975-76, Emporia (Kans.) U., 1977. Mem. Internat. Soc. Archtl. Artisans (pres., founder 1988—), Denver Cherry Creek Club (charter mem.), Rotary. Mem. Christian Science Ch. Home: 1520 King St Denver CO 80204 Office: OSearcaigh Ltd PO Box 310 Evergreen CO 80439-0310

SHARMA, NAGEEN, computer company marketing specialist; b. Delhi, India, Aug. 5, 1960; came to U.S. in 1982; s. Girdhari Lal and Nirmal (Shridar) S.; m. Amita Kharbanda Sharma, Nov. 20, 1987. BSEE, U. Delhi, 1981; MSEE in Computers, U. Md., 1984; MBA in Mktg., National U., 1988. Project engr. Siements, Delhi, India, 1981-82; sr. mktg. engr. Intel. Corp., Folsom, Calif., 1984—. Home: 2754 Orchid St Fairfield CA 94533

SHARMAN, LINDA K., public relations director, educator; b. Hutchinson, Kans., Sept. 16, 1937; d. Walter R. and Violet A. (Wood) Clothier; m. G. Edward Sharman, Jr., Aug. 6, 1960; children: Christianne, Graham III, Brett. BA, Whitworth Coll., 1960. Advt. copywriter The Bon Marche, Spokane, Wash., 1960-63, The Cresent, Spokane, 1963-65; free-lance writer The Spokesman Rev., Spokane, 1965-72; pub. relations asst. Wash. Community Coll. Dist. 17, Spokane, 1971-72; pub. relations asst. dir. Whitworth Coll., Spokane, 1973-80, pub. relations dir., 1980—; bd. dirs. Pub. Relations Soc. of Am., Spokane, 1980-83. Editor: Government in Spokane County (Governor's award 1973), Whitworth Coll. Today periodical (recipient CASE Top Ten Tabloids gold medal award 1983, 85, silver medal 1984); scriptwriter: Leaves Have Fallen tv series (Wash. State Humanities Commn. Grant). Bd. dirs. Spokane Citizens for EXPO '74, 1971, community relations EXPO '74, 1973, United Way of Spokane County, 1985—, v.p. 1986-87; chair bldg. com. Millwood Presbyn. Ch., 1984-85. Recipient Exceptional Achievement award CASE Mindpower campaign, 1981, Adminstr. of Yr. award Whitworth Coll., 1985; nominee Vol. of Yr., United Way of Spokane County, 1986. Mem. Council for Advancement and Support of Edn. (bd. dirs. dist. VIII, 1982-87, conf. chmn., 1987; CASE participant 1988 Nat. Women's Forum), CASE Nat. Com. on Inst. Relations, 1984-85, Momemtum '88 (facilitator 1987), Leadership Spokane Strategies for '89 Ccnf., 1987, Leadership Spokane Alumni, 1984, Spokane Area C. of C. Centennial Com., 1984. Presbyterian. Office: Whitworth Coll W 300 Hawthorne Rd Spokane WA 99251

SHARMAN, WILLIAM, former basketball executive; b. Abilene, Tex., May 25, 1926; m. Joyce Sharman; children by previous marriage: Jerry, Nancy, Janice, Tom. Student, U. So. Calif. Basketball player Washington Capitols, 1950-51, Boston Celtics, 1951-61; coach Los Angeles/Utah Stars, 1968-71; coach Los Angeles Lakers, 1971-76, gen. mgr., 1976-82, pres., 1982-88. Author: Sharman on Basketball Shooting, 1965. Named to Nat. Basketball Assn. All Star First Team, 1956-59, 2d Team, 1953, 55, 60, All League Team, 7 times; named Coach of Year Nat. Basketball Assn., 1972, Naismith Basketball Hall of Fame, 1976. Office: 4511 Roma Ct Marina Del Rey CA 90292 *

SHARON, BATIA, food products executive; b. Jerusalem, Dec. 31, 1942; came to U.S., 1967; d. Victor and Haya (Salomon) Bornstein; 1 child, Ossie. BA in Sociology and Polit. Sci., Jerusalem U., 1967; PhD in Sociology, U. Wis., 1974. Asst. prof. U. Calif., Santa Cruz, 1974-79; research scientist HUMRRO, Alexandria, Va., 1979-83; v.p. ops and human resources Threshold Enterprises, Scotts Valley, Calif., 1984—; cons. to Santa Cruz arts orgns., 1977-79. Contbr. articles to profl. jours. Bd. dirs. Gateway Sch., Santa Cruz, 1985—. Served as sgt. Israeli Infantry, 1960-62. Nat. Endowment for the Arts grantee, 1979. Mem. Am. Personnel Adminstrs. Assn. Office: Threshold Enterprises 23 Janis Way Scotts Valley CA 95066

SHARON, TIMOTHY MICHAEL, physicist; b. Portsmouth, Va., Aug. 21, 1948; s. Lester Clark and Ruth May (Banister) S.; student Santa Ana Coll., 1966-68; B.A., U. Calif.-Irvine 1970, M.A., 1972, Ph.D., 1976; m. Carla Deon Colley, Dec. 17, 1977. Jr. specialist solid state theory U. Calif.-Irvine, 1976, research asst. radiation physics Med. Center and Sch. Medicine, 1976-77, cons. to attending staff Research and Edn. Found., 1976-77; mktg. physicist Varian Assos., Irvine, 1977-78; prin. engr., program mgr. Spectra Research Systems, Newport Beach, Calif., 1977-82; v.p. Brewer-Sharon Corp., Newport Beach, 1981-86, Micor Instruments, Inc., Irvine, Calif., 1983-86; pres., chief exec. officer Medelec Instruments Co., Inc., Newport Beach, 1986-88; pres. Pacific Crest Enterprises, El Toro, Calif., 1988; adj. faculty physics and engring. Columbia Pacific U., San Rafael, Calif., 1981-87; dean Sch. Engring., Newport U., Newport Beach, Calif., 1983-87; mem. adv. panel on pub. Am. Inst. Physics, 1974-75. Brython P. Davis univ. fellow, 1973-74. Mem. AAAS, Am. Phys. Soc., Brit. Interplanetary Soc. (asso. fellow), Am. Assn. Physicists in Medicine, IEEE, Assn. Advancement Med. Instrumentation, Smithsonian Instn., Am. Film Inst., Nat. Hist. Soc., Nat. Geog. Soc., Festival of Arts Laguna Beach, Mensa, Intertel, Sigma Pi Sigma, Phi Theta Kappa, Alpha Gamma Sigma. Clubs: Acad. Magical Arts, Magic Island, Club 33. Contbr. articles to profl. jours. Office: 25422 Trabuco Rd No 105/464 El Toro CA 92630-2740

SHARP, ANDREA LEA, screenwriter, songwriter; b. San Bernardino, Calif., July 2, 1957; d. Alexander John and Lavilla Geraldine (Miller) S. BA with honors, U. Calif., Berkeley, 1981; postgrad., UCLA, 1985--. Tech. editor, pub. coordinator Brown and Caldwell, Walnut Creek, Calif., 1982-83; paralegal Pillsbury, Madison & Sutro, San Francisco, 1983; diver Dan's Diving Service, Richmond, Calif., 1984; researcher Good Morning Am., N.Y.C., 1985; pres. A Sharp Entertainment, L.A., 1986—. Author: (screenplays) The Survival Formula, 1986, Jack and Jill, 1987, The Futures Trader, 1988; writer, producer, dir. The Futures Trader, 1988; songwriter. Recipient grant Nat. Endowment Humanities, Berkeley, Calif., 1981. Mem. Songwriters Guild Am., ASCAP (assoc.), NOW. Democrat. Office: A Sharp Entertainment PO Box 66874 Los Angeles CA 90066-2130

SHARP, DAVID LEE, advertising executive, consultant; b. Chgo., Apr. 18, 1952; s. Homer Glenn and Jo Ann (Harbour) S.; m. Christine Rowe, Oct. 18, 1975; children: Tara Ann, Erica Dana. B.S., Bradley U., 1974; M.S., U. Ill., 1975. Advt. exec. Caterpillar Tractor, Peoria, Ill., 1975-76; sales promotion supr. Armstrong Cork Co., Lancaster, Pa., 1976-78; sr. account exec. Kraft Smith Advt., Seattle, 1978-80; pres. Sharp, Hartwig Advt., Inc., Seattle, 1980—; chmn. Response Mktg., Inc., Seattle, 1982—; instr. Cornish Inst., 1980; cons. Simpson Timber Co., Port of Seattle. Trustee, Eastside Community Mental Health Ctr., 1983—; active Seattle Allied Arts, 1988—. Bus. Profl. Advt. Assn. (v.p. 1982-83), Intermarket Assn. Advt. Agy., Am. Assn. Advt. Agy. (gov. 1984—, vice chmn. 1984-85, chmn. 1986-87), Mutual Advt. Agy. Network (v.p. programs 1988—), Seattle Advt. Fedn. Republican. Methodist. Clubs: Wash. Athletic; Juanita Bay Athletic; Univ. Rotary (program chmn. 1982-83). Home: 11647 73d Pl NE Kirkland WA 98034 Office: 100 West Harrison Pla South Tower Ste 500 Seattle WA 98119

SHARP, JANE ELLYN, human resources director; b. Chgo., Jan. 5, 1934; d. Truman V. and Mildred L. (Switzer) Lasswell; m. David H. Sharp, July 24, 1965 (div. Aug. 1979); children: Michelle Lynn, Lisa Elizabeth. BBA, Coll. Santa Fe, 1985, MBA, 1988. Adminstrv. asst. San Diego State U., 1956-58; dir. classified personnel Grossmont (Calif.) Union High Sch. and Jr. Coll. Dist., 1959-62; legal asst. Stockly & Boone, Attys., Los Alamos, N.Mex., 1974-75; with adminstrn. Los Alamos (N.Mex.) Nat. Lab., 1976-78, pub. rels. specialist, 1978-81, asst. group leader, 1981-82, dep. group leader, 1982-83, asst. div. leader, 1983-84, office dir. protocol, 1984—. Mem. adv. bd. Youth Working for Youth, Los Alamos, 1985—; mem. Adults Working for Youth, Los Alamos, Bingaman Circle, Santa Fe Rail Link Task Force, 1987—, Los Alamos Community Devel. Com., 1989—. Recipient Woman at Work award Coun. on Working Women, 1984. Mem. Tri Area Assn. for Econ. Devel., Los Alamos Nat. Lab. Community Coun. (rep. exec. bd. 1986—). Democrat. Office: Los Alamos Nat Lab PO Box 1663 MS P368 Los Alamos NM 87544

SHARP, M. RUTH, marketing research company official; b. Princeton, Mo., June 14, 1953; d. Glen Dale and Melvina Irene (McWaid) S.; m. Steven M. Brooks, Sept. 4, 1982. BA, U. Mo., Kansas City, 1975; MA, U. N.Mex., 1982. Trust adminstr. Lincoln Trust Co., Englewood, Colo., 1977-79; controller analyst Allstate Ins. Co., Englewood, 1979-82; programming mgr. J.D. Power & Assocs., Westlake Village, Calif., 1983-85; data processing mgr. Plog Rsch. Inc., Reseda, Calif., 1985—; instr. Calif. Luth. Coll., Thousand Oaks, 1984. Libertarian. Home: 4071 Blackwood St Newbury Park CA 91320 Office: Plog Rsch Inc 18631 Sherman Way Reseda CA 91335

SHARP, PAMELA ANN, mining engineer; b. Pullman, Wash., Dec. 20, 1950; d. Robert Melvin and Vivian Lois (Steele) Olson; m. David William Sharp, June 16, 1973; children: Jaime David, Erik Scott. Student, Big Bend Community Coll., Moses Lake, Wash., 1969-70; BS in Zoology, Wash. State U., 1973; postgrad., Portland State U., 1976. Lab. technician The Carter Mining Co., Gillette, Wyo., 1977-79, lab. supr., 1979-80, quality control supr., 1980-81, engring. analyst, 1982-88; engr. quality control The Carter Mining Co., Gillette, 1988—. Supt. Campbell County Fair, Gillette, 1985-87. Mem. AIME, ASTM (proximate analysis chmn. 1985—, chmn. on-line analysis com.), Am. Water Ski Assn. (regular judge 1974—, eastern regional water ski trick record 1975, 3d nat. trick title 1962, state champion in tricks Wash., Idaho, Mont. 1961-73, 2d 1987 Western region women's III tricks). Republican. Presbyterian. Office: The Carter Mining Co PO Box 3007 Gillette WY 82717

SHARP, PEGGY AGOSTINO, educational educator; b. Portland, May 4, 1950; d. Ernest E. and Vra Juanita (Work) A.; m. John Lester Chamberlain; children: David, Catherine L. BA, U. Oreg., 1973, MA, 1974. Library media specialist Fern Ridge Pub. Schs., Veneta, Oreg., 1973-75, Lake Oswego (Oreg.) Pub. Schs., 1975-80; prof. edn. Portland State U., 1980—; cons. Bur. of Edn. and Rsch, Bellevue, Wash., 1985—; cons. numerous sch. dists. Author: ABC of Children's Book Activities, 1983; contbr. articles to profl. jours. Named Outstanding Young Educator, Fern Ridge Pub. Schs., 1975; recipient Evelyn Sibley Campman award, Oreg. Library Assn. Mem. Oreg. Ednl. Media Assn., Oreg. Staff Devel. Coun. (bd. dirs. 1988-89), Internat. Reading Assn. (bd. dirs. 1985-88). Democrat. Office: Portland State Univ PO Box 751 Portland OR 97207

SHARP, TIMOTHY MICHAEL, marketing executive, consultant; b. Pasadena, Calif., July 20, 1945; s. Donald Dean Sharp and Ruth Ann (Merrick) Steven; m. Kristin Lohr, June 15, 1967; children: Whitney Leigh, Spencer Chapin. BS in Bus., U. So. Calif., 1967. V.p. mktg. IEC-Suzuki Auto Importers, San Diego, 1969-71, pres., 1972-73; v.p., gen. mgr. Don Sharp Porsche and Audi, Carlsbad, 1979-84; nat. sales mgr. Toyota Racing Devel. U.S.A., Inc., Gardena, Calif., 1984-87; pres. T.M. Sharp Mktg., Inc., Rancho California, Calif., 1987-88; v.p. ASHA Corp, Santa Barbara, Calif., 1988—; gen. ptnr. Stephan and Sharp Design Group, Rancho California, 1987—; pres. Tri-City Auto Dealers Assn., Carlsbad, 1982-83, San Diego Co. Porsche Advt. Council, 1981-82. Stephen and Sharp Monocoque Bicycle (patented) exhibited at group show Soviet Union Exhibition Design USA, 1989. Named Top 10 Dealer in U.S.A., Peugeot N.Am., 1981; recipient #1 Service award Porsche/Audi U.S.A., Orange, Calif., 1981. Mem. Am. Mktg. Assn., Sportscar Club Am. (mfgr.'s council 1986, named Divisional Champion 1970, 76, 80, Pacific Coast Champion 1979-80). Republican. Christian Scientist. Home and Office: ASHA Corp 600 Ward Dr Ste C Santa Barbara CA 93111

SHARP, WALTER EUGENE, business owner; b. Colorado Springs, Colo., Sept. 25, 1947; s. Leonard Searight and Audra Pauline (Petty) S.; m. Beverly Inez Watson, Aug. 23, 1972; 1 child, Stephen Todd. BSBA, U. Denver, 1970, MBA, 1971. Advt. asst. Diamond-Time Co., Ltd., Tokyo, 1971-72; travel cons. Compass Travel, Denver, 1974-75, May D&F Travel, Denver, 1975-77; mgr. May D&F Travel, Thornton, Colo., 1977-81; pres. Trek Internat. Travel, Westminster, Colo., 1981—. Mem. Gideons Internat. (v.p. 1988), Pacific Asia Travel Assn., Am. Soc. Travel Agts., Pacific Area Travel Assn. (program chmn. Denver chpt. 1980-82, out-of-country chmn. 1982-86). Republican. Office: Trek Internat Travel 8440 Federal Blvd Westminster CO 80030

SHARPE, ROLAND LEONARD, retired engineering company executive, seismologist, consultant; b. Shakopee, Minn., Dec. 18, 1923; s. Alfred Leonard and Ruth Helen (Carter) S.; m. Jane Esther Steele, Dec. 28, 1946; children—Douglas Rolfe, Deborah Lynn, Sheryl Anne. B.S. in Civil Engring., U. Mich., 1947, M.S.E., 1949. Registered civil engr. and structural engr., Calif. Designer, Cummins & Barnard, Inc., Ann Arbor, Mich., 1947-48; instr. engring. U. Mich., 1948-50; exec. v.p. John A. Blume & Assocs., engrs., San Francisco, 1950-73; chmn., founder Engring. Decision Analysis Co., Inc., Cupertino, 1974-87; cons. earthquake engr., 1989—; mng. dir. EDAC, GmBH, Frankfurt, Germany, 1974-82; dir. EDAC; pres. Calif. Devel. & Engring. Co., Inc., Las Vegas, Nev., 1973-81. Author: (with J. Blume, E.G. Kost) Earthquake Engineering for Nuclear Facilities, 1971. Mem. Planning Commn., Palo Alto, 1955-60; mng. dir. Applied Tech. Council, Palo Alto, 1973-83; dir. Earthquake Engring. Research Inst., 1972-75, now mem.; project dir., editor Tentative Provisions for Devel. of Seismic Regulations for Buildings, 1978; tech. mgr., editor Data Processing Facilities: Guidelines for Earthquake Hazard Mitigation, 1987. Served with USMC, 1942-46. Fellow ASCE (chmn. dynamic effects com., 1978-80, exec. com. structural div. 1980-84, chmn. 1983); mem. Structural Engrs. Assn. Calif. (dir. 1971-73, chmn. seismology com. 1972-74), Structural Engrs. No. Calif. (dir. 1969-71), Am. Concrete Inst. (cited for contbn. to constrn. industry Engring. New Record, 1978-79, 86-87). Home: 10320 Rolly Rd Los Altos CA 94022

SHARPE-WORKER, ROBIN ANN, social worker; b. Santa Monica, Calif., Feb. 28, 1957; d. John Loftes and Marie Ann (Sartorio) Sharpe; m. John Stephen Worker. AA, Santa Ana Coll., 1980; BS in Social Work, Chapman Coll., 1982. Program asst. New Horizons Santa Ana (Calif.) Coll., 1978-81; social worker, discharge planner Chapman Hosp., Orange, Calif., 1981-82; hospice social worker Town & Country Home Nursing, Garden Grove, Calif., 1982-85; program coord., dir. ElderMed/United Western Med. Ctrs., Anaheim and Santa Ana, 1985—; dir. geriatrics United Western Med. Ctr., Anaheim and Santa Ana, 1988—. Chairperson Santa Ana Chamber Health Svcs. Task Force, 1988-89; mem. org. Adult Day Care Adv. Bd., 1988—; Rancho Santiago Coll./New Horizons Sr. Svcs. Adv. Bd., 1988—; mem. Vols. in Probation, Orange, Calif., 1975-78, Anaheim (Calif.) Chamber Health Svcs. com., 1986—; vol. English tchr. St. Norbert's Ch. for Vietnam Refugees, Orange, 1975-76; vol. counselor Orange Police Dept. Crisis Intervention, 1981-83. Mem. Nat. Assn. Social Workers, Oncology Social Workers Orange County, Sr. Round Table, Am. Soc. Aging, Nat. Council Aging. Democrat. Office: ElderMed Western Med Ctr 1001 N Tustin Ave Santa Ana CA 92705

SHARPTON, THOMAS, physician; b. Augusta, Ga., July 15, 1949; s. Thomas and Elizabeth (Dozier) S. BA, Northwestern U., 1971; MS, Stanford U., 1973, MD, 1977. Intern Martinez (Calif.) VAMC, 1977-78, resident, 1978-80; mem. staff Kaiser Permanente Med. Group, Oakland, Calif., 1980—; cons. Berkeley (Calif.) Free Clinic, 1977—; chmn. peer review Kaiser Permanente Med. Group, Oakland, 1985-86. Mem. Alameda County Profl. Adv. Com., Oakland, 1984-88, Alameda County AIDS Task Force, Oakland, 1985-88. Mem. ACP, Calif. Med. Assn., Alameda-Contra Costa Med. Assn., Mensa, Sigma Pi Sigma, Phi Beta Kappa. Democrat. Club: Phi Beta Kappa of No. Calif. Office: Kaiser PMG 280 W MacArthur Blvd Oakland CA 94611

SHATTUCK, ALFRED JOHN, writer, researcher; b. Middletown, N.Y., July 23, 1954; s. Alfred Joseph and Diane Patricia (Comeau) S.; m. Karen Diane Volpe, Dec. 31, 1976. Student, Orange County Community Coll., Middletown, 1974. Writer, author Prentice-Hall Publs., Englewood, N.J., 1984-85, Loompanics, Port Townsend, Wash., 1987—. Author: The Greener Pastures Relocation Guide, 1984, States Related, 1988; (with others) The Eden Seekers Guide, 1989. Tutor Cath. Charities, Middletown, 1972-74, Needs, Inc., Cheyenne, Wyo., 1982-83. Roman Catholic. Office: Greener Pastures PO Box 2712 Cheyenne WY 82003

SHATUSKY, PAUL WALTER, medical computer company executive; b. Coaldale, Pa., Sept. 30, 1935; s. Walter and Adele (Ripko) S.; m. Marion Ruth Colquhoun, Oct. 18, 1958; 1 child, Donna Shatusky Winig. Student, Fairleigh Dickinson U., 1960-63. Design prodn. engr. Ortho Industries, Paterson, N.J., 1961-64; gen. mgr. Nytronics Inc. Ore Div., Alpha, N.J., 1964-66, Nytronics Inc. Precision Resistor Div., Kutztown, Pa., 1966-68; group mktg. dir. Essex Electronics div. Nytronics Inc., Berkeley Heights, N.J., 1969-70; v.p. mktg. Darlington (S.C.) Corp. div. Nytronics Inc., 1970-72; pres., chief exec. officer Omnitec Corp. subs. Nytronics Inc., Phoenix, 1972-79; U.S. dir. ops. Plessey Communications, Phoenix, 1979-82; v.p .mktg. Am. Health Scis. Inc., Phoenix, 1982-84; pres., chief exec. officer Infodyne Corp., Englewood, Colo., 1985—, also bd. dirs.; bd. dirs. Intelligent Medicine, Englewood, Colo. Served with USN, 1953-57. Republican. Presbyterian. Home: 8722 S Westwind Ln Highlands Ranch CO 80126 Office: Infodyne Corp 13 Inverness Way S Englewood CO 80112

SHAVER, DENNIS GEORGE, retail executive; b. Council, Idaho, Sept. 21, 1949; s. Carl Hutchins and Georgia L. (Bruce) S.; m. Kathryn Kay Russell, Aug. 24, 1975; 1 child, Patterson Dennis. AB with honors, Stanford U., 1971, MBA, 1974. V.p. Shaver's, Inc., Boise, Idaho, 1974-80, pres., 1980—. Vice chmn. Stanford Keystone Campaign, 1987—; bd. dirs., chmn. bd. Am. Festival Ballet, Boise, 1983-86; bd. dirs. Sta. KAID-TV, Boise, 1983—; trustee Boise Art Mus, 1987—. Mem. Idaho Retailers (bd. dirs., chmn. bd. 1983-86), Lincoln Day Assn. (pres. 1988-89), Crane Creek C. of C. (bd. dirs.), Phi Beta Kappa. Republican. Methodist. Clubs: Crane Creek Country (pres. 1989), Arid. Lodges: Rotary, Masons. Avocations: traveling, skiing, golf. Home: 118 E Curling Dr Boise ID 83702 Office: Shaver's Inc PO Box 7278 705 S Eighth Boise ID 83707

SHAVER, NETHALIE COLLETTE, small business owner; b. Newberg, Oreg., May 23, 1945; d. Theodore R. and Nola (McPheron) Zlab; m. John M. Shaver, Dec. 6, 1971; children: James L., Douglas J. Grad., high sch., Newberg. Sec. Community Hosp., Newberg, 1965-67; pres. Rex Bulb Farms, Port Townsend, Wash., 1968—. Republican. Home: PO Box 774 Port Townsend WA 98368 Office: Rex Bulb Farms 4310 Hwy 20 Port Townsend WA 98368

SHAW, ARTHUR ORION, production coordinator, business consultant; b. Boston, Jan. 8, 1958; s. Robert Stetson Shaw and Laura Deane (Higgins) Field; m. Julia Marie Campbell, Feb. 28, 1987; children: Ryan Patrick Rowe, Meaghan Electra Campbell. BA, Oberlin Coll., 1982; postgrad., Calif. State-Stanislaus, Turlock, 1987—. Sports info. dir., pub. info. asst. Baldwin-Wallace Coll., Berea, Ohio, 1980-83; sales rep. Postal Instant Press, Santa Cruz, Calif., 1984-85; paramedic Riggs Ambulance Svc., Merced, Calif., 1985-86; prodn. coord. Polito Printers, Merced, 1988—; owner Shaw Bus. Support Systems, Merced, 1987--. Editor, pub. Capitola Chamber Newsletter, 1983-84, KUBB Country News, 1987-88. Communications chmn. Am. Heart Assn. Merced-Mariposa div., 1987-88. Mem. Kiwanis (publicity chmn. Merced club 1987-88). Republican. Home: 125 Columbia Ave Merced CA 95340

SHAW, CAROLE, editor; b. Bklyn., Jan. 22, 1936; d. Sam and Betty (Neckin) Bergenthal; m. Ray Shaw, Dec. 27, 1957; children: Lori Eve Cohen, Victoria Lynn. BA, Hunter Coll., 1962. Owner The People's Choice, Los Angeles, 1975-79; founder, editor-in-chief BBW Mag., Beverly Hills, Calif., 1979—; creator BBW label clothing line. Author: Come Out, Come Out Wherever You Are, 1982; singer: Capitol Records, Hilton Records, Rama Records, Verve Records, 1952-65; TV appearance: Ed Sullivan, Steve Allen, Jack Paar, Colgate Comedy Hour, George Gobel Show, 1957. Office: BBW: Big Beautiful Woman 9171 Wilshire Blvd #300 Beverly Hills CA 90210

SHAW, CHARLES ALDEN, engineering executive; b. Detroit, June 8, 1925; s. Fred Alden and Amy (Ellis) S.; m. Barbara Loveland, Mar. 9, 1963 (div. 1979); children: Amy Elizabeth, Polly Nicole; m. Jeanne Steves Partridge, Apr. 22, 1989. BS, Harvard U., 1945; MSEE, Syracuse U., 1958. Test and design engr. G.E., Syracuse-Schenectady, N.Y., 1947-51; mgr. semiconductor div. G.E., Syracuse-Schenectady, 1960-66; mgr. CAD sect. integrated cir. product dept. G.E., Syracuse, 1969-71, mgr. CAD ctr. solid state applied ops., 1971-78, mgr. computer supportsolid state applied ops., 1978-81; dir. CAD G.E. Intersil, Cupertino, Calif., 1981-88; chief engr. Onondaga Pottery Co., Syracuse, 1951-60; cons. to gen. dir. Bull-G.E., Paris, 1966-69; cons. in field Cuppertino, 1988-89; mgr. tech. program Cadence Systems, Santa Clara, Calif., 1989—. Trustee Hidden Villa, Los Altos Hills, Calif., 1986—; vol. technician KETH Channel 54 Pub. T.V., 1984—. Ensign, USN, 1942-45, PTO. Mem. Assn. Computing Machinery, IEEE, Design Automation Conf. (exec. bd. 1985—, chmn. spl. interest group 1986—), Harvard Club of Peninsula. Democrat. Unitarian. Home: 1815 Sinclair Dr Pleasanton CA 94566 Office: 2455 Augustine Dr Santa Clara CA 95054

SHAW, FREDERIC JOHN, psychotherapist, lawyer; b. Bklyn., July 29, 1920; s. John Harris and Sybil (Galt) S.; divorced; children: John Harris, Elizabeth Shaw Buckley. BA, Bklyn. Coll., 1941; JD, NYU, 1954; MA, Fairleigh-Dickinson U., 1977; MSW, Ariz. State U., 1980; PhD in Clin. Psychology, Internat. U., 1983. Bar: N.Y., Ariz., U.S. Supreme Ct. Flight capt. Am. Airlines, N.Y.C., 1945-80, dir. flight adminstrn., 1954-61; pvt. practice law N.Y. and Ariz., 1954—; pvt. practice psychotherapy Scottsdale, Ariz., 1972—; instr., psychotherapy Franciscan Renewal Ctr., Scottsdale, 1980—, resident Faculty Inst. Reality Therapy, 1981—; vis. lectr. Ariz. State U., Tempe, 1981—; adj. faculty Ottawa U., Phoenix, 1985—, Scottsdale Community Coll.; pres., bd. dirs. Profl. Corp., Ariz., 1977—; ops. cons. Nat. Rsch. Corp., Manhasset, N.Y., 1960-63. Author: (monograph) 50 Years After Kitty Hawk, 1954, (research study) Conciliation in Marriage, 1979. Counselor Sr. Citizens Ctr., Scottsdale, 1985—; sponsor Scottsdale Boys Club, 1983—. N.Y.U. scholar, 1952, 53, 54. Mem. Nat. Assn. Social Workers (cert. clin. social worker), Am. Assn. Marital and Family Therapy, Ariz. Soc. Clin. Social Work and Psychotherapy, Assn. Family Conciliation Cts., Acad. Cert. Social Workers, (bd. cert. diplomate psychiat. social work 1987), Allied Pilots Assn., Ariz. Bar Com. Law and Counseling, Am. Arbitration Assn. (div. mediator 1979—, mem. family dispute panel 1979—, cons. family law, domestic rels. 1980—), Airline Pilots Assn. (bd. dirs., rep. 1946-54), Masons (32nd degree), Phi Delta Phi. Lutheran. Office: 7505 E Angus Dr Scottsdale AZ 85251

SHAW, JEFFREY WILLIAM, internal auditor; b. Salt Lake City, Nov. 9, 1958; s. William R. Jr. and Janet (Engar) S.; m. Cynthia Roberts, July 3, 1984; children: Morgan, Lauren, Catherine. BA in Acctg., U. Utah, 1983. CPA, Nev. With audit div. Arthur Andersen & Co., Dallas, 1983-85; With audit div. Arthur Andersen & Co., Las Vegas, Nev., 1985-88; dir. internal audit SW Gas Corp., Las Vegas, 1988—. Active Boy Scouts Am., Dallas, 1985, Las Vegas, 1987—. Mem. AICPA, Nev. Soc. CPAs. Republican. Mormon. Office: SW Gas Corp PO Box 98510 Las Vegas NV 89193-8510

SHAW, LINDA, mayor; m. Lawrence Shaw; children: Jeff, Leslie, Natalie. BS in Edn., Abilene Christian U., 1962. Tchr. spl. edn., Belmar Elem. Sch., 1976—; mem. City Council, 1980-81, pres., 1982-83; mayor City of Lakewood, Colo., 1983—. Mem. Metro Cooperation Council, Council of Governments, Nat. League of Cities and Colo. Mcpl. League, Leadership Lakewood Steering Com.; mem. exec. bd. Colo. Mcpl. League; hon. bd. dirs. Jeffco Family YMCA; past pres. Jefferson Women's Polit. Caucus, Foothills Swim Club Bd. Dirs.; past chairwoman Build a Better Lakewood; past treas. Voice of Tchrs. for Edn., numerous other civic activities. Recipient Disting. Service award Denver Regional Council of Govts., 1987; named Woman of Yr. Metro West Bus. and Profl. Women, 1988. Mem. Lakewood South Jeffco C. of C. (elected Ofcl. of Yr. 1986), Phi Delta Kappa. Office: 445 S Allison Pkwy Lakewood CO 80226

SHAW, MARK HOWARD, religious organization administrator; b. Albuquerque, Aug. 26, 1944; s. Brad Oliver and Barbara Rae (Mencke) S.; m. Ann Marie Brookreson, June 29, 1968 (div. 1976); adopted children: Daniel Paul, Kathleen Ann, Brian Andrew; m. Roslyn Jane Ashton, Oct. 9, 1976; children: Rebecca Rae, Amanda Leith. BA, U. N.Mex., 1967, JD, 1969. Law clk. to presiding justice N.Mex. Supreme Ct., Santa Fe, 1969-70; ptnr. Gallagher & Ruud, Albuquerque, 1970-74, Schmidt & Shaw, Albuquerque, 1974-75; sr. mem. Shaw, Thompson & Sullivan P.A., Albuquerque, 1975-82; chief exec. officer United Ch. Religious Sci. and Sci. Mind Publs., Los Angeles, 1982—. Trustee 1st Ch. Religious Sci., Albuquerque, 1974-77, pres. 1977; trustee Sandia Ch. Religious Sci., Albuquerque, 1980-82, pres. 1981-82; trustee United Ch. Religious Sci., Los Angeles, 1981-82, chmn. 1982; trustee Long Beach (Calif.) Ch. Religious Sci., 1983-86, chmn. 1983-86; chmn. Bernalillo County Bd. Ethics, Albuquerque, 1979-82. Served as sgt. USMCR, 1961-69. Mem. Pres.'s Assn., Am. Mgmt. Assn. Home: 4039 Locust Ave Long Beach CA 90807 Office: United Ch Religious Sci 3251 W Sixth St Los Angeles CA 90020

SHAW, MARVIN CABRERA, religious studies educator; b. L.A., Mar. 27, 1937; s. Robert Campbell and Moena (Cabrera) S.; m. Jeanne Paul, Aug. 15, 1959; children: Colin, Megan. BA, Occidental Coll., 1959; MDiv, Union Theol. Sem., 1962; PhD, Columbia U., 1968. Prof. religious studies Mont. State U., Bozeman, 1968—. Author: The Paradox of Intention, 1987; contbr. articles to profl. publs. State chmn. Mont. Com. for Humanities, 1985; assoc. Danforth Found., 1978. Mem. Am. Acad. Religion, Collegium (pres. 1986—), Phi Kappa Phi. Democrat. Unitarian. Office: Mont State U Bozeman MT 59717

SHAW, MAX LEROY, securities trader, investment counselor, small business consultant; b. Scottsbluff, Nebr., Sept. 10, 1937; s. Clifford Dean Shaw and Nettie Francis Marguetite (Barger) T.; m. Annita Louise Shaw, June 29, 1968; 1 child, Justin Owen. AA in Personal Mgmt., Olympic Coll., 1975; BA in Psychology, U. Wash., 1984; MBA, City U., Bellevue, Wash., 1988. Enlisted USN, 1958; mgr. film theater USN, Midway Island, 1958-59; supr. aux power USS Sargo SS(N) 583 USN, Pearl Harbor, Hawaii, 1961-64; repairman USS Dace SS(N) 607 USN, New London, Conn., 1964-67; instr. tng. command submarine sch. USN, New London, 1967-70; supr. IC group and maintenance program USS Trout SS566 USN, San Diego, 1970-73, asst. maintenance program coord. USS Constellation CV 64, 1975-78, mgr. prodn. scheduling ship repair facility, 1978-79; ret. USN, 1979; owner, mgr. RV Venture, Silverdale, Wash., 1985—; securites salesman, investment counselor Linsco, Boston, 1987—; trustee LuQuasit Water Corp. Silverdale, 1975—. Mem. curriculum com. CK Sch. Dist., Silverdale, 1980-82; mem. Puget Power Consumer Task Force, Bremerton, Wash., 1988—. Mem. Nat. Assn. Securities Dealers (registered rep.). Methodist. Address: 6163 LuQuasit Trail NW PO Box 737 Silverdale WA 98383

SHAW, MICHAEL WARREN, marketing executive; b. N.Y.C., June 14, 1952; s. Milton Robert Shaw and Esther Ann (Lewis) Auster; m. Karina De Nazare Olegario, July 27, 1984. BFA, NYIT, 1974. Mgr. imports Masterfreight Internat. Corp., Chgo., 1977-80; mgr. exports Amerford Internat. Corp., L.A., 1981-82; mng. dir., owner Restricted Article Freight Forwarding, L.A., 1983—. Patentee in field. Mem. Fed. Maritime Commn., L.A. Air Cargo Assn., Cousteau Soc., Planetary Soc.

SHAW, PEGGY NAHAS, clergywoman; b. Merced, Calif., Feb. 3, 1958; d. Edward Nahas and Edith Candler (Stebbins) Paxman; m. Albert A. Polhamas, Sept. 18, 1977 (div. 1979); m. Michael Steven Shaw, May 25, 1980; children: Danica, Brandy Rae, Adria. Grad. high sch., Davis, Calif. Dianetics counselor Ch. Scientology Mission of Davis (Calif.), 1975-76, dir. processing, 1976-77, registrar, 1977-78, dissemination dir., 1978-82; dir. pub. svcs. Ch. Scientology Mission of Sacramento Valley, Davis, 1982-83, orgnl. exec., 1983-84, HCO exec., 1984-85; exec. dir. Ch. Scientology Missions Sacramento Valley-River Park-Chico, Vacaville, Calif., 1985—; also pres. bd. dirs. Ch. Scientology Missions Sacramento Valley-River Park-Chico, Vacaville, 1985—. Mem. Internat. Assn. Scientology (honor roll 1987). Home: 4343 Kenneth Blvd Fair Oaks CA 95628 Office: Ch of Scientology 1485 River Park Dr Sacramento CA 95815

SHAW, SALLY ANN, culinary school administrator; b. Medford, Oreg., Oct. 26, 1959; d. James Brice and Jane (Carson) S. BS, Oreg. State U., 1982. Advisor prospective students Oreg. State U., Corvallis, 1980-82; exec. asst. Stone Pub. Co., Honolulu, 1983-85; v.p. Calif. Culinary Acad., Inc., San Francisco, 1985—. Mem. Delta Delta Delta. Republican. Home: 2107 Rosemary Ct Petaluma CA 94954 Office: Calif Culinary Acad 625 Polk St San Francisco CA 94102

SHAW, TAMARA CHANNELL, advertising executive; b. Aurora, Ill., Feb. 21, 1961; d. William Edward and Janet Maxine (Mueller) C.; m. Kenneth Leon, July 11, 1987. BS, Ariz. State U., 1983. Mktg. coord. ARC, Phoenix, 1983-84; account exec. Walt Sweet Advt., Phoenix, 1984-85; pub. rels. dir. Loews Paradise Valley Resort, Scottsdale Ariz., 1985-86; account coord. Evans/Phoenix Advt., Inc., 1986—. Active Jr. League of Phoenix, AD-2 Phoenix. Mem. Ariz. State U. Alumni Assn., Alpha Chi Omega, Beta Omega Beta. Republican. Methodist. Office: Evans/Phoenix Advt Inc 2122 E Highland Phoenix AZ 85016

SHAW, WILLIAM EDWARD, computer scientist; b. Browning, Ill., Apr. 1, 1943; s. Daniel and Wilma Dolores (Mercer) S.; m. Nancy Ruth Titus, Jan. 30, 1968; children: William II, Daniel. BS, Bradley U., 1965. Chief, Electro-Optics sect. U.S. Army Material Test and Evaluation Directorate, White Sands, N.Mex., 1965-79; mgr. new products and systems IECC div. US Natural Resources, Vancouver, Wash., 1979-82; v.p. mktg. & product devel. FLIR Systems Inc., Portland, Oreg., 1982-87; dir. research & devel. Key Tech. Inc., Milton-Freewater, Oreg., 1987—; cons. Lamb Weston, Inc., Portland, Oreg., 1983. Contbr. articles profl. jours. Mem. Soc. Photo-Optical Instrumentation Engrs., Lions (high Rolls Mt. Park, N. Mex., v.p. 1978). Home: Rt 5 Box 340 Walla Walla WA 99362 Office: Key Tech Inc 517 N Elizabeth Milton-Freewater OR 97865

SHAWKEY, DEBORAH ANN, nurse; b. Akron, Ohio, Nov. 5, 1949; d. John Richard and Grace Evelyn (Crawford) S.; 1 child, Jenni L. RN, Good Samaritan Hosp., Phoenix, 1971; student, Ariz. State U., Tempe, 1967-71, 82-84, Mesa Community Coll., 1983-85. Asst. head nurse emergency dept., nursing supr. Good Samaritan Med. Ctr., Phoenix, 1971-78; supr. emergency dept. Downey (Calif.) Community Hosp., 1978; asst. head nurse cardiovascular ICU Good Samaritan Med. Ctr., Phoenix, 1979-81; asst. head nurse emergency dept. Mesa (Ariz.) Luth. Hosp., 1982-85; dir. nursing Portamedic Healthcare, Phoenix, 1988; critical care nurse Med-Pro, Inc., Phoenix, 1985—; cons. Med-Pro, Inc., Phoenix, 1988-89; bd. dirs. Desert Star Prodns., Tempe. Active Amnesty Internat., Christian Childrens Fund. Mem. Nat.

Homecare Assn., Nat. League Nursing. Democrat. Home: 418 N 5th St Apt O Tempe AZ 85281

SHAWSTAD, RAYMOND VERNON, computer specialist; b. Brainerd, Minn., Mar. 17, 1931; stepson Klaas Ostendorf, s. Ruth Catherine Hammond; student West Coast U., 1960-62, UCLA Extension, 1966-81, Liberal Inst. Natural Sci. and Tech., 1973-83, Free Enterprise Inst., 1973-83. Salesman, Marshalltown, Iowa, 1952-53; asst. retail mgr. Gamble-Skogmo, Inc., Waverly, Iowa, 1953-54, retail mgr., Iowa Falls, 1954-57; sr. programmer County of San Bernardino (Calif.), 1958-64; info. systems cons. Sunkist Growers, Inc., Van Nuys, Calif., 1965-75, sr. systems programmer, 1975—; univ. extension instr. UCLA, 1980-81; propr., artificial intelligence researcher Lang. Products Co., Reseda, Calif., 1980—; propr., fin. educator Pennyseed Mgmt. Co., Reseda, 1987—; cons., tchr. in field, 1961-63. Vol. VA Hosp., 1984—; bedside music therapist Vets, Adminstrn., 1984—; musician Project Caring, 1984-87; rep. U.S. Senatorial Bus. Adv. Bd., Calif., 1988—. Mem. L.A. VM User Group, Am. Def. Preparedness Assn., Res. Officers Assn., Jewish Vegetarian Soc., U.S. Naval Inst., Am. Math. Soc., Aircraft Owners and Pilots Assn., Math. Assn. Am. Author numerous software programs; editor VM Notebook of GUIDE Internat. Corp., 1982—. Mem. B'nai B'rith. Home: PO Box 551 Van Nuys CA 91408 Office: PO Box 1667 Reseda CA 91335

SHAWVER, DEBRA ANN, nurse; b. Fresno, Calif., Dec. 11, 1953; d. Sheldon Bruce Kaiser and Bonnie Lou (Wagy) Barnhart; m. Deryl Branch Shawver, Apr. 18, 1981; children: Bonnie Michelle, Todd Keton, Chad Meryl. Diploma, Allen Meml. Sch. Nursing, Waterloo, Iowa, 1975; BS in Nursing, SUNY, Albany, 1986. Nurse technician Allen Meml. Hosp., Waterloo, Iowa, 1974-75; staff nurse Allen Meml. Hosp., Waterloo, 1975-76; commd. 2d lt. U.S. Air Force, 1976, advanced through grades to maj., 1979; staff nurse, hosp. supr. U.S. Air Force, Barksdale AFB, La., 1976-80; asst. chief nurse U.S. Air Force Res., Barksdale AFB, 1981-84; emergency room supr. U.S. Air Force, Carswell AFB, Tex., 1980-82; officer in charge aeromed. staging tng. U.S. Air Force Res., Luke AFB, Ariz., 1984—; staff nurse Janamar Nurses Registry, Phoenix, 1986—; staff/charge nurse VA Hosp., Shreveport, La., 1980-84, VA Hosp. Med. Ctr., Phoenix, 1984-86; capt. spl. task force U.S. Air Force Res., Robins AFB, Ga. Mem. family support and arts ministry, First United Methodist Ch., Phoenix, 1986—. Mem. Am. Heart Assn., Am. Assn. Critical Care Nurses (treas. 1978-80, sec. 1980-81), Res. Officers Assn., Air Force Assn. Republican. Office: Janamar Nurses Registry Ste 205 77 E Columbus St Phoenix AZ 85012

SHAY, PETER YUNGCHING, investment company executive; b. Shanghai, China, July 17, 1934; came to U.S., 1974, naturalized, 1980; s. Chung Liu and Chi Chiou (Chen) S.; B.S., Cheng Kung U., 1958; M.S., Va. Poly. U., 1962; m. Jean Wu, Aug. 31, 1963; children—Shirley, Thomas, Dennis. Chief engr. Mayer Steel Pipe Mfg. Co., Tapei, Taiwan, 1963-65; v.p., plant mgr. Kuo Hwa Chem. Corp., Taiwan, 1965-77; pres. Golden Cosmos Investment Corp., Palos Verdes Estates, Calif., 1977—. Served to 2d lt. Engring. Corps., Republic of China, 1958-60.

SHCOLNIK, ROBERT MILTON, insurance company executive; b. South Bend, Ind., Aug. 21, 1938; s. Harry and Esther (Baim) S.; m. Linda K. Egleberry, Aug. 10, 1972; children: Scott, Keith, Carin. BS in Bus., Ariz. State U., 1960; student, Am. Savings & Loan Inst., 1961; diploma in ins., Hartford Ins. Group Ins. Group, 1965. Loan officer, branch mgr., asst. to the pres. Home Savings & Loan Assn., 1959-61; pres. Harris/Shcolnik & Assocs., Inc., Phoenix, 1961—; ptnr. Harris/Shcolnik Properties; v.p., bd. dirs. My Florist, Inc., 1970—; guest lectr. in ins. Phoenix Coll.; speaker Nat. Assn. Independent Ins. Agts. Nat. Conv. Contbr. articles to profl. jours.; designer interface mini-computer concept. Mem. nat. presidents circle Cen. Mutual Ins. Co., inter-circle, 1975-76, Ariz. Jonathan Trumbull Coun., Hartford Ins., 1979-80, Nat. Great Am. Ins. Agts. Adv. Coun., 1979-81, chmn. 1979, Pacer (agts. coun.) CNA Group, agts. coun. Cigna Ins.; former mem. Key Club, Continental Assurance Co.; past pres. Am. Savings and Loan Inst., Ariz.; bd. dirs. Jewish Community Ctr., 1980-86, v.p., exec. com., 1983-85; mem. combined ops. coun. Jewish Ctrs. Greater Phoenix, 1987-88. Named Outstanding Agt. of Yr. Maricopa County Assn. Independent Ins. Agts., 1973, 76-78; recipient Jewish Community Ctr. Disting. Svc. award, 1981, 83, 85. Mem. Ind. Ins. Agts. Ariz. (pres. 1985). Republican. Jewish. Office: Harris Shcolnik & Assocs 4808 N Central Ave Phoenix AZ 85012

SHEA, LADONNA REINER, airline pilot; b. Mpls., Sept. 15, 1948; d. Donald Albert and Harriet Elizabeth (Wookey) R.; m. Bill Allen (div. 1977); m. Michael Alan Shea. BA, UCLA, 1970. Flight attendant Pan Am. Airlines, N.Y.C., L.A. and Honolulu, 1970-79; flight instr. Assoc. Aviation Activity, Honolulu, 1979; pilot various airlines, Honolulu, 1979—; pilot, capt. Hawaiian Airlines, 1984—. Pres. Poncho Barnes Scholarship Fund., 1984—. Mem. Airline Pilots Assn. (chmn. grievance com. 1985, 88—), Internat. Soc. Assn. Woman Airline Pilots (capts. club), Happy Bottom Riding Club (pres. 1984—).

SHEA, MICHAEL ALAN, lawyer; b. Iowa City, Oct. 9, 1946; s. Robert Wallace and Florence (Foley) S.; m. La Donna Reiner, Mar. 3, 1979. BA, U. Iowa, 1968, JD, 1974; B in Lit., Oxford U., Eng., 1973. Bar: Hawaii 1974, U.S Tax Ct. 1974, U.S. Dist. Ct. Hawaii 1974, U.S. Ct. Appeals (9th cir.) 1974, U.S. Supreme Ct. 1983. From assoc. to ptnr. Cades, Schutte, Fleming & Wright, Honolulu, 1974-83; ptnr. Goodsill, Anderson, Quinn & Stifel, Honolulu, 1983—. Mem. Gov.'s adv. com. on adoption of Tax Reform Act, 1986; bd. dirs. Arts Council Hawaii, Honolulu, 1975—, Honolulu Community Theatre, 1976-82. Mem. ABA (exempt orgns. com. tax sect.), Hawaii Bar Assn. (chmn. tax sect. com. 1986, chmn. tax sect. 1988-89), Honolulu C. of C. (chmn. tax com. 1985-88, pub. health com., bd. dirs. 1987—). Clubs: Honolulu, Hawaii Yacht (Honolulu); Plaza. Home: 207 Koko Isle Circle Honolulu HI 96825 Office: Goodsill Anderson Quinn & Stifel PO Box 3196 Honolulu HI 96801

SHEAFFER, RICHARD ALLEN, electrical engineer; b. Bronxville, N.Y., May 30, 1950; s. Harold Aumond and Carol Lois (Henry) Sweet; children: Alan Michael Sheaffer, Russell Logan Sheaffer; m. Pamela Christine Clark, May 23, 1987. BSEE, Pa. State U., 1972; MSEE, U. So. Calif., 1975. Registered profl. engr., Calif., Fla. Elec. engr. So. Calif. Edison Co., Rosemead, 1973-79, 1980—, Harris Controls div., Melbourne, Fla., 1979-80; project leader summer nomogram study for Pacific and S.W. transfer subcom. Western Systems Coordinating Coun., 1988. Author: 1984 West-of-the-River Operating Study, 1985, December 22, 1982 Disturbance Study, 1983. Mem. IEEE (Power Engring. Soc.), Phi Eta Sigma. Episcopalian. Office: So Calif Edison Co 2244 Walnut Grove Ave PO Box 800 Rosemead CA 91770

SHECKLER, KIM REED, editor; b. Inglewood, Calif., May 23, 1957; d. George Edgar and Mary Louise (Letteriello) Reed; m. Dale Alan Sheckler, Dec. 4, 1982; children: Christopher David, Reed Alan. AA, El Camino Coll., 1982. RN, Calif. Mng. editor Calif. Diving News, Torrance, Calif., 1984—; RN Little Co. Mary Hosp., Torrance, 1986-89. Author: Southern California's Best Beach Divers, 1986, Diving and Snorkeling Guide to Southern California, 1986, Diving and Snorkeling Guide to the Channel Islands, 1986; pub. Underwater Hunting and Gathering, California Edition, 1987; dir. Scuba, The Dive Show, Torrance, 1988—. Mem. Divers Alert Network. Republican. Roman Catholic. Office: Calif Diving News/The Dive Show PO Box 11231 Torrance CA 90504

SHEEHAN, F. MICHAEL, information systems official; b. Melrose, Mass., Apr. 28, 1952; s. Francis M. and Mary E. (Driscoll) S. BS, U. Mass., 1974; MT, Berkshire Med. Ctr., Pittsfield, Mass., 1974; MEd, U. Oreg., 1983. Cert. med. technologist Am. Soc. Clin. Pathologists. Med. technologist Sacred Heart Gen. Hosp., Eugene, Oreg., 1975-82, dir. Sch. Med. Tech., 1982-84; info. systems analyst Pathology Cons., Eugene, 1984-86; mgr. info. systems Oreg. Med. Labs., Eugene, 1986—; prof. U. Oreg., Eugene, 1982-85. Roman Catholic.

SHEEHAN, TIMOTHY M., lawyer. BA in Econs., U. N.Mex., 1971; JD, U. Mich., 1973. Ptnr. Sheehan, Sheehan & Stelzner, P.A., Albuquerque, 1974—; adj. prof. law U. N.Mex., 1979—. Contbr. articles to profl. jours. Bd. dirs. Albuquerque Conservation Trust, 1987—, Albuquerque Boys' Club (hon.), 1982—, Friends of Art, 1987, Maxwell Mus., 1980, Explora A Children's Mus., 1986—, St. Charles Sch., 1976, pres. 1977-78; mem. sch. bd. Archdiocese of Santa Fe, 1977-79, v.p., 1979; chmn. lawyers div. United Way, 1985, chmn. youth task force City of Albuquerque, 1986; sec. Albuquerque Ctr. Inc., 1979-88; mem. cen. core schs. study com. Albuquerque Pub. Schs., 1982-83; chmn. edn. com. Greater Albuquerque C. of C., 1981, gen. counsel, 1982—; mem. exec. com. Great Southwest Council Boy Scouts Am., 1978-87; pres. Archibishop's Sch. Fund, 1979—; co-chmn. ann. fund drive Manzano Day Sch., 1986; v.p. N.Mex. Zool. Soc., 1985-86. Mem. Tom L. Popejoy Soc., Am. Arbitration Assn. (mem. constrn. industry arbitration panel, 1980—), B'nai B'rith (mem. Albuquerque adv. com. anti-defamation league, 1988). Home: 4118 Sunningdale NE Albuquerque NM 87110 Office: Sheehan Sheehan & Stelzner PA 707 Broadway NE PO Box 271 Albuquerque NM 87103

SHEEHAN, TOM LEONARD, electronics technician; b. Sidney, Mont., Mar. 15, 1950; s. Leonard and Lucille (Ruffatto) S.; m. Sharon M. Gustin, Dec. 29, 1978; children: Kerri, Brian, Devin. AA, Western Tech. Sch., Denver, 1970. With Monaghan Co. Inc., Denver, 1969-70; with ITT Felec Svcs., Thule, Greenland, 1976-78, Storage Tech. Corp., Louisville, Colo., 1978-79; sr. radar tech. RCA/OMS, Cape Newenham, Alaska, 1979-80; linear accelerator tech. Mt. States Tumor Inst., Boise, 1980—. With USAF, 1971-75. Roman Catholic. Office: Mountain States Tumor Inst 151 E Bannock Boise ID 83702

SHEETS, JOHN WESLEY, JR., research scientist; b. Jacksonville, Fla., Sept. 17, 1953; s. John Wesley and Alice Marie (Hagen) S.; m. Robin Adair Ritchie, June 27, 1987. BS in Zoology, U. Fla., 1975, MS in Materials Sci., 1978, PhD in Materials Sci., 1983. Grad. research asst. U. Fla., Gainesville, 1976-78, grad. research assoc., 1978-82; biomaterials engr. Intermedics Intraocular, Pasadena, Calif., 1982-84, mgr. biomaterials research, 1984-87; dir. research Pharmacia Ophthalmics, Pasadena, 1987-89; dir. product devel. IOLAB Corp., Claremont, Calif., 1989—; lectr. Calif. State Poly. U., Pomona, 1984. Contbr. articles to profl. jours. Mem. AAAS, Soc. Plastics Engrs., Am. Chem. Soc., Soc. Biomaterials, Jaycees, Sigma Xi, Tau Beta Pi, Alpha Sigma Mu, Mensa. Club: So. Calif. Gator Club (Los Angeles). Home: 2241 Brigden Rd Pasadena CA 91104 Office: IOLAB Corp 500 Iolab Dr Claremont CA 91711

SHEETS, NELSON FRANKLIN, sociology and communications educator; b. Mulberry, Ind., Nov. 5, 1936; s. Isaac Emmerson and Mamie Esther (Houk) S.; m. Ruth Esther Roland, June 5, 196l; children: Stephen, Michelle, Melody, Nelson D. BS, Ind. Wesleyan U., 1962; MS, Mankato State U., 1966; MSW, U. Minn., Duluth, 1976. Tchr. pub. schs., Mazeppa, Minn., 1962-65; prof. speech and sociology Ind. Wesleyan U., Marion, 1965-74; sr. social worker State of Minn., Mankato, 1976-79; prof. sociology and communications, dir. social work Point Loma Nazarene Coll., San Diego, 1979—, chmn. dept. sociology, 1982—. Editor: Shafts of Light for Dark Days, 1985; contbr. articles to religious publs. Mem. N.Am. Assn. Christians in Social Work, Nat. Tchrs. Assn. (campus membership chmn. 198.—), Calif. Tchrs. Assn. (campus membership chmn. 198l—), Assn. Small Colls. (campus membership chmn. 198l—). Republican. Home: 6612 Golfcrest Dr San Diego CA 92119

SHEETS, PAYSON DANIEL, anthropology educator, medical researcher; b. Boulder, Colo., Jan. 1, 1944; s. Charles D. and Charlene E. (Spaulding) S.; m. Francine Mandel, Dec. 19, 1971; children: Kayla Mandel, Gabrielle Mandel. BA, U. Colo., 1967, MA, 1969; PhD, U. Pa., 1974. Asst. prof. anthropology Calif. State U., Fresno, 1972-74; assoc. prof. U. Colo., Boulder, 1974-86, prof., 1986—; pres. Fracture Mechanics Ltd., Boulder, 1980—. Author: Archaology and Volcanism in Central America, 1983; editor: Volcanic Activity and Human Ecology, 1979. Grantee NSF, 1973—, Nat. Geographic Soc., 1979, 84. Mem. AAAS, Soc. Am. Archeology, Am. Anthropol. Assn., Colo. Archeol. Soc. Home: 520 Marine Boulder CO 80309 Office: U Colo Dept Anthropology CB 233 Boulder CO 80309

SHEFFIELD, JOHN JOSEPH (JACK SHEFFIELD), public relations executive; b. N.Y.C., Feb. 20, 1931; s. Robert N. and Helen Agnes (Stanton) S.; m. Marlene Elizabeth Weale. Student, Woodbury U., 1955. Freelance writer, reporter 1955-60; with pub. rels. Edward Gottlieb & Assoc., 1960-73, The Sheffield Co., 1973—; Chmn. bd. N.E. Valley Health Corp., L.A., 1974-83. Writer, producer in field. Mem. Calif. Dem. State Cen. Com., Little League, Youth Hockey Club. Mem. Pub. Rels. Soc. Am., U.S. C. of C. Home and Office: 7701 Atoll Ave North Hollywood CA 91605

SHEFFIELD, WILLIAM JENNINGS, former governor of Alaska; b. Spokane, Wash., June 26, 1928; s. William J. and Hazel L. (Kraudelt) S. Student pub. schs., Silverdale, Wash. With service dept. Sears, Roebuck & Co., Seattle, 1951-53; with sales and service depts. Sears, Roebuck & Co., Anchorage, 1953-60; owner, mgr. Sheffield Hotels, Anchorage, 1960-82; gov. State of Alaska, Juneau, 1982-86; dir. Alaska Title Guaranty, Nat. Bank Alaska. Regent Alaska Pacific U.; past chmn. Easter Seal Telethon, Anchorage; past pres. March of Dimes, Anchorage; mem. planning commn. City of Anchorage, 1960-63. Served with U.S. Army, 1946-49. Mem. Alaska C. of C. (past pres.), Alaska Visitors Assn. (past pres.). Democrat. Presbyterian. Lodges: Lions, Elks.

SHEFFLER, GEORGE JUSTUS, real estate developer and broker; b. L.A., Dec. 10, 1944; s. Russell Noble and Dorothy Katherine (Sutherland) S. AA, Golden West Coll., Huntington Beach, Calif., 1967; BS, East Tex. State U., 1970; postgrad., So. Meth.'U., 1972-73, U. So. Calif., 1977. Cert. real estate brokerage mgr., Ariz. Prin. Sheffler Properties, Phoenix, 1973—; v.p. Vans Improvement Co., Salome, Ariz., 1978-80, pres., chief exec. officer, 1980—, also bd. dirs. Chmn. Hunt County Rep. Com., Greenville, Tex., 1974-80; del. Young Rep. Nat. Conv., 1975; alt. del. Rep. Nat. Conv., 1976. Mem. Realtors Nat. Mktg. Assn., Am. Resort and Residential Assn., Nat. Assn. Home Builders (land devel. com. 1977-79), Real Estate Securities and Syndication Inst. (publs. com. 1977-78), Nat. Assn. Realtors, Ariz. Assn. Realtors, Carlsbad Bd. Realtors (com. chmn. 1982), Ariz. C. of C., McMullen Valley C. of C. (pres.-elect), Parker Area C. of C., UCLA Alumni Assn. (life), SCV, Ariz. Club (Phoenix), Optimists (life), Rho Epsilon. Republican. Episcopalian. Home: Hwy 60 Harcuvar Twp Salome AZ 85348 Office: Vans Improvement Co 3855 N 29th Ave St F Phoenix AZ 85017

SHEFRIN, DAVID KERN, physician; b. Oakland, Calif., Nov. 26, 1949; s. Leo H. and Melvina Olive (Stenson) S.; m. Stephanie Jane Linderman, May 5, 1977; children: Micheal, John, Stephen, Candice, Kimberly. Student, U. Calif., Davis, 1970; BS, SUNY, 1989; MD, Nat. Coll. Naturopathic Med., 1975. Pvt. practice naturopathic medicine Portland, Oreg., 1975-78; dir. Clymer Heart & Diabetic Trtmt. Ctr., Quaker Town, Pa., 1979-80; pvt. practice naturopathic medicine Great Falls, Mont., 1980-82; chmn. destiny slender ME Internat., Inc., Fremont, Calif., 1982-85; physician HemCare, Phoenix, 1985-88; dir. HemCare, Portland, 1988—. Author: Naturopathic Physicians Handbook-Cookbook, 1981. Mem. Ariz. Naturopathic Med. Assn. (v.p., bd. dirs. 1985-88).

SHEINBERG, HASKELL, metallurgist, ceramist; b. Houston, Dec. 12, 1919; s. Max and Leona S.; m. Beatrice Freeman, Oct. 13, 1946; children: Michael, Arthur. BSChemE, Rice U., 1941; postgrad., Los Alamos (N.Mex.) Inst., 1945-46. Progress engr. Consol. Steel Corp., Orange, Tex., 1941-44; chem. engr. U.S. Army, Los Alamos, 1945-46; powder metallurgist Los Alamos Nat. Lab., 1946—; cons. in field, 1973—. Patentee 17 inventions in field. Fellow Los Alamos Nat. Lab. Fellow Am. Soc. for Metals (chmn. local chpt.); mem. Am. Ceramic Soc. (v.p. local chpt.), Am. Powder Metallurgy Inst., The Metall. Soc., Am. Def. Preparedness Assn. Jewish. Home: 1343 47th St Los Alamos NM 87544 Office: Los Alamos Nat Lab PO Box 1663 G770 Los Alamos NM 87545

SHEINBERG, SIDNEY JAY, recreation and entertainment company executive; b. Corpus Christi, Tex., Jan. 14, 1935; s. Harry and Tillie (Grossman) S.; m. Lorraine Gottfried, Aug. 19, 1956; children: Jonathan J., William David. A.B., Columbia Coll., 1955; LL.B., Columbia U., 1958. Bar: Calif. 1958. Assoc. in law UCLA Sch. Law, 1958-59; with MCA, Inc., Universal City, Calif., 1959—, pres. TV div., 1971-74, corp. exec. v.p., 1969-73, corp. pres., chief operating officer, 1973—. Mem. Assn. Motion Picture and Television Producers (chmn. bd.). Office: MCA Inc 100 Universal City Pla Universal City CA 91608 *

SHELDON, MARK SCOTT, research engineer; b. Orange, Calif., May 19, 1959; s. Howard Lezurn and Vida Louise (Winegar) S.; m. Marti Reisman, Aug. 8, 1986. BS in Engring. and Applied Sci., Calif. Inst. Tech., 1981; MS in Mech. Engring., Cornell U., 1985. Research engr. Energy and Environ. Research Corp., Irvine, Calif., 1985—. Mem. ASME (assoc.). Democrat. Mem. Reorganized Ch. Jesus Christ Latter-Day Saints. Office: Energy and Environ Rsch Corp 18 Mason Irvine CA 92718

SHELLEY, SAVILLA MAY, nurse; b. Johnstown, Pa., Oct. 22, 1953; d. Stephen John Hayko; m. Gary Lee Shelley, Apr. 15, 1975. AD in Nursing, U. Nev. at Las Vegas, 1983. Seamstress Bestform, Johnstown, 1971; clk. Sands Hotel, Las Vegas, 1980-81; sec. Robert A. McNeil Corp., Las Vegas, 1981-82; nurse U. Med. Ctr., Las Vegas, 1984—. Seved as staff sgt. USAF, 1972-80. Republican. Roman Catholic. Home: 3215 S Rosanna St Las Vegas NV 89117

SHELLNUT, ALLEN JAY, teacher, artist; b. Long Beach, Calif., Feb. 9, 1932; s. Harrison Brady Shellnut and Doris Maxine (Sullivan) Ackerman; m. Margaret L. Padgett, June 15, 1952 (div. 1976); children: Sandra, Cindy, Terry, Kevin; m. Jeri Lee Stewart, Mar. 17, 1985. AA, Santa Rosa Jr. Coll., 1952; BA, San Jose State U., 1955; MA, Stanislaus State Coll., 1967. Cert. tchr., Calif. Tchr. Delhi (Calif.) Elem Sch., 1956-58, Atwater (Calif.) Sr. Elem. Sch., 1958-63; tchr. art, sci. Plumas Unified Sch. Dist., Quincy, Calif., 1963--. Established the first student art exchange between Russia, Costa Rica and Chester High Sch. in 1970. Mem. NEA, Plumas County Tchrs. Assn. (past pres.), Almanor Art Assn. (past pres.), Plumas County Art Soc., Calif. Tchrs. Assn. Home: 266 Richardson Way Chester CA 96020 Office: Chester Jr Sr High Sch PO Box 797 Chester CA 96020

SHELLY, FRANKLIN JEFF, investor; b. Bay City, Tex., Mar. 13, 1942; s. Franklin E. and Josephine (Anderson) S.; m. Lynne C. Cruickshank, Nov. 20, 1965; children: Jennifer Lynn, Heather Leigh. AA, Harbor Coll., 1963; BS in Mktg., Loyola U., Los Angeles, 1965. Owner, pres. Almar Corp., Palos Verdes, Calif., 1963-65; sales dir. I.B.M. Corp., Glendale, Calif., 1965-70; dir. nat. accounts W.T.C. Air Freight, Los Angeles, 1970-78; v.p. sales Travel Guard Inc., San Juan Capastrano, Calif., 1978-81; gen. mgr., lic. capt. Cormorant Cruises, New Port Beach, Calif., 1981-85; pres. Shelly Enterprises, Channel Islands, Calif., 1985—. Inventor wheeled suitcase and shrinkwrap damage frame. Dir. Project Mex.-Orphanage, Rolling Hills, Calif., 1984-86; mem. Palos Verdes City Council, 1976-77. Recipient Angel of Mercy award Girl Scouts, 1979. Fellow Sales Mktg. Execs. (dir. 1972-73, Top Sales award 1973); mem. Navy League (sr., v.p. 1976-77). Republican. Congregationalist. Clubs: King Harbor Yacht (Redondo Beach, Calif.) (social chmn. and bd. dirs. 1983—); Palos Verdes Breakfast (bd. dirs. 1979-82). Home: 3251 Harbor Blvd Channel Islands CA 93035 Office: Shelly Enterprises 1209 Via Coronel Palos Verdes CA 90274

SHELTON, AUSTIN JAMES (SONNY SHELTON), territorial legislator; b. Yigo, Guam, June 30, 1949; s. Austin James and Amanda (Guzman) S.; m. Eleanore Connelly (div. 1984); children: Melinda Nadine, Madeline Anne; m. Graciallа Rose Shinohara, June 15, 1985; 1 child, Austin James III. Grad. high sch., Agana, Guam. Businessman 1978-86; senator 19th Guam Legislature, Agana, 1987—. Mem. Asian-Pacific Parliamentarian's Union (secretariat-gen. 1987-89), Assn. of Pacific Island Legislatures. Democrat. Roman Catholic. Home: PO Box 803 Agana GU 96910 Office: 19th Guam Legislature PO Box CB-1 Agana GU 96910

SHELTON, FRANK HARVEY, physicist; b. Flagstaff, Ariz., Oct. 5, 1924; s. Mark Harvey and Jessie Frankie (Foster) S.; m. Lorene Gregory, Dec. 29, 1947; children—Jill Jeannette, Joyce Lynn, Gwen Elaine. B.S., Calif. Inst. Tech., 1949, M.S., 1950, Ph.D., 1953. Mem. staff Sandia Corp., Albuquerque, 1952-55; tech. dir. Armed Forces Spl. Weapons Project, Washington, 1955-59; mem. staff Kaman Nuclear Corp., Colorado Springs, Colo., 1959-65; v.p., chief scientist Kaman Scis. Corp., Colorado Springs, 1965—. Author papers in field. Served to 2d lt. AUS, 1943-46. Fellow Am. Phys. Soc.; mem. Sigma Xi. Methodist. Club: Winter Night (Colorado Springs). Home: 1327 Culebra Ave Colorado Springs CO 80903 Office: Kaman Scis Corp 1500 Garden of Gods Rd Colorado Springs CO 80907

SHELTON, JOEL EDWARD, clinical psychologist; b. Havre, Mont., Feb. 7, 1928; s. John Granvil and Roselma Fahy (Ervin) S.; m. Maybelle Platzek, Dec. 17, 1949; 1 child, Sophia. AB, Chico (Calif.) State Coll., 1951; MA, Ohio State U., 1958, PhD, 1960. Psychologist Sutter County Schs., Yuba City, Calif., 1952-53; tchr., vice prin. Lassen View Sch., Los Molinos, Calif., 1953-55; tchr. S.W. Licking Schs., Pataskala, Ohio, 1955-56; child psychologist Franklin Village, Grove City, Ohio, 1957; clin. psychologist Marion (Ohio) Health Clinic, 1958; intern Children's Mental Health Ctr., Columbus, Ohio, 1958-59; acting chief research psychologist Children's Psychiat. Hosp., Columbus, 1959-60; cons. to supt. schs. Sacramento County, Calif., 1960-63; mem. faculty Sacramento State Coll., 1961-69; clin. psychologist DeWitt State Hosp., Auburn, Calif., 1965; exec. dir. Children's Ctr. Sacramento, Citrus Heights, Calif., 1965-66, Gold Bar Ranch, Garden Valley, Calif., 1964-72; clin. psychologist El Dorado County Mental Health Ctr., Placerville, Calif., 1968-70; clin. psychologist Butte County Mental Health Ctr., Chico, 1970—, dir. dept. consultation, edn. and community services, 1974-85, outpatient supr., 1985-86; mgmt. cons. 1972—; advisor to pres. Protaca Industries, Chico, 1974—; exec. sec. Protaca Agrl. Research, 1974—; small bus. cons., 1983—. Mem. Am. Pychol. Assn., Western Psychol. Assn. Home: 1845 Veatch St Oroville CA 95965 Office: Butte County Mental Health 18-C County Ctr Dr Oroville CA 95965

SHELTON, MARY LOIS, teacher; b. Kermit, Tex., Dec. 10, 1949; d. James L. and Anna May (Tackle) Stidham; m. Marvin L. Burrows (div.); m. Robert Kent Shelton, May 21, 1983; children: Melisa, Jennifer, Scott. BE, Coll. of SW, 1985; ME, Eastern N.Mex. U., 1987. Cert. elem. tchr., N.Mex. Tchr. Hobbs (N. Mex.) Pub. Schs., 1985—; cons. Hobbs Pub. Schs., 1986—. Recipient Tchr. of the Month award Classroom Tchrs. Assn., 1987. Mem. Hobbs Assn. Classroom Tchrs. (sec. 1987, v.p. 1988-89, pres.-elect 1989—). Democrat. Roman Catholic. Home: 1130 Calle Sur St Hobbs NM 88240

SHELTON, ROBERT CHARLES, electronics engineer; b. Los Angeles, July 31, 1934; s. Weir Mitchell and Martalena (Scavarda) S.; BEE, Calif. State Poly. U., 1961; divorced; 1 son, Kevin Lyle. Ops. mgr. Halcyon, Palo Alto, Calif., 1971-74; mfg. mgr. Programmed Power, Menlo Park, Calif., 1974-78; pres. Shelton Electronics, Menlo Park, 1976—. Bd. dirs. Herbert Hoover Boys Club, Menlo Park; vol. Peninsula Meml. Blood Bank, St. Anthony Padua Dining Rm. Served with USN, 1952-56. Mem. IEEE, Profl. and Tech. Cons. Assn. Clubs: Elks (chmn. Palo Alto public relations); Rotary (bd. dirs., pres. 1981-82) (Menlo Park). Rsch. and publs. in telecommunication microwave and high energy physics, small computer systems and data communications; patentee various cryogenic and computer devices. Address: PO Box 2573 Menlo Park CA 94026 Office: 1259-351 El Camino Real Menlo Park CA 94025

SHELTON, TIMOTHY NEAL, teacher; b. Des Moines, Mar. 20, 1953; s. Howard Lee and Beverly Ann (Kessell) S. AA, Trinity Western Coll., 1976; BA, Trinity Coll., Deerfield, Ill., 1978; postgrad., Trinity Evang. Divinity Sch., Deerfield, Ill., 1979-81. Tchr. Des Moines Christian Sch., 1981-82; with telemktg. dept. Mark IV Pictures, Des Moines, 1982-84; tchr. Valley Christian High Sch., San Marcos, Calif., 1984-85, Victory High Sch., Carlsbad, Calif., 1985-87, Capistrano Valley Christian High Sch., San Juan Capistrano, Calif., 1987—. High sch. basketball coach for boys and girls, various schs. Mem. Evang. Tchr. Tng. Assn., Women's Basketball Coaches Assn. Democrat.

SHELTON, WANDA CAROL, nurse; b. Riverside, Calif., Jan. 2, 1956; d. Wallace Campbell and Erma Frances (Elliott) Wendelstadt; m. Rodney Jay Shelton, Feb. 16, 1980; 1 child from previous marriage, Wendy Mae Cox. Cert. in voc. nursing, United Health Careers, 1982; AS, San Bernardino Valley Coll., 1987. RN, Calif. Tchr. piano Fontana, Calif., 1969-75; underwriter Prudential Ins. Co., San Bernardino, Calif., 1977; newspaper editor Allied Constrn. Ind., San Bernardino, 1979-82; nursing asst. San Bernardino County Med. Ctr., 1982-83; voc. nurse Remedy Health Svcs., San Bernadino, 1983; voc. nurse Kaiser Permanente, Fontana, 1983-87, RN, 1987—. Mem. United Nurses Assn. Calif., Alpha Gamma Sigma, Grange Club, Order of Rainbow for Girls.

SHEN, NELSON MU-CHING, fiber optics communications scientist; b. Taiwan, Sept. 2, 1946; came to U.S., 1971; s. Mao-Chang and Ching (Chang) S.; m. Jane Chu; children: Helen Diana, Basil Francis. BS in Physics, Chung Yuan Christian U., Taiwan, 1968; MS in Physics, North Western State U., La., 1972; PhD in Physics, U. Tex., Dallas, 1977. Rsch. assoc. U. So. Calif., L.A., 1977-79; chief scientist Kaptron corp., Palo Alto, Calif., 1979-81; sr. engr. GTE Corp., Mountain View, Calif., 1981-82; sr. scientist Raychem Corp., Menlo Park, Calif., 1982—. Patentee in fiber optics; contbr. papers to profl. publs. Bd. dirs., trustee, Canaan Ch., Mountain View, 1986—. Mem. Optical Soc. Am., SPIE. Home: 3138 Louis Rd Palo Alto CA 94303 Office: Raychem Corp 181 Constitution Dr Menlo Park CA 94025

SHENG, SHINAN-CHUR STEVE, laser physicist, engineer; b. Hsinchu, Taiwan, Republic of China, Oct. 29, 1950; came to U.S., 1974; s. Paul Pin and Jin-Hwei (Chow) S.; m. Hsiao-Ching Cindy Yuen, Dec. 21, 1974; children: Amy, Alice. BS in Physics, Nat. Tsing Hwa U., Hsinchu, Taiwan, Republic of China, 1972; MS in Applied Physics, Stanford U., 1976, MEE, 1978, PhD in Applied Physics, 1980. Sr. laser physicist Spectra-Physics, Inc., Mountain View, Calif., 1979-86; engring. sect. mgr. Spectra-Physics, Inc., Mountain View, 1986-87, sr. engring. sect. mgr., 1987—. Patentee in field. Mem. IEEE. Office: Spectra-Physics 1250 W Middlefield Rd Mountain View CA 94039-7013

SHENK, DAVID WESLEY, customhouse broker; b. Ft. Collins, Colo., May 30, 1938; s. Edward Alton and Emily Virginia (Erickson) S.; m. Midred Leona Fisher, July 4, 1959; children: Stephanie Rene, Robert Michael. BS, Colo. State U., 1962. Cert. customhouse broker. Owner, pres. David W. Shenk and Co., L.A., 1969—. With USN, 1956-62. Named Man of Yr. Women United Internat., 1985. Mem. Barbara Sinatra Children's Ctr., Needy Children of Desert, The Desert Blind, Variety Club Internat. Home: 4189 Candleberry Ave Seal Beach CA 90740 Office: David W Shenk & Co 8610 Airport Blvd Los Angeles CA 90045

SHEP, ROBERT LEE, editor, publisher, textile book researcher; b. Los Angeles, Feb. 27, 1933; s. Milton and Ruth (Miller) Polen S. B.A., U. Calif.-Berkeley, 1955; student Royal Acad. Dramatic Art, London, 1956; B.Fgn. Trade, Am. Inst. Fgn. Trade, 1960. Asst. area mgr. fgn. dept. Max Factor, Hollywood, Calif., 1960-65; editor, pub. The Textile Booklist, Lopez Island, Wash., 1980-84; free-lance writer, book reviewer, library appraiser, book repairer. Author: Cleaning and Repairing Books, 1980, Cleaning and Care for Books, 1983, Bhutan - Fibre Forum, 1984; co-author: (annotated edit.) The Costume or Annals of Fashion, 1986, Dress and Cloak Cutter: Womens Costume 1877-1882, 1987; editor: The Handbook of Practical Cutting, 2d rev. edit., 1986; pub. Ladies' Guide to Needle Work, 1986. Art of Cutting and History of English Costume, 1987; pub. Civil War Era Etiquette, 1988, Ladies Self Instr., 1988; mem. editorial rev. bd. The Cutter's Rsch. Jour. Mem. Costume Soc. (London), Costume Soc. Am. (bd. dirs. 1985-87), Costume Soc. Ont., Australian Costume and Textile Soc., U.S. Inst. Theatre Tech. Home: Box 668 Mendocino CA 95460

SHEPARD, EARL ALDEN, government official; b. Aurora, Ill., Sept. 30, 1932; s. Ralph George and Marcia Louise (Phelps) S.; AS magna cum laude in Bus. Adminstrn. (fed. and local govt. employee scholar), Southeastern U., 1967, BS magna cum laude in Bus. Adminstrn., 1969; MBA (Ammunition Procurement Supply Agy. fellow), U. Chgo., 1974; m. Carolyn Mae Borman, Sept. 1, 1959; 1 son, Ralph Lyle. Chief program budget div. U.S. Army Munitions Command. Joliet, Ill., 1971-73; comptroller, dir. adminstrn. U.S. Navy Pub. Works Center, Gt. Lakes, Ill., 1973-77; dep. comptroller U.S. Army Electronics Command/U.S. Army Communications Electronics Materiel Readiness Command, Ft. Monmouth, N.J., 1977-79; dir. resource mgmt., comptroller, dir. programs U.S. Army White Sands Missile Range, N.Mex., 1979—; bd. dirs. 1st Nat. Bank Dona Ana County, 1987—; adv. com. Rio Grande Bancshares/First Nat. Bank of Dona Ana County, 1983-84. Bd. govs., Southeastern Univ. Ednl. Found., 1969-71; chmn. fin. com. No. Va. Assn. for Children with Learning Disabilities, 1966-67, treas., 1968-70; pres. West Long Branch (N.J.) Sports Assn., 1979. Mem. Assn. U.S. Army, Am. Soc. Mil. Comptrollers. Assn. Govt. Accts., Fed. Mgrs. Assn. Republican. Home: 2712 Topley Ave Las Cruces NM 88005 Office: Attention: STEWS-RM White Sands Missile Range NM 88002

SHEPARD, REESE ALSOP, educator; b. N.Y.C., Feb. 5, 1946; s. Edward Morse S. and Elizabeth Wendell (Yates) Ensign; m. Helen Margaret Bundle, Oct. 1, 1983; 1 child, Rex Edward. AB in Econs., Harvard Coll., 1967; MBA in Urban Devel., Stanford U., 1971; postgrad., U. Oreg., 1988—. Mgmt. cons. ABT Assocs., Inc., Cambridge, Mass., 1970-73; exec. dir. Boston Bus. Resource Ctr., 1973-76; pres. Teton Video Co., Jackson Hole, Wyo., 1976-84; dir. bus. devel. Cen. Oreg. Community Coll., Bend, 1984-87, chmn. vocat. and tech. edn., 1987—; founder Pacific Northwest Cons. Group, Bend, 1986. Editor: (with others) Your Marketing Plan, 1986. Pres. Students for Kennedy, 1968; VISTA vol. San Francisco Local Devel. Corp., 1968-69; bd. dirs. Common Cause, Boston, 1975-76, United Way, Deschutes County, Oreg., 1986-88. Recognized for long term counseling impact in Oreg. SBA, 1985-86. Mem. Nat. Assn. Indsl. Tech. (community coll. div. standards and accreditation com.). Democrat. Home: 1536 NW Quincy Ave Bend OR 97701 Office: Cen Oreg Community Coll 2600 NW College Way Bend OR 97701-5998

SHEPARD, WILLIAM FRANCIS, III, sales executive; b. Tulsa, Dec. 22, 1948; s. William F. and Wanda Maye (Parris) S.; m. Barbara Edwards, May 11, 1974. BS, So. Ill. U., 1972. Sales mgr. Wohl Shoe Co., San Mateo, Calif., 1972-78, Hustons, Berkeley, Calif., 1978-79, Gallettis, San Francisco, 1979-84, Stride Rite, San Mateo, 1984-87, Nordstrom, San Mateo, 1987—. Mem. Rep. Presdl. Task Force, 1986. Mem. Burlingame Jaycees, Jolly Corks, Elks (inner guard San Mateo 1987-88). Democrat. Episcopalian. Home: 800 Sea Spray Ln Apt 210 Foster City CA 94404-2425 Office: Nordstrom 5540 Winfield Blvd San Jose CA 95123

SHEPHERD, GEORGE WILLIAM, JR., political science educator; b. Shanghai, People's Republic of China, Oct. 26, 1926; came to U.S., 1936; s. George William and Clara Sargent Shepherd; m. Shirley Brower, June 1948; children: Mary-Claire, Holland, Sharon, Harold. BA, U. Mich., 1949; PhD, London Sch. Econs. and Polit. Sci., 1952; DDL, Mercy Coll., 1986. Advisor African Farmers Coop., Uganda, 1953-54; exec. sec. Am. Com. on Africa, N.Y.C., 1954—; lectr. polit. sci. Bklyn. Coll., 1956-58; asst. prof. polit. sci. St. Olaf Coll., Minn., 1958-60; asst. prof. internat. relations U. Denver, 1961-63, prof. internat. relations, 1965—; research assoc., Unitar, N.Y.C., 1972; lectr. USIA, Africa, 1979; pres. Africa Today Assocs., Denver and N.Y.C., 1979—. Author: They Wait in Darkness, 1956, Politics of African Nationalism, 1962, Nonaligned Black Africa, 1970, Anti-Apartheid, 1977, Human Rights in the Third World, 1985, The Trampled Grass, 1987; editor: Africa Today mag., 1966—. Active Environ. Def. Fund, Am. Friends Service Com. ; mem. adv. council Am. Com. Africa, 1958—; chmn. internat. relations com. Council for Social Action United Ch. of Christ., 1970-72, African Studies Assn. Conf., Denver, 1987; dirs. Consortium on Rights Devel. U. Denver, 1988—. Served with mil. communication, U.S., 1944-47. Fellow Unitar, 1973, Ford Found., 1973; grantee Soc. Sci. Research Council, 1984; recipient Pres.'s Medal award Hunter Coll. CUNY, 1988. Fellow: African Studies Assn., Internat. Studies Assn. Independent democrat. Congregationalist. Club: Tennis and Racquet (Denver). Home: 4838 N Lariat Dr Castle Rock CO 80104 Office: U Denver Grad Sch Internat Studies University Park Denver CO 80208

SHEPHERD, JAMES FRANKLIN, business owner; b. L.A., Mar. 3, 1949; s. Howard F. and Mary Anne (Ransford) S. BS in Physics, Calif. Polytech., Pomona, 1973. Safety dir. Utah Internat., Imlay, Nev., 1980-82; owner Winnemucca (Nev.) Gun & Sport, 1983—. Mem. Nev. State Rifle and Pistol Assn. (dir. 1978—), Winnemucca C. of C., Humboldt County Rod and Gun Club (pres. 1988—), Elks. Republican. Office: Winnemucca Gun & Sport 1100 W Winnemucca Blvd Winnemucca NV 89445

SHEPHERD, MARGARET ZELLER, health care administrator; b. Lancaster, Wis., Apr. 29, 1941; d. Leonard Franklin and Jane (Kress) Knudtson Z.; m. Leland Arthur Shepherd, Feb. 7, 1970; children: Benjamin, Jonathan. Diploma in nursing, Evanston Hosp., Northwestern U., 1962; BS in Nursing, U. Wash., 1965. Pub. health nurse Snohomish Health Dist., Everett, Wash., 1965-68; nursing supr. Visiting Nurse Assn., Everett, 1968-71; profl. services dir. Home Health Svcs. King County, Seattle, 1972-75; co-founder, exec. dir. Community Home Health Care, Seattle, 1975—; bd. dirs. Puget Sound Health Systems Agy., Seattle, 1981—, Pacific Health Assocs. Seattle, 1985—; chair govt. affairs Home Care Assn. Wash., Seattle, 1986—; mem. State Health Coordinating Council, Olympia, Wash., 1988—. Sr. svc. advisory bd. Blue Cross of Wash./Alaska, Seattle, 1987-89, U. Wash. Sch. Nursing, Seattle, 1987-89. Recipient Outstanding Service award Home Care Assn. Wash., 1987; named Invited Participant "Nursing in the 21st Century" Am. Nurses Found., 1987, Invited Participant "Nurse Leadership in the United Kingdom and the U.S." First Internat. Inst., 1987. Mem. Am. Nurses Assn. Home: 2231 11th Ave West Seattle WA 98119 Office: Community Home Health Care 100 W Harrison South Tower Seattle WA 98119-4144

SHEPHERD, SHELLEY ANN, journalist, consultant; b. Lorain, Ohio, Aug. 14, 1957; d. Richard Frank and Betty (Kotai) Pall; m. Randall Orvin Shepherd, Oct. 6, 1978; 1 child, Jennifer Michelle. BA in Communications, Brigham Young U., 1984. With sportswear sales dept. Mervyns, 1980-85; asst. mgr. Brook's Fashions, San Rafael, Calif., 1985-86; community editor Novato (Calif.) Advance Newspaper, 1986-89; pvt. practice pub. rels. cons. 1987—; with community rels. Novato Human Needs Ctr., 1988-89; cons. Bottom Line Devel., Novato, Telfer Chiesea Dunham Architects, Novato, Novato Ecumenical Housing, Bradley Video, North Bay Children's Ctr., Novato. Corr. Marin Ind. Jour. Active community rels., legis. adv. chair Novato Child and Family Task Force, 1986—; with publicity com. For Kids Sake Group, Novato, 1986-88; v.p. bd. Marin Therapy & Tng. Inst., Novato, 1987-88; program chair Teen Ctr. Com., Novato, 1988, Sister City Com., Novato, 1989—. Mem. Romance Writers Am., Friends of World Coll. West (red ribbon week com.), Novato C. of C. (newsletter com.), Soroptimist (pres., 1st v.p., community rels. chair, program chair). Reorganized Ch. of Jesus Christ Latter-day Saints. Home and Office: 1302 Kaehler St Novato CA 94945

SHEPHERD, SKEET, JR. (LYLE DEAN SHEPHERD), real estate broker; b. Salem, Oreg., July 10, 1935; s. Lyle Dean and Dorothy Ann (pillette) S.; m. Constance H. Destner, July 16, 1960; children: Kris A., Kyle D., Kerry J. BS, Willamette U., 1957. Lic. real estate broker, Oreg. Supr. State Farm Ins. Co., Salem, Oreg., 1957-62; salesman Prudential Ins., Salem, 1962-72; real estate sales Davis and Mooney Realtors, Salem, 1972-76; broker, owner Shepherd Realty, Salem, 1976—. Sgt. USAF, 1953-62. Mem. Salem Bd. Realtors, Oreg. Bd. Realtors, Nat. Bd. Realtors, Salem Multiple Listing Bur. (exec. com.), Salem Basketball Officials Assn. (commr.), Salem Baseball Umpires Assn. (past pres., past commr.), Salem Softball Umpires Assn. (past pres., past commr.), Ducks Unltd. (co-chmn. Salem chpt.), Civitan Club (pres. 1965-66). Democrat. Roman Catholic. Office: Shepherd Realty 1390 Capitol St NE Salem OR 97303

SHEPPARD, JOHN ROY, teacher; b. Winnemucca, Nev., Apr. 18, 1940; s. John Henry (Jack) and Eleanor Estelle (Fordin) S.; m. Sylvia May Shipp, June 10, 1963; children: Kelley Jean, Jack Robert. BA, Humboldt State Coll., 1964; MS, U. So. Calif., 1969. Cert. elem. tchr., Calif. Tchr. elem. Jacoby Creek Sch. Dist., Bayside, Calif., 1969-70; tchr. elem. McKinleyville (Calif.) Union Sch. Dist., 1970-82, master tchr., 1982—; mem. leadership team Humboldt County Office Edn., Eureka, Calif., 1986—; mentor Teacher Scis. Edn., 1984-85. Dir. Fieldbrook (Calif.) Community Svc. Dist., 1984—; fire chief Fieldbrook Vol. Fire Dept., 1988—. Named Fireman of Yr. Fieldbrook Vol. Fire Dept., 1985. Mem. NEA, Calif. Tchrs. Assn. Democrat. Roman Catholic. Office: McKinleyville Sch 2285 Central Ave McKinleyville CA 95521

SHER, DORA ROBERTA, insurance broker; b. Legnica, Poland, Oct. 3, 1946; came to U.S., 1962; d. Henry and Anna (Rajs) Polivoda. AA, Los Angeles Community Coll., 1968. Cert. Ins. Counselor, cert. Profl. Ins. Woman. Mktg. product devel. mgr. GMIS (Ins.), Los Angeles, 1979; br. mgr. Comstock Ins. Co., Foster City, Calif., 1980-84; dist. mgr. Calco Ins. Brokers, San Mateo, Calif., 1984-86; dir. of mktg. Frank B. Hall & Co., Fresno, Calif., 1986-87; ptnr. Buffo & Sher Ins. Services, Fresno, 1988--; sr. instr. Ins. Ednl. Assn., Los Angeles, 1970-80; speaker Western Ins. Info. Inst., 1980--. Sch. Principal Congregation Beth Jacob, Fresno, 1987-88. Mem. Nat. Assn. of Ins. Women, Soc. of Cert. Ins. Counselors, Nat. Assn. of Female Execs., Am. Soc. of Prfl. & Bus. Women, Profl. Ins. Agts. of Calif. & Nev. Republican. Jewish.

SHERIDAN, GEORGE EDWARD, manufacturing company executive; b. Emporia, Kans., July 4, 1915; s. George and Josephine Frances (Benson) S.; m. Edith Joye Card, July 4, 1940; 1 dau., Phyllis Lynne. Liberal arts student Coll. of Emporia, 1934-36; engring. student Nat. Schs., 1936-37, Los Angeles City Jr. Coll., 1937-38. Cert. mfg. engr.; registered profl. engr., Calif. With Douglas Aircraft, Santa Monica, Calif., 1939-40, Northrop Aircraft, Hawthorn, Calif., 1940-45; pres. Sheridan Products, Inc., Inglewood, Calif., 1940—. Active, YMCA, Inglewood, 1960—. Mem. Soc. Mfg. Engrs. (life, award 1979-80, Industrialist of Yr. 1982 past chmn.), U.S. Power Squadron, Am. Ordnance Def. Preparedness Assn., Nat. Rifle Assn., Smithsonian Associates, Cutting Tool Mfg. Assn., Nat. Fedn. Ind. Bus., Mech. Bank Collectors Am., Antique Toy Collectors Am. Republican. Quaker. Patentee double edge scraper. Home and Office: Sheridan Products Inc 27692 Via Rodrigo Mission Viejo CA 92692 Office: 1054 E Hyde Park Blvd Inglewood CA 90302

SHERK, WARREN ARTHUR, counselor, educator; b. Buffalo, July 12, 1916; s. Warren E. and Jennie (Taylor) S.; m. Martha Jean Kritzer, June 11, 1954; children: Elena E., Adra K., Lydian M., Warren M., Wilson E. Student Hiram Coll., 1934-35, U. Rangoon, Burma, 1938-39, Duke U., 1939-40; AB, Allegheny Coll., 1938; BD, Berkeley Bapt. Div. Sch., 1945, ThM, 1952; STD, Burton Sem., 1958. Minister, Meth. chs. in western N.Y., 1941-43; Protestant chaplain Ariz. State Prison, 1971-72; vis. prof. Iliff Sch. Theology, U. Denver, 1945-47; field sec. to Pearl S. Buck, 1948-49; minister edn., Indiana, Pa., 1949-51; minister Waitsburg Meth. Ch., Washington, 1951-52, Community Ch., Watertown, Mass., 1955-58, Savanna, Ill., 1958-59, Nogales (Ariz.) United Ch., 1960-61; exec. Dynamics Found., Tucson, 1962—; personal counselor, 1962—; faculty Phoenix Coll., 1963-66, Mesa Community Coll., Eastern Ariz. Coll., Pima Coll., 1963-78, Western Internat. U., 1984—; cons. spl. seminars Pepsi Cola Mgmt. Inst., 1967-68; dir. bus. and profl. seminars for execs., 1968—; lectr. U. Durham (Eng.), summer 1981, Iliff Sch. Theology, summer 1982, Elder Hostels, N.Y., summer 1983, St. Deinels Library, Wales, summer 1985, S.S. Rotterdam N.Y.C. to South Africa, 1984; founder, exec. sec. Valley of Sun Forum, Phoenix, 1963-67; coordinator Assoc. Bus. Execs. Phoenix, 1963-67. Author: Wider Horizons, 1941, Agnes Moorehead: A Biography, 1976, Pearl Buck, 1987; contbr. numerous articles to mags. Chmn. spl. gifts div. Maricopa County Heart Fund. Corporate mem. Perkins Sch. for the Blind; bd. dirs. Boston World Affairs Council, N.E. Assn. UN; hon. bd. govs., bd. dirs. Pearl S. Buck Found. Fellow Am. Acad. Polit. Sci., Am. Geog. Soc.; mem. Thoreau Soc., Emerson Soc., Watertown Hist. Soc., Pimeria Alta Hist. Soc., Maricopa Mental Health Assn., Internat. Winston Churchill Soc., Theodore Roosevelt Assn., Execs. Internat. (founder, exec. dir. 1967—), Nat. Assn. Approved Morticians (exec. sec. 1967-69), Internat. Platform Assn., Tucson Com. Fgn. Rels., Phoenix Com. Fgn. Relations, NCCJ, AAUP, The Newcomer Soc., Ariz. Club, Univ. Club, Kiva Club, Theta Chi. Republican. Address: 10032 N 8th St Phoenix AZ 85020

SHERLOCK, EMMANELL PHILLIPS, educator, painter; b. Monroe, La., Oct. 27, 1914; d. Clarence Leroy and Amy Wallace (Holmes) Phillips; B.A. in Edn., Northwestern La. U., 1939; M.A. in Elem. Edn., Calif. State U., Long Beach, 1966; m. Frank J. Sherlock, Sept. 3, 1948 (div. Feb. 1973); children—Patricia, Michael (twins), Dan. Classroom tchr. St. Tammany and Calcasieu Parishes, La., 1934-41, Orange, Tex., 1941-42; elec. engring. draftsman Consol. Steel, Orange, 1942-43, H. Newton Whitesley, Chgo., 1943-44, George G. Sharp, New Orleans, 1944-45; music tchr. Orange Public Schs., 1945-47; reading cons. Silver Burdett Publs., 1947-48; tchr., resource tchr. Cypress (Calif.) Elem. Sch. Dist., 1963-83. Cert. tchr., La., Tex., Calif.; cert. adminstr., supr., reading specialist, Calif. Mem. Calif. Tchrs. Assn., NEA, Calif. Reading Assn., Internat. Reading Assn., Orange County (Calif.) Reading Assn. (past exec. bd.), Assn. Supervision and Curriculum Devel. Home: 3701 Green Ave Apt D Los Alamitos CA 90720

SHERLOCK, JOSEPH MICHAEL, plastics manufacturing company executive; b. Phila., Aug. 5, 1943; s. Joseph Michael and Ann Marie (McNicholas) S.; m. Carol Jean Howell, June 18, 1966; children: Joseph Michael III, Kathleen Anne. BME, Villanova U., 1965. Devel. engr. Uniroyal, Inc., Phila., 1965-66; process engr. Rohm and Haas Co., Bristol, Pa., 1966-71; new product specialist Rohm and Haas Co., Phila., 1971-75, mktg. mgr., 1975-78; pres. Discovery Plastics, Inc., Tangent, Oreg., 1978—. Contbr. articles to mags. Vol. counselor Active Corps of Exec.-SBA, Salem, Oreg., 1986—. Mem. Nat. Fedn. Ind. Bus. Roman Catholic. Office: Discovery Plastics Inc 32140 Hwy 34 Tangent OR 97389

SHERMAN, ERIC, filmmaker, writer, educator; b. Santa Monica, Calif., June 29, 1947; s. Vincent and Hedda (Comorau) S.; B.A. cum laude, Yale U., 1968; m. Eugenia Blackiston Dillard, Apr. 1, 1978; children—Cosimo, Rocky. Film producer, dir., writer, photographer and editor; films include: Charles Lloyd—Journey Within, 1968; Paul Weiss—a Philosopher in Process, 1972; Waltz, 1980; Inside Out, 1982; Measure of America, 1983; Michael Reagan's Assault on Great Lakes, 1983; represented in film festivals N.Y.C. Melbourne, Australia, Bilbao, Spain, others; books include: (with others) The Director's Event, 1970; Directing the Film, 1976; Frame by Frame, 1987; pres. Film Transform; film tchr. Art Center Coll. Design, Pepperdine U., UCLA; guest lectr. Yale, Calif. Inst. Tech., U. So. Calif.; Andrew Mellon lectr. on arts Calif. Inst. Tech., 1977; contbr. numerous articles to film publs. and distbn. catalogues, book dedication; works include three oral histories for Am. Film Inst. under Louis B. Mayer Found. grant. Trustee Am. Cinematheque; bd. dir. Film Forum. Mem. Soc. Motion Picture and TV Engrs. (asso.), Assn. Ind. Video and Filmmakers, Univ. Film Assn., Assn. Visual Communicators, Nat. Alliance Media Arts Ctrs. Home: 2427 Park Oak Dr Los Angeles CA 90068 Office: 3755 Cahuenga W #B Studio City CA 91604

SHERMAN, GLENN HOWARD, electronics executive; b. Chgo., Mar. 9, 1943; s. Stanford H. and Mary Irene (Cunningham) S.; m. Inamaria Schoof, July 16, 1964; children: Thomas Steven, Martina Margot Irene. BSEE, U. Ill., 1968, MSEE, 1970, PhD in Elec. Engring., 1972. From sales, mktg. and tech. positions to v.p., dir. II-VI, Inc., Saxonburg, Pa., 1972-79; founder, pres., chmn., chief exec. officer Laser Power Corp., San Diego, 1979—. V.p. Assn. for Corp. Growth, San Diego, 1986-87. Served with U.S. Army, 1962-64. NSF fellow, 1968-72. Mem. IEEE, Lasers and Electro-Optics Soc., Optical Soc. Am., Laser Inst. Am., Soc. Optical Engring., Laser Assn. Am. (bd. dirs., founding pres. 1986—). Club: Lomas Santa Fe Country (Solana Beach, Calif.). Office: Laser Power Corp 12777 High Bluff Dr San Diego CA 92130

SHERMAN, GREG DEAN, consulting geologist; b. Denver, May 16, 1953; s. Harry Francis and Margaret (Hintz) S.; m. Linda Gail Bowman, Dec. 29, 1976; 1 child, Hollis Anna. BS, U. No. Colo., 1975; postgrad., N.Mex. Inst. Mining & Tech., Socorro, 1976-77. Cert. profl. geologist. Staff geologist Uranerz U.S.A., Inc., Casper, Wyo., 1975-76, Resource Assocs. of Alaska, Fairbanks, 1977; project geologist Dames & Moore, Denver, 1977-79; sr. project geologist Apache Energy & Minerals, Lakewood, Colo., 1979-82; pres. Tierra Cons., Inc., Lakewood, 1982-85; sr. geologist ATEC Assocs., Inc., Denver, 1985--. Contbr. articles to profl. jours. Mem. Am. Assn. Profl. Geologists, Soc. Mining Engrs., Assn. Engring. Geologists. Home: 8191 Storm King Peak Littleton CO 80127

SHERMAN, MARILYN C., financial analyst; b. Chgo., Mar. 3, 1961; d. Irvin Sheldon and Marlene Pearl (Altman) S. BS in Acctg., U. Ill., 1983; postgrad., Northwestern U., 1986-89. CPA, Ill. Auditor, sr. tax analyst Peat, Marwick, Mitchell and Co., Chgo., 1983-85; fin. analyst Harris Trust and Savs. Bank, Chgo., 1985-89; with The Mirage, Las Vegas, 1989—. Mem. AICPA, Ill. Soc. CPA's, Chgo. Soc. Women CPA's, Phi Kappa Phi, Beta Gamma Sigma. Office: The Mirage 3400 Las Vegas Blvd Las Vegas NV 89109

SHERMAN, MILDRED RUTH, educational institution professional; b. Glendale, Calif., Mar. 14, 1931; d. Bryan Boy and Melzena Martha (Peters) Murray; m. Richard R. Sherman, June 29, 1950; children: Bryana, Leeana, Richard M., Cindy R. Student, Glendale Coll., 1949. Sec. dept. phys. edn. Calif. State U. L.A., 1970-77, sec. dean's office, 1977, sec. Sch. Fine and Applied Arts, 1977-84, evaluation tech. Sch. Edn., 1984-87, credential analyst Sch. Edn., 1987—. Mem. Credential Counselors and Analysts Calif., Spellbinders Sq. Dance Club. Democrat. Office: Calif State U Los Angeles 5151 State University Dr Los Angeles CA 90065

SHERMAN, PERRY JAMES, aerospace engineer; b. Pitts., Oct. 26, 1959; s. Peter P. Sherman and Virginia Somerville. BS, Case Western Res. U., 1981; MA, Simon Greenleaf Sch. Law, 1989. Engr. Hughes Aircraft Co., Culver City, Calif., 1981-82; engr. materials and process Hughes Aircraft Co., Fullerton, Calif., 1982-84; engr. Advanced Systems div. Northrop Corp., Pico Rivera, Calif., 1984-86; sr. engr. Advanced Systems div. Northrop Corp., Pico Rivera, 1986—. Mem. Anaheim Origins Soc. (pres. 1986), Tau Beta Pi. Republican. Home: 2828 W Lincoln Ave #124 Anaheim CA 92801 Office: Northrop Corp 2828 W Lincoln Ave 124 Anaheim CA 92801

SHERMAN, RAY SCOTT, minister, writer; b. Milw., June 4, 1939; s. Ray Elwin and Kathryn Elise (Hatch) S.; m. Judith Ann Schroeder, June 15, 1960 (div. Jan. 1987); children: David Scott, Douglas Clark. BA, Lawrence U., 1960; MA, U. Hawaii, 1968. Ordained to ministry Unity Ch., 1970. Sr. minister Unity Ch. Spokane, Wash., 1970-74; nat. outreach dir. Assn. Unity Chs., Chgo., 1974-76; field services dir. Assn. Unity Chs., Unity Village, Mo., 1976-78, support services dir., 1978-79, exec. dir., 1979-80; sr. minister Unity Ch. Seattle, 1980—; cons., bd. dirs. Therma-Tron-X Inc., Sturgeon Bay, Wis., 1983—. Author: Meditation and Prayer, 1973, Small Prayers, 1988, (poetry) Gifts, 1983; contbr. numerous articles to mags. Bd. dirs. Puget Sound Big Sisters, Seattle, 1983—, Three Mountain Found., Lone Pine, Calif., 1986—; trustee Charles and Myrtle Fillmore Found., Unity Village, 1973—. Served to Capt. USAF, 1960-68. Club: Wash. Athletic. Lodge: Rotary. Office: Unity Ch of Seattle 200 8th Ave N Seattle WA 98109

SHERMAN, ROBERT, communications executive, producer; b. N.Y.C., Jan. 9, 1950; s. Allan Sherman and Dolores Miriam (Chackes) Golden. Student, San Fernando Valley State Coll., 1968, UCLA, 1969, Brandeis U., 1970. Co-owner, sec., treas., cons. Sta. KJQN AM-FM, Ogden, Utah; pres./founder The Television Company, 1970—, See Other Page, 1987—; pres./co-owner Curtain Call Productions, 1973—. Producer, co-creator Spellbinders, 1978, The Better Sex, 1977-78, Puzzlers, 1980, Blockbusters, 1980-82, 87, Star Words, 1983; assoc. producer Tattletales, 1974-78, co-producer, 1982; writer, assoc. producer Match Game, 1973-81; producer Password Plus, 1979-82 (Daytime Emmy as Outstanding Game Show 1981-82); exec. producer Match Game/Hollywood Sqs. Hour, 1983-84, Super Password, 1984—; exec. producer, creator Body Language, 1984-86; producer, creator Oddball, 1986; contbr. articles to profl. jours.; inventor dimmer control system. Mem. NATAS (Emmy award 1971-72), Mensa, Soc. Motion Picture and TV Engrs. Home: 1555 Rising Glen Rd Los Angeles CA 90069 Office: Mark Goodson Prodns 5750 Wilshire Blvd Los Angeles CA 90036

SHERMAN, ROBERT B(ERNARD), composer, lyricist, screenwriter; b. N.Y.C., Dec. 19, 1925; s. Al and Rosa (Dancis) S.; student UCLA, 1943; BA, Bard Coll., 1949; m. Joyce Ruth Sasner, Sept. 27, 1953; children: Laurie Shane, Jeffrey Craig, Andrea Tracy, Robert Jason. Popular songwriter, 1950-60, including Tall Paul, Pineapple Princess, You're Sixteen (Gold Record); songwriter Walt Disney Prodns., Beverly Hills, Calif., 1960-68, for 29 films including The Parent Trap, 1961, Summer Magic, 1963, Mary Poppins, 1964, That Darn Cat, 1965, Winnie The Pooh, 1965, Jungle Book, 1967, Bedknobs and Broomsticks, 1971; co-composer song It's A Small World, theme of Disneyland and Walt Disney World, Fla.; composer, lyricist United Artists, Beverly Hills, 1969—, songs for film Chitty, Chitty, Bang, Bang, 1969, Snoopy, Come Home!, 1972; song score Charlotte's Web, 1972; composer for Walt Disney's Wonderful World of Color, TV, 1961—; co-producer NBC-TV spl. Goldilocks, 1970; v.p. Musi-Classics, Inc.; co-producer, composer, lyricist stage musical Victory Canteen, 1971; composer-lyricist Broadway show Over Here, 1975; screenplay and song score Tom Sawyer, United Artists, 1972, Huckleberry Finn, 1974, The Slipper and the Rose, 1977, The Magic of Lassie, 1978. Served with inf. AUS, 1943-45; ETO. Decorated Purple Heart; recipient 2 Acad. awards best score for Mary Poppins, 1964, best song for Chim Chim Cheree, 1964; Grammy award, 1965; Christopher medal, 1965, 74; nine Acad. award nominations; Acad. award nomination for song score Bedknobs and Broomsticks, 1971, for best song The Age of Not Believing, 1971, others; 16 golden, 4 platinum and one diamond record album, 1965-83; first prize best composer song score Tom Sawyer, Moscow Film Festival, 1973, B.M.I. Pioneer award, 1977; Golden Cassette awards for Mary Poppins, Jungle Book, Bed Knobs and Broomsticks, 1983, Mouscar award Disney Studios. Mem. Acad. Motion Picture Arts and Scis. (exec. bd. music br. 12 yrs.), AFTRA, Nat. Acad. Rec. Arts and Scis., Composers and Lyricists Guild (exec. bd.), Writers Guild Am., Dramatists Guild, Authors League. Office: care Mike Conner Office 9030 Harratt St Los Angeles CA 90069

SHERMAN, WILLIAM CHARLES, structural engineer; b. Pitts., July 12, 1952; s. Herbert LeRoy and Ruth (Taylor) S; m. Cheryl Beth Mahlman, June 19, 1971; children: Lindsey Rebekah, Kelsey Ann. BSCE with honors, U. Colo., 1974. Registered Civil Engr. Alaska, Colo.; Registered Civil and Structural Engr. Ariz., Calif., Wash. Engr. Stone & Webster Engring. Corp., Denver, 1974-80, structural engr., 1980-87, sr. structural engr., 1987—; engr. second powerhouse Rock Island (Wash.) Hydroelectric Project, 1975-80; lead structural engr. stability analysis Osage Hydroelectric Project, Lake of the Ozarks, Mo., 1980-82, stability analysis Rocky Reach Hydroelectric Project, Wash., 1981-85, Bradley Lake Hydroelectric Project, Alaska, 1985—. Mem. ASCE, Am. Concrete Inst., Tau Beta Pi, Chi Epsilon. Democrat. United Ch. of Christ. Home: 6779 S Delaware St Littleton CO 80120 Office: Stone & Webster Engring 5500 Quebec St Englewood CO 80111

SHEROTSKY, PRISCILLA COLLEEN, illustrator; b. Greeley, Colo., May 6, 1943; d. Folke David and Bernice Evangeline (Larsen) Ekblad; m. George Demetrius Sherotsky, July 12, 1968; 1 child, Steven Michael. Student, U. Wash., 1962, Cornish Coll. of Arts, Seattle, 1962-65. Sales person Frederick & Nelson, Seattle, 1962-65; designer window displays Keegs Interiors, Seattle, 1965-68; designer Walter Darwin Teague, Inc., Renton, Wash., 1966-67; prin. Priscilla Sherotsky Illustration & Designs, Redmond, Wash., 1968—; docent Burke Mus. U. Washington, Seattle, 1973-76; space planning project coord., Interspace Design, Seattle, 1976; illustrator, designer; U. Washington med. illustration learning resources, Seattle, 1977. One woman show at Fredrick & Nelson Gallery, Tolles Gallery, 1978; represented in collections at Panaca- Bellevue Gallery Art Mus., Fry Mus. Northwest Artists. Cultural Arts Chmn. Mead Elem. Sch., Redmond, Wash., 1979-80; co-chmn. Art Exhibit Northwest Boy Choir, Seattle, 1981; vol. 2001 Rsch. & Devel., Lake Washington Sch. Dist., Kirkland, Wash.; sec. Lake Washington Sch. Dist. Citizen's Adv. Coun., Kirkland, 1985-86, legis. rep., 1987; legis. chmn. PTA, Redmond, Wash., 1987-88. Fellow Master Resources Coun. Republican. Episcopalian. Home: 3335 Sahalee Dr W Redmond WA 98053

SHERRARD, RAYMOND HENRY, government official; b. Chgo., Mar. 8, 1944; s. Henry Loren and Minnie Valeria (Elrod) S.; m. Marsha L. McDermid, 1967 (div. 1971). AA, Long Beach City Coll., 1965; BA, Calif. State U., 1967; grad., Treasury Dept. Law Enforcement, Washington, 1970. Spl. dep. U.S. Marshal, L.A., 1970; pres. RHS Enterprises, Cypress, Calif., 1981—; criminal investigator criminal investigation div. IRS, Santa Ana, Calif., 1969—; story cons. Charles Fries Prodns., Hollywood, Calif., 1976—; instr. Fed. Law Enforcement Tng. Ctr., Glynco, Ga., 1977—; screenwriter Orion TV, Century City, Calif., 1984—; tech. advisor Paramount Pictures, Hollywood, Calif., 1987—; dir. speaker panel IRS, Laguna Niguel, Calif., 1984-89. Author: Federal Law Enforcement Patches, 1983, Vol. 2, 1987, About Badges, 1987, Badges of the United States Marshals, 1989; contbr. articles to profl. jours. Recipient Presidential Commendation, Pres. U.S.A., Washington, 1980, Spl. Act award U.S. Treasury Dept., L.A., 1978, 87. Mem. Fed. Criminal Investigators Assn. (life, regional v.p. 1978-80), Assn. Fed. Investigators, Fed. Law Enforcement Officers Assn., Calif. Narcotic Officers Assn. (life, sec. 1974). Republican. Home: PO Box 5779 Garden Grove CA 92645

SHERRER, CHARLES DAVID, college dean, clergyman; b. Marion, Ohio, Sept. 21, 1935; s. Harold D. and Catherine E. (Fye) S. A.B., U. Notre Dame, 1958, M.A., 1965; S.T.L., Gregorian U., 1962; Ph.D., U. N.C., 1969. Ordained priest Roman Cath. Ch., 1961. Instr. English U. Portland, Oreg., 1963-64, asst. prof., 1969-74, chmn. dept., 1970-74, dean Grad. Sch., 1982-87, mem. Bd. Regents, 1986-87, acad. v.p., 1987—; pres. King's Coll., Wilkes Barre, Pa., 1974-81; dir. studies Holy Cross Fathers, Ind. Province, 1979-88. Office: U Portland Office of Acad Vice Pres Portland OR 97203

SHERRILL, BARBARA ANN BUKER, educator; b. Hamilton, Mont., July 11, 1952; d. Emery Orville and Helen (Hackett) Buker; m. Mark Warren SHerrill, Oct. 7, 1978; children: Kristopher Kain, Ashley Ann. BS in Elem. Edn., Western Mont. Coll., 1973, postgrad., 1984. Cert. tchr., Mont. Tchr. Ramsay (Mont.) Sch., 1974—; facilitator labor history workshop Internat. Brotherhood Teamsters, U. Wis., 1987, U. Calif. at Berkeley, 1988; writer, researcher, 1988—. Contbg. author: Teaching Labor Studies in the Schools, vol. 1, 1987, vol. 2, 1988. Parent vol. Silver Bow Ameteur Wrestling assn., Butte. Mem. AAUW, Am. Fedn. Tchrs., Mont. Fedn. Tchrs., AFL-CIO, Ramsay Fedn. Tchrs. (pres. 1975-79). Democrat. Episcopalian. Office: Sch Dist 3 Box 105 Ramsay MT 59748

SHERROW, GLENN C., management consultant; b. Alhambra, Calif., Jan. 28, 1939; s. Charles Carl and Evelyn June (McCaffery) S.; m. Karen Lee Oakes, Sept. 26, 1987. BA in Bus., U. Calif., Riverside, 1962. Sales rep. Gen. Foods, Bethesda, Md., 1962-63; sr. adjustor Kemper Ins. Group, Washington and L.A., 1965-69; we. regional mgr. Cuna Mut. Ins. Soc., Pomona, Calif., 1969-78; ptnr. Bob Jacobsen Assocs., Irvine, Calif., 1978-82; assoc. Gary Nelson Assocs., San Francisco, 1982-84; sr. assoc. Bridgegate Group, San Francisco, 1984—; pres. G & S Assocs., San Francisco, 1984—; bd. dirs. CPD, San Francisco, 1986-88. Bd. dirs. Native Sons of Golden West, Fairfax, Calif., 1988; precinct capt. Rep. Com. Diamond Bar, Calif., 1972. With U.S. Army, 1963-65. Republican. Office: Bridgegate Group 600 Montgomery 37th Fl San Francisco CA 94111

SHERRY, KATHLEEN SUSAN, state developmental disabilities consultant; b. Chgo., May 17, 1954. BA in Philosophy, Ariz. State U., 1988, BA in Psychology, 1988, postgrad. Cert. emergency med. technician. Behavioral & devel. skills trainer Muskegon Regional Ctr. for Devel. Disabilities, Muskegon, Mich., 1973-77; proprietor, portrait photographer, sales, pub. relations Tempe, Ariz., 1977-82; cons. Dept. Economic Security, Div. Developmental Disabilities State of Ariz., Tempe, 1979—. Mem. Ariz. Country Dancers Assn., Golden Key Nat. Honor Soc., Alpha Kappa Psi (historian Ariz. State U. 1989—). Home and Office: 937 S Acorn Tempe AZ 85281

SHERWOOD, ALLEN JOSEPH, lawyer; b. Salt Lake City, Sept. 26, 1909; s. Charles Samuel and Sarah (Abramson) Shapiro; m. Edith Ziff, Jan. 19, 1941; children—Mary (Mrs. John Marshall), Arthur Lawrence. Student, UCLA, 1927-30; AB, U. So. Calif., 1933, LLB, 1933. Bar: Calif. 1933, U.S. Supreme Ct. 1944. Pvt. practice law L.A., 1933-54, Beverly Hills, 1954—; legal counsel Internat. Family Planning Rsch. Assn., Inc., 1970-76; bd. dirs. Family Planning Ctrs. Greater L.A., Inc., 1968-84, pres., 1973-76. Mem. editorial bd. So. Calif. Law Rev., 1932-33. Contbr. articles to profl. jours. Mem. Calif. Atty. Gen.'s Vol. Adv. Coun. and its legis. subcom., 1972-78. Mem. Med.-Legal Soc. So. Calif. (bd. dirs. 1966-74), ABA, L.A. County Bar Assn., Beverly Hills Bar Assn., State Bar of Calif., Am. Arbitration Assn. (nat. panel arbitrators 1965—), Order of Coif, Tau Delta Phi, Brentwood Country Club (L.A.), Masons. Home: 575 Moreno Ave Los Angeles CA 90049 Office: 9033 Wilshire Blvd Penthouse Beverly Hills CA 90211

SHICKLE, PAUL EUGENE, educator; b. Bloomington, Ill., Aug. 29, 1927; s. Benjamin Wilson and Eathel Delores (Rowe) S. B.S., Ill. State U., 1949. Cert. secondary tchr., Calif. Tchr. San Marino Unified Sch. Dist., Calif., 1956—, head fgn. lang. dept., 1967—. Mem. performing arts council Music Ctr. Los Angeles County. Mem. Soc. Indian Pioneers, Filson Club, Calif. Classical Assn. (pres. so. sect. 1981-82), Modern and Classical Assn. So. Calif., Am. Council Study Fgn. Lang., Calif. Humanities Assn., Am. Acad. Religion, Nat. Tchrs. Assn., Calif. Tchrs. Assn., Assn. for Supervision and Curriculum Devel., Am. Classical Assn., Am. Acad. Polit. and Soc. Sci., Am. Acad. Polit. Sci., Am. Council for Arts, Ams. United for Separation Ch. and State, Ind. Hist. Soc., Bibl. Archaeology Soc., Calif. Assn. Supervision and Curriculum Devel., Am. Film Inst., Va. Geneal. Soc., Ky. Geneal. Soc., N.Am. Conf. Brit. Studies, History Sci. Soc., Oceanic Soc., Nelson County (Ky.) Hist. Soc., Smithsonian Assocs., Nat. Trust for Historic Preservation, Met. Mus. Art (nat. assoc.), Met. Opera Guild, Asia Soc., Zionist Orgn. Am., ACLU, Amnesty Internat., Ctr. for Study of Presidency, Clan Fraser Soc. North Am., Archeol. Inst. Am., Va. Country Civil War Soc., Nat. Park and Conservation Assn., UN Assn. of U.S., Soc. French Hist. Studies, Am. Com. for Irish Studies, Irish Cultural Ctr., Nat. Coun. Social Studies, Conf. Group for Cen. European History. Republican. Roman Catholic. Home: 2115 Leafwood Ln Arcadia CA 91006 Office: San Marino Unified Sch Dist 2701 Huntington Dr San Marino CA 91008

SHICOFF, STUART DENNIS, controller; b. Bklyn., Feb. 1, 1947; s. Ralph and Harriet (Rabinowitz) S.; m. Sherrie R. Scharf, Dec. 15, 1971 (div. Jan. 1987); 1 child, Scott D.; m. Joan H. Miller, Aug. 5, 1987. BS, U. Nev., 1976. Jr. acct. Chanslor, Barbieri & DeWitt, CPA's, Reno, 1976-78; auditor Magic Pan Restaurants, San Francisco, 1978-79; sr. acct. Van Keulen & Lumer, CPA's, San Francisco, 1979-80; mgr. bookkeeping King, White & Danielson, CPA's, Walnut Creek, Calif., 1980-85; contr.-treas. Ion Systems Inc., Berkeley, Calif., 1985—. Mgr. Concord (Calif.) Little League, 1983; coach Pleasant Hill (Calif.) Soccer Assn., 1983-84; den leader Boy Scouts Am., Concord, 1984. Cpl. USMC, 1966-69, Vietnam. Mem. Nat. Assn. Accts., Mensa, Toastmasters (Able Toastmaster award 1985 Concord chpt.), Diablo Rd. Runners Club (Walnut Creek). Democrat. Home: 2227 Bridgeport Way Martinez CA 94553 Office: Ion Systems Inc 2546 10th St Berkeley CA 94710

SHIDELER, ISABEL BETTS, retired state agency administrator; b. Laclede, Mo., Dec. 15, 1905; d. Oscar Frazellan and Kathryn (Byrd) Libby; m. Gerald R. Shideler, Sept. 6, 1977 (dec. 1986); children: Roger Staton, Jeanne Cross, Harvey Milton Staton. BA, U. Calif., Berkeley, 1959. Caseworker Fed. Transient Bur., Kansas City, Mo., 1934-35, Travelers Aid Soc., Kansas City, 1935-39; supr. Immigration and Naturalization Svc., Seagoville, Tex., 1939-43; caseworker supr. ARC, Ft. Worth, 1943-45, San Francisco, 1945-49; probation officer, group counselor Alameda County Probation Dept., San Leandro, Calif., 1952-57, County Probation Dept., Santa Rosa, Calif., 1957-59; supr. parole agts. Calif. Dept. Corrections, Oakland and San Francisco, 1960-71; correctional counselor III Calif. Dept. Corrections, Corona, 1971-72, ret., 1972. Vol. Dem. Cen. Com., Martinez, Calif., 1987-88; mem. Dem. Nat. Com., Washington, 1982—, Great Decisions '88, Walnut Creek, Calif., Secular Humanists East Bay, Alameda County, Calif., 1988. Mem. Acad. Polit. Sci., AARP (program chmn. Santa Cruz, chpt. 1975-77). Unitarian. Home: 1441 Creekside Dr #3070 Walnut Creek CA 94595

SHIDELER, ROSS PATRICK, language and comparative literature educator, author, translator, poet; b. Denver, Apr. 12, 1936; s. Byron H. S. and Trudy (Shideler). B.A., San Francisco State U., 1958; M.A., U. Stockholm, 1963; Ph.D., U. Calif., Berkeley, 1968. Instr. in comparative lit. U. Calif., Berkeley, 1967-68; asst. prof. English Hunter Coll., N.Y.C., 1968-69; asst. prof. Scandinavian lang. and comparative lit. UCLA, 1969-73, assoc. prof., 1973-79, prof., 1979—; chmn. program in comparative lit. 1979-86. Author: (monograph) Voices Under The Ground: Themes and Images in the Poetry of Gunnar Ekelof, 1973, Per Olov Enquist—A Critical Study, 1984; translator: (play) The Night of the Tribades (Per Olov Enquist), 1977; U.S. assoc. editor Swedish Book Rev., 1984—. Fellow NDFL, 1964; fellow NDEA, 1965; Fulbright-Hays fellow, 1966-67. Mem. MLA, Soc. Advancement Scandinavian Studies (exec. council 1985-89), Am. Comparative Lit. Assn. Office: UCLA Program in Comparative Lit Los Angeles CA 90024

SHIELDS, KENNETH WAYNE, accountant; b. Albuquerque, Sept. 12, 1950; s. Lorn Morris and Ethel Louise (Ramsey) S.; m. Charlotte Diane Price. BBA, U. N.Mex., 1973. CPA. Revenue agt. IRS, Washington, 1973-78, Farmington, N. Mex., 1978-81; staff acct. Britton Smith & Assocs., Farmington, 1981-84; ptnr. Smith, Shields & Willis, Farmington, 1984-86; prin. Kenneth W. Shields, CPA, P.C., Farmington, 1986—. City councilman City of Farmington, 1986-88; treas. River Reach Found. Mem. AICPA, N.Mex. Soc. CPAs. Republican. Home: 800 N Auburn Farmington NM 87401 Office: PO Box 2375 Farmington NM 87499

SHIELDS, NORMAN ROBERT, lawyer; b. Deadwood, S.D., Aug. 30, 1953; s. Elmer R. and Fay A. (Hanrahan) S. BA in Polit. Sci. with honors, Grinnell Coll., 1975; JD, U. Oreg., 1979. Bar: Oreg. 1979, U.S. Dist. Ct. Oreg. 1980. Law clk. Douglas County Cir. Court, Roseburg, Oreg., 1979-80; dep. dist. atty. County of Yamhill, McMinnville, Oreg., 1980-82; city atty. City of Woodburn, Oreg., 1982—. Office: City of Woodburn 270 Montgomery St Woodburn OR 97071

SHIELDS, WALTER W., management consultant; b. Spokane, Wash., Oct. 18, 1935; s. John S. and Mary L. (Wiley) S.; m. Shizuko Saito, Apr. 2, 1958 (div. Oct. 1978); children: Linda I., Theresa Ann, William Wiley, John William; m. Betty Ann Fetterhoff, Dec. 24, 1983; stepchildren: Brad, Brett, William, Bryant. Student in Bus. Adminstrn., Wash. State U. Dist. mgr. Universal Motor Club, Spokane, 1958-59; wholesale salesperson Berliner's, Spokane, 1959-60; dist. supr. Greyhound Lines, Inc., Phoenix, 1960-79; cons. Transp. Specialist, Spokane, 1979-80; transp. mgr. spl. svcs. Saudi Pub. Transport Co., Riyadh, Saudi Arabia, 1980-82; pvt. practice Spokane, 1982-87; mgmt. cons. Mgmt. Analysis, Spokane, 1987—; Ea. province transp. coord. Saudi Pub. Transport Co., 1981. Mem. citizen adv. com. on transp. for Spokane County, 1979-80; mem. adv. bd. Multiple-Sclerosis, Spokane, 1983-84. Sgt. USMC, 1953-58, Korea. Mem. U.S. Assn. for Small Bus. and Entrepreneurs, Internat. Coun. for Small Bus. Office: Mgmt Analysis W 222 Mission Ste 233 Spokane WA 99201

SHIELDS, WILLIAM MAURICE, wood products company executive; b. Vancouver, Wash., Feb. 24, 1937; s. Marshall Joseph and Pearl Elizabeth (Wardle) S; m. Catherine Diane D'Orsa, June 16, 1962; children—Debi, Janelle, Jackie. B.S. in Bus. Adminstrn., U. Oreg., 1959. Prodn. supt. Willamette Industries, Inc., Lebanon, Oreg., 1970-71, prodn. mgr., 1971-73; gen. prodn. mgr. Willamette Industries, Inc., Albany, Oreg., 1973-76; sr. v.p. Willamette Industries, Inc., Ruston, La., 1976-80; exec. v.p. Willamette Industries, Inc., Portland, Oreg., 1980—. Served to 1st lt. U.S. Army, 1960-62. Mem. Nat. Forest Products Assn. (bd. govs., chmn. bd. dirs.), Western Wood Products Assn. (bd. dirs. 1982—). Republican. Office: Willamette Industries Inc 1300 SW Fifth Ave Portland OR 97201

SHIFFMAN, MAX, mathematician, educator; b. N.Y.C., Oct. 30, 1914; s. Nathan and Eva (Krasilchick) S.; m. Bella Manel (div. 1957); children: Bernard, David. BS, CCNY, 1935; MS, NYU, 1936, PhD, 1938. Instr. math. St. John's U., N.Y.C., 1938-39, CCNY, 1938-42; researcher Dept. Navy, NYU, 1942-45; assoc. prof. math NYU, 1945-49; prof. math. Stanford U., Palo Alto, Calif., 1949-66; prof. Calif. State U., Hayward, 1967-81; owner, mathematician Mathematico, Hayward and San Francisco, 1970—. Contbr. articles to profl. jours. Blumenthal fellow, 1935-38. Mem. Am. Math. Soc., Math. Assn. Am., Soc. Indsl. and Applied Math. Home and Office: 16913 Meekland Ave 7 Hayward CA 94541

SHIFFMAN, MELVIN ARTHUR, surgeon, oncologist; b. Bklyn., Aug. 23, 1931; s. Albert and Eva (Krieger) S.; m. Pearl Asher, Aug. 28, 1955; children: Scott, Karen, Denise. BS in Biochemistry, Union Coll., 1949; student dental medicine, Harvard U., 1953-54; MD, Northwestern U., 1957; JD, Western State U., 1976. Bd. cert. surgeon. Intern Los Angeles County Hosp., 1957-58; resident VA Hosp., Long Beach, Calif., 1960-64; pvt. practice oncologic surgery, cosmetic and reconstructive surgery Anaheim, Calif., 1964; chief of surgery Anaheim Gen. Hosp., 1969; chief of surgery Tustin (Calif.) Community Hosp., 1974, also chief of staff, bd. dirs., 1974; pvt. practice med.-legal cons. Tustin, 1976; prof. surgery and oncology, St. Lucia (West Indies) Health Scis. U., 1982—; past chmn. bd. dirs. Monte Park Hosp., El Monte, Calif., 1975. Contbr. articles to med. jours. With USPHS, 1958-60. Fellow Internat. Biographical Assn., Internat. Coll. Surgeons, Am. Coll. Legal Medicine, Am. Soc. Cosmetic Breast Surgery, Inst. Bloodless Medicine and Surgery; mem. Soc. Head and Neck Surgeons, Am. Soc. Clin. Oncology, So. Calif. Acad. Clin. Oncology, Soc. Abdominal Surgeons, Am. Acad. Cosmetic Surgery, Soc. Liposuction Surgery, Internat. Soc. Cosmetic Surgery, Am. Soc. Law and Medicine, Orange County Oncologic Soc. (founder, pres. 1970), Am. Cancer Soc. (pres. Orange County chpt. 1971-73), Union Am. Physicians and Dentists (bd. dirs. Orange County chpt. 1988, pres. 1982-88, bd. dirs. Calif. Fedn. 1982-88), Safari Club. Office: 1706 E First St Ste D Tustin CA 92680-3883

SHIGENAKA, GARY, oceanographer; b. Lake Forest, Ill., Dec. 26, 1953; s. Joe Keichi and Mary Masuko (Shibata) S.; m. Amy Elizabeth Burk, June 10, 1988. BS, U. Wash., 1976, M Marine Affairs, 1987. Sci. aide rsch. and devel. Wash. Dept. Fisheries, Olympia, 1976; fisheries biologist fgn. fisheries observer program Nat. Marine Fisheries Svc., Seattle, 1977-78, biol. technician resource assessment and conservation div., 1978-79; chief biol. survey technician nat. ocean svc. NOAA, U.S. Dept. Commerce, Seattle, 1979-85; phys. scientist NOAA, U.S. Dept. Commerce, Washington, 1986-87; oceanographer NOAA, U.S. Dept. Commerce, Seattle, 1987—; tech. cons. Marine Rsch. Assocs., Seattle, 1982-86. Contbr. articles to profl. publs. Recipient Donald L. McKernan award Inst. for Marine Studies, U. Wash., 1988; Dean John A. Knauss Congl. fellow, 1986. Mem. Am. Inst. Fishery Rsch. Biologists, Oceanography Soc. (charter), Am. Geophys. Union, AAAS. Democrat. Home: 715-D Summit Ave E Seattle WA 98102 Office: US Dept Commerce NOAA 7600 Sand Point Way NE Seattle WA 98115

SHIMEK, DEAN TROY, mechanical engineer; b. Austin, Tex., Nov. 4, 1948; s. George Dean and Mary Ellen (White) S. AAS, Austin Community Coll., 1978, AS, 1978; BSME, U. Tex., 1982; postgrad., U. So. Calif., 1989. Mech. engr. USN Gage and Standards Ctr., Pomona, Calif., 1983-87, USN Warfare Assessment Ctr., Corona, Calif., 1987—. Chmn. Gage and Standards Ctr. savings bond drive USN, 1986; mgr. Navy Twilight Golf League, Pomona, 1985. Mem. Navy League (local chpt. program com., 1984), Precision Measurements Assn. (treas. 1987-88), Air and Space Smithsonian (charter), Ex-Student's Assn. U. Tex., Smithsonian Inst. (assoc.). Methodist. Home: 6846 Plum Way Rancho Cucamonga CA 91739 Office: USN NWAC C Code 306 Corona CA 91720-5000

SHIMMON, JOSEPH MALIEK, retired farmer, real estate developer; b. Urumia, Persia, Apr. 4, 1896; s. Joseph and Esther (George) S.; m. Florence Elma Taylor, Nov. 20, 1925; 4 children. Student, Columbia U., 1913-1915. With fgn. dept. Nat. City Bank, N.Y.C., 1920-23; farmer Turlock, Calif., 1923-25, Ripon, Calif., 1924-55; owner various rental properties Modesto, Calif., 1955—. 2d lt. USAAF, 1916-20. Mem. Elks. Republican. Episcopalian. Home: 3217 Whitehorse Ave Modesto CA 95350

SHIMOTSU, GARY RIKIKAZU, designer; b. Santa Monica, Calif., July 27, 1961; s. George and Yaeko (Yokome) S. BArch, U. So. Calif., 1985. Designer South Bay Enring. Corp., Palos Verdes Estates, Calif., 1984-88; graphic draftsman Am. Geotech. Co., Torrance, Calif., 1986—; project mgr. Donald E. Hendrickson, A.I.A., Palos Verdes Estates, 1987—. Mem. AIA (assoc.), Asian Am. Architects and Engrs., U. So. Calif. Archtl. Guild, Lions (pres. L.A. Internat. club 1988, Lion of Yr. award 1987). Republican.

SHINAR, THOMAS SHRAGA, travel company executive; b. Satu Mare, Roumania, Apr. 12, 1947; came to U.S., 1970; s. Yeno and Julianna (Fisch) S.; m. Miriam Csendes, Nov. 19, 1967; children: Ori, Doron. BA, Hebrew U., Jerusalem, 1970, MA, 1973. Dep. dir. Israel Tourist Office, N.Y.C., 1975-80; dir. Overseas div. Ministry Tourism, Jerusalem, 1970-75; sales mgr. Trade Winds Tours, Great Neck, N.Y., 1980-83, sales dir., 1983-87; v.p. sales and mktg. Trade Winds Tours, Newport Beach, Calif., 1987-89, Simplex Tours, 1989—. Served as cpl. Israeli Army, 1967. Decorated Six Day War award, 1967. Home: 5 Honeysuckle Irvine CA 92714

SHINBO, ROBERT, landscape architect; b. Seattle, June 20, 1948; s. Hachiro and May (Asai) S.; m. Sharron Chin, Feb. 25, 1968; 1 child, Roberta. B Landscape Architecture, U. Wash., 1971; M, Harvard U., 1973. Registered landscape architect Calif., Wash. Designer Sakuma James Peterson, Seattle, 1970-71; research asst. Harvard U., Cambridge, Mass., 1972-73; designer Sasaki Assocs., Watertown, Mass., 1973-76, SWA Group, Irvine, Calif., 1976-77; sr. assoc. Edaw Co., Newport Beach, Calif., 1977-78; prin. Robert Shinbo Assocs., Seattle, 1978—. Commr. Pike Place Market Hist. Commn., Seattle, 1988—; mem. King County Affordable Housing Task Force, 1986; fund-raiser U. Wash. College Architecture and Urban Planning. Recipient Nat. award Program for Energy Innovation of Wash. State Energy Office, 1986. Mem. Am. Soc. Landscape Architects (pres. Wash. chpt. 1985, Merit award 1986), Urban Land Inst., Am. Planning Assn., Lambda Alpha. Office: Robrt Shinbo Assocs 89 Virginia St Seattle WA 98101

SHINDLER, MERRILL KARSH, writer; b. N.Y.C., July 2, 1948; s. Joseph and Miriam (Karsh) S.; m. Deborah Ann Sroloff, Feb. 14, 1988. BA, CCNY, 1970; MFA, NYU, 1971. Entertainment editor San Francisco Bay Guardian, 1972-75; music editor Rolling Stone mag., San Francisco, 1976-79; head writer Am. Top 40/Casey's Top 40/America's Top Ten, L.A., 1979—; film critic Los Angeles mag., 1979—; restaurant critic Los Angeles Examiner, 1979—; editor Zagat Los Angeles Restaurant Survey, 1986—. Author: Best Los Angeles Restaurants Under $10, 1989; contbr. Gault-Millau Best of Los Angeles, 1988, Gault-Millau Best of Hong Kong, 1989; conbtr. articles to jours. Office: NAm Shindler 2226 Moreno Dr Los Angeles CA 90039

SHINN, DUANE, music publisher; b. Auburn, Calif., Nov. 13, 1938; s. Archie W. and Iola E. (Eisley) S.; m. Beverly J. Luman; children: Kurt, Kendra, Garin, Garth. BS, So. Oreg. State Coll., 1970, MS, 1977. Prin. Keyboard Workshop/Duane Shinn Pubs., Medford, Oreg., 1965—. Author, publisher numerous instructional audio and video cassettes on piano playing including Playing Standard Ballads on the Piano, Country-Western Piano, How to Transpose and Modulate, How to Accompany, How to Play Piano By Ear, Arranging Gospel Songs, numerous others; author: (book) Will Herk Go to Hell for Biting the Avon Lady. Office: Duane Shinn Publs Box 700 Medford OR 97501

SHINN, MARILYN CROSS, home economist; b. Balt., May 26, 1946; d. Eugene Grayson and Marian (Gosser) Cross. BS, Drexel U., 1968; secondary teaching cert., San Jose State U., 1970; elem. teaching credential, U. Calif., Santa Cruz, 1973; postgrad., U. Idaho. Tchr. Concord (Calif.) Sch. Dist., 1970-71, Loma Prieta Sch. Dist., Los Gatos, Calif., 1971-72, Redwood City (Calif.) Sch. Dist., 1972-78; instr. San Francisco State U., 1977-78; program coord. Boise (Idaho) Community Schs., 1979-80; extension home economist U. Idaho Extension Svc., Moscow, 1980—; cons., San Jose (Calif.) Sch. Dist., 1975-78, San Francisco Sch. Dist. 1978-79. Author home-study course; contbr. articles to profl. publs. Bd. dirs., El Ada Community Action Agy., Boise, 1986-88. Mem. Boise Home Economists (pres. 1988-89; Mary Campbell scholar 1987), Idaho Home Econs. Assn. (sec. 1985-87, pres. 1989—), Am. Home Econs. Assn., Idaho Assn. Extension Home Economists, Bay Dist Calif Home Econs. Assn. (pres. 1978), LWV (chair fed. agr. policy sect. Boise chpt. 1987-88), Soroptimists. Democrat. Roman Catholic. Home: 2284 Dalton Ln Boise ID 83704 Office: U Idaho Extension 5880 Glenwood St Boise ID 83714

SHINN, MICHAEL DENNA, pilot; b. Hutchinson, Kans., Dec. 22, 1950; s. Clarence Arthur and Mary Ellen (Hapgood) S.; m. Linda Ann Pace, Feb. 20,

1988. Student, Hutchinson Community Jr. Coll., Kans., 1969-71. Pilot Sunflower Equipment Co., Hutchinson, 1978-79, Internat. Homes, Hutchinson, 1979-81, Am. Fence Co., Phoenix, 1981-85; pilot, capt. Am. West Airlines, Phoenix, 1985—; instr. Am. West Airlines, Phoenix, 1986-88. Co-capt. Am. West Airlines Charter Dem. Pres. Campaign Tour, 1988. Home: 8563 E Garfield Scottsdale AZ 85257 Office: America West Airlines 222 So Mill Ave Tempe AZ 85281

SHINOMIYA, YAEKO, librarian; b. San Francisco, Apr. 15, 1936; d. Masao and Toshiko (Mukai) Iwawaki; m. Kazuichi Shinomiya, Dec. 20, 1958; children: Coco, Ken C. BA, U. Calif. Berkeley, 1957, MLS, 1960. Tchr. San Francisco Unified Sch. Dist., 1957-59; libr. Contra Costa County Library, Pleasant Hill, Calif., 1960-63, Solano County Library, Vallejo, Calif., 1973-79; asst. libr. The Tribune, Oakland, Calif., 1979-83, chief libr., 1983—. Named. Calif. Congress PTA's children's libr. fellow, 1959. Mem. Spl. Libr. Assn., Phi Beta Kappa. Office: The Tribune 409 13th St Oakland CA 94612

SHIPLETT, DARRELL DEE, librarian; b. Waco, Tex., July 22, 1952; s. Delona and Alyda Mae (Groth) S.; m. Cheryl Rebecca Roller, Sept. 3, 1976; children: Karmae, Jarrod. BS in Libr. Sci., Baylor U., 1975; MLS, UCLA, 1984. Cert. tchr., Tex. Media resource aid Waco Ind. Sch. Dist., 1976-78; tchr. Gholson (Tex.) Ind. Sch. Dist., 1978-79, 1st Christian Day Sch., Newhall, Calif., 1979-81; circulation supr. Calif. Inst. Arts, Valencia, 1981-84; tech. librarian Donald Clark Assocs., Edwards, Calif., 1984; rsch. libr. E.H. White & Co. NASA Ames-Dryden Flight Rsch. Facility Libr., Edwards, Calif., 1984-88; base libr. George AFB, Calif., 1988—. Republican. Baptist. Office: USAF Base Libr FL4812 George AFB CA 92334-5000

SHIPLEY, LILLIAN LOREEN, psychologist; b. Cleve., July 7, 1943; d. William and Dorothy A. (Haeberle) Fox; divorced; children: Trent Carter, Traci Christine. BS, Grand Canyon Coll., 1964; MA, No. Ariz. U., 1967; PhD, Ariz. State U., 1978. Lic. psychologist, Ariz. Exec. dir. Glenhaven, Glendale, Ariz., 1973-78, United Cerebral Palsy Assn. of Cen. Ariz., Phoenix, 1978-81; pvt. practice psychology Valley West Counseling Assocs., Phoenix, 1981—; cons. family violence prevention and clin. svcs. Ariz. Dept. of Econ. Security, Clifton and Morenci, 1982-86; mem. Greenlee County Task Force for Prevention Family Violence, 1982-84; mem. Community Coun. Bd., Phoenix, 1983-84; mem. policy com. Maricopa Coun. for Children, Youth and Family, 1982-84, chmn. 1983-84; bd. dirs. West Side Mental Health Svc., Glendale, 1980-83; mem. Greenlee County Task Force Prevention Family Violence, 1982-84; pres. Glendale Community Coun., bd. dirs. 1983. Adv. com. Ariz. Ctr. for Law in Pub. Interest, 1984—; bd. dirs. Westside Mental Health Svcs., 1980-83; ex-officio mem. Community Coun. Bd., 1983-84, Gov.'s Counc. for Children, Youth and Families, 1983-84; participant Ariz. Women's Town Hall, 1986, 88, panel chmn., 1987. Mem. Am. Psychol. Assn., Ariz. Psychol. Assn., Maricopa County Psychol. Assn., Soroptomists. Democrat. Mennonite. Office: Valley West Counseling Assocs 10000 N 31st Ave Ste A-104 Phoenix AZ 85051

SHIPP, LUCY ELIZABETH, real estate associate, teacher; b. N.Y.C., Oct. 26, 1940; d. Roy Ralph and Eloise (Barrangon) Yerger; m. Keifer P. Shipp II, Dec. 17, 1960 (div. Aug. 1985); children: Sharon Lynn, Catherine Ann, William Conrad. BS, U. Ariz., 1961; MEd, No. Ariz. U., 1984. Tchr. Yuma (Ariz.) Elem. Sch. Dist. I, 1965—; real estate assoc. Colleen Newman Realty, Inc., Yuma, 1985—. Mgr. Yuma 4-H Nat. Horse Show, 1970-86; sec. Yuma County Fair Bd., 1986-88; active Yuma County Planning and Zoning Commn., 1988—. Named Yuma County Tchr. Yr., 1989. Mem. Yuma Bd. Realtors (assoc.), Yuma Classroom Tchr. Assn., Ariz. Quarter Horse Breeders Assn., Am. Quarter Horse Assn., Am. Horse Shows Assn., Tri-Valley Horse Show Assn. (v.p. 1986-88, pres. 1989—), Phi Kappa Phi. Democrat. Home: 2275 Chico Ln Yuma AZ 85365 Office: Colleen Newman Realty Inc 2833 S Fourth Ave Yuma AZ 85364

SHIPPER, FRANK MARTIN, management educator, consultant, researcher; b. Martinsburg, W.Va., June 27, 1945; s. Paul Bishop and Lillian Foreman (Flagg) S.; m. Frances Irene Clarke, Dec. 19, 198l; children: Christopher, Ford, Jay. BSME, W.Va. U., 1968; MBA, U. Utah, 1973, PhD, 1978. Asst. prof. mgmt. Ariz. State U., Tempe, 1979-8l, assoc. prof., 1982—; human productivity cons. USN, Washington, 1980-8l; fair employment practices cons. numerous orgns. and lawyers, Ariz., 198l—; prin. investigator VA, Phoenix, 1986—. Author: Business Strategy for the Political Arena, 1984, Avoiding and Surviving Lawsuits, 1989; contbg. author: Strategic Planning and Management Handbook, 1987; contbr. numerous articles to profl. jours. Bd. dirs. East Valley Big Bros. Assn., Mesa, Ariz, 1983. Capt. USAF, 1968-72. Recipient outstanding paper award Southeastern Am. Inst. Decision Scis., 198l; Ariz. State U. grantee, 1979-82; Am. Assembly Collegiate Schs. Bus. fellow, 1980-8l. Mem. Internat. Assn. Quality Circles (bd. dirs. Phoenix chpt. 1983-85, pres. 1984-85), Am. Psychol. Assn., Acad. Mgmt., Decision Inst., Assn. for Quality and Participation, Morrison Inst. for Pub. Policy, Data Based Orgnl. Rsch. Group (co-founder, pres. 1979-80). Republican. Presbyterian. Office: Ariz State U Dept Mgmt Tempe AZ 85287

SHIPPER, TODD JEFFREY, communications executive; b. Detroit, Nov. 18, 1946; s. Norman N. Shipper and Evaline (Spring) Krasner; m. Sherry E. Brown, May 30, 1968 (div. 1969). AA, L.A. Valley Coll., 1970; student, Calif. State U., Northridge, 1970-72. Announcer various radio stas., 1967-73; salesman, mgr. Standard Shoes, Encino, Calif., 1973-76; asst. mgr. K-Mart, Westminster, Calif., 1976-77; salesman Contractors Lic. Sch., Van Nuys, Calif., 1977-80; dir. mktg. Columbia Sch. Broadcasting, Hollywood, Calif., 1980-84; owner, operator Nat. Broadcasting Sch., Las Vegas, Nev., Sacramento, Portland, Oreg., Seattle, 1984—; prin. Nat. Advt. Agy., Las Vegas, 1986—, Nat. Ednl. Cons., Las Vegas, 1986—. With USAF, 1965-67. Mem. Nat. Assn. Trade and Tech. Schs., Assn. Broadcasters. Democrat. Jewish. Office: Nat Broadcasting Sch 1771 E Flamingo Las Vegas NV 89119

SHIRAI, SCOTT, communications executive; b. Honolulu, June 5, 1942; s. George Yoshio and Thelma Takeko (Tominaga) M.; children: Todd, Kimberly, Lance, Lyle. MusB, U. Hawaii, 1983; exec. dir. news, reporter Sta. KHON-TV, Honolulu, 1974-81; asst. gen. mgr. Vanguard Investments, Berkeley, Calif., 1976-79; newscaster Sta. KPOI, Honolulu, 1979-80; news dir. Sta. KGU, Honolulu, 1981-82; owner Visual Perspectives, Kailua, Hawaii, 1981—; communications supr. Hawaiian Electric Co., Honolulu, 1982—. Bd. dirs., sec. Hawaii Com. For Freedom of Press, 1982—; bd. dirs. Mental Health Assn. in Hawaii, 1981—, Moanalua Gardens Found., 1981-84, Health and Community Services Council, 1982-86, Pohakupu Community Assn., 1984—, Friends of Father Damien, 1986; v.p. Mele Nani Singers, 1986—; mem. Mayors Adv. Com. on Mcpl. TV, 1987, Office of Hawaiian Affairs Pub. Relations Adv. Com., 1987, (all Honolulu). Recipient Jefferson award Honolulu Advertiser, 1985, Gold award Audio-Visual Producers Assn. Am., 1985, Audio-Visual Dept. of Yr. award Videography mag., 1986, Award of Excellence Nat. Hospice Orgn., 1987, Intre award Inst. Teleradial Atica Puerto Rico, Inc., 1988. Mem. Internat. TV Assn. (pres. 1983—), Am. Soc. Tng. and Devel., Am. Film Inst., AFTRA (bd. dirs. 1980-83), Pub. Relations Soc. Am., Hawaii Speakers Assn., Hawaii Film Bd., Honolulu Community Media Council. Clubs: Honolulu Press (bd. dirs. 1984—), Hui Luna (bd. dirs. 1986—) (Honolulu). Avocation: martial arts. Office: Hawaiian Electric Co 900 Richards St #214 Honolulu HI 96813

SHIRE, DAVID LEE, composer; b. Buffalo, July 3, 1937; s. Irving Daniel and Esther Miriam (Sheinberg) S.; m. Talia Rose Coppola, Mar. 29, 1970 (div.); 1 son, Matthew Orlando.; m. Didi Conn, Feb. 11, 1984. BA, Yale U., 1959. Film scores include The Conversation, 1974, The Taking of Pelham 1-2-3, 1974, Farewell, My Lovely, 1975, The Hindenburg, 1975, All the President's Men, 1977, Saturday Night Fever (adaptation and additional music), 1977, Norma Rae, 1979 (Acad. award for best original song It Goes Like It Goes), Only When I Laugh, 1981, The World According to Garp, 1982, Max Dugan Returns, 1983, 2010, 1984, Return to Oz, 1985, Short Circuit, 1986, 'Night, Mother, 1986, Vice Versa, 1988, Monkey Shines, 1988; TV scores include Raid on Entebbe, 1977 (Emmy nomination), The Defection of Simas Kudirka, 1978 (Emmy nomination), Do You Remember Love?, 1985 (Emmy nomination), Promise, 1986, Echoes in the Darkness, 1987, The Women of Brewster Place, 1989; theatre scores include: The Sap of Life, 1961, Graham Crackers, 1962, The Unknown Soldier and His Wife, 1967, How Do You Do, I Love You, 1968, Love Match, 1970, Starting Here, Starting Now, 1977, Baby, 1983 (Tony nominee best mus. and best original score); composer: Sonata for Cocktail Piano, 1965; recorded songs include Autumn, 1959, Starting Here, Starting Now, 1965, What About Today?, 1969, Manhattan Skyline, 1977, The Promise, 1978 (Acad. award nomination), It Goes Like It Goes, 1979 (Acad. award), With You I'm Born Again, 1979; albums include Saturday Night Fever, 1977 (Grammy award 1978), Starting Here, Starting Now, 1977 (Grammy nomination 1977), Baby, 1984, Return to Oz, 1985. With Army N.G., 1960-66. Mem. Composers and Lyricists Guild Am., Am. Fedn. Musicians, Broadcast Music Inc., Acad. Motion Picture Arts and Scis., Nat. Acad. Rec. Arts and Scis., Nat. Acad. TV Arts and Scis. Jewish. Office: care Laventhol & Horwath 2049 Century Pk E Ste 3700 Los Angeles CA 90067

SHIRE, HAROLD RAYMOND, legal educator, author; b. Denver, Nov. 23, 1910; s. Samuel Newport and Rose Betty (Herrmann) S.; m. Cecilia Goldhaar, May 9, 1973; children: Margaret, David, Donna, Darcy, Esti. MBA, Pepperdine U., 1972; LLD (hon.), 1975; JD, Southwestern U., L.A., 1974; M. in Liberal Arts, U. So. Calif., 1977; PhD in Human Behavior, U.S. Internat. U., San Diego, 1980. Bar: Calif. 1937, U.S. Dist. Ct. (so. dist.) Calif. 1939, U.S. Supreme Ct. 1978. Dep. dist. atty. L.A. County, Calif., 1937-38; asst. U.S. atty. So. Dist. Calif., L.A. and San Diego, Justice Dept., 1939-42; pvt. practice, L.A., 1946-56; pres., chmn. bd. Gen. Connectors Corp., U.S. and Eng., 1956-73; prof. mgmt. and law Pepperdine U., Malibu, Calif., 1974-75, U.S. Internat. U., San Diego, 1980-83; dir. Bestobell Aviation, Eng., 1970-74. Advisor U. S.C. Gerentology, Andrus Sch., pre-retirement tng., 1976-80; bd. dirs. Pepperdine U., 1974-80; nat. bd. govs. Union Orthodox Jewish Congregations Am., 1973—. With U.S. Army, 1942-46. Author: Cha No Yu and Symbolic Interactionism: Method of Predicting Japanese Behavior, 1980; The Tea Ceremony, 1984. Patentee aerospace pneumatics; invented flexible connectors. Decorated chevalier du vieux moulin (France); companion Royal Aero. Soc. (U.K.); recipient Tea Name Grand Master Soshitsu Sen XV Urasenke Sch., Kyoto, Japan, 1976. Mem. Am. Legion (svc. officer China #1). Republican. Office: PO Box 1352 Beverly Hills CA 90213

SHIREMAN, JOAN FOSTER, social work educator; b. Cleve., Oct. 28, 1933; d. Louis Omar and Genevieve (Duguid) Foster; m. Charles Howard Shireman, Mar. 18, 1967; 1 child, David Louis. BA, Radcliffe Coll., 1956; MA, U. Chgo., 1959, PhD, 1968. Caseworker N.H. Children's Aid Soc., Manchester, 1959-61; dir. research Chgo. Child Care Soc., 1968-72; assoc. prof. U. Ill., Chgo., 1972-85; prof. Portland (Oreg.) State U., 1985—; research cons. child welfare orgns., Ill., 1968-85; mem. adv. bd. Children's Service Div., Salem, Oreg., 1985—; lectr. U. Chgo., 1968-72. Co-author: Care and Commitment: Foster Parent Adoption Decisions, 1985; mem. editorial bd. Jour. Sch. Social Work, 1978-81; contbr. chpts. to books and articles to profl. jours. Bd. dirs. Oreg. chpt. Nat. Assn. for Prevention of Child Abuse, 1985-87. Grantee HEW, 1980-82, Chgo. Community Trust, 1982-86. Mem. Nat. Assn. Social Workers, AAUP, Citizens for Children, Acad. Cert. Social Workers, Council on Social Work Edn., Phi Beta Kappa. Home: 2535 SW Sherwood Dr Portland OR 97201 Office: Portland State U Grad Sch Social Work PO Box 751 Portland OR 97202

SHIRKEY, MARY PAMELA, fraternal organization administrator; b. Sacramento, Oct. 8, 1940; d. Royal George and Mary Cecilia (Flanagan) Brooke; m. James Herbert Shirkey Jr., Oct. 7, 1961; children: Erliene Cathrine, Brooke Ellen. Grad. High Sch., Sparks, Nev., 1958. Sec. to supt. Stone & Webster Engring. Co., Storey County, Nev., 1971-76; exec. sec. Holiday Hotel/Casino, Reno, 1979-83, Dolven, Larson Architects, Reno, 1977-79, JBA Cons. Engrs., Reno, 1979-83; adminstrv. asst. Multiple Sclerosis Soc., Reno, 1984; asst. mgr. Switzers, Reno, 1985-86; sales mgr. Holiday Hotel/Casino, Reno, 1986-87; pres. elect Supreme Emblem Club of U.S.A., nationwide, 1988—. Editor: (newsletter) Easter Seals Orgn., 1970-71. Mem. Supreme Emblem Club of U.S.A. (supreme rec. sec. 1981-82, supreme 4th v.p. 1984-85, supreme 3d v.p. 1985-86, supreme 2d v.p. 1986-87, supreme pres. elect 1987-88), Reno Emblem Club No. 372 (pres. 1975-76). Home: 3657 Willowdale Dr Sparks NV 89431

SHIRLEY, DAVID ARTHUR, laboratory director; b. North Conway, N.H., Mar. 30, 1934; m. Virginia Schultz, June 23, 1956; children: David N., Diane, Michael, Eric, Gail. BS, U. Maine, 1955, ScD (hon.), 1978; PhD in Chemistry, U. Calif.-Berkeley, 1959; D honoris causa, Free U. Berlin, 1987. With Lawrence Radiation Lab. (now Lawrence Berkeley Lab.), U. Calif., Berkeley, 1958—, assoc. dir., head materials and molecular research div., 1975-80, dir., 1980—, lectr. chemistry, 1959-60, asst. prof., 1960-64, assoc. prof., 1964-67, prof., 1967—, vice chmn. dept. chemistry, 1968-71, chmn. dept. chemistry, 1971-75. Contbr. over 300 rsch. articles. NSF fellow, 1955-58, 66-67, 70; recipient Ernest O. Lawrence award AEC, 1972, Humboldt award (sr. U.S. scientist), 1988, Dr.rer.nat. hc. Free Univ., 1987; listed by Sci. Citation Index as one of the world's 300 most cited scientists for work published during 1965-78. Fellow Am. Phys. Soc.; mem. Nat. Acad. Scis., Am. Chem. Soc., AAAS, Am. Acad. Arts and Scis., Sigma Xi, Tau Beta Pi, Sigma Pi Sigma, Phi Kappa Phi. Office: Lawrence Berkeley Lab 1 Cyclotron Rd Berkeley CA 94720

SHIRLEY, FEHL LORAYNE, educator; b. St. Louis, Nov. 28, 1918; s. Fehl Jesse and Myrtle (McGregor) S. BA, Hofstra U., 1943; MA, Wash. U., 1955; PhD, U. Ariz., 1966. Tchr. Bristol Sch., Webster Groves, Mo., 1953-55, Julia Keen Sch., Tucson, 1955-56, Mansfield Jr. High Sch., Tucson, 1956-59; tchr./counselor Rincon High Sch., Tucson, 1959-67; asst. prof. Ferris State U., Big Rapids, Mich., 1967-68; assoc. prof. U. Wis., Eau Claire, 1968-69; prof. Calif. State U., Northridge, 1969—; cons. L.A. Pub. Schs., 1972-73. Contbr. articles to profl. jours. and chpts. to textbooks. Recipient Outstanding Svc. award San Fernando Valley Reading Coun., 1971-73, Cert. of Appreciation So. Calif. Assn. of Childhood Edn., 1985. Mem. Internat. Reading Assn., Nat. Coun. of English Tchrs., Calif. Reading Assn. Democrat. Club: Calif. Writers (L.A.). Home: 8811 Canoga Ave Canoga Park CA 91304 Office: Calif State U 18000 Nordhoff St Northridge CA 91330

SHIRTCLIFF, JOHN DELZELL, oil jobber; b. Roseburg, Oreg., Mar. 2, 1948; s. Henry Marion and Sheila Nell (Delzell) S.; m. Connie Lee Cantrell, June 13, 1975; children: Darcie, Danielle, Andrew. BS, Oregon State U., 1970. Owner, mgr. Shirtcliff Oil Co., Myrtle Creek, Oreg., 1971—. Engr. Myrtle Creek (Oreg.) Vol. Fire Dept., 1971—; mem. Rep. Cen. Com., Roseburg, Oreg., 1982-88; chmn. Umpqua Community Coll. Budget Com., Roseburg, 1983—; bd. dirs. Mercy Hospice Roseburg, 1988—. 2nd lt. U.S. Army, 1970-71. Named Citizen of Year, Myrtle Creek City, 1986, Vol. of Year, Douglas County C. of C., 1987. Mem. Petroleum Marketers Assn. Am. (dir. Oreg. 1988), Oreg. Petroleum Marketers Assn. (v.p. legis. chmn. 1986, pres. 1987, PMAA dir. 1988), Lions, Elks, Masons. Republican. Office: Shirtcliff Oil Co 283 SW Western Ave PO Box 6003 Myrtle Creek OR 97457

SHIRVANI, HAMID, college dean; b. Tehran, Iran, Oct. 20, 1950; came to U.S., 1974, naturalized, 1986; s. Majid and Taji (Granpisheh) S.; m. Diane Lillian Wilk, Mar. 21, 1988. Diploma in architecture, Poly. of Cen. London, 1974; MArch, Pratt Inst., 1975; MA, Harvard U., 1978, Princeton U., 1979; PhD, Princeton U., 1980. Project designer London Borough of Barnet, 1973-74; prin. Techonokam Inc., Tehran and N.Y.C., 1975-77; asst. prof. architecture Pa. State U., 1979-82; prof., dir. grad. studies SUNY, Syracuse, 1982-85; prof., dir. Sch. Urban Planning and Devel. U. Louisville, 1985-86; dean Sch. of Architecture and Planning U. Colo., Denver, 1986—; prof., dir. Sch. Urban Planning and Devel. U. Louisville, 1985-86; prof. architecture U. Colo., Denver, 1986—, dean Sch. Architecture and Planning, 1986—. Author: Urban Design: A Comprehensive Reference, 1981, Urban Design Review, 1981, Urban Design Process, 1985; editor Urban Design Review, 1982-85, Urban Design & Preservation Quarterly, 1985-88; mem. editorial bd. The Jour. of Archtl. Edn., 1988-91, Avant Garde, 1988-91, Art & Architecture, 1974-78Jour. of Am. Planning Assn., 1982-88. Recipient Gold Medal in Architecture and Urbanism. Fellow Royal Geog. Soc.; mem. Archtl. Assn., Am. Soc. Landscape Architects, Am. Inst. Cert. Planners, Am. Planning Assn. (chmn. Urban Design Div. 1987-89, Disting. award 1984, Urban Design award 1985), Denver Athletic Club, Sigma Xi, Omicron Delta Epsilon, Tau Sigma Delta (Silver medal 1988), Tau Beta Pi, Sigma Lambda Alpha. Office: U Colo Sch Architecture & Planning 1200 Larimer St Denver CO 80204-5300

SHISHIDO, CALVIN M., private investigator; b. Honolulu, Aug. 24, 1933; s. Isamu and Kane (Seto) S.; children: Dale, Neala. BS, Florence State, 1961. Spl. agt. IRS, Pitts., 1962-65, FBI, Washington, 1965-84; pvt. investigator Honolulu, 1987—; spl. asst. to deputy dir. Harbors Div Dept. of Transp., Hawaii. Sgt. USAF, 1952-57. Mem. Soc. Former Spl. Agts. of FBI (chpt. chmn. Honolulu 1987-88), Lions (program chmn. San Francisco 1970-71), Jr. C. of C.

SHIVELY, JOHN TERRY, business executive; b. Middletown, N.Y., July 1, 1943; s. Marvin Rathfelder and Esther (Manning) Westervelt; adopted child, Harold Eugene Shively; B.A., U. N.C., 1965. Vol. worker VISTA, Bethel, Yakutat, and Fairbanks, Alaska, 1965-68; health planner Greater Anchorage Area Community Action Agy., 1968-69; health cons. Alaska Fedn. Natives, Anchorage, 1969; dep. dir. Rural Alaska Community Action Program, Anchorage, 1969-70, exec. dir., 1971-72; exec. v.p. Alaska Fedn. Natives, Anchorage, 1972-75; v.p. ops. NANA Regional Corp., Kotzebue, Alaska, 1975-77, NANA Devel. Corp., Anchorage, 1977-82, sr. v.p., 1982-83; chief of staff to gov. of Alaska, 1983-85; cons. bus. and govt., 1985-86; sr. v.p. NANA Regional Corp., Inc., 1986—, chmn., chief exec. officer United Bar Corp., United Bank Alaska, 1987-88; chmn. Alaska State Bd. Game, 1983-84. dir. Unicorp. Inc., United Bank of Alaska. Mem. Greater Anchorage Area Comprehensive Health Plan Council, 1969-75, chmn., 1969-75; founding mem. bd. dirs. Alaska Pub. Interest Research Group, 1974-75, 86—, chmn. 1987—; mem. Gov.'s Rural Affairs Council, 1971-76, Gov.'s Manpower Commn., 1971, Greater Anchorage Health Bd., 1969-75, Alaska Pipeline Edn. Com., 1973-74; vestry All St. Episcopal Ch., 1988—; bd. regents U. Alaska, 1979-83. Mem. Alaska Fedn. Natives. Democrat. Episcopalian. Home: PO Box 101758 Anchorage AK 99510 Office: NANA Regional Corp 4706 Harding Dr Anchorage AK 99503

SHIVELY, STEPHEN DENNIS, military officer, computer science educator; b. Riverside, Calif., Nov. 13, 1954; s. Deane S. and Jeanne D. (Swindells) S. BS in Computer Sci., Pa. State U., 1977; MS in Computer Systems, Boston U., 1983. Commd. 2d lt. USAF, 1977, advanced through grades to maj., 1988; test dir. Electronics Systems div. USAF, Bedford, Mass., 1977-79, project mgr., 1979-81; mgr. field program USAF Systems Command, Kaiserslantern, Fed. Republic of Germany, 1981-83; mgr. program USAF Space Command, Colorado Springs, Colo., 1983—; instr. computer sci. Regis Coll., Colorado Springs, 1984—. Mem. Smithsonian Air and Space Soc., IEEE (affiliate). Lutheran. Home: 8261 Caravel Dr Colorado Springs CO 80920 Office: Hdqrs Air Force Space Command Peterson AFB CO 80914

SHKURKIN, EKATERINA VLADIMIROVNA (KATIA SHKURKIN), social worker; b. Berkeley, Calif., Nov. 20, 1955; d. Vladimir Vladimirovich and Olga Ivanovna (Lisenko) S. Student, U. San Francisco, 1972-73; BA, U. Calif., Berkeley, 1974-77; MSW, Columbia U., 1977-79; postgrad., Union Grad. Sch., 1986. Cert. police instr. domestic violence, Alaska. Social worker Tolstoy Found., N.Y.C., 1978-79, adminstr., 1979-80; program supr. Rehab. Mental Health Ctr., San Jose, Calif., 1980-81; dir. service counselor Kodiak (Alaska) Crisis Ctr., 1981-82; domestic violence counselor Abused Women's Aid in Crisis, Anchorage, 1982-85; pvt. practice social work specializing in feminist therapy Susitna Therapy Ctr., Anchorage, 1985—; field instr. Abused Women's Aid in Crisis, Anchorage, 1983-88; expert witness Anchorage Mcpl. Cts., 1982—; interim faculty U. Alaska, Anchorage, summer 1985, fall 1988—, LaVerne U., Anchorage, spring 1986, fall, 1987, summer 1988, winter 1988—. Coordinator Orthodox Christian Fellowship, San Francisco, 1972-76; pub. speaker Abused Women's Aid in Crisis, Anchorage, 1982—; active nat. and local election campaigns, 1968—. Mem. Nat. Assn. Social Workers (cert.). Democrat. Russian Orthodox. Home: 3605 Arctic Blvd #768 Anchorage AK 99503-5704

SHLADOVER, STEVEN ELLIOT, transportation executive; b. N.Y.C., Feb. 15, 1950; s. Joel and Ida Shladover. SB, MIT, 1972, SM, 1974, ScD, 1978. Research asst. MIT, Cambridge, Mass., 1976-78, lectr., 1978; staff engr. Systems Control, Inc., Palo Alto, Calif., 1978-81; sr. engr. Systems Control Tech., Inc., Palo Alto, 1981-84, program mgr., 1984-86, dir. CAE systems, 1986, mgr., transp. systems engr., 1987—. Assoc. editor Jour. of Dynamic Systems, Measurement and Control, 1980-85; contbr. articles to profl. jours. Nat. mem. Met. Opera Guild, N.Y.C., 1973—; mem. San Francisco Opera Guild, 1979—, Mus. Soc., San Francisco, 1979, Common Cause, Washington, 1983—. Named one of the Outstanding Young Men of Am., U.S. Jaycees, 1983; fellow NSF, 1972-75. Mem. Am. Soc. Mech. Engrs. (assoc. editor 1980-85, program chmn. dynamic systems and control div. 1986, honors com. 1988—, sec. 1989—), Transp. Research Bd. (com. on new transp. systems and tech. 1988), MIT Alumni Assn.. Democrat. Office: Systems Control Tech Inc 2300 Geng Rd Palo Alto CA 94303

SHLENKER, SIDNEY L., professional basketball team executive. Attended, Tulane Univ. Former exec. v.p., chief oper. officer Astrodomain Corp., Houston, Tex.; founder PACE Mgmt. Corp.; sr. chmn. Allied Bank West Loop, Houston, Tex.; chmn. Grant Broadcasting System, Inc.; former pres. Houston Astros baseball club; former vice-chmn. Houston Rockets basketball club; majority owner, chmn. Denver Nuggets basketball team, 1985-89. Office: care Denver Nuggets McNichols Sports Arena PO Box 4658 Denver CO 80204 also: Allied Bank West PO Box 4401 Houston TX 77210 *

SHOAIB, KEMAL, bank executive; b. Jaunpur, India, Nov. 5, 1936; came to U.S., 1986; s. Mohammed and Iffat (Ara) S.; m. Tanveer Fatima Raza, Sept. 3, 1965; children: Salman Ali, Faizan Ali, Samia Zehra. B in Chemical Engring., Catholic U. Am., 1959; MS in Chemical Engring., MIT, 1960. Dir., plant mgr. Wyeth Labs. Pakistan Ltd., Lahore, Pakistan, 1960-66; dir., gen. mgr. Chemical Cons. Pakistan Ltd., 1966-69; exec. dir., exec. v.p. Commerce Bank Ltd., Pakistan, 1969-74; gen. mgr., exec. in charge Bank of Credit and Commerce Internat.-SA, London, 1974-86; chief exec. officer, chmn. bd. dirs. Independence Bank, Encino, Calif., 1986—. Dir. Boys Club of San Fernando Valley, Los Angeles, 1988, Shakespeare Globe Theatre, Los Angeles, 1988. Honoree Boys Club of San Fernando Valley, 1987. Clubs: Jonathan (los Angeles); Sind (Karachi, Pakistan). Office: Independence Bank 15910 Ventura Blvd #1400 Encino CA 91436

SHOCKLEY, WILLIAM BRADFORD, physicist, emeritus educator; b. London, Feb. 13, 1910; (Am. parents); s. William Hillman and May (Bradford) S.; m. Jean A. Bailey, 1933 (div. 1955); children: Alison, William Alden, Richard Condit; m. Emmy Lanning, 1955. B.S., Calif. Inst. Tech., 1932; Ph.D., M.I.T., 1936; Sc.D. (hon.), Rutgers U., 1956, U. Pa., 1955, Gustavus Adolphus Coll., Minn., 1963. Teaching fellow M.I.T., 1932-36; mem. tech. staff Bell Telephone Labs., 1936-42, 45, became dir. transistor physics research, 1954; dir. Shockley Semicondr. Lab.; pres. Shockley Transistor Corp., 1958-60; cons. Shockley Transistor unit Clevite Transistor, 1960-65; lectr. Stanford U., 1958-63, Alexander M. Poniatoff prof. engring. sci. and applied sci., 1963-75, prof. emeritus, 1975—; exec. cons. Bell Telephone Labs., 1965-75; dep. dir. research, weapons systems evaluation group Dept. Def., 1954-55; expert cons. Office Sec. War, 1944-45; vis. lectr. Princeton U., 1946; vis. prof. Calif. Inst. Tech., 1954-55; sci. adv., policy council Joint Research and Devel. Bd., 1947-49; sr. cons. Army Sci. Adv. Panel, 1951-63; dir. research Anti-submarine Welfare Ops. Research Group USN, 1942-44; researcher on energy bands of solids, ferromagnetic domains, plastic properties of metals; semicondr. theory applied to devices and device defects such as disclosations; fundamentals of electromagnetic energy and momentum; mental tools for sci. thinking, ops. research on human quality problems. Author: Electrons and Holes in Semiconductors, 1950, (with W.A. Gong) Mechanics, 1966; editor: Imperfections of Nearly Perfect Crystals, 1952; holder over 90 patents; inventor junction transistor. Recipient medal for Merit, 1946; Air Force citation of honor, 1951; U.S. Army cert. of appreciation, 1953; co-winner (with John Bardeen and Walter H. Brattain) Nobel Prize in Physics, 1956; Wilhelm Exner medal Oesterreichischer Gewerbeverein Austria, 1963; Holley medal ASME, 1963; Calif. Inst. Tech. Alumni Disting. Service award, 1966; NASA cert. of appreciation Apollo 8, 1969; Public Service Group Achievement award NASA, 1969; named to Inventor's Hall of Fame, 1974, Calif. Inventor's Hall of Fame, 1983, Infomart Info. Processing Hall of Fame, Dallas, 1988. Fellow AAAS; mem. Am. Phys. Soc. (O.E. Buckley prize 1953), Nat. Acad. Sci. (Comstock prize 1954), IEEE (Morris Liebmann prize 1952, Gold medal, 25th anniversary of transistor 1972, Medal of Honor 1980), Sigma Xi, Tau Beta Pi. Home: 797

Esplanada Way Stanford CA 94305 Office: Stanford U Stanford Electronics Labs Dept Elec Engring McC 202 Stanford CA 94305

SHOCTOR, JOSEPH HARVEY, barrister, producer, civic worker; b. Edmonton, Alta., Can., Aug. 18, 1922. BA, LLB, U. Alta., 1946, LLD (hon.), 1981; diploma in theatre adminstrn. (hon.), Grant McEwan Coll., 1986. Barrister, solicitor, sr. ptnr. Shoctor, Starkman & Ferguson, Edmonton; bd. dirs. 1st City Trust, 1st City Fin. Corp., Vancouver, B.C., Saxony Motor Hotel Ltd., Westward Motor Inn, Citadel Mortgage Corp. Ltd.; pres., exec. officer Harvey Holdings Ltd.; chmn. bd. dirs. Edmonton Downtown Development Corp. Founder, contbr. Downtown Edmonton newspaper; producer Broadway plays including Peter Pan, 1965, Henry, Sweet Henry, 1967, Billy, 1969, Hamlet, 1969; founder, pres., exec. producer, bldg. chmn., campaign chmn. Citadel Theater; producer Circle 8 Theatre, Civic Opera, Red Cross Entertainment; panelist pub. affairs talk show and sports forum. Active United Community Fund, 1968—; chmn. Downtown Devel. Corp., Edmonton, 1986; mem. Edmonton Jewish Welfare Bd.; past pres. Edmonton Jewish Community Council; past nat. sec. Federated Zionist Orgn.; past nat. v.p. United Israel Appeal, Inc.; past bd. dirs. Can. Council Jewish Welfare Funds; chmn. div. Brit. Commonwealth Games Found., 1978; bd. govs. Nat. Theatre Sch. of Can., officer Order of Can., 1986. Inducted into Cultural Hall of Fame, 1987; named Man of Hr., Sta. CFRN-TV, 1966, Citizen of Yr., B'nai B'rith, 1966, one of Twelve Top Albertans of the 70's, The Alberta Report; recipient Performing Arts award City of Edmonton, 1972, Theatre Arts Achievement award Province of Alta., 1975, Prime Minister's medal State of Israel, 1978, Builder of Community award City of Edmonton, 1979, Queen's Silver Jubilee medal, 1977, City of Edmonton Silver Ribbon award, 1985; The Shoctor Theatre named in his honor, 1976; Officer of the Order of Can., 1986; Edmonton Cultural Hall of Fame, 1987. Mem. Edmonton C. of C. Clubs: The Edmonton, The Centre, Eskimo Football (founder, past sec.-mgr.). Office: Shoctor Starkman & Ferguson, 1800 10104 103rd Ave, Edmonton, AB Canada T5J 4A4

SHOEMAKER, CAMERON DAVID JAMES, federal agency official; b. Honolulu, Dec. 15, 1940; s. John James and Belle Bird (Kellogg) S.; m. Catherine LaMayne Prevost, May 23, 1966 (div. 1969); 1 child, David James; m. Leona Martha Wohlwend, May 18, 1972; 1 child, Jennifer Lee. BA in Polit. Sci., The Citadel, 1963; MA in History, San Jose State U., 1972; postgrad., U. San Francisco. Commd. 2d lt. U.S. Army, 1963, advanced through grades to maj., 1971; fgn. area officer U.S. Army, U.S., Korea, Germany, 1972-84; ret. U.S. Army, 1984; mgmt. analyst Def. Lang. Inst., Monterey, Calif., 1985; ednl. tech. project mgr. Def. Lang. Inst., Monterey, 1985-86, dir. info. mgmt., 1986—; instr., Chapman Coll., Monterey, 1982-84, Monterey Inst., 1987; chmn. Asian Employment Program Com., Monterey, 1983-84; guest lectr., Naval Postgrad. Sch., Monterey, 1986-87; mem. Handicapped Individual Program Com., Monterey, 1986—. Contbr. articles to various publs. Pres., Creekside Community Assn., Salinas, Calif., 1985-86; mem. County Svc. Area Adv. Bd., Salinas, 1985-87, Flood Control Dist. Planning Com., Salinas, 1986-87. Decorated Silver Star medal. Mem. Royal Asiatic Soc., Fed. Mgrs.' Assn., Monterey Peninsula Scottish Soc. (treas. 1986—). Republican. Roman Catholic. Home: 22315 Capote Dr Salinas CA 93908 Office: Def Lang Inst ATFL-IM Presidio of Monterey CA 93944-5006

SHOEMAKER, HAROLD LLOYD, infosystem specialist; b. Danville, Ky., Jan. 3, 1923; s. Eugene Clay and Amy (Wilson) S.; A.B., Berea Coll., 1944; postgrad. State U. Ia., 1943-44, George Washington U., 1949-50, N.Y. U., 1950-52; m. Dorothy M. Maddox, May 11, 1947. Research physicist State U., Ia., 1944-45, Frankford Arsenal, Pa., 1945-47; research engr. N.Am. Aviation, Los Angeles, 1947-49, Jacobs Instrument Co., Bethesda, 1949-50; asso. head systems devel. group The Teleregister Corp., N.Y.C., 1950-53; mgr. electronic equipment devel. sect., head planning for indsl. systems div. Hughes Aircraft Co., Los Angeles, 1953-58; dir. command and control systems lab. Bunker-Ramo Corp., Los Angeles, 1958-68, v.p. Data Systems, 1968-69, corp. dir. data processing, 1969-75; tech. staff R & D Assocs., Marina Del Rey, Calif., 1975-85; info. systems cons., 1985—. Served with AUS, 1945-46. Mem. IEEE. Patentee elec. digital computer. Home: PO Box 3385 Granada Hills CA 91344

SHOEMAKER, SUSAN INEZ, city official; b. Albany, Ky., Feb. 10, 1940; d. John E. Cooper and Margaret (Lee) Arnold; m. Russell L. Shoemaker, June 21, 1958; 1 child, Steven Michael. BS, U. Ariz., 1965, MEd, 1967; EdD, Internat. Grad. Sch., St. Louis, 1983. Cert. tchr. Head bus. dept. Sahuarita (Ariz.) High Sch., 1965-68; tchr. Palo Verde High Sch., Tucson, Ariz., 1968-71; instr. U. Alaska, College, 1971-74, So. Oreg. State Coll., Ashland, 1974-76; instr. TV Sta. KOLB TV, Medford, Oreg., 1974-76; asst. prof. Iowa Western Community Coll., Shenandoah, Iowa, 1976-79; head med. sec. program Coll. Health Sci., Ministry of Health, Bahrain, Arabian Gulf, 1980-84; curriculum specialist Coll. Health Sci., Ministry of Health, Bahrain, 1984-87; curriculum/tng. coord. City of Phoenix Aviation Dept., 1988—; workshop facilitator WHO, 1985-86; curriculum/tng. cons., Bahrain, 1984-87. Author: Introduction to Business for High School Freshmen, 1969, Joy of Exercise, 1975; co-author: Teaching Strategies for Physicians, 1985. Recipient Outstanding Employee and Merit Increase award Ministry of Health, Coll. Health Scis., Bahrain, 1983. Mem. Am. Soc. Trainers and Developers, Internat. Women's Assn. (v.p. 1986-87), Beta Sigma Phi. Democrat. Mem. United Ch. of Christ. Home: 8207 E Redwing Rd Scottsdale AZ 85253 Office: City of Phoenix Aviation 3400 Sky Harbor Blvd Phoenix AZ 85034

SHOEMAKER, WILLIAM EDWARD, financial executive; b. Charleston, W.Va., Sept. 17, 1945; s. Robert Edward and Janet Elizabeth (Hoglund) S. BBA, U. Notre Dame, 1967. Assoc. buyer Proctor & Gamble, Cin., 1971; gen. mgr. Eastwind Inc., Anchorage, 1972-73; pres., operator Golden Horn Lodge, Inc., Bristol Bay, Alaska, 1973-79; treas. Hawley Resource Group, Inc., Anchorage, 1979-88; treas., chief fin. officer Golden Zone Resources, Inc., Campbell, Calif., 1988—; ptnr. Resort Mgmt. Corp., Anchorage, 1987—; bd. dirs. Golden Zone Resources, Inc. Bd. dirs. Anchorage Econ. Devel. Corp., 1988—. Served to lt. (j.g.) USN, 1967-71. Mem. Alaska Miners Assn., Alaska Vistors Assn., Quarter Deck Club (Anchorage). Republican. Home: 4811 Bishop Way Anchorage AK 99508 Office: Golden Zone Resources Inc 3001 S Winchester Blvd #12 Campbell CA 95008

SHOEN, EDWARD JOSEPH, transportation, insurance companies executive. s. Leonard and Anna (Carty) S. MBA, Harvard U. Pres., chmn. Amerco a Nev. Corp., Phoenix. Office: Amerco a Nev Corp 2727 N Central Ave Phoenix AZ 85004 *

SHOEN, PAUL, transportation company executive. s. Leonard and Anna (Carty) S. Pres. U-Haul Internat. Inc., Phoenix. Office: U-Haul Internat Inc 2727 N Central Ave Phoenix AZ 85004 *

SHOLLY, KATHLEEN ANN, real estate appraiser; b. Milw., Apr. 9, 1957; d. Russell Edward and Katherine Barbara (Pietuch) Jacobsen; m. Kirk Alan Sholly, Sept. 3, 1977; children: Christine Renee, Rebecca Anne, Amy Mae. Grad. high sch., Phoenix. Exec. sec. Glen's Appraiser Svc., Glendale, Ariz., 1976-78; exec. sec., jr. landscape designer L.K. Wong Sprinklers/Westside Landscaping Co., Glendale, 1978-80; jr. landscape designer Landscaping Co., Glendale, 1980-81; appraiser Appraisal Scis., Ltd., Phoenix, 1982-88, John L. Loper, A.S.A., Phoenix, 1985—, Southwest Right of Way Svcs., Inc., Phoenix, 1988—; cons., Glen's Appraisal Svcs., Phoenix, 1985—. Mem. Native Seeds/SEARCH. Mem. Internat. Right of Way Assn. (newsletter editor 1988—), Am. Soc. Appraisers, Urban Land Inst. Republican. Office: Ste 135 10050 N 25th Ave Phoenix AZ 85021

SHOLTIS, JOSEPH ARNOLD, JR., nuclear safety engineer, military officer; b. Monongahela, Pa., Nov. 28, 1948; s. Joseph and Gladys (Frye) S.; m. Cheryl Anita Senchur, Dec. 19, 1970; children: Christian Joseph, Carole Lynne. BS in Nuclear Engring. (Disting. Mil. Grad.), Pa. State U., 1970; diploma Air Univ., 1977; MS in Nuclear Engring., U. N.Mex., 1977, postgrad., 1978-80. Lic. sr. reactor operator NRC, 1980-84. Mathematician, statistician, mine safety analyst U.S. Bur. Mines, Pitts., 1968-70; commd. 2d lt. U.S. Air Force, 1970, advanced through grades to lt. col. 1988; nuclear research officer Fgn. Tech. Div., U.S. Air Force, Wright-Patterson AFB, Ohio, 1971-74; chief space nuclear safety sect. Air Force Weapons Lab., Kirtland AFB, N.Mex., 1974-78; mil. mem. tech. staff, project officer Sandia Nat. Labs., Albuquerque, 1978-80; chief radiation sources div., reactor facility dir. Armed Forces Radiobiology Rsch. Inst., Bethesda, Md., 1980-84; program mgr. SP 100 space reactor power system devel. program U.S. Dept. Energy, Germantown, Md., 1984-87; chief analysis and evaluation br., nuclear power and sources div. Directorate Nuclear Surety, Kirtland AFB, N.Mex., 1987—; space shuttle nuclear payload safety assessment officer Air Force Weapons Lab., Kirtland AFB, 1976-78; instr. med. effects nuclear weapons Armed Forces Radiobiology Rsch. Inst., Bethesda, 1980-85, mem. reactor and radiation facility safety com., 1980-85; faculty, lectr. Uniformed Svcs. Univ. Health Scis., Bethesda, 1982-87; chmn. Power System Subpanel Intragency Nuclear Safety Rev. Panel assessments of Galileo and Ulysses space missions, 1988—; instr. Inst. for Space Nuclear Power Studies U. N.Mex., 1987—. Author: (with others) LMFBR Accident Delineation, 1980, Military Radiobiology, 1987; also articles, chpts. in books. U.S. del., tech. advisor UN Working Group on Nuclear Power Sources in Outer Space, 1984-88; mem. Multimegawatt Space Reactor Power Project safety adv. com., 1988—; pres. Fort Detrick Cath. Parish Community, Md., 1984. Decorated Def. Meritorious Service medal (2), Air Force Commendation medal (3), Nat. Def. Service medal, U.S. Army Reactor Comdr. Badge. Mem. Am. Nuclear Soc. (Best Paper 1977), ASME, AIAA, AAAS, N.Y. Acad. Scis., Sigma Xi. Republican. Avocations: hunting, fishing, baseball, camping, motorcycle touring. Office: Directorate Nuclear Surety Detachment I Air Force Inspection and Safety Ctr Kirtland AFB NM 87117-5000

SHOMER, JON ARTHUR, venture capital company executive; b. Cleve., June 28, 1943; s. John Arthur and Drusilla (Spece) S.; m. Marilyn Gale Lebold, June 13, 1964; children: Jon Scott, Robert Bradley. BS, Case Inst. Technology, 1965; MS, Case Western Res. U., 1966. Mem. advanced prodn. team computer div. GE, Phoenix, 1966-69; founder mem. Capex Corp. (now Computer Assocs. Inc.), Phoenix, 1969-83; sr. v.p., dir. Terak Corp. (now Calcomp), Phoenix, 1983-85; spl. ltd. ptnr. HMS Capital, Menlo Park, Calif., 1983—, HMS Capital Ptnrs., Menlo Park, 1983—; pres., chief exec. officer, bd. dirs. Multi-Systems Inc., Phoenix, 1986-87; chief exec. officer Tech. Enterprises, Phoenix, 1987—; pres., ptnr. Ariz. Ventures, Phoenix, 1988—; bd. dirs. Analog Design Tools Inc., Sunnyvale. Author, co-author computer software. Mem. Phoenix High Tech. Adv. Coun., 1982-86; founder mem. Ctr. for Innovation, Phoenix, 1987—. Mem. Assn. for Computer Machinery. Republican. Office: Technology Enterprises 218 W Royal Palm Rd Phoenix AZ 85021

SHOMER, ROBERT BAKER, employee benefit consultant; b. Lakewood, Ohio, Aug. 26, 1943; s. John Edward and Margaret Jeannette (Yeager) S.; BA in Psychology, Cen. Wash. State U., 1966; m. Phyllis B. Newman, Apr. 25, 1985; children: Adam. Jessica, Jaclyn. Brokerage Supr. Aetna Life and Casualty Co., San Francisco, 1971-73; regional dir. Hartford Variable Annuity Co., 1973-75; dir. deferred compensation dept. Galbraith & Green, Inc., Tempe, Ariz., 1976-79, v.p., 1980-82; sr. v.p. Fred S. James, 1983-86; exec. v.p. mktg./nat. accounts Alta Health Strategies, Inc., Salt Lake City, 1986—. Served as capt. USAF, 1967-71. Home: 9733 S Quail Ridge Rd Sandy UT 84092 Office: Alta Health Strategies Inc 2614 S 1935 W Salt Lake City UT 84119

SHONK, ALBERT DAVENPORT, JR., b. Los Angeles, May 23, 1932; s. Albert Davenport and Jean Spence (Stannard) S.; BS in Bus. Adminstrn., U. So. Calif., 1954. Field rep. mktg. div. Los Angeles Examiner, 1954-55, asst. mgr. mktg. and field supr. mktg. div. 1955-56, mgr. mktg. div., 1956-57; account exec. Hearst Advt. Svc., Los Angeles, 1957-59; account exec., mgr. Keith H. Evans & Assos., San Francisco, 1959-65; owner, pres. Albert D. Shonk Co., L.A., 1965—; pres., Signet Circle Corp., Inc., 1977-81, dir., 1962-81, hon. life dir., 1977-86. Bd. dirs., sec., 1st v.p. Florence Crittenton Svcs. of Los Angeles, exec. v.p., 1979-81, pres., 1981-83, chmn. bd., 1983-85, hon. life dir., 1986—; founding chmn. Crittenton Assos. Recipient Medallion of Merit Phi Sigma Kappa, 1976, Founders award, 1961. Mem. Advt. Club Los Angeles, Bus. and Profl. Advt. Assn., Pubs. Rep. Assn. of So. Calif., Nat. Assn. Pubs. Reps. (past v.p. West Coast 1981-83), Jr. Advt. Club Los Angeles (hon. life; dir., treas., 1st v.p.), Trojan Club, Skull and Dagger, U. So. Calif., USC Assocs., Inter-Greek Soc. (co-founder, hon. life mem. and dir., v.p. 1976-79, pres. 1984-86), Phi Sigma Kappa (dir. grand council 1962-70, 77-79, grand pres. 1979-83, chancellor 1983-87, court of honor , life, trustee, v.p. meml. found. 1979-84, pres. 1984, trustee pres. Phi Sigma Kappa found. 1984—), Alpha Kappa Psi, Los Angeles Club. Home: 3460 W 7th St Los Angeles CA 90005 Office: Albert Shonk Co 3156 Wilshire Blvd Ste 7 Los Angeles CA 90010

SHOOK, SANDRA LEE, marketing executive; b. Lewiston, Idaho, Mar. 10, 1958; d. Donal Lee and Bonita May (Berry) S. BS in Mktg./Mgmt., U. Idaho, 1981, postgrad., 1981-82. With R.W. Engring., Lewiston, Idaho, 1981; fin. sales rep. First Security Bank, Boise, 1983-84, mgmt. trainee, sales mgr., 1984-86, mktg. officer, 1986-87, mktg./tng. officer, asst. v.p., 1988—. Pub. rels. dir. Hugh O'Brien Youth Found., Boise, 1985-88; mem. membership com. Jr. League of Boise, 1989. Nat. Assn. Bank Women state scholar, 1987; named one or the Outstanding Woman Yr., 1986, 87. Mem. Nat. Assn. Bank Women (v.p./programming membership chmn. 1986-87, pres. 1987-88, v.p. 1989, numerous others), Daus. of the Nile. Republican. Office: First Security Bank Idaho PO Box 7069 Boise ID 83730

SHORE, ERLE MICHAEL, educator; b. Wichita, Kans., Apr. 3, 1935; s. Chester Kleinfelter and Eunice Cora (Wallace) S.; m. Sally June Dye Kowalczyk, June 2, 1962 (div. 1972); children: John Michael (dec.), Walter Frederick, Beverly Ann, Charles George, Loarrain K. BS in Edn., Bus., Ea. Mont. Coll., 1978, MS in Spl. Edn., Guidance Counseling, 1980; postgrad., No. Mont. Coll., 1980, Idaho State U., 1983-84. Cert. tchr., counselor, Idaho. Instr., cons. No. Cheyenne Sch. Dist. 6, Lame Deer, Mont., 1973-76; cons., tech. writer Mont. Coll. of Mineral Scis. and Tech., Butte, 1974-78; instr. coping skills Billings (Mont.) Sch. Dist. 2, 1979-82; instr., counselor Idaho State Youth Svcs. Ctr., St. Anthony, 1983-85; sch. counselor Shoshone-Bannock Tribe, Ft. Hall, Idaho, 1985-86; tchr. basic skills Canyon Vocat. Ctr., Nampa, Idaho, 1986-87; instr. Boise State U., 1988—; prin. St. Peters Sch., Ontario, Oreg., 1989—; dir. aerospace edn., Idaho Wing, Civil Air Patrol, Boise, 1986—. Author, editor occupational tng. courses, 1976, 78. Cons. Landmarks, Hist. Dist. Com, Billings, 1976. Served with USAF. Mem. Idaho Sch. Counselors Assn., Idaho Assn. of Individual Psychology, Aircraft Owners and Pilots Assn., Mont. Pilot's Assn., Am. Legion, Lions, Elks. Democrat. Roman Catholic. Home: 616 S 15th Ave Caldwell ID 83605

SHORE, SAMUEL COLEMAN, small business owner; b. Winnipeg, Man., Can., July 12, 1954; s. Manly Moses and Helen (Melnyk) S. Student, Valley Coll., 1972-74. Mgr. Keepers Industries, Canoga Park, Calif., 1975-76, Iberia Jewelry, Los Angeles, 1976-77; gen. mgr. Personal Atty. Service, Van Nuys, Calif., 1978-86; owner S.A.M. Atty. Service, Van Nuys, 1986—. Mem. Calif. Assn. Process Servers and Photocopiers. Jewish. Office: SAM Atty Svc 14416 Victory #116 Van Nuys CA 91401

SHORES, DONALD LEWIS, JR., communications educator; b. Bentonville, Ark., Mar. 9, 1952; s. Donald Lewis Sr. and Lois Irene (Wynne) S.; m. Mary Kathleen Burton, Nov. 17, 1973; children: April, Robyn, Holly. BA, Harding U., 1974; MS, Murray State U., 1977; PhD, U. Fla., 1981. News dir. KWCK, Inc., Searcy, Ark., 1973-76; teaching asst. Murray State U., Murray, Ky., 1976-77; assoc. minister Ch. of Christ, Gainesville, Fla., 1977-79; news editor WAKA, Gainesville, 1979; teaching asst. U. Fla., Gainesville, 1979-81; assoc. prof. communications, chairperson Pepperdine U., Malibu, Calif., 1981—; cons. Communications Cons. Svcs., Agoura, Calif., 1983-86. Mem. Malibu Twp. Coun., 1982-84; coach Malibu Youth Sports, 1989. Mem. Speech Communication Assn. Assn. for Edn. in Journalism & Mass Communication, Hollywood Radio TV Soc., Calif. Intercollegiate Press Assn., Phi Kappa Phi. Mem. Ch. of Christ. Office: Pepperdine U Communication Div Malibu CA 90265

SHORT, BYRON DAY, data processing company executive; b. Honolulu, Jan. 2, 1961; s. Leonard Ray Short and Jane (Moses) Ward; m. Yvonne Janette Espinosa, Aug. 21, 1982. Student, Colo. U., 1979-80. Sales exec. Academy Ford, Colorado Springs, 1980-82, Phil Long Ford, Colorado Springs, 1982-85; founder, chief exec. officer Automatic Follow-Up Systems, Inc., Colorado Springs, 1985—. Author: (integrated computer program) Autopilot, 1985. Recipient Free Enterprise award Charter Swap, Colorado Springs, 1988. Home: 14545 River Oaks Dr Colorado Springs CO 80921 Office: Automatic Follow-Up Systems Inc 7222 Commerce Center #212 Colorado Springs CO 80919

SHORT, DARLENE SUE, nurse; b. Upland, Calif., Apr. 19, 1958; d. Frederick Whitman and Dorothy Belle (Dungan) French; m. Larry Short, Aug. 10, 1979; children: Nathaniel, Amanda. BS in Nursing, Biola U., 1981. RN, Calif. Nurse La Habra Community Hosp., Calif., 1981; nurse San Antonio Community Hosp., Upland, Calif., 1981--, house supr., 1988--. Republican.

SHORT, DAVID BRUCE, business owner, consultant; b. Phoenix, Jan. 27, 1953; s. Billy E. and Ethel E. (Barker) S.; m. Laura A. Staehli, Aug. 20, 1988; children: Nicole, Amy, Michael. AA in PreArchitecture, Shasta Community Coll., Redding, Calif., 1973; BS in Constrn. Engring., Calif. Polytech. State U., 1977, MS in Computer Sci., 1978. Programmer, analyst Standard Oil Co. of Calif., San Francisco, 1978-80, data base support analyst, 1980-81; project engr. Chevron Corp., San Ramon, Calif., 1981-84; gen. ptnr. Auto Serve Computer Svcs., Walnut Creek, Calif., 1984-86; chief ops. officer Martha Damboise Bio Kosmetik, Concord, Calif., 1986-88; owner, cons. Delta Cons. and Assocs., Antioch, Calif., 1986—; co-chair piping com. Intergraph Users Group, Huntsville, Ala., 1983-84; computer scientist Lawrence Livermore (Calif.) Nat. Lab., 1989—. Scoutmaster Boy Scouts Am., Antioch, 1980-85, dist. tng. chair, 1985-86, team coach, 1985—. Recipient Dist. Merit award Boy Scouts Am., 1985, God and Svc. award 1st Christian Ch., 1986. Mem. Nat. Computer Graphics Assn. (membership com. 1984-85), Toastmasters Internat. (area gov. 1985). Republican. Home and Office: 4472 Deerfield Dr Antioch CA 94509

SHORT, HEDLEY VICARS ROYCRAFT, retired bishop; b. Toronto, Ont., Can., Jan. 24, 1914; s. Hedley Vicars and Martha (Parke) S.; m. Elizabeth Frances Louise Shirley, Apr. 14, 1953; children: Martha, Elizabeth, Janet, Margaret, Desmond. B.A., U. Toronto, 1941; L.Th., Trinity Coll., Toronto, 1943, B.D., 1945, D.D., 1964; D.D. (hon.), U. Emmanuel, St. Chad, 1985. Ordained deacon Anglican Ch. of Can., 1943 ordained priest Anglican Ch. of Can., 1944, consecrated bishop Anglican Ch. of Can., 1970. Asst. curate ch. Toronto, 1943-46; jr. chaplain St. Michael's Cathedral, Coventry, Eng., 1946-47; lectr., sr. tutor, dean of residence Trinity Coll., Toronto, 1947-51; rector Cochraine, Ont., 1951-56, St. Catharines Ch., Ont., 1956-63; canon Diocese of Niagara, 1963-70; dean, rector St. Alban's Cathedral, Prince Albert, Sask., Can., 1963-70; archdeacon of Prince Albert 1966-70, bishop of Sask., 1970-85; pres. council Coll. Emmanuel, St. Chad; chancellor U. Emmanuel Coll., Saskatoon, chmn. doctrine and worship coms., 1971-83; vis. prof. Emmanuel Coll., St. Chad, 1982; mem. no. devel. adv. council Gov. of Sask., 1985-86. Chmn. high sch. bd., Cochrane, 1953-56, Prince Albert, 1970; chmn. bd. dirs. Prince Albert Community Coll., 1974-77; mem. No. Devel. Adv. Council, Govt. of Sask. Named hon. fellow Coll. Emmanuel and St. Chad, 1980.

SHORT, JAMES GORDON, medical supply company executive, pathologist; b. N.Y.C., Oct. 16, 1931; s. James Joseph and Ruth (Gordon) S.; m. Lovina Aletha Tibbets, Aug. 22, 1954; children: James Gordon Jr., Barry Kevin. BA, Loma Linda U., Riverside, Calif., 1952, MD, 1956. Diplomate Am. Bd. Pathology. Postdoctoral fellow biochemistry dept. U. Utah, Salt Lake City, 1959-64; resident in pathology Holy Cross Hosp., Salt Lake City, 1964-67, asst. pathologist, 1967-70; dir. labs. Valley West Hosp., Granger, Utah, 1970-74; cons. Intermountain Lab., Midvale, Utah, 1974-78; cons. pathologist Meml. Hosp., Rock Springs, Wyo., 1974-78; med. dir. BSD Med. Corp., Salt Lake City, 1978-82; pres. Brevis Corp., Salt Lake City, 1978—; cons., licensor Lipshaw Corp., Detroit, 1985—. Inventee histology and infection control; contbr. articles to profl. jours. Mem. AIDS Adv. Com., Salt Lake City, 1988—; lobbyist for anti-tobacco legis. Utah State Legislature, 1985—; mem., past chair Coalition for a Tobacco-Free Utah, Salt Lake City, 1985—. Lt. USPHS, 1957-59. Fellow Am. Coll. Pathologists, Am. Soc. Clin. Pathologists; mem. Utah Med. Assn. (chair environ. health com. 1985-88), Canyon Racquet Club. Republican. Adventist. Home: 4305 Brockbank Way Salt Lake City UT 84124 Office: Brevis Corp 3310 S 2700 E Salt Lake City UT 84109

SHORT, MARY CHRISTINE, bank commission official; b. Chehalis, Wash., Dec. 15, 1947; d. John Paul and Charlotte Louise (Koschmann) Hoyt; m. Roy Lawrence Short, June 24, 1971 (div. Mar. 1977). BS, Seattle U., 1970. Salesperson Designer Fabrics, Bellevue, Wash., 1968-71, Nordstrom, Seattle, 1971-72; mgr. dept. Joseph Magnins, Reno, 1972-74; dir. tng. Weinstock's, Reno, 1974-76; asst. v.p., officer comml. loans Nev. Nat. Bank, Reno, 1976-83; dep. commr. Nev. Fin. Insts. Dept., Carson City, 1983-86; supt. banks Ariz. State Banking Dept., Phoenix, 1986—; chmn. state liaison com. Fed. Fin. Insts. Exam Council, Washington, 1988—, Inst. Supervisory Edn., Washington, 1986—, also trustee; vice chmn. dist. V Conf. State Bank Suprs., Washington, 1987—. Bd. dirs. Esperanca, Phoenix, 1986—, Friends Phoenix Pub. Library, 1986—. Named to Outstanding Young Women Am., 1983, 84. Mem. Nat. Assn. Bank Women, Nat. Assn. Credit Union Suprs., Nat. Assn. Consumer Credit Adminstrs., Internat. Assn. Fin. Planning (adv. council 1987—), Am. Council State Savs. Suprs. (bd. dirs.). Democrat. Lutheran. Club: Toastmasters (pres.). Office: Ariz State Banking Dept 3225 N Central Ave Ste 815 Phoenix AZ 85012

SHORT, ROBERT ALLEN, psychological researcher; b. Denver, Sept. 8, 1949; s. Lloyd Raymond and Margaret Elizabeth (Berkhimer) S.; m. Janet Carnell, July 12, 1980; children: Sarah Jean, Gregory Robert. BS in Psychology, U. Colo., 1971; MS in Biobehavioral Sci., U. Conn., 1974; MA in Psychology, U. Denver, 1982, PhD, 1985. Rsch. psychologist U. Colo. Health Sci. Ctr., Denver, 1974-84; rsch. scientist U. Wash. Primate Field Sta., Medical Lake, Wash., 1984—; mem. adj. faculty dept. psychology Eastern Wash. U., Cheney, 1987—; biostatis. cons., health rsch. and edn. ctr. Wash. State U., Spokane, 1989—. Contbr. articles to profl. jours. Office: U Wash Primate Field Sta Medical Lake WA 99022

SHORT, ROBERT HENRY, retired utility executive; b. Klamath Falls, Oreg., Oct. 15, 1924; s. Judge Haywood and Henrietta Luella (Lyon) S.; m. Ruby Madalyn Rice, Aug. 1, 1946; children—Robert L., Victoria (Mrs. Gregory Baum), Casey. BS in Journalism, U. Oreg., 1950; PhD in Humane Letters (hon.), Linfield Coll., 1984. City editor Klamath Falls Herald and News, 1950-52; dir. pub. rels. Water and Elec. Bd., Eugene, Oreg., 1952-55; mgr. pub. info. Portland Gen. Electric Co., Oreg., 1955-57, asst. to chmn., 1957-62, v.p., 1962-71, sr. v.p., 1971-73, exec. v.p., 1973-77, pres., 1977-80, chmn. bd., chief exec. officer, 1980-88, ret., 1989; bd. dir. First Interstate Bank of Oreg. Bd. dirs. Oreg. Ind. Colls. Found., Oreg. United Way; trustee Oreg. Grad. Ctr., Willamette U., St. Vincent Hosp. and Med. Ctr. With USNR, 1942-45. Mem. Astoria Country Club, Portland Golf Club, Arlington Club. Home: 1210 SW 61st Ct Portland OR 97221

SHORT, WILLIAM HARRY, manufacturing company executive; b. Peoria, Ill., May 22, 1940; s. Walter and Juvarian (Jacobson) S.; m. Nancy Carol Shively, Sept. 25, 1982; children: Alan Bradley, Brenda Marie. BS, Bradley U., 1964, MBA, 1965. Cons. Profl. Mgmt., Phoenix, 1965-66; plant acct. Rogers Corp., Chandler, Ariz., 1967-69, div. contr., 1970-77, product line mgr., 1978-79; div. mgr. Rogers Corp., Mesa, Ariz., 1979—. Patentee power and cooling method for integrated circuits, 1986. Bd. dirs. United Way, Chandler, Ariz., 1970-75, Tri-City Mental Health, Mesa, Ariz., 1970-78. Mem. Assn. Corp. Growth. Lutheran. Club: Rotary (Chandler). Office: Rogers Corp Box 4000 Chandler AZ 85244

SHORTLIFFE, EDWARD HANCE, internist, medical information science educator; b. Edmonton, Alta., Can., Aug. 28, 1947; s. Ernest Carl and Elizabeth Joan (Rankin) S.; m. Linda Marie Dairiki, June 21, 1970; children: Lindsay Ann, Lauren Leigh. AB, Harvard U., 1970; PhD, Stanford U., 1975, MD, 1976. Diplomate Am. Bd. Internal Medicine. Intern Mass. Gen. Hosp., Boston, 1976-77; resident Stanford Hosp., Palo Alto, Calif., 1977-79; asst. prof. medicine Stanford U. Sch. Medicine, Palo Alto, 1979-85, assoc. prof., 1985—, chief div. gen. internal medicine, 1988—; pres. SCAMC, Inc. (Symposium of Computer Applications in Med. Care), Washington, 1988-89; mem. tech. adv. bd. Teknowledge, Inc., Palo Alto, 1983-88; advisor Nat. Bd. Med. Examiners, Phila., 1987—. Editor: Rule-Based Expert Systems, 1984, Readings in Medical Artificial Intelligence, 1984; developer several medical computer programs including MYCIN, 1976 (Grace M. Hooper award Assn. Computing Machinery). Recipient Young Investigator award Western Soc. Clin. Investigators, 1987; rsch. grantee Nat. Libr. of Medicine, 1979-84; NIH scholar, 1971-76, Kaiser Family Found., 1983-88. Mem. Am. Assn. for Artificial Intelligence, Soc. for Med. Decision Making, Inst. Medicine, Am. Soc. for Clin. Investigation, Am. Coll. of Med. Informatics. Office: Stanford U Sch Medicine Med Computer Sci Group 300 Pasteur Dr Stanford CA 94305-5479

SHOWLEY, LON DUANE, lawyer; b. Rochester, Ind., May 3, 1944; s. Harold D. and Doveda G. (Rouch) S.; 1 child, Matthew. BA, Butler U., 1966; JD, Ind. U., 1969. Bar: Ind. 1970, Calif. 1972. Dep. atty. gen. State of Ind., Indpls., 1969-71; sole practice, San Diego, 1972—; instr. Cabrillo Pacific Coll. of Law, San Diego, 1972-75. Mem. Calif. Bar Assn., San Diego Bar Assn., San Diego County Bar (chmn. estate planning, trust and probate sect. 1985). Home: 1450 Hidden Mesa Trail El Cajon CA 92019 Office: 530 B St Ste 1750 San Diego CA 92101

SHREEVE, JEAN'NE MARIE, chemist, educator; b. Deer Lodge, Mont., July 2, 1933; d. Charles William and Maryfrances (Briggeman) S. B.A., U. Mont., 1953, D.Sc. (hon.), 1982; M.S., U. Minn., 1956; Ph.D., U. Wash., 1961; NSF postdoctoral fellow, U. Cambridge, Eng., 1967-68. Asst. prof. chemistry U. Idaho, Moscow, 1961-65; asso. prof. U. Idaho, 1965-67, prof., 1967-73, acting chmn. dept. chemistry, 1969-70, 1973, head dept., and prof., 1973-87, assoc. v.p. research and grad. studies, prof. chemistry, 1987—; Lucy W. Pickett lectr. Mt. Holyoke Coll., 1976; mem. Nat. Com. Standards in Higher Edn., 1965-67, 69-73. Editorial bd.: J. Fluorine Chem., 1970, J. Heteroatom Chemistry, 1988, Accounts Chem. Research, 1973-75, Inorganic Synthesis, 1976—; contbr. articles to chem. jours. Recipient Distinguished Alumni award U. Mont., 1970; named Hon. Alumnus U. Idaho, 1972; recipient Outstanding Achievement award U. Minn., 1975, award for creative work in fluorine chemistry, 1978; Sr. U.S. Scientist award Alexander von Humboldt Found., 1978; Excellence in Teaching award Chem. Mfrs. Assn., 1980; U.S. hon. Ramsay fellow, 1967-68; Alfred P. Sloan fellow, 1970-72. Mem. Am. Chem. Soc. (Garvan medal), AAUW (officer Moscow br. 1962-69), Phi Beta Kappa, Sigma Xi, Phi Kappa Phi. Office: U Idaho Univ Rsch Office Moscow ID 83843

SHREVE, THEODORE NORRIS, construction company executive; b. St. Louis, Feb. 14, 1919; s. Truxtun Benbridge and Beulah (Dyer) S.; B.S., U. Colo., 1942; m. Caroline Prouty, Jan. 7, 1943; children—Sara Ann Caile Shreve, Suzanne Godfrey Shreve, Theo Carol. Sec., treas. Trautman & Shreve, Inc., Denver, 1946-68, pres., 1965-86, chmn. bd., 1984—; pres. 4030 Corp., 1984—. Mem. Colo. U. Found. Bd., 1988—; Rep. County Assembly, 1962. Served with USNR, 1942-45. Registered profl. engr., Colo. Mem. Mech. Contractors Assn., Colo. Soc. Profl. Engrs., Rotary, Gyro Club, Denver Country Club, Sigma Phi Epsilon. Republican. Episcopalian. Home: 1510 E 10th Ave #13W Denver CO 80218 Office: Trautman & Shreve 4406 Race St Denver CO 80216

SHRONTZ, FRANK ANDERSON, airplane manufacturing executive; b. Boise, Idaho, Dec. 14, 1931; s. Thurlyn Howard and Florence Elizabeth (Anderson) S.; m. Harriet Ann Houghton, June 12, 1954; children: Craig Howard, Richard Whitaker, David Anderson. Student, George Washington U., 1953; LLB, U. Idaho, 1954; MBA, Harvard U., 1958; postgrad., Stanford U., 1969-70. Asst. contracts coordinator Boeing Co., Seattle, 1958-65, asst. dir. contract adminstrn., 1965-67, asst. to v.p. comml. airplane group, 1967-69, asst. dir. new airplane program, 1969-70, dir. comml. sales operations, 1970-73, v.p. planning and contracts, 1977-78; asst. sec. Dept. Air Force, Washington, 1973-76, Dept. Def., Washington, 1976-77; v.p., gen. mgr. 707/727/737 div. Boeing Comml. Airplane Co., Seattle, 1978-82, v.p. sales and mktg., 1982-84; pres. Comml. Airplane Co. Boeing Div., Seattle, 1986—; pres., chief exec. officer The Boeing Co., Seattle, 1986—, chmn., chief exec. officer, 1988—; bd. dirs. Ctr. for Strategic and Internat. Studies, 1986; mem. adv. bd. Stanford Bus. Sch., 1986; mem. The Bus. Council, 1987. Mem. Bus. Roundtable (policy com.). 1st lt. AUS, 1954-56. Mem. Phi Alpha Delta, Beta Theta Pi. Clubs: Rainier, Overlake Golf and Country, Columbia Tower. Home: 8434 W Mercer Way Mercer Island WA 98040 Office: Boeing Co 7755 E Marginal Way S Seattle WA 98108

SHROPSHIRE, DONALD GRAY, hospital executive; b. Winston-Salem, N.C., Aug. 6, 1927; s. John Lee and Bess L. (Shouse) S.; m. Mary Ruth Bodenheimer, Aug. 19, 1950; children: Melanie Shropshire David, John Devin. B.S., U. N.C., 1950; Erickson fellow hosp. adminstrn., U. Chgo., 1958-59. Personnel asst. Nat. Biscuit Co., Atlanta, 1950-52; asst. personnel mgr. Nat. Biscuit Co., Chgo., 1952-54; adminstr. Eastern State Hosp., Lexington, Ky., 1954-62; asso. dir. U. Md. Hosp., Balt., 1962-67; adminstr. Tucson Med. Center, 1967-82, pres., 1982—; Pres. Tucson Hosps. Med. Edn. Program, 1970-71, sec., 1971-86; pres. So. Ariz. Hosp. Council, 1968-69; bd. dirs. Ariz. Blue Cross, 1967-76, chmn. provider standards com., 1972-76; chmn. Healthways Inc., 1985—; bd. dirs. First Interstate Bank of Ariz. Bd. dirs., exec. com. Health Planning Council Tucson, 1969-74; chmn. profl. div. United Way Tucson, 1969-70, vice chmn. campaign, 1988; chmn. dietary services com., vice chmn., 1988. Md. Hosp. Council, 1966-67; bd. dirs. Ky. Hosp. Assn., 1961-62, chmn. council profl. practice, 1960-61; past pres. Blue Grass Hosp. Council; trustee Assn. Western Hosps., 1974-81, pres., 1979-80; mem. accreditation Council for Continuing Med. Edn., 1982-87, chmn., 1986; bd. govs. Pima Community Coll., 1970-76, sec., 1973-74, chmn., 1975-76, bd. dirs. Found., 1978-82, Ariz. Bd. Regents, 1982-87, sec., 1983-86, pres. 1987-88; mem. Tucson Airport Authority, 1987—; v.p. Tucson Econ. Devel. Corp., 1977-82; bd. dirs. Vol. Hosps. Am., 1977-88, treas., 1979-82; mem. Ariz. Adv. Health Council, 1976-78; bd. dirs. Tucson Tomorrow, 1983-87, Tucson Downtown Devel. Corp., 1988—; dir. Mus. No. Ariz., 1988—. Named to Hon. Order Ky. Cols.; named Tucson Man of Yr. 1987; recipient Disting. Svc. award Anti-Defamation League B'nai B'rith, 1989. Mem. Am. Hosp. Assn. (nominating com. 1983-86, trustee 1975-78, ho. dels. 1972-78, chmn. coun. profl. svc. 1973-74, regional adv. bd. 1969-78, chmn. joint com. with Nat. Assn. Social Workers 1963-64), Ariz. Hosp. Assn. (bd. dirs. 1967-72, pres. 1970-71), Ariz. C. of C. (bd. dirs. 1988—), Assn. Am. Med. Colls. (mem. assembly 1974-77), Tucson C. of C. (bd. dirs. 1968-69), United Comml. Travelers, Nat. League Nursing, Ariz. Acad. (bd. dirs. 1982, treas. 1985), Pima County Acad. Decathlon Assn. (dir. 1983-85), Tucson Community Coun. Baptist (ch. moderator, chmn. finance com., deacon, ch. sch. supt., trustee). Club: Rotarian. Home: 5301 E Grant Rd Tucson AZ 85712 Office: PO Box 42195 Tucson AZ 85733

SHROPSHIRE, HELEN MAE, historian; b. Prosser, Nebr., May 7, 1909; d. William Pearl and Dicy Belle (Myer) Stafford. Grad., Rogers Bus. Coll., Everett, Wash., 1928. Co-owner Camera Exchange, Pacific Grove, Calif., 1947-62; co-owner, photographer, writer Shropshire Film Prodns., Pacific Grove, 1950-76; pilot, co-owner Monarch Aviation, Monterey, Calif., 1962-63; co-founder, mgr. Calif. Heritage Guides, Monterey, Calif., 1971—. Mem. Ninety Nines Inc. (life). Republican. Home: PO Box 534 Pacific Grove CA 93950 Office: Calif Heritage Guides 10 Custom House Pla Monterey CA 93940

SHUBERT, GREGORY DONALD, mathematics educator; b. Pontiac, Ill., Dec. 5, 1953; s. Donald William and Marjorie Eileen (Degroodt) S.; m. Piper Lynne Aune, June 14, 1980; 1 child, Katherine Leigh Aune. BA, Ill. Wesleyan U., 1976; MS, Cornell U., 1978. Software engr. Hewlett-Packard Co., Ft. Collins, Colo., 1978-86; pvt. practice cons. Ft. Collins, 1986—; instr. math. Front Range Community Coll., Ft. Collins. Mem. Computer Soc. of IEEE. Republican. Home and Office: 1200 Dorchester Ct Fort Collins CO 80525

SHUBERT, GUSTAVE HARRY, research executive, social scientist; b. Buffalo, Jan. 18, 1929; s. Gustave Henri and Ada Shubert (Smith) S.; m. Rhea Brickman, Mar. 29, 1952; children—Wendy J., David L. B.A., Yale U., 1948; M.A., NYU, 1951. Staff mem. Lincoln Lab., MIT, 1955-57; adminstr. systems engring. Hycon Eastern, Inc., Paris, 1957-59; with RAND Corp., Santa Monica, Calif., 1959—, corp. v.p. domestic programs, 1968-75, sr. corp. v.p. domestic programs, 1975-78, sr. corp. v.p., 1978-89, trustee, 1973-89, sr. fellow, corp. advisor and adv. trustee, 1989—; dir. Inst. Civil Justice, 1979-87, sr. fellow, corp. advisor, adv. trustee, 1989—; trustee N.Y.C. Rand Inst., 1972-79, pres., 1972-73; trustee Housing Allowance Offices of Brown County and South Bend, Ind., 1973-80; mem. adv. council Sch. Engring., Stanford U., 1976-79; mem. policy adv. com. Clin. Scholars Program, UCLA; mem. program evaluation and methodology div. U.S. GAO, 1986—; adv. Commn. on Professionalism ABA, 1985-87; mem. Calif. jud. system com. Los Angeles County Bar Assn., 1984-85. Mem. Nat. Acad. Scis. Com. on Evaluation of Poverty Research. Served with USAF, 1951-55. Decorated Air medal with 2 oak leaf clusters, Commendation medal. Mem. Am. Judicature Soc. (bd. dirs. 1987—), Inst. Strategic Studies (London), World Affairs Council (L.A.), Council on Fgn. Rels., AAAS, Commonwealth Club of San Francisco, Town Hall Club of Calif., Jonathan Club, Yale Club (N.Y.C.). Home: 13838 Sunset Blvd Pacific Palisades CA 90272 Office: RAND Corp 1700 Main St Santa Monica CA 90406

SHUBINSKI, RAYMOND, planetarium director; b. Pikeville, Ky., Apr. 27, 1951; s. Jacob and Claris (Justice) S.; m. Carol Weckwerth, Aug. 16, 1975; children: Jennifer Carol, Julie Anna. BA in Humanities, Mich. State U., 1975, MA in Communication Arts, 1982. Phys. sci. curator Lafayette (La.) Nat. History Mus. and Planetarium, 1977-79; curator Kelly Planetarium, Charlotte (N.C.) Nat. Mus., 1979-80; dir. Pink Palace Mus. Planetarium, Memphis, 1980-85, Flandrau Planetarium, U. Ariz., Tucson, 1985—. Contbr. articles to profl. mags. Assoc. mem. U. Ariz. Near East Ctr. Mem. Internat. Plaetarium Soc., Am. Assn. Mus., Nat. Assn. Watch and Clock Collectors. Home: 7684 N Hopdown Tucson AZ 85741 Office: U Ariz Flandrau Planetarium Cherry at University Blvd Tucson AZ 85721

SHUBSDA, THADDEUS A., bishop; b. Los Angeles, Apr. 2, 1925. Grad., St. John's Sem. Ordained priest Roman Catholic Ch., 1950. Ordained titular bishop of Trau and aux. bishop of Los Angeles 1977-82; apptd. bishop of Monterey Calif., 1982—. Office: 580 Fremont Blvd PO Box 2048 Monterey CA 93940 *

SHUE, EUGENE WILLIAM, professional basketball coach; b. Balt., Dec. 18, 1931; m. Sandy Shue; children: Susan, Linda, Greg. Player Philadelphia Warriors, NBA, 1954, New York Knicks, 1954-56, 62-63, Fort Wayne Pistons, 1956-57, Detroit Pistons, 1957-62; player Baltimore Bullets, 1963-64, coach, 1966-73; coach Philadelphia 76ers, 1973-78, San Diego Clippers, 1978-80, Washington Bullets, 1980-86, Los Angeles Clippers, 1987-89. Named NBA Coach of Yr., 1969, 82; mem. NBA All-Star Team, 1958-62. Office: Los Angeles Clippers 3939 S Figueroa Los Angeles CA 90037 *

SHULER, SALLY ANN SMITH, telecommunications company executive; b. Mt. Olive, N.C., June 11, 1934; d. Leon Joseph and Ludia Irene (Montague) Simmons; m. Henry Ralph Smith Jr., Mar. 1, 1957 (div. Jan. 1976); children: Molly Montague, Barbara Ellen, Sara Ann, Mary Kathryn; m. Harold Robert Shuler, Aug. 2, 1987. BA in Math., Duke U., 1956; spl. studies, U. Liège, Belgium, 1956-57; postgrad. in bus. econs., Claremont Grad Sch., 1970-72. Mgr. fed. systems Gen. Electric Info. Services Co., Washington, 1976-78; mgr. mktg. support Gen. Electric Info. Services Co., Rockville, Md., 1978-81; dir. bus. devel. info. tech. group div. Electronic Data Systems, Bethesda, Md., 1981-82; v.p. mktg. optimum systems div. Electronic Data Systems, Rockville, 1982-83; v.p. planning and communications Electronic Data Systems, Dallas, 1983-84; exec. dir. comml. devel. U.S. West Inc., Englewood, Colo., 1984—. Recipient Gen. Electric Centennial award, Rockville, 1978. Fellow Rotary Internat. Found.; mem. Phi Beta Kappa, Tau Psi Omega, Pi Mu Epsilon. Democrat. Presbyterian. Home: 1626 S Syracuse St Denver CO 80231 Office: U S West 7800 E Orchard Rd Englewood CO 80111

SHULKIN, JEROME ROBERT, insurance brokerage executive; b. Chgo., Mar. 13, 1929; s. Dave H. and Belle (Oland) S.; m. Audrey Claire Stearns, Dec. 30, 1941; children: Michael B., Marc A., Pamela J. Shulkin Ruzi. BA, BS, U. Nebr., 1950. Owner, mgr. Shulkin-Miller Agy., Denver, 1957-60, 1st Security Ins. Agy., Denver, 1960-85; exec. v.p. Rolliins Burdick Hunter Colo., Denver, 1985—. Capt. USAF, 1950-53. Home: 6550 E Colorado Dr Denver CO 80224

SHULL, HARRISON, chemist, educator; b. Princeton, N.J., Aug. 17, 1923; s. George Harrison and Mary (Nicholl) S.; m. Jeanne Louise Johnson, 1948 (div. 1962); children: James Robert, Kathy, George Harrison, Holly; m. Wil Joyce Bentley Long, 1962; children: Warren Michael Long, Jeffery Mark Long, Stanley Martin, Sarah Ellen. A.B., Princeton U., 1943; Ph.D., U. Calif. at Berkeley, 1948. Assoc. chemist U.S. Naval Research Lab., 1943-45; asst. prof. Iowa State U., 1949-54; mem. faculty Ind. U., 1955-79, research prof., 1961-79, dean Grad. Sch., 1965-72, vice chancellor for research and devel., 1972-76, dir. Research Computing Center, 1959-63, acting chmn. chemistry dept., 1965-66, acting dean arts and scis., 1969-70, acting dean faculties, 1974; mem. faculty, provost, v.p. acad. affairs Rensselaer Poly. Inst., 1979-82; chancellor U. Colo., Boulder, 1982-85; prof. dept. chemistry U. Colo., 1982-88; provost Naval Postgrad. Sch., 1988—; asst. dir. research, quantum chemistry group Uppsala (Sweden) U., 1958-59; vis. prof. Washington U., St. Louis, 1960, U. Colo., 1963; founder, supr. Quantum Chemistry Program Exchange, 1962-79; chmn. subcom. molecular structure and spectroscopy NRC, 1958-63; chmn. Fulbright selection com. chemistry, 1963-67; mem. adv. com. Office Sci. Personnel, 1957-60; chmn. First Gordon Research Conf. Theoretical Chemistry, 1962; mem. com. survey chemistry Nat. Acad. Sci., 1964-65; mem. adv. panel chemistry NSF, 1964-67; mem. adv. panel Office Computer Activities, 1967-70, cons. chem. information program, 1965-71, mem. adv. com. for research, 1974-76; mem. vis. com. chemistry Brookhaven Nat. Lab., 1967-70; mem. adv. com. Chem. Abstracts Service, 1971-74; dir. Storage Tech. Corp.; chief of Naval Ops. Exec. Panel, 1984-88. Asso. editor: Jour. Chem. Physics, 1952-54; editorial adv. bd.: Spectrochimica Acta, 1957-63, Internat. Jour. Quantum Chemistry, 1967—, Proc. Nat. Acad. Scis, 1976-81; cons. editor, Allyn and Bacon.; Contbr. articles to profl. jours. Trustee Argonne U. Assn., 1970-75, Asso. Univs., Inc., 1973-76, U. Rsch. Assn., 1984-89, Inst. Defense Analysis, 1984—. Served as ensign USNR, 1945. NRC postdoctoral fellow phys. scis. U. Chgo., 1948-49; Guggenheim fellow U. Uppsala, 1954-55; NSF sr. postdoctoral fellow, 1968-69; Sloan research fellow, 1956-58. Fellow Am. Acad. Arts and Scis. (v.p. 1976-83, chmn. Midwest Center 1976-79), Am. Phys. Soc.; mem. Nat. Acad. Scis. (com. on sci. and public policy 1969-72, council, exec. com. 1971-74, chmn. U.S.-USSR sci. policy subgroup for fundamental research 1973-81, naval studies bd. 1974-79, chmn. Commn. on Human Resources 1977-81, nominating com. 1978), Am. Chem. Soc., AAAS, Assn. Computing Machinery, Royal Swedish Acad. Scis. (fgn. mem.), Royal Acad. Arts and Scis. Uppsala (corr. mem.), Phi Beta Kappa, Sigma Xi, Phi Lambda Upsilon. Club: Cosmos (Washington). Office: Naval Postgrad Sch Provost Code 01 Monterey CA 93943-5000

SHULOCK, CHARLES MARTIN, state agency administrator; b. Jeannette, Pa., Aug. 1, 1952; s. Charles N. and Helen Marie (Kantorczyk) S.; m. Nancy Joan Borow, July 12, 1980; children: Ellen Claire, Anne Marion. BA in English, Georgetown U., 1975; MS in Pub. Policy, U. Calif., Berkeley, 1978. Program analyst Office of Legis. Analyst, Sacramento, 1978-83; asst. to sec. Calif. Environ. Affairs Agy., Sacramento, 1984—; environ. affairs rep. Chem. Emergency Planning and Response Commn., Sacramento, 1987—, Gov.'s Biotech. Task Force, Sacramento, 1986—; mem. intergovtl. coordinating com. Santa Clara project U.S. EPA, 1986-88; staff to fiscal com. Gov.'s Task Force on Toxics, Waste and Tech., Sacramento, 1987. Mem. Assn. Resource and Environ. Economists, Assn. State Title III Program Officials. Office: Calif Environ Affairs Agy 1102 Q St Sacramento CA 95814

SHULTZ, EMMET LAVEL, oil company executive; b. Blackfoot, Idaho, Apr. 23, 1934; s. Emmet Franklin and Alba Elizabeth (Larsen) S.; m. Joan C. Kirby, Nov. 7, 1953; children: Joanne M., Jeanette G.; m. Marilyn Barney, Aug. 4, 1978. Asst. to pres. Flying Diamond Corp., Salt Lake City, 1973-74; pres., also bd. dirs. Shuhart Industries, Inc., Salt Lake City, 1974-75; v.p. Hunstman Chem. and Oil Corp., Salt Lake City, 1975-76; exec. v.p. Huntsman Coal Corp., Salt Lake City, 1975-76; pres., chmn. bd. Gulf Energy Corp., Salt Lake City, 1976—, Channel Energy Corp., 1983—, Kita Corp., 1985—, Inst. for Adept Health Rsch., Inc., 1988—. Bd. Dirs. Ballet West, 1980-83, Utah Symphony, 1980-83. Served with USN, 1952-56. Republican.

SHULTZ, JOHN DAVID, lawyer; b. Los Angeles, Oct. 9, 1939; s. Edward Patterson and Jane Elizabeth (Taylor) S.; m. Joanne Person, June 22, 1968; children: David Taylor, Steven Matthew. Student Harvard Coll., 1960-61; BA, U. Ariz., 1964; JD, Boalt Hall, U. Calif.-Berkeley, 1967. Bar: N.Y. 1968, Calif. 1978. Assoc. Cadwalader, Wickersham & Taft, N.Y.C., 1968-77; ptnr. Lawler, Felix & Hall, Los Angeles, 1977-83, mem. exec. com., chmn. planning com., co-chmn. recruiting and hiring com.; ptnr. Morgan, Lewis & Bockius, Los Angeles, 1983—, mem. ptnr. lateral entry com., mgmt. com.; chmn. profl. evaluation com., practice devel. com., chmn. recruiting com.; sec., counsel Copy Tech., Inc., 1971-73; trustee St. Thomas Ch., N.Y.C., 1969-72, Shore Acres Point Corp., Mamaroneck, N.Y., 1975-77; mem. adv. bd. Internat. and Comparative Law Center, Southwestern Legal Found., 1981—. Mem. Republican Nat. Com. Mem. Assn. Bar City N.Y., State Bar Calif., N.Y. State Bar Assn., ABA, University (Los Angeles), Phi Delta Phi, Sigma Chi. Episcopalian. Office: Morgan Lewis & Bockius 801 S Grand Ave 22d Fl Los Angeles CA 90017-3189

SHULTZ, MARTIN LOWELL, corporate public affairs executive, consultant; b. Cleve., Aug. 14, 1944; s. Albert H. and Marie (Solomon) S.; m. Linda Valerie Morris; children: Deborah, Robyn. BA in Edn., Ariz. State U., 1965, MA in Edn. Adminstrn., 1966; postgrad., UCLA, 1968, Harvard U., 1973. Cert. Edn. Adminstrn., Ariz. Dir. of edn. Osborn Sch. Dist., Phoenix, 1966-73; exec. asst. Mayor's Driggs/Barrow/Hance, Phoenix, 1973-77; dir. sales, mktg. and promotion Phoenix Suns Profl. Basketball Orgn., Phoenix, 1977-79; public affairs exec. Ariz. Pub. Svc. Co., Phoenix, 1979—; fin. cons. Ariz. State Legis., Phoenix, 1970-72; chmn. budget and fin. com. SAMCOR, Phoenix, 1987—; pres. Pub. Affairs Profls. of Ariz., Phoenix, 1988-89; v.p. govt. affairs Edison Electric Inst., Washington, 1988-89. Contbr. articles to profl., civic and co. publs. Pres. Samaritans: Samaritan Health Svc., Phoenix, 1981; chmn., bd. dirs. Anti Deformation League, Phoenix, 1986—; chmn. Citizens Transp. Coun., Phoenix, 1980—. Recipient JCC Community Svc. award, Cens. of Greater Phoenix, 1981; Valley Leardership, Valley Leadership Inc., 1983; named Outstanding Young Man of Ariz., Phoenix JC's, 1976-77. Mem. Ariz. C. of C., Phoenix C. of C., Soc. Fellow ADL. Republican. Jewish. Home: 3020 W Krall Phoenix AZ 85017

SHULTZ, ROBERT LARRY, civil engineer, contracting officer; b. Abbrington, Pa., Aug. 28, 1946; s. I. Robert M. and Dorothy Marion (Faust) S.; m. Cynthia Gene Rhodes, Aug. 24, 1968; children: Martha G., Robert F., Timothy M., Peter A. BSCE, Tufts U., 1968; MS in Fin. Mgmt., Naval Post Grad. Sch., Monterey, Calif., 1979. Registered civil engr., Calif. Commd. ensign USN, 1969, advanced through grades to comdr., 1986; asst. ops. officer Mobile Constrn. Bn. USN, N.Y., 1969-71; pub. works officer USN, Holy Loch, Scotland, 1971-74; officer in charge McMurdo Sta. USN, Antarctica, 1974-75; asst. resident officer in charge of constrn. Marine Corps Base, Camp Pendleton, Calif., 1975-77; asst. aquisition officer Naval Facilities Engring. Command, Chesapeake div., Washington, 1979-81; exec. officer Mobile Constn. Bn. Forty, San Francisco, 1981-83; asst. pub. works officer Marine Corps Base, El Toro, Calif., 1983-86; resident officer in charge of constrn. Marine Corps Air Sta., Camp Pendleton, 1986—. Scout leader Boy Scouts Am., Orange County, 1984-86, San Diego, 1986-88. Served to cdr USN, 1963—. Decorated Combat Action ribbon, Meritorious Svc. medal. Mem. U.S. Naval Inst. Lutheran. Office: Navy Contracts Office P O Box 209 Oceanside CA 92054

SHUMAN, THOMAS ALAN, correctional operations executive, consultant; b. Fairmont, W.Va., Dec. 31, 1946. BA, N.Mex. State U., 1969, 73; postgrad., U. N.Mex., 1988. Mgr. Drum Appliance, Inc., Las Cruces, N.Mex., 1971-75; classification supr. N.Mex. Corrections Dept., Santa Fe, 1976-80, mgmt. analyst supr., 1981-83, dir. classification, 1983-84, dep. sec., 1984-87; pres. Correctional Data Systems, Santa Fe, 1987—; owner Desktop Publ. Co., Santa Fe, 1988—; cons. Nat. Inst. Corrections, Washington, 1988, Am. Correctional Assn., Md., 1987—. Mem. Smithsonian Inst., U.S. Naval Inst. Served to lt. U.S. Army, 1969-71, Vietnam. Decorated Bronze Star, Presdl. Commendation. Republican. Presbyterian. Office: Correctional Data Systems 2728 Via Venado Santa Fe NM 87505

SHUMATE, CHARLES ALBERT, physician; b. San Francisco, Aug. 11, 1904; s. Thomas E. and Freda (Ortmann) S.; B.S., U. San Francisco, 1927, H.H.D., 1976; M.D., Creighton U., 1931. Pvt. practice dermatology, San Francisco, 1933-73, ret., 1973; asst. clin. prof. dermatology Stanford U., 1956-62; pres. E Clampus Vitus, Inc., 1963-64; hon. mem. staff St. Mary's Hosp. Mem. San Francisco Art Commn., 1964-67, Calif. Heritage Preservation Commn., 1963-67; regent Notre Dame Coll. at Belmont, 1965-78, trustee, 1977—; pres. Conf. Calif. Hist. Socs., 1967; mem. San Francisco Landmarks Preservation Bd., 1967-78, pres., 1967-69; trustee St. Patrick's Coll. and Sem., 1970-86. Served as maj. USPHS, 1942-46. Decorated knight comdr. Order of Isabella (Spain); knight Order of the Holy Sepulchre, knight of St. Gregory, knight of Malta. Fellow Am. Acad. Dermatology; mem. U. San Francisco Alumni Assn. (pres. 1955), Calif. Book Club (pres. 1969-71), Calif. Hist. Soc. (trustee 1958-67, 68-78, pres. 1962-64), Soc. Calif. Pioneers (dir. 1979—). Clubs: Bohemian, Olympic, Roxburghe (pres. 1958-59) (San Francisco); Zamorano (Los Angeles). Author: Life of George Henry Goddard; The California of George Gordon, 1976, Jas. F. Curtis, Vigilante, 1988, Francisco Pacheco of Pacheco Pass, 1977; Life of Mariano Malarin, 1980; Boyhood Days: Y. Villegas Reminiscences of California 1850s, 1983, The Notorious I.C. Woods of the Adams Express, 1986, Rincon Hill and South Park, 1988. Home: 1901 Scott St San Francisco CA 94115 Office: 490 Post St San Francisco CA 94102

SHUMWAY, FORREST NELSON, corporation executive, lawyer; b. Skowhegan, Maine, Mar. 21, 1927; s. Sherman Nelson and Agnes Brooks (Mosher) S.; m. Patricia Ann Kelly, Aug. 12, 1950; children: Sandra Brooks, Garrett Patrick. Student, Deerfield (Mass.) Acad., 1943-45; B.A., Stanford U., 1950, LL.B., 1952; LL.D. (hon.), U. So. Calif., 1974, Pepperdine U., 1978. Bar: Calif. 1952. Staff Office County Counsel, Los Angeles, 1953-57; sec. Signal Oil & Gas Co., Los Angeles, 1959-61, gen. counsel, 1961-64, group v.p. operations, 1963-64, pres., 1964-68; pres., chief exec. officer The Signal Cos., 1968-80, chmn. bd., chief exec. officer, 1980-85; vice chmn. Allied-Signal Inc., 1985-87, also bd. dirs.; dir. Transamerica Corp., First Interstate Bancorp, Am. Pres. Cos. Ltd., Clorox Co. Trustee U. So. Calif. Served to 1st lt. USMCR, 1945-46. Mem. ABA, State Bar Assn. Calif., Phi Delta Theta. Clubs: Cypress Point (Pebble Beach, Calif.); California (Los Angeles); Newport Harbor Yacht (Newport Beach, Calif.); Tuna (Avalon, Calif.); Bohemian (San Francisco); San Diego Yacht, La Jolla Country. Lodges: Masons, Shriners. Office: 11255 N Torrey Pines Rd La Jolla CA 92037-1059 *

SHUMWAY, JIM, secretary of state; b. Tempe, Ariz., July 8, 1939; m. Lurline Johnson; 3 children. Student, Brigham Young U., Ariz. State U. Asst. to voting machine custodian Maricopa County Election Dept., 1961-70; acting dir. elections Maricopa County, asst. elections dir.; election dir. Pima County, 1976-80; elections officer for Sec. of State State of Ariz., 1980-88, apptd. Sec. of State, 1988—; mem. bilingual adv. panel Fed. Election Commn. Clearinghouse on Election Adminstrn., mem. various standing coms. including Bus., Govt. and Licensing, and Voter Edn. and Registration; condr. Congressional Recount of Ind.'s 8th Dist. for U.S. House Adminstrn. Com., 1985. Mem. Nat. Assn. Secs. of State. Office: Office Sec of State 1700 W Washington W Wing Phoenix AZ 85007

SHUMWAY, NORMAN D., congressman; b. Phoenix, July 28, 1934; m. Luana June Schow; children: Jennifer, Neal, Perry, Tyler, Stuart, Brenda. A.A., Stockton Coll., 1954; B.S., U. Utah, 1960; J.D., Hastings Coll. Law, U. Calif., 1963. Bar: Calif. 1964. Practice law Downey, Calif.; formerly partner firm Cavalero, Bray, Shumway & Geiger; mem. 96th-101th Congresses from 14th Calif. Dist., 1979—. Mem. San Joaquin County Bd. Suprs., 1974-78, chmn. bd., 1978; past chmn. Goodwill Industries of San Joaquin Valley, Inc.; bd. dirs. Goodwill Industries Am.; former bishop, missionary to Japan Ch. Jesus Christ of Latter-day Saints. Office: Longworth House Office Bldg Rm 1203 Washington DC 20515 *

SHUMWAY, NORMAN EDWARD, surgeon, educator; b. Kalamazoo, Mich., 1923. M.D., Vanderbilt U., 1949; Ph.D. in Surgery, U. Minn., 1956. Diplomate: Am. Bd. Surgery, Am. Bd. Thoracic Surgery. Intern U. Minn. Hosps., 1949-50, med. fellow surgery, 1950-51, 53-54, Nat. Heart Inst. research fellow, 1954-56, Nat. Heart Inst. spl. trainee, 1956-57; mem. surg. staff Stanford U. Hosps., 1958—, asst. prof. surgery, 1959-61, assoc. prof., 1961-65, prof., 1965—, head div. cardiovascular surgery Sch. Medicine, 1974—; Frances and Charles D. Field prof. Stanford U., 1976—. Served to capt. USAF, 1951-53. Mem. AMA, Soc. Univ. Surgeons, Am. Assn.

Thoracic Surgery, Am. Coll. Cardiology, Transplantation Soc., Samson Thoracic Surg. Soc., Soc. for Vascular Surgery, Alpha Omega Alpha. Office: Stanford U Med Ctr Dept Cardiovascular Surgery 300 Pasteur Dr Stanford CA 94305 *

SHUPP, DAVID FRANKLIN, psychiatrist; b. Pitts., Aug. 17, 1926; s. Asher F. and Marguerite (Menges) S. Student, Antioch Coll., 1944-46; MD, UCLA, 1954. Pvt. practice, San Francisco and Sausalito, Calif., 1958—; from physician specialist to sr. psychiatrist Community Mental Health, San Francisco, 1985—. Author: Mission Mental Health Center, 1968. Fellow Am. Psychiat. Assn.; mem. Am. Group Psychiat. Assn., San Francisco Med. Soc. Repubilcan. Home and Office: 199 Santa Rosa Ave Sausalito CA 94965 Office: 915 Ashbury San Francisco CA 94965

SHUSTER, JEFFREY JAMES, business executive; b. Grand Rapids, Mich., Oct. 21, 1955; s. James C. and Mary Ann Shuster; m. Daly K. Gedanic, Oct. 5, 1985. BA in Telecommunications, Mich. State U., 1978. Profl. ski instr. Steamboat Ski Corp., Steamboat Springs, Colo., 1978-80; account exec. Sta. KZZX-FM, Albuquerque, 1980-81, Sta. KGGM-TV, Albuquerque, 1981-83; sales mgr. Sandia Advt., Albuquerque, 1983-86; account exec. The Wright Edge/Competitive Edge, Albuquerque, 1986-87; pres., owner Handiwork, Inc., Albuquerque, 1987—; advt. cons. Bob Myers RV Ctr., Inc., Albuquerque, 1985—. Percussionist Grand Rapids Youth Symphony, Grand Rapids, Mich., 1970-73; percussion instr. Highland High Sch. Marching Band, Albuquerque, 1982; vol. recruiter Mich. State U. Albuquerque, 1987. Mem. Profl. Ski Instructor Am. (assoc., cert. instr.), Mich. State U. Alumni Band, U.S. Ski Assn.

SHUTTLEWORTH, NATALIE OWNBEY, marketing management and software consultant; b. Athens, Tenn., Oct. 22, 1945; d. John B. and Nellie (Broyles) Ownbey; m. Richard W. Shuttleworth, Aug. 31, 1968 (div. 1983). BA in Music and Math., U. Tenn., 1968, MS in Computer Sci., 1976. Jr. systems analyst Alcoa (Tenn.) Aluminium Co., 1969-70; computer programmer nuclear div. Union Carbide Co., Oak Ridge, Tenn., 1969-70, systems programmer, analyst, 1970-71; project leader, sofware developer Lawrence Livermore (Calif.) Lab., 1974-78; unit and sect. mgr. Tymshare, Inc., Cupertino, Calif., 1978-82; product mgr. Apple Computer, Inc., Cupertino, 1982-83; data communications product mktg. mgr. for Europe Apple Computer, Paris, 1983-84; dir. mktg. Acorn Computers, Ltd., Cambridge, Eng., 1984-86; owner, mgr. Shuttleowrth & Assocs., Saratoga, Calif., 1986—; bd. dirs. Calif. Collector Series, Inc., San Francisco. Leader Girls Scouts U.S., 1965—. Mem. CAP. Mem. Internat. Mgmt. Cons. Assn. (assoc.), Assn. for Computing Machinery, Greenpeace, Internat. Fund for Animal Welfare, Amnesty Internat., ACLU, CARE, Common Cause, Sierra Club (life), Commonwealth Club, Phi Beta Kappa, Phi Kappa Phi. Home: 1 Panorama Dr San Francisco CA 94131 Office: Shuttleworth & Assocs 20764 4th St Ste 8 Saratoga CA 95070

SIART, WILLIAM ERIC BAXTER, banker; b. Los Angeles, Dec. 25, 1946; s. William Ernest and Barbara Vesta (McPherson) Baxter; m. Noelle Ellen Reid, Sept. 17, 1966; children—Shayne Allison, Tiffany Ann. B.A. in Econs., U. Santa Clara, 1968; M.B.A., U. Calif., Berkeley, 1969. With Bank of Am., 1969-78; v.p. corp. banking Bank of Am., Brussels, 1977-78; sr. v.p. charge mktg. Western Bancorp, Los Angeles, 1978-81; pres., chief operating officer First Interstate Bank of Nev. N.A., Reno, 1981-82; formerly pres., chief exec. officer First Interstate Bank of Nev. N.A., 1982—; now chmn., pres., chief exec. officer First Interstate Bank Calif., L.A., also bd. dirs. Trustee U. Nev.-Reno Found.; bd. dirs. Sierra Arts Found. Mem. Am. Bankers Assn. (mem. govt. relations council), Reno-Sparks C. of C. (dir.). Republican. Roman Catholic. Office: First Interstate Bank Calif 707 Wilshire Blvd Los Angeles CA 90017 *

SIBBING, THOMAS JOHN, manufacturing company executive; b. Long Beach, Calif., Oct. 11, 1957; s. Raymond John and Mary (Therese) S.; m. Terri Dieana Smithey, Feb. 20, 1988; 1 child, Kimberly Ann. Machinist Emco Machine Co., Fullerton, Calif., 1976-77; quality foreman Sargent Industries-Pico, City of Industry, Calif., 1977-79; gen. foreman Sargent Industries-Pico, 1979-82; engring. technician Sargent Industries-Pico, Seattle, 1982-84; mgr. Sargent Industries-Pico, Long Beach, 1984-85, BF Goodrich, Long Beach, 1985-88, Apeiron Tech., El Segundo, Calif., 1988-89; pres. Karrior Equipment Corp., El Segundo, 1989—; pres. Condo Homeowners Assn., Redondo Beach, 1988—. Mem. SAFE. Home: 720 Meyer Ln 105 Redondo Beach CA 90278

SICILIAN, JAMES MICHAEL, research engineer; b. Bronx, N.Y., May 25, 1947; s. Leonard James and Veronica Patricia (Reinwald) S. BS, MIT, 1969; MS, Stanford U., 1970, PhD, 1973. Tech. editor C.S. Draper Lab., Cambridge, Mass., 1968-69; research analyst Savannah River Lab., Aiken, S.C., 1973-76; staff Los Alamos (N.Mex) Scientific Lab, 1976-79, asst. group leader, 1979-80; sr. scientist Flow Science, Inc., Los Alamos, 1980-87, sec. of corp., 1987—. Mem. Cultural Ctr. Advisory Com., Los Alamos, 1987—, Park and Recreation Bd., Los Alamos, 1989—; treas. N.Mex. Theater Assn., 1983-85; pres. Los Alamos Little Theater, 1978-79. Recipient AEC spl. fellowship, U.S. AEC, 1969-72. Mem. AAAS, ASME, Sigma Xi. Office: Flow Science Inc 1325 Trinity Dr Los Alamos NM 87544

SICILIANO, A. VINCENT, banker; b. Washington, July 19, 1950; s. Rocco Carmine and Marion Stiebel; m. Susan Campbell; 1 child, Michael Carmine. BA, Stanford U., 1972, BS, 1972; MLA, U. Calif., Berkeley, 1976. Spl. asst. Dept. Commerce, U.S. Govt., Washington, 1972-73; energy planner, spl. cons. Calif. Coastal Commn., San Francisco, 1974; various positions with Bank Am., Manila, Singapore, 1976-84; v.p., mgr. corp. banking office Bank Am., San Diego, 1984-86; pres., chief exec. officer Internat. Savs. Bank, San Diego, 1986—. Contbr. articles to profl. jours. Chmn. Internat. Trade Commn., San Diego, 1988—; vice-chmn. Mus. Photographic Arts, San Diego, 1984—. Honoree Anglo-Am. Successor Generation Program, John Hopkins Sch. Advanced Internat. Studies and Royal Inst. Internat. Affairs, 1987. Republican. Office: Internat Savs 1455 Frazee Rd Ste 204 San Diego CA 92108

SICKLER, STEPHEN ROBERT, infosystems specialist; b. Syracuse, N.Y., Oct. 14, 1958; s. Robert Allen Sickler and Marlette Anne (Tappan) Frye. BA, U. Calif., San Diego, 1980. Sales rep. Unisys, Irvine, Calif., 1980-83; sr. sales rep. Control Data, Irvine, 1983-85; account exec. McCormack and Dodge, L.A., 1985—; guest speaker N.Mex. Personnel Assn., 1988, Profl. Assn. Diving Instrs. New Orleans, 1983. Author: (short stories) A Day in the Sun, 1988. Mem. Human Resource Systems Profls. (guest speaker 1987). Home: 2687 Orange Ave # C Costa Mesa CA 92627 Offcie: McCormack and Dodge 5933 W Century Blvd #1100 Los Angeles CA 90045

SIDELL, ROBERT A., cosmetics executive; b. Phila., Aug. 3, 1937; s. Sidney J. and Bertha F. (Fried) S.; m. Andrea F. Cook, Apr. 16, 1960; children: Jerry, Robyn, David. Student, L.A. Community Coll., 1957-59. Ind. make-up artist North Hollywood, Calif., 1962--; pres. Stage Ten Cosmetics, Inc., North Hollywood, 1972-78, Calif. Cosmetics, Inc., Chatsworth, 1985--; bd. dirs. CCI Internat. Advt., Chatsworth, Cadvision, Inc., Chatsworth. Pub., The Artisan, 1968-71. With USN, 1955-57. Mem. Nat. Acad. TV Arts and Scis. (awards com. 1985—, Founders award St. Jude's Children's Hosp. 1989), Internat. Alliance of Theatrical and Stage Employees, Acad. Motion Picture Arts and Scis. Republican. Jewish. Office: Calif. Cosmetics Inc 21100 Lassen St Chatsworth CA 91311

SIDEY, S. DEAN, electronic engineer, satellite systems engineer; b. Riverton, Wyo., July 16, 1953; m. Alane Joy Willis, Jan. 13, 1977 (div. Jan. 1984); m. Linda Diane Benson, Sept. 12, 1987. AS, Casper Coll., 1973; BSEE, U. Colo., 1975; MSEE, Ariz. State U., 1980. Registered profl. engr., Calif. Design engr. Collins Radio Group Rockwell Internat., Cedar Rapids, Iowa, 1975-77; sr. design engr. Motorola Govt. Electronics, Scottsdale, Ariz., 1977-80; staff engr. Magnavox Govt. & Electronics Co., Torrance, Calif., 1980-81; sr. staff engr. Hughes Aircraft Co., Fullerton, Calif., 1981—. Mem. Hughes Mgmt. Club, Hughes Archery Club (sec. 1983). Office: Hughes Aircraft Co GSG PO Box 3310 Bldg 675 MS CC241 Fullerton CA 92634

SIDNEY, WILLIAM WRIGHT, aerospace company executive; b. Anaconda, Mont., Dec. 31, 1929; s. Paul and Lily Maud (Wright) S.; divorced; children: Kay Elise, Paul Daniel. Student U. Calif., Berkeley, 1953-56. Supr. prodn. Kaiser Aerospace, San Leandro, Calif., 1953-57, project engr., 1957-67, chief engr., 1967-69, gen. mgr., 1969-77; pres. Kaiser Aerotech, San Leandro, Calif., 1977—, Kaiser Space Products, Pueblo, Colo., 1988—. With USN, 1948-52. Recipient NASA Pub. Svc. medal 1981. Mem. U. Calif. Alumni Assn., Smithsonian Assocs., Nat. Audubon Soc., Am. Mus. Natural History. Home: 6025 Ridgemont Dr Oakland Hills CA 94619 Office: 880 Doolittle Dr San Leandro CA 94577

SIDWELL, ROBERT WILLIAM, immunologist, educator; b. Huntington Park, Calif., Mar. 17, 1937; s. Robert Glen and Eva Amalie (Gordy) S.; m. Rhea Julander, May 31, 1957; children: Richard Dale, Jeanette Kathleen, David Eugene, Cynthia Diane, Michael Jason, Robert Odell. B.S., Brigham Young U., Provo, Utah, 1958; M.S., U. Utah, 1961, Ph.D., 1963. Head serology, ricketts and virus research Epizoology Lab., U. Utah, 1958-63; head virus div. So. Research Inst., Birmingham, Ala., 1963-69; head dept. virology ICN Nucleic Acid Research Inst., Irvine, Calif., 1969-72; head div. chemotherapy ICN Nucleic Acid Research Inst., 1972-75, dir. inst., 1975-77; prof. animal, dairy and vet. scis. Utah State U., Logan, 1977—; mem. faculty U. Ala. Med. Sch., 1968-69; dir. antiviral and AIDS rsch. programs Utah State U., Logan; bd. dirs. antiviral and AIDS rsch. programs Utah State U., Logan; lectr. in field. Editorial bd.: Antimicrobial Agts. and Chemotherapy, 1972—, Chemotherapy, 1974—, Jour. Antiviral Research, 1980—; Contbr. articles to profl. jours. Mem. Nibley (Utah) City Planning and Zoning Commn., 1978-80; mem. steering com. Irvine Sch. Bd., 1972, chmn. health edn. awareness forum, 1975. Recipient E. Wynne Thorne Research award Utah State U., 1987, Silver Beaver award Boy Scouts Am., 1987; Gov.'s medal for Sci. and Tech., Utah State U., 1988; scholar Order of Eagles, 1954, Dept. Interior, 1954. Fellow Infectious Disease Soc. Am.; mem. AAAS, Am. Assn. Univ. Profs., Am. Assn. Immunologists, Soc. Exptl. Biology and Medicine, Pan Am. Med. Assn., Internat. Soc. Chemotherapy, Inter-Am. Soc. Chemotherapy (exec. sec. 1985—), Am. Soc. Microbiology, Am. Soc. Virology, Nat. Assn. Colls., Tchrs. in Agriculture, Am. Assn. U. Profs., Sigma Xi. Home: 162 Quarter Circle Dr Nibley UT 84321 Office: Utah State U Dept Animal Dairy & Vet Sci Logan UT 84322-5600

SIDWELL, STEPHEN RICHARD, industrial operations executive; b. Orange, Calif., July 31, 1948; s. Max Rainford and Goldie Severna (Hansen) S.; m. Lynn Kinzer, May 24, 1969 (div. 1988); children: Tiffany, Lynn, Ryan Stephen; m. Eileen Speer, Jan. 1, 1989; stepchildren: Amy and Sarah Paulson. BSBA, U. Nebr., 1975. Inspection supr. Sq. D Corp., Lincoln, Nebr., 1971-75; sr. quality engr. Black & Decker Corp., Tarboro, N.C., 1976-77; with Amerock Corp., Rockford, Ill., 1978-84, 87-88; dir. new product and new bus. devel. Amerock Corp., Rockford, 1983-84, dir. internat. sourcing, 1987-88; v.p. internat. product devel. Embassy Indsl. Corp., L.A., 1985-87; v.p. internat. ops. Kingport Indsl. Corp., Santa Barbara, Calif., 1989—. With U.S. Army, 1969-71. Mem. Am. Soc. Quality Control (vice-chmn. Rockford chpt. 1979). Republican. Office: Kingport Indsl Corp 1203 De La Vinn St Santa Barbara CA 93101

SIEBE, CAROL ANN, educator; b. Petaluma, Calif., Aug. 30, 1946; d. Ernest Henry and Minnie Ann (Maffia) Corda; m. Norman Thomas, Mar. 21, 1970; children: David Henry, Meredith Ann. BA, U. San Francisco, 1968; teaching credential, 1970. Elem. tchr. Two Rock Sch., Petaluma, 1970-72, 75—, supr. primary curriculum, 1986—. Leader Wilson 4-H Club, Petaluma, 1981; softball coach Petaluma Girl's Softball Assn., 1984-85; active Children's Home Soc., Petaluma. Mem. AAUW (sec. Petaluma chpt. 1975-76), Delta Kappa Gamma (2d v.p. Gamma Tau chpt. 1988—). Republican. Roman Catholic.

SIEGAL, MARVYN EMANUEL, real estate broker; b. N.Y.C., Apr. 27, 1930; s. Bernard A. and Gussie (Ulitzky) S.; m. Susan B. Sahud, June 5, 1955; children: Floyd Gary, Anita Carol Collom, Paul Jay. BSEE, CUNY, 1952; MSEE, U. Pa., 1961; cert. in advanced mgmt., U. Chgo., 1968. Registered profl. engr., N.J., Mass.; lic. real estate broker, Calif. Engr. RCA Corp., Cherry Hill, N.J., 1954-57; sr. engr. Gen. Dynamics Corp., Rochester, N.Y., 1957-58; project engr. Philco Corp., Camden, N.J., 1959-62; mgr. EW & radar Philco Corp., Burlington, Mass., 1962-70; mgr. systems Philco Corp., Camden, 1970-72; v.p. Litton Systems Div., College Park, Md., 1972-75; pres. Suma Mgmt. Sciences, Encino, Calif., 1975-78, Marv Siegal & Co., Inc., Tarzana, Calif., 1978—. Author: Telephone Cost Reduction, 1976; contbr. articles to profl. jours.; inventor frequency control system. Lt. U.S. Army, 1952-54, Korea. Mem. IEEE (sr. mem.), Nat. Assn. Realtors, Assn. Old Crows (chpt. v.p. 1967-68, chpt. pres. 1968-70). Republican. Jewish. Office: Marv Siegal & Co Inc 5959 Topeka Dr Tarzana CA 91356

SIEGEL, ERIC RICHARD, public affairs director, researcher; b. Glen Ridge, N.J., Mar. 25, 1946; s. Ernest I. and Beatrice (Berman) S.; m. Christine Anderson, May 27, 1980; children: Erika, Brett. BA, UCLA, 1968, MA, 1970, MLS, 1981. Library asst. UCLA, 1975-80, research asst. African studies ctr., 1980-81, bibliographer African studies, 1981-82; researcher UCLA Office of Pub. Affairs, 1982-83, asst. dir. research, 1983-85, dir. research, 1985—; faculty mem. CASE major donor research conf., 1988—. Author: A Bibliography for the Study of African Politics, Vol. 3, 1983. Bd. dirs. devel. com. Junipero Serra High Sch., Gardena, Calif., 1985-87; mem. bus. adv. bd. Community Counseling Services, Los Angeles, 1987—. Fulbright-Hayes fellow, 1973, NDEA fellow, 1972, 74. Mem. Am. Prospect Research Assn. Democrat. Office: UCLA Pub Affairs Research 405 Hilgard Ave Los Angeles CA 90024

SIEGEL, GILBERT BYRON, educator; b. L.A., Apr. 19, 1930; s. Morris De Sagar and Rose (Vancott) S.; m. Darby Day Smith, Oct. 16, 1954; children: Clark Byron, Holly May. BS in Pub. Adminstrn., U. So. Calif., 1952, MS in Pub. Adminstrn., 1953; PhD in Polit. Sci., U. Pitts., 1964. Adminstrv. analyst, mgr. County of L.A., 1954-57; vis. asst. prof. U. So. Calif., Tehran, Iran, 1957-59; asst. prof. U. So. Calif., Rio de Janeiro, Brazil, 1961-63; from assoc. prof. to prof. and assoc. dean U. So. Calif., L.A., 1964—; instr. grad. sch. of pub. and internat. affairs U. Pitts., 1959-61; cons. UN, N.Y.C., Bangkok, 1969, 81, USAid, Panama, 1986, govt. of Brazil, 1961, 70, 76, 77. Author: Breaking With Orthodoxy in Public Administration, 1980, Public Personnel Administration, 1985. Sgt. U.S. Army, 1952-54. NSF grantee, 1987. Mem. Am. Soc. for Pub. Adminstrn., Internat. Personnel Mgmt. Assn. (editorial bd. 1987—), So. Calif. Personnel Mgmt. Assn. (bd. dirs. 1983—), Pi Sigma Alpha, Pi Alpha Alpha, Acacia Fraternity. Democrat. Home: 208 N Poinsettia Ave Manhattan Beach CA 90266 Office: U So Calif Sch Pub Admin Los Angeles CA 90089-0041

SIEGEL, JAY STEVEN, chemistry educator; b. Inglewood, Calif., Aug. 16, 1959; s. Erwin and Jeanne (Strzesak) S. BS, Calif. State U., Northridge, 1980; MA, Princeton U., 1982, PhD, 1985. Researcher Princeton (N.J.) U., 1981-83, 84-85, Eidgenossische Technishche Hochschule, Zürich, Switzerland, 1983-84, U. Louis Pasteur, Strasbourg, France, 1985-86; asst. prof. U. Calif., San Diego, 1986—; observer, mem. com. on stereochemistry Internat. Union of Pure and Applied Chemists, 1985—. Contbr. articles to sci. jours. Calif. State scholar, 1977-70; Swiss U. grantee, 1983-84, NSF-CNRS Sci. Exchange grantee, 1985-86; named Presdl. Young Investigator NSF, 1988—. Mem. Am. Chem. Soc., N.Y. Acad. Scis., Sigma Xi. Home: 236 Calle de Madera Leucadia CA 92024 Office: U Calif San Diego Dept Chemistry B-014 La Jolla CA 92093

SIEGEL, JONATHAN, film director, editor and writer; b. New Brunswick, N.J., June 14, 1953; m. Cindera Che, Apr. 14, 1984. BFA, NYU, 1975; MFA, Am. Film Inst., Beverly Hills, Calif., 1980. Ind. film dir., editor Hollywood, Calif., 1980—. Dir., writer The Silver Crown, 1980 (grand prize U.S.A. Film Fest 1980), also dance videos, 1980—; writer screenplay Thicker Than Blood, 1988. Mem. NYU West Coast Alumni Group. Home and Office: 1006 S Hi Point St Los Angeles CA 90035

SIEGEL, LES, radio producer; b. L.A., July 17, 1955; s. Herb and Mary Berman S. BA, Calif. State U., Northridge, 1978; MA, Columbia Coll., Hollywood, Calif., 1980. Salesman Swank Motion Pictures, L.A., 1980-87; radio producer KABC Radio, L.A., 1987—. Democrat. Jewish. Home: 8451 W 4th St Los Angeles CA 90048 Office: KABC Radio 3321 S La Cienega Blvd Los Angeles CA 90016

SIEGEL, RONNIE SWIRE, landscape architect, artist; b. N.Y.C., Feb. 27, 1953; d. Irving and Roslyn (Potisman) Swire; m. Peter Howard Siegel, July 4, 1976. BA cum laude, Colgate U., 1975; M. Landscape Arch., U. Pa., 1978. Lic. Landscape architect, N.Y. Landscape architect Arnold Assocs., Princeton, N.J., 1977, Edward Gaudy, South Nyack, N.Y., 1978; cons. Cen. Park Task Force, N.Y.C., 1979; landscape architect Vreeland & Guerriero, P.C., N.Y.C., 1979-81, Haines Lundberg Waehler, N.Y.C., 1981-82; prin. Swire Siegel, Upper Grandview, N.Y., 1982—, Pasadena, Calif., 1987—. Group shows Colgate U., Hamilton, N.Y., 1972, 74, U. Pa. Grad. Sch. Fine Arts, Phila., 1977, Met. Mus. Art, N.Y.C., 1981, Harvard U. Grad. Sch. Design, Cambridge, 1983; prin. works include North Ave. Park, N.Y.C., P.S. 52 playground, S.I., Frank Frontera Park, Queens, N.Y., N.J. Ave. Park, Bklyn. Mem. Am. Soc. Landscape Architects, Nat. Trust Hist. Preservation. Avocations: painting, photography, travel, tennis, swimming. Home and Office: Swire Siegel 2312 Dudley St Pasadena CA 91104

SIEGELE, MICHAEL LYNN, data processing administrator; b. Emporia, Kans., June 10, 1956; s. Milton H. and Bernice (Lynn) S.; m. Rita Jo Childers, Jan. 10, 1981; children: Chase M., Chance M. BBA, Emporia State U., 1980. Vault teller Citizens Nat. Bank and Trust, Emporia, 1977-79; teller Emporia State Bank and Trust, 1979-81; data ctr. ops. adminstrn. Rocky Mountain Bankcard System, Inc., Denver, 1981—; mem. pres.'s club Rocky Mountain Bankcard System Inc., 1988. Mem. Internat. Facility Mgmt. Assn. Home: 1058 S Alkire Lakewood CO 80228 Office: Rocky Mountain Bankcard System Inc 950 17th St Denver CO 80202

SIEGERT, RICK ALAN, infosystems specialist; b. Santa Monica, Calif., June 22, 1949; s. Benjamin O. and Doris B. (Markoff) S.; m. Janet Eileen Parsons, Sept. 19, 1984. BFA, Calif. Inst. Arts, 1971. Editor Voice News, Eugene, Oreg., 1972-73, sr. editor, 1973-74; systems trainee Bur. Land Mgmt., Lakewood, Colo., 1976-78; programmer Hosp. Data Svcs., Englewood, Colo., 1978-79; programmer/analyst Samsonite Corp., Denver, 1979-80; systems analyst Mountain Bell Corp., Denver, 1980-85; v.p. Inovative Solutions Corp., Aurora, Colo., 1985; payroll analyst Rocky Mountain Orthodontics, Denver, 1985-87; programmer/analyst II Guaranty Nat. Ins. Co., Englewood, 1987—; cons., speaker in field. Bd. dirs. Whispering Pines West Condo. Assn., Denver, 1983, 85; vol. Douglas County Parents of Handicapped Students, Castle Rock, Colo., 1988. Recipient Scholar award Colo. Dept. Higher Edn., 1986; scholar Calif. Inst. Arts, 1971. Mem. Internat. Fantasy Gaming Soc. (bd. dirs. 1982-84), Audubon Soc., World Wildlife Fedn. Democrat. Jewish. Home: 977 Mountain View Dr Castle Rock CO 80104

SIEGFRIED, LORI RAE, electrical and interior designer; b. Sioux Falls, S.D., Jan. 6, 1963; d. Neal R. and June E. (Mayer) S. BS Interior Architecture, Ariz. State U., 1986. Elec. designer Burgett & Assocs., Inc., Phoenix, 1986-88, Sullivan-Durand, Inc., Phoenix, 1988--. Mem. Illuminating Engrs. Soc. Republican. Lutheran. Office: Sullivan-Durand Inc 5060 N 40th St Ste 203 Phoenix AZ 85018

SIEGMUND, JAMES WILSON, auditor; b. Salem, Oreg., Sept. 26, 1942; s. Wilson N. and Margaret I. (Savage) S.; m. Pamela F. Oakes, Oct. ll, 1986; children: Gina, Jamie. BS, Pepperdine Coll., 1970. Cert. appraiser, Calif. Auditor-appraiser Riverside County, Riverside, Calif., 1973-85; internal auditor Super Shops Inc., San Bernardino, Calif., 1985--. With USAF, 1963-67. Office: Super Shops Inc Box 8457 San Bernardino CA 92412-8457

SIEH, JOHN S., international marketing professional; b. N.Y.C., Oct. 18, 1956; s. John Sieh and Olga (Barragan) Sibley. Student, U. Complutense de Madrid, 1976-77; BA in Polit. Sci. with honors, UCLA, 1978; M in Thesis, Oxford U., 1979; M of Internat. Mgmt., Am. Grad. Sch. of Internat. Mgmt., 1979. Cert. dairy engr., Pa. Advisor prodn. control Dreyer's Grand Ice Cream, Oakland, Calif. and Guangzhou, People's Republic of China, 1981-82; mktg. mgr. far east Dreyer's Grand Ice Cream, Hong Kong, 1982-84; mgr. exports Deutsch Engineered Connecting Devices, Banning, Calif., 1986-87; specialist cellular communications Motorola, Inc., Anaheim, Calif., 1985-88; internat. project mgr. Mid-Pacific Seafoods, Inc., L.A., 1988—; lectr. English and bus. U. Hong Kong, 1982-84; cons. export, Europe, Asia, Am., 1981—. Contbr. articles to profl. jours.; actor various TV commercials, 1982-84. Mem. People's Lobby, 1976-80; bd. dirs. Orange County Young Reps., Costa Mesa, Calif., 1985-87; bd. dir., newsletter editor Orange County Young Politicians; instr., Bridging the Gap Inmate Remedial Program, L.A., 1977-78; active UCLA Comic Relief Homeless Health Ctr. Benefit, 1988-89. AGSIM grantee, 1979. Mem. Am. Mgmt. Assn., Hong Kong Mgmt. Assn., Soc. Advancement of Sci., Amnesty Internat., Soc. Advancement of Mgmt., Orgn. Latino American (bus. mgr.), Chi Psi. (sec. publs. editors and alumni corp.). Roman Catholic. Home: 308 Via Pato San Clemente CA 92672

SIEMERS, REBECCA JANE, software engineer; b. Mason City, Iowa, Aug. 18, 1959; d. Paul Herbert and Betty Jane (Hagstrom) Potter. BS in Math., BS in Computer Engring., Iowa State U., 1981; MSEE, Stanford U., 1985. Software devel. engr. Hewlett-Packard co., Cupertino, Calif., 1981-82, project mgr., 1982-86; mgr. software engring. Microsensor Tech., Fremont, Calif., 1986—. Mem. rev. bd. Jour. Clin. Enginring., 1984—. Mem. IEEE, Phi Beta Kappa, Sigma Xi, Tau Beta Pi, Eta Kappa Nu (pres. 1980-81). Home: 1303 Hillview Ct Roseville CA 95661 Office: Microsensor Tech Inc 41762 Christy St Fremont CA 94538

SIEMON-BURGESON, MARILYN M., education administrator; b. Whittier, Calif., Nov. 15, 1934; d. John Roscoe and Louise Christina (Secoy) Mason; m. Carl J. Siemon, Aug. 18, 1956 (div. Oct. 1984); children: Timothy G., Melanie A. Siemon Imes; Troy M.; m. James K. Burgeson, Jan. 24, 1987. BA, U. Redlands, 1956; MA, Pacific Oaks Coll., 1975; postgrad., Point Loma Coll., 1979-80. Cert. elem. and early childhood tchr. Tchr. Sierra Madre (Calif.) Community Nursery Sch., 1970-79; tchr. parent edn. and music Pasadena (Calif.) Unified Schs., 1977-79, project coordinator, 1980-81, tchr. curriculum resource dept., 1982-83, head tchr., Washington Children's Ctr., 1983—. Active Arcadia, Calif. Bicentennial Commn., 1974-76; life mem. Sierra Madre Sch. PTA, also chpt. liaison; chmn. Pasadena Foothill Consortium on Child Care, 1987—; mem. Child Care Coalition, Pasadena. Ednl. Professions Devel. fellow Pacific Oaks Coll., Pasadena, 1969. Mem. Nat. Assn. Edn. Young Children, So. Calif. Assn. Edn. Young Children (grantee 1970), Child Care Info. Service (bd. dirs., chmn. parent edn. and family affairs 1986—), Women Ednl. Leadership (asst. program v.p.), AAUW (co-chmn. Math.-Sci. Conf. 1983, chair Coll./Univ. Relations 1988—, grantee 1982, 83), Delta Kappa Gamma (pres. 1986-88). Republican. Episcopalian. Home: 2266 Kinclair Dr Pasadena CA 91107 Office: Washington Children's Ctr 130 Penn St Pasadena CA 91103

SIERCKS, RANDOLPH LAVERNE, chairman and educator computer science department; b. Hollywood, Calif., Aug. 13, 1946; s. LaVerne George and Neva V. (Mitchell) S.; m. Nicia Lenore Weiss, Aug. 15, 1976; 1 child, Stephen Jeffrey. BS, Calif. State U., Pomona, 1969. Cert. tchr., Calif. Instr. L.A. Unified Schs., 1969-81; mgr. tech. edn. dept. MAI Basic Four, Inc., Tustin, Calif., 1981-85; div. mgr. edn. Sunar Haverman, Inc., Cleve., 1985-87; chair computer sci. dept. The Buckley Sch., L.A., 1987—; cons. The Oak Creek Ranch, Ojai, Calif., 1977-80. Vice pres. Casas Verdes, Palos Verdes, Calif., 1984, pres., 1985. Mem. Am. Soc. Tng. and Devel., L.A. Agriculture Tchrs. Assn., assn. Composer Tchrs., Computer Using Educators Calif., Oxford, Braemar Country Club. Home: 18624 Cassamdra St Tarzana CA 91356 Office: The Buckley Sch 3900 Stansbury Ave Sherman Oaks CA 91413-5949

SIEVERS, JUDY LOUISE, lumber company executive, controller, treasurer; b. Everett, Wash., May 27, 1942; d. Ralph Clarence and Peggy Joyce (Martin) Hershaw; m. John Henry Sievers, Aug. 31, 1972; children: Larry W. Jr., Lon Gregory, Lena Marie, Lee Edgar. Grad. high sch., Arlington, Wash. Harvest truck driver Twin City Foods, Stanwood, Wash., 1957-60; pvt. practice in comml. art Arlington and Everett, Wash., 1960-69; mem. floral staff Peg's Floral Shop, Arlington, 1961-68; receptionist Reinell Boat Co., Marysville, Wash., 1969; log inventory, asst. to controller Buse Timber & Sales, Inc., Marysville, 1969-84; store owner Clearwood Community Assn., Yelm, Wash., 1984-86; controller Brazier Forest Products, Inc., Tacoma, 1984-86, 89; controller, corp. treas. Arlington Forest Products, Inc., Arlington and Tacoma, 1986-89, controller, 1989—. Tchr. Trinity

Episcopal Ch., Everett, 1978; mem. Bald Hills Fire Dept., Yelm, 1984-86. Office: Arlington Forest Products Inc PO Box 3189 Arlington WA 98223

SIFTON, MICHAEL CLIFFORD, broadcasting executive; b. Toronto, Ont., Can., Jan. 21, 1931; s. Clifford and Doris Margaret (Greene) S.; m. Heather Ann McLean, Sept. 8, 1956; children: Clifford McLean, Michael Gregory, Derek Andrew. Student, U. Western Ont., 1950-54. Pres. Armadale Co. Ltd., Armadale Enterprises Ltd., Regina Leader-Post Ltd., Armadale Pubs. Ltd. (Saskatoon Star-Phoenix), Armadale Communications Ltd. (CKIT-FM Radio, Regina, Radio CKWG-FM, Winnipeg), Toronto Airways Ltd., Radio CKOC, Hamilton; pres. McLean Highland Chevrolet-Oldsmobile Ltd.; dir. Phoenix Leasing Ltd., Eastern Ont. Broadcasting (CFJR). Named hon. col. 411th Air Res. Squadron, 1975; recipient Can. Forces Decoration. Clubs: Toronto, Toronto and North York Hunt, Toronto Polo (pres.), Saskatoon, Canadian, Empire, Assiniboia. Office: Star Phoenix, 204 5th Ave N, North Saskatoon Can S7K 2P1 *

SIGBAND, NORMAN BRUCE, management communication educator; b. Chgo., June 27, 1920; s. Max and Bessie S.; m. Joan C. Lyons, Aug. 3, 1944; children: Robin, Shelley, Betsy. B.A., U. Chgo., 1940, M.A., 1941, Ph.D., 1954; L.H.D. (hon.), De Paul U., 1986. Asst. prof. bus. communication De Paul U., 1946-50, assoc. prof., 1950-54, prof., 1954-65; prof. mgmt. communication U. So. Calif., 1965—, chmn. dept. mktg., 1970-72; assoc. dean U. So. Calif. (Sch. Bus.), 1975-80, disting. prof. emeritus, 1989—; Disting. Centennial lectr. U. Tex., Austin, 1986; cons. to industry; speaker, condr. workshops, seminars in field; Scholar in Residence, Va. Commonwealth U., 1987, DePaul U., 1988; Disting. emeritus prof. U. So. Calif., 1989,. Author: books, including Practical Communication for Everyday Use, 25th printing, 1954, Effective Report Writing for Business, Industry and Government, 1960, Communication for Management, 1970, Communicacion Para Directivos, 1972, Management Communication for Decision Making, 1972, Communication for Management and Business, 1976, 5th edit., 1989, Communicating in Business, 1981, 3d edit., 1989; gen. editor: books, including Harcourt Brace Jovanovich Bus. Series; contbr. numerous articles to profl. jours., mags. Served to capt. AUS, 1942-46, ETO. Decorated Bronze Star; recipient Excellence in Teaching award U. So. Calif., 1975, Dean's award, 1972, Outstanding Educator award, 1973, Disting. Emeritus award, 1989. Fellow Am. Bus. Communication Assn. (pres. 1964-65); mem. Internat. Communication Assn., Acad. Mgmt., Anti-Defamation League, Hadassah Assocs., Blue Key, Phi Kappa Phi, Alpha Kappa Psi, Beta Gamma Sigma. Democrat. Jewish. Home: 3109 Dona Susana Dr Studio City CA 91604 Office: U So Calif Health Sci Campus 1985 Zonal Ave Los Angeles CA 90007

SIGGSON, ALBERT NATHAN, aircraft company executive; b. Phila., Sept. 22, 1928; s. Nathan Harry and Grace Elizabeth (Fenester) S.; m. Marjorie Jane Lindblom, July 17, 1966; children: Larry Jay, Randal Roy, Gary Norman. AA, Long Beach City Coll., 1957; BS cum laude U. Phoenix, Irvine, Calif., 1983. Standards engr. Standards, Northrop, Nortronics, Hawthorne, Calif., 1966-67; sr. electronic engr. standards Hughes, Fullerton, Calif., 1967-68; lead engr. standards ITT/Gilfillan, Van Nuys, Calif., 1968-69; sr. standards engr. Northrop Aircraft, Hawthorne, Calif., 1969-82, Northrop B-2 div., Pico Rivera, Calif., 1982-83, design specialist, 1983-86, mgr. data and pubs., 1986-89, engr. specialist, 1989—, mem. corp. metrication com., and B-2 div. mgmt. club; instr. blueprint reading evenings El Camino Coll., Torrance, Calif., 1980-86. Served with USN, 1946-49. Registered mfg. engr., Calif.; lifetime cert. mfg., standards and metrication engr. Fellow Inst. Advancement Engrng., U.S. Metric Assn.; mem. Soc. Mfg. Engrs. (sr. mem., chmn. Long Beach chpt. 1972-73, internat. award of merit and citation, numerous others), Standards Engrng. Soc., U.S. Metric Assn., Am. Soc. Testing and Materials, U.S. Metric Assn. (charter chmn. South Bay chpt. 1975-76), U. Phoenix Network for Profl. Devel. (charter), Sigma Xi. Lutheran. Author books on metrication; contbr. articles to profl. jours.

SIGMAN, MELVIN MONROE, psychiatrist; b. N.Y.C., Dec. 15, 1935; s. Irving and Lillian (Pearlman) S. BA, Columbia U., 1956; MD, SUNY, N.Y.C., 1960; postgrad., William Alanson White Analytic Inst., N.Y.C., 1969. Staff psychiatrist Hawthorne (N.Y.) Cedar Knolls Sch., 1966-68; pvt. practice psychiatry N.Y.C., 1966-72, Fresno, Calif., 1974-87; staff psychiatrist Fresno County Dept. of Health, 1974-87, Psychol. Svcs. for Adults, L.A., 1987—; attending staff psychiatry Bellevue Hosp., N.Y.C., 1966-68; cons. N.Y. Foundling Hosp., N.Y.C., 1966-72; assoc. attending staff Roosevelt Hosp., N.Y.C., 1967-72; asst. clin. prof U. Calif. San Francisco, Fresno, 1977; chmn. cen. Calif. com. Columbia Coll. Nat. Alumni Secondary Schs. Served to capt. USAF, 1961-63. Fellow Royal Soc. Health, Am. Orthopsychiat. Assn.; mem. Am. Psychiat. Assn., Hollywood Spa Calif. Fresno Racquet. Office: Psychol Svcs for Adults 11755 Wilshire Blvd Ste 1840 Los Angeles CA 90025

SIGNORELLI, PHILIP JOSEPH, III, educator, costumer; b. Bklyn., May 23, 1941; s. Philip Jr. and Catherine Elizabeth (Natoli) S. BA, Calif. State U., L.A., 1963, MA, 1967; student, Otis Art Inst., 1979-83; MFA, UCLA, 1984. Costume designer and tchr. Drake U., Des Moines, Iowa, 1969-72, L.A. Valley Coll., Van Nuys, Calif., 1973-83, Calif. State U., Fresno, 1984-85; key costumer Columbia TV, Burbank, Calif., 1981; costumer ABC Circle Films, L.A., 1985-86, Disney Studios, Burbank, 1986-87; key costumer Paramont Studios, Hollywood, Calif., 1987, Universal Studios, Burbank, 1987-88, Warner Bros. TV, Burbank, 1988—; workshop tchr. U. Wis., Madison, 1971-72, Drake U., 1973-77. Costumer for TV shows: (1987-89) A Different World, Star Trek: The Next Generation, (1986-87) Big Foot, Double Agent, (1985) Moonlighting, (1980-82) Cheers, Family Ties, Mork and Mindy, Bosum Buddies, Cagney and Lacey, Fantasy Island, Just the Ten of Us; contbr. articles to profl. jours. With U.S. Army, 1963-66. Don Post Studio study grant Drake U., 1971, Berman's Costume study grant Drake U., 1970. Fellow Costumers Union (local 705), Costume Soc. Am. (Region 5 bd. dirs. 1986-86), U.S. Inst. Theatre Tech., Speech Communication Assn. (nat. conv. workshop tchr. 1971), Am. Theatre Assn. (nat. conv. workshop tchr. 1971). Democrat. Roman Catholic. Home: 519 Raleigh St #G Glendale CA 91205

SIGOLOFF, SANFORD CHARLES, retail executive; b. St. Louis, Sept. 8, 1930; s. Emmanuel and Gertrude (Breliant) S.; m. Betty Ellen Greene, Sept. 14, 1952; children: Stephen, John David, Laurie. B.A., UCLA, 1950. Cons. AEC, 1950-54, 57-58; gen. mgr. Edgerton, Germeshausen & Grier, Santa Barbara, Calif., 1958-63; v.p. Xerox Corp., 1963-69; pres. CSI Corp., Los Angeles, 1969-70; sr. v.p. Republic Corp., Los Angeles, 1970-71; chief exec. officer Kaufman & Broad, Inc., Los Angeles, 1979-82; chmn., pres., chief exec. officer Wickes Cos. Inc., Santa Monica, 1982—. Contbr. articles on radiation dosimetry to profl. jours. Bd. govs. Cedars-Sinai Hosp. Served in USAF, 1954-57. Recipient Tom May award Nat. Jewish Hosp. and Research Ctr., 1972. Mem. AAAS, Am. Chem. Soc., AIAA, Am. Nuclear Soc., IEEE, Radiation Research Soc. Office: Wickes Cos Inc 3340 Ocean Park Blvd Santa Monica CA 90405 *

SIGURDSON, LARRY LEROY, advertising, public relations executive; b. Seaside, Oreg., June 16, 1950; s. Clarence Edwin and Beverly Mable (U'Renn) S.; m. Carolyn Lena Foote, July 5, 1980. AA, Clatsop Community Coll., 1979; BS in Journalism, BS in Polit. Sci., U. Oreg., 1980; postgrad., Syracuse U., 1980. Reporter, photographer Oreg. Daily Emerald, Eugene, 1979-80; dir. pub. relations Crawford Advt., Syracuse, N.Y., 1980-81; aviation info. specialist Port of Portland, Oreg., 1981; account exec. Sta. KEED Radio, Eugene, 1981-83; account rep. Sr. News Newspapers, Eugene, 1984; dir. community relations, advt. and spl. event promotion Umpqua Community Coll., Roseburg, Oreg., 1984-87; adv. dir., pub. relations, media buyer Cen. Valley Toyota Dealers' Assn., Inc., Fresno, Calif., 1987—. Editor, pub. (catalog) Umpqua Community Coll., 1985-86, 86-87; asst. editor: Oreg. N.G., Salem, 1979-84; contbr. articles to profl. jours.; photographer various pubs. Precinct committeemen Douglas County Rep. Cen. Com., Roseburg, 1986-87, mem. exec. bd., 1986-88; cons. Bruce Long for Congress, Eugene, 1984; vol. Ross Anthony for Congress, Eugene, 1982; chmn. speakers bur. Douglas County United Way, 1986-87. Served with USN, 1969-74. Named State V.P. of Yr., Oreg. Jaycees, Salem, 1975-76; recipient Pres.'s Cup award Clatsop Community Coll. Mem. Roseburg C. of C., Fresno Advt. Fedn. (mem. newsletter adv. com. 1988-89, nominating com. 1989, bd. dirs. 1989—), Douglas County Pub. Relations Roundtable (v.p., pres. elect 1987). Baptist. Office: Cen Valley Toyota Dealers Assn 4995 E Anderson Fresno CA 93727

SIKORA, JAMES ROBERT, educational business administrator; b. Sacramento, July 8, 1945; s. George Robert and Marian Frances (Fears) S.; m. Marie Lynore Nyarady, June 22, 1968. BEE, U. Santa Clara, 1967; postgrad., U. Calif.-Santa Cruz, 1979--. Electronic engr. GTE-Sylvania, Santa Cruz, 1967-69; systems analyst GTE-Sylvania, 1969-71; sr. support analyst GTE-Sylvania, Mt. View, Calif., 1971-73; bus. systems coordinator Santa Clara County Office Edn., San Jose, Calif., 1973-76; dir. dist. payroll, personnel svcs. Santa Clara County Office Edn., 1976-85, dir. dist. bus. svcs., 1985—; cons. records mgmt. County Santa Clara, San Jose, 1982. Author, co-editor Howdy Rowdy Memorial, 1979. Mem. Assn. Records Mgrs. and Adminstrs. (v.p. 1983-86), Pub. Agy. Risk Mgmt. Assn., Calif. Assn. Sch. Bus. Ofcls. (subsec. pres. 1984-85, bd. dirs. 1987--), Norwegian Elkhound Assn. (pres. 1977-79), Amnesty Interant., Am. Dog Owners Assn., Jaycees, Sierra Club,. Libertarian. Roman Catholic. Home: 400 Coon Heights Rd Ben Lomond CA 95005 Office: Santa Clara County Office Edn 100 Skyport Dr MC 252 San Jose CA 95005

SIKORA, WARREN, lawyer; b. Chgo., May 6, 1921; s. Paul Arthur and Mae Theresa (Hampl) S.; m. Jean Pessell, Nov. 20, 1943; children: Paul Elliott, Catherine Ann, Michael Warren. BA, U. Chgo., 1942, MBA, 1946; JD, UCLA, 1952. Bar: Calif. 1953, U.S. Dist. Ct. (cen. dist.) Calif. 1953, U.S. Ct. Appeals (9th cir.) 1960, U.S. Supreme Ct. 1962. Acct. Arthur Andersen, Los Angeles, 1946-47, Roberts & Coombs, Los Angeles, 1947-49; assoc. Paul Hastings & Janofsky, Los Angeles, 1952-54; ptnr. Rutan & Tucker, Santa Ana, Calif., 1954-66, Sikora & Price Inc., Santa Ana, 1966—. Served to capt. USMCR, 1942-46. Mem. ABA (chmn. sales and fin. trans. com. tax sect. 1987). Republican. Episcopalian. Clubs: Santa Ana Country, LaQuinta Country. Lodges: Masons, Shriners, Elks. Home: 2 Little River Circle Corona Del Mar CA 92625 Office: Sikora & Price Inc 2913 Pullman PO Box 15707 Santa Ana CA 92705

SIL, NARASINGHA PROSAD, history educator; b. Calcutta, India, Dec. 11, 1937; came to U.S., 1971; s. Umes Chandra and Tripura Sundari (Chander) S.; m. Sati Makhija, Aug. 12, 1965; 1 child, Jayashree. BA with honors, U. Calcutta, 1959, MA, 1963; MEd, U. Oreg., 1973, MA, 1974, PhD, 1978. Lectr. Vidyasagar Coll., India, 1962-63, Chandernagore Coll., India, 1963-64; tchr. Imperial Govt. Ethiopia, Addis Ababa, 1967-71; prin. edn. officer Nigerian Fed. Ministry Edn., Lagos, 1975-77; asst. prof. history U. Oreg., Eugene, 1979-80; assoc. prof. U. Benin, Nigeria, 1980-86; asst. prof. Western Oreg. State Coll., Monmouth, 1987—; vis. asst. prof. Oreg. State U., Corvallis, 1980; vis. prof. U. Oreg., Eugene, 1986. Author: Kautilya's Arthasastra: A Comparative Study, 1985, William Lord Herbert of Pembroke: Politique and Patriot, 1988; contbr. articles, book revs. to profl. jours. Mem. Am. Hist. Assn., Renaissance Soc. Am., N.Am. Conf. of British Studies, Inst. Hist. Studies, Hist. Soc. Nigeria. Hindu. Home: 288 E Jackson Apt #3 Monmouth OR 97361 Office: Western Oreg State Coll Monmouth Ave Monmouth OR 97361

SILACCI, HELEN BERNADETTE, nurse; b. Hanford, Calif., Apr. 19, 1943; d. Antone P. and Mary P. (Portugal) Silveira; m. Gary E. Silacci, Dec. 2, 1966; children: Gary Jr., Nicole, Brent. BS in Nursing, Calif. State U., Fresno, 1966; postgrad., San Jose (Calif.) State U., 1971, U. San Francisco, 1976, U. Santa Cruz, 1983-86, Golden Gate U., 1989—. Cert. fin. planner, Calif. Pub. health nurse Santa Clara County Health Dept., San Jose, 1967-69; sch. nurse Morgan Hill (Calif.) Unified Sch. Dist., 1969—; family life edn. tchr. Cen. High Sch., 1986—; fin. planner Silacci Enterprises, Morgan Hill, 1986—; tchr. family life edn. Cen. High Sch., 1986—; trainer health edn. Editor Nutrition Edn. Newsletter for Community, 1979-83. Officer Alice In Wonderland chpt. Children's Home Soc., Morgan Hill, 1970—; instr. first-aid ARC, San Jose, 1970-78; commr. health City of Morgan Hill, 1974-78; coordinator Berkeley Health Edn. Project for Schs., 1977-82; mem. health task force Santa Clara County Sch., 1978-82; mem. Citizens Against Drug Abuse, Morgan Hill, 1980—; chairperson fin. com. St. Catherine's Parish, Morgan Hill, 1983-86; area chairperson Bellamine Coll. Preparatory; mem. Calif. for Drug Free Youth, 1986—. Recipient Health Edn. award Santa Clara County, 1978; Calif. State Dept. Edn. grantee, 1980-83. Mem. Internat. Assn. for Fin. Planning, Nat. Assn. Sch. Nursing, Nat. Comml. Fin. Assn., Calif. Sch. Nurses Orgn. (chairperson nomination com. Bay Coast sect. 1976-78, chairperson membership com. 1978-80, 83-86, bd. dirs. 1980-83, chairperson research com. 1981-83, treas. 1987—, Outstanding Leadership award 1983-85), Santa Clara County Sch. Nurses Assn. (various offices 1970-80). Republican. Office: Silacci Enterprises PO Box 68 Morgan Hill CA 95037

SILBAR, RICHARD ROBERT, nuclear physicist, knowledge engineer; b. Milw., Sept. 19, 1937; s. Robert G. and Ruth Anne (Papke) S.; m. Margaret Lincoln, Jan. 19, 1963. BS, U. Mich., 1959, MS, 1960, PhD, 1963. Instr., rsch. assoc. Johns Hopkins U., Balt., 1963-65; asst. rsch. prof. Cath. U. Am., Washington, 1965-67; staff mem. Los Alamos Nat. Lab., 1967—; vis. prof. SUNY, Stony Brook, 1976, U. Mass., Amherst, 1985; program mgr. for nuclear physics Dept. Energy, Germantown, Md., 1981-82. Mem. Am. Phys. Soc. (life), Am. Assn. for Artificial Intelligence. Office: Los Alamos Nat Lab Dept T-5 MS 8283 POB 1663 Los Alamos NM 87545

SILBAUGH, PRESTON NORWOOD, savings and loan consultant, lawyer; b. Stockton, Calif., Jan. 15, 1918; s. Herbert A. and Della Mae (Masten) S.; m. Maria Sarah Arriola; children—Judith Ann Freed, Gloria Stypinski, Ximena Carey Braun, Carol Lee Morgan. A.B. in Philosophy, U. Wash., 1940; J.D., Stanford U., 1953. Bar: Calif. With Lockheed Aircraft Corp., 1941-44, Pan Am. World Airways, 1944, Office Civilian Personnel, War Dept., 1944-45; engaged in ins. and real estate in Calif., 1945-54; mem. faculty Stanford Law Sch., 1954-59, asso. prof. law, 1956-59, asso. dean, 1956-59; chief dep. savs. and loan commnr. for Calif., 1959-61, bus. and commerce adminstr., dir. investment, savs. and loan commr., mem. gov.'s cabinet, 1961-63; dir. Chile-Calif. Aid Program, Sacramento and Santiago, 1963-65; chmn. bd. Beverly Hills Savs. & Loan Assn., Calif., 1965-84; dir. Wickes Cos., Inc.; chmn. bd., pres. Simon Bolivar Fund, Del Mar, Calif.; of counsel firm Miller, Boyko & Bell, San Diego. Author: The Economics of Personal Insurance, 1958; also articles. Mem. pres.'s real estate adv. com. U. Calif., 1966—; mem. Beverly Hills Pub. Bldg. Adv. Com., 1970—. Served with USMCR, 1942-43. Mem. ABA, San Diego County Bar Assn., Soc. Internat. Devel., U.S., Nat., Calif. Savs. and Loan Leagues, Inter-Am. Savs. and Loan Union, Internat. Union Building Socs., U. Wash., Stanford Alumni Assns., Calif. Aggie Alumni Assn., Order of Coif, Phi Alpha Delta. Clubs: Commonwealth (San Francisco), Town Hall (Los Angeles). Home: Costenera del Sur, Zapallar Chile

SILBERGELD, JEROME LESLIE, art historian, educator; b. Highland, Ill., Apr. 25, 1944; s. David and Sabina Silbergeld; m. Michelle DeKlyen, June 27, 1970; children: David, Emily. BA in History, Stanford U., 1966, MA in History, 1967, PhD in Art History, 1974; MA in Art History, U. Oreg., 1972. Vis. asst. prof. dept. art history U. Oreg., Eugene, 1974-75; from asst. prof. to prof. U. Wash., Seattle, 1975—; chmn. art history dept. U. Wash., Seattle, 1988—. Author: Chinese Painting Style, 1982 (Soc. for Tech. Achievement award 1983), Mind Landscapes: The Painting of C.C. Wang, 1987; editor, translator: Chinese Painting Colors (Yu Fei'an) 1988; contbr. articles to profl. jours. Grantee Nat. Endowment for Humanities, 1981, J. Paul Getty Trust, 1987. Mem. Assn. Asian Studies, Coll. Art Assn. Office: U Wash Dept Art History DM-10 Seattle WA 98195

SILBERMAN, IRWIN ALAN, public health physician; b. Newport News, Va., Sept. 1, 1932; s. Henry and Toby (Weiss) S.; m. Mitsue Fukuyama, May 7, 1964 (div. July 1984); children: Denise, Donn, Daniel, Dean, Dana. BA, U. Calif., Berkeley, 1953; MD, U. Calif., San Francisco, 1956; MS, U. No. Colo., 1980. Intern L.A. County Harbor Gen. Hosp., Torrance, Calif., 1956-57; resident in ob-gyn. L.A. County Harbor Gen. Hosp., Torrance, 1957-61; commd. USAF, 1961, advanced through grades to col., 1971; staff obstetrician-gynecologist Tachikawa (Japan) Air Base, 1963-65; chief ob-gyn. Mather Air Force Base, Sacramento, 1965-66; chief aeromed. services Yokota Air Base, Tokyo, 1966-68; dir. base med. services Itazuke Air Base, Fukuoka, Japan, 1968-70, Kirkland Air Force Base, Albuquerque, 1970-72; chief hosp. services USAF Hosp. Davis-Monthan, Tucson, 1972-81; ret. USAF, 1981; med. dir. CIGNA Healthplan of Fla., Tampa, 1981-83; chief women's clinic H.C. Hudson Comprehensive Health Ctr., Los Angeles, 1983-85; dir. maternal health and family planning programs Los Angeles County Dept. Health Services, Los Angeles, 1985—; mil. cons. to surgeon-gen., USAF, Tucson, 1980-81; bd. dirs. Los Angeles Regional Family Planning Council, Perinatal Adv. Council of Los Angeles Communities. Chmn. health profls. adv. com. March of Dimes, Los Angeles, 1988; camp physician Boy Scouts Nat. Jamboree, Fort Hill, Va., 1985. Recipient Meritorious Service medal, USAF, 1972, 81, Air Force Commendation medal, 1980, Air medal, 1969. Fellow Am. Coll. Obstetricians and Gynecologists, Am. Coll. Physician Executives; mem. Am. Acad. Med. Dirs., Am. Pub. Health Assn., So. Calif. Pub. Health Assn. (governing council 1988—). Home: 2228 Flintridge Dr Glendale CA 91206 Office: LA County Dept Health Svcs 313 N Figueroa St Los Angeles CA 90012

SILBERT, AMY FOXMAN, clinical art therapist; b. Augusta, Ga., July 11, 1953; d. Elliott and Anita Foxman; m. Philip Silbert, Sept. 6, 1987; 1 child, Sean Kenneth. BA in Design, UCLA, 1976; postgrad., Loyola Marymount U., 1988—. Art dir., advt. mgr. Unico Am. Corp., L.A., 1976-78; freelance graphic artist, art specialist, tchr. 1979-82; vol. coord., tchr. Craft and Folk Art Mus., L.A., 1983-86; art specialist Art Reach, UCLA Calif. Arts Coun., 1983-84; editor in chief Grad. Achievement Preparation Svc., Santa Monica, Calif., 1985-87; tchr. coordinator art exhibit Hebrew Union Coll., Los Angeles, 1984; guest children's TV programs, 1970-84. Gov. intern U.S. Congress, Washington, 1973. Recipient 1st Place award traffic light design City Monterrey, Calif., 1973. Democrat. Jewish. Office: PO Box 2238 Culver City CA 90230

SILBERT, STEPHEN DAVID, entertainment company executive, lawyer; b. Los Angeles, Sept. 4, 1942; s. Bernard M. and Irene (Katz) S.; m. Susan Carp, Sept. 10, 1967 (div. 1973); 1 child, Tracy L. BA, Claremont McKenna Coll., 1964, M in Bus. Econs., 1965; JD, U. Calif., Berkeley, 1967. Bar: Calif. 1968. Assoc. Wyman, Bautzer, Christensen, Kuchel & Silbert, Los Angeles, 1967-70, ptnr., 1970-85, of counsel, 1985—; chmn. exec. com. United Artists Corp., Beverly Hills, Calif., 1985-86; pres., chief operating officer MGM/UA Communications Co., Beverly Hills, from 1986, now consultant. Mem. ABA, Calif. Bar Assn. Office: MGM/UA Communications Co 450 N Roxbury Dr Beverly Hills CA 90210 *

SILL, ALEXIS MATTOS, computer company executive; b. Rio de Janeiro, Apr. 15, 1949; came to U.S., 1956, naturalized, 1960; s. Bev Arthur and Gigi Lino (Mattos) S.; m. Sandra Sarah Ann Heaslip, Aug. 24, 1974; children: Courtney Jane, Alexis Ryan, Colin George. Student Golden Gate U., San Francisco. Sales mgr. United Calif. Bank, San Francisco, 1971-77; sales exec. Automatic Data Processing, Inc., San Francisco, 1977-84;nat. sales exec. Digital Research, Inc., Santa Clara, Calif., 1984—; pres. Mega Distbg., Sausalito, Calif. Served with USMCR, 1969-71. Republican. Home: 200 Via Lerida Greenbrae CA 95054 Office: Digital Rsch Inc 4401 Great America Pkwy Ste 200 Santa Clara CA 95054

SILLER, FREDERICK H., engineering educator; b. Regina, Sask., Can.; s. Joseph J. and Helen M. (Boyd) S.; children: Cameron Boyd, Heidi Christine. BSEE, U. Sask., Saskatoon, Can., 1962; MBA, U. Western Ont., London, Can., 1966, PhD, 1972. Cert. profl. engr. Engr. A.C.A., Ltd., Toronto, Ont., Can., 1962-65; prof. U. B.C., Vancouver, Can., 1969—. Contbr. articles to acad. jours. Office: U BC, 2053 Main Mall, Vancouver, BC Canada V6T 1Y8

SILVA, JOHN PHILIP COSTA, newspaper editor; b. Providence, Jan. 19, 1951; s. Silvano Costa and Florence Josephine (Russo) S.; m. Deborah Helen Radovsky, May 8, 1977; children: Daniel David, Matthew Philip. BA in Journalism, U. R.I., 1973. Staff writer Providence Jour.-Bull., 1973-79; staff writer Miami (Fla.) News, 1979-81, asst. city editor, 1981-82; city editor Lexington (Ky.) Herald-Leader, 1982-84; night city editor L.A. Herald Examiner, 1984-85, assignment editor, 1985-87; asst. mng. editor met.-state news Ariz. Daily Star, Tucson, 1987—. Recipient 1st place for spot news UPI Newspapers New Eng., 1977. Mem. Nat. Assn. Hispanic Journalists, Investigative Reporters and Editors Assn. Home: 9433 N Albatross Dr Tucson AZ 85741 Office: Ariz Daily Star 4850 S Park Ave Tucson AZ 85714

SILVA, MARY E., librarian; b. Seattle, Aug. 30, 1957; d. Theodore and Ruth Pauline (Kolk) S. BA in French, U. Wash., 1978, MLS, 1979, Cert. Library Automation, 1988. Cert. librarian, Wash. Librarian City U., Bellevue, Wash., 1981-86, Boeing Computer Services, Seattle, 1986—; instr. City U., Bellevue, 1984-85. Mem. Pacific Northwest Library Assn., Assn. Coll. and Research Libraries, ALA, Beta Phi Mu, Phi Beta Kappa. Home: 10442 Forest Ave S Seattle WA 98178

SILVA, RICHARD EDWARD, dentist; b. Berkeley, Calif., Mar. 5, 1952; s. Edward Raymond and Dora Marget (Godinez) S.; m. Ivy Emily Memmer, May 17, 1986. AA, Chabot Jr. Coll., Hayward, Calif., 1972; BS, Calif. State U., Hayward, 1975; BS, DDS, U. Calif., San Francisco, 1981. Dentist assoc. Dr. Thom Charron, San Francisco, 1980-81, Dexter Massa, DDS, San Jose, Calif., 1981-82, 84-86, Hui Dental Group, Oakland, Calif., 1982-83, Youthful Tooth, Inc., Oakland, 1983-84, South San Jose Dental Group, 1986-88; gen. practice dentistry Castro Valley, Calif., 1988—. Assoc. advisor Explorers, Boy Scouts Am., San Leandro, Calif., 1976-81. Fellow Acad. Gen. Dentistry; mem. ADA, Calif. Dental Assn., U. Calif. at San Francisco Alumni Assn. Republican. Roman Catholic. Lodge: Elks. Office: 20353 Lake Chabot Rd Suite 109 Castro Valley CA 94546

SILVA, ROBERT OWEN, protective service official; b. La Junta, Colo., Sept. 5, 1935; s. Owen Delbert and Gertrude H. (Kerr) S.; m. Meredith Ann Ginn, Dec. 18, 1953; children—Edward, Andrew, Colleen. Student Pueblo Jr. Coll., 1953, FBI Nat. Acad., 1975, Police Found. Exec. Program, 1979-80. Cert. peace officer, Colo. Police officer Pueblo Police Dept., Colo., 1958-66, sgt., 1966-72, capt., 1972-77, chief of police, 1977—, dir. Colo. Police Officers Standards and Tng. Bd. dirs. Salvation Army, Pueblo, Easter Seals Soc., Pueblo, Community Corrections Bd., Pueblo, Served with U.S. Army, 1955-57. Mem. Pueblo Community Coll. Criminal Justice Adv. Bd., Leadership Pueblo Steering Com., Pikes Peak Community Coll. Criminal Justice Program (chmn. adv. bd. 1981), Organized Crime Strike Force (bd. dirs. 1977-84, chmn. 1982, 83, 84); Colo. Assn. Chiefs of Police (pres. 1984-85), Rocky Mountain Info. Network (chmn. bd. dirs. 1986—), Presbyterian (elder). Lodges: Kiwanis (bd. dirs. 1982-84), Elks. Office: Pueblo Police Dept 130 Central Main St Pueblo CO 81003 *

SILVA, STANLEY ALBERT, construction company executive; b. San Luis Obispo, Calif., June 25, 1937; s. Tony Thomas and Julia Ruth (Brooks) S.; m. Connie Marie Marsella, Aug. 8, 1959 (div. Apr. 1978); 1 child, Stacey; m. Ann Spenser Moyer, Dec. 12, 1982; stepchildren: Carl, Lisa, Angela, Steven. Student, Fresno State U., 1956-58; BS, Ariz. State U., 1960. Cert. profl. estimator. Chief estimator Harris Constrn., Fresno, Calif., 1960-72, Nielsen-Nickles Co., Sacramento, 1972-75, Robert G. Fisher Co., San Diego, 1975-78, Colo. Pacific Constructors, San Diego, 1978-80; chief estimator, project mgr. Constrn. Mgmt. Services, San Diego, 1980-82; chief estimator, v.p. Holvick Constrn., Sunnyvale, Calif., 1982-88, also bd. dirs. Bd. dirs. Big Bros., Fresno, 1975-78, San Diego, 1978-81. Scholar Associated Gen. Contractors of Ariz., Tempe, 1958. Mem. ASCE, Am. Soc. Profl. Estimators (v.p. 1985-86), Am. Soc. Cost Engrs., Project Mgmt. Inst. Republican. Roman Catholic. Club: Toastmasters (Fresno). Lodges: Kiwanis, Elks. Home: 3036 Hounds Estates Ct San Jose CA 95135

SILVER, BARNARD STEWART, mechanical engineer, consultant; b. Salt Lake City, Mar. 9, 1933; s. Harold Farnes and Madelyn Cannon (Stewart) S.; B.S. in Mech. Engrng., MIT, 1957; M.S. in Engrng. Mechanics, Stanford U., 1958; grad. Advanced Mgmt. Program, Harvard U., 1977; m. Cherry Bushman, Aug. 12, 1963; children—Madelyn Stewart, Cannon Farnes. Engr. aircraft nuclear propulsion div. Gen. Electric Co., Evandale, Ohio, 1957; engr. Silver Engrng. Works, Denver, 1959-66, mgr. sales, 1966-71; chief engr. Union Sugar div. Consol. Foods Co., Santa Maria, Calif., 1971-74; directeur du complexe SODESUCRE, Abidjan, Ivory Coast, 1974-76; supt. engrng. and maintenance U and I, Inc., Moses Lake, Wash., 1976-79; pres. Silver Enterprises, Moses Lake, 1971-88, Silver Energy Systems Corp., Moses Lake, 1980—; pres., gen. mgr. Silver Chief Corp., 1983—; pres. Silver Corp., 1984-86, Silver Pubs., Inc., 1986—; v.p. Barnard J. Stewart Cousins Land

Co., 1987-88; instr. engring. Big Bend Community Coll., 1980-81. Explorer adviser Boy Scouts Am., 1965-66, chmn. cub pack com., 1968-74, chmn. scout troop com., 1968-74, vice chmn. Columbia Basin Dist., 1986—; pres. Silver Found., 1971-84, v.p., 1984—; ednl. counselor MIT, 1971-88; pres. Chief Moses Jr. High Sch. Parent Tchr. Student Assn., 1978-79; missionary Ch. of Jesus Christ of Latter-day Saints, Can., 1953-55, W. Africa, 1988—; 2d counselor Moses Lake Stake Presidency, 1980-88; bd. dirs. Columbia Basin Allied Arts, 1986-88. Served with Ordnance Corps, U.S. Army, 1958-59. Decorated chevalier Ordre National (Republic of Ivory Coast); registered profl. engr., Colo. Mem. ASME, Assn. Energy Engrs., AAAS, Am. Soc. Sugar Beet Technologists, Internat. Soc. Sugar Cane Technologists, Am. Soc. Sugar Cane Technologists, Sugar Industry Technicians, Nat. Fedn. Ind. Bus.; Utah State Hist. Soc. (life), Mormon Hist. Assn., Western Hist. Assn., Univ. Archeol. Soc. (life), Sigma Xi (life), Pi Tau Sigma, Sigma Chi, Alpha Phi Omega. Republican. Mormon. Lodge: Kiwanis. Home: 4391 S Carol Jane Dr Salt Lake City UT 84124 Office: Silver Chief Corp Rte 32 86 Easy St Moses Lake WA 98837 also: Silver Energy Systems Corp 140 W Moore Ave Hermistone WA 98837

SILVER, LAWRENCE ALAN, psychiatric social worker; b. Highland Park, Mich., Oct. 10, 1946; s. Herbert Martin Silver and Edna (Keller) Stotzky; m. Hollis Lee Dec, May 2, 1981. BA, Wayne State U., 1971; MSW, U. Mich., 1974. Lic. clin. social worker, Calif. Clin. social worker Detroit Psychiatric Inst., 1974-76, St. Joseph Mercy Hosp., Pontiac, Mich., 1976, VA Mental Hygiene Clinic, San Diego, Calif., 1977; direct svcs. supr. Harmonium, Inc., San Diego, 1978; social worker County of San Diego, Dept. of Social Svcs., 1978-80; sr. psychiatric social worker County of San Diego, Hillcrest Inpatient Unit, 1980-85, County of San Diego, E. County Mental Health, El Cajon, Calif., 1985-89; supervisory social worker Navy Family Svc. Ctr., San Diego, 1989—; oral commr. Bd. Behavioral Sci. Examiners, Calif., 1979; edn. liaison, County of San Diego, E. County Mental Health, 1988-89. Sustaining mem. Republican Nat. Com., 1988-89. Mem. Nat. Assn. Social Workers (state del. 1976, chmn. in-service edn. 1976). Republican. Home: 1029 Park Hill Dr Escondido CA 92025 Office: Family Support Center Murphy Canyon Housing Naval Station San Diego CA 92123

SILVER, SUE ANN, real estate broker; b. Manitowoc, Wis., July 29, 1945; d. Jerome Theodore and Verona (Schmidt) Wegner; m. Gerald Neil Silver (div. 1981); 1 child, Victoria Anne. BA, U. Wis., 1968. Lic. real estate broker, Calif. Sales cons. Coldwell Banker, Sherman Oaks, Calif., 1968-79; sales assoc. Jerry Berns Assocs., Encino, Calif., 1977-79; broker assoc. White House Properties, Woodland Hills, Calif., 1979-82; pres. Sue Silver & Assocs., Inc., Calabasas, Calif., 1982—. Troop ldr. Brownies, Girl Scouts Am., 1985-88; exec. com. Blind Children's Ctr. of L.A., 1987-88. Mem. San Fernando Valley Bd. Realtors (profl. stds. com. 1972-77), Inst. Resdl. Mktg., Delta Gamma (So. Calif. coordinating com. pres. 1986-88, alumnae pres. 1985-89). Republican. Presbyterian. Home: 22983 Paul Revere Dr Calabasas CA 91302

SILVERBERG, LEWIS HENRY, lawyer; b. L.A., Nov. 1, 1934; s. Milton Henry and Marjorie Vella (Coates) S.; m. Amelia Francis Backstrom, June, 9, 1959 (div. 1979); children: Stephen, Richard, Donna; m. Alice Ellen Deakins, Mar. 9, 1979. BA, Pomona Coll., 1955; JD, UCLA, 1958. Bar: Calif. 1959, U.S. Supreme Ct. 1966. Pvt. practice San Diego, 1959—; acted co-trustee bankruptcy reorganizations; acted receiver with commr. of corps; bd. dirs. pub. and privately held businesses; gen. ptnr. and investor in real estate investments; arbitrator Superior Ct.; speaker CEB on real estate seminars, probate panels; referee Calif. inheritance tax and probate, 1972-88. Mem. San Diego Zool. Soc., San Diego Opera Assn., San Diego Epilepsy Soc., San Diego County Burn Inst.; chmn. New Theatre Fund, U. Calif., San Diego, Judicial Nominees Evaluation Com., 1984. Mem. Pomona Coll. Alumni Assn. (bd. dirs.), UCLA Law Alumni Assn. (bd.dirs.), numerous pub., charitable and ednl. inst. Republican. Office: 3252 5th Ave San Diego CA 92103

SILVERBERG, ROBERT, author; b. N.Y.C.; s. Michael and Helen (Baim) S.; m. Barbara Brown, 1956; m. Karen Haber, 1987. B.A., Columbia U., 1956. Author: novels Thorns, 1967, The Masks of Time, 1968, Hawksbill Station, 1968, Nightwings, 1969, To Live Again, 1969, Tower of Glass, 1970, The World Inside, 1971, Son of Man, 1971, A Time of Changes, 1971, Dying Inside, 1972, The Book of Skulls, 1972, Born With the Dead, 1974, Shadrach in the Furnace, 1976, Lord Valentine's Castle, 1980, Majipoor Chronicles, 1982, Lord of Darkness, 1983, Valentine Pontifex, 1983, Gilgamesh the King, 1984, Tom O'Bedlam, 1985, Star of Gypsies, 1986, At Winter's End, 1988, To the Land of the Living, 1989; non-fiction Lost Cities and Vanished Civilizations, 1962; The Great Wall of China, 1965, The Old Ones: Indians of the American Southwest, 1965, Scientists and Scoundrels: A Book of Hoaxes, 1965, The Auk, the Dodo and the Oryx, 1966, The Morning of Mankind: Prehistoric Man in Europe, 1967, Mound Builders of Ancient America: The Archaeology of a Myth, 1968, If I Forget Thee, O Jerusalem: American Jews and the State of Israel, 1970, The Pueblo Revolt, 1970, The Realm of Prester John, 1971. Recipient Hugo award World Sci. Fiction Conv., 1956, 69, 87; Nebula award Sci. Fiction Writers Am., 1970, 72, 75, 86. Mem. Sci. Fiction Writers Am. (pres. 1967-68). Address: Box 13160 Station E Oakland CA 94661

SILVERBERG, STUART OWEN, obstetrician, gynecologist; b. Denver, Oct. 14, 1931; s. Edward M. and Sara (Morris) S.; B.A., U. Colo., 1952, M.D., 1955; m. Joan E. Snyderman, June 19, 1954 (div. Apr. 1970); children—Debra Sue Owen, Eric Owen, Alan Kent; m. 2d, Kay Ellen Conklin, Oct. 18, 1970 (div. Apr. 1982); 1 son, Cris S.; m. 3d, Sandra Kay Miller, Jan., 1983. Intern Women's Hosp. Phila., 1955-56; resident Kings County Hosp., Bklyn., 1958-62; practice medicine specializing in obstetrics and gynecology, Denver, 1962—; mem. staff Luth. Hosp., Rose Med. Ctr., St. Josephs Hosp., Denver; mem. staff St. Anthony Hosp., chmn. dept. obstetrics and gynecology, 1976-77, 86-87; clin. instr. U. Colo. Sch. Medicine, Denver, 1962-72, asst. clin. prof., 1972-88, assoc. clin. prof., dir. gynecol. endoscopy and laser surgery, 1988—; v.p. Productos Alimenticos, La Ponderosa, S.A.; dir., chmn. bd. Wicker Works Video Prodns., Inc.; cons. Ft. Logan Mental Health Center, Denver, 1964-70; mem. Gov.'s Panel Mental Retardation, 1966; med. adv. bd. Colo. Planned Parenthood, 1966—, Am. Med. Center, Spivak, Colo., 1967—. Mem. Colo. Emergency Resources Bd., Denver, 1965—. Served to maj. AUS, 1956-58; Germany. Diplomate Am. Bd. Obstetrics and Gynecology. Fellow Am. Coll. Obstetricians and Gynecologists, ACS; mem. Am. Internat. fertility socs., Colo. Gynecologists and Obstetricians Soc., Hellman Obstet. and Gynecol. Soc., Colo. Med. Soc., Clear Creek Valley Med. Soc. (trustee 1978, 80, 87), Phi Sigma Delta, AMA, Flying Physicians Assn., Aircraft Owners and Pilots Assn., Nu Sigma Nu, Alpha Epsilon Delta. Jewish. Mem. editorial rev. bd. Colo. Women's Mag.; editor-in-chief Physicians Video Jour., 1984—. Office: 8407 Bryant St Westminster CO 80030

SILVERMAN, CAROL ANN, interior designer; b. Bishop, Calif., Sept. 9, 1936; d. Ivan W. and Laura Harriet (Critchett) Wilson; m. James R. Silverman, Sept. 7, 1957; children: Denise Lynn, Michele Jeanene, Heather Gwenn, Todd Shawn. AA, Sacramento City Coll., 1956; grad., Sacramento State Coll., 1957; BA, San Francisco State U., 1958; postgrad., U. Calif., Davis, U. Calif., Berkeley, Am. River Coll., Sierra Coll. Prin. Environ. Design, Sacramento, 1970—. Elder Fremont Presbyn. Ch., Sacramento; active Jr. Mus. Sponsors, Sacramento. Mem. Am. Soc. Interior Designers (assoc.), Illuminating Engring. Soc., Designers Lighting Forum. Office: Environ Design 777 Campus Commons Rd Ste 160 Sacramento CA 95825

SILVERMAN, JEFFREY NEAL, writer; b. N.Y.C., Apr. 21, 1950; s. Murray and Rosalind (Rosel) S. Student, Union Coll., 1968-69; AB, Vassar Coll., 1972. Reporter Washington Star, 1977-78, N.Y. Daily News, 1978; contbr. Sta. KABC Radio, L.A., 1981-82; corr. Cable News Network, L.A., 1980-82; columnist L.A. Herald Examiner, 1978-82; contbg. editor US Mag., L.A., 1985-87; corr. Chgo. Tribune, L.A., 1983-87; arts and entertainment editor L.A. Herald Examiner, 1987—; cons. Entertainment Tonight, L.A., 1980-82. Contbr. articles to mags.; actor: (film) Exposed, 1983, Fever Pitch, 1985, Field of Dreams, 1989; producer (TV): I Love Your Perfect (ABC), 1989. Mem. Amnesty Internat., ACLU. Recipient Nat. Feature Writing award, Hearst Corp., 1988. Mem. Writers Guild of Am., SAG, PEN, Sigma Delta Chi. Jewish.

SILVERMAN, JEROME, psychologist; b. Bklyn., July 15, 1936; s. Harry and Gertrude (Adelman) S. BA, Boston U., 1958, MA, 1959; PhD, U. Pitts., 1962. Lic. psychologist, Calif. Clin. psychologist Calif. Youth Authority, Whittier, 1962-63, Los Angeles County Gen. Hosp., L.A., 1963-68; pvt. practice clin. psychology and psychodiagnostic testing L.A., 1968—; asst. prof. Sch. Medicine U. So. Calif., L.A., 1963-68; ptnr. Venti Real Estate Group, Monterey Park, Calif., 1982; bd. dirs. Golden Security Thrift & Loan, Alhambra, Calif.; cons. on drug abuse legislation Calif. Assembly, 1986-89. Democrat. Jewish. Home and Office: 320 S Garfield Ave Alhambra CA 91801

SILVERMAN, PAUL HYMAN, zoologist, former university official; b. Mpls., Oct. 8, 1924; s. Adolph and Libbie (Idlekope) S.; m. Nancy Josephs, May 20, 1945; children: Daniel Joseph, Claire. Student, U. Minn., 1942-43, 46-47; B.S., Roosevelt U., 1949; M.S. in Biology, Northwestern U., 1951; Ph.D. in Parasitology, U. Liverpool, Eng., 1955, D.Sc., 1968. Research fellow Malaria Research Sta., Hebrew U., Israel, 1951-53; research fellow dept. entomology and parasitology Sch. Tropical Medicine, U. Liverpool, 1953-56; sr. sci. officer dept. parasitology Moredun Inst., Edinburgh, Scotland, 1956-59; head dept. immunoparasitology Allen & Hanbury, Ltd., Ware, Eng., 1960-62; prof. zoology and veterinary pathology and hygiene U. Ill., Urbana, 1963-72; chmn. dept. zoology U. Ill., 1964-65, head dept. zoology, 1965-68; sr. staff mem. Center for Zoonoses Research, 1964; prof. biology, head div. natural scis. Temple Buell Coll., Denver, 1970-71; prof. biology, chmn. dept. biology, acting v.p. research, v.p. research and grad. affairs, assoc. provost for research and acad. services U. N.Mex., 1972-77; provost for research and grad. studies SUNY, Central Adminstrn., Albany, 1977-79; pres. Research Found., SUNY, Albany, 1979-80, U. Maine, Orono, 1980-84; fellow bio. and med. div. Lawrence Berkeley Lab., U. Calif. Berkeley, 1984-86, acting div. head, 1986-87; adj. prof. med. parasitology Sch. Pub. Health U. Calif.-Berkeley, 1986, assoc. lab. dir. for life scis., dir. Donner Lab., 1987—, dir. Systemwide Biotech. Rsch. and Edn. Program, 1989—; cons., examiner Middle States Assn. Schs. and Colls., Commn. Colls. and Univs., North Central Assn. Colls. and Secondary Schs., 1964—; chmn. Commn. on Instns. Higher Edn., 1974-76; adj. prof. U. Colo., Boulder, 1970-72; Fulbright prof. zoology Australian Nat. U., Canberra, 1969; adjoint prof. biology U. Colo., Boulder, 1970-72; examiner for Western Assn. Schs. and Colls., Accrediting Commn. for Sr. Colls. and Univs., Calif., 1972—; mem. bd. Nat. Council on Postsecondary Accreditation, Washington, 1975-77; faculty apointee Sandia Corp., Dept. Energy, Albuquerque, 1974-81; project dir. research in malaria immunology and vaccination AID, 1965-76; project dir. research in Helminth immunity USPHS, NIH, 1964-72; sr. cons. to Ministry Edn. and Culture, Brasilia, Brazil, 1975—; cons. to U.S. Senator George Mitchell, Maine; adv. on malaria immunology WHO, Geneva, 1967; bd. dirs. Inhalation Toxicology Research Inst., Lovelace Biomed. and Environ. Research Inst., Albuquerque, 1977—; mem. N.Y. State Gov.'s High Tech. Opportunities Task Force; chmn. research and rev. com. N.Y. State Sci. and Tech. Found.; mem. pres.'s council New Eng. Land Grant Univs.; mem. policies and issues com. Nat. Assn. State Univs. and Land Grant Colls.; bd. advs. Lovelace-Bataan Med. Center, Albuquerque, 1974-77; adv. com. U.S. Army Command and Gen. Staff Coll., Ft. Leavenworth, Kans., 1983-84; corporator Bangor Savs. Bank. Contbr. articles to profl. jours.; patentee process for prodn. parasitic helminth vaccine. Bd. dirs. Historic Albany Found.; chmn. Maine Gov.'s Econ. Devel. Conf.; chmn. research rev. com. N.Y. State Sci. and Tech. Found. Fellow Royal Soc. Tropical Medicine, Hygiene, N. Mex. Acad. Sci.; mem. Am. Soc. Parasitologists, Am. Soc. Tropical Medicine and Hygiene, Am. Soc. Immunologists, Brit. Soc. Parasitology (council), Brit. Soc. Immunologists, Soc. Gen. Microbiology, Soc. Protozoologists, Am. Soc. Zoologists, Am. Inst. Biol. Scis., AAAS, N.Y. Acad. Scis., N.Y. Soc. Tropical Medicine, Greater Bangor C. of C. (dir.), Sigma Xi, Phi Kappa Phi. Club: B'nai B'rith. Office: U Calif Berkeley Donner Lab Berkeley CA 94720

SILVERN, LEONARD CHARLES, engineering executive; b. N.Y.C., May 20, 1919; s. Ralph and Augusta (Thaler) S.; m. Gloria Marantz, June 1948 (div. Jan. 1968); 1 son, Ronald; m. 2d, Elisabeth Beeny, Aug. 1969 (div. Oct. 1972); m. Gwen Taylor, Nov. 1985. BS in Physics, L.I. U., 1946; MA, Columbia U., 1948, EdD, 1952. Tng. supr. U.S. Dept. Navy, N.Y.C., 1939-49; tng. dir. exec. dept. N.Y. Div. Safety, Albany, 1949-55; resident engring. psychologist Lincoln Lab. MIT for Rand Corp., Lexington, 1955-56; engr., dir. edn., tng., rsch. labs. Hughes Aircraft Co., Culver City, Calif., 1956-62; dir. human performance engring. lab., cons. engring. psychologist to v.p. tech. Northrop Norair, Hawthorne, Calif., 1962-64; prin. scientist, v.p., pres. Edn. and Tng. Cons. Co., L.A., 1964-80, Sedona, Ariz., 1980, pres. Systems Engring. Labs. div., 1980—; cons. hdqrs. Air Tng. Command USAF, Randolph AFB, Tex., 1964-68, Electronic Industries Assn., Washington, 1963-69, Edn. R and D Ctr., U. Hawaii, 1970-74, Ctr. Vocat. and Tech. Edn., Ohio State U., 1972-73, Coun. for Exceptional Children, 1973-74, Canadore Coll. Applied Arts and Tech., Ont., Can., 1974-76, Centro Nacional de Productividad, Mexico City, 1973-75, N.S. Dept. Edn., Halifax, 1975-79, Aeronutronic Ford-Ford Motor Co., 1975-76, Nat. Tng. Systems Inc., 1976-81, Nfld. Pub. Svc. Commn., 1978, Legis. Affairs Office USDA, 1980, Rocky Point Techs., 1986; adj. prof. edn., pub. adminstrn. U. So. Calif. Grad. Sch., 1957-65; vis. prof. computer scis. U. Calif. Extension Div., L.A., 1963-72. Dist. ops. officer, disaster communications svc. L.A. County Sheriff's Dept., 1973-75, dist. communications officer, 1975-76; bd. dirs. SEARCH, 1976—; mem. adv. com. West Sedona Community Plan of Yavapai County, 1986-88; councilman City of Sedona, 1988—; rep. COCOPAI, 1988—; vol. earth team Soi Conservation Svc., U.S. Dept Agr., 1989—; Verde Resource Assn., 1988—, Group on Water Logistics. Served with USNR, 1944-46. Registered profl. cons. engr., Calif. Mem. IEEE (sr.), Am. Psychol. Assn., Am. Radio Relay League (life), Nat. Solid Waste Mgmt. Symposium (chmn. publs. com. 1988-89), Friendship Vets. Fire Engine Co. (hon.), Soc. Wireless Pioneers (life), Quarter Century Wireless Assn. (life), Sierra Club, Sedona Westerners., Assn. Bldg. Coms. (chmn. bd. dirs. Sedona, 1986—), Nature Conservancy, Ariz. Ctr. Law in Pub. Interest. Contbg. editor Ednl. Tech., 1968-73, 81-85; reviewer Computing Revs., 1962—. Contbr. numerous articles to profl. jours. Office: PO Box 2085 Sedona AZ 86336

SILVERSTEIN, JOSEPH HARRY, musician; b. Detroit, Mar. 21, 1932; s. Bernard and Ida (Katz) S.; m. Adrienne Shufro, Apr. 27; children—Bernice, Deborah, Marc. Student Curtis Inst. Music, 1945-50; hon. doctoral degrees Tufts U., 1971, Rhode Island U., 1980, Boston Coll., 1981, New Eng. Conservatory, 1986. Violinist, Houston Symphony Orch., Phila. Orch.; concert-master Denver Symphony Orch., Boston Symphony Orch.; formerly chmn. string dept. New Eng. Conservatory Music; also chmn. faculty Berkshire Music Sch.; mem. faculty Boston U. Sch. Music, Yale U. Sch. Music; music dir. Boston Symphony Chamber Players, Boston U. Symphony Orch., Chautauqua (N.Y.) Instn., 1987—; interim music dir. Toledo Symphony Orch.; prin. guest condr. Balt. Symphony Orch., 1981; condr. Utah Symphony; now mus. dir. Worcester Orch., Mass., until 1987. Recipient Silver medal Queen Elizabeth of Belgium Internat. contest, 1959, Naumberg found. award, 1960; named one of ten outstanding young men, Boston C. of C., 1962. Fellow Am. Acad. Arts and Scis. Address: care Utah Symphony Orch 123 W S Temple Salt Lake City UT 84101 *

SILVERTHORN, GLORIA JEAN, radio sales executive; b. Altadena, Calif., July 17, 1951; d. W. Keith and D. Jean (Coffey) Brownell; m. Louis J. Silverthorn, Apr. 12, 1970 (div. June 1973); m. Terry Lee Wendt, May 19, 1984. AA, Coll. of the Redwoods, 1974. Sales rep. Sta. KRED, Eureka, Calif., 1977-79; sales mgr. Sta. KPDJ, Eureka, 1979-82; sales rep. Sta. KXGO, Arcata, Calif., 1982-83; sales rep. Sta. KEWB-FM, Redding, Calif., 1983-84, sales mgr., 1984—; sales mgr. Sta. KRDG, Redding, 1987—. Mem. Earthwatch. Democrat. Mem. Ch. of Religious Sci. Office: Stas KEWB/KRDG 1330 Hartnell Ave Redding CA 96002

SILZEL, WAYNE WARWICK, finance company executive; b. Colfax, Wash., Apr. 15, 1936; s. Frank Milton Silzel and Florence Pymrel (Warwick) Silzel-Bivins; m. Mary Claire Ruddick, Nov. 7, 1959; children: John Warwick, Karen Elizabeth. BA in Econs., Whitman Coll., 1958; MBA, Pepperdine U., 1979. Mortgage loan rep. Pacific Mut. Life Ins. Co., Seattle, 1959-62, mortgage loan br. mgr., 1962-64, mortgage loan dist. mgr., 1964-69, 2d v.p. mktg., 1969-76, 2d v.p. nat. accounts, 1976-80, v.p., 1980-83; pres. Wayne W. Silzel Assoc., Orange, Calif., 1983—; mayor City of Villa Park, Calif., 1984-85. Planning com. and Council mem. and Mayor pro-term (1983, 88) of City Villa Park, Calif. Hats Off award Orange Unified Sch. Dist. Orange. Mem. Am. Inst. Real Estate Appraisers (instr.-lectr.), nat. Assn. Corp. Real Estate Execs., Am. Soc. Real Estate Counselors, Nat. Assn. Securities Dealers, Mortgage Bankers Assn. Am. Republican. Presbyterian. Club: Orange County Model T Ford. Home: 18202 Montana Circle Villa Park CA 92667 Office: 3111 N Tustin Ave #180 Orange CA 92665

SIMARD, RODNEY, literature and communications educator, media consultant; b. Ft. Smith, Ark., June 18, 1952; s. Houston H. and Dorothy (Turner) S. BA, Memphis State U., 1974; MA, Miss. State U., 1976; PhD, U. Ala., 1982. Instr. lit. Birmingham (Ala.) So. Coll., 1981-82; instr. lit. and communications Calif. State Coll., Bakersfield, 1982-86; asst. prof. lit. Calif. State U., San Bernardino, 1986—. Author: Postmodern Drama, 1984; gen. editor series American Indian Studies Peter Lang Pub., Inc., 1989—; assoc. editor Furniture Methods and Materials, 1973-74; editor Black Warrior Rev., 1979-80, Showtime, 1983-84; cons. editor Elan, 1988—; faculty editor The Pacific Rev., 1988—; contbg. editor: The Variorum Edition of the Poetry of John Donne, 1982-88; contbr. articles to profl. jours., anthologies, also other publs. Tribal mem. Cherokee Nation of Okla.; bd. dirs., v.p., mem. profl. adv. coun. Riverside (Calif.) and San Bernardino County Am. Indian Ctr. Mem. MLA, Gay Am. Indians, John Donne Soc., Inland Area Native Am. Assn. (adv. coun., cons. editor assn. newsletter), NAACP, Sigma Tau Delta, Phi Gamma Delta. Office: Calif State U Dept English San Bernardino CA 92407

SIMBURG, EARL JOSEPH, psychiatrist; b. Vonda, Sask., Can., Mar. 21, 1915; came to U.S., 1941; s. Joseph E. and Liza (Yurovsky) S.; m. Virginia Ronan, Feb. 10, 1958; children by previous marriage: Arthur, Melvyn, Sharon. Cert. medicine, U. Sask., Saskatoon, 1935; MDCM, McGill U., Montreal, Que., Can., 1938; grad., San Francisco Psychoanal. Inst., 1959. Diplomate Am. Bd. Psychiatry and Neurology. Intern Royal Victoria Hosp., Montreal, 1938-39; sr. physician Brandon (Can.) Hosp. Mental Diseases, 1939-41; resident Grace New Haven Hosp., 1941-43; pvt. practice psychiatry Berkeley, Calif., 1947—; mem. faculty San Francisco Psychoanalytic Inst.; instr. psychiatry Yale U., New Haven, 1941-43, U. Calif., San Francisco, 1949-59, Calif. Dept. Health, Berkeley, 1975-76; pres. med. staff Herrick Hosp. and Health Ctr., 1985. Contbr. articles to profl. jours. Served to major M.C. USAF, 1943-47. Fellow Am. Psychiat. Assn. (life); mem. AMA, Am. Psychoanalytic Assn. (life, cert.), Calif. Med. Assn., Alameda Contra Costa County Med. Assn. Home: 86 Tamalpais Rd Berkeley CA 94708 Office: 2006 Dwight Way Berkeley CA 94704

SIMCOX, CRAIG DENNIS, aeronautical engineer; b. Iowa Falls, Iowa, Sept. 18, 1939; s. Clair Mock and Alice Mae (Shane) S.; m. Molly A. H. Simcox, Aug. 4, 1961; child, Vichi Rae Simcox Smokoff. BS in Aero. Engring., Iowa State U., 1962; MS in Aero. and Astro., Stanford U., 1965; PhD, Purdue U., 1969; postgrad., Columbia U., 1981. Research scientist Ames Research Ctr., NASA, Moffett Field, Calif., 1962-65; instr., cons. Purdue U., West Lafayette, Ind., 1965-68; research mgr. Boeing Comml. Airplanes Co., Renton, Wash., 1969-75; lab. mgr. Boeing Comml. Airplanes Co., Seattle, 1975-85; chief engr. Boeing Comml. Airplanes Co., Everett, Wash., 1985—; chmn. numerous nat. and internat. confs. Assoc. editor Tech. Periodic Jur. Aircraft, 1978-87; contbr. articles to profl. jours. Vice pres. Somerset Assn., Bellevue, Wash., 1978-80; v.p. civic affairs Boeing Mgmt. Assn., Seattle, 1986-88. Fellow AIAA (chmn. 1976-77, dep. dir. 1978-84). Mem. Christian Ch. Home: 4640 132d Ave SE Bellevue WA 98006 Office: Boeing Comml Airplanes Co PO Box 3707 M/S OT74 Everett WA 98006

SIMEK, JANET LORRAINE, educator; b. Ellsworth, Kans., June 30, 1942; d. John Paul and Lorene Violet (Kopsa) S. BS in Edn., Emporia State U., 1964; MS in Edn. and Reading, U. Ariz., 1968, MS in Edn. Adminstrn., 1983. Tchr. Tucson Unified Sch. Dist., 1968-81, project asst., 1981, project specialist, 1988—; mem. right to read State of Ariz. Dept. Edn., 1974; pres. Tucson Area Reading Coun., 1981-82, Ariz. Reading Coun., 1985-86. Mem. Internat. Reading Assn., Phi Beta Kappa, Delta Kappa Gamma. Office: Tucson Unified Sch Dist PO Box 40400 Tucson AZ 85717

SIMEON, BETTIE L. ROSS, musician, composer, songwriter; b. Los Angeles, May 12, 1948; d. Jack Wayland Ross and Margaret Cregar (Stryker) McCartney; m. Omer Theodore Simeon; 1 child, Noelle Bezart; stepchildren: Leslie Syniec, Omer Theodore Simeon III, Eric Albert Simeon. Student in piano, music theory, Trinity Coll., London, Los Angeles, 1953-60; student, Calif. State U., Northridge, 1966-68, 69-71; student keyboard tech., Jamie Faunt Sch. Creative Music, 1979-81, 86-87; studies with Dr. Philip Springer, Eddy L. Manson, L.A., 1973-74. Keyboardist various bands, musicals, and plays; tchr. piano, pipe organ, organ, synthesizers, music theor; accompanist various sch. orchestras, choral groups; owner Kameon Prodns.; keyboardist Melissa Manchester U.S. Tour, 1980, Bellamy Bros. U.S. Tour, 1976; conductor Bellamy Bros. Fifth Ann. Tokyo Music Festival, 1976; pipe organist various So. Calif. chs., 1963—. Composed, played, performed music for Vogue 2000, 1986-87, (films) Have a Banana, 1985, Galaxy Express 999, 1985, Closing Night, 1984, (plays) Neon (A Vaudeville of Obsession), 1983, The Melville Boys, 1988; produced solo albums, The Alon Series, 1980, Romance Suite, 1982. Vol. 1st and 2nd ann. Baby Golf Classic for newborn intensive care unit Cedars-Sinai Med. Ctr., Los Angeles, 1984, 85. Named Donna Delle Fave Meml. scholar, 1970-71; recipient Frederick Chopin Piano award, 1966, Bank of Am. Music award, 1966, Grand Prize and 3 awards Music City Song Festival, 1988. Mem. ASCAP, Songwriters/Composers Assn. (pres. 1986—), Am. Guild Organists, Musicians Union Local 47, Nat. Acad. of Songwriters, Nat. Acad. of Recording Arts and Scis., L.A. Women in Music. Democrat. Office: Kameon Prodns PO Box 931689 Los Angeles CA 90093

SIMERVILLE, JAMES JASPER, occupational and environmental physician; b. Bend, Oreg., Sept. 15, 1939; s. George Melvin and Clara Louise (Jasper) S.; m. Carol Marie Smith, Dec. 26, 1961; children: Pamela Marie, Steven James, Jeffrey Alan. BS, Oreg. State U., 1961; MD, U. Oreg., 1965. Diplomate, Am. Bd. Pediatrics. Commd. 2d lt. USAF, 1964, advanced through grades to col., 1979; intern USAF Hosp. Travis, Travis AFB, Calif., 1965-66; resident USAF Hosp. Wilford Hall, Lackland AFB, Tex., 1966-68; chief pediatric svc. USAF, Westover AFB, Mass., Lakenheath, Eng., and Scott AFB, Ill., Eng., 1968-75; dir. med. edn. USAF Hosp. Scott, Scott AFB, 1975-84; cons. in pediatrics, then dep. comdr. U.S. Air Force Acad. Hosp., Colorado Springs, Colo., 1976-84; retired USAF, 1984; dir. Colorado Springs Sports Medicine Clinic, 1984-87, Colo. Ctr. Occupational Medicine, Colorado Springs, 1985—; med. cons. sports medicine program, Chapman Coll., Colorado Springs, 1983-88. Fellow Am. Acad. Pediatrics; mem. Am. Coll. Occupational Medicine, Am. Coll. Sports Medicine (regional chpt. pres. 1989), Am. Acad. Sports Physicians. Democrat. Roman Catholic. Office: Colo Ctr Occupational Med 6197 Lehman St Colorado Springs CO 80918

SIMINI, JOSEPH PETER, accountant, financial consultant, author, former educator; b. Buffalo, Feb. 15, 1921; s. Paul and Ida (Moro) S.; B.S., St. Bonaventure U., 1940, B.B.A., 1949; M.B.A., U. Calif.-Berkeley, 1957; D.B.A., Western Colo. U., 1981; m. Marcelline McDermott, Oct. 4, 1968. Insp. naval material Bur. Ordnance, Buffalo and Rochester, N.Y., 1941-44; mgr. Paul Simini Bakery, Buffalo, 1946-48; internal auditor DiGiorgio (Fruit) Corp., San Francisco, 1950-51; tax accountant Price Waterhouse & Co., San Francisco, 1953; sr. accountant Richard L. Hanlin, C.P.A., San Francisco, 1953-54; prof. accounting U. San Francisco, 1954-79, emeritus prof., 1983—; mem. rev. bd. Calif. Bd. Accountancy, 1964-68. Mem. council com. Boy Scouts Am., Buffalo, San Francisco, 1942-65, Scouters Key, San Francisco council; bd. dirs. United Bay Area Fund Drive, U. San Francisco, 1960, Nat. Italian Am. Found., Washington, 1979—. Served to ensign USNR, 1944-46. Recipient Bacon-McLaughlin medal St. Bonaventure U., 1940, Laurel Key, 1940; Outstanding Tchr. award Coll. Bus. Adminstrn., U. San Francisco, 1973; Disting. Tchr. award U. San Francisco, 1975, Joseph Peter Simini award, 1977. Crown Zellerbach Found. fellow, 1968-69; Gold Medal Associazione Piemontese nel Mondo, Turin, Italy, 1984; decorated Knight Order of Merit, Republic of Italy, 1982. C.P.A., Calif. Mem. Am. Inst. C.P.A.s, Calif. Soc. C.P.A.s (past chmn. ednl. standards, student relations com. San Francisco chpt.), Nat. Assn. Accts. (past pres. San Francisco chpt.), Am. Acctg. Assn., Am. Mgmt. Assn. (lectr. 1968-78), Am. Arbitration Assn. (comml. arbitrator), Delta Sigma Pi (past pres. San Francisco alumni club), Beta Gamma Sigma. Roman Catholic. Clubs: Serra (pres.

Golden Gate chpt.), Il Cenacolo (past pres.), Toastmasters (pres. Magic Word). Lodges: K.C., Rotary. Author: Accounting Made Simple, 1967, 2d rev. edit., 1987, Cost Accounting Concepts for Nonfinancial Executives, 1976, Become Wealthy! Using Tax Savings and Real Estate Investments, 1982, Balance Sheet Basics for the Nonfinancial Managers, 1989, Profit and Loss Statement Basics for Nonfinancial Mangers, 1989, Budgeting Basics for Nonfinancial Managers, 1989. Tech. editor, Accounting Essentials, 1972. Patentee Dial-A-Trig and Verbum Est card game. Home: 977 Duncan St San Francisco CA 94131 Office: PO Box 31420 San Francisco CA 94131

SIMKIN, PENELOPE PAYSON, physical therapist, childbirth educator; b. Portland, Maine, May 31, 1938; d. Thomas and Caroline Wood (Little) Payson; m. Peter Simkin, Aug. 9, 1958; children: Andrew, Caroline, Elizabeth, Mary. BA in English Lit., Swarthmore Coll., 1959. Cert. physical therapist. Staff physical therapist Furman Clinic Sch., Phila., 1961, N.C. Meml. Hosp., Chapel Hill, 1961-63; cons. in physical therapy Ft. Lawton Army Hosp., Seattle, 1963-64; childbirth educator Childbirth Edn. Assn. Seattle, 1968—; pres., editor Pennypress, Inc., Seattle, 1978—; mem. tchr. tng. team Childbirth Edn. Assn. Seattle, 1980—; childbirth educator Virginia Mason Hosp., Seattle, 1981—, Independent Home Birth Educator, Seattle, 1986—; bd. cons. Seattle Midwifery Sch., 1984—. Author: The Birth Partner, 1989; co-author: Pregnancy, Childbirth and the Newborn, 1984; co-editor: Birth--Through Children's Eyes, 1981, reprint 1984, Episiotomy & the Second Stage of Labor, 1984, 86; editorial bd. Birth: Issues in Perinatal Care and Edn., 1974—. Mem. obstetrical tech. adv. group Wash. State Dept. Social and Health Svcs., Olympia, 1979-81. Mem. Internat. Childbirth Edn. Assn. (v.p. 1976-78, bd. cons. 1986—), Am. Soc. Psychoprophylaxis in Obstetrics, Am. Physical Therapy Assn., Midwives Assn. Wash. State (sec. 1983-88, bd. dirs. 1983—, 1st annual award for contributions to midwifery 1984), Childbirth Edn. Assn. Seattle (pres. 1969-70). Office: Pennypress Inc 1100 23rd Ave E Seattle WA 98112

SIMMONS, BRADLEY WILLIAMS, pharmaceutical company executive; b. Paterson, N.J., Apr. 16, 1941; s. John Williams and Grace Law (Van Hassel) S.; m. Diane Louise Simmons, June 6, 1964 (div. May 1986); children: Susan, Elizabeth, Jonathan; m. Cheryl Lynne Westrum, Aug. 16, 1987. AB, Columbia U., 1963, BSChemE, 1964; MBA, NYU, 1974. Chem. engr. Pfizer, Inc., N.Y.C., 1969-73, analyst, 1973-76, dir. planning, 1976-79; dir., bus. analysis Bristol-Myers, N.Y.C., 1979-82, v.p., 1982-85; pres. Oncogen subs. Bristol-Myers, Seattle, 1985-87, sr. v.p. adminstrn., 1987—; adj. prof. Farleigh Dickinson U., Teaneck, N.J., 1974-84. Council mem. borough of Allendale, N.J., 1977-82; mem. Bergen County (N.J.) com., 1974-82. Served to lt. USN, 1964-69, Vietnam. Republican. Mem. Unity Ch. Office: Oncogen 3005 1st Ave Seattle WA 98121

SIMMONS, GEORGE FINLAY, educator; b. Austin, Tex., Mar. 3, 1925; s. George Finlay and Armede Victoria (Hatcher) S.; m. Hope Bridgeford, Sept. 11, 1954; 1 child, Nancy Bingham. BS, Caltech, 1946; MS, U. Chgo., 1948; PhD, Yale U., 1957. Instr. U. Chgo., 1947-50, U. Maine, Orono, 1950-52, Yale U., New Haven, 1952-56; asst. prof. U. R.I., Kingston, 1956-58, Williams College, Williamstown, Mass., 1958-62; assoc. prof. Colorado Coll., Colorado Springs, 1962-65, prof., 1965—. Author: Introduction to Topology & Modern Analysis, 1962, Differential Equations, 1972, Precalculus Math. In A Nutshell, 1981, Calculus With Analytic Geometry, 1985. Mem. Mathematical Assn. Am. Home: 1401 Wood Ave Colorado Springs CO 80907 Office: Colorado College Colorado Springs CO 80903

SIMMONS, JAMES MILLARD, state senator, credit company executive; b. Portland, Oreg., May 20, 1916; m. Margie French, 1938; children—James, Nancy. Student Willamette U., 1933-34; cert. in acctg. Oreg. Inst. Tech., 1938. Operator, mgr. family wholesale grocery bus., 1934-37; acct. Walter D. Whitecomb & Co., 1937-38; loan officer Caldwell Fin. Co., 1938-49; pres., owner Simmons Credit Co., Portland, 1950—; mem. Oreg. Senate, 1980—. Bd. dirs. Portland Rose Festival Assn., 1947—, Consumer Credit Counseling Service, 1968—; precinct committeeman Multnomah County Republican Com., 1955—, Washington County Rep. Com., 1955—. Served with U.S. Army, 1942-46. Mem. Portland C. of C. (mil. affairs com. 1954—, recreational resources com., 1950—).

SIMMONS, MICHAEL ANTHONY, pediatrics educator; b. Ft. Wayne, Ind., Aug. 9, 1941; s. William David and Mary Gretchen (Roe) S.; m. Margaret Clave Martindale, Aug. 17, 1963; children: Kristen, Jeffrey, Jennifer, Jason. AB, Harvard U., 1963, MD, 1967. Diplomate Am. Bd. Pediatrics, Am. Bd. Neonatal-Perinatal. Asst. prof. pediatrics U. Colo., Denver, 1974-77, assoc. prof. pediatrics, 1977; assoc. prof. pediatrics Johns Hopkins U., Balt., 1977-83, dep. dir. dept. pediatrics, 1981-83; prof., chmn. dept. pediatrics U. Utah Sch. Medicine, Salt Lake City, 1983—; chmn. sub-bd. Neonatal-Perinatal Medicine, Am. Bd. Pediatrics, Chapel Hill, N.C., 1983-88. Established investigator Am. Heart Soc., 1976-78. Served to major USAF, 1969-71. Fellow Am. Acad. Pediatrics; mem. Perinatal Research Soc. (pres.-elect 1986, pres. 1987), Soc. Pediatric Research, Am. Pediatric Soc., Western Soc. Pediatric Research Council (pres. 1988), Assn. Med. Sch. Pediatric Dept. Chmn. (sec./treas. 1986-88). Home: 4302 Adonis Dr Salt Lake City UT 84124 Office: U Utah Sch Medicine Dept Pediatrics 50 N Med Dr Salt Lake City UT 84132

SIMMONS, NOEL ALEXANDER, human resources executive, consultant; b. San Francisco, Dec. 28, 1947; s. Clifford Edgar and Mildred (Malchow) S.; m. Elaine Diane Meyer, July 27, 1974; children: Carly Michelle, Rebecca Marie. BA, U. Calif., Berkeley, 1971; MBA, San Francisco State U., 1973. Regional acctg. mgr. ITT Continental Bakery, San Francisco, 1973-75; regional personnel mgr. VWR Sci. Corp., San Francisco, 1976-79; indsl. rels. mgr. Signetics Corp., Sunnyvale, Calif., 1979-81; human resources dir. Eaton Corp., Sunnyvale, 1981-89; human resources cons. The Simmons Group, Belmont, Calif., 1989—. Mem. No. Calif. Football Officials Assn., Calif., 1971-75; advisor Jr. Achievement, San Mateo County, Calif., 1976-79; sec. Redwood City (Calif.) Shores Homeowners Assn., 1983. Capt. USAF, 1973-79. Mem. Labor Adjustment Bd., Am. Soc. Personnel Adminstrs., No. Calif. Human Resources Coun., Calif. Unemployment Ins. Coun., Santa Clara (Calif.) Valley Personnel Assn., Peninsula Employee Rels. Coun. Home: 645 Spar Dr Redwood City CA 94065-1151 Office: The Simmons Group Landmark Ctr 951-2 Old County Rd Ste 136 Belmont CA 94002

SIMMONS, ROY WILLIAM, banker; b. Portland, Oreg., Jan. 24, 1916; s. Henry Clay and Ida (Mudd) S.; m. Elizabeth Ellison, Oct. 28, 1938; children—Julia Simmons Watkins, Matthew R., Laurence E., Elizabeth Jane Simmons Hoke, Harris H., David E. Asst. cashier First Nat. Bank Layton, Utah, 1944-49; Utah bank commr. 1949-51; exec. v.p. Bank of Utah, Ogden, 1951-53; pres. Lockhart Co., Salt Lake City, 1953-64, Zion's First Nat. Bank, Salt Lake City, 1964-81; chmn. bd. Zion's First Nat. Bank, 1965—; chmn., chief exec. officer Zion's Utah Bancorp., 1965—; chmn. bd. Zion's Savs. & Loan Assn., 1961-69; pres. Lockhart Co., 1964—; bd. dirs. Salt Lake City br. Fed. Res. Bank San Francisco, 1971-77, Kennecott Copper Corp., 1964-81, Beneficial Life Ins. Co., 1964—, Hotel Utah, 1964-85, Utah Portland Cement Co., Mountain Fuel Supply Co., 1964—, Denver & Rio Grande R.R., 1964-83, Rio Grande Industries, 1964-85, Ellison Ranching Co., 1969—. Chmn. Utah Bus. Devel. Corp., 1969-80; mem. Utah State Bd. Regents, 1969-81. Mem. Salt Lake City C. of C. (treas. 1964-65), Sigma Pi. Republican. Mem. Ch. of Jesus Christ of Latter Day Saints. Home: Crestwood Rd Kaysville UT 84037 Office: Zions Utah Bancorp 1380 Kennecott Bldg Salt Lake City UT 84133

SIMMONS, TED CONRAD, writer; b. Seattle, Sept. 1, 1916; s. Conrad and Clara Evelyn (Beaudry) S.; student U. Wash., 1938-41, UCLA and Los Angeles State U., 1952-54, Oxford (Eng.) U., 1980; m. Dorothy Pauline Maltese, June 1, 1942; children—Lynn, Juliet. Drama critic Seattle Daily Times, 1942; indsl. writer, editor Los Angeles Daily News, 1948-51; contbr. Steel, Western Metals, Western Industry, 1951—; past poetry dir. Watts Writers Workshop; instr. Westside Poetry Center; asst. dir. Pacific Coast Writers Conf., Calif. State Coll. Los Angeles. Served with USAAF, 1942-46. Author: (poetry) Deadended, 1966; (novel) Middlearth, 1975; (drama) Greenhouse, 1977, Durable Chaucer, 1978, Rabelais and other plays, 1980, Dickeybird, 1981 (nominated TCG Palys-in-Progress award 1985), Alice and Eve, 1983, Deja Vu, Deja Vu, 1986, The Box, 1987, Ingrid Superstar, 1988; writer short story, radio verse; book reviewer Los Angeles Times; contbr. poetry to The Am. Poet, Prairie Wings, Antioch Rev., Year Two Anthology; editor: Venice Poetry Company Presents, 1972.

SIMMONS, VICTOR J., financial executive; b. Vallejo, Calif., June 17, 1945; s. Victor J. Simmons; 1 child, Miriam Victoria. BA, U. Nev., 1968. Bid coord. Dietary Products div. Am. Hosp. Supply Corp., Irvine, Calif., 1972-73; loan officer, appraiser Brentwood Savs., L.A., 1973-77; loan cons. Union Fed. Savs., L.A., 1978-79; mortgage broker Far West Mortgage, L.A., 1980-81; ins. agt. Met. Life Ins., L.A., 1981-84; mortgage, ins. broker Far West Mortgage, L.A., 1984-85; loan cons. Coast Savs., Beverly Hills, Calif., 1985—. Contbr. articles to profl. jours., 1967-71. 1st lt. USMCR, 1968-71. Democrat. Baptist. Home: 3503 W 85th St Inglewood CA 90305 Office: Coast Savs 9090 Wilshire Blvd #200 Beverly Hills CA 90211

SIMMONS, VIRGINIA RUTH MCCONNELL, writer; b. Nashua, Iowa, Jan. 27, 1928; d. Joseph Lyle and Ruth Eleanor (Mink) McCorison; children: Thomas Creston McConnell, Susan McConnell Sakys. BA, Oberlin Coll., 1949; MA, Adams State Coll., Alamosa, Colo., 1981. Instr. English U. Colo., Colorado Springs, 1965-68; assoc. editor Swallow Press, Denver, 1966; editor in chief Pruett Pub. Co., Boulder, Colo., 1968-70; assoc. editor, acting editor State Hist. Soc. Colo., Denver, 1970-72; columnist, feature writer various newspapers, Jiddah, Saudi Arabia and Alamosa, 1978—; owner Rabbitbrush Enterprises, Alamosa, 1986—. Author: Bayou Salado: The Story of the South Park (2d honor award Nat. Fedn. Press Women 1967), 1966, The San Luis Valley: Land of the Six-Armed Cross, 1980; co-author: Valley of the Cranes, 1988, others; contbr. articles to mags and profl. jours.; book reviewer. Recipient 1st honor award Nat. Fedn. Press Women, 1967. Mem. San Luis Valley Hist. Soc. (editor 1984-86, cert. recognition 1980, 87), Manitou Springs Hist. Soc. (hon. life). Office: Rabbitbrush Enterprises 719 2d St Alamosa CO 81101

SIMMONS, WILLIAM ALLEN, accountant; b. Roswell, N.Mex., Dec. 7, 1946; s. Lee William amd Marcelle (Deutsch) S.; m. Kathy Burttram, Apr. 18, 1969; children: Dana, Kenneth. BBA, U. N.Mex., 1969. CPA, N.Mex. From asst. to mgr. Peat, Marwick, Mitchell and Co., Santa Fe, 1969-80, ptnr., 1980-83; ptnr. Daymon and Assocs., Santa Fe, 1983—; speaker on taxation various orgns. Pres. Santa Fe Boys Club, 1985-86, New Vistas Program for Developmentally Disabled, Santa Fe, 1986. Mem. Am. Inst. CPAs, N.Mex. Soc. CPAs, Santa Fe C. of C. (treas. 1987-89; Commerce Dir. of Yr. award, 1988). Republican. Lodge: Civitan (Civitan of Yr. Santa Fe chpt. 1978-79). Home: 2640 Caminito Carlitos Santa Fe NM 87505 Office: Daymon and Assocs CPA 409 Saint Michaels Dr Santa Fe NM 87501

SIMMS, MARIA ESTER, health services administrator; b. Bahia Blanca, Argentina, Nov. 19, 1938; came to U.S., 1963; d. Jose and Esther (Guays) Barberio Esandi; m. Michael Simms, July 15, 1973; children: Michelle Bonnie Lee Carla, Michael London Valentine. Degree medicine, Facultad del Centenario, Rosario, Argentina, 1962; Physician Asst. Cert. (hon.), U. So. Calif., 1977. Medical diplomate. V.p. Midtown Svcs. Inc., Los Angeles, 1973—, AAA Med. Clinics Inc., Los Angeles, 1980—; sec.-treas. Han-Sim Corp., Los Angeles. V.P., editor The Ebell of Los Angeles, 1985-88. Fellow Am. Acad. Physicians' Assts.; mem. Bus. for Law Enforcement (northeast div.), Physicians for Soc. Responsibility, Mercy Crusade Inc., Internat. Found. for Survival Research, Supreme Emblem Club of U.S., Order of the Eastern Star, Flying Samaritans, Shriners.

SIMMS, THOMAS HASKELL, chief of police; b. Yuma, Ariz., Sept. 3, 1945; s. Jessie Lee and Mary Elizabeth (Servos) S.; m. Oct. 12, 1966 (div. July 1981); m. Virginia Lee David, Mar. 26, 1988; children: Thomas Haskell Jr., Julie Marie. BA, St. Mary's Coll., Moraga, Calif., 1981. Officer Mountain View (Calif.) Police Dept., 1972-76; police sgt. East Bay Parks, Oakland, Calif., 1976-79; police lt. Town of Moraga, Calif., 1979-84, chief police, 1984-86; chief police City of Piedmont, Calif., 1986—. Bd. dirs. Piedmont coun. Boy Scouts Am., 1988-89. Maj. U.S. Army, 1967-71, Vietnam. Mem. Calif. Chiefs Police Assn., Calif. Peace Officers Assn., Rotary, Kiwanis (pres. Morage 1982-83, Kiwanian of Yr. award 1983). Presbyterian. Office: Piedmont Police Dept 403 Highland Piedmont CA 94611

SIMNAD, MASSOUD T., engineering educator; b. Teheran, Iran, Mar. 11, 1920; came to U.S., 1948; s. Reza an Ferhunde (Magari) S.; m. Lenora Virginia Brown, May 28, 1954; childrne: Jeffrey, Virginia. BS, London U., 1942; PhD, U. Cambridge, Eng., 1946. Rsch. fellow U. Cambridge, 1945-48; postdoctoral fellow Carnegie-Mellow U., Pitts., 1949-50, mem. faculty, 1950-56; with Gen. Atomics, San Diego, 1956-81; adj. prof., cons. in engring. U. Calif., San Diego, 1981—; vis. prof. MIT, Cambridge, 1962-63; mem. tech. coms. U.S. Dept. Energy, 1970—; cons. in field. Author papers, monographs in field; patentee in field. Fellow Am. Nuclear Soc., Am. Soc. Metals, AAAs; mem. AIAA, Electrochem. Soc., Inst. on Global Conflict and Cooperation, World Affairs Council, UN Club, sierra Club. Home: 9712 Claiborne Sq La Jolla CA 92037 Office: U Calif Mail Code B-010 La Jolla CA 92093

SIMON, DANIEL JOHN, software engineer; b. Visalia, Calif., Oct. 3, 1960; s. Walter Eder and Annette Joy (Staich) S.; m. Annette Joy Webel, Aug. 15, 1987. BEE, Ariz. State U., 1982; MEE, U. Wash., 1987. Software engr. Boeing Aerospace Corp., Seattle, 1983—; grad. asst. Syracuse (N.Y.) U., 1988—. Foster parent Issaquah Youth & Family, 1983-87. Named Eastside Vol. of Yr., Eastside Human Services Council, 1987; recipient Heart to Youth award Friends for Youth, 1987. Republican. Mem. Apostolic Christian Ch. Home: 105E Kings Park Dr Liverpool NY 13090 Office: Syracuse U ECE Dept 111 Link Hall Syracuse NY 13244-1240

SIMON, DAVID HAROLD, public relations executive; b. Washington, Dec. 3, 1930; s. Isaac B. and Marjorie S. (Felstiner) S.; m. Ruth Lurie, Mar. 2, 1962; children: Rachel, Jessie. BEE, Cornell U., 1954. Mktg. engr. Sylvania Elec. Products, Inc., Boston, 1957-58; advt. mgr. Sylvania Elec. Products, Inc., Mountain View, Calif., 1958-60; regional sales engr. Sylvania Elec. Products, Inc., L.A., 1960-63; mgr. advt. and pub. rels. Electronic Splty. Co., L.A., 1963-66; corp. dir. advt. and pub. rels. Teledyne, Inc., L.A., 1966-67; pres. Simon/Pub. Rels., Inc., L.A., 1967—. Contbr. articles on pub. rels. to various publs. Res. dep. sheriff L.A. Sheriff's Dept., 1973—; mem. L.A. Olympic Citizen's Adv. Commn., 1980-84; commr. City of L.A. Cultural Affairs Commn., 1987—; trustee Calif. Chamber Symphony, 1981-84; mem., founder L.A. Philharmonic, 1984—; mem. Philharmonic Men's Com., 1986—. With USN, 1954-57. Mem. Pub. Rels. Soc. Am. (bd. mem. L.A. chpt.), Nat. Assn. Sci. Writers, Nat. Assn. Corp. Dirs. (founding pres. L.A. chpt.), Opera Buffs Inc. (bd. dirs. 1986-87), Mensa. Home: 13025 Weddington St Van Nuys CA 91401 Office: Simon McGarry Pub Rels Inc 11661 San Vicente Blvd Ste 903 Los Angeles CA 90049

SIMON, JAMES ROBERT, small business owner; b. Phila., July 18, 1947; s. Robert Louis and Helen (Dryfoss) S.; m. Susan Ornstein, Dec. 1, 1976. BA, Beloit Coll., 1969; MEd, Xavier U., 1972. Prin. Simon's & Prices Less Fashions, Casa Grande, Ariz., 1978—. Jewish. Office: Simon's Fashions Inc 1226 E Flerence Blvd Casa Grande AZ 85222

SIMON, NORTON WINFRED, industrialist; b. Portland, Oreg., Feb. 5, 1907; s. Myer and Lillian (Glickman) S.; m. Jennifer Jones, May 30, 1971; children by previous marriage: Donald Ellis, Robert Ellis (dec.). Student, U. Calif., Berkeley, 1923. Founder, former chief exec. officer Norton Simon Inc., N.Y.C.; founder, chief exec. officer 5 corp. founds. and 1 family found. Los Angeles; former dir., chmn. fin. com. Burlington No., Inc. Mem. Courtauld Inst., London; former mem. Carnegie Commn. on Future of Higher Edn., Nat. Programming Council; mem. Nat. Com. on U.S.-China Relations, Founding Friends of Can.; chmn. bd. dirs. The Founders, Los Angeles Music Center; affiliated Calif. Sch. Profl. Psychology; bd. dirs., trustee Norton Simon Mus., Pasadena, Calif., pres., until 1989; trustee Inst. Advanced Study, Princeton, N.J.; former bd. dirs. Reed Coll., Inst. Internat. Edn., Los Angeles County Mus. Art; former regent U. Calif.; mem. adv. bd. Columbia U.-McGraw Hill Lectures; fellow Pierpont Morgan Library, N.Y.C.; mem., past chmn. Calif. State Transp. Commn. Office: Norton Simon Mus 411 W Colorado Blvd Pasadena CA 91105 *

SIMON, RICHARD HEGE, lawyer; b. Englewood, Colo., Jan. 15, 1911, AB, U. Denver, 1934, JD, 1936. Bar: Colo. 1938, U.S. Supreme Ct. 1970. Pvt. practice, Englewood, 1941—; mem. Simon, Lee & Shivers and predecessors, 1942-49; ptnr. Simon, Kelley, Hoyt & Malone, 1967-69; ptnr. Simon, Eason, Hoyt & Malone, 1969-76; sole practice, 1977—; dist. atty. First Jud. Dist. Colo., 1941-49; dir. First Nat. Bank Englewood, Key Savs. and Loan Assn. Founder, pres., dir. Arapahoe County (Colo.) Fair Assn., 1946—; bd. dirs., pres. Sch. Dist 1, Arapahoe County; sec., pres., chmn. bd., gen. counsel Centennial Turf Club, Inc., 1949-83; bd. dirs., pres. Arapahoe Park, Inc., 1983—; trustee Denver Met. United Way; state and county chmn. Republican Central Com.; pres., trustee Iliff Sch. Theology, 1960-88; pres., dir. Arapahoe Mental Health Ctr., 1960-75, Arapahoe County Mile High United Way, 1958-74. Fellow Am. Bar Found.; mem. Arapahoe County Bar Assn. (rep. to bd. govs. Colo. Bar Assn. 1958-67) ABA, Colo. Bar Assn. (pres. 1969-70), Am. Judicature Soc. Clubs: Denver Athletic, Columbine Country.

SIMON, SHELDON WEISS, political science educator; b. St. Paul, Jan. 31, 1937; s. Blair S. and Jennie M. (Dim) S.; m. Charlann Lilwin Scheid, Apr. 27, 1962; 1 child, Alex Russell. BA summa cum laude, U. Minn., 1958, PhD, 1964; MPA, Princeton U., 1960; postgrad., U. Geneva, 1962-63. Asst. prof., then prof. U. Ky., 1966-75; prof. polit. sci. Ariz. State U., 1975—, chmn. dept., 1975-79, dir. Ctr. Asian Studies, 1980-88; vis. prof. George Washington U., 1965, U. B.C. Can., 1972-73, 79-80, Carleton U., 1976; cons. USIA, Research Analysis Corp., Am. Enterprise Inst. Pub. Policy Research, Hoover Instn., Orkand Corp.;. Author: The Asean States and Regional Security, 1982; Asian Neutralism and U.S. Policy, 1975, The Future of Asian-Pacific Security Collaboration, 1988. Editor: The Military and Security in the Third World, 1978; other books, research articles; contbr. chpts. to books. Mem. Com. Fgn. Relations, Phoenix, 1976—; bd. dirs. Phoenix Little Theater, 1976-79. Grantee Am. Enterprise Inst., 1974, Earhart Found., 1979, 81, 82, 84, 88; Hoover Instn. fellow, 1980, 85. Mem. Am. Polit. Sci. Assn., Assn. Asian Studies, AAUP, Internat. Studies Assn. (profl. ethics com. 1987—), Asia Soc. (contemporary affairs com. 1987—), Phi Beta Kappa. Democrat. Jewish. Home: 5630 Rocky Point Tempe AZ 85283 Office: Ariz State U Polit Sci Dept Tempe AZ 85287

SIMON, WILLIAM LEONARD, film writer; b. Washington, Dec. 3, 1930; s. Isaac B. and Marjorie (Felsteiner) S.; m. Arynne Lucy Abeles, Sept. 18, 1966; 1 child, Victoria Marie; 1 stepson, Sheldon M. Bermont. BEE, Cornell U., 1954; MA in Ednl. Psychology, Golden State U., 1982, PhD in Communications, 1983. Writer features and TV movies, documentary and indsl. films, TV programs 1958—; lectr. George Washington U., Washington, 1968-70; juror Council on Nontheatrical Events Film Festival, 1975—, Cindy Festival Blue Ribbon Panel, 1985—. Writer over 600 produced works for motion pictures and TV, including screenplays Fair Woman Without Discretion, Majorca, Swindle, A Touch of Love, Flight of Freedom II, Missing You. Pres. Foggy Bottom Citizens Assn., 1963-65; mem. exec. bd., 1965-69; v.p. Shakespeare Summer Festival, 1966-67, trustee, 1965-70; mem. interview com. Cornell U., 1987—. Served to lt. USN, 1954-58. Recipient 8 Golden Eagle awards Cine Film Festival, gold medal N.Y. Internat. Festival, gold medal Freedoms Found., IFPA Gold Cindy; awards Berlin, Belgrade and Venice film Festivals, numerous others. Mem. Nat. Acad. TV Arts and Scis. (gov. D.C. chpt. 1970-73), Writers Guild Am., Am. Film Inst., Internat. Documentary Assn., Rotary (bd. dirs., program chmn.), Eta Kappa Nu (chpt. pres. 1953-54), Tau Beta Pi. Republican. Home: 6151 Paseo Delicias PO Box 2048 Rancho Santa Fe CA 92067

SIMONDS, JOHN EDWARD, editor; b. Boston, July 4, 1935; s. Alvin E. and Ruth Angeline (Rankin) S.; m. Rose B. Muller, Nov. 16, 1968; children—Maximillian P., Malia G.; children by previous marriage—Rachel F., John B. B.A., Bowdoin Coll., 1957. Reporter Daily Tribune, Seymour, Ind., 1957-58, UPI, Columbus, Ohio, 1958-60; reporter, asst. city editor Providence Jour. Bull., 1960-65, Washington Evening Star, 1965-66; corr. Gannett News Svc., Washington, 1966-75; mng. editor Honolulu Star Bull., 1975-80, exec. editor, 1980-87, sr. editor, 1987—. Served with U.S. Army, 1958. Mem. Am. Soc. Newspaper Editors, AP Mng. Editors, Honolulu Press Club, Soc. Profl. Journalists. Home: 5316 Nehu Pl Honolulu HI 96821 Office: Honolulu Star Bull 605 Kapiolani Blvd Honolulu HI 96813

SIMONE, ALBERT JOSEPH, academic administrator; b. Boston, Dec. 16, 1935; s. Edward and Mary (DiGiovanni) S.; m. Carolie Roberta Menko, Nov. 7, 1959; children: Edward, Karen, Debra, Laura. BA, Tufts U., 1957; PhD, MIT, 1962. Lectr. Coll. Bus. Adminstrn., Northeastern U., Boston, 1958-59; instr. econs. MIT and Tufts U., Boston, 1959-60; asst. prof. Northeastern U., Tufts U., 1960-63; prof., dir. quantitative mgmt. program Coll. Bus. Adminstrn., Boston Coll., 1963-66; prof., head dept. quantitative analysis Coll. Bus. Adminstrn. U. Cin., 1968-72, dean Coll. Bus. Adminstrn., 1972-83; v.p. acad. affairs U. Hawaii, Honolulu, 1983-84, acting pres., 1984-85, pres., 1985—; served on, chaired numerous univ. coms.; program chmn. 1970 Nat. Conf. of Am. Prodn. and Inventory Control Soc.; mem. accreditation com. Am. Assembly Collegiate Schs. Bus., 1978-83, visits to U. Ky., Carnegie-Mellon U., 1982; session chmn. various profl. confs.; cons. statis. forecasting, prodn. scheduling and sample design models various cos. including Cin. Gas & Electric Co., Cin. Milacron, Kroger Co.; econ. and mgmt. cons. Atty. Gen.'s Office, State of Mass.; mem. council econ. advisors to Gov., Commonwealth of Mass. Author: Matematica Finita Con Aplicaciones A Las Ciencias Administrativas, 1969, Foundations of Contemporary Mathematics with Applications in the Social and Management Sciences, 1967, Probability: An Introduction with Applications, 1967; (with L. Kattsoff) Finite Mathematics with Applications in the Social and Management Sciences, 1965, (with R. Wessel and E. Willett) Statistics as Applied to Economics and Business, 1965; also articles. Bd. dirs. Cin. Ctr. Econ. Edn., Cin. Minority Contractors Assistance Corp., Goodwill Industries Inc. Rehab. Program in Data Processing; bd. dirs., exec. com. Jr. Achievement Cin., Cin. Better Bus. Bur.; mem. Stadium Authority, Aloha Stadium; bd. govs., exec. com. East-West Ctr.; trustee, exec. com. U. Hawaii Found.; vice chair, bd. dirs. Research Corp. of U. Hawaii. Fellow of grad. sch. U. Cin.; named Prof. of Yr., Delta Sigma Pi, Alpha Theta chpt. U. Cin., 1972. Fellow Am. Inst. Decision Scis. (v.p. publs. 1969-70, v.p. and student liaison 1972, pres. 1974-75; founding editor and editor-in-chief jour. 1970-72; Disting. Service award 1972); mem. Acad. of Mgmt., Am. Econ. Assn., Am. Inst. Indsl. Engrs., Am. Prodn. and Inventory Control Soc., Am. Statis. Assn., Assn. Computing Machinery, Econometric Soc., Fin. Execs. Inst., Inst. Mgmt. Sci., Ops. Research Soc. Am., Phi Beta Kappa, Beta Gamma Sigma. Office: U Hawaii 2444 Dole St Honolulu HI 96822

SIMONIAN, MARIAN LOUISE, nurse; b. St. Louis, Feb. 22, 1925; d. Edward Joseph and Helen Mary (Becker) Heller; m. Steven Peter Simonian Sr., Apr. 12, 1947; children: Steven Peter Jr., Kim Edward, Scott K. Paul. AA, Fresno (Calif.) City Coll., 1969. RN. Psychiat. RN Northside Psychiat. Hosp., Fresno, 1969-70; head nurse Bel Haven Convalescent Hosp., Fresno, 1970-72; team leader, ICU Sierra Hosp., Fresno, 1972-78; asst. dir. nurses Fresno Convalescent Hosp., 1978-81; founder, program dir. St. Agnes Adult Day Health Care Ctr., Fresno, 1981-83; dir. nurses Quality Care Nursing Svc., Fresno, 1983-86; RN supr. Newhart Convalescent Hosp., Fresno, 1986—; mem. St. Agnes Med. Ctr. Home Health Care Adv. Coun., 1976—, chmn. 1981-82; bd. dirs. San Joaquin Valley Health Consortium, Fresno, 1976-85. Active nursing edn. com. Am. Cancer Soc.; sec. Cancer League Fresno, 1975. Mem. Am. Nurses Assn., Alpha Gamma Sigma. Republican. Roman Catholic. Home: 422 W Ashcroft Fresno CA 93705

SIMONS, LYNN OSBORN, state education official; b. Havre, Mont., June 1, 1934; d. Robert Blair and Dorothy (Briggs) Osborn; B.A., U. Colo., 1956; postgrad. U. Wyo., 1958-60; m. John Powell Simons, Jan. 19, 1957; children—Clayton Osborn, William Blair. Tchr., Midvale (Utah) Jr. High Sch., 1956-57, Sweetwater County Sch. Dist. 1, Rock Springs, Wyo., 1957-58, U. Wyo., Laramie, 1959-61, Natrona County Sch. Dist. 1, Casper, Wyo., 1963-64; credit mgr. Gallery 323, Casper, 1972-77; Wyo. state supt. public instrn., Cheyenne, 1979—; mem. State Bds. Charities and Reform, Land Commrs., Farm Loan, 1979—; mem. State Commns. Capitol Bldg., Liquor, 1979—; Ex-officio mem. bd. trustees U. Wyo.; ex-officio mem. Wyo. Community Coll. Commn.; mem. steering com. Edn. Commn. of the States; adv. State Bd. Edn., 1971-77, chmn., 1976-77. Mem. LWV (pres. 1970-71), Am. Assn. Sch. Adminstrs., Council Chief State Sch. Officers, Wyo. Assn. Sch. Adminstrs. Democrat. Episcopalian. Home: Box 185 Cheyenne WY 82002 Office: Edn Dept Hathaway Bldg 2nd Fl Cheyenne WY 82001

SIMONS, MADALENE BIBB, stockbroker; b. Marion, Ind., Dec. 5, 1940; d. George and Dorothy Dolores (Neff) B.; divorced; children: Joanne Elinor, Charles Arthur. Grad., Marion High Sch., 1958. Stockbroker Hornblower & Weeks dba Shearson, Portland, Oreg., 1975-79, Merrill Lynch, Portland, 1979-84, Prudential-Bache, Portland, 1984—. Chairperson retirement bd. United Meth. Ministers, Portland, 1987-90. Republican. Methodist. Club: West Hills Racquet (Portland). Office: Prudential-Bache 2020 SW 4 Ave Portland OR 97201

SIMONS, ROBERT LOUIS, physician; b. Chgo.; s. David B. and Kate (Silverman) S.; m. Florence Newman, Sept. 15, 1945; children—Hardye, John, David, Peter. B.A., U. Ill., 1944, B.S., M.D., 1947. Intern, Cook County Hosp., Chgo., 1947-48, resident in internal medicine, 1949, 53-54, mem. staff, 1949-60; research assoc. Hektoen Inst., Chgo., 1953-54; dir. med. edn./med. affairs Louis A. Weiss Meml. Hosp., Chgo., 1954-60, mem. staff, editor Bull., 1960-76; practice medicine specializing in internal medicine, Chgo., 1960-76; med. dir. Robert Wood Johnson Found.; med. dir. Ross Loos Med. Group, Los Angeles, 1980, Ross Loos Med. Center, Los Angeles, 1981-83; clin. assoc. prof. medicine, legal postgrad. clinics and seminar leader U. Ill. Coll. Medicine, Chgo., 1960-76; med. dir. Gillette Co., Chgo., 1960-67; med. dir. Aetna Life and Casualty, 1983—; v.p., med. dir. Aetna Health-care Systems Inc., 1983—. Served with U.S. Army, 1944-46, USAF, 1950-52; Korea. Diplomate Am. Bd. Internal Medicine. Fellow Am. Coll. Physician Execs.; mem. AMA, Chgo. Med. Soc., Ill. Med. Assn., Am. Acad. Med. Dirs., Am. Group Practice Assn.; editorial bd. Med. Trial Technique Quar., 1960-76. Office: Aetna 201 N Civic Dr Walnut Creek CA 94596

SIMONSON, HAROLD PETER, English language educator; b. Tacoma, Wash., Dec. 27, 1926; s. Peter Hans and Hilma (Mork) S.; m. Carolyn Ady, Nov. 20, 1951; children: Eric, Greta, Peter. BA, EdB, U. Puget Sound, 1950; MA, Northwestern U., 1951, PhD, 1958; PhB in Divinity, U. St. Andrews, Scotland, 1972. From instr. to prof. English U. Puget Sound, Tacoma, 1955-68; prof. U. Wash., Seattle, 1968—; research fellow Princeton (N.J.) Theol. Sem., 1962-63. Author: The Closed Frontier, 1970, Jonathan Edwards, 1974, Radical Discontinuities, 1983, Prairies Within, 1987, Beyond The Frontier, 1989. Fulbright scholar, 1953-54; named hon. research fellow Yale Divinity Sch., 1983, hon. fellow Inst. for Advanced Studies in the Humanities U. Edinburgh, Scotland, 1984. Mem. Western Lit. Assn. (exec. bd. 1986-89), Wash. State Hist. Soc. (bd. curators 1981—). Home: PO Box 7487 Tacoma WA 98407 Office: U Wash Dept English GN-30 Seattle WA 98195

SIMONSON, IKE, construction company executive; b. Hollis, Okla., Nov. 13, 1934; s. Earl and Alice Magge (Owen) S.; m. Mildred Kastner, Aug. 11, 1951; children: Eugene, John, Debra, David. With Oil Field Constrn. Co., Inc., Bakersfield, Calif., 1968—, sales and mgr. constrn. projects, 1980-85, acting gen. mgr., 1985, exec. v.p., chief exec. officer, 1985—. Mem. Petroleum Club, Bakersfield County Club, Elks. Eagles. Office: Oil Field Constrn Co Inc 4042 Patton Way Bakersfield CA 93308

SIMONSON, KENNETH WAYNE, JR., restaurant financial executive; b. N.Y.C., July 5, 1955; s. Kenneth Wayne and Alyce (Baumgarten) S.; m. Ellen Andrea Meinzer, Sept. 17, 1983; 1 child, Andrea Elizabeth. AA, Mesabi Community Coll., Virginia, Minn., 1977; BS in Bus., U. Minn., 1979. Field underwriter Mut. N.Y., Mpls., 1979-80; budget analyst Motel 6 Inc., Santa Barbara, Calif., 1980-81, field acctg. mgr., 1981-82; office mgr. Traister's Ethan Allen Gallery, Ventura, Calif., 1982-83; fin. analyst Carrows Restaurants Inc., Santa Barbara, 1984-85; fin. reporting mgr. W.R. Grace Restaurant Co. Family Div. Carrows Restaurant, Santa Barbara, 1985-86, dir. fin. and acctg., 1987-88; pres. Adminstrv. Spltys., Inc. (dba Office Svcs. Unltd.), Santa Barbara, 1988—; pres. Office Svcs. Unltd., Santa Barbara, 1985—. Notary pub. State of Calif., Santa Barbara, 1986—. Mem. Nat. Restaurant Assn., Nat. Notary Assn. Democrat. Jewish. Office: Nanco Restaurants Inc 800 Miramonte Dr Santa Barbara CA 93109

SIMONSON, MICHAEL, lawyer, judge; b. Franklin, N.J., Feb. 5, 1950; s. Robert and Eleanor (Weiss) S. BA, U. Ariz., 1973; JD, Southwestern U., Los Angeles, 1976; LLM in Taxation, Washington U., St. Louis, 1978. Bar: Ariz. 1977, U.S. Dist. Ct. Ariz. 1979, U.S. Tax Ct. 1978. Bailiff, law clk. Superior Ct. Maricopa County Div. 2, Phoenix, 1976-77; sole practice, Scottsdale, Ariz., 1978-79; ptnr. Simonson, Groh, & Lindteigen, Scottsdale, 1979-81, Simonson & Preston, Phoenix, 1984-86, Simonson, Preston & Arbetman, 1986-87, Simonson & Arbetman, 1987—; judge pro tempore Mcpl. Ct., City of Phoenix, 1984—; adj. prof. Ariz. State U. Coll. Bus., Tempe, 1984—, Coll. for Fin. Planning, Denver, 1984—, Maricopa County Community Colls., 1984—, Western Internat. U., Phoenix, 1984—, Ottawa U., 1987—; prof. law Univ. Phoenix, 1985—, area chmn. legal studies, 1986—. Mem. Maricopa County Foster Child Care Rev. Bd. No. 17, 1978-81; pres. Camelback Mountainview Estates Homeowners Assn., 1980-81, Congregation Tiphereth Israel, 1979-81. Co-author: Buying and Selling Closely Held Businesses in Arizona, 1986, Commercial Real Estate Transactions, 1986. Mem. ABA (taxation sect., various coms.), State Bar Ariz. (cert. specialist in tax law), Maricopa County Bar Assn., Cen. Ariz. Estate Planning Council, Mensa. Democrat. Jewish. Club: Nucleus. Lodge: Masons. Office: Simonson & Arbetman 4645 N 32d St Ste 200 Phoenix AZ 85018

SIMONSON, MILES KEVIN, real estate executive; b. Monmouth, Ill., May 25, 1950; s. John E. and Margaret Katherine (Huston) S. BA, No. Ill. U., 1972. Sgt. DeKalb County Sheriff's Police, Sycamore, Ill., 1972-75; owner Kishwaukee Realty, DeKalb, 1976-78; v.p and chief ops. officer Realty World, Oak Brook (Ill.), Tampa (Fla.), Phoenix, St. Louis, 1978-84; pres., chief exec. officer Realty 500, Inc., Reno, 1985-87, also bd. dirs.; founder, owner Simonson Seminars, Long Beach, Calif., 1987—; bd. dirs. Realty 500 of No. Nev., Realty 500 Advt. Fund., Reno. Author: Professional Sales, 1985, Professional Listing, 1985. Office: Simonson Seminars 2180 Eucalyptus Ave Long Beach CA 90806

SIMONSON, SUSAN KAY, hospital administrator; b. LaPorte, Ind., Dec. 5, 1946; d. George Randolph and Myrtle Lucille (Opfel) Menkes; m. Richard Bruce Simonson, Aug. 25, 1973. BA with honors, Ind. U., 1969; MA, Washington U., St. Louis, 1972. Perinatal social worker Yakima Valley Meml. Hosp., Yakima, Wash., 1979-81, dir. patient support and hospice program, 1981—, dir. social svc., 1982—; Spanish instr. Yakima Valley Coll., Yakima, Wash., 1981—; pres. Yakima Child Abuse Council, 1983-85; developer nat. patient support program, 1981. Contbr. articles to profl. jours. Mem. Jr. League, Yakima; mem. adv. council Robert Wood Johnson Found. Rural Infant Health Care Project, Yakima, 1980, Pregnancy Loss and Compassionate Friends Support Groups, Yakima, 1982—, Teen Outreach Program, Yakima, 1984—. Recipient NSF award, 1967, discharge planning program of yr. regional award Nat. Glasrock Home Health Care Discharge Planning Program, 1987; research grantee Ind. U., 1968, Fulbright grantee U.S. Dept. State, 1969-70; Nat. Def. Edn. Act fellowship, 1970-73. Mem. AAUW, Soc. Med. Anthropology, Soc. Hosp. Social Work Dirs. of Am. Hosp. Assn. (regional award 1989), Nat. Assn. Perinatal Social Workers, Nat. Assn. Social Workers, Phi Beta Kappa. Office: Yakima Valley Meml Hosp 2811 Tieton Dr Yakima WA 98902

SIMPLOT, JOHN R., agribusiness executive; b. Dubuque, Iowa, Jan. 4, 1909; m. Esther Becker; children: Richard, Don, Scott, Gay Simplot Otter. Founder, chmn. J.R. Simplot Co., Boise, Idaho, 1941—; bd. dirs. Micron Technology, First Security Corp., Continental Life and Accident Co., Morrison-Knudsen, Inc. Former chmn. bd. trustees Coll. Idaho. Avocations: skiing, horseback riding, hunting, fishing. Pioneer in commercial frozen french fries. Office: J R Simplot Co 1 Capital Ctr PO Box 27 Boise ID 83707 *

SIMPSON, ALAN KOOI, senator; b. Cody, Wyo., Sept. 2, 1931; s. Milward Lee and Lorna (Kooi) S.; m. Ann Schroll, June 21, 1954; children—William Lloyd, Colin Mackenzie, Susan Lorna. B.S., U. Wyo., 1954, J.D., 1958; L.L.D. (hon.), Calif. Western Sch. of Law, 1983, Colo. Coll., 1986, Notre Dame U., 1987. Bar: Wyo. 1958, U.S. Supreme Ct. 1964. Asst. atty. gen. State of Wyo., 1959; city atty. City of Cody, 1959-69; partner firm Simpson, Kepler, Simpson & Cozzens (and predecessor), Cody, Wyo., 1959-78; mem. Wyo. Ho. of Reps., 1964-77, majority whip, 1973-75, majority floor leader, 1975-77, speaker pro tem, 1977; legis. participant Eagleton Inst. Politics, Rutgers U., 1971; mem. U.S. Senate from Wyo., 1978—, asst. majority leader, 1985-87, asst. minority leader, 1987—, ranking minority mem. vets. affairs com., ranking minority mem. nuclear regulation subcom., ranking minority mem. subcom. on immigration and refugee policy; guest lectr. London exchange program Regent's Coll., London, 1987. Formerly v.p., trustee N.W. Community Coll., Powell, Wyo., 1968-76; trustee Buffalo Bill Hist. Ctr., Cody; trustee Grand Teton Music Festival, Gottsche Found. Rehab. Ctr., Thermopolis, Wyo.; del. Nat. Triennial Episcopal Ch. Conv., 1973, 76. Recipient Nat. Assn. Land Grant Colls. Centennial Alum award U. Wyo., 1987. Mem. Wyo. Bar Assn., Park County Bar Assn., Fifth Jud. Dist. Bar Assn., Am. Bar Assn., Assn. Trial Lawyers Am., U. Wyo. Alumni Assn. (pres. 1962, 63, Disting. Alumnus award 1985), VFW (life), Am. Legion, Amvets. (Silver Helmet award). Lodges: Eagles, Elks, Masons (33 deg.), Shriners, Rotary (pres. local club 1972-73). Office: US Senate 261 Dirksen Senate Bldg Washington DC 20510 *

SIMPSON, ANDREA LYNN, energy communication executive; b. Altadena, Calif., Feb. 10, 1948; d. Kenneth James and Barbara Faries Simpson; m. John R. Myrdal, Dec. 13, 1986. BA, U. So. Calif., 1969, MS, 1983; postgrad. U. Colo., Boulder, 1977. Asst. cashier United Calif. Bank, L.A., 1969-73; asst. v.p. mktg. 1st Hawaiian Bank, Honolulu, 1973-78; v.p. corp. communications Pacific Resources, Inc., Honolulu, 1978—. Bd. dirs. Kapiolani Women's and Children's Hosp., 1988—, Hawaii Heart Assn., 1978-83, Child and Family Svcs., 1984-86 , Coun. of Pacific, Girl Scouts U.S., 1982-85, Arts Coun. Hawaii, 1977-81; trustee Hawaii Loa Coll., 1984-86; commr Hawaii State Commn. on Status of Women, 1985-87. Trustee Hawaii sch. for girls at LaPietra, 1989—; Bd. dirs. Honolulu Symphony Soc., 1985-87. Named Panhellenic Woman of Yr. Hawaii, 1979, Outstanding Woman in Bus. Hawaii YWCA, 1980, Outstanding Young Woman of Hawaii Girl Scouts Coun. of the Pacific, 1985, 86, Hawaii Legis., 1980. Mem. Am. Mktg. Assn., Pub. Rels. Soc. Am. (bd. dirs. Honolulu chpt. 1984-865, Silver Anvil award 1984), Pub. Utilities Communicators Assn. (Communicator of Yr. 1984), Honolulu Advt. Fedn. (Advt. Woman of Yr. 1984), U. So. Calif. Alumni Assn. (bd. dirs. Hawaii 1981-83), Outrigger Canoe Club, Pacific Club, Kaneohe Yacht Club, Rotary (state pub. rels. chmn. 1988—, Hawaii chpt.), Alpha Phi (dir. Hawaii), Hawaii Jaycees (Outstanding Young Person of Hawaii 1978). Office: Pacific Resources Inc 733 Bishop St Ste 3100 Honolulu HI 96813

SIMPSON, JAMES RAY, marketing executive; b. Chgo., Dec. 2, 1945; s. Ray Hamill and H. Donna (Blake) S.; m. Terri Ann Ferrantello, June 8, 1974; children: Justin James, Larkin Ann. BSEE, U. Ill., 1969; MBA, U. Santa Clara, Calif., 1978. Mem. tech. staff Watkins-Johnson Co., Palo Alto, Calif., 1969-71, project mgr., 1971-72; prodn. engr. Hewlett Packard, Palo Alto, 1972; prodn. engr. Hewlett Packard, Santa Rosa, 1973-74, applications engr., 1974-78, product support mgr., 1979-80, product mktg. and applications engr. mgr., 1980-88, mgr. market devel. and sales, 1988—. Vice pres. site coun. Steele Ln. Sch., Santa Rosa, 1985-87; functional team leader Affirmative Action Com., Rohnert Park, 1987--. Office: Hewlett Packard Signal Analysis 1212 Valleyhouse Dr Rohnert Park CA 94928

SIMPSON, JAY ANDREW, information science executive; b. St. Louis, Sept. 20, 1930; s. Jay Miller and Sarah Louise (peairs) S. BS, U. Ariz., 1953, MS in Math., 1962. Advanced systems analysis Teledyne Ryan Electronics, San Diego, 1956-59; cons. Boeing Co., Seattle, 1960-63; rsch. engr. Rockwell Internat., Downey, Calif., 1963; mathematician Numer Control Corp., San Diego, 1964, U.S. Dept. of Navy, Port Hueneme, Calif., 1965-66; prin. sci. Info. Rsch. Assocs., San Diego, 1966-79; specialist Sperry Corp., San Diego, 1979-81; ship schedule engr. Frank E. Basil Corp., Washington, 1981-85; pres., chief exec. officer LMS Inc., San Diego, 1985—. Author 40 rsch. papers. With USN, 1952-56. Mem. Masons. Republican. Presbyterian.

SIMPSON, JOHN W. (PETER), public administrator; b. Fairbanks, Alaska, Aug. 12, 1934; s. John Edward Simpson and Robina Annie (Greig) Pege; Patricia Sylling, May 31, 1957; 1 child, David Alan. Student, U. Wash., 1952-54, BA in Communications, 1956; student, San Francisco State U., 1954-55. Bur. chief Jefferson County Port Angeles (Wash.) Evening News, 1963-66; exec. dir. Clallam-Jefferson Community Action Council, Port Townsend, Wash., 1966-68; regional dir. Ednl. Projects Inc., Washington, 1968-69; project dir. Ctr. for Human Systems Inc., Washington, 1969-70, area tng. mgr., 1970-71; project mgr. Head Start Tng. Ctr. U. Md., College Park, 1971-76; dir. housing programs Clallam-Jefferson Action Council Inc., Port Townsend, 1978-81, exec. dir., 1981—; cons. NOVATA Inc., Reston, Va., 1976-78. Co-author: Years That Are Gone, 1978; editor: City of Dreams, 1986. Mem. Port Townsend City Arts Commn., 1983—; pres. Jefferson County Hist. Soc., Port Townsend, 1986-87, Wash. State Hist. Soc., Tacoma, 1988—; legis. chmn. Wash. Assn. Community Action Agys., Tacoma, 1987—. With USAF, 1956-58. Mem. Internat. Transactional Analysts Assn. (cert.). Home: 929 Maple Port Townsend WA 98368 Office: Clallam-Jefferson Community Action 802 Sheridan 1st Fl Port Townsend WA 98368

SIMPSON, NORVELL JAMES, human relations administrator; b. Rochester, N.Y., Mar. 25, 1931; s. Frank Douglas and Martha Perlina (Jentons) S.; m. Alice Elizabeth Saxton, July 11, 1953; children: Gary A., Sharon R., Leslie A. BA in Econs. and Bus., Park Coll., Kansas City, Mo., 1970. Prodn coordinator TRW/CE, Colorado Springs, Colo., 1971-72; community action dir. Pikes Peak Community Action Prog., Colorado Springs, 1972-79; property control mgr. TRW/EPI, Colorado Springs, 1980-85, small bus. and small disadvantaged bus. adminstr., 1986; human relations adminstr. Sch. Dist. #11, Colorado Springs, 1986—. Bd. dirs. Pikes Peak Community Action Prog., Colorado Springs, 1986—, Sch. Dist. #11, 1975-85. Served with USAF, 1949-71. Named Citizen of Yr. Omega Psi Phi, 1981-84; Lion award Colo. Edn. Assn., 1985. Mem. NAACP (life mem., dir. 1983—), Urban League, Tuskegee Airmen, Alpha Phi Alpha (Citizen of Yr. 1981-84, pres. 1977-79), Masons (33 Degree), Shriner (past potentate). Home: 4880 Topaz Dr Colorado Springs CO 80918 Office: Sch Dist 11 Colorado Springs CO 80918

SIMPSON, RHYNE, JR., land developer; b. Dallas, Oct. 7, 1937; s. Rhyne and Avis L. (Miller) S.; B.A., U. Tex., 1959; M.B.A., Harvard U., 1964; m. Kay Slaughter; children—Michael Rhyne, Martha Katherine, Zachary Booth, (stepchildren) James A. Nolte II, Jennifer Leigh Nolte, Kathleen Mary Nolte. Vice pres. Republic Gypsum Co., Dallas, 1964-68, pres., 1968-73; pres. Santa Fe Resources, Inc., New Mex., 1973—; Democrat. Presbyterian. Clubs: Santa Fe Polo; Harvard (N.Y.C.). Office: Santa Fe Resources Inc PO Box 306 Windelman AZ 85292

SIMPSON, RICHARD JOHN, municipal official; b. Greensburg, Pa., Oct. 23, 1953; s. Henry Theodore and Marceline (Krempasky) S.; m. Gail Montgomery, Jan. 10, 1977 (div. May 1981); m. Jeri Anne Sheely, July 10, 1981. BA, Calif. U. Pa., 1976, 78; cert., Pa. Police Acad., 1978. Asst. security supt. Rouse Svc. Co., Greensburg, 1971-77; asst. police chief Ellsworth (Pa.) Borough Police Dept., 1977-78; police officer Fallowfield Twp. Police Dept., Charleroi, Pa., 1978-80; police officer, trainer, instr., coord. field tng. Rock Springs (Wyo.) Police Dept., 1980—; rsch. asst. centennial com. Rock Springs Police Dept.; police instr. State of Wyo, 1982—; actor, cons. tng. films series theater dept. Western Wyo. Coll., Rock Springs, 1987-88. Editor quar. newsletter Blue Knights News Wyo., 1986—. Asst. basketball coach Spl. Olympics, Rock Springs, 1987. Recipient numerous commedations Rock Springs Police Dept., 1980—, Outstanding Law Enforcement Officer award, 1985, Disting. Svc. medal, 1987, Svc. medal 1988. Mem. Blue Knights Internat. Law Enforcement Motorcycle Club (pres. Wyo chpts. 1985—), Police Protective Assn. (v.p. 1984-85), Western Alliance Police Officers (v.p. 1985-87), Shooting Stars Motorcycle Club (pres. 1980-84), Calif. U. Pa. Alumni Assn., Internmountain World War II Reenactment Assn. Home: 103 Agate St Rock Springs WY 82901 Office: Rock Springs Police Dept 221 C Rock Springs WY 82901

SIMPSON, ROBERT CARL, electronics company executive; b. Rochester, N.Y., Nov. 16, 1951; s. Robert Carl and Dorothy Norma (Lutz) S.; m. Diane Marie Noel, Oct. 27, 1973; children: Robert Carl III, Kristen. BSME, Western Mich. U., 1973; MBA, Xavier U., Cin., 1979. Registered profl. engr., Fla. Mem. mfg. mgmt. staff GE, Cin., 1973-76; project engr. Cordis Corp., Miami, Fla., 1976-79; group project mgr. Physio-Control Corp., Redmond, Wash., 1979-82; mgr. corp. communications Opcon, Everett, Wash., 1982-84; dir. nat. sales Korry Electronics, Seattle, 1984--; cons. Competetive Edge, Redmond, 1983--. Mem. Am. Mgmt. Assn. Republican. Baptist. Home: 16506 164th Ave NE Woodinville WA 98072 Office: Korry Electronics 901 Dexter Ave N Seattle WA 98109

SIMPSON, VELMA SOUTHALL, insurance agent; b. Denver, Jan. 29, 1948; d. Herbert Eugene and Gladys Jane (Pasquale) Southall; m. Stephen Wayne Simpson, Aug. 24, 1968; children: Sarah, Anna, Benjamin. BA, Colo. State U., 1971; postgrad., U. Denver, 1975-76. Adminstv. asst. Dacono (Colo.) Police Dept., 1981-83; community svcs. coord. Jefferson County, Golden, Colo., 1983; agt. Allstate Ins. Co., Longmont, Colo., 1983—. Active Mountain Prarie coun. Girl Scouts U.S., St. Vrain Hist. Soc., Family Extension, Community Food Share, Longmont Coalition for Women in Crisis. Democrat. Home: 99 Baylor Longmont CO 80501 Office: Allstate Ins Co 1600 N Hover D-3 Longmont CO 80501

SIMPSON, WILLIAM ARTHUR, insurance company executive; b. Oakland, Calif., Feb. 2, 1939; s. Arthur Earl and Pauline (Mikalasic) S.; m. Nancy Ellen Simpson, Mar. 31, 1962; children—Sharon Elizabeth, Shelley Pauline. B.S., U. Calif.-Berkeley, 1961; postgrad. Exec. Mgmt. Program, Columbia U. C.L.U. Br. mgr. Occidental Life of Calif., Los Angeles, 1965-73, v.p. agys., 1976-79; v.p. mktg. Countrywide Life, Los Angeles, 1973-76; pres., chief exec. officer Vol. State Life, Chattanooga, Tenn., 1979-83; exec. v.p. Transam. Occidental Life Ins. Co., Los Angeles, 1983-86, pres., 1986-88, pres., chief oper. officer, 1988—, also bd. dirs. Pres. Chattanooga coun. Boy Scouts Am., 1982, bd. dirs., L.A., 1983, v.p., 1983-85, vice-chmn, chmn. L.A. Area, 1988; pres. bd. councillors L.A. County Am. Cancer Soc.; trustee Calif. Med. Ctr. 1st lt. U.S. Army, 1961-64. Mem. Am. Soc. CLUs, Life Ins. Mktg. and Rsch. Assn. (bd. dirs. 1986—). Republican. Presbyterian. Lodge: Rotary. Office: Transam Occidental Life Ins Co 2101 Terminal Annex Los Angeles CA 90051

SIMPSON, WILLIAM BRAND, economist, educator; b. Portland, Oreg., Nov. 30, 1919; s. John Alexander and Janet Christie (Brand) S.; m. Ruth Laura Decker, June 12, 1957. B.A. in Math., Reed Coll., 1942; M.A. in Stats., Columbia U., 1943; Ph.D. in Econs., Claremont Grad. Sch., 1971. Exec. dir. Cowles Commn. Research Econs., Chgo., 1948-53; co-founder, bd. dirs. Inst. Social and Personal Relations, Oakland, Calif., 1955-61; prof. econs. Calif. State U., Los Angeles, 1958—; econs. cons. higher edn. Served with CIC, U.S. Army, 1943-46. Fellow Nat. Social Sci. Research Council; mem. ACLU; Econometric Soc. (internat. sec. 1948-52); AAUP (state pres. 1975-76, nat. council 1978-81, com. govt. relations 1982-88, state chmn. com. issues and policy 1981—), Am. Econs. Assn., Am. Assn. Higher Edn., Western Econ. Assn., Congress Faculty Assns., United Scottish Socs. So. Calif., Sierra Club (Los Angeles chpt.), Phi Beta Kappa. Democrat. Unitarian. Mng. editor, co-editor, Econometrica, 1948-53; contbr. articles to profl. jours. Home: PO Box 1456 South Pasadena CA 91031 Office: Calif State U Los Angeles CA 90032

SIMPSON, YVETTE, management consultant; b. Johannesburg, Transvaal, Republic of South Africa, Sept. 15, 1954; came to U.S., 1982; d. Jack and Shirley Ellen (Gordon) S. Grad. high sch., Republic of South Africa. Sec. Unilever (Lever Bros.), Republic of South Africa, 1974-76; councillor, mgr. Churchill Personnel, Republic of South Africa, 1977-78; pres. Park Ave. Placements, Republic of South Africa, 1978; coordinator human resources Mercedes Datakor, Republic of South Africa, 1980-82; pres. Simpson, Age & Cons., Inc., Los Angeles, 1982—. Mem. Nat. Assn. Women Execs. Office: Simpson Cons 2265 Westwood Blvd #918 Los Angeles CA 90064

SIMS, DARRELL BRUCE, oral and maxillofacial surgeon; b. Long Beach, Calif., Aug. 15, 1953; s. Darrell Leroy and Caroline (Manning) S.; m. Robin Renee Real, May 29, 1982. BA in Biology, U. Calif., San Diego, 1977; DDS, U. Tex., San Antonio, 1982; cert. oral and maxillofacial surgery, U. Tex., 1986; postgrad., Baylor U. Med. Ctr., Dallas, 1987. Pvt. practice. Mem. Am. Dental Assn., Am. Assn. Oral and Maxillofacial Surgeons, Am. Cleft Palate Assn., Ariz. Dental Soc., Ariz. Dental Implant Ctr., Rotary. Republican. Presbyn. Office: 737 E Glandale D Phoenix AZ 85020

SIMS, DAVID LEWIS, statistician; b. Rock Springs, Wyo., May 29, 1939; s. John Clifford and Annie (Smail) S.; m. Amy Marie Dunn, Sept. 5, 1959; children: Joan Marie, Susan Kay. BS, U. Wyo., 1962. Survey statistician Bur. of Census, Denver, Boston, 1962-63; statistician Air Res. Personnel Ctr., Denver, 1963-66; statistician Air Force Acctg. and Fin. Ctr., Denver, 1966-76, supervisory statistician, 1976—. Mem. Am. Soc. Quality Control (sect. mgmt. program chmn. 1986-88, recertification chmn. 1989), Am. Soc. Mil. Comptrollers, Air Force Assn., Windsor Gardens Evening Optimist Club (Just Say No chmn. 1987-88, personnel mgr. pancake breakfasts 1986-88). Roman Catholic. Home: 12406 E Kentucky Ave Aurora CO 80012 Office: Air Force Acctg & Fin Ctr AFAFC/AJQS Denver CO 80279-5000

SIMS, ROBERT CARL, university dean; b. Ft. Gibson, Okla., Dec. 26, 1936; s. Carl Raymond and Irene (Weatherford) S.; m. Elizabeth Ann Crow, June 3, 1963; children: Sarah, Barry, Todd. BA, Northeastern Okla. State Coll., 1963; MA, U. Okla., 1965; PhD, U. Colo., 1970. Asst. prof. history Boise State U., 1970-73, assoc. prof., 1973-79, prof., 1979—, dean Sch. Social Scis. and Pub. Affairs, 1985—. Author: Idaho's Governors, 1978; editorial bd. Idaho Yesterdays mag., 1980—; contbr. articles to mags. Commr. Boise City Planning and Zoning Commn., 1979-85, chmn., 1983-85. With U.S. Army, 1958-61. Mem. Assn. for the Humanities in Idaho. Democrat. Unitarian. Home: 1210 Harrison Blvd Boise ID 83702 Office: Boise State U Sch Soc Sci & Pub Affairs 1910 University Dr Boise ID 83725

SIMS, WILLIAM ROBERT, broadcasting executive; b. Globe, Ariz., Sept. 13, 1940; s. William Harlan and Edna Mae (Whitaker) S.; m. Linda Elizabeth Thomas, July 30, 1960; children: Cheryl Robin, Shannon Lynne. Student, U. N.Mex. Cert. radio mktg. cons. V.p., gen. mgr. Modcom Corp., Casper, Wyo., 1962-69; pres., chief exec. officer Wycom Corp., Laramie, Wyo., 1969-81; chmn., chief exec. officer Classic Media, Inc., Santa Fe, 1981—. Nat. bd. dirs. Jaycees, Tulsa, 1969; pres. Laramie C. of C., 1974. Named one of Outstanding Young Men of Am., 1973, Outstanding Grad. Albuquerque High Sch., 1979, Jaycees Internat. Sen., 1976; recipient Disting. Service award U. Wyo., 1986. Mem. Radio Advt. Bur., Nat. Broadcasters Assn. (bd. dirs. 1976-80, pres. Wyo. chpt. 1972, pres. Rocky Mountain chpt. 1974). Office: Classic Media Inc 121 Sandoval Santa Fe NM 87501

SIMSHAUSER, DUANE K., teacher; b. Colorado Springs, Colo., Feb. 18, 1937; s. Arthur R. and Elizabeth A. (Watson) S.; m. Hazel M. Zimmerer; children: Roger, Lance R., Vanessa M.; m. Julie Kay Bigger, Aug. 3, 1968. BE, Eastern Wash. U., 1959; MEd, Calif. Luth. U., 1974. Cert. secondary tchr. Tchr. art Colville Unified Sch. Dist., Wash., 1959-61; tchr. Lancaster (Calif.) Unified Sch. Dist., 1961-63, Mound Sch. Dist., Ventura, Calif., 1963-66; tchr. Ventura (Calif.) Unified Sch. Dist., 1966-80, tchr. 6th grade, 1980-82, math. tchr., 1982--. Seaman USNR, 1955-63. Mem. Calif. Tchrs. Assn., Ventura Unified Tchrs. Assn. Democrat. Home: 980 Grand Ave Fillmore CA 93015

SIMUNICH, MARY ELIZABETH HEDRICK (MRS. WILLIAM A. SIMUNICH), public relations executive; b. Chgo.; d. Tubman Keene and Mary (McCamish) Hedrick; student Phoenix Coll., 1967-69, Met. Bus. Coll., 1938-40; m. William A. Simunich, Dec. 6, 1941. Exec. sec. sales mgr. KPHO radio, 1950-53; exec. sec. mgr. KPHO-TV, 1953-54; account exec. Tom Rippey & Assos., 1955-56; pub. relations dir. Phoenix Symphony, 1956-62; co-founder, v.p. Paul J. Hughes Pub. Relations, Inc., 1960-65; owner Mary Simunich Pub. Relations, Phoenix, 1966-77. Pub. relations dir. Walter O. Boswell Meml. Hosp., Sun City, Ariz., 1969-85; instr. pub. relations Phoenix Coll. Evening Sch., 1973-78. Bd. dirs. Anytown, Ariz., 1969-72; founder, sec. friends Am. Geriatrics, 1977-86. Named Phoenix Advt. Woman of Year, Phoenix Jr. Advt. Club, 1962; recipient award Blue Cross, 1963; 1st Pl. award Ariz. Press Women, 1966. Mem. Internat. Assn. Bus. Communicators (pres. Ariz. chpt. 1970-71, dir.), Pub. Relations Soc. Am. (sec., dir. 1976-78), Am. Soc. Hosp. Pub. Relations (dir. Ariz. chpt. 1976-78), Nat., Ariz. press women. Club: Phoenix Press. Home: 4133 N 34th Pl Phoenix AZ 85018

SINCLAIR, WILLIAM DONALD, church official; b. Los Angeles, Dec. 27, 1924; s. Arthur Livingston and Lillian May (Holt) S.; m. Barbara Jean

Hughes, Aug. 9, 1952; children: Paul Scott, Victoria Sharon. BA cum laude, St. Martin's Coll., Olympia, Wash., 1975; postgrad. Emory U., 1978-79. Commd. 2d lt. USAAF, 1944, advanced through grades to col., USAF, 1970; served as pilot and navigator in Italy, Korea, Vietnam and Japan; ret., 1975; bus. adminstr. First United Methodist Ch., Colorado Springs, Colo., 1976-85; bus. adminstr. Village Seven Presbyn. Ch., 1985-87; bus. adminstr. Sunrise United Meth. Ch., 1987—; vice-chmn. council fin. and adminstrn. Rocky Mountain conf. United Meth. Ch., U.S.A., 1979-83. Bd. dirs. Chins-Up Colorado Springs, 1983—, Pikes Peak Performing Arts Ctr., 1985—; pres. Pioneers Mus. Found., 1985—. Decorated Legion of Merit with oak leaf cluster, D.F.C. with oak leaf cluster, Air medal with 6 oak leaf cluster, Dept. Def. Meritorious Service medal, Vietnam Cross of Gallantry with Palms. Fellow Nat. Assn. Ch. Bus. Adminstrs. (nat. dir., regional v.p., v.p. 1983-85, pres. 1986-87; Ch. Bus. Adminstr. of Yr. award 1983), Colo. Assn. Ch. Bus. Adminstrs. (past pres.), United Meth. Assn. Ch. Bus. Adminstrs. (nat. sec. 1978-81), Christian Ministries Mgmt. Assn. (dir. 1983-85), USAF Acad. Athletic Assn. Clubs: Colorado Springs Country, Plaza, Garden of the Gods. Lodge: Rotary (pres. Downtown Colorado Springs club 1985-86), Order of Daedalians. Home: 3007 Chelton Dr Colorado Springs CO 80909 Office: Village Seven Presbyn Ch 2655 Briargate Blvd Colorado Springs CO 80920

SINCOFF, STEVEN LAWRENCE, air force officer, computer systems chief; b. N.Y.C., Apr. 17, 1948; s. Murray B. and Lillian (Goldberg) S.; m. Constance Marie Onori, Jan. 17, 1970; children: Kristina Lynne, Carolyn Suzanne. BSChemE, N.J. Inst. Tech., 1969, MSChemE, 1972; PhD in Analytical Chemistry, Ohio State U., 1980. Commd. 2d lt. USAF, 1969, advanced through grades to lt. col., 1987; fuels mgmt. officer USAF, Albuquerque and Galena, Alaska, 1970-74; chem. engr. Aero. Systems Div., Wright-Patterson AFB, Ohio, 1974-77; assoc. prof. chemistry USAF Acad., Colorado Springs, Colo., 1980-84, dir. continuing edn. dept. chemistry, 1982-84; chief gas analysis lab. McClellan (AFB) Cen. Lab., Calif., 1984-88; exec. officer to comdr. Tech. Ops. Div. McClellan AFB, Calif., 1988-89, dir. computer communications systems. Tech. Ops. Div., 1989—; reviewer chemistry textbooks Saunders Pub., Phila., 1983-84. Mem. Am. Chem. Soc., Air Force Assn. Jewish. Home: 1863 Hidden View Ln Roseville CA 95661 Office: Tech Ops Div SC McClellan AFB CA 95652

SINES, RANDY DWAIN, business executive; b. Spokane, Jan. 16, 1948; s. Myron Jones and Paula Inez (Walls) S.; student Wash. State U., 1966-67, U. Wash., 1968-69; m. Irene Cheng, Mar. 18, 1981. With Boeing Co., 1967; with Winchell's Donut House, Inc. (merged with Denny's Restaurants), Seattle, 1968-71; owner, mgr. bakeries, Wash. and Mont., 1972-78; owner, mgr. Sonsine Inc., Great Falls, Mont., 1976-79; pres. Gardian Port Corp., Oxnard, Calif., 1980-82; pres., chmn. SNS Motor Imports, Inc., Oxnard, 1982—; chmn. Karakal Corp. of Ams., Ventura, Calif., 1986—; owner Dover Group, 1988—; owner Baker's "12". Recipient alumni grant Wash. State U., 1967; lic. water well contractor, Wash., Mont. Patentee sports apparatus, over 20 patents worldwide. Home: 5311 Gatewood Dr Klamath Falls OR 97603 Office: PO Box 7452 Klamath Falls OR 97602

SING, SANDIE FONG, elementary school educator; b. Oakland, Calif., July 30, 1949; d. Fong Hin Sing and Yuet Sen (Lee) Fong. AA, Modesto Jr. Coll., 1969; BA, Calif. State U.-Stanislaus, Turlock, 1972. Cert. Calif. Elem. Tchr. (life). Jewelry cons. Macy's, Modesto, Calif., 1979-81; tchr. Turlock (Calif.) City Sch. Dist., 1973—; mem. Calif. Internat. Studies Project tour to People's Rep. China and Rep. of Korea, 1987. Historian Stanislaus Reading Council, 1985-87; 2d v.p. PTA, 1986-87; sch. improvement program rep., Julien SIP Program, 1985-86; mem. Turlock Sch. Dist.'s Fine Arts Curriculum Com., policy bd. Project Internat. Multicultural Edn.; chmn. Turlock Unified Sch. Dist. Global Edn. Dist. Team; art commr. Turlock City Arts Commn., 1984—. Classroom Tchr. Instructional Improvement Program grantee, Turlock Sch. Dist., 1985—. Mem. Calif. Tchrs. Assn., AAUW, Stanislaus Chinese Assn. Office: Turlock Sch Dist Colorado and E Canal Turlock CA 95380

SINGER, JEFFREY ALAN, surgeon; b. Bklyn., Feb. 2, 1952; s. Harold and Hilda (Ginsburg) S.; m. Margaret Sue Gordon, May 23, 1976; children: Deborah Suzanne, Pamela Michelle. BA cum laude, Bklyn. Coll., 1973; MD, N.Y. Med. Coll., 1976. Diplomate Am. Bd. Surgery. Intern Maricopa County Gen. Hosp., Phoenix, 1976-77, resident, 1977-81, mem. teaching faculty, 1981—; trauma cons. John C. Lincoln Hosp., Phoenix, 1981-83; pvt. practice Phoenix, 1981-87; group pvt. practice Valley Surg. Clinics, Ltd., Phoenix, 1987—; sec.-treas. med. staff Humana Hosp. Desert Valley, Phoenix, 1987—, chief of surgery, 1985-87. Rep. precinct committeeman, Phoenix, 1986—. Fellow ACS, Internat. Coll. Surgeons, Southwestern Surgical Congress, Am. Soc. Abdominal Surgeons; Ariz. Med. Assn. (mem. legis. com. 1986—), AMA (bd. dirs. polit. action com. 1985—), Alpha Omega Alpha. Office: Valley Surg Clinics Ltd 4232 E Cactus Ste 209 Phoenix AZ 85032

SINGER, MARTIN BYRON, manufacturing executive; b. N.Y.C., Nov. 13, 1923; s. Nathaniel and Rose Minna (Lurie) S.; m. Nicole Berheim (div. 1970); children: Suzanne Karen, Michele, Martine Bettina; m. Mary Anne Elliott (div. 1979); 1 child, Bryan Evan. BA, Harvard U., 1947. Salesman, export mgr. Bay State Optical Co., Attleboro, Mass., 1947-53; v.p. research and devel. Soft-Lite Bay State Optical Co., Westbury, N.Y., 1953-55; pres. Harlequin Corp., N.Y.C., 1948-69, Harlequin West, Alhambra, Calif., 1969-74, Omni Optics, North Hollywood, Calif., 1973-83, MBS Optics Inc., Burbank, Calif., 1983—; cons. in field. Inventor: eyeglass frame, 1948. Served to 1st lt. U.S. Army, 1943-46, ETO. Democrat. Jewish. Club: Harvard (N.Y.C., Los Angeles). Home and Office: 421 S Lamer Burbank CA 91506

SINGER, MICHAEL HOWARD, lawyer; b. N.Y.C., Nov. 22, 1941; s. Jack and Etta (Appelbaum) S.; m. Saundra Jean Kupperman, June 1, 1962; children: Allison Jill, Pamela Faith. BS in Econs., U. Pa., 1962; JD, NYU, 1965, LLM in Taxation, 1968. Bar: N.Y. 1965, U.S. Ct. Claims 1968, U.S. Supreme Ct. 1969, U.S. Ct. Appeals (6th cir.) 1970, D.C. 1972, U.S. Tax Ct. 1972, Nev. 1973, U.S. Ct. Appeals (9th cir.) 1973. Law asst. Appellate Term Supreme Ct., N.Y.C., 1965-68; trial lawyer Ct. Claims Tax Div., Washington, 1968-72; tax lawyer Beckley, DeLanoy & Jemison, Las Vegas, 1972-74; ptnr. Oshins, Singer, Segal & Morris, Las Vegas, 1974-87; sole practice law Las Vegas, 1987; ptnr. Michael H. Singer Ltd., Las Vegas, 1987—. Pres. Las Vegas chpt. NCCJ, 1980-82. Mem. ABA, Nev. Bar Assn., Las Vegas Country Club, Ctr. Ct. Racquet Club. Democrat. Jewish. Home: 4458 Los Reyes Ct Las Vegas NV 89121 Office: 520 S 4th St 2d Fl Las Vegas NV 89101

SINGER, WILLIAM JAMES, real estate associate, consultant, teacher; b. St. Paul, Nov. 6, 1946; s. James Russell and Virginia F. (Hamlin) S. Student, U. Sweden, Lund, 1968; BA, U. Calif., Irvine, 1969; MA, U. Wis., 1971. Dir., founder UNI-PREP U. Calif., 1969-70, acting asst. dean, 1976-77; counselor U. Wis., Madison, 1970-71; v.p., chmn. bd. Legal Aid Warranty Fund, Santa Ana, Calif., 1971-73; pres. Pacific Guard Co., Anza, Calif., 1973-76; broker, owner Tierra del Sol Realty, Laguna Beach, Calif., 1978—; pres., chmn. bd., founder The Laguna Beach Psychic Inst., 1976—; pres., chmn. bd. Main Beach Investment Group, Inc., Laguna Beach, 1984—; chmn. bd. The Ultimate Cons. Group, Laguna Beach, 1986—. Author: Worlds in a Gourd, 1976; author, producer video The Spiritual Fitness Tape, 1988. Founder Mchts. Assn., Laguna Beach, 1985; official spokesperson Commn. to Recall City Coun., Laguna Beach, 1988; chmn. bd. The Healix Ctr., El Toro, Calif., 1985-88. Recipient Rene Descartes medal Consul Gen. of France, 1966, Spl. Commendation, Gov. and Bd. of Regents of Wis., 1971; Ford Found. fellow, 1970, Vilas Found. fellow, 1970. Mem. Nat. Assn. Realtors, Calif. Assn. Realtors, Laguna Beach Bd. Realtors. Home: 2107 Ocean Way Laguna Beach CA 92651 Office: Tierra del Sol Realty 213 Park Ave Laguna Beach CA 92651

SINGER-DELMONICO, RINA DAWN, information systems professional; b. Denver, Oct. 8, 1956; d. Paul and Billie Joyce (Dodd) S.; m. Kenneth John Delmonico Jr., Mar. 24, 1984. Student, U. No. Colo., 1978-79. Supr. customer svc. Gates Energy Products, Denver, 1974-77; programmer, analyst Gates Rubber Co., Denver, 1977-79; programmer, analyst Storage Tech. Corp., Louisville, Colo., 1979-80, staff programmer, analyst, 1980-81; mgr. applications software Uveon Corp., Denver, 1981-83; sr. programmer, analyst Petro-Lewis Corp., Denver, 1983-84, project mgr., 1984-85; mgr. Citicorp Systems Devel., Denver, 1985-87, v.p., 1987—; pres., owner KJ the DJ Co., Denver, 1986—; pres., owner Compu-Svc. Cons., Denver, 1980-88; instr. Community Coll. Denver, 1983-84. Mem. Am. Bus. Women's Assn., Denver C. of C. Home: 4774 Estes St Littleton CO 80123 Office: Citicorp Distbn Svc 183 Inverness Dr Englewood CO 80110

SINGH, KANWAR PARAMJIT, financial analyst; b. New Delhi, July 22, 1949; came to U.S., 1980; s. Harbans Singh and Kulwant Kaur (Sethi) Sahni; m. Baljit Kaur Kohli Sahni, Mar. 2, 1972; children: Gursimran Sahni, Sunena Sahni, Hanspreet Sahni. BA, Sri Guru Tegh Bahadur Khalsa Coll., New Delhi, 1971. Sales mgr. Weldon Sales Corp., New Delhi, 1971-72; ptnr. H. S. Sahni & Co., New Delhi, 1972-78; owner, mgr. Simpreena, Chandigarh, India, 1978-80; minister of religion Los Angeles, 1980-81; mgr. The Clothes Factory, Los Angeles, 1981-82; ins. agt. N.Y. Life Ins. Co., Los Angeles, 1982-86; fin. cons. Bebon Sahni, Los Angeles, 1986—; sales mgr. N.Y. Life Ins. Co., 1988—. Mem. Lanalu. Lodge: Optimists. Home: 7226 Ranchito Ave Van Nuys CA 91405 Office: NY Life Ins Co 20750 Ventura Blvd Ste 400 Woodland Hills CA 91364

SINGLETON, HENRY EARL, industrialist; b. Haslet, Tex., Nov. 27, 1916; s. John Bartholomew and Victoria (Flores) S.; m. Caroline A. Wood, Nov. 30, 1942; children: Christina, John, William, James, Diana. S.B., S.M., Mass. Inst. Tech., 1940, Sc.D., 1950. Vice pres. Litton Industries, Inc., Beverly Hills, Calif., 1954-60; chief exec. officer Teledyne Inc., Los Angeles, 1960-86; chmn. Teledyne Inc., 1960—. Home: 384 Delfern Dr Los Angeles CA 90024 Office: Teledyne Inc 1901 Ave of the Stars Los Angeles CA 90067 *

SINGLETON, LISA MICHELLE, civil engineer; b. Flint, Mich., Mar. 13, 1961; d. Robert Allan and Kay Jean (Huber) Bender; m. Mark Loring Singleton, May 19, 1984. BCE, Colo. State U., 1983; postgrad., Calif. State U., Fresno, 1987-88. Registered profl. engr., Calif. Civil engr. Yuma (Ariz.) Bur. Reclamation, 1983-84, Winzler & Kelly Consulting Engrs., Eureka, Calif., 1984-86; assoc. transp. engr. Calif. Dept. Transp., Fresno, 1987—. Sunday sch. tchr. First Christian Ch., Yuma, 1983-84, Ch. of the Highlands, Eureka, 1985-86; troop leader Yuma Girl Scouts U.S., 1983-84; high sch. sponsor, Sunday sch. tchr. North Fresno Christian Ch., 1987—. Mem. ASCE, Inst. Transp. Engrs., Toastmasters. Republican. Home: 764 Wood Duck Circle Fresno CA 93710

SINGLETON, MARGARET ELLEN, business and real estate appraiser, writer; b. Kansas City, Mo., Nov. 28, 1940; d. Daniel Robertson and Corinne Francis (Murchie) Neff; m. Seth Singleton, June 16, 1962 (div. Jan. 1983); children: Andrew, William; m. Jay Van Blarcom, June 27, 1988. Student, Radcliffe Coll., 1958-60; BA, George Washington U., 1962; postgrad., Yale U., 1962-63, 66-67, U. Alta., Edmonton, Can., 1970-71. Cert. Wis. Assessment Specialist. Supr. assessments Wis. Dept. Revenue, Fon du Lac, 1977-81; sr. appraiser Marshall & Stevens, Chgo., 1981-83; nat. mgr. real estate Arthur D. Little, Chgo., 1983-84; sr. real estate and fin. mgr. Arthur Andersen, Chgo., 1984-87; portfolio mgr. Indsl. Equity (Pacific), LaJolla, Calif., 1987-89; pres. G.R. Bill, 1989—; instr. Triton Coll., River Grove, Ill., 1986; bd. dirs. Pacific S.W. Corp. Contbg. author: (text book) Africa In Perspective, 1968; contbr. articles to profl. jour. Mem. task force Gov. Okla., 1986; lobbyist LWV, Wis. and Washington; asst. chmn. platform com. Wis. Dems. Fellow Woodrow Wilson Fellowship Found., 1962; scholar Nat. Merit Scholarship Found., 1958-62. Mem. Am. Inst. Real Estate Appraisers (nat. faculty mem. 1986-87, com. mem. 1984-86), Am. Soc. Appraisers (chmn. nat. com. 1982-86), Soc. Real Estate Appraisers (sr. real property appraiser). Democrat. Mem. Soc. Friends. Home: 12352 Escala Dr San Diego CA 92128-1209

SINGLETON, WILLIAM DEAN, newspaper publisher; b. Graham, Tex., Aug. 1, 1951; s. William Hyde and Florence E. (Myrick) S.; m. Adrienne Casale, Dec. 31, 1983; children: William Dean II, Susan Paige. Student, Tyler (Tex.) Jr. Coll., El Centro Coll., Dallas, U. Tex., Arlington. Various positions with The Dallas Morning News, Tyler Morning Telegraph, Wichita Falls Record News, and others, 1966-78; various positions with Albritton Communications Co., 1976-78, pres. newspaper div., 1978-83; pres. Gloucester County Times, Inc., 1983-85; pres. MediaNews Group, Inc., 1985-88, vice chmn., chief exec. officer, 1988—; chmn., publisher The Houston Post, 1988—. Baptist. Office: The Houston Post 4747 SW Frwy Houston TX 77001 also: care Denver Post PO Box 1709 Denver CO 80201 also: The Gloucester County Times 309 S Broad St Woodbury NJ 08096

SINGLETON, WILLIAM GEORGE, teacher, real estate associate, minister; b. Clovis, N.Mex., Jan. 4, 1945; s. Joseph Charles and Betty Jean (Russell) S.; m. Joan Marie Meadows, Aug. 22, 1970; children: Rebecca Marie, William Joshua, Tammy Rachel, Cody Caleb. Student, Lubbock (Tex.) Christian Coll., 1963-64, U. N.Mex., 1964-66; BS in Edn., Abilene (Tex.) Christian U., 1968; postgrad., Pepperdine U., 1981-84, N.Mex. Highlands U., 1970-71. Investigator FDA, Denver, 1971-76; preacher, speaker Chs. of Christ, Dallas, 1976-78, Livermore, Calif., 1979; with L.O.C. Equipment Co., Livermore, 1979-81; preacher Ch. of Christ, Lathrop, Calif., 1982—; tchr. pub. schs. Stockton, Calif., 1982—; real estate agt. Statewide Realty, Stockton, 1980—; co-owner Clovis Grain Processing, Ltd., 1987—; owner Apple Agy., Stockton, 1987; owner various mineral deposits and mines, Stockton. Contbr. articles to profl. jours. Vol. chaplain Deuel Vocat. Instn., Tracy, Calif., 1986—. With U.S. Army, 1968-70, Vietnam. Mem. NEA, Stockton Tchrs. Assn., Stockton Bd. Realtors. Republican. Home: 4149 N Center Stockton CA 95204 Office: Apple Agy 4555 N Pershing Ave #33-177 Stockton CA 95207

SINHA, ATIN KUMAR, aerospace engineer; b. Calcutta, India, Sept. 10, 1948; came to U.S., 1979; s. Gobinda Chandra and Sheela (Mitra) S.; m. Shukla Ghosh, May 13, 1975. BME with honors, Jadavpur U., Calcutta, 1970; MAeroE, Indian Inst. Sci., Bangalore, 1973; PhD in Aerospace Engring., U. Tenn., 1984. Engr. Indian Space Research Orgn., Trivandrum, 1973; scientist Nat. Aero. Lab., Bangalore, 1973-79; engr. Gates Learjet Corp., Wichita, Kans., 1984-85; sr. engr. Garrett Engine div. Allied Signal Aerospace Co. (formerly Garrett Turbine Engine Co.), Phoenix, 1985—. Contbr. articles to profl. jours. Mem. AIAA, Sigma Xi (assoc.). Home: 5038 S Hardy Apt 1018 Tempe AZ 85282 Office: Allied Signal Aerospace Co Garrett Engine Div 111 S 34th St M/S 93-364 503-4T Phoenix AZ 85010

SINHA, DIPEN N., physicist; b. Mosaboni, Bihar, India, Mar. 9, 1951; came to U.S., 1973; s. Mrigen and Narayani (Sinharoy) S.; m. Barbara Ann Rehor, Sept. 27, 1975; 1 child, Naveen Neil. BSc with hons., St. Xavier's Coll., Ranchi, India, 1970; MSc, Indian Inst. of Tech., Kharagpur, India, 1972; D.I.I.T., Indian Inst. of tech., Kharagpur, India, 1973; PhD in Physics, Portland State U., 1980. Grad. teaching asst. Portland State U., Portland, 1973-80; postdoctoral fellow Los Alamos Nat. Lab., Los Alamos, N.Mex., 1980-83; mem. of tech. staff Rockwell Internat., Anaheim, Calif., 1983-86; staff mem. physisist Los Alamos Nat. Lab., Los Alamos, N.Mex., 1986—; v.p. Physics Soc., Indian Inst. of Tech. Kharagpur 1972-73. Author: 20 articles on Physics in profl. jours.; patent author, Superlattice Strain Guage. Mem. Am. Physical Soc., Sigma Xi. Home: 112 Shirlane Pl Los Alamos NM 87544 Office: Los Alamos Nat Lab MS D429 Los Alamos NM 87545

SINNOTT, J. B., biomedical engineer; b. Wilkes-Barre, Pa., Apr. 9, 1964; s. A. Joseph and Roberta (Lewis) S. BS in Biomed. Engring., Ariz. State U., 1986. Product engr. Impra, Inc., Tempe, Ariz., 1987-88, devel. engr., 1988—; tech. cons. Vascular Implant Tech., Houston, 1988. Vol. Valley Big Bros., Phoenix, 1988—. Mem. Health Industry Bus. Communication Coun. (corr.). Republican. Roman Catholic. Office: Impra Inc 1625 W 3d St Tempe AZ 85281

SIOUKAS, JACK, financial advisor; b. Kastoria, Greece, Apr. 21, 1936; came to U.S., 1955; s. Anastasios Kyriakos and Nerantzia (Kopatsis) S.; m. Lillian Sutter, Apr. 28, 1968; children: Chris, Dean, Alex. BS, U. Ill., Chgo., 1960, DDS, 1962. Pvt. practice Sacramento, 1964; investor Jack Sioukas Investments, Sacramento, 1964—; pres. Lexington Homes Inc., Sacramento, 1986—, JAS Devel. Corp., Sacramento, 1986—. Founding mem. Dynamis, San Francisco, 1979; mem. Parish Council-Greek Orthodox Ch. Capt. USAF, 1962-64. Mem. ADA, Acad. Gen. Denstistry, Sacramento Dist. Dental Assn., Am. Hellenic Profl. Soc. No. Calif., Del Paso Country Club, NorthRidge Country Club. Republican. Home: 3331 American River Dr Sacramento CA 95864 Office: Sioukas Investments 7700 College Town Dr Ste 109 Sacramento CA 95826

SIPE, LYNN FOSTER, librarian; b. Denver, Nov. 4, 1942; d. Wilbur and Helen Ruth (Dressler) Sipe. BA in Internat. Relations, Am. U., 1964; MLS, Columbia U., 1966; MPA, Univ. So. Calif., 1975. Bibliog. searcher Univ. So. Calif. Libr., L.A., 1966-68, head, internat. & pub. affairs libr., 1968-84, acting asst. univ. libr. pub. svcs., 1984-86, asst. univ. libr. collection devel., 1986—. Author: Western Sahara A Comprehensive Bibliography, (with others) American Public Administration, a Bibliographic Guide to the Literature. Mem. ALA, Human Relations Area Files, Inc. (bd. dirs.), Research Libraries Group (collection mgmt. & devel. com.). Democrat. Home: 8175 Gould Ave Los Angeles CA 90046-1959 Office: Univ of So Calif University Park Los Angeles CA 90089-0182

SIPMA, ARTHUR, insurance company official, farmer; b. Friesland, The Netherlands, Sept. 7, 1932; came to U.S., 1948; s. John and Maria (Hoekstra) S.; m. Joan E. Dykstra, Mar. 21, 1965; children: Gretchen, Heidi, Anneke, Arjen. Student, Yosemite Jr. Coll., Modesto, Calif., 1965. Lic. ins. agt., Calif. Ptnr. dairy Ripon, Calif., 1951-55, owner, 1957-62; vol. Peace Corps, East Pakistan, 1962-64; with milk svc. dept. Jersey Crown Dairy, Manteca, Calif., 1964-67; agt. Calfarm Ins. Co., Escalon, Calif., 1967—. Chmn. Escalon United Way. With U.S. Army, 1955-57. Mem. Escalon C. of C. (bd. dirs. 1970-72), Lions (sec. Escalon 1981-89). Republican. Home: 19964 McHenry Ave Escalon CA 95320 Office: Calfarm Ins Co 1734 Main St Escalon CA 95320

SIPOS, CHIQUITA AGNES, community services consultant; b. Chgo., Apr. 21, 1939; d. Joaquin Angeles and Margaret Ross Arcala; m. Raymond E. Sipos, 1962 (divorced 1971); children: Sandra Rene, Stephanie Susan, Sheri Annette. AA, Pasadena City Coll., 1962; BA, Calif. State U., Los Angeles, 1967; BS in Law, Glendale U., 1978, JD, 1980. Bar: Calif. 1988. Playground dir. Melvindale (Mich.) Recreation Dept., 1958-59; probation attendant Los Angeles County Probation Dept., Commerce, Calif., 1961-62; group supr. Los Angeles County Probation Dept., El Monte, Calif., 1963-68; dir. Friendship Nursery Sch., El Monte, 1967-68; parole agent I Dept. Youth Authority, East Los Angeles, Calif., 1968-72; Parole Agent Specialist Dept. Youth Authority, Los Angeles, 1972-75, asst. supr., 1975-77; parole agent specialist Dept. Youth Authority, El Monte, 1977-78; cons. Dept. Youth Authority, Glendale, Calif., 1978—; instr. Dept. Youth Authority, Calif., 1975-87; cons. youth and criminal justice agys., Los Angeles County, 1980—; panel mem. Am. Probation Parole Assn., Boston, 1985; mem. Health and Welfare Agy. Filipino Advisory Comm., 1976-78, Los Angeles County Commn. comm. on Law, Soc. & Children's Rights, 1979. Tech. advisor: (film and video) Victim to Victimizer: Breaking the Cycle of Male Sexual Abuse, 1986. Commn. on Status Women Adv. Com., Sacramento, 1978-79. Recipient Women's Achievement award The East Los Angeles Community Union, 1976, Resolution award Calif. Legislature, Sacramento, 1976, Los Angeles County Bd. Suprs., 1982, commendation Californians Against Crime, Los Angeles, 1982. Mem. So. Calif. Juvenile Officers Assn., Am. Correctional Assn. (bd. govs. 1984-86, 88—), Los Angeles County Bar Assn. Juvenile Justice Commn., Calif. Probation Parole Correctional Assn. (pres. 1981-82), Am. Correctional Assn. (bd. govs. 1984-86). Democrat. Roman Catholic. Office: Dept of Youth Authority 143 S Glendale Ave Ste 305 Glendale CA 91030

SIRI, WILLIAM EMIL, physicist; b. Phila., Jan. 2, 1919; s. Emil Mark and Caroline (Schaedel) S.; m. Margaret Jean Brandenburg, Dec. 3, 1949; children: Margaret Lynn, Ann Kathryn. B.Sc., U. Chgo., 1942; postgrad. in physics, U. Calif.-Berkeley, 1947-50. Licensed profl. engr., Calif. Research engr. Baldwin-Lima-Hamilton Corp., 1943; physicist Manhattan Project Lawrence-Berkeley Lab., U. Calif. at Berkeley, 1943-45, prin. investigator biophysics and research, 1945-74; mgr. energy analysis program Lawrence Berkeley Lab., 1974-81; sr. scientist emeritus U. Calif., 1981—; exec. v.p. Am. Mt. Everest Expdn., Inc.; Field leader U. Calif. Peruvian Expdns., 1950-52; leader Calif. Himalayan Expdn., 1954; field leader Internat. Physiol. Expdn. to Antarctica, 1957; dep. leader Am. Mt. Everest Expdn., 1963. Author: Nuclear Radiations and Isotopic Tracers, 1949, papers on energy systems analyses, biophys. research, conservation and mountaineering. Pres. Save San Francisco Bay Assn., 1968-88; Bd. dirs. Sierra Club Found., 1964-78, Mountain Medicine Inst., 1988—; vice chmn. The Bay Inst., 1985—. Served to lt. (j.g.) USNR, 1950-59. Co-recipient Hubbard medal Nat. Geog. Soc., 1963, Elisa Kent Kane medal Phila. Geog. Soc., 1963, Sol Feinstone Environmental award, 1977. Mem. Am. Phys. Soc., Biophys. Soc., Am. Assn. Physicists in Medicine, Sigma Xi. Democrat. Lutheran. Clubs: Sierra (dir. 1955-74, pres. 1964-66, William Colby award 1975), American Alpine (v.p.), Explorers (certificate of merit 1964). Home: 1015 Leneve Pl El Cerrito CA 94530 Office: U Calif Lawrence Berkeley Lab 1 Cyclotron Rd Berkeley CA 94720

SIRIGNANO, WILLIAM ALFONSO, aerospace and mechanical engineer, educator; b. Bronx, N.Y., Apr. 14, 1938; s. Anthony P. and Lucy (Caruso) S.; m. Lynn Haisfield, Nov. 26, 1977; children: Monica Ann, Jacqueline Hope, Justin Anthony. B.Aero.Engring., Rensselaer Poly. Inst., 1959; Ph.D., Princeton U., 1964. Mem. research staff Guggenheim Labs., aerospace, mech. scis. dept. Princeton U., 1964-67, asst. prof. aerospace and mech. scis., 1967-69, assoc. prof., 1969-73, prof., 1973-79, dept. dir. grad. studies, 1974-78; George Tallman Ladd prof., head dept. mech. engring. Carnegie-Mellon U., 1979-85; dean Sch. Engring., U. Calif.-Irvine, 1985—; cons. industry and govt., 1966—; mem. emissions control panel Nat. Acad. Scis., 1971-73; lectr. and cons. NATO adv. group on aero. research and devel., 1967, 75, 80; chmn. nat. and internat. tech. confs.; chmn. acad. adv. council Indsl. Research Inst., 1985-88; mem. space sci. applications adv. com. NASA, 1985—, chmn. combustion sci. microgravity disciplinary working group. Assoc. editor: Combustion Sci. and Tech, 1969-70; tech. editor Jour. Heat Transfer, 1985—; contbr. articles to nat. and internat. profl. jours., also research monographs. United Aircraft research fellow, 1973-74. Fellow AIAA, ASME; mem. Combustion Inst. (treas. internat. orgn. and chmn. Eastern sect.), Soc. Indsl. Applied Math. Home: 3 Gibbs Ct Irvine CA 92715 Office: U Calif Sch Engring Irvine CA 92717

SISAM, DAVID MICHAEL, travel services executive; b. Salt Lake City, Apr. 26, 1961; s. Richard Lorne and Colleen M. (Moore) S. Pres. Mainstreet Travel, Inc., Salt Lake City, 1980-86; v.p. Beehive Travel Group, Salt Lake City, 1986—; tchr., advisor Utah Bus. Week, 1985-86. Mem. com. March of Dimes, Salt Lake City, 1983; chmn. bd. dirs. Ririe-Woodbury Dance Co., Salt Lake City, 1984-86; bd. dirs. Salt Lake City Responsibility Com. for Arts, 1986, 87. Mem. SAG, Salt Lake City C. of C. (pres.'s com. 1984). Home: 1942 N Grace Ave #112 Los Angeles CA 90068 Office: Beehive Travel Group 1130 West Center St North Salt Lake UT 84054

SISBARRO, LOUIS FREDERICK, automotive executive; b. Newark, Nov. 6, 1941; s. Louis and Florence (Gugliotta) S.; m. Patricia Lordy, July 11, 1964; children: Louis F. Jr., Daniel J., Nicole C. BS in Indsl. Engring., Gen. Motors Inst., 1964. Supr. Gen. Motors Corp., Linden, N.J., 1965-69; sales mgr. Glenn Wilson Buick-Oldsmobile, Fenton, Mich., 1969-74, v.p., 1974-81; pres. Owen Ops., Fenton, 1975-81; v.p. GM Rental (Budget Rent-a-Car), Boulder, Colo., 1978-80; pres. Sisbarro Buick-Pontiac-GMC, Las Cruces, N.Mex., 1981—, Sisbarro's Autoworld VW-Audi, Las Cruces, 1985—, Sisbarro Rental, Las Cruces, 1986-88, Sisbarro Ins., Las Cruces, 1986—. Pres. Holly (Mich.) Little League, 1979; bd. dirs. pres's. assocs. N.Mex. State U., 1983-86; bd. dirs., officer Aggie Sports Assn.; bd. councillors Citizen's Bank, 1987—. Recipient 5 Star Gen. award GMC Truck Co., 1987, Pontiac Master award Pontiac Motor Div., 1985-88. Mem. Nat. Auto Dealers Assn., Nat. Auto Dealers Assn. 20 Group (bd. dirs 1988), N.Mex. Auto Dealers Assn. (bd. dirs.), Fenton C. of C. (pres. 1979). Lodge: KC. Office: Sisbarro Buick-Pontiac-GMC 425 W Boutz Las Cruces NM 88005

SISEMORE, CLAUDIA, producer-director educational films and videos; b. Salt Lake City, Sept. 16, 1937; d. Darrell Daniel and Alice Larril (Barton) S. BS in English, Brigham Young U., 1959; MFA in Filmmaking, U. Utah, 1976. Cert. secondary tchr., Utah. Tchr. English, drama and writing Salt Lake Sch. Dist., Salt Lake City, 1959-66; tchr. English Davis Sch. Dist., Bountiful, Utah, 1966-68; ind. filmmaker Salt Lake City, 1972—; filmmakerin-residence Wyo. Coun. for Arts and Nat. Endowment for Arts, Dubois, Wyo., 1977-78; producer, dir. ednl. films Utah Office Edn., Salt Lake City, 1979—. Producer, dir. Beginning of Winning, 1984 (film festival award 1984), Dancing through the Magic Eye, 1986, Se Habla Espanol, 1986-87; writer, dir., editor Building on a Legacy, 1988, An Early Winter (film), 1989; artist (abstract acrylic) exhibited Phillips Gallery, numerous pvt. and pub. collections. Juror Park City (Utah) Arts Festival, 1982, Utah Arts Festival, Salt Lake City, 1982, Am. Film Festival, 1985-86, Best of West Film Festival, 1985-86; bd. dirs. Utah Media Ctr., Salt Lake City, 1981-87; mem. multi-disciplinary program Utah Arts Coun., Salt Lake City, 1983-87. Recipient award Utah Media Ctr., 1984, 85; Nat. Endowment for Arts grantee, 1978, Utah Arts Coun. grantee, 1980. Mormon. Office: Utah Office Edn 250 East 500 South Salt Lake City UT 84111

SISK, JAY MICHAEL, computer company owner; b. Newport News, Va., Nov. 25, 1945; s. James C. and Rebecca (Hodnett) S. BS, Va. Commonwealth U., 1971; MBA, U. Chgo., 1973. Social dir., entertainer Chamberlin Hotel, Ft. Monroe, Va., 1969-72; mktg. rep. IBM Corp., Chgo., Oakbrook, Ill., Mich, 1973-78; owner San Diego (Calif.) Software, 1978--, Michael Music, San Diego, 1978—, Computer Rents, San Diego, 1984—. Inventor word processing system computer software. Mem. San Diego Amiga Users Group. Office: Computer Rents 4934 Voltaire St San Diego CA 92107

SISSON, BARBARA ANN, real estate developer; b. Santa Monica, Calif., Oct. 25, 1940; d. Virgil George and Lucile Agnes (Brosnahan) Hutton; m. James Raymond, Mar. 13, 1971 (div. Sept. 1975). Cert. legal asst., U. W. Los Angeles, 1977. Sec. to purchasing agt. Ryan Aeronautical, San Diego, 1959-61; sec. to v.p. mktg. Capacitor Dept. ITT, Palo Alto, Calif., 1961-64; sec. to western regional mgr. Tex. Instrument, Santa Ana and Los Angeles, Calif., 1964-72; adminstrv. asst. to pres. MICA Corp., Culver City, Calif., 1972-77; real estate rep. KMart Corp., Covina, Calif., 1977-85; dir. devel. Diversified Shopping Ctrs., Costa Mesa, Calif., 1985—. Founding trustee Calif. Handicapped Skiers Found., Pasadena, 1984. Mem. Internat. Council Shopping Ctrs. (program com. 1985—). Republican. Roman Catholic. Home: 18724 Maplewood Cir Huntington Beach CA 92646

SISSON, JOHN ROSS, marine engineer; b. Everett, Mass., July 25, 1926; s. John Barkley and Nellie (Gronevoudt) S.; m. Alice Christine Wilson, Apr. 23, 1950; children: John C., Robin C. Lynam, Raymond C. BS in Marine Engring., U.S. Merchant Marine Acad., 1946. Marine supt. U.S. Steel, Pitts., 1956-59, Puerto Ordaz, Venezuela, 1959-63; devel. engr. Brookhaven Nat. Lab., L.I., N.Y., 1963-67; marine supt. Exxon Internat., Florham Park, N.J., 1967-84; dir. engring. Mil. Sealift Command (Pacific Fleet), Oakland, Calif., 1984—; marine surveyor Am. Bur. Shipping Puerto Ordaz, 1960-63. Served to lt. cmdr. USN, 1949-54. Home: 271 Calle La Mesa Moraga CA 94556 Office: Mil Sealift Command Pacific Bldg 310 Naval Supply Ctr Oakland CA 94625-5010

SITLER, BENJAMIN LEE, mechanical engineer; b. Harrisburg, Pa., May 14, 1955; s. Ralph Waldo and Dorothy Ellen (Waybright) S.; m. Genette Duea, May 7, 1978; children: Lauren Nicole, Benjamin Jacob. BME, U.S. Naval Acad., 1977. Commd. ensign USN, 1977, advanced through grades to lt., 1981; weapons officer, reactor controls officer USS Plunger, San Diego, 1977-82; flag lt., aide Comsubpac, Honolulu, 1982-84; resigned Comsubpac, 1984; account mgr. Raychem Corp., St. Louis, 1985-87, L.A., 1987—. Mem. coun. Westlake Luth. Ch., Calif., 1988. Mem. Electronic Connector Study Group. Republican. Office: Raychem Corp 14011 Ventura Blvd Ste 207E Sherman Oaks CA 91423

SIURU, WILLIAM DENNIS, JR., engineering journalist; b. Detroit, Jan. 29, 1938; s. William D. and Bertha Silvia (Lindfors) S.; children by previous marraige: Brian, Andrea. BSME, Wayne State U., 1960; MSAE, Air Force Inst. Tech., 1964; PhD, Ariz. State U., 1975. Commd. USAF, 1960, advanced through grades to col., 1981; adv. planner Space Systems Div. AFS, L.A., 1964-68; branch chief Wright-Patterson AFB , Fgn. Tech. Div., Ohio, 1968-71; br. chief Edwards AFB, A.F. Rocket Propulsion Lab., Ohio, 1974-76; asst. prof. U.S. Military Acad., West Point, 1976-79; comdr. Frank J. Seiler Rsch. Lab., USAF Acad., Colo., 1979-83; dir. flight systems engring. Wright-Patterson AFB, Aeronautical Systems Div., 1983-84; sr. rsch. assoc. U. Colo., Colo. Springs, 1985-88; pvt. practice journalism Colo. Springs, 1970—; v.p. engring. Space & Aeron. Scis., Inc., 1988—. Author six books on aviation, automobiles and more than 650 articles. Decorated Legion of Merit award, Meritorious Svc. medal USAF. Fellow AIAA; mem. Soc. Automotive Engrs., Assn. Automotive Journalists, Tau Beta Pi, Sigma XI. Home: 6341 Galway Dr Colorado Springs CO 80918

SIZEMORE, HERMAN MASON, JR., newspaper executive; b. Halifax, Va., Apr. 15, 1941; s. Herman Mason and Hazel (Johnson) S.; m. Connie Catterton, June 22, 1963; children: Jill, Jennifer. AB in History, Coll. William and Mary, 1963; postgrad., U. Mo., 1965; MBA, U. Wash., 1985. Reporter Norfolk (Va.) Ledger-Star, summers 1961, 62, 63; copy editor Seattle Times, 1965-70, copy-desk chief, 1970-75, asst. mng. editor, 1975-77, mng. editor, 1977-81, prodn. dir., 1981-83, asst. gen. mgr., 1984, v.p., gen. mgr., 1985, pres., chief operating officer, 1985—; vis. instr. Sch. Communications U. Wash., 1972-78; dir. Times Communications Co., Walla Walla Union-Bull, Inc.; mem. policyowner examining com. Northwestern Mut. Life Ins. Co., 1985, chmn., 1986. Bd. dirs. Seattle-King County Camp Fire Council, pres., 1989; mem. Pvt. Initiatives in Pub. Edn., 1987-88. Named Seattle Newsmaker of Tomorrow, 1978. Mem. AP Mng. Editors, Soc. Profl. Journalists, Allied Daily Newspapers of Wash., Am. Newspaper Pubs. Assn., U. Wash. Exec. MBA Alumni Assn. (pres. 1988), Wash. Athletic Club, Rainier Club. Methodist. Home: 2054 NW Blue Ridge Dr Seattle WA 98177 Office: Seattle Times Box 70 Seattle WA 98111

SJOGREN, JOANNA MARIE, cosmetics company executive; b. Portland, Oreg., May 4, 1935; d. Thomas Frank and Ethel Lou (Ormiston) Rich; m. Marvin W. Sjogren, July 1, 1955 (div. 1981); children: Eric David, Andrea Marie, Heidi Kristine. BS, U. Oreg., 1954, MBA, 1955, PhD, 1985. CPA; lic. psychologist Nev. Exec. asst. to pres. Columbia Pictures, Los Angeles, 1955-65; comptroller William N. Pennington, Reno, 1965-75; exec. sr. dir. Mary Kay Cosmetics Inc., Dallas, 1975—; freelance writer Reno, 1985—, pvt. practice psychology, 1985—; pres. ROTWANG, Reno and Los Angeles, 1987—; corp. sec. The Softerware Corp., Reno, 1987—. Author, psychologist seminars, 1985—. Pres. Nev. Opera Assn., Reno, 1986-88; chmn. Spl. Olympics, Reno, 1988-89; ptnr. Sierra Arts Found., Reno, 1986—; mem. Nev. Festival Ballet, Reno, 1986—, Rep. Nat. Com., 1984—. Named Rose Restival Princess, Portland, 1951, Woman of Yr., Beta Sigma Phi, 1963. Mem. AAUW, Bus. and Profl. Women, Smithsonian Instn., Mensa, Phi Beta Kappa, Delta Delta Delta. Presbyterian. Club: Over the Hill Gang. Home and Office: 2915 Susileen Dr Reno NV 89509

SJOLANDER, GARY WALFRED, physicist; b. Bagley, Minn., Dec. 5, 1942; s. Tage Walfred and Evelyn Mildred (Kaehn) S.; m. Joann Lorraine Tressler, June 18, 1966; 1 child, Toby Ryan. BS in Physics, U. Minn., 1970, MS in Physics, 1974, PhD in Physics, 1975. Rsch. assoc. U. Minn., Mpls., 1975-76; rsch. scientist Johns Hopkins U., Balt., 1977-78, sr. physicist, 1978-82; sr. engr. Westinghouse Electric Corp., Annapolis, Md., 1982-85; sr. group engr. Martin Marietta Astronautic Group, Denver, 1985—; pres. Cypress Improvement Assn., Inc., Saverna Park, Md., 1984-85; advisor Inroads/Denver, Inc., 1986-88. Author numerous articles in field. With USAF, 1960-64. Mem. Am. Phys. Soc., Am. Geophys. Union, AIAA, The Planetary Soc. Lutheran. Home: 811 W Kettle Ave Littleton CO 80120 Office: Martin Marietta Strategic Systems PO Box 179 Denver CO 80201

SKAAR, THOMAS CLIFFORD, construction executive; b. Ilwaco, Wash., Aug. 16, 1956; s. Clifford Linn and RoseAnn Margaret (Lentz) S.; m. Karla Jean Barden, Jan. 25, 1974 (div. Mar. 1982); m. Tracey Lee Munson, Sept. 11, 1982; children: Andrea Lynn, Brittany Lee. Student, Mt. Hood Community Coll., Gresham, Oreg., 1973-74. Grocery dept. mgr. Albertson's Food Stores, Inc., Portland, Oreg., 1974-78; v.p., dir. ops. Dierking Constrn., Inc., Portland, Oreg., 1978-80; owner Sunrise Homes, Inc., Portland, Oreg., 1980--. Mem. Homebuilders' Assn. (bd. dirs. 1983--, chmn. various coms. 1984-85, 88). Republican. Office: Sunrise Homes Inc 725 NE 102d Ave Portland OR 97220

SKAGGS, DAVID E., congressman; b. Cin., Feb. 22, 1943; s. Charles and Juanita Skaggs; m. Laura Driscoll, Jan. 3, 1987; 1 child from previous marriage, Matthew; stepchildren: Clare, Will. BA in Philosophy, Wesleyan U., 1964; student law, U. Va., 1964-65; LLB, Yale U., 1967. Bar: N.Y. 1968, Colo. 1971. Assoc. Newcomer and Douglass, Boulder, Colo., 1971-74, 77-78; prin. staff asst. Congressman Tim Wirth, Washington, 1975-77; ptnr. Skaggs, Stone & Sheehy, Boulder, 1978-86; mem. 100th, 101st Congresses from Colo. dist., Washington, 1987—; mem. Colo. Ho. of Reps., Denver, 1980-86, minority leader 1982-85. Served with USMC, 1968-71, Vietnam; maj. Res. Mem. Colo. Bar Assn., Boulder County Bar Assn. Democrat. Congregationalist. Office: US Ho of Reps 1723 Longworth Bldg Washington DC 20515

SKAGGS, L. SAM, retail company executive; b. 1922; married. With Am. Stores Co., Salt Lake City, 1945—, chmn. bd., chief exec. officer, from 1966, pres., chief exec. officer, until 1988, also bd. dirs.; chmn. Sav-On Drugs, Anaheim, Calif., bd. dirs. Served with USAAF, 1942-45. Office: Am Stores Co PO Box 9649 Newport Beach CA 92658 also: Am Stores Co 19100 Von Karman Ave Irvine CA 92715 *

SKAGGS, SAMUEL ROBERT, materials scientist; b. Philipsburg, Pa., June 23, 1936; s. Samuel Ralph and Martha Amelia (Montes) S.; m. Barbara Jan Hurley, Apr. 7, 1958; children: Russell, Cheryl, Michael, Teresa, Katherine. BSME, N.Mex. A&MA, 1958; MS in Nuclear Engring., U. N.Mex., Los Alamos, 1967; PhDChemE and Materials Sci., U. N.Mex., Albuquerque, 1972. Mech. engr. Argonne (Ill.) Nat. Lab., 1958-60; staff mem. Los Alamos (N.Mex.) Nat. Lab., 1960-61, 62-67, 71—, program mgr. materials and fossil energy, 1982-86, program mgr. armor protective systems, 1986—; program mgr. U.S. Dept. Energy, Germantown, Md., 1981-82; cons. USAF, 1970-80. Author 30 tech. pubs. in high temperature ceramics. Field coordinator N.Mex. State Search and Rescue Operation, 1961-87, patrol leader and regional dir. Rocky Mountain div. Nat. Ski Patrol, 1978-84. Served to lt. U.S. Army 1961-62, capt. Res. Mem. Am. Ceramic Soc. (life), AAAS. Roman Catholic. Home: Rte 11 Box 81E Santa Fe NM 87501 Office: Los Alamos Nat Lab PO Box 1663 K574 Los Alamos NM 87545

SKALAGARD, HANS MARTIN, artist; b. Skuo, Faroe Islands, Feb. 7, 1924; s. Ole Johannes and Hanna Elisa (Fredriksen) S.; came to U.S., 1942, naturalized, 1955; pupil Anton Otto Fisher, 1947; m. Mignon Diana Haack Haegland, Mar. 31, 1955; 1 dau., Karen Solveig Sikes. Joined U.S. Mcht. Marine, 1942, advanced through grades to chief mate, 1945, ret., 1965; owner, operator Skalagard Sq., Rigger Art Gallery, Carmel, 1966—; librarian Mayo Hays O'Donnel Library, Monterey, Calif., 1971-73; painter U.S. Naval Heritage series, 1973—; exhibited in numerous one-man shows including Palace Legion of Honor, San Francisco, 1960, J.F. Howland, 1963-65, Fairmont Hotel, San Francisco, 1963, Galerie de Tours, 1969, 72-73, Pebble Beach Gallery, 1968, Laguna Beach (Calif.) Gallery, 1969, Arden Gallery, Atlanta, 1970, Gilbert Gallery, San Francisco; group shows: Am. Artists, Eugene, Oreg., Robert Louis Stevenson Exhibit, Carmel Valley Gallery, Biarritz and Paris, France, David Findley Galleries, N.Y.C. and Faroe Island, Europe, numerous others; represented in permanent collections; Naval Post Grad. Sch. and Library, Allen Knight Maritime Mus., Salvation Army Bldg., Monterey, Calif., Robert Louis Stevenson Sch., Pebble Beach, Anenberg ARt Galleries, Chestlibrook Ltd.,; lectr. Bd. dirs. Allen Knight Maritime Mus., 1973—, mem. adv. and acquisition coms., 1973-77. Recipient Silver medal Tommaso Campanella Internat. Acad. Arts, Letters and Scis., Rome, 1970, Gold medal, 1972; Gold medal and hon. life membership Academia Italia dell Arti e del Honoro, 1980; Gold medal for artistic merit Academia d'Italia. Mem. Navy League (dir. Monterey), Internat. Platform Assn., Sons of Norway (cultural dir. 1974-75, 76-77). Subject of cover and article Palette Talk, 1980, Compass mag., 1980. Home: 25197 Canyon Dr Carmel CA 93923 Office: PO Box 6611 Carmel CA 93921 also: Dolores at 5th St Carmel CA 93921

SKAMAROCIUS, CAROLE MARY, realty company executive, writer; b. Toronto, Ont., Can., Feb. 3, 1936; came to U.S., 1952; d. Alexander Mitchell and Ethel May (Hart) Low; m. Richard Martin Dougherty, July 8, 1954 (div. Oct. 1973); children: Jill Ann Dougherty Greer, Jacquelyn A. Dougherty Strange, Douglas Michael; m. John Skamarocius, Feb. 3, 1979. Secretarial degree, Chapel Hill Secretarial Coll., 1964. Lic. real estate saleswoman, Calif. Office assoc. Student Placement Services, U. Calif., Berkeley, 1974-75; exec. sec. Mayor's Office, Municipality of Anchorage, 1978-80; realtor assoc. Century 21-Minton Realtors, Redding, Calif., 1987--. Columnist Tailinge from Trinity Ctr, 1977-78. Mem. Nat. Assn. Realtors, Calif. Assn. Realtors, Shasta County Bd. Realtors, Redding Legal Secs. Assn., Bus. and Profl. Women, Redding Writer's Forum. Republican. Home: 4501 Riverside Ave Apt 52 Anderson CA 96007 Office: Century 21-Minton Realtors 2986 Bechelli Ln Redding CA 96049

SKARDA, RICHARD JOSEPH, clinical social worker; b. Santa Monica, Calif., Jan. 2, 1952; s. Robert Ralph and Cathryn Marie (Tourek) S. AA, Los Angeles Valley Coll., Van Nuys, Calif., 1976; BA, U. Calif., Berkeley, 1978; MSW, UCLA, 1980. Lic. clin. social worker, Calif.; diplomate, Clin. Social work. Children's services worker Los Angeles County Dept. Children's Services, Panorama City, Calif., 1980-82; police service rep. Los Angeles Police Dept., 1982; psychiatric social worker Penny Lane, Sepulveda, Calif., 1983; children's services worker Ventura (Calif.) County Pub. Social Services Agy., 1983-85; head social work dept. Naval Med. Clinic, Port Hueneme, Calif., 1985—; part-time pvt. practice in clin. social work, Oxnard, Calif., 1987—. Served with USN, 1970-74. Mem. Nat. Assn. Social Workers (diplomate), Acad. Cert. Social Workers, Calif. Soc. Clin. Social Work, U. Calif. Alumni Assn. Democrat. Roman Catholic. Office: Naval Med Clinic Port Hueneme CA 93043

SKAVDAHL, RICHARD EARL, nuclear energy executive, nuclear engineer; b. Detroit, Nov. 24, 1934; s. Earl George and Ann (Zaplitny) S.; m. Patricia Ann Wolfe, May 9, 1959; children: Kristen Patricia, Karen Ruth, Eric Richard. SB in Chem. Engring., MIT, 1956; MS in Nuclear Engring., U. Mich., 1957; ScD in Nuclear Engring., MIT, 1962. Registered profl. engr., Calif. Sr. engr. Gen. Electric Co., Richland, Wash., 1962-64; unit mgr. Battelle Northwest, Richland, 1964-66; programs mgr. Gen. Electric Co., Sunnyvale, Calif., 1966-73, project mgr., 1973-78, mgr. projects, San Jose, Calif., 1978-83, mgr. waste mgmt. services, 1983-85, services gen. mgr. engring., 1985—; mem. vis. com. dept. nuclear engring. MIT, 1972-75. Contbr. articles to profl. jours. Mem. Am. Nuclear Soc., Sigma Xi, Phi Lambda Upsilon, Tau Beta Pi. Republican. Home: 927 Radcliffe Dr San Jose CA 95117 Office: Gen Electric Co 175 Curtner Ave San Jose CA 95125

SKEEN, JOHN KENNETH, sales executive; b. Taft, Calif., Sept. 20, 1941; s. Kenneth Charles and Mildred (Harman) S.; m. Michelle Lee Bailey, May. BA in Econs., Stanford U., 1963, MBA, 1966. Stockbroker J. Barth, San Francisco, 1966-70, Dean Writter, San Francisco, 1970-76; v.p., stockbroker Donaldson Lufkin & Jennette, San Francisco, 1976-79; gen. ptnr., dir. sales Montgomery Securities, San Francisco, 1979—; pres. Mill Valley Soc. Security Analysts, 1976. Contbr. Ed. 2s Chau for Congress, 1984; sponsor John Heinz for Senator. Mem. Inst. Investor Roundtable. Republican. Home: 3983 Happy Valley Rd Lafayette CA 94549 Office: Montgomery Securities 600 Montgomery Street San Francisco CA 94111

SKEEN, JOSEPH RICHARD, congressman; b. Roswell, N.Mex., June 30, 1927; s. Thomas Dudley and Ilah (Adamson) S.; m. Mary Helen Jones, Nov. 17, 1945; children: Mary Elisa, Mikell Lee. B.S., Tex. A&M U., 1950. Soil and water engr. Ramah Navajo and Zuni Indians, 1951; rancher Lincoln County, N.Mex., 1952—; mem. N.Mex. Senate, 1960-70; mem. 97th— Congresses from 2d N.Mex. Dist., 1981—, mem. appropriations com., sub-com. agr., ranking mem. treas.-postal svc.-gen. govt. Chmn. N.Mex. Republican Party, 1963-66. Served with USN, 1945-46; Served with USAFR, 1949-52. Mem. Nat. Woolgrowers Assn., Nat. Cattle Growers Assn., N.Mex. Woolgrowers Assn., N.Mex. Cattle Growers Assn., N.Mex. Farm and Livestock Bur. Republican. Roman Catholic. Clubs: Elks, Eagles. Office: 1007 Longworth House Office Bldg Washington DC 20515

SKELTON, THOMAS BERNARD, III, artist, designer; b. Brussels, May 18, 1946; came to U.S., 1947; s. Thomas Bernard and Mimie (Martinique) S.; m. Sylvia Jane Guzman, July 8, 1966; children: Renee, Todd. AA, Long Beach (Calif.) City Coll., 1972; BA in Design, Calif. State U., Fullerton, 1974. Prin., owner Tom Skelton Advt. Agy., Fresno, Calif., 1976—; freelance photographer, designer, artist, Fresno, 1974—. With USN, 1964-69, Vietnam. Recipient Golden Oak award Fresno Ad Fedn., 1986, 87, 88, Excellence award Board Report, 1986. Mem. Am. Rifle Assn. Republican. Home and Office: 3619 N Angus St Fresno CA 93726

SKENE, LAURENCE FARTHING, retired chemistry educator; b. Banks, Oreg., July 18, 1911; s. William and Mary (Hilts) S.; m. Rosa Mae Bateman, June 13, 1936; children: David Laurence, Louise Evelyn, Rosemary Skene Allen. Bs, Pacific U., 1933; MS, Oreg. State U., 1936. Prof. chemistry George Fox Coll., Newberg, Oreg., 1935-51, head dept. chemistry and natural sci., 1962-68; bldg. contractor Dundee, Oreg., 1951-82; fin. advisor Friends Cemetery, Newberg, 1980—. Pres. Am. Friends Service Com., Portland, 1940-65; supply officer UN Gaza (Palestine) unit, 1949. Mem. Am. Chem. Soc. Republican. Mem. Soc. Friends. Home: 8595 NE Worden Hill Rd Dundee OR 97115 Office: Newberg Friends Ch 305 N College Newberg OR 97132

SKEWES-COX, BENNET, accountant, educator; b. Valparaiso, Chile, Dec. 12, 1918; came to U.S., 1919, naturalized, 1943; s. Vernon and Edith Page (Smith) S-C.; B.A., U. Calif., Berkeley, 1940; M.A., Georgetown U., 1947; B.B.A., Golden Gate Coll., 1953; m. Mary Osborne Craig, Aug. 31, 1946; children—Anita Page McCann, Pamela Skewes-Cox Anderson, Amy Osborne Skewes-Cox (Mrs. Robert Twiss). Asst. to press officer Am. Embassy, Santiago, Chile, 1941-43; state exec. dir. United World Federalists of Calif., 1948-50; pvt. practice acctg., San Francisco, 1953—; asst. prof. internat. relations San Francisco State U., 1960-62; grad. researcher Stanford (Calif.) U., 1962-63, Georgetown U., Washington, 1963-65; pres. Acad. World Studies, San Francisco, 1969—; sec. Alpha Delta Phi Bldg. Co., San Francisco, 1957—; lectr. in field. Mem. Democratic state central com. Calif., 1958-60, fgn. policy chmn. Calif. Dem. Council, 1959-61, treas. Marin County Dem. Central Com., 1956-62; founder, 1st. chmn. Calif. Council for UN Univ., 1976—; compiler World Knowledge Bank; bd. dirs. Research on Abolition of War; treas. Marin Citizens for Energy Planning. Served as lt. (j.g.), USNR, 1943-46. Mem. Assn. for World Edn. (internat. council 1975—), Am. Soc. Internat. Law, Am. Polit. Sci. Assn., San Francisco Com. Fgn. Relations, Am. Acctg. Assn., Calif. State Univ. Profs., AAUP, Nat. Soc. Public Accts., Fedn. Am. Scientists, UN Assn., Internat. Polit. Sci. Assn. World Federalists Assn. (nat. bd. dirs.). Clubs: University, Commonwealth of Calif., Lagunitas Country. Author: The Manifold Meanings of Peace, 1964; The United Nations from League to Government, 1965; Peace, Truce or War, 1967. Home: Monte Alegre PO Box 1145 Ross CA 94957 Office: Acad World Studies 2820 Van Ness San Francisco CA 94109

SKIDMORE, DONALD EARL, JR., government official; b. Tacoma, Apr. 27, 1944; s. Donald E. and Ingeborg (Johnsrud) S.; BSc, Evangel Coll., 1968. With Dept. Social and Health Svcs., State of Wash., Yakima, 1967-74; quality rev. specialist Social Security Adminstrn., Seattle, 1974-76, program analyst, Balt., 1976-79, Seattle, 1979-81, quality assurance officer, mgr. Satellite office, Spokane, Wash., 1981-84, program analyst, Seattle, 1984—. Pres., bd. dirs. Compton Court Condo Assn., 1980-81; v.p., trustee Norwood Village, 1987—; vice chair ops. subcom., mem. citizen's adv. com. METRO, 1987-89; mem. citizen's adv. com. land use planning, Bellevue, Wash., 1988—. Office: 2201 6th Ave M/S RX-56 Seattle WA 98121

SKIDMORE, JOYCE THORUM, public relations/communications executive; b. Murray, Utah, Dec. 30, 1926; d. Rolla Arden and Alice Luetta (Fox) Thorum; m. E. Douglas Jacobsen, Mar. 20, 1956 (dec.); 1 son, Kelly Douglas Jacobsen; m. 2d, Clarence E. Skidmore, Aug. 9, 1969. B.S., U. Utah, 1950, postgrad., 1953-55; postgrad. U. So. Calif., 1964, U. Calif.-Irvine, 1973-74. Sales and promotion devel. JBL Internat., Los Angeles, 1959-69. Adminstrv. asst. world hdqrs. Toastmasters Internat., Santa Ana, Calif., 1973; adj. prof. communications Pepperdine U., 1974, developer human resources, Oran, Algeria, 1975; promotions coordinator Utah Bicentennial Project, Salt Lake City, 1976; editor Saga Weekly Post, and editor Children's Page, Stavanger and Bergen, Norway, 1976-78; press. sec. Utah Auditor's Office, Salt Lake City, 1979-81; pres., owner Joyce Skidmore Cons./Snowflake Prodns., pub. relations, communications and devel. in arts, bus., edn. and govt., Sandy, Utah, 1980—; Utah dir. Nat. Health Screening Coun. for Vol. Orgns., Bethesda, Md., 1982-83; adj. prof. Westminster Coll., 1978-79, Brigham Young U., 1978-89; cons. pub. relations, health costs and tourism C. of C. of Salt Lake Area; adj. prof. mktg. and communications Colo. Mountain Coll., 1985-86; bus. cons., prof. mktg. and communications Mountainwest Coll. Bus. and Brigham Young U., Salt Lake City; cons. Hema U.S.A., Westline and Bunell Inc.; guest dir. Westminster Theatre, 1974; guest dir./writer Cablevision, Newport Beach, Calif., 1975. Author: Happy Holidays, 1968; assoc. editor Utah Symphony newsletter; newsletter editor Nat. Auditor's Assn., 1979-81, State Auditor's Assn., 1979-81, Utah Health Fairs, 1982-83; journalist The Butler Banner; contbr. weekly columns to The Rifle Telegram; contbr. articles to Calif., Norwegian and Utah newspapers; initiated use of old copper from Utah Capitol dome as collector's item, 1980. Organizer Stavanger Theatre Guild and Workshops, 1977, Bookcliffs Arts and Humanities Council, 1984-86; originator, organizer Hurlburt Days, Grand Valley and Parachute, Colo.; initiator, dir.Reader's Theatre, Community Christmas Festival; fundraiser Utah Symphony Guild; dir. theatre Art Barn, Salt Lake City; mem. steering com. for first nat. competition Utah Playwriting Conf., Sundance, 1979-80; mem. local econ. devel. council.; polit. dist. del., 1986. Initiated invitation from Bergen Internat. Festival to Utah Symphony, 1981; campaign mgr. Mayor Lake Valley City (Utah), 1982; cons. Cottonwood Heights (Utah) Council, 1982-83; cons. to Utah pres. Instrumentation Soc. Am.; missionary leader Ch. of Jesus Christ of Latter-day Saints. Recipient Best Dir. statue, Colo., 2 Top Editor's awards Calif. Press Women, 1977, 4 writing awards 1977-78; Internat. Yr. of Child award Family Acad., San Francisco and Stavanger, 1979; Colo. Oscar award for Best Dir., 1986; nat. Zeta Phi Eta scholar, 1948; U. Utah fellow, 1953-55; So. Calif. Credit Assn. scholar, 1964. Mem. LWV (dist. pres. 1976), Pub. Relations Soc. Am. (student adv. 1980-82), Utah Press Women (6 writing awards 1979-81; 3d v.p. 1981-82), Instrument Soc. Am., Friendship Force Utah, MMB Reading Arts Soc. (v.p. devel.), Internat. Platform Assn., Daus. of Utah Pioneers. Avocations: historian, extensive genealogical research. Home and Office: 2629 Oak Creek Dr Sandy UT 84093

SKIFF, RUSSELL ALTON, plastic company executive; b. Waterford, Pa., Feb. 26, 1927; s. Albert Alton and Leah Gladys (Allen) S.; B.S., U. Pitts., 1950; m. Dolores Theresa Molnar, June 25, 1950; children—Russell James, Sandra Lee, Eric Alan, Rebecca Lynn. Metall. chemist Jones & Laughlin Steel Co., Alliquippa, Pa., 1950-51; research and devel. chemist Gen. Electric Co., Erie, Pa., 1951-57; mgr. tech. sales and plant operation Hysol Corp. of Calif., El Monte, 1957-60; sr. research engr. autonetics div. N.Am. Aviation, Downey, Calif., 1960-62; pres. Delta Plastics Co., Inc. (now Delta D.P.C., Inc.), Tulare, Calif., 1962—. Served with USAAF, 1944-46. Mem. Constrn. Specifications Inst. Republican. Presbyterian. Club: Exchange (past pres. Calif.-Nev. dist.). Lodge: Lions (dir.). Contbr. articles to profl. jours. Home: 15170 Avenue 260 Visalia CA 93277 Office: Delta DPC Inc 983 E Levin Tulare CA 93274

SKILLIN, THERESE JENO, elementary school teacher; b. San Jose, Calif., Feb. 16, 1956; d. Joseph John and Eloise Martha (Holden) Jeno; m. Robert Hance Skillin, Sept. 28, 1985; 1 child, Paul Holden. BA, San Francisco State U., 1978, MA, 1983. Cert. calif. multiple subject life tchr. Tchr. Lost Hills (Calif.) Union Sch., 1979-81, Panama Unified Sch. Dist., Bakersfield, Calif., 1981-85, Santa Paula (Calif.) Sch. Dist., 1985—; cons. Panama Unified Sch. Dist., 1984-85, Ventura County Farm Bus., Ventura, Calif., 1987-88. Mem. AAUW (mem. Camarillo Creative Arts Workshop 1988), Ventura County Reading Assn., Wasco Jr. Woman's Club (sec. 1982-83, v.p. 1983-84, dir. Annual Fun Run 1982-84, named Woman of Yr. 1982), Santa Paula Woman's Club, Petroleum Wives, Santa Barbara Cactus and Succulent Soc. Democrat. Roman Catholic. Home: 1220 Forest Dr Santa Paula CA 93060 Office: Santa Paula Sch Dist 410 Davis St Santa Paula CA 93060

SKILLING, JOHN BOWER, structural and civil engineer; b. Los Angeles, Oct. 8, 1921; s. Harold C. and Helen M. (Bower) S.; m. Mary Jane Stender, May 1, 1943; children: William, Susan, Ann. B.S., U. Wash., 1947. Design engr. W.H. Witt Co., Seattle, 1947-54; partner successor firm Worthington, Skilling, Helle and Jackson, Seattle, 1959-67, Skilling, Helle, Christiansen, Robertson, Seattle, 1967-82; chmn. successor firm Skilling Ward Rogers

Barkshire, Inc., Seattle, 1983-87, Skilling Ward Magnusson Barkshire, Inc.; mem. Bldg. Research Adv. Bd. Mem. Seattle Found.; mem. Seattle Municipal Art Commn., 1964-67. Fellow ASCE; mem. Nat. Acad. Engring., Am. Concrete Inst., Internat. Assn. Shell Structures, Internat. Assn. Bridge and Structural Engring., Soc. Am. Mil. Engrs., Structural Engrs. Assn. Wash., AIA (hon. mem. Seattle chpt.), Am. Inst. Steel Constrn. (adv. com.). Clubs: 101; Dean's, Pres.'s (Univ. Wash.). Home: 539 McGilvra Blvd E Seattle WA 98112 Office: Skilling Ward Magnusson Barkshire 2200 Unigard Financial Ctr Seattle WA 98161

SKILLMAN, ALLAN GEOFFREY, SR., dean; b. Everett, Wash., Feb. 4, 1937; s. Geoffrey R. and Rosa E. (Graham) S.; m. Julia Mary Scherer, June 16, 1964; children: Anne Melanie, Allan Geoffrey Jr. BS, Mont. State U., 1959, EdD, 1972; MS, U. Utah, 1964. Tchr. Hobson (Mont.) Pub. Sch., 1959-64; instr. Casper (Wyo.) Coll., 1965-66, 70-79, dean, 1979—; instr. Mont. State U., Bozeman, 1966-69; prin. N. Toole County High Sch., Sunburst, Mont., 1969-70; chmn. Wyo. Higher Edn. Computer Network, Laramie; bd. dirs. No. Rockies Consortium in Higher Edn., Boise, Idaho; mem. rev. com. U. Wyo., Laramie; title III program reviewer Miles Community Coll., Miles City, Mont., 1984, 85. Mem. bd. trustees Highland Pk. Community Ch., Casper, 1984-87, mem. ch. coun., 1987, 88. NSF grantee, 1962-675; State of Mont. scholar, 1955. Mem. Maths. Assn. Am. (v.p.), Golf League, Phi Delta Kappa. Republican. Home: 1701 Kingsbury Dr Casper WY 82609 Office: Casper Coll 125 College Dr Casper WY 82601

SKINNER, ANDREW CHARLES, history educator, religious writer; b. Durango, Colo., Apr. 25, 1951; s. Charles La Verne and Julia Magdalena (Schunk) S.; m. Janet Corbridge, Mar. 22, 1974; children: Cheryl Lyn, Charles Lon, Kelli Ann, Mark Andrew, Holly, Suzanne. BA with disting., U. Colo., 1975; MA with disting., Iliff Sch. of Theology, Denver, 1978; ThM, Harvard U., 1980; PhD, U. Denver, 1986. Group mgr. May Co. Dept. Store, Denver, 1980-83; assoc. studio dir. Talking Books Pub. Co., Denver, 1984-88; instr. history Metro. State Coll., Denver, 1984-88; prof. history Ricks Coll., Rexburg, Idaho, 1988—; visiting instr. ancient scripture, Brigham Young U., Provo, Utah, 1987; cons. U. Without Walls, Loretto Hgts. Coll., Denver, 1985-88. Author chpts. numerous books and encyclopaedia articles. Bishop Mormon Ch., Denver, 1986-88; varsity scout leader, Teton Parks Coun., Boy Scouts Am., Rexburg, 1988-89. Mem. Am. Historical Assn., Soc. Biblical Lit., Phi Theta Kappa, Phi Alpha Theta. Mormon. Office: Ricks Coll Dept of History 412 Smith Bldg Rexburg ID 83440

SKINNER, DANIEL PETERSON, insurance executive; b. Montpelier, Idaho, Feb. 16, 1956; s. Earnest Morgan and Mabel Clarinda (Peterson) S.; m. Laura Kay LeBaron, June 28, 1977; children: Lindsay, Daniel Jr., Stephanie, Scott. Grad. high sch., Mesa, Ariz. Cert. ins. counselor, accredited advisor ins. Acct. exec. LeBaron & Carroll, Inc., Mesa, 1977—, sales mgr., 1987—. Mem. Ind. Ins. Agts. Ariz. (membership dir. 1983-84), Ind. Ins. Agts. East Valley (pres. 1982-83, v.p. 1981-82, sec. 1980-81), Rotary (pres. 1986-87). Republican. Mormon. Office: LeBaron & Carroll Inc 1000 N Country Club Dr Mesa AZ 85214

SKINNER, GEORJA ANN, public relations executive; b. L.A., July 12, 1952; d. George Gordon and Pearl Theresa (Majoros) S. Student, Art Ctr. Coll. of Design, 1970, Los Angeles City Coll., 1970-71. Sound editor Wrather Corp., Hollywood, Calif., 1968-70; various positions Metromedia TV Inc., Hollywood, Calif., 1970-80; camera operator, script supr. Am. Film Inst., Hollywood, 1972-73; graphic artist NBC Broadcasting, Burbank, Calif., 1978; sound cons. Tandem Prodn., Hollywood, 1979; producer editor Waterstar Prodns., Hollywood, 1980; producer, dir., writer, editor Maui (Hawaii) Cable Vision/Camp Cable Vision, 1981; dir. mktg. Scotch Mist Charters, Lahaina, Hawaii and Maui, 1982-83; pub. relations coordinator Maui Marriott Resort, Kaanapali Beach, Hawaii, 1983; pres. Skinner Communications, Lahaina, 1983—, Maui, 1987—; sound cons. Lila Garrett Prodn., 1979, Writers Guild Am., 1979; stage mgr. Showtime, Inc., 1980; location mgr. Embassy TV, 1986; location/prodn. coordinator Warner Bros. TV, 1987, Vidio-Hits One/MTV, 1988; prodn. coordinator Rolfing Prodns./ Joe Hamilton Prodn., 1987; location coordinator New Century Entertainment, 1988. Mem. Maui Mayor's Motion Picture Coordinating Com. Mem. Hawaii Hotel Assn., Pub. Relations Soc. Am., Maui C. of C. Office: 180 Dickenson St #219 Lahaina HI 96761

SKINNER, HARRY BRYANT, orthopaedic surgery educator; b. Cleve., Oct. 13, 1943; s. Harry Bryant and Marion (Eastlick) S. BS, Alfred U., 1965; MS, PhD, U. Calif., Berkeley, 1970; MD, Med. U. S.C., 1975. Asst. prof. Youngstown (Ohio) State U., 1970-71; postdoctoral research assoc. Clemson (S.C.) U., 1971-72; lectr. Calif. State U., Sacramento, 1977-79; asst./assoc. prof. Tulane U., New Orleans, 1979-82; assoc. prof. orthopaedic surgery U. Calif., San Francisco, 1983-86, prof., 1986—; adj. asst./assoc. prof. Sch. Engring., Tulane U., New Orleans, 1979-82; dir. rehab. research and devel. VA Med. Ctr., San Francisco, 1983—. Mem. editorial bd. Orthopaedics jour., 1984-88, guest editor, 1985, Jour. Biomed. Materials Research, 1983—; contbr. articles to profl. jours. Grantee NIH, 1978-84, Nat. Inst. Dental Research, 1978-84, VA, 1978—, Schleider Found., 1980-82, Am. Fedn. Aging Research, 1986—. Fellow ACS, Am. Acad. Orthopaedic Surgeons; mem. Orthopaedic Research Soc., Soc. for Biomaterials (charter), Sigma Xi. Office: U Calif Dept Orthopaedic Surgery U-461 San Francisco CA 94143-0728

SKINNER, ILIHU BARNES, brokerage house executive; b. New Britain, Conn., Jan. 18, 1938; s. Harold Risley and Gertrude (Barnes) S.; m. Patricia Francis Roldan, Feb. 1962 (div. 1965); m. Lee R. Devel, Aug. 17, 1965; children: Matthew Todd, Amanda Milicant. BA, Hillsdale Coll., 1962. Stockbroker, v.p. Merrill Lynch, Inc., Tacoma, 1966—. Bd. dirs. Tacoma Philharm., 1987. 1st lt. USAF, 1962-66. Office: Merrill Lynch Inc PO Box 1338 Tacoma WA 98402

SKINNER, NANCY JO, recreation executive; b. Ogallala, Nebr., Nov. 5, 1956; d. Dale Warren Skinner and Beverly Jane (Fister) Berry. AA, Platte Community Coll., 1977; BS, U. Ariz., 1981; postgrad., U. Phoenix, 1985—. Sports specialist YWCA, Tucson, 1981, asst. dir. summer day camp, 1981, dir. health, phys. edn. and recreation, 1981-82; sr. recreation specialist Pima County Parks and Recreation Dept., Tucson, 1983, coordinator recreation program, 1983—; labor mgmt. quality of work life rep. Pima County Govt., 1987; dist. coordinator Atlantic Richfield Co. Jesse Owens Games, Tucson, 1986-89; adv. Pima County Health Dept. Better Health Through Self Awareness, 1982-83. Dir. tournament Sportsman Fund-Send a Kid to Camp, Tucson, 1984, 85, 86; dir. Labor Mgmt. Quality of Working Life com. Pima County govt., 1987; dist. coordinator Nat. Health Screening Council, Tucson, 1982-83, 84-85; event coordinator Tucson Women's Commn. Saguaro Classic, Tucson, 1984; mem. com. United Way, Tucson, 1982-83. Musco/APRF Graduate scholar. Mem. NAFE, Nat. Recreation & Parks Assn., Ariz. Parks & Recreation Assn. (treas. 1987, v.p. 1988, pres. 1988, 89, Tenderfoot award, 1984, cert.), Delta Psi Kappa (pres. U. Ariz. chpt. 1980-81). Democrat. Methodist. Office: Pima County Parks & Recreation Dept 1204 W Silverlake Rd Tucson AZ 85713

SKINNER, STANLEY THAYER, utility company executive, lawyer; b. Fort Smith, Ark., Aug. 18, 1937; s. John Willard and Irma Lee (Peters) S.; m. Margaret Olsen, Aug. 16, 1957; children—Steven Kent, Ronald Kevin. B.A. with honors, San Diego State U., 1960; M.A., U. Calif., Berkeley, 1961, J.D., 1964. Bar: Supreme Ct. Calif. bar 1965, U.S. Circuit Ct. Appeals for 9th Circuit bar 1965, 10th Circuit bar 1966. Atty. Pacific Gas and Electric Co., San Francisco, 1964-73; sr. counsel Pacific Gas and Electric Co., 1973, treas., 1974-76, v.p. fin., 1976, sr. v.p., 1977, exec. v.p., 1978-86, exec. v.p., chief fin. officer, 1982-85, vice chmn. bd., 1986—; dir. Pacific Gas and Electric Co., Pacific Gas Transmission Co., Alberta Natural Gas Corp. Calif. Ltd. Bd. dirs. Calif. Econ. Devel. Corp.; bd. dirs., former trustee United Way of Bay Area; trustee, former chmn. bd. dirs. Golden Gate U. Mem. Bankers Club San Francisco, San Francisco C. of C. (bd. dirs.), Calif. State Bar Assn., Pacific Coast Elec. Assn. (bd. dirs.), Pacific Coast Gas Assn., calif. State C. of C. (bd. dirs.). Republican. Presbyterian. Clubs: Bankers. Office: Pacific Gas & Electric Co 77 Beale St San Francisco CA 94106

SKLADAL, ELIZABETH LEE, elementary teacher; b. N.Y.C., May 23, 1937; d. Angier Joseph and Julia May (Roberts) Gallo; m. George Wayne Skladal, Dec. 26, 1956; children: George Wayne Jr., Joseph Lee. BA, Sweet Briar Coll., 1958; EdM, U. Alaska, 1976. Choir dir. Main Chapel, Camp Zama, Japan, 1958-59, Ft. Lee, Va., 1963-65; choir dir. Main Chapel and Snowhawk, Ft. Richardson, Alaska, 1968-70; elem. tchr. Anchorage (Alaska) Sch. Dist., 1970—. Active Citizens' Adv. Com. for Gifted and Talented, Anchorage, 1981-83, Music Com. Anchorage Sch. Dist., 1983-86; soloist Civic Opera Chorus, Anchorage, 1969—, Community Chorus, Anchorage, 1968-80; mem. choir First Presbyn. Ch., Anchorage, 1971—, deacon, 1988—. Named Am. Coll. Theater Festival winner Amoco Oil Co., 1974. Mem. Anchorage Concert Assn., Alaska Chamber Singers, Am. Guild Organists (former dean), Assn. Univ. Women. Republican. Presbyterian. Home: 1841 S Salem Dr Anchorage AK 99508

SKLANSKY, JACK, electrical engineering educator, researcher; b. N.Y.C., Nov. 15, 1928; s. Abraham and Clara S.; m. Gloria Joy Weiss, Dec. 24, 1957; children: David Alan, Mark Steven, Jeffrey Paul. B.E.E., CCNY, 1950; M.S.E.E., Purdue U., 1952; Eng.Sc.D., Columbia U., 1955. Research engr. RCA Labs., Princeton, N.J., 1955-65; mgr. Nat. Cash Register Co., Dayton, Ohio, 1965-66; prof. elec. engring. U. Calif.-Irvine, 1966—; pres. Scanicon Corp., Irvine, Calif., 1980—. Author: (with others) Pattern Classifiers and Trainable Machines, 1981; editor: Pattern Recognition, 1973, (with others) Biomedical Images and Computers, 1982; editor-in-chief: Machine Vision and Applications, 1987. Recipient best paper award Jour. Pattern Recognition, 1977; research grants NIH, 1971-84, Army Research, 1984—. Fellow IEEE; mem. Assn. Computing Machinery. Office: U Calif Dept Elec Engring Irvine CA 92717

SKLAR, HORACE JOSEPH, electronics engineering company executive; b. Havana, Cuba, Dec. 14, 1952; came to U.S. in 1960; s. Alfred Lee and Olga Maria (Ferrer) S.; m. Pamela Ann, May 21, 1975; children: Nicole Maria, Corinne Maria. BSEE, Princeton U., 1972; EE, MIT, 1975. Research and devel. engr. GTE Sylvania, Needham, Mass., 1975-78; engr. sci. level IV Rockwell/Collins Radio, Anaheim, Calif., 1978-81; engr. scientist ITT/DCD, San Diego, Calif., 1981-83; project mgr. TRW/Mead, San Diego, 1983-86; pres. Intech Processor Systems, Inc., San Diego, 1987--; owner Sklar Tech. Lab, San Diego, 1986--; cons. to numerous firms in Calif. and U.S. Patentee in field. Central leader, Neighborhood Coordinator for Land Improvement, San Diego, 1987; supporter, North County Blind Ctr., San Diego, 1986. Mem. IEEE. Christian. Home and Office: Sklar Tech Lab 1036 Landavo Dr Escondido CA 92077

SKLENAR, DAVID BRUCE, sales executive; b. Santiago, Cuba, Jan. 20, 1954; s. Richard Donald and Dorothy Ellen (Landrum) S. BS in Biology and Gen. Sci., U. Oreg., 1980. Reforestation technician U.S. Forest Svc., Oakridge, Oreg., 1975-80; sales rep. UpJohn Lab. Procedures, San Francisco, 1981; sr. sales rep. SmithKline Biosci. Labs., Seattle, 1982-85, dist. sales mgr., 1987-88; sales mgr. Associated Regional & Univ. Pathologists, Salt Lake City, 1988—. Sgt. U.S. Army, 1972-75. Mem. Nat. Geographic Soc., Clin. Lab. Mgrs. Assn., MENSA. Home: 531 NE 81st St Seattle WA 98115 Office: Associated Regional 390 Wakara Way Salt Lake City UT 84108

SKLOVSKY, ROBERT JOEL, physician, educator; b. Bronx, N.Y., Nov. 19, 1952; s. Nathan and Esther (Steinberg) S.; m. Michelle Sklovsky-Welch, Dec. 21, 1985. BS, Bklyn Coll., 1975; MA, Columbia U., 1976; PharmD, U. of Pacific, 1977; D in Naturopathic Medicine, Nat. Coll. Naturopathic Medicine, 1983. Intern Tripler Army Med. Ctr., Honolulu, 1977; prof. pharmacology Nat. Coll. Naturopathic Medicine, Portland, Oreg., 1982-85; pvt. practice specializing in naturopathy Clackamas, Oreg., 1983—; cons. State Bd. Naturopathic Examiners, Oreg., Hawaii, Clackamas County Sherriff's Dept.; cons. Internat. Drug Info. Ctr., N.Y.C., 1983—; cons. Albert Roy Davis Scientific Research Lab, Orange Park, Fla. 1986. Recipient Bristol Labs. award, 1983. Mem. Am. Assn. Naturopathic Physicians, N.Y. Acad. Sci., Soc. for Study of Biochem. Intolerance, Internat. Bio-oxidative Med. Found. Office: 10808 SE Hwy 212 Clackamas OR 97015

SKOOG, WILLIAM ARTHUR, oncologist; b. Culver City, Calif., Apr. 10, 1925; s. John Lundeen and Allis Rose (Gatz) S.; A.A., UCLA, 1944; B.A. with gt. distinction, Stanford U., 1946, M.D., 1949; m. Ann Douglas, Sept. 17, 1949; children—Karen, William Arthur, James Douglas, Allison. Intern medicine Stanford Hosp., San Francisco, 1948-49, asst. resident medicine, 1949-50; asst. resident medicine N.Y. Hosp., N.Y.C., 1950-51; sr. resident medicine Wadsworth VA Hosp., Los Angeles, 1951, attending specialist internal medicine, 1962-68; practice medicine specializing in internal medicine, Los Altos, Calif., 1959-61; pvt. practice hematology and oncology Calif. Oncologic and Surg. Med. Group, Inc., Santa Monica, Calif., 1971-72; pvt. practice med. oncology, San Bernardino, Calif., 1972—; assoc. staff Palo Alto-Stanford (Calif.) Hosp. Center, 1959-61, U. Calif. Med. Center, San Francisco, 1959-61; asso. attending physician U. Calif. at Los Angeles Hosp. and Clinics, 1961-78; vis. physician internal medicine Harbor Gen. Hosp., Torrance, Calif., 1962-65, attending physician, 1965-71; cons. chemistry Clin. Lab., UCLA Hosp., 1963-68; affiliate cons. staff St. John's Hosp., Santa Monica, Calif., 1967-71, courtesy staff, 1971-72; courtesy attending med. staff Santa Monica Hosp., 1967-72; staff physician St. Bernardine (Calif.) Hosp., 1972—, San Bernardino Community Hosp., 1972—; chief sect. oncology San Bernardino County Hosp., 1972-76; cons. staff Redlands (Calif.) Community Hosp., 1972-83, courtesy staff, 1983—; asst. in medicine Cornell Med. Coll., N.Y.C., 1950-51; jr. research physician UCLA Atomic Energy Project, 1954-55; instr. medicine, asst. research physician dept. medicine UCLA Med. Center, 1955-56, asst. prof. medicine, asst. research physician, 1956-59; clin. asso. hematology VA Center, Los Angeles, 1956-59; co-dir. metabolic research unit UCLA Center for Health Scis., 1955-59, 61-65; co-dir. Health Scis. Clin. Research Center, 1965-68, dir., 1968-72; clin. instr. medicine Stanford, 1959-61; asst. clin. prof. medicine, assoc. research physician U. Calif. Med. Center, San Francisco, 1959-61; lectr. medicine UCLA Sch. Medicine, 1961-62, assoc. prof. medicine, 1962-73, assoc. clin. prof. medicine, 1973—. Served with USNR, 1943-46, to lt. M.C., 1951-53. Fellow ACP; mem. Am., Calif. med. assns., So. Calif. Acad. Clin. Oncology, Western Soc. Clin. Research, Am. Fedn. Clin. Research, Los Angeles Acad. Medicine, San Bernardino County Med. Soc., Am. Soc. Clin. Oncology, Am. Soc. Internal Medicine, Calif. Soc. Internal Medicine, Inland Soc. Internal Medicine, Phi Beta Kappa, Alpha Omega Alpha, Sigma Xi, Alpha Kappa Kappa. Episcopalian (vestryman 1965-70). Club: Redlands Country. Contbr. articles to profl. jours. Home: 30831 Miradero Dr Redlands CA 92373 Office: 399 E Highland Ave Ste 201 San Bernardino CA 92404

SKOOR, JOHN BRIAN, art educator, art consultant; b. Mount Vernon, Wash., Dec. 14, 1939; s. George Nephi and Marie Elizabeth (Collins) S.; m. Susan Diane Waugh, June 17, 1972; children: Marie Elizabeth, Christine Elaine. AA in Edn., Graceland Coll., Lamoni, 1960; BA in Art, Cen. Wash. U., 1962, BA in Edn., 1965, MA in Art, 1969. Art instr. Delta (Mich.) Coll., Saginaw, 1977-79; instr. Renton (Wash.) Vocat. Tech. Inst., 1981-83; art instr. Green River (Wash.) Community Coll., Auburn, 1988—; cons. staff and development instr. various Seattle sch. dists., 1988—; adj. faculty Cen. Wash. U., 1984—, Seattle Pacific U., 1986—. Illustrator of religious curriculum texts, 1978-80; exhibited acrylic theol. paintings show, Independence, Mo., 1980. Guest speaker Alma (Mich.) Art Dept., 1977, Nat. Camping Assn., Detroit, 1979; elder Reorganized Ch. of Jesus Christ of Latter Day Saints, Seattle, 1966—, pastor, 1987—; bd. dirs. RLDS Ch. Creative Arts Festival, state of Mich., 1977. Mem. Wash. Alliance for Arts Edn. (commn. chmn. 1987—), Richland Art Tchrs. Assn. (pres. 1965-66), Tri-City Art Tchrs. Assn (pres. 1966-67). Home and Studio: 4830 S Morgan St Seattle WA 98118

SKOPIL, OTTO RICHARD, JR., judge; b. Portland, Oreg., June 3, 1919; s. Otto Richard and Freda Martha (Boetticher) S.; m. Janet Rae Lundy, July 27, 1956; children: Otto Richard III, Casey Robert, Shannon Ida, Molly Jo. BA in Econs., Willamette U., 1941, LLB, 1946, LLD (hon.), 1983. Bar: Oreg. 1946, IRS, U.S. Treasury Dept., U.S. Dist. Ct. Oreg., U.S. Ct. Appeals (9th cir.), U.S. Supreme Ct. 1946. Assoc. Skopil & Skopil, 1946-51; ptnr. Williams, Skopil, Miller & Beck (and predecessors), Salem, Oreg., 1951-72; judge U.S. Dist. Ct., Portland, 1972-79; chief judge U.S. Dist. Ct., 1976-79; judge U.S. Ct. Appeals (9th cir.), Portland, 1979—; chmn. com. adminstrn. of fed. magistrate system U.S. Jud. Conf., 1980-86; co-founder Oreg. chpt. Am. Leadership Forum. Hi-Y adviser Salem YMCA, 1951-52; appeal agt. SSS, Marion County (Oreg.) Draft Bd., 1953-66; master of ceremonies 1st Gov.'s Prayer Breakfast for State Oreg., 1959; mem. citizens adv. com., City of Salem, 1970-71; chmn. Gov.'s Com. on Staffing Mental Instns., 1969-70; pres., bd. dirs. Marion County Tb and Health Assn., 1958-61; bd. dirs. Willamette Valley Camp Fire Girls, 1946-56, Internat. Christian Leadership, 1959, Fed. Jud. Ctr., 1979; trustee Willamette U., 1969-71; elder Mt. Park Ch., 1979-81. Served to lt. USNR, 1942-46. Recipient Oreg. Legal Citizen of Yr. award, 1986, Disting. Alumni award Willamette U. Sch. Law, 1988. Mem. ABA, Oreg. Bar Assn. (bd. govs.), Marion County Bar Assn., Am. Judicature Soc., Oreg. Assn. Def. Counsel (dir.), Def. Research Inst., Assn. Ins. Attys. U.S. and Can. (Oreg. rep. 1970), Internat. Soc. Barristers, Prayer Breakfast Movement (fellowship council). Clubs: Salem, Exchange (pres. 1947), Illahe Hills Country (pres., dir. 1964-67). Office: US Ct of Appeals 232 Pioneer Courthouse 555 SW Yamhill St Portland OR 97204

SKOTHEIM, ROBERT ALLEN, museum director; b. Seattle, Jan. 31, 1933; s. Sivert O. and Marjorie F. (Allen) S.; m. Nadine Vail, June 14, 1953; children—Marjorie, Kris, Julia. BA, U. Wash., Seattle, 1955, MA, 1958, PhD, 1962; LLD, Hobart and William Smith Colls., Geneva, N.Y., 1975; LittD, Whitman Coll., 1988; LHD, Coll. Idaho, 1988, Occidental Coll., 1989; DFA, Willamette U., 1989. Prof. history U. Wash., 1962-63; prof. history Wayne State U., Detroit, 1963-66; prof. UCLA, 1966-67, U. Colo., Boulder, 1967-72; provost, dean faculty Hobart and William Smith Colls., 1972-75; pres. Whitman Coll., Walla Walla, Wash., 1975-88; dir. Huntington Library, art collections Botanical Gardens, San Marino, Calif., 1988—. Author: American Intellectual Histories and Historians, 1966, Totalitarianism and American Social Thought, 1971; Editor: The Historian and the Climate of Opinion, 1969; co-editor: American Social Thought: Sources and Interpretations, 2 vols, 1972. Guggenheim fellow, 1967-68. Mem. Phi Beta Kappa (hon.). Office: Huntington Libr Art Collections/Bot Gardens 1151 Oxford Rd San Marino CA 91108

SKOUSEN, OWEN D., marketing executive; b. Mesa, Ariz., Aug. 10, 1932; s. Vivian (O'Donnal) Redd; m. Nancy Carol Anderson, Nov. 9, 1957; children: Randy D., Tracy O., Carrie Jean. BA, Brigham Young U., 1957. Professional baseball player Boston Red Sox, 1957-60; coach Mesa (Ariz.) Jr. High Sch., 1957-62; store owner Baskin-Robbins, Mesa, 1962-64; sales mgr. Beaver Sales, Inc., Salt Lake City, 1964-69; v.p., distbr. Success Motivation Inst., Waco, Tex., 1969-76; pres., owner Reading and Learning Internat., Inc., Mesa, 1976—. Republican. Mormon. Office: Reading and Learning Internat Inc 127 W Juanita Ave Mesa AZ 85210

SKULSTAD, PAMELA JEAN, legal administrator; b. Seattle, Jan. 20, 1954; d. Thorvald Adolf Skulstad and Lillian Mary (Barnes) Koernig; 1 child, Camille Ashlea Clarke. AA in Legal Assistance, Edmonds Community Coll., 1985; BS in Legal Adminstrn., City U. Bellevue, Wash., 1987. Sec. Eyak Corp., Cordova, Alaska, 1975, 76, pres., 1980-82, acting chief exec. officer, 1987, cons., 1987-89, v.p. bd. dirs., 1989—, also bd. dirs.; sec. Prince William Sound Agr. Corp., Cordova, 1979, 83. Democrat. Russian Orthodox. Office: Eyak Corp PO Box 340 Cordova AK 99574

SKYLSTAD, WILLIAM S., bishop; b. Omak, Wash., Mar. 2, 1934; s. Stephen Martin and Renelde Elizbeth (Danzl) S. Student, Pontifical Coll., Josephinum, Worthington, Ohio; M.Ed., Gonzaga U. Ordained priest Roman Catholic Ch., 1960; asst. pastor Pullman, Wash., 1960-62; tchr. Mater Cleri Sem., 1961-68, rector, 1968-74; pastor Assumption Parish, Spokane, 1974-76; chancellor Diocese of Spokane, 1976-77; ordained bishop 1977; bishop of Yakima, Wash., 1977—. Office: 5301-A Tieton Dr Yakima WA 98908 *

SLACK, DONALD CARL, agricultural engineer, educator; b. Cody, Wyo., June 25, 1942; s. Clarence Ralbon and Clara May (Beightol) S.; m. Marion Arline Kimball, Dec. 19, 1964; children: Jonel Marie, Jennifer Michelle. BS in Agrl. Engring., U. Wyo., 1965; MS in Agrl. Engring., U. Ky., 1968, PhD in Agrl. Engring., 1975. Registered profl. engr., Ky., Ariz. Asst. civil engr. City of Los Angeles, 1965; research specialist U. Ky., Lexington, 1966-70; agrl. engring. advisor U. Ky., Tha Phra, Thailand, 1970-73; research asst. U. Ky., Lexington, 1973-75; from asst. prof. to assoc. prof. agrl. engring. U. Minn., St. Paul, 1975-84; prof. U. Ariz., Tucson, 1984—; tech. advisor Ariz. Dept. Water Resources, Phoenix, 1985—; cons. Winrock Internat., Morrilton, Ark., 1984, Water Mgmt. Synthesis II, Logan, Utah, 1985, Desert Agrl. Tech. Systems, Tucson, 1985—, Portek, Hermosillo, Mex., 1989—; deputy program support mgr. Research Irrigation Support Project for Asia and the Near East, Arlington, Va., 1987—. Contbr. articles to profl. jours. Mem. ASCE (Outstanding Jour. paper award, 1988), Am. Soc. Agrl. Engrs., Am. Geophys. Union, Am. Soc. Agronomy, Soil Sci. Soc. Am., Sigma Xi, Tau Beta Pi, Alpha Epsilon, Gamma Sigma Delta. Democrat. Lutheran. Home: 9230 E Visco Pl Tucson AZ 85710 Office: U Ariz Agrl Engring Dept 407 Shantz Bldg #38 Tucson AZ 85721

SLACK, JAMES MARSHALL, orthodontist; b. Shelby, Mont., June 8, 1942; s. John Howard and Margaret Dell (Oie) S.; m. Ann Louise Short, July 4, 1942; children: Donna, Jennifer, Kendra, John. BS, Wash State U., 1965; DDS, U. Wash., 1969; MS, U. Iowa, 1975. Orthodontist in pvt. practice Spokane, Wash., 1975--. Fund-raiser Boy Scouts Am., Spokane, 1988, Ferris High Sch., Spokane, 1987-88. Served to maj. U.S. Army, 1969-73. Mem. Am. Assn. Orthodontists, Pacific Coast Soc. Orthodontists, Am. Dental Assn., Spokane Dist. Dental Soc., Spokane C. of C. Republican. Lodge: Rotary. Club: bd. dirs. Cougar Club of Spokane, 1988. Home: 6110 S Helena Spokane WA 99223 Office: 418 E 30th Ave #3 Spokane WA 99203

SLADE, SANDRA LYNN, interior designer, educator, consultant; b. Seattle, April 22, 1946; d. Erwin R. Slade, M.D. and Leona Martha (Mears) S.; 1 son, David Slade Privette. B.F.A., U. Wash., 1969, M.F.A. in Interior Design, 1977. owner-designer Image West Inc., Boise, Idaho, 1971-76; asst. prof. interior architecture, U. Idaho, Moscow, 1977-81; asst. prof. interior design Wash. State U., Pullman, 1981-83; pvt. practice interior design, Seattle, 1983—; interior design mgr. Schemmer Assocs., Bellevue, Wash., 1988—; cons. health care, acad. facility design; profl. cons. Wilsonart Innova Design Competition, 1983-84. Recipient design award Institution Mag., 1980. Mem. Am. Soc. Interior Designers (cert. 1976), Interior Design Educators Council (NW regional dir.), Alpha Chi Omega. Republican. Episcopalian.

SLAPAK, GREGORY DONN, accounting and consulting firm executive; b. Berwyn, Ill., Apr. 26, 1951; s. Donald Frank and Alberta Elizabeth (Duffey) S. BS, U. Wis., La Crosse, 1973, MS, 1975. Coordinator Greek Affairs Rochester (N.Y.) Inst. Tech., 1975-77; dir. policies and procedures The Trane Co., La Crosse, 1977-80; dir. mktg. and pub. relations Hawkins, Ash, Baptie & Co., CPAs, La Crosse, 1981-84; dir. communications, mktg. and pub. relations Hood and Strong, CPAs, San Francisco, 1984-86; dir. mktg. Coopers and Lybrand, San Francisco, 1986—. Mem. editorial bd. CPA Mktg. Report, 1982—. Mem. bus. gifts. com. Embarcadero YMCA, San Francisco, San Francisco Symphony Orch.; field dir. Steve Gunderson for Congress, State of Wis., 1980, legis. dir. Congressman Steve Gunderson, Washington, 1981; campaign chmn. Sylvia Boma for Sheriff, La Crosse County, 1982, 84; mem. No. Calif. fund raising com. Pete Wilson for Senator, 1985-86, George Deukmejian for Gov., 1985-86; active membership com. San Francisco Rep., devel. com. Sta. KQED Radio-TV; bd. dirs., pres. Clay St. Homeowners Assn., United fund for The Arts, La Crosse, 1983-84, Coulee Council on Alcholism, La Crosse, 1983-84. Mem. AICPA, Am. Mkgt. Assn., Bay Area Sales and Mktg. Execs. Assn., Pub. Relations Soc., San Francisco C. of C. (small bus. com.), Sales and Mktg. Execs., Am. San Francisco Trees for an Urban Forest (pub. relations advisor), San Francisco C. of C. (small bus. com. 1984—), Rotary (dir. pub. affairs local chpt.), Kiwanis (Kiwanian of Yr. 1982). Home: 3140 Clay St San Francisco CA 94115 Office: Coopers and Lybrand 333 Market St Ste 2100 San Francisco CA 94105

SLATER, DON AUSTIN, shipyard executive, consultant; b. Bay City, Mich., May 27, 1938; s. William Stuart and Inez Fern (Hagen) S.; m. Sara Belva Sanford, Feb. 3, 1962; children: Shandra Sanford, Nathan Dorman. BS in Naval Architecture and Marine Engring., U. Mich. Naval architect Western Boat Bldg. Corp., Tacoma, 1964; exec. v.p. and gen. mgr. Star Marine Industries, Tacoma; gen. mgr. Shipyard div. Marine Iron Works, Tacoma; pres. and gen. mgr. Marine Industry N.W., Inc., Tacoma, 1976—;

cons. to various law firms, Wash. and N.J., 1975—; arbitrator Am. Arbitration Assn., 1985—. 1st v.p. Va. V Found., Seattlem 1986; bd. dirs. Puget Sound Marine Hist. Soc., 1978-80. Home: 30720 43d Ave SW Federal Way WA 98003 Office: Marine Industries NW Inc 313 E F St PO Box 1275 Tacoma WA 98401

SLATER, KAY ROSS, marketing and public relations specialist; b. Iowa City, Iowa, Sept. 20, 1942; d. Maurice Pershing and Dorothy (Mattheis) Ross; children: Daniel Larren, Sara Kay; m. Richard E. Slater, May 10, 1986. BA, San Diego State U., 1965; MBA, Nat. U., 1984. Cert. tchr., Calif. Tchr. San Diego Unified Sch. Dist., 1965-74; dir. mktg. staff Med. Svcs. Mktg., San Diego, 1974-81; mem. mktg. staff Mktg. Seminar Prodns., San Diego Foun. Med. Care, San Diego, 1982-84; dir. site ops. Western Health Cinics, Inc., San Diego, 1985-86; adminstr. Harbor Med. Ctr., Ventura, Calif., 1987—; owner, pres. Ross Resources & Assocsa., Simi Valley, Calif., 1984—; tchr. Moorpark (Calif.) Community Coll., 1986—; cons. mktg., pub. rels.; instr. Simi Valley Adult Sch.-ESL programs, 1988-89. Mem. Med. Group Mgmt. Assn., Soc. Healthcare Execs., Calif. Med. Group Mgrs., Soc. for Women in Health Adminstrn., Ventura C. of C., Am. Mktg. Assn., San Diego Soc. Med. Svc., La Amigos de Chicatas, Women's Internat. Ctr. (founding mem.). Republican. Methodist. Office: Ross Resources & Assocs 469 Quiet Ct Simi Valley CA 93065

SLATER, LEONARD, writer, editor; b. N.Y.C., July 15, 1920; s. Max and Jean (Lenobel) S.; m. Betty Moorsteen, 1946; children: Amy, Lucy. BA in Polit. Sci., U. Mich., 1941. Reporter, writer NBC News, Washington, 1941-44; news editor NBC News, N.Y.C., 1941-44; corr. Washington bur. Time mag., 1945-47; assoc. editor Newsweek mag., N.Y.C., 1947-59, corr. Eastern Europe and Middle East; bur. chief Newsweek mag., Los Angeles; sr. editor, columnist McCalls' mag., N.Y. and Europe, 1960-63; free-lance writer, editor 1963—. Author: Aly, 1965, The Pledge, 1970; contbr. articles to mags. Mem. Authors League of Am. Home: 4370 Arista Dr San Diego CA 92103 also: Binicalaf Minorca, Balearic Islands Spain

SLATON, ALICE MISRAHI, French language educator; b. Alexandria, Egypt, Feb. 11, 1944; came to U.S., 1962; d. Albert and Esther (Cohen) Misrahi; m. Stanley Alvin Slaton, Sept. 1, 1969; children: Ryan Nathan, Daniel Brett. BA, UCLA, 1965, MA, 1966, PhD, 1975. French lang. tchr. Santa Monica (Calif.) Coll., 1966-67, Beverly Hills (Calif.) Unified Sch. Dist., 1967-69; French lang. tchr. Ventura (Calif.) Coll., 1969—, instr. computer literacy, 1985—, chair ednl. tech., 1989—; research and devel. staff Ventura Coll., 1984—, devel. activities staff, 1985—. Jour. rep. for Computer-Assisted Lang. Instrn. Consortium Interactive Audio-Video Special Interest Group; designer, developer laser videodisc Interactions Audio-Visuelles, 1987, LAVIE, 1989; producer audio cassette Discover What Makes the French French, 1989; editor Interactive Video Monograph, 1988-89; contbr. articles on computer sci. to profl. jours. Mem. Internat. Interactive Communication Soc., Computer Assisted Lang. Instrn. Consortium, Ventura Coll. French Club (pres. 1985—). Office: Ventura Coll 4667 Telegraph Rd Ventura CA 93003

SLATTERY, THOMAS E., industrial gases company executive; b. Chgo., Aug. 2, 1935; s. James Frederic and Gladys Irene (Pratt) S.; m. Maxine Mary Beebe, Sept. 10, 1955; children: Mary Lynn, David Thomas. B.S. in Mech. Engring., Mich. State U., 1957. Various positions Union Carbide Corp., 1961-79; with strategic planning, mgmt. com. Union Carbide Corp., N.Y.C., 1974-75, v.p., gen. mgr. gases Linde div., 1975-77; v.p. mktg. Union Carbide Corp., 1977-79; pres. indsl. gases div., exec. v.p. Liquid Air Corp., San Francisco, 1979-84; chief operating officer Liquid Air Corp., 1984—, pres., chief exec. officer, 1986—; pres., chief exec. officer Air Liquide Am. Corp., Big Three Industries, Houston, 1988—. 1st lt. USAF, 1957-60. Mem. Orinda Country Club, Orindawoods Tennis Club. Office: Liquid Air Corp 2121 N California Blvd Walnut Creek CA 94596

SLAUGHTER, ALMA JEAN, educator; b. Oakland, Calif., Feb. 7, 1935; d. Ernest W. and Valeria Helen (Lengyel) Hansen; m. John Wayne Slaughter, Aug. 11, 1962 (dec.); children: David Wayne, Kenneth James. BA, San Jose (Calif.) State U., 1957. Tchr. Alasal Sch. Dist., Salinas, Calif., 1957-58, Pittsburg (Calif.) Unified Sch. Dist., 1958-62, Hayward (Calif.) Unified Sch. Dist., 1967-71; tchr. Annandale (Va.) Playcare, 1981-82, supr., 1982-85; tchr. Fairfax (Va.) County Office for Children, 1985—. Active PTA, Riverside Sch., Lakeside, Calif., 1971-75; exch. student parent Pacific Edn. & Cultural Exch., Honolulu, 1978-79, Youth for Understanding, Washington, 1980-81. Mem. Delta Zeta. Republican. Presbyterian.

SLAUGHTER, JOHN BROOKS, university administrator; b. Topeka, Mar. 16, 1934; s. Reuben Brooks and Dora (Reeves) S.; m. Ida Bernice Johnson, Aug. 31, 1956; children: John Brooks, Jacqueline Michelle. Student, Washburn U., 1951-53; B.S.E.E., Kans. State U., 1956, D.Sc. (hon.), 1988; M.S. in Engring, UCLA, 1961; Ph.D. in Engring. Scis, U. Calif., San Diego, 1971; D.Engring. (hon.), Rensselaer Poly. Inst., 1981; D.Sc. (hon.), U. So. Calif., 1981, Tuskegee Inst., 1981, U. Md., College Park, 1982, U. Notre Dame, 1982; D.Sci. (hon.), U. Miami, 1983, U. Mass., 1983, Tex. So. U., 1984, U. Toledo, 1985, U. Ill., 1986, SUNY, 1986; L.H.D. (hon.), Bowie State Coll., 1987; D.Sci., Morehouse Coll., 1988, Kans. State U., 1988; LLD (hon.), U. Pacific, 1989; DSc (hon.), Pomona Coll., 1989. Registered profl. engr., Wash. Electronics engr. Gen. Dynamics Convair, San Diego, 1956-60; with Naval Electronics Lab. Center, San Diego, 1960-75, div. head, 1965-71, dept. head, 1971-75; dir. applied physics lab. U. Wash., 1975-77; asst. dir. NSF, Washington, 1977-79; dir. NSF, 1980-82; acad. v.p., provost Wash. State U., 1979-80; chancellor U. Md., College Park, 1982-88; pres. Occidental Coll., Los Angeles, 1988—; bd. dirs., vice chmn. San Diego Transit Corp., 1968-75; mem. com. on minorities in engring. Nat. Research Council, 1976-79; mem. Commn. on Pre-Coll. Edu. in Math., Sci., and Tech. Nat. Sci. Bd., 1982-83; bd. dirs. Monsanto Co., Avery Internat., IBM, and Union Bank. Editor: Jour. Computers and Elec. Engring, 1972—. Bd. dirs. San Diego Urban League, 1962-66, pres., 1964-66; mem. Pres.'s Com. on Nat. Medal Sci., 1979-80; trustee Rensselaer Poly. Inst., 1982; chmn. Pres.'s Com. Nat. Collegiate Athletic Assn., 1986-88. Naval Electronics Lab Center fellow, 1969-70; Recipient Engring. Alumnus award UCLA, 1978; Disting. Service award NSF, 1979; Recipient Disting. Service in Engring. award Kans. State U., 1981; recipient UCLA Engring. Disting. Alumnus of Year, 1978, U. Calif.-San Diego Disting. Alumnus of Year, 1982. Fellow IEEE (chmn. com. on minority affairs 1976-80); mem. NAE, Nat. Collegiate Athletic Assn. (chmn. pres. commn.), Tau Beta Pi, Eta Kappa Nu, Alpha Phi Alpha. Office: Occidental Coll 1600 Campus Dr Los Angeles CA 90041 also: U Md College Park College Park MD 20742

SLAUGHTER, SHARON LOUISE, financial executive; b. Hawthorne, Calif., July 27, 1950; d. Jean Edward and Anastasia Elizabeth (Miles) Barry; m. Kenneth Leslie Slaughter, June 1970; children: Kenneth Brett, Kristine Marie, Bradley Edward,. Student, El Camino Coll., Torrance, Calif., 1958-70, Oxnard Coll., 1984. With Kresge Corp., Hawthorne, 1965, H&R Block, Hawthorne, 1966-67, Nova Art & Design, Hawthorne, 1968; salesperson, dept. supr. May Co., Torrance, 1969-70; operator Pacific Telephone, Inglewood, Calif., 1970-72; communication facilitator Pacific Telephone, Gardena, Calif., 1972-74; sales rep. Avon Co., Camarillo, Calif., 1979-80; with Speed Shore Systems, Moorpark, Calif., 1981-84, v.p., chief fin. officer, 1984—; Contbr. articles to profl. jours. Active Camarillo PTA, 1978—; bd. dirs. Los Colinas PTA, 1980-87; com. mem. LOs Colinas Grad, Com., 1985, co-chmn., 1987. Mem. Lambda Psi. Office: Speed Shore Systems Inc 4875 Spring Rd Moorpark CA 93021

SLEEMAN, THOMAS BARRETT, oil company executive; b. Chgo., May 3, 1932; s. Barrett Ayers and Marie J. (Henning) S.; m. Martha June Netzel, Aug. 29, 1953; children: Kevin, Daniel, Gary, Michael. BS in Acctg., U. Ill., 1954. CPA, Ill. Various positions Unocal Corp., Chgo., 1954-67; supr. corp. accts. Unocal Corp., Los Angeles, 1967-69, mgr. budgets, 1970-73, v.p. corp. planning, 1974-79; pres. Molycorp., Inc. subs. Unocal Corp., Los Angeles, 1979-85, Unocal Chems. div. Unocal Corp., Los Angeles, 1986—; sr. v.p. and dir. Unocal Corp., Los Angeles, 1988—; dir. Unocal Corp., 1988—. Office: Unocal Corp 1201 W 5th St PO Box 60455 Los Angeles CA 90060

SLEEPER, ELEANOR RUSSELL, real estate executive; b. Little Rock, Ark., Feb. 6, 1922; d. Everett Adams and Lena (Faisst) Ham; m. William Chapman Chilton, June 22, 1944 (dec. 1946); m. James Kirkendall Russell, March 8, 1952 (dec. 1970); children: Branch James, Kirk Everett, Lydia Russell McIntosh, Scott Ham; Donald C. Sleeper, Sept. 23, 1972. BS, Memphis State U., 1943. Mem. staff med. records U. Calif. Med. Sch., Berkeley, 1947-48; army hostess, program dir. Army. Spl. Services, Japan, 1948-49; real estate agt. Harry Parks Real Estate, 1950-52; prin. Realty Worl Eleanor Russell Realtors, Orinda, Calif., 1969—; registered rep. fin. planning and ins. Skaife & Co., Orinda, 1984—. Mem. Repub. Women's Club. Mem. AAUW, Contra Costa Bd. Realtors (dir. 1988), Cert. Bd. Realtors, Orinda C. of C., Nat. Assn. Realtors, Internat. Assn. Fin. Planning, Orinda Women's Investment Club, Soroptimists Internat. (liason Orinda City br.), Sleepy Hollow Book Club, Diablo Home Economists. Home: 129 Sleepy Hollow Ln Orinda CA 94563 Office: 16 Orinda Way Orinda CA 94563

SLIKER, TODD RICHARD, accountant, lawyer; b. Rochester, N.Y., Feb. 9, 1936; s. Harold Garland and Marion Ethel (Caps) S.; BS with honors (Ford Found. scholar), U. Wis., 1955; PhD, Cornell U., 1962; MBA, Harvard, 1970; JD, U. Denver, 1982; m. Gretchen Paula Zeiter, Dec. 27, 1963; children: Cynthia Garland, Kathryn Clifton. Bar: Colo. 1983. With Clevite Corp., Cleve., 1962-68, head applied physics sect., 1965-68; asst. to pres. Granville-Phillips Co., Boulder, Colo., 1970; v.p., gen. mgr. McDowell Electronics, Inc., Metuchen, N.J., 1970-71; pres. C.A. Compton, Inc., mfrs. audio-visual equipment, Boulder, 1971-77; chief acct. C&S Inc., Englewood, Colo., 1977-80, v.p., 1980-82; sole practice law, Boulder, 1983-88; mgmt. real estate, 1972—. Del., Colo. Rep. Assembly, 1974, 76; Rep. dist. fin. coordinator, 1974-75; precinct committeeman, 1974-86; chmn. Boulder County Rep. 1200 Club, 1975-79; mem. Colo. Rep. State Cen. Com., 1977-81, asst. treas., 1979-87; sect. corr. Harvard U., 1981—. Served to 1st lt. USAF, 1955-57. Recipient paper award vehicular communication group IEEE, 1966. Licensed real estate salesman, securities salesman; CPA, Colo. Mem. Colo. Soc. CPAs (govt. relations task force 1983-86), Colo. Bar Assn. (publs. com. 1982-84), Boulder County Bar Assn., Am. Phys. Soc., Optical Soc. Am. (referee Jour.), Sigma Xi, Phi Kappa Phi, Theta Chi, Beta Alpha Psi. Club: Colo. Mountain, Rotary. Contbr. articles to profl. jours. Patentee in field. Home: 1658 Bear Mountain Dr Boulder CO 80303

SLOAN, CLARENCE ARCHIBALD, JR., radiation effects test engineer; b. Kansas City, Mo., July 3, 1935; s. Clarence A. and Louis M. (Barton) S.; m. Patricia F. Egan, July 9, 1966; children: Mark, Maureen, Michael, Daniel. BSEE, San Diego Coll., 1971. Registered profl. engr., Calif. Electronic technician USN (USS Nautilus), New London, Conn., 1958-65, Gen. Atomic, San Diego, 1965-67; electronic technician Gulf Gen. Atomic, San Diego, 1967-71, electronic engr., 1971-73; test engr. Intelcom Radiation Tech., San Diego, 1973-80, chief test engr., 1980-86, project mgr., 1986—. Scout leader, Boy Scouts Am., San Diego, 1971—; lay chmn. Catholic Com. on Scouting, San Diego, 1986—. Recipient St. George medal, Catholic Com. on Scouting, San Diego, 1979, Dist. Order of Merit, Boy Scouts Am., San Diego, 1977, Silver Beaver award, 1988. Home: 5093 Dawne St San Diego CA 92117 Office: S-Cubed div of Maxell Labs 3020 Callan Rd San Diego CA 92121

SLOAN, EARLE DENDY, JR., educator; b. Seneca, S.C., Apr. 23, 1944; s. Earle Dendy Sr. and Sarah (Bellotte) S.; m. Marjorie Nilson, Sept. 7, 1971. BSChemE, Clemson U., 1965, MSChemE, 1972, PhD in Chem. Engring., 1974. Engr. Du Pont, Chattanooga, 1965-66, Seaford, Del., 1966-67; cons. Du Pont, Parkersburg, W.Va., 1967-68; sr. engr. Du Pont, Camden, S.C., 1968-70; postdoctoral fellow Rice U., 1975; prof. Colo. Sch. Mines, Golden, 1976—. Author: Clathrate Hydrates of Natural Gas, 1989. Scoutmaster local Cub Scouts; elder Presbyn. Ch., Golden, Colo., 1977-79. Mem. Am. Soc. Engring. Edn. (chmn. ednl. rsch. methods div. 1983-85), Am. Inst. Chem. Engrs., Am. Chem. Soc. Home: 2121 Washington Ave Golden CO 80401

SLOAN, F(RANK) BLAINE, lawyer, educator; b. Geneva, Nebr., Jan. 3, 1920; s. Charles Porter and Lillian Josephine (Stiefer) S.; m. Patricia Sand, Sept. 2, 1944; children—DeAnne Sloan Riddle, Michael Blaine, Charles Porter. AB with high distinction, U. Nebr., 1942, LLB cum laude, 1946; LLM in Internat. Law, Columbia U., 1947. Bar: Nebr. 1946, N.Y. 1947. Asst. to spl. counsel Intergovtl. Com. for Refugees, 1947; mem. Office Legal Affairs UN Secretariat, N.Y.C., 1948-78, gen. counsel Relief and Works Agy. Palestine Refugees, Beirut, 1958-60, dir. gen. legal div., 1966-78, rep. of Sec. Gen. to Commn. Internat. Trade Law, 1969-78, rep. to Legal Sub-com. on Outer Space, 1966-78; rep. UN Del. Vietnam Conf., Paris, 1973; rep UN Conf. on Carriage of Goods by sea, Hamburg, 1978; prof. internat. law orgn. and water law Pace U., 1978-87, prof. emeritus, 1987—. Cons. UN Office of Legal Affairs, 1983-84, UN Water Resources Br., 1983; supervisory com., Pace Peace Ctr. With AC, U.S. Army, 1943-46. Decorated Air medal. Mem. Am. Soc. Internat. Law, Am. Acad. Polit. and Social Sci., Am. Arbitration Assn. (panel of arbitrators), Order of Coif, Phi Beta Kappa, Phi Alpha Delta (hon.). Republican. Roman Catholic. Contbr. articles to legal jours. Home: HCR-68 Box 72 Foxwind-Forbes Park Fort Garland CO 81133 Office: 78 N Broadway White Plains NY 10603

SLOAN, GERALD EUGENE (JERRY SLOAN), professional basketball coach; b. Mar. 28, 1942; m. Bobbye; 3 children: Kathy, Brian, Holly. Student, Evansville Coll., Evansville, Ind. Professional basketball player, Baltimore, 1965-66, Chicago Bulls, NBA, 1966-7; head coach Chicago Bulls, 1979-82; scout Utah Jazz, NBA, Salt Lake City, 1983-84, asst. coach, 1984-88, head coach, 1988—; player 2 NBA All-Star games; named to NBA All-Defensive First Team, 1969, 72, 74, 75. Office: care Utah Jazz 5 Triad Ctr Ste 500 Salt Lake City UT 84180 *

SLOAN, LANNY GENE, municipal official; b. Denver, Aug. 30, 1945; s. Vincent Eugene and Leta Velma (Atwood) S.; m. Janet Cellen, July 5, 1968 (div. 1973). Student, U. Utah, 1963-68, Lewis-Clark State Coll., 1987—. Registered land surveyor, Idaho. Engr.'s technician Idaho Dept. Transp., Jerome, 1970-77; land surveyor Edwards-Howard-Martens, Engrs., Twin Falls, Idaho, 1977-80; project supt. J. Holley Constrn., Wells, Nev., 1981—; Dir. pub. works City of Jerome, 1982—; mem. adv. bd. N.W. Tech. Transfer Ctr., Olympia, Wash. Chmn. bd. dirs. Jerome City Library, 1986—; bd. dirs. Jerome County Airport, 1986—. Mem. Am. Pub. Works Assn., Am. Water Works Assn. (trustee intermountain sect. 1987—), Pacific N.W. Pollution Control Assn., Green Drake Soc. Office: City of Jerome 152 East Ave A Jerome ID 83338

SLOAN, MICHAEL DANA, management information systems manager; b. Santa Monica, Calif., Sept. 30, 1960; s. Avery and Beverly Rae (Krantz) S. BSBA in MIS, Calif. State U., Northridge, 1983; MBA, Pepperdine U., 1987. Programmer/analyst TICOR, Inc., L.A., 1979-80; data processing analyst Deluxe Check Printers, Inc., Chatsworth, Calif., 1980-83; fin. systems analyst Wismer & Assocs., Inc., Canoga Park, Calif., 1983-84; sr. systems analyst Coast Savs. & Loan, Granada Hills, Calif., 1984-86; microcomputer systems specialist Litton Industries, Woodland Hills, Calif., 1986-87; adminstrv. systems mgr. TRW, Inc., Redondo Beach, Calif., 1987—; cons., Data Most, Inc., Chatsworth, 1982-83, Home Savs. & Loan, North Hollywood, Calif., 1987, Micro Tech, L.A., 1987. Mem. U.S. Fencing Assn., Salle Gascon Fencing Club, Delta Sigma Pi. Republican. Office: TRW Space and Def One Space Park 110/2828 Redondo Beach CA 90278

SLOAN, ROBERT FRANCIS, management consultant; b. Los Angeles, June 19, 1935; s. Lafayette F. and Frances (Walsh) S.; B.A. in Zoology, UCLA, 1957; Ph.D. in Oral Radiology, Osaka Dental U., 1977; m. Paula Sy, Apr. 22, 1987; children—Patrick, Cristina, Brett. Research asso. U. Calif. Med.-Dental Sch., Los Angeles, 1957-67; founding pres. Rocky Mountain Data Systems, 1967-70; founding exec. dir. Found. Orthodontic Research, 1968-70; exec. dir. InterAm. Orthodontic Seminar, 1964-70; mgmt. cons., Calif., 1978; chmn. bd. Radiol. Mgmt. Communications, Ltd., ITA Ltd., prof. Grad. Sch. of Business, U.S. Internat. U., San Diego, 1977-79; producer documentary and tech. films. Served to capt. M.S.C., U.S. Army, 1957-69. Recipient Bronze N.Y. Film Festival award, 1973, 79, Chris award, 1965, 73, Cine awards, 1964, 65, 74. Mem. ADA, Brit. Inst. Radiology, AMA, Found. Orthodontic Research (hon.), Socieda de Brasileira de Foniatria (hon. mem.). Editor: (book) Craniofacial Radiological Diagnosis and Management, 1988; developer Dental Telesis, 1988. Home: 10342 Wilkins Ave Los Angeles CA 90024

SLOAN, STEPHEN, sales executive; b. Pasadena, Calif., Jan. 30, 1964; s. Peter O'Neil and Anna (Barczay) S.. BA, UCLA, 1986. Realtor assoc. Agt. Fred Sands Reators, Santa Monica, Calif., 1985-88; sales rep., mgmt. trainee South Coast Stationers, Costa Mesa, Calif., 1988--. Contbr. articles to profl. jours. Dir. home beautification Los Angeles Jr. C. of C., 1986. Named Mem. the Month Los Angeles Jr. C. of C., 1986. Office: South Coast Stationers 3590 Cadillac Ave Costa Mesa CA 92669

SLOANE, BEVERLY LEBOV, writer, consultant; b. N.Y.C., May 26, 1936; d. Benjamin S. and Anne (Weinberg) LeBov; AB, Vassar Coll., 1958; MA, Claremont Grad. Sch., 1975, postgrad., 1975-76; grad. exec. program. Sch. Mgmt., UCLA, 1982; grad. profl. pub. course, Stanford U., 1982; grad. intensive bioethics course Kennedy Inst. Ethics, Georgetown U., 1987, advanced bioethics course, 1988; grad. med. ethics sem., U. Wash., summer 1988; ethics fellow Loma Linda U. Med. Ctr., 1989; m. Robert Malcolm Sloane, Sept. 27, 1959; 1 dau., Alison Lori. Circulation librarian Harvard Med. Library, Boston, 1958-59; social worker Conn. State Welfare, New Haven, 1960-61; tchr. English, Hebrew Day Sch., New Haven, 1961-64; instr. creative writing and English lit. Monmouth Coll., West Long Branch, N.J., 1967-69; freelance writer, Arcadia, Calif., 1970—. Mem. public relations bd. Monmouth County Mental Health Assn., 1968-69; adv. council tech. and profl. writing dept. English, Calif. State U., Long Beach, 1980-82; v.p. Council of Grad. Students, Claremont Grad. Sch., 1971-72; mem. Foothill Health Dist. adv. coun., County of Los Angeles, 1987—, pres. 1989—, task force edn. and cultural activities, City of Duarte, 1987-88, strategic planning task force com.; rep. to Vassar Coll. Alumnae Assn. ann. meeting, 1989; cert. of appreciation City of Duarte 1988, County of Los Angeles 1988; campaign com. for pre-eminence, Claremont Grad. Sch., 1986-87; mem. exec. program network UCLA Grad. Sch. Mgmt., 1987—; trustee Ctr. for Improvement of Child Caring, 1981-83; mem. League Crippled Children, 1982—, chairwoman hostesses com., 1988—; bd. dirs. Los Angeles Commn. on Assaults Against Women, 1983-84; v.p. Temple Beth David, 1983-86; mem. community relations com. Jewish Fedn. Council Greater Los Angeles, 1985-87; bd. dirs. Los Angeles Commn. Assaults Against Women, 1983-84; del. Task Force on Minorities in Newspaper Bus., 1987— Coro Found. fellow, 1979. Fellow Am. Med. Writers Assn. (dir. 1980—, Pacific S.W. del. to nat. bd. 1980-87, chmn. various conv. coms., chmn. nat. book awards trade category 1982-83, chmn. Nat. Conv. Networking Luncheon 1983, 84, chmn. freelance and pub. relations coms. Nat. Midyr. Conf. 1983-84, workshop leader ann. conf. 1984, 85, 86, 87, nat. chmn. freelance sect. 1984-85, gen. chmn. 1985 Asilomar Western Regional Conf., gen. chmn. 1985, workshop leader 1985, program co-chmn. 1987, speaker 1988, program co-chmn. 1989), speaker 1985, 88, 89, nat. exec. bd. dirs. 1985-86, nat. adminstr. sects. 1985-86, pres.-elect Pacific Southwest chpt. 1985-87, moderator gen. session nat. conf. 1987, chairperson general session nat. conf., 1986-87, chairperson Walter C. Alvarez Meml. Found. award 1986-87); mem. Women in Communications (dir. 1980—, v.p. community affairs 1981-82, N.E. area rep. 1980-81, chmn. awards banquet 1982, sem. leader ann. nat. profl. conf., 1985, program adv. com. Los Angeles chpt. 1987, v.p. activities 1989—, chmn. Los Angeles chpt. 1st ann. Agnes Underwood Freedom of Info. Awards Banquet 1982, recognition award 1983, nominating com. 1982, 83, com. Women of the Press Awards luncheon 1988 Women in Communications awards luncheon 1988), Am. Assn. for Higher Edn., AAUW (legis. chmn. Arcadia br. 1976-77, books and plays chmn. Arcadia br. 1973-74, creative writing chmn. 1969-70, 1st v.p. 1975-76, networking chmn. 1981-82, chmn. task force promoting individual liberties 1987-88, Woman of Achievement award 1986, cert. of appreciation 1987), Coll. English Assn., Am. Pub. Health Assn., Calif. Press Women (v.p. programs Los Angeles chpt. 1982-85, pres. 1985-87, state pres. 1987-89, chmn. state speakers bur. 1989—, del nat. bd. 1989 —), AAUP, Internat. Communication Assn., N.Y. Acad. Scis., Ind. Writers So. Calif., Hastings Inst., AAAS, Am. Med. Writers Assn. (pres.-elect Pacific S.W. chpt. 1985-87, pres. 1987-89, nat. adminstr. sects. 1985-86, nat. exec. bd. dirs. 1985-86, chmn. nominating com. Pacific Southwest chpt., 1987—, workshop leader annual conf. 1ing com. Seminar on Med. Writing 1988, program planning com. for daylong program on med. writing in collaboration with Ind. Writers So. Calif., 1988, 89, topic leader Nat. Conf. Networking Breakfast 1988, del. nat. bd. 1989—), Nat. Fedn. Press Women, (bd. dirs. 1987-89, nat. co-chmn. task force recruitment of minorities 1987—, delegate 1987—, chmn. state women of achievement com. 1986-87), AAUW (chpt. Woman of Achievement award 1986, chmn. task force promoting individual liberties 1987-88, speaker 1987, recipient cert. of appreciation 1987), Soc. for Tech. Communication (workshop leader, 1985, 86), Kennedy Inst. Ethics, Soc. Health and Human Values, Assoc. Writing Programs. Clubs: Rotary of Duarte (chairwoman Rotary mag. 1988-89, mem. dist. friendship exch. com. 1988—), Women's City (Pasadena), Vassar of So. Calif., Claremont Colls. Faculty House, Pasadena Athletic, Stock Exchange of Los Angeles, Town Hall of Calif. (vice chmn. community affairs sect. 1982—, speaker, 1986, instr. Exec. Breakfast Inst., 1985-86, mem. study sect. council, 1986—). Author: From Vassar to Kitchen, 1967; A Guide to Health Facilities: Personnel and Management, 1971, 2d rev. edit., 1977; mem. adv. bd. Calif. Health Rev., 1982-83. Home and Office: 1301 N Santa Anita Ave Arcadia CA 91006

SLOANE, ROBERT MALCOLM, hospital administrator; b. Boston, Feb. 11, 1933; s. Alvin and Florence (Goldberg) S.; m. Beverly LeBov, Sept. 27, 1959; 1 dau., Alison. A.B., Brown U., 1954; M.S., Columbia U., 1958. Adminstrv. resident Mt. Auburn Hosp., Cambridge, Mass., 1957-58; med. adminstr. AT&T, N.Y.C., 1959-60; asst. dir. Yale New Haven Hosp., 1961-67; assoc. adminstr. Monmouth Med. Center, Long Branch, N.J., 1967-69; adminstr. City of Hope Nat. Med. Center, Duarte, Calif., 1969-80; pres. Los Angeles Orthopedic Hosp., Los Angeles Orthopedic Found., 1980-86; pres., chief exec. officer Anaheim (Calif.) Meml. Hosp., 1986—; mem. faculty Columbia U. Sch. Medicine, 1958-59, Yale U. Sch. Medicine, 1963-67, Quinnipiac Coll., 1963-67, Pasadena City Coll., 1972-73, Calif. Inst. Tech., 1973-85, U. So. Calif., 1976-79, clin. prof., 1987—, UCLA, 1985-87; chmn. bd. Health Data Net, 1971-73; pres. Anaheim (Calif.) Meml. Hosp., 1986—, Anaheim Meml. Devel. Found., 1986—. Author: (with B. L. Sloane) A Guide to Health Facilities: Personnel and Management, 1971, 2d edit., 1977; editorial and adv. bd.: Health Devices, 1972—; contbr. articles to hosp. jours. Bd. dirs. Health Systems Agy. Los Angeles County, 1977-78; Bd. dirs. Calif. Hosp. Polit. Action Com., 1979-87, vice chmn., 1980-83, chmn., 1983-85. Served to lt. (j.g.) USNR, 1954-56. Fellow Am. Coll. Hosp. Adminstrs.; mem. Am. Hosp. Assn., Hosp. Council So. Calif. (bd. dirs., sec. 1982, treas. 1983, chmn. elect 1984, chmn. 1985, past chmn. 1986, 89), Calif. Hosp. Assn. (bd. dirs., exec. com. 1984-86, 89), Vol. Hosps. Am. (bd. dirs. West chpt. 1986—). Home: 1301 N Santa Anita Ave Arcadia CA 91006 Office: 1111 W LaPalma Ave PO Box 3005 Anaheim CA 92803

SLOCUM, CHARLES BRUCE, guild administrator; b. Mt. Holly, N.J., July 15, 1958; s. Bruce and Dorothy (McCarraher) S. BS in Communications, Syracuse U., 1980; MBA, U. Pa., 1985. Supr. audience research ABC, Los Angeles, 1980-83; mgr. broadcast practices NBC, Burbank, Calif., 1985; sr. fin. analyst Paramount Pictures Corp., Hollywood, Calif., 1986-87; dir. indsl. analysis Writers Guild Am. West, West Hollywood, Calif., 1987—. Mem. Internat. Inst. Communications, Acad. TV Arts and Scis., Hollywood Radio and TV Soc. Presbyterian. Home: 1208 N Olive Dr Apt 211 West Hollywood CA 90069 Office: Writers Guild Am West 8955 Beverly Blvd West Hollywood CA 90048

SLOGGETT, BRUCE SCOTT, real estate development executive; b. Inglewood, Calif., July 13, 1951; s. Bruce Carrol and Mildred May (Lynn) S. BA, San Diego State U., 1974; MBA, Nat. U., 1978. Real estate broker Calif. Comml. Brokers, San Diego, 1977-81, Property Care, San Diego, 1981-84, Kirk-Taylor Ptnrs., San Diego, 1984-86; real estate developer San Diego Real Estate Devel. Corp., La. Jolla, Calif., 1986—; broker San Diego Exchangers, 1981—; instr. Mesa Coll., San Diego, 1981-83. Mem. San Diego Bd. Realtors. Republican. Home: 3125 Voltaire St San Diego CA 92106 Office: San Diego Real Estate Devel Corp 1250 Prospect St Ste 100 La Jolla CA 92037

SLOTA, RICHARD LEE, educator, poet; b. Orange, Calif., Mar. 17, 1947; s. John and Gretchen Roberta (Sanbury) S.; m. Patty Worland, Aug. 23, 1972 (div. Aug. 1973); m. Jean Laura Whelan, Jan. 7, 1978 (div. Dec. 1989); children: Will, Emily. BA in Theatre Arts, Calif. State U., San Francisco, 1972; BA in Psychology, Sonoma State U., 1977; MA in English, San Francisco State U., 1983. Psychiatric Eau Claire (Wis.) County Hosp., 1972-73; manpower analyst Sacramento-Yolo Employment and Tng. Agy.,

Sacramento, 1977-79; tech. writer, instr. writing Envirotech Operating Svcs., Fairfield, Calif., 1979—; tchr. children's poetry Pueblo Vista Alternative Sch., Napa, Calif., 1984—; bd . dirs. children's poetry contest Napa Spring Fair. Author: Letters from Jeanie's Grandmother, 1983, (poetry) Famous Michael, 1988. Served with U.S. Army, 1966-69. Democrat. Home: 2217 Marin St Apt D Napa CA 94559 Office: Envirotech Oper Svcs PO Box 488 Suisun City CA 94585

SLOVER, ARCHY F., chemist; b. Oshkosh, Wis., July 8, 1920; s. Archie F. and Josephine Petronella (Zindler); BA, UCLA, 1947; m. Mary Beatrice Corkill, May 25, 1946; 1 child, Mary Kay Slover Eckhardt. Devel. chemist Kelite Products Co., L.A., 1946-49; v.p., gen. mgr. Delco Chems. Inc., L.A., 1949-57; mgr. indsl. spltys. Pennwalt Corp., L.A., 1957-74; chemist Custom Chem. Formulators Inc., Cudahy, Calif., 1974—; mgr. Cherokee Chem. Co., Inc., Compton, Calif., 1976—; cons. in field. Capt. U.S. Army, 1942-46. Fellow AAAS, Am. Inst. Chemists; mem. Nat. Assn. Corrosion Engrs., Am. Chem. Soc., Am. Electroplaters Soc., USAF Assn., Soc. Advancement Material Process Engrs., Res. Officers Assn., Sigma Alpha Epsilon, Ky. Cols. Patentee in field. Address: 21 Hacienda Dr Arcadia CA 91006

SLUSSER, ROBERT WYMAN, aerospace company executive; b. Mineola, N.Y., May 10, 1938; s. John Leonard and Margaret McKenzie (Wyman) S.; BS, MIT, 1960; MBA, U. Pa., 1962; m. Linda Killeas, Aug. 3, 1968; children: Jonathan, Adam, Robert, Mariah. Assoc. adminstr.'s staff NASA Hdqrs., Washington, 1962-65; with Northrop Corp., Hawthorne, Calif., 1965—, adminstr. mktg. and planning dept., space labs., 1965-68, mgr. bus. and fin. Warnecke Electron Tubes Co. div., Chgo., 1968-71, controller Cobra Program Aircraft div., Hawthorne, 1971-72, mgr. bus. adminstrn. YF-17 Program, 1972-75, mgr. adminstrn. F-18/Cobra programs, also mgr. F-18 design to cost program, 1975-78, mgr. adminstrn. F-18L program, 1978-79, mgr. engring. adminstrn., 1980-82, acting v.p. engring., 1982, mgr. data processing, 1983-84, v.p. info. resources, 1985—; chief fin. officer, bd. dirs. So. Calif. Hist. Aviation Found., 1987—; bd. dirs. PDES, Inc., 1988—. Grumman Aircraft Engring. scholar, 1956-60. Fellow AIAA (assoc.); mem. So. Calif. Soc. Info. Mgmt. Home: 7270 Berry Hill Dr Rancho Palos Verdes CA 90274 Office: Northrop Aircraft Div 1 Northrop Ave Hawthorne CA 90250

SLUTSKY, ALAN MARTIN, dentist, health plan administrator; b. Wilmington, Del., Apr. 11, 1952; s. Leonard L. and Miriam (Alter) S.; m. Marilyn Jeanne Applin, June 16, 1974. AB, Harvard U., 1974; DMD, U. Pa., 1980, MBA, 1981. Instr. Sch. Dental Medicine U. Pa., Phila., 1978-80; spl. projects coord. ADA, Chgo., 1982-83; asst. coord. quality assurance Michael Reese Hosp. and Med. Ctr., Chgo., 1983-84; exec. dir. Portes Cancer Prevention Ctr., Chgo., 1984-86; chief adminstr. pvt. med. practice, Long Beach and L.A., 1987-88; pvt. practice gen. dentistry various locations, 1980—; v.p., adminstr. Community Dentaplan, Inc., Culver City, Calif., 1988—; cons., Am. Assn. Dental Examiners, Chgo., 1983—; seminar coord., Harbor Dental Soc., Long Beach, 1987. Contbr. to profl. publs. Regional screener, nat. rep. Am. Field Svc. Student Exchange, N.Y.C., 1970—; bd. dirs. Thorndale Beach South Condominium Assn., Chgo., 1984-86, Ocean Terr. Homeowners Assn., Long Beach, 1989—. Mem. ADA, Am. Assn. Dental Schs., Nat. Coun. Internat. Health, Physicians for Social Responsibility, Fedn. Dentaire Internat., Consumers Union. Home: PO Box 40296 Long Beach CA 90804

SMALL, LAWRENCE FARNSWORTH, history educator; b. Bangor, Maine, Dec. 30, 1925; s. Irving Wheelock and Geneva May (Turner) S.; m. Elfie Joan Ames, Aug. 9, 1947; children: Kathleen Ann, Linda Jean, Lawrence Farnsworth, Daniel Irving (dec.). B.D., Bangor Theol. Sem., 1948; B.A., U. Maine, 1948, M.A., 1951; Ph.D., Harvard, 1955. Ordained to ministry Congregational Ch., 1950; minister Paramus (N.J.) Congl. Ch., 1955-59; asso. prof. history Rocky Mountain Coll., Billings, Mont., 1959-61; prof. Rocky Mountain Coll., 1975—, dean of Coll., 1961-65, acting pres., 1965-66, pres., 1966-75; Chmn. Mont. commn. Higher Edn. Facilities Act, 1965-74; exec. dir. Mont. Assn. Chs. Author: Montana Passage, A Century of Politics on the Yellowstone, Journey with the Law, the Life of Judge William J. Jameson. Pres. Yellowstone County Council Chs., 1968-70; treas. Mont. Conf., United Ch. of Christ, 1970-73; chmn. bd. dirs. Western Independent Colls. Found.; bd. dirs. Community Concert Assn., Yellowstone County Mental Health Assn., Billings Citizens for Community Devel., Billings United Fund; trustee Billings Deaconess Hosp. Mem. Phi Beta Kappa, Phi Kappa Phi. Club: Kiwanis (pres. Billings). Home: 7320 Sumatra Pl RR 4 Billings MT 59106 Office: 1511 Poly St Billings MT 59102

SMALL, RICHARD F., county official, mechanical engineer, consultant; b. Buffalo, July 2, 1936; s. Frank and Rose (Cohn) S.; m. Marilyn A. Schroeder, Jan. 14, 1984; children: Scott, Mark, James. AS in Metallurgy, SUNY, Buffalo, 1957; BSME, Tri-State U., 1968; MBA, UCLA, 1973; JD, U. Calif., Irvine, 1974. Registered profl. engr., Calif., Ill., Fla., Eng., Italy. Engring. mgr. Worthington Corp., Buffalo, 1959-68; div. mgr. Pulsation Controls Corp., Santa Paula, Calif., 1968-70; project mgr. Pioneer Svc. & Engring. Corp., Chgo., 1970-72; mgr. internat. projects Bechtel Power Corp., Norwalk, Calif., 1972-74; v.p. VTN Corp., Irvine, 1974-76, Standard Rsch. Corp., Arcadia, Calif., 1977-78; dir. U.S. Dept. Energy, Oakland, Calif., 1976-77; sr. ptnr. Western Pacific Assocs., Costa Mesa, Calif., 1978-88; dir. architecture and engring. Orange County Gen. Svcs. Agy., Santa Ana, Calif., 1988—; sr. cons. Airesearch Mfg. Co., Torrance, Calif., 1980-85; contract cons. Rockwell Space Systems, Downey, Calif., 1980-81. Author: Energy Alternatives, 1976; contbr. numerous articles on energy to profl. jours.; patentee equipment for energy conversion. Counselor, advisor Phoenix House Found., Santa Ana, 1982. Sgt. U.S. Army, 1951-54, Korea, mem. Res. ret. Mem. Nat. Soc. Profl. Engrs., ASME, Am. Nuclear Soc., Am. Mgmt. Assn., Orange County Mfmt. Forum. Home: 26534 Monteil Mission Viejo CA 92691 Office: Orange County Gen Svcs Agy 14 Civic Ctr Santa Ana CA 92701

SMART, WILLIAM BUCKWALTER, newspaper editor; b. Provo, Utah, June 27, 1922; s. Thomas Laurence and Nellie (Buckwalter) S.; m. Donna Toland, July 15, 1945; children: William Toland, Melinda, Kristen, Thomas Toland, Alfred Lawrence. Student, U. Wyo., 1943-44, U. Utah, 1949-51; B.A., Reed Coll., 1948. Reporter Internat. News Service, Portland, Oreg., 1941-43; reporter The Oregonian, Portland, 1946-48, The Deseret News, Salt Lake City, 1948-52; chief editorial writer, editor The Deseret News, 1952-66, exec. editor, 1966-72, editor, gen. mgr., 1972-86, sr. editor, 1986—. Bd. dirs. Grand Canyon Trust, KUED; mem. Utah State Commn. on Excellence in Edn., Coll. Commn. N.W. Assn. Schs. and Colls., Provo-Jordan River Pkwy. Found.; mem. nat. adv. bd. Snowbird Inst. for Arts and Humanities; chmn. Utah Innovation Found.; mem. Utah Gov.'s Constn. Bicentennial Commn. Served to 1st lt., inf. AUS, 1943-46, PTO. Mem. Phi Beta Kappa, Sigma Delta Chi, Kappa Tau Alpha. Mem. Ch. of Jesus Christ of Latter-day Saints. Clubs: Bonneville Knife and Fork (Hidden Valley) (past pres.), Timpanogos (Hidden Valley), Fort Douglas (Hidden Valley); Aztec, Alta. Home: 55 Laurel St Salt Lake City UT 84103 Office: The Deseret News Box 1257 Salt Lake City UT 84110

SMEGAL, THOMAS FRANK, JR., lawyer; b. Eveleth, Minn., June 15, 1935; s. Thomas Frank and Genevieve (Andreachi) S.; m. Susan Jane Stanton, May 28, 1966; children: Thomas Frank, Elizabeth Jane. BS in Chem. Engring., Mich. Technol. U., 1957; JD, George Washington U., 1961. Bar: Va. 1961, D.C. 1961, Calif. 1964, U.S. Supreme Ct. 1976. Patent examiner U.S. Patent Office, Washington, 1957-61; staff patent atty. Shell Devel. Co., San Francisco, 1962-65; patent atty. Townsend and Townsend, San Francisco, 1965—, now mng. ptnr.; mem. U.S. del. to Paris Conv. for Protection of Indsl. Property. Pres. bd. dirs. Legal Aid Soc. San Francisco, 1982-84, Youth Law Ctr., 1973-84; bd. dirs. Nat. Ctr. for Youth Law, 1978-84, San Francisco Lawyers Com. for Urban Affairs, 1972—, Legal Svcs. for Children, 1980—, Legal Svcs. Corp., 1984—. Capt. Chem. Corps, U.S. Army, 1961-62. Recipient St. Thomas More award, 1982. Mem. ABA (vice-chmn. PTC sect.), Nat. Coun. Intellectual Property Law Assn. (chmn. elect 1988), Nat. Inventors Hall Fame (pres. 1988), Calif. Bar Assn. (v.p. bd. govs. 1986-87), Am. Patent Law Assn. (bd. dirs., pres. 1986), Internat. Assn. Intellectual Property Lawyers (dir.), Bar Assn. San Francisco, Patent Law Assn. San Francisco. Republican. Roman Catholic. Clubs: World Trade, Commonwealth, Olympic, Golden Gate Breakfast (San Francisco); Claremont (Berkeley); University (Washington). Contbr. articles to publs. in field. Office: Townsend & Townsend 1 Market Pla San Francisco CA 94105

SMELICK, ROBERT MALCOLM, investment banker; b. Phoenix, Mar. 27, 1942; s. Valentine and Mary Helen (McDonald) S.; m. Gail Paine Sterling, Dec. 10, 1979; children: Christopher Paine, Alexandra McBryde, Gillian Sterling. BA, Stanford U., 1964; MBA, Harvard U., 1968; postgrad. U. Melbourne (Australia), 1965-66. V.p. Kidder Peabody & Co., Inc., N.Y.C. and San Francisco, 1968-79; mng. dir. First Boston Corp., San Francisco, 1979-89; prin., founder Sterling Payot Co., San Francisco, 1989—; bd. dirs. King Broadcasting Corp., Seattle, Mayne Nickless Holdings. Republican. Episcopalian. Office: Sterling Payot Co One Montgomery St Telesis Tower Ste #110 San Francisco CA 94104

SMELSER, NEIL JOSEPH, sociologist; b. Kahoka, Mo., July 22, 1930; s. Joseph Nelson and Susie Marie (Hess) S.; m. Helen Thelma Margolis, June 10, 1954 (div. 1965); children: Eric Jonathan, Tina Rachel; m. Sharin Fateley, Dec. 20, 1967; children: Joseph Neil, Sarah Joanne. B.A., Harvard U., 1952, Ph.D., 1958; B.A., Magdalen Coll., Oxford U., Eng., 1954; M.A., Magdalen Coll., Oxford U., 1959; grad., San Francisco Psychoanalytic Inst., 1971. Mem. faculty U. Calif.-Berkeley, 1958—, prof. sociology, 1962—, asst. chancellor ednl. devel., 1966-68; assoc. dir. Inst. Internat. Relations, 1969-73, 80—, Univ. prof. sociology, 1972; dir. edn. abroad program for U. Calif., 1977-79; bd. dirs. Found. Fund for Research in Psychiatry, 1967-70; bd. dirs. Social Sci. Research Council, 1968-71, chmn., 1971-73; trustee Ctr. for Advanced Study in Behavioral and Social Scis., 1980-86, 87—, chmn., 1984-86; mem. subcom. humanism Am. Bd. Internal Medicine, 1981-85; editor Am. Sociol. Rev., 1962-65; adv. editor Am. Jour. Sociology, 1960-62; mem. com. econ. growth Social Sci. Research Council, 1961-65; chmn. sociology panel Behavioral and Social Scis. survey Nat. Acad. Scis. and Social Sci. Research Council, 1967-69; mem. com. on basic research in behavioral and social scis. NRC, 1980—, chmn., 1984-86, co-chmn., 1986—. Author: (with T. Parsons) Economy and Society, 1956, Social Change in the Industrial Revolution, 1959, Theory of Collective Behavior, 1962, The Sociology of Economic Life, 1963, 2d edit., 1975, Essays in Sociological Explanation, 1968, Sociological Theory: A Contemporary View, 1971, Comparative Methods in the Social Sciences, 1976, (with Robin Content) The Changing Academic Market, 1980, Sociology, 1981, 2d edit., 1984, 3d edit. 1987; editor: (with W.T. Smelser) Personality and Social Systems, 1963, 2d edit., 1971, (with S.M. Lipset) Social Structure and Mobility in Economic Development, 1966, Sociology, 1967, 2d edit., 1973, (with James Davis) Sociology, a Survey Report, 1969, Karl Marx on Society and Social Change, 1973, (with Gabriel Almond) Public Higher Education in California, 1974, (with Erik Erikson) Themes of Work and Love in Adulthood, 1980, (with Jeffrey Alexander et al) The Micro-Macro Link, 1987, Handbook of Sociology, 1988. Rhodes scholar, 1952-54; jr. fellow Soc. Fellows, Harvard U., 1955-58. Mem. Am. Sociol. Assn. (council 1962-65, 67-70, exec. com. 1963-65), Pacific Sociol. Assn. Home: 109 Hillcrest Rd Berkeley CA 94705

SMETTER, MARTIN, plastics company executive; b. Bklyn., Mar. 2, 1941; s. Fred Smetter and Cele (Rosenthal) Altman; m. Mary Elizabeth O'Neill, Jan. 17, 1970 (div. Jan. 1980); 1 child, Michael Anthony. MBA, Pepperdine U., 1972. Field engr. IBM Corp., L.A., 1965-67; account exec., stockbroker E.F. Hutton, Beverly Hills, Calif., 1967-69; dir. corp. devel. Tax Corp. Am., Inc., La Canada, Calif., 1969-70; mktg. rep. Mohawk Data Scis., L.A., 1970-72; porduct mgr. Vedtor Gen., Van Nuys, Calif., 1973; dir. corp. devel. TCA, Montrose, Calif., 1974-78; pres. Western Case, Inc., Tustin, Calif., 1978—. With USN, 1959-64. Mem. Balboa Yacht Club. Home: 503 Avenida Campo Newport Beach CA 92660 Office: Western Case Inc 14351 Chambers Rd Tustin CA 92680

SMILEY, DANIEL RAY, emergency medical services director, educator; b. San Jose, Calif., Sept. 5, 1956; s. Wayne Austin and Esther Ella (Weichert) S.; m. Beverly Ann Scheeler,. AS, Merced Coll., 1981; BS, Calif. State U., Fresno, 1983; MPA, San Francisco, 1987. Paramedic, emergency med. technician Riggs Ambulance, Merced, Calif., 1974-81; paramedic Jones Ambulance, Fresno, Calif., 1979-83; emergency med. services instr. Fresno County Dept. of Health, Fresno, 1981-83, dir. of emergency med. services, 1983-89; chief dep. dir. Calif. Emergency Med. Svcs. Authority, Sacramento, 1989—; lectr., faculty Fresno City Coll., 1982-83, Calif. State U., Fresno, 1987-88. Mem. Emergency Med. Services Adminstrn. Assn. of Calif. (pres. 1988-89). Republican. Mormon. Office: State of Calif Emergency Med Svcs Authority 1030 15th St Ste 302 Sacramento CA 95814

SMILEY, RICHARD MILLDRUM, leasing company executive, consultant; b. St. Petersburg, Fla., Apr. 22, 1928; s. Russell Glen and Rosila (Milldrum) S.; m. Beryl Jeanne Jensen, Sept. 21, 1956; children: Shannon, Kristin, Brett, Clayton. BA, U. Fla., 1950; BS, Am. Inst. Fgn. Trade, Glendale, Ariz., 1955. CLU. Staff mgr. IBM Corp., Chgo., 1969-73; sr. mktg. exec. IBM Corp., Los Angeles, 1973-84; v.p. Matrix Computer Co., Salt Lake City, 1984—. Rep. dist. chmn., Salt Lake City, 1986; pres. So. Calif. Sch. Adv. Council, Chatsworth, 1977. Served with U.S. Army, 1950-54. Fellow Life Ins. Mgmt. Inst.; mem. Am. Coll. Life Underwriters, Salt Lake City C. of C. (chmn. subcom. 1986), MENSA. Mormon. Lodge: Salt Lake Rotary. Home: 816 16th Ave Salt Lake City UT 84103 Office: Matrix Computer Funding Corp 6925 Union Park Ctr Midvale UT 84047

SMILEY, ROBERT WILLIAM, JR., investment banker; b. Lansing, Mich., Nov. 17, 1943; s. Robert William Sr. and Rebecca Lee (Flint) S. AB in Econs., Stanford U., 1970; postgrad., San Fernando Valley Coll. Law, 1973-75; MBA in Corp. Fin., City U. Los Angeles, 1979; LLB, LaSalle U., 1982. Bar: Calif. 1984. Sr. v.p. mktg. Actuarial Systems Inc., San Jose, Calif., 1972-73; founder, chmn. Benefit Systems Inc., Los Angeles, 1973-84, Brentwood Square Savs. and Loan, Los Angeles, 1982-84; chmn., chief exec. officer Benefit Capital Inc., Los Angeles, 1984-89, Ingelwood, Calif., 1989—; lectr. U. Calif. Extension, Los Angeles and Berkeley, 1977—; instr. Am. Coll. Life Underwriters. Editor, contbg. author: Employee Stock Ownership Plans: Business Planning, Implementation, Law and Taxation, 1989; contbg. author: The Handbook of Employee Benefits, 1984, 2d edit. 1989; contbr. articles to profl. jours. Mem. nat. adv. council, trustee Reason Found., Santa Monica, Calif., 1983—. Served with USn, 1961-64, Vietnam. Recipient Spl. Achievement award Pres.' Commn. on Pension Policy, 1984. Fellow Life Mgmt. Inst.; mem. Employee Stock Ownership Plan Assn. (founder, past pres., bd. dirs.), Assn. for Corp. Growth, Western and SW Pension Confs., Nat. Assn. Bus. Economists, ABA, Calif. Bar Assn. Office: Benefit Capital Inc 9920 S La Cienega Blvd 9th Fl Inglewood CA 90301

SMITH, ALBERT CROMWELL, JR., investments consultant; b. Norfolk, Va., Dec. 6, 1925; s. Albert Cromwell and Georgie (Foreman) S.; m. Laura Thaxton, Oct. 25, 1952; children: Albert, Elizabeth, Laura. BS in Civil Engring., Va. Mil. Inst., 1949; MS in Govtl. Adminstrn., George Washington U., 1965; MBA, Pepperdine U., 1975. Enlisted USMC, 1944, commd. 2d lt., 1949, advanced through grades to col., 1970; comdr. inf. platoons, companies, landing force; variously assigned staffs U.K. Joint Forces, U.S. Sec. Navy, Brit. Staff Coll., Marine Staff Coll.; adviser, analyst amphibious systems; ret., 1974; pres. A. Cromwell-Smith, Ltd., Charlottesville, Va., 1973, head broker, cons. A. Cromwell Smith, Investments, La Jolla and Coronado, Calif., 1975—. Bd. dirs. Republicans of La Jolla, 1975-76; vestryman St. Martin's Episcopal Ch., 1971-73. Decorated Legion of Merit with oak leaf cluster, Bronze Star with V device with oak leaf cluster, Air medal with 2 oak leaf clusters, Purple Heart. Mem. ASCE, Nat., Calif. assns. Realtors, San Diego, Coronado bds. Realtors, Stockbrokers Soc., So. Calif. Options Soc., SAR, Mil. Order Purple Heart. Club: Kona Kai. Author: The Individual Investor in Tomorrow's Stock Market, 1977; The Little Guy's Stock Market Survival Guide, 1979; Wake Up Detroit! The EVs Are Coming, 1982; The Little Guy's Tax Survival Guide, 1984; The Little Guy's Sailboat Success Guide, 1986, The Little Guy's Business Success Guide, 1988; contbr. articles to civilian and mil. publs. Office: 1001 B Ave Ste 319/320 PO Box 192 Coronado CA 92118

SMITH, ALBERT LEE, oil company executive; b. Bainville, Mont., Nov. 14, 1914; s. Charles Edward and Ruth Hattie (Leeson) S.; m. Edel Petersen, Dec. 31, 1941; children: Gary Lee, Debra Ann. Grad. high sch., Farmer, Mont. and Bainville. Grain supr. Triple A Farm Program, Great Falls, Mont., 1941-46; ptnr. Edmonson-Smith Real Estate, Great Falls, 1946-48; owner, operator Smith Agy., Great Falls, 1948-53; pres. Cloverleaf Petroleum, Great Falls, 1949-55; owner Al Smith Drilling, Newcastle, Wyo., 1956-70; pres. Accidental Oil Co. Inc., Newcastle, 1967—. Wyo. dir. Old West Trail Found., 1982—; exec. sec. Wyo. D&K Tourist, Newcastle, 1977—. Mem. Rotary, Kiwanis, Toastmasters (dist. gov. 1948). Republican. Methodist. Home: 20H Roundup Ave Newcastle WY 82701 Office: Accidental Oil Co Inc 5297 US Hwy 16 Newcastle WY 82701

SMITH, ALONZO DAVID, marketing executive; b. Detroit, Sept. 25, 1945; s. Robert Hugh and Roxie Minnie (Clowney) S.; m. Brenda Elizabeth Bryson, June 1, 1968; children: Donielle Catrice, Lia Nichole, Robert Hugh II. BA in Mktg., Detroit Coll. Bus., 1971; D (hon.), Napoleon Hill Acad., 1974. Shipping mgr. Chrysler Corp., Detroit, 1964-72; dist. mgr. Equitable Life Ins. Co., Detroit, 1972-74; HQ acct. rep. Chesebrough-Ponds, Inc., Greenwich, Conn., 1974-77; nat. mgr. Exxon Bus. Machines, L.A., 1977-79; sr. systems cons. Gen. Dynamics Corp., St. Louis, 1979-83; PBX acct. exec. U.S. West Info. Systems, Inc., L.A., 1983—; cons. various corps., Calif., 1984—; nat. accounts mgr. GTE Corp., 1985—. Pres. Orange County (Calif.) Jr. All-Am. Football League, Cerritos, 1982-84, Distributive Edn. Clubs Am., Detroit, 1972; active Cerritos Civic Leaders, 1981—; chmn. turstee bd. Curry Temple C.M.E. Ch., 1987—. Recipient Mayor's awards City of Cerritos, 1981-85, Pres.'s award Gen. Dynamics, L.A., 1979-81. Mem. Meth. Men's Club (Compton, Claif.). Methodist. Home: 19930 Harvest Way Cerritos CA 90701-6540 Office: US West Info Systems 680 Knox Torrance CA 90502

SMITH, A(NDREW) LEONARD, accountant, consultant; b. Denver, Sept. 7, 1949; s. Andrew L. and Elsie L. (Henke) S.; m. Aniko S. Szabo, June 14, 1986; 1 child, Andrew B. BS, Met. State Coll., Denver, 1976; postgrad., U. Colo., 1977-78. Auditor City of Denver, 1977-79; acct. King Soopers, Denver, 1979-81; mgr. acctg. Am. Home Video, Denver, 1981-83; treas. Estimatic Corp., Denver, 1983-84; pres. Mile High Info. Services, Denver, 1984—. Served with U.S. Army, 1969-72. Colo. Scholar's grantee Met. State Coll., 1971. Mem. Nat. Assn. Accts. (charter, v.p. Centennial chpt. 1986-87, pres. 1987-88). Episcopalian. Home: 600 Prairie Ridge Rd Highlands Ranch CO 80216 Office: Mile High Info Svcs 9101 E Kenyon #3400 Denver CO 80216

SMITH, ANDREW VAUGHN, telephone company executive; b. Roseburg, Oreg., July 17, 1924; s. Andrew Britt and Ella Mae (Vaughn) S.; m. Dorothy LaVonne Crabtree, Apr. 25, 1943; children: Janet L., James A. B.S. in Elec. Engring, Oreg. State U., 1950. Registered profl. engr., Oreg. With Pacific N.W. Bell Telephone Co., 1951-88; asst. v.p. ops. Pacific N.W. Bell Telephone Co., Seattle, 1965; v.p., gen. mgr. Pacific N.W. Bell Telephone Co., Portland, Oreg., 1965-70; v.p. ops. Pacific N.W. Bell Telephone Co., Seattle, 1970-78, pres., 1978-88; pres. ops. U.S. West Communications, 1988-89; exec. v.p. U.S. West Inc., 1989—; bd dirs. U.S. Bancorp, Portland, Unigard Mut. and Unigard Ins. Cos., Univar Corp., Seattle, Cascade Natural Gas, Seattle, Airborne Freight Corp., Seattle, VWR Corp., Seattle, Aldus Corp., Seattle. Trustee Oreg. State U. Found., U. Wash. Grad. Sch. Bus., 1985; chmn. bd. trustees U. Wash. Grad. Sch. Bus., 1984-85; gen. chmn. United Way of King County, 1980-81; trustee Wash. State Internat. Trade Fair; mem. Seattle Urban League. Served with USNR, 1943-46. Mem. Seattle C. of C. (chmn. 1985-86). Episcopalian. Clubs: Harbor, Washington Athletic, Seattle Yacht, Rainier, Overlake Golf and Country, Arlington, Multnomah (Portland), Columbia Tower (Seattle). Lodge: Masons. Office: US West Inc 1600 Bell Pla Rm 1802 Seattle WA 98191

SMITH, ARLYN GENE, management consultant; b. Rozel, Kans., Feb. 12, 1926; s. Glee Sidney and Bernice Mildred (Augustine) S.; m. Jacqueline Jane Houdyshell, March. 25, 1948; children: Arlyn G. II, Dana Gaye and Denise Kaye (twins). BS in Journalism, U. Kans., 1949. Editor Larned (Kans.) Chronoscope, 1949-50; ptnr., chief operating officer cattle and farming operation Kans., 1950-68; pvt. practice mgmt. cons. Larned, 1968-78, Tucson, Ariz., 1978—; dir. Glee Smith Cattle Co., Inc., Kans., 1970-76. Author (book): Agriculture: The Dynamic Years Ahead, 1970; columnist (mag.): $ and contbr. numerous articles to mags. and newspapers. Vol. advisor nonprofit orgns. and individuals; dist. fin. chmn. Boy Scouts Am., Kans., 1970; council fin. chmn. Girl Scouts U.S., Kans., 1968; mem. Kans. Com. Govt. Ethics, Topeka, 1971-73; mem. Repub. Cen. com., Kans., Ariz., 1960-80; adv. com. Kans. Geol. Survey, Topeka, 1977-78; assoc. Smithsonian Inst.; trustee Jordaan Meml. Libr. Lt. USNR, 1943-46, 51-53. Mem. Nat. Cattleman's Assn., Tucson C. of C., Tucson Exec.'s Assn. (bd. dirs. 1977-83, pres. 1983), Lions Club (charter pres.), Masons, Rotary (pres.), VFW, Am. Legion (comdr. Larned chtp.), Burning Bush Soc. Kans. Sch. Religion (vice-chmn.), Delta Tau Delta, Alpha Delta Sigma. Republican. Presbyterian. Home: 4620 N Avenida Ronca Tucson AZ 85715 Office: 5620 N Kolb Rd PO Box 65000 Tucson AZ 85740

SMITH, ARMISTEAD BURWELL, JR., retired banker and naval officer; b. Gastonia, N.C., Mar. 15, 1921; s. Armistead Burwell and Ruby (Gardner) S.; m. Margaret Pagliotti, Jan. 14, 1944; children—Sandra Smith Wallace, Armistead Burwell, Michael Spencer. Grad., Naval War Coll., Air War Coll.-USAF, Navy Postgrad. Sch., U. N.C., Chapel Hill. Lic. naval aviator. Enlisted U.S. Navy, 1941, served to capt., ret., 1972; trust banker Calif. First Bank, San Diego, 1972-86, advisor to pres., 1986-88; chmn. Calif. First Bank Capital Mgmt. Corp., La Jolla, Calif., 1983-86; dir. Calif. First Venture Capital Corp., Los Angeles, 1983-88; ret. Calif. First Venture Capital Corp., 1988. Chmn. bd. dirs. La Jolla Cancer Research Found., 1981—; trustee Powell Scholarship Fund, 1975—; bd. dirs. San Diego Aerospace Mus., 1976—, chmn., 1980—; foreman San Diego County Grand Jury, 1988—. Decorated Silver Star, Legion of Merit (2), D.F.C. with three clusters, Navy Meritorious Service medal, Air medals (8), Navy Commendation medal. Mem. Am. Fighter Aces Assn. (past pres.), Assn. Naval Aviation, Navy League, San Diego Zool. Soc., Early and Pioneer Naval Aviator's Assn. (golden eagles). Methodist. Clubs: Lomas Santa Fe Country; Naval Order of U.S.

SMITH, ARTHUR HUBERT, JR., retired golf professional; b. Cookeville, Tenn., Aug. 26, 1932; s. Arthur Hubert and Iva Thelma (Nabors) S.; m. Pamela V. King, Dec. 18, 1964. BS, Tenn. Technol. U., 1956. Golf profl. Cookeville Country Club, 1958-61, Sparta (Tenn.) Country Club, 1960-61, Arnold Ctr. Golf Club, Tullahoma, Tenn., 1962-72, Pinehurst (N.C.) Country Club, 1973, Concord Resort Hotel, Kiamesha Lake, N.Y., 1974-88; now ret. Author: Professional Approach, 1987. With U.S. Army, 1953-54. Mem. PGA (pres. Tenn. 1968-69, Southeastern Profl. of Yr. award 1968, Tenn. Profl. of Yr. award 1969, Nat. Profl. of Yr. award 1969, Merchandiser of Yr. award Met. sect. 1983), Desert Highlands Club. Democrat. Baptist. Home: 7238 E Joshua Tree Ln Scottsdale AZ 85253

SMITH, BARBARA KALO, communications, public relations and advertising executive; b. Lorain, Ohio, Dec. 24, 1950; d. George and Catherine Irene (Repko) K.; m. Robert Mathias Pangburn, May 26, 1973 (dec. July 1974); m. Paul Willis Smith III, Jan. 7, 1977. BA, U. Dayton, 1972. Edit. asst. Hotel and Restaurant Employees Union, Cin., 1973-74; editor Family Motor Coach Assn., Cin., 1974-76; advt. mgr. 3-T's RV Products, Inc., Van Nuys, Calif., 1977-80, 1985—; sec. Lexitron, Thousand Oaks, Calif., 1980-82; editor Micom Systems, Inc., Simi Valley, Calif., 1982-85. Recipient 1st pl. award, Nat. Labor Pubs., 1974. Mem. Internat. Assn. Bus. Communicators (Bronze Quill award 1985). Roman Catholic. Home: 16700 Gledhill St Sepulveda CA 91343 Office: 3-T's RV Products Inc 15216 Stagg St Van Nuys CA 91405

SMITH, BERNARD JOSEPH, civil engineer, consultant; b. Liverpool, Eng., Aug. 29, 1900; s. Thomas J. and Sarah Anne (Crum) S.; came to U.S., 1912, naturalized, 1930; student St. Edward's Coll., Liverpool, 1914-20; ed. Oxford U., Eng., 1918; B.Engring. with honors, U. Liverpool, 1923, M.Engring., 1926; m. Julia Susan Connolly, June 4, 1929; children—Bernard, Sarah Anne Kathleen, Maureen, Una, Aislin, Malachy, Joan, John. Pvt. tutor in math. and physics, Liverpool, 1923-24; field engr. Underpinning & Found. Co., N.Y.C., 1924; underground conduit engr. N.Y. and N.J. Bell Telephone Co., 1924-25, Ohio Bell Telephone Co., Toledo, 1925-26; asst. engr. to Alexander Potter, cons. engr. on water and sewerage systems, N.Y. and N.J., 1926-30; design engr. Humble Oil & Refining Co., Baytown, Tex., 1930-32; city mgr. and engr. City of Baytown, 1932-33, cons. engr., 1930-34; engr. examiner Pub. Works Adminstrn., Ft. Worth, 1935-37; dir. research and personnel City of Ft. Worth, 1938-42; acting state dir. and state planning engr. Tex. Pub. Works Res., 1942; asst. regional dir. and regional economist Nat. Housing Agy., hdqrs. Dallas, 1942-46; cons. engr. on water systems and town planning, Dallas, 1946-65; cons. tides and water resources, San Francisco, 1965—, also Aptos, Calif.; water commr. Santa Cruz County, Calif.; planning engr. and chief San Francisco Bay sect. U.S. Corps of Engrs., 1957-65; lectr. urban devel. Tex. Christian U., Ft. Worth, 1939-43; guest lectr. on town devel. Ala. Poly. Inst., 1940; instr. econs. and engring. So. Meth. U., Dallas, 1943-53; guest panelist Ann. Radio Conf., U. Okla., Norman, 1946; speaker on econs. and town planning to various civic and bus. groups, 1939—; v.p. Southwestern States Water Co., 1949-51. Mem. bd. govs. Dallas Fed. Reference Exchange, 1943-46. Registered profl. engr., Calif., N.J., Tex.; registered pub. surveyor, Tex. Fellow ASCE (com. city planning tng. for civil engrs. 1942); mem. Am. Waterworks Assn., AAAS, Am., Western econ. assns., Assn. Evolutionary Econs., History of Econs. Soc., County Louth (Eire) Archeol. Soc., Irish Lit. and Hist. Soc. of San Francisco (pres. 1959-62), Sierra Club. Club: Commonwealth of Calif. Contbr. articles and reports on water systems, flood control, urban devel. and pollution to profl. publs. Home: 1446 Day Valley Rd Aptos CA 95003 Office: PO Box 663 Aptos CA 95003

SMITH, BERNARD JOSEPH CONNOLLY, civil engineer; b. Elizabeth, N.J., Mar. 11, 1930; s. Bernard Joseph and Julia Susan (Connolly) S.; B.S., U. Notre Dame, 1951; B.S. in Civil Engring., Tex. A&M U., 1957; M.B.A. in Fin., U. Calif.-Berkeley, 1976; m. Josephine Kerley, Dec. 20, 1971; children—Julia Susan Alice, Teresa Mary Josephine, Anne Marie Kathleen. Asst. Bernard J. Smith, cons. engr. office, Dallas, 1947-57; hydraulic engr. C.E., U.S. Army, San Francisco, 1957-59, St. Paul dist., 1959-60, Kansas City (Mo.) dist., 1960-63, Sacramento dist., 1963-65; engr. Fed. Energy Regulatory Commn., San Francisco Regional Office, 1965—. Served with U.S. Army, 1952-54. Registered profl. engr., Calif., Mo.; lic. real estate broker, Calif. Mem. ASCE (sec. power div. San Francisco sect. 1969), Soc. Am. Mil. Engrs. (treas. Kansas City post 1962), Am. Econ. Assn., Nat. Soc. Profl. Engrs., Res. Officers Assn. (chpt. pres. 1973). Club: Commonwealth of Calif. Home: 247 28th Ave San Francisco CA 94121 Office: Fed Energy Regulatory Commn 333 Market St San Francisco CA 94105

SMITH, BERNARD RAYMOND, JR., aerospace engineer; b. Balt., May 14, 1947; s. Bernard Raymond Sr. and Verna Marie (Catania) S.; m. Barbara Anita Brumme, June, 1978 (div. July 1983); m. Denise Orstadius, June 30, 1984; children: Bernard Raymond III, Genevieve Marie. BS, U. Balt., 1970, postgrad., 1970; MA, Cen. Mich. U., 1977; MS, Ariz. State U., 1983. Systems analyst City of Balt., 1970-71; teaching asst. Ariz. State U., Tempe, 1981-82; engr. Singer Link, Higley, Ariz., 1982-84; sr. engr. McDonnell Douglas Helicopter Co., Mesa, Ariz., 1984-86, engring. mgr., 1986—; v.p. Aerotronics Cons., Scottsdale, Ariz., 1983-88. Capt. USAF, 1971-79. Mem. Eta Kappa Nu, Tau Beta Pi. Democrat. Roman Catholic. Home: 1747 E Garnet Ave Mesa AZ 85204 Office: McDonnell Douglas Co 5000 E McDowel Rd Mesa AZ 85205

SMITH, BETTY DENNY, civic worker; b. Centrlia, Ill., Nov. 12, 1964; d. Otto and Ferne Elizabeth (Beier) Hasenfuss; m. Peter S. Smith, Dec. 5, 1964; children: Carla Kip, Bruce Kimball. Student, U. Ill., 1950-52; student, L.A. City Coll., 1953-57, UCLA, 1985, U. San Francisco, 1982-84. Freelance fashion coordinator L.A., N.Y.C., 1953-58; tchr. fashion Rita LeRoy Internat. Studios, 1959-60; mgr. Mo Nadler Fashion, L.A., 1961-64; showroom dir. Jean of Calif. Fashions, L.A., 1986—; freelance polit. book reviewer for community newspapers, 1961-62; staff writer Valley Citizen News, 1963. Bd. dirs. Pet Assistance Found., 1969-76; founder, pres., dir. Vol. Services to Animals L.A., 1972-76; mem. County Com. To Discuss Animals in Research, 1973-74; mem. blue ribbon com. on animal control L.A. County, 1973-74; dir. L.A. County Animal Care and Control, 1976-82; mem. Calif. Animal Health Technician Exam. Com., 1975-82, chmn., 1979; bd. dirs. L.A. Soc. for Prevention Cruelty to Animals, 1984—; dir. West Coast Regional Office, Am. Humane Assn., 1986—; chief fin. officer Coalition for Pet Population Control, 1987-89; mem. Calif. Republican. Cen. Com., 1964-72, mem. exec. com., 1971-73; mem. Los Angeles County Rep. Cen. Com., 1964-70, mem. exec. com., 1966-70; chmn. 29th Congl. Cen. Com., 1969-70; sec. 28th Senatorial Cen. Com., 1967-68, 48th Assembly Dist. Cen. Com., 1965-68; mem. speakers bur. George Murphy for U.S. Senate, 1970; campaign mgr. Los Angeles County for Spencer Williams for Atty. Gen., 1966. Mem. Lawyers Wives San Gabriel Valley (bd. dirs. 1971-74, pres. 1972-73), Mannequins Assn. (bd. dirs. 1967-68), Internat. Platford Assn., L.A. Athletic Club, Town Hall, Delta Gamma, Pi Phi Theta. Home: 1766 Bluffhill Dr Monterey Park CA 91754

SMITH, BETTY GAIL, nuclear engineer; b. Chestnut, La., Aug. 5, 1944; d. Eula Nathan and Dorothy Jeweleen (Matthews) Keen; m. Paul B. Smith Sr., July 16, 1961; children: Juanita, Paul B. Jr., Paulette, Howard. Student, Idaho State U., 1979-86; BSE, U. Wash., 1988. Asst. office mgr. Parr Inc., Pocatello, Idaho, 1970-75; mgr. office Teds Chrysler Plymouth, Pocatello, 1975-79; mgr. office, dean's sec. Coll. Engring. Idaho State U., Pocatello, 1979-86; nuclear engr. Puget Sound Naval Shipyard, Bremerton, Wash., 1988—. Vol. Am. Cancer Soc.; Brownie leader Girl Scouts U.S. Republican. Baptist. Home: 3701 Phinney Bay Dr Bremerton WA 98312 Office: Puget Sound Naval Shipyard Nuclear Engring Dept Bremerton WA 98314

SMITH, BOBBY DALE, sales executive; b. Hobart, Okla., Dec. 5, 1948; s. Perry Merron and Zelma Louise (Williams) S.; m. Sue Ann Peters, Oct. 1970 (div. Dec. 1980) children: Shannon DeAnn, Ian Jerome, Casey Jean. Operator Sundance Mechanical, Albuquerque, 1985=86; sales dir. Barnett and Co., Albuquerque, 1986—. With USMC, 1967-69, Vietnam. Mem. Press Club (Albuquerque). Republican. Baptist. Home: 6419 Colleen Ave NE Albuquerque NM 87109

SMITH, BRIAN REXFORD, urban planner; b. St. Louis, Mo., Apr. 7, 1954; s. Fredrick A. and Joyce E. (Miller) S. MA, San Diego State U., San Diego, 1978; AB, U. Calif., Berkeley, 1976. Planning student intern County of San Diego, San Diego, Calif., 1977-78; planning technician City of Carlsbad, Carlsbad, Calif., 1978; environ. planner Prc toups Corp., La Jolla, Calif., 1979; asst. planner City of San Diego, 1979-80, City of Escondido (Calif.), 1980-88; planning dir. City of Vista (Calif.), 1988. Participant, Lead- San Diego, 1988; past Chmn., comm. mem., Orchids and onions community design awards program, San Diego, 1982-88; Jury Mem., Escondido C. of C.-Beautification Program, 1988. Calif. Assn. of Environ. Profl. (pres. 1987-89; dir. of profl. devel.), Am. Planning Assn. Democratic Protestant. Office: City of Vista Planning Div 600 Eucalyptus Ave Vista CA 92083

SMITH, BRUCE LAWRENCE, broadcasting executive; b. Duluth, Minn., Jan. 17, 1952; s. Bruce Robert and Hilda Francis (Schmidt) S. Student, Mich. Tech. U.; BA in Communications magna cum laude, U. Minn., 1973; MS in Radio/TV/Film, Miami U., Oxford, Ohio, 1974; MBA, Murray State U., 1979. Pub. affairs dir. Sta. KUMD-FM, Duluth, 1971-73; program dir. Sta. WGGL-FM, Houghton, Mich., 1975-77; gen. mgr. Sta. WKMS-FM, Murray, Ky., 1977-82, Sta. KSKA-FM, Anchorage, 1982-88, Sta. KUAC-TV-FM, Fairbanks, Alaska, 1988—; sec., treas. Alaska Pub. Radio Network, Anchorage, 1983-85; bd. dirs. Radio Reading Service, Anchorage. Vol. Alaska Congrl. Campaign, Anchorage, 1984, 86; v.p. Murray Civic Music Assn., 1979-82; bd. dirs. radio div. So. Ednl. Communications Assn., 1980-82, Alaska Ctr. for Environment, Anchorage, 1985—, Internship Program for Alaska, 1986—. Mem. Assn. MBA Execs., Anchorage Associated Broadcasters, Alaska Broadcasters Assn., Phi Kappa Phi, Alpha Epsilon Rho. Republican. Home: PO Box 82468 Fairbanks AK 99708 Office: Sta KUAC-TV/FM Univ Alaska Fairbanks AK 99775-1420

SMITH, BRUCE WARREN, photographer, writer; b. Myrtle Point, Oreg., Aug. 10, 1952; s. Warren Andrew and Enness Margaret (Hager) S.; m. Patricia Anne Thurston, Feb. 16, 1974. Student, Judson Baptist Coll., 1970-72, U. Oreg., 1982-84. Parts mgr. JI Case Co., sub-store, Coos Bay, Oreg., 1979-82; features editor Four Wheeler Mag., Canoga Park, Calif., 1984-85; tech. editor Four Wheeler Mag., Canoga Park, 1985-86, sr. editor, 1986-87, editorial dir., spl. publs. div., 1987-88, contbg. editor, 1988—; U.S. overseas editor 4x4 England, Brentwood, Eng., 1988—; field editor American Hunter Mag., Herndon, Va., 1987—; freelance writer, photographer Lancaster, Calif., 1988—; off-road racing press liason, GMC/Vista Group Pub. Relations, Van Nuys, Calif., 1989—, GM Truck Motorsports Pub. Rels. Rep.; contract pub. relations photographer, Chevrolet Truck and Bus. Pub. Relations, Warren, Mich., 1988—, Nissan Motorsports/Bob Thomas and Assocs., Redondo Beach, Calif., 1989—. Editor: Monster Trucks: The Poster Book, 1986 (Maggie award 1987). With U.S. Army, 1972-75. Mem. Soc. Profl. Journalists. Democrat. Home and Office: 43612 Easy St Lancaster CA 93535

SMITH, CAROLE, business executive; b. Stockton, Calif., Jan. 17, 1944; m. Albert Smith; children: Daniel, Terrie. Lic. cosmetician, pest control operator. Model Stockton, Calif., 1971-77, cosmetician, 1973-85; pres. J.C. Creations, Stockton, Calif., 1977-87, Area Wide Exterminators, Stockton, Calif., 1979—. commr. Stockton Planning Commn., 1987—; chmn. econ. devel., Stockton, 1988; mem. Econ. Outlook conf., Stockton, 1987-88; v.p. steering com. Asparagus Festival, 1988—; moderator Leadership Stockton, 1987; bd. dirs. Better Bus. Bur., Stockton, 1988, Pvt. Industry Council, Stockton, 1985—. Named Small Bus. Person of Yr. Greater Stockton C. of C., 1987; recipient Cert. Appreciation Pacific Gas and Electric Co., 1988, Cert. Appreciation Am. Cancer Soc., 1988. Mem. Nat. Pest Control Assn. (chmn. personnel com. 1987—), Bus. Leaders Club (pres. 1986), Stockton Bus. Devel., Greater Stockton C. of C. (v.p. 1988—), Stockton Visitor's and Conv. Bur. (v.p. 1988—), Stockton Women's Network (pres. 1987-88). Republican. Club: West Ln. (Stockton) (bd. dirs. 1987-88). Lodge: Rotary. Office: Area Wide Exterminators 2239 Country Club Blvd Stockton CA 95204

SMITH, CARROLL DEAN, transportation executive; b. Waitsburg, Wash., Mar. 29, 1928; s. Charles Alfred and Edith Ann (Wardrip) S.; m. Teresa Florence Shimizu, Aug. 30, 1948; children: Dean, Jacqueline Gomberg. BA, U. Wash., 1960; JD, Golden Gate U., 1988. Supr. transp. rate expert Calif. Pub. Utilities Commn., 1965—. Author: Development of Regulation of Trucking in California, 1987. Mem. San Anselmo Open Space Com., 1982-84. Mem. Am. Soc. Transp. and Logistics (bd. dirs.), Assn. Transp. Practitioners. Democrat. Home: 11 Elkhorn Way San Anselmo CA 94960 Office: Pub Utilities Commn 505 Van Ness Ave San Francisco CA 94102

SMITH, CARTER BLAKEMORE, broadcaster; b. San Francisco, Jan. 1, 1937; s. Donald V. and Charlotte M. (Nichols) S.; children: Carter Blakemore, Clayton M. AA, City Coll. San Francisco, 1958; BA, San Francisco State U., 1960; postgrad. N.Y. Inst. Finance, 1969-70; Assoc. in Fin. PLanning, Coll. for Fin. Planning, 1984. Announcer, Sta. KBLF, Red Bluff, Calif., 1954-56; personality Sta. KRE-KRE FM, Berkeley, Calif., 1958-63, Sta. KSFO, San Francisco, 1963-72, Sta. KNBR, San Francisco, 1972-83, Sta. KSFO, San Francisco, 1983-86, Sta. KFRC, San Francisco, 1986—; mem. faculty radio-TV dept. San Francisco State U., 1960-61. Mem. adv. bd. Little Jim Club Children's Hosp., 1968-71; bd. dirs. Marin County Humane Soc., 1968-73, San Francisco Zool. Soc., 1980—; trustee Family Service Agy. Marin, 1976-85; mem. alumni bd. Lowell High Sch. Recipient award San Francisco Press Club, 1965; named one of Outstanding Young Men in Am. U.S. Jaycees, 1972. Mem. Amateur Radio Relay League (life), Quarter Century Wireless Assn., Alpha Epsilon Rho. Office: Sta KFRC 500 Washington St San Francisco CA 94111

SMITH, CHARLES ANTHONY, businessman; b. Santa Fe, Sept. 16, 1939; s. Frances (Mier) Vigil; student various adminstrv. and law courses; m. Paula Ann Thomas, June 26, 1965; 1 dau., Charlene Danielle. Circulation mgr. Daily Alaska Empire, 1960-63; agt. Mut. of N.Y. Life Ins. Co., Juneau, Alaska, 1964-65; mng. partner Future Investors in Alaska and Cinema Alaska, Juneau, 1961-62; SE Alaska rep. K & L Distbrs., 1966-68; mgr. Alaska Airlines Newspapers, SE Alaska, 1969; dep. Alaska Retirement System, Juneau, 1970-71; apptd. dir. hwy. safety, gov.'s hwy. safety rep., Juneau, 1971-83; pres. Valley Service Ctr., Inc., 1984—. Alaska pres. Muscular Dystrophy Assn. Am.; pres. SE Alaska Emergency Med. Services Council, 1965-72. Served to capt. Army N.G., 1964—. Named Alaska Safety Man of Yr., 1977. Mem. Am. Assn. Motor Vehicle Adminstrs., Alaska Peace Officers Assn., Nat. Assn. Gov.s' Hwy. Safety Reps., N.G. Assn., Internat. Platform Assn. Roman Catholic. Club: Elks (Juneau). Author various hwy. safety manuals and plans, 1971—. Home: PO Box 493 Douglas AK 99824 Office: Pouch N Juneau AK 99811

SMITH, CHARLES RONALD COOPER, photographer, photojournalist; b. Plainview, Tex., Nov. 8, 1946; s. Otis Melvin and Jewell (Faith) S.; m. Patsy Louise Edgar, Nov. 25, 1974 (div. June 1979). Student, U. of Americas, 1964-65, San Antonio Coll., 1965-66, 68, New Sch. U., 1972-74. Photographer Lyncean Films, N.Y.C., 1974-78; freelance photographer various docations worldwide, 1969—; writer-photographer Rainbow Prodn., N.Y., 1976-82. Author: (screenplays) The Glass Soldier, 1985, The Mercenary, 1986. Sgt. US Army, 1966-68, Vietnam. Decorated Vietnamese Medal of Honor, ARVN, Vietnam, 1967, Combat Med. Badge, US Army, Vietnam, 1967, Army Commedation Medal, US Army, Vietnam, 1967-68, Silver Star Gallantry in Action medal, US Army, Vietnam, 1968, Purple Heart, 1967. Mem. Profl. Photographers of Am., Inc. Republican. Office: Cooper Smith PO Box 1382 Ross CA 94957-1382

SMITH, CHESTER, broadcasting executive; b. Wade, Okla., Mar. 29, 1930; s. Louis L. and Effie (Brown) S.; m. Naomi L. Crenshaw, July 19, 1959; children: Lauri, Lorna, Roxanne. Country western performer on Capitol records, TV and radio, 1947-61; owner, mgr. Sta. KLOC, Ceres-Modesto, Calif., 1963-81, Sta. KCBA-TV, Salinas-Monterey, Calif., 1981-86; owner, ptnr. Sta. KCSO-TV, Modesto-Stockton-Sacramento, Sta. KREN-TV, Reno, Nev., Sta. KBCP-TV, Paradise-Chico, Calif., Sta. KO7TA-TV, Santa Maria, Calif., Sta. KO9UF-TV, Morro Bay, Calif., 1986—. Mem. Calif. Broadcasters Assn. Republican. Mem. Christian Ch. original rec. Wait A Little Longer Please Jesus; named to Country Music Hall of Fame, Nashville, 1955, Western Swing hall of Fame, Sacramento, 1988.

SMITH, CHRISTINA MAYEM, sales manager; b. Redwood City, Calif., Jan. 19, 1962; d. Daniel Allen and Katherine McKay (Vellenga) S. AA in Social Sci., Foothill Coll., Los Altos, Calif., 1981. Sales mgr. Allen Tool Mfg. Inc., Mountain View, Calif., 1978-79; sales rep. Alex Lee Wallav, San Francisco, 1979-82, Danskin, Inc., L.A., 1982-84; mfrs. rep. Gilda Marx Industries, L.A., 1984-88; sales mgr. Western Region Rose of New Orleans, L.A., 1988-89; nat. sales mgr. Aviat Sportif, L.A., 1989—; cons. L.A. Sporting Club, 1987—; mktg. dir. Honey Locust Ranch, San Miguel, 1986-89. Photographer: newspaper photo essay Country Almanac, 1979. Republican. Home: 7504 Hollywood Blvd 4 Los Angeles CA 90046 Office: Aviat Sportif 110 E 9th St Ste C552 Los Angeles CA 90079

SMITH, CHRISTOPHER CASE, newspaper editor; b. Honolulu, July 22, 1934; s. Dudley Wall and Elizabeth McLean (Case) S.; m. Marjorie Anne Nurse, June 21, 1959; children: Suzanne Elizabeth, Patricia Louise (dec.), Sandra Kathleen. AB, Princeton U., 1956; MA, Stanford U., 1959. Adminstrv. asst. Calif. Assn. Ins. Agts., Berkeley, 1960-62; fin. writer The San Diego Union, 1962-68; asst. editor Bus. Week, Los Angeles, 1968-71; fin. editor The Honolulu Advertiser, 1971—. Bd. dirs. Pacific Found. for Cancer Research, Honolulu, 1984—. Served to lt. j.g., USNR, 1956-58. Recipient first prize media awards for econ. understanding Dartmouth Amos Tuck Sch., 1978. Mem. Soc. Profl. Journalists. Office: The Honolulu Advertiser 605 Kapiolani Blvd Honolulu HI 96813

SMITH, CRAIG SCOTT, internist, endocrinologist; b. San Francisco, July 16, 1951; s. Edward Joseph and Marjorie Loreen (Bruce) S.; m. Terri Ann Hughes, June 19, 1982; children: Rachel Deanna, Jessica Danielle. BS, Stanford U., 1973; MD, UCLA, 1977. Diplomate Am. Bd. Internal Medicine, Am. Bd. Endocrinology and Metabolism. Intern U. Calif. Med. Ctr., Davis, 1977-78, resident in internal medicine, 1978-80, fellow in endocrinology, 1980-82, asst. clin. prof. internal medicine, 1982—; practice medicine specializing in endocrinology and internal medicine Sacramento, 1982—. Mem. Calif. Med. Assn., Sacramento Soc. Internal Medicine, Sacramento-El Dorado Med. Soc. Office: Med Clinic Sacramento 3160 Folsom Blvd Sacramento CA 95816

SMITH, CYNTHIA GLYNN, data processor; b. Florence, Ala., Dec. 5, 1953; d. James Robert Smith and Evelyn (Dickinson) Riggs; m. Jerry Collins Scott, July 19, 1984. BS, Mid. Tenn. State U., 1976. Cert. data processor. Programmer, analyst mfg. systems SCI Systems, Inc., Huntsville, Ala., 1980-82, United Space Boosters, Inc., Huntsville, 1982-83; software engr. TRW, Inc., Huntsville, 1983-84; lead software engr. Lockheed Space Ops., Titusville, Fla., 1984-85; project leader for logistics Rockwell Internat., L.A. and El Segundo, Calif., 1985-87; project leader, data base analyst for logistics systems Northrop Co., L.A., 1987-89, Pico Rivera, Calif., 1987-89; programed analyst Am. Software Inc., Atlanta, 1989—. Named Young Careerist Lincoln County Bus. and Profl. Women, 1982, One of Outstanding Young Women of Am., 1982; recipient NASA Group Achievement award, 1984. Mem. Am. Prodn. and Inventory Control Soc. (cert.), Soc. Logistics Engrs., Nat. Mgmt. Assn. Home: 4131 Lincoln Ave Culver City CA 90230 Office: Am Software Inc 470 E Paces Ferry Rd NE Atlanta GA 30907

SMITH, CYNTHIA LEA, personnel and benefits administrator, consultant; b. Boise, Idaho, May 26, 1953; d. Ivan George and Artis Lavora (Shaw Bethel; m. Patrick J. Rutledge, May 11, 1972 (div. Aug. 1979); 1 child, Heidi; m. Jerry W. Smith, Dec. 5, 1981; 1 child, Nicole M. Student, Boise State U., 1971-83, 87-88. Owner, mgr. Fantasy Arts Co., Boise, 1975-77; sec., asst. Oppenheimer Cos., Boise, 1977-79; adminstrv. sec Foodways Nat., Inc. div. Gagliardi Bros., Inc., Boise, 1979-81, benefits adminstr., 1982--, personnel adminstr., 1985--; owner, operator N.W. Benefits Consulting, 1988--. Adv., bd. dirs. Child Care Connections, Boise, 1988--. Mem. Human Resource Assn. Treasure Valley. Home: 10612 W Treeline Ct Boise ID 83704 Office: Foodways Nat Inc 345 Bobwhite Ct Boise ID 83706

SMITH, D. DAVID, chamber of commerce executive; b. Bargesville, Ind., July 10, 1928; s. Donald Edgar and Velva (Whitehead) S.; m. Rachel Irene Maddux, Sept. 4, 1951; children: D. Gregory, Elizabeth A. BS in Bus., Ind. U., 1950. Asst. mgr. San Leandro (Calif.) C. of C., 1956-60; exec. mgr. Woodland (Calif.) C. of C., 1960-65; exec. v.p. Stockton (Calif.) C. of C., 1965—. Pres. Pvt. Industry Council, Stockton, 1981, Jr. Achievement San Joaquin, Stockton, 1986—, Stockton Hall of Fame Assn., 1985-86. Served to sgt. USAF, 1951-55. Named Stocktonian of Yr., Stockton Bd. Realtors, 1974. Mem. Calif. Assn. C. of C. Execs. (pres. 1971). Republican. Home: 1421 W Alpine Stockton CA 95204 Office: Greater Stockton C of C 445 W Weber Ave Ste 220 Stockton CA 95203 *

SMITH, DAVID ALLEN, insurance company executive; b. Hunstsville, Ala., Aug. 1, 1943; s. Clarence Theodore and Bernice (Snell) Smith; m. Michelle Haviland McCaffrey, June 1, 1964; 1 child, Eric Michael. BA, Calif. State U., L.A., 1969. Mgr. Allstate Ins. Co., L.A., 1969-81; v.p. Nat. Am. Ins. Co., Long Beach, Calif., 1982-86, First Calif. Property & Casualty Ins., Calabasas, Calif., 1987—; cons. various ins. cos. and law firms. Contbr. numerous environmental and outdoor articles. Vice chmn. Boy Scouts Am., L.A.; instr. ARC, Pasadena; vol. U.S. Forest Service, Angeles Nat. Forest, L.A. Recipient Silver Beaver award, Boy Scouts Am., L.A., 1986, award of merit, 1983, vigil honor, 1980; Vol. Service award, U.S. Forest Service, 1987. Mem. Blue Goose Internat. Republican. Presbyterian. Home: 961 Micheltorena St Los Angeles CA 90026 Office: First Calif P&C Ins 23621 Park Sorrento Calabasas CA 91302

SMITH, DAVID ASHER, data processing executive; b. Bklyn., Dec. 3, 1946; s. Samuel Harry and Adelle (Seftel) S.; m. Barbara Joan Suntup, Sept. 29, 1974 (div. May 1981); m. Rita Carol Patterson, Oct. 20, 1985. BS in Psychology, CCNY, 1977; MBA, San Jose State U., 1988. Programmer/analyst Control Data Corp., Sunnyvale, Calif., 1978-80; owner, operator Pet Way, San Jose, 1980-82; mgr. software Heald Bus. Coll., San Jose, 1982; mgr. data processing ICORE, Sunnyvale, 1982-84; software analyst Fairchild Research Ctr., Mountain View, Calif., 1985-86; software project mgr. Oximetrix, Mountain View, Calif., 1987—; owner, operator IDS, Campbell, Calif., 1987—; co-founder, treas Bay Area Mapics Users Group, San Francisco, 1984-85. Youth leader Friends Outside, San Jose, 1978—; chmn. Bikkur Cholim, San Jose, 1987—. Democrat. Jewish. Lodge: Optimists (pres. Palo Alto, Calif. chpt. 1986-87). Home and Office: 235 N Second St Campbell CA 95008

SMITH, DAVID ELVIN, physician; b. Bakersfield, Calif., Feb. 7, 1939; s. Elvin W. and Dorothy (McGinnis) S.; m. Millicent Buxton; children: Julia, Suzanne, Christopher Buxton, Christopher Buxton-Smith. Intern San Francisco Gen. Hosp., 1965; fellow pharmacology and toxicology U. Calif., San Francisco, 1965-67, assoc. clinical prof. occupational health and clinical toxicology, 1967—, dir. psychopharmacology study group, 1966-70; practice medicine specializing in toxicology and addictionology San Francisco, 1965—; physician Presbyn. Alcoholic Clinic, 1965-67, Contra Cost Alcoholic Clinic, 1965-67; dir. alcohol and drug abuse screening unit San Francisco Gen. Hosp., 2967-68; co-dir. Calif drug abuse info. project U Calif Med. Ctr., 1967-72; founder, med. dir. Haight-Ashbury Free Med. Clinic, San Francisco, 1967—; research dir. Merritt Peralta Chem. Dependency Hosp., Oakland, Calif., 1984—; chmn. Nat. Drug Abuse Conf., 1977; mem. Calif. Gov's. Commn. on Narcotics and Drug Abuse, 1977—; nat. health adviser to former U.S. Pres. Jimmy Carter; dir. Benzodiazepine Research and Tng. Project, Substance Abuse and Sexual Concerns Project, PCP Research and Tng. Project; cons. numerous fed. drug abuse agys. Author: Love Needs Care, 1970, The New Social Drug: Cultural, Medical and Legal Perspectives on Marijuana, 1971, The Free Clinic: Community Approaches to Health Care and Drug Abuse, 1971, Treating the Cocaine Abuser, 1985, The Benzodiazepines: Current Standard Medical Practice, 1986, Physicians' Guide to Drug Abuse, 1987; co-author: It's So Good, Don't Even Try it Once: Heroin in Perspective, 1972, Uppers and Downers, 1973, Drugs in the Classroom, 1973, Barbiturate Use and Abuse, 1977, A Multicultural View of Drug Abuse, 1978, Amphetamine Use, Misuse and Abuse, 1979, PCP: Problems and Prevention, 1981, Sexological Aspects of Substance Use and Abuse, Treatment of the Cocaine Abuser, 1985, The Haight Ashbury Free Medical Clinic: Still Free After all these Years, Drug Free: Alternatives to Drug Abuse, 1987, Treatment of Opiate Dependence, Designer Drugs, 1988, Treatment of Cocaine Dependence, 1988, Treatment of Opiate Dependence, 1988, others; also drug edn. films; founder, editor Jour. Psychedelic Drugs (now Jour. Psychoactive Drugs), 1967—; contbr. over 100 articles to profl. jours. Pres. Youth Projects, Inc.; founder, chmn. bd., pres. Nat. Free Clin. Council, 1968-72. Recipient Research award Borden Found., 1964, AMA Research award, 1966, Community Service award U. Calif. at San Francisco, 1974, Calif. State Drug Abuse Treatment award, 1984, Vernelle Fox Drug Abuse Treatment award, 1985. Mem. AMA (alt. del.), Am. Med. Soc. for Treatment of Alcoholism and Other Drug Dependencies, San Francisco Med. Soc., Am. Pub. Health Assn., Calif. Soc. Treatment of Alcohol and other Drug Dependencies (pres., bd. dirs.), Sigma Xi, Phi Beta Kappa. Methodist. Home: 289 Frederick St San Francisco CA 94131 Office: 409 Clayton St San Francisco CA 94117

SMITH, DAVID REEDER, physicist; b. Murray, Utah, Nov. 1, 1938; s. Clinton and Rhea (Reeder) S.; m. Kathleen M. Price, July 12, 1963; children: Tavian, Jared, Braniff. BS, U. Utah, 1963; MS, Purdue U., 1966, PhD, 1969. Asst. prof. S.D. Sch. of Mines and Tech., Rapid City, 1969-78, assoc. prof., 1978-87; vis. scientist Nat. Bur. Standards, Boulder, Colo., 1978-80, physicist, 1987—. Co-editor: Thermal Conductivity 18, 1985. NASA fellow, 1963-66. Mem. AAAS, Am. Assn. of Physics Tchrs., Am. Soc. for Testing and Materials, Sigma Xi. Republican. Mormon. Home: 1013 Alsace Way Lafayette CO 80026 Office: US Dept of Commerce NIST 325 Broadway Boulder CO 80303-3328

SMITH, DENNIS IVAN, electronics engineer; b. Great Falls, Mont., Mar. 12, 1952; s. Ivan Herbert and Shirley Jean (Erickson) S.; m. Suzanne Elizabeth Brown, May 21, 1976; children: Aaron Gregory, Nathan Andrew, Rebecca Lynn, Timothy Alexander, Walter Montgomery. BSEE, Mont. State U., 1974, MSEE, 1975. Design engr. Tektronix Inc., Beaverton, Oreg., 1974-84, sr. engr., 1984—. Home: 2220 SE Maple St Hillsboro OR 97123 Office: Tektronix Inc PO Box 500 MS 58-204 Beaverton OR 97077

SMITH, DENNY, congressman; b. Ontario, Oreg., Jan. 19, 1938; children: Maggie, Barrett, Ryan. B.A. in Polit. Sci., Willamette U., Salem, Oreg., 1961. Chmn. bd. Eagle Newspapers Inc.; co-pilot, flight engr. Pan Am. World Airways, 1967-76; mem. 97th-101st Congresses from 5th Oreg. Dist., 1981—; mem. house budget com., mil. reform caucus. Mem. exec. com. Nat. Republican Congl. Com. Served with USAF, 1965-66, Vietnam. Decorated Air medal with six oak leaf clusters. Mem. Vietnam Vets. Caucus, Oreg. Newspaper Pubs. Assn., Nat. Newspaper Assn., Young Pres. Orgn., Associated Oreg. Industries, Aircraft Owners and Pilots Assn., Beta Theta Pi. Office: Longworth House Office Bldg Rm 1213 Washington DC 20515 *

SMITH, DON CROSTON, JR., lawyer, publishing executive; b. Dodge City, Kans., Nov. 24, 1953; s. Don C. and Joyce (Harrison) S. BS in Journalism, U. Kans., 1976; JD, Washburn U., 1979. Bar: Kans. 1979, U.S. Dist. Ct. Kans. 1979. Asst. press sec. Gov. John Carlin, Topeka, 1979-81; assoc. Schmidt, O'Sullivan & Langley, Hutchinson, Kans., 1981; legal editor Shepard's/McGraw-Hill, Colorado Springs, 1982-85, sr. editor, 1985-87, mng. editor electronic pub., 1987, mgr. electronic pub., 1988—. Co-author: Handling Pregnancy and Birth Cases, 1983; contbg. author: Abortion, Medicine and the Law, 1986. Bd. dirs. Colo. Common Cause, 1985—, Penrose Hosp. Human Rights Com., Colorado Springs, 1986—. Mem. ABA, Phi Beta Kappa, Phi Kappa Phi. Democrat. Home: 1618 W Cheyenne Blvd Colorado Springs CO 80906 Office: Shepard's/McGraw Hill 420 N Cascade St Colorado Springs CO 80903

SMITH, DONALD E., broadcast engineer, manager; b. Salt Lake City, Sept. 10, 1930; s. Thurman A. and Louise (Cardall) S.; B.A. Columbia Coll., Chgo., 1955; B.S.; U. Utah, 1970; postgrad. U. So. Calif., U. Utah, PhD (hon.) Columbia Coll., 1985; m. Helen B. Lacy, 1978. Engr., Iowa State U., (WOI-TV), 1955-56; asst. chief engr. KLRJ-TV, Las Vegas, 1956-60; studio field engr. ABC, Hollywood, Cal., 1960; chief engr. Teletape, Inc., Salt Lake City, 1961; engring. supr. KUER, U. Utah, Salt Lake City, 1962—, gen. mgr., 1975-85. Free lance cinematography, 1950—; cons. engr. radio and TV prodns., 1965—. Mem. Soc. Motion Pictures and TV Engrs., Lambda Chi Alpha. Home: 963 Hollywood Ave Salt Lake City UT 84105

SMITH, DONALD EVANS, library consultant; b. Shenandoah, Iowa, Dec. 2, 1915; s. William Wesley and Bess Alice (Evans) S.; student Ricks Coll., 1939-40; BA, Hastings Coll., 1946; MLS, U. Wash., 1964. Tchr. English, librarian Tenino (Wash.) High Sch., 1950-51, Rochester (Wash.) High Sch., 1954-59; librarian North Thurston High Sch., Lacey, Wash., 1959-67; head librarian, coord. instructional materials Lakes High Sch., Lakewood Ctr., Wash., 1967-80; library cons., 1980—. Mem. awards com. Wash. Library Commn., 1964-66. With Signal Corps, AUS, 1942-45; to 1st lt., M.I., U.S. Army, 1951-54; to col. Wash. State Guard, 1971-80, now ret. Mem. Wash. Assn. Sch. Librarians (com. chmn.), Clover Park Edn. Assn. (com. chmn. 1970-71), Am. Legion, Phi Delta Kappa (del. nat. confs.). Home and Office: 4530 26th Loop SE Lacey WA 98503

SMITH, DONALD RICHARD, editor, publisher; b. Stockton, Calif., Aug. 20, 1932; s. Robert Gordon and Gertrude (Schweitzer) S.; m. Darlene Ruth Thomas, May 7, 1961; children: Douglas Robert, Deborah Renae. Student, Coll. Pacific, 1951, Delta Coll., 1951-52. Editor, pub. Calif. Odd Fellow & Rebekah, Linden, 1950—; editor Elk Grove (Calif.) Citizen, 1953-55; asst. dir. U.N. Pilgrimage for Youth, N.Y.C., 1956-59; editor, pub. Linden (Calif.) Herald, 1959-86, Lockeford (Calif.)-Clements Post, 1960-62, Internat. Rebekah News, Linden, 1963-86, INternat. Odd Fellow & Rebekah, Linden, 1986—. Author: From Stagestop to Friendly Community, 1976, Leadership Manual, 1980. Bd. dirs. Odd Fellow-Rebekah Youth Camp, Inc., Long Barn, Calif., 1959-61; chmn. Linden Rep. Com., 1962-66, Linden Centennial Observance, 1963, Linden Mcpl. Council, 1981—. Recipient Legion of Honor Order of Demolay, 1961, John R. Williams award S.J. Tchrs. Assn., 1963, 87, Golden Key award Stockton Tchrs. Assn., 1971, Achievement award County Bd. Suprs., 1970, Citizen of Yr. award Lions Internat., 1982. Mem. IOOF Internat. Press Assn., Internat. Press Assn. (pres. 1962-63), Desktop Pub. Assn., Boston Computer Soc., Linden Peters C. of C. (pres. 1968-69), S.J. Hist. Soc. (trustee 1986—). Methodist. Lodges: Lions, Odd Fellows (Calif.) (grand master 1958-59), Odd Fellows Internat. (sovereign grand master 1969-70). Home: 5350 N Harrison St Linden CA 95236 Office: Linden Publ 19033 E Main PO Box 129 Linden CA 95236

SMITH, DONNA, mayor, small business owner; b. Upper Darby, Pa., July 19, 1954; d. Dave and Theresa (McAleer) Fekay; m. Robert Howard Smith Jr., Dec. 1, 1951; children: Robert H. III, Sean M., Terence J. Grad. high sch., Pomona, Calif., 1970. Mayor City of Pomona, 1987—; owner Pomona Generator Co., 1976—. Pres. Simons Jr. High Sch. PTA, 1983-85; pres., sec. Pomona Youth Sports Com., 1983-85; mem. City Coun. Dist. 3, Pomona, 1985-87; mem. Garey High Sch. Booster Club, 1985—; mem. Hispanic youth task force; mem. econ. and human devel. com. SCAG Community, 1985-87; mem. Pomona Cen. Bus. Dist.; mem. policy com. Rapid Transit Dist.; vice chairperson Tri-City Mental Health; mem. Pomona Valley handicapped and sr. citizens com.; mem. exec. bd. Teen Outreach, ARC; mem. Old Baldy Coun. Boy Scouts Am. Named Women Achiever of 1985, Humanitarian of Yr., 1986; recipient PTA Honorary Service award 1985, PTA Honorary Lifetime Service award 1986. Mem. Calif. Elected Women's Assn., Pomona Bus. and Profl. Women's Assn., Pomona Hist. Soc., Pomona C. of C. (legis. action com., edn. com., city affairs com.), Pomona Jaycees (Disting. Svc. award 1988), Kiwanis, Fraternal Order of Police, Women of Moose. Republican. Mem. Ch. of God. Office: City of Pomona Office of Mayor 505 S Garey Ave Pomona CA 91766

SMITH, DONNIE LOUISE, nurse; b. Mountain Home, Idaho, Aug. 14, 1952; d. Bernard Armour and Lillian Doris (Lazzari) S.; children: Daniel Taylor, Drew Thomas. AA in Nursing, Solano Community Coll., 1973. RN, Calif. Staff nurse Woodland (Calif.) Clinic Med. Group, 1973-74, 79; office nurse Gaing W. Chan, MD, West Sacramento, Calif., 1974-76; staff nurse med.-surg. and critical care unit Woodland Meml. Hosp., 1976-79; staff nurse coronary care unit Santa Barbara (Calif.) Cottage Hosp., 1979-80; charge nurse critical care unit Northbay Med. Ctr., Fairfield, Calif., 1981-84, endoscopy nurse specialist, 1984-87; clin. coord. Sacramento Autologous Svc. Inc., Sacramento, 1987—. Mem. Rescue Now, Sacramento, 1985—. Recipient appreciation award Northbay Med. Ctr., 1987. Mem. Soc. Gastrointestinal Assts., Solano Community Coll. Profl. Registered Nurse Alumni (sec. 1986—). Democrat. Roman Catholic. Office: Sacramento Autologous Svc 225 30th St Sacramento CA 95816

SMITH, DWIGHT MORRELL, university chancellor, chemist; b. Hudson, N.Y., Oct. 10, 1931; s. Elliott Monroe and Edith Helen (Hall) S.; m. Alice Beverly Bond, Aug. 27, 1955; children—Karen Elizabeth, Susan Allison, Jonathan Aaron. B.A., Central Coll., Pella, Iowa, 1953; Ph.D., Pa. State U., 1957; ScD (hon.), Cen. Coll., 1986. Postdoctoral fellow, instr. Calif. Inst. Tech., 1957-59; sr. chemist Texaco Research Center, Beacon, N.Y., 1959-61; asst. prof. chemistry Wesleyan U., Middletown, Conn., 1961-66; asso. prof. Hope Coll., Holland, Mich., 1966-69; prof. Hope Coll., 1969-72; prof., chmn. dept. chemistry U. Denver, 1972-83, vice chancellor for acad. affairs, 1983-84, chancellor, 1984—. Editor Revs. on Petroleum Chemistry, 1975-78; contbr. articles to profl. jours.; patentee selective hydrogeneration. Chmn. Chs. United for Social Action, Holland, Mich., 1968-69; mem. Sch. Bd. Adv. Com., Holland, 1969-70; bd. commrs. Colo. Advanced Tech. Inst., 1984—; mem. adv. bd. United Way, Girl Scouts U.S., Freedoms Found. at Valley Forge, Inst. Internat. Edn., Jr. Achievement. DuPont fellow, 1956-57; NSF fellow Scripps Inst., 1971-72; recipient grants Research Corp., grants Petroleum Research Fund, grants NSF, grants Solar Energy Research Inst.; mem. ch. bds. or consistories Reformed Ch. Am., N.Y., Conn., Mich. Mem. Am. Chem. Soc. (chmn. Colo. 1976, sec. Western Mich. 1970-71, Colo. sect. award 1986), AAAS, Catalysis Soc., Soc. Applied Spectroscopy, Sigma Xi. Clubs: Denver; University (N.Y.); Metropolitan. Home: 7 Sunset Ln Littleton CO 80121 Office: U Denver Office of Chancellor 2301 S Gaylord St Denver CO 80208

SMITH, ED, photographic illustrator, consultant; b. Norfolk, Va., Nov. 14, 1937; s. Edgar Webster Summers and Ruby Evelyn (Stubbs) S.; m. Joanna Marie Sunseri, Sept. 15, 1964 (div. Dec. 1980); m. Georgia Lee Hartwell, June 21, 1986. Student, Johnson's Art Sch., Washington, 1961, Brook's Sch., Santa Barbara, Calif., 1970. Photographer, newspaper stringer Key West, Fla., 1952-54; freelance mag. photographer Arlington, Va., 1959-64; photographer Smith's Studio, Santa Barbara, 1964-70; dir., instr. Photo Illustration, Santa Barbara, 1970-74; owner, mgr. Ed Smith, Everett, Wash., 1974--; cons. Photonet, Osceola, Wis., 1981--, COMPU/PIX/Rental, Woodland Hills, Calif., 1981--. Capt. USAF, 1955-59. Mem. Internat. Soc. Photog. Illustrators (bd. dirs. Everett chpt. 1984--), Assoc. Photographers Internat. (Best of Yr. award 1983, 85, Merit award 1985, 87), Everett C. of C. Democrat. Buddhist. Office: 420 85th Pl SW Ste L-206 Everett WA 98204

SMITH, EDWARD CUTRER, physicist, engineer, consultant; b. Memphis, Sept. 19, 1922; s. Edward White and Blanche Clark (Cutrer) S.; m. Harriet Amanda Noel, Sept. 12, 1953; children: Walter Edward, Oscar Noel; stepson, Robert Tee Groom III. BA, U. Va., 1944, PhD, 1950. Physicist Oak Ridge (Tenn.) Nat. Lab., 1950-55; staff scientist Lockheed Ga. Co., Marietta, 1955-62; sr. scientist Advanced Research Corp., Atlanta, 1962-64, Hughes Aircraft Co., El Segundo, Calif., 1964-85; sr. staff engr. TRW-Def. Systems Group, Redondo Beach, Calif., 1985-88; cons. San Diego, 1988—. Contbr. articles to profl. jours. Lt. USNR, 1943-46. Mem. IEEE, Phi Beta Kappa, Sigma Xi. Republican. Episcopalian.

SMITH, ELVIN T., communications executive; b. Aztec, N.M., June 30, 1930; s. Orville V. and E. Avisa (Townsend) S.; m. Elaine C. Andersen, May 21, 1959; children: Eric T., Ellen C. BA, Ft. Lewis Coll., 1956. Sales exec. Sta. KOAT-TV, Albuquerque, 1962-75, sales mgr., 1975—; owner W.A. Group, Albuquerque, 1980-88. Photo dir. TV program Sandia Tram, 1970. Dir. Crime Stoppers, Albuquerque, 1988. Office: Sta KOAT-TV 3801 Carlisle NE Albuquerque NM 87107

SMITH, ERNEST EDWARD, taxi company executive, taximeter repairman; b. Little Rock, Aug. 25, 1944; s. Ernest Edward and Madelyn (Davis) S.; m. Paula Ann Scott, May 1, 1965; children: Michael Paul, Michelle Leann. Student, Riverside (Calif.) City Coll., 1966, Valley Coll., San Bernardino, Calif., 1967. Aircraft mechanic USAF, Calif. and Guam, 1962-66; silverbrazier Bourns Instruments, Riverside, 1966-68; foreman Loma Linda (Calif.) U., 1968-74; owner Paradise Taxi Co., Kailua-Kona, Hawaii, 1974—. Served with USAF, 1962-66. Recipient Best Taxi Service award Bartenders Ocean Breeze, Kailua-Kona, 1985. Republican. Seventh-Day Adventist. Home: 75-221 Aloha Kona Dr Kailua-Kona HI 96745 Office: Paradise Taxi PO Box 1715 Kailua-Kona HI 96740

SMITH, ERNEST KETCHAM, electrical engineer; b. Peking, China, May 31, 1922; (parents Am. citizens); s. Ernest Ketcham and Grace (Goodrich) S.; m. Mary Louise Standish, June 23, 1950; children: Priscilla Varland, Nancy Smith, Cynthia Jackson. BA in Physics, Swarthmore Coll., 1944; MSEE, Cornell U., 1951, Ph.D., 1956. Chief plans and allocations engr. Mut. Broadcasting System, 1946-49; with Nat. Bur. Standards, 1951-65; chief ionosphere research sect. Nat. Bur. Standards, Boulder, Colo., 1957-60; div. chief Nat. Bur. Standards, 1960-65; dir. aeronomy lab. Environ. Sci. Services Adminstrn., Boulder, 1965-67; dir. Inst. Telecommunication Scis., 1968, dir. univ. relations, 1968-70; assoc. dir. Inst. Telecommunications Scis. Office of Telecommunications, Boulder, 1970-72, cons., 1972-76; mem. tech. staff Jet Propulsion Lab. Calif. Inst. Tech., Pasadena, 1976-87; adj. prof. dept. Electrical Engring. U. Colo., Boulder, 1987—; vis. fellow Coop. Inst. Research on Environ. Scis., 1968; assoc. Harvard U. Coll. Obs., 1965-75; adj. prof. U. Colo., 1969-78, 87—; internat. vice-chmn. study group 6, Internat. Radio Consultative Com., 1958-70, chmn. U.S. study group, 1970-76; mem. U.S. commn. Internat. Sci. Radio Union, mem.-at-large U.S. nat. com., 1985—. Author: Worldwide Occurrence of Sporadic E, 1957; (with S. Matsushita) Ionospheric Sporadic E, 1962. Contbr. numerous articles to profl. jours. Editor: Electromagnetic Probing of the Upper Atmosphere, 1969. Served with U.S. Army, 1944-45. Recipient Diploma d'honneur, Internat. Radio Consultative Com., Internat. Telecommunications Union, 1978. Fellow IEEE, AAAS; mem. Am. Geophys. Union, Svc. Club, Kiwanis. Mem. United Ch. of Christ. Clubs: Harvard Faculty; University (Boulder); Athenaeum (Pasadena); Boulder Country. Home: 5159 Idylwild Trail Boulder CO 80301 Office: U Colo Dept Electrical Engring Campus Box 425 Boulder CO 80309

SMITH, EUGENE HERBERT, English professor; b. Framingham, Mass., Feb. 23, 1927; s. Hernert E. and Ida (Mills) S.; m. Marcia Miller, June 23, 1951; children: Sheila, Kenna, Maynard, Bradley, Naomi. BA, Oberlin Coll., 1950; MA, U. Wash., 1953, PhD, 1964. Tchr. Milton-Freewater (Oreg.) Sch. Dist., 1951-53, Longview (Wash.) Sch. Dist., 1954-58; rsch. coord. Office of Supt. Publ., Olympia, Wash., 1959-60; prof. U. Wash., Seattle, 1961—. Author: Teacher Preparation in Composition, (with others) Attitudes, Language and Change; contbr. articles to profl. jours. Sgt. U.S. Army, 1945-47. Recipient Eugene Smith Disting. Svc. award, Wash. State Council Tchrs. English. Mem. Nat. Council Tchrs. English (com. chairperson 1987—), Wash. State Council Tchrs. English (pres. 1964-65, 80-82). Democrat. Home: 2205 22d East Seattle WA 98112

SMITH, FORREST RANDALL, data processing executive; b. St. Charles, Ill., Mar. 27, 1951; s. Darrell Lemoine and Ruth Lavon (Jones) S.; m. Judith Ann Hollenbeck, May 29, 1969; 1 child, Denise Renee. Student, Parks Sch. Bus., 1969-70. Mgr. Gigantic Cleaners, Denver, 1969-70; with distbn. svcs. Kan-Nebr. Nat. Gas Co., Holdrege, Nebr., 1970-73; programmer, analyst Kan-Nebr. Nat. Gas Co., Phillipsburg, Kans., 1973-75; supr. property systems Fresno (Calif.) County, 1975-83; asst. v.p. application systems Gesco Corp., Fresno, 1983-86, v.p. application systems, 1986—. Democrat. Office: FIserv 1455 E Shaw Ave Fresno CA 93710

SMITH, FRAN KELLOGG, architectural lighting designer; b. Chgo., Oct. 28, 1940; d. James Hull and Jean Mathieson (Defrees) Kellogg; m. Frederick John Bertolone, July 3, 1976; children by previous marriages—Wayne E. McConnell III, Carol Jean McConnell, Scott Kellogg McConnell, Christina L. Smith. B.A., Pomona Coll., 1966; postgrad., Claremont Grad. Sch., 1966-68; B.S. in Interior Design, Woodbury U., 1973. Ptnr., lighting designer Omnia, Los Angeles, 1970-71; staff lighting cons. Black, Swarens & Okada, Los Angeles, 1972-73; founder, owner, operator Luminae Lighting Cons., Los Angeles, 1973-76; chmn. bd. Luminae Inc., Los Angeles and San Francisco, 1976-84; instr. interior design cert. program UCLA, 1980—, U. Calif., Berkeley, 1986; guest lectr. various seminars throughout U.S. Author: Bringing Interiors to Light, 1986; contbr. articles to Designers West, Miami Herald, Chgo. Tribune, Home Lighting and Accessories, New Shelter. Designer low voltage luminaire (Pacifica cert. of merit 1980). Author: Bringing Interiors to Light, 1986. Founder, charter pres. service sect. Faculty Wives Club, Calif. State U., Los Angeles, 1967, v.p., 1969; bd. dirs. Villa Esperanza Sch. for Retarded, Pasadena, Calif., 1969-72. Recipient 1st place award Los Angeles Art and Antiques Show, 1970, 2d place award Nat. Soc. Interior Designers, 1972, 1st place award for instns. Inst. Bus. Designers, 1974. Mem. Am. Soc. Interior Designers (2d place Halo award 1980, bd. dirs. No. Calif. 1980-81, liaison to Interior Designer Educators council 1981-83, Presdl. citation 1984, Chpt. citation 1985, del. to Nat. Council Interior Design Qualifications 1984-86), AIA (chpt. affiliate), Designers Lighting Forum (founder, charter pres. Los Angeles chpt. 1972-74), Internat. Assn. Lighting Designers, Illumination Engring. Soc. (CASI award 1976, Sol Cohn award 1984), Interior Design Eudcators Council (hon. life). Republican. Episcopalian. Club: Los Angeles Athletic. Home: 315 Orange St San Gabriel CA 91776 Office: Luminae 555 De Haro San Francisco CA 94107

SMITH, FRANK DOUGLAS, protective services official; b. Chgo., Dec. 10, 1949; s. Frank Morris and Evelyn (Bergstrom) S. Installer Western Electric Co., Chgo., 1968-74; adminstrv. asst. Calif. Plant Protection Security Systems, Elmhurst, Ill., 1974-78; supervisory agt. U.S. Border Patrol, Yuma, Ariz., 1978—. Served as sgt. U.S. Army, 1970-72. Republican. Office: US Border Patrol 350 1st St Yuma AZ 85364

SMITH, GAROLD DAVID, JR., architect-engineer; b. Colorado Springs, Colo., July 4, 1936; s. Garold David and Helen Louise (Sopko) S.; B.S., U. Colo. in Archtl. Engring., 1968; M.Arch., U. Colo., Denver, 1989; m. Mary Louise Mills, July 4, 1959; children—April Marie-Francine, Heather Anne-Elizabeth, Tiffanie Louise, Garold David III. Lic architect, Colo., N.Mex., Tex.; registered profl. engr., Colo., Tex. Prin., Garold D. Smith Jr., Colorado Springs, 1970-73; project coordinator architect, assoc. Page, Southerland & Page, med. cons., Austin, Tex., 1973-76; prin. Garold D. Smith Jr., AIA, Architect, Structural Engr., Passive Solar Cons., Colorado Springs, 1977-83; pres. Garold D. Smith, Jr. and Assocs., P.C.; 1983—; instr. Bemis Art Sch., 1980—. Bd. dirs. Colorado Springs Regional Bldg. Dept. Plumbing Com., 1979-83, Colorado Springs Fire Bd. Appeals, 1983-88. Mem. NSPE, AIA (past pres. S. Colo. chpt., sec. Colo. Soc. Architects 1983), Internat. Solar Energy Soc., Constrn. Specifications Inst., Internat. Platform Assn. Republican. Roman Catholic. Lodge: Sertoma. Home: 1213 High Point Lane E Colorado Springs CO 80904 Office: 102 E Pikes Peak Ste 306 Colorado Springs CO 80903

SMITH, GARY ANDERSON, state official; b. Monroe, Mich., Dec. 18, 1948; s. Grant Ulysses and Elsie Marie (Hayes) S.; m. Deborah Lynn Rod, Feb. 8, 1968 (div. 1975); children: Angela, Brian; m. Donna Lynn Hyatt, Dec. 29, 1978; children: Kristi Lundgren, Tracie Lundgren. AAS, Monroe County (Mich.) Community Coll., 1969; student, Glendale Community Coll., Ariz., 1983, Henry Ford Community Coll., Dearborn, Mich., 1973; BS in Engring., Ariz. State U., 1986. Electrician Ford Motor Co., Woodhaven, Mich., 1967-77; fire marshal Monroe Twp., 1973-75; safety tech. Uttly-James, Wyandotte, Mich., 1977-78; insp. II Ariz. Corp. Commn., Phoenix, 1979-81, utilities cons., 1981-84, chief pipeline safety, 1984-88, chief of safety, 1988—. Creator video tape: The Danger Beneath Us, 1985. Mem. ASTM, Nat. Assn. Pipeline Safety Reps., Nat. Assn. Regulatory Commrs., Nat. Assn. Corrosion Engrs., Nat. Fire Protection Assn. Democrat. Lutheran. Home: 4507 S Willow Dr Tempe AZ 85282 Office: Ariz Corp Commn 1200 W Washington Phoenix AZ 85007

SMITH, GARY RICHARD, software systems engineer, consultant; b. Salt Lake City, Nov. 30, 1952; s. Douglas Russell Smith and Orien Margaret (Anderson) Fairbanks; m. Lorie Lee Ingersoll, June 24, 1988. BEE, S.D. Sch. Mines and Tech., 1979, MEE, 1984; postgrad., U. Colo., Colorado Springs, 1984—. Test equipment engr. Collins Avionics, Cedar Rapids, Iowa, 1979-82; software systems engr. Tex. Instruments, Colorado Springs, 1984-87; software engr. CTA, Inc., Colorado Springs, 1987—. Served with USAF, 1972-76. Mem. IEEE, Assn. Computing Machinery, Mensa. Republican. Baptist. Office: CTA Inc 7150 Campus Dr Ste 100 Colorado Springs CO 80920

SMITH, GAYNL BEVERLY, hospice director, registered nurse; b. San Francisco, Nov. 19, 1940; d. Charles Homer and Gladys L. (Harvey) Smith; m. J. Vincent McCann, June 8, 1962 (div. May 1981); children: Kathleen Patricia, Kevin Patrick. RN, Johns Hopkins Hosp., 1962; BS, Johns Hopkins U., 1970; MDiv, San Francisco Theol. Sem., 1986. RN, Calif., Md. Asst. dir. nursing Washington Home for Incurables, 1971-73; staff nurse coronary care unit Doctors Hosp., Washington, 1973-74; dir. nursing Washington Home for Incurables, 1974; critical care float Sibley Meml. Hosp., Washington, 1975-83; RN, supr. Hillhaven Victorian Convalescent Hosp., San Francisco, 1984-87; chaplain Hospice, Contra Costa County Health Svcs., Martinez, Calif., 1984-85; nursing dir. and adminstr. Sisters of the Presentation Convent Infirmary, San Francisco, 1987-88; coord. symptoms control program Merrithew Meml. Hosp., Martinez, 1988—; mem. Concern for Dying, N.Y.C., 1985-89, AIDS Planning Com., Contra Costa County, Martinez, 1988-89, Bereavement Coalition, Contra Costa County, Concord, Calif., 1988-89; nursing cons. Sisters of the Presentation Convent Infirmary, San Francisco, 1988-89. Vice moderator Golden Gate Assn., United Ch. of Christ, San Francisco, 1986-87, First Congl. Ch., San Rafael, Calif., chair, 1988-89, pastor search com., 1987-89, min. of music, 1989—; active Girl Scouts, San Francisco, 1947-89. Mem. Assn. for Clin. Pastoral Edn., Oncology Nursing Soc., Am. Soc. on Aging, Found. Thanatology. Democrat. Office: Merrithew Meml Hosp Symptom Control Program 2500 Alhambra Ave Martinez CA 94553

SMITH, GENE CARLTON, aerospace engineer; b. York, Pa., Sept. 7, 1933; s. Charles Edward Jr. and Laretta May (Kohler) S.; m. Toshiko Niijima, June 7, 1960; children: Gene C. Jr., Sherry Mae. BS, BA, U. Redland, Redland, Calif., 1981. Radar tech. rep. Bendix, Can., Japan, Korea, 1957-63; computer engr. Bendix-Goddard Space Flight Ctr., Greenbelt, Md., 1963-64; experiment engr. Bendix-Mojave Sta., Barstow, Calif., 1964-75; operation mgr. Bendix-Application Tech. Satellite, Madrid, Spain, 1975-76; mgr., engr. Bendix-Oceangraphic System/PAC, Pearl Harbor, Hawaii, 1976-78; control ctr. mgr. Bendix-Deep Space Network, Pasadena, Calif., 1978-85; ops. engr. mgr. Bendix-Deep Space Network, Pasadena, 1985-87, sr. staff engr., 1987—. S/Sgt. USAF, 1953-56. Mem. Jaycees (chmn. Barstow chpt. 1968-70), Masons, Shriners. Republican. Lutheran. Home: 2837 Mataro St Pasadena CA 91107 Office: Bendix Field Engring Corp 1 Bendix Rd Columbia MD 21045

SMITH, GENEVIEVE GRANT, educational administrator; b. Meridian, Idaho, Dec. 3, 1922; d. Lawrence Jessie and Melitta Mae (Stiegelmeier) Grant; m. Jasper William Smith, Dec. 13, 1940; children—Lawrence Jasper, Lynda Jean, Eldon Howard, Stanley Dayle. AA, Boise Jr. Coll., 1957, BA, Northwest Nazarene Coll., 1964; MEd, Coll. Idaho, 1969. Classroom, vocal music tchr./coord. Boise (Idaho) Ind. Sch. Dist., 1957-73, adminstrv. team leader Lowell Sch., 1973-76; asst. prin. Garfield Sch., 1976-78; prin. Whitney Sch., 1978-85; dir. Capital Educators Fed. Credit Union, 1970-84, v.p., 1978-81, pres., 1981-84; co-founder 3 R's Found., reading workshops for tchrs. and parents; workshop instr., active dist., state edn. coms. Mem. Vista Neighborhood Housing Svcs.; chmn. supr. com. Capital Educators Fed. Credit Union, 1988-89, active Crisis Hot Line, active numerous fund-raising coms. Recipient Idaho Gem award Idaho Assn. Elem. Sch. Prins., Internat. Reading Assn. award, 1985, Spl. Svc. award Idaho State PTA, 1985, Life Merit award Idaho State PTA, Red Apple award Boise Sch. Dist., Boss of Yr. award Ada County Assn. Ednl. Office Personnel, 1983; named Disting. Citizen, Idaho Statesman Newspaper, 1985; grantee Title IV-C Match Program. Mem. Assn. Supervision and Curriculum Devel., Idaho Soc. Individual Psychology, Idaho Assn. Elem. Sch. Prins., Nat. Assn. Elem. Sch. Prins., Idaho Assn. Sch. Adminstrs., Boise Assn. Sch. Prins., Boise Edn. Assn., Idaho Edn. Assn., NEA, N.W. Women in Ednl. Adminstrn., Alumni Assn. Boise State U., Northwest Nazarene Coll. Assn., Yokefellows Assn., Ret. Tchrs. Assn. (v.p. 1988-89), NOW, Phi Delta Kappa, Delta Kappa Gamma, Phi Delta Lambda. Republican. Contbr. articles to local newspapers. Home: 2935 Caradoc Boise ID 83704

SMITH, GEORGE LARRY, analytical and environmental chemist; b. Beloit, Kans., Oct. 11, 1951; s. Richard Bailey and Vonda Ellene (Cox) S.; m. Charlene Janell Musgrove, Sept. 4, 1973; 1 child, Brian Lawrence. BA, Augustana Coll., 1973. Lab. technician Sanitary Dist. of Hammond, Ind., 1973; chemist Federated Metals Corp., Whiting, Ind., 1973-77; rsch. technician Air Pollution Technology, Inc., San Diego, 1978-80, environ. chemist, 1980-81, sr. tech. asst., 1981; staff chemist I Occidental Research Corp., Irvine, Calif., 1981-82, receiving chemist, 1982-84; processing chemist Chem. Waste Mgmt., Inc., Kettleman City, Calif., 1984-87, analytical chemist, 1987-89, wet analytical chemistry group leader, 1989—; lab. analyst for published article in environ. sci. and tech., 1981. bd. dirs. Apostolic Christian Missions, Inc., San Diego, 1978-82. Mem. Pentacostal Ch. Home: 205 E Merced Avenal CA 93204 Office: Chem Waste Mgmt Inc PO Box 471 Kettleman City CA 93239

SMITH, GERALD DAVID, labor relations professional; b. L.A., Dec. 9, 1932; s. George Joseph and Pearl (Zucker) S.; m. Rosita Cornell; children: Stuart Travis, Wenona Ann. BSc in Crop Sci., Calif. State U., Pomona, 1955; MBA, Calif. Western U., Santa Ana, 1976. Traffic mgr. Calif. Date Growers Assn., Indio, 1957-61; local office mgr. Calif. Dept. Employment, Blythe, 1961-76; dir. tng. and mgmt. consulting Agrl. Producers Assn., Valencia, Calif., 1976—; sec., Progressive Farmers, Blythe, 1963-76; bd. dirs., cons. Pacific Agricope, Blythe, 1976—. Author: Survival as a Farm Employer, 1976, Supervisor's Handbook: Citrus, 1978; patentee, melon harvester, citrus power chipper. Founder, pres. Palo Verde Day Care Ctr., Blythe, 1964-68; bd. dirs., sec. Soil Conservation Svc., Blythe, 1971-77; bd. dirs. Palo Verde Pub. Library, Blythe, 1986—. With U.S. Army, 1955-57. Kellogg Found. fellow, 1974. Mem. Agrl. Personnel Mgrs. Assn., Agrl. Leadership Assocs. (bd. dirs. 1974-77), Blythe C. of C. (bd. dirs. 1974-76). Republican. Home: 943 E Murphy St Blythe CA 92225 Office: Agrl Producers 25060 Stanford Ave Valencia CA 91355-3446

SMITH, GREGORY KENT, financial planner; b. Galesburg, Ill., Sept. 7, 1952; s. Ray Ira and Mary Helen (Mileham) S.; m. Debra Dee Vernon, Nov. 10, 1972; children: Gregory Trey, Casey Tyeler. AA in Acctg., Yavapai Community Coll., Prescott, Ariz., 1973; student, Coll. of the Canyon, Valencia, Calif., 1974-75, U. Calif., Long Beach, 1975; BS, U. Ariz., 1980. Acctg. technician VA, Prescott, 1972-73; canteen officer VA, Sepulveda, Calif. and Long Beach, 1973-76; sales rep. Philip Morris USA, Tucson, 1976-78; pres. Greg Smith & Assocs., Tucson, 1978—. Bd. dirs. Little League, Tucson, 1985-87. Served with U.S. Army, 1970-72, Vietnam. Decorated Flight Medal with "V" device; Cross of Gallantry, Presdl. Citation (Vietnam). Republican. Baptist. Lodge: Kiwanis (bd. dirs. Tucson club

1984-85). Home: 7841 N Paseo Monserrat Tucson AZ 85704 Office: Greg Smith & Assocs 4641 N 1st Ave Suite 1 Tucson AZ 85718

SMITH, HOWARD RUSSELL, manufacturing company executive; b. Clark County, Ohio, Aug. 15, 1914; s. Lewis Hoskins and Eula (Elder) S.; m. Jeanne Rogers, June 27, 1942; children: Stewart Russell, Douglas Howard, Jeanne Ellen Smith Akins. A.B., Pomona Coll., 1936. Security analyst Kidder, Peabody & Co., N.Y.C., 1936-37; economist ILO, Geneva, 1937-40; asst. to pres. Blue Diamond Corp., Los Angeles, 1940-46; pres., dir. Avery Internat. Corp., Pasadena, Calif., 1946-75, chmn. bd., 1975-84, chmn. exec. com., 1984—. Bd. dirs., past pres., chmn. Los Angeles Philharm. Assn.; bd. fellows Claremont Univ. Center; chmn. emeritus, bd. trustees Pomona Coll., Claremont, Calif.; past chmn. bd. Children's Hosp. Los Angeles, Community TV of So. Calif. (Sta. KCET), Los Angeles. With USNR, 1943-46. Home: 1458 Hillcrest Ave Pasadena CA 91106 Office: Avery Internat 150 N Orange Grove Blvd Pasadena CA 91103

SMITH, J. RICK, private investigator; b. Bethesda, Md., Sept. 10, 1951; s. James Elby and Margaret Rosalene (McCrobie) S.; m. Deborah Lynn Castania-Lloyd, Apr. 21, 1984; 1 child, Brittany Nicole. Student, Community Coll. Allegheny County, Monroeville, Pa.; cert. personnel mgmt., Community Coll. Allegheny County. Fugitive apprehension specialist Bail Bond Recovery Co., Pitts., 1974-81, Phoenix, 1981—; owner, operator G.S.I. Investigations, Phoenix, 1982—; terminal mgr. steel div. The Schreiber Systems Inc., Pitts., 1974-76, terminal mgr. air div., 1976-77, corp. nat. accounts mgr., 1977-79; exec. house security Hyatt Regency Corp., Phoenix, 1981; expert witness employers' personnel investigative matters and bail law. Mem. Ariz. Assn. Lic. Pvt. Investigators (editor state newsletter 1985-86, state treas. 1986, speaker's bur. chairperson 1986), West Valley Job Security Employers' Council (program chairperson 1988), Ariz. Employers' Council Inc. (assoc.), Nev. Assn. Lic. Investigators. Office: 4397 W Bethany Home Rd #1085 Glendale AZ 85301

SMITH, JACK, engineering educator, consultant; b. Morristown, N.J., Nov. 28, 1927; s. Samuel Smith; m. Charlene J. Smith; children: Suesanne, Charles. BSEE, U. Ariz., 1952, MSEE, 1958, PhD in Elec. Engring., 1964. Engr. Gen. Electric Co., N.Y.C., 1952-56; instr. U. Ariz., Tucson, 1956-64; assoc. prof. to prof. U. Tex., El Paso, 1964-86, asst. grad. dean, 1970-73, dean coll. engring., 1976-82; prof. Ariz. State U., Phoenix, 1986—; cons. Baltello Labs, U.S. Army. Contbr. articles to profl. jours.; inventor air borne instruments. With USN, 1945-48. Fellow NSF, Am. Soc. Engring. Edn.; mem. IEEE, Am. Soc. Engring. Edn., Am. Geophysical Union. Office: Ariz State U West Campus 2636 W Montebello Phoenix AZ 85023

SMITH, JAMES ALEXANDER, metal processing executive; b. Harvey, N.D., Jan. 16, 1926; s. James Kay MacKenzie and Palma Theresa (Johnson) S.; m. Cleo Lorraine, Sept. 1, 1948 (div. 1962); children: Deborah Kay Smith Hooper, Daryl Lynn Smith O'Neill, Darcey Amelia Smith Ryan; m. Louise Mae Hammer, July 21, 1979. BS, U. Minn., 1951. Ptnr., v.p. VIP, Phoenix, 1960-78; founder Therm-O-Low Inc., Phoenix, 1978-84; v.p., gen. mgr., founder and pres. 3XKryogenics, Phoenix, 1984-86; pres. Cryogenics Internat., Inc., Tempe, Ariz., 1987—; lectr. and speaker in field. Patentee in field. Staff sgt. U.S. Infantry, 1943-46, ETO, Japan. Mem. Soc. Mfg. Engrs. (Ariz. chpt. com. 1983, we. zone chmn. 1985), Pres.'s award 1984), Cryogenic Soc. Am., Am. Soc. Metals. Republican. Lutheran. Home: 4128 E Calle Redondo 73 Phoenix AZ 85018 Office: Cryogenics Internat Inc 915 S 52d St Ste 3 Tempe AZ 85281

SMITH, JAMES EDWARD, lawyer; b. Mpls., Mar. 13, 1952; s. James Edward Smith and Winifred Idella (Richardson) Flowers; m. Nancy Christine Gott, Feb. 14, 1974; children: Aria Denise, Beau Duncan. BA, U. Iowa, 1974; JD, U. San Diego, 1980. Bar: Calif. 1980, Nev. 1981, U.S. Dist. Ct. Nev. 1981, U.S. Ct. Appeals (9th cir.) 1982, U.S. Dist. Ct. (so. dist.) Calif., 1987. Law clk. to presiding judge Las Vegas, 1980-81; assoc. Harding & Dawson, Las Vegas, 1981-85; pvt. practice law Las Vegas, 1985—. Mem. allocations com., United Way, Las Vegas, 1989. Mem. Nat. Assn. Criminal Def. Lawyers (Nev. bar family law sect.), Clark County Bar Assn., Nev. Bar Assn., Calif. Bar Assn. Democrats. Office: 214 S Maryland Pkwy Las Vegas NV 89101

SMITH, JAMES EMORY, social worker, military officer; b. West Palm Beach, Fla., July 9, 1951; s. William Henry and Josephine (Everett) S. BA in Sociology with high honors, Hampton Inst., 1975; MSW, Va. Commonwealth U., 1977; M in Pub. Adminstrn., U. LaVerne, 1988. Lic. master social worker, Kans.; cert. clin. assoc. Social worker service to mil. families and vets. ARC, Richmond, Va., 1977-78; commd. 2d lt. U.S. Army, Ft. Riley, Kans., 1975; advanced through grades to maj. U.S. Army; unit social worker U.S. Army Retraining Brigade, Ft. Riley, 1978-80, asst. chief, social work div., 1980-82; chief community mental health U.S. Army, Ft. Greely, Alaska, 1982-83; chief army community service U.S. Army, Ft. Wainwright, Alaska, 1983-85, chief human resources div., 1985-86, dir. personnel and community activities, 1986, chief family support div., 1986-87; chief social work service Bassett Army Hosp., Ft. Wainwright, 1987-88; sr. social worker U.S. Army Correctional Activity, Ft. Riley, Kans., 1988-89, chief social work div., 1989—; field instr./adj. prof. dept. social work Kans. State U., Manhatten, 1979-82; field placement supr. social work, dept. psychology, sociology and social work U. Alaska, Fairbanks, 1983-84. Bd. dirs. Fairbanks Crisis Line, 1982-85, United Way of Greater Fairbanks, 1986-87. Recipient Expert Field Medical badge U.S. Army, 1981, Achievement medal U.S. Army, 1985. Fellow Menninger Found. (pres. council); mem. Nat. Assn. Social Workers, Acad. Cert. Social Workers (cert.), Nat. Assn. Black Social Workers, Va. Council on Social Welfare, Assn. of U.S. Army (bd. dirs. Polar Bear chpt. 1986-87), Nat. Soc. Scabbard and Blade, Soc. Hosp. Social Work Dirs., Am. Hosp. Assn., Nat. Network Social Work Mgrs. Club: Toastmasters (Tundra Talker chpt.).

SMITH, JANET MARIE, real estate executive; b. Jackson, Miss., Dec. 13, 1957; d. Thomas Henry and Nellie Brown (Smith) S. BArch, Miss. State U., 1981; MA in Urban Planning, CCNY, 1984. Draftsman Thomas H. Smith and Assocs. Architects, Jackson, Miss., 1979; mktg. coord. The Eggers Group, P.C. Architects and Planners, N.Y.C., 1980; program assoc. Ptnrs. for Livable Places, Washington, 1980-82; coord. asst. Lance Jay Brown, Architect and Urban Planner, N.Y.C., 1983-84; coord. architecture and design Battery Park City Authority, N.Y.C., 1982-84; pres., chief ops. officer Pershing Sq. Mgmt. Assn., L.A., 1985-89; dir. stadium lanning and devel. Balt. Orioles Meml. Stadium, 1989—; bd. dirs. Syska & Hennessy Inc., Engrs., N.Y.C., 1984—, Assn. Collegiate Schs. Architecture, Washington, 1979-82, Assn. Student Chpts. AIA, Washington, 1979-82. Guest editor: Urban Design Internat., 1985; assoc. editor: Crit, 1979-82; contbr. articles to profl. jours. Named Disting. Grad., Nat. Assn. State Univs. and Land Grant Colls., 1988, One of Outstanding Young Women of Am., 1982; recipient Spirit of Miss. award, Sta. WLBT, Jackson, 1987. Mem. AIA (assoc.), Urban Land Inst., Urban Design Adv. Coalition, So. Calif. Chpt. Soc. Archtl. Historians, L.A. Conservancy (docent), Toastmasters. Democrat. Episcopalian. Home: 3817 De Longpre Ave Los Angeles CA 90027-4729 Office: Balt Orioles Meml Stadium Baltimore MD 21218

SMITH, JEAN, interior design firm executive; b. Oklahoma City; d. A. H. and Goldy K. (Engle) Hearn; m. W. D. Smith, Dec. 2, 1939; children—Kaye Smith Hunt, Sidney P. Student Chgo. Sch. Interior Design, 1970. Vice pres. Billco-Aladdin Wholesale, Albuquerque, 1950—. Pres. Albuquerque Opera, 1979-83, advisor to bd. dirs.; active Civic Chorus, Cen. Meth. Ch.; pres. Inez PTA, 1954-55, life mem.; hon. life mem. Albuquerque Little Theater. Republican. Clubs: Albuquerque County, Four Hills Country, Daus. of the Nile (soloist Yucca Temple). Home: 1009 Santa Ana SE Albuquerque NM 87123 Office: Billco-Aladdin Wholesale 7617 Menaul NE Albuquerque NM 87123

SMITH, JEFF P., grocery and drug stores company executive; b. 1950. Attended, Utah State U. With Smith's Food & Drug Ctrs. (formerly Smith's Mgmt. Corp.), Salt Lake City, 1970—, v.p., then exec. v.p. purchasing ops. mktg., now pres., chief operating officer, dir. Office: Smith's Food & Drug Ctrs PO Box 30550 Salt Lake City UT 84104 *

SMITH, JEFFREY JOHN, public relations executive; b. Winchester, Mass., Apr. 28, 1951; s. Charles E. and Anne Marie (Overman) S.; m. Shaun Lea Gant, Aug. 20, 1988; children: Nathaniel Owen, Julia Colleen. BA in English, Holy Cross Coll., 1973; MEd, U. Mass., 1976. Tchr. English St. Sebastian's Prep. Sch., Newton, Mass., 1973-75, Falmouth (Mass.) High Sch., 1975-76; counselor Sun Valley Ranch/Adolescents, Missoula, Mont., 1976-78; sawyer Champion Internat., Missoula, 1978-80; community coord. Five Valleys Health Care, Missoula, 1981-83; project dir. Inst. Rockies, Missoula, 1984; freelance writer Missoula, 1983—; pub. info. coord. St. Patrick Hosp., Missoula, 1986—, writing cons., 1987—. Author: K. Ross Toole's Montana, 1985; editor Missoula Muse, Northwest Mileposts; contbr. numerous articles to profl. jours. Bd. dirs. Genesis House, Stevensville, Mont., 1979-80, Inst. of the Rockies, Missoula, 1984-85, Citizens Adv. Com. on Cable TV, 1983-89. Recipient Book of Yr. award Mont. Inst. of Arts, Billings, 1986. Democrat. Home: 216 Woodford Missoula MT 59801 Office: St Patrick Hosp 500 W Broadway Missoula MT 59802

SMITH, JEFFREY MACDONALD, manufacturing executive; b. Boston, July 2, 1947; s. Malcolm D. and Florence L. (Shaw) S.; m. Ellen C. Klinkenberg, Nov. 13, 1967; children: Timothy B., Peter G., Derek M., Andrew J., Brett A., Matthew B., Christopher E., Randall S. BSChemE, Northeastern U., 1970; MBA, U. Mich., 1974; JD, Ill. Inst. Tech., 1978. Bar: Ill. 1979, U.S. Dist. Ct. 1982. Prodn. developer engr. Dow Chem., Midland, Mich., 1970-72, asst. supt., 1972-74; sr. prodn. engr. Dow Chem., Joliet, Ill., 1974-76, asst. supt., 1976-78; plant mgr. Witco Chem., Chgo., 1978-81; group plant mgr. Purex Corp., Chgo., 1981-84; dir. environ. Purex Industries, Lakewood, Calif., 1984-86; v.p., adminstr. Purex Industries, Carson, Calif., 1986-89, pres., chief exec. officer, 1989—. Asst. dist. com. Boy Scouts Am., Joliet, 1974-84, troop commr. chmn., Mission Viejo, Calif., 1984—; twp. trustee Plainfield Bd. of Suprs., Joliet, 1980-84. Republican. Mormon. Home: 25432 Marina Cir Mission Viejo CA 92691 Office: Purex Industries Inc 535 Alondra Blvd Gardena CA 90248

SMITH, JEFFRY ALAN, public health administrator, physician, consultant; b. Los Angeles, Dec. 8, 1943; s. Stanley W. and Marjorie E. S.; m. Jo Anne Hague. BA in Philosophy, UCLA, 1967, MPH, 1972; BA in Biology, Calif. State U., Northridge, 1971; MD, UACJ, 1977. Diplomate Am. Bd. Family Practice. Resident in family practice WAH, Takoma Park, Md., NIH, Bethesda, Md., Walter Reed Army Hosp., Washington, Children's Hosp. Nat. Med. Ctr., Washington; dir. occupational medicine and environ. health Pacific Missile Test Ctr., Point Mugu, Calif., 1982-84; dist. health officer State Hawaii Dept. Health, Kauai, 1984-86; asst. dir. health County of Riverside (Calif.) Dept. Health, 1986-87; regional med. dir. Calif. Forensic Med. Group, Salines, Calif., 1987—. Fellow Am. Acad. Family Physicians; mem. AMA, Am. Occupational Medicine Assn., Flying Physicians, Am. Pub. Health Assn. Home: 112 Seafoam Ave Monterey CA 93940 Office: PO Box 3274 Salinas CA 93912

SMITH, JOHN KEVIN, accountant; b. Monroe, Oreg., Apr. 28, 1949; s. John and Vera Jane (Murray) S. Computer program certificate San Diego Coll. Bus., 1972; B.S., San Diego State U., 1978. Auditor, Atlas Corp., San Diego, 1976, Sheraton Corp., San Diego, 1976-77, Hyatt Corp., San Diego, 1977-78; acct. Hawthorne Machinery Co., San Diego, 1978-79; acct. Presto Foods, Inc., Los Angeles, 1979-81, also chief acct. subs. Jon Donaire Pastries, Inc. until 1981; sr. staff Van de Kamps, Los Angeles, 1981-83; chief acct. La. Pacific Corp., Huntington Beach, Calif., 1983—; owner, mgr. JKS Acctg. Service, Inc., Arcadia, Calif., 1982—. Served with U.S. Army, 1967-71; Vietnam. Mem. Nat. Assn. Accts. Am. Mgmt. Assn. Republican. Lodges: Masons, Rotary. Home and Office: Louisiana-Pac Corp PO Box 1505 Red Bluff CA 96080

SMITH, J(OHN) MALCOLM, political science educator; b. Vancouver, B.C., Can., Jan. 24, 1921; (parents Am. citizens); s. George John and Henrietta E. (Smith) S.; m. Connie Grace Shaw, June 2, 1943; children: Sheila C., Nancy L., Patricia L. BA, U. Wash., 1946; MA, Stanford U., 1948, PhD, 1951. Asst. prof. polit. sci. U. Calif., Riverside, 1945-57; instr. polit. sci. Stanford (Calif.) U., 1947-50; instr. pub. law and govt. Columbia U., N.Y.C., 1950-52; organizer World Affairs Coun., L.A., 1952-54; prof. polit. sci. Calif. State U., Hayward, 1965—; cons. Office of Sec. USAF, Washington, 1957-58, Commn. on Civil Rights, Washington, 1958-59; spl. asst. minority whip U.S. Senate, Washington, 1959-61; vis. prof. U. S.D., 1961-62, Ariz. State U., 1962-63; Merrill prof. Utah State U., 1976; mem. Ctr. for Study fo Presidency. Co-author: Powers of the President During Crisis, 1961, President and National Security, 1972; contbr. articles to profl. jours. Grantee Ford Found., 1955-56, John S. Sheppard, 1951-52. Mem. Acad. Polit. Sci., The Supreme Ct. Hist. Soc. Home: 2289 East Ave Hayward CA 94541 Office: Calif State U Dept Polit Sci Hayward CA 94542

SMITH, JOSEPH RONSTADT, food products executive, consultant; b. Tucson, Oct. 15, 1926; s. Harold Daniel and Marguerite (Ronstadt) S.; m. Joyce mcKeon, Sept. 9, 1950; children: Sally Carol, Allan Kent. BChemE, U. Colo., 1948, MS in Bus., 1950. Research asst., rocket project Dept. Physics, U. Colo., Boulder, 1949-50. chemist, group v.p. Pacific Vegetable Oil Corp., San Francisco, 1950-68; pres. Agricom Internat., San Francisco, 1968-81; pres. Oilseeds Internat., Ltd., San Francisco, 1981—, also bd. dirs. Contbr. articles to profl. jours., newsletters. Served with USNR, 1944-46. Mem. Am. Oil Chemists Soc., Nat. Inst. Oilseed Products (bd. dirs. 1966-86, pres. 1967-68). Club: World Trade (San Francisco). Home: 939 Carmel Ct Los Altos CA 94022 Office: Oilseeds Internat Ltd 885 Sansome Ste 100 San Francisco CA 94111

SMITH, JUNE MARY, vineyards executive; b. Oak Park, Ill., June 18, 1931; d. Edwin Richardson and Constance Margarita (Trimarco) Wright; m. James Raymond Smith, July 13, 1957; children: Jeffrey Ross, Bradford Louis, Jason James, Joy Marie. Grad. high sch., Oak Park. With mail room Sta. KNBH-TV, NBC, Hollywood, Calif., 1950-52; with front desk Anderson-McConnell Advt. Agy., L.A., 1952-53; with office and front desk depts. L.A. County Club, West Los Angeles, 1953-56; ins. clk. Leon Luxenberg, West Los Angeles, 1956-57; dep. clk. West L.A. Mcpl. Ct., 1957-59; order clk. Vivianne Woodward Cosmetics, Panorama City, Calif., 1960-61; cosmetic cons. El Toro, Calif., 1970-71; dir. pub. rels., co-owner Roudon-Smith Vineyards, Inc., Santa Cruz, Calif., 1971--. Co-author radio comml. 1988 (Silver award).; contbr. articles to trade mags. Recipient proclamation Santa Cruz Suprs. Bd., 1983. Mem. Santa Cruz County Winegrowers Assn. (v.p. 1987--), Santa Cruz Area Restaurant Assn. (events com. 1988--), Santa Cruz Mountain Vintners Assn., Santa Cruz Conv. and Visitors Coun., Scotts Valley C. of C., Aptos C. of C., Santa Cruz C. of C., Santa Clara C. of C., Monterey C. of C., Capitola C. of C., Rotary Internat./ Scotts Valley (fellowship chmn. 1988--). Republican. Roman Catholic. Office: Roudon-Smith Vineyards Inc 2364 Bean Creek Rd Santa Cruz CA 95066

SMITH, KATHLEEN MARIE CODY, accounting manager; b. Chgo., July 11, 1956; d. Edmund M. and Patricia A. (Maloney) Cody; m. Charles E. Smith, Feb. 19, 1983. BA, U. N.C., 1978. Asst. ops. mgr. Village Bank, Chapel Hill, N.C., 1978-83; acctg. mgr. Cons. Psychologist Press, Palo Alto, Calif., 1983-89, dir. ops., 1989—. Cardiopulmonary resuscitation instr. ARC, Palo Alto, 1987. Mem. Am. Payroll Assn., Nat. Audobon Soc. Office: Cons Psychologists Press 577 College Ave Palo Alto CA 94306

SMITH, KATHRYN JOYCE, secretarial service executive; b. Maud, Okla., Nov. 29, 1930; d. Elisha Alvin and Doris Louise (Kirk) Dooley; m. Richard A. Smith, Aug. 11, 1950; children—Rick L., John A., Kathy Keele. Student pub. schs., Boise. Steno-clk. Dept. Pub. Assistance, Boise, Idaho, 1948-49; officer Salvation Army, 1949-52; mem. duplicating dept. Suburban Gas Co., Pomona, Calif., 1960-63; sec. to headmistress Girls' Collegiate Sch., Claremont, Calif., 1964-66; steno-clk. FAA, Ontario, Calif., 1968-70; sec. spl. programs office, U. Redlands (Calif.), 1972-73, sec. various offices, 1975-81; owner The Word Co., Redlands. Active Variety Club Telethon; chpt. coordinator Food for All, Redlands. Mem. Nat. Assn. Secretarial Services, Nat. Assn. Female Execs., Soroptimist Internat. Sunrise Club (charter mem. Redlands chpt.). Republican. Mem. Ch. of Christ. Office: 408 E State St Ste B Redlands CA 92373

SMITH, KEITH LARUE, research co. exec.; b. Salida, Colo., Dec. 15, 1917; s. Leroy Holt and Verna Lea (Tunnell) S.; student Marion Coll., 1935-38; A.B. in Math., Ind. U., 1946; postgrad. DePauw U., 1946-47; M.A. in Internat. Affairs, Harvard U., 1955; M.P.A., Calif. State U.-Fullerton, 1979; m. Evelyn May De Bruler, Aug. 29, 1943; 1 son, Eric Douglas. Mil. intelligence research specialist Dept. of Army, Washington, 1951-60; staff engr. Librascope div. Gen. Precision, Inc., Glendale, Cal., 1960-61; sr. operations research analyst Space div. N.Am. Rockwell Corp., Downey, Cal., 1961-71; dir. research Am. Research Corp., Paramount, Calif., 1972—; instr. math. and polit. sci. DePauw U., 1946-47; cons. model bldg. and gaming techniques, 1960—; mgmt. cons., 1970—; instr. math. and sci. Verbum Dei High Sch., 1974-85 . Adult leader Boy Scouts Am., Long Beach, Calif., 1961-75. Treas., UN Council Harvard, 1947-49, Young Democratic Club, Arlington, Mass., 1949-50. Served to capt. USAAF, 1941-46; ETO. Recipient scholarship award Inst. World Affairs, 1947, Outstanding Efficiency award Dept. Army, 1960, Apollo 11 medallion NASA, 1970. Mem. Am. Mus. Natural History, Nat. Geog. Soc., Harvard Alumni Assn., Pi Sigma Alpha. Methodist. Mason. Research on lunar mission cartography, mil. operations research and war game model bldg. Home: 3451 Curry St Long Beach CA 90805

SMITH, KENNETH JAMES, hematologist; b. White Plains, N.Y., July 19, 1948; s. Henry James and Greta Elizabeth (Olson) S.; m. Catherine Horton, June 25, 1972; children: Patricia, Edward, Amy, David. AB, Fordham U., 1970; MD, Cornell U., 1974. Cert. Am. Bd. Internal Medicine, 1977, Med. Oncology Bd., 1978, Hemaldogy Bd., 1980. Intern then resident U. Pitts. Hosp., 1974-77; asst. prof. pathology and medicine U. N.Mex. Sch. Medicine, Albuquerque, 1980-86, assoc. prof., 1986—; assoc. med. dir. United Blood Svcs., Albuquerque, 1980—. Contbr. articles to sci. jours.; patentee blood product, 1988. Rsch. fellow U. Wash., 1977-80; rsch. grantee Blood Systems Rsch. Found., Inc., Ellis Pharm. Cons., Ortho Pharm., Inc., Rorer, Inc. Mem. Am. Heart Assn. (rsch. com. N.Mex. chpt., rsch. grantee), Am. Coll. Physicians, Am. Soc. Hematology, Am. Fedn. Clin. Rsch., Am. Assn. Blood Banks.. Democrat. Home: 1522 Wellesley Dr NE Albuquerque NM 87106 Office: U NMex Sch Medicine Dept Pathology Albuquerque NM 87131

SMITH, KENNETH MORRIS, magazine publisher, author; b. Berkeley, Calif., Sept. 1, 1949; s. Malcolm Kellogg Smith and Doris Jean (Fitzsimons) Harrison; m. Patricia Eileen Clyde, Dec. 31, 1983; children: Kimberly, Michael. Grad. high sch., Walnut Creek, 1967. Account exec. M.V Nursery, Inc., Sacramento, 1976-78; v.p. Energy Concepts, Ltd., Sacramento, 1978-80, C.A.F.P.A., Fair Oaks, Calif., 1980-81; publisher, founder, pres. Multi level Mktg. News, Inc., Sacramento, 1982—. Co-author: Financial Freedom Through Multilevel Marketing, 1983; publisher: The Best of M&M News, 1984. Mem. Nat. Assn. for Multilevel Mktg. (founder 1982), Multilevel Mktg. Internat. Assn., Direct Selling Assn., Calif. Alcohol Fuel Producers Assn. (v.p., co-founfer 1980). Libertarian. Unitarian. Office: MLM News Inc 7777 Sunrise Blvd #1800-333 Citrus Heights CA 95610-2300

SMITH, KEVIN CLAY, computer manufacturing executive; b. Colorado Spring, May 11, 1962; s. Graham Hardy and Nancy Louise (Wasson) S. BBA, U. Ariz., 1984. Database analyst Dept. of the Army Communications Command, Ft. Huachuca, Ariz., 1984; systems analyst E6&6 Energy Measurements, Las vegas, 1985-86; sr. cons. Myers Holum Inc., San Francisco, 1987; project leader Apple Computer, Cupertino, Calif., 1988—; computer systems cons. Daishowa Am., Port Angeles, Wash., 1987-88,. Usher, stage hand Community Theatre, Palo Alto, Calif., 1987—. Mem. Digital Equipment Computer Users Soc., Mgmt. Info. Systems. Office: Apple Computer 20525 Meriani Ave MS 25-B Cupertino CA 95014

SMITH, LE ROI MATTHEW-PIERRE, III, municipal administrator; b. Chgo., Jan. 11, 1946; s. Le Roy Matthew and Norma Buckner (McCamey) S.; m. Lois Divine, Jan. 30, 1969; 1 son, Le Roi Matthew Pierre. B.A. in Psychology, Idaho State U., 1969; Ph.D. in Psychology, Wash. State U., 1977. Instr. psychology Idaho State U., Pocatello, 1969-70, Wash. State U., Pullman, 1970-71; mem. faculty dept. psychology Evergreen State Coll., Olympia, 1971-81; equal opportunity officer Port of Seattle, 1981—; cons. in field. Bd. dirs. Thurston-Mason County Community Mental Health Ctr., Olympia; v.p., Idaho State Human Rights Commn., Bannock County, Idaho, 1968-70. Office Edn. fellow, 1969-70; U.S. Dept. Labor grantee, 1968; NSF grantee, 1972; Lilly Found. fellow, 1980. Mem. Am. Psychol. Assn., Am. Personnel and Guidance Assn., Wash. State Black Econs. and Edn. Conf., Assn. Black Psychologists, Am. Assn. of Affirmative Action Officers, Phi Delta Kappa. Democrat. Roman Catholic. Home: 761 S 45th St Tacoma WA 98408 Office: PO Box 1209 Seattle WA 98111

SMITH, LEE L., hotel executive; b. Long Beach, Calif., Oct. 15, 1936; s. Lowell Llake and Violet Margaret (Chrissman) S.; m. Sharon M.C. Lanahan, (div. 1977). AA, Long Beach City Coll., 1958; BAc in Music, Chapman Coll., 1965; postgrad., Calif. State U., Long Beach, 1966-67, U. Calif., Santa Barbara, 1974. Cert. tchr. Calif.; lic. ins. agt., Calif. Owner, mgr. Lee's Land Cattle Ranch, Cuyama Valley, Calif., 1960—; tchr. Cuyama Valley Schs., New Cuyama, Calif., 1967-79; owner, mgr. Cuyama Buckhorn Restaurant & Motel, New Cuyama, 1979-83; owner Allstate Ins. Agy., Desert Hot Springs, Calif., 1987—; owner, mgr. Caravan Resort Spa, Desert Hot Springs, 1983—. Violinist Bakersfield (Calif.) Symphony, 1967—, Brook String Quartet, Palm Springs, Calif., 1984—; dir. Planning Commn., Desert Hot Springs, 1985-87; chmn. Environ. Rev., Desert Hot Springs, 1986-88; mem. Redevel. Com., Desert Hot Springs, 1983-88; mem. exec. bd. growth and devel. Boys and Girls Club; bd. dirs. Food Now Program, 1988—. Mem. Am. Fedn. Musicians, Desert Hot Springs C. of C. (Bus. Person Yr. 1987), Breakfast Rotary (pres. 1987-88) Elks. Republican. Home: 66810 E 4th St Desert Hot Springs CA 92240 Office: Allstate Ins Co 66547 Second St Desert Hot Springs CA 92240

SMITH, LESTER MARTIN, broadcasting executive; b. N.Y.C., Oct. 20, 1919; s. Alexander and Sadie S.; m. Bernice Reitz, Sept. 28, 1962; 1 child, Alexander. B.S. in Bus. Adminstrn, NYU, 1940. Chief exec. officer Alexander Broadcasting Co., radio stas. in, Seattle, Portland, Oreg. and Spokane, 1954—; gen. partner 700 Investment Co.; past dir. Seattle C. of C.; past chmn. dir. Radio Advt. Bur. Served to maj. U.S. Army, 1942-46. Decorated Bronze Star. Mem. Nat. Assn. Broadcasters (past dir.), Oreg. Assn. Broadcasters (past pres.), Broadcast Pioneers. Clubs: Rotary (Seattle), Rainer (Seattle), Wash. Athletic (Seattle). Address: 700 112th NE Bellevue WA 98004

SMITH, LEWIS SPIVEY, controller; b. Madison County, Miss., Sept. 13, 1923; s. Arthur Perry and Matilda (Spivey) S.; m. Marie Giles, June 10, 1946; children: Evelyn, Lewis, Mary. Student, Holme Jr. Coll., 1948, Millsaps Coll., 1948-49. Nat. bank eaminer U.S. Treasury Dept., Washington, 1950-55; sr. acct. William Nader and Assocs., Jackson, Miss., 1955-65; controller Standard Cabinet Works Inc., Los Angeles, 1966—. Home: 15831 Wilmaglen Ave Whittier CA 90604 Office: 1800 E Washington Blvd Los Angeles CA 90021

SMITH, LINDA MARIE, financial company executive; b. Stanford, Calif., Apr. 25, 1961. BA, Stanford U., 1983. Analyst Marcus & Millichap, Palo Alto, Calif., 1984-86; project mgr. Trammell Crow, San Mateo, Calif., 1986-87; asset mgr. Sierra Capital Co., San Francisco, 1987—. Mem. Internat. Coun. Shopping Ctrs., Stanford Profl. Women (v.p. 1986—), Stanford San Francisco Club (pres. 1986—). Office: Sierra Capital Co Steuart St Tower Ste 1600 San Francisco CA 94105

SMITH, LOUISE EILEEN, toy manufacturing company executive; b. Hadley, Mass.; d. William J. and Anne (Canavan) S. BA in History, U. Mass. Analyst Lever Bros., N.Y.C., 1965-67; mgr. Chesebrough-Ponds, Greenwich, Conn., 1967-72; assoc. dir. Richardson-Merrill, Wilton, Conn., 1972-78; dir. Gen. Mills Co., N.Y.C., 1978-81; v.p. Mattel Toys, Hawthorne, Calif., 1982—. Mem. Am. Mktg. Assn., Advt. Research Found. Home: 344 31 St Hermosa Beach CA 90254 Office: Mattel Toys 5150 Rosecrans Ave Hawthorne CA 90250

SMITH, LUCINDA IRWIN, freelance writer; b. L.A., Sept. 20, 1952; d. Bernard Newell and Ruby (Irwin) S.; m. Jeffrey Allan Cohen, Dec. 8, 1977. BA, UCLA, 1974. Fashion and beauty editor Teen mag., L.A., 1978-80; west coast corr. Interiors mag., N.Y.C., 1980-83; freelance writer L.A.,

1983--. Author: Movie Palaces, 1980, Groving up Female, 1987, Women Who Write, 1989; contbr. articles to Modeling, Great Looks, Archtl. Digest, Home Entertainment, Millimeter mag. Debutante Nat. Charity League, L.A., 1970. Mem. PEN. Presbyterian.

SMITH, LYNWOOD STEPHEN, fisheries educator; b. Snohomish, Wash., Nov. 15, 1928; s. Stephen Johnson and Erna (von Lehe) S.; m. Betty Ann Mars, Sept. 15, 1951; children: Rebecca Jean, Peggy Lynn, Paul Kevin. BS in Biol. Edn., U. Wash., 1952, MS in Zoology, 1955, PhD in Zoology, 1962. Instr. biology Olympic Community Coll., Bremerton, Wash., 1955-60; asst. prof. zoology U. Victoria (B.C.), Can., 1962-65; from asst. prof. to prof. Sch. of Fisheries, U. Wash., Seattle, 1965—, assoc. dir. instrn., 1986—; vis. scientist Biol. Sta., Nemaino, B.C., Can., 1963-65, Cath. U. of Valparaiso, Chile, 1970; resource devel. project P.I., U.S. Agy. for Internat. Devel., Jakarta, Ambon, Indonesia, 1979-84. Author: Introductory Fish Physiology, 1981, Living Shores, 1975, Seashore Animals, 1962; contbr. articles to profl. jours. Mem. Shorelines Hearing Bd., Bothell, Wash., 1975-86. Grantee Fed. Water Pollution Control Adminstrn., 1966-70, U.S. Agy. for Internat. Devel., 1979-83, Wash. Sea Grant, 1981-84. Mem. AAUP, AAAS, Am. Fisheries Soc., Exptl. Aircraft Assn. Office: U Wash Sch Fisheries Seattle WA 98195

SMITH, MARILYN NOELTNER, science educator, consultant; b. Los Angeles, Feb. 14, 1933; d. Clarence Frederick and Gertrude Bertha (Smith) Noeltner; m. Edward Christopher Smith, Sept. 11, 1971. BA, Marymount Coll., 1957; MA, U. Notre Dame, 1966; MS, Boston Coll., 1969. Cert. tchr.; cert. community coll. tchr., Calif.; cert. adminstr., Calif. Tchr., chmn. sci. dept. Marymount High Sch., Santa Barbara, Calif., 1954-57, Los Angeles, 1957-58, 69-79; tchr., chmn. sci. and math. depts. Marymount High Sch., Palos Verdes, Calif., 1959-69; tchr., chmn. math. dept. Corvallis High Sch., Studio City, Calif., 1958-59; instr. tchr. tng. Marymount-Loyola U., Los Angeles, 1965-71, instr. freshman interdisciplinary program, 1970-71; tchr. math. Santa Monica (Calif.) High Sch., 1971-72; instr. math., chemistry, physics Santa Monica Coll., 1971—; tchr. sci. Beverly Vista Sch., Beverly Hills, Calif., 1972—; cons. Calif. State Sci. Framework Revision Com., Los Angeles, 1975; chmn. NASA Youth Sci. Congress, Pasadena, Calif., 1968-69, Hawaii, 1969-70; participant NASA Educators Conf. Jupiter Mission, Ames Research, San Francisco, 1973, NASA Educators Conf. Viking-Mars Ames Project, San Francisco, 1976-77, NASA Landsat Conf., Edward's AFB, Calif., 1978, NASA Uranus Mission, Pasadena, Calif., 1986. Author articles, books and computer programs on space and physics. Sponsor Social Service Club, Palos Verdes, 1959-69, moderator, sponsor ARC Youth Service Chmn., Beverly Hills, 1974-77, judge Los Angeles County Sci. Fair, 1969, mem. blue ribbon com. Nat. Acad. TV Arts and Scis., 1971—. Recipient Commendation in Teaching cert. Am. Soc. Microbiology, 1962, Salute to Edn. award So. Calif. Industry Edn. Council, 1962, Outstanding Teaching citationCons. Engrs. Assn. Calif., 1967, Cert. Honor, Silver Plaque Westinghouse Sci. Talent Search, 1963-68, Tchr. award Ford-Future Scientists of Am., 1968, Biomed. award Com. Advance Sci. Tng., 1971, Outstanding Tchr. award Los Angeles County Sci. Fair Com., 1975-76, Contbns. to Youth Service citation ARC, 1976-77, Outstanding Tchr. award Kiwanis Club Beverly Hills, 1987. Mem. We. Assn. Schs. and Colls. (vis. com. 1968, writing com. 1969—), Assn. Advancement Biomed. Edn. (pres. 1970-71), 1st Internat. Sci. Tchrs. Conf. (presider, evaluator 1977), Nat. Sci. Tchrs. Assn. (presider, evaluator 1976, chmn. contributed papers com. 1977-78), Beverly Hills Edn. Assn. Faculty Council (pres. 1980-81, 85-86), Chemist's Club, Calif. Statewide Math. Adv. Com., So. Calif. Industry Edn. Council, Calif. Assn. Chemistry Tchrs. (program chmn. 1960), Calif. Sci. Tchrs. Assn., Am. Chem. Soc., AAAS, South Bay Math. League (sec. 1967-68, pres. 1968-69, 72, 1969-70), Calif. Math. Council, Nat. Assn. Biology Tchrs. Republican. Roman Catholic. Home: 3934 Sapphire Dr Encino CA 91436 Office: Beverly Vista Sch 200 S Elm Dr Beverly Hills CA 91202

SMITH, MARK H., documentary producer, filmmaker; b. N.Y.C., Dec. 29, 1958; s. Arthur and Sandra (Scher) S. BS in Environ. Sci., U. Pa., 1982; BA in Film, Evergreen State Coll., 1983; MA in Journalism, NYU, 1988. Pilot 25 broadcast cos., U.S., Can., Mex., 1982—; prodn. mgr. Sta. KCWT-TV, Wenatchee, Wash., 1984-85; photojournalist Sta. WHQ-TV, Spokane, Wash., 1985-86; field producer CBS-TV, N.Y.C., 1986; producer PBS, N.Y.C. and Seattle, 1987-88; producer, cameraman PBS-WNET, Sta. KCTS-CBS, Seattle, 1988—; with Fellowship NYU, N.Y.C. 1988—; producer IXION, Seattle, 1987--; bd. dirs. N.W. Interactive, Seattle; cons. interactive learning IBM, 1988--; mktg. rep. Systems INFO Window, 1988--. Poducer doumentary Chernobyl, 1987. Recipient award for best feature N.W. Broadcasters, 1985, for best photog. essay, 1986. Mem. Airplane and Owners Assn., Wings Over Wash. Office: Fellowship NYU 10 Washington Pl New York NY 10033

SMITH, MARK LEE, architect; b. Los Angeles, Nov. 16, 1957; s. Selma (Moidel) Smith. BA in History of Architecture, UCLA, 1978, MA in Architecture, 1980. Lic. architect Calif., 1983, Nev., Oreg., Wash., Tenn., 1986. Designer, drafter John B. Ferguson and Assocs., Los Angeles, 1976-83, architect, 1983; pvt. practice architecture Los Angeles, 1984—. Contbr. articles to profl. jours. Regents scholar, U. Calif., Berkeley, UCLA, 1975-78; UCLA Grad. Sch. Architecture Rsch. fellow, 1979-80. Mem. AIA (treas. San Fernando Valley chpt. 1986, v.p. 1987, pres. 1988, Design award 1988, 89, dir. Calif. coun. 1989), Phi Beta Kappa. Office: 18340 Ventura Blvd #225 Tarzana CA 91356

SMITH, MARK MCCONAHA, venture capital executive; b. Redwood City, Calif., Oct. 10, 1958; s. Robert Ralph and Margaret (Fish) S. BA in Bus., Portland State U., 1984; MSBA in Internat. Bus., San Francisco State U., 1986. Asst. v.p. Futuretek Communications Inc., San Mateo, Calif., 1984-85; pres. Fashion Records Inc., San Francisco, 1985—, Flame Music Inc., San Rafael, 1987—; pres., chief exec. officer Richland Internat., Inc., 1987—; cons. for telecommunications and music industry, 1985. Contbr. articles to profl. jours. Address: 20-A Pimentel Ct Ste B Novato CA 94949

SMITH, MAUREEN MCBRIDE, chemist; b. Santa Monica, Calif., Mar. 4, 1952; d. Clayton Laird McBride and Luella (Sullivan) Boudreau; step-father Henry A Bourfeau; m. Gary Howard Cothran, July 27, 1974 (div. Apr. 1982); m. Guy Gordon Smith, Feb. 12, 1983; stepchildren: Keri Lynn, Scott Allen. BS magna cum laude, Calif. State Coll., San Bernardino, 1978, post-grad. Analytical chemist Chalco Engring., Edwards AFB, Calif., 1978-79, 82; microbiol. lab. tech. AVEK Water Agy., Quartz Hill, Calif., 1979-81, chemist, 1982—; instr. Antelope Valley Coll., Lancaster Calif., 1980-82. Mem. AAAS, Am. Chem. Soc. Office: Antelope Valley E Kern Water Agy 6500 W Ave N PO Box 3176 Quartz Hill CA 93536

SMITH, MELODY MELINDA, nurse; b. Benson, Ariz., May 6, 1962; d. Charles Matthew and Dorothy Eleanor (Henry) Jones; m. Richard Murray Smith, Oct. 16, 1981. AS in Nursing, Glendale (Ariz.) Community Coll., 1985. RN. Triage receptionist Cigna Urgent Care Ctr., Phoenix, 1983; counselor, phlebotomist, receptionist Family Enuresis Ctr., Phoenix, 1984; nurse Good Samaritan Med. Ctr., Phoenix, 1984—; mem. nursing diagnosis com., IV resource team, Good Samaritan Med. Ctr., Phoenix, 1986—. Contbr. articles to profl. journals. Organizer Hands Across Am., Phoenix, 1986. Rsch. grantee Sigma Theta Tau and Good Samaritan Med. Ctr. Nursing Rsch. Com., 1987. Mem. Nat. League Nursing, Assn. for the Continuance of Assoc. Degree Nursing. Republican. Home: 3637 W Laredo St Chandler AZ 85226

SMITH, MICHAEL ROBERT, chemical executive; b. Wilkes-Barre, Pa., Feb. 20, 1947; s. Robert M. and Mary (Stulak) S.; m. Kathryn L. Hadden, Aug. 24, 1979. BS in Acctg., King's Coll., 1968. Auditor CAB, Washington, 1970-72; supr. audit CAB, Los Angeles, 1975-78; auditor FCC, Washington, 1972-75; asst. controller Belmar Real Estate, Carson, Calif., 1978-84; mgr. acctg. FAA, Los Angeles, 1984-86; chief fin. officer Bayco Fin. Corp., Torrance, Calif., 1986-87; v.p. controller, gen. mgr. Samson Chem. Co., Gardena, Calif., 1987—. Served as sgt. USMC, 1968-70, Vietnam. Mem. Chem. Mktg. Assn., L.A. Soc. Coatings Tech., Aircraft Owners and Pilot Assn. Democrat. Roman Catholic. Home: 715 Prospect Ave Hermosa Beach CA 90254 Office: Samson Chem Co 1521 W 134th St Gardena CA 90249

SMITH, MICHAEL STEVEN, data processing executive; b. San Antonio, May 7, 1956; s. Columbus and Mary Patricia (Leahy) S. Student, San Bernardino Valley (Calif.) Coll., 1974-76, AS in Computer Scis., 1983; student, L.A. Community Coll., 1978-79, U. Md., 1980-81, City Colls. Chgo., 1980-81. Communications cons. Telephone Products Corp., San Bernardino, 1974-76; student svcs. advisor computer scis. lab. San Bernardino Valley Coll., 1982-83; assoc. programmer Aerojet ElectroSystems Corp., Azusa, Calif., 1983-85; mgr. data processing. Bonita Unified Sch. Dist., San Dimas, Calif., 1985—; analyst computer mktg. Pentamation Enterprises, Bethelehem, Pa., 1987—; cons. computer systems San Dimas, 1985—. With USN, 1976-82. Mem. Assn. for Computing Machinery, Digital Equipment Computer Users Soc. Office: 115 W Allen Ave San Dimas CA 91773

SMITH, MILTON RAY, computer company executive, lawyer; b. Pocatello, Idaho, Aug. 18, 1935; s. George William and Lettie (Denkers) S. AA, Long Beach (Calif.) City Coll., 1958; BS, Portland State U., 1962; MS, Oreg. State U., 1969; JD, Lewis & Clark Coll., 1970. Bar: Oreg. 1970, U.S. Dist. Ct. Oreg. 1970, U.S. Ct. Appeals (9th cir.) 1971, U.S. Supreme Ct. 1973. Tech. writer Northrop Corp., Hawthorne, Calif., 1957-58; engring. writer Tektronix Inc., Beaverton, Oreg., 1958-60, design engr., 1960-63, project engr., 1963-65, program mgr., 1966-70; asst. engring. mgr. Eldorado Electronics, Concord, Calif., 1965-66; ptnr. Acker, Underwood & Smith, Portland, Oreg., 1970-86; chmn., chief exec. officer Floating Point Systems Inc., Beaverton, 1986-87, pres., chief exec. officer, 1987-88, vice chmn., 1988—; bd. dirs. Flight Dynamics Inc., Portland. Bd. dirs. Oreg. Bus. Council, Portland, 1986—; mem. standing com. Northwestern Sch. Law, Portland, 1986—. Served with USN, 1952-56. Mem. ABA, Am. Electronics Assn. (exec. com. Oreg. chpt. 1987—), Am. Mgmt. Assn., Oreg. State Bar. Republican. Club: Founders (Portland). Office: Floating Point Systems Inc PO Box 23489 Portland OR 97223

SMITH, MONT JAMES, JR., military officer; b. Lawrence, Kans., Nov. 20, 1946; s. Mont James and Eleanor (Alicia) S.; m. Linda Jean Trail, June 6, 1968; children: Rebecca Lynn, Jeffrey Matthew. BS, USCG Acad., 1968; MS, U. West Fla., 1971. Cert. airline transport pilot; grad. numerous mil. courses, 1973-88. Commd. ensign USCG, 1968, advanced through grades to capt., 1988; deck watch officer USCGC Diligence, Key West, Fla., 1968-70; with USN Flight Sch., Pensacola, Fla., 1970-71; icebreaker recon officer aviation tng. ctr. USCG, Mobile, Ala., 1971-73; various pos. air sta. USCG, various cities, 1973-82; ops. officer air sta. USCG, Elizabeth City, NC, 1982-85; exec. officer air sta. USCG, Borinquen, Puerto Rico, 1985-88; commanding officer USCG, Kodiak, Alaska, 1988—. Contbr. articles to profl. publs. Asst. scoutmaster Boy Scouts Am., Borinquen, 1985-87; soccer coach USCG Youth Soccer League, Borinquen, Kodiak, 1985-88; asst. coach Youth Marksmanship Club, Kodiak, 1988—. Decorated Air medals, Joint Services Commendation medal, Commendation medals, Humanitarian Service medal; recipient Sikorsky Winged S award United Techs., 1973, Maritime Patrol Aviation award Assn. Naval Aviation, 1988. Mem. Nat. Rifle Assn., Kodiak Island C. of C., Rotary, Kodiak Island Sportsman's Assn. Republican. Roman Catholic. Home: 2 Parks Cir Kodiak AK 99615 Office: USCG Air Sta PO Box 33 Kodiak AK 99619

SMITH, NORMA GUEST, occupational health nurse; b. Lancaster, N.Y., June 2, 1925; d. Joseph Whitehouse and Norma Ethel (Montgomery) Guest; m. Gerald Francis Smith, Feb. 11, 1950 (dec. Apr. 1981); children: Gerald, Kathleen, Gordon, Mary, Dan, Ann, Joe, Elizabeth, Chris, Teresa. AA, W. L.A. Coll., 1977; BS, Chapman Coll., 1981, MA, 1985. RN; cert. occupational health nurse, teaching credential. Psychiat. nurse civ, L.A., 1947-48; clinic nurse L.A. City Health Dept., 1952-54; staff nurse Daniel Freeman Hosp., Inglewood, Calif., 1954-77; dir., instr. Centinela Valley Adult Edn., Hawthorne, Calif., 1974-77; occupational health nurse Flying Tiger Air Lines, L.A., 1977-86, Chevron Corp., El Segundo, Calif., 1986—. Vol. nurse ARC, L.A., 1964—; parish coun. St. Anastasia Cath. Ch., L.A., 1983-88, eucharistic minister, 1988—. Recipient Clara Barton Medallion ARC, 1972. Mem. St. Luke's Hosp. Alumnae Assn., Harbor Area Occupational Health Nurse Assn. Republican. Roman Catholic. Home: 8120 Fordham Rd Los Angeles CA 90045 Office: Chevron Corp 324 El Segundo Blvd El Segundo CA 90245

SMITH, OTTO J. M., electrical engineering educator; b. Urbana, Ill., Aug. 6, 1917; s. Otto Mitchell and Mary Catherine (Carr) S.; m. Phyllis P. Sterling, Sept. 3, 1941; children: Candace B., Otto J.A., Sterling M., Stanford D. BS in Chemistry, Okla. State U., 1938; BSEE, U. Okla., 1938; PhDEE, Stanford U., 1941. Registered profl. engr., Calif. Instr. elec. engring. Tufts U., Medford, Mass., 1941-43; assoc. prof. elec. engring. Denver U., 1943-44; research engr. Westinghouse Research Labs., Forest Hills, Pa., 1944-46; sr. research fellow econs. Monash U., Melbourne, Australia, 1966-67; prof. elec. engr. U. Calif., Berkeley, 1947—; chief engr. Smith and Sun, Berkeley, 1976—. Author: Feedback Control Systems, 1958; contbr. articles to profl. jours.; patentee in field. Dist. commr. Boy Scouts Am., Berkeley, 1949-53; trustee South Campus Community Ministry, Berkeley, 1968-70, Wesley Found., Berkeley, 1969-72. Guggenheim fellow, 1960. Fellow AAAS, IEEE; mem. Am. Soc. Engring. Edn., Soc. Social Responsibility Engring., Soc. Social Responsibility in Sci., Am. Solar Energy Soc., Internat. Solar Energy Soc., Am. Wind Energy Assn. Democrat. Methodist. Club: Berkeley City Commons (pres. 1963). Home: 612 Euclid Ave Berkeley CA 94708 Office: U Calif Dept Elec Engr & Computer Scis Berkeley CA 94720

SMITH, PATRICIA, Canadian provincial official. Mem. Province of Sask. Legis. Assembly; former minister of edn., now minister of energy and mines. Office: Sask Legis Assembly, Legislative Bldg, Regina, SK Canada S4S 0B3

SMITH, PATRICIA ANN, public relations consulant, educator; b. Chgo., June 7, 1933; d. Clarence Richard and Ruth Margaret (Jacobson) Nowack; m. Kurt E. Ferber, Feb. 14, 1954 (div.); m. Robert K. Hunsicker, June 28, 1968; children—Gail, Deborah, Kurt, Lori, Nancy, Janna; m. 3d, Kenneth Owler Smith, May 23, 1980. Student Cornell U., 1951-52; B.A., Centenary Coll., Hackettstown, N.J., 1983. Prodn. asst. Your Hit Parade Batten, Barton, Durstine & Osborne, 1953-54; pvt. practice polit. cons., 1954-66; legal sec., asst. Atty. John C. Cushman, 1966-68; field dep. L.A. County Assessor, 1968-69, pub. info. officer L.A. County Probation Dept., 1969-73; dir. consumer relations Fireman's Fund, San Francisco, 1973-76; pvt. practice pub. relations cons., 1976-77; spl. projects officer L.A. County Transp. Commn., 1977-78; tchr. Calif. State U.-Dominguez Hills, 1979-86; editor, writer Jet Propulsion Lab., 1979-80; pub. info. dir. L.A. Dept. Pub. Works, 1980-82; pub. info. cons. City of Pasadena, (Calif.), 1982-84; pub. relations cons., 1983—. Mem. First United Methodist Ch. Commn. on Missions and Social Concerns, 1983-89; bd. dirs. Depot, 1983-87; mem. devel. com. Pasadena Guidance Clinics, 1984-85. Recipient Pro award L.A. Publicity Club, 1978, Outstanding Achievement award Soc. Consumer Affairs Profls. in Bus., 1976. Mem. Pub. Relations Soc. Am. (accredited mem.; award for consumer program 1977, 2 awards 1984, Joseph Roos Community Service award 1985), Nat. Press Women (pub. relations award 1986), Calif. Press Women (awards 1974, 78, 83, 84, 85, community relations 1stplace winner 1986, 87, 88, 89), Nat. Assn. Mental Health Info. Offices (3 regional awards 1986). Republican. Clubs: Pasadena Women's City. Contbr. articles to profl. jours.

SMITH, PATRICK WELLS, emergency medical service executive and consultant; b. Mpls., Nov. 17, 1953; s. Ted and Margaret Smith; m. Linda Diane Seifert, Mar. 17, 1978; children: Michelle, Aaron, Danielle, Theodore. Paramedical sci., Methodist Hosp., St. Louis Park, Minn., 1974. Paramedic Smith Ambulance Svc., Mpls., 1975-78; county supr. Smith Ambulance Svc., 1978-80; dir. Hyatt Regency Hotel Disaster, Kansas City, Mo., 1981; asst. to med. dir. Emergency Physicians Found., Kansas City, 1982-83; asst. dir. Met. Ambulance Svc., Kansas City, 1981-82; cons. The 4th Party Inc., Miami, Fla., 1981-89; v.p. Eastern Paramedics, Syracuse, N.Y., 1985-88; chief exec. officer Mercy Ambulance Corp., San Francisco, 1988—; cons. The 4th Party, Pinnellas County, Fla., 1988—; numerous bd. positions Ft. Worth, 1987-88, Kansas City, Mo., 1981-83, Cornell Med. Ctr., N.Y.C., 1987-88. Den leader Boy Scouts Am., Reno, 1988. Mem. San Francisco Ambulance Assn. (bd. dirs. 1988—). Republican. Methodist. Home: 1175 LaGuardia Ln Reno NV 89511 Office: UPPER Mgmt Inc 240 Gentry Way Reno NV 89502

SMITH, PETER HOLLINGSWORTH, astronomer, researcher; b. N.Y.C., Dec. 2, 1947; s. Hugh Hollingsworth and Mary Maxine (Royhl) S.; m. Keith Ann Atkinson, Jan. 13, 1975 (div. June 1976); 1 child, Sara. BA, U. Calif., Berkeley, 1969; MS in Optics, U. Ariz., 1977. Rsch. assoc. Inst. for Astronomy, Honolulu, 1969-74; grad. asst. Optical Sci. Inst., U. Ariz., Tucson, 1975-77, rsch. specialist Lunar and Planetary Lab., 1978-87, 88—; optical engr. WYKO Corp., Tucson, 1987-88. Contbr. articles to profl. jours. Mem. Am. Astronomers Soc., Soc. Photo-Indsl. Engrs. Democrat. Office: U Ariz Lunar and Planetary Lab Tucson AZ 85721

SMITH, PETER WAYNE, photojournalist; b. San Diego, Jan. 29, 1951; s. Robert Vernon Goins and Esther Marie (Brumbaugh) Smith; m. Kathryn Sue Ogilvie (div. 1983). BA, Brooks Inst., 1974. Photographer Photo-Tec, Lemon Grove, Calif., 1969-73; darkroom technician Danforth Color Lab., Santa Barbara, Calif., 1972-73; prodn. supr. Pacific Mfg., Inc., Chula Vista, Calif., 1975-79; importer Coopersmith Mini Bits, Lemon Grove and Spring Valley, Calif., 1979-84; photojournalist Viewfinders, Lemon Grove, 1984—. Contbr. articles and photographs to Rail Classics Mag., Westways mag., San Diego mag., Pedco Reporter. Photographer Episcopal Diocese of San Diego, 1985-86, Am. Cancer Soc., San Diego, 1987—; judge San Diego County Fair, Del Mar, 1988; sec. ways and means Lemon Grove Hist. Soc., 1988; chmn. property com. Ch. of Good Shepherd, Bonita, Calif., 1985—. Mem. Assn. Photographers Internat., NRA (Mono Lake com.), Grove Hist. Soc. (sec. 1988-89), Lemon Grove C. of C. (bd. dirs. 1988-89). Democrat. Office: Viewfinders PO Box 913 Lemon Grove CA 92045

SMITH, PHILIP A., health care managment executive; b. Glasgow, Mont., May 18, 1946; s. Philip A. and Ann L. Smith; (div. Dec. 1979); children: Gillian, Jeremy, Zachary, Jonathan. BA, Sacramento State U., 1969; MSW, Wayne State U., 1971. Community organizer Family & Neighborhood Svcs., Wyandotte, Mich., 1971-72; exec. dir. Auburn (Wash.) Youth Resources, 1973-76; project coord., cons. Puget Sound Health Bd., Tacoma, 1977-78; tng. coord. Human Resources Coun., Missoula, Mont., 1979; program mgr. Social & Rehab. Svcs., Missoula, 1979-81; dir. community rels. Mont. Power Co., Missoula, 1981-89; dir. Mont. region Health Inventives Inc., Missoula, 1989—. Founder, coord. Clean Air Week, Missoula, 1985—; pres. Missoula Symphony Assn., 1989—; pres. Missoula Youth Homes, 1981-87; v.p., pres. Bikecentennial, Missoula, 1982—. Mem. Alliance of Missoula County Aging Programs (past pres.), Missoula Vol. Coun. (past pres.), Rattlesnake Edn. Coun. (past chmn. Missoula chpt.), Missoula C. of C. (bd. dirs. 1988—, George award 1988). Home: 638 Plymouth Missoula MT 59801

SMITH, PHILIP LINCOLN, artist, musician; b. Kansas City, Mo., Mar. 29, 1959; s. John Edward and Janet Lemay (Miller) S. Studies with William Crist, Barbara Mueller, Eric Bransby, John Gutowski, Marlin Rotach, Louis Cicotello and Stephen Gosnell. Co-founder, drummer, co-producer Glow, 1977—; announcer, disk jockey Sta. KCUR-FM, Kansas City, Mo., 1978; salesman Chabela's Artes A Mano, Kansas City, Mo., 1978; warehouseman J.C. Penney Co., Lenexa, Kans., 1979-80; creative/prodn. artist to sr. staff artist Spangler Printing Co., Kansas City, Kans., 1981-88; artist, cameraman, stripper Kaiwill USA Minuteman Press, Glendale, Calif., 1988—. Exhibited in group shows at ArtWestport Festival, Kansas City, Mo., 1988, Union Hills Art, Kansas City, Mo., 1987; designed and illustrated Riverrock's album cover Still 'live & Pickin, 1978. Named lifetime patron of arts Airbrush Digest mag., 1983; finalist Best Drummer Competition, 1982. Mem. ASCAP.

SMITH, RALPH EARL, virologist; b. Yuma, Colo., May 10, 1940; s. Robert C. and Esther C. (Schwarz) S.; m. Sheila L. Kondy, Aug. 29, 1961 (div. 1986); 1 child, Andrea Denise; m. Janet M. Keller, 1988. BS, Colo. State U., 1961; PhD, U. Colo., 1968. Postdoctoral fellow Duke U. Med. Ctr., Durham, N.C., 1968-70, asst. prof., 1970-74, assoc. prof., 1974-80, prof. virology, 1980-82; prof., head dept. microbiology Colo. State U., Ft. Collins, 1983-88, prof. microbiology, assoc. v.p. research, 1988—; cons. Bellco Glass Co., Vineland, N.J., 1976-80, Proctor & Gamble Co., Cin., 1985-86, Schering Plough Corp., Bloomfield, N.J., 1987-89. Contbr. articles to profl. jours.; patentee in field. Asst. scoutmaster Boy Scouts Am., Durham, 1972-82, com. mem., Ft. Collins, 1986—; mem. adminstrv. bd. 1st United Meth. Ch., Ft. Collins. Eleanor Roosevelt fellow Internat. Union Against Cancer 1978-79. Mem. Am. Soc. Microbiology, N.Y. Acad. Scis., Am. Soc. Virology, Am. Assn. Immunologists, Am. Assn. Avian Pathologists, Am. Assn. Cancer Rsch., Gamma Sigma Delta. Democrat. Methodist. Home: 2406 Creekwood Dr Fort Collins CO 80525 Office: Colo State U VP Rsch Fort Collins CO 80523

SMITH, RANDALL GENE, civil engineering company executive, public affairs consultant; b. Santa Ana, Calif., Apr. 1, 1947; s. Robert Hamilton and Margaret (Bottroff) S. BA, Calif. State U., Fullerton, 1969. Field rep. U.S. Congress, Washington, 1969-72; lobbyist So. Calif. Edison Co., Santa Ana, 1972-75; pres. Smith & Assocs., Santa Ana, 1975-80; sr. v.p. Van Dell & Assocs., Inc., Irvine, Calif., 1980—; pres. Smith Pub. Affairs, Irvine, 1982—. Bd. dirs. Orange County Housing Authority, 1970-75; bd. govs. Fairview State Hosp., Costa Mesa, Calif.; hon. del. Rep. Nat. Convs., 1984, 88. Mem. Pub. Rels. Soc. Am., Orange County Coast Assn. (v.p. 1986-88), Yorba Linda (Calif.) Country Club. Home: 18533 White Oak Yorba Linda CA 92686 Office: Van Dell & Assocs Inc 17801 Cartwright Rd Irvine CA 92714

SMITH, RAYMOND EDWARD, health care administrator; b. Freeport, N.Y., June 17, 1932; s. Jerry Edward and Madelyn Holman (Jones) S.; B.S. in Edn., Temple U., 1953; M.H.A., Baylor U., 1966; m. Lena Kathryn Jernigan Hughes, Oct. 28, 1983; children: Douglas, Ronald, Kevin, Doris Jean, Raymond. Commd. 2d lt. U.S. Army, 1953, advanced through grades to lt. col., 1973; helicopter ambulance pilot, 1953-63; comdr. helicopter ambulance units, Korea, 1955, Fed. Republic of Germany, 1961; various hosp. adminstrv. assignments, 1963-73; personnel dir. Valley Forge (Pa.) Gen. Hosp., 1966; adminstr. evacuation hosp., Vietnam, 1967; dep. insp. Walter Reed Gen. Hosp., Washington, 1970; dir. personnel div. Office of Army Surgeon Gen., Washington, 1971-73, ret., 1973; adminstr. Health Care Centers, Phila. Coll. Osteo. Medicine, 1974-76; dir. bur. hosps. Pa. Dept. Health, Harrisburg, 1976-79; contract mgr. Blue Cross of Calif., San Diego, 1979-88, Community Care Network, San Diego, 1989—. Decorated Bronze Star, Legion of Merit. Mem. Am. Hosp. Assn., Am. Legion, Ret. Officers Assn., Kappa Alpha Psi. Episcopalian. Club: Masons. Home: 7630 Lake Adlon Dr San Diego CA 92119 Office: Community Care Network 9265 Sky Park Cte San Diego CA 92123

SMITH, RAYMOND VICTOR, paper products manufacturing executive; b. Vancouver, B.C., Can., Apr. 28, 1926; s. Stanley Victor and Kathryn Stewart (Hunter) S.; m. Marilyn Joyce Meldrum, Oct. 17, 1947; children—Vicki, Kathi, Stan. Student, U. B.C., Banff Sch. Advanced Mgmt.; student Advanced Mgmt. Program, Harvard U. Trumpeter Dal Richards Band, 1942; ptnr. Warren McCuish Mens' Clothiers, 1947; sales rep. Vancouver Paper Box, 1949-54; with Home Oil Distbrs., 1954-57; with Kraft Paper & Board Sales, 1957-67, asst. mgr., 1961-65; newsprint rep. Powell River-Alberni Sales Corp., Pasadena, Calif., 1965-67; mgr. Powell River-Alberni Sales Corp., Pasadena, 1967-68; mgr. supply control and sales adminstrn. MacMillan Bloedel Ltd., Vancouver, 1968-70, gen. mgr., 1970-71, v.p. mktg. paper and pulp, 1971-73, v.p., gen. mgr. newsprint, 1973-77, group v.p. pulp and paper, 1977-79, sr. v.p. pulp and paper, 1979-80, pres., chief operating officer, 1980-83, chief exec. officer, 1983—; bd. dirs. Fibres Internat., Inc., Noranda Forest; bd. govs. Bus. Council B.C.; co-chmn. Newsprint Info. Com. Served with Can. Army, 1944. Clubs: Terminal City, Capilano Golf and Country, Vancouver. Office: MacMillan Bloedel Ltd, 1075 W Georgia St, Vancouver, BC Canada V6E 3R9

SMITH, RICHARD BOWEN, national park superintendent; b. Grandville, Mich., Mar. 8, 1938; s. William Jr. and Mary Elizabeth (Bowen) S.; m. Katherine Theresa Short, Sept. 21, 1980. BA in History, Albion Coll., 1960; MA in English, Mich. State U., 1967. Tchr. Grand Rapids (Mich.) Jr. High Sch., 1960-66; vol. Peace Corps, Asuncion, Paraguay, 1968-70; ranger Nat. Park Service, Yosemite, Calif., 1971-76; ranger. instr. Nat. Park Service, Grand Canyon, Ariz., 1976-78; ranger, legis. specialist Nat. Park Service, Washington, 1978-80; asst. supt. Nat. Park Service, Everglades, Fla., 1980-83; assoc. regional dir. ops. Nat. Park Service, Phila., 1984-86; supt. Nat. Park Service, Carlsbad Caverns, N.Mex., 1986-88; assoc. regional dir. ops. Nat. Park Service, Santa Fe, 1988—. Home: 9548 Bent Rd NE Albuquerque NM 87109 Office: Nat Park Svc 1100 Old Santa Fe Trail PO Box 728 Santa Fe NM 87504-0728

SMITH, RICHARD CLARK, city official; b. New Kinsington, Pa., Mar. 25, 1935; s. Ralph Burdette and Margaret Mary (Maracci) S.; A.S., El Paso Community Coll., 1971; m. Audrey Darlene Montgomery, Dec. 29, 1971; children—Richard Clark, Diane Kay, Gary Allen, David Mark, Carol Lynn. With Colorado Springs (Colo.) Fire Dept., 1962—, fire capt., 1969-77, bn. chief, 1977-78, div. chief, 1978-79, fire chief, 1979—; program dir. Fire Sci. Asso. Degree, El Paso Community Coll., 1969-72. Mem. Bd. Edn. El Paso County Sch. Dist. 2, 1973-79, treas., 1973-79. Mem. Internat. Assn. Fire Chiefs, Nat. Fire Protection Assn., Colo. Fire Chiefs Assn. Mem. Christian Ch. of Security. Club: Sertoma. Office: Colo Springs Fire Dept 31 S Weber St Colorado Springs CO 80903 *

SMITH, RICHARD KEANE, rehabilitation specialist; b. N.Y.C., Mar. 2, 1942; s. William Arthur Smith and Mary France (Nixon) Latessa; m. Lynda Ann Hart, May 30, 1980. BA in English, Bard Coll., 1965; MS in Rehab. Counseling, Calif. State U., Los Angeles, 1974; postgrad., U.S. Internat. U. Cert. rehab. counselor, registered psychol. asst. Eligibility worker L.A. County Dept. Pub. Social Svcs., 1969-74; case mgr. Portals House, L.A., 1974-75; pre-vocational counselor Rancho Los Amigos Med. Ctr., Downey, Calif., 1975-83; clin. coord. Transitional Living Ctr. Rancho Los Amigos Med. Ctr., L.A., 1984-87; vocat. coord. Head Injury Ctr. at Lewis Bay, Hyannis, Mass., 1983-84; program cons. Our House, Moreno Valley, Calif., 1987—; psychol. asst. various ctrs., Calif., 1986—; presenter various profl. confs. and workshops. Author: Exhibition Game, 1973; artist, composer Hand to Mouth, 1981; co-author various profl. publs. Bd. advisors So. Calif. Head Injury Found., Downey, Calif., 1988. Mem. Nat. Head Injury Found., Nat. Rehab. Assn., Traumatic Head Injury Profl. Assn. Calif., Am. Psychol. Assn. Office: Charter Counseling Ctr 14808 Pipeline Ave #105 Chino Hills CA 91709

SMITH, RICHARD LAWRENCE, industrial engineering educator; b. St. Louis, Apr. 5, 1933; s. Alfred William and Nannie Irene (Roberson) S.; m. Dixie Lou Koenig, Sept. 6, 1953; children—Robert, William, Dianne. A.A., Southwest Baptist Coll., Bolivar, Mo.; B.S.Indsl. Engring., Washington U., St. Louis; M.S. Indsl. Engring., Ohio State U., Columbus; Ph.D., Ariz. State U., Tempe. Engring. asst. McDonnell Aircraft Co., St. Louis, 1955-56; prin. engr. Battelle Meml Research Inst., Columbus, Ohio, 1956-60; mem. mgmt. staff Gen. Electric Co., Phoenix, 1960-67; prof., chmn. dept. indsl. and mgmt. systems engring. Ariz. State U., Tempe, 1967—; cons. Gen. Electric Co., Phoenix, 1967-70, Samaritan Health Services, Phoenix, 1970-85, Flori Corp., Phoenix, 1974-82, McDonnell Douglas Helicopter, Mesa, Ariz., 1985. Author research papers on indsl. engring., ops. research, systems engring. Bd. dirs. Northwest Phoenix YMCA, 1964-67; commr. Phoenix Babe Ruth Baseball, 1968-69; mem. bd. edn. Tempe Union High Sch. Dist., 1976-84; bd. trustees. Ariz. Sch. Bd. Assn. Ins., Phoenix, 1984-86, scholarship fund Am. Inds. Indsl. Engring., Atlanta, 1983—. Fellow Am. Inst. Indsl. Engring. (sr. mem., pres. local chpt. 1972); mem. Tech. Inst. Mgmt. Sci., Am. Soc. Engring. Educators. Republican. Home: 2116 E Geneva St Tempe AZ 85282 Office: Ariz State U Dept Indsl Engring Tempe AZ 85287

SMITH, ROBERT EARLE, artist, educator; b. L.A., Sept. 16, 1930; s. John Stanley and Bonnie (Earle) S.; m. Gwendolyn Joy Shockley; children: Fredrick Morris, Benjamin Andrew. AA, Los Angeles City Coll., 1950; BA, Pomona Coll., 1956; MA, Claremont Grad. Sch., 1964. Cert. tchr., Calif. Prof. art and photography Chaffey Community Coll., Rancho Cucamonga, Calif., 1956—. Dir. film, Andy Warhol, 1979, Sam Maloof, 1982; represented in group exhbn., Claremont Locals, 1985; contbg. author Portfolio Mag., Ontario, Calif., 1985; co-author musical composition, Baldy Mountain Blues 1987; pub. pen and ink illustrated calendars, Upland, Claremont, Rancho Cucamonga, 1986-89. Fulbright fellow, Italy, 1972. Mem. Ontario Mus. Art (trustee 1988—), Soc. Photographic Educators, Upland-Claremont-Corona C. of C. Democrat. Congregationalist. Office: Chaffey Community Coll 5885 Haven Ave Rancho Cucamonga CA 91701

SMITH, ROBERT FREEMAN, congressman; b. Portland, Oreg., June 16, 1931; m. Kaye Tomlinson, 1966; children: Christopher, Matthew, Tiffany. B.A., Willamette U., 1953. Mem. Oreg. Ho. of Reps., 1960-72, majority leader and speaker pro tem, 1964-66, speaker, 1968-72; mem. Oreg. Senate, 1972-82, Republican leader, 1978-82; mem. 98th-101st Congresses from 2d Oreg. Dist., 1982—; bd. dirs. Key Bank. Trustee Willamette U. Mem. Harney County C. of C. Lodges: Masons; Elks. Office: 118 Cannon House Office Bldg Washington DC 20515 *

SMITH, ROBERT GERALD, artist; b. Royal Oak, Mich., Nov. 8, 1928; s. Leon G. and Neva Eleanor (Knapp) S.; m. Elizabeth Louise Hursh, Aug. 18, 1949; children: Florence Louise, Renee Marise. BS in Art Edn., Mich. Normal Coll., 1953; postgrad., U. Tex., 1953, Famous Artist Schs., Westport, Conn., 1959-61, N.Mex. State U., 1969. Cert. secondary tchr., Mich. Advt. mgr. Record Pub. Co., Dallas, 1954; supr. Arthur Murray Dance Studio, Dallas and Wichita Falls, Tex., 1954-58; illustrator Stay Engraving & Humphrey Printing Co., Wichita Falls, 1955-56, Sta. KSYD-TV, Wichita Falls, 1957; tech. illustrator USAF, Wichita Falls, 1958-61; tech., sci. and indsl. illustrator USAF, Alamogordo, N.Mex., 1961-70, supervisory illustrator, 1970-76, base audio-visual mgr., 1977-85, EEO counselor, 1973-79, chief EEO counselor, 1980-83; owner, operator Robert's Roost, gallery, Alamogordo, 1977-81. Co-author, editor: The Different VisualAid, 1964; murals executed Old Art Bldg., Mich. State Normal Coll., 1952, Old Arthur Murray Dance Studio, Wichita Falls, 1957, Alamogordo C. of C. Bldg., 1974; co-inventor colored negative slide; group shows include Wichita Falls Art Assn Annual Show, 1955, 58, North Tex. Arts and Crafts Soc. Annual Exhibit, 1959-61, Alamogordo Art Assn., rotating exhibit Duert Aire Wotel, 1961, 69; permanent collections: literally hundreds of personal and family collections throught out the U.S. Canada, Mex. and Europe. Elder Westminster Presbyn. Ch., Alamogordo, 1978—. Sgt. USAF, 1946-49. Mem. Alamogordo Art Assn. (exhibit chmn., instr. drawing 1962-69), Gallery Assn. (exhibit chmn., instr. drawing, 1970-74), Alamogordo C. of C. (career day counselor 1970-82), Nat. Assn. Ret. Fed. Employees (life, Alzheimer's chmn. 1989—), Am. Assn. Ret. Persons, Gideons Internat. (N.Mex. v.p. 1982-83, leader zone 6, 1987—).

SMITH, ROBERT HAMIL, fund raiser, author; b. Oak Park, Ill., Nov. 8, 1927; s. Henry Garfield and Mary Ellen (Hamil) S.; student U. Denver, 1946-48, LLB, 1953, JD, 1960; m. Mary Helen Kingsley, Dec. 29, 1948; children: David H., Mark K., Steven H., Rebecca Anne Smith Quintana. Dep. clk. County Ct., City and County of Denver, 1948-53; with Colo. Ins. Group, 1953-59; mgr. claims dept. R.H. Smith & Assos., 1959-64; pres. Am. Bapt. Home Mission Soc., 1964-68; assoc. dir. devel. Ill. Wesleyan U., 1968-69; asst. to chancellor U. Calif., San Diego, 1969-77; exec. dir. devel. Scripps Clinic and Research Found., La Jolla, Calif., 1977-82, v.p. devel., 1982-88; pres. Cartographic Enterprises, 1981—; campaign dir. La Jolla Playhouse, 1989—; fund raising cons. deferred giving. Served with USNR, 1945. Mem. Nat. Soc. Fund Raising Execs., Internat. Yachting Fellowship of Rotarians (San Diego fleet comdr. 1979-81). Republican. Baptist. Club: Oceanside Yacht. Author: Guide to Harbors, Anchorages and Marinas So. and No. California edits., 1983.; The Physician as aFundraiser, 1984, Smith's Complete Guide to Maritime Museums in U.S./Canada, 1988. Home: PO Box 2785 Del Mar CA 92014 Office: R H Smith & Assocs PO Box 2785 Del Mar CA 92014

SMITH, ROBERT HOWARD, banker; b. Glendale, Calif., Sept. 3, 1935; s. James Howard and Marie Viana (Jenkins) S.; m. Loretta Marie Gesell, Feb. 8, 1958; children—Gregory (dec.), Jeffrey, Stephen, Sarah Beth. B.S. in Pub. Adminstrn., U. So. Calif., 1957; J.D., Van Norman U., Los Angeles, 1966. Various positions Security Pacific Bank, Los Angeles, 1961-66, mgr., 1969-71, regional v.p., 1971-74, sr. v.p., 1974-80, exec. v.p., 1980-84, vice chmn., from 1984, pres., chief exec. officer, 1987—; vice chmn. Security Pacific Bank & Security Pacific Corp, Los Angeles, 1984—. Served to lt. USN, 1958-61. Clubs: Jonathan (Los Angeles); Annandale Golf (Pasadena, Calif.). Home: 1617 Fairmount Ave LaCanada CA 91011 Office: Security Pacific Corp 333 S Hope St Los Angeles CA 90071 *

SMITH, RODNEY ELLWOOD, coast guard officer; b. Eugene, Oreg., Aug. 8, 1946; s. Fred. W. and Alvina (Ruth) S.; m. Gayla P. Grier, June 27, 1970; children: Cameron Cody, Paige Carrinne. BS, U. Oreg., 1968; MS, Naval Postgrad. Sch., 1974. CPA. Commd. officer USAG, 1969; advanced through grades to comdr. 1984; instr. Kodiak Community Coll., Alaska, 1980-82; systems cons. Bellevue, Wash., 1986—. Mem. AICPA, Am. Soc. Mil. Comptrollers. Home: 7033 82d Ave SE Mercer Island WA 98040 Office: USCG 1519 Alaskan Way Seattle WA 98134

SMITH, ROGER WILLIAM, engineer, accountant, business consultant; b. Quantico, Va., Sept. 26, 1945; s. Jacob Francis and Melba Louise (Taylor) S.; m. Donna Lynn Brasher Smith, June 15, 1968; children: Elliott Landry, Kendra Leigh. Student, U. Va., 1965; BS in Aero. Engring., Miss. State U., 1968, BS in Indsl. Mgmt., 1968. Cons. Arthur Andersen & Co., S.C., Houston, 1968-70, sr. cons., 1970-73; mgr. Arthur Andersen & Co., S.C., Portland, Oreg., 1973-80, ptnr., 1980-89; pres. Rubicon West, Inc., Lake Oswego, Oreg., 1989—; acting dir. Oreg. Econ. Devel. Dept., Salem, 1987. Author: Strategic Management for Bankers, 1984; contbr. numerous banking articles for Am. Banks to The Bankers mag. Chmn. Oreg. Econ. Devel. Com., 1987—. Sgt. Army N.G., 1968-74. Mem. Portland C. of C., Portland Ambs., Japan-Western U.S. Assn., Soc. Strategic Mgmt. (internat. bd. dirs. the planning forum 1984—), Planning Execs. Inst. (pres. 1983-84, Portland Chpt.) Japan-Am. Soc., City Club (Portland). Republican. Presbyterian. Office: Rubicon West Inc One Centerpointe Dr Ste 270 Lake Oswego OR 97035

SMITH, ROSS QUENTIN, defense electronics systems consultant; b. Nacogdoches, Tex., June 22, 1959; s. Roger Qumil and Mary Hilda (Taylor) S. BS in Computer Engring., U. Tex., 1982. Control systems engr. E.I. duPont de Nemours, Victoria, Tex., 1981-82; research and devel. engr. Geotronics Corp., Austin, Tex., 1982-83; sr. rsch. and devel. engr. Ford Aerospace and Communications Corp., Palo Alto, Calif., 1983-86; def. systems cons., advanced programs, C3I product mktg. mgr. ORI/Intercon Systems Corp., Sunnyvale, Calif., 1986—. Patentee in field. Recipient Ethics in Engring. award Hutchinson Found., 1983; Kmiecik fellow Brookview Inst., 1985. Mem. IEEE, Optical Soc. Am., Assn. Computing Machinery, Soc. Photographic and Imaging Engrs., Order of Leon, Hedonism Internat. Home: 169 Waverly St #C Palo Alto CA 94301

SMITH, RUSSELL EVANS, U.S. judge; b. Butte, Mont., Nov. 16, 1908; s. Ernest Clifford and Florence (Evans) S.; m. Mary Ruth Larison, June 21, 1931; children: Sonia Lee Zenk, Russell Evans Jr. LL.B. cum laude, U. Mont., 1931, LL.D. (hon.), 1980. Bar: Mont. 1931. Marshal, law clk. Mont. Supreme Ct., 1931-33; practiced in Cut Bank, Mont., 1933-35, Missoula, Mont., 1935-42, 45-66; counsel for Mont., OPA, 1942-43; judge U.S. Dist. Ct. for Mont., 1966—, chief judge, to 1978, sr. judge, 1978—; lectr. U. Mont. Law Sch.; Mem. Mont. Bd. Bar Examiners. Served to USNR, 1943-45. Mem. Mont. Bar Assn. (past pres. 1956), Alpha Tau Omega, Phi Delta Phi. Office: US Dist Ct PO Box 7219 Missoula MT 59807

SMITH, RUSSELL FRANCIS, transportation executive; b. Washington, Mar. 26, 1944; s. Raymond Francis and Elma Gloria (Daugherty) S.. Student East Carolina U., 1964, N.C. State U., 1964-65; BS with honors, U. Md.-Coll. Park, 1969, MBA, 1975. Exec. asst. mgr. Hotel Corp. Am. Internat. Inn and Mayflower Hotel, Washington, 1966-68; sr. venture capital cons. Initiative Investing Corp., Washington, 1968-69; pres., gen. mgr. Associated Trades Corp., Washington, 1970-74; cons. in fin., Greenbelt, Md., 1974-76; mng. cons. Bradford Nat. Corp., Washington, 1976-79; v.p. OAO Corp., Washington, 1979-81; ptnr. for fin. evaluation and ops. analysis Blake, Brunell, Lehmann & Co., Washington, 1981-86; v.p. mgmt. services adminstrn. United Airlines Services Corp., Lakewood, Colo., 1986—. Chmn. com. on wildlife Prince George Humane Soc., Hyattsville, Md., 1968-71, Soc. for Prevention Cruelty to Animals, Hyattsville. 1971-75. Served with U.S. Army, 1963-66. Decorated Silver Star medal, Bronze Star medal with V device, Purple Heart. Mem. Am. Fin. Assn., Ops. Research Soc. Am., Am. Acctg. Assn., N.Am. Soc. Corp. Planners, Internat. Assn. Math. Modeling, Assn. MBA Execs. (registered investment advisor), Beta Gamma Sigma, Beta Alpha Psi. Republican.

SMITH, RUSSELL LYNN, JR., engineer, consultant; b. Petaluma, Calif., Dec. 25, 1919; s. Russell Lynn and Marikka (Mikkelson) S.; m. Jean Margaret Austin, July 21, 1942; children: Lynn Suzanne, Dale Austin. Student, Stanford U., 1938-41; B.A., U. Hawaii, 1949. Registered profl. engr., Hawaii, Guam. Pilot, photogrammetric engr., surveyor R.M. Towill Corp., Honolulu, 1947-49; jr. engr. Austin & Towill, Honolulu, 1949-53; assoc. engr. H.A.R. Austin, Honolulu, 1953-56; v.p., sec. H.A.R. Austin & Assocs. Ltd., Honolulu, 1956-64; sec. Austin & Towill Ltd., Honolulu, 1957-59; v.p., treas. Austin, Smith & Assocs., Inc., Honolulu, 1959-75; pres. The Russ Smith Corp., Honolulu, 1975-84; chief engr., dir. pub. works City and County of Honolulu, 1985-86; pres. Smith, Young & Assocs. Inc., 1987—; mem. Honolulu Bd. Water Supply, 1985, 86; cons. on water supplies Pub. Utility Agy, Guam, 1966-74; chmn. Interprofl. Council on Environ. Design, U.S., 1982. Founder Hawaii Air N.G., 1946; mem. Gov.'s Com. on Yr. 2000, Hawaii; mem. budget rev. panel Aloha United Way, 1977-81. Served to 1st lt. A.C. U.S. Army, 1942-46, to lt. col. Air N.G. Decorated Air medal with oak leaf cluster; recipient Hawaii Engr. of Yr. award Hawaii Soc. Profl. Engrs., 1976, cert. of Merit Gov. Samuel W. King, Hawaii, 1956. Fellow ASCE (pres. Hawaii sect. 1961), Am. Cons. Engrs. Council (nat. pres. 1982-83, pres. Hawaii council 1970-71); mem. Water Pollution Control Fedn. (pres. Hawaii assn. 1967), Nat. Soc. Profl. Engrs., Engring. Assn. Hawaii (life), Hawaii Pub. Works Assn. (pres. 1985), Am. Water Works Assn., Am. Legion (vice commdr. Hawaii 1956). Republican. Clubs: Stanford (Hawaii) (pres. 1950-52); Pacific, Plaza. Lodge: Rotary. Home: 999 Wilder Ave #1102 Honolulu HI 96822 Office: Smith Young & Assocs Inc 3049 Ualena St Ste 1104 Honolulu HI 96819

SMITH, SAM CORRY, foundation executive; b. Enid, Okla., July 3, 1922; s. Chester Hubbert and Nelle Kate (Corry) S.; m. Dorothy Jean Bank, Sept. 21, 1945; children: Linda Jean, Nancy Kay, Susan Diane. Student, Phillips U., 1940-43; BS in Chemistry, U. Okla., 1947, MS in Chemistry, 1948; PhD in Biochemistry, U. Wis., 1951. Asst. and assoc. prof. U. Okla., Oklahoma City, 1951-55; assoc. dir. grants Research Corp., N.Y.C., 1957-65, dir., 1965-68, v.p. grants, 1968-75; exec. dir. M.J. Murdock Charitable Trust, Vancouver, Wash., 1975-88; foundation cons., 1988—; pres. Pacific Northwest Grantmakers Forum, 1983-84. Contbr. sci. articles to profl. jours. Trustee Nutrition Found., Washington, 1976-84, Internat. Life Scis. Inst., Washington, 1984-86; bd. councilors U. So. Calif. Med. Sch., Los Angeles, 1977-82; mem. adv. com. Coll. Natural Scis. Colo. State U., 1977-80. 1st lt. USAAF, 1943-45, ETO. Named Boss of Yr., Am. Bus. Women's Assn., 1982, Bus. Assoc. of Yr., 1983. Fellow AAAS; mem. Am. Chem. Soc., Am. Inst. Nutrition, Am. Inst. Biol. Scis., N.Y. Acad. Scis. Presbyterian. Home: 5204 DuBois Dr Vancouver WA 98661

SMITH, SAMUEL HOWARD, university administrator, plant pathologist; b. Salinas, Calif., Feb. 4, 1940; s. Adrian Reed and Elsa (Jacop) S.; m. Patricia Ann Walter, July 8, 1960; children: Samuel Howard, Linda Marie. BS in Plant Pathology, U. Calif., Berkeley, 1961, PhD, 1964. NATO fellow Glasshouse Crops Research Inst., Sussex, Eng., 1964-65; asst. prof. plant pathology U. Calif., Berkeley, 1965-69; assoc. prof. Pa. State U., Arendtsville, 1969-71; assoc. prof. Pa. State U., University Park, 1971-74, prof., 1974-85, head dept. plant pathology, 1976-81, dean Coll. Agr., dir. Pa. Agrl. Expt. Sta. and Coop. Extension Service, 1981-85; pres. Wash. State U., 1985—. Bd. dirs. Econ. Devel. Ptnrship. for Wash., 1986—. Mem. AAAS, Am. Phytopath. Soc., Nat. Assn. State Univs. and Land Grant Colls. (bd. dirs. commn. on vet. medicine 1986—), Gamma Sigma Delta, Alpha Zeta. Home: NE 755 Campus Ave Pullman WA 99163 Office: Wash State U 422 French Adminstrn Bldg Pullman WA 99164

SMITH, SCOTT RANDOLPH, sales executive; b. Culver City, Calif., Dec. 6, 1962; s. Floyd Randolph and Bonnie Louise (Horn) S. BA in Behavioral Sci., Calif. State U., 1986. Asst. buyer Macy's Calif., San Francisco, 1986-87; sr. sales rep. Friden-Alcatel, Hayward, Calif., 1987-88; med. sales rep. Bristol-Myers USPNG, Evansville, Ind., 1988-89; with San MAteo County Convention & Visitors Bur., San Francisco, 1989—. Mem. San Jose (Calif.) Postal Council, 1987-88. Mem. Cen. Valley Pharmacists Assn., MPI. Republican. Roman Catholic. Office: San Mateo County Conv & Visitors Bur 601 Gateway Blvd Ste 970 San Francisco CA 94080

SMITH, SELMA MOIDEL, lawyer, composer; b. Warren, Ohio, Apr. 3, 1919; d. Louis and Mary (Oyer) Moidel; 1 son from previous marriage: Mark Lee. Student Los Angeles City Coll., 1936-37, U. Calif., 1937-39, U. So. Calif., 1939-41; JD, Pacific Coast U., 1942. Bar: Calif. 1943, U.S. Dist. Ct. 1943, U.S. Supreme Ct. 1958. Gen. practice law; mem. firm Moidel, Moidel, Moidel & Smith. Field dir. civilian adv. com. WAC, 1943; mem. nat. bd. Med. Coll. Pa. (formerly Woman's Med. Coll. Pa.), 1953—, exec. bd., 1976-80, pres., 1980-82. Decorated La Order del Merito Juan Pablo Duarte (Dominican Republic). Mem. ABA, Calif. Bar Assn. (servicemen's legal com.), L.A. Bar Assn. (psychopathic ct. com.), L.A. Lawyers Club (pub. defenders com.), Nat. Assn. Women Lawyers (chmn. com. unauthorized practice of law, social commn. UN, regional dir. western states, Hawaii 1949-57, mem. jud. adminstrn. com. 1960, nat. chmn. world peace through law com. 1966-67), League of Ams. (dir.), Inter-Am. Bar Assn., So. Calif. Women Lawyers Assn. (pres. 1947, 48, chmn. Law Day com. 1966, subject of oral hist. project, 1986), State Bar Conf. Com., Coun. Bar Assns. L.A. County (charter sec. 1950), Calif. Bus. Women's Coun. (dir. 1951), L.A. Bus. Women's Coun. (pres. 1952), Calif. Pres.'s Coun. (1st v.p.), Nat. Assn. Composers U.S.A. (dir. 1974-79, ann. luncheon chmn. 1975), Nat. Fedn. Music Clubs (nat. vice chmn. for Western region, 1973-78), Calif. Fedn. Music Clubs (state chmn. Am. Music 1971-75, state conv. chmn. 1972), Docents of L.A. Philharmonic (v.p. 1973-83, chmn. Latin Am. community rels. 1972-75, press and pub. rels. 1972-75, cons. coord. 1973-75), Euterpe Opera Club (v.p. 1974-75, chmn. auditions 1972, chmn. awards 1973-75), ASCAP, Iota Tau Tau (dean L.A., supreme treas.), Plato Soc. of UCLA, 1981—, discussion leader UCLA Constitution Bicentennial Project, 1985-87. Composer: Espressivo-Four Piano Pieces (orchestral premiere at Nat. Mus. Women in the Arts 1989). Home: 5272 Lindley Ave Encino CA 91316

SMITH, SIDNEY PHILIP, protective services executive; b. San Mateo, Calif., Feb. 26, 1948; s. Arthur Jonathan and Ann Lucille (Stahlak) S. AA, Coll. of San Mateo, 1969; BA, San Jose State U., 1976; MA, Calif. State U., 1980. Police agt. Menlo Park (Calif.) Police Dept., 1969-74; dir. pub. safety Boys Town, Nebr., 1974-75; asst. police adminstr. Town of Belvedere, 1976-80, chief of police, 1980; pres. Systems for Pub. Safety, San Mateo, Calif., 1980-88; chief exec. officer Designs In Modern Learning, San Carlos, Calif., 1988—; instr. Santa Rosa Criminal Justice Tng. Ctr., 1978—, San Jose Evergreen Criminal Justice Ctr., 1981—; adminstrv. justice coord., Coll. of San Mateo, 1982-83. Author: Why Can't I Find Good Candidates Anymore, 1988; You've Found a Bomb-Now What? (audio cassette), 1981. Mem. Exploring com. local coun. Boy Scouts Am., 1984-85. Mem. Calif. Peace Officers Assn., Calif. Assn. Police Tng. Officers, Marin County Police Tng. Mgrs. Assn. (pres. 1979), Alpha Phi Omega (mem. nat. bd. dirs. 19 -80, Nat. Disting. Svc. award 1980). Republican. Episcopalian. Office: Designs In Modern Learning 1091 Industrial Rd Ste 250 San Carlos CA 94070

SMITH, STANFORD SIDNEY, state treasurer; b. Denver, Oct. 20, 1923; s. Frank Jay and Lelah (Beamer) S.; m. Harriet Holdrege, Feb. 7, 1947; children: Monta Smith Ramirez, Franklin Stanley. Student, Calif. Inst. Tech., 1941-42, Stanford U., 1942-43; BS, U.S. Naval Acad., 1946. Pres. Vebar Livestock Co., Thermoopolis, Wyo., 1961-89; mem. Wyo. Senate, 1974-76; pres. Wyo. Wool Growers, Casper, 1976-78; mem Wyo. ho. of reps., Cheyenne, 1978-82; treas. State Wyo., Cheyenne, 1983—; v.p. Wyo. Wool Growers, dir., 1976-82, Wyo. Prodn. Credit Assn., Casper, 1970-78. County commr. Hot Springs County, Wyo, 1966-74. Lt. USN, 1943-54. Decorated Bronze Star. Mem. Lions. Republican. Presbyterian. Office: State Capitol Dept Treasury Cheyenne WY 82002

SMITH, STEPHEN ALEXANDER, accountant; b. Springfield, Ill., Aug. 18, 1941; s. Roy Edward and Catherine (Saurer) S.; m. Marsha Jane Mugg, June 10, 1967; children: Alexandra, Danna. BS, U. Ill., Urbana, 1967, MBA, 1969. CPA, Colo. Staff acct. Ernst & Ernst, Chgo., 1969-73; pvt. practice Denver, 1973—. With U.S. Army, 1960-62. Home: 11844 W 28th Pl Lakewood CO 80215 Office: 6279 W 38th Ave Ste 3 Wheat Ridge CO 80033

SMITH, STEPHEN SINCLAIR, technology executive; b. Lakeview, Oreg., Oct. 16, 1947; s. S. Gordon and Mary Irene (Sinclair) S.; m. Paula Kay Smith, Aug. 15, 1970; children: Kyle Sinclair, Kendall Clairbrooke. BS in Indsl. Engring., Oreg. State U., 1969; MBA, Harvard U., 1972. Assoc. McKinsey & Co., Inc., San Francisco, 1972-74; mgr. Fairchild, Mountain View, Calif., 1974-77; v.p. Amdahl Corp., Sunnyvale, Calif., 1977-83; pres. Reference Tech., Inc., Boulder, Colo., 1983-87, SS Smith & Assocs., Palo Alto, Calif., 1987—, FAXplus Corp., Santa Clara, Calif., 1988—. Mem. Info. Industry Assn. (bd. dirs. 1986—), Assn. for Info. Image Mgmt. (bd. dirs. 1986—). Republican. Episcopalian.

SMITH, STEVEN LEE, electrical engineer; b. Phoenix, Dec. 30, 1958; s. Robert Harold and Lillian (Masko) S. BEE, Stanford U., 1981, MEE, 1982, MBA, 1987. Jr. engr. Delco Electronics div. Gen. Motors Co., Kokomo, Ind., summer 1979; Jr. engr. Delco Electronics div. Gen. Motors Co., Santa Barbara, Calif., summer 1980, assoc. engr., summer 1981; sr. assoc. engr. Gen. Products div. IBM, San Jose, Calif., 1982-87; sr. assoc. product planner IBM, Santa Clara, Calif., 1987–; intern. Subcom. on Space, Sci., and Applications U.S. Congress, Washington. Big bro. Stanford U.-Nat. Collegiate Athletic Assn. Vols. for Youth. N.C.A.A. nat. water polo champion, 1978, 80; Gen. Motors Corp. engring. scholar, 1981. Mem. IEEE, Nat. Space Soc., Aircraft Owners and Pilots Assn. Republican. Home: 6744 Leyland Park Dr San Jose CA 95120 Office: IBM 4900 Old Ironsides Santa Clara CA 95054

SMITH, STEVEN PAUL, opthalmologist; b. Fremont, Nebr., Feb. 8, 1952; s. Darrell Eugene and Dedrei Ann (Daharsh) S.; m. Marguerite Caroline Smith, Sept. 5, 1981. MD, UCLA, 1980. Intern Cedars-Sinai Med.Ctr., L.A., 1980-81; resident in ophthalmology U. Minn., Mpls., 1981-84; practice medicine specializing in ophthalmology Group Health Coop, Seattle, 1984—. Fellow Am. Acad. Ophthalmology, Wash. State Acad. Ophthalmology; mem. Pacific Coast Oto-Ophthal. Soc. Office: 200 15th Ave E Seattle WA 98112

SMITH, STEVEN SIDNEY, molecular biologist; b. Idaho Falls, Idaho, Feb. 11, 1946; s. Sidney Ervin and Hermie Phyllis (Robertson) S.; m. Nancy Louise Turner, Dec. 20, 1974. BS, U. Idaho, 1968; PhD, UCLA, 1974. Asst. research scientist Beckman Research Inst. City of Hope Nat. Med. Ctr., Duarte, Calif., 1982-84, staff Cancer Ctr., 1983—, asst. research scientist depts. Thoracic Surgery and Molecular Biology, 1985-87, assoc. research scientist, 1987—; cons. Molecular Biosystems Inc., San Diego, 1981-84. Contbr. articles to profl. jours. Grantee NIH, 1983—, Council for Tobacco Research, 1983—, March of Dimes, 1988—; Swiss Nat. Sci. Found. fellow Univ. Bern, 1968-73, Scripps Clinic and Research Found., La Jolla, Calif., 1978-82, NIH fellow, Scripps Clinic, 1979-81. Mem. AAAS, Pacific Slopes Biochem. Soc., N.Y. Acad. of Scis., Am. Soc. Cell Biology, Phi Beta Kappa. Republican. Office: City of Hope Nat Med Ctr 1500 E Duarte Rd Duarte CA 91010

SMITH, STUART ROBERT, foundation executive; b. South Amboy, N.J., Aug. 14, 1942; s. Stuart Conroy and Elizabeth Beatrice (Keenan) S.; m. Nancy Jo Roberts, Apr. 24, 1965; children: Mark Christopher, Melissa Jo. BA in Psychology, St. Vincent Coll., Latrobe, Pa., 1964; postgrad., Stanford U., 1986. Dist. exec. Raritan coun. Boy Scouts Am., Perth Amboy, N.J., 1965-68, Greater Niagara Frontier Coun., Buffalo, 1968-69; assoc. dir. devel. Canisius Coll., Buffalo, 1969-70; dir. devel. Kenmore (N.Y.) Mercy Hosp., 1971-74; dir. community rels. and devel. United Hosp., Port Chester, N.Y., 1974-77; exec. dir. Shadyside Hosp. Found., Pitts., 1977-79; exec. v.p. Samaritan Med. Found., Phoenix, 1979-87, pres., chief exec. officer, 1988—; cons. fundraising and golf tournaments. Contbr. articles to profl. jours., newsletters. V.p., bd. dirs. Crisis Nursery, Phoenix, 1987, 88, pres. elect 1989—; chmn. Fiesta Bowl Golf Classic, Phoenix, 1988, 89; mem. com. Fiesta Bowl, Phoenix, 1986--; bd. dirs. Dave Thomas Found., Farmington, N. Mex., Palms Clinic & Hosp. Found., Phoenix. Fellow Nat. Assn. Hosp. Devel. (nat. v.p. 1977-80, bd. examiners 1986—), Ariz. Assn. Hosp. Devel. (pres.-elect 1988-89), Nat. Soc. Fund Raising Execs. (cert., various offices local chpts.), Ladies Profl. Golf Assn. (sponsors bd., treas. 1988—), Moon Valley Country Club. Republican. Roman Catholic. Office: The Samaritan Charitable Trust 1441 N 12th St Phoenix AZ 85006

SMITH, TERESA SCHWEGMAN, educator educational administrator; b. Cin., Mar. 10, 1953; d. Jack R. and Norma (Bradley) Schwegman; m. E. Mark Smith, July 10, 1976; children: Aaron Lloyd, Evan Bradley. BS in

Elem. Edn., Miami U., Oxford, Ohio, 1975; postgrad., St. Nicholas Sch., London, 1979, Spring Valley Coll., Seattle, 1980, Seattle Pacific U., 1980. Tchr., dir. N.W. Learning Ctr., Kirkland, Wash. Office: NW Learning Ctr 13630 100th Ave NE Bldg 2 Kirkland WA 98034

SMITH, TERRENCE PAUL, economist; b. Providence, May 31, 1946; s. James Alphonsus Smith and Althea Maude (Davis) Nunes; m. Frances Claire Hornick, Apr. 3, 1982; 1 child, Gillian Catherine. BS in Zoology, U. R.I., Kingston, 1973; MS in Oceanography, U. R.I., Narragansett, 1978; PhD in Resource Econs., U. Md., 1989. Rsch. assoc. dept. resource econs. U. R.I., Kingston, 1977-80; rsch. assoc. dept. agrl. and resource econs. U. Md., College Park, 1980-83; economist North Pacific Fishery Mgmt. Coun., Anchorage, 1985—; pres. MicroSmith Computing, Anchorage, 1983—. Contbr. articles to sci. publs. Capt. U.S. Army, 1966-70, Vietnam. Recipient spl. achievement award North Pacific Fishery Mgmt. Coun., 1988. Mem. Am. Fisheries Soc., Am. Econ. Assn., Assn. Environ. and Resource Economists, Econometric Soc. Office: North Pacific Fishery Mgmt PO Box 103136 Anchorage AK 99510

SMITH, TERRY GORDON, electronics production manager; b. Cin., Aug. 7, 1937; s. Clifford John and Vivian Aileen (Stone) S.; m. Sylvia Ann Gehl, Jan. 20, 1959 (dec. Dec. 1984); children: Donald Melvin, Terri Ann. Student, Arizona State U.; BA, U. Phoenix, MA in Mgmt., MBA. Mgr., owner Pharmacy, Phoenix, 1959-65; mgr. Super X Pharmacy, Scottsdale, Ariz., 1965-70; supr. Motorola, Inc., Phoenix, 1966-71, prodn. mgr., 1971—; mgmt. lectr. U. Phoenix, 1984—. Author: Metal Finishing Safety Manual, 1975. Mem. World Electroless Nickel Soc., Am. Mgmt. Assn., Am. Electroplaters Soc., Am. Soc. for Metal, Assn. for Mfg. Excellence. Republican.

SMITH, THOMAS MATTHEW, securities trader; b. Hackensack, N.J., May 30, 1945; s. Arthur Joseph and Florence P. (O'Hara) S.; m. Elsa Torres, June 13, 1970; children: Christopher, Thomas. AB in Cursu Classico magna cum laude, St. Peters Coll., 1968; postgrad., NYU, 1968-70. Asst. v.p. 1st Jersey Nat. Bank, Jersey City, 1967-71, Franklin Nat. Bank, N.Y.C., 1971-74; sr. v.p. FCB Adv. Svcs., Inc., N.Y.C., 1974-78; v.p., regional mgr. Wismer Assoc., Inc., Breton Woods, N.J., 1978-79; v.p. trading Birr Wilson & Co., San Francisco, 1980-85; sr. v.p. Bateman Elcher Hill Richards, San Francisco, 1985-86; v.p. trading First Calif. Regional Securities, San Francisco, 1986-88; v.p. west coast A.F. Green & Co., Inc., Larkspur, Calif., 1988; v.p. Thomas F. White & Co., 1988-; chmn. bd., chief exec. officer Smith Culver, Inc., 1988-. Mem. Mcpl. Bond Club, Am. Sportsman, Wilderness Unltd. Home: 192 Ridgewood Dr San Rafael CA 94901 Office: Smith Culver Inc 700 Larkspur Landing Circle Ste 169 Larkspur CA 94939

SMITH, THOMAS WINSTON, cotton marketing executive; b. Crosbyton, Tex., Mar. 16, 1935; s. Lance L. and Willie Mae (Little) S.; m. Patricia Mae Zachary, Dec. 13, 1958; children—Janna Olean, Thomas Mark. B.S., Tex. A&M U., 1957; P.M.D., Harvard U., 1964. Various positions Calcot Ltd., Bakersfield, Calif., 1957-77, exec. v.p., pres., 1977—; v.p. Amcot, Inc., Amcot Internat., Inc., Bakersfield, 1977—, also bd. dirs.; v.p. Nat. Cotton Coun., Memphis; bd. mgrs. N.Y. Cotton Exchange, N.Y.C. Bd. dir. Greater Bakersfield Meml. Hosp.; mem. pres.'s adv. commn. Calif. State Coll., Bakersfield. Mem. Rotary.

SMITH, TURK, writer; b. Detroit, June 24, 1917; s. Talbot Truxtun and Constance (Fitch) S.; student U. Ariz., 1935-38; m. Leslie Collie, Apr. 4, 1942 (dec. 1972); children—Talbot Truxtun III, Chopeta Constance. Reporter, feature writer Ariz. Republic, Phoenix, 1952-84, automotive columnist, 1964-84; corr. Newsweek, 1952-64, USIA, 1952-79. Contbr. articles to mags. Home: 4825 E Picadilly St Phoenix AZ 85018 Office: 120 E Van Buren St Phoenix AZ 85002

SMITH, VIN, sports editor, business owner; b. Whittier, Calif., May 19, 1944; s. M. Clifford and Anna Eugenia (Hill) S.; m. Marthea Karen Callaham, May 15, 1969 (div. 1979); children: Jayare Smith, Eric Smith; m. Ginger Hammon, Oct. 20, 1984; children: Amy Michelle, Stacey Erin, Kellie Rae. Student, Columbia Sch. Broadcasting, San Francisco, 1967; AA, Cuesta Coll., 1974; grad., Am. Sch. of Piano Tuning, 1978. Sales mgr. Sta. KTAT, Frederick, Okla., 1967-69; owner Melmart Markets, San Luis Obispo, Calif., 1971-73, Am. Direct Sales, Grover City, Calif., 1973-79; instr. piano Valley View Acad., Arroyo Grande, Calif., 1977-78; instr. piano Long Piano Co., San Luis Obispo, 1977-79, piano technician, 1978-79; owner Chocolate Piano, Yreka, Calif., 1979—; instr. piano Makah India Tribe, Neah Bay, Wash., 1981-82; sports editor New Words Mag., Mt. Shasta, Calif., 1988—; cons., stress evaluator seminar Yreka Stress Therapy Clinic, 1986-87. Author: sports column New Words Mag., 1988—, 87-89; contbr. articles to profl. jours. Chmn. heart fund Tillman County, Okla., 1968; campaign worker Ken Jourdan for sheriff, Yreka, 1986. Recipient Cert. of Appreciation, Siskiyou County, 1988, Achievement award, 1988, Golden Poet award World of Poetry, Sacramento, 1989. Mem. Nat. Writers Club (chmn. student com. Yreka chpt. 1988), Author's Guild, Inc., Author's League of Am., Mystery Writers Am., Soc. Children's Book Writers, Jr. C. of C. (sgt.-at-arts Frederick chpt. 1967-69), Kiwanis, Moose. Home: 402 Turre #43 Yreka CA 96097 Office: Chocolate Piano Svcs PO Box 447 Yreka CA 96097

SMITH, WALDO GREGORIUS, former government official; b. Bklyn., July 29, 1911; s. John Henry and Margaret (Gregorius) S.; m. Mildred Pearl Prescott, July 30, 1935; 1 dau., Carole Elizabeth Smith Levin. Student CCNY, N.Y., 1928-29; B.S. in Forestry, Cornell U., 1933. Forester, Forest Service, U.S. Dept. Agr., Atlanta, 1933-41, Ala. Div. Forestry, Brewton, 1941-42; engr., civil engring. technician Geol. Survey, U.S. Dept. Interior, 1942-71, cartographic technician, 1972-75; chmn. Public Transp. Council, 1975—; aide to indiv. legislator Colo. State Legis. Internship Program, 1987—. Recipient 40 year Civil Service award pin and scroll; 42 Yr. Govt. Service award plaque. Registered profl. engr., Colo. Fellow Am. Congress Surveying and Mapping (life; sec.-treas. Colo. chpt. 1961, program chmn. 1962, reporter 1969, mem. nat. membership devel. com. 1973-74, rep. to Colo. Engring. Council 1976-77); mem. AAAS, Denver Fed. Center Profl. Engrs. Group (U.S. Geol. Survey rep. 1973-76, Engr. of Yr. award 1975), Nat. Soc. Profl. Engrs. (pre-coll. guidance com. 1986—), Profl. Engrs. Colo. (chpt. scholarship chmn. 1979—, advt. corr., service award 1983), Cornell U. Alumni Assn. (alumni secondary schs. com.), Common Cause, Colo. Engring. Council (chmn. library com. 1970—, spl. rep. Regional Transp. Dist., 1974-75; mem. sci. fair com. 1970-71; rep. ex officio Denver Pub. Library Found. Bd. Trustees 1975-80, Pres.' Outstanding Service award 1987), Fedn. Am. Scientists, Am. Soc. Engring. Edn., People for Am. Way., Environ. Concerns (chmn. com. 1988—). Contbr. proposals to science-for-citizens program and research applied to nat. needs program NSF. Contbr. articles to profl. jours. Home: 3821 W 25th Ave Denver CO 80211

SMITH, WILLARD GRANT, educational psychologist; b. Sidney, N.Y., June 29, 1934; s. Frank Charles and Myrtle Belle (Empet) S.; m. Ruth Ann Dissly, Sept. 14, 1957; children—Deborah Sue Henri, Cynthia Lynn Koster, Andrea Kay Richards, John Charles. BS, U. Md., 1976; MS, U. Utah, 1978, PhD, 1981. Cert. sch. psychologist, sch. adminstr., tchr., Utah. Rsch. asst. Med. Ctr., U. Utah, 1977, teaching asst. dept. ednl. psychology, 1976-78, rsch. cons. dept. edn., 1977; program evaluator Salt Lake City Sch. Dist.; program evaluator and auditor Utah State Bd. Edn., 1978; sch. psychologist Jordan Sch. Dist., Sandy, Utah, 1978-82, tchr., 1979-80; exec. dir. Utah Ind. Living Ctr., Salt Lake City, 1982-83; spl. edn. cons. Southeastern Edn. Svc. Ctr., 1983-85; psychologist Jordan Sch. Dist., Sandy, 1985—. Master sgt. USAF, 1953-76. Decorated Air Force Commendation medal with 2 clusters; recipient U. Md. scholastic achievement award, 1975. Mem. Am. Psychol. Assn., Nat. Assn. Sch. Psychologists, Am. Ednl. Rsch. Assn., Air Force Sgts. Assn., Ret. Enlisted Assn., Phi Kappa Phi, Alpha Sigma Lambda. Home: 6879 Maverick Circle Salt Lake City UT 84121 Office: Jordan Sch Dist 7500 S 1000 E Midvale UT 84047

SMITH, WILLIAM DAVID, real estate broker; b. Ypsilanti, Mich., Dec. 19, 1946; s. Charles William and Virginia May (Ford) S.; m. Judith Ellen Wilkiemeyer, Sept. 24, 1971 (div. Mar. 1983); children: Matthew, Joshua, Charity. BS, Mich. State U., 1970. Mgr. restaurant Westin Hotels, Chgo., 1970-71; with sales, mgmt. Real Estate One, Detroit, 1971-78; with mgmt. Stan Wiley Realtors, Portland, Oreg., 1978-79, Tarbell Realtors, Portland, 1979-81; real estate salesman Norris Beggs & Simpson, Portland, 1981—. Mem. fin. com. Frank Bearden for Supreme Ct., Portland, 1988; bd. dirs. Ladybug Children's Theater, Portland, 1985-87. Mem. Metro Portland Bldg. Owners and Mgrs. (trustee), Portland Bd. Realtors (bd. dirs.). Republican. Methodist. Clubs: Willamette Athletic, Oreg. Rd. Runners (Portland). Home: 4637 D SW Galewood Lake Oswego OR 97035 Office: Norris Beggs & Simpson 720 SW Washington #250 Portland OR 97205

SMITH, WILLIAM LARRY, sales executive; b. Wichita Falls, Tex., July 9, 1944; s. William L. and Thelma (Tanner) S.; 1 child, Kevin. BBA, Midwestern U., Wichita Falls, 1967. With sales depts. various airline cos. 1967-78; div. mgr. Eastern Airlines, Cleve. and Miami, Fla., 1978-81; asst. sr. v.p. mktg. Eastern Airlines, Miami, 1981-82; regional sales mgr., dir. Eastern Airlines, Houston and N.Y.C., 1982-85; v.p., gen. sales mgr. Sitmar Cruises, L.A., 1985-86, sr. v.p. mktg. and sales, 1986—. Mem. Cruise Lines Internat. Assn. (mktg. com. 1986—, mgmt. com. 1986—), Am. Soc. Travel Agts. Office: Princess Cruises 10100 Santa Monica Blvd #1800 Los Angeles CA 90067

SMITH, WILLIAM RAY, biophysicist, engineer; b. Lyman, Okla., June 26, 1925; s. Harry Wait and Daisy Belle (Hull) S. BA, Bethany Nazarene Coll., 1948; MA, Wichita State U., 1950; postgrad. U. Kans., 1950-51; PhD, UCLA, 1967. Engr., Beech Aircraft Corp., Wichita, Kans., 1951-53; sr. group engr. McDonnell Aircraft Corp., St. Louis, 1953-60; sr. engr. Lockheed Aircraft Corp., Burbank, Calif., 1961-63; sr. engr. scientist McDonnell Douglas Corp., Long Beach, Calif., 1966-71; mem. tech. staff Rockwell Internat., L.A., 1973-86, CDI Corp.-West, Costa Mesa, Calif., 1986-88, McDonnell Douglas Aircraft Corp., Long Beach, 1988—; tchr. math. Glendale Coll., Calif., 1972; asst. prof. math. and physics Pasadena Coll. (now Point Loma Coll., San Diego), 1960-62, Mt. St. Mary's Coll., L.A., 1972-73. Contbr. articles to sci. jours. Active L.A. World Affairs Coun.. Recipient citation McDonnell Douglas Corp., 1968; Tech. Utilization award Rockwell Internat., 1981; cert. of recognition NASA, 1982. Mem. AAAS, AIAA, N.Y. Acad. Scis., Calif. Acad. Scis., UCLA Chancellor's Assocs., Internat. Platform Assn., Internat. Visitors Coun. L.A., Town Hall Calif., Yosemite Natural History Assn., Sigma Xi, Pi Mu Epsilon. Republican. Presbyterian. Office: McDonnell Douglas Corp 3855 Lakewood Blvd Long Beach CA 90846

SMITH, WILLIAM RICHARD, city official, educator; b. N.Y.C., June 24, 1940; s. Harry John and Catharine Marie (Wheeler) S.; m. Judith Ann Carroll, Mar. 18, 1961; children: Shawn, Kevin, Susan, Kurt, Eric. BA, Iona Coll., 1962; MS, U.S. Naval Postgrad. Sch., Monterey, Calif., 1972; MPA with distinction, Golden Gate U., 1982. Commd. 2nd lt. USMC, 1962, advanced through grades to lt. col., 1978; mil. advisor Mil. Assistance Adv. Group, Saigon, Vietnam, 1970-72; budget analyst Hdqrs. USMC, Washington, 1972-76; comdg. officer Marine Barracks Mare Island, Vallejo, Calif., 1976-79; lectr. mgmt. sci. U.S. Naval Postgrad. Sch., 1979-82; ret. 1982; sr. adminstrv. analyst City of Monterey, 1982-84, asst. city mgr., 1986—; city adminstr. City of Sonora (Calif.), 1986—; instr. Golden Gate U., San Francisco, 1983—. Bd. dirs. Tuolumne County Community Svcs. Bd., Sonora, 1985-86, Monterey County AIDS Project Bd., 1987-88, Monterey Waste Mgmt. Dist. Bd., 1987—. Decorated Silver Star, Bronze Star medal with V, Purple Heart with oak leaf cluster, Meritorious Svc. medal. Mem. Internat. City Mgmt. Assn., Am. Soc. for Pub. Adminstrn. ((chmn. sec. 1982, v.p. 1983, pres. 1984, svc. award 1984), Am. Soc. for Personnel Adminstrn. (chpt. sec. 1983). Democrat. Roman Catholic. Home: 950 Madison St Monterey CA 93940 Office: City of Monterey City Hall Monterey CA 93940

SMITH, ZACHARY ALDEN, political science and public administration educator; b. Stanford, Calif., Aug. 8, 1953; s. Alden Wallace and Lelia (Anderson) S.; m. Lisa Friel, May 20, 1983. BA, Calif. State U., Fullerton, 1975; MA, U. Calif., Santa Barbara, 1979, PhD, 1984. dir. Ctr. for Island and Ocean Resources Mgmt. Adj. lectr. polit. sci. U. Calif., Santa Barbara, 1981-82; asst. prof. U. Hawaii, Hilo, 1982-87, assoc. prof., 1987-89; assoc. prof., dir. MPA program No. Ariz. U., Flagstaff, 1989—. Author: Groundwater Policy in the Southwest, Interest Group Interaction and Groundwater Policy, Groundwater and the Future of the Southwest, Groundwater in the West; contbr. numerous articles to profl. jours. Active campaign Jimmy Carter for Pres., 1976, campaign for various state propositions, 1970, 74, 76; elected to Orange County (Calif.) Dem. Cen. Com., 1976—. Research grantee U. Calif., Los Alamos (N.Mex.) Sci. Lab., Water Resources Ctr., Davis., Calif. Mem. Am. water Resources Assn., Am. Polit. Sic. Assn., Western Polit. Sci. Assn., Am. Soc. Pub. Adminstrn. Office: No Ariz U Dept of Polit Sci Flagstaff AZ 86011

SMITH, ZANE GREY, JR., association executive, forester; b. Albuquerque, Nov. 12, 1933; s. Zane Grey and Elsie Amelia (Lewis) S.; m. Betty Blake McLeish, Aug. 29, 1954; children: Timothy Zane and Kelly Ann. Student, U. N. Mex., 1951-52; BS in Forestry cum laude, U. Mont., 1955; postgrad., Cornell U., 1967-68. Forester USDA Forest Service, Oreg. and Wash, 1955-61; dist. ranger USDA Forest Service, Okanogan, Wash., 1961-65; job corps. ctr.dir. USDA Forest Service, Randall, Wash., 1965-66; staff asst. USDA Forest Service, Wash., 1966-68; forest supr. USDA Forest Service, Fresno, Calif., 1968-70, Eugene, Oreg., 1970-74; dir. recreaction USDA Forest Service, Wash., 1974-88; regional forester USDA Forest Service, San Francisco, 1978-88; Pacific field rep. Am. Forestry Assn., Springfield, Oreg., 1988—; policy bd. Bay Area Fed. Exec. Bd., San Francisco, 1978-88; bd. mem. Calif. Poly., San Luis Opispo (Calif.) Adv. Council,1982-88; chmn. Fed. Exec. Assn., Eugene, Oreg., 1972-74; mem. Western Fed. Regional Council, San Francisco, 1978-82. Contbr. articles to profl. jours. Team leader Nat. Recreation Strategy for U.S. Forest Service, 1988; bd. dirs. Boy Scouts Am., Fresno, Calif., Eugene, 1968-74, ARC, Eugne, 1970-74; bd. mem. Nature Conservancy, San Francisco, 1980-88. Served to capt. USAF, 1955-70. Recipient Managerial award Office of Personnel Mgmt., San Francisco, 1984, US/European Trails Exchange, The Walk Ways Ctr., Western Europe, 1988. Mem. Soc. of Am. Foresters (chpt. chmn. 1964). Home: 37899 Shenandoah Loop Springfield OR 97478-9748 Office: Am Forestry Assn 1516 P St NW Washington DC 20005

SMITH-BLUM, KAY, small business owner; b. Austin, Tex., Apr. 30, 1952; d. Clifford Dare and Maxine (Crooks) Smith; m. William Lawrence Blum, Oct. 25, 1981; children: Case Maxwell, Kyle Maurice, Bryce Clifford. BBA, U. Tex., 1974. Exec. trainee Neiman-Marcus, Dallas, 1974, asst. buyer, 1975-76, dept. mgr., 1977, buyer, 1978-80; mdse. mgr. Neiman-Marcus, Beverly Hills, Calif., 1980; co-owner Butch Blum, Seattle, 1981—; speaker Dallas Apparel Mart Trade Conf., Dusseldorf, Fed. Republic Germany, 1986, Women Plus Bus. Conf., Seattle, 1988. Chmn. advt., mktg. Downtown Seattle Assn., 1987-88; bd. dirs., mem. devel. com. West Wash. chpt. Arthritis Found., Seattle, 1982-88; bd. dirs. Seattle Acad. Arts and Scis., 1982-88; mem. adv. bd. Grad. Sch. Bus. U. Wash., 1987-88. Recipient Appreciation award Arthritis Found., 1984, Seattle Symphony, 1985-86. Democrat. Methodist. Office: Butch Blum 1408 Fifth Ave Seattle WA 98101

SMITHSON, EDDIE JOE, hotel executive; b. Clovis, N.Mex., Nov. 9, 1933; s. James Clyde and Ruby Laura (Powell) S.; m. Jackie Lou Hunt, Oct. 4, 1951; children—Samie Lou Martinez, Shari Lynn. Cert. hotel adminstr. Asst. mgr. Palms Motor Hotel, Las Cruces, N.Mex., 1965-66; gen. mgr. Diamond Jim's Restaurant, Albuquerque, 1966-69; mng. ptnr. Palms Motor Hotel, Las Cruces, N.Mex., 1969-74; regional dir. Don the Beachcomber, Dallas, 1974-75; gen. mgr. Holiday Inn, Las Cruces, 1975-77; mng. ptnr. Best Western of Las Cruces, 1977-83; v.p., mng. dir. La Fonda Hotel, Santa Fe, N.Mex., 1983-87; gen. mgr. Las Cruces Hilton, 1988; apptd. dir. N.Mex. Tourism & Travel, Santa Fe, 1988—. Mem. Gov.'s Econ. Devel. and Tourism Bd., N.Mex., 1981-87 , chmn. tourism com. 1986; bd. dirs. Pres. Assocs., N.Mex. State U., Las Cruces, 1982-83 (bd. dirs.); mem. Santa Fe Occupancy Tax Bd., Nat. Coun. State Travel Dirs. (bd. dirs. 1988). Mem. Am. Hotel and Motel Assn. (nat. dir. 1984—, cert. hotel adminstr.), N.Mex. Hotel and Motel Assn. (pres. 1983-84, Innkeeper of Yr. 1986), Santa Fe Lodger's Assn. (bd. dirs.), Las Cruces C. of C. (pres. 1979, Citizen of Yr. 1982, bd. dirs. 1973-80), N.Mex. Restaurant Assn. (pres. 1973-74, state dir. 1969-73, Restaurateur of Yr. 1980), N. Mex. State U. Found. (bd. dirs. 1988). Democrat. Methodist. Club: Skal Internat. (El Paso, Tex.) (pres. 1981-82). Home: 1810 Calle De Sebastian G-2 Santa Fe NM 87501 Office: NMex Econ Devel & Tourism Dept 1100 St Francis Dr Santa Fe NM 87503

SMITHWICK, RICHARD NEIL, dentist; b. India, Oct. 15, 1926; (parents Am. citizens); s. Richard Allen and Cathryn Clair (Clark) S.; m. Donna LaVelle, July 20, 1947 (div. 1974); children: Randall, Mark, Kimberlee, Lauren, Shari, Cindy; m. Cindy Lee Dickson, Oct. 1, 1977. BS, Pacific Union Coll., 1945; DDS, Univ. of the Pacific, 1948. Gen. practice dentistry Sunnyvale, Calif., 1948—. Contbr. articles to newspapers. Served to lt. (j.g.) USNR, 1951-53, Korea. Fellow Am. Coll. Dentists, Internat. Coll. Dentists; mem. ADA (trustee 1978-84), Calif. Dental Assn. (pres. 1970-71), Santa Clara County Dental Soc. (pres. 1961-62), Fedn. Dentaire Internat., Sunnyvale C. of C. Republican. Home: 7665 Woodborough Dr Granite Bay CA 95661 Office: 516 Remington Dr Sunnyvale CA 94087

SMOKER, MARK ROBERT, manufacturer representative; b. Phoenix, Sept. 13, 1957; s. Marion Robert and Beverly (Maunz) S.; children: Jessica Lynne, Melissa Marie. BSBA, Ariz. State U., 1981. Sales clk. Bashas Markets, Chandler, Ariz., 1976-84; retail mfr. rep. Couley Burcham, Phoenix, 1984-86; mfr. rep. Fort Howard Paper Corp., Green Bay, Wis., 1986—. Republican. Roman Catholic. Home and Office: 4401 E Hubbell #62 Phoenix AZ 85008

SMOKLER, PAUL EDWARD, environmental scientist, engineer, consultant; b. Washington, June 8, 1951; s. Melvin I. and Olga M.; m. Marta L. Katz, July 21, 1984. BA, UCLA, 1973, MPH, 1976, PhD in Environ. Sci., 1981. Research technician So. Calif. Coastal Water Research Proj., Los Angeles, 1973-75; USPHS tng. grantee 1975-76; staff environ. scientist Los Angeles County Sanitation Dists., Los Angeles, 1976-77; proj. physicist Jet Propulsion Lab., Pasadena, Calif., 1977; sr. proj. mgr. Ralph M. Parsons Co., Pasadena, Calif., 1978-81; proj. dir. Engring. Sci., Pasadena, Calif., 1981-87, dept. mgr., 1987--. Contr. articles on environ. sci., marine biology, medicine and mgmt. to profl. publs.; presentations on risk assessment and risk mgmt. Scaiff fellow UCLA, 1976-78. Mem. ASCE, AAAS, Nat. Assn. for Environ. Profls. (jour. reviewer 1985—), Environ. Sci. and Engring. Soc. (pres. 1987—), Air Waste Mgmt. Assn. Office: Engring Sci 100 W Walnut St Pasadena CA 91124

SMOLAN, RICK SCOTT, publisher, photographer; b. N.Y.C., Nov. 5, 1949; s. Marvin M. and Gloria (Claman) S. BA, Dickinson Coll., 1972. Photographer Life Mag., N.Y.C., 1974, Time Mag., N.Y.C., 1975-80; v.p. Contact Press Images, N.Y.C., 1975-80; photographer Nat. Geographic, Australia, 1977; pres. Day in the Life Inc., N.Y.C., 1981-86; cons. The Washington Post, 1982-83; pres. Lifetime Prodns., San Francisco, 1989—; cons. Apple Computer, San Francisco, 1989—; bd. dirs. Collins Publishers, San Francisco, 1986—. Creator photography book Day in the Life Series, 1981, art dir. A Day in the Life of Australia, 1982 (gold medal 1982), producer TV movie A Day in the Life of Hawaii, 1984 (honorable mention 1984). Named Man of Year Photog. Mktg. Assn., 1988, recipient Innovation in Photography award Am. Soc. of Mag. Photographers, 1986, esquire register award Esquire Mag., 1985, second place feature photo award Nat. Press Photographers Assn., 1987. Office: Lifetime Prodns PO Box 1189 Sausalito CA 94966-1189

SMOLENS, ROY WILKES, manufacturing executive; b. Phila., Aug. 23, 1928; s. Harry G. and Rosemary (Wilkes) S.; m. Louise Frederick, Nov. 3, 1956; children: Mark F., Roy W. Jr., Greg B. BS in Economics, Temple U., 1956. Mgmt. engr. U.S. Rubber Co., Phila., 1956-58; mgr. order entry U.S. Rubber Co., Passaic, N.J., 1958-61; mgr mfg. systems G.E. Ordnance Div., Pittsfield, Mass., 1961-62; mgr. mfg. adminstrn. G.E. Apollo Support Div., Daytona Beach, Fla., 1962-64; mgr. mfg. systems G.E. Computer Div., Phoenix, 1964-67, mgr. requisition svcs., 1967-69; acct. mgr. Bull Info. Systems, Inc., Phila., 1969-72; industry cons. Bull Info. Systems, Inc., Chgo., 1972-83; product mgr. Bull Honeywell Systems, Inc., Phoenix, 1983—. Contbr. articles to profl. jours. 1st lt. USAF 1948-53. Mem. Am. Production and Inventory Control Soc., Computer & Automated Systems Assn., Soc. Mfg. Engrs. Republican. Presbyterian. Office: Bull Info Systems Inc PO Box 8000 Phoenix AZ 85066

SMOLENSKY, EUGENE, economics educator; b. Bklyn., Mar. 4, 1932; s. Abraham and Jennie (Miller) S.; m. Natalie Joan Rabinowitz, Aug. 16, 1952; children: Paul, Beth. B.A., Bklyn. Coll., 1952; M.A., Am. U., 1956; Ph.D., U. Pa., 1961. Prof. econs. U. Wis., Madison, 1968-88, chmn. dept., 1978-80, 86-88; dir. Inst. for Research on Poverty, U. Wis., 1980-83; dean Grad. Sch. Pub. Policy U. Calif., Berkeley, 1988—. Author: Public Expenditures, Taxation and the Distribution of Income: The U.S., 1950, 61, 70, 77. Mem. com. on child devel. research and pub. policy Nat. Acad. Sci., Washington, 1982—, mem. com. on status of women in labor market, 1985—. Served with USN, 1952-56. Mem. Am. Econs. Assn. Democrat. Jewish. Home: 669 Woodmont Ave Berkeley CA 94708 Office: U Calif Dept Pub Policy 2607 Hearst Ave Berkeley CA 94720

SMOLLAN, DAVID LESLIE, tax practitioner; b. Middlesbrough, Eng., June 22, 1928; came to U.S., 1948, naturalized, 1954; s. Philip and Sarah (Freedman) S.; B.B.A., Woodbury Coll., 1950; m. Sheila Joy Glassman, Aug. 5, 1956 (dec.); children—Jeffrey, Debbie. Chief acct. Lucky Plastic Co., Inc., Los Angeles, 1951-64; self-employed tax practitioner, Encino, Calif, 1965—. Named Kiwanian of Yr., Pacoima Kiwanis Club, 1968; enrolled to practice before the IRS, 1967. Mem. Nat. Assn. Enrolled Agts. (pres. 1973-74), Calif. Soc. Enrolled Agts. Club: Kiwanis (pres. Encino 1985-86). Lodge: B'nai B'rith. Office: 7017 Hayvenhurst Ave Ste 5 Van Nuys CA 91406

SMOLUK, GERALDINE DENISE, biochemist; b. Montclair, N.J., July 7, 1959; d. George R. and Dolores M. (Kaporch) S.; m. Michael D. Crocker, Mar. 31, 1986. BS, McGill U., 1981; MS, U. Calif., San Diego, 1983, PhD, 1986. Rsch. scientist Biotrack Inc., Mountain View, Calif., 1986-87; sr. chemist Biotrack Inc., Mountain View, 1987-89; staff researcher Syntex (USA), Inc., Palo Alto, Calif., 1989—. Contbr. articles profl. jours., 1983-88. Named predoctoral trainee NIH, 1983-86. Mem. Am. Chem. Soc., Am. Assn. Clin. Chemists. Office: Syntex (USA) Inc R2-CAS 3401 Hillview Ave Palo Alto CA 94303

SMOOT, LEON DOUGLAS, university dean, chemical engineering educator; b. Provo, Utah, July 26, 1934; s. Douglas Parley and Jennie (Hallam) S.; m. Marian Bird, Sept. 7, 1953; children: Analee, LaCinda, Michelle, Melinda Lee. B.S., Brigham Young U., 1957; M.S., U. Wash., 1958, Ph.D., 1960. Registered profl. engr., Utah. Engr. Boeing Corp., Seattle, 1956; teaching and research asst. Brigham Young U., 1954-57; engr. Phillips Petroleum Corp., Arco, Idaho, 1957; engr., cons. Hercules Powder Co., Bacchus, Utah, 1961-63; asst. prof. Brigham Young U., 1960-63; engr. Lockheed Propulsion, Redlands, Calif., 1963-67; vis. asst. prof. Calif. Inst. Tech., 1966-67; asso. prof. to prof. Brigham Young U., 1967—, chmn. dept. chem. engring., 1970-77, dean Coll. Engring. and Tech., 1977—; dir. Advanced Combustion Engring. Research Ctr. (NSF), 1986—; cons. Hercules, Thiokol, Lockheed, Teledyne, Atlantic Research Corp., Raytheon, Redd and Redd, Billings Energy, Ford, Bacon & Davis, Jaycor, Intel Com Radiation Tech., Phys. Dynamics, Nat. Soc. Propellants and Explosives, France, DFVLR, West Germany, Martin Marietta, Honeywell, Phillips Petroleum Co., Exxon, Nat. Bur. Standards, Eyring Research Inst., Systems, Sci. and Software., Los Alamos Nat. Lab., others. Contbr. over 150 articles to tech. jours.; author 2 books on coal combustion. Mem. Am. Inst. Chem. Engrs., Am. Inst. Aeros. and Astronautics, Am. Soc. Engring. Edn., Combustion Inst., Research Soc. Am., Tau Beta Pi, Phi Lambda Epsilon, Sigma Xi. Republican. Mem. Ch. Jesus Christ of Latter-day Saints. Home: 1811 N 1550 East Provo UT 84604 Office: Brigham Young U 270 CB Provo UT 84602

SMOOT, WENDELL MCMEANS, JR., investment counselor; b. Salt Lake City, Jan. 15, 1921; s. Wendell M. and Rebecca (Clawson) S.; m. Barbara Davis, June 24, 1942; children—Wendell M. III, Margaret, David, John, Mary. B.A., U. Utah, 1942. Gen. ptnr. J.A. Hogle & Co., Salt Lake City, 1945-63, Goodbody & Co., N.Y.C., 1963-70; pres. Smoot, Miller, Cheney & Co., Salt Lake City, 1971—; dir. Grand Central, Inc. Pres. Great Salt Lake council Boy Scouts Am., 1968-70; chmn. Utah State Pioneer Meml. Theatre, 1978-79; pres. Mormon Tabernacle Choir. Served to capt., U.S. Army, 1942-45; ETO. Mem. Fin. Analysts Soc. Republican. Mem. Ch. of Jesus Christ of Latter Day Saints. Club: The Country. Lodge: Rotary.

SMOROWSKI, GERARD ANTHONY, JR., electrical engineer; b. Rockford, Ill., Nov. 20, 1952; s. Gerard Anthony and Victoria Jeanine (Muscato) S. BSEE, Calif. Poly. State U., 1978. Staff engr. Motorola, Inc., Scottsdale, Ariz., 1978—. With USAF, 1972-75. Mem. Etta Kappa Nu, GGGGG of A. Republican. Roman Catholic. Home: 531 Farmdale Mesa AZ 85210 Office: Motorola GEG 8201 E McDowell Rd Scottsdale AZ 85252

SMRCKA, ANTONIN KLEMENT JOSEF, university administrator, consultant; b. Humpolec, Czechoslovakia, June 17, 1931; came to Can., 1951; s. Antonin Karel Josef and Bozena (Kristufek) S.; m. Solanges Madeleine Gabrielle Domerson, June 28, 1958; 1 child, Julienne. BS, Concordia U., Montreal, Que., Can., 1957, BA, 1967; diploma in edn. McGill U., Montreal, 1971; PhD, U. N.Mex., 1978, cert. ednl. spl. adminstrn., 1984. Cert. tchr. N.Mex., Que.; cert. adminstr., N.Mex., Que. Sr. mktg. analyst Allied Chem. Co., Montreal, 1953-68; natural scis. coordinator, tchr. Vaudreuil High Sch., Que., 1968-73; tchr., supv. social scis. Pius X High Sch., Albuquerque, 1973-75; instr. ednl. found. U. N.Mex., Albuquerque, 1975-78; asst. to pres., planning and grants adminstr. and asst. prof. U. Albuquerque, 1978-84; v.p. for bus. affairs Coll. of Santa Fe, 1984-86; pres., dir. P.M.S., Inc., Albuquerque, 1981—; owner Profl. Mgmt. Svc., Quebec, 1963-73; reporter Czechoslovak Daily Herald, Chgo., 1987—. Exec. v.p., sec., treas. bd. trustees Am. U. of Les Cayes (Haiti), 1983-73; pres. bd. dirs. S.W. Maternity Ctr., Inc., Albuquerque, 1975; treas. Dorion Garden Community Council, Que., 1961. Named hon. mem. Ecole des Hautes Commerciales et Industrie, Port-Au-Prince, Haiti, 1971. Mem. Chem. Inst. Can., Can. Soc. for Chem. Engrs., AAUP, Assn. for Curriculum and Devel., Am. Accrediting Assn. of Retirement Ctrs. (trustee 1984-89, chmn. bd. trustees 1983-84), Greater Albuquerque C. of C., Optimist, Phi Delta Kappa. Republican. Roman Catholic. Home: 4224 Roma NE Albuquerque NM 87108 Office: Am U Les Cayes 1234 Massachusetts Ave NW Ste 819 Washington DC 20005

SMYSER, ADAM ALBERT, newspaper editor; b. York, Pa., Dec. 18, 1920; s. Adam Milton and Miriam (Stein) S.; m. Elizabeth Harrison Avery, Dec. 25, 1943 (dec. 1983); children: Heidi, Avery; m. Doris H. Prather, Apr. 24, 1984. B.A., Pa. State U., 1941. Rewrite man Pitts. Press, 1941-42; with Honolulu Star-Bull., 1946—, city editor, 1953-60, mng. editor, 1960-65, editor, 1966-75, editor editorial page, 1975-83, contbg. editor, 1983—; mem. Pulitzer Journalism Awards Jury, 1970. Author: Hawaii's Future in the Pacific: Disaster, Backwater or Future State?, 1988; former free lance writer: McGraw-Hill mags. Chmn. temporary commn. on statewide environ. planning, 1973; bd. dirs. Aloha United Fund, Friends of East-West Ctr., Oahu Cancer Soc., Found. for Study in Hawaii and Abroad, Aloha Week Hawaii, Nat. Council Crime and Delinquency, Goodwill Industries; chmn. steering com. Gov.'s Congress on Hawaii's Internat. Role, 1988. Lt. USNR, 1942-46, PTO. Recipient Distinguished Alumnus award Pa. State U., 1976. Mem. Hawaii C. of C., Council on Fgn. Relations, Hawaii Econ. Assn., Honolulu Social Sci. Assn., Honolulu Acad. Arts, Am. Soc. Newspaper Editors, Sigma Delta Chi. Clubs: Honolulu Press (named to Hall of Fame 1987), Honolulu Rotary. Home: 1052 Iiwi St Honolulu HI 96816 Office: Honolulu Star-Bull 605 Kapiolani Blvd Honolulu HI 96813

SMYSER, CHARLES ARVIL (SKIP SMYSER), senator, lawyer; b. Caldwell, Idaho, Nov. 14, 1949; s. Samuel H. and Mildred (Skelton) S.; m. Melinda Slovìaczek, Aug. 22, 1981; children: Lincoln William, Logan. BA, Ea. Wash. U., 1972; JD, Gonzaga U., 1977. Bar: Idaho 1977. Dep. pros. atty. Ada County, Boise, Idaho, 1977-79; dep. atty. gen. State of Idaho, Boise, 1979-80; ptnr. Connolly & Smyser, Boise and Parma, Idaho, 1980—; senator State of Idaho, 1982—. Mem. Idaho Ho. of Reps., Canyon County, 1980-82; bd. dirs. Idaho State Sch. and Hosp., Nampa, Calif., 1982-88. Capt. Q.M.C., U.S. Amry, 1972-74. Named Legis. of Yr. Idaho Prosecuting Atty.'s Assn., one of Outstanding Young Men of Am. U.S. Jaycees, 1977-86. Mem. Idaho State Bar Assn., Lions, Masons, Scottish Rite. Republican. Presbyterian. Office: Connolly & Smyser 134 S 5th Boise ID 83702 Address: Scotish Rite Shrine 26298 Lee Ln Parma ID 83660

SMYTH, DAVID SHANNON, real estate investor, commercial and retail builder and developer; b. Denver, May 13, 1943; s. William James and Constance Ruth (Sherman) S.; student Regis Coll., 1967-69, USAF Acad., 1961-65, U. No. Colo., 1965-67; m. Sharon Kaye Swiderski, Jan. 3, 1980; children—Julia Caitlin, Alexander Jeremiah, Matthew Davis; 1 son by previous marriage, Shannon David. Accountant, Colo. Nat. Bank, 1966-69; bus. analyst Dun & Bradstreet, 1969-70; pres., dir. Georgetown Valley Water & Sanitation Dist., 1973-74, Realists, Inc., 1973-74, Silver Queen Constrn. Co., 1973-74; v.p., sec., dir. Georgetown Assocs., Inc. (Colo.), 1970-74; pres., chief ops. officer Lincoln Cos., Denver, 1975-76; project mgr., sales mgr., prin. Brooks-Morris Homes, Fox Ridge, Colo., 1976-77; project mgr. U.S. West Homes, Denver, 1977-78; pres., dir. Denver Venture Capital, 1978-81; prin., dir., exec. v.p. Shelter Equities, Inc., 1982-87; prin., dir., exec. v.p. Comml. Constrn. Mgmt. Services, Inc., Shelter Equities, Inc., 1984-87; owner, dir., exec. v.p. Maple Leaf Realty Corp.; v.p., dir. Gibraltar Devel. Corp., Dominion Properties Ltd., 1978-82; investment dir. Van Schaack & Co., 1987—. Served with USAF, 1961-65. Lic. real estate broker. Home: 6093 E Briarwood Dr Englewood CO 80112 Office: Van Schaack & Co 370 17th St #505 Denver CO 80282

SMYTHE, EDWARD WILLIAM, communications and training company executive; b. Louisville, Dec. 11, 1941; s. Edward Joseph and Evelyn Pearl (Wheeler) S.; m. Sharon Stephanie Miller, Aug. 7, 1965; children: Stephen William, Shannon Stephanie. Student, Palomar Coll., 1960-64. Tech. artist Gen. Atomic Co., San Diego, 1959-75; pres. Smythe Graphics, Ltd., Del Mar, Calif., 1975-86; pres. Image Dynamics Inc., Sn Diego, 1986—, also bd. dirs.; lectr. in field. Mem. Soc. Tech. Communications. Office: Image Dynamics 5820 Oberlin Dr San Diego CA 92121

SNARE, CARL LAWRENCE, JR., business executive; b. Chgo., Oct. 25, 1936; s. Carl Lawrence and Lillian Marie (Luoma) S.; B.B.A., Northwestern U., 1968; postgrad. Roosevelt U.; postgrad. in econs. San Francisco State U., 1976-77. Cert. fin. planner. Asst. sec., controller Bache Halsey Stuart & Shields Inc. (now Prudential Bache), Chgo., 1968-73; controller Innisfree Corp. div. Hyatt Corp., Burlingame, Calif., 1973-76; cash mgr. Portland (Oreg.) Gen. Electric Co., 1976-79; chief fin. officer, controller Vistar Fin. Inc., Marina del Rey, Calif., 1979-82; v.p., treas. Carson Estate Co., Rancho Dominguez, Calif., 1988—; pres. Snare Properties Co., Rialto, Calif., 1984—, Snare Fin. Services Corp., Rialto, 1985—; registered investment advisor. C.P.A., real estate broker, cert. fin. planner, Calif. Mem. Am. Inst. C.P.A.s, Calif. Soc. C.P.A.s, Internat. Assn. Fin. Planners, Am. Inst. Fin. Planners. Founder Cash Mgmt. Assn., Portland, Oreg. Home: 1131 Wisteria Ave Rialto CA 92376 Office: 18710 S Wilmington Ave Ste 200 Rancho Dominguez CA 90220

SNASDELL, SUSAN KATHLEEN, computer company executive; b. St. Louis, July 17, 1948; d. Russell John and Gertrude Burnett (Gassman) S. BA, So. Nazarene U., 1972. Office adminstr. Lake, Van Dyke & Browne Med. Group, Pasadena, Calif., 1972-83; founder, ptnr., adminstr. ComputerEase, Oxnard, Calif., 1984—. Contbr. articles to profl. jours. Mem. NAFE, Better Bus. Bur., Oxnard C. of C. Office: ComputerEase 1201 Escalon Dr Oxnard CA 93035

SNELL, PAUL ALAN, SR., protective services official; b. L.A., June 14, 1957; s. Willie and Mary (Walker) S.; m. Rosalind Matthews, Nov. 24, 1975; children: Shannon Deniece, Paul Alan Jr. BA, Occidental Coll., 1979. Airport police officer L.A. Airport, 1982-84; police officer III L.A. Police Dept., 1984—; Democrat. Baptist. Democrat. Baptist.

SNELL, RICHARD, hotel company executive; b. Phoenix, Nov. 26, 1930; s. Frank L. and Elizabeth (Berlin) S.; m. Alice Cosette Wiley, Aug. 1, 1954. BA, Stanford U., 1952, JD, 1954. Bar: Ariz. Ptnr. firm Snell & Wilmer, Phoenix, 1956-81; pres., chmn., chief exec. officer Ramada Inc., Phoenix, 1981—; dir. Ariz. Public Service Co., Pinnacle West Capital Corp. Trustee Am. Grad. Sch. Internat. Mgmt., Phoenix; past pres. YMCA Met. Phoenix and Valley of Sun. Served with U.S. Army, 1954-56. Mem. ABA, Ariz. Bar Assn., Maricopa County Bar Assn. Republican. Lutheran. Clubs: Paradise Valley Country, John Gardiner's Tennis Ranch. Office: Ramada Inc 2390 E Camelback Rd Phoenix AZ 85016 *

SNELL, RICHARD MILAN, electrical engineer; b. Kalispell, Mont., Dec. 19, 1942; s. Robert and Hazel Magdalene (Smart) S.; m. Yvonne Marie Davis, June 5, 1965; children: Robin Lynn, David Alan. BSEE, Washington State U., 1966. Registered profl. engr. Mont. Asst. distbn. engr. Pacific Power and Light Co., Portland, Oreg., 1966-68; div. engr. Mont. Power Co., Great Falls, 1968-74; sr. engr. Mont. Power Co., Butte, 1974-76, sr. tech. engr., 1976-78, sect. head, distbn. engr., 1978—. Mem. IEEE, Northwest Electric Light and Power Assn. Baptist. Club: Butte Amateur Radio. Home: 324 Galaxy Dr Butte MT 59701-3973 Office: Mont Power Co 40 E Broadway Butte MT 59701-9334

SNETZER, MICHAEL ALAN, multi-industry executive; b. Denver, May 26, 1940; s. Robert Ellis and Kathryn (Wake) S.; m. Peggy Ann Sparks, Jan., 1964 (div. 1973); children: Michael Ellis, Gregory Alan; m. Deborah Kay Gee, Mar. 15, 1975; 1 child, Robert Adam. BS, U. Ark., 1963; MBA, So. Meth. U., 1969. Indsl. engr. Collins Radio Co., Dallas, 1966-69; v.p. fin. UCCEL Corp., Dallas, 1969-77; v.p. fin. Contran Corp., Dallas, 1977-84, exec. v.p., 1984-87; pres. Valhi, Inc., Dallas, 1987—; bd. dirs. NL Industries, Inc., Houston, Baroid Corp., Houston, Amalgamated Sugar Co., Ogden, Utah; chmn., dir. Medford (Oreg.) Corp. wholly owned sub. Valhi Inc. Served to capt. U.S. Army, 1963-66, Vietnam. Recipient Bronze star. Mem. Univ. Club. Republican. Methodist. Home: 18722 Campbell Rd Dallas TX 75252 Office: Valhi Inc 3 Lincoln Ctr 5430 LBJ Frwy Dallas TX 75240

SNIDER, LARRY LEE, surgeon; b. Shreveport, La., Dec. 31, 1945; s. Harold Everett and Dorothy (Speas) S.; m. Patricia Anselin, June 3, 1972; children: Jamie, Jordan. BS, U. Wyo., Laramie, 1968; DDS, Baylor U., 1972. Intern, then resident oral and maxillocacial surgery Parkland Meml. Hosp., Dallas, 1972-75; pvt. practice medicine specializing in oral and maxillofacial surgery Lakewood, Colo., 1975—; assoc. clin. prof. dentistry U. Colo., Denver, 1976—. Contbr. book Surgical Correction of Dennfacial Deformities, 1973. Bd. dirs. Am. Cancer Soc., Denver, 1976-79. Fellow Am. Assn. Oral-Maxillofacial Surgeons, Am. Coll. Oral-Maxillofacial Surgeons, Internat. Assn. Oral-Maxillofacial Surgeons; mem. ADA, Met. Denver Dental So., Psi Omega. Office: 2290 Kipling Lakewood CO 80215

SNIDER, PAUL RAYMOND, television director; b. L.A., June 15, 1952; s. Paul Rafael and Helen (Stoyka) S.; m. Kathleen Ann Zakarian, June 25, 1977; children: Evan Alexander, Paige Allison. AA in radio, TV, film, L.A. City Coll., 1973; BA in radio, TV, film, Calif. State U., Northridge, 1976. Prodn. asst. Lorimar Prodns., Calif., 1979-81, 2d asst. dir., 1981-84, 1st asst. dir., 1984-89; prodn. asst. Osmond TV, 1980; 2d asst. dir. MTM Prodns., 1983-84; 1st asst. dir. Stephen J. Cannell Prodns., 1985-87, Viacom Prodns., 1987-88, Lorimar Telepictures div. Lorimar Corp., 1988—. Mem. Dirs. Guild Am., Am. Film Inst. Republican.

SNOOK, JOHN MCCLURE, telephone company executive; b. Toledo, May 31, 1917; s. Ward H. and Grace (McClure) S.; m. Marjorie Younce (dec.); student Ohio State U., 1936-43. Instr. history, fine arts and scis. Ohio State U., Columbus; exec. v.p. Gulf Telephone Co., Foley, Ala., 1955-71, pres., 1971—. Chmn., Baldwin Sesquicentennial, 1969; mem. Baldwin County Bicentennial Commn.; pageant chmn., dir. Ft. Morgan Bicentennial Program, 1976; mem. hon. staff Gov. Ala., 1967—; past pres. Friends of Library Assn.; asso. sponsor Gulf Shores Mardi Gras Assn. Hon. a.d.c. lt. col. Ala.; hon. Ala. state trooper; recipient Citizen of Year award Gulf Shores, 1956-57. Mem. Ala.-Miss. Ind. Telephone Assn. (past pres.), Nat. Rifle Assn. (life), Am. Ordnance Assn., South Baldwin C. of C., Delaware County, Baldwin County (pres.) hist. assns., Defiance and Williams' Hist. Soc., Am. Mus. Nat. History Assn., Nat. Hist. Soc., Nat. Wildlife Fedn., Clan McLeod Soc., Smithsonian Assn., Am. Heritage Soc., Nat. Fedn. Blind, Ohio State Alumni Assn., Ala. Ind. Telephone Assn., Telephone Pioneers, Ind. Pioneers. Clubs: Lions (past pres.), Kiwanis (past pres.; asst. chmn. ann. Christmas Party and Parade). Office: Gulf Tel Co PO Box 670 Foley AL 36535

SNOOK, QUINTON, construction company executive; b. Atlanta, July 15, 1925; s. John Wilson and Charlotte Louise (Clayson) S.; student U. Idaho, 1949-51; m. Lois Mullen, Jan. 19, 1947; children—Lois Ann Snook Matteson, Quinton A., Edward M., Clayson S., Charlotte T. Rancher, Lemhi Valley, Idaho, 1942—; owner, mgr. Snook Constrn., Salmon, Idaho, 1952—; owner Snook Trucking, 1967—, Lemhi Posts and Poles, 1980—. Mem. Lemhi County Commn., Dist. 2, 1980—. Mem. Am. Quarter Horse Assn., Farm Bur., Nat. Rifleman's Assn., Am. Hereford Assn., Idaho Cattlemen's Assn. Republican. Episcopalian. Club: Elks. Home: Rte 1 Box 49 Salmon ID 83467

SNOW, DAVID WAYNE, computer security architect; b. Holyoke, Mass., Aug. 9, 1946; s. John Eaton and Ethel Nathalie (Coward) S.; m. Mary Lynne Vena, Feb. 23, 1969; children: Virginia Rosemary Wagner, Matthew John. BA, Clark U., 1968; MS, Johns Hopkins U., 1973. Cert. communication security analyst. Analyst Nat. Security Agy., Ft. George G. Meade, Md., 1968-73; mem. tech. staff Mitre Corp., Bedford, Mass., 1973-77; program mgr. Merdan Group, San Diego, 1977-81, Purvis Systems, San Diego, 1981-82; v.p. Compusec, Inc., San Diego, 1982-85; pres. Infosec Systems, San Diego, 1985—; author, instr. Integrated Computer Systems, Culver City, Calif., 1987—. With USMC, 1970. Scholar Clark U., 1964-68. Mem. Info. Systems Security Assn. (guest speaker 1988-89), Am. Soc. for Indsl. Security, IEEE, Armed Forces Communications and Electronics Assn. (guest speaker 1987). Republican. Christian Science. Office: INFOSEC Systems 9245 Sky Park Ct 210 San Diego CA 92123

SNOW, JEFFREY ELLIOTT, comptroller, accountant; b. Seattle, June 25, 1960; s. Sterling Elliott and Gloria (Phillipy) S. BA in Profl. Acctg., Ea. Wash. State U., 1984. CPA, Wash. Night auditor SE Rykoff, Spokane, Wash., 1982-83; asst. controller Wick Constn. Co., Seattle, 1984-85; sec., treas. Sound Elevator Co., Kirkland, Wash., 1985—. Bd. dirs. Bothell (Wash.) Downtown Mgmt. Assn., 1987—. Mem. Wash. State Soc. CPAs, Constrn. Fin. Mgmt. Republican. Lutheran. Home: 16294 39th Ave Seattle WA 98155 Office: Sound Elevator Co 506 7th Ave S Kirkland WA 98033

SNOW, KAREN MARIE, management information systems consultant; b. Camden, N.J., Aug. 15, 1962; d. Lewis Wendell and Patricia Ann (Sodja) S. BS, Tex. A&M U., 1984. Mgmt. info. cons. Andersen Cons. Arthur Andersen & Co., Dallas and L.A., 1984—. Vol. Calif. Spl. Olympics, L.A., 1986-88; mem. FOCUS Young Profls. Orgn. Multiple Sclerosis Soc., L.A., 1985—. Republican. Methodist. Office: Andersen Cons 990 W 190th St Ste 300 Torrance CA 90502

SNOW, MARCELLUS SCOWCROFT, economics educator; b. Ogden, Utah, Apr. 2, 1942; s. Marcellus Keyting and Charlene (Scowcroft) S.; m. Edwina Jo Burton, Mar. 27, 1967; children: David Burton, Jonathan Marcellus, Matthew Stephen. BA magna cum laude, U. Utah, 1965; MS, MIT, 1967; MA, Johns Hopkins U., 1969; PhD, U. Calif., Berkeley, 1974. Rsch. asst. World Bank, Washington, 1969; fin., polit. analyst Communications Satellite Corp., Washington, 1969-71, summer 1972; instr. econs. Calif. State U., San Francisco, 1972; rsch. asst. dept. econs. U. Calif., Berkeley, 1971-74; asst. prof. econs. U. Hawaii, Honolulu, 1974-79, assoc. prof., 1979-86, prof., 1986—; Fulbright rsch. prof. U. Bonn, 1980-81; vis. scholar Stanford U., summer 1983; cons. ITT, 1978, Dept. Commerce, 1979, Max Planck Inst., 1986-87. Author: International Commercial Satellite Communications, 1976, The International Telecommunications Satellite Orgn. (INTELSAT), 1987, INTELSAT: An Economic Assessment, 1988; co-editor: Economic and Policy Problems in Satellite Communications, 1977; editor: Marketplace for Telecommunications: Regulation and Deregulation in Industrialized Democracies, 1986; co-author: Telecommunication Economics and Internat Regulatory Policy, 1986; contbr. articles to profl. jours. Scoutmaster, Boy Scouts Am., Honolulu, 1984—. NSF fellow, 1965-68, NSF grantee, 1984; Harvard U. fellow, 1988. Mem. ABA (assoc.), Am. Econ. Assn., Pacific Telecommunications Council, Internat. Inst. Communications, Econometric Soc. (sec.-treas.), Hawaii Coun. Econ. Edn. Home: 4774 Aukai Ave Honolulu HI 96816 Office: U Hawaii Dept Econs 2424 Maile Way Honolulu HI 96822

SNOWDEN, DIANA EMILY, utility company executive; b. N.Y.C., Oct. 29, 1947; d. Joseph Philip and Barbara Ellen (O'Mara) Loftus; m. Arthur Holburn Snowden II, June, 1, 1968 (div. Dec. 1982); children: Kirsten M., Arthur Neilan III. BA, Trinity Coll., 1968; MA, U. Alaska, 1983. Asst. v.p., treas. Westwood Mgmt. Corp., Bethesda, Md., 1970-73; dir. employee relations Anchorage Sch. Dist., 1973-79; v.p. indsl. relations Alascom and Tel Utilities, Inc., Anchorage, 1979-81; commr. Alaska Pub Utilities Commn., Anchorage, 1981-85; exec. dir. PNUCC, Portland, Oreg., 1985-86; v.p. human resources Pacific Power and Light, Portland, 1986—; cons. Alaska Gas Pipeline Adv. Bd., Anchorage, 1985—. Commr. Alaska State Human Rights Commn., Anchorage, 1976-81, chairperson; mem. Alaska Adv. Bd. U.S. Commn. on Civil Rights, 1979-81; bd. dirs. Anchorage Youth Adv. Bd., 1974-76, Bus Youth Exchange, 1986—, Goodwill Industries Oreg., Greater Bus. Group on Health, 1986—. Mem. Nat. Assn. Regulatory Utility Commrs., 1981-84. Republican. Roman Catholic. Home: 4405 SW Coun Crest Dr Portland OR 97201 Office: Pacific Power and Light Co 920 SW 6th Ave Portland OR 97204

SNURE, DOUGLAS CONRAD, marketing executive; b. Triumph, Minn., July 15, 1934; s. Frank Hamilton and Esther Margaret (Gustafson) S.; m. Janice Marie Bartko, June 28, 1958; children: Craig, Dawn, Scott. BA in Econs., U. of Minn., 1959. Spl. agt. USN Intelligence, various cities, 1959-61; project adminstr. Honeywell Inc., West Covina, Calif., 1961-62, contracts rep., 1962-63, mktg. rep, 1963-64; mktg. rep Honeywell Inc., N.Y.C., 1964-65, Orlando, Fla., 1965-66; mktg. mgr. Honeywell Inc., Dallas, 1966-68; mgr. contract adminstrn. Honeywell Inc., Clearwater, Fla., 1968-73, program mgr., 1973-76, product mgr., 1976-77; mgr. bus. analysis Honeywell Inc., Mpls., 1977-79, dir. cust. spt., 1979-83, dir. mktg., 1983-87; v.p. mktg. Honeywell Inc., Phoenix, 1987—. Served to AO2 USN, 1952-55. Mem. Gen. Aviation Mfrs. Assn., Am. Helicopter Soc., Aircraft Owners & Pilots Assn. Republican. Lutheran. Club: Nat. Aviation. Home: 508 W Sweetwater Phoenix AZ 85029 Office: Honeywell Inc 5353 W Bell Rd Glendale AZ 85308

SNYDAL, LAURENCE RUSSELL, educator; b. Minot, N.D., July 26, 1938; s. Sigurdur Bjorneheddin and Bertha (Rasmussen) S.; m. Susan Louise Holmes, Dec. 27, 1968; children: Theodore Sigurd, Jonathan Solis. BA in History, San Jose State U., 1964; postgrad. in geography, U. Calif., Berkeley, 1966-68. Cert. tchr., Calif. Tchr. Berryessa Union Sch. Dist., San Jose, Calif., 1964-66, 74—, Happy Camp (Calif.) Sch. Dist., 1968-74. Author: Dinner, Diapers and Dad, 1984, New Fathers' Survival Guide, 1987; contbr. numerous poems to various mags. and anthologies. Pres. Happy Camp Library Bd., 1970-73; instr. new father's program El Camino Hosp., Mountain View, Calif., 1987—, San Jose Hosp., 1988—. With USAF, 1957-61. Hewlett-Packard Co. sci. grantee, 1986. Mem. Calif. Tchrs. Assn. Democrat. Office: Vinci Park Elem Sch 1311 Vinci Park Way San Jose CA 95131

SNYDER, ALLEGRA FULLER, dance educator; b. Chgo., Aug. 28, 1927; d. R. Buckminster and Anne (Hewlett) Fuller; m. Robert Snyder, June 30, 1951 (div. Apr. 1975, remarried Sept. 1980); children: Alexandra, Jaime. BA in Dance, Bennington Coll., 1951; MA in Dance, UCLA, 1967. Asst. to curator, dance archives Mus. Modern Art, N.Y.C., 1945-47; dancer Ballet Soc. of N.Y.C. Ballet Co., 1945-47; mem. office and prodn. staff Internat. Film Found., N.Y.C., 1950-52; editor, dance films Film News mag., N.Y.C., 1966-72; lectr. dance and film adv., dept. dance UCLA, 1967-73, chmn. dept. dance, 1974-80, acting chair, spring 1985, prof. dance and dance ethnology, 1973—; vis. lectr. Calif. Inst. of Arts, Valencia, 1972; co-dir. dance and TV workshop Am. Dance Fest., Conn. Coll., New London, 1973; dir. NEH summer seminar for coll. tchrs. Asian Performing Arts, 1978, 81; coord. Ethnic Arts Intercoll. Interdisciplinary program, 1974-83, acting chmn., 1986; vis. prof. performance studies NYU, 1982-83; hon. vis. prof. U. Surrey, Guildford, Eng., 1983-84; bd. dirs. Buckminster Fuller Inst.; cons. Thyodia Found., Salt Lake City, 1973-74; mem. dance adv. panel Nat. Endowment Arts, 1968-72, Calif. Arts Commn., 1974; mem. adv. screening com. Council Internat. Exchange of Scholars, 1979-82; mem. various panels NEH, 1979-85; mem. adv. bd. Los Angeles Dance Alliance, 1978-84; cons. dance film series Am. Film Inst, 1974-75. Dir. film Baroque Dance 1625-1725, in 1977; co-dir. film Gods of Bali, 1952; dir. and wrote film Bayanihan, 1962 (named Best Folkloric Documentary at Bilboa Film Festival, winner Golden Eagle award); asst. dir. and asst. editor film The Bennington Story, 1952; created films Gestures of Sand, 1968, Reflections on Choreography, 1973, When the Fire Dances Between Two Poles, 1982; created film, video loop and text Celebration: A World of Art and Ritual, 1982-83; supr. post-prodn. film Erick Hawkins, 1964, in 1973. Also contbr. articles to profl. jours. and mags. Adv. com. Pacific Asia Mus., 1980-84, Festival of the Mask, Craft and Folk Art Mus., 1979-84; adv. panel Los Angeles Dance Currents II, Mus. Ctr. Dance Assn., 1974-75; bd. dirs. Council Grove Sch. III, Compton, Calif., 1976-81; apptd. mem. Adv. Dance Com., Pasadena (Calif.) Art Mus., 1970-71, Los Angeles Festival of Performing Arts com., Studio Watts, 1970; mem. Technology and Cultural Transformation com., UNESCO, 1977. Fulbright research fellow, 1983-84; grantee Nat. Endowment Arts, 1981, Nat. Endowment Humanities, 1977, 79, 81, UCLA, 1968, 77, 80, 82, 85. Mem. Am. Dance Therapy Assn., Congress on Research in Dance (bd. dirs. 1970-76, chairperson 1975-77, nat. conf. chair 1972), Council Dance Adminstrs., Am. Dance Guild (chairperson com. awards, 1972), Soc. for Ethnomusicology, Am. Anthropol. Assn., Am. Folklore Soc., Soc. Anthropology of Visual Communication, Soc. Anthropol. Study of Play, Soc. Humanistic Anthropology, Calif. Dance Educators Assn. (conf. chair 1972), Los Angeles Area Dance Alliance (adv. bd. 1978-84, selection com. Dance Kaleidoscope project 1979-81), Fulbright Alumni Assn. Home: 15313 Whitfield Ave Pacific Palisades CA 90272 Office: UCLA Dept Dance 124 Dance Bldg Los Angeles CA 90024

SNYDER, BARBARA SHEPPARD, psychologist; b. Woodland, Calif., Nov. 14, 1930; d. Frederick Funston and Harriet Marian (Haas) Sheppard; m. Lloyd Robert Snyder; children: Julie Ann, Thomas Lloyd, James Paul, David Frederick. BA, U. Calif., Berkeley, 1952; MS, Calif. State U., Fullerton, 1969. Licensed ednl. psychologist, Calif. Tchr. Berkeley (Calif.) Unified Sch. Dist., 1952-53; psychologist Anaheim City (Calif.) Sch. Dist., 1969-71, North Salem (N.Y.) Cen. Sch. Dist., 1972-77, Somers (N.Y.) Cen. Sch. Dist., 1974-85, Mt. Diablo Unified Sch. Dist., Concord, Calif., 1986-. Active Community Adv. Bd., Yorktown Heights, N.Y., 1977-82. Mem. Nat. Assn. Sch. Psychologists, Calif. Assn. Sch. Psychologists, Mt. Diablo Sch. Psychologists Assn. Democrat. Presbyterian. Home: 26 Silverwood Ct Orinda CA 94563

SNYDER, DAVID L., film production designer; b. Buffalo, Sept. 22, 1944; s. Albert R. and Louise M. (Passero) S.; children: David Michael, Amy Lynne. Grad. high sch., Niagara Falls, N.Y. Ind. film prodn. designer Hollywood, Calif.; pres. Snyder Bros. Prodns., Inc., Hollywood. Art dir.: (films) In God We Trust, The Idolmaker, Blade Runner (Oscar nomination), Brainstorm; prodn. designer: (films) Strange Brew, Racing With the Moon, The Woman In Red, My Science Project, Pee-Wee's Big Adventure, Back to School, Armed & Dangerous, Summer School, Moving, She's Out of Control; assoc. producer film Cold Dog Soup. Mem. Soc. Motion Picture and TV Art Dirs., Acad. Motion Picture Arts and Scis., Nat. Acad. TV Arts and Scis. Democrat. Office: care The Gersh Agy 222 N Canon Dr Beverly Hills CA 90210

SNYDER, DAVID RICHARD, lawyer; b. Kalamazoo, Mich., Oct. 9, 1949; s. Richard E. and Margaret L. (Vanderplough) S.; m. Phyllis Alford, Aug. 14, 1971; children: Jason Richard, Carrie Lynn. BA with high honors, Mich. State U., 1971; JD with distinction, Cornell U., 1974. Bar: Calif. 1974. Assoc. Jenkins & Perry, San Diego, 1974-77, ptnr., 1978-83; ptnr. Aylward, Kintz & Stiska, San Diego, 1983-86, Luce, Forward, Hamilton & Scripps, San Diego, 1986—; adj. prof. Calif. Western Sch. Law, San Diego, 1982-84; lectr. Calif. Continuing Edn. of Bar, 1983—. Co-author: Drafting Legal Instruments, 1982; editor Cornell Law Rev., 1973-74. Bd. dirs. Boys' Club Chula Vista (Calif.), 1979-83; pres. Corpus Christi Parish Coun., Bonita, Calif., 1988—; vice chmn. Children's Hosp. Found., San Diego, 1989—. Mem. ABA (fed. securities law com. 1987—), State Bar Calif., San Diego County Bar Assn., Order of Coif., Phi Beta Kappa. Republican. Roman Catholic. Office: Luce Forward Hamilton et al 110 West A St San Diego CA 92101

SNYDER, DENNIS ROBERT, electronics executive; b. Rockeville Center, N.Y., Nov. 1, 1944; s. Edgar Joseph and Doris Edna (Bedell) S.; m. Angela Ann Wofford, July 10, 1976; children: Daisie Lynne, Richard Alan. AA,

Grossmont Coll., 1971; BSEE, San Diego State U., 1973; diploma, DeVry Inst. Tech., 1974; MBA, Fla. Inst. Tech., 1981; postgrad. in sr. mgmt. program, U. Fla., 1984-85. Test technician NCR, San Diego, 1968-72; systems design engr. Tex. Instruments, Dallas, 1973-74, NCR, Columbia, S.C., 1974-76; product planner Harris Semicondr., Melbourne, Fla., 1976-79; mktg. mgr. Motorola, Austin, Tex., 1979-82; strategic mktg. mgr. Harris Semicondr., Melbourne, Fla., 1982-85; pres., owner Bus. and Tech. Cons., Colorado Springs, 1986—; dir. product line microelectronics ctr. United Techs., Colorado Springs, Colo., 1986-88; cons., pres. Bus. and Tech. Cons., Colorado Springs, 1986—; dist. Watkins Products, Colorado Springs, 1987—; v.p. mktg. and sales OMUPE Tech., Montreal, Que., Can., 1988-89; pres., owner OMUPE Internat., Colorado Springs, 1988-89; cons. Dennis Snyder & Assocs., Austin, 1979-82. Contbr. articles to profl. jours. Capt. Rivershores East Assn., Indialantic, 1982-86; v.p. Brevard Zool. Soc., Melbourne, 1984-85. Served to sgt. USAF, 1965-68. Mem. IEEE (vice chmn. 1972-73), Mensa. Republican. Club: Computer (Austin) (v.p. 1981-82).

SNYDER, HOWARD ARTHUR, aerospace engineering sciences educator, industrial consultant; b. Palmerton, Pa., Mar. 7, 1930; s. Howard Franklin and Mary Rachel (Landis) S.; m. Nancy June Simon, Sept. 14, 1961 (div. Feb. 1975); m. Kaye Elizabeth Bache, Mar. 21, 1975. BS in Physics, Rensselaer Poly. Inst., 1952; MS in Physics, U. Chgo., 1957, PhD in Physics, 1961. From asst. prof. to assoc. prof. Brown U., Providence, 1961-68; prof. aerospace engring. U. Colo., Boulder, 1968—; cons. Storage Tech. Corp., Louisville, Colo., 1980-84, Ball Aerospace Systems, Boulder, 1984—. Contbr. articles to profl. jours. Served to lt. (j.g.) USN, 1948-55. Mem. Am. Phys. Soc. Club: Colo. Mountain (Denver). Home: 251 Gay St Longmont CO 80501 Office: U Colo Dept Aerospace Engring Sci Campus Box 429 Boulder CO 80309

SNYDER, JAMES KIMBALL, advertising executive; b. Montgomery, Ala., Sept. 9, 1949; s. Robert L. and Dove (Hudson) S.; m. Bridget Ursula Drake, Dec. 16, 1972 (div. 1988); 1 child, Andrea. BA, Auburn U., 1971, BS in Indsl. Design, 1976, MS in Indsl. Design, 1979. Indsl. designer Harry Lunstead Designs Inc., Kent, Wash., 1980; indsl. designer Lockheed Shipbldg. Corp., Seattle, 1981-83; prin. Snyder & Assocs., Issaquah, Wash., 1983—. Contbr. articles to profl. newspapers and mags. 1st lt. U.S. Army, 1971-73. Mem. Bus. Profl. Advt. Assn., Seattle Advt. Fedn. Office: Snyder & Assocs 22619 SE 64th Pl 220 Issaquah WA 98027

SNYDER, JAMES ROBERT, professional sports executive; b. Dearborn, Mich., Aug. 15, 1932; s. Bernard Joseph and Margaret Norine (Coughlin) S.; m. Gysele Marie Turcotte, Nov. 22, 1975; children: Debra, James, Scott, Fran. BS, Eastern Mich. U., 1960, MA, 1964. Profl. baseball player various orgns., 1952-64; tchr. Dearborn (Mich.) Schs., 1965-69; minor league mgr. Cin. and Phila., 1970-81; dir. player devel. Chgo. Cubs Orgn., 1982-86, coach, 1987; mgr. Seattle Mariners, 1988. Named Mgr. of Yr. Eastern Baseball League, Trois Rivieres, Que., Can., 1972, All-Star Mgr., 1972, 74. Roman Catholic. Home: 8613 Barkwood Dr Tampa FL 33615

SNYDER, JOHN JOSEPH, optometrist; b. Wonewoc, Wis., June 30, 1908; s. Burt Frederick and Alta Lavinia (Hearn) S.; A.B., UCLA, 1931, postgrad., 1931-32; postgrad. U. Colo., 1936, 38, 40, 41, U. So. Calif., 1945-46; B.S. in Optometry, Los Angeles Coll. Optometry, 1948, O.D., 1949. Tchr., La Plata County (Colo.) Pub. Schs., 1927-28; supt. Marvel (Colo.) Pub. Schs., 1932-33; tchr. Durango (Colo.) High Sch., 1933-41; pvt. practice optometry, Los Angeles, 1951-72, Torrance, Calif., 1972-78; now vacation and emergency relief optometrist. Former bd. dirs. Francia Boys' Club, Los Angeles; former pres. Exchange Club South Los Angeles, also sec. Mem. AAAS, Nat. Eye Research Found., Am. Inst. Biol. Scis., Am., Calif., Los Angeles County optometric assns., Internat. Biog. Assn. Republican. Home: 25937 Reynolds St Loma Linda CA 92354

SNYDER, KARL DANIEL, radio station executive; b. Louisville, Ky., Oct. 7, 1926; s. Gremm Karl and Monna Jean Snyder; m. Debra J. Johnson, Aug. 27, 1952; children: David, Randy, Jaque. BA in Philosophy, U. Montana, 1950. Mgr. Sta. KBMN, Bozeman, Mont., 1955; owner Sta. KQOI-FM, Great Falls, Mont., 1955-58, Sta. KRTV-TV, Great Falls, 1958-68; v.p. Village Bank, Great Falls, 1971-74; owner Import Depot and Freight House Supper Club, Great Falls, 1970-80; pres., gen. mgr. Sta. KCAP-AM/KZMT-FM, Helena, Mont., 1980—. Mem. Helena Ad Found. (pres. 1981), Helena C. of C. (pres. 1987). Club: Ad (pres. 1968). Lodge: Rotary (Pres. 1979). Home: 69 Cloverview Helena MT 59601 Office: Sta KCAP Box 1676 Helena MT 59624

SNYDER, KENNETH CLARENCE, aerospace company executive; b. Norton County, Kans., Mar. 20, 1929; s. Clarence Raymond and Elsie Ann (Klasna) S.; m. Nadene Louise Scott, Oct. 14, 1952; children: Kendra Caylene Snyder Uchida, Kari Ladene. BS in Bus., UCLA, 1957. Asst. to sr. components engr. Amelco, Inc., Santa Monica, Calif., 1957-59; engring. planner Litton Systems, Woodland Hills, Calif., 1959-62, engring. change analyst, 1962-64, sr. fin. analyst, 1964-65, program adminstrn., 1965-66; program mgr. Applied Tech., Inc., Palo Alto, Calif., 1966-67; mgr. bus. adminstrn. Teledyne Microelectronics, L.A., 1967-74, assoc. dir. bus. mgmt., 1975—; v.p., gen. mgr. NW Digital Systems, Bellevue, Wash., 1974-75. Served with USN, 1948-52, Korea. Republican. Home: 4714 E Escondido Ave Mesa AZ 85206 Office: Teledyne Microelectronics 12964 Panama St Los Angeles CA 90066

SNYDER, KENNETH DELE, geologist; b. Rifle, Colo., Sept. 26, 1949; s. Guy Cassius and Evelyn Ellen (Everett) S.; m. Ingela Marta Dahl, June 7, 1978; children: Emilia Kristina, Rebecca Linnea. BA, Western State Coll., Gunnison, Colo., 1971; MSc, U. Idaho, 1973; PhD, U. Nev., 1989. Cons. geologist Elko, Nev., 1987--; asst. geologist Bear Creek Mining, Reno, Nev., 1969; sr. geologist NL Industries, Golden, Colo., 1973-76; geologist fgn. subs. NL Industries, Italy, Ireland, Brazil, Eng., 1976-84; exploration mgr. NL Boroid, Elko, Nev., 1984-87; cons. geologist Elko, Nev., 1987--. Mem. Soc. Econ. Geologists, AIME, Soc. Exploration Geochemists, Geol. Soc. Nev. Republican. Home and office: 151 Maple St Elko NV 89801

SNYDER, KING CLAUDE, lawyer; b. Pitts., Nov. 12, 1957; s. Floyde Kenneth and Ruth Ann (Haigh) S. BA, U. Pitts., 1979, JD, 1982. Assoc. Jekel & Howard, Scottsdale, Ariz., 1984—; mem. Outdoor Dealers, Inc., Cornville, Ariz. Bd. dirs. Ariz. ArthritisFound., Phoenix. Mem. Scottsdale Bar Assn.(v.p. 1988—), Scottsdale C. of C. (chmn. 1987). Office: Jekel & Howard 4323 N Brown Ave Ste E Scottsdale AZ 85251

SNYDER, MARGARET JUDITH, writer; b. Luton, Bedfordshire, Eng., Mar. 11, 1940; came to U.S., 1964; d. Alan Ernest and Mable (Hartopp) Osborne; m. Lloyd Emerson Snyder, Sept. 26, 1964; children: Lloyd Alan, Angela Margaret, Tommy Lynne. Cert. in interior design, ICS, 1984; student, Ariz. Western Coll., 1985. Cashier, receptionist Automobile Assn., London, 1957-60; bookkeeper Butlins Hotel Resorts, Brighton, Eng., 1960-63; program coord. Hason Produce, Pasadena, Calif., 1980-81, 85-88; owner MJ Interiors, Yuma, Ariz., 1984. Columnist Yuma Daily Sun, 1977-82. Chmn. publicity Ocotilla dist. Boy Scouts Am., Yuma, 1977-83. Recipient Dist. Merit award Boy Scouts Am., Yuma, 1984. Mormon. Home: 896 Harvard St Yuma AZ 85365

SNYDER, RICHARD NEIL, lawyer; b. L.A., Aug. 27, 1944; s. Louis Morton Snyder and Bella (Horowitz) Karnot. B. in History, UCLA, 1968; postgrad., Hague Acad. Internat. Law, Netherlands, 1969; JD, U. Calif., San Francisco, 1971; postgrad., King's Coll., London, 1971. Bar: Calif. 1972, U.S. Supreme Ct. 1973, U.S. Tax Ct. 1974. Pvt. practice San Francisco, 1972-73; gen. counsel Inecon Corp., San Francisco, 1973-77; prof. law U. Calif. Hastings Coll. Law, San Francisco, 1974-77; pvt. practice San Francisco, 1977—. Author: Natural Law and Equity, 1973. Pres. Navy League of U.S., Marin Coun., Marin County (Calif.), 1989; assoc. gen. counsel Calif. Democratic Party, 1978-79; mem. Marin Republican Coun., Marin County, 1987—. Fellow Rockefeller Found., Villa Serbelloni, Italy, 1973, 75. Mem. State Bar Calif. (exec. com. real property law sect. 1988—, chmn. landlord-tenant subsect. 1985-87), Bar Assn. San Francisco, City Club (San Francisco). Democrat. Home: PO Box 457 Mill Valley CA 94942 Office: 126-128 Church St San Francisco CA 94114

SNYDER, STEVEN WAYNE, retail company executive; b. Lockhaven, Pa., Oct. 11, 1952; s. James Roland and Emma Jean S.; m. Patricia Ann Huebner, Nov. 25, 1977; children: Sondra Lynn, Steven Thomas. Grad. high sch. With City of Santa Clara, Calif., 1971-75, elec. dispatcher, 1975-84; elec. contractor Santa Clara, 1980—; owner Video Stop, San Jose, Calif., 1981—. With Calif. Army N.G., 1970-76. Office: Video Stop 1085 The Alameda San Jose CA 95126

SNYDER, WILLIAM HARRY, financial advisor; b. Newport, Pa., May 11, 1934; s. William Harry and Mary (Barner) S.; m. Irvil Kear, June, 1956 (div. 1961); 1 child, Geoffrey W.; m. Sandra Elizabeth Wolff, June 25, 1966; 1 child, Tara Elizabeth. BS in Indsl. Engring., Lehigh U., 1956; MS in Applied Stats., Rutgers U., 1961. Cert. fin. planner. Research engr. Johns-Manville Corp., Manville, N.J., 1956-61; indsl. engr., mgr. services and quality control Johns-Manville Corp., Nashua, N.H., 1961-69; mgr. phys. distbn. Johns-Manville Corp., N.Y.C., 1969-72; mgr. div. and corp. planning. Johns-Manville Corp., Denver, 1972-82; dir. corp. devel. Manville Corp. (formerly Johns-Manville Corp.), Denver, 1982-85; prin. Snyder Fin. Services, Littleton, Colo., 1985—; bd. dirs. Manville Employees Fed. Credit Union, Denver. Patentee process for making chalkboard; author: (with others) Standard Handbook of Plant Engineering, 1983. Served as 2d lt. U.S. Army, 1957-58. Mem. Internat. Assn. for Fin. Planners, Inst. of Cert. Fin. Planners, Pi Kappa Alpha (pres. 1954-55). Republican. Methodist. Lodge: Mason. Home and Office: Snyder Fin Svcs 1952 Ridge Rd Littleton CO 80120

SNYDER, WILLIAM REGIS, JR., construction company executive; b. Pitts., Mar. 14, 1954; s. William R. Sr. and Laverne V. (Krebs) S.; m. Nancy Mary Meglio, May 31, 1980; children: Sarah Elizabeth, William Joseph. Student, U. Pitts., Pa. State U., McKeesport, Mesa Community Coll. Checker Three Rivers Drafting Co., Pitts., 1973-75; estimator, project mgr. Plasteel Products, Washington, Pa., 1975-77; draftsman Siciliano Interiors, Pitts., 1977-78; engineered inside salesman Steelite, Inc., Pitts., 1978-80; assoc. Ariz. Joist & Deck Co., Scottsdale, 1980-82; sales mgr. George D. Widman, Inc., Gardena, Calif., 1982-83, mgr. Ariz. ops., 1983-84; pres. WRS & Assocs., Inc., Tempe, Ariz., 1984—. Mem. Mfrs. Agts. Nat. Assn., Constrn. News West. Office: WRS & Assocs Inc PO Box 24664 Tempe AZ 85282

SNYDER, WILMER ROY, nutrition company executive; b. Osseo, Mich., Aug. 11, 1939; s. Herman Dale and Reva (McComb) S.; m. Janet Louise Irving; children: Jamie, Wilmer Jr., Monte, Ryan. BA in Foods & Nutrition, Andrews U., 1962; MS in Food Adminstrn., Loma Linda U., 1969. Registered dietitian. Food svc. dir. Walla Walla Coll.nc., College Place, Wash., 1963-69; food svc. dir. P.D. Food Svc. Inc., La Sierra Campus, Loma Linda U., Riverside, Calif., 1969-71, Versitron Industries, Laurelwood Acad., Gaston, Oreg., 1971-73; food svc. dir. & area coord. Versitron Industries, Rio Lindo Acad., Healdsburg, Calif., 1973-77; area v.p. dir. Versitron Industries, Riverside, Calif., 1977-79; field v.p. Versitron Industries, 1979-85; regional v.p. Div. We. Health Resources, Versitron Industries, Riverside, 1983-85; v.p. nursing & retirement cts. product line Div. We. Health Resources, Versitron Industries, 1985-86; v.p. ednl. ops. Nutri-Group Inc., Roseville, Calif., 1986—; regional coord. so. hosps. Nutri-Group Inc., 1987—. Mem. Am. Dietitic Assn., Seventh-Day Adventist Dietitic Assn. (treas. 1981-85). Republican. Office: Nutri Group Inc 658 Commerce Dr Roseville CA 95678

SO, KENNETH THAY, aerospace engineer; b. Phnom Penh, Peoples Republic of Kampuchea, Dec. 16, 1952; came to U.S., 1973; s. Bun Hor So and Laam Tan; m. Theany Kimchandabot Kim, July 12, 1980; children: Elizabeth Kaliyan, Jacqueline Chakrya. BSChemE, U. Tenn., 1978. Engr. Ampex Corp., Redwood City, Calif., 1978-79, Rockwell Internat., Downey, Calif., 1979—; rep. from Rockwell to NASA Langley Research Ctr., Hampton, Va., 1986-87. Contbr. articles to profl. jours. Recipient Rockwell Internat. award, NASA award. Mem. Phi Kappa Phi, Tau Beta Pi. Republican. Buddhist. Office: Rockwell Internat 12214 Lakewood Blvd Mail Code AC85 Downey CA 90241

SOAVE, JAMES MICHAEL, food distribution executive; b. Detroit, July 31, 1954; s. John Thomas and Rose Delores (Serocki) S.; m. Carol Elizabeth Gillespie, July 30, 1976; children: James Michael Jr., Thomas John. AS, Macomb Community Coll., Warren, Mich., 1974; student, Oakland U., 1972-77. Produce mgr. Chatham Supermarkets Inc., Warren, 1972-79; sales mgr. Grocers Packaging Supply Inc., Detroit, 1979-82; v.p., gen. mgr. T.M. Morley Inc., East Detroit, Mich., 1982-86, Morley Candy Makers West Inc., Tempe, Ariz., 1986—; bd. dirs. Little Caesars Pizza DBA Morley Enterprises, Crofton, Md., T.M. Morley Inc., Roseville. Sponsor Am. Heart Assn.; mem. Econ. Club Detroit. Mem. Ariz. Police Officers Assn., Chandler (Ariz.) C. of C. Republican. Roman Catholic. Club: Cadillac of Am. Home: 16240 S 32d Pl Phoenix AZ 85044 Office: Morley Candy Makers West Inc 1840 W Drake Dr #101 Tempe AZ 85283

SOBEL, RICHARD STEPHEN, pediatric dentist; b. Cleve., Apr. 10, 1943; s. Murray and Matty (Mostoff) S. BA, Queens Coll., 1965; DDS, SUNY, 1967. Resident in pediatric dentistry Childrens' Hosp. Med. Ctr., Boston, 1967-70; fellow in pediatric dentistry Harvard U., Boston, 1967-70; faculty clinic U. Pacific Sch. Dentistry, San Francisco, 1971-73, practice dentistry specializing in pediatrics, 1973-76, asst. prof., 1974—; dir. pediatric dentistry residency program Childrens' Hosp. Med. Ctr., Oakland, Calif., 1974-82; practice dentistry specializing in pediatrics San Leandro, Calif., 1982-84; chief sect. pediatric dentistry Mt. Zion Hosp., San Francisco, 1982-87; practice dentistry specializing in pediatrics Antioch (Calif.) Pediatric Dentistry, 1984—; lectr., asst. prof. U. Calif. Sch. Dentistry, San Francisco, 1972-75, 1979—; cons. VA Hosp., Highland Hosp., Travis AFB, 1978-87. Author: (with others) Dental Genetics, 1978, 1980, Treatment of Hemophiliac, 1979, Pediatric Clinics, 1982, Child Abuse, 1984, Pediatric Dentistry, 1984; contbr. articles to profl. jours. Founder Bay Area Guidance Council for the Disabled, San Francisco, Oakland; chairperson Childrens Health Week, San Francisco, 1974-75, adv. com. Exploration, San Francisco, 1987; active USPHS Fed. Med. Ctr., Springfield, Mo., 1966. Mem. ADA, Calif. Dental Assn., Am. Soc. Dentistry Children, Calif. Soc. Dentistry Children (treas. 1976-82, pres. 1984-85), Am. Soc. Human Genetics, Internat. Assn. Dental Rsch., Calif. Soc. Pediatric Dentists (exec. bd. 1980-82, treas. 1987, sec. 1988, v.p. 1989—), Soc. Cranio Facial Genetics, Am. Assn. Hosp. Dentistry, Harvard U. Alumni Assn., Queens Coll. Alumni Assn. Office: Antioch Pediatric Dentistry 2901 Lone Tree Way Antioch CA 94509

SODERQUIST, ELDA GLENDOR, counselor; b. Madison, Minn., Aug. 29, 1923; d. Leonard Zious and Geneva S. (Retrum) Thompson; m. Ronald V. Soderquist, June 2, 1951; children: Lynn, Philip, Ann. RN, U. Minn., 1945; BA in English, Upsala Coll., 1970; MA in Social Sci., Azusa Pacific Coll., 1976. Lic. marriage, family and child counselor. Nurse U. Minn. Hosp., Mpls., 1945-47; parish worker Luth. Ch. of Good Sheperd, Mpls., 1948-50; counselor U. Minn., Hamlin and McCalester Coll., St. Paul, 1950-51; nurse Luth. Med. Ctr., Bklyn., 1951-52; tchr. Simi Valley (Calif.) Sch. Dist., 1970-74; counselor Calif. Family Study Ctr., Westlake Village, 1974-76; supr. Family Counseling Ctr. of the Oaks, Westlake Village, 1976-86, dir., 1983—; founder, bd. dirs. Calif. Open Door Counseling Ctr., Westlake Village. Pres. Human Relations Council, Northfield, Minn., 1965-67; chmn. UNICEF drive, Jersey City, 1958-60; tchr. Assertion & Parenting Classes, Thousand Oaks, Calif., 1977-87; leader hypnosis seminar, Sidney, Australia, 1980. Mem. Am. Assn. Marriage and Family Therapists, Calif. Assn. Marriage and Family Counselors, AAUW, Conejo Women in Bus., Ventura County Dem. Club. Lutheran. Office: Family Counseling Ctr 141 Duesenberg Dr #9 Westlake Village CA 91362

SOELDNER, J. STUART, physician, educator; b. Boston, Sept. 22, 1932; s. Frank and Mary Amelia (Stuart) S.; m. Elsie Irene Harnish, Aug. 25, 1962; children: Judith Marie, Elizabeth Anne, Stephen J.D. BS magna cum laude, Tufts U., 1954; Dr.med., Dalhousie U., Halifax, N.S., 1959. Diplomate Am. Bd. Med. Examiners; lic. Med. Coun. Can. Intern then resident Victoria Gen. Hosp., Halifax, 1958-61; from instr. medicine to assoc. prof. medicine Harvard U., Boston, 1964-87; prof. medicine Davis Med. Ctr. U. Calif., Sacramento, 1987—. Contbr. over 280 sci. publs. Founding mem. med. bd. Juvenile Diabetes Found., N.Y.C. Recipient Sci. award Juvenile Diabetes Found., 1973, U.S. Sr. Scientist, Von Humboldt Found., 1975; fellow Pfizer Traveling, 1973. Mem. Am. Physiol. Soc., Am. Soc. Clin. Investigation, Am. Diabetes Assn. (mem. profl. edn. com. 1975-81, 83-85, bd. dirs., 1982-85), Columbian Assn. Internal Medicine (corresponding), New Eng. Diabetes Assn., Am. Fedn., Clin. Rsch., European Assn. Study of Diabetes, Endocrine Soc., Soc. Experimental Biology and Medicine, Assn. Advancement Med. Instrumentation, Am. Soc. Artificial Internal Organs, Internat. Soc. Artificial Organs, Dalhousie Med. Alumni Assn. (bd. dirs. Can. 1977—), Alpha Omega Alpha. Democrat. Roman Catholic. Office: Diabete Clin Rsch Unit 1625 Alhambra Blvd Ste 2901 Sacramento CA 95816

SOFFER, NANCY CLAIRE, sales executive, marketing executive; b. Milw., Jan. 27, 1954; d. Morris and Helen (Lerner) S. BA in Psychology, San Diego State U., 1976. Dir. travel Maritz Travel Co., St. Louis, 1976-78; rep. group sales Zool. Soc. San Diego, 1976-80; dir. western regional sales TraveLodge Internat., San Diego, 1980-81; dir. sales and mktg. Sunrise Hotels, Irvine, Calif., 1981-84; dir. sales, mktg. Associated Hosts, Beverly Hills, Calif., 1984-85, Beverly Hills Ramada Hotel, 1985-86; v.p. sales, mktg. Internat. Innkeepers, South Laguna, Calif., 1986—; cons. NCS Mktg., Los Angeles. V.p. Highland Park Homeowners Assn., Mission Viejo, Calif., 1987—. Mem. Nat. Tour Assn., Meeting Planners Internat., Hotel Sales and Mgmt. Assn. (assoc. bd. mem.), Direct Mktg. Assn. Democrat. Jewish. Office: Internat Innkeepers Inc 3 Monarch Bay Pla Ste 206 South Laguna CA 92677

SOFFER, PHILIP J., technical writer; b. N.Y.C., Feb. 19, 1954; s. Paul and Florence (Hoffman) S.; m. Asuncion Ramos, Nov. 16, 1986; 1 child, Jessica Shannon. BS, Southwest U., New Orleans; MS, NRI Inst., Washington. Pres. Barrets Schs. Inc., N.Y.C., 1980-85; ind. tech. writer Chatsworth, Calif., 1985—; lectr. in field. Author: Robotics, 1988; contbr. articles to profl. jours. Mem. San Fernando Bd. Realtors, Calif. Assn. Realtors, Nat. Assn. Realtors. Home: 21735 Wahoo Trail Chatsworth CA 91311

SOFOS, STEPHANY LOUISE, real estate executive; b. Honolulu, Sept. 16, 1954; d. Thomas A. and Catherine B. (Seros) S. BA in History, U. Hawaii at Manoa, 1976. Assoc. Chaney Brooks Realty, Inc., Honolulu, 1976-77; supr. property/mgr. shopping ctr. Hawaii Mgmt. Corp., Honolulu, 1977-79; mgr. mktg. and customer relations Kaiser Devel. Co., Honolulu, 1979-82; gen. mgr. Kuhio Mall, Honolulu, 1982-86; pres. SL Sofos and Co., Ltd., Honolulu, 1986—. Mem. Nat. Assn. Realtors, Inst. Real Estate Mgmt. (cert. property mgr., bd. dirs. Hawaii chpt. 1987), Internat. Council Shopping Ctrs. (cert. shopping ctr. mgr.), Bldg. Owners and Mgrs. Assn. Greek Orthodox. Clubs: Honolulu, Outrigger Canoe, Oahu Country (Honolulu). Office: 610 Ward Ave Ste 204 Honolulu HI 96814

SOHNEN-MOE, CHERIE MARILYN, management consultant; b. Tucson, Jan. 2, 1956; d. D. Ralph and Angelina Helen (Spiro) Sohnen; m. James Madison Moe, Jr., May 23, 1981. BA, UCLA, 1977. Rsch. asst. UCLA, 1975-77; ind. cons. L.A., 1978-83; cons. Sohnen-Moe Assocs., Tucson, 1984—. Author: Business Mastery, 1988; contbr. monthly column of publ. Work Issues and Options, 1987—. Vol. Am. Cancer Soc., Tucson, 1984—; charter mem. Civitan-El Conquistador, Tucson, 1986-87; mem. Ariz. Sonora Desert Mus., Tucson. Mem. Resources for Women, Women in Tucson, NOW, Am. Soc. Tng. and Devel. (dir. mem. svcs. 1988, Outstanding Achievement award 1988), Tucson Met. C. of C., Sierra Club. Office: Sohnen-Moe Assocs 3906 W Ina Rd #200-264 Tucson AZ 85741

SOKOLOFF, ALEXANDER DIMITROVITCH, biology educator; b. Tokyo, Japan, May 16, 1920; came to U.S., 1938; s. Dimitri Fyodorovitch and Sofia Alexandrovna (Solovieff) S.; m. Barbara B. Bryant, June 24, 1956; children: Alexandra, Elaine A., Michael A. AA, UCLA, 1943, AB, 1948; PhD, U. Chgo., 1954. Instr. Hofstra U., L.I., N.Y., 1955-56, asst. prof., 1956-58; geneticist W.H. Miner Agrl. Research Inst., Chazy, N.Y., 1958-60; assoc. research botanist UCLA, 1960; assoc. research geneticist U. Calif., Berkeley, 1961-66, research geneticist, 1966-68; assoc. prof. Calif. State U., San Bernardino, 1965-66, prof. biology, 1966—. Author: Genetics of Tribolium, 1966, The Biology of Tribolium, vol. 1., 1972, vo. 2, 1975, vol. 3, 1977; mem. editorial bd.: Jour. Stored Product Research, 1965—; assoc. editor: Evolution, 1972-74, Jour. Advanced Zoology, 1980—; editor Tribolium Info. Bull., 1960—. Served to sgt. USAAF, 1942-46. Research grantee USPHS, 1961, NSF, 1957-59, 67-69, 69-71, 71-73, Army Research Office 1973-76, 79. Fellow Royal Entomol. Soc. of London; mem. Soc. Study of Evolution, Genetics Soc. Am., Am. Genetic Assn., Am. Soc. Naturalists, Am. Soc. Zoologists, Genetics Soc. Can., Japanese Soc. Population Ecology, Entomol. Soc. Am., Sigma Xi. Democrat. Lodge: Elks. Home: 3324 Sepulveda San Bernardino CA 92404 Office: Calif State U 5500 N University Pkwy San Bernardino CA 92407

SOKOLOFF, BURTON ZELIG, pediatrician; b. Cleve., Feb. 12, 1931; s. William and Belle (Brown) S.; m. Marilyn Kline, Feb. 10, 1952; children: Michelle, Lauren, Scott, Kevin. BS, UCLA, 1952; MD, St. Louis U., 1958. Asst. clin. prof. pediatrics UCLA Sch. Health Scis., 1964—; dir. Pediatric Affiliates Med. Gorup, Inc., Canoga Park, Calif., 1970—; cons. in field. Author: (with others) Developmental-Behavioral Pediatrics, 1983; contbr. articles to profl. jours. Advisor United Way Com. on Foster Care, L.A., 1985-88. Capt. U.S. Army, 1959-62. Recipient Endowment Award for Children, Am. Acad. Pediatrics, 1981, Humanitarian Efforts Cert., Valley Beth Shalom Temple, 1976. Fellow Am. Acad. Pediatrics; mem. Am. Pub. Health Assn., AMA. Democrat. Jewish. Office: Pediatric Affiliates Med 7345 Med Ctr Dr Canoga Park CA 91307

SOKOLOV, JACQUE JENNING, cardiologist, corporate medical director; b. L.A., Sept. 13, 1954; parents: Albert I. and Frances (Burgess) S. BA in Medicine magna cum laude, U. So. Calif., 1974, MD with hons., 1978; postgrad., Mayo Clinic, Rochester, Minn., 1978-81, U. Tex., Dallas, 1981-83. Med. diplomate. Cardiologist, nuclear cardiologist Health Sci. Ctr. U. Tex., 1981-84; chief med. officer Baylor Healthcare Enterprises Wellness & Lifestyle Corp., Dallas, 1985-87; dir. healthcare dept., corp. med. dir. So. Calif. Edison Co., Rosemead, Calif., 1987—; health care strategic planning cons. Procter & Gamble, Southwestern Bell, AT&T, Wang, Rosewood Corp., Dallas, 1985-87. Contbr. to articles in profl. jours. Mem. L.A. Coalition. Grantee NIH, Bethesda, Md., 1983. Mem. L.A. C. of C. Office: So Calif Edison Co 8631 Rush St Rosemead CA 91770

SOLA, JOHN CARL, marketing executive; b. Finale, Emilia, Italy, Feb. 10, 1924; came to U.S., 1926; s. John Maurice and Carolina (Venturi) S.; m. Phyllis Elaine (Fries), May 22, 1952; children: Gregory, David, Michael, William. BA, U. Colo., 1950; MA, Boston U., 1951; postgrad., UCLA, 1952. Pres. Audio Asoscs., Pasadena, Calif., 1954-79; sales mgr. A.L. Romano Wine Distributor, Los Angeles, 1979-81; mgr. western region Mirassou Vineyards, San Jose, Calif., 1981-85; owner, operator Western Vintage Mktg., Los Angeles, 1986—. Served as cpl. U.S. Army, 1943-45. Mem. Wine & Food Soc. Hollywood. Home: 1865 E Mountain St Pasadena CA 91104-4013 Office: Western Vintage Mktg PO Box 91-1132 Los Angeles CA 90091-1132

SOLBERG, WARREN RICHARDS, computer engineer; b. Riverside, Calif., Nov. 12, 1935; s. Lester Kenneth and Ida Mae (Richards) S.; m. Patricia R. Cullinan, Aug. 26, 1961; 1 child: Maryann Rose. BSEE, U. Calif., Berkeley, 1959. Staff engr. Hughes Aircraft Co., Culver City, Calif., 1962-68, IBM Corp. Fed. Systems, Manassas, Va. and Westlake, Calif., 1968-83; owner, mgr. Concept Eighty Three, Manassas, 1978-87; sr. engr. Rail Co. at U.S. Navy Air Test Ctr., Patuxent River, Md., 1987-88; resident mgr. U.S. Customs at Lockheed, Burbank, Calif., 1988; owner, mgr. Computer Potato, Burbank, 1988—; project engr. Rockwell Internat., El Segundo, Calif., 1988—. Served to lt. (j.g.) USN, 1959-62. Mem. U. Calif. Alumni Assn. (life). Republican. Lutheran. Home: 617 N Illinois Ct #16 El Segundo CA 90245 Office: Computer Potato 201 N Douglas St El Segundo CA 90245

SOLDNER, PAUL EDMUND, ceramist, educator; b. Summerfield, Ill.; s. Grover and Beulah (Geiger) S.; m. Virginia I. Geiger, June 15, 1947; 1 child, Stephanie. BA, Bluffton Coll., 1946; MA, U. Colo., 1954; MFA, L.A. County Art Inst., 1956. Tchr. art Medina (Ohio) County Schs., 1946-47; supr. art, asst. county supr. Wayne County Schs., Wooster, Ohio, 1951-54;

tchr. adult edn. Wooster Coll., 1952-54; vis. asst. prof. ceramics Scripps Coll., 1957-66, prof., 1970—; prof. Claremont (Calif.) Grad. Sch., 1957-66, prof., 1970—; prof. U. Colo., Boulder, 1966-67, U. Iowa, Iowa City, 1967-68; pres. Soldner Pottery Equipment, Inc., Aspen, Colo., 1956-77; mem. steering com. Internat. Sch. Ceramics, Rome, 1965-77; advisor Vols. for Internat. Assistance, Balt., 1966-75; craftsman, trustee Am. Craft Coun., N.Y.C., 1970-74, trustee emeritus, 1976-77; dir. U.S. sect. World Craft Coun., 1970-74; dir. Anderson Ranch Ctr. for Hand Art Sch., 1974-76; speaker 6th Internat. Ceramics Symposium Syracuse, 1989; participant Internat. Russian Artists Exchange Program, Riga, Latvia, 1989; cons. in field; originator Am. Raku philosophy and techniques in ceramics. Author: Kilns and Their Construction, 1965, Raku, 1964; contbr. articles to profl. jours.; subject of 5 films; 155 one-man shows including Cantini Mus. Modern Art, Marseille, France, 1981, Thomas Segal Gallery, Boston, 1982, Elements Gallery, N.Y., 1983, Louis Newman Gallery, L.A., 1985, Susan Cummins Gallery, Mill Valley, Calif., 1989, Great Am. Gallery, Atlanta, 1986, Patricia Moore Gallery, Aspen Colo., 1987, Coleg Prifysgol Cymru, Aberystwyth, Wales, 1987, Joan Hodgell Gallery, Sarasota, Fla., 1988, Esther Saks Gallery, Chgo., 1986, 88, El Camino Gallery Art, Toraance, Calif., 1987, San Antonio Art Ctr., San Angelo, Tex., 1988; group shows include Nelson-Atkins Mus., Kansas City, Mo., 1983, Los Angeles Mcpl. Art Gallery, 1984, 27th Ceramic Nat. Exhibition, Everson Mus. Art, Syracuse, N.Y., 1986, Victoria & Albert Mus., London, 1986, Chicago Internat. New Art Forms Exposition, 1986, Hanover Gallery, Syracuse, N.Y., 1987, L.A. County Mus. of Art, 1987, Crain/Wolov Gallery, Tulsa, 1987, Contem Crafts Gallery, Portland, Oreg., 1988, Oakland (Calif.) Art Mus., 1988, Munson Gallery, Santa Fe, 1988, Japanese Influence on Am. Ceramics, Everson Mus., Syracuse, N.Y., 1989; works in permanent collections, Nat. Mus. Modern Art, Kyoto, Japan, Victoria and Albert Mus., London, Smithsonian Instn., Washington, Los Angeles County Mus. Art, Oakland Art Mus., Everson Mus. Art, Syracuse Australian Nat. Gallery, Taipei Fine Arts Mus.; curator Mirror Images Exhibit, Craft Alliance Gallery, St. Louis, 1989. Served with U.S. Army, 1941-46. Decorated Purple Heart; grantee Louis Comfort Tiffany Found., 1966, 72, Purple Heart. Grantee Nat. Endowment for Arts, 1976, Colo. Gov.'s award for the Arts & Humanities, 1975; voted one of Top Twelve Potters World-Wide, Ceramics Monthly mag., 1981; Scripps Coll. Faculty Recognition award, 1985; named Hon. Mem. Coun., Nat. Coun. on Edn. for Ceramic Arts, 1989. Fellow Collequim of Craftsmen of the U.S.; mem. Internat. Acad. Ceramics, Nat. Coun. on Edn. for Ceramic Arts. Home: PO Box 90 Aspen CO 81612

SOLHEIM, JAMES K., aerospace executive; b. Alton, Ill., June 16, 1937. BS, U. So. Calif., 1960. V.p., gen. mgr. Metal Bellows div. Parker Hannifin, Moorpark, Calif. NASA pub. svc. medal, 1983. Mem. ASM, Soc. Mfg. Engrs. Office: Parker Metal Bellows 200 Science Dr Moorpark CA 93021

SOLINSKY, LEONARD P., accountant; b. Pitts., May 1, 1935; s. Joseph Antohony and Amalia H. (Hajduk) S.; m. Margaret M. Petrancosta, May 30, 1959; children: Joseph A., Philip L., Keith R., Devin E., James B., Marianne M. Student, Duquesne U., 1962-63. Pvt. practice acctg., life ins. sales Solinsky & Assocs., Pitts., 1964-72, Tucson, 1972—. V.p. St. Vincent De Paul Soc., Tucson; pres. St. Francis De Sales Conf., Polio Epic, Tucson. Mem. Nat. Soc. Pub. Accts., Nat. Assn. Tax Practitioners. Lodge: Elks. Office: Solinsky & Assocs 1103-05 S Sherwood Village Dr Tucson AZ 85710

SOLIS, HILDA LUCIA, educational administrator; b. Los Angeles, Oct. 20, 1957; d. Raul and Juana (Sequiera) S.; m. Sam H. Sayyad, June 26, 1982. BA in Polit. Sci., Calif. State Poly U., 1978; MA in Pub. Adminstrn., U. So. Calif., 1981. Interpreter Immigration and Naturalization Service, Los Angeles, 1977-79; editor-in-chief White House Office Hispanic Affairs, Washington, 1980-81; mng. analyst Office Mgmt. and Budget, Washington, 1981; field rep. Assemblyman Art Tores, Los Angeles, 1982; dir. Calif. Student Opportunity and Access, Whittier, 1982—; chief cons. South Coast Consortium, L.A., 1985—; mem. South Coast Ednl. Opportunity Pers. Consortium. Corr. Sec. Friendly El Monte (Calif.) Democratic Club, 1986-; mem. credentials com. Calif. Dem. Com., 1987-; trustee Rio Hondo Community Coll. Recipient Meritorious Service award Dept. Def., 1981, Young Careerist award El Monte Bus. and Profl. Women, 1987; Nat. Edn. Inst., Kellogg Found. fellow, 1984-85. Mem. Western Assn. Ednl. Opportunity Pers. (sec. bd. dirs. 1986—), Comision Feminil de Los Angeles (bd. dirs. 1983-84, edn. chmn.), Women of Moose. Roman Catholic. Home: 11724 Roseglen St El Monte CA 91732 Office: Calif Student Opportunity and Access 9401 S Painter St Whittier CA 90605

SOLLARS, GARY MICHAEL, emergency physician; b. Detroit, July 8, 1947; s. Paul Joseph and Irene Alexandra (Cecot) S.; m. Halina Josephine Czerniejewski, Oct. 3, 1981; children: Claire Mikhaila, Kendra Elizabeth. AB honors, U. Detroit, 1969; MD, U. Mich., 1974. Diplomate Am. Bd. Emergency Medicine (examiner 1983-). Resident in emergency medicine U. Chgo., 1974-77; attending staff Northwestern Meml. Hosp., Chgo., 1977-85, assoc. chief sec. emergency medicine, 1979-85; pvt. practice Phoenix, 1985—; attending staff Mesa (Ariz.) Luth. Hosp., 1985—, Valley Luth. Hosp., Mesa, 1985—, Boswell Meml. Hosp., Sun City, Ariz., 1987—, Del Webb Meml. Hosp., Sun City, 1987; lectr. in field, 1977—; cons. med. dept. People's Energy Corp., Chgo., 1979-85; med.-legal case reviewer, Chgo., 1983-85; physician advisor Health Systems Adv. Group, Phoenix, 1988—. Author: (with others) Quality Assessment in the Emergency Department, 1984; contbr. articles to med. jours. Pub. service appearances various radio and TV stas., Chgo., 1978-83. Fellow Am Coll. Emergency Physicians (bd. dir. Ariz. chpt. 1988—, alt. counselor 1988—); mem. Ariz. Med. Assn. (Physician of Day resource person for Ariz. Ho. of Reps. 1988—), Soc. Tchrs. Emergency Medicine, Hastings Ctr.-Inst. Soc., Ethics, and Life Scis. Roman Catholic. Office: Emergency Physicians Inc 1741 E Morten Ave Ste C-1 Phoenix AZ 85020

SOLOMON, A. MALAMA, state legislator; b. Honolulu, Mar. 3, 1961; d. Randolph Folau Solomon and Flora Beamer. B.Ed., U. Hawaii-Manoa, 1972, M.A., 1973; B.A., U. Hawaii-Hilo, 1974; Ph.D., Oreg. State U., 1980. Market and sales mgr. beef cattle Kohala Farms, from 1972; lectr. U. Hawaii-Hilo, 1973-75; program coordinator Aloha Week Festivals Inc., 1977-87. Trustee, Office Hawaiian Affairs, 1980-82; mem. Hawaii Senate, Dist. 3, 1983—. Native Am. Ford fellow, 1976-80; recipient Outstanding Community Service award Hilo Coll., 1973-75; Outstanding Leadership award Council Hawaiian Civic Clubs, 1982; named Outstanding Woman of Yr., Hawaii Nat. Women's Week, 1982. Mem. Kohala Community Assn., Dist. Council Hawaiian Civic Clubs. Congregationalist. Office: State Senate State Capitol Honolulu HI 96813 Home: PO Box 219 Kapaau HI 96755

SOLOMON, JULIUS OSCAR LEE, pharmacist, hypnotherapist; b. N.Y.C., Aug. 14, 1917; s. John and Jeannette (Krieger) S.; student Bklyn. Coll., 1935-36, CCNY, 1936-37; BS in Pharmacy, U. So. Calif., 1949; postgrad. Long Beach State U., 1971-72; Southwestern Colls., 1979, 81-82; PhD, Am. Inst. Hypnotherapy, 1988; m. Sylvia Smith, June 26, 1941 (div. Jan. 1975); children: Marc Irwin, Evan Scott, Jeri Lee; m. 2d, Ana Maria C. MacFarland, Apr. 5, 1975; children: George, Anamaria, Gabriella, Arthur. Cert. hypnotherapist; cert. hypnoanaesthesia therapist. Dye maker Fred Fear & Co., Bklyn., 1935; apprentice interior decorator Dorothy Draper, 1936; various jobs, N.Y. State Police, 1940-45; rsch. asst. Union Oil Co., 1945; lighting cons. Joe Rosenberg & Co., 1946-49; owner Banner Drug, Lomita, 1949-53, Redondo Beach, Calif., 1953-72, El Prado Pharmacy, Redondo Beach, 1961-65; pres. Banner Drug, Inc., Redondo Beach, 1953-72, Thrifty Drugs, 1972-74, also Guild Drug, Longs Drug, Drug King, 1976-83; pres. Socoma, Inc. doing bus. as Lee & Ana Pharmacy, 1983-86, now Two Hearts Help Clinic, 1986—. Charter commr., founder Redondo Beach Youth Baseball Council; sponsor Little League Baseball, basketball, football, bowling; pres. Redondo Beach Boys Club; v.p. South Bay Children's Health Ctr., 1974, Redondo Beach Coordinating Coun., 1975; founder Redondo Beach Community Theater, 1975; active maj. gift drive YMCA, 1975; mem. SCAG Com. on Criminal Justice, 1974, League Calif. Environ. Quality Com., 1975; mem. Dem. State Cen. Com., Los Angeles County Dem. Cen. Com.; del. Dem. Nat. Conv., 1972; chmn. Redondo Beach Recreation and Parks Commn.; mem. San Diego County Parks Adv. Commn., 1982; mem. San Diego Juvenile Justice Commn., 1986—; mem. San Diego County Adv. Com. Adult Detention, 1987—; mem. human resource devel. com., pub. improvement com. Nat. League of Cities; v.p. Redondo Beach Coordinating Coun.; councilman, Redondo Beach, 1961-69, 73-77; treas. 46th Assembly Dist. Coun.; candidate 46 Assembly dist. 1966; nat. chmn. Pharmacists for Humphrey, 1968, 72; pres. bd. dirs. South Bay Exceptional Childrens Soc., Chapel Theatre; bd. dirs. so. div. League Calif. Cities, U.S.-Mex. Sister Cities Assn., Boy's Club Found. San Diego County, Autumn Hills Condominium Assn. (pres.), Calif. Employee Pharmacists Assn., Our House, Chula Vista, Calif., 1984—; mem. South Bay Inter-City Hwy. Com., Redondo Beach Round Table, 1973-77; mem. State Calif. Commn. of Californias (U.S.-Mexico), 1975-78; mem. Chula Vista Safety Commn., 1978, chmn., 1980-81; chmn. San Diego County Juvenile Camp Contract Com., 1982-83; mem. San Diego County Juvenile Delinquency Prevention Commn., 1983-85, 89—, San Diego County Juvenile Justice Commn., 1986—, San Diego County Adv. Com. for Adult Detention, 1987—; spl. participant Calif. Crime and Violence Workshop; mem. Montgomery Planning Commn., 1983-86. With USCGR, 1942-45. Recipient Pop Warner Youth award, 1960, 1962, award of merit Calif. Pharm. Assn., 1962, award Am. Assn. Blood Banks, 1982. Diplomate Am. Bd. Diplomates Pharmacy Internat. Fellow Am. Coll. Pharmacists (pres.); mem. South Bay Pharm. Assn. (pres.), South Bay Councilmans Assn. (founder, pres.), Palos Verdes Peninsula Navy League (charter), Am. Legion, U. So. Calif. Alumni Assn. (life), Assn. Former N.Y. State Troopers (life), AFTRA, Am. Pharm. Assn., Nat. Assn. Retail Druggists, Calif. Pharmacists Assn., Calif. Employee Pharmacist Assn. (bd. dirs. 1980-81), Hon. Dep. Sheriff's Assn., San Ysidro C. of C. (bd. dirs. 1985-87), Fraternal Order of Police, San Diego County Fish and Game Assn., Rho Pi Phi (pres. alumni). Club: Trojan (life). Lodges: Elks (life), Masons (32 deg.; life), Lions (charter mem. North Redondo). Established Lee and Ana Solomon award for varsity athlete with highest scholastic average at 10 L.A. South Bay High Schs. in Los Angeles County and 3 San Diego area South Bay High Schs.

SOLOMON, PAUL ALAN, environmental and analytical chemist; b. Boston, Dec. 14, 1956; s. Maurice and Ethel (Goodman) S.; m. Jocelyn Ileen Kritzer, June 9, 1985. BS in Chemistry with honors, U. Md., 1978; PhD in Chemistry, U. Ariz., 1984. Teaching asst. U. Ariz., Tucson, 1978-79, research asst., 1979-83, research assoc., 1983-84; research scientist Calif. Inst. Tech., Pasadena, 1984-88; chemist, air quality specialist technol. and ecol. services Pacific Gas and Electric, San Ramon, Calif., 1988—; cons. Tex. A&M U., Austin, Environ. Monitoring Services Inc., Newbury Park, Calif., Calif. Air Resources Bd., El Monte, Calif., 1986-87. Contbr. articles to profl. jours. Biochemistry scholar NSF, 1973; recipient John C. Ingang award U. Md., 1978. Mem. AAAS, Am. Inst. Chemists, Am. Chem. Soc. (Coryell award in Basic and Applied Nuclear Chemistry 1978), Am. Geophys. Union, No. Calif. Ion Chromatography Users Group, Air Pollution Control Assn., Alpha Chi Sigma, Phi Eta Sigma. Democrat. Jewish. Home: 4486 Sweet Shrub Ct Concord CA 94521 Office: Pacific Gas and Electric 3400 Crow Canyon San Ramon CA 94583

SOLORIO, CHRISTINA LYNN, loan officer; b. Hollister, Calif., June 18, 1963; d. Joseph L. and Dorothy Diane (Atwood) S.; 1 child, Sharon Elaine. BA, U. of the Pacific, 1985. Dist. sales rep. Calif. State Lottery, Sacramento, 1985-86; account exec. Calif. Fed. Savs., Concord, 1986-87; loan rep. Great Am. Savs., Pleasant hill, Calif., 1987-88; loan agt. Wells Fargo Bank, Orinda, Calif., 1988; loan officer Gibraltar Savs. & Loan, Pleasanton, Calif., 1988-89; sales assoc., fin. planner Cooper Fin. Group, Concord, Calif., 1989—. Mem. Nat. Assn. for Treas. (treas. 1986-88), Profl. Saleswomen, Perfect Strings Classical Music Lovers Club. Democrat. Roman Catholic. Home: 1400 Contra Costa 42 Pleasant Hill CA 94523 Office: Cooper Fin Group Willow Way Ste 210 Concord CA 94520

SOLOW, HERBERT FRANKLIN, film producer, writer; b. N.Y.C., Dec. 14, 1930; s. Morris David and Frances Louise (Birnbaum) S.; m. Maxine Debra Turner, Aug. 6, 1954 (div. 1974); children: Jody, Bonnie, Jamie. AB, Dartmouth Coll., 1953. Agt. William Morris Agy., N.Y.C., 1954-58; dir., exec. NBC, N.Y.C., 1958-59, Los Angeles, 1958-60, CBS, Los Angeles, 1961-63; v.p. Desilu Studios, Los Angeles, 1964-69; v.p. prodn. Paramount TV, Los Angeles, 1969; v.p. worldwide prodn. Metro-Goldwyn-Mayer, Los Angeles, 1969-73; pres. Solow Prodn. Co., Los Angeles, 1976-79; v.p. Sherwood Prodns., Los Angeles, 1980-83; ind. producer, writer Los Angeles, 1984—. Mem. Writers Guild Am., Dirs. Guild Am., Acad. Motion Picture Arts and Scis., Acad. TV Arts and Scis.

SOLOW, ROBERT A., physician; b. Newark, Sept. 11, 1925; m. Marilyn Ames, Dec. 25, 1949; children: Lawrence, Jay, Lee Howard, Bruce Alan, Brian Keith, Margaret Ames. AA, Princeton U., 1944; MD, N.Y. Med. Coll., 1948. Diplomate Am. Bd. Psychiatry and Neurology. Intern Jersey City Med. Ctr., 1948-49; resident in psychiatry Winter VA Hosp., Topeka, Kans., 1949-52; fellow Menninger Found. Sch. Psychology, Topeka, Kans., 1949-52; staff psychiatrist Topeka State Hosp., 1952; attending staff psychiatrist Mt. Sinai Hosp., Los Angeles, 1956-59; child psychiatrist Reiss Davis Child Study Ctr., 1955-70; vis. staff psychiatrist U. Calif. Hosp. and Clinics, Los Angeles, 1958-86, UCLA Neuropsychiat. Inst., 1958—; mem. courtesy staff Westwood Hosp., Los Angeles, 1960-77; mem. tchg. staff Menninger Found. Sch. Psychiatry, 1958-62, asst clinical prof. psychiatry, 1962-69, assoc. clinical prof., 1969-78, clinical prof., 1978—; med. examiner State of Calif.; ind. med. examiner State of Calif. Dept. Indsl. Med.; med. adv. com. Musular Dystrophy Assn. Am., 1955-80. Co-author: The Joys and Sorrows of Parenthood, 1973, Speaking Out for Psychiatry, 1987; mem. editorial bd. Adolescent Psychiatry, 1969-76. Chmn. exec. com. Boy Scouts Am., L.A. chpt., 1968-74. Capt. M.C., USAF, 1952-54. Recipient Silver Bruin award Boy Scouts Am., 1969, Hon. Svc. award Calif. Congress Paretns and Tchrs., 1970. Fellow Am. Psychiat. Assn. (life), Am. Soc. for Adolescent Psychiatry (life), So. Calif. Psychiat. Soc. (life, past. pres.), So. Calif. Soc. for Adolescent Psychiatry (life), Am. Coll. Psychiatrists, Am. Assn. Social Psychiatry, World Assn. for Social Psychiatry; mem. Internat. Assn. for Adolescent Psychiatry (exec. bd.), Group for Advancement of Psychiatry (editorial bd.), Calif. Med. Assn. (past chmn. sect. on psychiatry), So. Calif. Soc. Child Psychiatry (past pres.), Physicians for Social Responsibility, Calif. Soc. Indsl. Medidine and Surgery, AAAS (editorial rev. bd. Am. Jour. Psychiat. Hosp. and Community Psychiatry). Club: Mountainsgate Country. Office: 152 Lasky Dr Beverly Hills CA 90212

SOLTISIAK, CHRISTINA ANN, management consultant; b. Bridgeport, Conn., Sept. 22, 1945; d. Frank Edward and Ann Georgiana (Pjura) Tomek; m. Aug. 31, 1967 (dec. 1986); 1 child, Scott William Soltisiak; m. Steven Earl Howell, Apr. 25, 1987. AA, Bryant Coll., 1965. Exec. sec. Glass Tite Mfg., Providence, 1965-67; legal sec. Robert D. Moilanen, Atty., Vancouver, Wash., 1974-77; exec. asst., sales and mktg. Devel. Svcs. Corp., Portland, Oreg., 1978-83; mgmt. cons. Exec. Forum, Vancouver, 1983—. Bd. edn. Grace Luth. Ch., Vancouver, 1988-89; mem. Clark County YWCA, Columbia River Economic Devel. Coun. Recipient Customer Care award U.S. Army C.E., 1989. Mem. Am. Soc. Tng. and Devel., C. of C. Democrat. Lutheran. Office: Exec Forum 404 E 15th St Ste 7 Vancouver WA 98663

SOMERMEYER, HERBERT FREDERICK, consulting patent lawyer; b. Balaton, Minn., Nov. 27, 1928; s. Augustus Gerhard and Selma Dora (Freuchte) S.; m. Lois Marie Mitchell, Aug. 1, 1954; 1 child, Randy James. Student, Gustavus Adolphus Coll., 1946-47; BSEE, Iowa State U., 1950; JD cum laude, William Mitchell Coll., 1957. Bar. Minn. 1957, Colo. 1972. Patent engr. Sperry Rand Corp. (Univac Div.), St. Paul, 1952-57; patent atty. Carlson & Hazle, Mpls., 1957-59; patent counsel Sperry Rand Corp. (Univac Div.), St. Paul, 1959-65; sr. atty. Sperry Rand Corp., N.Y.C., 1965-67; patent atty. Mueller Aichele & Rauner, Phoenix, 1967-69; sr. atty. IBM, Boulder, Colo., 1969-78; cons. atty. IBM, Tucson, 1978-87; sole practice Tucson, 1987—. Served to lt. U.S. Army, 1951-52. Mem. IEEE, Am. Intellectual Property Law Assn. Lutheran. Home and Office: 8421 E Fernhill Dr Tucson AZ 85715

SOMERVILLE, ROGER JAMES, military officer, civil engineer; b. Kalispell, Mont., May 18, 1947; s. James Paul and Verna (Roe) S. BSCE, Mont. State U., 1970. Registered profl. engr., Idaho. Commd. 2d lt. U.S. Army, 1971—, advanced through grades to lt. col.; engr. co. comdr. 16th Combat Engr. Bn., Furth, Fed. Republic of Germany, 1976-77; asst. prof. Rose-Hulman Inst. Tech., Terre Haute, Ind., 1978-81; project engr. C.E., Twin Falls, Idaho, 1981-83; engring. project mgr. C.E., Walla Walla, Wash., 1983-84; dir. logistics U.S. Army Mil. Community, Nurnberg, Fed. Republic of Germany, 1984-85; asst. div. engr. 1st Armored Div., Ansbach, Fed. Republic of Germany, 1986-87; brigade engr. 177th Armored Brigade, Ft. Irwin, Calif., 1987-88, brigade dep. comdr., 1988—. Mem. Assn. U.S. Army, Soc. Am. Mil. Engrs. (v.p. 1986-87), Elks. Republican. Roman Catholic. Office: US Army 177th Armored Brigade Fort Irwin CA 92310-5001

SOMMERHALDER, JOHN EDWARD, real estate company executive; b. Milw., Feb. 20, 1934; s. Arnold Henry and Alma Josephine (Wolter) S.; m. Susan Helen Steinke, Nov. 17, 1956; children: Lisa, Thomas, Linda Sue, Steven. BS, Regis Coll., 1960; cert. in urban policy, Brookings Instn., 1968. V.p., gen. mgr. Rio Rancho Estates, Albuquerque, 1964-70; pres. Tenneco West, Inc., Bakersfield, Calif., 1970-73; v.p. housing div. Wylain, Inc., Dallas, 1973-74; v.p. real estate and land devel. Dale Bellamah Corp., Albuquerque, 1975-76; pres. Aetna Diversified Properties, Scottsdale, 1975-80, Transcontinental Properties, Scottsdale, Ariz., 1980-83, MCO Properties, Inc., Fountain Hills, Ariz., 1983—; pres. Horizon Corp., Fountain Hills, 1983—, also bd. dirs.; bd. dirs. Fountain Hills Bank. Pres. March of Dimes, Albuquerque, 1968, United Way Fund, Bakersfield, 1971; dir. econ. devel. com. State of Calif., Bakersfield, 1971-73. Served with USMC, 1953-54. Mem. Lloyds of London, Fountain Hills C. of C., Calif. C. of C. (bd. dirs., officer 1965-74), Fountain Hills Men's Club. Republican. Roman Catholic. Office: MCO Properties Inc PO Box 17795 Fountain Hills AZ 85268

SOMMERNESS, MARTIN DAVID, journalism educator, media law consultant; b. Fergus Falls, Minn., Dec. 17, 1954; s. Martin Duane and Gertrude L. (Titus) S. B.A., Mich. State U., 1977, M.A., 1979; J.D., Wayne State U., 1981. Bar: Ariz. 1982, U.S. Dist. Ct. Ariz. 1982. Staff writer Traverse City Record-Eagle, Mich., 1972-77, writer, editor State News, East Lansing, Mich., 1972-76; sr. editor Lansing Chronicle, Mich., 1976-77; teaching asst. Mich. State U., East Lansing, 1977-78; shift supr. Free Legal Aid Clinic, Detroit, 1980-81; atty. intern Wayne County Neighborhood Legal Services, Inkster, Mich., 1980-81; asst. prof. No. Ariz. U., Flagstaff, 1981-87, assoc. prof., 1987—, adminstrv. asst. to dean, 1984-85; cons. Flagstaff Arts Festival, 1984-85, Hopi Tribal Housing Authority, 1983, Phoenix chpt. Pub. Realtions Soc. Am., 1983; legal counsel No. Ariz. Com. against Strip Mining, 1982, Kachina Village Fire Bd., Flagstaff, 1982. Editor: Great American Communications Connection, 1982. Author and editor: Communications America, 1983. Author: Free to Inform: A Beginning Journalist's Survival Guide to Self-Preservation in Media Law, 1989. Pres. Lutheran Campus Ministry Flagstaff, 1982-89. Recipient Gen. Mgr.'s award East Lansing State News, 1976; Bur. Nat. Affairs scholar, 1981; Doctoral Honors fellow U. Ga., 1987. Mem. Western Social Sci. Assn. (program coordinator 1983), Assn. Edn. in Journalism and Mass Communications, Am. Judicature Soc., Ariz. Humanities Council (grant co-dir. 1983-84), Sigma Delta Chi (Mark of Excellence award 1976, chpt. v.p. 1982—). Republican. Home: 4350 Spring Meadows Circle Flagstaff AZ 86004 Office: No Ariz U Box 6001 Flagstaff AZ 86011

SOMMERS, MASON ANDREW, psychologist; b. L.A., Apr. 18, 1956; s. Richard H. and Dione Elyse (Kallin) S. BA cum laude, UCLA, 1978; MA, Calif. Sch. Profl. Psychology, 1980, PhD, 1982. Lic. clin. psychologist. Staff therapist Ross-Loos Med. Ctr., Torrance, Calif., 1980-81; psychology intern Glendale Adventist Med. Ctr., Torrance, Calif., 1981-82; psychol. asst. Barry S. Lieberman, Beverly Hills, Calif., 1982-86; pvt. practice Beverly Hills, 1986-; cons. in field. Bd. dirs. Westside Women's Health Ctr., Santa Monica, Calif., 1986-88, Gay & Lesbian Community Svcs. Ctr., Hollywood, 1988-. Cedars and Sinai Med. Ctr. scholar, 1975. Mem. Am. Psychol. Assn., Calif. Psychol. Assn., Soc. Psychol. Study Gay and Lesbian Issues. Democrat. Jewish. Office: 416 N Bedford Dr #208 Beverly Hills CA 90210

SOMORJAI, GABOR ARPAD, chemist, educator; b. Budapest, Hungary, May 4, 1935; came to U.S., 1957, naturalized, 1962; s. Charles and Livia (Ormos) S.; m. Judith Kaldor, Sept. 2, 1957; children: Nicole, John. B.S. in Chem. Engring, U. Tech. Scis., Budapest, 1956; Ph.D., U. Calif., Berkeley, 1960. Mem. research staff IBM, Yorktown Heights, N.Y., 1960-64; prin. investigator materials and molecular research div. Lawrence Berkeley Lab., Calif., 1964—; mem. faculty dept. chemistry U. Calif.-Berkeley, 1964—, assoc. prof., 1967-72, prof., 1972—, Miller prof., 1978; unilever prof. dept. chemistry U. Bristol, Eng., 1972; vis. fellow Emmanuel Coll., Cambridge, Eng., 1969; Baker lectr. Cornell U., 1977. Author: Principles of Surface Chemistry, 1972, Chemistry in Two Dimension, 1981; mem. editorial bd. Jour. Solid State Chemistry, 1976—, Progress in Solid State Chemistry, 1973—, Nouveau Jour. de Chimie, 1977-80, Colloid and Interface Sci., 1979—, Catalysis Revs., 1981, Jour. Phys. Chem., 1981—, Langmuir, 1985—, Jour. Applied Catalysis, Advances in Catalysis; editor in chief Catalysis Letters, 1988—; contbr. articles to profl. jours. Recipient Emmett award Am. Catalysis Soc., 1977, Kokes award John Hopkins U., 1976, Albert award Precious Metal Inst., 1986, Sr. Disting. Scientist award Alexander von Humboldt Found., 1989; Guggenheim fellow, 1969. Fellow Am. Phys. Soc., AAAS; mem. Am. Acad. Arts and Scis., NAS, Am. Chem. Soc. (chmn. colloid and surface chemistry 1981, Surface and Colloid Chemistry award 1981, Peter Debye award 1989), Am. Phys. Soc., Catalysis Soc. N.Am. Office: U Calif Dept Chemistry Berkeley CA 94720 Home: 665 San Luis Rd Berkeley CA 94707

SONDAK, BRADLEY WAYNE, sports editor; b. Far Rockaway, N.Y., Apr. 7, 1962; s. Norman Edward and Eileen Lorraine (Miller) S. BS, San Diego State U., 1984. Sports editor San Diego Weekly News, 1984-, Inn Rm. Mag., 1985-87, Coast Dispatch, Encinitas, Calif., 1987-; on-the-spot reporter The Sports Network, Phila., 1986-; sportswriter Coast Dispatch, Encinitas, Calif., 1986-87; cons. KGTV Channel 10 Sports Dept., San Diego, 1986-; sports commentator Sta. KVSD, Carlsbad, Calif., 1988—. Contbr. articles to profl. jours. Home: 6344 Lake Lomond Dr San Diego CA 92119 Office: Coast Dispatch 687 First St Encinitas CA 92024

SONDEREGGER, ROBERT CARL, data processing executive; b. Baden, Aargau, Switzerland, Aug. 19, 1948; came to U.S. 1973; s. Arnold A. and Annemarie (Grob) S.; m. Joanna G. Moss, Aug. 24, 1980; children Morgan Arthur, Lauren Rose. Baccalaureat, Collegio Papio, Ascona, Switzerland, 1968; MS in Physics, Fed. Inst. Tech., Zurich, Switzerland, 1973; PhD in Mech. Engring., Princeton U., 1977. Research assoc. Swiss Inst. Nuclear Research Villigen, Aargua, 1973; vis. lectr. U. Calif., Berkeley, 1977-78; staff scientist III Lawrence Berkeley Lab, Berkeley, 1977-78, group leader, 1978-83, dep. program leader, 1983-84; founder, pres. Morgan Systems Corp., Berkeley, 1984-88, sr. v.p. research and devel., 1988-; cons. Gen. Mills, Inc., Mpls., 1982-83, Building Research Establishment, Garston, Watford, U.K., 1981, Azienda per il Risparmio dell' Energia, Rome, Italy, 1981-82. Contrb. articles to profl. jours. Guggenheim fellow, 1975. Mem. AAAS, ASHRAE, ASTM. Home: 560 San Luis Rd Berkeley CA 94707 Office: Morgan Systems Corp 1654 Solano Ave Berkeley CA 94707

SONE, PHILIP GEARY, health psychologist; b. Detroit, Jan. 16, 1949; s. Geary Masami and Monica Kazuko (Itoi) S. BA in Psychology and Sociology, Bowling Green U., 1971; MA in Clinical Psychology, W. Ga. Coll., 1974; PhD in Psychology, Ariz. State U., 1981. Cert. psychologist, nat. counselor. Family psychologist Family Service Ctr., Canton, Ohio, 1974-77; counselor and trainer Ariz. State U., Tempe, 1977-79; health psychologist Mesa Luth. Hosp., 1979-86, Health Psychology & Counseling Assocs., Phoenix and Mesa, 1983—, Rehab. Medicine Assocs., Ariz. Phys. Medicine, Mesa, 1986—; trainer, med. staff, Phoenix Gen. Hosp., 1984; cons., trainer ITT Courier, Inc., Phoenix, 1985, Garrett Pneumatic Industries, Inc., Phoenix, 1985, Coen Engring., Inc., Phoenix, 1985. Mem. Am. psychol. Assn. (health psychology div.), Am. Assn Counseling and Devel., Ariz. Assn. for Health Psychology, Phoenix Group for Study of Chronic Pain,. Presbyterian. Office: Ariz Phys Medicine & Rehab 445 W 5th Pl Ste E Mesa AZ 85201

SONNE, THELMA ELIZABETH (LISA SONNE), producer, freelance writer and record producer; b. Pasadena, Calif., July 21, 1956; d. Roscoe Newbold and Ann Miriam (Vierhus) S. BA, Stanford U., 1978, MA, 1983. Broadway shows mgr. San Francisco, 1978-79; dir. student devel. Stanford U., Calif., 1980; writer, producer, Calif., 1983—; pres. Mira Prodns., Los Angeles, 1988—; cons. Arts & Scis. Prodns., San Francisco; freelance photographer, 1986-88. Editor: Engines of the Mind, 1980-82; co-writer various TV prodns. including Faces of Culture, 1983 (Emmy cert.), Broken Rainbow (1986 academy award winner); producer current works including Maestros in Moscow (broadcast-video program with Gregory Peck); The

Moscow Sessions, 1986—; (recording) Rhapsody in Russia - A Gershwin Celebration, 1988—. Nicholl Fellow Stanford U., 1980. Mem. Live Oaks Tennis Club. Office: Mira Prodns 30473 Mulholland Hwy Los Angeles CA 91301

SONNEBORN, DANIEL ATESH, composer, ethnomusicologist, producer; b. Chgo., Oct. 31, 1949; s. Curt Lewis and Annette (Lubove) S.; m. Patrizia Pallaro, Sept. 21, 1986; 1 child, Samuel Clement. AB in Music with honors, U. Calif., Santa Cruz, 1982; MA in Music Theory, U. Calif., San Diego, 1984; Degree in Philosphy, UCLA, 1988. Music dir., composer Company Theatre Found., L.A., 1970-72, ProVisional Theatre, L.A., Theater Workshop Boston, 1973-76, James Joyce Meml. Liquid Theatre, Paris, London, 1972; prodn. mgr. Music Ctr. L.A. Forum Lab, Hollywood, Calif., 1972-73; producer Cosmic Mass, World Spiritual Summit Conf., UN, N.Y.C., 1975; freelance composer, producer L.A., San Francisco, 1976-84; teaching asst. U. Calif., La Jolla, 1982-84; teaching assoc., researcher music dept. UCLA, 1984-88; project mgr. 360 (Degrees) Prodns., San Rafael, Calif., 1988—; cons. Kuper Advt., Boulder, Colo., 1986. Composer: Dominus Marlowe: A Play on Dr. Faustus, 1972 (Best Show of Yr. award 1972), Class, 1976 (Best Show of Yr. award 1976). President's fellow U. Calif., Santa Cruz, 1981-82, grad. fellow UCLA, 1984-85, NDEA Title VI fellow UCLA, 1986-87; grantee Nat. Endowment for Arts, 1970-76, also Rockefeller Found., Ford Found., Calif. Council on Arts, Mass. Council on Arts, Bezalel Found. Mem. Soc. for Ethnomusicology, Internat. Council for Traditional Music, Am. Fedn. Musicians. Democrat. Home: 1586 Sir Francis Drake Blvd Apt 6 San Anselmo CA 94960 Office: 360 Degrees Prodns PO Box 3472 San Rafael CA 94912

SONNIKSEN, JANET W., education educator; b. Portland, Oreg., Nov. 7, 1942; d. Edward Conrad and Edith Geneve (Matson) Wyss; m. Scott Thomas Sonniksen, Nov.18, 1967 (div. 1976); 1 child, Lara W. Student architecture, U. Oreg., 1960-62; BS, Portland State U., 1963-66, postgrad., 1971-72. Cert. tchr., Oreg. Art tchr. Beaverton (Oreg.) Sch. Dist. #48, 1966-69, 76-83; designer J & J Designs, Concord, Calif., 1983—; ptnr. J & J Designs, Concord, 1985—; art tchr. Beaverton Sch. Dist. #48, 1985—. Artist: sculpture, Useful Objects, NW Exhibit '76, Jurors' Award. Art Tchr. Coordinator Congl. Student Art Exhibn., Les Aucoin Dist., 1988; coordinator Oreg. Art Edn. Student art exhibit "Youth Art Month" Portland, 1988. Named Mentor Tchr., Beaverton Sch. Dist. and Portland State U., 1987-88. Mem. Oreg. Art Edn. Assn., Nat. Art Edn., Beaverton Edn. Assn., Oreg. Edn. Assn., Nat. Edn. Assn. Republican. Office: Beaverton Sch Dist 48 PO Box 200 Beaverton OR 97075

SONSTELIE, RICHARD ROBERT, utilities executive; b. Ottawa, Ont., Can., Mar. 31, 1945; s. Robert Daniel and Valerie Marjorie (St. Laurent) S.; m. Cynthia Louise Prussing, Sept. 19, 1970; children: Marit K., Jennifer A. BS, U.S. Mil. Acad., 1966; MS in Nuclear Engring., MIT, 1968; MBA, Harvard U., 1974. Commd. 2d lt. U.S. Army, 1966, advanced through grades to capt., served in Vietnam, 1966-72, resigned, 1972; staff mem., project mgr. Los Alamos (N.Mex.) Sci. Labs., 1969-72; with Puget Sound Power and Light Co., Bellevue, Wash., 1974-80, v.p. engring. and ops., 1980-83, sr. v.p. fin., 1983-85, exec. v.p., 1985-87, pres., 1987—, also bd. dirs. Mem. Mcpl. League, Wash. State Job Tng. Coordinating Council, Olympia, 1984-88; bd. dirs. Jr. Achievement of Greater Puget Sound, Seattle, 1985—, chmn., 1986-87; bd. dirs. Seattle Sci. Ctr., 1987—; bd. trustees Bellevue Community Coll., 1985—; civilian aide to sec. of army, 1987—; mem. Vietnam Vets. Leadership Program. Decorated Bronze Star. Mem. Edison Electric Inst., Seattle C. of C., West Point Soc. Puget Sound (pres.). Lodge: Rotary. Home: 5 Brook Bay Mercer Island WA 98040 Office: Puget Sound Power & Light Puget Power Bldg PO Box 97034 M/S 15 Bellevue WA 98009

SONTHEIM, KENNETH RUSSELL, land use planner, consultant; b. Lyons, N.Y., Nov. 2, 1951; s. Max Russell and Edna May (Goosen) S. BSBA, Colgate U., 1973. Restauranteur Snowmass (Colo.) Corp., 1973-75, acctg. mgr., 1975-76, comml. ops. dir., 1976-79; project mgr. The Snowmass Co., Ltd., 1979-85; pres. Snowmass Land Co.; v.p. devel. The Snowmass Co., Ltd., 1985—; cons. The Snowmass Club Partnership, 1980—, Investors Real Estate Investment Co., Richmond, Va., 1987-89. Mem. com. Town of Snowmass-Mcpl. Code, 1978-79, Keep Snowmass Beautiful, 1983, Snowmass Codes, 1987; bd. dirs. Anderson Ranch Arts Found., 1984, Snowmass Resort Assn., 1982-87, Country Club Townhomes Assn., 1980-85. Mem. Urban Land Inst. Home: 4000 Brush Creek Rd PO Box 5349 Snowmass Village CO 81615

SORBY, DONALD LLOYD, university dean; b. Fremont, Nebr., Aug. 12, 1933; s. Lloyd A. and Orpha M. (Simmons) S.; m. Jacquelyn J. Burchard, Nov. 7, 1959; children—Thomas, Sharon. B.S. in Pharmacy, U. Nebr., 1955; M.S., U. Wash., 1958, Ph.D., 1960. Dir. pharm. services U. Calif., San Francisco, 1970-72; chmn. dept. pharmacy practice Sch. Pharmacy, U. Wash., Seattle, 1972-74; dean Sch. of Pharmacy, U. Mo., Kansas City, 1974-84, Sch. of Pharmacy, U. Pacific, Stockton, Calif., 1984—. Contbr. articles in field to profl. jours. Assoc. fellow Am. Coll. Apothecaries; mem. Am. Pharm. Assn., Am. Assn. Colls. of Pharmacy (pres. 1980-81), Fedn. Internat. Pharmaceutique, Calif. Pharm. Assn., Acad. Pharm. Scis., Calif. Soc. Hosp. Pharmacists, Assn. Pharm. Scis., Sigma Xi, Phi Kappa Phi, Rho Chi. Home: 4362 Yacht Harbor Dr Stockton CA 95204 Office: U Pacific Sch Pharmacy Stockton CA 95211

SOREF, DROR, film producer, director; b. Haifa, Isreal, July 23, 1950; s. Jack Soref and Lili Konforty; m. Su Falcon, Dec. 20, 1980; 1 child, Oren Alexander. BA, U. Haifa, 1974; postgrad., U. So. Calif., L.A., 1976-77. Devel. exec. A Brilliant Film Co., Hollywood, Calif., 1979-80; story analyst Joe Wizan Prodns., Century City, Calif., 1982-83; dir. devel. Inter-Planetary Prodns., Studio City, Calif., 1984; pres. Orbit Entertainment, Inc. at Paramount Studios, Hollywood, 1986—. Dir. (film) Platinum Blonde, 1987, (music video) I Love Rocky Road, 1983; line producer (TV series) Hitchhiker, 1983; co-producer (film) The Long Run, 1982, numerous TV commls. for internat. market. Lt. Isreali Army, 1968-71, 73-74. Mem. Dirs. Guild Am. Office: Orbit Entertainment Inc Paramount Studios 5555 Melrose Ave Hollywood CA 90038

SOREN, DAVID, archaeology educator and administrator; b. Phila., Oct. 7, 1946; s. Harry Friedman and Erma Elizabeth (Salamon) Soren; m. Noelle Louise Schattyn, Dec. 22, 1967. B.A., Dartmouth Coll., 1968; M.A., Harvard U., 1972, Ph.D., 1973. Cert. Rome Classics Ctr. Curator of coins Fogg Art Mus., Cambridge, Mass., 1972; asst. prof. U. Mo., Columbia, 1972-76, assoc. prof., dept. head, 1976-81; prof. archaeology U. Ariz., Tucson, 1982-83, dept. head, 1984-89; guest curator, lectr. Am. Mus. Natural History, N.Y.C., 1983—; creator, dir. Kourion excavations, Cyprus, 1982—, Portugal, 1983-84; pot cons., field dir. Tunisia Excavations Chgo. Oriental Inst./Smithsonian Instn., 1973-78; creator/dir. Am. Excavations at Lugnano, Italy, 1988. Co-author: Kourion: Search for a Lost Roman City, 1988, Corpus des Mosaiques de Tunisie, 1972, 76, 80, 86, monograph on Cyprus, Carthage: A Mosaic of Ancient Tunisia, 1987; author 2 books on film: Unreal Reality, 1978, Rise and Fall of Fantasy Film, 1980, History of Carthage, 1989; producer film A Mosaic of Ancient Tunisia, 1987; editor: Excavations at Kourion I, 1987; creatir/guest curator internat. traveling exhbn. Carthage: A Mosaic of Ancient Tunisia, 1987-92; contbr. articles to profl. jours.; subject of Nat. Geographic spl. Archeological Detectives, 1985. NEH research grantee, 1979; featured articles on his work, Newsweek, Connoisseur, Nat. Geographic, others. Fulbright grantee, Lisbon, 1983; recipient Cine Golden Eagle, 1980, Angenieux Film award, Indsl. Photog. Mag., 1980, Outstanding American Under 40 award C. Johns Hopkins/Britain's Royal Inst. Internat. Affairs, 1985; named Outstanding American Under 40 Esquire mag., 1985; named hon. Italian Citizen, Lugano, Italy, 1989. Mem. Archaeol. Inst. Tucson (pres. 1983—), Am. Sch. Oriental Research (dept. rep. 1981—), Nat. Geog. Soc. (project dir. 1983-84), Luso-Am. Commn. (citation 1983-84), Explorer's Club. Office: U Ariz Dept Classics 371 MLB Tucson AZ 85721

SORENSEN, DEBRA LYNNETTE, computer training executive; b. Austin, Tex., Jan. 16, 1954; d. T.D. and Dolores E. (Walton) Williams; m. Audun I. Sorensen, June 10, 1972; children: Shawn M., Emily L. Student, Kelsey-Baird Bus. Sch., Spokane, Wash., 1972-73, Spokane Community Coll., 1974, Lane Community Coll., Eugene, Oreg., 1976, 79, 86-87, U. Oreg., 1986—. Secretarial and word processing positions various, 1972-77; word processing mgr. Lane Council of Govts., Eugene, 1977-80; sales and tng. various word processing/computer vendors, Eugene, 1980-84; owner, mgr. Automation Plus, Eugene, 1984—; user svcs. mgr., computing and info. svcs. dept. Eugene Sch. Dist., 1987—; served on numerous panels related to word processing/computers for bus. and edn., including establishment of courses at Lane Community Coll., Eugene, 1979. Chmn. Lane County Affirmative Action Com., Eugene, 1980-82, Lane Community Coll. Women's Adv. Com., Eugene, 1980-82; Bethel Sch. Dist. #52 Budget Com., Eugene, 1980-84, bd. dirs., 1984—; vice chmn. Lane Coun. of Govts., 1984-89, chmn., 1989—. Bd. Dirs., Eugene, 1984—; Young Bd. Members Caucus Nat. Sch. Bd., 1986; pres. Willamette High Sch. Band Parents' Orgn., 1987-88; mem. Talented and Gifted Students Adv. Com., 1987—. Recipient scholarship Spokane Ednl. Secs. Assn., 1972. Mem. Eugene Word Processing Assn. (salary survey com. 1978, area dir. Willamette Valley chpt. 1977), Adminstrv. Mgmt. Soc. Republican. Mem. Ch. of Christ. Office: Automation Plus 3800 Barger Dr Eugene OR 97402

SORENSEN, IRMA RACHEL, postmaster; b. Manti, Utah, July 5, 1928; d. Warren Rex and Rachel (Petersen) Mellor; m. Bernard Mortimer Sorensen, May 24, 1949; children: Morris Bernard, Sherwin Marty, Lane Rex, Len Warren, Jarvis Lynn, Wayne Hal, Kevin Ned, Lu Ann Lesa. Student, Brigham Young U., 1946-48. Flex clk. U.S. Postal Svc., Gunnison, Utah, 1967-84; officer in charge U.S. Postal Svc., Gunnison, 1982, postmaster, 1984—; mem., recorder Mgmt. Involvement/Quality of Work Life U.S. Postal Svc., Fish Lake Dist., Utah, 1987-89. Recipient 2nd Miller award Boy Scouts Am., Gunnison Dist., 1972, Ephraim Region, 1978; scholar Brigham Young U., 1946. Mem. Am. Legion Aux. (sec. Gunnison chpt. 1976-89, pres. 1989—). Mormon. Home: 665 S Main St Gunnison UT 84634-0136 Office: US Postal Service 25 W Center Gunnison UT 84634

SORENSEN, JACKI FAYE, aerobic dance company executive, choreographer; b. Oakland, Calif., Dec. 10, 1942; d. Roy C. and Juanita F. (Bullon) Mills; m. Neil A. Sorensen, Jan. 3, 1965. B.A., U. Calif., 1964. Cert. tchr., Calif. Ptnr., Big Spring Sch. Dance, 1965; tchr. Pasadena Ave. Sch., Sacramento, 1968; founder, chmn. bd. dirs., choreographer Jacki's Inc., Northridge, Calif., 1969—; cons., lectr. on phys. fitness. Author: Aerobic Dancing, 1979, Jacki Sorensen's Aerobic Lifestyle Book, 1983; choreographer numerous dance exercises for records and videocassettes. Trustee Women's Sports Found. Recipient Diamond Pin award Am. Heart Assn., 1979; Individual Contbn. award Am. Assn. Fitness Dirs. in Bus. and Industry, 1981; Spl. Olympics Contbn. award, 1982; Contbn. to Women's Fitness award Pres.'s Council Phys. Fitness and Sports, 1982; Healthy Am. Fitness Leader award U.S. Jaycees, 1984; Lifetime Achievement award Internat. Dance Exercise Assn., 1985; New Horizons award Caldwell (N.J.) Coll., 1985; Legend of Aerobics award City Sports mag., 1985; Pres. Council award Calif. Womens' Leadership Conf., 1986; Hall of Fame award Club Industry mag., 1986. Mem. Am. Coll. Sports Medicine, AAHPERD, Nat. Intramural and Recreation Assn., AFTRA. Office: Jacki's Inc 19420 Business Center Dr Northridge CA 91324

SORENSEN, JOHN CHRISTIAN, technical writer; b. Chgo., Feb. 17, 1929; s. Johannes Marius and Jensine Elizabeth (Jensen) S.; m. Jane Henry Lowenbach, Sept. 21, 1957 (Div. May 21, 1966); 1 child, Jule Lise; m. Sally Locke Johnson, Feb. 28, 1970 (div. Oct. 21, 1984); 1 child, Brittany Noelle. Student, North Park Coll., 1951, Regis Coll., Dana Coll., Augustana Coll.; grad., DeVry Tech. Inst. Colo. real estate license; broadcast engr. license. Acting unit supr. Martin Marietta Denver Aero., Denver, 1962-66; sr. tech. writer H.L. YOH McDonnell Douglas, St. Louis, 1966-67; publ. suspr. Data Products Card Equipment, Englewood, Colo., 1967-71; writing unit supr. Storage Technology Corp., Louisville, Colo., 1971-73; software documentation supr. Potomac Rsch. Data Communications, Colorado Springs, Colo., 1973-78; writing unit supr. Ford Aerospace, Colorado Springs, 1979-80; publ. supr. Martin Marietta Aerospace Div., Denver, 1980-87; sr. tech. writer US WEST Communications, Englewood, 1987. Emergency coord. ARC, Adams County, 1965; sec. Indian Hills (Colo.) Water Dist., 1966-73; engr. Indian Hills Vol Fire Dept., 1966-73, Southwest Adams County Fire Dept., Westminster, Colo., 1962-65, N. Leyden Vol. Fire Dept., Rosemont, Ill., 1959-62; coord. emergency svcs. mission Colo. Wing CAP; mem. Sankey Search & Rescue Unit, United Rescue Unit Cave and Mines. Mem. Denver Danes. Lutheran. Home: PO Box 914 Indian Hills CO 80454

SORENSEN, WALTER FACCOU, JR., graphic designer, artist; b. Los Angeles, Feb. 11, 1926; s. Walter Faccou and Sena S.; m. Carol Jeanne Burrow, Sept. 9, 1945; children: Jeffrey Lynn, Bruce Allen, Dane Steven. Cert., Art Ctr. Sch., Los Angeles, 1951. Owner Walt Sorensen Studio, Santa Ana, Calif., 1951-71; artist/designer Disneyland, Anaheim, Calif., 1967-71; art supr. Walt Disney World, Lake Buena Vista, Fla., 1971-83; owner Walt Sorensen Studio, Roseville, Calif., 1983—; pres. Soc. of Designers and Illustrators, Santa Ana, 1963-65. Pres. Isle of Catalina Homeowners, Orlando, Fla., 1975; co-chmn. Neighborhood Watch, Roseville, Calif., 1985-88; mem. Advent Luth. Ch. Council, Citrus Heights, Calif., 1987—. Served to corp. USAF, 1944-46. Mem. Roseville C. of C. Republican. Club: Contando (pres. 1965-68). Home and Office: Walt Sorensen Studio 1300 Ridgecrest Way Roseville CA 95661

SORENSON, CRAIG ALLEN, business executive; b. Belle Fourche, S.D., Mar. 11, 1954; s. LaMoine Charles and Verla Leulla (Twombley) S.; m. Vicki Ann Fitzgerald, Nov. 28, 1981; children: Joshua, Amanda, Carin, Casey. AS, NW Community Coll., Powell, Wyo., 1974; BS in Agrl. Engring., U. Wyo., 1978. Reclamation engr. Decker (Mont.) Coal Co., 1978-81; contract adminstr. Am. Line Builders Inc., Dayton, Wash., 1981-83; exec. owner SE Inc., Deaver, Wyo., 1983—; bd. dirs. SE Inc., 1983—, Calif.-Wyo. Ventures West, Inc., Blythe, Calif. Council mem. Town of Deaver, 1984-88, mayor elect, 1988, mayor 1989—; vol. fireman Frannie, Wyo., 1984—; bd. dirs. joint powers bd. Shoshone Mcpl. Water System. Mem. Power and Communication Contractors Assn., Wyo. Assn. Municipalities (voting del. 1988). Republican. Lutheran. Lodge: Eagles. Home: 727 Rd 1 Deaver WY 82421

SORKIN, DAN, broadcaster, flight instructor; b. Hinsdale, Ill., Apr. 6, 1927; s. Harry and Dorothy (Rosenzweig) S.; m. Margaret Jane Calhoun, Dec. 24, 1973 (div. Oct. 1977); children: Bruce, Vikki, Brian; m. Jo Adele Miller, Oct. 2, 1981; children: Jennifer, Kirsten. Cert. engring., U. Wis., 1944; BS, U. Ill., 1950. Radio personality Sta. WCFL, Chgo., 1951-62; TV announcer Bob Newhart, NBC-TV, Burbank, Calif., 1962; co-owner, check pilot Great Lakes Airlines, Chgo., 1963; radio personality Sta. KSFO, San Francisco, 1964-72; audio and video producer Synanon Corp., Badger, Calif., 1968—; pres. GFFC, Inc., Badger, 1987—. With USAAF, 1945-47, CBI. Mem. Aircraft Owners and Pilots Assn., AFTRA. Home and Office: 50300 Hwy 245 PO Box 42 Badger CA 93603

SOROM, TERRY ALLEN, ophthalmic surgeon; b. Lanesboro, Minn., Jan. 9, 1940; s. Martin John and Elvira (Lodahl) S.; m. Suzanne A. Johnson, children: Martin, Jeb, Abraham, Theodore. BS, Luther Coll., 1962; MD, U. Minn.-Mpls., 1966. Diplomate Am. Bd. Ophthalmology. Intern. U. Oreg., Portland, 1967, resident in ophthalmology, 1969-73; ophthalmic surgeon Eye and Ear Clinic, Inc., Wenatchee, Wash., 1973—. Charter trustee Wenatchee Visitor and Conv. Bur., 1980; bd. dirs. Blue Cross Wash., and Alaska; pres. Wenatchee Valley Coll. Found., 1986-88. Capt. M.C., USAF, 1967-69. Mem. AMA, Am. Acad. Ophthalmology, Contact Lens Assn. Ophthalmology, Am. Intraocular Implant Soc., Wash. State Acad. Ophthalmology (trustee 1978-80), Oregon Ophthalmologic Alumni Assn. (pres. 1988—), Greater Wenatchee Found. (bd. dirs.), Chelan-Douglas County Med. Assn. Republican. Lutheran. Office: Eye & Ear Clinic Wenatchee Inc PS 600 Orondo Ave PO Box 3027 Wenatchee WA 98801

SOROY, MICHAEL, service executive; b. Bronnoy, Norway, Oct. 2, 1950; came to U.S., 1979; s. Michael Nordanger and Ymbjorg (Wang) S. MS in polit. sci., U. Oslo, 1978. Product mgr. Four Winds Travel, N.Y.C., 1979-81; contracts mgr. Unitours, Los Angeles, 1981-83; sr. cons. Internat. Tour Cons., Los Angeles, 1983--. Author: Introduction to the Travel Business, 1978. Mem. Internat. Assn. Skal Clubs. Home: 14004 Palawan Way Ph #10 Marina Del Ray CA 90292 Office: Internat Tour Cons 8939 Sepulveda Blvd #220 Los Angeles CA 90045

SORRELL, JAMES ROBERT, astronautics, electronics, aerospace, mining and agriculture consultant; b. San Antonio, Apr. 22, 1944; s. Howard Clifton and Pearl (Secrist) Doolittle; m. Trudy Kay Cressy, Apr. 22, 1979; children: Abby Anne, Alissa Rose, Benjamin Alan. BS, Southwestern U., 1966; MA, UCLA, 1969. News dir. Stas. KFXD and KSPD, Pacific Northwest Broadcasting, Boise, Idaho, 1973-78; newspaper columnist Valley News, Rexburg, Idaho, 1977; dir. Revelation, IR&D, Boise, Idaho, 1979—; radio reporter covering launch of Apollo 15, Cape Kennedy, 1971, launch of Skylab Space Sta., Cape Kennedy, 1973, launch of Apollo-Soyuz (US-USSR), Cape Kennedy, 1975; NASA pool writer USS New Orleans for landing of 2d Skylab crew, 1973; only reporter on bd. final U.S. comml. whaling voyage, 1971, published in Environ. Quality mag., 1972; speaker N.Y. Graphics, 1985. Tchr. Boise Schs. Night Edn., 1975-82; bd. dirs. Crisis Line, Boise, 1982-83; state chmn. Statue of Liberty Fund, Idaho, 1984-86, bd. dirs. Internat. Space Adv. Council, 1985—; adminstr. Faith Community Ch.; mem. Idaho Centennial Com., 1986—. Home and Office: PO Box 8509 #27033 Boise ID 83707-2509

SORRENTINO, BETTY ROBINSON, nurse; b. Freemansburg, W.Va., Apr. 29, 1935; d. Elmer Truman and Iva Lou (Wiant) Robinson); m. Frank Sorrentino, May 31, 1959 (div. 1983); 1 child, Gina Louise. Diploma in Nursing, We. Pa. Hosp., 1955; BS, Calif. State U., L.A., 1980; MS, Loma Linda (Calif.) U., 1983. RN, Calif., Pa. Staff nurse We. Pa. Hosp., Pitts., 1955-56, St. Clair Hosp., Pitts., 1956-57, L.A. County Gen. Hosp., 1957-59, Whittier (Calif.) Hosp., 1970-82; nursing supr. intensive care unit Santa Ana (Calif.) Hosp. Med. Ctr., 1983-84, mgr. nursing edn., infection control nurse, 1984-87; staff nurse French Hosp. Med. Ctr., San Luis Obispo, Calif., 1988--; instr. Cuesta Coll., San Luis Obispo, 1988--; speaker in field. Fellow Am. Assn. Critical Care Nurses (cert., speaker 1988--); mem. Phi Kappa Phi, Sigma Theta Tau. Republican. Methodist. Home: 1490 4 Descanso St San Luis Obispo CA 93401

SORRENTINO, GILBERT, English language educator, novelist, poet; b. Bklyn., Apr. 27, 1929; s. August E. and Ann Marie (Davis) S.; m. Victoria Ortiz; children: Jesse, Delia, Christopher. Student, Bklyn. Coll., 1949-51, 54-56. In various positions 1947-70; including reins. clk. Fidelity and Casualty Co., N.Y.C., 1947-48; freight checker Ace Assembly Agy., N.Y.C., 1954-56; packer Bennett Bros. Inc., N.Y.C., 1956-57; messenger Am. Houses, Inc., N.Y.C., 1948-49; shipping-room supr. Thermo-fax Sales, Inc., Queens, N.Y., 1957-60; editor Grove Press, N.Y., 1965-70; tchr. Columbia U., 1966, Aspen Writers Workshop, 1967, Sarah Lawrence Coll., 1972, The New Sch. for Social Rsch., From 1976; Nat. Endowment for Humanities chair in lit. U. Scranton, 1979; prof. English Stanford U. (Calif.), 1982—. Author: books The Darkness Surrounds Us, 1960, Black and White, 1964, The Sky Changes, 1966, The Perfect Fiction, 1968, Steelwork, 1970, Imaginative Qualities of Actual Things, 1971, Corrosive Sublimate, 1971, Splendide-Hotel, 1973, Flawless Play Restored, 1974, A Dozen Oranges, 1976, White Sail, 1977, Sulpiciae Elegidia/Elegiacs of Sulpicia, 1977, The Orangery, 1978, Mulligan Stew, 1979, Aberration of Starlight, 1980, Selected Poems, 1958-80, 1981, Crystal Vision, 1981, Blue Pastoral, 1983, Something Said: Essays, 1984, Odd Number, 1985, Rose Theatre, 1987. With U.S. Army, 1951-53. Recipient Samuel Fels award in fiction Coordinating Coun. Lit. Mags., 1974, John Dos Passos prize, 1981, Am. Acad. and Inst. Arts and Letters award in Lit., 1985; John Simon Guggenheim Meml. fellow, 1973-74, 87-88; Creative Artists Pub. Svc. Program grantee, 1974-75; Nat. Endowment for Arts grantee, 1975-76, 1978-79. Mem. PEN Am. Ctr.

SORRENTINO, RALPH DOMINIC, systms analyst; b. Bklyn., Sept. 22, 1948; s. Frank and Julia (Iaconi) S.; m. Milena Dorothy Mitten, May 19, 1973; 1 child, Nicole. BSEE, Clarkson U., 1970. Mem. engring. staff Western Electric/Bell Telephone Labs., Whippany, N.J., 1970-74; mem. info. systems staff Western Electric Co., Aurora and Englewood, Colo., 1974-80; mem. sr. staff info. systems AT&T, Aurora and Englewood, 1980—. Home: 1455 S Zeno St Aurora CO 80017 Office: AT&T 7979 E Tufts Ave Englewood CO 80111

SORROCHE, ELIZABETH HUFFMAN, engineer, jeweler; b. Goldsboro, N.C., Mar. 30, 1959; d. Leo Earl and Marion (Dominguez) Huffman; m. Jeff Huffman Sorroche, Jan. 8, 1983. AS in Elec. Engring Tech., N. Mex. State U., 1979, BSEE Tech., 1982. Cert. Engr. Technologist, N. Mex. Engring staff asst. surface physics Sandia Nat. Labs., Albuquerque, 1982-84; sr. tech. asst. surface physics 1984-87, sr. tech. asst. surface metallurgy, 1987—. Named one of Outstanding Hispanic Srs., Soc. Hispanic Engrs., 1982; recipient Outstanding Sr. Woman award AAUW, 1982. Mem. Nat. Inst. for Cert. in Engring. Techs., Am. Vacuum Soc., Sandia Women's. Republican. Mem. Christian Ch. Home: Box 13A Mountain Home Estates Tijeras NM 87059 Office: Sandia Nat Labs Div 1834 PO Box 5800 Albuquerque NM 87185

SORTOR, BRETT VAN DYKE, army officer; b. Oakland, N.J., Jan. 25, 1963; s. John B. and Marcia (Whipple) S. BSME, U.S. Mil. Acad., 1985. Commd. 2d lt. U.S. Army, 1985, advanced through grades to lst lt., 1986; inf. platoon leader 4th bn. 87th Inf. Regt., Schofield Barracks, Hawaii, 1986-88; with 3d brigade 25th Inf. Div., Schofield Barracks, 1988—. Mem. Assn. U.S. Army, Les Amis du Vin, Hawaii Bicycle League, Phi Kappa Phi. Republican. Home: 98-708 Iho Pl Apt 303 Aiea HI 96701 Office: HHC 3d Brigade Schofield Barracks HI 96857

SORVOJA, MARKKU, banker; b. Ylivieska, Finland, Oct. 23, 1955; came to U.S., 1957; s. Martti and Signe Helena (Valli) S. BBA, U. Alaska, 1984. Auditor, acct. KMG-Main Hurdman, Fairbanks, Alaska, 1985-86; loan rev. officer Nat. Bank Alaska, Anchorage, 1986-87, tax analyst, 1987—; bd. dirs., sec. Sorvoja Corp., Fairbanks. Republican. Lutheran. Home: 830 E 45th Ct Anchorage AK 99503 Office: Nat Bank Alaska 301 W Northern Lights Blvd Anchorage AK 99503

SOSA, DAN, JR., chief justice supreme court; b. Las Cruces, N.Mex., Nov. 12, 1923; s. Dan and Margaret (Soto) S.; m. Rita Ortiz, Aug. 31, 1950; 7 children. BSBA, N.Mex. State U., 1947; JD, U. N.Mex., 1951. Bar: N.Mex. 1951. Tchr., coach, public schs. Mesilla, N.Mex., 1947-48; pvt. practice law Las Cruces, 1952-75; judge Las Cruces City Ct., 1952-55; spl. agt. Office of Price Stblzn., 1951-52; asst. dist. atty., then dist. atty. N.Mex. 3d Jud. Dist., 1956-64; spl. asst. atty. gen. for prosecution capital criminal cases Dept. Justice, 1965-66; justice N.Mex. Supreme Ct., 1975-89, chief justice, 1989—. 1st lt. AC U.S. Army, 1942-45. Democrat. Roman Catholic. Office: NMex Supreme Ct PO Box 848 Santa Fe NM 87504

SOSS, ALEXANDER LESTER, marketing and business professional, consultant; b. Cleve., Nov. 2, 1938; s. Lester A. and Elizabeth (Osiecki) S.; m. July 10, 1971; div. Aug, 1984. Student, Stanford U., 1969, U. So. Calif., 1975. Asst. to chancellor CSUN, 1966-68; regional mgr. South Bay U.S. Census, L.A., 1969-70; treas. United Rep. Fin. Com. L.A. County, L.A., 1970-73; v.p. St. Johns & Talmadge, L.A., 1973-79; dir. mktg. Showcase U.S.A., L.A., 1979-80; pvt. practice cons. L.A., 1980—; bd. dirs. CIS, Inc., 1985—. Contbr. poetry to mags., articles to profl. jours. Chmn. bd. SCAG/DWP SFV Groundwater Contamination Commn., 1981-83; mem. Roosvelt Ctr. Am. Policy Studies (San Fernando Valley Citizens Assembly 1988—), Ctr. Entreprenurial Mgmt., 1987—, Tierra del Sol Found., Sunland (bd. dirs. 1981-83). U.S. Army, 1961-69. Recipient honorary resolutions by Calif. legislature, L.A. County Bd., L.A. City Coun., L.A. Dept. Water and Power and others. Mem. Order of AHEPA (pres. Beverly Hills, nat. del.), Nat. Football Found. Hall Fame, San Fernando Valley Pub. Rel. Round Table (pres. 1978-79), L.A. Pub. Affairs Officers Assn., Am. Soc. Pub. Adminstrn., Pub. Rels. Soc. Am., Splty. Equipment Mfrs. Assn., Export Mgrs. Assn., Calif. C. of C. (small bus. task force), San Fernando Valley C. of C. (v.p., bd. dirs. 1975-81), Van Nuys Area C. of C., Soc. Blue Key, Phi Mu Alpha, Pi Sigma Alpha, Sigma Chi. Lutheran. Office: 13347 Victory Blvd Ste 105 Van Nuys CA 91401

SOSSAMAN, JAMES J., state legislator; b. Phoenix, July 17, 1932; s. Jasper H. and Faith Carolyn (Mather) S.; m. Carolyn Sue Peters, Dec. 12, 1953; children—Kimberlee, Stephen, Scott. Student, Ariz. State U., 1950-52. Mem. Ariz. Ho. of Reps., 1969—, majority whip, 1976-84, speaker, 1985-87, senator, 1987—. Precinct committeeman City of Higley, Ariz., 1958—; mem. Queen Creek Sch. Bd., Ariz., 1965-80. Lt. USN, 1952-56, Korea. Recipient Outstanding Young Farmer award Flying Farmers, 1966, Legislator of Yr. award Ariz. Students' Assn., 1977, 78, Disting. Citizen award U. Ariz., 1979, hon. state farmer degree Future Farmers Am., 1980. Mem. Am. Legis. Exchange Council, Western Conf. Council State Govts., Maricopa County Farm Bur. (pres.), Ariz. Cotton Growers Bd. (agriculturalist for 1986). Republican. Methodist. Home: 19105 E Ocotillo Higley AZ 85236 Office: Office State Senate 1700 W Washington St Phoenix AZ 85007

SOTER, NICHOLAS GREGORY, advertising agency executive; b. Great Falls, Mont., Apr. 26, 1947; s. Sam Nick and Bernice (Bennett) S.; m. Kathleen Lyman, Feb. 20, 1970; children: Nichole, Erin, Samuel Scott, Kara, Stephen Andrew, Riley Kyle. BS, Brigham Young U., 1971. With McLean Assocs., Provo, Utah, 1970-75; chmn. bd., chief exec. officer Soter Assocs. Inc., Provo, 1975—; founder, pres. RS Corp., 1986-88, Plum C Corp., 1988; instr. advt. Utah Tech. Coll., Provo, 1971-75, Brigham Young U., Provo, 1980-84. Publisher: Journal of Joseph, 1979, Journal of Brigham, 1980, LaVell Edwards, 1980, Amos Wright, 1981, Moments in Motherhood, 1981, What It Means to Know Christ, 1981, Mormon Fortune Builders, 1982, Utah History, 1982; contbr. articles to profl. jours. Active Utah Valley Pub. Communications Council for Ch. Jesus Christ of Latter-day Saints, 1982-87; mem. adv. council. Monte L. Bean Life Sci. Mus., 1987-89; Rep. dist. chmn.; v.p. exec. com. Am.'s Freedom Festival at Provo, 1989—; jury chmn. Coun. for Advancement and Support of Edn., 1989. Recipient N.Y. Art Dir.'s The One Show award, Salt Lake Art Dirs. Communications Assn. of Utah Valley award. Mem. Utah Advt. Fedn., Pub. Rels. Soc. Am., Communications Assn. Utah Valley (past pres.), Provo C. of C. (bd. dirs.), Innisbrook Network of Advt. Agys. (pres. 1986-87). Home: 1728 S 290 E Orem UT 84058 Office: Soter Assocs Inc 209 N 400 W Provo UT 84601

SOTIROS, JAMES THOMAS, university administrator; b. San Diego, June 14, 1951; s. John James and Helen (Rigopoulos) S.; m. Stephanie Lee Johnston, May 2, 1982. BA cum laude, Claremont Men's Coll., 1975. Campaign div. dir. United Way, San Diego, 1978-81; dir. corp. and found. relations U. San Diego, 1981-86, dir. ann. fund, 1986-87, dir. devel., 1987—; mem. pres's. adv. council U. San Diego, 1988—. Active parish council Sts. Constantine and Helen Ch., Encinitas, Calif., 1984—, chmn. bldg. com., 1986—. Mem. Council for Advancement and Support Edn., Nat. Soc. Fundraising Execs. Greek Orthodox. Home: 11754 Calle Vivienda San Diego CA 92128 Office: U San Diego Alcala Park San Diego CA 92110

SOUKUP, JEANNE D'ARCY, nurse; b. Burbank, Calif., July 8, 1961; d. Vincent Joseph and Mary Theresa (D'Arcy) S. BA cum laude, Loyola Marymount U., L.A., 1983; AA, Mt. St. Mary's Coll., L.A., 1987, BS, 1988. RN, Calif. Clin. nurse I Children's Hosp. L.A., 1988—; clin. nurse L.A. County Pub. Health Dept., 1988—. Vol. AIDS Project L.A., 1989—. Mem. Amnesty Internat., Loyola Marymount Alumni Assn., Mt. St. Mary's Alumni Assn., Alpha Tau Delta Alumni Assn., Delta Epsilon Sigma. Republican. Roman Catholic.

SOURAPAS, STEVE JAMES, manufacturing executive; b. Seattle, Mar. 29, 1935; s. James and Angelika (Stavrou) S.; children: Angela, Alicia. Salesman Northwest Bottling Co., Seattle, 1958-61, sales supr., 1961-68, sales mgr., 1968-77, pres., gen. mgr., 1977—. Served with U.S. Army, 1956-57. Mem. Nat. Assn. Can. Dry Franchise Bottlers (pres. 1987—, bd. dirs.), Royal Crown Bottlers Assn. (bd. dirs. 1984—), Dr. Pepper Bottlers Assn. (state rep. 1983—), Wash. Soft Drink Assn. (pres. 1987—, bd. dirs.), Assn. of Wash. Bus., Com. for Litter Control and Recycling, Seattle C. of C., Tacoma C. of C. Republican. Greek Orthodox. Office: NW Bottling Co 1136 Albro Pl South Seattle WA 98108

SOUTH, JOSHIE ANN, educator; b. Tokyo, Feb. 21, 1953; d. Lawrence Lloyd and Yoshi (Kawamura) S.; m. Kent Roger Hein, July 19, 1975 (div. 1980). BA, Pacific U., 1975; MA, Ea. Wash. U., 1989; postgrad., Pratt Inst., N.Y. Tchr. Spokane (Wash.) Art Sch., 1981—. Mem. Calligraphic Soc. (pres. 1981-84).

SOUTHWARD, ROCK ALLEN, lawyer; b. Tiffin, Ohio, July 31, 1950; s. Stanton Clay and Dorothy Ann (Warfel) S. BS, Bowling Green State U., 1972; JD, U. Toledo, 1982. Counselor Non-Commn. Officers Assn., Colorado Springs, Colo., 1983; sole practice Columbus, Ohio, 1984-86; real estate specialist, U.S. Postal Service, San Bruno, Calif., 1986—. Scripps-Howard scholar, 1972. Mem. ABA, Ohio Bar Assn., Bar Assn. of San Francisco, Phi Alpha Delta, Rho Sigma Mu, Kappa Tau Alpha. Democrat. Methodist.

SOUTHWARD, WALTER WILLIAM, public relations company executive; b. Pitts., July 16, 1936; s. Walter William and Hilda (Geider) S.; m. Leilani Akoni, Mar. 30, 1963. Student, Marshall U., 1957-59. Reporter Herald-Dispatch, Huntington, W.Va., 1957-59; reporter, asst. Sunday editor Hilo (Hawaii) Tribune-Herald, 1959-62; asst. Sunday editor Honolulu Advertiser, 1962-63; Big Island bur. chief Honolulu Advertiser, Hilo, 1963-70; mgr. pub. affairs Waikoloa, Hilo, 1970-77; pvt. practice pub. relations Hilo, 1977—; various sportscasting and freelance writing assignments, 1957—. Pres. Hilo Nat. Little League, 1966-68, Big Island Women's Softball League, 1968-73, Waikoloa Village Assn., 1971-74; head coach Hilo Comets Women's Softball Team, 1970-88, U. Hawaii at Hilo Athletic Boosters, 1976-77. With U.S. Army, 1954-57. Named Booster of Yr. U. Hawaii at Hilo, 1974. Mem. Am. Numismatic Assn. (life), Pub. Relations Soc. Am., Geothermal Resources Council, Hawaii Island C. of C. (pres. 1982-83), Big Island Coin Club (pres. 1964), Big Island Press, Lions, Hilo Yacht Club. Home: 94 Pakalana St Hilo HI 96720 Office: PO Box 251 Hilo HI 96721

SOUTHWICK, CHARLES HENRY, zoologist, educator; b. Wooster, Ohio, Aug. 28, 1928; s. Arthur F. and Faye (Motz) S.; m. Heather Milne Beck, July 12, 1952; children: Steven, Karen. B.A., Coll. Wooster, 1949; M.S., U. Wis., 1951, Ph.D., 1953. NIH fellow 1951-53; asst. prof. biology Hamilton Coll., 1953-54; NSF fellow Oxford (Eng.) U., 1954-55; faculty Ohio U., 1955-61; assoc. prof. pathobiology Johns Hopkins Sch. Hygiene and Pub. Health, Balt., 1961-68; prof. Johns Hopkins Sch. Hygiene and Pub. Health, 1968-79; assoc. dir. Johns Hopkins Internat. Ctr. for Med. Rsch. and Tng., Calcutta, India, 1964-65; chmn. dept. environ., population and organismic biology U. Colo., Boulder, 1979-82, prof. biology, 1979—; researcher and author publs. on animal social behavior and population dynamics, influences animal social behavior on demographic characteristic mammal populations, primate ecology and behavior, estuarine ecology and environmental quality; mem. primate adv. com. Nat. Acad. Sci.-NRC, 1963-75, com. primate conservation, 1974-75; mem. Gov.'s Sci. Adv. Com. State of Md., 1975-78; mem. com. on rsch. and exploration Nat. Geog. Soc., 1979—. Editor: Primate Social Behavior, 1963, Animal Aggression, 1970, Nonhuman Primates in Biomedical Research, 1975, Ecology and the Quality of Our Environment, 1976, Global Ecology, 1985; Ecology and Behavior of Food-Enhanced Primate Groups, 1988. Recipient Fulbright Rsch. award India, 1959-60. Fellow AAAS, Acad. Zoology, Animal Behavior Soc.; mem. Am. Soc. Zoologists, Ecol. Soc. Am., Am. Soc. Mammalogists, Am. Soc. Primatology, Internat. Primatology Soc., Internat. Soc. Study Aggression.

SOWELL, WILLIAM HILTON, marketing professional; b. L.A., Mar. 26, 1956; s. William Raymond and Helen (Hilton) S.; m. LyndaLee Jones, July 27, 1985 (div. 1987); children: William Nicholas Hilton, Ashlee Kristen; m. Lynette Kent, Dec. 24, 1988; stepchildren: Jean-Marc and Nathalie Anne Corredor. Student, U. Okla., 1976-77; BA in Communications, Calif. State U., Dominguez Hills, 1981; MBA in Mktg., U. So. Calif., L.A., 1985; postgrad., Calif. Coast U., 1987—. Cert. tchr., Calif. Paramedic Midwest City (Okla.) Meml. Hosp., 1974-76, Norman (Okla.) Fire Dept., 1976-77, L.A. County Fire Dept., 1977-81; pres. Paramedic Svcs. Ltd., Redondo Beach, Calif., 1978-81; dir. mktg. Barnett-Raus Advt., Inc., Torrance, Calif., 1981-82; sales mgr. Intertek Svcs. Corp., Rolling Hills, Calif., 1982-84; regional mgr. Intertek Svcs. Corp., Sunnyvale, Calif., 1982-85; v.p. mktg. Vendor Surveillance Corp., Irvine, 1985-87; mgr. sales and mktg. Redhill Med. Mgmt. Group, Santa Ana, Calif., 1988—; mem. affiliate faculty, Am. Heart Assn., L.A., 1977-82; cons., U.S. Testing, Hoboken, N.J., 1988—. Writer teleplay for TV series Emergency, 1978; author: Lincoln County Rescue Squad, 1981. Instr. CPR, first aid, ARC, L.A. and Santa Ana. Mem. Am. Mktg. Assn., Med. Mktg. Assn., Am. Soc. Quality Control. Republican. Office: Redhill Med Mgmt Group 2871 S Pullman St Santa Ana CA 92705

SOWELL, WILLIAM RAYMOND, aerospace management engineer; b. Maud, Okla., Mar. 11, 1928; s. William Thomas Sowell and Blanche Hardaway; m. Helen LaDawn Hilton, Dec. 24, 1950; 1 child, William Hilton. BSME, Okla. Baptist U., 1950; BSAE, Calif. Aero Tech. Inst., Glendale, 1952; M Engring., U. So. Calif., 1958; M Ocean Engring., UCLA, 1966. Program mgr. Rockwell Internat., L.A., 1952-70; v.p. Ocean Environments, Inc., St. Thomas, Virgin Islands, 1970-73, Royal Industries, Thompson Div., Carson, Calif., 1973-75; cons. Intercontinental Mgmt., Inc., Torrance, Calif., 1976-79; gen. mgr. Nat. Engring. Svcs. and Mktg., Jeddah, Saudi Arabia, 1980-84; dir. contracts Murdock, Inc., Compton, Calif., 1984—. Author technical papers. With USMC, 1946-47, PTO, China. Recipient Menta Martin award, Inst. Aeronautical Scis., L.A., 1952. Mem. Nat. Contract Mgmt. Assn. (bd. dirs. 1987-88). Republican. Covenant Ch. Home: 2744 Via Campesina Palos Verdes Estates CA 90274

SOWERS, DENNIS TURNER, food service executive; b. Hays, Kans., May 30, 1941; s. Harry C. and Vivian M. (Turner) S.; m. Mary Jo Van Eaton, Nov. 5, 1959; children: Susan, Mitzi, Sandra. Grad. high sch., Oakley, Kans. Mgr. Greyhound/Prophet Foods, Glenwood Springs, Colo., 1968-71, Golden, Colo., 1971-74; mgr. Greyhound/Prophet Foods, Northglenn, Colo., 1974-75, adminstrv. asst., 1975-76; dist. mgr. Profl. Foodservice Mgmt., Northglenn, 1976-80; owner DM Premier Mgmt., Inc., Northglenn, 1980-87; v.p., gen. mgr. DM Premier Mgmt./Dobbs, Broomfield, Colo., 1987-88, Dobbs Food Service/Morrison's Custom Mgmt., Broomfield, 1988—. Century mem. Boy Scouts Am., Denver, 1980—. Democrat. Roman Catholic. Home: 11246 Lewistown St Commerce City CO 80022

SOWERWINE, ELBERT ORLA, JR., chemical engineer; b. Tooele, Utah, Mar. 15, 1915; s. Elbert Orla and Margaret Alice (Evans) S.; B. in Chemistry, Cornell U., 1937, Chem. Engr., 1938; m. Norma Borge; children—Sue-Ann Sowerwine Jacobson, Sandra Sowerwine Montgomery, Elbert Orla 3d, John Frederick, Avril Ruth Taylor, Albaro Francisco, Octavio Evans, Zaida Margaret. Analytical chemist Raritan Copper Works, Perth Amboy, N.J., summers 1936, 37; rsch. chem. engr. Socony-Vacuum Oil Co., Paulsboro, N.J., 1938-43; prodn. supr. Merck & Co., Elkton, Va., 1943-45; asst. plant mgr. U.S. Indsl. Chems. Co., Newark, 1945-48; project engr. and rsch. dir. Wigton-Abbott Corp., Newark, 1948-50, Cody, Wyo., 1950-55; cons. engring., planning, indsl. and community devel., resource evaluation and mgmt. Wapiti, Wyo., also C.Am., 1955-80. Commr. N.J., Boy Scouts Am., 1938-43; mem. Wapiti and Park County (Wyo.) Sch. Bds., 1954-58; bd. dirs. Mont. State Planning Commn., 1959-61; exec. bd. Mo. Basin Rsch. and Devel. Coun., 1959-61. Fellow Am. Inst. Chemists; mem. Am. Inst. Chem. Engrs., Am. Planning Assn., Nicaraguan Assn. Engrs. and Architects. Libertarian. Mem. Christian Ch. Researcher desulfurization of petroleum products, process control, alternate energy projects; patentee in petroleum and chem. processes and equipment. Home: Broken H Ranch Wapiti WY 82450 Office: Sowerwine Cons Wapiti WY 82450

SOX, STEPHEN EDWARD, engineer; b. Palo Alto, Calif., Mar. 17, 1965; s. Edward Ellis and Josephine (Delgado) S. BSME, U. Pacific, 1988. Engr. in training Naval Energy & Environ. Support Activity, Port Hueneme, Calif., 1985-86; asst. engr. Westinghouse Electric Co., Sunnyvale, Calif., 1987-88; engr. Huges Aircraft Co., El Segundo, Calif., 1988—. Mem. Am. Soc. Machanical Engrs. (sec. 1987, treas. 1986), Tau Beta Pi, Phi Kappa Phi Honor Soc., Palo Alto Ski. Democrat.

SPADE, GEORGE ELDRED, II, miliatry officer; b. Norfolk, Va., Nov. 29, 1955; s. George Eldred Sr. and Geneva Joyce (Underwood) S.; m. Laura Isabel Spade. BS, Wayland Bapt. U., 1984, MBA, 1986. Pass and ID clk. 64th Police Squadron USAF, Reese AFB, Tex., 1978-81; with supply adminstrn. 64th Supply Squadron USAF, Reese AFB, 1981-86; dir. patent affairs USAF Clinic/SGR Los Angeles AF Sta., 1986—; Mem. Credit com. Reese Fed. Credit Union, Lubbock, Tex., 1981-84. Mem. Air Force Assn., Am. Coll. Healthcare Execx., Toastmaster (pres. sounding bd., 1984, admin. v.p. Area 7, 1985). Republican. Roman Catholic. Home: 1409 Garfield Wichita Falls TX 76309 Office: USAF 3790 Medical Svc Tng Wing Sheppard AFB TX 76309

SPADOTTO, BEVERLY THERESE, editor; b. Syracuse, N.Y., July 11, 1951; d. Ted and Beverly Jean (Loughlin) S.; BA in Journalism, George Washington U., 1973; MA, U. So. Calif., 1975. Dir. pub. relations D'Arcy-MacManus & Masius, advt., Los Angeles, 1976-78; editor Rangefinder mag., Santa Monica, Calif., 1978-81; communications editor CIGNA Healthplans of Calif., Glendale, Calif., 1982-85; dir. communications U.S. Adminstrs., Inc., 1985—; owner BTS Prodns., Los Angeles, 1988—. Mem. Western Publs. Assn., Publicity Club Los Angeles, Sigma Delta Chi. Democrat. Roman Catholic. Home: 410 S Hobart Blvd Los Angeles CA 90020

SPAETH, JOSEPH LOUIS, lawyer; b. Buffalo, Feb. 20, 1940; s. Joseph L. and Carolyn M. (Deibel) S.; m. Sparkie Weisberger, Feb. 18, 1984. AB, Hamilton Coll., 1961; JD, SUNY, Buffalo, 1969. Bar: N.Y. 1970, Calif. 1972; cert. criminal law specialist, Calif. Staff acct. Arthur Young & Co., San Francisco, 1970-72; atty. San Francisco Office Pub. Defender, 1973-81, head trial atty., supr. misdemeanor and felony attys., 1981—, mng. atty. juvenile div., 1983—; instr. criminal procedure Lincoln U. Law Sch., San Francisco, 1987, 88; mem. Jud. Coun. Adv. Com. on Juvenile Ct. Law, 1988—; lectr. on juvenile law to legal assns., also Nat. Coun. Juvenile and Family Ct. Judges, Calif. Ctr. for Jud. Edn. and Rsch. Mem. tech. adv. com. San Francisco Dept. Social Svcs.; chmn. AB90 Youth Svcs. Task Force, San Francisco, 1989—; mem. San Francisco Mayor's Task Force on Dependent Children, 1987—; mem. out-of-home care task force-populations working com. Health and Welfare Agy., San Francisco, 1987-88. Lt. (j.g.) USNR, 1961-66. Mem. State Bar Calif. (com. on juvenile justice, 1988—), Calif. Pub. Defenders Assn. (rep. chief victim witness jud. adv. com. 1987-88, select com. on children and youth task force 1987—, bd. dirs. 1989—), San Francisco Bar Assn., San Francisco Child Abuse Coun., Olympic Club. Democrat. Office: Office Pub Defender 375 Woodside Ave Rm 118 San Francisco CA 94127

SPAFFORD, MICHAEL CHARLES, artist; b. Palm Springs, Calif., Nov. 6, 1935. B.A., Pomona Coll., 1959; M.A., Harvard U., 1960. One man shows include Seattle Art Mus., 1982, U. Puget Sound, Tacoma, Wash., 1973, Tacoma Art Mus., 1975, Utah Mus. Fine Arts, Salt Lake City, 1975, Francine Seders Gallery, Seattle, 1965—; exhibited in group shows at Wilcox Gallery, Swarthmore Coll., Pa., 1977, Seattle Art Mus., 1977, Am. Acad. and Inst. Arts and Letters, N.Y.C., 1980, 83, Seattle Art Mus., 1980, Kobe, Japan, 1981, Eastern Wash. U., 1982, Henry Art Gallery, 1982. Recipient Prix de Rome, 1967-69, award Am. Acad. and Inst. Arts and Letters, 1983; Louis Comfort Tiffany Found. grantee, 1965-66. Home: 2418 E Interlaken Blvd Seattle WA 98112 *

SPAGHT, EILEEN PEARL, real estate company executive; b. Coos Bay, Oreg., Nov. 15, 1940; d. John Victor and Florence Francis (Carr) Koski; m. Melvin Ellis Spaght, Oct. 31, 1964; children: Kelvin M., Kenneth V. Grad. high sch., Coos Bay, Oreg. Office mgr. Hoffman Jewelers, Coos Bay, 1958-63; owner, operator Ken-Kel Park (Sports Complex), Coos Bay, 1969-76; adminstrv. asst. Homart Devel., Mesa, Ariz., 1985—. Mem. Mesa Southwest Museum. Republican. Office: Homart Devel 2104 Fiesta Mall Mesa AZ 85202

SPAGON, PATRICK DENIS, statistical consultant; b. Rome, N.Y., Nov. 25, 1945; s. John Edward and Louise Antionette (Bolognese) S.; m. Sue-Ann Joe, Nov. 22, 1986; children: Brandon, Michael. BS, U. Ariz., 1968; MS, U. Calif., Berkeley, 1969; PhD, Stanford U., 1981. Mem. tech. staff Bell Tel. Rsch. Labs., Whippany and Holmdel, N.J., 1968-72; teaching fellow, grad. asst. dept. indsl. engring. Stanford U., Palo Alto, Calif., 1973-77; instr. dept. indsl. engring., mgmt. sci. The Technological Inst. Northwestern U., Evanston, Ill., 1978-79; quality assurance mgr. mjg. div. Hewlett-Packard, Palo Alto, 1981; assoc. prof. sch. bus. San Francisco State U., 1981-85; statistical methods cons. FMC Corp., Santa Clara, Calif., 1985-89; sr. statistical cons. BBN Corp., Mountain View, Calif., 1989—. Mem. Am. Soc. for Quality Control, Am. Statis. Assn., Inst. Indsl. Engrs., Inst. Mgmt. Scis., IEEE. Office: BBN Corp 2121 Landings Dr Mountain View CA 94043

SPAHLE, MICHAEL THOMAS, engineer, volunteer; b. Montclair, N.J., Oct. 20, 1952; s. Thomas Patrick Spahle and Maryanne (Dowd) Cutlip; m. Susan Janice Nieminski, Aug. 23, 1975; children: Matthew Peter, Nicholas Adam, Julia Marguerite. AS in Elem. Edn., Essex County Community Coll., 1973; BS in Liberal Arts, Ariz. State U., 1988, postgrad., 1988—. Engring. change coord. ITT Courier Terminal Systems, Inc., Tempe, Ariz., 1976-84; configuration and data specialist Motorola, Inc., GED, Scottsdale, Ariz., 1984-87; configuration engr. Allied Signal Aerospace Co., GAPD, Phoenix, 1987—; contract data adminstr. Lear Sigler, Santa Monica, Calif., 1985. Tribal chief Scottsdale-Paradise Valley YIG, Scottsdale, 1988—; chair planning com. Greater E. Phoenix Neighborhood Assn., 1986, mem. exec. search com., 1987; mgr. pub. rels. com. Linda Nadolski for City Coun., Phoenix, 1988. Sgt. USAF, 1976-82. Mem. Ariz. Alliance Health and Phys. Edn., Scottsdale Bike Club, Golden Key Nat. Honor Soc. (past pres.), Phoenix Velodeom Assn. Home: 5432 E Pinchot Phoenix AZ 85018 Office: Allied Signal Aerospace Co 2739 E Washington St PO Box 5227 Phoenix AZ 85010

SPAHLINGER, DAVID A., savings and loan executive; b. Metropolis, Ill., Jan. 12, 1939; s. Melvin and Gertrude (Chaney) S.; m. Leta Southard, Sept. 28,1972 (div. Feb. 1984); m. Helen Lee, July 23, 1984. BS in Acctg., Washington U., St. Louis, 1963; MBA, U. So. Calif., 1977. Mgr. acctg. Greater Ariz. Savs. and Loan, Phoenix, 1963-64; sr. v.p., chief fin. officer Far West Fin. Corp., Newport Beach, Calif., 1964-75; v.p., mgr. acctg. div. Security Pacific Nat. Bank, L.A., 1975-80; exec. v.p., chief fin. officer Am. City Bank, L.A., 1980-83, Cen. Savs. and Loan Assn., San Diego, 1983-86; sr. v.p., chief fin. officer Am. Diversified Savs. Bank, Costa Mesa, Calif., 1986-88; pres. Standard Pacific Savs., Newport Beach, 1988—, bd. dirs. Mem. Beta Gamma Sigma. Republican. Office: Standard Pacific Savs 4590 MacArthur Blvd Newport Beach CA 92630

SPAIN, CARYN ANN, management consultant; b. Houghton, Mich., June 6, 1957; d. James D. and Patricia (Mann) S.; m. Carl Raymond Haglund, May 8, 1987. BA in Interpersonal Communication, U. Mont., 1982; MA in Communication, U. N.Mex., 1984. Instr. U. N.Mex., Albuquerque, 1982-84; pres., cons. Applied Communication Concepts, Seattle, 1984—; cons. Weyerhaeuser, Tacoma, 1985-86, Boeing Computer Services, Seattle, 1985-88, Boeing Comml. Airplane, Seattle, 1987-88. Recipient U. N.Mex. Top 10% Teaching Asst. award Bd. Regents, Albuquerque, 1983, Number One Teaching Asst. award Internat. comml. Assn., Honolulu, 1985. Assn. Tng. and Devel. (chmn., mgr. devel. 1982), Assn. Quality and Prodn., Women's Bus. Exchange.

SPAKE, GARY GERARD, information systems specialist; b. Mpls., Dec. 17, 1945; s. Lyle Floyd Spake and Jenny Sophia (Matson) Heston. AA, Fullerton Jr. Coll., 1965. Electronic technician N.Am. Rockwell Corp., Anaheim, Calif., 1966-70; engring. aid Trivex Datapac, Santa Ana, Calif., 1970-73; applications engr. Plessey MicroSystems, Irvine, Calif., 1974-77; product mgr. Remex div. Ex-Cell-O Corp., Irvine, 1977-81; supr. systems support Moxon Electronics, Anaheim, 1981-86; mgr. systems group Intermec Corp., Tustin, Calif., 1986—. Mem. Smithsonian Inst., Great Outdoors Club (pres.-v.p. 1982-85), Perris Valley Skydiving Soc. (advt. com. 1986). Office: Intermec W 1542 Edinger Ave Suite C Orange CA 92680

SPAL, EDWARD SCOTT, marketing executive; b. Anchorage, June 8, 1953; s. Edward Charles and Lorraine Joan (Morrison) S.; m. Patricia Mary Ralph, Mar. 18, 1978; children: Scott Edward, Michael Patrick. AA, Fullerton Jr. Coll., 1973; BS, San Diego State U., 1975. Sales trainee Simmons Co., San Francisco, 1976; sales trainee Simmons Co., L.A., 1976, sales rep., 1976-77; sales rep. Simmons Co., Salt Lake City, 1977-79; account mgr. Simmons Co., Fresno, Calif., 1979-84; key account exec. Simmons Co., Seattle, 1984-87, regional mktg. mgr., 1987—.

SPALDING, JOSEPH GERARD, marketing specialist; b. Buffalo, N.Y., Sept. 13, 1952; s. John Robert and Ruth Marie (White) S.; m. Francene Michele Spalding, Mar. 29, 1975; children: James Ryan, Bridgette Denise, Suzanne Alathaire. BS in Mech. Engring., UCLA, 1975; MA in Bus. Econs., U. Calif., Northridge, 1975. With product acquisition dept. Mellonics Info. div. Litton Industries, Canoga Park, Calif., 1975-76; pres. Pride Maintenance div. Palmer Assocs., Northridge, 1977-86; gen. mgr. Aircraft Components div. Hudson Gen. Corp., Northridge, 1987—; research adv. panel Aviation Week, 1988--. Contbr. articles to local newspapers, 1982. Active Cousteau Soc., Nat. Geog. Soc., Nat. Air and Space Mus., Green Peace, 1988--. Served with U.S. Army, 1969-72. Decorated Bronze Star. Mem. Air Transport Assn., Northridge C. of C. Republican. Roman Catholic. Home: 6049 Lake Lindero Dr Agoura Hills CA 91301 Office: Hudson Gen. 19525 Business Ctr Dr Northridge CA 91324

SPANG, SARA CROSBY, publisher; b. Boston, Dec. 21, 1947; d. Carl Francis and Ruth Mary (Patterson) S.; m. Uzi Y. Bar-Gadda, Sept. 19, 1981; children: Rachel Ruth, David Carl. BA, U. Pa., Phila., 1969; PhD, Temple U., 1983. Rsch. assoc. Inst. for the Future, Menlo Park, Calif., 1979-81; mktg. mgr. Tymshare, Cupertino, Calif., 1981-83; founder Target Techs., Menlo Park, 1983-85, Spang Robinson, Menlo Park, 1985-88; founder, prin. John Wiley & Sons (formerly Spang Robinson Wiley), Menlo Park, 1988—. Contbr. articles to profl. jours. Grantee Ford Found., 1974-76, Nat. Sci. Found., 1974-76, Am. Inst. Pakistan Studies, 1974-76. Mem. IEEE, Palo Alto Jr. League. Republican. Office: Spang Robinson Wiley 1050 Chestnut St Ste 203A Menlo Park CA 94025

SPANGLER, TONY RAY, educational administrator; b. Lancaster, Ohio, Aug. 24, 1963; s. Weldon Alfred and Wanda Imogene (Romine) S.; m. Marilu Schmitt, Mar. 23, 1985; children: Trystan Anthony, Kyle Brannon. Student in electronics, Lancaster Vocat. Inst., 1979-81. Bench technician Montgomery Ward, Kenosha, Wis., 1984, Advanced TV, Sacramento, Calif., 1985-86; electronics instr. Sierri Hi-Tech, Sacramento, 1986-87, computer instr., 1988-89, head instrn., 1988—; trade advisor electronic vocation Folsom (Calif.) Prison, 1988—. Mem. Calif. State Electronics Assn. (bd. dirs. 1988—). Republican. Office: Sierra Hi Tech 10561 Old Placerville Rd Sacramento CA 95827

SPANIER, ALLEN BENSON, JR., mortgage company executive; b. Denver, Jan. 20, 1949; s. Allen B. and Georgia (Benton) S. BA in Bus., U. Colo., 1971, postgrad., 1972-77. V.p. Investors Service Co., Denver, 1971-75; loan officer Capitol Life Ins. Co., Denver, 1975-77; owner Spanier Co., Denver, 1975--; asst. v.p. Colo. Nat. Mortgage, Denver, 1979-84; pres. Wallace Moir Co., Denver, 1984--. Supporting vol. Ptnrs. in Progress, Inc., Denver, 1987; bd. dirs. Kendrick Lake Homeowners Assn., Lakewood, Colo., 1971-72. Scholarship Colo. Assn. Realtors, 1970. Mem. Mortgage Bankers Assn. of Am., Colo. Mortgage Bankers Assn. (comml. com. 1983--), Toastmasters (Denver) (Pres. 1976), Hobie Fleet 61 (Denver). Republican. Episcopalian. Home: 10842 W Evans Ave Lakewood CO 80227 Office: Wallace Moir Co 1777 S Harrison Ste 507 Denver CO 80210

SPANN, KATHARINE DOYLE, marketing, communications executive; b. Holton, Kans.; d. Edward James and Josephine (Hurla) Doyle; m. Hugh J. Spann (div. Feb. 1952); 1 dau., Susan Katharine. BS, Emporia State Coll. V.p. Bozell & Jacobs Advt. (formerly L.C. Cole Co.), San Francisco, 1951-76; pres. Katharine Doyle Spann Assos., 1977—; propr. Kate's Vineyard, Napa Valley, Calif.; exec. producer TV shows Doctors News Conf., The Ben Alexander Show, Land of Jazz, 1956—; communications counsel to health professions, 1970—. Bd. dirs. Heritage Fund, Napa Valley Opera House. Named Advt. Woman of Year, 1962; recipient El Capitan award Peninsula chpt. Pub. Relations Soc. Am., 1962, 66, Am. Silver Anvil award, Pub. Relations Soc. Am., 1962, 66, Excellence award Publicity Club of Bay Area, 1966. Mem. exhbn. com. San Francisco Fine Arts Museums. Mem. Am. Soc. Enology, Am. Inst. Wine and Food, Napa Valley Women in Wine, Calif. Vintage Wine Soc. (wine com.), Conferie des Chevaliers du Tastevin (events com.), Delta Sigma Epsilon. Club: Metropolitan (San Francisco). Home: 1447 S Whitehall Ln Saint Helena CA 94574

SPANN, STEPHEN ALLISON, civil engineer, state official; b. Albuquerque, May 22, 1941; s. Ben Allison and Doris Lovern (Carson) S.; m. Annemie Weinelt, July 24, 1970; children: Stefan Oliver, Christopher Andrew. BS in Civil Engrin., Colo. State U., 1969; MPA, U. Denver, 1984. Registered profl. engr., Colo. Project engr. Continental Pipeline Co., Ponca City, Okla., 1969-71; sr. engr. W.W. Wheeler & Assocs., Denver, 1971-73,

Batchley & Assocs., Denver, 1973-76; chief design rev. and constrn. inspection unit for dam safety Colo. Div. Water Resources, Denver, 1976—; bd. dirs. S.R.M. Corp., Denver; exec. sec. Como (Colo.) Civic Assn., 1982—. Mem. 208 Water Quality Com., Fairplay, Colo., 1986; chmn. Upper South Platte Water Conservancy Dist., Fairplay, 1986. Fellow Soc. Am. Mil. Engrs. (bd. dirs. 1985—); mem. U.S. Com. on Large Dams, Am. Soc. Pub. Adminstrn. Home: 4801 S Galapago St Englewood CO 80110 Office: Colo Div Water Resources 1313 Sherman St Rm 818 Denver CO 80203

SPANO, JOSEPH, actor; b. San Francisco; s. Vincent D. and Virginia Jean (Carpenter) S.; m. Joan Zerrien. B.A., U. Calif.-Berkeley, 1967. actor with South Coast Repertory, Los Angeles, Los Angeles Actors Theatre, numerous prodns. with Berkeley Repertory Theatre. Star TV series Hill Street Blues, 1981-87 (Emmy award nomination 1983); appeared in films American Graffiti, 1973, Terminal Choice, The Enforcer, Roadie, The Incredible Shrinking Woman, Northern Lights; various TV series guest appearances; producer, actor (stage prodn.) Dracula, A Musical Nightmare, Los Angeles, N.C., San Francisco; rec. Ed McBain novels for Simon Schuster. Office: care EV Assocs 9056 Santa Monica Blvd #307 Los Angeles CA 90069

SPANOS, ALEXANDER GUS, professional football team executive; b. Stockton, Calif., Sept. 28, 1923; m. Faye Spanos; children: Dean, Dea Spanos Economou, Alexis Spanos Ruhl, Michael. LLD (hon.), U. Pacific, 1984. Chmn. bd. dirs. A.G. Spanos Constrn. Inc., Stockton, Calif., 1960—, A.G. Spanos Properties Inc., Stockton, Calif., 1960—, A.G. Spanos Mgmt. Inc., Stockton, Calif., 1967—, A.G. Spanos Enterprises Inc., Stockton, Calif., 1971—, A.G. Spanos Devel. Inc., Stockton, Calif., 1973—, A.G. Spanos Realty Inc., Stockton, Calif., 1978—, A.G. Spanos Jet Ctr. Inc., Stockton, Calif., 1980—, A.G.S. Fin. Corp., Stockton, Calif., 1980—; pres., chmn. bd. dirs. San Diego Chargers, 1984—. Former trustee Children's Hosp., San Francisco, San Francisco Fine Arts Mus.; trustee Eisenhower Med. Ctr., Rancho Mirage, Calif.; hon. regent U. Pacific, Stockton, 1972-82; gov. USO, Washington, 1982—. Served with USAF, 1942-46. Recipient Albert Gallatin award Zurich-Am. Ins. Co., 1973, Horatio Alger award Horatio Alger Found., 1982, medal of Honor Statue of Liberty-Ellis Islan Found., 1982. Mem. Am. Hellenic Ednl. Progressive Assn., Calif. C. of C. (bd. dirs. 1980-85). Republican. Greek Orthodox. Office: San Diego Jack Murphy Stadium PO Box 20666 San Diego CA 92120 also: A G Spanos Constrn Co 1341 W Robinhood Dr Stockton CA 95207 *

SPARKS, IRVING ALAN, Biblical scholar, educator; b. Ft. Wayne, Ind., June 15, 1933; s. James Edwin and Isabelle Mildred S.; A.B., Davidson (N.C.) Coll., 1954; B.D., Union Theol. Sem., Richmond, Va., 1959; S.T.M., Lancaster (Pa.) Theol. Sem., 1970; Ph.D., Claremont (Calif.) Grad. Sch., 1970; m. Helen Daniels, Sept. 3, 1954; children—Lydia Isabelle Sparksworthy, Leslie Bishop, Robin Alan. Lectr. philosophy and religion LaVerne (Calif.) Coll., 1965-69; asst. prof. religion Claremont Grad. Sch., 1970-74, assoc. dir. Inst. Antiquity and Christianity, 1970-74; mem. faculty San Diego State U., 1974—, prof. religious studies, 1980—, chmn. dept. religious studies, 1983—, assoc. dean grad. div. and research, 1974-83; founder/pres. Inst. Bibl. Studies, 1983—; cons. photog. archival conservation of Dead Sea Scrolls in Jerusalem, 1980; mem adv. bd. Inst. Antiquity and Christianity, 1974—. Trustee, Claremont Collegiate Sch., 1970-75, pres., 1972-74; trustee, mem. exec. com. Ancient Bible Manuscript Ctr., 1981—. Fellow Lilly Found., 1964-65, Layne Found., 1965-66; disting. vis. scholar James Madison U., 1982. Mem. Am. Soc. Papyrologists, Soc. Bibl. Lit., Phi Beta Delta. Author: The Pastoral Epistles: Introduction and Commentary, 1981, Exploring World Religions: A Reading and Writing Workbook, 1986; editor Studies and Documents; contbr. articles on papyrology and bibl. studies to scholarly jours. Office: San Diego State U San Diego CA 92182

SPARKS, JACK NORMAN, dean of college; b. Lebanon, Ind., Dec. 3, 1928; s. Oakley and Geraldine Ruth (Edrington) S.; m. Esther Lois Bowen, Apr. 11, 1953; children: Stephen Michael, Robert Norman, Ruth Ann, Jonathan Russell. BS, Purdue U., 1950; MA, U. Iowa, 1951, PhD, 1960. Tchr. math. Leyden Community High Sch., Franklin Park, Ill., 1954-58; rsch. asst. U. Iowa, Iowa City, 1958-60; assoc. prof. applied stats., dir. bur. of rsch. U. No. Colo., Greeley, 1960-65; assoc. prof. ednl. psychology Pa. State U., State Coll., 1965-68; dir. corr. Campus Crusade for Christ, San Bernardino, Calif., 1968-69; dir. Christian World Liberation Front, Berkeley, Calif., 1969-75; pastor, ch. overseer New Covenant Apostolic Order, Berkeley, 1975-77; dean St. Athanasius Acad. Orthodox Theology, Santa Barbara, Calif., 1977-87, St. Athanasius Coll., Santa Barbara, 1987—; cons. Measurement Rsch. Ctr., Iowa City, 1959-60, Western States Small Schs. Project, Greeley, 1962-65, Colo. Coun. on Edn. Rsch., Denver, 1963-65. Author: Letters to Street Christians, 1971, The Mind Benders, 1977, 79, The Resurrection Letters, 1978, The Preaching of the Apostles, 1987; editor: Apostolic Fathers. Trustee Rock Mont Coll., Denver, 1962-77, Thomas Nelson Co., Nashville, 1977-78. 1st lt. U.S. Army, 1952-54. Mem. Am. Scientific Affiliation, Assn. Orthodox Theologians, Conf. on Faith and History, Phi Delta Kappa (Epsilon chpt. pres. 1959-60). Democrat. Orthodox Christian. Home: 885 Fortuna Ln Santa Barbara CA 93117 Office: St Athanasius Coll 6778 Pasado Rd Santa Barbara CA 93117

SPARKS, LEE PHILIP, publishing company executive; b. Denver, Dec. 12, 1957; s. Charles William and Marian Neva (Zeigler) S. BA summa cum laude, Phillips U., 1980. Editor-in-chief Group Books, Loveland, Colo., 1981-87; dir. devel. Group Pub., Loveland, 1988—. Co-author: (books) Student Plan-It Calendar, 1988, Training Teenagers for Peer Ministry, 1988; editor: (books) Youth Group How-To Book, 1981, Fast Forms for Youth Ministry, 1987. Active Habitat for Humanity, Loveland, 1987—; coun. mem. King of Glory Luth. Ch., Loveland, 1986-87. Mem. Evang. Christian Pubs. Assn. Republican. Office: Group Pub 2890 N Monroe Loveland CO 80538

SPARKS, RICHARD HARRY, aerospace systems engineer, program manager; b. Owatonna, Minn., July 27, 1935; s. Harry Lee and Viola Julia (Barwald) S.; m. Geraldine Ann Shay, July 20, 1957 (wid. 1970); children: David, Joan; m. Carol Marie Moore, June 9, 1972; children: Deborah, Mark, Cherith. BA in Electrical Engring., U. Minn., 1958; MBA, UCLA, 1965. Rsch. engr. North Am. Aviation, L.A., 1958-61; mem. technical staff Space Tech. Labs., Renondo Beach, Calif., 1961-63; engring. sect. head TRW Space Tech. Labs., Redondo Beach, Calif., 1963-67; v.p. engring.and ops. Elpower Corp., Santa Ana, Calif., 1968-70; mgr., electronics devel. labs. McCulloch Corp., L.A., 1970-73; dept. mgr. Space Power Systems TWR, Redondo Beach, 1974-79; mgr. space systems engring. TRW Space & Tech. Group, Redondo Beach, 1980-87; program mgr., space systems programs TWR SPace & Tech. Group, Redondo Beach, 1987—; battery cons., Westminster, Calif., 1967-75; lectr. Sch. of Engring., San Jose, Calif., 1983-87. Author, editor: Sealed-Cell NIckel Cadmium Battery Applications Manuel, 1979; inventor in field. Asst. Scout Master Boy Scout of Am., Westminster, 1970-75. Mem. Inst. Electrical and Electronics Engrs., Am. Inst. Aeronautics and Astronautics, Armed Forces Communications and Electronics Assn. Republican. Home: 474 Palos Verdes Blvd Redondo Beach CA 90277

SPARKS, WALTER CHAPPEL, horticulturist, educator; b. New Castle, Colo., Aug. 22, 1918; s. Lester Elroy and Jean Ivene (Murray) S.; m. Barbara Ferne Gardner, May 31, 1942; children: Robert, Richard, Eugene. Student, Western State Coll., 1936-37; BS, Colo. State U., 1941, MS, 1943; postgrad., U. Minn., 1945, Wash. State U., 1949, 56-57; DSc (hon.), U. Idaho, 1984. Instr., head dept. agr. Pueblo Jr. Coll., 1941; grad. asst. Colo. State U., 1941-43, instr. horticulture, 1943-44, asst. prof., 1944-47, asso. prof., 1947; asso. horticulturist U. Idaho, Aberdeen, 1947-57; acting supt. Aberdeen br. Agrl. Expt. Sta., 1951, 57, 65, horticulturist, 1957—, research prof. horticulture, 1968—, prin. liaison coordinator for potato program, 1976—; exchange prof. Research Inst., Kolding, Denmark, 1972-73; adviser and lectr. on potato problems to various fgn. govts.; cons., adv., Israel, 1980, Philippines, 1981, Jamaica, 1988; dir. Postharvest Inst. Perishables, 1980—. Contbr. articles to profl. jours. Recipient 50th Anniversary medal Fed. Land Banks, 1967; Distinguished Service award for service to Potato Industry of Idaho Gov. of Idaho, 1967; named to Hall of Fame Potato Mus. Brussels, 1977; recipient Alumni Service award, 1980, Disting. Faculty award Phi Kappa Phi, 1980; spl. recognition for numerous contbns. to Idaho agr., 1984; elected to Idaho Agrl. Hall of Fame, 1983; Eldred L. Jenne research fellow, 1957. Mem. AAAS, Am. Inst. Biol. Scis., Am. Soc. Hort. Sci. (life), European Assn. Potato Research, N.W. Assn. Horticulturists, Entomologists and Plant Pathologists, Idaho Acad. Sci., Nat. Potato Research and Edn. Found. (cert. appraciation seed potato storage tech. 1986), N.W. Food Processors Assn. (Disting. Service award, 1987), N.W. Fieldman's Assn. (Disting. Agrl. Service award, 1987), Potato Assn. Am. (life mem., past pres., dir.), Western Regional Potato Improvement Group (past pres.), C. of C., Scabbard and Blade, Sigma Xi (Outstanding Research Paper award 1974), Gamma Sigma Delta (Outstanding Research Worker award 1977, award of merit 1978), Alpha Zeta, Beta Beta Beta, Epsilon Rho Epsilon. Club: Rotary. Home: 234 N 1st St Aberdeen ID 83210 Office: U Idaho Rsch and Extension Ctr Aberdeen ID 83210

SPARROW, DONALD WALLACE, JR., data processing executive; b. Chapel Hill, N.C., June 2, 1951; s. Donald Wallace Sr. and Jean Carolyn (Pressley) S.; m. Kalla Diane Jordan, Aug. 15, 1981; children: Donald III, Jeffrey, Brian. BA in Math., U. N.C., 1982; MA in Computer Resource Mgmt., Webster U., 1988. Analyst Nat. Security Agy., Ft. Meade, Md., 1980; test mgr. B-1B System Program Office Directorate of Test and Evaluation, Wright Patterson AFB, Ohio, 1982-86; lead analyst Command, Control, Communications and Intelligence Systems Hdqrs. Air Force Operational Test and Evaluation Ctr., Kirtland AFB, N.Mex., 1986—. Author computer program Literacy Volunteers of Albuquerque Data Base Management and Tracking System, 1988. Vol., project leader data base mgmt. system devel. Literacy Vols. of Albuquerque. Capt. USAF. Mem. Company Grade Club, Officers Coun. Club. Office: HQ AFOTEC Kirtland AFB NM 87117

SPAS, APRIL LOUISE, marketing professional; b. Springville, N.Y., Apr. 3, 1950; d. Edward John and Faith (Ellis) Ferry S.; m. Krzysztof K. Burhardt, Jan. 26, 1985. BA, SUNY, Fredonia, 1973. Sales rep. Travenol Labs., Buffalo, 1974-76; mktg. dir. Snyder-Darien Corp., Buffalo, 1976-80; sales rep. 3M Co., Buffalo, 1980-83; sr. market devel. coordinator 3M Co., St. Paul, 1983-85, mktg. supr., 1985-88, mktg. supr. dental products div., 1988—.

SPATARO, LUCIAN PETER, manufacturing company executive; b. Baton Rouge, Mar. 8, 1957; s. Lucian Peter and Dorothy Estelle (DiBiase) S. Student, Ohio U., 1975-77; BS in Bus. Adminstrn., U. Ariz., 1979. Indsl. engr. GATES Lear Jet Corp., Tucson, 1979-81, prodn. mgr., 1981-83; indsl. engr. mgr. Unitronics, Inc., Tucson, 1983-85; program mgr. Cin. Electronic, 1985-87; dir. Prissa, Hermosillo, Sonora, Mex., 1987-88; v.p. Prime Shelter, Inc., Nogales, Ariz., 1988—; cons. in field, 1986—; lectr. Ariz.-Sonora Commn./Prissa, 1986—. Creator MFR Software System, 1987. Active Big Bros., Tucson, 1985—. Mem. Am. Soc. Quality Control, Am. Inst. Indsl. Engrs., Am. Productivity, Inventory Control Soc., P. A. Diving Instrs., Delta Sigma Pi, Sigma Chi Alumni. Clubs: Yacht, 20-30 (Tucson). Office: Prime Shelter Inc 5620 N Kolb #173 Tucson AZ 85715

SPAULDING, JOHN PIERSON, public relations executive, marine consultant; b. N.Y.C., June 25, 1917; s. Forrest Brisbine and Genevieve Anderson (Pierson) S.; m. Eleanor Rita Bonner, Aug. 18, 1947; children: Anne Spaulding Balzhiser, John F., Mary T.; m. 2d, Donna Alene Abrescia, May 15, 1966. Student Iowa State Coll., 1935-36, Grinnell Coll., 1936-38, U. Chgo., 1938-39. Reporter, Chgo. City News Bur., UPI, 1939-40; editor Cedar Falls (Iowa) Daily Record, 1940-41; picture editor Des Moines Register & Tribune, 1941-42, 47-50; pub. relations dir. Motor Club Iowa, Davenport, 1950-51; commd. 2d. lt. USAF, 1942, advanced through grades to maj., 1947, recalled, 1951, advanced through grades to lt. col.; ret., 1968; v.p. Vacations Hawaii, Honolulu, 1969-70; dir. pub. relations, mgr. pub. relations services Alexander & Balwin, Inc., Honolulu, 1970-76; mgr. community relations Matson Navigation Co., Honolulu, 1976-81. Pres., Econ. Devel. Assn., Skagit County, Wash., 1983-85; mem. Anacortes (Wash.) Sch. Bd., 1982-88; mem. Gov.'s Tourism Devel. Council, 1983-85; mem. adv. com. State Ferry System, 1982—; chmn. Everett chpt. S.C.O.R.E., 1984-86. Decorated Air medal. Mem. Pub. Relations Soc. Am. (pres. Hawaii chpt. 1974), Hawaii Communicators (pres. 1973), Nat. Def. Transp. Assn. (pres. Aloha chpt. 1980-81, Disting. Service award 1978-79), Air Force Assn., Anacortes C. of C., Sigma Delta Chi (life). Clubs: Propeller (pres. Port of Honolulu 1979-80), Honolulu Press, Fidelgo Yacht, Hawaii Yacht, Royal Hawaiian 400 Yacht (comdr. 1977-81), Rotary. Home: 6002 Sands Way Anacortes WA 98221

SPAULDING, ROBERT EDWARD, systems planning engineer; b. Charleston, S.C., Mar. 27, 1939; s. David Claud and Inez Pearl (Weeks) S.; m. Wilgefort Elfride Lohr, Oct. 7, 1960 (div. 1984); 1 child, Andrea Patricia; m. Linda Darlene Mills, Dec. 29, 1984; 1 stepchild, Brad B. Huie. AAS in Computer Sci., Wilbur Wright Coll., Chgo., 1974; AA in Bus., U. Md., 1974, BS in Bus., 1976; EdM, Boston U., 1979. Enlisted U.S. Army, 1957, advanced through grades to chief warrant officer, 1979, ret., 1981; program mgr. United Techs., Orlando, Fla., 1982-84; v.p. mktg. Vector Telcom, Inc., Sacramento, 1984-86; reliability engr. Planning Rsch. Corp., McLean, Va., 1986-87; sr. systems engr. Gen. DataCom Systems, Tampa, Fla., 1987-88; systems planning engr. Lockheed Tech. Ops. Co., Sunnyvale, Calif., 1988—; prof. Golden Gate U., San Francisco, 1986—, Cochise Community Coll., Sierra Vista, Ariz., 1986-87. Author: (with others) Resource Manual for Domestic Violence for the State of Virginia, 1981. Decorated Legion of Merit. Mem. Nat. Assn. Radio and Telecommunications Engrs., Warrant Officers Assn., Nat. Panel Consumer Arbitrators. Republican. Episcopalian. Home: 85 Bing Dr #30 Santa Clara CA 95051 Office: Lockheed Tech Ops Co PO Box 61687 Sunnyvale CA 94088

SPEAR, JEFFREY ALLAN, graphic designer; b. Balt., Nov. 28, 1955; s. Louis J. and Hortense (Bloom) S. BFA, U. Ariz., 1977. Graphic designer Gruen Assocs./Architects, L.A., 1977-78, Pereira Assocs./Architects, L.A., 1978-79, Spear Design and Assocs., Santa Monica, Calif., 1979-81, Earle Palmer Brown Advt., Washington, 1981-82; graphic designer, creative dir. Jeffrey Spear Design and Mktg., Santa Monica, 1982—. Recipient Merit award Art Dirs. Club of N.Y., N.Y.C., 1985, cert. of design excellence Print Mag., 1987, Desi award Graphic Design USA, 1988. Mem. Type Dirs. Club, Am. Inst. Graphic Arts, Art Dirs. Club L.A. (v.p. 1987-88, cert. of merit, 1987), Acad. Magical Arts. Democrat. Jewish. Home and Office: Jeffrey Spear Design & Mktg 1228 Eleventh St #201 Santa Monica CA 90401

SPEAR, STEPHEN LOUIS, data processing executive; b. Boston, Feb. 6, 1943; s. Arthur S. and Phyllis (Grossman) S.; m. Susan H. Auslander, June 26, 1966; children: Joshua M., Ben G. Student, Lehigh U., 1960-63, Rutgers U., 1963-70. Programmer Chubb & Son Inc., Short Hills, N.J., 1961-64; program counselor Bell Telephone Labs., Whippany, N.J., 1964-66; supr. systems support The Singer Co., Wayne, N.J., 1966-76; sr. teleprocessing analyst Transcon Lines, El Sequndo, Calif., 1976-77; mgr. corp. systems Twentieth Century Fox, Beverly Hills, Calif., 1977-85; info. services mgr. Carnation Dairies, Los Angeles, 1985, mgr. info./automation services div., 1987—. Developer computer system, TV Print Syndication, integrated bus. process control system. Mem. Am. Motorcyclists Assn., Nat. Street Rod Assn, TRW Motorcycle Club. Office: Carnation Dairies 7301 District Blvd Bakersfield CA 93313

SPEARE, DANIEL BERNARD, broadcasting company executive, consultant; b. Los Angeles, July 29, 1929; s. Frederick H. Speare and Fannie (Goldstein) Speare Rosenberg; m. Mary Magidow, Sept. 11, 1948; children—Eric, Ellen, Marc. Student Profl. Radio and TV Sch., Calif., 1946-48; B.S. in Pub. Relations, UCLA, 1974. Program dir., news dir. Sta. KREO, Indio, Calif., 1950; dir. pub. relations, speech instr. Frederick H. Speare Radio-TV Sch., Los Angeles, 1950-52, pres., 1952-56; program dir. Sta. KGFJ, Los Angeles, 1956-57; program dir., sales staff Sta. KAFY, Bakersfield, Calif., 1957-58, Sta. KLYD, Bakersfield, 1958-62; v.p., gen. mgr. Sta. KGEE, Bakersfield, 1962-76; pres., chief exec. officer Dan B. Speare Broadcast Enterprises, Inc., KPMC Radio, Bakersfield, 1976—. Bd. dirs. YMCA, Bakersfield. pres. Temple Beth El, Bakersfield, 1972-73. Served with USN, 1948-50. Recipient Radio Mmgt. award Nat. Assn. Broadcasters, 1973, cert. of appreciation Fgn. Govts. Press Assn., 1976, honor citation Americanism Edn. League, 1980, Toastmasters award, Bakersfield, 1981. Mem. Broadcast Pioneers, Kern County Broadcasters, Advt. Club Bakersfield, Bakersfield C. of C. (bd. dirs. 1976-78). Republican. Jewish. Club: Exchange (bd. dirs. 1983-84, pres.-elect 1988-89) (Bakersfield). Lodge: Elks. Home: 4912 Panorama Dr Bakersfield CA 93306 Office: Sta KPMC 230 Truxton Ave Bakersfield CA 93301

SPEARS, WILLIAM JEFFREY, electronics product manager; b. Seattle, Aug. 8, 1954; s. Robert Stanley and Mary Francis (Bailey) S.; m. Anne Lightfoot, Oct. 2, 1976. BS in Geol. Sci., U. Wash., 1976; BSEE, Cogswell Coll. North, Kirkland, Wash., 1989. Application engr. Terra Tech. Corp., Redmond, Wash., 1984-86; sr. applications engr. Integrated Circuits, Inc., Redmond, 1984-86; product sales mgr. Integrated Circuits, Inc., 1986-89; mgr. program Interpoint Corp., Redmond, 1989—. With USN, 1976-83. Mem. Internat. Soc. Hybrid Microelectronics, U.S. Naval Inst. Republican. Baptist. Home: 13431 NE 119th Way Redmond WA 98052 Office: Interpoint Corp 10301 Willows Rd Redmond WA 98052

SPECK, ROBERT CHARLES, geological engineer; b. Bklyn., June 15, 1944; s. Charles Ernest and Helen Gertrude (York) S.; m. Pia Rey Polanco, July 4, 1971; 1 child, Stephen Ruben. BA, Franklin and Marshal Coll., 1968; BS, U. Missouri, Rolla, 1974, MS, 1975, PhD, 1979. Geologist Peace Corps, Dominican Republic, 1968-70; resident geologist Geokinetics, Inc., Dominican Republic, 1970-72; project geologist Hanson-Rodriguez, S.A., Dominican Republic, 1972-73; staff engr. GAI Cons., Inc., Pitts., 1979-84; assoc. prof., dept. chmn. U. Alaska, Fairbanks, 1984—. Contbr. articles to profl. jours. Mem. Assn. Engring. Geologists (sect. vice chmn. 1985—), Soc. Mining Engrs., Am. Inst Profl. Geologists (lic.), Internat. Soc. for Rock Mechanics, Tau Beta Pi, Sigma Gamma Epsilon. Home: 3030 Forrest Dr Fairbanks AK 99709 Office: U Alaska Dept Mining & Geol Engring Fairbanks AK 99775-1190

SPECTOR, HAROLD, real estate developer, financier; b. Boston, Mar. 8, 1921; s. Mier I. and Ann R. (Kamins) S.; m. Joan L. Smith, May 7, 1967; 1 child, Pamela S. Ankerman. Student, New Eng. Conservatory Music; JD, Northeastern U., Boston, 1941. With chem. dept. Amfac, Honolulu, 1949-51; credit mgr. Hawaii Builders Supply, Honolulu, 1951-53; ptnr. Island Lumber Co., Honolulu, 1953-56; owner Aloha Lumber Co., Honolulu, 1956-62; v.p. Loyalty Enterprises, Honolulu, 1962-75; pres. Hadley-Spector, Inc., Honolulu, 1975—, Spector Holdings, Ltd., Honolulu, 1978—; owner Liliha Sq. Shopping Ctr.; chmn., chief exec. officer Cosmos Investment Co. of Japan (USA); ptnr. Ramada Renaissance Hotel, Maui, Hawaii. Mem. Gov.'s Task Force for Harbors and Airports, 1976-80, Dist. Export Coun., 1979. Capt. U.S. Army, 1942-49. Mem. Union League, Plaza Club. Jewish. Home: 141 Poloke Pl Honolulu HI 96822 Office: Hadley Spector Inc 745 Fort St Ste 205 Honolulu HI 96813

SPEED, JOHN WILLIAM, city official, fire chief; b. Fresno, Calif., July 8, 1935; s. John Moody and Dorothy Ann (Lucas) S.; student Diablo Valley Coll., 1963-64, Contra Costa Coll., 1965-67, Solano Community Coll., 1968; m. Virginia H. Polk, Oct. 8, 1958; children—Dorothy Sue, Valorie Lynn, Lorilee. With Vallejo (Calif.) Fire Dept., 1961-71, 73-76, fire chief, 1973-76; fire chief Tracy (Calif.) Fire Dept., 1971-73; fire chief Aurora (Colo.) Fire Dept., 1976—; instr. fire sci. Solano Coll., 1968-75. Mem. adv. bd. Salvation Army, Aurora, 1976—. Served with USAF, 1952-61. Mem. Nat. Fire Protection Assn., Internat. Fire Chiefs Assn., Colo. State Fire Chiefs Assn., Met. Fire Chiefs Assn. Democrat. Episcopalian. Clubs: Masons, Shriners. Office: City of Aurora Fire Dept 1470 S Havana St Aurora CO 80012

SPEER, GARY DOUGLAS, career military officer; b. Gadsden, Ala., Apr. 4, 1950; s. James Ralph and Anne Louise (Barnes) S.; m. Catherine Marie Tucker, Apr. 19, 1974. BS, U.S. Mil. Acad., 1972; MA in Mgmt., Webster U., St. Louis, 1982. Commd. 2d lt. U.S. Army, 1972, advanced through grades to lt. col., 1988; co. exec. officer, rifle platoon leader 1st battalion 503d Inf. U.S. Army, Ft. Campbell, Ky., 1973-74, 75th Inf., 1974-76; battalion logistics officer U.S. Army, Ft. Campbell, 1976-77; battalion logistics officer 1st Battalion 46th Inf. U.S. Army, Erlangen, Fed. Republic Germany, 1978-79; co. comdr. Co. B U.S. Army, Erlangen, 1979-81; Latin Am.-Africa desk officer Hdqrs. Dept. Army U.S. Army, Washington, 1982-84; batallion exec. officer 2d Battalion 75th Ranger Regt. U.S. Army, Ft. Lewis, Wash., 1984-87; brigade exec. officer 3d brigade 9th Inf. div. U.S. Army, Ft. Lewis, 1987-88, battalion comdr. 2d Battalion 60th Inf., 1968—. Decorated Meritorious Svc. medal with 4 oak leaf clusters. Home: Quarters 2315 Clark Rd Fort Lewis WA 98433 Office: US Army 2d Battalion 60th Inf Fort Lewis WA 98433

SPEICHER, KIRK ALLEN, orthodontist; b. Wilkes-Barre, Pa., May 2, 1949; s. Frank Parry and Treveryan Beatrice (Williams) S.; m. Shelley Weisberger, Oct. 8, 1972; 1 child, Jared Michael. BA, Bucknell U., 1971; DDS, Temple U., 1976; cert. pediat. dentistry, UCLA, 1978; cert. orthodontics, U. Minn., 1982. Asst. prof. U. Ky., Lexington, Ky., 1978-80; gen. practice dentistry Mpls., 1981-82; pediatric dentistry, orthodontics Affiliated Childrens Dental Specialists, Phoenix, 1982-84; practice orthodontic dentistry Chandler, Ariz., 1984--. Trustee Temple Emanuel of Tempe. Am. Fund for Dental Health fellow, 1980-81, NIH fellow, 1977-78. Mem. ADA, Am. Assn. Orthodontists, Ariz. Orthodontic Study Group, Am. Acad. Pediatric Dentists, Cen. Ariz. Dental Soc. (com. chmn.), Chandler C. of C., Ariz. State Dental Assn., Pacific Coast Soc. Orthodontists, Ariz. State Orthodontic Soc., Ariz. Craniomandibular Group, Rotary. Office: Chandler Orthodontic Cons 335 N Alma Sch Rd Ste D Chandler AZ 85224

SPEIGHT, JOHN BLAIN, lawyer; b. Cheyenne, Wyo., May 29, 1940; s. Jack B. and Kathryn Elizabeth (Schmidt) S.; m. Sally Karolee Sullivan, Aug. 20, 1960 (div. Apr. 1977); children: Sheryl, Tricia, Jackie; m. Carol Ann McBee, Sept. 16, 1979. BA, U. Wyo., 1962, JD, 1965. Bar: Wyo. 1965. Atty. Standard Oil Calif., 1965-67; asst. atty. gen. State of Wyo., Cheyenne, 1967-69, adminstrv. legal asst. to gov., 1969-71, atty. for reorgn. com., 1969-71; asst. U.S. atty. litigation div. Dist. Wyo., Cheyenne, 1971-72; ptnr. Hanes, Carmichael, Johnson, Gage & Speight, Cheyenne, 1972-75, Hathaway, Speicht, Kunz, Trautwein & Barrett, Cheyenne, 1976--; cons. to sec. interior Dept. Interior, Washington, summer, 1975; mem. Commn. for Uniform State Laws, 1986--; chmn. Wyo. Jud. Supervisory Commn., 1986--. Chmn. Wyo. Republican. Com., 1973-75; bd. dirs. various civic orgns. Recipient numerous awards for civic activities. Mem. ABA, Wyo. Bar Assn., Laramie County Bar Assn., ATLA, Wyo. Trial Lawyers Assn., Young Men's Literary Club. Roman Catholic. Home: 4021 Snyder St Cheyenne WY 82001 Office: Hathaway Speight Kunz 2424 Pioneer Ave Ste 402 PO Box 1208 Cheyenne WY 82003

SPEISER, BURTON LYLE, radiation oncologist; b. N.Y.C., Jan. 24, 1946; s. Morris and Mollie (Chtive) S.; m. Jeanne Michelle Speiser, Dec. 21, 1968; children: Michael Lawrence, Leonard Robert, Lisa Jennifer. AB in Biology, Queens Coll., 1966; MD, N.J. Coll. Medicine, Newark, 1970; MS in Radiation Biology, U. Rochester, 1977. Diplomate Am. Bd. Radiology, Therapeutic Radiology. Intern Manhattan VA Hosp., N.Y.C., 1970-71; assoc. dir. radiation LDS Hosp., Salt Lake City, 1976-79; resident in radiation oncology U. Rochester, 1971-74; asst. prof. radiation oncology Ind. U., Indpls., 1979-80; dir. radiation oncology St. Joseph's Med. Ctr., Phoenix, 1980—. Pres. Phoenix unit Am. Cancer Soc., 1987. Maj. M.C., USAF, 1974-76. Mem. AMA, Am. Soc. Therapeutic Radiologists and Oncologists, Am. Coll. Radiology, Am. Soc. Clin. Oncologists, N.Y. Acad. Scis., Sigma Xi. Republican. Office: St Joseph's Med Ctr 350 W Thomas Rd Phoenix AZ 85013

SPEISER, THEODORE WESLEY, astrophysics, planetary and atmospheric sciences educator; b. Del Norte, Colo., Nov. 23, 1934; s. Alfred Theodore and Virginia Melva (Pickens) S.; m. Patricia Jane McCrummen, June 10, 1956; children: Tanya Lee, Kelly Ann, Tetria Ava. BS, Colo. State U., 1956; MS, Calif. Inst. Tech., 1959; PhD, Pa. State U., 1964. Asst. prof. U. Colo., Boulder, 1969-74, assoc. prof., 1974-85, prof. astrophysics, planetary and atmospheric scis., 1985—; cons. NOAA, Boulder, 1970—. Contbr. articles to profl. jours. Served to capt. U.S. Army, 1960-61. Recipient U.S. Sr. Scientist award A.V. Humboldt Found., 1977; Fulbright fellow, 1956. Mem. Am. Geophys. Union (local br. v.p. 1986-87, pres. 1987—). Home: 2335 Dartmouth Ave Boulder CO 80303 Office: U Colo/Dept of Astrophysics Planetary & Atmospheric Scis C Box 391 Boulder CO 80309

SPELLMAN, DOUGLAS TOBY, advertising executive; b. Bronx, N.Y., May 12, 1942; s. Sydney M. and Leah B. (Rosenberg) S.; BS, Fairleigh Dickinson U., 1964; m. Ronni I. Epstein, Jan. 16, 1966 (div. Mar. 1985); children: Laurel Nicole, Daren Scott; m. Michelle Ward, Dec. 31, 1986. Media buyer Doyle, Dane, Bernbach, Inc., N.Y.C., 1964-66, Needham, Harper & Steers, Inc., N.Y.C., 1966; media supr. Ogilvy & Mather, Inc.,

N.Y.C., 1967-69; media dir. Sinay Advt., Los Angeles, 1969-70; chief ops. officer S.H.H. Creative Mktg., Inc., Los Angeles, 1969—; assoc. media dir. Warren, Mullen, Dolobowsky, Inc., N.Y.C., 1970—; dir. West Coast ops. Ed Libov Assocs., Inc., Los Angeles, 1970-71; media supr. Carson/Roberts Advt. div. Ogilvy & Mather, Inc., Los Angeles, 1971-72; assoc. media dir. Ogilvy & Mather, Inc., Los Angeles, 1972-73; media dir. Vitt Media Internat., Inc., Los Angeles, 1973-74; v.p., dir. West Coast ops. Ind. Media Services, Inc., Los Angeles, 1974-75; owner Douglas T. Spellman, Inc., Los Angeles, 1975-77, pres., chmn. bd., 1977-82; pres., chief operating officer Douglas T. Spellman Co. div. Ad Mktg., Inc., Los Angeles, 1982-85; pres., chief exec. officer, chmn. bd. Spellbound Prodns. and Spellman Media divs. Spellbound Communications, Inc., Los Angeles, 1984-86; gen. ptnr. Faso & Spellman, Los Angeles, 1984-86; chief operating officer, pres. Yacht Mgmt. Internat., Ltd., Los Angeles, 1984-86; v.p. media Snyder, Longino Advt. div. Snyder Advt., Los Angeles, 1985-86; advt./media cons., Los Angeles, 1986—; guest lectr. sch. bus UCLA, 1975, U. So. Calif., 1976. Served with U.S. Army Res. N.G., 1964-69. Mem. Aircraft Owners and Pilots Assn., Nat. Rifle Assn., Phi Zeta Kappa, Phi Omega Epsilon. Jewish. Clubs: Rolls Royce Owners, Mercedes Benz Am., Aston Martin Owners. Office: PO Box 180 Beverly Hills CA 90213

SPELLMAN, JOHN DAVID, electrical engineer; b. Beaver Dam, Wis., July 27, 1935; s. John Joseph and Elsie Marguerite (Schultz) S.; B.S. in Elec. Engring., U. Wis., 1959; m. Kathleen Burns King, May 26, 1972; stepchildren—Kathleen Biegel, Karen Silva, Kimberly Lyon. Jr. engr., part time, Malleable Iron Range Co., Beaver Dam, 1952-59; mem. tech. staff Rockwell Internat., Anaheim, Calif., 1961-85, lead engr., 1969-78, 81-85; mgr. ground instrumentation ops. unit Rockwell Internat., Vandenberg AFB, 1985—; cons. Data Processing, Santa Maria, Calif., 1965. Served to 1st lt. Signal Corps, AUS, 1959-61. Recipient U.S. Army Accomodation award, 1961, USAF Outstanding Achievement award for Civilian Personnel. Mem. Assn. Computing Machinery, Air Force Assn., Res. Officers Assn. Clubs: Birnam Wood Golf (Montecito, Calif.); Santa Maria Country. Contbr. publs. on minutemen data systems, PCM Telemetry systems. Home: 642 Meadowbrook Santa Maria CA 93455 Office: PO Box 5181 Vandenberg AFB CA 93437

SPELTS, RICHARD JOHN, lawyer; b. Yuma, Colo., July 29, 1939; s. Richard Clark and Barbara Eve (Pletcher) S.; children—Melinda, Meghan, Richard John. B.S. cum laude, U. Colo., 1961, J.D., 1964. Bar: Colo. bar 1964, U.S. Supreme Ct. bar 1968. With Ford Motor Internat., Cologne, Fed. Republic Germany, 1964-65; legis. counsel to U.S. Senator, 89th and 90th Congresses, 1967-68; minority counsel U.S. Senate Subcom., 90th and 91st Congresses, 1968-70; asst. U.S. atty., 1st asst. U.S. atty Dist. of Colo., 1970-77; owner, pres. Spelts and Robinson P.C., Denver, 1977—. Recipient cert. for outstanding contbns. in drug law enforcement U.S. Drug Enforcement Adminstrn., 1977; spl. commendation for criminal prosecution U.S. Dept. Justice, 1973; spl. commendation for civil prosecution, 1976. Mem. Colo. Bar Assn. (gov. 1976-78), Fed. Bar Assn. (chmn. govt. torts seminar 1980), Denver Bar Assn., Leadership Denver, Colo. Trial Lawyers Assn., Order of Coif. Republican. Presbyterian. Club: Denver Law.

SPENCE, CLYDETTE WEAVER, nursing educator, deacon; b. Houston, Mar. 15, 1934; d. Clyde and Isabelle Alma (Coignard) Weaver; m. James Thorsvig Spence, June 11, 1966; children: James Theodore, Mariette Elizabeth, Christopher LUke. Diploma in Nursing, Lillie Jolly Sch. Nursing Meml. Hosp.; BS, U. Houston, 1962; postgrad., U. London, 1963-64, Ctr. Diaconate, Oreg., 1987. RN, Tex., Oreg.; ordained to ministry Episcopal Ch. Dir. nursing Annie Wright Sem., Tacoma, 1965; milieu therapist U. Wash. Med. Sch. Hosp., Seattle, 1965-66; staff nurse Virginia Mason Hosp., Seattle, 1966-67, Lebanon (Oreg.) Community Hosp., 1975-76, Albany (Oreg.) Gen. Hosp., 1976-79; dir. staff devel. Linn Care Ctr., Albany, 1979-84; instr. Linn-Benton Community Coll., Albany, 1987—; deacon Ch. Good Samaritan, Corvallis, Oreg., 1987—; Mem. task force to organize Sch. Theology Diocese of Oreg., 1987—, Diocesan Conv. Planning Com., Oreg., 1988. Chmn. bd. dirs. Linn County March of Dimes, Albany, 1978-79; bd. dirs. Linn-Benton Aging Svcs. Inc. Episcopalian. Home: 37037 Gore Dr Lebanon OR 97355 Office: Ch Good Samaritan 333 NW 35th Corvallis OR 97330

SPENCE, OWEN EDWARD, manufacturing executive; b. Baker, Oreg., Sept. 18, 1935; s. Owen Edward and Dorothy Evelyn (Robison) S.; m. Nancy Gay Walters, Feb. 15, 1962 (div. Nov. 1984); children: Micheal, Kathy, Kelley, Shawn, Barry, Randy. Student, Portland State U., 1953-55, Sacramento City Coll., 1966-68, Humphrey's Sch. Law., 1969-70. Installer Hubbard's Drapery Service, Portland, Oreg., 1955-63, Bruener's Home Furnishings, Sacramento, Calif., 1963-75; head installer J.C. Penney Co., Portland, 1975-79, mgr. fabrication, 1979-81, sales mgr., 1981-84, mgr. ops./personnel, 1984-87, asst. mgr. fabrication, 1987—. Served with Oreg. NG, 1953-56. Methodist. Club: Corsa Oreg. (Portland) (pres. 1976-77, editor 1975-77). Home: 12500 SE River Rd Apt #10 Milwaukie OR 97222 Office: JC Penney Co 1020 SE Market St Portland OR 97214

SPENCER, ARTHUR CHAMPLIN, III, librarian; b. Portland, Oreg., June 18, 1938; s. Arthur Champlin and Mary (Chamberlain) S. BA, Lewis and Clark Coll., 1960; MA, U. Oreg., 1964, MLS, 1969; postgrad. Portland State U., 1965-66. Ref. and catalogue librarian Oreg. Hist. Soc., Portland, 1969-83; librarian Hist. Preservation League Oreg., Portland, 1983-84, Broome Oringdulph O'Toole Rudolf & Assocs., Architects, Portland, 1984—; parish archivist Trinity Episc. Ch., Portland, 1973-79. Newsletter editor Oreg. Preservation Resource Ctr., 1984-85; staff mem. Northwest Examiner, Portland, 1986—; contbr. articles on preservation to local jours. Sec., Oreg. Performing Arts History Com., 1965-75; mem. Portland Hist. Landmarks Commn., 1970-78, Portland Hist. Resources Com., 1981-83; bd. dirs. Northwest Portland Ministries, 1985-87; vestryman St. Mark's Episc. Ch., Portland, 1985—; active hunger projects. Nat. Trust Hist. Preservation grantee, 1966; recipient cert. of recognition Gutman Rehab. Programs, Portland, 1973; Multnomah County election ofcl. Mem. Soc. Archtl. Historians, Soc. Archtl. Librarians, Northwest Mus. Nat. History Assn., Episc. Laymen's Soc. Oreg., Phi Alpha Theta. Avocations: urban archtl. walking tours, genealogy. Home: 2065 NW Flanders St #502 Portland OR 97209-1126 Office: 733 NW 20th Ave Portland OR 97209-1397

SPENCER, CAROL BROWN, public information officer; b. Normal, Ill., Aug. 26, 1936; d. Fred William and Sorado (Gross) B.; m. James Calvin Spencer, Dec. 18, 1965 (div. July 1978); children: James Calvin Jr., Anne Elizabeth. BA in English, Calif. State U., Los Angeles, 1964, MA in Pub. Adminstrn., 1986. Cert. secondary edn. tchr., Calif. Corr. Ashland (Ohio) Times Gazette, 1975-78; tchr. English Seneca Vocat. High Sch., Buffalo, 1966-70; pub. info. officer City of Pasadena, Calif., 1979—. Editor: Pasadena In Focus monthly mcpl. publ., 1984-86, N.W. Bulletin quarterly mcpl. publ., 1985-86. Sec., bd. dirs. Calif. Music Theatre, 1987—; bd. dirs. Pasadena Beautiful Found., 1984—, Pasadena Cultural Festival Found., 1983-86; mayoral appointee Strategic Planning Adv. Com., Pasadena, 1985-86; chmn. pub. events com., United Way Los Angeles County. Mem. Pub. Relations Soc. Am., Calif. Assn. Pub. Info. Ofcls. (exec. bd., Paul Clark Achievement award 1986), Mcpl. Mgmt. Assts. of So. Calif., City/County Communications and Mktg. Assn. (bd. dirs. 1988—, pres. 1989—), Kiwanis. Democrat. Anglican. Home: 6026 Encinita Ave Temple City CA 91780 Office: City of Pasadena 100 N Garfield Pasadena CA 91109

SPENCER, CHARLES ALLEN, security and investigation company executive; b. Bossivain, Va., Oct. 8, 1941; s. James Henry and Elizabeth (Palmer) S.; m. Linda Lou Repass, Jan. 25, 1961 (div. Jan. 1975); 1 child, Charles Allen Jr.; m. Janet Lee Whittington, Apr. 28, 1984. AA, U. Md., 1977, BS, 1981. Cert. in law enforcement, bus. mgmt., pvt. investigator. Teller Nat. Savs. & Trust, Washington, 1960-63, Nat. Bank Washington, 1963-68; officer Metro Police Dept., Washington, 1966-67, Prince George's County Police Dept., Marlboro, Md., 1967-83; ret. 1983; mgr. Pinkerton's, Phoenix, 1983-85; gen. mgr. Dictoguard Security & Investigations, Phoenix, 1985—; cons. mfrs., lawyer and homeowner assns., Phoenix, 1983—. Named Policeman of Month, Prince George's County Police Dept., 1968, 70, Merit award, 1981. Mem. Am. Soc. for Indsl. Security, Ret. Police Officers Assn., Fraternal Order of Police, Chandler C. of C. (cons. 1983—, ambassador 1987—). Republican. Baptist. Home: 21445 S 158th St Chandler AZ 85249 Office: Dictoguard Security & Investigations 2711 N 24th St Ste 12 Phoenix AZ 85008

SPENCER, DICK, III, magazine publisher; b. Dallas, Jan. 28, 1921; s. Richard and Jessie (Burden) S.; m. Jo Anne Nicholson, July 24, 1943 (div. May, 1983); children: Barbara Jo Spencer Corpolongo, Richard Craig (dec.), Debra Jean.; m. Vivian King, June 4, 1983. B.A., U. Iowa, 1942. With promotion dept. Look mag., 1945-47; editor info. service, instr. Sch. Journalism U. Iowa, 1948-50; publs. editor U. Colo., Boulder, 1950-51; editor Western Horseman mag., Colorado Springs, 1951-69; pub. Western Horseman mag., 1969—. Author: Editorial Cartooning, 1949, Pulitzer Prize Cartoons, 1951, Beginning Western Horsemanship, 1959, Intermediate Western Horsemanship, 1960, Horse Breaking, 1967. Served with AUS, 1942-45, ETO. Decorated Purple Heart with 2 oak leaf clusters, Bronze Star with oak leaf cluster, Combat Inf. badge, Parachutist badge. Mem. Sigma Delta Chi, Alpha Tau Omega. Methodist. Clubs: Pikes Peak Range Riders, Desert Caballeros. Home: 14050 Roller Coaster Rd Colorado Springs CO 80921 Office: Western Horseman Mag 3850 N Nevada Ave Colorado Springs CO 80907 *

SPENCER, DOUGLAS LLOYD, chemist, manufactuing executive; b. Berkeley, Calif., July 19, 1952; s. Alma Glenn and Anna Lea (Lloyd) S.; A.A., Diablo Valley Coll., 1971; B.S., Brigham Young U., 1974; m. Connie Jeanette Whitesel, Aug. 23, 1974; children—Jeanette Dawn, Jared Douglas, Jilissa Annette, Janine Marie, Janelle Renee, Jeffrey Brian. Lab. instr. chemistry dept. Brigham Young U., 1973-74; lab. asst., computer cons. Hartley Internat., Provo, Utah, 1974; rsch. chemist Dow Chem. Western div., Pittsburg, Calif., 1975-80; pres. Sunset Distbg., Inc., El Dorado Hills, Calif., 1980-82; pres. Maier & Assocs., Inc., Brentwood, 1982-83; pres. Doug Spencer & Assocs., Brentwood, 1983—. Mem. Brentwood Planning Commn., 1980-81; missionary, dist. zone leader Eastern States Mission, 1971-73. Rossmoor residents scholar, 1969-71, Brigham Young U. scholar, 1973-74. Mem. Nat. Eagle Scout Assn., Alpha Gamma Sigma (Calif. state treas. 1970), Liahona Club. Republican. Mormon. Home: 6500 Wagon Loop Placerville CA 95667 Office: Doug Spencer & Assocs 4961 Windplay Dr Ste A El Dorado Hills CA 95630

SPENCER, JUNE MARTHA, dress shop owner; b. Boston, May 29, 1928; d. James Eric and Florence (Roebuck) Spencer; m. James Donald MacShane, Feb. 2, 1949 (div. 1954: children: Douglas and Don (twins), Jenna; m. Robert G. Jessath, July 4, 1956 (div.). PhD, U. Alta., Can., 1977; Dr.Metaphysics, U. Metaphysics, L.A., 1981. Owner J.M. Spencer, Custom Dress Designer, N.Y.C., 1954-64; tchr., counsellor, lectr. 1st Church of Religious Sci., San Jose, 1978-83; owner J.M. Spencer Unltd., Cupertino, Calif., 1982—. Contbr. articles to profl. jours.

SPENCER, RICHARD JAY, appliance store executive; b. Ogden, Utah, Nov. 16, 1952; s. Albert Mark and Doris Mae (Harris) S.; m. JoAnn Laterza, Nov. 22, 1975; 1 child, MaryAnn. Greenskeeper Nordic valley Golf Course, Eden, Utah, 1969-70; installer Mark-A-Newt Appliance Inc., Ogden, 1968-72, appliance technician, 1973-75, pres., gen. mgr., 1978-89; appliance technician Freeport Ctr. Whirlpool Corp., Clearfield, Utah, 1971-73; instr. State Vocat. Ctr., Ogden, 1976-78; cons. Intermountain Appliance Supply, Salt Lake City, 1977-78; procurement specialist Erro Precision Corp., Ogden, 1987-88; dir. No. Utah Appliance Retailers, 1986-89. Scout master Boy Scouts Am., North Ogden, 1980-81; campaign vol., Utah Rep. Party, Ogden, 1980-81. Mem. Intermountain Electrical Assn., Nat. Small Bus. Assn., Utah Council of Small Bus., Utah Electrical Assn., Better Bus. Bur., Nordic Valley Golf Assn., Elks. LDS. Home: 212 W 3325 North North Ogden UT 84414 Office: Mark-A-Newt Appliance Inc 2855 Washington Blvd Ogden UT 84401

SPENCER, STUART KRIEG, public relations executive; b. Phoenix, Feb. 20, 1927; s. Albert Kenneth and Beulah (Krieg) S.; m. Joan A. Spencer (div. Dec. 1987); children: Karen Gwen, Steven Krieg. Student, E. Los Angeles Jr. Coll.; BA, Los Angeles State Coll., 1951. Dir. recreation City of Alhambra, Calif., 1951-59; pres. Spencer-Roberts Assocs., Irvine, Calif., 1961—. Served in U.S. Navy, 1945-46. Recipient Presdl. Citizens medal Pres. Ronald Reagan, 1989. Mem. Am. Assn. Polit. Cons. Republican. Office: Spencer-Roberts Assocs 17702 Cowan St Ste 106 Irvine CA 92714

SPENSKO, SALVACION VARGAS, power company manager; b. Manila, Jan. 14, 1953; came to U.S., 1980; d. Balbino T. and Rosario (Santelices) V.; m. Leo Stanley Spensko, June 12, 1983. A in Sectl. Adminstrn., U. East, Manila, 1971; BA, Western State U., Doniphan, Mo., 1987, MA in Bus. Adminstrn., 1987. Exec. sec. Sulo Restaurant, Makati, Philippines, 1971-72; tour guide, asst. mgr. Super Travel Philippines, Subic Bay, 1972-74; exec. sec. Tourist Philippines, Manila, 1974-75; freelance performing artist Okayama, Japan, 1975, Conty Prodns., Western Europe, 1976-79; exec. sec. Security Pacific Bank, San Francisco, 1981, Bechtel Western Power Corp., San Francisco, 1981-86; office mgr. Bechtel Power Corp., San Francisco, 1986—; proprietor, gen. mgr. Salve Vargas Prodns., Pacifica, Calif., 1984—; instr. Modern Performing Arts, New Concept in Minus-One Music. First pres., founder Calolbon Civic Assn. U.S.A., Pacifica, 1987—, chmn. bd., 1987-89. Mem. Pacifica C. of C., NAFE, Nat. Notary Assn., Bechtel Employees Club (dir. 1986, social v.p. 1986), Employee Svcs. (sec., dir. Golden Gate chpt. 1988-89). Home: 659 Hickey Blvd Pacifica CA 94044 Office: Bechtel Employees Club 50 Beale St San Francisco CA 94044

SPERRY, ROGER WOLCOTT, neurobiologist, educator; b. Hartford, Conn., Aug. 20, 1913; s. Francis B. and Florence (Kraemer) S.; m. Norma G. Deupree, Dec. 28, 1949; children: Glenn Tad, Janeth Hope. B.A., Oberlin Coll., 1935, M.A., 1937, D.Sc. (hon.), 1982; Ph.D., U. Chgo., 1941, D.Sc. (hon.), 1977; D.Sc. (hon.), Cambridge U., 1972, Kenyon Coll., 1979, Rockefeller U., 1980. Research fellow Harvard and Yerkes Labs., 1941-46; asst. prof. anatomy U. Chgo., 1946-52, sect. chief Nat. Inst. Neurol. Diseases of NIH, also asso. prof. psychology, 1952-53; Hixon prof. psychobiology Calif. Inst. Tech., 1954-84, Trustee prof. Emeritus, 1984—; research brain orgn. and neural mechanism. Contbr. articles to profl. jours., chpts. to books.; Editorial bd.: Behavioral Biology. Recipient Oberlin Coll. Alumni citation, 1954; Howard Crosby Warren medal Soc. Exptl. Psychologists, 1969; Calif. Scientist of Year award Calif. Mus. Sci. and Industry, 1972; award Passano Found., 1973; Albert Lasker Basic Med. Research award, 1979; co-recipient William Thomas Wakeman Research award Nat. Paraplegia Found., 1972, Claude Bernard sci. journalism award, 1975, Disting. research award Internat. Visual Literacy Assn., 1979; Wolf Found. prize in medicine, 1979; Nobel prize in physiology or medicine, 1981, Realia award Inst. for Advanced Philos. Research, 1986. Fellow AAAS, Am. Acad. Arts and Scis., Am. Psychol. Assn. (recipient Distinguished Sci. Contbn. award 1971); mem. Royal Acad. (fgn. mem.), Nat. Acad. Scis., Am. Physiol. Soc., Am. Assn. Anatomists, Internat. Brain Research Orgn., Soc. for Study of Devel. and Growth, Psychonomic Soc., Am. Soc. Naturalists, Am. Zool. Soc., Soc. Developmental Biology, Am. Philos. Soc. (Lashley prize 1976), Am. Neurol. Assn. (hon.), Soc. for Neurosci., Internat. Soc. Devel. Biologists, AAUP, Pontifical Acad. Scis., Inst. for Advanced Philos. Research (Realia award 1986), Sigma Xi. Office: Calif Inst Tech 1201 E California St Pasadena CA 91125

SPEYER, JAMES A., entrepreneur; b. Chgo., Sept. 25, 1950; s. Lester D. Speyer and June (Heller) Rose; m. Teresa Fronczek, May 1973 (div. 1983); 1 child, Maxwell. BSEE, Carnegie-Mellon U., 1982, MSEE, 1983, MBA, 1985. Elec. engr. Magnavox Research Labs., Torrance, Calif., 1975-78; v.p. Tennsco Corp., Dickson, Tenn., 1978—; pres. Midwest Folding Products Mfg. Corp. and Midwest Folding Products Sales Corp., Chgo., 1978—, Western Wholesale Appliances Inc., Escondido, Calif., 1987—. Mem. Exptl. Aircraft Assn. Republican. Office: Western Wholesale Appliances Inc 1234 Simpson Way Escondido CA 92024

SPICER, ROBERT JOHN, information systems specialist; b. Santa Monica, Calif., Sept. 30, 1940; s. Stanley and Elizabeth (Gardener) S.; m. Linda Ann Pao, Feb. 20, 1960; children: David, Sheryl, Bryan. AA, Coll. San Mateo, 1962; BS, San Jose State U., 1966; MBA, U. Santa Clara, 1974. EDP mgr. Varian Assocs., Palo Alto, Calif., 1966-74; mgmt. info. systems mgr. Litronix, Cupertino, Calif., 1974-75, Carter Hawley Hale Stores Inc., Santa Clara, Calif., 1975-77, Siliconix, Santa Clara, 1977-81; mgmt. info. systems dir. Nat. Semiconductor Corp., Santa Clara, 1981—; EDP curriculum advisor Evergreen Jr. Coll, San Jose, Calif., 1978-79. Mem. Data Processing Mgrs. Assn. (cert., mem. exam com. 1968-69). Club: Sea Ray Boat (No. Calif.).

SPIEGEL, ABRAHAM, savings and loan association executive; b. 1906. Chmn. Columbia Savs. and Loan Assn., Beverly Hills, Calif., also bd. dirs. Office: Columbia Savs & Loan Assn 8840 Wilshire Blvd Beverly Hills CA 90211 *

SPIEGEL, ALBERT ALEXANDER, lawyer; b. McKeesport, Pa., Mar. 9, 1916; m. Bernice Spiegel; 4 children. BA, U. Pitts., 1937; JD, Harvard U., 1940. Bar: Calif. 1946. Sole practice Los Angeles, 1946—; sec., bd. dirs. Beaumont Meadows, Inc. Hon. chmn. B'nai B'rith Hillel Commn.; mem. nat. campaign cabinet United Jewish Appeal; bd. dirs. Am. Joint Jewish Distbn. Com., United HIAS Service, Jewish Fedn. Council Greater Los Angeles, Santa Monica Hosp. Found.; mem. bd. overseers The Jewish Theol. Sem. Am.; hon. chmn. bd. govs. U. Judaism; mem. mat. governing council Am. Assn. Jewish Edn.; mem. exec. com. Am. Friends of Hebrew U. western region; spl. advisor to Pres. Ronald Reagan on matters of concern to Jewish community, 1981-83. Home: 211 Spalding Dr Beverly Hills CA 90212 Office: 2050 S Bundy Dr Ste 225 Los Angeles CA 90025

SPIEGEL, RONALD STUART, insurance company executive; b. Chgo., Sept. 12, 1942; s. Arthur I. and Elaine M. (Young); m; Carol J. Lieberthal, July 25, 1964; children: Eric, Elissa. BA, Calif. State U., Los Angeles, 1966. Pres. Newhouse Automotive, Los Angeles, 1966-78; agt. N.Y. Life Ins. Co., Santa Fe Springs, Calif., 1978-82, sales mgr., 1982-86, assoc. gen. mgr., 1986-88, gen. mgr., 1989—; v.p. Cerritos Valley Br. Life Underwriters Assn. of Los Angeles, 1984-86, pres., 1987-88. Pres. Temple Shalom, West Covina, Calif., 1975-77, 88—, treas., 1978-83; pres. Jewish Fedn. Council Eastern Region, Los Angeles, 1986-88, v.p., 1984-85. Mem. Am. Soc. CLU's, Gen. Agts. and Mgrs. Assn., Airline Owners and Pilots Assn. Democrat. Lodge: Kiwanis. Home: 1720 Orchard Hill Ln Hacienda Heights CA 91745 Office: NY Life Ins Co 10100 Pioneer Blvd #110 Santa Fe Springs CA 90670

SPIER, LUISE EMMA, film editor, director; b. Laramie, Wyo., Aug. 22, 1928; d. Louis Constantine Cames and Vina Jane Cochran; m. John Spier, Sept., 1957 (div. 1962). Student, U. Wyo., 1947, U. Calif., Berkeley, 1948-53. Head news film editor Sta. KRON-TV, San Francisco, 1960-70, film editor, 1980—; freelance film editor, director San Francisco, 1970-80, 83—. Edited and directed numerous news specials and documentaries, including The Lonely Basque, Whaler, The American Way of Eating. Recipient numerous awards for film editing and directing, including Cine Golden Eagle, Best Med. Res. Film award John Muir Med. Found., Chris Statuette, Bronze and Silver Cindy awards Info. Film Producers Am. Democrat. Episcopalian.

SPIES, KAREN BORNEMANN, writer, education consultant; b. Renton, Wash., Sept. 5, 1949; d. William Edward and Aina Jeanette (Johnson) Bornemann; m. Allan Roy Spies, July 18, 1970; children: Karsten, Astrid. BA, Calif. Luth. U., Thousand Oaks, 1970; MEd, U. Wash., 1974. Vice prin., tchr. Lake Washington Sch. Dist., Kirkland, Wash., 1971-79; tchr. various pub. schs. N.J., 1979-82; kindergarten tchr. Mt. Park Sch., Lake Oswego, Oreg., 1982-84; writer, seminar leader, cons. Wash., 1984-87, Oreg., 1984-87, Littleton, Colo., 1987—; editorial cons. Knute Lee of Luth. Bible Inst., Issaquah, Wash., 1987; lectr. in field; ski instr., various locations, 1974-87, Copper Mt. Resort, Colo., 1987—. Author: Family Activities for the Christmas Season, 1988, Denver: The Mile High City, 1988, Raffi: The Children's Voice, 1989; contbr. articles to profl. jours. Organist Wooden Cross Luth. Ch., 1977-79. Title III grantee, 1974. Mem. Soc. of Children's Book Writers, AAUW, Mensa, Profl. Ski Instrs. Am., Pi Lambda Theta. Republican. Lutheran.

SPILLERS, ROBERT V., savings and loan executive; b. Perkins, Okla., Oct. 13, 1911; s. Noah Robert and Mary Alice (Lemons) S.; m. Neva Roxie Moore, Aug. 4, 1938. Student, Tonkawa Jr. Coll., 1933-35, Springfield Coll., 1935-37. Real estate appraiser Eureka Savs. and Loan Assn., San Francisco, 1956-61; loan officer Lytton Savs. and Loan Assn., Palo Alto, Calif., 1961-65; asst. v.p. bus. devel. Sacramento Savs. and Loan Assn., Redwood City, Calif., 1965—. Active Redwood City Council, 1948-60, retirement bd. San Mateo County, Calif., 1973-77, YMCA, Redwood City, 1948-89. Mem. Redwood City C. of C., Elks. Home: 1054 Whipple Ave Redwood City CA 94062 Office: 961 Woodside Rd Ste D Redwood City CA 94061

SPILLMAN, MICHELLE A., school system administrator; b. Fort Collins, Colo., July 17, 1963; d. Richard F. and Nancy A. (Harold) S. BA in Elem. and Spl. Edn., U. N.C., 1986, MA Spl. Edn., 1988. Jr. vol. Poudre Valley Hosp., Ft. Collins, Colo., 1977-80; child care aide Kiddie Koll., Ft. Collins, Colo., 1980-82; vol. Foothills-Gateway Rehab., Ft. Collins, Colo., 1982; toddler tchr. Countryside Montessori, Ft. Collins, Colo., 1983-85; student tchr. Foothills-Gateway Rehab., Ft. Collins, Colo., Shepardson Elem. Sch., Ft. Collins, 1986; day care dir. Foothills Day Care Ctr., Ft. Collins, 1986; supr. line Foothills-Gateway Rehab., Ft. Collins, 1986-87, supr. evaluator, 1987-89; supr. evaluator Ryan Elem. Sch., Lafayette, Colo., 1989—. TV poller Boulder (Colo.) Dem. Party, 1988; vol. Boulder County Safehouse, 1989, Boulder Community Hosp., 1989; mem. Coun. for Exceptional Children, Coun. for Children with Behavioral Disorders. Recipient Academic award U. No. Colo., 1982-85. Mem. Nat. Assn. Edn. Young Children. Democratic. Presbyterian. Home: 3250 O Neal Circle #J27 Boulder CO 80301 Office: Ryan Elem Sch Boulder Valley Sch Dist 1405 Centaur Village Dr Lafayette CO 80026

SPINALE, JOSEPH MICHAEL, business consultant; b. Cambridge, Mass., Apr. 20, 1947; s. Joseph Michael Spinale; m. Lori Lynnell Moorehead, May 12, 1988; children: Scott, Wendy, Brandi, Tony, Jessica. BA in Psychology, Calif. State U., Long Beach, 1977, MS in Orgnl. Psychology, 1979. Mgr. mgmt. devel. Taco Bell div. Pepsico, Irvine, Calif., 1979-84; cons. Saga Corp., Menlo Park, Calif., 1985-86; western regional dir. Restaurant Devel. Corp., Cleve., 1987; pres. Getting There, Huntington Beach, Calif., 1987-89; mgr. Vision Sports, Inc., Santa Ana, Calif., 1988—. Contbr. articles, poems to profl. publs. Mem. Am. Soc. Tng. and Devel., Phi Kappa Phi.

SPINDEL, REVA DARLENE, accounting executive; b. Springfield, Ill., June 8, 1960; d. Jack Clark Payne and Arlene Francis (Holstein) Payne; m. Philip David Spindel, July 8, 1979. BS with highest distinction, Denver Tech. Coll., 1987. With telecommunications Franklin Life Ins. Co., Springfield, Ill., 1979-81; adminstrv. asst. DO of Cen. and So. I., Springfield, 1981-84; policy adminstr. Bart Automotive Service Corp., Springfield, 1984-86; acctg. exec. Ferguson Homes Inc., Arvada, Colo., 1986—; pres., chief exec. officer Bus. Organizational Services Inc., Arvara, Colo., 1988 (bd. dirs. 1988—). Republican. Office: Ferguson Homes Inc 6275 Simms St Suite 200 Arvada CO 80003

SPINDLER, PAUL, public relations executive; b. Chgo., May 2, 1931; s. Isaac Edward and Sophia (Stein) S.; divorced; children: Kevin, Makayla, Cyd, Jeffrey. BA in Journalism, Temple U., 1952. Reporter Akron Beacon Jour., Akron, Ohio, 1955-58, San Francisco Examiner, 1958-59; editor Santa Clara (Calif.) Daily Jour., 1959-63; dir. pub. affairs Litton Industries, Inc., Beverly Hills, Calif., 1963-68; dir. pub. relations Internat. Industries, Beverly Hills, 1968-70; pres. Paul Spindler & Co., L.A., 1970-75; exec. v.p. Manning Selvage & Lee, Inc., N.Y.C., 1975-85; pres. The Spindler Co., L.A., 1985-87; pres. Western div. GCI Group, L.A., 1987—. Cpl. U.S. Army, 1952-54. Mem. Pub. Relations Soc. Am. (chmn. L.A. counselors group 1987-88), Nat. Investor Relations Inst., Fin. Analysts Fedn., Mountain Gate Country Club (L.A.). Democrat. Jewish. Office: GCI Group 6100 Wilshire Blvd #840 Los Angeles CA 90048

SPINO, ALBERT BENJAMIN, JR., insurance executive; b. Salida, Colo., July 21, 1927; s. Albert B. Spino and Helen I. Carroccia; m. Helen I. Miller, Apr. 14, 1948; children: Terry Lee, Mark Steven. Student, Western State Coll., 1946-48. Sales rep. Stapleton Chevrolet, Salida, 1959-61; sales mgr. Findlay Oldsmobile, Las Vegas, 1961-74; owner, pres. Haas & Spino Ins.,

Las Vegas, 1974—. Served with USNAF, 1943-45. Mem. Prof. Ins. Agt., Ind. Ins. Agts., Showboat Country Club, Las Vegas Country Club, Painted Desert Golf Club (Las Vegas), Elks, Am. Legion. Democrat. Roman Catholic. Home: 8105 Golfers Oasis Dr Las Vegas NV 89129 Office: Hass & Spino Ins 1200 S 4th St Ste J Las Vegas NV 89104

SPINWEBER, CHERYL LYNN, research psychologist; b. Jersey City, July 26, 1950; d. Stanley A. And Evelyn M. (Pfleger) S.; m. Michael E. Bruich, June 18, 1977; children: Sean Michael Bruich, Gregory Alan Bruich. AB with distinction, Cornell U., 1972; PhD in Exptl. Psychology, Harvard U., 1977. Lic. psychologist, Calif. Asst. prof. psychiatry Tufts U. Sch. Medicine, Medford, Mass., 1977-79; asst. dir. sleep lab. Boston State Hosp., 1973-79; dep. head dept. behavioral psychopharmacology Naval Health Research Ctr., San Diego, 1978-86, head dept. behavioral psychopharmacology, 1986—; research asst. prof. dept. psychiatry Uniformed Services U. of the Health Scis., Bethesda, Md., 1985—; lectr., workshop instr. U. Calif. San Diego, La Jolla, Calif., 1979-81, vis. lectr. 1979-86; adj. assoc. prof. San Diego State U. Grad. Sch. Pub. Health, 1984—; courtesy clin. staff appointee dept. psychiatry Naval Hosp., San Diego, 1984—. Contbr. articles to profl. jours. Scholar Cornell U., Ithaca, N.Y., 1968-72, West Essex Tuition, 1968-72, Cornell U. Fedn. Women, 1917-72, Harvard U., 1972-73, 74-76, NDEA Title IV, 1973-74; postdoctoral associateship Nat. Research Council, 1978-80. Fellow Clin. Sleep Soc.; mem. Am. Men and Women of Sci., Sleep Research Soc. (exec. com. 1986—), Am. Psychol. Assn., Western Psychol. Assn. (sec., treas. 1986—), Calif. Sleep Soc., Sigma Xi. Office: Naval Health Rsch Ctr Naval Hosp Sleep Lab San Diego CA 92134-5000

SPIRA-SOLOMON, DARLENE JOY, industrial chemist, researcher; b. Walnut Creek, Calif., Feb. 7, 1959; d. Erwin Irving and Beverly Sue (Davis) Spira; m. Edward Ira Solomon, Sept. 15, 1984. BS, Stanford U., 1980; PhD, MIT, 1984. Rsch. asst. Beckman Instruments, Palo Alto, Calif., 1978-79; rsch. assoc. MIT, Cambridge, 1980-84; rsch. assoc. Stanford (Calif.) U., 1982-84, asst. in instrn. FT-IR spectroscopy, 1982-83; rsch. scientist Hewlett-Packard Labs., Palo Alto, 1984—. Contbr. numerous articles to profl. jours. Coll. recruiter Hewlett-Packard, 1985—; co-chairperson Hewlett-Packard Tech. Women's Conf., 1988; workshop coord. Expanding Your Horizons Conf., Humboldt State U., 1987. Fellow chemistry dept. MIT, 1980-82, Stanford U., 1976-80. Mem. Am. Chem. Soc., Sigma Xi, Phi Beta Kappa. Office: Hewlett Packard Labs PO Box 10490 Palo Alto CA 94303-0971

SPIRTOS, NICHOLAS GEORGE, lawyer, financial company executive; b. Youngstown, Ohio, Mar. 19, 1950; s. George Nicholas Spirtos and Tulla (Palaologos) Waldron; m. Andrea Carel DeFrane, Aug. 19, 1979. BA in Physics, UCLA, 1969, MA in Biochemistry, 1974, JD, 1978. Bar: Calif., 1978. Intelligence analyst 1969-72; dir. product devel. Adolph's Food Products, Burbank, Calif., 1972-73; asst. to pres. Eckel Research and Devel., San Fernando, Calif., 1973-74; dep. State Public Defender Los Angeles, 1977-82; sole practice Pacific Palisades, Calif., 1982—; exec. v.p. Gen. Counsel Compesation Strategies Group, Santa Ana, Calif., 1988—; pro bono legal counsel Junipero Serra High Sch., Gardena, Calif., 1987-88; cons. U.S. Govt., 1982—. Patentee solubilization of Sodium CMC at room temperature, 1972. Founder, fund raiser Pacific Multiple Sclerosis Research Found., Beverly Hills, Calif., 1982—, coordinator with Reed Neurology Ctr. at UCLA. Mem. State Bar of Calif. Democrat. Greek Orthodox. Office: 845 Via de la Paz Ste A-219 Pacific Palisades CA 90272

SPITALERI, VERNON ROSARIO, newspaper publisher, manufacturing company executive; b. Pelham, N.Y., Aug. 2, 1922; s. Rosario S. and Martha (Landerer) S.; m. Marjorie A. Ferrar, Oct. 14, 1952; children—Marc, Eric, Kris, Lynn. B.S., Carnegie Inst. Tech., 1942. Mgr. mech. dept. Am. Newspaper Pubs. Assn., N.Y.C., 1946-53; research dir., gen. adminstr. Miami Herald and Knight Newspapers (Fla.), 1953-57; chmn. bd., pres. Sta-Hi Corp., Newport Beach, Calif., 1957-74; chmn. bd. Sta-Hi Color Service, Sta-Hi Europe, Brussels, Concrete Floats-Huntington Engring. Corp., Huntington Beach, Calif.; editor, pub. Laguna Beach (Calif.) News-Post, 1967-81; pres. Laguna Pub. Co., Nat. Newspaper Found.; dir. Suburban Newspapers Am. ; chmn. bd. Victory Profl. Products, Mango Surfware. Pres., Boys Club, Laguna Beach; mem. citizens adv. com. Laguna Beach; pres. Laguna Beach Library Bd., Laguna Playhouse, Laguna Coordinating Council; bd. dirs. Sta-Hi Found.; dir. Opera Pacific. Served to lt. comdr. USNR, 1942-46. Decorated Purple Heart. Mem. Am. Mgmt. Assn., Nat. Newspaper Assn. (dir.), Calif. Newspaper Pubs. Assn. (dir.), Laguna Beach C. of C. (dir.), Alpha Tau Omega. Republican. Roman Catholic. Club: Dama Point Yacht. Office: 23011 Moulton Pkwy Laguna Hills CA 92653

SPITHILL, PATRICK LYALL, service company executive; b. Spokane, Wash., May 13, 1952; s. Jack Randolph and Alma Catherine (McLaughlin) S.; m. Patricia Ann Green, Jan. 29, 1974 (div. July 1982); stepchildren: Gary Allen, Howard Glen; m. Janelle Ruth Bordeleau, June 10, 1986. Grad., High Sch., Ellensburg, Wash.; Student, Cen. Wash. State Coll., 1970-72, U. Oregon, 1972; MscD (hon.), U. Metaphysics, Ventura, Calif., 1987. Entertainer various clubs, theatres, U.S.A. and Canada, 1970-78; salesperson various retail music stores, Oreg. and Wash., 1978-79; dist. sales mgr. Mfrs. Centre Holland, Elk Grove Village, Ill., 1979-81; salesman, mgr. Gould Music, Seal Beach, Calif., 1981-83; dist. sales mgr. Penning Music, Westminster, Calif., 1983-84, Midco Internat., Effingham, Ill., 1984-87; pub. relations adminstrv. asst. Tracey Locke Advt., Denver, 1987; pres. Spithill and Assocs., Larkspur, Colo., 1987—; profl. speaker devel. tng. seminars, 1987—. Author: (audio cassette) Letting Others Know You're Listening, 1987. Mem. Toastmasters Internat. Democrat. Office: Patrick Spithill and Assocs PO Box 503 Midlothian TX 76065

SPITZ, LEWIS WILLIAM, historian, educator; b. Bertrand, Nebr., Dec. 14, 1922; s. Lewis William and Pauline Mary (Griebel) S.; m. Edna Marie Huttenmaier, Aug. 14, 1948; children: Stephen Andrew, Philip Mathew. AB, Concordia Coll., 1944; MDiv, Concordia Sem., 1946; MA, U. Mo., 1947; PhD, Harvard U., 1954, DD, 1977, LLD (hon.), 1978; LlD (hon.), Wittenberg U., 1983; LittD (hon.), Harvard U., 1988. With U. Mo., Columbia, 1953-60, assoc. prof. history, 1958-60; Fulbright prof. U. Mainz, Fed. Republic of Germany, 1960-61; prof. history Stanford (Calif.) U., 1960—, William R. Kenan Jr. prof., 1974—, assoc. dean humanities and scis., 1973-77; vis. prof. Harvard U., Cambridge, Mass., 1964-65; dir. rsch. Ctr. for Reformation Rsch., Clayton, Mo., summer 1964, mem. bd. control, 1973—; sr. fellow Southeastern Medieval and Renaissance Inst., Duke U., summer 1968; vis. prof. Barnard Coll., 1980-81; sr. fellow Inst. Advance Study Princeton U., 1979-80. Author: Conrad Celtis-The German Arch-Humanist, 1957, The Religious Renaissance of the German Humanists, 1963, Life in Two Worlds-A Biography of William Sihler, 1968, The Renaissance and Reformation Movements, 2 vols., 1987, Humanismus und Reformation in der deutschen Geschichte, 1980; The Protestant Reformation, 1517-1559, 1985; mem. editorial bd.: Soundings, 1973-79, Ch. History, 1982-86; mng. editor: Archive for Reformation History, 1968-76. Recipient Harbison award for teaching Danforth Found., 1964; Guggenheim fellow, 1956; Nat. Endowment for Humanities sr. fellow, 1965; Am. Council Learned Socs. fellow, 1971; Huntington Library fellow, 1959; Inst. Advanced Study Princeton fellow, 1979-80; Pew Found. fellow, 1983. Fellow Am. Acad. Arts and Scis.; mem. Am. Soc. Reformation Rsch. (pres. 1963-64), Am. Hist. Assn., No. Calif. Renaissance Soc. (pres. 1964-65), Am. Soc. Ch. History (pres. 1976-77). Home: 827 Lathrop Dr Stanford CA 94305 Office: Stanford U Dept History Stanford CA 94305

SPITZER, MATTHEW L., retail store executive; b. Pitts., June 20, 1929; s. Martin and Ruth G. S.; student U. Buffalo, 1948-50; children—Mark, Edward, Eric, Joseph. Product line mgr. Gen. Dynamics, Rochester, N.Y., 1962-67; dir. contracts Friden div. Singer, San Leandro, Calif., 1968-69; asst. v.p. Talcott Computer Leasing, San Francisco, 1970-71; pres. Spitzer Music Co., Hayward, Calif., 1972—; chmn. bd. Leo's Audio and Music Techs., Oakland, Calif. Clubs: Commonwealth, Masons, Mensa. Office: 5447 Telegraph Ave Oakland CA 94541

SPITZKA, ROBERT E., engineering company executive, mechanical engineer; b. LaCross, Kans., Nov. 21, 1931; s. Bruno Joseph and Elizabeth Sophia (Togie) S.; m. Peggy Lucille Farnsworth, July 9, 1960; children: Carolyn, Jan Marie. BS, Purdue U., 1953; MBA, Calif. State U., Sacramento, 1970. Registered profl. engr., Calif., Va. Chief engr. Spitzka Industries, Sacramento, 1955-60; from mem. staff to v.p. McDonnell Douglas Astro, Rancho Cordova, Calif., 1960-70; program analyst Office of Legis. Analyst, Sacramento, 1970-75; program dir. Calif. Solid Waste Mgmt. Bd., Sacramento, 1975-78; mng. engr. Brown & Caldwell Cons. Engrs., Walnut Creek, Calif., 1978-83; pres. Water & Energy Mgmt., Inc., Danville, Calif., 1983—; mech. engr. McDonnell Douglas, 1960-70; cons. Brown & Caldwell, et al, Walnut Creek, 1978-83. Contbr. articles to profl. jours. Tech. advisor Grass Roots Solid Waste and Environ. Group, Sacramento, 1977; tech. advisor dept. community svcs. Cit of Milpitas, Calif., 1988; mem. Gov. Regan's Steering Com., Sacramento, 1968. With U.S. Army, 1953-55. Mem. ASME (v.p. 1987-88, pres. San Francisco chpt. 1988—), Calif. Soc. for Hosp. Engrs., Internat. Cogeneration Soc., Purdue U. Alumni Assn., Beta Gamma Sigma. Republican. Roman Catholic. Home: 79 Hillmont Pl Danville CA 94526

SPIVAK, JACQUE R., bank executive; b. San Francisco, Nov. 5, 1929; d. Robert Morris and Sadonia Clardine Breitstein; m. Herbert Spivak, Aug. 26, 1960; children—Susan, Donald, Joel, Sheri. B.S., U. So. Calif., 1949, M.S., 1950, M.B.A., 1959. Mgr. Internat. Escrow, Inc., Los Angeles, 1960-65, Greater Los Angeles Investment Co., 1965-75; mgr. escrow Transam. Title Ins. Co., Los Angeles, 1975-78; mgr. escrow, asst. v.p. Wells Fargo Bank, Beverly Hills, Calif., 1979-80; adminstr. escrow, v.p. 1st Pacific Bank, Beverly Hills, 1980-85; escrow adminstr. Century City Savs. & Loan Assn., Los Angeles, 1986-87; pres. Producers Escrow Corp., Beverly Hills., 1987—. Recipient awards PTA, Girl Scouts U.S.A., Jewish Fedn. Los Angeles, Hadassah. Mem. Calif. Escrow Assn., Nat. Assn. Bank Women, Inst. Trustees Sales officers. Republican. Jewish. Office: Producers Escrow Corp 9328 Civic Ctr Dr Beverly Hills CA 90210

SPIVEY, BRUCE E., opthalmology educator, health association executive; b. Cedar Rapids, Iowa, Aug. 29, 1934; s. William Loranzy and Grace Loretta (Barber) S.; children: Lisa, Eric; m. Patti Birge Tyson, Dec. 20, 1987. B.A., Coe Coll., 1956; M.D., U. Iowa, 1959, M.S., 1964; M.Ed., U. Ill., 1969; hon. doctorate Sc., Coe Coll., 1978. Diplomate: Am. Bd. Ophthalmology. Asst. prof. U. Iowa Coll. Medicine, Iowa City, 1966, assoc. prof., 1966-71; dean Sch. Med. Scis. U. Pacific, San Francisco, 1971-76; prof., chmn. dept. ophthalmology Pacific Med. Ctr., San Francisco, 1971-87, pres., chief exec. officer, dir., 1976—; exec. v.p., chief exec. officer Am. Acad. Ophthalmology, San Francisco, 1978—; pres., chief exec. officer Calif. Healthcare System, Bay area, 1986—; dir. Ophthalmic Pub. Co., Chgo., 1977—; v.p. Am. Bd. Med. Specialties, 1978-82, pres., 1980-82; chmn. bd. dirs. Vol. Hosps. of Am.-Northern Calif., 1985-87; mem. nat. adv. eye council NEI, NIH, 1987—. Editor: Ophthalmology for Medical Students; contbr. over 100 articles to profl. jours.; inventor instruments for eye surgery. Bd. dirs. Pacific Vision Found., San Francisco, 1977—, U.S.-China Ednl. Inst., 1978—; trustee Coe Coll., 1985—; active VA, Washington, 1987—. Served to capt. U.S. Army, 1964-66. Decorated Bronze Star; recipient Emile Javal Gold medal Internat. Contact Lens Council, San Francisco, 1982, Gradle medal Pan-Am. Assn. Ophthalmol., others. Fellow Am. Acad. Ophthalmology (Disting. Service award 1972, Sr. Honor award 1986), Am. Bd. Ophthalmology (dir. 1975-83), ACS; mem. AMA, Am. Opthalmol. Soc., Academia Ophthalmol. Internationalis, Internat. Congress Opthalmol. (sec.-gen. 1978-82). Republican. Presbyterian. Clubs: Pacific-Union; University (San Francisco). Home: 1800 Gough #4 San Francisco CA 94109 Office: Pacific Med Ctr 2340 Clay St PO Box 7999 San Francisco CA 94120

SPIZIZEN, LOUISE MYERS, musician, composer, critic; b. Lynn, Mass.; d. Louis Samuel and Lillian D. (Gordon) Myers; m. Eugene R. Schlesinger, June 19, 1948 (div.); children: Louis M., Thomas R., Kenneth G., Kathryn Ann; m. John Spizizen, Apr. 26, 1968. AB, Vassar Coll., 1949; MA, U. Calif., San Diego, 1972. Cert. instr., Calif. Composer, mus. dir. Interplayers, Inc., N.Y.C., 1949-51, Dorothea Spaeth Dancers, N.Y.C., 1949-51, Invisible Theatre, Tucson, 1980—; freelance and staff music writer La Jolla (Calif.) Light, 1974-79; staff music critic Tucson Weekly, 1984—; tchr., lectr. music history and lit., Conn., Calif., Ariz., 1960—; annotator, lectr. Norwalk (Conn.) Symphony, Sta. WNLK-FM, 1962-65; scriptwriter, panelist L.A. Philharm., San Diego Symphony, 1975-79; music panelist Calif. Arts Council, 1978; teaching-performance resident Chinese Ministry Arts Edn., 1985. Harpsichordist La Jolla Chamber Orch., 1972—, Solisti de Alcala, Old Globe Theatre, Basically Baroque Ensembles, San Diego, 1972—, Anna Magdalena Bach Quartet, Tucson, 1972—, Tucson Symphony Orch., 1982—, Ariz. Opera, Phoenix and Tucson, 1982—; composer works include Weary with Toil, 1970; contbr. articles and revs. to mus. publs. and newspapers. Founder, artistic dir. San Diego Mini-Concerts, Inc., 1972; bd. dirs. Ariz. Mini-Concerts, Inc., Tucson, 1980—; music program com. Tucson Symphony Orch., 1988—. NARAS grantee, 1988. Mem. Music Critics Assn., Early Music Am. (founding), Am. Fedn. Musicians, Ariz. Composers Forum (composer designee), Ariz. Early Music Soc. (founding), Ariz. Music Tchrs. Assn. (pres. 1985-86), Nat. Soc. Arts and Letters. Home and Office: 2540 Camino La Zorrela Tucson AZ 85718

SPOEHEL, JERRI HOSKINS, volunteer agency executive; b. Oak Park, Ill., Mar. 13, 1932; d. George Alex and Myrtle Jean (McBean) Hoskins; BA in English cum laude, Coll. Wooster, 1953; m. Edwin H. Spoehel, Apr. 16, 1955; children: Ronald Ross, Jacqueline Jean. Instr., Success-Plus, 1974; columnist Daily News, San Fernando Valley, Van Nuys, Calif., 1970-85; community rels. dir. Sta. KCSN-FM, Nat. Pub. Radio, Northridge, Calif., 1975-85; exec. dir. Vol. Ctr. of San Fernando Valley, 1985-89; sec. Vol. Ctrs. of So. Calif.; mem. Pres. Assocs. Calif. State U., Northridge; panelist/seminar instr. Nat. Devel. Conf., Corp. Pub. Broadcasting. Recipient Nat. Abe Lincoln Merit award So. Bapt. Radio and TV Commn.; named Disting. Citizen of Northridge; other awards. Mem. AAUW (pres.), Pub. Rels. Roundtable, Dirs. Vols. in Agys., Soroptimists (pres.), Northridge Cultural Arts Club. Mem. Unity Ch.

SPOEHR, ALEXANDER, anthropologist, retired educator; b. Tucson, Aug. 23, 1913; s. Herman Augustus and Florence (Mann) S; m. Anne Dinsdale Harding, Aug. 2, 1941; children—Alexander Harding, Helene Spoehr Clarke. A.B., U. Chgo., 1934, Ph.D., 1940; D.Sc. (hon.), U. Hawaii, 1952. From asst. curator to curator Field Mus., Chgo., 1940-53; dir. Bishop Mus., Honolulu, 1953-62; prof. Yale U., New Haven, 1953-62; chancellor East-West Ctr., Honolulu, 1962-63; prof. anthropology U. Pitts., 1964-78, prof. emeritus, 1978; U.S. mem. South Pacific Commn., 1957-60; mem. Pacific sci. bd. NRC, Washington, 1955-61, chmn. 1958-61. N.Am. and Pacific ethnological and archaeol. researcher. Contbr. numerous articles to profl. jours. Trustee Bishop Mus., 1981-84; Served to lt. USNR, 1942-45. Fellow Am. Anthropol. Assn. (pres. 1965), AAAS; mem. Nat. Acad. Scis., Sigma Xi. Home: 2548 Makiki Heights Dr Honolulu HI 96822

SPOELSTRA, JON, professional basketball executive. s. Watson Spoelstra; m. Lisa Spoelstra; children: Monica, Erik. Grad. in communications, U. Notre Dame. With Portland (Oreg.) Trail Blazers, NBA, 1979—, now sr. v.p., gen. mgr. Office: Portland Trail Blazers Llyod Bldg Ste 950 700 NE Multnomah St Portland OR 97232 *

SPOFFORD, ROBERT HOUSTON, advertising executive; b. N.Y.C., Apr. 3, 1941; s. Robert Knowlton and Linda P. (Houston) S.; m. Susan Allerton, Aug. 29, 1964; children: Margaret, Robert Christopher. BEE, Cornell U., 1964. Account exec. Batton, Barton, Durstine and Osborn, N.Y.C., 1964-71, v.p., account supr., 1971-78; v.p., mgmt. supr. Batton, Barton, Durstine and Osborn, Mpls., 1978-80; sr. v.p. Batton, Barton, Durstine and Osborn, N.Y.C., 1981-86; exec. v.p., dir. client svc. Batton, Barton, Durstine and Osborn, L.A., 1986—. Contbr. articles to profl. jours. Committeeman Dem. Cen. Com., Westchester County, N.Y., 1974-78. Mem. Am. Mktg. Assn., Western States Advt. Agy. Assn., Manhattan Country Club. Unitarian. Home: 449 35th St Manhattan Beach CA 90266 Office: Batton Barton et al 10960 Wilshire Blvd Los Angeles CA 90024

SPOONER, ELAINE MARGARET, information services director; b. Woodsville, N.H., Mar. 22, 1952; d. Parker Jonas and Marilyn Blanche (Foss) S. BA, Boston U., 1978. Project leader John Hancock Life Ins., Boston, 1971-77; project mgr. Union Bank, L.A., 1977-78; systems analyst Warner Bros, Burbank, Calif., 1978-80; dir. mgmt. info. systems, facilities div. 20th Century Fox, Beverly Hills, Calif., 1980-83; sr. cons., prodn. automation mgr. MCA, Inc., Universal City, Calif., 1983-87; dir. info. svcs. MCA TV Group, Universal City, 1988—. Mem. Assn. Entertainment Industry Computer Profls. (bd. dirs. 1984-88), NAFE, Women in Film, Acad. TV Arts and Scis. Office: MCA Inc 100 Universal City Pla Universal City CA 91608

SPOOR, JAMES EDWARD, company executive; b. Rockford, Ill., Feb. 19, 1936; s. Frank Kendall and Genevieve Eileen (Johnson) S.; B.S. in Psychology, U. Ill., 1958; m. Nancy E. Carlson, Sept. 8, 1962; children—Sybll K., Kendall P., Andrea K., Marcie K. Personnel mgr. Nat. Sugar Refining Co., N.Y.C., 1960-64, Pepsico, Inc., N.Y.C., Auburn, N.Y., 1964-67; mgr. internat. personnel Control Data Corp., Mpls., 1967-75; v.p. personnel and employee relations Vetco, Inc., Ventura, Calif., 1975-79; v.p. employee relations Hamilton Bros. Oil Co., Denver, 1979-84; pres. Spectrum Human Resource Systems Corp., 1984—; cons., speaker on human resources. Mem. adv. bd. Salvation Army, 1978-79; chmn. Spl. Commn. for Ventura County Bd. Suprs., 1978; mem. task force on human resources Colo. Sch. Mines, 1983. Served with U.S. Army, 1958-60. Mem. Am. Soc. Personnel Adminstrn. (contbg. author handbook), Assn. for Human Resource Systems Profls., Colo. Soc. Personnel Adminstrn. Republican. Episcopalian. Clubs: Denver, Masons, Shriners, Lions. Contbg. author: Am. Soc. Personnel Adminstrn. Personnel and Indsl. Relations Handbook.

SPORCK, CHARLES E., electronic products manufacturing company executive; b. 1928. B.S. in Mech. Engring., Cornell U. With semiconductor div. Fairchild Camera and Instrument Co., 1949-67; pres., chief exec. officer Nat. Semiconductor Corp., Santa Clara, Calif., 1967—, also dir. Office: Nat Semiconductor Corp 2900 Semiconductor Dr Santa Clara CA 95051 *

SPRAGUE, PETER JULIAN, semiconductor and computer company executive; b. Detroit, Apr. 29, 1939; s. Julian K. and Helene (Coughlin) S.; m. Tjasa Krofta, Dec. 19, 1959; children: Carl, Steven, Kevin, Michael. Student, Yale U., 1961, MIT, 1961, Columbia U., 1962-66. Chmn. bd. dirs. Nat. Semiconductor Corp., Santa Clara, Calif.; bd. dirs. GEO Internat. Corp. Trustee Strang Clinic. Club: Yale. Home: 249 Undermountain Rd Lenox MA 01240 Office: Indata Corp 645 Fifth Ave 4th Fl New York NY 10022 also: Nat Semiconductor Corp PO Box 58090 Santa Clara CA 95052

SPRAGUE, RODERICK, III, anthropologist, educator; b. Albany, Oregon, Feb. 18, 1933; s. Roderick and Mary Curtis (Willis) S.; m. Linda Ferguson, May 28, 1975; children: Roderick IV, Katherine K., Frederick L., Alexander W. BA, Wash. State U., 1955, MA, 1959; PhD, U. Ariz., 1967. Staff archaeologist Wash. State U., Pullman, 1965-67; asst. prof. U. Idaho, Moscow, 1967-69, head dept. anthropology, 1968-81, dir. anthropology lab., 1968—, assoc. prof., 1969-72, prof. anthropolgy, 1972—; fgn. expert Inner Mongolia U., Huhhot, Peoples Republic of China, 1986-87; bd. trustees N.W. Sci. Assn., 1968-71. Co-author: A Bibliography of Glass Trade Beads in North America, 1980; editor N.W. Anthrop. Rsch. Notes jour., 1970—. With U.S. Army, 1956-58. Fellow Am. Anthrop. Assn., AAAS; mem. Soc. for Hist. Archaeology (sec., treas. 1971-74, pres. 1976, rev. editor 1977—), Soc. for Am. Archaeology, Sigma Xi (pres. local chpt. 1980). Office: U Idaho Lab Anthropology Moscow ID 83843

SPRAINGS, VIOLET EVELYN, psychologist; b. Omaha, Aug. 1, 1930; d. Henry Elbert and Straunella (Hunter) S.; A.B., U. Calif., Berkeley, 1948, M.A., 1951, postgrad., 1960-64; Ph.D., U. San Francisco, 1982. Tchr., Oakland (Calif.) Public Schs., 1951-58; psychologist Med. Edn. Diagnostic Ctr., San Francisco, 1959-62; dir. psychol. edn. and lang. services Calif. Dept. Edn., 1963-71; asst. prof. San Francisco State U., 1964-71; assoc. prof. ednl. psychology Calif. State U., Hayward, 1971-79; dir. Lang. Assocs., Orinda, Lafayette and Redwood City, 1971-79; psychologist in pvt. practice, 1962—; dir. Western Women's Bank, Sprainas Acad.; mem. adv. bd. Bay Area Health Systems Agy.; instr. U. Calif., Berkeley extension, 1964—; mem. oral bd. for Ednl. Psychologists, 1972—; mem. Calif. Dept. Task Force on Psychol. Assessment, 1987—. mem. adv. com. Foothill Jr. Coll. Dist. Recipient Phoebe Apperson Heart award San Francisco Examiner, 1968. Mem. Am. Psychol. Assn., Internat. Neuropsychol. Assn. (charter), Calif. Psychol. Assn., Calif. Assn. Sch. Psychologists and Psychometrists, Western Psychol. Assn., Nat. Council Negro Women, AAUP, Delta Sigma Theta, Psi Chi, Pi Lambda Theta. Contbr. articles to profl. jours. Home: 170 Glorietta Blvd Orinda CA 94563 Office: 3408 Deer Hill Rd Lafayette CA 94549

SPRAKER, LEONARD CHARLES, real estate developer; b. Little Falls, N.Y., Aug. 29, 1939; s. Leonard Francis and Mary Frances (Stegich) S.; m. Elizabeth Nina Setticase, Aug. 19, 1967; children: Kiersten Mary, Larissa Renee, Leonard Joseph. AAS in Electronics, Mohawk Valley Community Coll., Utica, N.Y., 1960; BA in Econs., Utica Coll., 1968; MBA, Rochester Inst. Tech., 1977. Customer svcs. mgr. GE, Utica, 1970-72; product cost acct. Xerox Corp., Rochester, N.Y., 1973-76, corp. auditor, 1976-78; ops. mgr. Xerox Corp., Phoenix, 1979-81, sales mgr., 1981-82; fin. programs mgr. Honeywell Corp., Phoenix, 1978-79; v.p. Great Western Bank, Phoenix, 1982-83; corp. customer svcs. mgr. Intel Corp., Phoenix, 1983-85; real estate developer, investor Glendale, Ariz., 1986—. Commiteeman Rep. party, Utica, 1967-70. Served with U.S. Army, 1961-64. Mem. Glendale Bd. Realtors. Home: 10021 N 50th Ave Glendale AZ 85302 Office: 8024 N 51st Ave Ste 3 Glendale AZ 85302

SPREITER, JOHN ROBERT, mechanical and aerospace engineering educator; b. Oak Park, Minn., Oct. 23, 1921; s. Walter F. and Agda E. (Hokanson) S.; m. Brenda Owens, Aug. 7, 1953; children: Terry A., Janet L., Christine P., Hilary M. B in Aero. Engring., U. Minn., 1943; MS, Stanford U., 1947, PhD, 1954. Research scientist Ames Research Ctr. NASA, Moffett Field, Calif., 1943-62, chief theoretical studies br., 1962-69; prof. applied mechanics and aeros. and astronautics Stanford (Calif.) U., 1968—; lectr. Stanford U., 1951-68; cons. Nielsen Engring. and Research Inc., Mountain View, Calif., 1968-85, RMA Aerospace, Mountain View, 1985—. Contbr. numerous articles to profl. jours. Served with USN, 1944-46. Fellow AIAA, Royal Astron. Soc.; mem. Am. Geophys. Union, Am. Phys. Soc., Sigma Xi, Tau Beta Pi, Tau Omega. Democrat. Clubs: Saratoga (Calif.) Tennis (treas. 1955-65); Fremont Hills Country (Los Altos Hills, Calif.). Home: 1250 Sandalwood Ln Los Altos CA 94022 Office: Stanford U Div Applied Mechanics Stanford CA 94305

SPREITZER, CYNTHIA ANN, computer programming professional; b. Chgo., July 16, 1953; d. John Herbert and Patricia Virginia (Tieman) S. BS in Math., Loyola U., Chgo., 1975. Cert. data processor, 1986. Sr. Arthur Andersen and Co., Chgo., 1975-80; lead analyst Larimer County, Ft. Collins, Colo., 1980—. Mem. Assn. Inst. Cert. Computer Profls., Computer Security Inst., Data Processing Mgmt. Assn. Roman Catholic. Home: 610 Grove Ct Loveland CO 80537 Office: Larimer County PO Box 1190 Fort Collins CO 80522

SPRENKLE, PETER MCKEE, site education executive; b. Lansing, Mich., Jan. 14, 1937; s. William Howard and Elisabeth McPherson (McKee) S.; m. June ElsieSprenkle. BBA, U. Miami, 1957. Systems engr. mktg. IBM Corp., Conn., 1957-65; with edn. fin., planning dept. IBM Corp., N.Y.C., 1965-77; new products dept. IBM Corp., Boulder, Colo., 1977-80; materials mgmt. planner IBM Corp., Boulder, 1980-84, prodn. mgr., 1984-85, indsl. engring. mgr., 1985-87, site edn. mgr., 1987—. Bd. dirs. YMCA, Boulder, 1988—; founder Boulder Valley Girsl Softball Assn., 1978, pres. 1978-81, treas. 1981—; pres. Bd. Edn., Ossining, N.Y. Mem. Kiwanis (bd. dirs. Foothills chpt. 1987—). Republican. Baptist. Home: 330 Hopi Pl Boulder CO 80303

SPRINGER, CHARLES EDWARD, state justice; b. Reno, Feb. 20, 1928; s. Edwin and Rose Mary Cecelia (Kelly) S.; m. Jacqueline Sirkegian, Mar. 17, 1951; 1 dau., Kelli Ann. B.A., U. Nev., Reno, 1950; LL.B., Georgetown U., 1953; LL.M., U. Va., 1984. Bar: Nev. 1953, D.C. 1953. Pvt. practice Reno, 1953-80; atty. gen. State of Nev., 1962; legis. legal adv. to gov. State of Nev., 1958-62; legis. bill drafter Nev. Legislature, 1955-57; mem. faculty Nat. Coll. Juvenile Justice, Reno, 1978—; juvenile master 2d Jud. Dist. Nev., 1973-80; judge Supreme Ct. Nev., Carson City, 1981—; chmn. Jud. Selection Commn., 1981—; trustee Nat. Council Juvenile and Family Ct. Judges, 1983-85; mem. faculty U. Nev., Reno, McGeorge Sch. Law, 1982—. Served with AUS, 1945-47. Recipient Outstanding Contbn. to Juvenile Justice award Nat. Council Juvenile and Family Ct. Judges, 1980. Mem. Am. Judicature Soc., Am. Trial Lawyers Assn., ABA. Office: Nev Supreme Ct Capitol Complex 100 N Carson St Carson City NV 89710

SPRINGER, GERALD WILLIAM, sales executive; b. Amherst, Ohio, Nov. 13, 1943; s. Raymond W. and Ione J. (Myers) S.; m. Marilyn F. Gregg, Aug. 28, 1971. BBA, Kent State U., 1966. Dist. sales mgr. Flintkote Co., Kent, Ohio, 1970-72, US Gypson Co., Denver, 1972-75, Ameron Corp., Denver, 1975-79; nat. sales mgr. Blue Bird Internat. Co., Englewood, Colo., 1979-81; sales mgr. Smith & Wesson, Golden, Colo., 1981-85; pres. The West & Assocs., Inc., Golden, 1985—. Served with Ohio N.G., 1963-67. Jeffco Posse Club. Republican. Congregationalist. Office: The West and Assocs Inc 4895 Easley Rd Golden CO 80403

SPRINGER, KARL GOERGE, religious organization administrator; b. N.Y.C., Oct. 20, 1949; s. Gustave and Florence (Hacker) S.; m. Jane Anne Condon, June 10, 1978 (div. 1981). BA, Brandeis U., 1971; DD, Naropa Inst., 1977. Ordained to ministry, Vajradhatu Buddhist Assn., 1977. Dir. Karme Choling Retreat Str., Barnet, Vt., 1971-75; dir., chief exec. officer Naropa Inst., Boulder, Colo., 1975-77; v.p. Vajradhatu Internat., Boulder, 1977—; exec. dir. U.S. Com. UN Lumbini Project, Boulder, 1983—; founder, co-chmn. Am. Buddhist Congress, L.A., 1986—; bd. dirs. Karma Triyana Dharmachakra, Woodstock, N.Y., San Luis Valley Tibetan Project, Crestone, Colo., World Resources Com., Bangkok; regional dir. World Fellowship Buddhists, Bangkok. Compiler, dir. Asian Art Exhbn.. MIT, 1974; contbr. articles to to mags. Del. UN Conf. on Disarmament and Devel., N.Y.C., 1987. Mem. UN Assn., UN Assn. in India, Acad. Polit. Sci. Democrat. Home: 1135 10th St Boulder CO 80302 Office: Vajradhatu Internat 1345 Spruce St Boulder CO 80302

SPRINGER, PAUL DAVID, lawyer, motion picture company executive; b. N.Y.C., Apr. 27, 1942; s. William W. and Alma (Markowitz) S.; m. Mariann Frankfurt, Aug. 16, 1964; children: Robert, William. BA, U. Bridgeport, 1963; JD, Bklyn. Law Sch., 1967. Bar: U.S. Dist. Ct. (so. and ea. dists.) N.Y. 1968, U.S. Ct. Appeals (2d cir.) 1970, U.S. Supreme Ct. 1973. Assoc. Johnson & Tannenbaum, N.Y.C., 1968-70; assoc. counsel Columbia Pictures, N.Y.C., 1970; assoc. counsel Paramount Pictures, N.Y.C., 1970-79, v.p., theatrical distbn. counsel, 1979-85, sr. v.p., chief resident counsel East Coast, 1985-87; sr. v.p., asst. gen. counsel Paramount Pictures, Los Angeles, 1987—. Trustee West Cunningham Park Civic Assn., Fresh Meadows, N.Y., 1978—. Mem. ABA, Assn. of Bar of City of N.Y. Office: Paramount Pictures Corp 5555 Melrose Ave Los Angeles CA 90038-3197

SPRINGER, SALLY PEARL, university administrator; b. Bklyn., Mar. 19, 1947; d. Nathaniel Margulies and Fanny (Schoen) S.; m. Hakon Hope; children: Erik Jacob Hope, Mollie Liv Hope. BS, Bklyn. Coll., 1967; PhD, Stanford U., 1971. Postdoctoral fellow Stanford U. Med. Sch., Calif., 1971-73; asst. prof. SUNY-Stony Brook, 1973-78, assoc. provost, 1981-85, assoc. prof., 1978-87; exec. asst. to chancellor U. Calif., Davis, 1987—. Author (with others): Left Brain, Right Brain, 1981 (Am. Psychol. Found. Disting. Contbr. award 1981), 2d edit., 1985, 3d edit., 1989; How to Succeed in College, 1982; contbr. articles to profl. jours. Mem. Internat. Neuropsychol. Soc., Behavior Genetics Assn., Psychonomic Soc., Acoustical Soc. Am. Office: U Calif Office Chancellor Davis CA 95616

SPRINGER, WILMA MARIE, elementary educator; b. Goshen, Ind., Jan. 13, 1933; d. Noah A. and Laura D. (Miller) Kaufman; m. Walter Frederick Springer, May 25, 1957; children: Anita Daniel, Timothy, Mark. BA, Goshen Coll., 1956; MS, Bradley U., 1960. Tchr. Topeka (Ind.) Elem. Sch., 1956-57, Metamora (Ill.) Grade Sch., 1957-59, Bellflower (Calif.) Unified Sch. Dist., 1960-61, 68-89, Jefferson Elem. Sch., Bellflower, 1989—; chairperson gifted and Talented Edn. Lindstrom Elem. Sch., Lakewood, Calif., 1986-89, Regional Ednl. TV Adv. Council, Lakewood, 1985-87; stage mgr. Hour of Power T.V., Crystal Cathedral, 1983—; mem. Calif. State Program Quality Rev. Team, 1989—. Contbr. articles in field. Campaigner Sch. Bd. Mem., 1984, Bellflower City Council, 1988, State Senator and Assemblymen, 1986-87; petition circulator, State Initiatives, 1987-88; mem. Women's Ministries of Crystal Cathedral, Garden Grove, Calif. (bd. dirs. 1978-88, recipient Cathedral Star 1985). Classroom Tchrs. Instructional Improvement Program grantee, State of Calif., 1986-87; recipient Recognition award Regional Ednl. TV Adv. Council, 1986. Mem. Bellflower Edn. Assn. (elem. dir. 1986-88, treas. 1988-89, v.p. 1989—), Calif. Tchrs. Assn. (del. 1986-87), Nat. Edn. Assn. (del. nat. conv. 1986, 87), AAUW. Republican. Mem. Reformed Churches of Am. Home: 3180 Marna Ave Long Beach CA 90808 Office: Jefferson Elem Sch 10027 E Rose St Bellflower CA 90706

SPROUL, JOHN ALLAN, public utility executive; b. Oakland, Calif., Mar. 28, 1924; s. Robert Gordon and Ida Amelia (Wittschen) S.; m. Marjorie Ann Hauck, June 20, 1945; children: John Allan, Malcolm J., Richard O., Catherine E. A.B., U. Calif., Berkeley, 1947, LL.B., 1949. Bar: Calif. 1950. Atty. Pacific Gas & Electric Co., San Francisco, 1949-52, 56-62, sr. atty., 1962-70, asst. gen. counsel, 1970-71, v.p. gas supply, 1971-76, sr. v.p., 1976-77, exec. v.p., 1977-89, cons., 1989—; gen. counsel Pacific Gas Transmission Co., 1970-73, v.p., 1973-79, chmn. bd., 1979-89, also bd. dirs.; atty. Johnson & Stanton, San Francisco, 1952-56; bd. dirs. Alta. and So. Gas Co. Ltd., Alta. Natural Gas Co. Ltd., Oreg. Steel Mills, Inc. Bd. dirs. Hastings Coll. of Law. Served to 1st lt. USAAF, 1943-46. Mem. Calif. Bar Assn., Am. Gas Assn., Pacific Coast Gas Assn. Clubs: Engineers, World Trade (San Francisco); Commonwealth, Bohemian, Pacific-Union, Orinda Country. Home: 8413 Buckingham Dr El Cerrito CA 94530 Office: Pacific Gas & Electric Co 245 Market St Rm 1421 San Francisco CA 94106

SPROUSE, JOHN ALWYN, retail executive; b. Tacoma, Nov. 23, 1908; s. Robert Allen and Jenne (Glaessel) S.; m. Mary Louise Burpee, Dec. 27, 1932 (dec. June 1954); children—Lucy (Mrs. Clyde B. Fletcher), Robert Allen II, John Edward; m. Barbara Barker, May 22, 1955 (dec. July 1983). Student, U. Oreg., 1926-28. With Sprouse-Reitz Stores Inc., Portland, Oreg., 1928—, asst. to pres., 1945-61, pres., 1961-74, chmn. bd., 1974-86, hon. chmn., 1986—; Expert cons. to Q.M. Gen., 1943-45. Mem. U.S. Power Squadron, USCG Aux., Delta Upsilon. Clubs: Rotarian. (Portland), Yacht (Portland), Arlington (Portland), Multnomah (Portland). Office: Sprouse-Reitz Stores Inc PO Box 8996 1411 SW Morrison St Portland OR 97208-8996

SPROUSE, ROBERT ALLEN, II, retail chain store executive; b. Portland, Oreg., Dec. 25, 1935; s. John Alwyn and Mary Louise (Burpee) S.; m. Frances Carolyn Russell, June 22, 1957. Student, Williams Coll., 1953-57. With Sprouse-Reitz Stores Inc., Portland, 1957—; buyer, sec. Sprouse-Reitz Stores Inc., 1963-69, v.p., 1969-73; pres. —, 1973—; chief exec. officer Sprouse-Reitz Stores Inc., 1986—; also bd. dirs. Active Jr. Achievement, Good Samaritan Hosp. Found. Mem. Chief Execs. Orgn., Portland Met. C. of C., Theta Delta Chi. Republican. Episcopalian. Clubs: Multnomah Athletic (Portland); Arlington. Lodge: Rotary. Office: Sprouse-Reitz Stores Inc PO Box 8996 Portland OR 97208-8996

SPRUNGL, JANICE MARIE, nurse; b. Brooklyn, Ohio, Mar. 9, 1960; d. Donald Edward and Delores Jane (Slys) S. BS in Nursing, U. Akron, 1982. Lic. nurse, Ohio. Commd. 1st lt. U.S. Air Force, 1982, advanced through grades to capt., 1986; clin. nurse Med. Ctr. Keesler U.S. Air Force, Biloxi, Miss., 1982-86; charge nurse Med. Ctr. Keesler U.S. Air Force, 1986-88; charge nurse U.S. Air Force Acad. Hosp. U.S. Air Force, Colorado Springs, Colo., 1988—. Vol., Spl. Olympics, Keesler AFB, 1983-87; fundraiser, Biloxi unit Am. Cancer Soc., 1984. Mem. Ohio Nursing Assn., Soc. Peripheral Vascular Nursing, Air Force Assn.

SPUND, LANI CHARLES, banker, managment information systems executive; b. Los Angeles, Dec. 17, 1948; d. Allen and Ann Spund; m. June Lundstrom, Sept. 12, 1979. BS in Indsl. Mgmt., San Diego State U., 1972, MBA, 1979; PhD, Calif. Western U., 1973; M in Pub. Acctg., Calif. State U., Long Beach, 1977. Lic. master USCG. Chief exec. officer Ribbitt Enterprises, San Diego, Calif., 1968-72; mfg. mgr. Max Factor, Hawthorne, Calif., 1972-75; MIS dir. Campbell Industries, San Diego, 1975-78; dir., prin. Gottfried Cons. (ACME), Los Angeles, 1978-83; sr. v.p. Citicorp, Los Angeles and London, 1983-88; dir. global systems Architecture, Apple Computer, 1989—; bd. dirs. Spund Corp, Los Angeles, Fgn. Property Mgmt. Inc., London, Foolproof Marine, Los Angeles, chief exec. officer, 1984—; mem. staff Ford Milpedas Psychology Study, Los Angeles, 1969; mem. faculty UCLA Sch. Bus. and Mgmt., 1983, U. So. Calif. Grad. Sch. Bus., Los Angeles, 1980. Author: CETA Effectiveness Measurement System, 1975. Mem. Am. Prodn. and Inventory Control Soc., Inc. (cert.). Home: 11011 Seven Hills Dr Tujunga CA 91042

SREENIVASAN, KRISHNAMACHAR, computer scientist; b. Tumkur, Karnataka, India, May 1, 1937; came to U.S., 1960; s. Tirumale Krishnamachar and Vedavalli (Iyengar) K.; m. Padma Raman, Sept. 8, 1967; children: Mukund, Meera. BE, U. Mysore, Bangalore, 1957; MS, Indian Inst. Sci., Bangalore, 1959; PhD, U. Pa., 1967. Postdoctoral fellow U. Pa., Phila., 1967-69; sr. computer analyst RCA Corp., Cinnaminson, N.J., 1969-72; mem. tech. staff The Mitre Corp., Bedford, Mass., 1972-77; sr. computer architect Amdahl Corp., Sunnyvale, Calif., 1977-79; sr. computer scientist SRI, Internat., Menlo Park, Calif., 1979-81; project leader Ford Aerospace Corp., Palo Alto, Calif., 1981-84; project mgr. GE/CALMA, Milpitas, Calif., 1984-87; mem. tech. staff Hewlett-Packard, Inc., Cupertino, Calif., 1987—; lectr. Boston U., 1974-76, San Jose (Calif.) State U., 1983-85. Home: 2156 Bellview Dr Palo Alto CA 94303

SRIVASTAVA, KARUNESH, electrical engineer; b. Bareilly, Up, India, July 13, 1943; arrived in U.S., 1969; s. Shiam Bahadur and Hansmukhi S.; m. Manishi Srivastava, 1973; children: Ritesh, Sumeet. BSc, Bareilly Coll., 1961; BEE, Roorkee (India) U., 1967; MEE, USC, 1971. Registered profl. engr., Calif. Elec. test engr. AEI, Fullerton, Calif., 1971-72; elec. engr. D.M.J.M. Corp., L.A., 1973-74, Parsons Corp., Pasadena, Calif., 1974-78, Santafe Internat. Corp., Alhambra, Calif., 1978-86; cons. engr. K.S. Cons. Engrs., Laguna Hills, Calif., 1986—; pres. K.S. Cons. Engr., Laguna Hills. Mem. IEEE, NSPE, Soc. Mil. Engrs., Calif. Soc. Profl. Engrs. Home: 25771 Terra Bella Laguna Hills CA 92653 Office: KS Cons Engrs PO Box 3767 Laguna Hills CA 92654

SROUFE, J. PARKER, systems integration executive; b. Pasco, Wash.; s. James Parker and Helen Louise (Marsh) S.; m. Evelyn Therese Graves, June 23, 1965. BA in Econs., U. Wash., 1965. CPA, Wash. Indsl. engr. Boeing Co., Seattle, 1966-74; supr. Peat Marwick & Mitchell, Seattle, 1971-77; v.p. Princess Tours, Seattle, 1977-78; v.p., chief fin. officer Unico, Inc., Seattle, 1978-83; pres. Parker Sroufe Assocs., Seattle, 1983-86; chmn., chief exec. officer ESCA Corp., Bellevue, Wash., 1986—; mem. vis. com. sch. engrs. U. Wash., Seattle, 1988. Chmn., bd. trustees Seattle Children's Home, 1979-85. Served as sgt. AUS, 1968. Mem. Wash. Soc. CPAs, Fin. Exec. Inst., Wash. Athletic Club. Club: Wash. Athletic. Home: 2111 Broadmoor Dr Seattle WA 98112 Office: ESCA Corp 13208 Northrup Way Bellevue WA 98005

STAATS, MARK EDWARD, restaurant manager; b. Milw., Dec. 6, 1964; s. Earl M. and Barbara J. (Bachman) S. Student, No. Ariz. U., 1989. Mgr. in tng. Kinney Shoe Corp., Mesa, Ariz., 1980-87; restaurant mgr. Cafe Espress, Flagstaff, Ariz., 1987-89; asst. mgr. Clark House Fine Dining Restaurant, Flagstaff, 1989—. Home: 606 S Elden St Flagstaff AZ 86001

STACEY, PAUL F(RICK), JR., controller; b. Salem, Mass., Sept. 4, 1951; s. Paul F.and Josephine F. (Kelleher) S.; m. Jean Eaves, Mar. 8, 1980. BS with honors, Bently Coll., 1973. Auditor Def. contract Agy., Lynn, Mass., 1972-73, Arthur Andersen & Co., Boston, 1973-76; acct. Friendly Ice Cream Corp., Wilbraham, Mass., 1976-77; contr. Bobby McGee's U.S.A., Inc., Phoenix, 1977-79; v.p., contr. Western Farm Mgmt. Co., Western Commodities Co., Visalia, Calif., 1979-80; fin. cons. Stacey & Stacey, Visalia, Calif., 1981—; treas., contr. Visalia Citrus Packing Group, 1985—. Recipient Cert. Achievement Mass. Soc. CPA's, 1973. Mem. Nat. Assn. Accts. (manuscript dir. 1972-73). Republican. Home: 12716 Ave 328 Visalia CA 93291 Office: Visalia Citrus Packing Group PO Box 2800 Visalia CA 93291

STACKLIN, CHRISTOPHER ANTHONY, chemical engineer; b. San Diego, Feb. 14, 1960; s. Howard Anthony and Mary Regina (Masako Fukuda) S. BS in Chem. Engring., Calif. State Poly. U., Pomona, 1984. Printed cir. fabricant Hewlett Packard Co., San Diego, 1977-78; structural-archtl. engring. technician Fluor Tech., Inc., Irvine, Calif., 1979-80, control systems engring. technician, 1981, process systems engring. technician, 1982, cost and scheduling engring. technician, 1983, control systems engr., 1984, process engr., 1985-86; reliability availability and maintainability engr. Advanced Tech. div. Fluor Daniel, Inc., Irvine, Calif., 1986—; computer cons. KPT, Newport Beach, Calif., 1987—. Contbr. articles to profl. publs. Mem. Am. Inst. Chem. Engrs., Inventors Workshop Internat. Republican. Office: Fluor Daniel Inc 3333 Michelson Dr Irvine CA 92730

STACKPOLE, MICHAEL AUSTIN, writer; b. Wausau, Wis., Nov. 27, 1957; s. James Ward and Janet Marie (Kerin) S. BA in History, U. Vt., 1979. Store mgr. Flying Buffalo, Inc., Scottsdale, Ariz., 1979-80, game designer, editor, 1981-83, prodn. coordinator, 1984-86; cons. Coleco Industries, Hartford, Conn., 1980-81; freelance writer, designer Phoenix, 1986—; creative cons. Interplay Prodns., Costa Mesa, Calif., 1987—, Fasa Corp., Chgo., 1988—; mem. Game Speakers Bur., Game Mfrs. Assn., Plano, Tex., 1988. Author: Warrior: En Garde, Warrior: Riposte, 1988, Warrior: Coupé, Lethal Heritage, 1989; author, designer computer game: Wasteland, 1988 (Best Adventure Game of Yr. 1988); author game: Stormhaven, 1983 (Best Adventure of Yr. 1983); contbr. articles to profl. jours. Chmn. Phoenix Skeptics, 1988—. Mem. Acad. Gaming Arts and Design, Acad. Game Critics (exec. dir. 1981—), Sci. Fiction Writers Am., Small Press Writers and Artists Orgn. Democrat. Roman Catholic. Home: 3816 E McDowell Apt 204 Phoenix AZ 85008-4328 Office: Flying Buffalo Inc 8192 E Thomas Scottsdale AZ 85251

STADLEY, PAT ANNA MAY GOUGH (MRS. JAMES M. STADLEY), author; b. El Paso, Tex., Aug. 31, 1918; d. Thomas and Leona (Plitt) Gough; A.A., Chaffey Jr. Coll., 1936; m. James M. Stadley, Aug. 15, 1936; children—William T., Jerry M. Author books, anthologies, short stories published in over 15 fgn. langs., works include: The Black Leather Barbarians, 1960; Autumn of a Hunter (Edgar Allen Poe spl. award 1970, produced as The Deadly Hunt TV Friday Night Movie Week 1971), 1970; The Deadly Hunt; 1977; The Murder Hunt, 1977; also numerous short stories including The Doe and The Gantlet, 1957, The Waiting Game, 1961, Kurdistan Payload, 1962, Something for the Club, 1963, The Big Measure, 1976, The Tender Trap, 1977, The Stranger, 1980. Democrat. Mem. Christian Ch. Clubs: Calif. Writers (v.p. 1967) (Citrus Heights), Calif. Writers (v.p. 1967—), Mystery Writers Am. Home: 6439 Donegal Dr Apt 2 Citrus Heights CA 95610

STAEHLE, ALAN WALLACE, county police and public safety official; b. Rochester, N.Y., Mar. 13, 1941; s. Henry C. and Isabel M. Staehle. Student, U. Colo., 1959-60, U. Colo., 1973-74. Cert. Peace Officer, Colo., Peace Officer Tng. Instr., Colo. Patrolman Boulder Police Dept., 1968-70, supr., 1971; capt. patrol Boulder County Sheriff's Dept., 1972, 74-76, capt. communications, 1973, capt. detectives, 1977-82, undersheriff, 1983—; chmn. automation task force, Boulder County, 1983. Named Officer of Month Boulder Jaycees, 1968; recipient Disting. Service award Boulder Optimists, 1981. Mem. AMA, Internat. Assn. Chiefs of Police, World Space Found. (founding), Planetary Soc., Smithsonian Instn., Am. Mus. Natural History, Nat. Sheriffs Assn., Cousteau Soc., Colo. Hist. Soc., Denver Mus. Natural History, Trout Unltd., Air and Space Smithsonian (charter). Office: Boulder County Sheriff's Dept 1777 6th St Boulder CO 80302

STAEHLE, ROBERT L., foundation executive; b. Rochester, N.Y., Apr. 22, 1955; s. Henry Carl and Isabel Montgomery S. BS in Aero. and Astronautic Engring., Purdue U., 1977. Prin. investigator Skylab Expt. ED-31 (bacteria aboard Skylab), NASA/Marshall Space Flight Center, Huntsville, Ala., 1972-74; student trainee engring. Skylab Expt. ED-31 (bacteria aboard Skylab), NASA/Marshall Space Flight Center, 1974-77; sci. observation analyst Caltech/Jet Propulsion Lab., Pasadena, Calif., 1977-78; engr. advanced projects group 1978-84, mem. tech. staff system integration sect. of Space Sta., 1984-87, mem. tech. staff and space sta., user ops. team leader, 1987-88; technical mgr. Jet Propulsion Lab., Pasadena, Calif., 1988—; prin. founder, pres. World Space Found., South Pasadena, Calif., 1979—; founding dir. So. Calif. Space Bus. Roundtable, 1987—. Contbr. articles to profl. jours. bd. dirs. Calif. Inst. Tech. YMCA, 1987—. Nat. Space Club Goddard scholar, 1977; Charles A. Lindbergh Fund grantee, 1986. Fellow Brit. Interplanetary Soc.; mem. AIAA, Tau Beta Pi, Sigma Gamma Tau. Office: World Space Found PO Box Y South Pasadena CA 91030

STAFFORD, J. FRANCIS, archbishop; b. Balt., July 26, 1932; s. F. Emmett and Mary Dorothy S. Student, Loyola Coll., Balt., 1950-52; B.A., St. Mary's Sem., Balt., 1954; S.T.B., S.T.L., Gregorian U., Rome, 1958; M.S.W., Catholic U., 1964; postgrad., Rutgers U., 1963, U. Wis.-Madison, 1969, St. Mary's Sem. and Univ., Balt., 1973-75. Spiritual moderator Ladies of Charity Ch., Balt., 1966-76; spiritual moderator Soc. St. Vincent de Paul, Balt., 1965-76; urban vicar Archdiocese of Balt., 1966-76, monsignor, 1970, vicar gen., auxiliary bishop, 1976-83; bishop Diocese of Memphis, 1983-86; archbishop Archdiocese of Denver, 1986—; dir. Assn. Cath. Charities, Balt., 1966-76; archdiocesan liaison to Md. Cath. Conf., Balt, 1975-78; Oriental Orthodox/Roman Cath. consultation Nat. Cath. Conf. Bishops, 1977-85, com. on doctrine, 1978-82, vice chmn. ecumenical and interreligious affairs com., 1986—, chmn. ecumenical and interreligious affairs com., 1987—; co-chmn. bilateral dialogue Roman Cath./World Meth. Council, 1977-86; chmn. Bishops' com. marriage and family life U.S. Cath. Conf., 1978-84; mem. gen. Synod Bishops, Vatican City, 1980. Contbr. articles to profl. jours. Bd. trustees Good Samaritan Hosp., Balt., 1973-76, St.Thomas Theol. Sem., chmn. 1987—, Blue Cross of Md., Inc., 1973-76, Balt. Urban Coalition, 1970-75; mem. bd. Sch. Social Work and Planning U. Md., 1973-76. Recipient Father Kelly Alumni award Loyola High Sch., 1978; Alumni Laureate, Loyola Coll., 1979. Mem. World Methodist Conf. Roman Catholic Dialogue (co-chmn. 1977-86), Oriental Orthodox Roman Catholic Consultation, (co-chmn. 1977-85), Nat. Conf. Cath. Bishops, Lutheran Roman Catholic Dialogue. Office: Archdiocese of Denver 200 Josephine St Denver CO 80206

STAFFORD, JOHN MICHAEL, banker; b. Colorado Springs, Colo., Oct. 22, 1940; s. John Michael and Alice (Daugherty) S.; m. Loretta B. Martin, Nov. 30, 1960 (div. Apr. 1974); children: Cynthia, Gregory; m. C. Diane Edgar, Aug. 16, 1980; stepchildren: Bradley, John. Degree Grad. Sch. Banking, U. Colo., 1972. Credit mgr. Am. Fin. Co., Glassboro, N.J., 1963-65; adjustment mgr. 1st Camden (N.J.) Nat. Bank, 1965-68; exec. v.p. Cen. Bank-Colorado Springs, 1968-82; pres. Cen. Bank-Chapel Hills, Colorado Springs, 1982, Cen.Bank-Academy Blvd., Colorado Springs, 1982-86; v.p., div. dir. Cen. Bancorp Colo., Denver, 1986—; chmn. bd. dirs. Cen. Banks Aurora, Chatfield, Centennial and Inverness, Colo., 1985-86, Cen. Banks North Denver, Broomfield, Westminster, Colo., 1987—; mem. First Bank System (Minn.). Mem. El Paso Club, Lone Tree Country Club, Colo. State Banking Bd. Roman Catholic. Home: 9873 Greensview Circle Littleton CO 80124 Office: Cen Bancorp Colo 1515 Arapahoe St Denver CO 80202

STAFFORD, KENNETH ROGER, university administrator; b. Twin Falls, Idaho, Jan. 29, 1949; s. Roger and Corinne (McBeth) S.; m. Kristie Kunau, June 10, 1971. BSBA, U. Idaho, 1971, MS in Econs., 1975. Statistician U. Idaho, Moscow, 1974-75, asst. dir. MIS, 1975-80, fiscal officer, 1980-88, dir. adminstrv. svcs., 1988—; cons. in field. Author: Economic Impact of Higher Education, 1975, numerous MIS computer systems. Recipient Alumni award of Faculty Excellence U. Idaho Alumni Assn., 1986, 88. Mem. Gamma Sigma Delta, Elks. Office: U Idaho Coll Agriculture Moscow ID 83843

STAFFORD, NORMAN SHERIDAN, sales executive; b. Galveston, Tex., June 7, 1944; s. Norman and Jean (Colgate) S.; divorced; children: Darrin G., Martin G. Student, Middlesex Coll., 1977. Svc. technician Nat. Cash Register, Fairfield, Conn., 1971-73; svc. mgr. Rockwell Internat., Berlin, Conn., 1973-77; svc. technician Diversified Data System, Tucson, 1977-80, svc. mgr., 1980-85; project mgr., 1985-87, Ea. region sales engr., 1987-88; sales engr. Four Corners Tech., Scottsdale, Ariz., 1988—; del. Nat. Conf. of Standards Labs., 1987-88. With USAF, 1963-71. Mem. Am. Soc. Quality Control, Telecommunications Assn. Republican. Methodist. Home: 9031 E Calle Norlo Tucson AZ 85710 Office: Four Corners Tech 7802 E Gray Rd Scottsdale AZ 85260

STAFFORD, STEPHEN L., sales executive; b. Beeville, Tex., June 21, 1953; s. G.L. (Bill) and Florita Lou (Young) S.; 1 child, Robert Len. BA, West Tex. State U., Canyon, 1976. Foreman Wagner-Brosier Ranch, Canyon, Tex., 1974-77; lab tech. Getty Oil Co., Big Spring, Tex., 1977-82; acct. mgr. Calgon Corp., Carlsbad, N.Mex., 1982—. Republican. Mem. Ch. of Christ. Home and Office: 1025 N Halagneno Carlsbad NM 88220

STAHL, CHARLES JEFFREY, greeting card company executive; b. Maysville, Ky., Mar. 29, 1957; s. James Eugene and Josephine (Ryan) S. BBA, U. Ky., 1979. Sales rep. Am. Greetings, Lexington, Ky., 1980-82; field sales mgr. Am. Greetings, Cleve., 1982-84, sales placement adminstr., 1984-85; Pacific area sales mgr. Am. Greetings, Honolulu, 1985-89; regional dir. sales ops. Am. Greetings, N.Y.C., 1989—. Home: 6750 Hawaii Kai #102 Honolulu HI 96825 Office: Am Greetings 10500 American Rd Cleveland OH 41144

STAHL, JACK LELAND, state official, real estate company executive; b. Lincoln, Ill., June 28, 1934; s. Edwin R. and Edna M. (Burns) S.; m. Carol Anne Townsend, June 23, 1956; children—Cheryl, Nancy, Kellea. B.S. in Edn., U. M.Mex., 1957. Tchr. Albuquerque Public Schs., 1956-59; pres. House Finders, Inc., Albuquerque, 1959-65; v.p. N.Mex. Savs. & Loan Assn., Albuquerque, 1965-67; chmn. bd. Hooten-Stahl, Inc., Albuquerque, 1967-77; pres. The Jack Stahl Co., Albuquerque, 1977—; N.Mex. Ho. of Reps. The Jack Stahl Co., 1969-70; mem. N.Mex. Senate, 1981-86; lt. gov. State of N.Mex., 1987—. Mem. exec. bd. Great S.W. coun. Boy Scouts Am., 1982—; bd. dirs. Better Bus. of N.Mex., 1968-82, pres., 1975-76; trustee Univ. Heights Hosp., 1980-85; vice chmn. N.Mex. Bd. of Fin., 1987—, N.Mex. Community Devel. Coun., 1987—. Named Realtor of Yr., Albuquerque Bd. Realtors, 1972. Mem. Nat. Assn. Realtors, Nat. Homebuilders Assn., N.Mex. Amigos. Republican. Methodist. Clubs: 20-30 (pres. 1963-64), Rotary. Office: 1911 Wyoming Blvd NE Albuquerque NM 87112

STAHL, LESLIE DIANE, desktop publishing company owner; b. Chgo., June 13, 1952; d. Dennis Jay and Mary Catherine (Cooper) Hulet; m. David M. Stahl, Oct. 30, 1983. Cert. in Engring. Drawing, Chgo. Tech. Coll., 1972. Typesetter, illustrator Argonne (Ill.) Nat. Lab., 1971-73; advt. asst./artist Elgin Watch Co., Chgo., 1973-74; mgr. pubs. Irvine (Calif.) Sensors Corp., 1974-80; graphic artist Rockwell Internat., Anaheim, Calif., 1980-83; specialist CADD system Seattle Computer Products, 1983-84; tech. writer Boeing Computer Svcs., Seattle, 1986-87; pres., owner Documents Unlimited Co., Enumclaw, Wash., 1987-88; technical editor Electronic Data Systems, Enumclaw, 1988—; computer cons. various organizations. Author CAD/CAM User's Guide, 1987, CD/ROM User's Guide, 1988; editor Annual Research Report, Boeing IR&D, 1987; editor, publisher CD/ROM Database, 1988; typographer Engineering Mechanics, 1974; contbr. jour. Soc. for Tech. Communication. Leader Girl Scouts U.S., Chgo., 1965-70. Mem. Nat. Computer Graphics Assn. Republican. Mem. Pentecostal Ch. Home: 24316 SE 473rd St Enumclaw WA 98022

STAHL, RICHARD G. C., journalist, editor; b. Chgo., Feb. 22, 1934; m. Gladys C. Weisbecker; 1 child, Laura Ann. Student, Northwestern U., U. Ill., Chgo. Editor Railway Purchases and Stores Mag., Chgo., 1960-63; editor pub. rels. dept. Sears Roebuck & Co., Chgo., 1963-68; dir pub. rels. dept. St. Joseph's Hosp. Med. Ctr., Phoenix, 1968-72; v.p. pub. rels. dept. Consultation Svcs., Inc., Phoenix, 1972-73; creative dir. Don Jackson and Assoc., Phoenix, 1973; editor, pub. rels. mgr. Maricopa County Med. Soc., Phoenix, 1974-76; mng. editor Ariz. Hwys. mag., Phoenix, 1977—. Regional editor: (travel guides) Budget Travel, 1985, USA, 1986, Arizona, 1986; freelance writer and editor. Mem. Soc. Profl. Journalists. Office: Ariz Hwys Mag 2039 W Lewis Ave Phoenix AZ 85009

STAHLER, JOHN PATRICK, video security equipment manufacturer; b. Malden, Mass., Jan. 28, 1957; s. Robert Walter and Dorothy Stahler. Student in elec. engring., San Diego State U., 1975-78. Engring. asst. Teledyne Ryan Aero. Co., San Diego, 1975-76, jr. design engr., 1976-78; sr. design engr. Pacific Aerosystem, Inc., San Diego, 1978-79, cons., 1979-80; sr. design engr. Robot Rsch., Inc., San Diego, 1978-82, chief engr.,

1982-84, pres., 1984—. Contbr. articles to profl. jours.; inventor color slow scan video signal transl., monochrom compatible color slow scan TV system, fractional cycle time-amplitude modulation. Mem. So. Calif. High Tech. Execs. Network. Office: Robot Rsch Inc 5636 Ruffin Rd San Diego CA 92123

STAHLHUTH, PAUL HENRY, aerospace engineer; b. Detroit, Jan. 10, 1927; s. Arthur Henry and Mayme (Salsbury) S.; m. Janet Ellen Pyke, Jan. 28, 1950; children: Judith Lee, Mark Allen, Beth Ann. BS in Aerospace Engring., Wayne State U., Detroit, 1950. Engr. Allison div. GM, Speedway, Ind., 1950-52; engr. Ford Motor Co., Dearborn, Mich., 1952-56; engring. sect. mgr. Sundstrand Turbo Div., Denver, 1956-66; prin. engr. Ford Aerospace, Newport Beach, Calif., 1966—; cons. engr. Dental Product Devel. Patentee in field; contbr. articles to profl. jours. Mem. Mensa, Calif. Carvers Guild, Calif. Kayak Friends. Republican. Lutheran. Home: 26612 Espalter Dr Mission Viejo CA 92691 Office: Ford Aerospace Ford Rd Missle Controls Dept Newport Beach CA 92658

STAIBLE, FRED ELLIS, education and technical consulting company executive; b. Denver, Aug. 19, 1948; s. Edward William and Patricia (Cox) S.; m. Karleen Sue Goodner, Jan. 24, 1970; children: Jeremy, Kara. BS, Colo. Sch. Mines, 1970. Registered profl. engr., Tex. Prodn. engr. Union Carbide Corp., Seadrift, Tex., 1970-74; plant engr. El Paso Products Co., Odessa, Tex., 1974-77; engring. supt. El Paso LNG Service Co., Arzew, Algeria, 1977-81, Roy M. Huffington, Inc., Bontang, Indonesia, 1981-86; v.p. ops. Fibertein Corp., Wheat Ridge, Colo., 1987-88; pres. Egal T Ltd., Arvada, Colo., 1989—. Named Young Engr. of Yr. West Tex. Soc. Profl. Engrs., 1977. Mem. Am. Inst. Chem. Engrs. Office: Egal T Ltd PO Box 5248 Arvada CO 80005

STALBERG, CHRISTIAN ERIC, infosystems specialist; b. Monterey, Calif., Aug. 28, 1955; s. Herman Reimers and Gladys Aileen (Holme) S.; m. Paula Pam Spertus, Aug. 9, 1978 (div. 1982); 1 child, Ian Hamal. BA in Environ. Studies and Planning, Sonoma State U., 1988. Energy policy analyst County of Sonoma, Santa Rosa, Calif., 1982-83; energy analyst Energetics, Berkeley, Calif., 1984-86; adminstr. EcoNet Farallones Inst., Occidental, Calif., 1984-87; v.p. tech. group Diversified Network Applications, Inc., Santa Rosa, 1987--; planning coun. Internat. Informatics Access, Dallas, 1986--; cons. communications Pan Am. Health Orgn., Washington, 1987, Internat. Diabetes Fedn., Brussels, 1988. Bd. dirs. Ptnrs. Ams., San Francisco, 1988. Recipient Commendation ARC, 1986. Home: PO Box 1028 Forestville CA 95436 Office: Diversified Network Applications Inc PO Box 5374 Santa Rosa CA 95402

STALL, STUART MURRAY, sales executive; b. Coronado, Calif., Jan. 27, 1954; s. Anthony A. and Joan Ruth (Kuck) S. BA, San Diego Community Coll., 1984; BSBA, San Diego State U., 1987. Maitre'd, mgr. Chez Loma, Coronado, 1977-88; adminstr., salesperson Semco, San Diego, 1988, regional mgr., 1988—. Co-founder Prof. Paintings Schs. Am., 1989—. Recipient Citizenship medal Am. Legion, 1988. Mem. Nat. Assn. Advancement Jet Boarding (pres. 1987-88). Home: 764 Orange Ave Coronado CA 92118 Office: Semco 591 Camino de la Reina San Diego CA 92108

STALLARD, GEORGE THOMAS (DUKE STALLARD), retail store owner; b. Lakin, Kans., Oct. 1, 1937; s. George Aubry and Gladys Agnes (Prather) S.; m. Carolyn Diane Flower, Mar. 18, 1967. Student, Colo. State U., 1955-56; cert. of agriculture, Lamar (Colo.) Community Coll., 1958-60; student, Adams State Coll., Alamosa, Colo., 1963, 67. Parts mgr. Irrigation and Power Co., Greeley, Colo., 1965-67; owner, mgr. Shelpers, Inc., Roswell, N.M., 1967-87; bd. dirs. Tabosa Devel. and Tng. Ctr., Roswell; cons. numerous establishments in N.M. including N.M. Rehab. Ctr. and Ea. N.M. Med. Ctr. Vice chmn. Gov.'s Com. Concerns of Handicapped, Sante Fe, 1981-87; past pres. Roswell Area Com. Concerns of Handicapped, 1978-79; rep. Nat. Conf. for Coalition of Handicapped, Houston, 1978; life mem. Disabled Am. Vets., Roswell, Paralized Vets. Am.; mem. Agrl. Council Chaves County, Roswell. Served with U.S. Army, 1961-66. Recipient Outstanding Handicapped New Mexican N.M. Gov.'s Com. Concerns of Handicapped, 1983; agrl. scholarship Lamar Coll., 1958. Republican. Methodist. Clubs: Roswell Sertoma, Paralized Vets. Am., Disabled Am. Vets. Lodges: Elks, York Rite, Scottish Rite, Masons, Shriners. Home: Rte 1 227 Peaceful Valley Roswell NM 88201-9801

STALLINGS, GENE CLIFTON, professional football coach; b. Paris, Tex., Mar. 2, 1935; s. Eugene C. and Neil (Moye) S.; m. Ruth Ann Jack, Dec. 1, 1956; children: Anna Lee, Laura Nell, John Mark, Jacklyn Ruth, Martha Kate. B.S., Tex. A&M U., 1958. Asst. football coach U. Ala., 1958-64; head football coach, dir. athletics Tex. A&M U., 1964-72; asst. coach Dallas Cowboys, 1972-85; head football coach St. Louis Cardinals (now known as Phoenix Cardinals), 1986—; dir. Bank of A&M, College Station, Tex., Rolling Internat., Inc., Dallas; Spalding sports cons. Mem. Sam Houston council Boy Scouts Am.; trustee Abilene (Tex.) Christian U. Named 1983 Dallas Father of the Yr.; elected to Tex. A&M U. Hall of Fame, 1982. Mem. Nat. Assn. Collegiate Dirs. Athletics, Am. Football Coaches Assn., Fellowship Christian Athletes. Mem. Ch. of Christ. Office: Phoenix Cardinals 515 N 48th St Phoenix AZ 85008 *

STALLINGS, RICHARD H., congressman; b. Ogden, Utah, Oct. 7, 1940; s. Howard J. and Elizabeth (Austin) S.; m. Ranae Garner, Sept. 5, 1963; children—Richard H., Sallianne, Daniel. B.S., Weber State Coll., 1965; M.S., Utah State U., 1968; student, Colo. Coll., 1968. Tchr. Bonneville High Sch., Ogden, Utah, 1964-69; prof. Ricks Coll., Rexburg, Idaho, 1969-79, chmn. dept. history, 1979-84; mem. 99th, 100th, 101st Congresses from 2d Idaho dist., Washington, 1985—. Office: Ho of Reps Office House Mems Washington DC 20515

STAMES, WILLIAM ALEXANDER, realtor, cost mgmt. exec.; b. Douglas, Ariz., Mar. 26, 1917; s. Alex Basil and Teresa (Ruis) S.; AA, Long Beach Coll., 1941; postgrad. U. Calif., Berkeley, 1962-64; cert. mgmt. practices Naval Officers CIC Sch., Glenview, Ill., 1955; grad. Real Estate Inst., Calif.; m. Marguerite Winifred Nelson, June 11, 1943; 1 child, Wynn Lorain. Owner, Stames Beverage Co., Brawley, Calif., 1945-50; liaison engr. Lockheed Missiles & Space Co., Sunnyvale, Calif., 1958-60, liaison engr. sr., 1960, adminstr., 1960-62, staff adminstr., 1962-63, liaison engr., sr., design engr. sr., 1965-76; owner, mgr. Cost Reduction Equipment Sales & Tech., Sunnyvale, 1967-76; realtor Cornish & Carey, 1988—. Comdr. USNR, 1941-69, ret., World War II, Korea, Vietnam. Decorated D.F.C., Air medal with two gold stars, Presdl. citation. Mem. Am. Mgmt. Assn., Mountain View Real Estate Bd. (pres.), Calif. Assn. Realtors (bd. dirs.), Tailhook Assn. Clubs: Commonwealth San Francisco, Ret. Officers (past pres. Peninsula chpt.), Lions. Author: Polaris Electrical Subsystems Design History, 1964; Poseidon Subsystem Invention, 1971. Home: 1060 Coronado Ave Coronado CA 92118 Office: 341 Castro St Mountain View CA 94041 also: Cornish and Carey Real Estate 2754 Middlefield Rd Palo Alto CA 94306

STAMM, RICHARD WILLIAM, podiatrist; b. Meadville, Pa., July 9, 1944; s. William Henry and Norma Marie (Bertocci) S.; m. Maria Johnine Avdellas, June 16, 1968; children: Aileen Johnine, William Tarkington. AA, Hershey Jr. Coll., 1965; BA, Washington and Jefferson Coll., 1967; D Podiatric Medicine, Ohio Coll. Podiatric Medicine, 1978. Resident in podiatric surgery Cleve. Foot Clinic, 1978-79; practice medicine specializing in podiatry Family Foot Care, Albuquerque, 1979—. Contbr. articles to profl. jours. Bd. dirs. Albuquerque Wild Turkey Fedn., 1984-88, SVC, 1984-88, Bernalillo Chpt. Am. Diabetes Assn., 1985-88, Albuquerque Vis. Nurse Found., 1983-88, pres. bd. dirs., 1985-86, Hospice and Home Care Found., 1989—; mem. citizens adv. council Albuquerque Pub. Schs., 1985-86. Served with U.S. Army, 1967-71, Vietnam. Fellow Am. Coll. Foot Orthopedists; mem. Am Coll. Podopediatrics (sec. 1988-89), Am. Podiatric Med. Assn. (ho. of del. 1982—), N.Mex. Podiatric Med. Assn. (pres. 1984-88, Appreciation awards 1981, 85, 86), Am. Diabetes Assn. (bd. dirs. Albuquerque chpt. 1986-88). Republican. Greek Orthodox. Lodge: Rotary. Home: 1700 Father Sky NE Albuquerque NM 87112 Office: Family Foot Care 10555 Montgomery NE Ste 80 Albuquerque NM 87111

STAMOLIS, MICHAEL GEORGE, marketing executive; b. Seattle, July 8, 1966; s. George John and Linda (Fehring) S. BA, U. Calif., Irvine, 1988. Account rep. Xerox Corp., Costa Mesa, Calif., 1988—. Vol., Am. Diabetes Assn., 1987—. Named Outstanding Young Man of Am., 1986, 87, 88; Kappa Sigma scholar, 1986-87. Mem. Univ. Club, Phi Alpha Delta. Republican. Greek Orthodox. Home: 658 Veneto Irvine CA 92714 Office: Xerox Corp 180 E Ocean #224 Long Beach CA 90802

STAMPER, MALCOLM THEODORE, aerospace company executive; b. Detroit, Apr. 4, 1925; s. Fred Theodore and Lucille (Cayce) S.; m. Marion Philbin Guinan, Feb. 25, 1946; children: Geoffrey, Kevin, Jamie, David, Mary, Anne. Student, U. Richmond, Va., 1943-44; B.E.E., Ga. Inst. Tech., 1946; postgrad., U. Mich., 1946-49. With Gen. Motors Corp., 1949-62; with Boeing Co., Seattle, 1962—; mgr. electronics ops., v.p., gen. mgr. turbine div. Boeing Co., 1964-66; v.p., gen. mgr. Boeing Co. (747 Airplane program), 1966-69, v.p., gen. mgr. comml. airplane group, 1969-71, corp. sr. v.p. ops., 1971-72; pres. Boeing Co., 1972-85, vice chmn., 1985—; bd. dirs. Travelers Ins. Cos., Nordstrom Co., Chrysler Corp.; trustee The Conf. Bd., 1988—. Chmn. Wash. State U.S. Treasury Savs. Bond Campaign, Boy Scouts Am. Devel. Fund State of Wash., Variety Club Handicapped Children Telethon.; candidate U.S. Ho. of Reps., Detroit, 1952; trustee Seattle Art Mus., Conference Bd., 1988; nat. bd. dirs. Smithsonian Assocs.; trustee The Conf. Bd., 1988. With USNR, 1943-46. Named Industrialist of Year, 1967; recipient Educator's Golden Key award, 1970, Elmer A. Sperry award, 1982, AIEE award, Ga. Inst. Tech. award, Sec. Dept. Health and Human Services award. Mem. Nat. Alliance Businessmen, Phi Gamma Delta. Office: Boeing Co 7755 E Marginal Way S Seattle WA 98108

STANBACK, ELIEHUE, public accountant; b. Byhalia, Miss., May 25, 1918; s. Clint and Eva (McGowan) S.; m. Sophronia M. Thompson, Dec. 7, 1936 (div. 1939); m. Ellen Richmond, July 18, 1941 (div. Feb. 1962); children: Eliehue Jr., William Earl, DeLores Ann, Alice Marie; m. Celia Anne Davis, Mar. 9, 1962; children: Gwendolyn Ann, Sandra Renee, Anthony, Mildred Cynthia, Eric. Student, Cen. YMCA Coll., Chgo., 1936-37; degree in higher accountancy, Henderson Bus. Coll., 1949-50; student, LeMoyne Coll., 1951-52; cert. pub. accountancy, LaSalle Extension U., 1961, LLB, 1979; postgrad., Mt. San Antonio Coll., Walnut, Calif., 1979-80, Calif. State Poly. U., Pomona, 1969-83. Registered pub. acct. Founder, editor, pub. Indsl. Leader, Chgo. and Memphis, 1939—; U.S. railway mail clk. U.S. Mail, Memphis, 1943-49; pvt. practice acctg. Memphis, 1950—; carrier U.S. Mail, Pomona and Ontario, Calif., 1965-77. Candidate for Tax Assessor, Memphis, 1959; pres. Memphis, Shelby County and Tenn. Voters Assn., 1959-63, civil rights activist 1949-63; chmn. bd. Binghampton Civic League, Memphis, 1958-63. Served as pvt. U.S. Army, 1942-43. Mem. Soc. of Calif. Accts. (bd. dirs. Tri County Chpt. 1982-84), Nat. Soc. Pub. Accts., Nat. Assn. Letter Carriers, Disabled Am. Vets., Pomona Valley Amatuer Astronomers, Postal Sportsmen Rod and Gun Club. Republican. Methodist. Office: Stanback's Bus Mgmt & Tax Svcs 1230 Cromwell St Pomona CA 91768

STANDEFER, HOUSTON LEA, structural engineer; b. Fresno, Calif., Dec. 26, 1920; s. Huse Frank and Myrtle (Kenyon) S.; m. Rose Venegas (dec. Jan. 1986); children: George H., Linda J., Teresa A.; m. Avis Warness, 1988. BCE, U. So. Calif., 1944. Registered profl. engr., Calif., Nev. Design engr. George Fosdyke, Los Angeles, 1944-47; owner H.L. Standefer, Cons., Los Angeles, 1947—. Mem. Structural Engrs. Assn. (assoc.). Republican. Office: H L Standefer 18455 Burbank Blvd #304 Tarzana CA 91356

STANDIFER, DAVID BERRIS, physical therapist; b. Salem, Oreg., Jan. 23, 1959; s. Larry Walter and Mary (Polales) S.; m. Teresa Lynne Eaves, Aug. 14, 1982; children: Jennifer Lynne, David Berris Jr. BS in Biology, Williamette U., 1981; BS in Physical Therapy, U. Puget Sound, 1986. Lic. physical therapist. Staff physical therapist Physical Therapy Specialists, Tacoma, Wash., 1982-86; clin. dir. SCORE Physical Therapy, Tacoma, 1987-89; mem. staff Bend (Oreg.) Physical Therapy, 1989—; phsycial therapy con., Competitive Edge Fitness Inst., Tacoma, 1987-89. Mem. Am. Physical Therapy Assn. (sports medicine sect.), Oreg. Physical Therapy Assn. Republican. Methodist. Home: 594 Riverside Blvd Bend OR 97701 Office: Bend Physical Therapy 2275 NE Doctors Dr Bend OR 97701

STANDRING, JAMES DOUGLAS, real estate developer; b. Fresno, Calif., Dec. 2, 1951; s. James Robert Pusey and Jacquelin (Moore); m. Paula Jean Monson, Oct. 27, 1972; children: Craig Douglas, Ryan Scott, Melinda Jean, Kevin Paul. BS, Calif. State U., Fresno, 1975. Pres. Westland Industries, Inc., Portland, Oreg., 1976—; ptnr. Aloha Land and Cattle, Inc., Portland, 1982—; bd. dirs. Homebuilders Assn., Metro Portland, Oreg. State Homebuilders Assn., Portland, Nat. Assn. Homebuilders, Washington; v.p. Homebuilders Assn. Metro Portland, 1988—. Bd. dirs. Tualitin Valley Econ. Devel. Corp., Portland, 1988-89; co-founder, dir. People for Washington County Charities, Beaverton, Oreg., 1985-88. Mem. Tualitin Valley Econ. Devel. Commn., Multnomah Athletic Club, Portland City Club, BPOE. Republican. Episcopalian. Home: 5 Nansen Summit Lake Oswego OR 97035 Office: Aloha Land/Cattle Co 2720 17th Pl Forest Grove OR 97116

STANFIELD, MICHAEL DEAN, realtor, real estate developer; b. Hillsdale, Mich., Jan. 28, 1943; s. Walter Emanuel and Dorothy (Hoose) S. BA, U. Fla., 1966; JD, Golden Gate U., 1973. Pres., owner Stanfield & Co. Realtors, San Francisco, 1974—. Mem. San Francisco Bd. Realtors, Nat. Assn. Realtors. Clubs: Prsidio Golf, San Francisco Tennis. Home: 306 Locust St San Francisco CA 94118 Office: Stanfield & Co 2960 Van Ness Ave San Francisco CA 94109

STANFORD, JACK ARTHUR, biological station administrator; b. Delta, Colo., Feb. 18, 1947; s. LeRoy and Wilma (Tucker) S.; children: Jake, Chriss. BS in Fisheries Sci., Colo. State U., 1969, MS in Limnology, 1971; PhD in Limnology, U. Utah, 1975. Fisheries biologist Alaska-Fish and Game, Dillingham, 1968-69; rsch. biologist and limnologist instr. U. Mont., Bigfork, 1973-74, dir. Flathead Lake Biol. Sta., 1980—; research prof. zoology U. Mont., Missoula, 1983-86; prof. N. Tex. State U., Denton, 1974-81; panelist div. biotic system NSF, Washington, 1985-89. Editor: Ecology of Regulated Streams, 1979; co-editor Internat. Newsletter on Regulated Stream Limnology, 1981—; mem. bd. editors Regulated Rivers: Research and Management, 1985—; contbr. 65 articles to profl. jours. Advisor Nature Conservancy, Boulder, Colo., 1982—. Named Bierman Prof. Ecology U. Mont., 1986—; grantee N. Tex. State U., EPA, U.S. Army, U.S. Bur. Reclamation, NSF, U.S. Nat. Park Svc. Mem. Mont. Acad. Sci., Am. Soc. Limnology and Oceanography, Ecol. Soc. Am., N.Am. Benthological Soc. (exec. com. 1979, 1988-89), AAAS. Home and Office: Flathead Lake Biol Sta 311 Bio Station Ln Polson MT 59860

STANFORD, ROBERT AUGUST, editor; b. Akron, Ohio, Mar. 16, 1927; s. George Frederick and Margaret Hannah (Ruthenberg) S. BA with honor, U. Akron, 1956; lic. et arts et lettres avec mention bien, U. Paris, 1958. Asst. to pres. Dover Pubs., N.Y.C., 1962-64; copy editor McKinsey & Co., N.Y.C., 1965-66; gen. mgr. Burt Franklin Pubs., N.Y.C., 1967-68; dep. dir., adv. bd. N.Y.C. Dept. Social Services, 1968-78; mng. editor, co-owner N.Y. Native Newspaper, 1981-82; editor-in-chief In Touch Pubs., North Hollywood, Calif., 1984—; field ops. asst. U.S. Census Bur., Manhattan, N.Y.C.; part-owner That New Mag., Inc., NYC. Vol. Congresswoman Bella S. Abzug, N.Y.C., 1970-76. Served with signal corp U.S. Army, 1950-52. Mem. Nat. Honor Soc. Secondary Schs., Phi Sigma Alpha. Democrat. Mem. United Ch. Christ. Home: 6842 Fulton St #7 North Hollywood CA 91605 Office: In Touch Pubs Internat Inc 7216 Varna St North Hollywood CA 91605

STANGELAND, ROGER EARL, retail chain store executive; b. Chgo., Oct. 4, 1929; s. Earl and Mae E. (Shaw) S.; m. Lilah Fisher, Dec. 27, 1951; children: Brett, Cyndi Stangeland Meili, Brad. Student, St. Johns Mil. Acad., 1943-47, Carleton Coll., 1947-48; B.S., U. Ill., 1949-51. With Coast to Coast Stores, Mpls., 1960-78, pres., 1972-77; sr. v.p., exec. v.p. Household Merchandising, Chgo., 1978-84; chief exec. officer, chmn. bd. Vons Grocery Co., Los Angeles, 1984-85; chmn., chief exec. officer The Vons Cos., Inc., El Monte, Calif., 1986—; bd. dirs. Coast to Coast Stores Inc., Denver, Frank Purcell Co., Kansas City, Mo. Chmn. Wauconda (Ill.) Bd. Edn., 1957-60, Hopkins (Minn.) Bd. Edn., 1968-74; bd. dirs. Claremont (Calif.) U. Ctr. & Grad. Sch., 1986. Mem. Food Mktg. Inst. (bd. dirs.), Food Employer Council (bd. dirs.), Mchts. & Mfrs. Assn. (bd. dirs.). Clubs: Jonathan (Los Angeles). Home: 842 Oxford Rd San Marino CA 91108 Office: The Vons Cos Inc 10150 Lower Azusa Rd El Monte CA 91731

STANGLE, DONAVON WAYNE, telecommunications marketing executive; b. Vancouver, Wash., Oct. 24, 1944; s. Norbert Martin Stangle and Grave Lavelle (Deetz) Morehead; m. Eva Constance Young, June 28, 1969 (div.); children: Jessica, Laura. BBA in Acctg., U. Wash., 1967, MBA in Adminstrv. Theory, 1969. Owner, pres. ind. film co. Seattle, 1965-85, Donavon Telecommunications Group, Inc., Seattle, 1983-87; chmn., chief exec. officer Operator One Am., Inc., 1987--; co-owner, pres. Boondocks Restaurants, Inc., Seattle, 1972-79; cons. Com-Co Communications Cons., Inc., Seattle, 1969-72, Girvan's Restaurants, Seattle, 1986-87; corp. sec. Red. Robin Restaurants, Inc., Seattle, 1973-79; spl. fin. cons. Republic of Turkey, Geneva and London, 1982. Fundraiser local polit. campaigns; bd. dirs. PONCHO, Seattle, 1976-82.

STANISZEWSKI, HENRY ROBERT, environmental engineer; b. Phila., Nov. 25, 1951; s. Harry Robert and Dorothy Rita (Cervonka) S.; m. Ellen Louise Martin, Dec. 30, 1977; children: Kristen, Melissa. BS, Drexel U., 1974. Area engr. Hooker Chems. & Plastics, Niagara Falls, N.Y., 1974-78; devel. engr. Great Salt Lake Minerals and Chems., Little Mountain, Utah, 1978-83; environ. engr. Utah Power & Light, Castle Dale, Utah, 1983—. Mem. Am. Chem. Soc., Am. Inst. Chem. Engrs., Internat. Hazardous Materials Assn., KC. Democrat. Roman Catholic. Home: 950 Wadleigh Ln Price UT 84501 Office: Utah Power & Light PO Box 569 Castle Dale UT 84513

STANLEY, EMORY DAY, JR., maritime consultant; b. Los Angeles, Aug. 29, 1913; s. Emory Day and Eva (Cooper) S.; m. Marguerite Mountcastle, May 15, 1953 (dec. Dec. 1984); children: Rowena Stanley Jaap, Joan Stanley Maroulis, Marilyn Stanley Hamilton; m. Susan Gerrard, June 23, 1988. BS, U.S. Naval Acad., 1935; Advanced Mgmt. Cert., Harvard U., 1949. Enlisted USNR, 1935, advanced through grades to rear adm., 1963, ret., 1966; sec. SEA USE Council, Pacific Northwest and Hawaii, 1967-86; cons., prin. Stanley Assocs., Seattle, 1987—; sec. Def. Distbn. Coun., Washington, 1948-51. Chmn. 44th Dist. Dem. Com., Seattle, 1967-69. Democrat. Episcopalian. Clubs: Army-Navy (Washington); N.Y. Yacht; Rainier, Propeller (Seattle). Lodge: Masons.

STANLEY, FORREST EDWIN, fund raiser, educational administrator; b. Bakersfield, Calif., Sept. 6, 1942; s. James Edwin and Lucile Haworth (Sloan) S.; student U. Calif., Los Angeles, 1960-63, M.S., 1970; B.S., Calif. State U., Northridge, 1969; m. Suzanne Roberts, June 15, 1968 (div. 1984); children—John Forrest, Cheryl Suzanne; m. Virginia Louise Sorenson, Jan. 18, 1987. Sr. clk. So. Calif. Gas Co., 1963-65, programmer analyst, 1965-70; fin. analyst Continental Bldgs. Co., Burbank, Calif., 1970-72; fin. analyst McKinsey & Co., Inc., Los Angeles, 1972-74; analyst Unionamerica Advisors, Beverly Hills, Calif., asst. v.p., asst. treas., 1974-75; dir. alumni and devel. Grad. Sch. Mgmt., UCLA, 1976-80; dir. spl. campaigns U. Calif., Berkeley, 1980-84; dir. devel. U. Colo., Colorado Springs, 1984-86; dir. devel. pub. affairs, Calif. State U., Bakersfield, 1987—; v.p. U. Colo. Found., Inc., 1984-86. Mem. Am. Inst. Cert. Computer Profls., Assn. for Computing Machinery, Council for Advancement and Support of Edn., UCLA Mgmt. Alumni Assn. (v.p. 1974, pres. 1975-77), Sons Am. Colonists, Mensa, Lambda Chi Alpha (UCLA alumni chpt. pres. 1974-77, treas. 1977-80). Clubs: North Kern. Office: PO Box 10705 Bakersfield CA 93389-0705

STANLEY, JAMES LEE, composer, recording artist; b. Phila., Apr. 30, 1946; s. Clyde James and Mary Grace (Borio) S.; m. Eveline Yolande Knossen, Sept. 23, 1987. Student, L.A. City Coll., 1969-71, Calif. State U., Northridge, 1971-72. Owner, mgr. The Folk Ghetto, Norfolk, Va., 1965; recording artist RCA/Woodn Nickel, L.A., 1972-74, MCA/Regency Records, L.A., 1980-81, Jollye Roger Records, L.A., 1981-83, Takoma Records, L.A., 1984-85, Beachwood/Capitol, L.A., 1985—; touring musician throughout U.S., 1975-80; music dir. for spl. prodns., CBS-TV, L.A., 1987-89; ind. record producer, L.A., 1986—. Writer, producer, artist for record albums: James Lee Stanley/JLS Too, 1973, Three's the Charm, 1974, Midnight Radio, 1980, Eclipse, 1982, Racing the Moon, 1984, JLS-Live, 1986, Simpatico, 1988. Sgt. USAF, 1965-69. Mem. AFTRA, Musicians Union, Hacks. Office: Beachwood Records Ste 810 6253 Hollywood Blvd Los Angeles CA 90028

STANLEY, JOHN LANGLEY, political science professor; b. Boston, Nov. 16, 1937; s. John Willis and Marion (Langley) S.; m. Charlotte Whitcomb Colony, Nov. 28, 1964; children: John Colony, Andrea Page, Marjorie Page. BA, Kenyon Coll., 1960; postgrad., Cambridge (Eng.) U., 1960-61; PhD, Cornell U., 1966. Asst. prof. polit. sci. U. Calif., Riverside, 1965-71, assoc. prof., 1971-80, prof., 1981—; vis. lectr. Hertford Coll., Oxford (Eng.) U., 1986; adv. editor Transaction Books, New Brunswick, N.J., 1976—; mem. editorial bd. Cahiers Georges Sorel, Paris, 1983—. Author: The Sociology of Virtue, 1981; editor, translator: From George's Sorel, 1976, The Illusions of Progress By Georges Sorel, 1969; contbr. articles to profl. jours. Woodrow Wilson Found. fellow, 1961, NEH fellow, 1970. Mem. Am. Polit. Sci. Assn., Am. Soc. for Polit. and Legal Philosophy, Polit. Studies Assn., United Oxford and Cambridge U. Club. Democrat. Episcopalian. Office: U Calif Dept Polit Sci Riverside CA 92521

STANLEY, MARION EDWARD, editor; b. Aurora, Nebr., Jan. 31, 1903; s. Marion Francis and Ethzelda (Rush) S.; m. Pauline Gund, Oct. 18, 1927 (dec. June 1983); children: Michael, David; m. Gloria Ifland. AB, U. Nebr., 1926, LLD, 1966. Reporter AP, Chgo., 1928, Atlanta, 1929, N.Y.C., 1930, 36-38, London, 1931-32, Denver, 1932-33, Kansas City, Mo., 1934-35; created concept for new newspaper 1939-40, freelance writer, 1941; coord. Inter-Am. Affairs U.S. Govt., dir. activities and publs., dep. dir. Office of War Info.; with pub. relations dept. Earl Newsome and Co., 1944-45, Standard Oil of N.J., 1945-47; exec. editor Esquire, N.Y.C., 1947-48; dir. pub. affairs NBC, N.Y.C., 1950-68. Author: Thomas Forty, 1947, The Rock Cried Out, 1949. Mem. Century Club, Cosmos Club.

STANLEY, MARLYSE REED, horse breeder; b. Fairmont, Minn., Sept. 19, 1934; d. Glenn Orson and Lura Mabel (Ross) Reed; m. James Arthur Stapleton, 1956 (div. 1976); 1 child, Elisabeth Katharene; m. John David Stanley, Oct. 22, 1982. BA, U. Minn., 1957. Chmn. bd. dirs. Sitting Rock Spanish Arabians, Inc., Greensboro, N.C., 1978-81; pres. Sitting Rock Spanish Arabians, Inc., Hollister, Calif., 1981—; bd. dirs. Glenn Reed Tire Co., Fairmont, Minn. Contbr. articles to horse jours. Mem. Internat. Arabian Assn. (bd. dirs. region 10, Minn. and Wis., 1973-76, nat. chmn. hunter-jumper com. 1976-81), Minn. Arabian Assn. (bd. dirs. 1972-75), Am. Paint Horse Assn. (nat. bd. dirs. 1967-70). Republican. Episcopalian. Avocations: fox hunting, fishing, breeding and importing Arabian horses.

STANLEY, MAURICE DUDLEY, JR., manufacturing executive; b. Atlanta, Jan. 2, 1940; s. Maurice Dudley and Sarah Claudia (Bryan) S.; m. Miriam Paige Bennington, July 9, 1961; children: Elizabeth Bryan, John Lawrence, Michael Paige. BS, U.S. Naval Acad., 1961; MS, U.S. Naval Postgrad. Sch., 1973. Lic. comml. pilot, naval aviator. Commd. ensign USN, 1961, advanced through grades to comdr., 1976, ret., 1981; pres. Stanley Yachts, Inc., Oak Harbor, Wash., 1981-87; tng. analyst Allen Corp. of Am., Oak Harbor, 1987—; pres. Tech. Mgmt. Corp., Oak Harbor, 1986—; adj. instr. Chapman Coll. Oak Harbor, 1987—, Embry-Riddle Aero. U., Oak Harbor, 1981—. Vice. chmn. planning commn. City of Oak Harbor, 1987—; orgn. chmn. Downtown Devel. Council, Oak Harbor, 1988—. Decorated Air medals, Navy Commendation. Mem. U.S. Naval Inst., Tailhook Assn., Oak Harbor Yacht Club (vice comdr. 1989—, bd. dirs. 1981-87), Navy League, Oak Harbor C. of C. (pres., bd. dirs. 1981—). Republican. Home: 11468 115th St NW Oak Harbor WA 98277

STANLEY, PATRICK EDWARD, engineer; b. Ft. Lewis, Wash., Mar. 9, 1949; s. Richard Fielding and Avis Louise (Dustin) S.; m. Karen Lynn, June 25, 1977; children: Ryan, Erin. BS in Mech. Engring. Tech., Mont. State U., 1976. Registered profl. engr., Wash. Engr. process/project Stauffer Chem. Co., Butte, Mont., 1976-80; engr. maintenance Stauffer Chem. Co., Butte, 1980-85, Rockwell Internat. Hanford Co., Richland, Wash., 1986-87, Westinghouse Hanford Co., Richland, 1987—. Served in U.S. Navy, 1969-73. Roman Catholic. Home: 5143 Owl Ct West Richland WA 99352 Office:

Westinghouse Hanford Co Maint Engrg Mail Stop S4-65 PO Box 1970 Richland WA 99352

STANNARD, DAPHNE EVON, nurse; b. New Haven, Oct. 12, 1963; d. Jerry Wilmert and Katherine Evon (Moore) S. BSN, Vanderbilt U., 1986. RN, Calif. Critical care extern U. Mich. Med. Ctr., Ann Arbor, 1985, critical care nurse, 1986-87; recovery rm. nurse U. Calif. Med. Ctr., L.A., 1987; pub. health nurse Home Care Ptnrs., L.A., 1988; nurse ICU N.J.J., San Francisco, 1988; clin. nurse II Cedars-Sinai Med. Ctr., L.A., 1988—. mem. productivity com. Cedars-Sinai Med. Ctr., 1988—. Mem. Am. Nurses Assn., Nat. Am. Assn. Critical Care Nurses (L.A. chpt.), Calif. Assn. Critical Care Nurses, Calif. Nurses Assn. (chmn. anti-rct campaign L.A. chpt. 1988—), Soc. Critical Care Medicine, Omicron Delta Kappa. Home: 6610 Orange St #7 Los Angeles CA 90048 Office: Cedars-Sinai Med Ctr 8700 Beverly Blvd Los Angeles CA 90048

STANNARD-FRIEL, DONALD LEROY, college dean, sociologist; b. N.Y.C., Apr. 27, 1943; s. David LeRoy and Florence Evelyn (Harwood) Stannard; m. Natalie Guyol, Nov. 7, 1966 (div. 1970); children: Rachel Stannard Jones, Matthew Stannard; m. Kathleen Marie Friel, June 14, 1974; children: Sean, Jessica. BA, San Francisco State U., 1970, MA, 1971; PhD, U. Calif., Davis, 1978. Mental health counselor McAuley Neuropsychiat. Inst., San Francisco, 1968-74; lectr. sociology San Francisco State U., 1973-79, Santa Rita Rehab. Ctr., Pleasanton, Calif., 1975-76, Fed. Correctional Instn. for Women, Pleasanton, 1978; asst. prof. Coll. Notre Dame, Belmont, Calif., 1978-82, assoc. prof., 1982-87, dean faculty, 1983—, prof., 1987—; cons. strategic planning Mayor's Task Force on Children, San Francisco, 1987—, other orgns. Author: Harassment Therapy: A Case Study of Psychiatric Violence, 1981; contbr. articles to profl. jours. Speaker Mental Patients' Rights, 1978—; organizer Social Justice Symposium and Events, San Francisco, Belmont and Santa Cruz, Calif., 1978—; community conciliator Good Life Alliance, San Francisco, 1984. Mem. Clin. Sociology Assn., Humanistic Sociology Assn. Democrat. Roman Catholic. Home: 255 Connecticut St San Francisco CA 94107 Office: Coll Notre Dame Coll Arts & Scis 1500 Ralston Ave Belmont CA 94002

STANTON, BETHELENE, nurse; b. Perkins, Okla., Sept. 21, 1931; d. John David and Virginia Ann (Clayton) Riggs; m. Edward Arthur Stanton, Aug. 20, 1970. AA, San Joaquin Delta, 1976, ADN, 1978, RN, 1980. Cert. nurse specialist. Medication nurse Stockton (Calif.) State Hosp., 1978-80, unit supr., 1980-81; mental health charge nurse San Joaquin County Dept. Mental Health, Stockton, 1981-83; nursing supr. Stanislaus County Dept. Mental Health, Modesto, Calif., 1983—; design cons. Stanislaus County Psychiat. Mental Health Unit, Modesto, 1985—; expert witness J.G. Haro Law Offices, Miami, Fla., 1987.; cons. Harbor View Psychiat. Hosp., Miami, 1988. Staff mem. State Sen. Dan McGorquodale campaign, Modesto and Sacramento, 1986-88, Pat Paul for Supr. campaign, Modesto, 1988. Mem. DAV Aux., Am. Nursing Assn., Calif. Nursing Assn. (chmn. spl. interests groups 1988), Forensic Mental Health Assn. Calif. Democrat. Methodist. Office: Stanislaus County Heroin Treatment Program 800 Scenic Dr Modesto CA 95350

STANTON, JAMES LOCKE, publishing executive; b. Houston, Jan. 12, 1945; s. Robert John and Mary Louise (Locke) S.; m. Jolanne Elizabeth Luchak, Jan. 12, 1980; children: Matthew, James, George. BA, Harvard U., 1967, MBA, 1973. Project dir. Indonesia Cons. Ltd., Jakarta, 1973-74; mng. dir. APA Prodns., Hong Kong, 1974-75; chmn., chief exec. officer Seavex Ltd., Boston, Hong Kong, 1976-85; pres. J.L. Stanton & Co., Seattle, 1985—; bd. dirs. Mainland Corp., Tulsa, N.W. Expansion Capital, Seattle. Lt. USN, 1967-70. Mem. Wash. Software Assn., Harvard Club, Royal Hong Kong Yacht Club, Tanglin Club, Mercer Island Beach Club. Republican. Roman Catholic. Office: JL Stanton & Co Inc 800 Fifth Ave Suite 240 Seattle WA 98104

STANTON, ROBERT GLENN, association executive; b. Rapid City, S.D., June 11, 1944; s. Robert Marion and Clara Lucille (Roark) S.; m. Linda Lucille Dunn, Feb. 19, 1966; children: Stacey, Stephanie, Nicole. AA, Valencia Community Coll., 1975, AS, BS, Fla. Tech. U., 1977. Investigator security div. Walt Disney World Co., Orlando, Fla., 1971-78; conv. services exec. sales div. Walt Disney World Co., Orlando, 1978-83; assoc. dir. Am. Soc. Aesthetic Plastic Surgery, Long Beach, Calif., 1983-85; exec. dir. Am. Soc. Aesthetic Plastic Surgery, Long Beach, 1985—. Asst. scoutmaster Boy Scouts Am., Rapid City, S.D., 1961-64, eagle jr. scout. Capt. U.S. Army, 1965-71, Vietnam. Decorated Silver Star, Bronze Star, Cross of Gallantry, Rep. Vietnam; Dr. Phillips Found. scholar, 1974, Am. Spirit Honor medal. Mem. Am. Soc. Assn. Execs., So. Calif. Soc. Assn. Execs. (chmn. program com. 1987—, bd. dirs. 1988—, scholar 1985), Meeting Planners Internat., Profl. Conv. Mgmt. Assn., Bixby Knolls Area Bus. Assn. (bd. dirs., treas. 1984-88, pres. 1985-87), VFW. Republican. Methodist. Office: Am Soc Aesthetic Plastic Surgery 3922 Atlantic Ave Long Beach CA 90807

STANTON, WILLIAM JOHN, JR., marketing educator; b. Chgo., Dec. 15, 1919; s. William John and Winifred (McGann) S.; m. Imma Mair, Sept. 14, 1978; children by previous marriage: Kathleen Louise, William John III. B.S., Ill. Inst. Tech., 1940; M.B.A., Northwestern U., 1941, Ph.D., 1948. Mgmt. trainee Sears Roebuck & Co., 1940-41; instr. U. Ala., 1941-44; auditor Olan Mills Portrait Studios, Chattanooga, 1944-46; asst. prof., asso. prof. U. Wash., 1948-55; prof. U. Colo., Boulder, 1955—; head mktg. dept. U. Colo., 1955-71, acting dean, 1963-64; assoc. dean U. Colo. (Sch. Bus.), 1964-67; vis. prof. summers U. Utah, 1946, 1949, U. Calif., Berkeley, 1950, Los Angeles, 1957; mktg. cons. to various bus. firms and govt. agys., 1950—. Author: Economic Aspects of Recreation in Alaska, 1953, (with Richard H. Buskirk) Management of the Sales Force, 7th edit, 1987 (also Spanish transl.), (with others) Challenge of Business, 1975, (with C. Futrell) Fundamentals of Marketing, 8th edit, 1987 (also Spanish, Portuguese and Indonesian transls.); (with M.S. Sommers and J.G. Barnes) Can. edit. Fundamentals of Marketing, 4th edit., 1985 Australian edit. (with K. Miller and R. Layton), 1986, Italian edit. (with R. Varaldo); mem. editorial bd. Jour. Mktg, 1963-69. Mem. Am., So., Southwestern, Western mktg. assns., Beta Gamma Sigma. Roman Catholic. Home: 1445 Sierra Dr Boulder CO 80302 Office: U Colo Campus Box 419 Boulder CO 80309

STAPLES, GREY SKIPWITH, infosystems consultant; b. Raleigh; s. Grey Skipwith Staples Sr.; children: Grey III, Lissa Melinda. BS in Physics, CUNY, 1964; MEE, Ariz. State U., 1971. Cert. data processor, computer programmer. Pres. Camelback Systems, Inc., Scottsdale, Ariz., 1982—; cons. in field. Office: Camelback Systems Inc PO Box 1509 Scottsdale AZ 85252

STAPLES, JOHN NORMAN, III, lawyer; b. Durham, N.C., Aug. 1, 1946; s. Norman Appleton Staples and Elizabeth (Stewart-Richardson) Smith; m. Lila Banks James, May 18, 1968; children: Susan Banks, John William, James Nicholas. BA in English, Trinity Coll., 1968; JD, Pepperdine U., 1976. Bar: Calif. 1976. Assoc. Law Offices Donald B. Black, L.A., 1976-79, Walker, McClure, Bohnen & Brehmer, Monterey, Calif., 1979-83; ptnr. Millard, Tourangeau, Morris & Staples, Carmel, 1983—; bd. dirs. Household Bank, N.A., Salinas, Calif. Bd. dirs. Monterey Peninsula United Way, 1980-83, Planned Parenthood Monterey County, 1986—; chmn. bd. dirs. All Sts. Episcopal Day Sch., Carmel Valley, Calif., 1986—; trustee Monterey Peninsula Mus. Art. Capt. USMC, 1968-73, maj. USAFR. Mem. ABA, Monterey County Bar Assn., Calif. Bar Assn., Calif. Assn. Ind. Schs. (trustee's com. 1986—), Pacheco Club (Monterey), Old Capital Club (Monterey), Cypress Point Club. Republican. Episcopalian. Office: 6th and Dolores Sts PO Box 5427 Carmel CA 93921

STAPLETON, SHIRLEY WAUTERS, real estate executive; b. Boise, Idaho, June 17, 1936; d. Charles Edward Lee and Eleanor L. (Swiggart) Noble; m. Bruce F. Wauters, May 23, 1986. A in Liberal Arts, DeAnza Coll., Cupertino, Calif., 1975; BS in Bus. Mgmt. summa cum laude, Ariz. State U., 1979. Lic. realtor assoc. Founder, dir. Women's Opportunity Ctr., Cupertino, 1970-73; owner, pub. Ariz. Women's Yellow Pages, Inc., Scottsdale, Ariz., 1973-80; pvt. practice cons. Cupertino, 1967-73, Scottsdale, Ariz., 1973-83; ptnr. The Weigelt Co., Inc., Phoenix, 1973-87; br. mgr. B. Rich, Inc., Tempe, Ariz., 1987, R. Richard Vick, Inc., Scottsdale, 1987-88; v.p. real estate sales TransWestern Consol. Realty, Inc., Phoenix, 1988—. Mem. Women in Comercial Real Estate, Ariz. State U. Alumni.

STAPP, CATHERINE HANCE, designer; b. Saint Albans, Vt., Jan. 15, 1953; d. James Edward and Jean (Munton) Hance; m. Paul Stapp, Oct. 25, 1980 (div.). AA, L.A. Valley Coll., Van Nuys, Calif., 1976; BA, Calif. State U., Northridge, 1979, postgrad., 1979-81. Pvt. practice Sherman Oaks, Calif., 1983—; designer, creator Stamp Designs, 1983—. Designer Prelude Mag. cover, 1987. Mem. Am. Topical Assn., Calif. Bus. Womens Assn. Democrat. Roman Catholic. Office: Stamp Designs PO Box 5002 Sherman Oaks CA 91423

STARING, GRAYDON SHAW, lawyer; b. Deansboro, N.Y., Apr. 9, 1923; s. William Luther and Eleanor Mary (Shaw) S.; m. Joyce Lydia Allum-Poon, Sept. 1, 1949; children: Diana Hilary Agnes, Christopher Paul Norman. Student, Colgate U., 1943-44; A.B., Hamilton Coll., 1947; J.D., U. Calif.-Berkeley, 1951. Bar: Calif. 1952, U.S. Supreme Ct. 1958. Atty. Office Gen. Counsel, Navy Dept., San Francisco, 1952-53; atty. admiralty and shipping sect. U.S. Dept. Justice, San Francisco, 1953-60; assoc. Lillick McHose & Charles, San Francisco, 1960-64, ptnr., 1965—; titulary mem. Internat. Maritime Com.; bd. dirs. Marine Exchange at San Francisco, 1984-88, pres. 1986-88; instr. pub. speaking Hamilton Coll., 1947-48. Assoc. editor: Am. Maritime Cases, 1966—; contbr. articles to legal jours. Mem. San Francisco Lawyers Com. for Urban Affairs, 1972—; bd. dirs. Legal Aid Soc., San Francisco, 1974—, v.p., 1975-80, pres., 1980-82. Served with USN, 1943-46, comdr. Res. ret. Fellow Am. Bar Found., Am. Coll. Trial Lawyers; mem. ABA (chmn. maritime ins. com. 1975-76, mem. standing com. on admiralty law 1976-82, 86—, ho. of dels. 1986—), Fed. Bar Assn. (pres. San Francisco chpt. 1968), Bar Assn. San Francisco (sec. 1972, treas. 1973), Calif. Acad. Appellate Lawyers, Maritime Law Assn. U.S. (exec. com. 1977-88, v.p. 1980-84, pres. 1984-86), Brit.-Am. C. of C. (bd. dirs. 1987—), World Trade Club San Francisco, Propeller Club of U.S. Republican. Episcopalian. Home: 195 San Anselmo Ave San Francisco CA 94127 Office: 2 Embarcadero Ctr Ste 2600 San Francisco CA 94111

STARK, FORTNEY HILLMAN, JR. (PETE STARK), congressman; b. Milw., Nov. 11, 1931; s. Fortney Hillman Sr. and Dorothy M. (Mueller) S.; children: Jeffrey Peter, Beatrice Ann, Thekla Brumder, Sarah Gallun; m. Carolyn Wente. BS, MIT; MBA, U. Calif. Teaching asst. MIT, Cambridge, 1953-54; prin. Skaife & Co., Berkeley, Calif., 1957-61; founder Beacon Savs. & Loan Assn., Antioch, Calif., 1961; pres., founder Security Nat. Bank, Walnut Creek, Calif., 1963-72; mem. 93d-101st Congresses from 9th Calif. dist., 1973—; mem. ways and means com, mem. D.C. com., mem. select com. on narcotics. Bd. dirs. ACLU, 1971, Common Cause, 1971, Starr King Sch., Housing Devel. Corp.; adv. com. Contra Costa County Coalition; del. Dem. State Cen. Com.; trustee Calif. Dem. Council. Capt. USAF, 1955-57. Mem. Delta Kappa Epsilon. Office: US Ho of Reps 1125 Longworth Bldg Washington DC 20515

STARK, FRANKLIN CULVER, lawyer; b. Unityville, S.D., Apr. 16, 1915; s. Fred H. and Catherine (Culver) S.; m. Alice C. Churchill, Sept. 16, 1941 (dec. May 1975); children: Margaret C., Wallace C., Judith C., Franklin Culver; m. Carlyn Kaiser Stark, July 18, 1976. J.D., Northwestern U., 1940; A.B., Dakota Wesleyan U., 1937, LL.D., 1959. Bar: Ill. 1940, U.S. Supreme Ct. 1945, U.S. Tax Ct. 1945, U.S. Ct. Appeals (10th cir.) 1945, Calif. 1946; cert. taxation law specialist, Calif. Assoc. firm Sidley, McPherson, Austin & Burgess, Chgo., 1940-41, Fitzgerald, Abbott & Beardsley, Oakland, Calif., 1946-47; sr. mem. firm Stark, Wells, Rahl, Field & Schwartz, Oakland, 1947—; lectr. comml. law U. Calif. Sch. Bus., 1946-66. Editor: Ill. Law Rev, 1939-40; Contbr. articles to legal publs. Staff Office Gen. Counsel, OPA, Washington, 1941-42; bd. dirs. Merritt Peralta Found., Claremont Sch. Theology, Dakota Wesleyan U., Fred Finch Youth Ctr., 1970-82, Calif.-Nev. United Meth. Found., 1974-80, Oakland Meth. Found., 1952-82; chmn. bd. trustees Calif.-Nev. Meth. Homes, 1966-73; pres. Oakland Council of Chs., 1954-56; charter mem. World Peace Through Law Ctr.; former nat. pres. Campaign for UN Reform; nat. pres. Ctr. for UN Reform Edn. Served with USNR, 1942-45. Named Alumnus of Year for notable achievement Dakota Wesleyan U., 1966. Mem. Am., Calif., Alameda County bar assns., Oakland C. of C., Am. Trial Lawyers Assn., Phi Kappa Phi, Pi Kappa Delta, Phi Alpha Delta, Order Coif. Methodist. Clubs: Lakeview (Oakland); Commonwealth (San Francisco). Lodges: Masons; Shriners. Home: 333 Wayne Ave Apt E Oakland CA 94606 Office: Stark Wells Rahl Field & Schwartz 1999 Harrison St Ste 1300 Oakland CA 94612 also: Peri Exec Centre 2033 N Main St Ste 900 Walnut Creek CA 94596

STARK, JACK EVERETT, national park official; b. Arkansas City, Kans., Aug. 27, 1931; s. Daniel Crenshaw and Audra Maxine (Woolridge) S.; m. Gail Karlene White, Dec. 16, 1956; children: Jennifer, Cynthia, John. B.S., Colo. State U., 1954. Park ranger Nat. Park Service, 1957-67; supt. Platt Nat. Park, Sulphur, Okla., 1967-71, Everglades Nat. Park, Homestead, Fla., 1971-76; regional dir. North Atlanta Region, Nat. Park Service, Boston, 1975-79; supt. Grand Teton Nat. Park, Moose, Wyo., 1979—. Served to lt. USNR, 1954-57. Named Conservationist of Yr. Tropical Audubon Soc., Miami, Fla., 1970; recipient Meritorious Service Dept. Interior, 1982, Dept. Interior Disting. Svc. award Sec. Interior, 1988. Mem. Sigma Chi. Lodge: Rotary. Office: Grand Teton Nat Pk PO Drawer 170 Moose WY 83012

STARK, JACK LEE, college president; b. Urbana, Ind., Sept. 26, 1934; s. Lynn C. and Helen (Haley) S.; m. Jil Carolyn Harris, June 14, 1958; children: Janet, Jeffrey, Jennifer, Jonathan. BA, Claremont McKenna Coll., 1957; hon. degree, Redlands U., LDH, 1973. Asst. to pres. Claremont (Calif.) McKenna Coll., 1961-70, pres., 1970—; bd. dirs. Angeles Corp., Los Angeles. Chmn. Pomona Valley Community Hosp., Region II United Way, El Monte, Calif.; bd. dirs. Foothill Country Day Sch., Claremont. Served to capt. USMCR, 1957-60. Mem. Assn. Ind. Calif. Colls. and Univs. (chmn.), Ind. Colls. So. Calif. (bd. dirs.), Western Coll. Assn. (bd. dirs.). Club: California (Los Angeles). Office: Claremont McKenna Coll Office of the Pres Bauer Ctr Claremont CA 91711 *

STARK, MARTIN J., management consultant; b. N.Y.C., May 29, 1941; s. Nathan and Lola (Belmont) S.; m. Shigemi Matsumoto, Apr. 27, 1967; AA Glendale Coll., 1960; BA, Calif. State U., 1966; postgrad. San Fernando Valley Coll. Law, 1967-70. Systems analyst Industrial Electronic Engrs., Van Nuys, Calif., 1969-71; sales mgr., 1971-73; sales rep. Columbia Artists Mgmt., Inc., N.Y.C., 1973-78, sales mgr., 1978-79, v.p. bus. affairs, mgr. data processing, 1979-82; dir. corp. affairs Kolmar-Luth Entertainment, Inc., N.Y.C., 1982-84; pres. Oryx Corp., N.Y.C., 1984-85; exec. v.p. Asco Aerospace Products, Inc., El Segundo, Calif., 1985-87; exec. v.p. Internat. Engine Parts, Inc., Chatsworth, Calif., 1987—; pres. Stark & Assocs., Northridge, Calif., 1985—; lectr. Calif. State U., Long Beach; cons. City of N.Y., Memory Data Software, IEPO, Inc., and others. Mem. Opera Guild of So. Calif., Am. Symphony Orch. League, Assn. Coll., Univ. and Community Arts Adminstrs., Internat. Soc. Performing Arts Adminstrs., Am. Mgmt. Assn., Northridge C. of C., Chatsworth C. of C., Delta Upsilon. Avocations: sports cars, antiques, travel. Home: 18342 Chatham Ln Northridge CA 91326

STARK, MILTON DALE, sports organization executive; b. Fellows, Calif., Apr. 28, 1932; s. Ernest Esco and Ruth Hazel (Keeney) S.; m. Katherine Margaret Boyd, Dec. 17, 1955 (div. June 1978); children: Mark Boyd, Kimberly Kay, Matthew Scott, Martin Dean; m. Diana Lynn Mead, July 26, 1980; 1 child, Ryan. AA, Taft Coll., 1956; BA, Whittier Coll., 1958, MEd, 1963. Cert. edni. adminstr., Calif. Sec. Western Softball Congress, Hollywood, Calif., 1962-70; commr. Internat. Softball Congress, Anaheim Hills, Calif., 1966-75, sec., 1975-83, exec. dir., 1983—; sports cons. Whittier (Calif.) News, 1959-70. Editor in chief Softball Illus. mag., 1966-69; contbr. articles to softball mags. Served with USAF, 1951-55. Named to Internat. Softball Congress Hall of Fame, 1981. Republican. Home and Office: Internat Softball Congress 6007 E Hillcrest Circle Anaheim Hills CA 92807

STARK, RAY, motion picture producer. m. Fran Stark. Student, Rutgers U. Publicity agt, lit. agt.; talent agt. Famous Artist Agy., to 1957; co-founder Seven Arts Prodn. Co., 1957; Ind. film producer 1966—. Producer: (films) The World of Suzie Wong, 1960, The Night of the Iguana, 1964, Reflections in a Golden Eye, 1967, Funny Girl, 1968, The Owl and the Pussycat, 1970, Fat City, 1972, The Way We Were, 1973, Funny Lady, 1975, The Sunshine Boys, 1975, Murder By Death, 1976, Smokey and the Bandit, 1977, The Goodbye Girl, 1978, The Cheap Detective, 1978, California Suite, 1978, Chapter Two, 1979, The Electric Horseman, 1979, The Hunter, 1980, Seems Like Old Times, 1980, Annie, 1981, Nothing in Common, 1986, Peggy Sue Got Married, 1986, The Secret of My Success, 1987, Biloxi Blues, 1988, others. Recipient Thalberg award Acad. Motion Picture Arts and Scis., 1980. *

STARKEY, HARRY CHARLES, geologist; b. Wheeling, W.Va., Dec. 10, 1925; s. Burtice Johannes and Mary Irene (Hilton) S.; BS, W.Va. U., 1950; m. Ruth Woods, May 16, 1964. With U.S. Geol. Survey, 1955-84, geologist specializing in clay mineralogy, Denver, 1958-84. With inf. U.S. Army, 1944-46. Mem. Clay Minerals Soc., Mensa. Methodist. Research in clay mineralogy, ion-exchange in clay and zeolites, chem. reactions involving clays; contbr. articles to profl. jours. Home: 1636 S Yarrow Ct Lakewood CO 80226

STARKWEATHER, FREDERICK THOMAS, data processing executive; b. Sioux City, Iowa, Feb. 24, 1933; s. Fred Ervin and Gertrude Faye (Madden) S.; m. Margot Glassen, Nov. 19, 1959; children: Thomas Frederick, Jerry Russell, Michael Glassen. BA in Math. and Physics, U. Nebr., Omaha, 1955. Mathematician Flight Determination Lab., White Sands Missile Range, N.Mex., 1955-56; supervisory mathematician Analysis & Computation, White Sands Missile Range, N.Mex., 1956-81; chief Data Scis. Div. Nat. Range Ops., White Sands Missile Range, N.Mex., 1981—; Nat. council rep. Am. Def. Preparedness Assn., Washington, 1980—; pres. White Sands Pioneer Group, White Sands Missile Range, 1983-86; bd. dirs. Assn. U.S. Army, Washington. Author hist. and genealog. books; contbr. book reviews and articles to newspapers and mags. Chmn. El Paso (Tex.) City Planning Commn., 1980-84; bd. dirs. El Paso County Hist. Soc., 1983-87; mem. El Paso County Hist. Commn., 1983—. Served with USAR, 1955-63. Recipient Profl. Secs. Internat. Exec. of Yr. award, 1987; named Disting. Alumnus U. Nebr., Omaha, 1985; named to Hon. Order of St. Barbara U.S. Field Artillery Assn., 1988; recipient Conquistador City of El Paso award, 1980, Civilian Svc. award Dept. of Army, 1989, Comdr.'s award for pub. svc., 1989, Comdr.'s award for civilian svc., 1989; cited for Svcs. to Mankind Sertoma, El Paso chpt., 1985. Mem. Fed. Mgrs. Assn. (bd. dirs.), Freedom Found. at Valley Forge (pres. El Paso chpt., George Washington Hon. medal 1982), El Paso C. of C. (assoc. dir. 1984—, bd. dirs.), Hon. Order Saint Barbara, U.S. Field Artillery Assn., Tau Kappa Epsilon (Hall of Fame 1986). Club: Toastmasters (dist. gov. 1970-71). Lodge: Masons. Home: 8010 Tonto Pl El Paso TX 79904 Office: Nat Range Ops Chief Data Scis Div White Sands Missile Range NM 88002

STARR, DAVID, makeup company executive, beauty expert, author; b. L.A., Oct. 4, 1950. Student biol. sci. and medicine, Stanford U., 1966; BFA, UCLA, 1972. Owner, makeup artist David Starr Enterprises, San Francisco and L.A., 1971-80; dir. mktg., makeup artist Chanel Beauty-West Coast, San Francisco, 1980-81; owner, mgr. David Starr Makeup Ctr., San Francisco, 1984—; cons. Motown Records-Artist Advancement, L.A., 1974, Sta. KGO-TV, 1987-88, Sta. KCRA-TV, Sacramento, 1988; beauty judge Miss Gilroy (Calif.) Pageant, 1986, Miss Oakland (Calif.) Pageant, 1988. Fund-raiser Pacific Presbyn. Hosp., Project Open Hand, San Francisco, 1987—, San Francisco Zool. Soc.; mem. San Francisco Opera Guild, Mus. of Modern Art. Named Best Makeup Artist, Harper's Bazaar, 1987, San Francisco mag., 1987, 88, Achievment award Doer's Scotch, 1988. Mem. San Francisco C. of C., San Francisco Tennis Club. Office: 166 Geary St Penthouse San Francisco CA 94108

STARR, GARY, solar energy company executive; b. San Francisco, Sept. 18, 1955; s. Louis and Bernadine (Shapiro) S.; m. Susan Bryer, Oct. 25, 1986; 1 child, Brian. BS in Environ. Consulting, U. Calif., Davis, 1977. Cert. educator community colls., Calif. Mem. staff Calif. Energy Commn., Sacramento, 1977; project mgr. NSF, Davis, 1977-78; owner Natural Systems, Clearlake, Calif., 1978-80; exec. v.p., mgr. R&D Sunwind Ltd., Sebastopol, Calif., 1980-83; pres. Solar Electric Engring., Inc., Petaluma, Calif., 1983-88, Solar Electric, Rohnert Park, Calif., 1988—; instr. Santa Rosa (Calif.) Jr. Coll., U. Calif., Davis, Analy Adult Edn., Lake County (Calif.) Integrated Sci. Project; cons. City of Davis and others; lobbyist Calif. Solar Tax Credit; participant, fundraiser Project Survival; inventor, researcher in field. Designer, installer solar energy systems; contbr. articles to profl. jours. Pres.'s Fund scholar U. Calif.; NSF grantee, 1977; recipient Sci. award of Merit LCIP, 1979, Suntherm Home award PG&E, 1980. Home: 4620 Hessel Rd Sebastopol CA 95472 Office: Solar Electric 175 Cascade Ct Rohnert Park CA 94928

STARR, GORDON GREGORY, management consultant; b. Ravenna, Ohio, Nov. 28, 1944; s. Leighton Paul and Vivian Lavern (Wilson) S.; m. Lily Harootunian, July 6, 1969. BA, Allegheny Coll., 1966; MBA, Stanford U., 1968. Dir. Stanford U., Stanford, Calif., 1971-75; mgr. est, an edn. orgn, Washington, San Francisco and Chgo., 1975-78; pres. Computer Land Europe, Luxembourg, 1978-81; v.p. Computer Land Corp., Haywood, Calif., 1981; sr. v.p. Computer Land Corp., Hollywood, 1981-85; chief executive officer, pres. Fredkin Enterprises, Boston, 1985-86; v.p. TTI, Greenbrae, Calif., 1986-88; owner Starr & Assocs., San Francisco, 1988—. Vol. The Hunger Project, San Francisco, 1978—, Werner Erhard & Assocs., San Francisco, 1974—; founder, The Moscow Marathon, San Francisco, 1985—. Mem. Stanford Alumni Assn. Home: 2030 Steiner St San Francisco CA 94115

STARR, GRIER FORSYTHE, pathologist; b. Jamestown, N.D., Oct. 6, 1926; s. Earl Grier and Grace (Forsythe) S.; m. Virginia Lucille Heidinger, June 25, 1948; children: William Grier, Joan Elizabeth Starr Ferguson. BS cum laude, Jamestown (N.D.) Coll., 1947; MD, Northwestern U., 1951; MS in Pathology, U. Minn., 1956. Diplomate Nat. Bd. Med. Examiners, 1952, Minn., Mich. and Oreg. state bds., Am. Bd. Pathology in Clin. Pathology, 1956, and in Pathol. Anatomy, 1957;. Intern Evanston (Ill.) Hosp., 1951-52; sr. resident in pathology Henry Ford ,Hosp., Detroit, 1955-56; fellow in pathology Mayo Clinic, Rochester, Minn., 1952-55, cons. surgical pathology, 1956-59; cons., pathologist Lab. Pathology and Pathology Cons., Eugene, Oreg., 1959—, pres., 1973-85; mem. staff McKenzie-Willamette Hosp., Springfield, Oreg., 1959—; mem. staff Sacred Heart Gen. Hosp., Eugene, Oreg., 1959—, chief of staff, 1969-71, dir. labs., 1973-81; chmn. bd., chief ops. officer Oreg. Consol. Labs., Eugene, Oreg., 1986-89; bd. dirs. Oreg. Blue Cross-Blue Shield, Portland, 1985—; affiliate in pathology Oreg. Health Scis. Ctr., Portland, 1972-88; assoc. prof. U. Oreg., Eugene, 1986. Contbr. articles to profl. jours. Served with USN, 1944-46. Fellow Am. Coll. Pathologists, Am. Soc. Clin. Pathologists; mem. AMA, Lane County Med. Soc. (pres. 1984-85), Am. Soc. Cytology, Internat. Acad. Pathologists, Pacific NW Soc. Pathologists (pres. 1979-80), Oreg. State Soc. Pathologists, Am. Soc. Dermatopathology (chmn. 1984, peer review com. 1976—). Republican. Presbyterian. Home: 2455 S Louis Ln Eugene OR 97405 Office: Pathology Cons PO Box 369 Eugene OR 97440

STARR, MELVIN LEE, counselor; b. N.Y.C., Mar. 17, 1922; s. Herman and Martha (Aberman) S.; m. Eileen Ferne Kagan, Sept. 7, 1947; children: Marianne, Lisa Caren. BBA, U. Miami, 1947; postgrad. Columbia U., 1949-53, U. Denver, 1955-56, Ariz. State U., 1956-57; MA, U. Ariz., 1950; EdD, Western Colo. U., 1974. Faculty, adminstrn. Tucson Pub. Schs., 1950—; tchr. Doolen Jr. High Sch., 1951-53, counselor high sch., 1953-62, asst. prin. Alice Vail Jr. High Sch., 1962-64, Catalina High Sch., 1964-68; prin. Rincon High Sch., 1968-71, Tucson High Sch., 1971-74; asst. supt. Tucson Pub. Schs., 1974-78, assoc. supt., 1978-82; pvt. practice family counseling. Mem. Tucson Mayor's Com. on Human Relations, 1969—; mem. Ariz. state com. Anti Defamation League, 1971; Ariz. state adv. bd. Good Shepherd Sch. for Girls, 1971; mem. Dem. Cen. Com., Pima City, Ariz., 1968—; bd. dirs., Mobile Meals of Tucson, Pima County Bd. Health, So. Ariz. Girl Scouts U.S. Council; chmn. Tucson Community Ctr. Commn.; bd. dirs. Amigos dos los Americanos, AnyTown, Ariz., Lighthouse YMCA, Beacon Found., Big Bros., NCCJ, Jr. Achievement, Tucson Community Center, Pacific Western region Anti-Defamation League, Handmaker Nursing Home Pima County, United Way, CODAC, Planned Parenthood, Girl Scouts Am., Ariz. Mobile Meals, Epilepsy Soc. So. Ariz., Drug Abuse and Alcohol Consortium; adv. bd. Tucson Free Med. Clinic; bd. dirs. Los Ninos Crisis Center. Mem. Ariz. Assn. Student Teaching (state treas.), NEA, Ariz. Interscholastic Assn. (pres. conf. 1971, legis. council), Ariz. Personnel and Guidance Assn., Nat. Assn. Secondary Sch. Prins., Am. Assn. Sch. Adminstrs., Assn. Supervision and Curriculum Devel., Ariz. Sch. Adminstrs., Phi Epsilon Pi, Phi Delta Kappa.

Home: 7101 E River Canyon Rd Tucson AZ 85715 Office: PO Box 30163 Tucson AZ 85751

STARR, ROBERT IRVING, plant physiologist, chemist; b. Laramie, Wyo., Dec. 11, 1932; s. George Herman and Meriel Louise (Spooner) S.; m. Lavon Fabricius, June 10, 1956; children: Deborah Ann, Kenneth Irving. BS in Chemistry, U. Wyo., 1956, MS in Soil and Biochemistry, 1959, PhD in Plant Physiology and Chemistry, 1972. Ordained deacon, Presbyn. Ch. Chemist Shell Chem. Corp., Dominguez, Calif., 1956-57; biochemist Bur. Sport Fisheries and Wildlife, Denver, 1960-63; plant physiologist U.S. Bur. Sport Fisheries and Wildlife, Denver, 1968-74; plant physiologist Colo. State U., Ft. Collins, 1963-64, chemist, 1965-68, mem. environ. faculty dept. botany and plant pathology, 1973—; analytical chemist FDA, Denver, 1964-65; environ. scientist coal mining U.S. Geol. Survey, Denver, 1974-77, chief environ. tech. unit, 1977-78; chief biol. and ecol. scis. br. Office of Surface Mining U.S. Dept. Interior, Denver, 1979-81, sr. tech. coord., cons. environ. chemistry, 1984—; cons. in environ. chemistry and fin. planning/real estate, 1982-84. Reviewer Jour. Agrl. Food Chemistry, 1970; editor, Reclamation Rev., 1981; contbr. articles to profl. jours. Served to 1st lt., AUS, 1957-64. Fellow Am. Inst. Chemists; mem. AAAS, Am. Chem. Soc., Nat. Water Well Assn., Sigma Xi. Club: Ft. Collins Swimming.

STARRETT, MARY BETH, television talk show co-host; b. Bklyn., Sept. 3, 1954; d. Kenneth J. and Roslyn (Gabriele) S. Student, Wagner Coll., 1972-74; BS cum laude, Emerson Coll., 1976; postgrad., Guilford Tech., 1977-78. Health reporter/news anchor WGHP TV, High Point, N.C., 1976-79; news anchor KVOS TV, Bellingham, Wash., 1979-80; mag. show host KATU TV, Portland, 1980—, TV talk sho co-host, 1980—. Bd. dirs. Harmony House, Portland, 1987-88; mem. Oreg. Coalition to Free POW's, 1988—. Recipient Oreg. Chiropractic Physicians Annual Citizens award, 1984. Libertarian. Office: Sta KATU TV 2153 NE Sandy Blvd Portland OR 97207

STARRFIELD, SUMNER GROSBY, astrophysics educator, researcher; b. L.A., Dec. 29, 1940; s. Harold Ernest and Eve (Grosby) S.; m. Susan Lee Hutt, Aug. 7, 1966; children: Barry, Brian, Sara. BA, U. Calif., Berkeley, 1962; MA, UCLA, 1965, PhD, 1969. From lectr. to asst. prof. Yale U., New Haven, 1967-71; rsch. scientist IBM, Yorktown Heights, N.Y., 1971-72; asst. prof. Ariz. State U., Tempe, 1972-75, assoc. prof., 1975-80, prof., 1980—; vis. assoc. prof. Steward Observatory, Tucson, 1978-79; vis. staff mem. Los Alamos (N.Mex.) Nat. Lab., 1974—. Author numerous scientific papers. Grantee Ariz. State U., 1973, NSF, 1974—, NASA, 1981—; Los Alamos Summer fellow, 1974, 89. Fellow Royal Astron. Soc.; mem. Internat. Astron. Union, Am. Astron. Soc. (high energy astrophysics div., mem. publs. bd. 1978-81), Am. Physical Soc. (astrophysics div.). Office: Ariz State U Dept Physics Tempe AZ 85287-1504

STARSKY, SCOTT DAVID, retail executive; b. Rochester, N.Y., July 17, 1957; s. Edward Henry and Thelma Tamarra (Toledo) S.; m. Bonnie Lynnette Starsky, June 19, 1988. Student, Clarkson Coll., 1975-76; BSChemE, U. Colo., 1982. Engr. Nat. Bur. Standards, Boulder, Colo., 1979-82; prin., retail computer salesperson and pres. Star Enterprises Inc, Louisville, Colo., 1982—; computer cons., Louisville, Colo., 1982—. Mem. Am. Internat. Chem. Engring. Soc., SWAP (dir. newsletter, treas.). Democrat. Jewish. Home: 328 S Taft Ct Louisville CO 80027 Office: Star Enterprises Inc 318 S McCaslin Blvd Louisville CO 80027

STASER, BETTY JO, model; b. Santa Ynez, Calif., Dec. 6, 1921; d. Rudolph Frederick and Josephine (Estelle) Thies; m. Bruce Ingle Staser, June 6, 1944; children: Merry Anna, Jeffrey Bruce, John Rud. BE, U. Alaska, 1943, postgrad., 1975-76; postgrad., U. So. Calif., L.A., 1942, U. So. Calif., Berkeley, 1954. High sch. tchr. Vass (N.C.) Sch. Dist., 1945; projectionist U.S. Army, Lathrop, Calif., 1945-46; tchr. jr. high sch. Elsinore (Calif.) Sch. Dist., 1955, Ft. Bragg (N.C.) Sch. Dist., 1956-57; pvt. practice interior design Honolulu, 1972-79; model Hensley Agy., Anchorage, 1982—; v.p. Star Cruise, Anchorage, 1988—; model Nordstroms A.C. Bang, Anchorage, 1982—; hostess Miss Am. Padgent, Anchorage, 1986-87; judge Miss Co-ed Am. Padgent, Anchorage, 1987; nat. title holder Beauties of Am. age group 60 and over, 1987-88; apptd. Anchorage Women's Commn. by Mayor, 1989. Mem. Anchorage Women's Club, Symphony League. Mem. Am. Legion Aux., Pioneers of Alaska. Home: 1351 Hillcrest Dr #306 Anchorage AK 99503 Office: Hensley Agy 500 W 27th Ste 4 Anchorage AK 99503

STASIO, FRANK JOHN, computer software company executive; b. Sapporo, Japan, July 13, 1952; came to U.S., 1966; s. Francis J. and Hisayo (Kawakami) S.; m. Kelly Michelle Floyd, May 30, 1986. BBA, Northeastern U., 1977. Asst. officer Bank of New England, Boston, 1977-81; asst. v.p. Rainier Nat. Bank, Seattle, 1981-83; asst. v.p. Portland (Oreg.) Regional Office Bank of Boston, 1983-84; mng. ptnr. Seneca Fin. Co., Seattle, 1984-87; pres., founder Prometheus Software Co., Seattle, 1987—. Vol. Northwest Harvest, Seattle. Club: Wash. Athletic. Home: 8605 Meridian Ave N Seattle WA 98103 Office: Prometheus Software Bank of California Center Ste 3140 Seattle WA 98164

STASTNY, JOHN SHELBY, accountant; b. Ely, Nev., Nov. 21, 1938; s. John James and Doris Christine (Larsen) S.; m. Mary Ellen Cressall, Sept. 5, 1940; children: Karin Lyn, Mark Alan, Kristin Lee, Katie Lynette, Matthew Aaron. BS in Acctg., U. Utah, 1963. CPA, Alaska. Staff acct. Arthur Young & Co., L.A., 1963-68; tax mgr. Arthur Young & Co., Anchorage, 1971-74, dir. tax, 1971-82, tax prin., 1974-77, tax ptnr., 1977-82; sr. tax ptnr. Ernst & Whinney, Anchorage, 1987—; chmn. Alaska Bd. Pub. Accountancy, Juneau, 1985-86. Pres. Common Sense for Alaska, 1980-81, Resource Devel. Coun. for Alaska, 1988-; treas. Anchorage Community Mental Health Assn., 1988-. Mem. AICPA (mem. coun. 1977-78), Alaska Soc. CPAs (pres. Anchorage 1977-78, Outstanding CPA award 1979), Nat. Assn. State Bd. Accountancy (bd. dirs. 1983-86), Rotary. Republican. Mormon. Office: Ernst & Whinney 301 W Northern Lights Blvd Ste 601 Anchorage AK 99503

STATEN, SAMUEL GREGORY, bookkeeper; b. Carthage, Tex., Nov. 17, 1953; s. Alton B. and Haru (Butler) S.; m. Dolores Ann Kennedy, July 3, 1982; 1 child, Candace. Student, Wiley Coll., 1972-73, Seattle Pacific U., 1973-76. Graphic artist, reporter Medium newspaper, Seattle, 1977-80; staff inventory control Preservative Paint Co., Seattle, 1980-82; meter technician City of Marshall, Tex., 1986-87; office mgr., bookkeeper South End Seattle Community Orgn., 1987—; assoc. minister Prince of Peace Bapt. Ch., Seattle, 1986—. Author: Book of Life, 1987. Musician Total Experience Gospel Choir, Seattle, 1977—. Recipient hon. mentions Music City Song Festival. Democrat. Baptist. Home: 1131 Yakima Ave S Seattle WA 98144

STATES, MITCHELL HUGH, management development consultant, educator; b. San Francisco, Mar. 20, 1945; s. Hugh Wilson and Frances (Peters) S. BS in Bus., Calif. Poly. State U., San Luis Obispo, 1967; MBA in Mgmt. Sci., U. Nev., 1974; postgrad. and ABD in bus., U. Ariz., 1975-80; PhD, CCU, 1988. Coord. Coll. Rels. Atlantic Richfield Co., L.A., 1969-76; prof. mgmt. Calif. State U., Chico, 1980-84; mgmt. devel. cons. Pacific Gas & Electric Co., Diablo Canyon Nuclear Power Plant, San Luis Obispo, 1984—; mem. faculty Calif. Poly. State U., San Luis Obispo, 1984—; mem. faculty, advisor U. Ariz., Tucson, 1975-80; registered orgn. devel. cons.; cons. in field, 1976—. Named Disting. Alumnus, Calif. Poly. State U., 1972, Outstanding Bus. Tchr. U. Ariz., Tucson, 1977, Outstanding Mgmt. Tchr. Calif. State U., Chico, 1982, 84. Mem. Acad. Mgmt. (doctoral consortium 1979), Sigma Iota Epsilon, Beta Gamma Sigma, Pi Alpha Alpha.

STATHIS, JAMES GEORGE, dentist; b. Chgo., Dec. 17, 1958; s. Silas Louis and Helen Christine (Futris) S. BS in Chemistry, Biology, U. Pacific, 1981; DDS, Northwestern U., 1985. Pvt. practice Santa Barbara, Calif., 1985--. Recipient Student award Am. Acad. Periodontology, 1985. Mem. ADA, Calif. Dental Assn., Santa Barbara-Ventura County Dental Soc., Odd Fellows.

STEA, DAVID, urban planner, educator; b. Bklyn., Dec. 12, 1936; s. Armand and Henriette (Lipsky) S. BS, Carnegie Inst. Tech., 1957; MS, U. N.Mex., 1960; PhD, Stanford U., 1964. Human factors engr. Sandia Corp., Albuquerque, 1957-60; engring. psychologist Lockheed Missiles & Space Corp., Sunnyvale, Calif., 1961; asst. prof. geography and psychology Clark U., Worcester, Mass., 1967-69, assoc. prof., 1969-71; assoc. prof. architecture, urban design and planning UCLA, 1971-74, prof., 1974-82; disting. prof. architecture U. Wis., Milw., 1982-88, sr. scientist Urban Rsch. Ctr., 1982-86; adj. prof. planning U. N.Mex., 1986—; dir. Internat. Ctr. for Built Environ., Santa Fe, 1985—; Enrique O. Aragon disting. prof. Univ. Nacional Autonoma de Mex., 1989—; vis. scholar Latin Am. Inst., U. N.Mex., 1987-89; co-founder Miniversity, 1970; cons. Navajo Nation and Pima/Maricopa Salt River Community, 1974—, Fed. U. Tech., Yola, Nigeria, 1982-84, Inst. Am. Indian Arts, 1983—; vis. prof. architecture Mid. East Tech. U., Turkey, 1981, U. Melbourne, 1982, U. Autónoma de Baja Calif., Mex., 1983, Gadjah Mada U., Yogyakarta, Indonesia, 1986. Author: Environmental Mapping; co-editor: Maps in Minds, Ethnoscapes; mem. editorial bd. Environ. and Behavior, 1969-80, Human Ecology, 1971-76, Jour. Environ. Psychology and Non-Verbal Behavior, 1976-80, Jour. Environ. Psychology, 1980—, Geog. Rsch. Forum, 1982—. Cons. community planning Sawtelle Community, Los Angeles, 1972-75, Confederated Tribes of the Umatilla, 1980, San Ysidro del Norte, N.Mex., 1985—, Costilla, N.Mex., 1987, Tierra Amarilla, N.Mex., 1988, AIA Regional/Urban Design Assistance Team program, 1976—. Grantee NSF, 1961-64, Social Sci. Research Council, 1966-67, Shell Found., 1969, U.S. Dept. Edn., 1968-71, 85-88. Mem. AIA (assoc.), Sociedad Interamericana de Psicolog'88a, Sociedad Interamericana de Planificación, Internat. Assn. Impact Assessment, Soc. for Intercultural Edn. Tng. and Rsch. Office: UNAM Cividad Universitaria, Dept Psicologia Ambiental, Mexico City 04510, Mexico

STEAD, DOLORES EILEEN, social worker; b. Port Townsend, Wash., Nov. 30, 1929; d. Clinton Henry and Louise Anna (Clippinger) Morey; m. Robert E. Stead, Aug. 5, 1961; children: Susan, Elizabeth. BA, Seattle Pacific U., 1952; MSW, U. Wash., 1959. Lic. NASW, ACSW. Counselor Salvation Army Family Bur., Seattle, 1958-59; psychiat. social worker Dept. of Instns., Port Townsend, 1959-61; sch. social worker Tacoma (Wash.) Pub. Schs., 1961-62; youth, family counselor Youth Service Bur., Federal Way, Wash., 1978-79; probation counselor King County Probation Service, Federal Way, 1984—. Chmn. coordinating com. Fed. Way, 1961-64; bd. dirs. Presby. Counseling Service, Seattle, 1964-67; vol. Fed. Way Pub. Schs., 1970-84. Named Citizen of Month, Federal Way C. of C., 1975. Mem. AAUW (v.p. Fed. Way chpt. 1980-81), Nat. Assn. Social Workers, Nat. Council on Alcoholism. Home: 29852 Marine View Dr SW Federal Way WA 98023

STEAD LEE, POLLY JAE See LEE, PALI JAE

STEARNS, MARY, lawyer; b. N.Y.C., Feb. 8, 1952; d. Richard Wendell and Irene (Kusmin) S.; m. James Edward Clemons, July 25, 1980. BA, Calif. State U., 1975, teaching credential, 1976; JD, Loyola U., 1979. Bar: Calif. 1979, U.S. Dist. Ct. (cen. dist.) Calif. 1983, U.S. Dist. Ct. (so. dist.) Calif. 1984. Owner Law Offices of Mary Stearns, West Covina, Calif., 1980-82, L.A., 1982-87; ptnr. Stearns & Clemons, L.A., 1988—. Mem. Calif. State Bar. Democrat. Office: Stearns & Clemons 3250 Wilshire Blvd Ste 1750 Los Angeles CA 90010

STEARNS, STEWART WARREN, charitable association executive; b. Denver, Apr. 8, 1947; s. Vinton H. and Marjorie L. (Tedro) S.; BS, Ea. N.Mex. U., 1970; MA, No. Ill. U., 1973; postgrad. SUNY, Albany, 1974—; m. Marjorie L. Fuller, Jan. 25, 1969; children—Theresa Lyn, Gregory Robert. Mng. editor Studies in Linguistics, DeKalb, Ill., 1972-73; instr. No. Ill. U., DeKalb, 1972-73; cons. AID, Guatemala, 1973-74; instr. Skidmore Coll., Saratoga Springs, N.Y., 1975; OAS fellow, Guatemala, 1976-77; asst. dir. Chaves County Community Action Program, Roswell, N.Mex., 1977-78; exec. dir. United Way Chaves County, Roswell, 1978-83, Levi Strauss Found., 1983-85; exec. dir. Community Trust of Met. Tarrant County, 1985-88; exec. dir. Sarasota County Community Found., 1989—. NDEA fellow, Dallas, 1970-71. Mem. Nat. Soc. Fund Raising Execs.

STEARS, JOHN CAMERON, physician, neuroradiologist; b. Lynn, Mass., Jan. 3, 1928; s. Ernest LeBaron and Sarah Venables (Smallwood) S.; children: Robert L.G., Anne E., Jane K. BA, U. Toronto, 1950, MD, 1954. Pvt. practice Heron Bay South, Ont., 1955-59; resident radiology Washington U., St. Louis, Mo., 1959-62; fellow neuroradiology Washington U., St. Louis, 1962-64, instr., 1964-66; asst. prof. U. Colo., Denver, 1966-71, assoc. prof., 1971-87, prof., 1987—. Contbr. articles to profl. jours. Capt. Can. Army, 1951-55. Mem. Am. Soc. Neuroradiology, Western Soc. of Neuroradiology. Home: 3305 S Newport St Denver CO 80224-2823 Office: U Colo Health Sci Ctr Dept Radiology 4200 E Ninth Ave Denver CO 80262

STEBBINGS, GEORGE DONALD, JR., professional society administrator; b. Wyandotte, Mich., Dec. 19, 1945; s. George Donald Sr. and Betty Jane (Farotte) S.; m. Joanne Marie Dangel, Sept. 1967 (div. Apr. 1981); m. Kim Linker, Apr. 1981; children: Brian James, Mark Andrew. BSBA, Ferris State Coll., 1968. Cert. pers. cons. Asst. br. mgr. Old Kent Bank & Trust Co., Grand Rapids, Mich., 1968-69; sales agt. Allstate Ins. Co., Ann Arbor, Mich., 1969-76; v.p. ASOSA Pers., Phoenix, 1976-84; legal placement dir. Legal Placement Svc., Inc., Phoenix, 1984—. Contest chmn., state and nat. confs., Vocat. Indsl. Clubs of Am., Phoeniz, 1986-88; mem. adv. com. Phoenix Community Coll., Glendale Community Coll. and Acad. of Bus; co-chmn. Job Svc. Employers Com., 1989. Mem. Nat. Assn. Pers. Cons. (co-chmn. job svc. employers' com. 1989), Ariz. Assn. Pers. Cons. (pres. 1988-89), Ariz. Assn. Pers. Cons. (various offices since 1978), Nat. Assn. of Bar Execs. (chmn. placement com. 1986—), Toastmasters Internat. (adminstrv. lt. gov. 1986-87, Ariz. chpt.). Democrat. Roman Catholic. Home: 1231 W Barrow Dr Chandler AZ 85224 Office: Legal Placement Svc Inc Maricopa County Bar Ctr 333 W Roosevelt Phoenix AZ 85003

STEBBINS, GEORGE MCKINLEY, construction company executive; b. Merced, Calif., Nov. 15, 1957; s. George Norton and Mildred Ann (Wigdaul) S.; m. Kathleen Mary Callanan, June 16, 1984; children: Michael Paul, Christina Marie. Assoc. in Tech., Ft. Steilacoom Community Coll., 1978; student, U. Puget Sound, 1978-81; BSBA, Evergreen State Coll., 1985; student, N.Y. Inst. Tech., 1986-89. Cert. fire systems evaluation systems surveyor, 1982. Restaurant mgr. 3 brs. 1975-78; engring. draftsman VA Med. Ctr., Tacoma, 1978-81; engring. technician VA Med. Ctr., Portland, Oreg., 1981—; cons. Norton McKinley, Vancouver, Wash., 1985—. Youth leader St. James Cath. Ch., Vancouver, 1981—. With USCGR, 1978—. Mem. Am. Fedn. Govt. Employees, KC. Home: 15212 NE 18th Ave Vancouver WA 98686 Office: VA Med Ctr Portland PO Box 1034 Portland OR 97207

STEBLAY, CRAIG DOUGLAS, real estate executive, entrepreneur; b. San Bernardino, Calif., Mar. 1, 1948; s. Ralph Edward and Grace J. (Rhody) S.; m. Amina Marie Nickell, Sept. 28, 1968; children: Lavee, Kari Ann, Jennifer. V.p. Phototron Corp., San Bernardino, Calif., 1982—, also dir.; sec., treas. Sunmass Corp., Phoenix, Ariz., 1986—; pres. Sunmass Corp., Phoenix, 1987—. Served with USMC, 1969-71. Lodge: Knights of Malta (named Knight of Honor 1984), Cedam Internat.

STECKEL, BARBARA JEAN, city financial officer; b. L.A., Mar. 9, 1939; d. John Herschel and Bernice Evelyn (Selstad) Webb Banta; m. Jimmie Raeburn Lugenbeel, Feb. 16, 1957 (div. 1962); Leanna Virgina, Debra Lynn; m. Dale Robert Steckel, Mar. 16, 1962; 1 child, Richard Alan. AA in Bus., Anchorage Community Coll., 1975; BBA, U. Alaska, Anchorage, 1980. City clk., treas. City of Kotzebue, Alaska, 1973-74, city mgr., treas., 1974-76; grants adminstr. Municipality of Anchorage, Alaska, 1976-79, contr., 1979-82, mcpl. mgr., 1982-84, chief fiscal officer, 1984-87; fin. dir., treas. City of Riverside, Calif., 1988—; bd. dirs. ICMA Retirement Corp., Riverside Community Ventures Corp. Mem. adv. coun. sch. bus. and pub. adminstrn. U. Alaska, Anchorage, 1982-85; bd. dirs. Anchorage Parking Authority, 1984-87, Police and Fire Retirement System Mcpl. of Anchorage, 1982-87, chmn. 1986; devel. com. mem. Am. Heart Assn., Anchorage, 1987. Mem. Govt. Fin. Officers U.S. and Can., Govt. Fin. Officers U.S. and Can. (bd. dirs. 1984-87), Mcpl. Fin. Officers of Alaska (pres. 1981-82), Nat. Assn. Accts. (bd. dirs. 1976-87), Am. Soc. Women Accts., Calif. Soc. Mcpl. Fin. Officers (chmn. cash mgmt. com. 1989—), Mcpl. Treas. Assn., Calif. Mcpl. Treas. Assn., Internat. City Mgrs. Assn., U. Alaska Alumni Assn., Soroptomist, Elks, Moose. Home: 6947 Gladys Rd Riverside CA 92506 Office: City of Riverside 3900 Main Riverside CA 92522

STECKEL, RICHARD J., oncologist, educator; b. Scranton, Pa., Apr. 17, 1936; s. Morris Leo and Lucille (Yellin) S.; m. Julie Raskin, June 16, 1960; children—Jan Marie, David Matthew. B.S. magna cum laude, Harvard U., 1957, M.D. cum laude, 1961. Diplomate: Am. Bd. Radiology. Intern UCLA Hosp., 1961-62; resident in radiology Mass. Gen. Hosp., Boston, 1962-65; clin./research asso. Nat. Cancer Inst., 1965-67; mem. faculty UCLA Med. Sch., 1967—, prof. radiol. scis. and radiation oncology, dir. Jonsson Comprehensive Cancer Ctr., 1974—; pres. Assn. Am. Cancer Insts., 1981. Author two books, over 100 articles in field of radiology and cancer diagnosis. Fellow Am. Coll. Radiology; mem. Radiol. Soc. N. Am., Am. Roentgen Ray Soc., Assn. Univ. Radiologists. Office: UCLAMed Ctr Jonsson Comprehensive Cancer Ctr 10833 LeConte Ave Los Angeles CA 90024

STECKLER, PHYLLIS B., publishing company executive; b. N.Y.C.; d. Irwin H. and Bertha (Fellner) Schwartzbard; m. Stuart J. Steckler, June 3, 1956; children: Randall, Sharon Steckler Slotky. BA, Hunter Coll., 1954; MA, NYU, 1957. Editorial dir. R.R. Bowker Co., N.Y.C., 1954-69, Crowell Collier Macmillan Info. Pub. Co., N.Y.C., 1969-71, Holt Rinehart & Winston Info. Systems, N.Y.C., 1971-73; pres., chief exec. officer Oryx Press, Scottsdale, Ariz., 1973-76, Phoenix, 1976—. Chair adv. coun. Ariz. Ctr. for the Book; exec. com. Friends of Librs.; mem. exec. com. ednl. resources info. com. U.S. Dept. Edn. Elected to Hunter Coll. Hall of Fame, 1985. Mem. ALA, Spl. Library Assn., Ariz. Library Assn., Am. Soc. for Info. Sci. (bd. dirs.), Info. Industry Assn. (co-chmn. west coast com.), Univ. Club. Home: 5024 N 45th Pl Phoenix AZ 85018 Office: Oryx Press 2214 N Central at Encanto Phoenix AZ 85004

STEED, JOHN ARTHUR, JR., medical technologist; b. Seattle, Jan. 15, 1953; s. John Arthur and Roberta Louise (Rapp) S.; m. Jennifer Ann Fowler, Jan. 27, 1979 (div. Oct. 1980); m. Diane Marie Carey, July 8, 1989. BS in Botany, BA in Zoology, U. Wash., 1976, BS in Med. Tech., 1978. Med. technologist Grays Harbor Community Hosp., Aberdeen, Wash., 1978-81, asst. lab. supr., med. technologist, 1981—. Mem. Am. Soc. Clin. Pathologists. Home: 209 Karr St Hoquiam WA 98550 Office: Grays Harbor Community Hosp Lab 915 Anderson Dr Aberdeen WA 98520

STEED, WILLIAM LEE, ceramic tile company executive; b. Los Angeles, July 18, 1934; s. Lee R. and Mary Caroline (Banks) S.; m. Geraldine Ann Murphy, Feb. 11, 1956; children: Edward L., Colleen, William Jr., Heather, Amanda. Grad. high sch., Idaho Falls, Idaho. Cert. tile cons. Installation foreman SelecTile Inc., Los Angeles, 1959-69; tile contactor, cons. William L. Steed Tile Inc., Ventura, 1969—. Active Joint Apprenticeship Com., Los Angeles, Orange and Ventura Counties, 1977—. Served with U.S. Army, 1956-58. Mem. Associated Tile Contractors (bd. dirs. 1977-84, pres. 1979), Western States Ceramic Tile Contractors Assn. (pres. 1981-88, Tile Contractor of Yr. 1981), Ceramic Tile Inst. (Golden Tile award 1982). Republican. Roman Catholic. Office: PO Box 3259 Ventura CA 93006

STEEL, DAWN, movie production company executive; b. N.Y.C., Aug. 19, 1946; m. Charles Roven; 1 child, Rebecca. Student in mktg., Boston U., 1964-65; student in mktg., NYU, 1966-67. Sportswriter Major League Baseball Digest and NFL, N.Y.C., 1968-69; editor Penthouse Mag., N.Y.C., 1969-74; pres. O'Dawn, Inc., N.Y.C., 1975-78; merchandising cons. Playboy mag., N.Y.C., 1978-79; v.p. merchandising Paramount Pictures, N.Y.C., 1979-80; sr. v.p. prodn. Paramount Pictures, Los Angeles, 1980-85, pres. prodn., 1985-87; pres. Columbia Pictures, 1987—; mem. bd. trustees Am. Film Inst. Served as prodn. co. pres. for numerous feature films including, Flashdance, Footloose, Top Gun, Star Trek IV, Beverly Hills Cop II, The Untouchables, Fatal Attraction, 1985-87. Active Neil Bogart Cancer Found., Calif. Abortion Rights Action League, Los Angeles, AIDS Project Los Angeles. Mem. Acad. Motion Picture Arts and Scis. Office: Columbia Pictures Office of Pres Columbia Pla Burbank CA 91505

STEELE, CRAIG ALAN, electronics company administrator; b. San Rafael, Calif., Mar. 28, 1945; s. Robert Carley and Pauline Mildred (Post) S.; m. Sharon Marie Bolen, May 8, 1970 (separated); children: Sean Alan, Shannon Lee. AB in Art, Sacramento State Coll., 1968. Sales exec. Ad Type Typogradners, Sacramento, 1968-69; cameraman, layout artist Healdsburg (Calif.) Tribune, 1971-73; graphic designer Hewlett-Packard Co., Santa Rosa, Calif., 1973-83, supr. facilities, 1983—; cons. in field. Served with USNR, 1969-71, Vietnam. Mem. Internat. Facilities Mgmt. Assn. (treas. 1987, Ann. Achievement award 1985). Republican. Lodge: Masons. Office: Hewlett-Packard Co 1412 Fountaingrove Pkwy Santa Rosa CA 99403

STEELE, DAVID ARTHUR, school system administrator; b. Everett, Wash., Sept. 2, 1942; s. V. Wilson and Margaret Helen (Warren) S.; m. Valaura Jean Barger, Aug. 24, 1963; children: David Samuel, Daniel Paul. BS, Ea. Mont. Coll., 1966; MS, Mont. State U., 1971; postgrad., U. Wash., 1988—. Cert. sch. supt. Tchr. bus. Aberdeen (Wash.) Sch. Dist., 1967-68; tchr. adult edn. Olympia (Wash.) Vocat. Tech. Inst., 1969-71; tchr. bus. North Thurston High Sch., Lacey, Wash., 1968-72; area vocat. dir. Olympia/North Thurston Schs., Olympia, 1972-74; dir. vocat. edn. North Thurston Schs., Lacey, Wash., 1974-79, dir. facilities planning, 1979-80, adminstr. secondary edn., 1980-83, asst. supt. schs., 1983—; dir. State Supt. Internship Program, Olympia, 1983—; owner, cons., prof. Devel. Svcs, Lacey, 1983—. Mem. bd. elders Lacey Bapt. Ch., 1981—. Recipient Pres. award North Thurston Kiwanis, Lacey, 1980, Pres. award Wash. Vocat. Assn., Spokane, 1979. Mem. Wash. Assn. Sch. Adminstrs. (leadership award 1988), Wash. Coun. Econ. Edn. (bd. mem. 1983—, Lacey Rotary (bd. dirs. 1986—), Phi Delta Kappa. Baptist. Office: North Thurston Schs 305 College St NE Lacey WA 98506

STEELE, ELLEN LIVELY, business development executive, publishing executive; b. Fayette County, W.Va., Jan. 22, 1936; d. Alfred French and Sarah Ellen (Pritchard) L.; student N.Mex. State U., 1962-74; m. Henry Gilmer Steele, July 20, 1981; children: Gregory Benjamin Pake, Seana Ellen Pake. Civilian adminstrv. officer Dept. Army, White Sands Missile Range, N.Mex., 1962-67; mgr. Kelly Services Inc., Las Cruces, N.Mex., 1967-85; pres. Lively Enterprises, Inc., Las Cruces, 1967-76; sec., treas. Adam II, Ltd., Las Cruces, 1973-77; pres. Symposium Internat. Inc., Las Cruces, 1977-78, Asset & Resource Mgmt. Corp., Organ, N.Mex., 1978-83; lit. agt., prin. Ellen Lively Steele & Assocs., 1979—; mng. partner AVVA III, Las Cruces, 1981-82, Internat. Alliance Sports Ofcls., Las Cruces, 1982—; mng. ptnr. Steele Lehnert, 1986-88; pres., chief exec. officer Steele Svcs., Inc., Las Cruces, 1988—; ptnr., exec. producer Triple L Prodns., 1986—; chief exec. officer Nithra Corp., 1989—; dir. mktg. Los Cruces Conv. and Visitors Bur., 1984-85; dir. Santa Rosa Resources Corp., Denver; exec. GASCO Internat. Inc., Las Cruces, 1981-82; mem. N.Mex. State Senate, 1985-89, co-chmn. higher edn. reform com., 1985, 86, mem. interim coms., jud. com., edn. com., criminal justice com., Human Needs & Aids com., vice chmn. Children and FAmily Needs and Human Svcs., 1988; mem. nat. conf. state legislatures; N.Mex. Federated Rep. Women, Am. Legis. Exchange Commn.; mem. task force El Paso Electric Co. Rate Moderation; mem. firearms preemtion statute rev.; pres. N.Mex. Film Found., Inc., 1987-88. Served with USAF, 1954-57. Mem. Internat. Assn. Fin. Planners, Sales and Mktg. Execs. Internat., Am. Mgmt. Assn., DAR, La Croisee des Chemins Bruxelles, Belgium, Order Eastern Star, Picacho Hills Country (co-chmn. bd. dirs. 1980-84) (Las Cruces). Episcopalian. Home: PO Drawer 447 Organ NM 88052

STEELE, KELLEY DAWN, military personnel; b. Marshall, Mo., Aug. 22, 1958; d. Clyde and Dorthy (Dehil) S. Med. asst. Kans. U. Med. Ctr., 1984-85; mil. adminstr. USN, Vallejo, Calif., 1985-86; with counseling and assistance USN, Vallejo, 1986-87, staff civil engr., 1987-88; ocean system tech. analyst Centervill Beach, USN, Ferndale, Calif., 1988—; dept. career counselor USN, Centervill Beach, 1988. Leader Girls Scouts U.S.A., Kansas City, Mo., 1984-85, counselor summer camp, Hot Springs, Ark., 1983. Decorated Good Conduct medal. Mem. Nat. Mus. Women Arts, Smithsonian Inst., POW-MIA. Democrat. Roman Catholic. Home: 441 16st St Fortuna CA 95540 Office: Naval Facility Centervill Beach Ferndale CA 96636

STEEN, ALAN MORTON, vintager; b. Rock Island, Ill., June 16, 1928; s. Isador H. and Eva Ruth (Friedman) Finkelstein; m. Charlene B. Bernstein, Nov. 5, 1961; children: Eva, Larry, Sarah. BS in Biochemistry, U. Ill., 1949; MS in Physiology, U. Chgo., 1952; BS in Medicine, U. Ill., Chgo., 1953, MD, 1958. Diplomate Am. Bd. Plastic and Reconstructive Surgery. Pvt.

practice Torrance, Calif., 1964-83; pres., owner Whitehall Ln. Winery, St. Helena, Calif., 1983—. Mem. Am. Soc. Plastic and Reconstructive Surgery, Am. Soc. for Exptl. Biology, Med. Friends of Wine Club. Office: Whitehall Ln Winery 1563 Saint Helens Hwy Saint Helena CA 94574

STEEN, ATLE, real estate developer; b. Hamar, Norway, July 12, 1946; s. Odd and Marit Alice (Løvheim) S.; m. Katherine Jo Alexander, Dec. 2, 1987. BS in Architecture, MIT, 1970, MS in Naval Architecture, degree in Ocean Engring., 1974. Sr. ocean engr. Kennecott Exploration Inc., San Diego, 1974-80; sr. staff engr. TRW Corp., Redondo Beach, Calif., 1980-82, section head, 1982-87; project mgr. Alpine Park, Moraga, Calif., 1987—. Mem. Prometheus Soc. Home: 1396 Summit Ave Cardiff CA 92007 Office: Alpine Park 370 Park St Ste 5 Moraga CA 94556

STEEN, MARY BETH, non-profit health agency executive; b. L.A., Feb. 15, 1959; d. Robert Givens and Victoria Mary Patricia (Ramsay) S. BSBA in Mktg., San Diego State U., 1981. Promotions dir. Firstworld Travel, San Diego, 1979-81; assoc. product mgr. ICN Pharms., Covina, Calif., 1982-83; account exec. TNT/Skypak, Inc., San Francisco, 1983-84; account mgr. Krupp/Taylor USA, Marina Del Rey, Calif., 1984-87; dir. ann. support programs ALS Assn., Woodland Hills, Calif., 1987-88, v.p. devel., 1988—. Fund raiser L.A. Music Ctr., 1986, 87. Mem. Nat. Vol. Health Agys. (chmn. program and devel. com. 1987—), Nat. Soc. Fund Raising Execs., L.A. C. of C., Execs. South Bay (co-founder). Mem. Unity Ch. Office: ALS Assn 21021 Ventura Blvd Ste 321 Woodland Hills CA 91364

STEEN, PAUL JOSEPH, broadcasting executive; b. Williston, N.D., July 4, 1932; s. Ernest B. and Inez (Ingebrigtson) S.; m. Judith Steen; children—Michael M., Melanie. BA, Pacific Luth. U., 1954; MS, Syracuse U., 1957. Producer, dir. Sta. KNTV, San Jose, Calif., 1957-58, Sta. KVIE, Sacramento, 1958-60; asst. prof. telecommunications Pacific Luth. U., Tacoma, 1960-67; dir. ops. Sta. KPBS San Diego State U., 1967-74; gen. mgr. 1974—, prof. telecommunications and film, 1974—, dir. univ. telecommunications; co-chmn. Office of New Tech. Initiatives. Dir. (tel. program) Troubled Waters (winner Nat. Ednl. TV award of excellence 1970). With AUS. Named Danforth Assoc. Mem. Pacific Mountain Network (bd. dirs., v.p.), NATAS, Assn. Calif. Pub. TV Stas. (pres.), Pi Kappa Delta. Home: 4930 Campanile Dr San Diego CA 92115-2331 Office: San Diego State U Sta KPBS-TV San Diego CA 92182

STEENBEKE, HENRY MAURICE, electronics company executive; b. N.Y.C., Feb. 24, 1933; s. Henry M. and Josephine (Geoghan) S.; m. Patricia A. Caumont, Oct. 11, 1958; children: John, Michael, Michelle, Linda. BSEE, Manhattan Coll., 1958; MBA, Hofstron U., Hempstead, N.Y., 1965. Design engr. Airborne Instruments Lab., Melville, N.Y., 1958-60; engr., sales engr., product mgr., regional mgr., mktg. mgr. North Am. Philips, N.Y., R.I., 1960-70; distbn. ops. mgr. Fairchild Semiconductor, Mt. View, Calif., 1970-76; distbr. sales mgr. Motorola Semiconductor, San Jose, Calif., 1976-80; sales mgr. Bell Industries, Sunnyvale, Calif., 1980-81; div. gen. mgr. Marshall Industries, Sunnyvale, 1981-84; v.p. northwest region Marshall Industries, Milpitas, Calif., 1984—. With USN, 1952-56. Republican. Roman Catholic. Office: Marshall Industries 336 Los Coches St Milpitas CA 95035

STEERE, LOIS KAY, flight information analyst; b. Grove City, Pa., Aug. 6, 1952; d. Ernest Jacob and Mary Ann (McQuiston) LeGrand; m. David Frank Steere, Sept. 21, 1974. BA, Point Park Coll., Pitts., 1977. Receptionist Vee Neal Aviation, Inc., Pitts., 1978-80; pilot, traffic reporter radio Forbes Trail Aviation, Inc., West Mifflin, Pa., 1980-81; flight instr. to chief flight instr. Allegheny Beechcraft, West Mifflin, Pa., 1981-85; flight instr. Whalon Aviation, Broomfield, Colo., 1986; flight info. analyst Jeppesen-Sanderson, Inc., Englewood, Colo., 1987—; instr., safety dir. 99's Colo. chpt., Denver, 1987—. Mem. Aircraft Owners and Pilot's Assn., Denver Air Ctr. Club, Country of the air Club. Democrat. Office: Jeppesen-Sanderson Inc 55 Inverness Dr E Englewood CO 80112-5498

STEERS, CAROL KRAATZ, import shop executive; b. Olmsted, Ill., Oct. 14, 1923; d. Roy R. and Cecil (Earnhart) Kraatz; m. Fred L. Steers, June 6, 1949; children: Scott, Stacey, Stuart, Spencer. BA, U. Ill., 1948, MS, 1949. Tchr. various schs., 1948-50; social worker various orgns., 1950-54; prin., owner Mesa Imports, Golden, Colo., 1975--. Fellow Jefferson County Rep. Women, Golden, 1986--, Applewood Homeowners Assn., Golden, 1960--, Denver Art Mus., 1980--. Named Bus. Woman of Yr. Swap-Foothills, 1981; recipient Best of Denver award Westword, 1988. Mem. Applewood Bus. Owners (bd. dirs. 1982--), Asian Art Assn., Jefferson County C. of C. Unitarian Universalist. Home: 14815 Foothill Rd Golden CO 80401 Office: Mesa Imports 1921 Youngfield Golden CO 80401

STEERS, SANDY, management consultant; b. Indpls., July 9, 1952; d. Russell Dean and Charlotte (Cain) Thornberry; m. Louis Leonardus Steers, Aug. 10, 1973 (div. Sept. 1976); m. Michael Linsley, Dec. 6, 1986. Student, Purdue U., 1970-72; BA in Biology, UCLA, 1975. Engring. technician NASA-Dryden Flight Research Ctr., Edwards AFB, Calif., 1971-76; programmer analyst Byron Jackson, Commerce, Calif., 1976-79; field analyst Harris Corp., Culver City, Calif., 1979-80; sr. systems analyst Prime Computer, Irvine, Calif., 1980-82; founder, pres. Lorien Systems, Long Beach, Calif., 1982—; mem. adv. coun. SBA, L.A., 1988—. Contbr. articles to profl. publs. Mem. planning com. Minority and Women Bus. Devel. Conf., Long Beach, 1987—; charter founder L.A. Found. for Women, 1988. Recipient Entrepreneur award City of Long Beach, 1988; cert. of commendation SBA, 1988; named. Dist. Women Bus. Adv. of Yr. SBA, 1989. Mem. Nat. Assn. Women Bus. Owners (pres. L.A. chpt. 1987-88, nat. mgmt. info. svcs. chmn. 1988—), Long Beach C. of C. (women's coun.), L.A. Area C. of C., Calif. Small Bus. United. Home: 6230 Parima St Long Beach CA 90803 Office: Lorien Systems 5030 E 2nd St Ste 200 Long Beach CA 90803

STEFFAN, WALLACE ALLAN, entomologist, educator, museum director; b. St. Paul, Aug. 10, 1934; m. Sylvia Behler, July 16, 1966; 1 child, Sharon. B.S., U. Calif.-Berkeley, 1961, Ph.D., 1965. Entomologist dept. entomology Bishop Mus., Honolulu, 1964-85, head diptera sect., 1966-85, asst. chmn., 1979-85; dir. Idaho Mus. Natural History, Idaho State U., Pocatello, 1985—, U. Ala. Mus., 1989—; prof. biology U. Ala Fairbanks, 1989—; mem. grad. affiliate faculty dept. entomology U. Hawaii, 1969-85; liaison officer Bishop Mus., Mus. Computer Network, 1980-85; reviewer NSF, 1976—; mem. internat. editorial adv. com. World Diptera Catalog, Systematic Entomology Lab., U.S. Dept. Agr., 1983—; mem. affiliate faculty biology, Idaho State U., 1986—; bd. dirs. Idaho State U. Fed. Credit Union, 1986—; mem. Ft. Hall Replica Commn., 1986—. Acting editor Jour. Med. Entomology, 1966; assoc. editor Pacific Insects, 1980-85. Judge Hawaii State Sci. and Engring. Fair, 1966-85, chief judge sr. display div., 1982, 83, 84; v.p. Ahuimanu P.T.A., 1977; mem. vestry St. Christophers Episcopal Ch., 1974-76; bd. dirs. Kamehameha Fed. Credit Union, 1975-77, chmn., mem. supervisory com., 1980-84. Served with USAF, 1954-57. Grantee NIH, 1962, 63, 67-74, 76-81, 83-85. U.S. Army Med. Research and Devel. Command, 1964-67, 73-74, NSF, 1968-76, 83-89, City and County of Honolulu, 1977, U.S. Dept. Interior, 1980, 81. Mem. Entomol. Soc. Am. (mem. standing com. on systematics resources 1983-87), Am. Mosquito Control Assn., Pacific Coast Entomol. Soc., Soc. Systematic Zoology, Hawaiian Entomol. Soc. (pres. 1974, chmn. coms. 1966-85, editor procs. 1966), Hawaiian Acad. (councillor 1976-78), Entomol. Soc. Wash., Pocatello C. of C. (adv. bd. Conv. Visitors Bur. 1989), Sigma Xi. Office: U Ala Mus 907 Yukon Dr Fairbanks AK 99775-1200

STEFFANY, ALO WILLIAM, territorial senator; b. Fagasa, Am. Samosa, Oct. 22, 1911; s. Josef and Pepe Alo (Taisi) S.; m. Fiti Kereti, July 14, 1950; 15 children. Supt. Matson Navigation Co., Pago Pago, Am. Samoa; harbor master Govt. of Am. Samoa, wharf supt.; lic. capt., engr. Steffany Shipping, Govt. of Am. Samoa; owner Steffany's Inter-Island Shipping, Pago Pago; senator Govt. of Am. Samoa, Pago Pago, 1974—, chmn. power and energy com., mem. govt. ops. com., agr. com., transp. and communications com. Mem. London Missionary Soc. Home: PO Box 21 Fagasa AS 96799 Office: Am Samoa Legislature Pago Pago AS 96799

STEFFEN, THOMAS LEE, state supreme court justice; b. Tremonton, Utah, July 9, 1930; s. Conrad Richard and Jewel (McGuire) S.; m. Lavona Ericksen, Mar. 20, 1953; children—Elizabeth, Catherine, Conrad, John, Jennifer. Student, U. So. Calif., 1955-56; BS, U. Utah, 1957; JD with honors, George Washington U., 1964; LLM, U. Va., 1988. Bar: Nev. 1965, U.S. Dist. Ct. Nev. 1965, U.S. Tax Ct. 1966, U.S. Ct. Appeals 1967, U.S. Supreme Ct. 1977. Contracts negotiator U.S. Bur. Naval Weapons, Washington, 1961-64; private practice Las Vegas, 1965-82; justice Supreme Ct. Nev., Carson City, 1982—. Mem. editorial staff George Washington U. Law Rev., 1963-64; contbr. articles to legal jours. Bd. dirs. So. Nev. chpt. NCCJ, 1974-75; mem. exec. bd. Boulder Dam Area coun. Boy Scouts Am., 1979-83; chmn. Nev. State-Fed. Jud. Coun., 1986—; bd. visitors Brigham Young U., 1985—. Recipient merit citation Utah State U., 1983. Mem. Nev. Bar Assn. (former chmn. So. Nev. med.-legal screening panel), Nev. Trial Lawyers Assn. (former dir.). Republican. Mem. Ch. of Jesus Christ of Latter-day Saints. Office: Nev Supreme Ct 100 N Carson St Carson City NV 89710

STEFFENHAGEN, JULIAN LEAL, JR., mechanical engineer; b. Boston, Sept. 19, 1943; s. Julian Leal and Jeanne (Garrity) S.; m. Karen A. Billard, Jan. 17, 1943 (div. 1976); children: Jay L., Justin R. BS in Mech. Engring., U. Mich., 1966, MS in Mech. Engring., 1967, MBA, 1969. Mktg. mgr. Transidyne Gen., Ann Arbor, Mich., 1974-79; mktg. specialist Beckman Instruments, Brea, Calif., 1979-80, mktg. mgr., 1980-85, program mgr., 1985-86, strategic market mgr., 1986-87, mgr. investor rels., 1988—. Mem. Biomed. Mktg. Assn., Am. Assn. Clin. Chemistry. Home: 73 Lakeview Irvine CA 92714 Office: Beckman Instruments 200 S Kraemer Brea CA 92621

STEFFES, LARRY MICHAEL, accountant; b. Mosinee, Wis., June 1, 1947; s. Henry Harold and Verna Mary (Gorski) S.; m. Leslie Jane Starkweather, Nov. 28, 1970; 1 child, Brooke Ellen. BBA, U. Wis., Oshkosh, 1970. CPA, Ariz. Supr. auditor U.S. Dept. Health & Human Services, Madison, Wis., 1970-80; EDP audit mgr. CUMIS Ins. Soc., Madison, 1980-84; v.p. fin. Ariz. Fed. Credit Union, Phoenix, 1984-85; pres. Steffes Consulting, Phoenix, 1985—. Mem. Am. Inst. CPAs, Ariz. Soc. CPAs, Inst. Internal Auditors (cert. internal auditor), EDP Auditors Found., Inst. Mgmt. Cons. Office: Steffes Cons PO Box 47596 Phoenix AZ 85068

STEFFEY, EUGENE PAUL, veterinary medicine educator; b. Reading, Pa., Oct. 27, 1942; s. Paul E. and Mary M. (Balthaser) S.; m. Marcia Ann Matzelle, June 10, 1967; children: Michele A., Bret E., Michael R., Brian T. Student, Muhlenberg Coll., 1960-63; D in Vet. Medicine, U. Pa., 1967; PhD, U. Calif., Davis, 1973. Diplomate Am. Coll. Vet. Anesthesiologists (pres. 1980). NIH spl. research fellow U. Calif., San Francisco, 1973; asst. prof. U. Calif., Davis, 1974-77, assoc. prof., 1977-80, prof. vet. medicine, 1980—, also chmn. dept. vet. surgery; mem. scientific reviewers Am. Jour. Vet. Research, Schaumburg, Ill., 1984-87. Contbr. numerous articles to profl. jours. NIH fellow, 1972-73, anesthesiology research fellow U. Calif. Med. Ctr., 1973. Mem. NIH, AVMA, Am. Coll. Vet. Anesthesiologists, Am. Physiol. Soc., Am. Soc. Pharmacology Exptl. Therapeutics, Am. Soc. Anesthesiologists, Assn. Vet. Anaesthetists Gt. Britain and Ireland, Calif. Soc. Anesthesiologists, Comparative Respiratory Soc., Internat. Anesthesia Research Soc., Pa. Vet. Med. Assn., Soc. Edn. Anesthesia, Sigma Xi, Phi Zeta. Office: U Calif Dept Surgery Sch Vet Medicine Davis CA 95616

STEFFEY, RICHARD DUDLEY, land use consultant; b. Plymouth, Ind., Apr. 13, 1929; s. Albert Otto and Ethel (Williams) S.; m. Evelyn Jean Brunn, Apr. 5, 1952 (div. Nov. 4, 1985); children: Janet, Diane, Steffey-Smith, Kay; m. Barbara Mae Clark, Nov. 28, 1985. Student, Northwestern U., 1949-51. Mgmt. trainee, mgr. Lockheed Aircraft Corp., Burbank, Calif., 1953-59; asst. mgr., registered rep. Schnabacher & Co., Palo Alto, Calif., 1959-63; v.p. Colby's, Northbrook, Ill., 1963-67; pres. Steffey Fruit Ranch, Temecula, Calif., 1967-85; chmn., pres., chief exec. officer Steffey Ltd., Temecula, 1985—. Dir., pres. Rancho Calif. Water Dist., Temecula, 1974-79, 85—(Distinguished Svc. award 1979); dir. Elsinore Murrieta Anza Resource Conservation Dist., Temecula, 1977-81, 86—; commr., chmn. Riverside (Calif.) County Planning Commn., 1980-85 (Distinguished Svc. award 1985); commr. Local Agy. Formation Comm., Riverside, 1986—. With USAF, 1951-53.

STEFONIC, LARRY EUGENE, food products distribution executive; b. Deadwood, S.D., Feb. 9, 1939; s. Martin J. and Reba Lavern (Wallace) S.; m. W. Christine Trunner, Aug. 15, 1964 (div.); children: Reba Dee, Larry Martin; m. Anna Ruth Peterson, Oct. 10, 1979; children: John, Jim, Ann. Sales mgr. Keebler Co., Pocatello, Idaho, 1964-72; pres. Lions Candy Corp., Pocatello, 1972-83, Orawheat Distributorship, Pocatello, 1977-81, Capitol Distbg., Inc., Boise, 1987--; ind. real estate broker Pocatello, 1983-87; owner Gooding (Idaho) Trailer Ct., 1974-76, Coll. Market, Pocatello, 1974-76, Jefferson St. Market, Pocatello, 1974-76,Clarks Cookies, Pocatello, 1981-83, Pretzel Factory, Pocatello, 1982-86, Bengel Auto, Pocatello, 1983-84. With USN, 1957-61. Mem. Nat. Candy Wholesaler Assn., Idaho Candy and Tobacco Assn. (v.p.). Roman Catholic. Home: 3923 N Marcliffe Pl Boise ID 83704

STEGEMEIER, RICHARD JOSEPH, oil company executive; b. Alton, Ill., Apr. 1, 1928; s. George Henry and Rose Ann (Smola) S.; m. Marjorie Ann Spess, Feb. 9, 1952; children: Richard Michael, David Scott, Laura Ann, Martha Louise. BS in Petroleum Engring., U. Mo., Rolla, 1950, cert. petroleum engr. (hon.), 1981; MS in Petroleum Engring., Tex. A&M U., 1951. Registered profl. engr., Calif. Various nat. and internat. positions with Unocal Corp. (formerly Union Oil Co.), Los Angeles, 1951—, v.p. sci. and tech. div., 1978-80, sr. v.p. corp. devel., 1980-85, pres., chief operating officer, 1985—, chief exec. officer, 1988—, also bd. dirs. Patentee in field. Pres. World Affairs Council of Orange County, 1980-81; chmn. Brea (Calif.) Blue Ribbon Com., 1979-80; mem. math sci.-engring. adv. council Calif. State U., Fullerton; mem. chem. adv. council Calif. State U., Long Beach; bd. dirs. YMCA, Los Angeles, Martin Luther Hosp. Med. Ctr. Fellow Tenn. Gas Transmissions Co., 1951; recipient Engring. Merit award Orange County Engring. Council, 1980, Outstanding Engr. Merit award, Inst. Advancement Engring., 1981. Mem. Am. Petroleum Inst., Soc. Petroleum Engrs (lectr. 1978). Republican. Roman Catholic. Club: California (Los Angeles). Office: Unocal Corp PO Box 7600 Los Angeles CA 90051 *

STEIMNETZ, WILLIAM QUINBY, business executive, consultant; b. Dobbs ferry, N.Y., Jan. 6, 1932; s. Richard Bird and Charlotte (Quinby) S.; m. Judith Chapman, Sept. 30, 1967; children: Melinda, Robert, James, Liana. BA, Cornell U., 1953; BFT, Am Grad. Sch. Internat. mgmt., 1956; MBA, Harvard U., 1967. Sales and advt. mgr. for North Latin Am. Miles Labs., 1957-60; internat. mgr. Proprietary div., Norwich Pharmacal Co., N.Y.C., 1960-63; Latin Am. mgr. Andrew Jergens Co., Cin., 1963-65; pres. Internat. Bus. Cons., San Juan, Porto Rico, 1967-74, William Steinmetz Assocs., San Francisco, 1974-80, Chapman Williams, San Francisco, 1980--. Mem. Rep. Cen. Com. San Francisco, Marin and Sonoma Counties; v.p., bd. dirs. Internat. Visitors Ctr., San Francisco, 1986--; Rep. candidate for U.S. House of Reps., Calif. 6th cong. Dist. 1988. Lt. (j.g.) USN, 1953-55. Mem. Calif. Assn. Personnel Cons. (bd. dirs. San Francisco chapt.), San Francisco C. of C. (consular affairs com.), World Affairs Council, Family Club. Episcopalian. Home: 610 Wanda Ln Mill Valley CA 94941

STEIN, ARTHUR OSCAR, pediatrician; b. Bklyn., Apr. 3, 1932; s. Irving I. and Sadie (Brander) S.; A.B., Harvard U., 1953; M.D., Tufts U., 1957; postgrad. U. Chgo., 1963-66; m. Judith Lenore Hurwitz, Aug. 27, 1955; children—Susan, Jeffrey, Benjamin. Intern U. Chgo. Hosps., 1957-58, resident, 1958-59; resident N.Y. Hosp.-Cornell U. Med. Center, 1959-61; practice medicine specializing in pediatrics, 1963—; instr. pediatrics U. Chgo., 1963-66, asst. prof. pediatrics, 1966-70; mem. Healthguard Med. Group, San Jose, Calif., 1970-72; mem. Permanente Med. Group, San Jose, 1972—; asst. chief pediatrics Santa Teresa Med. Center, 1979-87; clin. instr. Santa Clara Valley Med. Center, Stanford U., 1970-72. Served to capt., M.C., AUS, 1961-63. USPHS Postdoctoral fellow, 1963-66. Fellow Am. Acad. Pediatrics. Jewish (v.p. congregation 1969-70, pres. 1972-73). Clubs: Light and Shadow Camera (pres. 1978-80) (San Jose); Central Coast Counties Camera (v.p. 1980-81, pres. 1981-82), Santa Clara Camera. Co-discoverer (with Glyn Dawson) genetic disease Lactosylceramidosis, 1969. Home: 956 Redmond Ave San Jose CA 95120 Office: Kaiser/Permanente Med Group 260 Internat Circle San Jose CA 95119

STEIN, JAY SCOTT, lawyer, consultant; b. Chgo.. BA, No. Ill U., 1984, JD, 1984. Councilman City of Dekalb, Ill., 1983-87; assoc. Nixen, Lewis and Foltz P.C., Riverside, Calif.; pres. Stein & Assocs., Riverside; mem. Dekalb Human Relations Commn., 1983-87, Dekalb County Dem. Cen. Com.; county rep. Ill. Dem. Conv. Mem. ABA (mem. individual rights and responsibilities sect.), Ill. Bar Assn., Calif. Bar Assn., Decalogue Soc. Lawyers, Lambda Sigma. Office: Stein & Assocs PO Box 942 Riverside CA 92502

STEIN, JEFFREY HOWARD, dentist; b. N.Y.C., Nov. 16, 1960; s. Arthur Oscar and Judith Lenore (Hurwitz) S.; m. Beth Ann Brown, Aug. 12, 1984; 1 child, Michelle Ilana. BA, U. of the Pacific, 1983; DDS, U. So. Calif., 1987. Pvt. practice dentistry Palmdale, Calif., 1987—. Mem. ADA, Calif. Dental Assn., L.A. Dental Soc., Alpha Omega. Democrat. Home: 25886 Parma Ct Valencia CA 91355

STEIN, KENNETH MICHAEL, motion picture producer; b. Cleve., Apr. 2, 1957; s. LeRoy and Leatryce June (Jacobs) S. BA in Communications, Pepperdine U., 1979. Agt. trainee William Morris Agy., Beverly Hills, Calif., 1982-83; personnel asst. Allan Carr, Beverly Hills, 1983-84; agt. Hamper-Neafsey, London, 1984-85, Eisenbach, Inc., Los Angeles, 1985-86; owner Pimlico Prodns., Los Angeles, 1986—. Producer film The Drifter, 1988. Democrat.

STEIN, PHILIP LAWRENCE, community college dean; b. L.A., May 26, 1939; s. Sidney G. and Rae (Rhine) S.; m. Carol Ann Freed, July 4, 1965; childern: Amy Jean, Rebecca Lynne. BA, UCLA, 196l, MA, 1963. Prof. anthropology L.A. Pierce Coll., Woodland Hills, Calif., 1965-80, asst. dean, 1980-86, dean, 1986—. Co-author: Physical Anthropology, 1974, 4th edit., 1989. Fellow Am. Anthrop. Assn. Office: LA Pierce Coll 6201 Winnetka Ave Woodland Hills CA 91371

STEIN, RICHARD ALLEN, theatre director; b. Sacramento, Mar. 16, 1953; s. Bernard George and Iris (Trueheart) S.; m. Alison Archer Bly, Sept. 6, 1981. BA, Columbia U., 1976; MA, Syracuse U., 1978. Assoc. producer Contemporary Theatre, Syracuse, N.Y., 1978-81; faculty mem. Syracuse (N.Y.) U., 1976-81; exec. dir. Oswego County Coun. on Arts, Fulton, N.Y., 1978-80; sales promotion mgr. Syracuse Symphony Orch., 1980-81; dir. mktg. and pub. rels. The Fla. Orch., Tampa Bay, 1981-82; dir. Lincoln Theater, U. Hartford (Conn.), 1982-87; mng. dir. Grove Shakespeare Festival, Garden Grove, Calif., 1987—; panel mem. New Eng. Found. for Arts, Cambridge, Mass., 1983-87, Western States Arts Found., Santa Fe, N.Mex., 1987; panel mem., cons. Conn. Commn. on the Arts, Hartford, Conn., 1983-87; emissary Internat. Theatre Inst., Seoul, South Korea, 1988; participant Leadership Greater Hartford, 1985-86. Stage dir.: Teibele and Her Demon, 1986, Seascape, 1987; producer: Albertine, In Five Times, 1986, 1987 (Conn. State Arts awards); contbr. articles to profl. jours. Pres. WRVO-FM Pub. Radio Adv. Bd., Oswego, N.Y., 1981-82; mem. Oswego County CETA Adv. Bd., Oswego, 1981-82; mem. John Wayne Airport Arts Task Force, County of Orange, Calif., 1989. NEH fellow, Columbia U., N.Y.C., 1984. Mem. Sierra Club, Garden Grove C. of C. (v.p. 1989—), Garden Grove Sister City Assn. (v.p. 1988—). Democrat. Jewish. Office: Grove Shakespeare Festival 12852 Main St Garden Grove CA 92640

STEIN, ROBERT KENNETH, JR., infosystems specialist; b. Hackensack, N.J., May 21, 1933; s. Robert Kenneth and Marian Gertrude (Ackert) S.; m. Joan Marie Olympius, Mar. 3, 1957; children: Robert K. III, Gregory Harold Stein. BS in Mil. Sci., U.S. Mil. Acad., 1956; M in Engring. Adminstrn., George Washington U., 1972. Commd. 2d lt. USAF, 1956, advanced through grades to col., ret., 1983; with USAF, various locations, 1956-75; air attache U.S. embassy USAF, Rabat, Morocco, 1975-78; dir. intelligence systems Europe USAF, Ramstein AFB, Fed. Republic Germany, 1978-81; dir. mission control Milstar prog. office USAF, Los Angeles, 1981-83; bus. mgr. Northrop Electronics Div., Hawthorne, Calif., 1983-85, dep. program mgr., 1985-87; dir. systems engring. ops. Gen Research Corp., El Segundo, Calif., 1987—. Recipient Legion of Merit, Disting. Flying Cross, Meritorious Service medal, Air medal; Spl Achievement award Royal Morocco Air Force. Mem. Nat. Geographic Soc., Smithsonian Instn., AIAA. Republican. Office: Gen Rsch Corp 240 N Nash St El Segundo CA 90245

STEIN, SHELDON, hospital administrator; b. N.Y.C., Oct. 17, 1953; s. Robert and Muriel (Schumansky) Jacobs; m. Susan Adams, Sept. 5, 1981; children: Kesha, Brandyn, Colleen. AS, Manhattan County Coll., 1974; BS, SUNY, Stony Brook, 1977; MBA, U. Colo., 1989. Sr. respiratory therapist Nassau Hosp., Mineola, N.Y., 1973-77; cardiovascular technician Presbyn. Hosp., Denver, 1977-78; clin. instr. St. Anthony's Hosp., Denver, 1978-79; dir. respiratory care Mercy Med. Ctr., Denver, 1979-84; dir. respiratory care Univ. Hosp., Denver, 1984-86, program adminstr., 1986—. Bd. dirs Am. Lung Assn., Denver, 1984-86; mem. adv. bd. Front Fange Community Coll., Westminster, Colo., 1984—. Mem. Am. Assn. Respiratory Care (mem. state credential com. 1987), Colo. State Respiratory Therapy (pres. 1981-83), Phi Theta Kappa. Home: 204 DeFrance Way Golden CO 80401 Office: Univ Hosp 4200 E 9th Ave Denver CO 80262

STEINBACH, LYNNE SUSAN, radiologist, educator; b. San Francisco, Dec. 28, 1953; d. Howard Lynne and Ilse (Rosengarten) S.; m. Eric Franklin Tepper, Aug. 14, 1977; 1 child, Mark Evan. Student, Vassar Coll.; BA, Stanford U., 1975; MD, Med. Coll. Pa., 1979. Intern Coll. Medicine and Dentistry N.J., Newark, 1979-80; resident radiology N.Y. Hosp.-Cornell Med. Ctr., N.Y.C., 1980-83; fellow musculoskeletal radiology Hosp. Spl. Surgery Cornell Med. Ctr., N.Y.C., 1983-84; asst. prof. radiology U. Calif., San Francisco, 1984—. Contbr. articles on radiology, chpts. on musculoskeletal radiology to profl. publs. Mem. Radiologic Soc. N.Am., Am. Assn. Women Radiologists (mem.-at-large 1987-88, pres. San Francisco chpt. 1987-88), Am. Roentgen Ray Soc., Soc. Magnetic Resonance Imaging, Assn. Univ. Radiologists, Soc. Magnetic Resonance Imaging in Medicine. Democrat. Jewish. Home: 6 Burrell Ct Tiburon CA 94920

STEINBECK, JOHN WITHERUP, II, educational administrator; b. St. Louis, Feb. 14, 1931; s. John William and Fayne Harriet (Witherup) S.; B.A. magna cum laude, Westminster (Mo.) Coll., 1952; postgrad. law U. Mich., Ann Arbor, 1952-53; M.A., Ind. U., 1955, postgrad., 1960-61; Ph.D., La Jolla U., 1983; m. Jeanette Palmer Hubbard, June 16, 1962; children—Jeffrey Alan, John Witherup, Sarah Jane Bunker. Tchr., Judson Sch., Scottsdale, Ariz., 1954-55; research tchr., counselor Imperial Valley Coll., El Centro, Calif., 1955-56; tchr., chmn. dept. social studies Citrus Coll.; tchr. Azusa (Calif.) High Sch., 1957-60; master tchr. Morton Jr. Coll., Cicero, Ill., 1961-63; instr. Ind. U., Bloomington, 1960-61; founder, owner, dir., headmaster The Villa Sch., Casa Grande, Ariz., 1964—. Pres., The Villa Sch. Found. Edn., Inc., 1973—. Mem. S.A.R., Ariz., So. Ariz. assns. ind. acad. schs., English Speaking Union, Phi Gamma Delta, Phi Alpha Theta. Episcopalian. Mason. Home: 3640 N Toltec Rd Toltec AZ 85231 Office: The Villa-Oasis Sch PO Box 1218 Casa Grande AZ 85222

STEINBERG, DANIEL, preventive medicine physician, educator; b. Windsor, Ont., Can., July 21, 1922; came to U.S., 1922; s. Maxwell Robert and Bess (Krupp) S.; m. Sara Murdock, Nov. 30, 1946 (dec. July 1986); children—Jonathan Henry, Ann Ballard, David Ethan. B.S. with highest distinction, Wayne State U., 1941, M.D. with highest distinction, 1944; Ph.D. with distinction (fellow Am. Cancer Soc. 1950-51), Harvard U., 1951. Intern Boston City Hosp., 1944-45; physician Detroit Receiving Hosp., 1945-46; instr. physiology Boston U. Sch. Medicine, 1947-48; joined USPHS, 1951, med. dir., 1959; research staff lab. cellular physiology and metabolism Nat. Heart Inst., 1951-53, chief sect. metabolism, 1956-61, chief of lab. metabolism, 1962-68; lectr. grad. program NIH, 1955, mem. sci. adv. com. ednl. activities, 1955-61, com. chmn., 1955-60; mem. metabolism study sect. USPHS, 1959-61; chmn. heart and lung research rev. com. B Nat. Heart, Lung and Blood Inst., 1977-79; vis. scientist Carlsberg Labs., Copenhagen, 1952-53, Nat. Inst. Med. Research, London, 1960-61, Rockefeller U., 1981; pres. Lipid Research Inc., 1961-64, adv. bd., 1964-73; prof. medicine, head div. metabolic disease Sch. Medicine, U. Calif., San Diego and La Jolla; also program dir. basic sci. medicine Sch. Medicine, U. Calif., 1968—. Former editor Jour. Lipid Research; mem. editorial bd. Jour Clin. Investigation, 1969-74, Jour. Biol. Chemistry, 1980-84, Arteriosclerosis, 1980—; exec. editor Analytical Biochemistry, 1978-80; contbr. articles to profl. jours. Bd. dirs. Found. Advanced Edn. in Scis., 1959-68, pres., 1956-62, 65-67. Served to capt. M.C. AUS, World War II. Mem. Nat. Acad. Scis., AAAS, Am.

Acad. Arts and Scis., Am. Heart Assn. (mem. exec. com. council on arteriosclerosis 1960-63, 65-73, chmn. council arteriosclerosis 1967-69), Fedn. Am. Scientists (exec. com. 1957-58), Am. Soc. Biol. Chemists, Am. Soc. Clin. Investigation, Assn. Am. Physicians, Am. Fedn. Clin. Research, AMA, European Atherosclerosis Discussion Group, Am. Physiol. Soc., Alpha Omega Alpha. Home: 7742 Whitefield Pl La Jolla CA 92037 Office: U Calif San Diego Dept Medicine La Jolla CA 92093

STEINBERG, HOWARD, chemical company executive; b. Chgo., Aug. 23, 1926; s. Leo and Hattie (Seskind) S.; m. Eve Taubman, Feb. 10, 1946; children—Gary, Erik, Lisa. B.S., U. Ill., 1948; PhD, UCLA, 1951. AEC postdoctoral fellow MIT, 1951-52; research chemist Aerojet Gen. Corp., Azusa, Calif., 1952; research asso. UCLA, 1952-53; collaborator U.S. Dept. Agr., Pasadena, Calif., 1953-54; with U.S. Borax Research Corp., Anaheim, Calif., 1954—; dir. chem. research U.S. Borax Research Corp., 1961-63, v.p., 1963-69, pres., 1969—; v.p. U.S. Borax & Chem. Corp., Los Angeles, 1969—; dir. U.S. Borax & Chem. Corp., 1973—; mem. sci. and engring. adv. council Calif. State U., Fullerton, 1964—. Author: Organoboron Chemistry, Vol. 1, 1964, Vol. 2, 1966; also articles.; Co-editor: Progress in Boron Chemistry, Vol. 1, 1964, Vol. 2, 1970, Vol. 3, 1970; patentee in field. Served with USAAF, 1945. Mem. Am. Chem. Soc., Soc. Chem. Industry, Indsl. Research Inst., AIME, Brit. Chem. Soc., Sigma Xi, Pi Mu Epsilon, Phi Lambda Upsilon. Home: 1401 Miramar Dr Fullerton CA 92631 Office: US Borax & Chem Corp 3075 Wilshire Blvd Los Angeles CA 90010

STEINBERG, JOAN EMILY, educator; b. San Francisco, Dec. 9, 1932; d. John Emil and Kathleen Helen (Montgomery) S.; B.A., U. Calif.-Berkeley, 1954; Ed.D., U. San Francisco, 1981. Tchr., Vallejo (Calif.) Unified Sch. Dist., 1959-61, San Francisco Unified Sch. Dist., 1961—, tchr. life and phys. sci. jr. high sch., 1978-85, 87—, sci. cons., 1985-87. Fulbright scholar U. Sydney (Australia), 1955-56; recipient Calif. Educator award, 1988, Outstanding Educator in Teaching award U. San Francisco Alumni Soc., 1989. Mem. Audubon Soc., Nat. Wildlife Fedn., Oceanic Soc., Nature Conservancy, Astron. Soc. Pacific, Am. Fedn. Tchrs., AAAS, Calif. Acad. Scis., Calif. Malacozool. Soc., Nat. Sci. Tchrs. Assn., Elem. Sch. Sci. Assn. (sec. 1984-85, pres. 1986-87), Calif. Sci. Tchrs. Assn., Internat. Reading Assn., Sigma Xi. Democrat. Contbr. articles to profl. jours. Home: 424 43d Ave San Francisco CA 94121 Office: San Francisco Unified Sch Dist San Francisco CA 94102

STEINBERG, WARREN LINNINGTON, school principal; b. N.Y.C., Jan. 20, 1924; s. John M. and Gertrude (Vogel) S.; student U. So. Calif., 1943-44, UCLA, 1942-43, 46-47, BA, 1949, MEd, 1951, EdD, 1962; m. Beatrice Ruth Blass, June 29, 1947; children: Leigh William, James Robert, Donald Kenneth. Tchr., counselor, coach Jordan High Sch., Watts, Los Angeles, 1951-57; tchr. athletic coordinator Hamilton High Sch., Los Angeles, 1957-62; boys' vice prin. Univ. High Sch., Los Angeles, 1962-67, Crenshaw Hig Sch., Los Angeles, 1967-68; cons. Ctr. for Planned Change, Los Angeles City Sch., 1968-69; instr. edn. UCLA, 1965-71; boys' vice prin. LeConte Jr. High Sch., Los Angeles, 1969-71, sch. prin., 1971-77; adminstrv. cons. integration, 1977-81; prin. Gage Jr. High Sch., 1982-83, Fairfax High Sch., 1983—. Pres. Athletic Coordinators Assn., Los Angeles City Schs., 1959-60; v.p. P-3 Enterprises, Inc., Port Washington, N.Y., 1967-77, Century City (Calif.) Enterprises, 1966-88. Vice pres. B'nai B'rith Anti-Defamation League, 1968-70; mem. adv. com. Los Angeles City Commn. on Human Relations, 1966-71, 72-76, commr., 1976—, also chmn. edn. com.; pres. Los Angeles City Human Relations Commn., 1978-87; mem. del. assembly Community Relations Conf. of So. Calif., 1975—; mem. citizens adv. com. for student integration Los Angeles Unified Sch. Dist., 1976-79; chmn. So. Calif. Drug Abuse Edn. Month com., 1970. Bd. dirs. DAWN, an anti-narcotics youth group. Served with USMCR, 1943-46. Recipient Beverly Hills B'nai B'rith Presdl. award, 1965; commended Los Angeles City Council, 1988. Mem. West Los Angeles Coordinating Council (chmn. case conf., human relations), Beverly-Fairfax C. of C. (bd. dirs. 1986-88). Lodges: Lions (dir. 1960-62), Kiwanis. Contbr. articles on race relations, youth behavior to profl. jours. and newspapers. Home: 2737 Dunleer Pl Los Angeles CA 90064 Office: Fairfax High Sch 450 N Grand Ave Los Angeles CA 90054

STEINBOCK, JOHN T., bishop; b. Los Angeles, July 16, 1937. Student, Los Angeles Diocesan sems. Ordained priest Roman Cath. Ch., 1963. Aux. bishop Diocese of Orange, Calif., 1984-87; bishop Diocese of Santa Rosa, Calif., 1987—; titular bishop of Midila 1984. Office: Diocese of Santa Rosa 547 B St PO Box 1297 Santa Rosa CA 95402 *

STEINBRECHER, STEVEN ALAN, county official, data processor, consultant; b. Sacramento, Apr. 18, 1949; s. Eugene Raymond Steinbrecher and Bette Lee (Myers) Eggleston; m. Glenda Lee Freitas, Feb. 22, 1969 (div. 1980); 1 child, Shawna Lynn; m. Susan Gayle Bostick, Aug. 17, 1985. BA, Calif. State U., Sacramento, 1977; postgrad., Kennedy Govt. Sch., Harvard U., 1980; MPA, Calif. State U., Stanislaus, 1982. Mgr. mgmt. info. services City of Stockton (Calif.), 1978-80; mgr. data processing San Joaquin County Health Care Services, Stockton, 1980-88; dir. data processing San Joaquin County, Stockton, 1988—. Defensive coordinator East Side Lions Football Club, Pop Warner Youth Football, Stockton, 1981-85. With USAF, 1970-74. Named Mgr. of Yr., San Joaquin County Health Care Services, 1987. Mem. Am. Soc. for Pub. Adminstrn., Data Processing Mgmt. Assn. Democrat. Roman Catholic. Home: 2632 Meadowlake Dr Stockton CA 95207 Office: San Joaquin Courthouse 24 A Hunter St Rm 5 Stockton CA 95202

STEINER, DALE NORMAN, dentist; b. Watseka, Ill., Feb. 8, 1957; s. Norman Edgar and Rosalie (Henke) S.; m. Tracy Lee Arnold; children: Cara, Christa. BS in Biology, Ariz. State U., 1979; DMD, So. Ill. U., 1983. Pvt. practice Chandler, Ariz., 1984--. Mem. adv. bd. Desert Samaritan Hosp., Mesa, Ariz., 1986--, Salvation Army, Chandler, 1987--. Ariz. Bd. Regents scholar, 1975-79. Mem. ADA, Dental Assn., Cen. Ariz. Dental Soc., Mortar Bd., Alpha Lambda Delta. Republican. Lutheran. Home: 680 N Chippewa St Chandler AZ 85224 Office: 78 W Ray Rd Ste A Chandler AZ 85224

STEINER, GREIG WILLIAM, artist, interior designer; b. L.A., Aug. 9, 1934; s. Everett August and Violette (Gerard) S.; m. Ann Carolyn Hale, July 6, 1963. AA, Mt. San Antonio Coll., 1960; B Theater Arts, Pasadena Playhouse, 1960. Co-owner Shirley Greig Originals, L.A., 1951-52; tchr. art Baldwin Park (Calif.) Sch. Dist., 1952-55, 57-58; dancer, entertainer USO, ARC, Calif., 1952-60; art dir. Tacoma Little Theater, 1957; art and tech. dir. Dark Horse Players, Estes Park, Colo., 1959-62, Pasadena (Calif.) Playhouse Coll. and Theater, 1960-62, Gilmore Brown Play Box Theater, Pasadena, 1960-61; assoc. artist Dave Stirling Studios, Rocky Mountain National Park, Colo., 1962-68; owner, mgr. Greig Steiner Gallery, Estes Park, 1967—; workshop demonstrator, art show judge and juror, Colo., 1962--; lectr. R & D Frame Sch., Ft. Collins, Colo., 1982--. Designer over 300 shows for stage and TV, 1952—; bronze sculpture at U.S. Air Force Acad., Colorado Springs, Colo., U. Colo., Boulder, Harry S. Truman Library, Independence, Mo.; murals executed oil paintings Children's Hosp., Denver, 1974, Nat. Park Service Regional Hdqrs., Denver, 1974, 75, Citrus Coll., Azusa, Calif., 1974, 76, 82. Pres. Estes Park Jaycees, 1966-67. With AUS, 1955-58, Korea. Home and Office: PO Box 1671 Estes Park CO 80517

STEINER, KENNETH DONALD, bishop; b. David City, Nebr., Nov. 25, 1936; s. Lawrence Nicholas and Florine Marie (Pieters) S. B.A., Mt. Angel Sem., 1958; M.Div., St. Thomas Sem., 1962. Ordained priest Roman Catholic Ch., 1962, bishop, 1978; asso. pastor various parishes Portland and Coos Bay, Oreg., 1962-72; pastor Coquille Ch., Myrtle Point, Powers, Oreg., 1972-76, St. Francis Ch., Roy, Oreg., 1976-77; aux. bishop Diocese of Portland, Oreg., 1977—; vicar of worship and ministries and personnel dir. clergy personnel Portland Archdiocese. Democrat. Office: 2838 E Burnside St Portland OR 97214

STEINER, RANDALL WILLIAM, construction executive; b. Washington, Dec. 12, 1946; s. William J. and Barbara M. (Grady) S.; m. Aug. 12, 1967 (div. Sept. 1980); children: Melissa K., Jessica B. BS, Chaminade U., 1985. Commd. 2nd lt. U.S. Army, 1966, advanced through grades to capt., 1969, ret., 1972; electrician Ace Electric Co., Honolulu, 1974-78; designer, gen. contractor Ranco, Honolulu, 1978—. Mem. Honolulu Club.

STEINER, RICHARD RUSSELL, conglomerate executive; b. Chgo., Feb. 26, 1923; s. Frank Gardner and Ruth (Cowie) S.; m. Colleen M. Kearns, Dec. 6, 1949; children—Robert C., Kevin K., Sheila M. B.A., Dartmouth Coll., 1948. With Steiner Corp., Salt Lake City, 1948—; divisonal dir., v.p. Steiner Corp., 1951-59, pres., 1959—; dir. Am. Uniform Co. Served with USAAF, 1942-46. Decorated D.F.C. Mem. Phi Beta Kappa. Clubs: Alta, Salt Lake Country. Office: Steiner Corp 505 E S Temple St Salt Lake City UT 84102

STEINHARDT, LINDA LORENE, educator; b. Medford, Oreg., June 10, 1945; d. Arvel Lee and Lorene Rosabelle (Babcock) Nash; m. Cecil Byron Johnson, July 29, 1967 (div. 1974); 1 child, Michael Dewey; m. Daniel Frederick Steinhardt, Mar. 17, 1984. BS in Edn., U. Oreg., 1967; MS in Edn., So. Oreg. State Coll., 1978. Cert. tchr., Oreg. Recreation dir. Springfield (Oreg.) Parks Dept., 1966-67; tchr. Harrisburg (Oreg.) Sch. Dist., 1967-68, Franklin Elem. Sch., Boise, Idaho, 1968-73, Jefferson Elem. Sch., Medford, Oreg., 1974—. Dir., Jefferson Elem. Chorus, 1974-86; jr. choir dir. Ascension Lutheran Ch., 1979-81; vice-chmn. Citizen's Planning Adv. Com., Medford, 1980—, Medford Historic Commn., 1986-89, chmn. 1989—. Mem. NEA, Oreg. Edn. Assn., Medford Edn. Assn. (bldg. rep. 1975-79, mem. negotiations team 1977-79), So. Oreg. Music Tchrs. (chmn. 1975-76), Medford Jr. Women's Club, Parents Without Ptnrs., AAUW.

STEINHAUER, LOREN CLIFFORD, physicist; b. Eugene, Oreg., June 18, 1944; s. Kenneth Wilbur and Evangeline Grace (Benton) S.; m. Carol Louise Finkbeiner, Aug. 19, 1967; children: David, Jonathan. BS in Aeronautics, U. Wash., Seattle, 1966, MS in Aeronautics, 1967, PhD in Aeronautics, 1970. Acting asst. prof. dept. aeronautics and astronautics U. Wash., Seattle, 1971; instr. maths. dept. MIT, Cambridge, Mass., 1971-73; prin. rsch. scientist Spectra Tech., Inc., Bellevue, Wash., 1973—; recording sec. Magnetic Fashion Adv. Com., 1988—. Resident assoc. editor: The Physics of Fluids Jour., 1984—; contbr. articles to profl. jours. Mem. Am. Phys. Soc. (exec. com. div. plasma physics 1983-84), IEEE (exec. com. plasma scis. and applications 1988—), Tau Beta Pi. Baptist. Office: Spectra Tech Inc 2755 Northrup Way Bellevue WA 98004

STEINHAUSER, SHELDON E., communal executive, educator, consultant; b. N.Y.C., Aug. 11, 1930; s. Charles W. and Helen (Rosenstein) S.; m. Frances Goldfarb, June 30, 1953 (div. 1963); children: Karen, Lisa Steinhauser Hackel; m. Janice M. Glass, May 2, 1965; children: Shayle, David, Susan Hirschman. BS, Long Island U., 1963. Community cons. Anti-Defamation League, Columbus, Ohio, 1951-57; regional dir. Anti-Defamation League, Denver, 1957-85, dir. nat. field services, 1977-85, dir. nat. community services div., 1979-81, western area dir., 1975-85; exec. dir. Allied Jewish Fedn. of Denver, Denver, 1985—; asst. prof. sociology Metropolitan State Coll., Denver, 1971—; arbitrator Am. Arbitration Assn., Denver, 1988—; pres. Anti-Defamation League Profl. Staff Assn.,1967-70; chmn. Intergroup Agy. Orgn., Denver, 1963, cons. EEOC. Leader Congressional Missions to Egypt and Israel, 1982, 83; staff dir. Mission to Israel, 1987; mem. Denver Anti-Crime Council; chmn. Mountain States Inst. of Judaism, Denver, 1958-59; pres. Adult Edn. Council of Metropolitan Denver; community adv. bd. Jr. League of Denver. Recipient MLKing, Jr. Humanitarian award Colo. MLKing Commn., Denver, 1986, 1st annual Human Rels. award Colo. Civil Rights Commn., Denver, 1965, Humanitarian award NAACP, Denver, 1980, Gallery of Fame award, Denver Post, Denver, 1979, 80, Leadership award Denver Cen. Br. NAACP, 1980. Mem. Assn. Jewish Community Orgn. Profl., Colo. Jewish Reconstructionist Fedn., B'Nai Brith Lodge (Columbus, v.p. 1957), B'Nai Brith Lodge, Denver, KC. Office: Allied Jewish Fedn 300 S Dahlia Ste 300 Denver CO 80222

STEINKE, LETHA MAY, nurse; b. Springfield, Oreg.; d. Walter Lewis Lawrence and Bertha Julia (Zellmer) S.; divorced. AA in Humanities and Sci., Columbia Basin Coll., Pasco, Wash., 1975; BA in Human Resources, George Fox Coll., Newburg, Oreg., 1988. Cert. nursing instr., Oreg., Wash. Nurse Alcohol Detoxification Ctr., Pasco, 1975-76, Hillcrest Convalescent Ctr., Pasco, 1976-77, Kennewick (Wash.) Gen. Hosp., 1977-79; dir. nursing services Life Care Ctrs., Richland, Wash., 1979-83, Sheridan (Oreg.) Care Ctr., 1983-88; pres., coordinator Oreg. Health Care Nurses Adminstrn., McMinnville, 1983-88. Author: (instrn. manual) Medication Aide Certification Program, 1988. Recipient Young Career Woman of Yr. Bus. and Prodl. Women, 1976. Mem. Soroptimist (sec., corresponding sec., com. chmn.). Republican. Lutheran. Club: Toastmasters.

STEINKE, RANDALL LEE, architect; b. Belvidere, Ill., Feb. 21, 1956; s. Richard Carl Jr. and Virginia Joyce (Smith) S. BArch., U. Ill., 1978, MArch., 1980. Registered architect, Ill., Colo. Architect Seigfreid, Johnson Edward AIA, Rockford, Ill., 1973-74, J. Robert Lofton & Assocs., Rockford, 1978-79, Metz, Train, Youngren Inc., Chgo., 1980-81, Davis & Assocs. Architects and Cons., Chgo., 1982-84, Pouw & Assocs. Inc., Denver, 1984-85, RMA Architects Alley Constrn., Denver, 1985-86; ptnr. Devel. Design Consortium, Denver, 1986—; vis. instr. Denver Tech. Coll., 1986-87. Author: (computer space program) Space Planning Package, 1983. Mem. task force Blueprint for Colo., Denver, 1987. Recipient Earl prize, U. Ill., 1978. Office: Devel Design Consortium 1999 Broadway Ste 3135 Denver CO 80202

STEINMAN, JOHN FRANCIS, psychiatrist; b. N.Y.C., May 5, 1916; s. David Barnard and Irene Stella (Hoffman) S.; m. Helen G. Meyer (div. 1963); children: James, Judith, Jill; m. Roxane Bear (div. 1972); m. Ellen M. Sears, Nov. 16, 1985. AB with hons., Columbia U., 1936, MD, 1940. Diplomate Am. Bd. Psychiatry and Neurology. Intern Strong Meml. Hosp., Rochester, N.Y. and Cin. Gen. Hosp., 1940-43; resident psychiatry Nebr. Psychiat. Inst., 1948, 58, R.I. Med. Ctr., 1961; psychiatrist, dir. Lincoln (Nebr.) and Lancaster County Child Guidance Ctr., 1948-61; instr. pediatrics, psychiatry and neurology U. Nebr., Lincoln, 1951-52; postdoctoral fellow in psychiatry Yale U., New Haven, Conn., 1962-64; psychiatrist U. Conn., Storrs, 1964-69, Community Mental Health Services, San Francisco, 1971-79; pvt. practice psychiatry San Francisco, 1979—. Delgate, chmn. Nebr. health com. White House Conf. Children and Youth, Washington, 1960. Served to capt. M.C., AUS, 1943-46, PTO. Mem. Am. Psychiat. Assn. (life), Am. Orthopsychiat. Assn., N.Y. Acad. Scis., Phi Beta Kappa. Home and Office: 164 Otsego Ave San Francisco CA 94112

STEINMAN, LISA MALINOWSKI, English literature educator, writer; b. Willimantic, Conn., Apr. 8, 1950; d. Zenon Stanislaus and Shirley Belle (Nathanson) Malinowski; m. James A. Steinman, Apr. 1968 (div. 1980); m. James L. Shugrue, July 23, 1984. BA, Cornell U., 1971, MFA, 1973, PhD, 1976. Asst. prof. English Reed Coll., Portland, Oreg., 1976-82, assoc. prof., 1982—; cons. NEH, Washington, 1984-85; bd. dirs. Portland Poetry Festival. Author: Lost Poems, 1976, Made in America, 1987, All That Comes To Light, 1989; editor Hubbub Mag., 1983—; contbr. articles to profl. jours. Fellow Nat. Endowment for Arts, 1984, Oreg. Arts Commn., 1983-84, NEH, 1983, Danforth Found., 1971-75; recipient Pablo Neruda award, 1987; Rockefeller Found. scholar, 1987-88. Mem. MLA, Poets and Writers Pen. Home: 5344 SE 38th Ave Portland OR 97202 Office: Reed Coll Dept English 3203 SE Woodstock Ave Portland OR 97202

STEINMANN, JOHN COLBURN, architect; b. Monroe, Wis., Oct. 24, 1941; s. John Wilbur and Irene Marie (Steil) S.; m. Susan Koslosky, Aug. 12, 1978. BArch., U. Ill., 1964; postgrad. Ill. Inst. Tech., 1970-71; Project designer C.F. Murphy Assocs., Chgo., 1968-71, Steinmann Architects, Monticello, Wis., 1971-73; design chief, chief project architect State of Alaska, Juneau, 1973-78; project designer Mithun Assos., architects, Bellevue, Wash., 1978-80; owner, prin. John C. Steinmann Assos., Architect, Kirkland, Wash., 1980—; bd. dirs. Storytell Internat.; lectr. Ill. Inst. Tech., 1971-72; prin. works include: Grant Park Music Bowl, Chgo., 1971, Menomonee Falls (Wis.) Med. Clinic, 1972, Hidden Valley Office Bldg., Bellevue, 1978, Kezner Office Bldg., Bellevue, 1979, The Pines at Sunriver, Oreg., 1980, also Phase II, 1984, Phase III, 1986, The Pines at Sunriver Lodge Bldg., 1986, 2d and Lenora highrise, Seattle, 1981, Bob Hope Cardiovascular Research Inst. lab. animal facility, Seattle, 1982, Wash. Ct., Bellevue, 1982, Anchorage Bus. Park, 1982, Garden Townhouses, Anchorage, 1983, Vacation Internationale, Ltd. corp. hdqrs., Bellevue, 1983, Vallarta Torre III, Puerto Vallarta, Mex., 1987, Torres Mazatlan (Mex.) II, 1988, Canterwood Townhouses, Gig Harbor Wash., 1988, also pvt. residences. Served to 1st lt. C.E., USAR, 1964-66; Vietnam. Decorated Bronze Star. Registered architect, Wash., Oreg., Calif., N.Mex., Ariz., Utah, Alaska, Wis., Ill. Mem. AIA, Am. Mgmt. Assn., Nat. Council Archtl. Registration Bds., Alpha Rho Chi. Republican. Roman Catholic. Clubs: U. Wash. Yacht, Gig. Address: 4316 106th Pl NE Kirkland WA 98033

STEINMETZ, JAMES WILLIAM, pharmacist; b. Ashland, Wis., May 18, 1949; s. Edward Thomas and Virginia Anne (Paiement) S.; m. Myra Larson, Feb. 18, 1974 (div. May 1976); m. Louise Ann Memmer, Jan. 20, 1989. BS in Pharmacy, Ferris State U., 1972. Pharmacist Albany Med. Ctr., Albany, N.Y., 1972-73; pharmacist, mgr. Lane Drug Co. (Peoples), Flint, Mich., 1973-74, S.S. Kresge Co. (K-Mart), Pueblo, Colo., 1974-77; chief exec. officer K & S Constrn. Co., Inc., Glenwood Springs, Colo., 1978-85; pharmacist, mgr. Sundance Drug Co., Inc., Snowmass Village, Colo., 1985-87; pharmacist, owner Basalt Clinic Pharmacy, Basalt, Colo., 1987—; cons. Family Physicians Clinic, Snowmass Village, 1985—. Inventor sure-rod blind tie. Co-founder Basalt Downtown Orgn., 1988. Fellow Colo. Phamacal Assn.; mem. Nat. Assn. Retail Druggist's, Assn. Independent Pharmacy. Home: 0318 W Sopris Creek Rd Basalt CO 81621 Office: Basalt Clinic Pharmacy 160 Midland Ave Basalt CO 81621

STEINMETZ, SEYMOUR, pediatrician; b. Czechoslovakia, Oct. 6, 1934; s. Nathan and Gisela (Perl) S.; m. Ronnie P. Simons, June 24, 1973. BA, Yeshiva U., N.Y.C., 1956; MD, Albert Einstein Coll. Medicine, Bronx, N.Y., 1960. Diplomate Am. Bd. Pediatrics. Intern UCLA Hosp., L.A., 1960-61, resident pediatrician, 1961-62; chief resident pediatrician Montetiore Hosp., Bronx, N.Y., 1964-65; fellow child psychiatry Jacobi Hosp., Bronx, N.Y., 1966-67; pvt. practice Great Neck, N.Y., 1966-74, Fremont (Calif.) Pediatric Med. Group, 1974—; fellow Albert Einstein Coll. With USAF, 1962-64. Fellow Am. Acad. Pediatrics, Am. Bd. Pediatrics. Office: Fremont Pediatric Med Group 3755 Beacon Ave Fremont CA 94538

STELLMACHER, HERBERT BOB, real estate appraiser; b. Dallas, June 11, 1914; s. Herbert and Marie (Bielstein) S.; m. Willetta Sherrill, Sept. 6, 1952 (div. Feb. 1986). BA, U. Tex., Austin, 1935; MBA, So. Meth. U., 1952. Cert. appraiser, sr. real estate appraiser. Salesman Stellmacher & Clark, Dallas, 1938-42; ptnr. Stellmacher & Son, Dallas, 1945-52; instr. Ill. Tech., Chgo., 1952-53; asst. prof. U. Houston, 1953-54, N. Tex. State U., Denton, 1954-58; prof. U. Hawaii, Honolulu, 1958-79; appraiser Bishop Trust Co., Honolulu, 1980-84; staff appraiser Stellmacher & Sadoyama, Honolulu, 1984—; cons. Pan Am. Airways, N.Y.C., Europe, 1965-66. Author: Marketing Cases, 1976, Cases in real Estate Practice, 1980; contbr. articles in field to profl. jours. Mem. Environ. Quality Commn. State Hawaii, 1980-81. Lt. USNR, 1942-45, PTO, Korea, China. Found. for Econ. Edn. fellow, 1965. Mem. Am. Inst. Real Estate Appraisers, Internat. Soc. Real Estate Appraisers, Hawaii Assn. Realtors, IBDA Club. Lutheran. Home: 2416 Ferdinand Ave Honolulu HI 96822 Office: Stellmacher & Sadoyama Ltd 1109 C Maunakee St Honolulu HI 96817

STELLMACHER, RICHARD A., real estate appraiser; b. Dallas, Dec. 12, 1953; s. H. Bob and Willetta (Sherrill) S.; m. Jennifer Lund, July 11, 1981; 1 child, Robert John. BBA, U. Hawaii, Manoa, 1976; SRPA, Hawaii, 1980, MAI, 1981. Registered real estate appraiser. Researcher and staff appraiser Hastings, Martin, Hallstrom & Chew, Honolulu, 1976-79; v.p. Hastings, Martin, Conboy & Braig, 1980-84; pres. Stellmacher & Sadoyama, Ltd., 1984--. Contbr. articles in field to profl. jours. Past pres. Hawaii Chapter, Am. Inst. Real Estate Appraisers; past. pres. Hawaii Chapter, Internat. Soc. Real Estate Appraisers. Mem. Hawaii Assn. Realtors, Honolulu Bd. Realtors, Oahu Country Club (Honolulu), Pacific Club (Honolulu). Home: 2210 Halulu Way Honolulu HI 96822 Office: Stellmacher & Sadoyama Ltd 1109-C Maunakea St Honolulu HI 96817

STEMMER, JAY JOHN, safety engineer, consultant; b. Wilkes-Barre, Pa., Apr. 29, 1939. BSCE, N.J. Inst. Tech., 1962; MBA, Calif. State U., Long Beach, 1969. Registered profl. engr., Calif.; cert. safety profl.; cert. hazard control mgmt. Engr. Factory Mut., N.J., 1973-77; cons. McKay & Assoc., Calif., 1977-81, Index Research, Calif., 1981-83, Fireman's Fund, Calif., 1983-85, AIG Cons., Calif., 1985-87; sr. cons. Argonaut, Calif., 1987—; assoc. prof. Sierra Coll., Los Angeles, 1979-80. Author: Medical Manual of Industrial Toxicology, 1965, Latin America, A Study of Air Transport Development and Potential in the Decade Ahead, 1970. Served to lt. USAF, 1962-65. Mem. NSPE, Calif. Soc. Profl. Engrs., Am. Soc. Safety Engrs., Am. Risk and Ins. Assn., Bd. Motion Pictures and TV Engrs., Screen Actors Guild, Actors Equity Assn., AFTRA. Home: 1517 E Garfield Ave #84 Glendale CA 91205

STENBERG, SHELDON LEROY, accountant; b. Rapid City, S.D., Feb. 5, 1957; s. Erland LeRoy and Mary Ann (Marquess) S. BBA, U. S.D., 1979. CPA, S.D. Jr. staff acct. dept. legis. audit State of S.D., Pierre, 1979-81; sr. staff acct. Sayler Thorstenson & Co., Rapid City, S.D., 1981-88; corp. audit supr. Alumax, Inc., San Mateo, Calif., 1988; sr. auditor Wells Fargo & Co., San Francisco, 1988—. Mem. AICPA, S.D. Soc. CPAs (pub. rels. com. 1984—, pres. Black Hills chpt. 1986, 87), Inst. Internal Auditors, Cosmopolitan Club, Elks. Republican. Lutheran. Home: 310 Channing Way #119 San Rafael CA 94903

STENEHJEM, MICHELE ANN, historian, owner research consulting firm; b. Schenectady, N.Y., Dec. 1, 1948; d. William Keenan and Elva Margaret (Trumblay) Flynn; div.; children: Jason, James, Danielle. BA in Sociology, SUNY, Cortland, 1970; MA in History, SUNY, Albany, 1971, PhD in History, 1975. Grad. asst. History Dept. SUNY, Albany, 1971-74; edn. info. staff N.Y. State Edn. Dept. Bicentenniel Commn., Albany, N.Y., 1974-75; historical lib. Chgo. Hist. Soc., 1975-76; lectr., program coord. Capital U., Columbus, Ohio, 1986-87; asst. curator Ohio Hist. Soc., Columbus, 1987-88; owner History View. Author: An American First: John T. Flynn and the America First Committee, 1976, The Henford Nuclear Reservation and Its Vicinity: 1805-1988, Historic Survey: Proposed Route ot the Fiber Optics Cable; planner: Exhibit and Script, Post World War II Sect. History Mall, Ohio Hist. Soc., 1988. V.p. (suburban) YWCA metro Denver, 1980-83; vol. PTO, Littleton, Colo, 1981-84, PTO, Dublin, Ohio, 1984-87. Recipient Dissertation Rsch. Grant, Inst. for Humane Studies, Menlo Park, Calif.1973, Rsch. Grant, Am. Assn. State and Local History, Nashville, Tenn., 1988-89. Mem. Am. Hist. Soc., Am. Assn. Mus., Pacific Northwest Historians Guild, Wash. State Hist. Soc., History of Sci. Soc. (Columbia chpt.), Northwest Environ. Studies Assn. Office: 325 Casey Ave Richland WA 99352

STENFORD, LEIF MARTIN, real estate broker; b. Ketchikan, Alaska, Sept. 6, 1959; s. John Martin and Judith Ann (Cramer) S. AA in Humanities, Ketchikan Community Coll., 1983. Bookkeeper, clk. Stenford Corp., Ketchikan, 1968-82; rampservice Alaska Airlines, Ketchikan, 1982-84; salesman real estate Tongass Realty, Inc., Ketchikan, 1985—. Vol. Lloyd Jones Alaska State Sen. Campaign, Ketchikan, 1985. Republican. Mem. Christian and Missionary Alliance. Lodge: Rotary. Home: 2221 3d Ave #4 Ketchikan AK 99901 Office: Tongass Realty Inc 431 Dock St Ketchikan AK 99901

STENSTROM, MICHAEL KNUDSON, civil engineering educator; b. Anderson, S.C., Nov. 28, 1948; s. Edward Farnum and Virginia Frances (Garrett) S.; m. Linda Ann Moxley, Aug. 15, 1974 (div. Nov. 1976); m. Margaret Merle Allen, Jan. 13, 1977. BSEE, Clemson U., 1971, MS in Environ. Engring., 1972, PhD in Environ. Engring., 1976. Registered profl. engr., Calif. Project mgr. Amoco Oil Co., Naperville, Ill., 1975-77; asst. prof. civil engring. UCLA, 1977-81, assoc. prof., 1981-84, prof., 1984—, dir. Engring. Computer Ctr., 1985—; cons. on pollution control to numerous cos. and state and city govts. Contbr. articles to profl. jours. Chmn. sci. adv. bd. Heal-the-Bay, L.A., 1987-88. With USAF, 1969-70. Recipient numerous grants. Mem. ASCE (Walter L. Huber award 1989), Am. Acad. Environ. Engrs., Assn. Environ. Engring. Profs., Water Pollution Control Fedn., Internat. Assn. on Water Pollution Rsch. and Control, Am. Chem. Soc., Blue Key, Sigma Xi, Tau Beta Pi. Democrat. Home: 1829 S Crescent Heights Los Angeles CA 90035 Office: UCLA 4173 Boelter Hall Los Angeles CA 90024-1600

STENTZ, STEVEN THOMAS, researcher, systems analyst; b. Sidney, Nebr., May 4, 1951; s. Howard William and Orletha Maxine (Gardner) S.;

m. Patricia Marie Thompson, Oct. 9, 1971 (div. 1979); 1 child, Carrie Lee. BA magna cum laude, We. Wash. U., 1979; MS, U. Wash., 1982, doctoral postgrad., 1982-85. Counselor Auburn (Wash.) Youth Svcs., 1977-79, Renton (Wash.) Area Youth Svcs., 1980; research analyst Dept. Social & Health Svcs., Olympia, Wash., 1981-82; computer, rsch. cons. U. Wash., Seattle, 1982-85, instr., 1986; instr. We. Wash. U., Bellingham, 1986-88; systems analyst S. Stentz & Assocs., Olympia, 1981—; researcher Wash. Supreme Ct., Olympia, 1986—; Mem. Human Subjecs Rev. Com. U. Wash., Seattle, 1982-85; cons. King County Dept. of Youth Svcs., Seattle, 1984-88, Wash. Assn. Rehab. Psychologists, Seattle, 1983-88, King County Health Planning Coun., Seattle, 1983-84. Contbr. articles to profl. jours.; author software reference manuals. Speaker Assn. Hosp. Adminstrs., 1983-86, Coun. on Social Work Edn., Detroit, 1983, Alliance for Children, Youth & Families, Seattle, 1986. With U.S. Army, 1971-72.

STEPANEK, JOSEPH EDWARD, industrial development consultant; b. Ellinwood, Kans., Oct. 29, 1917; s. Joseph August and Leona Mae (Wilson) S.; m. Antoinette Farnham, June 10, 1942; children: Joseph F., James B., Antoinette L., Debra L. BSChemE, U. Colo., 1939; DEng in Chem. Engring., Yale U., 1942. Registered profl. engr., Colo. Engr. Stearns-Roger Mfg., Denver, 1939-45; from asst. to assoc. prof. U. Colo., Boulder, 1945-47; from cons. to dir. UN, various countries, 1947-73; cons. internat. indsl devel., U.S.-China bus. relations Boulder, 1973—; bd. dirs. 12 corps., 1973—. Author 3 books on indsl. devel.; contbr. 50 articles to profl. jours. Exec. dir. Boulder Tomorrow, 1965-67. Recipient Yale Engring. award Yale Engring. Assn., 1957, Norlin award U. Colo. 1978, Annual award India League of Am., 1982. Mem. AAAS. Democrat. Unitarian. Club: Yale (N.Y.C.). Home: 1622 High St Boulder CO 80302

STEPHAN, KATHRYN MARIE, weaver, designer; b. Perth Amboy, N.J., June 8, 1957; d. Robert Walter and Marie Elizabeth (Trost) S. BA, Glassboro State Coll., 1979. Apprentice weaver, then head weaver Sunflower Studios, Grand Junction, Colo., 1979-81; prin. Kathryn Stephan Studios, Steamboat Springs, Colo., 1981—; head weaver Arianthe/Kris Studios, Steamboat Springs, 1983-85; instr. weaving and dying, Mesa Coll., Western Colo. Ctr. for Arts, both Grand Junction, 1982. Mem. Am. Crafts Coun., Steamboat Springs Arts Coun., Nature Conservancy, Wilderness Soc. Democrat. Office: Kathryn Stephan Studios PO Box 774492 Steamboat Springs CO 80477

STEPHAN, LARRY KEITH, associate dean of students; b. Piqua, Ohio, June 24, 1951; s. Walter John and Barbara Delores (Allen) S.; m. Brenda Sue Hinger, Apr. 17, 1971; children: Alisha, Joshua. BA in Edn., Ohio No. U., 1974; postgrad., U. Colo., 1974-75. Sales rep. Dinner Bell Foods, Troy, Ohio, 1974; grad. asst. U. Colo., Boulder, 1974-76; tchr. Victoria (Australia) Dept. Edn., Cobram, 1976-78, Piqua Bd. Edn., 1978-79; athletic dir. Embry-Riddle Aero. U., Prescott, Ariz., 1979-86, assoc. dean students, 1986—; presenter Ednl. Leadership Devel., 1985-87. Mem. com. parks and Recreation Devel. Commn., Prescott, 1987, mem. adv. com., 1982-85; bd. dirs. Prescott YMCA, 1982-85, sec., 1983-85. Mem. Nat. Assn. Campus Activities (coordinator 1983-85, mem. com. 1987-88), Nat. Intramural Recreational Sports Assn., AAHPER. Lutheran. Club: Aeromech. Athletic (Prescott) (pres. 1985-87). Home: 2958 Quartz Dr Prescott AZ 86301 Office: Embry-Riddle Aero U 3200 N Willow Creek Rd Prescott AZ 86301

STEPHANY, GARY ROBERT, environmental health professional; b. San Diego, June 1, 1938; s. Joseph Robert and Kathleen (Vdink) S.; div.; children: Kristin, Erik. BS in Geology, San Diego State U., 1963; cert. mgmt. by objective, Calif. Environ. Health Assn., 1977; cert. mgmt. tng., San Diego County, 1980; cert.hazardous waste mgmt, Ariz. State Health Dept., 1982. Registered sanitarian, Calif.; cert. technician vertebrate vector, mosquito and terrestrial invertebrate control, Calif. Sanitarian Environ. Health Svcs. San Diego County Dept. Health Svcs., San Diego, 1963-87, chief Environ. Health Svcs., 1981-87, dir. Environ Health Svcs., 1987—; lectr. in field; chmn. tech. adv. coun., So. Calif. Hazardous Waste Mgmt. Project, chmn. solid waste com., Dirs. Environ. Health, San Diego; chmn. solid waste enforcement adv. coun., Calif. Waste Mgmt. Bd., Sacramento; instr., San Diego State U., 1988-89; guest lectr. ednl. instns. Author waste mgmt. procedure manuals. Bd. dirs., I Love A Clean San Diego, 1989; co-chmn. San Diego Internat. Hist. Fair, 1984-86. Mem. San Diego Hist. Soc., San Diego Maritime Assn., Dirs. Environ. Health, Nat. Environ. Health Assn., Calif. Environ. Health Assn., San Diego Assn. Geologists, Geol. Soc. Am., Rotary, San Diego Yacht Club. Republican. Presbyterian.

STEPHENS, BRODIE ROBERTSON, architect; b. San Francisco, May 2, 1961; s. Terry Robertson and Alice (Kent) S.; m. Stephanie Ann Tambe, Jan. 10, 1987. BArch, U. Calif., 1984. Designer Whisler-Patri Architects, San Francisco, 1984-86, Associated Architects, Oakland, Calif., 1986; architect Naval Facilities Engring. Command, Oakland, 1986—; graphic designer Berkeley Crisis Pregnancy Ctr.; Trinity Fellowship, Berkeley, 1984-88. Mem. Alpha Gamma Omega. Baptist. Office: Naval Pub Works Ctr PO Box 24003 Oakland CA 94111

STEPHENS, CHARLES WILLIAM, aerospace consultant, electronic engineer; b. Liberal, Kans., July 26, 1930; s. Ernest Virgil and Thelma Dorleska (Keating) S.; m. Mary B. Hoofnagle, Aug. 31, 1952; children—Craig A., Cathy J., Kirk M. B.S.E.E., U. Kans., Lawrence, 1952; postgrad. engring. studies, Bell Telephone Labs., N.Y.C., 1953-54. Mem. tech. staff Bell Telephone Labs. Inc., Whippany, N.J., 1953-54; v.p., dep. gen. mgr. Electronics & Def. Sector, TRW Inc., Redondo Beach, Calif., 1957-86, aerospace consultant, 1986—; mem. adv. bd. dept. elec. and computer engring. U. Kans., 1980—, mem. adv. bd. Sch. Engring., 1981—; mem. bd. counselors sch. engring., U. So. Calif.; chmn. telecommunications and computer applications bd. Nat. Research Council, 1988—. Bd. mgrs. Torrance-South Bay Area YMCA, Calif., 1982; mem. Rolling Hills Covenant Ch., Calif., 1984—. Served with U.S. Army, 1954-56; Army Ballistic Missile Agy. Mem. Nat. Acad. Engring., AIAA, IEEE, Electronic Industries Assn. (bd. govs. 1983-86, bd. dirs. gov. div. 1983-86), Am. Men and Women of Sci., Sigma Xi, Sigma Pi Sigma, Eta Kappa Nu, Tau Beta Pi, Sigma Tau. Home: 2707 W 233 St Torrance CA 90505

STEPHENS, DONALD R(ICHARDS), banker; b. San Francisco, June 28, 1938; s. Donald Lewis and Anona Marie (O'Leary) S.; m. Christina Brinkman, Sept. 11, 1971; children—Lane B., Justin H., Nicholas W., Adam H. B.S., U. So. Calif., 1961; J.D., Hastings Coll., 1969. Pres. Campodonico & Stephens, San Francisco, 1963-65; pres., owner Union Investment Co., San Francisco, 1966-69; assoc. Law Offices of Louis O. Kelso, 1969-72; individual practice law, San Francisco, 1972-77; pres. D.R. Stephens & Co., San Francisco, 1976—; chmn., chief exec. officer Bank of San Francisco, 1978—, also bd. dirs.; bd. dirs. A.I.F.S., Inc., Skouras Pictures, Lincoln N.L. Realty. Bd. dirs. Bay Area Coun.; trustee St. Francis Meml. Hosp., San Francisco, 1976-82; mem. policy adv. bd. U. Calif. Mem. Urban Land Inst., World Bus. Coun., Bohemian Club, Calif. Club. Republican. Presbyterian. Avocation: tennis.

STEPHENS, FREDRIC MILO, transportation executive; b. Laredo, Tex., Sept. 24, 1955; s. Albert Milo and Wanda Joann (White) S. BA in Polit. Sci., U. N.Mex., 1977; MBA, U. Fla., 1987. Commd. ensign USN, 1977, pilot trainee, 1977-79, maintenance officer, patrol plane comdr., 1979-82, instr. pilot, 1982-85; resigned 1985; pilot Northwest Airlines, Inc., Mpls., 1985—. Mem. Airline Pilots Assn., Naval Inst., Experimental Aircraft Assn. Republican. Presbyterian. Home: PO Box 571 Peralta NM 87042

STEPHENS, GEORGE EDWARD, JR., lawyer; b. Lawrence, Kans., Mar. 26, 1936; s. George Edward and Mary Helen (Houghton) S.; m. Gretel Geiser, Dec. 31, 1965; children: Thaddeus Geiser, Edward Houghton, Mary Schoentgen. Student, U. Colo., Boulder, 1954-57, U. Colo. Sch. Medicine, Denver, 1957-59; LLB, Stanford U., 1962. Bar: Calif. 1963, U.S. Dist. Ct. (cen. dist.) Calif. 1963, U.S. Ct. Appeals (9th cir.) 1971. Law clk. to judge U.S. Dist. Ct., Los Angeles, 1962-64; ptnr. Pollock & Palmer, Los Angeles, 1964-69, Gates, Morris, Merrill & Stephens, Los Angeles, 1969-72, Paul, Hastings, Janofsky & Walker, Los Angeles, 1972—; Mem. coordinating council on Lawyer Competence, Conf. Chief Justices, 1983-86; chmn. porbate sect. Los Angeles County Bar Assn., 1979-80. Nat. chmn. Stanford (Calif.) U. Law Fund Quad Program, 1980-87; mem. bd. visitors Stanford Law Sch., 1982-85; founder Mus. Contempory Art, Los Angeles, 1982. Recipient Stanford Assocs. award, 1982. Fellow Am. Bar Found., Am. Coll. Probate Counsel, Internat. Acad. Probate and Trust; mem. ABA (chmn. standing com. specialization 1979-82, rep. to coordinating council on lawyer competence 1982-87), Stanford Law Soc. (pres. 1972-73). Episcopalian. Clubs: Chancery (Los Angeles), Annandale Golf (Pasadena, Calif.), Valley Hunt (Pasadena). Office: Paul Hastings Janofsky & Walker 555 S Flower 22nd Fl Los Angeles CA 90071

STEPHENS, GUY MORGAN, magazine editor; b. St. Helens, Oreg., Sept. 12, 1947; s. Lloyd E. and Uldene H. (Morgan) S.; m. Candace J. Johnston, Feb. 18, 1949 (div. Dec. 1986). BA, Met. State Coll., Denver, 1976; MBA, U. Colo., 1985. Sports editor Montrose Daily Press, Montrose, Colo., 1977-78; asst. city editor Longmont Daily Times-Call, Longmont, Colo., 1978-80; with pub. affairs Am. TV & Communications, Englewood, Colo., 1980-84; editor Satellite Communications Mag., Englewood, 1984—; program dir. Satellite Communications Users Conf., Englewood, 1984—; pub. presenter on satellite related topics, various confs., 1984—. With Nat. Guard, 1966-72. Mem. Soc. of Satellite Profls. Internat. (pres. Rocky Mountain chpt. 1987—). Democrat. Home: 1055 Steele St Denver CO 80206 Office: Cardiff Publishing 6300 S Syracuse Way 650 Englewood CO 80111

STEPHENS, JACK, writer, photographer; b. Huntington Park, Calif., Dec. 1, 1936; s. Herman Franklin and Ruth Thekla (Burleson) S.; m. Kristi Marie Kellogg, Feb. 14, 1987. BA, Wash. State U., 1962. With D'Velco, Lawndale, Calif., 1952-54; reporter/editor Daily Evergreen, Pullman, Wash., 1959-62, Ferndale Record, Wash., 1961; morn. edit. editor Idaho Falls Post-Register, 1962; reporter Maui (Hawaii) News, 1963-67; instr. Maunaolu Coll., Makawao, Hawaii, 1967-73; reporter Pacific Bus. News, Honolulu, 1969-72; owner Aquarius Ent., Wailuku, 1968—. Author: Maui Now, 1969; contbr. articles to profl. jours.; writer/photographer Sci. Digest, 1966, Nat. Parks Mag., 1967, Ariz. Hwys. Mag., 1988-89. With USAF, 1955-58. Mem. Soc. Profl. Journalists. Home: 53 Central Ave #15 Wailuku HI 96793

STEPHENS, JOHN DICKSON, III, engineer; b. Palo Alto, Calif., Mar. 8, 1954; s. John Dickson Jr. and Maryjane (Yardley) S. BS, Calif. Poly. State U., 1986. Mfg. engr. Ford Aerospace & Communications Corp., Palo Alto, 1987-88, Tandem Computers, Inc., Cupertino, Calif., 1988--. Democrat. Episcopalian. Home: 910 Rockefeller Dr Apt 14A Sunnyvale CA 94087

STEPHENS, LARRY DEAN, engineer; b. Sterling, Colo., Sept. 1, 1937; s. John Robert and Shirley Berniece (Rudel) S.; m. Carol Ann Wertz, Sept. 1, 1957 (div. May 1975); children: Deborah Lynn, Janell Diane, Dana Larry. BS in Engring., Colo. State U., 1960; MBA, U. Colo., 1967. Registered profl. engr., Colo. Engr. Bur. Reclamation, Denver, 1960—; exec. v.p. U.S. Com. on Irrigation and Drainage, Denver, 1971—; exec. dir. U.S. Com. on Large Dams, Denver, 1986—. Served with USNG, 1961-62. Mem. Council on Engring. and Sci. Soc. Execs., Am. Water Found (exec. v.p. 1984—). Republican. Methodist. Home: 1625 Larimer St #1505 Denver CO 80202 Office: USCID PO Box 15326 Denver CO 80215

STEPHENS, PHILIP HAMILTON, company executive, consultant; b. Oakland, Calif., Sept. 4, 1927; s. Raymond Hamilton and Harriet (Peck) S.; m. Cherie Ann Mashburn, Jan. 30, 1954; children: Tracy, Norman. Student, U. San Francisco, 1953; BA, U. Calif., Berkeley, 1957. Mktg. div., research div. Standard Oil Calif., San Francisco, 1948-50, acctg. and mktg. researcher, 1951-53; regional acct. mgr. Ampex Corp., Redwood City, Calif., 1957-61; mgr. nat. acctg. Ampex Corp., Redwood City, 1962-65, mgr. internat. acctg., 1966-69, mgr. internat. planning, 1977--; accounts dir. Toamco-Japan, Tokyo, 1970-76; cons. Stephens Group, Palo Alto, Calif., 1977--. Author: (radio show) It Was a Dark and Stormy Night, 1973, (book) Letters on Our Times, 1986. Chmn. Cub. Scouts com. Boy Scouts Am., Menlo Park, Calif., 1968-70; dir. Democrats for McCloskey, Palo Alto, 1976-80. Sgt. U.S. Army, 1945-47. Mem. Am. Mgmt. Inst., San Alma Assn. (bd. dirs. 1981--), Mensa, Am. Apt. Owners Assn., U.S. Power Squadron (comdr. Tokyo 1975), U. Calif.-Berkeley Alumni Assn. Episcopalian. Office: Ampex Corp 401 Broadway Redwood City CA 94063

STEPHENS, RAND L., lawyer; b. Seattle, Mar. 21, 1947; s. Jack Edward and Trula Yvonne (Allison) S.; children: Eric F., Wendy L. JD, San Francisco U., 1984. Bar: Calif. 1985. Asst. mgr. Transam., El Cerrito, Calif., 1971-73; br. mgr. Avco Fin. Svcs., Yakima, Wash., 1973-76; credit mgr. Milens of Calif., Oakland, 1976-83; ptnr. Huffaker, Huffaker & Stephens, Antioch, Calif., 1984-87; pvt. practice Antioch, 1985—; dir. Milens Fed. Credit Union, Oakland, Calif., 1978-83. Dir. Youth Baseball, Brentwood, Calif., 1986. Mem. Calif. Trial Lawyers Assn. (legis. rev. com. 1987-88), Contra Costa County Bar Assn., Rusty Bindings Ski Club (Walnut Creek, Calif., singles league rep. 1988-89), Alameda County Bar Assn. Office: 1407 A St Ste D Antioch CA 94509

STEPHENS, RICHARD DALE, banker, real estate and insurance agency executive; b. Del Norte, Colo., Aug. 20, 1932; s. Charles William and Evelyn Aileen (Mount) S.; m. Virginia Lee Brown, June 29, 1951; children: Charles J., Candace S., Julia A. Cert. in real estate law, Parriot Del Monte Sch., Jackson, Wyo., 1978. Lic. real estate broker, ins. agt., Wyo. Owner, mgr. service sta. Standard Oil Co., Pine Bluffs, Wyo., 1953-56; owner, mgr. Stephens Ins., Pine Bluffs, 1958--, Stephens Realty, Pine Bluffs, 1970--; pres. Farmers State Bank, Pine Bluffs, 1978--; also bd. dirs. Farmers State Bank. Councilman, Town of Pine Bluffs, 1969-75, mayor, 1975-79. With USAF, 1950-54, Korea. Mem. Wyo. Bankers Assn., Wyo. Jaycees (treas., v.p. 1960-64), Masons, Order Eastern Star, Lions (pres. Pine Bluffs lodge 1978-79). Republican. Methodist. Office: Farmers State Bank 103 E 2d St Pine Bluffs WY 02082

STEPHENS, STANLEY GRAHAM, governor, cable television company executive; b. Calgary, Alta., Can., Sept. 16, 1929; s. Joseph and Margaret (Farrelly) S.; m. Ann Hanson, 1954; children: Alana, Carol Ann. Grad., West Can. High Sch., Calgary, 1947. V.P., sec. Radio Sta. KOJM, Havre, Mont., from 1965; pres. Big Sky TV Cable Inc., Sidney, Mont., 1968—, Glasgow TV Cable Inc., 1968—, Community TV Inc., Havre, 1968—; mem. Mont. State Senate, 1969-72, 75-87, pres. senate, 1983-85, minority floor leader, 1985-87; gov. of Montana 1989—. Del. Republican Nat. Conv., 1976. Served with U.S. Army, 1951-53, Korea. Mem. Am. Legion. Lutheran. Lodges: Masons; Shriners; Elks. Office: Office of Gov Capitol Sta Rm 204 Helena MT 59620 *

STEPHENS, WAYNE J., construction company executive; b. Odgen, Utah, Apr. 30, 1949; s. Garth J. and Lavon (Staker) S.; m. Jacqueline Vern Kenealy Stephens, Aug. 25, 1973; children: Prinny D., Matthew J. BA in Psychology, Utah State U., 1971. Project mgr. Specification Steel, Colton, Calif., 1971-73; chief executive officer, pres. Kimko Corp., San Bernardino, Calif., 1973—. Mem. Am. Welding Soc. Republican. Mormon. Home: 441 W Emerson Upland CA 91786

STEPHENS, WILLIAM JAMES, army officer, communications specialist; b. Detroit, May 30, 1937; s. James Willard and Edythe Viola (Harris) S.; m. Jacqueline Younger, Apr. 2, 1963; children: Leslie Diane, Patricia Elaine. BS, Eastern Mich. U., 1960; MS, So. Ill. U., 1968; cert. U.S. Army Command and Gen. Staff Coll., 1973, U.S. Army Signal Sch., 1960, 64, Indsl. Coll. Armed Forces, 1981. Commd. 2d lt. U.S. Army, 1960, advanced through grades to col., 1981; project officer Orgn. Joint Chiefs of Staff, 1978-80, dep. asst. chief of staff, 1981-82; dir. communications Armed Forces Inauguration Com., 1984-85; comdr. dep. chief staff Communications-Electronics, U.S. Army Communications Command, Mil. Dist. of Washington, 1984-85; comdr. Pentagon Telecommunications Ctr., 1982-85, brigade comdr. U.S. Army Info. Systems Command Ops. Command, The Pentagon, 1982-85, mil. asst. for info. Office Asst. Sec. of Army for Fin. Mgmt., The Pentagon, 1985; comdr. USAIS Engring. Support Activity, Ft. Huachuca, Ariz., 1985-87; chief of staff USA ISEC, 1987; Supreme Hdqrs. Allied Powers Europe liaison officer, Continental U.S. exec. to Supreme Allied Comdr. Europe, 1987-88; dep. dir. for policy and strategy Office for Sec. of the Army Directorate for Info. Systems Command Control Communications and Computers The Pentagon, 1988—. Advisor Transatlantic council Explorer Scouts, 1960-64; mem. service team Nat. Capitol Area council Explorer Scouts, 1968-71; asst. dist. commr. Belgium and Netherlands, Boy Scouts Am., 1974-76. Decorated Legion of Merit, Bronze Star with oak leaf cluster, Def. Meritorious Service medal with two oak leaf clusters, Joint Service Commendation medal with 2 oak leaf clusters, Meritorious Service medal with oak leaf cluster, Air medal. Mem. Armed Forces Communications-Electronics Assn., Assn. U.S. Army, U.S. Army Signal Officers Assn., 101st Airborne Div., Ft. Huachuca Assn. (pres. 1986-87), Eastern Mich. U. Alumni Assn. (Disting. Alumni award 1985), Indsl. Coll. Armed Forces Alumni Assn., SHAPE Officers Assn. Episcopalian. Club: Lettermen's (Eastern Mich. U.). Lodges: Masons, Shriners. Inducted Eastern Mich. U. Athletic Hall of Fame, 1987. Avocations: basketball; tennis; jogging; horseback riding. Home: 11004 Clara Barton Dr Fairfax Station VA 22039

STEPHENS, WILLIAM LEONARD, university dean; b. Covington, Ky., Apr. 19, 1929; s. Leonard Edwin and Mary Blanche S.; m. Claire Neall, Apr. 12, 1957. B.A. with honors, Calif. State U., Sacramento; Ph.D. in Microbiology, U. Calif., Davis, 1963. Research asst. U. Calif., Davis, 1957-63; mem. faculty Calif. State U., Chico, 1963—; prof. biol. scis. Calif. State U., 1970—, chmn. dept., 1968-74; dean Calif. State U. (Coll. Natural Scis.), 1977—; researcher in bacterial pigments, microbial metabolism. Served with USN, 1950-54. Mem. Am. Soc. Microbiology, Sigma Xi. Home: 1661 Oak Vista Chico CA 95926 Office: Calif State U Coll Natural Scis Chico CA 95929

STEPHENS, WILLIAM THOMAS, mining and forest products company executive. married. BS, U. Ark., 1965, MS, 1966. Various mgmt. positions Manville Forest Products Corp., from 1963; asst. to pres., then sr. v.p., pres. forest products group Manville Corp., Denver, exec. v.p. fin. and adminstrn., from 1984, now pres., chief exec. officer. Office: Manville Corp Manville Pla 717 S 17th Denver CO 80202 also: Manville Corp PO Box 5108 Denver CO 80217 *

STEPHENSON, HERMAN HOWARD, banker; b. Wichita, Kans., July 15, 1929; s. Herman Horace and Edith May (Wayland) S.; m. Virginia Anne Ross, Dec. 24, 1950; children: Ross Wayland, Neal Bevan, Jann Edith. BA, U. Mich., 1950; JD with distinction, U. Mo., Kansas City, 1958. Bar: Kans. 1958. Mem. fgn. dept. City Nat. Bank, Kansas City, Mo., 1952-54; asst. sec. City Bond & Mortgage Co., Kansas City, 1954-59; with Bank of Hawaii, Honolulu, 1959—, asst. cashier, 1960-62, v.p., 1962-68, sr. v.p., 1968-72, exec. v.p., 1972-80, pres., dir., 1980-89; v.p., treas. Bancorp. Hawaii, Inc., Honolulu, 1978-80, pres., dir., 1980-89, chmn., chief exec. officer, 1989—; chmn., bd. dir. Bank of Hawaii Investment Mgmt. Co., Hong Kong, Ltd., Bancorp Bus. Systems of Hawaii, Inc.; v.p., chmn. bd. dirs. Bancorp Fin. of Hawaii, Inc., Bancorp. Fin. of Hawaii-Guam, Inc., Bancorp Ins. Agy. of Hawaii, Inc., Bancorp Investment Adv. Svcs., Inc., Bancorp Leasing of Hawaii, Inc., Bancorp Life Ins. Co. of Hawaii, Inc., Bank of Hawaii International, Inc., Bankoh Adv. Corp., Bankoh Corp, First Nat. Bank of Ariz., Hawaii Fin. corp. (Hong Kong) Ltd., Hawaiian Hong Kong Haldings, Ltd., Hawaiian Trust Co., Ltd., Investors Pacific Ltd., Fiji; pres., bd. dirs. Bancorp Charitable Found., Bank of Hawaii Internat. Corp. N.Y.; bd. dirs. Bancorp Hawaii Svc. Corp., Banque de Novelle-Caledonie, Banque de Tahiti, S.I.L., Inc. Chmn. urban renewal com. Oahu Devel. Conf., 1966-68, mem. comprehensive planning com., 1970-71; trustee, past pres. Tax Found. Hawaii; former trustee Hawaii Conf. Found., United Ch. of Christ; mem. bd. govs. Honolulu Symphony, Maunalani Hosp.; former chmn., bd. dirs. Aloha United Way; co-chmn. Ellison Onizuka Meml. Scholarship Fund Com.; bd. regents U. Hawaii; mem. U. Hawaii Found. Served with U.S. Army, 1950-52. Mem. ABA, Am. Bankers Assn. (past chmn. exec. com. housing and real estate fin. div., dir. 1976-77, mem. governing coun. 1976-77, mem. govt. rels. coun. Banking Leadership Conf.), Kans. Bar Assn., Mortgage Bankers Assn. Hawaii (past pres.), Hawaii Bankers Assn. (pres. 1984-85), U.S.-Japan Bus. Coun., Pacific Asia Travel Assn. (Hawaii chpt., assoc.), Navy League of U.S., Hawaii Bus. Roundtable, Janpan-Hawaii Econ. Coun., Am. Res. City Bankers, Kappa Sigma, Pi Eta Sigma, Pres. Club, Oahu Country Club, Pacific Club, Waialae Country Club, Rotary. Office: Bancorp Hawaii Inc 111 S King St PO Box 2900 Fin Pla of Pacific Honolulu HI 96813

STEPHENSON, IRENE HAMLEN, biorhythm analyst, consultant, editor, teacher; b. Chgo., Oct. 7, 1923; d. Charles Martin and Carolyn Hilda (Hilgers) Hamlin; m. Edgar B. Stephenson, Sr., Aug. 16, 1941 (div. 1946); 1 child, Edgar B. Author biorhythm compatibilities column Nat. Singles Register, Norwalk, Calif., 1979-81; instr. biorhythm Learning Tree Open U., Canoga Park, Calif., 1982-83; instr. biorhythm character analysis 1980—; instr. biorhythm compatibility, 1982—; owner, pres. matchmaking service Pen Pals Using Biorhythm, Chatsworth, Calif., 1979—; editor newsletter The Truth, 1979-85, Mini Examiner, Chatsworth, 1985—; researcher biorhythm character and compatibility, 1974—, selecting a mate, 1985—, biorhythm column True Psychic Inquirer, 1989—, True Astrology Forecast, 1989—; author: Learn Biorhythm Character Analysis, 1980; Do-It-Yourself Biorhythm Compatibilities, 1982; contbr. numerous articles to mags; frequent guests clubs, radio, TV. Office: Irene Hamlen Stephenson PO Box 3893 WW Chatsworth CA 91313

STEPHENSON, JEAN MARIE, teacher; b. Phoenix, Nov. 22, 1954; d. Norman Eugene and Virginia Dare (Frost) Stephenson. AA, Phoenix Coll., 1974; BAE, Ariz. State U., 1976, MAE, 1981. Phys. edn. and gymnastics tchr. Camelback High Sch., Phoenix, 1977-78, Sutton Elem. Sch., Phoenix, 1978-80; adaptive phys. edn. tchr. Isaac Sch. Dist., Phoenix, 1980-87; multiple handicap tchr. Butler Elem. Sch., Phoenix, 1987—; spl. Olympic dir. Isaac Sch. Dist., 1980-87; archery coach Phoenix Coll., 1977-81; archery instr., 1977-81. Active PTA, Phoenix, 1987—. Named Woman Athlete of the Yr., Ariz. Republic Newspaper, 1976; mem. Ariz. State U. Hall of Fame. Mem. NEA, Ariz. Edn. Assn., Ariz. Interscholastic Assn., Phi Delta Kappa. Republican. Office: Butler Sch 3843 W Roosevelt Phoenix AZ 85009

STEPHENSON, JOSEPH WALLER, writer; b. Chgo., Nov. 8, 1913; s. George Blaine and Amanda (Waller) S.; m. Marjorie Jane Oakes, Jan. 17, 1942; children: Timothy, Wendy. MA, San Jose State U., 1956. Registered landscape architect, Calif. Author: The Gardener's Directory, 1960; columnist Indoor Citrus Soc.; writer on foods, horticulture, travel. Served as sgt. U.S. Army, 1940-45, ETO, PTO. Fellow Royal Horticultural Soc. Mem. Soc. Friends. Home and Office: 14878 Heather Dr San Jose CA 95124

STEPHENSON, LARRY KIRK, strategic planner, management and geography educator; b. Seattle, Sept. 22, 1944; s. Norman Eugene and Virginia Dare (Frost) S.; m. Tamara Leah Ladin, June 24, 1967; children: Mathew Alan, Leah Anela. BS, Ariz. State U., 1966, MA, 1971; PhD, U. Cin., 1973; Manpower research analyst Employment Security Commn. of Ariz., 1969-70; asst. prof. dept. geography U. Hawaii, Hilo, 1973-76, assoc. prof., 1976-78, chmn. dept., 1975-77; vis. lectr. dept. geography Ariz. State U., 1978, adj. assoc. prof., 1979—; planner Ariz. Dept. Health Services, Phoenix, 1978-84; vis. assoc. prof. dept. geography, area devel. and urban planning U. Ariz., 1978; strategic plannner City of Glendale, Ariz., 1984—. Mem. faculty U. Phoenix, 1979—; adj. prof. Golden Gate U., 1981—; ptnr. Urban Research Assocs., Phoenix, 1981—; adj. prof. Coll. St. Francis, 1982—. Mem. Hawaii Island Health Planning Council, 1974-78; mem. Glendale Community Colls. Pres.'s Council, 1986—. Served with U.S. Army, 1966-68. NDEA fellow, 1971-72. Mem. Am. Inst. Cert. Planners, Am. Planning Assn., Assn. Am. Geographers, Ariz. Planning Assn. (pres. 1987—), Southwest Profl. Geog. Assn., Lambda Alpha. Unitarian. Author books in field; contbr. chpts. to textbooks, articles to profl. jours. Home: 306 W Encanto Blvd Phoenix AZ 85003 Office: 5850 W Glendale Ave Glendale AZ 85301

STEPHENSON, MICHAEL DAVID, chemical engineer, freelance photographer; b. Huntington, N.Y., July 5, 1957; s. Thomas Edgar and Helen Julia (Mizzoni) S. BA in Chemistry, SUNY, Potsdam, 1979; MSChemE, Iowa State U., 1982. Grad. asst. Ames Labs., 1979-82; assoc. chem. engr. Ill. State Geol. Survey, Champaign, 1983-88; sr. engr. Solar Turbines Inc., San Diego, 1988—. Contbr. articles to profl. jours. Rsch. fellow NSF, 1978. Mem. Am. Chem. Soc., Am. Inst. Chem. Engrs. Home: 2045 1/2 Oliver Ave San Diego CA 92109 Office: Solar Turbine Inc PO Box 85376 San Diego CA 92138

STEPHENSON, ROBERT BAIRD, energy company executive; b. Washington, Jan. 20, 1943; s. Orlando Worth and Martha Ann (Kostelak) S.; m. Sheryl Ann Fish, Jan. 10, 1967; children: Brie Danielle, Eric Baird. BS in Mech. Engring., Purdue U., 1965; MS in Nuclear Engring., U. Mich., 1970, MBA, 1972. Engr. Jersey Nuclear Co., Inc., Boston, 1972-74; engr., mgr. Exxon Nuclear Co., Inc., Richland, Wash., 1974-80; mng. dir. Exxon Nuclear GmbH, Lingen, Fed. Rep. Germany, 1980-83; mktg., sales staff Exxon Nuclear Co., Inc., Bellevue, Wash., 1983-85, v.p. adminstn., 1986; v.p. comml. div. Exxon Nuclear Co., Inc., Belleville, 1987; pres., chief exec. officer, chmn. EPID, Inc., San Jose, Calif., 1985-86; pres., chief exec. officer Advanced Nuclear Fuels Corp., Bellevue, Wash., 1988—; also bd. dirs. Advanced Nuclear Fuels Corp., Bellevue, 1986—. Lt., U.S. Navy, 1965-70. Mem. Am. Nuclear Soc., Overlake Country Club. Office: Advanced Nuclear Fuels Corp 600 108th Ave NE Bellevue WA 98004

STEPHENSON, TONI EDWARDS, publisher, investment management executive; b. Bastrop, La., July 23, 1945; d. Sidney Crawford and Grace Erleene (Shipman) Little; BS, La. State U., 1967; enrolled owner/pres. mgmt. program Harvard Bus. Sch.; m. Arthur Emmet Stephenson, Jr., June 17, 1967; 1 dau., Tessa Lyn. ; pres., dir. Gen. Communications, Inc., Denver; sr. v.p., founder Stephenson & Co., Denver, 1971—, Stephenson Mcht. Banking, 1980—; gen. ptnr. Viking Fund; ptnr. Stephenson Properties, Stephenson Ventures, Stephenson Mgmt. Co.; pres., dir. Globescope Corp.; underwriting mem. Lloyd's of London; founder, dir. Charter Bank & Trust. Pub. Denver Bus. Mag., Denver Mag., Development Sales Catalog, Colorado Book, Law Enforcement Product News; former dir. The Children's Hosp., St. Joseph's Hosp. Past pres. Children's Hosp. Assn. Vols. Mem. Harvard Bus. Sch. Clubs of Colo., So. Calif. and Orange County, Colo. Press Assn., Denver Advt. Fedn., DAR, Delta Gamma. Clubs: Rancho Mirage (Calif.), Annabel's (London), Thunderbird Country, Denver Petroleum. Office: Gen Communications Inc 100 Garfield St Denver CO 80206

STEPOVICH, MICHAEL LEO, orthodontist; b. Fairbanks, Alaska, Nov. 17, 1929; s. Mike and Vuka (Radovich) S.; A.B., San Jose State U., 1956; D.D.S., Marquette U., 1961; M.S., St. Louis U., 1964; m. Arline Audry Gentry, June 10, 1956; children—Michael John, Matthew James, Dean Alexander, Lynn Diane. Intern, USPHS Hosp., Fort Worth, 1961-62; pvt. practice orthodontics, San Jose, Calif., 1964—; mem. staff Good Samaritan Hosp., San Jose. Pres., Orthodontic Edn. and Research Found., St. Louis, 1969; bd. dirs. Tweed Found. for Orthodontic Research, 1978-84, pres. Western sect., 1985-87. Served with AUS, 1953-54; PTO. Diplomate Am. Bd. Orthodontists. Mem. Am., Calif., Santa Clara County dental assns., Am. Assn. Orthodontists, Pacific Coast Soc. Orthodontists (pres. Central sect. 1975), Angle Soc., DeMolay, Interfrat. Council San Jose State U. Alumni (chmn. 1966), Omicron Kappa Upsilon, Delta Upsilon. Contbr. articles to profl. jours. Home: 19557 Arden Ct Saratoga CA 95070 Office: 4110 Moorpark Ave San Jose CA 95117

STEPP, CHRISTINE, stock broker; b. Hopkinsville, Ky., May 3, 1959; d. John Allen Jr. and Flora Ann (Couglass) Jacks. BS, U. Evansville, 1981, MBA, 1983. Sales clk. The Ltd., Evansville, 1982-83; asst. mgr. The Ltd., Newark, Calif., 1983-84; Mktg. rep. Xerox Corp., Santa Clara, Calif., 1984-86; account rep. Xerox Corp., Oalkand, Calif., 1986-87; investment rep. FN Investment Ctr. affiliate 1st Nationwide Bank, Oakland, 1987—. Youth instr. Allen Temple Bapt. Ch., Oakland, 1983-84; bd. dirs. Project Interface, Oakland, 1985-86; speaker Solano Community Coll., Vacaville, Calif., 1986, Bay Area Urban League, Oakland, 1986. Mem. Nat. Black MBA Assn. (staff writer 1985-87, Com. of Yr. award, newsletter com. 1986), Bay Area Black Profls. (outstanding young woman Am., 1983-84, 86). Democrat. Office: 1st Nationwide Bank 1325 Broadway Oakland CA 94612

STEPP, GEORGE ALLAN, JR., state official; b. Inglewood, Calif., Apr. 26, 1922; s. George Allan and Ida Johanna (Wehselau) S.; m. Margit Lindblad, Oct. 15, 1966; 1 dau., Elizabeth. B.A., U. Hawaii, 1948, M.A. in Govt., 1950. Personnel technician and adminstr. Hawaii Dept. Civil Service, Honolulu, 1950-59; asst. dir. research Hawaii Employers Council, Honolulu, 1959-61; mgmt. services adminstr. Hawaii State Dept. Budget and Fin., Honolulu, 1961-88; mgmt. cons. DHB Inc., Honolulu, 1988—. Served with USCG, 1942-45, to comdr. Res. (ret.), 1952-82. Mem. Western Govtl. Research Assn. (pres. 1971-72), Am. Soc. Pub. Adminstrn., Am. Mgmt. Assn., Am. Cons. League. Res. Officers Assn. of U.S. Democrat. Home: 2999 Kalakaua Ave Honolulu HI 96815 Office: DHB Inc 1173 Lunalilo Home Rd Honolulu HI 96825

STERBICK, PETER LAWRENCE, I, lawyer; b. Tacoma, Nov. 12, 1917; s. Anton John and Pearl (Medak) S.; children: Marilyn, Lawrence, Thomas, David, Colleen. BBA, U. Wash., 1941, LLB, 1948. Bar: Wash. 1949. Adjuster Gen. Accidenty Ins. Co., Seattle, 1948-49, Farmers Ins. Group, Tacoma, 1949-50; dep. pros. atty. Pierce County, Tacoma, 1950-51; ptnr. Sterbick and Sterbick, Tacoma, 1951-57, Sterbick, Manza, Moceri and Sterbick, Tacoma, 1958-72, Sterbick, Abel and Sterbick, Tacoma, 1972—. 2d lt. USAAF, 1943-45. Mem. Wash. Bar Assn., Tacoma-Pierce County Bar Assn., Kiwanis, KC, Elks. Roman Catholic. Home: 3143 Olympic Blvd W Tacoma WA 98466 Office: Sterbick Abel & Sterbick 15 Oregon Ave Ste 303 Tacoma WA 98409

STERLING, DONALD T., professional basketball team executive; b. Chgo.. Owner Los Angeles (formerly San Diego) Clippers, Nat. Basketball Assn. Office: care Los Angeles Clippers Los Angeles Meml Sports Arena 3939 S Figueroa St Los Angeles CA 90037 *

STERMER, DUGALD ROBERT, designer, illustrator, writer, consultant; b. Los Angeles, Dec. 17, 1936; s. Robert Newton and Mary (Blue) S.; m. Jeanie Kortum; children: Dugald, Megan, Chris, Colin. B.A., UCLA, 1960. Art dir., v.p. Ramparts mag., 1965-70; freelance designer, illustrator, writer, cons. San Francisco, 1970—; founder Pub. Interest Communications, San Francisco, 1974; pres. Frisco Pub Group Ltd. Cons. editor Communication Arts mag., Palo Alto, Calif., 1974—; designer Oceans mag., 1976-82; editor: The Environment, 1972, Vanishing Creatures, 1980; author: The Art of Revolution, 1970, Vanishing Creatures, 1980; designer 1984 Olympic medals; illustration exhbn. Calif. Acad. Scis., 1986. Bd. dirs. Delancey St. Found., 1976—; mem. Grand Jury City and County San Francisco. Recipient various medals, awards for design and illustration nat. and internat. design competitions. Mem. Soc. Publ. Designers, Am. Inst. Graphics Arts, San Francisco Soc. Communicating Arts. Office: 1844 Union St San Francisco CA 94123

STERN, ARTHUR PAUL, electronics manufacturing company executive, electrical engineer; b. Budapest, Hungary, July 20, 1925; came to U.S., 1951, naturalized, 1956; s. Leon and Bertha (Frankfurter) S.; m. Edith M. Samuel; children: Daniel, Claude, Jacqueline. Diploma in Elec. Engring., Swiss Fed. Inst. Tech., Zurich, 1948; MSEE, Syracuse U., 1955. Mgr. electronic devices and applications lab. Gen. Electric Co., Syracuse, N.Y., 1957-61; dir. engring. Martin Marietta Corp., Balt., 1961-64; dir. ops. Bunker Ramo Corp., Canoga Park, Calif., 1964-66; v.p., gen. mgr. advanced products div. Magnavox, Torrance, Calif., 1966-79, pres. Magnavox Advanced Products and Systems Co., Torrance, 1980—; vice chmn., bd. dirs. Magnavox Govt. and Indsl. Electronics Co., Ft. Wayne, Ind.; non-resident staff mem. MIT, 1956-59; instr. Gen. Elec. Bus. Mgmt., 1955-57. Chmn. engring. div. United Jewish Appeal, Syracuse, 1955-57; mem. adv. bd. dept. elec. engring. U. Calif., Santa Barbara, 1980—; mem. Sch. Engring. Adv. and Devel. Council Calif. State U., Long Beach, 1985—. Co-author: Transistor Circuit Engineering, 1957, Handbook of Automation, Computation and Control, 1961; also articles; U.S., fgn. patentee in field. Fellow AAAS, IEEE (pres. 1975, bd. dirs., officer 1970-77, guest editor spl. issue IEEE Trans. on Circuit Theory 1956, invited guest editor spl. issue Procs. IEEE on Integrated Electronics 1964, Centennial medal 1984). Jewish. Office: Magnavox Advanced Products & Systems Co 2829 Maricopa St Torrance CA 90503

STERN, DANIEL DAVID, conductor; b. Locarno, Switzerland, July 28, 1943; came to U.S., 1949, naturalized, 1955; s. Frans Martin and Dorette (Tchenio) S.; children: Rebecca, Frances. Mus.B., Eastman Sch. Music, Rochester, N.Y., 1965; Mus.M. (NDEA fellow), U. Oreg., 1969, Mus.D. (NDEA fellow), 1973. String specialist Salem (Oreg.) public schs., 1965-67; conducter Am. Festival Ballet, Boise, Idaho, 1987—; asst. prof. music N.Mex. Highlands U., 1971-74. Asst. condr., U. Oreg. Symphony Orch., 1968-71, music dir., Boise (Idaho) Philharm., also, Boise Civic Opera, 1974-88, condr.-in-residence, Boise State U., 1974-79, founder, 1975, since dir., Sun Valley, also Idaho music festivals; recipient performers cert. conducting U. Oreg. 1971. Bd. dirs. Idaho Civic Ballet, 1977-79; Religious leader Beth Israel Congregation, Boise, 1981-83. Mem. Am. Symphony Orch. League, Condrs. Guild. Club: Boise Rotary.

STERN, DARRYL R., psychiatrist; b. Milw., June 6, 1942; s. Jack and Viola (Newman) S.; m. Helen B. Sheps, Jan. 22, 1966; children: Ariann N., Miles B. BS, U. Wis., 1963, MD, 1967. Diplomate Am. Bd. Psychiatry and Neurology. Resident in psychiatry U. Wis. dept. Psychiatry, Madison, 1968-71; dir. Mental Health Clinic, Camelback Hosp. Mental Health Ctr., Scottsdale, Ariz., 1973-75; pvt. practice medicine specializing in psychaitry Tempe, Ariz., 1975—; cons. Camelback Hosp. Day Trtmt. Prog. Scottsdale, 1985-87; chmn. dept. psychiatry Desert Samaritan Hosp., Mesa, Ariz., 1987—; med. dir. adult svcs. Desert Vista Hosp., Mesa, 1987—. Maj. USAF, 1971-73. Mem. AMA, Am. Psychiatric Assn., Acad. Psychosomatic Medicine, Am. Assn. Geriatric Psychiatry, Am. Acad. Psychiatrists in Alcoholism and Addictions. Office: 2034 E Southern Ave Tempe AZ 85282

STERN, G. CHRIS, engineer; b. Tucson, Jan. 15, 1950; s. G. Charles and Elsie W. Stern; m. Diana G. Harbour (div. 1983); 1 child, Jonathan B. BS in Engring. Physics, U. Ariz., 1973; MBA, U. Utah, 1976. Process engr. Alcoa Aluminum Corp., Rockdale, Tex., 1977-79; engr., mgr. IBM Corp., Tucson, 1979—. Author Play On the Outside, 1986, PORP, 1988. Assoc. dir. Tucson Writers' Conf., 1986—; treas. Ariz. Kidney Found., Tucson, 1987-88, Friends of Tucson Pub. Library, 1987—; sec. bd. dirs. Chax Press., Tucson, 1987—. Capt. USAF, 1973-77. Named to Outstanding Young Am., U.S. Jaycees, 1981. Mem. Soc. Materials and Process Engrs., Internat. Brotherhood Magicians. Home: 1546 Plaza de Lirios Tucson AZ 85745 Office: IBM 67H/061-1 Tucson AZ 85744

STERN, GERALD M., lawyer, oil company executive; b. Chgo., Apr. 5, 1937; s. Lloyd and Fannye (Wener) S.; m. Linda Stone, Dec. 20, 1969; children: Eric, Jesse, Maia. B.S. in Econs., U. Pa., 1958; LL.B. cum laude, Harvard, 1961. Bar: D.C. 1961, U.S. Supreme Ct. 1971. Trial atty. civil rights div. U.S. Dept. Justice, 1961-64; assoc. firm Arnold & Porter, Washington, 1964-68; ptnr. Arnold & Porter, 1969-76; founding ptnr. Rogovin, Stern & Huge, Washington, 1976-81; exec. v.p., sr. gen. counsel Occidental Petroleum Corp., Washington, 1981-82, Los Angeles, 1982—; also bd. dirs.; bd. dirs. Occidental Petroleum Corp. Author: The Buffalo Creek Disaster, 1976; co-author: Southern Justice, 1965. Bd. dirs. Occidental Petroleum Corp., Facing History and Ourselves Nat. Found., Inc., Bet Tzedek. Mem. ABA. Office: Occidental Petroleum Corp 10889 Wilshire Blvd Los Angeles CA 90024

STERN, JAMES COPER, sales executive; b. N.Y.C., Dec. 12, 1925; s. George Charles and Ruth (Coper) S.; m. Judith Vinson, Oct. 31, 1963 (div. Mar. 1974); children: Hillary Anne, Renee Jean; m. Ruth Nussbacker Szold, Aug. 22, 1982. BA, NYU, 1949. Trainee, exec. asst. Gardner Advt. Co., N.Y.C., 1949-50; advt. mgr. NOPCO Chem. Co., Harrison, N.J., 1950-53; account exec. Ziv TV Programs, N.Y.C., 1954-56; sales rep. United Artists Associated, N.Y.C., 1957-61; v.p., sales mgr. Allied Artists TV, N.Y.C., 1961-70; exec. v.p., gen. sales mgr. ITC Entertainment, Inc., Studio City, Calif., 1970—. Cpl. U.S. Army, 1944-46, ETO. Mem. Internat. Radio and TV Soc., Nat. Assn. TV Program Execs., Ind. TV Program Execs. Republican. Jewish. Home: 8787 Shoreham Dr Apt 1202 West Hollywood CA 90069 Office: ITC Entertainment Group 12711 Ventura Blvd Studio City CA 91604

STERN, RICHARD OLAV, airlines executive, social sciences researcher; b. Syracuse, N.Y., Apr. 4, 1951. Diploma, U. Oslo, 1971; BA, SUNY, Potsdam, 1972; MA, SUNY, Binghamton, 1974, PhD, 1980. Rsch. assoc. U. Alaska, Fairbanks, 1975-78; historian land titles Alaska Div. Land and Water Mgmt., Anchorage, 1979-81; archaeologist Alaska Dept. Natural Resources, Anchorage, 1982-83; regional supr. Alaska Dept. Fish and Game, Nome, 1984-86; gen. mgr. Bering Air, Inc., Nome, 1986—; mem. loan com. North Country Credit Union, Nome, 1988—. Sr. author: Eskimos, Reindeer and Land, 1978; co-author: A Bibliography of Alas kan Archaeology, 1987. Mem. Arctic Inst. N.Am. (life), Alaska Air Carriers Assn. (bd. dirs. 1987—), CAP-Anvil Mt. Squadron (sr.). Office: Bering Air Inc Box 1650 Nome AK 99762

STERN, STANLEY, psychiatrist; b. N.Y.C., Apr. 5, 1933; s. Frank and Gussie S.; children: Marcus F., David S. BA cum laude, N.Y. U., 1953; MD, SUNY, 1957. Intern Ohio State U. Hosp., Columbus, 1957-58; resident in psychiatry Inst. Living, Hartford, Conn., 1958-60, Austen Riggs Ctr., Stockbridge, Mass., 1960-61; psychoanalytic tng. We. New Eng. Inst. for Psychoanalysis, New Haven, Conn., 1965-73; asst. clin. prof. psychiatry Yale U., New Haven, Conn., 1975-81; assoc. clin. prof. psychiatry U. Calif., San Diego, 1982-84; pvt. practice New Haven, 1965-82, La Jolla, Calif., 1982-84, Phoenix, 1984—; staff psychiatrist USAF, Eglin AFB, Fla., 1961-63; mem. faculty San Diego Psychoanalytic Inst., 1983-84; pres. Ariz. Psychoanalytic Study Group, Phoenix, 1986-88, Phoenix Psychoanalytic Study Group, 1986-88; lectr., presenter, participant seminars and conferences in field. Contbr. article to profl. jours. Trustee, Gesell Inst., New Haven, 1986-88, Ctr. for the Exceptional Patient, New Haven; bd. dirs. ACLU. Capt. USAF, 1961-63. Mem. Am. Coll. Psychoanalysts (cert.), Am. Psychoanalytic Assn. (cert.), Am. Psychiatric Assn., Am. Acad. Psychoanalysts, Irene Josselyn Group Advancement of Psychoanalysis, So. Calif. Psychoanalytic Inst. and Soc. (faculty), San Diego Psychoanalytic Inst., Council for the Advancement of Psychoanalysis (treas. 1972-73, pres.-elect 1973-74, pres. 1974-75, councillor 1975-80), Phi Beta Kappa, Beta Lambda Sigma, Psi Chi. Home and Office: 3352 E Camelback Ste D Phoenix AZ 85018

STERN, STEVEN ALAN, investment banker; b. Chgo., Dec. 5, 1943; s. Sidney J. and Leona (Bernstein) S.; m. Helena Kerner, July 12, 1975; children: Jeremy, Jessica. AB, Brandeis U., 1965; postgrad. Columbia U. Grad. Sch. Bus., 1965-66. CPCU, Ill. Trust officer, First Nat. Bank Chgo., 1966-69; ptnr., Equicon, Inc., Chgo., 1970-74; coordinator Singer for Mayor, Chgo., 1974-75; mgr. underwriting policy CNA Ins., Chgo., 1976-79; project dir. Gov.'s Blue Ribbon Panel, Denver, 1979-81; dir. capital budget State of Colo., Denver, 1981-82; exec. dir. Ctr. Bus. and Econ. Forecasting, U. Denver, 1982-85; v.p. pub. finance, Kirchner, Moore & Co., Denver, 1986—; mem. adv. task force to capital devel. com. Colo. Gen. Assembly, 1985-87, chmn. adv. task force subcom. on privatization, 1986-87; mem. adv. council Colo. Advanced Tech. Inst., 1986—; guest lectr., 1982—; adv. task forces on capital budgeting, transp. Denver C. of C., 1980—. Speaker annual meetings Nat. Assn. State Mental Health Program Dirs., 1987—, Nat. Assn. State Mental Retardation Program Dirs., 1987, Nat. Assn. State Alcohol and Drug Abuse Dirs., 1988. Author: Colorado Capital Investment Budget, 1982; (with others) Colorado; Investing in the Future, 1981; editor: Techniques of Economic Research, 1981. Speaker, Adopt-A-Sch., Denver Pub. Schs., 1983, 86, numerous other orgns.; participant Leadership Denver, 1983-84; sec.-treas. Colo. Student Obligation Bond Authority, 1984-86, also bd. dirs.; bd. dirs. Circus Arts Found., 1985-86; chmn. devel. com. Stanley Brit. Primary Sch., Denver, 1984; mem. Denver Baseball Commn., 1987—; bd. dirs., chmn. corp. gifts Epilepsy Found. Chgo., 1977-79. Mem. Denver Zool. Soc., Denver Childrens Mus., Denver Mus. Natural Hist., Wilderness Soc., Brandeis U. Alumni Assn., NAACP (life), Colo. Mcpl. Bond Dealers Assn. (chmn. legis. affairs com. 1987), Denver C. of C. Democrat. Jewish. Office: Kirchner Moore & Co 717 17th St Ste 2500 Denver CO 80202

STERNE, CHARLES, III, financial executive; b. Phila., Mar. 25, 1947; s. Charles and Jean (Harris) S.; m. Oct. 18, 1969 (div. 1981); children: Emily, Carly. BA with hons. & distinc., Pa. State U., 1969. Sr. estate planning officer, trust officer Girard Bank, Phila., 1969-81; v.p. new bus. devel. Mellon Bank Nat. Assn., Phila., 1983-87; v.p. fin. and adminstrn., sec.-treas. Internat. Found. for Edn. and Self-Help, Phoenix, 1988—; cons. IFESH, Phila., 1984-88. Co-founder, pres. Plowshares, Inc., Germantown, Pa., 1978-81; trustee First United Meth. Ch., Germantown, 1978-81; bd. dirs. Crime Prevention Assn., Phila., 1972-88; pres. Pa. council Boys Clubs of Am., 1983-84. Mem. First Mond. Club(pres. 1987-88). Office: IFESH 5040 E Shea Blvd #260 Scottsdale AZ 85254

STERNHAGEN, CHARLES JAMES, therapeutic radiologist; b. Glasgow, Mont., Oct. 15, 1933; s. Joseph Peter and Mary Catherine (Carignan) S. BA, Carroll Coll., 1956; MD, Loyola U., 1959. Intern St. Joseph Hosp., South Bend, Ind., 1959-60; resident U. Okla., Oklahoma City, 1969-72; instr. environ. health Health Scis. Ctr. U. Okla., 1968-72, instr. radiation oncology, 1972; asst. prof. radiology Cancer Rsch. and Treatment Ctr. U. N.Mex.-Los Alamos Sci. Lab., 1971-75, assoc. prof., 1976-78; chief radiation oncology Lovelace Bataan Med. Ctr., Albuquerque, 1972-78; dir. Cancer Therapy Ctr. Providence Hosp., Anchorage, 1978—; state surgeon N.Mex. N.G., 1973-76, Alaska Air N.G., 1988—. Contbr. articles to profl. jours. Pres.-elect State of Alaska div., Am. Cancer Soc., 1982, nat. med. del. , 1986—. Col. USAR, 1964—. Lederle Rsch. fellow, 1956, recipient various grants. Fellow Am. Pub. Health Assn., Royal Soc. Health (London); mem. AMA, AAAS, Am. Endocurietherapy Soc., Am. Soc. Preventive Oncology, Okla. Acad. Environ. Health Scis., Alaska State Med. Assn. (councillor, conv. chmn.), Am. Soc. Therapeutic Radiologists, Am. Coll. Radiology, Am. Soc. Clin. Oncology, Am. Roentgen Ray Soc., Am. Assn. for Cancer Rsch., Health Physics Soc. (ethics com.), Internat. Radiation Protection Assn., Radiation Rsch. Soc., Radiol. Soc. N.Am., Am. Radium Soc., N.Mex. Soc. Radiology, Anchorage Med. Soc. Office: 3200 Providence Blvd Anchorage AK 99504

STERZER, ALBERT LEROY, aerospace engineer; b. Salt Lake City, June 8, 1938; s. Albert John and Ruby Agnes (Anderson) S.; m. Donna Lee Holmes, Sept. 13, 1961 (div. Dec. 1976); children: Terri, Cindi; m. Virginia Marie Webb, Mar. 19, 1977; children: Sara, Joseph, Michael, Rachael. BSEE, U. Utah, 1965; MS in Systems Engring., Calif. State U., Fullerton, 1970. Instr. Utah Trade Tech. Sch., Salt Lake City, 1964-65; field engr. Rockwell Internat., Groton, Conn., 1965-68; customer tng. specialist Rockwell Internat., Anaheim, Calif., 1968-72, project engr., 1975-83; mgr. Trident tng. program Data Design Labs., Cucamonga, Calif., 1972-75; program mgr. All Bann Enterprises, Anaheim, 1983-86; project mgr. Litton Guidance and Control Systems, Woodland Hills, Calif., 1986-88; reliability engr. Salt Lake City, 1988—. Mem. Nat. Mgmt. Assn. (pres. Anaheim chpt. 1982-83), Navy League (sec. Upland, Calif. 1974), Litton Mgmt. Club, Toastmasters (pres. Anaheim 1976-77, Able Toastmaster award Santa Ana, Calif. 1978). Republican. Mormon. Home: 4902 S Hidden Cove Dr Taylorsville UT 84123 Office: Litton Guidance-Ctl Systems 22ll W N Temple St Salt Lake City UT 84116

STETSON, JEFFREY PAUL, educator, playwright; b. N.Y.C., June 5, 1948; s. John Howard and Isabella (Calvanese) S.; m. Carmen Elisia Hayward, June 21, 1980. BA, Framingham State Coll., 1973; EdM, Boston U., 1974, ABD, 1978. Dir. affirmative action Mass. State Coll. System, Boston, 1974-79; dean faculty and staff affairs Calif. State U., Long Beach, 1979-87, dir. pub. affairs & U. relations, 1986—. Playwright: The Meeting, 1987, Louis B. Mayer award, 8 NAACP Theatre awards, And the Men Shall Also Gather, 1988, Fraternity, Winner Nat. Multi-cultural Festival, 1988, Fathers and Other Strangers, 1989, Theodore Ward award. Mem. Urban League, NAACP; pres. Black Alliance for Scholarship in Edn., 1982-87, Concerned Helpers Inner City Endeavors, 1985-89. Recipient Outstanding Black Educator's award, Urban Learning Ctr., 1973; Whitney Young Jr. Fellowship, Boston U., 1974, CHOICE award for community svc., L.A., 1985. Mem. L.A. Black Playwrights (founding mem.), Dramatists Guild, Writers Guild of Am. Democrat. Home: 14005 Palawan Way #210 Marina Del Rey CA 90292 Office: Calif State Univ 400 Golden Shore Long Beach CA 90802

STEVENS, DAVID, economics educator; b. Burbank, Calif., Jan. 26, 1926; s. Frederick and Alpheus (Perkins) S.; 1 child, David Fancher. B.A., Whitman Coll., 1947; M.B.A., Stanford U., 1949. Asst. prof. Okla. State U., 1949-51; asst. prof. econs. Whitman Coll., Walla Walla, Wash., 1951-54; asso. prof. Whitman Coll., 1954-56, prof., 1956-67, Roger and David Clapp prof. of econ. thought, 1958—, dean adminstrn., 1954-64, chmn. faculty, 1982-85; vis. prof. Glasgow U., Scotland, 1964-66, sr. research fellow, 1980—; instr. Am. Inst. Banking. Author: Adam Smith and the Colonial Disturbances, 1976; Editor: The Wedderburn Manuscript In Adam Smith: Correspondence, 1977. Commr. Regional Planning Commn., Walla Walla County, 1960-64; chmn. Walla Walla County chpt. ARC, 1961-63, 75-77. Served to lt. J.G. U.S. Navy, 1943-46. Mem. Am. Econ. Assn., Western Econ. Assn., History of Econ. Soc. Episcopalian. Clubs: Columbia Tower, Rainier (Seattle). Home: 602 Boyer Ave Walla Walla WA 99362 Office: Whitman Coll Walla Walla WA 99362

STEVENS, DIANE KAY, nurse; b. Portland, Oreg., Sept. 11, 1959; d. Larry Donn and Geraldine Rose (Reiswig) Smith; m. Barry Clayton Stevens, Feb. 14, 1982; 1 child, Andrew Lee. BSN, Walla Walla Coll., 1981. RN, Oreg. Nurse Portland Adventists Med. Ctr., 1981--, New Nursing Concepts, Portland, 1984-85. Republican. Office: Portland Adventist Med Ctr 10123 SE Market St Portland OR 97216

STEVENS, EDWARD FRANKLIN, college president; b. Newcastle, Wyo., Sept. 7, 1940; s. Edward Downey and Esther Elizabeth (Watt) S.; m. Linda Elaine Loewenstein, June 3, 1962; children: Carla, Cathy. Student, U. Denver, 1959-60; BA in Edn. cum laude, Nebr. Wesleyan U., 1963; MA, U. Nebr., 1967; PhD, U. Minn., 1983. Tchr., head basketball coach Alvo-Eagle (Nebr.) High Sch., 1963-64, Madison (Nebr.) High Sch., 1964-65; asst. basketball coach U. Nebr., Lincoln, 1965-67; coach, asst. prof. edn. Augustana Coll., Sioux Falls, S.D., 1967-71; v.p., gen. mgr. tng. Iseman div. U.S. Ind., Sioux Falls, 1971-74; chief devel. officer Sioux Falls Coll., 1974-79, asst. prof. then prof., 1980-83; exec. v.p. Kearny (Nebr.) State Coll. Found., 1979-80; pres. George Fox Coll., Newberg, Oreg., 1983—. Chmn. campaign Yamhill County United Way, Newberg, 1988; bd. commrs. Newberg Community Hosp., 1988-89. NDEA fellow, 1965; recipient Young Alumni Achievement award, Nebr. Wesleyan U., 1973, Leadership Fellows award, Bush Found., St. Paul, 1976. Mem. Nat. Christian Coll. Cons. (chmn. 1987-88), Nat. Assn. Intercollegiate Athletics (exec. com. 1988-89), Oreg. Ind. Colls. Assn. (chmn. 1986-87), Oreg. Ind. Colls. Found. (bd. dirs. 1988), Rotary. Republican. Mem. Soc. Friends. Office: George Fox Coll Office of Pres Newberg OR 97132

STEVENS, ELEANOR SANDRA, professional services executive; b. Oklahoma City, Nov. 1, 1932; d. Benjamin Franklin and Mary Lou (Smith) Williams; children: Fred W., Nathandra, Benjiman, Ola Enaid. AS in medicine, Fresno State U., 1954; student Fresno Adult Edn., Los Angeles Trade Tech., 1972-73. Radio disc jockey, Fresno, Calif., 1954-55; bookkeeper Los Angeles County Assessor, 1961-69; supervisor Holzman-Begue Real Estate Co., Los Angeles, 1969-73; dist. mgr. United Systems, Inc., Los Angeles, 1973-77; pub. relations cons. Harold G. Simon & Assoc., Vernon, Calif., 1977-81; pres. Stevens Personalized Services, Los Angeles, 1982—. Recipient cert. profl. devel. State of Calif., 1983. Mem. Van Nuys Women's Referral Service, Torrance Bus. Mgmt. Assn., Los Angeles Good Neighbor Council, Nat. Assn. Female Execs. Mem. Ch. of God Holiness. Lodge: Order of Eastern Star. Office: 4614 S Western Ave Los Angeles CA 90062

STEVENS, HALLEY ORVILLE, mechanical engineer; b. Laramie, Wyo., Aug. 17, 1948; s. Howard Le Roy and Darlene Fae (Brown) S.; m. Kathleen Long, June 28, 1975 (div. Feb. 1977); m. Marsha JoLene Haun, Feb. 22, 1980; children: Christopher Mark. BSME, Ariz. State U., 1974. Registered profl. engr. Ariz., Utah. Analyst Wastach div. Thiokol Corp., Brigham City, Utah, 1974-77; project engr. Govt. Electronics div. Motorola Corp., Scottsdale, Ariz., 1977-79; engr. ARC Tech. Services, Phoenix, 1979-82; lead ballistician Talley Def. Systems, Mesa, Ariz., 1982-84, mgr. of analysis, 1984—. Bd. dirs. Mesa Eastern Little League, 1984—. Mem. ASME. Democrat. Methodist. Home: 4423 E Fairfield Mesa AZ 85205 Office: Talley Def Sytems 3501 N Greenfield Rd PO Box 849 Mesa AZ 85201

STEVENS, RANDOLPH J., lawyer; b. Midland, Mich., Apr. 16, 1950; s. Dale Robert and Patricia Ann (Davis) S.; m. Susan Stevens, June 12, 1971; children: Amanda, Matthew. BA in Rhetoric, U. Oreg., 1972, JD, 1980. Instr. Bend High Sch., Bend, Oreg., 1973-77; instr. U. Oreg., Eugene, 1972-79; legis. asst. Oreg. Legis. Assembly, Salem, 1979; ptnr. Cegavske, Seitz & Stevens, Roseburg, Oreg., 1981-86, Tamblyn & Bush, Portland, Oreg., 1986-87, Bolliger, Hampton & Tarlow, Portland, 1987-88, Eckley & Assocs., Salem, 1987-88, Thetford, Stevens, Mario & Schmit, Lake Oswego, Oreg., 1988-89, Thetford, Stevens & Schmit, Lake Oswego, Oreg., 1989—. Editor: Energy Policy Analysis, 1978. Mem. Portland BXB Officials Assn., 1986—; bd. dirs. Pub. Health Internat., Roseburg, 1983-87. Mem. Oreg. Trial Lawyers Assn., Oreg. State Bar, Rotary (Rotary Internat. group study exchange, Iceland, 1985), Phi Delta Kappa (pres. Cen. Oreg. chpt. 1976-77), Phi Delta Phi (Chase Inn magister 1979-80). Democrat. Methodist. Office: Thetford Stevens & Schmit 4550 Kruse Way Ste 175 Lake Oswego OR 97035

STEVENS, ROBERT BOCKING, scholar, college administrator, lawyer; b. U.K., June 8, 1933; naturalized, 1971; s. John Skevington and Enid Dororthy (Bocking) S.; m. Katherine Booth, Dec. 23, 1985; 1 child, Robin; children by previous marriage: Carey, Richard. BA, Oxford U., 1955, BCL, 1956, MA, 1959, DCL, 1984; LLM, Yale U., 1958; LLD (hon.), N.Y. Law Sch., 1984, Villanova U., 1985, U. Pa., 1987. Barrister-at-law London, 1956; tutor in law Keble Coll. Oxford U., 1958-59; asst. prof. law Yale U., 1959-61, assoc. prof., 1961-65, prof., 1965-76; provost, prof. law and history Tulane U., 1976-78; pres. Haverford Coll., 1978-87; chancellor U. Calif., Santa Cruz, 1987—; vis. prof. U. Tex., 1961, U. East Africa, 1962, Stanford U., 1966; cons. UN, HEW, U.S. Dept. State. Author: The Restrictive Practices Court, 1965, Lawyers and the Courts, 1967, In Search of Justice, 1968, Income Security, 1970, Welfare Medicine in America, 1974, Law and Politics, 1978, The Law School, 1983. Rockefeller Found. grantee, 1962-64, Ford Found. grantee, 1962-64, 73-74, Nat. Endowment for the Humanities grantee, Nuffield Found. grantee, Russell Sage Found. grantee, 1967-68; Hon. fellow Keble Coll. Oxford U., 1985. Mem. Nat. Council on Humanities. Clubs: Oxford and Cambridge (London); City (San Francisco). Home: U Calif University House Santa Cruz CA 95064 Office: U Calif Office Chancellor Santa Cruz CA 95064

STEVENS, STEPHEN EDWARD, psychiatrist; b. Phila.; s. Edward and Antonia S.; BA cum laude, LaSalle Coll., 1950; MD, Temple U., Phila., 1954; LLB, Blackstone Sch. Law, 1973; m. Isabelle Helen Gallacher, Dec. 27, 1953. Intern, Frankford Hosp., Phila., 1954-55; resident in psychiatry Phila. State Hosp., 1955-58; practice medicine specializing in psychiatry Woodland Hills, Calif., 1958-63, Santa Barbara, Calif., 1970-77; asst. supt. Camarillo (Calif.) State Hosp., 1963-70; cons. ct. psychiatrist Santa Barbara County, 1974-77; clin. dir. Kailua Mental Health Ctr., Oahu, Hawaii, 1977—. Served with M.C., USAAF. Diplomate Am. Bd. Psychiatry and Neurology. Fellow Am. Geriatrics Soc. (founding); mem. Am. Acad. Psychiatry and Law, AMA, Am. Psychiat. Assn., Am. Legion, DAV (Oahu chpt. 1), Caledonia Soc., Am. Hypnosis Soc., Am. Soc. Adolescent Psychiatry, Hawaiian Canoe Club, Honolulu Club, Elks, Aloha String Band (founder and pres.). Home: PO Box 26413 Honolulu HI 96825 Office: 45-691 Keaahala Rd Kaneohe HI 96744

STEVENS, THEODORE FULTON, senator; b. Indpls., Nov. 18, 1923; s. George A. and Gertrude (Chancellor) S.; m. Ann Mary Cherrington, Mar. 29, 1952 (dec. 1978); children—Susan B., Elizabeth H., Walter C., Theodore Fulton, Ben A.; m. Catherine Chandler, 1980; 1 dau.; Lily Irene. B.A., U. Calif. at Los Angeles, 1947; LL.B., Harvard U., 1950. Bar: Calif., Alaska, D.C., U.S. Supreme Ct. bars. Pvt. practice Washington, 1950-52, Fairbanks, Alaska, 1953; U.S. atty. Dist. Alaska, 1953-56; legis. counsel, asst. to sec., solicitor Dept. Interior, 1956-60; pvt. practice law Anchorage, 1961-68; mem. Alaska Ho. of Reps., 1965-68, majority leader, speaker pro tem, 1967-68; U.S. senator for Alaska 1968—, asst. Rep. leader, 1977-85. Served as 1st lt. USAAF, World War II. Mem. ABA, Alaska Bar Assn., Calif. Bar Assn., D.C. Bar Assn., Am. Legion, VFW. Lodges: Rotary, Pioneers of Alaska, Igloo #4. Home: PO Box 879 Anchorage AK 99501 Office: US Senate 522 Hart Senate Bldg Washington DC 20510

STEVENSON, EDMOND CHARLES, small business owner; b. Stockton, Calif., Mar. 5, 1946; s. Edmond Robert and Helen Mary (Trulson) S.; m. Karen Stevenson, Mar. 14, 1974 (div. Jan. 1978); m. Ruth Daniela Tompkins, Apr. 19, 1979. AA, Foothill Coll., Los Altos Hills, Calif., 1966; BS, Calif. State U., Hayward, 1974. Asst. to v.p. Union Termina Warehouse, L.A., 1971-72; mgr. Pacific Motor Trucking Co., Burlingame, Calif., 1972-85; owner Jet Photo Lab., Sherman Oaks, Calif., 1985—. 1st lt. USMC, 1967-71, ret. maj., USMCR, 1988. Mem. Pasadena Tournament Roses, La Canada Flintridge Tournament Roses (v.p. 1988--), Navy League (pres. 1984-85), Kiwanis, Masons. Office: Jet Photo Lab 14120 Ventura Blvd Sherman Oaks CA 91423

STEVENSON, FRANCES GRACE, small business owner; b. Colorado Springs, Colo., Aug. 4, 1921; d. Albert Earl and Grace Margaret (Cahill) Storey; m. Robert Louis Stevenson, Oct. 23, 1943; children: Donald Maurice, Nancy Jean, Richard Dean, James Kirk. Grad. high sch., Las Vegas, Nev. Owner, mgr. Francie's Fancies, Napa, Calif., 1973-78, Cheyenne, Wyo., 1979—. Organizer Citizens Com. for Sylvan Dist. Schs., Citrus Heights, Calif., 1954; mem. Napa (Calif.) County Dem. Cen. Com., 1966-78, chmn., 1975-78; hdqrs. chmn. McGovern for Pres., Napa, 1972; mem. Calif. State Dem. Cen. Com., 1975-78; chmn. Klee for U.S. Congress, Napa County, 1976, Brown for Gov., Napa County, 1976; candidate 2d Congl. Dist. Calif. Assembly, 1976; elector Carter for U.S. Pres., Napa County, 1976. Mem. Am. Cut Glass Assn., Am. Carnival Glass Assn., Am. Bell Assn., Cheyenne C. of C. Episcopalian. Home and Office: 1715 Van Lennen Cheyenne WY 82001

STEVENSON, GENE CRAIG, dentist; b. Loma Linda, Calif., July 22, 1949; s. Charles Walter and Loretta Emmagene (George) S.; m. Yun Lu Hsu, Feb. 24, 1985. BA in Biology, Calif. State U., Northridge, 1971; postgrad., Oxford U., 1971-72; DDS, U. So. Calif., 1978; MPhil in History, Somerset U., Ilminster, Eng., 1988. Pvt. practice Glendale, Calif., 1978-81, Carmel, Calif., 1979-82, Watsonville, Calif., 1982-83; dentist Armed Forces Hosp. Saudi Arabia Ministry Def. and Aviation, Dhahran, 1983—; instr. Sch. Dentistry U. So. Calif., Los Angeles, 1978-79; mem. emergency room staff Monterey (Calif.) Peninsula Community Hosp., 1979-83. Contbr. articles to hist. jours. Co-founder Thubten Dhargye Ling Tibetan Ctr., Los Angeles, 1978. Calif. State U. internat. program scholar Oxford U., 1971-72. Mem. Fedn. Dentaire Internationale (lectr. 72d World Dental Congress, Helsinki 1984), ADA, Calif. Dental Assn., Internat. Naval Rsch. Orgn. (assoc.), U.S. Naval Inst., Am. Businessmen's Assn., Delta Sigma Delta. Office: Armed Forces Hosp, PO Box 570, Dhahran Airport, Dhahran 31932, Saudi Arabia

STEVENSON, JAMES RICHARD, radiologist, lawyer; b. Ft. Dodge, Iowa, May 30, 1937; s. Lester Lawrence and Esther Irene (Johnson) S.; m. Sara Jean Hayman, Sept. 4, 1958; children: Bradford Allen, Tiffany Ann, Jill Renee, Trevor Ashley. BS, U. N.Mex., 1959; MD, U. Colo., 1963; JD, U. N.Mex. 1987. Diplomate Am. Bd. Radiology, Am. Bd. Nuclear Medicine, Am. Bd. Legal Medicine; Bar: N.Mex. 1987, U.S. Dist. Ct. N.Mex. 1988. Intern U.S. Gen. Hosp., Tripler, Honolulu, 1963-64; resident in radiology U.S. Gen. Hosp., Brook and San Antonio, Tex., 1964-67; radiologist, ptnr. Van Atta Labs., Albuquerque, 1970-88, Radiology Assocs. of Albuquerque, 1988—, Civerolo, Hansen & Wolf, Albuquerque, 1988-89; adj. asst. prof. radiology U. N.Mex., 1970-71; pres. med. staff AT & SF Meml. Hosp., 1979-80, chief of staff, 1980-81, trustee, 1981-83. Author: District Attorney manual, 1987. Participant breast screening, Am. Cancer Soc., Albuquerque, 1987-88; dir. profl. div. United Way, Albuquerque, 1975. Maj. U.S. Army 1963-70, Vietnam. Decorated Bronze Star. Allergy fellow, 1960. Fellow Am. Coll. Radiology (councilor 1980-86), Am. Coll. Legal Medicine, Am. Coll. Nuclear Medicine; mem. AMA (Physicians' Recognition award 1969—), Albuquerque Bar Assn., Am. Coll. Nuclear Physicians (charter), Soc. Nuclear Medicine (v.p. Rocky Mountain chpt. 1975-76), Am. Inst. Ultrasound in Medicine, N.Am. Radiol. Soc., N.Mex. Radiol. Soc. (pres. 1978-79), N.Mex. Med. Soc. (chmn. grievance com.), Albuquerque-Bernalillo County Med. Soc. (scholar 1959), Nat. Assn. Health Lawyers, ABA (antitrust sect. 1986—), N. Mex. State Bar, Albuquerque Bar Assn., Sigma Chi. Republican. Methodist. Club: Albuquerque Country. Lodges: Elks, Masons, Shriners. Home: 3333 Santa Clara Dr SE Albuquerque NM 87106 Office: Van Atta Imaging Ctr A-6 Med Arts Sq 801 Encino Pl NE Albuquerque NM 87102

STEVENSON, LANI LEE, nurse; b. Seoul, Korea, Feb. 7, 1961; came to U.S., 1961; d. John Donald and Marian Ruth (Lusk) S. BS in Nursing, Ariz. State U., 1983. R.N., Calif., Ariz. Staff nurse Good Samaritan Hosp., Phoenix, 1983-85, Kenneth Norris Jr. Cancer Ctr., L.A., 1985-89; rsch. protocol coord. U. So. Calif. Cancer Ctr., L.A., 1987-89; staff nurse Cedars-Sinai Comprehensive Cancer Ctr., L.A., 1989—. Mem. Oncology Nursing Soc. (cert.), Sigma Theta Tau. Republican. Lutheran. Home: Apt 103 843 4th St Santa Monica CA 90403 Office: Cedars-Sinai Comprehensive Cancer Ctr 8700 Beverly Blvd Los Angeles CA 90069

STEVENSON, PATRICIA ANN, elementary educator; b. Longview, Wash., July 12, 1948; d. Richard Marion and Phyllis (Lilley) Barge; m. Clifford Lynn Stevenson, July 13, 1974; 1 child, Sherri Lynlee-Deann. Assoc. in Liberal Arts, Tacoma (Wash.) Community Coll., 1968; BEd, Cen. Wash. U., 1971, cert., 1976. Substitute tchr. Puyallup (Wash.) Sch. Dist., 1971-73, Tacoma Sch. Dist., 1971-73, Sumner (Wash.) Sch. Dist., 1971-73, North Franklin Sch. Dist., Connell, Wash., 1975--; custom decorator J. C. Penney, Tacoma, 1972-73; purchasing sales rep. Singer Co., Tacoma, 1973-74, Kennewick, Wash., 1974-81; sales rep. Sterling Recreation Orgn., Richland, Wash., 1981-84. Site coordinator Am. Heart Assn., Mesa, Wash., 1988. Ednl. grantee North Franklin Sch. Dist., 1988. Mem. NEA, Wash. Edn. Assn., North Franklin Edn. Assn., Sigma Tau Alpha. Mormon. Home: 70 Canal Dr Mesa WA 99343 Office: Mesa Elem Sch Pepiot Rd Mesa WA 99343

STEVENSON, RICHARD GRAY, III, dentist; b. Long Beach, Calif., July 9, 1958; s. Richard Gray and Carla (Wood) S.; m. Victoria Puthumana, Sept. 15, 1985; 1 child, Richard Gray IV. BS, UCLA, 1982, DDS, 1986. Lic. dentist, Calif. Paramed. vol. Project Nepal, Palo Alto, Calif., 1979-80; dental rschr. Va. Med. Ctr., Sepulveda, Calif., 1980-83; pvt. practice Laguna Niguel, Calif., 1986—, Santa Ana, Calif., 1987—. Active Youth Evolving Solutions, Palo Alto, 1980, Creative Initiative Found., Palo Alto, 1976-82, Students for Global Awareness, UCLA, 1980-82, Beyond War, Palo Alto, 1985—. Mem. ADA, Acad. Gen. Dentistry, Am. Soc. Dentistry for Children, Calif. Dental Assn., Orange County Dental Soc., Crown Pacific Dental Study Club (co-pres. 1986—), Implant Dentistry Orange County Study Club (sec. 1988—), Lions (dir. 1987-88), Delta Sigma Delta (v.p. 1984-86). Office: 32241 Crown Valley Pkwy Ste 200 Laguna Niguel CA 92677

STEVENSON, ROBERT MURRELL, music educator; b. Melrose, N.Mex., July 3, 1916; s. Robert Emory and Ada (Ross) S. AB, U. Tex., El Paso, 1936; grad., Juilliard Grad. Sch. Music, 1938; MusM, Yale, 1939; PhD, U. Rochester, 1942; STB cum laude, Harvard U., 1943; LittB, Oxford (Eng.) U.; Th.M., Princeton. Instr. music U. Tex., 1941-43, 46; faculty Westminster Choir Coll., Princeton, N.Y., 1946-49; faculty research lectr. UCLA, 1981, mem. faculty to prof. music, 1949—; vis. asst. prof. Columbia, 1955-56; vis. prof. Ind. U., Bloomington, 1959-60, U. Chile, 1965-66; cons. UNESCO, 1977. Author: Music in Mexico, 1952, Patterns of Protestant Church Music, 1953, La musica en la catedral de Sevilla, 1954, 85, Music before the Classic Era, 1955, Shakespeare's Religious Frontier, 1958, The Music of Peru, 1959, Juan Bermudo, 1960, Spanish Music in the Age of Columbus, 1960, Spanish Cathedral Music in the Golden Age, 1961, La musica colonial en Colombia, 1964, Protestant Church Music in America, 1966, Music in Aztec and Inca Territory, 1968, Renaissance and Baroque Musical Sources in the Americas, 1970, Music in El Paso, 1970, Philosophies of American Music History, 1970, Written Sources For Indian Music Until 1882, 1973, Christmas Music from Baroque Mexico, 1974, Foundations of New World Opera, 1973, Seventeenth Century Villancicos, 1974, Latin American Colonial Music Anthology, 1975, Vilancicos Portugueses, 1976, Josquin in the Music of Spain and Portugal, 1977, American Musical Scholarship, Parker to Thayer, 1978, Liszt at Madrid and Lisbon, 1980, Wagner's Latin American Outreach, 1983, Spanish Musical Impact Beyond the Pyrenees, 1250-1500, 1985; contbg. editor: Handbook Latin Am. Studies, 1976—; editor: Inter-Am. Music Rev, 1978—; contbr. to: New Grove Dictionary of Music and Musicians, 9 other internat. encys. Served to capt. U.S. Army, 1943-46, 49. Decorated Army Commendation ribbon; fellow Ford Found., 1953-54; Gulbenkian Found., 1966, 81; Guggenheim, 1962; NEH, 1974; recipient Fulbright research awards, 1958-59, 64, 70-71, 88-89, Carnegie Found. teaching award, 1955-56, Gabriela Mistral award OAS, 1985; Heitor Lobos Jury award OAS, 1988, Gold medal Sociedad Espanola de Musicología, 1985; Orgn. Am. States medal, 1986, Cert. Merit Mexican Consulate San Bernardino, Calif., 1987. Mem. Am. Musicological Soc. (hon. life, Pacific SW chpt.), Real Academia de Bellas Artes, Hispanic Soc. Am., Am. Liszt soc. (cons. editor), Heterofonia (cons. editor). Office: UCLA Dept Music 405 Hilgard Ave Los Angeles CA 90024

STEWARD, HAL DAVID, correspondent; b. East St. Louis, Ill., Dec. 2, 1918; s. Owen Bob and Margaret Alice (Martin) S.; m. Dawn Jochebed Bentata, Aug. 18, 1945 (dec. Apr. 1968). BS, Boston U., 1961; LLB, LaSalle Ext. U., 1949; PhD, Columbia Pacific U., 1979. Commd. sgt. U.S. Army, 1937, advanced through ranks to lt. col., ret., 1961; reporter Los Angeles Examiner, 1961-62, San Diego Union, 1962-64; writer San Diego, 1964-69, 72-74; asst. dir. dept. human resources devel. State of Calif., Sacramento, 1970-71; exec. editor The Daily Chronicle, Centralia, Wash., 1975-78; writer Denver, 1982—; roving corr. Newsletter on Newsletters, Rhinebeck, N.Y., 1985—; flight instr. Elma (Wash.) Airport, 1981-82; adjunct faculty Columbia Pacific U., 1981—. Author: The Successful Writer's Guide, 1970, Money-making Secrets of The Millionaires, 1972; contbr. articles to nat. mags. Asst. to Lt. Gov. Calif., 1971. Decorated Bronze Star medal with oak leaf cluster. Mem. Army and Navy Club, Nat. Press Club (Washington). Home and Office: 4725 W Quincy Ave Denver CO 80236

STEWARD, PATRICIA ANN RUPERT, real estate executive, management consultant; b. Panama City, Panama, Apr. 20, 1945 (parents Am. citizens); d. Paul S. and Ernestina M. (Ward) Rupert; grad. Sch. of Mortgage Banking, Grad. Sch. of Mgmt., Northwestern U., 1979; m. Robert M. Levine, Oct. 28, 1978; children by previous marriage: Donald F. Steward, Christine Marie Steward. V.p. Assoc. Mortgage & Investment Co., Phoenix, 1969-71; v.p., br. mgr. Sun Country Funding Corp., Phoenix, 1971-72, Freese Mortgage Co., Phoenix, 1972-74, Utah Mortgage Loan Corp., Phoenix, 1974-81; pres. Elles Corp., 1982—, Elles Mgmt. Corp., 1987—, Elles Approvals Corp., 1987—; founder, The Elles Group, 1987; condr. numerous seminars on mortgage fin. State chmn. Ariz. Leukemia Dr., 1977-78, mem. exec. com., 1979-80; troop leader Cactus Pine council Girl Scouts U.S.A., 1979-80; bd. dirs. Nat. Mental Health Assn., 1986-87, Ariz. Mental Health Assn., pres., 1986-87, bd. dirs., treas. Maricopa Mental Health Assn., 1984-85, v.p., 1985-86, pres., 1986-87; apptd. by state supreme ct. to Ariz. Foster Care Rev. Bd., 1984—, chairperson Bd. 8, 1986-87. Recipient cert. of appreciation Multiple Listing Svc., Phoenix Bd. Realtors, 1975, Multiple Listing Service, Glendale Bd. Realtors, 1977. Lic. mortgage broker, Ariz. Mem. Ariz. Mortgage Bankers Assn. (dir. 1981-82, chmn. edn. com. 1981-82, founder continuing edn. seminar series 1981), Young Mortgage Bankers Assn. (chmn. exec. com. 1980-81), Cen. Ariz. Homebuilders Assn. Republican. Author: A Realtors Guide to Mortgage Lending, 1972. Office: Elles Corp 320 E McDowell Rd Ste 100 Phoenix AZ 85004

STEWART, CYNTHIA FAYE, computer network official, educator; b. Las Cruces, N.Mex., Sept. 27, 1949; d. Louis Barragon and Joyce Aleen (Jetton) Cooper; m. Eugene H. Stewart, Jan. 21, 1978; children: Jeffrey Russell, Jason Bryan, Michelle Renee Pendergrass. BA in Edn., Ariz. State U., 1974. Personal computer network cood. Tanner S.W. div. APAC, Inc., Phoenix, 1986—; instr. Maricopa County Community Coll. Dist., Phoenix, 1986—. Office: Tanner SW Inc 701 N 44th St Phoenix AZ 85008

STEWART, ISAAC DANIEL, JR., Utah Supreme Court justice; b. Salt Lake City, Nov. 21, 1932; s. Isaac Daniel and Orabelle (Iverson) S.; m. Elizabeth Bryan, Sept. 10, 1959; children: Elizabeth Ann, Shannon. B.A., U. Utah, 1959, J.D., 1962. Bar: Utah 1962. Atty. Dept. Justice, 1962-65; asst. prof., then asso. prof. U. Utah Coll. Law, 1965-70, chmn. curriculum com., 1967-69; ptnr. firm Jones, Waldo, Holbrook & McDonough, Salt Lake City, 1970-79; justice Utah Supreme Ct., 1979-86, 88—, now assoc. chief justice, 1986-88; lectr. in field; mem. Utah Bd. Oil, Gas and Mining, 1976-78, chmn., 1977-78; Utah rep. Interstate Oil Compact Commn., 1977-78, exec. com. 1978-79; mem. adv. com. rules of procedure Utah Supreme Ct., 1983—. Contbr. articles to legal jours. Chmn. subcom. on legal rights and responsibilities of youth Utah Gov's Com. on Youth, 1972; pres. Salt Lake Chpt. Council Fgn. Relations, 1982; mem. Salt Lake City C. of C., 1974-79, mem. govtl. modernization com., 1976-78; missionary for Mormon Ch. in Fed. Republic Germany, 1953-56; bd. dirs. U. Utah Alumni. Named Apellate Judge of Year, 1986. Mem. ABA, Am. Judicature Soc., Utah Bar Assn. (com. on law and property 1967-69, com. on specialization 1977-78, pub. relations com. 1968-69, chmn. com. on antitrust law 1977-78, com. on civil procedure reform 1968, Appellate Judge of Yr. 1986), Salt Lake County Bar Assn., U. Utah Alumni Assn. (bd. dirs. 1985—), Phi Beta Kappa, Order of Coif, Phi Kappa Phi, Sigma Chi (Significant Sig award 1987). Office: Utah Supreme Ct 332 State Capitol Bldg Salt Lake City UT 84114

STEWART, JAMES MEREDITH, systems engineering executive; b. Northampton, Mass., Mar. 22, 1942; s. James Edward Woodson and Juanita (Hampton) S.; m. Shirley Bradsher, Aug. 10, 1978. BS in Aeronautical Tech., Boston U., 1964; MS in Systems Mgmt., U. So. Calif., 1977. Lic. comml. pilot. Commd. 2d lt. USAF, 1964, advanced through grades to col., 1981; test pilot Hdqrs. Aerospace Def. Command, Colorado Springs, Colo., 1971-73; chief standardization and evaluation 49 Fighter Interceptor Squadron, Griffiss AFB, N.Y., 1974-77; chief aerospace def. The Pentagon, Washington, 1977-82; dir. ops. 36 Tactical Fighter Wing, Bitburg AFB, Fed. Republic Germany, 1983-84, vice comdr., 1984-85; dir. operational requirements Hdqrs. USAF Europe, Ranstein AFB, Fed. Republic Germany, 1985-88; ret. USAF, 1988; pres. Tech. Vectors Inc., Colorado Springs, 1988—. Decorated D.F.C., Legion of Merit, Air medal with 11 oak leaf clusters. Mem. Nat. Security Indsl. Assn., Armed Forces Communication & Electronic Assn. Republican. Methodist. Home: 3071 Banjo Dr Colorado Springs CO 80918 Office: Technology Vectors Inc PO Box 62247 Colorado Springs CO 80962-2247

STEWART, JAMES VAHL, business owner; b. Osceola, Wis., July 11, 1947; s. Vahl J. and Virginia (Stocker) S.; m. Mary D. Zutefern, June 16, 1985. Student, U. Wis., Eau Claire, 1965-68, U. Wash., Seattle, 1968-69, Los Angeles Coll. Optometry, 1969-71. Pres. Wet Whisker Inc., Coupeville, Wash., 1969-83, SBC, Vashon Island, Wash., 1983—. Recipient Package Design Creativity award Art Direction mag., 1986, Excellence award Seattle Design Assn., 1985, Honor award Seattle chpt. AIA, 1985, ADDY award Helena (Mont.) chpt. Advt. Fedn., 1987. Mem. Seattle C. of C. Republican. Methodist. Clubs: Swift Creek Hunt (Clam Fork, Mont.) (pres. 1983-88); P-51 (Quinns Hot Spring, Mont.). Home: PO Box 964 Vashon WA 98070 Office: SBC Dugans Country Bldg #1 on Ctr Vashon WA 98070

STEWART, JOHN FORBES, investment counselor; b. San Francisco, Apr. 8, 1929; s. John Loftus and Katherine (Forbes) S.; m. Ann Churchman, June 20, 1953; children: Douglas C., Derek F. BA, Lake Forest (Ill.) Coll., 1951; postgrad. in bus., San Jose State Coll., 1956-57. Exec. trainee Bank of Am., San Francisco, 1956; registered rep. Dean Witter & Co., Palo Alto, Calif., 1957-65; investment counselor John F. Stewart & Co., Palo Alto, 1965-67, Los Actos, Calif., 1970—; portfolio mgr. Wells Fargo Bank, San Francisco, 1967-68; instnl. rep. Glore, Forgan, Staats, San Francisco, 1968-70; mem. adv. bd. Transition Capital, Palo Alto, 1988—; cons. in field. 1st lt. USAF, 1952-55. Mem. Rotary, (bd. dirs. Los Actos chpt. 1978-80), Los Altos Golf and Country Club. Republican. Christian Scientist. Home: 13075 Alta Ln S Los Altos Hills CA 94022 Office: John F Stewart Investments 444 1st St Los Altos CA 94022

STEWART, KATHRYN BOOTH, marketing executive; b. Durham, N.C., Apr. 4, 1946; d. John Edward and Swannie Mae (Bailey) Booth; m. John Merlin Stewart (div. May 1988); 1 child, Ian Roe. BA, Meredith Coll., 1968; MA, N.C. State U., 1976. Tchr. Mt. Pleasant (S.C.) High Sch./Jr. Coll., 1970-74; exec. recruiter Mgmt. Recruiters, Norfolk, Va., 1975; sales rep. IBM Corp., Norfolk, 1976-79; systems laser specialist IBM Corp., Newport Beach, Calif., 1979-81; mktg. mgr. Xerox Corp., El Segundo, Calif., 1981-83, mktg. program mgr., 1983-85; v.p. mktg. Digital Compositions Systems, Phoenix, 1985-86; pres. Market Match, Inc., Yorba Linda, Calif., 1986-88; v.p. sales and mktg. Interlink Electronics, Santa Barbara, Calif., 1989—; conf. chmn. Inst. for Graphic Communications, Boston, 1986. Contbr. articles to newspapers and mags. Mem. Ctr. for Entrepreneurial Mgmt., Jr. Women's Club. Republican. Home: 3750 Forest Glen Rd Yorba Linda CA 92686

STEWART, LARRY R., engineer, financial director, consultant; b. Rock Springs, Wyo., Mar. 26, 1948; s. Raymond Melvin and Mary Jane (Fillin) S.; m. Della Jean Warren, Aug. 25, 1967; children: Stephanie M., Kara K., Gina R., Laura J. BS in Engrng., U. Wyo., 1970, MS in Engrng., 1972. Registered profl. engr., Ariz., Colo., Idaho, Mont., N.Mex., Oreg., Tex., Utah, Wyo. Mgr. apt. Willey Enterprises, Laramie, Wyo., 1966-70; grad. asst. U. Wyo., Laramie, 1970-72; systems analyst Dept. Def., Corona, Calif., 1972-73; engr. Mountain Bell, Cheyenne, Wyo., 1973-77; adminstr. Mountain Bell, Denver, 1977-79; mgr. Mountain Bell, Englewood, Colo., 1979-84; dist. mgr. Mountain Bell, Denver, 1985-87; dir. Bell TRICO Services, Englewood, 1984-85, U.S. West CGI, Denver, 1987—; mem. adv. bd. U. Wyoming Grad. Sch., Laramie, 1970-72; IOF co-chair AT&T/Bell System, Basking Ridge, N.J., 1980-83; curriculum advisor Network Tng., Englewood, 1980-83; fin. advisor Employee Suggestion Plan, Denver, 1984-86. Editor (coll. mag.) Enginews, 1970. Pres. Maplewood Homeowners, Arvada, Colo., 1986; key chair United Way, Denver, 1988. Served with USAF, 1970-76. Mem. IEEE, Nat. Soc. Profl. Engrs. Republican. Mormon. Lodge: Optimist (lt. gov. of Colo./Wyo. Dist.). Home: 10940 W 65 Way Arvada CO 80004 Office: US West Communications 1801 California MBC 2950 Denver CO 80202

STEWART, PAULA IRENE, principal; b. Evansville, Ind., Apr. 3, 1946; d. Carl F. and Mildred I. (Wilsman) Koeing; m. Milton Roy Stewart, June 15, 1968. BS in Elem. Edn., Ind. U., 1968, MS in Elem. Edn., 1971. Cert. elem. tchr., Oreg. Tchr. elem. schs. Ind., 1968-87; vice prin. Reynolds Sch. Dist., Trouldale, Oreg., 1980-81; prin. Estacada (Oreg.) Grade Sch., 1988-. Mem. Confederation Oreg. Sch. Adminstrs., Women Ednl. Assn., Multnomah Athletic. Democrat. Home: 2840 SW Champlain Dr Portland OR 97201 Office: Estacada Grade Sch PO Box 519 Estacada OR 97023

STEWART, ROBERT CHARLES, JR., real estate company executive, lumber company executive; b. Palo Alto, Calif., Feb. 18, 1955; s. Robert Charles and Bernadette Ann (Johnson) S.; m. Jacqueline Helen Reed, June 25, 1983. AA, De Anza Coll., 1976; BS, San Jose State U., 1979. Constrn. materials salesman Pine Cone Lumber Co., Sunnyvale, Calif., 1983—; salesman G.I.A. Real Estate, Campbell, Calif., 1988—. Past v.p., treas. Cystic Fibrosis Research, Inc. Office: GIA Real Estate 441 N Central Ave Ste 5 Campbell CA 95008

STEWART, RODNEY LEE, retired naval officer, seminar leader; b. Albuquerque, Aug. 8, 1928; s. Melvin Lloyd and Martha Lee (Capron) S.; m. Beverly June Park, Apr. 17, 1948; children: David Lloyd, Gayle Suzanne. BA in English Lit., U. N.Mex., 1951; postgrad., U.K. Nat. Defense Coll., 1968; student exec. seminar fgn. policy, State Dept., 1974-75. Commd. ensign USN, 1951, advanced through grades to capt., 1981, ret., 1981, head internat. policy br. Politico-Mil. Affairs Directorate Office Chief Naval Ops., 1972-74; dir. vulnerability Def. Nuclear Agy. Dept. Def., Washington, 1977-79; dep. dir. Identification-Friend, Foe or Neutral Joint Task Force Dept. Def., Albuquerque, 1979-81; ret. USN, 1981; S.W. regional mgr. PE Systems Inc., Albuquerque, 1981-82; v.p. Parks Coll., Albuquerque, 1982-84; sr. staff mem. The BDM Corp., Albuquerque, 1984-87, dir. personnel and adminstrn., 1987-89; mgmt. cons., adminstrn. Jaynes Corp., Albuquerque, 1987-89; chmn. Navy Recruiting Dist. Assistance Council, Albuquerque, 1982—. Bd. dirs. Found. for Free Enterprise Edn., Albuquerque, 1987—; mem. N.Mex. adv. com. U.S. Civil Rights Commn., 1988—, mem. fgn. relations com., Albuquerque, 1982—; vice-chmn. City-County Unification Task Force, Albuquerque, 1984-85; chmn. city bd. Sister Cities and pres. Albuquerque Sister Cities Found., 1989—. Decorated Legion of Merit, Bronze Star medals (2). Mem. Nat. Speakers Assn., Armed Forces Communications and Electronics Assn., Navy League U.S. (state pres. 1986-88), Navy League N.Mex. Council (pres. 1989—), U.S. Naval Inst., Internat. Test and Evaluation Assn., N.Mex. Personnel Assn., Greater Albuquerque C. of C., Soc. Preservation and Encouragement Barbershop Quartet Singing in

Am. Republican. Methodist. Clubs: Assn. Old Crows, Albuquerque TIP (pres. 1983-84), Toastmans (v.p. 1973-74). Lodge: Kiwanis (pres. 1986-87). Home: 1133 Marigold Dr NE Albuquerque NM 87122

STEYER, RANDY CARL, rental company executive; b. Nashville, Nov. 24, 1950; s. Lorenz Winfield and Darlene Shirley (Kraeger) S.; m. Belinda Adele Bostheder, July 13, 1985; 1 child, Gary. BS, Coll. Notre Dame, Belmont, Calif., 1973. Asst. ops. mgr. Leaseametric, Foster City, Calif., 1971-80; equipment sales mgr. U.S. Instrument Rentals, San Mateo, Calif., 1980--. Mem. Elks. Home: 301 Portola Dr San Mateo CA 94403

STICH, SALLY SIMON, educator, newspaper columnist, writer; b. Omaha, Apr. 18, 1950; d. Stuart E. and Esther (Fox) Simon; m. Thomas M. Stich, Aug. 9, 1975; children: Max, Sarah. BA in French, U. Denver, 1972; MA in English, U. Colo., 1983. Cert. tchr., Colo. Tchr. St. Mary's Acad., Englewood, Colo., 1973-79; instr. writing U. Colo., Denver, 1980—; columnist Family Fun, Denver Post, 1986—, edn. cons., 1987—; freelance writer, 1986—. Author: Writing with Today's Text, 1987. Mem. women's com. Brandeis U., Denver, 1983—; bd. dirs. Herzl Jewish Day Sch., Denver, 1988—. Named Tchr. of Yr., St. Mary's Acad., 1976-77. Mem. Denver Women's Press Club, Colo. Authors League. Democrat. Home: 3227 S Niagara St Denver CO 80224 Office: Denver Post 650 15th St Denver CO 80202

STICKEL, FREDERICK A., publisher; b. Weehawken, N.J., Nov. 18, 1921; s. Fred and Eva (Madigan) S.; m. Margaret A. Dunne, Dec. 4, 1943; children—Fred A., Patrick F., Daisy E., Geoffrey M., James E., Bridget A. Student, Georgetown U., 1939-42; BS, St. Peter's Coll., 1943. Advt. salesperson Jersey Observer daily, Hoboken, N.J., 1945-51; retail advt. salesperson Jersey Jour., Jersey City, 1951-55; advt. dir. Jersey Jour., 1955-66, publisher, 1966-67; gen. mgr. Oregonian Pub. Co., Portland, Oreg., 1967-72, pres., 1972—, publisher, 1975—. Bd. regents U. Portland; mem. adv. bd. Portland State U.; bd. dirs. Portland Rose Festival Assn., United Way Oreg.; chmn. Portland Citizens Crime Commn. Capt. USMC, 1942-45. Mem. Assn. for Portland Progress (dir.), Portland C. of C. (dir.), Oreg. Newspaper Pubs. Assn. (past pres.), Pacific N.W. Newspaper Assn. (pres.), Am. Newspaper Pubs. Assn., University Club, Multnomah Athletic Waverley Country Club, Arlington Club, Rotary. Office: Oregonian Pub Co 1320 SW Broadway Portland OR 97201

STICKNEY, ROBERT ROY, fisheries educator; b. Mpls., July 2, 1941; s. Roy E. and Helen Doris (Nelson) S.; m. LuVerne C. Whiteley, Dec. 29, 1961; children: Robert Roy, Marolan Margaret. BS, U. Nebr., 1967; MA, U. Mo., 1968; PhD, Fla. State U., 1971. Cert. fisheries scientist. Research assoc. Skidaway Inst. Oceanography, Savannah, Ga., 1971-73, asst. prof., 1973-75; asst. prof. Texas A&M U., College Station, 1975-78, assoc. prof., 1978-83, prof., 1983-84; prof. zoology, dir. Fisheries Research Lab., So. Ill. U., Carbondale, 1984-85; dir. Sch. of Fisheries U. Wash., Seattle, 1985—; chmn. S-168 com. So. Regional Coop. Research Project, 1981-84. Author: Principles of Warmwater Aquaculture, 1979, Estuarine Ecology of the Southeastern United States and Gulf of Mexico, 1984; editor Culture of Non-Salmonid Freshwater Fisheries, 1986, Reviews in Aquatic Sciences; contbr. articles to profl. jours. Served with USAF, 1959-63. Mem. AAAS, Am. Fisheries Soc. (pres. fish culture sect. 1983-84, Tex. Aquaculturist of Yr. 1979), Am. Inst. Fish Research Biologists (past Tex. div. dir.), Am. Inst. Nutrition, World Aquaculture Soc. (bd. dirs.), Am. Soc. Limnology and Oceanography, Western Region Aquaculture Consortium (chmn., bd. dirs. 1987). Home: 17507 NE 133 Redmond WA 98052 Office: U Wash Sch Fisheries WH-10 Seattle WA 98195

STIEHL, KURT JOHN, bank executive; b. Santa Maria, Calif., Jan. 10, 1949; s. John Albert and Adele Marie (Baeressen) S.; m. Anne Marie Marguerite Royet, Nov. 14, 1981; 1 child, Christopher Michel John. BA, UCLA, 1972; cert., U. Sorbonne, Paris, 1973; M Internat. Bus., Monterey Inst. Internat. Study, 1980. Mgr. wine sales various cos., San Francisco, 1974-78; v.p. Wells Fargo Bank, N.A., San Francisco, 1981—. San Luis Obispo (Calif.) hdqrs. mgr., Eugene McCarthy presdl. campaign, 1968; vestry fin. chmn., All Saints Episcopal Ch., Palo Alto, Calif., 1988—. Mem. Vintners Club San Francisco. Democrat. Home: 221 N Rengstorff Ave Mountain View CA 94043 Office: Wells Fargo Bank NA 464 California St San Francisco CA 94111

STIFEL, FREDERICK BENTON, pastor, biochemist, nutritionist; b. St. Louis, Jan. 30, 1940; s. Carl Gottfried and Alma J. (Clark) S.; m. Gail Joane Stewart, Aug. 10, 1963; children: Tim, Faith, Seth, Elizabeth. BS, Iowa State U., 1962, PhD, 1967; MDiv., Melodyland Sch. Theol., Anaheim, Calif., 1979. Ordained to ministry Evang. Presbyn. Ch., 1981. Lab. supr., research chemist U.S. Army Med. Research and Nutrition Lab., Denver, 1968-74, Letterman Army Inst. Research, San Francisco, 1974-76; intern pastor Melodyland Christian Ctr., Anaheim, 1979-80; assoc. pastor Faith Presbyn. Ch., Aurora, Colo., 1980—; chmn. Care of Candidates Com., Presbytery of West, Denver, 1985-88; bd. dirs. Christian Family Services, Aurora; v.p. Love, Inc. of Metro Denver; regional coordinator Nat. Assn. Single Adult Leaders. Contbr. clin. med. and nutritional articles to profl. jours. Del. Iowa State Rep. Conv., Des Moines, 1964, Colo. State Rep. Conv., Denver, 1984; mem. parent adv. council, IMPACT drug intervention team Rangeview High Sch., Aurora, 1985—; vice chmn. Young Life com. Marin County, Calif., 1974-76. Served to capt. U.S. Army Med. Service Corps, 1967-70. Recipient Sci. Achievement award U.S. Army Sci. Conf., West Point, N.Y., 1968, 70. Mem. Am. Inst. Nutrition, Am. Soc. Clin. Nutrition, Am. Sci. Affiliation, Evang. Theol. Soc., Phi Eta Sigma, Phi Kappa Phi, Alpha Zeta, Gamma Sigma Delta, Kappa Sigma, Sigma Xi. Home: 3492 S Blackhawk Way Aurora CO 80014 Office: Faith Presbyn Ch 11373 E Alameda Ave Aurora CO 80012

STIGLICH, JACOB JOHN, JR., engineering consultant; b. Milw., Dec. 21, 1938; s. Jacob John Sr. and Augusta (Prezel) S. BSME, Marquette U., 1961; PhD, Northwestern U., 1970. Chief engr. Boride Products, Traverse City, Mich., 1971-74; mgr. ceramic materials Valeron Corp., Madison Heights, Mich., 1974-76; group leader, asst. dir. tech. Eagle Picher, Miami, Okla., 1976-78; program mgr. San Fernando Lab., Pacoima, Calif., 1978-84; tech. specialist Aerojet Ordnance Co., Tustin, Calif., 1984-85; cons. Sierra Madre, Calif., 1985—. Contbr. articles to profl. jours.; patentee in field. Served to col. Ordnance Corps, USAR, 1961—. Mem. AIME, Am. Soc. Metals, Am. Ceramic Soc., Mensa, Sigma Xi. Office: Ultramet 12173 Montague St Pacoima CA 91331

STILES, JOYCE ANN, nurse; b. Everett, Mass., Oct. 13, 1943; d. Paul Arnom and Myrtle Marion (Sylvester) Connor; m. Robert Lee Stiles, June 10, 1972; children: Kimberly, Mark, Jason. Diploma in Nursing, New Eng. Bapt. Hosp. Sch., Mass., 1964; BSN cum laude, Calif. State U., L.A., 1987. RN, Mass., Calif. Mgr. venereal disease clinic Boston U. Hosp., 1972-74; charge nurse surg. dept. Downey (Calif.) Community Hosp., 1976-80, med., surg. nurse, pub. health nurse, case mgr., 1981—; clin. supr. surg. dept. City of Hope Hosp., Duarte, Calif., 1980-81. Active Boy Scouts Am. Mem. AAUW, Golden Key, Greenpeace, Phi Kappa Phi. Democrat. Congregationalist. Home: 8339 Albia St Downey CA 90242

STILES, LESTER WARREN, mechanical engineer; b. Wilton, N.Y., Jan. 17, 1927; s. Elton Warren and Bertha Estela (Chase) S.; m. Lorraine Shirley Gratto; children: David James, Julia Anne. BS, Rensselaer Polytechnic Inst., 1958. Engring. asst. Gen. Electric Co., Hudson Falls, N.Y., 1953-57; mech. engr. Crocker Burbank, Fitchburg, Mass., 1958-64; mgr. research and devel. instrumentation Weyerhaeuser Co., Tacoma, Wash., 1964—. Patentee in methods of forming paper. Served with U.S. Navy, 1945-52, ETO. Mem. Instrument Soc. Am. (gen. chmn. 1988). Republican. Home: 37004 32nd Ave S Auburn WA 98001 Office: Weyerhaeuser Co WTC 1B14 Tacoma WA 98447

STILL, BARRY NOEL, general contracting company executive, consultant; b. St. Louis, Jan. 29, 1946; s. Arthur John and Miriam Louise (Kellenberger) S.; m. Karen Elizabeth Thummel, Mar. 9, 1974; children: Brian Edward, Elizabeth Erin. BSCE, U. Ala., 1969. Registered profl. engr., Alaska. Engr. Chgo. Bridge & Iron Co., Birmingham, Ala., 1969; city engr. City of Kodiak (Alaska), 1973-76; v.p. Brechan Enterprises, Inc., Kodiak, 1977—; pres. Lash Corp., Kodiak, 1977—. Lt. USN, 1969-72. Mem. Profl. Engrs. Kodiak, Rotary (pres. Kodiak 1988-89). Office: Lash Corp 2705 Mill Bay Rd Kodiak AK 99615

STILLMAN, ALFRED WILLIAM, JR., design/support engineer; b. Biloxi, Miss., Sept. 11, 1942; s. Alfred William and Marie Ann (Hengen) S.; AA, Am. River Coll., 1966; BSEE, Calif. Poly. State U., 1970, BS in Applied Math., 1970, MS in Applied Math., 1973; ME in Indsl. Engring., Tex. A. and M. U., 1976; postgrad. elec. engring. N.J. Inst. Tech., 1977; PhD in Mgmt., Calif. Coast U., 1984; children: Shannon Lynn, Laura Marie. Cert. profl. logistician, instr. Calif. Community Colls. Engring. intern U.S. Army Material Command, Texarkana, Tex., 1973-75, electronic systems staff maintenance engr., Ft. Monmouth, N.J., 1975-77, mil. tactical data system integrated logistics support mgr. Office of Project Mgr., ARTADS, Ft. Monmouth, 1977-78, tactical ADP ILS Mgr., ILS dir. CORADOM, Ft. Monmouth, 1978-79, engring. mgr. regional dist. office Office of Project Mgr., Firefinder, Hughes Aircraft Co., Fullerton, Calif., 1979-80; prof. systems acquisition mgmt. Dept. Def. Systems Mgmt. Coll., Ft. Belvoir, Va., 1980-82; integrated logistics support engring. specialist, advanced systems div. Northrop Corp., Pico Rivera, Calif., 1982-83; program mgmt. rep. space systems group Rockwell Internat., Downey, Calif., 1983-84; product assurance project engr. Space Sta. Systems div. Rockwell Internat., Downey, Calif., 1984-85; mgr. product support, 1985-86; sr. mgr. ILS, Amex Systems, Inc., Compton, Calif., 1986—; bd. dirs. ILS NavCom Def. Electronics Inc., El Monte, Calif.;pres. AWS Assocs. Calif., Inc., Huntington Beach, 1983—; corp. v.p., div. pres. HOPE Assocs., Inc., Huntington Beach, 1983—. With USAF, 1962-66. Mem. IEEE, Am. Mgmt. Assn., Am. Inst. Indsl. Engrs. (sr.) Soc. Logistics Engrs. (sr.), Am. Def. Preparedness Assn., Am. Security Council, Acacia, Tau Beta Pi. Presbyterian. Home: 10115 Valley Blvd Ste 263 El Monte CA 91731 Office: 4323 Arden Dr El Monte CA 91731

STILLMAN, JOHN ALLEN, lawyer; b. Mpls., Dec. 20, 1940; s. David and Rose (Spitalnick) S.; m. Myra Lee Gould, Aug. 29, 1965; children: Jamy, Michael. BA, San Francisco State U., 1965; JD, U. So. Calif., 1968. Bar: Calif. 1968. Dep. dist. atty. Los Angeles County, 1968-84; spl. asst. U.S. Atty.'s Office, 1982-84; ptnr. Good, Wildman, Hegness & Walley, Newport Beach, Calif., 1984--. Pres. Huntington Harbor Cancer League, 1982; chmn. bd. dirs. Orange County unit Am. Cancer Soc., 1988--; officer, founder Orange County Wellness Community, 1988--; bd. dirs. United Way Orange County, 1988--. Democrat. Jewish. Office: Good Wildman Hegness & Walley 5000 Campus Dr Newport Beach CA 92660

STILSON, BRUCE WAINWRIGHT, lawyer; b. Spokane, Wash., Dec. 13, 1933; s. Leslie Adelbert and Alice (Turner) S.; m. Valerie Jelenfy, Apr. 19, 1961 (div. 1981); children: Guy W., Gregory B. AB, Stanford U., 1955, JD, 1957. Bar: Calif. 1957. Law clk. Calif. Ct. Appeals, San Francisco, 1957-58; ptnr. Skelly, Lack & Stilson, San Francisco, 1958-68; pvt. practice San Rafael, Calif., 1968—. Mem. editorial bd. Stanford Law Rev., 1956-57. Bd. dirs. Trauma Found., San Francisco, 1980—, Marin Civic Ballet, San Rafael, 1986—. Mem. ABA, State Bar Calif., San Francisco Bar Assn., Marin Bar Assn. Home: 1229 Idylberry Rd San Rafael CA 94903 Office: 880 Las Gallinas San Rafael CA 94903

STILSON, WALTER LESLIE, radiologist, educator; b. Sioux Falls, S.D., Dec. 13, 1908; s. George Warren and Elizabeth Margaret (Zager) S.; m. Grace Beall Bramble, Aug. 15, 1933 (dec. June 1984); children: Carolyn G. Palmieri, Walter E., Judith A. Stirling; m. Lula Ann Birchel, June 30, 1985. BA, Columbia Union Coll., 1929; MD, Loma Linda U., 1934. Diplomate Am. Bd. Radiology, Nat. Bd. Med. Examiners. Intern White Meml. Hosp., Los Angeles, 1933-34; resident radiology Los Angeles County Gen. Hosp., 1934-36; instr. radiology Loma Linda (Calif.) U. Sch. Medicine, 1935-41, asst. prof., 1941-49, exec. sec. radiology, 1945-50, assoc. prof., 1949-55, head dept. radiology, 1950-55, prof. radiology, 1955-83, chmn. dept. radiology, 1955-69, emeritus prof., 1983—; chief radiology service White Meml. Hosp., Los Angeles, 1941-65, Loma Linda U. Med. Ctr., 1966-69; chmn. dept. radiologic tech. Sch. Allied Health Professions, 1966-75, med. dir. dept. radiologic tech., 1975-83. Contbr. articles to health jours. Fellow Am. Coll. Radiology; mem. AAAS, Los Angeles Radiol. Soc. (sec. 1960-61, treas. 1961-62, pres. 1963-64), Radiol. Soc. N.Am., Am. Roentgen Ray Soc., N.Y. Acad. Sci., Inland Radiol. Soc. (pres. 1971), Alpha Omega Alpha. Republican. Adventist. Home: 25045 Crestview Loma Linda CA 92354 Office: Loma Linda Radiology Group Inc 11234 Anderson St Loma Linda CA 92354

STINI, WILLIAM ARTHUR, anthropologist, educator; b. Oshkosh, Wis., Oct. 9, 1930; s. Louis Alois and Clara (Larsen) S.; m. Mary Ruth Kalous, Feb. 11, 1950; children—Patricia Laraine, Paulette Ann, Suzanne Kay. B.B.A., U. Wis., 1960, M.S., 1967, Ph.D., 1969. Planner cost acct. Kimberly-Clark Corp., Niagara Falls, N.Y., 1960-62; asst. prof. Cornell U., Ithaca, N.Y., 1968-71; assoc. prof. Cornell U., 1971-73, U. Kans., Lawrence, 1973-76; prof. anthropology U. Ariz., Tucson, 1976—; head dept. anthropology U. Ariz., 1980—; panelist anthropology program NSF, 1976-78; cons. NIH, 1974—. Author: Ecology and Human Adaptation, 1975; Nature, Culture and Human History - A Biocultural Introduction to Anthropology, (with Davydd J. Greenwood), 1977; Physiological and Morphological Adaptation and Evolution, 1979; editor-in-chief Am. Jour. Phys. Anthropology, 1983-89 ; assoc. editor Nutrition and Cancer, 1981—; cons. editor Collegium Antropologicum, 1985—; contbr. articles to profl. jours. Mem. Gov.'s Adv. Council on Aging, State of Ariz., 1980-83. Nat. Inst. Dental Research tng. grantee, 1964-68; Clark Found. grantee, Cornell U., 1973; fellow Linacre Coll., Oxford, 1985. Fellow AAAS (steering group sect. H 1987—), Am. Anthrop. Assn., N.Y. Acad. Sci.; mem. Am. Assn. Phys. Anthropologists (exec. com. 1978-81, pres. 1988—), Soc. Study Human Biology, Human Biology Council (exec. com. 1978-81), Soc. Study Social Biology, Am. Inst. Nutrition, Am. Soc. Aging, Sigma Xi. Home: 6240 N Camino Miraval Tucson AZ 85718 Office: U Ariz Dept Anthropology Tucson AZ 85721

STINSON, JIM, writer, consultant; b. Pitts., Oct. 7, 1937; s. James Emerson and Mary Campbell (Maize) S.; m. Sue Ellen Wilkinson, Apr. 17, 1965; children: Alexander Adrian, Virginia Elizabeth. BA, Harvard U., 1959; MFA, UCLA, 1971. Author: (novels) Double Exposure, 1985, Low Angles, 1986, Truck Shot, 1989. Mem. Authors Guild Am., Mystery Writers Am., Internat. Assn. Crime Writers, PEN Ctr. West. Home: 252 Annandale Rd Pasadena CA 91105

STIRLING, CHRISTOPHER, commercial real estate development company executive; b. Ft. Benning, Ga., Dec. 28, 1954; s. Taylor Stirling and Jean-Margaret (Ritter) Albaum; m. Xristina Karen Grammatikas, July 16, 1983. BA, U. Redlands, 1977; MBA, U. So. Calif., 1979. Asst. to exec. v.p. M.J. Brock & Sons, Inc., Los Angeles, 1979-83; v.p. Angeles Corp., Los Angeles, 1983-85; sr. devel dir. Homart Devel. Co., Los Angeles, 1985--. Founding sponsor Arts in Los Angeles Program Sta. KCRW, pub. radio, 1986; mem. adv. bd. Los Angeles Housing Authority, 1986, mem. dean's council Grad. Sch. Urban Planning, UCLA, 1987--. Mem. Los Angeles C. of C. West (bd. dirs. 1985--, developer task force), Pasadena Athletic Club (Calif.). Office: Homart Devel Co 11755 Wilshire Blvd Los Angeles CA 90025

STIRM, EUGENE ROBERT, artist, graphic arts company executive; b. Portland, Oreg., Jan. 6, 1945; s. Robert Adolf and Matilda Herminia (Niehaus) S.; m. Patricia Dale Button; Feb. 25, 1972; children: Malinda, Daniel, Mark. AA in Fine Arts, West Valley Coll., Campbell, Calif., 1965; postgrad., San Jose (Calif.) State Coll., 1965-66; BA in Comml. Art, N. Am. Coll., 1969; cert., Word of Faith Bible Coll., Dallas, 1983. Ordained minister of the Gospel. Art dir. Joston's Pub. Co., Visalia, Calif., 1972-76; owner, prin. Word Print Shop, Ivanhoe, Calif., 1976-79; freelance artist Orange County, Calif., 1979-85; pastor Christ's Love Fellowship Ch., Corina, Calif., 1980-85; gen. mgr. Menu Printers Inc., Orange, Calif., 1985-87; v.p., ptnr. Stirm/Collins & Assocs., Inc., Anaheim, Calif., 1987—; lectr. in field. Author: Israel, Is Your Fig Tree Budding?, 1978. Founder, Coarsegold (Calif.) Artist Assn., 1972-74; advisor Yorba Linda (Calif.) Light Opera, 1988—. Recipient Fine Arts award Bank of Am., 1963, Strathmore Graphics Gallery Gold award, 1989. Mem. Printing Industry Am., Am. Orchid Soc. (editor newsletter 1984). Republican. Presbyterian. Home: 4665 School St Yorba Linda CA 92686 Office: Stirm/Collins & Assocs Inc 1015 E Vermont Anaheim CA 92805

STITCH, SHARON ANNE, city official; b. Peoria, Ill., Jan. 27, 1947; d. Herbert Leroy and Rilla Ann (Loughridge) Fahlberg; m. Malcolm Lane Stitch, Dec. 30, 1975; children: Wendy Jade, Amy Elizabeth. Student, Western Ill. U., 1965-67. Flight attendant Am. Airlines, Chgo., 1969-75; planner Boeing Computer Svcs., Richland, Wash., 1976-80; exec. asst. to v.p. fin. Airtron, Morris Plains, N.J., 1983; commr. Richland Housing Authority, 1984—. Membership chmn. Jefferson Sch. PTA, Richland, 1988-89, pres., 1989—. Mem. Desert Ski Club (treas. 1978), Zonta (treas. Richland 1988-89, v.p. Tri-Cities club 1989—). Republican. Episcopalian. Home: 2315 Camas Ave Richland WA 99352

STITNIZKY, JOHN LOUIS, hospital services administrator; b. Chgo., Oct. 10, 1939; s. John and Laura Lucille (Elzroth) S.; m. Yasuko Terada, June 2, 1961; children: Janet Laura, Diane Lynn, Sherry Jean. BA in Bus., Chaminade U. of Honolulu, 1977, postgrad., 1980-81. Enlisted USN, 1956, advanced through grades to sr. chief, ret., 1977; ins. underwriter Conn. Mut., Honolulu, 1977-80; gen. mgr. Waikiki Grand Hotel, Honolulu, 1980-81; auditor, night mgr. Outrigger Hotel, Honolulu, 1981-86; asst. dir. environ. svcs. St. Mary Med. Ctr. United Health Services, Inc., Long Beach, Calif., 1987-88; dir. environ. svcs. Fairview Devel. Ctr., Costa Mesa, Calif., 1988-89, Camarillo State Hosp., 1989—. Big brother Big Bros. of Hawaii, Honolulu, 1975-76; del. Rep. Conv., Honolulu, 1980. Mem. Navy League of U.S. (sec., v.p. 1978-79, Sailor of Yr. award 1977), Am. Legion (comdr., dist. vice comdr. Post 56 1979), Fleet Res. (bd. dirs. br. 46 1978), VFW, Nat. Rifle Assn. (cert.), Elks. Lutheran. Office: United Health Svcs Inc 1878 S Lewis Rd Camarillo CA 93010

STITT, ROBERT RHEA, electrical engineer; b. Mpls., Dec. 5, 1941; s. Rhea Emerson and Katherine May (Knoop) S.; m. Kay Frances Reinartz, Sept. 4, 1965 (div. July 1980); m. Marcia Elston, Dec. 28, 1985; stepchildren: Marisa, Lisa, Rachel. BSEE, Mont. State U., 1965. Equipment engr. Boeing Comml. Airplane, Seattle, 1965-69; maintenance engr. Sparton S.W., Albuquerque, 1969-70; facilities elec. engr. Molybdenum Corp. Am., Questa, N.Mex., 1970-71; design engr. Gen. Mills, Mpls., 1972-73; sr. facilities engr. Boeing Aerospace, Seattle, 1975-80; sr. facilities engr. fabrication div. Boeing Comml. Airplane, Auburn, Wash., 1980-88; prin. engr. Boeing Comml. Airplane, Auburn, 1988—. Editor, co-author: Cave Gating, 1975; editor: SpeleoDigest, 1983; contbr. articles to profl. jours. Dir., pres. N.W. Folklife Festival, Seattle, 1980-85; joint venturer Cave Rsch. Found., Columbus, Ohio, 1975-81. Mem. Instrument Soc. Am., Nat. Speleological Soc. (dir. 1973-85, exec. v.p. 1977-78, pres. 1981-83, Cert. of Merit 1975, Outstanding Svc. award 1986), Seattle Folklore Soc. (dir., pres. 1978-85), N.W. Cave Rsch. Inst. (pres. 1987—). Democrat. Office: Boeing Comml Airplane PO Box 3707 MS 57-04 Seattle WA 98124

STIVER, SAN JUAN, biologist; b. Henderson, Nev., Mar. 27, 1952; s. William Harvey and Sara Lois (Johnson) S.; m. Debra Jean Kingsporn,. BS, U. Mont., 1974. Exotic bird biologist Nev. Dept. Wildlife, Yerington, 1975-76; research biologist Nev. Dept. Wildlife, Ely, 1976-78, nongame biologist, 1978-81; staff biologist Nev. Dept. Wildlife, Reno, 1981—; computer programmer Nev. Wildlife Record Book, Reno, 1985—; Wildlife researcher Xingjiang Province, People's Republic of China, Summer; cons. internat. wildlife mgmt. Am. Ecol. Union , Washington, 1987—. Contbr. articles to profl. publs. Mem. The Wildlife Soc. Office: Nev Dept Wildlife 1100 Valley Rd Reno NV 89520

STOBBE, LESLIE HAROLD, publishing executive; b. Kent, B.C., Can., June 7, 1930; s. Peter John and Marie E. (Harder) S.; m. Rita Laurine Langemann, Sept. 7, 1956; children: Carol June, Gerald Lane. BTh, Mennonite Brethren Bible Coll., 1955. Editor Mennonite Observer, Winnipeg, Can., 1955-59; tchr. Mennonite Ednl. Inst., Clearbrook, B.C., Can., 1959-60; selling fl. supr. Moody Bible Inst. Bookstore, Chgo., 1960-62; editor Christian Bookseller Mag., Chgo. and Wheaton, Ill., 1962-66; editorial dir. Cambridge Pubs., Winnipeg, 1966-70; editor-in-chief Moody Press, Chgo., 1970-78; v.p., editorial dir. Christian Herald Books & Book Clubs, Chappaqua, N.Y., 1978-82; editorial dir. Here's Life Pubs., Inc., San Bernardino, Calif., 1982-85, pres., 1985—; cons. Mennonite Brethern Bd. of Christian Lit., Fresno, Calif., 1970-80; bd. dirs. Voice of Calvary Ministries, Jackson, Miss. Author: Preteen Bible Exploration, 1980, (with others) Managing Your Emotions, 1981, When a Good Man Falls, 1985, Reconcilable Differences, 1985. Pres. San Bernardino City Grand Opera, 1984-85. Mem. Evang. Christian Pubs. Assn. Office: Here's Life Pubs 2700 Little Mountain Dr San Bernardino CA 92405

STOCKDALE, RONALD ALLEN, grocery company executive; b. Aplington, Iowa, Apr. 28, 1934; s. Carl Robert and Mildred Louise (Gerhardt) S.; m. Carol Ann Hermeier, Dec. 23, 1956; children—Bryan Ross, Russell Allen, Paul Roderick. B.S. in Commerce, State U. Iowa, 1958. C.P.A. Auditor Arthur Andersen & Co., Chgo., 1958-63; controller Super Food Services, Bellefontaine, Ohio, 1963-66, Mountain States Wholesale Co., Boise, Idaho, 1966-69; exec. v.p., sec. West Coast Grocery Co., Tacoma, 1969-82, pres., chief operating officer, 1982-87, chief exec. officer, 1988—; bd. dirs. Profit Sharing Council Am., Chgo., 1977-83. Trustee Humana Hosp.-Tacoma, 1985-87, San Francisco Theol. Sem., 1987—; mem. adv. bd. Sch. Bus. Adminstrn., Pacific Luth. U., 1986—. Served with U.S. Army, 1954-56. Mem. AICPA, Fin. Execs. Inst. Republican. Presbyterian. Home: 2720 Soundview Dr W Tacoma WA 98466 Office: W Coast Grocery Co PO Box 1834 Tacoma WA 98401

STOCKING, BEAU CAROL DIANE, optometrist; b. Arlington, Va., Feb. 28, 1949; d. John Howard and June Lillian (Mathurin) Stapf. m. Reginald Angus Stocking, Mar. 6, 1976. B.S., Whittier Coll., 1970; postgrad. U. So. Calif., 1970-72; O.D., So. Calif. Coll. Optometry, 1976. Lic. optometrist, Calif. Optometrist USAF, 1976-79; gen. practice optometry, Burbank, Calif., 1980—. Served to capt., USAF, 1976-79. Mem. Calif. Optometric Assn., Am. Optometric Assn. Republican. Episcopalian. Office: 2915 W Magnolia Blvd Burbank CA 91505

STOCKING, SHERL DEE, retail executive; b. Boise, Idaho, Aug. 20, 1945; s. Parley Dean and Iola Merrill (Linford) S.; m. Debra Lynn Hunt, Sept. 5, 1982. BS, Brigham Young U., 1968. Automotive specialist Bradshaw Auto Parts, Provo, Utah, 1964-68, J.C. Penney Co., Salt Lake City, 1969-70; store mgr. Uniroyal Tire Co., Salt Lake City, 1970-71; corp. tng. coordinator Uniroyal Tire Co., Houston, 1971, corp. advt. coordinator, 1972; store supr. Uniroyal Tire Co., Norfolk, Va., 1973-76; mgr. automotive dept. K-Mart Corp., Rapid City, S.D., 1976-79; dist. mgr. automotive dept. K-Mart Corp., N.Mex., 1979-80; mgr. Service Mdse. subs. K-Mart Corp., Denver, 1980-88; pres., owner S. & H. Svcs. Inc., Denver, 1988—. Pres. Quail Crossing Homeowner Assn., Denver, 1986—. Mem. Samuel Hall Soc. Republican. Mormon. Home: 870 W 134th Ave Denver CO 80234 Office: 870 W 134th AVe Denver CO 80234

STOCKLEY, WILLIAM HENRY, equipment appraisal service company executive; b. Halifax, N.S., Can., Aug. 23, 1921; came to U.S., 1925; s. James George and Maryann (Slattery) S.; m. Thelma Eckblade, Nov. 15, 1949 (div. July 1976); children: Victoria, James, Stephen, Britta, Thomas. Student, Hemphill Diesel Sch., L.A., 1940, U. Calif., Berkeley, 1943. Mgr. Berglund Tractor & Equipment Co., Willits, Calif., 1945-70; owner, mgr. Stockley Equipment Appraisal Svc., Willits, 1970—; cons. Rainbow Agrl. Svcs., Ukiah, Calif., 1984—. Mem. Willits Airport Commn., 1962-66. Sgt. AUS, 1940-45, PTO. Mem. Willits C. of C. (bd. dirs. 1960-64), Rotary (pres. Willits 1964), Elks. Home: 20518 Hwy 101 PO Box 612 Willits CA 95490 Office: Rainbow Agrl Svcs 276 E Clay St Ukiah CA 95482

STOCKLIN, MICHAEL JOHN, marketing executive; b. Havre, Mont., Nov. 25, 1943; s. Arthur Louis Stocklin and Margaret Eleanor Quinlan Anderson; m. Carol Jean Neufeld, July 29, 1972; 1 child, Timothy Patrick. BS, Rocky Mountain Coll., 1968. Gen. mgr. Sta. KTVM-TV, Butte, Mont., 1979-87, Sta. KCFW-TV, Kalispell, Mont., 1979-87, Sta. KECI-TV, Missoula, Mont., 1979-87, Eagle Communication, Inc., Missoula, 1979-87; v.p. Precht TV Assn., L.A., 1985-87; gen. mgr. Sta. KIEM-TV, Eureka, Calif., 1985-87; pres. Running Bear Communications, Kalispell, 1987—,

Stocklin Enterprises, Inc., Kalispell, 1987—, Media and Mktg., Inc., Kalispell, 1988—. Producer TV series Artist and Their Art (Chgo. Film Festival award 1979); producer, host TV show Helen Humes: Jazz Singer, 1978. Pres. Flathead Festival of Arts, Whitefish, Mont., Friends of Flathead Valley Community Coll., Kalispell; pres. Flathead Arts Council, Kalispell, Northwest Mt. Historical Village and Mus., Kalispell. Served with U.S. Army, 1968-69. Recipient 2d Pl. Editorial award Pacific Northwest Journalism Soc., 1979, 1st Place award, 1982. Mem. Rotary, Kalispell Club. Home: 248 Fifth Ave E Kalispell MT 59901 Office: Media & Mktg 69 N Main Kalispell MT 59901

STOCKNER, ROBERT CHRISTIAN, engineer; b. North Charleroi, Pa., July 8, 1952; s. James Robert and Patricia Dean (Galbraith) S.; m. Virginia Athena Kaloyeros, July 5, 1981. BA, Sonoma State U., Rohnert Park, Calif., 1983; postgrad., Pepperdine U., 1985, Calif. State U., Northridge, Calif., 1989—. Program control analyst Hughes Aircraft Co., El Segundo, Calif., 1984-85; refinery ops. Chevron, USA, Corp., El Segundo, 1985-86; svc. engr. Lockheed Aeronautical Systems Co., Burbank, Calif., 1986—. Coach Petaluma Youth Softball, Calif., 1983; econ. instr. Jr. Achievement, Encino, Calif., 1987; alt. rep. Engrs. & Sci. Guild, Burbank, 1987—. With USN, 1974-78, With USNR, 1983—. Mem. Soc. Logistics Engrs., Lockheed Mgmt Assn. (v.p. internat., Redondo Beach), Masons, Soc. Auto. Engrs. (assoc.). Republican. Protestant. Home: 17423 Chatsworth St Granada Hills CA 91344 Office: Lockheed Aero Systems Co PO Box 551 Burbank CA 91520-6446

STOCKS, CHESTER LEE, JR., health care executive; b. Montgomery, Ala., Oct. 8, 1928; s. Chester Lee and Evelyn (Cooley) S.; m. Mary Gwendoline Hase, June 5, 1954; children: Susan, Bradley Hase, Charles Lee, Sally. B.S., Auburn U., 1949; M.H.A., Washington U., St. Louis, 1955. Resident Baylor U. Med. Center, Dallas, 1954-55; adminstrv. asst. Baylor U. Med. Center, 1955-57, asst. adminstr., 1957-63; exec. v.p. Good Samaritan Hosp. and Med. Center, 1963, Portland, Oreg., 1963-89; pres. Legacy Health Systems, Portland, 1989—; Preceptor grad. programs in hosp. adminstrn. U. Calif., U. Iowa, Washington U.; lectr., participant programs on health care; mem. exec. com. Oreg. Regional Med. Programs, 1966-74, v.p., 1969-76; mem. Oreg. Commn. on Nursing, 1969-75, Oreg. Health Manpower Commn., 1966-73, Comprehensive Health Planning Assn. Met. Portland, 1969-76, Oreg. Health Commn. Siting Com., 1974-77; dir. Oreg. Med. Polit. Action Com., 1974-77; Oreg. chmn. Wash. U. devel. program, 1967-70. Trustee Fred Hutchison Cancer Center, Seattle, 1972-79, Oreg. Comprehensive Cancer Center, 1973-75, Blue Cross Oreg., 1965—; pres. Oreg. Hosp. Found., 1979; mem. vestry Trinity Episc. Ch., 1983-86. Served to 1st lt. USAF, 1950-53. Recipient Disting. Alumnus award Washington U., 1989. Fellow Am. Coll. Health Care Execs. (regent 1969-75, gov. 1975-78, chmn. 1979); mem. Assn. Western Hosps. (trustee, pres. 1973-74), Am. Hosp. Assn. (trustee 1984-87, various coms. 1965—), Oreg. Assn. Hosps. (pres. 1967-68, trustee 1973-76), Portland Council of Hosps. (pres. 1966-67), Greater Portland Area Hosp. Council (pres. 1983), NW Oreg. Council Hosps. (exec. com. 1980-83), Tex. Hosp. Assn. (hon.), Portland C. of C. (bd. dirs. 1967-69), Nat. Assn. for Practical Nurse Edn. and Service (trustee 1960-86), Voluntary Hosps. Am. (bd. dirs. 1988-89), Am. health Care Systems (bd. dirs. 1989—), Voluntary Hosps. Am. Enterprises (bd. dirs. 1986-89), Protestant Hosp. Assn., Nat. League for Nursing, Pi Kappa Alpha. Episcopalian (dir. William Temple House 1965-70). Clubs: Rotarian. (Portland), Multnomah Athletic (Portland), Arlington (Portland). Home: 282 NW Macleay Blvd Portland OR 97210 Office: Legacy Health Care Systems 500 NE Multnomah Portland OR 97232

STOCKTON, RICHARD BRADLEY, electronics specialist; b. Sheffield, Nottinghamshire, Eng., Jan. 31, 1946; s. Everett Nance and Joyce Elizabeth (Spinks) S.; m. Carol Ann Bartkowski, Dec. 23, 1970; children: Dawn, Mary, Robert. AA, U. Md., 1982; BS, SUNY, Albany, 1986, Park Coll., 1988; MPA, Golden Gate U., 1989. Mil. intelligence specialist U.S. Air Force, various locations, 1964-74, with electronic warfare mgmt., 1974-84; mil. analyst Bell. Tech. Ops., Tucson, 1984-85; project officer U.S. Army Intelligence Ctr., Ft. Huachuca, Ariz., 1985-87; rsch. specialist U.S. Army Electronic Proving Ground, Ft. Huachuca, 1987—. Decorated Air medals, Meritorious Svc. medal, Air Force Commendation medals, 1974-84. Mem. VFW, Air Force Assn., Armed Forces Communications Electronics Assn., Assn. Old Crows (sec. 1984-85). Episcopalian. Home: 4632 N Melpomene Way Tucson AZ 85749

STOCKWELL, MARY LOU, interior designer; b. Biloxi, Miss., Jan. 21, 1938; d. Olaf and Esther (Schwoeglar) Gullickson; children: Lisa, John. Student, UCLA, 1965-66. Pvt. practice interior designing Westwood, Beverly Hills, Playa del Rey, Calif., 1962-72; designer Arthur Valdes Ltd., Newport Beach, Calif., 1973; asst. designer Circa Designs, Newport Beach, Calif., 1974; ptnr. M.L. Stockwell Interiors, Laguna Beach, Calif., 1975-85, 86—; owner, operator La Vie Chere, Laguna Beach, Calif., 1985; ptnr. Opulent Affaires, Laguna Beach, 1987—. Home and Office: 1524 S Coast Hwy Laguna Beach CA 92651

STODDARD, STEPHEN DAVIDSON, state senator, ceramic engineer; b. Everett, Wash., Feb. 8, 1925; s. Albert and Mary Louise (Billings) S.; m. Joann Elizabeth Burt, June 18, 1949; children: Dorcas Ann, Stephanie Kay. Student, Tacoma Coll., 1944, Conn. Coll., 1946; B.S., U. Ill., 1950. Asst. prodn. supr., asst. ceramic engr. Coors Porcelain Co., Golden, Colo., 1950-52; ceramics-powder metallurgy sect. leader Los Alamos (N.Mex.) Sci. Lab., U. Calif., 1952-80; pres., treas. Materials Tech. Assocs., Inc.; Cons. Ceramic Age Mag., 1958-60, Nuclear Applications for Ceramic Materials, 1958-60; Jury commr. Los Alamos County, 1969; justice of peace 1956-62; mem. Los Alamos Sch. Adv. Council, 1966; mcpl. judge 1976-77; chmn. Los Alamos Ordinance Rev. Com., 1958; Mem. Republican County and State Central Com., 1955—; county commr. Los Alamos, N.Mex., 1966-68; mem. Los Alamos County Planning Commn., 1962-63, N.Mex. State Senate, 1981—; bd. dirs. Bank of Los Alamos, 1982—. Patentee in field. Bd. dirs. Sangre de Cristo council Girl Scouts Am., 1965-71, N.Mex. chpt. Nature Conservancy, 1987—, Southwestern Assn. on Indian Affairs, Inc., 1987—. Served with AUS, 1943-46. Decorated Bronze Star medal, Purple Heart, Combat Inf. badge; recipient Disting. Alumni award U. Ill. Coll. Engring., 1986. Fellow Am. Ceramic Soc. (treas. 1972-74, pres. 1976-77, disting. life mem. 1984), Am. Inst. Chemists; mem. Nat. Inst. Ceramic Engrs. (PACE award 1965, Greaves Walker award 1984), Am. Soc. Metals, U. Ill. Alumni Assn. (Honor award 1986), Sigma Xi, Alpha Tau Omega. Episcopalian. Clubs: Masons, Shriners, Elks, Kiwanis (pres. 1963-64, dist. dep. grand exalted ruler 1968-69, lt. gov. 1968-69), Los Alamos Golf Assn. (dir. 1964-66). Home: 326 Kimberly Ln Los Alamos NM 87544 Office: PO Box 11 Los Alamos NM 87544

STODDARD, SUSAN, research firm executive, consultant; b. Modesto, Calif., May 11, 1942; d. Howard Augustus and Doris Ruth (Anderson) S.; m. Otto Pflueger Jr., June 12, 1970(div. 1977); children: Jeffrey, Justin. AB, U. Calif., Berkeley, 1964, M of City Planning, 1968, PhD, 1982. Evaluator Ctr. for Ind. Living, Berkeley, 1973-74; teaching asst. U. Calif., Berkeley, 1971-75; assoc. Sedway Cooke, Planners, San Francisco, 1971; v.p. sales Berkeley Planning Assocs., 1976-85; chmn., co-founder Inst. for the Study of Family, Work and Community, Berkeley and Corte Madera, Calif., 1985—; pres. Info Use, Corte Madera, 1984—; adj. faculty U. San Francisco, 1985—. Author: Independent Living: Emerging Issues, 1978, Software Tools of Rehabilitation Managers, 1987. Bd. dirs. Larkspur Isle Condominium Assn., 1983—, pres., 1986—. Grantee Mott Found., 1986, 3 yr. expert systems Nat. Inst. Disability and Rehab. Research, 1988. Mem. Nat. Women's Polit. Caucus, Am. Planning Assn. (charter, chmn. human svcs. and planning div. 1983-85), Am. Inst. Cert. Planners (charter, profl. devel. trainer 1985—), Am. Mgmt. Assn. (on-site trainer 1985—). Democrat. Office: Info Use 1995 University Ave Ste 227 Berkeley CA 94704

STOEBE, THOMAS GAINES, university chairman, material science educator; b. Upland, Calif., Apr. 26, 1939; s. Wallace Theodore and Martha Thomas (Gaines) S.; m. Jessica Rae Trout, June 20, 1959 (div. Jan. 1981); children: Brian, Paul, Diane; m. Janet Eleanor Dumm, Aug. 7, 1982. BS, Stanford U., 1961, MS, 1963, PhD, 1965. Instr. Imperial Coll., London, Eng., 1965-66; from asst. to assoc. prof. U. Wash., Seattle, 1966-75, prof., 1975—, assoc. dean, 1982-87, chmn. dept. materials sci. and engring., 1987—; vis. prof. U. Sao Paulo, Brazil, 1972-73; fellow USAF Materials Lab, Wright Patterson AFB, 1975. Patentee direct response dosimeter system; contbr. numerous tech. articles to profl. jours. Bd. dirs. Wash. Math., Engring., Sci. Achievement Program, Seattle, 1984—. Spl. fellow Atomic Energy Commn. Mem. Am. Soc. Engring. Edn. (young faculty award, 1972, Western Electric award, 1977), Am. Phys. Soc., Materials Research Soc., The Metall. Soc. (chmn. No. Pacific sect. 1973), Am. Ceramic Soc. Club: PRO Sports (Redmond, Wash.). Home: 11106 NE 38 Pl Bellevue WA 98004 Office: U Wash Roberts Hall FB-10 Seattle WA 98195

STOEN, J. THOMAS, energy company executive, land developer, investor; b. Milw., June 20, 1939; s. Joel A. and Lucile V. (Oliver) S.; m. Sara Peterson (div. 1980); children: Eric Thomas, Erin Kristen. BA, Wheaton (Ill.) Coll., 1961. V.p. Columbia Savs., Denver, 1964-72; pres. Crown Properties, Denver, 1972-74, Columbia Corp., Denver, 1972-74, Cimmaron Corp., Colorado Springs, Colo., 1974-79; chmn. Pacific Energy and Minerals Ltd., Colorado Springs, 1979-87; pres. Remington Oil and Gas Co., 1986—; bd. dirs. Bristol Trading Co., Vancouver, B.C., Can. Served to lt. U.S. Army, 1961-64. Clubs: Garden of the Gods, Broadmoor Golf (Colorado Springs); Castles Pines Golf Club (Castle Rock, Colo.). Home: 8 Pourtales Rd Colorado Springs CO 80906

STOIK, LLOYD JOHNSON, insurance company executive; b. Fargo, N.D., Nov. 27, 1961; s. Lloyd Palmer and Mary Lee (Johnson) S. BA, Colo. State U., 1984. Dept. underwriter Chubb Group Ins. Cos., Denver, 1985-87; dept. mgr. Chubb Group Ins. Cos., Newport Beach, Calif., 1987—, coord. mgmt. adv. com., 1985-87. Editor Trade Winds, 1987—. Home: 779 Amigos Way Newport Beach CA 92658 Office: Chubb Group Ins Cos 4695 MacArthur Ct Ste 600 Newport Beach CA 92658

STOKDYK, JOHN ELLIS, insurance company executive; b. Berkeley, Calif., July 26, 1931; s. Ellis Adolph and Virginia Lundy (Gibsn) S.; m. Arlene Burnett, Apr. 1964. Student, U. Calif., 1949; BA, Yale U., 1953; MBA, Harvard U., 1957. Mgr. programming Hewlett Packard Co., Palo Alto, Calif., 1957-68; dir. ins. Teledyine Inc., Century City, Calif., 1968-73; pres., dir. Travel Air Ins. Co., Wichita, Kans., 1973-86; dir. ins. Lear Siegler Inc., Santa Monica, Calif., 1986-87; nat. risk mgr. Toyota Motor Sales U.S.A., Inc., Torrance, Calif., 1987—; bd. dirs. Travel Air Ins. Co. Mem. Kans. Assn. Commerce & Industry, Topeka 1978-86, Gen. Aviation Mfg. Mem. Soc. Certified Property & Casualty Underwriters, Risk & Ins. Mgmt. Assn., L.A. Risk Ins. Mgmt. Soc. (dir. 1970-72). Republican. Presbyterian. Home: 1358 Avenida De Cortez Pacific Palisados CA 90272 Office: Toyota Motor Sales USA Inc 19001 S Western Ave Torrance CA 90509

STOKES, JOHN DENNIS, physician; b. Tacoma, June 26, 1946; s. John Franklin and Mildred (Trump) S.; m. Gayle Eileen Weeden, Dec. 20, 1969; children: Jonathan Patrick, Michael Stephen. BA, Ind. U., 1968; MS, Loyola U., 1973; MD, U. Ill., Chgo., 1976. Diplomate Nat. Bd. Med. Examiners, Am. Bd. Internal Medicine, Am. Bd. Endocrinology and Metabolism. Resident, fellow U. Calif., Irvine, 1976-81; practice medicine specializing in endocrinology and internal medicine San Clemente, Mission Viejo, Calif., 1981—; instr. OC paramedic program, 1977—; lectr. CME program and diabetes edn. South Coast Med. Ctr., Mission Community Hosp., San Clemente Hosp, 1981—, chmn. dept. medicine, 1988-89; with Western Med. Ctr., 1982—, chmn. code blue com., 1984-88. E. James scholar U. Ill. Med. Ctr., Chgo., 1973-76. Mem. ACP, AAAS, AMA (del. Hosp. Systems Mgmt. Soc. 1985, 88), Am. Chem. Soc., Am. Heart Assn., Am. Diabetes Assn., Internat. Diabetes Fedn., Am. Assn. Diabetes Educators, Am. Fedn. Clin. Research, Calif. Med. Assn., Orange County Med. Assn., Am. Soc. Internal Medicine. Methodist. Office: 647 Camino de Los Mares #234 San Clemente CA 92672 other: 27800 Medical Ctr Rd #257 Mission Viejo CA 92691

STOLLER, FRANCES, retired university administrator; b. L.A., May 6, 1922; d. Morris and Edith (Mogilner) Plotkin; m. David S. Stoller, Dec. 26, 1943; children: Stephen Paul, Sharon Anne, Jonathan Michael. BA, Calif. State U., Fullerton, 1973, MPA, 1981. Registrar for extended edn. Calif. State U., Fullerton, 1974-86; ret. 1986—. Mem. Placentia (Calif.) Round Table, 1986--. Mem. AAUW (treas. Placentia-Yorba Linda br. 1986-88), Continuing Learning Experience. Home: 326 Patrician Ln Placentia CA 92670

STOLPMAN, THOMAS GERARD, lawyer; b. Cleve., June 2, 1949; s. Joseph Eugene and Katherine Ann (Berry) S.; m. Marilyn Heise, Aug. 17, 1974; children: Jennifer, Peter. BA, UCLA, 1972; JD, Los Angeles, 1976. Bar: Calif. 1976, U.S. Dist. Ct. (cen. dist.) Calif. 1976, U.S. Dist. Ct. (ea. dist.) Calif. 1985. Ptnr. Carriage Trade Parking Service, Los Angeles, 1970-76, Silver, McWilliams, Stolpman, Mandel & Katzman, Wilmington and Los Angeles, Calif., 1976—. Editor-in-chief The Forum, 1978-84, The Advocate legal jour., 1984-87; contbr. articles to profl. jours. Bd. dirs. Miraleste Recreation and Park Dist., Rancho Palos Verdes, Calif., 1982—, Citizens Against Forced Annexation, Rancho Palos Verdes, 1978-83; del. Rancho Palos Verdes Council of Homeowners Assns., 1979-86, v.p. 1986; v.p., gov. Miraleste Assn., Rancho Palos Verdes, 1976-82. Named Trial Lawyer of Yr. So. Calif., Verdictum Juris, 1984. Mem. L.A. Trial Lawyers Assn. (bd. govs. 1979-83, pres.-elect, 1988, pres. 1989), Calif. Trial Lawyers Assn. (bd. govs. 1987—, exec. com. 1989—), Assn. Trial Lawyers of Am., Am. Bd. Trial Advocates, Nat. Bd. Trial Advocacy (cert.), L.A. Bar Assn., South Bay Bar Assn., Long Beach Bar Assn. Democrat. Roman Catholic. Office: Silver McWilliams Stolpman Mandel & Katzman 1121 N Avalon Blvd PO Box 1118 Wilmington CA 90744-3598

STOLTENBERG, CARL HENRY, university dean; b. Monterey, Calif., May 17, 1924; s. George L. and Eloise (Hyatt) S.; m. Rosemary Johnson, Apr. 20, 1973; children by previous marriage—Bruce C., Gail L., Susan I., Paul L., Shirley J.; stepchildren—Michael Johnson, Jillean Johnson. B.S., U. Calif.-Berkeley, 1948, M.F., 1949; Ph.D., U. Minn., 1952. Instr. U. Minn., 1949-51; asst. prof. Duke U., 1951-56; forest economist U.S. Forest Service, Washington, 1956; chief div. forest econs. research N.E. Forest Expt. Sta., Forest Service, USDA, Upper Darby, Pa., 1956-60; head dept. forestry Iowa State U., 1960-67; dean, prof. Oreg. State U. Coll. Forestry, Corvallis, 1967—; mem. adv. bd. Coop. Forestry Research, USDA, 1963-67, 86—, mem. adv. com. for state and pvt. forestry, 1970-74; mem. Oreg. Bd. Forestry, 1967-87, chmn., 1974-83; bd. dirs. Resources for Future, 1980—. Author: Research Planning for Resource Decisions, 1970. Served with AUS, 1943-45, ETO. Mem. AAAS, Soc. Am. Foresters (pres. 1988, past mem. council, com. chmn.), Forest Products Research Soc., Am. Econ. Assn., Sigma Xi, Xi Sigma Pi. Methodist. Home: 7890 NW Ridgewood Dr Corvallis OR 97330 Office: Oreg State U Coll of Forestry Corvallis OR 97331

STOLZ, NEIL N., financial services company executive; b. Ottawa, Kans., June 28, 1935; s. Norbert E. and Vida M. Stolz; m. Patricia L. Stolz, June 22, 1963; children: Sherilyn, Darryl. BS, U. Ariz., 1961. Personnel asst. Am. Savs. and Loan Assn., Whittier, Calif., 1962-66; asst. v.p. personnel Equitable Savs. and Loan Assn. (now Gt. Western Bank), L.A., 1966-68; v.p. adminstrn. Fin. Fedn., Inc. (now Gt. Western Bank), L.A., 1968-83; sr. v.p. corp. planning Gt. Western Bank, Beverly Hills, Calif., 1983-84; exec. v.p., chief adminstrv. officer Fin. Corp. of Am., Irvine, Beverly Hills, 1985—. Mem. adv. bd. U. of Pacific Bus. Sch., Stockton, Calif., 1986—. Mem. Stockton C. of C. (bd. dirs. 1986—), Palos Verdes Golf Club (bd. dirs. 1982-86), Palos Verdes Tennis Club. Republican. Home: 2512 Via Amador Palos Verdes CA 90274 Office: Fin Corp Am 18401 Von Karman Ave Irvine CA 92715

STOMPRO, KEITH HAROLD, mortgage broker; b. Casselton, N.D., June 15, 1947; s. Harold I. and Mildred Josephine (Gylland) S. BA, U. N.D., 1970. With Valley Nat. Bank Ariz., Phoenix, 1973-83; v.p. Corp. Fin. Assocs., Phoenix, 1983-84; pres. Stompro & Assocs., Ltd., Phoenix, 1984—. Author and publisher newsletter Rate Update, 1987—. First lt. U.S. Army, 1970-72. Mem. Phoenix Metro. C. of C., Ariz. Multihousing Assn., Ariz. Commercial Mortgage Bankers Assn. (founding dir. 1987—), Soc. for The Arts, Mansion Club, Sigma Chi. Lutheran. Office: Stompro & Assocs Ltd 4747 N 7th St Ste 416 Phoenix AZ 85014

STONE, BRINTON HARVEY, retired university official; b. Balt., Mar. 30, 1907; s. Harvey Brinton and Ethel (Hoffman) S.; m. Margaret Keeler, Aug. 19, 1933 (dec. Dec. 1975); children: Gregory B., David M., Melinda, Nancy E. AB, Johns Hopkins U., 1927, postgrad., 1928-32; MA, Columbia U., 1937. Asst. to pres. Haverford (Pa.) Coll., 1942-45; asst. to pres., dean men Alfred (N.Y.) U., 1946-48; asst. to v.p. U. Chgo., 1948-51; asst. to pres. Beloit (Wis.) Coll., 1951-52; exec. dir. Assoc. Colls. Ill., Chgo., 1952-53; v.p. Coll. of Idaho, Caldwell, 1953-54, Boise (Idaho) Jr. Coll., 1955-56; mem. staff higher edn. survey U. Calif., Berkeley, 1956-58, coll. and univ. placement adviser, 1958-74; ret. 1974. Author advice and info. commentaries.

STONE, DAVID ULRIC, management executive; author; b. Santa Cruz, Calif., Feb. 4, 1927; s. Ernest Marshall and Grace (Stone) S.; student Theol. Ministry Sch., San Jose, Calif., 1945-48; grad. Real Estate Inst., Nat. Inst. Real Estate, 1964; m. Iva Dell Frazier, July 20, 1947; children—Katherine LaVerne, Russell Keith, Susan Marie. With E.M. Stone Realty, San Jose, 1945-48; mgr. Broadway-Hale Co., San Jose, 1948-52; sales mgr. William Perry Co., San Francisco, 1952-56; gen. mgr., ptnr. Stone & Schulte, Inc., San Jose, 1956-66; pres., chmn. bd. dirs. Stone Inst., Los Gatos, Calif., 1966; chmn. bd. Sunchoke Internat., Inc 1983—, Custom One Internat. Inc., 1986—; pres. The Mktg. Forum, Inc., Mpls., 1986—; dir. Realty Programming Corp. St. Louis; chmn. bd. dirs. Custom One Internat., Inc., Mpls.; pres. Sunchoke Internat. San Juan Bautista, Calif, 1984. Named Realtor of Yr. Homes for Living Network, 1982. Mem. Nat. Inst. Real Estate Brokers (faculty mem. 1965—), Nat. Assn. Real Estate Bds. (chmn. joint task force 1966-68), Builder's Mktg. Soc. (founder, chmn. 1985), Calif. Real Estate Assn. (dir.), Nat. Assn. Home Builders (award 1960, Sales Mgr. of Year 1960, chmn. joint task force 1966-68, faculty mem. Inst. Residential Mktg. 1982—), The Builder Marketing Soc. (founder, chmn. bd.). Author: How to Operate a Real Estate Trade-In Program, 1962; Training Manual for Real Estate Salesmen, 1966; Guaranteed Sales Plan for Realtors and Builders, 1968 New Home Sales Training Course; The Professional Approach To Selling Real Estate; How To Communicate with Persuasive Power; How to Sell New Homes and Environmental Communities; How to Market and Sell Condominiums; How to Hire, Train and Motivate Real Estate Salespeople, How to Profitably Manage a Real Estate Office, 1977; The Road to Success in Real Estate, 1978; New Horizons in Real Estate, 1980; New Home Sales, 1982, Sales Power: American Sales Masters, 1986, The Gold Series, 1986, New Home Marketing, 1988. Home: 236 Camino Del Cerro Los Gatos CA 95030

STONE, DONALD D., investment and sales executive; b. Chgo., June 25, 1924; s. Frank J. and Mary N. (Miller) Diamondstone; student U. Ill., 1942-43; B.S., DePaul U., 1949; m. Catherine Mauro, Dec. 20, 1970; 1 child, Jeffrey. Pres., Poster Bros., Inc., Chgo., 1950-71, Revere Leather Goods, Inc., Chgo., 1953-71; owner Don Stone Enterprises, Chgo., 1954—; v.p. Horton & Hubbard Mfg. Co., Inc. div. Brown Group, Nashua, N.H., 1969-71, Neevel Mfg. Co., Kansas City, Mo., 1969-71. Mem. adv. bd. San Diego Opera; founder Don Diego Meml. Scholarship Fund; mem. bd. overseers U. Calif., San Diego, chancellor's assoc.; mem. exec. bd. Chgo. Area council Boy Scouts of Am. Served with U.S. Army, 1943-46. Clubs: Bryn Mawr Country (Lincolnwood, Ill.) (dir.), Carlton, La Jolla Beach and Tennis, La Jolla Country, Del Mar Thoroughbred. Home: 8240 Caminito Maritimo La Jolla CA 92037

STONE, GENE, writer, editor; b. N.Y.C., Oct. 6, 1951; s. Henry and Babette Laura (Rosmond) Stone. BA, Harvard U., 1974. Sr. editor Harcourt Brace Co., N.Y.C., 1976-80, Bantam Books, N.Y.C., 1980-82, Esquire Mag., N.Y.C., 1982-85; West Coast editor Simon & Schuster, L.A., 1986; cons. editor L.A. Times, 1986; editor-in-chief Calif. Mag., L.A., 1987; freelance writer L.A., 1987--; dir. pub. course Rice U., Houston, 1980; cons. New Age jour., Boston, 1986, Inc. Mag., Boston, 1986. Columnist, Premiere mag., 1988. Tchr. Peace Corps, W. Africa, 1974-76. Mem. Phi Beta Kappa.

STONE, GREGORY LINCOLN, photographer; b. Fort Sill, Okla., July 23, 1967; s. Wentworth Lincoln and Betty Louise (Ekman) S.; m. April Lynn Schalamon, Oct. 29, 1988. Grad., Monta Vista High Sch., Cupertino, Calif., 1985. Tech. support engr. Apple Computer, Inc., Cupertino, 1987—; photographer Joint Solutions Mktg., Cupertino, 1987—. Head photographer mag. Answer Source. Office: Joint Solutions Mktg 20370 Towne Center Ln B-245 Cupertino CA 95129

STONE, JAMES ROBERT, surgeon; b. Greeley, Colo., Jan. 8, 1948; s. Anthony Joseph and Dolores Concetta (Pietrafeso) S.; m. Kaye Janet Friedman, May 16, 1970; children: Jeffrey, Marisa. BA, U. Colo., 1970; MD, U. Guadalajara, Mex., 1976. Diplomate Am. Bd. Surgery. Intern Md. Gen. Hosp., Balt., 1978-79; resident in surgery St. Joseph Hosp., Denver, 1979-83; practice medicine specializing in surgery Grand Junction, Colo., 1983-87; staff surgeon, dir. critical care Va. Med. Ctr., Grand Junction, 1987-88; dir. trauma surgery and critical care St. Francis Hosp., Colorado Springs, Colo., 1988—; asst. clin. prof. surgery U. Colo. Health Sci. Ctr., Denver, 1984—; pres. Stone Aire Cons., Grand Junction, 1988—. Contbr. articles to profl. jours.; inventor in field. Bd. dirs. Mesa County Cancer Soc., 1988-89, Colo. Trauma Inst., 1988—. Colo. Speaks out on Health grantee, 1988. Fellow Denver Acad. Surgery, Southwestern Surg. Congress, Am. Coll. Chest Physicians, Am. Coll. Surgeons (trauma com. Colo. chpt.); mem. Soc. Critical Care (task force 1988—). Roman Catholic. Home: 15 Stanwell Colorado Springs CO 80906 Office: St Francis Hosp 825 E Pikes Peak Ave Colorado Springs CO 80903

STONE, JENNIFER JOAN, nurse; b. Banning, Calif., Feb. 1, 1957; d. Wilbur Fred and Joan Marie (Linton) Newbold. BS, Azusa Pacific U., 1979. RN. Staff nurse Tri-City Hosp., Oceanside, Calif., 1979-80; staff nurse med./surg. San Gorgonio Pass Meml. Hosp., Banning, 1980-81; dir. nursing Meadowbrook Convelescent Hosp., Hemet, Calif., 1981-82; staff nurse intensive care unit Redlands (Calif.) Community Hosp., 1982—. Mem. Am. Assn. Critical Care Nurses. Republican. Baptist.

STONE, JOYCE ELIZABETH, interior designer; b. Sheboygan, Wis., May 5, 1938; d. Arthur Edgar and Evangeline M. (Zimmerman) Jensen; m. Neal Dwayne Stone, Aug. 25, 1956; children: Earl Dwayne, Karen Luann Johnson. AA, El Camino Coll., Gardena, Calif., 1972; BS, Pepperdine U., 1974. Sec., bus. mgr. Thomas Ramo Wooldrige, Redondo Beach, Calif., 1962-80; owner Duraclean Home Services, Rancho Palos Verdes, Calif., 1975—; interior designer A Personal Touch, Torrance, Calif., 1985—. Republican. Home: 6023 Scotmist Dr Rancho Palos Verdes CA 90274

STONE, LINDA, sales executive, broadcaster, writer; b. Atlanta, Nov. 11; student Forrell Sch. Entertainment Arts, 1960-61, Phoenix Coll., 1960-61, Ga. State U., 1962-63. Owner, Acad. Playhouse of Entertainment Arts, Charleston, S.C., 1969-70; promotion mgr. WUSN-TV, Charleston, 1967-69; promotion mgr., broadcaster Sta. KPHO-TV, Phoenix, 1970-78; creative dir. KJJJ and KXTC Radio Stas., 1978-79; promotion dir., pub. svc. dir. Sta. KTAR-KBBC-FM, Phoenix, 1980-81; v.p. sales and promotion Aerolight Flight Devel., Inc., Mesa, Ariz., 1982-83; pilot, dir. Svcs. Superstition Mountain Airpark, 1982-83; program and advt. dir. Short Excursions in Ariz.; freelance writer, TV producer, 1984-86; coord. promotion svcs. premium incentives buyer The Dial Corp., 1987. Author children's books; contbr. articles to various jours. and publs. including: Phoenix mag., Ariz. Sports News Weekly, Ariz. Host; instr. communication Ariz. State U., 1977. Mem. Broadcast Promotion Assn., Acad. TV Arts and Scis., Am. Women in Radio and TV (past bd. dirs.), Phoenix Press Club, LWV, Mu Rho Sigma (life). Editor: Ad-Libber, Phoenix Ad Club, 1975-76. Address: PO Box 2313 Phoenix AZ 85002

STONE, NORMAN CLEMENT, psychologist, foundation administrator; b. Evanston, Ill., Apr. 28, 1939; s. W. Clement and Jessie Verna (Tarson) S.; m. Norah Grace Sharpe, June 1, 1986; children: Bryan C., Norman Clifford, Mark C., Amy M. ABA, Nichols Jr. Coll., 1959; BA, Stanford U., 1962; PhD, Wright Inst., 1985. Pvt. investor, 1964—; gen. ptnr., founder San Francisco Venture Capital, 1970-76; trustee, co-founder Nueva Day Sch. and Learning Center, Hillsborough, Calif., 1967-76; psychotherapist Bay View Hunter's Point Found. for Community Improvement Mental Health Ctr., San Francisco, 1981—; pres. W. Clement and Jessie V. Stone Found., San Francisco Friends of the Homeless.

STONE, ROBERT MAURICE, lawyer; b. Great Lakes, Ill., Apr. 6, 1956; s. Herman and Leah Sara (Horberg) S.; m. Kathleen Ferguson, Jan. 23, 1981; children: Alexander, Brian. BA, UCLA, 1978; JD, U. Calif., San Francisco, 1982. Bar: Calif. 1982, U.S. Dist. Ct. (no. dist.) Calif. 1982, U.S. Dist. Ct. (cen. dist.) Calif. 1983, U.S. Dist. Ct. (ea. dist.) Calif. 1985. Assoc. atty. Simon, McKinsey & Miller, Long Beach, Calif., 1983—; cons. Long Beach City Coll., 1985—. Mem. ABA, Long Beach Bar Assn., Los Angeles County Bar Assn., Phi Alpha Delta. Democrat. Jewish. Office: Simon McKinsey & Miller 2750 Bellflower Blvd Ste 100 Long Beach CA 90815

STONE, SAMUEL ALAN, petroleum engineer, oil company official; b. Uravan, Colo., May 1, 1951; s. Theodore Harold and Mary Lou (Tomlinson) S.; m. Louise Marie Morell, Aug. 1, 1978; children: Karen Christine, Ryan Christopher. BS, Colo. Sch. Mines, 1974; MS, U. Mo., Rolla, 1982. Petroleum engr. Amoco Prodn. Co., Liberal, Kans., 1981-84; sr. petroleum engr. Amoco Prodn. Co., Denver, 1984-88, sr. gas mktg. rep., 1988—. Team organizer ann. drive Kidney Found., Denver, 1987-88; keyworker United Way, Denver, 1987. Capt. U.S. Army, 1974-81. Mem. Soc. Petroleum Engrs. (sect. sec. 1982-83, chmn. 1983-84, mem. nat. com. 1987—), Am. Soc. for Engring. Mgmt. (charter), Rocky Mountain Natural Gas Assn., Natural Gas Assn. Okla. Republican. Home: 11471 Cimarrona Peak Littleton CO 80127 Office: Amoco Prodn Co 1670 Broadway Denver CO 80201

STONE, TEENA MARIE, land corporation executive; b. Victoria, Tex., June 30, 1948; d. Allison Joseph and Vivian Marie (Tull) Hyak; m. Daniel Stone, July 3, 1982 (dec. 1985). Diploma in cosmetology, Papacs Beauty Sch., 1966; student, West Covina Coll., 1973. Mgr. Robert Houlihan, M.D., Pasadena, Calif., 1978-81; tchr. Western Coll. of Medicine, Van. Nuys, Calif., 1979-80; order desk operator Transo Envelope Co., Glendale, Calif., 1981-83; exec. adminstr. Edmund and Connie Chein, M.D., Beverly Hills, 1984-87; cons. acct. Charleen Chase, Beverly Hills, 1987; cons. sales Franklin B. Kirkbride, Inc., N.Y.C., 1987; pres. TNT Oley a Land Corp., Glendora, Calif., 1988—. Mem. NAFE. Republican. Home and Office: 136 N Grand Ave #206 West Covina CA 91791

STONE, THOMAS EDWARD, transportation executive; b. Charleston, W.Va., Jan. 18, 1952; s. George Edward and Latrice Joy (Gully) S.; m. Cheryl Ann Knapton, Jan. 20, 1982 (div. Apr. 1984); 1 child, Johnathan Steven (dec.). Student, So. Ill. U., 1982, U. Albuquerque, 1983, Chapman Coll., 1984. Constrn. asst. W.H. Smith's Kitchen Specialities, St. Albans, W.Va., 1969-70; enlisted U.S. Air Force, 1970, advanced through grades to tech. sgt., 1983, ret., 1987; pres. Stone Transp., Albuquerque, 1987-88; cons. transp. Albuquerque Nissan, 1988—. Post advisor Boy Scouts Am., Albuquerque, 1977-86, com. chmn. 1984; leader 4-H Clubs Am., Kanawha County, W.Va., 1966-70. Mem. Nat. Search and Rescue Assn., Icelandic Life Saving Assn. (hon. life), NRA (life). Democrat. Methodist. Home: 900 Country Club Dr Rio Rancho NM 87124 Office: Albuquerque Nissan 1318 4th St Albuquerque NM 87112

STONE, WILLIAM, JR., ophthalmologist; b. N.Y.C., Mar. 1, 1916; s. William and Gabriella S.; m. Margaret Saunders Fyles, Jan. 22, 1963; children: Heather Fyles, Hollice Fyles. BA, Columbia U., 1937, MD, 1941. Diplomate Am. Bd. Ophthalmology. Asst. resident in neurology Colombia U., N.Y.C., 1941-42; intern Lenox Hill Hosp., N.Y.C., 1942-43; resident Mass. Eye & Ear Inst., Boston, 1947-49, dir. eye research lab., 1949-64, asst. surgeon, 1950-64; pres. Nat. Inst. Sci. Research, Los Angeles, 1968—; assoc. clin. prof. Loma Linda U., Los Angeles, 1965-71, U. So. Calif., Los Angeles, 1967-71; cons. C.R. Bard, Murray Hill, N.J., 1975-80, Gambro Inc., 1980—; pres. Am. Membrane Corp., 1970—. Inventor plastic artificial cornea. Pres. Bishops Sch. Fathers Club, La Jolla, 1984-85, La Jolla Homeowners Summit, 1986. Served to maj. Air Surgeons Office, 1943-47. Recipient Bronze medal for original research AMA, 1950. Mem. U. Calif San Diego Chancellors Club. Clubs: Rancho Santa Fe Tennis (Calif.); La Jolla Beach and Tennis.

STONEHOUSE, JAMES ADAM, lawyer; b. Alameda, Calif., Nov. 10, 1937; s. Maurice Adam and Edna Sigrid (Thuesen) S.; m. Marilyn Jean Kotkas, Aug. 6, 1966; children: Julie Aileen, Stephen Adam. AB, U. Calif., Berkeley, 1961; JD, Hastings Coll. Law, U. Calif., San Francisco, 1965. Bar: Calif. 1966. Assoc. Hall, Henry, Oliver & McReavy, San Francisco, 1966-71; ptnr. firm Whitney, Hanson & Stonehouse, Alameda, 1971-77; pvt. practice, Alameda, 1977-79; ptnr. firm Stonehouse & Silva, Alameda, 1979—; judge adv. Alameda council Navy League, 1978—. Founding dir. Alameda Clara Barton Found., 1977-80; mem. Oakland (Calif.) Marathon-Exec. Com., 1979; mem. exec. bd. Alameda council Boy Scouts Am., 1979—, pres., 1986-88, Lord Baden-Powell Merit award, 1988; mem. Nat. council Boy Scouts Am., 1986—; trustee Golden Gate Scouting, 1986—, treas. 1989—; bd. dirs. Lincoln Child Ctr. Found., 1981-87, pres., 1983-85. Named Boss of Yr. Alameda Jaycees, 1977; Coro Found. fellow in pub. affairs, 1961-62. Mem. ABA, State Bar Calif., Alameda County Bar (vice chmn. com. office econs., 1977-78). Republican. Roman Catholic. Club: Commonwealth. Lodges: Rotary (dir. club 1976-78), Elks (past exalted ruler, all state officer 1975-76, all dist. officer 1975-77, 78-79) (Alameda). Home: 2990 Northwood Dr Alameda CA 94501 Office: Stonehouse & Silva 512 Westline Dr Ste 300 Alameda CA 94501

STONER, BARTINE ALBERT, JR., advertising executive; b. Trenton, N.J., Apr. 18, 1926; s. Bartine Albert and Estella (Hart) S.; m. Elizabeth Ann Bond, Mar. 18, 1949 (div. 1973); children: Bartine Albert III, Jonathan West; m. Madeleine Ruskin, 1973. B.S., Princeton U., 1948. With Westinghouse Electric Corp., Boston, Newark and Phila., 1948-56; account exec. N.W. Ayer & Son, Inc., Phila., 1956-65; v.p., dir. account service N.W. Ayer & Son, Inc., 1965-67; dir., exec. v.p., gen. mgr. N.W. Ayer & Son, Inc., Phila. region, 1967-73; dir. internat. ops. N.W. Ayer & Son, Inc., N.Y.C., 1974-76; also bd. dirs. N.W. Ayer & Son, Inc.; pres. Ayer Baker Advt., Seattle, 1974-75; mng. dir. Ayer Barker Hegemann Internat. B.V., London, 1976-79; pres., chief exec. officer Ayer, Jorgensen, Macdonald, Los Angeles, 1979-80; exec. v.p., dir. N.W. Ayer Inc.; pres. N.W. Ayer Inc. (Western div.), 1981-83, chmn., chief exec. officer, 1983—; dir., pres. Settembrini and Tecchio ABH Internat., Milan, Italy, 1976-79; Charles Barker, Gmbh, Frankfurt, Fed. Republic of Germany, 1978-79; dir Moussault ABH Internat., Amsterdam, Holland and Antwerp, 1976-79, O'Hara, Hannigan and Reid, ABH Internat., Toronto, 1975-76. Bd. dirs. Greater Phila. Movement, 1973-74, Elwyn Inst.-Hosp., 1967-76; bd. pensions U.P. Ch. U.S.A., 1971-76; pres., trustee Internat. Assn. Shipboard Edn.; mem. Town Hall Calif., Los Angeles, The Founders of Music Ctr., Los Angeles, Museum Contemporary Art, Los Angeles, Los Angeles County Art Mus., Natural History Mus. Los Angeles County. Served to lt. (j.g.) USNR, 1944-46. Mem. Pa. Soc., Princeton Club of So. Calif., Greater Los Angeles C. of C., Los Angeles World Affaris Council, Japan Am. Soc. Presbyterian (elder). Clubs: Phila. Racquet; Hurlingham (London); Princeton (N.Y.C.); Jonathan (Los Angeles), Rotary (Los Angeles), Riviera Tennis (Los Angeles). Home: 10475 Wyton Dr Los Angeles CA 90024 Office: N W Ayer & Co 888 S Figueroa St 12th Fl Los Angeles CA 90017 also: 1345 Ave of the Americas New York NY 10019

STOODY, JOHN ROBERT, II, mink rancher; b. Delta, Colo., July 28, 1950; s. John Robert and Helen Pauline (Karcher) S.; m. Karen Elaine Cribbs,Aug. 14, 1971; children: Cullen Marshall, Britta Laree. BA, Adams State Coll., 1972; MA, U. No. Colo., 1978. Cert. tchr., Colo. Tchr. East Elem. Sch., Craig, Colo., 1977-78; mgr. Stoody Fur Farms, Inc., Delta, Colo., 1978-84; owner, mgr. John Stoody Furs, Delta, 1984—. Chmn., Delta County Sch. Accountability Com., 1989. With U.S. Army, 1973-75. Mem. Colo. Fur Breeders Assn., Fur Farm Animal Welfare Coalition. Republican. Methodist. Home and Office: John Stoody Furs 1236 G Rd Delta CO 81416

STORCH, DONN MARVIN, air force officer, chemistry educator; b. Cin., Aug. 27, 1950; s. Robert Walter and M. Elise (Minster) S.; m. Beverly Sue Mattie, July 6, 1974; children: David Brian, Jennifer Sue, Heather Lynn. BS in Chem., U. Cin., 1972, MS in Chem., 1974; PhD in Chemistry, U. Tex., 1985. Commd. 2d lt. USAF, 1974, advanced through grades to maj.; computer oper. system designer Communications Computer Programming Ctr., Tinker AFB, Okla., 1975-78; asst. prof. chemistry U.S. Air Force Acad., Colo., 1978-82, dir. rsch., 1984-88, tenure assoc. prof., 1988-89, tenure prof., 1989—; adj. prof. Colo. Tech. Coll., Colorado Springs, Colo., 1985-88; cons. in field. Designer computer programs; contbr. articles to profl. publs. Leader Pikes Peak coun. Boy Scouts Am., 1985—. Named to Outstanding Young Men Am. Mem. Am. Chem. Soc., Air Force Assn., Colorado Springs Computer User Group, Phi Kappa Phi. Mem. Christian Ch. (Disciples of Christ). Office: USAFA/DFC Dept Chemistry USAF Academy CO 80840

STOREVIK, TERRY ROBERT, executive search company executive; b. San Diego, Jan. 7, 1943; s. Oscar and Lois Valentine (Hatter) S.; m. Patricia Ann Reilly, Dec. 29, 1973; children: Matthew Damian, Andrew Christopher, Kathryn Teresa. BS magna cum laude, Calif. State U., San Diego, 1965, postgrad., 1970-72. CPA, Calif. Dist. mgr. retail stores Firestone Tire & Rubber Co., L.A., 1965-69; dir. adminstrn. Touche Ross & Co., CPAs, San Diego, 1969-72; dir. Exec. Offices Touche Ross & Co., CPAs, N.Y.C., 1974-76; regional personnel dir. for midwest and so. regions Laventhol & Horwath, CPAs, Dallas, 1972-74; pres., founder Acctg. Resources Internat., Inc., San Diego, 1976—; leader, speaker seminars for acctg. firms, colls. and univs. Contbr. articles to various publs. Mem. Am. Inst. CPAs, Calif. Soc. CPAs, Nat. Assn. Accts. (bd. dirs. 1970-72, Most Valuable Mem. award 1971), Laguna Niguel Tennis and Racquet Club. Republican. Office: Acctg Resources Internat Inc 2670 Del Mar Heights Rd Ste 213 Del Mar CA 92014

STOREY, BRIT ALLAN, historian; b. Boulder, Colo., Dec. 10, 1941; s. Harold Albert and Gladys Roberta (Althouse) S.; m. Carol DeArman, Dec. 19, 1970; 1 child, Christine Roberta. AB, Adams State Coll., Alamosa, Colo., 1963; MA, U. Ky., 1965, PhD, 1968. Instr. history Auburn (Ala.) U., 1967-68, asst. prof., 1968-70; dep. state historian State Hist. Soc. Colo., Denver, 1970-71, acting state historian, 1971-72, rsch. historian, 1972-74; hist. preservation specialist Adv. Coun. on Hist. Preservation, Lakewood, Colo., 1974-88; sr. historian Bur. Reclamation, Lakewood, 1988—. Contbr. articles to profl. publs. Mem. Nat. Coun. Pub. History (sec. 1987), Orgn. Am. Historians (chmn. com. 1982-86), Victorian Soc. Am. (bd. dirs. 1977-79), Western History Assn. (chmn. com. 1982-85). Home: 7264 W Otero Ave Littleton CO 80123-5639 Office: Bur Reclamation D-5520 Bldg 67 Denver Fed Denver PO Box 25007 Denver CO 80225-0007

STORM, BETTY LUNNAM, small business owner; b. Santa Monica, Calif., Dec. 3, 1940; d. Robert Lincoln and Leona Amey (Halterman) Lunnam; m. James Patrick Storm, June 25, 1960; 1 child, Amey Diane. Grad. high sch., Santa Monica, Calif. V.p. Santa Monica (Calif.) Bank, 1958-83; pres. BST Escrow Inc., Santa Monica, 1984—; instr. Santa Monica Coll., 1978-84. chmn. Affiliate Com. Santa Monica Bd. Realtors, 1974, Women's Council Santa Monica C. of C., 1977. Mem. Escrow Inst., Calif. Escrow Assn. Office: BST Escrow Inc 528 Arizona Ave #315 Santa Monica CA 90401

STORM, DONALD JOHN, archaeologist, historian; b. Bradford, Pa., Nov. 20, 1947; s. John Ross and Jean Lamar (Frederick) S. AA, Yuba Coll., 1967; BA, Sacramento State U., 1972; postgrad., Calif. State U., Sacramento, 1972-74,, Calif. State U., Chico, 1980, U. Nev., Reno, 1988-89. Instr. Marysville (Calif.) Joint Unified Sch. Dist., 1977-78; state archaeologist Calif. Dept. Parks and Recreation, Sacramento, 1981-84; owner North Yuba Contracting, Oregon House, 1984-87; archaeologist Elko dist. Nev. Bur. Land Mgmt., Elko, 1988; archaeol. tech. Tahoe Nat. Forest, Camptonville, Calif., summer 1980; archaeol. cons. Oregon House, Calif., 1976-88, 88—; instr. Yuba Coll., Marysville, Calif., 1976-88, 88—; archaeologist Elko dist. Nev. Bur Land Mgmt., Elko, summer 1988. Activist various conservation/environ. groups. With U.S. Army, 1967-70. Mem. Soc. Am. Archaeology, Soc. Hist. Archaeology, Soc. for Calif. Archaeology, Calif. Hist. Soc., Nat. Trust for Historic Preservation. Home: PO Box 552 Oregon House CA 95962 Office: PO Box 552 Oregon House CA 95962

STORM, JAMES EUGENE, psychoanalyst; b. San Diego, Feb. 12, 1941. BA, Pomona Coll., 1962; MD, U. Calif., San Francisco, 1971. Diplomate Am. Bd. Psychiatry and Neurology. Intern Herrick M. Hosp., Berkeley, Calif., 1971-72; resident U. Calif., San Francisco, 1972-75, Mt. Zion, San Francisco, 1975-77; pres. J.S. Profl. Corp., San Francisco, 1977—; asst. prof. U. Calif., San Francisco, 1977—. Mem. Internat. Psychoanalytic Assn., Am. Psychoanalytic Assn., San Francisco Psychoanalytic Assn.

STORMENT, JOHN HERMAN, health facility administrator; b. Eugene, Oreg., July 17, 1940; s. John Wilson Alexander and Alvena Viola (Clum) S.; m. Beverly Ann Rutherford, Oct. 6, 1966; children: Julia Anne Bancroft, John Thomas, Jason Rutherford. BS in Adminstrn., George Washington U., 1972; MS in Pub. Adminstrn., U. Colo., 1975; AS, Umpqua Community Coll., Roseburg, Oreg., 1983. Lic. nursing home adminstr., Oreg. Enlisted U.S. Navy, 1958, advanced through grades to lt. comdr., 1978; advisor med. services to Vietnamese, Navy and Marine Corps. Mil. Adv. Group U.S. Navy, Saigon, Socialist Republic of Vietnam, 1972-73; analyst mgmt. Office Civilian Health and Med. Uniformed Services, Denver, 1973-75; dep. dir. Naval Regional Med. Ctr., Camp Pendleton, Calif., 1975-79; ret. U.S. Navy, 1979; surveyor health Oreg. State Health Div., Portland, Oreg., 1980-81, 85; adminstr. Coos Bay (Oreg.) Care Ctr., 1985-86; interim adminstr., cons. various nursing homes, 1982-88; adminstr. Dallas (Oreg.) Nursing Home Inc., 1988—; instr. San Diego State U., 1975-78, Umpqua Community Coll., Roseburg, Oreg., 1984-86; dir. Nurses Unlimited, Eugene, Oreg., 1987-88; chmn. bd. Shangri-La Corp., Salem, Oreg., 1987. Recipient 1st class Staff Service medal Republic of South Vietnamese Navy, 1973. Mem. Am. Hosp. Assn., Oreg. Assn. Homes Aging, Bay Area C. of C. (dir. 1985—), Oreg. Health Care Assn., Ret. Officers Assn., Fleet Res. Assn., Disabled Am. Vets., Am. Legion. Republican. Baptist. Home: 2066 NW Luth St Roseburg OR 94770 Office: Nurses Unltd 1200 Executive Pkwy Ste 250 Eugene OR 97401

STORMES, ROBERT LEWIS, JR., investment banker; b. Fulton, N.Y., Nov. 17, 1934; s. Robert L. Sr. and Marie Josephine (Roy) S.; m. Tanya Ross, Aug. 22, 1959; children: Lori Stormes Largent, Lisa M., Robert L. III. BS, Lemoyne Coll., 1960. Adminstrn. mgr. IBM, Denver, 1962-66, various adminstrn., 1967-74, acct. mgr., sales, 1975-78, sr. acct. mgr., 1978-81; pres. Stormes Sales Cons., Englewood, Colo., 1981-82; acct. exec. Kirchner Moore, Denver, 1982-83; sr. acct. exec. Drexel Burnham Lambert, Denver, 1983-85; v.p. Advanced Securities, Englewood, 1986-88; exec. v.p., ptnr. Shearwater Fin. Corp., Englewood, 1988—; cons. Swiss Security Vaults, Denver, 1981-82. V.p. Walnut Hills Civic Assn., Englewood, 1963-65; pres. Walnut Hills Preschool Assn., Englewood, 1970-72, Walnut Hills Community Ctr., Englewood, 1972-74. With U.S. Army, 1955-57. Mem. Denver Bronco Club (treas. 1977-78), QB Club, Denver (pres. 1979-80). Republican. Presbyterian. Office: Shearwater Fin Corp 3333 South Bannock Ste 930 Englewood CO 80110

STORMONT, CLYDE JUNIOR, laboratory company executive; b. Viola, Wis., June 25, 1916; s. Clyde James and Lulu Elizabeth (Mathews) S.; m. Marguerite Butzen, Aug. 31, 1940; children: Bonnie Lu, Michael Clyde, Robert Thomas, Charles James, Janet Jean. BA in Zoology, U. Wis., 1938, PhD in Genetics, 1947. Instr., lectr. then asst. prof. U. Wis.-Madison, 1946-50; asst. prof. dept. vet. microbiology U. Calif.-Davis, 1950-54, assoc. prof., 1954-59, prof., 1959-73, prof. dept. reprodn., 1973-82, prof. emeritus, 1982—; chmn. Stormont Labs., Inc., Woodland, Calif., 1981—. Contbr. articles to profl. jours. Lt. (j.g.) USNR, 1944-46, PTO. Fulbright fellow, 1949-50, Ellen B. Scripps fellow, 1957-58, 64-65. Mem. AAAS, Am. Genetic Assn., Genetics Soc. Am., Nat. Buffalo Assn., N.Y. Acad. Sci., Am. Soc. Human Genetics, Soc. Exptl. Biology and Medicine, Internat. Soc. for Animal Genetics, Sigma Xi. Office: Stormont Labs Inc 1237 E Beamer St Ste D Woodland CA 95695

STORSTEEN, LINDA LEE, librarian; b. Pasadena, Jan. 26, 1948; d. Oliver Matthew and Susan (Smock) Storsteen. AB cum laude in History, UCLA, 1970, MA in Ancient History, 1972, MLS, 1973. Librarian, Los Angeles Pub. Library, 1974-79; city librarian Palmdale City Library (Calif.), 1979—. Adv. bd. So. Calif. Inter-Library Loan Network, Los Angeles, 1979-80; commr. So. Calif. Film Circuit, Los Angeles, 1980—; council South State Coop. Library System, 1981—, chmn., 1982-83, 85-86, 87-88, chmn., 1987-88; pres. So. Calif. Film Circuit, 1985-86; rec. sec. So. Antelope Valley Coordinating Council, Palmdale, 1983-84. Mem. ALA, Calif. Library Assn., Pub. Libraries Exec. Assn. So. Calif., Am. Saddle Horse Assn., Pacific Saddlebred Assn., So. Calif. Saddle Bred Horse Assn. (bd. dirs.), Chinese Shar-Pei Club of Am. Home: PO Box 129 Palmdale CA 93550 Office: Palmdale City Libr 700 E Palmdale Blvd Palmdale CA 93550

STOTLER, ALICEMARIE H., federal judge; b. Alhambra, Calif., May 29, 1942; d. James R. and Loretta M. Huber; m. James A. Stotler, Sept. 11, 1971. BA, U. So. Calif., 1964, JD, 1967. Bar: Calif. 1967, U.S. Dist. Ct. (no. dist.) Calif. 1967, U.S. Dist. Ct. (cen. dist.) 1973, U.S. Supreme Ct., 1976. Dep. Orange County Dist. Atty.'s Office, 1967-73; mem. Stotler & Stotler, Santa Ana, Calif., 1973-76, 83-84; judge Orange County Mcpl. Ct., 1976-78, Orange County Superior Ct., 1978-83, U.S. Dist. Ct. (cen. dist.) Calif., Los Angeles, 1984—. Active numerous civic orgns. Mem. ABA (jud. adminstrn. div., litigation sect.), Fed. Judges Assn. (bd. dirs. 1988—), 9th Cir. Judges Assn., Nat. Assn. Women Judges, Orange County Bar Assn. (mem. numerous coms., Franklin G. West award, 1984, Judge of Yr., 1978), Calif. Judges Assn. (mem. numerous coms.), Orange County Trial Lawyers Assn. (bd. dirs. 1975). Office: 751 W Santa Ana Blvd #405 Santa Ana CA 92701

STOTT, BRIAN, software company executive; b. Eccles, Eng., Aug. 5, 1941; came to U.S., 1983; s. Harold and Mary (Stephens) S.; m. Patricia Ann Farrar, Dec. 3, 1983. BSc, Manchester U., 1962, MSc, 1963, PhD, 1971. Asst. prof. Middle East Tech. U., Ankara, Turkey, 1965-68; lectr. Inst. Sci. and Tech., U. Manchester (Eng.), 1968-74; assoc. prof. U. Waterloo (Ont., Can.), 1974-76; cons. Electric Energy Rsch. Ctr. Brazil, Rio de Janeiro, 1976-83; prof. Ariz. State U., Tempe, 1983-84; pres. Power Computer Applications Corp., Mesa, Ariz., 1984—; cons. in field. Contbr. numerous articles to rsch. publs. Fellow IEEE. Office: Power Computer Applications 1930 S Alma School Rd C-204 Mesa AZ 85210

STOTT, JAMES CHARLES, chemical company executive; b. Portland, Oreg., Sept. 5, 1945; s. Walter Joseph and Rellalee (Gray) S.; m. Caroline Loveriane Barnes, Dec. 7, 1973; children: William Joseph, Maryann Lee. BBA, Portland State U., 1969. Ops. mgr. Pacific States Express, Inc., Portland, 1970-73; bus. mgr. Mogul Corp., Portland, 1974-80; v.p. Market Transport, Ltd., Portland, 1980-85; pres., founder, chmn. bd. dirs. Chem. Corp. Am., Portland, 1985—, also bd. dirs.; bd. dirs. Market Transport, Ltd., Portland; chmn. bd. dirs. Carolina Industries, Portland. Mem. TAPPI. Republican. Roman Catholic. Club: University (Portland). Home: 18321 Wood Thrush Cir Lake Oswego OR 97035 Office: Chem Corp Am 2525 SE Ninth Ave Portland OR 97202

STOTT, JOHN FRANCIS, insurance professional; b. Butte, Mont., Oct. 22, 1956; s. William Alfred and Frances Delores (Leary) S.; m. Pamela Bothwell, Apr. 18, 1981; children: Jocelyn, Caitlin. BS, U. Utah, 1979; postgrad., Oreg. State U., 1980-81. Claims cons. Saif Corp., Portland, Oreg., 1983-85; investigations supr. Saif Corp., Portland, 1985-86, ins. cons., 1986-88; account exec. Rolling, Burdick, Hunter, Portland, 1988—. Mem. Soc. Cert. Ins. Counselors. Democrat. Home: 7275 SW 167th Pl Beaverton OR 97007 Office: Rollins Burdick Hunter 1211 SW 5th Ave Portland OR 97225

STOTT, PETER WALTER, trucking company executive; b. Spokane, Wash., May 26, 1944; s. Walter Joseph and Rellalee (Gray) S. Student Portland State U., 1962-63, 65-68, U. Americas, Mexico City, 1964-65. Founder, chmn. bd. dirs. Market Transport Ltd., Portland, Oreg., 1969—; chmn. bd. dirs., officer United Express Ltd.; chmn. bd., chief exec. officer, prin. Crown Pacific, Ltd. Bd. dirs. Sunshine div. Portland Police Bur. With USAR, 1966-72. Mem. Nat. Football Found. and Hall of Fame, Oregon Sports Hall of Fame (bd. dirs.), Oreg. Trucking Assn., Western Hwy. Inst. (area dir.), Internat. Platform Assn. Republican. Roman Catholic. Clubs: Mazamas, Multnomah Athletic, Univ. Office: Market Transport Ltd 110 N Marine Dr Portland OR 97217

STOUGH-REIMEL, M. SUZANNE, artist; b. Terre Haute, Ind., Nov. 11, 1945; d. Harry and Betty Jane (Vaughn) Stough; m. Gordon Lee Reimel. BS, Ind. State U., 1970; cert. fine arts, painting, Herron Art Inst. of Ind. U., Indpls., 1967. Graphic artist U. Hawaii, Honolulu, 1970-83; freelance graphics designer Honolulu, 1976-86; owner, artist Stough-Reimel/Hawaii, Honolulu, 1986—. Exhibitions in Royal Gallery, Honolulu, 1988, Artloft, Honolulu, 1988, Village Galleries, Lahaina, Hawaii, 1988, Pacific Island Arts, Haleiwa, Hawaii, 1989; artist numerous pastel paintings. Recipient scholarship, Ind. U., Indpls., 1963-67; grantee State of Ind., 1967. Mem. Hawaii Watercolor Soc., Northwest Pastel Soc., Assn. Hawaii Artists (newsletter editor 1986-87 (1st pl. award 1986, Best of Show 1987, Grumbacher award 1988). Democrat.

STOUGHTON, HERBERT WARREN, geodetic engineer; b. Ann Arbor, Mich., Aug. 29, 1940; s. Herbert Baker and Theresa Agnes (Swab) S.; m. Catherine Wyman Dolan, May 15, 1970; 1 child, Sean Dolan. BSE in Civil Engring., U. Mich., 1963, MSE in Geodetic Engring., 1970, PhD in Civil Engring., 1980. Registered profl. engr., N.Y., Wyo.; lic. profl. land surveyor, Mich., N.Y., Ohio, Pa., Vt., W.Va., Wyo.; cert. photogrammetrist. Jr. civil engr. Atwell-Hicks, Inc., Ann Arbor, Mich., 1964; project surveyor O'Brien & Gere Cons. Engrs. and Surveyors, Syracuse, N.Y., 1965-66; jr. and asst. engr. Met. Water Dist. So. Calif., L.A., 1966-69; teaching asst., lectr. U. Mich., Ann Arbor, 1969-73; asst. prof. SUNY, Alfred, 1973-79; geodesist Dept. Def., Cheyenne, 1980—; cons. geodetic engr., Ann Arbor, Almond, N.Y., Cheyenne, 1971—; lectr. geodetic engring. seminars, 1971—. Author 5 books; contbr. numerous articles and book revs. to profl. jours. Coach, referee Cheyenne Youth Soccer, 1981-88; vol. various civic orgns. NSF grantee, 1970, Ford Found. grantee, 1971. Mem. Am. Congress on Surveying and Mapping, Am. Soc. Photogrammetry and Remote Sensing, Can. Inst. Surveying, Am. Geophys. Union, Profl. Land Surveyors Wyo. (state pres. 1987-88), Tau Beta Pi, Chi Epsilon. Roman Catholic. Home: 2821 Carey Ave Cheyenne WY 82001

STOUT, ELAINE CAROL, chiropractor; b. Sharpsville, Pa., Jan. 6, 1939; d. John Paul and Mary (Niec) Velky; m. Raymond S. Stout, Dec. 31, 1961 (dec. 1985); 1 child, John. D of Chiropractic Medicine, Palmer Coll., Davenport, Iowa, 1981. Lic. chiropractor, Wash., Pa. Women's reporter Sharon (Pa.) Herald, 1956-60; acctg. clk. D.K. MacDonald Ins. Brokers, Seattle, 1962-67; corr. reporter Everett (Wash.) Herald, 1969-72; editor Granite Falls (Wash.) Press, 1969-72; owner Soda Fountain, Granite Falls, 1970-72; with Home Interior & Gifts, Davenport, 1978-81; chiropractor Stout Chiropractic, Arlington, Wash., 1981—. Named Woman of Yr. Beta Alpha, 1988, Delta Pi. Mem. Sacro Occipital Rsch. Soc. Internat., Am. Legion, Soroptimists, Delta Pi (Woman of Yr. 1974), Beta Sigma Phi (Woman of Yr. 1988). Roman Catholic. Home and Office: 432 West Ave Arlington WA 98223

STOUT, ERNEST GORDON, water ski manufacturing company executive; b. Moran, Kans., Apr. 25, 1913; s. Raymond Theron and Ival Atena (Boatwright) S.; m. Helen Keller Sterling, Feb. 20, 1936 (div. 1973); children: Claudette Stout Blank, Valarie Stout Rerecich; m. Lilliam Corrine Stocker, Mar. 31, 1973. BS in Mech. Engring., NYU, 1935, MS in Aero. Engring., 1939; cert. systems engring., Lockheed Inst., 1965. Registered profl. engr. mech., Calif. Chief naval research Convair div. Gen. Dynamics Corp., San Diego, 1936-55; mgr. Wash. ops. Ralph M. Parsons Co., Pasadena, Calif., 1955-61; div. mgr. advanced design Lockheed Corp., Burbank, Calif., 1961-66, dir. transp. systems, 1966-74; pres. Stout-Stocker Assocs., Glendale, Calif., 1974-78, Hydro-Ski Corp., San Diego, 1978—; chmn. seaplane subcom. NASA, 1944-57; cons. Ops. Research, Inc., Silver Springs, Md., 1976-82. Author: Hydrodynamics and Hull Design, 1942; contbr. articles to tech. publs.; designer 1st supersonic seaplane; patentee hudro-ski marine vehicle. Bd. dirs. Parkway Manor Home Owners Assn., La Mesa, Calif., 1983—. Served to lt. comdr. USN, 1944-45 PTO, ETO. Recipient citation of achievement NYU, 1955. Fellow AIAA (v.p. 1953, Lawrence Sperry award 1941, Sylvanus A. Reed award 1953); mem. Nat. Security Indsl. Assn. (antisubmarine warfare adv. com. 1954-70), Aerospace Mus., Admiral's Club (N.Y.C.), Masons, Tau Beta Pi, Psi Upsilon. Home and Office: 7780 Parkway Dr Apt 1601 La Mesa CA 92042

STOUT-ABARIOTES, KAREN REBA, industrial hygiene consultant; b. Dover, N.J., Mar. 5, 1952; d. Koehler Sheridan and Phyllis Adell (Storer) Stout; m. Nickolas George Abariotes, Jan. 1, 1984. BS in Med. Tech., U. Mont., 1974; BS in Environ. Engring., Mont. Coll. Mineral Sci.-Tech., Butte,

1975. Environ. health engr. Kennecott Copper Corp., Salt Lake City, 1975-76; environ. engr., indsl. hygienist Kaiser Aluminum & Chem. Corp., Spokane, Wash., 1976-81; indsl. hygienist compliance State of WAsh., Dept. Labor and Industries, Spokane, 1982-83, indsl. hygienist, cons., 1983—. Recipient Gov.'s Club award Dept. Labor and Industries, Olympia, Wash., 1986, Labor and Industries Quality Team award, 1986, We Inspire Safety and Health award, 1987. Mem. Am. Indsl. Hygiene Assn. Office: Wash Dept Labor-Industries E 3901 Main St TAF-C33 Spokane WA 99220

STOVALL, M. SCOTT, insurance company executive; b. McCook, Nebr., Aug. 1, 1946; s. Charles William and Esther Marie (Peterson) S.; m. Carol Champion, Apr. 17, 1971 (div. 1974). BS, So. Oreg. Coll., 1968. Loan officer SELCO Credit Union, Eugene, Oreg., 1971-72; comml. equipment loans NW Acceptance Corp., Eugene, Oreg., 1972-73; sales Cascade Title Co., Eugene, Ore., 1973-76; sales mgr. Pioneer Title Co., Eugene, Ore., 1976-80; owner, mgr. Evergreen Land Title Co., Springfield, Oreg., 1980—; dir. Springfield Escrow, Inc. Ore., 1975-88, cons. TitleScan Software. Patentor: Invention, Cutting Tool Guide 1982 (Patent award); Author:. Dir. Springfield Utility Bd., Ore. 1988—. With U.S. Army, 1968-70. Mem. Am. Land Title Assn., Oreg. Land Title Assn., Am. Escrow Assn. Republican. Office: Evergreen Land Title Co 1317 N 18th St Springfield OR 97477

STOY, WERNER, photojournalist; b. Detroit, Feb. 2, 1912; s. Karl Walter August and Johanna (Jardon) S.; m. Janet Broadbent Stoy, Feb. 23, 1940 (dec. Sept. 1980); m. Mary Clark Stoy, Feb. 15, 1985. Student, Art Ctr. Sch., L.A., 1933. Office and clerical L.A. Times, Advt. dept., 1928-38; pvt. practice L.A., Hollywood, Calif., 1935-38; feature and promotion photographer San Francisco Examiner, 1939-40; photographer various publs., Honolulu, 1940-50; founder, pres. Camera Hawaii, Inc. Studio, Honolulu, 1950-85; photojournalist Nat. mags., Books, U.S. and Internat., 1940—; photo illustrator Original Hawaiian calendar, 1966—; speaker U. Hawaii. One-man traveling photo show, 1938; photographer slide show Fifty Years of Photography. Vol. photographer and relief pilot Los Medicos Voladores - The Flying Doctors; vol. photographer internat. relief group, Mauretania, North Africa. Recipient Spl. Advt. Recognition award Advt. Assn. of Hawaii, 1982. Mem. Nat. Press Photographers Assn., Am. Soc. Mag. Photographers, Rotary Club, Rotary Internat. (Paul Harris fellow, 1988), Honolulu Ad Club.

STRACHAN, W. BRUCE, Canadian provincial official; b. Winnipeg, Man., Can., July 22, 1941; s. William James and Callie Robson (Partridge) S.; m. Beverley Bostock, Sept. 7, 1964; children: William Dean, Jody Carol. Student, Coll. of New Caledonia, Prince George, B.C., 1971-73. Profl. musician 1959-71; pub. rels. officer Coll. of New Caledonia, Prince George, B.C., 1973-79; mem. legis. assembly Province of B.C., Prince George South, 1979—; dep. speaker B.C. Legis., Victoria, 1982-86, min. intergovernmental rels., 1986-87, min. environ. and parks, 1987-88, govt. house leader, 1986-88; min. of state of cariboo region 1988—. Mem. Rotary. Mem. Social Credit Party. Presbyterian. Home: 3789 Rosia Rd, Prince George, BC Canada V2N 2J2 Office: BC Legislature, Parliament Bldgs, Victoria, BC Canada V8V 1X4

STRACZYNSKI, JOSEPH MICHAEL, writer; b. Paterson, N.J., July 17, 1954; s. Charles and Evelyn (Pate) S.; m. Kathryn May Drennan, Sept. 30, 1983. AA in Interdisciplinary Studies, Southwestern Coll., 1975; BA in Clin. Psychology, San Diego State U., 1976, BA in Sociology, 1978. Acad. counselor San Diego State U., 1974-75, orientation counselor, 1974-76; editor Racquetball News, El Cajon, Calif., 1975-77; spl. corr. Daily Californian, El Cajon, 1977-78; entertainment editor KSDO-AM Newsradio, San Diego, 1978-80; freelance writer Calif.; host Hour 25 Sta. KPFK-FM, Los Angeles, 1987—; artistic dir. Airstage Radiodrama Prodns., San Diego, 1979-80; spl. corr. Los Angeles Times, San Diego Bur., 1977-79, TV Cable Week, Time Inc., Los Angeles, 1981-82, Tales from the New Twilight Zone, 1989; creative writing instr. San Diego State U., 1977-78; staff writer Filmation Studios, Reseda, Calif., 1984-85; story editor DIC Enterprises, Encino, Calif., 1985-86, Landmark Entertainment, Hollywood, Calif., 1986-87, London Films, Hollywood, 1987-88; devel. writer TMS Enterprises, 1985-87, Nelvana Entertainment, 1988, Warner Bros., 1988—. Author: (novel) Demon Night, 1988, shortstories appearing in Amazing Stories mag., numerous articles, plays, radio dramas, TV shows including He-Man and the Masters of the Universe, She-Ra, Princess of Power, Jayce and the Wheeled Warriors, CBS Storybreak, Nighmare Classics V: The Next Chapter; story editor: The Real Ghostbusters, Captain Power and the Soldiers of the Future, The Twilight Zone, The Waiting Darkness, 1989, Shattered Lives; contbg. editor Writer's Digest, 1981—, Twilight Zone mag., 1983—; creator: Aragon and the Wuff, ABC-TV, Bablyon 5, United TV Network, 1989. Mem. citizen's com. People for the Am. Way, Washington, 1985—. Mem. Writers Guild of Am. West, Horror Writers of Am., Animation Writers Am., Sci. Fiction Writers Am., Psi Chi. Democrat.

STRAHAN, JULIA CELESTINE, electronics company executive; b. Indpls., Feb. 10, 1938; d. Edgar Paul Pauley and Pauline Barbara (Myers) Shawver; m. Norman Strahan, Oct. 2, 1962 (div. 1982); children: Daniel Keven, Natalie Kay. Grad. high sch., Indpls. With EG&G/Energy Measurements, Inc., Las Vegas, Nev., 1967—; sect. head EG&G Co., 1979-83, mgr. electronics dept., 1984—. Mem. Am. Nuclear Soc. Home: 5222 Stacey Ave Las Vegas NV 89108 Office: EG&G PO Box 1912 Las Vegas NV 89125

STRAHLER, ARTHUR NEWELL, former geology educator, author; b. Kolhapur, India, Feb. 20, 1918; s. Milton W. and Harriet (Brittan) S.; m. Margaret E. Wanless, Aug. 10, 1940; children: Alan H., Marjorie E. A.B., Coll. Wooster, 1938; A.M., Columbia U., 1940, Ph.D. (Univ. fellow), 1944. Faculty Columbia U., 1941-71, prof. geomorphology, 1958-68, adj. prof. geology, 1968-71, chmn. dept. geology, 1959-62. Author: Physical Geography, rev, 1975, The Earth Sciences, rev. edit., 1971, Introduction to Physical Geography, rev. edit., 1973, Planet Earth, 1971, Environmental Geoscience, 1973, Introduction to Environmental Science, 1974, Elements of Physical Geography, 2d edit., 1979, 3d edit., 1984, 4th edit., 1989, Principles of Earth Science, 1976, Principles of Physical Geology, 1977, Geography and Man's Environment, 1977, Modern Physical Geography, 1978, 3d edit., 1987, Physical Geology, 1981, Science and Earth History--The Evolution/Creation Controversy, 1987. Fellow Geol. Soc. Am., Am. Geog. Soc.; mem. Am. Geophys. Union, Phi Beta Kappa, Sigma Xi. Home: 1039 Cima Linda Ln Santa Barbara CA 93108

STRAIN, JOHN THOMAS, electronics engineer; b. Raymondville, Mo., Oct. 25, 1939; s. Thomas and Lillie (Merckling) S.; m. Bonnie J. Cline, 1967 (div. 1980); children: Robert Vidmar, Anthony Vidmar. BSEE, U. Mo., Rolla, 1964. Electronics technician Exec. Aircraft Co., Kansas City, Mo., 1960-61; electronic engrng. technician Wilcox Electric Co., Kansas City, 1963, sr. electronics technician, 1964-67; sr. electronics technician Exec. Aircraft Co., 1964; electronic engrng. tech. Gianni Voltex Co., San Diego, 1967-68; electronic fabricator Bendix Atomic Energy Commn., Kansas City, 1968; electronics engr. Electronic Research Corp., Overland Park, Kans., 1968-69, Monitor Products Co., South Pasadena, Calif., 1969-73, NBC, Burbank, Calif., 1973--. Designed and developed original TV stereo encoder; responsible (with Ron Estes) for audio engrng. for first recorded stereo TV program (nominated for Emmy 1983); co-developer first DIP style crystal controled oscillator for use in computer and areospace industries. With USAF, 1964-65. Home: 6450 Clybourn Ave North Hollywood CA 91606 Office: NBC 3000 W Alameda Ave Burbank CA 91523

STRAIT, LINDSY EDWARD, computer systems executive, consultant; b. Delta, Colo., Nov. 4, 1955; s. Lindsy Dean and Diana Pearl (Wright) S. BA, MWC U. Va., 1980; grad. cert., Computer Sci. Sch., Quantico, Va., 1981; MS, U. So. Calif., 1984. Commd. ensign USMC, 1980, advanced through grades to capt., 1982—; tech. dir. Software AG of N. Am., L.A., 1984-86; asst. v.p. Profl. Hosp. Svcs., L.A., 1986-89; v.p. Interpractice Systems, San Francisco, 1989—; pres., founder Sytem Builder Assoc., Irvine, Calif., 1986—, Cognizance Tech. Systems, Marin, Calif., 1989—. Author and Presentor: Strategic Technology Initiatives, 1988. Recipient Outstanding Presentor, Data Gen. Worldwide Systems Supplier, USMCR. Mem. Nat. Riffle Assn., Marine Corps Meml. Assn., Assn. Computer Machinery, IEEE, Digital Cons. Assoc. (advisory bd. mem. 1984—), Homeowners Assn. (pres. 1982-84), Nat. Honor Soc., Elks. Home: 329 Via La Cumbre Greenbrae CA 94904

STRAKA, GEORGE JOHN, police chief; b. Hazleton, Pa., Mar. 14, 1937; s. George and Mary (Orach) S.; m. Gloria Helen Newton, Feb. 18, 1956; children—Leslie Anne, Stephen John. A.A., Fullerton Jr. Coll., 1964; B.A. in Police Sci., John F. Kennedy U., 1972, M.A. in Pub. Adminstrn., 1975; grad. FBI Nat. Acad., 1980. Advanced cert. peace officer's standards and tng., Calif. Police officer, Fullerton, Calif., 1958-65; police officer, Concord, Calif., 1966-68, police sgt., 1968-71, police lt., 1971-81, police chief, 1981—; instr. No. Calif. Peace Officer's Acad., 1965-72. Mem. exec. bd. Mt. Diablo Council Boy Scouts Am., 1981—. Served with USMC, 1954-57. Mem. Internat. Assn. Chiefs Police, FBI N.Am. Assn., Calif. Police Chiefs Assn., Calif. Peace Officers Assn. Republican. Lutheran. Club: Century (Concord). Office: Concord Police Dept Willow Pass and Parkside Concord CA 94519 *

STRALING, PHILLIP FRANCIS, bishop; b. San Bernardino, Calif., Apr. 25, 1933; s. Sylvester J. and Florence E. (Robinson) S. B.A., U. San Diego, 1963; M.S. in Child and Family Counseling, San Diego State U., 1971. Ordained priest Roman Catholic Ch., 1959, consecrated bishop, 1978. Mem. faculty St. John Acad., El Cajon, Calif., 1959-60, St. Therese Acad., San Diego, 1960-63; chaplain Newman Club, San Diego State U., 1960-72; mem. faculty St. Francis Sem., San Diego, 1972-76; pastor Holy Rosary Parish, San Bernardino, 1976-78; bishop Diocese of San Bernardino, 1978—; pub. Inland Catholic newspaper, 1979—; bd. dirs. Calif. Assn. Cath. Campus Ministers, 1960s; exec. sec. Diocesan Synod II, 1972-76; Episcopal vicar San Bernardino Deanery, 1976-78. Office: Diocesan Pastoral Ctr 1450 North D St San Bernardino CA 92405

STRAM, RON, tax adviser; b. Santa Monica, Calif., July 28, 1950; s. John Dominic Strambini and Christina Mary Stram; m. Christine Sierko, Apr. 8, 1972 (div. 1975). BA, U. Calif., Santa Barbara, 1970. Tax interviewer Kirley Tax Svc., San Bernardino, Calif., 1977; tax adviser Triple Check, Inc., Bellflower, Calif., 1977-80, 81-82; tax specialist, asst. prodn. mgr. Computer Sci. Corp., Eagle Rock, Calif., 1980-81; tax adviser Bus. Record Svc., Ventura, Calif., 1983-85; ind. tax adviser Camarillo, Calif., 1985—; agt., Vistar, Inc., Marina Del Rey, Calif., 1989—. Roman Catholic. Home and Office: 3108 Village St Camarillo CA 93010

STRAND, RAY WALTER, general contractor; b. Seattle, July 23, 1924; s. Arvid O. and Antonia (Sjogren) S.; m. Luella Oak, Oct. 1948 (div. 1959); m. Ruby Good, Jan. 8, 1960; children: Timothy Ray, Donald Brent. Student, U. Wash., 1945-48. Ptnr. Strand & Sons, Seattle, 1939-54; chief executive officer, pres. Strand Inc., Seattle and Bellevue, Wash., 1954—. Staff sgt. U.S. Army Air Corps, 1943-45. Mem. Assn. Gen. Contractors, Wash. Athletic Club, Bellevue Athletic Club. Republican. Congregational. Home: 5800 Princeton NE Seattle WA 98105

STRAND, ROBERT, sculptor; b. Chgo., Aug. 15, 1936; s. J.A.O. and Mabel (Hanisch) S.; m. Sharon Kaiser, Nov. 30, 1970 (div. 1985). Student, Brown U., 1958, R.I. Sch. Design. Owner, pres. Strand & Co., San Francisco, 1975—. Mem. adv. com. Mayor San Francisco, 1985-88; adv. bd. Citywide Alcohol Com. 1st lt. USMC, 1959-62. Mem. Univ. Club, Brown Club, Olympic Club. Republican. Office: Strand & Co 2911 Pine St San Francisco CA 94115

STRAND, ROGER GORDON, federal judge; b. Peekskill, N.Y., Apr. 28, 1934; s. Ernest Gordon Strand and Lisabeth Laurine (Phin) Steinmetz; m. Joan Williams, Nov. 25, 1961. AB, Hamilton Coll., 1955; LLB, Cornell U., 1961; grad., Nat. Coll. State Trial Judges, 1968. Bar: Ariz. 1961, U.S. Dist. Ct. Ariz. 1961, U.S. Supreme Ct. 1980. Assoc. Fennemore, Craig, Allen & McClennen, Phoenix, 1961-67; judge Ariz. Superior Ct., Phoenix, 1967-85, U.S. Dist. Ct. Ariz., Phoenix, 1985—; assoc. presiding judge Ariz. Superior Ct., 1971-85; lectr. Nat. Jud. Coll., Reno, 1978-87. Past pres. cen. Ariz. chpt. Arthritis Found. Served to lt. USN, 1955-61. Mem. ABA, Ariz. Bar Assn., Maricopa County Bar Assn., Nat. Conf. Fed. Trial Judges, Phi Delta Phi, Aircraft Owners and Pilots Assn. Lodge: Rotary. Home: 5825 N 3rd Ave Phoenix AZ 85013 Office: US Dist Ct US Courthouse & Fed Bldg 230 N 1st Ave Rm 3013 Phoenix AZ 85025

STRANDE, CARL ANGELO, construction company executive; b. Hibbing, Minn., Mar. 7, 1937; s. Julius A. and Loretta M. (Cusciotto) S.; m. M. Sam Strande, 1982. BS in Geol. Engring, S.D. Sch. Mines, 1962. With Morrison-Knudsen Co., Inc., 1959-66; mgr. pipeline constrn.div. Morrison-Knudsen-River, Ft. Worth, 1967-77, internat. v.p., 1977-81, retired, 1981. Mem. Soc. Petroleum Engrs., World Dredging Assn., Soc. Am. Mil. Engrs., Am. Petroleum Inst., Am. Arbitration Assn. Lodge: Elks. Home: PO Box 1276 Golden CO 80402-1276

STRANG, GARY LEONARD, architect; b. Oakland, Calif., Nov. 24, 1956; s. Carl Carmen and Lillian Ann (Riskin) S. BS, U. Calif., Davis, 1982; MArch, U. Calif., Berkeley, 1985. Registered architect, Calif., Registered landscape architect, Calif. Architect, landscape architect Sam Davis FAIA Architects, Berkeley, Calif., 1985-86; architect, landscape architect Stanley Saitowitz Architecture, San Francisco, 1986-87, Daniel Solomon & Assoc., San Francisco, 1987--; lectr. U. Calif. Davis, 1986--. Contbr. articles to profl. publs. Home: 1403 Scenic Ave Berkeley CA 94708

STRANGE, RICHARD EUGENE, conductor, music educator; b. Hutchinson, Kans., Sept. 14, 1928; s. Virgil and Dorothy (Lusk) S.; m. Marian Lucille Box; children: Steven Lynn, Phillip Michael. MusB in Edn., Wichita U., 1950; MusM in Edn., U. Colo., 1957; D Mus. Arts, Boston U., 1962. Tchr. music Clifton (Kans.) High Sch., 1951-57; asst. band dir. Boston U., 1957-59; asst. prof. music Tex. State Coll. A&I, Kingsville, 1959-60; dir. bands W.Va. U., Morgantown, 1960-61, Carnegie-Mellon U., Pitts., 1961-74, Ariz. State U., Tempe, 1974—; condr. Carnegie (Pa.) Civic Symphony, 1961-74, Butler (Pa.) County Symphony, 1965-74, Tempe Symphony Orch., 1975—; adjudicator, condr. mus. groups worldwide. Music reviewer: (mags.) Sch. Musician, Bandworld, 1987—. With U.S. Army, 1950-51. Recipient Outstanding Contbn. to the Arts award Tempe City Coun., 1984; Faculty Rsch. grantee Ariz. State U., 1986, 88. Mem. Am. Bandmasters Assn. (pres. 1985-86), Coll. Band Dirs. Nat. Assn. (pres. 1989-91), Music Educators Nat. Assn. (life), Kappa Kappa Psi (life). Office: Ariz State U Sch Music Tempe AZ 85287

STRANGWAY, DAVID WILLIAM, geologist, university president; b. Can., June 7, 1934. B.A. in Physics and Geology, U. Toronto, 1956, M.A. in Physics, 1958, Ph.D., 1960. Sr. geophysicist Dominion Gulf Co. Ltd., Toronto, 1956; chief geophysicist Ventures Ltd., 1956-57, sr. geophysicist, summer 1958; research geophysicist Kennecott Copper Corp., Denver, 1960-61; asst. prof. U. Colo., Boulder, 1961-64, M.I.T., 1965-68; mem. faculty U. Toronto, 1968-85, prof. physics, 1971-85, chmn. dept. geology, 1972-80, v.p., provost, 1980-83, pres., 1983-84; pres. U. B.C., 1985—; chief geophysics br. Johnson Space Center, NASA, Houston, 1970-72, chief physics br., 1972-73, acting chief planetary and earth sci. div., 1973; vis. prof. geology U. Houston, 1971-73; interim dir. Lunar Sci. Inst., Houston, 1973; vis. com. geol. scis. Brown U., 1974-76, Meml. U., St. John's, Nfld., 1974-79, Princeton U., 1980-86. v.p. Can. Geosci. Council, 1977; chmn. proposal evaluating team Univs. Space Research Assos., 1977-78, Ont. Geosci. Research Fund, 1978-81; Pahlavi lectr. Govt. of Iran, 1978; cons. to govt. and industry, mem. numerous govt. and sci. adv. and investigative panels. Author numerous papers, reports in field. Mem. Premier's Council Sci. and Tech. Recipient NASA Exceptional Sci. Achievement medal, 1972; hon. mem. Can. Soc. Exploration Geophysicists. Fellow Royal Astron. Soc., Royal Soc. Can.; mem. Soc. Exploration Geophysicists (Virgil Kauffman Gold medal 1974), Geol. Assn. Can. (pres. 1978-79, Logan medal), Can. Geophys. Union (chmn. 1977-79, J. Tuzo Wilson medal 1987), Am. Geophys. Union (sect. planetology sect. 1978-81), European Assn. Exploration Geophysicists, Soc. Geomagnetism and Geoelectricity Japan, Can. Geosci. Council (pres. 1980), AAAS, Can. Exploration Geophysicists, Soc. Exptl. Geophysics (hon.), Bus. Council of B.C. *

STRASBURGER, JOHN HUNTER, lawyer; b. Dallas, Nov. 18, 1937; s. Henry W. and Anita June (Hunter) S.; m. Laura J. Fleming, June 4, 1960; children: Carol, Sue, Beth, Jennifer. BA, U. Tex., 1959, LLB, 1961; MA, Johns Hopkins Sch. Advanced, 1964. Bar: Tex. 1961, Wash., 1964. Ptnr. Short, Cressman & Burgess, Seattle, 1964--. Office: Short Cressman & Burgess 999 3d Ave Seattle WA 98104

STRASSER, WILLIAM CARL, JR., educator; b. Washington, Feb. 4, 1930; s. William Carl and Minnie Elizabeth (Saxton) S.; m. Jeanne Carol Peake, Sept. 17, 1954 (div.); children: Sheryl Lynn, Keith Edward, Robert Carl; m. Jane Anne Gunn, Nov. 25, 1978. BA, U. Md., 1952, MA, 1954, PhD, 1961. Asst. dean, asst. prof. Sch. Edn., SUNY, Buffalo, 1962-64; specialist ednl. adminstrn. U.S. Office Edn., Washington, 1964-65; asst. dir. profl. pers. Montgomery County (Md.) Pub. Schs., 1965-66; acting pres, exec. dean Montgomery Community Coll., Rockville, Md., 1966-67, prof., 1978-86, pres., prof. emeritus, 1986—; vis. scholar U. Calif., Berkeley, 1977-79; cons. Middle States Assn. Colls. and Secondary Schs., 1975—. Contbr. poetry and articles to jours. Mem. Gov.'s adv. coun. Md. Higher Edn. Facilities, 1977-79; del. UNESCO Conf. Africa, 1961; participant 50th Anniversary Conf. Fgn. Policy Assn. U.S., 1968; mem. Montgomery County Community White House Conf. on Aging, 1971; v.p. Md. Coun. Community Coll. Presidents, 1971-72, 75-77; pres., v.p. Jr. Coll. Coun. Middle Atlantic States, 1969-72; founder Coun. Chief Exec. Adminstrs., 1973-75; exec. com. President's Acad., 1975-77. With AUS, 1954-55. Recipient Cert. Disting. Citizenship Gov. of Md., 1979; Silver medallion for Outstanding Svc. Montgomery Coll. Bd. Trustees, 1986; postdoctoral fellow in coll. adminstrn. U. Mich., 1961-62; Danforth Found. study grantee, 1972, Ford Found. study grantee, 1972; Ford Found. grantee, 1974-75. Mem. Am. Assn. Jr. Colls. (chmn. nat. comm. on instrn. 1969-71, nat. assembly 1973), AAUP, Am. Assn. Higher Edn., Montgomery County C. of C. (Disting. Svc. award 1979), Phi Kappa Phi, Omicron Delta Kappa, Pi Delta Epislon, Phi Eta Sigma, Phi Delta Kappa. Democrat. Unitarian-Universalist. Home: 285 E 2020 North Provo UT 84604

STRATI, TONY J., accountant. BBA in Acctg., U. Notre Dame, MBA in Acctg. CPA, N.Mex. With Peat Marwick Main & Co., Albuquerque, ptnr., 1981—; conductor practice groups on local government and education. Bd. dirs. Greater Albuquerque C. of C. (mem. fin. com., vice-chmn. membership affairs div.), active United Way, Rehabilitation Ctr. Mem. AICPA, N.Mex. Soc. CPAs (past. bd. dirs.), Rotary. Office: Peat Marwick Main & Co 20 First Pla Bldg Albuquerque NM 87102

STRATTON, HAL, state attorney general; b. Muskogee, Okla., Dec. 6, 1950; s. Mr. and Mrs. H. Duane S. BS in Geology, U. Okla., 1973, JD, 1976. Bar: N.Mex., Okla., U.S. Dist. Ct. N.Mex., U.S. Dist. Ct. (we. dist.) Okla., U.S. Ct. Appeals (10th cir.), U.S. Supreme Ct. Spl. asst. dist. atty. Bernalillo County Dist. Atty.'s Office, Albuquerque, 1978; mem. N.Mex. Ho. Reps., 1979-86, mem. house jud. com., 1979-86, chmn. house jud. com., 1985-86, mem. house energy and natural resources com., 1979-82, 85-86, vice-chmn. house energy and natural resources com, 1981-82, mem. house transp. com., 1983-84, mem. house rules and order of bus. com., 1981-82, mem. radioactive waste consultation com., 1979-81, mem. N.Mex. mortgage fin. authority oversight com., 1983-84, mem. N.Mex. workmens compensation com., 1986; assoc. Coors, Singer and Broullire, Albuquerque, 1977-81; ptnr. Stratton and Barnett, Albuquerque, 1981-86; atty. gen. State of N.Mex., 1987—; mem. N.Mex. Supreme Ct. com. on rules governing magistrate cts., mcpl. cts. and met. ct., 1984-86; mem. N.Mex. Jud. Council, 1981-82. Sec./treas., bd. dirs. N.Mex. Rep. legis. campaign com., 1981-85; state counsel Rep. Nat. Com., 1984—; mem. juvenile justice project adv. bd. Rose Inst., Claremont-McKenna Coll., 1984—, Bur. of Land Mgmt. Citizens Adv. Com., Albuquerque, 1983-86; state dir. The Conservative Caucus; state chmn. Nat. Tax Limitation Com., 1981—, Citizens for Am., 1984-87; founding chmn. N.Mexicans for Tax Limitation. Phillips petroleum scholar, 1969, Union Oil of Calif. scholar, 1969-73, George Wyatt Brown scholar, 1972-73; recipient George Wyatt Brown award, 1971-72. Mem. Council of State Govts. (western conf. 1981-84), Nat. Conf. of Commrs. on Uniform State Laws, 1985-86. Office: Office of Atty Gen PO Drawer 1508 Santa Fe NM 87504-1508 *

STRATTON, WILLIAM EDGAR, educator; b. Akron, Ohio, Mar. 5, 1941; s. Edgar H. and Helen Lenore (Biggs) S.; m. Dena Kae Everett, Aug. 4, 1973; children: Jeffrey, Andrew, Jill. BSME, Carnegie Mellon U., 1963, MS in Indsl. Adminstrn., 1965; PhD in Orgn. Behavior, Case Western Reserve U., 1974. Vol. U.S. Peace Corps., Columbia, 1967-69; systems analyst City of Cleve., 1969-70; prof. Idaho State U., Pocatello, 1974—. Contbr. articles to profl. jours. Mem. Acad. Mgmt., Am. Soc. Personnel Adminstrn., Am. Soc. Tng. Devel., Am. Sociol. Assn. Democrat. Methodist. Home: 17 Columbia Pocatello ID 83201 Office: Idaho State U Coll Bus Pocatello ID 83209

STRAUB, DEBRA ANN, naval officer; b. Indpls., Aug. 17, 1953; d. Jack Franklin and Betty Jean (Stevens) S. BS, Ind. State U., 1975; MS, Naval Postgrad. Sch., 1984. Commd. officer USN, 1976, advanced through grades to lt. comdr., 1986; computer systems analyst Def. Communications Agy., Washington, 1977-80, Ft. Ritchie, Md., 1980-82; communications and ops. officer Naval Communication Sta., Keflavik, Iceland, 1984-85; plans and programs officer U.S. Comdr.-in-Chief Pacific, Camp H.M. Smith, Hawaii, 1985-88; exec. officer Naval Communication Sta., Bangor, Wash., 1989—; instr. math. continuing edn. program U. Hawaii, Honolulu, 1985-88. Decorated D.S.M. with one oak leaf cluster. Mem. Armed Forces Communications and Electronics Assn. (assoc. bd. dirs. 1981-82, class dir. 1982-86, v.p. publicity Hawaii chpt. 1987-88, Disting. Young AFCEAN award 1981). Democrat. Presbyterian. Home: 114 NE Tracy Ave Bremerton WA 98310 also: 446 Rudder Rd Naples FL 33940 Office: Naval Communication Sta Puget Sound Naval Submarine Base Bangor Silverdale WA 98315-5600

STRAUB, THOMAS JEFFERSON, III, financial consulting firm executive, educator; b. Stockton, Calif., Apr. 13, 1942; s. Thomas Jefferson Jr. and Lenore (Grimes) S.; m. Susan Eileen Rose, Aug. 24, 1968; children—Lynn, Heidi. A.B., Stanford U., 1963; M.B.A. with gt. distinction, Nat. U., San Diego, 1976. Cert. flight instr. Dir. devel. Children's Hosp., San Diego, 1967-68; dir. tng. Fotomat Corp., La Jolla, Calif., 1968-70, dir. new markets, 1970-71; chief exec. officer Rush Press, Inc., San Diego, 1971-75; pres. Profit Mgmt. Consultants, San Diego, 1975—; assoc. prof. Nat. U., San Diego, 1976—; dir. Microprobe, Inc., Price Products, Inc., Aeronet, Inc. Pres. Stanford Young Republicans, 1960; pres. Internat. Aerospace Hall of Fame, San Diego. Served to lt. USN, 1963-67; Vietnam. Mem. Inst. Mgmt. Acctg. (cert.), Inst. Cert. Mgmt. Accts. (cert.). Episcopalian. Club: San Diego Yacht. Office: Profit Mgmt Cons 1050 Rosecrans St San Diego CA 92106

STRAUS, LEONARD H., retail company executive; b. 1914; married. LL.B., Harvard U., 1938. With Thrifty Corp., Los Angeles, 1945—, officer legal dept., from 1948, chmn., 1979—, now chief exec. officer, also dir. Served with USCG, 1943-45. Office: Thrifty Corp Worldway Postal Ctr PO Box 92333 Los Angeles CA 90009 *

STRAUS, MARK ALAN, employee benefit consultant; b. Bridgeport, Conn., Aug. 21, 1943; s. Robert N. and Sylvia Lee (Gray) S.; m. Cherri Gruber, Sept. 12, 1965; children: Eric, Darren. BA in History, Dartmouth Coll., 1966. Group ins. underwriter Prudential Ins. Co., Newark, 1966-69, L.A., 1969-75; employee benefits cons. Alexander & Alexander Cons. Group, L.A., 1975—. Mem. Am. Mgmt. Assn., Employee Benefit Planning Assn. (pres. 1980-81, bd. dirs. 1976-83). Club: L.A. Athletic. Office: Alexander & Alexander Cons Group 3333 Wilshire Blvd #900 Los Angeles CA 90010

STRAUSS, DENNIS RONALD, chemist; b. San Diego, Oct. 20, 1953; s. Arnold Gerald and Marion Elaine (Richards) S. BS in Chemistry, San Diego U., 1975; postgrad., U. Calif., 1975-78. Staff assoc. Rockwell Internat. Sci. Ctr., Thousand Oaks, Calif., 1978-80; technical specialist Rockwell Internat. Sci. Ctr., Thousand Oaks, 1980-85, rsch. specialist, 1985—. Mem. Materials Rsch. Soc., Ventura Amiga Users Exch. Club (founding pres.). Democrat. Office: Rockwell Internat Sci Ctr 1049 Camino Dos Rios Thousand Oaks CA 91360

STREET, DIANE DYER, acupuncturist; b. Salt Lake City, Oct. 22, 1931; d. Howard and Jeannette (Darcey) Dyer; m. George Magallon, Oct. 21, 1952 (div. 1973); children: Christopher, Michele, Cynthia, Laura, Paula. BS in Nursing, Golden West Coll., Huntington Beach, Calif., 1973. RN, Calif.; lic.

acupuncturist. Nurse Capistrano By the Sea Hosp., Dana Point, Calif., 1973-75, South Coast Med. Ctr., 1975-88; pvt. practice nursing specializing in acupuncture Encinitas, Calif., 1987--. Mem. Encinitas C. of C., Calif. Acupuncture Alliance, Am. Assn. Acupuncture and Oriental Medicine, Letip Internat. Home and Office: 1152 Devonshire Dr Encinitas CA 92024

STREET, ROBERT LYNNWOOD, civil and mechanical engineer; b. Honolulu, Dec. 18, 1934; s. Evelyn Mansel and Dorothy Heather (Brook) S.; m. Norma Jeanette Ensminger, Feb. 6, 1959; children: Brian Clarke (dec.), Deborah Lynne, Kimberley Anne. M.S., Stanford U., 1957, Ph.D. (NSF grad. fellow 1960-62), 1963. Mem. faculty Stanford U. Sch. Engring., 1962—, prof. civil engring., asso. chmn. dept., 1970-72, chmn. dept., 1972-80, prof. fluid mechanics and applied math., 1972—; assoc. dean research Sch. Engring., 1971-83, vice provost for acad. computing and info. systems, 1983-85, vice provost and dean of research and acad. info. systems, 1985-87, v.p. for info. systems, 1987—, acting provost, 1987; vis. prof. U. Liverpool, Eng., 1970-71; trustee Univ. Corp. Atmospheric Research, 1983—, chmn. sci. programs evaluation com., 1981, treas. corp., 1985, vice chmn. bd., 1986, chmn. bd., 1987-90; bd. dirs. UCAR Found., 1987—; cons. in field. Author: The Analysis and Solution of Partial Differential Equations, 1973; co-author: Elementary Fluid Mechanics, 6th edit, 1982; asso. editor: Jour. Fluids Engring, 1978-81; author articles in field; mem. editorial bds. profl. jours. Served with C.E.C., USN, 1957-60. Sr. postdoctoral fellow Nat. Center Atmospheric Research, 1978-79; sr. Queen's fellow in marine sci., Australia, 1985; fellow N.E. Asia-U.S. Forum on Internat. Policy at Stanford U., 1985-89. Mem. Am. Soc. Engring. Edn., ASCE (chmn. publs. com. hydraulics div. 1978-80, Walter Huber prize 1972), ASME (R.T. Knapp award 1986), Am. Geophys. Union, The Oceanographic Soc., Phi Beta Kappa, Sigma Xi, Tau Beta Pi. Office: Stanford U Info Resources Redwood Hall Jordan Quad Stanford CA 94305-4120

STREETER, DANIEL DENISON, biomedical and biomechanical engineer; b. Bklyn., Feb. 8, 1925; s. Daniel Denison and Gladys Marie (Rudolph) S.; m. Patricia Engle, Aug. 9, 1956 (div.); 2 children; m. Hazel Dionne, Aug. 8, 1981 (div. Aug. 1982). SB in Mech. Engring., MIT, 1946; SM in Mech. Engring., 1951; PhD in Biomech. Engring., Cath. U. Am., 1969. Registered profl. engr., Wash. Mech. engr. Douglas Aircraft Corp., El Segundo, Calif., 1946, Lago Oil & Transp. Co., Aruba, The Netherlands and West Indies, 1948-50; teaching asst. mech. engring. dept. MIT, Cambridge, 1951-52; research asst. in charge High Temperature Torsional-Creep Lab., MIT, Cambridge, 1951-52; vis. prof. mech. engring. U. Rangoon, Burma, 1952-54, Tulane U., New Orleans, 1982, Purdue U., West Lafayette, Ind., 1954-55; stress analyst Boeing Co., Seattle, 1955-65; spl fellow cardiovascular tng. program U. Wash. Sch. Medicine, Seattle, 1965-66, research fellow pathology dept., 1969-71, research assoc. pathology dept., project dir. left ventricular fiber geometry unit, 1971-76; USHPS trainee Nat. Heart Inst., Bethesda, Md., 1966-68; on spl. assignment cardiology div. Children's Orthopedic Hosp., Seattle, 1976-81; engring. cons. to Burma, Am. embassy, Burma, Knappen, Tippets, Abbetts & McCarthy, engrs., N.Y.C., 1952-54. Scoutmaster Boy Scouts. Mem. Order of Arrow.

STREETER, EUGENE CLARENCE, university administrator, museum director, educator; b. Fond du Lac, Wis., Apr. 14, 1924; s. Clarence L. and Lillian R.S. 1 adopted son, Vincent J. DeMarco-Streeter. B.A., Brooks Inst. Photography, 1965. Civilian adv. U.S. Army, Fond du Lac, 1951-63; faculty Brooks Inst. Photography, Santa Barbara, Calif., 1965—, chmn. colortech. dept., 1967-80, v.p., 1970-72, 78—, prof. history of photography, 1982-84; pres. Brooks Photographic Research and Devel. Found., 1977—; dir., curator Western States Mus. Photography, Santa Barbara, 1977—; nat. exec. committeeman State of Wis. AMVETS, 1952-55; mem. registrars com. Western Region Mus. Dirs. Served with U.S. Army, 1942-51, to maj. Res. ret., 1951-67. Decorated Bronze Star. Mem. Western Photog. Collectors Assn., Soc. Tchrs. Profl. Photography, Assn. Ind. Colls. and Schs. (accreditation liaison officer 1984—), Am. Soc. Camera Collectors, Camera Collectors Assn. Cen. Calif., Smithsonian Inst. (assoc.). Home: 1323 Rialto Ln Bel Air Knolls Santa Barbara CA 93105 Mailing Address: Brooks Inst Photography 801 Alston Rd Santa Barbara CA 93108

STREETER, PATRICIA ELLEN, educator; b. Detroit, Nov. 16, 1936; d. Edward William and Helen Katherine (Thiele) Hare; m. Earl Louis Streeter, June 20, 1958; 1 child, Michelle Lynn. BA, Whittier Coll., 1958; MEd, UCLA, 1963; EdD, Brigham Young U., 1976. Cert. elem. tchr., K-8, adminstrv. credential, life adult edn. credential, Calif. Tchr. Guam Pub. Schs., Agana, 1959-60; tchr. L.A. Unified Schs., 1961-78, bi-lingual coordinator, 1979-80, reading specialist, 1980-82; learning lab specialist, adult div. L.A. Unified Sch. Dist., 1977-83, bilingual tchr., 1982-89, ESL instr., 1983-89, educator, 1989—; career day chmn., Montague Street Sch., Pacoima, Calif., 1986—; bd. dirs. Kollege Bound Kids, Montague, Pacoima, Young Astronauts, Pacoima. Contbr. articles to profl. jours. Program chmn. UCLA Bd. dirs. Grad Sch. of Edn., 1988-89; patron McGowan Theater Arts, UCLA, 1966-89; bd. dirs. Whittier Coll. West Alumni Club, 1987-89. Recipient scholarship, UCLA, Thomas Language Sch., 1981; grantees, L.A. Edn. Partnership, 1987-89, Montague Street Sch., Pacoima, Calif., 1989, Assn. of Calif. Sch. Administrator's, Calif. Ednl. Initiatives Fund. Mem. Tarzana Taxpayers Assn., Pi Lambda Theta (pres. Santa Monica chpt. 1987-89, v.p. region IV, 1986-88, v.p. so. chpts. 1986-88, treas. south chpt. 1985-86, v.p. Santa Monica 1985-87), Citizen Band Club, Alpha Delta (pres. UCLA chpt. 1989—). Republican. Congregational. Home: 18331 Tarzana Dr Tarzana CA 91356

STREITWIESER, ANDREW, JR., chemistry educator; b. Buffalo, June 23, 1927; s. Andrew and Sophie (Morlock) S.; m. Mary Ann Good, Aug. 19, 1950 (dec. May 1965); children—David Roy, Susan Ann; m. Suzanne Cope Beier, July 29, 1967. A.B., Columbia U., 1949, M.A., 1950, Ph.D., 1952; postgrad. (AEC fellow), MIT, 1951-52. Faculty U. Calif.-Berkeley, 1952—, prof. chemistry, 1963—; researcher on organic reaction mechanisms, application molecular orbital theory to organic chemistry, effect chem. structure on carbon acidities, f-element organometallic chemistry; cons. to industry, 1957—. Author: Molecular Orbital Theory for Organic Chemists, 1961, Solvolytic Displacement Reactions, 1962, (with J.I. Brauman) Supplemental Tables of Molecular Orbital Calculations, 1965, (with C.A. Coulson) Dictionary of Pi Electron Calculations, 1965, (with P.H. Owens) Orbital and Electron Density Diagrams, 1973, (with C.H. Heathcock) Introduction to Organic Chemistry, 3d edit, 1985; also numerous articles.; co-editor: Progress in Physical Organic Chemistry, 11 vols, 1963-74. Recipient Humboldt Found. Sr. scientist award, 1976, Humboldt medal, 1979, Cope scholar award, 1989. Fellow AAAS; mem. NAS, Am. Chem. Soc. (Calif. sect. award 1964, award in Petroleum Chemistry 1967, Norris award in phys. organic chemistry 1982, Cope scholar award 1989), Royal Soc. Chemistry, AAAS, Am. Acad. Arts and Scis., German Chem. Soc., Phi Beta Kappa, Sigma Xi. Office: U Calif Dept Chemistry Berkeley CA 94720

STRELL, JOHN JOSEPH, educator; b. Urbana, Ill., June 7, 1943; s. John Jr. and Rose (Novak) S.; m. Sharon Studdard, Dec. 28, 1965 (div. July 1984); children: Jay S., Jeb N.; m. Janet Ann Ellis, Aug. 6, 1985; children: Melissa K. Farrow, James Farrow. BS, Colo. State U., 1965; MEd, U. Ariz., 1970. Tchr.-coach Ampitheater Sch. Dist., Tucson, 1965-68, 85—, Barrington (Ill.) Sch. Dist., 1968-78; dir. tng. Mex. Foods div. Gen. Foods Corp., Denver, 1978-83; dir. creative concept. devel. Howard Johnson Restaurants, North Quincy, Mass., 1983; dir. tng. and devel. Mister Steak Restaurant Group, Denver, 1984. Democrat. Presbyterian. Home: 1581 W Oak Shadows Dr Tucson AZ 85737 Office: Canyon Deloro High Sch 25 W Calle Concordia Tucson AZ 85737

STREMBITSKY, MICHAEL ALEXANDER, school administrator; b. Smoky Lake, Alta., Can., Mar. 5, 1935; s. Alec and Rose (Fedoretz) S.; m. Victoria Semeniuk, Aug. 12, 1954; children: Michael, William-John. BA, U. Alta., 1955, BEd, 1958; MA, Columbia U., 1968, MEd, 1972, LLD, 1989. With Edmonton (Alta.) pub. schs., now supt. of schs. Bd. dirs. Glenrose Hosp. Mem. Am. Assn. Sch. Adminstrs., Am. Mgmt. Assn., Am. Sch. Bus. Ofls., Assn. for Supr. and Curriculum Devel., Can. Assn. Sch. Adminstrs., Can. Coll. Tchrs., Can. Edn. Assn., Conf. Alba. Sch. Suptds., Alberta Tchr's Assn., Pub. Sch. Admstrs. Assn., Council Ednl. Facility Planners Internat., Edmonton C. of C., Edmonton-Harbin (China) Friendship Soc., Edmonton Edn. Soc., U. Alta. Faculty Edn. Alumni Assn., Large City Sch. Supts., Nat. Assn. Ednl. Negotiators, Nat. Assn. Elementary Sch. Prins., Nat. Ukranian Profl. Bus. Club, Phi Delta Kappa. Lodge: Rotary. Office: Edmonton Pub Schs, Ctr for Edn, 1 Kingsway, Edmonton, AB Canada T5H 4G9

STRESS, JAMES WILLIAM, JR., chemical executive, consultant; b. Chgo., Mar. 18, 1954; s. James William Sr. and Therase (Aprile) S.; m. Renee Cynthia Penton, June 5, 1976; children: James T.A., Mikla Nichole. BS in Premed, Ill. Benidictine Coll., 1976. Dist. rep. Nalco Chem. Co., Casper, Wyo., 1979-81; area mgr. Nalco Chem. Co., Casper, 1981-83; dist. mgr. Nalco Chem. Co., Denver, 1985—. Mem. Nalco Dist. Mgrs. Assn. Office: Nalco Chem Co 165 S Union Blvd Ste 560 Littleton CO 80210

STRETZ, LAWRENCE ALBERT, chemical engineer; b. Santa Rita, N.Mex., Oct. 5, 1946; s. Charles and Myrtle Belle (Gray) S.; m. Paula Elaine Rogers, Sept. 10, 1966; 1 child, Curtis Charles. BS, N.Mex. State U., 1969; MS, Iowa State U., 1971, PhD, 1973. Registered profl. engr., N.Mex. Engr. Consumer's Power, Jackson, Mich., 1973-74; engr. El Paso Products Co., Odessa, Tex., 1974-78; staff mem. Los Alamos Nat. Lab., Los Alamos, N.Mex., 1978-85; sect. leader Los Alamos Nat. Lab., 1985—. Contbr. articles to profl. jours. Mem. Los Alamos Sch. Bd., 1989—. Mem. Am. Inst. Chem. Engrs., Sigma Xi. Republican. Baptist. Office: Los Alamos Nat Lab Box 1663 MS C920 Los Alamos NM 87545

STRICHARTZ, JAMES LEONARD, lawyer; b. N.Y.C., Feb. 5, 1951; s. Morris Harvey and Estelle (Flatow) S.; m. Cheryl Rene Johnson, July 10, 1982. BA in Urban Studies, U. Mich., 1973, M in Pub. Policy, 1976, JD, 1977. Bar: Mich. 1977, D.C. 1978, Wash. 1980. Law clk. Mich. Ct. Appeals, Detroit, 1977-78; assoc. atty. Weinrich, Gilmore & Adolph, Seattle, 1978-79; gen. counsel The 13th Regional Corp., Seattle, 1979-81; pvt. practice Seattle, 1981—; bd. dirs., pres. Community Assns. Inst., Seattle, 1988; mem. Senate Judiciary Com. Condominium Law Task Force, Seattle, 1986-89, Condominium Act Statutory Revision Com., 1987-89. Pres., bd. dirs. Fremont Community Health Clinic, 1982-83, 45th St. Community Health Clinic, 1984-89; gen. counsel, trustee Wash. Trust for Hist. Preservation, 1982-87; mem. Corp. Coun. For The Arts, 1987-88, Coun. for Corp. Responsibility, 1984—. Mem. ABA, Wash. State Bar Assn., D.C. Bar Assn., Wash. State Community Assns. Inst. (chmn. 1988, speaker 22d, 23rd Nat. Conf. 1987, pres.-elect 1988-89, pres. 1989—), Coll. Club (Seattle). Democrat. Unitarian. Office: 200 W Mercer St #511 Seattle WA 98119

STRICKLER, JEFFREY HAROLD, pediatrician; b. Mpls., Oct. 14, 1943; s. Jacob Harold and Helen Cecelia (Mitchell) S.; m. Karen Anne Stewart, June 18, 1966; children: Hans Stewart, Liesl Ann. BA, Carleton Coll., 1965; MD, U. Minn., 1969. Diplomate Am. Bd. Pediatrics. Resident in pediatrics Stanford (Calif.) U., 1969-73; pvt. practice Helena, Mont., 1975—; chief staff Shodair Children's Hosp., Helena, 1984-86; dir. maternal-child health Lewis and Clark County, Helena, 1978-88. Mem. Mont. Gov.'s Task Force on Child Abuse, 1978-79; mem. steering com. Region VIII Child Abuse Prevention, Denver, 1979-82; bd. dirs. Helena Dist. 1 Sch. Bd., 1982-88, vice chmn., 1985-87. Maj. M.C., USAF, 1973-75. Fellow Am. Acad. Pediatrics (vice chmn. Mont. chpt. 1981-84, chmn. 1984-87, mem. nat. nominating com. 1987—, chmn. 1989—, Wyeth award 1987); mem. Mont. Med. Assn., Rotary (youth exchange chmn. dist. 539, 1984-88, pres. Helena 1988-89). Office: Helena Pediatric Clinic 1300 N Montana Helena MT 59601

STRICKSTEIN, HERBERT JERRY, lawyer; b. Detroit, Sept. 4, 1932; s. Samuel and Leah (Freedman) S.; m. Elaine Frances Cohen, Aug. 22, 1963; children: Jaynee Esther, Jill Rose. AA, UCLA, 1952; BS in Law, U. So. Calif., 1954, JD, 1956. Dep. judge adv. USAF, 1957-60; dep. city atty. L.A., 1960-61; assoc. Axelrad, Seville & Ross, 1961-65; ptnr. Iliff & Strickstein, 1965-72; pvt. practice Herbert J. Strickstein Law Corp., L.A., 1972—. Contbr. numerous articles to profl. jours. Commr. Small Craft Harbor Comm., Marina del Rey, Calif., 1983—. Mem. Calif. Dept. Real Estate (sub. advisors com.), State Bar Calif. Assn. (real property sec.), L.A. County Bar Assn., Braemar Country Club. Office: 2049 Century Park E #1200 Los Angeles CA 90067

STRINGER, JAMES DALE, JR., telecommunications company executive; b. West Point, Miss., Jan. 25, 1938; s. James Dale and Rachel Joyce (Beaird); m. Kathryn Joyce Merrill, May 30, 1963; children: Elizabeth, Christopher, Donald, Murl, Matthew, Rebecca. BS in Math., U. Ariz., 1963; postgrad., Drexel U., 1976-77. With RCA Computers, 1966-67; tech. staff Hughes Aircraft, 1967-68; mgr. software devel. Lockheed Electronics, 1968-69; mgr. regional systems engr. Digitial Scientific, 1969-72; sr. tech. staff Martin Marietta Aerospace, 1972-74; with RCA Missiles and Radar, Morrestown, N.J., 1974-76, Equipment div. Raytheon Co., Wayland, Mass., 1977-78, Def. Systems div. Computer Scis. Corp., Moorestown, 1978-79, Xten Svcs. div. Xerox Corp., Long Beach, Calif., 1979-80; mgr. advanced devel., corp. telecommunications Hughes Aircraft Co., Woodland Hills, 1980-85; with Network Svcs. Group div. Boeing Computer Svcs. Co., Seattle, 1985—; founder, pres. Exotel, Inc., 1983-85; mgmt. cons., 1976—; del. to Def. Sci. Bd. Workshop, 1977; guest lectr. Software Summit, London, 1981. Patentee in field; cited in Datamation mag., 1971, Bus. Week mag., 1983, Wall St. Jour., 1988; contbr. articles to profl. jours. Former Scoutmaster Boy Scouts Am., Edison (N.J.) Council; mem. Neighbos Council No. 1, City of Simi Valley, Calif. With Signal Corps AUS, 1959-66. Mem. IEEE (Computer Soc., Areospace Soc.), Nat. Security Indsl. Assn. (chmn. Software Com., 1976-79). Republican. LDS. Home: 17240 SE 47th St Issaquah WA 98027 Office: Boeing Computer Svcs Network Svcs Group MS7R-90 PO Box 24346 Seattle WA 98124-0246

STRINGER, WILLIAM JEREMY, university official; b. Oakland, Calif., Nov. 8, 1944; s. William Duane and Mildred May (Andrus) S.; BA in English, So. Meth. U., 1966; MA in English, U. Wis., 1968, PhD in Ednl. Adminstrn., 1973; m. Susan Lee Hildebrand; children: Shannon Lee, Kelly Erin, Courtney Elizabeth. Dir. men's housing Southwestern U., Georgetown, Tex., 1968-69; asst. dir. housing U. Wis., Madison, 1969-73; dir. residential life, asso. dean student life, adj. prof. Pacific Luth., Tacoma, 1973-78; dir. residential life U. So. Calif., 1978-79, asst. v.p., 1979-84, asst. prof. higher and post-secondary edn., 1980-84; v.p. student life Seattle U., 1984—. Bd. dirs. N.W. area Luth. Social Services of Wash. and Idaho, pres. elect, 1989. Danforth Found. grantee, 1976-77. Mem. Am. Assn. Higher Edn., Nat. Assn. Student Personnel Adminstrs. (bd. dirs. region V), Am. Personnel and Guidance Assn., Phi Eta Sigma, Sigma Tau Delta, Phi Alpha Theta. Lutheran. Author: How to Survive as a Single Student, 1972; The Role of the Assistant in Higher Education, 1973. Home: 4553 169th Ave SE Issaquah WA 98027 Office: Seattle U Seattle WA 98122

STRISOWER, BEVERLY BOUTELL, information specialist; b. Ypsilanti, Mich., Oct. 13, 1923; d. William G. and Helen Marie (McLane) Boutell; m. Edward H. Strisower, Aug. 14, 1948; children: Suzanne, Paul E., John M., Edwin R. AB, Ea. Mich. U., 1945. Research assoc. U. Calif., Berkeley, 1948-61, 71-81, info. specialist, 1981-86; owner Geo Info., Orinda, Calif., 1986--. Contbr. articles on energy, earth scis. and medicine to profl. jours. Mem. AAAS. Office: Geo Info 28 Las Cascadas Orinda CA 94563

STRITTMATTER, PETER ALBERT, astronomer, educator; b. London, Eng., Sept. 12, 1939; came to U.S., 1970; s. Albert and Rosa S.; m. Janet Hubbard Parkhurst, Mar. 18, 1967; children—Catherine D., Robert P. B.A., Cambridge U., Eng., 1961, M.A., 1963, Ph.D., 1967. Staff scientist Inst. for Astronomy, Cambridge, Eng., 1967-70; staff scientist dept. physics U. Calif.-San Diego, La Jolla, Calif., 1970-71; assoc. prof. dept. astronomy U. Ariz., Tucson, 1971-74, prof. dept. astronomy, 1974—; dir. Steward Observatory, Tucson, 1975—; mem. staff Max Planck Inst. Radio-astronomy, Bonn, W. Germany, 1981—. Contbr. articles to profl. jours. Recipient Sr. award Humboldt Found., 1979-80. Fellow Royal Astron. Soc.; mem. Am. Astron. Soc., Astronomische Gesellschaft. Office: U Ariz Steward Obs Tucson AZ 85721

STRIZEK, GENE, county official; b. Fond du Lac, Wis., Mar. 3, 1958; s. John Joseph and Dorothy Margaret (Bastian) S.; m. Theresa Mary Sherlock, Apr. 23, 1982; children: Amy Morgan, Lauren Stephanie. AS, U. Wis.-Fond du Lac, 1978; BBA, U. Wis.-Oshkosh, 1980. CPA, Ariz. Staff acct. Young, Peachin & Co., CPAs, Tucson, 1980-81; sr. tax preparer Beneficial Income Tax Svc., Tucson, 1982; revenue field auditor Ariz. Dept. Revenue, Tucson, 1982-87; internal auditor Pima County Govt., Tucson, 1987-88; fund acct. Pima County Govt., 1988--. Mem. Ariz. Soc. CPAs, Nat. Assn. Accts. (dir. newsletter Tucson chpt. 1988--), Saguaro Golf Club. Republican. Lutheran. Home: 1450 S Coati Dr Tucson AZ 85713 Office: Pima County Fin Dept 130 W Congress St Tucson AZ 85701

STROBER, LAWRENCE STEVEN, electronics executive; b. N.Y.C., Aug. 26, 1942; s. Robert and Ray (Ramer) S.; m. Glenda Elliot Barter, Dec. 8, 1967; children: Jeremy David, Zachary Matthew. BBA, Bucknell U., 1964; MBA, Hofstra U., 1971. Dir. Strober Investment Group, San Rafael, Calif., 1965—; founder, v.p. Direct, Inc., Sunnyvale, Calif., 1979-81; v.p. sales Micropro Internat. Corp., San Rafael, 1981-83; founder Agoura Internat., Tokyo, 1985—; founder, pres. Know How, Inc., San Francisco, 1982-84; exec. v.p. Schuchardt Software Systems, San Rafael, 1984-85; founder, v.p. Concise Computer Corp., Nashua, N.H., 1985-86; v.p. Ariel Electronics, Inc., Sunnyvale, 1986—; cons. in field. Dir. Gerstle Park Neighborhood Assn., San Rafael, 1983—. Served to 1st lt. U.S. Army, 1965-67. Home: 17 Redwood Dr San Rafael CA 94901

STROBERG, JON ERIC, military officer; b. Oak Park, Ill., Dec. 18, 1952; s. Hubert Frederic and Arlyn Elaine (Gillon) S.; m. Sally Ann D'Angelo, Feb. 1, 1976; 1 child, Kevin David. BS in Aviation Mgmt., Auburn U., 1974; MBA, Embry-Riddle, 1983. Commd. USAF, 1974, advanced through grades to major, 1986; student pilot USAF, Columbus AFB, Miss., 1976-77, T-38 instr. pilot, 1977-81; squad plans officer USAF, Spangdahlem AB, Fed. Republic Germany, 1981-82, chief victor alert div., 1982-83, wing flight examiner, 1983-84; standardization/evaluation liaison officer USAF, George AFB, Calif., 1984-85, flight comdr., 1985-87, asst. ops. officer, 1987-88, chief weapons and tactics, 1988—; exchange officer Royal Air Force, 1989—. Mem. Daedalians, High Desert Flight, Air Force Assn., War Eagle Flying Team, Alpha Eta Rho (pres. gamma chpt. 1972-74). Republican.

STROM, PETER GORDON, data processing executive; b. Seattle, July 9, 1958; s. Clarence Gordon and Nancy Jean (Helland) S.; m. Ellen Jean Stenerson, Aug. 30, 1980; children: Christopher Gordon, Karin Marie, Lise Ann. BS, Pacific Luth. U., 1980; postgrad., Utah State U., 1981-82. Research biologist NSF, Manhattan, Kans., 1979; grad. asst. Utah State U., Logan, 1981-82; expediter Morton Thiokol, Inc., Brigham City, Utah, 1982-83; computer system specialist Morton Thiokol, Inc., 1983-84; sr. tech. analyst Project Software & Devel., San Francisco, 1984-86; account mgr. Project Software & Devel., 1986-88, br. mgr., 1988—. Precinct chmn. Rep. Party, Concord, Calif., 1988; elder First Luth. Ch., Concord, 1985-88. Mem. Sons of Norway. Republican. Lutheran. Office: Project Software & Devel 4 Embarcadero San Francisco CA 94111

STROM, SHIRLEY LONGETEIG, civic worker; b. Craigmont, Idaho, Jan. 28, 1931; d. Iver J. and Frances Willard (Mason) Longeteig; m. Robert C. Strom, June 15, 1952; children: Kristin, Trina, Camber. BA with honors, U. Idaho, 1952. Mem. Idaho Rep. Com., 1954-58, mem. exec. com., 1976-84; del. Nat. Rep. Conv., 1968, 72; mem. Craigmont Planning and Zoning Commn., 1965-70, justice of peace, 1967-70; trustee Lewis County Library Dist., 1980—, past chmn.; mem. adv. coun. Coll. Letters and Sci., U. Idaho, Moscow, 1986—, chmn. mem. centennial com. for library, 1988—; chmn. Idaho Women's Polit. Caucus, 1975, Higher Edn. Polit. Action Com., 1987—; mem. Idaho Humanities Coun., 1988—; mem. community adv. coun. Lewiston (Idaho) Morning Tribune, 1988-89. Recipient cert. of appreciation Lewis County Rep. Com., 1984. Mem. NOW, Nat. Women's Polit. Caucus, U. Idaho Alumni Assn. (bd. dirs. 1977-84, pres. 1982-83, Alumni Svc. award 1988), Library Assocs. U. Idaho, Lewis County Hist. Soc., Order Eastern Star (grand Esther 1970), Pi Gamma Mu.

STROMEI, FRANK C., insurance agent, real estate developer; b. Raton, N.Mex., Dec. 19, 1940; s. Frank T. and Mozella (LaDella) S.; m. Linda Faye Kyle, June 11, 1972; children: Shane K., Sunni DeAndra. B Humanities, U. N.Mex., 1963. CLU. Tchr. N.Mex. Schs., Albuquerque, 1962-67; ins. agt. Albuquerque, 1968-74, State Farm Inc., Albuquerque, 1974—; real estate developer Shasun Cos., Albuquerque, 1974—; artist Albuquerque, 1966—, writer, 1973—; bank organizer Allied Bancorp., Albuquerque, 1987—; rancher Hornado Lakes Ranch, Engle, N.Mex., 1982—; pub. speaker Motivation Systems, Albuquerque, 1980—. Pres. Rio Rancho (N.Mex.) Polit. Action Bd., 1980-85, Ranchers Econ. Bd., Albuquerque, N.Mex., 1981-82. Recipient Yearling award N.Mex. Life Underwriters, 1974; named Civitan of Yr., 1982. Mem. Rio Rancho C. of C., West Side Life Agts. Democrat. Roman Catholic. Home: Box 2050 Corrales NM 87048

STRONG, GARY EUGENE, librarian; b. Moscow, Idaho, June 26, 1944; s. Authur Dwight and Cleora Anna (Nirk) S.; m. Carolyn Jean Roetker, Mar. 14, 1970; children: Christopher Eric, Jennifer Rebecca. BS in Edn., U. Idaho, 1966; AMLS, U. Mich., 1967. Adminstrv. and reference asst. U. Idaho, 1963-66; extension librarian Latah County Free Library, Moscow, 1966; head librarian Markeley Residence Library, U. Mich., 1966-67; library dir. Lake Oswego (Oreg.) Public Library, 1967-73, Everett (Wash.) Public Library, 1973-76; asso. dir. services Wash. State Library, Olympia, 1976-79; dep. state librarian Wash. State Library, 1979-80; state librarian Calif. State Library, Sacramento, 1980—; chief exec. Calif. Library Services Bd., 1980—; founder, bd. dirs. Calif. State Library Found., 1982—; bd. dirs. No. Regional Library Bd., 1983—; mem. adv. bd. Ctr. for Book in Libr. of Congress, 1983-86; mem. nat. adv. com. Libr. of Congress, 1987-89; chmn. adv. bd. Calif. Libr. Constrn. and Rennovation Bond, 1989—; vis. lectr. Marylhurst Coll., Oreg., 1968, Oreg. Div. Continuing Edn., 1972; lectr. and cons. in field. Host, producer: cable TV Signatures program, 1974-76, nationwide videoconfs. on illiteracy, censorship, 1985; editor Calif. State Library Found. Bull., 1982—(H.W. Wilson Periodical award, 1988), Western Americana in the Calif. State Library, 1986, On Reading-In the Year of the Reader, 1987; contbr. articles to profl. jours.; editor, designer and pub. of various books; author: On Reading-in the Year of the Reader, 1987. Bd. dirs., v.p. Pacific N.W. Bibliog. Ctr., 1977-80; bd. dirs. Thurston Mason County Mental Health Ctr., 1977-80, pres., 1979-80; bd. dirs. Coop. Library Agy. for Systems and Services, 1980—, vice chmn., 1981-84; bd. dirs. Sr. Services Snohomish County, 1973-76, HISPANEX (Calif. Spanish lang. data base), 1983-86; bd. govs. Snohomish County Hist. Assn., 1974-76; mem. Oreg. Council Public Broadcasting, 1969-73; mem. psychiat. task force St. Peters Hosp., Olympia, 1979-80; co-founder Calif. Ctr. for the Book, bd. dirs., 1987—; mem. adv. bd. Calif. State PTA, 1981-86. Recipient Disting. Alumnus award U. Mich., 1984; Disting. Service award Calif. Literacy Inc., 1985; Oreg. Library scholar, 1966, Spl. Achievement award Literacy Action, 1988. Mem. ALA (legis. com. 1980-82, Commn. on Freedom and Equality of Access to Info. 1983-86), Library Adminstrn. and Mgmt. Assn. (dir. 1980-86, pres. 1984-85), Oreg. Library Assn. (hon. life mem., pres. 1970-71), Pacific N.W. Library Assn. (hon. life mem., pres. 1978-79), Calif. Library Assn. (govt. relations com. 1980—), Chief Officers of State Library Agys. (pres. 1984-86), Western Coun. of State Librs. (v.p. 1989—), Everett Area C. of C. (bd. dirs. 1974-76). Clubs: Book of Calif., Press of San Francisco, Sacramento Book Collectors, Roxburghe. Office: Calif State Libr PO Box 942837 Sacramento CA 94237

STRONG, GAY, industrial relations and human resources executive; b. Santa Monica, Calif., Jan. 13, 1930; d. Claude Roderick and Katherine Anna (Brown) Riley; student UCLA, 1947-49; A.A., Pierce Coll., Los Angeles, 1969; B.A. in English, Calif. State U.-Northridge, 1973; m. Duane Gordon Strong, Aug. 20, 1949; children—Philip, Katherine, Patricia, Barbara. With credit office, store ops., then asst. personnel mgr. Builders Emporium, Van Nuys, Calif., 1969-74, personnel mgr., 1974-78; dir. indsl. relations GC Internat., Hawthorne, Calif., 1978-81; personnel mgr. Lok Products Co., Fullerton, Calif., 1981-82; chief exec. officer Asset Recovery, Santa Monica, Calif., 1982-83; dir. Human Resource Targeted Coverage, Inc., Glendora, Calif., 1983-89, editor house organ, 1983-89; dir. human resources Aero Alloys, GC Internat., 1989—. Republican. Editor Builders Emporium house organ, 1972-78. Office: 18405 S Santa Fe Ave Rancho Dominguez CA 90221

STRONG, GERALDINE ANNE, library manager; b. San Francisco, Feb. 22, 1943; d. Gerald Richard and Ann (Freeman) O'Melveny; m. Douglas Michael Strong; children: Michael Phillip, David Richard, Patricia Anne. BA, Gonzaga U., Spokane, 1965; MLS, U. Md., 1973. Cert. librarian, Wash. Library clk. Dept. Pub. Libraries, Rockville, Md., 1971-72, children's librarians, 1973-84; youth svcs. coord. Sno-Isle Regional Library System, Marysville, Wash., 1985—; guest lectr. U. Washington and U. Md. Co-author nat. competencies for children's librarians; author bibliographies. Mem. Snohomish County Childre's Commn., Everett, Wash., 1987—. Mem. ALA, Wash. Library Assn., Seattle Storytellers, Freedom to Read Found., Beta Phi Mu. Democrat. Roman Catholic. Home: 18624 94th Ave W Edmonds WA 98020 Office: Sno Isle Regional Library Box 148 Marysville WA 98270

STRONG, GLENN WILLIAM, building contractor, consultant; b. East Orange, N.J., Oct. 26, 1949; s. Harold Thomas and Elaine Elsie (Landgraber) S.; m. Dale Ellen Klieback, June 15, 1980; 1 child, Ashley Jordan. Student communications, U. Tex., El Paso, 1967-68. Carpenter Alco Builders, New Providence, N.J., 1968-72; constrn. supr. Sanddollar Constrn. Co., Santa Cruz, Calif., 1973-86; chief exec. officer Sea Hawk Enterprises, Inc., Santa Cruz, 1986—; owner, mgr. Sea Hawk Constrn. Co., Santa Cruz, 1986—; industry expert, expert witness Calif. Contractor's Lic. Bd., Sacramento, 1987—; bd. dirs. Santa Cruz County Builders Exchange, 1988—. Mem. Internat. Conf. Bldg. Ofcls. (profl.), Nat. Assn. Gen. Contractors, Constrn. Specifications Inst., Western Regional Master Builders. Democrat. Methodist. Office: Sea Hawk Enterprises Inc PO Box 797 Santa Cruz CA 95061

STRONG, JOHN CHARLES, yacht repair company and epoxy supply company exec; b. Eugene, Oreg., May 30, 1947; s. Charles Henderson and Isabelle Margaret (Browne) S.; m. F. Suzanne Kacprzynski, Feb. 1, 1978 (div. Dec. 1987). AA in Communications, Mt. Hood Community Coll., 1975; BS in Communications, San Francisco State U., 1977. Announcer, producer Sta. KZEL-FM, Eugene, 1969-71; prodn. mgr. GE, Eugene, 1971-76; newswriter, producer Group W Broadcasting Inc., San Francisco, 1976-77; master control dir. Fisher Broadcasting Inc., Seattle, 1978-83; owner, mgr. Yachtcare Maintenance Mgmt., Seattle, 1982—, Sigma Yachts Ltd.,, Seattle, 1985—, Sigma Supply Co., Seattle, 1987—; pres., chief exec. officer Sigmar Corp., Seattle, 1985—. Contbr. articles to consumer yachting newsletter. Founding bd. dirs. Phinney Neighborhood Assn., Seattle, 1982. With USCG, 1987—. Mem. Am. Boatbuilders and Repairers Assn., N.W. Marine Trade Assn., Am. Boat and Yacht Coun., Better Bus. Bur., Alfa Romeo Owners Club, Northwest Riggers Sailing Club. Democrat. Office: Sigmar Corp 4300 11th Ave NW Seattle WA 98107

STRONG, MAYDA NEL, psychologist, educator; b. Albuquerque, May 6, 1942; d. Floyd Samuel and Wanda Christmas (Martin) Strong; 1 child, Robert Allen Willingham. BA in Speech-Theatre cum laude, Tex. Western Coll., 1963; EdM, U. Tex., Austin, 1972, PhD in Counseling Psychology, 1978; lic. clin. psychologist, Colo., 1984; cert. alcohol counselor III, Colo., 1987. Asst. instr. in ednl. psychology U. Tex., Austin, 1974-78; instr. psychology Austin Community Coll., 1974-78, Otero Jr. Coll., La Junta, Colo., 1979—; dir. outpatient and emergency services S.E. Colo. Family Guidance and Mental Health Ctr., Inc., La Junta, 1978-81; pvt. practice psychol. therapy, La Junta, 1981—; exec. dir. Pathfinders Alcohol Dependency program, 1985—. Del. to County Dem. Conv., 1988. Co-star The Good Doctor, 1980, On Golden Pond, 1981, Plaza Suite, 1987, Otero Jr. Coll. Players, 1987, Chase Me Comrade, 1989. AAUW fellow, 1974-76. Mem. Bus. and Profl. People (legis. chairperson 1982-83, NES chmn. 1982—), Colo. Psychol. Assn. (legis. chmn. for dist.). Contbr. articles in field to profl. publs. Author poems in Chinook: Paths through the Puzzle, Decisions, Passion. Home: 500 Holly Ave PO Box 177 Swink CO 81077 Office: #21 Town Square Mall La Junta CO 81050

STRONG, PETER HANSEN, lawyer; b. Ann Arbor, Mich., Mar. 1, 1952; s. James Kilroy and Ruthann (Hansen) S.; m. Nancy J. Klaphaak, Dec. 14, 1974. BA, U. Ariz., 1972; JD, Stanford U., 1975. Bar: Calif. Assoc. Thelen, Marrin, Johnson & Bridges, L.A., 1975-77, Fenwick, Stone, Davis and West, L.A., 1977-82; ptnr. Griffin and Strong, L.A., 1982—; judge pro tem L.A. County Mcpl. Ct., 1982—. Pres. Foothill Friends of Music, Pasadena, 1987, dir. 1988—. Mem. ABA, L.A. County Bar Assn., Assn. Bus. Trial Lawyers, L.A. Athletic Club. Office: Griffin and Strong 700 South Flower St Los Angeles CA 90017

STRONG, ROBERT GEORGE, sales engineer, marketing consultant; b. Rochester, N.Y., Sept. 23, 1916; s. Robert H. and Sadie E. (McNeil) S.; m. Dorothy M. Reimer, Sept. 28, 1939; 1 child, Susan Diane Evans. ME, Rochester Inst. Tech., 1936; grad., U. Rochester, 1938. Govt. project supr. Stromberg Carlson Co., Rochester, 1937-41; pres. Strong Appliance Industries, Danbury, Conn., 1942-48; cons. to gen. mgr. Allan B. DuMont Labs., East Paterson, N.J., 1948-51; asst. chief engr. Bendix Aviation Corp., North Hollywood, Calif., 1951-55; sales mgr. F. Somers Paterson Co., L.A., 1955-57; v.p., gen. mgr. Western div. Keco Industries, Santa Ana, Calif., 1957-71, mktg. cons., 1978—; pres. Strong Industries, San Juan Capistrano, Calif., 1971—, Honolulu, 1975—; cons., mktg. and acquisitions for environ. control industry, 1978—; mktg. mgr. Keco Industries, Inc., Florence, Ky. Designer, developer household and indsl. electric can opener. Mem. Am. Soc. Refrigerating Engrs., Am. Ordnance Assn., Air Force Assn., Instrument Soc. Am., Am. Soc. Plastic Engrs., SAE, Mfrs. Agents Nat. Assn. address: 1328 Calle Emilia San Clemente CA 92672

STRONG, WILLIAM LEE, former manufacturing company executive; b. Jacksonville, Fla., Sept. 17, 1919; s. William M. and Hedwig C. (Ulm) S.; m. Betty Jean Stream, Dec. 13, 1941; children—William Lee, Thomas B., Robin E. Strong Vandever. AB in Econs., Occidental Coll., 1942; MBA, Harvard U., 1947. Budget dir. Byron-Jackson div. Borg Warner Corp., Los Angeles, 1954-56, controller, 1956-57; budget dir. Consol. Freightways, Inc., Menlo Park, Calif., 1957-60, treas., chief fin. officer, 1960-62; v.p. fin., treas., dir. Packard-Bell Electronics Corp., Los Angeles, 1962-65; treas. Allis-Chalmers Mfg. Co., Milw., 1965-68; v.p., treas. Continental Can Co., Inc., (now Continental Group, Inc.), 1968-75; sr. v.p., chief fin. officer Firestone Tire & Rubber Co., Akron, Ohio, 1976-77, exec. v.p., dir., 1978-81; dir. Transatlantic Fund, U.S. Life Corp.; guest lectr. various grad. bus. schs., other groups. chmn. bd. advisors Sch. Acctg. U. So. Calif. Served to lt. comdr. USN, 1942-54; PTO. Mem. Treas. Club N.Y., Phi Gamma Delta. Clubs: Harvard Bus. Sch. (N.Y.C.), Tennis (Rancho San Clemente). Home: 4020 Calle Marlena San Clemente CA 92672

STRONGIN, DAVID ADOLPH, real estate broker; b. N.Y.C., Jan. 17, 1931; s. William and Rose Hannah (Fliesler) S.; divorced; children: Timothy Scott, Terry Wayne, Barbara Kathleen, Paul Douglas; m. Nancy Louise Aanestad Strongin, Aug. 25, 1973. Real estate broker Timber/Lake Realty, Incline Village, Nev., 1973; pres. Diamond Peak Co., Incline Village, Nev., 1978; pres. Ties Honor Found., Incline Village, 1987—. Author: short stories, poems; former editor: Das Sitzmark. Former pres. Incline Village Little Theater; founding mem. North Lake Tahoe Symphony Assn.; founding chmn. C-Right Com. With U.S. Army. 1948-69. Decorated Confrerie des Chevalier du Tastevio (comdr.). The Ret. Officers Assn., Tyrolian Village Homeowners Assn., AUSA, Vietnam Vet. Am. Am. Legion, Incline Village C.of C., Nat. Assn. Realtors (broker mem.). Episcopalian. Clubs:Tahoe Racquet (founding mem.); Incline Village Ski; Walley's Hot Springs Resort and Country; Rotary (pres.). Office: Ties of Honor Drawer ZZ Incline Village NV 89450

STROOCK, THOMAS FRANK, state senator; b. N.Y.C., Oct. 10, 1925; s. Samuel and Dorothy (Frank) S.; B.A. in Econs., Yale U., 1948; m. Marta Freyre de Andrade, June 19, 1949; children—Margaret, Sandra, Elizabeth, Anne. Landman Stanolind Oil & Gas Co., Tulsa, 1948-52; pres. Stroock Leasing Corp., Casper, Wyo., 1952—, Alpha Exploration, Inc., 1980—; partner Stroock, Rogers & Dymond, Casper, 1960-82; dir. Wyo. Bancorp., Cheyenne, First Wyo. Bank, Casper; mem. Wyo. Senate, 1967-69, 71-75, 79—, chmn. appropriations com. 1983, co-chmn. joint appropriations com., 1983—, mem. mgmt. and audit com. P; mem. steering com. Edn. Commn. of States. Pres. Natrona County Sch. Bd., 1960-69; pres. Wyo. State Sch. Bds. Assn., 1965-66; chmn. Casper Community Recreation, 1955-60; chmn. Natrona County United Fund, 1963-64; chmn. Wyo. State Republican Com., 1975-78; chmn. Western States Rep. Chmn. Assn., 1977-78; chmn. Wyo. Higher Edn. Commn., 1969-71; mem. Nat. Petroleum Council, 1972-77; chmn. trustees Sierra Madre Found. for Geol. Research, New Haven; chmn. Wyo. Nat. Gas Pipeline Authority 1987-88; bd. dirs. Ucross Found., Denver; mem. Nat. Pub. Lands Adv. Council, 1981-85. Served with USMC, 1943-46. Mem. Rocky Mountain Oil and Gas Assn., Petroleum Assn. Wyo. Republican. Unitarian. Lodge: Kiwanis. Clubs: Casper Country; Casper Petroleum; Denver. Office: PO Box 2875 Casper WY 82602

STROOP, WILLIAM GEORGE, neurology and pathology educator; b. Klamath Falls, Oreg., June 17, 1952; s. John William and Constance Salome (Truchan) S.; m. Janice Louise Brandenburg, June 22, 1974; 1 child, Miriam Elizabeth. BS, Oreg. State U., 1975; PhD, U. Calif., San Francisco, 1981. Staff research assoc. dept. neurology U. Calif. Sch. Medicine, San Francisco, 1975-78, predoctoral fellow dept. pathology, 1978-81, research asst. dept. medicine, 1980-81; postdoctoral fellow The Slow Virus Group The Wistar Inst., Phila., 1981-83, sec., 1982-83; postdoctoral fellow U. Penn., Phila., 1981-83; instr. dept. neurology U. Utah, Salt Lake City, 1983-84, instr. dept. pathology, 1983-85, asst. prof. dept. neurology, 1984-89, faculty mem. program in neurosci., 1984—, asst. prof. dept. pathology, 1985-89, assoc. prof. depts. pathology, neurology, 1989—; coordinator Neurol. Diseases Tissue Ctr., U. Utah Med. Sch., 1983—; mem. research safety subcom. Research Adminstrn. Service, VA Med. Ctr., Salt Lake City, 1984-88, animal research subcom., 1984—, research and devel. com., 1986-89; grant reviewer NSF, 1984-85; mem. VA Merit rev. bd. for neurobiology; ad hoc mem. NIH site visit team, 1985. Reviewer Sci., Jour. Neuropathology and Exptl. Neurology, Infection and Immunity, Annals of Neurology, Jour. Infectious Diseases; contbr. articles to profl. jours., chpts. to books. founder, sec. Fairway Park Neighborhood Assn., Pacifica, Calif., 1979-81. Walter H. Beane Meml. scholar, 1970-74; Earl C. Anthony fellow U. Calif., 1980-81; recipient Nat. Research Service award U. Penn. Sch. Medicine, 1981-83, prin. investigator grant U. Utah, 1983-84, 1984-85, 1987, VA Merit Rev., 1985—, UHPHS grant, 1987—, Superior Performance award VA, 1985, 86, 87, 88. Mem. AAAS, Am. Assn. Neuropathologists, Am. Soc. Microbiology, Am. Soc. Neurologic Investigation, Am. Soc. Virology, N.Y. Acad. Scis., Soc. Exptl. Biology and Medicine, Sigma Xi. Roman Catholic. Home: 8126 S Scandia Circle Sandy UT 84093 Office: VA Med Ctr Neurovirol Rsch 500 Foothill Dr Salt Lake City UT 84148

STROTTMAN, KENNETH JAMES, marketing executive; b. Cin., Mar. 2, 1949; s. Louis Milton and Beatrice Ann (Oberle) S.; m. Barbara Jo Monch, June 2 1972; children: Kenneth Matthew, Charles Benjamin, Peter Lucas. BBA in Mktg., U. Notre Dame, 1971; MBA in Mktg., U. Cin., 1972. Brand mgr. Bristol-Myers Co., Cin., 1972-75; sales and mktg. mgr. Sunmark, Inc., St. Louis, 1975-76; group mktg. mgr. Borden, Inc., Chgo., 1976-80; v.p. mktg. Mattel, Inc., Hawthorne, Calif., 1980-83; pres. Strottman Mktg., Inc., Irvine, Calif., 1983-. Office: Strottman Mktg Inc 38 Corporate Park Irvine CA 92714

STROUB, STEPHEN FRANK, construction executive; b. Montclair, N.J., Mar. 8, 1948; s. Stephen N. Stroub and Alice (Zuch) Stroub Campbell. BS, Stockton State Coll., 1976. Owner, pres. Stroub Builders, Brigantine, N.J., 1976-82; real estate assoc. Lang Real Estate, Brigantine, 1978-81; owner, chief exec. officer Stroub Constrn., Inc., Sausalito, Calif., 1983—. Mem. Nat. Assn. Remodeling Industry, U.S. Yacht Racing Union, San Francisco Yacht Club. Home and Office: 254 Glen Dr Sausalito CA 94965

STROUP, ELIZABETH FAYE, librarian; b. Tulsa, Mar. 25, 1939; d. Milton Earl and Lois (Buhl) S. BA in Philosophy, U. Wash., 1962, MLS, 1964. Intern Libr. of Congress, Washington, 1964-65; asst. dir. North Cen. Regional Libr., Wenatchee, Wash., 1966-69; reference specialist Congl. Reference div. Libr. of Congress, Washington, 1970-71, head nat. collections Div. for the Blind and Physically Handicapped, 1971-73, chief Congl. Reference div., 1973-78, dir. gen. reference, 1978-88; city libr., chief exec. officer Seattle Pub. Libr., 1988—; cons. U.S. Info. Svc., Indonesia, Feb. 1987. Mem. adv. bd. KCTS 9 Pub. TV, Seattle, 1988—; bd. visitors Sch. Librarianship, U. Wash., 1988—; bd. dirs. Wash. Literacy, 1988—. Mem. ALA (pres. reference and adult svcs. div. 1986-87, div. bd. 1985-88), Wash. Libr. Assn., D.C. Libr. Assn. (bd. dirs. 1975-76), City Club, Ranier Club. Office: Seattle Pub Libr 1000 4th Ave Seattle WA 98104

STROZIER, WENDELL, nuclear medical technologist; b. St. Louis, Sept. 21, 1952; s. Harvey and Hattie Beatrice (Bell) S.; m. Juanita L. Watts, Sept. 1983. A.A., Los Angeles City Coll., 1977; B.S., Calif. State U., 1980; postgrad. U. Redlands, 1980-81; diploma Excel Security Acad., 1982. Distbr. Amway Products, Los Angeles, 1979-85; radiol. technologist USAFR, North AFB, Calif., 1974-78; nuclear medicine staff technologist NuclearMedico Services, Van Nuys, Calif., 1977-81, nuclear medicine mgr., Los Angeles, 1981; staff technologist Kaiser Permanente of West Los Angeles, 1982—; call technologist Meml. Hosp., Gardena, Calif., 1982—; regional mgr. A.L. Williams, 1985—; rep. Mass. Indemnity and Life Ins. Co. and First Am. Nat. Securities, Inc., 1986—; pres. The Akili Network; lectr. in field. Vol., UCLA Med. Ctr., 1979-80; counselor Watts Labor Community Action Com., 1982; union steward Local 399 Hosp. and Service Employees Union AFL-CIO, 1986—. Served with USAF, 1972-73. Mem. Soc. Nuclear Medicine, Am. Mgmt. Assn., Am. Legion, NRA (cert. instr.). Club: Kaiser Employee. Home: PO Box 88184 Los Angeles CA 90009 Office: 2310 La Cienaga Blvd Los Angeles CA 90019

STRUCK, JEANNE PATRICIA, teacher; b. Peabody, Mass., Aug. 14, 1935; d. Sheldon Reynold Bishop and Madelyn (Patten) Ginkel; m. Jerome Frederick Struck, Mar. 24, 1956; children: Timothy J., Michael A., Carrie J., Daniel P., Katherine A., Susan E. BS, Iowa State, 1958; MS, Drake U., 1979. Tchr. phys. edn. West Des Moines (Iowa) Community Sch., 1971-75, educator spl. needs, 1975-88, coach synchio swim, 1971-88; coach synchio swim Des Moines Aquamaids, 1979-88; judgenorth zone U.S. Synchro Swim, Indpls, 1982—; nat. meet mgr. U.S. Synchro Swim, Inc., Indpls., 1982—, nat. bd. review, 1985—; dept. chair Valley High Sch., West Des Moines, 1979-88, curriculum coun., 1986-88. Mem. platform com. Rep. Party, Polk Co., 1984—; pres. West Des Moines Coun. of Sch., 1970; PTA pres., 1969; mem. Community Edn. Adv. Coun., 1986-72. Named Coach of Year Iowa Girls High Sch. Athletic Union, 1983. Mem. Nat. Edn. Assn., Iowa State Edn. Assn., West Des Moines Edn. Assn., Coun. for Exceptional Children, Assn. for Children Learning Disabilities. Home: 5936 Paseo Ventoso Tucson AZ 85715

STRUCK, MONTE LYNN VON, management consultant; b. LaGrange, Oreg., Jan. 28, 1950; s. Grant L. and Jennie I. (Perry) S.; m. Denise Lewis (div. 1986); 1 child, Jennifer. BA in Communications, Oreg. State U., 1972; BArch, U. Oreg., 1977. Agt. William Morris Agy., L.A., 1971-74; gen. mgr. KFMT Radio, LaGrande, 1974-77; v.p. Ketco Devel. Corp., Portland, Oreg., 1977-79; dir. comml. design constrn. Robert Randall Co., Portland, 1979-80; gen. mgr. DSDE Engrs./Designers, Portland, 1980-83; project adminstr. Project Mgmt. Svcs., Bellevue, Wash., 1983-84; dir. constrn. Plaid Pantry Food Stores, Portland, 1984-87; dir. ops. Project Mgmt. Group, Portland, 1987—; cons. in field. Mem. Jaycees (pres. LaGrande chpt. 1975). Republican. Mormon. Office: Project Mgmt Group 3853 SW Scholls Ferry Rd Portland OR 97221

STRUHL, STANLEY FREDERICK, real estate developer; b. Bklyn., Oct. 10, 1939; s. Isidore and Yvette (Miller) S.; BS with honors in Engring., UCLA, 1961, MBA in Data Processing, 1963; m. Patricia Joyce Wald, Feb. 26, 1966; children: Marc Howard, Lisa Lynn. Mem. tech. staff Hughes Aircraft Co., Fullerton, Calif., 1963-65; sr. assoc. Planning Research Corp., Los Angeles, 1965-70; mgr. corporate info. systems Logicon, Inc., Torrance, Calif., 1970-73; mgr. operations analysis System Devel. Corp., Santa Monica, Calif., 1973-77; gen. partner TST Developers, Canyon Country, Calif., 1977-81; pres. Struhl Enterprises, Inc., Northridge, Calif., 1977-85; owner Struhl Properties, Northridge, 1979—. Mem. planning sub. com. 12th council dist., Los Angeles, 1986—. Lic. real estate broker, Calif. Mem. Assn. For Computing Machinery, San Fernando Valley Bd. Realtors, Tau Beta Pi, Beta Gamma Sigma, Alpha Phi Omega. Home: 17074 Knapp St Northridge CA 91325

STRUNK, HAROLD KENNETH, insurance company executive; b. McCreary County, Ky., June 23, 1933; s. Obal Edmund and Matilda L. (New) S.; m. Nancy Lou Patton, June 12, 1954; children: Nancy Karen, Melanie Ann, Kenneth Wayne. Student, Ga. Inst. Tech., 1951-54; BA in Psychology, Calif. State U., Fullerton, 1967; M in Social Welfare, UCLA, 1969, MPH, 1970, DrPH, 1972. Asst. chief adult and child health Alameda County Health Dept., Oakland, Calif., 1972-74; exec. dir. United Found. Med. Care, San Francisco, 1974-78; project dir. PSRO Support Ctr. for Calif., San Francisco, 1974-78; exec. dir. Take Care Health Maintenance Orgn. div. Blue Cross, Oakland, 1978-80; sr. health planner Arabian Bechtel Corp., Ltd., Jubail, Saudi Arabia, 1980-82; hosp. adminstr. Saudi Arabian Ministry of Def., Dhahran, 1982-84, Nat. Med. Enterprises, Taif, Saudi Arabia, 1984-85; physician recruiter Hosp. Staffing Systems, Pleasanton, Calif., 1986-87; regional mgr. hosp. relations Blue Shield of Calif., San Francisco, 1987—. Contbr. articles to profl. jours. With U.S. Army, 1954-56; commdr. Med. Service Corps USNR, 1977—. Mem. Healthcare Execs. No. Calif., Assn. Mil. Surgeons U.S., Am. Pub. Health Assn., Naval Res. Assn., World Affairs Coun., Middle East Inst., Sigma Phi Epsilon. Republican. Presbyterian. Club: Commonwealth (San Francisco). Home: 4365 Clovewood Ln Pleasanton CA 94566 Office: Blue Shield of Calif 2 Northpoint San Francisco CA 94133

STRUTZEL, J(OD) C(HRISTOPHER), escrow company executive; b. L.A., Sept. 20, 1947; s. James Rudolph and Charlotte Elizabeth (Weiss) S.; m. Christine Melba Kemp, Dec. 28, 1969; children: Jason James, Jess Warren. BS in Bus. Mgmt., Calif. State U., Long Beach, 1970. Bellman Edgewater Hyatt House Hotel, Long Beach, 1970, night auditor, 1970-71; asst. mgr. Sands Resort Hotel, Palm Springs, Calif., 1971-72; gen. mgr. Sands Resort Hotel, Palm Springs, 1972-73; sales coordinator Bendix Home Systems, Santa Fe Springs, Calif., 1973-74; loan rep. J.E. Wells Fin. Co., L.A., 1974-75; v.p. Express Escrow Co., Huntington Beach, Calif., 1976-78; pres., chmn. bd., bd. dirs. Express Escrow Co., Westminster, Calif., 1978—; pres., chmn. bd., bd. dirs. Elsinore (Calif.) Escrow, Inc., 1977-79; bd. dirs. Sorrel Devel., Redondo Beach, Calif.; expert witness on escrow, litigation and cons., 1982—. Contbr. articles to trade publs. Campaign treas. Californians to Elect Ted Cook, 1982; bd. dirs. publicity chmn. Fountain Valley (Calif.) Youth Baseball, 1986-87. Recipient J.E. Wells Meml. award, 1988. Mem. Escrow Agts. Fidelity Corp. (bd. dirs. 1983—), Calif. Manufactured Housing Assn. (treas., bd. dirs. 1984-86), Calif. Manufactured Housing Inst. (bd. dirs. 1986—, treas. 1986-87, Polit. Action Com. Man of Yr. award 1988, Orange County chpt. Man of Yr. award 1988). Republican. Office: Express Escrow Co 14441 Beach Blvd Ste 100 Westminster CA 92683

STUART, DAVID EDWARD, anthropologist, columnist; b. Calhoun County, Ala., Jan. 9, 1945; s. Edward George and Avis Elsie (Densmore) S.; B.A. (Wesleyan Merit scholar 1965-66), W.VA. Wesleyan Coll., 1967; M.A. in Anthropology, U. N.Mex., 1970, Ph.D., 1972, postdoctoral student, 1975-76; m. Cynthia K. Morgan, June 14, 1971. Research assoc. Andean Center, Quito, Ecuador, 1970; continuing edn. instr. anthropology U. N.Mex., 1971, research archeologist Office Contract Archeology, 1974, research coordinator, 1974-77, asst. prof. anthropology, 1975-77, assoc. prof. anthropology, 1984—, asst. v.p. acad. affairs, 1987—; asst. prof. Eckerd Coll., St. Petersburg, Fla., 1972-74; cons. archeologist right-of-way div. Pub. Service Co. N.Mex., Albuquerque, 1977-78; cons. anthropologist Bur. Indian Affairs, Albuquerque, 1978, Historic Preservation Bur. N.Mex., Santa Fe, 1978-81, Nat. Park Service, 1980, Albuquerque Mus., 1981; sr. research assoc. Human Systems Research, Inc., 1981-83, Quivira Research Center, Albuquerque, 1984-86; bd. dirs. Table Ind. Scholars, 1979-83, pres., bd. dirs. Rio Grande Heritage Found., Albuquerque and Las Cruces, 1985-87; advisor Human Systems Research, Inc., Tularosa, N.Mex., 1978-80, Albuquerque Commn. on Hist. Preservation, 1984-86. Grantee Eckerd Coll., 1973, Historic Preservation Bur., 1978-80. Essayist award N.Mex. Humanities Council, 1986. Mem. Am. Anthrop. Assn., Royal Anthrop. Inst. Gt. Britain, N.Mex. Archeol. Council, N.Mex. Press Assn., Albuquerque Archeol. Soc. (pres. 1986-88), Descs. Signers Declaration Independence, Sigma Xi, Phi Kappa Phi. Presbyterian. Co-author: Archeological Survey: 4 Corners to Ambrosia, N.Mex., 1976, A Proposed Project Design for the Timber Management Archeological Surveys, 1978, Ethnoarcheological Investigations of Shepherding in the Pueblo of Laguna, 1983; Author: Prehistoric New Mexico, 1981, 2d edit., 1984, 3d edit., 1988, Glimpses of the Ancient Southwest, 1985, The Magic of Bandelier National Monument, 1989, others; columnist New Mexico's Heritage, 1983-87, others. Editor: Archeological Reports, No. 1, 1975, No. 2, 1981. Address: U NMex Dept Anthropology Albuquerque NM 87131

STUART, DOROTHY MAE, artist; b. Fresno, Calif., Jan. 8, 1933; d. Robert Wesley Williams and Maria Theresa (Gad) Tressler; m. Reginald Ross Stuart, May 18, 1952; children: Doris Lynne Stuart Willis, Darlene Mae Stuart Cavalletto, Sue Anne Stuart Peters. Student, Calif. State U., Fresno, 1952-53, Fresno City Coll., 1962-64. Artist, art judge, presenter demonstrations at schs., fairs and art orgns. Calif., 1962—. Graphics, oils and watercolor group shows include: M.H. De Young Mus., San Francisco, 1971, Charles & Emma Frye Mus., Seattle, 1971, Calif. State U.-Fresno tour Peoples Republic China, 1974. Winner 53 art awards, 1966—. Mem. Soc. Western Artists (bd. dirs. 1968-74, v.p. 1968-70), AAUW, Fresno Womens Trade Club (bd. dirs. 1986-89, pres. 1988-89), Fresno Art Ctr. Mus., Fresno Met. Mus., Native Daus Golden West Fresno. Republican. Home and Office: 326 S Linda Ln Fresno CA 93727

STUART, GERARD WILLIAM, JR., corporate executive; b. Yuba City, Calif., July 28, 1939; s. Gerard William and Geneva Bernice (Stuke) S.; student Yuba Jr. Coll., 1957-59, Chico State Coll., 1959-60; A.B., U. Calif., Davis, 1962; M.L.S., U. Calif., Berkeley, 1963; m. Lenore Frances Loroña, 1981. Rare book librarian Cornell U., 1964-68; bibliographer of scholarly collections Huntington Library, San Marino, Calif., 1968-73, head acquisitions librarian, 1973-75; sec.-treas., dir. Ravenstree Corp., 1969-80, pres., chmn. bd., 1980—; pres., chmn. bd. William Penn Ltd., 1981—. Lilly fellow Ind. U., 1963-64. Mem. Bibliog. Soc. Am., Phi Beta Kappa, Alpha Gamma Sigma, Phi Kappa Phi. Clubs: Rolls-Royce Owners; Grolier (N.Y.C.); Zamorano (Los Angeles). Home: 500 E Country Club Dr Yuma AZ 85365 Office: 2424 W 5th St Yuma AZ 85364

STUART, JERRY LEON, electronic engineering consultant; b. Tulsa, May 1, 1932; s. Leon Howard and Margaret Jane (Samson) S.; m. Donna Jane Wilson, Mar. 15, 1958; children: Laurel Lynn, Mara Jan. BS in Geophysical Engring., U. Tulsa, 1953; MS in Electrical Engring., Calif. Inst. Tech., 1955. Registered profl. engr., Calif. Research engr. Jet Propulsion Lab., Pasadena, Calif., 1955-60, sr. research engr., 1960-62, engring. group supr., 1962-66, research group supr., 1966-68; mem. tech. staff Jet Propulsion Lab., Pasadena, 1968-73; ind. cons. systems design Grass Valley, Calif., 1968—; cons. Biometric Specialties, Santa Ana, Calif., 1965-68, Beckman Instruments, Fullerton, 1967. Contbr. numerous articles to profl. jours.; patentee in field. Served with USN, 1951-57. U. Tulsa scholar, 1949; recipient Patent award NASA, Pasadena, 1972. Mem. IEEE. Republican. Home: 3817 Stanford Dr Oceanside CA 92056

STUART, ROBERT HENRY, professional services company executive; b. Artesia, N.Mex., Dec. 20, 1929; s. James Austin and Mary Ella (Hight) S.; m. Jane R. Hodgson, Apr. 5, 1958; children: Laura R., Elizabeth H., Anne M., M. Angela. BA, U. N.Mex., 1953; MBA, U. Ala., 1968. Chief tactical systems div. USAF Studies & Analyses, Pentagon, Washington, 1974-77; dir. analysis USAF Test and Evaluation, Kirtland AFB, N.Mex., 1977-79; dir. The BDM Corp., Albuquerque, 1979-83, asst. v.p., 1984-87, v.p., 1987—. Served to col. USAF, 1953-79. Mem. Ops. Rsch. Soc. Am., Mil. Ops. Rsch. Soc., Beta Gamma Sigma, Phi Delta Theta. Republican. Episcopalian. Home: 13548 Cedarbrook Ave NE Albuquerque NM 87111

STUBBERUD, ALLEN ROGER, engineering educator; b. Glendive, Mont., Aug. 14, 1934; s. Oscar Adolph and Alice Marie (LeBlanc) S.; m. May B. Tragus, Nov. 19, 1961; children: Peter A., Stephen C. B.S. in Elec. Engring, U. Idaho, 1956; M.S. in Engring, UCLA, 1958, Ph.D., 1962. From asst. prof. to assoc. prof. engring. UCLA, 1962-69; prof. elec. engring. U. Calif., Irvine, 1969—; assoc. dean engring. U. Calif., 1972-78, dean engring., 1978-83; chief scientist U.S. Air Force, 1983-85; dir. Electrical Communications and Systems Engring. div. NSF, 1987-88. Author: Analysis and Synthesis of Linear Time Variable Systems, 1964, (with others) Feedback and Control Systems, 1967; assoc. editor: IEEE Transaction on Automatic Control. Contbr. articles to profl. jours. Recipient USAF Exceptional Civilian Service medal, 1985. Fellow IEEE (centennial medal 1984), AIAA (assoc.), AAAS; mem. Ops. Research Soc. Am., Sigma Xi, Sigma Tau, Tau Beta Pi, Eta Kappa Nu. Home: 19532 Sierra Soto Rd Irvine CA 92715 Office: U Calif Dept Elec Engring Irvine CA 92717

STUBBLEFIELD, THOMAS MASON, agricultural economist, educator; b. Taxhoma, Okla., Apr. 16, 1922; s. Temple Roscoe and Martha Lacy (Acree) S.; BS, N.Mex. State U., 1948; MS, A. and M. Coll. Tex., 1951, PhD, 1956; postgrad. U. Ariz., 1954; m. Martha Lee Miller, Mar. 7, 1943; children: Ellen (Mrs. Richard Damron), Paula (Mrs. James T. Culbertson), Thommye (Mrs. Gary D. Zingsheim). Specialist cotton mktg. N.Mex. State U., 1948; extension economist, then asst. agrl. economist U. Ariz., Tucson, 1951-58, from assoc. prof. to prof., 1958-64, prof. and agrl. economist, 1964-83, emeritus prof., 1983—, acting asst. dir. agrl. expt. sta., 1966-68, asst. to dir. sta., 1973-74, chief party Brazil contract, 1968-70. Mem. Pima Council Aging, 1974-77, 83-89; chmn. adv. com. Ret. Sr. Vol. Program, Pima County, 1974-77, 80-89. Chmn. bd. Saguaro Home Found. With AUS, 1942-45. Mem. Soc. Range Mgmt. Author bulls. Home: 810 Calle Milu Tucson AZ 85706

STUBBS, DANIEL GAIE, management consultant; b. Charleston, S.C., Nov. 13, 1940; s. Daniel Hamer and Esther Virginia (Garlow) S.; m. Sherrill Ann Sloan, July 8, 1984; children: Kimberly, Allison, Don; student U. Fla., 1959-60; B.A., W.Va. U., 1965; postgrad. Temple U., 1965-67. Tchr., Sch. Dist. of Phila., 1965-67; rep. Am. Fedn. Tchrs., Washington, 1967; exec. sec. Calif. State Coll. Council, Am. Fedn. Tchrs., AFL-CIO, Los Angeles, 1967-68; rep. Am. Fedn. Tchrs., AFL-CIO, Los Angeles, 1968-69, dir. orgn. Balt. Tchrs. Union, 1969-70; employee relations specialist Calif. Nurses Assn., Los Angeles, 1971-72; exec. dir. United Nurses Assn. Calif., Los Angeles, 1972-74; labor relations cons. Social Services Union, Service Employees Internat. Union, Local 535, AFL-CIO, Los Angeles, 1974-76; exec. dir. Met. Riverside UniServ Unit, Calif. Tchrs. Assn., 1976-79, exec. dir. San Bernardino/Colton Uniserv Unit, 1979-80; gen. services adminstr. Housing Authority, City of Los Angeles, 1980-82; cons. Blanning & Baker Assocs., Tujunga, Calif., 1983-84; asst. exec. dir. adminstrv. services Los Angeles Housing Authority, 1984-86; mgmt. con., Los Angeles, 1986—; lectr. in field. Served with U.S. Army, 1961-62. Recipient W.Va. U. Waitman Barbe Prize for creative writing, 1965. Mem. So. Calif. Indsl. Relations Research Assn., Orange County Indsl. Relations Research Assn., Indsl. Relations Research Assn., UCLA Inst. Indsl Relations Assn., Soc. of Profls. in Dispute Resolution. Presbyterian. Club: Town Hall of Calif. Home: 3200 Fairesta St #11 La Crescenta CA 91214

STUBBS, RODNEY E., aerospace engineer; b. Denver, Oct. 27, 1946; s. Jack and Anita L. (Carter) S.; divorced 1981; children: R. Daryl, Ryan S.; m. Donna J. Smoot, June 17, 1981; children: Joan B., Jennifer E., Jill L., Kenneth B. BS in Engring. Scis., USAF Academy, 1968; MS in Ops. Rsch., Ariz. State U., 1972. Commd. 2d lt. USAF, 1968, advanced through grades to capt.; exec. officer DCS personnel USAF, Andrews AFB, Md., 1975-78; chief prog. control USAF, Elgin AFB, Fla., 1978-79; resigned USAF, 1979; integration planner Martin Marietta Strategic Systems, Denver, 1979-81; project engr., peacekeeper Martin Marietta Vandenberg (AFB) Ops., Calif., 1981-84; mgr. small intercontinental ballistic missile test Martin Marietta Strategic Systems, Denver, 1985-88; mgr. plans and adminstrn. Martin Marietta Comml. Titan Inc., Denver, 1988; mgr. total quality mgmt. Martin Marietta Space Launch Systems, Denver, 1989—. Author: ICBM Nuclear Hardness, 1970; contbr. articles to profl. jours. Coach and referee Columbine Soccer Assn., Littleton, Colo., 1984—. Home: 7292 S Moore Ct Littleton CO 80127 Office: Martin Marietta PO Box 179 MS-DC 1420 Denver CO 80201

STUBENBERG, JAMES ARTHUR, lawyer; b. Honolulu, Mar. 9, 1944; s. Arthur David and Ann Idell (Simms) S.; m. Lynne Elizabeth Wong, Feb. 4, 1983; children: Eric, Melissa, Seth. BBA, So. Meth. U., 1966; JD, Loyola Marymount U., 1970. Bar: Hawaii 1970, U.S. Supreme Ct. 1977. Sr. ptnr. Stubenberg, Shinn & Durrett, Honolulu, 1974—; bd. dirs. Swire Properties, Ltd., Honolulu, Dynasty Travel, Honolulu. Arbitrator Circle Ct. Hawaii, Honolulu, 1985—. Mem. ABA, Hawaii Bar Assn., Internat. Bar Assn., Am. Judicature Soc., Waikiki Yacht. Club. Democrat. Congregationalist. Office: Stubenberg Shinn & Durrett 1250 Pauahi Tower 1001 Bishop St Honolulu HI 96813

STUDLEY, HELEN ORMSON, artist, poet, writer, designer; b. Elroy, Wis., Sept. 8, 1937; d. Clarence Ormson and Hilda (Johnson) O.; m. William Frank Studley, Aug. 1965 (div. 1981); 1 son, William Harrison. Owner RJK Original Art, Sherman Oaks, Calif., 1979—; designer Aspen Series custom greeting cards and stationery notes, lithographs Love is All Colors, 1982; represented in numerous pub. and pvt. collections throughout U.S., Can., Norway, Sweden, Austria, Germany, Eng., France; author poetry Love is Care, Changes, 1988. Active Luth. Brotherhood, Emmanuel Luth. Ch. Honors include display of lithograph Snow Dreams, Snow Queens at 1980 Winter Olympics, Lake Placid, N.Y., lithograph Summer Dreams, Summer Queens at 1984 Summer Olympics, Los Angeles; named finalist in competition for John Simon Guggenheim fellowship. Mem. Soc. Illustrators, Am. Watercolor Soc., Internat. Soc. Artists, Internat. Platform Assn., Calif. Woman's Art Guild. Club: Sons of Norway. Office: RJK Original Art 5020 Hazeltine Ave Sherman Oaks CA 91423

STUKALO, CAROL JOAN, educational administrator; b. Placerville, Calif., Aug. 26, 1935; d. Austin Frank and Carolina (Watt) McLellan; m. Gary Walter Highley, Aug. 13, 1955 (div. July 1972); children: Kathryn Marie, Linda Jean; m. Clifford Victor Stukalo, June 21, 1975. AB, Calif. State U., Chico, 1958; MA, Calif. State U., Sacramento, 1983. Cert. gen. elem. credential, learning handicapped and severely handicapped credential, resource specialist. Tchr. Corning (Calif.) Elem. Sch., 1958-59, Tahoe-Truckee Unified Sch., Kings Beach, Calif., 1960-62; tchr., math coordinator Camino (Calif.) Elem. Sch., 1967-76; tchr. spl. edn. El Dorado County Office Edn., Placerville, 1980-82, math cons., 1970-75; resource specialist Pioneer Elem. Sch., Somerset, Calif., 1982—; instr. U. Calif., Davis, part-time 1969-72. Co-author metric activity cards. Vice pres. El Dorado County Friends Abused Children, 1984-85. Named Outstanding Sol. Edn. Tchr. El Dorado County, Spl. Edn. Local Plan Area, 1984, Calif. State U., Chico scholar, 1982. Mem. Council for Exceptional Children (chpt. pres. 1987-88), Internat. Reading Assn., Delta Kappa Gamma (area dir. 1987—), Pi Lambda Theta. Democrat. Lutheran. Home: PO Box 760 Diamond Springs CA 95619 Office: PO Box 8 Somerset CA 95684

STULL, MICHAEL RAY, manufacturing executive; b. Elkhart, Ind., May 13, 1959; s. Raymond Dean and Sharon Kay (Wright) S. BS, Purdue U., 1985; postgrad., Pepperdine U., 1988--. Foreman Young Door Co., Plymouth, Ind., 1985; prodn. control coordinator McDonnell Douglas Aircraft Co., Torrance, Calif., 1985-86, prodn. control mgr., 1986-88, customer rep. C17 program, 1988--. Republican. Methodist. Home: care Larsons Marina 1046 S Seaside Ave Terminal Island CA 90731 Office: McDonnell Douglas M/C C6-54 Normandie & 190th Torrance CA 90501

STULTS, MARION BERDETTE, electrical engineer; b. Huntington, Ind., Aug. 23, 1925; s. Earle Waldorf Stults and Neta Bernice (Decker) Ball; m. Ruth Freida Uhlig, Feb. 14, 1953 (dec. July 1968); children: Rick David, Rebecca Lea; m. Susan Anne Knust, Jan. 31, 1970; children: Molly Kay, Sarah Lynn. BSEE, Ind. Inst. Tech., 1956. Engr. Internat. Telephone and Telegraph, Ft. Wayne, Ind., 1956-60; sr. engr. Sperry Phoenix (Ariz.) Co., 1960-62; sr. electronic engr. Kaiser Aero and Electric Corp., Phoenix, 1962-68; head quality and reliability engring. Atlantic Research Corp., Green River, Utah, 1968-69; sr. reliability engr. Magnavox Corp., Ft. Wayne, 1969-74; sr. electronic engr. U.S. Army Info. Systems Engring., Ft. Huachuca, Ariz., 1974-88; prin. engr. Bell Tech. Ops., Sierra Vista, Ariz., 1988—. Mem. Bisbee (Ariz.) Arts and Humanities Council, 1985-88; chaplain Bisbee Gideons, 1980-83; pres. Full Gospel Businessmen, Bisbee, 1985-86. Served with USMC, 1942-49, PTO. Democrat. Methodist. Lodges: Elks, Lions. Home: 132 Calle de Rosas Bisbee AZ 85603 Office: Bell Tech Ops 999 E Fry Blvd Sierra Vista AZ 85635

STUMBLES, JAMES RUBIDGE WASHINGTON, multinational company executive; b. Salisbury, Zimbabwe, Aug. 13, 1939; came to U.S., 1980; s. Albert R.W. and Mary Dallas (Atherstone) S.; m. Vyvienne Clare Shaw, Dec. 19, 1964; children: Christopher, Timothy, Jonathan. BA, U. Cape Town, Republic of South Africa, 1960, LLB, 1962. Adv. Supreme Ct. of S. Africa. Mng. dir. Pritchard Services Group of South Africa, Johannesburg, 1972-80; dir. security, pres. subs. security cos. Pritchard Services Group Am., Columbus, Ohio, 1980-83; sr. v.p., pres. subs. Mayne Nickless/ Loomis Corp., Seattle, 1984-87; v.p. N.W. Protective Svc. Inc., Seattle, 1987—. Sec. Boy Scouts, Johannesburg, 1978-80. Episcopalian. Clubs: Rand (Johannesburg), Mercer Island (Wash.) Country. Lodges: Rotary, Kiwanis, Round Table (officer 1969-80). Office: NW Protective Svc Inc 2700 Elliott Way Seattle WA 98101

STUMMAN, RUSSELL GEORGE, accountant; b. Mar. 7, 1955; s. Henry Edward and Gwendolyn May (Baxter) S.; m. Beverly Elizabeth Schafer, May 5, 1984. BS, San Diego State U., 1979. Acctg. mgr. JC Systems, Inc., San Diego, 1979--; cons. RGS Svcs., San Diego, 1984--. Mem. Am. Mgmt. Assn. (assoc.), Am. Inst. Profl. Bookkeepers, Zool. Soc. San Diego. Office: JC Systems Inc 11175 Flintkote Ave San Diego CA 92121

STUMP, BOB, congressman; b. Phoenix, Apr. 4, 1927; s. Jesse Patrick and Floy Bethany (Fields) S.; children: Karen, Bob, Bruce. B.S. in Agronomy, Ariz. State U., 1951. Mem. Ariz. Ho. of Reps., 1957-67; mem. Ariz. Senate, 1967-76, pres., 1975-76; mem. 95th-101st Congresses from 3d Ariz. Dist., 1976—; mem. numerous govt. coms. With USN, 1943-46. Mem. Am. Legion, Ariz. Farm Bur. Republican. Seventh-day Adventist. Office: 211 Cannon House Office Bldg Washington DC 20515 also: 230 N First Ave Rm 5001 Phoenix AZ 85025

STUMP, D. MICHAEL, librarian; b. Santa Monica, Calif., Dec. 22, 1947; s. H. Walter and Margaret June (Stetler) S. B.A. in History, Pasadena Coll., 1971; M.L.S., U. So. Calif., 1977. Library asst. Calif. Inst. Tech., Pasadena, Calif., 1970-74; librarian First Baptist Ch. of Van Nuys, Calif., 1974-81, 1982-87, Laurence/2000, Van Nuys, 1981-82; Van Nuys Christian Coll., 1975-76, Hillcrest Christian Sch., Granada Hills, Calif., 1987—. Asst. scoutmaster San Fernando council Boy Scouts Am., 1970-73. Named to Outstanding Young Men Am. U.S. Jaycees, 1976. Mem. Spl. Libraries Assn., Am. Assn. Sch. Librarians, Evang. Ch. Library Assn. (So. Calif. chpt.). Republican. Baptist. Office: Hillcrest Christian Sch 17531 Rinaldi St Granada Hills CA 91344

STURETT, MICHAEL STEVEN, laser engineering manager; b. Canton, OH, Mar. 5, 1950; s. Angelo Joseph and Florence Ellen (Casteel) S.; m. Cynthia Kay Mercier, Mar. 18, 1972; children: Todd, Jeff. BS in Elec. Tech., Akron U., 1972. Project engr. Marlite Div. Masonite, Dover, Ohio, 1972-73; test engr. supr. Diebold Inc., Newark, Ohio, 1973-75; quality control engr. Diebold Inc., Newark, 1975-76, product liaison engr., 1976-78, mfr. engr. leader, 1978-80; sr. product engr. Micro-Rel/Medtronic, Tempe, 1982—, laser trim engr., 1982—. Team mgr. Mesa (Ariz.) Southwestern Little League, 1983—, pres., 1985-86, , Mesa Parent Youth Athletic Assn., 1987. Mem. Internat. Soc. Microelectronics. Club: Motorola 4-Wheel. Office: Micro-Rel/Medtronic 2343 W 10th Pl Tempe AZ 85281

STURGULEWSKI, ARLISS, state senator; b. Blaine, Wash., Sept. 27, 1927; B.A., U. Wash. Mem. Assembly Municipality of Anchorage; vice chmn. New Capital Site Planning Commn., mem. Capital Site Selection Com.; chmn. Greater Anchorage Area Planning and Zoning Commn.; mem. Alaska State Senate, 1978—. Rep. nominee Office Gov. Alaska, 1986. Address: Alaska State Senate Juneau AK 99811

STUTZ, DERRYL LANDRATH, aerospace engineer; b. Chgo., Dec. 21, 1948; s. Louis Fred and Louise Martha (Dennis) S.; m. Kompat Jantakud, Mar. 15, 1975 (div. 1986); children: Peter, Nancy; m. Chuenjit Jantakud, Dec. 30, 1986. BS in Aerospace Engring., U. Ill., Chgo., 1971; postgrad., Def. Lang. Inst., Monterey, Calif., 1972. CIRIS engr., 6585 Test Group, Guidance div. U.S. Dept. Defense, Holloman AFB, N.M., 1983-87; adv. ref. sys. devel. engr., 6585 Test Group, Guidance div. U.S. Dept. Defense, Holloman AFB, 1987—. Contbr. articles to profl. jours. Capt. USAF, 1971-83. Decorated Vietnam Gallantry Cross, Air Force Commendation medal. Mem. AIAA. Office: 6585 Test Group/GDE Holloman AFB NM 88330-5000

STYLES, BEVERLY, entertainer; b. Richmond, Va., June 6, 1923; d. John Harry Kenealy and Juanita Russell (Robins) Carpenter; m. Wilbur Cox, Mar. 14, 1942 (div.); m. Robert Marascia, Oct. 5, 1951 (div. Apr. 1964). Studies with Ike Carpenter, Hollywood, Calif., 1965—; student, Am. Nat. Theatre Acad., 1968-69; studies with Paula Raymond, Hollywood, 1969-70. Freelance performer, musician, 1947-81; owner Beverly Styles Music, Joshua Tree, Calif., 1971—. Composer (sheet music) Joshua Tree, 1975, I'm Thankful, 1978, Color Chods, 1989; records include The Perpetual Styles of Beverly, 1978, Wow, Wow, Wow, 1986; performer (album) The Primitive Styles of Beverly, 1977. Mem. ASCAP (Gold Pin award), Am. Fedn. Musicians. Republican. Office: PO Box 615 Joshua Tree CA 92252-0615

STYRT, PAUL JOSEPH, orthodontist; b. Encino, Calif., Oct. 8, 1958; s. Robert Jay and Florence Gail (Rudnick) S. BA, U. Calif., San Diego, 1980; MPH, Harvard U., 1985, Doctor of Dental Medicine, 1985; MS, UCLA, 1988. Cert. Orthodontics and Pedodontics, 1988. Research assoc. U. Calif., La Jolla, 1978-79, academic tutor, 1979-80; research assoc. Sch. of Dental Medicine Harvard U., Cambridge, Mass., 1984-85; staff dentist, scholar Neuropsychiatric Inst. UCLA, 1985-86; resident in pediatric dentistry U. Calif., Los Angeles, 1985-86, sr. orthodontic resident, 1986-87; pvt. practice in orthodontics and pediatric dentistry Univ. Towne Dental Group, San Diego, 1987—. Vol. Los Angeles Multiple Sclerosis Soc., 1988, Boston Multiple Sclerosis Soc., 1983-85, Physicians for Social Responsibility, Boston and Los Angeles, 1984-85, 85-88. W.K. Kellog Found. fellow Harvard U., 1984-85. Mem. Am. Assn. Orthodontists, Am. Acad. Pediatric Dentistry, Am. Soc. Dentistry for Children, Am. Acad. Dental Radiology, Pacific Coast Soc. Orthodontists, Alpha Omega. Republican. Jewish. Office: 5627 Oberlin Dr #100 San Diego CA 92121

SU, SHIAW-DER, nuclear engineer; b. Tainan, Republic of China, Jan. 20, 1945; came to U.S., 1969; s. Hsin-Chun and King-New (Chen) S.; m. Shi-Ju Wang, June 30, 1968; children: Eastor Y., Wesley Y. BS, Nat. Tsing Hua U., Republic of China, 1968; MS, Purdue U., 1971. Registered profl. nuclear engr., Calif. Engr. Burns & Roe Inc., Oradell, N.J., 1971-72; prin. Gen. Atomics, San Diego, Calif., 1972—. Mem. Am. Nuclear Soc., Sigma Xi (assoc.). Home: 12870 Pine Meadow Ct San Diego CA 92130 Office: Gen Atomics PO Box 85608 San Diego CA 92138

SU, YUNCAI, management executive; b. Pangkalpinang, Bangka, Indonesia, Feb. 6, 1938; came to U.S., 1980; s. Hon Djin Su and Nyo Moi Chen; m. Guiming Li, Apr. 9, 1966. BS, Beijing Petroleum Inst., China, 1963-68; postgrad., Columbia U., N.Y.C., 1982-84. Researcher Beijing (China) Petroleum Acad. Sci. & Rsch., 1963-70; engr. Jing Men Refinery, Hubei, China, 1970-76, Luoyang Petroleum Sci. & Design Inst., Honan, China, 1976-78; engr. Mineral Petroleum Industry div. Bur. Fgn. Affairs, Beijing, 1978-80; engr. China Nat. Offshore Oil Corp., Beijing, 1980-82, mgr., 1984-85; div. chief China Internat. Trust & Investment Corp., Beijing, 1985-86; pres. Citifor, Inc., Seattle, 1986—; participant Exec. Program for Internat. Mgr., N.Y.C. 1980, summer assoc.; vis. scholar Columbua U. Bus. Sch., N.Y.C., 1982-84. Mem. China Petroleum Sci. Assn., Columbia Tower Club (Seattle). Office: Citifor Inc 701 Fifth Ave Seattle WA 98014

SUAREZ, CARLOS WILLIAM, microcomputer consulting company executive; b. Havana, Cuba, June 25, 1960; came to U.S., 1960; s. Ernesto and Marta (Inferian) S. BS in Aero. Engring., Ga. Inst. Tech., 1982; MS in Mech. Engring., Stanford U., 1985. Pres. MacMemory, Inc., San Jose, Calif., 1985-87, Suarez Cons. Co., Cupertino, Calif., 1988—. Served with USN, 1978-80. Mem. Am. Electronics Assn. Democrat. Office: Suarez Cons Co 1996C Olivewood Dr Cupertino CA 95014

SUAREZ, OSCAR, insurance company executive; b. Havana, Cuba, Aug. 31, 1955; came to U.S., 1961; s. Oscar and Consuelo Suarez; m. Beverly A. Teague, Dec. 30, 1977 (div. Aug. 1986); children: Holly Amber, Gabriel Oscar; m. Wendy L. Sherratt. B of Acctg., Fla. Atlantic U., 1977; M of Acctg., U. Denver, 1979. Auditor WOMETCO Enterprises, Miami, Fla., 1977-78; dir. auditing Blue Cross/Blue Shield of Colo., Denver, 1980-81; asst. v.p. auditing Gt.-West Life Assurance Co., Englewood, Colo., 1982-89; asst. v.p.-individual fin. Gt. West Life Assurance Co., Englewood, 1989—. Bd. dirs. Arapahoe Retarded Citizens Assn., 1988—. Mem. Inst. Internal Auditors (cert., sec. Denver chpt. 1981-82, treas. 1982-83, v.p. 1983-84, pres. 1984-85, bd. dirs. 1981-85, 86—), Colo. Assn. Commerce and Industry. Roman Catholic. Home: 7489 S Ivy Way Englewood CO 80112 Office: Great-West Life Assurance Co 8515 E Orchard Rd Englewood CO 80111

SUAREZ-ROGERS, BARBARA JEANNE, pathology supervisor; b. Detroit, Jan. 3, 1938; d. Henry Walter and Vera Kathleen (Cole) Rogers; m. Ralph John Suarez (dec. 1975); children: William, Charles, Michael, Robert. Student, U. Paris, 1984, Wayne State U., 1984; AA, Harbor Coll., 1985. Supr., instructional coordinator Harbor UCLA Med. Ctr., Torrance, Calif., 1974—; owner Photos by Rogers, 1960-65; photo colorist Van Gogh Studio, Chgo. Office: Harbor UCLA Med Ctr 1000 W Carson Torrance CA 90509

SUAZO, LAWRENCE ERIC, dentist, military officer; b. Bethal, Alaska, May 1, 1961; s. Victor Leonard and Caroline (Trujillo) S.; m. Sandra Rue Mars. Student, U. N.Mex., 1983; DDS, U. Mo., Kansas City, 1987. Pvt. practice Durango, Colo., 1987-88; commd. lt. U.S. Navy, 1988; dentist br. dental clinic Naval Air Sta., Lemoore, Calif., 1988--. Mem. ADA, Colo. Dental Assn., San Juan Dental Soc., Am. Student Dental Assn., Acad. Gen. Dentistry. Democrat. Office: Naval Air Sta Br Dental Clinic Lemoore CA 93246

SUBACH, JAMES ALAN, infosystems company executive, consultant; b. Lawrence, Mass., Mar. 24, 1948; s. Anthony John and Bernice Ruth (Pekarski) S. m. Marilyn Butler, Feb. 16, 1980. BS with distinction, U. Maine, 1970; MS, U. Ariz., 1975, PhD, 1979. Vis. scientist NASA Johnson Space Ctr., Houston, 1977-79; rsch. assoc. Baylor Coll. Medicine, Houston, 1977-79; pres. Subach Ventures, Inc., San Antonio, 1980-84, JAS & Assocs., Inc., Phoenix, 1984—, C.I.O., Inc., Phoenix, 1987—. Assoc. editor Jour. Applied Photog. Engring., 1973-78; author software Gen. Acctg. System, 1987; bus. computing columnist, 1987. Pres. Forest Trails Homeowners Assn., Phoenix, 1987-88. Mem. Toastmasters (treas. Phoenix 1984), Tau Beta Pi, Sigma Pi Sigma. Republican. Office: CIO Inc 3615 N 16th St Ste 4 Phoenix AZ 85016

SUBRAMANIAN, SUNDARAM, electronics engineer; b. Emaneswaram, Madras, India, July 9, 1934; came to U.S., 1968; s. Sundaram and Velammal (Subbiah) S.; m. Hemavathy Vadivelu, Feb. 18, 1968; children: Anand Kumar, Malathy. BE, Madras (India) U., 1959; PhD, Glasgow (Scotland) U., 1967; MBA, Roosevelt U., Chgo., 1977. Research engr. Zenith, Inc., Chgo., 1968-75; project engr. Motorola, Inc., Chgo., 1975-77; prof. Chapman Coll., Orange, Calif., 1977-78; cons. MCS, Orange, 1978-80; project engr. Endevco, San Juan Capistrano, Calif., 1980-84; project mgr. Unisys Corp., Rancho Santa Margarita, Calif., 1984—; bd. dirs. P.S.B. Inc., Torrance, Calif., 1984—. Patentee in field. Bd. dirs. Tamil Nadu Found. Inc., Balt. and Washington, 1976-79; pres. S. India Cultural Assn., Villa Park, Calif., 1977-78. Mem. IEEE, Inst. Environ. Sci. (sr.). Office: Unisys Corp 30200 Bandaras Rancho Santa Margarita CA 92688

SUBRAMANYA, SHIVA, aerospace systems engineer; b. Hole-Narasipur, India, Apr. 8, 1933; s. S.T. Srikantaiah and S. Gundamma; m. Lee. S. Silva, Mar. 3, 1967; children: Paul Kailas, Kevin Shankar. BSc, Mysore U., Bangalore, India, 1956; MSc, Karnatak U., Dharwar, India, 1962; postgrad., Clark U., 1963; MBA, Calif. State U., Dominguez Hills, 1973; D in Bus. Adminstrn., PhD in Bus. Adminstrn., Nova U., 1986. Sr. scientific officer AEC, Bombay, India, 1961-63; chief engr. TEI, Newport, R.I., 1964-67; prin. engr. Gen. Dynamics Corp., San Diego, 1967-73; asst. project mgr. def. and systems group TRW, Colorado Springs, Colo., 1973-87; asst. project mgr. space and def. group TRW, Redondo Beach, Calif., 1987—. Contbr. over 100 articles to profl. jours. V.p. VHP of Am., Berlin, Conn., 1984-88; pres. IPF of Am., Redondo Beach, 1981-88; appointed to Atomic Energy Commn., India. Mem. Armed Forces Communications and Electronics Assn. (v.p.-elect Rocky Mountain chpt. 1986—, Meritorious service award 1985), Am. Acad. Mgmt. Hindu. Home: 2115 Shelburne Way Torrance CA 90503 Office: TWR Def and Space Group 1 Space Park Redondo Beach CA 90278

SUCRE, VICTOR WILLY, musician; b. La Paz, Bolivia, Aug. 18, 1950; came to U.S., 1971; s. Jose Sucre Pozo and Rogelia (Varas) Sucre; m. Sarah McClellan Hartshorne, Feb. 26, 1974; children: Gabriel Benjamin, Nicolas Andrew, Peter Emmanuel. Diploma, Principe de Paz, La Paz, 1970. Violinist, violist Nat. Symphony Bolivia, La Paz, 1964-71; violist Can. Symphony Orch., Montreal, Que., Can., 1972-74, Calgary (Alta., Can.) Philharm., 1975-76, N.Mex. Symphony Orch., Albuquerque, 1976-78, 81—; conductor Albuquerque Philharmonia, 1976-87; violist, conductor La Paz Chamber Orch., 1978-79.

SUDDOCK, FRANCES SUTER THORSON, educator; b. Estelline, S.D., Oct. 23, 1914; d. William Henry and Anna Mary (Oakland) Suter; m. Carl Edwin Thorson, July 6, 1941 (dec. Apr. 1976); children: Sarah Thorson Little, Mary Frances; m. Edwin Matthew Suddock, Aug. 7, 1982 (dec. 1986). BA, U. No. Iowa, 1936; postgrad., Syracuse U., 1940-41, U. Iowa, 1946; MA, Antioch U., San Francisco, 1981. Cert. tchr. Tchr. various high schs., Correctionville and Eagle Grove, Iowa, 1936-38, 38-40, 41-43, 45-47; chief clk. War Price and Rationing Bd., Eagle Grove, 1943-45; instr. (part time) Eagle Grove Jr. Coll., 1953-61; adminstr. Eagle Grove Pub. Library, 1961-77; tchr. Will Schutz Assocs., Muir Beach, Calif., 1987—; facilitator indep. grief workshops, Anchorage, 1989—. Keynote speaker Nat. Widowed Persons Conf. of Am. Assn. Retired Persons, 1988. Vol., trainer widowed persons svc. Am. Assn. Retired Persons, 1989—, retired sr. vol. program, Anchorage, 1988—; bd. dirs. Mental Health Ctr. N. Iowa, Mason City, Iowa, 1959-76; Eagle Grove Community Chest, 1960, Help Line, Inc., Ft. Dodge, Iowa, 1976-77; chmn. Community Mental Health Fund, Eagle Grove, 1966-73; charter pres. Eagle Grove Concerned, Inc., 1973-77, active various civic drives. Mem. Am. Soc. on Aging, Alaska Assn. of Gerontology, PEO, Kappa Delta Pi. Home: 333 'M' St Apt 404 Anchorage AK 99501

SUDDUTH, CHARLES GRAYSON, geotechnical engineer; b. Oxnard, Calif., Sept. 16, 1935; s. Charles Franklin and Leilla Eunice (Johnson) S. B.S., U. So. Calif., 1958, M.S., 1963, M.P.A., 1979. Registered profl. engr., Calif. Civil engring. asst. Los Angeles County Flood Control Dist., Los Angeles, 1963-64, sr. civil engring. asst., 1964-65, civil engring. assoc., 1965-66, assoc. civil engr., 1967-70; civil engr. II, Los Angeles County, 1970-80, supervising civil engr. III, 1980—; mem. Geotech. Engring. Application Rev. Com., Sacramento, 1987-88; Geotech. Engring. Tech. Adv. Com., Sacramento, 1988—; Calif. Bd. Registration Profl. Engrs., Land Surveyors. Mem. ASCE (Daniel Mead prize for assoc. mems. 1971), Assn. Engring. Geologists, Am. Pub. Works Assn., Am. Water Works Assn., Nat. Soc. Profl. Engrs., Calif. Soc. Profl. Engrs. Presbyterian. Home: 1851 Boca Ave Los Angeles CA 90032 Office: Dept Pub Works LA County 900 S Vermont Ave Alhambra CA 91803

SUDEKUM, WILLIAM ANTHONY, JR., military officer; b. Nashville, Sept. 9, 1949; s. William Anthony Sr. and Muriel May (Breaux) S.; m. Jo Anne Tavel, May 15, 1971; 1 child: Bradley Allan. BS in Edn., Memphis State U., 1971; postgrad., Chapman Coll., 1987—. Commd. 2d lt. USAF, 1971, advanced through ranks to maj., 1983; student navigator USAF, Mather AFB, Calif., 1972-73; instr. navigator USAF, Minot AFB, N.D., 1973-78; evaluator navigator USAF, RAF Mildenhall, Eng., 1978-81, wing exec. officer, 1981-82; br. chief mission devel. USAF, Beale AFB, Calif., 1982-85, wing inspections officer, 1985-87, div. chief logistics plans, 1987—. Bd. dirs. Yuba-Sutter United Way, Marysville, Calif, 1988—; coach youth soccer league; coach, umpire Little League Baseball. Mem. Air Force Assn., Yuba-Sutter C. of C. (exec. bd.). Roman Catholic.

SUDLER, BARBARA WELCH, historical society administrator; b. Honolulu, Apr. 20, 1925; d. Leo F. and Barbara Lloyd (Petrikin) Welch; m. James Stewart Sudler, Dec. 30, 1950 (dec. 1982); children—Eleanor, James S.; m. William H. Hornby, Oct. 22, 1983. B.A., U. Colo., 1944. Exec. adminstr. Historic Denver, 1974-79; exec. dir. Colo. Hist. Soc., Denver, 1979-81, pres., 1981—; historic preservation officer State of Colo., Denver, 1983—; dir. Women's Bank, Denver. Editor: Nothing Is Long Ago, 1975. Bd. dirs. Denver Symphony Assn., 1983-86, Met. State Coll. Found; mem. Colo. Tourism Adv. Bd. Recipient Soroptimist award, 1980, Contbn. to

Arts award Big Sisters, 1981, Contbns. to Community award AIA, 1982, Community Service award U. Colo., 1986, James Grafton Rogers award, 1987. Mem. Am. Antiquarian Soc., Nat. Conf. State Historic Preservation Officers, Colo. Hist. Records Commn., Colo. Commn. on Bicentennial of Constitution, Martin Luther King Jr. Holiday Commn. Republican. Episcopalian. Clubs: Denver Country, University. Lodge: Rotary. Home: 180 High St Denver CO 80218 Office: State Hist Soc Colo 1300 Broadway St Denver CO 80203

SUDOLCAN, CATHERINE ELEAINE, artist; b. Glendale, Calif., Aug. 14, 1953; d. Joseph Jack Sudolcan and Betty Eleaine (Budway) Stanley; m. Michael Anthony Buttitta, Apr. 1, 1978 (div. Apr. 1982). Student, Pierce Jr. Coll., 1971-75, Am. Animation Inst., North Hollywood, Calif., 1982-83, Otis/Parsons, Los Angeles, 1984—, UCLA, 1985—. With animation dept., painter Hanna-Barbera Studios, Hollywood, Calif., 1977-78, Ralph Bakshi Prodns., Hollywood, 1978; visual effects artist Universal Studios, Universal City, Calif., 1978-85; visual effects artist, ops. mgr. Illusion Arts, Inc., Van Nuys, Calif., 1985—; instr. aerobics Family Fitness Ctr., Beverly Hills, Calif., 1983-86; prodn. asst. Group Repertory Theatre, 1985; free-lance theatrical costume designer, 1985—; accessories designer Catherine's Masquerade, Los Angeles, 1987—. Patron mem. Los Angeles County Mus. Art, 1988—. Profiled as illusionist, La Style Mag., May, 1987. Mem. Motion Picture Screen Cartoonists. Home: 595 S Ogden Dr Los Angeles CA 90036 Office: Illusion Arts Inc 7002 Sophia Ave Van Nuys CA 91406

SUE, ALAN KWAI KEONG, dentist; b. Honolulu, Apr. 26, 1946; s. Henry Tin Yee and Chiyoko (Ohata) S.; m. Ginger Kazue Fukushima, Mar. 11, 1972; 1 child, Dawn Marie. BS in Chemistry with honors, U. Hawaii, 1968; BS, U. Calif., San Francisco, 1972, DDS, 1972. Film editor, photographer Sta. KHVH-TV ABC, Honolulu, 1964-71; staff dentist Strong-Carter Dental Clinic, Honolulu, 1972-73; dentist Waianae Dental Clinic, Honolulu, 1972-73; pvt. practice Pearl City, Hawaii, 1973—; dental dir. Hawaii Dental Health Plan, Pearl City, 1987—; dental cons. Calif. Dental Health Plan, Tustin, 1987—; mem. exec. bd. St. Francis Hosp., Honolulu, 1976-78, chief dept. dentistry, 1976-78. Mem. West. Honolulu Sub-Area Health Planning Coun., 1981-84; mem. plan devel. com. Hawaii Statewide Health Coordinating Coun., Hawaii, 1981-84; mem. dental task force Hawaii Statewide Health Coordinating Coun., 1980; vol. oral cancer sreening program Am. Cancer Soc.; v.p. Pearl City Shopping Ctr. Merchants Assn., 1975-84. Regent's scholar U. Calif., San Francisco, 1968-72. Fellow Acad. Gen. Dentistry; mem. ADA, Hawaii Dental Assn. (bd. trustee 1978-80), Pierre Fauchard Acad., Honolulu County Dental Soc. (pres. 1982), Porsche Club (Honolulu), Pantera Owners Club, Mensa Club, Mercedes Benz Club. Democrat. Office: Dental Image Specialists 850 Kam Hwy Ste 116 Pearl City HI 96782

SUE, LAWRENCE GENE, statistician; b. Portland, Oreg., Sept. 22, 1939; s. Henry Lock Sue and Dorothy Helen (Wong) Chung. BS in Math., Brigham Young U., 1967, MS in Statistics, 1973. Assoc. engr. Boeing Co., Seattle, 1967-69; math. statistician Ultrasystems Inc., Hill AFB, Utah, 1974-77; mem. tech. staff TRW Systems, Hill AFB, 1977-81; sr. staff engr. Motorola Inc., Phoenix, 1981-84, mgr. engring., 1984-85, statis. engr., 1985—; statis. cons. Motorola Semiconductor Research and Devel. Lab., Phoenix, 1985—; instr. Rio Salado Community Coll., Phoenix, 1984—, Brigham Young U. Extension, Salt Lake City, 1975-81, Highline Coll., Midway, Wash., 1967-69. Single adult adminstr. Ch. Jesus Christ Latter-day Saints, Salt Lake City, 1973-81; voting del. Salt Lake County Rep. Conv., 1973. Mem. Am. Statis. Assn. (2d v.p. Utah chpt., pres. Ariz. chpt. 1988—), Am. Soc. Quality Control (vice chair Phoenix sect. 1989—), Sigma Xi. Home: 2308 W Sagebrush Dr Chandler AZ 85224

SUEKER, JULIE, civil engineer; b. Pitts., Sept. 6, 1960; d. Keith Hayles and Betty Lorraine (Freeman) S. BArch, Carnegie-Mellon U., 1983; MCE, U. Colo., 1986. Draftsman Commandaros, Architect, Pitts., 1982-83; lab. technician U. Colo., Boulder, 1984; rsch. asst. Energy and Resource Cons. (RCG/Hagler, Bailly Inc.), Boulder, 1984-85, engr., 1986—. Contbr. articles to profl. jours. ASHVACE scholar, 1984. Mem. ASME. Home: 2637 Valmont Rd Apt 27 Boulder CO 80302 Office: RCG/Hagler Bailly Inc 207 Canyon Blvd Ste 301 Boulder CO 80302

SUESS, MICHAEL ANDREW, small business owner; b. Sleepy Eye, Minn., Nov. 29, 1930; s. Peter James and Agnes Amelia (Pinzka) S.; m. Oct. 10, 1955 (div. Apr. 1988); children: Katherine, Anthony, Timothy, Patricia, Maryellen, Frances Ann. Student, Dunwoody Inst., Mpls., 1950, USAF Acad., 1951, Fla. So. U., 1954. Cert. master baker. Ptnr., owner Al's Bakery, Sleepy Eye, Minn., 1955-58; owner Model Bake Shop, Worthington, Minn., 1958-60; mgr. bakery dept. Super Valu Store, Worthington, 1960-67; mgr. production Dixie Bake Shop, Sioux Falls, S.D., 1967-71; mgr. bakery dept. Smitty's, Phoenix, 1971-86; pres., owner Maas Products Corp., Phoenix, 1987—. Mem. adv. bd. Metro Tech. Vocat. Sch., Phoenix, 1966—. Mem. Retail Bakers Am. (state councilman Ariz.). Republican. Roman Catholic. Home and Office: MAAS Products Corp 5023 W Clarendon Phoenix AZ 85031

SUGANO, DEAN HIDEKI, restaurant executive, entrepreneur; b. Chgo., Feb. 17, 1964; s. Mark Kiyoshi and Irene Kyoko (Kurihara) S. BS, Cornell U., 1989. Pres. Takao Restaurant, San Clemente, Calif., 1980—; chmn. Sugano Corp., San Clemente, 1983—. Republican. Home: 161 Bundy Rd Ithaca NY 14850 Office: Takao Restaurant 425 N El Camino Real San Clemente CA 92672

SUGIKI, SHIGEMI, physician; b. Wailuku, Hawaii, May 12, 1936; s. Sentaro and Kameno (Matoba) S.; A.B., Washington U., St. Louis, 1957, M.D., 1961; m. Bernice T. Murakami, Dec. 28, 1958; children—Kevin S., Boyd R. Intern St. Luke's Hosp., St. Louis, 1961-62, resident ophthalmology, Washington U., St. Louis, 1962-65; chmn. dept. ophthalmology Straub Clinic, Honolulu, 1965-70; chmn. dept. ophthalmology Queen's Med. Center, Honolulu, 1970-73, 80-83, 88—; assoc. clin. prof. ophthalmology Sch. Medicine, U. Hawaii, 1973—. Served to maj. M.C., AUS, 1968-70. Decorated Hawaiian NG Commendation medal, 1968. Fellow ACS; mem. Am., Hawaii med. assns., Honolulu County Med. Soc., Am. Acad. Ophthalmology, Contact Lens Assn. Opthalmologists, Soc. Eye Surgeons, Pacific Coast Oto-Ophthal. Soc., Pan-Pacific Surg. Assn., Am. Soc. Cataract and Refractive Surgery, Internat. Assn. Ocular Surgeons, Am. Soc. Contemporary Ophthalmology, Washington U. Eye Alumni Assn., Hawaii Ophthal. Soc., Research To Prevent Blindness. Home: 2398 Aina Lani Pl Honolulu HI 96822 Office: 1380 Lusitana St Suite 714 Honolulu HI 96813

SUINN, RICHARD MICHAEL, psychologist; b. Honolulu, May 8, 1933; s. Maurice and Edith (Wong) S.; m. Grace D. Toy, July 26, 1958; children: Susan, Randall, Staci, Bradley. Student, U. Hawaii, 1951-53; B.A. summa cum laude, Ohio State U., 1955; MA in Clin. Psychology, Stanford U., 1957, PhD in Clin. Psychology, 1959. Lic. psychologist, Colo. Counselor Stanford U., 1958-59; research assoc. Stanford U. Med. Sch., 1964-66; asst. prof. psychology Whitman Coll., 1959-64; assoc. prof. U. Hawaii, 1966-68; prof. Colo. State U., 1968—, head dept. psychology, 1973—; cons. in field; psychologist U.S. Ski Teams, 1976 Olympic Games, U.S. Women's Track and Field, 1980 Olympic games; mem. sports psychology adv. com. U.S. Olympic Com., 1983—; mem. Colo. Bd. Psychologist Examiners, 1984-86; reviewer NIMH, 1977-80. Author: The Predictive Validity of Projective Measures, 1969, Fundamentals of Behavior Pathology, 1970, The Innovative Psychological Therapies, 1975, The Innovative Medical-Psychiatric Therapies, 1976, Psychology in Sport: Methods and Applications, 1980, Fundamentals of Abnormal Psychology, 1984, Seven Steps to Peak Performance, 1986; editorial bd.: Jour. Cons. and Clin. Psychology, 1973-86, Jour. Counseling Psychology, 1974—, Behavior Therapy, 1977-80, Behavior Modification, 1977-78, Jour. Behavioral Medicine, 1978—, Behavior Counseling Quar, 1979-83, Jour. Sports Psychology, 1980—; author: tests Math. Anxiety Rating Scale. Mem. City Council, Ft. Collins, 1975-79, mayor, 1978-79; mem. Gov.'s Mental Health Adv. Council, 1983, Colo. Bd. Psychologist Examiners, 1983-86. Recipient cert. merit U.S. Ski Team, 1976; NIMH grantee, 1963-64; Office Edn. grantee, 1970-71. Fellow Am. Psychol. Assn. (bd. ethnic minority affairs 1981-83, chmn. 1982-83, mem. edn. and tng. bd. 1985-87, chmn. 1986, 87, mem. policy and planning bd. 1987—), Behavior Therapy and Research Soc. (charter); mem. Assn. Advancement Psychology (trustee 1983-86), Assn. Advancement Behavior Therapy, (sec.-treas. 1986-89), Asian Am. Psychol. Assn. (bd. dirs. 1983-88), Am. Bd. Behavior Therapy (bd. dirs. 1987—), Phi Beta Kappa, Sigma Xi. Home: 808 Cheyenne Dr Fort Collins CO 80525 Office: Colo State U Dept Psychology Fort Collins CO 80523

SUITT, TRACY TALBOT, hospital administrator; b. N.Y.C., Mar. 2, 1961; d. William Wallace and Kathryn (Staley) S. BA, Smith Coll., 1983. Adminstrv. asst. pediatric dept. N.Y. Hosp. Cornell Med. Ctr., N.Y.C., 1985-87; adminstr. adolescent medicine U. Calif., San Francisco, 1987—. Office: U Calif 400 Parnassus San Francisco CA 94143

SULICH, VASSILI, artistic director; b. Island of Brac, Yugoslavia, Dec. 29, 1929; came to U.S., 1964; s. Thomas and Vjekoslava (Orlandini) Sulic. From co. mem. to Dancer Etoile various dance cos., Paris, 1952-64; prin. dancer Broadway prodn. Follies Bergere, N.Y.C., 1964; prin. dancer, ballet master Las Vegas prodn. Follies Bergere, 1964-72; ind. choreographer Europe and U.S., 1964—; artistic dir. Nev. Dance Theatre, Las Vegas, 1972—. Choreographer: Suite Lyrique, Oedipe roi, Idomeneo with Luciano Pavarotti; creator, choreographer numerous dance works including Mantodea, Walls in the Horizon, Cinderella; prin. dancer: La Dryade, L'Echelle, Combat, Cyrano de Bergerac, Lovers of Teruel; performer (TV show) Geraldine starring Geraldine Chaplin. Named Outstanding Individual Artist Gov. of Nev., 1981, Disting. Nevadan U. Nev. Bd. Regents, 1987. Office: Nev Dance Theater 4505 S Maryland Pkwy Las Vegas NV 89154 *

SULLIVAN, BOETIUS HENRY, III, realtor, management consultant; b. Chgo., Feb. 3, 1952; s. Boetius Henry Jr. and Marcaline (Block) S.; m. Jacquylin Lou. Student, Ottawa (Kans.) U., 1971-73, Macalester Coll., 1973-74; BS, U. Colo., 1976. Asst. dir. Boulder (Colo.) Resevoir, 1979-80; realtor Full Circle Co., Aurora, Colo., 1980-81; realtor, mgmt. cons. Perry & Co., Denver, 1981—. Mem. Denver Bd. Realtors, Community Assns. Inst. Republican. Roman Catholic. Club: Arlberg (Winter Port, Colo.). Home: 552 Humboldt St Denver CO 80218 Office: Perry & Co 101 S Madison St Denver CO 80209

SULLIVAN, BONITA JEAN, manufacturing executive; b. Middletown, Conn., Sept. 2, 1946; d. Peter John and Agnes (Romanik) Kowal; m. James Kevin Sullivan, Oct. 28, 1967; children: Sean, Tara. BS, Simmons Coll., 1968; MBA, Portland State U., 1979. Real estate assoc. Tarbell Co., Portland, 1977-79; with Tektronix, Inc., Beaverton, Oreg., 1980—; procurement policies mgr. Tektronix, Inc., Beaverton, 1982-83, procurement commodities and ops. mgr., 1983-85, div. procurement mgr., 1985-86, mktg. accounts mgr., 1986-87, dir. corp. procurement, 1987—; lectr. in field. Contbr. articles to profl. jours. Adv. Bd. Electronic Buyer's News Purchasing Mgmt mag. Manhassett, N.Y., 1987—; bus. advisor Concordia Coll., Portland, 1987—; asst. local and reg. Track and Field Youth. Mem. Assn. for Mfg. Excellence, Assn. for Inventory and Prodn. Control, MAPI, Eastside Athletic (Milw., Oreg.), Portland Masters Track. Roman Catholic. Office: Tektronix Inc PO Box 500 M/S 19-020 Beaverton OR 97077

SULLIVAN, CORNELIUS WAYNE, marine biology researcher, educator; b. Pitts., June 11, 1943; s. John Wayne and Hilda Sullivan; m. Jill Hajjar, Oct. 28, 1966; children: Shane, Preston, Chelsea. BS in Biochemistry, Pa. State U., 1965, MS in Microbiology, 1967; PhD in Marine Biology, Scripps Inst. Oceanography, 1971. Postdoctoral fellow Scripps Inst. Oceanography, La Jolla, Calif., 1971-74; asst. prof. marine biology U. So. Calif., Los Angeles, 1974-80, assoc. prof., 1980-85, dir. marine biology sect., 1982—, prof., 1985—; vis. prof. U. Colo., Boulder, 1981-82, MIT, Cambridge, 1981-82; field team leader Sea Ice Microbial Communities Studies, McMurdo Sound, Antarctica, 1980-86; chief scientist/cruise coordinator Antartic Marine Ecosystem Resarch at the Ice Edge Zone Project, Weddell Sea, 1983, 86, 88; mem. BIOMASS Working Party on Pack-Ice Zone Studies, 1983-86, ecol. research rev. bd. Dept. Navy, 1982-85; So. Ocean Ecology Group Specialist Sci. Com. on Antarctic Research; chmn. SCOR working group 86 "Sea Ice Ecology" sci. com. on oceanic research. Editorial bd. Jour. Microbiol. Methods, 1982-85, Polar Biology, 1987—; contbr. articles to profl. jours. USPHS fellow; recipient Antarctic Service Medal of U.S., NSF, 1981. Mem. Nat. Acad. Sci. (polar research bd., 1983-86, chmn. com. to evaluate polar research platforms, 1985—). Office: U So Calif Dept Biol Scis University Pk Los Angeles CA 90089-0371

SULLIVAN, DANIEL J., artistic director; b. Wray, Colo., June 11, 1940; s. John Martin and Mary Catherine (Hutton) S.; children—John, Rachel M. B.A., San Francisco State U. Actor, Actor's Workshop, San Francisco, 1963-65; actor, dir. Lincoln Center Repertory, N.Y.C., 1965-73; dir. numerous regional theatres, 1973-79; resident dir. Seattle Repertory Theater, 1979-81, artistic dir., 1981—; instr. acting Calif. Inst. Arts, Valencia, 1973-74. Translator play, The Mandrake, 1984. Recipient Drama Desk award N.Y. Theatre Critics, 1972. Mem. Nat. Endowment for Arts, Theatre Panel Communications Group (bd. dirs. 1982—), Democrat. Office: Seattle Repertory Theatre 155 Mercer St Seattle WA 98109 *

SULLIVAN, DAVID LAWRENCE, JR., industrial insulation manufacturing company executive; b. Chgo., Aug. 2, 1945; s. David Lawrence and Agnes (Shea) S.; m. Mary Kathleen Weitkamp, Aug. 10, 1968. BS, St. Benedict's Coll., Atchison, Kans., 1967. Sales rep. Owens-Corning Fiberglas, St. Louis, 1971; resident sales mgr. Owens-Corning Fiberglas, Des Moines, 1972-73; product mgr. Owens-Corning Fiberglas, Toledo, 1973-74, mktg. mgr., 1974-76; gen. mgr. Borden Inc., Columbus, Ohio, 1976-81; mktg. dir. Kinnear div. Harsco, Columbus, 1981-83; pres. Rockwool Industries, Inc., Denver, 1983-86; pres., chief exec. officer Partek N. Am., Denver, 1986—; cons. in field; chmn. bd. dirs. Partek Insulation Ltd., Sarnia, Ont., Can.; bd. dirs. Nat. Awards Mfg. Inc., Dayton, Ohio, World Trade Ctr.; bd. dirs., info. com. Nat. Inst. Building, Washington, 1980-81. Served to 1st lt. U.S. Army, 1968-71, Vietnam. Mem. Denver C. of C. (mem. task force internat. com.), Am. Mgmt. Assn. (chairperson, pres. assn. course), Glenmoor Country club, Pinehurst County club (Denver). Republican. Roman Catholic. Office: Partek N Am 6400 S Fiddlers Green Circle Ste 1850 Englewood CO 80111

SULLIVAN, EDWARD HOLDEN, JR., financial services executive; b. Shreveport, La., Oct. 5, 1941; s. Edward Holden and Florence (Tierney) S.; m. Lisa Rimer, June 24, 1977; 1 child, Shannon E. BS in Bus. Mgmt., LaSalle U., 1972. Pres., chief exec. officer Caballero Loan Svc., Inc., El Paso, Tex., 1966-74; dir. mktg. and advt. Richardson (Tex.) Savs. and Loan, 1974; mgr. regional sales and mktg. Depositors Portrait Svcs. Internat. div. Chromalloy Am. Corp., St. Louis, 1974-79; sales rep. Fla. Software Svcs., Altamonte Springs, 1979-80; dist. mgr. J.B. Steelman, Inc., Altamonte Springs, 1980-82; dir. sales Systematics, Inc., Little Rock, 1982-85; dir. nat. accounts UCCEL Corp., Dallas, 1985-86; div. mgr., chief exec. officer Security Pacific Fin. Systems, Phoenix, 1986-87; div. mgr. Security Pacific Info. Svcs. Corp., Denver, 1987-88; pres., chief exec. officer One Card Mktg., Inc., Culver City, Calif., 1988-89; pres. sales div. Dot Systems, Inc., Denver, 1989—. Recipient Community Svc. award Optimists, 1973. Mem. Am. Bankers Assn., Ind. Bankers of Am. (assoc.), Mortgage Bankers Assn., Bank of Adminstrn. Inst. (assoc.), Consumer Bankers Assn. (participating), U.S. Savs. League, Denver C. of C. Roman Catholic. Clubs: Memphis Petroleum; Greenwood Athletic (Englewood, Colo.); Glenmoor Country (Denver). Home: 5411 S Geneva St Englewood CO 80111 Office: Dot Systems Inc 10730 E Bethany Dr Ste 204 Aurora CO 80014

SULLIVAN, GEORGE ANDERSON, orthodontist; b. Bon Aqua, Tenn.; s. Joe Marble and Ruby Christine (Luther) S.; m. Edith Melvina Timmons, May 11, 1957; children: Scott Patrick, Shawn Michael. AS, Henry Ford Community Coll., Dearborn, Mich., 1957; student, Eastern Mich. U., 1958-59; DDS, U. Mich., 1963, MS, 1966. Diplomate Am. Bd. Orthodontics. Pvt. practice specializing in orthodontics Phoenix, 1966—; pres. Ammons Meml. Dental Clinic, Phoenix, 1979-80. Chmn. Phoenix Meml. Hosp., 1977-80.Served with USNR, 1955-63. Mem. Am. Assn. Orthodontics, Cen. Ariz. Dental Soc., Ariz. State Dental Assn., ADA, Ariz. Orthodontic Soc., Pacific Coast Soc. Orthodontics, Optimist Club (pres. Phoenix chpt. 1967-68), Lions (pres. 1972-73), Elks. Republican. Office: 4909 N 44th St #E Phoenix AZ 85018

SULLIVAN, GERALD JAMES, insurance company executive; b. Olympia, Wash., Sept. 30, 1937; s. John F. and Elizabeth J. (Yater) S.; B.B.A., U. Wash., 1959; M.B.A., Wharton Sch. U. Pa., 1966; m. Wendy D. Edmunds, Sept. 2, 1987; children—Gerald James, Thomas, Katheleen, Shannon. Security analyst Hartford Ins. Group (Conn.), 1966-67; chief dep. ins. commr. State of Wash., Olympia, 1967-68; sec. John F. Sullivan Co., Seattle, 1968-71; pres. Walker Sullivan Co., Los Angeles, 1971-80, chmn., 1979; chmn. bd., pres. Gerald J. Sullivan & Assocs., Inc., ins. brokers, 1980—; mem. exec. com., chmn. security com. Calif. Surplus Lines Assns., San Francisco, 1974; mem. NAIC Industry Adv. Com. on Surplus Lines Laws and Reins. Served to capt. USAF, 1959-64. C.P.C.U., C.L.U. Roman Catholic. Clubs: Wilshire Country, Pauma Valley Country, Jonathan, Calif., Stock Exchange, K.C. Author: Trends in International Reinsurance Affecting American Reinsurers, 1966. Office: 800 W 6th St Los Angeles CA 90017

SULLIVAN, JAMES DENNIS, construction executive; b. Evanston, Ill., Mar. 5, 1938; s. John Federick and Dorothy (Horter) S.; m. Karen L. Kelly. Estimator, v.p. A&M Insulation Co., Chgo., 1959-87; chief exec. v.p., treas., dir. Overhill Land & Devel. Co., Scottsdale, Ariz., 1987; chief exec. officer, v.p., treas., dir. R.J. Cole Builders Inc., Scottsdale, 1987; prin. Overhill Land & Devel. Co., Scottsdale, 1987—. With USAF, 1961-65. Mem. Western Soc. Engrs. Republican. Roman Catholic. Address: Overhill Land & Devel Co 4416 N Scottsdale Rd #434 Scottsdale AZ 85251

SULLIVAN, JAMES JEROME, lawyer, consultant; b. Fargo, N.D., Feb. 23, 1943; m. Roberta Jean Ranes, Nov. 8, 1980; children: Kristen, Eric, Amy, Jason. PhB, U. N.D., 1966, JD, 1970. Bar: N.D. 1970, Wash. 1982. Atty. Northwestern Nat. Life Ins. Co., Mpls., 1970-73; regional counsel Econ. Devel. Admin. of U.S. Dept. Commerce, Seattle, 1973—; sole practice Bellevue, Wash., 1986—. Editor, contbr. articles to numerous periodicals. Recipient numerous legal awards, 1973-88. Mem. Wash. State Bar Assn. (mem. editorial adv. bd. 1984-88, lawyer assistance program 1989—). Home: 11110 NE 38th Pl Bellevue WA 98004 Office: US Dept Commerce 915 Second Ave Ste 1856 Seattle WA 98174

SULLIVAN, JAMES KIRK, forest products company executive; b. Greenwood, S.C., Aug. 25, 1935; s. Daniel Jones and Addie (Brown) S.; m. Elizabeth Miller, June 18, 1960; children: Hal N., Kim J. BS in Chemistry, Clemson U., 1957, MS, 1964, PhD, 1966; PSE, MIT, 1975. Prodn. supr. FMC Corp., South Charleston, W.Va., 1957-62; tech. supt. FMC Corp., Pocatello, Idaho, 1966-69; mktg. mgr. FMC Corp., N.Y.C., 1969-70; v.p. govtl. and environ. affairs Boise Cascade Corp., Idaho, 1971—; dir. Key Bank Idaho. Contbr. articles to profl. jours.; patentee in field. Mem. Coll. of Forest and Recreation Resources com. Clemson U., Idaho Found. for Pvt. Enterprise and Econ. Edn., Idaho Rsch. Found., Inc., adv. com. Idaho Task Force on Higher Edn.; chmn. adv. bd. U. Idaho Coll. Engring., pub. affairs com. NAM; pres. Bishop Kelly Found.; chmn. centennial campaign U. Idaho; trustee Idaho Children's Emergency Fund, Bishop Kelly High Sch.; past chmn. Bronco Athletic Assn. 1st lt. U.S. Army, 1958-59. Mem. Am. Inst. Chem. Engrs., Am. Chem. Soc., Am. Inst. Chem. Engrs., Am. Paper Inst. (govtl. affairs com.), Bus. Week Found. (chmn. Bus. Week 1980), Bus. Roundtable (environ. com.), Idaho Assn. Commerce and Industry (bd. dirs.), C. of C. of U.S. (pub. affairs com.). Republican. Home: 5206 Sorrento Circle Boise ID 83704 Office: Boise Cascade Corp One Jefferson Sq Boise ID 83728

SULLIVAN, JOHN LOUIS, JR., search company executive; b. Macon, Ga., Aug. 27, 1928; s. John Louis and Elizabeth (Macken) S.; m. Barbara Boyle, Aug. 17, 1974; children: John, Katherine, Betsy, Ted. A.B. in Econs., Duke U., 1950; M.B.A., U. Pa., 1957; postgrad. Advance Mgmt. Program, Harvard U., 1975. Br. mgr. IBM, Phila., 1962-63; mgr. edn. IBM, Endicott, N.Y., 1963-64; asst. to pres. Data Processing Div. IBM, White Plains, N.Y., 1965-67; dist. mgr. Data Processing Div. IBM, Washington, 1967-69; mgr. eastern and fed. regions Memorex Corp., 1969-71; v.p. mktg. Infonet div. Computer Sci. Corp., El Segundo, Calif., 1971-75; exec. v.p. Fin. Service Group-ADP Inc., Clifton, N.J., 1975-77; sr. v.p. Heidrick & Struggles Inc., San Francisco and Los Angeles, 1977-82, dir., 1977-82, office mgr., 1979-82; v.p., mng. dir., mem. exec. com. Korn-Ferry Internat., Los Angeles, 1982—, now pres. Bd. dirs., mem. exec. com. March of Dimes, Los Angeles County; bd. regents Mount St. Mary's Coll., Los Angeles. Served to lt. (j.g.) USN, 1950-53. Mem. Harvard U. Bus. Sch. Alumni Assn. (dir.). Democrat. Clubs: Regency (Los Angeles); Bankers (San Francisco); Flint Canyon Tennis, Atheneum; Mission Hills (Rancho Mirage); Calif. Yacht (Los Angeles). Office: Korn Ferry Internat 101 Federal St Boston MA 02110 also: Korn Ferry Internat 1800 Century Park E Los Angeles CA 90067

SULLIVAN, KRISTIN LESLIE, political worker; b. Mpls., Dec. 21, 1957; d. Richard Leslie and June Harriet (Runsberg) Ruud; m. Ronald Gerard Sullivan, Apr. 25, 1987. BS, No. Ariz. U., 1980. Reporter Sierra Vista (Ariz.) Herald-Dispatch, 1974-78; legal sec. Thikoll, Johnston & Rosen, Tucson, 1978; intern Ariz. Ho. of Reps., Phoenix, 1980; paralegal Ariz. Atty. Gen.'s Office, Phoenix, 1980-82; dir. govt. affairs Ariz. Assn. Realtors, Phoenix, 1982-89; cons. Phoenix, 1989—. Precinct committeeman Maricopa County, Phoenix, 1984-86, dep. registrar, 1984—; mem. steering com. local polit. campaigns, 1986, 88, Cactus Wren Rep. Women. Mem. Am. Soc. Assn. Execs., Phi Kappa Phi. Republican. Lutheran. Home and Office: 6009 N 10th Pl Phoenix AZ 85014 Office: Ariz Assn Realtors 4414 N 19th Ave Phoenix AZ 85015

SULLIVAN, LARRY ALAN, lawyer; b. Madison, Wis., Dec. 13, 1951; s. James Francis and Muriel Germaine (Weeks) S.; m. Patricia Ann Sully, Nov. 24, 1979; children: Susan Elizabeth, Kelsey Marie. BA, U. Va., 1974; JD, U. Oreg., 1978. Bar: Oreg. 1978. Dep. dist. atty. Malheur County, Vale, Oreg., 1978-80; assoc. Combs, Tharp & Pierce, Ontario, Oreg., 1980-82; ptnr. Pierce & Sullivan, Ontario, 1982-84, Schroeder, Hutchens & Sullivan, Vale, 1984-88, Sullivan & Powell, Vale, 1988—; atty. City of Vale, 1986-88; bd. atty. Vale Oreg. Irrigation Dist., 1988—. Chmn. Malheur County Dems., Ontario, 1983-86; bd. dirs. Small Bus. Devel. Ctr., Ontario, 1984-88. mem. Oreg. Bar Assn., Malheur County Bar Assn. (treas. 1978-82). Home: 1083 NW 2d Ave Ontario OR 97914 Office: Sullivan & Powell 280 A St E PO Box 220 Vale OR 97918

SULLIVAN, MARK THOMAS, photographer, graphic artist; b. L.A., June 7, 1950; s. Martin and Patricia (Davidson) S.; m. Cristye Lee Rhodes, Oct. 11, 1980; children: Dallas, Austin; 1 child by previous union, Justin. Student, Pasadena City Coll., 1968-69, U. So. Calif., L.A., 1983-84. Asst. to curator of photography, staff photographer Pasadena (Calif.) Art Mus., 1969-71; freelance photographer 1979—; staff photographer L.A. Free Press, 1973-77; art dir. On Location mag., L.A., 1977-78; head camera dept. Diener, Hauser, Bates Advt., L.A., 1978-82; asst. to comml. photographer Ron Slenzak Studios, L.A., 1982; head camera dept. CBS TV network, L.A., 1982-87, Backer, Spielvogel, Bates Advt., L.A., 1987—; photographer, Midnight Spl., NBC, 1975-77. Photographic work pub. in Rolling Stone, Playboy, Time mag., numerous others. Mem. Valencia (Calif.) Traffic Safety Awareness Com., 1986-88. Home: 25664 Alicante Dr Valencia CA 91355-2266 Office: Backer Spielvogel Bates Inc 5700 Wilshire Blvd Ste 475 Los Angeles CA 90036

SULLIVAN, MARY KATHLEEN, nurse; b. Kansas City, Kans., Oct. 4, 1961; d.Robert W. and Ann J. (Cindrich) S. BS in Nursing, Creighton U., 1983. RN, Mo., Ariz., Kans., Nebr.; cert. psychiatric mental health nursing/ Staff nurse Western Mo. Mental Health Ctr., Kansas City, 1983-84, Kansas City VA Hosp., 1984-85; shift supr. Ariz. State Hosp., Phoenix, 1986; staff nurse Camelback Hosp., Phoenix, Scottsdale, 1985-87, Carl T. Hayden VA Hosp., Phoenix, 1987—; mem. quality assurance com. Carl T. Hayden VA Hosp., 1988—. Mem. Am. Nurses Assn. (mem. coun. psychiat. and mental health), Ariz. Nurses Assn. Roman Catholic.

SULLIVAN, MAURICE FRANCIS, biologist; b. Butte, Mont., Feb. 16, 1922; s. John G. and Abigail Philomina (Lowney) S.; m. Sheila Hamill, Oct. 1, 1951; children: Ellen, John, Kevin, Cornelius, Kathleen, Brian. BS, Mont. State U., 1950; PhD, U. Chgo., 1955. Scientist GE, Richland, Wash., 1955-60, sr. scientist, 1962-65; postdoctoral rsch. Med. Rsch. Coun., Harvell, Eng., 1962-65; mgr. Battelle Meml. Inst., Richland, Wash., 1965-71, staff scientist, 1971—. Contbr. articles to profl. jours. Fellow Am. Assn. Scientists; mem. Radiation Rsch. Soc., Am. Physiol. Soc. Democrat. Roman Catholic. Home: 2125 Harris Richland WA 99352

SULLIVAN, MICHAEL EVAN, investment and management company executive; b. Phila., Dec. 30, 1940; s. Albert and Ruth (Liebert) S.; BS, N.Mex. State U., 1966, MA (Ednl. Research Tng. Program fellow), 1967; BS, U. Tex., 1969; MBA, U. Houston, 1974; MS, U. So. Calif., 1976, MPA, 1977, PhD in Adminstrn., 1983; BS in Acctg., U. La Verne, 1981. Sr. adminstrv. and tech. analyst Houston Lighting & Power Co., 1969-74; electronics engr. U.S. Govt., Point Mugu, Calif., 1974-77; mem. tech. staff Hughes Aircraft Co., El Segundo, Calif., 1977-78; staff program adminstr. Ventura div. Northrop Corp., Newbury Park, Calif., 1978-79; div. head engring. div. Navastrogru, Point Mugu, 1979-82; br. head, div. head spl. programs Pacific Missile Test Ctr., (Calif.), 1983—; head operational systems integration office and assignments CNO-Dir. Research, Devel., and Acquisition in the Pentagon, Washington, 1987-88; pres., chmn. bd. Diversified Mgmt. Systems, Inc., Camarillo, Calif., 1978—. Author: The Management of Research, Development, Test and Evaluation Organizations; Organizational Behavior Characteristics of Supervisors-Public versus Private Sectors, Organizational Behavior Characteristics of Supervisors, Public versus Private Sectors; Self-Actualization in RDT & E Organizations; Self-Actualization in a Health Care Agency; others. V.p., bd. dirs. Ventura County Master Chorale and Opera Assn; bd. dirs. Southern Calif. Assn. of Pub. Adminstrn. (also mem. fin. com., programs com., student aid com.). Served with U.S. Army, 1958-62. Ednl. Research Info. Clearing House fellow, 1965-67. Mem. Am. Math. Soc., Math. Assn. Am., Am. Statis. Assn., IEEE, IEEE Engring. Mgmt. Soc., Am. Soc. Pub. Adminstrn., So. Calif. Assn. Pub. Adminstrn. (bd. dirs., various coms.), Am. Personnel and Guidance Assn., Fed. Mgrs. Assn., Am. Assn. Individual Investors, Mcpl. Mgmt. Assts. So. Calif., Acad. Polit. Sci., Assn. M.B.A. Execs., Phi Kappa Phi, Pi Gamma Mu. Home: PO Box 273 Port Hueneme CA 93041 Office: PO Box 447 Camarillo CA 93010

SULLIVAN, MICHAEL J., governor of Wyoming, lawyer; b. Omaha, Sept. 23, 1939; s. Joseph Byrne and Margaret (Hamilton) S.; m. Jane Metzler, Sept. 2, 1961; children: Michelle, Patrick, Theresa. BS in Petroleum Engring., U. Wyo., 1961, JD, 1964. Assoc. Brown, Drew, Apostolos, Barton & Massey, Casper, Wyo., 1964-67; ptnr. Brown, Drew, Apostolos, Massey & Sullivan, Casper, 1967—; gov. State of Wyo., Casper, 1987—. Trustee St. Joseph's Children's Home, Torrington, Wyo., 1986-87; bd. dirs. Natrona County Meml. Hosp., Casper, 1976-86. Mem. ABA, Wyo. Bar Assn., Assn. Trial Lawyers Am., Wyo. Trial Lawyers Assn. Democrat. Roman Catholic. Lodge: Rotary (pres. Casper club). Home: 5001 Central Ave Cheyenne WY 82002 Office: Office of Gov State Capitol Cheyenne WY 82002-0010 *

SULLIVAN, PATRICK ALLEN, strategic management educator; b. Peoria, Ill., Oct. 31, 1932; s. Francis Richard and Carmela Marie (Smith) S.; m. Gwendolyn Jo Herndon, Aug. 25, 1958; children: Richard John, Sharon Louise Little, Patrick Michael, Cecelia Anne, Catherine Marie Markee. BCE, Marquette U., 1955; MBA, San Diego State U., 1975; DBA, U.S. Internat. U., San Diego, 1988. Engr. USMC, 29 Palms, Calif., 1958-63; engr. USN, San Diego, 1963-67, mgmt. analyst, 1967-88; asst. prof. strategic mgmt. U.S. Internat. U., San Diego, 1988—; ptnr. Sullivan and Assocs. Mgmt. Cons., San Diego, 1988-89. Pres. St. Aus X Ch. Parish Coun., Chula Vista, Calif., 1984. 1st lt. USMC, 1955-58. Mem. ASCE, Inst. Indsl. Engrs., Acad. Mgmt., Strategic Mgmt. Soc., K.C., Chi Epsilon, Tau Beta Pi, Sigma Iota Epsilon, Beta Gamma Sigma. Democrat. Roman Catholic. Home: 98 E Emerson St Chula Vista CA 92011

SULLIVAN, ROBERT EDWARD, lawyer; b. San Francisco, May 18, 1936; s. Edward C. S. and Mary Jane (Sullivan); m. Maureen Lois Miles, June 14, 1958 (dec. 1972); children: Teresa Ann, Andrew Edward, Edward Braddock. BS, U. San Francisco, 1958; LLB, U. Calif-Berkeley, 1961. Bar: Calif. 1962. Assoc. Pillsbury, Madison & Sutro, San Francisco, 1963-70, ptnr., 1971—; lectr. bus. law Calif. Continuing Edn. Bar and Practicing Law Inst.; mem. com. corps. State Bar Calif., 1979-82, chmn., 1981-82; mem. exec. com. bus. law sect., 1982-85, vice chmn., 1983-84, chmn., 1984-85, advisor, 1985-86; v.p., treas., dir. MPC Ins., Ltd. Contbr. articles to profl. jours. Served to 1st lt. U.S. Army, 1961-63. Mem. ABA, San Francisco Bar Assn. Democrat. Roman Catholic. Club: Bankers (San Francisco). Office: Pillsbury Madison & Sutro 225 Bush St San Francisco CA 94104-2105

SULLIVAN, ROBERT JAMES, electrical contractor, owner trailer park, mayor; b. Warren, Ohio, July 6, 1942; s. Robert Dan and Edith Nora (Fisher) S.; m. Emily Scott Romberg, June 11, 1972 (div. Oct. 30, 1978); m. Krista J. Sangster, Feb. 15, 1986. BSBA, U. Denver, 1971. Cert. electrical contractor, N.Mex. Asst. mgr. Laguna Vista Lodge, Eagle Nest, N.Mex., 1966-74; mgr. Laguna Vista Lodge, Eagle Nest, 1975-81; owner, operator Lost Eagle Trail Park, Eagle Nest, 1972—, Alpine Electric, Eagle Nest, 1985—. Councilman Eagle Nest Village Govt., 1978-88, mayor, 1988—; fire chief, Eagle Nest Fire Dept., 1974—, emergency med. technician, 1973-84; mem. Fire Protection Adv. Bd., 1985-89, Hazardious Material Planning Bd., 1988-89. Sr. chief petty officer USNR, 1966—. Mem. Eagle Nest C. of C. (pres. 1987-89), Better Bus. Bur. (arbitrator 1986-88, sr. arbitrator 1987-89). Republican. Home and Office: 201 Therma Dr Eagle Nest NM 87718

SULLIVAN, ROBERT SCOTT, architect; b. Alexandria, La., Sept. 8, 1955; s. Robert Wallace and Harriette Henri (Fedric) S. BA cum laude, Tulane U., 1979, BArch, 1979. Registered architect, N.Y. Staff architect Cavitt, McKnight, Weymouth, Inc., Houston, 1979-81, Hardy, Holzman, Pfeiffer Assocs., N.Y.C., 1981-83; ptnr. Sullivan, Briggs Assocs., N.Y.C., 1983-86; project architect Butler, Rogers, Baskett, N.Y.C., 1985-86; prin. R. Scott Sullivan AIA, Berkeley, Calif., 1986—; cons. Neometry Graphics, N.Y.C., 1983-86, dir, 1986—; dir. Middleton/Sullivan Inc., Alexandria, 1981—. Works include specific design projects at N.Y. Hist. Soc. exhibit Grand Cen. Terminal, N.Y.C., 1982, The Pingry Sch., Bernards Twp., N.J., 1982, Arts Ctr. at Oak Knoll Sch., Summit, N.J., 1985. Vestryman St. Mark's Episc. Ch., Berkeley, 1988—. Mem. AIA, Calif. Council Architects, Archtl. League N.Y.C., English Speaking Union, Nat. Trust for Hist. Preservation, Victorian Soc. in Am., Tau Sigma Delta. Democrat. Office: 1060 Sterling Ave Berkeley CA 94708

SULLIVAN, STEPHEN JEROME, psychologist; b. Wilmington, N.C., Apr. 13, 1943; s. Jerome John and Ann Elizabeth (Holmes) S.; m. Carol Lynn Fischer, May 22, 1982. BA, St. John's U., 1965; MA, Cath. U. Am., 1968, PhD, 1971. Dir. dept. psychology Fairview Hosp. and Tng. Ctr., Salem, Oreg., 1971-74; psychologist Salem, 1974—. Adv. bd. Salem Airport, 1983-88, chmn. 1985-86; bd. dirs. Salem Area Mass Transit Dist., 1987-89. Mem. Am. Psychol. Assn., Oreg. Psychol. Assn., Oreg. Pilots Assn. Office: 635 Church St NE Salem OR 97301

SULLIVAN, STUART FRANCIS, anesthesiologist, educator; b. Buffalo, July 15, 1928; s. Charles S. and Kathryn (Duggan) S.; m. Dorothy Elizabeth Faytol, Apr. 18, 1959; children: John, Irene, Paul, Kathryn. BS, Canisius Coll., 1950; MD, SUNY, Syracuse, 1955. Diplomate Am. Bd. Anesthesiology. Intern O State Univ. Hosp., 1955-56; resident Columbia Presbyn. Med. Ctr., 1958-60; instr. anesthesiology Coll. Physicians and Surgeons Columbia U., N.Y.C., 1961-62; assoc. Columbia U., N.Y.C., 1962-64, asst. prof., 1964-67, assoc. prof., 1967-73; prof., vice chmn. dept. anesthesiology Sch. Medicine UCLA, 1973—. Served to capt. M.C., USAR, 1956-58. Fellow NIH, 1960-61; recipient research career devel. award NIH, 1966-69. Mem. Assn. Univ. Anesthetists, Am. Physiol. Soc., Am. Soc. Anesthesiologists. Home: 101 Foxtail Dr Santa Monica CA 90402 Office: UCLA Sch Medicine Dept Anesthesiology Los Angeles CA 90024-1778

SULLIVAN, THOMAS JUDE, life insurance company executive; b. Eugene, Oreg., Oct. 24, 1955; s. William Gilbert and Teresa K. (Rowe) S.; m. Donna Lee Goergen, Dec. 23, 1982; children: Aaron Thomas, Penny Marie. BA, U. Oreg., 1978. Tennis coach Springfield High Sch., Oreg., 1973-77; tennis profl. Casa Grande Tennis Club, Arix., 1978; phys. edn. tchr. Springfield (Oreg.) Sch. dist., 1978-79; sp. agt. Northwestern Mutual Life Ins. Co., Eugene, Oreg., 1980—. Pres. Mid-Oreg. Execs., Eugene, 1986-87; cons. Jr. Achievement, Eugene, 1987—; mem. fund raising bd. Eugene Arts Found. Endowment, 1984—; fund raiser Mar. of Dimes, Eugene, 1984—; co-chmn. Eugene-Springfield Campaign United Way, 1982-84. Mem. U. Oreg. Alumni Assn. (bd. dirs. 1984-85), Nat. Assn. Underwriters, Oreg. Assn. Life Underwriters, Eugene Assn. Life Underwriters, Internat. Assn. Fin. Planners., Downtown Athletic Club (Eugene), Rotary. Republican. Roman Catholic. Home: 2172 Fireside Ct Springfield OR 97477 Office: 1358 Oak St Ste 3 Eugene OR 97401

SULLIVAN, THOMAS MILTON, mining company executive, inventor; b. San Diego, July 2, 1954; s. Thomas Marshall and Mary Evelyn (Walker) S. Grad. high sch., San Diego. Chief exec. officer Sullivan Mining Corp., San Diego, 1980—. Patentee mining methods, fiber coating ad composites, ratcheting box end wrench, hydraulic mining method, coated carbon fiber reinforced composites, armored glove fingers. Alt. del. Rep. Nat. Conv., 1980; mem. steering com. Bentley for 77th Assembly Dist. campaign, San Diego, 1988.

SULLIVAN, TIMOTHY REESE, broadcasting executive; b. Los Angeles, June 15, 1938; s. Charles Gardner and Ann Beatrice (May) S.; B.S., U. Ariz., 1961; M.B.A., Pepperdine U., 1978; m. Nancy Lee Robbins, July 6, 1967; children—Kelly Ann, John Casey. Vice-pres., West Coast mgr. Metro Radio Sales, Los Angeles, 1968-71; gen. sales mgr. Sta. KIAC, Los Angeles, 1971-72; v.p., dir. sales Metromedia Radio West Coast, 1972-73; v.p., gen. mgr. Sta. KHJ, Los Angeles, 1973-79; gen. mgr. Sta. KHTZ, 1978-80; v.p., gen. mgr. Sta. KMGG, Los Angeles, 1980-84; pres. Anaheim Broadcasting, Calif., 1984—. Mem. radio adv. com. U. So. Calif.; mem. exec. bd. Los Angeles March of Dimes, treas., 1977-79; mem. exec. bd. Pacific Palisades YMCA, 1978. Served with USMC, 1961-65. Mem. Nat. Assn. Broadcasters, Nat. Radio Broadcasters Assn., So. Calif. Broadcasters Assn. (chmn. 1980-81), Sigma Alpha Epsilon. Republican. Presbyterian. Club: Los Angeles Country, Beach. Office: Anaheim Broadcasting 1190 E Ball Rd Anaheim CA 92805

SULLIVAN, WILLIAM JAMES, university president; b. Freeport, Ill., Dec. 20, 1930; s. Arlend Eugene and Bessie (Burton) S. B.A. in Philosophy, St. Louis U., 1954, M.A. in Philosophy, 1956, Ph.L., 1956; S.T.L., Faculté de Theologie, Lyons, France, 1962; M.A., Yale U., 1966, M.Phil. in Religious Studies, 1967, Ph.D. in Religious Studies, 1971; D.D. (hon.), Concordia Sem. in Exile, 1977. Tchr. classical lang. Creighton Prep. Sch., 1955-58; asst. prof. theology Marquette U., 1967-71; dean Sch. Div., St. Louis U., 1971-75; provost Seattle U., 1975-76, pres., 1976—; bd. dirs. Internat. Fedn. Catholic Univs., 1978-88, Maryville Coll., 1972-75, Am. Council Edn., 1978-81, U. San Francisco, 1976-84; founder, bd. dirs. Wash. Student Loan Guaranty Assn.; trustee Carnegie Found. Advancement of Teaching, 1985—; mem. Wash. State Higher Edn. Facilities Authority, 1984—. Contbr. articles on theology, edn. and cultural topics to profl. jours., popular publs. Bd. dirs. World Without War Council, Seattle, 1978-81; bd. dirs. Seattle United Way, 1979-81, Creighton U., 1982-86, Loyola U. Chgo., 1983-87; chmn. host com. 1990 Goodwill Games, 1986—. Recipient Edmund Campion award Campion High Sch., 1970; Pope John XXIII award Viterbo Coll., 1979; Brotherhood award NCCJ, 1981; Recipient Torch of Liberty award Anti-Defamation League, B'nai B'rith. Mem. Assn. Cath. Colls. and Univs. (bd. dirs. 1986—), Nat. Assn. Ind. Colls. and Univs. (bd. dirs. 1983-86), Assn. Jesuit Colls. and Univs. (bd. dirs. 1986—), Wash. Friends Higher Edn., Ind. Colls. Wash., Seattle C. of C. (dir. 1979-82, 88—). Catholic. Clubs: Rainier, Seattle Yacht, Columbia Tower (bd. dirs.), University (Seattle). Lodge: Rotary (Seattle). Home and Office: Seattle U 12th & E Columbia Seattle WA 98122

SULMAN, A(BRAHAM) MICHAEL, data processing company executive, consultant; b. Phila., July 18, 1936; d. Philip Victor and Bertha (Weisfeld) S.; m. Rochelle Beverly Chanen, Dec. 24, 1959; children: Stacy Beth, L. Erik P. BS, Temple U., 1958; AM, U. Pa., 1963; PhD, U. Pitts., 1972. Trust adminstr. Mellon Bank, Phila., 1958-63; asst. prof. Carnelie-Mellon U., Pitts., 1968-77; chief exec. officer Data Availability Svcs., Inc., Tucson, 1977—; pres. Sheriden Park, Inc., Pitts., 1971-77; adj. asst. prof. Sch. Medicine, U. Pitts., 1972-77; adminstr. history of sci. Hunt Found, 1972-75; curriculum cons. Sch. for Advanced Jewish Studies, Pitts., 1973-77; chmn. adult edn. Jewish Community Ctr., Pitts., 1974-76; exec. dir. Congregation Anshei Israel, Tucson, 1982-86. Editor: Judaism in Secular World, 1976; contbr. articles and revs. to scholarly publs. Chmn. Jewish Com. on Scouting, Tucson, 1978-87; commr. Boy Scouts Am., Tucson, 1978-86; v.p. Tucson Hebrew Acad., 1979-82; bd. dirs. Tucson Jewish Community Ctr., 1980-82. Mellon Found. rsch. fellow, 1965-68, Social Sci. Rsch. Found. rsch. fellow, 1968, Falk Found. rsch. fellow, 1974. Mem. Nat. Assn. Synagogue Adminstrs. (chmn. EDP com. 1984), Profl. Photographers Am., Am. Historica Assn., Assoc. Photographers Internat. Home and Office: 5121 E 6th St Tucson AZ 85711

SULMEISTERS, TALIVALDIS KARLIS, aerospace engineer; b. Riga, Latvia, June 30, 1935; came to U.S., 1951; s. Karlis and Vallija Reta (Eikerts) S.; m. Valda Arija Heine (div. July 1977); children: Walter Karl, Peter Tal; m. Dorothy Marie Hild, July 4, 1977. BSEE, U. Colo., 1962; postgrad., U. Santa Clara, 1963-64. Quality engr. Martin Marietta, Denver, 1958-62; design engr. Lockheed Missiles & Space Co., Sunnyvale, Calif., 1962-64; sect. chief Johnson Space Ctr. div. NASA, Houston, 1964-67; engring. mgr. Martin Marietta, Denver, 1967—; instr. Red Rocks Community Coll., Denver, 1976—. Served with USAF, 1954-58, Korea. Mem. Elect. and Electronics Engrs., Talavija Club (pres. Colo. chpt. 1969—). Republican. Lutheran. Home: 12894 Hwy 285 Conifer CO 80433

SUMIDA, GERALD AQUINAS, lawyer; b. Hilo, Hawaii, June 19, 1944; s. Sadamu and Kimiyo (Miyahara) S.; m. Sylvia Whitehead, June 23, 1970. AB summa cum laude, Princeton U., 1966, cert. in pub. and internat. affairs, 1966; JD, Yale U., 1969. Bar: Hawaii 1970, U.S. Dist. Ct. Hawaii 1970, U.S. Ct. Appeals (9th cir.) 1970, U.S. Supreme Ct. 1981. Research assoc. Ctr. Internat. Studies, Princeton U., 1969; assoc. Carlsmith, Wichman, Case, Mukai & Ichiki, Honolulu, 1970-76, ptnr., 1976—; mem. cameras in courtroom evaluation com. Hawaii Supreme Ct., 1984—. Mem. sci. and statis. com. Western Pacific Fishery Mgmt. Council, 1979—; mem. study group on law of armed conflict and the law of the sea Comdr. in Chief Pacific, U.S. Navy, 1979-82; pres. Pacific and Asian Affairs Council Hawaii, 1982—, bd. govs., 1976—, Paul S. Bachman award, 1978; chmn. internat. com. Hawaii chpt. ARC, 1983—, bd. dirs., 1983; vice chmn. Honolulu Com. on Fgn. Relations, 1983—; pres., dir., founding mem. Hawaii Ocean Law Assn., 1978—; mem. Hawaii Adv. Group for Law of Sea Inst., 1977—; pres. Hawaii Inst. Continuing Legal Edn., 1979-83, dir., 1976—; pres., founding mem. Hawaii Council Legal Edn. for Youth, 1980-83, dir., 1983—; chmn. Hawaii Commn. on Yr. 2000, 1976-79; mem. Honolulu Community Media Council, exec. com., 1976-84, legal counsel, 1979-83; bd. dirs. Hawaii Imin Centennial Corp., 1983—, Hawaii Pub. Radio, 1983-88, Legal Aid Soc. Hawaii, 1984. Mem. Pacific Alliance Trade and Devel., 1984—; founding gov. Ctr. Internat. Comml. Dispute Resolution, 1987—; exec. v.p., chmn. rules and procedures Pacific Rim Found., 1987—; exec. com. Pacific Islands Assn., 1988—. Recipient cert. of appreciation Gov. of Hawaii, 1979, resolutions of appreciation Hawaii Senate and Ho. of Reps., 1979; grantee Japan Found., 1979. Mem. ABA, Hawaii Bar Assn. (pres. young lawyers sect. 1974, v.p. 1984), Japan-Hawaii Lawyers Assn., Am. Soc. Internat. Law, Japan-Hawaii Lawyers Assn., Hawaii C. of C. (energy com. 1981-87, chmn. 1985-87), Am. Judicature Soc., AAAS, Asia Pacific Lawyers Assn., Phi Beta Kappa. Democrat. Clubs: Yale (N.Y.C.); Plaza (Honolulu); Colonial (Princeton). Author: (with others) Legal, Institutional and Financial Aspects of An Inter-Island Electrical Transmission Cable, 1984, Alternative Approaches to the Legal, Institutional and Financial Aspects of Developing an Inter-Island, Electrical Transmission Cable System, 1986; editor Hawaii Bar News, 1972-73; contbr. chpts. to books. Home: 1130 Wilder Ave #1401 Honolulu HI 96822 Office: Pacific Tower 1001 Bishop St Honolulu HI 96813 also: Carlsmith Wichman Case Mukai Ichiki 1001 Bishop St Pacific Tower Ste 2200 Honolulu HI 96813

SUMMERS, SUSAN LUEDTKE, retail executive; b. Wausau, Wis., Dec. 21, 1959; d. Gerald Leonard and Bonnie Mae (Olson) Hollman; m. Charles John Summers, July 2, 1988. Student, Middlebury (Vt.) Coll., 1980, Instituto Internat., Madrid, Spain, 1980-81; BA, Lake Forest (Ill.) Coll., 1982. Account coord. Internat. Travel Svc., Deerfield, Ill., 1982-83; export coord. ACCO Internat., Inc., Wheeling, Ill., 1983-86; mgr. import and export Simon Mktg., Inc., L.A., 1986—. Mem. Fgn. Trade Assn., Nat. Assn. Female Execs. Republican. Lutheran.

SUMSION, HENRY THEODORE, mining company executive; b. Chester, Utah, Mar. 7, 1912; s. Henry Lacelle and Phoebe Ellen (Barlow) S.; m. June Hayes, Aug. 27, 1938; children: Robert Scott, Brent Spencer, Sharon Janine, Shauna Susan. BS in Metall. Engring., U. Utah, 1938; MS in Mining Engring., U. Ala., 1939; PhD in Metall. Engring., U. Utah, 1949. Engr. Bur. Mines, 1939-42; asst. physicist U. Calif., 1946-47, U. Utah, 1947-49; sr. engr. Carborundum Co., 1949-51; research assoc. Knolls Atomic Power Lab., Gen. Electric Co., 1951-56, nuclear fuels engr. atomic power equipment dept., 1956-57; research scientist Lockheed Missiles and Space Co., Palo Alto, Calif., 1957-62, Ames Research Ctr., NASA, Moffett Field, Calif., 1962-84; instr. engring. U. Calif. Berkeley Extension, 1955-57. Contbr. articles to profl. jours. Patentee in field. Served to capt. USAF, 1942-46. Recipient Commendation, USN, 1959, Apollo Achievement award NASA, 1969, Legion of Honor. Fellow Am. Inst. Chemists, N.Y. Acad. Scis.; mem. AIME, Am. Soc. Metals, AAAS, Sigma Xi, Tau Beta Pi, Phi Kappa Phi. Mormon. Home: 5378 Harwood Rd San Jose CA 95124

SUN, CHRISTOPHER I-CHUM, architect, minister; b. Nov. 29, 1953; s. Ki-Tung and Gloria Liang-Hui (Kuo) S.; m. Sue-Ling Shirley Chen, May 28, 1977; children: Abraham, Annabel. BArch, Chung Yuan Christian U., 1977; MArch, U. Calif., Berkeley, 1980; MA in Theology, Fuller Theol. Seminary, Pasadena, Calif., 1984; PhD, Calif. Grad. Sch. Theology, 1987. Lic. architect, Calif. Designer Total Engring. Cons., 1977; curator Chih-Ching Library, 1978-79; project mgr. D.L. & Assocs., L.A., 1980-82; sr. designer H.R. Architect, L.A., 1982, R.M. & Assocs., Santa Monica, Calif., 1983-84; owner, exec. Millennium Architect, Alhambra, Calif., 1984—; mem. U. Calif.-Berkeley Coll. Environ. Design Coun., 1986—. Author (books) Closer, Closer, 1982, Creationism versus Evolutionism, 1983. Bible tchr. Bapt. Ch., L.A., 1980-81, assoc. pastor, Van Nuys, 1983-84; youth dir. Evang. Ch., Torrance, 1982-84; founder, exec. Kingdom of God Ministry, L.A., 1984—. Mem. AIA. Office: PO 3126 Los Angeles CA 90051

SUN, JAMES DEAN, toxicologist, consultant; b. Denver, Feb. 8, 1951; s. Yun Pei and Jung (Tung) S.; m. Ann Marie Dereschuk, Mar. 31, 1974. BS in Biochemistry, U. Calif., Davis, 1973; PhD in Biochemistry, U. Calif., Riverside, 1978; postdoctoral, Chem. Industry Inst., 1978-80. Rsch. asst. U. Calif., Riverside, 1974-75, 76-78, teaching asst., 1975-76; inhalation toxicologist Lovelace Inhalation Toxicology Rsch. Inst., Albuquerque, 1980—; study dir. Nat. Toxicology Program on Ferrocene, Albuquerque, 1988—. Contbr. articles to profl. jours. Mem. Soc. of Toxicology, Mountain W. Soc. Toxicology (counciler 1988—), N.Y. Acad. Sci., Nat. Acad. Sci. (com. on fire toxicology Washington chpt. 1985-87), TI Computer Group (pres. Albuquerque chpt. 1987—). Republican. Presbyterian. Office: Lovelace Inhalation Inst PO Box 5890 Albuquerque NM 87185

SUND, JOHN LEONARD, lawyer, state legislator, business executive; b. Ketchikan, Alaska, Feb. 14, 1949; s. Otto Arthur and Karen (Berre) S.; m. Kathleen A. MacKinnon, Aug. 7, 1971; children: Kevin, Theresa. BA in History, Polit. Sci. and Edn., Western Wash. U., 1971; JD, Lewis and Clark Coll., 1974. Bar: Alaska 1974, U.S. Dist. Ct. Alaska 1975, U.S. Ct. Appeals (9th cir.) 1976. Ptnr., Ellis, Sund & Whittaker, Ketchikan, 1974-79; chief counsel to speaker Alaska Ho. of Reps., Juneau, 1979-81; pres. Waterfall Group Ltd., Ketchikan, 1981-84; mem. Alaska Ho. of Reps., 1984-88, chmn. house judiciary com., 1987-88; ptnr. Silver Lining Seafoods, Ketchikan, Alaska, 1981—; apptd. Gov.'s Com. for Study of Bodily Injury Reparations, 1978-79, Fisheries Ctr. Study Com., 1980-81. Chmn. Ketchikan Overall Econ. Study Com., 1977-79. Mem. ABA, Alaska Bar Assn., Am. Judicature Assn. Democrat. Club: Sons of Norway (Ketchikan).

SUND, KIRK ALFRED, dentist; b. Aberdeen, Wash., Nov. 21, 1951; s. Eric Alfred and Lois LaVaughn (Bittinger) S. BA in Zoology, U. Wash., 1977, BS in Dental Hygiene, 1977, DDS, 1987. Assoc. dentist Timothy E. Wandell, Hoquiam, Wash., 1987—. Home: 808 4th St Hoquiam WA 98550 Office: 401 7th St Hoquiam WA 98550

SUNDARAM, SHANMUGHA N., consulting engineer; b. Coimbatore, India, Aug. 25, 1930; came to U.S., 1963; s. Nanjappa Chettiar and Chinnammal Nanjapa; m. Indira Mani, July 11, 1956; children: Senthil Kumar, Siva Kumar. BEngring., Govt. Coll. Tech., Coimbatore, 1952; MTech, Indian Inst. Tech., Kharagpur, 1959; PhD, Purdue U., 1967. Chief structural engr. Longardner Assocs., Indpls., 1967-69, 70-72; bridge engr. Beam, Longest & Neff, Indpls., 1972-73; project engr. Bellante, Clauss, Miller and Nolan, Scranton, Pa., 1973-75; program devel. engr. Ariz. Dept. Transp., Phoenix, 1975-78; project engr. Magadini-Alagia Assocs., Phoenix, 1978-82; consulting engr. Sundaram Engring., Mesa, Ariz., 1983—; assoc. prof. Calif. State U.-L.A., 1983. Contbr. papers to profl. publs. Fellow ASCE; mem. Am. Concrete Inst. (mem. tech. com. 1981—), Am. Soc. Engring. Edn., Rotary. Democrat. Hindu.

SUNDBERG, EDGAR LEONARD, land management executive, manufacturing executive; b. Boston, May 30, 1920; s. Mattias Algot and Ruth (Nystrom) S.; m. Ruth Olive Kinsman, Feb. 19, 1944; children: Richard Lee, Heidi Lynn. AA, New Eng. Sch. Art, 1946. Asst. chief clk. Singer Sewing Machine Co., Boston, 1939-41, 46; sales engr. Coast Pro-Seal & Mfg. Co., L.A., 1947-52; founder, ptnr. Deccofelt Products Co., Glendora, Calif., 1952-63; pres., chief exec. officer, chmn. bd. dirs. Deccofelt Corp., Glendora, 1963-81; pres. Dazey Mfg. Corp., Glendora, 1963-75; pres., chief exec. officer Sundberg Mgmt. Corp., Seal Beach, Calif., 1981—; co-ptnr. Casa del Norte Apts., La Habra, Calif., 1987—; ltd. ptnr. Sun-State Corp., Burbank, Calif., 1988—; cons. mfg. Deccofelt Corp., Glendora, 1982—. Founder Bob Hope Cultural Ctr. for the Arts, Palm Desert, Calif., 1987—; trustee Glendora Meth. Ch., 1970-73, Long Beach (Calif.) Meth. Ch., 1982-84; mem. Kona (Hawaii) Cen. Union Ch., Palm Desert Presbyn. Ch. Sgt. USMC, 1942-45, PTO. Mem. Marina del Ray C. of C. (dir. 1974), USN League (life), Am. Legion Desert Horizons Country Club (current bd. dirs.), Calif. Yacht Club (commodore 1973), Transpacific Yacht Club, So. Calif. Yacht Assn. (bd dirs. 1974), Huntington Harbour Yacht Club (bd. dirs. 1979-80), Assn. Santa Monica Bay Yacht Club (bd. dirs. 1975), Rotary (internat dir. 1980). Republican. Methodist. also: 78-7070 Alii Dr Kailua-Kona HI 96740 Office: Sundberg Mgmt Corp 239 Seal Beach Blvd Ste C Seal Beach CA 90740

SUNDEL, HARVEY H., marketing research analyst and consultant; b. Bronx, NY, July 24, 1944; s. Louis and Pauline (Brotman) S. BBA, St. Mary's U., San Antonio, 1969, MBA, 1970; PhD, St. Louis U., 1974. Asst. dir. research Lone Star Brewery, San Antonio, 1970-71; cons. Tri-Mark, Inc., San Antonio, 1972-73; asst. prof. mktg. Lewis and Clark Coll., Godfrey, Ill., 1973-74; asst. prof. mktg. Met. State Coll., Denver, 1974-77, chmn., prof. mktg., 1977-86; pres. Sundel Research, Inc., Denver, 1976—; cons. Frederick Ross Co., Denver, 1979-84, US West Direct, Denver, 1986—, Monsanto Chems. Co., St. Louis, 1985—, Mountain Bell, Denver, 1979-88, U.S. West Communications, Denver, 1988—, AT&T, 1986—, Holmdel, 1986—, Melco Industries, 1987—. Contbr. papers and proceedings to profl. jours. Com. mem. Mile High United Way, Denver, 1975-80. Jewish. Home: 1616 Glen Bar Dr Lakewood CO 80215 Office: Sundel Rsch Inc 1150 Delaware Denver CO 80204

SUNDIN, ROBERT LYNN, civil engineer, retired military officer; b. Youngstown, Ohio, Oct. 1, 1942; s. Carl Albert and Mary Jane (Watkins) S.; m. Angela D'Addio, June 18, 1966; children: Christine Laura, Gregg Robert. BCE, USCG Acad., 1964, U. Ill., 1969. Enlisted USCG, 1964, advanced through grades to comdr., 1978; comdg. officer U.S. Coast Guard Cutter Point Slocum, Republic of Vietnam, 1967-68; civil engr. 7th Coast Guard Dist., Miami, Fla., 1969-71; facility engr. Coast Guard Base, San Juan, P.R., 1971-72; asst. to chief civil engr. 1st Coast Guard Dist., Boston, 1972-75; chief resources sect. Coast Guard Hdqr., Washington, 1975-79; chief civil engr. 13th Coast Guard Dist., Seattle, 1979-83; planning and mgmt. chief Facilities Design Ctr., Seattle, 1983-84; retired USCG, Seattle, 1984; planning and project dir. John Graham Assoc., Seattle, 1984—. Contbr. articles to profl. jours. Recipient Navy Commendation V medal, 1968, Comdt.'s Commendation award, Washington, 1979, USCG Commendation medal, Seattle, 1984. Fellow Soc. of Am. Mil. Engrs. (pres. 1987, v.p. 1989—), Puget Sound Coast Guard Officers Assn., U. Ill. Alumni Assn., Coast Guard Acad. Alumni., KC. Republican. Roman Catholic. Home: 18725 SE 45th St Issaquah WA 98027 Office: John Graham Assoc 520 Pike St Ste 1100 Seattle WA 98101

SUNDIN, THEODORE ALAN, military officer, engineer; b. Mpls., Nov. 30, 1932; s. August Theodore Sundin and Evelyn Mable (Emerson) Sheaff; m. Judith Adell, Apr. 28, 1962 (div. Aug. 1977); children: Brian, Charles; m. Michelle Madonna, Mar. 31, 1983; children: Kristie Scofield, Tracie Scofield. B in Mech. Engring., U. Minn., 1955. Registered mech. engr. Enlisted USAF, 1955; advanced through grades to col. USAF, USAFR, 1962; engr. USAF, Carswell AFB, Tex., 1955-58; test engr. Convair, Ft. Worth, Tex., 1958-59; sr. engr. Delco Electronics, GMC, Santa Barbara, Calif., 1959-71; freelance cons. Ashland, Oreg., 1971-77; mgr. Comptech Research Inc., Santa Barbara, 1977-81; sr. staff engr. Martin Marietta, Vandenberg AFB, Calif., 1981-83; system program dir. USAF, Tyndell AFB, Fla., 1983-87; engr. Martin Marietta, Denver, 1987—; v.p. Avaition Hall of Fame, Dayton, Ohio, 1974-77. appointed to bldg. commn. Ashland (Oreg.) City Govt., 1976-77. Decorated Legion of Merit, USAF. Mem. Am. Inst. Aeronautics and Astronautics (sr.) (sect. chmn. 1979-83, cert. 1983, mem. tech. com. 1986—), La. Engring. Soc., Air Force Assn. (life), Res. Officers Assn. (life), Rotary. Avocations: boating, classic autos, home restoration.

SUNDIN, WESLEY NORMAN, social welfare administrator; b. Omaha, Jan. 31, 1944; s. Carl Petrus and Esther (Schaefer) S.; m. Ruth Alice Davenport, July 24, 1965; children: Shana, Marie, Erik, Heather. BA, Asbury Coll., 1966. Comdg. officer The Salvation Army, various cities, currently Denver, 1968—. Contbr. articles to popular mags. Exec. com. Billy Graham Crusade, Denver. Lodge: Kiwanis (dir. Columbine chpt., Littleton, Colo., 1987-88). Office: The Salvation Army 4505 W Alameda Denver CO 80219

SUNDRY, CATHIE LEE, sales representative; b. Kalamazoo, Mar. 27, 1946; d. James William Gilmartin and Geraldine Ann (Minckler) Jones; m. Charles Wayne Sundry, Nov. 20, 1977; children: Haakon Barrett, Cailin Dael. BSN cum laude, U. Pitts., 1968. RN; cert. pub. health nurse, Calif. Staff, charge nurse Magee Women's Hosp., Pitts., 1968-71; head nurse, unit dir. St. Vincent's Hosp., Portland, Oreg., 1971-73; instr., head nurse obstetrics Queens Med. Ctr., Honolulu, 1974-78; med. surg. instr. Kapiolani Community Coll., Honolulu, 1980-81; operating room, office nurse Plastic Surgeons Med. Group, Grossmont, Calif., 1982-83; med. sales rep., instr. Total Pharm. Care, Inc., San Diego, 1985—; instr. Pitts. Organ. for Childbirth Edn., Pitts, 1969-71; panel coordinator, Hawaii Nurses Assn., Honolulu, 1975. Mem. Am. Soc. Parenteral and Enteral Nutrition, Intravenous Nurses Soc., Coun. of Long Term Care Nurses of Calif. Lutheran. Home: 778 Baylor Ave Chula Vista CA 92013 Office: Total Pharm Care Inc 11021 Via Frontera Ste 203 San Diego CA 92127

SUNLIGHT, CAROLE, psychologist; b. DuBois, Pa., Aug, 19; d. Andy and Mary Ann Gaborick; Med. Tech., Carnegie Coll., 1959; BA in Psychology, Cleve. State U., 1971; MA in Psychology (Univ. scholar), Pepperdine U., 1973; PhD in Psychology, U.S. Internat. U., 1980. Med. technologist Doctors Piercy, Fertig, Schneider and Doran, Cleve., 1959-67; chief technologist med. dept. U.S. Steel Corp., Lorain, Ohio, 1967-69; office mgr. dept. philosophy and religious studies Cleve. State U., 1969-70; counselor Gardena Valley Counseling Service, Gardena, Calif., 1971-72; clin. intern Pepperdine U. psychology clinic, 1972-73; testing technician Norco-Corona (Calif.) Sch. Dist., 1973; dir. treatment services Unfinished Symphony Ranch, Inc., Agoura, Calif., 1973-77; pvt. practice, Westlake Village, Calif., 1977-78; staff Kaiser Permanente Mental Health Center, 1977—; pvt. practice, Torrance, Calif., 1980—; speaker in field. Bd. dirs. COMOSI Mental Health, Thousand Oaks, Calif., 1977-78. Registered med. technologist. Mem. Am. (sects on psychology of women, clin. neuropsychology, Calif. Psychol. Assn., Los Angeles County (newsletter editor 1982-84) Psychol. Assn., Am. Med. Technologists (Ohio State Soc. Publ. award 1972), Calif. Neuropsychol. Soc., Psychologists for Social Responsibility, NOW, Psi Chi. Office: 9449 Imperial Hwy Downey CA 90242 also: 19000 Hawthorne Blvd Ste 300 Torrance CA 90503

SUNTHARALINGAM, GNANALINGAM, physics educator; b. Colombo, Sri Lanka, June 10, 1924; came to U.S., 1984; s. Chellappah and Kanagambihai (Canagasabai) S.; m. Pushpaletchimy Kasippillai, Sept. 9, 1949; children: Anandan, Lakshmi, Arjavan, Dhanya, Anandi. BS, U. Ceylon, Colombo, Sri Lanka, 1945; BA, U. Cambridge, England, 1948; MA, U. Cambridge, 1951, PhD, 1954. Fellow (Title A) Trinity Coll., Cambridge U., England, 1952-55; sr. lectr. in elec. engring. U. Ceylon, Sri Lanka, 1955-60; chief exec. officer Paranthan Chemicals Corp., Sri Lanka, 1960-62; head sect. applied physics and electronics Ceylon Inst. Sci. and Indsl. Rsch., Sri Lanka, 1962-83; vis. rsch. assoc. U. Ill., Champaign, 1984-85; adj. prof. physics U.S. Naval Postgrad. Sch., Monterey, Calif., 1985—; sr. postdoctoral resident rsch. assoc. NASA Goddard Space Flight Ctr., Greenbelt, Md., 1971-72; chmn. Sri Lanka Overseas Branch of IEE, Colombo, 1975-76; gen. pres. Sri Lanka Assn. for the Advancement of Sci., Colombo, 1983. Mem. Gov.-Gen.'s Commn. on Tech. Edn., Sri Lanka, 1961-63; chmn. Panel for Tamil Music, Dancing & Folk Music, Arts Coun. Sri Lanka, 1969-70; mem. coun. U. Peradeniya, Sri Lanka, 1979-82; bd. dirs. Sri Lanka Broadcasting Corp., 1981-83. Recipient Award for Sci. Achievement, Nat. Sci. Coun. Sri Lanka, 1981, Vidya Jyothi, Pres. of Sri Lanka, 1986. Fellow IEE London, Nat. Acad. Sci. Sri Lanka; mem. IEEE (sr. mem.). Hindu. Home: 469 Larkin St 5 Monterey CA 93940 Office: US Naval Postgrad School Sloat Ave Monterey CA 93943

SUPER, PAUL JONATHAN, contact lens specialist; b. Johannesburg, South Africa, Sept. 29, 1957; came to U.S., 1977; s. Selwyn and Cynthia (Cohen) S.; m. Tessa Susan Margot Levy, Feb. 14, 1985. BS, U. Houston, 1979, OD, 1981; vision tng. residency, SUNY, N.Y.C., 1985-86. Assoc., ptnr. Prof. Selwyn Super, Johannesburg, South Africa, 1981-85; asst. clin. prof. SUNY, N.Y.C., 1985-86; assoc. Drs. Farkow & Kassalow, P.C., N.Y.C., 1986-87, Dr. Melvin Remba, L.A., 1987-88; prin. Paul J. Super OD Inc., L.A., 1988-89; cons. Med. Aviation Soc., 1983-85, Contact Lens Industry, 1987-89. Contbr. articles to profl. jours. Fellow Am. Acad. Optometry; mem. Med. Aviation Soc., Am. Optometric Assn. Jewish.

SUPLIZIO, SAMUEL VICTOR, finanical services executive; b. DuBois, Pa., Sept. 14, 1932; Carter, Cynthia Lee, Samuel Paul, Thomas Eugene. BE, U. N.Mex., 1954. Profl. baseball player N.Y. Yankees Orgn., 1953-56; mgr. minor league team Los Angeles Dodgers Baseball Team, Thomasville, GA., 1957; pres. Home Loan & Investment Co., Grand Junction, Colo., 1957; scout, instr. Milw. Brewers Baseball Team, 1975—; bd. dirs. Cen. Bank, Grand Junction, 1984—l coach 1982 World Series. Speaker in field; contbr. articles to profl. jours. Chmn. Nat. Jr. Coll. Baseball World Series, Grand Junction, 1959—, Hilltop House Rehab. Ctr., 1963-67, Colo. Easter Seal, 1969; trustee Mesa Jr. Coll., Grand Junction, 1971-74; fin. chmn. Colo. Repub. Com., Denver, 1981-82; mem. Salvation Army Bd., 1967—. Recipient Disting. Service award Jaycees, Grand Junction, 1963, W.P. "Dutch" Fering award of merit U.S. Baseball Fedn., N.Y., 1985; named to All Sports Hall of Fame, DuBois Pa. Booster Club, 1968, Baseball Hall of Fame Nat. Jr. Coll. Athletic Assn., Colo. Springs, 1985. Mem. Am. Baseball Coaches Assn. (award of merit 1985), Ind. Insurers Colo. (bd. dirs. 1980-87, outstanding service award 1985-86), Ind. Insurors Colo. (pres. 1986), Club 20 (pres. 1982), U.S. C. of C. (v.p., dir. 1968-70), Grand Junction C. of C. (bd. dirs. 1969-72), Bookcliff Knife & Fork Club (pres. 1966—). Roman Catholic. Lodges: Elks, KC, Kiwanis (pres. Bookcliff chpt. 1973), Fellowship of Christian Athletes. Home: 2625 H Rd Grand Junction CO 81506 Office: Home Loan 145 N 4th Grand Junction CO 81501

SURAWICZ, CHRISTINA MATHILDA, physician; b. Munich, Jan. 4, 1948; d. Barys and Frida (Vanklaveren) S.; m. James Butler Bushyhead. BA, Barnard Coll., 1969; MD, U. Ky., 1973. Resident in medicine U. Wash. Affiliated Hosp., Seattle, 1973-76, asst. prof. medicine, 1981-86, assoc. prof. medicine, 1986—. Contbr. articles to profl. jours. Fellow Am. Coll. Physicians, Am. Coll. Gastroenterology; mem. AMA. Office: Harborview Med Ctr 325 9th Ave Seattle WA 98104

SURFACE, STEPHEN WALTER, water treatment chemist; b. Dayton, Ohio, Feb. 25, 1943; s. Lorin Wilfred and Virginia (Marsh) S.; m. Suzanne MacDonald, Aug. 29, 1964 (div.); 1 child, Jennifer Nalani; m. Sinfrosa Garay, Sept. 16, 1978; children: Maria Lourdes, Stephanie Alcantara. BS, Otterbein Coll., 1965; MA, U. So. Calif., 1970; postgrad., U. Hawaii, 1971. Tchr. Hawaii State Dept. Edn., Honolulu, 1970-71; staff chemist Del Monte Corp., Honolulu, 1971; head chemist USNPearl Harbor, Honolulu, 1971-76, staff chemist, 1976—. Contbr. articles to profl. jours. Recipient DuPont Teaching award, U. So. Calif., 1966. Fellow Internat. Biog. Assn., Am. Inst. Chemists; mem. Am. Chem. Soc., Am. Water Works Assn., N.Y. Acad. Scis., Sigma Zeta, Phi Lambda Upsilon. Democrat. Methodist. Home: 94-1139 Noheaiki St Waipahu HI 96797-4138 Office: Naval Facilities Engring Command Pacific Div Pearl Harbor HI 96860-7300

SURISKEY, JO ANN, organization administrator; b. Denver, Aug. 29, 1949; d. John and Minnie Helen (Coutts) S. BA in Elem. Edn., Western State Coll., Gunnison, Colo., 1970, MA in Elem. Edn., 1975. Cert. tchr. Colo., N.Mex. Dance tchr. Hope Moore Dance Studio, Englewood, Colo., 1962-67; tchr. Denver Pub. Schs., 1972-73, Truth or Consequences (N.Mex.) Elem. Sch., 1973-83, Mt. Calvary Luth. Sch., Denver, 1983-84, Gilpin Grammar Sch., Denver, 1985-86, Child Motivation Ctr., Lakewood, Colo., 1986-87; acct. Woodlawn, Harvey, McGraw, Denver, 1987; med. soc. VA, Denver, 1987—. Mem. AAUW (life), Sierra County Edn. Assn. (SW dist rep. 1974-83, SW dist treas. 1981-82). Republican. Lutheran. Office: VA 1055 Clermont St Denver CO 80222

SURWILL, BENEDICT JOSEPH, JR., college dean, educator; b. Chgo., Oct. 8, 1925; s. Benedict Joseph and Emily (Zemgolis) S.; m. Frances May Welling, Oct. 16, 1948; children: Thomas, Benedict, Robert, Patricia. BS in Edn., Ariz. State Coll., 1951, MS in Edn., 1954; EdD, U. Colo., 1962. Elem. tchr. Winnetka (Ill.) Pub. Schs., 1958-61; jr. high sch. prin. Champaign (Ill.) Pub. Schs., 1961-63; dir. Campus Sch. SUNY, Buffalo, 1963-68; dean. Sch. Edn. Ea. Mont. Coll., Billings, 1968—; chmn. dean's council Mont. Univ. System, 1974; mem. Mont. Supt.'s Adv. Com. on Tchr. Edn. and Cert., 1969—, chmn., 1972-73; mem. ednl. forum State Supt. of Pub. Instrn., 1977—, Mont. Rural Youth Adv. Council, Billings, 1979—; lectr. in field. Editor: A Critical Examination of American Education, 1985; mem. editorial bd., contbg. editor Jour. Creative Behavior, 1966—. Co-chmn. cancer drive Billings chpt. Am. Cancer Soc., 1988—, Mont. State Cham Cancer Crusade, 1989. With inf. U.S. Army. Recipient Am. Assn. of Coll. for Tchr. Edn. award, 1972, Presdl. citation Ill. Assn. Sch. Adminstrs., 1973. Mem. Nat. Council Accreditation Tchr. Edn. (mem. standards com., mem. multicultural edn. com. 1977, bd. appeals 1980-83, bd. examiners 1988—), Phi Delta Kappa, Kappa Delta Pi, Yellowstone Country Club, Elks. Home: 5864 Sam Snead Trail Billings MT 59106 Office: Ea Mont Coll Sch Edn 1500 N 30th Billings MT 59101

SUTHERLAND, BRUCE, composer, pianist; pupil Halsey Stevens, Ellis Kohs, Ethel Leginska, Amparo Iturbi; b. Daytona Beach, Fla.; s. Kenneth Francis and Norma (Williams) S.; Mus.B., U. So. Calif., 1957, Mus.M., 1959. Harpsichord soloist with Telemann Trio in concert tour, 1969-70; tchr. master class for pianists U. Tex., Austin, 1971; dir. Bach festivals Music Tchrs. Assn. Calif., 1972-73, dir. Artists of Tomorrow Music Festivals Music Tchrs. Assn. Calif., 1984—, competitions performed in numerous contemporary music festivals in U.S., 1957—; piano faculty Calif. State U. at Northridge, 1977—; adjudicator music competitions and auditions Nat. Guild Piano Tchrs., others; dir. Brentwood-Westwood Symphony ann. competition for young artists, 1981—; composer: Allegro Fanfara for Orch., world premiere conducted by José Iturbi with Bridgeport Symphony Orch., 1970; Saxophone Quartet, 1971; Quintet for Flute, Strings, Piano, 1972; Notturno for Flute and Guitar, 1973; also string trio, piano and vocal works. Recipient grand prize Internat. Competition Louis Moreau Gottschalk, 1970; Stairway of Stars award Music Arts Soc., Santa Monica, 1973; named one of Los Angeles' Finest Piano Tchrs., New West Mag., 1977. Mem. Nat. Assn. Am. Composers and Condrs., Music Tchrs. Nat. Assn., Music Tchrs. Assn., Calif. Assn. Profl. Music Tchrs., Pi Kappa Lambda.

SUTHERLAND, DOUGLASS B., tent and awning company executive, mayor; b. Helena, Mont., May 2, 1937; s. Chris and Marie Sutherland; m. Grace Sutherland, Sept. 5, 1986; children: Karen, Scott. B.A., Central Wash. U., 1959. Program specialist Boeing Co., Tacoma, Wash., 1960-71; owner, pres. Tacoma Tent & Awning, Inc., 1971—. Bd. dirs., chmn. Puget Sound Air Pollution Control Agy.; bd. dirs. Tacoma-Pierce County Bd. Health, Tacoma-Pierce County Employment and Tng. Consortium; mayor City of Tacoma, 1982—. Mem. Assn. Wash. Cities, Tacoma-Pierce County C. of C. Republican. Lodge: Rotary. Office: Tacoma Tent and Awning Inc 121 N G St Tacoma WA 98403 also: Office of the Mayor 747 Market St Suite 1220 Tacoma WA 98402 *

SUTHERLAND, JEROME DOUGLAS, radiologist; b. Denver, Jan. 24, 1937; s. Donald Clarence and Hypatia (Slusser) S.; m. Ella Mae McCormick, Apr. 24, 1961; children: Jason, Charles, Michael. MD, U. Colo., Denver, 1961. Diplomate Am. Bd. of Radiology, Am. Bd. of Nuclear Medicine. Intern So. Pacific Hosp., San Francisco, 1961-62; resident in radiology Beth Israel Hosp., Boston, 1962-63; resident U. Colo., Denver, 1963-65; radiologist St. Joseph and Porter Hosp., Denver, 1965-84, Porter Hosp. and Swedish Hosp., Denver, 1984—; also dir nuclear medicine Porter Hosp., Denver; mem. Radiology Imaging Assocs., Englewood, Colo.; asst. clin. prof. radiology U. Colo. Contbr. articles to profl. jours. With U.S. Army, 1966-67. Fellow Am. Coll. Radiology; mem. AMA, Colo. Med. Soc., Soc. Nuclear Medicine, Radiol. Soc. of N.Am., Rocky Mountain Med. Soc., Colo. Med. Soc., Denver Country Club, Grand Lake Yacht Club. Republican. Home: 1198 S Franklin Denver CO 80210 Office: 3576 S Logan Englewood CO 80110

SUTHERLAND, JOHN ELLIOTT, writer, producer, educator; b. Williston, N.D., Sept. 11, 1910; s. Ronald and Adelaide Mae (Elliott) S.; student U. N.D., 1929-30; B.A., UCLA, 1937; m. Lysiane Wagner, 1952; children: Ronald, Eric, Diane. Grad. dir. dramatics and debate UCLA, 1938; prodn. mgr., writer, dialogue dir. Walt Disney Prodns., 1939-40; free-lance screenplay writer, Hollywood, 1941; writer-producer-dir. U.S. Army Signal Corps, other govtl. agys., 1941-45; writer, producer animated cartoons United Artists, Metro Goldwyn Mayer, 1946-55, live-action entertainment films Eagle Lion Motion Pictures Distributor, 1955-56; pres. John Sutherland Prodns., Los Angeles, 1946—, also Sutherland Learning Assos.; producer entertainment programs for ABC and CBS TV, 1972-76; writer, producer health multimedia learning systems U.S. Office of Edn. Housing Edn. Welfare, 1969-73, Capt. Kangaroo program CBS-TV, 1972-73. Mem edn. group Nat. Arthritis Commn., 1975; bd. visitors Grad. Sch. Edn. UCLA, 1974. Creator Thumper characfer in film Bambi, Walt Disney Prodns., 1939-40. Recipient 250 awards for creative excellence in documentary and ednl. films from domestic and internat. film festivals, 1950—; Sesquicentennial award for creative contbns. ednl. films U. Mich., 1967. Co-author, writer, original story: (feature film) Flight Command, 1941; co-author (hist. novel) The Valiant, 1955. Conceived and produced 1st multi-media learning systems in continuing med. edn. Div. Nursing, USPHS, 1969-70. Address: 8700 Reseda Blvd Ste 108 Northridge CA 91324

SUTHERLAND, LOWELL FRANCIS, lawyer; b. Lincoln, Nebr., Dec. 17, 1939; s. Lowell Williams and Doris Genevieve (Peterson) S.; A.B., San Diego State Coll., 1962; LL.B., Hastings Coll. Law, 1965; m. Sandra Gaylynne Stengel, June 12, 1965; children—Scott Thorpe, Mark James, Sandra Doris. With Cooper, White & Cooper, attys., San Francisco, 1963-66; admitted to Calif. bar, 1966; with Wien & Thorpe, attys., El Centro, 1966-67; ptnr. Wien, Thorpe & Sutherland, El Centro, 1967-74, Wien, Thorpe, Sutherland & Stamper, 1973-74, Sutherland, Stamper & Feingold, 1974-77, Sutherland & Gerber, 1977—; ptnr. Sutherland & Sutherland, Ivy Shoppe; Mem. Am., Calif., Imperial County Bar Assns., Am., Calif. (Recognition of Experience awards), San Diego (named Outstanding Trial Lawyer April 1981, Oct. 1983, Trial Lawyer of Yr. 1982), Trial Lawyers Assns., Thurston Soc., Nat. Bd. Trial Advs. (diplomate), Am. Bd. Trial Advocates (assoc.), Theta Chi. Mem. editorial staff Hastings Law Jour., 1964-65. Home: 1853 Sunset Dr El Centro CA 92243 Office: 300 S Imperial Ave 7 El Centro CA 92243

SUTTER, HARVEY MACK, consultant, engineer; b. Jennings, La., Oct. 5, 1906; s. Josiah Harvey and Effie Relief (Murray) S.; AB, U. Wichita, 1932; m. Julia Genevieve Wright, Sept. 19, 1936; children: James Houston, Robert Mack, Julia Ann Boyd, John Norman. Design and prodn. engr. Boeing Aircraft, Wichita, Kans., 1936-38; supr. arts, crafts and coop. activities Bur. Indian Affairs, U.S. Dept. of Interior, 1938-42, chief procurement br. Bur. of Reclamation, Washington, 1946-54, chief div. procurement and property mgmt., 1954-58; asst. to adminstr. Bonneville Power Adminstrn., 1958-61, asst. to chief engr., 1962-66; cons. engr., 1967—; analyst, chief prodn. service WPB, Denver, 1942-44; chief div. supply C.E., Denver, 1944-46. Mem. exec. bd. Portland area Boy Scouts Am. Recipient Silver Beaver award. Presbyterian. Mem. Nat., Western woodcarvers assns., Internat. Wood Collectors Soc., Electric of Oreg. Author or co-author books and articles on woodcarving. Home: 3803 SE Carlton Portland OR 97202

SUTTER, JOHN ORVAL, foundation executive; b. University City, Mo., Jan. 13, 1926; s. Orval Charles and Anne (Bernat) S.; m. Doris Frances Ake, June 30, 1956; children: Ann Wellwood, John Gordon. BS in Fgn. Svc., Wash. U., St. Louis, 1948, AM, 1948; postgrad., Yale U., 1951-52; PhD, Cornell U., 1959. Vice consul Am. Consulate Gen., Shanghai, People's Republic of China, 1949-50, Am. Consulate, Surabaya, Indonesia, 1950-51; diplomatic sec. econ. affairs Am. Embassy, Jakarta, Indonesia, 1952-54; chief rsch. analyst for Indonesia U.S. Dept. of State, Washington, 1955; with The Asia Found., 1959—; rep. The Asia Found., Malaysia, 1967-71, Indonesia, 1969-73, 82-84; dir. program mgmt., grant adminstr. The Asia Found., San Francisco, 1974-82, 85—; cons. from Nat. Acad. Scis. to Indonesian Coun. Scis., Jakarta, 1959. Author: Indonesianisasi: Politics in a Changing Economy, 1959, Scientific Facilities & Information Services in the Republic of Indonesia, 1961, Scientific Facilities & Information Services in the Republic of Vietnam, 1961; editor: quar. No. Calif. World Federalist, 1987—. Staff sgt. U.S. Army, 1944-46. Decorated Bronze Star; Ford Found. fellow, 1955-57. Mem. Assn. Asian Studies, World Affairs Coun. No. Calif., Ripon Soc., World Federalist Assn. No. Calif. (dir. 1989—, v.p. No. Calif. region 1988—), Malaysian-Am. Soc. (v.p. 1968-70), Indonesian-Am. Soc. U.S. (v.p. 1966-67), Selangor, Am. (Jarkarta), Phi Eta Sigma. Republican. Home: 884 Flaxberry Ln San Rafael CA 94903 Office: The Asia Found 465 California St 14th Fl San Francisco CA 94104

SUTTLES, VIRGINIA GRANT, advertising executive; b. Urbana, Ill., June 13, 1931; d. William Henry and Lenora (Fitzsimmons) Grant; grad. pub. schs., Mahomet, Ill.; m. John Henry Suttles, Sept. 24, 1977; step-children—Linda Suttles, Peg Suttles La Croix, Pamela Suttles Diaz, Randall. Media estimator and Procter & Gamble budget control Tatham-Laird, Inc., Chgo., 1955-60; media planner, supr. Tracy-Locke Co., Inc., Dallas and Denver, 1961-68; media dir., account exec. Lorie-Lotito, Inc., 1968-72; v.p., media dir. Sam Lusky Assos., Inc., Denver, 1972-86; ind. media buyer, 1984—; mktg. asst. mktg. dept. Del E. Webb Communities, Inc., Sun City West, Ariz., 1985-88, with telemarketing sales dept., 1989—; lectr. sr. journalism class U. Colo., Boulder, 1975-80; condr. class in media seminars Denver Advt. Fedn., 1974, 77; Colo. State U. panelist Broadcast Day, 1978, High Sch. Inst., 1979, 80, 81, 82, 83. Founder, Del E. Webb Meml. Hosp. Found. Mem. Denver Advt. Fedn. (dir. 1973-75, program chmn. 1974-76, 80-82, exec. bd., v.p. ops. 1980-81, chmn. Alfie awards com. 1980-81, advt. profl. of Yr. 1981-82), Denver Advt. Golf Assn. (v.p. 1976-77, pres. 1977-78), Colo. Broadcasters Assn., Sun City West Bowling Assn. (bd. dirs. 1987-88), Sun City West Women's Social Club. Republican. Congregationalist. Club: Denver Broncos Quarterback. Home: 21022 Sunglow Dr Sun City West AZ 85375 Office: Dell E Webb Communities Inc PO Box 1705 Sun City AZ 85372-1705

SUTTON, BARBARA JEAN, financial planner; b. Fremont, Nebr., Apr. 12, 1949; d. James Lawrence and Beth Elaine (Dunn) Heywood; m. Byron Lee Sutton, Aug. 8, 1970 (div. Nov. 1980). BA in Edn., Wayne State Coll., Nebr., 1970; MEd, U. Nebr., 1976. Tchr. Genoa (Nebr.) Sch. Dist., 1970-74, Ashland-Greenwood (Nebr.) Unified Sch. Dist., 1974-77; fin. planner Profl. Planning Assocs. Ltd., Phoenix, 1978—, v.p., 1980—. Contbr. articles to profl. jours. Mem. adv. bd. Phoenix Econ. Growth Corp., 1988—; bd. dirs. Valley Citizens League, 1987—; founding pres. Community Treatment Program, 1981-85; sec., pres. Phoenix Local Devel. Corp., 1986—; treas., 2d v.p. Phoenix City Club, 1986—. Mem. Am. Soc. CLUs and Chartered Fin. Cons's. (bd. dirs. Phoenix chpt. 1986-87), Nat. Assn. Health Underwriters, Greater Phoenix Assn. of Life Underwriters. Republican. Home: 3059 E Rose Ln Phoenix AZ 85016 Office: Profl Planning Assocs Ltd 1661 E Camelback Rd Ste 100 Phoenix AZ 85016

SUTTON, BARBARA POWDERLY, marketing executive; b. Scranton, Pa., Oct. 29, 1940; d. Eugene Thomas and Kathryn Dorothy (Loftus) Powderly; m. Ronald Lewis Sutton, Jan. 7, 1984 (div. Feb. 1985). Student, Miami (Fla.)-Dade Jr. Coll., 1960. Asst. controller Oak Ridge, Inc., Hialeah, Fla., 1959-63; v.p., media dir. Harold Gardner Assocs., Inc., Miami Beach, Fla., 1963-67; media dir., adminstrv. asst. Stern, Hays & Lang Advt., Inc., Miami, 1967-69; exec. asst. Los Angeles Times, 1969-71; media dir., adminstrv. asst. Greenman Advt., Inc., Hollywood, Fla., 1971-73; asst. to gen. mgr. Sta. WGMA-FM, Hollywood, 1974; with acctg. and settlement dept. Fed. Res. Bank, Miami, 1974-75; bus. mgr. Impart Pub. Corp., Reno, 1975-76; adminstrv. asst., office mgr. Edn. Advancement Inst., Reno, 1976-78; ind. contractor Du-Bar Internat., Reno, 1979-80; pres. Capitol Advt., Reno, 1980-81; dir. media Mktg. Systems Internat., Reno, 1981-82; owner Dolphin Secretarial Service, Reno, 1982-88, Dolphin Services, Reno, 1982—, Powderly Assocs., Reno, 1982—; pres. Bus.-Promotional Services, Inc., Reno, 1986-89; speaker Mktg. Fedn., Inc., N.Y.C., 1986; seminar developer and presenter Advt. and Mktg. for Small Bus., U. Nev. Small Bus. Devel. Ctr., 1987-88. Bd. dirs. March of Dimes, Reno, 1981-82, Teen View Home, Reno, 1987; mem. Presdl. Task Force, Washington, 1983-85; mem. Reno Commn. on Status of Women Reno Women's Network, 1987-88; active Gov. Conf. for Women. Named one of 2,000 Women of Achievement, London, 1971. Mem. Nat. Assn. Female Execs., Am. Soc. Profl. and Exec. Women, Mem. Entrepreneurial Women of Reno (rec. sec., bd. dirs. 1987-88), Bridge Club. Republican. Roman Catholic.

SUTTON, GEORGE WALTER, research laboratory executive, professional engineer; b. Bklyn., Aug. 3, 1927; s. Jack and Pauline (Aaron) S.; m. Evelyn D. Kunnes, Dec. 25, 1952; children—James E., Charles S., Richard E., Stewart A. B. Mech. Engring. with honors, Cornell U., 1952; M.S., Calif. Inst. Tech., 1953, Ph.D. magna cum laude, 1955. Rsch. scientist Lockheed Missile Co., 1955; rsch. engr. Space Sci. Lab. GE, 1955-61, mgr. magnetohydrodynamic power generation, 1962-63; vis. Ford prof. MIT, 1961-62; sci. adviser Hdqrs. USAF, 1963-65; with Avco Rsch. Lab., 1965—, dir. laser devel., 1971—; v.p. Avco Everett Rsch. Lab., Everett, Mass., 1972-82; v.p., tech. dir. Helionetics Laser div. Avco Everett Rsch. Lab., San Diego, 1983-86, v.p., tech. dir., 1985-86; v.p. JAYCOR, San Diego, 1986—; spl. cons. Energy Agy., 1977-79, Arms Control Agy., 1986; lectr. magnetohydrodynamics U. Pa., 1960-63, Stanford, 1964; spl. research on ablation of heat protection for ICBM and high energy lasers. Author: Proceedings 4th Symposium Engineering Aspects of Magnetohydrodynamics, 1964, (with A. Sherman) Engineering Magnetohydrodynamics, 1965, Direct Energy Conversion, 1966; editor-in-chief: Jour. Am. Inst. Aeros. and Astronautics, 1967—; contbr. 72 articles to profl. jours. Served with USAAF, 1945-47. Recipient Arthur Flemming award for outstanding govt. service, 1965. Fellow AIAA (chmn. plasmadynamics tech. com., Thermophysics award 1980, Disting. Service award 1988), ASME, AAAS; mem. Symposium Engring. Aspects Magnetohydrodynamics (pres.). Office: PO Box 85154 San Diego CA 92138

SUTTON, JACK REDELL, food products executive; b. N.Y.C., Oct. 7, 1942; s. Jack R. and Lillian Roth (Fischer) Sutton; m. Sandra L. Wryats, June 1, 1960 (div. Jan. 1972); children: Glenn E., Robert E., Charles R.; m. Marilyn Joyce Westerfield, Apr. 28, 1972; children: Shannon M., Julie A. Student, Shoreline Coll., 1962-63. Dist. mgr. Safeway Stores, Inc., Seattle, 1960-79; sr. v.p. Sea Galley Store, Inc., Mtlk. Terr., Wash., 1979-82; owner Chick n Spuds Restaurants, Everett, Wash., 1982-84; sr. v.p. Am. Restaurants, Ventura, Calif., 1984-86; exec. v.p. Haircuts Co., Milw., 1986-87; pres. Plush Pippin Co., Federal Way, Wash., 1987—; bd. dirs. Lockmane, Inc., Lynnwood, Wash., 1985-87. Mem. Rotary, Edmonds, Wash., 1969-72, Everett, Wash., 1977-79. Republican. Methodist. Home: 1077 SW 326th St Federal Way WA 98023 Office: Plush Pippin Corp 31620 23rd Ave S Ste 318 Federal Way WA 98003

SUTTON, MARCELLA FRENCH, interior designer; b. Prague, Czechoslovakia, Sept. 4, 1946; came to U.S., 1952, naturalized, 1956; d. Eugen E. and Frances V. (Pruchovia) French; BS in Profl. Arts, Woodbury U., 1971; m. Michael D. Sutton, Feb. 11, 1978; 1 child, Kevin Christopher. Mgr. design dept. W. & J. Sloane, Beverly Hills, Calif., 1972-76; project dir. Milton I. Swimmer, Beverly Hills, 1977-78; owner, interior designer Marcella French Designs, Woodland Hills and La Crescenta, Calif., 1969—; v.p.

Shepherd of the Valley Sch., mem. fund raising com.; property mgmt. coordinator, interior designer Home Savs. and Loan., State of Calif., Los Angeles, 1979-82; regional premises officer, asst. v.p. regional hdqrs. Bank of Am., Los Angeles, 1981-86; v.p. M.D. Sutton Ins. Agy.; prin. designer Marcella French Designs, Woodland Hills; cons. pvt. residences. Mem. fund raising com. City of Canoga Park, 1987-88; active Young Reps; treas. West Hills Baseball Aux., 1989—. Recipient various scholarships.

SUTTON, MILO WILTON, newspaper publishing executive; b. Hartford, Kans., Dec. 24, 1928; s. Joseph Bernard and Genevieve Loraine (Campbell) S.; m. Erna Doreen Clemmer, Dec. 18, 1946; children—Cynthia, Janet, Rita, Debbie, Wendy, Michael. Student Kans. State Tchrs. Coll., 1948-50, UCLA, 1969. Mem. Kans. Ho. of Reps., 1950-54; adv. mgr. Emporia (Kans.) Times, 1949-52; reporter Emporia Gazette, 1953-54; owner, pub. Salina (Kans.) Advertiser-Sun, 1954-59; with advt. and editorial depts. Los Angeles Mirror-News, 1959-60; promotion mgr. South Bay Daily Breeze, Torrance, Calif., 1960-74; dir. promotion and research Dallas Times Herald, 1974-77; dir. mktg. services, mem. operating com. Los Angeles Herald Examiner, 1977-84; mktg. mgr. for spl. projects Los Angeles Times, 1984—; internat. lectr. Bd. dirs., regional pres. Kans. Press Assn., 1956-57. Served with USN, 1946-48. Mem. Internat. Newspaper Mktg. Assn. (internat. bd. dirs. 1975-79, 85-88, pres. So. region 1976-77, pres. Western region 1984-85, internat. v.p. 1986-87, internat. pres. 1989—), Advt. Club Los Angeles. Lutheran. Author numerous trade mag. articles. Home: 415 2nd St Hermosa Beach CA 90254 Office: Times Mirror Sq Los Angeles CA 90053

SUTTON, RAY FREDERICK, automotive executive; b. Canton, Ohio, Dec. 9, 1931; s. Louis Ray and Kathleen Mary (Troske) S.; m. Marceline Brunner, Aug. 28, 1949; children: Thomas R., Cynthia. Grad. high sch., Canton. Owner Sutton Enterprises, Canton, 1953-56; sales exec. Salta Pontiac, Long Beach, Calif., 1956-58, McKenzie Ford, Long Beach, Calif., 1958-60, Friendly Rambler, Redwood City, Calif., 1960-63, E.Z. Davis, Redwood City, 1963-67; ptnr. Swift Dodge, Sacramento, 1967-75; owner Anchorage Chrysler, 1975—. With U.S. Army, 1945-48. Mem. Dealer CMC, Alaska Chrysler-Plymouth Dealers Assn., CMC Honor Soc., Pentastar, Ramcharger Soc., Eagle Club, Pacemakers Club, Charger Club. Republican. Office: Anchorage Chrysler Ctr Inc 2601 E 5th Ave Anchorage AK 99501

SUTTON, THOMAS C., insurance company executive; b. Atlanta, June 2, 1942; m. Marilyn Sutton; children: Stephen, Paul, Matthew, Meagan. BS in Math. and Physics, U. Toronto, 1965; postgrad., Harvard U., 1982. With Pacific Mut. Life Ins. Co., Newport Beach, Calif., 1963—, actuarial asst., 1966-69, successively asst. actuary, assoc. actuary, asst. v.p., 2d v.p., v.p. individual ins., 1969-80, successively v.p. individual fin., sr. v.p. corp. devel., exec. v.p. individual ins., 1980-87, pres., 1987—, also bd. dirs.; mem. affiliates adv. bd. U. Calif. Irvine Grad. Sch. Mgmt. Trustee South Coast Repertory; bd. dirs. Ind. Colls. So. Calif. Fellow Soc. of Actuaries (mem. numerous coms.); mem. Am. Acad. Actuaries (com. on dividend prins. and practices, 1978), Pacific States Actuarial Club, L.A. Actuarial Club (sec. 1974-75, pres. 1978-79). Office: Pacific Mut Life Ins Co 700 Newport Ctr Dr Newport Beach CA 92663

SUVER, JAMES DONALD, health administration educator, accountant; b. Swords Creek, Va., Oct. 21, 1931; s. Van Dola and Marcia Ellen (Davis) S.; m. Margaret Louise Schindler, Mar. 21, 1958 (div. 1977); children: James A., Amanda M.; m. Jean Claire Cooper, Dec. 31, 1979. BBA, Calif. State Coll., Sacramento, 1962; MBA, Harvard U., 1965, DBA, 1971. Cert. mgmt. acct. Enlisted U.S. Air Force, 1949, advanced through grades to col., 1975; dir. mil. pay Air Force Acctg. and Fin. Ctr., Denver, 1973-75; ret., 1975; prof. acctg. U. Colo.-Colorado Springs, 1975-81, prof. health adminstrn. Health Scis. Ctr., 1978-81; prof. health policy and adminstrn. U. N.C. Sch. Pub. Health, Chapel Hill, 1981-84, dir. masters program, 1982-84; dir. program health adminstrn. U. Colo., Denver, 1984-86, assoc. dean, 1984-88; dir. health adminstrn. programs, 1988—; cons. in field. Bd. dirs. Peak Health, Ltd., Colorado Springs, Colo., 1981-87; treas. Triangle Hospice, Chapel Hill, 1982-84, dir., chmn. fin. com. Rocky Mountain Multiple Sclerosis Ctr., 1985—, sec., treas., 1986—, bd. dirs., 1984-88; chmn., bd. dirs. Assn. Univ. Programs in Health Adminsrt., 1989; exec. bd. Health Adminstrn. div. Acad. Mgmt. Served to col. USAF, 1949-75, Korea, Vietnam. Decorated D.F.C., Legion of Merit, Air medal (6), Bronze Star; recipient Outstanding Teaching award U. Colo., 1977, 78, 81; Disting. Vis. Scholar Series, Calif. State Coll., Sacramento, 1985. Fellow Health Care Fin. Mgmt. Assn.; mem. Nat. Assn. Acctg. (Cert. of Merit 1977-79), Am. Pub. Health Assn., Assn. Govt. Acctg. (Disting. Research award 1978), Am. Acad. Med. Dirs., Med. Group Mgmt., Am. Hosp. Assn. Republican. Roman Catholic. Author: Management Accounting for Health Care Organizations, 1981, 85, Financial Management Concepts and Applications for Health Care Provider, 1984, 89; contbr. articles in field to profl. publs. Home: 7878 W 110th Dr Westminster CO 80020 Office: U Colo Coll Bus Box 165 1200 Larinier St Denver CO 80204-5300

SUYETSUGU, GRACE TAMIKO, nurse; b. San Mateo, Calif., Feb. 16, 1957; d. Frank Takiji and Mitsuka (Shimizu) S. BS magna cum laude in Nursing, San Francisco State U., 1979. RN, Calif. Charge nurse med./surg. unit Peninsula Hosp. and Med. Ctr., Burlingame, Calif., 1979-84; staff nurse ICU, 1984-88; charge nurse ICU, 1988—. Mem. Nat. Nurses Assn., Calif. Nurses Assn., Am. Assn. Critical Care Nurses. Democrat. Buddhist. Avocations: traveling, photography, cooking, needlework, sports. Home: 3682 Bobwhite Terr Fremont CA 94555 Office: Peninsula Hosp and Med Ctr 1783 El Camino Real Burlingame CA 94010

SUZAKI, KIYOSHI, management executive; b. Ichikawa, Chiba, Japan, Apr. 5, 1948; s. Matsujiro and Fusako (Sawaji) S.; m. Barbara Louise Suzaki, Apr. 15, 1988; 1 child, Peter Kenji. BSEE, Waseda U., Tokyo, 1971; MBA, Stanford U., 1981. Engr., dep. mgr. Toshiba Corp., Tokyo, 1971-81; cons. Boston Cons. Group, Tokyo, 1981-83; mng. assoc. Theodore Barry and Assocs., L.A., 1983-84; prin. Arthur Young and Co., L.A., 1985-88; pres. Eucalyptus Group, Pacific Palisades, Calif., 1985—; chmn. Suzaki-Lochridge and Co., Boston, 1988—; bd. dirs. Fireplace Mfrs., Inc., Santa Ana, Calif. Author: Produire Juste a Temps, 1986, The New Manufacturing Challenge, 1987, (in Japanese) Just-in-Time Revolution, 1987; patentee pressure suppression system, also others. Mem. Assn. for Mfg. Excellence (editorial bd. 1984—), Am. Supplier Inst. (steering com. 1988—), Am. Prodn. and Inventory Control Soc. Home and Office: 1137 El Medio Ave Pacific Palisades CA 90272

SUZUKI, GEORGE MASAYASU, aerospace company executive; b. Culver City, Calif., May 27, 1928; s. Satoshi and Tsuneko (Ohtsuki) S.; m. Kaoru Fukumisu, Nov 23, 1958; children: Michael M., Irene S., Carol M. BS in Engring., U. Calif., L.A., 1954, postgrad., 1960-64; MBA, Pepperdine U., 1980. Project engr. flight test ctr. USAF, Edwards AFB, Calif., 1954-56; rsch. engr. Rockwell Internat. Corp., Canoga Park, Calif., 1956-60, supr., 1961-63, project engr., 1964-70, project mgr., 1970-80, advisor bus. devel., 1980-85, program mgr., 1985-89, program dir., 1989—, instr., 1961—; mem. Aviation Week Rsch. Adv. Panel, 1985—. Fellow AIAA (assoc., nat. subcom. 1972-73, 25-yr. Svc. award 1979), Nat. Mgmt. Assn. Office: Rockwell Internat Corp 6633 Canoga Ave Canoga Park CA 91303

SVEC, RICHARD STANLEY, insurance executive; b. L.A., Oct. 16, 1942; s. Stanley F. and Dorothy E. (Whaley) S.; m. Barbara A. Gerzin, Sept. 24, 1966; 1 child, David M. BA, St. Mary's Coll., 1964. Jr. underwriter Fireman's Fund Ins. Co., San Francisco, 1965-67; sales rep. Fireman's Fund Ins. Co., L.A., 1967-69; surety mgr. Fireman's Fund Ins. Co., San Jose, Calif., 1969-77; surety mgr. Alexander & Alexander, San Jose, 1977-81, v.p., 1981-88, sr. v.p., 1988—. Contbr. articles to profl. jours. Bd. dirs. Almaden Valley Youth Athletic Assn., San Jose, 1971-80. Mem. Assoc. Gen. Contractors (chmn. mktg. com. 1989—), Nat. Assn. Surety Bond Producers, Bldg. Industry Assn., San Jose Athletic Club. Home: 7007 Quail Cliff Way San Jose CA 95120 Office: Alexander & Alexander 1530 Meridian Ave Ste 300 San Jose CA 95125

SVIKHART, EDWIN GLADDIN, equipment manufacturing executive; b. Chgo., July 12, 1930; s. Edwin Gabriel and Mildred Charlotte (Slapnicka) S.; m. Joann Barbara Frisk, Aug. 22, 1954; children: David E., Robert E. BA, Beloit (Wis.) Coll., 1952; postgrad., Bradley U., 1957-59. Western fin. mgr. Caterpillar Tractor Co., Peoria, Ill., 1956-66; chief fin. officer Berglund Inc., Napa, Calif., 1966-71; chief fin. officer, treas. Galion (Ohio) Mfg. Co., Galion, 1971-77; chief operating officer constrn. equip. internat. div. Dresser Industries, Columbus, Ohio, 1977-81; chief operating officer Rocky Mountain Machinery Co., Salt Lake City, 1981-87; chief oper. officer Constrn. Equipment Corp., Salt Lake City, 1989—; investor, cons., 1987—; chief oper. officerMet-Tek, Inc., Salt Lake City, 1989—; bd. dirs. Sabre Systems, Inc., Salt Lake City. V.p., bd. dirs. Galion Community Ctr., 1973-75; elder, personnel chmn. 1st Presbyn. Ch., Salt Lake City, 1981-83. Served to lt. (j.g.) USN, 1952-56. Named an Outstanding Young Man of Am., U.S. C. of C., 1966. Mem. Nat. Assn. Accts., Mountain W. Venture Capital Club (founder). Republican.

SWADLEY, STEPHEN ELLIS, employee benefits administrator; b. Muncie, Ind., July 15, 1949; s. Ellis C. and Catherine (Janney) S.; m. Carolyn Sue Bryant, June 20, 1969. BA, U. Maine, 1971, MPA, 1974; MBA, Boise State U., 1985. Employee rep. Maine State Employees Assn., Augusta, 1972-73, asst. exec. dir., 1973-74; exec. dir. Idaho Pub. Employees Assn., Boise, 1974-81; adminstr. Idaho Div. Ins. Mgmt., Boise, 1981-85; employee benefits mgr. Simpson Timber Co., Seattle, 1985-87; client svcs. mgr. United Administrators, Inc., Seattle, 1987—. Mem. Western Pension Conf., Employee Benefits Planning Assn., Am. Assn. Individual Investors. Office: United Administrators 201 Queen Anne Ave N Ste 100 Seattle WA 98109

SWAGEL, DENNIS JAY, lawyer; b. N.Y.C., May 25, 1946; s. Harry R. and Sah Belle (Fisher) S.; student Harvard U., 1966; certificat de langue pratique U. Paris, 1967; AB (Dana scholar), Hamilton Coll., 1968; JD, Fordham U., 1971; postgrad. U. So. Calif. Sch. Law, Los Angeles, 1976, 79. Bar: N.Y. 1972, Calif. 1974. Law clk. firm Lord, Day & Lord, N.Y.C., 1969; legal asst. Legal Aid Soc., N.Y.C., 1969-70; law clk. Greenbaum, Wolff & Ernst, N.Y.C., 1970-71; ptnr. Casa de Cynjaden Co., Cypress, Calif., 1972-73; assoc. firm William J. Bluestein, Beverly Hills, Calif., 1974; ptnr. firm Bluestein, Heimbach & Swagel, Beverly Hills, 1975; sole practice, Los Angeles, 1975-84, Beverly Hills, Calif., 1984—. Active Environ. Def. Fund; dir.-at-large, 1st tenor, grants mgr. Valley Master Chorale; benefactor Da Camera Soc.; friend Joffrey Ballet, Los Angeles Theatre Ctr.; sponsor Mark Taper Forum Scholarship, Statue of Liberty Found., World Wildlife Fund, Chrystic Inst., Natural Resources Def. Coun., Discovery Fund for Eye Rsch., Cousteau Soc., People for the Ethical Treatment of Animals, The S.W. Mus., Gene Autry Western Heritage Mus. Mem. ABA, Los Angeles County Bar Assn., Beverly Hills Bar Assn., Assn. Trial Lawyers Am., Calif. Trial Lawyers Assn., Los Angeles Trial Lawyers Assn., Lawyers Club Los Angeles, Fordham Law Alumni Assn., Am. Film Inst., U.S. Olympic Soc., ACLU, Los Angeles County Mus. Art, Los Angeles Contemporary Exhbns., Greater Los Angeles Zoo Assn., Mus. Contemporary Art Los Angeles, Town Hall, Internat. Platform Assn., Nat. Trust Hist. Preservation, Am. Guild Authors and Gomposers, Sierra Club. Democrat. Jewish. Club: B'nai B'rith. Home: 4329 Latona Ave Los Angeles CA 90031

SWAGEL, LORIN MARC, ophthalmologist; b. N.Y.C., Nov. 27, 1941; s. Harry Robert and Sahbelle (Fisher) S.; m. Carol Francine Goldsmith, June 28, 1964; children: David, Eric. BA, Hamilton Coll., 1963; MD, Albany Med. Coll., 1967. Intern Hosp. of Good Samaritan Med. Ctr., L.A., 1967-68; resident in ophthalmology N.Y. Eye and Ear Infirmary, N.Y.C., 1968-71; practice medicine specializing in ophthalmology Mesa, Ariz., 1973—. Maj. M.C., U.S. Army, 1971-73. Fellow Am. Acad. Ophthalmology, ACS; mem. Am. Soc. Cataract and Refractive Surgery, Ariz. Ophthal. Soc., Phoenix Ophthal. Soc. (sec.-treas. 1976-78). Republican. Jewish. Office: Swagel Wootton Eye Ctr 636 W Southern Ave Mesa AZ 85210

SWAN, KENNETH CARL, physician and surgeon; b. Kansas City, Mo., Jan. 1, 1912; s. Carl E. and Blanche (Peters) S.; m. Virginia Grone, Feb. 5, 1938; children: Steven Carl, Kenneth, Susan. A.B., U. Oreg., 1933, M.D., 1936. Diplomate: Am. Bd. Ophthalmology (chmn. 1960-61). Intern U. Wis., 1936-37; resident in ophthalmology State U. Iowa, 1937-40; practice medicine specializing in ophthalmology Portland, Oreg., 1945—; staff Good Samaritan Hosp.; asst. prof. ophthalmology State U. Iowa, Iowa City, 1941-44; asso. prof. U. Oreg. Med. Sch., Portland, 1944-45, prof. and head dept. ophthalmology, 1945-78; Chmn. sensory diseases study sect. NIH; mem. adv. council Nat. Eye Inst.; also adv. council Nat. Inst. Neurol. Diseases and Blindness. Contbr. articles on ophthalmic subjects to med. publs. Recipient Proctor Rsch. medal, 1953; Disting. Svc. award U. Oreg., 1963; Meritorious Achievement award U. Oreg. Med. Sch., 1968; Howe Ophthalmology medal, 1977; Aubrey Watzek Pioneer award Lewis and Clark Coll., 1979, Disting. Alumnus award Oreg. Health Scis. U. Alumni Assn., 1988, Disting. Svc. award, 1988; named Oreg. Scientist of Yr. Oreg. Mus. Sci. and Industry, 1959. Mem. Assn. Research in Ophthalmology, Am. Acad. Ophthalmology (v.p. 1978, historian), Soc. Exptl. Biology and Medicine, AAAS, AMA, Am. Ophthal. Soc. (Howe medal for distinguished service 1977), Oreg. Med. Soc., Sigma Xi, Sigma Chi (Significant Sig award 1977). Home: 4645 SW Fairview Blvd Portland OR 97221 Office: Oreg Health Scis U Portland OR 97201

SWAN, RICHARD ALAN, executive recruiter; b. Hollywood, Calif., May 5, 1944; s. Morris George and Mary Theresa (Fenusz) S.; m. Carol Ann Jacobs, Apr. 15, 1967; children: David Michael, Jennifer Marie, Matthew Richard. BS in Indsl. Mgmt., U. So. Calif., 1966; MS in Health Care Adminstrn., Trinity U., 1970. Adminstrv. resident Tucson (Ariz.) Med. Ctr., 1971; assoc. cons. A.T. Kearney and Co. Inc., Chgo., 1971-72; v.p. Tribrook Group Inc., Oakbrook, Ill., 1972-82; dir. program and spl. studies div. James A. Hamilton Assocs. Inc., Dallas, 1982-83; v.p. corp. devel. Vincentian Health Services, L.A., 1983-88; v.p., dir. healthcare group Boyden Internat., L.A., 1988—. Contbr. articles to profl. jours. Served to capt. Med. Service Corps, U.S. Army, 1967-69. Fellow Am. Assn. Hosp. Cons., Am. Coll. Healthcare Execs.; mem. Soc. Hosp. Planning and Mktg., So. Calif. Soc. Hosp. Planners (charter), Health Care Execs. of So. Calif., Am. Hosp. Assn. Republican. Roman Catholic. Office: Boyden Internat 800 S Figueroa St Ste 700 Los Angeles CA 90017

SWANER, PAULA MARGETTS, clinical psychologist; b. Salt Lake City, Nov. 23, 1927; d. Sumner Gray and Pauline (Moyle) M.; m. Leland Scowcroft, May 22, 1951; children: Leland S., Jr., Sumner Margetts, Paula June Swaner-Sargetakis. BA in Eng. Lit., U. Utah, 1949, MA in Eng. Lit., 1972, MS in Ednl. Psychol., 1978, PhD in Clin. Psychology, 1986. Lic. clin. psychologist, Utah. Psychotherapist Granite Mental Health Ctr., Salt Lake City, 1978-80; postdoctoral intern Mental Health Unit, Juvenile Ct., Salt Lake City, 1984-87; pvt. practice Salt Lake City, 1986—; cons. CPC Olympus View Hosp., Salt Lake City, 1988—; affiliate, admitting privileges Western Inst. Neuropsychiatry, Salt Lake City, 1989—. Lector, All Saints Episcopal Ch., Salt Lake City. Mem. Am. Psychol. Assn., Utah Psychol. Assn., Wasatch Mountain Club. Democrat. Episcopalian. Office: Paula M Swaner 1775 E 4500 S Salt Lake City UT 84124

SWANSON, ARTHUR ARNE, marketing consultant; b. Joliet, Ill., Dec. 23, 1931; s. Everett Arthur and Margaret Caroline (Wright) S.; m. Nancy Clare Lange, Aug. 25, 1956; children: Paul, Steven, Douglas, Gregg, Matthew. BA, U. Ill., 1957. Dir. personnel Campana Corp., Batavia, Ill., 1959-65; mgr. benefit adminstrn. Thor Power Tool Co., Aurora, Ill., 1965-66; mgr. personnel Grede Foundries, Inc., Kingsford, Mich., 1966-75; with real estate sales dept. Real Estate North, Inc., Iron Mountain, Mich., 1975-79; real estate salesman Doug Johns Real Estate, Kalispell, Mont., 1979-85; mgr. personnel Precision Rolled Products, Inc., Reno, 1985-88; mktg. cons. Garland Homes, Victor, Mont. Advisor Jr. Achievement, Aurora, 1965; bd. dirs. C. of C., Iron Mountain, 1969-70. With U.S. Army, 1952-54, Korea. Mem. Nev. Mfrs. Assn., Western Indsl. Nev., No. Nev. Personnel Assn., Tri-City Indsl. Club (pres. 1964-65). Home: Victor MT 59875

SWANSON, DONALD ALAN, geologist; b. Tacoma, July 25, 1938; s. Leonard Walter and Edith Christine (Bowers) S.; m. Barbara Joan White, May 25, 1974. BS in Geology, Wash. State U., 1960; PhD in Geology, Johns Hopkins U., 1964. Geologist U.S. Geol. Survey, Menlo Park, Calif., 1965-68, 71-80, Hawaii National Park, 1968-71; sr. geologist Cascades Volcano Obs. U.S. Geol. Survey, Vancouver, Wash., 1980—, rsch. scientist-in-charge, 1986-89; cons. U.S. Dept. Energy, Richland, Wash., 1979-83; volcanologist New Zealand Geol. Survey, Taupo, 1984; advisor Colombian Volcano Obs., Manizales, 1986. Assoc. editor Jour. Volcanolgy and Geothermal Research, 1976—; editor Bull. of Volcanology, 1985—; contbr. numerous articles to profl. jours. Recipient Superior Service award U.S. Geol. Survey, 1980, Meritorious Service award U.S. Dept. Interior, 1985; postdoctoral fellow NATO, 1964-65. Fellow Geol. Soc. Am.; mem. AAAS, Am. Geophys. Union, Sigma Xi. Home: 15710 NE 31st Ave Vancouver WA 98686 Office: US Geol Survey 5400 MacArthur Blvd Vancouver WA 98661

SWANSON, EDWIN ARCHIE, business educator; b. Boone County, Nebr., July 5, 1908; s. Andrew E. and Alma (Nordgren) S.; student George Washington U., 1933-34; B.S., Nebr. State Tchrs. Coll., Kearney, 1932; M.S., U. So. Calif., 1936, Ed.D., 1949; m. Fern E. Anderson, Aug. 25, 1933; children—Edwin Burton, John LeRoy. Elementary, high sch. tchr., Nebr., 1925-35; instr. Fullerton Jr. Coll., 1936-37, 38-39; teaching and research fellow in edn. U. So. Calif., 1935-36, instr. edn. and commerce, 1937-38; asso. prof., dept. head Ariz. State Coll., 1939-46; prof. bus. San Jose (Calif.) State U., 1946-79, emeritus prof. bus., 1979—, chmn. dept., 1957-68. Vis. faculty mem., summer sessions U. Tenn., Woman's Coll. U. N.C., Armstrong Coll., Colo. State Coll., U. So. Calif., U. Fla. Editor: New Media in Teaching the Business Subjects, 1965; editorial bd. Nat. Bus. Edn. Quar., 1939-48, editor, 1939-41. Mem. AAUP, AAAS, Am. Mgmt. Assn., Nat. (pres. 1950-51, mem. and chmn. publs. com. and editorial bd. 1959-62, editor Yearbook 1965), Western (pres. 1954-55, gen. program chmn. conv. 1965), Cal. bus. edn. assns., NEA, Calif. Tchrs. Assn., Phi Delta Kappa (chpt. pres. 1945-46, 54-55, area coordinator 1955-66), Kappa Delta Pi, Pi Omega Pi, Delta Pi Epsilon (mem. nat. commn. bus. and econ. edn. 1964-65, mem. bd. govs. for research and devel. in bus. edn. 1968-74), Gamma Rho Tau, Xi Phi, Phi Kappa Phi (chpt. pres. 1956-57). Presbyn. Club: Commonwealth (San Francisco). Contbr. publs. in field. Home: 2390 Mazzaglia Ave San Jose CA 95125

SWANSON, KELLY HANSEN, lawyer; b. Middletown, Conn., Nov. 19, 1946; s. Carl Everett and Charlotte (Weston) S.; m. Carolyn McLaughlin, Aug. 2, 1976; children: Jennifer, Julie, Victoria. BA, U. Ill., 1971; JD, U. Ark., 1974. Bar: Ark. 1974, Nev. 1974, U.S. Dist. Ct. Nev. 1974, U.S. Ct. Appeals (9th cir.) 1974, U.S. Tax Ct. 1979. Atty., law clk. Clark County Pub. Defender, Las Vegas, Nev., 1974-76; pres. Kelley H. Swanson, Chartered, Las Vegas, 1976--. With USAF, 1964-68. Mem. ABA, ATLA, Nev. Trial Lawyers Assn., State Bar Nev. (fee. dispute com. 1977-86). Mormon. Office: Kelly H Swanson Chartered 1200 S Eastern St Las Vegas NV 89104

SWANSON, LEE RICHARD, computer security executive; b. Mpls., Apr. 21, 1957; s. Donald Jerome and Wildie (Greenwood) S.; m. Amy Jane Shutkin, Jan. 1, 1980. BS, U. Minn., 1983. Owner, prin. Environ. Landforms, Inc., Minnetonka, Minn., 1974-80; v.p. Blomfield-Swanson, Inc., Minnetonka, 1981-85; contractor Citicorp Card Acceptance Svcs., Seattle, 1986-88; owner, pres. Room Svcs. Computers, Bellevue, Wash., 1988—. Vol. Eastside Literacy Coun., Bellevue, 1987—. Libertarian. Office: Room Svc Computers 1075 Bellevue Way NE Ste 453 Bellevue WA 98004

SWANSON, RICHARD CLYDE, paint manufacturing company executive; b. St. Louis, Nov. 27, 1939; s. Clyde William and Audrey Marie (Dickson) S.; m. Ruth Lett, July 23, 1973. BS in Chem. Engring., U. Mo., Rolla, 1962. Engr. Monsanto Corp., St. Louis, 1962-65; mfg. supr. Monsanto Corp., 1965-68; mfg. supt. Monsanto Corp., Seattle, 1968-70; gen. supt. Monsanto Corp., Nitro, W.Va., 1970-74; dir. ops. Cordova Chem., Sacramento, 1974-76; v.p. ops. Cordova Chem., 1976-80, The Flecto Co., Inc., Oakland, Calif., 1980-85; v.p., gen. mgr., dir. Flecto Coatings Ltd., Richmond, B.C., Can., 1985—; trustee, asst. chmn. Paintmakers Health & Welfare Trust, Paintmakers Pension Trust, Oakland. Mem. Calif. Mfrs. Assn., Bus. Coun. B.C., Can. Mfrs. Assn., Commonwealth Club Calif., Emeryville Industries, Diablo Country Club. Republican. Presbyterian. Home: PO Box 56 Diablo CA 94528 Office: The Flecto Co 1000 45th St Oakland CA 94828

SWANSON, RICHARD WILLIAM, operations research analyst; b. Rockford, Ill., July 26, 1934; s. Richard and Erma Marie (Herman) S.; B.S., Iowa State U., 1958, M.S., 1964; m. Laura Yoko Arai, Dec. 30, 1970. Ops. analyst Stanford Research Inst., Monterey, Calif., 1958-62; statistician ARINC Research Corp., Washington, 1964-65; sr. scientist Booz-Allen Applied Research, Vietnam, 1965-67, Los Angeles, 1967-68; sr. ops. analyst Control Data Corp., Honolulu, 1968-70; mgmt. cons., Honolulu, 1970-73; exec. v.p. SEQUEL Corp., Honolulu, 1973-75; bus. cons. Hawaii Dept. Planning and Econ. Devel., Honolulu, 1975-77, tax research and planning officer Dept. Taxation, 1977-82; ops. research analyst U.S. Govt., 1982—. Served with AUS, 1954-56. Mem. Hawaiian Acad. Sci., Sigma Xi. Home: 583 Kamoku St Apt 3505 Honolulu HI 96826 Office: HQ PACAF/OA Hickam AFB HI 96853

SWANSON, ROBERT A., genetic engineering company executive; b. N.Y.C., Nov. 29, 1947; s. Arthur John and Arline (Baker) S.; m. Judy Church, Sept. 2, 1980. S.B., M.I.T., 1970, S.M. in Mgmt, 1970. Asst. treas. Citicorp Venture Capital Ltd., N.Y.C., 1970-74; partner Kleiner & Perkins Venture Capital Partnership, San Francisco, 1975; chief exec. Genentech, Inc., South San Francisco, Calif., 1976—. Mem. corp. MIT; bd. dirs. San Francisco Mus. Modern Art, San Francisco Ballet Assn., Tech. Ctr. Silicon Valley. Named Entrepreneur of Year Chgo. Research Dirs. Assn., 1981; Gold medal chief Exec. for Biotech. industry Wall Street Transcript, 1984. Mem. Am. Chem. Soc., Am. Soc. Microbiology, Royal Swedish Acad. Engring. Scis., AAAS. Office: Genentech Inc 460 Point San Bruno Blvd South San Francisco CA 94080 *

SWANSON, ROBERT KILLEN, management consultant; b. Deadwood, S.D., Aug. 11, 1932; s. Robert Claude and Marie Elizabeth (Kersten) S.; m. Nancy Anne Oyaas, July 19, 1958; children: Cathryn Lynn, Robert Stuart, Bart Killen. B.A., U. S.D., 1954; postgrad., U. Melbourne, Australia, 1955. With Gen. Mills, Inc., Mpls., 1955-58, 71-79, v.p., 1971-73, group v.p., 1973-77, exec. v.p., 1977-79; with Marathon Oil Co., Findlay, Ohio, 1958-60; sr. v.p., dir. Needham, Harper & Steers, Inc., Chgo., 1961-69; joint mng. dir. S. H. Benson (Holdings) Ltd., Eng., 1969-71; pres., chief operating officer Greyhound Corp., Phoenix, 1980; chmn., chief exec. officer Del E. Webb Corp., Phoenix, 1981-87; chmn. RKS Inc., Phoenix, 1987—; bd. dirs. Grossman's, Inc., Conzept Internat. Trustee Scripps Clinic and Rsch. Found., Ariz. State U. Found.; bd. dirs. Phoenix Art Mus., Ariz. chpt. Am. Cancer Soc., Univ. S.D. Found. 2nd lt. U.S. Army, 1955. Fulbright scholar, 1954-55; Woodrow Wilson scholar. Mem. U.S. Coun. Fgn. Rels., U.K. Dirs. Inst., U.S. Internat. Scholars Assn. Episcopalian. Club: Phoenix Country. Lodge: Masons. Office: RKS Inc 3003 N Central Ave Ste 1800 Phoenix AZ 85012

SWARD, JEFFREY EDWIN, infosystems specialist; b. Milw., Jan. 16, 1953; m. Andrea J. Lankow, June 7, 1975. MusB, Calif. State U., Fullerton, 1975, BA in Math., 1976, MusM, 1978; studied photography at Calif. State U., Fullerton, Newport Sch. Photography, Orange Coast Coll., and Yosemite Workshop. Computer programmer State of Calif., Fullerton, 1971-78; mem. tech. staff Computer Scis. Corp., Santa Ana, Calif., 1978-80; sr. programmer analyst Figgie Internat., Anaheim, Calif., 1980-81; applications systems specialist TRW, Orange, Calif., 1981-89; sr. programmer analyst Times Mirror Cable TV, Irvine, Calif., 1989—; freelance photographer, 1971—. Photographs exhibited at various local shows, 1987—. Choir dir. Garden Grove (Calif.) United Ch. of Christ, 1973-76; oboist Fullerton Civic Light Opera, 1974-87; oboist, English hornist Chapman Symphony, 1984-89. Fine Arts scholar Bank of Am., 1971. Mem. L.A. Ctr. Photog. Studies, Westminster Viewfinders, Phi Kappa Phi, Phi Kappa Lambda. Home: PO Box 7019 Huntington Beach CA 92615

SWARNER, SYLVIA MARTHA, nurse; b. Sacramento, Mar. 15, 1955; d. Arnold Joseph and Elisabeth (Hartmann) Guallini; m. David Lee Swarner, Nov. 1, 1980; children: Christopher Glenn, Jessica Reneé. Nursing diploma, Sacramento City Coll., 1978. RN, Calif. ICU nurse Sutter Community Hosp., Sacramento, 1978--. Mem. Quality Assurance Com., 1987--, Standards Critical Care Com., 1985--. Mem. Am. Assn. Critical Care Nurses. Home: 9512 Country Roads Dr Sacramento CA 95827

SWARNER, THOMAS HERBERT, newspaper publisher; b. Corvallis, Oreg., Apr. 4, 1941; s. James Herbert and Ella M. (Day) S.; m. Sylvia Joan Thompson, Aug. 26, 1962; children: Ronald Thomas, Kenneth Michael,

Deborah Lynn. BA in Journalism/Advt., U. Wash., 1965. Rep. advt. Ranger Pub. Co., Tacoma, Wash., 1964-65; mgr. sales Ranger Pub. Co., Tacoma, 1965-69, v.p., 1969-73; pres. and pub. Mil. News Pub., Tacoma, 1973—; owner, corp. officer Grays Mgmt. Inc., Tacoma, 1985—. Dir. Pierce County Econ. Task Force, 1986-87, Crime Stoppers Inc. Tacoma/Pierce County, 1986—; mem. Republican Presl. Task Force, Washington, 1982—. Mem. Soc. Profl. Journalists, Am. Soc. Travel Agts., Air Force Assn. (dir. 1983-88), Assn. U.S. Army (dir. 1974-88), Am. Newspaper Pub. Assn., Lakewood Area C. of C. (dir. 1984-87), Tacoma Photographic Soc. (numerous awards 1985-87, dir./treas. 1985-88), Rotary (Paul Harris fellow 1985, 87, dir, 1986-88). Office: Mil News Pub PO Box 98801 Tacoma WA 98499

SWARTHOUT, JOHN VANLEWEN, brokerage house professional; b. Tampa, Fla., July 18, 1945; s. John Max and Mary A. (Cianfoni) S.; m. Kathleen A. Deal, Aug. 19, 1984; 1 child; Jaime Michaela. Student, U. Washington, 1963-65, U. Utah, 1965; BA, Portland State U., 1967; MA, Ind. U., 1968. Cert. fin. planner; lic. securities broker, commodities broker. Instr. polit. sci. Tacoma Community Coll., 1968-73; mgmt. coordinator, personnel dir. Multnomah County, Portland, Oreg., 1973-75; indsl. engring. cons. Ritchie & Assoc., Los Angeles, 1976-77; personnel mgr. AAR Western Skyways, Troutdale, Oreg., 1977-80; stockbroker Kidder Peabody & Co., Portland, 1980-85, cons., 1985-88; equity mgr. ManEquity Inc., Portland, 1985-89; owner John Swarthout & Assocs., Investment Advisors, Portland, 1989—; instr., Portland State U., 1973-75. Bd. dirs. Am. Heritage Assn., Lake Oswego Oreg., 1984—. Nat. Def. Fgn. Lang. fellow U. Utah, 1965, NSF fellow Ind. U., 1967-68. Mem. Western Polit. Sci. Assn., Northwest Polit. Sci. Assn., Theta Delta Phi, Sigma Nu. Clubs: City, Willamette Athletic (Portland), Western Fitness and Racquet. Home and Office: 6970 SW Gable Pkwy Portland OR 97225

SWARTZ, CRAIG CHARLES, electronic engineer; b. Erie, Pa., Feb. 20, 1956; s. Frank Charles and Gladys May (Fleming) S. BSEE, W.Va. U., 1978. Electronic design engr. Motorola, Phoenix, 1979-82, Martin Marietta, Denver, 1983-85; pvt. practice Denver, 1986-87; electronic design engr. Tangent Engring., Denver, 1988—. Patentee in field. Office: Tangent Engring 40 Inverness Dr E Ste 90 Englewood CO 80112

SWARTZ, DONALD HOWARD, organizational change consulting company executie; b. Harrisburg, Pa., Oct. 8, 1931; s. Howard Franklin and Esther (Kaylor) S.; children: William, Jann, Joan; m. Anna Louise Stock, July 21, 1981; 1 child, Regeena. BS in Mech. Engring., Lehigh U., 1953. Supr. engr. tng. York Corp., Pa., 1953-55; product mgr. York Corp., 1955-58; mgr. sales devel. York div. Borg Warner Corp., 1958-68; mgr. mgmt. devel. Weyerhaeuser Co., Tacoma, 1968-72; mgr. tng. Weyerhaeuser Co., 1972-75; pres. Effectiveness Resources Group Inc., Federal Way, Wash., 1973--; dir. Systems Renewal Inst., Federal Way, 1979--; chmn. Systems Renewal Inst. Corp., Federal Way, 1987--. Author tng. courses. Recipient silver editorial award Nat. Soc. Sales and Tng. Execs., 1968, gold editorial award, 1971. Mem. Am. Soc. Tng. & Devel., Soc. Creative Change, Internat. Cons. Found. Republican. Lutheran. Office: Effectiveness Resource Grp 32506 40th Ct SW Federal Way WA 98023

SWARTZ, RAY, data processing executive; b. Glendale, Calif., May 3, 1952; s. Albert and Ethel S.; m. Rita Risser, May 2, 1982. BA, U. Calif., Irvine, 1974; MBA, U. Calif., Berkeley, 1981. Mng. dir. Berkeley Decision Systems, Santa Cruz, Calif., 1981—; adj. lectr. U. Santa Clara, 1982-84; vis. lectr. U. Calif., Santa Cruz, 1984-87, India-sponsored by NIIT, 1988. Author: Doing Business with C, 1989; editor conf. proceedings, Modeling and Simulation, 1984; columnist Answers on UNIX, 1989—. Coach Community Basketball League, Santa Cruz, 1987. Mem. Soc. for Computer Simulation (bd. dirs. 1985--, sec. 1988--), Inst. Mgmt. Sci., USENIX. Office: Berkeley Decision/ Systems 803 Pine St Santa Cruz CA 95062

SWARTZ, TERESA ANNE, marketing educator, researcher, consultant; b. Port Alleghany, Pa., May 3, 1953; d. Robert Wilson and Geraldine Elizabeth (Hess) S. B.S. in Edn., Clarion State Coll., 1974, M.B.A., 1977; Ph.D. in Bus. Adminstrn., Ohio State U., 1981. Cert. secondary tchr., Pa. High sch. tchr. Bradford Area Schs., Bradford, Pa., 1975-76; grad. asst. Clarion State Coll., Pa., 1976-77; research, teaching assoc., Ohio State U., Columbus, 1977-80; lectr. Ariz. State U., Tempe, 1980-81, asst. prof., 1981-86, assoc. prof., 1986—; mktg. cons., Tempe, 1981—; vis. prof. Dailey and Assocs., L.A., 1983. Mem. Am. Mktg. Assn. (mem. Phoenix bd. dirs. 1982-85, nat. bd. dirs., v.p. elect western region 1985-86, v.p. 1986-87), Assn. Consumer Research, Am. Acad. Advt., Acad. Mktg. Sci., Am. Psychol. Assn., Beta Gamma Sigma. Republican. Avocations: golf, tennis, travel, softball. Office: Ariz State U Dept Mktg Tempe AZ 85287

SWARTZWELDER, JOHN JOSEPH, writer; b. Seattle, Feb. 8, 1949; s. John Joseph Sr. and Gloria Mae (Matthews) S. Student, U. Wash., 1967. Writer various advt. agys., Chgo., Los Angeles, Houston, 1970-85; comedy writer TV shows Saturday Night Live, N.Y.C., 1985-86, David Brenner Show, N.Y.C., 1987; freelance writer TV episodes for shows Women in Prison, Mr. President, The Dictator, The Simpsons, Los Angeles, 1987—. Recipient numerous advt. awards. Mem. Writers Guild Am. East, AFTRA. Home: 14311 Addison St #209 Sherman Oaks CA 91423

SWATEK, MIKE ALLEN, engineer; b. Agana, Guam, Apr. 28, 1958; s. James Allen Swatek and Tommie Lou (Mitchell) Howard; m. Leslie Patricia Knight, Aug. 10, 1985. BSME, U. Okla., 1986. Designer City Engrs. Office, Oklahoma City, 1976-80, Transworld Drilling Co., Oklahoma City, 1980-82; engring. mgr. Positech Corp., Ruthven, Iowa, 1985-87; propulsion systems engr. Rockwell Internat.-Rocketdyne, Canoga Park, Calif., 1987—; pres. New Age Engring. and Design, Granada Hills, Calif., 1988—. Bd. mem. GT Homeowners Assn., Granada Hills, Calif., 1989. Coll. Bowl scholarship, Gen. Electric, 1984, Meml. scholarship, U. Okla., 1983, scholarship, Cities Service Corp., 1982. Mem. ASME, Planetary Soc., Tau Beta Pi, Pi Tau Sigma. Democrat. Unitarian. Home: 17221 Chatsworth #112 Granada Hills CA 91344

SWATEK, WILLIAM CYRIL, medical services executive; b. St. Louis, Jan. 10, 1920; s. Cyril William and Agnes Rose (Stratmann) S.-Coyle; m. Rose Larson Swatek, Apr. 17, 1946; children: Claude M., Pamela D. Swatek-Tripp. Student, Stanford U., 1944; MD, Loma Linda U., 1949. Diplomate Am. Bd. Pathology. Resident in pathology Loma Linda (Calif.) U. Med. Ctr., 1949-52; chmn. pathology dept. Framingham (Mass.) Union Hosp., 1954-58, Washington Adventist Hosp., Takoma Park, Md., 1958-68; pres. med. staff Washington Adventist Hosp., Takoma Park, 1967-68; chmn. pathology dept. St. Joseph Mercy Hosp., Pontiac, Mich., 1969-73; pres. Clin. Diagnostic Services Corp., Loma Linda, Calif., 1969—; chmn. pathology dept. Grenada (Miss.) Lake Med. Ctr., 1974-78. Contbr. articles to med. jours. Chmn. Am. Cancer Soc., Montgomery County, Md., 1959-62, chmn. pathology sect. D.C. Med. Soc., 1967; pres. med. staff Washington Adventist Hosp., 1967-68, N. Panola Regional Med. Ctr., Sardis, Miss., 1980-81. Served to capt. USAF, 1952-54. Armed Force Inst. Pathology fellow, 1952-53, emeritus fellow Am. Coll. Pathologists, 1987, Am. Soc. Clin. Pathologists, 1987, Chirurgical Faculty and Md. Med. Soc., 1987. Mem. AMA. Adventist. Home: 31 Loop Rd Indian Point Georgetown ME 04548 Office: Clin Diagnostic Svcs Corp PO Box 7060 Loma Linda CA 92354

SWEAT, BRUCE PIERRE, electronic technologist; b. Colfax, Wash., Jan. 18, 1950; s. John Bruce Sweat and Pierrette Christian (Decremps) Gustafson; m. Cheryl Leigh Cox, Mar. 8, 1975; children: Jonathan Colin, Christopher Bruce. Pres. Summit Industries, Spokane, Wash., 1981-84; bd. dirs. Ebtek, Inc., Spokane, 1984—, v.p., 1988; v.p. O.A. Sys, Inc, Spokane, 1984—; cons. Lighting Consortium, Spokane, 1988. Inventor switched capacitive ballast for discharge lamps, electronic ballast for vapor lamps. Mem. Electronic Industry Evaluation Panel, Illuminating Engring. Soc. Office: Ebtek Inc N 910 Washington Ste 216 Spokane WA 99201

SWEENEY, CHRISTOPHER LEE, applied mathematics engineer; b. Denver, Oct. 14, 1959; s. Roger Lee Sweeney and Beverly Ann (Wagoner) Good; m. Susan Ann Merrell, May 24, 1986. Student, Community Coll. Denver; grad., U. Colo., 1988. Technican Ball Computer Products, Boulder, Colo., 1978-82, devel. engr., 1982-83; devel. engr. Ball Electronic Systems, Westminster, Colo., 1983—. Inventor in field. Mem. Eta Kappa Nu, Tau Beta Pi. Home: 9836 Jellison St Westminster CO 80020 Office: Ball Electronic Systems Div 9300 W 108th Circle Westminster CO 80020

SWEENEY, DANIEL BRYAN, JR., financial adviser, pension fund administrator; b. Providence, Oct. 23, 1946; s. Daniel Bryan Sr. and Clara Perene (Hodgdon) S.; m. Carol Jane Weir, June 18, 1966; children: Heather, Holly. AS in Electronic Engring., San Mateo Community Coll., 1969. CLU. Tax specialist Northwestern Nat. Life, Minn., 1974-81; pres. Dan Sweeney & Assocs., Inc., Bellevue, Wash., 1981—; pres., trustee Davis-Bacon Pension Adminstrn., Inc., Bellevue, 1987—. Author: Investment Planning Ideas, 1983. With USN, 1964-70. Mem. Internat. Assn. Fin. Planners, Eastside Estate Planning Coun., Masons, Elks. Office: Davis-Bacon Pension Adminstrn 11911 NE First St #102 Bellevue WA 98005

SWEENEY, J. GRAY, American art historian, educator; b. Jacksonville, Fla., Nov. 20, 1943; s. John M. and Mary (Gray) S.; m. Karrie J. Knecht, Aug. 24, 1981; 1 child, James Gray Flournoy. BA magna cum laude, U. N.Mex., 1968; MA, Ind. U., 1969, PhD, 1975. From asst. prof. to assoc. prof. Grand Valley State Coll., Allendale, Mich., 1971-85; guest curator Muskegon Mus. Art, Mich., 1978-83, Grand Rapids Art Mus., Mich., 1976, 77, 81; rsch. assoc. Tweed Mus. Art, Duluth, Minn., 1980-82; sr. fellow Nat. Mus. Am. Art, Smithsonian Inst., Washington, 1984-85; prof. Dept. Art History Ariz. State U., 1986—. Author, curator exhbn. and catalog Themes in American Painting, 1977, Artists of Grand Rapids, 1981, Great Lakes Marine Painting, 1983, Bela Petheo, 1985, Artists of Mich., 1987, Morning of a New Day: The West inImage, Object and Myth, 1989. Author: Tweed Museum of Art, 1982; Muskegon Museum of Art, 1980. Grantee Ind. U., 1970-71, Kress Found. Ind. U., 1967-68, Ford Found. U. N.Mex., 1966-68. Fellow Smithsonian Inst. Am. (sr.); mem. Coll. Art Assn. Am., Am. Assn. Museums Avocation: sailing. Office: Ariz State U Dept Art History Tempe AZ 85287

SWEENEY, RICHARD JAMES, economics educator; b. San Diego, Jan. 13, 1944; s. John Joseph and Catherine Scott (Spahr) S.; m. Joan Zita Long, June 19, 1965; children: Robin Scott, Erin Michaela. BA, UCLA, 1965; PhD, Princeton U., 1972. Acting asst. prof. econs. UCLA, 1968-71; asst. prof. Tex. A&M U., College Station, 1971-73; dep. dir. office of internat. monetary research U.S. Dept. Treasury, Washington, 1973-77; Charles M. Stone prof. econs. and fin. Claremont (Calif.) McKenna Coll., 1977-89, chmn. dept. econs., 1987-89; dean, prof. internat. fin. Georgetown U., Washington, 1989—; Sullivan vis. assoc. prof. econs. U. Va., Charlottesville, 1975; vis. prof. bus. adminstrn. Dartmouth Coll., Hanover, N.H., 1979. Author: Principles of Microeconomics, Macroeconomics, 1980, Wealth Effects and Monetary Theory, 1988; author/editor Exchange Rates, Trade and the U.S. Economy, 1985, A Macro Theory with Micro Foundations, 1974; contbr. articles to profl. jours. Fellow NSF 1966-68, Woodrow Wilson Found. 1965; grantee Gen. Electric Found., 1980, Mid.-Am. Found., 1987, Earhart Found., 1988. Mem. Western Econ. Assn. (editor Econs. Inquiry jour. 1984—), Am. Econ. Assn., Am. Fin. Assn., Western Fin. Assn., Phi Beta Kappa. Democrat. Office: Georgetown U Sch Bus Adminstrn Washington DC 20057

SWEET, ANDREW ARNOLD, psychologist; b. Mt. Kisco, N.Y., Aug. 26, 1956; s. John Stevens and Deana (Baron) S.; m. Nancy Rainwater, May 19, 1984; 1 child, Adrienne Elizabeth Sweetwater. BS, SUNY, Oneonta, 1978; Psychology D., Denver U., 1982. Lic. psychologist. Asst. prof. U. Colo., Greeley, 1982-83; pvt. practice Behavior Therapy Inst., Aurora, Colo., 1982—; clin. supr. Wallace Village for Children, Broomfeild, Colo., 1983-84; clin. affiliate sch. profl. psychology U. Denver, 1983—; clin. psychologist Human Performance Inst., Lakewood, Colo., 1985-87. Co-author: Behavior Therapy Outcome, 1986, Anxiety & Stress Disorders, 1987; contbr. articles to profl. jours. Mem. Colo. Psychol. Assn., Am. Psychol. Assn., Assn. for Advancement Behavior Therapy, Am. Psychol. Soc. Democrat. Home: 1900 Leyden St Denver CO 80220 Office: Behavior Therapy Inst 3000 S Jamaica Ct Aurora CO 80014

SWEET, GEORGE ELLIOTT, geophysicist, author; b. Denver, Sept. 26, 1904; s. Leroy F. and Bertie Belle (Cooper) S.; m. Mildred Robison, Oct. 13, 1932 (dec. Aug. 1976); 1 child, J. Eric. BS, U. Okla., 1927, MS, 1928; postgrad. Harvard U., 1940-41. Cert. geophysicist, Calif. Party chief Geophys. Research Corp., Houston, 1928-32; chmn. bd. Am. Seismograph Co., Oklahoma City, 1932-40; pres. Sweet Geophys. Co., Malibu, Calif., 1945—. Author: Shakespeare, The Mystery, 1956; Gentleman in Oil, 1966; The History of Geophysical Prospecting, Vol. I, 1966, Vol. II, 1969; The Petroleum Saga, 1971; Seven Dramas from Seven Centuries, 1978; Beginning of the End, 1982; Murder by Guess, 1984. Pres. Santa Monica Pony League, Calif., 1958-59. Lt. USNR, 1942-45. Named Valedictorian U. Okla., 1927. Mem. Soc. Exploration Geophysicists, Am. Assn. Petroleum Geologists, Acacia, Phi Beta Kappa, Alpha Chi Sigma, Sigma Delta Psi, Harvard-Radcliffe Club of So. Calif. Home: 502 Georgina Ave Santa Monica CA 90402

SWEET, JOHN WILLIAM, retired metallurgist; b. Seattle, May 6, 1910; s. Roy William and Sara Veronica (Brown) S.; m. Mary Elizabeth Pierce, Aug. 26, 1939; children: Elizabeth Ann, John Robert. BS, U. Wash., 1934. Registered profl. engr., Wash. Design engr. The Boeing Airplane Co., Seattle, 1935-37; test engr. The Boeing Airplane Co., 1937-42, metall. engr., 1942-45, chief metallurgist, 1946-70, ret., 1970. Fellow Am. Soc. Metals. Republican. Roman Catholic. Home: 1605 5th Ave Hillside House 301 Seattle WA 98109

SWEET, VICKI CHARLA, nurse; b. Oceanside, Calif., June 22, 1952; d. Phillip Edward and Toni (Sewall) Vedder; m. John Roger Sweet, Feb. 3, 1973; children: Jeremy, Kyle. AA in Nursing, Saddleback Coll., 1985; BS in Health Sci., U. Redlands, 1987; postgrad., U. LaVerne. RN, Calif.; cert. community coll. tchr., BCLS and ACLS instr. Asst. childbirth instr., parent educator Orange County (Calif.) Childbirth Edn. Assn., 1976-81; emergency med. technician San Clemente (Calif.) Hosp., 1981-84, staff nurse emergency rm., 1985-87; coord. emergency dept. San Clementa (Calif.) Hosp., 1987—; instr. health scis. Saddleback Coll., Mission Viejo, Calif., 1987—; affiliate faculty, Orange County chpt. Am. Heart Assn., 1983—. Bd. dirs. Palisades PTA, Capistrano beach, 1979-87, San Clemente Little League, 1981-86, Capistrano Beach Community Assn., 1988—. Mem. Orange County Emergency Nurses Assn. (bd. dirs. 1986—), Am. Assn. Critical Care Nurses, Orange County Emergency Dept. Suprs. (sec. 1988). Democrat. Methodist. Office: San Clemente Hosp 654 Camino de los Mares San Clemente CA 92672

SWEETMAN, JOSEPH DAVID, JR., manufacturing company executive; b. Passaic, N.J., Jan. 30, 1948; s. Joseph David and Alice Evans (Timmerman) S.; m. Donna Lee Carbone, May 5, 1974. BS in Physics, San Diego State U., 1977; MBA, Santa Clara U., 1985. Engr. Signetics Corp., Sunnyvale, Calif., 1977-78, mgr. quality/reliability assurance, 1978-82; mgr. quality assurance SEEQ Tech., San Jose, Calif., 1982-84, dir. quality and reliability, 1984-86, dir. mil. programs, 1986—; module task group chmn. Jedec com.-13 Electronics Industries Assn./Joint Electronic Devices Engring. Coun., Washington, 1988—, chmn. task group Statis. Process Control, 1986-88. Contbr. articles to profl. publs. With USN, 1968-72. Mem. IEEE (floating gate standards com. 1984—), Am. Soc. Quality Control (statistics task group 1984—), Nat. Space Soc., Phi Beta Kappa. Republican. Office: SEEQ Tech Inc 1849 Fortune Dr San Jose CA 95131

SWENSON, CURTIS FLOYD, sales executive; b. Seattle, Aug. 24, 1953; s. Floyd A. and Lorraine (Sorenson) S.; m. Valerie Pack, Sept. 5, 1979; children: Joshua Curtis, Justin Anthony, Nicholas Ray, Danielle Janette. BS, Brigham Young U., 1978; MBA, Wash. State U., 1980. Sales rep. Procter & Gamble Distbg. Co., Portland, Oreg., 1980-81; dist. field rep. Procter & Gamble Distbg. Co., Chgo., 1981-82, unit mgr., 1983-85; unit mgr. Procter & Gamble Distbg. Co., Portland, 1985-89; chain mgr. nat. accounts Procter & Gamble Distbg. Co., Dallas, 1989—; moderator New Rep. Tng. Course, Procter & Gamble Co., Cin., 1982, 83, 84, 85, 86, 88. Asst. scoutmaster Boy Scouts Am., Portland, 1981, Chgo., 1982-85; pres. elder's quorum LDS Ch., Portland, 1986—. Recipient Life Scout award, Duty to God award Boy Scouts Am., Seattle, 1971. Mem. Brigham Young U. Mgmt. Soc. Republican. Home: 10232 SW 59th Pl Portland OR 97219 Office: Procter & Gamble Distbg Co 500 108th Ave NE Ste 1600 Bellevue WA 98004

SWENSON, ERICK NOAK, data processing executive, retired naval officer; b. Rochester, N.Y., June 12, 1926; s. Noak and Hulda Josephina (Sjellberg) S.; m. Annette Miller, Nov. 22, 1959; 1 child, Erika Margaret. BEE, U. Rochester, 1950; postgrad. U. Pitts., 1950-51, USN Postgrad. Sch., 1960-62. Registered profl. electrical engr., Calif. Enlisted USN, 1944, commd. ensign, 1951, advanced through grades to capt., 1975; electronics div. officer USS Missouri, 1951-52; ships supt. U.S. Navy Yard, San Francisco, 1952-53; quality control engr. Naval Ordnance div. Eastman Kodak Co., Rochester, N.Y., 1953-57; asst. Naval Tactical Data System project officer Dept. Navy, Washington , 1957-60, buships tech. rep. St. Paul, 1962-65, Naval Tactical Data System project officer, Washington, 1965-75, ret., 1975; sr. scientist Hughes Aircraft Co., Fullerton, Calif., 1975-76, project mgr., 1976—; served as mil. adv. to NATO Indsl. Adv. Group on Naval Command and Control; coordinated naval command and control matters for U.S. and Allied Navies and involved in fgn. mil. sales; co-designer Naval Tactical Data System used world-wide for combat warships; instigated update of combat weapons system USN Iranian destroyers (KIDD class); pres. Physical Evaluation Bd., U.S. Navy, Washington, 1969-75; Pres. 1st Luth. Ch., Fullerton, Calif., 1981-83; mem. Mil. Service Academy Rev. Bd., 39th Congl. Dist., Fullerton, 1982—. Decorated Meritorious Service Medal; recipient Value Engr. award Hughes Aircraft Co., 1980, Naval Bd. Crest, Australian Dept. Def., 1975; N.Y. State Regents scholar 1946-50. Mem. IEEE, Am. Soc. Naval Engrs. (chmn. Long Beach/ Greater Los Angeles sect. 1987-88), Navy League of the U.S., Am. Def. Preparedness Assn., Nat. Railway Hist. Soc., USS Missouri Assn., Am. Battleship Assn., Fleet Res. Assn., U.S. Naval Inst., Australian Naval Inst., Res. Officers Assn., Ret. Officers Assn., Tailhook Assn. Home: 2073 Smokewood Ave Fullerton CA 92631 Office: Hughes Aircraft Co 1901 W Malvern Fullerton CA 92634

SWENSON, KATHLEEN SUSAN, music and art teacher; b. Reno, Nev., Oct. 23, 1938; d. Harold Ruthaford McNeil and Hollyce Margaret (Scruggs) McNeil Biggs; m. James Michael Phalan, 1956 (div. 1974); children: David Michael, Jeanine Louise Phalan Lawrence, Gregory Shaun; m. Gerald Allen Swensen, Nov. 1976 (div. 1987); stepchildren: Craig Allen, Sarah Ann, Eric Sander. Student, U. Nev., Reno, 1956-58, Foothill Coll., 1966-68; AA, West Valley Coll.; BA, U. Calif., Santa Cruz, 1983. Concert pianist Nev.,Calif, 1950-64; pvt. piano instr. various locations, 1963—, pvt. art instr., 1970—, pvt. astrology instr., 1973—; founder, pres. AAM Triple Arts, Aptos, Calif., 1974—. Producer, instr. art instrn. videos. Mem. Soc Western Artists, Calif. Piano Tchrs. Assn., Los Gatos Art Assn. (pres. 1985-86), Saratoga Contemporary Artists (v.p. 1984-85), Nat. League Am. Pen Women (honorarian 1985). Republican. Episcopalian. Home and Office: AAM Triple Arts 3000 Wisteria Way Aptos CA 95003

SWERDA, PATRICIA FINE, artist, author, educator; b. Ft. Worth, Aug. 10, 1916; d. William Emerson and Margaret Ellen (Cull) Fine; B.S. cum laude, Tex. Woman's U., 1941; grad. Ikenobo U., Tokyo, 1965-66, Ikenobo Dojo, Kyoto, Japan, 1976, 77, 83; m. John Swerda, July 7, 1941; children—John Patrick James, Susan Ann Mary Swerda Foss, Margaret Rose Swerda Yovino. Pres. N.W. Sakura chpt. Ikenobo Ikebana Soc., Redmond, Wash., 1960—; exhibited ikebana in one-woman shows including: Bon Marche, Tacoma, 1966, Seattle, 1967, 85, Gallery Kokoro, Seattle, 1972-78; exhibited in group shows including: Takashimaya Dept. Store, 1965, 77, 83, 85, Matsuzakaya Dept. Store, Tokyo, 1966, Ikenobo Center, Kyoto, 1966, 77, Seattle Art Mus., 1974-80, Sangyo Kaikan, Kyoto, 1976, Burke Mus., U. Wash., ann. Cherry Blossom Festival, Seattle; demonstrations in field for various groups. Master of Ikebana of Ikenobo Ikebana Soc., Kyoto. Trustee, pres. Bellevue Sister Cities Assn. 1985-88. Mem. Ikenobo Ikebana Soc., Bonsai Clubs Internat., Puget Sound Bonsai Assn., Japan-Am. Soc., Seattle Rose Soc., AAUW. Democrat. Russian Orthodox. Author: Japanese Flower Arranging: Practical and Aesthetic Bases of Ikebana, 1969; Creating Japanese Shoka, 1979, Art Deco / Free Style Ikebana; contbr. articles to mags. in field; creator, Ikenobo Gardens, Redmond; numerous radio and TV appearances. Home and Office: 23025 NE 8th St Redmond WA 98053

SWIFT, AL, congressman; b. Tacoma, Sept. 12, 1935; m. Paula Jean Jackson, 1956; children—Amy, Lauri. Student, Whitman Coll., 1953-55, Central Wash. U., 1956; 57. Broadcaster; public affairs dir. Sta. KVOS-TV; adminstrv. asst. to U.S. rep. Lloyd Meeds, 1965-69, 77; mem. 96th-101st Congresses from 2d Wash. dist., 1979—; mem. Bellingham (Wash.) City Charter Revision Com.; chmn., mem. Bellingham Citizens Adv. Com.; mem. Bellingham Housing Authority. Democrat. Office: 1502 Longworth House Office Bldg Washington DC 20515

SWIFT, WALTER LE GRAND, III, realtor; b. Pasadena, Calif., Sept. 23, 1947; s. Walter Le Grand Jr. and Mary Elizabeth (Bumbaugh) S.; m. Suzette Carol Boyles, Sept. 23, 1967 (div. Jan. 1981); children: Suzette Carol Lyon, Walter IV; m. Shelia Coleen Coleman, July 14, 1981. AA, Pasadena City Coll., 1968; student, Mt. Shasta Coll., 1973. Prodn. supr. Resiflex Labs., Covina, Calif., 1968-72; owner Wonder World Snack Bar, Redding, Calif., 1972-74; real estate sales agt. Medley Realty, Redding, 1973-76; v.p. br sales mgr, real estate sales agt. Forest E. Olson Inc. subs. Coldwell Banker, Oxnard, Calif., 1976-77; real estate sales mgr. Forest E. Olson Inc. subs. Coldwell Banker, Ventura County, Calif., 1977-83, Drosten Properties Corp., Camarillo, Calif., 1983-84, Coldwell Banker, Thousand Oaks, Calif., 1985-88; real sales agt. Coldwell Banker, Camarillo, 1988—. Mem. Realtors Nat. Mktg. Inst. (real estate brokerage coun.), Nat. Assn. Realtors, Calif. Assn. Realtors. Republican. Lodges: Kiwanis (pres. Camarillo chpt. 1986-87), Moose. Office: Coldwell Banker Real Estate 302 N Lantana Ste 41 Camarillo CA 93010

SWIGERT, ROB, writer, educator; b. Chgo., Jan. 7, 1941; s. Eugene and Ruth (Robison) S.; m. Margaret Jane Bugas, Mar. 26, 1969; children: Saramanda Nell, Tess Miranda. BA, Princeton U., 1962; PhD, SUNY, Buffalo, 1972. Assoc. prof. San Jose (Calif.) State U., 1972—; cons. Spectrum Holobyte, Alameda, Calif., 1986—. Author: Little America, 1977, A.K.A. A Cosmic Fable, 1978, The Time Trip, 1979, The Book of Revelations, 1981, Vector, 1986, Portal, 1988; (computer software) Portal, 1988, Toxin, 1989. Mem. Mystery Writers Am., Sci. Fiction Writers Am., Author's Guild. Democrat. Home and Office: 770 Bear Gulch Rd Woodside CA 94062

SWIHART, H. GREGG, real estate company executive; b. San Francisco, Sept. 25, 1938; s. Lawson Benjamin and Violet Mary (Watters) S.; B.A., U. Ariz., 1958; postgrad. U. Heidelberg (W.Ger.), 1958-59, Harvard U., 1959-60; M.A., Boston U., 1961; postgrad. U. Freiburg (West Germany), 1961-65; m. Ilse Paula Rambacher, Dec. 24, 1958; children—Tatjana Etta, Brett Marc, Natascha Theda. Stock broker Walston & Co., Tucson, 1966-71; with Solot Co., Tucson, 1971-74; pres. Cienega Properties, Inc., property mgmt. and investment, Tucson, 1975-77; pres. GT Realty Assocs., Ltd., Tucson, 1977—. Mem. Tucson Com. Fgn. Relations, 1973—; pres. Forum for Greater Outdoors, 1977-79; bd. dirs. Tucson Mus. Art, 1968-74, pres. 1969-70; pres. and trustee Canelo Hills Sch., 1977-79. Cert. property mgr. Mem. Tucson Bd. Realtors, Inst. Real Estate Mgmt. (pres. Tucson-So. Ariz. chpt. 1982, mem. nat. governing council 1985-87), Inst. Real Estate Mgmt. (governing council 1985-87, Porperty Mgr. of Yr. award So. Ariz. chpt. 1988), Realtors Nat. Mktg. Inst. Clubs: Harvard (pres. 1973-74), Active 20-30 (pres. 1969), Downtown Tucson. Home: PO Box 555 Tunnel Springs Ranch Sonoita AZ 85637 Office: 660 N Swan Tucson AZ 85711

SWIHART, JOHN MARION, aircraft manufacturing company executive; b. New Winchester, Ohio, Dec. 27, 1923; s. Harry Miron and Fay I. (Cress)

S.; m. Gail G. Carter, Nov. 8, 1986; children from previous marriages: Vicki Ann, John Richard, Thomas Marion, Mark Andrew, Karen Lee, Laurie Christine, Stacey Anne. B.S. in Physics, Bowling Green State U., 1947; B.S. in Aero. Engring., Ga. Inst. Tech., 1949, postgrad., 1951-53; postgrad., U. Va., 1951-53. Asst. group leader propulsion group NASA, 1956-58, group leader spl. projects, 1958-59, head advanced configurations group aircraft, 1959-62, chief large supersonic tunnels br., 1962; with Boeing Co., 1962—; dep. dir. internat. sales Boeing Co., Renton, Wash., 1974-75; v.p. Japan Boeing Internat. Corp. Boeing Co., Tokyo, 1973-74; program mgr. 7X7 Boeing Co., Kent, Wash., 1975-76; dir. new airplane product devel., sales, mktg. Boeing Co., Seattle, 1976-78; dir. product devel., sales mktg. Boeing Co., 1978-79, v.p. U.S., Can. sales, 1979-83, v.p. govt. tech. liaison, 1983-85, corp. v.p. airplane market analysis, 1985; corp. v.p. internat. affairs Boeing Co., Seattle, 1985-89; ret. Contbr. over 100 articles to profl. jours. Served to 1st lt. USAAF, 1943-45. Decorated D.F.C., Air medal with 3 oak leaf clusters; recipient Wright Bros. Meml. Lectureship award, 1987. Fellow AIAA (chmn. aircraft design com. 1970-72, chmn. Pacific N.W. sect. 1969-70, gen. chmn. aircraft systems and design meeting 1977, pres.-elect), Royal Aero. Soc.; mem. Am. Ordnance Assn., Japan-Am. Soc. (pres. 1978-79), Wash. State China Rels. Coun. (pres.-elect), Nat. Ctr. Advanced Techs. (pres. 1989—). Office: Boeing Co PO Box 3707 Seattle WA 98124

SWIHART, TIMOTHY A., chiropractor; b. Bluffton, Ind., Apr. 9, 1953; s. Hilden Chester William and Doris Eileen (Alexander) S.; m. Betty Lou Thompson, Aug. 1, 1975; children: Alexander, Serena, Ian-Luke. Student, Purdue U., 1975-77; D of Chiropractic Medicine, Palmer Coll., 1980. Diplomate Am. Bd. Chiropractic Medicine. Intern Palmer Coll. Chiropractics, Davenport, 1979-80; pvt. practice medicine specializing in chiropractics Ontario, Calif., 1986—; assoc. dir. Mendenhall Chiropractic Clinic, Riverside, Calif., 1984-86. Editor: Inland Empire, 1988. Leader Boy Scouts Am., Upland, Calif., 1987-88; speaker Gideons Internat., Corona, Calif., 1981—. Served with U.S. Army, 1972-74. Named Superachiever Chiropractic Achievers Mag., 1988. Mem. Am. Chiropractic Assn., Calif. Chiropractic Assn., San Bernadino Chiropractic Soc., Parker Research Found., Practice Mgmt. Assn. (Cornerstone, Chancellor, Comdr., Baron, Earl, Marquis, Duke, Master awards 1986-88), Palmer Coll. Alumni Assn. (chmn. ednl. career seminar 1980-81), Chiropractic Assn. Ariz. (pub. relations dir. 1982-83), Dist. 19 Chiropractic Assn. (del. 1982), Tucson C. of C. (legis. com. 1983). Republican. Mem. Reformed Ch. Am. Home: 2393 N Euclid Upland CA 91786 Office: Swihart Chiropractic Clinic 2537 S Euclid Ave Ontario CA 91762

SWINDELLS, WILLIAM, JR., lumber and paper company executive; b. 1930; married. B.S., Stanford U., 1953. With Willamette Industries, Inc., Portland, Oreg., 1953—; sr. v.p. prodn., mktg. bldg. materials Willamette Industries, Inc., until 1978, exec. v.p., 1978-80, pres. forest products div., 1980-82, pres., chief exec. officer, 1982—, also dir., chmn., 1984—; dir. Oreg. Bank, Portland. Office: Willamette Industries Inc First Interstate Tower 1300 SW 5th Ave Portland OR 97201 *

SWINDLER, DARIS RAY, physical anthropologist, forensic anthropologist; b. Morgantown, W.Va., Aug. 13, 1925; s. George Raymond and Minnie Mildred (McElroy) S.; m. Kathryn Pardo, Nov. 10, 1977; children: Gary, Darece, Linda, Dana, Bruce, Geoffry, Jason. AB, W.Va. U., 1950; MA, U. Pa., 1952, PhD, 1959. Instr. Cornell Med. Sch., N.Y.C., 1956-57, W.Va. Med. Sch., Morgantown, 1957-59; asst. prof. Med. Coll. S.C., Charleston, 1959-64; assoc. prof. Mich. State U., East Lansing, 1964-68; prof. phys. anthropology, comparative primate anatomy, dental anthropology U. Wash., Seattle, 1968—; cons. King County Med. Examiner, Seattle, 1968—; vis. sr. scientist Com. on Scholarly Communications with People's Republic China, 1987-88. Author: A Racial Study of the West Nakani of New Britain, 1962, Dentition of Living Primates, 1976, Systematics, Evolution and Anatomy, Comparative Primate Biology; (with C.D. Wood) Atlas of Primate Gross Anatomy, 1973 (Gov's. award 1973), (with J. Sirianni) Growth and Development of Pigtailed Macaque, 1985. Served with USN, 1943-46. Recipient Alexander von Homboldt Sr. U.S. Scientist award, Frankfurt, Fed. Republic Germany, 1982-83. Mem. AAAS, Am. Assn. Phys. Anthropologists (v.p. 1976-78), Internat. Primatology Soc., N.Y. Acad. Sci., Italian Primatological Assn., Sigma Xi. Office: U Wash Dept Anthropology Seattle WA 98195

SWINEFORD, THOMAS DERALD, banker; b. Oklahoma City, Dec. 31, 1940; s. Derald Thomas and Mary (Good) S.; m. Janis Jane Bunch, Mar. 24, 1983; children: Stuart Thomas, Scott Alan. BA, U. Okla., 1964, MA, 1967. With Liberty Nat. Bank & Trust Co., Oklahoma City, 1965-74; sr. v.p. Penn Sq. Bank N.A., Oklahoma City, 1974-79, 81-82, Citizens Nat. Bank & Trust Co., Oklahoma City, 1979-80; v.p. Citizens Nat. Bank & Trust Co., 1980-81; liquidation asst. FDIC, 1982; v.p. United Okla. Bank, 1983; pres., chief exec. officer First Security Bank & Trust Co., Oklahoma City, 1984-85, Gunnison Bank & Trust Co., Colo., 1985—. Mem. Rotary. Republican. Presbyterian. Office: Gunnison Bank & Trust Co PO Box 119 Gunnison CO 81230-0119

SWINERTON, WILLIAM ARTHUR, building and construction company executive; b. San Francisco, Dec. 12, 1917; s. Alfred Bingham and Jane Thomas (Hotaling) S.; m. Mary Nichols Clark, June 5, 1943; children: Leslie Engelbrecht, Susan McBaine, James B., Sarah Blake. B.S., Yale, 1939; postgrad., Stanford, 1940. With Swinerton & Walberg Co., San Francisco, 1940-88, ret. Served with USMCR., 1940-46. Decorated Bronze Star. Clubs: Pacific Union, Burlingame Country. Home: PO Box 620265 Woodside CA 94062 Office: Swinerton & Walberg Co 100 Pine St San Francisco CA 94111

SWING, WILLIAM EDWIN, bishop; b. Huntington, W.Va., Aug. 26, 1936; s. William Lee and Elsie Bell (Holliday) S.; M. Mary Willis Taylor, Oct. 7, 1961; children—Alice Marshall, William Edwin. B.A., Kenyon Coll., Ohio, 1954-58; D.Div. (hon.), Kenyon Coll., 1980; M.A., Va. Theol. Sem., 1958-61, D.Div., 1980. Ordained priest Episcopal Ch. Asst. St. Matthews Ch., Wheeling, W.Va., 1961-63; vicar St. Matthews Ch., Chester, W.Va., 1963-69, St. Thomas Ch., Weirton, W.Va., 1963-69; rector St. Columbias Episcopal Ch., Washington, 1969-79; bishop Episcopal Ch. Calif., San Francisco, 1980—; chmn. bd. Ch. Div. Sch. of the Pacific, 1983-84; founder, chmn. Episcopal Found. for Drama, 1976—. Republican. Home: 2006 Lyon St San Francisco CA 94115 Office: Episcopal Ch Diocesan Office 1055 Taylor St San Francisco CA 94108 *

SWINGLE, DONALD MORGAN, physicist, meteorologist, consultant; b. Washington, Sept. 1, 1922; s. Louis Morgan and Anna Pearl (Fenby) S.; m. Hazel Elizabeth O'Hara, Mar. 5, 1943; children: Donald Morgan, Donna Beth, Jonathan Warne. MS, NYU, 1947; MA, Harvard U., 1948, M of Engring. Sci., 1949, PhD, 1950; MBA, George Washington U., 1962. Cert. Indst. Coll. Armed Forces, 1962. Commd. 2nd lt. U.S. Army, 1944, advanced through grades to lt. col., 1964, research and devel. project officer, 1944-46; radio engr. Signal Corps Lab. U.S. Army, Ft. Monmouth, N.J., 1946-47; research asst. Harvard U., Cambridge, Mass., 1949-50; physicist Signal Corps Lab., Ft. Monmouth, N.J., 1950-66; sr. scientist Atmospheric Sci. Lab. U.S. Army Electronics Command, Ft. Monmouth, N.J., 1966-71, sr. scientist Exploratory and Engring. Devel. Tech Area, 1971-74, Spl. Sensors Tech. Area, Combat Surveillance, 1974-78; research physicist, cons. U.S. Army, White Sands Missile Range, N.M., 1978-80. Mem. Army Research Council, 1964-65. U.S. mem. Commn. for Instruments and Methods of Obs., World Meteorol. Orgn., UN, 1952-72. Fellow N.Y. Acad. Scis., AIAA (assoc. mem. com. on unidentified flying objects 1965-75); mem. Am. Meteorol. Soc., IEEE (sr.), Am. Geophys. Union, AAAS, Am. Mgmt. Assn., Nat. Soc. Profl. Engrs., Mensa, N.M. Research Inst. Methodist. Home: 1765 Pomona Dr Las Cruces NM 88001-4919 Office: PO Box 160 Las Cruces NM 88004-0160

SWINSKY, DANA ALISON, architect; b. N.Y.C., Apr. 4, 1962; d. Morton and Florence (Pincus) S.; m. Christopher Glen Cantelmo, Mar. 6, 1988. BA, Yale U., 1984; MArch, So. Calif. Inst. Architecture, 1989. Draftsperson James Di Maria Assocs., N.Y.C., 1984; assoc. Ari Bahat Architects, N.Y.C., 1984-86; with prodn. Architrave, Los Angeles, 1987—; tchr. aide So. Calif. Inst. Architecture, 1987—. Mem. editorial bd. Offramp (mag. of the arts), 1988—. Recipient Kaplan scholarship in sci. and architecture, 1988. Democrat. Jewish. Home: 621 Ocean dr Manhattan Beach CA 90026

SWINTON, JEFFREY CHEEVER, lawyer; b. Salt Lake City, June 22, 1947; s. Kenneth Perry and Venice (Cheever) S.; m. Heidi Sorensen, Apr. 14, 1972; children: Cameron, Daniel, Jonathan, Ian. BA, U. Utah, 1971, JD, 1974. Bar: Utah 1974, U.S. Ct. Appeals (10th cir.) 1985, U.S. Supreme Ct. 1985. Ptnr. Stringham, Larsen, Mazuran & Sabin, Salt Lake City, 1974-79, Larsen, Mazuran & Verhaaren, Salt Lake City, 1984-85, Jensen & Swinton, Salt Lake City, 1986-87; sr. v.p. Ruti-Sweetwater, Inc., Salt Lake City, 1979-84; ptnr., v.p., bd. dirs. Woodbury, Jensen, Kesler & Swinton, Salt Lake City, 1988—. Assoc. editor Utah Bar Jour., 1973-74; editor Summation: Jour. Utah Law, 1973. Chmn., v.p., del. Salt Lake City Rep. Com., 1975-88; trustee Bus. Industry Community Edn. Partnership, Salt Lake City, 1979-80; mem. panel judges Utah Pub. Employees Assn., 1980-83, 85-87; bd. dirs., v.p. Work Activities Ctr. for Handicapped Adults, Salt Lake City, 1987—; dist. chmn. Boy Scouts Am., Salt Lake City, 1987—. Mem. ABA, U. Utah Law Sch. Alumni Assn. (treas., trustee 1979-83), Am. Trial Lawyers Assn., Young Alumni Assn. U. Utah (pres. 1981-83), Ft. Douglas Country Club, Soc. Bar and Gavel (pres. 1976-78), Beehive, Owl and Key, Skull and Bones. Mormon. Home: 1211 East 100 South Salt Lake City UT 84102 Office: 265 East 100 South Salt Lake City UT 84111

SWINTON, RICHARD BRUCE, lawyer; b. Honolulu, Apr. 28, 1950; s. David Bruce and Jean B. (McGregor) S. BA in Econs. and Bus. Adminstrn., U. Redlands, 1972; JD, Calif. Western Sch. Law, San Diego, 1975. Bar: Calif. 1975, Hawaii 1976, Alaska 1977, Guam 1982; CPA, Calif. Atty. State of Alaska Dept. Revenue, Anchorage, 1977; acct. Bigler, hawkins & Obendorf, CPA's, Anchorage, 1977-78, Diehl Evans & Co., CPA's, Escondido, Calif., 1978-80; assoc. Law Offices John Bohn, Agana, Guam, 1980-83; atty., acct. Guam Landowners Assn., Inc., Agana, 1980-83; acct. U.S. Dept. Def., Synnyvale, Calif., 1985; atty., acct. U.S. Dept. Def., Burbank, Calif., 1987—, PMJ Enterprises, Reno, Nev., 1985-87; cons. PMJ Enterprises, 1987—. Mem. State Bar Calif. Assn., Hawaii State Bar Assn., Alaska Bar Assn., Guam Bar Assn., Archaeol. Inst. Am., L.A. County Mus. Art, Smithsonian Inst., Sierra Club. Home: 1710 Avenida del Mundo Apt 1502 Coronado CA 92118

SWIONTKOWSKI, MARC FRANCIS, orthopedist; b. Elizabeth, N.J., Sept. 15, 1951; s. William Robert and Agnes Eileen (Baker) S.; m. Beth Ellen, Sept. 2,. BA, Calif. State U., 1973; MD, U. So. Calif., 1979. Gen. surgeon Univ. Wash., Seattle, 1979-80, orthopaedic residence, 1980-84; orthopedic cons. KIlimanjoro Christian Med. Ctr., Moshi, Tanzania, 1984; research assoc. Lab. for Experiment, Davos, Swit.; asst. prof. Vanderbilt Univ. Surgery, Nashville, 1985-86; assoc prof. Vanderbilt Univ., Nashville, 1986-88; assoc. prof. Univ. Wash., Seattle, 1988—. Fellow, Am. Acad. Orthopadic Surgery, Soc. Internat. Chgo. (chmn.), Orthapedic. Democrat. Office: Harborview Med Ctr 325 9th Ave Seattle WA 98104

SWISTOK, JOHN EDWARD, electrical engineer; b. Lordstown, Ohio, June 18, 1933; s. John and Matilda Margaret (Mathe) S.; AA, Long Beach City Coll., 1959; BS in Elec. Engring., U. Calif., Berkeley, 1961; m. Nancy Ann Miloch, Mar. 29, 1955; children: John Robert, Paula Marie Swistok Elston, Roberta Paula, Diana Nannette, Nancy Ann, Robert John, Vetura Roberta. Rsch. engr. Autonetics, Anaheim, Calif., 1961-62; engr. Nortronics, Anaheim, 1962-63; elec. engr. Gen. Dynamics, Pomona, Calif., 1963-64; sr. engr. Northrop Corp., Newbury Park, Calif., 1968-69, Hawthorne, Calif., 1969-74; sr. engr. Litton Industries, Woodland Hills, Calif., 1964-68; engring. specialist Litton Industries, 1974-76; reliability engring. specialist Northrop Corp., Hawthorne, Calif., 1977—. Tchr., Religious Sci. Jr. Ch., 1971—. With USN, 1952-56; Korea. Mem. IEEE, Northrop Mgmt. Club. Home: 2037 N Chouteau St Orange CA 92665 Office: One Northrop Ave Hawthorne CA 90250

SWIZER, JOHN WARREN, airport administrator; b. Sacramento, Mar. 15, 1945; s. John Herman and Julia Suzanne (Kraushar) S.; m. Janet Ann Redick, Aug. 14, 1968; children: Angela, Michelle. Student, Sacramento City Coll., 1963-64, San Jose City Coll., 1971-72. Mktg. rep. Delta Air Lines, Inc., San Francisco, 1970-78; area mgr. Air Logistics Inc., Lake Charles, La., 1978-88; mgr. Nut Tree-Solano County Airport, Vacaville, Calif., 1988—. With U.S. Army, 1965-70, Vietnam. Mem. Calif. Assn. Airport Execs. (exec.), Vietnam Helicopter Pilots Assn., DAV (life), Masons, Shriners. Republican. Lutheran. Home: 512 Wintergreen Ct Vacaville CA 95687 Office: Nut Tree Airport 301 County Airport Rd Vacaville CA 95688

SWOAP, DAVID BRUCE, government relations firm executive; b. Kalamazoo, Aug. 12, 1937; s. Orlo Frederick and Aileen Esther (Hempy) S. B.A. in Govt. with honors, Denison U., 1959; M.A. in Govt, Claremont Grad. Sch., 1961; D.Sci. (hon.), U. Osteo. Medicine and Health Scis., Des Moines, 1981. Asst. sec. Calif. State Personnel Bd., Sacramento, 1972-73; chief dep. dir., acting dir. Calif. State Dept. Social Welfare, Sacramento, 1973; dir. Calif. State Dept. Social Welfare, 1973-74, Calif. State Dept. Benefit Payments, 1974-75; sr. research asso. Republican Study Com., U.S. Ho. of Reps., Washington, 1975-76; profl. staff mem. U.S. Senate Com. on Fin., Washington, 1976-79; legis. dir. U.S. Senator William L. Armstrong, Washington, 1979-81; undersec. Dept. Health and Human Services, Washington, 1981-83; sec. health and welfare State of Calif., Sacramento, 1983-85. Elder Presbyn. Ch.; bd. dirs. Friends of SOS Children's Villages, Inc., 1975—. Rotary Club Found. fellow, 1961-62. Mem. United Council on Welfare Fraud, Wycliffe Assn., Rotary, Club of San Francisco, Phi Beta Kappa, Delta Upsilon. Republican. Office: Franchetti & Swoap One Market Pla Steuart St Tower Ste 1210 San Francisco CA 94105

SYDNOR, ROBERT HADLEY, state government geologist; b. Whittier, Calif., July 1, 1947; s. Thurston Edward and Mary Edith (Thompson) S.; m. Nancie Jeanne Neubert, Mar. 29, 1986; 1 child, Christopher. B.A., Whittier Coll., 1969; M.S., U. Calif.-Riverside, 1975. Registered geologist, Calif., Oreg., Alaska, Ariz.; cert. engring. geologist, Calif., Oreg. Asst. petroleum geologist Mobil Oil Corp., Anchorage, 1970-71; staff engring. geologist Leighton & Assocs., Irvine, Calif., 1973-77; assoc. engring. geologist Orange County, Laguna Niguel, Calif., 1977-79; sr. engring. geologist VTN Corp., Irvine, 1979; chief engring. geologist R&M Cons., Inc., Irvine, 1979-82; supervising geologist Calif. Div. Mines and Geology, Sacramento, 1982—; mem. exam. com. Calif. State Bd. of Registration for Geologists and Geophysicists, Sacramento, 1977—, chmn., 1978. Contbr. many cons. reports on landslides and seismicity . Mem. alumni scholarship com. U. Calif.-Riverside, 1978-86; mem. City of Los Angeles Grading Appeals Bd., 1979-84; alt. mem. County of Orange Grading Appeals Bd., 1980-84. Donnel Foster Hewett fellow U. Calif., 1972. Mem. Calif. Acad. Sci. (life), Assn. Engring. Geologists (assoc. editor Bull. 1979-86, chmn. So. Calif. sect. 1979-80), Geol. Soc. Am., Seismol. Soc. Am. (life), Am. Assn. Petroleum Geologists, Am. Inst. Profl. Geologists, Nat. Assn. Geology Tchrs., Arctic Inst. N.Am. (life), ASTM, Am. Geophys. Union (life), Sigma Gamma Epsilon (life). Republican. Home: 4930 Huntridge Ln Fair Oaks CA 95628-4823 Office: Calif Div Mines and Geology 630 Bercut Dr Sacramento CA 95814-0131

SYERS, WILLIAM EDWARD, manufacturing company executive; b. DeKoven, Ky., Feb. 26, 1926; s. John Benedict and Mary Helen (Watson) S.; student Lockyear's Bus. Coll., Evansville, Ind., 1950-52; m. Veda Marie Swisher, Dec. 23, 1950; children: David Bruce, Drew Edward. With Internat. Harvester Co., Evansville, Ind., 1946-52, IBM, 1952-68, subs. Svc. Bur. Corp., 1968-70; with Teledyne Econ. Devel. Co., Phoenix, 1970—, dir. adminstrv. svcs., 1979—, asst. ctr. dir., 1980—. With Q.M.C., AUS, 1946-48. Mem. Adminstrv. Mgmt. Soc. (pres. Phoenix chpt. 1977-78, dir. 1978-79), Phoenix C. of C. Republican. Mem. Ch. of Christ. Office: Teledyne Econ Devel Co 518 S 3d St Phoenix AZ 85004

SYKE, CAMERON JOHN, lawyer; b. Oak Park, Ill., Jan. 29, 1957; s. A. John and Rosemarie (Grasso) S.; m. Susan Royer, Jan. 2, 1982; children: Caroline, Jared. BSBA cum laude, U. Denver, 1977, LLM in Taxation, 1986; JD with honors, DePaul U., 1982. Bar: CPA, Colo. 1983, U.S. Tax Ct. 1985. Acct. Touche, Ross, Chgo., 1978-79, Denver, 1980-83; investment broker Boettcher & Co., Denver, 1983-84; CPA Laventhol & Horwath, Denver, 1984-85; assoc. Roath & Brega, Denver, 1985-87; ptnr. Hopper, Kanouff, Smith, Peryam & Terry, Denver, 1987—; adj. prof. U. Denver, 1985; instr. Colo. Soc. CPA's, 1986-87; lectr. Nat. Bus. Inst., 1986-87. Candidate councilman City of Denver, 1987. Mem. Colo. Bar Assn., Colo. Soc. CPA's. Republican. Presbyterian. Home: 3284 S Elmira Denver CO 80231 Office: Hopper & Kanouff 1610 Wynkoop #200 Denver CO 80202

SYKES, RANDOLPH JOSEPH, banker, management consultant, business analyst; b. Pasadena, Calif., Jan. 26, 1951; s. Joseph Francis and Marguerite Ann (Rickard) S. BA in Philosophy, Loyola U., L.A., 1973. Vice pres. Bank Am. NT&SA, San Francisco, 1975--; prin. Sykes Dahl Cons. Group, San Francisco, 1981-85; mng. dir. Dolphin Circle, Mill Valley, Calif., 1986--; exec. dir. Kauai Life Clarity Inst., Hanalei, Hawaii, 1987--. Author: Charting Your Goals: Personal Life-Goals Planner, 1988. Mem. City Club San Francisco (founding). Office: 645 Northern Mill Valley CA 94941

SYME, DAVID MICHAEL, data processing executive; b. Alexandria, Va., Aug. 17, 1959; s. Sherman Leonard and Marilyn Elaine (Egenes) S.; m. Catherine Joan Holmes, June 26, 1988. BA, U. Calif., Berkeley, 1981; MBA, San Francisco State U., 1984; JD, U. San Francisco, 1987. Field rep. Gen. Motors Acceptance Corp., Emeryville, Calif., 1981-82; computer analyst One Point Computer Corp., Walnut Creek, Calif., 1984-85; law clk. Calif. Supreme Ct., San Francisco, 1986; with Williams, Kelly, Pulverari and Skelton, Redwood City, Calif., 1986-87; owner, pres. Marathon Micro, Moraga, Calif., 1985—; bd. dirs. Calif. Aesthetics, Orinda, 1985—. Mem. Mensa. Home: 273 Scofield Dr Moraga CA 94556 Office: Marathon Micro 273 Scofield Dr Moraga CA 94556

SYMMES, DANIEL LESLIE, three-dimensional technology executive, producer, director; b. Los Angeles, June 26, 1949; s. Louis Leslie and Mary (Warkentine) S.; m. Joanne Iriye Masada, June 4, 1988. Student, Columbia Coll., Hollywood, Calif., 1970-71. Co-founder Stereovision Internat., Inc., North Hollywood, Calif., 1975-75; cons. Dimension 3e, Beverly Hills, Calif., 1975-87; pres., chmn. Spatial Techs. Inc., Hollywood, Calif., 1987—. Author: Amazing 3-D; contbr. numerous articles to profl. jours.; patentee 3-D TV; dir. photography local 659 IATSE. Mem. SMPTE. Office: Spatial Techs Inc 801 N LaBrea Ave Ste 104 Hollywood CA 90038

SYMMS, STEVEN DOUGLAS, senator; b. Nampa, Idaho, Apr. 23, 1938; s. Darwin and Irene (Knowlton) S.; children: Dan, Susan, Amy, Katy. B.S., U. Idaho, 1960. With Symms Fruit Ranch, Inc., Caldwell, Idaho, 1963-72; mem. 93d-96th Congresses from 1st Idaho Dist., U.S. Senate, 1980—; mem. Com. on Budget, Com. on Finance, Com. on Environment and Public Works, Joint Econ. Com., Nat. Republican Senatorial Com. Served with USMC, 1960-63. Office: US Senate 509 Hart Senate Bldg Washington DC 20510

SYMONDS, JOHN C., bank executive; b. Hinsdale, Ill., May 30, 1942; s. Cortlandt and Frances (Wood) S.; m. Maren Fristrup, Oct. 29, 1983. BA, Stanford U., 1964; MBA, Harvard U., 1968. Analyst fin. Hexcel Corp., Dublin, Calif., 1968-72; sr. v.p. Fed. Home Loan Bank, San Francisco, 1973-87; sr. v.p., chief fin. officer Allied Savs. Bank, Santa Rosa, Calif., 1987—. Lt. U.S. Navy, 1964-66. Home: 100 Thunderbird Ct Novato CA 94949

SYMONS, ROBERT SPENCER, electronic engineer; b. San Francisco, July 3, 1925; s. Spencer W. and Avesia (Atkins) S.; m. Alice Faye Smith, Dec. 21, 1960; children: Julia Ann, Robert Spencer Jr. BS, Stanford U., 1946, MS, 1948. Engr. Eitel-McCullough, Inc., San Bruno, Calif., 1947, Heinz & Kaufman, South San Francisco, 1948, Pacific Electronics Co., Los Gatos, Calif., 1949; sr. engring. mgr. Varian Assocs., Palo Alto, Calif., 1950-83; tech. dir. Litton Industries, San Carlos, Calif., 1983—. Patentee in field. Served to 1st lt. AUS, 1950-53. Fellow IEEE (assoc. editor Transactions on Electron Devices jour. 1980-83); mem. Phi Beta Kappa, Tau Beta Pi. Club: Commonwealth of Calif. Home: 290 Surrey Pl Los Altos CA 94022 Office: Litton Industries 960 Industrial Rd San Carlos CA 94070

SYNDER, MARGARET JUDITH, writer; b. Luton, Bedfordshire, Eng., Mar. 11, 1940; came to U.S., 1964; d. Alan Ernest and Mable (Hartopp) Osborne; m. Lloyd Emerson Synder, Sept. 26, 1964; children: Lloyd Alan, Angela Margaret, Tammy Lynne. Cert. in interior design, Internat. Corr. Sch., Stanton, Ariz., 1984; student, Ariz. Western Coll., 1985. Cashier, receptionist Automobile Assn., London, 1957-60; bookkeeper Butlins Hotel Resorts, Brighton, Eng., 1960-63; program coord. Honson Produce, Pasadena, Calif., 1980-81, 85-88; owner MJ Interiors, Yuma, Ariz., 1984, Gift World, Yuma, 1988—. Columnist Yuma (Ariz.) Daily Sun, 1977-82. Chmn. publicity Ocotilla Dist. Boy Scouts Am., Yuma, 1977-83; active Yuma Rep. Women's Club (v.p. 1984, publicity chmn., fund raiser, 1984, 85, 88, pres. 1989—). Recipient Dist. Merit award Boy Scouts Am., Yuma, 1984. Mormon. Office: Gift World 1215 8th St Ste A-3 Yuma AZ 85365

SYPULT, ROBERT LYNN, security services professional; b. Bloomington, Ill., Apr. 20, 1945; s. Francis Eugene and Dorothy Lucille (Freed) S.; m. Nancy Sue Case, July 30,1979 (div. 1987). BS, U. Airz., 1968. Contract adminstr. Motorola, Inc., Phoenix, 1970-73; spl. agt. FBI, Kansas City, Mo., 1973-78; mgr. corp. security Salt River Project, Phoenix, 1978-84; regional security mgr. Intel Corp., Phoenix, 1984-85; dir. security systems Phillips Petroleum Co., Bartlesville, Okla., 1985-87; dir. security So. Calif. Edison Co., Rosemead, 1987—; cons., Maricopa County Superior Cts., Phoenix, 1984-85. Author: Travel Safely Overseas, 1986. Mem. Crime Prevention Com., Mesa, Ariz., 1981-83; mem. adv. bd., Scottsdale (Ariz.) Community Coll., 1982-83. 1st lt. U.S. Army, 1968-70, Vietnam. Mem. Am. Soc. Indsl. Security (chpt. chmn. 1981-82), Chief Spl. Agts. So. Calif. (bd. dirs. 1987-88), Calif. Peace Officers Assn., Internat. Assn. Chiefs of Police, Peace Officers Assn. L.A. County. Republican. Office: So Calif Edison Co 2244 Walnut Grove Ave Rosemead CA 91770

SYPUTA, ROBERT WAYNE, electronics company executive; b. Chgo., Nov. 30, 1950; s. Phillip Joseph and Leola Murial (Palmer) S. BS in Elec. Engring., So. Tech. Inst. (name changed to So. Coll. Engring. div. Ga. Inst. Tech.), 1979; MBA, Seattle U., 1985. Owner Blown-In-Insulation, Marietta, Ga., 1977-79; sales engr. Honeywell Comml. div., Seattle, 1979-82; sales engr., mgr. Centralab, Inc., Seattle, 1982-85; sales engr. Fairchild, Inc., Bellevue, Wash., 1985; pres. Microsafe, Inc., Kirkland, Wash., 1985—; v.p. mktg. Philipp Technologies Corp., Bellevue, Wash., 1988—. Inventor/patentee fiber optic theft alarm, 1985; author bus. plan, Microsafe Products Co., 1986. Vol. United Way, Seattle, 1985-86. Mem. Toastmasters. Republican. Lutheran. Office: 4850 156th Ave N E #282 Redmond WA 98052-9642

SYRETT, (JOHN) BARRY, airline pilot; b. Barkingside, Essex, Eng., June 15, 1934; came to U.S., 1966; s. John Victor and Molly Mackrell (Skelcher) S.; m. Cecile F. Boucher, June 15, 1957; children: Louise, Denise, Claire. Air traffic control asst. RAF, Uxbridge, Middlesex, Eng., 1952-54; pilot Aer Lingus, Dublin, Ireland, 1961-66; pilot, capt. Am. Airlines Inc., Los Angeles, 1966—. Flying Officer RCAF, 1955-60. Mem. Guild of Air Pilots and Air Navigators, London, Allied Pilots Assn. (bd. dirs. 1969-77, editor 1980-87). Republican. Roman Catholic. Home: 6341 Tarragon Rd Rancho Palos Verdes CA 90274

SYRING, JAMES JOHN, television news editor; b. N.Y.C., Oct. 4, 1942; s. John Joseph and Genevieve (Reynolds) S.; m. Virginia Catherine Zemaitis, July 20, 1968. BA in Mass Communications, SUNY, N.Y.C., 1975. V.p. Edna and Friends, Inc., N.Y.C., 1971-75; freelance editor Denver, 1975-76; chief editor Sta. KUSA-TV, Denver, 1976-80; news editor Sta. KCNC-TV, Denver, 1980—. Cpl. USMC, 1961-64. Recipient, Kodak award, Nat. Press Photographers Assn., 1976, Colo. Broadcasters award, Colo. Broadcasters Assn., 1988. Mem. NATAS (Emmy award 1973, regional Emmy, Denver, 1988), Colo. Hist. Soc., Colo. Archeol. Soc., Friends of Denver Library, Denver Art Mus. Democrat. Home: 3229 S Forest St Denver CO 80222 Office: Sta KCNC TV 1044 Lincoln St Denver CO 80203

SZABLYA, HELEN MARY, writer, language professional; b. Budapest, Pest, Hungary, Sept. 6, 1934; came to Can., 1957; d. Louis and Helen Hilda (Bartha) Kovacs; m. John Francis Szablya, June 12, 1951; children: Helen, Janos, Louis, Stephen, Alexandra, Rita, Dominique-Mary. Diploma in Sales, Mktg., U.B.C., 1962; BA in Fgn. Lang., Lit., Wash. State U., 1976. Freelance writer, translator 1967—; columnist Cath. News, Trinidad, W.I., 1980—; adult educator TELOS Bellevue (Wash.) Community Coll., 1987—; adult educator Pullman-Spokane (Wash.) Community Coll., 1976-80; faculty

Christian Writers' Conf., Seattle, 1983—, Pacific Northwest Writers' Conf., Seattle, Tacoma, 1987—. Author: (with others) Hungary Remembered, 1986 (Guardian of Liberty award 1986, George Washington Honor Gold medal, Freedoms Found. award 1988), 56-os Cserkészcsapat, 1986, numerous articles; translator: Emlé kezû nk, 1986, Mind Twisters, 1987. Recipient Nat. 1st place editorial Nat. Fedn. Press Women, 1987, Sen. Tom Martin Mem. award Pacific Northwest Writers Conf., 1979; grantee Hungarian Am. Assn. of Wash., 1986, Wash. Com. for Humanities, 1986. Mem. Wash. Press Assn. (pres. 1987-88, 1st and 2nd place awards, several editorial and profile awards 1983, 87, Communicator of Achievement award 1987), Authors Guild, Soc. for Profl. Journalists, Nat. Writers Club, Am. Translators Assn., Arpad Acad. (Gold medal 1987), AAUW, Sigma Delta Chi Soc. Profl. Journalists. Home and Office: 4416 134th Pl SE Bellevue WA 98006

SZABO, ROBERT JOSEPH, family entertainment company executive; b. San Jose, Calif., July 29, 1962; s. Joseph John and Katalin Rozalia Szabo. BS in Fgn. Svc., Georgetown U., 1983. Pres. Futuretainment, Inc., San Jose, 1983—. Adviser Jr. Achievement, Santa Clara County, Calif., 1980—; mem. Better Bus. Bur. Santa Clara. Mem. San Jose C. of C., Amusement and Music Operators Assn., Calif. Coin Machine Assn., Jaycees.

SZABO, SHARON LYNN, nurse; b. Cleve., Nov. 17, 1946; d. Joseph Steven and Margaret Minerva (Marigaard) S.; m. Ross Earl McFarland Jr., June 15, 1968 (div. June 1972). RN, Mt. Sinai Hosp. Sch. Nursing, 1967. Cert. operating room nurse. Asst. head nurse Mt. Sinai Hosp., Cleve., 1967-68; staff nurse operating room Cedars-Sinai Med. Ctr., Los Angeles, 1969-71; ob-gyn office nurse for med. office of Everett Wood, MD, Burbank, Calif., 1968-69; internal medicine office nurse for Martin Covel, MD, Beverly Hills, Calif., 1971-74; from. staff nurse to asst. head nurse U. Calif., San Francisco, 1974-85, cardiac surgery head, 1985-86, asst. head nurse, cardiac surgery, 1986-87, staff nurse, ambulatory surgery, 1987—; cons. Westervelt, Johnson, Nicholl, & Keller, Attys. at Law, Peoria, Ill., 1985—. Contbg. author: Alexander's Care of the Patient in Surgery. Mem. Assn. of Operating Room Nurses (chpt. treas. 1983-84, test specifications com. mem. of nat. cert. bd., 1979-81). Office: U Calif San Francisco Med Ctr 3d & Parnassus Aves San Francisco CA 94143

SZABO, ZOLTAN, medical science administrator; b. Szeged, Hungary, Oct. 5, 1943; came to U.S., 1967; s. Imre and Maria (Szikora) S.; m. Wanda Toy, Dec. 5, 1976; children: Eva, Maria. Student, U. Med. Sch., Szeged, 1962-65; PhD, Columbia Pacific U., 1983. Tech. dir. microsurgery lab. R.K. Davies Med. Ctr., San Francisco, 1972-80; dir. Microsurg. Research Inst., San Francisco, 1980—; research assoc. oral and maxillofacial surgery U. of the Pacific, San Francisco, 1980-83, adj. asst. prof., 1983—. Author: Microsurgery Techniques, vol. 1 1974, vol. 2 1984 (1st Place award for excellence in med. writing, 1982); contbr. chpt. books, articles to profl. jours. Served with U.S. Army, 1969-71, Vietnam. Recipient 1st prize sci. exhibit Am. Soc. Plastic and Reconstructive Surgeons, 1977, Cert. of Merit, AMA, 1978, Commendation, Accreditation Council for Continuing Med. Edn., 1984, Spl. Recognition award Cen. U. Venezuela Sch. Medicine, 1988. Fellow Internat. Coll. Surgeons; mem. Hungarian Gynecol. Soc. (hon.), Medico-Dental Study Guild of Calif., Internat. Microsurg. Soc., Am. Fertility Soc., Am. Soc. Reconstructive Microsurgery (assoc.), Soc. for Study of Impotence. Office: Microsurg Rsch Inst 153 States St San Francisco CA 94114

SZCZEPANIAK, WALTER (JOSEPH), health care facility executive; b. Bklyn., Oct. 3, 1940; s. Walter Charles and Caroline Elizabeth (Kowalska) S.; m. Grace Frances Peaty, Aug. 12, 1961; children: Mary Louise, Kathleen, Walter John, Florence, Donna Marie, Charles, Joseph, Michael, Terrence. BS, NYU, 1972; Cert. in Bank Adminstrn., U. Wis., 1972. CCM. Acctg. clk. Brown Bros. Harriman & Co., N.Y.C., 1959-75, asst. mgr., treas., 1976; staff asst. Samaritan Health Svc., Phoenix, 1978-85, dir. corp. fin., 1985—. Mem. Ariz. Cash Mgmt. Assn., Health Care Fin. Mgmt., Nat. Corp. Cash Mgmt. Assn. (bd. dirs. 1987—, mem. cert. coun. 1987—, mem. human resources com. 1988, cert.). Republican. Home: 4802 W Julie Dr Glendale AZ 85308 Office: Samaritan Health Svc 1441 N 12th St Phoenix AZ 85308

SZETO, HUNG, publisher; b. Hoyping, Canton, People's Republic of China, Sept. 8, 1936; s. Cheong Yee and Sau King(Kwan) S.; m. Sau Hing Chow, Jan. 27, 1962; children: Roland, Lisa, Nancy. B in adminstrn., Tsing Hua Coll., Hong Kong, 1969. Mgr. Far East Trade Ctr., Seattle, 1975-81; editor Seattle Chinese Post, 1981-86; pub. Asia Pub. Co., Seattle, 1986—. Contbg. pub., editor Chinese Bus. Jour. Mem. Chinese Restaurants Nat. Assn. (pres. 1987—). Office: Chinese Bus Jour 606 Maynard Ave S Ste 102 Seattle WA 98104

SZUTU, PETER CHENG, non-profit administrator; b. Beijing, Peoples Republic of China, Sept. 18, 1945; came to U.S., 1952; s. Gene Chan and Florence (Chiang) S.; m. Janice Rose Eldred, May 26, 1985. BA in Chemistry and Biology, U.S. Internat. U., 1972; MPH, U. Calif., Berkeley, 1981. Adminstr. Beach Area Community Clinic, San Diego, 1973-79; peer counseling U. Calif., Berkeley, 1979-81; spl. asst. State Dept. Health Services, Sacramento, Calif., 1980-82; exec. dir. Oakland (Calif.) Chinese Community Council, 1982-86; mgmt., planning cons. Calif., 1986—. Legis. cons. Bay Area Asian Health Alliance, Oakland, 1980-83; bd. dirs. Chinatown & Cen. Dist. Community Devel., Oakland, 1983-84; mem. State Adv. Council Refugee Affairs, Oakland, Sacramento, 1983-85; mem. steering com. City of 21st Century, Oakland, 1985-86. Served to sgt. USAF, 1966-70. Recipient Cert. of Appreciation, Pub. Adminstrn. U. So. Calif., 1981, Spl. Recognition award Vietnamese Fisherman's Assn., 1985. Mem. East Bay Forum on Refugee Affairs (chmn., pres. 1984-85), Fund Devel. Com. (bd. dirs. La Clinica de La Raza, Inc. chpt. 1982-84), Community Adult Day Health Services (bd. dirs. 1983-88), Nat. Council on Alternate Health (bd. dirs. 1974—). Democrat.

SZYNAKA, EDWARD M., library director, consultant; b. N.Y.C., Sept. 26, 1948; s. Edward J. and Catherine A. (Regan) S.; m. Diane Pickering; children—Edward, Andrew, Emily. B.A. in Polit. Sci., SUNY-Fredonia, 1972; M.L.A., Syracuse U., 1973. Dir. libraries, Massena, N.Y., 1972-75, Midland, Mich., 1975-80; dir. Pasadena (Calif.) Pub. Library, 1980—; mgmt. cons. Bd. dirs. ARC; active Big Bros. Served to lt. U.S. Army, 1966-68. Mem. ALA, Calif. Library Assn., Mich. Library Assn. Democrat. Roman Catholic. Club: Kiwanis. *

TABB, WILLIAM HOWARD, podiatrist; b. Bklyn., Oct. 27, 1951; s. Irving and Miriam (Feldman) T.; m. Patty Bernice Sokolecki, Aug. 19, 1973 (div. Jan. 1978); m. Carolyn Jean Stallard, Nov. 20, 1983. BSEE, Poly. Inst. Bklyn., 1972; postgrad., UCLA, 1974-76; BS in Basic Med. Sci., Calif. Coll. Podiatric Medicine, 1978, D Podiatric Medicine, 1979. Diplomate Nat. Bd. Podiatric Examiners. Staff engr. PRD Electronics, Syosset, N.Y., 1972-73; mem. tech. staff Hughes Aircraft Co., Culver City, Calif., 1973-76; preceptor Harbor Podiatric Group, Torrance, Calif., 1979-80; pvt. practice Torrance, 1980-81, Anaheim, Calif., 1982—; attending staff Riviera Hosp., Torrance, 1979-81, Bay Harbor Hosp., Harbor City, Calif., 1980-81, A. Claude Hudson County Clinic, L.A., 1980-81. Republican. Jewish. Home: 6930 E Avenida de Santiago Anaheim CA 92807 Office: Gericare Podiatry Group 6312 E Santa Ana Canyon 292 Anaheim CA 92807

TABOR-SMITH, VALERIE JEANENE, photographer, business owner; b. L.A., Dec. 1, 1953; d. Samuel Alton and Martha Jeanne (Smalley) Tabor; m. Robert Francis Smith Jr., Mar. 30, 1974. Student, Pasadena (Calif.) City Coll., 1972-74. Studio mgr. Tracy Studios, Granada Hills, Calif., 1976-78, Eli Studios, N. Hollywood, Calif., 1979-81; owner, photographer Valerie Tabor-Smith Fine Art and Photography, Granada Hills, 1980—; co-producer Vogager Video, N. Hollywood, 1985—. Represented in permanent collections Transam., L.A., Nat. Med. Enterprises, L.A., Fluor Corp., Irvine, Calif. Named Photographer of Yr., Profl. Photographer Orange County, 1983, 85. Mem. Profl. Photographers Am., Alliance Photog. Artists, Victorian Soc. Am. Home: PO Box 33122 Granada Hills CA 91344

TABRISKY, JOSEPH, radiologist, educator; b. Boston, June 23, 1931; s. Henry and Gertrude Tabrisky; BA cum laude, Harvard U., 1952; MD cum laude, Tufts U., 1956; m. Phyllis Eleanor Page, Apr. 23, 1955; children: Joseph Page, Elizabeth Ann, William Page. Flexible intern U. Ill. Hosp., 1956-57; resident in radiology Fitzsimons Army Hosp., 1958-60; instr. radiology Tufts U. Med. Sch., 1964-65; cons. radiologist Swedish Med. Center, Denver, 1966-68; chief radiologist Kaiser Found. Hosp., Harbor City, Calif., 1968-72; mem. faculty UCLA Med. Sch., 1972—, prof. radiol. scis., 1975—, vice chmn. dept., 1976—, exec. policy com. radiol. scis.; chmn. radiology dept. Harbor-UCLA Med. Ctr., 1975—, pres. faculty soc., 1979-80, exec. dir. MR/CT Imaging Ctr., 1985—; bd. dirs. Rsch. Ednl. Inst., Harbor Collegium/UCLA Found.; chief exec. officer Vascular Biometrics Inc.; steering com. Harvard U., 1952; cons. L.A. County Dept. Pub. Health; chmn. L.A. County Radiol. Standards Com., 1979. Mem. Harvard-Radcliffe Schs. Com.; bd. dirs., treas., Harbor-UCLA Med. Found.; chmn. UCLA Coun. for Ednl. Devel. Maj. M.C., U.S. Army, 1957-63. Diplomate Am. Bd. Radiology. Fellow Am. Coll. Radiology, Univ. Radcom Assn. (chief exec. officer 1987—); mem. Radiol. Soc. N. Am., Calif. Med. Assn., Calif. Radiol. Soc., L.A. Med. Assn., L.A. Radiol. Soc., Alpha Omega Alpha. Contbr. articles to med. jours. Office: 1000 W Carson St Torrance CA 90509

TACHER, SOL MICHAEL, broadcasting company executive, consultant; b. Seattle, Sept. 9, 1934; s. Morris and Zelda (Haleva) T.; m. Mimi Jean Aronson, Aug. 25, 1957 (div. 1972); children: Brad, Jeff, Carla, Greg, Kevin, Chris; m. Mary Ann Melchoir, Feb. 22, 1986. BA, U. Wash., 1957. Gen. mgr. Sta. KFKF, Bellevue, Wash., 1957-62, Sta. KOL-Goodson-Todman, Seattle, 1962-65; assoc. v.p. Simpson & Assocs., Seattle, 1965-68; pres., chief exec. officer Tacher Co. Inc., Seattle, 1968—. Chmn. Boys and Girls Club King County, Seattle, 1963. Mem. Radio Advt. Mgrs. (pres. Seattle 1962-64), Seattle Advt. Club (chmn. 1964-65), Wash. Athletic Club, Glendale Country Club (pres. 1986-88). Office: Tacher Co Inc 701 Dexter Ave N Seattle WA 98109

TACHOUET, JOHN JAMES, real estate executive; b. San Rafael, Calif., Feb. 11, 1943; s. John Jacques and Mary K. (Bailey) T.; m. Mary Elizabeth Bergevin, Aug. 21, 1971; children: Matthew John, Stephen James, Marie Elizabeth. BS, U. Oreg., 1964. Pres. The Equity Group, Inc., Beaverton, Oreg., 1984—, also bd. dirs.; bd. dirs. E.G. Devel., Inc., Beaverton, Mountain Devel., Inc., Portland, Oreg. Mem. Nat. Assn. Realtors (residential specialist cert. 1979, residential brokerage mgr. cert. 1985), Oreg. Assn. Realtors (bd. dirs., grad. realtors inst. 1975), Washington County Bd. Realtors (pres.), Multnomah Athletic Club. Office: The Equity Group Inc 1905 NW 169th Pl Beaverton OR 97006

TADDEUCCI, TERRY NICHOLAS, physicist; b. Hancock, Mich., Feb. 25, 1954; s. Nicholas Joseph and Carol Matilda (Lahti) T.; m. Debra Rae Langseth, July 2, 1977 (div. Aug. 1982); m. Karen Sue Denison, Mar. 2, 1985. BS in Physics, Mich. Tech. U., 1976; PhD in Physics, U. Va., 1980. Research assoc. Ohio U., Athens, 1980-84, U. Md., College Park, 1984-85; staff physicist cyclotron facility, Ind. U., Bloomington, 1985-86, Los Alamos (N.Mex.) Nat. Lab., 1986—; chmn. Ind. Cyclotron User's Group, Bloomington, 1988—. Mem. Am. Phys. Soc., AAAS. Club: Sierra (Santa Fe). Home: 220 Miramonte Santa Fe NM 87501 Office: Los Alamos Nat Lab Los Alamos NM 87545

TAFF, BARRY EDWARD, research scientist; b. Chgo.; s. Jacob and Ruth (Brown) T. AA, Los Angeles Community Coll., 1969; BA, Calif. State U., Northridge, 1972; MA, Goddard, 1975. Ptnr. Aeon Techs. Inc., Los Angeles, 1987—; cons. NIMH, Los Angeles, 1975-77, CIA, Los Angeles, 1972-74, Def. Advanced Rsch. Projects Agy., Los Angeles, 1972-75, Def. Lang. Inst., Los Angeles, 1972-75. Patentee in field. Home: 8665 Pickford St #8 Los Angeles CA 90035

TAFF, WARREN RUSSELL, psychiatrist; b. Newark, Apr. 6, 1947; s. Harry and Edith Joyce (Tobias) T.; m. Barbara Ann Zordan, Apr. 13, 1986. BA, Rutgers U., 1968; MD, Birmingham U., Eng., 1974; MPH, UCLA, 1977. Diplomate Am. Bd. Psychiatry and Neurology. Intern VA Hosp., Sepulveda, Calif., 1974-75; resident LAC-USC, 1975-78, Auckland Hosp., New Zealand, 1978, Royal Prince Alfred Hosp., Sydney, Australia, 1978; med. dir. adult svcs. Coll. Hosp., Cerritos, Calif., 1982—; ptnr. Brea (Calif.) Mental Health Assn., 1983—; chief of staff Coll. Hosp., Brea, 1984-86, assoc. med. dir., 1987-89, med. dir., 1989—; asst. clin. prof. U. So. Calif. Med. Sch., L.A., 1984—. Mem. Royal Coll. Psychiatrists of Eng. (treas. 1986—, pres. 1989—), Am. Psychiatric Assn. Office: College Hospital 10802 College Place Cerritos CA 90701

TAFFAE, PETER R., insurance executive; b. N.Y.C., Apr. 17, 1960; s. Robert Charles and Anita (Runkel) T. BA, Ithaca (N.Y.) Coll. Underwriter Chubb Group, Phila., 1982-84; underwriting mgr. Chubb Group, N.Y.C., 1984-86, L.A., 1986; asst. v.p. Marsh & McLennan, L.A., 1986—. Mem. World Affairs Council of L.A. Mem. Nat. Assn. Corp. Dirs. Office: Marsh & McLennan 3303 Wilshire Blvd Los Angeles CA 90010

TAFOYA, ARTHUR N., bishop; b. Alameda, N.Mex., Mar. 2, 1933; s. Nicholas and Rosita Tafoya. Ed., St. Thomas Sem., Denver, Conception (Mo.) Sem. Ordained priest Roman Cath. Ch., 1962. Asst. pastor Holy Rosary Parish, Albuquerque, 1962-65; pastor Northern N.Mex., from 1965, San Jose Parish, Albuquerque; rector Immaculate Heart of Mary Sem., Santa Fe; ordained bishop of Pueblo Colo., 1980—. Office: 1001 Grand Ave Pueblo CO 81003 *

TAFT, PETER R., lawyer; b. Cin., Mar. 3, 1936; s. Charles P. and Eleanor (Chase) T.; m. Diana F. Todd, Nov. 17, 1979; children: Travis Todd, Tyler Frost. B.A., Yale U., 1958, LL.B., 1961. Bar: D.C. 1963, Calif. 1969. Law clk. U.S. Ct. Appeals (5th cir.), 1961-62; law clk. to Chief Justice Earl Warren, U.S. Supreme Ct., 1962-63; assoc. Williams & Connolly, Washington, 1963-67, ptnr., 1967-69; asst. atty. gen. Land and Natural Resources div. Dept. Justice, Washington, 1975-77; ptnr. Munger Tolles & Olson, Los Angeles, 1969-75, 77—. Mem. D.C. Bar Assn., Calif. Bar Assn., Los Angeles Bar Assn., ABA. Republican. Episcopalian. Home: 17058 Ave de Santa Ynez Pacific Palisades CA 90272 Office: 355 S Grand St 35th Fl Los Angeles CA 90071

TAGERT, DAVID BRUCE, military officer; b. Holyoke, Mass., June 2, 1956; s. Hugh Billie and Sibyl Bernadine (Romero) T. BS in Animal Sci., Tex. A&M U., 1978; diploma, Squadron Officers Sch., Montgomery, Ala., 1984, Air Command and Staff Coll., 1985; MS in Ops. Mgmt., U. Ark., 1986. Commd. USAF, 1978, advanced through grades to maj., 1989; navigator 774th Tactical Airlift Squadron USAF, Dyess AFB, Tex., 1979-81; instr. navigator 16th Tactical Airlift Tng. Squadron USAF, Little Rock AFB, Ark., 1981-83, instr. navigator 34th Tech. Tng. Squadron, 1983-86; sr. navigator 1st Spl. Ops. Squadron USAF, Clark AB, The Philippines, 1986—. Author: (books) Satellite Navigator Simulator, 1984, Satellite Navigator Instructor Simulator, 1985. Decorated Longevity medal with Oak Leaf Cluster, USAF. Mem. Air Force Assn., Tex. A&M Former Students Assn., Stray Goose Assn., Am. Water Skiing Assn., Blackbird Assn., Air Commando Assn. Office: USAF 8th Spl Ops Squadron 912 Aloma Faye Ln Fort Walton FL 32548-3320

TAGGART, DENNIS D., physician; b. Logan, Utah, Sept. 19, 1938; s. DeVere Jerome and Faye (Hodges) T.; m. Karen Miller, June 29, 1966; children: Dennis, Pamela. BS, Utah State U., 1960; MD, George Washington U., 1963. Diplomate Am. Bd. Internal Medicine. Intership Wash. U., St. Louis, 1963-64, resident, 1964-65, fellow in nephrology, 1968-70, instr., 1970-71; resident U. N.Mex., Albequerque, 1965-66; asst. prof. U. Utah, Salt Lake City, 1971-74; chief of medicine Holy Cross Hosp., Salt Lake City, 1974-75, pres. med. staff, 1988—. Capt. U.S. Army, 1966-68, Vietnam. Mem. Salt Lake City Med. Soc., Utah State Med. Assn., Am. Coll. Physician, Am. Soc. Nephrology, Internat. Soc. Nephrology, Ft. Douglas Club. Office: 24 South 1100 E Ste 306 Salt Lake City UT 84102

TAGGART, SONDRA, financial planner, investment advisor; b. N.Y.C., July 22, 1934; d. Louis and Rose (Birnbaum) Hamov; children: Eric, Karen. BA, Hunter Coll., 1955. Cert. fin. planner, registered investment advisor; registered prin. Nat. Assn. Securities Dealers. Founder, dir. Copyright Service Bur., Ltd., N.Y.C., 1957-69; dir., officer Maclen Music, Inc., N.Y.C., 1964-69; pres. Westshore, Inc., pub. internat. bus. materials, Mill Valley, Calif., 1965-80; pres. securities broker dealer The Taggart Co. Ltd., 1981—; The Beatles, Ltd., 1964-69. Mem. Internat. Assn. Fin. Planners, Registry Fin. Planning Practitioners. Republican. Clubs: Bankers, Beverly Hills Country. Editor: The Red Tapes: Commentaries on Doing Business With The Russians and East Europeans, 1978. Office: 1875 Century Pk E #1400 Los Angeles CA 90067-2501

TAGLIO, LESLIE WYNN, cosmetic company executive; b. Inglewood, Calif., Sept. 29, 1954; d. Bud Peter E. and Georgia Mae Taglio. AA, Sierra Coll., 1974; BA in Retail Mgmt., U. Calif., Davis, 1976. Store mgr. Joseph Magnin, San Francisco, 1978-80; spl. events coordinator Macy's of Calif., San Francisco, 1980-81; ptnr. DR Assocs., San Francisco, 1981-88; account exec. Prestige Fragrances Ltd., San Francisco, 1984—; cons. Closetmaid Inc., Fla., 1984-86, Word Processing Svcs., San Francisco, 1986-87. Mem. San Francisco Vol. Symphony League, Jr. League of San Francisco, Am. Soviet Youth Orch. com., 1988; chairperson Children's Garden, San Francisco, 1985, Youth Advocates, San Francisco, 1986. Mem. Nat. Assn. Profl. Women, San Francisco Jr. C. of C., Delta Delta Delta. Club: Spinsters (San Francisco) (pres. 1987-88).

TAI, FLORENCE MARGARET, allergist; b. Jamaica, July 8, 1955; came to U.S., 1979.; d. Clarence and Daisy Blanche (Lim Hing) T. Degree in Premedicine, U. W.I., Jamaica, 1973, MD, 1978. Diplomate Am. Bd. Pediatrics, Am. Bd. Allergy and Immunology. Intern Princess Margaret Hosp., Nassau, Bahamas, 1978-79; resident in pediatrics N.Y. Med. Coll., N.Y.C., 1979-80, 81-82, Columbia Coll. Physicians and Surgeons, N.Y.C., 1980-81; clin. instr. pediatrics N.Y. Med. Coll., N.Y.C., 1982-83; fellow in allergy and immunology Wayne State U., Detroit, 1983-85; attending physician Covenant House, N.Y.C., 1982-83; allergy assoc. Troy (Mich.) Allergy Assocs., 1985-86; allergist Napa Valley Asthma & Allergy Clinic, Napa, Calif., 1987—. Fellow Am. Coll. Allergists; mem. Am. Acad. Allergy and Immunology, Allergy Assn. No. Calif. Roman Catholic. Office: Napa Valley Asthma Clinic 1155 Trancas St Napa CA 94558

TAIMUTY, SAMUEL ISAAC, physicist; b. West Newton, Pa., Dec. 20, 1917; s. Elias and Samia (Hawatt) T.; BS, Carnegie Mellon U., 1940; PhD, U. So. Calif., 1951; m. Betty Jo Travis, Sept. 12, 1953 (dec.); children: Matthew, Martha; m. Rosalie Richards, Apr. 3, 1976. Physicist, U.S. Naval Shipyard, Phila. and Long Beach, Calif., 1942-46; rsch. asst. U. So. Calif., 1947-51; sr. physicist U.S. Naval Radiol. Def. Lab., 1950-52, SRI Internat., Menlo Park, Calif., 1952-72; sr. staff engr. Lockheed Missiles & Space Co., Sunnyvale, Calif., 1972-89; cons. physicist, 1971—. Mem. Am. Phys. Soc., Masons, Sigma Xi. Episcopalian. Contbr. articles to sci. publs. Patentee in field. Home: 3346 Kenneth Dr Palo Alto CA 94303

TAJON, ENCARNACION FONTECHA (CONNIE TAJON), retired educator, association executive; b. San Narciso, Zambales, Philippines, Mar. 25, 1920; came to U.S., 1948; d. Espiridion Maggay and Gregoria (Labrador) Fontecha; m. Felix B. Tajon, Nov. 17, 1948; children: Ruth F., Edward F. Teacher's cert., Philippine Normal Coll., 1941; BEd, Far Eastern U., Manila, 1947; MEd, Seattle Pacific U., 1976. Cert. tchr., Philippines. Tchr. pub. schs. San Narciso and Manila, 1941-47; coll. educator Union Coll. Manila, 1947-48; tchr. Auburn (Wash.) Sch. Dist., 1956-58, Renton (Wash.) Sch. Dist., 1958-78; owner, operator Manila-Zambales Internat. Grill, Seattle, 1980-81, Connie's Lumpia House and Ethnic Restaurant, Seattle, 1981-84; founder, pres. Tajon-Fontecha, Inc., Renton, 1980—, United Friends of Filipinos in Am. Found., Renton, 1985—; founder Tajon Fontecha Permanent Scholarship Fund of The Philippine Normal Coll., 1978, U. Wash. Alumni Assn. Endowed Scholarship Fund, World Div. of the Gen. Bd. of Global Ministries of the United Meth. Ch., 1982-84. Bd. dirs. women's div. Global Ministries United Meth. Ch., 1982-84; bd. dirs. Renton Area Youth Services, 1980-85; mem. Mcpl. Arts Commn. Renton, 1980—; chair fundraising steering com. Washington State Women's Polit. Caucus, 1984—, gov. mem. Recipient spl. cert. of award Project Hope, 1976, U.S. Bicentennial Commn., 1976, UNICEF, 1977; named Parent of Yr. Filipino Community of Seattle, Inc., 1984. Mem. NEA, U. Wash. Alumni Assn. (life), U. Wash. Filipino Alumni Assn. (pres. Wash. State chpt. 1985-87), Renton Retired Tchrs. Assn., Wash. State Edn. Assn., Am. Assn. Retired Persons, Nat. Retired Tchrs. Assn., Renton Hist. Mus. (life), United Meth. Women, Pres.'s Forum, Alpha Sigma, Delta Kappa Gamma. Democrat. Home and Office: 2033 Harrington Pl NE Renton WA 98056

TAKAHASHI, WATARU, environmental consultant; b. Ewa, Hawaii, Aug. 20, 1925; s. Zenjiro and Matsuno (Kodama) T.; m. Nobuko Toyama, Sept. 17, 1955; 1 child, Ann Eiko. BA in Chemistry, U. Hawaii, 1957; MA in Chemistry, Ind. U., 1959. Organic chemist U.S. Argl. Research Service, Peoria, Ill., 1961-62; indsl. hygiene chemist Dept. Health, Honolulu, 1962-65; marine chemist U. Hawaii, Honolulu, 1965-70, field epidemiologist, 1971-82; cons. Aiea, Hawaii, 1982—. Contbr. articles to profl. jours. Served with U.S. Army, 1950-52, PTO. Mem. AAAS, Am. Chem. Soc., Phi Beta Kappa. Home and Office: 98-1996 Hoala St Aiea HI 96701

TAKASHIMA, HIDEO, lawyer, accountant; b. Kobe, Hyogo-Ken, Japan, Mar. 2, 1919; came to U.S., 1956; s. Yoshimitsu and Yoshie (Akagi) T.; m. Adrianna Elizabeth Selch Coe, Oct. 31, 1961 (div. Apr. 1984); children: James, George K., Oliver Sachio; m. Chizu Kojima, Mar. 14, 1986. Chartered acct., Kanagawa U., Yokohama, Japan, 1941; LLM in Criminal Law, Taihoku Imperial U., Japan, 1943; LLM in Bus. Law, Yale U., 1957; SJD in Antitrust Laws, NYU, 1959; postgrad., Yale U., 1961-62. Bar: D.C. 1973, U.S. Tax Ct. 1973, U.S. Ct. Appeals (D.C. cir.) 1973, N.J. 1974, U.S. Dist. Ct. N.J. 1974, U.S. Ct. Claims 1974, U.S. Ct. Appeals (3d cir.) 1977, U.S. Supreme Ct. 1977. Lectr. criminology Yen Ping Coll., Taipei, Taiwan, 1946-47; mgr. Taiwan br. Warner Bros. F.N. Pix, Inc., Taipei, 1947-52; with labor union activities dept. FOA MSM/C, Am. Embassy, Taipei, 1953-54; tax editor Prentice-Hall, Inc., Englewood Cliffs, N.J., 1961-66; editor-in-chief Washington Publs., Inc., N.Y.C., 1966-69; tax atty., editor Am. Inst. CPAs, N.Y.C., 1971-72; pres., Charles Hideo Coe, P.A., Jersey City, 1973—; dir. Coe & Coe, Inc., Park Ridge, N.J., 1973—; pvt. practice acctg., N.J. 1980—; U.S. del. U.S./Japan Bilateral Session: A New Era in Legal and Econ. Relations, Tokyo, Aug.-Sept., 1988, People to People legal del. to European countries to assist U.S. immigration law legislation, People to People legal del. to People's Republic China and USSR, 1989. Author: My Unsuspecting Formosa, 1944; editor-in-chief The Tax Barometer, 1966-69. Instr. Judo-Kendo New Milford (N.J.) Recreation Commn., 1963-69, Park Ridge Recreation Com., 1969-72, Pascack Valley Kendo Club, Park Ridge, 1969-71. Served to capt. Chinese Kuo-Min-Tang, Taipei, 1945. Yale Law Sch. fellow, 1956-57; N.Y. Law Sch. scholar, 1958, Prentice-Hall, Inc. scholar grad. div. NYU Sch. Law, 1961-63. Mem. Am. Immigration Lawyers Assn. (sec. N.J. chpt. 1978-83), Japanese Am. Assn. N.Y., Yale U. Law Sch. Alumni Assn., NYU Law Alumni Assn. Republican. Club: Yale. Mailing: 1425 S Falstone Ave Ste 1510 Hacienda Heights CA 91745

TAKASUGI, NAO, mayor, business developer; b. Oxnard, Calif., Apr. 5, 1922; s. Shingoro and Yasuye (Hayashi) T.; m. Judith Shigeko Mayeda, Mar. 23, 1952; children—Scott, Russell, Ronald, Tricia, Lea. B.S., Temple U., 1945; M.B.A., U. Pa. Wharton Sch., 1946. Mem. city council City of Oxnard, Calif., 1976-82, mayor, 1982—; bus. developer, cons. Mem., Oxnard Planning Commn., 1974-76; pres. World Trade Ctr. Assn., Oxnard. Mem. Ventura County Japanese Am. Citizens League, World Trade Ctr. Assn. (pres. Oxnard chpt.), U.S. Conf. Mayors (mem. nat. adv. bd.). Republican. Methodist. Club: Optimists (Oxnard). Home: 1221 El Portal Way Oxnard CA 93035 Office: City of Oxnard 305 N Third St Oxnard CA 93030

TAKASUGI, ROBERT MITSUHIRO, federal judge; b. Tacoma, Sept. 12, 1930; s. Hidesaburo and Kayo (Otsuki) T.; m. Dorothy O. Takasugi; children: Jon Robert, Lesli Mari. BS, UCLA, Los Angeles, 1953; LLB, JD, U. So. Calif., 1959. Bar: Calif. bar 1960. Practiced law Los Angeles, 1960-73; judge East Los Angeles Municipal Ct., 1973-75, adminstrv. judge, 1974, presiding judge, 1975; judge Superior Ct., County of Los Angeles, 1975-76; U.S. dist. judge U.S. Dist. Ct. for Central Dist. Calif., 1976—; nat. legal counsel Japanese Am. Citizens League; guest lectr. law seminars Harvard U. Law Sch. Careers Symposium; commencement speaker; mem. Legion Lex U. So. Calif. Law Center; chmn. Pub. Defs. Indigent Def. & Psychiat. Panel Com.; mem. Affirmative Action Com., Habeas Corpus-Death Penalty Com., Exec. Com., Jury Com., Settlement Rule Com., Adv. Com. on Codes of

Conduct of the Jud. Conf. of the U.S., 1988—. Mem. editorial bd. U. So. Calif. Law Rev., 1959; contbr. articles to profl. jours. Mem. Calif. adv. com. Western Regional Office, U.S. Commn. on Civil Rights. Served with U.S. Army, 1953-55. Recipient U.S. Mil. Man of Yr. award for Far East Theater U.S. Army, 1954; certificate of merit Japanese-Am. Bar Assn.; other awards; Harry J. Bauer scholar, 1959. Mem. U. So. Calif. Law Alumni (dir.). Office: US Dist Ct 312 N Spring St Los Angeles CA 90012

TAKATA, SAYOKO, educator; b. Los Angeles, July 12, 1937; d. Henry Takuji and Fujie (Udo) Nishi; m. Isao Jon Takata, Nov. 24, 1961; 1 child, Stephen Isamu. BA in Bus., U. No. Colo., 1959; M.Ed. in Vocat. Edn., Colo. State U., 1980. Life teaching cert., Colo. Tchr. home econs. Erie (Colo.) Jr. and Sr. High Sch., 1959-60; tchr. bus. and office edn. Manual High Sch., Denver, 1960-63, 68-78, chmn. dept., 1977-78; asst. bookkeeper Century Fixtures, Inc., Los Angeles, 1963-64; tchr. bus. and office edn. East High Sch., Denver, 1978-79; tchr. bus. and office edn. Met. Youth Edn. Ctr., Zuni Ctr., 1978-79; tchr. bus. and office edn. East extension, Denver, 1979—, chmn. dept., 1980—; mem. Colo. Spl. Needs Ad Hoc Com., 1980. Mem. Am. Vocat. Assn., Nat. Bus. Edn. Assn. (chmn. decorations NBEA conv. 1988), NEA, Colo. Educators For/About Bus. (treas. 1981-83, Profl. Merit award 1987), Internat. Soc. bus. Educators, Colo. Vocat. Assn., Mountain Plains Bus. Edn. Assn. (Colo. rep. 1986—), Denver Classroom Tchrs. Assn., Colo. Edn. Assn., Delta Pi Epsilon, Delta Kappa Gamma (asst. treas. 1986-88, treas. 1988—). Buddhist. Home: 561 W 87th Pl Denver CO 80221 Office: 3800 York St Bldg 1 Unit A Denver CO 80205

TAKEI, TOSHIHISA, otolaryngologist; b. L.A., Apr. 19, 1931; s. Taketomi and Mitsue (Hagihara) T.; m. Emiko Kubota, Jan. 25, 1955; children: H. Thomas, T. Robert. BA, UCLA, 1954; MD, Boston U., 1962. Diplomate, Am. Bd. Otolaryngology. Intern L.A. County Harbor Gen. Hosp., 1962-63; resident in otolaryngology L.A. County/U. So. Calif. Med. Ctr., 1963-67; staff physician Covina (Calif.) Ear, Nose & Throat Med. Group, 1968—; asst. prof. Sch. Medicine, U. So. Calif., L.A., 1968—. 1st lt. U.S. Army, 1955-56, Korea. Fellow Am. Acad. Otolaryngology, Royal Soc. Medicine. Republican. Buddhist. Office: Covina ENT Med Group Inc 236 W College St Covina CA 91723

TAKEUCHI, ROBIN KEIKO, interior designer, business owner; b. L.A., Feb. 5, 1960; d. Wayne Yushi and June Junko (Kobayashi) T. BA cum laude, UCLA, 1980. Interior designer Chaix and Johnson Internat., L.A., 1981-83, KOPI, Honolulu, 1983-85; assoc., prin. KOPI/Interiors, Honolulu, 1985-87; owner, prin. Interior Spaces, Honolulu, 1987—; asst. Grunwald Ctr. Graphic Arts, UCLA, 1978-80. Mem. ASID, Graphic Designers Assn., Theta Kappa Phi. Republican. Office: Interior Spaces 501 Kalihi St Ste 201 Honolulu HI 96819

TAKEUCHI, SYLVIA FUJIE, marketing executive; b. Portland, Oreg., Jan. 15, 1939; d. Thomas K. and Tomie (Miyake) T.; m. Donald D. Owens, Aug. 30, 1985. Student, Willamette U.; BABA, Portland State U., 1975. Cert. in internat. bus. Adminstrv. asst. Gov. Mark O. Hatfield, Salem, Oreg., 1960-63, Nelson Rockefeller and John D. Rockefeller III, N.Y.C., 1963-66, Senator Mark O. Hatfield, Washington, 1966-67; personnel dir. Donaldson, Lufkin & Jenrette, N.Y.C., 1967-70; sales rep. Boise Casdade, Portland, 1976-81; owner, gen. mgr. Far West Office Systems, Phoenix, 1981-86; cons. NBI"s The Office Pl., Seattle, 1987-88; pres. Customer Satisfaction Evaluations, Phoenix, 1988—. Chmn. Gov.'s Energy Policy, Salem, Oreg., 1983-85. Republican.

TAKLA, JOHN MICHAEL, dentist; b. Alexandria, Egypt, Nov. 4, 1960; s. Michael and Annie Takla. BS, U. Santa Clara, 1982; DDS, U. Pacific, 1985. Gen. practice dentistry San Mateo, Calif., 1985—. Mem. ADA, Calif. Dental Assn., San Mateo County Dental Soc. (chmn. directory com. 1987-88), Networks, U. Santa Clara Alumni Assn., U. Pacific Alumni Assn. Office: 400 N San Mateo Dr San Mateo CA 94401

TALARICO, CARMEN LOUIS, radiologist; b. Canton, Ohio, Aug. 25, 1952; s. Carmen Louis Sr. and Mary Elizabeth (Cagle) T.; m. Margaret Ann Roels, June 21, 1975; children: Leslie Elizabeth, Matthew Richard. BA in Biology magna cum laude, Cath. U. Am., 1974; MD cum laude, Ohio State U., 1979. Commd. 2d lt. U.S. Army, 1974, advanced through grades to maj., 1985; intern in surgery Walter Reed Army Med. Ctr., Washington, 1979-80, resident in radiology, 1980-83; pediatric radiology fellow Children's Hosp. Nat. Med. Ctr., Washington, 1983-85; chief pediatric radiology Fitzsimons Army Med. Ctr., Aurora, Colo., 1985—, chief imaging br., 1989—; radiology child abuse cons. USAF, Aurora, 1986—; dir. radiology student intern training Fitzsimons Army Med. Ctr., Aurora, 1986—. Mem. Soc. for Pediatric Radiology, Colo. Radiologic Soc., Am. Inst. Ultrasound in Medicine, Phi Beta Kappa. Democrat. Roman Catholic. Office: Fitzsimons Army Med Ctr E Colfax Ave Aurora CO 80045

TALBERT, MELVIN GEORGE, bishop; b. Clinton, La., June 14, 1934; s. Nettles and Florence (George) T.; m. Ethlelou Douglas, June 3, 1961; 1 child, Evangeline. BA, So. U., 1959; MDiv, Interdenominational Theol. Ctr., Gammon Theol. Sem., Atlanta, 1962; DD hon., Huston Tillotson Coll., Austin, 1972; LLD (hon.), U. Puget Sound, Tacoma, 1987. Ordained deacon, Meth. Ch., 1960 ordained elder, Meth. Ch., 1962 elected to episcopacy, United Meth. Ch., 1980. Pastor Boyd Chapel, Jefferson City, Tenn., 1960-61, Rising Sun, Sunrise, Tenn., 1960-61, St. John's Ch., L.A., 1961-62, Wesley Ch., L.A., 1962-64, Hamilton Ch., L.A., 1964-67; mem. staff So. Calif.-Ariz. Conf. United Meth. Ch., L.A., 1967-68; dist. supr. Long Beach dist. So. Calif.-Ariz. Conf. United Meth. Ch., 1968-73; gen. sec. Gen. Bd. Discipleship, Nashville, 1973-80; resident bishop Seattle area Pacific N.W. conf. United Meth. Ch., 1980-88, resident bishop San Francisco area Calif.-Nev. Conf., 1988—, sec. coun. bishops, 1988—; mem. exec. com. World Meth. Coun., 1976-81, 84—; mem. governing bd. Nat. Coun. Chs., 1980—; v.p., chmn. funding com. Gen. Commn. on Religion and Race, 1980-84, pres., 1984-88; chmn. Missional Priority Coordinating com. Gen. Coun. Ministries, 1980-84; mem. Gen. Commn. on Christian Unity and Interreligious Concerns, 1984—, African Ch. Growth and Devel. Com., 1981-84; sec. Coun. Bishops United Meth. Ch., 1988—. Mem. steering com. Student Non-Violent Coordinating com. Atlanta U. Ctr., 1960-61; trustee Gammon Theol. Sem., Atlanta, 1976—, U. Puget Sound, Tacoma, 1980-88 , Sch. Theology at Claremont, Calif., 1981-88, Pacific Sch. Religion, 1988—; bd. dirs. Glide Found., 1988—. Recipient award of merit for outstanding svc. in Christian edn. Gen. Bd. Edn., 1971; recipient Spl. achievement award Nat. Assn. Black Bus. Women, 1971; Nat. Meth. scholar, 1960; Crusade scholar, 1961. Mem. Theta Phi. Democrat. Home: 13816 Campus Dr Oakland CA 94605

TALBERT, RICHARD CLARK, management professional; b. Oak Park, Ill., Oct. 27, 1950; s. Austin Gertner and Kathryn Mary (Pokragac) T.; m. Patricia Parker, Mar. 16, 1974; children: Jeffrey, Kristin. Student, U. Ill., 1968-71. Cert. water specialist. Mgr. Rock Rd. Trailer, St. Louis, 1971-74; nat. dir. Narconon, Los Angeles, 1974-79; dealer Sunland Industries, Phoenix, 1981-85; pres., gen. mgr. Northland Purewater div. Northland Environ. Inc., Burbank, Calif., 1979-88; prin. Western Water Resources, Burbank, Calif., 1988—; pres. Northland Tech., Inc., 1987—. Co-author, editor booklet Narconon. Active Citizens' Commn. on Human Rights, 1973—, Narconon Get Am. Off Drugs, Los Angeles, 1983—, Campaign Crusade for Religious Freedom, Hollywood, 1985—, Way to Happiness Found., 1985—. Mem. Calif. Solar Energy Industries Assn., Los Angeles Solar Energy Industries Assn., Orange County Solar Energy Industries Assn., Bettter Bus. Bur., World Inst. of Scientology Enterprises, Water Quality Assn., Calif. C. of C., Burbank C. of C. Republican. Mem. Ch. Scientology. Office: Western Water Resources 5358 Cartwright Ave North Hollywood CA 91601

TALBOT, JOHN, journalism educator; b. N.Y.C., Jan. 24, 1930; s. John and Rosalie Blanche (Weill) T.; m. Susan Wells Anderson, July 15, 1952; children: Peter, Deborah. AB, Harvard U, 1951. With polit. affairs Dept. of Def., Washington, 1951-56; with flight ops. Trans World Airlines, N.Y.C., 1956-58; various positions Madison (Wis.) Newspapers, 1958-63; bus. mgr. The Muscatine (Iowa) Jour., 1963-65; gen. mgr. The Billings (Mont.) Gazette, 1965-70; pub. The Missoulian, Missoula, Mont., 1970-80; newspaper group mgr. Lee Enterprises Inc., Missoula, Mont., 1980-82, v.p., 1982-84; vis. instr. U. Mont., Missoula, 1985—. Pres. The Billings Symphony, 1966-67, The Missoula Symphony, 1971-72. Mem. Mendelssohn Club, Rotary. Home: 11 Greenbrier Dr Missoula MT 59802 Office: U Mont Journalism Sch Missoula MT 59812

TALBOTT, GEORGE ROBERT, physicist, mathematician, educator; b. San Diego, Oct. 1, 1925; s. George Fletcher and Mary (Lanz) T.; BA with honors, UCLA, 1960; DSc, Ind. No. U., 1973. Physicist, mem. tech. staff Rockwell Internat. Co., Anaheim, Calif., 1960-85; mem. faculty thermodynamics Pacific States U., 1971-77, prof., 1972-80, chmn. dept. math. studies, 1973-80; lectr. computer sci. Calif. State U., Fullerton, 1979—; cons. physics, computer sci.; disting. guest lectr. Brunel U., London, 1974, 76; spl. guest Forschungsbibliothek, Hannover, W. Ger., 1979; assoc. editor KRONOS jour., Glassboro (N.J.) U., 1978—; chief computer scientist and ednl. videotape dir. Specialized Software, Wilmot, Wis., 1982—. With M.C., U.S. Army, 1956. Recipient Vis. Scholar's award Western Mich. U., 1979. Mem. Am. Soc. Med. Technologists, Am. Math. Soc., Math. Assn. Am., Am. Soc. Clin. Pathologists (lic. med. lab. technologist). Buddhist. Author: Electronic Thermodynamics, 1973; Philosophy and Unified Science, 1977; co-inventor burner. Home: 4031 Charter Oak Dr Orange CA 92669

TALBOTT, RICHARD DAVID, physician; b. Jackson, Mich., Dec. 31, 1930; s. James Ernest and Ellen (McGowan) T.; m. Katherine Marie Bonney, June 18, 1983; children: James M., William J., Judith M. AB, Yale U., 1952; MD, Northwestern U., 1956. Diplomate Am. Bd. Orthopaedic Surgery. Intern Denver Gen. Hosp., 1956-57; resident St. Luke's Hosp., Denver, 1957-58, Lahey Clinic, Boston, 1958-59, Shriners Hosp. for Crippled Children, Springfield, Mass., 1959-60, Boston City Hosp., 1960-61; pvt. practice Orthopaedic Assocs., P.C., Denver, 1961-86; dir. dept. orthopaedic surgery Denver Gen. Hosp., 1987—. Home: Four Polo Field Ln Denver CO 80209 Office: Denver Gen Hosp Dept Orthopaedics 777 Bannock St Denver CO 80204

TALLEY, GREGORY BRENT, police officer, criminal justice educator; b. Indpls., Apr. 15, 1948; s. Richard Eugene and Vivian Jeanne (Goodman) T.; m. Susan Schofield, Aug. 13, 1970; children: Benjamin, Scott, Nanon, Justin, Megan. Student, Ricks Coll., 1970; BA, Coll. Santa Fe, 1981; cert., U. Va., 1984. Probation officer Johnson Superior Ct., Franklin, Ind., 1970-73; spl. dep. sheriff Marion County Sheriff's Office, Indpls., 1974-75; police officer Los Alamos (N.Mex.) Police Dept., 1975—, detective sgt., 1982—, capt., 1985—. Cubmaster Boy Scouts Am., 1986—; Rep. ward chmn., Los Alamos, 1980; bd. dirs. Family Recovery Ctr., Los Alamos, 1983-86, Family Council, Los Alamos, 1985-88; bishop Los Alamos Ward Ch. Jesus Christ of Latter-day Saints, 1987—. Named one of Outstanding Young Men of Am., U.S. Jaycees, 1983. Mem. FBI Nat. Acad. Assocs., Delta Phi Kappa. Mormon. Office: Los Alamos Police Dept 2500 Trinity Dr Los Alamos NM 87544

TALLEY, RICHARD WARREN, English educator; b. Monte Vista, Colo., Oct. 6, 1927; s. Wayne Orville and Dorothy Imogene (Fisher) T.; m. Margaret Ann Griffin, Apr. 3, 1949; 1 child, Richard Dale. BA, Adams State Coll., 1950, MA, 1961. Tchr. Phillips County High Sch., Holyoke, Colo., 1950-52, Fowler (Colo.) High Sch., 1952-57, La Junta (Colo.) High Sch., 1957-64; tchr. English Adams State Coll., Alamosa, Colo., 1964—. Pres. Rio Grande Arts Ctr., Alamosa, 1986—. Sgt. U.S. Army, 1945-46, Japan. Mem. NCTE, Rotary, Masons. Democrat. Episcopalian. Home: 88 Sierra Ave Alamosa CO 81101 Office: Adams State Coll Alamosa CO 81102

TALLMADGE, DIANE JOYCE, bookstore manager; b. Racine, Wis., May 10, 1934; d. Robert William and LuLu A (Steinike) Sperberg; m. Guy Kasten Tallmadge Jr. Sept. 12, 1957. BA, U. Wis., 1957; MA, 1957; MLS, UCLA, 1962. Ballet instr., choreographer Madison, Wis., 1952-57; tchr. pub. schs. Melbourne, Australia, 1957-58; ballet instr., choreographer Los Angeles, 1959-62; libr./physical sci. cataloger UCLA, 1962-64, Slavic lang. cataloger, 1964-66; docent libr. Stanford U. Mus., 1974--; mgr. Stanford U. Art Gallery Bookshop, 1985--. Bd. govs. Com. for Art, Stanford, 1985--; mem. Santa Monica and Westside Jr. Philharmonic, 1964-66. Mem. AAUW (pres. 1970-71), Phi Beta Kappa, Phi Kappa Phi, Beta Phi MU, Chi Omega. Republican. Congregationalist. Home: 446 Guadalupe Dr Los Altos CA 94022 Office: Stanford U Art Gallery The Gallery Bookshop Stanford CA 94305

TALLMADGE, GUY KASTEN, research psychologist; b. Milw., Mar. 2, 1932; s. Guy Kasten and Alice (LaBoule) T.; m. Diane Joyce Sperberg, Sept. 12, 1957. AB, Princeton U., 1954; MS, Purdue U., 1956, PhD, 1959. Rsch. scientist Douglas Aircraft Co., Santa Monica, Calif., 1959-61; mgr. behavioral psychology Humetrics div. Thiokol Chem. Corp., L.A., 1961-63; sr. assoc. Planning Rsch. Corp., L.A., 1963-65; dir. instrnl. methods Am. Insts. for Rsch., Palo Alto, Calif., 1965-73; v.p., pres. RMC Rsch. Corp., Mountain View, Calif., 1973-83, sr. v.p., 1987—; sr. v.p. SRA Techs., Mountain View, 1983-86. Contbr. articles to profl. jours. Fulbright scholar U. Melbourne (Australia), 1957-58. Mem. Am. Ednl. Rsch. Assn., Nat. Coun. on Measurement in Edn., Am. Evaluation Assn., Los Altos Golf and Country Club, Princeton Club No. Calif. Office: RMC Rsch Corp 2570 W El Camino Real Mountain View CA 94040

TALMADGE, MARY CHRISTINE, educator; b. Monticello, Ga., Nov. 6, 1940; d. Herbert Pope and Margaret (Allen) T.; m. Larry Benson, Aug. 10, 1962 (div. 1975). Student, Crawford W. Long Hosp. Sch. of Nursing, Atlanta, 1961; BSN, U. Dayton, 1966; MPH, U. Hawaii, 1971, PhD, 1989. RN. Staff charge nurse Crawford W. Long Hosp., Atlanta, 1961-62; instr. LPN program Dayton (Ohio) Bd. Edn., 1963-66; instr. Miami Valley Hosp. Sch. of Nursing, Dayton, 1967-69; clin. nurse specialist Hawaii State Hosp., Kaneohe, 1970-77, dir. nursing, 1978-80; adminstrv. asst. to dir. health Hawaii State Dept. of Health, Honolulu, 1977-78; clin. nurse specialist Windward Community Counseling Ctr., Kaneohe, 1980-83; asst. prof. U. Hawaii, 1983-85; assoc. prof., assoc. program dir. Hawaii Loa Coll., Kaneohe, 1987—; cons. Tokyo Women's Med. Coll. Sch. of Nursing, 1988—; local and internat. healthcare orgns. Sec., mem. Gov.'s Commn. on Mental Health and Criminal Justice, Honolulu, 1978-80; mem., chmn. Windward Oahu Svc. Area Bd. on Mental Health and Substance Abuse, Honolulu, 1985-86; candidate Neighborhood Bd. Kaneohe, 1988. Mem. Nat. League for Nursing, Am. Sociol. Soc., Sigma Theta Tau. Democrat. Methodist. Home: 44-30 Kaneohe Bay Dr Kaneohe HI 96744 Office: Hawaii Loa Coll 45-045 Kamehameha Hwy Kaneohe HI 96744

TALMADGE, PHILIP ALBERT, state senator, lawyer; b. Seattle, Apr. 23, 1952; s. Judson H., Jr., and Jeanne C. T.; m. Darlene L. Nelson, Sept. 6, 1970; children—Adam, Matthew, Jessica, Jonathan, AnnMarie. B.A. magna cum laude with honors in Polit. Sci., Yale U., 1973; J.D., U. Wash., 1976. Bar: Wash. 1976. Shareholder, Karr, Tuttle, Campbell, Mawer, Morrow and Sax, P.S., Seattle, 1976—; mem. Wash. Senate, 1978—, law and justice com., mem. senate ways and means com. Trustee, South Seattle Community Coll. Found.; bd. dirs. Seattle Consumer Credit Counseling Service; mem. Nature Conservancy Bd. Mem. Wash. State Bar Assn., Seattle-King County Bar Assn. Author: The Nixon Doctrine and the Reaction of Three Asian Nations, 1973; editor Law Rev., U. Wash., 1975-76; contbr. articles to legal publs.

TALMADGE, WOODDALL WELLS, lawyer; b. Portland, Oreg., May 14, 1958; s. Marion Lyman and Frances Louise (Wooddall) T. BA, Colgate U., 1980; JD, Cornell U., 1983. Bar: Oreg. 1983. Assoc. Miller, Nash, Wiener, Hager & Carlsen, Portland, Oreg., 1983-85, Weiss, DesCamp & Botteri, Portland, 1985—. Trustee, pres. N.W. Svc. Ctr., Portland, 1986—; trustee Boys and Girls Aid Soc. Oreg., 1987—. Mem. ABA, Oreg. Bar Assn., Multnomah County Bar Assn., University Club, Multnomah Athletic Club. Republican. Office: Weiss DesCamp & Botteri 111 SW Fifth Ste 2300 Portland OR 97204

TALMAGE, KENNETH KELLOGG, business executive; b. Morristown, N.J., Jan. 16, 1946; s. Edward Taylor Hunt Talmage Jr. and Dorothy (Rogers) Kaye; B.A., Claremont Men's Coll., 1968; M.B.A., Boston U., Brussels, 1976. Asso., Hon. Leonard K. Firestone, Los Angeles, 1973-74; attaché Am. Embassy, Brussels, 1974-77; mgmt. cons. strategic planning and fin. Arthur D. Little, Inc., Cambridge, Mass., 1977-80; sr. v.p. Boston Safe Deposit & Trust Co., 1980-87; pres., chief exec. officer Lloyd's Furs, Inc., Denver, Colo., 1987—. Trustee Island Inst., Vols. for Outdoor Colo., Breckenridge (Colo.) Outdoor Edn. Ctr.; advisor Hurricane Island Outward Bound Sch., Maine, chmn. bd. trustees, 1980-83. With USNR, 1968-69. Mem. The Country Club (Mass.), Somerset Club (Boston). Home: 1510 East 10th Ave Denver CO 80218 Office: Lloyd's Furs Inc 1543 Stout St Denver CO 80202

TAM, ROLAND FOOK SENG, physician; b. Honolulu, Feb. 19, 1946; s. William Kai Ing and Lydia (Chang) T.; m. Kathleen Ann Dos Santos, Aug. 9, 1987; 1 child, Tyler. BA, U. Hawaii, 1968; MD, U. Wash., 1972. Intern surgery Orange County Med. Ctr., Orange, Calif.; resident U. Calif., San Francisco; physician Pang Eye Ear Nose & Throat Clinic, Honolulu, 1977-80. Fellow Am. Bd. Otolaryngology; mem. AMA, Am. Acad. Facial Plastic & Reconstructive Surgery, Hi Soc. Otolaryngology, Hawaii Med. Assn., Honolulu County Med. Soc. Episcopalian.

TAMASHIRO, THOMAS KOYEI, electrical engineer; b. Paia, Maui, Hawaii, Aug. 4, 1926; s. Kokichi and Mashi (Shinyashiki) T.; BEE, Tri-State U., Angola, Ind., 1951, EE, 1964; m. Mary E. Oden; children: Cheryl M., Venita. Project engr. Jackson & Church Co., Saginaw, Mich., 1953-55; project mgr. Aerojet-Gen. Corp., Azusa, Calif., 1955-72; sr. staff engr. Aerojet Nuclear Corp., Idaho Falls, Idaho, 1972-75; project mgr. Allied Chem. Corp., Idaho Falls, 1976-79, Exxon Nuclear-Idaho, Idaho Falls, 1979-84; project mgr., sect. mgr. Westinghouse Idaho Nuclear Co., 1984—; lectr. in field. Mem. Am. Nuclear Soc. Club: Eagle Rock Amateur Radio. Lodges: Shriners, Masons. Home: 2514 W Barberry Ln Rte 9 Idaho Falls ID 83402 Office: Westinghouse Idaho Nuclear Co PO Box 4000 Idaho Falls ID 83403

TAMHANE, SHRIKANT KAMLAKAR, engineer, photographer; b. Bombay, Oct. 29, 1953; came to U.S., 1975; s. Kamlakar Vishwanath and Sudha (Ranadive) T. B in Tech., Indian Inst Tech., Bombay, 1975; MBA, U. Calif., 1984; MS, N.D. State U., 1978. Staff engr. IBM, San Jose, Calif., 1978—; research specialist Am. Crystal Sugar, Fargo, N.D., 1977-78; participant publs. and tech. presentations internat. confs. Bus. advisor Jr. Achievement, San Jose, Calif., 1980—. Mem., investment specialist, San Jose Real Estate Bd., 1979—. Office: Trans Estates Realty 5310 Monterey Hwy San Jose CA 95111

TAMKIN, CURTIS SLOANE, real estate development company executive; b. Boston, Sept. 21, 1936; s. Hayward and Etta (Goldfarb) T.; B.A. in Econs., Stanford U., 1958; m. Priscilla Martin, Oct. 18, 1975; 1 son, Curtis Sloane. Vice pres., treas., dir. Hayward Tamkin & Co., Inc., mortgage bankers, Los Angeles, 1963-70; mng. ptnr. Property Devel. Co., Los Angeles, 1970-82; pres. The Tamkin Co., 1982—. Bd. govs. Music Center Los Angeles, 1974—; pres. Los Angeles Master Chorale Assn., 1974-78; mem. vis. com. Stanford U. Libraries, 1982-86; bd. dirs. Los Angeles Philharm. Assn., 1985—. Served to lt. (j.g.) USNR, 1960-63. Mem. Founders League of Los Angeles (pres.), Los Angeles Jr. C. of C. (dir. 1968-69). Republican. Clubs: Burlingame Country, Los Angeles, University. Office: 3600 Wilshire Blvd Los Angeles CA 90010

TAMMANY, ALBERT SQUIRE, III, savings and bank executive; b. Paget, Bermuda, Aug. 21, 1946; s. Albert Squire Jr. and Marion Genevieve (Galloway) T.; m. Teresa Reznor, Sept. 8, 1973. BA Stanford U., 1968; MBA, U. Pa., 1973. Budget and planning officer Tuskegee Inst., Ala., 1973-74; budget analyst controllers dept. Chase Manhattan Bank, N.Y.C., 1974-75; v.p., div. controller Wells Fargo Bank, San Francisco, 1975-78, v.p., retail group controller, 1978-79; v.p., controller Imperial Bank, Los Angeles, 1979-81, sr. v.p. fin., 1981-83; exec. v.p., First Network Savs. Bank, Los Angeles, 1983-87, pres., 1987—; cons. Inst. for Services to Edn., Inc., 1973-74. Woodrow Wilson fellow U. Pa. Served with USMC, 1968-71. Wharton Pub. Policy fellow, 1972. Mem. Am. Bankers Assn. (trust ops. com.). Episcopalian. Clubs: Wharton, Stanford. Office: First Network Savs Bank 10100 Santa Monica Blvd Suite 500 Los Angeles CA 90067

TAMURA, NEAL NOBORU, dentist, consultant; b. Honolulu, May 3, 1953; s. Tony T. and Doris (Fujiki) T.; m. Liana N.N. Pang, May 31, 1980; 1 child, Randi M.A. BS in Biology with distinction, U. Mo., Kansas City, 1975; DDS, Northwestern U., 1985. Resident asst. in counselling U. Mo., Kansas City, 1974-75; emergency med. technician Pacific Ambulance, Honolulu, 1975-77, mgr. ops., mobile intensive care technician, 1977-79; gen. practice dentistry Honolulu, 1985—; cons. Nuuanu Hale Hosp., Honolulu, 1985—, dept. corrections State of Hawaii, 1987—. Vice chair mgmt. area hosps. State of Hawaii Bd. Commrs., Honolulu, 1987; mem. YMCA, Honolulu, 1987— (service award 1972, 73). Mem. ADA, Hawaii Dental Assn., Honolulu County Dental Soc. Democrat. Club: Papaniho Study (founder, sec. 1987—). Home: 2016 Metcalf St Honolulu HI 96822 Office: 1632 S King St Ste 100 Honolulu HI 96826

TAN, LILY, textile executive; b. Medan, Sumatra, Indonesia, Aug. 10, 1947; came to U.S., 1968; d. Eng Chuan and Sor Choo (Peh) T. BA, I.K.I.P., Medan, 1967, Gustavus Adolphus Coll., St. Peter, Minn., 1972; MM, U. So. Calif., Los Angeles, 1974. Adminstrn. officer Lloyds Bank, Los Angeles, 1974-80; v.p. Comml. Flooring Assn., Marina Del Rey, Calif., 1981-83; contract mgr. Harbinger Co., Los Angeles, 1983-86; v.p. regional sales Princeton Techs., Ltd., Los Angeles, 1986-87; dir. export services Bentley Mills, Inc., City of Industry, Calif., 1987—. Mem. Network Exec. Women in Hospitality. Office: Bentley Mills Inc 14641 E Don Julian Rd City of Industry CA 91746

TAN, WILLIAM LEW, lawyer; b. West Hollywood, Calif., July 25, 1949; s. James Tan Lew and Choon Guey Louie. BA, U. Pa., 1971; JD, U. Calif. Hastings Coll. Law, San Francisco, 1974. Bar: Calif. 1975, U.S. Dist. Ct. (cen. dist.) Calif. 1975, U.S. Ct. Appeals (9th cir.) 1975, U.S. Supreme Ct. 1979. Assoc. Hiram W. Kwan, Los Angeles, 1974-79; ptnr. Mock & Tan, Los Angeles, 1979-80; sole practice Los Angeles, 1980-81; ptnr. Tan & Sakiyama, P.C., Los Angeles, 1981-87, Tan, Sakiyama & Ohata, Los Angeles, 1987—; bd. dirs. Pacific Career Opportunities, Los Angeles, Am. Bus. Network, Los Angeles; pres., bd. dirs. Asian Research Cons., Los Angeles. Founder Asian Pacific Am. Roundtable, Los Angeles, 1981; chmn. bd. dirs. Leaderhip Edn. for Asian-Pacifics, Los Angeles, 1984; alt. del. Dem. Nat. Conv., San Francisco, 1984; mem. Calif. State Bd. Pharmacy, Sacramento, 1984, v.p., 1988—; mem. Los Angeles City and County Crime Crisis Task Force, Los Angeles, 1981, Los Angeles Asian Pacific Heritage Week Com., 1980—, Asian Pacific Women's Network, Los Angeles, 1981, Los Angeles City Atty.'s Blue Ribbon Con. of Advisors, 1981, community adv. bd. to Mayor of Los Angeles, 1984, allocations vol. liaison team health and therapy div. United Way, Los Angeles, 1986; bd. dirs. Chinatown Service Ctr., Los Angeles, 1983; conf. advisor U.S.-Asia, Los Angeles, 1981-83; atty. Los Angeles City Housing Adv. Com.; mem. Pacific Bell Consumer Product Adv. Panel; mem. community adv. bd. Sta. KCET-TV, PBS. Named one of Outstanding Young Men of Am., 1979. Mem. ABA (mem. numerous coms.), Calif. State Bar Assn. (vice chmn. com. ethnic minority relations 1983-85, chmn. pub. affairs com. 1981-82, mem. others), Los Angeles County Bar Assn. (vice chmn. 1980-82, mem. numerous coms.), So. Calif. Chinese Lawyers Assn. (pres. 1980-81, chmn., 1987-88, mem. various coms.), Minority Bar Assn. (chmn. 1981-82, sec. 1980-81, chmn. adv. bd. 1982-83), Asian Pacific Bar of Calif., Nat. Asian Pacific Am. Bar, Japanese Am. Bar Assn., Assn. Trial Lawyers Am., Bench and Bar Media Council, Calif. Trial Lawyers Assn., Soc. Intercultural Edn. (conf. coordinator, advisor panelist tng. and research com. 1983),. Office: Tan Sakiyama & Ohata 711 W College St Ste 610 Los Angeles CA 90012

TANAKA, JEANNIE E., lawyer; b. Los Angeles, Jan. 21, 1942; d. Togo William and Jean M. Tanaka. BA, Internat. Christian U., Tokyo, 1966; MSW, UCLA, 1968; JD, Washington Coll. Law, 1984. Bar: Calif. 1984, U.S. Dist. Ct. (cen., no. dists.) Calif. 1985, U.S. Ct. Appeals (ninth cir.) 1985, D.C. 1987. Instr. Aoyama Gakuin, Meiji Gakuin, Sophia U., Tokyo, 1968-75; with program devel. Encyclopedia Britannica Inst., Tokyo, 1976-78; instr. Honda, Mitsubishi, Ricoh Corps., Tokyo, 1975-80; with editorial dept. Simul Internat., Tokyo; assoc. Seki and Jarvis, Los Angeles, 1984-86, Jones, Day, Reavis & Pogue, Los Angeles, 1986-87, Reavis & McGrath, Los Angeles, 1987—. Active Japan-Am. Soc., L.A., 1984—, Asia Soc., L.A., 1984—, Japanese-Am. Citizens League, L.A., 1981; Japanese Am. Cultural and Community Ctr., 1986—, vol. Asian Pacific Am. Legal Ctr. of So. Calif., 1985-86. Mem. ABA, L.A. County Bar Assn., Japanese-Am. Bar Assn.,

Women Lawyers' Assn. of L.A., Asian Bus. League, Mensa. Democrat. Methodist. Home: 100 S Doheny #322 Los Angeles CA 90048

TANAKA, STANLEY KATSUKI, optometrist, consultant; b. Honolulu, Sept. 19, 1932; s. Tomikichi and Hatsue T.; m. Esther K. Kokubun, Oct. 31, 1959; children—Glen A., Fay M. Student U. Hawaii, 1950-52; B.S., U. Okla., 1952; O.D. magna cum laude (Jackson award), Ill. Coll. Optometry, 1956. Enlisted U.S. Army, 1957, advanced through grades to col. Res., 1981; optometrist Hawaii Permanente Med. Group, Honolulu, 1968—; cons. opthalmic firms. Named Hawaii Optometrist of Yr., 1984. Mem. Am. Optometric Assn., Hawaii Optometric Assn., Armed Forces Optometric Soc., Contact Lens Soc., Am. Optometric Found., Optometric Extension Program, Beta Sigma Kappa. Democrat. Club: Toastmasters. Home: 2645 Oahu Ave Honolulu HI 96822 Office: 1010 Pensacola St Honolulu HI 96814

TANDON, SIRJANG LAL, data processing executive; b. 1941; married. BS, Punjab U., India, 1959; BSME, Howard U., 1962; MBA, U. Santa Clara, 1970. Project engr. Beckman Co., 1965-66; staff & project engr. IBM Corp., 1966-68, Memorex Co., 1968-73; mgr. recording tech. Pertec Computer Corp., 1973-75; now chmn., chief exec. officer, dir. Tandon Corp., Chatsworth, Calif., also bd. dirs. Office: Tandon Corp 301 Science Dr PO Box 8025 Moorpark CA 93021 *

TANEN, NED STONE, motion picture company executive; b. Los Angeles, 1931. Grad., UCLA, 1954. With MCA Inc. (and subsidiaries); v.p. MCATTV, 1964-67; founder UNI Records, later MCA Records, 1967; exec. v.p. Universal City Records, Calif., 1967-69; v.p. MCA Inc., Universal City, 1967—; pres. Universal Theatrical Motion Pictures div., 1976; pres. Universal Picture div., 1979-82, also dir.; pres. motion picture group Paramount Pictures, 1985—; ind. producer 1982—. Served with USAF, 1950-52. Office: Motion Picture Group Paramount Pictures 5555 Melrose AVe Los Angeles CA 90038 *

TANG, THOMAS, judge; b. Phoenix, Jan. 11, 1922. B.S., U. Santa Clara, 1947, law student, 1948-50; LL.B. with distinction, U. Ariz., 1950. Bar: Ariz. 1950, Calif. 1951. Dep. county atty. Maricopa County, Ariz., 1953-57; asst. atty. gen. State of Ariz., 1957-58; judge Ariz. Superior Ct., 1963-70; mem. firm Sullivan, Mahoney & Tang, Phoenix, 1971-77; councilman City of Phoenix, 1960-62, vice mayor, 1962; judge U.S. Ct. of Appeals 9th Circuit, Phoenix, 1977—. Mem. State Bar Ariz. (bd. govs. 1971-77, pres. 1977), State Bar Calif. Office: US Ct Appeals 6412 US Courthouse & Fed Bldg 230 N 1st Ave Phoenix AZ 85025

TANIGUCHI, IZUMI, economics educator; b. Stockton, Calif., Feb. 3, 1926; s. Isamu and Sadayo (Miyagi) T.; m. Barbara Kazuko Nishi, June 11, 1960; children: Neal Izumi, Ian Kei. BBA, U. Houston, 1952, MBA, 1954; PhD, U. Tex., 1970. Statis. analyst Anderson Clayton and Co., Houston, 1953-54; instr., research assoc. U. Houston, 1956; teaching asst., research assoc. U. Tex., Austin, 1956-59, lectr. in econs., 1959-60; asst. prof. Econs. U. Mo., Columbia, 1960-63; asst. prof. Econs. Calif. State U., Fresno, 1963-70, dept. chmn., assoc. prof. Econs., 1971-74, prof. Econs., 1974-79, dept. chmn., prof. Econs., 1979—. Nat. v.p. Japanese-Am. Citizens League, San Francisco, 1974-76, gov. Cen. Calif. Dist. Council in Fresno, 1973-74, pres. Fresno chpt., 1971; active Beyond War, Fresno, 1985—; mem. Ednl. Innovation and Planning Commn., Sacramento, 1979-82, State Supr. of Instruction Council on Asian, Pacific Islander Affairs, Sacramento, 1984-85; mem. Adv. Bd. Sch. Edn. Calif. State U., Fresno, 1976—; mem. Legal Compliance Panel State Dept. Edn., Sacramento, 1974-79. Recipient Wall Street Jour. Achievement award U. Houston, 1952. Mem. Am. Econs. Assn., Southwestern Social Sci. Assn., Assn. Evolutionary Econs., Assn. Asian Studies, Western Social Sci. Assn., Phi Kappa Phi. Democrat. Clubs: U.S. Judo Fedn. (Fresno) (advisor), Japanese Lang. Sch. (pres. 1971). Home: 738 E Tenaya Way Fresno CA 93710 Office: Calif State U Fresno Dept of Econs Fresno CA 93740

TANIGUCHI, RAYMOND MASAYUKI, neurosurgeon; b. Waipahu, Hawaii, May 14, 1934; s. James Takeo and Yoshiko (Yamaguchi) T.; m. Helen Akiki Fujiyoshi, Oct. 6, 1971; 1 child, Stacy. Student, U. Hawaii, 1952-54; BA, Washington U., St. Louis, 1956; MD, Tulane U., 1960. Diplomate Am. Bd. Neurological Surgery, 1973. Rotating internship McLeod Infirmary, Florence, S.C., 1960-61; resident, gen. pathology and neuropath Duke Med. Ctr., 1961-62; resident in gen. surgery N.C. Baptist Hosp., 1962-63; resident in neurology Duke Med. Ctr., 1963-64; resident in clin. neurosurgery N.C. Baptist Hosp., 1964-65, Duke Med. Ctr., 1965-66, 68-70; clin. assoc. prof. U. Hawaii Sch. of Med., Honolulu, 1980—; pvt. practice, nuerosurgeon Honolulu, to date; 19; cons. in neurosurgery, Tripler Army Med. Ctr., Kaiser Found. Hosp., spl. physician cons. on spinal cord injury and trauma, Hawaii Med. Assn., Emergency Med. Svcs. Program, ADHOC com. on trauma, State of Hawaii, 1981-82. Contbr. articles to profl. jours. Capt. U.S. Army Med. Corps, 1966-68, Vietnam, Japan. Fellow, Am. Coll. of Surgeons, (chmn. credential com.); mem. Am. Assn. Neurological Surgeons, Pan Pacific Surgical Assn. (chmn. elect, bd. trustees); Congress of Neurological Surgeons, AMA, Hawaii Med. Assn. Office: 1380 Lusitana St 415 Honolulu HI 96813

TANIGUCHI, RICHARD RYUZO, building supplies company executive; b. Eleele, Hawaii, Oct. 21, 1913; s. Tokuichi and Sana (Omaye) T.; B.A., U. Hawaii, 1936; m. Sumako Matsui, July 22, 1939; children—Grace Fujiyoshi, Susan Penisten. Acctg. clk. Bank of Hawaii, 1935-36; treas., gen. mgr. Hawaii Pläning Mill, 1944-54; pres., gen. mgr. Hawaii Hardware Co., Ltd., Hilo, 1954—; pres., dir. Enterprises Hilo; v.p., dir. Hawaii Funeral Home. Chmn. Hawaii County CSC, 1950-56; vice chmn. Hawaii County Tidal Wave Adv. Com., 1961-68; vice chmn. Hawaii Council Tb and Health Assn., 1965; pres. Am. Cancer Soc., 1969-72, state bd. dirs., 1970-78; pres. Hilo Hongwanji Mission 1968-70, sr. adviser, 1972—; v.p. Hawaii State Hongwanji Mission, 1969—; mem. Hawaii Comprehensive Health Planning Com., 1970-72; gen. chmn. Kanyaku Imin Centennial Com., 1985. Named Hawaii Vol. of Year, Am. Cancer Soc., 1973, recipient Nat. award Am. Cancer Soc., 1978, Fifth Class Order of Sacred Treasure, Emperor of Japan, 1985. Mem. Am. Supply Assn., Nat. Plumbing Wholesalers Assn., Japanese C. of C. and Industry of Hawaii (pres. 1957), Hawaii (dir. 1958-59), Japanese (hon. dir.) chambers commerce, Hawaii Funeral Home (chmn. bd.), Hawaii Island Japanese Community Assn. (pres. 1983-85), Phi Kappa Phi, Pi Gamme Mu. Club: Waiakea. Lodge: Lions (treas., bd. dirs. 1956-60) Home: 572 Iwalani St Hilo HI 96720 Office: Hawaii Hardware Co 550 Kilauea Ave Hilo HI 96720

TANIGUCHI, TOKUSO, surgeon; b. Eleele, Kauai, Hawaii, June 26, 1915; s. Tokuichi and Sana (Omaye) T.; BA, U. Hawaii, 1941; MD, Tulane U., 1946; 1 son, Jan Tokuichi. Intern Knoxville (Tenn.) Gen. Hosp., 1946-47; resident in surgery St. Joseph Hosp., also Marquette Med. Sch., Milw., 1947-52; practice medicine, specializing in surgery, Hilo, Hawaii, 1955—; chief surgery Hilo Hosp.; teaching fellow Marquette Med. Sch., 1947-49; v.p., dir. Hawaii Hardware Co., Ltd. Capt. M.C., AUS, 1952-55. Diplomate Am. Bd. Surgery. Fellow Internat., Am. colls. surgeons; mem. Am., Hawaii med. assns., Hawaii County Med. Soc., Pan-Pacific Surg. Assn., Phi Kappa Phi. Contbr. articles in field to profl. jours. Patentee automated catheter. Home: 277 Kaiulani St Hilo HI 96720

TANIMOTO, GEORGE, agricultural executive, farmer; b. Gridley, Calif., Feb. 10, 1926; s. Hirokhi and Rewa TAnimoto; m. Hanami Yamasaki, Dec. 19, 1946; 1 child, Patricia. Grad. high sch., Newell, Calif. Dir. Kiwi Fruit Growers Calif., Sacramento, 1973, pres., 1973-80; chmn. Calif. Kiwi Fruit Commn., Sacramento, 1980-84, vice chmn., 1985-87, chmn., 1988-89; bd. dirs. Blue Anchor, Inc., Sacramento. Adv. commr. Butte County Agrl. Commn., Oroville, Calif., 1985-89. Mem. Gridley Sportsman Club (pres. 1975-78). Republican. Buddhist. Home: 948 River Ave Gridley CA 95948

TANIMOTO, STEVEN LARRY, computer science educator; b. Chgo., May 18, 1949; s. Taffee Tadashi and Mary-Mae Muriel (Whistler) T.; m. Gunnel Birgitta Neander, Sept. 19, 1981; children: Elise Marie, Anna Sofia. AB, Harvard U., 1971; PhD, Princeton U., 1975. Asst. prof. U. Conn., Storrs, 1975-77; asst. prof. U. Wash., Seattle, 1977-81, assoc. prof., 1981-87, prof., 1987—. Author: Elements of Artificial Intelligence, 1987 (Book of Month award 1987); patentee in field. Mem. IEEE (sr., computer soc., editor-in-chief transactions on pattern analysis and machine intelligence 1986—). Office: U Wash Dept Computer Sci FR-35 Seattle WA 98195

TANKE, THOMAS JOHN, engineer; b. Chgo., Mar. 17, 1944; s. Raymond and Catherine (Dybas) T.; m. Virginia Rae Coyne, July 3, 1965; children: Kimberly, Michael, Kelly, Carrie. BSME, U. Ill., Urbana, 1966; MSME, U. Wis., 1969; PhD in Bus. Adminstrn., U. Colo., Boulder, 1987. Registered profl. engr.; Calif., Ill., Tex., Colo. Loss prevention engr. Royal-Globe, Inc. Co., Chgo., 1966-69; corp. safety dir. Wright, Corp., Des Moines, 1969-72; loss prevention mgr. Green Construction Co., Pueblo, Colo., 1972-75; mgr. safety and emergency svcs. Kentron Internat., Pueblo, 1975-76; mgr., safety, quality and emergency svcs. U.S. Dept. Transp., Pueblo, 1976-81; mgr. project integration Kaiser, Engrs., Houston, 1981-83; project mgr. Kaiser, Engrs., L.A., 1983—. Contbr. articles profl. publs.; speaker profl. confs. Scoutmaster, Boys Scouts Am., Houston, 1981-83; mem. Assn. Retarded Citizens, Houston, 1982, Spl. Olympics, Ventura, Calif., 1987. Recipient Outstanding Achievement award, Am. Pub. Transit Assn., Washington, 1987, Award of Merit, U.S. Dept. Trans., Washington, 1980, Sr. Exec. Service designation, Office of Personnel Mgmt., Washington, 1980. Mem. Am. Soc. Safety Engrs. (pres. 1973-75), Nat. Safety Mgmt. Soc. (pres. 1974-78), Nat. Fire Protection Assn., Am. Mgmt. Assn., NSPE, Calif. Assn. Profl. Engrs. (sec. 1987), Am. Soc. for Quality Control (cert. quality examiner). Home: 1222 Lamont Ave Thousand Oaks CA 91362 Office: Kaiser Engrs Inc 403 W 8th St Los Angeles CA 90014

TANNER, DONNA WITTWER, speech pathologist; b. Ithaca, N.Y., Feb. 18, 1929; d. Eldon and Alice LaVerne (Tullis) Wittwer; m. Bernard Malan Tanner, Sept. 10, 1954; children: Gordon W., Mark W., Robert E., Edwin B., Charlene, Donnette, Leanne, David H. BA, Brigham Young U., 1950; MS, U. Utah, 1951. Tchr. lip reading and audiologist Salt Lake City Schs., 1951-53; speech pathologist Utah Soc. Crippled Children and Adults, 1953-54; audiologist Dist. Bd. of Health, Washington, 1954-55, VA, 1956-59; speech pathologist Children's Ct. Emotionally Disturbed Children, 1962-64, Primary Children's Hosp., 1963-64; gen. practice speech pathology Salt Lake City, 1964—; speech pathologist Children's Ctr., Salt Lake City, 1977—. Pres. Skyline PTSA, 1986-87. Mem. Am. Speech, Language and Hearing Assn., Utah Speech, Language and Hearing Assn. (sec. 1949-50), Gamma Phi Beta. Republican. Mormon. Home: 3911 S 3250 E Salt Lake City UT 84124 Office: Childrens Ctr 1855 Medical Dr Salt Lake City UT 84112

TANNER, JOHN DOUGLAS, JR., author, educator; b. Quantico, Va., Oct. 2, 1943; s. John Douglas and Dorothy Lucille (Walker) T.; m. Jo Ann Boyd, Jan. 1964 (div. Aug. 1966); 1 child, Lorena Desiree; m. Laurel Jean Selfridge, Dec. 19, 1967 (div. Oct. 1987); children: John DouglasIII, Stephen Douglas, Elizabeth Jane; m. Karen M. Olson, Apr. 16, 1988. BA, Pomona Coll., 1966; MA, Claremont Calif. Grad. Sch., 1968; postgrad., U. Calif., Riverside, 1976, 84-86, U. Calif., San Diego, 1984-87. Cert. tchr., Calif. Asst. swimming, water polo coach Pomona Coll., 1966-69; rsch. asst.history dept. Claremont Grad. Sch., 1967-69; assoc. prof. history Palomar Coll., San Marcos, Calif., 1969—; judge internat. history fair Calif. State U., San Diego, Universidad Autonoma de Baja Calif., Tijuana, Mex., 1985-86; speaker in field. Author: Olaf Swenson and his Siberian Imports jour., 1978 (Dog Writers Assn. Am. Best Series award 1979), Campaign for Los Angeles, 1846-47, 69; co-editor: Don Juan Foster, 1970; contbr. articles to profl. jours. Mem. citizens com. Fallbrook (Calif.) San. Dist., 1980; merit badge counselor Boy Scouts Am., 1975-85; Martin County Hist. Soc., Morgan County Hist. Soc., Fallbrook Hist. Soc., San Diego Opera Guild, San Diego Classical Music Soc., Opera Pacific Guild. Chautauqua fellow NSF, 1979. Mem. Custer Battlefield Hist. & Mus. Assn., The Westerners, Siberian Husky Am. (bd. dirs. 1974-78, 1st v.p. 1978-79), So. Calif. Siberian Husky (pres. 1972-79). Republican. Episcopalian. Home: 2810 E Live Oak Park Rd Fallbrook CA 92028 Office: Palomar Coll 1140 N Mission Rd San Marcos CA 92069

TANNER, KEVIN ROY, dentist; b. London, Aug. 11, 1956; came to U.S., 1966; s. Roy Henry and Hellen Jane (Nicole) T.; m. JoAnne Theresa Servinsky, Sept. 14, 1985; 1 child, Garin Joseph. BS, U. So. Calif., 1978; postgrad., Calif. Polytechnic U., 1979-80; DDS, U. Pacific, 1982. Resident Navy Hosp., Oakland, Calif., 1982-83; gen. practice dentistry Citrus Heights, Calif., 1985—. Active 1st Presby. Ch., Roseville, Calif., 1987-88; treas. Mermers Group, Roseville, 1987-88. Lt. USN, 1982-85. Decorated Navy Achievement medal. Fellow Acad. Gen. Dentistry; mem. ABA, Calif. Dental Assn., U. Pacific Alumni Assn., Calif. Polytechnic U. Alumni Assn., Sertoma (bd. dirs. Citrus Heights chpt. 1987-88), Omicron Kappa Upsilon, Tau Kappa Omega. Republican. Office: 7916 Pebble Beach Dr Citrus Heights CA 95616

TANNER, THOMAS WILLIAM, marketing executive; b. St. Louis, Aug. 7, 1952; s. William Eugene amd Betty (Helmering) T. BS in Computer Sci., U. Mo., Rolla, 1974; MBA, So. Ill. U., Edwardsville, 1982. Systems analyst City of St. Louis, 1972-76; adv. mktg. rep. Motorola Corp., San Bruno, Calif., 1976; sr. mktg. rep. Motorola Corp., 1976-87; prin. Dimensions in Health, Los Gatos, Calif., 1987-88, Corp. Wellness Systems, Inc., San Jose, Calif., 1988; mktg. execitove Omni Concepts, Inc., San Jose, 1988—. Vol. ARC, St. Louis and Calif., 1974-79; vice-chmn. Cambrian Community Council, San Jose, Calif., 1983-86, chmn., 1987—; mem. citizen adv. council Housing and Urban Devel., Santa Clara County, Calif., chmn., 1987—; planning commr. Santa Clara County, 1988, Overfels Parks Task Force, City of San Jose. Roman Catholic.

TANNO, RONALD LOUIS, dentist; b. San Jose, Calif., Dec. 17, 1937; s. George Anthony and Rose Marie (Manghisi) T.; m. Ellen Theresa Goodbread, Nov. 30, 1985. BS, Santa Clara U., 1959, DDS magna cum laude, 1963. Lic. DDS. Dentist Santa Clara County Health Dept., San Martin, Calif., 1965-67, Alameda County Health Dept., Oakland, Calif., 1965-67; pvt. practice San Jose, 1966—; dental cons. Found. Med. Care, San Jose, 1977-81, Dental Ins. Cons., Saratoga, Calif., 1980-88, Santa Clara County Sch. Dists. Dental Plan, San Jose, 1983-88; cons. quality rev. Delta Dental Plan Calif., San Francisco, 1983-88; mem. dental staff Los Gatos (Calif.) Community Hosp., 1978—, chief dental dept., 1983, 84. Capt. USAF, 1963-65. Mem. Santa Clara County Dental Soc., Calif. Dental Assn., Am. Dental Assn., Elks, Lions, Xi Psi Phi, Omicron Kappa Upsilon. Office: 1685 Westwood Dr #10 San Jose CA 95125

TANQUARY, JANICE RAE, lawyer; b. Hinsdale, Ill., Feb. 27, 1946; d. Raymond H. and Mary Elizabeth (Hadley)ûVavrinek; m. Fred T. Tanquary, Apr. 20, 1968 (div. May 1981); 1 child, Kimberly. BA, U. Denver, 1968, JD, 1976, LLM in Taxation, 1977. Bar: Colo. 1977. Assoc. Kutak, Rock & Huie, Denver, 1977-80; pvt. practice Denver, 1980--. Contbr. articles to profl. jours. Troop leader Girl Scouts U.S., Denver, 1979-84. Mem. Colo. Bar Assn. (citizenship com. 1977--, chmn. bicentennial com. 1987-88), U. Denver Alumni Assn. Office: 3300 E 1st Ave Ste 500 Denver CO 80206

TANZMANN, VIRGINIA WARD, architect; b. Tuxedo, N.Y., July 6, 1945; d. John A. Ward and Helen Pfund. BA in Architecture, Syracuse U., 1968, BArch, 1969. Registered architect, Calif., Nev. Intern architect Burke Kober Nicolais Archuleta, Los Angeles, 1969-72; project architect Daniel L. Dworsky & Assocs., Los Angeles, 1972-74, SUA, Inc., Los Angeles, 1974-75; staff architect So. Calif. Rapid Transit Dist., Los Angeles, 1975-78; prin. The Tanzmann Assocs., Los Angeles, 1978—. Prin. works include transp. facilities, retail stores, comml. and office facilities 6 railroad stations, Los Angeles to Long Beach Light Rail Transit, Convention Ctr. Expansion Team, Petroleum Lab. Chevron USA, Inc., El Segundo, Calif., Hyperion Treatment Plant UCLA Med. Ctr., Los Angeles Unified Sch. Dist., Los Angeles Dept. Water and Power. Work exhibited: Monterey Design Conf., Calif., 1981, 87. Pres. YWCA of Los Angeles, 1984-87, v.p. 1983-84; rec. sec. Vol. Ctr. Los Angeles, 1984-86; bd. dirs. Dorland Mountain Arts Colony. Mem. AIA, (state bd. dirs., Calif. coun. 1989—), Assn. Women in Architecture (v.p. 1986-87, pres. 1987-88), Archtl. Guild (treas. 1987-88, v.p. 1988-89), Architects Designers and Planners for Social Responsibility, L'Union International des Femmes Architectes. Office: The Tanzmann Assocs 820 E Third St Los Angeles CA 90013-1820

TAPANILA, GLEN ROBERT, information systems specialist; b. Duluth, Minn., July 17, 1947; s. Urho Matt and June Emma (Raunio) T.; m. Lynne Marie Yoshimasu, Dec. 10, 1970. BA magna cum laude, U. Minn., 1967; postgrad., U. Hawaii, 1967-71, U. Edmonton, Alta., Can., 1972-73. Info. systems specialist Dept. Info. Svcs., Olympia, Wash., 1974—. Contbr. numerous articles to profl. jours. Precinct officer Dem. Party, Tumwater, Mass., 1986-88. NDEA fellow U. Hawaii, 1970-71. Mme. Gamma Theta Epsilon, Psi Chi. Home: 316 Laurelhurst Dr Tumwater WA 98501 Office: Dept Info Svcs 1310 Jefferson Olympia WA 98504

TAPKING, DOUGLAS ALLEN, county government official; b. Downey, Calif., June 30, 1949; s. John Douglas and Loveday Jaennine (Ransier) T.; m. Karen Elaine Shipway, June 19, 1971; children: Eric Allen, Bridget Elaine. AA, Moorpark (Calif.) Jr. Coll., 1969; BA, Calif. State U., San Diego, 1972; MSA, Calif. State Coll., Dominquez Hills, 1977. Cert. housing mgr. Engring. aide City of Thousand Oaks (Calif.), 1967-69, City of La Mesa (Calif.), 1969-72; dir. owned housing Housing Authority, County of L.A., L.A., 1972-79; exec. dir. Housing Authority, County of Salt Lake, Salt Lake City, 1979—; mem. Govs. Housing Task Force, Salt Lake City, 1982. Rev. Com. United Way of the Great Salt Lake Are, 1989; chmn. Bollinger Scholarship Com., Washington, 1984-87; legis. action Utah Sportmans Alliance, Salt Lake City. Mem. Pub. Housing Authorities Dirs. Assn. (regional v.p., 1984—, treas., Washington, 1987-89), Nat. Assn. Housing and Redevel. Officials (legis. action com. 1988—), Home Builders of Greater Salt Lake (co-chmn. housing fin. com. 1988—), Greater Salt Lake C. of C. (leadership Utah 1986), Kiwanis. Lutheran. Office: Housing Authority County of Salt Lake 1962 South 200 East Salt Lake City UT 84115

TAPP, JESSE WASHINGTON, JR., physician, educator; b. N.Y.C., July 10, 1930; s. Jesse Washington Sr. and Isabel Converse (Dickey) T.; m. Marie Jean Glasse, July 10, 1952; children: Elizabeth, Jane, Cathleen, Jessie, Mary. BA, Stanford U., 1952; MD, U. Chgo., 1955; MPH, Harvard U., 1962. Diplomate Am. Bd. Preventive Medicine, Am. Bd. Family Practice. Rotating intern Alameda County Hosp., Oakland, Calif., 1955-56; family physician Presbyn. Nat. Missions, San Sebastian, P.R., 1956-61; asst. prof. U. Ky. Sch. Medicine, Lexington, 1962-68, assoc. prof., 1968-70; assoc. prof. U. Ariz. Sch. Medicine, Tucson, 1970-73, prof., 1973-79; chief physician svcs. Seattle-King County Dept. Pub. Health, 1979-80, dir., 1980-85, communicable disease control officer, 1985—; affiliate prof. dept. health svcs. U. Wash., Seattle, 1982—; vis. prof., hon. cons. St. Thomas Hosp. Med. Sch., London, 1968-69. Contbr. articles to med. jours. Milbank Meml. Fund faculty fellow. Mme. Am. Coll. Preventive Medicine (v.p. 1977, regent 1980-83), Internat. Epidemiol. Assn., Am. Pub. Health Assn., King County Med. Soc. Home: 4234 51st Ave NE Seattle WA 98105 Office: Seattle-King County Dept Pub Health 1200 Public Safety Blvd Seattle WA 98104

TAPP, RONALD GENE, insurance company executive; b. Bloomington, Ind., July 15, 1941; s. Wayne E. and Golda G. Tapp; student Ind. U., 1959-63; m. Helen L. Black, Sept. 24, 1977; children—Rhonda Jean, Randy G., Rita Jean. Printer, Phoenix Newspapers, Inc., 1972-76; ins. agt. Am. Republic Ins. Co., Phoenix, 1976-77; ins. agt. Minn. Protective Life Ins. Co., Phoenix, 1977-78, gen. agt., 1978-82, Southwestern regional mgr., 1978-82; sec.-treas. Internat. Benefit Cons., Ltd., 1981—; mktg. dir. Lincoln Benefit Life, 1982—; regional mgr. Pan Am. Life Ins. Co., 1983-85; pres. Empire-Am. Ins. Cons., Ltd., 1982—, Empire-Am. Bonding, Inc., 1985—. Republican precinct committeeman, also state committeeman for dist. 19. Served with U.S. Army, 1964-65. Recipient various profl. awards, 1977-81. Mem. Ariz. Public Employees Assn. (assoc.), Profl. Bail-Agts. Ariz. (pres. 1987—), Bail-Agts. of the U.S. (pres.'s coun. 1987—). Home: 144 E Bluefield Phoenix AZ 85022 Office: 4215 N 16th St Ste 2 Phoenix AZ 85016

TAPPAN, DAVID S., JR., engineering, construction, natural resources management company executive; b. Hainan, People's Republic of China, May 27, 1922; m. Jeanne Boone. B.A., Swarthmore Coll., 1943; M.B.A., Stanford U., 1948. With sales and engring. dept. U.S. Steel Corp., 1948-52; adminstrv. asst. to v.p. of sales Fluor Corp., 1952-59, v.p. domestic sales, 1959-62, v.p. domestic and internat. sales, 1962-68, also. bd. dirs., sr. v.p., 1968-71; pres. Fluor Corp., Irvine, Calif., 1987-88; chmn., chief exec. officer, dir. Fluor Corp., Irvine, 1988—; pres. Fluor Engrs. & Constructors Inc. (now named Fluor Daniel Inc.), 1971-76, vice chmn. bd., 1976-82, pres., chief operating officer, 1982-84, chmn., chief exec. officer, from 1984; bd. dirs. Genentech Inc., Allianz Ins. Co., The Nat. Council for U.S.-China Trade Inc., Los Angeles-Guangzhou Sister City Assn., Nat. Energy Found.; bd. overseas exec. council on fgn. diplomats and adv. com. Export-Import Bank of U.S. Bd. dirs. Nat. Bus. Com. for Arts; chmn. Orange County Orgn.; councillor U. So. Calif. Sch. Bus. and Adminstrn., Stanford U. Grad. Sch. Bus. Served to lt. (j.g.) USNR, 1943-46. Mem. Am. Petroleum Inst., Los Angeles C. of C. (vice chmn., bd. dirs.). Office: Fluor Corp 3333 Michelson Dr Irvine CA 92730

TAPPHORN, RALPH M., physicist; b. Grinnell, Kans., July 26, 1944; s. Tony H.a nd Clara M. (Broeckelman) T.; m. Karen L. Tapphorn, June 2, 1969; children: Janelle E., Carolyn M. BS in Physics, Ft. Hays State U., Kans., 1966; PhD in Nuclear Physics, Kans. State U., 1970. Postdoctoral assoc. Nat. Acad. Sci., Aberdeen Proving Grounds, Aberdeen, Md., 1970-72; sr. scientist Schlumbrger-Doll Research Ctr., Ridgefield, Conn., 1972-76; prog. mgr. Ball Aerospace Systems div., Boulder, Colo., 1976-82; pres. Tapphorn Conservation, Ltd., Grinnell, Kans., 1982-87; prin. scientist Lockheed Engring. & Sci. Co., Las Cruces, N.Mex., 1987—. Contbr. articles to profl. jours. Mem. APS. Home: 1224 Mages St Las Cruces NM 88005 Office: Lockheed Engring & Sci Co WSTF PO Drawer MM Las Cruces NM 88004

TARANIK, JAMES VLADIMIR, geologist, educator; b. Los Angeles, Apr. 23, 1940; s. Vladimir James and Jeanette Downing (Smith) T.; m. Colleen Sue Glessner, Dec. 4, 1971; children: Debra Lynn, Danny Lee. B.Sc. in Geology, Stanford U., 1964; Ph.D., Colo. Sch. Mines, 1974. Chief remote sensing Iowa Geol. Survey, Iowa City, 1971-74; prin. remote sensing scientist Earth Resources Observation Systems Data Ctr., U.S. Geol. Survey, Sioux Falls, S.D., 1975-79; chief non-renewable resources br., resource observation div. Office of Space and Terrestrial Applications, NASA Hdqrs., Washington, 1979-82; dean mines Mackay Sch. Mines, prof. geology U. Nev.-Reno, 1982-87; pres. Desert Research Inst., U. Nev. System, 1987—; adj. prof. geology U. Iowa, 1971-79; vis. prof. civil engring. Iowa State U., 1972-74; adj. prof. earth sci. U. S.D., 1976-79; program scientist for space shuttle large format camera expt. for heat capacity mapping mission, liaison Geol. Scis. Bd., Nat. Acad. Scis., 1981-82; team mem. Shuttle Imaging Radar-B Sci. Team NASA, 1983-88, mem. space applications adv. com. 1986-88; chmn. remote sensing subcom. SAAC, 1986-88; chmn. working group on civil space commercialization U.S. Dept. Commerce, 1982-84, mem. civil operational remote sensing satellite com., 1983-84; bd. dirs. Newmont Gold Co.; mem. NASA Space Sci. and Applications adv. com., 1988—; developer remote sensing program and remote sensing lab. for State of Iowa, ednl. program in remote sensing for Iowa univs.; Office Space and Terrestrial Applications program scientist for 2d space shuttle flight; terrestrial geologic applications program for NASA. Contbr. to profl. jours. Served with C.E. U.S. Army, 1965-67. Decorated Bronze Star medal.; recipient Spl. achievement award U.S. Geol. Survey, 1978, exceptional sci. achievement medal NASA, 1982; NASA prin. investigator, 1973, 1983-88; NDEA fellow, 1968-71. Fellow AAAS, Explorers Club, Geol. Soc. Am.; mem. Am. Assn. Petroleum Geologists, Soc. Mining Engrs., Am. Inst. Profl. Geologists (certified, pres. Nev. sect. 1985-87), AIAA (sr. mem.), Internat. Acad. Astronautics (academician), Am. Astronautical Soc. (sr. mem.), Soc. Exploration Geophysicists, Geosci. and Remote Sensing Soc. of IEEE (bd. dirs., geosat com.), Am. Soc. Photogrammetry (certified), Internat. Soc. Photogrammetry and Remote Sensing (pres. working group II/4 1976-80, working group VIII-5 non-renewable resources 1980-88), Sigma Xi, Phi Kappa Phi (life). Home: 3075 Susileen Dr Reno NV 89509 Office: U Nev System Desert Rsch Inst Pres' Office Reno NV 89512

TARDIFF, GARY ROBERT, chemical engineer; b. Laconia, N.H., Dec. 30, 1951; s. Conrad Ernest and Janette Virginia (Lerman) T.; m. Claire Lucille Samson, Aug. 30, 1974 (div. Nov. 1984); 1 son, Adam Thomas; m. Marie Gwen Mason, July 14, 1985. BS in Chem. Engring., U. N.H., 1974. Registered profl. engr., N.H. Chem. engr. DuPont Co., Wilmington, Del., 1974-76; process devel. engr. W. R. Grace Co., Nashua, N.H., 1976-81; prin. engr. Westinghouse Hanford Co., Richland, Wash., 1981—. Mem. Am. Inst. Chem. Engrs. Home: 2435 Michael Ave Richland WA 99352 Office: Westinghouse Handford PO Box 1970 55-80 Richland WA 99352

TARIN, WILLIAM MICHAEL, senior publications engineer; b. San Antonio, July 15, 1942; s. Joseph Walter and Dorothy Mae (Perry) T.; m. Elizabeth Ann Scout, Feb. 1, 1969; children: Dorothy Elizabeth, William Michael, Joseph Clement. BS in Info. Systems, Nat. Coll., 1988. Communications analyst USAF, Ft. Meade, Md., 1961-81; tech. writer Docu-Data Corp., Millersville, Md., 1981-83; document control mgr. Ford Aerospace & Communications Corp., Hanover, Md., 1983; data processing mgr. Dept. Defense, Ft. Meade, 1983-84; tech. writer Intercon Systems Corp., Aurora, Colo., 1984-87; sr. publ. engr. Lockheed Missiles & Space Co., Aurora, 1987—; cons. in field. Recipient Air Force Commendation Medal Air Force, 1967, 1979, 1981, Commendation Cert. Nat. Security Agy., 1977. Democrat. Methodist. Home: 5285 S Yampa St Aurora CO 80015 Office: Lockheed Missiles & Space 3151 S Vaughn Way Ste 300 Aurora CO 80014

TARIO, TERRY C(HARLES), broadcasting executive; b. Los Angeles, Aug. 28, 1950; s. Clifford Alexander and Marion Charlene (Olive) T.; m. Bonnie Leisen; 1 child, Brian Paul. Grad. high sch., Hermosa Beach, Calif., 1968. Gen. mgr. South Bay Power Tools, Hermosa Beach, 1973-76; broadcaster Sta. KEZJ AM/FM, Twin Falls, Idaho, 1976—; dir. mktg. Pet Complex, Boise and Salt Lake City, 1985—. Creator commls. John Lennon Meml. (Best of Yr. award 1982), Pets Unltd., 1983 (Best of Yr. award 1983), Depot Grill, 1984 (Best of Yr. award 1984), Eyecenter (Best of Yr. award 1986). Served with USN, 1968-72. Mem. BMI, Idaho State Broadcasters Assn., Advt. and Mktg. Cons. (pres.). Office: Stas KEEP/KEZJ 415 Park Ave Twin Falls ID 83301

TARLOV, ALVIN RICHARD, philanthropic foundation administrator, former physician, educator; b. Norwalk, Conn., July 11, 1929; s. Charles and Mae (Shelinsky) T.; m. Joan Hylton, June 12, 1956 (div. 1976); children: Richard, Elizabeth, Jane, Suzanne, David. BA, Dartmouth Coll., 1951; MD, U. Chgo., 1956. Intern Phila. Gen. Hosp., 1956-57; resident in medicine U. Chgo. Hosps., 1957-58, 62-63, research assoc., 1958-61; asst. prof. medicine U. Chgo., 1963-68, assoc. prof., 1968-70, prof., 1970-84, chmn. dept. medicine, 1969-81; chmn. nat. adv. com. on grad. med. edn. HHS, Washington, 1980; pres. Henry J. Kaiser Family Found., Menlo Park, Calif., 1984—. Served to capt. U.S. Army, 1958-61. Recipient Research Career Devel. award NIH, 1962-67; John and Mary Markle Found. scholar, 1966-71. Mem. ACP (master), Inst. Medicine of Nat. Acad. Scis. Office: Henry J Kaiser Family Found 2400 Sand Hill Rd Menlo Park CA 94025

TARR, RAYMOND FREDERICK, banker, consultant; b. Corvallis, Oreg., June 8, 1932; s. Raymond Porter Tarr and Ruth Viola Jacobsen; m. Donna Scheel, Feb. 10, 1956 (div. Feb. 1969); children: Raymond M., William P., Steven J., Sherri L.; m. Elaine Esther Patterson, Jan. 22, 1986. Student, Santa Ana (Calif.) Jr. Coll., 1951-53; BS in Indsl. Engring., U. Mont., 1956; MBA, UCLA, 1959. Cert. indsl. engr. Agt. U.S. Govt., 1961-83; pres. World Trade Bank, Valencia, Calif., 1985—; bd. dirs. Prison Industries, Valencia, 1985—; cons. President's Yacht Trust, Beverly Hills, Calif., 1987-88. Author: Social Problems in Prison, 1968. Pres. Eastside Little League, Pop Warner Football, Garden Grove, Calif., 1965-68.with USMC, Korea. Decorated Purple Heart, Silver Star; recipient Presidential Citation. Mem. Ex Offenders Union (pres. 1986—), Am. Correctional Assn., BPOE. Republican.

TARR, SANDRA DIANE, realtor; b. Great Falls, Mont., Sept. 12, 1944; d. Jack Joseph DiBetta and Shirley Gurina (Halverson) Dickson: m. Van Wye Tarr, June 1, 1963 (div. Oct. 9, 1985); 1 child, Branson Wye. Student, U. Mont., 1971. Ops. asst. IBM, Boulder, Colo., 1966-68; exporter Bonner Packing Co., Fresno, Calif., 1969-70; asst. to dean U. Mont., Missoula, 1971-77; realtor Lambros Realty, Missoula, 1977—. Pres. Hospice, Missoula, 1987-88; bd. dirs. Easter Seal Soc., Missoula, 1980-88, Mountain West Home Health Orgn., 1987-88; chmn. Easter Seal Telethon, Missoula, 1984. Recipient Outstanding Ability and Performance award, Missoula YMCA, 1988. Mem. Mont. Realtor Assn., Nat. Assn. of Realtors, Cert. Real Estate Specialist, Grad. Realtor Inst. Office: Lambros Realty 1001 Higgins Missoula MT 59801

TARSON, HERBERT HARVEY, university administrator; b. N.Y.C., Aug. 28, 1910; s. Harry and Elizabeth (Miller) T.; m. Lynne Barnett, June 27, 1941; 1 son, Stephen. Grad., Army Command Gen. Staff Coll., 1942, Armed Forces Staff Coll., 1951, Adavnced Mgmt. Sch. Sr. Air Force Comdrs., George Washington U., 1954; B.A., U. Calif., Los Angeles, 1949; Ph.D., U.S. Internat. U., 1972. Entered U.S. Army as pvt., 1933, advanced through grades to maj., 1942; transfered to U.S. Air Force, 1947, advanced through grades to lt. col., 1949; adj. exec. officer Ft. Snelling, Minn., 1940-42; asst. adj. gen. 91st Inf. Div., 1942-43; chief of personnel, advance sec. Comd. Zone, ETO, 1944-45; dir. personnel services 8th Air Force, 1946-47; dep. dir. dept. info. and edn. Armed Forces Info. Sch., 1949-51; dir. personnel services Japan Air Def. Force, 1951-53, Continental Air Command, 1953-62; dir. adminstrv. services, spl. asst. to Comdr. 6th Air Force Res. Region, 1962-64; ret. 1964; asst. to chancellor L.I. U., Brookville, 1964-69; dean admissions Tex. State Tech. Inst., San Diego Indsl. Center, 1970-72; v.p. acad. affairs Nat. U., San Diego, 1972-75; sr. v.p. Nat. U., 1975-88. Decorated Bronze Star medal with oak leaf cluster, Air Force Commendation medal with 2 oak leaf clusters. Fellow Bio-Med Research Inst.; mem. Doctoral Soc. U.S. Internat. U., Am. Soc. Tng., Devel., World Affairs Council, Air Force Assn., Navy League U.S., Pres.'s Assos. of Nat. U. (presidential life). Home: 4611 Denwood Rd La Mesa CA 92041 Office: Nat U 4141 Camino del Rio S San Diego CA 92108

TARTIKOFF, BRANDON, television network executive; b. L.I., N.Y., 1949; m. Lilly Samuels, 1982; 1 child, Calla Lianne. B.A. with honors, Yale U., 1970. With promotion dept. ABC TV, New Haven, Conn., 1971-73; program exec. dramatic programming Sta. WLS-TV (ABC), Chgo., 1973-76; mgr. dramatic devel. ABC TV, N.Y.C., 1976-77; writer, producer Graffiti; dir. comedy programs NBC Entertainment, Burbank, Calif., 1977-78, v.p. programs, 1978-80, pres., 1980—. Named 1 of 10 Outstanding Young Men Am. U.S. Jaycees, 1981; recipient Tree of Life award Jewish Nat. Found., 1986. Office: NBC-TV 3000 W Alameda Blvd Burbank CA 91523 *

TASAKA, MASAICHI, hospital executive; b. Hilo, Hawaii, Feb. 3, 1925; s. Sunao and Shizue (Katayama) T.; m. Toshiko Kohatsu, Aug. 30, 1952; children—Sharon Lei, Russell Ken. M.S. in Hosp. Adminstrn., Northwestern U., 1955. Bookkeeper, Francis Hiu & Co., 1948-50; bus. mgr. South Shore Hosp., 1950-53; asst. adminstr. Highland Park Hosp., 1955-64; asst. adminstr. Kuakini Med. Ctr., Honolulu, 1964-69, pres., 1969—; asst. prof. Sch. Pub. Health. Mem. Am. Hosp. Assn. (life), Am. Coll. Hosp. Adminstrs., C. of C. of Hawaii, Honolulu Japanese C. of C. Club: Lions. Office: Kuakini Med Ctr 347 N Kuakini St Honolulu HI 96817

TASKER, RICHARD EDWARD, consulting company executive; b. Syracuse, N.Y., July 16, 1952; s. Richard Duane and Eleanor Victoria (Kuhlman) T.; m. Janna Lynn Whitten, July 9, 1984; 1 child, Terra Sage. BS, Syracuse U., 1974; BArch, SUNY-Syracuse, 1975; MBA, U. Fla., 1981. Registered landscape architect, Colo. Contract adminstr., mgr. Cashin and Silverman, Mineola, N.Y., 1975-78; v.p. Cashin Assocs., Denver, 1978-84; pres. Forcon Internat. Ltd., Denver, 1984--. Contbr. articles to mags. Mem. planning bd. City Adv. Bd., Boulder, 1981-84. Mem. Am. Arbitration Assn., Am. Soc. Land Architects. Colo. Soc. Landscape Architects. Republican. Home: 2696 Newland Denver CO 80202 Office: Forcon Internat Ltd 1660 17th St Denver CO 80202

TASLER, JOSEPH WARD, transportation executive, consultant; b. Carrollton, Mo., Sept. 5, 1942; s. Joseph Francis and Roby Ann (Ward) T.; m. Pauline Ruth Lewis, July 27, 1967 (div. May 1988); children: Jonathan, Jason. Ticket agt. Continental Airlines, Kansas City, Mo., 1963-68; dir. passenger svcs. Continental Airlines, L.A., 1970-73, mgr. charter sales dept., 1973-83; v.p. ops. Charter Svcs., Inc., Albuquerque, 1983-86; pres. Tasler Aviation Svcs., Albuquerque, 1986—. Sec. Westlake Village (Calif.) Homeowners Assn., 1980-81. With U.S. Army, 1968-70. Republican. Home: 7215 General Kearney NE Albuquerque NM 87109 Office: Tasler Aviation Svcs PO Box 14851 Albuquerque NM 87191

TATA, GIOVANNI, museum curator; b. Taranto, Italy, Apr. 26, 1954; came to U.S., 1974, naturalized, 1982; s. Vito and Angela (Colucci) T.; m. Brenda Susan Smith, Feb. 14, 1978; children: Elizabeth Ariana, Katherine Allison. BS cum laude (scholar), Brigham Young U., 1977, MA, 1980; grad. cert. area studies U. Utah, 1980; PhD, 1986; postgrad. U. Turin (Italy), 1980-81. Archaeologist, Utah State Hist. Soc., Salt Lake City, 1979; instr. dept. langs. U. Utah, Salt Lake City, 1983-85; Mediterranean specialist Soc. Early Hist. Archaeology, Provo, Utah, 1978—; mus. curator Pioneer Trail State Park, Salt Lake City, 1982-83; instr. dept. art Brigham Young U., Provo, 1982-84; research fellow Direzione Generale per la Cooperazione Scientifica Culturale e Technica, Rome, 1980-81; research curator Utah Mus. Fine Arts, Salt Lake City, 1985—; chmn. 35th Ann. Symposium on the Archaeology of the Scriptures, 1986; pres. Transoft Internat., Inc., 1988—; dir. Taras Publs., Inc., 1987—. Republican. Mem. Ch. Jesus Christ of Latter-day Saints. Mem. Am. Assn. Mus.'s, Coll. Art Assn. Am., Utah Art History Assn., Utah State Hist. Soc. Home: PO Box 8414 Salt Lake City UT 84108 Office: PO Box 960 Orem UT 84057

TATE, DENNIS ARMFIELD, financial planner; b. Kimberly, Idaho, Apr. 30, 1931; s. Ernest W. and Lou Vernia (Savage) T.; m. Blanche Harper, Nov. 16, 1961; children: Shawna, Lisa, Stephanie. BA in Econs., U. Mont., 1958. Registered fin. planner. With Mutual of N.Y., 1961—; financial planner Mutual of N.Y., Missoula, Mont., 1976—. Contbr. numerous articles to profl. jours. First lt. AUS, 1951-53, 56-57, 60-61. Mem. Nat. Assn. Life Underwriters (dir. 1971-73, Health Quality award, Nat. Sales Achievement, Nat. Quality), Internat. Assn. Registered Fin. Planners, Nat. Assn. Registered Reps., Gen. Agts. Mgrs. Assn. (pres. 1973-74), SAR, Rotary, Masons, Shriners, Elks, U. Mont. Alumni Assn. Republican. Home and Office: 317 Westview Dr Missoula MT 59803

TATE, JERRY ALLEN, mechanical engineer; b. De Kalb, Ill., Mar. 10, 1956; s. Kenneth Jean and Doris Jean (Parks) T. BSME, Ariz. State U., 1983. Devel engr. assoc. Allied-Signal Fluid Systems Div., Tempe, Ariz., 1983-84; devel. engr. Allied-Signal Fluid Systems Div., Tempe, 1984-86, sr. devel. engr., 1986—. Co-inventor flow straightener for fluidic devices, 1984. Mem. Soc. Automotive Engrs., Am. Soc. Mech. Engrs., Phi Theta Kappa, Tau Beta Pi, Pi Tau Sigma. Republican. Club: Cen. Ariz. Trials, Inc. (Tempe) (pres. 1987-88).

TATE, SHARON LEE, educator; b. Glendale, Calif., July 19, 1943; d. Patrick Terrance and Irmgard (Bachler) Moore; m. Richard Stephen Kline, June 16, 1985; children by previous marriage: Allison Marie, Kevin Patrick. BS, UCLA, 1964, MA, 1969. Designer Carl Naftal Originals, L.A., 1965-68; asst. buyer J.W. Robinsons, L.A., 1968-70; head design dept. Fashion Inst. of Design & Merchandising, L.A., 1970-74; designer Grayce Baldwin Cons., L.A., 1975-78, Rhodes of Calif., L.A., 1978-82; asst. dean L.A. Trade-Tech. Coll., 1983--. Author: Inside Fashion Design, 1974, The Complete Book of Fashion Illustration, 1981, The Fashion Coloring Book, 1985. Mem. costume coun. L.A. County Mus. Art, 1970--. Mem. Fashion Grp. L.A. (dir. 1970--), L.A. Community Coll. Adminstrs. Assn., Western Horse Exhibitors Assn. Office: LA Trade Tech Coll 400 W Washington Blvd Los Angeles CA 90015

TATMAN, ROBIN REICH, pilot; b. Walnut Creek, Calif., July 21, 1959. AA with honors, Coll. San Mateo (Calif.), 1983; BS, Calif. State U., Hayward, 1985. Sr. patient service rep. Mills Meml. Hosp., San Mateo, 1981-87; pvt. practice flight instrn. West Valley Flying Club, San Mateo, 1986—. Vol. San Mateo Hist. Assn., 1975-82, Planned Parenthood, San Mateo, 1975-85. Mem. Aircraft Owners and Pilots Assn., Air and Space Smithsonian, Calif. Scholarship Fedn. (life mem.). Democrat. Club: Sierra.

TATUM, JOHN BENJAMIN, association executive; b. Anaheim, Calif., July 22, 1968; s. James William and Joni (Bayorek) T. Grad. high sch., Placentia, Calif. chaplain Calif. Assn. Disabled Ministries, La Mirada, 1984—, bd. dirs. disabled Hill Svc.Ministries, Ventura, Calif. Author: Handicapped Ministries, 1986; editor: Calif. Assn. for the Disabled Guide, 1986. Technician Nat. Found.Wheelchair Tennis, Tustin, Calif., 1984—; team walk rep. March of Dimes, Costa Mesa, Calif., 1984—; mem. telethon staff Muscular Dystrophy Assn., Costa Mesa, 1986—; bd. dirs. troop 999 Boy Scouts Am., 1986—. Fellow Calif. Assn. Disabled asst. dir., v.p. 1985—, pres. ops. 1986—, chaplain 1984—, Man of Yr. award 1987); mem. Toastmasters, Omega (founder Ventura, Calif.) Club. Home: 7761 E Northfield Ave Anaheim Hills CA 92807-2417 Office: Calif Assn Disabled 14742 Beach Blvd Ste 183 La Mirada CA 90638-4217

TATUM, THOMAS DESKINS, film and television producer, director; b. Pineville, Ky., Feb. 16, 1946; s. Clinton Turner and Gaynelle (Deskins) T.; m. Laura Ann Smith, Aug. 15, 1968 (div. 1974); m. Suzanne Pettit, Sept. 29, 1983; children: Rhett Cowden, Walker Edwin. Ba, Vanderbilt U., 1968; JD, Emory U., 1974. Bar: Ga. 1974, D.C. 1980. Spl. asst. City of Atlanta, 1974-76; dep. dir. fed. relations Fed. Relations Nat. League of Cities, Washington, 1977-78; dir. communications Office of Conservation and Solar Energy, Washington, 1979-80; chmn. exec. producer Tatum Communications, Inc., L.A., 1981—; chmn., pres. Western Film & Video, Inc., Telluride, Colo., 1987—. Producer feature film Winners Take All, 1987, producer, dir.: (documentary) Double High, 1982 (award), Maui Windsurf, 1983, (home video) Greenpeace in Action; various TV, cable, home video sports programs 1982-88. Dep. campaign mgr. Maynard Jackson, 1973, Jimmy Carter campaign, 1976, staff conf. Dem. Mayors, 1974-75, media cons. Greepeace, 1988; bd. dirs. Atlanta Ballet, v.p., 1975; nat. urban affairs coordinator Carter Mondale campaign 1976, mem. Carter Mondale transition team 1976-77. Mem. Ga. Bar Assn., Washington Bar Assn., Hollywood Film and TV Soc. Presbyterian. Office: Tatum Communications Inc 2920 W Olive Ave Ste 102 Burbank CA 91505

TAUB, BETSY ANN, manufacturing executive; b. N.Y.C., May 23, 1946; d. Morris and Lillian (Weinberg) T. BA, SUNY, New Paltz, 1967; MA, Columbia U., 1969; MBA, Santa Clara (Calif.) U., 1982. Tchr. N.Y.C. Elem. Schs., 1967-68; administr. asst. Marsteller Advt., N.Y.C., 1969-70; customer service positions various orgns., Calif., 1970-78; internat. mktg. asst. Fairchild Semiconductor, Palo Alto, Calif., 1978-84; customer service supr. VLSI Technology, Inc., San Jose, Calif., 1984-85; pub. relations coordinator Amdahl Corp., Sunnyvale, Calif., 1986-87; mktg. analyst Fujitsu Microelectronics, San Jose, 1987—. Mem. Peninsula Profl. Women's Network (bd. dirs. 1988), Assn. MBA Execs., Inc. Office: Fujitsu Microelectronics Inc 3545 N First St Bldg 3 San Jose CA 95134-1804

TAUBE, HENRY, chemistry educator; b. Sask., Can., Nov. 30, 1915; came to U.S., 1937, naturalized, 1942; s. Samuel and Albertina (Tiledetski) T.; m. Mary Alice Wesche, Nov. 27, 1952; children: Linda, Marianna, Heinrich, Karl. B.S., U. Sask., 1935, M.S., 1937, LL.D., 1973; Ph.D., U. Calif., 1940; Ph.D. (hon.), Hebrew U. of Jerusalem, 1979; D.Sc. (hon.), U. Chgo., 1983, Poly. Inst., N.Y., 1984, SUNY, 1985, U. Guelph, 1987; D.Sc. honoris causa, Seton Hall U., 1988, Seton Hall U., Debrecen, Hungary, 1988. Instr. U. Calif., 1940-41; instr., asst. prof. Cornell U., 1941-46; faculty U. Chgo., 1946-62, prof., 1952-62, chmn. dept. chemistry, 1955-59; prof. chemistry Stanford U., 1962—, Marguerite Blake Wilbur prof., 1976, chmn. dept., 1971-74; Baker lectr. Cornell U., 1965. Hon. mem. Hungarian Acad., Scis., 1988. Recipient Harrison Howe award, 1961; Chandler medal Columbia U., 1964; F.P. Dwyer medal U. N.S.W., Australia, 1973; Nat. medal of Sci., 1976, 77; Allied Chem. award for Excellence in Grad. Teaching and Innovative Sci., 1979; Nobel Prize in Chemistry, 1983; Bailar medal U. Ill., 1983; Robert A. Welch Found. Award in chemistry, 1983; Disting. Achievement award Internat. Precious Metals Inst., 1986; Guggenheim fellow, 1949, 55. Fellow Royal Soc. Chemistry (hon.); mem. Am. Acad. Arts and Scis., Nat. Acad. Scis. (award in chem. scis. 1983), Am. Chem. Soc. (Kirkwood award New Haven sect. 1965, award for nuclear applications in chemistry 1955, Nichols medal N.Y. sect. 1971, Willard Gibbs medal Chgo. sect. 1971, Disting. Service in Advancement Inorganic Chemistry award 1967, T.W. Richards medal NE sect. 1980, Monsanto Co. award in inorganic chemistry 1981, Linus Pauling award Puget Sound sect. 1981, Priestley medal 1985, Oesper award Cin. sect. 1986), Royal Physiographical Soc. of Lund (fgn. mem.), Am. Philos. Soc., Finnish Acad. Sci. and Letters, Royal Danish Acad. Scis. and Letters, Coll. Chemists of Catalonia and Beleares (hon.), Can. Soc. Chemistry (hon.), Hungarian Acad. Scis. (hon. mem.), Royal Soc. (fgn. mem.), Phi Beta Kappa, Sigma Xi, Phi Lambda Upsilon (hon.). Office: Stanford U Dept Chemistry Stanford CA 94305

TAUER, PAUL E., mayor, educator; b. 1941; m. Kate Tauer, 1963; 8 children. BS in Edn. Adminstrn., U. No. Colo. Tchr. Denver Pub. Schs., 1961-87. Mayor City of Aurora, Colo., 1987—, mem. Aurora City Coun., from 1981; mem. Adams County Coordinating Com., Gov.'s Met. Transp. Roundtable; active Aurora airport coms. Mem. Noise. Office: Office of Mayor 1470 S Havana St Aurora CO 80012

TAURA, Y., automobile company executive. Pres., chief exec. officer Mazda Motors of Am. (Cen.) Inc., Irvine, Calif. Office: Mazda Motors of Am Cen Inc 7755 Irvine Ctr Dr Irvine CA 92718 *

TAUSCHEK, TERRENCE ALAN, dentist, consultant; b. Cleve., June 29, 1948; s. Max Joseph and Marilyn (Kuhl) T.; m. Debora Jon Farr, June 10, 1972; children: Heather, Megan, Heidi. DDS, Marquette U., 1972. Staff dentist, resident USPHS Hosp., Seattle, 1972-73; staff dentist Alaska Native Med. Ctr., Anchorage, 1973-75; pvt. practice Anchorage, 1975—; mem. staff Surgery Ctr., Inc., 1979—, Providence Hosp., 1975—, chmn. dental staff 1985-86; contract dentist Indian health Svc., Kokhanok and Pedro Bay, Alaska, 1973—; cons., expert witness U.S. Govt. and State of Alaska, 1979—; mem. Alaska Bd. Dental Examiners, 1987—. Recipient svc. award Alaska Native Med. Ctr., 1975, commendation USPHS, 1986, Alaska State Legis., 1987. Mem. ADA, Alaska Dental Soc. (chmn. peer rev. com. 1979-84), South Dental Dist. Dental Soc. Office: Alaska Dental Assocs 1600 E Tudor Rd Ste 201 Anchorage AK 99507

TAUSCHER, WILLIAM YOUNG, pharmaceutical and cosmetic products executive; b. Hyattsville, Md., 1950; s. Gilbert Young and Dorcas (Jones) T.; m. Janet Mariani, Oct. 25, 1975; children: Lauren M., Joseph William. B.S., Yale U., 1972. With mktg. dept. IBM Co., Chgo., 1972-75; computer exec. MST Co., Chgo., 1975-78; pres. Western Textile Co., Chgo., 1978-79; pres. Foxmeyer Corp., Denver, 1979-85, chmn., from 1979; chmn. Computerland Corp., Pleasanton, Calif., 1987—, pres., 1988—; dir. Far Western, San Jose, Calif., Nat. Wholesale Druggists Assn., Washington. Office: Computerland Corp 5964 W Las Positas Blvd PO Box 9012 Pleasanton CA 94566 *

TAVARES, TERRY ALAN, aerospace designer; b. Hollywood, Calif., Feb. 13, 1943; s. Fred T. and Tami Keliihue (Mookini) T.; m. Carole Dene Gray (div. July 1986); children: Greggory Alan, Tam Kealoha; m. Linda Marie Guy. AA, Fullerton Coll., 1962. Sr. design specialist Hughes Aircraft, Fullerton, Calif., 1978-82, sr. devel. engr., 1982-87; sr. cad designer Pacific Electro Dynamics, Redmond, Wash., 1988—. Songwriter: Hey Let's Go Steady, 1961, Stompin' Time, 1961, Won't Somebody Touch Me, 1975, Green Hills of Seattle, 1982, Season's Greeting, 1984. Lobbyist Am. Citizenship Fund, Fullerton, 1980.

TAVEGGIA, THOMAS CHARLES, psychologist, educator; b. Oak Lawn, Ill., June 15, 1943; s. Thomas Angelo and Eunice Louise (Harriss) T.; m. Brigitte I. Adams, Jan. 23, 1965; children—Michaela, Francesca. BS, Ill. Inst. Tech., 1965; MA, U. Oreg., 1968, PhD, 1971. Prof., U. Oreg., Eugene, 1970, U. B.C. (Can.), Vancouver, 1970-73, U. Calif.-Irvine, 1973-74, Ill. Inst. Tech., Chgo., 1974-77; mgmt. cons. Towers, Perrin, Forster & Crosby, Chgo., 1977-80; ptnr. Manplan Cons., Chgo., 1980-81; ptnr. Coopers & Lybrand, San Francisco, 1981-86; ptnr. Touche Ross, San Francisco, 1986-88; prof. Calif. Sch. Profl. Psychology, Berkeley, 1989—. NDEA Title IV fellow, 1967-71; U. B.C. faculty research grantee, 1970, 71, 72. Mem. Acad. Mgmt., Am. Compensation Assn., Am. Soc. Personnel Adminstrn., Inst. Mgmt. Cons. Presbyterian. Author: (with R. Dubin and R. Arends) From Family and School To Work, 1967; (with Dubin) The Teaching-Learning Paradox: A Comparative Analysis of College Teaching Methods, 1968; (with Dubin and R.A. Hedley) The Medium May Be Related to the Message: College Instruction by TV, 1969; contbr. numerous articles to profl. jours. Home: 2188 Lariat Ln Walnut Creek CA 94596 Office: Calif Sch Profl Psychology 1001 Atlantic Ave Alameda CA 94501

TAVERNA, RODNEY ELWARD, retired marine corps officer, marketing company executive; b. Springfield, Ill., Aug. 8, 1947; s. Jerome Thomas and Virginia (Holcomb) T.; m. Cheryl Ann Walters, Sept. 4, 1968 (div. 1983); children: Lara Lyn, Melinda Marie, Ryan Thomas; m. Caroline Whiffen, Apr. 1985. BA, U. Mo., 1969; MBA in Fin., Nat. U., 1988. Commd. 2d lt., supply officer USMC, 1969, advanced through grades to maj., 1979; supply officer Central Svcs. Agy., Danang, Vietnam, 1970-71, Marine Air Control Squadron, Futenma, Okinawa, 1977-78; logistics officer Hdqrs. Marine Corps Recruit Depot, Paris Island, S.C., 1972-75; support officer Marine Barracks, Treasure Island, San Francisco, 1975-77; regimental supply officer 1st Marine Div., Camp Pendleton, Calif., 1978-79; brigade supply officer 1st Marine Brigade, Kaneohe Bay, Hawaii, 1980-82; exec. officer 1st Maintenance Bn., Camp Pendleton, 1982-85; asst div. supply officer 1st Marine Div., 1985-88; owner, mgr. Opportunities Unltd., Oceanside, Calif., 1985--; cons. Incentive leasing Corp., San Diego, 1985-86; founding mgr. Meditrend Internat., San Diego, 1987-88; founding dir. Am. 3-D Corp., 1989—, Henderson, Nev. Republican. Home and Office: 445 Via Emily Oceanside CA 92056

TAVROW, RICHARD LAWRENCE, lawyer, corporate executive; b. Syracuse, N.Y., Feb. 3, 1935; s. Harry and Ida Mary (Hodess) T.; m. Barbara J. Silver, Mar. 22, 1972; children—Joshua Michael, Sara Hallie. A.B. magna cum laude, Harvard U., 1957, LL.B., 1960, LL.M., 1961; postgrad., U. Copenhagen, 1961-62, U. Luxembourg, 1962. Bar: N.Y. bar 1961, U.S. Supreme Ct. bar 1969, Calif. bar 1978. Atty. W.R. Grace & Co., N.Y.C., 1962-66; asst. chief counsel Gen. Dynamics Corp., N.Y.C., 1966-68; chief counsel office of fgn. direct investments U.S. Dept. Commerce, Washington, 1969-71; ptnr. Schaeffer, Dale, Vogel & Tavrow, N.Y.C., 1971-75; v.p., sec., gen. counsel Prudential Lines, Inc., N.Y.C., 1975-78, also bd. dirs.; v.p., sec., gen. counsel Am. Pres. Lines, Ltd., Oakland, Calif., 1978-80, sr. v.p., sec., gen. counsel, 1982—, also bd. dirs.; sr. v.p., sec., gen. counsel Am. Pres. Cos., Ltd., Oakland, 1983—; also bd. dirs. Am. Pres. Cos., Ltd.; instr. Harvard Coll., 1959-61; lectr. Am. Mgmt. Assn., Practising Law Inst. Contbg. author: Private Investors Abroad - Problems and Solutions in International Business, 1970. Recipient Silver Medal award Dept. Commerce, 1970; Fulbright scholar, 1961-62. Mem. ABA, State Bar Calif., Internat. Bar Assn., Am. Soc. Internat. Law, Maritime Law Assn., San Francisco Bar Assn., Asia-Pacific Lawyers Assn., Transp. Lawyers Assn., Am. Steamship Owners Mut. Protection and Indemnity Assn. (dir.), Pacific Mcht. Shipping Assn. (dir., chmn. bd. dirs.), Am. Corp. Counsel Assn., Am. Soc. Corp. Secs. Inc., Assn. Transp. Practitioners, Harvard Law Sch. Assn., Navy League. Democrat. Jewish. Clubs: World Trade; Alpine Hills Swimming and Tennis; Lakeview (Oakland); Harvard (N.Y.C. and San Francisco); Concordia-Argonaut (San Francisco). Office: Am Pres Cos Ltd 1800 Harrison St Oakland CA 94612

TAY, DAVID YEE-CHAW, biochemist; b. Rangoon, Burma, June 28, 1953; came to U.S., 1982; s. Tze-Hwa and Tao-Tzu (Fang) T.; m. Julia Shing-Hung, July 27, 1982. BS in Pharmacy, Nat. Taiwan U., Taipei, 1978; MS in Chemistry, Eastern N.Mex. U., 1984. Registered pharmacist, Taiwan, Calif. Asst. leader Panlabs Taiwan, Ltd., Taipei, 1979-80; pharmacist Cen. Trust of China, Hwalien, Taiwan, 1980-81; research assoc. City of Hope Med. Ctr., Duarte, Calif., 1984—. Contbr. articles to profl. jours. Mem. Am. Chem. Soc. Home: 3818 Durfee Ave #2 El Monte CA 91732 Office: City of Hope Nat Med Ctr Dept Endocrinology Metabolism Diabetes 1550, E Duarte Rd Duarte CA 91010

TAYLOR, ANN, artist; b. Rochester, N.Y., Mar. 23, 1941. Student, Vassar Coll., 1958-61; BA, The New Sch. Social Research, 1962. Pvt. practice Scottsdale, Ariz. One-woman shows include Carl Solway Gallery, Cin., 1964, York Gallery, N.Y.C., 1967, Hunter Gallery, Aspen, Colo., 1970, Christopher Gallery, N.Y.C., 1975, 77, Miller Gallery, Cin., 1978, 83, Munson Gallery, Santa Fe., 1980, Oxford Gallery, Rochester, 1980, 84, 87, 88, C.G. Rein Galleries, Mpls., 1981, Scottsdale, Ariz., 1982, 85, Houston, 1983, Yuma (Ariz.) Art Ctr., 1984, Gallery Henoch, N.Y.C., 1984, Scottsdale Ctr. for Arts, 1985, Kauffman Galleries, Houston, 1986, Marilyn Butler Fine Art, Scottsdale, 1987, others; solo exhibition or solo traveling exhibition: Rochester Mus. and Scis. Ctr., 1984-85, Palm Springs Desert Mus., 1984-85, Yuma Art Ctr., 1984-85, Reed Whipple Cultural Ctr., 1984-85, Scottsdale Ctr. for the Arts, 1984-85, Beaumont Art Mus., 1984-85; exhibited in group shows at Indpls. Ctr. for Contemporary Art, Gallery of Modern Art, N.Y.C., Fine Art Ctr., Tempe, Ariz., Everson Mus., Syracuse,

N.Y., Walton-Gilbert Galleries, San Francisco, Adelle M. Fine Art, Dallas, Janet Fleischer Gallery, Phila., Peter M. David Gallery, Mpls., Mickelson Gallery, Washington, Julia Black Gallery, Taos, N.Mex., Palm Springs Desert Mus., Scottsdale Ctr. for the Arts, Ariz. State U.; represented in permanent collections Eastman Kodak Co., Bank of Am., Houston, Am. Express, Phoenix, Bausch & Lomb, Inc., Rochester, A.C. Nielsen Corp., Chgo., 1st Interstate Bank, Phoenix, Honeywell, Inc., Mpls., Xerox, Rochester, Lincoln Chase Trust Co., Rochester, Third Nat. Bank, Dayton, Ohio, Cen. Trust Co., Cin., Valley Nat. Bank, Phoenix, Butterfield Savs. & Loan, Santa Ana, Calif., Sohio Petroleum Co., Houston, A.C. Neilsen Corp., Chgo., others.

TAYLOR, BLAIR THOMAS, product design company executive; b. Oakland, Mich., Dec. 17, 1961; s. Edward F. and Gail E. (Toepher) T. BS, Art Ctr. Coll. Design, Pasadena, Calif., 1985. Chief designer Action Products, Inc., Tempe, Ariz., 1986-88; chief exec. officer Impact Design and Mfg. Corp., Laguna Niguel, Calif., 1987--; design cons. Columbia Pictures, Hollywood, Calif., 1985, Design West Inc., Mission Viejo, Calif., 1988--; designer Suzuki Co., L.A., 1983-84, Empire Entertainment Co., Hollywood, 1985. Patentee in field. Recipient Achievement award Detroit New Paper, 1979, 80; Lawrence Inst. Tech. scholar, 1980-81. Office: Impact Design and Mfg Group PO Box 7416 Laguna Niguel CA 92677

TAYLOR, BRENDA ELIZABETH, insurance agency manager; b. Des Moines, Aug. 28, 1955; d. Herbert R. and Elizabeth E. (Wolver) T.; m. Michael J. Ideker, 1979 (div. Sept. 1982); m. Gary A. White, Apr. 16, 1983. AA with honors, Mesa Community Coll., 1976. Office mgr. Lee Jones Ins. Agy., Scottsdale, Ariz., 1974-79, 82—; sec., bus. office Taipei (Taiwan) Am. Sch., 1979-82. Big sister, Big Sisters Am., Scottsdale, 1978. Mem. Women's Coun. Realtors (treas. 1984-86, sec. 1986-87), Scottsdale Bd. Realtors (affiliate chmn. 1987-88, MLS com. 1986-88, affiliate of yr. 1987, mem. edn. com. 1986-88). Republican. Methodist. Home: 9073 E Larkspur Dr Scottsdale AZ 85260 Office: Lee Jones Ins Agy 8630 E Via de Ventura Ste 110 Scottsdale AZ 85258

TAYLOR, BRIAN D., art and photography educator, artist; b. Tucson, June 14, 1954; s. Porter C. and Irene Francis (Munaretto) T.; m. Patrice Katherine Garrett, July 28, 1984. BA cum laude, U. Calif., San Diego, 1975; MA, Stanford U., 1976; MFA, U. N.Mex., 1979. Grad. asst. U. N.Mex., Albuquerque, 1976-79; assoc. prof. of Art San Jose (Calif.) State U., 1979—; lectr. various univs., workshops. One-man exhibits include San Jose Mus. Art, 1982, Susan Spiritus Gallery, Newport Beach, Calif., 1983, Ithaca (N.Y.) Coll., 1983, Houston Ctr. Photography, 1984, Nagase Photo Salon, Tokyo, Japan, 1985, Etherton Gallery, Tucson, U. Oreg. Art Mus., Eugene, 1986, James Madison U., Harrisonburg, Va., 1987, Monterey (Calif.) Peninsula Mus. Art, Northlight Gallery, Ariz. State U., Tempe, 1989; represented in permanent collections Bibliotheque Nationale, Paris, Victoria and Albert Mus., London, San Francisco Mus. Modern Art, Australian Photographic Soc., Victoria. Recipient resident artist's grant Polaroid Corp., 1989. Mem. AAUP, Soc. for Photog. Edn., Coll. Art Assn., Phi Kappa Phi, Phi Delta Kappa. Republican. Roman Catholic.

TAYLOR, BRUCE BARRY, physician assistant; b. Newark, Feb. 17, 1951; s. William Henry Taylor and Grace Taylor (Wheeler) Comrade; m. Lubow Irena Lojik, Dec. 18, 1971; children: Jason Matthew, Jared William, Erin Rebecca, Emily Christine, Jordan Bruce. AA, Englewood Cliffs (N.J.) Coll., 1974; BS in Anthropology and Health Scis., Brigham Young U., 1977; BS, SUNY, Stony Brook, 1980; MPH, U. Tenn., 1986. Supr. radiology Utah Valley Regional Med. Ctr., Provo, 1976-78; physician asst. Corpus Christi (Tex.) Health Dept., 1980-81, Nye Gen. Hosp., Tonopah, Nev., 1981-85, U. Ky. Dept. Preventative Medicine and Environ. Health, Lexington, 1985-87, Clinica Sierra Vista, Lamont, Calif., 1987—; cons. physician asst. Cypruss Minerals Co., Denver, 1986-87, Amselco Minerals, Denver, 1987. Contbr. articles to profl. jours. Counselor Harrogate, Tenn. Mormon Ch., 1986-87. Mem. Am. Registry Radiol. Technicians, Am. Pub. Health Assn., Am. Acad. Physician Assts., Nat. Commn. Cert. Physician Assts., Mine Safety and Health Adminstrn. Home: 212 Joelyle St Bakersfield CA 93312

TAYLOR, CHARLES WADE, physician; b. Ada, Okla., June 1, 1956; s. Silas Peter and Ileta Pat (Mitchell) T.; m. Susan Carol Dodd, June 13, 1982. BS in Chemistry, U. Okla., 1978, MD, 1982. Diplomate Nat. Bd. Med. Examiners, Am. Bd. Internal Medicine and Med. Oncology. Intern U. Okla., Oklahoma City, 1982-83, resident internal medicine, 1983-85; fellow med. oncology U. Ariz., Tucson, 1985-88, asst. prof. internal medicine, 1988—. Recipient Clin. Oncology Career Devel. award Am. Cancer Soc., 1988. Mem. AMA, ACP. Office: U Ariz 1501 N Campbell Ave Tucson AZ 85724

TAYLOR, DAVID, product marketing manager; b. South Bend, Ind., Dec. 9, 1957; s. Richard Wayne and Judith Kaye (Clarke) T.; m. Elizabeth Helen Christensen , Aug. 21, 1982; children: Stephen, Scott, Tracie. BS in Bus., Portland (Oreg.) State U., 1982. Line supr. Intel Corp., Portland, 1977-79; trainer Intel Corp., 1979-80, lab. mgr., 1980-83, ops. supr., 1983-85, product mgr., 1985-87, product mktg. mgr., 1988—. Contbr. articles on computer industry trends and mktg. to profl. jours. Mem. Am. Mktg. Assn. Republican. Roman Catholic. Home: 14730 SW Surrey Ct Beaverton OR 97006 Office: Intel Corp 5200 NE Elam Young, Co3-04 Hillsboro OR 97124

TAYLOR, DENNIS RILEY, chemist, researcher; b. Eureka, Calif., May 5, 1941; s. Walter Riley and Lenora May (Viale) T.; m. Georgie Ann Cherry, July 17, 1965; children: Noelani Ann, Sean Riley. AA, Am. River Jr. Coll., 1959-61; BS, U. Calif., Davis, 1963; PhD, U. Oreg., 1967. Sr. chemist, research chemist Texaco, Inc., Beacon, N.Y., 1968-74; mgr. research and devel. Filtrol, Inc., Los Angeles, 1974-80; mgr. rsch. and devel. Harshaw-Filtrol Co., Pleasanton, Calif., 1980-88; dir. rsch. and devel. Kaiser Ctr. for Tech., Pleasanton, 1988—; rsch. assoc. Engelhand Corp., Menlo Park, N.J. Contbr. articles to profl. jours.; patentee in field. Office: Kaiser Ctr for Tech PO Box 877 Pleasanton CA 94566

TAYLOR, DONALD J., oil industry executive. B. Com., U. Alta., 1955. Currently exec. v.p. Shell Can. Ltd., Calgary; pres. Shell Can. Products Ltd., Calgary. Office: Shell Can Ltd, 400 4th Ave SW, Calgary, AB Canada T2P 0J4

TAYLOR, DOUGLAS GRAHAM, Canadian provincial minister and member legislative assembly; b. Wolseley, Sask., Can., July 4, 1936; s. Robert Douglas and Isabella Roy (Graham) T.; m. Katherine Isabel Garden, Oct. 3, 1959; children—Robert Douglas, Katherine Isabel Marie, Susan Joan, Peter Samuel. B.Ed., U. Regina (Sask.), 1966, Diploma in Ednl. Adminstrn., 1972. Tchr. Kipling (Sask.) High Sch., 1962-64; prin. Wolseley High Sch., 1967-79; mem. Sask. Legis. Assembly for Indian Head-Wolseley, 1979—, minister of health, opposition house leader, 1979, opposition critic for edn. and continuing edn., minister of tourism and small bus., minister-in-charge Sask. Property Mgmt. Corp. (formerly dept. Supply and Services), Sask. Econ. Devel. Corp., No. Affairs Secretariat, Higher Control Bd., Liquor Commn.; mem Cabinet planning and priority coms.; Founder Qu'Appelle Valley Sci. Fair, Sask. Mem. Indian Head Superintendency Tchrs.' Assn., pres., Qu'Appelle Valley Prins.' Assn. Progressive Conservative. Mem. United Ch. of Canada. Club: Lions (Wolseley). Office: Legis Assembly, Legislative Bldg Rm 38, Regina, SK Canada S4S 0B3

TAYLOR, FREDERICK CLAYTON, infosystems specialist, consultant, musician; b. Spokane, Wash., July 2, 1954; s. David Edwards and Alice (Butterworth) T.; m. Linda Schoolcraft, Nov. 4, 1973 (div. July 1975); m. Katherine M.T. Chevrier, Nov. 8, 1980; children: Alexander, Diane. Student, Olympic Coll., Bremerton, Wash., 1972-73, Seattle Cen. Community Coll., 1980. Traffic mgr. Taylor-Edwards Warehouse & Transfer Co., Seattle, 1976-87, data processing mgr., 1984-87; computer cons. Taylor MISystems, Seattle, 1987—; gen. mgr. Taylor-Edwards, Inc., Seattle, 1987—. Author musical recording Court of Circe, 1982. Mem. Data Processing Mgmt. Assn., Am. Fedn. of Musicians, Percussive Arts Soc. Republican. Club: Wash. Athletic (Seattle). Office: Taylor-Edwards Inc 1930-6th Ave S #103 Seattle WA 98134

TAYLOR, GRAHAM, Canadian provincial government official. Minister of health Govt. of Saskatchewan, Regina, Can., 1982-86; minister of tourism, small bus. and cooperatives Govt. of Saskatchewan, Regina, 1986-88, minister of pub. participation, 1988—. Office: Cabinet of Sask, Legislative Bldg, Regina, SK Canada S4S 0B3

TAYLOR, HOWARD HARPER, lawyer; b. Detroit, June 5, 1926; s. Howard Francis and Helen (Hawken) T.; m. Mary L. Maddox, Mar. 28, 1953 (div. Oct. 1967); 1 child, Steven. BA, Stanford U., 1949, JD, 1951. Bar: Calif. 1952., U.S. Dist. Ct. (so. dist.) Calif. 1952. Sole practice San Diego, 1952—; instr. bus. law and real estate law Mesa Coll., San Diego, 1962—. Editor Stanford U. Law Rev., 1950-51. Served to petty officer 3d class USN, 1944-46, PTO. Mem. ABA, Calif. Bar Assn., San Diego County Bar Assn. Republican. Lodge: Masons, Shriners. Home: 980 Scott St San Diego CA 92106 Office: 1200 3d Ave Ste 1200 San Diego CA 92101

TAYLOR, IRVING, mechanical engineer, consultant; b. Schenectady, N.Y., Oct. 25, 1912; s. John Bellamy and Marcia Estabrook (Jones) T.; m. Shirley Ann Milker, Dec. 22, 1943; children: Bronwen D., Marcia L., John I., Jerome E. BME, Cornell U., 1934. Registered profl. engr., N.Y., Mass., Calif. Test engr. Gen. Electric Co., Lynn, Mass., 1934-37; asst. mech. engr. M.W. Kellogg Co., N.Y.C., 1937-39; sect. head engring. dept. The Lummus Co., N.Y.C., 1939-57; research engr. Gilbert and Barker, West Springfield, Mass., 1957-58, Marquardt Corp., Ogden, Utah, 1958-60, Bechtel, Inc., San Francisco, 1960-77; cons. engr. Berkeley, Calif., 1977—; adj. prof. Columbia U., 1950-60, NYU, 1950-60. Contbr. articles to profl. jours. Mem. ASME (life), Pacific Energy Assn., Soaring Soc. Am. (life), Sigma Xi (assoc.). Unitarian. Home: 1150 Keeler Ave Berkeley CA 94708

TAYLOR, JAMES ELLSWORTH, real estate executive, mortgage banker; b. San Diego, Mar. 21, 1953; s. Gerry Eugene and MAry (Wayne) T.; m. Susan Kneelange (div.); children: Joel Ellsworth, Kyle Houston; m. Sally Lucia Cobbs, Feb. 18, 1988. Student, Grossmont Coll., 1972-74; AS, Cuamaca Coll., 1977; student, San Diego State Coll., 1973-75, U. LaVerne, 1976. Lic. real estate broker, Calif.; cert. real estate appraiser, Calif. Owner T & H Tire Co., El Cajon, Calif., 1974-76; real estate agt. Century 21- Mt. Helix, LaMesa, Calif., 1976-78; broker, mgr. CalWest Properties, LaMesa, 1980-83; v.p. Westend Realty Corp., San Diego, 1983-85, exec. v.p., 1985-87; pres. J. Ellsworth and Assoc. Inc., LaMesa, 1987—; counsel mem. Grossmont Coll., El Cajon, 1974. Author: S.D. Foreclosure Manual, 1983. Mem. San Diego Multiple Listing Service, LaMesa C. of C., Appraisal Soc., Exchange Club (LaMesa). Republican. Lutheran. Office: J Ellsworth and Assoc Inc 7777 Alvarado Rd Ste 265 La Mesa CA 92041

TAYLOR, JAMES WALTER, marketing professor; b. St. Cloud, Minn., Feb. 15, 1933; s. James T. and Nina C. Taylor; m. Joanne Syktte, Feb. 3, 1956; children: Theodore James, Samuel Bennett, Christopher John. BBA, U. Minn., 1957; MBA, NYU, 1960; DBA, U. So. Calif., 1975. Mgr. research div. Atlantic Refining, Phila., 1960-65; dir. new product devel. Hunt-Wesson Foods, Fullerton, Calif., 1965-72; prof. mktg. Calif. State U., Fullerton, 1972—; cons. Chint/Day Advt., 1982—, Smithkline Beckman Corp., Phila. , 1972—, Govt. of Portugal, Lisbon, 1987—. Author: Profitable New Product Strategies, 1984, How To Create A Winning Business Plan, 1986, Competitive Marketing Strategies, 1986, The 101 Best Performing Companies In America, 1987, How to Write A Successful Advertising Plan, 1988, The Complete Manual for Developing Winning Strategic Plans, 1988, Every Manager's Survival Guide, 1989. Fulbright scholar Ministry of Industry, Lisbon, Portugal, 1986-87; recipient Merit award Calif. State U., 1986-89. Mem. North Am. Soc. Corp. Planners, Am. Mktg. Assn., Strategic Mgmt. Assn., Assn. for Consumer Research, Acad. Mktg. Sci. Home: 3190 Mountain View Dr Laguna Beach CA 92651 Office: Calif State U Dept of Mktg Nutwood at State College Fullerton CA 92634

TAYLOR, JEFFREY LYNN, engineer; b. Bellefontaine, Ohio, Oct. 16, 1952; s. Max A. and Kathryn (Strathman) T.; m. Ann L. Miller, June 8, 1974 (div. May 1987); children: Amanda, Abby; m. Georgann Seibert, May 6, 1989. BS, Wright's State U., Dayton, Ohio, 1975; MS, U. Dayton, 1985. Registered profl. engr., Ohio. Mech. design engr. Wright Patterson Air Force Base, Dayton, 1975-81; energy engr. Control Data Corp., Dayton, 1981-86; application engr. Control Data Corp., Los Alamos, N.Mex., 1986—; cons. Los Alamos Nat. Lab., 1986—. Mem. ASHRACE. Republican. Roman Catholic. Home: 956 Camino Oraibi Santa Fe NM 87501

TAYLOR, JENNIFER HO, nurse; b. L.A., Aug. 1, 1960; d. John Arthur and Frances (King) Ho; m. Gregory Michael Taylor, June 8, 1986. BS in Nursing, Loma Linda U., 1983. R.N., Calif. Pub. health nurse Riverside (Calif.) County, 1984-86; nurse cons. Aetna Life & Casualty Co., Portland, Oreg., 1986-87; home health nurse Carevision Home Health Agy., Ridgerest, Calif., 1987-88; pub. health nurse Kern County, Ridgecrest, 1988—; vol. vis. nurse, U.S. Navy Relief, China Lake, Calif., 1987—. Home: 1310 Ticonderoga St Ridgecrest CA 93555 Office: Kern County Dept Health 250 W Ridgecrest Blvd Ridgecrest CA 93555

TAYLOR, JOAN CITTY, bookkeeping service executive, artist; b. Amarillo, Tex., May 25, 1929; d. Noel Floyd Franklin and Gertrude Keith (Irby) Citty; m. Lawrence William Taylor, Oct. 30, 1948; children: Linda Kathleen Taylor Cook, Sara Lynne Taylor Wood, Jane Ellen Taylor Kelley, Laura Joan. BA, West Tex. State U., 1968, MA, 1975. Cert. tchr., Tex. Bookkeeper Roswell (N.Mex.) State Bank, 1948, JayTee Bookeeping Svc., Roswell, 1988—; tchr. Amarillo Ind. Sch. Dist., 1968-80; substitute tchr. Roswell Ind. Sch. Dist., 1980-82; art instr. Life Long Scholars Program, Roswell, 1982-85; part time instr. Ea. N.Mex. State U., Roswell, 1986—. One-man show Amarillo Savs. and Loan, 1966, Southwestern Pub. Svc. Ctr., Amarillo, 1969. Dir. publ. staff Crockett Jr. High Sch., Amarillo, 1971-80; phone mgr. Rep. Party, Roswell, 1986. Mem. Tex. State Tchrs. Assn. (life mem.), DAR, Roswell Story League, Phi Theta Kappa. Home and Office: 3300 Highland Rd Roswell NM 88201

TAYLOR, JOANN MALONE, research color scientist; b. Abington, Pa.. BS in Chemistry, Rensselaer Poly. Inst., 1981, MS in Chem. & Color Sci., 1983, Phd in Chem. & Color Sci., 1984. Research fellow Color Measurement Lab., Rensselaer Poly. Inst., Troy, N.Y., 1980-84; research scientist Tektronix, Inc., Beaverton, Oreg., 1985--. Contbr. articles to profl. jours. Mem. Inter. Soc. Color Council, Am. Chem. Soc., Soc. for Info. Display, Council for Optical Radiation Measurements, Sigma Xi, Phi Lambda Upsilon. Office: Tektronix Inc PO Box 500 M/S 50-320 Beaverton OR 97077

TAYLOR, JOHN FELTON, II (JACK TAYLOR), insurance company executive; b. San Francisco, Feb. 10, 1925; s. John Felton Sr. and Mary Madeline (Sicocan) T.; m. Wilburta Estelle Prather, Oct. 23, 1948; children: Stephanie, Sharon, Suzanne, Stacie, John III, Saundra, Shelby. BA, San Jose State U., 1950. Dist. mgr. Farmers Ins. Group Cos., San Jose, Calif., 1952--. Mem. bd. fellows U.Santa Clara. 1st lt. USAAF, 1943-46, PTO. Mem. Saratoga Men's Club (Calif.), La Rinconda Country Club (Los Gatos, Calif.), Spyglass Hill Country Club, Monterey Peninsula Country Club (Pebble Beach, Calif.), PGA West Country Club (La Quinta, Calif.). Republican. Roman Catholic. Home: 13177 Ten Oak Ct Saratoga CA 95070 Office: Farmers Ins Group Cos 1471 Saratoga Ave San Jose CA 95129

TAYLOR, KAREN TANDY, grants and development executive; b. Mpls., Apr. 10, 1963; d. Thomas Kenneth and Nancy Ann (Schrock) T. BA, Earlham Coll., 1985. Exec. sec. Pacific Northwest Ballet, Seattle, 1985--, grants coordinator, 1987--, grants mgr., 1988--. Contbr. articles to profl. newsletter, mags. Bd. dirs. Pride Found., Beyond Dance. Mem. Northwest Devel. Officers Assn.

TAYLOR, KENDRICK JAY, microbiologist; b. Manhattan, Mont., Mar. 17, 1914; s. William Henry and Rose (Carney) T.; B.S., Mont. State U., 1938; postgrad. (fellow) U. Wash., 1938-41, U. Calif. at Berkeley, 1952, Drama Studio of London, 1985; m. Hazel Marguerite Griffith, July 28, 1945; children: Stanley, Paul, Richard. Research microbiologist Cutter Labs., Berkeley, Calif., 1945-74; microbiologist Berkeley Biologicals, 1975-86. Committeeman Mount Diablo council Boy Scouts Am., 1955, dist. vice-chmn., 1960-61, dist. chmn., 1962-65, cubmaster, 1957, scoutmaster, 1966; active Contact Ministries, 1977-80; bd. dirs. Santa Clara Community Players, 1980-84; vol. instr. English as a Second Lang., 1979-80; vol. ARC Blood Ctr., VA Hosp., San Jose. Served with AUS, 1941-46, lt. col. Res., ret. Recipient Scout's Wood badge Boy Scouts Am., 1962; recipient Golden Diploma Mont. State U., 1988. Mem. Am. Soc. Microbiology (chmn. local com. 1953, v.p. No. Calif. br. 1963-65, pres. 1965-67), Sons and Daus. Mont. Pioneers. Presbyterian (trustee 1951-53, elder 1954—). Home: 550 S 13th St San Jose CA 95112

TAYLOR, KIM Y., physician; b. Salt Lake City, Apr. 27, 1937; s. Harris Dale and Edna (FAcer) T.; m. Carolyn Watrous, Sept. 19, 1958;. BA, U. Utah, 1958; MD, U. Utah, S.L.C., 1981. Medical intern L.D.S. Hosp., Salt Lake City, 1961-62; flight surgeon USAF, Lockbourn AFB, Ohio, 1962-64; resident in opthalmology U. Calif., San Francisco, 1964-65; fellow in ophthalmology U. Calif., Sacramento, 1964-67, resident in ophthalmology, 1966-67; ophthalmologist Salt Lake Clinic, 1967-69; pvt. practice ophthalmologist, Salt Lake City, 1969—; asst. clin. prof. ophthalmology U. Utah, Salt Lake City. Chmn. med. adv. bd. Nat. Soc. to Prevent Blindness, Salt Lake City, 1968-87. Fellow Am. Acad. Ophthalmology, Am. Bd. Ophthalmology, Am. Med. Assn. Republican. Home: 1650 E 1700 S Salt Lake City UT 84105 Office: 750 E 100 S Salt Lake City UT 84102

TAYLOR, LEIGHTON ROBERT, JR., museum administrator; b. Glendale, Calif., Nov. 17, 1940; s. Leighton Robert and Mary A. (Highberger) T.; m. Linda Louise Puder, Feb. 2, 1963; children: Leighton, Maria Louise. BBA, Occidental Coll., 1962; MS, U. Hawaii, 1965; PhD, Scripps Instn. Oceanography, 1972; MBA, Chaminade U., 1985. Mus. curator Scripps Instn. Oceanography, 1971-72; mem. grad. faculty dept. zoology U. Hawaii, Honolulu, 1972— , dir. Waikiki Aquarium, 1975-86; fishery biologist U.S. Fish and Wildlife Service, Honolulu, 1972-75; dep. exec. dir. Calif. Acad. Scis., San Francisco, 1986-88; research assoc. Calif. Acad. Scis. Contbr. articles to profl. jours. Bd. dirs. Lahaina Restoration Found., 1976—; pres. Hawaiian Islands Aquarium Corp., 1984-86. Fellow Am. Assn. Zool. Parks and Aquariums; mem. Bishop Mus. Assn., Hawaii Small Bus. Assn., Explorers Club, Western Soc. Naturalists, Am. Miscellaneous Soc. Clubs: Bohemian, Outrigger Canoe. Office: Leighton Taylor & Assocs PO Box 1417 Sausalito CA 94966

TAYLOR, LESLIE GEORGE, mining company executive; b. London, Oct. 8, 1922; came to U.S., 1925; s. Charles Henry and Florence Louisa (Renouf) T.; m. Monique S. Schuster, May, 1964 (div. 1974); children: Leslie G. Anthony II, Sandra J. Mira, Linda S. Marshall; m. Wendy Ann Ward, July 4, 1979. BBA, U. Buffalo, 1952. Asst. to pres. Kelsey Co., 1952-60; pres. Aluminum Industries and Glen Alden Co., Cin. and N.Y.C., 1960-63; pres., chmn. bd. dirs. DC Internat. (and European subs.), Denver, 1963-68; prin. Taylor Energy Enterprises, Denver, 1968—, Taylor Mining Enterprises, Denver, 1968—, Leslie G. Taylor and Co., Denver, 1968—; pres., bd. dirs. Lucky Break Gold, Inc. and Aberdeen Minerals, Ltd., Vancouver, B.C., Can.; del. Internat. Astronautical Soc., Stockholm, 1968, London, 1969, Speditur Conv., 1976. Mem. USCG Aux. Mem. Soc. Automotive Engrs., Denver Country Club, Shriners, Masons, Scottish Rites. Republican. Episcopalian. Office: 5031 S Ulster Pkwy Ste 200 Denver CO 80237

TAYLOR, LINDAJEAN THORTON, information systems executive; b. Cambridge, Mass., Apr. 16, 1942; d. Ferdinand and Hazel Irene (Towne) Karamanoukian; m. John Robert Thornton, Jan. 21, 1961; 1 child, John Robert; m. 2d, F. Jason Gaskell, Nov. 30, 1978. Cert. systems profl., quality analyst. AA in Bus. Adminstrn., West Los Angeles Coll., 1976; BS, West Coast U., 1978, MS in Bus. and Info. Scis., 1980. Cert. quality analyst, systems profl. Asst. to chief indsl. engr. Pitts. Plate Glass Co., Boston, 1960-64; corp. sec., gen. mgr. Seaboard Planning Corp., Boston, 1967-67, Los Angeles, 1969-72; prin. Tay-Kara Mgmt., Los Angeles, 1972-73; chief systems adminstrn. Comp-La, Los Angeles, 1973-74; mgr. systems analysis Trans Tech Inc., Los Angeles, 1974-77; mgr. software engring. and tech. audit depts. System Devel. Corp., Los Angeles, 1977-81; v.p. Gaskell and Taylor Engring., Inc., Los Angeles, 1981-86; pres. Taylor and Zeno Systems, Inc., 1986—; mem. faculty, sr. lectr. West Coast U., Los Angeles, 1980—; vis. lectr. sr. seminar Calif. Poly. U., Pomona, 1978, 87-89; del. 11th World Computing Congress, San Francisco, Internat. Fedn. Info. Processing; leader ednl. exchange del to People's Republic China; del. to 10th World Computing Congress, Internat. Fedn. Info. Processing, Dublin, Ireland, 1986; keynote speaker Hong Kong Computer Soc., Hong Kong Assn. for Advancement Sci. and Tech., 1987, NEC Inc. Software Engring. Lab., Tokyo, 1987. Appeared in 8 episodes of The New Literacy: An Introduction to Computers, Pub. Broadcasting System; mem. editorial bd.: Data Processing Quality jour. Chmn. bus. and profl. women's com. Calif. Rep. Cen. Com., 1974; mem. White House Com. on Workers Compensation, 1976; mem. fiscal adv. com. Santa Monica Unified Sch. Bd. Edn., 1979-81. Recipient Pub. Service award West Los Angeles C. of C., 1974. Mem. Assn. Women in Computing (pres. 1980-84, v.p. Los Angeles chpt. 1979-80), Nat. Computer Conf. (vice chmn., program com. 1980, mem. adv. com. 1983), Data Processing Mgmt. Assn. (v.p. South Bay chpt. 1979-80, bd. dirs. Los Angeles chpt. 1984, chmn. program com., media relations com. 1984 internat. conf., Individual Performance awards), IEEE (software engring. terminology task force 1980), Assn. Systems Mgmt. (sec. local chpt. 1974-75), EDP Auditors Assn., Assn. for Computing Machinery, Women in Mgmt., Nat. Assn. Women Bus. Owners, Ind. Computer Cons. Assn., Inst. for Cert. of Computer Profls. (cert., bd. dirs.). Office: Taylor & Zeno Systems Inc 2040 Ave of the Stars Ste 400 Los Angeles CA 90067

TAYLOR, LOUIS HENRY, laboratory geologist; b. Albion, Pa., Feb. 2, 1944; s. Stanley Mearl and Doris Aleen (Redfoot) T.; m. Mary Jean Soine, Dec. 21, 1971; 1 child, Taito Clayton. BS, Edinboro State Coll., 1965; MA, No. Ariz. U., 1971; MS, U. Ariz., 1977, PhD, 1984. Tchr. NW High Sch., Albion, 1965-71; instr. Cen. Ariz. Coll., Coolidge, Ariz., 1971-74; lab. geologist Texaco Inc., Midland, Tex., 1981-84, Denver, 1984—. Contbr. articles to profl. jours. Mem. Soc. Econ. Paleontologists and Mineralogists (sec. Permian Basin Sect. 1983), Western Interior Paleontological Soc. (pres. 1988), Am. Assn. Petroleum Geologists, Paleontology Soc., Soc. Vertebrate Paleontology, Rocky Mountain Assn. Geologists. Democrat. Home: 6266 W Coalmine Pl Littleton CO 80123 Office: Texaco Inc 4601 DTC Blvd Denver CO 80237

TAYLOR, MARGUERITE FAYE, academic administrator; b. Roswell, N. Mex., Feb. 23, 1935; d. John Robert and Alice Marguerite (Gordon) Wilhite; m. Liam R.A. McCurry III. BA in Journalism, U. N. Mex., 1974, MA in Pub. Adminstrn., 1976, PhD in Health Edn., 1980. Dir. med. ctr. pub. info. U. N. Mex., Albuquerque, 1976-80, dir. devel., pub. affairs, 1981-85; rsch. specialist NIH, Bethesda, Md., 1980-81; exec. dir. coll. advancement Stephens Coll., Columbia, Mo., 1985-86; exec. dir. univ. advancement Calif. State U., Sacramento, 1986—. chmn. Med. Alert Found., N. Mex., 1982-85; bd. dirs. Lovelace Health Plan, Albuquerque, 1982-85; pres. Nat. Health Agys. N. Mex., 1985. Recipient John P. McGovern scholarship Eta Sigma Gamma, 1979. Mem. Coun. Advancement and Support Edn. (judge 1985), Assn. Am. Med. Colls. (nat. sec. 1974-75, chmn. western region 1978), N. Mex. Wellness Assn. (bd. dirs. 1982-85), Am. Cancer Soc. (chmn. N. Mex. Smokeout 1982). Episcopalian. Home: 8366 Mediterranean Way Sacramento CA 95826 Office: Calif State U Sacramento CA 95819

TAYLOR, MARK, educational and telecommunications consultant; b. Linden, Mich., Aug. 15, 1927; s. George Wilton Huebler-Taylor and Constance (Page) Chinery. BA, U. Mich., 1950, MLS, 1952; MEd, U. So. Calif., 1972, PhD, 1976. Asst. libr. Elem. Sch. U. Mich., Ann Arbor, 1950-56; broadcaster Broadcasting Svc. U. Mich., Ann Arbor, 1950-56; dir. young adult svcs. Dayton (Ohio) and Montgomery County Pub. Libr., 1957-60; prof. Sch. Libr. Sci. U. So. Calif., L.A., 1960-70; children's book columnist L.A. Times, 1962-70; producer, performer CBS-Hollywood (Stas. KNXT, KNX-TV) Tell It Again program, L.A., 1962-64; author in residence for schs. and librs., nationwide, 1960—; founding mem. So. Calif. Coun. Lit. Children and Young People, L.A., 1961. Author: (children's books) Henry series, 1966-88, The Bold Fisherman, 1967, Time for Flowers, 1967, Old Woman and Pedlar, 1969, Old Blue, You Good Dog You, 1970, Wind in my Hand, 1970, Bobby Shafto's Gone to Sea, 1970, Time for Old Magic, 1970, Time for New Magic, 1971, Fisherman and Goblet, 1971, Lamb, Said the Lion, I am Here, 1972, Wind's Child, 1973, Jennie Jenkins, 1975, Case of Missing Kittens, 1978, Young Melvin on the Road, 1980, Cabbage Patch

Kids Books (4), 1983, Mr. Pepper Stories, 1984, Care Bear Cousins Books (2), 1984, Case of the Purloined Compass, 1985, Maxie's Mystery Files, 1987 (with Eleanore Hartson), Troll Family Stories (6), Cora Cow Tales (6), Adventures of Pippin (6), San Francisco Cat, 1987, Space Monster Mysteries (with Adams and Hartson), 1987, Beginning-to-Read Fairy Tales (with Hartson), 1987, God, I Listened: The Life Story of Eula McClaney, 1981, (film and TV) President is Missing, Manhattan Magic (The Jeffersons, Lion to Kill, Star Traveler, Summerwind, (textbooks) Understanding Your Language, 1968 (3 vol.), Pathfinder Series, 1978; contbr. articles to profl. jours. Recipient Dutton-Macrae award E.P. Dutton Pub., N.Y.C., 1956, award as author of an outstanding series of books So. Cal. Coun. Lit. for Children and Young People, 1977. Mem. ALA, PEN, ASCAP, AFTRA, Reading is Fundamental So. Calif. (chmn. bd. 1984—), Am. Ctr. Films and TV Children (juror 1985-86), Amnesty Internat., Freedom to Read Found., Internat. Reading Assn., Calif. Libr. Assn., Nat. Coun. Tchrs. English, Assn. Childhhod Edn. Internat., Ohio Libr. Assn., Mich. Libr. Assn., Am. Inst. Graphic Arts, Internat. Folk Music Coun., Am. Fedn. Musicians, Harp Soc. Am., So. Calif. Coun. Lit. Children and Young People (past v.p., founding mem.). Office: Jane Jordan Browne Multimedia Product Devel 410 S Michigan Ave Ste 724 Chicago IL 60605

TAYLOR, MARY ELIZABETH, dietitian; b. Medina, N.Y., Dec. 10, 1933; d. Glenn Aaron and Viola Hazel (Lansill) Grimes; m. Wilbur Alvin Fredlund, Apr. 12, 1952 (div. Jan. 1980); 1 child, Wilbur Jr.; m. Frederick Herbert Taylor, Mar. 15, 1981; children: Martha Dayton, Jean Grout, Beth Stern, Cindy Hey, Carol McLellan, Cheryl, Robert. BS in Food and Nutrition, SUCB, Buffalo, 1973; MEd in Health Sci. Edn. and Evaluation, SUNY, 1978. Registered dietitian, 1977. Diet cook Niagara Sanitorium, Lockport, N.Y., 1953-56; cook Mount View Hosp., Lockport, N.Y., 1956-60, asst. dietitian, 1960-73, dietitian, food svc. dir., 1973-79, cons. dietitian, 1979-81; instr. Erie Community Coll., Williamsville, N.Y., 1979-81; sch. lunch coord. Nye County Sch. Dist., Tonopah, Nev., 1982—; cons. dietitian Nye Gen. Hosp., Tonopah, 1983-88; adj. instr. Erie Community Coll., Williamsville, 1978-79; cons. Group Purchasing Western N.Y. Hosp. Administrs., Buffalo, 1975-79, vice-chmn. adv. com., 1976-78; cons. BOCES, Lockport, 1979-81. Nutrition counselor Migrant Workers Clinic, Lockports, 1974-80; mem. Western N.Y. Soc. for Hosp. Food Svc. Adminstrn., 1974-81; nutritionist Niagra County Nutrition Adv. Com., 1977-81. Recipient Outstanding Woman of the Yr. for Contributions in the field of Health award YWCA-UAW Lockport, 1981, Disting. Health Care Food Adminstrn. Recognition award Am. Soc. for Hosp. Food Svc. Adminstrs., Chgo., 1979, USDA award for Outstanding Lunch Program in Nev. and Western Region, 1986. Mem. Am. Dietitic Assn., Nev. State Dietitic Assn., So. Nev. Dietitic Assn., Nutrition Today Soc., Am. Sch. Food Svc. Assn. (bd. drs. 1987). Republican. Baptist. Home: 481 N Murphy PO Box 656 Pahrump NV 89041 Office: Nye County Sch Dist Mil Circle PO Box 113 Tonopah NV 89049

TAYLOR, MICHAEL JAMES, engineering and construction company executive; b. Des Moines, June 20, 1941; s. Robert Phillip and Evelyn (Brown) T.; m. Judith Brissette, Dec. 27, 1966; children: Jason Edmond, Bryan Michael, Jennifer Marie. BSCE, Carnegie Mellon, 1963; MSCE, Carnegie Mellon U., 1965. Registered profl. engr., Colo., Ill., Md., Mich., Minn., Mont., Nev., N.Mex., N.D., Ohio, Pa., Va., W.Va., Wyo. Engr. E. D'Appolonia, Pitts., 1964-65, from asst. project engr. to asst. project mgr., 1967-76; project mgr., v.p. tech. E. D'Appolonia, Denver, 1976-83; from v.p. to exec. v.p. Canonie Environ. Service Corp., Denver, 1983—. Contbr. articles to profl. jours.; chpts. to books; patentee in field. Served to lt. C.E., U.S. Army, 1965-67. Mem. ASCE, Am. Inst. Mining Engrs. Home: 9807 E Bayou Ridge Trail Parker CO 80134 Office: Canonie Environ Svc Corp 94 Inverness Terr E #100 Englewood CO 80112

TAYLOR, PATRICK JAMES, civil engineer; b. Gallup, N.Mex., Apr. 30, 1957; s. Herbert John and Barbara (Lebeck) T.; m. Amalia Elvira Barrios, Jan. 15, 1983. BSCE, Ariz. State U., 1979. Registered profl. engr., Calif. Civil and structural engr. Brooks Engring. Co., Fresno, Calif., 1980; structural engr. Structcon, Fresno, 1980-83, Nowak-Meulmester & Assocs., San Diego, 1983-85; prin. Patrick Taylor Cons., San Diego, 1985-86; civil and structural engr. Navy Pub. Works Ctr., San Diego, 1986—; cons. in field. Mem. PWC Architects and Engrs. Assn. Democrat. Episcopalian. Home: 7447 New Salem St San Diego CA 92126-2066 Office: Navy Pub Works Ctr Naval Sta PO Box 113 San Diego CA 92136

TAYLOR, PETER VAN VOORHEES, advertising and public relations consultant; b. Montclair, N.J., Aug. 25, 1934; s. John Coard and Mildred (McLaughlin) T.; BA in English, Duke U., 1956; m. Janet Kristine Kirkebo, Nov. 4, 1978; 1 son, John Coard III. Announcer, Sta. WQAM, Miami, 1956; announcer, program dir. Sta. KHVH, Honolulu, 1959-61; promotion mgr. Sta. KPEN, San Francisco, 1962; with Kaiser Broadcasting, 1962-74, GE Broadcasting Co., 1974-78; program/ops. mgr. Sta. KFOG, San Francisco, 1962-66; mgr. Sta. WXHR AM/FM, Cambridge, Mass., 1966-67; gen. mgr. Sta. WJIB, Boston, 1967-70; v.p., mgr. FM div. Kaiser Broadcasting, 1969-72; v.p., gen. mgr. Sta. KFOG, San Francisco, 1970-78; pres. Taylor Communications, 1978—, No. Calif. Broadcasters Assn., 1975-77, Broadcast Skills Bank, 1975-76. Trustee, WDBS, Inc., Duke U., 1974-80; bd. dirs. San Francisco Better Bus. Bur., 1976-78, 89—. Lt. USCGR, 1957-63. Mem. Nat., Internat. Radio Clubs, Calif. Hist. Soc., Mus. Assn., Calif. Broadcasters Assn., San Francisco Symphony, Bay Area Publicity Club, San Francisco Advt. Club, Pub. Rels. Soc. Am., Worldwide TV/FM Dx Assn., Advt. Tennis Assn. (pres. 1975-77), San Francisco Tennis Club, Marina Tennis Club, Circle de L'Union Club, Olympic Club, Bacchus Club, The Family Club, Rotary (bd. dirs. 1988—, dist. pub. rels. chmn. 1986—). Home: 2614 Jackson St San Francisco CA 94115-1123 Office: 490 Post St Penthouse San Francisco CA 94102-1308

TAYLOR, QUINTARD, JR., history educator; b. Brownsville, Tenn., Dec. 11, 1948; s. Quintard and Grace (Brown) T.; m. Carolyn E. Fain, Aug. 2, 1969; children: Quintard III, Jamila E., William M. BA, St. Augustine's Coll., Raleigh, N.C., 1969; MA, U. Minn., 1971, PhD, 1977. Instr. history U. Minn., Mpls., 1970-71, Gustavus Adolphus Coll., St. Peter, Minn., 1971; asst. prof. hist. Wash. State U., Pullman, 1971-75; cons. Sta. KWSU-TV, Pullman, 1978-79; prof. hist. Calif. Poly State U., San Luis Obispo, Calif., 1977--; vis. Fulbright prof., Univ. Lagos, Nigeria, 1987-88; cons. Afro Am. Cultural Arts Ctr., Mpls., 1977-79, Gt. Plains Black Mus., Omaha, 1980-84, Black Am. West Mus., Denver, 1980-85. Contbr. articles to hist. jours. Mem. Martin Luther King, Jr. Meml. Scholarship Fund, San Luis Obispo, 1980-86; scoutmaster Boy Scouts Am., San Luis Obispo, 1983-84; mem. San Luis Obispo County Democratic Central Com., 1986-88. Recipient Meritorious Performance and Profl. Promise award, Calif. Poly. State U., 1986; Danforth Found. Kent fellow, 1974-76. Mem. Am. Hist. Assn., Assn. for Study Afro Am. Life and History, So. Conf. on Afro-Am. Studies (adv. bd.), African Studies Assn., Pacific Coast Africanist Assn., Golden Key, Alpha Phi Alpha. Presbyterian. Office: Calif Poly State U History Dept San Luis Obispo CA 93401

TAYLOR, R. MYCHEL, nurse; b. June 4, 1954; d. Payton III and Peggy Geneva (Morrison) T. RN, Fresno City Coll., 1989; student, Fresno State U. Profl. model Calif., 1978—; night supr. Sunnyside Hosp., Fresno, 1984—; AIDS care specialist Calif., 1980—; group leader, AIDS Support, Calif., 1985—. Author songs and poetry. Home and Office: 5965 129 E Shields Ave Fresno CA 93726

TAYLOR, RICHARD EDWARD, physicist, educator; b. Medicine Hat, Alta., Can., Nov. 2, 1929; came to U.S., 1952; s. Clarence Richard and Delia Alena (Brunsdale) T.; m. Rita Jean Bonneau, Aug. 25, 1951; 1 child, Norman Edward. B.S., U. Alta., 1950, M.S., 1952; Ph.D., Stanford U., 1962; Docteur honoris causa, U. Paris-Sud, 1980. Boursier Lab. de l'Accelerateur Lineaire, Orsay, France, 1958-61; physicist Lawrence Berkeley Lab., Berkeley, Calif., 1961-62; staff mem. Stanford Linear Accelerator Ctr., Calif., 1962-68, assoc. dir., 1982-86, prof., 1968—. Fellow Guggenheim Found., 1971-72, von Humboldt Found., 1982. Fellow Am. Phys. Soc. (council, div. particles and fields 1983-84), Royal Soc. Can.; mem. AAAS. Office: Stanford Linear Accelerator Ctr PO Box 4349 Bin 96 Stanford CA 94309

TAYLOR, ROBERT H., rehabilitation company executive; b. N.Y.C., Mar. 18, 1951; s. Donald and Miriam (Lasky) Schneider; m. Beth M. Cypress, Oct. 28, 1979 (div. 1985); m. Therese A. Thomson, Jan. 24, 1987; children: Aubrey, Aryn. BA, Hawthorne Coll., 1972; MA, NYU, 1975. Rehab. counselor, supr. United Cerebral Palsy N.Y.C., 1972-78; dir. adult programs Nassau Ctr. Developmentally Disabled, Woodbury, N.Y., 1978-79; rehab. specialist Injury Mgmt. and Rehab Corp., South San Francisco, Calif., 1979-80; dist. mgr. Injury Mgmt. and Rehab Corp., Phoenix, 1980-84; pres. Vocat. Diagnositcs, Inc., Phoenix, 1984—; vocat. rehab. expert witness, Ariz., Calif., Nev., N.Mex., 1979—; rehab. rep. Calif. Div. Ind. Accts., San Francisco, 1979—; rehab. cons., The Greyhound Corp., Phoenix, 1980—; rehab. counselor, Wash. Dept. Labor and Industry, Olympia, 1988—. Mem. Nat. Assn. Rehab. Practitioners in Pvt. Sector, Ariz. Assn. Rehab. Profls., La mancha Racquet Club, Plaza Club. Republican. Home: 457 E Lamar Rd Phoenix AZ 85012 Office: Vocat Diagnostics Inc C308 4621 N 16th St Phoenix AZ 85016

TAYLOR, ROBERT REED, financial consulting executive; b. Wichita, Kans., Mar. 24, 1944; s. Dayton Reed and Verla Rose (Moody) T.; m. Rosemary Wheeler, June 10, 1972; children: James Reed, John Andrew, Robert David, Samuel Denny. BA, U. Colo., 1966; cert. Portuguese lang., Birgham Young U., 1966. Cert. shopping ctr. mgr. Missionary Ch. of Jesus Christ of Latter-day Saints, Sao Paulo, Brazil, 1966-68; dist. sales mgr. R. H. Hinkley Co. div. Grolier Co., Denver, 1971-72; shopping ctr. mgr. Clark Fin. Corp., Salt Lake City, 1972-74, Collier, Heinz & Assocs., Salt Lake City, 1974-77; gen. property mgr. The Equitable Life Assurance Soc., Salt Lake City, 1977-82; pres. Promanco Property Cons., Salt Lake City, 1982—; gen. mgr, v.p. North Star Mall, div. The Rouse Co., San Antonio, 1982-86; dir. property mgmt. Collier, Heinz & Assocs., Salt Lake City, 1986—; property cons. various commercial property owners, 1982—; Utah real estate salesman Varner Real Estate, Salt Lake City, 1986—. Unit commr. dist. one Boy Scouts Am., San Antonio, 1984-86, troop com. chmn., Boutiful, Utah, 1986-88, scoutmaster, 1988—. With U.S. Army, 1969-71. Recipient Best Actor award North Canyon Stake Latter-day Saints Ch., Bountiful, 1988. Mem. Internat. Coun. Shopping Ctrs. (panel mem., speaker 1972—), Bldg. Owners and Mgrs. Assn., Internat. Real Estate Mgrs. Assn., Bountiful C. of C., Phi Delta Theta (chpt. sec. 1964-65). Republican. Office: Collier Heinz & Assocs 370 E 500 South Ste 100 Salt Lake City UT 84111

TAYLOR, RONALD J., biology educator; b. Victor, Idaho, Oct. 16, 1932; s. George G. and Elva A. (Drake) T.; m. Gloria M. Wood, May 26, 1955; children: Ryan J., Rhonda L. Ripplinger. BA, Idaho State U., 1954; MS, U. Wyo., 1960; PhD, Wash. State U., 1964. Asst. prof. biology Western Wash. U., Bellingham, 1964-72, prof. biology, 1972—, chmn. dept., 1985—. Author: Sagebrush Country, 1975, Mountain Wildflowers of the Pacific Northwest, 1976, Rocky Mountain Wildflowers, 1979; editor: Mosses of North America, 1978. Served to 1st lt. USAF, 1954-59. Mem. AAAS (bd. dirs. Pacific div. 1983—), Torrey Bot. Club, Bot. Soc. Am., Am. Soc. Plant Taxonomy (past pres.), N.W. Sci. Assn. (past pres.), Wash. Native Plant Soc. (pres. 1985-87), Sigma Xi (past chpt. pres.). Home: 4241 Northwest Rd Bellingham WA 98226 Office: Western Wash U Dept of Biology Bellingham WA 98225 *

TAYLOR, SCOTT DOUGLAS, publishing company official, infosystems specialis; b. Salt Lake City, Apr. 12, 1954. BS in Mktg., U. Utah, 1975; MBA in Fin., U. Colo., 1978. Corp. fin. analyst Manville Corp., Denver, 1978-80; sr. product design analyst Standard & Poor's Compustat, Englewood, Colo., 1980-82, corp. planning systems analyst, 1982-84, mgr. product ech., 1984--; developer CD-ROM McGraw-Hill Corp., Englewood, 1987--, editor newsletter Update, 1987--. H.G.B. Gould Meml. scholar U. Colo., 1977-78. Mem. Planning Forum (bd. dirs. Denver chpt. 1984--). Office: McGraw-Hill Corp 7400 S Alton Ct Englewood CO 80112

TAYLOR, SCOTT L., property management executive; b. Seattle, Apr. 1, 1960; s. Peter Leslie and Margaret Ann (Dodd) T.; m. Lisa Christine Cole, June 30, 1984. BA, Wash. State U., 1982. CPA, Ariz.; lic. real estate broker, Ariz. Staff acct. Touche Ross & Co., Seattle, 1982-85; v.p. Goodman Mgmt. Group, Phoenix, 1985—. Office: Goodman Mgmt Group 1730 E Northern #122 Phoenix AZ 85020

TAYLOR, STEVE HENRY, zoologist; b. Inglewood, Calif., Mar. 18, 1947; s. Raymond Marten and Ardath (Metz) T.; 1 child, Michael Travis. B.A. in Biology, U. Calif.-Irvine, 1969. Animal keeper Los Angeles Zoo, 1972-75, assoc. curator, 1975-76; children's zoo mgr. San Francisco Zoo, 1976-81; zoo dir. Sacramento Zoo, 1981—. Bd. dirs. Sacramento Soc. Prevention Cruelty to Animals, 1983-87, Sacremento Red Cross, 1988—. Fellow Am. Assn. Zool. Parks and Aquariums (infant care diet advisor 1979, 85, bd. dirs. 1987—, chmn. pub. edn. com., 1987-89, Outstanding Service award); mem. Sierra Club, Audubon Soc., Animal Use and Care Adminstrn. Democrat. Lodge: Rotary. Home: 443 De Mar Dr Sacramento CA 95831 Office: Sacramento Zoo 3930 W Land Park Sacramento CA 95822

TAYLOR, STEVEN GRAY, geologist; b. El Paso, Nov. 17, 1955; s. Elwyn D. and Francine O. (Gray) T.; m. Shaunna Lynn Newell, Nov. 29, 1980; children: Brandon James, Bryan Paul. BS in Geology, Adams State Coll., Alamosa, Colo., 1978; MBA, Regis Coll., Denver, 1987. Mine geologist Homestake Mining, Grants, N.Mex., 1978-79; exploration geologist Cotter Corp., Golden, Colo., 1979-82, mine geologist, 1982-84, chief geologist, 1984—. Home: 3713 W 99th Ave Westminster CO 80030

TAYLOR, T. RABER, lawyer; b. Colorado Springs, Colo., Dec. 31, 1910; s. Ralph Franklin and Mary Catherine (Burns) T.; m. Josephine Loretto Reddin, Sept. 20, 1938; children: Mary Therese, Carol Anne, Margaret Claire, Josephine R., Rae Marie, Kathleen Mae, Anne Marie. BA magna cum laude, Regis Coll., 1933; JD, Harvard U., 1937. Bar: Colo. 1937, U.S. Dist. Ct. Colo. 1937, U.S. Tax Ct. 1938, U.S. Ct. Appeals (10th cir.) 1940, U.S. Supreme Ct. 1950. Pvt. practice law Denver. Bd. dirs. Denver Cath. Charities, 1946-71; v.p. Nat. Conf. Cath. Charities, 1956-57, 69-75; mem. gov.'s com., White House Conf. on Children and Youth, 1971. Lt. comdr. USNR, 1943-45, NATOUSA, ETO. Knight Order St. Gregory, 1971, Equestrian Order of Holy Sepulchre of Jerusalem, 1973; recipient St. Vincent de Paul medal St. John's U., Jamaica, N.Y., 1971, St. Thomas More award Cath. Lawyers Guild Denver, 1981. Fellow Am. Coll. Probate Counsel; mem. ABA, Colo. Bar Assn., Denver Bar Assn., Denver Estate Planning Coun. (pres. 1962-63), Greater Denver Tax Counsel Assn., Sierra Club Denver, Denver Athletic Club. Home: 790 Fillmore St Denver CO 80206 Office: 250 Century Bank Pla 3300 E 1st Ave Denver CO 80206

TAYLOR, TIMOTHY DAVIES, psychologist; b. Tacoma, Jan. 25, 1945; s. Thomas Gibson and Eleanor Jane (Davies) T.; B.A., Central Wash. U., 1968; M.A., U. Puget Sound, Tacoma, 1975; Ph.D., U.S. Internat. U., 1980. Tchr. schs. in Wash., 1968-72; v.p. Tom Taylor Ins. Brokers, Tacoma, 1972-81; pvt. practice psychology, Tacoma, 1981—. Vice chmn. Pierce County March of Dimes, 1977-78, chmn., 1980; active Tacoma-Pierce County YMCA; assoc. chmn. United Way Pierce County, 1981-82. Mem. Ind. Ins. Agts. and Brokers Am., Family Service Assn. Am., Profl. Ins. Agts. Wash., Am. Psychol. Assn., Am. Assn. Marriage and Family Therapy. Democrat. Clubs: W. Tacoma Optimist (pres. 1977, Optimist of Yr. award 1977), Elks. Home: 4412 N 27th St Tacoma WA 98407 Office: Trust Office Bldg 808 N 2d St Tacoma WA 98403

TAYLOR, WALTER WALLACE, lawyer; b. Newton, Iowa, Sept. 18, 1925; s. Carrol W. and Eva (Greenly) T.; A.A., Yuba Coll., 1948, A.B., 1950; M.A., U. Calif., 1955, J.D., McGeorge Coll. Law, 1962; m. Mavis A. Harvey, Oct. 9, 1948; children—Joshua Michael (dec. 1980), Kevin Eileen, Kristin Lisa, Jeremy Walter, Margaret Jane, Melissa E., Amy M. Adminstrv. analyst USAF, Sacramento, 1951-53; personnel, research analyst Calif. Personnel Bd., Sacramento, 1954-56; civil service, personnel analyst, chief counsel, gen. mgr. Calif. Employees Assn., Sacramento, 1956-75; staff counsel, chief profl. standards Calif. Commn. Tchr. Credentialing, 1975-88, ret. 1988; tchr. discipline civil service, personnel cons. Served USCGR, 1943-46. Mem. Calif. State Bar, Am., Sacramento County bar assns. Democrat. Author: Know Your Rights, 1963-64. Home: 4572 Fair Oaks Blvd Sacramento CA 95862

TAYLOR, WARREN, JR., construction company, consultant; b. Columbus, Ohio, Mar. 10, 1958; s. Warren and Judy Lynn (Pickens) T.; m. Jennifer Ann Ward, Aug. 2, 1980; children: Nicholas John, Wendy Michele. Student, Golden West Coll., 1977-78, Orange Coast Coll., 1979, Long Beach State U., 1979. Foreman R.A. Taylor Constrn. Co., Norwalk, Calif., 1979-80; facilities engr. Ultrasystems Inc., Irvine, Calif., 1980-83; v.p. AFM Constrn. Inc., Santa Ana, Calif., 1983--; RMO Fast Trac Constrn. Co., Huntington Beach, Calif., 1988--; cons. rec. studios and constrn., 1987--. Mem. 20/30 Club. Republican. Baptist.

TAYLOR, WILLIAM HENDERSON, communications executive; b. Sandusky, Ohio, Jan. 17, 1945; s. William Donald and Virginia (Hays) T.; m. Bridget Ann Hand, Apr. 19, 1980; children: Ashley Ann, Austin Hays. AB, Hillsdale (Mich.) Coll., 1967; MA, U. Mich., 1970. Cert. tchr., Mich., Ohio, N.Y. Assoc. dir. admissions Hillsdale Coll., 1967-72; div. mgr. Bloomingdale's, N.Y.C., 1973-76; sr. pers. analyst Office Ct. Adminstr. State of N.Y., N.Y.C., 1973-76; dist. mgr. Proving Ground, Susan Ives, Ups-N-Down, Cleve., 1976-78; regional mgr. Nat. Alliance Bus., San Francisco, 1978-83; account dir. Carlson Learning Co., Gardena, Calif., 1983-88; v.p. DeSalvo & Diehl, Tustin, Calif., 1988—; cons. Pvt. Industry Coun., Torrance, Calif, 1980-83, San Francisco, 1979-83. Recipient Youth Svcs. awards City of Torrance, 1983, City of Oakland, Calif., 1982, City of San Francisco, 1982, 83. Mem. Alpha Tau Omega, Lambda Iota Tau. Office: DeSalvo & Diehl Inc 1800 Wilshire Ave Santa Ana CA 92707

TAYLOR, WILLIAM MALCOLM, executive recruiter; b. South Hiram, Maine, June 18, 1933; s. William Myers and Gladys Marie (Weldy) T.; m. Carrie Mae Fiedler, Aug. 31, 1957 (div. Sept. 1980); children: William Stephan, Alyson Marie, Eric Fiedler; m. Elizabeth Van Horn, June 18, 1983. BA in Liberal Arts, Pa. State U., 1956; MEd in Sci., U. N.C., 1961. Cert. secondary sch. tchr. Chemistry and biology tchr. Coral Shores High Sch., Tavernier, Fla., 1961-62; park naturalist Nat. Park Service, Everglades Nat. Park, Fla., 1962-65; tech. editor Nat. Park Service, Washington, 1965-67; chief naturalist Nat. Park Service, Canyonlands Nat. Park, Utah, 1967-71; environ. edn. specialist western regional office Nat. Park Service, Calif., 1971-77; programs devel. dir. Living History Ctr., Novato, Calif., 1981-83; ptnr. Van Horn, Taylor & Assocs., Santa Cruz, Calif., 1983—. Originator: (ednl. program) Environ. Living Program, 1973 (Calif. Bicentennial Commn. award 1974, Don Perryman award Calif. Social Studies Council, 1975, Calif. Conservation Council award 1975). Dir. Novato Environ. Quality Commn., 1973-76; mem. Calif. Conservation Council, 1973-76; pres. docents Long Marine Labs. U. Calif., Santa Cruz; sponsor Foster Parents. Mem. AAAS, Assn. Ind. Recruiters, Mensa. Clubs: Santa Cruz Bird, West Valley Flying, Air Life Line. Home and Office: 4209 Smith Grade Rd Santa Cruz CA 95060

TAYLOR-HUNT, MARY BERNIS BUCHANAN, educator, artist; b. Marion, Ind., Aug. 16, 1904; d. Walter Scott and Nora Elizabeth (Kinslear) B.; m. Robert Rush Taylor, Jan. 26, 1929 (dec. Mar. 1975); m. Ralph Van Nice Hunt, May 20, 1978; stepchildren: Penelope Clark, Diane Stockmar. AB in English, UCLA, 1926; MA in Drama, U. So. Calif., 1931. Tchr. speech and dramatics Los Angeles City Schs., 1929-44; vol. instr. Ikebana (Japanese Flower Arranging) Huntington Library, San Marino, Calif., 1957—,; produced Japanese Festival at Huntington Library, for Olympic Fine Arts Festival in L.A., 1984. represented in permanent collection at Japanese House in Japanese Garden at Huntington Library, 1957—. Recipient Golden Crown award Arts Council, Pasadena. Mem. L.A. Soc. Ikenobo (bd. dirs. 1987-88, 89), San Marino League (fine arts projects), Valley Hunt Club, Calif. Club. Republican. Mem. Christian Ch. Club: San Marino League (founding pres. 1954-55). Home: 1300 Sierra Madre Blvd San Marino CA 91108

TEAGUE, CATHERINE LYNNE, real estate brokerage executive; b. Phoenix, Aug. 13, 1951; d. Arthur and Pauline (Choloduik) Hatton; m. David Lynn Teague, Apr. 15, 1972; children: Jill Lynne, Kevin Phillip. MA in Sales, Tom Hopkins Internat. U., 1987; student, Prof. Inst. Real Estate, Scottsdale. Lic. real estate broker, Ariz. Personnel dir. Maricopa County Med. Soc., Phoenix, 1982-84; real estate salesperson Prine Ariz. Realty, Phoenix, 1984-85; owner, chief exec. officer Chelsey Internat. Inc., Desert Hills, Ariz., 1985—. Inventor in field. Sec. Valley Bus. Alliance, Desert Hills Improvement Assn., 1985-87; founder Desert Hills Community Found.; bd. dirs. Northwest Theater Project; mem. Maricopa County Bd. Adjusters, 1989—. Mem. Soc. Profl. and Exec. Women, Phoenix Bd. Realtors (co-founder Apache Peak News), Nat. Assn. Realtors, Ariz. Assn. Realtors, Soroptomists. Home: 35039 N Central Ave Phoenix AZ 85027 Office: Chelsey Realty 515 E Carefree Hwy Phoenix AZ 85027

TEAGUE, LAVETTE COX, JR., educator, systems consultant; b. Birmingham, Ala., Oct. 8, 1934; s. Lavette Cox and Caroline Green (Stokes) T.; student Auburn U., 1951-54; B.Arch., MIT, 1957, M.S.C.E., 1965, Ph.D., 1968; M.Div. with distinction, Ch. Div. Sch. Pacific, 1979; cert. systems profl., 1985—. Archtl. designer Carroll C. Harmon, Birmingham, 1957, Fred Renneker, Jr., Birmingham, 1958-59; architect Rust Engring. Co., Birmingham, 1959-62, Synergetics, Inc., Raleigh, N.C., 1962-64, Rust Engring. Co., Birmingham, 1964-68; research asst., inst., research assoc. MIT, Cambridge, 1964-68; dir. computer services Skidmore, Owings & Merrill, San Francisco, Chgo., 1968-74; postdoctoral fellow UCLA, 1972; adj. assoc. prof. architecture and civil engring. Carnegie-Mellon U., Pitts., 1973-74; archtl. systems cons., Chgo., 1974-75, Berkeley, Calif., 1975-80, Pasadena, Calif., 1980-82, Altadena, Calif., 1982—; lectr. info. systems Calif. State Poly. U., Pomona, 1980-81, prof., 1981—; Fulbright lectr., Uruguay, 1985. Co-author: Structured Analysis Methods for Computer Information Systems, 1985. Recipient Tucker-Voss award M.I.T., 1967; Fulbright scholar, 1985. Mem. AIA (Arnold W. Brunner scholar 1966), Assn. Computing Machinery, Sigma Xi, Phi Eta Sigma, Scarab, Scabbard and Blade, Tau Beta Pi, Chi Epsilon. Episcopalian. Home: 1696 N Altadena Dr Altadena CA 91001 Office: 3801 W Temple Ave Pomona CA 91768

TEARSE, JAMES EDWARD, ophthalmologist; b. Honolulu, Feb. 19, 1956; s. Herbert and Claire Tearse. BS, Stanford U., 1978; MD, Baylor Coll. Medicine, 1982. Diplomate Am. Bd. Ophtholmology. Intern Baylor Affiliated Hosps., Houston, 1982-83; resident in ophthalmology U. Tex., Dallas, 1983-86; fellow in ophthalmology Project ORBIS, N.Y.C., 1986; pvt. practice Palo Alto, Calif., 1987; ophthalmologist Redwood Med. Clinic, Redwood City, Calif., 1988—; clin. instr. Stanford U., Calif., 1987—. Recipient Eagle Scout award Boy Scouts Am., 1969; Am. Field Svc. Internat. scholar, 1973. Mem. AMA, Am. Acad. Ophthalmology, San Mateo County Med. Soc., Calif. Med. Assn. Democrat. Roman Catholic. Office: Redwood Med Clinic 2900 Whipple Redwood City CA 94062

TEBO, STEPHEN DWANE, real estate investment and development company, store fixtures manufacturer's representative; b. Hays, Kans., Aug. 22, 1944; s. John W. and Lorene (Depew) T.; m. Elaine King, Feb. 22, 1963 (div. jan. 1977); children: Brenda, Bonnie, Brad. BS in Math., Ft. Hays State Coll., 1967; MS in Computer Sci., U. Mo., Rolla, 1968. Owner, mgr. Tebo Coin Co., Boulder, Colo., 1968-79, Tebo Store Fixtures, Boulder, 1968—, Tebo Leasing Co., Boulder, 1971—, Tebo Devel. Co., Boulder, 1973—. Fin. chmn. boulder County Rep. Com., 1982-86; nat. del. Colo. Rep. Com., 1984; bd. dirs. Downtown Boulder, Inc., Boulder Arts Commn. Named Outstanding Young Man in Am., 1973, Alumni of Yr., Ft. Hays U., 1978; recipient Bronze Baton award Boulder Philharm. Orch., 1987. Mem. Boulder C. of C. Home: 3645 Cholla Ct Boulder CO 80302 Office: Tebo Devel Co PO Box T Boulder CO 80306

TEDDER, WILLIAM RANDALL, III, sales engineer; b. Salinas, Calif., June 10, 1957; s. William Randall Jr. and Edna Claire (Johnson) T. AB in Genetics, U. Calif., Berkeley, 1980. Cert. CPR tchr., Calif. Tutor Hartnell Community Coll., Salinas, 1982; tchr. Salinas Union High Sch. Dist., 1982-84; sales engr. Filtrex Inc., Hayward, Calif., 1984-85; tchr. San Mateo (Calif.) Union High Sch. Dist., 1985-86; tech. specialist indsl. filtration and heating products Montgomery Bros. Inc., Burlingame, Calif., 1986-87; sales engr. Mensco, Inc., Fremont, Calif., 1988—; cons. Western Analytical Products, San Francisco, 1987-88, in fields of filtration and chromatography. Bd. dirs. Salinas Lyceum, 1983. Recipient U. Calif. Berkeley Grant in Aid, 1975-76, fee grant U. Calif., Berkeley, 1975-76; Calif. State scholar, Berkeley, 1976-78. mem. AAAS, N.Y. Acad. Scis., Calif. Alumni Assn., Mensa (chmn. local bylaw com. 1983, editor newsletter 1982). Republican. Presbyterian. Office: PO Box 14176 Fremont CA 94539

TEDFORD, CHARLES FRANKLIN, biophysicist; b. Lawton, Okla., June 26, 1928; s. Charles E. and Loula B. (Waters) T.; m. Julie Reme Sauret, Sept. 15, 1951; children: Gary Franklin, Mark Charles, Philip John. BS with distinction in Chemistry, S.W. Tex. State U., 1950, MS, 1954; postgrad. in radiobiology Reed Coll., 1957, in biophysics U. Calif., Berkeley, 1961-63. Enlisted USN, 1945-47, commd. ensign, 1950, advanced through grades to capt., 1968; biochemist U.S. Naval Hosp., San Diego, 1953-54, U.S. Naval Biol. Lab., Oakland, Calif., 1954-56; sr. instr., radiation safety officer Nuclear, Biol. and Chem. Warfare Def. Sch., Treasure Island, Calif., 1956-61; asst. chief nuclear medicine div. Navy Med. Sch., Bethesda, Md., 1963-66; adminstrv. program mgr. radiation safety br. Bur. Medicine and Surgery, Washington, 1966-72; dir. radiation safety and health physics program Navy Regional Med. Center, San Diego, 1972-74; mgr. Navy Regional Med. Clinic, Seattle, 1974-78, ret., 1978; dir. radiation health unit Ga. Dept. Human Resources, Atlanta, 1978-79; dir. Ariz. Radiation Regulatory Agy., Tempe, 1979—; elected chmn. Conf. Radiation Program Dirs., 1987. Decorated Legion of Merit, Meritorious Service medal. Mem. Health Physics Soc., Am. Nuclear Soc. Contbr. articles on radiation safety to profl. publs.

TEDFORD, JACK NOWLAN, III, construction executive, small business owner; b. Reno, Jan. 1, 1943; s. Jack Nowlan Jr. and Elizabeth (Kolhoss) T.; m. Nancy Joanne Stiles, Feb. 27, 1971; children: Jack Nowlan IV, James Nathan. BS, U. Nev., 1966, MBA, 1969. Bus. mgr. Los Angeles Bapt. Coll., Newhall, Calif., 1969-71; v.p. Jack N. Tedford, Inc., Fallon, Nev., 1971—; owner/broker Tedford Realty, Fallon, 1974—; owner/mgr. Tedford Bus. Systems, Fallon, 1978—; bd. dirs. Masters Coll., Newhall, Calif., 1972—. Author numerous computer programs. Active Selective Service Local Bd., Fallon, 1971-76; chmn. City of Fallon Bd. Adjustment, 1975—, Chuchill Co. Reps., Fallon, 1976-80; mem. exec. com. Nev. Reps., 1976—; del. Rep. Nat. Conv., Detroit, 1980, Dallas, 1984. Mem. Assn. Gen. Contractors, Nat. and State Bd. Realtors, Internat. Slurry Seal Assn., Nev. Motor Transport Assn. Republican. Baptist. Lodge: Rotary (bd. dirs. 1969-71). Home: 115 N Bailey Fallon NV 89406 Office: 235 E Williams Ave PO Box 1505 Fallon NV 89406-1505

TEECE, DAVID JOHN, economics and management educator; b. Marlborough, New Zealand, Sept. 2, 1948; came to U.S., 1971; s. Allan Teece. BA, U. Canterbury, Christchurch, N.Z., 1970, MA in Commerce, 1971; MA in Econs., U. Pa., 1973, PhD, 1975. Asst. prof. Stanford U., 1975-78, assoc. prof., 1978-82; prof. U. Calif., Berkeley, 1982—, dir. Ctr. Rsch. in Mgmt., 1983—. Author: Profiting from Innovation, 1986, and numerous other articles and books. Mem. Am. Econ. Assn. Office: U Calif 554 Barrows Hall Berkeley CA 94720

TEED, DAVID SAMUEL, consumer products distributor executive; b. Penang, Malaysia, Mar. 24, 1954; came to U.S., 1987; s. Samuel Richard and Bette (Mamouney) T.; m. Maureen Lynn Cunningham, July 28, 1984; children: Sarah Lindsey, Emily Morgan. Matriculation, Guildford Grammer Sch., Perth, West Australia, 1971; law, Royal Melbourne Inst. of Tech., 1977. Barrister, solicitor Ellison, Hewison & Whitehead, Melbourne, 1974-78, Cetnar, Teed & Hale, Melbourne, 1978-84; mng. dir. Capvest Group, Australia, Can., 1986-88; pres. Pacvest Capital Inc., Australia, Can., 1986-88; chmn. of the bd. Core-Mark Internat., Can., U.S., 1987—; dir. Capvest Ltd., Australia, 1986—, Corporate Pacific Ltd., Australia, 1986—, Pacvest Capital Inc., Can., 1986—, Great Eastern Internat. Inc., U.S., 1986—. Chmn. Melbourne Fed. Electrate-Liberal Party of Australia, 1979-84. Fellow Inst. Dirs. Australia, mem. Australian Inst. Mgmt., Law Inst. Victoria.

TEEL, DALE, utility company executive; b. Sesser, Ill., Oct. 11, 1925; s. Lester N. and Ruth (Martin) T. B.S. in Chem. Engring., U. Ill., 1946. With chem. div. U.S. Rubber Co., Naugatuck, Conn., 1946-47, plantations div., Penang, Malaya, 1948-52; asst. gen. sales mgr., mgr. Hawaii br. Honolulu Gas Co., Honolulu and Hilo, 1952-60; pres. Anchorage Natural Gas Corp., Anchorage, 1960-88, Alaska Pipeline Co., Anchorage subs. Seagull Energy Corp., 1974-88; cons. Energy Internat., Inc., Bellevue, Wash., 1989—. Served with USNR, 1943-45. Office: Alaska Pipeline Co PO Box 6288 3000 Spanard Rd Anchorage AK 99503

TEERLINK, J(OSEPH) LELAND, real estate developer; b. Salt Lake City, July 16, 1935; s. Nicholas John and Mary Luella (Love) T.; student U. Utah, 1953-55; m. Leslie Dowdle, Nov. 5, 1975; children: Steven, David, Andrew, Suzanne, Benjamin. Sales rep. Eastman Kodak Co., Salt Lake City, 1960-69; founder Graphic Systems, Inc., Salt Lake City, 1969-82, pres., 1969-79, chmn. bd., 1979-82; founder Graphic Ink Co., Salt Lake City, 1973, pres., 1975-79, chmn. bd., 1979-82; founder G.S.I. Leasing Co., Salt Lake City, 1975, pres., 1975-82; chmn. bd. Graphic Systems Holding Co., Inc., Salt Lake City, 1978-82; dir. leasing and acquisitions Terra Industries, Inc., real estate developers, 1982-86, ptnr., 1986—. Bd. dirs. ARC, Salt Lake City, 1979-82; vice consulate of the Netherlands for Utah, 1977—; mem. active corps of execs., SBA, 1979-83. Named Small Businessman of the Yr. for Utah, SBA, 1978. Mem. Graphic Arts Equipment and Supply Dealers of Am. (dir. 1978-82), Printing Industry of Am., Nat. Assn. Indsl. and Office Parks (pres. Utah chpt., 1986-87), Nat. Fedn. Ind. Businessmen, Million Dollar Club (life). Republican. Mormon. Home: 2984 Thackeray Pl Salt Lake City UT 84108 Office: 6925 Union Park Ctr Midvale UT 84047

TEETERS, CLARENCE, salt company manager; b. Mt. Pleasant, Pa., Dec. 22, 1933; s. Clarence and Edna Marie (Grimm) T.; student U. Toledo, 1952-55, U. So. Calif., 1978; m. Sandra Jean Ulery, Aug. 2, 1958; children: Deanna Marie, Douglas James. Buyer, mgr. Tiedtkes, Toledo, 1955-60; sales rep. Morton Salt Co., 1960-69, dist. sales mgr., No. Calif., Nev., Hawaii, 1969-78; mgr. consumer products Leslie Salt Co., Newark, Calif., 1978—. Mem. The Illuminators, San Francisco Sales Mgrs. Club, Masons. Republican. Presbyterian. Address: 7200 Central Ave Newark CA 94560

TEETS, JOHN WILLIAM, diversifed company executive; b. Elgin, Ill., Sept. 15, 1933; s. John William and Maudie T.; m. Nancy Kerchenfaut, June 25, 1965; children: Jerri, Valerie Sue, Heide Jane, Suzanne. Student, U. Ill. Pres., ptnr. Winter Garden Restaurant, Inc., Carpenterville, Ill., 1957-63; v.p. Greyhound Food Mgmt. Co.; pres. Post Houses, Inc., and Horne's Enterprises, Chgo., 1964-68; pres., chief operating officer John R. Thompson Co., Chgo., 1968-71; pres., chief operating officer Restaurant div., also corp. v.p Canteen Corp., Chgo., 1971-74; exec. v.p., chief operating officer Bonanza Internat. Co., Dallas, 1974-76; chmn., chief exec. officer Greyhound Food Mgmt., Inc., Phoenix, 1976; group v.p. food service Greyhound Corp., Phoenix, 1976-81, group v.p. services group, 1980-81, vice chmn., 1980-82, chmn., chief exec. officer, 1981—, now also pres. and dir.; chmn., pres. Armour & Co., from 1981; chief exec. officer Dial Corp., Phoenix; chmn., chief exec. officer Greyhound Food Mgmt. Inc., Phoenix, 1982—; chmn. Greyhound Support Svcs. Inc., Phoenix; vice chmn. President's Conf. on Foodservice Industry; mem. adv. bd. Phoenix and Valley of Sun Conv. and Visitors Bur., 1979-82. Recipient Silver Plate award, Golden Plate award Internat. Foodservice Mfrs. Assn., 1980. Mem. Nat. Automatic Mdsg. Assn., Nat. Restaurant Assn., Nat. Inst. Foodservice Industry (trustee), Am. Mgmt. Assn., Christian Businessmen's Assn. (chmn. steering com. 1977), Nat. Speakers Assn. Club: Arizona. Office: The Greyhound Corp Greyhound Tower Sta 3103 Phoenix AZ 85077 *

TEGELER, DOROTHY, writer; b. Effingham, Ill., Oct. 12, 1950; d. Albert Bernard and Mildred Elizabeth (Haarmann) T.; children: Paul Anthony, Laura Ann. BS cum laude, Ill. State U., 1971. Cert. elem. tchr., Ill. Tchr. Camp Point Sch. Dist., Golden, Ill., 1971-72; elem. career devel. specialist McKnight Pub. Co., Bloomington, Ill., 1972-74; sales rep. Bobbs Merrill Pub. Co., Indpls., 1981-82; tchr. Lincoln Coll., Lincoln, Ill., 1980-82; employee communications adminstr. Ill. Farm Bur., Bloomington, Ill., 1982-84; freelance writer Phoenix, 1972—; pres. Fiesta Books Inc., Phoenix, 1987—. Author: Retiring in Arizona 1987, Hello Arizona 1987, Moving to Arizona 1988; contbr. articles to popular mags. Dep. Registrar Dem. Party Phoenix, 1987-88. Mem. Internat. Assn. Small Pubs., Pubs. Mktg. Assn., Ariz. Authors Assn. (pres. 1987-88). Office: 7250 N 16th St Ste 409 Phoenix AZ 85020

TEITEL, MARTIN, foundation director; b. Passaic, N.J., July 3, 1945; s. Sidney Teitel and Blanche Migden; m. Mary Jeanette Harrington, May 9, 1980; children: Jason, Julia Ruth, Samuel Cullen. BA, U. Wis., 1967; MSW, San Diego State U., 1977. Intern Am. Friends Service Com., Phila., 1967-69, from asst. dir. to dir. overseas refugee program, 1969-72; field dir. Am. Friends Service Com., Vientiane, Laos, 1974-75, Indochina rep., 1974-75; dir. Asia programs Am. Friends Service Com., Phila., 1972-75; dir. West coast Council on Econ. Priorities, San Francisco, 1977-78; field dir. West The Youth Project, San Francisco, 1978-80; exec. dir. C.S. Fund, Freestone, Calif., 1981—. Contbr. articles to profl. jours. Mem. Nat. Network Grantmakers.

TEITZ, RICHARD STUART, museum director; b. Fall River, Mass., July 18, 1942; s. Alexander George and Lucille T.; m. Elaine Tallmadge Osborn, 1962; children: Rebecca Eve, Jessica Ann, Alexander Osborn. A.B., Yale U., 1963; M.A., Harvard U., 1965. Asst. curator Fogg Art Mus., Harvard U., 1964-65; curatorial asst. Worcester (Mass.) Art Mus., 1965-67, asst. dir., 1969-70, dir., 1970-81; dir. Hood Mus. of Art, Dartmouth Coll., Hanover, N.H., 1981-84, Denver Art Mus., 1984—; dir. Wichita Art Mus., 1967-69; lectr. Boston Archtl. Center, 1964-65; instr. Clark U., 1966-67; asso. dir. Etruscan Found., Siena, 1965, 66—; prof. art Dartmouth Coll., 1981-84; bd. dirs. Ava Gallery, N.H. Visual Artists Coalition. Author: Masterpieces of Etruscan Art, 1967, Art of the Victorian Era, 1969; also articles. Mem. Assn. Art Mus. Dirs., Archaeol. Inst. Am., Internat. Council Mus., Coll. Art Assn. Clubs: Yale (N.Y.C. and Colo.), Denver Athletic. Home: 1968 Ivy St Denver CO 80220 Office: Denver Art Mus 1000 W 14th Avenue Pkwy Denver CO 80204

TEJI, DARSHAN SINGH, city official; b. Ferozepore, India, Aug. 18, 1925; came to U.S., 1969; s. Hardial Singh and Daropadi Teji; m. Gurdip Kaur Harnam, Apr. 21, 1951; children—Jagjit Singh, Manjit Kaur. B.S., U. Punjab (India), 1946; B. Engring., U. Rajputana (India), 1950; M. Engring., U. Toronto (Can.), 1968. Registered profl. engr., Can., Ariz. Tech. advisor Shell Oil Co., New Delhi, India, 1957-64; mech. engr. Found. Co. of Can., Toronto, 1964-67; application engr. FECO Co., Cleve., 1969-70; chief engr. Gasway Corp., Chgo., 1970-72; sr. facilities engr. Motorola Inc., Phoenix, 1972-78; energy conservation mgr. City of Phoenix, 1978—. Author tech. papers. Recipient Gov.'s award for Spl. Achievement Ariz. State, 1983. Mem. Assn. Energy Engrs. (sr.; pres. 1984-85, energy man of yr. award 1982); ASME, ASHRAE, Am. Inst. Chem. Engrs. Home: 8813 N 86th St Scottsdale AZ 85258 Office: City of Phoenix 2631 S 22d Ave Phoenix AZ 85009

TELLEP, DANIEL MICHAEL, mechanical engineer; b. Forest City, Pa., Nov. 20, 1931. B.S. in Mech. Engring. with highest honors, U. Calif., Berkeley, 1954, M.S., 1955; grad. Advanced Mgmt. Program, Harvard U., 1971. With Lockheed Missiles & Space Co., 1955—, chief engr. missile systems div., 1969-75, v.p., asst. gen. mgr. advanced systems div., 1975-83, exec. v.p., 1983-84, pres., 1984—, 1986—; chmn., chief exec. officer Lockheed Corp., 1989—; cons. in field. Contbr. article to profl. jours. Fellow AIAA (Lawrence Sperry award 1964, Missile Systems award 1986), Am. Astronautical Soc.; mem. Nat. Acad. Engring., Sigma Xi, Pi Tau Sigma, Tau Beta Pi. Office: Lockheed Corp 4500 Park Granada Blvd Calabasas CA 91399

TELLER, DAVIDA YOUNG, psychology, physiology and biophysics educator; b. Yonkers, N.Y., July 25, 1938; d. David Aidan and Jean Marvin (Sturges) Young; m. David Chambers Teller, June 18, 1960 (div. May 1986); children: Stephen, Sara. BA, Swarthmore Coll., 1960; PhD, U. Calif., Berkeley, 1965. Lectr., research prof. U. Wash., Seattle, 1965-69, asst. prof. psychology, physiology and biophysics, 1969-71, assoc. prof., 1971-74, prof., 1973—; research affiliate Regional Primate Research Ctr., Child Devel. and Mental Retardation Ctr.; mem. com. on vision Nat. Acad. Scis.-Nat. Research Council, 1971—, vision research program com. Nat. Eye Inst. and NIH, 1973-76, Assn. Research in Vision and Ophthalmology, program com. Visual Psychophysics and Physiol. Optics, 1973-75, visual scis. B study sect. NIH, 1981-85, chmn. 1983-85; U. Wash. appointments include chmn. Univ. Com. on Vision, 1971; mem. Univ. Council on Women, 1971-76, Faculty Senate Spl. Com. on Faculty Women, 1972-75, ad hoc com. Evaluation of Dir. of Black Studies Program, 1976, faculty adv. bd. Women Studies, 1980-82, ad hoc com. to search for Chmn. Psychology, 1981, standing com. Women Studies, 1982-83, faculty senate council on Grants and Contract Research, 1985—, Univ. Acad. Council, 1986—; dept. psychology appoints include Exec. Com., 1973-75, 77-79; chmn. Budget and Facilities Com., 1979-81; mem. ad hoc com. Staff Employment, 1982-83; honors advisor and dir. Honors Program, 1982—; mem. planning com. 1984-87; reviewer for the following granting agys. NSF, Exptl. Psychology and Visual Sci. B Study Sects. of NIH, Nat Research Council of Can., U.S.-Israel Binational Sci. Found., The Thrasher Research Fund; visited sites for Nat. Inst. Neurol. Diseases and Stroke, Nat. Eye Inst., Vision B. Study Sect. Mem. editorial bd. Infant Behavior and Development, 1981-85, Behavioral Brain Research, 1984-87, Vision Research, 1985—, Clinical Vision Sciences, 1986-87; contbr. numerous articles to profl. jours.; patentee in field. Recipient Sabbatical award James McKeen Cattell Fund, 1981-82. Fellow AAAS, Optical Soc. Am. (dir.-at-large 1989); mem. Assn. Research in Vision and Ophthalmology, Assn. Women in Sci., Am. Acad. Ophthalmology (Glenn Fry award 1982). Office: U Wash Dept Psychology NI-25 Seattle WA 98195

TELLO, DONNA, accounting company executive; b. Annapolis, Md., Mar. 23, 1955; m. Gregory Tello, July 5, 1975 (div. 1978); m. Dennis R. Thompson, Apr. 1, 1987; children: Jesse Elliott Timothy Tello, Kimbrelle Shey Thommasson. Owner, tax strategist Tax Savers, San Diego, 1981—; owner, mgr. All Around Bookkeeping, San Diego, 1983—. Libertarian party candidate for state assembly, 1984. Mem. Internat. Platform Soc., Inland Soc. Tax. Cons., Nat. Taxpayers Union, Nat. Assn. Enrolled Agts., Calif. Assn. Enrolled Agts., Mensa (columnist on taxes in monthly newsletter, treas. San Diego chpt. 1985-87), Camelopard Club (co-founder), Toastmasters (v.p. edn. Liberty chpt. 1987). Home: 5932 Michael St San Diego CA 92116 Office: 4114 Adams Ave San Diego CA 92116

TEMIANKA, HENRI, violinist, conductor; b. Greenock, Scotland, Nov. 19, 1906; came to U.S., 1940; s. Israel and Fanny (Hildebrand) T.; m. Emmy Cowden, Jan. 28, 1943; children: Daniel, David. Ed., Rotterdam, Berlin, Paris; grad., Curtis Inst., 1930; PhD (hon.), DFA (hon.), Pepperdine U., 1986. Founder, artistic dir. Calif. Chamber Symphony Orch., Los Angeles, 1960—; head violin dept., summer master classes Santa Barbara Music Acad. of West, 1952; artistic adviser Nat. Fedn. Music Clubs; vis. prof. U. Calif. at Santa Barbara, 1960-65; lectr. univs.; prof., music dir. Calif. State U. at Long Beach, 1964-74, prof. emeritus, 1974—; lectr. UCLA; cons. Ford Found. Debut, N.Y.C., 1928, Europe, 1930, soloist with, John Barbirolli, George Szell, Vaughan Williams, Sir Adrian Boult, Fritz Reiner, Otto Klemperer, also with, Amsterdam Concertgebouw Orch., philharm. orchs. of, Warsaw, The Hague, Rotterdam, London, Brussels, Monte-Carlo, Geneva, Stockholm, Copenhagen, Helsinki; toured, Russia at govt. invitation, 1935, 36, founded, Temianka Chamber Orch., London, 1936, toured, U.S., 1942—, leader, Paganini String Quartet, 1946-66; produced, wrote, narrated series ednl. motion pictures commd. by, Ednl. TV Center, 1956; guest condr., Los Angeles Philharmonic Orch., 1958-59, 59-60, U.S. tour of 40 concerts with, Temianka Little Symphony, 1960, 61, 64, concert tours, Europe, Orient, S.Am., Can., 1960—; concert tours with Temianka Virtuosi, U.S. and Hong Kong, 1980, 82, 85; Author: Facing the Music, 1973; contbr. to magazines. Adviser Young Musicians Found. Served with overseas br. OWI, 1942-44. Decorated officier des Arts et Lettres (France). Home: 2915 Patricia Ave Los Angeles CA 90064 Office: Calif Chamber Symphony Soc PO Box 64425 Los Angeles CA 90064

TEMKO, ALLAN BERNARD, writer; b. N.Y.C., Feb. 4, 1924; s. Emanuel and Betty (Alderman) T.; m. Elizabeth Ostroff, July 1, 1950; children: Susannah, Alexander. A.B., Columbia U., 1947; postgrad, U. Calif., Berkeley, 1949-51, Sorbonne, 1948-49, 51-52. Lectr. Sorbonne, 1953-54, Ecole des Arts et Metiers, Paris, 1954-55; asst. prof. journalism U. Calif., Berkeley, 1956-62; lectr. in city planning and social scis. U. Calif., 1966-70; prof. art Calif. State U., Hayward, 1971-80; lectr. art Stanford U., 1981, 82; architecture critic San Francisco Chronicle, 1961—, art editor, 1979-82; archtl. planning cons. Author: Notre Dame of Paris, 1955, Eero Saarinen, 1962; contbr. articles to U.S. and fgn. mags. and newspapers; West Coast editor, Archtl. Forum, 1959-62. Served with USNR, 1943-46. Recipient Gold medal Commonwealth Club Calif., 1956, journalism award AIA, 1961, Silver Spur award, 1985, 1st prize in archtl. criticism Mfrs. Hanover/Art World, 1986, Critic's award Mfrs. Hanover/Art World, 1987, Profl. Achievement award Soc. Profl. Journalists, 1988; Rockefeller Found. grantee, 1962-63; Twentieth Century Fund grantee, 1963-66; Guggenheim fellow, 1956-57; Nat. Endowment for the Arts grantee, 1988. Office: San Francisco Chronicle San Francisco CA 94119

TEMPEST, RICHARD BLACKETT, state senator, general contractor; b. Salt Lake City, Oct. 4, 1935; s. John Henry and Kathryn (Blackett) T.; m. Ruth Ottosen, Sept. 8, 1958; childrn: Robert, Lynne Anne, Michael, Mathew, David. BS, U. Utah, 1959. Sec.-treas. The Tempest Co., Murray, Utah, 1960—; senator Utah State Senate, Salt Lake City, 1987—; bd. dirs. Sta. KUED, Salt Lake City. With U.S. Army, 1958-59. Mem. Associated Gen. Contractors (past sec.-treas.). Republican. Mormon. Office: Office State Senate State Capitol Salt Lake City UT 84114 also: The Tempest Co 4681 S 300 West Murray UT 84107

TEMPLIN, KATHLEEN ANN, nursing educator; b. Santa Monica, Calif., June 13, 1947; d. Charles Richard and Marion Elizabeth (Taylor) Allen; children: Christine, Joanna. BS in Nursing, Georgetown U., 1969; M. Nursing, U. Calif., L.A., 1981. RN, Calif. Intensive care nurse St. Vincent Charity Hosp., Cleve., 1969-77, UCLA Med. Ctr., 1977-79, Meml. Med. Ctr., Long Beach, Calif., 1982; asst. prof. nursing Calif. State U., Long Beach, 1982—; cons. and educator in field. Contbg. author Nursing Care Planning Guides. Mem. Am. Assn. Critical Care Nurses, Honor Soc. of Nursing, Sigma Theta Tau Internat. (chpt. pres. 1986-87), Iota Eta (chpt. v.p. 1988—). Roman Catholic.

TENNANT, SAMUEL MCKIBBEN, aerospace systems company executive; b. Feb. 1, 1928; s. Richard Grenville and Margaret Louise (McKibben) T.; m. June Ann Fleischer, June 20, 1953; children: Samuel McKibben Jr., Ann Tennant Boehler, Catherine Tennant Jacobi. BME, MIT, 1950; MME, Purdue U., 1951. Vibration engr. Change Vought Aircraft Corp., Dallas, 1951-52; group engr. dynamics and computations Temco Aircraft Corp., Dallas, 1952-58; sr. staff engr. Titan Space Tech. Labs., Redondo Beach, Calif., 1958-61; assoc. group dir. advanced planning Aerospace Corp., El Segundo, Calif., 1961-66, group dir. engring. manned orbiting lab., 1966-69, v.p., gen. mgr. advanced orbital systems div., 1969-84, group v.p. programs, 1984-87, pres., chief exec. officer, 1987—; cons. Los Alamos (N.Mex.) Nat. Lab. Patentee total knee prosthesis. Mem. sci. adv. bd. USAF, 1984-88; mem. sci. adv. group Air Force Logistics Ctr. Mem. AIAA. Office: Aerospace Corp 2350 E El Segundo Blvd El Segundo CA 90245

TENNANT, TIMOTHY DON, producer; b. Chgo., Aug. 14, 1951; s. Donald George and Barbara Jean (Fuller) T. Student, Roosevelt U., 1969; AA, Lincoln Coll., 1970; student, Am. Acad. Art, Chgo., 1971, Art Ctr. Coll. Design, Pasadena, 1972. Editor, prodn. mgr. Filmfair Inc., Studio City, Calif., 1972-74; prodn. head west coast Lippert, Saviano Inc., Chgo., 1974-75; exec. producer Associated Filmmakers Internat., 1975-78; producer, prodn. mgr. Harmony Pictures Inc., L.A., 1980-83; producer motion pictures Snowball, Inc., MGM, L.A., 1983-84, Inst. Nautical Ark., Coll. Station, Tex., 1984-85; pres. Berdis-Tennant Entertainment, L.A., 1985—; producer motion pictures New World Pictures, L.A., 1987—; producer Kadokawa Prodns., 1988—; cons. Quaker Oats Co., Chgo., 1983, various film studios, 1977—; music video dir. A&M Records, Hollywood, Calif., 1978-80; exec. producer Paramount Studios, Hollywood, 1985. Producer, dir. Feels So Good (Clio award) 1979, Chgo. Advt. (Internat. award) 1980, U.S. TV Comml. (Internat. award) 1982; producer, prodn. mgr. various commls. (Clio award) 1976-83. Recipient Gold Statue Telly Awards, 1987, Silver Statue award, 1988, Gold Medal award N.Y. Film Festival, 1987, Spl. Gold Jury award Houston Film Festival, 1987. Mem. Dirs. Guild Am. (prodn. mgr., asst. dir. 1975—), Assoc. Filmmakers Internat. (sr. v.p., exec. producer 1975-79). Republican. Office: Berdis-Tennant Entertainment 1956 N Cahuenga Blvd Hollywood CA 90028

TENNEN, KEN, property management executive, commercial arbitrator; b. Belmont Shore, Calif., June 30, 1949; s. Morris and Clair (Rose) T.; m. Diane Janet Sussman, Dec. 25, 1982; children: Sterling M., Skyler Alexander. Cert. counseling, UCLA, 1973; lic., U. Los Ams., Cholula Puebla, Mex., 1975; MA, Georgetown U., 1977. Cons. Booz Allen & Hamilton, Washington, 1974-77; real estate investor Multinat. Corp., L.A., 1977-86; owner, mgr. Share-Tel Internat. Hostels, Venice Beach, Calif., 1986-; bd. dirs., chief exec. officer Suntree Townhomes, Tarzana, Calif. Mem. Happy Valley Sch. Bd., Ojai, Calif., 1988—. Home and Office: Share-Tel Internat Hostels 20 Brooks Ave Venice Beach CA 90291

TENNEY, ROBERT IMRODEN, chemical executive; b. Decatur, Ill., Nov. 15, 1910; s. Ralph Mead and Susanne (Imroden) T.; m. Sigrid S. Carlson, July 27, 1935; children: Sally-Sue Tobias, Carla T. Applegate, Lynne N. Lufen. BS in Chemistry, U. Ill., 1932. Product mgr. Rockford (Ill.) Brewing Co., 1932-34; chemist Best Malt Products Co., Chgo., 1934-36; tech. dir., v.p. Wahl-Henius Inst., Chgo., 1936-41, pres., 1941-58; v.p., tech. dir. Fleischman Matling Co., Chgo., 1958-66, exec. v.p., 1966-86; v.p. Tenney Assocs., Winnetka, Ill., 1968—, Bio Pure, Inc., Dolton, Ill., 1980—. Lt. col. U.S. Army. Fellow AAAS, Am. Soc. for Quality Control; mem. Am. Chem. Soc. (emeritus), Inst. Food Technologists, Am. Soc. Brewing Chemists (pres.), Master Brewers Assn., Chgo. Chemists Club, Theta Chi. Home: 25801 S Cloverland Dr Sun Lakes AZ 85248

TENNEY, WILLIAM FRANK, pediatrician; b. Shreveport, La., June 5, 1946; s. William Bonds and Pat (Patton) T.; m. Elizabeth Carter Steadman, Oct. 4, 1973; children: Amy Karen, William Allen. BA, Vanderbilt U., 1968; MD, La. State U., New Orleans, 1972. Diplomate Am. Bd. Pediatrics, sub-Bd. Pediatric Nephrology. Intern Grady Meml. Hosp., Atlanta, 1972-73; resident in pediatrics Emory U. Affiliated Hosps., Atlanta, 1973-74, fellow in pediatric nephrology and inorganic metabolism, 1974-76; practice medicine specializing in pediatric nephrology St. Helens, Oreg., 1976-79, Shreveport, 1979-85, Seattle, 1985—; mem. staff Children's Orthopedic Hosp. and Med. Ctr., Seattle; chief dept. pediatrics Swedish Hosp. Med. Ctr., Seattle, 1987—; clin. asst. prof. pediatrics La. State U. Sch. Medicine, 1979-85, U. Wash. Sch. Medicine, Seattle, 1985—; chmn. Renal com. Schumpert Med. Ctr., Shreveport, 1982, co-chmn. 1979-81, mem. 1983-84, co-dir. Renal Dialysis Unit, 1979-84, mem. renal transplantation com., 1984; cons. pediatric nephrology Shriner's Hosp. Crippled Children, Shreveport, 1979-84, Shreveport Regional Dialysis Ctr., 1979-84, Bossier Dialysis Ctr., Bossier City, La., 1983-84, Natchitoches (La.) Dialysis Facility, 1984. Author: (with others) Pediatric Case Studies, 1985; contbr. articles to profl. jours. Mem. Union Concerned Scientists, Cambridge, Mass., 1986—, Internat. Physicians for Prevention of Nuclear War, Boston, 1986—. Fellow Am. Acad. Pediatrics; mem. Am. Soc. Pediatric Nephrology, North Pacific Pediatric Soc., AMA, Wash. State Med. Assn., Internat. Soc. Peritoneal Dialysis, Empirical Soc. Emory U., King County Med. Soc., AAAS, Northwest Renal Soc., Southwest Pediatric Nephrology (mem. study group 1981-84). Home: 1133 16th Ave E Seattle WA 98112 Office: 1221 Madison St Seattle WA 98104

TENNISON, DON, entertainer; b. Dallas, Aug. 4, 1950; s. Ross R. Tennison and June Marie (Hibbard) Underwood; m. Mary Alice Ledeen, Nov. 30, 1968; children: Kenneth Donald, Ronald Brian. Grad., Palomar Coll., 1978. Newsman Tex. State Network, Ft. Worth, 1974-75; news dir. Sta. KCLE, Cleburne, Tex., 1976-77; keyboardist Marty Robbins Enterprises, Nashville, 1980-82; producer von Allman Advt. Agy., Nacogdotches, Tex., 1983-84; rec. artist Dean Records, Escondido, Calif., 1985; songwriter Don Tennison Music, Escondido, 1985. Writer numerous songs. Served as cpl. USMC, 1969-72. Mem. Broadcast Music, Inc. Republican.

TENNYSON, GEORG BERNHARD, educator; b. Washington, July 13, 1930; s. Georg B. and Emily (Zimmerli) T.; m. Elizabeth Caroline Johnstone, July 13, 1953; children: Cameron, Holly. BA, George Wash. U., 1953, MA, 1959; MA, Princeton U., 1959, PhD, 1963. Instr. English U. N.C., Chapel Hill, 1962-64; asst. prof. to prof. English UCLA, 1964—. Author: Sartor Called Resartus, 1965, An Introduction to Drama, 1969, Victorian Devotional Poetry, 1981, A Carlyle Reader, 1984, Nature and the Victorian Imagination, 1977, Victorian Literature: Prose and Poetry (2 vols.), 1976; contbr. articles to profl jours.; editor: Nineteenth Century Fiction, 1971, Nineteeth Century Literature, 1983. With U.S. Army, 1954-56. Fullbright fellow, Freiburg, Germany, 1953-54, Guggenheim fellow, Guggenheim

Found., London, 1970-71. Mem. MLA (chmn. Victorian sect. 1973), Philological Assn. of Pacific Coast (chmn. English 2 1969), Carlyle Soc. (Edinburgh). Republican. Anglican. Office: UCLA Dept English 405 Hilgard Ave Los Angeles CA 90024-1530

TENORIO, PEDRO PANGELINAN, government official; b. Saipan, Mariana Islands, Apr. 18, 1934; m. Sophia Tenorio; 8 children. Student, Territorial Coll. of Guam (now U. Guam). Formerly sch. tchr., bus. exec; former mem. Congress of Micronesia, also Marianas Dist. Legis.; v.p. Senate, chmn. program com. 1978-80, pres. Senate, 1980-82; gov. No. Mariana Islands, 1982—. Republican. Roman Catholic. Office: Office of Gov Civic Ctr, Susupe Saipan MP 96950

TENZER, MICHAEL L., housing development executive; b. N.Y.C., May 7, 1930; s. Sigmund and Rose (Weiss) T.; m. Jacqueline Newmark, Aug. 7, 1952; children—Gary, Marc. Grad. Art Ctr. Coll. Design, 1949. Photojournalist Look mag., 1949-50; free-lance photographer, pub. relations UN, 1950-51; mgr. brand mktg. Modern Globe, Inc., 1953-57; gen. sales mgr. Berkshire Hosiery Mills, Reading, Pa., 1957-60; mktg. mgr. intimate apparal div. Kayser-Roth Corp., N.Y.C., 1960-63; sr. v.p., dir. Larwin Group, Inc., Beverly Hills, Calif., 1963-74; pres. single family div. Tenzer & Co., Inc., Beverly Hills, 1975-76; chmn. bd., pres., chief exec. officer, dir. Leisure Tech., Los Angeles, 1976—; bd. dirs. policy adv. bd. Ctr. for Real Estate and Urban Econs., U. Calif., Berkeley; mem. Nat. Housing Conf. Past regional chmn. Crescent Bay council Boy Scouts Am., 1966-68, chmn. exec. com., exec. bd. Ocean Ctr. council, 1987; bd. trustees Art Ctr. Coll. of Design; mem. Ocean County (N.J.) council Boy Scouts Am., Los Angeles council Boy Scouts Am.; mem. Pres. Carter's Housing Task Force; trustee, chmn. bd. emeritus Young Musicians Found.; trustee Friends of Music, U. So. Calif., 1971-79, Washington Inst. for Near East Policy; bd. dirs. Am. Youth Symphony, 1974-80; Los Angeles Music Ctr. Opera; founder Met. Opera; Gold Circle founder Los Angeles Music Ctr.; chmn. bd. dirs. Am.-Israel Cultural Found., trustee Art Ctr. Coll. Design in Pasadena, Calif. and Art Ctr. Coll. of Design-Europe based in Vevey, Switzerland; bd. dirs. John Douglas French Found. for Alzheimer's Disease; mem. Am.-Israel Polit. Action Com. Served with Signal Corps, AUS, 1951-52. Recipient Top Performer award Housing mag., 1968, Disting. Eagle Scout award Nat. council Boy Scouts Am., 1982, Inst. Human Relations civic achievement award Am. Jewish Com., 1984, Nat. Humanitarian award Nat. Jewish Hosp., Denver, 1985; named Chief Exec. Officer of Yr., Fin. World's, 1987, Ann. Gala honoree Am.-Israel Cultural Found., 1987. Mem. Urban Land Inst. (fed. policy com.), Nat. Assn. Home Builders (conv. housing, mortgage banking coms. 1965-73). Office: Leisure & Tech Inc 12233 W Olympic Blvd Los Angeles CA 90064

TEPPER, R(OBERT) BRUCE, JR., lawyer; b. Long Branch, N.J., Apr. 1, 1949; s. Robert Bruce and Elaine (Ogus) T.; m. Belinda Wilkins, Nov. 26, 1971; children—Laura Katherine, Jacob Wilkins. A.B. in History, Dartmouth Coll., 1971; J.D. cum laude, St. Louis U., 1976, M.A. in Urban Affairs, 1976. Bar: Mo. 1976, Calif. 1977, Ill. 1978, U.S. Ct. Appeals (7th cir.) 1978, (8th cir.) 1976, (9th cir.) 1978, U.S. Dist. Ct. (cen., no. and so. dists.) Calif. 1978. Asst. gen. counsel St. Louis Redevel. Authority; 1976-77; assoc. Goldstein & Price, St. Louis, 1977-78, Loo, Merideth & McMillan, Los Angeles, 1978-82; sole practice, Los Angeles, 1982-84; ptnr., litigation supr. Kane, Ballmer and Berkman, Los Angeles, 1984—; spl. counsel to Solano County, San Diego, Santa Barbara, Hermosa Beach, Anaheim, Bakersfield, Culver City, Lynwood, Norwalk, Redondo Beach, Oceanside, Ontario, Pasadena, Moreno Valley, West Covina, Whittier, Glendale and Hawthorne, Calif.; spl. counsel redevel. agy. City L.A.; judge pro tempore Los Angeles County Mcpl. Ct., 1983—; grader State Bar Calif., 1980-84. Assoc. editor St. Louis U. Law Jour., 1974-76. Contbr. articles to legal jours. Grad fellow St. Louis U., 1973-76. Mem. Los Angeles County Bar Assn., Assn. Bus. Trial Lawyers, ABA. Republican. Jewish. Clubs: So. Calif. Dartmouth (bd. dirs. 1980-83), Los Angeles Athletic (Los Angeles). Home: 10966 Wrightwood Ln Studio City CA 91604 Office: Kane Ballmer & Berkman 354 S Spring St Ste 420 Los Angeles CA 90013

TERBELL, THOMAS GREEN, JR., bank officer; b. N.Y.C., Oct. 22, 1938; s. Thomas Green Terbell and Louise (Boone) Peterson; m. Melinda Farris, June 17, 1960 (div. June 9, 1972); children: Elizabeth Louise, Alison Virginia, Jennifer Ellen; m. Yolanda Irene Mezey, June 10, 1972; children: Heather Irene, Thomas Green III. BA in Econs., Stanford U., 1960; MBA in Fin., Harvard U., 1962. Dir. mktg., co-owner Albin Enterprises, Inc. div. Jack Built Toys, Burbank, Calif., 1962-64; mgmt. trainee to asst. v.p. Security Pacific Bank, Los Angeles, 1964-69; acting dir. and then dir. Pasadena (Calif.) Art Mus., 1969-71; prin. Terbell Assocs., Pasadena, 1971-72; asst. v.p., then v.p. and gen. mgr. Security Pacific Nat. Bank, Los Angeles, Hong Kong, Tokyo, London, Chgo., San Francisco and Los An, geles, 1972—; mem. exec. com. Bank of Canton, Hong Kong, 1975-76; mem. No. Calif. exec. com. Security Pacific Nat. Bank, San Francisco, 1984-86. Trustee Pasadena Art Mus., 1968-71, Am. Sch. in Japan, 1976-80; treas. San Mateo County Jr. Hockey Club, 1986-87; alternate mem. Rep. State Cen. Com., 1966-68. Republican. Episcopalian. Clubs: American (Hong Kong), Valley Hunt (Pasadena). Office: Security Pacific Bank H12-60 333 S Hope St Los Angeles CA 90071

TERNEUZEN, ROGER MICHAEL, television station executive; b. Chgo., July 20, 1946; s. Robert Louis and Edith (Silverstein) T.; divorced; children: Sandra, Jennifer. Student, Calif. State U., Sacramento, 1964-66, Oxnard Coll., 1968-70, Moorpark Coll., 1982, Ventura Coll., 1986-87. Owner, mgr. Dutchman's Boogie, Ventura, Calif., 1974-79; sales mgr. Chevrolet Co., Oxnard, Calif., 1979-8l; gen. mgr. Storer Communications Co., Westlake Village, Calif., 1981-87; dir. ops., Sta. KADY-TV, Riklis Broadcasting Co., Oxnard, 1987—; sta. mgr. Sta. KBBL-TV Riklis Broadcasting Co., Palm Springs, Calif., 1988—; cons. to cable TV industry, 1987—. Commr. Ojai (Calif.) Redevel. Agy., 1981-83; pres. Tri County chpt. Muscular Dystropy Assn., Santa Barbara, 1987-88. With USAF, 1966-70. Mem. Cen. Coast Cable Club, Conejo Valley C. of C. (bd. dirs. 1985-87), Rotary (sec. Ojai 1985-87). Republican. Home: PO Box 8627 Palm Springs CA 92263 Office: PO Box 8627 Palm Springs CA 92263

TERRA, DALE EDWARD, personnel executive; b. Berkeley, Calif., July 16, 1948; s. Albert Lewis Terra and Norma (Angeles) Bernardi; m. Robin Davison, Aug. 24, 1976 (div. 1978); m. Diane Mae Sahkari, July 3, 1983; 1 child, Dana Miglietto. Student, Coll. of Redwoods, 1968-70, Solano State Coll., Fairfield, CAlif., 1980-82; BA, Calif. State U., Sacramento, 1974, postgrad., 1977. Mgr. security Burns Internat. Security Svcs., Inc., Concord, Calif., 1974-76; rsch. asst. Calif. State U., Sacramento, 1976-77; grad. student asst. Calif. State Pers. Bd., Sacramento, 1976-77, staff svcs. analyst, 1977-80, test validation and devel. specialist, 1980-84, pers. selection cons., 1984-89; mgr. Dept. Corrections, Sacramento, 1989—; pers. cons. Orange County Corrections Dept., Orlando, Fla., 1988—. Contbr. reports to profl. publs. Sgt. USAF, 1966-70, Vietnam. Mem. Internat. Pers. Mgmt. Assn., Pers. Testing Coun., NOW, Phi Kappa Phi, Psi Chi. Home: 336 Chisum Ave Rio Linda CA 95673

TERRACINA, STEPHEN JOSEPH, naval officer; b. Opelousas, La., Sept. 7, 1956; s. Joseph Jr. and Madeline W. (Andrepont) T. BA, N.E. La. U., 1978; degree, Monterey Peninsula Coll., 1986; degree gen. bus., Adminstrn. of Justice, 1986. Tchr. Opelousas High Sch., 1978-79; commd. ensign USN, 1979, advanced through grades to lt., 1985; recruiting officer USN, Jacksonville, Fla., 1989—. Democrat. Roman Catholic. Office: Naval Air Recruiting Box 4 NAS Jacksonville FL 32212-0004

TERRANCE, JOHN, art director; b. St. Louis, Aug. 17, 1959; s. Raymond Jacob and Mary Lillian (McWay) Bregenzer. Student, Ind. U., 1983. Photojournalist Burlington (Vt.) Free Press subs. Gannett Pub. Co., 1983-85; photojournalist designer Ft. Myers (Fla.) News Press subs. Gannett Pub. Co., 1985-86; art dir. World and Health Communications subs. Ogilvy & Mather, N.Y.C., 1986-87, Computer Reseller subs. Thomson Retail Press, L.A., 1987-88, SanyoFisher (USA) Corp., Chatsworth, Calif., 1988—; editor in-chief ARBUTUS Yr. Book, Bloomington, Ind., 1982-83; photojournalist JB Pictures Ltd., N.Y.C., 1987—. Recipient Photo award AP, 1984, 85. Mem. Nat. Press Photographers Assn. (treas. Ind. chpt. 1981-83), Art Dirs. Club N.Y., Art Dirs. Club L.A. Democrat. Home: 1850 N Whitley Ave Apt 506 Hollywood CA 90028 Office: Sanyo Fisher (USA) Corp 21350 Lassen St Chatsworth CA 91311

TERRANOVA, PATRICIA HELEN, treasurer; b. Tacoma, Mar. 25, 1952; d. Donald John and Alicia Katherine (Rose) Marcan; m. Richard James McDonald, Aug. 28, 1971 (div. 1974); 1 child, Christopher Ryan; m. Anthony James Terranova, July 3, 1986. A.Acctg., Ft. Steilacoom Coll., Tacoma, 1974. Contract adminstr. Titan Pacific Corp., Ft. Lewis, Wash., 1974-77; office mgr. Sequoia Supply, Tacoma, 1977-78; treas., chief fin. officer Woodworth & Co., Inc., Tacoma, 1978—. Active PTA, Tacoma, 1978—. Mem. Credit Execs. of Puget Sound, Women in Constrn. Republican. Roman Catholic. Office: Woodworth & Co Inc 1200 E D St Tacoma WA 98421

TERRELL, A. JOHN, university telecommunications director; b. Pasadena, Calif., Dec. 27, 1927; s. Harry Evans and Elizabeth (Eaton) T.; m. Elizabeth Schalk, June 6, 1949; children—Patricia Elyse, Marilee Diane, John Scott. Student, Chaffey Coll., 1947-48; B.B.A., U. N. Mex., 1952. Communications cons. Mountain States Tel. & Tel., Albuquerque, 1951-56; mgr. office and communications services A.C.F. Industries, Inc., Albuquerque, 1956-62; mgr. communications and services Norton Simon Industries, Inc., Fullerton, Ca., 1962-68; v.p. gen. mgr. Wells Fargo Security Guard Service Div. Baker Industries, Fullerton, Ca., 1968-71; adminstrv. mgr., budget adminstr. Hyland div. Baxter-Trevenol Labs. Inc., Costa Mesa, CA, 1971-77; exec. v.p. Am. Tel. Mgmt. Inst Inc., Newport Beach, Calif., 1977-78; telecommunications dir. UCLA, 1978-89, retired, 1989. Contbr. articles to profl. jours. Republican. candidate for state rep., Albuquerque, 1960; precinct chmn. and mem. Bernalillo County Rep. Central Com., 1961-62; Rep. candidate for N. Mex. State Bd. Edn., 2nd Jud. Dist., 1962; colonial aide-de-camp Gov. N. Mex., Santa Fe, 1968. Served with U.S. Mcht. Marine, 1944-45, U.S. Army, 1946-47, USAR, 1947-50. Mem. Nat. Assn. Accts. (dir. 1967-77) (Most Valuable mem. 1974-75), Telecommunications Assn., Am. Legion, Am. Legion Yacht Club , VFW. Episcopalian. Lodges: Greater Irvine Lions (charter pres. 1975-76), Albuquerqué Jaycees (v.p., treas. 1956-62). Home: 1725 Port Charles Pl Newport Beach CA 92660-5319

TERRELL, DALE PAUL, data processing executive; b. Flint, Mich., May 30, 1940; s. Sedgwick Edward and Goldie (Brown) T.; m. Barbara Jean Purdo, Jan. 8, 1971; children: Jeffrey, Melanie. BA, Albion (Mich.) Coll., 1961. With IBM Grand Rapids, Mich., 1962-64; sys. engr. IBM, Oak Park, Mich., 1966-69; dir. fin. sys. U. Computing Co., Troy, Mich., 1969-75, U.C.C., Dallas, 1975-79; sys. mgr. Security Pacific Automation, Los Angeles, 1979--. Home: 25626 Barganca Ct Valencia CA 91355

TERRELL, HOWARD BRUCE, psychiatrist; b. Cleveland, Calif., Feb. 19, 1952. BS magna cum laude, Calif. State U., Hayward, 1974; MD, U. Calif., San Diego, 1980. Intern. Kaiser Found. Hosp., Oakland, Calif., 1980-81; resident in psychiatry U. Calif., San Francisco/Fresno, 1982-85; staff psychiatrist Kings View Corp., Reedley, Calif., 1985-87, sr. staff psychiatrist, 1987-88, dir. outpatient psychiatry, 1988-89; dir. affective disorders program CPC Sierra Gateway Hosp., Clovis, Calif., 1989—. Contbr. articles to profl. jours. Mem. Am. Coll. Forensic Psychiatry, Am. Acad. Psychiatry and the Law, Am. Psychiat. Assn., U. Calif.-San Francisco-Fresno Psychiat. Residency Program (alumni pres. 1985—). Office: 3100 Willow Ave Ste102 Clovis CA 93612

TERRELL, W. GLENN, university president; b. Tallahassee, May 24, 1920; s. William Glenn and Esther (Collins) T.; divorced; children: Francine Elizabeth, William Glenn III. BA, Davidson Coll., 1942, LLD (hon.), 1969; MS, Fla. State U., 1948; PhD, State U. Iowa, 1952; LLD (hon.), Gonzaga U., 1984, Seattle U., 1985. Instr., then asst. prof. Fla. State U., Tallahassee, 1948-55; asst. prof., then assoc. prof., chmn. dept. psychology U. Colo., Boulder, 1955-59, assoc., acting dean Coll Arts and Scis., 1959-63; prof. psychology, dean Coll. Liberal Arts and Scis., U. Ill. at Chgo. Circle, 1963-65, dean faculties, 1965-67; pres. Wash. State U., Pullman, 1967-85, pres. emeritus, 1985—; Pres. Nat. Assn. State Univs. and Land-Grant Colls., 1977-78; cons. The Pacific Inst., Seattle, 1987—. Contbr. articles to profl. jours. Served to capt. inf. U.S. Army, 1942-46, ETO. Recipient Disting. Alumnus award U. Iowa, 1985. Fellow APA; mem. Am. Psychol. Assn., AAAS, Sigma Xi, Phi Kappa Phi. Home: 2320 43 E #305A Seattle WA 98112 Office: The Pacific Inst 1201 Western Ave Seattle WA 98101

TERRERI, FRANK JOHN, lawyer; b. New Castle, Pa., Apr. 25, 1922; s. Edward and Nancy (Christopher) T.; m. Evelyn Leasure, Jan. 9, 1943 (div. 1963); children: Bonnie Lee Mucrief, Laura Jean Horacek. BS, Youngstown U., 1951; JD, Western State U., Fullerton, Calif., 1971. Bar: Calif. 1972. Claims staff Allstate Ins., Santa Ana, Calif., 1963-73; trial atty. Thomas Moore & Assocs., L.A., 1973-74; ptnr. Stroschein & Terreri, Santa Ana, 1974-75, Terreri & Pozzi, Santa Ana, 1976-80; pvt. practice Newport Beach, Calif., 1980-86, Corona Del Mar, Calif., 1986—; judge pro tem Orange County Superior Ct., Santa Ana, 1978--; arbitrator Orange County Superior Ct., Santa Ana, 1983--, Am. Arbitration Assn., L.A., 1974-76. Advisor, bd. dirs. Vols. in Parole, Westminister, Calif., 1985--. With AUS, 1943-45, ETO. Decorated Bronze Star medal. Mem. Oragne County Trial Lawyers, Orange County Bar Assn., Orange County Am. Italian Renaissance Found. (bd. dirs. 1988), Phi Alpha Delta, Lex Romana (pres. 1985). Presbyterian. Office: 2121 E Coast Hwy Ste 280 Corona Del Mar CA 92625

TERRES, EDWARD TODD, computer systems analyst; b. Phila., Dec. 20, 1935; s. Edward A. and Irene Steritt (Todd) T.; m. Mary Stuart Taylor, Feb. 1958 (div. June 1973); 1 child, Nora Todd. BA in History, Am. U., 1961, postgrad in computer sci., 1966-69. Various fin. mgmt. and computer system positions Naval Facilities Engring. Command, Washington, 1961-73; controller, officer in charge of construction, Trident Naval Facilities Engring. Command, Bremerton, Wash., 1973-81; dir. Field Data Systems Office, Port Hueneme, Calif., 1981--. Transp. chmn., exec. com. mem. Calif. Strawberry Festival, Oxnard, 1986--; co-chmn. Oxnard 4th of July Street Fair, 1988--; mem. Oxnard Adv. Council, 1988. Served with USAF, 1956-59. Home: 518 E Bard Rd Oxnard CA 93030 Office: USN Constrn Bn Ctr Port Hueneme CA 93043

TERRI, MARIE URSULA, real estate professional; b. Tehran, Iran, Oct. 20, 1943; came to U.S., 1955; d. George and Urszula (Paproczka) Domanski; m. Marshall Lee Enyart, Aug. 24, 1963 (div. 1974). Student, U. Hawaii, 1985-86, 88. Lic. real estate assoc., Calif., Hawaii. Mgr., coord. rels. Shaklee Corp., San Francisco, 1968-76; assoc. various real estate firms, Cupertino, Calif., 1978-83, Locations, Inc., Kaneohe, Hawaii, 1988—; with Kailua (Hawaii) Realty; writer, researcher, cons. Preservation of Modern and Ancient Hawaiian Culture, Moloka'i, Hawaii, 1984-88; mem. adv. bd. NaPu'u Wai-Hawaiian Heart Study, Moloka'i, 1986-87; pres. bd. trustees The Moloka'i Found., 1985—. Fundraiser, Aloha United Way, Moloka'i, 1986; sec., bd. dirs. Hui Imi Na'au, Moloka'i, 1985-87. Mem. NAFE, Smithsonian Inst., Nature Def. Fund, Sierra Club. Home: PO Box 4932 Kaneohe HI 96744 Office: Kailua Realty 130 Kailua Rd Kailua HI 96734

TERRY, DALE RANDOLPH, controller; b. Phila., Jan. 15, 1947; s. Richard Arthur Terry and Anne (Schwab) Williams; m. (Polly) Elides Isabel Ramos, June 16, 1974; children: David, Joseph, Tamera, Kurt. BS in Hotel Adminstrn., Cornell U., 1970; MBA, Golden Gate U., 1978. Food svc. mgr. Svc. Systems, Davis, Calif., 1976-80; food svc. dir. Svc. Systems, Davis, 1980-81; fin. analyst Del Monte, San Francisco, 1981-85; system adminstr. Chaminade, Santa Cruz, Calif., 1985-87; contr. Charter at Beaver Creek (Colo.), 1987-88, Manor Vail (Colo.) Condominium Assn., 1988—. Scoutmaster Eagle, Colo. Boy Scouts Am., 1988. With U.S. Army, 1972-75. Recipient On My Honor award Mormon Ch. Mem. Cornell Soc. Hotelmen. Republican. Home: PO Box 329 Edwards CO 81632

TERRY, ROBERT DAVIS, educator, neuropathologist; b. Hartford, Conn., Jan. 13, 1924; m. Patricia Ann Blech, June 27, 1952; 1 son, Nicolas Saul. A.B., Williams Coll., 1946; M.D., Albany (N.Y.) Med. Coll., 1950. Diplomate: Am. Bd. Pathology, Am. Bd. Neuropathology. Postdoctoral tng. St. Francis Hosp., Hartford, 1950, Bellevue Hosp., N.Y.C., 1951, Montefiore Hosp., N.Y.C., 1952-53, 54-55, Inst. Recherches sur le Cancer, Paris, France, 1953-54; sr. postdoctoral fellow Inst. Recherches sur le Cancer, 1965-66; asst. pathologist Montefiore Hosp., 1955-59; assoc. prof. dept. pathology Einstein Coll. Medicine, Bronx, N.Y., 1959-64; prof. Einstein Coll. Medicine, 1964-84, acting chmn. dept. pathology, 1969-70, chmn., 1970-84; prof. depts. neuroscis. and pathology U. Calif.-San Diego, 1984—; mem. study sect. pathology NIH, 1964-68; study sects. Nat. Multiple Sclerosis Soc., 1964-72, 74-78; mem. bd. sci. counselors Nat. Inst. Neurol. and Communicative Disorders and Stroke, NIH, 1976-80, chmn., 1977-80; mem. nat. sci. council Huntington's Disease Assn., 1978-81; mem. med. and sci. adv. bd. Alzheimer's Disease Soc., Inc., 1978-88. Editorial adv. bd.: Jour. Neuropathology and Exptl. Neurology, 1963-83, 85-88, Lab. Investigation, 1967-77, Revue Neurologique, 1977-87, Annals of Neurology, 1978-82, Ultrastructural Pathology, 1978-86, Am. Jour. Pathology, 1985—. Served with AUS, 1943-46. Recipient Potamkin prize for Alzheimer Research, 1988. Mem. Am. Assn. Neuropathologists (pres. 1969-70), N.Y. Path. Soc. (v.p. 1969-71, pres. 1971-73), Am. Soc. Exptl. Pathology, Am. Neurol. Assn., Am. Acad. Neurologists. Office: U Calif San Diego Dept Neuroscis La Jolla CA 92093

TERRY, STEVEN SPENCER, mathematics educator, consultant; b. Hoodriver, Oreg., July 9, 1942; s. Steven Bliss and Kathryn (Spencer) T.; m. Vivian Hickman, Aug. 20, 1964; children: Yvette, Kathryn, S. Matthew, Spencer, Stuart, Heather. BS, Utah State U., 1964, MS, 1967. Tchr. math Clayton Jr. High, Salt Lake City, 1964-67, 29 Palms (Calif.) High Sch., 1967-68; tchr. math, coach Yucca Valley (Calif.) High Sch., 1968-76; prof. math. Ricks Coll., Rexburg, Idaho, 1976—. Author: (textbook) Elementary Teachers' Math, 1985. Pres. City Council Yucca Valley, Calif., 1972-76, water bd., fire streets bd., lighting bd., recreation bd.; judge Jr. Miss Contests, Idaho; officer Baseball Assn., Madison County, Idaho. Named one of Outstanding Young Men of Am. Jaycees, 1976; recipient Outstanding Tchr. award San Bernardino and Riverside Counties, Calif., 1976, Outstanding Secondary Educator, 1974, 75. Mem. Am. Math. Assn. Two Yr. Colls. (v.p. 1980-86), Outstanding Contribution award 1982, 84, 86, co-chair Summer Inst. at Ricks Coll. co-chair 1988 Conv.), Nat. Coun. Tchrs. of Math., NEA (life), Phi Delta Kappa (life, sec. 1974-76, Outstanding Contribution award 1984). Republican. Mormon. Home: 221 S 2d E Rexburg ID 83440 Office: Ricks Coll Rexburg ID 83440

TERWEDO, SHANNON MARY, healthcare executive; b. Denver, May 19, 1958; d. Edward Dean and Donna Marie (O'Leary) Richardson; m. John Carlo DeConcini, May 29, 1982 (div. 1986); m. Randal John Terwedo, Apr. 25, 1987. BS, U. Ariz., 1980, MPA, 1984. Projects planning mgr. Ariz. Health Care Cost Containment System, Phoenix, 1984, spl. asst. to med. dir., 1985; dir. Phoenix Health Plan, 1985-88; corp. dir. managed care St. Luke's Health System, Phoenix, 1988—. Mem. Am. Cancer Soc., Hispanic Leadership Inst., Group Health Assn. Mem. Group Health Assn. Am. Home: 16027 S 41st Pl Phoenix AZ 85044 Office: St Lukes Health System 1800 E Van Buren Phoenix AZ 85006

TERWILLIGER, ROBERT ALAN, county government official, lawyer; b. Middletown, N.Y., Sept. 11, 1947; s. Clarene Lawrence and Anne Jenny (Gregory) T.; m. Marilyn Elizabeth Walsh, July 29, 1972; children: Catherine Anne, Matthew Muir. BA, SUNY, Stony Brook, 1969; MPA, SUNY, Albany, 1970; JD, U. Puget Sound, 1977. Bar: Wash. 1977. Adminstrv. asst. Coll. of Arts and Scis. SUNY, Albany, 1972-74; dep. pros. atty. Snohomish County, Everett, Wash., 1978-80; assoc. Breskin, Robbins and Bastian, Seattle, 1980-82; chief dep. Snohomish County Auditor's Office, Everett, 1983—. Co-chmn. allocations com. United Way of Snomohish County, Everett, 1988—; vice chair 44th Legis. Dist., Snomohish County, 1985—; bd. dirs. Pub. Edn. Fund, Edmonds, Wash., 1988—. Democrat. Presbyterian. Office: Snohomish County Auditor 3000 Rockefeller Ave Everett WA 98201

TERZIAN, JAMES RICHARD, marketing executive; b. L.A., Mar. 9, 1961; s. Carl Richard and Lynne (Morgan) T. Student, Oxford U., 1981; AB, U. Calif., Berkeley, 1984. Polit. cons. Mayor Brian O'Toole and Sen. Becky Morgan, Calif., 1984; senate cons. Calif. State Senate Select Com. Bus. Devel., Sacramento, 1985-86; cons. various bus. devel. and fundraising firms Sacramento and Santa Rosa, Calif., 1986-88; with exec. office Terzian Internat. Group (TIGR), Santa Rosa, 1987—. Mem. Royal Oak Found., Boy Scouts Am.; assoc. mem. Calif. Rep. Cen. Com. Named to Order of St. Dunstan Episc. Ch., 1979. Mem. Soc. Creative Anachronism, Order of De Molay, Am. Gem. Soc., Golden Nuggets, Phi Kappa Alpha. Home and Office: PO Box 4739 Santa Rosa CA 95402

TESTA, GREGORY SISTO, JR., sales executive; b. Elizabeth, N.J., Jan. 30, 1943; s. George Sisto Sr. and Carmen Ann (Muro) T.; m. Rosalind Arline Paolello, Sept. 12, 1964; children: Debora Diana (dec.), Darius. BA in Chemistry and Chem. Engring., Northwestern U., 1965; MBA in Mktg. and Mgmt., Fairleigh Dickinson U., 1971. Inside sales rep. Beckman Instruments, Inc., Fullerton, Calif., 1965-66, sr. sales rep., 1966-74, dist. sales mgr., 1974-82, nat. bio-rsch. planning mgr., 1982-84, bioanalytical sales planner, 1984, mgr. nat. accounts and export sales, 1984-86; sr. v.p., chief exec. officer, div. mgr. Heraeus, Inc. Indsl. Products, South Plainfield, N.J., 1986—. Home: 10092 Knuth Circle Villa Park CA 92667

TESTA, STEPHEN MICHAEL, geologist, consultant; b. Fitchburg, Mass., July 17, 1951; s. Guiseppe Alfredo and Angelina Mary (Petitto) T.; m. Lydia Mae Payne, July 26, 1986; 1 child, Brant Ethan Gage. AA, Los Angeles Valley Jr. Coll., Van Nuys, 1971; BS in Geology, Calif. State U., Northridge, 1976, MS in Geology, 1978. Registered geologist, Calif., Oreg.; cert. profl. geol. scientist., Idaho, Alaska. Engring. geologist R.T. Frankian & Assocs., Burbank, Calif., 1976-78, Bechtel, Norwalk, Calif., 1978-80, Converse Cons., Seattle, 1980-82; sr. hydrogeologist Ecology Environment, Seattle, 1982-83; sr. geologist Dames & Moore, Seattle, 1983-86; v.p. west coast ops. Engring. Enterprises, Long Beach, Calif., 1986—. Editor: Geologic Field Guide to the Salton Basin, 1988, Environmental Concerns in the Petroleum Industry, 1989; contbr. numerous articles to profl. jours. Mem. Am. Inst. Profl. Geologists (profl. devel. com. 1986, continuing edn. com., program chmn., 1988—, Presidential Cert. of Merit, 1987), Geol. Soc. Am., Am. Assn. Petroleum Geologists, AAAS, Assn. Ground Water Scientists and Engrs., Assn. Engring. Geologists, Mineral. Soc. Can., Hazardous Materials Research Inst., Calif. Water Pollution Control Assn., Sigma Xi. Home: 29351 Kensington Dr Laguna Niguel CA 92677 Office: Engring Enterprises 21818 S Wilmington Ave Ste 406 Long Beach CA 90816

TETLOW, WILLIAM LLOYD, computer executive; b. Phila., July 2, 1938; s. William Lloyd and Mary Eleanor (Ferris) T.; m. Amber Jane Riederer, June 13, 1964; children: Jennifer Kay, Rebecca Dawn, Derek William. Student, Cornell U., 1956-60; B in Gen. Edn., U. Omaha, 1961; MA, Cornell U., 1965, PhD, 1973. Dir. instl. research Cornell U., Ithaca, N.Y., 1965-70; dir. planning U. B.C., Vancouver, Can., 1970-82; dir. NCHEMS Mgmt. Products, Boulder, Colo., 1982-85; pres., dir. Vantage Info. Products, Inc., Boulder, 1985-87; pres., propr. Vantage Computer Services, Boulder, 1986—; cons. various univs. U.S., Can. and Australia, 1970—. Editor/ author: Using Microcomputers for Planning and Decision Support, 1984; contbr. numerous articles to profl. jours. Served to 1st lt. AUS, 1961-63. Recipient U. Colo. medal, 1987. Mem. Assn. Inst. Research (sec. 1973-75, v.p. 1980-81, pres. 1981-82). Republican. Lodges: Concordia, Tsawwassen. Home: 3650 Smuggler Way Boulder CO 80303 Office: Vantage Computer Svcs PO Box 1857 Boulder CO 80306-1857

TETZLAFF, KELLY RICHARD JOHN, banker; b. L.A., Nov. 2, 1954; s. Frederick August and Ellilian May (Dalquest) T.; m. Laureen Teresa McKee, Sept. 10, 1978; children: Jason Thomas William, Jared Stephen Michael, Jerilyn Kristine. Grad. high sch., Upland, Calif. Svc. technician S.W. Gas Corp., Bullhead City, Ariz., 1975-80; minister of youth Riviera Bapt. Ch., 1980-82; field sales rep. N.Y. Life Ins. Co., 1982-83; personnel interviewer Flyash Haulers Inc., 1983; loan collector lst Interstate Bank Ariz., 1983-84; asst. br. mgr. lst Interstate Bank Ariz., Lake Havasu City, 1984-86; br. mgr. lst Interstate Bank Ariz., Parker, 1986--. Pres. Mohave Valley Youth Ctr.; dist. commnr. London Bridge coun. Boy Scouts Am., 1984-886; chmn. bd. deacons Desert View Bapt. Ch., 1987--; chmn. Parker Area Econ. Devel. Com., 1986--; mem. La Paz County Indsl. Devel. Authority. Sgt. U.S. Army N.G., 1972-75. Mem. Rotary. Office: lst Interstate Bank Ariz 100l Arizona Ave PO Box 9l0 Parker AZ 85344

TEVRIZIAN, DICKRAN M., JR., federal judge; b. Los Angeles, Aug. 4, 1940; s. Dickran and Rose (Mooradian) T.; m. Geraldine Tevrizian, Aug. 22,

1964; children: Allyson Tracy, Leslie Sara. BS, U. So. Calif., 1962, JD, 1965. Tax acct. Arthur Andersen and Co., Los Angeles, 1965-66; atty., ptnr. Kirtland and Packard, Los Angeles, 1966-72; judge Los Angeles Mcpl. Ct., Los Angeles, 1972-78, State of Calif. Superior Ct., Los Angeles, 1978-82; ptnr. Manatt, Phelps, Rothenberg & Tunney, Los Angeles, 1982-85, Lewis, D'Amato, Brisbois & Bisgaard, Los Angeles, 1985-86; judge U.S. Dist. Ct., Los Angeles, 1986—. Office: US Dist Ct 312 N Spring St Los Angeles CA 90012

TEYSSIER, EDWARD MATTHEW, manufacturing executive, engineer; b. San diego, June 29, 1954; s. Leonard Edward and Monica E. T. BSEE, U. Calif., Berkeley, 1977, BS in Nuclear Engring., 1977; MSEE, Calif. State U., Northridge, 1983. Design engr. Avantek, Inc., Santa Clara, Calif., 1977-79; project engr. Amplica, Inc., Newbury Park, Calif., 1979-84; pres. Microwave Solutions, Inc., National City, Calif., 1984—. Mem. IEEE, Bachelor Club. Home: 855 Muirlands Dr La Jolla CA 92037 Office: Microwave Solutions Inc 3200 Highland Ave B1-3A National City CA 92050

THACKER, RICHARD THOMAS, JR., cable television company executive, consultant; b. Everett, Wash., Mar. 31, 1931; s. Richard Thomas and Gertrude Dagmar (Skrondal) T.; m. Nancy Lurvey, June 17, 1956 (div. 1966); children: Randi Liann, Richard Thomas III; m. Joyce D. Reed, Sept. 12, 1968. Student, Oreg. State Coll., 1949-51; BS in Speech, U. Oreg., 1953. Mgmt. trainee Meier & Frank Dept. Store, Portland, Oreg., 1956-57; dir. guest relations ABC TV Network, Hollywood, Calif., 1957-59; account exec. TV sales advt. Blair TV, L.A., 1959-64; sales mgr. Eastman TV, Hollywood, 1964-68; dir. mktg. Color TV City, Houston, 1968-71; account exec.TV advt. sales Gaylord Broadcasting Co., Houston, 1971-80; pres. Success Shop, Houston, 1980-82; sales mgr. cable advt. Malloy Broadcasting Cod., Houston, 1982-86, Palmer Cablevision Co., Palm Desert, Calif., 1986--. Capt. U.S. Army, 1953-55. Mem. Rotary. Home: PO Box 1078 La Quinta CA 92253 Office: Palmer Cablevision Co 41-725 Cook St Palm Desert CA 92260

THAGARD, SHIRLEY STAFFORD, sales and marketing executive; b. Detroit, Nov. 29, 1940; d. Walter Jay Stafford and Marjorie Gertrude (LaRa) Stafford Goode; children: Grayson Jay, Devon Charles. Assoc. Bus., Webber Coll., 1961; cert. Pierce Coll., 1973. Dir. pub. relations Miami Herald, Fla., 1963-67; pres. Thagard Enterprises, Woodland Hills, Calif., 1980—; v.p. mktg. R.T. Durable Med. Products, Inc., Miami, also Woodland Hills, 1983-85; investment cons., lectr. investments Palisades Fin. Services, Sherman Oaks, Calif., 1985-86; v.p. real estate investments, M.W. Palmer and Assocs., 1986-87, with real estate sales dept. Country Club West Realtors, 1987—; ind. lectr. women's issues and children's health care, 1980—. Editor, pub. Pediatric Network, 1980-85. Contbr. articles to various jours. Creator Med. Moppets healthcare teaching tools, 1983. Chairperson Los Angeles County Mental Health (Expressing Feelings), 1985-87; ind. lobbyist for child abuse legislation Calif. Legislature, 1985—. Recipient commendation Los Angeles City Council, 1983, Calif. Congresswoman Bobbi Fiedler, 1984. Mem. Nat. Assn. Female Execs., San Fernando Valley Bd. Realtors, Assn. Care of Children's Health, Am. Bus. Women's Assn., Pilot Internat. (pub. relations com. 1985-86, San Fernando Valley club commendation 1985), Nat. Assn. Edn. Young Children, Direct Mktg. Council Los Angeles. Avocations: travel, writing.

THAL, MICHAEL LEWIS, teacher; b. Oceanside, N.Y., Feb. 28, 1949; s. Herman Leon and Vivian (Friedman) T.; m. Daphna Oded, Dec. 23, 1980; children: Channie Anne, Koren Ellen. BA in History, U. Buffalo, 1971; MA in Elem. Edn., Wash. U., 1973; MA in Reading, Calif. State U., Northridge, 1978. Cert. elem., sec. tchr., reading specialist. Tchr. L.A. Unified Sch. Dist., L.A., 1973-78; dir. edn. Readwrite Ednl. Program, Newport Beach, Calif., 1978-80; tchr. Montobello (Calif.) Unified Sch. Dist., 1980-85; tchr., dept. chmn. Glendale (Calif.) Unified Sch. Dist., 1985—; instr. The Learning Annex, L.A., 1986-89; sales rep. World Book, Inc., Chgo., 1986—; chmn. Parent-Tchr.'s Adv. Council, Roosevelt Jr. High Sch., Glendale, 1986—, reading dept.; reader Glendale Unified Sch. Dist., 1986—. Contbr. articles to profl. jours. Treas. Orgn. for Advancement of Space Industrialization and Settlements, L.A., 1978-80; bd. dirs. Glendale Beautification Project, 1987. Mem. Glendale Tchrs. Assn., Calif. Tchrs. Assn., NEA, Sports Connection. Republican. Jewish. Home: 9007 Cresta Dr Los Angeles CA 90035 Office: Roosevelt Jr High Sch 1017 S Glendale Ave Glendale CA 91205

THALER, MANNING MICHAEL, pediatrics educator; b. Poland, Sept. 29, 1934; came to U.S., 1965; s. Morris and Fanny Thaler; m. Libby L. Fuss, Jan. 24, 1966; children: Eva, Joshua. MD, U. Toronto, Can., 1958. Prof. pediatrics U. Calif., San Francisco, 1967—, also dir. pediatric gastroenterology and nutrition; bd. dirs. U. Calif., San Francisco, 1967—. Contbr. articles to profl. jours. and chpts. to books. Pres. Holocaust Ctr. of No. Calif., San Francisco, 1982. Josiah Macy Jr. Found. scholar, 1974. Mem. Am. Soc. Biol. Chemists, Am. Pediatric Soc., Am. Soc. Clin. Investigation, Assn. for Study Liver Disease, Soc. Pediatric Research, Am. Gastroenterol. Assn. Office: U Calif M680 San Francisco CA 94143-0136

THALER, NANCY MOHNEY, psychotherapist; b. New Castle, Pa., Nov. 4, 1953; d. Willis Robert and Lillian Marie (Snyder) Mohney; m. James Lynn Oglesbee, Oct. 30, 1971 (div. Jan. 1975); m. Maximillan Werner Thaler, Mar. 5, 1977; children: Linda Christine, Scott Warren, Lisa Michele, Wyatt Michael. AA in Psychology, Spokane Falls Community Coll., 1982; BS in Psychology, Ea. Wash. U., 1984, MS in Clin. Psychology, 1986; postgrad., Calif. Sch. Profl. Psychology, 1987—. Realtor Wash., 1975-85; psychotherapist Spokane (Wash.) Community Mental Health Clinic, 1985-86; teaching intern Ea. Wash. U., Cheney, 1986; psychology intern Calif. Men's Colony, San Luis Obispo, 1986-87, Atascadero-San Luis Obispo Community Mental Health Clinic, 1987-88; doctoral intern Astacadero (Calif.) State Hosp., 1988—. Mem. Calif. Psychol. Assn., NOW, Psi Chi. Democrat. Lutheran. Home: 841 Tulare Pismo Beach CA 93449 Office: Atascadero State Hosp PO Box A Atascadero CA 93423

THALKEN, MARGARET MARY, magazine executive; b. Nebr., Nov. 8, 1932; d. William Gustav and Jane Francis (Flynn) T. BA, Mt. St. Mary's Coll., 1954. Editor West coast Glamour mag., L.A., 1954-64; exec. editor Glamour mag., N.Y.C., 1965-68; fashion dir. Eastern Airlines, N.Y.C., 1968-72; mdse. editor Vogue mag., N.Y.C., 1972-74, travel mgr., 1974-85; mgr. West House & Garden mag., Beverly Hills, Calif., 1985-88; mgr. pacific Condé Nast International, 1988—; mem. Fashion Group, L.A. Bd. dirs. Calif. Hist. Soc., L.A., L.A. Orphanage Guild. Roman Catholic. Home: 578 S Ogden Dr Los Angeles CA 90036

THALL, RICHARD VINCENT, school administrator; b. San Francisco, Sept. 12, 1940; s. Albert Vincent and Alice Stella (O'Brien) T.; m. Ellyn Marie Wisherop, June 15, 1963; children: Kristen Ellyn, Richard Vincent Jr. AA, City Coll. San Francisco, 1961; BA, San Francisco State Coll., 1964; MA, San Francisco State U., 1971. Cert. elem. tchr., Calif.; cert. secondary tchr., Calif.; cert. community coll. tchr., Calif. Tchr. biology San Francisco Unified Sch. Dist., 1965-66; tchr. biology Mt. Diablo Unified Sch. Dist., Concord, Calif., 1966-79, program coordinator, 1979—; ranger/naturalist State of Calif., Brannan Island, 1973-78; naturalist Adventure Internat., Oakland, Calif., 1979-81; lectr. Princess Cruise Lines, Los Angeles, 1982-84, Sea Goddess, 1986—, Sun Lines, 1987—; Am. biology tchr., 1976; speaker commencements U. Calif., Berkeley, 1989. Author: Ecological Sampling of the Sacramento-San Joaquin Delta, 1976; Water Environment Studies Program, 1986; co-author: Project MER Laboratory Manual, 1982. Mem. Contra Costa County (Calif.) Natural Resources Commn., 1975-78, vice-chmn., 1977-78; active Save Mt. Diablo, Concord, 1969-76, v.p., 1974-75; mem. citizens com. Assn. Bay Area Govt. Water Quality, 1979-82, vice-chmn., 1980-82; active John Marsh Home Restoration Com., Martinez, Calif., 1977-78; mem. edn. adv. com. Marine World/Africa USAd, Vallejo, Calif., 1988—; troop com. chmn. Boy Scouts Am., Concord, 1984-86, asst. scoutmaster, 1985-87. Recipient Recognition and Excellence cert. Assn. Calif. Sch. Adminstrs., 1984, Wood Badge award Boy Scouts Am., 1986; grantee State Calif., 1982, 84. Mem. AAAS, Nat. Assn. Biology Tchrs., Nat., Audubon Soc., Am. Mus. Natural Hist., Nat. Geog. Soc., Smithsonian Instn. (assoc.). Republican. Roman Catholic. Home: 1712 Lindenwood Dr Concord CA 94521 Office: Mt Diablo Unified Sch Dist 1936 Carlotta Dr Concord CA 94519

THAMES, TROY LYNN, security company executive, consultant; b. Plainview, Tex., Sept. 18, 1953; s. Jesse Thomas and Betty Jean (Bradley) T.; m. Terri Joyce Billings, Apr. 7, 1979; children: Christopher Dustin, Michael Kent, Amanda Dawn. BS, U.S. Mil. Acad., West Point, N.Y., 1976. Commd. 2d lt. U.S. Army, Colorado Springs, Colo., 1976; advanced through grades to capt. U.S. Army, 1976-80, resigned, 1986; mgr. trainee Allied Security, Inc., Houston, 1986; br. mgr. Allied Security, Inc., San Antonio, 1986-87, Phoenix, 1987—. Mem. Am. Soc. Indsl. Security. Republican. Baptist. Office: Allsafe Security Inc 3150 N 24th St Ste 200 Phoenix AZ 85016

THARP, PATRICIA HELENE, travel agency executive; b. N.Y.C., July 15, 1939; d. Louis John and Frances (Souchetloff) Gallo; m. Charles Eugene Tharp, Aug. 1, 1974; children: Deborah Sardine, Jami Kong, Cari Ortiz, Gary Tharp. Student, U. Nev., 1968-69, Breech Acad., 1972; cert., Wellesley Coll., 1986. Mgr. Valley Travel Co., Las Vegas, 1971-74, Passport To Better Travel, Honolulu, 1975-77; v.p., gen. mgr. Global Travel Ctr., Inc., Kahuliu, Hawaii, 1979—. Contbr. articles to profl. jours. Conv. del. Rep. Com., Maui, Hawaii, 1988. Mem. Assn. Retail Travel Agts., Am. Soc. Travel Agts., Pacific Assn. Travel Agts., NAFE, Inst. Cert. Travel Cons. Home: 2727 Keikilani St Pukalani HI 96768

THATCHER, REGINALD, real estate broker; b. Los Angeles, June 18, 1927; s. Howard Russell and Regina (Cremer) T.; m. Nancy Dale Hemmings, Nov. 27, 1954; 1 child, Kimberly Dale. Student, Chouinard, Los Angeles, 1939-44, UCLA Extension, West Los Angeles, 1951-66, Glendale Community Coll., 1980. Cert. real estate appraiser. Sales mgr. Stewart-Warner Microcircuits, Los Angeles, 1968-70; ptnr. and mfgs. rep. Compar L.A., Gardena, Calif., 1970-72; sales engr. De Angelo-Rothman & Co., Culver City, Calif., 1972-73; dist. sales mgr. Teledyne Semiconductor, Hawthorne, Calif., 1973-74; v.p. V & L Assocs., Encino, Calif., 1974-76; regional sales mgr. Triridge Corp., Goleta, Calif., 1976; realtor assoc. Pro Realty Inc., Glendale, Calif., 1976-78, O.E. Higgs Realtor, Glendale, 1978; sole proprietor Thatcher Enterprises, Glendale, 1978—; founder, past pres. Glendale (Calif.) Eschangors, 1979-85; dir., treas. Inst. for Cryobiological Ext., Glendale, 1979—; dir. Glendale Bd. Realtors, 1981-83. Contbr. numerous articles to profl. mags.; inventor wrist worn cardiotachometer, catamaran airboat. Bd. dirs. Glendale Regional Arts Coun., 1981. Mem. Nat. Assn. Realtors, Nat. Coun. of Exchangors, Nat. Assn. Real Estate Appraisers, Comml. Investment Real Estate Coun., Realty Investment Assn. Calif., San Fernando Valley Exchangor, Glendale C. of C., Rotary (sr. citizens com. Glencale 1981). Office: Thatcher Enterprises 318 E Glenoaks Blvd #101 Glendale CA 91207-2012

THATCHER, STEPHEN RICHARD, aerospace business manager; b. Orange, Calif., June 5, 1945; s. Robert Wilson and Margaret Elizabeth (Estus) T.; m. Gail Elizabeth Gray, June 10, 1967 (div. Feb. 1982); children: Wendy Marie, Robert Paul, Thomas David James, Stephen Richard Jr., Brian Louis; m. Barbara Lorraine McBride, May 16, 1987. AA, Orange Coast Coll., 1965; BA, Calif. State U., Fullerton, 1967, MA, 1970. Life Teaching Credential (Calif. Secondary). Adminstrv. aide to city mgr. City of Santa Ana, Calif., 1969-70; asst. city adminstr. City of Lawndale, Calif., 1970-72; asst. city mgr., redevel. dir. City of Cerritos, Calif., 1972-77; city mgr., redevel. dir. City of Antioch, Calif., 1977-79; pres. SRT Assoc., Antioch, 1979-81; city mgr., redevel. dir. City of Santee, Calif., 1981-82; logistics bus. mgr. Rockwell Internat. Corp., Downey, Calif., 1983—; instr. Calif. State U., Long Beach, 1974-77, Calif. State U., Dominguez Hills, 1975-77; dir. Western Govt. Research Assoc., Long Beach, 1978-79. Petty officer USN, 1967-68. Recipient award of Merit Nat. Aeronautics and Space Adminstrn, Commendation for Outstanding Professionalism Calif. State Assembly. Mem. Internat. City Mgmt. Assn., Nat. Mgmt. Assn., Nat. Contract Mgmt. Assn., Inst. Cert. Profl. Mgrs. (cert.). Republican. Roman Catholic. Office: Rockwell Internat Corp 12214 Lakewood Blvd Downey CA 90241

THAXTON, VERA, home economics educator; b. Wenatchee, Wash., Aug. 15, 1933; d. Charles Clay and Ruth Ellen (Parsons) T. A.A., Mt. San Antonio Coll., 1954; B.A., San Diego State U., 1956; M.S., U. Ill.-Urbana, 1958. Cert. secondary tchr., Calif. Child welfare worker I, Lucas County (Ohio) Child Welfare, Toledo, 1958-60; home econs. instr. Bridgewater (Va.) Coll., 1960-62; licensing caseworker I, Los Angeles County Dept. Charities, Bur. Licensing, 1962-63; home econs. tchr. Pomona (Calif.) Unified Sch. Dist., 1963-69, Sonora (Calif.) High Sch., 1969-71, Banning (Calif.) High Sch., 1971-73, Coachella High Sch., Thermal, Calif., 1974—. Sec., La Quinta Property Owners Assn., 1979-82, 83-84. Mem. AAUW, Am. Home Econs. Assn., Calif. Home Econs. Assn. (dist. past pres., treas.), Future Homemakers Am. (sponsor), Fgn. Affairs Council. Republican. Presbyterian. Club: U. Ill. Alumni (past treas.). Home: PO Box 85 La Quinta CA 92253 Office: 83-800 Airport Blvd Thermal CA 92274

THAYER, DONALD WAYNE, healthcare company executive; b. Nebraska City, Nebr., Nov. 22, 1948; s. Harry Wayne and Eileen Anna (Broers) T.; m. Sandra Darlene Bond, June 6, 1967 (div. Sept. 1969); m. Janis Shapiro, June 16, 1979; children: Neil L. Haber, Shannon K., J. David. BA in Biol. Sci., Calif. State U., Dominguez Hills, 1971, MBA in Fin., 1978. Contracts adminstr. Action Industries, Inc., Woodland Hills, Calif., 1973-76; dir. adminstrn. Inter-Con Security Systems, Inc., Alhambra, Calif., 1976-78; sr. fin. analyst Nat. Med. Enterprises, Inc., Santa Monica, Calif., 1978-79, asst. dir. fin., 1979-80, dir. fin., 1980, asst. v.p., 1980-83, v.p. acquisition and devel., 1983--. Mem. mgmt. and fin. com. Am. Heart Assn., L.A., 1982-88, also chmn. fund raising adv. com., 1985-87, exec. com., bd. dirs., treas.; bd. dirs. Sr. Peer Counseling Ctr., Santa Monica, 1988--. With U.S. Army, 1971-73. Mem. Am. Mgmt. Assn., Hosp. Fin. Assn., Civitans (life, So. Calif. citizenship award). Republican. Presbyterian. Home: 7800 Bobbyboyar Ave West Hills CA 91304 Office: Nat Med Enterprises Inc 2600 Colorado Blvd Santa Monica CA 90406

THAYER, HANFORD, consulting engineer; b. Maple Island, Minn., Sept. 12, 1909; s. Nap Bon and Ida May (Purchase) T.; m. Lois Mae Foster, June 12, 1934; children: Roger Hanford, Diane Mae (Mrs. Robert Anthony Hill), Alden Bon, Shirley Anne. BSCE, Iowa State U., 1935. Registered profl. engr., Wash. Field engr. constrn. Stone & Webster Engring. Corp., Rock Island Dam, Wash., 1935-36; field engr. Bur. Fisheries, Seattle, 1936; jr. engr., asst. engr. design and constrn. migratory fish program Grand Coulee Dam project Bur. Reclamation, Fish and Wildlife Svc., Seattle, 1939-41; regional engr. Bur. Reclamation, Fish and Wildlife Svc., Portland, Oreg., 1941-42; asst. engr. Office of Div. Engrs., CE U.S. Army, Portland, 1942; assoc. engr. and supervising civil engr. Office of Div. Engrs., CE U.S. Army, Seattle, 1942-62, flood plain planning engr., 1962, sr. army project coord., chief archtl. engring. sect., 1963-67; dir. rsch. and devel. Quinton-Budlong Engring. Corp., Seattle, 1967-69, asst. v.p., 1969-70; cons. engr., planner, mgr. Tudor Engring. Co., 1970-76; mgr. Thayer Studio, Seattle, 1972-76; mem. Puget Sound Engring. Council, chmn., 1959; v.p. Nat. Advanced Tech. Mgmt. Conf., 1962-70; primary organizer Radiation Biol. Lab. U. Wash., 1943-46; project liaison Manhattan Atomic Project, 1943-46; researcher Herbert Hoover Oral History Program, 1967-70. Bd. dirs. Useless Bay Colony, 1985-88; pres. Useless Bay Condo Assn., 1975-88; mem. Island County Fire Bd., 1985-88, Rep. Nat. Com. Lt. CE USAR, 1934-40. Fellow ASCE (life mem., pres. Seattle chpt. 1956, named Engr. of Yr. 1960), Soc. Am. Mil. Engrs. (life, pres. Seattle chpt. 1950, nat. dir. 1952-67, regional v.p. 1967-76, Engr. of Yr. 1959-60, highest nat. gold medal award 1974); mem. NSPE, NRA, Newcomen Soc. N.Am., Wash. Soc. Profl. Engrs. (dir. 1970-71), Allied Arts of Seattle, Metric Assn., Seattle Area Indsl. Coun., Kiwanis. Mem. Ch. of Christ. Republican. Clubs: Seattle Engrs.; Wenatchee (Wash.) Fencing (pres. 1937-39); Cascade Sportsmens Rifle (pres. 1951); Progressive (bd. dirs. Whidbey Island, Wash. chpt.). Home: 5674 S McDonald Dr #202 Langley WA 98260

THAYER, JAMES NORRIS, financial corporation executive; b. Janesville, Wis., July 9, 1926; s. James Norris and Hazel (VanWormer) T.; m. Sylvia Lucille Kittell, June 26, 1948; children: Scott Norris, Diane Marie, Bradley Raymond. B.S., UCLA, 1948. With Prudential Ins. Co. Am., 1948-55; with William R. Staats & Co., 1955-65, partner, 1960-65; sr. v.p. Glore Forgan-Wm. R. Staats Inc., 1965-67; treas. Lear Siegler, Inc., 1967—, v.p., 1969—, sec., 1972—, sr. v.p. fin., 1977-87; pres., chief exec. officer Gibraltar Fin. Corp., Beverly Hills, Calif., 1988—; bd. dirs. Bunker Hill Income Securities. Bd. dirs., treas. Hathaway Home Children, Highland Park, Calif., 1956-62. Served with USAAF, 1944-47. Mem. UCLA Alumni Assn. (pres. 1982-84), Delta Sigma Phi, Beta Gamma Sigma. Clubs: Bel Air Country, Regency (Los Angeles). Home: 305 S Camden Dr Beverly Hills CA 90212 Office: Gibraltar Fin Corp 9111 Wilshire Blvd Beverly Hills CA 90210

THAYER, ROBERT LOUAYN, JR., printing and packaging company executive; b. Highland, Ill., Oct. 1, 1960; s. Robert L. and Karen S. (Clayton) T. Grad. high sch., LaCrescenta, Calif. Owner Am. Wholesale Jewelry, Camarillo, Calif., 1984-86; product, prodn. mgr. Software Pub. and Packaging Ind., Camarillo, 1986-88; v.p. Rolt Corp. dba Austin Pub. Svcs., Thousand Oaks, Calif., 1988—; cons., Thousand Oaks, Calif., 1980—. Composer: Because We're Lovers, 1978. Mem. Internat. Natural Bodybldg. Assn., Am. Entrepreneurs Assn. (Achievement award 1985). Republican. Office: Austin Pub Svcs 2219 Thousand Oaks Blvd Ste 202 Thousand Oaks CA 91362

THAYER, SUSAN ELIZABETH, jewelry company executive; b. Waterloo, Iowa, Sept. 3, 1954; d. Robert Howard and Glennes Agnes (Burger) Jamerson; m. Jack Stephen Thayer, Nov. 8, 1981; stepchildren: Nicole Rene, Christopher Stephen. Student, U. No. Iowa, 1972-76, Ariz. State U., 1977-78. Registered jeweler Gemological Inst. Am. Saleswoman, mgr. Schilling Jewelers, Cedar Falls, Iowa, 1970-76; saleswoman Weisfields Jewelers, Scottsdale, Ariz., 1976-79; saleswoman, mgr. Otto Schmieder & Son Jewelers, Phoenix, 1979-83, v.p., gen. mgr., 1983—. Vol. Am. Heart Assn., Phoenix, 1980—; edn. advisor Am. Cancer Soc., Phoenix, 1987—. Mem. Am. Gemological Soc. (registered jeweler, nat. membership coord., 1986—), Ariz. Guild of Am. Gemological Soc. (v.p. 1984-86, pres., 1986-88), Am. Gem Trade Assn. (chmn. retailers 1988—), Phoenix C. of C. Roman Catholic. Office: Otto Schmieder & Son Jewelers Park Cen Mall W Phoenix AZ 85013

THAYER, WILLIAM WENTWORTH, hematologist, medical oncologist; b. L.A., Mar. 17, 1926. AB with distinction, Stanfor (Calif.) U., 1949, MD, 1954. Diplomate Am. Bd. Internal Medicine. Intern in straight medicine Stanford U. Hosp., San Francisco, 1953-54, asst. resident clinic svc. medicine, 1954-55; resident in medicine VA Hosp., Boston, 1955-56; sr. resident in hematology Boston City Hosp., 1956-57; pvt. practice Stockton, Calif., 1958-72; chief div. hematology and oncology, asst. chief of medicine Harkness Community Hosp. (So. Pacific Hosp.), San Francisco, 1973-75; pvt. practice San Francisco, 1975-81; dir. dept. gen. and consultive medicine City of Hope Nat. Med. Ctr., Duarte, Calif., 1981-85; pvt. practice Monterey Park, Calif., 1986; physician dept. hematology and med. oncology CIGNA Healthplans of So. Calif., L.A., 1986—; mem. teaching staff San Joaquin Gen. Hosp., Stockton, 1958-72; asst. clin. prof. medicine U. Calif., San Francisco, 1973-81, assoc. prof. medicine, 1981; instr., mem. resident staff teaching program Presbyn. Hosp. of Pacific Med. Ctr., San Francisco, 1981; reader all bone marrow exams. San Joaquin Gen. Hosp., Stockton, 1962-72; staff physician, specialist Laguna Honda Hosp., San Francisco, 1971-81; mem. dept. gen. and consultive medicine City of Hope Nat. Med. Ctr., 1981-86. Contbr. articles to profl. jours. Chmn. cancer com., dir. tumor bd. and tumor registry French Hosp., San Francisco, 1978-81; chmn. library support com. City of Hope Nat. Med. Ctr., Duarte, 1982-86, chmn. med. records com., 1983-85; chmn. nutritional support subcom. CIGNA Hosp., L.A., 1987—, mem. tissue and transfusion com., 1987-88, chmn. tissues and transfusion com., 1989—, dir. tumor registry, 1989—. Mem. AMA, Am. Fedn. for Clin. Rsch., Calif. Med. Assn., San Joaquin County Med. Soc., Am. Soc. for Internal Medicine, Calif. Soc. for Internal Medicine, San Francisco County Med. Soc., No. Calif. Acad. Clin. Oncology (chartered), ACP (life fellow), Calif. Acad. Medicine, Calif. Tissue Culture Assn., So. Calif. Bone and Mineral Rsch., So. Calif. Acad. Clin. Oncology, Phi Beta Kappa, Phi Rho Sigma. Home: 3634 Yorkshire Rd Pasadena CA 91107

THEBEAU, ROBERT STEPHEN, hospital administrator; b. St. Louis, Nov. 19, 1939; s. John Stephen and Victoria Minerva (Lambrechts) T.; m. Ashley Elizabeth Moore, Feb. 10, 1962; 1 child, Eden A. AA, Harris Tchr.'s Coll., 1959; BBA, S.E. Mo. State Coll., 1961; M in Health Adminstrn., Washington U., 1971. Asst. exec. dir. St. Mary's Health Ctr., St. Louis, 1971-74; adminstrv., exec. dir. Med. Ctr., Independence, Mo., 1974-80; regional dir. Hosp. Affiliates Mgmt., Independence, Mo., 1980-81; regional v.p. Hosp. Corp. Am., Kansas City, Mo., 1981-82; v.p. ops., corp. officer Am. Med. Ctrs., Nashville, 1982-83, Surgical Care Affiliates, Inc., Nashville, 1983-85; chief operating officer Penrose Hosp., Colorado Springs, Colo., 1985-88; sr. v.p. Penrose/St. Francis Healthcare, Colorado Springs, Colo., 1987-88; chmn., chief exec. officer Interstate Health and Health Care Providers, Colorado Springs, Colo., 1988—; chmn. bd. dirs. Interstate Healthcare Providers; bd. dirs. Penrose Hosp. Found., Colorado Springs. Bd. dirs. United Fund, Colorado Springs; devel. chmn. Am. Heart Assn.; community advisor Jr. League, Colorado Springs, 1988. Lt. col. USAR, 1961—. Mem. Am. Coll. Healthcare Execs., Am. Hosp. Assn., Cath. Hosp. Assn., Colo. Hosp. Assn. (mem. legis. com.), Gates Plaza Club, Rotary.

THEIS, JOAN C., accountant; b. Flushing, N.Y., Feb. 22, 1948; d. Phillip Martin and Juanita Elizabeth (Weigelt) Brown; m. John H. Theis, Jr., Mar. 24, 1979; children: Mathew, Jacqueline. BA, U. Denver, 1970, MA, U. Colo., 1978; BS summa cum laude, Met. State Coll., Denver, 1984. CPA, Colo.; cert. master tchr., Colo. Tchr. Englewood (Colo.) Pub. Schs., 1976-82; acct. Diane D. Blackman, CPA, Denver, 1984-88, Tanner, Dirks & Co., Inc., CPAs, Denver, 1988—. Pres., bd. dirs. Denver Birth Ctr., 1989—; pres. Englewood Educators, 1981-82. Mem. AICPA, Colo. Soc. CPAs, Phi Beta Kappa. Office: Tanner Dirks & Co Inc CPAs 999 Jasmine Denver CO 80220

THEOBALD, WILLIAM LOUIS, botanist; b. N.Y.C., Feb. 12, 1936; s. William Walter and Helen Elizabeth (Garcin) T. BS in Agrl. Research, Rutgers U., 1958, MS in Horticulture, 1959; PhD in Botany, UCLA, 1963. Lectr. U. Calif., Santa Barbara, 1963-65; NSF postdoctoral fellow Royal Botanic Gardens, Kew, Eng., 1965-66; postdoctoral fellow Harvard U., Cambridge, Mass., 1966-67; asst. prof. biology Occidental (Calif.) Coll., 1967-71; assoc. prof. botany U. Hawaii, Honolulu, 1971-75; dir. Nat. Tropical Bot. Garden, Lawai, Hawaii, 1975—. Recipient Outstanding Tchr. award Occidental Coll., 1971, Silver Medal Mass. Hort. Soc., 1982. Mem. Bot. Soc. Am., Hawaiian Bot. Soc. (v.p. 1973, pres. 1974), Am. Assn. Bot. Gardens and Arboreta. Presbyterian. Office: Nat Tropical Bot Garden PO Box 340 Lawai HI 96765

THEURER, BYRON W., aerospace engineer; b. Glendale, Calif., July 1, 1939; s. William Louis and Roberta Cecelia (Sturgis) T.; m. Sue Ann McKay, Sept. 15, 1963 (div. 1980); children: Karen Marie, William Thomas, Alison Lee. BS in Engring. Sci., USAF Acad., 1961; MS in Aero. Sci., U. Calif., Berkeley, 1965; postgrad., U. Redlands, Calif. Commd. USAF, 1961, advanced through grades to lt. col., ret. 1978; project officer Space Shuttle Devel. Prog., Houston, 1971-76; chief of test F-15 System Prog. Office, Wright Patterson AFB, Ohio, 1976-78; sr. engr. Veda, Inc., Dayton, 1979-81, Logicon Inc., Dayton, 1981-83; project mgr. Support Systems Assocs., Inc., Dayton, 1983-84, CTA Inc., Ridgecrest, Calif., 1985—; cons. in field. Decorated Silver Star, D.F.C., Air Medals (16); named Officer of the Yr., Air Force Flight Test Ctr., Edwards AFB, 1970. Mem. Air Force Assn., Assn. Old Crows, USAF Acad. Assn. Grads. (nat. bd. dirs. 1972-75, chpt. pres. 1981-83). Republican. Episcopalian. Home: 521 N Randall St Ridgecrest CA 93555 Office: CTA Inc 900 Heritage Dr Ridgecrest CA 93555

THEURER, HANS D., JR., financial consultant; b. N.Y.C., Jan. 15, 1935; s. Hans D. Theurer Sr. and Adele Margaret (Hughes) DeBruin; m. Nancie S. Boardman, June 6, 1964; children: John D., David E. BS in Mgmt., Ind. U., 1970, MBA, 1971. Instr. Monmouth (Ill.) Coll., 1971-75; sr. auditor Amfac, Inc., San Francisco, 1978-80; chief fin. officer Zadocorp Internat., San Francisco, 1980-84; v.p. IPF Enterprises, Inc., Indio, Calif., 1988—; pres. Janus Group, Inc., Redwood City, Calif., 1984—. Author: (with others) Proposal to Restructure Social Security System, 1975. With U.S. Army. Republican. Unitarian. Home and Office: 231 Laurie Meadows Dr #157 San Mateo CA 94403

THIBODEAU, PHILLIP ELDRIDGE, electrical engineer; b. Mt. Vernon, Ill., Dec. 20, 1945; s. Joseph Alcid and Lucille (Ervine) T.; m. Julia Eleanor McConnell, Aug. 3, 1968. BSE, Calif. State U., Fullerton, 1975. Staff Rockwell Internat., Anaheim, Calif., 1975-83; mgr. aerospace Internat. Rectifier, El Segundo, Calif., 1985-86; scientist Hughes Aircraft Co., El Segundo, Calif., 1986—; prin. P.E.T. Consulting, Venice, Calif., 1975—. Author: (with others) Text on Mosfets, 1987; contbr. articles on power electronics profl. jours. Sgt. USAF, 1963-67. Mem. IEEE (sr. mem.), Air Force Assn., Naval Inst., Soc. Aerospace Engrs. (power panel). Democrat. Home: 703 Marco Pl Venice CA 90291 Office: Hughes Aircraft Co R 35 A1292 El Segundo CA 90245

THIEL, JOHN WILLIAM, aeronautical engineer; b. St. Paul, Apr. 14, 1940; s. William Herman Frederick and Helen Lillian (Heifort) T.; m. Jeanine Bourven, Sept. 28, 1963; children: Natalie, Audrey. Student, USN Schs. Command, Great Lakes, Ill., 1959, 63, USN Guided Missile Sch., Dam Neck, Va., 1962-63. Enlisted USN, 1959, advanced through ranks to chief warrant officer 4, ret., 1979; fire control technician USS Dyess, Charleston, S.C., 1959-63; missile radar technician USS King, San Diego, 1963, USS R.K. Turner, San Diego, 1963-66; missile radar instr. USN Guided Missile Sch., Mare Island, Calif., 1966-67; fire control officer USS MacDonough, Charleston, 1967-70, Naval Ordnance Missile Test Facility, N.Mex., 1970-73, USS Norton Sound, Port Hueneme, Calif., 1973-77; ordnance officer USN Naval Weapons Sta., Fallbrook, Calif., 1977-79; missile flight tester Gen. Dynamics, Pomona, Calif., 1979—. Home: 160 Taylor Rd Las Cruces NM 88005 Office: Gen Dynamics PO Box 10 White Sands Missile Range NM 88002

THIELE, JOAN ELIZABETH, nurse, educator; b. Dallas, July 5, 1940; d. Felix Charles and Julia Elizabeth (Jackson) T. BS in Nursing, Tex. Woman's U., 1962; MS in Nursing, Case Western Res. U., 1965; PhD, Ariz. State U., 1973. RN. Staff nurse Univ. Hosps., Cleve., 1962-63; instr. Tex. Woman's U., Dallas, 1965-66; asst. prof. U. No. Colo., Greeley, 1966-71, Ariz. State U., Tempe, 1973-75; assoc. prof. nursing Intercollegiate Ctr. Nursing Edn., Spokane, Wash., 1986—; mem. grad. faculty Idaho State U., Pocatello, 1976-86. Editor, author: Drug Dosages, 1974; contbr. articles to profl. jours. Named Disting. Tchr. Idaho State U., 1981, 83, 84; HHS grantee, 1985. Mem. Am. Nurses Assn., Nat. League Nursing Forum (program com. 1985-86), Soc. Rsch. Nursing Edn. (nominating com. 1987-89), Wash. Nurses Assn., Sigma Theta Tau (grantee 1987, Nurse Excellence award 1989), Spokane Wood Carvers (sec., treas. 1987—). Office: Intercollegiate Ctr Nursing W 2917 Fort Wright Dr Spokane WA 99204

THIELSCHER, KARL LEAVITT, JR., marketing director; b. Buffalo, Sept. 2, 1929; s. Karl L. and Adele (Duhrssen) T.; m. Antoinette Sandhofer, Mar. 17, 1955; 1 child, Jeffrey David. BS in Bus. Adminstrn., Dartmouth Coll., 1952. Unit mgr. Procter & Gamble, Cin., 1955-65; v.p. mktg./sales P. Ballantine & Sons, Newark, 1965-69; mgr. western div. Gallo Winery, Modesto, Calif., 1970-71; v.p. mktg./sales Lammt Winery, Bakersfield, Calif., 1971-77; dir. mktg./sales Wine Imports Am., Hawthorne, N.J., 1977-81, Giumarra Vineyards, Bakersfield, 1981—; guest lectr. Calif. State U., Bakersfield, 1987-88. Served to lt. U.S. Army, 1953-55. Republican. Episcopalian. Home: 4041 Country Club Dr Bakersfield CA 93306

THIERIOT, RICHARD TOBIN, publisher; b. San Francisco, Jan. 18, 1942; s. Charles de Young and Barbara Mary (Tobin) T.; m. Angelica Maria Reynal, Sept. 30, 1972; children: Charles de Young, II, Richard Reynal; stepchildren—Juan P. Withers, Simon Withers. B.A., Yale U., 1963; M.B.A., Stanford U., 1969. Reporter, Camden (N.J.) Courier-Post, 1963-64; asso. editor San Francisco Chronicle, 1969-77, editor, pub., 1977—; treas. Chronicle Pub. Co., 1969-77, pres., 1977—. Served with USMCR, 1964-67. Mem. Am. Newspaper Pubs. Assn., AP, Am. Soc. Newspaper Editors, Am. Press Inst., Calif. Press Assn., Calif. Newspaper Pubs. Assn., Sigma Delta Chi. Office: Chronicle Pub Co 901 Mission St San Francisco CA 94103 *

THIES, DAVID BYRON, chemist, researcher; b. Cottage Grove, Oreg., May 8, 1945; s. Byron O. and Muriel Leora (Dickinson) T.; m. Robin Marie Robinette, Jan. 23, 1971 (div. Sept. 1975); 1 child, Laurie. AS, Lane Community Coll., Eugene, Oreg., 1969; BS in Biology, U. Oreg., 1971; postgrad., Oreg. State U., 1973-74. Med. researcher VA Hosp., Albany, N.Y., 1972-73; cons. Water Analysis and Cons., Eugene, 1974-77; chemist, applied research dept. J.H. Baxter Co., Eugene, 1978—. Served with U.S. Army, 1963-66. Mem. ASTM, Am. Chem. Soc., Western Dry Kiln Assn. (com. chmn. 1984-85), Am. Water Works Assn., Am. Wood Preservers' Assn. Democrat. Office: J H Baxter Co 85 Baxter St PO Box 10797 Eugene OR 97440

THIESEN, GREGORY ALAN, accountant; b. Denver, Apr. 24, 1958; s. Gene Duane and Virginia Ruth (Haas) T.; m. Karen Elise McGrew, Aug. 17, 1984; children: Jeffrey Richard, Jeremy Eugene. BS in Bus., U. Colo., 1980. CPA, Colo. Sr. mgr. Ernst & Whinney, Denver, 1980—. Mem. MIT Enterprise Forum Colo. (exec. com. 1987—), Denver Athletic Club. Office: Ernst & Whinney 4300 Republic Pla Denver CO 80202

THIGPEN, JOE DENNARD, management consultant; b. Gainesville, Fla., June 22, 1942; s. Joe Dennard and Doris (Young) T. BA, U. Fla., 1966, postgrad., 1972, PhD, 1974; MS, George Washington U., 1970. Vol. Peace Corps, Santa Catarina, Brazil, 1963-65; counseling psychologist U. Fla., Gainesville, 1972-73; exec. dir. Suicide and Crisis Intervention Ctr., Gainesville, 1973-75; dir. Alachua County Crisis Ctr., Gainesville, 1975-79, v.p. western region, 1986-88; mgmt. cons. Gehlhausen Ruda and Assocs., Chgo., 1979-86; adj. prof. U. Fla., Gainesville, 1974-79. Author: (contbr.) Psychological Assessment of Suicidal Risk, 1974; cons. editor Suicide and Life-Threatening Behavior jour., 1982-88; contbr. articles to profl. jours. Pres. Alachua County Council on Child Abuse, Gainesville, 1978-79. Served with U.S. Army, 1966-69. Mem. Am. Assn. Suicidology (cert. examiner, treas. 1981-83, bd. dirs. 1981-85, pres. 1983-84, Edward Shneidman Young Contributor award, 1980), Am. Assn. Counseling and Devel. Democrat. Methodist. Home: 800 W First St Apt 2308 Los Angeles CA 90012

THISSELL, CHARLES WILLIAM, lawyer; b. Sioux Falls, S.D., Nov. 23, 1931; s. Oscar H. and Bernice Grace Janet (Olbertson) T.; m. Leila Amoret Rossner; Jan. 24, 1959; children—Amoret Gates, William Richards. B.A., Augustana Coll., Sioux Falls, 1953; J.D., U. Calif.-Berkeley, 1959. Bar: Calif. 1960, U.S. Dist. Ct. (no. and ea. dists.) Calif. 1960, Ct. Appeals (9th cir.) 1966, U.S. Claims Ct. 1974, U.S. Ct. Appeals (D.C., 5th cirs.) 1985, U.S. Supreme Ct. 1985. Cert.in trial advocacy Nat. Bd. Trial Advocacy. Trial counsel Calif. Dept. Transp. San Francisco, 1959-66; atty. law dept. Pacific Gas and Electric Co., San Francisco, 1966—; instr. San Francisco Law Sch., 1962-63; arbitrator Superior Cts. San Francisco and Marin County, 1979—. Vice chmn. Marin County Republican Central Com., 1983-84; pres. Marin County Rep. Council, 1981-82; chancellor, vestry mem. St. Luke's Episcopal Ch., San Francisco, 1979-82. Served to lt. (j.g.) USNR, 1953-56; comdr. Ret. Mem. ABA, San Francisco Bar Assn. (chmn. trial lawyers sect. 1974), Am. Arbitration Assn., Am. Judicature Soc. Clubs: Commonwealth of Calif. (chmn. environ. energy sect. 1981-83), Engineers (San Francisco). Home: 2 Garden Rd Ross CA 94957 Office: Pacific Gas and Electric Co Law Dept 77 Beale St San Francisco CA 94106

THOBURN, LELAND CRAIG, marketing executive, financial consultant; b. Cambridge, Mass., May 10, 1953; s. Norman Leroy and Joy Kathleen (Haber) T.; m. Carol Ann Bailey, Dec. 21, 1979; children: Anastasia Ruth, Kendall Robert. Grad. high sch., North Hollywood, Calif. Accounts payable exec. Bullock's, Los Angeles, 1974-77; pub. relations exec. Ch. of Scientology, Los Angeles, 1977-82; dir. new venture Royal & Assocs., Beverley Hills, Calif., 1983-87; dir. mktg. Exec. Software, La Crescenta, Calif., 1988; fin. cons. Royal & Assocs., Beverly Hills, 1988. Libertarian. Scientologist. Office: Exec Software 2219 Broadview Glendale CA 91208

THOLEN, JANET GAIL, artist; b. Los Angeles, Sept. 26, 1948; d. Robert William and Adele (Chadwick) T. BA, Whittier Coll., 1970; MFA, Claremont Grad. Sch., 1978. One-woman shows include Tortue Gallery, Santa Monica, Calif., 1984, Long Beach City Coll., Calif., 1986, Koplin Gallery, Los Angeles, 1988; numerous group shows including Exchange Show, Fine Arts Gallery, U. Calif., Irvine, 1977, Small Images Exhbn., Santa Barbara City Coll., Calif., 1978, All Paper Work, Las Vegas Art Mus., 1979, Contemporary Works on Paper, Sierra Nevada Mus. of Art, Reno, Nev., 1981, Fall Show V, Art Rental Gallery, Los Angeles, 1982, 10-10-10, Los Angles Inst. Contemporary Art, 1983, In Celebration, Summer Group Exhibit, Tortue Gallery, Santa Monica, 1984, New Directions/Calif. Painting, Visual Arts Ctr. Alaska, Anchorage, 1985, Lawyers Collect, Loyola Law Sch. Gallery, Los Angeles,1986. Claremont Grad. Sch. fellow, 1976-78, Nat. Endowment for the Arts Visual Artist fellow, 1985-86. Home and Studio: 1321 Maltman Ave Los Angeles CA 90026

THOMAS, CHARLES CARLISLE, JR., nuclear technologist; b. Rochester, N.Y., Aug. 18, 1925; s. Charles Carlisle and Pleasantine Virginia (Doan) T.; m. Marilynn Bee Smih, Dec. 1, 1945; children: Charles C. III, Frank C., Jeffrey C., Jonathan C. BS in Chemistry, U. Iowa, 1947; MS, U. Rochester, 1950. Prin. chemist Battelle Meml. Inst., Columbus, Ohio, 1953-55; fellow engr. Westinghouse Electric, Pitts., 1955-60; nuclear chemist Quantum, Inc., Wallingford, Conn., 1960-62; research mgr. Western N.Y. Nuclear Research Ctr., Buffalo, 1962-72; dir. NSTF SUNY, Buffalo, 1972-78; staff mem. Los Alamos (N.Mex.) Nat. Lab., 1978—; vis. prof. Tsing Hua U., Hsin Chu, Taiwan, 1964-65; prin. Nuclear Tech. Cons., Santa Fe, N. Mex., 1986—; instr. No. N.Mex. Community Coll., Espanola, 1987—. Author: (with others) Handbook of Nuclear Safeguards and Measurement Methods, 1983; contbr. articles to profl. jours. Active Repub. County Com., Santa Fe, 1985—. Fellow Am. Nuclear Soc. (chmn. BMD 1988—); mem. Am. Chem. Soc., Health Physics Soc. (plenary), Inst. Nuclear Materials Mgmt. (sr.). Home: 3373 La Avenida de San Marcos Santa Fe NM 87505 Office: Los Alamos Nat Lab Group 05-2 Mail Stop F 508 Los Alamos NM 87545

THOMAS, CHARLES WILLIAM, II, urban studies educator; b. Md., Apr. 26, 1926; s. Charles W. and Estella Thomas; m. Shirley Wade, Aug. 30, 1958; children: Charles William III, Shawn. BS, Morgan State Coll., 1951; MA, John Carroll U., 1955; PhD, Western Res. U., 1961. With Highland View Cuyahoga County Hosp., Cleve., 1955-63, acting dir. sheltered workshop research project, 1956-58, co-prin. investigator, dir. aging research project, until 1963; asst. prof., dir. counseling services and personnel devel. Job Corps Ctr., U. Oreg., 1963-66; evaluation design analyst, dir. edn. and tng. South Central Multipurpose Health Service Ctr., U. So. Calif., 1966-69; assoc. prof. community medicine U. So. Calif., Los Angeles, 1966-69; prin., dir. Ctr. for Study Racial and Social Issues, Los Angeles, 1969-71; prof. urban studies and planning U. Calif.-San Diego Third Coll., La Jolla, 1977—, coordinator urban studies and planning, 1977-82; lectr. John Carroll U., 1961-63, Calif. State Coll., Los Angeles, 1967-68, Calif. State Coll., Dominguez Hills, 1970, Claremont Coll. Black Studies Ctr., 1970-71; vis. prof. counseling psychology Ariz. State U., 1970-71; vis. scientist Am. Psychol. Assn., 1979-80, Assn. Black Psychologists, 1969-70; mem. Calif. Psychology Examining Commn.; active Calif. Bd. Edn., 1975-79; facilitator, chmn. pro tem Nat. Ad Hoc Com. on Homicidal Violence Among Blacks; facilitator for devel. Nat. Black Mental Health Workers Assn.; founder, coordinator Ann. Conf. on Issues in Ethnicity and Mental Health; speaker, cons. in field. Contbr. articles, chpts. to profl. publs., popular mags. Served with AUS, 1944-46. Recipient Father of Black Psychology award Black Students' Psychol. Assn., 1970; cert. recognition Nat. Assn. Sch. Psychologists, 1971; commendation Mayor San Diego, 1976; legis. commendation State of Ohio, 1979; Legal Aid Soc. San Diego award, 1979; Outstanding Contbn. award So. Regional Edn. Bd. Community Clin. Psychology Project, 1980; commendation Christ Ch. of San Diego, 1980; San Diego Black Achievement award in sci., 1981, in journalism, 1983; Charles W. Thomas psychology scholarship established in his honor at Morgan State U., 1976; named to Scroll of Honor for Ednl. Leadership, Omega Psi Phi, 1979; Jesse Smith Noyes fellow John Carroll U.; Cleve. Found. fellow Western Res. U.; Danforth assoc., 1979; vis. scholar Howard U. Inst. Urban Affairs, 1979-80; Spl. Achievement award Morgan State U., 1986, Disting. Alumni award Nat. Equal Opportunity Assn. for Higher Edn. Fellow Am. Psychol. Assn. (chmn. edn. and tng. bd. 1971-72, chmn. task force on master's level edn. 1973); mem. Calif. State Psychol. Assn., Nat. Acad. TV Arts and Scis., AAAS (adv. body), Council for Advancement Psychol. Profession and Scis. (gov. 1969), Assn. Black Psychologists (founding chmn. 1968, hon. nat. chmn.), Black Action Council San Diego (hon.), NAACP (pres. San Diego chpt. 1977, San Diego chpt. Outstanding Service award 1976), Nat. Acad. Black Scientists (chmn.). Republican. Home: 610 Bradford Rd El Cajon CA 92021 Office: U Calif-San Diego Third Coll/Dept Urban Studies & Planning D-009 La Jolla CA 92093

THOMAS, CHRISTOPHER PEARCE, lawyer; b. Phila., Apr. 4, 1945; s. Eliot Burnham and Lillian Eleanor (Pearce) T.; m. Sarah Jane Silverstein, Dec. 15, 1966; children: Jennifer Jane, Wendy McLean. BA in Biology, Amherst Coll., 1966; JD, N.Y. U. Law Sch., 1969. Bar: Oreg. 1969. Law clk. to presiding judge U.S. Dist. Ct., Dist. of Oreg., Portland, 1969-70; exec. asst. to pres. Oreg. State Senate, Salem, 1971; assoc., ptnr. Kell, Alterman, Runstein & Thomas Attys., Portland, 1970-75; spokesman, legal counsel Oregonians for Nuclear Safeguards, Portland, 1976; city atty. City of Portland, Oreg., 1977-84; pvt. practice Portland, 1985—. Editor-in-chief Annual Survey of American Law, 1969. Coord. Beyond War Found., Portland, 1983—; treas. Amigos de las Americas, Portland, 1985—; mem. Com. on Bar, Press, Broadcast, Oreg., 1988—. Democrat. Office: 2000 SW First Ave Ste 400 Portland OR 97201

THOMAS, CLAUDEWELL SIDNEY, psychiatric educator; b. N.Y.C., Oct. 5, 1932; s. Humphrey Sidney and Frances Elizabeth (Collins) T.; m. Carolyn Pauline Rozawsky, Sept. 6, 1958; children: Jeffrey Evan, Julie-Anne Elizabeth, Jessica Edith. BA, Columbia U., 1952; MD, SUNY, Downstate Med. Ctr., 1956; MPH, Yale U., 1964. Diplomate Nat. Bd. Med. Examiners, Am. Bd. Psychiatry. From instr. to assoc. prof. Yale U., New Haven, 1963-68, dir. Yale tng. program in social community psychiatry, 1967-70; dir. div. mental health service programs NIMH, Washington, 1970-73; chmn. dept. psychiatry U.M.D.N.J., Newark, 1973-83; prof., chmn. dept. psychiatry Drew Med. Sch., 1983—; prof., vice chmn. dept. psychiatry UCLA, 1983—; cons. A.K. Rice Inst., Washington, 1978-80. Author: (with B. Bergen) Issues and Problems in Contemporary Soc., 1966; editor: (with R. Bryce LaPorte) Alienation in Contemporary Society, 1976; mem. editorial bd. Internat. Jour. Mental Health, Adminstrn. In Mental Health, Social Psychiatry Internat., World Jour. Psychosynthesis. Served to capt. USAF, 1959-61. Fellow: Am. Psychoanalytic Assn. (hon.), Am. Psychiat. Assn., Am. Pub. Health Assn., Royal Soc. Health, N.Y. Acad. Sci., N.Y. Acad. Medicine; mem. Am. Sociol. Assn. Home: 30676 Palos Verdes Dr E Rancho Palos Verdes CA 90274 Office: Charles R Drew Med Sch Dept Psychiatry 1720 E 120 St AFH Bldg Los Angeles CA 90059

THOMAS, CRAIG LYLE, congressman; b. Cody, Wyo., Feb. 17, 1933; s. Craig E. and Marge Oweta (Lynn) T.; m. Susan Roberts; children: Peter, Paul, Patrick, Alexis. BS, U. Wyo., 1955; LLB, LaSalle U., 1963. Exec. v.p. Wyo. Farm Bur., Laramie, 1960-69; asst. legis. dir. Am. Farm Bur., Wash., 1969-71; dir. nat. resource Am. Farm Bur., Chgo., 1971-75; gen. mgr. Wyo. Rural Elec. Assn., from 1975; mem. Wyo. Ho. of Reps., 1985-1989, 101st Congress from Wyo., 1989—. Former chmn. Natrona County (Wyo.) Rep. Com.; state rep. Natrona County Dist.; del. Rep. Nat. Conv., 1980. Capt. USMC. Mem. Am. Soc. Trade Execs., Masons. Methodist. Home: 3907 Dorset Casper WY 82601 Office: US Ho of Reps Longworth House Office Bldg Washington DC 20515 *

THOMAS, DARRELL DENMAN, lawyer; b. Lake Cormorant, Miss., Sept. 10, 1931; s. Darrell Dane and Maggie Adele (McKay) T.; m. Dora Ann Bailey, Feb. 12, 1957 (div. 1988). BS, Memphis State U., 1957; JD, U. Denver, 1960. Bar: Colo. 1960, U.S. Dist. Ct. Colo. 1960, U.S. Supreme Ct. 1967, U.S. Ct. Appeals (10th cir.) 1971. Law clk. to presiding justice U.S. Dist. Ct., Colo., 1960-61; ptnr. Mills & Thomas, Colorado Springs, Colo., 1961-65; pvt. practice Colorado Springs, 1965—; U.S. commr. U.S. Dist. Ct., 1961-71, U.S. magistrate, 1971—. Pres. Colorado Springs Symphony, 1979-82; v.p. Colorado Springs Symphony Orch. Found. With U.S. Army, 1952-54. Mem. ABA, Colo. Bar Assn., El Paso County Bar Assn., Nat. Council U.S. Magistrates, El Paso Club (dir. 1985-88), Broadmoor Golf Club, Garden of the Gods Club, Plaza Club, Masons, Shriner. Republican. Office: 115 E Vermijo St Colorado Springs CO 80903

THOMAS, (JOHN) DAVID, musician, composer; b. Muncie, Ind., Mar. 30, 1951; s. John Charles and Phyllis Lorraine (Wear) T.; m. Rosalie Faith Baldwin, July 27, 1974; children: Bethany Carol, Mark David. Student, Purdue U., 1969-71; BS, Ball State U., 1976. Musician, composer Indpls. and Phoenix, 1955-88; photographer Indpls., 1964-84; budget analyst USAFAC, Indpls., 1976-84; co-leader, keyboardist, sound technician JETSTREAM, Indpls., 1979-83; sound technician audio visual Valley Cathedral Ch., Phoenix, 1987; musician. composer Mountlake Terrace, Wash., 1988—; pianist Wrigley Mansion, Phoenix, 1988, Boulders Resort, Carefree, Ariz., 1987, Clarion Inn/McCormick's Ranch, Scottsdale, Ariz., 1986; synthesist/key bass, Pinnacle Peak Patio, Scottsdale, Ariz., 1984, Dee Dee Ryan, Apache Junction, Ariz., 1984-86. Poet Penpoints, 1969; composer music and lyrics Someday, 1969, Death of Rock and Roll, 1970 (Outstanding Musician award 1969), Infinity, 1970-71, Night Visions, 1973, Jubilee in F, 1989, over 125 compositions, songs and themes. Musician Castleview Bapt. Ch. Indpls., 1975-84, Valley Cathedral Ch., Phoenix, 1986-87; actor T.C. Howe High Sch., Indpls., 1969; mem. Am. Contract Bridge League, Indpls., 1969. GM scholar Purdue U., Palmer Meml. scholar Ball State U.; recipient Eagle Scout award Boy Scouts Am., 1966, God and Country award, 1965; Gen. Motors scholar, Detroit, 1969. Mem. ASCAP, Mensa., Am. Contract Bridge League, U.S. Chess Fedn. Home: 21706 52d Ave W Mountlake Terrace WA 98043 Office: Baldwin Agy 20306 15th Ave NE Seattle WA 98105

THOMAS, DAVID EDWIN, marketing executive; b. Phoenix, Apr. 17, 1935; s. Albion Clarence and Lucille (Nichols) T.; m. Mildred Reese, Aug. 18, 1958 (div. Feb. 1977); children: Brian, Bruce; m. Patricia Pauline Fallmer, Apr. 23, 1977; children: Todd, Shawnell. BS in Econs., U. Redlands, 1957. V.p. Haskell-Thomas, Inc., Phoenix, 1960-68; pres. Zesbaugh-Thomas, Inc., Seattle, 1968-77, Thomas Archtl. Products, Inc., Seattle, 1977-87; mktg. mgr. Constrn. Specialties, Inc., Mill Creek, Wash., 1987—; v.p. Constrn. Specifications Inst., 1987-88. Lt. U.S. Navy, 1957-60. Fellow The Constrn. Specifications Inst., Mill Creek Country. Republican. Methodist. Office: Conspec Systems Inc 16000 Bothell Everett Hwy Mill Creek WA 98012

THOMAS, DAVID STANLEY, sales executive; b. Malad, Idaho, July 4, 1946; s. Stanley and Erma (Peterson) T.; m. Rochelle Skinner, Sept. 27, 1974; children: Aaron, Adam, Amanda. BS in Acctg., Brigham Young U., 1969. Ptnr. Emporium Gift Shop and Union Block Inc., Provo, Utah, 1971-73; prin. Keith Warshaw & Co., Salt Lake City, 1973-79; regional sales mgr. Eddie Parker Sales, Dallas, 1979-84; dir. mktg. Country Cozy's Inc, Paramount, Calif., 1984—. Mem. Nat. Fedn. Ind. Businessmen, Am. Legion. Republican. Mormon. Home: 13126 San Felipe St La Mirada CA 90638 Office: Country Cozy's Inc 16443 Illinois Ave Paramount CA 90723

THOMAS, DELBERT DALE, engineering executive; b. Portland, Oreg., June 14, 1930; s. Theodore C. and Esther E. (Kemnitz) T.; m. Phyllis B. Bartlett, Jan. 8, 1949; children—James, Leonard, Stephen, Timothy, Susan. Student San Jose City Coll., Santa Rosa Community Coll., 1950-51. Lic. contractor, Calif., Ariz., Nev. Pres., Shale Devel. Corp. Redlands, Calif., 1976—; pres. Energy '80 Scientific, Inc., Redlands, 1981—; chmn. bd. Impex, Inc., Redlands, 1982—; developer indsl. projects Govt. of Pakistan. cons. on elec. co-generation systems; speaker on air conditioning and refrigeration. Awarded 3rd place Inventor of Yr., Inventors Workshop Internat., 1976. Mem. Am. Soc. Heating Air Conditioning and Refrigerating Engrs, Tri County Chpt. ASHRAE (refrigeration com.). Republican. Baptist. Mech. contractor on space shuttle assembly facility, Palmdale, Calif., 1973. Author: Practical Ductwork Estimating, Synfuel, Vulcan II, Practical Energy Conservation, Practical Mechanical Contracting; patentee in field of synthetic fuels; inventor in field. Home: 1522 Cameo Dr Redlands CA 92373 Office: Impex Inc 313 High St Redlands CA 92373

THOMAS, EDWARD DONNALL, physician, educator; b. Mart, Tex., Mar. 15, 1920; s. Edward E. and Angie (Hill) T.; m. Dorothy Martin, Dec. 20, 1942; children: Edward Donnall, Jeffery A., Elaine. B.A., U. Tex., 1941, M.A., 1943; M.D., Harvard U., 1946. Diplomate: Am. Bd. Internal Medicine. NRC fellow medicine dept. biology MIT, 1950-51; instr. medicine Harvard Med. Sch., Boston; also hematologist Peter Bent Brigham Hosp., 1953-55; research asso. Cancer Research Found., Children Med. Center, Boston, 1953-55; physician in chief Mary Imogene Bassett Hosp., also asso. clin. prof. medicine Coll. Physicians and Surgeons, Columbia U., 1955-63; prof. U. Wash. Sch. Medicine, Seattle, 1963—; researcher and author numerous publs. on hematology, marrow transplantation, biochemistry and irradiation biology. Mem. Nat. Acad. Scis., Am. Soc. Clin. Investigation, Assn. Am. Physicians, Am. Soc. Hematology, Am. Fedn. Clin. Research, Internat. Soc. Hematology, Am. Assn. Cancer Research, Western Assn. Physicians, Am. Soc. Clin. Oncology, Transplantation Soc. Office: Fred Hutchingson Cancer Rsch Ctr 1124 Columbia St Seattle WA 98104

THOMAS, EDWARD FRANCIS, JR., synthetic fuel executive; b. N.Y.C., Feb. 19, 1937; s. Edward Francis and Helen Katherine (Baker) T.; m. Barbara Joyce Mahler, Mar. 23, 1975 (div. 1980); children: Edward, Diana. BA, Va. Mil. Inst., 1959; MBA, NYU, 1970. Asst. v.p. Citibank, N.A., N.Y.C., 1962-70; sr. fin. analyst Atlantic Richfield Co., N.Y.C., 1970-73; nat. sales mgr. Easton-Mahler Corp., N.Y.C., 1973-80; exec.v.p. Superfuel Inc., Phoenix, 1980-83; asst. v.p. The Ariz. Bank, Yuma, 1983-85; sr. v.p. Lumber Country, Inc., Tucson, 1985-87; exec. v.p. Synergistic Energy Systems, Inc., Phoenix, 1987—; cons. in field; instr., Keystone Coll., Marywood Coll., Ariz. Western Coll., Webster U. Bd. dirs., Boys & Girls Club, Yuma, 1983-85, Cocopah Indian Tribe Econ. devel. Com., Somerton, Ariz., 1983-85, Cath. Community Svcs., Tucson, 1985-87, Episc. Community Svcs., Tucson, 1985-87, Tucson Boys' Chorus, 1985-87, Sahuaro coun. Girl Scouts U.S., 1985-87, Interfaith Coun. for Homeless, Tucson, 1985-87, Mayor's Community Partnership for Homeless, Tucson, 1985-87; exec. com. Yuma Econ. Devel. Com., 1983-85. 1st lt. U.S. Army, 1960-62. Mem. Yuma Leadership, Ariz. Assn. Indsl. Developers, Rotary, Masons. Home: 1645 E Thomas Rd Phoenix AZ 85016 Office: Synergistic Energy Systems 3850 E Freiss Dr Phoenix AZ 85032

THOMAS, ESTHER MERLENE, educator; b. San Diego, Oct. 16, 1945; d. Merton Alfred and Nellie Lida (Von Pilz) T. AA, Grossmont Coll., 1966; BA, San Diego State U., 1969; MA, U. Redlands, 1977. Cert. elem. and adult edn. tchr. Tchr. Cajon Valley Union Sch. Dist., El Cajon, 1969—. Contbr. articles to profl. jours. Mem. U.S. Senatorial Club, Washington, 1984—; mem. Lakeside (Calif.) Centennial Com., 1985-86; hon. mem. Rep. Presl. Task Force, Washington, 1986. Mem. Nat. Tchrs. Assn., Calif. Tchrs. Assn., Cajon Valley Educators Assn., Christian Bus. and Profl. Women, Lakeside Hist. Soc. Republican. Home: 13594 Hwy 8 Apt 3 Lakeside CA 92040 Office: Flying Hills Elem Sch 1251 Finch St El Cajon CA 92020

THOMAS, ETHEL COLVIN NICHOLS (MRS. LEWIS VICTOR THOMAS), educator; b. Cranston, R.I., Mar. 31, 1913; d. Charles Russell and Mabel Maria (Colvin) Nichols; Ph.B., Pembroke Coll. in Brown U., 1934; M.A., Brown U., 1938; Ed.D., Rutgers U., 1979; m. Lewis Victor Thomas, July 26, 1945 (dec. Oct. 1965); 1 child, Glenn Nichols. Tchr. English, Cranston High Sch., 1934-39; social dir. and adviser to freshmen, Fox Hall, Boston U., 1939-40; instr. to asst. prof. English Am. Coll. for Girls, Istanbul, Turkey, 1940-44; dean freshman, dir. admission Women's Coll. of Middlebury, Vt., 1944-45; tchr. English, Robert Coll., Istanbul, 1945-46; instr. English, Rider Coll., Trenton, N.J., 1950-51; tchr. English, Princeton (N.J.) High Sch., 1951-61, counselor, 1960-62, 72-83, coll. counselor, 1962-72, sr. peer counselor, 1986—. Mem. NEA, AAUW, Nat. Assn. Women Deans Adminstrs. and Counselors, Am. Assn. Counseling and Devel., Bus. and Profl. Women's Club (named Woman of Yr., Princeton chpt. 1977), Met. Mus. Art, Phi Delta Kappa, Kappa Delta Pi. Presbyn. Clubs: Brown University (N.Y.C.); Nassau.

THOMAS, GRACE FERN, psychiatrist; b. Gothenburg, Nebr., Sept. 23, 1897; d. George William and Martha C. (Johnson) T. BS, U. Nebr., 1924; MA, Creighton U., 1926; MD, U. So. Calif., 1935; postgrad., U. Colo., 1942-43, Inst. of Living, 1943, U. So. Calif., 1946, UCLA, 1947-50, Columbia U., 1953; MA in Religion, U. So. Calif., 1968. Diplomate Am. Bd. Psychiatry and Neurology. Instr. chemistry, biology Duchesne Coll., 1924-27; lab. technician various hosps., 1927-32; intern L.A. County Hosp., 1934-35; resident physician Riverside County Hosp., 1935-36; resident psychiatrist L.A. County Psychopathic Hosp., 1936-37; staff psychiatrist Calif. State Hosp. System, 1937-42, Glenside San., 1943-44; pvt. practice neuropsychiatry, Long Beach, Calif., 1946-51; chief mental hygiene clinic VA, Albuquerque, 1951-54; dir. psychiat. edn. Miss. State Hosp., Jackson, 1955; dir. Stark County Guidance Ctr., Canton, Ohio, 1956-58; dir. Huron County Guidance Center, Norwalk, Ohio, 1958-61, Arrowhead Mental Health Ctr., San Bernardino, Calif., 1962-64; dir. Mendocino County Mental Health Svcs., Ukiah, Calif.,

1964-65; chief psychiat. edn. Porterville (Calif.) State Hosp., 1965-66; dir. Tuolumne County Mental Health Svcs., Sonora, Calif., 1966-70; psychiatrist-cons. Emanuel Hosp. Mental Health Ctr., Turlock, Calif., 1970-71; pvt. practice psychiatry, Turlock, 1970-73, Modesto, Calif., 1973—; cons. psychiatrist Stanislaus County Mental Health Dept., Modesto, 1972-73; alienist to Stanislaus County Superior Ct., Modesto, 1972—; psychiatrist-cons. Cath. Social Svc. Agy., 1974-78. Ordained to ministry United Meth. Ch., 1968. Capt. M.C., AUS, 1944-46. Fellow Am. Psychiat. Assn.; mem. AMA, Stanislaus Med. Soc., Central Calif. Psychiat. Assn., Inst. Religion and Health, Am. Med. Women's Assn. Am. Legion, AAUW, Soroptimists, Phi Delta Gamma, Phi Beta Kappa, Sigma Xi, Phi Kappa Phi, Nu Sigma Phi. Methodist. Home: 2001 LaJolla Ct Modesto CA 95350 Office: 1130 Coffee Rd Ste 8B Modesto CA 95355

THOMAS, HAYWARD, manufacturing company executive; b. Los Angeles, Aug. 9, 1921; s. Charles Sparks and Julia (Hayward) T.; m. Phyllis Mary Wilson, July 1, 1943; children: H. David, Steven T. BS, U. Calif., Berkeley, 1943. Registered profl. engr. Staff engr. Joshua Hendy Corp., Los Angeles, 1946-50; prodn. mgr. Byron Jackson Co., Los Angeles, 1950-55; mgr. mfg. Frigidaire div. Gen. Motors Corp., Dayton, Ohio, 1955-70; group v.p. White Motor Corp., Cleve., 1971-73; sr. v.p. Broan Mfg. Co., Hartford, Wis., 1973-85; pres. Jensen Industries, Los Angeles, 1985-87; retired 1987. Served to lt. USNR, 1943-46. Mem. Soc. Mfg. Engrs. (chmn. mfg. mgmt. council 1984-86). Republican. Episcopalian. Home: 1320 Granvia Altamira Palos Verdes Estates CA 90274

THOMAS, HERBERT CUSHING, JR., physician, teacher; b. Charlotte, N.C., Oct. 6, 1941; s. Herbert Cushing and Doris (Roberts) T.; m. Laureen Thompson, June 9, 1961 (div. 1983); children: Steven, Michael; m. Catherine Anne Campbell, Feb. 11, 1989. BA, U. Colo., 1963, MD, 1967; MS, U. Wash., 1976. Resident in surgery Swedish Hosp., Med. Ctr., Seattle, 1972-73; resident in otolaryngology U. Wash., Seattle, 1973-77; fellowship in otology Ear Rsch. Inst., L.A., 1977-78; pvt. practice Seattle, 1978—; attending physician Children's Hosp. and Med. Ctr., Seattle, 1985—; pres. Surgical Specialist, Inc., Seattle, 1988—. With USN, 1967-72. Mem. AMA, Am. Acad. Otolaryngology, King County Med. Soc., Seattle Surg. Soc., N.W. Acad. Otolaryngology. Office: 4540 Sand Point Way NE Seattle WA 98105

THOMAS, HOWARD PAUL, civil engineer, consultant; b. Cambridge, Mass., Aug. 20, 1942; s. Charles Calvin and Helen Elizabeth (Hook) T.; m. Ingrid Nybo, Jan. 4, 1969; children: Kent Michael, Lisa Karen, Karina Michelle. BS in Engring., U. Mich., 1965, MS in Engring., 1966. Registered profl. engr., Alaska, Calif. Engr. Ove Arup & Ptnrs., London, 1966-67; project engr. Woodward-Clyde Cons., San Francisco, 1967-73; assoc. Woodward-Clyde Cons., Anchorage, 1975-89; spl. cons. Cowiconsult Cons., Copenhagen, 1973-75; prin. engr. Harding-Lawson Assocs., Anchorage, 1989—; chmn. Nat. Tech. Council Cold Regions Engring., 1988-89, chmn. com. program and publs., 1982-84; chmn. 4th Internat. Conf. Cold Regions Engring., Anchorage, 1986. Contbr. articles to profl. jours. Mem. Resource Devel. Council, Anchorage, 1985—. Named Alaskan Engr. Yr., 1986. Mem. NSPE, ASCE (pres. Anchorage chpt. 1985-86), Internat. Soc. Soil Mechs. and Found. Engring., Soc. Am.'s Mil. Engrs., Cons. F grs. Council of Alaska (pres. elect 1988—), Project Mgmt. Inst., Anchorage C. of C. Lutheran. Club: Toastmasters (Anchorage) (pres. 1984). Lodge: Sons of Norway. Home: 2611 Brittany Dr Anchorage AK 99504 Office: Harding Lawson Assocs 601 E 57th Pl Anchorage AK 99518

THOMAS, HOWARD RASMUS, economist, consultant; b. Preston, Idaho, Sept. 2, 1943; s. Franklin Howard and Lydia Sena (Rasmussen) T.; m. Judith Ann Hines, Apr. 14, 1962 (div. Oct. 1975); children: Carrie Lynn, Preston Howard, Michael Todd, Cami Nicole; m. Elnora Mecham, May 10, 1988; stepchildren: Julie Ann Gale Hill, Darren Gale, Kevin Donald Gale, Tanya Jolyne. BS, Utah State U., 1966, MS, 1968; PhD, Oreg. State U., 1974. Economist Econ. Research Service, USDA, Corvallis, Oreg., 1967-84; economist, planner Soil Conservation Service, USDA, Boise, 1984-85; economist Soil Conservation Service, USDA, Portland, Oreg., 1985—; economist, planner H.R. Thomas & Assocs., Camas, Wash., 1985—; assoc. prof. Oreg. State U., Corvallis, 1975—. Contbr. articles and other publs. in field. Recipient Cert. of Merit, Econ. Research Service, Washington, 1983, Adminstrv. Spl. Merit award, 1983. Mem. Am. Agrl. Econs. Assn., Wash. Agrl. Econs. Assn., Soil and Water Conservation Soc. (edn. chair 1986-87). Mormon. Home: 1235 NE 6th Ave Camas WA 98607 Office: Soil Conservation Svc 511 NW Broadway Rm 248 Portland OR 97209

THOMAS, JACK WARD, wildlife biologist; b. Fort Worth, Sept. 7, 1934; s. Scranton Boulware and Lillian Louise (List) T.; m. Farrar Margaret Schindler, June 29, 1957; children: Britt Ward, Scranton Gregory. BS, Tex. A&M U., 1957; MS, W.Va. U., 1969; PhD, U. Mass., 1972. Wildlife biologist Tex. Game & Fish Commn., Sonora, 1957-60, Tex. Parks & Wildlife Dept., Llano, 1961-66; research biologist U.S. Forest Service, Morgantown, W.Va., 1966-69, Amherst, Mass., 1970-73, LaGrande, Oreg., 1974—. Author, editor: Wildlife Habitats in Managed Forests, 1979 (award The Wildlife Soc. 1980), Elk of North America, 1984 (award The Wildlife Soc. 1985); contbr. numerous articles to profl. jours. Served to lt. USAF, 1957. Recipient Conservation award Gulf Oil Corp., 1983, Earle A. Childs award Childs Found., 1984, Disting. Svc. award USDA, Disting. Citizen's award, E. Oreg. State Coll. Fellow Soc. Am. Foresters; mem. The Wildlife Soc. (cert., pres. 1977-78, Oreg. chpt. award 1980, Arthur Einarsen award 1981, Spl. Services award 1984), Am. Ornithol. Union, Am. Soc. Mammalogists, Lions, Elks. Office: US Forest Service Rt 2 Box 2315 La Grande OR 97850

THOMAS, JAMES ROBERT, physician in maternal and fetal medicine; b. Lodi, Calif., Nov. 22, 1948; s. Harold Morse and Lillian Bertha (Litvin) T.; m. Mona Lee Mason, June 1, 1969; adopted children: Sarah Marie, Jesse Lee-Hwan, Hannah Shereé, Joseph Michael. BS, Loma Linda U., 1970, MD, 1977; PhD, U. Calif., 1974. Cert. Am. Bd. Ob-Gyns, Nat. Bd. Med. Examiners. Resident in ob-gyn Yale U., New Haven, 1978-82; fellow maternal-fetal medicine U. Vt., Burlington, 1982-84; dir. maternal-fetal medicine U. S.D., Sioux Falls, 1984-87, asst. prof. ob-gyn, 1984-87, assoc. prof., 1987; dir. maternal and fetal medicine Flagstaff (Ariz.) Med. Ctr., 1987—, chmn. dept. ob-gyn, 1988—. Mem. Ariz. Perinatal Trust, 1987—; bd. dirs. Women's Ctr. Against Domestic Violence. Fellow Am. Coll. Ob-Gyn (Mead Johnson Clin. Rsch. fellow 1984); mem. AMA, Soc. Perinatal Obstetrics, Am. Inst. Ultrasound, Wine Club Sioux Falls (charter pres. 1984-85), Alpha Omega Alpha. Home: RR 4 Box 736A Mount Elden Rd Flagstaff AZ 86001

THOMAS, JOHN VAL, architect; b. San Diego, Feb. 26, 1943; s. H. Clay and Doris Thelma (Speir) T.; m. Dorothy Jean Rawlings, June 5, 1966 (div. 1984); 1 child, Leli Dael. BA, BArch, Rice U., 1966; MArch, U. Pa., 1972. Registered architect, Wash., Pa. Project mgr. Preston Bolton & Assocs., Wilson Morris Crane & Anderson, Houston, 1968-70; ptnr., dir. David A. Crane & Ptnrs., Inc., Phila., 1972-74; devel. mgr. Pike Place Market Preservation Devel. Authority, Seattle, 1974-79; prin., dir. Cardwell/Thomas & Assocs. Architects, Seattle, 1979—; prin. Val Thomas Inc., Seattle, 1979—; lectr. U. Wash., Seattle, 1979-88, mem. profl. council Coll. Architecture & Urban Design, 1987—. Exhibited at White House Nat. Endowment for Arts, 1985. Mem. Mayor's Downtown Housing Task Force, Seattle, 1984—, Allied Arts of Seattle, 1978—, numerous city planning task force coms. Served as lt. USNR, 1966-70. Recipient Nat. Honor award Nat. Trust Hist. Preservation, 1985, Mayor's Small Bus. award, City of Seattle, 1987. Mem. AIA (Seattle Honor award 1988), Tau Sigma Delta. Democrat. Episcopalian. Office: Val Thomas Inc 1221 2d Ave Ste 300 Seattle WA 98119

THOMAS, KEITH VERN, bank executive; b. Provo, Utah, Oct. 21, 1946; s. Vern R. and Lois (Doran) T.; m. Sherrie Hunter, Oct. 7, 1969; children: Genevieve, Joshua, Rachel, William, Rebecca. AA, Dixie Coll., 1969; BS, Brigham Young U., 1971; MBA, St. Mary's Coll., 1980. Examiner Fed. Home Loan Bank Bd., San Francisco, 1971-79, field mgr., 1979-84, asst. dir., 1984-85; sr. v.p., dir. examinations and supervision Fed. Home Loan Bank, Seattle, 1985-88; exec. v.p. and chief operating officer Frontier Savings Assn., Las Vegas, Nev., 1988-89, pres., 1989—; bd. dirs., v.p. Thomas Mgmt. Corp., Cedar City, Utah, 1979—; bd. dirs. Inst. Fin. Edn., San Francisco, Calif., 1982-85; bd. trustees Nev. Sch. of the Arts, 1988—; sec. Nev. League Savs. Insts., 1988—. Editor: Real Estate Textbook, 1983-84. dir. Nev. Community Found. Recipient Outstanding Service award, Fed. Home Loan Bank Bd., 1976, 77, 85, Disting. Service award, Fed. Home Loan Bank Bd., 1981; named Outstanding Instr. Inst. Fin. Edn. 1984. Mem. Nat. Assn. Rev. Appraisers and Mortgage Underwriters, Brigham Young U. Mgmt. Soc. Republican. Mormon. Office: Frontier Savs Assn 1860 E Sahara Ave Las Vegas NV 89104

THOMAS, LARRY, information systems consultant; b. Watertown, N.Y., Aug. 17, 1942; s. George Edward and Rea Adelle (Coolidge) Coons; 1 child, Lawrence Prohaska. BA in Bus. Adminstrn., U. Wash., 1979. Owner, gen. mgr. K & M Corp., Olympia, Wash., 1971-73; adminstr. Community Coll. Dist. 12, Olympia, 1973-77; pvt. practice Seattle, 1977-81; mgr. infosystems Manus Computer Services, Seattle, 1981-83, Interchecks, Seattle, 1984-87; instr. computer sci. Highline Community Coll., Seattle, 1987—; infosystems cons. Thomas and Assocs., Seattle, 1987—; cons. Nat. Assn. Trade and Tech. Schs., Washington, 1987—. Mem. adv. bd. Highline Community Coll., 1986—. Mem. Data Processing Mgmt. Assn. (bd. dirs.). Office: Thomas Cons Box 30698 Seattle WA 98103-0698

THOMAS, LAURA MARLENE, artist, social services; b. Chico, Calif., Apr. 29, 1936; d. Boyd Stanley Beck and Lois Velma (Behrke) Lyons; m. Charles Rex Thomas,. AA in Fine Arts, Sacramento City Coll., 1978; BA in Fine Arts, Calif. State U., 1981. Tchrs. asst. Hanford Elem. Sch., Hanford, Calif., 1963-68; asst. dir. RSVP: Retired Sr. Vol. Program, Hanford, 1971-74; dir. of Art Bank Sacramento City Coll., Sacramento, 1976-78; pub. asst. Student Activities Calif. State Univ., Sacramento, 1978-81; antique dealer pvt. practice, Sacramento, 1981--, arts and crafts bus., 1976--; social worker Cath. Social Svcs., Sacramento, 1985--. Artist: weaving, Double Image, 1977, 2nd Place 1977; ceramic sculptor, Bird. Charter mem. YWCA, Sacramento, 1972, Folsum Hist. Soc., 1988. Cert. of appreciation, Carmellia City Ctr. Adv. Council, Sacramento, 1986. Mem. Statue of Liberty-Ellis Island Found., 1985, North Shore Animal League (Benefactors award 1985), Calif. State U. Alumni Assn., Hanford Sportsman Club (v.p. 1963-68). Republican. Protestant. Home: 2721 I St #8 Sacramento CA 95816 Office: Cath Social Svcs 1121 9th St Sacramento CA 95814

THOMAS, LAWRENCE EUGENE, academic library director; b. York, Pa., Dec. 8, 1931. BS in Composition, Julliard Sch., 1954; MFA in Composition, Brandeis U., 1957; MLS, Ind. U., 1961. Asst. head circulation Columbia U., N.Y.C., 1961-63; chief circulation services Dartmouth Coll., Hanover, N.H., 1964-67; asst. librarian U. Tex. Med., San Antonio, 1967-69; AUL Coll. Devel. and Pub. Service Simon Fraser U., Burnaby, B.C., Can., 1970-80; university librarian Seattle U., 1980—; adj. faculty music Seattle U., 1983; cons. Bowdoin Coll., Brunswick, Maine, 1966, McDowell Colony, Peterborough, N.H., 1964, Eastern Oreg. State Coll., 1987. Mem. ALA. Office: Seattle U Lemieux Libr Seattle WA 98122

THOMAS, LEO, pension, insurance and executive compensation consultant; b. Los Angeles, July 5, 1947; s. Leonard and Rose (Morris) T.; m. Bernice Roberts, Aug. 19, 1969; 1 child, Tod. BA, Occidental Coll., Los Angeles, 1968. With pub. relations com. Dem. Party, Los Angeles, 1968-69; ins. agt. Prudential Co., Los Angeles, 1969-77; fin. estate mgr. Hansch Fin. Group, Los Angeles, 1970—; pres. Thomas Fin. and Ins. Services, Inc., Los Angeles, 1980—; cons. Fin. Adv. Clinic, Los Angeles, 1982-84, Fin. Digest, Los Angeles, 1983-88, Life Ins. Leaders Round Table, Los Angeles, 1984-86. Contbr. articles to profl. jours. Mem. Nat. Tax Limitation Com., Washington, 1982-85, So. Poverty Law Council, Atlanta, 1982-88; charter mem. Statue of Liberty-Ellis Island Found., 1984-88; past pres. Young Dems., 1967. Named Agt. of Yr., Los Angeles Life Underwriters, 1983, 84, 85. Mem. Internat. Assn. Fin. Planners, Am. Soc. CLU's, Internat. Forum, Top of the Table, First Fin. Resources Group. Jewish. Lodge: Kiwanis (bd. dirs. Los Angeles chpt. 1983-85). Office: Thomas Fin and Ins Svc Inc 5900 Wilshire 17 Los Angeles CA 90036

THOMAS, LYNN R., sculptor; b. San Francisco, Jan. 6, 1943; d. Joseph and Emma Rita (Webber) Mitchelson; m. Clifford Miller Hickman; children: Christina Lynn, Diana Lynn; m. Ralph Sylvester Thomas, Mar. 3, 1982. Student, Santa Monica City Coll., 1961-62, San Fernando Valley Coll., 1962-63; studied with, Milba Lloyd, London. Med asst. Dr. Omar John Fareed, Los Angeles, 1960-62; sec. City NAT. bANK, Los Angeles, 1962-64, Gulf Oil Corp., Los Angeles, 1965-67, ARC, Santa Barbara, Calif., 1967-69. Exhibited Gallery Americana, Carmel, Calif., Montecito Fine Arts Gallery, Santa Barbara, Calif., Jeanine's Art Gallery, Los Olivos, Calif., 1988, Pemberton & Oakes Fine Arts Gallery, 1988; prin. works include terra cotta bust of Mother Teresa, 1981, Pres. Reagan, also others; designer of various recognition awards and commns. Active St. Vincent's Sch., Santa Barbara, 1982--, Hospice Santa Barbara, 1986--, Seton Sch., Santa Barbara, 1986. Mem. Sculptors Guild. Roman Catholic. Home and Studio: 1118 Deer Trail Ln Solvang CA 93463

THOMAS, MICHAEL EARL, mortgage broker, investment manager; b. Honolulu, Mar. 1, 1953; s. Earl Jr. and Lula Elfreda (Patterson) T.; m. Patti Jo South, Aug. 29, 1981; children: Corey Lou, Casey Michael. AA, Saddleback Coll., 1973; BA, Calif. State U., Fullerton, 1981. Pres. Thomas & Assocs. Investment Mgmt., Costa Mesa, Calif., 1975-87; pres., chief exec. officer Equity Investment Fund, Inc., Tustin, Calif., 1987—; cons. Bryan Family Trust Found., Sacramento, 1982-83, Mission Viejo Nat. Bank, 1986-87. Contbr. articles to profl. mags. Bd. dirs. Loma Linda (Calif.) U. Found. Trust, 1988—. Mem. Calif. Ind. Mortgage Brokers Assn., Calif. Assn. Realtors, Nat. Assn. Realtors, Masons (deacon 1974-75). Office: Equity Investment Fund Inc 145 W Main St #100 Tustin CA 92680

THOMAS, NANCY MARIE, advertising company executive; b. Denver, Dec. 21, 1947; d. Edwin Leo and Teresa Margaret (Elper) Doherty; m. Hans Herbert Ufert, June 8, 1968 (div. Nov. 1979); children: Stephan Hans, Kelly Marie; m. John Thomas, Jan. 1, 1988. Student, Community Coll. Denver, Idaho State U. Nurse Kaiser Permanente Health Orgn., Denver, 1972-75; sales mgr. Sta. KSEI, Pocatello, Idaho, 1976-78; sales and mktg. dir. Holiday Inn, Pocatello, 1979-80; sales mgr., gen. sales mgr. Sta. KPVI-TV, Pocatello, 1980-83; prin. Intermedia, Pocatello, 1984—. Producer, dir. (TV comls.) Hydrotube Summer Just Went Indoors, 1984 (Idaho State Broadcasters Assn. award 1984). Named an Outstanding Young Woman of Am., 1982. Mem. Pocatello Advt. Fedn. (pres. 1981-82, bd. dirs. 1982-85, v.p. 1980-81), Idaho State U. Vocat. Home Econs. Adv. Com. Roman Catholic. Home and Office: 200 S Main Suite L Pocatello ID 83204

THOMAS, PAUL MASSENNA, JR., retail executive, investment holding company executive; b. Darby, Pa., Sept. 7, 1935; s. Paul Massenna Sr. and Leota L. (Errett) T.; m. Eloise Whitney Fletcher, Aug. 28, 1957; children: Carolyn, Peter, James. Student, San Diego State U., 1953-55, U. Calif., various locations, 1955-56, 78-70. Licensed realtor Calif. Ptnr., founder Thomas Fletcher Nicol Co., San Diego, 1968-80; pres., founder Sierra S.W. Cos., San Diego, 1980—; chmn., co-owner Nat. Theme Prodn., San Diego, 1982—; owner, mng. ptnr. Thomas Jaeger Winery, San Diego, 1988—; bd. dirs., founder Rancho Santa Fe Nat. Bank. Owner, curator Mus. Show of posters since 1896 of Olympic athletes in Art. Bd. dirs. Rancho Santa Fe Assn., 1988—; trustee Rancho Santa Fe Youth, Rancho Santa Fe Community Found., also founding mem., Rancho Santa Fe Little League, La Jolla Theater Arts Found., La Jolla Country Day Sch., Fountain Valley Sch., Colorado Springs; ruling elder Rancho Santa Fe Presbyn. Ch. Mem. Confrerie des Chevaliers de Tastevin (La Jolla chpt.). Republican. Clubs: Rancho Santa Fe Garden, Rancho Santa Fe Golf, Rancho Santa Fe Supper. Lodge: Rotary (Paul Harris fellow), Internat. Order St. Hubert (knight officer), Los Ancianos. Office: Nat Theme Prodns 1843 Hotel Circle S Ste 300 San Diego CA 92108

THOMAS, RICHARD SAVAGE, aerospace executive; b. Washington, Feb. 21, 1936; s. Ernest Alvin and Regina (Savage) T.; m. Elizabeth Campbell, Feb. 14, 1962; children: Richard, Ernest, Eleanor. BS ME, U. Notre Dame, 1958; MBA, U. So. Calif., 1978; JD (hon.), UCLA, 1980; ArtsD (hon.), U. Md., 1982. Registered profl. engr. Commd. USN, 1958, advanced through grades to capt.; dir. internat. mktg. Gen. Dynamics, San Diego, 1980-86; pres. Tomcon, La Jolla, Calif., 1986—. Recipient Silver Star, Bronze Star, Disting. Flying Cross, Purple Heart. Republican. Lodges: Masons, K.T. Home: 7051 Caminito La Benera La Jolla CA 92037

THOMAS, ROBERT CHESTER, sculptor, art educator; b. Wichita, Kans., Apr. 19, 1924; s. Chester and Alma (Mead) T.; m. Eleanor Louise Brand, July 15, 1944; children—Robin Louise, Elizabeth Catherine. Studies with Ossip Zadkine, Paris, 1948-49; B.A., U. Calif.-Santa Barbara, 1951; M.F.A., Calif. Coll. Arts and Crafts, 1952. Prof. sculpture U. Calif., Santa Barbara, 1954—; executed life size bronze figure U. Calif., Santa Barbara, 1967, sculpture J. Magnin store, Century City, 1966, fountain, Montecito, 1968; represented in permanent collection Hirshhorn Mus., Washington, Whatcom Mus., Bellingham, Wash., Santa Barbara Mus., U. Calif., Santa Barbara. Served with USAAF, 1943-46; ETO. Recipient Bronze medal City of Los Angeles, 1949, Silver medal Calif. State Fair, 1954. Home: 38 San Mateo Ave Goleta CA 93117 Office: U Calif Dept Art Santa Barbara CA 93106

THOMAS, ROBERT LANCEFIELD, psychiatrist; b. Forest Grove, Oreg., Feb. 23, 1909; s. Horace Estes and Georgia (Lancefield) T.; student Reed Coll., 1926-27; AB with distinction, Stanford U., 1930; MD cum laude, Harvard, 1933; children: Randolph Woodson, Suzanne Chilton, Robert W., Barbara Jelen, Gwen Thomas. Diplomate Am. Bd. Surgery. Intern, Mass. Gen. Hosp., Boston, 1933-36; fellow Lahey Clinic, Boston, 1936-37; practice medicine, specializing in surgery, Portland, Oreg., 1937-42, Oakland, Calif., 1946-64, Whitefield, N.H., 1964, Nev. Test Site, AEC, 1964-66; med. dir. Yolo Gen. Hosp., Woodland, Calif., 1966-67, Yerington, Nev., 1967-68; asst. med. dir. Multnomah Med. Svc. Bur., Portland, 1938-42; med. dir. Hosp. Svc. of Calif., Oakland, 1948-58; resident psychiatry Napa-Sonoma State Hosps., 1969-72; staff psychiatrist Napa State Hosp., 1972-80, 84-88; practice medicine, specializing in psychiatry, 1969-80; with Rehab. Mental Health Svcs., San Jose, 1980-84. Capt. M.C., USNR, 1938-69; Res., 1938-42, 46-69; PTO. Decorated Asiatic Pacific medal with 4 bronze stars. Fellow ACS; mem. Am. Psychiat. Assn., Huguenot Soc., Order First Families Va., Soc. Mayflower Descs. (mem.-at-large exec. com. gen. soc. 1972-75, surgeon gen. 1969-72, gov. Calif. soc. 1970-73, gov. gen. 1975-78), Soc. of Cincinnati in State of R.I., Hereditary Order Descs. Colonial Govs., Jamestowne Soc., Soc. Calif. Pioneers, SAR, Sons and Daus. Oreg. Pioneers, Naval Order U.S., Sovereign Colonial Soc., Ams. of Royal Descent, Barons of Magna Charta, Soc. Descs. Colonial Clergy, Alden Kindred Am., Order of Crown in Am., Sons of Colonial New England, Phi Beta Kappa, Alpha Omega Alpha, Phi Gamma Delta, Nu Sigma Nu, U. Calif. Faculty Club, Order Am. Armorial Ancestry. Home: 41359 Whitecrest Ct Fremont CA 94539-4529 Office: Napa State Hosp Imola CA 94558

THOMAS, ROGER PARRY, interior designer, art consultant; b. Salt Lake City, Nov. 4, 1951; s. E. Parry and Peggy Chatterton T.; m. Marilyn Harris Hite, Nov. 21, 1976 (div. Apr. 1979); m. H. Andrea Wahn, Nov. 20, 1982; 1 child, Andrew Chatterton. Student Interlochen Arts Acad., 1969; B.F.A., Tufts U., 1973. Pres. Miller-Thomas, Inc., Las Vegas, 1973-76; v.p. Yates-Silverman, Inc., Las Vegas, 1976-81; v.p. design Atlandia Design a Golden Nugget Co., Las Vegas, 1981—; curator Valley Bank Nev. Fine Art Collection. Bd. dirs. Nev. Dance Theatre; mem. McCarren Arts Adv. Bd., dir. Nev. Inst. Contemporary Art. Republican. Mem. Ch. of Jesus Christ of Latter-day Saints. Clubs: Sports Club, Country (Las Vegas). Office: Atlandia Design 3380 Arville St Las Vegas NV 89102

THOMAS, SAMUEL FINLEY, psychiatrist; b. Paris, France, Oct. 2, 1913 (parents Am. citizens); s. Edward Russell and Elisabeth (Finley) T.; A.B., Princeton, 1935; M.D., Columbia, 1940; m. Ruth Larson, May 21, 1976; 1 dau. by previous marriage, Susan Faith. Intern St. Lukes Hosp., N.Y.C., 1940-41, resident 1941-42, Neurol. Inst. N.Y., 1942-43; practice medicine specializing in neurology and psychiatry, N.Y.C., 1946—; mem. staff Neurol. Inst., N.Y.C., 1946—, attending neurologist, 1975-80, cons. emeritus, 1980—, clin. prof. neurology, 1975-80; mem. staff St. Luke's Hosp., N.Y.C., 1946-80, attending physician neurology, 1955-80, attending psychiatrist, 1975; cons. physician and psychiatrist emeritus, 1980—. Served to maj., M.C., USAAF, 1943-46. Mem. A.M.A., N.Y. County Med. Soc., Am. Psychiat. Assn., N.Y. Neurol. Soc., N.Y. Acad. Medicine. Republican. Episcopalian. Clubs: Ambassador Athletic (Salt Lake City); Am. Alpine (N.Y.C.); Wasatch Mountain (Salt Lake City). Contbr. articles to med. jours., poetry to popular mags. and newspapers. Address: 123 2d Ave Salt Lake City UT 84103

THOMAS, SHARI LEE, restaurant purveyor; b. Cheyenne, Wyo., Mar. 13, 1946; d. Robert Gene and Laurella Florence (Hearing) T. B in Music Edn., Pacific U., 1969. Asst. mgr. Morrison's, Inc., Mobile, Ala., 1972-73; food, beverage dir. Holiday Inn, Charlotte, N.C., 1973-74; asst. mgr. Triton Investments Co. dba McDonalds, Greensboro, N.C., 1974-76; eletronic technician Tektronix, Inc., Beaverton, Oreg., 1977-84; gen. mgr. Triple R Ranch, Cornelius, Oreg., 1984-88; chief exec. officer Classic Country Rabbit Co., Hillsboro, Oreg., 1988—. 1st lt. USMC, 1969-72, Res. 1976. Named Women of Yr. Arg. Mushaw Ctr., 1986. Mem. Am. Rabbit Breeders Assn., Tri-county Farm Fresh Foods, Hillsboro Farmers Market (dir. 1987-88), Chef di Cuisine Soc., Pacific U. Alumni Assn. (exec. coun. 1989—). Republican. Lutheran. Office: Classic Country Rabbit Co PO Box 1412 Hillsboro OR 97123

THOMAS, SHARLA MARIE, utility company technician; b. Missoula, Mont., June 12, 1950; d. Kenneth Charles and Mary Grace (Caras) T. Student, U. Mont., 1986—. Meter reader Mont. Power Co., Missoula, 1976-77, groundman, 1977-78, apprentice lineman, 1978-81, div. technician, 1981—. Republican. Mormon.

THOMAS, STEVE D., info-system specialist; b. Butte, Mont., Aug. 8, 1951; s. William James and Catherine (Murphy) T.; m. Kathy Ann McCarthy, Aug. 22, 1971; children: Shawn, Heather. Programmer analyst Anaconda Co., Butte, 1973-81, systems analyst, 1981-82; systems programmer ARCO Metals, Columbia Falls, Mont., 1982-83, supr. ops. and tech. support, 1983-85; supr. of mgmt. info. systems Columbia Falls Aluminum Co., Columbia Falls, 1985—. Office: CFAC 2000 Aluminum Dr Columbia Falls MT 59912

THOMAS, TERESA ANN, microbiologist, educator, consultant; b. Wilkes-Barre, Pa., Oct. 17, 1939; d. Sam Charles and Edna Grace T. B.S. cum laude, Coll. Misericordia, 1961; M.S. in Biology, Am. U. Beirut, 1965; M.S. in Microbiology, U. So. Calif., 1973. Tchr., sci. supr., curriculum coord. Meyers High Sch., Wilkes-Barre, 1962-64, Wilkes-Barre Area Public Schs., 1961-66; research assoc. Proctor Found. for Research in Ophthalmology U. Calif. Med. Ctr., San Francisco, 1966-68; instr. Robert Coll. of Istanbul (Turkey), 1968-71, Am. Edn. in Luxembourg, 1971-72, Bosco Tech. Inst., Rosemead, Calif., 1973-74, San Diego Community Coll. Dist., 1974-80; prof. math.-sci. div. Southwestern Coll., Chula Vista, Calif., 1980—,pres. acad. senate, 1984-85, del., 1986—; mem. steering com. project CREATE Southwestern Coll.-Shanghai Inst. Fgn. Trade; coord. Southwestern Coll. Great Teaching Seminar, 1987, 88, coord. scholars program, 1988—; mem. exec. com. Acad. Senate for Calif. Community Colls., 1985-86, Chancellor of Calif. Community Colls. Adv. and Rev. Council Fund for Instrnl. Improvement, 1984-86; adj. asst. prof. Chapman Coll., San Diego, 1974-83; asst. prof. San Diego State U., 1977-79; chmn. Am. Colls. Istanbul Sci. Week, 1969-71; mem. adv. bd. Chapman Coll. Community Center, 1979-80; cons. sci. curriculum Calif. Dept. Edn., 1986—; mem. Chula Vista Internat. Friendship Commn., 1987-90; pres. Internat. Relations Club 1959-61; mem. San Francisco World Affairs Council, 1966-68; chmn. land use, energy and wildlife com. Congressman Duncan Hunter's Environ. Adv. Council, 1982-84; v.p. Palomar Palace Estates Home Owners Assn., 1983-85, pres. 1987—. mem. editorial rev. bd. Jour. of Coll. Sci. Teaching, NSTA, 1988—. NSF fellow, 1965; USPHS fellow, 1972-73; recipient Excellence in Edn. award Nat. Inst. Staff and Orgnl. Devel., 1989; recognized at Internat. Conf. Teaching Excellence, Austin, 1989, ; Pa. Heart Assn. research grantee, 1962; named Southwestern Coll. Woman of Distinction, 1987. Mem. Am. Soc. Microbiology, Nat. Sci. Tchrs. Assn. (life, internat. com., coord. internat. honors exchange lectr. competition sponsored with Assn. Sci Educators Great Britain, 1986), Nat. Assn. Biology Tchrs., Soc. Coll. Sci. Tchrs. (Calif. membership coordinator 1984—), S.D. Zool. Soc., Calif. Tchrs. Assn., NEA, Am. Assn. Community and Jr. Colls., MENSA, Arab Am. Med. Assn., Am.-Lebanese Assn. San Diego (chmn. scholarship com., pres. 1988—), Am. U. of Beirut Alumni and Friends of San Diego (1st v.p. 1984—) Kappa Gamma Pi (pres. Wilkes-Barre chpt. 1963-64, San Francisco chpt. 1967-68), Sigma Phi Sigma, Phi Theta Kappa (advisor Southwest Conf. chpt. 1989). Club: Am. Lebanese Syrian Ladies (pres. 1982-83). Office: Southwestern Coll 900 Otay Lakes Rd Chula Vista CA 92010

THOMAS, VERNEDA ESTELLA, perfusionist; b. Chgo., June 21, 1936; d. Russel Huston and Verneda (Williams) T. BS, Graceland Coll., Lamoni, Iowa, 1973. Cardiovascualr technician Michael Reese Hosp., Chgo., 1962; cardiopulmonary technician Chgo. State Tuberculosis Sanitorium, Chgo., 1962-66, Loyola U. Sch. Medicine, Maywood, Ill., 1966-68; physiology technician Loyola U. Sch. Medicine, 1968-69; med. technologist Cook County Hosp., Chgo., 1969-71; rsch. assoc. Queen's Med. Ctr., Honolulu, 1973-78; intra aortic balloon pump technician Queen's Med. Ctr., 1973—; perfusionist for pvt. med. practice Honolulu, 1978-82; perfusionist Mid Pacific Perfusion, Honolulu, 1982—; referee, U.S. Volleyball Assn., 1978. Contbr. articles to med. publs. Mem. U.S. Pan-Am. high jump team, Mex., 1955; mem. U.S. Olympic volleyball team, Tokyo, 1964. Mem. Am. Soc. Cardiopulmonary Technology, Am. Bd. Cardiovascular Perfusion. Baptist. Home: 217 Prospect St Honolulu HI 96813 Office: Psicor Inc 16818 Via del Campo Ct San Diego CA 92127

THOMAS, VICKY LYNNE, counselor; b. Cocoa Beach, Fla., Mar. 12, 1954; d. Robert Milo and Doreen Victoria (Rasmussen) Watkins; m. James Edward Thomas, Aug. 16, 1980; 1 child, Megan Amelia. BS in Rehab., Ea. Mont. Coll., 1976; MEd in Counseling, Boston U., 1985. Social services dir. Orchard Park Rehab. Ctr., Tacoma, 1976-80, Puyallup (Wash.) Manor Rehab. Ctr., 1980-81; social worker Tacoma Luth. Home, 1981-82; social service dir. U.S. Army Community Services, Wurzburg, Fed. Republic Germany, 1982-84; quality assurance coordinator U.S. Army Med. Ctr., Wurzburg, Fed. Republic Germany, 1984-85; career counselor Pacific Luth. U., Tacoma, 1986-88. Bd. dirs. Adult Literacy Council, Tacoma Community House, 1987-88; fed. women's program mem. U.S. Govt. Civil Service Workers, Wurzburg, 1982-85; mem. Child Protection Services, San Antonio, 1986; geriatric adv. bd. Alzheimer's Support Club, Tacoma, 1981. Mem. Nat. Council Family Relations, Nat. Assn. Student Employment Adminstrs., Wash. State Student Employment Adminstrs., Toastmasters Internat. (v.p. Wurzburg 1984-85, Competent Toastmaster award, 1985), Jobs Daughters (honored queen 1971). Home: 13523 108th Ave Ct E Puyallup WA 98374 Office: Jr Achievement Greater Puget Sound Seattle WA 98101 also: 600 Stewart St 212 Pla 600 Bldg Seattle WA 98101

THOMAS, VIOLETA MARIA DE LOS ANGELES, real estate broker; b. Buenos Aires, Dec. 21, 1949; came to U.S., 1968; d. Angel and Lola (Andino) de Rios; m. Jess Thomas, Dec. 23, 1974; 1 child, Victor Justin. BA, Pine Manor Coll., 1970; BBA, U. Bus. Adminstrn., Buenos Aires, 1971. Mgr. book div. Time-Life, N.Y.C., 1970-74; real estate broker First Marin Realty, Inc., Mill Valley, Calif., 1985—. Bd. dirs. City of Tiburon, Calif., 1987—, Art and Heritage Commn., Tiburon. Named Woman of Yr. City of Buenos Aires, 1977. Home: PO Box 662 Tiburon CA 94920

THOMAS, WILLIAM ELWOOD (WILL THOMAS), newspaper editor; b. Willows, Calif., Feb. 5, 1932; s. Ralph E. and Bertha A. (Adam) T.; B.S. in Agrl. Journalism, Calif. State Poly. U., 1956; m. Nancy Rae Eisenbeiss, Aug. 27, 1955; children—William Scott, Brian Edward, Bradley Westlund, Karen Jessica. Reporter, Merced (Calif.) Sun-Star, 1956-57; patrolman-clk. Willows (Calif.) Police Dept., 1957-58; staff announcer, news dir. KHSL-TV and Radio Sta., Chico, Calif., 1958-60; editor Lakeport (Calif.) Record-Bee, 1960-66, North County Publs., San Mateo Times Newspaper Group, South San Francisco, 1966—. Active San Mateo coun. Boy Scouts Am., 1970-71; pres. Benjamin Franklin Jr. High Sch. PTA, 1971-72, del. state conv., 1971, 76; pres. Broadmoor Property Owners Assn., 1976-77. With U.S. Army, 1953-55. Recipient Hon. Svc. award Jefferson Coun. of PTA, 1976. Mem. Peninsula Press Club, South San Francisco C. of C. (past mem. bd. dirs.). Republican. Home: 723 87th St Colma CA 94015 Office: 1331 San Matoe Ave S San Francisco CA 94080

THOMAS, WILLIAM ESMANT, JR., air force officer; b. Euclid, Ohio, July 3, 1958; s. William Esmant and Frances Alice (Buttolph) T. BS, Miami U., 1980; MS, Air Force Inst. Tech., 1985. Commd. USAF, 1980, advanced through grades to capt.; lauch and integration mgr. Space Div. Los Angeles, 1980-84; project officer Weapons Lab. Albuquerque, 1986—. Mem. Air Force Assn., Jr. Officers Group (chmn. 1987). Mem. Ch. of Christ. Home: 10616 Pennyback Park Dr NE Albuquerque NM 87123 Office: USAF Weapons Lab Kirtland AFB NM 87117

THOMAS, WILLIAM F., newspaper editor; b. Bay City, Mich., June 11, 1924; s. William F. and Irene Marie (Billette) T.; m. Patricia Ann Wendland, Dec. 28, 1948; children: Michael William, Peter Matthew, Scott Anthony. BS, Northwestern U., 1950, MS cum laude, 1951; LHD (hon.), Pepperdine U., Los Angeles. Asst. chief copy editor Buffalo Evening News, 1950-55; editor Sierra Madre (Calif.) News, 1955-56; reporter, asst. city editor, then city editor Los Angeles Mirror, 1957-62; asst. city editor, then met. editor Los Angeles Times, 1968-71, editor, 1971-72, editor, exec. v.p., 1972—. Served with U.S. Army, 1943-46. Office: LA Times Times Mirror Sq Los Angeles CA 90053

THOMAS, WILLIAM MARSHALL, congressman; b. Wallace, Idaho, Dec. 6, 1941; s. Virgil and Gertrude T.; m. Sharon Lynn Hamilton, Jan., 1967; children: Christopher, Amelia. B.A., San Francisco State U., 1963, M.A., 1965. Mem. faculty dept. Am. govt. Bakersfield (Calif.) Coll., 1965-74, prof., 1965-74; mem. Calif. State Assembly, 1974-78, 96th-101st Congresses from 18th, now 20th Calif. Dist.; vice chmn. Nat. Republican Congl. Com. Western Region; mem. Ho. of Reps. Ways and Means Com.; Mem. del. to Soviet Union, by Am. Council Young Polit. Leaders, 1977; chmn. Kern County Republican Central Com., 1972-74; mem. Calif. Rep. Com., 1972-80; del. Republican Party Nat. Conv., 1980, 84, 88. Office: 2402 Rayburn House Office Bldg Washington DC 20515 *

THOMAS, WILLIAM RICHARD, retired financial executive; b. Sacramento, Apr. 13, 1920; s. Raymond Joseph and Annie (Clemence) T.; m. Jane Dunning Lasher, Nov. 3, 1964; children: Paul Kenneth, Susan Jane; children by previous marriage: William Richard, Robert Charles, Alan James. B.S., U. Calif. at Berkeley, 1941. Accountant Gen. Mills, Inc., 1941-42; with Cutter Labs., Inc., Berkeley, Calif., 1945-67; v.p. finance Cutter Labs., Inc., 1957-67; also dir.; pres., dir. Optical Coating Lab., Inc., Santa Rosa, 1967-68; v.p. Pacific Lighting Corp., 1968-73, sr. fin. v.p., 1973-77; sr. v.p. fin. and adminstrn. Global Marine Inc., 1977-85, also dir.; dir. AeroViornment, Bank of The West, San Francisco. Served to lt. USNR, 1942-45, PTO. Mem. Fin. Execs. Inst. (nat. pres. 1966), U. Calif. Bus. Adminstrn. Alumni Assn. (past pres.). Lutheran. Home: 2701 Paseo del Mar Palos Verdes Estates CA 90274

THOMASMA, KENNETH RAY, author, storyteller; b. Grand Rapids, Mich., Sept. 2, 1930; s. Peter E. and Freda Louise (Jones) T.; m. Barbara Joan Veurink, June 16, 1955; 1 child, Daniel Ross. AB in Elem. Edn., Calvin Coll., 1953; MA, U. Mich., 1958. Tchr. Grand Rapids Pub. Schs., 1953-58, 64-70, prin., 1958-64, 72-74, media specialist, 1972-77; assoc. prof. Grand Valley State U., Allendale, Mich., 1970-72; tchr. Teton County Schs., Jackson, Wyo., 1977-87; producer Travelog Films, Grand Rapids, 1960-75; dir. Ken-O-Sha Nature Ctr., Grand Rapids, 1964-74. Author: Naya Nuki: Girl Wyo Ran, 1983 (Indian Paintbrush award 1986), Soun Tetoken: Nez Perce Boy, 1984, Om-Kas-Toe of the Blackfeet, 1986. Mem. citizen's adv. com. Jackson Pub. Schs., 1978, 81, 87. Served with USN, 1950-51. Named Citizen of Yr., Jackson C. of C., 1988. Mem. Mich. PTA (life). Baptist. Home: Box 2863 Jackson WY 83001

THOMASON, GAIL ANN, small business coordinator; b. Denver, June 22, 1947; d. Galen Arthur and Eva Mary (Lenzen) T.; 1 child, John Folsom Hallett II; m. James H. Harmon, Sept. 30, 1972. BA magna cum laude, Colo. State U., 1980, MA in Teaching, 1982. Owner, ptnr. BCA Resources Tng., Ft. Collins, Colo., 1983-86; arts cons. Raeburn House Gallery, Palm Springs, Calif., 1986-87; instr. Colo. State U., U. Colo., Boulder, 1983-86; tng. cons. McGraw-Hill, N.Y.C., 1985-86. Author/editor Colo. State U. research bull., 1984. Hist. restoration photographer Jr. League, Ft. Collins, 1985-86; head Zonta sponsored battered women's safehouse project, 1985-86. Mem. AAUW, NAFE (leadership program 1985-86), Delta Zeta Alumnae Assn., Panhellenic Alumnae Assn. Episcopalian. Lodge: Zonta. Home: 2663 Victoria Park Dr Riverside CA 92506 Office: Riverside C of C 4261 Main St Riverside CA 92501

THOMAS-SANCHEZ, AMY LEE, nurse; b. Davenport, Iowa, Mar. 15, 1955; d. Raymond Milton Jr. and Doris May (Johnston) Thomas; m. Manuel Frank Sanchez, Apr. 29, 1983; 1 child, Raymond Daniel. AA, Ill. Cen. Coll., 1976; AS, U. Albuquerque, 1979. RN, N.Mex. Staff nurse Presbyn. Hosp., Albuquerque, 1979, staff nurse, rehab. nurse for brain damaged babies newborn nursery, 1981-84; staff nurse U. N.Mex. Hosp., Albuquerque, 1980-81; charge nurse, emergency coord. LaVida Llena Retirement Ctr., Albuquerque, 1984; maternity nurse Heights Gen. Hosp., Albuquerque, 1984-87; cons. nursing Neuro Infant Rehab. and Stimulation, Albuquerque, 1985—; instr. childbirth maternal and infant project U. N.Mex., Albuquerque, 1987-88. Playwright Whose Child is This, 1986; songwriter The Unmailed Letter; author poems. Arranger, tenor Thomas Family Singers, 1974—; poet, co-arranger Gospel Chapel Radio Ministries, 1980—. Mem. Assn. Rehab. Nurses, Gospel Music Assn., Alpha Mu Gamma. Republican. Mem. Assembly of God. Home: 12012 Golden Gate NE Albuquerque NM 87111 Office: Neuro Infant Rehab Stimulation PO Box 14452 Albuquerque NM 87191

THOMASSON, GEORGE ORIN, physician, insurance company executive; b. Davenport, Iowa, Dec. 22, 1937; s. Loris and Elsie Mae (Parker) T.; m. Dorothy Jane Adams, Nov. 25, 1962 (div. 1978); m. Jacqueline Jean Heilman, July 6, 1984; children: Laura, William, Patrick, David, Elizabeth. BA, North Tex. State U., 1959; MD, U. Tex., Dallas, 1962; postgrad., U. Ga., 1976. Cert. pub. mgr. Intern. U. Ark. Med. Ctr, 1962-63; residence USPHS, 1963-65; pvt. practice Russellville, Ark., 1965-66; instr. U. Fla. Med. Sch., Gainesville, 1966-71; univ. physician U. Ga., Athens, 1971-73; dist. health officer Ga. Dept. Human Resources, Athens, 1973-78; asst. prof. U. Colo. Health Scis. Ctr., Denver, 1978-83; risk mgr. Med. Liability Cons. Program, Denver, 1983-88; v.p. risk mgmt. COPIC Ins. Co., Denver, 1988—; med. dir. Alachua County Head Start Project, Gainesville, 1968-71; med. cons. Robert Woods Johnson Sch. Health Project, Denver, 1978-80, Clin. Reference Systems Inc., Englewood, Colo., Colo. Lt. Gov.'s Rural Coun., 1983-86; bd. dirs. Pricare, Inc., Englewood. Contbr. articles to med. publs. Cons. Gilpin County Health Ctr., Black Hawk, Colo., 1983-85, Clinica Compasina, Lafayette, Colo., 1984-87, Colo. Health Dept., 1984—. Recipient outstanding contbn. award Colo. Hosp. Assn., 1985. Mem. Am. Assn. Med. Systems and Informatics, Am. Acad. Med. Dirs., AMA, Colo. Med. Assn. (chmn. community health issues coun., Presdl. commendation 1987), Denver Med. Soc. (pub. health com. 1985—, Presdl. gold star 1986), Am. Coll. Physian Execs. Democrat. Episcopalian. Office: COPIC Ins Co 5575 DTC Pkwy Englewood CO 80111

THOMFORD, WILLIAM EMIL, engineer, consultant; b. San Francisco, Mar. 15, 1927; s. Emil George and Anna Marie (Robohm) T.; m. Irene Shapoff, Mar. 21, 1948; children: Elaine Margaret, John William. AA, City Coll. San Francisco, 1949; BA, U. Calif., Berkeley, 1951; postgrad., Stanford U., 1967. Registered profl. engr., Calif. Various positions So. Pacific Transp. Co., San Francisco, 1951-80, mgr. research and test, 1981-83; prin. Transp. Cons. Services, Millbrae, Calif., 1983—; tech. cons. Sumitoma Corp. Am., San Francisco, 1983-87, Am. Pres. Lines, Oakland, Calif., 1984, Greenbriar Leasing Corp., Portland, Oreg., 1985—, Nippon Sharyo USA, Inc., N.Y.C., 1987—. Designer Hydra-Cushion, 1954 (Henderson medal, 1964), automotive parts rail car, 1957, rail car for 30 autos (Best Design in Steel award Am. Iron and Steel Inst., 1971), double stack car for 10 Intermodal Standards Orng. containers, 1980, fiberglas covered hopper car, 1982. Served with USN, 1944-46. Fellow ASME; mem. NSPE, Assn. Am. Railroads, Car Dept Officers' Assn. Lutheran. Club: Engrs. (San Francisco), Pacific Railway (San Francisco). Home and Office: 1176 Glenwood Dr Millbrae CA 94030

THOMPSON, ALICE ABBOTT, interior designer; b. Long Beach, Calif., June 23, 1933; d. Clell Eugene Abbott and Madelon Gail (Erter) Jacobs; m. Robert Benton Thompson, Nov. 22, 1955; children: Amy, Jennifer, Caroline (dec.), Robert Benton Jr. Student, Penn Hall Jr. Coll., Chambersburg, Pa. Designer Leland-Thompson Inc., Dayton, Ohio, 1978-80; pres., owner R. Thompson & Co., Vail, Colo., 1980-88; freelance interior designer, owner Evergreen, Colo., 1988—. Mem. Jr. League Dayton, 1956-88. Republican. Presbyterian. Office: PO Box 2954 Evergreen CO 80439 also: 3560 Hwy 74 Ste B-10 Ctr Evergreen CO 80439

THOMPSON, ARLENE RITA, nursing educator; b. Yakima, Wash., May 17, 1933; d. Paul James and Esther Margaret (Danroth) T. BS in Nursing, U. Wash., 1966, Masters in Nursing, 1970, postgrad., 1982—. Staff nurse Univ. Teaching Hosp., Seattle, 1966-69; mem. nursing faculty U. Wash. Sch. Nurses, Seattle, 1971-73; critical care nurse Virginia Mason Hosp., Seattle, 1973—; educator Seattle Pacific U. Sch. Nursing, 1981—. Contbr. articles to profl. jours. USPHS grantee, 1969; nursing scholar Virginia Mason Hosp., 1965. Mem. Am. Assn. Critical Care Nurses (cert.), Am. Nurses Assn., Am. Heart Assn., Nat. League Nursing, Sigma Theta Tau, Alpha Tau Omega. Republican. Presbyterian. Home: 2320 W Newton Seattle WA 98199 Office: Seattle Pacific U 3307 3d Ave West Seattle WA 98199

THOMPSON, BENJAMIN VEERLAND, army officer; b. Newport, Va., June 22, 1956; s. Veerland Fredrick and Henritta (Jackson) T.; children: Benjamin V., Brandon V. Student, W.Va. State Coll., 1974-79. Commd. 2nd lt. U.S. Army, 1979, advance through grades to capt., 1983; supply officer 44th Med. Brigade, Ft. Bragg, N.C., 1979-81; student flight 6th AVN Co., Ft. Rucker, Ala., 1981-82; sect. officer 377th Med. Co. Air Ambul, Yong San, Republic of Korea, 1982-83, 237th Med. DET Air Ambul, Ft. Ord, Calif., 1983-86; student 6th AVN Co., Ft. Rucker, 1986-87; operation officer 54th Med. DET Air Ambul, Ft. Lewis, Wash., 1987—. Coord. MAST 54th Med. DET, 1987—; local pres. NAACP, 1971-74. Decorated Flight Wings, Army Achievement medal, Army Svc. Ribbon, Overseas Svc. Ribbon, ARCOM. Mem. Pershing Rifles (pres. 1978-79), Scabbard & Blade, W.Va. State Coll. Head Cheerleader, Gospel Cavalier (pres. 1974-79, bd. dirs. 1975-79), W.Va. State Coll. Alumni. Methodist. Home: PO Box 33945 Tacoma WA 98433 Office: 54th Med Det Fort Lewis WA 98433

THOMPSON, BETTY JANE, small business owner; b. Ladysmith, Wis., Nov. 18, 1923; d. Edward Thomas and Mayme Selma (Kratwell) Potter; m. Frederick Sturdee Thompson, Apr. 19, 1945 (div. Apr. 1973); children: Denise Alana, Kent Marshall; m. J.R. Critchfield, Feb. 14, 1977 (div. 1987). Student, Jamestown (N.D.) Coll., 1946-47, U. Calif., Long Beach, 1964-69; AA, Orange Coast Coll., 1976; postgrad., Monterey Peninsula Coll., 1979-80; SBA Cert., Hartnell Coll., 1982. Cert. fashion cons. Owner, mgr., buyer Goodview (Minn.) Food Mart, 1947-50; dist. mgr. Beauty Counselor of Minn., Winona County, 1951-61; Boy Scout liaison J.C. Penney Co., Newport Beach, Calif., 1969-72; dept. mgr. and buyer boyswear At Ease, Newport Beach, 1972-77; mgr. Top Notch Boys Wear, Carmel, Calif., 1977-83, propr., 1984-88; owner, mgr. Top Notch Watch, Sun City, Ariz., 1989—; v.p., chmn. Don Loper Fashion Show, 1967, pres., 1968, bd. dirs., 1969. Co-editor Aux. Antics mag., 1965. Vol. fund raising leadership Family Svc. Assn., Orange County, Calif., 1962-69, other orgns.; chmn. publicity, study group, Sunday sch. tchr., Congl. Ch., Winona, Minn., 1956-58, fellwoship pres., Santa Ana, Calif., 1963-65; pres. Goodview Civic Club, 1948. Recipient Athena award Panhellenic Assn. Orange City, Calif., 1968, El Camino Real Dist. Svc. award Orange Empire coun. Boy Scouts Am., Baden-Powell award, Outstanding Leadership award, El Camino Real Dist., Calif., 1972J. Ringling North award, 1949; named Outstanding Svc. Vol. Family Svc. Assn., 1969. Mem. Carmel Bus. Assn. Home and Office: 10048 Hawthorn Dr Sun City AZ 85351

THOMPSON, BRUCE RUTHERFORD, judge; b. Reno, July 31, 1911; s. Reuben Cyril and Mabel (McLeran) T.; m. Frances Ellen Creek, Sept. 11, 1938; children: Jeffrey, Judith, Harold. A.B., U. Nev., 1932; LL.B., Stanford U., 1936. Bar: Nev. 1936. Practiced in Ren; asst. U.S. atty. Dist. Nev., 1942-52; spl. master U.S. Dist. Ct., Reno, 1952-53; judge U.S. Dist. Ct. Nev., Reno, 1963—. Mem. Nev. State Planning Bd., 1959—, chmn., 1960-61; bd. regents U. Nev. Mem. Am. Judicature Soc. (dir.), ABA, State Bar Nev., Am. Coll. Trial Lawyers, Am. Law Inst., Alpha Tau Omega. Democrat. Baptist. Club: Elks. Home: 1550 Plumb Ln Reno NV 89509 Office: US Dist Ct 300 Booth St Reno NV 89509

THOMPSON, CHUCK, computer consultant; b. Steubenville, Ohio, Mar. 6, 1959; s. Charles E. and June (Bowers) T.; m. Kimberly Ann Vankirk Thompson, July 19, 1986. Nat. sales mgr. L. M. Engring., Youngstown, Ohio, 1982-87; sales cons. West L.A. Music, L.A., 1987—; programmer, Atlantic Starr, L.A., 1987—. Republican. Lutheran. Home: 5409 3 Yarmouth Ave Encino CA 91316 Office: West LA Music 11345 Santa Monica Blvd Los Angeles CA 90025

THOMPSON, CLAYTON HOWARD, computer engineer; b. Albert Lea, Minn., Aug. 29, 1939; s. Howard Truman and Bernice Nelsena (Munson) T.; m. George Ann Devault, Mar. 5, 1961 (div. Aug. 1979); children: Clayton, David; m. Karen Joan Dahlinger Baughman, Apr. 6, 1985; stepchildren: Kit, Juliana. BS in Computer Sci., Colo. State U., 1973, MBA, 1974. Enlisted USAF, 1959, advanced through grades to lt. col., ret., 1980; chief computer resources div. USAF, Wright Patterson, Ohio, 1976-80; sr. software engr. Hughes Aircraft Co., El Segundo, Calif., 1980-81; software mgr. Contel Info. Systems, Dayton, Ohio, 1981-82, Ford Aerospace Corp., Colorado Springs, Colo., 1982-86, Northrop Corp., L.A., 1986—. Mem. Assn. Computing Machinery, IEEE, Phi Kappa Phi, Beta Gamma Sigma. Home: 300 Pebble Beach Dr Thousand Oaks CA 91320 Office: Northrop Corp 1515 Rancho Conejo Blvd Newbury Park CA 91320-0500

THOMPSON, CRAIG SNOVER, corporate communications executive; b. Bklyn., May 24, 1932; s. Craig F. and Edith (Williams) T.; m. Masae Sugizaki, Feb. 21, 1957; children: Lee Anne, Jane Laura. Grad., Valley Forge Mil. Acad., 1951; B.A., Johns Hopkins U., 1954. Newspaper and radio reporter Easton (Pa.) Express, 1954-55, 57-59, Wall St. Jour., 1959-60; account exec. Moore, Meldrum & Assocs., 1960; mgr. pub. relations Cen. Nat. Bank of Cleve., 1961-62; account exec. Edward Howard & Co., Cleve., 1962-67; v.p. Edward Howard & Co., 1967-69, sr. v.p., 1969-71; dir. pub. relations White Motor Corp., Cleve., 1971-76; v.p. pub. relations No. Telecom Inc., Nashville, 1976-77, White Motor Corp., Farmington Hills, Mich., 1977-80; v.p. corp. communications White Motor Corp., 1980-81; dir. exec. communications Rockwell Internat. Corp., Pitts., 1981-86, El Segundo, Calif., 1986—. Bd. dirs. Shaker Lakes Regional Nature Center, 1970-73. Served to 1st lt., inf. U.S. Army, 1955-57. Mem. Pub. Relations Soc. Am. (accredited), Alumni Assn. Valley Forge Mil. Acad. (bd. dirs. 1988—). Office: Rockwell Internat Corp 2230 E Imperial Hwy El Segundo CA 90245

THOMPSON, DAVID ALLEN, artist; b. Buffalo, June 4, 1941; s. David Allen and Ruth (Mitchell) T.; div., 1981; children: David, Ann, Austin, James. BA, Wagner Coll., 1964; MFA, Calif. Coll. of Arts and Crafts, 1967; MAT, Wesleyan U., 1968. Tchr. Coll. Prep. Sch., Oakland, Calif., 1971-76, Town Sch. for Boys, San Francisco, 1982-85; artist Calif., 1985—; vis. artist Wesleyan U., Middletown, Conn., 1968. Exhibited in group shows, Ruth Sherman Gallery, N.Y.C., 1965, CCAC Gallery, Oaklnad, Calif., 1967, Davison Art Ctr. Wesleyan U., Middletown, Conn., 1969, Hoover Gallery, San Francisco, 1971, Comsky Callery, L.A., 1973, Erica Williams Gallery, Seattle, 1975, Woodland (Calif.) Community Art Ctr., 1975, Genesis Gallery, N.Y.C., 1977, Circle Gallery, N.Y.C., 1978, Elizabeth Ives Bartholet Gallery, N.Y.C., 1978, ADI Gallery Pier 39, San Francisco, 1979, Marshall-Meyers Gallery, San Francisco, 1980, Greenwood Gallery, Seattle, 1982, TM Artworks, San Francisco, 1984, Columbia (Mo.) Coll., 1988; represented in permanent collections, USIA, IBM Corp., Delta Airlines, Transamerica Corp., Itel Corp., Manning Assocs., many others in U.S., Europe, Japan. Finalist Am. Artist mag., 1978. Mem. Ctr. for Visual Arts (bd. dirs. 1979-81), Buffalo Fine Arts Acad., Pro Arts, Coll. Art Assn., 45th St. Artists' Co-op. Presbyterian. Home and Office: 1420 45th St Emeryville CA 94608

THOMPSON, DAVID CHARLES, SR., logistician; b. Oneonta, N.Y., Jan. 27, 1942; s. Gordon George and Evelyn Beatrice (Michaels) T.; m. Carol Anne Peele, Dec. 24, 1976; children: David Charles Jr., Robert Edward. BS in Mgmt., U. La Verne, 1989. Mgr. Hughes, West Covina, Calif., 1968—; bd. dirs. Honeywell West Coast Fed. Credit Union, Azusa, Calif. Officer Glendora (Calif.) Police Aux., 1972-74; agt. South Pasadena Police Res., 1978-82; active Foothill Apt. Owners Assn., Pasadena, Calif., 1979—. Served with USN, 1960-68. Mem. Soc. Logistics Engrs., NRA, The Rogues Club (chief Arcadia, Calif. chpt. 1987-88), Elks. Republican. Home: 6792 Country Club Dr La Verne CA 91750 Office: Hughes 1200 E San Bernardino Rd West Covina CA 91790

THOMPSON, DAVID JOHN, chief of police, attorney; b. New Tredegar, Great Britain, Dec. 29, 1930; came to U.S., 1947; s. Leander and Rose (Seal) T.; m. June Lillian Douglas, May 4, 1951; children: Barbara June, Terry Susan. AA, L.A. City Coll., 1956; BS, Calif. State U., L.A., 1959; JD, Glendale Coll. Law, 1974. Bar: Calif. With Glendale (Calif.) Police Dept., 1956—, police capt., 1973-82, police chief, 1982—; Mem. adv. bd. Glendale Adventist Med. Ctr., 1985—, U. So. Calif. Delinquency Control, Los Angeles, 1986—. Post dir. Glendale council Boy Scouts Am., 1982—; mem. Citizens for Law and Order, Glendale, 1980. With USAF, 1951-54. Recipient Law Enforcement Commendation medal SAR, San Fernando, Calif., 1988; named Man of Yr., Montrose Shopping Pk. Assn., 1984, Citizen of Yr., Glendale Bd. Realtors, 1987. Mem. Calif. Bar Assn., Calif. Peace Officers Assn., Internat. Assn. Chiefs of Police, Glendale Criminal Justice Council (pres. 1984—), Kiwanis (bd. dirs. Glendale chpt. 1983—), Elks. Republican. Office: Glendale Police Dept Office of the Chief 140 N Isabel St Glendale CA 91206-4382

THOMPSON, DAVID WHEELER, bank executive; b. Milw., Feb. 6, 1952; s. Marshall Joseph Thompson and Betty Mae (Bolson) Hunt; m. Cynthia Louise Burton, July 1, 1972; children: Juliet Genevieve, Jennifer Elaine, William Wheeler. BS in TV Prodn., San Diego State U., 1975. Audio visual specialist Bank of Am., San Francisco, 1975-77, Wells Fargo Bank, San Francisco, 1975-77, Bank of Calif., San Francisco, 1975-77; audio visual specialist Security Pacific Bank (formerly Rainier Bank), Seattle, 1977-80, mgr., visual communications, 1980-84; asst. v.p. and mgr., video communications First Interstate Bank of Wash., Seattle, 1985—. Producer: (film) The Perils of Paychecks, 1988 (Gold medal, 1988, Silver Plaque, 1988, Silver Reel, 1989, Blue Ribbon 1989); exec. producer: (video) We Work Hard for the Money, 1987 (Gold Camera award 1988), Use NACE Before You Pack, 1987 (Silver Plaque, 1988, Golden Reel 1989). Recipient Bronze Cindy, Visual Communications Assn., L.A., 1987. Mem. Internat. TV Assn. (chmn. internat. membership 1988-89, regional v.p. 1987-89, chmn. festival adv. bd. 1987-88, internat. video festival 1986-87, internat. v.p. 1989—, Service awards 1987, 89; Silver Reel awards 1985, 86, 89, Golden Reel award 1984, 89). Republican. Mormon. Office: First Interstate Bank Wash 999 Third Ave 7th Fl Seattle WA 98104

THOMPSON, DENNIS PETERS, plastic surgeon; b. Chgo., Mar. 18, 1937; s. David John and Ruth Dorothy (Peters) T.; m. Virginia Louise Williams, June 17, 1961; children: Laura Faye, Victoria Ruth, Elizabeth Jan. BS, U. Ill., 1957, BS in Medicine, 1959, MS in Physiology, MD, 1961. Diplomate Am. Bd. Surgery, Am. Bd. Plastic Surgery. Intern Presbyn.-St. Lukes Hosp., Chgo., 1961-62; resident in gen. surgery Mayo Clinic, Rochester, Minn., 1964-66, fellow in gen. surgery, 1964-66; resident in gen. surgery Harbor Gen. Hosp., Los Angeles, 1968-70; resident in plastic surgery UCLA, 1971-73, clin. instr. plastic surgery, 1975-82, asst. clin. prof. surgery, 1982—; practice medicine specializing in plastic and reconstructive surgery, Los Angeles, 1974-78, Santa Monica, Calif., 1978—; chmn. plastic surgery sect. St. John's Hosp., 1986—; mem. staff Santa Monica Hosp., UCLA Ctr. Health Scis., Brotman Med. Ctr.; chmn. dept. surgery Beverly Glen Hosp., 1978-79; pres. Coop. of Am. Physicians Credit Union, 1978-80, bd. dirs., 1980—, chmn. promotion com., 1983—, treas., 1985—. Contbr. articles to med. jours. Moderator Congl. Ch. of Northridge (Calif.), 1975-76, chmn. bd. trustees, 1973-74, 80-82. Am. Tobacco Inst. research grantee, 1959-60. Fellow ACS; mem. AMA (Physicians Recognition award 1971, 74, 77, 81, 84, 87), Calif. Med. Assn., Los Angeles County Med. Assn. (chmn. bylaws com. 1979-80, chmn. ethics com. 1980-81, sec.-treas. dist. 5 1982-83, program chmn. 1983-84, pres. 1985-86), Pan-Pacific Surgical Assn., Am. Soc. Plastic Surgeons, Calif. Soc. Plastic Surgeons (chmn. bylaws com. 1982-83, chmn. liability com. 1983-85, councilor 1988—), Los Angeles Soc. Plastic Surgeons (sec. 1980-82, pres. 1982-89), Lipoplasty Soc. N.Am., UCLA Plastic Surgery Soc. (treas. 1983-84), Am. Soc. Aesthetic Plastic Surgery, Western Los Angeles Regional C. of C. (bd. dirs. 1981-84, 86-89, chmn. legis. action com. 1978-80), Santa Monica C. of C., Phi Beta Kappa, Alpha Omega Alpha, Nu Sigma Nu, Phi Kappa Phi. Republican. Office: 2001 Santa Monica Blvd Santa Monica CA 90404

THOMPSON, DENNIS ROY, information management executive; b. Chgo., Apr. 11, 1939; s. Roy Gustav and Charlotte Rose (Schultz) T.; m. Donna Tello; children: Jesse, Kimbrelle. BSEE with honors, U. Ill., 1964; MS in Bus. Adminstrn., UCLA, 1967. Ops. research cons. Dart Industries, Los Angeles, 1969-70; pres. Seahill, Inc., Los Angeles, 1971-72; dir. credit analysis Comml. Credit Co., Balt., 1973-77; pres. Epicom, Inc., San Diego, 1978—; pub. RFP Publs., 1983-85; lectr. data processing and computer sci. San Diego Community Coll. Patentee matchbook. Founder and past chmn. UNIX/C SIG, San Diego; sec., Annapolis (Md.) Libertarians, 1975; 1988 Libertarian Candidate for Calif. 44th Congl. Dist. Served with U.S. Army, 1959-61. Mem., Assn. Computing Machinery, IEEE, Data Processing Mgmt. Assn., Mensa. Club: Toastmasters (Able Toastmaster 1987). Office: RFP Publs 3647 Fairmount Ave San Diego CA 92105

THOMPSON, DWIGHT ALAN, vocational rehabilitation specialist; b. Monterey Park, Calif., Mar. 2, 1955; s. Irvin Edward and Lydia (Busch) T.; m. Irene Anita Arden, June 18, 1977; children: Dwight Christopher, Meredith Irene. BA in Social Welfare, U. Wash., 1978, MSW, 1980. Registered vocat. rehab. counselor, Wash. and Oreg.; diplomate in clin. social work; cert. social worker, Wash. Houseparent Parkview Home for Exceptional Children, Seattle, 1976-77; rsch. analyst Wash. State Ho. Reps., Olympia, 1979-81; v.p. The James L. Groves Co., Everett, Wash., 1982-86; exec. dir. Evaluation & Tng. Assocs., Seattle, 1984-86; pres., owner Rehab. & Evaluation Svcs., Seattle, 1986—; social work officer 50th Gen. Army Reserve Hosp., Seattle, 1982-87; aide-de-camp 2d Hosp. Ctr., San Francisco, 1986-88; practicum instr. U. Wash., 1985—, officer pub. affairs., 1988—. Co-author Correction Study Report, 1981. Registered lobbyist Wash. State, 1983-87; conf. pres. St. Vincent de Paul Soc., 1975-78; lt. Thurston County Fire Dist #6, East Olympia, Wash., 1980-83; alumni rep. COS Track Com. U. Wash., 1984-87; primary candidate Dem. Primary for State Rep., Renton, Wash., 1984. Mem. Nat. Assn. Rehab. Profls. (pvt. sector, cert. ins. rehab. specialist), Acad. Cert. Social Workers, Nat. Assn. Social Workers (cert.), Profl. Rehab. Orgn. Wash., Wash. Self-Insurers Assn. (legis. com., chair vocat. issues subcom.), Assn. Mil. Surgeons Am., Res. Officers Assn., Theta Xi (pres. 1975-77). Roman Catholic. Home: 16136 41st Ave NE Seattle WA 98155 Office: Rehab & Evaluation Svcs 1723 8th Ave N Seattle WA 98109

THOMPSON, EDGAR J., musician, educator. BS in Physics and Math., Brigham Young U.; MA in Music, Calif. State U., Long Beach; PhD in Choral Music Edn., U. Utah; studies with Frank Pooler, Newell B. Weight. Asst. dir. Choral Activities Calif. State U., Long Beach; mem. faculty U. Utah, 1978, chmn. Music dept., conductor Univ. A Cappella Choir, 1979—; mus. dir. Utah Symphony Chorus, 1982—; conductor clinics, guest conductor in field. Producer film on new choral literature and techniques, 1972; developer computer program to teach fundamental music skills. Mem. Music Educators Nat. Conf., Utah Music Educators Assn., Am. Choral Dirs. Assn. (past state pres.). Office: U Utah Music Dept 204 Gardner Hall Salt Lake City UT 84112

THOMPSON, EDWARD K., III, political assistant, information specialist; b. Honolulu, Sept. 17, 1958; s. Edward K. Jr. and Dora I. (Kusunoki) T. BA, U. Hawaii, 1984. Program specialist office lt. gov. State of Hawaii, Honolulu, 1984-86, legis. aide state ho. of reps., 1985, com. clk. ho. edn. com., 1986, com. clk. ho. transp. com., 1987, info. specialist statewide volunteer services office gov., 1987-88; elections clk., Office of City Clk. Honolulu, 1985; polit. asst., Dem. Nat. Com., Washington, 1988. Chmn. Liliha and Kapalama Neighborhood Bd., Honolulu, 1985-87, Assn. Hawaiian Civics Clubs, Honolulu, 1987; 2nd vice chmn. Hawaiian Civic Political Action Com., Honolulu, 1987; exec. v.p. Am. Mktg. Assn. (U.H. Chpt.) 1980-81; com. mem. State Dem. Party, 1985-88, Honolulu Neighborhood Housing Services, Inc., 1987, Young Dem. Hawaii, 1987; dir. Kalihi-Palama Community Council, 1987. Named State Exec. intern Office Lt. Gov., 1984. Episcopalian. Office: Dem Nat Com 430 S Capital St Washington DC 20003

THOMPSON, EVON LEE, mortgage loan officer; b. Balt., Dec. 1, 1946; d. Edward W. and Altia (Nixon) Lee; m. Nathan Beams, Nov. 1, 1981 (div. 1987); 1 child, Christopher M. BS, Morgan State Coll., Balt., 1968; MBA, Atlanta U., 1969. Pub. svc. employment coord. City of Oakland, Calif., 1971-75; dep. dir. recreation, parks and community svc. City of Berkeley, Calif., 1975-79; with Fox and Carskadon Realtors, Hayward, Calif., 1979-83; mortgage broker Canty & Assocs., Hayward, 1984—. Active Bay Area Big Sisters, 1975-80. Ford Found. fellow, 1968; Morgan State Coll. grantee, 1962-64. Mem. Am. Mktg. Assn. (sec. 1965-68), Soc. for Advancement of Mgmt. (chartered), Morgan State Coll. Alumni Assn. (v.p. 1985—), Hope Acad. Parents Assn., Alpha Kappa, Chi Psi Sigma. Republican. Methodist. Home: 2751 D St Hayward CA 94541

THOMPSON, GARY WAYNE, civilian military employee; b. Bemidji, Minn., Mar. 18, 1947; s. Irvin Wilfred and Delores Georgine (Erickson) T.; m. Aleta Lucille Davidson, Mar. 13, 1974 (div. 1982); 1 child, Kelly. Student, Sierra Coll., Rocklin, Calif., 1972-85, Am. River Coll., Sacramento, 1972-85. Stock handler USAF Directorate of Distbn., McClellan AFB, Calif., 1966, material processor, 1968-72, insp., 1972-77, supr. 1st line, 1977-79, supr. 2d line, 1979-83, supr. 3d line, 1983-88, br. chief, 1988—. With U.S. Army, 1966-68, including Vietnam. Recipient Outstanding Fed. Svc. award Sacramento Fed. Exec. Assn., 1988. Republican. Baptist. Home: 10830 Tims Ln Elverta CA 95626 Office: USAF Directorate of Distbn McClellan AFB CA 95652

THOMPSON, GEORGE ALBERT, geophysics educator; b. Swissvale, Pa., June 5, 1919; s. George Albert Sr. and Maude Alice (Harkness) T.; m. Anita Kimmell, July 20, 1944; children: Albert J., Dan A., David C. BS, Pa. State U., 1941; MS, MIT, 1942; PhD, Stanford U., 1949. Geologist, geophysicist U.S. Geol. Survey, Menlo Park, Calif., 1942-76; asst. prof. Stanford (Calif.) U., 1949-55, assoc. prof., 1955-60, prof. geophysics, 1960—, chmn. geophysics dept., 1967-86, chmn. geology dept., 1979-82, Otto N. Miller prof. earth scis., 1980-89, dean sch. earth scis., 1987-89; Chmn., mem. sci. plan commn. EDGE Seismic Reflection Consortium, Houston, 1986—. Author over 100 research papers. Cons. adv. com. reactor safeguard, Nuclear Regulation Commn., Washington, 1974—; bd. earth sci., Nat. Res. Coun., 1986-88; bd. dirs. Inc. Reasearch Inst. for Seismology, Washington, 1984—. Served with USNR, 1944-46. Recipient G.K. Gilbert award in seismic geology, 1964; NSF postdoctoral fellow, 1956-57; Guggenheim Found. fellow, 1963-64. Fellow AAAS, Geol. Soc. Am. (council mem., 1983-86, George P. Woollard award, 1983), Am. Geophys. Union; mem. Seismol. Soc. Am., Soc. Exploration Geophysicists, Soc. Econ. Geologists. Home: 421 Adobe Pl Palo Alto CA 94306 Office: Stanford U Geophysics Dept Stanford CA 94305

THOMPSON, GORDON, JR., judge; b. San Diego, Dec. 28, 1929; s. Gordon and Garnet (Meese) T.; m. Jean Peters, Mar. 17, 1951; children—John M., Peter Renwick, Gordon III. Grad., U. So. Calif., 1951, Southwestern U. Sch. Law, Los Angeles, 1956. Bar: Calif. bar 1956. With Dist. Atty.'s Office, County of San Diego, 1957-60; partner firm Thompson & Thompson, San Diego, 1960-70; U.S. dist. judge So. Dist. Calif., San Diego, 1970—, chief judge, 1984—. Mem. Am. Bd. Trial Advocates, ABA, San Diego County Bar Assn. (v.p. 1970), Delta Chi. Club: San Diego Yacht. Office: US Dist Ct 940 Front St San Diego CA 92189

THOMPSON, GREG ALAN, computer sciences consulting executive; b. Palo Alto, Calif., Sept. 15, 1955; s. Jack Edward and Elaine Irene (Palmer) T.; m. Michelle Marie Barnes, Dec. 26, 1987; children: Amy, Beth, Julie, Kimberly. BSEE and Computer Sci., MIT, 1977. Cons. engr. Informatics-PMI Ames Rsch. Ctr. NASA, Moffett Field, Calif., 1975-78; prin. software specialist Digital Equipment Corp., Santa Clara, Calif., 1978-83; lead engr. computer aided design-CAM ctr. Digital Equipment Corp., 1982; lead cons. engr., mgr. Interlink computer Scis., Inc., Fremont, Calif., 1983—. Bank of Am. and Hertz Found. scholar, 1973. Mem. IEEE Computer Soc., Bay Area MIT Alumni. Office: Interlink Computer Scis Inc 47370 Fremont Blvd Fremont CA 94538

THOMPSON, HAVELOCK, pedatrician; b. L.A., Jan. 15, 1934; s. Roy Towner and Ora Frances (Frith) T.; m. Sandra Sue Stahler, July 3, 1952 (div. Jan. 1985); children: Stephen F., Rex W., Melanie A., Clayton L. BA, U. Colo., 1956, MD, 1961. Intern, then resident in pediatrics U. Colo., Denver, 1961-63; resident U. Wash., Seattle, 1963-64; fellow in genetics U. Oreg., Portland, 1964-65, instr. pediatrics, 1965-67; asst. prof. U. Calif., Los Angeles, 1967-69, assoc. prof., 1976-78; assoc. prof. W.Va. U., Morgantown, 1969-75; assoc. prof. human devel. Mich. State U., Lansing, 1975-76; chmn. pediatrics Kern Med. Ctr., Bakersfield, Calif., 1976-78; med. dir. Kern Regional Ctr., Bakersfield, 1978-81; clinic physician Kern County Health Dept., Bakersfield, 1981-82; pvt. practice medicine specializing in pediatrics and med. genetics Bakersfield, 1982-85; pvt. practice medicine specializing in pediatrics Big Bear Lake (Calif.) Med. Group, 1986; cons. pediatrics Dhanran (Saudi Arabia) Health Ctr., 1986-87; pvt. practice pediatrics Lancaster and Palmdale, Calif., 1988—; Diplomate Am. Bd. Pediatrics. Contbr. articles to profl. jours. Fellow Am. Acad. Pediatrics, Mem. Am. Soc. Human Genetics, Sigma Xi, Phi Sigma, Alpha Omega Alpha. Republican. Office: Sierra Med Group 44469 10th St W Lancaster CA 93534

THOMPSON, HERBERT ERNEST, tool and die company executive; b. Jamaica, N.Y., Sept. 8, 1923; s. Walter and Louise (Joly) T.; student Stevens Inst. Tech., 1949-51; m. Patricia Elaine Osborn, Aug. 2, 1968; children: Robert Steven, Debra Lynn. Foreman, Conner Tool Co., 1961-62, Eason & Waller Grinding Corp., 1962-63; owner Endco Machined Products, 1966-67, Thompson Enterprises, 1974—; pres. Method Machined Products, Phoenix, 1967; pres., owner Quality Tool, Inc., 1967—. Served to capt. USAAF, 1942-46. Decorated D.F.C., Air medal with cluster. Home: 14009 N 42d Ave Phoenix AZ 85023 Office: 4223 W Clarendon Ave Phoenix AZ 85019

THOMPSON, HUNTER STOCKTON, author, editor, journalist; b. Louisville, July 18, 1939; s. Jack R. and Virginia (Ray) T.; 1 child, Juan. Carribean corr. Time mag., 1959, N.Y. Herald Tribune, 1959-60; South Am. corr. Nat. Observer, 1961-63; West Coast corr. The Nation, 1964-66; columnist Ramparts, 1967-68, Scanlan's, 1969-70; nat. affairs editor Rolling Stone, 1970-84; global affairs corr. High Times, 1977-82; columnist San Francisco Examiner, 1985—; editor at large Smart, 1988—; polit. analyst European mags. Tempo, Time Out, Nieuwe Revu, 1988—. Author: Prince Jellyfish, 1960, Hell's Angels, 1966, The Rum Diary, 1967, Fear and Loathing in Las Vegas, 1971, Fear and Loathing On the Campaign Trail '72, 1973, The Great Shark Hunt, 1977, (with Ralph Steadman) The Curse of Lono, 1983, collected articles Generation of Swine, 1988; creator Gonzo journalism. Mem. Sheriff's Adv. Com., Pitkin County, Colo., 1976-81; a judge Nat. Book Awards, 1975; mem. nat. adv. bd. NORML, 1976—; exec. dir. Woody Creek Rod and Gun Club, Overseas Press Club, U.S. Naval Inst., Air Force Assn. Mem. Kona Coast Marlin Fisherman's Assn., Vincent Black Shadow Soc. Clubs: Key West, Press, Hong Kong Fgn. Corrs. Office: ICM 40 W 57th St New York NY 10019 *

THOMPSON, JAMES BRUCE, national park administrator; b. Toledo, Iowa, Dec. 27, 1937; s. Irvin Warren and Ruth Marian (Elston) T.; m. Janice Ruth Huizinga, Aug. 24, 1957; children: Samantha Ruth, Ian Bruce. Student, U. Iowa, 1955-56; BS, U. Wyo., 1959; postgrad., George Washington U., 1966-67. Park ranger Rocky Mountain Nat. Park, Estes Park, Colo., 1960-65, supt., 1984—; park mgr. Jewel Cave Nat. Monument, Custer, S.D., 1965-66; program analyst Nat. Park Service, Washington, 1966-69; assoc. regional dir. Pacific NW region Nat. Park Service, Seattle, 1976-78; dep. regional dir. Rocky Mountain region Nat. Park Service, Denver, 1978-84; supt. Theodore Roosevelt Nat. Park, Medora, N.D., 1969-72, Death Valley (Calif.) Na^. Monument, 1972-76; mem. numerous task forces on info. mgmt. and data systems. Author: Geology of Jewel Cave, 1967. Trustee Estes Park Music Festival Found., 1987—; v.p. Longs Peak Highland Festival, Estes Park, 1985-87. Named One of Outstanding Young Men of Am., 1971; recipient Meritorious Service award Dept. of Interior, 1980. Lodge: Rotary. Office: Rocky Mountain Nat Pk Estes Park CO 80517

THOMPSON, JAMES HAROLD, judge; b. Chgo., Aug. 15, 1927; s. Robert Bruce and Jimmie Lee (Walls) T.; m. Jean Fay Ruttenbur, Sept. 21, 1953; 1 child, Irene Lee. BS in Pub. Adminstrn., The Am. Univ., 1958, LLB, 1961. Bar: D.C. 1962, Nev. 1963. Chief counsel Nev. Dept. Hwys., 1965-70; atty. gen. State of Nev., 1971-78, spl. dep. atty. gen., 1979-81, judge 2d jud. dist., 1981-83, judge Reno Justice Ct., 1983—; rep. State of Nev. to U.S. Supreme Ct. in Calif. vs. Nev. boundary litigation, 1979-81. Past mem. editorial bd. Better Roads mag., 1968-69; contbr. articles to profl. jours. With U.S. Army, 1946-47, 51-53. Recipient Am. Jurisprudence prize for Excellence in Trusts. Mem. Washoe County Bar Assn., First Jud. Dist. Bar Assn. (v.p. 1967-68), Am. Arbitration Assn. (nat. constrn. panel), Delta Theta Phi. Democrat. Methodist. Home: 136 Greenridge Dr Reno NV 89509

THOMPSON, JAMES HOMER, insurance agent, educator; b. Henrietta, Tex., Sept. 11, 1926; s. James Hite and Virginia (Marberry) T.; student U. Okla., 1944-45; Ph.B., U. Chgo., 1947, M.B.A., 1950; M.S. in Fin. Services, Am. Coll., Bryn Mawr, Pa., 1980; m. Ilene Kriss, Mar. 17, 1979; children by previous marriage—Julie A., Laurie J. Dist. sales mgr. Studebaker Corp., South Bend, Ind., 1951-55; assoc. gen. agt. State Mut. Life Assurance Co. Am., Denver, 1955—; instr. U. Colo. 1964—; mem. bd. Nat. C.L.U. Inst. Recipient J. Stanley Edwards award Colo. Ins. Industry, 1985, Alumni Service Citation, U. Chgo., 1987; Inst. Mem. cabinet U. Chgo.; mem. Colo. Ins. Adv. Bd., 1980—. C.L.U., C.P.C.U. Bd. dirs. Adult Edn. Council of Met. Denver, 1977. Mem. Am. Soc. C.L.U.s (v.p. Rocky Mountain chpt. 1967, pres. 1968-69, regional v.p. 1972-73), Denver Assn. Life Underwriters (dir. 1963-66). Home: 180 Ivanhoe St Denver CO 80220 Office: 44 Cook St Denver CO 80206-5898

THOMPSON, JAMES WILLIAM, lawyer; b. Dallas, Oct. 22, 1936; s. John Charles and Frances (Van Slyke) T.; BS, U. Mont., 1958, JD, 1962; m. Marie Hertz, June 26, 1965; children: Elizabeth, Margaret, John. Acct., Arthur Young & Co., N.Y.C., summer 1959; instr. bus. adminstrn. Eastern Mont. Coll., Billings, 1959-60, U. Mont., Missoula, 1960-61; admitted to Mont. bar, 1962; assoc. Cooke, Moulton, Bellingham & Longo, Billings, 1962-64, James R. Felt, Billings, 1964-65; asst. atty. City of Billings, 1963-64, atty., 1964-66; ptnr. Felt, Speare & Thompson, Billings, 1966-72, McNamer, Thompson & Cashmore, 1973-86, McNamer & Thompson PC, 1986—; bd. dirs. Associated Industries, Inc. Mem. Billings Zoning Commn., 1966-69; v.p. Billings Community Action Program (now Dist. 7 Human Resources Devel. Council), 1968-70, pres., 1970-75, trustee, 1975—; mem. Yellowstone County Legal Services Bd., 1969-70; City-County Air Pollution Control Bd., 1969-70; pres. Billings Symphony Soc., 1970-71; bd. dirs. Billings Studio Theatre, 1967-73, Mont. Inst. of Arts Found., 1986-89, Downtown Billings Assn., 1986—; mem. Diocesan exec. council, 1972-75; mem. Billings Transit Commn., 1971-73; mem. City Devel. Agy., 1972-73; bd. dirs. United Way, Billings, 1973-81. C.P.A., Mont. Mem. ABA, State Bar Mont., Yellowstone County Bar Assn. (bd. dirs. 1983-87, pres. 1985-86), Mont. Soc. CPAs, C. of C., Elks, Kiwanis, Sigma Chi (pres. Billings alumni assn. 1963-65). Episcopalian. Home: 123 Lewis Ave Billings MT 59101 Office: Transwestern 1 Bldg Billings MT 59101

THOMPSON, JESSE JACKSON, university educator, clinical psychologist; b. Sangar, Calif., July 26, 1919; s. Lewis Elmer and Lucy Jane (Hamilton) T.; m. Clara Lucile Roy, Feb. 4, 1945; children: Lyle Blair, Carolrae, Jon Royal, Mark Alan. BA, Santa Barbara State Coll., 1941; MS in Edn., U. So. Calif., 1947, PhD, 1957. Lic. psychologist, speech pathologist, Calif. Prof. communicative disorders Calif. State U., Long Beach, 1956-79, dir. ctr. for health manpower edn., 1970-74; pvt. practice in clin. psychology Westminster, Calif., 1979—; adv. bd. Speech and Lang. Devel. Ctr., Buena Park, Calif., 1966—; cons. Orange County Schs., Santa Ana, Calif., 1969-71, Child Devel. Clinic, Long Beach, 1961-64, Head Start Program, Compton, Calif., 1967-72. Co-author: Talking Time, 1951, Speech Ways, 1955, Phonics, 1962, Rhymes for Fingers and Flannel Boards, 1962, 85. pres. Orange County Community Action Coun., Santa Ana, 1970-71; chmn. bd. dirs. Orange County-Long Beach Health Consortium, Santa Ana, 1974, vol. AIDS Response Program, Garden Grove, Calif., 1987—, coord. mental health svcs., 1988—. Capt. U.S. Army, 1941-46. Fellow Am. Speech, Lang. and Hearing Assn.; mem. Calif. Speech, Lang. and Hearing Assn. (pres. 1959-60), Christian Assn. for Psychol. Studies, Assn. Emeritii Profs. Democrat. Home: 13282 Cedar St Westminster CA 92683

THOMPSON, JOHN LESTER, bishop; b. Youngstown, Ohio, May 11, 1926; s. John Lester and Irene (Brown) T.; m. Shirley Amanda Scott, Aug. 1, 1951; children: Amanda, Ian. B.A., Youngstown Coll., 1948; S.T.B., Episcopal Theol. Sch., Cambridge, Mass., 1951. Ordained priest Episcopal Ch., 1951; curate, then rector chs. Ohio, Oreg. and Calif., 1951-78; bishop Episcopal Diocese No. Calif., Sacramento, 1978—; trustee Ch. Divinity Sch. Pacific, Berkeley, Calif. Pres., Oreg. Shakespeare Festival, 1955-56, chmn. bldg. com. for outdoor theatre, 1957-58. Served with USNR, 1943-46. Office: PO Box 161268 Sacramento CA 95816

THOMPSON, JOSEPH FRANCIS, insurance loss control consultant; b. Newburgh, N.Y., Feb. 23, 1957; s. Gordon R. and Florence (Kavanaugh) T. Student, Dutchess Community Coll., 1975-76; AAS, Rockland Community Coll., 1978. Cons. loss control Kemper Ins. Co., Melville, N.Y., 1979-80, Continental Ins. Co., Glens Falls, N.Y., 1981-84, Genesis Custom Homes, Inc., Los Angeles; sr. cons. loss control Fireman's Fund Ins. Co., Los Angeles, 1985—; pres., bd. dirs., cheif fin. officer, chief exec. officer Genesis Custom Homes, Inc., Los Angeles, 1986—; profl. instr. open water scuba diving. Vol. firefighter Vails Gate (N.Y.) Fire Co., 1973-80. Mem. Am. Soc. Safety Engrs. Republican. Home: 6627 Burnet Ave Van Nuys CA 91405 Office: Firemans Fund Ins Co 3223 W 6th St Los Angeles CA 90020

THOMPSON, KATHY HELEN, personnel administrator; b. Portland, Oreg., Feb. 14, 1947; d. Wesley Van and Louise Lorenz (Austin) Dill; 1 child, Elissa Lee. BA, U. Calif., Santa Barbara, 1978; MA, Calif. State U., Northridge, 1980. Head composition br. Naval Ship Weapon Systems Engring. Sta., Port Hueneme, Calif., 1977-79; personnel specialist Pacific Missile Test Ctr., Point Mugu, Calif., 1979-82, dir. learning ctr., 1982-84, in employee devel., 1984-86, tng., classification officer Naval Sta., Long Beach, Calif., 1986—; profl. speaker in field. Contbr. articles on tech. and gen. subjects to publs. Mem. NAFE, Am. Soc. Tng. and Devel., Bus. and Profl. Women (woman of achievement award Coast Dist., Calif. 1982, named outstanding woman of year 1981), Fed. Mgrs. Assn. (named outstanding fed. mgr. 1981, tng. advisor), Internat. Tng. in Communication (named outstanding toastmistress 1981, recipient numerous awards and speech contests) (Point Mugu). Office: Code 009 Naval Sta Long Beach CA 90822

THOMPSON, LARRY ALAN, state agency administrator; b. Columbus, Ohio, May 10, 1949; s. Robert W. and Pauline Z. (Markley) T.; m. Betsy Lee Row, Sept. 4, 1981; children: Derek Robert, Tracy Lee. BS in Acctg., Ohio State U., 1973. Cert. pub. acct., 1986. Auditor Ohio Dept. Taxation, Columbus, 1973-82, supr. sales tax, 1978-82, dist. mgr., 1982-86; acting asst. dir. Ariz. Dept. Revenue, Phoenix, 1987-88, sales tax adminstr., 1986—. With U.S. Army N.G. Mem. Am. Inst. CPAs, Ohio Soc. CPAs, Ariz. Soc CPAs, Big Brothers Am., Mason. Home: 4902 E Everett Dr Phoenix AZ 85254

THOMPSON, LINDA INGRID, membership director; b. Birkenfeld, Germany, Mar. 10, 1962; d. Darrell Kenneth and Ingrid Charlotte (Kofke) T. Student, Cochise Coll., 1982—. Salesperson Sierra Vista (Ariz.) Jewelers, 1980-85; asst. mgr. D.L.L. Jewelers, Sierra Vista, 1985-86; membership dir. Sierra Vista C. of C., 1986—; chamber ambassador Sierra Vista C. of C., 1986—. Recipient Certificate of Appreciation Sierra Vista C. of C., 1988, Outstanding Young Women Am., 1988. Mem. Sierra Vista Rotary (Special Olympics, 1987-88), Sierra Vista Kiwanas.

THOMPSON, LOHREN MATTHEW, oil company executive; b. Sutherland, Nebr., Jan. 21, 1926; s. John M. and Anna (Ecklund) T.; children—Terence M., Sheila M., Clark M. Ed., U. Denver. Spl. rep. Standard Oil Co., Omaha, 1948-56; v.p. mktg. Frontier REF. co., 1967-68; mgr. mktg. U.S. region Husky Oil Co., Denver, 1968-72; v.p. Westar Stas., Inc., Denver, 1967-70; pres., chmn. bd. Colo. Petroleum, Denver, 1971—. Served with USAAF, 1944-46. Mem. Colo. Petroleum Council, Am. Petroleum Inst., Am. Legion. Democrat. Lutheran. Clubs: Denver Petroleum, Denver Oilman's Lodge: Lions. Home: 2410 Spruce Ave Estes Park CO 80517 Office: Colo Petroleum 4080 Globeville Rd Denver CO 80216

THOMPSON, LOREN EDWARD, petrophysical consultant, publisher; b. Salem, W.Va., May 8, 1937; s. Loren Edward and Ruby Mildred (Flanagin) T.; m. Marilyn Jo Kibbler, Jan. 23, 1958 (div. 1976); children: Martha, Michael, Scott; m. Sally Fleming Woosley, Nov. 23, 1984; children: Stephanie, Dwight, Marygale, Paul, George Dial. BS in Geology, Marietta Coll., 1960; MS in Geology, Ohio U., 1963; postgrad, Colo. Sch. Mines. Geophysicist Phillips Petroleum Co., Bartlesville, Okla., 1963-67; sr. petrophysicist Marathon Oil Co. Rsch. Ctr., Littleton, Colo., 1967-81; sr. cons. Sci. Software, Inc., Denver, 1981-82; pres. Loren E. "bud" Thompson, Inc., Lakewood, Colo., 1982—. Editor, pub.: (newsletter) "bud's" Logging Lines, 1983—. Mem. Soc. Profl. Well Log Analysts, Soc. Exploration Geophysicists, Soc. Petroleum Engrs., Denver Well Log Soc. (past pres.), Am. Radio Relay League.

THOMPSON, MALCOLM FRANCIS, electrical engineer; b. Charleston, S.C., Sept. 2, 1921; s. Allen R. and Lydia (Brunson) T.; BS, Ga. Inst. Tech., 1943, MS, 1947; postgrad. MIT, 1947-49; m. Ada Rose O'Quinn, Jan. 20, 1943 (dec. 1987); children: Rose Mary, Nancy Belle, Susan Elizabeth, Frances Josephine. Instr. dept. elec. engring. Mass. Inst. Tech., 1947-49; research engr. Autonetics Co., Anaheim, Calif., 1949-70; tech. dir. SRC div. Moxon, Inc., Irvine, Calif., 1970-73; engring. mgr., mgr. computers and armament controls. Northrop Aircraft Div., Hawthorne, Calif., 1973-87; ind. cons., 1987—. Served to capt. AUS, 1943-46. Mem. IEEE, Nat. Geog. Soc., Nat. Rifle Assn., Am. Ordnance Assn., Eta Kappa Nu. Patentee in field. Home and Office: 1602 Indus St Santa Ana CA 92707

THOMPSON, MARGARET THERESE, manufacturing executive; b. Fontana, Calif., Jan. 26, 1950; d. Joseph Robert and Margaret Mary (McKinney) Benchwick; m. Jeffrey Lee Thompson, Sept. 8, 1973; children—Kristen Ashley, Cara Lauren. AA, Moorpark Jr. Coll., 1970; BS in Nursing, BA in Psychology, Calif. State U.-Los Angeles, 1974; MS in Health Adminstrn., Calif. State U.-Northridge, 1981. Rsch. asst. L.A. County Probation Dept., 1972-74; head nurse, group counselor Glendale (Calif.) Adventist Med. Ctr., 1974-76, quality assurance coord., 1976-80, nursing unit coord., definitive observation unit, 1980-84; assoc. prof. Calif. State U.-Northridge, 1983—; dir. L.A. br. Nat. In-Home Health Svcs., 1984-85, v.p. internal ops., 1985-86; prin. B&T Innovations, Inc., 1986-87, Fin. Svcs., 1987—; cons. West Coast Med. Mgmt. Assocs., Westlake Village, Calif., 1979—. NIMH scholar, 1972-74. Home: 2212 Richey Dr La Canada Flintridge CA 91011 Office: 35 N Lake Ave Ste 600 Pasadena CA 91101

THOMPSON, MARK DUAINE, electrical engineer; b. Blue Island, Ill., July 4, 1956; s. James Alvin and Nella (Frances) T.; m. Cynthia Lee Zelasko, Sept. 24, 1977; children: James Irwin, Rebecca Louise. BSEET, DeVry Inst. Tech., Chgo., 1977; MSEE, U. N.Mex., 1983. Mem. tech. staff Sandia Nat. Labs., Albuquerque, 1977-83; field application engr. Intel Corp., Albuquerque, 1983-89; application engring. mgr. Alliance Electronics, Albuquerque, 1989—; cons. systems div. BFANM, Albuquerque, 1982-83. Contbr. articles to tech. publs. Bell & Howell scholar, 1974-77. Republican. Baptist. Office: Alliance Electronics 11030 Cochitise Albuquerque NM 87123

THOMPSON, MARY JEAN, interior designer, furniture designer; b. Salem, Oreg., Aug. 6, 1935; d. Lester Wayne and Bernis Laverne (Nelson) Schrunk; m. Newton L. Thompson, July 5, 1962 (div.); children—Craig L., Brooks D., K. Inga, Heidi A. B.A. cum laude in Music, Lewis and Clark Coll., 1957; B.A. cum laude in Interior Design, U. Utah, 1969. Designer, Clark Leaming Co., Salt Lake City, 1967-69; pres. Thompson Design Assocs., Inc., Reno, 1970—; pres. Faile Thompson Wardrobe Systems, 1987—. Bd. dirs. Community Concerts, 1975-76, Washoe Landmark Preservation, 1976-82, Sierra Nev. Mus. of Art, 1980—; co-chmn. Nev. Gov.'s Conf. for Women, 1988-89. Founding pres. parents' coun. Sch. Med. U. Nev. Recipient McGraw Edison Lighting Excellence award, 1978; AIA honor award, 1981. Mem. Am. Soc. Interior Designers (cert. 1970, Merit award ASID/Wilsonart design competition 1983, design excellence award Calif. cen. chpt. 1988, design award ASID/Nat. Assn. Mirror Mfgs. 1987), Nat. Assn. Mirror Mfrs. (design award 1987), AIA (affiliate mem., dir. No. Nev. chpt. 1981-82). Interiors include: Truckee Meadows Community Coll., 1976, Reno Internat. Airport, 1981, Sparks Family Hosp., 1982, Harrah's Tahoe, 1983-84, Wellington (Fla.) Regional Med. Ctr., 1986, Inland Valley

(Calif.) Med. Ctr., 1986, Roseville (Calif.) Community Hosp., 1986, U. Calif. Davis Med. Ctr. Interiors featured in Designers West Mag., Dec. 1983, Interior Design Mag., Dec. 1983, Contract Mag., Feb. 1984, 88, Restaurant & Hotel Design, 1987.

THOMPSON, MAXINE ETHEL, social worker, poet; b. Detroit, June 17, 1951; d. Mervin McKinley and Artie Mae (Jackson) Vann; m. Horace Thompson, Jr., Sept. 11, 1971; children: Horace Thompson III, Tamaira, Aaron. BA, Wayne State U., 1973. With data control dept. Detroit Traffic Ct., 1973-74; foster care worker Detroit Dept. Children's Svcs., 1974-79; social worker Delinquency Svcs., Detroit, 1979-81; with Infoline, El Monte, Calif., 1982-84; social worker L.A. Dept. Children's Svcs., 1984—, E.R.I.C. vol., mem. emergency respiratory com., 1985-87; workshop moderator Info. Referral Svcs., El Monte, 1984. Author: (poetry) Love's Quiver, 1985, Hidden's Treasure, 1986, Circumcision of Heart, 1987, Badness Blinders, 1988. Minister Jehovah's Christian Witness, Detroit, 1979—. Recipient Honorable Mention Ebony's First Writing Contest Short Story, 1989. Office: Dept Children Svcs 3965 S Vermont Los Angeles CA 90039

THOMPSON, MILTON EARL, protective services official; b. Vincentown, N.J., Apr. 15, 1931; s. Milton and Margaret (Van Bibber) T.; divorced; children: Randa Lee, Carolyn Gayle, Gregory Douglas, Eric Van; m. Carol Lynne Kincaid, Mar. 10, 1973; children: Cynthia Ann Sevier, Kristin Noel Sevier. AA in Fire Sci., San Jose City Coll., 1976; BA in Pub. Service, U. San Francisco, 1977; M in Pub. Adminstrn., Golden Gate U., 1983. Fire fighter Palo Alto (Calif.) Fire Dept., 1953-58; fire fighter San Jose (Calif.) Fire Dept., 1959-85, asst. fire chief, 1975-85; mgr. emergency services Santa Clara County, San Jose, 1985—; instr. fire sci. San Jose City Coll., 1968-71, Mission Coll., Santa Clara County, 1985—. Fund raiser YMCA, San Jose, 1977—; mem. adv. council Salvation Army ARC, San Jose, 1976—. Served with USN, 1949-53. Recipient Spl. Recognition award City of San Jose, 1985. Mem. County Emergency Services Assn. Republican. Lodges: Kiwanis, Rotary. Home: 131 College Ave Los Gatos CA 95030 Office: Santa Clara County 70 W Hedding St San Jose CA 95110

THOMPSON, NEIL BRUCE, foundation executive; b. Tuscaloosa, Ala., Oct. 14, 1941; s. Donald Eugene and Jean (Beecher) T.; m. Diane Sorrita Ramsey, Aug. 13, 1966; children: Marnie, Karina. BA, Rutgers U., 1963; MS, San Diego State U., 1974. Enlisted USN, 1965, advanced through grades to lt. comdr., 1965-86, pub. affairs officer, 1965-70; dep. dir. USN Pub. Affairs Office Midwest, Chgo., 1970-72; pub. affairs officer Carrier Div. 5/CTF-77 USN, 1972-73; pub. affairs officer Taiwan Def. Command USN, Taipei, 1975-78; pub. affairs officer USN, Bklyn., 1978-81, exec. officer, 1980-81; pub. affairs officer Naval Postgrad. Sch. USN, Monterey, Calif., 1981-86; ret. USN, 1986; exec. dir. Monterey County Spl. Olympics, 1986-88; dir. Monterey County Food Bank, 1988—. Co-chmn. Fleet Week, Monterey, 1987; active Leadership Monterey Peninsula, 1987-88; commr. City of Marina Planning Commn., 1988-89; bd. dirs. Monterey County Homeless Coalition, 1989—; commr. Monterey County Social Svcs. Commn., 1989—. Mem. Navy League U.S. (bd. dirs. Monterey Peninsula council 1987-89), Devel. Execs. Network. Republican. Home: 3126 Shoemaker Pl Marina CA 93933 Office: Monterey County Food Bank 125-A Sun St Salinas CA 93901

THOMPSON, PATSY KAY, educator; b. Colusa, Calif., July 8, 1936; d. Earl Robert and Glenna Beatrice (Reische) Kay; m. Richard Merritt Thompson, May 27, 1977; children by previous marriage: Karen Kay Hodges, William Geoffrey Bodle. BA, U. Calif., Berkeley, 1967; MA, Holy Names Coll., 1972. Tchr. Mt. Diablo Sch. Dist., Concord, Calif., 1967-83; tchr. resource specialist Pollock Pines (Calif.) Sch. Dist., 1983—; storyteller trainer Word Weavers Inc., San Francisco, 1985—; innkeeper The James Blair House, 1983-88; instr. Chapman Coll. Chmn. hist. adv. com., Placerville, Calif., 1987. Mem. AAUW (program chmn. 1987—), Calif. Reading Assn., Internat. Reading Assn. (presenter 1989 conf.), U. Calif. Alumni Assn., Delta Kappa Gamma. Democrat. Home: 2985 Clay St Placerville CA 95667

THOMPSON, PHILIP MASON, museum director; b. N.Y.C., June 9, 1942; s. William R. and Marie J. (Buckovecky) T.; m. Vilja Maria Horner, Sept. 4, 1966; children: Philip Jr., Tyra. BA, Ariz. State U., 1969, MA, 1986. Asst. dir. Phoenix Art Mus., 1971-73, Phila. Mus. Art, 1973-78; dir. devels. and community affairs Phoenix Meml. Hosp., 1978-81; dir. devels. St. Joseph's Hosp., Phoenix, 1981-83; dir. Mus. No. Ariz., Flagstaff, 1983—; nat. adv. bd. practitioners No. Ariz. U., Flagstaff, 1986; bd. dirs. Western Mus. Conf., Ariz. Mus. Assn. Mem., vice chmn. Ariz. Hist. Gov.'s Adv. Commn., Phoenix, 1984—; mem. steering com. BLOC Grant Program, 1980-83. Served with U.S. Army, 1963-66. Mem. Am. Assn. Mus., Am. Anthropol. Assn., Sigma Xi. Republican. Presbyterian. Club: Continental Country (Flagstaff). Home: Rte 4 Box 718 Flagstaff AZ 86001 Office: Mus No Ariz Rte 4 Box 720 Flagstaff AZ 86001

THOMPSON, RAYMOND KERMIT, architect, engineer; b. Seaside, Oreg., Aug. 27, 1905; s. Herschel V. and Anna Mathilde (Schirmer) T.; m. Lillian Myrtle Polly Povey, Jan. 5, 1929; children: Kermit Duncan, Priscilla Ann Elizabeth. BArch, U. Oreg., 1929; MS, MIT, 1932. Registered architect Oreg., Wash., Idaho, Ohio, N.Y., Conn.; registered profl. engr., Conn. With design bur. mech. engring. dept. Bklyn. Edison Co., 1930-31; pvt. practice architecture Pittsfield, Mass., 1938-42, Portland, Oreg., 1948-53; ptnr. Thompson & Thompson AIA, Portland, 1953—; assoc. prof. sch. engring. U. Portland, 1965-83; assoc. prof. architecture Ohio State U., Columbus, 1946-48; mem. architecture faculty Wentworth Inst., Boston, 1932-42. Served to lt. comdr. USN, 1942-46. Mem. AIA (sec. Oreg. chpt. 1950), Am. Soc. Engring. Edn. (vice chmn. N.W. region 1967), SAR (trustee nat. chpt. 1988-89, pres. Oreg. chpt. 1987-88, v.p. 1985-86, pres. Portland chpt. 1984-85). Republican. Methodist. Home: 806 SW Vista Ave Portland OR 97205 Office: Thompson & Thompson AIA 320 SW Stark St Portland OR 97204

THOMPSON, RICHARD EARL, artist; b. Oak Park, Ill., Sept. 26, 1914; s. Abijah Snyder and Vera (Koster) T.; m. Mary Munn, June 25, 1937; children—Richard Earl, Bruce, Daniel. Student Chgo. Acad. Fine Arts, 1930-31, Am. Acad. Art, Chgo., 1932-33, Chgo. Art Inst., 1944. Instr., Am. Acad. Art, Chgo., 1935-37; comml. artist Coca Cola, Anheuser-Bush, Standard Oil and Miller Brewing Co., 1937-59; artist in residence U. Wis.-Rhinelander, 1980; numerous one-man exhibits include: Veldman Galleries, Milw., 1970-71, 73, 75, 77, Wild Life Art Gallery, Minocqua, Wis., 1971, John P. Klep Galley, Houston, 1971-74, Richard Thompson Gallery, San Francisco, 1977, 79, 81; group exhbns. include: Vincent Price Collection Fine Art, 1965, Peter Darro Galleries, Chgo., 1969; mus. shows include: Berstorm Art Ctr., Neenah, Wis., 1965, Leigh Yawkey Woodson Art Mus., Wausau, Wis., 1979, R.W. Norton Art Gallery, Shreveport, La., 1982; represented in mus. and corp. collections: Continental Ill. Bank, Chgo., de Sasset Art Gallery and Mus. of U. Santa Clara, Calif., Leigh Yawkey Woodson Art Mus., Lewer Agy., Kansas City, Mo., Marquette U. Collection, Mills Coll., Milw. Jour., Naval Art Collection of Pentagon, Washington, New Britain Mus. Am. Art, R.W. Norton Art Gallery, Robert Louis Stevenson Acad. Collection, Carmel, Calif., Southland Fin. Corp., Irving, Tex., Southland Corp., Dallas, Wis. Meml. Park, Milw., Wood County Nat. Bank, Wisconsin Rapids, Wis. Recipient 1st hon. mention award Salmagundi Club, N.Y.C., 1981. Club: Salmagundi. Subject of book: Richard Earl Thompson—American Impressionist, a Prophetic Odyssey in Paint (Patricia Jobe Pierce), 1982. Office: Richard Thompson Gallery 80 Maiden Ln San Francisco CA 94108

THOMPSON, ROBERT JAMES, chemical engineer, petroleum company executive; b. Olds, Alta, Can., Oct. 16, 1937; came to U.S., 1977.; s. Roy Bradley and May Winnefred (McGill) T.; m. Mar. 14, 1964 (div. Nov. 1986); children: Teresa, Stephen, Morgan. BSc in Chem. Engring., U. Idaho, 1964. Jr. engr. Tidewater Oil Co., Martinez, Calif., 1963-64; plant mgr. Gt. Can. Oil Sands,, Ft. McMurray, Alta, 1964-70; prodn. mgr. Aquitaine Co. Can., Calgary, Alta, 1970-77; pres. Can. West, Tempe, Ariz., 1977-81; gen. mgr. Canterra Petroleum Inc., Denver, 1981--. Patentee in field, Can. Mem. Assn. Profl. Engrs. Geologists & Geophysicists of Alberta. Republican. Office: Canterra Petroleum Inc 1625 Broadway Ste 600 Denver CO 80202

THOMPSON, ROGER CRAIG, manufacturing company executive; b. Detroit, July 22, 1941; s. Wilford George and Lucille (Watson) T.; m. Victoria Renee Baughn, July 3, 1964; children: Laura, David, Douglas, Jeanette, Sharon. Student bus. adminstrn., Colo. State U., 1959-60, Brigham Young U., Liae, Hawaii, 1961; student fin. and mktg., Ariz. State U., 1963-64. Mgmt. trainee Theo. H. Davies & Co., Ltd., Honolulu, 1961-62; div. mgr. Sears, Roebuck & Co., Phoenix, 1964-67; program mgr. Talley Def. Systems, Mesa, Ariz., 1968-69; area mgr. Fotomat Corp., Phoenix, 1970-71; mktg. mgr. Fotomat Corp., La Jolla, Calif., 1972-73; regional dir. Fotomat Corp., Stamford, Conn., 1974-79; v.p., co-owner Biesemeyer Mfg. Corp., Mesa, 1980—; mem. adv. bd. Powermatic div. Houdaille Industries, McMinnville, Tenn., 1985-86; lectr. Brigham Young U., Provo, Utah, 1988—. Bd dirs. YMCA, Mesa, 1987—, Mesa Symphony Orch. Assn., 1988—; dir. El Tour de Tucson, 1988—; chmn. Project Eagle, Boy Scouts Am., Mesa, 1988—; mem. adv. bd. Mesa Crime Prevention, 1989. Recipient Addy award Phoenix Advt. Club, 1988. Mem. Wood Machinery Mfg. Assn. Am. (bd. dirs. 1987—). Republican. Mormon. Home: 1717 E Ivy Glen Mesa AZ 85203 Office: Biesemeyer Mfg Corp 216 S Alma School Rd Mesa AZ 85210

THOMPSON, RONALD EDWARD, lawyer; b. Bremerton, Wash., May 24, 1931; s. Melville Herbert and Clara Mildred (Griggs) T.; m. Marilyn Christine Woods, Dec. 15, 1956; children—Donald Jeffery, Karen, Susan, Nancy, Sally, Claire. B.A., U. Wash., 1953, J.D., 1958. Bar: Wash. 1959. Asst. city atty. City of Tacoma, 1960-61; pres. firm Thompson, Krilich, LaPorte & Tucci, P.S., Tacoma, 1961—; judge pro tem Mcpl. Ct., City of Tacoma, Pierce County Dist. Ct., 1972—; dir. Air Gemini, Inc. Chmn. housing and social welfare com. City of Tacoma, 1965-69; mem. Tacoma Bd. Adjustment, 1967-71, chmn., 1968; mem. Tacoma Com. Future Devel., 1961-64, Tacoma Planning Commn., 1971-72; bd. dirs., pres. Mcpl. League Tacoma; bd. dirs. Tacoma Pierce County Cancer Soc., Tacoma-Pierce County Heart Assn., Tacoma-Pierce County Council for Arts, Econ. Devel. Council Puget Sound, Tacoma Youth Symphony, Kleiner Group Home, Tacoma Community Coll. Found., Pierce County Econ. Devel. Corp.; precinct committeeman Republican party, 1969-73. Served with AUS, 1953-55; col. Res. Recipient Internat. Community Service award Optimist Club, 1970, Patriotism award Am. Fedn. Police, 1974, citation for community service HUD, 1974, Disting. Citizen award Mcpl. League Tacoma-Pierce County. Mem. Am. Arbitration Assn. (panel of arbitrators), ABA, Wash. State Bar Assn. , Tacoma-Pierce County Bar Assn. (sec. 1964, pres. 1979, mem. cts. and judiciary com. 1981-82), Assn. Trial Lawyers Am., Wash. State Trial Lawyers Assn., Tacoma-Pierce County C. of C. (dir., exec. com., v.p., chmn.), Downtown Tacoma Assn. (com. chmn.), Phi Delta Phi, Sigma Nu. Roman Catholic. Clubs: Variety (Seattle); Lawn Tennis, Tacoma, Optimist (Tacoma). Home: 817 N Yakima Ave Tacoma WA 98403 Office: 524 Tacoma Ave S Tacoma WA 98402

THOMPSON, SANDRA JEAN, educational administrator; b. San Diego, Apr. 5, 1958; d. Robert Ellert Thompson and Joan Carol (McNeil) Schaaf. BBA magna cum laude, Nat. U., 1987, MBA in Legal Studies, 1988. Lic. real estate salesperson, Calif. Jr. clk.-typist San Diego County Office Edn., San Diego, 1976-77; intermediate clk.-typist San Diego County Office Edn., 1977-78, sec. II, 1978-84, adminstrv. sec. I, 1984-86, adminstrv. sec. II, 1986-87, bus. asst., 1987—. Bd. dirs. Dollars for Scholars, San Diego, 1987—. Recipient achievement award, Bank Am., San Diego, 1976, Free Enterprise Bus. award, Greater San Diego Industry-Edn. Council, 1976; named Woman of Achievement, San Diego County Office Edn., 1981, Employee of Yr., 1982. Mem. Calif. Assn. Sch. Bus. Ofcls. Republican. Methodist. Office: San Diego County Office Edn 6401 Linda Vista Rd San Diego CA 92111

THOMPSON, SHERMAN LEE, producer; b. Perris, Calif., Jan. 13, 1934; s. Leo and Anna Margart (Schwarz) T. Student, Chouinard Art Inst., 1957-60. Staff artist Churchill Films, Inc., Hollywood, Calif., 1960-64; prod. mgr. Murakami-Wolf Sweason Films, Hollywood, 1964-72; prod. supr. Focus Films Inc., N.Y.C., 1972-74; producer Film Fair, Inc., Studio City, Calif., 1974-78; exec. producer Murakami-Wolf Sweason Films, Hollywood, 1978-80; bd. dirs. Camera Services Inc., Burbank, Calif., 1980-81; sr. producer Ogilvy & Mather Advt., Los Angeles, 1981--; animation instr. Art Ctr. Sch. Design, Los Angeles, 1968-70. Mem. Acad. TV Arts and Sci. Office: Ogilvy & Mather 5757 Wilshire Blvd Los Angeles CA 90036

THOMPSON, TERENCE WILLIAM, lawyer; b. Moberly, Mo., July 3, 1952; s. Donald Gene and Carolyn (Stringer) T.; m. Caryn Elizabeth Hildebrand, Aug. 30, 1975; children: Cory Elizabeth, Christopher William. BA in Govt. with honors and high distinction, U. Ariz., 1974; JD, Harvard U., 1977. Bar: Ariz. 1977, U.S. Dist. Ct. Ariz. 1977, U.S. Tax Ct. 1979. Assoc. Brown & Bain P.A., Phoenix, 1977—; legis. aide Rep. Richard Burgess, Ariz. Ho. of Reps., 1974; mem. bus. adv. bd. Citibank Ariz. (formerly Great Western Bank & Trust, Phoenix), 1985-86. Mem. staff Harvard Law Record, 1974-75; rsch. editor Harvard Internat. Law Jour. , 1976; contbr. articles to profl. jours. Mem. Phoenix Mayor's Youth Adv. Bd. 1968-70, Phoenix Internat. Active 20-30 Club, 1978-81, sec. 1978-80, Valley Leadership, Phoenix, 1983-84, citizens task force future financing needs City of Phoenix, 1985-86; deacon Shepherd of Hills Congl. Ch, Phoenix, 1984-85; pres. Maricopa County Young Dems., 1982-83, Ariz. Young Dems., 1983-84, sec. 1981-82, v.p. 1982-83; exec. dir. Young Dems. Am., 1985, mem. exec. com. 1983-85; sec. Ariz. Dem. Com., 1984-87; bd. dirs. City Phoenix Mcpl. Ctr. Corp., 1987—, sec., 1987—. Fellow Ariz. Bar Found.; mem. ABA, State Bar Ariz. (vice chmn. internat. law sect. 1978, coun., securities law sect. 1988—), Maricopa County Bar Assn., Nat. Assn. Bond Lawyers, Am. Acad. Hosp. Attys., Blue Key, Phi Beta Kappa, Phi Kappa Phi, Phi Eta Sigma. Home: 202 W Lawrence Rd Phoenix AZ 85013 Office: Brown & Bain PA PO Box 400 Phoenix AZ 85001

THOMPSON, TERESA JOAN, health science facility adminstra; b. Princeton, Ind., May 16, 1951; d. Kenneth Eldon Ikeler and LaDonna Joan (Cravens) Walton; m. Charles A. AAS, Kankakee Community Coll., 1979. Nurses aid Various Nursing Homes, Watseka, Ill., 1969-79; dir. nurses Frankfort Terr. Nursing Home, Frankfort, Ill., 1979-81, Our Lady Victory Nursing Home, Bourbonnais, Ill., 1981-83; adminstra. Momence Meadows Nursing, Center, Ill., 1983-87; dir. ops. Premier Mgmt., Beverly Hills, Calif., 1987--.

THOMPSON, VAN E., electrical engineer; b. Kilgore, Tex., Dec. 13, 1940; s. William Lawsonand and Katie May T.; m. Mary E. Hauet, Mar. 24, 1978; children: Charlotte, Gina, Jennifer, Evan. BEE, Tex. A. and M. U., 1963; M. Mgmt. Sci., West Coast U., L.A., 1978. Test/evaluation engr. Gen. Dynamics, Pomona, Calif., 1963-75, sys. engr., 1975-80, mktg. engr., 1980-85; project engr. Gen. Dynamics-VSD, Cucamonga, Calif., 1985—. Mem. IEEE, Am. Def. Preparedness Assn., Nat. Security Indsl. Assn. Republican. Office: Gen Dynamics 10900 4th St Rancho Cucamonga CA 91730

THOMPSON, VIRGINIA LOU, agricultural products supplier and importer; b. Malcolm, Iowa, July 15, 1928; d. Isaac Cleveland and Viola (Montgomery) Griffin; m. Alfred Thompson, Mar. 1, 1946; children—Michael Duane, Cathryn Lynn, Steven Curtis, Laura Lue. Student Phoenix Coll., 1962, Phoenix-Scottsdale Jr. Coll., 1973-74. With sales dept. Trend House, Phoenix, 1962-67; importer World Wide Imports, Ft. Collins, Colo., 1974-79; owner, mgr. Windsor Elevator Inc. (Colo.), 1979—; participant in trade shows, seminars. Pres. Am. Luth. Ch. Women, 1973-74. Mem. Nat. Grain and Feed Assn., Colo. Grain and Feed Assn., Rocky Mountain Bean Dealers, Colo. Cattle Feeders Assn., Western U.S. Agrl. Assn., Rice Millers Assn. Democrat. Lutheran. Clubs: Christian Women (Greeley, Colo.); Order of Eastern Star (Iowa). Home: 1627 Adriel Dr Fort Collins CO 80524 Office: PO Box 147 Windsor CO 80550

THOMPSON, WILLIAM BENBOW, JR., physician, educator; b. Detroit, July 26, 1923; s. William Benbow and Ruth Wood (Locke) T.; m. Constance Carter, July 30, 1947 (div. Feb. 1958); 1 child, William Benbow IV; m. Jane Gilliland, Mar. 12, 1958; children: Reese Ellison, Belinda Day. AB, U. So. Calif., 1947, MD, 1951. Diplomate Am. Bd. Ob-Gyn. Resident Gallinger Mun. Hosp., Washington, 1952-53; resident George Washington U. Hosp., Washington, 1953-55; asst. ob-gyn. La. State U., 1955-56; asst. clinical prof. UCLA, 1957-64; assoc. prof. U. Calif.-Irvine Sch. Med., Orange, Calif., 1964—; dir. gynecology U. Calif.-Irvine Sch. Med., 1977—, vice chmn. ob-gyn., 1978--; assoc. dean U. Calif.-Irvine Coll. Med., Irvine, 1969-73. Inventor: Thompson Retractor, 1976; Thompson Manipulator, 1977. Bd. dirs. Monarch Bay Assn. Laguna Niguel, Calif. 1969-77, Monarch Summitt II A ssn. 1981-83. With U.S. Army, 1942-44, PTO. Fellow Am. Coll. Ob-Gyn., Am. Coll. Surgeons, Los Angeles Ob-Gyn. Soc. (life), Orange County Gynecology and Obstetrics Soc. (hon.), Capistrano Bay Yacht Club (commodore 1975). Office: UCI Med Ctr OB/GYN 101 City Dr Orange CA 92668

THOMPSON, WILLIAM PAUL, JR., aerospace company executive; b. Elmira, N.Y., June 3, 1934; s. W. Paul and Helen Katharine (Bruce) T.; m. Sally W. Lessig, Aug. 1955 (div. Apr. 1977); children: Helen W., Bruce A., Leila E., Judith A.; m. Anne Stevenson, Dec. 11, 1977. BS in physics, Yale U., 1955; MS in Physics, Lehigh U., 1957, PhD in Physics, 1963. Research and teaching asst. Lehigh U., Bethlehem, Pa., 1955-61; instr. Moravian Coll., Bethlehem, 1957-58, Los Angeles Trade-Tech., Bethlehem, 1967; mem. tech. staff labs Aerospace Corp, Los Angeles, 1961-68; head dept. reentry systems Aerospace Corp., San Bernardino, Calif., 1968-72; assoc. group dir. Aerospace Corp., Los Angeles, 1972-79, dir. space tech., 1979-81, dir. aerophysics lab, 1981—. Contbr. articles to profl. publs., chpt. to books. Bd. dirs. minority engring. program UCLA, 1987—. Fellow AIAA (assoc., mem. laser tech. com. 1986-89, chmn. 1989—); mem. Am. Phys. Soc., Sigma Xi. Republican. Episcopalian. Home: 361 Glen Summer Rd Pasadena CA 91105 Office: Aerospace Corp M5-742 Box 92957 Los Angeles CA 91105

THOMPSON, WILLIAM RANDALL, international relations educator; b. Great Falls, Mont., July 30, 1946; s. William Wesley and Jacquelyn May (Risley) T.; m. Karen Anne Rasler, Aug. 15, 1981. BA, U. Wash., 1968, MA, 1969, PhD, 1972. From asst. prof.to prof. Fla. State U., Tallahassee, 1973-83; prof. Claremont (Calif.) Grad. Sch., 1983—, prof., chmn., 1986-87; vis. prof. U. Minn., Mpls., 1972-73, U. Ariz., Tucson, 1982; asst. program dir. NSF, Washington, 1979. Author: (monograph) The Grievances of Military Coup-Makers, 1973, On Global War: Historical=Structural Approaches to World Politics, 1988; (with others) The Comparative Analysis of Politics, 1978; Sea Power in Global Politics, 1494-1993, 1988, War and State Making: The Shaping of the Global Powers, 1989; co-editor: Rhythms in Politics and Economics, 1985; editor Contending Approaches to World System Analysis, 1983; mem. editorial bd. Am. Jour. Polit. Sci., 1982-85, Jour. Politics, 1982—, Internat. Studies Notes, 1983—, Western Polit. Quarterly, 1984-87, Internat. Interactions, 1984—, Internat. Polit. Economy Yearbook, 1987—; contbr. articles to profl. jours. Fellow NIMH, 1972-73; grantee Nat. Acad. Scis., 1971-72, NSF, 1982-85, 85-87. Mem. Am. Polit. Sci. Assn., Internat. Studies Assn., Inter-Univ. Seminar on Armed Forces and Soc. Home: 4045 La Junta Dr Claremont CA 91711 Office: Claremont Grad Sch Ctr for Politics and Policy Claremont CA 91711

THOMPSON LYONS, KELTON RAE, advertising executive; b. Oklahoma City, Oct. 23, 1959; d. Kenneth Wayne and Barbara Ann (Mitchell) Thompson; m. Brad Edward Lyons, Nov. 29, 1985. BS, Iowa State U., 1982. Corp. trainee Meredith Corp., Des Moines, 1982-83; acct. exec. Meredith Corp., San Francisco, 1983—. Mem. Women in Communications, San Francisco Mag. Reps., Young Profl. Women, Am. Cancer Soc., Sigma Delta Chi (rsch. assoc. travel and tourism), Kappa Alpha Theta Alumnae Assn. (v.p. 1984-85, pres. 1986-87, alumnae dist. IX pres. 1988-89).

THOMPSON-MONASTERO, JUDY, personnel consultant; b. Fall River, Mass., Apr. 28, 1948; d. Eldredge Humphrey and Patricia (McLeod) Leeming; m. Michael Bennett Thompson, Feb. 19, 1970 (div. Apr. 1978); 1 child, William Bennett; mm. Robert Joseph Monastero, Apr. 24, 1987. Student, Coll. William and Mary, 1968-69; AA in Math., Colby Jr. Coll., 1968. Mgr. sales dept. Tupperware, Fairfax, Va., 1971-73; adminstrv. asst. Leboeuf, Leiby & MacRae, Washington, 1973-74; mgr. sales dept. CRM/Random House Books, San Diego, 1974-76; mgr. dist. sales Avon Products, San Diego, 1976-78; sr. recruiter Dunhill San Diego, 1978-81; pres., owner Fin. Search Cons., Inc., San Diego, 1981—. Mem. vol. PSI World. Mem. Nat. Assn. Accts. (v.p. mem.). Office: Fin Search Cons Inc 3750 Convoy St #106 San Diego CA 92111

THOMSEN, PAULA JOAN, marketing consultant; b. Long Beach, Calif., Dec. 1, 1961; d. Peter Steven Polchert and Joan Marilyn (Perrin) Rockwell; m. Mark Thomas Thomsen, Jan. 17, 1981 (div. Jan. 1987), 1 child, Abby Marie. Student, Calif. State U., 1979-81, Inst. Children Lit., Conn., 1987—. Dist. mgr. sales Olan Mills, Inc., Scottsdale, Ariz., 1982-84; mgr. retail merchandising Max Factor and Co., Hollywood, Calif., 1984-87; sr. account exec. Transworld Systems, Inc., Long Beach, Calif., 1987-89; mktg. cons. Sebastian Internat., Chatsworth, Calif., 1989—. Active mem. PTA, Long Beach, 1986—, World Wildlife Fund, Washington, 1986—. Mem. Nat. Assn. Female Execs., Cousteau Soc., Smithsonian Assn, Amnesty Internat., Met. Mus. Art. Republican. Roman Catholic. Home: 822 E Carson St Long Beach CA 90807-2903 Office: Sebastian Internat 20362 Plummer St Chatsworth CA 91311

THOMSETT, MICHAEL CHRISTOPHER, author, lecturer; b. Brighton, Sussex, Eng., Mar. 31, 1948; s. Ronald George Thomsett and Rose Karin (Walbaum) Glasgow; m. Linda Lee Dinnocenzo, July 1, 1967; children: Michael P., Eric J. Grad. high sch., Mill Valley, Calif. Acctg. clk. Jordano's, Inc., Santa Barbara, Calif., 1968-69; acct. Pacific Nat. Life Assurance, San Francisco, 1969-70; pvt. practice acctg. San Rafael, Calif., 1970-74; acct. Western Traveler's Life Ins., San Rafael, 1974-76, Utah, Internat., San Francisco, 1976-78; pvt. practice cons. part-time San Rafael, 1978-84, freelance writer, 1978—. Author: Builders Guide to Accounting, 1978, Fundamentals of Bookkeeping and Accounting, 1980, Builders Office Manual, 1981, Contractor's Year-Round Tax Guide, 1983, Computers: The Builders New Tool, 1985, Investment and Securities Dictionary, 1986 (Outstanding Acad. Book award 1987, 88), Homeowner's Money Management, 1987, How to Buy a House, Condo or Co-op., 1987, Little Black Book of Business Math, 1988, Contractor's Growth and Profit Guide, 1988, Little Black Books of Budgets and Forecasts, 1988, Real Estate Dictionary, 1988, Little Black Book of Business Reports, 1988, Little Black Book of Business Letters, 1988, The Complete Guide to Selling Your Home, 1988, Bookkeeping for Builders, 1989, Insurance Dictionary, 1989, How to Sell Your Home for Top Dollar, 1989, Save Money on Your Home Mortgage, 1989, Investor Factline, 1989; contbr. numerous articles to profl. jours. Republican. Home and Office: 3864 Robby Ct Bellingham WA 98226

THOMSON, BARBARA JEANNE, purchasing executive; b. Cardiff, Calif., Feb. 10, 1929; d. Zack Rowden and Zula Mae (Tuckness) Taylor; m. Robert Allyn San Clemente, Feb. 8, 1946 (div. Aug. 1954); children—Robert Allyn Jr., Frances Irene, Michael George; m. Seeth Lyle Thomson, Aug. 7, 1954; 1 child, David Seeth. Grad. high sch., Encinitas, Calif. Various positions Gen. Dynamics Convair, San Diego, 1957-73; purchasing agt. Systems, Sci. & Software, San Diego, 1973-78; sr. buyer Gen. Dynamics Electronics, San Diego, 1978-80; sr. buyer LSI Products div. TRW, San Diego, 1980-84, purchasing mgr., 1984—. Named Employee of Yr., Gen. Dynamics Electronics, San Diego, 1978. Mem. Ry. Hist. Soc. (sec. San Diego 1957-60), Pacific Beach Model R.R. Club (sec. 1955-65), Nat. Assn. Female Execs., Nat. Mgmt. Assn., San Diego Hospice Assn. Democrat. Avocations: model railroading; photography; baseball; football. Home: 3204 McGraw St San Diego CA 92117 Office: TRW LSI Products Div 4243 Campus Point Ct San Diego CA 92121

THOMSON, FRANK WILLIAM, urban planner; b. N.Y.C., May 30, 1946; s. William Emile and Sophie (Loehle) T.; m. Rochelle Lenore Spiegel, Feb. 12, 1972; children: Paige Judith, Scott William. BS in Econ., St. John's U., 1970; BS in Architecture, U. Ariz., 1980, MS in Urban Planning, 1981. Research asst. U. Ariz., Tucson, 1978-81; planning dir. Ruiz Engring., Tucson, 1981-84; v.p. Carter Assoc., Tucson, 1984-86; v.p. urban planning Jerry Jones & Assoc., Tucson, 1986—. Mem. So. Ariz. Homebuilders Assn., Tucson C. of C., Am. Planning Assn., Ariz. Planning Assn. (bd. dirs. 1985-87, So. Ariz. Sect. 1985-87), Am. Inst. Cert. Planners. Office: Jerry Jones & Assoc 35 E Toole Ave Tucson AZ 85702

THOMSON, GRACE MARIE, nurse, minister; b. Pecos, Tex., Mar. 30, 1932; d. William McKinley and Elzora (Wilson) Olliff; m. Radford Chaplin, Nov. 3, 1952; children: Deborah C., William Earnest. Assoc. Applied Sci., Odessa Coll., 1965; extension student U. Pa. Sch. Nursing, U. Calif., Irvine, Golden West Coll. RN, Calif., Okla., Ariz., Md., Tex. Dir. nursing Grays Nursing Home, Odessa, Tex., 1965; supr. nursing Med. Hill, Oakland, Calif.; charge nurse pediatrics Med. Ctr., Odessa; dir. nursing Elmwood Extended Care, Berkeley, Calif.; surg. nurse Childrens Hosp., Berkeley; med-surg.

charge nurse Merritt Hosp., Oakland, Calif.; adminstr. Grace and Assocs.; advocate for emotionally abused children; active Watchtower and Bible Tract Soc.; evangelist for Jehovah's Witnesses, 1954—.

THOMSON, JEFFREY RICHARD, scenography professor; b. Mpls., Aug. 21, 1942; s. Richard Harry and Catherine Virginia (Gallagher) T.; m. Jean Marie Thomsen, Aug. 10, 1978. BA in Art, Ripon (Wis.) Coll., 1965; MA in Theatre, U. Wash., Seattle, 1970; MFA in Theatre, Wayne State U., 1981. Resident designer Potlatch Playhouse, Bainbridge Island, Wash., 1966-68; design instr. U. Wyo., Laramie, 1968-70; resident designer Raleigh (N.C.) Little Theatre, 1971-73; design instr. Macalester Coll., St. Paul, 1973-78; design lectr. U. Mich., Flint, 1978-81; assoc. prof. scenography Ariz. State U., Tempe, 1981—; resident designer Childsplay, Inc., Tempe, 1983—; scene designer Ariz. Theatre Co., Tucson, 1988—; design cons. Sunbelt Scenic Studios, Phoenix, 1984-88, Timberline Prodns., Phoenix, 1985-89; theatre cons. Childsplay, Inc., Tempe, 1984—, Actors Theatre of Phoenix, 1988—; vis. designer U.S. Internat. U., San Diego, 1986-88. Designer play Wild Oats (Best of Region 1980), Liquid Skin (Best of Yr. 1988). Mem. United Scenic Artists Am. (bd. dirs.). Home: 1911 E Pebble Beach Dr Tempe AZ 85282 Office: Ariz State U Theatre Tempe AZ 85287-2002

THOMSON, PARVIN DARABI, electronics company executive; b. Tehran, Iran, Sept. 16, 1941; came to U.S., 1964; d. Esmaiel and Eshrat (Dastyar) Darabi; m. Robert Thomson, Nov. 25, 1967 (div. 1975); 1 child, Romin Pete. BSEE, Calif. State U., Northridge, 1971; MSEE, U. So. Calif., 1975; MBA, Pepperdine U., 1979. Design engr. Singer Librascope Co., Burbank, Calif., 1971-73, Hughes Aircraft Co., L.A., 1973-78; program mgr. Applied Tech. Co., Sunnyvale, Calif., 1978-83, cons., 1985-86; program mgr. Ford Aerospace Co., Palo Alto, Calif., 1983-84, EM Systems Co., Fremont, Calif., 1984-85; pres., founder PT Enterprises, Inc., Mountain View, Calif., 1985—; cons. AEG, Aktiengesellschaft, Fed. Republic Germany, 1985—. Mem. Soc. Women Engrs. (industry adv. chmn. 1983), Assn. Old Crows. Office: PT Enterprises Inc 1235 Pear Ave Ste 111 Mountain View CA 94043

THOMSON, ROBERT STEPHEN, travel service executive; b. Charles City, Iowa, May 10, 1955; s. Robert Lee and Janan (McQuillen) T.; m. Christine Barbara Hollister, June 3, 1978; 1 child, Robert Francis. BS with honors, U. Iowa, 1977, MBA, 1977. Supr. community ctr. City of Eugene, Oreg., 1977-81; dir. recreation Town of Manchester, Conn., 1981-84; owner, mgr. Avenida Travel Svcs., Laguna Hills, Calif., 1984—; v.p., Le Tip, Mission Viejo, Calif., 1984—. Mem. Saddleback Valley (Calif.) Planning Commn., 1984-85. Grantee, Bur. Land Mgmt., 1983. Mem. Am. Soc. Travel Agts., Travel Industry Mktg. Enterprise (bd. dirs. 1987-88), Assn. Retail Travel Agts., Cruise Lines Internat. Assn., Saddleback Regional C. of C. v.p. 1989—), Rotary (pres. Laguna Hills club 1989—). Republican. Roman Catholic. Office: Avenida Travel Ste N10 24351 Ave Carlota Laguna Hills CA 92653

THOMSON, THYRA GODFREY, former state official; b. Florence, Colo., July 30, 1916; d. John and Rosalie (Altman) Godfrey; m. Keith Thomson, Aug. 6, 1939 (dec. Dec. 1960); children—William John, Bruce Godfrey, Keith Coffey. B.A. cum laude, U. Wyo., 1939. With dept. agronomy and agrl. econs. U. Wyo., 1938-39; writer weekly column Watching Washington pub. in 14 papers, Wyo., 1955-60; planning chmn. Nat. Fedn. Republican Women, Washington, 1961; sec. state Wyo. Cheyenne, 1962-86; mem. Marshall Scholarships Com. for Pacific region, 1964-68; del. 72d Wilton Park Conf., Eng., 1965; mem. youth commn. UNESCO, 1970-71, Allied Health Professions Council HEW, 1971-72; del. U.S.-Republic of China Trade Conf., Taipei, Taiwan, 1983; mem. lt. gov.'s trade and fact-finding mission to Saudi Arabia, Jordan, and Egypt, 1985. Bd. dirs. Buffalo Bill Mus., Cody, Wyo., 1987—. Recipient Disting. Alumni award U. Wyo., 1969, Disting. U. Wyo. Arts and Scis. Alumna award, 1987; named Internat. Woman of Distinction, Alpha Delta Kappa; recipient citation Omicron Delta Epsilon, 1965, citation Beta Gamma Sigma, 1968, citation Delta Kappa Gamma, 1973, citation Wyo. Commn. Women, 1986. Mem. N.Am. Securities Adminstrs. (pres. 1973-74), Nat. Assn. Secs. of State, Council State Govts. (chmn. natural resources com. Western states 1966-68), Nat. Conf. Lt. Govs. (exec. com. 1976-79). Home: 3102 Sunrise Rd Cheyenne WY 82001

THOMSON, WILLIAM EDWARD, JR., lawyer, city mayor; b. Sharon, Pa.; m. Carol J. Krieg, Aug. 25, 1961; children: William III, Elizabeth, Steven. BSChemE, Bucknell U., 1957; JD, Georgetown U., 1963. Bar: Va. 1963, Ohio 1964, Calif. 1970, U.S. Dist. Ct. (cen. dist.) Calif. 1970, U.S. Ct. Appeals (9th cir.) 1970, U.S. Supreme Ct. 1983. Ptnr. Lyon and Lyon, L.A., 1969—. Mayor City of Pasadena, Calif., 1988—, vice-mayor, 1986-88, bd. dirs., 1981—; mem. Tournament of Roses Assn., 1974—. Recipient Arts Merit award Pasadena Com. Arts Ctr. Mem. ABA, Calif. Bar Assn., L.A. County Bar Assn. Office: City of Pasadena 100 N Garfield Ave Pasadena CA 91109

THOMSON, WILLIAM ENNIS, theorist, author; b. Ft. Worth, May 24, 1927; s. William Tell and Ruby Florence (Schwarz) T.; m. Elizabeth Anne Everett, Sept. 11, 1948; children: Carol Anne, Mark William, Laurie Elizabeth, John Everett. MusB, North Tex. State U., 1948, MusM, 1949; PhD, Ind. U., 1952. Prof. music Sul Ross State U., Alpine, Tex., 1951-60, Ind. U., Bloomington, 1961-69; Kulas prof. Case Western Res. U., Cleve., 1969-73; dir. grad. studies U. Ariz., Tucson, 1973-75; chmn. dept. SUNY-Buffalo, 1975-80; dean sch. music U. So. Calif., L.A., 1980-86 ; mem. music panel Nat. Endowment for Arts, Washington, 1970-74, policy com. Contemporary Music Project, Washington, 1963-73; cons. N.Y. State Arts Coun., 1976-80; editor and cons. Hawaii Music Project, 1969—. Author: Introduction to Music Reading, 1965; Advanced Music Reading, 1969; Introduction to Music as Structure, 1971; Music for Listeners, 1979; co-author: Materials and Structure of Music, 1963-65, Schoenberg's Error, 1989. V.p. bd. dirs. Buffalo Philharmonic, 1978-80; mem. bd. dirs. Pasadena Chamber Orch., 1980-82; trustee Young Musicians Found., L.A., 1981—. With USN, 1945-46. Composer-in-residence grantee Ford Found., 1960-61; named Outstanding Educator Case Western Res. U., 1971, U. Ariz., 1974. Democrat. Office: U So Calif Sch Music Los Angeles CA 90089-0851

THOR, RICHARD MARQUETTE, automotive executive; b. Seattle, Mar. 3, 1931; s. Russell Johnston and Hazel (Stowe) T.; m. Ann Lee Shingleton, July, 13, 1959; children: Daniel M., Michael R. B in Econs., U. Wash., 1954; MSW, U. So. Calif., 1958. Cert. social worker; lic. clin. social worker, Calif. Stock trader Blythe & Co., Seattle, 1954-56; clin. social worker Calif. Youth Authority, Los Angeles, 1958-60; asst. dir. relocation Community Redevel., Los Angeles, 1960-64, dir. relocation, 1966-68; asst. to dean Sch. Social Work U. So. Calif., Los Angeles, 1964-66; pres. Russ Thor, Inc., Torrance, Calif., 1968—; clin. social worker Los Angeles Psychiat. Services, Rush Clinic, 1960-65; social work cons. Juvenile Div. Project, Redondo Beach, Calif., 1984—; instr. U. So. Calif. Delinquency Control Inst., 1965, bd. councilors; instr. UCLA Crisis Intervention, 1966; mem. adv. coun. Sch. Mgmt. Calif. State U., Dominguez Hills. Elder Presbyn. Ch., Palos Verdes, Calif., 1986; chmn. adv. bd. Salvation Army, 1986. Served with USAF, 1951-52. Mem. Nat. Assn. Social Workers (registered), Am. Internat. Automotive Dealers Assn. (state chmn. 1986), South Bay Student Attendance Rev. Bd., South Bay Free Clinic (bd. dirs. exec. com. 1986—), Little County Mary Hosp. Centurian Bd. (pres. 1984—). Republican. Presbyterian. Lodge: Rotary.

THORDARSON, DONALD JEFFREY, real estate broker; b. Winnipeg, Man., Can., Sept. 28, 1952; came to U.S., 1957; s. John Donald and Betty Jean (Wasson) T.; m. Bridget Ann Patton, Oct. 29, 1988. BS in Bus., U. So. Calif., 1977. Real estate salesman W.H. Daum, Daumcorp. Daum Johnstown Am., Los Angeles, 1978—; owner Donald J. Thordarson, Inc., Los Angeles, 1983—. Mem. Am. Indsl. Real Estate Assn. Republican. Lutheran. Office: Daum Johnstown Am 20920 Warner Ctr Ln C Woodland Hills CA 91367

THORDARSON, WILLIAM, hydrogeologist; b. N.Y.C., Mar. 14, 1929; s. William and Lillian (Hirsch) T. BA, Columbia U., 1950; postgrad., U. Kans., Lawrence, 1953-55; MA, U. Colo., 1987. Hydrogeologist U.S. Geol. Survey, Denver, 1955—. Author: Perched Groundwater, Nevada, 1965, Hydrogeology Great Basin, Nevada, 1974, Hydrogeology of Test Wells, 1983, Hydrogeologic Monitoring, Nevada, 1985. Served with U.S. Army, 1950-52. Mem. AAAS, Geol. Soc. Am., Am. Assn. Petroleum Geologists, Am. Geophys. Union, Assn. Groundwater Scientists and Engrs., Am. Water Resources Assn., Am. Inst. Profl. Geologists (cert.), Am. Inst. Hydrology (cert.), Assn. Engring Geologists, Internat. Assn. Mat. Geologists.

THOREN-PEDEN, DEBORAH SUZANNE, lawyer; b. Rockford, Ill., Mar. 28, 1958; d. Robert Roy and Marguerite Natalie (Geoghegan) Thoren; m. Steven E. Peden, Aug. 10, 1985. BA in Philosophy and Polit. Sci., U. Mich., 1978; JD, U. So. Calif., 1982. Bar: Calif. 1982. Assoc. Bushkin, Gaines & Gaims, L.A., 1982-84, Rutan & Tucker, Costa Mesa, Calif., 1984-86; counsel First Interstate Bank Calif., L.A., 1986—. Supervising editor U. So. Calif. Entertainment Law Jour., 1982, 1983 Entertainment Publishing, 1983, 1984, Arts Handbook, 1988. Mem. ABA, State Bar Calif. Office: First Interstate Bank Calif 707 Wilshire Blvd Rm W20-1 20th Fl Los Angeles CA 90017

THORINGTON, GLYNE UNDINE, research scientist; b. West Indies, Barbados, Jan. 20, 1941; came to U.S., 1964; d. Charles and Enid Undine (Husbands) T. BS, Andrews U., 1969; MS, U. Conn., 1971; PhD, Boston U., 1980. Tchr. Modern High Sch., St. Michael, Barbados, 1960-61; biology tchr. Alexandra Sch., St. Peter, Barbados, 1961-64; sci. tchr. Westledge Sch., Simsbury, Conn., 1971-73; postdoctoral fellow Oxford U., Eng., 1980-81; postdoctoral fellow Loma Linda (Calif.) U., 1981-85, research scientist, 1985—; presenter papers Internat. Collegium on Endosymbiosis and Cell Research, Tubingen U., Fed. Republic of Germany, 1980, Am. Soc. Cell Biology, Kansas City, Mo., 1984; invited speaker Internat. Symposia, U. Calif., Irvine, 1984. Contbr. articles to profl. jours. Macy's scholar Marine Biol. Sta., 1977-78; grad. scholar Boston U., 1979-80. Fellow N.Y. Acad. Sci., Sigma Xi. Adventist. Office: Loma Linda U Dept Physiology & Pharmocology Loma Linda CA 92350

THORNBURY, WILLIAM MITCHELL, lawyer, law educator; b. Kansas City, Mo., Feb. 11, 1944; s. Paul Cobb and Marguerite Madellaine (Schulz) T.; m. Joy Frances Barrett, Feb. 2, 1973; children: Barrett Mitchell, Adele Frances. BA, UCLA, 1964; JD, U. So. Calif., 1967, postgrad. 1967-69. Bar: Calif. 1968, U.S. Dist. Ct. (cen. dist.) Calif. 1968, U.S. Dist. Ct. (no. dist.) Calif. 1973, U.S. Dist. Ct. (so. dist.) Calif. 1980, U.S. Dist. Ct. (ea. dist.) Calif. 1980, U.S. Ct. Appeals (9th cir.) 1973, U.S. Ct. Claims 1980, U.S. Ct. Internat. Trade, 1981, U.S. Ct. Customs and Patent Appeals 1980, U.S. Ct. Mil. Appeals 1980, U.S. Supreme Ct. 1973, U.S. Ct. Appeals (Fed. cir.) 1984. Dep. L.A. County Pub. Defender, 1969—, dep.-in-charge traffic ct., 1982-84, supervising atty. Juvenile Svcs. div., 1984, dep. in charge, Inglewood, Calif., 1984-85; legal asst. prof. Calif. State U., L.A., 1983—; mem. adv. com. on alcohol determination State Dept. Health, 1984—; appointed to apprenticeship council by Gov. Deukmejian State of Calif., 1986—, chmn. equal opportunity com. 1987—; chmn., vice chmn. Santa Monica Fair Election Practices Commn., Calif., 1981-85; advisor on drunk driving Calif. Pub. Defenders Assn., 1984—; alt. mem. L.A. County Commn. on Drunk Driving, 1983-84; mem. steering com. Santa Monica Coalition, nominations com., 1984—; bd. dirs. Westside Legal Svcs., 1984-86, v.p., 1986-87, pres., 1987-88. Columnist Calif. Defender; editor Drunk Driving Manual, 1984; contbr. article to Forum. Exec. bd. dirs. Santa Monica Young Rep., 1967-72, pres. 1972-73, treas. 1973-75, bd. dirs. 1968-72; del., precinct chmn., registration chmn. L. A. County Young Rep., 1968-70; chmn. legal com. L.A. County Rep. Cen. Com., 1977-81, 83-85; chmn. jud. evaluation com., 1978-80; pres. Santa Monica Rep. Club 1986-88, bd. dirs., 1966—; bd. dirs. West L.A. Rep. Club, 1986—; mem. Beverly Hills Rep. Club, Rep. State Cen. com., 1983-85, assoc. mem., 1980-83, 86—, Non-Partisan Candidate Evaluating Coun., Inc. (bd. dirs. 1980-86, v.p. 1986-89, pres. 1989—); mem. Pasadena Rep. Club, 1984—; bd. dirs. Santa Monicans Against Crime, 1979—; chmn. 44th Assembly Dist. Rep. Cen. Com. 1974-87; chmn. Western part of L.A. County for George Murphy for U.S. Senate, 1970, John T. LaFollette for Congress, 1970; campaign chmn. Donna A. Little for City Council, 1984; adv. Pat Geffner for City Council, 1979, 81; campaign mgr. Experienced Coll. Team, 1983. Recipient Outstanding Chmn. award Los Angeles County Rep. Party, 1974, sec.-treas. 1968-75, chmn. legal com. 1977-82, 83-85; named Outstanding Service to Rep. Party Legal Counsel, 1978; recipient award Am. Assn. UN, 1961. Mem. ABA, L.A. County Bar Assn. (vice chmn. indigent and criminal def. com., jud. evaluation com. 1986-88, 2d vice chmn. 1989—, criminal justice com. 1986—, criminal law and law enforcement com., 1986-87), Santa Monica Bar Assn. (trustee 1976-77, 79-87, chmn. legis. and publicity com., chmn. jud. evaluation com. 1982-84, pres.-elect 1984, pres. 1985-86, del. to state bar conv. 1974-88, liaison to L.A. County Bar Assn. 1986-87, chmn. legis. com. 1983-84, 88), L.A. County Pub. Defenders Assn. (advisor, bd. dirs. 1980-88), Calif. Pub. Defenders Assn. (advisor), Santa Monica Hist. Soc., San Fernando Valley Criminal Bar Assn. (membership chmn. 1986—, bd. trustees 1986—, treas. 1987-88, pres.-elect 1988-89, pres. 1989—, chmn. judicial evaluations com. 1988), Assn. Trial Lawyers Am., Supreme Ct. Hist. Soc., Nat. Legal Aid and Defenders Assn., Nat. Assn. Criminal Def. Attys., Acad. Criminal Justice Scis., U. So. Calif. Law Alumni Assn., UCLA Alumni Assn., N.Y. Acad. Scis., Am. Assn. Polit. Sci., Criminal Law sect. of State Bar of Calif., Am. Soc. Criminology (life), Western Region Criminal Law Educators, Santa Monica C. of C. (inebriate task force 1980), Calif. Hist. Soc., Santa Monica Coll. Patron's Assn., Nat. Assn. Criminal Def. Counsel, Navy League (life, bd. dirs. 1979—, legis. chmn. 1982, judge adv. 1983-89, 2d vice chmn. 1989—), Ne), Calif. Rifle and Pistol Assn. (life).

THORNGATE, JOHN HILL, physicist; b. Eau Claire, Wis., Dec. 23, 1935; s. John Harold and Dorothy Geraldine (Maxon) T.; m. Carole Joan Rye, Aug. 5, 1956; children: FayAnne, John, Sharon. BA, Ripon Coll., 1957; MS, Vanderbilt U., 1961, PhD, 1976. Insp. U.S. Atomic Energy Commn., Oak Ridge, Tenn., 1959; physicist Oak Ridge Nat. Lab., ž, 1960-78, Lawrence Livermore (Calif.) Nat. Lab., 1978--. Inventee determining Radon in air, stable pulsed light source, fast neutron solid state dosimeter, method of improving BEO as a thermoluminescent dosimeter. Mem. Am. Phys. Soc., Health Physics Soc., IEEE, Sigma Xi. Office: Lawrence Livermore Nat Lab L-386 PO Box 5505 Livermore CA 94550

THORNSJO, DOUGLAS FREDRIC, insurance company executive, lawyer, consultant; b. Mpls., July 10, 1927; s. Adolph Fredric and Agnes Emily (Grynikewski) T.; m. Barbara Jean Bachmann, Aug. 10, 1950; children: Claudia, Douglas Fredric Jr. BS, U. Minn., 1948, JD, 1951. Bar: Maine, Minn., N.Y., U.S. Dist. Ct. Maine, U.S. Dist. Ct. (so. dist.) N.Y., U.S. Ct. Appeals (2d and 8th cirs.), U.S. Supreme Ct. Of counsel Dewey, Ballentine, et al, N.Y.C., 1951-52, 54-55; spl. counsel Investors Diversified Svcs., Mpls., 1955-61; chief exec. officer Midwest Tech. Devel. Corp., Thornsto, Smith & Johnson, Mpls., 1961-66; sr. v.p., counsel Union Mut. Life Ins. Co., Portland, Maine, 1966-76, Bradford Nat. Corp., N.Y.C., 1976-83; 1st sr. v.p. Dime Savs. Bank N.Y., N.Y.C., 1984-88; vice chmn., chief operating officer Gen. Svcs. Life Ins. Co., Novato, Calif., 1987—, also bd. dirs.; bd. dirs. Agoil, Inc., Secaucus, N.J., Internat. Life Investors Ins. Co., N.Y.C. Author: The Mutual Company-Use of a Downstream Holding Company in Process of Self-Analysis, 1973; contbr. numerous articles to mags. Bd. dirs. Nat. Multiple Sclerosis Soc., N.Y.C., 1980—, Eureka Theater Co., San Francisco, 1989—. With U.S. Mcht. Marines, 1945-47; lt. USNR, 1952-54. Mem. ABA, Am. Corp. Counsel Assn. (pres. N.Y. chpt. 1987-88), Nat. Assn. Bus. Economists, Lotos Club (N.Y.C.). Home: 1 View Ridge Novato CA 94949 Office: Gen Svcs Life Ins Co PO Box 7952 San Francisco CA 94120-9722

THORNTON, DEAN DICKSON, airplane company executive; b. Yakima, Wash., Jan. 5, 1929; s. Dean Stoker and Elva Maud (Dickson) T.; m. Joan Madison, Aug. 25, 1956 (div. Apr. 1978); children—Steven, Jane Thornton; m. Mary Shultz, Nov. 25, 1981; children—Volney, Scott, Peter, Todd Richmond. B.S. in Bus., U. Idaho, 1952. C.P.A., Wash. Acct. Touche, Ross & Co., Seattle, 1954-63; treas., controller Boeing Co., Seattle, 1963-70; various exec. positions Boeing Co., 1974-85; pres. Boeing Comml. Airplane Co., 1985—; sr. v.p. Wyly Co., Dallas, 1970-74; bd. dirs. Seafirst Corp, Prin. Fin. Group. Bd. dirs. YMCA, Seattle, 1966-68, Jr. Achievement, Seattle, 1966-68; chmn. Wash. Council on Internat. Trade, Seattle, 1984-87. Served to 1st lt. USAF, 1952-54. Named to U. Idaho Alumni Hall of Fame. Mem. Phi Gamma Delta. Republican. Presbyterian. Clubs: Rainier, Seattle Tennis, Seattle Yacht, Conquistadores de Cielo. Home: 1602-34 Ct W Seattle WA 98199 Office: Boeing Co PO Box 3707 Seattle WA 98124

THORNTON, JAMES SCOTT, medical association executive; b. Detroit, Aug. 23, 1941; s. Thomas George and Iris Irene (Malcolm) T.; m. Diana Louise Barker, Nov. 18, 1961; children: James Scott Jr., Christian Stuart. BA, U. Olso, 1972, Eastern Wash. U., 1976; MS, Eastern Wash. U., 1977. Commd. ensign USAF, 1961, advance through grades to master sgt., 1972; flight comdr. USAF, S.E. Asia, 1964-66; med. adminstr. USAF, Fairchild AFB, Wash., 1966-68, 72-73, Oslo, 1968-72; resigned USAF, 1973; pres. N.W. Tng. Cons., Spokane, Wash., 1973-78; exec. dir. Am. Heart Assn., Spokane, 1978-83; exec. v.p. Am. Heart Assn., San Jose, Calif., 1983—; adj. instr. Eastern Wash. U., C. Cheney, 1977-80; cons., speaker J. S. Thornton Assocs., San Jose, 1983—; v.p. field svcs. Calif. Affiliate, 1987—. Fellow Heart Assn. Staff Soc.; men. Assn. United Way Agys. (pres. San Jose chpt. 1987-88), No. Calif. Soc. Assn. Execs. (bd. dirs., chmn. South Bay chpt. 1987—), Am. Motorcyclist Assn., Rotary, Rider Touring Club (Agoura, Calif.). Office: Am Heart Assn 3003 Moorpark Ave San Jose CA 95128

THORNYCROFT, ANN CATHERINE, artist; b. Petersfield, Hampshire, Eng., Feb. 29, 1944. BA, Cen. Sch. of Art, London, 1966; diploma, Chelsea Sch. of Art, London, 1968. One woman shows include Rosamund Felsen Gallery, L.A., 1979, 80, 81, W. Beach Cafe, Venice, Calif., 1981, Thomas Babeor Gallery, La Jolla, Calif., 1982, Ochi Gallery, Boise, Idaho, 1985, Royce Gallery, Miami, Fla., 1988, Four Seasons Hotel, Newport Beach, Calif., 1989, Linda Cathcart Gallery, Santa Monica, Calif.; exhibited in group shows at Music Ctr., 1986, Cedars-Sinai Med. Ctr., 1985, James A. Doolittle Theatre, 1985, The Works Gallery, 1984, 89; represented in numerous pub. and pvt. collections; contbr. articles to profl. jours. Nat. Endowment for the Arts fellow, 1982.

THORP, CHARLES PHILIP, minister; b. San Francisco, Nov. 27, 1949; s. Robert Jay and Natalie Ann (Lotti) T. Student, San Francisco State U., 1970-71, Diablo Valley Jr. Coll., 1983-84; PhD (hon.), Siberian Inst. Devel. Resources, USSR, 1979. Ordained minister, The Church For Unity And Service, 1979. Cons. EST, San Francisco, 1973-75; counsellor SDSI, San Francisco, 1976-78; founder, minister The Church For Unity And Service, San Francisco, 1979—; cons. Rivendell Sch., San Francisco, 1976-78; host Radio Free Religion, Sta. KWUN, Concord, Calif., 1985. Author: Quotes from the Inner Door, Vol. 1-3, 1980-88. Mem. Child Abuse Coun. of Contra Costa County. Mem. Am. Humanist Assn. (counsellor 1974-83), COAST User Group (pres. 1986-88), San Francisco State GLF (founder and chmn. 1970-71). Democrat. Mem. Progressive Charismatic. Home and Office: 1015 Esther Dr Ste A Pleasant Hill CA 94523-4301

THORP, EDWARD OAKLEY, investment management company executive; b. Chgo., Aug. 14, 1932; s. Oakley Glenn and Josephine (Gebert) T.; B.A. in Physics, UCLA, 1953, M.A. (NSF fellow 1954-55), 1955, Ph.D. in Math., 1958; m. Vivian Sinetar, Jan. 28, 1956; children—Raun, Karen, Jeffrey. Instr., UCLA, 1958-59, C.L.E. Moore instr. MIT, 1959-61; asst. prof., then assoc. prof. math. N.Mex. State U., 1961-65; mem. faculty U. Calif., Irvine, 1965—, prof. math., 1967-78, prof. mgmt., 1978-82; pres. Oakley Sutton Mgmt. Corp., investments, 1972—; v.p. Oakley Sutton Securities Corp., 1972—; gen. ptnr. Princeton/Newport Ptnrs., MIDAS Advisors. Grantee NSF, 1962-64, Air Force Office Sci. Research, 1964-74. Fellow Inst. Math. Stats.; mem. Am. Math. Soc., Math. Assn. Am., Phi Beta Kappa, Sigma Xi. Author: Beat The Dealer: A Winning Strategy for the Game of Twenty-One, rev. edit., 1966; Elementary Probability, 1966; The Mathematics of Gambling 1984; co-author: Beat The Market, 1967; The Gambling Times Guide to Blackjack, 1984; columnist Gambling Times, 1979-84. Office: 3 Civic Pla Ste 100 Newport Beach CA 92660

THORPE, GARY STEPHEN, chemistry educator; b. Los Angeles, Mar. 9, 1951; s. David Winston and Jeanette M. (Harris) T.; m. Patricia Marion Eison, Apr. 13, 1949; children: Kristin Anne, Erin Michelle. BS, U. Redlands, 1973; MS, Calif. State U., Northridge, 1975. Tchr. L.A. Schs., 1975-80, L.A. Community Colls., 1976-81, Beverly Hills (Calif.) High Sch., 1980—; pres. 21st Century Software, L.A., 1984—. Recipient Commendation, L.A. County Bd. Supers., 1983, 84, Commendation Beverly Hills City Council, 1983, 84, Resolution of Commendation, State of Calif. Senate and Assembly, 1983, 84, Cert. Appreciation, L.A. County Bd. Edn., 1984-85, Cert. Appreciation, Gov. George Deukmejian, Sacramento, 1984-85. Mem. Am. Chem. Soc. (Selected as Outstanding Chemistry Tchr. of So. Calif. 1989), NEA, Calif. Tchrs. Assn., Phi Delta Kappa. Republican. Lutheran. Lodge: Masons. Home: 6127 Balcom Ave Reseda CA 91335 Office: 21st Century Software Inc 1888 Century Park E Los Angeles CA 90067

THORPE, JAMES, humanities scholar; b. Aiken, S.C., Aug. 17, 1915; s. J. Ernest and Ruby (Holloway) T.; m. Elizabeth McLean Daniells, July 19, 1941; children: James III, John D., Sally Jans-Thorpe. A.B., The Citadel, 1936, LL.D., 1971; M.A., U. N.C., 1937; Ph.D., Harvard U., 1941; Litt.D., Occidental Coll., 1968; L.H.D., Claremont Grad. Sch., 1968; H.H.D., U. Toledo, 1977. Instr. to prof. English Princeton, 1946-66; dir. Huntington Library, Art Gallery and Bot. Gardens, San Marino, Calif., 1966-83; sr. research assoc. Huntington Library, San Marino, Calif., 1966—. Author: Bibliography of the Writings of George Lyman Kittredge, 1948, Milton Criticism, 1950, Rochester's Poems on Several Occasions, 1950, Poems of Sir George Etherege, 1963, Aims and Methods of Scholarship, 1963, 70, Literary Scholarship, 1964, Relations of Literary Study, 1967, Bunyan's Grace Abounding and Pilgrim's Progress, 1969, Principles of Textual Criticism, 1972, 2d edit., 1979, Use of Manuscripts in Literary Research, 1974, 2d edit., 1979, Gifts of Genius, 1980, A Word to the Wise, 1982, John Milton: The Inner Life, 1983, The Sense of Style: Reading English Prose, 1987. Served to col. USAAF, 1941-46. Decorated Bronze Star medal.; Guggenheim fellow, 1949-50, 65-66. Fellow Am. Acad. Arts and Scis., Am. Philos. Soc.; mem. MLA, Am. Antiquarian Soc. Democrat. Episcopalian. Clubs: Zamorano, Twilight. Home: 1199 Arden Rd Pasadena CA 91106 Office: Huntington Libr San Marino CA 91108

THORPE, JOHN NATHAN, electrical contractor; b. Oakland, Calif., May 18, 1934; s. Carl V. and Margaret B. Thorpe; m. Betty J. Stout, Mar. 9, 1967; children: Nathan Wade, Matthew John. BA, Calif. State U., Chico, 1958. Lic. contractor Calif. Pres., Kutz-Hall-Thorpe Contractors, Chico, Calif., 1966-83; pres. Agri Electric, Chico, 1983—. Bd. dirs., chmn. Durham Parks & Recreation; dir. Durham Irrigation Dist. Mem. Phi Kappa Tau, Iota Sigma. Lodge: Elks (past exalted ruler Chico). Office: Agri Electric 11011 Midway Chico CA 95926

THORSEN, CARL THOR, maintenance engineer; b. Sandefjord, Norway, Dec. 7, 1932; came to U.S., 1980; s. Thor Kristian and Alfhild (Aadne) T.; m. Grethe Lise Sorensen, July 29, 1961; children: Thor Aadne, Lene Naomi. BSME, Koping (Sweden) Inst. Tech., 1954. Whaling sta. works mgr., Falkland Islands Compania Argentina de Pesca, Buenos Aires, 1954-67; maintenance supt. Ertsberg Copper Mining project Freeport Indonesia, Inc., Irian Jaya, Indonesia, 1971-79; maintenance supt., engr. Jerritt Canyon Gold Mining project Freeport-McMoran Gold Co., Elko, Nev., 1980—; marine surveyor, Norwegian Veritas, Falkland Islands, 1959-67, Indonesia, 1974-79. Mem. Falkland Islands Assn. Home: 3152 Scenic View Dr Elko NV 89801 Office: Freeport McMoran Gold Co Mountain City Star Rte Elko NV 89801

THORSEN, JAMES HUGH, aviation director, airport manager; b. Evanston, Ill., Feb. 5, 1943; s. Chester A. and Mary Jane (Currie) T.; BA, Ripon Coll., 1965; m. Nancy Dain, May 30, 1980. Asst. dean of admissions Ripon (Wis.) Coll., 1965-69: adminstrv. asst. Greater Rockford (Ill.) Airport Authority, 1969-70; airport mgr. Bowman Field, Louisville, 1970-71; asst. dir. St. Louis Met. Airport Authority, 1971-80; dir. aviation, airport mgr. City of Idaho Falls (Idaho), 1980—. Bd. dirs. Crime Stoppers, 1987—. Named hon. citizen State of Ill. Legislature, 1976, Ky. Col.; FAA cert. comml. pilot, flight instr. airplanes and instruments. Mem. Am. Assn. Airport Execs. (accredited airport exec.), Internat. NW Aviation Council, Greater Idaho Falls C. of C. (bd. dir. 1986—), Mensa, Sigma Alpha Epsilon. Home: 1270 First St Idaho Falls ID 83401 Office: Mcpl Airport Idaho Falls ID 83401

THORSON, JAMES LLEWELLYN, English educator; b. Yankton, S.D., Jan. 7, 1934; s. James Albert and Doris Reece (Burgi) T.; m. Barbara Gay Jelgerhuis, Sept. 6, 1957 (div. 1970); m. Connie Capers, June 6, 1970. BS in Edn., Nebr. U., 1956, MA, 1961; PhD, Cornell U., 1966; MA (hon.), Oxford U., Oxford, England, 1976. Instr. English U. Nebr., Lincoln, 1961-62; asst.

prof. U. N.Mex., Albuquerque, 1965-70; assoc. prof. U. N.Mex., 1970-84; vis. prof. U. Kiril i Metodij, Skopje, Yugoslavia, 1971-72, U. Wurzburg, Wurzburg, Fed. Republic of Germany, 1983; prof. English U. N.Mex., Albuquerque, 1984—; vis. prof. U. Munster, Munster, Fed. Republic of Germany, 1985-86; lectr. USIA, Yugoslavia, Denmark, Czechoslovakia, Fed. Republic of Germany, England, 1971. Editor: Yugoslav Perspectives on American Literature, 1980, Humphry Clinker, 1983, (with Connie Thorson) A Pocket Companion for Oxford, 1988. Lt. USN, 1956-59. Fulbright professorship Skopje, 1971-72, Munster, 1985-86. Mem. Modern Lang. Assn., AAUP (pres. U. N.Mex. chpt. 1968-70), Old Mems. Jesus College Oxford, Am. Soc. for Eighteenth-Century Studies (patron), Wig and Pen Club (London). Democrat. Home: 1411 Columbia NE Albuquerque NM 87106 Office: U New Mexico Dept of English Albuquerque NM 87106

THORSTAD, BRUCE HARDY, magazine editor; b. Mpls., Apr. 16, 1946; m. Ruth Pederson, Oct. 1, 1967; 1 child, Holly Dana. BA, U. Wis., 1973; postgrad., U. Iowa, 1974-75. Editor Holiday Inn Companion, Friedrichsdorf, Fed. Republic Germany, 1975-78, Overseas Life Mag., Friedrichsdorf, Fed. Republic Germany, 1975-78; editor Off Duty, Frankfurt, Fed. Republic Germany, 1978-80, Costa Mesa, Calif., 1980—; copywriter, cons. SCM Walton Printing, Buena Park, Calif., 1984—. Contbr. articles to profl. jours. Home: 17349 Los Amigos Circle Fountain Valley CA 92708 Office: Off Duty Mag 3303 Harbor Blvd Ste C-2 Costa Mesa CA 92626

THREDGOLD, JEFF KEVIN, bank economist; b. Ogden, Utah, Feb. 25, 1951; s. Kevin Arnold and Donna Jean (Taylor) T.; m. 1971 (div. 1985); children: Amy Leigh, Christopher Jeffrey, Shawn Arnold, Michelle Suzanne; m. Lynnette Oliphant, Jan. 24, 1986; 1 child, Kacey Lynne. BS, Weber State Coll., 1973; MS in Econs., U. Utah, 1981. Bank trainee Security Pacific Nat. Bank, L.A., 1973; v.p., staff economist Key Bank of Utah, Salt Lake City, 1973—; v.p., economist western states div. KeyCorp, Seattle, 1987—; adj. prof. fin., U. Utah, Salt Lake City, 1985—; instr. MBA program Westminster Coll. of Salt Lake City, 1981—. Mem. Nat. Assn. Bus. Economists (treas. Utah chpt. 1983-85, pres. 1985-86). Republican. Mormon. Office: Key Bank of Utah 50 S Main St Ste 1900 Salt Lake City UT 84144

THREET, DOUGLAS FLOYD, publishing company executive, clergyman; b. Honeygrove, Tex., Nov. 14, 1944; s. Floyd J. and Bonnie May (Butler) T.; m. Jane Ellen Vickery, Aug. 17, 1969; children: Sara, Aimee, Ryan. BA, Pepperdine U., 1966, MA, 1968, MA in Theology, 1977; MA, UCLA, 1976; MBA, Santa Clara U., 1983. Lic. marriage, family and child counselor, Calif. Commentator Ch. of Christ program Sta KMST-TV, Monterey, Calif., 1971-74; adminstr. Convalescent Hosp., Watsonville, Calif., 1974-76; sr. minister Ch. of Christ, San Jose, Calif., 1976-84; mgr. product mktg. and research Pacific Bell, San Francisco, 1984-85; sales mgr. Pacific Bell Directory, Santa Clara, Calif., 1985-88; regional sales mgr. Pacific Bell Directory, San Francisco, 1988--; dir. Daybreak Youth Camp, Felton, Calif., 1978-83. Mem. Am. Mktg. Assn., Am. Assn. for Marriage and Family Therapy (clin. mem.), Calif. Assn. Mariage and Family Therapists. Office: Pacific Bell Directory 303 2d St San Francisco CA 94107

THRELKELD, STEVEN WAYNE, civil engineer; b. LaJolla, Calif., Feb. 22, 1956; s. Willard Wayne and Sylvia Eileen (Daugherety) T.; m. Sheree Leslie Chabot, Nov. 17, 1984; 1 child, Tristan David. BS in Geophysics, San Diego State U., 1985. Geophys. trainee Western Geophys., Bakersfield, Calif., 1985; civil engr. Dee Jaspar & Assocs., Bakersfield, 1986, Bement, Dainwood & Sturgeon, Lemon Grove, Calif., 1987, Calif. Dept. Transp., San Diego, 1988—; comml. scuba diver, San Diego, 1987-88. Photo editor Montezuma Life Mag., San Diego, 1981; portrait photographer Coast Prodns., San Diego, 1975. Mem. Profl. Engrs. in Calif. Govt. Christian Ch. Home: 4262 Bancroft Dr La Mesa CA 92041

THROCKMORTON, REX DENTON, lawyer; b. Lima, Ohio, June 4, 1941; s. Francis and Jane (Corwin) T.; m. Barbara Catherine Poore, July 21, 1962; children: Scott, John. BS, Denison U., 1963; JD, Ohio State U., 1965. Bar: Ohio 1966, N. Mex. 1971, U.S. Dist. Ct. N. Mex. 1971, U.S. Ct. Appeals (10th cir.) 1973. Assoc. Squire, Sanders & Dempsey, Cleve., 1965-66; ptnr., bd. dirs. Rodey, Dickason, Sloan, Akin & Robb, P.A., Albuquerque, 1971—, chmn. comml. litigation dept., 1985--. Editor Ohio State Law Jour., 1965. Pres. Albuquerque Civic Light Opera Assn., 1985. Capt. JAGC, USAF, 1966-71. Mem. ABA, N. Mex. Bar Assn., Albuquerque Bar Assn. (bd. dirs. 1980-83, pres. 1982), N. Mex. Bar Found., Tanoan Country Club. Republican. Home: 9109 Luna del Oro NE Albuquerque NM 87111 Office: Rodey Dickason Sloan Akin & Robb PO Box 1888 Albuquerque NM 87103

THROPAY, JOHN PAUL, radiation oncologist; b. L.A., Aug. 1, 1949; s. Adam Joseph and Marianita (Lopez) T.; m. Maricela Oropeza Rojas, Sept. 2, 1972; children: John Adams, Natalie Sarah, Jacquelyn Grace. BS in Chemistry, UCLA, 1971, MD, 1975. Diplomate Am. Bd. Radiology. Intern L.A. County/U. So. Calif. Med.Ctr., 1975-76, resident in radiation oncology, 1976-79, instr. radiation therapy, 1983, 85; spl. tng. in endocurietherapy Calif. Med. Group, Inc., L.A., 1979-80; practice medicine specializing in radiation oncology Montebello, Calif., 1980—; mem. staff, trustee Beverly Hosp., Montebello Midway Hosp.; staff Community Hosp., Huntington Park, Greater El Monte Hosp., Monterey Park Hosp., Queen of Angels Hosp., Presbyn. Hosp., Linda Vista Community Hosp., Temple Hosp., L.A.; co-chmn. Hollywood Community Hosp., L.A. Community Hosp. Mem. ABA, Calif. Med. Assn., L.A. County Med. Assn., Am. Coll. Radiology, Am. Cancer Soc., Am. Endocurietherapy Soc., Am. Soc. Therapeutic Radiologists and Oncologists, L.A. Radiol. Soc., So. Calif. Radiation Therapy Assn., Assn. Medicos Hispanos Calif. (adv. bd.). Office: Beverly Oncology & Imagin 120 W Beverly Blvd Montebello CA 90640

THUMS, CHARLES WILLIAM, designer, consultant; b. Manitowoc, Wis., Sept. 5, 1945; s. Earl Oscar and Helen Margaret (Rusch) T. B. in Arch., Ariz. State U., 1972. Ptnr., Grafic, Tempe, Ariz., 1967-70; founder, prin. I-Squared Environ. Cons., Tempe, Ariz., 1970-78; designer and cons. design morphology, procedural programming and algorithms, 1978—. Author: (with Jonathan Craig Thums) Tempe's Grand Hotel, 1973, The Rossen House, 1975; (with Daniel Peter Aiello) Shelter and Culture, 1976; contbg. author: Tombstone Planning Guide, 5 vols., 1974. Office: PO Box 3126 Tempe AZ 85280-3126

THURSTON, RALPH LLOYD, business manager, consultant; b. Des Moines, Apr. 3, 1952; s. Ray Lealand and Leatrice Ione (Babcock) T.; m. Joyce Lynn Weinberg, Aug. 28, 1982; children: Randall Lloyd, Rebecca Lynn. AA, Long Beach City Coll., 1973; BS, Calif. Polytech. U., Pomona, 1976. Cons. SBA, L.A., 1976; internal auditor Van Ordt Inc., Ontario, Calif., 1976-77; branch acct. Comtronn Corp., Santa Ana, Calif., 1978; office mgr. Barovich Konecky Braun Schwartz & Kay, Beverly Hills, Calif., 1979; controller Sheppard Mullin Richler & Hampton, L.A., 1980-85, Biles & Cook Adminstrs., No. Hollywood, Calif., 1986; bus. mgr. Psychol. Svcs., Inc., Glendale, Calif., 1987—; cons. David Blake Films, W. Hollywood, Calif., 1986-87, Sessions Payroll Mgmt., Burbank, Calif., 1987-88, Dadco Inc., Long Beach, Calif., 1987-88. Pres. Kings Villas Home Owners Assn., W. Hollywood, Calif., 1986-87; treas., bd. deacons Covenant Presbyn. Ch., 1970-72. Mem. Assn. Legal Adminstrs., Am. Mgmt. Assn., Crescenta Valley C. of C. (pres. 1989, dir. 1988). Republican. Presbyterian. Home: 6922 Day St Tujunga CA 91042 Office: Psychol Svcs Inc 100 W Broadway #1100 Glendale CA 91210

TIBBETS, ROBIN FRANK, freelance writer; b. Alanreed, Tex., Nov. 7, 1924; s. Marvin Frank and Hazel Kenneth (Porter) T.; m. Dorothy Louise McMahan, Sept. 15, 1952; children: Marlin D., Judith L. BS, McMurry Coll., 1950. Various reporter, photographer positions Daily News and Daily Spokesman, Pampa, Tex., 1946-52; publ. dir. McMurray Coll. and Abilene (Tex.) High Sch., 1953-57; city editor Carlsbad (N. Mex.) Current-Argus, 1957-59; mng. editor Free Press, Colorado Springs, Colo., 1959-64; city editor Gazette-Telegraph, Colorado Springs, 1964-65, Standard-Examiner, Ogden, Utah, 1968-69; feature writer 1970-77, sports columnist, 1977-87, freelance writer, 1987—. Contbr. various articles to mags. Bd. dirs. Colo. Schs. for Deaf/Blind, Colorado Springs, 1963-67; mem. Colo. Manpower Adv. Com., Colorado Springs, 1963-65, Pikes peak or Bust Rodeo Com., Colorado Springs, 1964, Ogden (Utah) Pioneer Days Exec. Com., 1967-77. Recipient 3rd Place Typography award N. Mex. Press Assn., 1959, Outstanding Citizenship award Am. Heritage Found., 1961, Appreciation award McKay-Dee Council, 1969, Award of Excellence Ogden City Council, 1973, First Place award Utah-Idaho Assoc. Press Assn., 1979. Mem. Sigma Delta Chi. Republican. Baptist. Home and Office: 1444 N 250 W Sunset UT 84015-2850

TICE, PAUL, emergency physician; b. Rochester, Minn., Jan. 5, 1947; s. George and Eunice (Anderson) T.; m. Jody DeLay, Sept. 8, 1975; children: Jennifer, Jonathan, Whitney. BS, Grinnell (Iowa) Coll., 1968; MD, U. Calif., San Diego, 1972. Diplomate Am. Bd. Emergency Medicine. Intern Providence Hosp., Seattle, 1972-73; emergency physician Everett (Wash.) Gen., Providence Hosps., 1973-75; pvt. practice Mason City, Iowa, 1976; emergency physician Harrison Meml. Hosp., Bremerton, Wash., 1976—; dir. med. program Kitsap (Wash.) Co. Emergency Med. Svcs., 1986—. Fellow Am. Coll. Emergency Physicians; mem. Am. Heart Assn. (chpt. bd. dirs. 1987—), Nat. Assn. Emergency Physicians, Kitsap Co. Med. Soc., Wash. State Med. Assn, Sierra Club. Home: 142 Alta Dr Bremerton WA 98310 Office: Harrison Meml Hosp 2520 Cherry St Bremerton WA 98310

TIDWELL, JOSEPH PAUL, JR., chief aviation and product safety/flight safety parts program; b. Tuscaloosa, Ala., Oct. 29, 1943; s. Joseph Paul and Jeanette (Steinwinder) T.; m. Susan Kay White, Oct. 3, 1970; children: Joseph Paul III, James Boland, Heather Loran, Shawn Damon. A.S., NYU, 1978, BS, 1984; postgrad. Murray (Ky.) State U., 1984-85, Embry Riddle Aero. U., 1986—. Lic. pilot rotorcraft, cert. safety mgr., safety exec. Commd. aviation ops. officer U.S. Army, 1976, advanced through grades to maj., 1985; aviation safety officer Ft. Campbell, Ky., 1982-85, Chun Chon, Korea, 1981-82; chief aviation and product safety/flight safety parts programs McDonnell Douglas Helicopter, Co., Mesa, Ariz., 1985—. Developer safety engring., safety cons., safety instr. Webelos den leader Clarksville council Cub Scouts Am., Tenn., 1983-85; asst. scout master Clarksville council Boy Scouts Am., 1983-85, scoutmaster Mesa council, 1985—; bd. dirs., vice-chairperson External Affairs S.W. Health and Safety Congress, 1985-86. Decorated Purple Heart, Meritorious Service medal, recipient Den Leaders Tng. Key Middle Tenn. council Boy Scouts Am., 1985, Woodbadge Beads Middle Tenn. Council Boy Scouts Am., 1985. Named Scoutmaster of Yr., Mesa Dist., Theodore Roosevelt Council Boy Scouts Am., 1986, award of merit Mesa Dist. 1988.. Mem. Am. Soc. Safety Engrs. (profl.; Safety Officer of Month award 1985, chmn. awards and elections Ariz. chpt. 1985-87), Army Aviation Assn. Am. (air assault chpt. exec. treas. 1983-85, Aviation Safety Officer of Yr. award 1984), U.S. Army Warrant Officer's Assn. (Ky.-Tenn. chpt. pres. 1984-85, Disting. Service plaque 1984, Cert. of Merit for Disting. Achievement in Youth Leadership Devel. Men of Achievement, Cambridge, Eng., 1987. World Safety Orgn. (affiliate), Internat. Soc. Air Safety Investigators), Aviation Edn. Coun. of Ariz. (com. mem.). Republican. Roman Catholic. Lodge: WIPALA WIKI, Order of Arrow. Avocations: golfing, camping, cycling. Home: 2338 E Javelina St Mesa AZ 85204 Office: McDonnell Douglas Helicopter Co 5000 E McDowell Rd Mesa AZ 85205

TIEDEMANN, DALE MERRIT, infosystems specialist; b. Milw., Dec. 4, 1944; s. Edward H.J. and Dorothy F. (Vedner) T.; m. Dixie L. White, May 2, 1970. AA in Data Processing, Milw. Inst. Tech., 1973; BA in Mgmt., U. Phoenix, 1984. Assoc. systems analyst Globe Union, Milw., 1969-70; programmer, analyst Clark Oil & Refining, Milw., 1970-73; systems analyst Am. Petrofina, Dallas, 1973-77, electronic data processing auditor, 1977-78; cons. Arthur D. Little, Phoenix, 1978-80; mgr. electronic data processing auditing Am. Express, Phoenix, 1980-84; dir. mgmt. info. systems auditing Greyhound Corp., Phoenix, 1984—. Mem. Electronic Data Processors Auditors Assn. (v.p. 1980-82), Info. Systems Security Assn. Office: The Greyhound Corp 111 W Clarendon #817 Phoenix AZ 85077

TIEDMAN, PAUL GERALD, aerospace engineer; b. Syracuse, N.Y., July 7, 1961; s. Alan Clarence and Janet Ann (Marter) T. BA in Computer Sci., SUNY, Potsdam, 1983; MA in Computer Resource Mgmt., Webster U., 1987, MBA, 1988. Software engr. Gen. Electric, Syracuse, 1984-85; engr. Martin Marietta, Denver, 1985-87, sr. engr., 1987--. Home: 3046 G West Prentice Ave Littleton CO 80123 Office: Martin Marietta PO Box 179 Denver CO 80201

TIERNAN, S. GREGORY, educator; b. San Francisco, May 9, 1936; s. Earl Peter and Elisabeth L. (Tichenor) T. BA in Philosophy, Gonzaga U., 1961; MA in English, Loyola U., L.A., 1968; MA in Philosophy, Santa Clara U., 1969. Prof. English West Valley Community Coll., Saratoga, Calif., 1968-74; chmn. philosophy dept., prof. English Mission Coll. of L.A., 1974-76; prof. English, prof. philosophy Santa Clara Mission Coll., 1977—. Co-author: Responsibility of Financial Freedom, 1989; author: Christian Objectivism--A New Lifestyle, 1989, Carrillion, 1989, The Responsibility of Being Financially Free. Founder, pres. Dynamic Christ Leadership Program, 1971—; founder, chmn. Visionaries in Action, San Jose, Calif., 1987—; co-founder, chmn. Ctr. for Responsible Actions, San Jose, 1988—; v.p. Total Image Corp., San Diego, 1982-86; div. v.p. Champions of Pvt. Enterprise, San Diego, 1979-82; assoc. mem. Republican Cen. Com., San Jose, 1973, speakers bur., 1971-73. Named Keynote Speaker, Ariz. Hosp. Assn., 1974. Mem. Faculty Assn. Community Colls. Republican. Home: 806 Jackson St Santa Clara CA 95050 Office: Ctr for Responsible Action 3080 Olcott St 202B Santa Clara CA 95054

TIETZ, WILLIAM JOHN, JR., university president; b. Chgo., Mar. 6, 1927; s. William John and Irma (Neuman) T.; children: Karyn Elizabeth, William John, Julia Wells. BA, Swarthmore Coll., 1950; MS, U. Wis., 1952; DVM, Colo. State U., 1957; PhD, Purdue U., 1961, DSc, 1982. Research assoc. Baxter Labs., Morton Grove, Ill., 1952-53; instr., then assoc. prof. Purdue U., 1957-64; faculty Colo. State U., 1964-77, prof., chmn. physiology and biophysics, 1967-70, v.p. student and univ. relations, 1970-71; dean Colo. State U. (Coll. Vet. Medicine and Biomed. Scis.), 1971-77; assoc. dir. Colo. State U. (Agr. Expt. Sta.), 1975-77; pres. Mont. State U., Bozeman, 1977—; dir. First Bank of Bozeman; mem. Gov.'s Com. on Econ. Devel., 1984—; mem. Mont. Sci. and Tech. Alliance, 1985—; chmn. bd. Intermountain Community Learning and Info. Service, 1987—, NW Commn. of Schs. and Colls., Commn. on Colls., 1982—. Bd. dirs. Children's House, Montessori Sch., 1966-70, chmn., 1968-70; bd. dirs. Colo. State U. Found., 1970-71, Colo. chpt. Am. Cancer Soc., 1976-79; mem. research bd. Denver Zool. Soc., 1975-77; treas. Mont. Energy Research and Devel. Inst., 1977—, v.p., 1978-80, pres., 1981-83; bd. dirs. Greater Mont. Found., 1979—; mem. Mont. Com. for Humanities, 1980-83; mem. div. research resources adv. council NIH, 1979-82; trustee Yellowstone Park Found., 1981—. Served with USNR, 1945-46. Recipient Service award Colo. Vet. Med. Assn., 1976. Mem. Larimer County Vet. Med. Assn. (pres. 1968-69), Am. Assn. Vet. Physiologists and Pharmacologists (pres. 1971-72), Am. Physiol. Soc., Sigma Xi, Phi Zeta (sec.-treas. 1970-71), Assn. Am. Colls. Vet. Medicine (chmn. council of deans 1975-76), Phi Kappa Phi, Phi Sigma Kappa, Omicron Delta Kappa, Beta Beta Beta. Office: Mont State U Office of Pres Bozeman MT 59717 *

TIFFANY, MARIAN CATHERINE, real estate broker, social worker; b. Seattle, Dec. 22, 1919; d. Evald Martiness and Amy Myrtle (Wampler) Petersen; m. William Robert Tiffany, Nov. 5, 1943; children: Susan Margaret, Ruston William (dec.), Lisa Ann Amy, William W. BA in Social Work, U. Wash., 1974. Dir. social svcs. Wash. Villa Care, Inc., Seattle, 1973-74; instr., coord. sr. adult edn. North Seattle Community Coll., 1974-84; real estate saleswoman William Bruce Co., Seattle, 1984-86, Richard James Realtors, Seattle, 1986—; cons. to families of aging parents, Seattle, 1989—. V.p. U. Wash. Faculty Wives, 1966; mem. dept. health Seattle-King County North Social Ctr., 1982-83, chairwoman, 1983-84. Democrat. Methodist. Home: 7076 NE 163d St Bothell WA 98011

TIFFANY, TED WALLACE, school principal; b. Glendale, Calif., Jan. 11, 1935; s. Edward and Marie Tiffany; m. Sue C. Denny, 1954 (div. 1971); children: Randal, Teri, Pam; m. Darlene R. Tang, July 27, 1973; children: Darryn, David. BA, Occidental Coll., 1957; MA, Calif. State U., L.A., 1964. Tchr. jr. high sch. Glendale Unified Sch. Dist., 1957-63, tchr. high sch., 1964-70, football, basketball and golf coach, athletic dir., 1967-70, vice prin. high sch., 1970-75, prin. jr. high sch., 1975-82, prin. high sch., 1982—; mem. Commn. on Athletics, Calif. Community Coll. Assn., 1986-. Trustee Glendale Coll, 1981—, pres., 1989; bd. dirs. Indsl. Edn. Coun., 1983--, Glendale br. Am. Heart Assn. 1987—, Glendale Community Coll. Found., 1984—. Named to Basketball Hall of Fame, Occidental Coll., 1985. Mem. Assn. Calif. Sch. Adminstrs. (charter), Glendale Schs. Mgmt. Assn. (pres. 1977), Glendale C. of C., Occidental Coll. Athletic Alumni Assn. (pres. 1981—), Kiwanis (pres. Glendale 1984-85). Republican. Presbyterian. Office: Glendale Unified Sch Dist 223 N Jackson St Glendale CA 91206

TIGGES, JAMES GENE, space planner, interior designer; b. Estherville, Iowa, June 24, 1962; s. Eugene Vernon and Mary Johanna (Vaske) T. BA with distinction, Iowa State U., 1984. Space planner, prodn. mgr. Archtl. Interiors, Phoenix, 1984-86; pres., prin. Integrated Design Systems Inc., Phoenix, 1986—; condr. space planning seminars, Phoenix, 1987—. Mem. Interior Designers' Efforts for Ariz. Legis., 1987—. Mem. Inst. Bus. Designers, Am. Soc. Interior Designers (exam. chmn. 1988, chpt. presdl. citation 1987). Republican. Roman Catholic. Office: Integrated Design Systems Inc 2141 E Highland Ave #138 Phoenix AZ 85016

TILLERY, BILL W., physics educator; b. Muskogee, Okla., Sept. 15, 1938; s. William Earnest and Bessie C. (Smith) Freeman; m. Patricia Weeks Northrop, Aug. 1, 1981; 1 child, Elizabeth Fielding; children by previous marriage: Tonya Lynn, Lisa Gail. B.S., Northeastern U., 1960; M.A., U. No. Colo., 1965, Ed.D., 1967. Tchr. Guthrie Pub. Schs., Okla., 1960-62; tchr. Jefferson County schs., Colo., 1962-64; teaching asst. U. No. Colo., 1965-67; asst. prof. Fla. State U., 1967-69; assoc. prof. U. Wyo., 1969-73, dir. sci. and math. teaching ctr., 1969-73; assoc. prof. dept. physics Ariz. State U., Tempe, 1973-75, prof., 1976—; cons. in field. Author: (with Ploutz) Basic Physical Science, 1964; (with Sund and Trowbridge) Elementary Science Activities, 1967, Elementary Biological Science, 1970, Elementary Physical Science, 1970, Elementary Earth Science, 1970, Investigate and Discover, 1975; Space, Time, Energy and Matter: Activity Books, 1976; (with Bartholomew) Heath Earth Science, 1984; (with Bartholomew and Gary) Heath Earth Science Activities, 1984, 2d edit. 1987, Heath Earth Science Teacher Resource Book, 1987, Heath Earth Science Laboratory Activity, 1987; editor Ariz. Sci. Tchrs. Jour., 1975—, Ariz. Energy Edn., 1978—. Fellow AAAS; mem. Nat. Sci. Tchrs. Assn., Ariz. Sci. Tchrs. Assn., Assn. Edn. of Tchrs. in Sci., Nat. Assn. Research in Sci. Teaching. Republican. Episcopalian. Home: 8986 S Forest Ave Tempe AZ 85284 Office: Ariz State U Dept Physics Tempe AZ 85287

TILLSON, STEPHEN ALFRED, endocrinologist; b. Flint, Mich., Dec. 29, 1940; s. Harry Alfred and Mary Eva (Hartwig) T.; m. Judith Ann Osterloh, Dec. 30, 1961 (div. June 1978); children: David Alfred, Michael Thomas; m. Elizabeth Tiebout, Nov. 28, 1985. BS, Calif. State Poly Coll., Pomona, 1962; MS, U. Mo., 1965; PhD, Purdue U., 1969; MBA, St. Mary's Coll., 1988. Postdoctoral fellow Worcester Found., Shrewsbury, Mass., 1970; dir. toxicology Alza Corp., Palo Alto, Calif., 1970-78; dir. lab. Cen. Ariz. Vet. Lab., Casa Grande, 1978-81; mgr. clins. Syntex Med. Diagnostics, Palo Alto, 1981—; cons. Los Olivos Med. Lab., Los Gatos, Calif., 1982-84. Author: Immunologic Methods in Steroid Determination, 1970, Research on Steroids IV, 1970, Advances in Steroid Biochemistry and Pharmacology, 1974, Clinical Experience with the Progesterone Uterine Therapeutic System, 1978. Mem. AAAS, Soc. Study Reproduction, N.Y. Acad. Sci., Endocrine Soc., Pacific Coast Fertility Soc. Republican. Baptist. Home: 409 F Cork Harbour Circle Redwood City CA 94065 Office: Syntex Diagnostics 900 Arastradero Rd Palo Alto CA 94304

TILSWORTH, TIMOTHY, environmental and civil engineering educator; b. Norfolk, Nebr., Apr. 6, 1939; s. Brooke and Mildred (Palmer) T.; m. Joanne Novak, Apr. 19, 1966 (div. Jan. 1984); children: Craig Scott, Patrick Joseph; m. Debbie J. May, July 20, 1984. BSCE, U. Nebr., Lincoln, 1967; PhD, U. Kans, 1970. Registered profl. engr., Alaska. Instr. U. Nebr., Lincoln, 1967; prof. environ. quality and civil engring. U. Alaska, Fairbanks, 1970—, asst. to pres. for acad. affairs, 1976-78; owner Alaska Arctic Environ. Services, Fairbanks, 1972—, DJT's Shelties Delight, Fairbanks, 1985—; project mgr. superconducting super collider proposal State of Alaska, Fairbanks, 1987-88. Chmn. exec. com. Cowper for Gov. Alaska, Fairbanks, 1986. Recipient commendation State of Alaska, 1988. Mem. Assn. for Environ. Engring. Profs., ASCE (Outstanding Service award 1975), Am. Water Works Assn. Water Pollution Control Fedn., Chi Epsilon. Roman Catholic. Home: 1900 Raven Dr Fairbanks AK 99709 Office: U Alaska Civil Engring Dept 306 Tanana Dr Fairbanks AK 99775

TILTON, BARRY CHRISTOPHER, electrical engineer; b. Lubbock, Tex., May 29, 1963; s. Frederick Elmore and Julia (Pilgrim) T.; m. Rebecca Rene Rust, Aug. 23, 1986. BS in Elec. Engring., U. So. Calif., 1985; postgrad., Northrop U., 1988. Commd. 1st lt. USAF, 1985; project officer Space div. USAF, El Segundo, Calif., 1985-87, engr. space based interceptor program, 1987-88; staff phenomenologist space based interceptor program USAF, Lawndale, Calif., 1987-88; staff action officer comdrs. action group USAF, Los Angeles, 1988—; chmn. steering group Space Based Interpretor Phenomenology, El Segundo, 1987-88; mem. steering group Strategic Def. Initiative Office Phenomenology, Washington, 1987-88. Mem. IEEE, Soc. Photo-Optic Instrument Engrs., Air Force Assn., The Planetary Soc. Republican. Home: 20553 S Vermont St Apt 4 Torrance CA 90502 Office: USAF SD/CSX 92960 PO Box 92960 Los Angeles CA 90005

TILTON, RONALD WILLIAM, naval officer; b. Brookline, Mass., Dec. 28, 1944; s. John Walter and Audrey Muriel (Rice) T.; m. Eve April Cushing, May 12, 1982 (div. 1984). BA in Mgmt., Jacksonville U., 1967; cert., Naval War Coll., 1979, Air U., 1985; MS in Systems Mgmt., U. Southern Calif., 1985. Commd. ens. USN, 1967, advanced through grades to comdr., 1982; sr. pilot evaluator Atlantic Fleet Patrol Squadron Thirty, Jacksonville, Fla., 1975-78; patrol plane comdr., maintenance officer Patrol Squadron 17, Barbers Point, Hawaii, 1980-82; ops. and plans officer Commander in Chief Pacific, Camp H.M. Smith, Hawaii, 1982-84; comptroller Naval Air Sta., Barbers Point, 1984-86; exec. officer, chief test pilot NAVPRO, Lockheed Aero. Systems Co., Burbank, Calif., 1986—. Loaned exec. United Way, Jacksonville, 1975. Mem. Naval Air Exec. Inst., Order of Daedalians, Phi Delta Theta. Republican. Home: PO Box 10031 Burbank CA 91510-0031 Office: NAVPRO Lockheed Aero System PO Box 551 Burbank CA 91520

TILUS, DARRELL DUANE, electrical engineer; b. Buffalo, S.D., May 5, 1943; s. Waino and Anna Mary Tilus; m. Nancy Lee Barlow, Aug. 29, 1964; children: Duane Tod, Troy Darrell. BSEE, Mich. Tech. U., 1967; MA, Webster U., St. Louis, 1978. Avionics engr. Trans World Airlines, Kansas City, Mo., 1967-70, project elec. engr., 1972-86; elec. engr. Black & Veatch Cons. Engrs., Kansas City, 1971-72; sr. quality engr. McDonnell Douglas Helicopter Co., Mesa, Ariz., 1986-87, mem. tech. staff IV elec. design engr., 1987—. Active Nashua Sch. Bldg. Com., Kansas City, 1973-75; mem. bldg. com. Northland Cathedral Ch., Kansas City, 1970-75; dir. edn. Tiffany Fellowship Ch., Kansas City, 1979-84, bd. dirs., 1984-86; bd. dirs. Red Mountain Christian Ctr., Mesa, 1989—. Mem. IEEE. Republican. Mem. Assembly of God Ch. Home: 2668 E Fountain St Mesa AZ 85213 Office: McDonnell Douglas Helicopter Co 5000 E McDowell Rd Mesa AZ 85205

TIMM, JERRY ROGER, retail grocery chain executive; b. Nampa, Idaho, Apr. 16, 1942; s. Sheldon A. and Beulah M. (Bell) T.; m. Wandalee Miller, June 22, 1963; children—Bryan Lee, Michelle Ann. B.S. in Acctg, U. Idaho, 1965; student, Stanford Fin. Mgmt. Program, 1986. C.P.A., Idaho. With Touche Ross & Co. (C.P.A.), 1965-73; mgr. Touche Ross & Co. (C.P.A.), Boise, Idaho, 1973; asst. controller to controller corp. div. Albertson's, Inc., Boise, 1973-76; controller Albertson's, Inc., 1976-81, v.p. and controller, 1981—; pres., dir. Albertson's Fed. Credit Union, 1976-84; past chmn. Idaho Bd. Accountancy. Bd. dirs. Boise Family YMCA, 1978-81; chmn., dir. Boise chpt. ARC, 1986—; campaign chmn. United Way of ADA County, Inc., 1985, pres. elect 1986, pres. 1987; bd. dirs. Associated Taxpayers of Idaho, Inc., 1983—. Mem. Am. Inst. C.P.A.s, Nat. Assn. Accts. (past pres. Boise chpt.), Idaho Soc. C.P.A.s. Lutheran. Lodges: Boise Capital Lions (pres. 1970-83), Boise Sunrise Rotary (v.p. 1984—). Office: Albertson's Inc PO Box 20 Boise ID 83726

TIMMERHAUS, KLAUS DIETER, chemical engineering educator; b. Mpls., Sept. 10, 1924; s. Paul P. and Elsa L. (Bever) T.; m. Jean L. Mevis, Aug. 3, 1952; 1 dau., Carol Jane. BS in Chem. Engring, U. Ill., 1948, MS, 1949, PhD, 1951. Registered profl. engr., Colo. Process design engr. Calif. Rsch. Corp., Richmond, 1952-53; extension lectr. U. Calif., Berkeley, 1952; mem. faculty U. Colo., 1953—, prof. chem. engring., 1961—, asso. dean engring., 1963-86, dir. engring. rsch. ctr. coll. engring., 1963-86, chmn. aerospace dept., 1979-80, chmn. chem. engring. dept., 1986—; chem. engr. cryogenics lab. Nat. Bur. Standards, Boulder, summers 1955,57,59,61; lectr. U. Calif. at L.A., 1961-62; sect. head engring. div. NSF, 1972-73; cons. in field. Bd. dirs. Colo. Engring. Expt. Sta., Inc., Engring. Measurements Co., both Boulder. Editor: Advances in Cryogenic Engineering, vols. 1-25, 1954-80; co-editor: Internat. Cryogenic Monograph Series, 1965—. Served with USNR, 1944-46. Recipient Disting. Svc. award Dept. Commerce, 1957; Samuel C. Collins award outstanding contbns. to cryogenic tech., 1967; George Westinghouse award, 1968; Alpha Chi Sigma award for chem. engring. rsch., 1968; Meritorious Svc. award Cryogenic Engring. Conf., 1967; R.L. Stearns Profl. Achievement award U. Colo., 1981; Disting. Pub. Svc. award NSF, 1984. Fellow AAAS; mem. Nat. Acad. Engring., Am. Astron. Soc., Am. Inst. Chem. Engrs. (v.p. 1975, pres. 1976, Founders award 1978, Eminent Chem. Engr. award 1983, W. K. Lewis award 1987), Am. Soc. for Engring. Edn. (bd. dirs. 1986-88, 3M Chem Engring. div. award 1980), Internat. Inst. Refrigeration (v.p. 1979-87, pres. 1987—, U.S. nat. commn. 1983—, pres. 1983-86, W.T. Pentzer award 1989), Austrian Acad. Sci., Cryogenic Engring. Conf. (chmn. 1956-67, bd. dirs. 1956—), Sigma Xi (v.p. 1986-87, pres. 1987-88, bd. dirs. 1981-89), Sigma Tau, Tau Beta Pi, Phi Lambda Upsilon. Home: 905 Brooklawn Dr Boulder CO 80303

TIMMINS, JAMES DONALD, investment banker; b. Hamilton, Ont., Can., Oct. 3, 1955; came to U.S., 1979; s. Donald G. and Myrna L. (Seymour) T. BA, U. Toronto, 1977; JD, Queen's U., 1979; MBA, Stanford U., 1981. Investment banker Wood Gundy, Toronto, 1980, Salomon Bros., San Francisco, 1981-84; mng. dir. and chief exec. officer McKewon & Timmins, San Diego, 1984-87; ptnr. Hambrecht & Quist, San Francisco, 1987—. Mem. Olympic Club of San Francisco. Home: 402 Stephen Rd San Mateo CA 94403 Office: Hambrecht & Quist 1 Bush St San Francisco CA 94104

TIMMINS, WILLIAM MONTANA, II, management educator; b. Salt Lake City, Mar. 13, 1936; s. William Montana and Mary Brighton T.; m. Theda Laws, Oct. 14, 1960; children: William Montana III, Clark Brighton, Laurel, Sally, Rebekah. BS, U. Utah, 1960, PhD, 1972; MA, Harvard U., 1962; postdoctoral student, UCLA, 1973. Asst. to gov. State of Utah, Salt Lake City, 1966-69; asst. v.p. U. Utah, Salt Lake City, 1969-71; dir. interstate projects Utah Bd. Edn., Salt Lake City, 1971-74; prof. mgmt. Brigham Young U., Provo, Utah, 1974—; chmn. of bd. TCI, Inc., Paris; vice chmn. Pioneer Valley Hosp., West Valley, Utah, 1985-88; chmn. Mountain View Hosp., Payson, Utah; bd. dirs. Nat. Congress Hosp. Governing Bds., Washington, 1984-88. Author: Career Education (vols. I and II), 1971, Guide to Improved Employee Relations, 1984, International Economic Policy Coordination, 1985, Nonsmoking in the Workplace, 1989; editor: Comprehensive Educational Planning, 1972; contbr. articles to profl. jours. Chmn. Salt Lake County Youth Services Ctr., 1979-80. Recipient Silver Beaver award Boy Scouts Am., 1974, Carnation Silver Bowl Community Services Council, 1978; Redd fellow Redd Ctr. Brigham Young U., 1982. Mem. Utah Hosp. Assn. Salt Lake City (trustee 1985—, Outstanding Trustee award 1988), Am. Soc. Pub. Adminstrn. (bd. dirs. 1983-85, com. mem. 1981-86), Soc. Profls. in Dispute Resolution, Am. Arbitration Assn., Nat. Assn. Civil Service Commrs. (hon., life, pres. 1982-83), Rocky Mountain Pub. Employer Labor Relations Assn. (v.p. 1980-83), Utah Assn. Civil Service Commrs. (pres. 1979-80), Internat. Personnel Mgmt. Assn. (publs. com. 1985—), Phi Kappa Phi. Republican. Mormon. Office: Brigham Young U 772 Tanner Bldg Provo UT 84602

TIMMONS, WILLIAM MILTON, cinema arts educator; b. Houston, Apr. 21, 1933; s. Carter Charles and Gertrude Monte (Lee) T.; m. Pamela Cadorette, Dec. 24, 1975 (div. 1977). BS, U. Houston, 1958; MA, UCLA, 1961; PhD, U. So. Calif., 1975. Child actor Houston Jr. Theater, 1945-46; staff announcer Sta. KMCO, Conroe, Tex., 1951-52; prodn. asst. Sta. KUHT-TV, Houston, 1953-54, 56-57; teaching fellow UCLA, 1960-61; ops. asst. CBS-TV, Hollywood, Calif., 1961-62; prof. speech and drama Sam Houston State U., Huntsville, Tex., 1963-67; chmn. dept. cinema Los Angeles Valley Coll., Van Nuys, Calif., 1970—; producer Sta. KPFK, Los Angeles, 1959-60, 1983—; pub. Acad. Assocs., L.A., 1976—; proofreader, cons. Focal Press Pub. Co., N.Y.C., 1983—. Author: Orientation to Cinema, 1986; contbr. articles to mags.; producer, dir.: (radio program) Campus Comments, 1963-67, numerous ednl. films, 1963—. Mem. Am. Rationalists Assn., St. Louis, 1974, Com. for Sci. Investigation of Claims of the Paranormal, Los Angeles, 1976, Humanist Friendship Ctr., Los Angeles, 1987. Served with USNR, 1954-56. Named Hon. Tex. Ranger, State of Tex., Austin, 1946; U. Houston scholar, 1957. Mem. Am. Fedn. Tchrs., Soc. Motion Picture and TV Engrs., Assn. for Ednl. and Communications Tech., Am. Film Inst., Univ. Film and Video Assn., Assn. Visual Communicators, Soc. for Scholary Pub., Mensa, U. So. Calif. Cinema-TV Alumni Assn., Red Masque Players, Alpha Epsilon Rho, Delta Kappa Alpha. Democrat. Office: LA Valley Coll 5800 Fulton Ave Van Nuys CA 91401

TIMMRECK, JOE EDWARD, data processor; b. Longview, Wash., Oct. 8, 1950; s. Carmin C. and Betty (Snyder) T.; m. Janet Clipp; 1 dau., Jennifer. A.A. in Computer Sci., Lower Columbia Coll., 1970; student Weber State Coll., 1971-74. Engr. technician Ultrasystems, Ogden, Utah, 1973-75; system programmer St. Benedict's Hosp., Ogden, 1975-77; system analyst Jackson County (Oreg.), 1978-79; data processing mgr. Medford (Oreg.) Sch. Dist. 549C, 1979-83; writer, bus. cons. The Key Found., Point Roberts, Wash., 1987—. Founder, pres. Human Potentials Unltd., Medford, 1981-87; pub. The Obelisk, Medford, 1982-87. Mem. Am. Mgmt. Assn., Oreg. Assn. Ednl. Data Systems. Home and Office: 1905 Province Rd Point Roberts WA 98281

TIMMRECK, THOMAS C., health sciences and health administration educator; b. Montpelier, Idaho, June 15, 1946; s. Archie Carl and Janone (Jensen) T.; m. Ellen Prusse, Jan. 27, 1971; children: Chad Thomas, Benjamin Brian, Julie Anne. AA, Ricks Coll., 1968; BS, Brigham Young U., 1971; MEd, Oreg. State U., 1972; MA, No. Ariz. U., 1981; PhD, U. Utah, 1976. Program dir. Cache County Aging Program, Logan, Utah, 1972-73; asst. prof. div. health edn. Tex. Tech U., Lubbock, 1976-77; asst. prof. dept. health care adminstrn. Idaho State U., Pocatello, 1977-78; program dir., asst. prof. health services program No. Ariz. U., Flagstaff, 1978-84; cons., dir. grants Beth Israel Hosp., Denver, 1985; assoc. prof. dept. health scis. and human ecology, coordinator grad. studies, coordinator health adminstrn. and planning Calif. State U., San Bernardino, 1985—; pres. Health Care Mgmt. Assocs., 1985—; presenter at nat. confs. Author: Dictionary of Health Services Management, rev. 2d edit., 1987, editorial bd. Jour. Health Values, 1986—; contbr. numerous articles on health care adminstrn. to profl. jours. Vice chmn., bd. dirs. Inland Counties Health System Agy. Served with U.S. Army, 1966-72, Vietnam. Mem. Assn. Advancement of Health Edn., Am. Acad. Mgmt., Assn. Univ. Programs in Health Care Adminstrn., Healthcare Forum. Republican. Mormon. Office: Calif State U Dept Health Scis and Human Ecology San Bernardino CA 92407

TINAGLIA, MICHAEL ANTHONY, graphic designer; b. Chgo., June 14, 1962; s. Anthony John and Rose (Morano) T.; m. Jennifer Anne Johannes, Nov. 30, 1985; 1 child, Joshua Michael. Student, Bethany Coll., 1981-82, Wichita State U., 1982. Security officer RTL Investigations, Boulder, Colo., 1982-83; acct. exec. D&K Printing, Inc., Boulder, Colo., 1983-85; asst. coach Boulder High Sch., 1985; v.p. sales Edison Press, Inc., Englewood, Colo., 1985-86; pres. Hesdorfer Assocs, Denver, 1986-87; owner, exec. Tinaglia Design, Denver, 1987—. Graphic artist: Internat. V II, 1987, U.S Olympic Com., Denver, 1989; creative dir.: Internat. V VIII, 1988. Vol. Boys Clubs Metro Denver, 1988. Recipient Harry C. Eckoff award Nat. Golf Found., 1988. Republican. Mem. Evang. Free Ch. Office: Tinaglia Design 6505 E Amherst Ave Denver CO 80224

TINDLE, CHARLES DWIGHT WOOD, broadcasting company executive; b. Bryn Mawr, Pa., Jan. 13, 1950; s. Charles Wood and Nancy (Sapp) T. Student, Kenyon Coll., 1968-71. Pres. Dwight Karma Broadcasting, Mesa, Ariz., 1971-76, Natural Broadcasting System, Mesa, 1976-79; producer, fellow Am. Film Inst. Ctr. for Advanced Film Studies, 1979-80; pres. Network 30, Scottsdale, Ariz., 1985—; owner Sta. KDKB-AM-FM, Mesa, Sta. KSML-FM, Lake Tahoe, Calif., Sta. KNOT-AM-FM, Prescott, Ariz., Sta. KBWA, Williams, Ariz. Recipient Peabody award U. Ga., 1976. Republican. Episcopalian. Home: 4959 E Red Rock Dr Phoenix AZ 85018 Office: Network 30 Inc 4416 N Scottsdale Rd #605 Scottsdale AZ 85251

TINKER, GRANT A., broadcasting executive; b. Stamford, Conn., Jan. 11, 1926. Student, Dartmouth Coll. With radio program dept. NBC, 1949-54; TV dept. McCann-Erickson Advt. Agy., 1954-58, Benton & Bowles Advt. Agy., 1958-61; v.p.-programs West Coast, NBC, 1961-66; v.p. in charge programming West Coast, NBC, N.Y.C., 1966-67; v.p. Universal TV, 1968-69, 20th-Fox, 1969-70; pres. Mary Tyler Moore (MTM) Enterprises, Inc., Studio City, Calif., 1970-81; chmn. bd., chief exec. officer NBC, Burbank, Calif., 1981-86; independent producer Burbank, Calif., 1986—. Office: care NBC-TV 3000 W Alameda Blvd Burbank CA 91523 *

TINNIN, THOMAS PECK, real estate professional; b. Albuquerque, May 15, 1948; s. Robert Priest and Frances (Ferree) T.; m. Jamie Tinnin Garrett, Dec. 12, 1986; 1 child, Megan Ashley. Student, U. Md., 1969-72; BA, U. N.Mex., 1973. Ins. agt. Occidental Life of Calif., Albuquerque, 1972-78; gen. agt. Transamerica-Occidental Life, Albuquerque, 1978—; pres. Tinnin Investments, Albuquerque, 1978—, Tinnin Enterprises, Albuquerque, 1978—, Tinnin Real Estate & Devel., Albuquerque, 1989—; mem. N.Mex. State Bd. Fin., Santa Fe, 1985-87; del., White House Conf. on Small Bus., Washington, 1986; bd. dirs. Albuquerque Econ. Devel., 1987-88. Bd. dirs., St. Joseph's Hosp., Albuquerque, 1984-86; pres. N.Mex. Jr. Livestock Investment Found., Albuquerque, 1988—. Mem. N.Mex. Life Leaders Assn., Albuquerque C. of C. (bd. dirs. 1978-84), N.Mex. Life Underwriters Assn., Albuquerque Country Club. Republican. Presbyterian. Home: 2312 Calle de Estavan Albuquerque NM 87104 Office: Tinnin Enterprises 20 First Pla Ste 518 Albuquerque NM 87110

TIPPMAN, PAMELA CANDIECE, museum executive; b. Amityville, N.Y., Jan. 7, 1950; d. Scott and Eleanor Josephine Tippman. BFA in Sculpture, Calif. State U.-Long Beach, 1976, teaching credential, 1978, museology cert., 1985. Tchr. Bolsa Grande High Sch., Garden Grove, Calif., 1979-80; substitute tchr. Garden Grove Unified Sch. Dist., 1980-85; intern Met. Mus. Art, N.Y.C., 1985; photog. svcs. sec., rights and reprodns. asst. L.A. County Mus. Art, 1985-87, asst. registrar outgoing loans, 1987--; tchr. ceramics Beverly Hills (Calif.) Adult Sch., 1986--. Photographer: Rip Rap, 1984; author: Anders Zorn Rediscovered, 1985. Mem. Am. Assn. Mus. (registrar's com. western region 1987--). Office: LA County Mus Art 5905 Wilshire Blvd Los Angeles CA 90036

TIPPY, ALAN CLAY, banker; b. Albuquerque, Nov. 6, 1953; s. Marshall Wayne and Dorothy Nell (Matthews) T. BA with distinction, U. N.Mex., 1976; M. Internat. Mgmt., Am. Grad. Sch. Internat. Mgmt., Glendale, Ariz., 1979. Asst. mgr., diamond gemologist Feathers Jewelers, Albuquerque, 1977-78; diamond gemologist Grunewald and Adams, Scottsdale, Ariz., 1980; front office supr. Sheraton Palace Hotel, San Francisco, 1980-84; adminstrn. mgr. Bank of Am., San Francisco, 1985—. Mem. The Experiment in Internat. Living, Fed. Republic Germany, 1971. Mem. Gemological Inst. Am. (cert.), San Francisco Ballet Assn., San Francisco Opera Guild, Phi Alpha Theta. Libertarian. Presbyterian. Home: 26 Carl St San Francisco CA 94117 Office: Bank of Am BASE Div 2000 Clayton Rd Concord CA 94520

TIPTON, GARY LEE, personal services company executive; b. Salem, Oreg., July 3, 1941; s. James Rains and Dorothy Velma (Dierks) T.; BS, Oreg. Coll. Edn., 1964. Credit rep. Standard Oil Co. Calif., Portland, Oreg., 1964-67; credit mgr. Uniroyal Inc., Dallas, 1967-68; partner, mgr. bus. Tipton Barbers, Portland, 1968—. Mem. Rep. Nat. Com., 1980—, Sen. Howard Baker's Presdl. Steering Com., 1980; apptd. Deputy Dir. Gen., Internat. Biog. Ctr., Cambridge, England, 1987—; mem. U.S. Congl. adv. bd. Am. Security Council, 1984-88. Recipient Key to Internat. Biog. Cen., Cambridge, U.K., 1983, World Culture prize Accademia Italia, 1984, Presdl. Achievement award, 1982, cert. disting. contbn. Sunset High Sch. Dad's Club, 1972, 73. Fellow Internat. Biog. Assn. (life, Key award 1983) (U.K.); mem. Sunset Mchts. Assn. (co-founder, treas. 1974-79, pres. 1982-83), Internat. Platform Assn., Smithsonian Assocs., Council on Fgn. Relations (vice chmn. steering com. Portland 1983-84, chmn. Portland com. on fgn. relations 1984-86), UN Assn. (steering com. UN day 1985). Office: Tipton Barbers 1085 NW Murray Rd Portland OR 97229

TIPTON, JAMES CEAMON, resort executive; b. Ardmore, Okla., Jan. 8, 1939; s. James Marcus Tipton and Georgia Muriel (Terrell) Freiberger; m. Ruth Eve Green, May 1, 1971; children by previous marriage: Martha, Marcus. BA in Bus., East Cen. U., 1961. Contr. Aetna Life & Casualty Co., various locations, 1962-72; pension regional mgr. Aetna Life & Casualty Co., Oakland, Calif., 1972-74; pension mgr. Aetna Life & Casualty Co., Salt Lake City, 1974-77, San Jose, Calif., 1974-77; owner, mgr. Valhalla Resort and Vacation Homes, Estes Park, Colo., 1981—. With U.S. Army, 1961. Mem. Estes Park Accommodations Assn. (pres., bd. dirs. 1986-87). Republican. Methodist. Home and Office: PO Box 1439 Estes Park CO 80517

TISCHNER, RICHARD LAWRENCE, aeronautic engineer; b. Balt., Sept. 1, 1950; s. Eric and Ruth Marie (Hohlweg) T.; m. Marie Ellen Hartsock, Oct. 11, 1986. BS, Va. Poly. Inst., 1972, MS, 1974. Mem. tech. staff space div. Rockwell Internat., Downey, Calif., 1974—. Mem. AIAA, Sierra Club. Democrat. Methodist. Office: Rockwell Internat 12214 Lakewood Blvd Downey CA 90241

TISDALE, DOUGLAS MICHAEL, lawyer; b. Detroit, May 3, 1949; s. Charles Walker and Violet Lucille (Battani) T.; m. Patricia Claire Brennan, Dec. 29, 1972; children—Douglas Michael, Jr., Sara Elizabeth, Margaret Patricia, Victoria Claire. B.A. in Psychology with honors, U. Mich., 1971, J.D., 1975. Bar: Colo. 1975, U.S. Dist. Ct. Colo. 1975, U.S. Ct. Appeals (10th cir.) 1976, U.S. Supreme Ct. 1979. Law clk. to chief judge U.S. Dist. Ct. Colo., Denver, 1975-76; assoc. Brownstein, Hyatt, Farber & Madden, P.C., Denver, 1976-81, ptnr., 1981-87, dir., 1988—; bd. dirs. Warner Devels., Inc., Vail, Colo.; lectr. Law Seminars, Inc., 1984—, Continuing Legal Edn. in Colo., Inc., 1984—, Nat. Bus. Insts., 1985—, ABA Nat. Insts. 1988; Colo. Law-Related Edn. Coordinator, 1982-88. Mem. ABA (mem. litigation sect. trial evidence com. 1981—, vice chmn. real property sect. com. on enforcement of creditors rights and bankruptcy 1984—, vice chmn. real property sect. com. on pub. edn. concerning the lawyers role 1984-87, chmn. 1987—, chmn. real property sect. sub-com. on foreclosures in bankruptcy 1982—), Colo. Bar Assn. (conv. com. 1979-88), Denver Bar Assn. (jud. adminstrn. com. 1978—), Am. Judicature Soc., Assn. Trial Lawyers Am., Colo. Trial Lawyers Assn., Law Club of Denver (sec. 1984-85), Phi Alpha Delta, Phi Beta Kappa. Democrat. Roman Catholic. Home: 4662 S Elizabeth Ct Cherry Hills Village CO 80110 Office: Brownstein Hyatt Farber & Madden 410 17th St Denver CO 80202

TISS, GEORGE JOHN, pediatrician, educator; b. Weiser, Idaho, Aug. 24, 1925; s. George Joseph and Mildred Gwendolyn (Barham) T.; m. Catherine Cassady, June 6, 1968; children: Randy, Carolyn, Danny, Mary, Andy. BS, U. Oreg., 1950, MD, 1954. Diplomate Am. Bd. Pediatrics. Intern U. Oreg. Hosps. and Clinics, Portland, 1954-55, resident in pediatrics, 1955-57; practice medicine specializing in pediatrics Visalia (Calif.) Med. Clinic, 1957—, chmn. bd., 1959-70; specialist Care Medico, Malaysia, 1969, Indonesia, 1976; specialist Managua, Nicaragua, 1979; cons. Keweah Delta Dist. Hosp., Visalia, Tulare (Calif.) Dist. Hosp., Tulare County Hosp.; chmn. 1st Rubella mass immunization program in U.S., Tulare, 1969; chmn. Visalia Comprehensive Health Planning Bd., 1973-74; mem. bd. consortium San Joaquin Valley, 1975—; co-chmn. Calif. Immunization adv. com., 1973-76, chmn., 1976-77, chmn. Toddler Immunization adv. com., Calif., 1983—; asst. clin. prof. pediatrics U. Calif., San Francisco. Mem. sch. bd. Liberty Sch., 1980—. Served with USAAF, 1945-46. Recipient Lyda M. Smiley award Calif. Assn. Sch. Nurses, 1981. Mem. AMA, Calif. Med. Assn., Tulare County Med. Soc. (pres. 1969-70), Am. Acad. Pediatrics, West Coast Allergy Soc., L.A. Pediatric Soc., Calif. Thoracic Soc., Am. Legion. Am. Coll. Allergy, Christian Med. Soc. (missions to Mex. 1987, Dominican Republic 1988). Office: 5400 W Hillsdale Rd Visalia CA 93277

TO, TERESA HELLEN, accountant; b. Saigon, Vietnam, Nov. 11, 1962; came to U.S., 1978; d. Tan and Dung Thieu (Giang) T. B in Acctg., Wichita State U., 1985. CPA, Kans. Sales assoc. Dillard's Dept. Store, Wichita, Kans., 1981-84; software programmer Burroughs Corp., Wichita, 1984-85; staff acct. Kirkpatrick, Sprecker & Co., Wichita, 1985-87; tax cons. Ernst & Whinney, L.A., 1987-89, sr. tax cons., 1989—. Mem. AICPA. Home: 712 E Ross Ave Alhambra CA 91801 Office: Ernst & Whinney 515 S Flower Ste 2800 Los Angeles CA 90071

TOADVINE, JOANNE ELIZABETH, physical therapy foundation executive; b. Covington, Ky., Nov. 29, 1933; d. Ralph and Myrtle (Wasson) Bailer; children: Daniel, Michael, Patrick, Michell, Joseph. Student, St. Benedict Coll. Bus. Sch., 1948; PhD, U. for Humanistic Studies, Las Vegas, Nev., 1986. Cert. rehab. technician in functional elec. stimulation, Nev. Founder, pres. Help Them Walk Again Found., Inc., Las Vegas, 1976—. Contbr. articles to profl. jours. Mem. State of Nev. Dem. Cen. Com., Clark Clunty (Nev.) Dem. Cen. Com. Recipient Humanitarian award Chiropractic Assn. of Ariz., Channel 3 Spirit award, Humanitarian award Dr. Otto Kestler; named to Honorable Order Ky. Colonels, Mother of Yr. Clark County, 1988. Mem. Am. Acad. of Neurol. Orthopedic Surgeons (nat. coordinating council on spinal cord injury), Nat. Coordinating Coun. on Spinal Cord Injury, Las Vegas C. of C. (Women's Achievement award in health care), VFW, NAFE, The Pilot Club Internat. Office: Help Them Walk Again Found 5300 W Charleston Blvd Las Vegas NV 89102

TOBEY, MICHAEL EARL, manufacturing executive; b. Pasadena, Calif., Oct. 31, 1943; s. J. Earl and Andrée (DeCuyas) T.; m. Cheryl Ewbank, 1966 (div. 1973); children: Gregory, Tina; m. Susan J. Zavick, Aug. 9, 1974; 1 child, Brian. AA in Police Sci., Los Angeles Valley Coll., 1969; BA in Pub. Adminstrn., Calif. State U., Los Angeles, 1972. Police officer Glendale (Calif.) Police Dept., 1966-69; investigator Los Angeles County Dist. Atty., 1969-81; pres. Custom Racing Products, Inc., Atascadero, Calif., 1981—. Mem. Atascadero Planning Commn., 1988—. Served with USN, 1964-66, Vietnam. Mem. Radio Control Car Mfrs. Assn. (pres. 1985-87), Radio Control Hobby Trade Assn. (v.p. 1986—). Republican. Lodges: Elks, Rotary. Office: Custom Racing Products Inc 3250 El Camino Real Atascadero CA 93422

TOBIAS, CHRISTOPHER ORD, software company executive; b. Phila., Aug. 17, 1962; s. Joel Allen Tobias and Lucy Cresap (Beebe) T. Student, Reed Coll., 1980-82. Mgr. DaVinci Personal Tech., Portland, Oreg., 1982-84, Computer One, Portland, 1984-85; ptnr. PC Profls., Portland, 1985-87; devel. mgr. Somex, Lake Oswego, Oreg., 1987—; bd. dirs. Oreg. Computer Cons., Portland, 1986-87. Contbr. articles to profl. jours. Mem. Am. Seed Trade Assn. Office: Somex 587 SW 3d Lake Oswego OR 97034

TOBIAS, CYNTHIA LEE, data processing executive; b. Dayton, Ohio, July 6, 1945; d. Raymond Wilbur and Dorothy Virginia Tobias; m. Riaz Ahmed Gondal, July 4, 1981. BS in Lang., Georgetown U., 1967; MA in Sociology, U. Chgo., 1969, PhD, 1977; MS in Indsl. Engring., U. Ariz., 1986. Lectr. Bayero U., Kano, Nigeria, 1977-78; cons. 1979—; research assoc. U. Ariz., Tucson, 1984-87, dir. Office Med. Computing, Coll. Medicine, 1987—. Contbr. articles to profl. jours. NIMH fellow, 1969-72, OAS fellow, 1975-76. Mem. Am. Sociol. Assn., Inst. Indsl. Engrs., Human Factors Soc. (treas. 1988—), Soc. Women Engrs. (v.p. 1987-88). Democrat. Home: PO Box 42064 Tucson AZ 85733

TOBIN, KIEFER A., acoustical engineer, consultant; b. Honolulu, Oct. 24, 1937; s. Albert and Mary Helen (Jordan) T.; m. Sharlene Tobin, June 23, 1960; children: Mari, Kerri, Shawn. BS, Oreg. State U., 1960; MS, Naval Postgrad. Sch., 1977. Ensign U.S. Navy, 1960, mgr. submarine silencing program, 1977-80, ret., 1980; sr. engr., scientist Tracr Inc., Austin, Tex., 1980-84; pres. W. Sound Assocs., Bremerton, Wash., 1984—; instr. Chapman Coll., Silverdale, Wash., 1982—. Mem. Acoustical Soc. Am. (pres. NW chpt. 1982-83). Lodge: Rotary. Office: West Sound Assocs 202 Pacific Ave Bremerton WA 98310

TOBIN, ROBERT MANFORD, JR., karate educator; b. Idaho Falls, Idaho, Feb. 17, 1958; s. Robert Manford and Marilyn Hilma (Harju) T. BS in Fin. and Acctg., U. Colo., 1979. Asst. instr. taekwon-do U. Colo., Boulder, 1977-85, head instr., 1985—, instr. basketball team, 1985-88; fin. mgr. Tobin Engrs. & Constructors, Longmont, Colo., 1979-80, gen. mgr., 1981-82; gen. mgr. Roofguard of Colo., Longmont, 1981-83; oximetry researcher Biox-B.T.I.-Ohmeda Boulder, Boulder and Louisville, Colo., 1984—; instr. Sereff Taekwo-Do, Broomfield, Colo., 1984-85. Contbr. articles to various publs. Del. Colo. Dem. Com., 1980, Boulder County Dem. Com., 1984. Mem. U.S. Taekwon-Do Fedn. (test bd. 1985—, bd. dirs. 1986—), Internat. Taekwon-Do Fedn. (1st and 4th degree black belts). Presbyterian. Home: 1841 19th St Uranus Boulder CO 80302 Office: Ohmeda Boulder 1315 W Century Dr Louisville CO 80027

TOBIN, WILLIAM JOSEPH, newspaper editor; b. Joplin, Mo., July 28, 1927; s. John J. and Lucy T. (Shoppach) T.; m. Marjorie Stuhldreher, Apr. 26, 1952; children—Michael Gerard, David Joseph, James Patrick. BJ, Butler U., 1948. Staff writer AP, Indpls., 1947-52, news feature writer, N.Y.C., 1952-54, regional membership exec., Louisville, 1954-56, corr., Juneau, Alaska, 1956-60, asst. chief of bur., Balt., 1960-61, chief of bur., Helena, Mont., 1961-63; mng. editor Anchorage Times, 1963-73, assoc. editor, 1973-85, gen. mgr., 1974-85, v.p., editor-in-chief, 1985—; bd. dirs. Enstar Corp., 1982-84. Mem. devel. com. Anchorage Winter Olympics, 1984—, bd. dirs. Anchorage organizing com., 1985—; bd. dirs. Alaska Council on Econ. Edn., 1978-84, Boys Clubs Alaska, 1979-83, Anchorage Symphony Orch., 1986-87, Blue Cross Wash. and Alaska, 1987—; mem. adv. bd. Providence Hosp., Anchorage, 1974—, chmn., 1980-85. Served to sgt. AUS, 1950-52. Mem. Am. Soc. Newspaper Editors, AP Mng. Editors Assn., Alaska AP Mems. Assn. (pres. 1964), Anchorage C. of C. (bd. dirs. 1969-74, pres. 1972-73), Alaska World Affairs Council (pres. 1967-68), Soc. Profl. Journalists, Phi Delta Theta. Clubs: Alaska Press (pres. 1968-69), Commonwealth North (Anchorage). Home: 2130 Lord Baranof Dr Anchorage AK 99517 Office: Anchorage Times PO Box 40 Anchorage AK 99510

TOBKIN, VINCENT HENRY, venture capitalist, lawyer; b. Pelican Rapids, Minn., July 4, 1951; s. Henry Edward and Kathryn Mary (Johnson) T.; m. Christine Marie Anderson, Aug. 28, 1976; children: Gregory, Carolyn. BS, MS, MIT, 1973; MBA with high distinction, JD, Harvard U., 1977. Bar: N.Y. Elec. engr. Fairchild Semicondr. Co., Calif., 1969-74, Hewlett-Packard Co., 1969-74; founder Kodon, Inc., Wellesley, Mass., 1971-72; mgmt. cons. MC Kinsey & Co., N.Y.C., 1976-84; mgmt. cons. MC Kinsey & Co., San Francisco, 1979-84, ptnr., 1983-84; v.p. Wood River Capital, Calif. and N.Y., 1984—, Prospect Group, N.Y.C., 1985-88; gen. ptnr. Sierra Ventures Mgmt. Co., Menlo Park, Calif. and N.Y.C., 1984—, Sierra Ventures II, Menlo Park, 1988—; bd. dirs. Stratacom, Inc., Campbell, Calif., Lab Support Inc., Woodland Hills, Calif., BioRecovery Systems Inc., Las Cruces, N.Mex., Advanced Technology Materials, New Milford, Conn., Automated Compliance Systems, Flemington, N.J., Altran, Sunnyvale, Calif., Advantage Prodn. Tech. Inc., Sunnyvale. Editor: (mag.) Tech. Engring. News, 1969-73. Hughes fellow, 1973. Mem. IEEE, Assn. Computing Machinery, Assn. Old Crows, Oceanic Soc., Tau Beta Pi, Eta Kappa Nu. Republican. Roman Catholic. Clubs: Lincoln's Inn (Cambridge), Hasty Pudding (Cambridge); Commonwealth (San Francisco). Home: 2644 Webster St San Francisco CA 94123 Office: Sierra Ventures 3000 Sand Hill Rd Bldg 1 Ste 280 Menlo Park CA 94025

TOBUREN, LARRY HOWARD, research physicist; b. Clay Center, Kans., July 9, 1940; s. Howard H. and Beulah (Boyd) T.; m. Lana L. Henry, June 16, 1962; children: Debra L., Tina L. BA, Emporia State U., 1962; PhD, Vanderbilt U., 1968. Research scientist Battelle Northwest Lab., Richland, Wash., 1967-80, mgr. radiol. research, 1980—; adj. assoc. prof. U. Wash., 1982—. Contbr. articles to profl. jours. Fellow Am. Phys. Soc.; mem. AAAS, Radiation Research Soc., Internat. Radiation Physics Soc. Home: 226 Wallace Richland WA 99352 Office: Battelle NW Lab PO Box 999 Richland WA 99352

TODD, HARRY WILLIAMS, aircraft propulsion system company executive; b. Oak Park, Ill., 1922. BSME, U. So. Calif., 1947, BS, 1948, MBA, 1950. With Rockwell Internat., Pitts., 1946-76, former v.p. ops.; pres., chmn., chief exec. officer, bd. dirs. The L.E. Myers Co., Pitts., 1976-80; with Rohr Industries, Inc., Chula Vista, Calif., 1980—, pres., chief operating officer, 1980-82, pres., chief exec. officer, chmn., 1982—, now chmn., chief exec. officer, 1989—, also bd. dirs.; bd. dirs. Pacific Scientific, Helmnich &

Payne. Served with U.S. Army, 1944-46. Office: Rohr Industries Inc PO Box 878 Chula Vista CA 92012 *

TODD, LISA MAY, city official; b. Lincoln, Nebr., Nov. 10, 1954; d. Dale Dean and Delores May (Brammer) Bergantzel; m. Stephen Karl Todd, May 15, 1976. BA, Seattle Pacific U., 1986. Med. receptionist Lincoln Clinic, Inc., 1976-79; adminstrv. asst. Inter-Mountain Clinic, Salt Lake City, 1979-82; libr. med. records Magnolia Convalescent Hosp., Riverside, Calif., 1983-84; leader spl. recreation City of Mountlake Terrace, Wash., 1985-86, coord. spl. recreation, 1986—; advisor to bd. dirs. Sno-King, Mountlake Terrace, 1986—. Merit scholar U. Utah, 1982. Mem. Nat. Coun. for Therapeutic Recreation. Methodist. Home: 23602 28th Pl W Brier WA 98036 Office: Sno-King Spl Recreation 5303 228th St SW Mountlake Terrace WA 98043

TODD, MAYLON JERRY, dentist, military officer; b. Palestine, Tex., Sept. 24, 1942; s. Maylon Percell Todd and Nell (Dansby) Durrett; m. Joy E. Neary, Aug. 22, 1961 (div.); m. Ida Baty, July 6, 1985; children: Hollianne E., Tyler D. DDS, Creighton U., 1968; MS, George Washington U., 1975. Commd. capt. U.S. Army, 1968, advanced through grades to col., 1983; gen. dentist Ft. Monroe, Va., 1968-69, Vietnam, 1970-71, Fed. Republic Germany, 1971-74; resident in endodontics George Washington U., Washington, 1974-75, Ft. Lewis, Wash., 1975-76; endodontic mentor Ft. Hood, Tex., 1976-81; endodontist Ft. Polk, La., 1981-85, Honolulu, 1985--. Contbr. articles to dental jours. Coach Little League, Harker Heights, Tex., 1978-80; v.p. Harker Heights Recreation Assn., 1978-79. Decorated Bronze Star. Mem. ADA, Am. Assn. Endodontists (diplomate), European Soc. Preventive Dentistry, S.W. Soc. Forensic Dentistry. Home: 619 Dawson Rd Wahiawa HI 96786 Office: Dental Clinic Schofield Barracks HI 96786

TODD, WILLIAM JAMES, aerospace researcher; b. Milw., Aug. 11, 1948; s. Sanford William and Marion Eleonore (Hass) T.; m. Linda Lucille Edgren, June 12, 1971; children: Anna, Kenneth. Student, U. Wis., Milw., 1966-67; BA, Valparaiso U., 1970; MA, Ind. State U., 1972; diploma in photointerpretation, Internat. Inst. Aerial Survey and Earth Scis., Enschede, The Netherlands, 1974. Research geographer Lab. Applications of Remote Sensing Purdue U., West Lafayette, Ind., 1972-73; application scientist Technicolor Graphic Services Inc., EROS Data Ctr., U.S. Geol. Survey, Sioux Falls, S.D., 1974-78; project mgr. Technicolor Graphic Svcs., Inc., Ames Research Ctr. NASA, Moffett Field, Calif., 1978-80; research analyst Lockheed Missiles & Space Co., Sunnyvale, Calif., 1980—. Contbr. articles to profl. jours. Mem. Am. Soc. Photogrammetry and Remote Sensing, Armed Forces Communications and Electronics Assn., Planetary Soc., IEEE (geosci. and remote sensing soc.), Sierra Club, Nature Conservancy, Gamma Theta Upsilon, Sigma Gamma Epsilon. Republican. Home: 6615 Winterset Way San Jose CA 95120 Office: Lockheed Missiles and Space Co 1111 Lockheed Way Sunnyvale CA 94088

TODD COPLEY, JUDITH ANN, materials scientist and mechanical engineering educator; b. Wakefield, West Yorkshire, Eng., Dec. 13, 1950; came to U.S., 1978; d. Marley and Joan Mary (Birkinshaw) Booth; m. David Michael Todd, June 17, 1972 (div. June 1981); m. Stephen Michael Copley, Aug. 3, 1984. BA, Cambridge (Eng.) U., 1972, MA, PhD, 1977. Research asst. Imperial Coll. Sci. and Tech., London, 1976-78; research assoc. SUNY, Stonybrook, 1978; research engr. U. Calif., Berkeley, 1979-82; asst. prof. materials sci. and mech. engring. U. So. Calif., Los Angeles, 1982—; mem. task force Materials Property Council, N.Y.C., 1979—. Contbr. articles to profl. jours. Recipient Faculty Research award Oak Ridge (Tenn.) Nat. Lab., 1986,Brit. Univs. Student Travel award 1972, Brit. Fedn. Univ. Women award 1972; Kathryn Kingswell Meml. scholar 1972. Mem. AIME (research award, 1983), ASTM, Soc. Women Engrs. (sr.), ASM Internat. (chmn. Los Angeles chpt. 1986-87, council mem. materials sci. div. 1984—), Electron Microscopy Soc. Am., Assn. Women in Sci., Hist. Metallurgy Soc., Nat. Soc. Corrosion Engrs. (Seed Grant award 1983), Microbeam Analysis Soc. Home: 4029 Via Nivel Palos Verdes Estates CA 90274 Office: U So Calif Dept Materials Sci Los Angeles CA 90089-0241

TOFFEL, PAUL HASKELL, maxillofacial surgeon, educator; b. Los Angeles, Mar. 3, 1943; s. Harry and Estelle Charlotte (Kandel) T.; m. Beverly Diane Peterson, June 12, 1965; children—Nicole, Hope, Erica. Student Stanford U., 1961-62; M.D., U. So. Calif., 1968. Intern, Los Angeles County-U. So. Calif. Med. Center, 1968-69, resident in otolaryngology, 1969-73; practice medicine specializing in otolaryngology and maxillofacial surgery, Los Angeles, 1975—; mem. staff Daniel Freeman Med. Center, Centinela Valley Med. Center, Orthopedic, Verdugo Hills hosps.; clin. assoc. prof. U. So. Calif. Med. Sch., 1974—; mem. med. emergency team Los Angeles County Sheriff's Dept., 1973—; head facial plastics div., med. adv. com. Calif. Athletic Commn.; chief med. officer equestrian events 1984 Los Angeles Olympiad. Served to lt. comdr. M.C., USNR, 1973-75. Fellow Am. Acad. Otolaryngology, Soc. Mil. Otolaryngologists, A.C.S., Am. Acad. Facial, Plastic and Reconstructive Surgery; mem. AMA, Calif., Los Angeles County med. assns., Salerni Collegium. Office: 2080 Century Park E Ste 610 Los Angeles CA 90067 also: 1808 Verdugo Blvd Ste 420 Glendale CA 91208

TOFTNESS, CECIL GILLMAN, lawyer, consultant; b. Glasgow, Mont., Sept. 13, 1920; s. Anton Bernt and Nettie (Pedersen) T.; m. Chloe Catherine Vincent, Sept. 8, 1951. A.A., San Diego Jr. Coll., 1943; student Purdue U., Northwestern U.; B.S., UCLA, 1947; J.D., Southwestern U., 1953. Bar: Calif. 1954, U.S. Dist. Ct. (so. dist.) Calif. 1954, U.S. Supreme Ct. 1979. Sole practice, Palos Verdes Estates, Calif., 1954—; dir., pres., chmn. bd. Fisherman & Mchts. Bank, San Pedro, Calif., 1963-67; dir., v.p. Palos Verdes Estates Bd. Realtors, 1964-65. Chmn. Capital Campaign Fund, Richstone Charity, Hawthorne, Calif., 1983. Served to lt. (j.g.) USN, 1938-46, ETO, PTO. Named Man of Yr., Glasgow, 1984. Mem. South Bay Bar Assn., Southwestern Law Sch. Alumni Assn. (class rep. 1980—), Internat. Physicians for the Prevention of Nuclear War (del. 7th World Congress, 1987), Themis Soc.-Southwestern Law Sch., Schumacher Founder's Circle-Southwestern Law Sch. (charter). Democrat. Lutheran. Lodges: Kiwanis (sec.-treas. 1955-83, v.p., pres., bd. dirs.), Masons, K.T. Participant Soc. Expedition thur the N.W. Passage. Home: 2229 Via Acalones Palos Verdes Estates CA 90274 Office: 2516 Via Tejon Palos Verdes Estates CA 90274

TOGO, YUKIYASU, automotive executive; b. Yokohama, Kanagawa, Japan, Nov. 13, 1924; came to U.S., 1983; s. Kinji Togo and Nobuko Watanabe; m. Misako Togo, Apr. 2, 1948; children: Yukinori, Yumi. Gen. mgr. Toyota Motor Sales, Tokyo, Japan, 1976-78, assoc. dir., 78-79, dir., 1979-80; pres. Toyota Can. Inc., Ontario, Can., 1980-82; dir. Toyota Motor Corp., Aichi, Japan, 1982, mng. dir., 1982-83; pres. Can. Auto Parts Toyota Inc., B.C., Can., 1983—; pres., chief exec. officer Toyota Motor Sales U.S.A. Inc., Torrance, Calif., 1983—; pres. Toyota Motor Credit Corp., Torrance, Calif., 1989—, Toyota Motor Ins. Svcs., Torrance, Calif., 1989—, Toyota Aviation USA Inc., Torrance, Calif., 1989—. Bd. dirs. Los Angeles World Affairs Coun., 1989. Office: Toyota Motor Sales USA Inc 19001 S Western Ave PO Box 2991 Torrance CA 90509

TOKAR, DANIEL, mining company executive; b. Detroit, Nov. 27, 1937; s. Alex and Olga (Leme) T.; m. Marian Carol Wilson, Dec. 10, 1970 (div. 1981); 1 child, Jonathan Wilson; m. Taffy Jill Stubbs, Sept. 19, 1986. BS in Engring., Boston U., 1962, MBA, 1964. With Ford Motor Co., Dearborn, Mich., 1964-67; fin. analyst Sperry Corp., N.Y.C., 1967-68; mgr. acctg. Am. Motors Corp., Southfield, Mich., 1969-74; controller Gen. Vehicle, Inc., Livonia, Mich., 1974-75; pres. Motor City Container, Romulus, Mich., 1975-80; dir. fin. planning Mountain States Mineral Enterprises, Inc., Tucson, 1981—; chmn. Addax Corp., Livonia, 1976-79; freelance cons., 1979—; bd. dirs. Zytex Corp., Tucson, 1980—; teaching fellow Boston U., 1962-64; assoc. faculty Henry Ford Coll., Dearborn, 1969-79; adj. prof. U. Phoenix, 1980-82, Pima Coll., Tucson, 1988—. Trustee local ch., Detroit, 1971-79; chmn. fin. com. local ch., Tucson, 1985-87. Mem. Engring. Soc. Detroit. Democrat. Unitarian. Home: 1830 N Norton Ave Tucson AZ 85719 Office: Mountain States Mineral Enterprises 4370 S Fremont Ave Tucson AZ 85714

TOKIOKA, FRANKLIN MAKOTO, investment company executive; b. Honolulu, Nov. 17, 1936; s. Masayuki and Harue (Fujiyoshi) T.; m. Suzanne M. Sears, Dec. 11, 1965; children: Franklin M. II, Dana M. BA, Williams Coll., 1958; MBA, Stanford U., 1960. Exec. v.p., sec. Nat. Mortgage and Fin. Co., Ltd., Honolulu, 1960—; sr. v.p., sec. Island Ins. Co., Ltd., Honolulu, 1969—; pres. Mut. Fin. Co., Ltd., Honolulu, 1971—, Nat. Securities and Investment, Inc., Honolulu, 1975—; bd. dirs. 1st Interstate Bank, Oceanic Cablevision, Inc., Honolulu, Intelect, Inc., Honolulu. Bd. dirs. Young People's Support Ctr., Honolulu, Boy Scouts Am., Honolulu, Sex Abuse Treatment Ctr. Recipient Silver Beaver award Boy Scouts Am., 1984. Clubs: Honolulu, Waialae Country. Home: 925 Waiholo St Honolulu HI 96821 Office: Nat Mortgage Fin Co Ltd 1022 Bethel St Honolulu HI 96813

TOKOFSKY, JERRY HERBERT, film producer; b. N.Y.C., Apr. 14, 1936; s. Julius H. and Rose (Trager) T.; m. Myrna Weinstein, Feb. 21, 1959 (div.); children: David, Peter; m. Fiammetta Bettuzzi, 1960 (div.); 1 child, Tatianna; m. Karen Oliver, Oct. 4, 1981. BS in Journalism, NYU, 1955, LLD, 1959. Talent agt. William Morris Agy., N.Y.C., 1953-59; v.p. William Morris Agy., L.A., 1959-64; v.p. prodn. Columbia Pictures, L.A., 1964-69, Paramount Pictures, London, 1970, MGM, London, 1971; pres. Jerry Tokofsky Prodns., L.A., 1972-82; exec. v.p. Zupnik Enterprises, L.A., 1982—. Producer (films) Where's Poppa, 1971, Born to Win, 1972, Dreamscape, 1985, Fear City, 1986, Wildfire, 1988, Glengarry Glen Ross, 1989. With U.S. Army, 1959, res. 1959-63. Named Man of Yr. B'nai Brith, 1981; recipient L.A. Resolution City of L.A., 1981. Mem. Variety Club Internat. Office: Zupnik Enterprises 9229 Sunset Blvd Ste 818 Los Angeles CA 90069

TOLAND, FREDERICK MORGAN, insurance broker; b. Detroit, Feb. 3, 1939; s. Wayne Carlton and Alice (Morgan) T.; m. Diane Susan Kilian, June 19, 1976; children by previous marriage: Frederick Morgan, Jeffrey Pierce, Christopher Reynick, Alexander Joseph; children by present marriage: Scott Hamilton, Katherine Elise. BSBA, U. So. Calif., 1966. CPCU. Underwriter, spl. agt. Ins. Co. N.Am., L.A., 1961-63; solicitor Keystone Bond & Ins. Svc., Pasadena, Calif., 1963-66; ptnr. Joseph P. Kesler Co. Ins. Svc., Long Beach, Calif., 1966-71; exec. v.p. Frank B. Hall Co. of Calif., L.A., 1971-83; pres. Emmett & Chandler of So. Calif., L.A., 1983-86; chmn. bd. Oland Internat. Ins. Brokers, Inc., L.A., 1986—. Mem. Nat. Assn. Casualty Surety Agts., CPCU Assn., Nat. Taxpayers Union, Conservative Caucus, Newcomen Soc. U.S., Rotary. Libertarian. Episcopalian. Office: Oland Internat Ins Brokers Inc 655 S Hope St 8th Fl Los Angeles CA 90017

TOLENTINO, CASIMIRO URBANO, lawyer; b. Manila, May 18, 1949; came to U.S., 1959; s. Lucio Rubio and Florence (Jose) T.; m. Jennifer Masculino, June 5, 1982; 2 children: Casimiro Masculino, Cristina Cecelia Masculino. BA in Zoology, UCLA, 1972, JD, 1975. Bar: Calif. 1976. Gen. counsel civil rights div. HEW, Washington, 1975-76; regional atty. Agrl. Labor Relations Bd., Fresno, Calif., 1976-78; regional dir. Sacramento and San Diego, 1978-81; regional atty. Pub. Employment Relations Bd., Los Angeles, 1981; counsel, west div. Writers Guild Am., Los Angeles, 1982-84; dir. legal affairs Embassy TV, Los Angeles, 1984-86; sole practice Los Angeles, 1986—; mediator Ctr. Dispute Resolution, Santa Monica, Calif., 1986—; asst. chief counsel Dept. of Fair Employment and Housing, State of Calif. Editor: Letters in Exile, 1976; contbr. articles and revs. to Amerasia Jour. Chmn. adv. bd. UCLA Asian Am. Studies Ctr., 1983—; chmn. bd. Asian Pacific Legal Ctr., Los Angeles, 1983—; pres. bd. civil service commrs., City of Los Angeles, 1984—. Mem. State Bar Calif. (exec. com. labor law sect. 1985—), Los Angeles County Bar Assn., Minority Bar Assn. (sec. 1984-85), Philippine Lawyers of So. Calif. (pres. 1984—, Award of Merit 1982). Democrat. Roman Catholic.

TOLL, CHARLES HULBERT, construction executive; b. Los Angeles, June 30, 1931; s. Charles Hulbert Sr. and Kathryn (Burrows) T.; m. Barbara Jean Tressler, Mar. 5, 1955; 1 child, Wendy Warren Toll Greene. Grad. high sch., North Hollywood, Calif. Various positions The Flinkote Co., Blue Diamond, Nev., 1965-67, works mgr., 1967-75; v.p. The Grail Co., Santa Ana, Calif., 1975-78, H.G. Toll Co., El Segundo, Calif., 1978-80; pres. H.G. Toll Co., Scottsdale, Ariz., 1980-89, Toll Constrn., Scottsdale, Ariz., 1989—. Republican. Episcopalian. Office: Toll Constrn Co 7762 E Gray Rd Scottsdale AZ 85260

TOLLEY, JOHN STEWART, state transportation administrator, urban planner; b. Greenville, Miss., Feb. 3, 1953; s. Frank Edward and Rachel Lee (Roberts) T. BA, U. Alaska, 1977; M in Urban Planning, Princeton U., 1979. Research asst. Princeton (N.J.) U., 1978-79; planner transp. Alaska Dept. Transp., Anchorage, 1979-81, mgr. statewide planning, 1982-84, chief of planning, 1985—. Mem. AIA, Am. Planning Assn., Transp. Research Bd. of Nat. Acad. Scis. (mem. various coms.). Home: 1200 I St #416 Anchorage AK 99501

TOLLIVER, ELLA MAE, college counselor, consultant; b. Vallejo, Calif., May 10, 1946; d. Harry and Josephine (Buckner) Clark; m. John Oliver Tolliver, Mar. 16, 1963; children: Vivian Hazzard, John Jr., Lisa. BA, Sonoma State U., 1983; MS, Hayward State U., 1985. Cert. counselor and instr., Calif. Specialist manpower County of Solano, Fairfield, Calif., 1974-78; specialist student Peralta Community Coll. Dist., Oakland, Calif., 1984-87; counselor, instr. Solano Community Coll., Suisun, Calif., 1983—; co-dir. Step Up Stream, Vallejo, 1980—, Women's Koinonia, Vallejo, 1984—; cons. Solano Coll., 1983—. Contbr. articles Youth Concerns, 1986, 88. Bd. dirs. Inner-City Org., Vallejo, 1980-81; leader Berea Young Adults, Vallejo, 1986—; vol. presdl. campaign, Oakland, 1984. Named Tchr. of Yr. Golden Gate Acad., Oakland, 1984. Democrat. Seventh-Day Adventist. Home: 3030 Potrero Way Fairfield CA 94533

TOLLIVER, JAMES DAVID, JR., aerospace engineer; b. Long Branch, N.J., Dec. 27, 1938; s. James David and Daisy E. (Brabham) T.; m. Evelyn C. Davis, Jan. 16, 1965 (div. 1982); children: Yvette, James D. III; m. Rachel Evelyn Thornton, June 14, 1986. BS in Law, Glendale U., 1974; postgrad., UCLA, 1965-72, cert. numerical analysis, 1968. Mem. staff Cambridge (Mass.) electron accelerator div. Harvard U. and MIT, 1963-64; mem. staff Cyclotron lab. UCLA, 1964-73; system engr. Honeywell Systems Co., West Covina, Calif., 1977-80, Magnavox Systems Co., Torrance, Calif., 1980-86, Teledyne Systems Co., Northridge, Calif., 1986—; speaker at profl. seminars. With USMC, 1958-62. Mem. Elec. Discharge and Elec. Over Stress Soc., Toastmasters Internat. (pres. Magnavox Toastmasters, Torrance, 1985-86). Home: 1634 Stearns Dr Los Angeles CA 90035

TOM, CLARENCE YUNG CHEN, city and county official; b. Honolulu, Jan. 25, 1927; s. John Chong and Dorothy Oi Fook (Ing) T.; m. Vivian Kam Oi Lum, July 19, 1969; children: Claire-Anne, Karen-Anne, Patricia-Anne. BS in Chem. Engring., Purdue U., 1947, MS in Chem. Engring., 1957; M City Planning, Harvard U., 1959. Chem. engr. Libby, McNeill & Libby, Honolulu, 1947-50, 52-54; planner City and County Honolulu, 1958—, chief environ. and plans assessment br. dept. gen. planning, 1980—; mem. Hawaii Census Tract Com., 1960—. Jr. warden St. Mary's Ch., Honolulu, 1970-82; vestryman Ch. Holy Nativity, Honolulu, 1984-86. Served with U.S. Army, 1950-52, Korea. Mem. Hawaii Govt. Employees Assn. (steward 1971-72, 81-82, alt. steward 1988). Democrat. Home: 2911-A Koali Rd Honolulu HI 96826

TOM, CREIGHTON HARVEY, aerospace engineer, consultant; b. Oakland, Calif., Mar. 29, 1944; s. Harvey and Katherine (Lew) T. BS in Forestry, U. Calif., Berkeley, 1966; MS in Stats., Colo. State U., 1972, PhD in Computer Sci., 1978. Sr. environ. analyst HRB-Singer, Inc., Ft. Collins, Colo., 1977-78; staff scientist Sci. Applications, Golden, Colo., 1979-80; cons. Golden, 1981; scientist, specialist ConTel Info. Systems, Littleton, Colo., 1981-84; sr. staff engr. Hughes Aircraft Co., Aurora, Colo., 1984—; shuttle astronaut cand. NASA, Houston, 1980; cons. to companies and schs. Contbr. articles to profl. jours. Adviser CAP, Golden, 1981—; mem. YMCA. Served to maj. U.S. Army, 1966-67, with Res. 1967—. Decorated Bronze Star and Air medals, U.S. Army, 1967. Mem. Am. Soc. Photogrammetry, AAAS, NRA, Mensa, Intertel, Sigma Xi, Xi Sigma Pi, Phi Kappa Phi. Republican. Methodist. Home: 7951 S Cedar St Littleton CO 80120 Office: Hughes Aircraft Co 16800 E CentreTech Pkwy Aurora CO 80111

TOM, LAWRENCE, computer engineer; b. L.A., Jan. 21, 1950; s. Tommy Toy and May (Fong) T. BS, Harvey Mudd Coll., 1972; JD Western State U., San Diego, 1978. Design engr. Rockwell Internat., L.A., 1972-73; design engr. Rohr Industries, Inc., Chula Vista, Calif., 1973-76, sr. design engr., 1980, computer graphics engring. specialist, 1980-83, chief engring. svs., 1989—; pvt. practice design engring. cons., L.A., 1975-77; sr. engr. Rohr Marine, Inc., Chula Vista, 1977-79; chief exec. officer Computer Aided Tech. Svcs., San Diego, 1983-87; software cons. Small Systems Software, San Diego, 1984-85; computer graphics engring. specialist TOM & ROMAN, San Diego, 1986-88; dir. western region Computervision Users Group, 1986-88, vice chmn. 1988—; cons. in field. George H. Mayr Found. scholar, 1971; Bate Found. Aero. Edn. scholar, 1970-72. Mem. Aircraft Owners and Pilots Assn. Office: 7770 Regents Rd Ste 113-190 San Diego CA 92122

TOM, STANLEY JOHNATHAN., technical writer; b. Los Angeles, Dec. 9, 1959; s. Yee Q. and Dora M. (Chan) T. BA, UCLA, 1983; MA, U. Ariz., 1984. Tech. writer McDonnell Douglas, Long Beach, Calif., 1984-89, computer systems trainer, 1989—. Cons. Multiple Sclerosis Soc. So. Calif., 1985; docent Mus. Contemporary Art, Los Angeles, 1984—. Home: 4682 Pinecrest Cir Huntington Beach CA 92649 Office: Douglas Aircraft Co 3855 Lakewood Blvd Long Beach CA 90846

TOMASSON, HELGI, dancer, choreographer, dance company executive; b. Reykjavik, Iceland, 1942; m. Marlene Rizzo, 1965; children: Kristin, Erik. Student, Sigridur Arman, Erik Bidsted, Vera Volkova, Sch. Am. Ballet, Tivoli Pantomime Theatre, Copenhagen. Debut with, Tivoli Pantomime Theatre, 1958; with Joffrey Ballet, 1961-64; soloist Harkness Ballet, 1964-70; prin. dancer, N.Y.C. Ballet, 1970-85; artistic dir. San Francisco Ballet, 1985—; choreographer Ballet d'Isoline, 1983, others. Decorated Order of Falcon (Iceland), 1974; recipient Silver medal Internat. Moscow Ballet Competition, 1969. Office: care San Francisco Ballet 455 Franklin St San Francisco CA 94102 *

TOMBACK, JEFFREY MICHAEL, advertising executive, consultant; b. Bklyn., June 13, 1948; s. Michael Wolf and Sheila (Goldberg) T.; m. Gloria Bonita Miller, June 13, 1985; 1 child, Jordan Michael. BBA, U. Miami, 1971. Salesperson M.W. Samara Inc., N.Y.C., 1973-79; v.p. sales Walter W. Cribbins, San Francisco, 1980-86; pres. Miller Tomback Corp., San Francisco, 1986—. Mem. Ad Splty. Industry, Splty. Advt. Assn. Internat., Golden Gate Ad Splty. Assn., San Francisco Club, Sausalito Yacht Club, Commonwealth Club. Jewish. Office: Miller Tomback Corp 1902 Divisadero San Francisco CA 94115

TOMLIN, WILLIAM STEVEN, artist; b. Dallas, Aug. 29, 1947; s. Billy Jim and Mary Louise (Dendinger) T.; m. Perett Cota, Aug. 15, 1980 (div.). AA, Chaffie Coll., 1970; BA, Claramont Coll., 1972, MFA, 1975. Art prof. Contemporary Art Inst., Dallas, 1978-83; art dealer Tomlin Fine Arts, Santa Monica, 1984—. Mem. Nat. Assn. Appraisers, Restorers of So. Calif. Home: 301 Marine St Santa Monica CA 90405 Office: Tomlin Fine Arts 301 Marine St Santa Monica CA 90405

TOMLINSON-KEASEY, CAROL ANN, psychology educator; b. Washington, Oct. 15, 1942; d. Robert Bruce and Geraldine (Howe) Tomlinson; m. Charles Blake Keasey, June 13, 1964; children: Kai Linson, Amber Lynn. BS, Pa. State U., 1964; MS, Iowa State U., 1966; PhD, U. Calif., Berkeley, 1970. Lic. psychologist, Calif. Asst. prof. psychology Trenton (N.J.) State Coll., 1969-70, Rutgers U., New Brunswick, N.J., 1970-72; assoc. prof. U. Nebr., Lincoln, 1972-77; prof. U. Calif., Riverside, 1977—, assoc. dean coll. humanities and social scis., 1986-88. Author: Child's Eye View, 1980, Child Development, 1985; also numerous chpts. to books; articles to profl. jours. Recipient Disting. Tchr. award U. Calif., 1986. Mem. Am. Psychol. Assn., Soc. Rsch. in Child Devel., Riverside Aquatics Assn. (pres. 1985). Office: U Calif Dept Psychology Riverside CA 92521

TOMPKINS, DOUGLAS, apparel company executive; m. Susie Tompkins, 1963; children: Quincey, Summer. Founder, owner North Face, North Beach, Calif., 1964-69; pres. Esprit de Corps Internat., San Francisco, 1969—. Recipient Design Leadership award Am. Inst. Graphic Arts, 1987. Office: Esprit de Corps Internat 900 Minnesota St San Francisco CA 94107 *

TOMPKINS, JEANNIE KAY, teacher; b. Portage, Wis., Feb. 8, 1944; d. Matt and Ivy (Lee) Keiller; m. Robert Jay Tompkins, June 18, 1967; children: Troy M., Lee M. BA, U. Ariz., 1966, MEd, 1970. Tchr. spl. edn. Moreno Valley Sch. Dist., Sunnymead, Calif., 1966-67; tchr. educationally handicapped Centralia Sch. Dist., Buena Park, Calif., 1967-68; pupil appraisal rm. tchr. Tucson Unified Sch. Dist., 1968-69, learning disabilities resource tchr., 1969-70; learning disabilities tchr., diagnostician Grace Christian Sch., Tucson, 1979—; organizer, dir. Attention Deficit Disorders Support Group for Parents, Tucson, 1988. Mem. Young Reps., Tucson, 1972-76. Govt. scholar, 1970. Mem. Ariz. Coun. for Learning Disabilities, Coun. for Exceptional Children. Republican. Home: 600 S Avenida Los Reyes Tucson AZ 85748

TOMPKINS, SUSIE, apparel company executive; m. Douglas Tompkins, 1963; children: Quincey, Summer. Design cons. Esprit de Corps Internat., San Francisco. Office: Esprit de Corps Internat 900 Minnesota St San Francisco CA 94107 *

TOMSKY, JUDY, fundraiser; b. Oklahoma City, Nov. 28, 1959; d. Mervin and Helen (Broude) T. Student, Hebrew U. of Jerusalem, 1979-80; BA in Liberal Studies, Sonoma State U., 1981. Internat. tour group dir. Kibbutz Yahel, Israel, 1981-83; telemktg. supr., mktg. and advt. coordinator The Sharper Image, San Francisco, 1983-85; br. mgr., acct. exec. advt. Marin Express Ltd., Corte Madera, Calif., 1986; spl. events coordinator, fundraiser Sausalito, Calif., 1987-88; regional coordinator Pacific Northwest Jewish Nat. Fund, San Francisco, 1988—. Democrat. Home and Office: 214 Bayview St #8 San Rafael CA 94901

TONARELY, ELINOR JANE, administrative officer; b. Fullerton, Calif., Aug. 27, 1958; d. Paul Hubert Crews Sr. and Nancy Elizabeth (Batson) Crews; m. John Paul Tonarely, Aug. 9, 1980. AA in Dramatic Arts, Mesa Coll., 1980. Asst. mgr. Cathy Jean, San Diego, 1980-81, Joel's, San Diego, 1981-82; teller with new accounts Mitsui Mfrs. Bank, San Diego, 1982-83; with platform utility dept. Mitsui Mfrs. Bank, Hollywood, Calif., 1983-84; loan sec. La Jolla (Calif.) Bank & Trust Co., 1984-86; loan adminstr. Scripps Bank, La Jolla, 1986-88, sr. loan adminstr., 1988-89, adminstrv. officer, 1989—. Vol. Sta. KPBS, San Diego, 1987-88, Off the Wall St. Dance, La Jolla, 1988. Recipient Presdl. Citation. Republican. Office: Scripps Bank 7817 Ivanhoe Ave La Jolla CA 92037

TONDREAU, BEVERLY FRANCIS, computerized teleprompting service executive; b. Los Angeles, Dec. 2, 1945; d. Thomas Francis and Beverly Green (Goodrich) Hanley; m. William P. Tondreau, Oct. 26, 1968 (div. Feb. 1971); m. Thomas M. Feldman, Mar. 1988. B.A. in Art, Immaculate Heart Coll., 1967. Dir. rental promotions Compu-Prompt, Hollywood, Calif., 1984, v.p. ops., 1984—; reporter Nat. Pub. Radio, Washington; ind. producer various prodns., Hollywood, 1985—, comedy cons.; comedy writer for Joan Rivers; performer as Blanche Avalanche. Mem. Internat. Documentary Assn., Nat. Assn. Female Execs., Women in Film, Assn. Entertainment Industry Computer Profls. Democrat. Avocations: hiking; writing. Home: 3221 Fernwood Ave Los Angeles CA 90039

TONELLI, EDITH ANN, art gallery director, art historian; b. Westfield, Mass., May 20, 1949; d. Albert Robert and Pearl (Grubert) T. B.A., Vassar Coll., 1971; M.A., Hunter Coll., 1974; Ph.D., Boston U., 1981; grad., Mus. Mgmt. Inst. U. Calif.-Berkeley, 1981. Arts curriculum coordinator Project SEARCH, Millbrook, N.Y., 1972-74; curator DeCordova Mus., Lincoln, Mass., 1976-78; dir. art gallery, asst. prof. art U. Md., College Park, 1979-82, dir. mus. studies program, 1979-82; project dir. Summer Inst. Artists U. Md., 1981-82; dir. Frederick S. Wight Art Gallery, 1982—; adj. asst. prof. art UCLA, 1982—; reviewer pub. programs NEH, 1977—. Author exhbn. catalogs. Fellow Nat. Endowment Arts, 1981; predoctoral fellow Smithsonian Instn., 1979; doctoral and teaching fellow Boston U., 1974-76; mem. Helen Squire Townsend fellow Vassar College, 1971-72; recipient dissertation award Boston U. Vis. Com., 1979. Mem. Am. Assn. Museums, Coll. Art Assn., Women's Caucus for Art, Am. Fedn. Arts(advisor profl. tng.), Assn. Art Mus. Dirs. (trustee 1987—), Am. Studies Assn., Art Table Inc. Office: UCLA Wight Art Gallery 1100 Gallery Bldg 405 Hilgard Los Angeles CA 90024

TONELLO-STUART, ENRICA M., political economist; b. Monza, Italy, Dec. 20, 1926; d. Alessandro P. and Maddalena M. (Marangoni) Tonello; m. Albert E. Smith, May 14, 1947 (div. 1964); m. Charles L. Stuart, Feb. 14, 1975. BA in Internat. Affairs, Econs., U. Colo., 1961; MA, Claremont Grad. Sch., 1966, PhD, 1971. Sales mgr. Met. Life Ins. Co., 1974-79; pres. E.T.S. Research and Devel., Inc., 1977—; dir. internat. studies program Union U., Los Angeles-Tokyo, 1975-83; lectr. internat. affairs and mktg. UCLA Extention, Union U.; chief exec. officer E.T.S. Worldwide Seminars, 1986—. Pub., editor Tomorrow Outline Journal, 1963—, The Monitor, 1988; pub. World Regionalism--An Ecological Analysis, 1971, A Proposal for the Reorganization of the United Nations, 1966, The Persuasion Technocracy, Its Forms, Techniques, and Potentials, 1966, The Role of the Multinationals in the Emerging Globalism, 1978. . Bd. dirs. Caesarea World Monument; mem. Los Angeles World Affairs Council; organized first family assistance program Langley AFB Tactical Air Command, 1956-58. Recipient vol. service award VA, 1956-58, ARC service award, 1950-58. Mem. Corp. Planners Assn. (treas. 1974-79), Investigative Reporters and Editors, World Future Soc. (pres. 1974—), Nat. Assn. Bus. Economists, World Future Soc., US-China Journalists Fellowship Assn. (founder, pres. 1984—), Los Angeles C. of C., Palos Verdes C. of C., Italian Heritage Found. (pub. relations agt.), Pi Sigma Alpha, Sigma Delta Chi. Clubs: Los Angeles Press, San Francisco Press. Lodge: Zonta (chmn. internat. com. South Bay).

TONG, RICHARD DARE, anesthesiologist; b. Chgo., Oct. 20, 1930; s. George Dare and June (Jung) T.; student U. Calif., Berkeley, 1949-52; MD, U. Calif., Irvine, 1956; postgrad. UCLA, 1965-67; m. Diane Helene Davies, Apr. 12, 1970; children: Erin, Jason. Intern, Phoenix Gen. Hosp., 1956-57; resident in anesthesiology UCLA, 1965-67; pvt. practice, Lakewood, Calif., 1967—; clin. instr. UCLA Sch. Medicine, 1968—. Dep. sheriff reserve med. emergency team, L.A. County. With USNR, 1947-53. Diplomate Am. Bd. Anesthesiology. Fellow Am. Coll. Anesthesiology; mem. Am. Soc. Anesthesiologists, AMA, Calif. Med. Assn., L.A. County Med. Assns. Democrat. Office: 3700 South St Lakewood CA 90712

TONG, SIU WING, computer programmer; b. Hong Kong, Hong Kong, May 20, 1950; came to U.S., 1968; BA, U. Calif., Berkeley, 1972; PhD, Harvard U., 1979; MS, U. Lowell, 1984. Research assoc. Brookhaven Nat. Lab., Upton, N.Y., 1979-83; software engr. Honeywell Info. Systems, Billerica, Mass., 1984-85; sr. programmer, analyst Hui Computer Cons., Orinda, Calif., 1985—. Vol. tchr. Boston Chinatown Saturday Adult Edn. Program of Tufts Med. Sch., 1977-79. Muscular Dystrophy Assn. fellow, 1980-82. Mem. AAAS, IEEE, Assn. Computing Machinery, N.Y. Acad. Scis. Home: 131 Chilpancingo Pkwy Apt 265 Pleasant Hill CA 94523 Office: Hui Computer Cons and Svcs Inc 4 Orinda Way Ste 110B Orinda CA 94563

TONICK, ILLENE, clinical psychologist; b. Bronx, N.Y.; d. Benjamin and Mollie (Airov) T.; m. Michael S. Levine, May 30, 1984. BA, SUNY-Stony Brook, 1973; MS, U. Utah, 1979, PhD, 1981. Staff psychologist Neuropsychiat. Inst., UCLA, 1980-82, asst. clin. prof. dept. psychiatry, 1984—; clin. supr. Ctr. Legal Psychiatry, L.A., 1982-83; dir. Psychology Licensing Workshops, L.A., 1983—; pvt. practice psychology, L.A., 1982—. Dir. Acad. Rev. Psychol. Lic. Workshops., L.A., 1983—. Contbr. articles to profl. jours. NIMH fellow, 1973-76, Solomon Baker fellow 1979-80. Mem. Am. Psychol. Assn., Nat. Register Health Providers in Psychology, So. Calif. Psychotherapy Affiliation, Phi Kappa Phi. Office: 941 Westwood Blvd Ste 221 Los Angeles CA 90024

TONINI, LEON RICHARD, sales professional; b. Pittsfield, Mass., May 16, 1931; s. John Richard and Mabel Grayce (Rushbrook) T.; B.A. in Mgmt., U. Md., 1951; m. Helen Jo, Aug. 15, 1966; 1 son, John Richard, II. Enlisted in U.S. Army, 1947, advanced through grades to master sgt., 1968; service in W.Ger., Vietnam; ret., 1974; dir. vets. employment and assistance Non-Commd. Officers Assn., San Antonio, 1974-75; supr. security Pinkerton's Inc., Dallas, 1975-78; gen. mgr. civic center Travelodge Motor Hotel and Restaurant, San Francisco, 1978-85; sales representative Vernon Co., 1985—. Chmn. San Francisco Vets. Employment Com., 1981. Served as sgt. maj. Calif. N.G., res. Decorated Bronze Star; Republic Vietnam Honor medal 2d class. Mem. San Francisco Hotel Assn. (dir.), Non-Commd. Officers Assn. (dir. Calif. chpt.), Am. Legion, Regular Vets. Assn. (nat. sr. vice comdr.), Amvets, Patrons of Husbandry. Republican. Baptist. Club: Masons. Home and Office: 205 Collins St Apt 9 San Francisco CA 94118

TONJES, MARIAN JEANNETTE BENTON, reading educator; b. Rockville Center, N.Y., Feb. 16, 1929; d. Millard Warren and Felicia E. (Tyler) Benton; m. Charles F. Tonjes (div. 1965); children: Jeffrey Charles, Kenneth Warren. BA, U. N.Mex., 1951, cert., 1966, MA, 1969; EdD, U. Miami, 1975. Dir. recreation Stuyvesant Town Housing Project, N.Y.C., 1951-53; tchr. music., phys. edn. Sunset Mesa Day Sch., Albuquerque, 1953-54; tchr. remedial reading Zia Elem. Sch., Albuquerque, 1965-67; tchr. secondary devel. reading Rio Grande High Sch., Albuquerque, 1967-69; research asst. reading Southwestern Coop. Ednl. Lab., Albuquerque, 1969-71; assoc. dir., vis. instr. Fla. Ctr. Tchr. Tng. Materials U. Miami, 1971-72; asst. prof. U.S. Internat. U., San Diego, 1972-75; prof. edn. Western Wash. U., Bellingham, 1975—; vis. prof. adult edn. Palamar (Calif.) Jr. Coll., 1974; reading supr. Manzanita Ctr. U. N.Mex., Albuquerque, 1968; mem. numerous coms. at Western Wash. U.; dir. summer study in Eng. at Oxford U., 1975—; speaker, cons. in field. Author: (with Miles V. Zintz) Teaching Reading/Thinking Study Skills in Content Classrooms, 2d rev. edit. 1987; contbr. articles to profl. jours. Mem. English Speaking Union/Dartmouth House, London. Recipient Disting. Tchr. award Western Wash. U., 1981; TTT grantee; NDEA fellow Okla. State U. Mem. Am. Reading Forum (chmn. bd. dirs. 1983-85), Internat. Reading Assn. (travel interchange and study tours com. 1984-86, non-print media and reading com. 1980-83, workshop dir. S.W. regional conf. 1982, 85, English Speaking Union tchr. yr. com. 1988—, Outstanding Reading Tchr. Educator Award com. 1988—), Nat. Assn. Primary Edn. (Eng.), Nat. Council Tchrs. English, United Kingdom Reading Assn. (speaker), PEO (past local pres.), English Speaking Union, Phi Delta Kappa (local chpt. nominating com. 1984, alt. del. 1982), Delta Delta Delta. Republican. Office: Western Wash U Dept Edn Bellingham WA 98225

TONTZ, JAY LOGAN, university dean; b. Balt., July 20, 1938; s. E. Logan and Charlotte (Mullikin) T.; m. Frances Anne Deems, June 26, 1982; 1 child, Michelle Anne. B.A., Denison U., 1960; M.S., Cornell U., 1962; Ph.D., U. N.C., 1966. Asst. prof. U.S. Air Force Acad., 1966-69; asst. to prof. Calif. State U., Hayward, 1969—, acting assoc. dean, 1970-72, chmn. dept. econs., 1972-73, acting dean, 1973-74, dean Sch. Bus. and Econs., 1974—. Trustee St. Rose Hosp., Hayward, Calif., 1979-85, chmn. bd. trustees, 1981-85. Mem. Nat. Assn. Drs. in U.S., Am. Econ. Assn., Western Econ. Assn., Rotary (pres. Hayward chpt. 1986-87), Omicron Delta Epsilon, Delta Sigma Pi. Home: 602 Lomond Circle San Ramon CA 94583 Office: Calif State U Sch Bus and Econs Hayward CA 94542

TOOKEY, ROBERT CLARENCE, consulting actuary; b. Santa Monica, Calif., Mar. 21, 1925; s. Clarence Hall and Minerva Maconachie (Anderson) T.; BS, Calif. Inst. Tech., 1945; MS, U. Mich., 1947; m. Marcia Louise Hickman, Sept. 15, 1956; children: John Hall, Jennifer Louise, Thomas Anderson. Actuarial clk. Occidental Life Ins. Co., Los Angeles, 1945-46; with Prudential Ins. Co. Am., Newark, 1947-49; assoc. actuary in group Pacific Mut. Life Ins. Co., Los Angeles, 1949-55; asst. v.p. in charge reins. sales and service for 17 western states Lincoln Nat. Life Ins. Co., Ft. Wayne, Ind., 1955-61; dir. actuarial services Peat, Marwick, Mitchell & Co., Chgo., 1961-63; mng. partner So. Calif. office Milliman & Robertson, cons. actuaries, Pasadena, 1963-76; pres. Robert Tookey Assos., Inc., 1977—. Committeeman troop 501 Boy Scouts Am., 1969-72. Served to lt. (j.g.) USNR, 1943-45, 51-52. Fellow Soc. Actuaries, Conf. Actuaries in Pub. Practice; mem. Am. Acad. Actuaries, Pacific States Actuarial Club, Pacific Ins. Conf. Clubs: San Gabriel Country; Rotary (Pasadena); Union League (Chgo.). Home and Office: 1249 Descanso Dr La Canada-Flintridge CA 91011

TOOLE, CLYDE ROWLAND, JR., physicist; b. Seattle, July 24, 1933; s. Clyde Rowland and Esther Stanun (Magnuson) T.; m. Hazel Ruth Coppess, June 15, 1957; children: Kelli, Shauna, Erin, Megan. BS in Physics, U. Wash., 1955; postgrad., U. Idaho, 1956-60. Research physicist Phillips Petroleum, Idaho Falls, Idaho, 1955-59; spl. power excursion reactor test facility, ops. mgr. Phillips Petroleum, Idaho Falls, 1959-68, Aerojet Nuclear, Idaho Falls, 1968-71; power burst facility, ops. mgr. EG&G, Inc., Idaho Falls, 1971-75, power burst facility mgr., 1975-77, tech. asst. to loft facility mgr., 1977-81; rep. to fed. lab. consortium Idaho Nat. Engring. Lab., Idaho Falls, 1981-85; mgr., exploratory rsch. and devel. EG&G, Inc., Idaho Falls, 1985—; gen. chmn. 8th Topical Mtg. on Tech. of Fusion Energy, Salt Lake City, 1988; cons. Dept. of Energy, Buffalo, N.Y., 1969; lectr. U. Wash., Seattle, 1968, Naval Officer's Tng., Idaho Falls, 1966. Contbr. articles to profl. jours. Vice-chmn. Idaho Sch. Bd., Dist. #91, Idaho Falls, 1979—; bd. dirs. Idaho Falls Aquatic Ctr., 1987—; chmn. Idaho Falls Youth/Adult Assn., 1978; precinct com. Republican Party, Idaho Falls, 1968-72. Mem. Am. Nuclear Soc. (program com. 1978, chmn. Idaho sect. 1985-86, Exceptional Service award 1980), Idaho Acad. Sci., Pinecrest Golf Assn., Sigma Alpha Epsilon. Republican. Episcopalian. Home: 356 Redwood Dr Idaho Falls ID 83401 Office: EG&G Inc PO Box 1625 Idaho Falls ID 83415

TOOLEY, CHARLES FREDERICK, communications executive, consultant; b. Seattle, Sept. 29, 1947; s. Creath Athol and Catherine Ella (Wainman) T.; m. Valerie Adele Gose, Mar. 7, 1981; children: Paige Arlene Higdon, Marni Higdon Tooley. BA, Lynchburg Coll., 1968. Producer, stage mgr., tech. dir. various theatre cos. and performing arts orgns., Ala., Fla., Va., N.Y., Ariz., 1965-74; field underwriter N.Y. Life Ins. Co., Billings, Mont., 1974-77; market adminstr. Mountain Bell Telephone Co., Butte and Billings, Mont., 1978-83; pres. BCC Inc., Billings, Mont., 1983—. Active Mont. Arts Council, 1982—; Billings/Yellowstone County Centennial, 1981-82, steering com. Mont. Cultural Advocacy, 1982—, bd. Yellowstone 89ers, 1987—, commn. Christian Chs. in Mont., 1983—, Billings Com. Fgn. Relations; elder Cen. Christian Ch., Billings, chmn. trustees, 1983-85; dir. Mont. Dem. Exec. Bd., 1982-87; adv. bd. Salvation Army, Billings., 1984—; del. Dem. Nat. Conv., 1980; Dem. candidate Mont. Ho. Reps., 1986; mem. Billings City Coun., 1989—. Sgt. U.S. Army, 1969-72, Vietnam. Mem. Disciples of Christ. Club: Toastmasters (div. gov.'s. cup. 1978). Lodges: Kiwanis (bd. dirs. 1981-88), Masons, Shriners, Elks. Home: 502 Alderson Billings MT 59101 Office: BCC Inc PO Box 555 Billings MT 59103

TOOLEY, WILLIAM LANDER, real estate development company executive; b. El Paso, Tex., Apr. 23, 1934; s. William Lander and Virginia Mary (Ryan) T.; m. Reva Berger, Mar. 5, 1966; children: William Ryan, Patrick Boyer, James Eugene. BA, Stanford U., 1956; MBA, Harvard U., 1960. Treas., mgr. Pickwick Hotel Co., San Diego, 1960-63, David H. Murdock Devel. Co., Phoenix, 1963-67; ptnr. Ketchum, Peck & Tooley, L.A., 1967-74; chmn. Tooley & Co., investment builders, L.A., 1974--; bd. dirs. Fed. Res. Bank San Francisco; dir. Nat. Realty Com., Washington, 1975--. Trustee Loyola Marymount U., L.A., 1975-82, bd. regents, 1982--, mem. task force, 1988--; bd. dirs. Internat. Leadership Ctr., Dallas, 1988--. Lt. (j.g.) USNR, 1956-58. Mem. Urban Land Inst., Calif. Club, Calif. Yacht Club, Lambda Alpha. Office: 3303 Wilshire Blvd Los Angeles CA 90010

TOON, LEONARD EUGENE, chiropractor; b. San Fernando, Calif., Dec. 19, 1932; s. Lester F. and Bessie M. (Rucker) T.; m. Jillian D. Gibbs, May 14, 1975, (div. Mar. 1979); children: Donna J., Susan J. D Chiropractic, L.A. Chiropractic, 1956. Diplomate Am. Bd. Chiropractic Orthopedists. Pvt. practice, chiropractic Chatsworth, Calif., to date; treas., Am. Bd. Chiropractic Orthopedists, 1981—. Mem. Am. Coll. Chiropractic Orthopedists (pres. 1980), Council on Chiropractic Orthopedics (pres. 1985-86); fellow Acad. Chiropractic Orthopedists (sec. 1980—). Office: 20529 Devonshire St Chatsworth CA 91311

TOOR, JON, engineering executive; b. Phoenix, Sept. 2, 1960; s. Jeanne Ann Stolberg. BSME, BA in Econ., Stanford U., 1983. Founder Toor Furniture Corp., L.A., 1977-83; mgr. mech. analysis Seagate Tech., Scotts Valley, Calif., 1983—; bd. dirs. Salyer Aviation, Watsonville, Calif. Contbr. articles to profl. jours.; inventor single-point head mount, composite-structure capstan. Home: 14120 Shadow Oaks Way Saratoga CA 95070 Office: Seagate Tech 900 Disc Dr Scotts Valley CA 95066

TOOTELL, THOMAS EDWARD, lawyer; b. Trenton, N.J., Mar. 20, 1948; s. Robert William and Katherine (Crooks) T.; m. Janet Lee Apgar, Dec. 28, 1984; children: Tony, Jesse. BSBA, Lehigh U., 1970; JD, Southwestern, Los Angeles, 1973. Bar: Calif. 1973. Assoc. Kirtland and Packard, Los Angeles, 1973-82; ptnr. Tuverson and Hillyard, Los Angeles, 1982—. Mem. Am. Bd. Trial Advs. (assoc.). Home: 1129 First St Hermosa Beach CA 90254 Office: Tuverson and Hillyard 12400 Wilshire Blvd Los Angeles CA 90025

TOPHAM, DOUGLAS WILLIAM, writer, consultant; b. Hollywood, Calif.; s. Ollie Austin and Harriet Winifred (Scott) T. BS, Stanford U., 1964, AM, 1965. Cert. secondary tchr., Calif. Tchr. The Principia, St. Louis, 1969-72; instr. Can. Coll., Redwood City, Calif., 1973-74; writer Varian Assocs., Palo Alto, Calif., 1977, Four-Phase Systems Inc., Cupertino, Calif., 1977-80, MicroPro Internat., San Rafael, Calif., 1980-81, Zentec Corp., Santa Clara, Calif., 1981-85; contract writer various cos., 1985—, TeleVideo Systems Inc., Sunnyvale, Calif., 1988-89; freelance Santa Clara, Calif., 1989—; cons. ABC-TV, Burbank, Calif., 1974. Author: WordStar Training Guide, 1981, UNIX and XENIX, 1985 (Small Computer Book of Month 1985), UNIX and XENIX System V, 1989, Using WordStar, 1988, World Perfect, 1989. Bd. dirs. Las Brisas Condominium Assn., 1983, 88, Christian Sci. Ch., 1988—. Capt. USAF, 1965-69. Acad. scholar Stanford U., 1960-64. Mem. Authors Guild, Writers Connection, Nat. Writers Union. Republican.

TOPJON, ANN JOHNSON, librarian; b. Los Angeles, Dec. 2, 1940; d. Carl Burdett and Margaret Elizabeth (Tildesley) Johnson; children: Gregory Eric and Cynthia Elizabeth (twins). BA, Occidental Coll., 1962; MLS, UCLA, 1963. Reference asst. Whittier (Calif.) Pub. Library, 1973-78; pub. services and reference librarian Whittier Coll., 1981--. Faculty research grantee Whittier Coll., 1987-88. Mem. Calif. Academic and Rsch. Librs., AAUW (Whittier br. 1968-77, Brea-La Habra br., Calif. 1977—, chmn. lit. group, 1977—, chmn. scholarship fund raising 1988-89). Office: Whittier Coll Wardman Libr 7031 Founders Hill Rd Whittier CA 90608

TOPP, ALPHONSO AXEL, JR., environmental scientist, consultant; b. Indpls., Oct. 15, 1920; s. Alphonso Axel and Emilia (Karlsson) T.; m. Mary Catherine Virtue, July 7, 1942; children: Karen, Susan, Linda, Sylvia, Peter, Astrid, Heidi, Eric, Megan, Katrina. BS in Chem. Engring., Purdue U., 1942; MS, UCLA, 1948. Registered health physicist, N.Mex. Commd. 2d lt. U.S. Army, 1942, advanced through grades to col., 1966, ret., 1970; environ. scientist Radiation Protection Sect., State of N.Mex., Santa Fe, 1970, program mgr., licensing and registration sect., 1978, chief radiation protection bur., 1981-83; cons., 1984—. Decorated Legion of Merit, Bronze Star with 2 oak leaf clusters. Mem. Health Physics Soc., Conf. Radiation Control Program Dirs. (emeritus), Sigma Xi, Rotary. Republican. Presbyterian. Home and Office: 872 Highland Dr Los Osos CA 93402

TORDOFF, JOHN T., civil engineer; b. Corpus Christi, Tex., June 18, 1947; s. John J. and Harriet J. (Andrews) T.; children: Tobia S., Amanda J. BSCE, Marquette U., 1970. Civil engr. State of Wis., Wisconsin Rapids, 1970-71; pvt. practice engr. Moclips, Wash., 1971-74; civil engr. State of Alaska, Juneau, 1974-76; pvt. practice engring. Priest River, Idaho, 1976-81; civil engr. Tongass Nat. Forest, Ketchikan, Alaska, 1981-84, Badlands Nat. Park, Interior, S.D., 1984-86, Nat. Park Service, Lakewood, Colo., 1986—. Office: Nat Park Svc 12795 W Alameda Pkwy Box 25287 Denver CO 80225

TORELL, JOHN RAYMOND, III, banker; b. Hartford, Conn., July 10, 1939; s. Raymond John and Gertrude May (Bent) T.; m. Anne A. Keller, Feb. 17, 1962; children: John Raymond, Anne Elizabeth, Susan Allgood. BA, Princeton U., 1961. With Mfrs. Hanover Trust Co., N.Y.C., 1961—, asst. sec., 1964-67, asst. v.p., 1967-70, v.p. nat. div., 1970, v.p. credit dept., 1970-71, v.p. corp. planning, 1971-72, sr. v.p. planning, mktg. and spl. products, 1973-75, sr. v.p., dep. gen. mgr. retail banking, 1975-76, exec. v.p. met. div., 1976-78, vice chmn., dir., 1978-82, pres., dir., 1982-88; exec. vice chmn., dir. Mfrs. Hanover Corp. (parent), N.Y.C., from 1982, pres., until 1988; chmn., chief exec. officer Calfed Inc., Los Angeles, Ca., 1988—; chmn. Calif. Fed. Savs. and Loan, Los Angeles, Ca., 1988—; dir. Am. Home Products, N.Y. Telephone, Reins Corp., Econ. Captial Corp., N.Y.C. Bd. dirs. Juilliard Mus. Found. Served with USN, 1962. Republican. Clubs: Blind Brook, Siwanoy Country, Bronxville Field. Home: 16 Birchbrook Rd Bronxville NY 10708 Office: Calfed 5670 Wilshire Blvd Los Angeles CA 90036 *

TOREN, ROBERT, photojournalist; b. Grand Rapids, Mich., Oct. 9, 1915; s. Clarence J. and Helen (Holcomb) T.; student Winona Sch. Profl. Photography, 1957, West Coast Sch. Photography, 1959-62; m. Miriam Jeanette Smith, July 17, 1940. Photographer, Harris and Ewing, Washington, 1938-39, Versluis Studios, Grand Rapids, Mich., 1939-43, prodn. mgr., 1940-43; owner, photographer Toren Galleries, San Francisco, 1946-70; photographer Combat Tribes of World, Rich Lee Orgn., 1978-84, Darien jungle expdn. Am. Motors, 1979; feature writer Auburn (Calif.) Jour., El Dorado Gazette, 1983-87. One man shows various univs.; prints in permanent collections: Photog. Hall of Fame, Coyote Point Mus., San Mateo County Hist. Mus.; photog. column San Mateo Times; lectr. Am. Pres. Lines, Coll. San Mateo, Peninsula Art Assn., Mendicino Art Center. Historian City of Foster City; vice chmn. Art Commn. Foster City. Trustee, West Coast Sch.; bd. dirs. Foster City Art League, Hillbarn Theatre, San Mateo County Arts Council; mem. art com. San Mateo County Fair, 1979-87 ; coordinator, dir. Georgetown (Calif.) Mountain Mus., 1982—. Served from pvt. to staff sgt. AUS, 1943-46. Mem. Calif. Writers (br. pres.), Profl. Photographers Am. Presbyn. Author: Peninsula Wilderness. Illustrator: The Tainted Tree, 1963. Editor: The Evolution of Portraiture, 1965; The Western Way of Portraiture, 1965, Conquest of the Darien, 1984. Home: 3140 Cascade Trail Cool CA 95614

TORKLEP, LYNLEE (LINDA LEE TORKLEP), educational educator; b. Rochester, N.Y., Mar. 15, 1942; d. Donald Webster and Marjorie Elizabeth (Loeffler) Crombie; m. Hans Arthur Torklep, Nov. 28, 1964; children: Tracianne Nicole, Tamara Kirsten. BS, Cornell U., 1964; MS, Nova U., 1983. Cert. tchr., vocat. tchr., Wash. Tchr. Auburn (Wash.) Sch. Dist., 1965-67; ctr. dir. Children's Ctr. Kent (Wash.), 1979-87, Daybridge Learning Ctrs., Renton, Wash., 1987; mng. dir. Children's World Learning Ctrs., Renton, 1987—; on-site trainer Renton Vocat. Tech. Inst., 1981-87, mem. child care specialist adv. bd., 1982-84; validator Nat. Acad. Early Childhood Programs, Washington, 1986. Mem. occupational adv. com. Highline Community Coll., Midway, Wash., 1979-81; del. Seattle-Managua Sister Cities, 1986. Recipient cert. of appreciation Renton Vocat. Inst. Tech., 1982, 83, 84, Highline Community Coll., 1986. Mem. Nat. Assn. for Edn. Young Children, Assn. Childhood Edn. Internat. Republican. Lutheran. Office: World Learning Ctrs 11010 SE 176th St Renton WA 98055

TORRENCE, LINDA LEE, child care director, consultant; b. San Diego, Oct. 31, 1945; d. William and Ardis May (Todd) Hamry; m. John Robert Torrence, June 30, 1973; children: Leslie, Steven, Karen, David, Lori, Angie. Cert. child devel., San Diego Community Coll., 1974. Bookkeeping clk. Bank of Am., San Diego, 1963-64; underwriting asst. Ins. Co. N.Am., 1964-71; dir. nursery and presch. 1st Bapt. Ch. of Mira Mesa, San Diego, 1971-78; dir., founder Christian Care Presch., San Diego, 1975-79, Rainbow of Love Presch., San Diego, 1979—; chmn. Community Coll. Adv. Bd., San Diego, 1976-87, chairperson, 1987—; treas. Ch. Related Early Childhood Edn. Fellowship, San Diego, 1976-86, retreat dir., 1980-86. Mem. bldg. com. 1st Bapt. Ch. of Mira Mesa, 1971-76; trainer, educator Regional Occupation Program, 1980, 81, 82, 83, 84, 85. Mem. Nat. Assn. for Edn. of Young Children, Nat. Assn. Childcare Profls., Child Care Info. Exch. Panel 100 Experts, Job's Daughters (guardian sec. 1981-85), Scottish Rite Women's Assn. Republican. Home: 13283 Gabilan Rd San Diego CA 92128 Office: Rainbow of Love Presch 4955 Conrad Ave San Diego CA 92117

TORRES, ALLAN HENRY, computer company executive; b. Los Angeles, Apr. 15, 1952; s. Henry Sanchez and Rachel (Rodela) T.; m. Linda Kay Brown, Dec. 30, 1986; 1 child, Lauren Rochelle. AS, Calif. State U., Los Angeles, 1971-73; BS, U. So. Calif., 1979. Fin. planner Prudential Ins. Co., Ventura, Calif., 1975-76; account mgr. GE, Portland, Oreg., 1977; v.p., bus. mgr., co-owner Burbank (Calif.) Race & Coachworks, Inc., 1977—; prototype and devel. engr. Cray Research, Inc., Chippewa Falls, Wis., 1979-80; sr. engr. Cray Research, Inc., Albuquerque, 1980-81, sales rep., 1981-83; account mgr. Cray Research, Inc., Boulder, Colo., 1983-86; account exec. Digital Equipment Corp., Santa Fe, 1986-88; sales mgr. Thinking Machines Corp., Cambridge, Mass., 1988—; cons. PBM & Assocs. Inc., Boulder, 1985-86. Mem. AIAA, Soc. Exploration Geophysicists, Soc. Petroleum Engrs. Methodist. Home and Office: Thinking Machines Corp 271 Loma Entrada Santa Fe NM 87501

TORRES, ESTEBAN EDWARD, congressman, business executive; b. Miami, Ariz., Jan. 27, 1930; s. Esteban Torres and Rena Baron (Gomez) T.; m. Arcy Sanchez, Jan. 22, 1955; children: Carmen D'Arcy, Rena Denise, Camille Bianca, Selina Andre, Esteban Adrian. AA, East Los Angeles Coll., 1960; grad., Calif. State U., Los Angeles, 1963; postgrad., U. Md., 1965, Am. U., 1966; PhD (hon.), Nat. U., 1987. Chief steward United Auto Workers, local 230, 1954-63, dir. polit. com., editor, 1963; organizer, internat. rep. United Auto Workers (local 230), Washington, 1964; asst. dir. Internat. Affairs Dept., 1975-77; dir. Inter-Am. Bureau for Latin Am., Caribbean, 1965-67; exec. dir. E. Los Angeles Community Union (TELACU), 1967-74; U.S. ambassador to UNESCO, Paris, 1977-79; chmn. Geneva Grp., 1977-78; chmn. U.S. del. Gen. Conf., 1978; spl. asst. to pres. U.S., dir. White House Office Hispanic Affairs, 1979; mem. 98th-101st Congresses from 34th Dist. Calif.; pres., chmn. bd. Internat. Enterprise and Devel. Corp., Washington; campaign coordinator Jerry Brown for Gov., 1974; Hispanic coordinator Los Angeles County campaign Jimmy Carter for Pres., 1976; mem. Sec. of State Adv. Group, 1979-81; v.p. Nat. Congress Community Econ. Devel., 1973-74; pres. Congress Mex.-Am. Unity, 1970-71, Los Angeles Plaza de la Raza Cultural Center, 1974; dir. Nat. Com. on Citizens Broadcasting, 1977; cons. U.S. Congress office of tech. assessment, 1976-77; del to U.S. Congress European Parliament meetings, 1984—; ofcl. congl. observer Geneva Arms Control Talks; treas. Congl. Hispanic Caucus, 1989—; speaker Wrights Del. to USSR, 1987. Contbr. numerous articles to profl. jours. Co-chmn. Nat. Hispanic Dems., 1988—; bd. visitors Sch. Architecture U. Calif. at Los Angeles, 1971-73; bd. dirs. Los Angeles County Econ. Devel. Com., 1972-75, Internat. Devel. Conf., 1976-78. Served in AUS, 1949-53, ETO. Recipient various awards for public service. Mem. Americans for Dem. Action (exec. bd. 1975-77). Office: Longworth Office Bldg Rm 1740 Washington DC 20515

TORRES, MAYDEAN KAU'IONAMOKU LING HOW, architect; b. Honolulu, Mar. 15, 1960; d. Alfred Lopez and Maydelle Puukoa (Kawai) T. AA, Kapiolani Community Coll., 78-80; postgrad., Honolulu Community Coll., 81; BArch, U. Hawaii, 1988. Clk., typist U.S. Army Corps Engrs., Honolulu, 1981-82; clk. U. Hawaii, Honolulu, 1984-85; engring. aid U.S. Army Corps Engrs., Honolulu, 1982—; architect intern, U.S. Army Engrs., Honolulu, 1982—; architect U.S. ARmy Corps. Engrs., 1989—. Active Hist. Hawaii Found. and Nat. Trust for Hist. Preservation. Recipient Group Project Design Merit award AIA, 1988. Mem. Am. Inst. Architecture Students (v.p. 1984-85, pres. 1985-86, Outstanding Chpt. award 1985). Office: US Army Corps Engrs Bldg 230 Honolulu HI 96858

TORRES, ROBERTO HIRAM, nuclear engineer; b. Santurce, P.R., Nov. 16, 1951; s. Manuel Augusto and Irma Isabel (Diaz) T.; m. Lillian Vicent Platon, Jan. 8, 1977; children: Melisa Cristina, Alejandro Roberto. BS in Engring. Physics, Cornell U., 1973; MS in Nuclear Engring., U. Calif.-Berkeley, 1974. Engr. nuclear energy div. GE, San Jose, Calif., 1974-80, sr. engr. nuclear energy div., 1980—; prog. mgr. restart testing Gen. Elec. Nuclear kEnergy Div., San Jose, Calif., 1985. Home: 397 Bangor Ave San Jose CA 95123 Office: GE 175 Curtner Ave San Jose CA 95125

TORREY, JAMES FRANCIS, media consultant; b. Detroit, Feb. 15, 1950; s. James Doolin and Agnes Marie (O'Shea) T.; 2 children. BA in Social Sci., Mich. State U., 1972. Reporter Sta. WITL-AM-FM, Lansing, Mich., 1973-74, Sta. WILX-TV, Lansing, 1974-77, The Ariz. Republic, Phoenix, 1980—, 1980-88; with Opus Enterprises, Phoenix, 1988—. Editor Charlotte Rep.-Tribune, Mich., 1977-80. Recipient Best Use of Graphics 1st pl. award Mich. Press Assn., 1979, Best Enterprise award Mich. Press Assn., 1980, Best of Phoenix award New Times, 1983. Mem. ACLU, Inst. Community Journalism (charter, bd. dirs.), Ariz. Press Club (Spot News Reporting award 1984), Sigma Delta Chi (chmn. com. 1979). Roman Catholic. Office: Opus Enterprises 1617 W Willetta St Phoenix AZ 85007

TORRIGLIA, THOMAS ANTHONY, publishing company executive; b. San Francisco, Feb. 8, 1953; s. Guido and Geraldine Rose (Merovingo) T. BA in English, St. Mary's Coll., Moraga, Calif., 1975. Copywriter San Francisco Guide mag., 1975-79; tech. writer various cos. Bay Area, Calif., 1979--; prin. Pierce, Beach & Assocs., San Francisco, 1988--; freelance entertainment journalist 1985--. Author: The Nightime Good Time Guide to San Francisco and the Bay Area, 1987;. Recipient Milliken award, St. Mary's Coll., 1975. Mem. Nat. Assn. Songwriters, Soc. Tech. Writers, Media Alliance, Olympic Club. Republican. Roman Catholic. Office: Pierce Beach & Assocs 2269 Chestnut St Ste 183 San Francisco CA 94123

TOSTENRUD, DONALD BOYD, banker; b. Estherville, Iowa, Mar. 24, 1925; s. O.M. and Irene (Connell) T.; m. Arlene Girg, Jan. 12, 1950; children: Eric, Amy. B.B.A., U. Minn., 1948; grad., Rutgers U. Grad. Sch. Banking, 1957. Nat. bank examiner Mpls., 1948-57; v.p. First Nat. Bank Black Hills, Rapid City, S.D., 1958-59; with Ariz. Bank, Phoenix, 1959—, exec. v.p., 1967-69, sr. exec. v.p., 1969-71, pres., 1971-78, chmn. bd., chief exec. officer, 1978-87, chmn. bd., chmn. exec. com., 1987-88, chmn. emeritus, chmn. exec. com., 1988—; pres. COMPAS 6; bd. dirs. Samcor, Security Pacific Nat. Bank & Corp. Trustee Phoenix Art Mus., pres., 1980-82; bd. fellows Center for Creative Photography, U. Ariz., Tucson; trustee Grand Central Art Galleries, Inc., N.Y.C., Am. Grad. Sch. Internat. Mgmt., Ariz. Heart Inst., Scottsdale Artists Sch. Inc. Served with AUS, 1943-45. Mem. Ariz. Commn. on Arts, Western Art Assos., Tucson C. of C. (past pres.), Ariz. Bankers Assn. (dir., past pres.), Am. Bankers Assn. (governing council, past dir.). Home: 3059 E Marshall Phoenix AZ 85016 Office: Ariz Bancwest Corp 101 N 1st Ave Phoenix AZ 85003

TOTH, ELIZABETH LEVAY, educational organization executive, lawyer; b. Woodbridge Twp., N.J.; d. Nicholas and Elizabeth (Nagy) Levay; m. Frederick Louis Toth; children: Frederick Albert, Thomas Franklin. BA, Rutgers U., 1970; JD, Seton Hall U., 1973; LLM, NYU, 1980. Bar: N.J. 1973. Mgr., dispatcher Tri-R-Bus Svc., Inc., Metuchen, N.J., 1959-71; arbitration atty. Robert J. Casulli, East Orange, N.J., 1973; mediator, hearing officer N.J. Pub. Employment Relations Commn., Trenton, 1973-74; assoc. dir. employee relations Woodbridge (N.J.) Twp. Pub. Schs., 1974-81; dir. govt. and community relations Ariz. Sch. Bd. Assn., Phoenix, 1981-85; exec. dir. Greater Phoenix Ednl. Mgmt. Coun., 1985—; participant Insts. for Orgnl. Mgmt., San Jose (Calif.) State U., 1985—. Mem. community adv. bd. Sta. KAET-TV, Ariz. State U., Tempe, 1985—; pres-elect North Community Behavioral Health Ctr. (merged into Terros Community Mental Health Orgn. 1988), Phoenix, 1984-88, bd. dirs. 1988—; arbitrator Better Bus. Bur., Phoenix, 1987—. Recipient plaque and pub. recognition North Community Behavioral Health Ctr., 1987. Mem. Am. Soc. Assn. Execs., Ariz. Soc. Assn. Execs. (bd. dirs. 1987-88, Exec. of Yr. award 1987), Soc. Profls. in Dispute Resolution (sec. 1986-87), Pub. Affairs Profls. Ariz., Corp Bus. and Profl. Women's Club, Rutgers U. Alumni Club of Phoenix, Alumni Club of Ariz., Phi Alpha Delta, Alpha Sigma Lambda. Home: 3142 W Marconi Ave Phoenix AZ 85023 Office: Greater Phoenix Ednl Mgmt Coun 415 E Grant St Ste 209 Phoenix AZ 85004

TOTH, JOSEPH MICHAEL, JR., astronautical engineer; b. Somerville, N.J., Mar. 8, 1935; s. Joseph Michael and Anna Theresa (Horvath) T.; m. Ann Todd Carlton, Aug. 22, 1959; children: Joseph Michael III, Sarah Ann, Deborah Lynn. Student, Lafayette Coll., 1951-53; BS, MIT, 1956; MS, U. Ariz., 1965, postgrad., 1965-68. Registered profl. engr., Colo. Design engr. U.S. Steel Corp., Fairless Hills, Pa., 1956-58; rsch. assoc. U. Ariz., Tucson, 1958-61; design engr. McDonnell Douglas Corp., Huntington Beach, Calif., 1961-72; program mgr. Martin Marietta Astronautics Group, Denver, 1972—. Contbr. articles to profl. jours.; patentee in field. Mem. ASTM (com. D-30, composites), Soc. for Advancement of Material and Process Engring., AIAA (mem. materials and structures standards panel), MIL-HDBK-17 Coordination Group. Home: 4551 N Lariat Dr Castle Rock CO 80104 Office: PO Box 179 Denver CO 80201

TOTMAN, RICHARD CURTIS, title company executive; b. Lancaster, Wis., Apr. 14, 1917; s. Curtis Reul and Vera (McDonald) T.; m. Rosemary Wills, Mar. 19, 1944; children: Charles, Lisa, Sandra, Cathy, Pamela. BS, U. Wis., Madison, 1939; MBA, U. Chgo., 1952. Asst. treas. Curtiss Candy Co., Chgo., 1946-50; dist. sales mgr. Dole Valve Co., Chgo., 1950-56; sales mgr. Rahr Malting Co., Manitowoc, Wis, 1956-58; v.p. The Ariz. Bank, Phoenix, 1958-64; stock broker Bache & Co., Phoenix, 1964-71; v.p. Stewart Title & Trust, Phoenix, 1971-76; sales mgr. Minn. Title, Phoenix, 1976-86; dir. mktg. Founders Title, Phoenix, 1986—. Pres. Ariz. Bus. Alliance, Phoenix, 1984, 88, Phoenix Mus. Theatre, 1975; bd. dirs. Scottsdale (Ariz.) Artists' Sch., 1985. Lt. col., USAAF. Mem. Ariz. Club, Plaza Club, Dons of Ariz. (pres. 1970-71), Phoenicians (pres. 1972-73). Republican. Episcopalian. Home: 7117 E Jenan Dr Scottsdale AZ 85254 Office: Founders Title 333 E Osborn St Phoenix AZ 85012

TOTTEN, ALFRED EDWARD, educator; b. L.A., June 19, 1938; s. Tracy Hall and Phyllis Sarah (Jarvis) T.; m. Sumako Ann Yoshida, Apr. 27, 1969; children: Albert, Gregory, Sonia. BA, U. Hawaii, 1965, MA, 1968. Cert. community coll. instr., Calif. Data processor City of L.A. Dept. of Water and Power, 1956-59; instr. ESL Tezukayama Coll., Nara, Japan, 1968-72; adminstrv. asst. County of L.A. Pub. Defender, 1974-85; typesetter Berlitz Trans. Svcs., Woodland Hills, Calif., 1985; bookkeeper Pacific Asia Mus., Pasadena, Calif., 1986-87; instr. bus. English, math, acctg., computer literacy and word processing Glendale (Calif.) Coll. Bus., 1987—. Contbr. articles to Tezukayama Coll. Jour., 1969-72. Served with U.S. Army, 1962-64. Republican. Anglican. Home: 8271 Glencrest Dr Sun Valley CA 91352 Office: Glendale Career Coll 1021 Grandview Ave Glendale CA 91201

TOTTEN, GEORGE OAKLEY, III, political science educator; b. Washington, July 21, 1922; s. George Oakley Totten Jr. and Vicken (von Post) Totten Barrois; m. Astrid Maria Anderson, June 26, 1948 (dec. Apr. 1975); children: Vicken Yuriko, Linnea Catherine; m. Lilia Huiying Li, July 1, 1976; 1 child, Blanche Lemes. Cert., U. Mich., 1943; A.B., Columbia U., 1946, A.M., 1949; M.A., Yale U., 1950, Ph.D., 1954; docent i Japanologi, U. Stockholm, 1977. Lectr. Columbia U., N.Y.C., 1954-55; asst. prof. MIT, Cambridge, 1958-59, Boston U., 1959-61; assoc. prof. U. R.I., Kingston, 1961-64; assoc. prof. polit. sci. U. So. Calif., Los Angeles, 1965-68, prof., 1968—, chmn. dept., 1980-86; dir. East Asian Studies Ctr. U. So. Calif., 1974-77; dir., founder U. So. Calif.-UCLA Joint East Asia Ctr., 1976-77; vis. prof. U. Stockholm, 1977-79, dir. Ctr. Pacific Asia Studies, 1985—. Author: Social Democratic Movement in Prewar Japan, 1966, Chinese edit., 1987; co-author: Socialist Parties in Postwar Japan, 1966, Japan and the New Ocean Regime, 1984; co-editor, author: Developing Nations: Quest for a Model, 1970 (Japanese edit. 1975); co-translator: Traditional Government in Imperial China, 1982. Mem. U.S.-China People's Friendship Assn., Washington, 1974—, mem. Com. on U.S.-China Relations, N.Y.C., 1975—; chmn. Los Angeles-Pusan Sister City Assn., Los Angeles, 1976-77; bd. dirs. Los Angeles-Guangzhou Sister City Assn., 1982—; mem. council of dirs. Japan-Am. Soc. Los Angeles, 1981—. Served to 1st lt. AUS, 1942-46, PTO. Social Sci. Research Council fellow, 1952-53; Ford Found. grantee, 1955-58; NSF grantee, 1979-81; recipient Plaque for program on Korean studies Consulate Gen. of Republic of Korea, 1975. Mem. Assn. for Asian Studies, Am. Polit. Sci. Assn., Internat. Polit. Sci. Assn., Internat. Studies Assn., Japanese Polit. Sci. Assn. Presbyterian. Club: U. So. Calif. Faculty (Los Angeles). Home: 5118 Village Green Los Angeles CA 90016 Office: U So Calif Dept Polit Sci University Pk Los Angeles CA 90089-0044 also: U Stockholm, Ctr Pacific Asia Studies, Stockholm S-10691, Sweden

TOULOUSE, JAMES RAYMOND, lawyer; b. Albuquerque, Apr. 14, 1919; s. Joseph Harrison and Laura Belle (Cauger) T.; m. Charlotte Johnson, Aug. 30, 1941; children: Carmie Lynn, Charlotte Mary, Laura Lee, Leigh Ann, Samantha McAnally. AB, U. N.Mex., 1941; JD, GeorgetownU., 1949. Reporter, sports writer Albuquerque Tribune, 1938-43; prtnr. McAtee & Toulouse, Albuquerque, 1949, McAtee, Toulouse, Marchiondo, Ruud & Walters, Albuquerque, 1959, Toulouse, Ruud, Gallagher & Walters, Albuquerque, 1966, Toulouse, Moore & Walters, Albuquerque, 1969, Toulouse & Moore, Albuquerque, 1972, Toulouse, Krehbiel & DeLayo, Albuquerque, 1973, Toulouse, Toulouse & Garcia, Albuquerque, 1979—. Representer rights of Am. Indians and Spanish Ams.; mem. Albuquerque NAACP Def. Fund. Petty officer USN, 1943-46. Mem. ABA, Am. Bd. Trial Advs., Am. Trial Lawyers Assn., Albuquerque Bar Assn., N.Mex. Bar Assn. (1st ever courageous Advocacy award 1987), N.Mex. Trial Lawyers Assn. (trial atty. 1988), NAACP (civil rights atty., award 1986), Westerners. Democrat. Presbyterian. Office: Toulouse & Assocs 2403 San Mateo #9 W Albuquerque NM 87110

TOUR, ROBERT LOUIS, opthalmologist b. Sheffield, Ala., Dec. 30, 1918; s. R.S. and Marguerite (Meyer) T. Chem.E., U. Cin., 1942, M.D., 1950. Intern, U. Chgo. Clinics, 1950-51; resident U. Calif. Med. Center-San Francisco, 1951-54; practice medicine, specializing in ophthalmology, San Francisco, 1954-76, Fairbanks, Alaska, 1976-79, Phoenix, 1979—; mem. staff Boswell Meml. Hosp.. Del Webb Meml. Hosp.; clin. prof. ophthalmology U. Calif.-San Francisco, 1974-76. Served to maj. AUS, 1942-45. Diplomate Am. Bd. Ophthalmology. Fellow ACS, Am. Acad. Ophthalmology; mem. AMA, Ariz. Ophthal. Soc., Phoenix Ophthal. Soc., Calif. Assn. Ophthalmology, Contact Lens Assn. Ophthalmologists, Pacific Coast Oto-Ophthal. Soc., Ariz. Med. Assn., Maricopa County Med. Soc. , F.C. Cordes Eye Soc., Sigma Xi, Nu Sigma Nu, Alpha Tau Omega, Tau Beta Pi, Alpha Omega Alpha, Phi Lambda Upsilon, Omicron Delta Kappa, Kappa Kappa Psi. Clubs: Masons, K.T., Lions. Shriners. Home: 1016 E Lois Ln Phoenix AZ 85020

TOVAR, NICHOLAS MARIO, mechanical engineer; b. Ogden, Utah, Jan. 18, 1960; s. Gerdo and Alice (Martinez) T.; m. Suzanne Oxborrow, Sept. 17, 1982; children: Ashley, Nicholas Brock, Clinton Gregory. BS in Logistics Mech. Engring., Weber State Coll., 1986; postgrad. in mech. engring., Nat. U., 1988—. Warehouseman R.C. Wiley & Son Co., Syracuse, Utah, 1982-85; logistics controller Utah-Idaho Supply Co., Salt Lake City, 1985-86; assoc. engr. Aerojet TechSystems Co., Sacramento, 1986-87, engr., 1988—. Republican. Mormon. Home: 2360 Cobble Oak Ct Rancho Cordova CA 95670 Office: Aerojet TechSystems Co PO Box 13222 Dept 9790 Bldg 2019 Sacramento CA 95813

TOVEY, WELDON REYNOLDS, college dean, engineering educator; b. Malad City, Idaho, Oct. 19, 1938; s. Lester Malcolm and Edith (Raynolds) T.; m. Vicki Rae Bowman, July 15, 1964; children: Kristina, Bradley, Kimberli, Daniel, Camille, Laura Lee. BSME, U. Idaho, 1961, MEd, 1964; EdD, Brigham Young U., 1971. Instr. engring. U. Idaho, Moscow, 1962-64, asst. prof., 1965-71, assoc. prof., asst. dean, 1971-76, prof., asst. dean, 1976-80, prof., assoc. dean, 1980—. Author: Engineering Analysis and Design, 1974, Engineering Graphics Problems, 1975. Bishop LDS Church, Moscow, 1968-74; counselor LDS Church Stake Presidency, Pullman, Wash., 1974-80; pres. LDS Church Stake, Pullman, 1980—. Mem. Am. Soc. for Engring. Edn. (Western Electric Fund award 1971), Tau Beta Pi, Sigma Tau, Phi Delta Kappa. Republican. Home: 1130 E 7th St Moscow ID 83843 Office: U Idaho Coll Engring Moscow ID 83843

TOWE, THOMAS EDWARD, lawyer; b. Cherokee, Iowa, June 25, 1937; s. Edward and Florence (Tow) T.; m. Ruth James, Aug. 21, 1960; children: James Thomas, Kristofer Edward. Student, U. Paris, 1956; BA, Earlham Coll., 1959; LLB, U. Mont., 1962; LLM, Georgetown U., 1965. Ptnr. Towe, Ball, Enright & Mackey, Billings, Mont., 1967-71; legislator Mont. House of Rep., Billings, 1971-75, Mont. State Senate, Billings, 1975-87; served on various coms. Mont. Senate, 1973-87. Contbr. articles to law revs. Pres. Alternatives, Inc. Halfway House, Billings, 1985-86; mem. adv. com. Mont. Crime Control Bd. 1973-78, Youth Justice council, 1981-83; mem. State Dem. Exec. com., 1969-71, Yellowstone County Dem. Exec. Com., 1969-73; mem. Billings Friends Meeting Ch.; bd. dirs. Mont. Consumer Affairs Council, Regional Community Services for the Devel. Disabled, 1975-77, Rimrock Guidance Found., 1975-80, Vols. of Am., Billings, 1984-89, Youth Dynamics Inc., 1989—. Capt. U.S. Army, 1962-65. Mem. Mont. Bar Assn., Yellowstone County Bar Assn., Am. Hereford Assn., Billings C. of C., Optimists. Mem. Soc. of Friends. Home: 2739 Gregory Dr S Billings MT 59102 Office: 2525 Sixth Ave N Billings MT 59101

TOWERS, ROY LANGE, JR., buyer; b. Hayward, Calif., May 6, 1955; s. Roy Lange and Julie (Santos) T.; m. Peggy Louise Renk, July 20, 1985. MA, Calif. State U., Hayward, 1984. Cert. purchasing mgr. Contract specialist U. Calif., Berkeley, 1984--. Office: U Calif 2510 Channing Way #7 Hayward CA 94720

TOWEY, RICHARD EDWARD, economics professor; b. Mount Kisco, N.Y., Sept. 22, 1928; s. William Joseph and Anna Margaret (Rumse) T.; m. Mary Ann Franusich, June 12, 1954 (dec. Mar. 1988); 1 child, John Patrick. BS, U. San Francisco, 1954; MA, U. Calif., Berkeley, 1957, PhD, 1967. Economist Fed. Reserve Bank of San Francisco, San Francisco, 1957-60; econ. prof. Oreg. State Univ., Corvallis, Oreg., 1962—; economist Fed. Deposit Ins. Corp., Washington, 1968-70. Cpl. U.S. Army, 1948-49, 1950-51. Named Earhart Fellow, Univ. Calif., Berkeley, 1961-62. Mem. Am. Econ. Assn., Am. Fin. Assn., Western Econ. Assn. Roman Catholic. Office: Dept Econ Oreg State Univ Corvallis OR 97331

TOWNE, DOROTHEA ALICE, chiropractor; b. Easton, Ill., Feb. 1, 1910; d. Elnathan and Fairy Alice (Downey) T. D.C., Cleveland Chiropractic Coll., Los Angeles, 1954, Ph.C., 1955, B.S., 1977; student U. Wash., 1928-30; B.A. magna cum laude, U. So. Calif., 1946. Indsl. relations dir. Standard Paper Box Corp., Los Angeles, 1943-54; asso. dean acad. affairs Cleveland Chiropractic Coll., 1956-75, dean, tchr., 1976-82, dir. clin. scis., 1972-78, emerita, 1981—; naturopath, 1986—; lectr. in field; numerous radio and TV appearances. Composer: (with L. Mayberry) The Presidents Parade. Contbr. to poetry anthologies. Recipient numerous awards including appreciation award San Francisco Bay Research Assn., C.S. Cleveland, Sr., award for outstanding service, 1984. Fellow Internat. Chiropractors Assn., Idaho Assn. Naturopathic Physicians (bd. dirs. 1986, 87-88), Gamma Phi Beta, Psi Chi, Sigma Chi Psi. Address: E 508 Eaton Ave Spokane WA 99218

TOWNER, GEORGE RUTHERFORD, writer; b. N.Y.C., Sept. 15, 1933; s. Rutherford Hamilton and Marion (Washburn) T.; m. Danielle Lemoine, Apr. 30, 1985; children: Stephane, Diane, Philip, Claire. BA, U. Calif., 1955, MA, 1956. Asst. dir. Kaiser Found., Richmond, Calif., 1958-60; rsch. engr. Advanced Instrument Corp., Richmond, Calif., 1960-61; pres. Berkeley Instruments, Oakland, Calif., 1962-67; chmn. bd. Towner Systems Corp., San Leandro, Calif., 1968-78; cons. Towner Systems Corp., San Leandro, 1968-78; sr. writer Apple Computer, Computer, Cupertino, Calif., 1987—. Inventor: Teladvisor Data System, 1962 (awarded 3 Patents 1966-76),. Recipient award of Merit Soc. Technical Communication 1985, 1988. Mem. Soc. Technical Communication, Assn. Computing Machinery, Mensa. Home: 814 Gail Ave Sunnyvale CA 94086 Office: Apple Computer 20525 Mariani Ave Cupertino CA 95014

TOWNER, LARRY EDWIN, transportation company executive; b. Gallup, N.Mex., Sept. 27, 1937; s. Edwin Robert and Esther Kathryn (Kern) T.; m. D. Yvonne Turner, Mar. 12, 1966; children: Kristina Kay, Jennifer Kate. BS in Tech. Mgmt., Am. U., Washington, 1976. Project mgr. Wolf Research, Houston, 1965-66, Gulton SRG, Arlington, Va., 1966-67; dep. for database devel. USN, Washington, 1967-79; mgr., BTP teleprocessing RCA, Cherry Hill, N.J., 1979-80; mgr., data base adminstrn., solid state div. RCA, Somerville, N.J., 1980-82; mgr., systems devel. Hughes Aircraft, El Segundo, Calif., 1982—. Author: Ads/Online Cookbook, 1986IDMS/R, A Professionals Guide, 1989; contbr. articles to profl. jours. Treas. Va. Hills Recreation Assn., Alexandria, 1970-72, pres. 1975-77; active Civil Air Patrol, Alexandria, 1968-79; bd. dirs. Northwest Citizens Radio Emergency Service, Spokane, Wash., 1960-63. Recipient Meritorious Service award Civil Air Patrol, 1976. Mem. IDMS User Assn. (bd. dirs.) (Outstanding Service award, 1984), Hughes Mgmt. Club, Amateur Radio Relay League. Methodist. Home: 8702 Delray Circle Westminster CA 92683 Office: Hughes Aircraft Co S64/C403 PO Box 92919 Los Angeles CA 90009

TOWNES, CHARLES HARD, physics educator; b. Greenville, S.C., July 28, 1915; s. Henry Keith and Ellen Sumter (Hard) T.; m. Frances H. Brown, May 4, 1941; children: Linda Lewis, Ellen Screven, Carla Keith, Holly Robinson. B.A., B.S., Furman U., 1935; M.A., Duke U., 1937; Ph.D., Calif. Inst. Tech., 1939. Mem. tech. staff Bell Telephone Lab., 1939-47; assoc. prof. physics Columbia U., 1948-50, prof. physics, 1950-61; exec. dir. Columbia Radiation Lab., 1950-52, chmn. physics dept., 1952-55; provost and prof. physics MIT, 1961-66, Inst. prof., 1966-67; v.p., dir. research Inst. Def. Analyses, Washington, 1959-61; prof. physics U. Calif. at Berkeley, 1967-86, prof. physics emeritus, 1986—; Guggenheim fellow, 1955-56; Fulbright lectr. U. Paris, 1955-56, U. Tokyo, 1956; lectr., 1955, 60; dir. Enrico Fermi Internat. Sch. Physics, 1963; Richtmeyer lectr. Am. Phys. Soc., 1959; Scott lectr. U. Cambridge, 1963; Centennial lectr. U. Toronto, 1967; Lincoln lectr., 1972-73, Halley lectr., 1976; dir. Gen. Motors Corp.; mem. Pres.'s Sci. Adv. Com., 1966-69, vice chmn., 1967-69; chmn. sci. and tech. adv. com. for manned space flight NASA, 1964-69; mem. Pres.'s Com. on Sci. and Tech., 1976; researcher on nuclear and molecular structure, quantum electronics, interstellar molecules, radio and infrared astrophysics. Author: (with A.L. Schawlow) Microwave Spectroscopy, 1955; author, co-editor: Quantum Electronics, 1960, Quantum Electronics and Coherent Light, 1964; editorial bd.: (with A.L. Schawlow) Rev. Sci. Instrument, 1950-52, Phys. Rev, 1951-53; bd.: (with A.L. Schawlow) Phys., Rev, 1951-53, Jour. Molecular Spectroscopy, 1957-60, Procs. Nat. Acad. Scis, 1978—; contbr. articles to sci. publs.; patentee masers and lasers. Trustee Calif. Inst. Tech., Carnegie Instn. of Washington, Pacific Sch. Religion; mem. corp. Woods Hole Oceanographic Instn. Recipient numerous hon. degrees and awards, including; Nobel prize for physics, 1964; Stuart Ballantine medal Franklin Inst., 1959, 62; Thomas Young medal and prize Inst. Physics and Phys. Soc., Eng., 1963; Disting. Public Service medal NASA, 1969; Wilhelm Exner award Austria, 1970; Niels Bohr Internat. Gold medal, 1979; Nat. Sci. medal, 1983, Berkeley citation U. Calif., 1986; named to Nat. Inventors Hall of Fame, 1976, Engring. and Sci. Hall of Fame, 1983. Fellow Am. Phys. Soc. (council 1959-62, 65-71, pres. 1967, Plyler prize 1977), Optical Soc. Am. (hon., Mees medal 1968), IEEE (medal of honor 1967), Calif. Acad. Scis.; mem. Am. Philos. Soc., Am. Astron. Soc., Am. Acad. Arts and Scis., Nat. Acad. Scis. (council 1969-72, 78-81, chmn. space sci. bd. 1970-73, Comstock award 1959), Société Française de Physique (council 1956-58), Royal Soc. (fgn.), Pontifical Acad. Scis., Max-Planck Inst. for Physics and Astrophysics (fgn. mem.). Office: U Calif Dept Physics Berkeley CA 94720

TOWNSEND, JEFFREY FRED, winery executive, infosystems specialist; b. Bklyn., Aug. 20, 1953; s. Richard F. Townsend and Blanche Horgan; m. Jan M. Pathroff, Nov. 10, 1984. BS in Acctg., Rider Coll., 1975; MBA in Fin., Fairleigh Dickinson U., Madison, N.J., 1978. Project mgr. IMS Internat., N.Y.C., 1976-79; dir. research Dun and Bradstreet, N.Y.C., 1979-80, dir. mgmt. info. systems, 1980-83; mgmt. cons. N.Y.C., 1983-84; dir. info. resources Gallo Winery, Modesto, Calif., 1984-88, dir. sales and mktg. support, 1988—. Inventor in field. Mem. Data Processing Mgmt. Assn., Am. Info. Assn., Assn. for Computing Machinery, Assn. Systems Mgmt. (speaker), Food Mktg. Inst., Am. Assn. Artificial Intellience. Home: 2624 Nassau Circle Modesto CA 95355 Office: Gallo Winery PO Box 1130 Modesto CA 95351

TOWNSEND, LARRY DARWYN, commercial printer; b. Marysville, Calif., Nov. 25, 1959; s. Lawrence Wayne Townsend and Yvonne (Holsey) Godfrey; m. Karen Faye Chappell, June 4, 1983; 1 child, Jennifer Lynn. Grad. high sch., Fed. Republic Germany, 1976. Fly boy/jogger Sacramento Suburban Newspapers, 1979, rolltender, 1979-81; rolltender Treasure Chest Advt. Inc., Sacramento, 1981-82, 2d pressman, 1982-83, 1st pressman, 1983-85, press foreman, 1985-86, tech. trainer, 1986—. Recipient Eagle Scout, Boy Scouts Am., 1977, Order of the Arrow, 1976. Home: 1147 Ravine View Dr Roseville CA 95678 Office: Treasure Chest Advt Inc 1201 Shore St West Sacramento CA 95691

TOWNSEND, RUSSELL HENRY, lawyer; b. Ft. Lewis, Wash., Dec. 27, 1949; s. Peter Lee and Irma Matilda (Greisberger) T.; m. Patricia Susan Parks, Feb. 9, 1985; children: Alexander Peter, Jennifer Sabrina. BS, Calif. Maritime Acad., 1971; JD, Lincoln U., San Francisco, 1979. Bar: Calif., U.S. Dist. Ct. (no. and ea. dists.) Calif. Title examiner Western Title Ins. Co., Oakland, Calif., 1972-74; clk. Garrison, Townsend, Hall and predecessor, San Francisco, 1974-79; ptnr. Amberg & Townsend, San Francisco, 1980-83, Townsend and Bardellini, San Francisco, 1983-87, Townsend, Bardellini, Townsend and Wechsler, San Francisco, 1988—. Lt.j.g. USNR, 1971-75. Mem. State Bar Calif. Republican. Home: 5 Mae Ct Novato CA 94947 Office: Townsend Bardellini et al 201 Spear St Ste 1550 San Francisco CA 94105

TOWNSEND, SUSAN ELAINE, social service institute administrator, hostage survival consultant; b. Phila., Sept. 5, 1946; d. William Harrison and Eleanor Irene (Fox) Rogers; m. John Holt Townsend, May 1, 1976. BS in Secondary Edn., West Chester State U., 1968; MBA, Nat. U., 1978; PhD in Human Behavior, La Jolla U., 1984. Biology tchr. Methacton Sch. Dist., Fairview Village, Pa., 1968-70; bus. mgr., analyst profl. La Jolla Research Corp., San Diego, 1977-79; pastoral asst. Christ Ctr. Bible Therapy, San Diego, 1980-82, also bd. dirs.; v.p., pub. relations World Outreach Ctr. of Faith, San Diego, 1981-82, also bd. dirs.; owner, pres., cons. Townsend Research Inst., San Diego, 1983—; teaching assoc. La Jolla U. Continuing Edn., 1985-86. Author: Hostage Survival-Resisting the Dynamics of Captivity, 1983; contbr. articles to profl. jours. Religious vol. Met. Correctional Ctr., San Diego, 1983—, San Diego County Jail Ministries, 1978—. Served to comdr. USN, 1970-76, USNR, 1976—. Mem. Naval Res. Assn. (life), Res. Officers Assn. (Outstanding Jr. Officer of Yr. Calif. chpt. 1982), Navy League U.S. (life), West Chester U. Alumni Assn., Nat. U. Alumni Assn. (life), La Jolla U. Alumni Assn., Gen. Fedn. Women's Clubs (pres. Peninsula club 1983-85, pres. Parliamentary law club 1984-86, Past Pres.' Assn.), Calif. Fedn. Women's Clubs (v.p.-at-large San Diego dist. 25 1982-84). Office: 1060 Alexandria Dr San Diego CA 92107

TOWNSLEY, JUSTIN L., JR., commercial real estate executive; b. Cin., June 3, 1950; s. Justin L. and Hilda H. (Quigg) T.; m. Phyllis M. Gilpatrick Townsley, Apr. 21, 1973; children: Blake Cameron, Courtland Garrett. BS in Economics, USAF Acad., 1972; MS in Economics, U. Pitts., 1973. Cert. fin. planner, fin. specialist USAF, Dayton, Ohio, 1973-76; fin. mgr. USAF, Dayton, 1976-77; mgmt. and fin. cons. Riverton, Wyo., 1978-86; asset mgr. LaSalle Ptnrs., Denver, 1986—; fin. cons. Gold Shield Mining, Denver, 1986—. Author: A Development Plan for Indian Tribes Controlling Mineral Reserves, 1984. Council mem. Colo. Assn. of Commerce and Industry, Denver, 1987-88. Capt. USAF, 1976-77. Mem. Inst. of Cert. Fin. Planners. Office: LaSalle Ptnrs Ltd 100 S 5th St Ste 490 Minneapolis MN 55402

TOYER, RICHARD HENRY, accountant; b. Snohomish, Wash., Aug. 6, 1944; s. Henry James Toyer and Bertha Maud (Darrow) Gilmore; m. Jean Ann Moore, July 1, 1966; 1 child, David K. BS in Acctg., Cen. Wash. U., 1973. CPA. Staff acct. Moss, Adams and Co., Everett, Wash., 1973-74, sr. staff acct., 1975-77; prin. Toyer and Assocs., Everett, Wash., 1977—. Mayor City of Lake Stevens, Wash., 1983—, city councilman, 1977-83; state treas. Wash. Jaycees, 1975-76; pres. Snohomish Jaycees, 1974-75; mem. Snohomish County Estate Planning Council. Served as sgt. U.S. Army, 1965-67, Vietnam. Mem. Am. Inst. CPAs, Wash. Soc. CPAs. Lutheran. Home: 2401 116th Ave NE Lake Stevens WA 98258 Office: 3201 Broadway Ste C Everett WA 98201

TOYOMURA, DENNIS TAKESHI, architect; b. Honolulu, July 6, 1926; s. Sansuke Fujimoto and Take (Sata) T.; m. Akiko Charlotte Nakamura, May 27, 1949; children—Wayne J., Gerald F., Amy J., Lyle D. BS in Archtl. Engring., Chgo. Tech. Coll., 1949; cert., U. Ill., Chgo., 1950, 53, 54; student, Ill. Inst. Tech., Chgo., 1953-54; cert., U. Hawaii-Dept. Def., Honolulu, 1966-67, 73. Registered architect, Ill., Hawaii; lic. real estate broker, Ill. Designer, draftsman James M. Turner, Architect, Hammond, Ind., 1950-51, Wimberly and Cook, Honolulu, 1952, Gregg, Briggs & Foley, Architects, Chgo., 1952-54; architect Holabird, Root & Burgee, Architects, Chgo., 1954-55, Loebl, Schlossman & Bennett, Architects, Chgo., 1955-62; prin. Dennis T. Toyomura, AIA, Architect, Honolulu, 1963-83, Dennis T. Toyomura, FAIA, Architect, Honolulu, 1983—; fallout shelter analyst Dept. Def., 1967—; cert. analyst multi-distaster design, Dept. Def., 1973; cert. value engr. NAVFACENGCOM, Gen. Svc. Adminstrn, U.S.A., 1988; cons. Honolulu Redevel. Agy., City and County of Honolulu, 1967-71; sec., bd. dir. Makiki of Hawaii, Honolulu, 1972-74; bd. dirs. Pacific Canal Hawaii, 1972; mem. steering com. IX world conf. World Futures Studies Fedn., U. Hawaii, 1986; conf. organizer pub. forum 10th Hawaii Conf. in High Energy Physics, U. Hawaii, 1985; appointments rsch. corp U. Hawaii, 1986—; mem.

Hawaii State Found. on Culture and the Arts, 1982-86; mem. Gov.'s Com. on Hawaii Econ. Future, 1984; archtl. mem. Bd. Registration for Profl. Engrs., Architects, Land Surveyors and Landscape Architects, State of Hawaii, 1974-82, sec. 1980, vice chmn. 1981, chmn., 1982; mem. Nat. Coun. Engrng. Examiners, 1975-82; mem. Nat. Coun. Archtl. Registration Bds., Western region del. 1975-82, nat. del. 1976-82. Ecclesiastical del. commr. state assembly, Synod of Ill., United Presbyn. Ch. U.S.A., 1958, alt. del. commr. nat. gen. assembly, 1958, del. commr. L.A. presbytery, 1965; bd. session 2d Presbyn. Ch., Chgo., 1956-62, trustee, 1958-62; trustee 1st Presbyn. Ch., Honolulu, 1964-66, 69-72, sec., 1965, bd. sessions, 1964-72, 74-79; founding assoc. Hawaii Loa Coll., Kaneohe, 1964; mem. adv. commn. drafting tech. Leeward Community Coll., U. Hawaii, 1965—; bd. dirs. Lyon Arboretum Assn., U. Hawaii, 1976-77, treas., 1976. With U.S. Army, 1945-46. Recipient Human Resources of U.S.A. award Am. Bicentennial Rsch. Inst., 1973; Outstanding Citizen Recognition award Cons. Engrs. Coun. Hawaii, 1975, Cert. Appreciation Gov. of Hawaii, 1982, 86, commendation, 1983; resolution and cert. commendation Hawaii Ho. of Reps. and Senate, 1983. Fellow AIA (Coll. Fellows 1983, bd. dirs. Hawaii Soc. 1973-74, treas. 1975, Pres.'s Mahalo award 1981, Fellows medal); mem. AAAS (life), Acad. Polit. Sci., Am. Acad. Polit. and Social Scis., N.Y. Acad. Scis., Chgo. Art Inst., Chgo. Natural History Mus., Honolulu Acad. Arts, Nat. Geog. Soc., Coun. Ednl. Facility Planners Internat. (bd. govs. N.W. region 1980-86), Bldg. Rsch.Inst. (adv. bd. of Nat. Acad. Sci.), Ill. Assn. Professions, ASTM, Constrn. Specifications Inst., Constrn. Industry Legis. Orgn. (bd. dirs. 1973-81, 83—, treas. 1976-77), Japan-Am. Soc., Hawaii State C. of C. (bd. dirs. 1984-87), U. Hawaii Kokua O'Hui, O'Nahe Popo (bd. dirs. 1984—), Hawaii-Pacific Rim Soc. (bd. trustees 1988—), Alpha Lambda Rho, Kappa Sigma Kappa, Pres. Club Hawaii Loa Coll., Pres. Club U. Hawaii, Malolo Mariners Club (purser 1964, skipper 19865, Hawaii),. Home: 2602 Manoa Rd Honolulu HI 96822 Office: Dennis T Toyomura FAIA Architect 1370 Kapiolani Blvd Honolulu HI 96814

TOYOOKA, LAURA L., public relations executive; b. Atlanta, Jan. 21, 1961; d. Donald Leslie and Eleanor Jane (Hill) Spanton; m. John Arthur Toyooka, May 26, 1983. BS in Journalism, U. Md., 1982; MA in Communications, U. West Fla., 1984; postgrad., Western State U., Fullerton, Calif., 1987. Pub. relations asst. Fed. Home Loan Mortgage Corp., Washington, 1982; writer Whiting Tower, Milton, Fla., 1984-85; pub. relations aaccount exec. asst. Investor Communications Systems, Irvine, Calif., 1985-86; pub. relations freelancer Thomas Wilch Assocs., Irvine, 1986; pub. relations coordinator Green Martin Nevins, Costa Mesa, Calif., 1986-87; pub. relations and mktg. coordinator Fidelity Nat. Title, Irvine, 1987-88; v.p. bus. devel. Terra Escrow, Irvine, 1988; cofounder, v.p. Yates-Hill Rsch. Inc., Mission Viejo, Calif., 1988—. Vol. Orange County Performing Arts Ctr. Triathlon Com., 1988. Mem. Bldg. Industry Assn., Nat. Assn. Female Execs., Nat. Soc. Hist. Preservation. Republican. Methodist. Office: PO Box 3622 Mission Viejo CA 92690

TOZZER, CHARLES PHILLIP, dentist; b. Honolulu, July 24, 1953; s. Leroy Charles and Patricia (Anderson) T.; m. Karen Norton, Mar. 11, 1978; children: Lauren Anderson, Meredith Beattie. BA in Chemistry, Emory U., 1975; DDS, U. N.C., 1979. Lic. dentist, Calif., N.C. Pvt. practice Irvine, Calif., 1981—; internat. lectr. Kulzer, Inc., Irvine, 1984—; cons. 1984—. Dentist Share Ourselves Dental Clin., Costa Mesa, Calif., 1988; tribe chief YMCA Indian Princesses, Irvine, 1988. Mem. ADA, Calif. Dental Assn., Orange County Dental Soc., Irvine Med./Dental Soc. (bd. mem. 1987-89). Republican. Office: 14785 St Ste 112 Irvine CA 92720

TRACY, GEORGE WILLIAM, JR., manufacturing executive, engineer; b. Cin., Aug. 4, 1944; s. George William Sr. and Helen Mary (Lauber) T.; m. Donna Rae Fellerman, July 15, 1967; children: Andrea Jean, James Patrick. BSME, U. Cin., 1967, MS, 1970. Registered profl. engr., Calif. Tech. rep. Joy Tech., L.A., 1970-72, staff engr., 1972-73, test engr. supr., 1973-75, mgr. svc., 1975-78, svc. and results mgr., 1978-87; project mgr. Joy Tech., Glendale, Calif., 1987-88, tech. mgr. internat., 1988--; chmn. West Covina (Calif.) Waste Mgmt. Com., 1984--; vice chmn. ABMA/IGCI Joint Tech. Com., Washington, 1982--. Served with U.S. Army, 1967-69. Mem. ASME (vice chmn. Power Test Code 40, mem. Power Test Code 28, 38), Air Pollution Control Assn. Republican. Home: 808 S Cajon West Covina CA 91791 Office: Joy Tech Western Prescrip 404 Huntington Dr Monrovia CA 91016

TRACY, MARCUS RICHARD, printer; b. Seattle, Nov. 8, 1957; s. Donald Raymond and Marcia Jane (St. Pierre) T. Student, Cornish Coll. Printer Resprographics Northwest Inc., Seattle, 1981—. Vol. designer Chicken Soup Brigade, Seattle, 1988. Home: 207 12th Ave E Seattle WA 98102

TRAGER, RUSSELL HARLAN, publishing company executive; b. Cambridge, Mass., Sept. 26, 1945; s. Nathan Allan and Shirley (Gibbs) T.; m. V. Jan Adams, Aug. 19, 1968 (div. July 1975); 1 child, Eric Todd; m. Edna Marie Sanchez, Feb. 16, 1980; 1 child, Felice Rosanne. AA, Newton Jr. Coll., 1965; BS, U. Miami, 1968; postgrad., Harvard U., 1968-69. Account rep. Hervic Corp., Sherman Oaks, Calif., 1972-75, Canon USA, Lake Success, N.Y., 1975-78; key account sales rep. Yashica Inc., Glendale, Calif., 1978-79; sales rep. Region I United Pubs. Corp., Beverly Hills, Calif., 1979-81, sales mgr., 1981-83; regional pres. United Pubs. Corp., Carson, Calif., 1983-86, region v.p., 1986-88; v.p. sales United Pubs. Corp., Beverly Hills, 1988—. Home: 1201 11th St Manhattan Beach CA 90266 Office: United Pubs Corp 8383 Wilshire Blvd Beverly Hills CA 90201

TRAHERN, GEORGE EUGENE, real estate appraiser/owner, insurance agent; b. Grants Pass, Oreg., June 29, 1936; s. Eugene Goodyear and Lela Marie (Feldmaier) T.; m. Darlene Irma Taylor, Dec. 22, 1956; children: Karen Marie Bodeving, Eugene Lyle, Keith Charles. BS, U. Oreg., 1960. Owner, dealer, gen. mgr. Trahern Motors, Inc., Grants Pass, Oreg., 1960-68, John Day, Oreg., 1969-71; asst. mgr. Keith Roberts Ford, Cottage Grove, Oreg., 1959-60; dep. assessor Josephine County, Grants Pass, 1971-73, county assessor, 1973-81; owner, appraiser Trahern Real Estate Appraiser, Grants Pass, 1981—; owner, dealer, gen. mgr. N.Valley Auto Ctr., Inc., Grants Pass, 1985-87; ins. agt. Siskiyou Agy., Medford, Oreg., 1988-89. Capt., sec. Josephine County Sheriff's Mounted Posse, Grants Pass, 1971-88; rep. Oreg. Legis. Assembly, Salem, Oreg., 1981-88, senator, 1988; commr. Grant County Planning Commn., Canyon City, Oreg., 1969-71; bd. dirs. shooting sports com. Oreg. 4-H Club, Corvallis, Oreg., 1966-87. With USN, 1952-54, USNR, 1954-62. Recipient 3 Quality Dealer awards Chrysler Corp., 1961, 62, 64, Merit award Internat. Harvester, Inc., 1964, Pentstar Club award Chrysler Corp., 1986. Mem. Nat. Assn. Real Estate Appraiers (cert.), Nat. Assn. Life Underwriters, Grants Pass C. of C., Josephine County Hist. Soc. (bd. dirs. Grants Pass chpt. 1975-88), Grants Pass Knife & Fork Club (pres. 1978-79), Rotary, Order of Eastern Star (worthy patron 1966-67). Republican. Methodist (past pastor parish rels., bd. dirs.). Home and Office: 4011 Williams Hwy Grants Pass OR 97527

TRAINA, CYNTHIA MARIE, Public relations consultant; b. Rockford, Ill., Oct. 27, 1957; d. Vincenzo Lorenzo and Carol (Anselmo) T. BA, Rockford Coll., 1977. Research asst. Ctr. for Regional Tech. Polytechnic U. of N.Y., Bklyn., 1978-79; research asst. Resource Planning Assocs., Washington, 1979-80; campaign coordinator Anderson for President, Washington, 1980; account exec. Orsborn Group, P.R., San Francisco, 1980-82; Traina Public Relations San Francisco, 1982--. Office: 3875 21 St San Francisco CA 94114

TRAMONTANA, CHARLES STEPHEN, hospital administrator; b. Brookville, Pa., July 12, 1952; s. Joseph Anthony and Betty Mae (Finerty) T.; 1 child, Stephen; m. Donna Peterson; stepchildren: Zac Peterson, Adam Peterson. Registered Radiologic Technologist, Presbyn.-U. Hosp., Pitts., 1972. Radiology staff technologist Childrens' Hosp., Pitts., 1972-73; clin. instr. radiology St. Joseph Mercy Hosp., Ann Arbor, Mich., 1973-78; mgr. radiology svcs. Mercy Med. Ctr., Durango, Colo., 1978-88, dir. materials mgmt., 1988—. Mem. Am. Healthcare Radiology Adminstrs. (edn. chmn. Western Region 1986-88), Am. Registry Radiologic Technologists, Am. Assn. Purchasing Mgmt., Am. Soc. Hosp. Materials Mgrs., Rotary. Methodist.

TRANQUADA, ROBERT ERNEST, medical school dean, physician; b. Los Angeles, Aug. 27, 1930; s. Ernest Alvro and Katharine (Jacobus) T.; m. Janet Martin, Aug. 31, 1951; children: John Martin, James Robert, Katherine Anne. B.A., Pomona Coll., 1951; M.D., Stanford U., 1955; D.Sc. (hon.), Worcester Poly. Inst., 1985. Diplomate: Am. Bd. Internal Medicine. Intern in medicine UCLA Med. Center, 1955-56, resident in medicine, 1956-57; resident Los Angeles VA Hosp., 1957-58; fellow in diabetes and metabolic diseases UCLA, 1958-59; fellow in diabetes U. So. Calif., 1959-60, asst. prof. medicine, 1959-63, assoc. prof., 1963-67, prof., chmn. dept. community medicine, 1967-75; med. dir. Los Angeles County/U. So. Calif. Med. Center, 1969-74; regional dir. Central Region, Los Angeles County Dept. Health Services, 1975-76; assoc. dean UCLA, 1976-79; chancellor/dean U. Mass. Med. Sch., 1979-86; dean Sch. Medicine Univ. So. Calif., 1986—. Contbr. numerous articles to profl. publs. Trustee Pomona Coll., 1969—, vice chmn., 1987—; mem. bd. fellows Claremont U. Ctr., 1971-79; corporator Worcester Art Mus., 1980-86; bd. dirs. Nat. Med. Fellowships, Inc., 1973—, chmn., 1980-85; trustee Charles Drew U. Medicine and Sci., 1986—, Orthopaedic Hosp., 1986—, Barlow Hosp., 1986—, Hollywood Presbyn. Hosp., 1987-89; bd. dirs. Worcester Acad., 1984-86, Worcester County Inst. for Savs., 1982-86. Milbank faculty fellow, 1967-72. Fellow Am. Antiquarian Soc.; mem. AMA, Am. Diabetes Assn., Western Soc. Clin. Investigation, Los Angeles County Med. Assn., Los Angeles Acad. Medicine, Calif. Med. Assn., Inst. Medicine of Nat. Acad. Scis., Am. Assn. Advancement Sci., Phi Beta Kappa, Sigma Xi, Alpha Omega Alpha. Office: U So Calif Sch Medicine Office Dean 2025 Zonal Ave Los Angeles CA 90033

TRAPANI, RALPH JAMES, highway engineer; b. Buffalo, May 21, 1952; s. Ralph James and Estelle (Silvaroli) T.; m. Barbara Hicks, June 8, 1974. BS in Archtl. Engrng., U. Colo., 1974. Registered profl. engr., Colo. Hwy. engr. Colo. Dept. Hwys., Glenwood Springs, 1975-80, project mgr., 1980—; cons. Hicks & Assoc., Glenwood Springs. Contbr. articles to profl. jours. Pres. Glenwood Springs Soccer Assn., 1988—. Mem. ASCE, Nat. Soc. Profl. Engrs. Home: 1194 137 Rd Glenwood Springs CO 81601 Office: Colo Dept Hwys PO Box 1430 Glenwood Springs CO 81601

TRAPINI, JAN DIANE, nurse; b. St. Joseph, Mich., Feb. 24, 1953; d. Joseph Michael and Helen Eleanore (Vigansky) D'Agostino; m. Vincent Frank Trapini, Oct. 4, 1986. BSN, Nazareth Coll., 1976. Staff nurse Borgess Med. Ctr., Kalamazoo, 1976-78, critical care nurse, 1978-84; head nurse ICU Sun Coast Hosp., Largo, Fla., 1985-86; dir. nursing Vital Care Nursing Svcs., Inc., Fountain Valley, Calif., 1986-88; discharge planner Fountain Valley Regional Hosp. and Med. Ctr., 1988--. Republican. Lutheran. Home: 39 Navarre Irvine CA 92715 Office: Fountain Valley Regional Hosp and Med Ctr 17100 Euclid Fountain Valley CA 92708-8010

TRASK, LINDA ANN, sales executive; b. Cambria Heights, N.Y., Oct. 13, 1956; d. Lewis Volkert and Ethel May (Sheid) T. Cert. Transp., Delta Coll., 1985. Office mgr. Roofers Supply, Modesto, Calif., 1978-80; terminal mgr. Prouty Trucking, Modesto, 1980-82; mgr. Cert. Transpn., Modesto, 1982-86; mgr. regional sales Provisioners Express, Modesto, 1987—; Mem. Cen. Valley Transpn., Modesto, 1987—.

TRASK, ROBERT CHAUNCEY RILEY, author, lecturer, foundation executive; b. Albuquerque, Jan. 2, 1939; s. Edward Almon Trask and Florence Jane (White) Jones; m. Katie Lucille Bitters (div. 198l); m. Mary Jo Chiarottino, Dec. l, 1984. Student pub. schs., San Diego. Lic. master sea capt. Entertainer, singer, comedian 1964--; founder, pres. Nat. Health & Safety Svcs., San Francisco, 1968-7l, ARAS Found., Bellevue, Wash., 1978—; capt., dive master San Diego Dive Charters, 1972-75; sr. capt., dive master Pacific Sport Diving Corp., Long Beach, Calif., 1975-77; lectr., bus. cons. 1978—; cons., tng. developer Nissan, Gen. Dynamics, AT&T, religious orgns., also other corps., 1978--. Author: (manual) Tulip, 197l; Living Free, 1982, God's Phone Number, 1987, also seminar manuals. Mem. SAG. Office: ARAS Found 1380 156th St NE Ste 2060 Bellevue NE 98007

TRAUGOT, DEBRA, employment agency manager; b. Ridgewood, N.J., Aug. 10, 1956; d. Fortunato Vincent and Rose (Petracca) DeSimone; m. William H. Wholey, Aug. 14, 1983 (div. Jan. 1988); m. Kenneth Traugot, Mar. 17, 1989. Student, Bergen Community Coll., Paramus, N.J., 1981-82, Ramapo Coll., Mahwah, N.J., 1984, Chubb Inst., 1983. Office mgr. United Bur. Investigation, Paramus, N.J., 1977-78; office supervisor Oradell (N.J.) Animal Hosp., 1978-81; personnel adminstr. Brandon Systems Corp., Clifton, N.J., 1981-85; technical recruiter Citicorp, N.Y.C., 1985-87; br. mgr. Brandon Systems Corp., Los Angeles, 1987—. Mem. Nat. Assn. Temporary Services. Republican. Roman Catholic. Office: Brandon Systems Corp 3600 Wilshire Blvd Ste 830 Los Angeles CA 90010

TRAUTENBERG, GERALD ANTHONY, chemical company executive; b. Newark, Dec. 10, 1935; s. Anthony and Catherine (Galik) T.; m. Nancy Ann Hecker, 1987; children from previous marriage: Laurie Jean, Carol Ann, Christopher Neal. AB, Rutgers U., 1959, MS in Biochemistry, 1964. Biochemist Bristol Myers, Hillside, N.J., 1958-62; product mgr. Drew Chem. Corp., Parsippany, N.J., 1962-72; tech. service mgr. Betz Labs., Calif., Wash., 1973-78; ptnr. Process Products N.W., Bellevue, Wash., 1979-85; U.S. mgr. Com Cor Group sub. Esso-Can., Bellevue, 1986—; bd. dirs. Fitness Network Am., Bellevue, 1985—. Contbr. tech. papers to sci. publs. V.p. Bellevue Ski Council, 1983—; mem. Metro-Seattle Water Quality adv. com., 1989—. Mem. TAPPI. Home: PO Box 5052 Bellevue WA 98009 Office: Com Cor Group Sub Esso Can, 1035 Derwent Way, New Westminster, BC Canada V3M 5R4

TRAVERS, JUDITH LYNNETTE, human resource executive; b. Buffalo, Feb. 25, 1950; d. Harold Elwin and Dorothy (Helsel) Howes; m. David Jon Travers, Oct. 21, 1972; 1 child, Heather Lynne. BA in Psychology, Barrington Coll., 1972; cert. in paralegal course, St. Mary's Coll., Moraga, Calif., 1983; postgrad., Southland U., 1982-84. Exec. sec. Sherman C. Weeks, P.A., Derry, N.H., 1973-75; legal asst. Mason-McDuffie Co., Berkeley, Calif., 1975-82; paralegal asst. Blum, Kay, Merkle & Kauftheil, Oakland, Calif., 1982-83; exec. v.p. Western Med. Personnel Inc., Concord, Calif., 1983—; pres. All Ages Sitters Agy., Concord, 1986—. Vocalist record album The Loved Ones, 1978. Vol. local Congl. campaign, 1980, Circle of Friends, Children's, Hosp. No. Calif., Oakland, 1987—; mem. Alameda County Sheriff's Mounted Posse, 1989, Contra Costa Child Abuse Prevention Coun., 1989. Mem. NAFE, Am. Assn. Respiratory Therapy, Calif. Soc. Respiratory Care, Am. Mgmt. Assn., Gospel Music Assn., Palomino Horse Breeders Am., DAR, Barrington Oratorio Soc., Commonwealth Club Calif., Nat. Trust Hist. Preservation, Alpha Theta Sigma. Republican. Baptist. Home: 3900 Brown Rd Oakley CA 94561 Office: Western Med Pers Inc 1820 Galindo St Ste 225 Concord CA 94520

TRAVERS, RICHARD JOSEPH, instrumentation company executive, consultant; b. San Francisco, Oct. 11, 1936; s. Richard Joseph and Grace Isabelle (Zurcher) T.; m. Jane Ellen Wagner, Nov. 27, 1957 (div. Oct. 1977); children: Joseph Richard, James Edward, Richard Joseph, Donald John; m. Marie Viola White, Oct. 15, 1978. BS, U. San Francisco, 1958, GS, 1960. Engrng. mgr. T.A. Pelsue Co., Englewood, Colo., 1970-7l, Nederland (Colo.) Mobil & Electric Co., 197l-75, M.D.C. Corp., Crossville, Tenn., 198l-85; maintenance supt. Coors Container Co., Golden, Colo., 1975-77; mine foreman and examiner Stauffer Chem. Co., Green River, Wyo., 1977-79; assoc. prof. Western Wyo. Coll., Rock Springs, 1979-8l; elec. supr. Project Constrn. Corp., Frontier, Wyo., 1986; tng. supr. Chevron Chem. Co., Rock Springs, 1986-87; v.p. dir. Crickett Controls Corp., Salt Lake City, 1987--; tng. cons. Arco, Sunoco, Bridger Coal Co., Green River, 1977-8l; supervising engr. Kilborn Internat., Elko, Nev., 1988. Patentee umbrella pop up tent. Mem. Crime Stoppers, Green River, 198l. Capt. U.S. Army, 1958-60. Mem. Instrument Soc. Am. (sr., pres. 1987-88, tng. cons. 1988, Svc. award 1988), Internat. Assn. Elec. Insps., Am. Radio Relay League, Air Force Assn. (life), NRA, Sweetwater Country Club. Republican. Mormon. Home: 1155 Mountain View Dr Green River WY 82935

TRAVERSO, PEGGY BOSWORTH, speech pathologist; b. Stockton, Calif., Nov. 1, 1938; d. James Everett Bosworth and Jeanne (Owens) Sturla; divorced; children: Gregory, Douglas. BA, Stanford U., 1960; MA in Early Childhood Edn., Calif. State U., Sacramento, 1989. Cert. tchr., Calif. Speech therapist Stockton Unified Sch. Dist., 1960-65, 77--; mem. early childhood adv. com. San Joaquin Delta Coll., 1985—, children's svcs. coordinating commn. of San Joaquin County, 1989—; tchr. Lincoln Presbyn. Nursery Sch., Stockton, 1968-70; owner, mgr. restaurants, Stockton, 1969-77. Speaker Child Abuse Prevention Coun., Stockton, 1981--, pres. bd. dirs., 1982-84. Recipient Sammy Davis Jr. award Child Abuse Prevention Coun., 1987. Mem. Calif. Speech-Lang. Hearing Assn., Calif. Children's Lobby. Office: Harrison Sch 3203 Sanguinetti Ln Stockton CA 95205

TRAVIS, JOHN RICHARD, mechanical engineer; b. Billings, Mont., Sept. 3, 1942; s. Lynn E. and Dorothy (Howard) T.; m. Carole M. Lahti, Aug. 1, 1963 (div. 1980); children: Kristi Ann, Patti Sue; m. Linda M. Hasenbank, May 24, 1985; 1 child, Jason Allan. BSME with hons., U. Wyo., 1965; MS, Purdue U., 1969, PhD, 1971. Registered profl. engr., N.Mex. Instr. engrng. sci. U. Wyo., Laramie, 1965-66; instr. fluid mechanics Purdue U., Lafayette, Ind., 1970-71; staff Argonne (Ill.) Nat. Lab., 1971-73, Los Alamos (N.Mex.) Nat. Lab., 1973—; summer staff Argonne Nat. Lab., Idaho Falls, Idaho, 1965, Battelle Meml. Inst., Columbus, Ohio, 1966; cons. in field; official U.S. Cons. to Internat. Atomic Energy Agy. on nuclear reactor safety issues, Vienna, 1984—; official U.S. Del. to Fed. Republic of Germany on nuclear reactor safety issues, 1989—. Contbr. articles to profl. jours. Nat. Ctr. Atmospheric Rsch. fellow, 1970. Mem. ASME, Am. Nuclear Soc., Los Alamos Ski Club, Sigma Xi, Sigma Pi Sigma, Sigma Tau, Elks. Home: 121 LaSanda Rd Los Alamos NM 87544 Office: Los Alamos Nat Lab Group N6 MS-K557 Los Alamos NM 87545

TRAYLOR, CLAIRE GUTHRIE, state senator; b. Kansas City, Mo., Jan. 18, 1931; d. Frank and Janet Guthrie; m. Frank A. Traylor, 1954; children: Nancy, Frank, Susan, David. BS, Northwestern U., 1952; MA, Washington U., St. Louis, 1955. Primary sch. tchr., 1955-57; mem. Colo. Ho. of Reps., 1978-82, majority caucus chmn., 1980-82; mem. Colo. State Senate, 1982—, chair bus. affairs and labor, 1987—, capital devel. com., 1988; mem. health, environ. and insts. audit com., 1987—; mem. Colo. Commn. on Aging, Colo. Commn. on Children and Families, Colo. Housing Fin. Authority Bd., Colo. Guaranteed Student Loan Bd., Colo. Indsl. Commn. Adv. Com., Colo. Internat. Trade Adv. Commn., Colo. Capital Complex Commn., Wheat Ridge, Golden, Arvada, Lakewood, Jefferson County, Rep. Cen. Coms., del. rules com. Rep. Nat. Com., 1988; Jr. League, Clear Creek (Colo.) Valley Med. Aux., pres. bd. Highland West-Highland So. (Colo.). Presbyterian. Mem. C. of C., Nat. Conf. State Legislators (dir. western region), Women's Network (chair human resource com. 1988-89), vice chair internat. trade com.). Office: Colo State Senate State Capitol Bldg Denver CO 80203

TRAYLOR, WILLIAM ROBERT, publisher; b. Texarkana, Ark., May 21, 1921; s. Clarence Edington and Seba Ann (Talley) T.; m. Elvirez Traylor, Oct. 9, 1945; children: Kenneth Warren, Gary Robert, Mark Daniel, Timothy Ryan. Student, U. Houston, 1945-46, U. Omaha, 1947-48. Div. mgr. Lily-Tulip Cup Corp., N.Y.C., 1948-61; asst. to pres. Johnson & Johnson, New Brunswick, N.J., 1961-63; mgr. western region Rexall Drug & Chem. subs. Dart Industries, L.A., 1963-67; pres. Prudential Pub. Co., Diamonds Springs, Calif., 1967—; cons. printing industry, 1976—. Author: Instant Printing, 1976, Successful Management, 1979, Quick Printing Encyclopedia, 1982, 7th edit., 1988. With USCG, 1942-45. Named Man of Yr. Quick Printing Mag., 1987. Mem. Nat. Assn. Quick Printers (hon. lifetime), C. of C., Kiwanis, Toastmasters. Democrat. Office: Prudential Pub Co 7089 Crystal Blvd Diamond Springs CA 95619

TREANOR, WALTER JOHN, physician; b. County Tyrone, No. Ireland, May 14, 1922; came to U.S., 1949, naturalized, 1954; s. Hugh and Marion (deVine) T.; M.D., Nat. U. Ireland, 1947; Diplomate Am. Bd. Phys. Medicine & Rehab.; m. Mary Stewart, Dec. 29, 1971; children: James P., Wanden, Dona, June. Intern, St. Mary's Hosp., San Francisco, 1949-52; resident Mayo Found., Rochester, Minn.; practice medicine specializing in rehab. medicine, Santa Rosa, Calif.; emeritus prof. medicine U. Nev., Reno, 1979—. Served to capt., M.C., U.S. Army, 1953-55. Fellow ACP, Royal Soc. Medicine; mem. Am. Acad. Neurology, Internat. Med. Soc. Paraplegia, Am. Acad. Phys. & Rehab. Medicine. Republican. Contbr. articles to profl. jours. Home: 1370 Spring St Santa Rosa CA 95404

TRECKEME, CLAUDEA MITCHELL, healthcare consultant; b. Milw., Sept. 20, 1945; d. William Pokrass and Elizabeth Anne (Packard) Mitchell; m. Thomas John Treckeme, June 10, 1967; 1 child, Craig Andrew. AA, Consumnes River Coll., 1978. Sr. healthcare systems analyst Computer Sci. Corp., Sacramento, 1979-88; healthcare cons. Sacramento, 1988--. Contbr. articles to profl. publs. Vol. Sacramento Child Abuse Coun., 1986. Mem. Profl. Women's Assn., Orgn. Nuclear Freeze, Mensa, Rainbow Girls. Democrat. Jewish. Office: 4424 G Pkwy Sacramento CA 95823

TREDER, ALFRED JAMES, aerospace engineer; b. Chgo., July 5, 1940; s. Ralph Aloysius and Marie Magdalen (Seaman) T.; m. Mary Angela Jaaska, May 9, 1964; children: Anne, Susan, Barbara, Patricia, Lisa, Laura. BEE, Marquette U., 1963. Devel. engr. Honeywell Aerospace Div., Mpls., 1962-69; tech. staff TRW Systems Group, Redondo Beach, 1969-71; sr. engr. Cal Tech Jet Propulsion Lab., Pasadena, 1971-80; prin. engr. Boeing Aerospace Div., Seattle, 1980—. Contbr. articles to profl. jours. Mem. AIAA, Inst. Navigation, K.C. Bowling League (pres. 1978-80). Roman Catholic. Home: 28327 183d Ave SE Kent WA 98042 Office: Boeing Aerospace Box 3999 MS 8C-47 Seattle WA 98124-2499

TREFNY, JOHN ULRIC, physics educator; b. Greenwich, Conn., Jan. 28, 1942; s. Ulric John and Mary Elizabeth (Leech) T.; m. Beverly Jane Robin, Mar. 18, 1967; 1 child, Benjamin Robin. BS, Fordham U., 1963; PhD, Rutgers U., 1968. Research assoc. Cornell U., Ithaca, N.Y., 1967-69; asst. prof. physics Wesleyan U., Middletown, Conn., 1969-77; asst. prof. physics Colo. Sch. Mines, Golden, 1977-79, assoc. prof., 1979-85, prof. 1985—, dir. Amorphous Materials Ctr., 1986—, assoc. dean of research, 1988—; cons. Solar Energy Research Inst., Golden, Energy Conversion Devices, Troy, Mich., various other cos. Contbr. articles to profl. jours. Recipient AMOCO Teaching award AMOCO Found., 1984. Mem. Am. Ceramic Soc., Am. Phys. Soc., Am. Assn. Physics Tchrs., Colo. Assn. Sci. Tchrs. (bd. dirs. 1986—), Sigma Xi, Sigma Pi Sigma. Avocations: golfing, traveling, whiskey. Home: 14268 W 1st Ave Golden CO 80401

TREGARTHEN, TIMOTHY DORAN, journalist, economics educator; b. Riverside, Calif., Nov. 25, 1945; s. Doran Woodrow and Ethel Mae (Geabhart) T.; m. Karen Sue Angel, June, 1967 (div. 1971); m. Nancy L. Sidener, Aug. 23, 1971 (div. 1985); m. Suzanne Jo Schroeder, Aug. 3, 1985; children: Doran Richard, Brittany Grace. BA in Econs., Calif. State U., 1967; MA in Econs., U. Calif., Davis, 1970, PhD in Econs., 1972. Lectr., U. Calif., Davis, 1970-71; asst. prof. econs. U. Colo., Colorado Springs, 1971-76, assoc. prof., chmn. dept., 1976-78, prof., chmn. dept. 1981-85; vis. prof. The Colo. Coll., 1981-87; chmn. bd. dirs. The Wright-Ingraham Inst., Colo. Springs, 1982—. Author: Food, Fuel and Shelter, 1978; editor The Margin mag., 1985—; syndicated columnist, 1984-88. Chmn., El Paso Country Planning Commn., Colorado Springs, 1981-83, Nat. Multiple Sclerosis Soc., Colo. Springs, 1984. Woodrow Wilson Found. fellow, 1967; recipient Disting. Teaching award, U. Colo., 1976, 81, 86. Mem. Am. Econ. Assn., Atlantic Econ. Assn., Western Econ. Assn. Democrat. Home: 1075 Applewood Dr Colorado Springs CO 80907-4605 Office: U Colo Dept Econs Colorado Springs CO 80933

TREHARNE, JOHN EDWARD, automobile executive; b. Bklyn., Jan. 26, 1939; s. Donald Eugene Treharne and Majorie F. (Leavers) Cameron; m. Shirley A. Kittock, Dec. 31, 1958 (div. 1983); children: Bradford C., James Douglas. Student, Boise Jr. Coll., 1957-58. Gen. mgr. Gem State Motors, Boise, Idaho, 1963-73, Peterson Toyota and Peterson Jeep/Eagle, Boise, Idaho, 1973—; sec., treas. Idaho Toyota Dealers, Boise 1983—, Better Bus. Bur. Treasure Valley, Boise, 1988—. Vol. Parole Officer Idaho State Parole Dept., Boise 1971-72; asst. chmn. Ada County United Way; co-host Arthritis Telethon, 1989—; bd. dirs. Idaho chpt. Arthritis Found., 1989—. Republican. Office: Peterson Toyota 1201 Main St Boise ID 83702

TREIGER, IRWIN LOUIS, lawyer; b. Seattle, Sept. 10, 1934; s. Sam S. and Rose (Steinberg) T.; m. Betty Lou Friedlander, Aug. 178, 1957; children: Louis H., Karen I., Kenneth B. BA, U. Wash., 1955, JD, 1957; LLM in Taxation, NYU, 1958. Bar: Wash. 1958, D.C. 1982, U.S. Dist. Ct. (we. dist.) Wash., U.S. Ct. Appeals (9th cir.), U.S. Supreme Ct. Assoc. Bogle & Gates, Seattle, 1958-63, ptnr., 1964—. Sec. Jewish Fedn. of Greater Seattle, 1982—; chmn. Mayor's Symphony Panel, 1986, Corp. Council for the Arts,

1987-88; pres. Seattle Symphony Found., 1986—; trustee, vice-chmn. Cornish Coll. of the Arts, 1987—. Fellow Am. Coll. of Tax Counsel; mem. ABA (chmn. taxation sect. 1988—), Seattle State Bar Assn. (chmn. taxation sect. 1975), Greater Seattle C. of C. (gen. counsel 1987—), Rainier Club (trustee Seattle 1985-88). Jewish. Office: Bogle & Gates 601 Union St Seattle WA 98101

TREIMAN, JOYCE WAHL, artist; b. Evanston, Ill., May 29, 1922; d. Rene and Rose (Doppelt) Wahl; m. Kenneth Treiman, Apr. 25, 1945; 1 child, Donald. A.A., Stephens Coll., 1941; B.F.A. (grad. fellow 1943), State U. Iowa, 1943. Vis. prof. San Fernando Valley State Coll., 1968; lectr. UCLA, 1969-70; vis. prof. State U. Calif., Long Beach, 1977. One-man shows include Paul Theobald Gallery, Chgo., 1942, John Snowden Gallery, Chgo., 1945, Art Inst. Chgo., 1947, North Shore Country Day Sch., Winnetka, Ill., 1947, Fairweather-Garnett Gallery, Evanston, 1950, Edwin Hewitt Gallery, N.Y.C., 1950, Palmer House Galleries, Chgo., 1952, Glencoe (Ill.) Library, 1953, Elizabeth Nelson Gallery, Chgo., 1953, Charles Feingarten Gallery, Chgo., 1955, Cliff Dwellers Club, Chgo., 1955, Fairweather-Hardin Gallery, Chgo., 1955, 58, 73, 81, 86, Marian Willard Gallery, N.Y.C., 1960, Felix Landau Gallery, Los Angeles, 1961, 64, La Jolla (Calif.) Mus., 1962-72, Forum Gallery, N.Y., 1963, 66, 75, 81, Adele Bednarz Gallery, Los Angeles, 1969-71, 74, Palos Verdes (Calif.) Art Mus., 1976, Mcpl. Art Gallery L.A., 1978, monotypes UCLA, 1979, drawings Art Inst. Chgo., 1979, Tortue Gallery, Santa Monica, Calif., 1980, 83, 86, Schmidt-Bingham Galery, N.Y.C., 1986, 88, Portland (Oreg.) Art Mus., 1988, Rochester Meml. Art Gallery, 1988, U. So. Calif. L.A., 1988, U. So. Calif. Retrospective, 1987, L.A., Rochester Meml. Art Gallery, Rochester, N.Y., 1988, Portland (Oreg.) Art Mus., 1988; numerous exhbns. including Carnegie Internat., 1955, 57, Met. Mus., 1950, Whitney Mus., 1951, 52, 53, 58, Art Inst. Chgo., 1945-59, John Herron Art Inst., 1953, Library of Congress, 1954, Cocoran Gallery, 1957, Pa. Acad. Fine Arts, 1958, Mus. Modern Art, 1962, Am. Acad. Arts and Letters, N.Y.C., 1974, 75, 76, Retrospective Exhbn., Mcpl. Art Gallery, Los Angeles, 1978; represented in permanent collections Kemper Ins. Co., Chgo., Met Mus. Art, N.Y.C., Denver Mus. Art, State U. Iowa, Ill. State Mus., Long Beach (Calif.) Mus., Whitney Mus. Am. Art, N.Y.C., Tupperware Art Mus., Orlando, Fla., Art Inst. Chgo., Utah State U., Abbott Labs., Oberlin Allen Art Mus., Internat. Mineral Corp., Pasadena Art Mus., U. Calif. at Santa Cruz, Grunwald Found., UCLA, Santa Barbara Mus. Art, Calif., Oakland Mus., Calif., Security Pacific Nat. Bank, Los Angeles, Rochester (N.Y.) Art Mus.; pub. collections include Art Inst. Chgo., Whitney Mus., Met. Mus., Santa Barbara (Calif.) Mus., Portland (Oreg.) Mus. Recipient numerous awards including Logan purchase prize Art Inst. Chgo., 1951, Martin B. Cahn prize, 1959, 60, Pauline Palmer prize, 1953, Saratosa Am. Painting Exhbn. award, 1959, Ford Found. purchase prize, 1960, Purchase prize Ball State Coll., 1961, prize La Jolla Art Mus., 1961, Purchase prize Pasadena Art Mus., 1961; Tiffany fellow, 1947-48; Tupperware Art Fund fellow, 1955; Tamerind Lithography fellow, 1961. Address: 712 Amalfi Dr Pacific Palisades CA 90272

TREINEN, SYLVESTER WILLIAM, bishop; b. Donnelly, Minn., Nov. 19, 1917; s. William John and Kathryn (Krausert) T. Student, Crosier Sem., Onamia, Minn., 1935-41; B.A., St. Paul's Sem., 1943. Ordained priest Roman Cath. Ch., 1946; asst. pastor Dickinson, N.D., 1946-50; sec. to bishops Ryan and Hoch, 1950-53; asst. pastor Cathedral Holy Spirit, Bismarck, N.D., 1950-57; chancellor Diocese Bismarck, 1953-59; asst. pastor St. Anne's Ch., Bismarck, 1957-59; pastor St. Joseph's Ch., Mandan, N.D., 1959-62; bishop Boise, Idaho, 1962—. Address: 420 Idaho St PO Box 769 Boise ID 83701 *

TREIT, ELROY MALCOLM, clergyman; b. Wilkie, Sask., Can., Mar. 6, 1933; s. Henry and Hilda (Rosnau) T.; m. Carol Jean Schneider, Jan. 29, 1960; children—Jonathan, Matthew, Marla Jean. AA, Concordia Coll., 1953, BA, 1954; BD, Concordia Sem., 1959; MS in Sociology, Simon Fraser U.; DDiv, Brock U., 1989. Ordained to ministry Luth. Ch., 1959. Pastor Parish Killarney Park Luth. Ch., Vancouver, B.C., Can., 1959—; 2d v.p. Alta.-B.C. Dist. Luth. Ch. of Can., 1970-88, dir. fund raising, 1971-86; family life dir. Alta.-B.C. Dist. Luth. Ch. of Can. (Western Region), 1972-76; pres. Luth. Ch. of Can., 1977-88, now hon. pres.; mem. Fed. Family Life Bd.; counsellor ABC Dist. for women's orgns.; lectr. in seminars on human sexuality. Researcher, author publs. in philately. Bd. dirs Vancouver YMCA, 1961-76; adv. B.C. Human Resources Dept., 1976-79. Mem. Profl. Counsellors Assn. of Province B.C., Luth. Laymen's League, Luth. Women's Missionary League (counsellor). Conservative. Home: 3871 Hurst St, Burnaby, BC Canada V5J 1M4 Office: 3022 E 49th St, Vancouver, BC Canada V5J 1K9

TREMBLAY, KENNETH RICHARD, JR., housing educator; b. Quonset Point, R.I., Apr. 2, 1953; s. Kenneth Richard and Joyce Henderson (Brown) T.; m. Irene Elizabeth Hasse, May 30, 1981; 1 child, Rick. BA, U. Alaska, 1973; MA, Wash. State U., 1977, PhD, 1980. Asst. prof. U. Nebr., Lincoln, 1980-82, U. Ark., Fayetteville, 1982-85; assoc. prof. housing and interior design Colo. State U., Ft. Collins, 1985—; mktg. cons. Ameristar, Inc., Little Rock, 1986—. Author: (with others) American Housing Dream, 1983; editor: Energy Conservation, 1981; co-editor: Social Aspects of Housing, 1989. Dir. Office on Aging, Ft. Collins, Colo., 1988. Mem. Am. Assn. Housing Educators (dir. Manhattan, Kans., 1984-86), Internat. Assn. for Housing Sci., Am. Home Econ. Assn., Policy Studies Orgn., Rural Sociological Soc., Sigma Xi, Omicron Nu, Alpha Kappa Delta. Republican. Methodist. Home: 2642 Pampas Dr Fort Collins CO 80526 Office: Colorado State University Consumer Sciences Fort Collins CO 80523

TREMBLY, DENNIS MICHAEL, musician; b. Long Beach, Calif., Apr. 16, 1947; s. Fred Lel and Jewel Fern (Bouldin) T. Student, Juilliard Sch. Music, 1965-68. Asst. adj. prof. U. So. Calif., 1981—. Bass player, 1959—, with Los Angeles Philharmonic Orch., 1970-73, co-prin. bass, 1973—. Recipient 2d pl. Internat. Solo Bass competition, Isle of Man, 1978. Mem. Internat. Soc. Bassists. Office: LA Philharm Orch 135 N Grand Ave Los Angeles CA 90012

TRENNERT, ROBERT ANTHONY, JR., historian, educator; b. South Gate, Calif., Dec. 15, 1937; s. Robert Anthony Sr. and Mabel Valentine (Chesnut) T.; m. Linda Lee Griffith, July 31, 1965; children: Robert Anthony III, Kristina M. BA, Occidental Coll., 1961; MA, L.A. State Coll., 1963; Phd, U. Calif., Santa Barbara, 1969. Asst. prof. Temple U., Phila., 1967-74; Asst. prof. Ariz. State U., Tempe, 1974-76, assoc. prof., 1976-81, prof. history, 1981—, chmn. dept. history, 1986—; chmn. Ariz. Hist. Sites Rev. Com., 1985-88. Author: Alternative to Extinction, 1975, Indian Traders on Middle Border, 1981, Phoenix Indian Sch., 1988. Bd. dirs. Ariz. Hist. Found. Mem. Orgn. of Am. Historians. Home: 2047 E Ellis Ave Tempe AZ 85202 Office: Ariz State U Dept of History Tempe AZ 85287

TRENT, THOMAS MICHAEL, semiconductor company executive; b. Des Moines, Iowa, Oct. 6, 1945; s. Voight Beason and Millicent Inas (Fenton) T.; m. Marsha Kay Dean, Aug. 2, 1969 (div. 1976); children—Cherelynne, Amy Camille. B.S.E.E., Kans. State U., 1973; M.S.E.E., Ariz. State U., 1976, M.B.A., 1980. Maintenance technician AT&T, Dodge City, Kans., 1963-69; design engr. Motorola, Inc., Mesa, Ariz., 1973-80; design engr. Micron Tech., Boise, 1980-83, engring. mgr., 1983-86; v.p. research and devel., chief tech. officer, 1986—. Served with U.S. Army, 1967-68. Republican. Episcopalian. Office: Micron Tech Inc 2805 E Columbia Rd Boise ID 83706

TRESCHER, SUSAN, lawyer; b. Glendale, Calif., Dec. 18, 1928; d. F. George and Susan T. (O'Shea) T. BA, U. Calif., Berkeley, 1950; LLB, Harvard U., 1955. Bar: Calif. 1955, U.S. Dist. Ct. (so. dist.) Calif. 1956, U.S. Ct. Appeals (9th cir.) 1957, U.S. Supreme Ct. 1970. Staff atty. Columbia Pictures Corp., Hollywood, Calif., 1955-56; law clk. U.S. Dist. Ct., Los Angeles, 1956-58; cons. atty. Fund for the Republic, Berkeley, 1958-60; research atty. Continuing Edn. of the Bar, U. Calif., Berkeley, 1960-63; chief dep. county counsel County of Santa Barbara, Calif., 1964-82; sole practice Santa Barbara, 1982—. Editor: Legal Aspects of Competitive Business Practices, 1961. Mem. Dem. Cen. Com., Santa Barbara, 1970. Mem. Calif. Bar Assn., Calif. Women Lawyers (bd. dirs. 1980-82, 83-85, v.p. 1981-82), Legal Aid Found. Santa Barbara County (bd. dirs. 1985-89, v.p. 1988-89, pres. 1989—), Bus. and Profl. Women's Found. (v.p. Mar Vista Santa Barbara chpt. 1986-87). Home: One Mesa Ln Santa Barbara CA 93101 Office: 211 E Victoria St #A Santa Barbara CA 93101

TREVITHICK, RONALD JAMES, financial planner; b. Portland, Oreg., Sept. 13, 1944; s. Clifford Vincent and Amy Lois (Turner) T.; m. Delberta Russell, Sept. 11, 1965; children: Pamela, Carmen, Marla, Sheryl. BBA U. Wash., 1966. CPA, Alaska, N.C., Va., La. Mem. audit staff Ernst & Ernst, Anchorage, 1966, 68-70; pvt. practice acctg., Fairbanks, Alaska, 1970-73; with Touche Ross & Co., Anchorage, 1973-78, audit ptnr., 1976-78; exec. v.p., treas., bd. dirs. Veco Internat., Inc., 1978-82; pres., bd. dirs. Petroleum Contractors Ltd., 1980-82; bd. dirs. P.S. Contractors A/S, Norcon, Inc., OFC of Alaska, Inc., V.E. Systems Services, Inc., Veco Turbo Services, Inc., Veco Drilling, Inc., Vemar, Inc., 1978-82; with Coopers & Lybrand, Anchorage, 1982-85; field underwriter, registered rep. New York Life Ins., 1985—; instr. acctg. U. Alaska, 1971-72; lectr. acctg. and taxation Am. Coll. Life Underwriters, 1972, instr. adv. sales Life Underwriters Tng. Coun., 1988-89; bd. dirs. Aetna Devel. Corp., 1985-86. Div. chmn. United Way, 1975-76, YMCA, 1979; bd. dirs., fin. chmn. Anchorage Arts Council, 1975-78, Am. Diabetes Assn., Alaska affiliate, 1985—, chmn. bd. 1988-89, Am. Heart Assn., Alaska affiliate, 1986-87. With U.S. Army, 1967-68. Mem. AICPA, Alaska Soc. CPAs, Petroleum Accts. Soc. (bd. dirs. Alaska 1976; nat. tax com. 1978-80), Fin. Execs. Inst. (pres. Alaska chpt. 1981-83), Internat. Assn. Fin. Planners, Am. Soc. CLUs, Nat. Assn. Life Underwriters, So. Alaska Assn. Life Underwriters, Alaska Assn. Life Underwriters (sec., treas. 1987—), Million Dollar Roundtable, Rotary, Beta Alpha Psi. Clubs: Alaska Goldstrikers Soccer; Petroleum; Rainier. Home: 4421 E Huffman Rd Anchorage AK 99516 Office: 1400 W Benson Blvd Anchorage AK 99503

TREYBIG, JAMES G., computer company executive; b. 1940. Mkgt. mgr. Hewlett-Packard Co., 1968-72; with Kleiner and Perkins, 1972-74; with Tandem Computer Inc., Cupertino, Calif., 1974—, now pres., chief exec. officer, dir. Office: Tandem Computers Inc 19333 Vallco Pkwy Cupertino CA 95014 *

TRIBBLE, RICHARD WALTER, brokerage executive; b. San Diego, Oct. 19, 1948; s. Walter Perrin and Catherine Janet (Miller) T.; m. Joan Catherine Sliter, June 26, 1980. BS, U. Ala., Tuscaloosa, 1968; student, Gulf Coast Sch. Drilling Practices, U. Southwestern La., 1977. Stockbroker Shearson, Am. Express, Washington, 1971-76; ind. oil and gas investment sales, Falls Church, Va., 1976-77; pres. Monroe & Keusink, Inc., Falls Church and Columbus, Ohio, 1977-87; institutional investment officer FCA AssetMgmt., 1983-85; fin. cons. Merrill Lynch Pierce, Fenner & Smith, Inc., Phoenix, 1987-89, cert. fin. mgr, fin. cons., 1989—. Served with USMC, 1969-70. Mem. Renaissance Athletic Club. Republican. Methodist. Office: 2929 E Camelback Rd Phoenix AZ 85016

TRIBKEN, CRAIG LEWIS, real estate executive; b. Bklyn., Apr. 9, 1953; s. Everett Robert and Carol (Deane) T.; m. Bridget Fuqua. BS, Ariz. State U., 1976. With sales dept. Grubb and Ellis, Phoenix, 1976-81, Iliff Thorn and Co., Phoenix, 1981-84; regional dir. BetaWest Properties, Phoenix, 1984-86; ptnr. Heitel, Tribken and Marshall, Phoenix, 1986—. Steering com. Community Devel. Block Grant, Phoenix, 1982-86; chmn. bd. adjustment City of Phoenix, 1989—, Encanto Village Planning Com., Phoenix, 1989—; active Valley Leadership, Phoenix, 1984—, Futures Forum Planning Com., Phoenix, 1989—, Arts Dist. Adv. Com., Phoenix, 1989—. Mem. Ariz. Acad. Democrat. Home: 10 E Orange Phoenix AZ 85012 Office: Heitel Tribken & Marshall 777 E Thomas #210 Phoenix AZ 85004

TRIER, WILLIAM CRONIN, medical educator, plastic surgeon; b. N.Y.C., Feb. 11, 1922; s. John and Anne (Cronin) T.; m. Kathleen Emily Renz, June 14, 1947; children: William Cronin, Peter L. AB, Dartmouth Coll., 1943; MD, N.Y. Med. Coll., 1947. Diplomate Am. Bd. Surgery, Am. Bd. Plastic Surgery (dir. 1976-82, vice-chmn. 1981-82). Intern St. Agnes Hosp., White Plains, N.Y., 1947-48; intern Grasslands Hosp., Valhalla, N.Y., 1948-49, resident in surgery, 1949-50; commd. lt. (j.g.) USN, 1948, advanced through grades to capt., 1964; asst. med. officer USS Midway and USS Wasp, 1950-52; residen in surgery St. Albans Hosp., L.I., N.Y., 1952-55; fellow plastic surgery Washington U. Barnes Hosp., St. Louis, 1956-58; mem. plastic surgery staff Naval Hosp., St. Albans, 1958-60; chief plastic surgery Naval Hosp., Phila., 1960-63; chief plastice surgery Nat. Naval Med. Ctr., Bethesda, Md., 1963-67; asst. prof. surgery, plastic surgery U. N.C., Chapel Hill, 1967-69, prof. surgery, plastic surgery, 1976-85, prof. dental ecology Sch. Dentistry, 1976-85; assoc. prof., chief plastic surgery U. Ariz. Coll. Medicine, Tucson, 1969-76; prof. surgery U. Wash. Sch. Medicine, Seattle, 1985—; mem. com. on study evaluation procedures Am. Bd. Med. Specialties, 1981-85, sci. adv. com. Contbr. articles to profl. jours. Bd. dirs., pres. Pima County unit and Ariz. divs. Am. Cancer Soc., 1970-76, bd. dirs. N.C. div., pres. Orange County (Calif.) unit, 1976-82. Mem. ACS, Am. Assn. Plastic Surgeons (historian 1973-76, v.p. 1984-85, pres.-elect 1985-86, pres. 1986-87), Am. Soc. Plastic and Reconstructive Surgeons, Am. Soc. Aesthetic Plastic Surgery (at large bd. dirs. 1979-81, treas. 1984-87), Am. Soc. Maxillofacial Surgeons, Am. Acad. Pediatrics, Am. Cleft Palate Assn. (pres. 1980-81), Am. Cleft Palate Found. (pres. 1984—), Gamma Delta Chi, Alpha Kappa Kappa. Episcopalian. Home: 7701 Lakemont Dr NE Seattle WA 98115 Office: U Wash Sch Medicine Dept Surgery RF-25 Seattle WA 98195

TRIFFET, TERRY, college dean; b. Enid, Okla., June 10, 1922; B.A., U. Okla., 1945; B.S., U. Colo., 1948, M.S., 1950; Ph.D. in Structural Mechanics, Stanford U., 1957; married; 3 children. Instr. engring. U. Colo., 1947-50; gen. engr. rocket and guided missile research U.S. Naval Ordnance Test Sta., 1950-55; gen. engr. radiol. research, head radiol. effects br. U.S. Naval Radiol. Def. Lab., 1955-59; assoc. prof., then prof. mech. and materials sci. Mich. State U., 1959-76; assoc. dean research Coll. Engring., U. Ariz., Tucson, 1976-84, acting dean, 1984, 87; prof. materials sci. engring., dir. NASA/UA Space Engring. Resch. Ctr., 1988—; mem. apex com. U.S. Naval Research Labs., 1959-65; cons. to govt. and industry. Grantee Australian Research Grants Com., 1966-67, 72-73. Mem. Am. Phys. Soc., Am. Math. Soc., Soc. Engring. Sci., Soc. Industry and Applied Math., IEEE, AIAA, Assn. Computing Machinery. Address: U Ariz Coll Engring Tucson AZ 85721

TRIFONIDIS, BEVERLY ANN, opera company manager, accountant; b. Dallas, Dec. 19, 1947; d. Philo McGill and Mary Elizabeth (Sikes) Burney; m. Paul Douglas Spikes, June, 1968 (div. 1976); m. Chris Trifonidis, August 1979 (div. 1986); 1 child, Alexandra. BBA, U. Tex., 1971, M in Profl. Acctg., 1976. CPA, Tex. Mgmt. trainee J.C. Penney Co., Austin, Tex., 1971-72; acctg. clk. SW Ednl. Devel. Lab., Austin, 1972-73; editorial asst. Jour. of Mktg., Austin, 1974-76; staff auditor Hurdman & Cranstoun, CPA's, San Francisco, 1976; instr. acctg. U. Tex., San Antonio, 1976-77; lectr. acctg. Simon Fraser U., Burnaby, B.C., Can., 1978-79, 81-84; gen. mgr. Vancouver (Can.) Opera, 1984—. Bd. dirs. United Way, 1988—. Mem. Am. Inst. CPA's, Tex. Soc. CPA's. Presbyterian. Office: Vancouver Opera, 1132 Hamilton St, Vancouver, BC Canada V6B 2S2

TRIGG, CHARLES WILDERMAN, writer; b. Balt., Feb. 7, 1898; s. Samuel Holland and Mary E. (Wilderman) T.; grad. Balt. Poly. Inst., 1914; B.S. in Chem. Engring., U. Pitts., 1917; M.A., U. So. Calif., 1931, M.S., 1934, postgrad., 1950-55; postgrad. U. Calif. at Los Angeles, 1936-38; m. Ida Faye Conner, Dec. 17, 1932 (dec. Aug. 1973); m. 2d, Avetta Hoffman Danford, Jan. 11, 1975. Fellow Mellon Inst. Indsl. Research, Pitts., 1916-20; chemist, prodn. mgr. King Coffee Products Corp., Detroit, 1920-23; sales promotion mgr. John E. King Coffee Co., Detroit, 1923-24; with E.R. Bohan Paint Co., Los Angeles, 1924-27; tchr. Los Angeles Pvt. High Sch., 1927-30; asso. prof. chemistry Cumnock Coll., Los Angeles, 1930-36, dean men, 1936-38; tchr. Eagle Rock High Sch., Los Angeles, 1938; coordinator Air Corps Inst., 1941-43; instr. East Los Angeles Jr. Coll., 1945-46; instr. Los Angeles City Coll., 1938-43, 46-49, coordinator, 1949-50, asst. dean, 1950-55, dean instruction, 1955-63, dean emeritus, prof. emeritus, 1963—; lectr. U. So. Calif., 1946, 59-60. Served to lt. comdr. USNR, 1943-45. Named Eagle Scout Boy Scouts Am., 1914. Mem. Math. Assn. Am. (sect. chmn. 1952-53; mem. nat. bd. govs. 1953-56), Nat. Council Tchrs. Math., Sch. Sci. and Math. Assn., Assn. Los Angeles Jr. Coll. Adminstrs. (pres. 1957-58), Sigma Xi, Alpha Chi Sigma, Phi Lambda Upsilon, Phi Delta Kappa, Pi Mu Epsilon, Alpha Mu Gamma. Author: Mathematical Quickies, 1967. Mem. editorial bd. Los Angeles Math. Newsletter, 1954, Jour. Recreational Math., 1971—. Mem. editorial staff Math. Mag., 1949-63. Contbr. numerous articles to profl. jours. Book reviewer, 1961—. Patentee in the field of instant coffee. Address: 2404 Loring St San Diego CA 92109

TRIGIANO, LUCIEN LEWIS, physician; b. Easton, Pa., Feb. 9, 1926; s. Nicholas and Angeline (Lewis) T.; m. Christy; children: Lynn Anita, Glenn Larry, Robert Nicholas. Student Tex. Christian U., 1944-45, Ohio U., 1943-44, 46-47, Milligan Coll., 1944, Northwestern U., 1945, Temple U., 1948-52. Intern, Meml. Hosp., Johnstown, Pa., 1952-53; resident Lee Hosp., Johnstown, 1953-54; gen. practice, Johnstown, 1953-59; med. dir. Pa. Rehab. Center, Johnstown, 1959-62, chief phys. medicine and rehab., 1964-70; fellow phys. medicine and rehab. N.Y. Inst. Phys. Medicine and Rehab., 1962-64; dir. rehab. medicine Lee Hosp., 1964-71, Ralph K. Davies Med. Center, San Francisco, 1973-75, St. Joseph's Hosp., San Francisco, 1975-78, St. Francis Meml. Hosp., San Francisco, 1978-83; asst. prof. phys. medicine and rehab. Temple U. Sch. Medicine; founder Disability Alert. Served with USNR, 1944-46. Diplomate Am. Bd. Phys. Medicine and Rehab. Mem. AMA, A.C.P., Pa., San Francisco County Med. socs., Am. Acad. Phys. Medicine and Rehab., Am. Congress Phys. Medicine, Calif. Acad. Phys. Medicine, Nat. Rehab. Assn., Babcock Surg. Soc. Author various med. articles. Home: 1050 Northpoint St San Francisco CA 94109 Office: 2000 Van Ness Ste 506 San Francisco CA 94109

TRIMBLE, THOMAS JAMES, utility company executive; b. Carters Creek, Tenn., Sept. 3, 1931; s. John Elijah and Mittie (Rountree) T.; m. Glenna Kay Jones, Sept. 3, 1957; children: James Jefferson, Julie Kay. BA, David Lipscomb Coll., 1953; JD, Vanderbilt U., 1956; LLM, NYU, 1959. Bar: Tenn. 1956, Ariz. 1961, U.S. Dist. Ct. Ariz. 1961, U.S. Dist. Ct. D.C. 1963, U.S. Ct. Appeals (10th cir.) 1971, U.S. Supreme Ct. 1972, U.S. Ct. Appeals (9th cir.) 1975. From assoc. to ptnr. Jennings, Strouss & Salmon, Phoenix, 1960-85, mng. ptnr., 1985-87; sr. v.p., gen. counsel S.W. Gas Corp., Las Vegas, Nev., 1987—. Mem. editorial bd. Vanderbilt U. Law Rev., 1954-56. Mem. Pepperdine U. Bd. Regents, Malibu, Calif., 1981—, sec., mem. exec. com., 1982—; mem. bd. visitors Pepperdine Sch. Law, Malibu; pres. Big Sisters Ariz., Phoenix, 1975, bd. dirs., 1970-76; chmn. Sunnydale Children's Home, Phoenix, 1966-69, bd. dirs., 1965-75; pres. Clearwater Hills Improvement Assn., Phoenix, 1977-79, bd. dirs., 1975-80; trustee Nev. Sch. of Arts, 1988—. Served to 1st lt. JAGC, USAF, 1957-60. Fellow Ariz. Bar Found. (founding); mem. ABA, Ariz. Bar Assn. (editorial bd. Jour. 1975-80), Am. Gas Assn. (legal sect. mng. com.), Pacific Coast Gas Assn. (legal adv. com. 1987—), Energy Ins. Mut. Ltd. (bd. dirs. 1988—), Order of Coif, Phi Delta Phi. Republican. Mem. Ch. Christ. Club: Spanish Trail Country (Las Vegas). Lodge: Kiwanis (pres. Phoenix 1972-73). Home: 5104 S Turnberry Ln Las Vegas NV 89113 Office: SW Gas Corp 5241 Spring Mountain Rd PO Box 98510 Las Vegas NV 89193-8510

TRIMINGHAM, DIANE MARIE, dentist; b. Concord, Calif., July 10, 1960; d. Jack Lawrence and Carol Jean (Jamieson) T. BA, U. Calif., 1982; DDS, Case We. Res. U., Cleve., 1986. Pvt. practice in dentistry Santa Rosa, Calif., 1986—. Mem. ADA, Calif. Dental Assn., Redwood Empire Dental Soc., Am. Assn. Women Dentists. Democrat. Office: 76 Doctors Park Dr Santa Rosa CA 95405

TRIPATHI, AMIT, manufacturing executive; b. Kanpur, India, June 15, 1853; came to U.S., 1974; s. Uma Kant and Prafull (Kumari) T.; m. Clara Lu, July 3, 1987; 1 child, Anjali. BSME, Indian Inst. Tech., Kanpur, 1974; MSME, Howard U., 1976; MS in Nuclear Engring., Oreg. State U., 1979; postgrad., Calif. Inst. Tech., 1982. Cons. engr. Engring. & tech. Svcs., Allahabad, India, 1973-74; sr. engr. Parsons Corp., Pasadena, Calif., 1979-84; with Xerox Corp., El Segundo, Calif., 1984-89, mgr. systems strategy, integration and host software mktg., 1989—; engring., data processing cons. ERDA, NRC, NIH, State of Calif., others, 1979-84. Contbr. articles to profl. jours. Recipient Health Physics award, Health Physics Soc., 1978. Mem. ACM, Am. Nuclear Soc. (chpt. v.p. 1975-76, Outstanding Paper award 1977), Mensa. Office: Xerox Corp 101 Continental Blvd El Segundo CA 90245

TRIPPY, DONALD R., illustrator; b. Denver, May 19, 1934; s. Fred Esta and Agnes Wilma (Van Duesen) T.; m. Mary Catherine Karnes, Jan. 27, 1961; children: Lynn Mary, Matthew Allen. Student, Colo. Inst. of Art, 1956-59. Illustrator tng. aids Ft. Carson Co., Colorado Springs, Colo., 1964-65; illustrator, supr. aerospace def. command USAF, Colorado Springs, 1965-74; illustrator, supr. graphics tactical fighter weopens ctr. USAF, Nellis AFB, Nev., 1974—, chief of graphics, 1979—. Mem. tech. skills adv. com. Clark County Sch. Dist., Nev., 1987-88; bd. dirs. Las Vegas (Nev.) Art Mus., 1987-88, Desert Sculptors, Las Vegas, 1988; mem. adv. bd. Clark County Community Coll., 1987-88. Democrat. LDS Ch. Home: 4027 Maple Hill Rd Las Vegas NV 89115 Office: USAF Tactical Fighter Weopens Ctr Nellis AFB NV 89191-5000 also: Las Vegas Art Mus 3333 W Washington Las Vegas NV 89107

TRISKA, BRADLEY FRANK, sales executive; b. Sewickley, Pa., Mar. 13, 1950; s. Frank and Mary Florence (Copy) T.; m. Linda Carol Freno, Aug. 25, 1973; 1 child, Tawny Lin. BSBA in Mktg., Robert Morris Coll., 1973. With Kellogg Sales Co., various locations, 1973—; met. dist. mgr. Kellogg Sales Co., L.A., 1979-82, unit mgr., 1982-84; dir. div. sales Kellogg Sales Co., St. Louis, 1984-87, L.A., 1987—. Mem. Food Industry Sales Mgrs. Club. Republican. Mem. Assemblies of God Ch. Office: Kellogg Sales Co Ste 590 7755 Center Ave Huntington Beach CA 92647

TRISKA, JAN FRANCIS, political science educator; b. Prague, Czechoslovakia, Jan. 26, 1922; came to U.S., 1948, naturalized, 1955; s. Jan and Bozena (Kubiznak) T.; m. Carmel Lena Burastero, Aug. 26, 1951; children: Mark Lawrence, John William. J.U.D., Charles U., Prague, 1948; LL.M., Yale U., 1950, J.S.D., 1952; Ph.D., Harvard U., 1957. Co-dir. Soviet treaties Hoover Instn., Stanford, Calif., 1956-58; lectr. dept. polit. sci. U. Calif.-Berkeley, 1957-58; asst. prof. Cornell U., Ithaca, N.Y., 1958-60; assoc. prof. Stanford U., Calif., 1960-65, prof. polit. sci., 1965—, assoc. chmn. dept., 1965-66, 68-69, 71-72, 74-75. Co-author: (with Slusser) The Theory, Law and Policy of Soviet Treaties, 1962, (with Finley) Soviet Foreign Policy, 1968, (with Cocks) Political Development and Political Change in Eastern Europe, 1977, (with Ike, North) The World of Superpowers, 1981, (with Gati) Blue Collar Workers in Eastern Europe, 1981, Dominant Powers and Subordinate States, 1986; bd. editors: East European Quar. Comparative Politics, Internat. Jour. Sociology, Jour. Comparative Politics, Studies in Comparative Communism, Soviet Statutes and Decisions, Documents in Communist Affairs. Recipient Research award Ford Found., 1963-68; fellow NSF, 1971-72; Fulbright-Hays faculty research fellow, 1973-74; fellow Woodrow Wilson Internat. Ctr. for Scholars, 1980-81. Mem. Am. Polit. Sci. Assn. (sec. pres. conf. on communist studies 1970-76), Assn. Advancement Slavic Studies (bd. dirs. 1975-83), Am. Soc. Internat. law (exec. council 1964-67), Czechoslovak Soc. Arts and Scis. (pres. 1978-80). Democrat. Club: Fly Fishers (Palo Alto, Calif.). Home: 720 Vine St Menlo Park CA 94025 Office: Stanford U Dept Polit Sci Stanford CA 94305

TROAN, JANET LILLIAN, accountant; b. Mpls., Oct. 7, 1934; d. William Edward and Lillian (Bering) Cook; m. John Trygve Troan, Mar. 21, 1953; children: Gordon, Janine. BS in Acctg., Mpls. Sch. Bus., 1958; postgrad., Anoka-Ramsey Coll., Coon Rapids, Minn., 1963-66, Phoenix Coll., 1982-85. Controller Sanford, Inc., Mpls., 1955-67; account mgr. Troan Fin. Services, Phoenix, 1971-80; sec., bd. dirs. Five Star Corp., Phoenix, 1980—. Treas. Federated Women's Club, Coon Rapids, 1965-69; pres. Federated Women's Club, Phoenix, 1977-81; sec. Coon Rapids Dems., 1963-68; dep. registrar Phoenix Dems.; precint com. Ariz. Dems. Recipient Outstanding Achievement award Ariz. Dems., 1984. Lutheran. Lodge: Sons of Norway. Home: 2403 W Cortez Ave Phoenix AZ 85029 Office: Five Star Enterprises Inc 10635 N 19th Ave Phoenix AZ 85029

TROAN, JOHN TRYGVE, lawyer, financial executive; b. Mpls., Nov. 6, 1932; s. Trygve and Blanche Maggie (Goff) T.; m. Janet Lillian Cook, March 21, 1953; 2 children: Gordon Trygve, Janine Henderson. BSL, U. Minn., 1959, JD, 1961; PhD, John Marshall U., Chgo., 1963. Bar: Minn. 1961, U.S. Supreme Ct. 1970. Prosecutor, criminal tax div. U.S. Govt., 1961-68; atty. Troan Law Firm, Coon Rapids, Minn., 1968-71; tax atty., chief exec. officer Five Star Enterprises, Inc., Phoenix, 1971—; arbitrator Phoenix Better Bus. Bur., 1981—. Contbr. articles to profl. jours. Commr. Coon Rapids Planning and Zoning Commn., 1965-69; mem. Village Planning Com., Phoenix, 1974—; mem. State Dem. Cen. Com., Minn. and Ariz., 1968—; mem. ct. discipline Evang. Luth. Ch. in Am., Grand Canyon Synod. Adminstrv. officer USAF, 1951-55. Mem. Nat. Assn. Tax Consultors, Phoenix C. of C.,

Internat. Jaycees (senator Minn. and Ariz. 1966—), Am. Legion. Democrat. Lutheran. Office: Five Star Enterprises Inc 10635 N 19th Ave Phoenix AZ 85029

TROCINO, FRANK MERRILL, interior designer; b. Sidney, N.Y., Dec. 28, 1956; s. Frank Samuel and Merilyn (Budlong) T.; m. Patricia Ann Mariani, May 14, 1988. B Interior Design, U. Oreg., 1984. Designer A.C. Martin & Assocs., Los Angeles, 1985-86, Kober, Cedargreen, Rippon, Los Angeles, 1986-87; project mgr. United Bus. Interiors, Los Angeles, 1987--; prin. FMT Environs, Altadena, Calif., 1986--. Home: 949 Marcheta St Altadena CA 91001

TRONE, DONALD LEROY, electronic design and manufacturing company executive; b. Durango, Colo., Jan. 23, 1937; s. Ralph Eugene and Mary Grace (Mosty) T;. m. Harriet Ann Jessing, July 2, 1960; children: Bob, Donna, Charlotte. BA, Ft. Lewis Coll., 1964; MSEE, N.Mex. State U., 1970. Mgr. svc. dept. Sears, Roebuck & Co., Santa Fe, N.Mex., 1964-67; asst. student teaching N.Mex. State I., Las Cruces, 1967-70; project engr. microwave devel. EG&G, Alburquerque, 1970-76; founder, gen. mgr. Miletus Assoc., Inc., Alburquerque, 1976—; founder, chief exec. officer Cybertronics, Inc., 1985—; curriculum advisor Albuquerque Tech. Vocat. Inst. With USN, 1955-59. Mem. Soc. Photo-Optical Instrumentation Engrs., Eta Kapp Nu. Republican. Roman Catholic. Home: 5903 Princess Jeanne St NE Albuquerque NM 87110 Office: 3876 Hawkins NE Albuquerque NM 87109

TROTTER, F(REDERICK) THOMAS, university president; b. Los Angeles, Apr. 17, 1926; s. Fred B. and Hazel (Thomas) T.; m. Gania Demaree, June 27, 1953; children—Ruth Elizabeth, Paula Anne (dec.), Tania, Mary. AB, Occidental Coll., 1950, DD, 1968; STB, Boston U., 1953, PhD, 1958; LHD, Ill. Wesleyan U., 1974, Cornell Coll., 1985, Westmar Coll., 1987; LLD, U. Pacific, 1978, Wesleyan Coll., 1981; EdD, Columbia Coll., 1984; LittD, Alaska Pacific U., 1987. Exec. sec. Boston U. Student Christian Assn., 1951-54; ordained elder Calif.-Pacific, Methodist Ch., 1953; pastor Montclair (Calif.) Meth. Ch., 1956-59; lectr. So. Calif. Sch. Theology at Claremont, 1957-59, instr., 1959-60, asst. prof., 1960-63, assoc. prof., 1963-66, prof., 1966, dean, 1961; prof. religion and arts, dean Sch. Theology Claremont, 1961-73; mem. Bd. Higher Edn. and Ministry, United Meth. Ch., 1972-73, gen. sec., 1973-87; pres. Alaska Pacific U., Anchorage, 1988—; dir. Third Nat. Bank, Nashville, Inst. for Antiquity and Christianity at Claremont. Author: Jesus and the Historian, 1968, Loving God with One's Mind, 1987, weekly column local newspapers; editor-at-large: Christian Century, 1969-84. Trustee Dillard U. Served with USAAF, 1944-46. Kent fellow Soc. for Values in Higher Edn., 1954; Dempster fellow Meth. Ch., 1954. Mem. University Club, Rotary Internat. (Anchorage Downtown), Commonwealth North. Office: Alaska Pacific U Office Pres 4101 University Dr Anchorage AK 99508

TROVATO, JAMES DAVID, JR., computer consulting executive; b. Pitts., Sept. 27, 1955; s. James D. and Virginia (Lang) T.; m. Kimberly Ann Merwin, July 5, 1986. BS in Bus. Systems Analysis, Indiana U. of Pa., 1977. Programmer Amtrak, Washington, 1977-78; programmer, analyst Computer Corp. Am., Washington, 1978-79; cons. Lambda Tech., Inc., San Francisco, 1979-80; sr. programmer, analyst Itel Corp., San Francisco, 1980-81; cons. San Francisco, 1981-83; pres. Innovative Directions, Inc., San Francisco, 1983—. Mem. Wang Users Group, Model 204 DBMS Users Group. Democrat. Roman Catholic. Home and Office: Innovative Directions Inc 5 Eugenia Ave San Francisco CA 94110

TROVER, ELLEN LLOYD, lawyer; b. Richmond, Va., Nov. 23, 1947; d. Robert Van Buren and Hazel (Urban) Lloyd; m. Denis William Trover, June 12, 1971; 1 dau., Florence Emma. A.B., Vassar Coll., 1969; J.D., Coll. William and Mary, 1972. Asst. editor Bancroft-Whitney, San Francisco, 1973-74; owner Ellen Lloyd Trover Atty.-at-Law, Thousand Oaks, Calif., 1974-82; ptnr. Trover & Fisher, Thousand Oaks, 1982-89; pvt. practice law, Thousand Oaks, 1989—. Editor: Handbooks of State Chronologies, 1972. Trustee, Conejo Future Found., Thousand Oaks, 1978—, vice chmn., 1982-84, chmn., 1984-88; pres. Zonta Club Conejo Valley Area, 1978-79; trustee Hydro Help for the Handicapped, 1980-85. Mem. Conejo Simi Bar Assn. (pres. 1979-80, dir. 1983-85), Ventura County Bar Assn. (state del. 1984), State Bar Calif., Va. State Bar, Phi Alpha Delta. Democrat. Presbyterian. Home: 11355 Presilla Rd Camarillo CA 93010 Office: 1107E Thousand Oaks Blvd Thousand Oaks CA 91362

TROWBRIDGE, JEFFREY ARTHUR, financial planning company executive; b. Mpls., Dec. 5, 1950; s. Donald Truman and Margaret Louise (Terry) T.; m. Wynne Eileen Mackenthun, Aug. 20, 1983; children: Christopher, Brittany. BS in Edn., U. Minn., 1974; MBA in Fin., U. Denver, 1983. Tchr. Cook County High Sch., Grand Marais, Minn., 1974-76; gen. mgr. Mountain Food Svcs., Breckenridge, Colo., 1976-8l; v.p. Asset Mgmt. Group, Denver, 1983-89; chief exec. officer PB & J, Inc., Englewood, Colo., 1989—; bd. dirs. PB&J Inc., Denver. Home: 2125 Grove St Denver CO 80211 Office: PB & J Inc 8745 E Orchard Rd Ste 525 Englewood CO 80111

TRUE, DIEMER, state senator, trucking company executive; b. Cody, Wyo., Feb. 12, 1946; s. Henry Alfonso and Jean (Durland) T.; B.S., Northwestern U., 1968; m. Susie Lynn Niethammer, Aug. 28, 1967; children—Diemer Durland, Kyle Shawn, Tara Jeanine, Tracy Lynn. With Black Hills Trucking, Inc., Casper, Wyo., 1970—, v.p., 1974—; v.p. Toolpushers Supply Co., Casper, 1981—; dir. Hilltop Nat. Bank, Mountain Plaza Nat. Bank; mem. Wyo. Ho. of Reps., 1972-76; mem. Wyo. Senate, 1976—, senate majority fl. leader, 1989—, mgmt. coun., 1988—; adv. bd. U. Wyo. Enhanced Oil Recovery Inst., senate rules and procedures coms.; mem. governing bd. Coun. State Govts., 1979—; mem. Coun. of State Govts. suggested state legis. com. and coun. of State Govt. exec. com., Am. Legis. Exch. Coun., 1974-76. Pres. Natrona County United Way, 1976; mem. bus. adv. coun. Coll. Commerce and Industry U. Wyo. With AUS, 1968. Mem. Wyo. Trucking Assn. (dir. 1972-80, pres. 1983-85), Ind. Petroleum Assn. Am. (bd. dirs.), Rocky Mountain Oil and Gas Assn. (chmn. transp. com.), Nat. Assn. Mfrs. (bd. dirs.), Western Hwy. Inst. (bd. dirs.). Republican. Methodist. Office: PO Box 2360 Casper WY 82602

TRUE, HENRY ALFONSO, JR., entrepreneur; b. Cheyenne, Wyo., June 12, 1915; s. Henry A. and Anna Barbara (Diemer) T.; m. Jean Durland, Mar. 20, 1938; children: Tamma Jean (Mrs. Donald Hatten), Henry Alfonso, III, Diemer D., David L. BS in Indsl. Engring. with honors, Mont. State Coll., 1937; PhD in Engring. with honors, Mont. State U., 1983; LLD (hon.), U. Wyo., 1988. Roustabout, pumper, foreman The Tex. Co., 1937-45, supt. drilling and prodn. for Wyo., 1945-48; mgr. Res. Drilling Co., 1948-51, pres., 1951-59; ptnr. True Drilling Co. and True Oil Co., Casper, Wyo., 1951—; v.p., sec. Toolpushers Supply Co., 1952-53, pres., 1954—; v.p., sec. True Svc. Co., 1953, pres., 1954-70; pres. True Bldg. Corp., 1956-67, Smokey Oil Co., 1975—, Belle Fourche Pipeline Co., 1957—, Black Hills Trucking, Inc., 1977—; owner True Ranches, Inc., 1957-76, pres., 1977-86; pres. True Oil Purchasing Co., 1977-81, True Geothermal Drilling Co., 1981—, True Wyo. Beef, 1987—; ptnr. Eighty-Eight Oil Co., 1955—, Double Four Ranch Co., 1980—, True Geothermal Energy Co., 1981—, True Ranches, 1983—; chmn. Powder River Oil Shippers Svc., Inc., 1963-67; pres. Camp Creek Gas Co., 1964-77; v.p. George Mancini Feed Lots, Brighton, Colo., 1964-72; v.p. Black Hills Marketers, Inc., 1966-72, pres., 1973-80; v.p. White Stallion Ranch, Inc., Tucson, 1965—; pres. Res. Oil Purchasing Co., 1972-73; bd. dirs. Midland Fin. Corp., U. Wyo. Rsch. Corp.; chmn. Hilltop Nat. Bank, 1977—, Mountain Plaza Nat. Bank, 1980—; mem. Wyo. adv. com., 1965-84; mem. exec. com. Wyo. Oil Industry Com., 1958-74, treas., 1958-59, pres. 1960-62; dir. Rocky Mountain Oil Show, 1955; mem. adv. bd. Internat. Oil and Gas Edn. Ctr., 1964—, vice chmn., 1969-73; mem. natural gas adv. coun. Fed. Power Commn., 1964-65, mem. exec. adv. com., 1971-74; mem. exec. co. com. Gas Supply Com., 1965-69, vice chmn., 1967-69; mem. adv. coun. Pub. Land Rev. Commn., 1965-70; dir. U.S. Bus. and Indsl. Coun., 1971—, exec. com., 1974—; mem. Nat. Petroleum Council, 1962— , nat. oil policy com., 1965, vice chmn., 1970-71, chmn., 1972-73; mem. Rocky Mountain Petroleum Industry Adv. Com., Fed. Energy Office, 1973-77; hon. dir. Mountain Bell, bd. advisors, 1965-84; mem. Wyo. Com. Newcomen Soc. U.S., 1974—. Chmn. advance gifts com. United Fund; mem. Wyo. com. Newcomer Soc. of U.S., 1974—, chmn. advanced gifts; nat. assoc. Boys Clubs Am., 1964-69, hon. chmn. local chpt. 1971; trustee Casper Air Terminal, 1960-71, pres. 1964-65, 67-68; mem. research fellows Southwestern Legal Found., 1968—; trustee U. Wyo., 1965-77, pres. bd., 1971-73, mem. adult edn. and community svc. coun., 1961-64; bd. govs. Western Ind. Colls. Found., 1963-65; nat. trustee Voice of Youth, 1968; bd. dirs., trustee Nat. Cowboy Hall of Fame and Western Heritage Ctr., 1975—, pres. bd., 1978-80, chmn., 1980-82; dir. Mountain State Legal Found., 1977—, exec. com. 1984—, chmn. bd. 1988—, Nat. Legal Ctr. for the Pub. Interest, 1988—; trustee steering committee Wyo. Heritage Soc., 1979—, sec.-treas. 1988—; Buffalo Bill Meml. Assn., 1983—; Wyo. state fin. chmn. Reagan-Bush campaign '84. Named Oil Man of Yr., 1959, recipient Honored Citizen award, 1964, Casper C. of C.; Chief Roughneck of Yr. award, Lone Star Steel award 1965, ann. Indsl. award Wyo. Assn. Realtors, 1965, Pierre F. Goodrich Conservation award Polit. Econ. and Rsch. Ctr., 1982; named Disting. Businessman for Small Bus. Mgmt., 1966-67, recipient Alumni Medallion U. Wyo., 1978; named to Wisdom Hall Fame; named Exec. of Year Teton chpt. Profl. Secs. Internat., 1985. Mem. Internat. Assn. Drilling Contractors (dir. 1950—), Am. Petroleum Inst. (dir. 1960—, exec. com. 1970—, Gold Medal for Disting. Svc. award 1985), Rocky Mountain Oil and Gas Assn. (treas. 1954-55, v.p. Wyo. 1956-58, dir. 1950—, pres. 1962-63, exec. com. 1954—, hon. mem., 1978), Ind. Petroleum Assn. Am. (v.p. Wyo. 1960-61, exec. com. 1962—, pres. 1964-65; Russell B. Brown Meml. award 1975), Rocky Mountain Petroleum Pioneers, Wyo. Storoleum (dir. 1954), U.S. C. of C. (dir. 1975-81), Casper C. of C., All-Am Wildcatters, 25 Year Club Petroleum Industry, Ind. Petroleum Assn. Mountain States (Rocky Mountain Wildcatter of Yr. award 1982), Petroleum Assn. Wyo. (dir. 1974—), Am. Judicature Soc. (mem. com. justice 1976), Sigma Chi (Significant Sig award, 1981), Beta Gamma Sigma (hon. mem., 1971 Alpha chpt. Wyo.), Masons, Shriners, Elks. Republican. Episcopalian (vestry 1960-62). Office: Belle Fourche Pipeline Co 895 W Rivercross Rd PO Drawer 2360 Casper WY 82602

TRUEBLOOD, BENNETT M., aeronautical engineer; b. Enumelaw, Wash., Jan. 8, 1964; s. Leslie Laroy and Elizabeth (Skillman) T.; m. Catherine A. Gwynn, Oct. 1, 1988. BS in Aeronautical and Astronautical Engring., U. Wash., 1986, MS, 1987. Mem. tech. staff Rocketdyne div. Rockwell Internat., Canoga Park, Calif., 1987—. Mem. AIAA, Chatsworth (Calif.) C. of C. Home: 9950 Jordan #15 Chatsworth CA 91311 Office: Rockwell Internat 6633 Canoga Ave Canoga Park CA 91367

TRUETT, HAROLD JOSEPH, III, lawyer; b. Alameda, Calif., Feb. 13, 1946; s. Harold Joseph and Lois Lucille (Mellin) T.; m. Kathleen Truett, Dec. 5, 1970 (div. July 1982); 1 child, Harold Joseph IV; m. Anna V. Billante, Oct. 1, 1983; 1 child, James S. Carstensen. BA, U. San Francisco, 1968, JD, 1975. Bar: Calif. 1975, Hawaii 1987, U.S. Dist. Ct. (we., ea., so., no., and cen. dists.) Calif. 1976, U.S. Dist. Ct. Hawaii 1987, U.S. Ct. Appeals (9th cir.) 1980, U.S. Supreme Ct. 1988. Assoc. Hoberg, Finger et al, San Francisco, 1975-78, Bledsoe, Smith et al, San Francisco, 1979-80, Abramson & Bianco, San Francisco, 1980-83, Ingram & Dykman, San Rafael, Calif., 1983-86; mem. Ingram & Truett, San Rafael, 1987—. Mem. Marin Dem. Coun., San Rafael, 1983—. Lt. USN, 1967-72. Mem. ABA, Hawaii Bar Assn., Assn. Trial Lawyers Am., Calif. Bar Assn. (com. for adminstrn. of justice), San Francisco Bar Assn., Marin County Bar Assn. (programs and legis. coms., del. state bar meeting), Calif. Trial Lawyers Assn., Lawyers Pilots Assn. Roman Catholic. Home: 1349 Vallejo St San Francisco CA 94109

TRUFFAUT, MICHELLE, director; b. San Francisco, Nov. 17, 1942; d. Louis and Eve (Schefski) Mardecich. Student, U. Calif., Berkeley, 1964-65; MFA, Am. Film Inst., 1989. Freelance performer U.S., Eng. and France, 1965-72; pub. rels. asst. Am. Conservatory Theatre, San Francisco, 1972-74; producing and artistic dir. San Francisco Repertory Theatre, San Francisco, 1974-87; artistic dir. San Francisco Shakespeare Festival, 1986-87; freelance filmmaker, dir. L.A., 1987—; mem. adv. bd. Theatre Communications Bay Area, San Francisco, 1983-86. Dir. in field; dir., adapter play Animal Farm Orwell, 1984, Lulu-Wiedkino 1985; writer, dir. screenplay Ralph's Arm, 1988. Recipient Best Directing and Best Prodn. Achievement award Bay Area Critics Circle, 1984, 86, Outstanding Best Directing and Best Prodn. Achievement award Bay Area Critics, 1986, Best Directing award Dramalogue, 1984. Democrat. Jewish.

TRUHAN, WAYNE KEITH, supermarket chain executive; b. New Milford, N.J., Sept. 1, 1954; s. Richard and Dorothea Audrey (Miller) T.; m. Jodi Ann Leoning, Oct. 16, 1982; children: Matthew Wayne Richard, Tiffany Naomi. BSBA, Calif. State U., Long Beach, 1978. Retail systems coordinator Boys Markets, Inc., L.A., 1980--, energy mgr., 1982--. Recipient award of merit in energy conservation L.A. Dept. Water and Power, 1983. Mem. Assn. Energy Engrs. (Energy Mgr. of Yr. for So. Calif. 1987), Assn. Profl. Energy Mgrs. Republican. Office: Boys Markets Inc 5532 Monte Vista Highland Park CA 90042

TRUJILLO, JOHN RUSSELL, geologist; b. Montrose, Colo., May 26, 1950; s. Sam and Rebecca (Vasquaz) T.; m. Rosalyn Ann River, Sept. 5, 1970; children: John Elwood, Valerie Rose, Corinne Rebecca. BS, Ft. Lewis Coll., 1972. Geologist, engr. Idarado Mining Co., Ouray, Colo., 1972-78; chief mine geologist Ranchers Exploration & Devel. Corp., Ouray, 1981-84, Atlas Precious Metals Corp., Ohio City, Colo., 1985-86; pvt. practice cons. mining geologist Ouray, 1986-87; dist. mgr. Am. Gold Resources Corp., Lakewood, Colo., 1988—; capt. San Juan Mine Rescue Coop., Ouray, 1981-85, dir., 1981-88; instr. Mine Safety and Health Adminstrn., Ouray, 1982-86. Instr. hunter safety Colo. Div. of Wild Life, Ouray, 1981-85. Mem. Soc. Mining Engrs., San Juan Miners Assn., Chief Ouray Gun Club (sec. 1972-78). Republican. Roman Catholic. Home: 964 1/2 3d St Ouray CO 81427 Office: Am Gold Resources Corp 134 Union Blvd Lakewood CO 80228

TRUJILLO, JOSEPH BEN, insurance company executive; b. Santa Fe, Sept. 26, 1947; s. Jose Benito and Annette (Jaramillo) T.; m. Marcelle K. Johnson, Dec. 11, 1976. BA, Wichita State U., 1969; MA, N.Mex. Highlands U., 1972; MBA, U. Phoenix, Denver, 1986. Sales mgmt. trainee Conn. Gen. Co., Bloomfield, 1973-76; sales agt. Conn. Mut. Ins. Co., Hartford, 1976-78; owner, mgr. Larimer Ins. Group, Denver, 1978-84, JBT Fin. Group, Denver, 1984—; CLU, fin. cons. Pres. Rep. Nat. Hispanic Assembly Colo., 1983, Heritage Village Homeowners Assn., Littleton, Colo., 1984-85; co-chmn. Colo. Gov.'s Latin Am. Task Force, 1988—; mem. Colo. Airport Task Force, 1988—, Colo. Econ. Devel. Task Force, Denver, 1988—. Mem. Nat. Assn. Life Underwriters, Colo. Assn. Life Underwriters, Denver Assn. Life Underwriters, Am. Soc. CLU's, Million Dollar Round Table (life), Colo. Hispanic C. of C. (pres. 1985-87, Man of Yr. award 1987). Roman Catholic. Office: JBT Fin Group 7555 E Hampden Ave Ste 104 Denver CO 80231

TRUJILLO, STEPHEN MICHAEL, physicist; b. Culver City, Calif., Mar. 5, 1932; s. Richard Martin and Lena Rue (Kirby) T.; m. Josefina Caravaca, Aug. 22, 1959. BSEE, U. Kans., 1958; PhD in Physics, U. London, 1975. Staff scientist Convair div. Gen. Dynamics, San Diego, 1958-69, Gulf Gen. Atomic Corp., San Diego, 1969-70; vis. rsch. fellow U. London, 1970-75; prin. physicist IRT Corp., San Diego, 1975-80; cons., tech. advisor Gen. Atomic Co., San Diego, 1980; sr. physicist Internat. Nuclear Energy Co., San Diego, 1981-83; staff scientist S-cubed div. Maxwell Labs. Inc., San Diego, 1983-88, sr. staff scientist, 1988—; cons., tech. advisor Alcoa Def. Systems, San Diego, 1984—. Mem. IEEE, Am. Phys. Soc., Inst. Physics (Eng.), N.Y. Acad. Scis., Old Crows Club. Republican. Home: 5931 Bellevue Ave La Jolla CA 92037 Office: Maxwell Labs Inc 9244 Balboa Ave San Diego CA 92123

TRUJILLO-MOPHETT, LORI SUE, fashion designer; b. Albuquerque, Oct. 3, 1958; d. Donald Daniel and Carol Louise (Anderson) Trujillo; m. Walter Roy Mophett, Aug. 22, 1987. AA, Fashion Inst., Los Angeles, 1980; BA in Art, Calif. State U., Long Beach, 1988. Designer So. Calif. Pleating Co., Los Angeles, 1981-83; owner, designer Fashion by Design, Rancho Palos Verdes, Calif., 1983—, Gentleman's Choice, San Pedro, Calif., 1985—; designer Anvil Cases, Rosemead, Calif., 1989—; judge sr. fashion show Los Angeles Trade Tech. Sch., 1982; artist. Mem. Mus. Contemporary Art. Recipient 2d place award Nat. Home Sewing contest, 1984, 2d place painting award Harbor Art Show, Los Angeles Harbor Coll., 1984. Mem. Fashion Inst. Alumni Assn. Home: 729 24th St #15 San Pedro CA 90731

TRUONG, HOA PHU, lawyer, consultant; b. Saigon, Republic Vietnam, Mar. 17, 1953; s. Loc P. Troung and D. Sam T. Hau; m. Vy T. Le, May 26, 1980; children: Heather , Michael. Bachelor's, U. San Francisco, 1975; JD, U. West Los Angeles, 1987. Lic. real estate broker, mortgage banker, Calif. Exec. v.p. Resco Realty, Inc., San Jose, 1979-84; house counsel Golden Coast Fin. Group, Garden Grove, Calif., 1987—. Recipient Am. Jurisprudence award, 1986. Mem. Calif. Trial Lawyers Assn. Los Angeles Trial Lawyers Assn. Republican. Buddhist. Office: Golden Coast Fin Group 11752 Garden Grove Blvd Ste 223 Garden Grove CA 92643

TRUSSEL, HAROLD JUNIOR, school principal; b. Montpelier, Idaho, July 4, 1936; s. William and Wanda Matilda (Jaussi) T.; m. Vilate Gardner, Jan. 21, 1961; children—Reed William, Bryan Gardner, Allison. B.S., U. Utah, 1963, M.S., 1968, Ednl. Specialist, 1972; postgrad. U. Fla., 1977. Tchr., South High Sch., Salt Lake City, 1970-73; acting prin. SE Jr. High Sch., Salt Lake City, 1972-73; prin. Lincoln Jr. High Sch., Salt Lake City, 1974-75, Jordan Intermediate Sch., Salt Lake City, 1975-78, Bryant Intermediate Sch., Salt Lake City, 1978-84, West High Sch., Salt Lake City, 1984—; chmn. Utah State Middle Sch. Com., 1981-83, Utah Jr. High Adv. Com., 1984—, High Sch. Prins. Salt Lake City Sch. Dist., 1988-89; dir. Nat. Tchr. Corps, Salt Lake, 1976-78. Organizer, officer Freedom Clubs for Am., Salt Lake City, 1979—; coach Little League Baseball, Salt Lake City, 1968-70; mem. Town Council Meeting, Salt Lake City, 1976; mem., speaker Utah Pub. Productivity Fair, 1983; mem. Gov.'s Criminal and Juvenile Justice Commn., 1987—. Recipient Valley Forge Freedoms Found. medal, 1983; named Best High Sch. Prin. Utah, Utah Holiday Mag., 1985, Outstanding Prin. of Yr. for State of Utah state P.T.A., 1989. Mem. Salt Lake Adminstrs. Exec. Council, Salt Lake Assn. Secondary Sch. Adminstrs. (chmn. adminstr. edn. com. 1981-82, chmn. profl. rights and responsibility com. 1979-80), Nat. Assn. Secondary Sch. Prins., Phi Delta Kappa. Lodge: Kiwanis (Bonneville, Internat.). Address: West High Sch 241 N 300 W Salt Lake City UT 84103

TRUSSELL, GRAYSON LEE, management consultant; b. Albuquerque, 1941; m. Jotina E. Huxford; 1 child, Heather Renee. BBA, U. N.Mex., 1963, MBA summa cum laude, 1984. Sr. acct./auditor Denhan & Co., Albuquerque, 1969-71; mgr. fin. acctg. and cost acctg. EG&G Inc., Albuquerque, 1971-72; ptnr., sec.-treas., comptroller Jaynes Corp., Albuquerque, 1972-75; comptroller, fin. mgr. DAR Tile and Carpeting Co., Albuquerque, 1975-77; comptroller, gen. fin. and ops. mgr. Luther Constrn. Co. and Luther Investment Co., Albuquerque, 1977-78; ptnr., sec.-treas. Constrn. Contracting & Mgmt. Inc., Albuquerque, 1982-83, Diginetics Inc., Albuquerque, 1982-84; assoc., sec.-treas., comptroller Bohannan-Huston Inc., Albuquerque, 1978-84; owner, ptnr. Johnson-Trussell Co., Albuquerque, 1984—; bd. dirs. Homecare Enterprises Inc., N.Mex.; adj. instr. U. N.Mex., mem. adv. council sch. mgmt. Co-Author: Entrepreneurial Development Guide, 1984, Managing for Profit and Change, 1986, Creating the Service Vision, 1988. Bd. dirs., sec. St. Francis Gardens, Inc.; bd. dirs., exec. com., past v.p., chmn. small bus. roundtable Albuquerque C. of C.; bd. dirs. Quality of Life Coalition, Inc. Capt. USN, Vietnam, 1966-69, also, USNR. Decorated Nat. Def. medal, Viet Nam Service medal, Viet Nam Campaign medal with 3 stars, Meritorious Svc. medal. Mem. Navy League U.S. (pres.), Naval Res. Assn., Assn. Naval Aviation, Kiwanis, Phi Kappa Phi. Home: 8808 Hilton Ave NE Albuquerque NM 87111 Office: The Johnson-Trussell Co 8205 Spain NE Ste 111 Albuquerque NM 87109

TRUSSELL, R(OBERT) RHODES, environmental and sanitary engineer; b. National City, Calif; s. Robert L. and Margaret (Kessing) T.; m. Elizabeth Shane, Nov. 26, 1969; children—Robert Shane, Charles Bryan. BSCE, U. Calif.-Berkeley, 1966, MS, 1967, PhD, 1972. With J.M. Montgomery Cons. Engrs., Pasadena, Calif., 1972—, v.p., 1977, sr. v.p., 1986, dir. applied tech., 1980—. Mem. com. on water treatment chems. Nat. Acad. Sci., 1980-82, mem. com. 3d part cert., 1982-83, com. on irrigation-induced water quality problems, 1985—, chmn. subcom. on treatment; mem. U.S./German research com. on corrosion of water systems, 1984-85; mem. U.S./Dutch research com. on organics in water, 1982-83; mem. U.S./USSR research com. on water treatment, 1985—. Mem. joint editorial bd. Standards Methods for Examination of Water and Wastewater, 1980-89; mem. editorial adv. bd. Environ. and Sci. and Tech., 1977-83; contbr. articles to profl. publs. Mem. Am. Water Works Assn. (mem. editorial adv. bd. jour. 1987—), Water Pollution Control Fedn., Internat. Water Pollution Research Assn., Am. Chem. Soc., Am. Inst. Chem. Engrs., Nat. Assn. Corrosion Engrs., Sigma Xi. Office: 250 N Madison PO Box 7009 Pasadena CA 91109-7009

TRUTA, MARIANNE PATRICIA, oral and maxillofacial surgeon; b. N.Y.C., Apr. 28, 1952; d. John J. and Helen Patricia (Donnelly) T.; m. William Christopher Donlon, May 28, 1983. BS, St. John's U., 1974; DMD, SUNY, Stonybrook, 1977. Intern The Mt. Sinai Med. Ctr., N.Y.C., 1977-78, resident, 1978-80, chief resident, 1980-81; asst. prof. U. of the Pacific, San Francisco, 1983-85, clin. asst. prof., 1985—; asst. dir. Facial Pain Rsch. Ctr., San Francisco, 1986—; pvt. practice oral and maxillofacial surgery Peninsula Maxillofacial Surgery, South San Francisco, Calif., 1985—, Burlingame, Calif., 1988—. Mem. Am. Assn. Oral Maxillofacial Surgeons, Am. Dental Soc. Anesthesiology, Am. Soc. Cosmetic Surgery, Am. Assn. Women Dentists, Western Soc. Oral Maxillofacial Surgeons. No. Calif. Soc. Oral Maxillofacial Surgeons. Office: Peninsula Maxillofacial Surgery 1860 El Camino Real Ste 300 Burlingame CA 94010

TRYBUL, THEODORE N., government official; b. Chgo., Apr. 12, 1935; s. Theodore and Sophie T.; m. Barbara Reynolds, Aug. 22, 1959; children—Catherine, Barbara, Adrienne, Diane, Theodore. B.S. in Mech. Engring., U. Ill., 1957; M.S. in Mech. Engring, U. N.Mex., 1963; D.Sc. magna cum laude, George Washington U., 1976. Research staff Sandia (N.Mex.) Labs., 1957-64; engring. group supr. Gen. Dynamics Corp.; project mgr. Aerospace Corp., San Bernardino, Calif., 1965-67; program dir. Raytheon Co., Bedford, Mass., 1967-68; div. chief USA Advanced Materiel Concepts Agy., AMC, Washington, 1968-74; dir. TECOM, Md.; project mgr. electronic warfare programs, advanced programs div. Hughes Aircraft Co., Los Angeles, 1983-87; dir. quality assurance USN, North Island, CA, 1987—; prof. engring. George Washington U., 1976-83, Am. U., 1978-83, Calif. State Coll.; prof. mgmt. U. No. Colo.; prof. system scis. U. So. Calif.; mem. USN Bur. Weapons Adv. Council, joint study group on Mil. Resource Allocation Methodology, Army Sci. Bd. Author: Operations Research, 1968, Systems Analysis, 1971, Systems Engineering, 1974; contbr. numerous articles to profl. jours.; patentee in field. Pres. Gunston Sch. PTA, Lorton, Va., Aquia Harbor Assn., Hollowing Point Potomac River Estates Assn., Assn. Sea Pines Plantation Oroperty Owners, Inc.; mem. council Our Lady of Angels Ch., Woodbride, Va. Served with U.S. Army, 1959-61. Recipient Marquette U. Scholarship award, U. Ill. Scholarship Key, U. N.Mex. Math. award, George Washington U. teaching fellowship, U.S. Govt. Long Term Tng. award. Mem. Internat. Soc. Tech. Assessment, Indsl. Research Inst., World Future Soc., Washington Acad. Sci., Armed Forces Mgmt. Assn., Military Ops. Research Soc. (chmn. research and devel.), Washington Ops. Research Council, AAAS (sci. reviewer, mem. govt. fluidics coordination group, standardization, reliability and fabrication com.), Am. Soc. Mil. Comptrollers, ASME, Am. Def. Preparedness Assn. (needs analysis and effectiveness analysis coms.), Assn. U.S. Army, Soc. Computer Simulation (chmn.), Sigma Xi, Kappa Mu Epsilon, Pi Tau Sigma, Tau Beta Pi. Roman Catholic. Clubs: Sea Pines, Millionaire's, KC. Home: 1820 Avenida del Mundo Coronado CA 92118

TRYBUS, RAYMOND J., academic dean, psychologist; b. Chgo., Jan. 9, 1944; s. Fred and Cecilia (Liszka) T.; m. Sandra A. Noone, Aug. 19, 1967; children: David, Nicole. BS, St. Louis U., 1965, MS, 1970, PhD, 1971. Lic. psychologist, Md., D.C., Calif. Clin. psychologist Jewish Vocat. Svc., St. Louis, 1968-71; clin. psychologist Gallaudet U., Washington, 1971-72, rsch. psychologist, 1972-74, dir. demographic studies, 1974-78, dean grad. studies and rsch., 1984-88; assoc. provost, prof. psychology Calif. Sch. of Profl. Psychology, 1988—. dean Gallaudet Rsch. Inst., 1978-84; cons. Mental Health Ctr. for Deaf, Lanham, Md., 1982-88 , Congl. Rsch. Svc., 1982-84 , McGill U. Nat. Study Hearing Impairment in Can., 1984-88 . Contbg. author: The Future of Mental Health Services for the Deaf, 1978, Hearing-impaired Children and Youth with Devel. Disabilities, 1985; editor Jour. Am. Deafness and Rehab. Assn. Grantee NIMH, Spencer Found., Tex. Edn. Agy., W.K. Kellogg Found. Mem. Am. Assn. Univ. Adminstrs. (bd. dirs.), Assn. Internat. Assn. Study of Interdisciplinary Rsch., Am. Psychol. Assn., Soc. Rsch. Adminstrs., AAAS, Acad. San Diego Psychologists. Roman Catholic. Home: 6342 Cibola Rd San Diego CA 92120 Office: 6212 Ferris Square San Diego CA 92121

TRYTTEN, STEVEN EARL, lawyer; b. Ann Arbor, Mich., Nov. 11, 1952; s. J. Perry and Joyce M. (Haworth) T.; m. Karen M. Saewert, Jan. 5, 1975 (div. 1979); m. Patricia L. Farrell, Dec. 31, 1983; children: Tawnia L., Hilary L. BS in Communications, U. Ill., 1974, JD, 1978. Bar: Ill. 1978, Calif. 1983; CPA, Ill. Tax acct., fin. planner Coopers and Lybrand, Chgo., 1978-81; sole practice Chgo., 1981-83, Los Angeles, 1985—; fin. planner Bank of Am., Los Angeles, 1983-85. Author various visual aids and software. Mem. Ill. Bar Assn., Calif. Bar Assn., ABA, Los Angeles County Bar Assn., Am. Inst. CPAs. Republican. Office: 6735 Forest Lawn Dr Suite 206 Los Angeles CA 90068

TRZYNA, THADDEUS CHARLES, academic institution administrator; b. Chgo., Oct. 26, 1939; s. Thaddeus Stephen and Irene Mary (Giese) T.; divorced; 1 child, Jennifer. BA in Internat. Relations, U. So. Calif., 1961; PhD in Govt., Claremont Grad. Sch., 1975. Vice consul U.S. Govt., Elisabethville, Katanga, Zaire, 1962-63; consul U.S. Govt., Leopoldville, Republic of Congo, 1963-64; sec. Nat. Mil. Info. Disclosure Policy Com. U.S. Govt., Washington, 1964-67; pres. Calif. Inst. Pub. Affairs, Claremont, 1969—; mem. steering com., commn. sustainable devel. Internat. Union for Conservation of Nature and Natural Resources, 1983—; chmn. Calif. Forum on Hazardous Materials, 1985-88, Calif. Farmlands Project Task Force, 1981-84; cons. U.S. and Calif. State Agys. on environ. policy, cons. on devel. of natural resources Univ. for Peace, Costa Rica; lectr. internat. relations, Pomona Coll. Author: The California Handbook, rev. 5th edit. 1987. Mem. Am. Fgn. Service Assn., Sierra Club (v.p. 1975-77, chmn. internat. com. 1977-79). Democrat. Unitarian. Office: Calif Inst Pub Affairs PO Box 10 Claremont CA 91711

TSANG, CANDY, real estate associate; b. Canton, Fah Yuen, China, Dec. 29, 1954; d. Foo and Wan Yum (Gong) T. BS in Bus. & Mktg., Fresno State U., 1981. Store mgr. Fair Mart, Caruthers, Calif., 1981-83; acctg. clk. San Francisco Museum Soc., 1983-85; skycap ITS Internat. Total Svc., San Francisco, 1985-87; sales assoc. Century 21 Herd & Co., Daly City, Calif., 1987—. Mem. San Francisco Bd. Realtor, San Mateo County Bd. Realtor. Office: Century 21 Herd & Co 100 Skyline Plaza Daly City CA 94015

TSANG, CHIT-SANG, engineering educator; b. Hong Kong, Mar. 24, 1952; came to U.S., 1971; s. Chu-Pang and Siu-Han (Ho) T.; m. Jiuan-Min Chang, June 16, 1979; children: Anita Huey-En, Serena Huey-Ning. BS, La. State U., 1974; MS, Ohio State U., 1976; PhD, U. So. Calif., 1982. Network control engr. RCA Am. Communications Corp., Piscataway, N.J., 1976-77; software engr. Digital Equipment Corp., Maynard, Mass., 1977-79; sr. system engr. Lincom Corp., Los Angeles, 1980-88; assoc. prof. Calif. State U., Long Beach, 1988—. Deacon First Evangelical Ch., Glendale, Calif., 1984—. Mem. IEEE, Tau Beta Pi, Eta Kappa Nu. Home: 6413 N Lemon Ave San Gabriel CA 91775 Office: Calif State U Dept Elec Engring Long Beach CA 90840

TSAO, CHICH-HSING ALEX, electrical engineer; b. Taipei, Taiwan, Republic of China, Feb. 8, 1953; arrived in U.S., 1976; m. Hsiao-Jen Ni, May 20, 1978: children: Bohr-Young, Bihn-Young. BEE, Nat. Taiwan U., 1974; MEE, Duke U., 1978; PhD, U. Ill., 1981. Sr. engring. specialist Ford Aerospace Corp., Palo Alto, Calif., 19816. Contbr. articles to profl. jours.; inventor microstrip antennas, 1987. Mem. IEEE. Home: 20567 Brookwood Ln Saratoga CA 95070 Office: Ford Aerospace Corp 3825 Fabian Way Palo Alto CA 94303

TSCHANZ, DAVID WERNER, epidemiologist; b. Bridgeport, Conn., Nov. 21, 1952; s. Alfred Werner and Frances Ann (Konecny) T.; m. Cynthia Leigh Eckert, Oct. 20, 1979; children: Karl Martin, Eric David. BA, St. Louius U., 1974; MA, U. Bridgeport, 1979; MS in Pub. Health, U. S.C., 1985. Dir. communicable diseases S.C. Dept. Health, Lancaster, 1982-86; mgr. infectious disease Ariz. Dept. Health Svcs., Phoenix, 1986--; mem. Phoenix Sick Child Care Com., 1987--. Contbr. articles on communicable diseases to profl. jours. Tee-ball coach NW Phoenix Parks and Recreation Dept., 1986-- . USPHS scholar, 1981-83. Mem. Am. Pub. Health Assn., Soc. for Pediatric Epidemiologic Rsch., Soc. for Epidemiologic Rsch. Roman Catholic. Home: 4155 W Evans Dr Phoenix AZ 85023 Office: Ariz Dept Health Svcs 3008 N 3d St Phoenix AZ 85023

TSCHIRHART, JOHN THOMAS, economist, educator; b. N.Y.C., Oct. 23, 1946; s. John A. and Mary Ellen (McManus) T.; m. Linda R. Stanley, 1987; children: Deborah, Daniel. BS, Johns Hopkins U., 1970; MS, Purdue U., 1972, PhD, 1975. Instr. Purdue U., West Lafayette, Ind., 1973-75; asst. prof. SUNY, Buffalo, 1975-78; assoc. prof. U. Wyo., Laramie, 1978-81, prof., 1982—. Author: Regulation of Natural Monopolies, 1988; contbr. articles to profl. jours. Midshipman USN, 1964-66. Mem. Am. Econs. Assn. Home: 59 Corthell Laramie WY 82071 Office: U Wyo Dept Econs University Station Box 3985 Laramie WY 82071

TSE, FELIX YAN-TAK, data processing executive; b. Canton, People's Republic China, July 29, 1956; came to U.S., 1970; s. Abraham Tse; m. Mary Choi-Ngo Yapp, Aug. 2, 1976; children: Alan, Victoria. Student, City Coll. San Francisco, 1974-76, Community Coll. San Francisco, 1986-87. With data processing dept. Bank of Am., San Francisco, 1975-79, sr. computer operator, acting supr., 1979-83, computer facilities and ops. mgr., 1983--. Mem. Alpha Gamma Beta.

TSEU, FRED K., insurance company executive; b. Hunan, Peoples Republic of China, Nov. 19, 1923; came to U.S., 1930; s. Joseph Y. and Lillian (Choy) T.; m. Alice Y. Chu Tseu, Dec. 16, 1946 (div. Mar. 1958); 1 child, Eygenia; m. Edna K. Loo, Apr. 8, 1959; children: Steven F., Deborah M., Lori A. Chartered life underwriter. Sales agt. Security Life and Accident Co., Denver, 1947-53; asst. mgr. ins. sales Fin. Security Life, Honolulu, 1953-54; br. mgr. ins. sales Standard Ins. Co., Portland, Oreg., 1954-55; pres, mgr. ins. sales Guardian of Hawaii, Ltd., Honolulu, 1955—. St. chmn. com. Life Underwriters Polit. Action, 1978—; commr. neighborhood Boy Scouts Am., 1956; youth counselor YMCA, 1959-60; vol. solicitor Am. Heart Assn., ARC, 1950—; team leader Aloha United Way, 1968-80. With USN, 1942-45, WWII, 1950-51, Korea. Decorated Pacific Theatre medal, Am. Def. medal, Victory medal. Mem. Honolulu Assn. Life Underwriters (chmn. mem. com. 1949, legis. com. 1950), Wast Honolulu Assn. of Life Underwriters (chmn. 1976-78), Gen. Agt. and Mgr. Assn. (mem. com. 1985), Am. Soc. CLU's, Assn. Ind. Brokerage Agys. Republican. Home: 530 Ulukou St Kailua HI 96734 Office: Guardian of Hawaii Ltd 850 Richards St Ste 504 Honolulu HI 96813

TSUCHIYA, MASAHIRO, computer company executive; b. Kobe, Japan, May 23, 1948; s. Kiyoshi and Shizuko (Saito) T. BS, Konan U., Kobe, 1965; PhD, U. Tex., 1972. Prof. computer sci. Northwestern U., Evanston, Ill., 1973-74; prof. U. Calif., Irvine, 1974-76, U. Hawaii at Manoa, Honolulu, 1976-79; pres. Computer Progress Unltd., Honolulu, 1977-80; mgr. Def. Systems Group TRW, Inc., Redondo Beach, Calif., 1980-87; pres. Sypex Internat. Co., Kailua, Hawaii, 1986—. Contbr. over 30 articles to profl. jours. Mem. Computer Soc. of IEEE (sr.). Home and Office: PO Box 1199 Manhattan Beach CA 90266-8199

TSUCHIYA, TAKUMI, agronomy educator; b. Ajimu-cho, Oita-Ken, Japan, Mar. 10, 1923; came to U.S., 1968; s. Torao and Masao Tsuchiya; m. Chiyoko Kukushima, Feb. 20, 1953; children: Keiko, Noriko. BAgr, Gifu Ag. Coll., 1943, Kyoto Imperial U., 1947; DAgr, Kyoto U., 1960. Cytogeneticist Kihara Inst. for Biol. Rsch., Yokohama, Japan, 1957-63; postdoctoral fellow U. Man., Winnepeg, Can., 1963-64; cytogeneticist Children's Hosp., Winnepeg; rsch. assoc. U. Manitoba, Winnepeg, 1965-68; assoc. prof. agronomy Colo. State U., Ft. Collins, 1968-73, prof., 1973—; chmn. genetics com. Am. Barley Workers Conf., 1969—; presenter, lectr. seminars in field. Editor: Barley Genetics Newsletter; mem. editorial bd. Cereal Rsch. Communication; contbr. over 400 articles to sci. jours., chpts. to books. Recipient Oliver P. Pennock Achievement Disting. Svc. award Colo. State U., 1986, Faculty Achievement award Burlington-No., 1987. Fellow Am. Soc. Agronomy, Crop Sci. Soc. Am. (Crop Sci. Rsch. award 1986), Japan Soc. for Promotion of Sci. (fgn. sci.); mem. Genetics Soc. Japan (hon. fgn.), Am. Genetic Assn., Soc. Econ. Botany, Can. Genetics Soc., Internat. Soc. Cytology (standing collaborator), Sigma Xi (hon. scientist award 1987), Kappa Phi, Phi Kappa Phi, Gamma Sigma Delta. Home: 1617 Lakeridge Ct Fort Collins CO 80521 Office: Colo State U Dept Agronomy Fort Collins CO 80523

TSUKASA, KIMURA, electronics executive; b. Yokohama, Japan, May 15, 1935; s. Mitsugu and Chiyo (Sato) K.; m. Chieko Saito, Oct. 22, 1961; children: Naomi, Keigo. 2nd class radio officer, Sendai Radio Communication Sch, 1955; 1st class radio officer, Inst. Merchant Marine, 1958. Radio officer Inui Steam Ship Co., Kobe, Japan, 1955-61; tech. instr. Sony Service Co., Tokyo, Japan, 1962-67; sales mgr. Sony Corp. Internat. Div., Tokyo, 1968-71; managing dir. Sony Service Ctr., Antwerp, Belgium, 1971-78; pres. Sony Consumer Service Co., U.S.A., 1979-85; dir. gen. Sony Magnetic Products of Europe, Paris, France, 1985-87; gen. mgr. Sony Customer Service Group, Tokyo, 1987-88; sr. v.p. Sony Corp. Am., Ontario, Calif., 1988—. Home: 643 Promontory Dr East Newport Beach CA 92660 Office: Sony Corp of Am 2940 E Inland Empire Blvd Ontario CA 91764

TUBBS, WILLIAM REID, JR., public service administrator; b. Johnson Air Base, Japan, June 1, 1950; s. William Reid and Roberta Daisy (Krenkel) T.; m. Ellen Lee Duccini, May 19, 1984. BA, Calif. State U., Sacramento, 1973, MPA, 1981. Assoc. analyst exec. dept. County of Sacramento, 1975-84, program coordinator emergency ops., 1984-85; adminstrv. dir. mental health services Sacramento Mental Health Ctr., 1985—. Chmn. Cable TV Adv. Commn., West Sacramento, 1987—. Lt. (j.g.) USCGR. Mem. Am. Soc. Pub. Adminstrn., Res. Officers Assn., U.S. Naval Inst. Republican. Home: 1012 Rogers St West Sacramento CA 95605 Office: Sacramento Mental Health Ctr 2150 Stockton Blvd Sacramento CA 95817

TUBIS, SEYMOUR, painter, printmaker, sculptor, educator; b. Phila., Sept. 20, 1919; student Temple U., 1937-39, Phila. Mus. Sch. Art, 1941-42, Art Students League of N.Y., 1946-49; Academie Grande-Chaumiere, Paris, 1949-50, Instituto d'Arte, Florence, Italy, 1950; student of Hans Hofmann, N.Y.C., 1951. Pvt. tchr. art, N.Y.C., Rockport, Mass., 1948-60; tchr. art, summer program Bd. Edn., Great Neck, N.Y., 1949; asst. instr. Art Students League of N.Y., 1948, 49, Bklyn. Mus. Sch. Art, 1950-51; instr. N.Y.C. Adult Edn. Program, 1950-52; head dept. fine arts, instr. printmaking, painting and design Inst. of Am. Indian Arts, Santa Fe, 1963-80. One-man shows at Galerie St. Placide, Paris, 1950, Lowe Found. Galleries, N.Y.C., 1953, 55, Taft Sch., Conn., 1953, La Chapelle Gallery, Santa Fe, 1960, Mus. N.Mex., Santa Fe, 1964, Accents Gallery, Cleve., 1966, U. Calgary (Alta., Can.), 1967, Jamison Galleries, Santa Fe, 1967, N.Mex. State Library, Santa Fe, 1968, Coll. of Santa Fe, 1969, The New West, Albuquerque, 1969, 71, 72, 73, Gallery Contemporary Art, Taos, 1969, Antioch Coll., Balt. and Washington, 1973, Pacific Grove (Calif.) Art Ctr., 1983, Tobey C. Moss Gallery, L.A., 1986-89, Associated Am. Artists, N.Y.C., 1986-89, Warner Roberts Gallery, Palo Alto, 1987, Bluecreek West Gallery, Denver, 1989, numerous others; exhibited in group shows at Library of Congress, Carnegie Inst., Bklyn. Mus., Pa. Acad. Fine Arts, Dallas Mus. Art, Syracuse U., Royal Soc., London, Eng., Hofstra Coll., Asso. Gallery Art, Detroit, Riverside Mus., N.Y.C., Met. Mus. Art, N.Y.C., Seattle Art Mus., Dept. Interior, Dept. State Embassies Program, Mus. Modern Art, N.Y.C., Mus. of N.Mex., St. John's Coll., Santa Fe, Mus. Internat. Folk Art, Santa Fe, Pa. State Coll., Wichita Art Assn., John F. Kennedy Center for Performing Arts, Washington, also others; represented in permanent collections Library of Congress, Soc. Am. Graphic Artists, Met. Mus. Art, Pa. State Coll., U. Ariz., U. Calgary, Art Students League N.Y., U.S. Dept. Interior, Antioch Coll., Georgetown U., Boston Pub. Library, also numerous pvt. collections; artist-cons. N.Y. World-Telegram and Sun, 1955-59, St. John's Coll., 1960, Mus. of N.Mex., 1960, N.Y. Times, 1961-63; research grantee U. Ariz., U. Calif.-Santa Barbara. Recipient 1st prize in painting, Newspaper Guild N.Y., purchase award Mus. of N.Mex.; Nat. Endowment Arts grantee, 1980. Mem. Soc. Am. Graphic Artists (1st prize in etching), Art Students League N.Y., Coll. Art Assn. Home and Office: 1531 S Flamingo Way Denver CO 80222

TUCCELLI, CHERI FRANCES, computer executive, business owner; b. L.A., July 22, 1960; d. Anthony Cosmo and Georgia (Davis) T. V.p. Precision Payroll, L.A., 1975—; payroll cons. L.A. Olympic Organizing Com., 1984; pres., payroll and systems cons. Century City Messenger, L.A., 1986—. Recipient Accomadation for Excellent Achievement, L.A. Olympic Com., 1984. Office: Precision Payroll 8100 Balboa Van Nuys CA 91406

TUCCIO, SAM ANTHONY, aerospace executive, physicist; b. Rochester, N.Y., Jan. 15, 1939; s. Manuel Joseph and Phillis (Cannizzo) T.; m. Jenny Laprell Elvington, May 1, 1982; children: David Samuel, Karen Ann, Rebecca Jean. BS, U. Rochester, 1965. Research physicist Eastman Kodak Co., Rochester, 1965-72; program mgr. Lawrence Livermore (Calif.) Labs., 1972-75; sr. physicist Allied Corp., Morristown, N.J., 1975-81; gen. mgr. Allied Laser Products Div., Westlake Village, Calif., 1981-84; sr. bus. mgr. Northrop Corp., Hawthorne, Calif., 1984—. Patentee in field; contbr. numerous articles to profl. jours. Recipient IR 100 award Indsl. Rsch. Assn., 1971. Republican. Methodist. Home: 27 Malaga Pl W Manhattan Beach CA 90266 Office: Northrop Corp 2301 W 120th St Hawthorne CA 90250

TUCK, MICHAEL RAY, technical services executive; b. Pocatello, Idaho, Aug. 9, 1941; s. Amos R. and Phyllis (Day) T.; m. Heather K. Fowler, Oct. 22, 1962; children: Lisa M., Jennifer A., Mark. BS in Math., Idaho State U., 1964; MS in Math., U. Idaho, 1971. Programmer analyst Argonne Nat. Labs., Idaho Falls, Idaho, 1964-69; computer scientist Argonne Nat. Labs., Idaho Falls, 1969-76; engr., mgr. computer div. Montana Energy Inst., Butte, Mont., 1976-81; v.p. MultiTech Inc. div. MSE Inc., Butte, 1981-82, pres., 1982-83; vice pres. MSE Inc., Butte, 1983—; cons. TMA Assocs., Butte, 1982-83. Bd. dirs. Jr. Achievement of Butte, Port of Mont., Mont. Trade and Comml. Devel. Ctr., Inc. Mem. Am. Soc. Data Processing Profls., Butte C. of C. (bd. dirs.), Mont. Data Processing Soc., Exch. Club, Continental Club (pres. local chpt.). Methodist. Office: MSE Inc PO Box 4078 Butte MT 59701

TUCK, RAYMOND R., JR., college president; b. June 9, 1934; m. Marjorie Gay Tuck; children: Russell R. III, Catherine Elizabeth. BS in Chemistry, Union U., 1956; MS in Biology, Vanderbilt U., 1957, PhD in Curriculum and Instrn., 1971; study, Wash. U., 1960-61. Instr. biology, asst. coordinator Korean Tchr. Edn. Program George Peabody Coll. Vanderbilt U., Nashville, 1957-59; tchr. biology, chmn. sci. dept. University City (Mo.) Sr. High Sch., 1960-63, from asst. prin. to prin., 1963-70; prin. Parkway North Sr. High Sch., St. Louis County, Mo., 1971-78; asst. supt. Parkway Sch. Dist., St. Louis County, 1979-81, assoc. supt., 1981-84; pres. Calif. Bapt. Coll., Riverside, 1984—. Contbr. articles to profl. jours. Bd. dirs. Opera Assn., ARC, pres. 1989—; active Bapt. Ch., local hosp. assn. bd., local edn. com.; World Affairs Coun. Mem. Calif. Bapt. Hist. Soc. (bd. dirs.), Calif. Bapt. Devel. Found. (bd. dirs.), Am. Assn. Sch. Adminstrs., Am. Assn. Pres.' of Ind. Colls. and Univs., Inland Empire Higher Edn. Coun. (pres. 1987-88), Kappa Delta Pi, Phi Delta Kappa. Lodge: Rotary. Office: Calif Bapt Coll 8432 Magnolia Ave Riverside CA 92504

TUCKER, CHARLES CYRIL, information systems consultant; b. N.Y.C., Mar. 7, 1942; s. Bernard Anthony and Charlotte Yvonne (Carron) T.; m. Sue Ann Rasmuson, Apr. 11, 1970; children: Michele, Christine. BS in Mech. Engring., U. Santa Clara, 1964, MBA, 1968. Mktg. rep. IBM, L.A., 1968-72; sr. assoc. McKinsey & Co., L.A., 1972-76; v.p. planning and info. services 20th Century-Fox, L.A., 1977-81; v.p. planning and corp. devel. MSI Data Corp., Costa Mesa, Calif., 1981-83; sr. v.p. planning and control 1st Interstate Services Co., Torrance, Calif., 1983-88; sr. mgr. Nolan, Norton & Co., L.A., 1988—; mem. product adv. bd. Teradata Corp., L.A., 1980-83; chmn. computers and info. systems adv. bd. Grad. Sch. Mgmt. UCLA, 1984-85. Served to 1st lt., U.S. Army, 1964-66, Korea. Mem. Soc. for Info. Mgmt. Roman Catholic. Home: 30201 Cartier Dr Rancho Palos Verdes CA 90274 Office: Nolan Norton & Co 725 S Figueroa St Los Angeles CA 90017

TUCKER, JOE WAVERLIA, JR., manufacturing executive; b. Dallas, July 29, 1942; s. Joe W. and Ethlyn (Hendricks) T.; m. Judith Julia Staghelin, Dec. 6, 1969. BBA, North Tex. Y., 1966; postgrad., So. Meth. U., 1970, Harvard U., 1985-86. Various pos. Tex. Instruments, Dallas, 1969-80, Honeywell Optoelectronics, Richardson, Tex., 1980-88; v.p., gen. mgr. United Detector Tech., Hawthorne, Calif., 1988—. With U.S. Army, 1963-65. Republican. Episcopalian. Office: United Detector Tech 12525 Chadron Ave Hawthorne CA 90250

TUCKER, JOEL LAWRENCE, aviation company executive; b. Berkeley, Calif., Feb. 23, 1932; s. Lawrence Otis Tucker and Edythe Lauretta (Pye) Connolly; m. Constance Nadine Finnick, Oct. 19, 1951 (div. Sept. 1975); 1 child, John Lawrence. BS, U. Wash., 1953. Statistician Bell Telephone System, Seattle, 1953-61, AID, Washington, 1961-64; dir. sales Boeing Comml. Airplanes, Seattle, 1965-87; pres. J.E.T. Cons. Ltd., Kirkland, Wash., 1987—; mng. dir. Lorad Boeing Ltd., Hamilton, Bermuda, 1988-89. Chmn. Citizens Sch. Adv. Coun., Bellevue, Wash., 1969-71. With U.S. Army, 1954-56. Republican. Presbyterian. Office: JET Cons Ltd PO Box 2146 Kirkland WA 98083-2146

TUCKER, LINDA WISE, real estate operations manager; b. Prospect, Tenn., Oct. 3, 1955; d. Johnnie Ester and Hattie Will (Gatlin) Wise; m. Marc Lory Tucker, June 9, 1979. BS, U. Ala., Florence, 1977. Fin. counselor U. Tenn. Hosp., Memphis, 1978-81; credit mgr. Wilson Electronics, Las Vegas, 1981-82; office mgr. Upjohn Healthcare Services, Abilene, Tex., 1982-83, Computer Optical Products, Chatsworth, Calif., 1983-84; ops. mgr. Merrill Lynch Realty, Woodland Hills, Calif., 1984—; v.p. Marlin Corp., Las Vegas, Nev., 1980—, Futura Services, Woodland Hills, 1988—. Mem. LWV. Mem. NAFE, Nat. Assn. Meeting Planners, Lead's Club. Home: 22291 Cass Ave Woodland Hills CA 91364-3009 Office: Merrill Lynch Realty 26541 Aquora Rd Ste #180 Calabasas CA 91302

TUCKER, MARSHALL DANIEL, retail company executive, accountant; b. Dresden, Tenn., Mar. 30, 1932; s. Marshall Jackson and Julia Isabell (Travis) T.; m. Gloria Shelwitt, Aug. 27, 1957; children: Susan, Karen, Mark. BA, U. Tenn., 1954. Corp. fin. analyst Mead Corp., Dayton, Ohio, 1966-70, asst. treas., 1977-79; dir. planning Mead Interiors, Dayton, 1971-74; controller Mead Corp.-Stanley, Stanleytown, Va., 1975-76; v.p., chief fin. officer McJunkin Corp., Charleston, W.Va., 1979-84, Dixon Paper Co., Denver, 1984—. Bd. dirs., treas. Charleston Symphony Orch. Served with U.S. Army, 1956-57. Mem. Fin. Exec. Inst. Lodge: Rotary. Home: 5528 S Iris St Littleton CO 80123 Office: Dixon Paper Co 410 Raritan Way Denver CO 80244

TUCKER, MELVILLE, film company executive; b. N.Y.C., Mar. 4, 1916. Student, Princeton U. Purchasing agt. Consol. Labs., N.Y.C., 1934-36; sound effects and picture editor Republic Prodns., Inc., 1936-38, asst. prodn. mgr., 1st asst. dir., 1938-42, asst. producer, 1946, assoc. producer, 1947-52; producer Universal, 1952-54, exec. v.p., 1955-70; producer Verdon Prodns., 1971—. Producer: (feature films) The Missourians, Thunder in God's Country, Rodeo King and the Senorita, Utah Wagon Train, Drums Across the River, Black Shield of Falworth, A Warm December, Uptown Saturday Night, 1972, Let's Do It Again, 1975, A Piece of the Action, 1977; exec. producer: (feature films) Stir Crazy, 1980, Hanky Panky, 1982, Fast Forward, 1985. Served with U.S. Army, 1942-46. Office: Verdon Cedric Prodns Inc 9350 Wilshire Blvd Ste 310 Beverly Hills CA 90212

TUCKER, PATRICIA ANN KELLY, corporate professional; b. Kansas City, Mo., Sept. 22, 1953; d. Leland Keith and Pauline Delphi (Duffek) Elliott; m. James Edward Kelly, June 7, 1980 (div. July 1986); 1 child, Ian Daniel; m. Steven Craig Tucker, May 7, 1988. AA in Applied Sci., Penn Valley Community Coll., Kansas City, 1973; BA in Mgmt., U. Phoenix, 1988, Cert. in Concentration in Mktg., Indsl. Rels., 1988; Degree in Med. Record Sci., Bapt. Meml. Hosp., Kansas City, 1973. Sr. accredited record tech. surg. unit Kansas City (Kans.) Gen. Hosp., 1973-76; office mgr. family practice ctr. North Kansas City Meml. Hosp., Kansas City, Mo., 1976-78; sr. accredited record technician Bethany Med. Ctr., Kansas City, Kans., 1980-82; dir. med. records, utilization rev. coord. Bryans Meml. Extended Care Ctr., Phoenix, 1983-84; dir. admissions med. records and utilization rev. coord. Basic Am. Med., Inc., Glendale, Ariz., 1984-85, asst. administr., 1984-85, dir. resident svcs., 1985-86; pvt. practice cons. Kel-Tuk Enterprises, Phoenix, 1986—. Mem. Am. Med. Record Assn., Ariz. Med. Record Assn. (membership com. 1988-89), Nat. Assn. Female Execs. Republican. Roman Catholic. Office: Kel-Tuk Enterprises 15222 N 23d Ln Phoenix AZ 85023

TUCKER, RONALD JAY, manufacturing company executive; b. Long Beach, N.Y., Oct. 24, 1948; s. William and Sally Ruth (Sonin) T.; m. Sharon Jo Ingersoll, Feb. 6, 1971; children: Michelle, Matthew. BS in Mgmt., Rensselaer Poly. Inst., 1971; postgrad., U. Conn., 1981-84. Supr. Baker/Beech-Nut Inc., Canajoharie, N.Y., 1973-74; distbn. engr. Frito-Lay, Inc., Elmhurst, Ill., 1974-76; shipping mgr. Frito-Lay, Inc., Wooster, Ohio, 1976-78; mgr. distbn. svcs. H. J. Heinz, Pitts., 1978-79, The Stanley Wks., Farmington, Conn., 1979-84; distbn. mgr. Stanley-Proto Indsl. Tools, Covington, Ga., 1984-87; plant mgr. Stanley-Proto Indsl. Tools, Portland, Oreg., 1987—. Lt. (j.g.) USNR, 1971-73. Office: Stanley Proto Indsl Tools 10330 SE 32nd Ave Portland OR 97222

TUELL, JACK MARVIN, bishop; b. Tacoma, Nov. 14, 1923; s. Frank Harry and Anne Helen (Bertelson) T.; m. Marjorie Ida Beadles, June 17, 1946; children—Jacqueline, Cynthia, James. B.S., U. Wash., 1947, LL.B., 1948; S.T.B., Boston U., 1955; M.A., U. Puget Sound, 1961; D.D., Pacific Sch. Religion, 1966; LLD, Alaska Pacific U., 1980. Bar: Wash. 1948; ordained to ministry Meth. Ch., 1955. Practice law with firm Holte & Tuell, Edmonds, Wash., 1948-50; pastor Grace Meth. Ch., Everett, Wash., 1950-52, South Tewksbury Meth. Ch., Tewksbury, Mass., 1952-55, Lakewood Meth. Ch., Tacoma, 1955-61; dist. supt. Puget Sound dist. Meth. Ch., Everett, 1961-67; pastor 1st United Meth. Ch., Vancouver, Wash., 1967-72; bishop United Meth. Ch., Portland, Oreg., 1972—, Calif.-Pacific Conf., United Meth. Ch., L.A., 1980—; Mem. gen. conf. United Meth. Ch., 1964, 66, 68, 70, 72; pres. coun. of Bishops United Meth. Ch., 1989-90. Author: The Organization of the United Methodist Church, 1970. Pres. Tacoma U.S.O., 1959-61, Vancouver YMCA, 1968; v.p. Ft. Vancouver Seamens Cnt., 1969-72; vice chmn. Vancouver Human Rels. Commn., 1970-72; pres. Oreg. Coun. Alcohol Problems, 1972-76; Trustee U. Puget Sound, 1961-73, Vancouver Meml. Hosp., 1967-72, Alaska Meth. U., Anchorage, 1972-80, Willamette U., Salem, Oreg., 1972-80, Willamette View Manor, Portland, 1972-80, Rogue Valley Manor, Medford, Oreg., 1972-76; pres. nat. div. bd. global ministries United Meth. Ch., 1972-76, pres. ecumenical and interreligious concerns div., 1976-80, Commn. on Christian Unity and intereligious concerns, 1980-84, Gen. Bd. of Pensions 1984—, Calif. Coun. Alcohol Problems, 1985-88. Jacob Sleeper fellow, 1955. Club: Rotarian. Office: The United Meth Ch 472 E Colorado Blvd PO Box 6006 Pasadena CA 91102

TUFTS, ROBERT B., registrar; b. Cleve., Nov. 5, 1940; s. Robert L. and Dora Mae (Yingling) T.; m. Nancy Intihar, June 22, 1968; children: Therese, Kevin R. BA cum laude, Cleve. State U., 1967; MA, Case Western Res. U., 1972; postgrad., U. Akron, 1973-76. Admissions counselor Cleve. State U., 1967-69, asst. registrar, 1969-70; asst. registrar Youngstown (Ohio) State U., 1970-73; asst. registrar U. Akron (Ohio), 1973-75, assoc. registrar, 1975-78; registrar Portland (Oreg.) State U., 1978—; com. mem. Park Recreation Adv. Bd., W. Linn., Oreg., 1981-84. Served with U.S. Army, 1959-62m Korea. Mem. Oreg. Assn. Registrars and Admissions Officers (current sec., treas.), Pacific Assn. Collegiate Registrars and Admissions Officers (mem. program com. 1986-87), Am. Assn. Collegiate Registrars and Admissions Officers (mem. facilities planning mgmt. com., 1975-78, chmn. of com. 1977-78), Nat. Assn. Coll. and Univ. Bus. Officers, Theta Rho. Democrat. Mem. Unitarian Ch. Home: 4981 Prospect St West Linn OR 97068 Office: Portland State U PO Box 751 Portland OR 97207

TUHOLSKI, ELIZABETH MURRAY, nurse, educator; b. Portsmouth, Va., Oct. 20, 1956; d. William Michael and Nora (Bryan) Murray; m. Richard Allen Tuholski, July 3, 1983; 1 child, Eric William. BS in Nursing, Northeastern U., 1979. RN, Calif.; cert. Advanced Cardiac Life Support. Staff nurse Centinela Hosp., Inglewood, Calif., 1979-80, staff nurse ICU, 1981-86, clin. instr., coord. diabetic teaching, 1987—; charge nurse Little Co. Mary Hosp., Torrance, Calif., 1980-81; instr. nursing ICU Calif. State U., L.A., 1987—, Am. Heart Assn., 1987—; mem. Advanced Cardiac Life Support Provider, 1988—; tchr. prepatory classes for RN state bd. exams. Democrat. Roman Catholic. Home: 4934 W 137th Pl Hawthorne CA 90250 Office: Centinela Hosp 555 E Hardey St Inglewood CA 90307

TUKEY, HAROLD BRADFORD, JR., horticulture educator; b. Geneva, N.Y., May 29, 1934; s. Harold Bradford and Ruth (Schweigert) T.; m. Helen Dunbar Parker, June 25, 1955; children: Ruth Thurbon, Carol Tukey Schwartz, Harold Bradford. B.S., Mich. State U., 1955, M.S., 1956, Ph.D., 1958. Research asst. South Haven Expt. Sta., Mich., 1955; AEC grad. research asst. Mich. State U., 1955-58; NSF fellow Calif. Inst. Tech, 1958-59; asst. prof. dept. floriculture and ornamental horticulture Cornell U., Ithaca, N.Y., 1959-64, assoc. prof., 1964-70, prof., 1970-80; prof. urban horticulture U. Wash., Seattle, 1980—, dir Arboreta, 1980—, dir. Ctr. Urban Horticulture, 1980—; cons. Internat. Bonsai mag., Electric Power Research Inst., P.R. Nuclear Ctr., 1965-66; lectr. in field; mem. adv. com. Seattle-U. Wash. Arboretum and Bot. Garden, 1980—, vice chmn., 1982; vis. scholar U. Nebr., 1982; vis. prof. U. Calif.-Davis, 1973; mem. various coms. Nat. Acad. Scis.-NRC; bd. dirs. Arbor Fund Bloedel Res., 1980—, pres., 1983-84. Mem. editorial bd. Jour. Environ. Horticulture. Pres. Ithaca PTA; troop advisor Boy Scouts Am., Ithaca. Served to lt. U.S. Army, 1958. Recipient B.Y. Morrison award USDA, 1987; NSF fellow, 1958-59; grantee NSF, 1962, 75, Bot. Soc. Am., 1964; hon. dr. Portuguese Soc. Hort., 1985. Fellow Am. Soc. Hort. Sci. (dir. 1970-71); mem. Internat. Soc. Hort. Sci. (U.S. del. to council 1971—, chmn. commn. for amateur horticulture 1974-83, exec. com. 1974—, v.p. 1978-82, pres. 1982-86), Internat. Plant Propagators Soc. (eastern region dir. 1969-71, v.p. 1972, pres. 1973, internat. pres. 1976), Am. Hort. Soc. (dir. 1972-81, exec. com. 1974-81, v.p. 1978-80, citation of merit 1981), Bot. Soc. Am., N.W. Horticulture Soc. (dir. 1980—), Arboretum Found. (dir. 1980—), Sigma Xi, Alpha Zeta, Phi Kappa Phi, Pi Alpha Xi, Xi Sigma Pi. Presbyterian. Lodge: Rotary. Home: 3300 E Saint Andrews Way Seattle WA 98112 Office: U Wash Ctr for Urban Horticulture GF-15 Seattle WA 98195

TULL, ANN HINDS, federal agency administrator; b. Denver, Aug. 26, 1938; d. Ervin Arthur and Pauline Elizabeth (Wright) Hinds; m. Robert William Tull, Sept. 7, 1963 (div. 1980); children: Linda Margaret, Paula Evelyn. BS Med. Tech., U. Colo., 1960; MA in Mgmt., Supervision, Central Mich. U., 1977. Med. technologist Presbyn. Hosp., Denver, 1960-62; research microbiologist Fitzsimmons Army Med. Ctr., Denver, 1962-78; mgmt. asst. U.S. SBA, Denver, 1978-82; internat. trade specialist U.S. Dept. Commerce, Denver, 1982—. Contbr. articles to tech. publs. Deacon, Montview Blvd. Presbyn. Ch., Denver, 1969-72; bd. dirs. Collegiate Sch. Denver, 1976-77. Mem. Am. Soc. Clin. Pathologists (cert. med. technologist), Jr.League Denver (com. mem., conf. del.), Kappa Kappa Gamma. Republican.

TULL, GLENDA LOIS, contract development manager; b. Dallas, Jan. 12, 1954; d. John Scott and Wava (Lafon) Hahn; m. John Weldon Tull, Dec. 8, 1973 (div. Aug. 1981); children: Shannon Christine, Kristin Rose. Student, Riverside Community Coll., 1972-73. Sec. County of San Bernardino Planning and Devel., San Bernardino, Calif., 1972-73; clk. and police sec. Rathdrum (Idaho) City, 1974-76; police sec. Post Falls (Idaho) Police Dept., 1980-83; adminstrv. sec. Corona (Calif.) Community Hosp., 1984-86, mgr. contract devel., 1987—. Mem. Female Execs. Am. Office: Corona Community Hosp 800 S Main St Corona CA 91720

TULLER, WENDY JUDGE, educational foundation administrator; b. Cranston, R.I., Dec. 17, 1943; d. Alfred Carmen and Anna Louise (Waterman) Judge. A.B., Brown U., 1965; M.L.S., U. R.I., 1969. Librarian, Providence Public Schs., 1965-69; mgr. various locations Xerox Corp., 1969-75; mgr. Carter Hawley Hale Stores, Inc., Los Angeles, 1976; cons. Sibson & Co., Inc., Princeton, N.J., 1976-78; coordinator Atlantic Richfield Co., Los Angeles, 1978-87; pres. Found. for Ednl. Excellence, 1987—. Mem. Am. Soc. Personnel Adminstrn., Am. Soc. Tng. and Devel., Internat. Assn. Personnel Women, AAUW (v.p. local chpt. 1979-80). Club: Los Angeles Athletic. Home: 222 S Figueroa St Los Angeles CA 90012

TULLIS, DAVID ALLEN, municipal official, safety consultant; b. Madison, S.D., Sept. 10, 1938; s. Ralph and Millie Grace (Hanneman) T.; m. Celia Kathleen Hagan (div. 1970); children: Christine Louise, David Bradford; m. Linda Pauline Sweat, Sept. 10, 1972; 1 child, Larry Allan. Student, U. Wash., 1963, Centralia (Wash.) Coll., 1969, South Sound Coll., 1975. Customer engr. IBM Corp., Seattle, 1963-69; bus. machine technician State of Wash., Olympia, 1969-77, safety compliance officer, 1977-80, sr. safety compliance officer, 1980-83; safety officer City of Tacoma, 1983—; mem. Employers Elec. Safety Commn., State of Wash., 1983—; chmn. utilities panel Gov.'s Conf. on Safety, State of Wash., 1985-86. Scoutmaster Boy Scouts Am., Olympia, 1977. Served with U.S. Army, 1959-62. Mem. Am. Water Works Assn. (chmn. northwest sect. 1985—), Am. Soc. Safety Engrs., Am. Pub. Power Assn. Lodge: Elks. Home: 2111 Tina Ct SE Olympia WA 98503 Office: City of Tacoma PO Box 11007 Tacoma WA 98411

TULLOCH, JAMES MACDONALD, insurance executive; b. Racine, Wis., Mar. 5, 1924; s. Thomas MacDonald and Mabel (Peterson) T.; m. Shirley Jordan, May 19, 1943; children: Tara Nancy, Thomas Scott, Gail Jean. BA, Charleton Coll., 1949. Underwriter Federated Mut. Ins. Co., Owatoma, Minn., 1949-53; casualty underwritng mgr. Integrity Mut. Casualty Inc. Co., Appleton, Wis., 1953-57; actuarial and underwriting mgr. Nat. Farmers Union Ins. Cos., Denver, 1957-67, dir. research and planning, 1967-68; actuary Dairyland Ins. Co., Madison, Wis., 1968-69; v.p., actuary Dairyland Ins. Co., Madison, 1969-71; pres. Dairyland Ins. Co., Scottsdale, Ariz., 1971-85; also dir, ret., 1985; bd. dirs. Dairyland County Mut. Ins. Co., Sentry Life Ins. Co., United Bank. Bd. dirs. Scottsdale YMCA, Dairyland Found., Scottsdale Bapt. Ch.; deacon Grace Bible Ch., Sun City, Ariz., 1988. Served with USAF, 1942-46, PTO. Mem. Nat. Assn. Independent Insurer (dirs., Am. Mgmt. Assn., Phoenix Met. C. of C., Rotary, Ariz. Country Club, Camelback Golf, Mesa Country Club, Briarwood Country Club. Republican. Home: 13438 Stardust Blvd Sun City West AZ 85375

TUMMOND, ALISON SUZANNE, commercial insurance underwriter; b. Flushing, N.Y., Nov. 21, 1963; d. Joseph Peter and Claire Sara (Berkow) Paradiso; m. Raymond Dale Tummond, May 25, 1985. BS cum laude, Ariz. State U., 1986. Credit analyst Am. Express Co., Phoenix, 1982-85; adminstrv. asst. IBM Corp., Phoenix, 1985-86; comml. underwriter Safeco Ins. Cos., Phoenix, 1986-87, Federated Ins. Co., Phoenix, 1987—. Vol. Adaptive Swim Program, Santa Barbara, Calif. 1986, Valley Big Bros./Big Sisters Program, Scottsdale, 1987. Mem. Ariz. State U. Alumni Assn., Phi Theta Kappa, Sigma Iota Epsilon. Republican. Home: 7748 E Peppertree Ln Scottsdale AZ 85253

TUNISON, ELIZABETH LAMB, education educator; b. Belfast, Northern Ireland, Jan. 7, 1922; came to U.S., 1923; d. Richard Ernest and Ruby (Hill) Lamb; m. Ralph W. Tunison, Jan. 24, 1947 (dec. Apr. 1984); children: Eric Arthur, Christine Wait, Dana Paul. BA, Whittier Coll., 1943, MEd, 1963. Tchr. Whittier (Calif.) Schs., 1943-59; tchr. T.V pub. schs. So. Calif. Counties, 1960-75; dir. curriculum Bassett (Calif.) Schs., 1962-65; elem. sch. prin. Rowland Unified Schs., Rowland Heights, Calif., 1965-68; assoc. prof. edn. Calif. State Poly. U., Pomona, 1968-71; prof. Whittier Coll., 1971-88, prof. emerita, 1988—. Recipient Whittier Coll. Alumni Achievement award 1975; Helen Hefernan scholar 1963. Mem. Assn. Calif. Sch. Adminstrs. (chmn. higher edn. com. 1983-86, pres. region XV 1981-83, Wilson Grace award 1983), AAUP, Delta Kappa Gamma. Lodge: P.E.O. (chaplain 1975-77). Home: 5636 Ben Alder Whittier CA 90601 Office: Whittier Coll 13406 E Philadelphia Whittier CA 90601

TUNNEY, MICHAEL MARTIN, product certification manager; b. Port Dahlousie, Ontario, Can., July 9, 1948; came to U.S., 1952; s. Martin Bernard and Dorothy Alice Tunney (Colburn) T.; m. Constance Mary Walczak, Oct. 14, 1967; 1 child, Sean Patrick. Program support rep. IBM, Ithaca, N.Y., 1967-75; staff systems programmer Amdahl Deutschland GMBH, Munich, 1976-78, Amdahl U.K., London, 1978-79; branch mgr. Amdahl Corp., Denver, 1979-81; div. ops. mgr. Amdahl Edn. & Profl. Svcs. Div., Santa Clara, Calif., 1981-84; mgr. product certification Amdahl Corp., Sunnyvale, Calif., 1984—; ptnr. Flare Investors, San Jose, Calif., 1983-84, Innovative Security Systems Inc., San Jose, Calif., 1989—. Mem. Jaguar Assn. Group. Libertarian. Universal Life. Home: 2011 Park Royal Dr San Jose CA 95125 Office: Amdahl Corp 1250 E Arques Ave Sunnyvale CA 94086

TUOSTO, VANCE WOODY, marriage, family and child counselor; b. Landstuhl, Germany, June 15, 1957; d. Floyd William Woody and Sondra Phyllis (Fern) Pauly; m. Louis Joseph Tuosto, Aug. 9, 1980; children: Nicholas Ryan, Jessica Danielle. BA, U. Calif., Santa Cruz, 1982; MA, Azusa Pacific U., 1984. Marriage, family and child counselor intern U. Calif., Santa Cruz, 1984, Relational Resources, Inc., Scotts Valley, Calif., 1986—. Mem. Christian Assn. for Psychol. Studies, Calif. Assn. of Marital and Family Therapists, Am. Assn. of Counseling and Devel. Republican. Home: 3925 Adar Ln Soquel CA 95073

TUPIN, JOE PAUL, hospital medical director, psychiatry educator; b. Comanche, Tex., Feb. 17, 1934; m. Betty Thompson, June 19, 1955; children: Paul, Rebecca, John. BS in Pharmacy, U. Tex., 1955, postgrad., 1955; MD, U. Tex., Galveston, 1959, Wash. Sch. Psychiatry, 1962, NIH Grad. Sch., 1962-64. Lic. psychiatrist, Tex., Calif. Intern U. Calif. Hosps., San Francisco, 1959-60; resident U. Tex. Med. br., Galveston, 1960-62, asst. prof. psychiatry, 1964-68, mem. staff John Sealy Hosp., 1964-69, dir. psychiatric consultation service, 1965-66, dir. psychiatric research, 1965-69, asst. dean medicine, 1967-68, assoc. prof., 1968-69, assoc. dean, 1968-69; resident NIMH div NIH, 1963-64; assoc. prof. psychiatry U. Calif., Davis, 1969-71, mem. staff Davis Med. Ctr., 1969—, vice-chmn. dept. psychiatry, 1970-76, prof., 1971—, acting chmn. dept. psychiatry, 1977, acting dir. admissions sch. medicine, 1977-78, chmn. dept. psychiatry, 1977-84; cons. staff St. Mary's Infirmary, Galveston, 1967-69, Moody House Retirement Home for the Aged, Galveston, 1967-69, VA Hosp., Martinez, 1977-82, Yolo Gen. Hosp., 1980—; dir. psychiatric consultation service U. Calif., Davis, 1969-74, co-director 1974-77; vis. prof. King's Coll. Med. Sch., London, 1974; acting dir. admissions sch. medicine, U. Calif., Davis, 1977-78; chief div. mental health U. Calif. Davis Med. Ctr., 1977-84, also mem. quality care com., 1979-85, chmn. com., 1981-85; med. dir. and assoc. dir. Hosp. and Clinics U. Calif., Davis, 1984—. Referee and book reviewer numerous pubs.; mem. sci. editorial bd. Am. Jour. Forensic Psychiatry, 1985—, Jour. Clin. Psychopharmacology, 1981—, Psychiatry, 1985, Tex. Reports on Biology and Medicine, 1965-67, 68-69; Western Jour. Medicine, 1979—; contbr. numerous articles to profl. jours. Mem. Academically Talented Child com. Galveston City Sch. Bd., 1966-67; chmn. bd. dirs. William Temple Found., Galveston, 1967-68; bd. dirs. Citizens for Advancement of Pub. Edn., Galveston, 1967-69, pres., 1968-69, Moody House Retirement Home for the Aged, 1968, Cal Aggie Athletic Assn., 1978-82; mem. Davis Master Plan com., 1971. Served to lt. commdr. USPHS, 1962-64, with Res. 1964-80. Recipient Career Teaching award NIMH, 1964-66; named to Friars Soc. U. Tex., 1954; Mosby scholar U. Tex., Ginsberg fellow Group for Advancement of Psychiatry, 1960-62, Nat. Found. Infantile Paralysis fellow, 1957; grantee U. Tex. Med. br., 1964-69, NIMH, 1965-68, 69-77, U. Calif. Davis and Sacramento Med. Ctr., 1973-77, U. Calif. Davis, 1969-77, 73—. Fellow Am. Psychiat. Assn., Am. Coll. Psychiatrists (mem. com., editorial com.); mem. AMA, Yolo County Med. Assn. (chmn. credentials com. 1974-75, nominating com. 1980-84), Calif. Med. Assn. (sec. psychiatry sect. 1977-78, 78-79, sci. adv. panel on psychiatry 1975—, psychiatry adv. sect. 1977—, sci. adv. bd. 1978-80), Titus Harris Soc., Cen. Calif. Psychiat. Soc. (chmn. mem. com. 1970-73, pres. 1976), AAAS, Soc. Health and Human Values (exec. council 1970-73), Am. Acad. Psychiatry and the Law, AAUP, West Coast Coll. Biol. Psychiatries Com., Sigma Xi, Rho Chi, Alpha Omega Alpha. Home: 1108 Kent Dr Davis CA 95616 Office: U Calif Davis Med Ctr 2315 Stockton Blvd Med Staff Office Sacramento CA 95817

TURBEVILLE, DANIEL EUGENE, III, geography educator; b. La Grande, Oreg., July 20, 1945; s. Daniel Eugene Jr. and Dorothy Lucille (Cole) T.; m. Diane Jean Weller, June 3, 1972; children: Daniel Eugene IV, Debra Elise, David Edward. BS, U. S.C., 1968; MA, Western Wash. U., 1976; PhD, Simon Fraser U., Burnaby, B.C., Can., 1985. Asst. prof. geography Eastern Oreg. State Coll., La Grande. Author: Historic Bellingham Buildings, 1977, The Electric Railway Era, 1979, (with others) Early Industries, 1980, Whatcom County in Maps, 1983. Served to lt. comdr. USNR, 1968—. Office: Ea Oreg State Coll La Grande OR 97850

TUREK, BRAD HENRY, real estate executive; b. Northridge, Calif., Jan. 8, 1956; s. Robert Joseph and Shirley Joan (Pogacnik) T. BA, U. Calif., Santa Barbara, 1979. Indsl. real estate broker Ashwill-Burke Co., Woodland Hills, Calif., 1979-81, The McDonald Co., Woodland Hills, 1981-82; account exec., tech. cons. AT&T, Santa Ana, Calif., 1983-87; equity ptnr. Super Mgmt. Services, Santa Ana, 1987—; cons. in field. Project mgr. Anaheim Redevel. Agy., 1988. Republican. Lodge: Rotary. Home: 3910 Channel Pl Newport Beach CA 92663 Office: Super Mgmt Svcs 1580 E Edinger Ave Ste L Santa Ana CA 92705

TURK, PENELOPE BRYANT, educator; b. Washington, July 2, 1941; d. David Logan and Marjorie Lenore (Hull) B.; m. Robert Louis Turk, Mar. 25, 1964; children: Marjorie Carol, Susan Elizabeth. BA, UCLA, 1963, MA, 1964. Secondary teaching credential, Calif. Tchr. English Venice High Sch., L.A., 1964-66, Iowa City High Sch., 1966-67, Montgomery Middle Sch., El Cajon, Calif., 1983-84; tchr. for gifted students Murray Manor Elem. Sch., La Mesa, Calif., 1977-79; tchr. English, chmn. dept. Greenfield Jr. High Sch., El Cajon, 1984—. Elder, deacon Fletcher Hills Presbyn. Ch., El Cajon, 1973—; pres. Friends El Cajon Library, 1974-76, now life mem.; trainer Girl Scouts U.S.A., San Diego, 1975—. Recipient hon. service award El Cajon PTA, 1978, Woman of Action award Soroptimist Internat., El Cajon, 1979, Thanks Badge, San Diego council Girl Scouts U.S.A., 1984; fellow San Diego Area Writers Project, 1987, Calif. Lit. Project, 1988. Mem. Nat. Council Tchrs. English, Calif. Assn. Tchrs. English, NEA, Calif. Tchrs. Assn., Greater San Diego Council Tchrs. English, San Diego Reading Assn., Toastmasters (El Cajon) (past pres., Able Toastmaster award 1983), Phi Delta kappa. Home: 1760 Key Ln El Cajon CA 92021 Office: Greenfield Jr High Sch 1495 Greenfield Dr El Cajon CA 92021

TURK, RUDY HENRY, museum director; b. Sheboygan, Wis., June 24, 1927; s. Rudolph Anton and Mary Gertrude (Stanisha) T.; m. Wanda Lee Borders, Aug. 4, 1956; children: Tracy Lynn, Maria Teresa, Andrew Borders, Jennifer Wells. BS in Edn., U. Wis., 1949; MA in History, U. Tenn., 1951; postgrad., Ind. U., 1952-56. Instr. art history, gallery dir. U. Mont., Missoula, 1957-60; dir. Richmond (Calif.) Art Ctr., 1960-65; asst. dir. San Diego Mus. Art, 1965-67; dir. Ariz. State U. Art Mus., 1967—; from assoc. prof. to prof. art Ariz. State U., 1967-77; bd. dirs., pres. Friends of Mexican Art, Ariz., 1988—; mem. Ariz. Commn. Arts and Humanities, 1980-84. Painter, works exhibited in solo and group exhbns.; mus. cons., juror, art cons., art lectr; author: (with Cross and Lamm) The Search for Personal Freedom, 2 vols., 1972, 76, 80, 85, Merrill Mahaffey: Monumental Landscapes, 1979, Udinotti, 1973, (with others) Scholder, 1983, also commentaries. Bd. dirs. Chandler Arts Com., 1983-86, Tempe Arts Com., 1987-89; hon. fellow Am. Craft Coun., 1988. With USN, 1945-46. Recipient Merit award Calif. Coll. Arts and Crafts, 1965, Senator's Cultural award State of Ariz., 1987; named Hon. Ariz. Designer Craftsman, 1975; Fulbright scholar, U. Paris, 1956-57. Mem. Am. Assn. Mus., Western Assn. Art Mus. (Golden Crate award 1974), Phi Alpha Theta, Phi Kappa Phi. Democrat. Roman Catholic. Home: 760 E Courtney Ln Tempe AZ 85284 Office: Ariz State U Art Mus Fine Arts Ctr Tempe AZ 85287

TURLEJ, ZBIGNIEW STANISLAW, film producer, director; b. Tarnow, Poland, Oct. 27, 1954; came to U.S., 1984; s. Jan and Filomena (Gofron) T. MS in Electronics Engring., Mining and Metal U., Krakow, Poland, 1978; MA in Art History, Jagiellon U., Krakow, 1984; MFA in Film Prodn., U. So. Calif., 1988. Pres. Univ. Art History Soc., Krakow, 1980-83, Ars Longa Corp., Los Angeles, 1986—, Turlej Film Inst., Los Angeles, 1988—; chmn. Turlej Corp., Los Angeles, 1987; creative v.p. Early Bird Films, Los Angeles, 1986—. Dir. experimental film Summer Dreams, 1987; editor documentary film Wise Guys, 1986 (Focus 1st prize, 1987); dir. photography feature film Shattered, 1987. Recipient Rosenberg Screenwriting award, 1988. Office: Ars Longa Corp 616 W 32d St Los Angeles CA 90007

TURLEY, JAMES HOWARD, small business owner; b. Joliet, Ill., Jan. 10, 1944; s. Paul Garnet and Elizabeth (Enslow) T.; m. Nancy E. Schick, Oct. 28, 1967; children: Michael James, Melissa Elizabeth. BA, U. Ill., 1967. Tchr. jr. high social studies Schaumburg Ill. Sch. Dist., 1967-70; owner Autotech Enco, Denver, 1970-71, Turley & Co. Real Estate, Denver, 1971-76; ptr. and co-founder Harvest Restaurants, Boulder, Colo., 1975-85; pres. Turley & Co., Denver, 1970—. Regional coord. Beyond War Movement, Denver, 1985-88, vol. com. svc, 1985-88. Office: Turley & Co 535 16th St Ste 600 Denver CO 80202

TURLEY, KEITH L., holding company executive; b. Mesa, Ariz., June 16, 1923; s. Ora Elmer and Zella Exa (Thurman) T.; m. Dorothy Rae Welton, Sept. 2, 1950; children: Sue Ann, Cinda Jane, Nancy Lynn, Robert. B.A., Ariz. State U., 1948. With Central Ariz. Light & Power Co., Phoenix, 1948-51, Stanolind Oil & Gas Co., Okla., 1951; with Ariz. Pub. Service Co., Phoenix, 1952-87, v.p. marketing, 1967-69, exec. v.p. customer services, 1969-72, exec. v.p., gen. mgr., dir., 1972-73, pres., chief exec. officer, 1974-81, pres., chmn. bd., 1981-82, chief exec. officer, 1982-87, chmn. bd., 1982—; chief exec. officer Pinnacle West Capital Corp., Phoenix, 1987—. Dir. Central Ariz. Project, 1971—; chmn. Phoenix Commn. on Housing, 1972; trustee Heard Mus.; bd. dirs. Sun Angel Found. Lt. (j.g.) USNR, 1943-47. Recipient Alumni Service award Ariz. State U., 1971. Mem. Edison Electric Inst. (dir.), Ariz. State U. Alumni Assn. (pres. 1966), Paradise Valley Country Club. Office: Pinnacle W Capital Corp PO Box 52132 Phoenix AZ 85072-2132

TURLEY, MARK C., television director; b. St. Louis, Aug. 26, 1949; s. Paul W. and Mary C. (Austin) T.; m. Judy Anne Mugford, May 10, 1986; 1 child, Bryan. Student, U. Hawaii, 1967-71; student, Am. Film Inst., L.A., 1981-82. Dir., cameraman Sta. KHVH-TV, ABC, Honolulu, 1967-71; cameraman Sta. KHON-TV, NBC, Honolulu, 1972-73; producer, dir. Sta. KITV-TV, ABC, Honolulu, 1973-77; sr. producer, dir. Hawaii Pub. TV, PBS, Honolulu, 1977-82; directing fellow Am. Film Inst., L.A., 1981-82; asst. Robert Towne, Screenwriter, L.A., 1983-84; broadcast analyst We. Internat. Media, L.A., 1985-88; dir. Sta. KCOP-TV, L.A., 1985—. Recipient Silver award Internat. Film & TV Festival N.Y., 1978. Fellow Am. Film Inst. Alumni Assn. Democrat.

TURMAN, GEORGE, former lieutenant governor Montana; b. Missoula, Mont., June 25, 1928; s. George Fugett and Corinne (McDonald) T.; m. Kathleen Hager, Mar. 1951; children—Marcia, Linda, George Douglas, John, Laura. B.A., U. Mont., 1951. Various positions Fed. Res. Bank of San Francisco, 1954-64; mayor City of Missoula, 1970-72; mem. Mont. Ho. of Reps. from (Dist. 18), 1973-74; Mont. Pub. Service commr. (Dist. 5), 1975-80; lt. gov. State of Mont., 1981-88, resigned; apptd. Pacific NW Electric Power & Conservation Council, 1988. Served with U.S. Army, 1951-53. Decorated Combat Inf. badge. Address: 1300 Stuart St Helena MT 59601

TURNAGE, JEAN A., chief justice; b. St. Ignatius, Mont., Mar. 10, 1926. JD, Mont. State U., 1951. Bar: Mont. 1951, U.S. Supreme Ct. 1963. Formerly ptnr. Turnage, McNeil & Mercer, Polson, Mont.; formerly Mont. State senator from 13th Dist.; pres. Mont. State Senate, 1981-83; chief justice Supreme Ct. Mont., 1985—. Mem. Mont. State Bar Assn. Office: Mont Supreme Ct 215 N Sanders T Justice Bldg Rm 414 Helena MT 59620

TURNBOW, JOE FOSTER, physician, consultant; b. Little Rock, May 3, 1950; s. Robert Lawson and Sue Turnbow; m. Terry Lee Waldeisen, June 10, 1978; 1 child, Robert. Student, Hendrix Coll., 1968-70, U. Ark., 1970-71; MD, U. Ark., Little Rock, 1975. Diplomate Am. Bd. Emergency Medicine. Emergency physician Mercy Med. Ctr., Denver, 1976-79, Aurora (Colo.) Community Hosp., 1979-80, Porter Meml. Hosp., Denver, 1980-81; cons. emergency med. adminstrn. Denver Emergency Physicians, 1981-86; dir. emergency medicine Union Med. Ctr., El Dorado, Ark., 1986-87; dir. urgent care Boulder (Colo.) Med. Ctr., P.C., 1987—; pres. Emergency Care Cons., El Dorado, 1986—; asst. clin. prof. U. Ark. for Med. Scis., Little Rock, 1986—; dir. Vail (Colo.) Emergency Med./Critical Care Conf., 1982-85; advisor Haley Paramedics Ambulance, Denver, 1981-83; affiliate faculty Advanced Cardiac Life Support, Colo./Ark., 1982—; mem. Colo. Blue Cross/Blue Shield Med. Rev. Bd., Denver, 1982-86; speaker various med. seminars. Bd. dirs. Nat. Emergency Medicine Polit. Action Com., Dallas, 1985—, Beth Israel Hosp., Denver, 1985-86; mem. med. adv. com. U.S. Congressman Beryl Anthony, 1987; dir. adult forum 1st United Meth. Ch., Boulder, 1988. Fellow Am. Coll. Emergency Physicians (govt. affairs com. 1983—, speaker numerous seminars, councillor Colo. chpt. 1985-86, bd. dirs. 1983-85); mem. AMA, Colo. Med. Soc. (emergency med. care physician adv. com. 1977-85, 87—). Home: 945 Parkway Dr Boulder CO 80303-2849 Office: Boulder Med Ctr 2750 Broadway Boulder CO 80302

TURNBULL, ANTHONY ROBERT, financial executive; b. Ealing, Middlesex, Eng., Nov. 22, 1944; came to U.S., 1987; s. James Robert and Mabel Olive (Ward) T.; m. Irene Beneke, Aug. 17, 1968 (div. 1988); 1 child, Penelope Irene; m. Diane Lynn Bennett, Oct. 22, 1988; children: Laura Chandler Young, Sara Beth Young. Clk. Midland Bank Ltd., London, 1962-67; officer Commonwealth Bank Corp., Sydney, Australia, 1967-69; office mgr. Kraft Foods Ltd., Sydney, 1969-72; acct. Allan C. Smith & Co., Ltd., Sydney, 1972-73; cost acct. Cottees Gen. Foods, Ltd., Sydney, 1973-77; fin. controller Stauffer Australia, Ltd., Sydney, 1978-88; fin. planner Diversified Securities, Ltd., El Toro, Calif., 1988-89; contr. Med. Clinics, Inc., San Diego, 1989—. Liaison officer U.S.A. Athletic Team, Pacific Conf. Games, Canberra, Australia, 1977; rep. Australia-World Vet. Games Track and Field, Rome, 1985, Melbourne, 1989, Eugene, 1989. Fellow Inst. Fin. Accts.; mem. Nat. Assn. Security Dealers, Chartered Inst. Bankers. Mem. Anglican Ch. Home: 7336-198 Mission Dam Terr Santee CA 92071 Office: Med Clincs Inc 3500 Estudillo St San Diego CA 92110

TURNER, DAVID SCOTT, sound diagnostics executive; b. Everett, Wash., July 12, 1952; s. Robert Scott and Carol Jean (Hein) T.; m. Michelle Louise Aicher, Feb. 2, 1980; 1 child, Ryan Scott. BS in Fin., U. Puget Sound, 1970-74. Lending officer Bank of Everett, 1974-77; asst. v.p., regional br. mgr. Pioneer Bank, Lynnwood, Wash., 1977-84; exec. v.p. Sound Diagnostics, Everett, 1984—. Com. mem. Am. Heart Assn., Everett, 1987, bd. dirs., 1989—; mem. Snohomish County Econ. Devel. Coun., 1987-88. Mem. Everett C. of C., Cascade Club, Everett Golf and Country Club. Home: 2517 51st St SW Everett WA 98203 Office: Sound Diagnostics 1602 Hewitt Ave Ste 608 Everett WA 98201

TURNER, DEAN EDSON, education educator, minister; b. Tyrone, Okla., May 24, 1927; s. Jesse Lee and Cora May (Luman) T.; m. Nancy Margaret Roche, Aug. 12, 1964; children: Taos Lee, Summer Marie. BA, Centro de Estudios Universitarios, Mexico City, 1953-55; MEd, Adams State Coll., 1959; PhD in Philosophy and History of Edn., U. Tex., 1966. Cert. tchr., Colo.; ordained to ministry Disciples of Christ Ch., 1967. English tchr. Instituto Taylor Comercial, Mexico City, 1953-55; Spanish tchr. Anchorage High Sch., 1956-58, Carmichael (Calif.) High Sch., 1958, Farmingdale (L.I.) High Sch., 1961, Rye (N.Y.) High Sch., 1963-64; prof. Spanish Sullins Women's Coll., Bristol, Va., 1962-63; prof. sociology, Spanish U. Md., 1959-61; prof. founds. of edn. U. No. Colo., Greeley, 1966—. Author: The Autonomous Man, 1970, Commitment to Care, 1978, The Einstein Myth, 1979 (Alt. Book of Month award 1979); co-author: Classrooms in Crisis, 1986, Benevolence, 1988. Served to sgt. U.S. Army, 1950-52. Recipient Tchrs. Who Care award Channel 4, Denver, 1986, Lucille Harrison Outstanding Tchr. of Yr. award U. No. Colo., 1983. Mem. Soc. Christian Philosophers, Soc. Christian Ethics, Christian Educators Assn. Internat. Home: 1708 37th Ave Greeley CO 80634 Office: U No Colo Greeley CO 80639

TURNER, ERMELINDA MIGUELITA, nurse; b. Manila, May 8, 1932; came to U.S., 1968; d. Francisco Luis and Elvira Victorina (Carrion) San Juan; m. Jeffrey Scott Turner; Nov. 10; 1 child, Marie Lourdes Teresa. Student, Mapua Inst. Tech. & F.E.U., Manila; Diploma Nursing, Claire Hall Hosp., Putney Hosp., 1960-62, 1965. Nurse Dominican Hosp., Santa Cruz, Calif., 1968-69; surg. nurse Stanford (Calif.) Med. Ctr., 1969-70, Kaiser Med. Permanete, Redwood City, Calif., 1970-80; nurse Juvenile Hall Clin., Santa Clara County, San Jose, 1985—; midwife I, St. Helier Hosp., Surry, Eng., 1967-68. Vol. Sunnyvale Sch. Dist., 1970-71. Mem. RN Profl. Assn., Calif. Nursing Assn., RN Eng. and Wales. Republican. Roman Catholic. Home: 206 Twin Lake Dr Sunnyvale CA 94089 Office: Juvenile Hall Clin Santa Clara County Valley Med Ctr San Jose CA 95128

TURNER, FRAN JEAN, management consultant; b. Ogden, Utah, Sept. 5, 1940; d. Wilmer Harrison and Bernice (Kendell) Taylor; m. Larry Michael Turner, Nov. 6, 1970; children: Larry Kirk, Kristilyn, Douglas Michael,

Leslie Todd. AS, Weber State Coll., 1964. With admintrv. dept. Comml. Security Bank, Ogden, Utah, 1964-68, TRW Inc., Ogden, 1968-70, Comml. Security Bank, Ogden, 1970-73; bd. dirs. Mary Kay Cosmetics, Utah, Idaho, Calif., 1973-77; computation directorate U. Calif. Lawrence Livermore Nat. Lab., Livermore, Calif., 1977-89, with mgmt., 1983—; pres. L.M. Turner Internat. Inc., Auburn, Calif., 1985—, also bd. dirs., 1981—; program dir. U.S. Dept. Energy Sci. Honors Program at U. Calif. Lawrence Livermore Nat. Lab., 1985-88; instr. Dataspan, 1985—. Mem. Alamo Improvement Assn., 1981—, Alamo PtA, 1981—; coordinator Nat. Urban League conf.. San Francisco, 1986, OEO/Affirmative Action, U. Calif. Livermore Nat. Lab., 1983—. Mem. Am. Mgmt. Assn., U. Calif. Women's Assn. Democrat. Mormon. Office: L M Turner Internat Inc 10594 Combie Rd Auburn CA 95603

TURNER, GEOFFREY WHITNEY, information security consultant; b. Highland Park, Ill., Sept. 4, 1948; s. Stansfield and Patricia (Busby) T.; m. Roberta Marie Tidball, Sept. 28, 1969; children: Scott Whitney, Grant Stansfield, Katherine Cass. BA, Oreg. State U., 1973; MA, Naval Postgrad Sch., 1979. Commd. ensign USN, 1973, advanced through grades to comdr., 1982; communications officer USS La Moore County (LST 1194) USN, Norfolk, Va., 1974-76; Soviet navy analyst Naval Ops. Intelligence Ctr. USN, Washington, 1976-77; spl. asst. to nat. intelligence officer CIA, Washington, 1977; intelligence officer Task Force 61 Mediterranean Sea, 1979-80; intelligence officer USS Carl Vinson (CVN-70) USN, Alameda, Calif., 1983-85; chief target systems br. Joint Strategic Target Planning Staff USN, Omaha, 1980-83; ret. USN, 1985; comdr. USNR, 1988—; v.p. Bank Am., San Francisco, 1985-88; sr. mgmt. systems cons. SRI Internat., Menlo Park, Calif., 1988—; chmn. data encryption com. Am. Nat. Standards Inst., Washington, 1986—, mem. fin. svcs. security com, 1986—; mem. Internat. bd. editors Computers and Security, Netherlands, 1987—; mem. steering com. Nat. Computer and Telecommuncations Security Coun., Washington, 1987—. Decorated Def. Meritorious Svc. medal. Mem. Info. Systems Security Assn., Armed Forces Communications and Electronics Assn. Office: SRI Internat 333 Ravenswood Ave Menlo Park CA 94025

TURNER, HAL WESLEY, state agency administrator; b. Winchester, Mass., Nov. 18, 1932; s. Wesley Francis and Anna Louise (Hodgkins) T.; m. Patricia Frances Heastan, Mar. 31, 1984; children: Julie, Karen. BA, Sioux Falls (S.D.) Coll., 1955. Mem. tech. and mgmt. staff Boeing Computer Svcs., Seattle, 1958-69; mgr. prodn. systems Kennecott Copper Corp., Salt Lake City, 1970-71; dir. MIS State of Idaho, Boise, 1971-74, adminstr. of budget, 1974-77; sales assoc. White Riedel Realtors, Boise, 1978-81; chief dep. state auditor Idaho State Auditor's Office, Boise, 1981—; pres., Student Loan Fund Idaho, Inc., Fruitland, 1978—. With U.S. Army, 1955-57. Mem. Nat. Assn. State Auditors, Comptrollers, Treasurers, Elks, Broadmore Country Club. Democrat. Methodist. Home: 3512 S Brookshore Pl Boise ID 83706 Office: State Auditors Office 700 W State St Boise ID 83720

TURNER, HERBERT BRANCH, designer, builder, artist; b. Mt. Vernon, N.Y., Mar. 20, 1926; s. Oscar Oliver and Irene (Branch) T.; m. Marysa Senn, Oct. 5, 1956 (div.) children: Brent Stockton, Rachel. BS, U.S. Military Acad., 1949. Designer, artist Herbert Turner Designs, Del Mar, Calif., 1952—; prin. Turner Construction, Del Mar, 1954-80, Turner & Assoc., Del Mar, 1968—. Featured in Am. Artist Mag., 1962; exhibited in group shows at Laguna Beach Art Mus., La Jolla Mus., Tex. Fine Arts Assn., Audibon Artist, N.Y.C., Allied Artist, N.Y.C., Purdue U. Chmn. Pub. Access TV Channel 37, Del Mar, Calif., 1984—, Flood Control Com., San Diego County, 1986—; dir. Artists' Space at South Fair, Del Mar, 1987—; mem. Escondido Devel. Adv. Com., 1988—. With U.S. Army, 1945-49. Recipient Citation A.I.A., Sunset Mag., San Francisco, 1974; award of Excellence Builder Industry Assn., 1982, Historic Preservation award, Save Our Heritage Orgn., San Diego, 1984. Mem. Assn. Bldg. Contractors (bd. dirs., legis. chmn. 1976-77), San Diego Mus. Artists' Guild. Republican. Methodist. Home: 606 Zuni Dr Del Mar CA 92014

TURNER, JAMES EDWARD, senior civil technician; b. Charleson, W.Va., Apr. 4, 1941; s. Theo Leslie and Hazel Leona (Jones) T.; m. Shirley Juanita Wayne, May 25, 1963; children: James Dean, David Wayne. Student, Charleston U., 1959-61; student, Aurora Community Coll., Aurora, Colo., 1982, 84; cert. of completion, Morris Harvey Coll., Aurora, 1984. With hwy. engring. Michael Baker, Jr., Inc., Charleston, 1959-77; civil designer Stearns Catalytic Corp., Denver, 1978-86; drafter HDR Infrastructure, Denver, 1986; sr. civil technician Howard Needles Tammen & Bergendorff, Phoenix, 1986—. Scoutmaster troop 766 Boy Scouts Am., Beaver, Pa., 1977, asst. scoutmaster troop 188, Denver, 1984. Mem. Am. Inst. Design and Drafting (profl. mem.), United Methodist Men (pres. Beaver chpt. 1972-77, Denver chpt. 1979-84). Methodist. Home: 8008 W Highland Ave Phoenix AZ 85033 Office: Howard Needles Tammen & Bergendorff 2207 E Camelback Ste 400 Phoenix AZ 85016

TURNER, JEFFREY ALAN, construction executive; b. Indpls., Jan. 5, 1959; s. James Herbert Turner and Roxie Roberta (Groth) West; m. Kimberly Jo Collier, May 31, 1980; children: Justin Alan, Danielle Nicole, Evan James. BS in Constrn. Mgmt., Purdue U., 1981. Estimator P.R. Duke Constrn., Indpls., 1980-81; estimator, project mgr. Kitchell Corp., Phoenix, 1981-84; v.p., chief operating officer Project Control Co., Phoenix, 1984—. Active met. facilities com. YMCA, Phoenix, 1988—, constrn. adv. com. Ariz. State U., Phoenix, 1988—. Mem. Project Mgmt. Inst., Pointe Racquet Club. Republican. Office: Project Control Co 4343 E Camelback Rd Ste 300 Phoenix AZ 85018

TURNER, JERRY, artistic director. BA, U. Colo., MA; PhD in Theater, U. Ill. Educator U. Ark., Wash. State U., Pullman, 1956-57; assoc. prof. drama, dept. head Humboldt State U., Arcata, Calif., 1957-64; chmn. dept. drama U. Calif., Riverside, 1964-70; artistic dir. Oreg. Shakespearean Festival, Ashland, 1971—. Director numerous plays including Richard II, On the Verge, Three Sisters, King Lear, The Revenger's Tragedy, Translations, 'Tis Pity She's a Whore, Ah Wilderness!, Wild Oats, Doctor Faustus, Timon of Athens; translator, dir. The Wild Duck, Mother Courage, Night of the Tribades, Brand, Dance of Death, The Father. Office: Oreg Shakespeare Festival Office of Artistic Dir Ashland OR 97520

TURNER, JERRY MARSHALL, school system administrator; b. Hohenwald, Tenn., Sept. 3, 1944; s. Marshall Lewis and Freeda Elizabeth (Tatum) T.; m. Martha Anne McCann; children: Marle Kristen, Jerry William, Jordan Wesley, Suzannah Elizabeth, Brenton Russell. AA, Martin Jr. Coll., Pulaski, Tenn., 1964; BA, Magna Union Coll., Barbourville, Ky., 1966; MA, Vanderbilt U., Nashville, Tenn., 1969, PhD, 1971. Asst. prof. German Ga. So. Coll., Statesboro, 1969-72, Mercer U., Macon, Ga., 1972-78; mktg. assoc. The Ga. Bank, Macon, 1978-80; dean of adm. Tift Coll., Forsyth, Ga., 1981-83; adminstrv. rep. Crandall Coll., Macon, Ga., 1983-85; dir. Am. Tech. Inst., Amarillo, Tex., 1985-86; v.p. mktg. Am. Tech. Coll., Tulsa, 1986-87; dir. The Constrn. Sch., Denver, 1988—; propriety sch. cons. Denver 1987--. Mem. Colo. Pvt. Schs. Assn. (bd. trustees), Civitan Club (lt. gov. areas IV and VI S. Ga. chpt. 1971-72, gov. 1974, Civitan of Yr. 1971). Methodist. Home: 8055 Johnson Court Arvada CO 80005 Office: The Constrn Sch 2246 Federal Blvd Denver CO 80211

TURNER, JOHN FREELAND, state senator, rancher; b. Jackson, Wyo., Mar. 3, 1942; s. John Charles and Mary Louise (Mapes) T.; m. Mary Kay Brady, 1969; children—John Francis, Kathy Mapes, Mark Freeland. B.S. in Biology, U. Notre Dame, 1964; postgrad. U. Innsbruck, 1964-65, U. Utah, 1965-66; M.S. in Ecology, U. Mich., 1968. Rancher, outfitter Triangle X Ranch, Moose, Wyo.; chmn. bd. dirs. Bank of Jackson Hole; photo-journalist; state senator from Sublette, Teton County, pres. Wyo. Senate, 1987-89, chmn. legis., chmn. minerals bus. and econ. develops com., vice chmn., Sec. of Interior's Nat. Parks adv. bd.; statewide coordinating Task Force U. Wyo., exec. commn. State Reps., adv. council Coll. Agriculture U. Wyo.; mem. Teton Sci. Sch. Bd.. Nat. Wetland Forum, 1983, 87; mem. exec. com. Council of State Govt.; chmn. Pride in Jackson Hole Campaign, 1986; bd. dirs. Wyo. Waterfowl Trust. Mem. Western River Guides Assn., Jackson Hole Guides and Outfitters. Named Citizen of Yr. County of Teton, 1984; recipient Nat. Conservation Achievement award Nat. Wildlife Fedn., 1984. Author: The Magnificent Bald Eagle: Our National Bird, 1971. Republican. Roman Catholic. Address: Triangle X Ranch Moose WY 83012

TURNER, JOHN WALTER, investor; b. Cleve., June 4, 1923; s. John H. and Dessa (Walter) T.; m. Marion T. Taylor, Feb. 3, 1945; 1 child, Leslie Ann. Student, N.Mex. Mil. Inst., 1942-43, U. N.Mex., 1943-44. With Davis, Skaggs & Co. investment bankers, San Francisco, 1946-49; S.W. rep. Axe Securities Corp., 1949-52; founder, pres., chmn. bd. Eppler Guerin & Turner, Inc., 1952-73; pres. N.Y. Stock Exch., Dallas, 1952-65, chmn. bd., 1965-73; bd. dirs. United N.Mex. Fin. Corp., El Chico, Inc., 1st So. Trust Co., Banctec, Inc., Dallas, Comml. Metals Col, Computer Lang. Rsch., Inc., Highland Park Cafeterias, Inc., Fin. Securities Advs., Inc., Nashville; past gov. Am. Stock Exchange, Midwest Stock Exch., Vicorp Restaurants, Denver, Golden Era Svcs., Inc., Houston; past chmn. Tex. State Securities. Trustee St. Vincent Hosp., Santa Fe, N.Mex.; bd. dirs. Santa Fe Community Found., Santa Fe Inst. Fine Arts. With USNR, 1943-46, PTO. Mem. Ind. Petroleum Assn. Am., N.Mex. Rsch. and Devel. Inst. (bus. adv. group), Am. Brahman Breeders Assn., Dallas Security Dealers Assn., Inst. Bus. Appraisers, Nat. Assn. Corp. Dlrs., N.Mex. Mil. Inst. Alumni Assn., Sigma Chi (life), Chuck Wagon Trial Riders N.Mex. Club, Dallas Country Club, Dallas Petroleum Club, Kiva Club. Home: RR 9 PO Box 62T Santa Fe NM 87505 Office: 2001 Bryan Tower Ste 2874 Dallas TX 75201

TURNER, JULIANNE DYE, film and tape production executive; b. Dayton, Ohio, Aug. 10, 1954; d. Edward Thomas and Phyllis (Dye) T.; m. James N. Stuart, Aug. 20, 1988. BA, U. Utah, 1976. Theatre prodn. stage mgr. and prodn. mgr. free lance, San Francisco, 1977-81, theatre producer, 1981; freelance TV stage mgr. San Francisco, 1981—; asst. dir. and prodn. mgr. film and tape prodn. free lance, San Francisco, 1985—. Recipient Best Musical Prodn. award L.A. Dramalogue, San Francisco, 1981. Mem. Dirs. Guild Am. (chmn. San Francisco coordinating com. exec. bd. 1987—), Actor's Equity Assn. (vice chmn. and mem. Bay Area adv. com. 1984-88), Film Arts Found., Film Tape Coun. Democrat.

TURNER, LILLIAN ERNA, nurse; b. Coalmont, Colo., Apr. 22, 1918; d. Harvey Oliver and Erna Lena (Wackwicz) T. BS, Colo. State U., 1940, Columbia U., 1945; cert. physician asst., U. Utah, 1978. Commd. 2d lt. Nurse Corps, U.S. Army, 1945; advanced through grades to lt. comdr. USPHS, 1964; dean of women U. Alaska, Fairbanks, 1948-50; head nurse Group Health Hosp., Seattle, 1950-53; adviser to chief nurse Hosp. Am. Samoa, Pago Pago, 1954-60; head nurse Meml. Hosp., Twin Falls, Idaho, 1960-61; shift supr. Hosp. Lago Oil & Transport, Siero Colorado, Aruba, 1961-63; chief nurse, adviser Truk Hosp., Moen, Ea. Caroline Islands, 1972-74; nurse adviser Children's Med. Relief Internat., South Vietnam, 1974-75; physician's asst. U. Utah, 1976-78, Wagon Circle Med. Clinic, Rawlins, Wyo., 1978—. Mem. Wyo. Acad. Physician Assts. (bd. dirs. 1982—), Am. Acad. Physician Assts., Nat. Assn. Physician Assts. Home: Park View Apts Apt A Rawlins WY 82301 Office: Wagon Circle Med Clinic 2012 Elm St Rawlins WY 82301

TURNER, MICHAEL SETH, public relations director, radio educator; b. San Diego, July 28, 1948; s. Charles Irwin and Lee (Yomin) T., m. Marlene Carol Meyer, Sept. 7, 1981. BS, San Diego State U., 1970; MS, Iowa State U., 1971. Instr. U. Nebr., Omaha, 1971-72; news dir. Sta. KFJM-AM-FM, Grand Forks, N.D., 1972-78; sta. mgr. Sta. KUOP-FM, Stockton, Calif., 1978-79; dir. pub. relations Sta. KCSN-FM, Northridge, Calif., 1980—; cons. Calif. State U., Northridge, 1987. Host, producer radio shows Morning Journal, 1972-78, L.A. Connection, 1980-87; freelance restaurant critic, 1986—. Bd. dirs. Pine-to-Prairie Girl Scout Council, 1972-78; bd. dirs. Grand Forks Jaycees, 1972-78; bd. dirs. North Hills Jaycees, 1980-84; bd. dirs. Northridge Recreation and Parks Festival, 1982-84. Participant Rotary Internat. Group Study Exchange, Philippines, 1978; named one of Outstanding Young Men of Am., U.S. Jaycees, 1982-84. Mem. So. Calif. Broadcasters, Pub. Interest Radio and TV Ednl. Soc. (pres. 1984-87), Publicity Club Los Angeles (pres. 1988—). Home: 10341 Canoga Ave Unit 29 Chatsworth CA 91311

TURNER, PAUL EDWIN, psychologist; b. Livingston, Tex., Sept. 7, 1951; s. Jack Edwin and Virginia Pauline (Pedigo) T.; m. Shannon Deen McKinney, Aug. 19, 1972. B.S. in Psychology, Tex. A. and M. U., 1972, M.S., 1974; Ph.D., U. Miss.-University, 1978. Dir., Central Peninsula Mental Health Ctr., Kenai, Alaska, 1978-84; pvt. practice, 1984—; sec. Bd. Psychologists and Psychol. Assoc. Examiners, 1980-86. Contbr. articles to profl. jours. Mem. City of Kenai Planning & Zoning, 1981-82, Kenai Library Commn., 1983—; bd. dirs. Cook Inlet Council on Alcohol Abuse, 1980, Pickle Hill Pub. Broadcasting. Health and Social Services Mental Health Devel. Disability grantee, 1978-84. Mem. Alaska Psychol. Assn. (pres. 1985), Am. Psychol. Assn., Alaska Mental Health Dirs. Assn. (pres. 1981, sec.-treas. 1984), Assn. for Advancement of Behavior Therapy. Club: Runners Anonymous. Home: PO Box 270 Kenai AK 99611 Office: 605 Main Kenai AK 99611

TURNER, RALPH HERBERT, sociologist, educator; b. Effingham, Ill., Dec. 15, 1919; s. Herbert Turner and Hilda Pearl (Bohn) T.; m. Christine Elizabeth Hanks, Nov. 2, 1943; children: Lowell Ralph, Cheryl Christine. B.A., U. So. Calif., 1941, M.A., 1942; postgrad., U. Wis., 1942-43; Ph.D., U. Chgo., 1948. Research assoc. Am. Council Race Relations, 1947-48; faculty UCLA, 1948—, prof. sociology and anthropology, 1959—, chmn. dept. sociology, 1963-68; chmn. Acad. Senate U. Calif. System, 1983-84; bd. dirs. Founds. Fund for Rsch. in Psychiatry; vis. summer prof. U. Wash., 1960, U. Hawaii, 1962; vis. scholar Australian Nat. U., 1972; vis. prof. U. Ga., 1975, Ben Gurion U., Israel, 1983; vis. fellow Nuffield Coll. Oxford U., 1980; disting. vis. prof. Am. U., Cairo, Egypt, 1983; adj. prof. China Acad. Social Scis., Beijing, People's Republic China, 1986; faculty research lectr. UCLA, 1986-87. Author: (with L. Killian) Collective Behavior, 1957, 2d edit., 1972, 3d edit., 1987, The Social Context of Ambition, 1964, Robert Park on Social Control and Collective Behavior, 1967, Family Interaction, 1970, Earthquake Prediction and Public Policy, 1975, (with J. Nigg, D. Paz, B. Young) Community Response to Earthquake Threat in Southern California., 1980, (with J. Nigg and D. Paz) Waiting for Disaster, 1986; editorial cons., 1959-62; editor: Sociometry, 1962-64; acting editor: Ann. Rev. of Sociology, 1977-78; assoc. editor, 1978-79, editor, 1980-86; adv. editor: Am. Jour. Sociology, 1954-56, Sociology and Social Research, 1961-74; editorial staff: Am. Sociol. Rev., 1955-56; assoc. editor: Social Problems, 1959-62, 67-69; cons. editor: Sociol. Inquiry, 1968-73, Western Sociol. Rev., 1975-79; editorial bd. Mass Emergencies, 1975-79, Internat. Jour. Critical Sociology, 1974—, Symbolic Interaction, 1977—. Mem. behavioral scis. study sect. NIH, 1961-66, chmn., 1963-64; dir.-at-large Social Sci. Research Council, 1965-66; chmn. panel on pub. policy implications of earthquake prediction Nat. Acad. Scis., 1974-75, also mem. earthquqke study delegation to Peoples Republic of China, 1976; Mem. com. social edn. and action Los Angeles Presbytery, 1954-56. Served to lt. (j.g.) USNR, 1943-46. Recipient Faculty prize Coll. Letters and Scis. UCLA, 1985; Faculty Research fellow Social Sci. Research Council., 1953-56; Sr. Fulbright scholar U.K., 1956-57; Guggenheim fellow, U.K., 1964-65. Mem. Am. Sociol. Assn. (council 1959-64, chmn. social psychology sect. 1960-61, pres. 1968-69, chmn. sect. theoretical sociology 1973-74, chmn. collective behavior and social movements sect. 1983-84, Cooley-Mead award 1987), Pacific Sociol. Assn. (pres. 1957), Internat. Sociol. Assn. (council 1974-82, v.p. 1978-82), Soc. Study Social Problems (exec. com. 1962-63), Am. Acad. Arts and Scis., Soc. for Study Symbolic Interaction (pres. 1982-83, Charles Horton Cooley award 1978), AAUP. Home: 1126 Chautauqua Blvd Pacific Palisades CA 90272 Office: UCLA 405 Hilgard Ave Los Angeles CA 90024

TURNER, RONALD LEE, assistant to the manufacturing executive; b. Denver, Nov. 4, 1947; s . Howard Lee and Gail Francis (Crane) T.; m. Donna Arlene Turk, Sept. 1976. BSBA, U. Denver, 1969. Sr. acct. Coopers & Lybrand, L.A., 1969-72; sr. auditor City Investing Co., Beverly Hills, Calif., 1972-74; internal audit mgr. Warner Communications Inc., N.Y.C., 1974-76; internat. audit mgr. Warner Communications Inc., London, 1976-78; dir. fin. systems Elektra Asylum Records, L.A., 1978-79; dir. internal audit Gen. Automation Inc., Anaheim, Calif., 1979-81; v.p. internal audit Browning-Ferris Industries, Houston, 1981-88; mgr. internal audit Teledyne Inc., L.A., 1988, asst. to corp. treas., 1988—. Mem. AICPA, Calif. Soc. CPAs, Inst. Internal Auditors. Home: PO Box 34310 Los Angeles CA 90034 Office: Teledyne Inc 1901 Avenue of the Stars #1800 Los Angeles CA 90069

TURNER, ROSS JAMES, investment corporation executive; b. Winnipeg, Man., Can., May 1, 1930; s. James Valentine and Gretta H. (Ross) T.; children: Ralph, Rick, Tracy Lee. U. Man. Extension, 1951, Banff Sch. Advanced Mgmt., 1956. Various sr. operating and mgmt. positions Genstar Corp., San Francisco, 1961-76, chmn./pres., chief exec. officer, 1976-86, also bd. dirs.; chmn. Genstar Investment Corp., San Francisco, 1986—; chmn., bd. dirs. Rio Algom Ltd., Gt. West Life Assurance Co., Fed. Industries Ltd.; bd. dirs. Blue Shield of Calif., Guy F. Atkinson Co. of Calif., Oxford Properties Can. Ltd., Western Corp. Enterprises Inc. Vice chmn. bd. dirs. YMCA, San Francisco; mem. Bay Area Internat. Forum. Fellow Soc. Mgmt. Accts. Can.; mem. San Francisco C. of C. (past chmn., dir.), Toronto Club, Vancouver Club, World Trade Club, Pacific Union Club, Rancho Santa Fe Golf Club, Peninsula Golf and Country Club, Mt. Royal Club. Office: Genstar Investment Corp 801 Montgomery San Francisco CA 94133

TURNER, WARREN AUSTIN, health association administrator; b. Berkeley, Calif., Dec. 21, 1926; s. Warren Mortimer and Rebecca Oline (Noer) T.; m. Daune Mackay, Mar. 29, 1952; children: Daune Scott Marable, Warren Adair, Alan Corey. BA, U. Calif., Berkeley, 1950, BS, 1952, MPH, 1958. Pub. acct. Price Waterhouse, San Francisco, 1951-52, A.W. Blackman, CPA, Las Vegas, 1952-56; asst. adminstr. Marin Gen. Hosp., San Rafael, Calif., 1958-60; assoc. dir. UCLA Hosp., 1960-68; founding adminstr. Walter O. Boswell Meml. Hosp., Sun City, Ariz., 1968-81; pres. Sun Health Corp., Sun City, 1981—; bd. dirs. Multi Hosp. Mutual Ins. Co., Bannackburn, Ill. Served with USN, 1944-46. Mem. Ariz. Hosp. Assn. (pres., chmn., 1977-78), AHA Governing Council for Aging and Long-Term Care Ariz., Cooperative Purchasing Assn. (pres. 1981-82, 87), Phoenix Regional Council (past pres.), Ariz. Acad., Ariz. State Health Planning Council, Assn. High Medicare Hosps. (chmn. 1988—), Lakes Club, Rotary. Republican. Office: Sun Health Corp 13180 N 103d Dr Sun City AZ 85372

TURNER, WILLIAM CHAPMAN, lawyer; b. Omaha, Feb. 18, 1944; s. Chapman and Grace Mary (Blair) T.; m. Kathern Petersen, Nov. 29, 1980; children: Angela, Jason, Joshua. BS, Emory U., 1966, JD, 1969; LLM, Georgetown U., 1971. Bar: Ga. 1969, D.C. 1969, Nev. 1976, Calif. 1977. Trial lawyer SEC, Washington, 1971-75; asst. U.S. atty. Dept. Justice, Las Vegas, 1975-87; assoc. Beckley, Singleton, Delaney & Jemison, Las Vegas, 1985-87, Cohen, Lee, Johnson, Merialdo, Las Vegas, 1988—; spl. asst. U.S. atty., Las Vegas, 1972-75, assigned to Watergate com., Dept. Justice, 1971-73. mem. Ga. Bar Assn., Nev. Bar Assn., Calif. Bar Assn., D.C. Bar Assn., Clark County Bar Assn., Phi Gamma Delta, Phi Delta Phi. Home: 7630 S Spencer St Las Vegas NV 84123 Office: 870 Cal Fed Bldg 301 E clark St Las Vegas NV 89123

TURNER, WILLIAM COCHRANE, international management consultant; b. Red Oak, Iowa, May 27, 1929; s. James Lyman and Josephine (Cochrane) T.; m. Cynthia Dunbar, July 16, 1955; children: Scott Christopher, Craig Dunbar, Douglas Gordon. BS, Northwestern U., 1952. Pres., chmn. bd. dirs. Western Mgmt. Cons., Inc., Phoenix, 1955-74, Western Mgmt. Cons. Europe, S.A., Brussels, 1968-74; U.S. ambassador, permanent rep. OECD, Paris, 1974-77, vice chmn. exec. com., 1976-77, U.S. rep. Energy Policy Com., 1976-77; mem. U.S. dels. internat. meetings, 1974-77, western internat. trade group U.S. Dept. Commerce, 1972-74; chmn. Argyle Atlantic Corp., Phoenix, 1977—; chmn. European adv. council, 1981-88, Asia Pacific adv. council AT&T Internat., 1981-88; mem. European adv. council IBM World Trade Europe, Africa, Mid. East Corp., 1977-80; mem. Asia Pacific adv. council Am. Can Co., 1981-85, Gen. Electric of Brazil adv. council Gen. Electric Co., Coral Gables, Fla., 1979-81, Caterpillar of Brazil adv. council Caterpillar Tractor Co., Peoria, Ill., 1979-84, Caterpillar Asia Pacific Adv. Council, 1984—, U.S. adv. com. Trade Negotiations, 1982-84; bd. dirs. Goodyear Tire & Rubber Co., Akron, Ohio, 1978—, Salomon Inc., N.Y.C., 1980—, Atlantic Inst. Found., Inc., 1984—, mem. internat. adv. council Avon Products, Inc., N.Y.C., 1985—; mem. Spencer Stuart adv. council Spencer Stuart and Assocs., N.Y.C., 1984—; chmn., mem. internat. adv. council Advanced Semiconductor Materials Internat. NV., Bilthoven, The Netherlands, 1985-88; bd. dirs. The Atlantic Council of the U.S., Washington, 1977—; co-chmn. internat. adv. bd. Univ. of Nations, Pacific & Asia Christian U., Kona, Hawaii, 1985—; bd. dirs. World Wildlife Fund/U.S., 1983—, The Conservation Found., 1985—; bd. govs. Joseph H. Lauder Inst. Mgmt. and Internat. Studies, U. Pa., 1983—; trustee Heard Mus., Phoenix, 1983-86, mem. adv. bd., 1986—; trustee Am. Grad. Sch. Internat. Mgmt., 1972—, chmn. bd. trustees, 1987—; bd. govs. Atlantic Inst. Internat. Affairs, Paris, 1977-88; adv. bd. Ctr. Strategic and Internat. Studies, Georgetown U., 1977-81; mem. European Community-U.S. Businessmen's Council, 1978-79; bd. govs. Am. Hosp. of Paris, 1974-77; trustee Nat. Symphony Orch. Assn., Washington, 1973-83, Am. Sch., Paris, 1976-77, Orme Sch., Mayer, Ariz., 1970-74, Phoenix Country Day Sch., 1971-74; mem. nat. councils Salk Inst., 1978-82; mem. U.S. Adv. Com. Internat. Edn. and Cultural Affairs, 1969-74; nat. rev. bd. Ctr. Cultural and Tech. Interchange between East and West, 1970-74; mem. vestry Am. Cathedral, Paris, 1976-77; pres., bd. dirs. Phoenix Symphony Assn., 1969-70; chmn. Ariz. Joint Econ. Devel. Com., 1967-68; exec. com., bd. dirs. Ariz. Dept. Econ. Planning and Devel., 1968-70; chmn. bd. Ariz. Crippled Children's Services, 1964-65; treas. Ariz. Rep. Com., 1956-57; chmn. Ariz. Young Rep. League, 1955-56. Recipient East-West Ctr. Disting. Service award, 1977. Mem. U.S. Council Internat. Bus. (trustee, exec. com.), U.S.-Japan Bus. Council, Council Fgn. Relations, Council of Am. Ambassadors, Nat. Adv. Council on Bus. Edn., Council Internat. Edn. Exchange, Phoenix 40, Met. Club, Links Club (N.Y.C.), Plaza Club (Phoenix), Paradise Valley (Ariz.) Country Club, Bucks Club (London). Episcopalian. Office: 4350 E Camelback Rd Ste 240-B Phoenix AZ 85018

TURNER, WILLIAM WEYAND, author; b. Buffalo, N.Y., Apr. 14, 1927; s. William Peter and Magdalen (Weyand) T.; m. Margaret Peiffer, Sept. 12, 1964; children: Mark Peter, Lori Ann. BS, Canisius Coll., 1949. Spl. agt. in various field offices FBI, 1951-61; free-lance writer Calif., 1963—; sr. editor Ramparts Mag., San Francisco, 1967—; investigator and cons. Nat. Wiretap Commn., 1975. Author: The Police Establishment, 1968, Invisible Witness: The Use and Abuse of the New Technology of Crime Investigation, 1968, Hoover's F.B.I.: The Men and the Myth, 1970, (with Warren Hinckle and Eliot Asinof) The Ten Second Jailbreak, 1973, (with John Christian) The Assassination of Robert F. Kennedy, 1978, (with Warren Hinckle) The Fish is Red: The Story of the Secret War Against Castro, 1981. Contbg. author: Investigating the FBI, 1973. Contbr. articles to popular mags. Dem. candidate for U.S. Congress, 1968. Served with USN, 1945-46. Mem. Authors Guild, Internat. Platform Assn., Press Club of San Francisco. Roman Catholic. Home and Office: 163 Mark Twain Ave San Rafael CA 94903

TURNER-MCFARLAND, ALICE ELIZABETH, librarian; b. Saskatoon, Sask., Can., Oct. 16, 1925; d. John Ross and Annie Louise (Jackson) Turner; m. R.B. McFarland, 1985. BA, U. Sask., 1946; BLS, McGill U., 1950. Librarian, U. Man. (Can.), Winnipeg, 1950-52; childrens librarian Saskatoon Pub. Library, 1952-53, head reference dept., 1953-61, asst. chief librarian, 1961-80, chief librarian, 1981—. Office: Saskatoon Pub Libr, 311 23d St E, Saskatoon, SK Canada S7K 0J6

TUROFF, MARSHALL A., consulting company executive; b. Chgo., July 9, 1927; s. Nat and Bertha (Leavitt) T.; m. Gloria Auerbach, May 6, 1951 (div. Apr. 1983); children: Sara Ann, Barbara, Charles; m. Barbara Phillips, Apr. 18, 1983. BSc, Roosevelt Coll., 1950; MBA, U. Chgo., 1954. Asst. mgr. mktg. research Signode Steel Strapping Co., Chgo., 1951-55; mgr., mktg. research Precision Scientific Co., Chgo., 1955-56; dir., mktg. research Ohmite Corp., Skokie, Ill., 1956-57; cons. Booz, Allen & Hamilton, Chgo., 1957-60; pres., chief executive officer Turoff Industries, Ltd., Chgo., 1960-78, Jomar Warehousing Co., Chgo., 1966-78; pres. Photonic Environmental Corp., Chgo., 1972-78, Turoff Consulting Svcs., Chgo., 1978—. Treas. Jewish Vocational Service, Chgo., 1978-79, sec. 1979-80, v.p. 1980-81); pres. North Cen. Home Owners Assn., Skokie, Ill., 1963-65; mem. Bd. Zoning, Skokie, 1961-63. With U.S. Army Air Corps, 1945-46. Mem. Am. Soc. Profl. Cons. (pres. Midwest div. 1980-83), Am. Statistical Assn., Am. Mktg. Assn., Packaging Inst., USA (Chmn. and Excellence awards 1982). Republican. Jewish. Office: Turoff Consulting Svcs Inc PO Box 5740 Scottsdale AZ 85261

TURRENTINE, HOWARD BOYD, U.S. district judge; b. Escondido, Calif., Jan. 22, 1914; s. Howard and Veda Lillian (Maxfield) T.; m. Virginia Jacobsen, May 13, 1965; children: Howard Robert, Terry Beverly. A.B., San Diego State Coll., 1936; LL.B., U. So. Calif., 1939. Bar: Calif. 1939. Practiced in San Diego, 1939-68; judge Superior Ct. County of San Diego, 1968-70; judge U.S. Dist. Ct. for So. Dist., Calif., San Diego, 1970—. Served with USNR, 1941-45. Mem. ABA, Fed. Bar Assn., Am. Judicature Soc. Office: US Dist Ct 940 Front St San Diego CA 92189

TURRENTINE, LYNDA GAYLE, interior designer; b. Carrizozo, N.Mex., Apr. 12, 1941; d. Edward Franklyn and Lora Olive (Allen) Adams; m. Frank George Turrentine, Sept. 5, 1961 (div. 1974); 1 child, Teri Lynn. BA, U. North Tex., 1964. Cert. interior design. Interior Designer Marsh and Assoc., Denton, Tex., 1964-65, Stewart Office Supply, Dallas, 1965-66, The Paper Mill, Las Cruces, N.Mex., 1966-74; gen. mgr. and interior designer Design Plaza, Las Cruces, 1974-79; acct. rep. Cholla Bus. Interiors, Tucson, 1979-80; owner Interior Concepts, Tucson, 1980-87; owner, interior designer Interior Concepts, affiliated with Friedman, Keim, McFerror Architects, Tucson, 1987—; Speaker at several univs.; judge portfolios U. Ariz., 1983, 85; com. chmn. Designer Showhouse, Tucson, 1983, 84, 86, 88. Mem. Arts council, Las Cruces, 1977-79, PTA, Las Cruces, 1977-84; cookie chmn., Girl Scouts, Las Cruces, 1978; mem. ch. choir. Mem. Am. Soc. Interior Designers (pres. 1981-83, nat. bd. dirs. 1981-83, 1987-89, Presdl. citation), Ariz. S. Chpt. Am. Soc. Interior Designers (treas. 1983-85, bd. dirs. 1981-8, Medalist award 1985), Las Cruces C. of C., Tucson C. of C., Sahuraro Bus (bd. dirs. Tucson 1981-88). Republican. Methodist. Office: Interior Concepts Affiliates 655 N Alvernon Way #100 Tucson AZ 85711

TUSSEY, WALTER F., banker; b. Altoona, Pa., Aug. 22, 1932; s. Paul Kemmler and Emily Margaret (Frisch) T.; m. Etsuko Hashimoto; children: Teri, Kathleen, Douglas, Martin. BS, Pacific Western U., 1987. With Bank of Am., 1955-71; country ops. officer Bank of Am., Saigon, Vietnam, 1971-74; regional ops. officer Bank of Am., Agana, Guam, 1974-75; chief auditor Insular Bank of Asia and Am., Manila, The Philippines, 1976-78; project mgr. Bank Duta Ekonomi, Jakarta, Indonesia, 1978-80; ops. adminstr. Bank Am., London, 1981-82; mgr. ops. and adminstrn. Alahli Comml. Bank, Manama, Bahrain, 1983-86; v.p. Bank of Am., San Francisco, 1987—. With USAF, 1951-54. Mem. Aircraft Owners and Pilots Assn., Am. Legion (vice commdr. San Francisco chpt. 1957), Bavarian Aid Soc., Irish-Am. Club (Altoona). Republican. Lutheran. Home: 4119 Third Ave Altoona PA 16602 Office: Bank of Am 555 California St San Francisco CA 94105

TUTTLE, FRANK LINDSTROM, advertising consultant; b. Myton, Utah, Jan. 1, 1929; s. Harold Overston and Nellie Anna (Lindstrom); m. Marjorie Magee, Sept. 4, 1949 (div. 1968); children: Jeffrey Steven, Tracy Lynn Kafkafi; m. Sandra Marquis, Aug. 29, 1970. BJ, U. Mo., 1951. Mgr. Video Prodns., Inc., Denver, 1952-53; dir. Sta. KOMU-TV, Columbia, Mo., 1953-56; dir. radio/TV Bruce Brewer Advt., Mpls., 1956-59; comml. product supr. Procter & Gamble, Cin., 1959-64; exec. v.p. Filmex, Inc., Los Angeles and N.Y.C., 1965-67; pres. Wakeford/Orloff, Inc., Los Angeles, 1967-77, The Film Tree, Inc., Los Angeles, 1977-87; cons. Bird, Bonette, Stauderman, Los Angeles, 1987—. Dir. Calif. Tax Reform, Los Angeles, 1986. Petty officer 3d class USN, 1946-48. Mem. Assn. Assn. Ind. Comml. Producers (pres. 1978-80, nat. bd. dirs. 1978—), Mountain Gate Country Club. Home and Office: 11724 Brookdale Ln Studio City CA 91604

TUTTLE, PHILLIP MAURICE, health services adminstrator; b. Pontiac, Mich., Sept. 2, 1937; s. Silas James (Ted) and Jewel Inez (Bishop) Tuttle; m. Betty A. Maas, Apr. 2, 1961; children: Sharon White, Michael Maas. AA, Hannibal (Mo.) LaGrange Coll., 1959; student, U. Kansas City, 1961, Carthage (Ill.) Coll., 1961-62. Lic. practical nurse, cardiovascular technologist. Dept. head Cen. Services Menorah Med. Ctr., Kansas City, Mo., 1961-61; athletic trainer Carthage Coll., 1961-63; with Cardiovascular testing Meml. Hosp., Carthage, 1963—, dir. clin. services, 1986—; physician asst. James E. Coeur, Carthage, 1984—. Mem. Carthage Vol. Fire Dept., 1970-75. Mem. Am. Heart Assn. (bd. dirs. 1987-88, Certificate of Appreciation), Am. Cardiology Technologist (bd. dirs. 1978-80, Plaque of Distinction 1980), Am. Arthritis Assn., Am. Coll. Sports Medicine, Hancock County Heart Assn. (bd. dirs. 1987—), Hancock County Gun Club. Republican. Presbyterian.

TUTTLE, RICHARD GLEN ELLISON, management consultant; b. Wichita, Kans., Oct. 3, 1935; s. Laburn Lorn and Mary Frances (Scott) T.; m. Wanda Louise Holmes, May 27, 1955; children: Lori Jean, Richard Scott, Terri Lynn, Michael Howard. Student, U. Oreg., 1957-59; PhD in Clin. Hypnotherapy, Am. Inst. Hypnotherapy, 1987. Risk mgr. Ross Island Sand and Gravel Co., Portland, Oreg., 1979-84; pres., exec. dir. Saratoga Pacific Corp., Beaverton, Oreg., 1984—; cons. Richard G. Tuttle and Assocs., Beaverton, 1984—. Served with USMC, 1953-57. Mem. Vets. of Safety, Am. Soc. Safety Engrs. (1st v.p. Portland chpt. 1974-75, pres. 1975-76, v.p. Region I, 1977-79). Republican. Lutheran.

TUTTLE, STEPHANIE ELLEN, entertainment company executive; b. Pensacola, Fla., Feb. 1, 1954; d. William Edwin and Lillian Patricia (Kastuck) T. Student, Beaver Coll., 1972-76. Asst. account exec. McCaffrey & McCall, Inc., N.Y.C., 1978-79, account exec., 1980-82; dir. advt. services ABC Entertainment Ctr., Los Angeles, 1982-86, mgr. dramatic devel., 1986-87, dir. dramatic series programming, 1987—. Mem. Los Angeles Arts Council. Mem. Acad. Arts and TV Soc. Episcopalian. Office: ABC Entertainment Ctr 2040 Avenue of Stars Los Angeles CA 90067

TUVESON, CHRISTOPHER ARCHER, company official, consultant; b. Riverside, Calif., Apr. 26, 1944; s. Leo Lewis and Margaret Helen (Linde) T.; m. Dianne F. Safholm, Feb. 4, 1967 (div. Nov. 1986); children: Carrie Ann, Jennifer Lee; m. Afton Susan Auld, Apr. Il, 1987. BSEE, Stanford U., l966, MS in Indsl. Engring., 1972. Prodn. engr. Hewlett-Packard Co., Palo Alto, Calif., 1965-70, prodn. supr., 1970-73; prodn. mgr. Hewlett-Packard Co., Santa Rosa, Calif., 1973-75, facilities engr., 1975-78, engring. supr., 1978-84; facilities mgr. Hewlett-Packard Co., Santa Rosa, 1984—; facilities cons. Electroscale Corp., Santa Rosa, 1978-79, Nortec Corp., Richland, Wash., l980, Mawson Computers, Santa Rosa, 1985—. Pres. Jr. Achievement Sonoma County, Santa Rosa, 1976, 86; bd. dirs. Sonoma County Alliance, 1978-82. Recipient bronze leadership award Nat. Jr. Achievement, 1979. Mem. Internat. Facilities Mgmt. Assn., Rohnert Park C. of C. (pres. 1986), Santa Rosa C. of C. (bd. dirs. 1979-8l). Democrat. Methodist. Home: 24l8 Rancho Cabeza Dr Santa Rosa CA 95404 Office: Hewlett-Packard Co l2l2 Valley House Dr Rohnert Park CA 94928

TVEDT, JOSEPH ARNOLD, JR., municipal judge; b. Cocoa, Fla., Jan. 21, 1944; s. Joseph Arnold and Donna Patricia (Ogden) Tvedt. BA in Chemistry, Ariz. State U., 1968, JD, 1971. Bar: Ariz., 1971. Asst. city atty. City of Phoenix, 1972-81; sole practice Phoenix, 1981—; judge protem Phoenix Mcpl. Ct., 1982—. Reserve patrolman Ariz. Dept. Pub. Safety, 1980; mem. City of Phoenix AIDS Task Force, 1988. Office: 1642 N 24th St Phoenix AZ 85008-3504

TWIGG-SMITH, THURSTON, newspaper publisher; b. Honolulu, Aug. 17, 1921; s. William and Margaret Carter (Thurston) Twigg-S.; m. Bessie Bell, June 9, 1942 (div. Feb. 1983); children: Elizabeth, Thurston, William, Margaret, Evelyn.; m. Laila Roster, Feb. 22, 1983. B.Engring., Yale U., 1942. With Honolulu Advertiser, 1946—, mng. editor, 1954-60, asst. bus. mgr., 1960-61, pub., 1961-86; pres., dir., chief exec. officer Honolulu Advertiser, Inc., 1962—; pres., dir., chief exec. officer Persis Corp.; chmn. Asa Properties Hawaii, Shiny Rock Mining Corp.; bd. dirs. Am. Savs. Bank, Hawaiian Electric Industries, Inc., Hawaiian Electric Company, Tongg Pub. Co., Am. Fin. Svcs., Inc. Trustee Punahou Sch., Old Sturbridge Inc., Honolulu Acad. Arts, The Contemporary Mus., Hawaii. Served to maj. AUS, 1942-46. Mem. Honolulu C. of C. Clubs: Waialae (Honolulu), Pacific (Honolulu), Oahu (Honolulu). Office: PO Box 3110 Honolulu HI 96802

TWIST, ROBERT LANPHIER, farmer, rancher, cattle feeder; b. Memphis, Dec. 27, 1926; s. Clarence C. and Edith G. Twist; student Springfield (Ill.) Jr. Coll., 1943; B.S. in Agr., U. Ill., 1950; postgrad. U. Edinburgh (Scotland); 1 dau., Marilyn Edith. Owner, operator farm lands, Twist, Ark., 1949—, Bow Fiddle Ranch, Laramie, Wyo., 1961—, Lost Creek Ranch, Masters, Colo., 1963, Rolling T Ranch, Ft. Morgan, Colo., 1965—, R.L. Twist Ranches Cattle Feeding Enterprises, Greeley, Colo. and Ft. Morgan, 1974—; prin. R.L. Twist Land & Investments, Paradise Valley, Ariz., 1974—; Rocker M Ranch, Douglas, Ariz., 1981—; cons. agrl. mgmt. Justice of Peace, Twist, Ark., 1954. Served with USAAF, 1944-46. Mem. Colo. Farm Bur., Wyo. Farm Bur., Nat. Cattlemen's Assn. (charter). Republican. Presbyterian. Home: 4612 E Sparkling Ln Paradise Valley AZ 85253

TWOMLEY, BRUCE CLARKE, lawyer, state official; b. Selma, Ala., Jan. 23, 1945; s. Robert Clarke and Eleanor Jane (Wood) Anderson T.; m. Sara Jane Minton, June 13, 1979. BA in Philosophy, Northwestern U., 1967; LLM, U. Calif., San Francisco, 1970; postgrad. Nat. Jud. Coll., Reno, Nev., 1983, 88. Bar: Calif. 1972, Alaska 1973, U.S. Dist. Ct. Alaska, 1973, U.S. Ct. Appeals (9th cir.) 1982. VISTA vol., Anchorage, 1972-73; lawyer Alaska Legal Services Corp., Anchorage, 1973-82; commr. Alaska Comml. Fisheries Entry Commn., Juneau, 1982-83, chmn., 1983—; mem. Gov.'s Fisheries Cabinet, 1983—; cons. IRS, Sta. WNED-TV, Buffalo, 1988. Recipient Alaska Legal Services Disting. Service award, 1983. Mem. Juneau Racquet Club (adv. bd. 1989—), Kappa Sigma (pres. interfraternity council 1966-67). Home: PO Box 020972 Juneau AK 99802-0972 Office: Alaska Comml Fisheries Entry Commn PO Box KB Juneau AK 99811

TYCHOWSKI, CHRISTOPHER ROMAN, engineer; b. Chorzow, Poland, Sept. 20, 1937; came to U.S., 1973; s. Theodor and Mari Jadwiga (Napierala) T.; m. Slavomira Maria Zbierska, Sept. 16, 1975 (div. March 1979). Bachelors Degree, Poznan (Poland) Tech. Coll., 1958; Masters Degree, Poznan Politechnik, 1965; PhD, Warsaw (Poland) Inst. Tech., 1972. Sr. project engr. Warsaw Inst. Tech., 1969-73; project engr. Arthur G. McKee, San Mateo, Calif., 1974-76; pvt. practice cons. Phoenix, 1976-78; civil engr. W.B.C. Cons., Phoenix, 1978-79; project engr. Peter A. Lendrum Architects, Phoenix, 1979-80; sr. structural engr. Sullivan-Mason, Inc. Architects-Engrs., Phoenix, 1981-83; plans rev. engr. City of Phoenix Bldg. Safety Dept., 1981-83; sr. project engr. Magadini Alagia Assoc., Phoenix, 1983-84; pres. C.R.T. Corp., Phoenix, 1984—; realtor Realty Experts, Inc., Phoenix, 1987—; pres. Alliance Bldg. Corp., Phoenix, 1988—, Acorn Bldg. Corp.; exec. v.p. Gemcraft Constrn. Co., Inc., Phoenix, 1988—. Patentee in field. Recipient Recognition awards, Polish Assn. of Architects, 1968, 70, Tech. Excellence award Polish Normalization Com., 1971, Best Sports Pub. of Yr. award Polish Nat. Olympic Com., 1972. Mem. Am. Inst. Steel Constrn., Structural Engrs. Assn., Phoenix Bd. Realtors. Republican. Roman Catholic. Home: 2537 E Coolidge St Phoenix AZ 85016 Office: CRT Corp 2401 N 32d St Ste B Phoenix AZ 85008

TYLER, DARLENE JASMER, dietitian; b. Watford City, N.D., Jan. 26, 1939; d. Edwin Arthur and Leola Irene (Walker) Jasmer; BS, Oreg. State U., 1961; m. Richard G. Tyler, Aug. 26, 1977; children: Ronald, Eric, Scott. Clin. dietitian Salem (Oreg.) Hosp., 1965-73; sales supr. Sysco Northwest, Tigard, Oreg., 1975-77; clin. dietitian Physicians & Surgeons Hosp., Portland, Oreg., 1977-79; food svc. dir. Meridian Park Hosp., Tualatin, Oreg., 1979—. Registered dietitian. Mem. Am. Dietetic Assn., Oreg. Dietetic Assn., Portland Dietetic Assn., Am. Soc. Hosp. Food Svc. Adminstrs. Episcopalian. Home: 12800 SE Nixon Ave Milwaukie OR 97222 Office: 19300 SW 65th St Tualatin OR 97062

TYLER, FREEMAN RUSSELL, pathologist; b. Taunton, Mass., Apr. 23, 1925; s. Freeman Lester and Fannie Bell (Wilson) T.; m. Helen Elaine Rice, June 11, 1950; children: Lawrence, Reginald, Patricia, Loretta. BA, Atlantic Union Coll., 1950; MD, Loma Linda U., 1954. Diplomate Am. Bd. Pathology. Intern Porter Meml. Hosp., Denver, 1954-55, resident in pathology, 1956-59; resident in pathology VA Hosp., Denver, 1955-56, Salem (Mass.) Hosp., 1959-60; chief pathology New Eng. Meml. Hosp., Stoneham, Mass., 1960-85; pathology cons. VA Hosp., Bedford, Mass., 1966-68; pathologist Bangkok Adventist Hosp., Thailand, 1968-69, 72-73; retired 1985. With USN, 1943-46, PTO. Fellow Mass. Med. Soc., Coll. Am. Pathologists; mem. Soc. Nuclear Medicine, AMA (sr.). Seventh Day Adventist. Home: 7921 S Bemis St Littleton CO 80120

TYLER, GAIL MADELEINE, nurse; b. Dhahran, Saudi Arabia, Nov. 21, 1953 (parents Am. citizens); d. Louis Rogers and Nona Jean (Henderson) T. AS, Front Range Community Coll., Westminster, Colo., 1979; BS in Nursing, U. Wyo., 1989; RN Ward sec. Valley View Hosp., Thornton, Colo., 1975-79; nurse Scott and White Hosp., Temple, Tex., 1979-83, Meml. Hosp. Laramie County, Cheyenne, Wyo., 1983-89; dir. DePaul Home Health, 1989—. Avocations: collecting international dolls, sewing, reading, traveling.

TYLER, KENDALL LEE, retail executive; b. Clovis, N.Mex., Jan. 14, 1963; s. Charles Robert and Joyce Marie (Broska) T. Student, No. Ariz. U., 1981-83; BA in Communication, Ariz. State U., 1985. Phys. edn. instr. John Hancock Acad., Mesa, Ariz., 1983-84; dept. mgr. Platt Music/Diamond's Dept. Stores, Ariz., 1985; mdse. distbn. mgr. Platt Music Corp., Torrance, Calif., 1985-86; buyer home electronics Platt Music Corp., Torrance, 1986-87; regional sales mgr. Dillard's Dept. Stores, Tempe, Ariz., 1987—. Libertarian.

TYLER, NEAL EVANS, criminal justice educator, consultant; b. Hartford, Conn., June 8, 1954; s. Cleon Adrein and Dorthery (Weir) T.; m. Janet Kay Weibe, Aug. 22, 1981; children: Ryan D., Janeal N. AS, Manchester Community Coll.,, 1978. Police officer Canon City, Colo;, 1981--; owner, instr. coordinator for criminal justice acad, Canon City, 1981--, police trainer, 1081--, state dir. U.S. Police Defensive Tactics Assn., Strongsville, Ohio, 1985--, nat. trainer, 1981--; chmn. Nat. Law Enforcement Hall of Fame, Strongsville, 1986--. Chmn. Explorer Scouts, Canon City, 1988. Mem. Nat. Sheriff's Assn., Southwestern Law Enforcement Assn. Home: 751 Windsor Canon City CO 81212 Office: Criminal Justice Acad 2951 E Hwy 50 Canon City CO 81212

TYLER, RICHARD CURTIS, JR., restaurant executive; b. Hammond, Ind., Mar. 17, 1946; s. Richard Curtis and Bernadine (Morrison) T.; m. Deborah Jan Kindy, Oct. 1, 1968 (div. 1982); 1 child, Richard Curtis III. BS in Mass Communications, Manchester (Ind.) Coll., 1971; postgrad., Ind. U., 1971-73. Various hospitality pos. 1967-73; restaurant mgr. Little Zagreb Inn, Bloomington, Ind., 1973-75; gen. mgr. Pancho Villa's Restaurant, Bloomington, 1975-78, Great Am. Railroad, Tucson, Ariz., 1978-79; asst. gen. mgr. The Tack Room, Tucson, 1979-84, v.p., gen. mgr., 1986—; dir. food and beverage, resident mgr. Westward Look Resort, Tucson, 1984-86; owner, v.p. V.K.T. Mgmt. Co., Tucson, 1986—. Sgt. U.S. Army, 1967-69. Named one of Outstanding Young Men Am., 1973. Mem. Am. Inst. Wine and Food, Brotherhood of Knights of Vine (master knight), Am. Legion. Republican. Office: The Tack Room 2800 N Sabino Cyn Tucson AZ 85715

TYLKA, CATHERINE M., nurse; b. Cleve., July 11, 1948; d. Paul William and Dannie Dean (Truberville) Roshetko; m. Michael S. Tylka, Jan. 21, 1969; children: Michael S. Jr., Wendy Lee. AS in Nursing, Ariz. Western Coll., 1982; BA, U. Phoenix, 1987. RN, Ariz.; cert. advanced cardiac life support instr., trauma nurse specialist, instr. verified trauma nurse core provider. Emergency RN Yuma (Ariz.) Regional Med. Ctr., 1982-84, U. Med. Ctr., Tucson, 1984-86; emergency charge nurse Northwest Hosp., Tucson, 1986-87; clin. nurse leader El Dorado Hosp., Tucson, 1985-86, emergency supr., 1987—; tutor Ariz. Western Coll., Yuma, 1983-84; assoc. faculty Pima Community Coll., Tucson, 1986—. Mem. Emergency Nurses Assn. (pres. 1986-87, trauma nursing chair 1986-88, chair govt. affairs 1989—), Am. Assn. Critical Care Nurses. Home: 4414 E Cerrada del Charro Tucson AZ 85718

TYMAN, MARY JO, social worker; b. Saskatoon, Sask., Can., Jan. 9, 1963; came to U.S., 1965; d. Paul Myron and Aimee Jane (Perkins) T. BS, Metropolitan State U., 1988. Counselor Family Tree, Denver, 1985-88; social work assoc. Univ. Hosp., Denver, 1988—; case mgr. Adams County Mental Health Ctr., Commerce City, Colo., 1988—; cons. Care Unit, Denver, 1987-88. Vol. Rocky Mountain Human Soc., Denver, 1987-88. Mem. Nat. Orgn. Human Services. Office: Adams County Mental Health Ctr 4371 E 72d Ave Commerce City CO 80022

TYRRELL, ELEANORE DAY, medical research administrator; b. Phila., Aug. 9, 1938; d. Peter Aloysius Tyrrell and Elsie Amelia Day. BA in Psychology, U. Richmond, 1960; MA in Psychology, Pepperdine U., 1980. Rsch. assoc. U. Pa. Med. Sch., Phila., 1961-62; with UCLA, 1962—, rsch. assoc. to lab. supr. to co-adminstr. Marijuana Rsch. Program, 1973-77, now project coord. program in psychiatry, law and human sexuality Neuropsychiatric Inst., 1987—; exec. dir. Ctr. for Drug Edn. and Brain Rsch., L.A., 1987-88; cons. Beverly Hills Headache and Pain Med. Group, L.A., Los Alamos (N.Mex.) Nat. Labs., SUNY-Stony Brook, Southern Calif. Neuropsychiatric inst., La Jolla, Southern Calif. Ctr. for Sleep Disorders, Santa Monica, others. Contbr. articles and rsch. papers to profl. jours. Pres. The Opera Assocs., L.A.; dir. publicity and pub. rels. L.A. and western regions Met. Opera Nat. Coun. Auditions. Mem. Psi Chi. Home: 1436 Butler Ave Los Angeles CA 90025

TYSON, JOHN, television reporter, range management consultant; b. Bethlehem, Pa., May 4, 1945; s. John Lever Tyson and Josephine (Falcone) Straub; m. Donna Tyson, Sept. 30, 1967 (div. 1979); children: Julie Lynn, Marlene Michel; m. Linda S. Tyson, Dec. 3, 1979. AA, Santa Rose Jr. Coll., 1972. Announcer Sta. KTHS, Berryville, Ark., 1980-81, Sta. KSRN, Reno, 1982-83; reporter Sta. KTVN, Reno, 1983-84, anchorman, 1984-85; corr., cons. Armed Forces Radio and TV System, Dept. Def., C. Am., 1985-87; state reporter Sta. KOLO-TV, Reno, 1987--; media cons., lectr., Reno, 1987-- . Newspaper columnist Range Rider, 1983--. Range mgmt. officer Storey County Sheriff's Dept., 1987--. Sgt. USAF, Vietnam. Decorated Vietnamese Cross Gallantry. Republican. Lutheran. Home: 169 16th Pleasant Valley Elko NV 89801 Office: Sta KOLO-TV 4850 Ampere Dr Reno NV 89510

TYSON, ROYCE DON, teacher; b. Colorado Spring, June 28, 1941; s. Mark and Lohraine (Ramey) T.; m. Coralie Ann Dungan, July 31, 1965; children: Troy Niles, Todd Courtney. BA, U. Colo., Boulder, 1963; MEd in Reading, U. Colo., Denver, 1977. Cert. sec. tchr. Russian tchr. Jefferson County Pub. Schs., Lakewood, Colo., 1964—; co-chmn. Green Mountain Area Sch. Bond, Jefferson County, 1976; adult tutorial program, Teaching English as Second Language, Denver, 1975-77; tour dir. Soviet Union Student Tours, Lakewood, 1970—. Author: Oral Russian Language, 1967; co-author: Jr. High Russian Curriculum, 1967—. Spkr. Kiwanis and other civic clubs, Lakewood, Wheatridge, Colo.; Grand Marshall, Lakewood on Parade, 1981; church elder and song leader, Non-Denominational Ch.; mem. Task Force of Colo. Dept. Edn., Denver. Grantee, Russian Language Inst., Carneigie Found., Finland, Russia, 1963, grad. sch. U. Calif. Berkeley, 1963-64; named Colo. Tchr. of Yr., Dept. of Edn., Denver Post, Encyclopedia Britannica, 1981; recipient coordinator's award, Jefferson County Pub. Sch., 1983. Mem. Jefferson County Edn. Assn. (rep.), NEA, Am. Council Tchrs. of Russian, Colo. Council of Fgn. Language Tchrs. Democrat. Office: Everitt Jr High Sch 3900 Kipling St Wheat Ridge CO 80033

TYSSELAND, TERRY LAWRENCE, division manager; b. Fargo, N.D., Oct. 28, 1941; s. Milford Selner and Lucile Margaret (Oehlke) T.; m. Shirley Ann Thompson, May 4, 1968. BS, U.S. Merchant Marine Acad., 1964. Plant mgr. Gulf Atlantic Distbn. Services, Arlington, Tex., 1965-80; v.p. and western regional mgr. Trammell Crow, Commerce, Calif., 1980-86; div. mgr. Southland Distbn. Ctr., San Bernardino, Calif., 1986—. Republican. Lutheran. Clubs: Newport (Calif.) Sailing; Redlands (Calif.) Country. Office: Southland Distbn Ctr 4472 Georgia Blvd San Bernardino CA 92407-1857

TYTLER, LINDA JEAN, marketing executive, state legislator; b. Rochester, N.Y., Aug. 31, 1947; d. Frederick Easton and Marian Elizabeth (Allen) Tytler; m. George Stephen Dragnich, May 2, 1970 (div. July 1976). AS, So. Sem., Buena Vista, Va., 1967; student U. Va., 1973; student in pub. adminstrn. U. N. Mex., 1981-82. Spl. asst. to Congressman John Buchanan, Washington, 1971-75; legis. analyst U.S. Senator Robert Griffin, Washington, 1975-77; ops. supr. Pres. Ford Com., Washington, 1976; office mgr. U.S. Senator Pete Domenici Re-election, Albuquerque, 1977; pub. info. officer S.W. Community Health Service, Albuquerque, 1978-83; cons. pub. relations and mktg., Albuquerque, 1983-84; account exec. Rick Johnson & Co., Inc., Albuquerque, 1983-84; dir. mktg. and communications St. Joseph Healthcare Corp., 1984-88; mem. N.Mex. Ho. of Reps., Santa Fe, 1983—, vice chmn. appropriations and fin. com., 1985-86, interim com. on children and youth, 1985-86, mem. edn. com., transp. com., interim com. environ., land use and solid waste, 1989—; adv. mem. legis. edn. study com.; chmn. Rep. caucus, 1985-88; chmn. legis. campaign com. Rep. Party; mem. hosp. cost containment task force Nat. Conf. State Legislatures; del. to Republic of China, Am. Council of Young Polit. Leaders, 1988. Bd. dirs. N. Mex. chpt. ARC, Albuquerque, 1984. Recipient award N.Mex. Advt. Fedn., Albuquerque, 1981, 82, 85, 86, 87. Mem. Am. Soc. Hosp. Pub. Relations (cert.), Nat. Advt. Fedn., Soc. Hosp. Planning and Mktg., Am. Mktg. Assn. Republican. Baptist.

TZAVELLA-EVJEN, HARA, classics educator; b. Pireus, Greece, June 27, 1936; came to U.S., 1966; d. Adam and Markella (Polymeri) Tzavellas; m. Harold D. Evjen, Jan. 30, 1967; 1 child, Harald. BA, U. Athens, Greece, 1959, PhD, 1970. Tchr. classics Pearce Coll., Athens, 1960-66; lectr. U. Colo., Denver, 1966-69; asst. prof. classics U. Colo., Boulder, 1966-67, 70-73, assoc. prof., 1973—; dir. excavation at Lithares Greek Archaeol. Service, Thebes, 1970-77. Author: The Winged Creatures in Aegaean Art, 1970, Lithares, 1984, Lithares An Early Helladic Settlement, 1985; contbr. articles to profl. jours. Mem. Archaeol. Inst. Am., Am. Philol. Assn., Archaeol. Soc. Athens, Classical Assn. Middle West and South, Assn. Greek Writers, Greek Archaeol. Soc. (dir. excavation at Chaeroneia 1983—). Home: 2123 4th Boulder CO 80302 Office: U Colo Dept of Classics Boulder CO 80309

UDALL, MORRIS KING, congressman; b. St. Johns, Ariz., June 15, 1922; s. Levi S. and Louise (Lee) U.; m. Ella Royston (dec.), 1968; children by previous marriage: Mark, Judith, Randolph, Anne, Bradley, Katherine. LL.B. with distinction, U. Ariz., 1949. Bar: Ariz. 1949. Ptnr. firm Udall & Udall, Tucson, 1949-61; chief dep. county atty. Pima County, 1950-52, county atty., 1953-54; lectr. labor law U. Ariz., 1955-56; mem. 87th-101st Congresses, 2d Dist. Ariz., 1961—; chmn. House Com. on Interior and Insular Affairs; vice chmn. Com. on Post Office and Civil Service; vice chmn. Office Tech. Assessment; mem. Com. on Fgn. Affairs; a founder Bank of Tucson, 1959, former dir.; former chmn. bd. Catalina Savs. and Loan Assn.; chmn. Ariz. Com. for Modern Cts., 1960. Author: Arizona Law of Evidence, 1960, Education of a Congressman, 1972; co-author: The Job of the Congressman, 1966. Del. Democratic Nat. Conv., 1956; chmn. Ariz. delegation, 1972, Ariz. Volunteers for Stevenson, 1956; candidate for Dem. nomination for Pres., 1976; keynote speaker Dem. Nat. Conv., 1980. Served to capt. USAAF, 1942-46, PTO. Mem. ABA, Ariz. Bar Assn. (bd. govs.), Pima County Bar Assn. (exec. com.), Am. Judicature Soc., Am. Legion, Phi Kappa Phi, Phi Delta Phi. Office: 235 Cannon House Office Bldg Washington DC 20515 *

UDEVITZ, NORMAN, publishing executive; b. Cheyenne, Wyo., Jan. 22, 1929; s. Jay and Edith (Stienberg) U.; m. Marsha Rae Dinner, Dec. 17, 1960; children: Jane, Kathryn, Andrew. Student, U. Colo., 1946-49. With Cheyenne Newspapers Inc. Cheyenne, 1949-54; editor-pub. Wyo. Buffalo, Cheyenne, 1954-63; account supr. Tilds & Cantz Advt. Agy., L.A., 1963-66; exec. v.p. Fitzgerald, Maahs & Miller, L.A., 1966-71; staff writer The Denver Post, 1971-88; dir. pubs. Am. Water Works Assn., Denver, 1988—. Sgt. USNG, 1950-53. Named Colo.'s Outstanding Journalist, U. Colo., 1977; recipient Pulitzer Prize Gold medal Columbia U., 1986. Mem. Investigative Reporters and Editors Inc., (bd. dirs. 1978-80, 81-83), The Newspaper Guild (McWilliams award 1976, 77). Jewish. Home: 4677 E Euclid Ave Littleton CO 80121 Office: Am Water Works Assn 6666 W Quincy Ave Denver CO 80235

UDICK, ROBERT E., newspaper executive; b. Colorado Springs, Colo., May 27, 1922; s. Albert Earl and Edna (Young) U. Student, Colo. Coll. Staff corr. Rocky Mountain News, Denver, 1947-49, United Press, Denver and Santa Fe, 1950-51; war corr. United Press, Korea, 1951-53; later became mgr. Hong Kong and Manila burs.; then mgr. for Southeast Asia, hdqrs., Singapore; editor, pub. Bangkok World, until 1967; pub. Pacific Daily News, Agana, Guam, until 1985; cons. Gannett Co., Inc., 1985—; Mem. civilian adv. bd. 8th Air Force; mem. Navy League, Guam Stock Exchange. Bd. regents U. Guam. Served with Coast Arty., Inf., Signal Corps, World War II. Mem. Fgn. Corr. Assn. Thailand (pres.), Phi Delta Theta. Club: Rotary. Office: Pacific Daily News PO Box DN Agana GU 96910

UDWADIA, FIRDAUS ERACH, engineering educator, consultant; b. Bombay, Aug. 28, 1947; came to U.S., 1968.; s. Erach Rustam and Perin P.

(Lentin) U.; m. Farida Gagrat, Jan. 6, 1977; children: Shanaira, Zubin. BS, Indian Inst. Tech., Bombay, 1968; MS, Calif. Inst. Tech., 1969, PhD, 1972; MBA, U. So. Calif., 1985. Mem. faculty Calif. Inst. Tech., Pasadena, 1972-74; asst. prof. engrng. U. So. Calif., Los Angeles, 1974-77, assoc. prof., 1977-83, prof. mech. engrng., civil engrng. and bus. adminstrn., 1983-86; prof. engrng, bus. adminstrn. U. So. Calif., 1986—; also bd. dirs. Structural Identification Computing Facility U. So. Calif.; cons. Jet Propulsion Lab., Pasadena, Calif., 1978—, Argonne Nat. Lab., Chgo., 1982-83, Air Force Rocket Lab., Edwards AFB, Calif., 1984—. Contbr. articles to profl. jours. Bd. dirs. Crisis Mgmt. Ctr., U. So. Calif. NSF grantee, 1976—. Mem. AIAA, ASCE, Am. Acad. Mechanics, Soc. Indsl. and Applied Math., Seismological Soc. Am., Sigma Xi (Earthquake Engring. Research Inst., 1971, 74, 84). Home: 2100 S Santa Anita Arcadia CA 91006 Office: U So Calif University Park 364 DRB Los Angeles CA 90089-1114

UEHLING, BARBARA STANER, educational administrator; b. Wichita, Kans., June 12, 1932; d. Roy W. and Mary Elizabeth (Hilt) Staner; m. Stanley Johnson; children: Jeffrey Steven, David Edward. B.A., U. Wichita, 1954; M.A., Northwestern U., 1956, Ph.D., 1958; hon. degree, Drury Coll., 1978; LL.D. (hon.), Ohio State U., 1979. Mem. psychology faculty Oglethorpe U., Atlanta, 1959-64, Emory U., Atlanta, 1966-69; adj. prof. U. R.I., Kingston, 1970-72; dean Roger Williams Coll., Bristol, R.I., 1972-74; dean arts scis. Ill. State U., Normal, 1974-76; provost U. Okla., Norman, 1976-78; chancellor U. Mo.-Columbia, 1978-86, U. Calif., Santa Barbara, 1987—; sr. vis. fellow Am. Council Edn., 1987; cons. higher edn. State of N.Y., 1973-74; cons. North Central Accreditation Assn., 1975-86; mem. nat. educator adv. com. to Comptroller Gen. U.S., 1978; mem. commn. on mil.-higher edn. relations Am. Council on Edn., 1978-86; bd. dirs. Merc Bancorp, Inc., 1979-86, Meredith Corp., 1980—. Author: Women in Academe: Steps to Greater Equality, 1978; contbr. articles to profl. jours. Bd. dirs., chmn. Nat. Ctr. Higher Edn. Mgmt. Systems; bd. dirs. Am. Council on Edn., 1979-83, treas., 1982-83; trustee Carnegie Found. for Advancement of Teaching, 1980-86, Santa Barbara Med. Found. Clinic, 1989—; mem. adv. com. Nat. Ctr. for Food and Agrl. Policy; bd. dirs. Resources for the Future; mem. NCAA Select Com. on Athletics, 1983-84, NCAA Presdl. Commn.; pres. elect Western Coll. Assn.; mem. Nat. Council on Ednl. Research, 1980-82; mem. Bus.-Higher Edn. Forum, Am. Council on Edn. Social Sci. Research Council fellow, 1954-55; NSF fellow, 1956-57; NIMH postdoctoral research fellow, 1964-67; named one of 100 Young Leaders of Acad. Change Mag. and ACE, 1978; recipient Alumni Achievement award Wichita State U., 1978, Alumnae award Northwestern U., 1985. Mem. Am. Assn. Higher Edn. (dir. 1974-77, pres. 1977-78), Western Coll. Assn. (pres.-elect 1988), Internat. Com. for Study of Ednl. Exchange (chair 1988—), Sigma Xi. Office: U Calif Cheadle Hall Santa Barbara CA 93106

UHDE, LARRY JACKSON, labor union administrator; b. Marshalltown, Iowa, June 2, 1939; s. Harold Clarence and Rexine Elizabeth (Clemens) U.; m. Linda-Lee Betty Best, Nov. 9, 1960; children: Mark Harold, Brian Raymon. Student, Sacramento City Coll., 1966, Am. River Coll., Sacramento, 1975. Equipment supr. Granite Constrn., Sacramento, 1962-69; truck driver Iowa Wholesale, Marshalltown, Iowa, 1969-70; mgr. Reddy & Essex, Inc., Sacramento, 1970-71; dispatcher Operating Engrs. Local Union 3, Sacramento, 1971-73; tng. coord. Operating Engrs. Joint Apprenticeship Com., Sacramento, 1973-83, apprenticeship div. mgr., 1983-87, adminstr., 1987—; chmn. First Women in Apprenticeship Seminar, 1972; com. mem. Sacramento Gen. Joint Apprenticeship Com., 1973-74; rep. Sacramento Sierra's Bldg. and Constrn. Trades Coun., 1973-75; com. mem. Valley Area Constrn. Opportunity Program, 1974-77. Contbr. articles to trade papers. Mgr., v.p. Little League, 1971-75; co-chmn. Fall Festival St. Roberts Ch., 1973-75; v.p. Navy League Youth Program, 1978-81; instr. ARC, 1978-87; counselor United Way 1980—; bd. mem. County CETA Bd., 1981-82; coun. mem. Calif. Balance of State Pvt. Industry Coun., 1982-83, Sacramento Pvt. Industry Coun., 1982-83; coord. Acholic Recovery Program, 1984—. With USN, 1956-60. Mem. We. Apprenticeship Coords. Assn. (exec. dir. 1987—), Calif. Apprenticeship Coords. Assn. (statewide dir. 1987—), U.S. Apprenticeship Assn., Sacremento Valley Apprenticeship Tng. Coords. Assn. (rep.), Rancho Murieta Country Club, U.S. Golf Assn., Bing Maloney Golf Club. Democrat. Roman Catholic. Office: Operating Engrs Apprentice 7388 Murieta Dr Rancho Murieta CA 95683

UHL, CHARLES DANIEL, JR., marketing executive; b. Anaconda, Mont., Dec. 13, 1938; s. Charles Daniel Sr. and Mayme Patti Uhl; m. Vera Ruggles, Jan. 20, 1959; children: Kimberly Ann, Kenneth D., Angela L. BA, Mont. State Coll., 1960. Sales mgr. Reiters Marina, Billings, Mont., 1964-74; v.p. Alphenhaus Sports Motors, Great Falls, Mont., 1974-79, Avitel, Inc., Great Falls, 1979-84; nat. sales mgr. M/A-Com, Hickory, N.C., 1984-86, Gen. Instrument Corp., San Diego, 1986—; v.p. Nat. Satellite Distbrs., 1980-81. With USN, 1956-58. Republican. Roman Catholic. Office: Gen Instrument Corp 6262 Lusk Blvd San Diego CA 92121

UHL, PHILIP EDWARD, marine artist; b. Toledo, Aug. 19, 1949; s. Philip Edward and Betty Jean (Mayes) U. Student, Dayton Art Inst., 1967-68, Art Students League, 1974. Creative dir. Ctr. for Civic Initiative, Milw., 1969-71; art dir. Artco Advt. Agy., Honolulu, 1972-73; artist, photographer Assn. Honolulu Artists, 1974-77; pres. Uhl Enterprises div. Makai Photography, Honolulu, 1977—, Videoscapes div. Channel Sea TV, Honolulu, 1977—; cons. Pan Am. Airways, N.Y.C. and Honolulu, 1979-84, ITTC Travel Ctr., Honolulu, 1982-83, Royal Hawaiian Ocean Racing Club, Honolulu, 1985-86, Sail Am.-Am.'s Cup Challenge, Honolulu, 1985-86. Co-producer video documentary White on Water, 1984 (Emmy 1984), Racing the Winds of Paradise (Golden Monitor award Internat. TV Assn. 1989); producer Joy of Life (recipient Golden Monitor award Internat. TV Assn. 1988); pub., art dir. mags., promotional publs. Pan Am. Clipper Cup, 1980, 82, 84 and Kenwood Cup, 1986; photographer: (book) Nautical Quarterly (Soc. Publ. Designers award 1984); contbr. numerous articles, photos to yachting publs. vol. VISTA, 1969-71. Mem. Am. Soc. Mag. Photographers, U.S. Yacht Racing Union, Royal Hawaiian Ocean Racing Club (cons.), Royal Corinthian Yacht Club, Waikiki Yacht Club. Mem. Am. Film Inst., Internat. Platform Assn., Soc. Internat. Nautical Scribes, Honolulu Creative Group, U.S. Yacht Racing Union, Royal Hawaiian Ocean Racing Club (cons.), Royal Corinthian Yacht Club, Waikiki Yacht Club. Office: UHL Enterprises 1750 Kalakaua Century Ctr Ste 3-757 Honolulu HI 96826

UHLANER, JULIUS EARL, psychologist; b. Vienna, Apr. 22, 1917; came to U.S., 1928; naturalized 1928; s. Benjamin and Ethel U.; m. Vera Kolar, Sept. 3, 1949; children: Carole Jean, Lorraine Marie Hendrickson, Robert Theodore. BS, CUNY, 1938; MS, Iowa State U., 1941; PhD, NYU, 1947. Indsl. psychology asst. Ford Motor Co., Dearborn, Mich., 1940-41; rsch. asst. Iowa State U., Ames, 1940-41; rsch. assoc. NYU, 1941-42; asst. dir. tng. N.Y. State div. Vets. Affairs, N.Y.C., 1946-49; with U.S. Army Rsch. Inst., Washington, 1947-78, tech. dir., 1964-78; chief psychologist U.S. Army, Washington, 1964-78; adj. prof. psychology George Washington U., 1971—; v.p. Perceptronics, Inc., Woodland Hills, Calif., 1978-81; pres. Uhlaner Cons., Inc., Encino, Calif., 1981—. Author: Psychological Research in National Defense Today, 1964; cons. editor Jour. Applied Psychology, 1970—; contbr. articles to profl. jours. Served with USAF, 1944-46. Recipient Presdl. Mgmt. Improvement award, 1978. Fellow Am. Psychol. Assn. (pres. div. mil. psychology 1969-70), Human Factors Soc., Washington Acad. Scis., Iowa Acad. Scis., Ops. Rsch. Soc. Am.; mem. Cosmos Club, Psi Chi. Home and Office: 4258 Bonavita Dr Encino CA 91436

UHLMAN, THOMAS MICHAEL, electronics company executive; b. N.Y.C., Mar. 14, 1947; s. Rudolph E. and Hilde B. (Igersheimer) U.; m. Elizabeth C. Thomas, Sept. 24, 1988. AB in Polit. Sci., U. Rochester, 1968; PhD in Polit. Sch., U. N.C., 1975; MS in Bus., Stanford U., 1983. Asst. prof., then assoc. prof. polit. sci. U. Mo., St. Louis, 1975-80; dir. productivity improvement U.S. Dept. Edn., Washington, 1981-82; dir. Pres.'s Commn. on Indsl. Competitiveness, Washington, 1983-85; dir. corp. devel. Hewlett-Packard Co., Palo Alto, Calif., 1985—. Author: Racial Justice, 1977. Mem. Planning Execs. Forum of Conf. Bd., Machinery and Allied Products Inst. (council planning execs. 1986--). Office: Hewlett Packard Co Corp Devel Dept 3000 Hanover St Palo Alto CA 94304

UHRICH, RICHARD BECKLEY, hospital executive, physician; b. Pitts., June 11, 1932; s. Leroy Earl and Mabel Hoffer (Beckley) U.; m. Susan Kay Manning, May 25, 1985; children by previous marriage—Mark, Karen, Kimberly. B.S., Allegheny Coll., 1954; M.D., U. Pa., 1958; M.P.H., U. Calif.-Berkeley, 1966. Diplomate: Am. Bd. Preventive Medicine. Intern Lancaster Gen. Hosp., (Pa.), 1958-59; commd. asst. surg. USPHS, 1959, advanced through grades to med. dir., 1967; resident U. Calif., 1965-66; various adminstrv. positions regional and service unit levels Indian Health Services, until 1971; dir. div. programs ops. Indian Health Service, Health Services Adminstrn. USPHS, Washington, 1971-73; assoc. dir. div. profl. resources Office Internat. Health, Office Asst. Sec. for Health, HEW, Washington, 1973-74; assoc. dir. for program devel. and coordination Office Internat. Health, 1974-78; dir. Phoenix Indian Med. Ctr. and Phoenix Services Unit, 1978-81, ret., 1982; sr. adminstr. Good Samaritan Med Ctr., Phoenix, 1981-82, chief exec. officer, 1982—; mem. Phoenix Regional Hosp. Council, 1981—, pres., 1982-83; bd. dirs. Med. Ctr. Redevel. Corp., Phoenix; v.p. Samaritan Redevel. Corp., 1983—. Bd. dirs. Phoenix Symphony Orch., 1984—, Ariz. Sr. Olympics Bd., 1985—. Recipient Meritorious Service medal USPHS, 1973; recipient citation USPHS, 1973, Commd. Officers award, 1981. Mem. Ariz. Hosp. Assn. (bd. dirs. 1980-86, chmn. council on planning 1980-81, council on human resources 1982-83, council on patient care 1983-84, fin. com. 1984—), Am. Coll. Health Care Adminstrs., Am. Pub. Health Assn. Clubs: Arizona, University, Camelback Country (Phoenix). Office: Good Samaritan Med Ctr PO Box 2989 Phoenix AZ 85062

UHT, AUGUSTUS KINZEL, computer engineering educator; b. N.Y.C., July 19, 1955; s. Charles Frederick and Carol (Kinzel) U. BS, Cornell U., 1977, MEE, 1978; PhD, Carnegie-Mellon U., 1985. Registered profl. engr., N.Y., Pa. Assoc. engr. IBM, Hopewell Junction, N.Y., 1978-80; sr. assoc. engr. IBM, 1980-82; teaching intern dept. elec. and computer engring. Carnegie-Mellon U., Pitts., 1983; grad. asst., then vis. asst. prof. Carnegie-Mellon U., 1983-86; asst. prof. dept. computer sci. and engring. U. Calif.-San Diego, La Jolla, 1986—; mem. sci. adv. bd. Parallex Co., San Diego, 1988—. Contbr. to profl. publs.; inventor in computer concurrency field. Mem. IEEE, Assn. Computing Machinery, NSPE, Pitts. Cornell Alumni (head secondary schs. com. 1984-85). Office: U Calif San Diego Dept Computer Sci Engring C 014 La Jolla CA 92093

UKROPINA, JAMES ROBERT, energy company executive, lawyer; b. Fresno, Calif., Sept. 10, 1937; s. Robert J. and Persida (Angelich) U.; m. Priscilla Lois Brandenburg, June 16, 1962; children—Michael Steven, David Robert, Mark Gregory. A.B., Stanford U., 1959, M.B.A., 1961; LL.B., U. So. Calif., 1965. Bar: Calif. 1966, D.C. 1980. Assoc. firm O'Melveny & Myers, Los Angeles, 1965-72; partner O'Melveny & Myers, 1972-80; exec. v.p., gen. counsel Santa Fe Internat. Corp., Alhambra, Calif., 1980-84, dir., 1981-86; exec. v.p., gen. counsel Pacific Enterprises, Los Angeles, 1984-86, pres., dir., 1986—; bd. dirs. Security Pacific Corp., Lockheed Corp., Pacific Mut. Life Ins. Co.; lectr. in field. Editor-in-chief: So. Calif. Law Rev, 1964-65. Trustee Occidental Coll.; mem. adv. council Stanford Bus. Sch.; mem. Calif. Econ. Devel. Corp. Bd. Served with USAF, 1961-62. Mem. Am. Bar Assn., Calif. Bar Assn., Los Angeles County Bar Assn., Beta Theta Pi. Club: Calif. Office: Pacific Enterprises 801 S Grand Ave Los Angeles CA 90017

ULCH, BRYAN DEE, product development executive; b. Lansing, Mich., Apr. 12, 1948; s. Shirley Dee and Donna Mary U.; m. Madelyn Deborah Reckon, Oct. 10, 1971; 1 child, Jordan Michael. BSEE, Calif. Poly. U., 1971. Pilot capt. U.S. Army, 1971-75; research and devel. mgr. Rusco Electronic Systems, Glendale, Calif., 1975-77; projects mgr. FMC Corp. Agro Electronics, San Jose, Calif., 1977-80; v.p. Anchor Automation Inc., Chatsworth, Calif., 1980-; chief engr. Security Control System Inc., Chatsworth, Calif., 1984-; cons. in field. Facility dir. Congregation Beth Shalom, Valencia, Calif., 1982. Democrat. Jewish. Lodge: BPOE Elks. Home: 24576 Peachland Ave Santa Clarita CA 91321 Office: Anchor Automation Inc 20675 Bahama St Chatsworth CA 91311

ULF, FRANKLIN EDGAR, trust company executive; b. Pitts., Aug. 12, 1931; s. Franklin Edgar Jr. and Elizabeth (Carnes) U.; m. Betsy Roberts, Feb. 14, 1953; children: Bonnie, Brian. BA in Econs., Pomona Coll., Claremont, Calif., 1953; MBA in Fin., U. So. Calif., 1960. Fin. analyst Union Oil Co. of Calif., L.A., 1956-60; pres., chief exec. officer, co-founder Am. Investment Counseling, L.A., 1960-73; v.p., dir. of mktg. Scudder, Stevens & Clark, L.A., 1973-82; pres., chief exec. officer U.S. Trust Co. of Calif. N.A., L.A., 1982—; bd. dirs. Standard Ins. Co., Portland. Mem. exec. bd. L.A. Area Coun. Boy Scouts Am.; mem. adv. bd. Calif. Mus. Sci. and Industry; bd. dirs. Queen of Angels/Hollywood Presbyn. Med. Ctr.; chmn. bd. dirs. Pacific Homes Corp.; trustee Pomona Coll., San Francisco Theol. Sem.; elder San Marino Community Presbyn. Ch. Lt. USN, 1953-66. Mem. Investment Counsel Assn. Am. (chartered investment counselor), Western Pension Conf. Republican. Lodges: Rotary (L.A.) (pres. #5 1981-82). Clubs: Jonathan, San Gabriel Country, The Calif. Office: US Trust Co of Calif NA 555 S Flower St #2700 Los Angeles CA 90071-2429

ULLE, KARL FRANK, JR., architect, product designer; b. San Diego, Nov. 14, 1951; s. Karl Frank and Sherill Colleen (Cosby) U.; m. Barbara Marie Cagliero, Jan. 10, 1981; 1 child, Nicholas Adam. AA, Southwestern Coll., Chula Vista, Calif., 1973; BA, San Diego State U., 1975; MArch., So. Calif. Inst. Architecture, 1987. Owner, prin. Furniture Design & Reconstrn.Co., Pacific Beach, Calif., 1979-80; constrn. carpenter Furniture Design & Reconstrn.Co., San Diego, 1980-81; computer aided technician Deardorff & Deardorff Engring., San Diego, 1982-83; owner, mgr. Design Svcs., Northridge, Calif., 1984; project coord., computer aided design mgr. John Ash, A.I.A. & Assocs., L.A., 1985-86; project mgr. Marc Tarasuck, A.I.A. & Assocs., San Diego, 1987-89, Henry Hester, A.I.A. & Assocs., La Jolla, Calif., 1989—. Fund raiser Am. Cancer Soc.; mem. San Diego Hist. Soc., San Diego Zool. Soc. Mem. AIA (assoc.). Republican. Home: 1012 Country Club Dr Escondido CA 92025 Office: Henry Hester AIA & Assocs PO Box 1739 La Jolla CA 92038

ULLIMAN, JOSEPH JAMES, forester, educator; b. Springfield, Ohio, July 19, 1935; s. Joseph James Sr. and Iola Mae (Roth) U.; m. Barbara Blessing Gish, Apr. 29, 1961; children: Kathryn Nicole, Barbara Anne, Mark Joseph. BA in English, U. Dayton, 1958; MF in Forest Mgmt., U. Minn., 1968, PhD in Forest Mgmt., 1971. Research asst. U. Minn., Mpls., 1966-68, from instr. to asst. prof., 1968-74; mem. staff land use planning Willamette Nat. Forest, Eugene, Oreg., 1973; from assoc. prof. to prof. U. Idaho, Moscow, 1974—; dir. U. Idaho FWR Remote Sensing Ctr.; co-dir. U. Idaho Remote Sensing Research Unit, Moscow, assoc. dean 1988-89, dept. head of forest resources, 1989—; cons. USAID, 1979—. Contbr. numerous articles on forestry and remote sensing to profl. jours. and books. Chmn. Natural Resources Com., Moscow, 1980-81, Environ. Commn., South St. Paul, Minn., 1972-74; pres. Moscow Swim Team Parents Assn., 1976. Mem. Am. Soc. Photogrammetry and Remote Sensing (pres. Minn. chpt. 1974, dep. dir. 1983-85, Ford Bartlett award 1981), Soc. Am. Foresters (counselor 1981-84, chmn. remote sensing working group 1982-84), Internat. Soc. Photogrammetry (chmn. working group 1981-84). Democrat. Roman Catholic. Home: 2226 Weymouth St Moscow ID 83843 Office: U Idaho Coll of Forestry Moscow ID 83843

ULLMAN, CORNELIUS GUMBEL, conservation consultant; b. Cleve., Sept. 14, 1906; s. Lee J. and Daisy (Gumbel) U.; B.S. in Econs., U. Calif. at Berkeley, 1928; M.S. in Agr., U. Calif. at Davis, 1934; m. Robie Jenkins, Jan. 24, 1936; children—Cornell, Lorna, Maury. Area agronomist soil conservation service U.S. Dept. Agr., 1935-41, dist. conservationist, 1941-50; field rep. Calif. Soil Conservation Commn., Sacramento, 1950-57; program coordinator div. soil conservation Calif. Dept. Conservation, Ventura, 1957-68, resource conservationist, 1967-68; resource conservation cons., 1968—. Recipient Cert. of Appreciation U.S. Dept. Agr., 1988. Fellow Am. Geog. Soc.; mem. Am. Geophys. Union, AAAS, Western Soc. Soil Sci., Soil Conservation Soc. Am., Sigma Xi. Republican. Club: Commonwealth of Calif. Home and Office: 50 Debussy Ln Ventura CA 93003

ULLMAN, DANA GREGORY, educational administrator; b. L.A., Dec. 22, 1951; s. Sanford and Estelle Nancy (Pulvers) U. BA, U. Calif., Berkeley, 1975, MPH, 1978. Dir. Homeopathic Ednl. Services, Berkeley, Calif., 1975—; publisher North Atlantic Books, Berkeley, 1979—; pres., founder Found. for Homeopathic Edn. & Rsch., 1986—; conf. organizer U. Calif. Berkeley Extension, 1981. Author: Homeopathy: Medicine for the 21st Century, 1988; co-author: Everybody's Guide to Homeopathic Medicine, 1984, Medical Self-Care book award, 1985. Fellow San Francisco Found., 1977-78, grantmaker, 1977-78; mem. Media Alliance, 1983—; fundraiser Dem. Party, 1972; advisor Elmwood Inst., Berkeley, 1986—. Mem. Am. Pub. Health Assn., Soc. Pub. Health Edn., Nat. Ctr. Homeopathy (bd. dirs., Washington, 1985—), Internat. Found. for Homeopathy, Assn. for Humanistic Psychology (exec. bd. dirs. 1986—), Calif. Bd. Med. Quality Assurance (cons. 1980-81). Office: Homeopathic Ednl Svcs 2124 Kittredge St Berkeley CA 94704

ULLRICH, MAGDALENE MARIE, nursing administrator; b. Hammond, Ind., June 27, 1957; d. Howard William and Theresa Ruth (Michuda) U. A in Nursing, Purdue U. N.W., Hammond, 1977; BS, Coll. St. Francis, Joliet, Ill., 1987. Critical care mgr. St. Mary Med. Ctr., Gary, Ind., 1980-83; Medicare coordinator Kimberly Nurses, El Paso, Tex., 1983-84; regional supr. Med. Health Care Services, El Paso, 1984-86; nursing supr. Landmark Med. Ctr., Inc., El Paso, 1986—. Mem. Nat. Assn. Female Execs. Democrat. Roman Catholic. Home: 125 Torrey Pines PO Box 1003 Santa Teresa NM 88008

ULMER, HAROLD WILLIAM, electronic engineer, manufacturing company executive; b. Los Angeles, Oct. 1, 1912; s. Henry Charles and Elizabeth Anna (Baumetz) U.; m. Olga Katherine Koehlert, Jan. 2, 1943 (dec. Aug. 1988); children: Janice Irene, Ronalee Anne Ulmer Elsberry, James R. (dec.). Student Pasadena City Coll., 1930-31, student Oceanside-Carlsbad Coll., 1934-35, Palomar Coll., 1962. Registered profl. engr., Calif. Sr. vacuum tube engr. Fed. Telegraph Co., Newark, 1942; sect. head power tube div. Raytheon Mfg. Co., Waltham, Mass., 1942-45; research engr. Convair, San Diego, 1946-51; pres., chief engr. Vacuum Tube Products, Oceanside, Calif., 1951-58, dir., 1955-58; electron tube div. mgr. Hughes Aircraft Co., Los Angeles, 1959; pres., chief engr. H.W. Ulmer Co., Oceanside, 1960-64; chief engr. M U Inc., Oceanside, 1965—, pres., dir., 1965-83. Contbr. articles to profl. jours. Author engring. manuals. Mem. IEEE (sr., life), Calif. Soc. Profl. Engrs. (charter), NSPE, Am. Soc. Quality Control, Am. Vacuum Soc. Republican. Methodist. Club: Palomar Radio (North San Diego County). Home: 2550 Pahvant St Oceanside CA 92054

ULOSEVICH, STEVEN NILS, military officer, educator; b. Tampa, Fla., Nov. 19, 1947; s. Steven Anthony and Coragene (Paulson) U.; m. Pamela Elmeda Locke, June 27, 1970; children: Christina, Garrett. BA, U. N.C., Greensboro, 1969; MBA, Webster U., 1981. Commd. USAF, 1970; advanced through grades to majo; ops. officer Detachment 5, 40th Aero. Rescue and Recovery Squadron/MAC, 1975; instr. pilot 96th Flying Tng. Squadron, Air Tng. Command, 1976-77; class comdr. 82d Student Squadron/ATC, 1977-78; project officer Women in Undergrad. Pilot Tng. Test Program, 1979; chief Life Support Br. Hdqrs., 1979-81; exec. officer Air Tng. Command's Contingency Support Staff, 1981; comdr. Detachment 2, 3636th Combat Crew Tng. Wing, 1981-83; chief Acad. Tng. Br., 12th Student Squadron, 1984-85, Life Support Systems Div. Hdqrs. Pacific Air Forces, Hickam AFB, Hawaii, 1985—; adj. faculty Embry-Riddle Aero. U., Honolulu, 1988—. Contbr. articles to profl. jours. Mem. Am. Security coun., Washington, 1979—, nat. adv. bd., 1981—; state advisor U.S. Congl. Adv. Bd., 1981—; mem. U.S. Def. Com., 1982—. Mem. Survival and Flight Equipment Assn. (chpt. v.p. 1980-81, pres. 1986-88), Air Force Assn., Mil. Order World Wars, Order of Daedalians. Home: 629 Sperry Loop Wahiawa HI 96786

ULRICH, DELMONT MARION, physician; b. Connell, Wash., Jan. 22, 1919; s. Otto Carl and Hannah M. (Zimmerman) U.; m. Doris Pauline Swanson, Mar. 25, 1946; children: Beverly, James, Dean. Student, U. Wash., 1937-40; BS, U. Minn., 1941, MD, 1944. Diplomate Am. Bd. Internal Medicine. Intern Milw. County Hosp., 1944, resident internal medicine, 1944-46; practice medicine specializing in internal medicine Seattle, 1949—; assoc. clin. prof. medicine U. Wash., Seattle, 1950—; pres. med. staff Providence Hosp., Seattle, 1968-69. Served to capt. AUS, 1946-48. Mem. AMA, Seattle Acad. Medicine, NW Soc. Clin. Research, Wash. State Soc. Internat. Medicine (pres. 1956-57), Theta Chi, Phi Rho Sigma. Republican. Episcopalian. Club: Seattle Yacht. Home: 5017 NE Laurelcrest Ln Seattle WA 98105

ULRICH, PAUL GRAHAM, lawyer, author, editor; b. Spokane, Nov. 29, 1938; s. Donald Gunn and Kathryn (Vandercook) U.; m. Kathleen Nelson Smith, July 30, 1982; children—Kathleen Elizabeth, Marilee Rae, Michael Graham. B.A. with high honors, U. Mont., 1961; J.D., Stanford U., 1964. Bar: Calif. 1965, Ariz. 1966, U.S. Supreme Ct. 1969, U.S. Ct. Appeals (9th cir.) 1965. Law clk. judge U.S. Ct. Appeals, 9th Circuit, San Francisco, 1964-65; assoc. firm Lewis and Roca, Phoenix, 1965-70; ptnr. Lewis and Roca, 1970-85; pres. Paul G. Ulrich PC, Phoenix, 1985—; owner Pathway Enterprises, 1985—; judge pro tem Ariz. Ct. Appeals Div. 1, Phoenix, 1986; instr. Thunderbird Grad. Sch. Internat. Mgmt., 1968-69, Ariz. State U., Coll. Law, 1970-73, 78, Scottsdale Community Coll., 1975-77, also continuing legal edn. seminars. Author: Applying Management and Motivation Concepts to Law Offices, 1985; editor, contbr.: Arizona Appellate Handbook, 1978—; Working with Legal Assistants, 1980, 81; Future Directions for Law Office Management, 1982; People in the Law Office, 1985-86; contbg. editor Law Office Economics and Management, 1984—; contbr. numerous articles to profl. jours. Mem. Ariz. Supreme Ct. Task Force on Ct. Orgn. and Adminstrn., 1988—; bd. visitors Stanford U. Law Sch., 1974-77. Served with U.S. Army, 1956. Recipient continuing legal edn. award State Bar Ariz., 1978, 86, Harrison Tweed Spl. Merit award Am. Law Inst./ABA, 1987. Fellow Ariz. Bar Found. (founding 1985—); mem. ABA (chmn. selection and utilization of staff personnel com., econs. of law sect. 1979-81, mem. standing com. legal assts. 1982-86, co-chmn. joint project on appellate handbooks 1983-85, co-chmn. fed. appellate handbook project 1985-88, chmn. com. on liaison with non-lawyer orgns. Econs. of Law Practice sect. 1985-86), Ariz. Bar Assn. (chmn. econs. of law practice com. 1980-81, co-chmn. lower ct. improvement com. 1982-85, co-chmn. Ariz. Appellate handbook project 1976—), Maricopa County Bar Assn., Calif. Bar Assn., Am. Law Inst., Am. Judicature Soc. (Spl. Merit Citation 1987), Phi Kappa Phi, Phi Alpha Delta, Sigma Phi Epsilon. Republican. Presbyterian. Home: 107 E El Caminito Rd Phoenix AZ 85020 Office: 3030 N Central Ave Ste 1000 Phoenix AZ 85012

UMEZAWA, HIROOMI, physics educator, researcher; b. Saitama-ken, Japan, Sept. 20, 1924; came to Can., 1975; s. Junichi and Takako (Sato) U.; m. Tamae Yamagami, July 30, 1958; children: Rui, Ado. B of Engring., U. Nagoya, Japan, 1947, DSc in Physics, 1952. Research asst. U. Nagoya, 1947-53, assoc. prof., 1953; assoc. prof. U. Tokyo, 1955, prof., 1960-64; prof. U. Napoli Inst. Theoretical Physics, Italy, 1964-66; prof. U. Wis., Milw., 1967-67, disting. prof., 1967-75; dir. Inst. Theoretical Physics, Helsinki, Finland, 1965; group leader on structure of matter Centre of Nat. Research Naples div., Italy, 1964-66; Killam Meml. prof. sci., prof. physics U. Alta., Edmonton, Can., 1975—; vis. prof. U. Wash., Seattle, 1956, U. Md., College Park, 1957, U. Iowa, Iowa City, 1957, U. Marseille, France, 1959. Mem. editorial bd. Physics Essays, NRC Can.; contbr. numerous articles to profl. jours. ICI fellow U. Manchester, Eng., 1953-55; Lady Davis Sr. scholar, Israel, 1989; Two books published in honor of his 60th birthday, 1985, 86. Fellow N.Y. Acad. Scis., Am. Phys. Soc., Royal Soc. Can. Office: U Alta, Dept of Physics, Edmonton, AB Canada T6G 2J1

UMILE, LAUREL FLANDERS, psychotherapist; b. Longmont, Colo., Aug. 15, 1942; d. Laurence Burdette and Eleanor (Carlson) F.; m. Anthony Umile, July 4, 1965; children: Mark Anthony, Barbara Lynette. BA, U. Colo., 1960; postgrad., U. Calif., Berkeley, 1965, MSW, 1969. Lic. clin. social worker, Colo. Caseworker Colo. Dept. Social Services, Boulder, 1969-70, 1975-79, supr. III, 1979-81, adminstr. IV, 1981-85; adoption caseworker Friends for All Children, Boulder, 1973-75; pvt. practice psychotherapy Longmont, Colo., 1985—; instr. intro. to social work Lees Jr. Coll., Jackson, Ky., 1970; trainer Family Resource Ctr., Boulder, 1974; field instr. Colo. State U., Ft. Collins, 1982, Denver U., 1983; presenter child abuse workshops, 1983-84. Cellist Longmont Symphony Orch., 1972-83; vol. Planned Parenthood, San Francisco, 1966, Telegraph Hill Neighborhood Ctr., San Francisco, 1965; chmn. Colo. Adoption Coalition, 1987; vol. pilot project Futurist Century Sch., 1986; trustee Flanders Found., 1975—. Mem. Nat. Assn. Social Workers (diplomate), Boulder Psychiat. Inst. (affiliate), St. Vrain Women's Connection, Audubon Soc., Sierra Club, Longmont Assn.

for Helping Profls., Attender Soc. of Friends, Phi Beta Kappa. Democrat. Office: 2919 17th St Ste 207 Longmont CO 80501

UMLAND, PAULINE SAWYER, realtor; b. Salem, Mass., June 14, 1903; d. Arthur Franklin and Nellie Susan (Page) Sawyer; m. E. Eugene Umland, Aug. 26, 1932 (dec. May 1969); children: Gretchen Umland Kingsbury, Peter S., Diana Umland Bos. BBA, Boston U., 1925, MBA, 1928. Fin. sec. Walnut Hill Sch., Natick, Mass., 1927-29; buyer Jordan Marsh Co., Boston, 1929-31, R.H. White Co., Boston, 1931-32; sec.-treas. Umland & Co. Advt., San Francisco, 1949-54, Umland-Eastman-Becker Advt., San Francisco, 1954-58; assoc. Rochex & Rochex Realtors, San Mateo, Calif., 1958-77, Jane Powell, Realtor, San Mateo, Calif., 1977—. Vol. Mills Hosp. Aux.; mem. life McKinley Sch. PTA, Peninsula Braille Transcribers Guild. Mem. AAUW, Nat. Assn. Realtors, Calif. Assn. Realtors, San Mateo-Burlingame Bd. Realtors (Realtor Assn. of Yr. award 1987), Gamma Phi Beta. Republican. Methodist. Home: 416 Villa Terr Apt 1 San Mateo CA 94401 Office: Jane Powell Realtor 255 Baldwin Ave San Mateo CA 94401

UMPHRES, JERRY DARMOND, senior electronics technologist; b. Utopia, Tex., Dec. 26, 1931; s. Johnnie D. and George Ann (Cavitte) U.; m. Annette Ruth Hooten, Jan. 29, 1954 (div. Feb. 1974); children: Jerry Darmond Jr., Dana Leigh; m. Constance Elizabeth Ross, May 14, 1976; 1 child, Jolie Danielle. Sr. technologist Northrop-Ventura, Newbury Park, Calif., 1957-63; sr. technician space div. Chrysler Corp., New Orleans, 1963-65, Lockheed Elec. Co., Clearlake City, Tex., 1965-66; sr. technologist EG & G Inc., Albuquerque, 1966-75; technician III Dinalectron Corp., Hollaman Air Force Base, N.Mex., 1975-76, Mo. Research Labs Inc., Aluquerque, 1976; sr. technologist U. Calif., Los Alamos, N.Mex., 1976—. Bd. dirs., pres. bd. Los Alamos County Coun. on Alcoholism, 1982-88. Sgt. USMC, 1950-54, Korea. Mem. IEEE, Civitan, Masons. Republican. Home: 718 43rd St Los Alamos NM 87544 Office: Univ California Los Alamos Nat Lab Los Alamos NM 87545

UNDERWOOD, RALPH EDWARD, computer systems engineer; b. Houston, Sept. 26, 1947; s. Harry Anson and Ethel Jackson Underwood; m. Linda Sue Merkel, Apr. 10, 1976. BS in Biology, Baker U., 1969; JD, Washburn U., 1973; MS in Computer Sci., Kans. U., 1984. Bar: Kans, 1973. Free-lance stock and options trader Prairie Village, Kans., 1974-79; mem. staff BDM Corp., Leavenworth, Kans., 1982-84; sr. research and devel. engr. Ford Aerospace and Communications Corp., Colorado Springs, Colo., 1984-87, subcontract adminstr., 1987-89; engr. Computer Tech. Assocs., Colorado Springs, 1989—. Patentee in field. Mem. ABA, IEEE, Armed Forces Communications and Electronics Assn., Kans. Bar Assn., Upsilon Pi Epsilon, Sigma Phi Epsilon (social chmn. 1968, asst. ho. mgr. 1968, sec./treas. sr. council 1969), Phi Alpha Delta. Office: Computer Tech Assocs 7150 Campus Dr Ste 100 Colorado Springs CO 80920

UNDERWOOD, THOMAS WOODBROOK, communications company executive; b. Royal Oak, Mich., Nov. 29, 1930; s. Elmer and Della Marie (Zimmer) U.; m. Louise Virginia, May 24, 1953 (dec. Feb. 1979); children: Ann Marie Underwood Shuman, Dan and Dave (twins). BAS in Elec. Engring., Milw. Sch. Engring., 1957. Service analyst, writer ITT Gillfillan, Los Angeles, 1958-60; sr. tech. editor, writer Smithkline Beckman, Fullerton, Calif., 1960-78; tech. com. mgr. Smithkline Beckman, Brea, Calif., 1978-85; pres. Tranwood Communications, Santa Ana, Calif., 1985—. Tech. editor, writer manuals for manned space flights to Mars and the moon. Served to staff sgt. USAF, 1950-54, Korea. Mem. Soc. Tech. Communications (sr., treas. 1966, 88), Am. Med. Writers Assn, U.S. C. of C., Santa Ana C. of C. Democrat. Methodist. Office: Tranwood Communications 2122 S Grand Ste L Box 15101 Santa Ana CA 92705

UNGAR, RICHARD JAMES, construction executive; b. Cin., Aug. 2, 1949; s. Richard Gidding and Joan (Salinger) U.; m. Ricki Krauss, Apr. 24, 1977; children: Cameron Bernard, Bradley Todd. BBA, U. Ky., Lexington, 1971. V.p. Ultima Corp., Cin., 1971-75; account exec. Merrill Lynch, Phoenix, 1975-77, Dean Witter Reynolds, Sun City, Ariz., 1977-78; bd. dirs., treas. Joric Corp., Scottsdale, Ariz., 1979—; pres., chief exec. officer, treas. Moon Valley Enterprises, Phoenix, 1978-80; mgr. constrn. Delcon Devel., Inc., Tempe, Ariz., 1981-83; pres., chief exec. officer, treas. Bedford West Devel., Inc., Phoenix, 1983—. Mem. Ariz. Contractors Assn. (bd. dirs., treas. 1987—).

UNGER, ARLENE KLEIN, employee assistance coordinator; b. Bklyn., May 12, 1952; d. Eli and Harriet Barbara (Shapiro) Klein; m. Stefan Howard Unger, Aug. 19, 1979; 1 child, Max Elias. BS with distinction, Emerson Coll., 1974; MS, So. Conn. State Coll., 1976, Calif. State U., Hayward, 1981; postgrad., Western Grad. Sch. Psychology, Palo Alto, Calif., 1987—. Site adminstr., teaching specialist Severely Delayed Langs. Program Santa Clara (Calif.) County, 1976-81; language-movement counselor Peninsula Children's Ctr., Palo Alto, 1981-83; marriage, family and child counselor Woodside (Calif.) Psychol. Services, 1983-84; dir. tng. and sales Human Resource Services Employee Assistance Program, Sunnyvale, Calif., 1984-86; pvt. practice psychol. counseling Palo Alto, 1984-86; regional Employee Assistance mgr. Occupational Health Services, Sunnyvale, 1986—; mental health counselor, instr. Foothill Coll., Los Altos, Calif., 1984-85; exec. dir. Sunnyvale Childrens' Arts and Movement Program, 1979-81, Cafe Motek, 1976-81; vol. instr. in music and movement Ohlone Sch., Palo Alto, 1986—; founder, pres. Boutique Supply, Palo Alto, 1985—; frequent speaker to groups, orgns. Active Palo Alto Docent. Mem. Assn. for Counseling and Devel., Assn. Labor Mgmt. Adminstrs. and Cons. on Alcoholism (conf. chair Santa Clara chpt. 1987—), Calif. Assn. Marriage and Family Counselors, Assn. Tng. and Devel., Am. Dance Therapy Assn. Clubs: Palo Alto Run, Santa Clara Decathlon. Home: 2250 Webster Ave Palo Alto CA 94301

UNGER, LES, automotive executive; b. Chgo., Jan. 18, 1943; s. Hunt Herman and Anni (Lawrence) U.; m. Sherry Jeanne Sarginson, July 31, 1964; children: Amy, Holly, Kelly. BBA, Northwestern U., 1964, MBA in Mktg., 1967. Field mgr. Ford Motor Co., Dallas, 1967-70, bus. mgmt. mgr., 1973-74, instr. Ford Mktg. Inst., 1972-73, mgr. light truck merchandising, 1974-75; asst. mgr. sales tng. Toyota Motor Sales, U.S.A., Torrance, Calif., 1980-83, mgr. nat. motorsports div., 1984—. Fellow Internat. Motor Sports Assn., Sports Car Club Am., So. Calif. Off-Road Race Enthusiasts, High Desert Racing Assn. Republican. Methodist. Office: Toyota Motor Sales USA 19001 S Western Torrance CA 90509

UNGS, TIMOTHY JOHN, aerospace medicine physician, coast guard officer; b. Dyersville, Iowa, Feb. 8, 1952; s. David Harold and Helen Mae (Phelps) U. BS, Oreg. State U., 1973; MD, U. Oreg., 1977; MS, Wright State U., 1987. Diplomate Am. Bd. Preventive Medicine. Commd. officer USPHS, 1978, advanced through grades to comdr.; med. officer USCG, Kodiak, Alaska, 1978-80; flight surgeon USCG, Port Angeles, Wash., 1980-85, Kodiak, 1987—; mem. resident faculty Wright State U., Dayton, Ohio, 1985-87, asst. clin. prof. aerospace medicine, 1987—. Contbr. articles to med. jours. Recipient physician's recognition award AMA, 1980, 83, 86, 89. Fellow Am. Coll. Preventive Medicine, Aerospace Med. Assn. (assoc.); mem. Am. Acad. Family Practice, Assn. Mil. Surgeons U.S., Human Factors Soc. Office: USCG Support Ctr Box 2 - Medical Kodiak AK 99619

UNRUH, DAN A., education educator; b. Clatskanie, Oreg., Feb. 21, 1930; s. Alexander J. and Katherine Ethel (Bates) U. BS, Oreg. Coll. Edn., 1952; MEd, U. Oreg., 1957; EdD, Columbia U., 1966; postgrad., U. Wash., 1969-70, 81-82, U. Oxford, Eng., 1973-74. Cert. tchr. and adminstr., Wash. Music tchr. Newport (Oreg.) Pub. Schs., 1952-55; music cons. Lake Oswego (Oreg.) Pub. Schs., 1955-57; edn. supr. State of Oreg., Salem, 1957-64; prof. edn. Cen. Wash. U., Ellensburg, 1965—; evaluator numerous schs., sch. dists.; reviewer manuscripts in sch. law. Contbr. articles to profl. jours. Mem. NEA, Wash. Edn. Assn., Assn. Supervision and Curriculum Devel., Nat. Orgn. on Legal Problems of Edn., Phi Delta Kappa. Office: Cen Wash U Dept Edn Ellensburg WA 98926

UNSOELD, JOLENE, congresswoman; b. Corvallis, Oreg., Dec. 3, 1931. Dir. U.S. Info. Svc. English Lang. Inst., Kathmandu, Nepal, 1965-67; mem. Wash. Ho. of Reps., 1985-88, 101st Congress from 3d Dist. Wash., 1989—. Office: US Ho of Reps Office House Mems Washington DC 20510 *

UPADHYAYA, SHRINIVASA KUMBHASHI, agricultural engineer, educator; b. Kumbhashi, India, Feb. 27, 1950; came to U.S., 1976; s. Krishna G. and Satyabhama G. (Bhat) U.; m. Jayashree S. Hebbar, Jan. 17, 1977; children: Arun, Amar. B Tech. with honors, Indian Inst. Tech., Kharagpur, 1972; MS, U. Man., Can., 1975; PhD, Cornell U., 1979. Research and devel. engr. Vicon Ltd., Bangalore, India, 1972-73; asst. prof. U. Agrl. Scis., Hebbal, Bangalore, 1973-74; research asst. agrl. engring. U. Man., 1974-75; teaching, research asst. agrl. engring. Cornell U., Ithaca, N.Y., 1976-79, research assoc. agrl. engring., 1979-81; asst. prof. agrl. engring. U. Del., Newark, 1981-83; asst. prof. agrl. engring. U. Calif., Davis, 1983-87, assoc. prof., 1987—. Contbr. numerous agrl. engring. papers to jours.; patentee in field. Energy Research grantee Univ. Wide Energy Research Group, 1985-86, 87, 88 Compactions Research grantee Kerney Found., 1986—, traction research grantee Good Yr. Rubber Co., 1986-87, Kelly Springfield Tire Co., 1986; U. Man. fellow, 1975. Mem. AAAS, Am. Soc. Agrl. Engrs. (Paper award 1982), Sigma Xi. Office: U Calif Dept Agrl Engring Davis CA 95616

UPHAM, STEADMAN, associate dean; b. Denver, Apr. 4, 1949; s. Albert Tyler and Jane Catherine (Steadman) U; m. Margaret Anne Cooper, Aug. 21, 1971; children: Erin Cooper, Nathan Steadman. BA, U. Redlands, 1971; MA, Ariz. State U., 1977, PhD, 1980. Dist. sales mgr. Ind. News Co. Inc., Los Angeles, 1971-72; regional sales mgr. Petersen Pub. Co, Los Angeles, 1972-74; archeologist, researcher Bur. Land Mgmt., Phoenix, 1979; research asst. Ariz. State U., Tempe, 1979-80; chief archeologist Soil Sytems Inc., Phoenix, 1980-81; chief archeologist N.Mex. State U., Las Cruces, N.Mex., 1981-85, asst. prof. to assoc. prof., 1982-87, assoc. dean, 1987—; interim dir. Cultural Resources Mgmt. div, N.Mex. State U., Las Cruces, 1988. Author: Politics and Power, 1982; editor: Computer Graphics in Archaeology, 1979, Mogollon Variability, 1986, The Sociopolitical Structure of Prehistoric SW Societies, 1988. Contbr. articles to profl. jours. Advanced seminar grantee Sch. of Am. Research, 1987, research grantee NSF, 1979, 1984-85, Hist. Preservation grantee State of N.Mex., 1982-84. Republican. Lodge: Rotary. Office: NM State U Grad Sch Box 3G Las Cruces NM 88003

UPP, JEFFREY FRANKLIN, oil company official, accountant; b. San Angelo, Tex., Jan. 30, 1964; s. Franklin Herbert and Tellie Frances (McWilliams) U. BBA in Acctg., Abilene Christian U., 1986. Acct. Arthur Andersen & Co., Ft. Worth, 1986-88; area mgr. Auto Fuel Co., Phoenix, 1988—. Republican. Mem. Ch. of Christ. Office: Auto Fuel Co 7736 E Peppertree Ln Scottsdale AZ 85253

UPTON, HUBERT MABERY, family physician; b. Omaha, May 14, 1925; s. Hubert Allen and Mildred (Mabery) U.; m. Celeste Upton, Aug. 28, 1948; children: Hugh, Bruce, Gary, Janice. BS, U. Calif., Berkeley, 1944; MD, U. Rochester, 1951. Intern U.S. Naval Hosp., Oakland, Calif., 1951-52; resident U.S. Naval Hosp., Madre Island, 1952, San Mateo Community Hosp., 1953-54; pvt. practice Mountain View, Calif., 1954—; chief staff El Camino Hosp., 1962-63, chief dept. gen. practice, 1962-63; assoc. prof. family and community medicine Stanford Med. Sch., 1974-89, prof. family and community medicine, 1989—; mem. adv. com. family practice residency, 1974-76; conductor workshops in field. Contbr. articles to profl. jours. Mem. Am. Acad. Family Practice (chmn. membership svcs. 1988, bd. dirs. 1986—), Calif. Acad. Family Physicians (dir. 1966-75, pres. 1980-81), Calif. Inst. Family Medicine (pres. 1984—), Alpha Sigma Phi, Alpha Omega Alpha. Office: 253 Franklin St Mountain View CA 94041

URBANO-BROWN, AUDREY MARIE, physician; b. Norristown, Pa., June 18, 1956; d. Marino Augustus and Ortrud Johanna (Lippoldt) Urbano; m. James Randall Brown, May 10, 1986. BS magna cum laude, Davidson Coll., 1978; MD, U. N.C., Chapel Hill, 1983. Diplomate Am. Bd. Emergency Medicine. Intern Montefiore Hosp., Pitts., 1983-84; resident Charlotte Meml. Hosp., Charlotte, N.C., 1984-86; resident in emergency medicine U. Meml. Hosp., Charlotte, 1985-86; staff physician in emergency dept. Gallup Indian Med. Ctr., Gallup, N.Mex., 1986—, Rehobeth McKinley Hosp., Gallup, 1986—; asst. prof. emergency medicine U. N.Mex., Albuqueque, 1988—; med. dir. Tohatchi (N.Mex.) EMS, 1988-89. Contbr. articles to med. jours. Asst. surgeon USPHS, 1986-89. Recipient scholarships, Joseph Moore McConnell and Charles A. Dana, Davidson Coll., 1974-78, Firestone Tire and Rubber Co., 1974-78. Mem. Am. Coll. Emergency Physicians, AMA, U. N.C. Alumni Assn., Davidson Coll. Alumni Assn., Sierra Club, Natural Resources Defense Counsel, Phi Beta Kappa, Phi Delta Epsilon (Miami) (sec. 1979-81). Roman Catholic. Office: U N Mex Dept Emergency Medicine 670 Camino de Salid NE Albuquerque NM 87131

URBANSKI, DOUGLAS JAMES, film and theater producer; b. Somerville, N.J., Feb. 17, 1957; s. Roman and Diane (Rustic) U. BFA, NYU, 1979. Sr. v.p. prodn. The IndieProd Co. div. Carolco Pictures, L.A., 1987-88; co-mng. dir. Boston's Met. Ctr., 1982-84; cons. Miami Opera, 1981-84, Houston Grand Opera, 1981-84. Producer Broadway plays including Whodunnit, Show Boat, 1981-83 (6 Tony nominations), Beethoven's Tenth, 1983-84, The Woman of Independent Means, 1983-84 (L.A. Critics award), Strange Interlude, 1984-85 (6 Tony nominations), Benefactors, 1984 (Winner Best Play Drama Critics Circle award 1984), Wild Honey, 1986; London plays including, Strange Interlude, Aren't We All, 1984-85, Benefactors, 1985-86, The Caine Mutiny Court Marshall, 1986, Sweet Bird of Youth, 1986-87, The Way of the World, 1986-87, Wild Honey, 1986-87 (9 Olivier awards, Evening Standard award), Blithe Spirit, 1987 (3 Tony nominations). Mem. Players Club. Roman Catholic. Also: PO Box 691763 Los Angeles CA 90069

URE, KIM MARIE, computer programmer/analyst; b. Pueblo, Colo., Oct. 28, 1958; d. LeRoy John and Catherine O. (Hernandez) U. BBA, U. So. Colo., 1980, BS in Computer Sci., 1983. Lab. asst., computer operator U. So. Colo. Computer Ctr., Pueblo, 1976-80; auditor Inventory Auditors, Pueblo, 1980-81; programmer, operator Westburne Supply, Inc., Pueblo, 1981-82; sr. data entry operator Pueblo Data Ctr., Pueblo, 1982-84; sec. data processing Colo. State Jud. Dept., Denver, 1984-85, programmer, 1985—. Vol. tutor Adult Learning Resource Ctr., Denver, 1988. Mem. Rocky Mountain Wang Users Group. Democrat. Roman Catholic. Club: Friends (Denver). Home: 11951 E Ohio Ave Aurora CO 80012 Office: Colo State Jud Dept 1301 Pennsylvania Ave Ste 300 Denver CO 80203

URELL, TIMOTHY WILLIAM, osteopathic physician; b. Key West, Fla., Feb. 11, 1954; s. John Patrick and Madeline (Ryan) U.; m. Gail Diane Schilling, Aug. 31, 1974. BS in Psychology, Ariz. State U., 1977, MA in Psychology, 1978; DO, Coll. Osteo. Medicine and Surgery, Des Moines, 1983. Intern Naval Hosp., Oakland, Calif., 1983-84; pvt. practice Yuma, Ariz., 1986—. Lt. USN, 1983-86. Mem. Am. Osteo. Assn., AMA, Am. Coll. Osteo. Gen. Practitioners. Office: 1812 S 8th Ave Yuma AZ 85364

URENA-ALEXIADES, JOSE LUIS, electrical engineer; b. Madrid, Spain, Sept. 5, 1949; s. Jose L. and Maria (Alexiades Christodulakis) Urena y Pon. MSEE, U. Madrid, Spain, 1976; MS in Computer Science, UCLA, 1978. Rsch. asst. UCLA, 1978; systems analyst Honeywell Info. Systems, L.A., 1978-80; mem. tech. staff Jet Propulsion Lab., Pasadena, Calif., 1980—. Contbr. various articles to profl. jours. Mem. IEEE, IEEE Computer Soc., IEEE Communications Soc., Assn. for Computer Machinery, World Federalist Assn., Spanish Profl. Am. Inc. Roman Catholic. Home: 904 Dickson St Marina del Rey CA 90292 Office: Jet Propulsion Lab 4800 Oak Grove Dr Pasadena CA 91109

URI, GEORGE WOLFSOHN, accountant; b. San Francisco, Dec. 8, 1920; s. George Washington and Ruby (Wolfsohn) U.; m. Pamela Dorothy O'Keefe, May 15, 1961. A.B., Stanford U., 1941, I.A., 1943, M.B.A., 1946; postgrad., U. Leeds, Eng., 1945. C.P.A., Calif.; Chartered Fin. Cons.; Cert. Fin. Planner. Mem. acctg., econs. and stats. depts. Shell Oil Co., Inc., San Francisco, 1946-48; ptnr. Irelan, Uri, Mayer & Sheppie, San Francisco; pres. F. Uri & Co., Inc., Athos Corp., Irelan Accountancy Corp.; instr. acctg. and econs. Golden Gate Coll., 1949-50. Contbr. articles to profl. jours. Chmn. San Rafael Redevel. Adv. Com., 1977-78, mem., 1978—; bd. dirs. San Francisco Planning and Urban Renewal Assn., 1958-60. Served with AUS, 1942-46, to col. Res. (ret.). Recipient Key Man award San Francisco Jr. C. of C.; Meritorious Service medal Sec. of Army, 1978. Mem. AICPA, Inst. Mgmt. Scis. (treas. No. Calif. chpt. 1961-62), Calif. Soc. CPA's (sec.-treas. San Francisco chpt. 1956-57, dir. 1961-63, state dir. 1964-66, mem. Forbes medal com. 1968-69, chmn. 1969-71), Am. Econs. Assn., Nat. Assn. Accts., San Francisco Estate Planning Council (dir. 1965-68), Am. Statis. Assn., Am. Soc. Mil. Comptrollers, Execs. Assn. San Francisco (pres. 1965-66), Inst. Cert. Mgmt. Accts. (cert. mgmt. acctg., Disting. Performance cert. 1978), Inst. Cert. Fin. Planners, Am. Soc. CLUs and Chartered Fin. Cons., Am. Soc. Mil. Comptrollers. Clubs: Engrs. San Francisco, Commonwealth, Stanford, Rafael Racquet; Army and Navy (Washington). Home: 11 McNear Dr San Rafael CA 94901 Office: 100 Pine St Ste 2000 San Francisco CA 94111

URIBE, CHARLES, school system administrator; b. N.Y.C., Feb. 9, 1937; s. Pablo and Ramona (Gonzales) U.; m. Saiko Hanamaki, June 17, 1957; children: Charles Jr., Raymond. AA, USAF Community Coll., 1966; BA, U. Nebr., 1969; MBA, Golden Gate U., 1981; PhD, Century U., 1989. Cert. tchr. K-12, adult community coll.; cert. adminstr. community coll., pvt. postsec. schs. Enlisted USAF, 1953, retired, 1976; mgr. Household Fin. Corp., Woodland, Calif., 1976-78; dean of instruction Acad. Bus. Colls., Sacramento, 1978-79; credit mgr. JC Penney, Sacramento, 1980-81; vocat. supr. Sacramento Job Corps., 1981-83; mgr. Hertz Corp., Sacramento, 1983-85; student services/fin. aid dir. Apollo Tech. Coll., Sacramento, 1985-86; clinic mgr. Ednl. Clinics, Inc., Sacramento, 1986—; instr. part-time Grant Adult Sch., Sacramento, 1981—; cons. in field., 1987—. Bd. dirs. Youth for Ednl. and Econ. Devel.; council mem. Sacramento Job Corps; mem. Neighborhood Networking Orgn., Greater Avenues for Independence; coord. Sacramento and Yolo Counties Joint Action in Community Svcs. Decorated Bronze Star. Mem. Non-Commd. Officers Assn. Office: Ednl Clinics Inc 811 Grand Ave Ste A Sacramento CA 95838

URMER, MICHELLE RANDI, banker; b. Austin, Tex., Nov. 12, 1955; d. Albert Heinz and Diane Hedda (Leverant) U. BS, UCLA, 1976, MBA, 1983; MEd, U. So. Calif., 1978. Dir. edn. Comprehensive Care Corp., Newport Beach, Calif., 1979-81; loan officer Wells Fargo Bank, San Francisco, 1983-85; asst. v.p. Wells Fargo Bank, Walnut Creek, Calif., 1985-87, v.p., 1987—. Mem. Nat. Assn. Bank Women (bd. dirs. Walnut Creek chpt. 1987—), Women in Bus., Contra Costa Coun.

URQUIDI-MACDONALD, MIRNA, physicist; b. Tuxtla, Chis, Mexico, July 8, 1946; came to U.S., 1983; d. Jose and Miriam (Fernandez) U.; m. Francois Gouin, July 22, 1972 (div. 1984); 1 child, Nahlin Gouin; m. Digby D. Macdonald, July 6, 1985. BA in Physics and Math., Instituto Tecnologeco y de Estudios Supercores de Monterrey, Mex., 1969; MA, Faculte d'Orsay, Orsay, France, 1970; PhD in Plasma Physics, Faculte d'Orsay, Orsay, France, 1972. Scientist U. of Paris VI- Pierre et Marie Curie, Paris, 1972-75, Instituto de Ingenieria, Mexico, 1975-77, Comision Federal de Electricidad, Mexico, 1977-79, Secretaria de Agricultura y Hobras Publicas-Direccion General de Agueas, Mexicali, B.C., 1980-81, Intituto de Investigaciones Electricas, Mexicali, B.C., 1981-83, Fontana Corrosion Ctr.-Ohio State U., Columbus, 1983-84, SRI Internat., Menlo Park, Calif., 1984—. Author: Evaporation, 1980; contbr. articles to sci. publs. Mem. Material Rsch. Soc., Math. Soc., Electrochem. Soc. Home: 44406 Arapaho Ave Fremont CA 94539 Office: SRI Internat 333 Robenswood Ave Menlo Park CA 94025

URSIN, BJARNE ELLING, manufacturing company executive; b. Bridgeport, Conn., Aug. 8, 1930; s. Bjarne and Esther (Schiott) U.; student Oberlin Coll., 1949-51; BS in Physics, MIT, 1957; m. Mary Elizabeth Locke, July 26, 1969; children: Stephanie, Lara, Matthew, Jonathan, Teri, Kristian. Project engr. Raytheon, Andover, Mass., 1957-60; prin. investigator Gen. Dynamics, San Diego, 1960-62; sr. scientist Philco-Ford, Newport Beach, Calif., 1962-67; with McDonnell Douglas Corp., Huntington Beach, Calif., 1967-76, sr. ops. project mgr., mgr. mfg., 1967-76; prodn. mgr. Eldec Corp., Lynnwood, Wash., 1976-78; v.p. mfg. TCS Inc., Redmond, Wash., 1978-80; bd. dir. new bus. Data I/O Corp., Redmond, 1980-82; prodn. mgr. Atex Inc., A Kodak Co., 1982-83; quality assurance systems mgr. Boeing Electronics Co., Seattle, 1983—; assoc. Coldwell Banker Co., 1981-83, Wallace and Wheeler Realty, 1984—; owner Westechnology, Bellevue, Wash., 1980—; co-owner Lighthouse Interiors, 1982—; community chmn. City of Huntington Beach, 1975-76. With AUS, 1951-53, Korea. Recipient NASA Team award Saturn/Apollo, 1975, Nasa Design VIP award Skylab, 1976, Cert. Appreciation, McDonnell Douglas, 1976. Mem. Am. Assn. Physics Tchrs., AIAA, AASS, U.S. Internat. Sailing Assn., Am. Mgmt. Assn. Republican. Roman Catholic. Clubs: Bahia Corinthian Yacht (bd. dir. 1972-76, rear commodore 1974, vice commodore 1975, commodore 1976) (Corona Del Mar); Royal Norwegian Yacht (Oslo); Balboa Bay; Seattle Yacht, U.S. Power Squadron, MIT of Puget Sound (bd. dir. 1979—). Home: PO Box 1218 Mercer Island WA 98040 Office: PO Box 596 Mercer Island WA 98040 Office: PO Box 6968 Bellevue WA 98008

USELMANN, DONALD PETER, II, retail executive; b. Madison, Wis., Sept. 30, 1951; s. Donald Peter and Mary Lucille (Armstrong) U.; m. Debra Jean Kozuszek, May 4, 1974; children: Amanda Marie, Donald Peter III. BBA, U. Wis., Madison, 1974. Asst. buyer Famous-Barr, St. Louis, 1974-75, dept. mgr., 1975-76, assoc. buyer, 1976-77, buyer, 1977-78, sr. buyer, 1978-79; asst. gen. mgr. Saks Fifth Ave., Boston, 1980-81; gen. mgr. Saks Fifth Ave., Short Hills, N.J., 1981-83, Cin., 1984-85, San Francisco, 1986—. V.p. mktg. Cin. Symphony Orch. Assn., 1985; chmn. tng. United Way of the Bay Area, San Francisco, 1987; chmn. teamwalk March of Dimes, San Francisco, 1987. Mem. Union Sq. Assn. (pres. 1989—), Retail Merchants Assn. (past pres. 1988), Convention and Visitors Bur. (bd. dirs. 1987—), Downtown Assn. (bd. dirs. 1988—), Better Bus. Bur. (bd. dirs. 1987—). Republican. Roman Catholic. Office: Saks Fifth Ave 384 Post St San Francisco CA 94108

USHER, RONALD LEE, county official; b. Wenatchee, Wash., Sept. 14, 1935; s. Harlan King and Lida Marie (Hall) U.; m. Nancy Jean Mallon, Dec. 30, 1961; children: Bradley, Eric, Craig, Michael. BBA, U. Puget Sound, 1957; M in Govtl. Adminstrn., U. Pa., 1959; PhD in Pub. Adminstrn., Golden Gate U., 1980. Adminstrv. intern City of Vallejo (Calif.), 1958-59, asst. city mgr. and personnel dir., 1962-65; adminstrv. analyst Sonoma County, Santa Rosa, Calif., 1959-62; town mgr. Town of Corte Madera (Calif.), 1965-70; city and borough mgr. City and Borough of Juneau (Alaska), 1970-74; city mgr. City of Mill Valley (Calif.), 1974-75; dir. health and human svcs. Marin County, San Rafael, Calif., 1975-78; dir. health Sacramento County, Sacramento, 1978—; professorial lectr. Golden Gate U., San Francisco and Sacramento, 1977—; asst. prof. Calif. State U., Sacramento, 1978-88; cons. Placer County Grand Jury, Auburn, Calif., 1981; asst. clin. prof. U. So. Calif., Sacramento, 1983-84. Contbr. articles to profl. jours. Bd. dirs. Community Svcs. Planning Coun., Sacramento, 1978—, Parent Support Program, Sacramento, 1984-87, Golden Empire Hypertension Coun., 1987—; exec. couple Sacramento Marriage Encounter, 1988-89. Recipient Exceptional Svc. in Pub. Health award Taxpayers League Sacramento County, 1988. Mem. Am. Soc. for Pub. Adminsrn. (chpt. pres. 1972-73, 86-87), Calif. Conf. Local Mental Health Dirs. (exec. bd. 1981-86), County Health Execs. Calif. (exec. bd. 1988-89). Office: Sacramento Co Health Dept 3701 Branch Center Rd Sacramento CA 95827

USHIJIMA, JEAN MIYOKO, city official; b. San Francisco, Feb. 14, 1933; d. Toyoharu George and Frances Fujiko (Misumi) Miwa; m. Tad E. Ushijima; 1 child, Carol M. BS, U. San Francisco, 1981. City clk. City of Beverly Hills, Calif., 1973—. Bd. dirs. West Los Angels Japanese Am. Citizens League, 1979—, pres., 1988—, also chmn. bd.; bd. dirs. Leadership Edn. for Asian Pacifics, 1985—. Named City Clk. of Yr., 1989. Mem. Acad. Advanced Edn., City Clks. Assn. Calif. (pres. 1986), Calif. Women in Govt. (program chmn. 1978-79), Leadership Edn. for Asian Pacific (chmn. bd. 1987), League Calif. Cities (adminstrv. services com. 1982-86), Internat. Inst. Mcpl. Clks. (bd dirs. 1988). Avocations: reading, Japanese dancing. Office: City Clerk 450 N Crescent Dr #102 Beverly Hills CA 90210

USIAK-RADI, ARLENE ANN, video production executive; b. Woodland, Calif., Apr. 7, 1932; d. Samuel Usiak and Anna (Hulka) U.; m. Bob J. Radi, May 11, 1988; children: Cindy L. Huntley, Darch S. Brennan, Erika B. BA, U. Calif., Davis, 1982; postgrad., Sonoma State U., 1982, Sacrameto State U., 1989—. Mgr. Town House Gift Store and Post Office, Napa, Calif., 1976-79; asst. to Mayor C. Demmon, Vallejo, Calif., 1979; asst., assoc. Panache Fashions, Napa, 1979-87; pvt. practice video prodn. Napa, 1987—; honor's rep. Am. Sociol. Assn., 1982—; camerman, switcher Channel 5B Prodn., Napa, 1986—. counselor Abuse Counsel, Napa; del. state conv. Status Women Commn., Dist. 2, Sacramento, 1986—, mem. 1986-87; bd.

mem. Luth. Ch. the Redeemer, 1976; pres., reorganizer Northwood Parent Faculty Club, 1972, 74. Recipient Cert. Appreciation, Napa Valley Unified Sch. Dist., 1973. Democrat. Home and Office: PO Box 83 Napa CA 94559-0083

USINGER, MARTHA PUTNAM, educator; b. Pitts., Dec. 10, 1912; d. Milo Boone and Christiana (Haberstroh) Putnam; m. Robert Leslie Usinger, June 24, 1938 (dec. Oct. 1968); children: Roberta Christine, Richard Putnam. AB cum laude, U. Calif., Berkeley, 1934; postgrad., Oreg. State U., 1936, U. Ghana, 1970, Coll. Nairobi, 1970. Tchr. Oakland (Calif.) Pub. Schs., 1936-38; tchr. Berkeley (Calif.) Pub. Schs., 1954-57, dean West Campus, counselor, 1957-78; lectr., photographer. Mem. Berkeley Retired Tchrs. Congregationalist.

USINGER, RICHARD PUTNAM, dentist; b. Oakland, Calif., Sept. 26, 1947; s. Robert Leslie and Martha Boone (Putnam) U.; m. Lynne Journigan, Sept. 16, 1978; children: Clay, Corbin. BA, U. Pacific, 1969; DDS, U. So. Calif., 1973. Pvt. practice, Concord, Calif., 1973—; mem. med. staff John Muir Meml. Hosp., Walnut Creek, Calif.; expert examiner Calif. State Bd. Dental Examiners, 1988—. Mem. Contra Costa Dental Soc. (bd. trustees 1984-85), ADA, Calif. Dental Assn., Acad. Gen. Dentistry, So. Calif. Acad. Oral Pathology, U. So. Calif. Alumni Assn., U. Pacific Alumni Assn., SAR, Los Medicos Volodores, Century Club. Office: 2991 Treat Blvd Ste G Concord CA 94518

USUI, LESLIE RAYMOND, clothing executive; b. Wahiawa, Hawaii, Feb. 2, 1946; s. Raymond Isao and Joyce Mitsuyo (Muramoto) U.; m. Annie On Nor Hom, Oct. 23, 1980; 1 child, Atisha. BA in Zool., U. Hawaii, 1969, MA in Edn., 1972. Cert. tchr., Hawaii. Flight steward United Airlines, Honolulu, 1970; spl. tutor Dept. Edn., 1971-73; v.p. Satyuga, Inc., Honolulu, 1974-80; pres. Satyuga, Inc., 1980—; also bd. dirs.; cons. Hawaii Fashion Guild, 1978-79. Composer: Song to Chenrayzee, Song to Karmapa. Co-founder, bd. dirs. Kagyu Thegchen Ling Meditation Ctr., 1974—, Maitreya Inst., 1983-86; bd. dirs. Palpung Found., 1984-88, U.S. Senatorial Bus. Adv. Bd., Washington, 1988. Mem. Hawaii Bus. League, Nat. Fedn. Ind. Bus. Republican. Buddhist. Home: 1417 Laamia Pl Honolulu HI 96821 Office: Satyuga Inc 248 Mokauea St Honolulu HI 96819

UTLEY, ROBERT MARSHALL, historian; b. Bauxite, Ark., Oct. 31, 1929; s. Don Williams and Valeria (Hanley) U.; m. Lucille Alvia Dorsey, May 5, 1956 (div.), m. Melody Webb, Nov. 12, 1980. BS, Purdue U., 1951; MA, Ind. U., 1952, degree (hon.), 1983; degree (hon.), Purdue U., 1974, U. N.Mex., 1976. Historian Joint Chiefs Staff Dept. Def., Washington, 1954-57; regional historian Nat. Park Svc., Santa Fe, 1957-64; from chief historian to asst. dir. Nat. Park Svc., Washington, 1964-77; deputy dir. Adv. Coun. on Historic Preservation, Washington, 1977-80; freelance historian Sante Fe, N.M., 1980—; bd. dirs. Eastern Nat. Park and Monument Assn., Phila. 1978-87, chmn., 1986-87. With U.S. Army, 1952-57. Recipient Wrangler award Nat. Cowboy Hall of Fame, Oklahoma City, 1988, 89. Mem. Western History Assn. Home and Office: 5 Vista Grande Ct Santa Fe NM 87505

UTMAN, CRAGG BRIEN, mortgage banker; b. Abington, Pa., Sept. 5, 1952; s. Richard Eugene and Doreen June (Heron) U.; m. Annette Marie Drake, Dec. 5, 1981; children: Cragg Brien II, Wilson Taylor. Student, Pitzer Coll., 1971-72, U. Calif., San Francisco, 1972-73, U. Calif., Berkeley, 1973-74. Lic. real estate agt. V.p. Wells Fargo Mortgage, Upland, Calif., 1978-81, Rainier Mortgage, Monterey, Calif., 1981-82, Crocker Mortgage, Irvine, Calif., 1982-83, Am. Savs., Upland, 1983-84; pres. Western Relocation Services, Montclair, Calif., 1985; v.p. Santa Barbara Savs., Anaheim, Calif., 1985-87, Bank of Palm Springs, Calif., 1987—. Mem. Civil Air Patrol, Palm Springs, 1988. Mem. Desert Contractors Assn., Bldg. Industry Assn., Mortgage Bankers Assn., Rotary (Rancho Mirage). Republican. Lutheran. Home: 2563 Verona Rd Palm Springs CA 92262 Office: Bank of Palm Springs-BankCal 601 E Tahquitz Way Palm Springs CA 92262

UTTER, CHARLES ARVIN, insurance agent; b. Dickinson, N.D., Mar. 31, 1946; s. Arvin C. and Lorraine (Zeren) U.; m. Phyllis Renee Kopp, June 3, 1972; children: Megan, Joseph, Anne. BA in History, St. John's U., 1968. CLU. Tchr., coach St. Gertrude's High Sch., Raleigh, N.D., 1968-72, 73-74, Corvallis (Oreg.) High Sch., 1972-73, Bismarch (N.D.) High Sch., 1974-75; agt. N.Y. Life Ins., Bismarck, 1975-78; sales mgr. N.Y. Life Ins., Fargo, N.D., 1978-79; agt. N.Y. Life Ins., Lisbon, N.D., 1979-80, CF&R Fin. Services, Longmont, Colo., 1980—. Candidate Longmont City Council, 1985; chmn. recall com., Longmont, 1986; coordinator David Bath for Congress Campaign, 1988; active Long Range Planning Commn., Longmont, 1987—; sec. Longmont Found., 1987—. Named Cross Country Coach of Yr., N.D. High Sch. Avtivities Assn., 1971. Mem. Longmont Assn. Life Underwriters (sec. treas. 1982-83, bd. dirs. 1981-83), Million Dollar Round Table, Am. Soc. CLU and Chartered Fin. Cons. Republican. Roman Catholic. Office: CF&R Fin Svcs 850 23d Ave Longmont CO 80501

UTTER, ROBERT FRENCH, judge; b. Seattle, June 19, 1930; s. John and Besse (French) U.; m. Elizabeth J. Stevenson, Dec. 28, 1953; children: Kimberly, Kirk, John. B.S., U. Wash., 1952; LL.B., 1954. Bar: Wash. 1954. Pros. atty. King County, Wash., 1955-57; individual practice law Seattle, 1957-59; ct. commr. King County Superior Ct., 1959-64, judge, 1964-69; judge Wash. State Ct. Appeals, 1969-71; judge Wash. State Supreme Ct., 1971—, chief justice, 1979-81; lectr. in field; leader comparative law tour Peoples Rep. in China, 86, 87, 88; adj. prof. constl. law U. Puget Sound, 1987, 88. Editor books on real property and appellate practice. Pres., founder Big Brother Assn., Seattle, 1955-67; pres., founder Job Therapy Inc., 1963-71; mem. exec. com. Conf. of Chief Justices, 1979-80, 81-86; pres. Thurston County Big Bros./Big Sisters, 1984. Named Alumnus of the Year Linfield Coll., 1973, Disting. Jud. Scholar, U. Ind., 1987. Mem. ABA, Am. Judicature Soc. (Herbert Harley award 1983, sec. 1987—, 1st v.p., mem. exec. com.), Order of Coif. Baptist. Office: Wash Supreme Ct Temple of Justice Olympia WA 98504

UTTERSTROM, JOHN RAYMOND, missiles systems executive; b. Vancouver, B.C., Can., Oct. 8, 1922; s. John and Gertrude Wilhemina (Hanson) U.; m. Mary Agnes Deffries, Sept. 24, 1947; children—Vicki Ann, Thomas Raymond, Mary Susan, Kathy Jo. B.S.E.E., U. Wash., 1948. With Boeing Co., Seattle, 1948-83, successively analyst, successively group leader, dept. head, chief engr., dir. engring., program mgr., 1948-80, v.p. Missile Systems div., 1980-83; pres. Boeing Mgmt. Assn. Pres. bd. dirs. Wash. State Spl. Olympics. Served to lt., USAAF, 1942-45. Recipient Ann. Honors, Aviation Week, 1961. Fellow AIAA (assoc. dir. Outstanding Aerospace Engring. award 1980, Wright Meml. Lectureship 1985, Edward Wells award 1984); mem. Sigma Xi, Tau Beta Pi. Clubs: Overlake Golf and Country (Bellevue, Wash.); Seattle Yacht. Patentee AC modulation suppressor. Deceased Dec. 1986. Home: 9830 Shoreland Dr SE Bellevue WA 98004

UYEDA, LANCE DEN, city official, management consultant; b. Denver, July 24, 1943; s. John Noritsugu and Etsuko Francis (Kawata) U.; m. Susie Yoshie Takahashi, Jan. 30, 1970; children: Craig, Shelley, Lauren, Scott. AA, Foothill Coll., 1963; BA in Environ. Health, San Jose Stae Coll., 1967, MA, 1973. Environ. health sanitarian Santa Clara County Health Dept., San Jose, Calif., 1967, 69-79; housing sanitarian City of San Jose, 1979—, code enforcement supr., 1979—; instr. health Foothill Coll., Los Altos Hills, Calif., 1974-79, San Jose City Coll., 1979-80; propr., mgr. Lance Uyeda Co., Los Altos, Calif., 1979—. Bd. dirs. Tri City Assn., Los Altos, 1978, baseball commr., 1982; v.p. fin. Los Altos Aquatic Club, 1981; asst. commr. region 45, Am. Youth Soccer Orgn., Los Altos, 1987-89. With U.S. Army, 1967-69. Mem. Assn. Pub. Adminstrs., Calif. Environ. Health Assn. (chmn. pub. rels. No. chpt. 1974-75), Santa Clara County Environ. Health Assn. (pres. 1975-76). Democrat. Methodist. Home: 2133 Sierra Ventura Dr Los Altos CA 94022 Office: City of San Jose 801 N lst St San Jose CA 95110

UYEHARA-ISONO, JUNE MIEKO, audiologist, consultant; b. Honolulu, Nov. 28, 1953; d. Donald Masuo and Yoshika (Torigoe) Uyehara; m. Gary Akira Isono, June 23, 1979; children: Sean, Catherine. BS, U. Hawaii, 1974; MS Clin. Competence in Audiology, Purdue U., 1977. Audiologist Honolulu Med. Group, 1977-80; audiologist, pres. Audiol. Cons. and Services, Honolulu, 1980—. Fellow Am. Acad. Dispensing Audiologists; mem. Am. Speech-Lang.-Hearing Assn., Alexander Graham Bell Assn., St. Regulatory Bd. of Hearing Aid Dealers (chmn. 1979-89). Office: Audiol Cons & Svcs 1380 Lusitana #209 Honolulu HI 96813

UZZELL, GREGORY WAYNE, manufacturer's representative company executive; b. Little Rock, Mar. 22, 1962; s. David Lee and Betty Jean (Fritts) U. BBA in Fin., Tex. A&M U., 1985. Agt. Kosich Ins. Agy., Lafayette, Calif., 1985-87; mfr's rep. Diablo Pacific Corp., Long Beach, Calif., 1987--. Republican. Baptist. Home: 1609 Ximeno Ave Apt 160 Long Beach CA 90804 Office: Diablo Pacific Corp 2750 Bellflower Blvd Ste 212 Long Beach CA 90815

V., NAOMI See KELLEY, BRIDGET ANN

VACHAL, TRACY, speciality contracting company owner; b. Bellvue, Wash.; parents: John Douglas and Wendy Hazel (Tait) V. Grad., High Sch., Bellevue. Mgr. Presige Offices Inc., 1980-82; sec. northwest region Datapoint Corp., 1981-83; chief estimator Postal Spltys., Bellevue, 1981-84, owner, mgr., 1984-88; owner, mgr. Archtl. Spltys. & Products, Seattle, 1988—. Home and Office: 2724 NE 45th St Ste 485 Seattle WA 98105

VACHON, ROGATIEN ROSAIRE (ROGIE VACHON), professional ice hockey executive; b. Palmarolle, Que., Can., Sept. 8, 1945; m. Nicole Vachon; children: Nicholas, Jade, Mary Joy. Goaltender Montreal (Que) Canadiens, NHL, 1966-72, Los Angeles Kings, NHL, 1972-78, Detroit Red Wings, NHL, 1978-80, Boston Bruins, 1980-82; asst. coach Los Angeles Kings, 1982-84, gen. mgr., 1984—. Co-recipient Vezina Trophy, 1968. Office: care LA Kings 3900 W Manchester Blvd PO Box 17013 Inglewood CA 90306 *

VACKAR, DAVID MARVIN, rancher, consultant; b. Lubbock, Tex., Aug. 24, 1949; s. Marvin I. and Joreta Clois (Smith) V.; m. Rebecca Jo Allen, Nov. 26, 1971; children: Dana Kristin, Julie Christine. BS, Tex. A&M U., 1971. Regional sales mgr. Kalo Industries, Albany, Ga., 1972-74; ranch mgr. Simmental Breeders, Ltd., Cardston, Alta., Can., 1974-77; rancher, owner Buena Vaca Ranch, Glenwood, N.Mex., 1977—; natural resource analyst U.S. Senator Jeff Bingaman, Albuquerque, 1987—. Mem. Catron County Sch. Dist 1, Reseve, N.Mex., 1981-86; field coord. N.Mex. State Police Search and Rescue, Reserve, 1982—; chief Glenwood Fire & Rescue, 1980-83; chmn. Catron County Commn., Reserve, 1982-86, S.W. N.Mex. Coun. of Govts., Silver City, 1985-86. Recipient Merit award N.Mex. Cattle Growers Assn., 1986, Svc. award S.W. N.Mex. Coun. of Govts., 1986, Svc. award Gila Nat. Forest Permitters Assn., 1987. Mem. Soc. for Range Mgmt., Acad. Polit. Sci. Home: Rt 10 Box 530 Glenwood NM 88039 Office: US Senator Jeff Bingaman 500 Gold SW Albuquerque NM 57102

VACTOR, ALMA KANE, service executive; b. Cleve., July 7, 1925; d. Marvin A. and Fan (Morgenstern) Kane; m. David C. Vactor, Oct. 8, 1944 (dec. 1984); children: Drew, Wendy Sekovich, Jill Gunzel. Student, Syracuse U., 1942-44, Western Reserve U., 1945-47. Owner, operator, v.p. Rancho Del Rio, Inc., Tucson, 1945—, food cons., 1950-65; owner, operator The Tack Room Restaurant, Tucson, 1965—; tchr. cooking U. Ariz. Health Scis. Ctr., 1970—, Brandeis U., 1970—; owner, v.p., sec. K&V Water Co., 1963—; gen. ptnr. Rancho Del Rio Ltd. Ptnrship., 1984—. Bd. dirs. Fan Kane Research Fund Brain Injured Children, 1955—. Mem. Tucson Panhellenic (pres. 1965-76). Office: Rancho Del Rio 2800 Sabino Canyon Rd Tucson AZ 85715

VAGNEUR, KATHRYN OTTO, accountant, rancher; b. Aurora, Ill., Feb. 23, 1946; d. Harold William and Afton (Bryner) Otto; m. Gerald Ronald Terwilliger, Oct. 19, 1968 (div. 1974); 1 dau., Jocelyn Marie; m. Clyde O. Vagneur, Aug. 24, 1979. BS in Math., U. Utah, 1968; MS in Agribus. Mgmt., Ariz. State U., 1979. CPA, Colo. Computer systems designer U. Utah Libraries, Salt Lake City, 1966-68; rsch. asst. in computer systems Carnegie-Mellon U., 1968-70; owner, mgr. Evening at Arthurs Restaurant, Aspen, Colo., 1973-76; self-employed tax cons. Phoenix, 1977-78; with Touche Ross & Co., Colorado Springs, Colo., 1978-82; ptnr., fin. mgr. V Bar Lazy V Ranch, Peyton, Colo., 1978—; ptnr. Vagneur & Firth, Colorado Springs, 1982—; pres. The Marlwood Corp., Colorado Springs; chmn. Excellence in Bus. Seminar Series, 1987-88. Chmn. bd. dirs. Pikes Peak Ctr.; del. Rep. State Conv., 1982, White House Small Bus. Conf., 1986; bd. dirs. Springs Into Action Econ. Devel. Strategy, 1987-88, Pvt. Industry Council, 1988—; mem. Gov.'s Econ. Devel. Action Council, 1988—, trustee 1988—; 4-H leader; advisor Colo. Small Bus. Devel. Ctrs., 1988—. Mem. Am. Inst. CPAs, Nat. Soc. Accts. for Coops., Colo. Soc. CPAs, Nat. Assn. Accts., Jr. League, Am. Salers Assn., Nat. Cattlemen's Assn. (featured speaker 1986 Beef Profit Conf.), Nat. Fedn. Ind. Bus., Colorado Springs C. of C. (com. chmn.), Am. Quarter Horse Assn., Beta Alpha Psi, Alpha Zeta. Author: A Financial Analysis of Cooperative Livestock Marketing, 1978; contbr. articles to mags. Home: 14725 Jones Rd Peyton CO 80831 Office: Vagneur & Firth 830 N Tejon Ste 303 Colorado Springs CO 80903

VAGNINI, LIVIO LEE, chemist, forensic consultant; b. North Bergen, N.J., Apr. 26, 1917; s. Frank S. and Margaret (Avondo) V.; m. Daniele Hogge, Sept. 29, 1949; children: Frank, Stephen, Eric. BS in Chemistry, Fordham U., 1938; postgrad., U. Md. Med. Sch., 1938-39. Chemist H.A. Wilson Co. div. Englehard Industries, Inc., 1940-42; chief chemist U.S. Army Graves Registration, Liege, Belgium, 1946-48; chief forensic chemist U.S. Army Criminal Investigation Lab., Frankfurt, Fed. Republic Germany, 1948-60; sr. chemist FDA, Washington, 1960-62, CIA, Washington, 1963-73; project engr. Mitre Corp., McLean, Va., 1973-75; staff scientist Planning Research Corp., McLean, 1975-77; program dir. L. Miranda Assocs., Washington, 1978-81; forensic cons. Carmel, Calif., 1981--. Contbr. articles to profl. publs. Mem. Fort Ord, Calif. Retiree Coun., 1988, 89—. Lt. col. AUS, 1942-46. Decorated Bronze Star. Fellow Am. Inst. Chemists, Am. Acad. Forensic Scis.; mem. Internat. Soc. Blood Transfusion, Internat. Soc. Forensic Scientists, Ret. Officers Assn. (pres. Monterey County chpt. 1985), Sons in Retirement (pres. Pebble Beach br. 1986), Am.-Scandinavian Soc. (1st v.p., program dir. Monterey County 1989). Roman Catholic. Home: 26069 Mesa Dr Carmel CA 93923

VAGT, CRAIG D., accountant; b. Seattle, July 29, 1947. BS, U. Oreg., 1969; JD, Golden Gate U., 1976, MS in Taxation, 1987. Staff Peat Marwick Main & Co., San Francisco, 1977-86, ptnr., 1986—.

VAHIDI, VIRASB, electrical engineer; b. Tehran, Iran, Feb. 24, 1967; came to U.S., 1984; s.Manouchehr and Delara (Sarafi) V. BS, U. Calif., San Diego, 1988. Engr. Dibble Electronics, San Diego, 1989—. Mem. Persian Club, L'Alliance Francaise, Biomed. Engring. Soc. Home: 9663 Easter Way San Diego CA 92121 Office: Dibble Electronics 3670 Ruffin Rd San Diego CA 92123

VAIL, LUKI STYSKAL, financial consulting firm executive; b. Los Angeles, June 7, 1937; d. Ladislav Jakup and Lucia Marie (Matulich) Styskal; children by previous marriage—Thomas Lad, Jerome David, Tricia Marie. B.S. in Mktg., Loyola-Marymount U., Los Angeles, 1959. Registered securities prin. Nat. Assn. Securities Dealers. Mem. Inst. Cert. Fin. Planners, Western Pension Conf., Internat. Assn. Fin. Planners.

VALA, ROBERT DONALD (DONALD ROBERT MANN), artist; b. Berkeley, Calif., Apr. 19, 1930; s. Robert H. and Nell (Curry) Mann. Student, Coll. Arts & Crafts, Oakland, Calif., 1947, Art Student League, N.Y.C., 1950; BA, U. Calif.-Berkeley, 1951. Designer Ballet Russe, Europe, 1952, San Francisco Opera, 1953-56, San Francisco Ballet, 1953-56, Spanish Dance Co., Santa Cruz, Calif., 1986—, Patri Nader Co., Santa Cruz, Calif., 1986—; artist-in-residence, tchr. Calif. State U., Sacramento, 1987. Multi-media one-man shows include: Art Dirs. Gallery, N.Y.C., 1963, Galeries Raymond Duncan, Paris, 1963, Madison Gallery, N.Y.C., 1964; group shows include: UN Bldg., N.Y.C., 1970, Bohman Gallery, Stockholm, 1965, Arlene Lind Gallery, San Francisco, 1987, Will Stowe Gallery, San Francisco, 1987; represented in comml. installations and numerous pvt. collections. Recipient Prix de Paris, L'Art Modern Mus., 1962, 1st prize Salon 50 States, N.Y.C., 1963. Home: 440 Cliff Dr Aptos CA 95003

VALADEZ, ANNA MARIE, manufacturing executive, educator; b. Balinger, Tex., June 21, 1949; d. Joshua Benjamin and Margaret (Holquin) V. BA, Pepperdine U., Malibu, Calif., 1977; M in Human Resources, U. San Francisco, 1989. With Columbia Broadcasting Co., Fullerton, Calif., 1967-68, Beckman Instruments, Fullerton, 1968-69, Pepperdine U., 1969-76, Mgmt. Labs. Am., L.A., 1976-77; mgmt. assoc. Security Pacific Nat. Bank, L.A., 1978; tchr. Normandie Christian Sch., L.A., 1978-79; adminstr. Talentos de Salud Internat., Guatemala, 1979-80; sr. pension adminstrv. asst. William M. Mercer, Inc., L.A., 1980-82; employment interviewer Employment Devel. Dept., L.A., 1983-85; bilingual sec. Setco, Inc., Anaheim, Calif., 1985—; project adminstr. periodical On-the-Wall Birmingham, 1980. Author: pamphlet Power for Today, 1975. Internship, supr. Kenny Hahn's Community Project, L.A., 1977; Spanish instr. Community Project by Dean of Women, Pepperdine U., 1975. With Calif. Air N.G., 1985—. Recipient Bronze medal City of Anaheim, 1988. Mem. NAFE, Nat. Notary Pub. Assn. Democrat. Mem. Ch. of Christ. Office: SETCO Inc 4875 E Hunter Ave Anaheim CA 92817

VALDEZ, ARNOLD, dentist; b. Mojave, Calif., June 27, 1954; s. Stephen Monarez Jr. and Mary Lou (Esparza) V. BS in Biol. Sci., Calif. State U., Hayward, 1976; BS in Dental Sci. and DDS, U. Calif., San Francisco, 1982; MBA, Calif. State Poly. U., 1985; postgrad., U. So. Calif. Pvt. practice specializing in temporomandibular joint and Myofascial Pain Dysfunction Disorders Pomona, Calif., 1982—, Claremont, Calif., 1982—; mem. adv. com. dental assisting program Chaffey Coll., Rancho Cucamonga, Calif., 1982—. Vol. dentist San Antonio Hosp. Dental Clinic, Rancho Cucamonga, 1984-85, Pomona Valley Assistance League Dental Clinic, 1986—. Mem. ADA, Calif. Dental Assn., Tri-County Dental Soc. (co-chmn. mktg. 1986, chmn. sch. screening 1987, Golden Grin award), Acad. Gen. Dentistry, U. Calif.-San Francisco Alumni Assn., Psi Omega, Delta Theta Phi. Democrat. Roman Catholic. Home: 125 E Artesia St Pomona CA 19767 Office: 410 W Baseline Rd Claremont CA 91711

VALDEZ, LUIS, playwright, actor, director. married; three children. D of Arts (hon.), Columbia Coll., Chgo. Founder, dir., actor El Teatro Campesino, San Juan Bautista, Calif., 1965—. Playwright, dir.: (stage and film) Zoot Suit, 1978 (Disting. Prodn. award L.A. Drama Critics Circle, 8 Outstanding Achievement in Theater awards Drama-Logue); writer, dir., actor (TV screenplay, stage musical) Corridos! Tales of Passion and Revolution (Best Musical, 10 awards San Francisco Bay Area Theatre Critics Circle, 1983), 1987; writer (screenplays) Carmina Burana, La Carpa de Los Rasquachis, Gringo Viejo, Which Way Is Up?, La Bamba; playwright: I Don't Have to Show You No Stinking Badges; dir., actor 5 European tours to World Theatre Festival, Nancy, France, Festival Nations, Paris, others. Rockefeller Found. Artist-in-Residence grantee Mark Taper Forum, L.A., 1977; recipient Off-Broadway Obie award, 1969, L.A. Drama Critics Circle award, 1969, 72. Mem. Calif. Arts council (founding). Office: El Teatro Campesino 705 4th St PO Box 1240 San Juan Bautista CA 95045

VALDEZ, ROBERT OTTO BURCIAGA, health policy analyst; b. San Antonio; s. Santiago E. and Gloria (Burciaga) V.; m. Mary Elizabeth Winter; children: Ariel Carlos, Graciela Elena. AB, Harvard U., 1978; Master of Health Svcs. Adminstrn., U. Mich., 1980; PhD, Rand Grad. Sch., 1985. Econ. analyst The RAND Corp., Santa Monica, Calif., 1980-85, health policy analyst, 1985—; asst. prof. sch. of pub. health UCLA, 1985—; cons. Western Consortium Pub. Health, Berkeley, 1986—, Coronado Communication, L.A., 1987—; pres. S.W. Inst., L.A., 1988—. Contbr. articles to profl. jours. Bd. mem. Minority AIDS Project, L.A., 1988—; advisor L.A. Dept. Pub. Works, 1986-87, L.A. Dept. Health, 1984-85. Predoctoral fellow Bush Program in Child Devel. and Social Policy, U. Mich., 1979-80; vis. scholar Stanford Ctr. Chicano Rsch., Palo Alto, Calif., 1985-88. Fellow Am. Coll. Healthcare Execs.; mem. Am. Pub. Health Assn. (governing coun. 1982-84), Assn. Pub. Policy Analysis and Mgmt., Assn. Health Svcs. Rsch., Population Assn. Am. Roman Catholic. Office: The RAND Corp 1700 Main St Santa Monica CA 90406

VALDEZ, VINCENT EMILIO, artist; b. Mora, N.Mex., Mar. 15, 1940; s. Jose Bartolo Valdez and Maria Natividad (Nolan) Henderson; children: Trevor, Tiffney. Student, U. Wyo. Detective Laramie (Wyo.) Police Dept., 1964-84; free-lance artist Laramie, 1983—. Mem. Nat. Sculpture Ctr. With U.S. Army, 1964-68. Recipient Best of Show award Wildlife and Western Art Exhbn., Milw., 1985, 3d Pl. sculpture award George Phippen Meml. Art Show, Prescott, Ariz., 1986. Mem. Laramie Art Guild. Office: Vince Valdez Studio PO Box 581 Laramie WY 82070

VALENTI, FREDERICK ALAN, actor, screenwriter; b. Wiesbaden, Fed. Republic of Germany, Feb. 24, 1967; s. Fred and Arietta Maxinne (Deline) V. BA in Theater Arts, San Francisco State U., 1988. Model Kim Dawson Agy., Dallas, 1982-84; actor W. Press Agy., San Francisco, 1984—; play dir. Children's Theater Workshop, San Francisco, 1987—. Actor: (film) This is Spinal Tap, 1984, (play) Breaking New Ground, 1986 (Critics award 1986); screenwriter The Hip Guys, 1988. Organizer San Francisco Youth for a Better Day rally, 1987; spokesman Just Say No to Drugs campaign, San Francisco, 1987, 88. Recipient Youth in Film award Acad. Motion Picture Arts and Scis., 1984. Fellow Screen Actors Guild, Actors Equity Assn. Democrat. Roman Catholic. Home and Office: Valenti Prodns 334 Infantry Terr San Francisco CA 94129

VALENTINE, CAROL ANN, director educational program, consultant; b. Mt. Clemens, Mich., Dec. 5, 1942; d. Joseph Eldon and Erna Fredericka (Brandt) V.; married; children: Christopher, David. BA, U. Mich., 1964, MA, 1965; PhD, Pa State U., 1971. Tchr. Oak Park (Ill.)-River Forest High Sch., 1965-67; research assoc. U. Md., College Park, 1967; dir. grants Pa. State U., State College, 1967-78; asst. prof. Oreg. State U., Corvallis, 1970-74; vis. prof. U. Oreg., Eugene, 1974-75; assoc. prof. Ariz. State U., Tempe, 1975-85, assoc. dir. women's studies, 1985—; cons. Tempe, 1975—. Author: First Impressions, 1980, Women and Communicative Power. Bd. dirs. Tempe Pub. Library, 1984—. Named Outstanding Woman, Ford Motor Co., Phoenix, 1987. Mem. Zeta Phi Eta. Democrat. Presbyterian. Home: 2607 S Forest Ave Tempe AZ 85282 Office: Ariz State U Comfac Tempe AZ 85287

VALENTINE, CHRISTINE SPICER JONES, counselor; b. Newbury, Berks, Eng., Jan. 20, 1942; came to U.S., 1964; d. Percy W. and Mary E. (Brooks) Spicer; m. Robert H. Jones, Dec. 17, 1965 (dec. Nov. 1972); m. Stephen Valentine III, May 11, 1974; stepchildren: Stephen, Cary, John, Samuel, Sarah. Student, Reading Tech. Coll., Dull Knife Coll. Cert. chem. dependency counselor, Mont. Med. rsch. counselor technician histology dept. radiobiol. unit Atomic Energy Rsch. Establishment, Harwell, Eng., 1958-62, med. rsch. counselor tech. genetics dept., 1962-64; head tchr. Headstart Program No. Cheyenne Headstart, Birney, Mont., 1969-72; counselor No. Cheyenne Recovery Ctr., Lame Deer, Mont., 1979-82, sr. counselor, 1982—. Photographer color prints. Mem. No. Cheyenne Interdisciplinary Core Team, IHS Clinic, Lame Deer, 1986-89; coordinator St. Judes Bikeathon, Birney, 1987, 88; leader 4-H, Birney, 1966-71. Recipient Svc. award No. Cheyenne Bd. Health, Lame Deer, 1987, Community Svc. award No. Cheyenne Tribe Community Com., Lame Deer, 1988. Mem. Photographic Inst. Billings. Mem. Ch. of Eng. Home: Box 547 Birney MT 59012 Office: No Cheyenne Recovery Ctr Box 857 Lame Deer MT 59043

VALENTINE, JAMES WILLIAM, geology educator, author; b. Los Angeles, Nov. 10, 1926; s. Adelbert Cuthbert and Isabel (Davis) V.; m. Grace Evelyn Whysner, Dec. 21, 1957 (div. 1972); children—Anita, Ian; m. Cathryn Alice Campbell, Sept. 10, 1978 (div. 1986); 1 child, Geoffrey; m. Diane Mondragon, Mar. 16, 1987. B.A., Phillips U., 1951; M.A., UCLA, 1954, Ph.D., 1958. From asst. prof. to assoc. prof. U. Mo., Columbia, 1958-64; from assoc. prof. to prof. U. Calif.-Davis, 1964-77; prof. geol. scis. U. Calif.-Santa Barbara, 1977—. Author: Evolutionary Paleoecology of the Marine Biosphere, 1973; editor: Phanerozoic Diversity, 1985; co-author: Evolution, 1977, Evolving, 1979; also numerous articles, 1954—. Served with USNR, 1944-46; PTO. Fulbright research scholar, Australia, 1962-63; Guggenheim fellow Yale U., Oxford U., Eng., 1968-69; Rockefeller Found. scholar in residence, Bellagio, Italy, summer 1974; grantee NSF, NASA. Fellow Am. Acad. Arts and Scis., AAAS, Geol. Soc. Am.; mem. Nat. Acad. Scis., Paleontol. Soc. (pres. 1974-75). Home: 475F Cannon Green Dr Goleta CA 93117 Office: U Calif Dept Geol Scis Santa Barbara CA 93106

VALENTINE, MARTYANN PENBERTH, management consultant; b. Pottsville, Pa., Mar. 11, 1949; d. Floyd James and Martha Helen (Chivinski)

Penberth; m. Steven T. Valentine, Oct. 25, 1980; children: Jennifer P., Jessica M. BSN, U. Pa., 1973; MS, U. Calif., San Francisco, 1977; MPH, U. Calif., Berkeley, 1979. Cert. nursing adminstr. Mgmt. cons. W.L. Ganong Co., L.A., 1977-80; dir. edn. Daniel Freeman Hosp., L.A., 1980-85; dir. nursing Lakeview Med. Ctr., Lakeview Terrace, Calif., 1985-86, Serra Meml. Hosp., Sun Valley, Calif., 1986-87; chief exec. officer Cooper-Valentine & Assocs., Inc., L.A., 1987—. Author: Health Planning for Nurse Managers, 1984; contbr. articles to profl. jours.; contbr. to: Nursing Management by Ganong, 1980, Creative Problem Solving, 1981. Mem. Calif. Soc. Nursing Svc. Adminstrs., Health Care Edn. Coun. L.A. (pres. 1985-86), Sigma Theta Tau. Home: 189 Bell Canyon Rd Bell Canyon CA 91307 Office: Cooper Valentine & Assocs PO Box 8966 Calabasas CA 91302

VALENZUELA, FERNANDO, professional baseball player; b. Navajoa, Sonora, Mexico, Nov. 1, 1960; m. Linda, Dec. 29, 1981; chidlren: Fernando, Ricardo, Linda. Pitcher Mexican Leagues, 1978-79, minor league, 1979-80, Los Angeles Dodgers, Nat. League, 1980—; mem. Nat. League All-Star Team, 1981-86, World Series championsip team, 1981. Recipient Cy Young Meml. award Nat. League, 1981, Silber Bat Nat. League , 1983, Gold Glove Nat. League, 1986; named Rookie of the Yr. Nat. League, Rookie of Yr. Baseball Writers' Assn. Am., 1981. Office: LA Dodgers 1000 Elysian Park Ave Dodger Stadium Los Angeles CA 90012 *

VALFER, ERNST SIEGMAR, psychologist; b. Frankfurt-Main, Germany, July 4, 1925; came to U.S., 1941; s. Hermann Heinrich and Frieda (Kahn) V.; m. Lois Brandwynne, July 8, 1961; children: Rachel, Lilah. AA, City Coll., San Francisco, 1948; BS, U. Calif.-Berkeley, 1950, MS, 1952, PhD, 1965. Lic. psychologist, registered profl. engr., Calif. Supr. indsl. planning Naval Air Rework Facility, Alameda, Calif., 1952-57; rsch. scientist Maritime Cargo Transp. Conf., NRC, Washington, 1957-60, sci. dir., 1960-62; assoc. rsch. engr. U. Calif.-Berkeley, 1961-64, sr. lectr., 1965-68; dean, prof. J.F. Kennedy U., Martinez, Calif., 1970-73; adj. sr. fellow cons. Inst. Indsl. Rsch., UCLA, 1973-83; dir. mgmt. scis. USDA-Forestry Svc., Berkeley and Washington, 1962-88, chief mgmt scientist, 1988—; counselor, cons., Berkeley, 1966—; cons. govt., pvt. orgns., individuals. Author: (with P.B. Buck and Harvey C. Panze) San Francisco Port Study, 1964, (with L.E. Davis and Alfred W. Clark) Experimenting with Organizational Life, 1976; contbr. articles in field to profl. jours. Pres., Agy. for Jewish Edn., Oakland, Calif., 1982-85; v.p. Hillel Found., Berkeley, 1988—; bd. dirs. various orgns. in Bay Area, 1970—. Lt., U.S. Army, 1944-46, ETO. Recipient several awards USDA-Forestry Svc., NAS-NRC, 1960—. Mem. Am. Bd. Profl. Psychology, Am. Psychol. Assn., Inst. Indsl. Engrs. (spl. recognition award 1958), Inst. Mgmt. Scis., Sigma Xi, Alpha Pi Mu. Jewish. Home: 2621 Rose St Berkeley CA 94708-1920 Office: USDA Forest Svc PO Box 245 Berkeley CA 94701-0245

VALINE, FREDERICK CHRIST, JR., systems engineer, applied mathematician; b. Sacramento, July 7, 1944; s. Frederick Christ and Nadine (Duncan) V.; m. Helen Petraki, Apr. 23, 1949; children: Barbara Rene, Thomas Nicholas. BA in Math., St. Anselms Coll., Manchester, N.H., 1973; MS in Systems Mgmt., U. So. Calif., 1977. Electronic technician Philco-Ford Co., Palo Alto, Calif., 1970-74; satellite ops. specialist Lockheed Missile & Space Co., Sunnyvale, Calif., 1974-79; rsch. specialist Lockheed Missile & Space Co., Sunnyvale, 1979-81, 83-84, system test engr., 1981-83, staff engr., 1984—. Sgt. USAF, 1966-70. Mem. Nat. Mgmt. Assn. Republican. Roman Catholic.

VALINES, A. IRENE, student affairs associate; b. Washington, Oct. 28, 1958; d. David Lynn and Velma Irene (Bailey) Clodfelter; m. Francisco Alberto Valines IV, July 30, 1983. BA in Psychology, U. N.C., Charlotte, 1981; MEd, U. Fla., 1983; postgrad. in higher ednl. adminstrn., Wash. State U., 1988—. Grad. hall dir. Div. Housing, U. Fla., Gainesville, 1981-83; intern Syracuse U., 1982; summer conf. unit mgr. dept. housing and food service Tex. Tech U., Lubbock, 1984, residence hall dir., 1983-86, instr. resident asst. tng., 1984-86; receptionist, travel cons. trainee The Travel Studio, Pullman, Washington, 1986-87; program asst. fin. aid Wash. State U., Pullman, 1986-88, grad. staff asst. div. student svcs., 1988—. Mem. Am. Coll. Personnel Assn., Tex. Women's Network (bd. dirs. region III), Assn. Coll. and Univ. Housing Officers, Am. Personnel and Guidance Assn., Nat. Assn. Student Personnel Adminstrs., Nat. Assn. for Campus Activities, Scottish Heritage Soc., Sigma Kappa, Phi Lambda Theta, Kappa Delta Pi. Democrat. Avocations: cross-stitching, traveling, photography, stamp collecting. Home: PO Box 2794CS Pullman WA 99165 Office: Wash State U Div Student Svcs Pullman WA 99164-7204

VALLERGA, VALERIE GENE, educational psychologist; b. Oakland, Calif., May 30, 1953; d. John B. and Theresa (Rossi) V. BA, St. Mary's Coll., Moraga, Calif., 1975; MA, 1978. Pupil personnel services credential, U. Calif., Davis, 1980, sch. psychologist credential, 1981, lic. ednl. psychologist, Calif. Audit clk. Montgomery Ward Co., Walnut Creek, Calif., 1974-76; intern psychologist Fairfield (Calif.)-Suisun Unified Sch. Dist., 1980-81; sch. psychologist Hemet (Calif.) Unified Sch. Dist., 1981—. Telephone counselor, Contra Costa Crisis and Suicide Intervention Ctr., Walnut Creek, Calif., 1977-78. Mem. Nat. Assn. Sch. Psychologists, Calif. Assn. Sch. Psychologists. Roman Catholic. Office: Hemet Unified Sch Dist 2350 W Latham Ave Hemet CA 92343

VALONE, KEITH EMERSON, clinical psychologist; b. Austin, Tex., Aug. 3, 1953; s. James Floyd and Elizabeth Niles (Emerson) V.; m. Leona Marie Lagace, July 22, 1978; 1 child, Kyle Stephen James. BA, U. So. Calif., 1975; MA, U. Ill., 1979, PhD, 1981. Lic. psychologist, Calif. Pvt. practice Pasadena, Calif., 1983—; clin. asst. prof. dept. psychology Fuller Theol. Sem., Pasadena, Calif., 1984-85; asst. clin. prof. dept. psychology UCLA, 1984-87; chief psychology svc. Las Encinas Hosp., Pasadena, 1988. Contbr. articles to profl. jours. Mem. Am. Psychol. Assn., Calif. State Psychol. Assn., Rotary, Phi Beta Kappa. Episcopalian. Office: 960 E Green St #342 Pasadena CA 91106

VALSAMAKIS, HELEN, food executive; b. L.A., May 31, 1953; d. Christopher and Marina (Laokaitis) V. Grad. high sch. Pres. Renaissance Bakeries, Inc., Laguna Beach, Calif., 1976—. Author: The Renaissance Cookbook, 1988. Republican. Russian Orthodox. Home: 22081 Susan Ln Huntington Beach CA 92646

VAN ARSDALE, JAMES, mayor; m. Eva Van Arsdale; three sons. B.S.B.A., U. Colo. Various sales mgmt. positions mktg. dept. Conoco, 1948-81; mayor City of Billings, Mont., 1984—; past chmn. Billings City Council. Bd. dirs. Mont. League Cities and Towns, Deaconess Hosp. Served with USN. Methodist. Office: City of Billings Office of Mayor PO Box 1178 Billings MT 59103 *

VAN ARSDEL, PAUL PARR, JR., allergist, educator; b. Indpls., Nov. 4, 1926; s. Paul Parr and Ellen (Ewing) Van A.; m. Rosemary Thorstenson, July 7, 1950; children: Mary Margaret, Andrew Paul. BS, Yale U., 1948; MD, Columbia U., 1951. Diplomate Am. Bd. Internal Medicine, Am. Bd. Allergy and Immunology. Intern Presbyn. Hosp., N.Y.C., 1951-52; resident in medicine Presbyn. Hosp., 1952-53; research fellow in medicine U. Wash. Sch. Medicine, Seattle, 1953-55, instr. medicine, 1956-58, from asst. prof. to prof. medicine, 1958--, head allergy sect., 1956--; spl. fellow in allergy, Boston U., Columbia U., N.Y.C., 1955-56; mem. staff Univ. Hosp., Seattle, chief of staff, 1983-85; assoc. staff Harborview Med. Ctr., Seattle; cons. Children's Hosp., Seattle VA Hosp. Contbr. to profl. publs. V.p., bd. dirs. Community Assn., Iron Springs, Wash., 1980-82. Served with USN, 1945-46. Fellow Am. Acad. Allergy and Immunology (pres. 1971-72), ACP; mem. AMA (alt. del. 1972--), Assn. Am. Med. Colls., Phi Beta Kappa, Sigma Xi, Alpha Omega Alpha. Home: 4702 NE 39th St Seattle WA 98105 Office: Univ Hosp Dept Medicine Seattle WA 98195

VAN ARSDOL, MAURICE DONALD, JR., sociologist, educator; b. Seattle, May 4, 1928; s. Maurice Donald and Madge (Belts) V.; m. Marian Clide Gatchell, Aug. 18, 1950; 1 child, Pece Durcinovski. B.A. in Sociology, U. Wash., 1949, M.A., 1952, Ph.D., 1957. Research asst. Office Population Research U. Wash., Seattle, 1950-54, pre-doctoral assoc., 1953-57; asst. prof. dept. sociology U. So. Calif., Los Angeles, 1957-61, research coordinator youth studies ctr., 1959-60, assoc. prof. sociology, 1961-65, prof. sociology, 1965—, dir. population research lab., 1965—; vis. prof. dept. sociology U. Hawaii, Honolulu, 1966, Stockholm U., Sweden, 1978, 82; cons., lectr. in field. Co-author: Mortality Trends in the State of Washington, 1955, The Population of Bahrain, 1978, Changing Roles of Arab Women in Bahrain, 1985; contbr. chpts. to books, articles to profl. jours. Served with U.S. Army, 1952-53. Grantee in field from numerous profl. orgns. Fellow AAAS, Am. Sociol. Assn. (conf. com. 1963); mem. Internat. Union Sci. Study of Population, Population Assn. Am., Pacific Sociol. Assn. (adv. council 1965-68), Alpha Kappa Delta, Lambda Alpha. Office: Population Rsch Lab 3716 S Hope St RAN 385 Los Angeles CA 90007

VANASEK, JAMES GEORGE, commercial banker; b. Chgo., Jan. 20, 1944; s. James Harold and Virginia Edna (Von Asch) V.; m. Deborah Ann Zaccagnini, Nov. 28, 1975. AB, Ind. U., 1966; MBA, Penn State U., 1968. Sr. v.p. Pitts. Nat. Bank, 1968-79, Banc Ohio Nat. Bank, Columbus, 1979-84; exec. v.p. First Interstate Bank of Ariz., Phoenix, 1984—; bd. dirs. Robert Morris Assocs., Phoenix, Assn. for Corporate Growth, Phoenix. Sgt. U.S. Army Res., 1968-74. Mem. Phi Beta Kappa. Republican. Home: 13720 N 85th Pl Scottsdale AZ 85260 Office: 1st Interstate Bank Ariz NA 1st Interstate Bank Pla 100 W Washington St Phoenix AZ 85038-9743

VAN ASPEREN, MORRIS EARL, banker; b. Wessington, S.D., Oct. 5, 1943; s. Andrew and Alyce May (Flagg) Van A.; m. Anne Virginia Merritt, July 2, 1966; 1 child, David Eric. BS in Math., U. Okla., 1966; MBA, Pepperdine U., 1979. Mgr. western dist. Svc. Rev. Inc., Northbrook, Ill., 1970-77; v.p. Hooper Info. Systems Inc., Tustin, Calif., 1977-78; v.p., chief fin. officer ATE Assocs. Inc., Westlake Village, Calif., 1978-84; mgmt. cons. Thousand Oaks, Calif., 1984—; sr. v.p. Nat. Bank Calif., L.A., 1986—; bd. dirs. Packaging Corp. Am., L.A. Nat. advocate fin. svcs. SBA, 1989. Lt. USN, 1966-70. Mem. Nat. Assn. Govt. Guaranteed Lenders, Robert Morris Assocs. Office: Nat Bank Calif 145 S Fairfax Ave Los Angeles CA 90036

VANBLARICOM, JANICE L., interior designer; b. Yakima, Wash.; m. D.P. VanBlaricom, Mar. 25, 1978. BA, U. Wash., 1971. Interior designer-in-residence Bellevue, Wash., 1972—. Trustee, Seattle Found., Pacific Northwest Ballet, Overlake Hosp. Found., Wash. State Film Coun.; trustee, founding pres. Bellevue Allied Arts Coun.; bd. dirs. Bellevue Downtown Park Citizens, Wash. State Arts Alliance; commr., chmn. City of Bellevue Arts Commn.; Seattle Ctr. Adv. Commr.; hon. bd. dirs. Bellevue Philharmonic. Mem. Bellevue Art Mus. (past bd. dirs.), Seattle-King county Hist. soc., Mus. Flight, Pioneer Assn. Wash., Seattle Design Ctr., Columbia Tower Club (founder), Lakes Club (founder).

VAN BRUGGEN, RICHARD JAMES, civil engineer; b. Edwards AFB, Calif., Sept. 28, 1957; s. Richard and Jean Ellen (Murless) Van B.; m. Laura Lin Lovgren, May 21, 1983. BS in Engring. cum laude, UCLA, 1980, MS in Engring., 1981. Registered civil engr., Calif. Civil engr. U.S. Army Corps of Engrs., Los Angeles, 1981-84; sr. engr. Harding Lawson Assocs., Novato, Calif., 1984-88; project engr. Camp, Dresser & McKee, Inc., Walnut Creek, Calif., 1988-89; ind. cons. Vallejo, Calif., 1983—; lectr. Loyola Marymount U., Los Angeles, 1983-84. Contbr. articles to profl. jours. Mem. ASCE, Tau Beta Pi. Republican. Office: 3435 Hazelwood St Vallejo CA 94591

VAN BUTSEL, MICHAEL RANDY, real estate developer; b. Alma, Nebr., Dec. 7, 1952; s. Julius Alfonso and Margaret Lucille (McCorkle) Van B., m. Linda Kay Hagerman, Oct. 9, 1976 (div. Jan. 1985); children: Vanessa, Stephanie, Jamie. BA, U. Nebr., 1975. Lic. real estate rep. Asst. to v.p. cen. adminstrn. U. Nebr., Lincoln, 1975-76; architect Consol. Architects Engrs., Omaha, 1976-77; project mgr. Dana, Larson, Roubal Architects, Phoenix, 1977-79; mktg. dir. Dick, Fristohe Architects, Phoenix, 1979-81; mktg. mgr. Lendrum Design Group, Phoenix, 1981-85; owner Developers Mgmt. Group, Phoenix, 1985-86; mktg. mgr. Turner Constrn., Phoenix, 1986-87; v.p. devel. The Bay Plaza Co., St. Petersburg, Fla., 1987—. Commnr. Housing Commn., City of Phoenix; mem. Paradise Valley Planning Bd.; pres. The Mariners for Senator John McCain, Phoenix; surrogate speaker for Congressman Eldon Rudd, Phoenix. Mem. Urban Land Inst., Leadership St. Petersburg, Valley Leadership (Phoenix). Republican.

VANCE, CARRIE TEMPLE, nurse; b. Jackson, Miss., Nov. 20, 1944. A.A. in Nursing, San Joaquin Delta Coll., Stockton, Calif., 1974; BA in Health Service Adminstrn., St. Mary's Coll., Moraga, Calif., 1978; MS in Nursing Adminstrn. and Music, PhD in Music Performance, Columbia Pacific U., 1985. Lic. nurse, Calif. Staff nurse Dameron Hosp., Stockton, Calif., 1976-77, charge nurse, 1977-80, supr. nursery, 1980—. Mem. San Joaquin Gen. Hosp. Delta Coll. Nurse Alumni Assn., Soc. Nursing Service Adminstrs., Nat. Assn. Female Execs., Columbia Pacific U. Alumni Assn., Nat. Assn. Neonatal Nurses, St. Mary's Coll. Alumni Assn. Seventh-day Adventist. Office: Dameron Hosp Assn 525 W Acacia St Stockton CA 95203

VANCINA-SCOTT, EDLYN JEAN, skin care consultant, problem solver; b. Joliet, Ill., Jan. 3, 1954; d. Edward Joseph and Marilyn Sophia (Fleischauer) V.; m. Joseph Lawrence Scott, May 12, 1986. BS in Edn., No. Ariz. U., 1976. Cons. skin care Mary Kay Cosmetics, Dallas, 1980-85; make-up artist Christian Dior, El Segundo, Calif., 1985—; make-up cons. Biotherm Cosmetics, 1986—; resident make-up artist Janet Sartin Inc., N.Y.C., 1988; promotional rep. Clientele, Inc., Miami, Fla., 1988-89; cons., promotional rep. Parfums Stern, N.Y.C., 1989—; asst. mktg. Halston Fragrance, 1987, Deneuve Fragrance, 1987, Ralph Lauren Fragrance, 1987, Fendi Fragrance, 1987; mem. career mktg. bd. Mademoiselle mag., N.Y.C., 1987—. Mem. Am. Bus. Women's Assn., Flagstaff, Ariz. C. of C. (hon. Sawdust Art Festival Queen), Order Sons and Daus. Italy. Episcopalian. Home and Office: 22024 Antigua Mission Viejo CA 92692

VAN CITTERS, ROBERT LEE, medical educator, physician; b. Alton, Iowa, Jan. 20, 1926; s. Charles and Wilhemina (Heemstra) Van C.; m. Mary E. Barker, Apr. 9, 1949; children: Robert, Mary, David, Sara. A.B., U. Kans., 1949; M.D., U. Kans. Med. Ctr., Kansas City, 1953; Sc.D. hon., Northwestern Coll., Orange City, Iowa, 1977. Intern U. Kans. Med. Ctr., Kansas City, 1953-54, resident, 1955-57, fellow, 1957-58; research fellow Sch. Medicine, U. Wash., Seattle, 1958-61, asst. prof. physiology and biophysics, 1962-65, assoc. prof, 1965-70, prof., 1970—; prof. medicine Sch. Medicine, U. Wash., 1970—, assoc. dean Sch. Medicine, 1968-70, dean Sch. Medicine, 1970-81; mem. staff Scripps Clinic and Research Found., La Jolla, Calif., 1961-62; exchange scientist joint U.S.-U.S.S.R. Sci. Exchange, 1962; mem. Liason Commn. on Med. Edn., Washington, 1981-85; mem. nat. adv. research council NIH, Bethesda, Md., 1980-83; mem. Va. Spl. Med. Adv. Commn., 1974-78, chmn., 1976-78; mem. various com.s NIH, Bethesda, Md. Contbr. numerous articles to profl. jours. Bd. dirs. Pacific Sci. Ctr., Seattle; bd. dirs. Wash. State Heart Assn. Served to 1st lt. U.S. Army, 1943-46, PTO; to capt. M.C., USAF, 1953-55. Recipient research career devel. USPHS. Fellow AAAS; mem. Assn. Am. Med. Colls. (adminstrv. bd. and exec. council 1972-78, Disting. Service mem.), Am. Coll. Cardiology (Cummings medal 1970), Nat. Acad. Sci. Inst. Medicine, Am. Heart Assn., Wash. State Med. Assn. (hon. life). Club: Rainier (Seattle). Office: U Wash Sch Medicine Seattle WA 98195

VAN COTT, JEFFREY MARK, manufacturing company executive; b. Lakewood, Ohio, Dec. 1, 1945; s. John F. and Shirley H. Van C.; BS in engring., Oreg. State U., 1973, BS in Bus., 1973; divorced; children: Dustin Mark, Rachel Jean, Jill Anne. Mfg. trainee Unadilla (N.Y.) Silo Co., 1958-66; owner JM Van Cott Trucking, Unadilla, 1966-70; exec. v.p., treas., Unadilla Silo Co., Inc., 1973-85, Unadilla Laminated Products Co., 1973-85; v.p. Am. Laminators, Eugene Oreg., 1985—; panelist Am. Arbitration Assn., 1983—. Chmn. fin. Methodist Ch., Unadilla, 1976-79; dir. Sidney Hosp., 1981-85. Mem. Am. Inst. Timber Constructor (dir. 1980—, treas. 1983-84, v.p. 1984-85, pres. 1985-86), Am. Mgmt. Assn., Am. Wood Preservers Inst., C. of C., Forest Products Research Soc., Midstate Mgmt. Assn., Rotary, (Paul Harris fellow), Elks. Avocations: competitive running, fishing, traveling. Home: PO Box 10154 Eugene OR 97440 Office: Am Laminators PO Box 1839 Eugene OR 97440

VAN DAM, R. PAUL, attorney general. m. Randi Wagner; 2 children. Grad., U. Utah, JD, 1966. Bar: Utah. Dep. county atty. Salt Lake County, county atty., from 1974; dep. dist. atty, atty. gen. of Utah, 1989—; adj. prof. litigation techniques U. Utah Law Sch. Mem. Nat. Dist. Attys. Assn. (cons.). Office: Office of Atty Gen 236 State Capitol Salt Lake City UT 84114

VAN DE KAMP, ANDREA LOUISE, academic administrator; b. Detroit, July 28, 1943; m. John K. Van De Kamp; 1 child, Diana. BA, Mich. State U., 1966; MA, Columbia U., 1972. Dir. recruitment Columbia U., N.Y.C., 1968-71; asst. dean admissions Dartmouth Coll., Hanover, N.H., 1971-74; assoc. dean admissions Occidental Coll., L.A., 1974-77; exec. dir. Internat. Acad. Estate Trust Law, L.A., 1976-79, Coro Found., L.A., 1977-80; dir. devel. Mus. Contemporary Art, L.A., 1980-81; dir. pub. affairs Carter Hawley Hale Stores, Inc., L.A., 1981-87; pres. Ind. Colls. So. Calif., L.A., 1987-89; v.p., mng. dir. west coast Sotluley's N.Am., Beverly Hills, Calif., 1989—. Bd. dirs., KCET, L.A., L.A. County Mus. Art; bd. dirs., officer, Music Ctr. Operating Co., L.A.; co-chmn. Arts Task Force, L.A.; mem. L.A. 2000. Mem. L.A. Pub. Affairs Officers' Assn. (chmn. 1987-88), Women in Pub. Affairs, Town Hall, Ind. Coll. Fund Am. Democrat. Office: 308 N Rodeo Dr Beverly Hills CA 90210

VAN DE KAMP, JOHN KALAR, state attorney general; b. Pasadena, Calif., Feb. 7, 1936; s. Harry and Georgie (Kalar) Van de K.; m. Andrea Fisher, Mar. 11, 1978; 1 child, Diana. BA, Dartmouth U., 1956; JD, Stanford U., 1959. Bar: Calif. 1960. Asst. U.S. atty. Los Angeles, 1960-66, U.S. atty., 1966-67; dep. dir. Exec. Office for U.S. Attys., Washington, 1967-68, dir., 1968-69; spl. asst. Pres.'s Commn. on Campus Unrest, 1970; fed. pub. defender for Los Angeles 1971-75; dist. atty. Los Angeles County, 1975-83; atty. gen. State of Calif., 1983—; mem. Commn. on Jud. Appointments, Peace Officers Standards and Tng. Commn. Mem. Calif. Dist. Attys. Assn. (past pres.), Nat. Dist. Attys. Assn. (past v.p.), Peace Officers Assn. Los Angeles County (past pres.), Nat. Assn. Attys. Gen. (mem. exec. com.), Conf. Western Attys. Gen. (pres. 1986). Office: Office Atty Gen 3580 Wilshire Blvd Ste 800 Los Angeles CA 90010

VAN DEN BERG, JAN BEETS, real estate developer, consultant; b. Eindhoven, The Netherlands, Dec. 22, 1930; came to U.S., 1940; s. Pieter and Cornelia (Beets) Van Den B.; m. Diana G. Grupe, June 22, 1954 (div. 1985); children: Gloria, Cornelia, Julia; m. Diane M. Pelletier, Sept. 22, 1985; 1 child, Pieter Mathieu. BA, Wesleyan U., Middletown, Conn.; 1953; MBA, Stanford U., 1955. Assoc. McKinsey & Co., Inc., N.Y.C., 1959-63; prin. McKinsey & Co., Inc., London, 1963-66; dir. McKinsey & Co., Inc., Amsterdam, The Netherlands, 1966-72, N.Y.C., 1972-73, London, 1973-377, Stamford, Conn., 1977-88; pvt. practice real estate devel., Sisters, Oreg., 1988—. Lt. USNR, 1955-58. Republican. Home and Office: Cascade Meadow Ranch Sisters OR 97759

VANDENBERG, JOHN DONALD, entomologist; b. Benton Harbor, Mich., Jan. 24, 1954; s. Robert Landis and Madelaine Louise (Westendorf) V.; m. Alice C. L. Churchill, Oct. 8, 1983. B.S. with Honors, U. Mich., 1975; M.S., U. Maine, 1977; Ph.D., Oreg. State U., 1982. Grad. research asst. U. Maine, Orono, 1975-77; grad. teaching asst. Oreg. State U., Corvallis, 1977-78, grad. research asst., 1978-82; postdoctoral assoc. Boyce Thompson Inst., Ithaca, N.Y., 1982-83; research entomologist Agrl. Research Service, U.S. Dept. Agr., Beltsville, Md., 1983-87, research leader Agrl. Research Service, Logan, Utah, 1987—; equal employment opportunity counsellor, 1985-87, sec.-treas., chmn. sci. seminar com., 1984-87. Contbr. articles to profl. jours. Pacific N.W. Regional Chalkbrood Program grantee, Moscow, Idaho, 1978-82; U.S. Forest Service Expt. Sta. and Maine Dept. Conservation grantee, Orono and Augusta, 1976-77. Mem. Soc. for Invertebrate Pathology, Entomol. Soc. Am., Am. Soc. for Microbiology, Sigma Xi, Gamma Sigma Delta. Avocations: singing, guitar-playing, softball coaching, gardening. Office: USDA-ARS Utah State U Bee Biology and Systematics Lab Logan UT 84322-5310

VANDENBERG, PETER RAY, magazine publisher; b. Geneva, Ill., Sept. 8, 1939; s. Don George and Isabel (Frank) V.; m. Kathryn Stock, June 1973 (div. Apr. 1977). BBA, Miami U., 1962. Creative adminstr. E.F. McDonald Incentive Co., Dayton, Ohio, 1966-73; mfrs.' rep. Denver, 1974-75; mgr. Homestake Condominiums, Vail, Colo., 1975-76; desk clk. Vail Run Resort, 1976-77; sales rep. Colo. West Advt., Vail, 1977-79, pres., 1980-83; pres. Colo. West Publ., Vail, 1983—. With U.S. Army, 1963-66.

VANDENBERG, ROBERT LEE, service industry executive; b. Kenosha, Wis., May 5, 1951; s. Neil Lawrence and Alzora Rosalie (Woodward) V.; m. Jane Louise McPike, Aug. 25, 1973 (div. 1989); children: Timothy Neil, Jeffrey Lee. Grad. high sch., Kenosha. Engring. tech. Parko Electronics, Santa Ana, Calif., 1973-74; field svc. engr. Leeds & Northrup, North Wales, Pa., 1974-78; service mgr. Instrument Pers., Long Beach, Calif., 1978-81; v.p. Am. Instrument Svc. Corp., San Dimas, Calif., 1981—. Active Grand Prix Race Com., Del Mar, Calif., 1988. Sgt. USMC, 1969-73. Mem. Instrument Soc. Am. (sr.), Benicia Yacht Club, U.S. Power Squadron. Republican. Office: Am Instrument Service Corp 100 W Foothill San Dimas CA 91773

VANDENBERGHE, RONALD GUSTAVE, accountant, real estate developer; b. Oakland, Calif., July 1, 1937; s. Anselm Henri and Margaret B. (Bygum) V.; B.A. with honors, San Jose State Coll., 1959; postgrad. U. Calif. at Berkeley Extension, 1959-60, Golden Gate Coll., 1961-63; CPA, Calif.; m. Patricia W. Dufour, Aug. 18, 1957; children: Camille, Mark, Matthew. Real estate investor, pres. VandenBerghe Fin. Corp., Pleasanton, Calif., 1964—. Instr. accounting U. Cal., Berkeley, 1963-70; CPA, Pleasanton, 1963—. Served with USAF. Mem. Calif. Soc. CPAs. Republican. Presbyterian. Mason (Shriner). Home: PO Box 803 Danville CA 94526 Office: 20 Happy Valley Rd Pleasanton CA 94566

VAN DE POEL, JEFFREY PAUL, data processing executive; b. San Francisco, Nov. 6, 1957; s. John Frederick and Dorothy Agnes (Kern) Van De P.; m. Karen Jean Wentworth, July 12, 1986; 1 child, Andrew Paul. BS in Info. Systems, San Diego State U., 1981. Programmer, analyst Ins. Co. the West, San Diego, 1981-83, Security Pacific Fin. Corp., San Diego, 1983-84; programmer, analyst XYCOR, Inc., San Diego, 1984-85, project leader, 1985-86; programming mgr. ESC Adminstrs., San Diego, 1986-87; v.p. systems, programming Aztec Computer Svcs., San Diego, 1988-89; systems mgr. AVCO Fin. Svcs., Irvine, Calif., 1989—. Office: AVCO Fin Svcs 3349 Michelson Dr Irvine CA 92715-1606

VANDERFORD, FRANK JOSIRE, engineer; b. Moose Lake, Minn., Oct. 19, 1921; s. William and Mary (Flaa) V.; m. Eleanor Marie Gibis, Feb. 8, 1945; children: Constance, Gail, Deborah. Cert. in Electronics, U. Minn., 1952. Engr. Remington Rand Univac, St. Paul, 1955-59, Collins Radio Co., Newport Beach, Calif., 1959-69, Control Data Corp., Santa Ana, Calif., 1969-71; staff engr. Hughes Aircraft Co., Fullerton, Calif., 1971—. Served with USN, 1940-46. Mem. Nat. Rep. Senatorial Com., U.S. Senatorial Club, Rep. Presdl. Task Force (charter), World War II Submarine Vets., Nat. Rifle Assn. Mem. Assembly of God Ch.

VANDERGRIFF, JERRY DODSON, computer store executive; b. Ft. Leonard Wood, Mo., Nov. 6, 1943; s. Oliver Wyatt Vandergriff and Mary Ella (Perkins) Myers; m. Donna Jean Niehof, Aug. 14, 1976 (div. Nov. 1987); children: Robert Lee II, William Oliver. BS in Bus., Emporia State U., 1974. Customer svc. mgr. Pictures, Inc., Anchorage, 1975-83, v.p., gen. mgr., 1983-87; gen. mgr. Pictures-The Computer Store, Anchorage, 1987—. Bd. dirs. Community Schs. Coun., Anchorage, 1986-87, govs. coun. on edn., 1989, Romig Jr. High Sch., 1989-90. With USN, 1961-64. Mem. VFW, Moose. Republican. Home: 3831 Balchen Dr Anchorage AK 99517-2446 Office: Pictures-The Computer Store 8ll W 8th Ave Anchorage AK 99501-3495

VANDERHOFF, ROBERT EDWARD, sales executive; b. Atlantic City, Apr. 8, 1955; s. Lester Lamont and Phyllis Ruth (Rest) V.; m. Carol Ann Rambo, June 10, 1978; children: Kylie Nicole, Robert Jordan, Jared Robert. BA, Messiah Coll., 1977. Sales rep. Westinghouse Electric Supply Co., Harrisburg, Pa., 1977-80, Phoenix, 1980-82, Boise, Idaho, 1984-86, Riverside, Calif., 1986—; sales specialist Amp Product Corp., Washington, 1982-84. Recipient Hank Rich Meml. award Atlantic City Exchange Club, 1973; named to Top Performer Club, Wesco, Riverside, Calif., 1987. Republican. Baptist. Home: 5639 Argyle Ave San Bernardino CA 92404 Office: Westinghouse Electric 3233 Trade Center Dr Riverside CA 92507

VANDERLINDEN, CAMILLA DENICE DUNN, quality assurance development and management executive, educator; b. Dayton, July 21, 1950; d. Joseph Stanley and Virginia Danley (Martin) Dunn; m. David Henry VanderLinden; Oct. 10, 1980; 1 child, Michael Christopher. Student, U. de Valencia, Spain, 1969; BA in Spanish and Secondary Edn., U. Utah, 1972, MS in Human Resource Econs., 1985. Asst. dir. Davis County Community Action Program, Farmington, Utah, 1973-76; dir. South County Community Action, Midvale, Utah, 1976-79; supr. customer service Ideal Nat. Life Ins. Co., Salt Lake City, 1979-80; mgr. customer service Utah Farm Bur. Mutual Ins., Salt Lake City, 1980-82; quality assurance analyst Am. Express Co., Salt Lake City, 1983-86, quality assurance and human resource specialist, 1986-88; mgr. quality assurance & engring. Am. Express Co., Denver, 1988—; adj. faculty Westminster Coll., Salt Lake City, 1987-88. Vol. translator Latin Am. community. Republican. Office: Am Express Info Svcs Co Integrated Payments Systems Div 181 Inverness Dr W Englewood CO 80112-3100

VAN DER MEULEN, JOSEPH PIERRE, neurologist; b. Boston, Aug. 22, 1929; s. Edward Lawrence and Sarah Jane (Robertson) VanDer M.; m. Ann Irene Yadeno, June 18, 1960; children—Elisabeth, Suzanne, Janet. A.B., Boston Coll., 1950; M.D., Boston U., 1954. Diplomate: Am. Bd. Psychiatry and Neurology. Intern Cornell Med. div. Bellevue Hosp., N.Y.C., 1954-55; resident Cornell Med. div. Bellevue Hosp., 1955-56; resident Harvard U., Boston City Hosp., 1958-60, instr., fellow, 1962-66; assoc. Case Western Res. U., Cleve., 1966-67; asst. prof. Case Western Res. U., 1967-69, assoc. prof. neurology and biomed. engring., 1969-71; prof. neurology U. So. Calif., Los Angeles, 1971—; also dir. dept. neurology Los Angeles County/U. So. Calif. Med. Center; chmn. dept. U. So. Calif., 1971-78, v.p. for health affairs, 1977—, dean Sch. Medicine, 1985-86; vis. prof. Autonomous U. Guadalajara, Mex., 1974; pres. Norris Cancer Hosp. and Research Inst., 1983—. Contbr. articles to profl. jours. Mem. med. adv. bd. Calif. chpt. Myasthenia Gravis Found., 1971-75, chmn., 1974-75, 77-78; med. adv. bd. Amyotrophic Lateral Sclerosis Found., Calif., 1973-75, chmn., 1974-75; mem. Com. to Combat Huntington's Disease, 1973—; trustee Calif. Hosp. Med. Ctr., Good Hope Med. Found., Eisenhower Med. Ctr., Doheny Eye Hosp., House Ear Inst., Los Angeles Hosp. Good Samaritan, Children's Hosp. of Los Angeles, Thomas Aquinas Coll.; bd. dirs. Assn. Acad. Health Ctrs., The Scott Newman Found; pres. Scott Newman Ctr. Served to lt. M.C. USNR, 1956-58. Nobel Inst. fellow Karolinska Inst., Stockholm, 1960-62; NIH grantee, 1968-71. Mem. Am. Neurol. Assn., Am. Acad. Neurology, Los Angeles Soc. Neurology and Psychiatry (pres. 1977-78), Mass., Ohio, Calif. med. socs., Los Angeles Acad. Medicine, Alpha Omega Alpha (councillor). Home: 39 Club View Ln Rolling Hills Estates CA 90274 Office: U So Calif 1985 Zonal Ave Los Angeles CA 90033

VANDER MOLEN, JACK JACOBUS, industrial facility planner, consultant; b. Assen, Drenthe, Netherlands, May 28, 1916; came to U.S., 1947, naturalized 1952; s. Evert Moll and Victorina Sweelssen; m. Ina Mary Auerbach, 1946. ME, M.T.S., Haarlem, 1940; postgrad., Ariz. Tech., 1982—. Draftsman, designer Fokker Aircraft, Amsterdam, Netherlands, 1939-40; asst. plant mgr. Bruynzeel's Deuren Fabriek, Zaandam, Netherlands, 1941-44; civilian mgr. Allied Hdqrs. Rest Ctrs., Maastricht, Amsterdam, Netherlands, 1944-45; cen. staff tech. efficiency and orgn. Philips Radio, Eindhoven, Holland, 1945-47; indsl. engr. N.Am. Philips, Dobbs Ferry, N.Y., 1947-48; supr. methods and standards Otis Elevator Co., Yonkers, N.Y., 1948-51; staff engr., material handling and distbn., cons. Drake, Startzman, Sheahan & Barclay, N.Y.C., 1951-55; mgr. material handling, engring. Crane Co., Chgo., 1955-60; assoc., cons. A.T. Kearney & Co., Inc., Chgo., 1960-67; pres., cons. J.J. Vander Molen & Co., Internat., Oak Park and Sun City, Ill., Ariz, 1967—. Conceptual developer of plants, warehouses and terminals, computerized conversion of inventory requirements into space requirements for food chains. With U.S. Army, 1940-45; with Can. Army, 1944-45. Mem. ASME, Internat. Materials Handling Soc. (nat. dir., past pres. Chgo. chpt). Republican. Presbyterian.

VANDERSANDE, JOHAN, mechanical engineer; b. Amsterdam, The Netherlands, Sept. 27, 1946; came to U.S., 1972; s. Doede and Helena M. (Spoel) V.; m. Evelyne M. Perrot, Jan. 9, 1971; children: Vanessa Y., Antony D. BSc. in Mech. Engring., U. of Tech., Delft, The Netherlands, 1968, MSc. in Food and Refrigeration Engring., 1971. Research fellow N.Y. Blood Ctr., N.Y.C., 1972-73, assoc. dir., 1973-80, dir. mfg., 1980-83, plant mgr., 1984-86; dir. engring. Baxter/Hyland div., Glendale, Calif., 1986—. Contbr. articles to profl. jours. With Dutch Army, 1971-72. Mem. Parenteral Drug Assn. Home: 25433 Via Alcira Valencia CA 91355

VANDERSPEK, PETER GEORGE, management consultant; b. The Hague, Netherlands, Dec. 15, 1925; came to U.S., 1945; s. Pieter and Catherine Johanna (Rolf) V.; m. Charlotte Louise Branch, Aug. 18, 1957. Student, Tilburg (Netherlands) U., 1944; MA in Econs., Fordham U., 1950, PhD in Econs., 1954; postgrad., George Washington U., 1967-68. Internat. economist Mobil Oil Corp., N.Y.C., 1956-59; mgr. internat. market rsch. Celanese Corp., N.Y.C., 1959-63; internat. economist Bethlehem (Pa.) Steel Corp., 1964-65; sr. tech. adviser Battelle Meml. Inst., Washington, 1965-66; indsl. adviser Inter-Am. Devel. bank, Washington, 1967-69; economist Fed. Res. Bank, N.Y.C., 1970-72; mgr. internat. market rsch. Brunswick Corp., Skokie, Ill., 1973-76; mgr. advanced planning Sverdrup Corp., St. Louis, 1979-87; cons. Sverdrup Corp., 1988—; pres. OBEX, Inc., San Luis Obispo, Calif., 1988—. Contbr. to profl. publs. Thomas J. Watson fellow, IBM-Fordham U., 1945-49. Mem. Nat. Assn. Bus. Economists, Mensa. Home: 1314 Vega Way San Luis Obispo CA 93401 Office: Sverdrup Corp 13723 Riverport Dr Maryland Heights MO 63043

VANDER TOP, ROGER DEAN, certified public accountant; b. Slayton, Minn., Nov. 28, 1953; s. John and Christina (Drooger) V.T.; m. Alicia Marie Veenendaal, Sept. 5, 1984. AS, Southwestern Tech., Canby, Minn., 1973. CPA, S.D., Calif. Staff acct. Bernell J. McGinnis, C.P.A., Sioux Falls, S.D., 1973-76, John Lane Accountancy Corp., Modesto, Calif., 1976-81; pvt. practice Modesto, 1981—; treas. Modesto Patriots Youth Football, 1983-88, Inland Soc. Tax Cons., Modesto, 1983. Coach Modesto Youth Soccer Assn., 1986; sponsor Bel Passi Youth Baseball, Modesto, 1983-88. Mem. Calif. Soc. CPA's, Modesto C. of C. Democrat. Office: 720 13th St Ste B Modesto CA 95354

VANDER VELDEN, CHERYL MARIE, federal agency administrator; b. Rhinelander, Wis., Jan. 29, 1962; d. Thomas Clifford and Carol Elizabeth (Braun) Vander V. BSBA, U. Mont., 1984. Teaching asst. Sch . Bus. U. Mont., Missoula, 1982; student trainee U.S. Forest Svc., Missoula, 1984-85; resource specialist Nezperce Nat. Forest U.S. Forest Svc., Grangeville, Idaho, 1985; resource specialist Clearwater Nat. Forest U.S. Forest Svc., Orofino, Idaho, 1985-88; supervisory resource specialist U.S. Forest Svc., Orofino, 1988--; treas., del. Internat. Tng. in Communications, Orofino, 1985--. Mem. AAUW (co-sec.), Nat. Honor Soc. Republican. Roman Catholic. Office: US Forest Svc 12730 Hwy 12 Orofino ID 83544

VANDER ZALM, WILLIAM NICK, government official; b. Noordwykerhout, Holland, May 29, 1934; came to Canada, 1947; s. Wilhelmus Nicholaas and Agatha C. (Warmerdam) van der Zalm; m. Lillian Vander Zalm, June 27, 1956; children: Jeffrey, Juanita, Wim, Lucia. Student pub. schs., Holland and Canada. Pres. Art Knapp Nurseries Ltd., 1956—; alderman Surrey Mcpl. Council, 1965-69, mayor, 1969-75; Minister of Human Resources Provinical Legis. for Social Credit Party, 1975-78; Minister Mcpl. Affairs and Minister of Urban Transit Authority (name now B.C. Transit) B.C., 1978-82; Minister of Edn. and Minister responsible for B.C. Transit 1982-83; founder Fantasy Garden World, Richmond, Can., 1983; Premier of B.C. and leader of B.C. Social Credit Party Victoria, B.C., Can., 1986—. Mem. B.C. C. of C. (pres. 1986). Roman Catholic. Home: 19003-88 Ave, Surrey, BC Canada V3S 5X7 Office: Office of Premier, Legislature Bldg, Victoria, BC Canada V8V 4R3

VAN DE VEERE, KATHLEEN DAILEY, foundation administrator; b. Seattle, Nov. 8, 1935; d. Joseph Anderson and Dorothy Mable (Burke) Dailey; m. Warren Craig Van De Veere, Dec. 22, 1957; children: Mary Kathleen, Joseph Earl. AA, U. Calif., Berkeley, 1955; BS, U. Calif., San Francisco, 1958; M in Pub. Adminstrn., U. Denver, 1983. RN, Calif., Colo., registered pub. health nurse, Colo. Clk. typist U.S. Army, White Sands Missile Range, N.Mex., 1958-59; community health nurse Dept. Health Santa Clara County, San Jose, Calif., 1959-61, Orange County, Santa Ana, Calif., 1961-63; sch. nurse Garden Grove (Calif.) Unified Sch. Dist., 1964-72, Huntington Beach (Calif.) Union High Sch. Dist., 1972-75; program dir. Tri-County Dist. Dept. Health, Thorton, Colo., 1977-83; dir. svc. and rehab. Colo. div. Am. Cancer Soc., Denver, 1984—. Mem. Arvada (Colo.) Ctr. Chorale, 1978—. Mem. Oncology Nursing Soc., Mile Hi Cloggers. Republican. Office: Am Cancer Soc Colo Div 2255 S Oneida Denver CO 80224

VAN DE VEN, FLORIS GERARD HELENA, physical therapist; b. Haarlem, Netherlands, Jan. 13, 1956; came to U.S., 1982; s. Jan Willem and Lucia (Angenent) Van de V.; m. Leslie Fernandez, Apr. 23, 1988. Grad., SAFA Acad. for Phys. Therapy, Amsterdam, Netherlands, 1979. Registered phys. therapist, Calif. Staff therapist Univ. Hosp. Free Univ., Amsterdam, 1979-82; staff and chief therapist Phys. Therapy Assocs., Wharton, Tex., 1982-85; dir. phys. therapy dept. Daniel Freeman Hosp., Inglewood, Calif., 1985-86; pvt. practice Colusa, Calif., 1986--; instr. sch. nursing Free U., 1981-82, SAFA Acad. for Phys. Therapy, 1981-82. Mem. Am. Phys. Therapy Assn., Lions (sec. Colusa chpt. 1988). Home: 418 8th St PO Box 176 Colusa CA 95932 Office: 199 E Webster St Colusa CA 95932

VANDEVENTER, JANICE LEIGH, cartographer, flight instructor; b. Long Beach, Calif., Aug. 10, 1944; d. Owen Jerome and Laurence Elizabeth (Monninger) V.; B.A. in Geography, UCLA, 1966. Cartographer, Automobile Club So. Calif., Los Angeles, 1966-70, sr. cartographer, 1970-72, research coordinator, 1972-74, chief cartographer, supr. 1974—; flight instr. Falcon Air, Long Beach, 1975—. Recipient FAA Safety Pin, 1974. Active choir New Life Community Ch., Artesia, Calif. Mem. Am. Congress Surveying and Mapping, Nat. Computer Graphics Assn., Los Angeles Area C. of C., Aircraft Owners and Pilots Assn., Sweet Adelines, Goldenaires Quartet (lead singer, group named novice quartet champions 1982), UCLA Alumni Assn., Alpha Xi Delta. Home: 5141 E Burnett St Long Beach CA 90815 Office: Automobile Club So Calif 2601 S Figueroa St Los Angeles CA 90007

VANDIVER, GERALDINE M., construction company executive; b. Yakima, Wash., June 29, 1926; d. Iroxel Leroy and Dorothy (Strachan) Tennant; m. John H. Vandiver, June 21, 1951; children: Dean H., Roger A., Mary D., Mark J. BA in Math., Wash. State U., 1948, EdB, 1949. Dean of women, faculty phys. and health edn. Yakima Valley Coll., 1949-50; tchr. Franklin Sch., Yakima, 1950-51; ptnr. John H. Vandiver Constrn., Yakima, 1951—. Active Yakima Co. Unit Pro-Am., 1976—. Mem. Woman's Century Club (pres. 1987-88, 89), Yakima Rep. Women (pres 1983, 84, 87, 88), Phi Theta Kappa. Address: 701 S 27th Ave Yakima WA 98902

VANDIVER, ROBERT SANFORD, telecommunications company executive; b. Barksdale Field, La., Apr. 2, 1937; s. William Marion and Mattie Katherine (Tiller) V.; m. Patricia Gail Kelly, Feb. 10, 1956; children: Cynthia Ann, Kathleen. AA, U. Md., 1973; BA, SUNY, Albany, 1975; MS, Golden Gate U., 1985, MPA, 1986. Enlisted U.S. Army, 1955, commd. lt., 1967, advanced through grades to maj., 1978, served worldwide, 1978; materiel mgr. Pima County Sheriff Dept., Tucson, 1979-81; task leader Computer Scis. Corp., Sierra Vista, Ariz., 1981-83, Mandex, Inc., Sierra Vista, 1983-86; project mgr. Planning Rsch. Corp., Sierra Vista, 1986—; adj. faculty, Cochies Coll., Sierra Vista, 1987—, Golden Gate U., San Francisco, 1988—; instr. Sch. Pub. Adminstrn., Ariz. State U., Tucson, 1988—. Co-editor, South Vietnam Boy Scout Handbook, 1965. Troop leader, Boy Scouts Am., various locations, 1956—; lt. col. CAP, Tucson, 1977—. Decorated Legion of Merit, Bronze Star medal; recipient Silver Beaver award, Boy Scouts Am., 1977. Mem. Nat. Property Mgmt. Assn., Soc. Logistics Engrs., Armed Forces Communications Electronics Assn., Am. Soc. Pub. adminstrn., Co. Mil. Historians. Lutheran. Home: 8345 E Cypress Point Ln Tucson AZ 85710 Office: Planning Rsch Corp 1001 Executive Dr Sierra Vista AZ 85635

VAN DOREN, LEOH HUGH, finance company executive; b. Wenatchee, Wash., May 13, 1931; s. Hugh Louis and Florence (Betty) V.; m. Jean Marie Bonham, Aug. 18,. BA in History, Econ., Wash. State U., 1956; MA in History, Polit. Sci, U. Nev., 1960. Tchr. Brewster (Wash.) Sch. Dist., 1956-57; tchr., counsler Washoe County Sch. Dist., Reno, Nev., 1957-60; tchr Anchorage (Ala.) Sch. Dist., 1960-61; counselor Yakima (Wash.) Sch. Dist., 1961-64; instr., asst. dean Treas. Valley Coll., Ontario, Oreg., 1964-68; dean Honolulu Community Coll., 1968-70; exec. pres., pers. dir. Community Coll. Div., Reno, 1970-77; v.p., dean Big Bend Coll., Moses Lake, Wash., 1977-80; budget dir. Mason County Commr., Shelton, Wash., 1980-82; dir., fin., grant Shelton Sch. Dist. No. 309, 1982--. Bd. dirs. Health Ins. Coop. , Olympia, 1987--, Ind. Relation Mason Gen. Mem. Jaycees, Reno Little League, Wash. Assn. Sch. Bus. Officer. Shelton. Home: 706 Holly Ln Shelton WA 98584

VAN DORN, PETER DOUGLAS, accountant; b. Craig, Colo., June 28, 1941; s. Perry Douglas and Gloria Marjorie (Miller) Van D.; m. Joyce Lucille Swanson, Aug. 9, 1964; children—Douglas, Stephen, Marsha. Student Colo. State U., 1959-60; B.S., U. Colo., 1969. C.P.A., Colo., Wyo., La., N.C. With Touche Ross & Co., Denver, 1969-86, ptnr., 1978-86, nat. dir. banking, 1979-86, founder, mng. ptnr. Van Dorn & Bossi, Broomfield, Colo., 1986—. Treas. Colo. Children's Chorale . Served with Army NG, 1963-69. Mem. Am. Inst. CPAs, Colo. Soc. CPAs, Wyo. Soc. CPAs. Republican. Baptist. Clubs: Ranch Country (Westminister), U. Colo. Alumni Dirs.; 26 (Denver) ; U. Colo. Alumni Dirs. Home: 4280 Creek Dr Broomfield CO 80020 Office: Van Dorn & Bossi 760 Burbank St Broomfield CO 80020

VANDOVER, JACK ALLEN, senior principle engineer; b. Oakland, Calif., June 14, 1947; s. C.R. and Theresa (Jazenbak) V.; m. Ellen Dawn Benefield, Oct. 19, 1977. BS in Math., Hampden Sydeny Coll., 1969; AA in Computer Sci., Coleman Coll., San Diego, 1976; MS in Computer Sci., West Coast U., 1980. Programmer J. H. Elliot Co., Washington, 1969-70; sr. computer scientist Computer Scis. Corp., San Diego, 1977. Served with USN, 1970-76. Mem. Assn. for Computing machinery, Nat. Mgmt. Assn., Cabrillo Internat. Folk Dancers (chmn. 1981-82). Office: Computer Scis Corp 4045 Hancock St San Diego CA 92110

VAN DREAL, GEORGE, educator, artist; b. Denver, Oct. 19, 1931; s. Ira Ari and Marguereet (Déleve) Van D.; children: Edward, John. BS, Colo. State U., 1963; MA, Fresno State Coll., 1967. Art illustrator, meter reader Colo. Cen. Power, Englewood, 1952-58; tech. illustrator Martin Co., Englewood, 1958-61; specification rev. engr. Martin Marietta, Littleton, Colo., 1962-63; tchr. Kern County High Sch., Bakersfield, Calif., 1963—; cons. artist, 1975—. Author (booklet) Fun and Inexpensive Physical Science Labs, 1986; editor in field. With USAF, 1950-51. Recipient Disting. Teaching award Nat. Sci. Tchrs. Assn., 1987, Nat. Assn. of Microbiologists teaching award, 1975, various art awards U. Calif.-Davis, Calif. Expo., Sacramento, Oklahoma City Ann. Open Exhibit. Mem. NEA, Calif. Tchrs. Assn. (named Inventive Tchr. of Yr. 1972), Calif. Assn. for the Gifted (Regional Tchr. of Yr. 1989), Fla. Painting Soc. (Overall award 1979), Guild of Natural Sci. Illustrators, Greenpeace, Artists Guild, Englewood Jaycees (state chmn.), Bakersfield Art Assn. (v.p. 1978, 79), Phi Delta Kappa. Presbyterian. Home: 1757 Camino Primavera Bakersfield CA 93306

VAN DRUNEN, SCOTT WILLIAM, accountant, treasurer; b. Phoenix, Jan. 31, 1961; s. Gilbert P. and Phyllis Anne (Mauro) VanD.; m. Julie Anne Griffin, Dec. 29, 1984. BS in Fin., Ariz. State U., Tempe, 1984; MBA in Bus., U. Phoenix, 1987. Credit analyst The Dial Corp., Phoenix, 1984-86, fin. acct., 1986-87, sr. acct., 1987—; treas., co-owner Jotmon, Inc., PHoenix, 1986—. Mem. Ariz. State U. Alumni Assn., Phi Gamma Delta (social chmn. 1981-82). Republican. Roman Catholic. Home: 3328 N 17th Dr Phoenix AZ 85015 Office: 15101 N Scottsdale Rd Scottsdale AZ 85260

VAN DUSEN, ANN BRENTON, writer; b. Blackfoot, Idaho, June 15, 1919; d. Henry Kirk and Margaret Mary (Burrell) Williams; divorced; children: Delbert Wayne, Brenton John (dec.). Student art history, Univ. of Ams., Mexico City, 1976-78; cert., Famous Writer's Sch., 1981; BA in English, Coll. Idaho, 1985. Cert. tchr., Idaho. Elem. tchr. rural sch. dist. Meridian, Idaho, 1940-42. Author: Who's Depressed?, 1984 (Strata merit award 1984). Coord. Am. Cancer Soc., Boise, 1954-69; com. chmn. Idaho Mental Health Assn., 1962-68; vol. Caldwell (Idaho) Hosp. Aux. Mem. PEO (pres. Meridian 1983-85). Republican. Mem. Ch. Religious Sci. Home: 1907 Idaho Ave Caldwell ID 83605

VAN DUZER, ASHLEY MACMILLAN, III, marketing company executive, consultant; b. Cleve., June 19, 1948; s. Ashley MacMillan Van Duzer and Virginia (Hosford) Jones; m. Mary Elizabeth Hrake, Aug. 17, 1985; 1 child, Amy Daisy Hosford. BA, Claremont McKenna Coll., 197l; MBA, Stanford U., 1976. Owner, mgr. San Luis Obispo (Calif.) Moving Co., 1983-86, Ashley's Dog & Catalog, Harmony, Calif., 1986, Advanced Image Mktg., Harmony, 1987—. Republican. Episcopalian. Home and Office: PO Box 2525 Harmony CA 93435

VANE, EDWIN THOMAS, broadcasting company executive; b. N.Y.C., Apr. 29, 1927; s. Edwin T. and Marie (Beilman) V.; m. Claire A. Vane, Oct. 7, 1950; children: Richard, Christopher, Timothy, B. Paul. BA, Fordham U., 1948; MBA, NYU, 1951. Various positions including page, audience promotion and sales promotion NBC, N.Y.C., 1945-61, mgr. daytime programs, 1961-64; dir. daytime programs ABC, N.Y.C., 1964-66, v.p. daytime programs, 1966-67, v.p. nighttime programs prodn., 1967-72, v.p. nat. program dir., 1972-79, v.p. network program affairs, 1979; pres., chief exec. officer Group W Productions, Los Angeles, from 1979; mem. program producers and distbrs. com. Mem. Acad. TV Arts and Scis. (bd. govs.), Internat. Radio and TV Soc. (bd. dirs.), Programming Panels and Display Circuits (treas.).

VANE, SYLVIA BRAKKE, anthropologist, cultural resource management company executive; b. Fillmore County, Minn., Feb. 28, 1918; d. John T. and Hulda Christina (Marburger) Brakke; m. Arthur Bayard Vane, May 17, 1942; children—Ronald Arthur, Linda, Laura Vane Ames. A.A., Rochester Jr. Coll., 1937; B.S. with distinction, U. Minn., 1939; student Radcliffe Coll., 1944; M.A., Calif. State U.-Hayward, 1975. Med. technologist Dr. Frost and Hodapp, Willmar, Minn., 1939-41; head labs. Corvallis Gen. Hosp., Oreg., 1941-42; dir. lab. Cambridge Gen. Hosp., Mass., 1942-43, Peninsula Clinic, Redwood City, Calif., 1947-49; v.p. Cultural Systems Research, Inc., Menlo Park, Calif., 1978—; pres. Ballena Press, Menlo Park, 1981—; cons. cultural resource mgmt. So. Calif. Edison Co., Rosemead, 1978-81, San Diego Gas and Elec. Co., 1980-83, Pacific Gas and Elec. Co., San Francisco, 1982-83, Wender, Murase & White, Washington, 1983—, Yosemite Indians, Mariposa, Calif., 1982-84, San Luis Rey Band of Mission Indians, Escondido, Calif., 1986—, U.S. Ecology, Newport Beach, Calif., 1986—, Riverside County Flood Control and Water Conservation Dist., 1985—. Author: (with L.J. Bean), California Indians, Primary Resources, 1977, The Cahuilla and the Santa Rosa Mountains, 1981. Contbr. chpts. to several books. Bd. dirs. Sequoia Area council Girl Scouts U.S., 1954-61; bd. dirs., v.p., pres. LWV, S. San Mateo County, Calif., 1960-65, cons. San Francisco council Girl Scouts U.S., 1962-69. Fellow Soc. Applied Anthropology; mem. Southwestern Anthrop. Assn. (program chmn. 1976-78, newsletter editor 1976-79), Am. Anthropology Assn., Soc. for Am. Archaeology. Mem. United Ch. of Christ. Office: Ballena Press 823 Valparaiso Ave Menlo Park CA 94025

VAN EECKHOUT, EDWARD MATHIAS, mining and geological engineer, researcher; b. Fargo, N.D., Dec. 25, 1945; s. Edward Cornelius and Rose (Tuchscherer) Van E.; m. Mary Alice Svendsen, June 15, 1967; children: Barbara Sue, Mark Edward. B in Geol. Engring., U. Minn., 1967, PhD, 1974; MS, U. Chgo., 1974. Registered profl. engr., Mont. Rsch. engr. Conoco, Ponca City, Okla., 1974-76; mining engr. U.S. Bur. Mines, Twin Cities, Minn., 1976-77; from asst. to assoc. prof. mining dept. Mont. Tech., Butte, 1977-85; staff mem., tech. coord. earth and space scis. div. Los Alamos (N.Mex.) Nat. Lab., 1985—; cons. in field. Contbr. articles to profl. jours. Trustee Butte Sch. Bd., 1983-84; bd. dirs. Mont. Tech. Found. Bd., Butte, 1984-85; mem. Sangre de Cristo Chorale, Santa Fe, 1986—. 1st lt. U.S. Army, 1969-71, Vietnam. Mem. Soc. Mining Engrs. (v.p. 1964—, sec., treas. 1980-850, Internat. Soc. Rock Mechanics, Am. Underground Space Assn., ASCE, Rotary (pres. Butte chpt. 1978-85, pres. Los Alamos chpt. 1985—). Home: 100 Venado Los Alamos NM 87544 Office: Los Alamos Nat Lab MS D446 Los Alamos NM 87545

VAN FLEET, WILLIAM MABRY, architect; b. Point Richmond, Calif., Jan. 22, 1915; s. Harvey Lorenz and Allie O'Dell (Taylor) Van F.; A.B., U. Calif., Berkeley, 1938; m. Colette Sims, Apr. 26, 1940; children—Christine, Ellen, Peter. Pvt. practice architecture, Eureka, Calif., 1951—; lectr. design Humboldt (Calif.) State U., 1965-66; ptnr. William & Colette Van Fleet, 1954—; prin. works include: Del Norte County Courthouse and Library, Crescent City, Calif., 1957, Freshwater (Calif.) Elementary Sch., 1954, Lee residence, Sunnybrae, Calif., 1962, Zane Jr. High Sch., Eureka, 1965, offices for Brooks-Scanlon Lumber Co., Bend, Oreg., 1967. Chmn., No. Humboldt Vocat. Council, 1964-65, Humboldt County Scenic Resources Com., 1965; pres. Humboldt-Del Norte Mental Health Soc., 1970-71; mem. Humboldt County Community Services Ctr. 1970, Humboldt Arts Council, 1970, Humboldt County Energy Adv. Com., 1979; chmn. Eureka Beautification Com., 1969, Humboldt Sr. Retirement Homes Com., 1979—; bd. dirs. Humboldt County Assn. Retarded Children, 1960-68, Humboldt Family Service Ctr., 1970, Redwoods United Workshop, 1973, Open Door Clinic, 1973, Coordinating Council Human Services Humboldt County, 1976, Calif.-Oreg. Community Devel. Soc., 1980—; mem. Humboldt Energy Adv. Com., 1980—, Eureka City Housing Adv. Bd., 1982. Recipient Merit award HHFA, 1964, 1st Honor award Pub. Housing Adminstrn., 1964, Gov. Calif. Design award, 1966, Outstanding Service award Far West Indian Hist. Soc., 1973, Man of Year award Redwood region Nat. Audubon Soc., 1976, resolutions of commendation Calif. State Senate and Assembly, 1982. Mem. AIA, Net Energy Assn. (dir.), Humboldt Native Plant Soc., Redwood Art Assn. (pres. 1970), Sierra Club (dir. 1972), Fifty-Plus Runners Assn. (1st place in age group Nat. Fifty-Plus Runners Meet 1981). Unitarian. Clubs: Kiwanis (pres. Eureka 1976-77; Disting. Service award 1968); Six Rivers Running (dirs., All-Am. awards 1987). Participant in various marathons and races, including Internat. Marathon, Sacramento, 1983 (1st in 65-69 age group), World Vet. Championships Marathon, Rome, Italy, 1984 (1st in U.S., 8th in World, 70-74 age group), Fifty-Plus 5 mile run, Stanford, Calif., 1985 (1st in 70-74 age group, 2d all-time nationally), course records (70-74 age group) 300-meters and 5-kilometer runs Masters Hayward Classic Track & Field Meet, Eugene, Oreg., 1988, set new nat. record for age 73 in Hale Marathon, San Francisco, 1988; others. Home: 71 Old Forest Ln Eureka CA 95501 Office: 818 3d St Eureka CA 95501

VAN HOOMISSEN, GEORGE THOMAS, manufacturing company executive; b. Portland, Oreg.; s. George Albert and Ruth Madeleine (Niedermeyer) Van H. BA in Econs., Princeton U., 1986. Fin. analyst Tektronix, Inc., Beaverton, Oreg., 1984, mfg. analyst, 1985, project mgr., 1986, product line mktg. mgr., 1987; pres. Columbia Body & Equipment Co., Portland, 1987-88; v.p., gen. mgr. Phase One Mfg., Inc., Milwaukie, Oreg., 1988—. Home: 2381 NW Flanders St No 2 Portland OR 97210 Office: Phase One Mfg Inc 2441 SE Stubb St Milwaukie OR 97222

VAN HORSSEN, CHARLES ARDEN, manufacturing executive; b. Mpls., June 28, 1944; s. Arden Darrel and Margaret E. (Ellingsen) V H.; m. Mary Katherine Van Kempen, Sept. 11, 1967 (div. 1975); children: Lisa, Jackie; m. Mary Ann Pashuta, Aug. 11, 1983; children: Vanessa, Garrett. BSEE, U. Minn., 1966. Design engr. Sperry Univac, Mpls., 1966-68; sr. project engr. Sperry Univac, Salt Lake City, 1975-80; systems engr. EMR Computer, Mpls., 1968-75; pres. A&B Industries Inc., Phoenix, 1980—. Mem. Ariz. Tooling and Machining Assn. (bd. dirs., v.p. 1987-89). Republican. Episcopalian. Office: A&B Industries Inc 9233 N 12th Ave Phoenix AZ 85021

VAN HOUTEN, GENE STEVEN, industrial engineering executive; b. Chgo., June 18, 1946; s. Eugene Kazimier and Ann Geraldine (Durica) V.; m. Eileen Marie Meister, June 15, 1974; children: Steven, Heather, Kristopher. AA/AS, Riverside (Calif.) City Coll., 1973; student Calif. Poly. U., 1979-81; BS, U. Redlands, 1982, BSBA, 1983, MA in Bus. Adminstrn/Mgmt., 1983. Spl. equipment design and assembly engr. Deutsch Co., Banning, Calif., 1967-74; mgr. indsl. engring. Sunkist Growers Inc., Ontario, Calif., 1974—, owner, president, chief exec. officer; gen. mgr. Digmor Inc., Redlands, Calif., Pacific Attachments, Inc.; mem. Calif. Senatorial Productivity Rev. Bd. Scoutmaster Boy Scouts Am., 1983. Recipient So. Calif. Edison Energy Mgmt. award, 1982; cert. of appreciation Productivity Council of S.W., 1982. Mem. Am. Concrete Inst., IEEE, Presdl. Energy Adv. Council, Am. Inst. Indsl. Engrs. (pres. Inland Empire chpt.), Soc. Mfg.

Engrs., Nat. Council of Farmer Co-ops (rep.), Sunkist Growers Suprs. Club (pres.), Internat. Assn. Quality Circles, Assn. Standards and Research, Am. Mgmt. Assn., Kiwanis (Ontario and Riverside, Calif.). Democrat. Home: 5042 Red Bluff Rd Riverside CA 92503

VANHOUTEN, RUTGER ARN, forester; b. Apeldoorn, Netherlands, July 15, 1944; came to U.S., 1962; s. Herman Johan and Rudolphine Johanna (Enger) vanH.; m. Katherine Rosalie Wafstet, Aug. 28, 1965; children: Joanne Marie, Karla Kay, Michael William. BA, U. Mont., 1969, MA, 1974. Forestry technician Clearwater Nat. Forest U.S. Forest Svc., Orofino, Idaho, 1973-78; forester, forest mgr. Nez Perce Tribe, Lapwai, Idaho, 1979—; Nez Perce del. to Intertribal Timber Coun., Warm Springs, Oreg., 1980-85, bd. dirs., 1985—; mem. People to People Ambassadors Tour, forestry, People's Republic China, 1986. Contbr. articles to profl. publs. Bd. dirs., Sch. Dist. 341, Lapwai, 1979-87, chmn., 1982-87. Mem. Soc. Am. Foresters (sec.-treas. Snake River chpt. 1982, vice chmn., 1983, chmn. 1984), Am. Forestry Assn. Home: Rte 1 Box 133A Lapwai ID 83540 Office: Nez Perce Tribe PO Box 365 Lapwai ID 83540

VAN KEMPEN, TIES HAROLD, environmental consultant; b. Jakarta, Indonesia, Sept. 2, 1949; came to U.S., 1981; s. Harold Egon August and Laura Marie V.; divorced. BA in Geography with honors, U. Western Australia, Perth, 1972; Diploma Environ. Studies, Macquarie U., Sidney, Australia, 1978. Environ. analyst Environ. Resources of Australia Pty, Ltd., Perth, Australia, 1972-73, Nat. Systems Rsch. Pty, Ltd., Sydney, Australia, 1973-74; project mgr. P.A. Mgmt. Cons. Pty, Ltd., Sydney, 1974-75, Dames & Moore, Sydney, 1975-81; assoc. Dames & Moore, Santa Barbara, Calif., 1981-86; v.p. L.D. Attaway & Assoc., Inc., San Rafael, Calif., 1986-88; regional mgr. Westec Svcs. Inc., San Rafael, 1988-89; sr. scientist Woodward-Clyde Cons., Oakland, Calif., 1989—. Contbr. articles to profl. jours. Mem. Assn. Environ. Profls. Home: 490 Canal St #9 San Rafael CA 94901 Office: Woodward-Clyde Cons 500 12th St Ste 100 Oakland CA 94607-4014

VAN KOMEN, GEORGE JOHAN WILLIAM, physician; b. Amsterdam, The Netherlands, July 4, 1944; came to U.S., 1949; s. Egbert and Maria C. (Van Maare) Van K.; m. Susan C. Smith, Aug. 9, 1968; children: Marguerite J., Anne E. BS, U. Utah, 1968; MD, Bowman Gray U., 1972. Diplomate Am. Bd. Internal Med. Intern LDS Hosp., Salt Lake City, 1972-73, resident, 1973-75; ptnr. Internal Med. Assocs., Salt Lake City, 1975-89, Bryner Clinic, Salt Lake City, 1989—; bd. dirs. LDS Hosp., Salt Lake City, pres. med. staff, 1987. Chmn. Alcohol Policy Coalition, Salt Lake City, 1988—. Mem. AMA, Am. Coll. of Physicians, Utah Med. Assn. (chmn. controlled substances com. 1988—). Republican. Mormon. Home: 1415 Chancellor Way Salt Lake City UT 84108 Office: Bryner Clinic 745 E 300 S Salt Lake City UT 84102

VANLENGEN, CRAIG ALAN, computer educator; b. Grundy Ctr., Iowa, Aug. 4, 1948; s. Ben H. and Gladys V. (Freese) V.; m. Lila Ileen Pilkington, Nov. 29, 1969; 1 child, Lori Ileen. AA, Ellsworth Coll., 1971; BSBA, U. Colo., Colorado Springs, 1976, MBA, 1981; EdD, No. Ariz. U., 1988. CPA, Colo. Acct. Fox and Co. CPAs, Colorado Springs, Colo., 1976-79; asst. city auditor Colorado Springs, Colo., 1979-81; asst. prof. Mesa Coll., Grand Junction, Colo, 1981-83; computer instr. No. Ariz. Univ., Flagstaff, 1983--. Served as Sgt. U.S. Army, 1967-70. Mem. Am Inst. CPAs, Assn. Supervision and Curriculum Devel. Presbyterian. Office: No Ariz U Box 15066 Flagstaff AZ 86011

VAN LEUVEN, ARTHUR EDWIN, JR., financial services executive; b. Redlands, Calif., Nov. 13, 1925; s. Arthur Edwin and Bessie Lee (Gotcher) Van L.; m. Charlotte Adele Miller, Apr. 21, 1946. Student, Kans. State Coll. at Pittsburg, 1944-45, U. Kan., 1945-46; Exec. Degree in Credit and Financial Mgmt, Stanford, 1962-64. Field rep. Transam. Fin. Corp. (previously Pacific Fin. Corp.), Los Angeles, 1947-48; office mgr. Transam. Fin. Corp. (previously Pacific Fin. Corp.), 1948-52, credit supr., 1952-55, supr. operations, 1955-59, mgr. dist., 1959-62, various home office positions, 1962-66, v.p. region, 1967-69, v.p. adminstrn., 1969-72, exec. v.p., 1972-77, pres., chief exec. officer, 1977—, mem. exec. com., 1972—, also dir.; exec. v.p. Transam. Corp.; dir. Transam. Title Ins. Co., 1980—; dir. Transam. Investment Services Inc., Transam. Realty Services, Transam. Equipment Leasing Co., Transam. Interway, Transam. Occidental Life Ins. Co, Transam. Ins. Co., Transam. Corp. Served with USNR, 1943-46. Office: Transam Fin Group Inc 1150 S Olive St Los Angeles CA 90015

VAN LIGTEN, RAOUL FREDRIK, optics scientist, physicist; b. Bandung, Indonesia, Sept. 27, 1932; came to U.S., 1960; s. C. Robert W. and Liliana C.F. (Juch) van L.; m. Suzanne M. Gaucher, Feb. 22, 1986; children: Gwendolin A., Kerry A. Hovey, Carol M. Hovey, Rudy, Ronnie. B in Engring. Physics, Delft Inst. Tech., 1956, M in Engring. Physics, 1957; PhD in Physics, U. Paris Sorbonne, 1972. Project mgr. Nat. Rsch. Council, Delft, The Netherlands, 1956-60; rsch. physicist Am. Optical Co., Southbridge, Mass., 1960-61, 63-73; dir. R & D Am. Optical Co., Basle, Switzerland, 1973-76; dept. head R & D Itek Corp., Lexington, Mass., 1961-63; gen. mgr., co-founder Polycore Optical, Singapore, Singapore, 1976-82; vis. prof. Nat. U. Singapore, Singapore, 1982-86; dir. ops. Younger Optics, L.A., 1986—; Mem. study group USAF Systems Command, Woods Hole, Mass., 1966, 67; mem. Sci. Coun. Singapore, 1980-84, mem. exec. com., 1984-86; mem. adv. com. Singapore Ministry Trade and Industry. Contbr. articles on holography to profl. jours.; patentee on holography and progressive addition lenses. Fellow Optical Soc. Am., Soc. Photo-optical Instrumentation Engrs. (Karl Fairbanks Meml. award. 1969). Home: 18921 Capense St Fountain Valley CA 92708

VAN LINT, VICTOR ANTON JACOBUS, physicist; b. Samarinda, Indonesia, May 10, 1928; came to U.S., 1937; s. Victor J. and Margaret (DeJager) Van L.; m. M. June Woolhouse, June 10, 1950; children: Lawrence, Kenneth, Linda, Karen. BS, Calif. Inst. Tech., Pasadena, 1950, PhD, 1954. Instr. Princeton (N.J.) U., 1954-55; staff mem. Gen. Atomic, San Diego, 1957-74; physics cons. San Diego, 1974-75; staff mem. Mission Research Corp., San Diego, 1975-82, 83—; spl. asst. to dep. dir. sci. and tech. Def. Nuclear Agy., Washington, 1982-83. Author, editor: Radiation Effects in Electronic Materials, 1976; contbr. articles to profl. jours. Served with U.S. Army, 1955-57. Recipient Pub. Service award NASA, 1981. Fellow IEEE. Republican. Mem. United Ch. of Christ. Home: 1032 Skylark Dr La Jolla CA 92037

VAN MAERSSEN, OTTO L., aerospace engineer, consulting firm executive; b. Amsterdam, North Holland, The Netherlands, Mar. 2, 1919; came to U.S., 1946; s. Adolph L. and Maria Wilhelmina (Edelmann) V.; m. Hortensia Maria Velasquez, Jan. 7, 1956; children: Maria, Patricia, Veronica, Otto, Robert. BS in Chem. Engring., U. Mo., Rolla, 1949. Registered profl. engr., Tex., Mo. Petroleum engr. Mobil Oil, Caracas, Venezuela, 1949-51; sr. reservoir engr. Gulf Oil, Ft. Worth and San Tome, Venezuela, 1952-59; acting dept. mgr. Sedco of Argentina, Comodoro Rivadavia, 1960-61; export planning engr. LTV Aerospace and Def., Dallas, 1962-69, adminstr. ground transp. div., 1970-74, engr. specialist new bus. programs, 1975-80; mgr. cost and estimating San Francisco/Alaska LYV Aerospace and Def., Dallas, 1981-84; owner OLVM Cons. Engrs., Walnut Creek, Calif., 1984—; cons. LTV Aerospace and Def., Walnut Creek, 1984—. Served with British Army, 1945, Germany. Mem. SPE (sr.). Democrat. Roman Catholic. Clubs: Toastmasters (Dallas), (sec./treas. 1963-64), Pennywise (Dallas) (treas. 1964-67). Home: 1649 Arbutus Dr Walnut Creek CA 94595 Office: OLVM Cons Engrs 1649 Arbutus Dr Walnut Creek CA 94595

VAN MICHAELS, CHRISTOPHER, research engineer; b. Bulgaria, Feb. 14, 1924; came to U.S., 1967; s. Miho and Dragana (Ivanova-Dragneva) van M.; m. Anna Atanasova Vakarelyisky, Apr. 24, 1955; children: Diana Michaels, Julien Michaels. Grad. in theoretical and nuclear physics, U. Paris, 1962-66; diploma in physics, geophysics, chemistry, U. Sofia, Bulgaria, 1949; MSci of Research, Acad. Scis., Sofia, 1955. Research engr., physicist, indsl. chemist Sci. Research Inst. of Bulgaria Acad. Scis., Sofia, 1949-60; research engr. ESCOA Corp., Phoenix, 1967-73; pres. Montex Corp., Los Angeles, 1974—; cons. in physics, indsl. chemistry, math. Discovered the rotary ctrs. of the ellipse; patentee elliptic engines and compressors, bladeless turbines, gasiform engine pistons, internally cooling thermodynamic cycles, fuel alloys process for mfg. hydrocarbons, process for converting cellulose into edible flour, resonance quanto-ionic propulsion concept and contbrns. in Bulean Algebra, thermodynamic state of molecular and nuclear Benzentropy; contbr. articles to profl. jours. Recipient Magnavox award, 1974. Mem. Internat. Physics Assn. Home: 1850 N Cherokee Ave Los Angeles CA 90028

VANN, ROBERT LEWIS, engineer; b. Santa Monica, Calif., May 13, 1938; s. Lewis B. and Ruby L. (Roby) V.; m. Nancy J. Gay, Aug. 10, 1957; children: Robert, Nina, Ruby, Judy. BSEE, Western State U., 1964. Registered profl. engr., Calif. Cable design engr. Hughes Aircraft Co., Culver City, Calif., 1959-67; system engr. TRW Systems, Redondo Beach, Calif., 1967-71; sr. engr. TRW Systems, Redondo Beach, 1973-79, engring. mgr., 1981—; sect. head Litton Data Systems, Van Nuys, Calif., 1971-73; dept. mgr. Litton Data command Systems, Agoura, Calif., 1979-81; engring. adv., Electronic Connector Study Group, Inc., Deerfield, Ill., 1982—. Lt. Law Enforcement Mounted Posse, L.A., 1980—; leader 4H Youth, Thousand Oaks, 1973-81; commr. Boy Scouts Am., L.A., Ventura, Calif. With USN, 1955-62. Mem. Calif. Peace Officers Assn. Republican. Baptist.

VANNESS, CALVIN HANN, architect; b. Oxford, Ohio, June 19, 1926; s. LeRoy and Susan Christine (Hann) V. BArch, Miami U., Oxford, Ohio, 1950; postgrad., Creative Guidelines, Phoenix, 1975. Registered architect, Ariz. Apprentice builder Le Roy Vanness, Contractor, Oxford, 1926-50; archtl. draftsman Wright Patterson AFB, Dayton, Ohio, 1951, Zeller & Hunter, Architects, Springfield, Ohio, 1952, Nax Mercer, Architect, Yellow Springs, Ohio, 1953, Robert Johnson, Architect, Phoenix, 1954, Herb Green, Architect, Phoenix, 1955, Charles Polacek, Architect, Phoenix, 1956; architect, owner Calvin H. Vanness, Architect, Phoenix, 1957—; minister, counselor House of th Dawn Ch., Phoenix, 1971—; founder, dir. House of the Dawn Ch., Phoenix, 1971—; counselor self hypnosis, Phoenix; tchr. Kriya Yoga, Phoenix. Author: Rainbows and Rhapsodies, 1988. Deacon Met. Community Ch., Phoenix, 1967-73; mem. S.W. dist. bldgs. and locations com. Meth. Ch., Ariz., Calif., Nev., 1965. With U.S. Army, 1946-48, ETO. Recipient Bldg. award of distinction City of Tempe (Ariz.), 1977. Mem. Constrn. Specifications Inst., AIA, New Age Alliance Chs., Order of Omega, Creative Guidelines, Phys. Fitness Club, Ande's Club, Sun Bear Medicine Circle, Reevis Mountain Native Am. Gathering. Republican. Home: 2141 E Palm Ln Phoenix AZ 85006 Office: 2141 E Palm Ln Phoenix AZ 85006

VANNIX, C(ECIL) ROBERT, programmer, systems analyst; b. Glendale, Calif., June 14, 1953; s. Cecil H. Jr. and Gloria Jenny (Zappia) V.; married, 1980; 1 child, Robert Jeremy. AS in Plant Mgmt., BS in Indsl. Arts, Loma Linda U., 1977; AS in Info. Systems, Ventura City Coll., 1985. Instr. indsl. arts Duarte (Calif.) High Sch., 1977-79, Oxnard (Calif.) High Sch., 1979-81; computer cons. Litton Data Comand Systems, Agoura, Calif., 1976-81, sr. engr. instr., 1981-85; computer cons. McLaughlin Research Corp., Camarillo, Calif., 1976-77, sr. program analyst, 1985-88; sr. program analyst Computer Software Analysts, Camarillo, Calif., 1988—. Recipient Spl. Achievement award One Way Singers, Glendale, 1975. Republican. Adventist. Clubs: Apple PI Computer, Litton Computer (pres. 1975-76). Home: 407 Appletree Ave Camarillo CA 93010 Office: Computer Software Analysts 165 Durley Ave Camarillo CA 93010

VAN NOY, TERRY WILLARD, insurance company executive; b. Alhambra, Calif., Aug. 31, 1947; s. Barney Willard and Cora Ellen (Simms) V.; m. Betsy Helen Pothen, Dec. 27, 1968; children: Bryan, Mark. BS in Bus. Mgmt., Calif. State Poytechnic U., 1970. CLU. Group sales rep. Mutual of Omaha, Atlanta, 1970-74, dist. mgr., 1974-77; regional mgr. Mutual of Omaha, Dallas, 1977-82; nat. sales mgr. Mutual of Omaha, Omaha, Neb., 1982-83; v.p. group mktg. Mutual of Omaha, Omaha, 1983-87; div. dir. Mutual of Omaha, Orange, Calif., 1987—. Presenter: Health Ins. Assn. of Am., Chgo, 1984, Life Insur Mktg. & Rsch. Assn., San Francisco, 1987. Vice chmn. Morning Star Luth. Ch., Omaha, 1987. Mem. Am. Soc. CLUS, Orange County Employee Benefit Coun. Republican. Home: 381 S Smokeridge Terr Anaheim Hills CA 92807 Office: Mut of Omaha 333 S Anita Dr Ste 650 Orange CA 92668

VAN NUYS, ANDREE ANNIE, artist; b. Cholet, France, Jan. 23, 1946; came to U.S., 1970; d. Jean André Lucien Bahu and Bernadette Graveleau; m. Donald Warren Van Nice, June 5, 1972. Licence ès lettres, U. Rennes, France, 1967; Maitrise ès lettres, U. Nantes, France, 1969; MS, Montana State U., 1972, BA, 1978; MFA, Nova Scotia Coll. Art and Design, 1980. Workshop leader Mont. Inst. Arts, 1981, juror, 1981. Represented in galleries Mont., Colo., Ariz., Calif.; exhibited in group shows at Renwick Gallery, Smithsonian Inst., 1981. Recipient 1st prize Student Art Show at Mont. State U., 1978, Judges award Marietta (Ohio) Nat. Competition, 1981. Mem. Am. Craft Council. Democrat. Home and Office: 1011 Poplar Missoula MT 59802

VAN PATTEN, DENIS J., insurance agency executive; b. Lincoln, Nebr., May 29, 1947; s. Jack and Jean Marie (Dirks) Van P.; m. Gwen Joy Gilmer, Apr. 10, 1971; children: James Russell, Melody Christine. BS, Principia Coll., Elsah, Ill., 1969; postgrad., Purdue U., 1981, Am. Coll., 1986. With K-Mart, Cheyenne, Wyo., 1971-72; store mgr. Brooks Cameras, Cheyenne, Wyo., 1972-80; owner, prin. Fin. Mgmt. Advantage, Cheyenne, Wyo., 1981--, Van Patten Ins. Agy., Cheyenne, Wyo., 1980--; bd. dirs. Mountain View Meml. Park Cemetery, Cheyenne; v.p./treas. Internat. Bus. Tech., Cheyenne, 1988--, Cheyenne Tech., 1988--. Active Boy Scouts Am. With USN, 1969-70. Recipient Nat. Sales Achievement award Nat. Assn. Life Underwriters, 1982-87. Mem. Am. Soc. CLU's and Chartered Fin. Cons., Southeastern Wyo. Assn. Life Underwriters (pres. 1986-88), C. of C., Lions. Republican. Christian Scientist. Home: 210 Lafayette Blvd Cheyenne WY 82009 Office: Van Patten Ins Agy 721 E 16th St Cheyenne WY 82001

VAN PELT, W(ESLEY) AUSTIN, clergyman, educator; b. Rahway, N.J., Aug. 24, 1930; s. Charles Wesley and Grace Elizabeth (DeHart) Van P.; m. Elenor Kramer, June 11, 1952; children: Mary, Anne, Peter, David. BA, Maryville Coll., 1952; MDiv, Louisville Presbyn. Sem., 1955; MA, U. Denver, 1964, PhD, 1970. Ordained to ministry United Presbyn. Ch., mem. faculty Maryville (Tenn.) Coll., 1954-57, Sheldon Jackson Jr. Coll., Sitka, Alaska, 1957-59; gen. mgr. Sta. KSEW, 1959-61; pastor, New Castle, Pa., 1961-63; asst. prof. sociology Peru State Coll., 1964-68; dean Arapahoe Community Coll., Littleton, Colo., 1969-75, instr. sociology, 1976-87; pastor 1st Presbyn. Ch., Leadville, Colo., 1987—; interim pastor chs., Colo., Alaska, Utah, Wyo., 1984—; adj. prof. U. Denver, 1976, McCormick Theol. Sem., Chgo., 1979-81. Mem. NEA, Colo. Edn. Assn., Presbytery of Denver. Office: 1st Presbyn Ch PO Box 498 Leadville CO 80461

VAN PUTTEN, DONALD JOHN, aerospace engineer, researcher; b. Paterson, N.J., May 11, 1934; s. John and Hazel Harriet (Liggett) Van P.; m. Patricia Ann Hulshorst, Nov. 12, 1960; children: Steven Douglas, Karen Sue. Diploma, Acad. Aeros., 1955; BS in Engring. Tech., Northrop U., 1978. Mem. tech. staff Rockwell Internat., Columbus, Ohio, 1955-69; El Segundo, Calif. Rockwell Internat., 1969-78; sr. tech. specialist Aircraft div. Northrop Corp., Hawthorne, Calif., 1978-82, mgr. advanced structural concepts, 1982-84, sr. tech. specialist, 1988—; project engr. Northrop Advanced Systems div., Pico Rivera, Calif. Northrop Corp., 1984-88. Recipient Collier Trophy Nat. Aero. Assn. U.S.A., 1976. Mem. Tau Alpha Pi. Republican. Home: 26617 Indian Peak Rd Rancho Palos Verdes CA 90274 Office: Northrop Corp Aircraft Div 1 Northrop Ave Hawthorne CA 90250

VAN REMMEN, ROGER, advertising executive; b. Los Angeles, Sept. 30, 1950; s. Thomas J. and Elizabeth (Vincent) V.; m. Mary Anne Montague, Sept. 11, 1976. B.S. in Bus., U. So. Calif., 1972. Account mgr. BBDO, Los Angeles, 1972-78; account mgr. Dailey & Assocs. Advt., Los Angeles, 1978—, v.p., mgmt. supr., 1980-84, sr. v.p., 1985—; dir. Aux. Aids Inc., Richstone Family Ctr. Chmn. adv. bd. El Segundo (Calif.) First Nat. Bank; bd. dirs. Advt. Emergency Relief Fund. Mem. Univ. So. Calif. Alumni Assn., Advt. Club of Los Angeles. Roman Catholic. Home: 9 Arbolado Ct Manhattan Beach CA 90266 Office: Dailey & Assocs 3055 Wilshire Blvd Los Angeles CA 90010

VAN RENNES, JERRY WAYNE, electronics engineer; b. Orange, Calif., May 4, 1941; s. Henry and Ann (Van Leeuwen) VanR.; m. Geneva Ione Allbee, Mar. 3, 1967; children: Geri Lynn, Scott Allen. BS in Mech. Engring., Ariz. State U., 1979. Chem. technician Gould Nat. Battery, St. Paul, 1962-63; process technician Sperry Univac, St. Paul, 1964-67; technician IC Dickson Electronics, Scottsdale, Ariz., 1967-71; tchr., trucker various orgns., Phoenix, 1971-72; trucker, mfg. rep. Lorts Mfg., Phoenix, 1972-73; free-lance trucker, cons. Phoenix, 1973-79; sr. engr. Dale Electronics, Norfolk, Nebr., 1979-84, Intel Corp., Chandler, Ariz., 1984—. Mem. Internat. Soc. for Hybrid Microelectronics (local chpt. sec. 1985—), Am. Soc. for Testing Materials (chair subcom. task force 1985—). Methodist. Home: 1229 W Linda Ln Chandler AZ 85224 Office: Intel Corp 145 South 79th St Chandler AZ

VAN SANT, DAVID EUGENE, school system administrator; b. Tuscola, Ill., Apr. 21, 1950; s. Arthur D. and Martha (O'Neill) Van S.; m. Shary Stafford, Aug. 11, 1979; children: Zachary, Sean, Evan. BA, St. John's U., 1968; MA, Ill. State U., 1973. Asst. prin. Ft. Lupton (Colo.) Schs., 1976-79, dir. curriculum, 1979-85; asst. supt. Moffat County Schs., Craig, Colo., 1985—; pvt. practice cons. Distance Learning, Craig, 1986—; bd. dirs. Kellogg Learning Resource Ctr., Interstate Consortium, Ogden, Utah. Bd. dirs. Weld County Human Svcs., Greeley, Colo., 1981-85, Learning Resource Ctr., Craig, 1986—, Moffat County United Way, Craig, 1987—. Climax Molybdenum Corp. fellow, 1976. Mem. Colo. Assn. Sch. Execs., Am. Assn. Curriculum Developers, Colo. Assn. Curriculum Developers, Ft. Lupton C. of C. (bd. dirs. 1980-84), Rotary (pres. 198-485, bd. dirs. 1985—). Republican. Roman Catholic. Home: 2910 Pinon Circle Craig CO 81625 Office: Moffat County Schs 775 Yampa Ave Craig CO 81625

VAN SCHOIK, DOUGLAS RICK, biologist, educator; b. Columbus, Ohio, Feb. 9, 1950; s. Dickson Moore and Olive Hill (Oberst) Van S.; m. Joyce S. Crosthwaite, Sept. 30, 1980; children: Jolie Alexandra Taliaferro, Rachel Whitney. BS, U.S. Naval Acad., 1972; MS, San Diego State U., 1981; PhD, Duke U., 1982. Commd. ens. USN, 1972, advanced through grades to lt., 1976, resigned, 1977; pres. S.W. Rsch. Assocs., Cardiff, Calif., 1981—; mem. bus. devel. staff Lockheed Marine Systems, San Diego, 1986—; assoc. prof. Palomar Coll., San Marcos, Calif., 1985—. Democrat. Mem. Soc. of Friends. Home and Office: 1842 Westminster Cardiff CA 92007

VAN SEVENTER, A., accountant; b. Amsterdam, The Netherlands, Sept. 25, 1913; came to U.S., 1940; s. A. and Maria (van Dijk) van S.; m. Ruth E. Smith, Nov. 5, 1949; children: Antony, Ronald E. AB, U. Amsterdam, 1934; MBA, Stanford U., 1949; PhD, U. Mich., 1966. Acct. C.A. Gall and Co., N.Y.C., 1940-41, Credit Suisse, N.Y.C., 1941, Haskins and Sells, San Francisco, 1949, Philip A. Hershey, San Francisco, 1949, O.M. Beaver CPA, Anchorage, 1950, Beaver and van Seventer CPAs, Anchorage, 1950-62; pvt. practice acctg. Anchorage and Palo Alto, Calif., 1957-62; vis. lectr. taxation Eastern Mich. U., Ypsilanti, 1963; instr. acctg. Cleary (Mich.) Coll., 1963; instr., lectr. acctg. U. Mich., Ann Arbor, 1963-66; asst. and assoc. prof. acctg. San Jose (Calif.) State U., 1966-76; prof. acctg. San Francisco State U., 1976-84; pres. Bay Books Publishing, Palo Alto, Calif., 1976—; instr. acctg. Anchorage Community Coll., 1954-62. Author: The History of Accountancy - translation, 1976, 2nd edit., 1986, Intermediate Accounting Problems, 1973, 3rd edit. 1981; editor: Accounting Bibliography, 1986; contbr. articles to profl. jours. Sec. Alaska Bd. Pub. Accountancy, 1953-57. With USAAF, 1942-45. Lybrand fellow, 1965; decorated French Medal of Honor in Bronze. Mem. AICPA, Am. Acctg. Assn., Acad. Acctg. Historians, Calif. Soc. CPAs, Peninsula Symphony, Phi Beta Kappa (pres. No. Calif. chpt. 1980-81), Rotary.

VAN SIEGMAN, ROBERT LEWIS, landscape contractor; b. Palo Alto, Calif., Jan. 14, 1947; s. Henry and Kathryn Irene (Johnson) Van S.; m. Nancy Ellen Cleese, July 6, 1968; 1 child, Christopher Hans. BS, Calif. State Poly. U., 1972. Chief estimator Valley Crest Landscape, Inc., Pleasanton, Calif., 1971-83; owner, mgr. Landscaping & Design, Dublin, Calif., 1983--. Deacon, Christian & Missionary Alliance Ch., Paradise, Calif., 1986. With U.S. Army, 1967-69. Mem. Am. Assn. Landscape Designers, Gamma Sigma Delta. Republican. Mem. Assemblies of God Ch. Office: Landscaping and Design 46 Rickenbacker Circle Livermore CA 94550

VANSTRALEN, ERIC, title insurance company executive; b. Montebello, Calif., Dec. 4, 1952; s. Albert Phillip and Evelyn Ruth (Murray) VanS.; m. Linda K. Hunt, June 30, 1972 (div. Feb. 1976); 1 child, Katrina Meagan; m. Diane Alene Laizure, May 18, 1980; children: Heather Annalisa, Rebecca Lynn, Candice Marie. Student, Long Beach City Coll., 1971, 75, Solano Community Coll., Fairfield, Calif., 1980-83, U. Calif., Davis, 1981-82. Los Angeles County mgr. Title-Tax, Inc., L.A., 1976-80; title searcher, examiner 1st Am. Title Co., Fairfield, 1980-82; mgr. title ops. Transam. Title Ins. Co., Walnut Creek, Calif., 1982-87, Stewart Title Calif., Santa Ana, 1987; mgr. Southbay area N.Am. Title Co., Torrance, Calif., 1987—. Rescue sgt. Long Beach (Calif.) Search and Rescue Team, 1970; chief Tribe of Tahquitz Boy Scouts Am., 1970-71, activities dir. Camp Tahquitz, Barton Flats, Calif., 1971, dir. mountain man program, Long Beach, 1975. With USN, 1972-75. Recipient appreciation award Exchange Club, Concord, Calif., 1986. Mem. Calif. Land Title Assn. (speakers' bur. 1986-87), Calif. Escrow Assn., Calif. Trustees Assn. Republican. Episcopalian. Office: NAm Title Co 3655 Torrance Blvd Ste 450 Torrance CA 91792

VAN TAMELEN, MARY RUTH, councilman; b. Holland, Mich., Oct. 20, 1930; d. Cornelius and Dorothy Mae (Reif) Houtman; m. Eugene E. van Tamelen; children: Jane Elizabeth, Carey Catherine, Peter Gerrit. BS, U. Wis., 1952, MS, 1953. Free-lance writer, editor Los Altos Hills, Calif.; planning commn. City of Los Altos Hills, 1978-82, councilmem., 1982—, mayor, 1983-84, 86-87. Author: New Directions in English; editor: Bioorganic Chemistry; indexer various books, flim producer monthly series Access TV, Los Altos. Cons. Foothills Festival Arts, Los Altos Hills, 1986—; pres. Community Services Agy., Mountain View, Calif., 1985-87, bd. dirs., 1983—; bd. dirs. Community Health Awareness Council, Mountain View, 1982—. Mem. AAUW. Home: 23570 Camino Hermoso Los Altos Hills CA 94022

VAN TASSELL, JAN, film producer, director; b. Indpls., Sept. 30, 1943; s. Raymond and Bethel (Holmes) Van T.; divorced, 1976; 1 child, Jon. Student, Diablo Valley Coll., 1969-79, Berkeley (Calif.) Film House, 1980. Cameraman Sierra Motion Pictures, Pleasant Hill, Calif., 1976-80, KTVN-TV, Reno, 1980-82; producer, dir. TFL Entertainment, Alamo, Calif., 1980—. Producer, dir.: (films) Death Machines, Weapons of Death, Falcon Claw, Herbie Goes to Monte Carlo, The Tounament, One Way Out, 1986, Jungle Wolf, 1986, Flask: A Hard Way to Live, 1988, Blind Date, 1988, and numerous others. Mem. Film Art Found. Democrat. Unitarian. Office: TFL Entertainment 3158 Danville Blvd Alamo CA 94507

VAN TIEL, WOUTER JAN, financial analyst, publisher; b. Amsterdam, The Netherlands, Dec. 12, 1960; came to U.S., 1981; s. Johannes and Dagmar (Wenz) Van T. BBA, Schiller Internat. U., Heidelberg, Fed. Republic Germany, 1981; M Fin., Am. Grad. Sch. Internat. Mgmt., 1983. Underwriter Am. Internat. Group, N.Y.C., 1983-86; fin. rep. D.E.F. Leasing, San Diego, 1986-87; fin. analyst Indsl. Indemnity, San Diego, 1987-88, sr. fin. analyst, 1988—; computer cons., N.Y.C., 1984-86. Author: Credit Solutions Portfolio, 1987, Mortgage Interest Reduction Techniques, 1989. Mem. Toastmasters. Home: 818 Kingston Ct San Diego CA 92109 Office: Indsl Indemnity 3255 Camino Del Rio S San Diego CA 92108

VANTINE, MICHAEL ROY, sales executive; b. Santa Barbara, Calif., Sept. 22, 1946; s. Roy Lee and Fleta Jeraldine (Campbell) V.; m. Patricia Ann Kalberg, June 27, 1970; children: Kristin, Kathryn Anne. BA, Pepperdine U., 1969; MDiv, Fuller Theol Sem., 1976. Comml. teller Bank Am., Los Angeles, 1969-70; tchr. So. Calif. Christian Sch., Hawthorne, 1970; pharmacy technician Calif. Hosp. Med. Ctr., Los Angeles, 197073, pharmacy supr., 1973-76; profl. services Pacific Health Resources, Los Angeles, 1976-77; mgr. Travenol Labs Parenterals/Div., Baxter, Seattle, 1977-82, special care rep., 1982, dist. mgr., 1982-87; dist. mgr. Caremark Homecare/Div. Baxter, 1987--; assoc. minister Ch. of Christ, Westchester, Calif., 1974-76; sales trainer Travenol Labs, Seattle, 1979-82; bd. dirs. Young Life, Lake Wash. Sch. Dist., 1987--. Republican. Home: 12720 NE 113th Pl Kirkland WA 98033 Office: Caremark Plus 1855 Business Center Dr San Bernardino CA 92408

VAN TUYLE, ROBERT WOODING, health care facilities company executive; b. Manchester, Ill., 1912. Student, Univ of Cincinnati, MIT. Chmn., chief exec. officer Beverly Enterprises, Pasadena, Calif.; dir. Jacobs Engring. Group, Inc., Alpha Microsystems. Office: Beverly Enterprises Inc 99 S Oakland Ave Pasadena CA 91101 *

VAN VALKENBURG, HOLLI BEADELL, administrator; b. Blue Island, Ill., Dec. 25, 1950; d. Robert Morton and Vivian (Doberstein) Beadell; m. Gerard William Van Valkenburg, May 26, 1984. BS, U. Nebr., 1973; cert. paralegal, Colo. Paralegal Inst., 1978. Child care counselor Father Flanagan's Boys Home, Boys Town, Nebr., 1974-77; service rep. Blue Cross & Blue Shield, Denver, 1977-78; escrow asst. Transamerica Title, Denver, 1978; paralegal Pendleton & Sabian, P.C., Denver, 1978-84, Isaacson, Rosenbaum, Spiegleman, Woods & Levy, P.C., Denver, 1984-88; adminstr. Pan-Terra, Inc., Kirkland, Wash., 1988—; dir. Rocky Mountain Legal Assistance Assn., Denver, 1979-82. Recipient Betty King Grainger scholarship for Excellence in Journalism, U. Nebr., 1970. Mem. Alpha Chi Omega (newsletter editor 1970-73), Univ. Club. Home: 13245 100th Pl NE Kirkland WA 98034 Office: Pan-Terra Inc 624 8th St S Kirkland WA 98034

VAN VALKENBURGH, FRANKLIN BUTLER, photographer; b. Annapolis, Md., Feb. 5, 1919; s. Franklin and Marguerite (Horne) Van V.; m. Loraine Elizabeth Shaw, Jan. 3, 1942; children: Franklin, Chares Frederick, Marguerite Loraine, Edward, Janette Elizabeth, Robert. Student, Ga. Inst. Tech., Atlanta, 1937-39, San Diego City Coll., 1954. Instr. USN Gen. Line Sch., Monterey, Calif., 1951; photographer Baron of Coronado, Calif.; photographer Calif. Hall of Fame, 1988. Lt. comdr. USN, 1942-46, PTO, 50-54, Korea. Recipient 14 Achievement merits Profl. Photos Am., 1988, Calif. Svcs. awards, 1988. Mem. Profl. Photographers San Diego (past pres. 1976), Profl. Photographers Calif. (sec. 1974-75, treas. 1983-85, 1st v.p. 1986-87), Profl. Photographers Inland Empire (past pres. 1975—), Nat. Assn. Van Valkenburgh Family. Office: Baron of Coronado PO Box 441 Coronado CA 92118

VAN VELDHUIZEN, PHILIP ANDROCLES, mathematics and statistics educator; b. Hospers, Iowa, Nov. 6, 1930; s. Andrew and Elizabeth (Oordt) Van V.; m. Deborah Susan Judwin, Mar. 7, 1984; children: Robert, Jay, Varina, Heather. BA, Central Coll., 1952; MS, Iowa U., 1960; postgrad., U. Colo., Boulder, 1952-54, Iowa State, 1965-66. Instr. Central Coll., Pella, Iowa, 1956-59; asst. prof. Calif. State U., Sacramento, 1960-63; prof. math and stats. U. Alaska, Fairbanks, 1963—, emeritus, 1988—; vis. prof. Coll. Idaho, Caldwell, 1982-83; cons. alaska Dept. Edn., Juneau, 1963—; instr. Quantitative Litarary Program, Alaska, 1984—; lectr. in field. Author curriculum materials, papers for profl. orgns.; author, lead actor television series on metric system., 1980. Mem. Fairbanks Sch. Bd., 1978-81; bd. dirs. Tanana Valley State Fair, Fairbanks, 1984-87, Chena-Gold Stream Fire and Rescue, Fairbaks, 1984-87. Served with U.S. Army, 1954-56. Mem. Am. Statis. Assn., Nat. Council Tchrs. Math., Math. Assn. Am. Office: U Alaska Fairbanks AK 99775

VAN VOORHEES, KENNETH ALLEN, marketing executive; b. Omaha, Oct. 16, 1951; s. Loren Wendell and Dolores Jean (Surratt) Voorhees. BS, U. Wash., 1974, MBA, 1978. Sci. computer programmer U. Wash., Seattle, 1976-78, lectr., 1978-80; program coord. Small Bus. Inst., U. Wash., Seattle, 1977-80; lectr. U. So. Calif., L.A., 1980-82, Pepperdine U., Malibu, Calif., 1982-83; contracts adminstr. Flow Industries, Kent, Wash., 1983-84; mktg. rep. Hewlett-Packard, Bellevue, Wash., 1984-88; pvt. practice cons. L.A. and Seattle, 1978-80, 88--. Mem. Data Processing Mgmt. Assn., Wash. Athletic, Beta Gamma Sigma. Home: 719 N 48th St Seattle WA 98103

VAN VOORHIS, THOMAS, lawyer; b. Great Falls, Mont., Feb. 24, 1930; s. George E. and Ruthe (Williams) V.; AA, U. Calif., 1955; LLB, JD, Hastings Coll. Law, 1959; m. Eleanor Cooper, Mar. 21, 1958; children: Kevin, Karen, Thomas. Admitted to Calif. bar, 1960; pres. Campbell & Van Voorhis, Walnut Creek, Calif., 1960-82; of counsel Van Voorhis & Skaggs, 1982-85; of counsel McCutchen, Brown, Doyle & Enersen, 1985—; judge pro tem Walnut Creek-Danville Municipal Ct., 1974-82; pres. Domino II Cattle Co., Walnut Creek, 1971-86; v.p. Blackhawk Devel. Co., Danville, Calif., 1972-75; corp. sec., dir. RWC Calif. Co., Danville, 1975-85, RWC Nev. Co., Reno; sec., dir. Woodhill Devel. Co., Danville, 1976-85; dir. First Security Savs. Bank. Pres. Rep. Assembly, Walnut Creek, 1964. Bd. dirs. Walnut Creek (Cal.) Action for Beauty Council, Pacific Vascular Found., 1986. Served with USAF, 1950-54. Mem. State Bar Calif., ABA (com. on devel. and mgmt. real estate 1975—), Contra Costa Bar Assn., Internat. Assn. Fin. Planning. Office: 1855 Olympic Blvd Walnut Creek CA 94596

VAN WAGENEN, STERLING, film producer, director; b. Provo, Utah, July 2, 1947; s. Clifton Gray and Donna Anna (Johnson) Van W.; m. Marilee Jeppson; children: Sarah, Kristina, Arthur, William, Hugh, Andrew. BA, Brigham Young U., 1972. Media coord. Utah Arts Coun., Salt Lake City, 1976-78; exec. dir. U.S. Film Festival, Park City, Utah, 1978-80; exec. dir. Sundance Inst., Salt Lake City, 1980-84, v.p., 1984-86; asst. dir. L.A. Music Ctr., 1971, script reader Creative Mgmt. Assocs., 1971. Dir.: (plays) King Lear, 1974, Othello, 1984, Hamlet, 1972, The Flies, 1970, (film) Christmas Snows, Christmas Winds (2 regional Emmy awards); producer: (films) Faith of an Observer 1984, The Trip to Bountiful, 1986, Yosemite: The Fate of Heaven, 1988. Office: Del Rio Films 9 Exchange Pl Ste 1120 Salt Lake City UT 84111

VAN-WHY, REBECCA RIVERA, counseling administrator; b. Casa Blanca, N.Mex., Sept. 14, 1932; d. Charles and Doris (Thompson) Rivera; m. Raymond Richard Van-Why, Aug. 27, 1955; children: Raymond R., Ronald R., Randall R. BS, U. N.Mex., 1959. Tchr. Bur. of Indian Affairs, Albuquerque, 1960-62, guidance counselor, 1969—, tchr., supr., 1973-74, acting dir. student life, 1987; head tchr. Laguna (N.Mex.) Headstart OEO, 1967-69, acting dir., 1969. Recipient Cert. of Recognition, Sec. of Interior, 1975, Cert. of Appreciation, State of N.Mex., 1986; named honoree Internat. Women's Day, U. N.Mex., 1987. Republican. Home: 6328 Cuesta Pl NW Albuquerque NM 87120 Office: Bur of Indian Affairs 9169 Coors Blvd NW Albuquerque NM 87184

VANZI, MAX BRUNO, editor; b. Ferrara, Italy, Sept. 24, 1934; s. Lambert S. Vanzi and Helen (Larimer) Hughes; m. Lynn A. D'Costa; children: Linda, Victor. A.B. in Journalism, U. Calif., Berkeley, 1959. Reporter Oroville (Calif.) Mercury, 1959-60; reporter UPI, Seattle, 1960-64, San Francisco, 1960-64, Japan, India, Pakistan, 1964-67; editor, correspondent UPI, Hong Kong, 1967-68; mgr. Southeast Asia UPI, Singapore, 1969-75; editor for Tex. UPI, Dallas, 1975-77; editor for Calif. UPI, San Francisco, 1977-81, gen. editor for Pacific div., 1981-84; editor Los Angeles Times, Washington Post News Service, Los Angeles, 1984-86; asst. met. editor Los Angeles Times, 1986—. Co-author: Revolution in the Philippines: The United States in a Hall of Cracked Mirrors, 1984. Served with USAF, 1953-55. Am. Press Inst. fellow Reston, Va., 1980; recipient cert. excellence Overseas Press Club. Am., N.Y.C., 1983. Office: LA Times Times Mirror Sq Los Angeles CA 90053

VARELA, GEORGE G., city official; b. Los Angeles, May 25, 1947; m. Terryl A. Varela; children: Cynthia Kathleen, Eric Jason. BA, Whittier Coll., 1970; MPA, Calif. State U., Fullerton, 1975; postgrad., UCLA, Calif. Inst. Tech. Community coll. instr. credential, Calif. Adminstrv. asst. City of Montebello (Calif.), 1970-73; personnel dir. City of Chino (Calif.), 1973-77, City of West Covina (Calif.), 1977-81; asst. city mgr. City of Covina, 1981--; speaker to profl. orgns. Coach Chino Am. Youth Soccer Orgn., 1980-82, Chino Little League and Pony Baseball, 1980-84; pres. Don Lugo High Sch. Booster Club, 1982-83. Recipient award for outstanding service in local govt. Calif. Assembly, 1977. Mem. Am. Soc. for Pub. Adminstrn., Internat. City Mgmt. Assn., So. Calif. Personnel Mgmt. Assn. (bd. dirs. 1977), San Gabriel Valley Labor Relations Assn. (pres. 1973), League Calif. Cities (task force 1972, 74), Whittier Coll. Hispanic Alumni Assn. Home: 13423 Netzley Pl Chino CA 91710

VARGA, STEVEN CARL, reinsurance company official; b. Columbus, Ohio, Jan. 19, 1952; s. Stephen Thomas and Eva Jeney V.; BA in Psychology and Philosophy magna cum laude, Carthage Coll., 1977, MSA with honors Cen. Mich. U., 1986; m. Michelle L. Auld, Nov. 17, 1973; children—Zachary Steven, Joshua Lewis. Svc. mgr. Chem-Lawn Corp., Columbus, 1972-75; respiratory therapist St. Catherine's Hosp., Kenosha, Wis., 1975-77; policy analyst Nationwide Ins. Cos., Columbus, 1978-79, asst. mgr. Corp. Tng. Ctr., 1979-86; dir. ednl. tng. Sullivan Payne Co., Seattle, 1986-88, asst. v.p. human resources, 1989—. Mem. civic action program com., 1979—, Nat. Mental Health Assn., 1972—; v.p. Kenosha County chpt., 1975-77; mem. Franklin County (Ohio) Mental Health Assn., 1978—. Rhodes scholar, 1976-77. Mem. Am. Soc. Tng. and Devel., Soc. Broadcast Engrs., Internat. TV Assn., Am. Psychol. Assn., Am. Mgmt. Assn., Soc. of Ins. Trainers and Educators (chmn. regional area planning com.), Am. Film Inst., Carthage Coll. Alumni Assn., Phi Beta Kappa, Psi Chi. Home: 12111 SE 46th Ctd Bellevue WA 98006 Office: Sullivan Payne Co 1501 4th Ave Seattle WA 98101

VARGAS, MICHAEL PAUL, college administrator; b. San Jose, Calif., Apr. 10, 1947; s. Donald Joseph and Dollie Martha (Fuhrmann) V. BA in Art, San Jose State U., 1969; MA in History of Art, Ohio State U., 1972; MA in Museology, John F. Kennedy U., 1979. Cert. tchr. community colls., Calif. Instr. art history Coll. of Dayton (Ohio) Art Inst., 1973-75, Mission Coll., Santa Clara, Calif., 1977-84; instl. dean Mission Coll., Santa Clara, 1984—. Author (exhibition catalog): Life and Times of Elizabeth Boott Duveneck, 1980, A System for the Classification and Cataloging of Art Slides and Photographs, 1980. Advisor Triton Mus. Art, Santa Clara, 1983—; mem. Heritage Preservation Commn., Sunnyvale, Calif., 1983-87. Office: Mission Coll 3000 Mission College Blvd Santa Clara CA 95054

VARNES, DAVID JOSEPH, engineering geologist; b. Howe, Ind., Apr. 5, 1919; s. David Joseph and Florence (Culmer) V.; m. Helen Dowling, Mar. 21, 1943 (dec. Mar. 1964); m. Katharine Lutz Buck, Aug. 30, 1966. BS with honors, Calif. Inst. Tech., Pasadena, 1940; postgrad., Northwestern U., 1941. Registered profl. engr., Colo., geologist, Calif. Branch geologist U.S. Geol. Survey, various locations, 1941-60; branch chief U.S. Geol. Survey, 1961-64, research geologist, 1965—; lectr., researcher U.S. Geol. Survey-Academia Sinica Co-op, Szechuan-Yunnan, People's Republic China, 1984; lectr. advisor, Chinese U. Devel. Project II, Changchun, People's Republic China, 1987. Named Outstanding Scientist, Denver Fed. Exec. Bd., 1987; recipient Disting. Svc. award Dept. Interior, 1975. Fellow Geol. Soc. Am. (recipient Burwell award 1970, 76), Geol. Soc. London; mem. Internat. Assn. Engring. Geology, Am. Assn. Advancement Sci, Assn. Engring. Geologists. Methodist, Episcopalian. Office: US Geol Survey MS 966 Box 25046 Denver CO 80225

VARNES, RICHARD STEPHEN, communications executive; b. Denver, Jan. 5, 1949; s. David Joseph and Helen Edith (Dowling) V.; m. Joan Roberts Carroll, Nov. 22, 1980; 1 child, Andrew Dowling. BA, U. Colo., 1971; MPA, U. Colo, Denver, 1984. Dir. of young adult svcs. Boulder (Colo.) Pub. Lib., 1976-78, dir. media & programming, 1978-85; dir. ops. Mcpl. Channel 28, Boulder, Colo., 1986—; cons. Cable TV, Boulder, Colo, 1979—; mng. ptnr. Somerset Partnership, Somerton, Somerset UK, 1985—; pres. Buying in Britain, Boulder Colo., 1985-87. Contbr. articles and reviews to TV pubs. Bd. dirs. Colo. Music Festival, Boulder, 1980-86, Boulder Ctr. for the Visual Arts, 1980-86; trustee U. of Colo. Artist Series, Boulder, 1986—. Recipient of both state and fed. grants, 1982-88. Mem. Am. Lib. Assn., Nat. Assn. Telecommunications Officers and Advisors (founding mem.), NATAS, Flatirons Country Club. Office: Mcpl Channel 28 1000 Canyon Blvd Boulder CO 80302

VARRELMANN, ROBERT GALE, architect; b. Los Angeles, Aug. 5, 1947; s. Gale L. and Jane E. (Weller) V.; m. Diane Slibsager, Sept. 8, 1968; children: Erik Steven, Sheri Louise, Jason Robert. BArch, Calif. Poly., 1971. Registered architect, Calif. Draftsman/designer James Dodd & Assoc., Sacramento, 1973-74, Churchill-Zlatunich Architects, San Jose, Calif., 1974, Hawley-Stowers & Assocs., San Jose, 1975, Higgins & Root Architects, Los Gatos, Calif., 1975-76, The Griffin/Joyce Assoc., San Jose, 1976, Oscar E. Sohns Arch., Los Gatos, 1976-79; owner/prin. Varrelmann Design, San Jose, 1979—. Mem. Better Bus. Bur.; mgr. little league, 1980-83, 87-88; coach San Jose Girls Soccer, 1982-83; active Cub Scouts, 1982, 87, 88. Served to Capt., U.S. Army, 1971-73. Recipient Cert. of Appreciation Future Bus. Leaders of Am., 1982, 85, Cert. of Appreciation Seicho-No-le Truth of Life Ctr., San Jose, 1982. Mem. AIA, Better Bus. Bur., Valle del Sur Art Guild, Morgan Hill Art Guild (Artist of Yr. 1977). Republican. Methodist.

VARTANIAN, HAIK, construction executive; b. Yerevan, Armenia, Dec. 29, 1961; came to U.S., 1971; s. Kevork Nazareth and Virgine (Tashchian) V. BS in Engring., U. So. Calif., 1984. Prin. Cal Five Constrn, Inc., Glendale, Calif., 1985—; chmn. Tensor Group, Glendale, 1986-. Home: 345 Pioneer Dr #505W Glendale CA 91203 Office: Cal Five Constrn Inc 600 W Broadway No 220 Glendale CA 91204

VASCONCELOS, CARLOS GERMANO ZIVIANI, credit union executive; b. Belo Horizonte, Minas Gerais, Brazil, July 1, 1947; came to U.S., 1966; s. Carlos Noronha and Hilza (Ziviani) V. BA, U. Calif., Riverside, 1979; PhD, U. Calif., Berkeley, 1983. Librarian Press Enterprise, Riverside, Calif., 1970-79, San Francisco Chronicle, 1979-82; asst. mgr. Printing and Pub. Employees Credit Union, Riverside, 1982-85, chief exec. officer, 1985—; pres. Germano Ziviani Inc., Los Angeles, 1981—; bd. dirs. Consumer Credit Counselors, Riverside, 1986—, Share Guaranty Corp. of Calif. Mem. Credit Union League (chpt. bd. govs. 1986—), Phi Beta Kappa, Santa Barbara Polo Club. Roman Catholic. Office: Printing/Pub Employees CrUn 3630 13th St Riverside CA 92501

VASQUEZ, FRIDA, oil company executive; b. Lima, Peru, Sept. 28, 1951; d. Edwin and Frida (Ruesta) V. BS in Civil Engring., Universidad Catolica del Peru, 1973. Planning engr. Petroleos Del Peru, Lima, 1974-75, civil works design engr., 1975-78; prodn. stats. engr. Occidental Peruana Inc., Lima, 1979-82, systems support to reservoir engr., 1982-85, tech. systems programmer, analyst, 1985—. Mem. Internat. Revolver Club. Roman Catholic. Home: Lopez de Ayala 221, Lima 41, Peru Office: Occidental Peruana Inc PO Box 11174 Bakersfield CA 93309

VASQUEZ, KATHY LORRAINE, electrical engineer; b. Albuquerque, Nov. 21, 1964; d. Chester Gerald and Augustina Romo (Holguin) Claghorn; m. Steven Thomas Vasquez, Nov. 26, 1988. BS, N.Mex. State U., 1987. Elec. engr. trainee Naval Underwater Systems Ctr., New London, Conn., 1983-84, Naval Surface Weapons Ctr., Dahlgren, Va., 1985-86; mem. tech. staff TRW-WSGT, Las Cruces, N. Mex., 1987—. Democrat. Roman Catholic. Home: 830 Stagecoach Dr Las Cruces NM 88001

VASQUEZ, TONY E., physician; b. Fresno, Calif., Apr. 15, 1953; s. Tony L. and Mary E. Vasquez. BA, Calif. State U., Fresno, 1976; MD, U. Calif., Irvine, 1983. Diplomate Am. Bd. Nuclear Medicine. Intern Long Beach (Calif.) Vets. Adminstrn. Hosp., 1983-84; resident U. Calif. San Diego Med. Ctr., 1984-87, assoc. physician, 1987-88; gen. practice medicine Gould Med. Foumd., Modesto, Calif., 1988—. Patentee in field. Recipient Silver Tongue award Meml. Hosp., 1988, Vincent P. Carroll, Jr. Meml. Rsch. award U. Calif. Irvine, 1983. Mem. Calif. Med. Assn., Soc. Nuclear Medicine. Republican.

VAUGHAN, ELIZABETH CROWNHART, historian; b. Madison, Wis., Jan. 9, 1929; d. Jesse George and Hildegarde L. (Wooll) Crownhart; m. Thomas J. G. Vaughan, June 16, 1951; children: Meagan Becker, Margot Riordan-Eva, Stephen, Cameron Tyler. BA, U. Wis., 1950; MA, Portland State U., 1970. Script writer Wis. State Broadcasting System, Madison, 1951-53; women's program dir. Westinghouse KEX, Portland, Oreg., 1954-56; chief Russian desk Oreg. Hist. Soc., Portland, 1972-80, chief fgn. archives, 1980-85, coord. North Pacific studies, 1985-88; exec. dir. North Pacific Studies Ctr., Portland, 1988—; bd. dirs. First Interstate Bank Oreg., Portland, 1977—, Nordstrom Inc., Seattle, 1977—; treas. Salar Enterprises, Portland, 1968-88, pres., 1988—. Editor, translator: Explorations of Kamchatka, 1972, End of Russian Am., 1979, Russia's Conquest Siberia, 1985, Russia's Penetration North Pacific, 1988. Bd. dirs. Oreg. Ind. Coll. Found., Portland, 1981—, Oreg. Symphony Assn., Chamber Music N.W., Portland, Portland Opera Assn., 1989—; founder Young Audiences Oreg., Portland, 1964. Recipient Aubrey Watzek award, Lewis & Clark Coll., 1974. Fellow Royal Geog. Soc.; mem. Am. Com. on East-West Accord, North Am. Falconers Assn., Internat. Trade and Commerce Inst. (bd. dirs.), Am Assn. Slavic and East European Studies, Phi Kappa Phi, Town Club, Univ. Club. Office: Oreg Hist Soc 1230 SW Park Ave Portland OR 97205

VAUGHAN, JAMES ARTHUR, JR., surgeon; b. Sherman, Tex., Aug. 16, 1914; s. James Arthur and Nola Beatrice (Lawrence) V.; B.S., East Tex. State Coll., 1947, M.S., 1950; D.O., Chgo. Coll. Osteopathy, 1951; M.D., Calif. Coll. Medicine, 1962; m. Betty Ruth Brecheen, June 19, 1942 (dec.); children: J.A., James A. III; m. 2d, Betty Jo Stewart, Nov. 14, 1958 (div.); 1 dau., Karen. Intern Dallas Osteo. Hosp., 1951-52; pvt. practice, Dallas, 1952-63; assoc. Antelope Valley Med. Clinic, 1963-77; practice medicine, 1977-86; vice chief staff Lancaster Community Hosp., 1968, chief of staff, 1980-86; staff mem. Antelope Valley Hosp.; bd. dirs. Dallas Osteo. Hosp. until 1963; mem. adv. com. LVN Sch. Nursing until 1963. Served from seaman 2d class to lt. comdr. USNR, 1941-46, now lt. comdr. ret. Decorated Air medal with 1 gold star; recipient Disting. Service award CAP. Mem. AMA, Los Angeles County Med. Assn., Ret. Officers Assn. (life), Nat. Aero. Assn., Flying Doctors Soc. Africa (life), D.A.V. (life), Am. Legion (life), VFW (life), Sigma Tau Gamma, Iota Tau Sigma, Sigma Sigma Phi. Mason (32 deg., Shriner); mem. Order Eastern Star, Amaranth. Democrat. Episcopalian. Club: Caterpillar. Office: Box 2988 Lancaster CA 93539-2988

VAUGHAN, THOMAS JAMES GREGORY, historian; b. Seattle, Oct. 13, 1924; s. Daniel George and Kathryn Genevieve (Browne) V.; m. Elizabeth Ann Perpetua Crownhart, June 16, 1951; children: Meagan, Margot, Stephen, Cameron. BA, Yale U., 1948; MA, U. Wis., 1950, doctoral residence, 1951-53; LittD, Pacific U., 1969; LLD, Reed Coll., 1975. Exec. dir. Oreg. Hist. Soc., Portland, 1954—; editor-in-chief Oreg. Hist. Quar., 1954—; adj. prof. Portland State U., 1968—; chmn. bd. Salar Enterprises, Ltd.; bd. dir. Am. Heritage Pub. Co., 1976—; film producer, 1958-76. Author: A Century of Portland Architecture, 1967, Captain Cook, R.N, The Resolute Mariner: An International Record of Oceanic Discovery, 1974, Portland, A Historical Sketch and Guide, 1976, 2d edit., 1983, Voyage of Enlightenment: Malaspina on the Northwest Coast, 1977; editor: Space, Style and Structure: Building in Northwest America, 2 vols., 1974, The Western Shore, 1975, Ascent of the Athabasca Pass, 1978, Wheels of Fortune, High and Mighty, 1981, Soft Gold, 1982, To Siberia and Russian America, Vols. I, II and III, also others.; mem. adv. bd. Am. Heritage Mag., 1977—. First chmn. Oreg. State Com. for Humanities, NEH, 1969—; 1st chmn. Gov.'s Adv. Com. on Historic Preservation Oreg., 1970—; sec. Oreg. Geog. Names Bd., 1958—; adviser 1000 Friends of Oreg., 1972—; lay mem. Oreg. State Bar Disciplinary Rev. Bd., 1975—; vice chmn. adv. panel Nat. Endowment Arts, 1975—; mem. Nat. Hist. Publs. and Records Commn. Matrix, 1975-76. Served with USMC, 1942-45; historian laureate State of Oreg., 1989. Decorated comdr. Order Brit. Empire; recipient Aubrey Watzek award Lewis and Clark Coll., 1975; Edith Knight Hill award, 1977; recipient Disting. Svc. award U. Oreg., 1980, Portland State U., 1985, Pres. medal Portland State U., 1988, Tom McCall Broadcasting award, 1981; English Speaking Union grantee, 1961. Fellow Royal Geog. Soc.; mem. Am. Assn. State and Local History (bd. dir. 1955-74, pres. 1976—), Am. Assn. Mus. (coun., exec. com.), Nat. Trust Historic Preservation (adv. coun.), City Club (Portland, bd. govs.), Univ. Club (Portland, bd. govs.). Home: 2135 SW Laurel St Portland OR 97201 Office: Oreg Hist Soc 1230 SW Park Ave Portland OR 97205

VAUGHAN, WARREN TAYLOR, JR., psychiatrist; b. Portola Valley, Calif., Aug. 24, 1920; s. Warren Taylor and Emma Elizabeth (Heath) V.; m. Cecil Todd Knight, Dec. 19, 1942 (div. 1958); children: W. Taylor III, Christopher, Todd Jameson; m. Clarice Helm Haylett, Aug. 16, 1960; children: Richard Haylett, Jennifer Anne. BS, Harvard U., 1942, MD, 1943. Diplomate Am. Bd. Psychiatry. Resident Boston U. Sch. Medicine, 1946-48; fellow child psychiatry Judge Baker Guidance Ctr., Boston, 1948-50; from rsch. fellow to asst. prof. Harvard U. Sch. Pub. Health, Boston, 1950-59; asst. clin. prof. U. Colo. Sch. Medicine, Denver, 1959-60; from assoc. clin. prof. to lectr. in psychiatry Stanford U., Palo Alto, Calif., 1966—; chmn. dept. psychiatry Peninsula Hosp., 1968-69; cons. in field. Contbr. articles to profl. jours. Dir. mental hygiene Mass. Dept. Mental Helth, Boston, 1952-59; chmn. com. Futures Planning Council, 1967-74; bd. dirs. Planned Parenthood, 1987—. Capt. AUS, 1944-46. Recipient Svc. award NIMH, 1976. Fellow Am. Psychiatric Assn., Northern Calif. Psychiatric Assn. (pres. 1970-71), Am. Orthopsychiatric Assn., Am. Acad. Child and Adolescent Psychiatry; mem. Group for Advancement Psychiatry, Am. Coll. Psychiatry (emeritus). Republican. Episcopalian. Home: 41 Stonegate Rd Portola Valley CA 94025 Office: 1720 Marco Polo Way Burlingame CA 94010

VAUGHN, MARK ROY, mechanical engineer; b. Albuquerque, Oct. 27, 1957; s. Harold Roy and Mary Joanne (Tawzer) V.; m. Leslie Gail White, Dec. 30, 1979; children: Kristina Lee, James Roy. BS, U. N.Mex., 1979; MS, U. Tex., 1983, PhD, 1985. Engr. in tng., N.Mex. Engr. Ctr. for Electro Mechanics, Austin, Tex., 1983-85; mem. tech. staff, engr. Sandia Nat. Labs., Albuquerque, 1985—. Patentee: Bearing, 1987. Mem. ASME, Tau Beta Pi, Eta Kappa Nu, Phi Eta Sigma. Republican. Presbyterian. Office: Sandia Nat Labs Div 9142 Albuquerque NM 87185

VAUGHN, SUSAN ELIZABETH, writer; b. Rockville Ctr., N.Y., Oct. 7, 1959; d. Rose Marie Maloni. Student, Pa. State U., 1976-78, Golden Gate U., 1983. Freelance writer San Francisco, 1983-86, L.A., 1987—; fin. analyst Union Oil, San Francisco, 1979-83; bur. chief Time, Inc., L.A., 1986; instr. journalism UCLA Extension, 1988. Contbr. articles to mags. and newspapers including People, McCalls, L.A. Times, Time, Cosmopolitan; author: screenplay A Cheerleader's Story (1st Place winner Diane Thomas award UCLA 1989). Ford Found. scholar, 1977, Mary C. Abrams scholar, 1977, Nat. Merit scholar, 1983; recipient Pres.'s Freshman award Pa. State U., 1976. Home: PO Box 10987 Beverly Hills CA 90213-3987

VAUS, STEVEN TIMOTHY, music composer, producer; b. L.A., Apr. 7, 1952; s. James Arthur and Alice Rosealba (Park) V.; m. Barbara Ellen Samilson, Apr. 3, 1982; children: Chelsea, Amanda, Emily. Student, Eisenhower Coll., 1970-71. Composer United Artists Music, L.A., 1979-80; exec. v.p. pub. relations Youth Devel., Inc., San Diego, Calif., 1981-84; owner music studio San Diego, 1984—; mem. mktg. com. Old Globe Theater, San Diego, 1986-87, Excel, San Diego, 1986-88. Composer, producer USN Blue Angels theme song, 1988, America's Cup theme song, 1986-88, White House theme Just Say No, 1985. Mem. Rep. Nat. Com., Washington; dir. Multiple Sclerosis, San Diego, 1988, Crime Stoppers, San Diego, 1987-88; officer, San Diego Police Reserves, 1984—. Named Outstanding Citizen Jr. C. of C., 1985, 86, Headliner of the Yr. San Diego Press Club, 1986; recipient Silver Microphone award San Diego Press Club 1987. Mem. Advt. Club of San Diego, Am. Soc. Composers and Publs., Nat. Acad. TV Arts and Scis., Peace Officers Rsch. Assn. of Calif. Republican. Presbyterian. Office: 9590 Chesapeake Dr San Diego CA 92123

VAUX, DORA LOUISE, sperm bank official, consultant; b. White Pine, Mont., Aug. 8, 1922; d. Martin Tinus and Edna Ruth (Pyatt) Palmlund; m. Robert Glenn Vaux, Oct. 25, 1941; children: Jacqueline, Cheryl, Richard, Jeanette. Grad. high sch., Bothell, Wash. Photographer Busco-Nestor Studios, San Diego, 1961-68; owner, mgr. Vaux Floors & Interiors, San Diego, 1968-82; cons., mgr. Repository for Germinal Choice, Escondido, Calif., 1983—. Mem. Escondido Country Club, Escondido Fish and Game Club. Republican. Home: 1255 LaCienega San Marcos CA 92069 Office: Found for Advancement Man 450 S Escondido Blvd Escondido CA 92025

VAWTER, DONALD, personnel management consultant; b. Spokane, Wash., May 19, 1920; s. Edgar F. and Lina M. V.; student polit. sci. Wash. State U., 1946-49; m. Margaret Schroeder, May 5, 1950; children—Charlotte, Sara. Supr. employee services Wash. State Employment Service, Seattle, 1950-58; employment mgr. Sundstrand Data Control, Redmond, Wash., 1958-72; profl. recruiter DBA Bellevue Employment Agy., Bellevue, Wash., 1972-73; personnel mgr., workers compensation adminstr. Crown Zellerbach, Omak, Wash., 1973-82; bd. dirs. Pacific N.W. Personnel Mgmt. Assn. 1974-78; apptd. Gov's. Svcs. Coun., 1977-83; treas. econ. devel. corp. North Okanogan County, 1984—. Served with USCGR, 1942-46, 50-53, comdr. Res. ret., 1968. Mem. Am. Soc. Personnel Adminstrn. (accredited personnel mgr.). Clubs: Elks, Grey W (Wash. State U.). Home: PO Box 296 Tonasket WA 98855

VAWTER, ROY GLENN, research company executive, engineer; b. Denver, Aug. 10, 1938; s. Roy G. and D. Jean (Cole) V.; m. Terry Lynn Stine, Oct. 27, 1961; children: Kathleen Ann, John Christopher. BS, Colo. Sch. Mines, 1960; postgrad. advanced mgmt., Harvard U., 1977. Registered profl. engr., Utah, Colo. Engr. Marathon Oil Co., Bakersfield, Calif., 1961-64; sr. v.p. Tosco Corp., Denver and Los Angeles, 1964-83; pres. Leesburg Land & Mining, Denver, 1983-84; mgmt. cons. Denver, 1984-86; v.p. Western Research Inst., Laramie, Wyo., Washington, 1986--; bd. dirs. VIP Travel Coins., Inc., Aurora, Colo. Author: contbr. articles to profl. jours., chpt. to book; patentee: flapper valve assembly, horizontal retort with solid heat transfer medium, apparatus and method for heating a plurality of solids. Precinct chmn. Bakersfield Republican Com., 1962; mem. grand Valley (Colo.) Town Council, 1968; chmn. mining sect. United Way, Denver, 1984-85. Mem. Soc. Petroleum Engrs. (chpt. pres. 1959-60), Am. Inst. Chem. Engrs., Rocky Mountain Oil and Gas Assn., (chmn. com. on oil shale 1981-82), Harvard Bus. Sch. Club (Denver), Masons. Episcopalian. Office: Western Rsch Inst PO Box 3395 Laramie WY 82071

VEAL, DONALD LYLE, former university president, aircraft instrumentation executive and researcher, educator; b. Chance, S.D., Apr. 17, 1931; s. Boyd William and Esther Mabel (Iverson) V.; m. Bonita Dale Larson, May 8, 1953; children: Sherrill, Barbara. B.S.C.E., S.D. State U., 1953; M.S.C.E., U. Wyo., 1960, Ph.D. in Civil Engring., 1964. Lic. profl. engr. Wyo. Asst. prof. civil engring. U. Wyo., 1964-66, assoc. prof., 1966-71, prof., 1971—, head dept. atmospheric sci., 1971-76, 77-80, v.p. research, 1980-81, acting pres., 1981-82, pres., 1982-87; dir. nat. hail research expt. Nat. Ctr. Atmospheric Research, Boulder, Colo., 1976-77; trustee Univ. Corp. for Atmospheric Research, Boulder, 1978—; chmn. Univ. Corp. for Atmospheric Research, 1980-82; commr. Western Interstate Commn. for Higher Edn., Salt Lake City, 1981-87; mem. ROTC adv. com. U.S. Army Command and Gen. Staff Coll., Fort Leavenworth, Kans., 1982-87; dir. Particle Measuring Systems, Inc., Boulder, 1982—, pres., 1987—; dir. First Interstate Bank, Laramie, Wyo., 1974—; mem. Nat. Acad. Scis.-NRC panel on low-altitude wind variability. Mem. Brees Field Airport Authority, Laramie, 1962-76; pres. Bress Field Airport Authority, 1964-76; mem. Wyo. Congl. Award Council, 1983; pres. Western Athletic Conf. Found., 1983—. Served to 1st lt. USAF, 1953-57. Recipient Disting. Alumnus U. S.D., 1983. Fellow Am. Meteorol. Soc.; mem. Nat. Soc. Profl. Engrs., Am. Soc. Engring. Edn., ASCE, Weather Modification Assn., N.Y. Acad. Scis., Sigma Xi. Lodge: Rotary (Laramie). Office: Particle Measuring Systems Inc 1855 S 57th Ct Boulder CO 80301 *

VEASEY, COLUMBUS, JR., library administrator; b. Memphis, Aug. 22, 1935; s. Columbus and Grace Marie (Jackson) V.; m. Joan Marie Ingram, Mar. 31, 1956; children: Byron Keith, Janet Lynn. BSBA, Syracuse U., 1963; MBA, U. Dayton, 1970; MPA, U. Denver, 1980, PhD, 1985. Cert. data processor. Commd. USAF, 1955, advanced through grades to maj., 1975, ret., 1975; head. acad. computer support dept. Air Force Inst. Tech., Dayton, 1968-72; chief large group display br. N.Am. Aerospace Def. Command, Colorado Springs, 1972-75; exec. asst. to exec. dir. Western Interstate Commn. on Higher Edn., Boulder, Colo., 1975-77; mgr. fin. infosys. and no. ops. Regional Transp. Dist., Denver, Boulder, 1977-80; mgr. sys. devel. Colo. Dept. Social Svcs., Denver, 1980-82; mgr. fin. info. sys. Stearns-Catalytic Corp., Denver, 1984-86; dir. fin. Denver Pub. Library, 1986—. Dist. capt. Denver Dem. Party, 1985—, vice chmn., 1989—; v.p. Kappa Towers Sr. Citizens Housing, Denver, 1984—; chmn. fin. com. Colo. Black Roundtable, Denver, 1986—, Kappa Housing, Inc., 1989—; mem. fund raising com. Rocky Mt. Adoption Exchange, Denver, 1987—; mem. Mayor's Black Adv. Coun., Denver, 1986—. Fellow Phi Delta Kappa, Sigma Iota Epsilon; mem. Kappa Alpha Psi (treas. 1985—, Named Man of the Yr. 1980). Democrat. Presbyterian. Office: Denver Pub Libr 3840 York St Unit 1 Denver CO 80205-2165

VEATCH, JOHN WILLIAM, speech pathologist; b. Mitchell, S.D., Dec. 9, 1923; s. William Homer and Helen Gwendolyn (Lowther) V.; m. Doris Lavelle Guthrie (dec. 1978); children: Dean, Joan; m. Winnifred Ann Sawin, Aug. 6, 1982; children: Shaun, Monicah. BA in Speech, Wash. State U., 1946, BEd, 1951; MA in Speech, U. Wash., 1950; DEd, U. Idaho, 1970. Pvt. practice speech pathology Spokane, Wash., 1950-79; pvt. practice speech pathology and ednl. cons. Tacoma, 1980—; lectr. in speech pathology Gonzaga U., Spokane, Wash., 1963-70; adj. prof. Wash. State U., 1972-77, Applied Psychology, Eastern Wash. U., 1977; chief exec. officer and dir. research. Espial Inst., Tacoma, 1982—; mem. home health adv. bd. Spokane County Health Dept., past. pres. Wash. State Health Dept. Crippled Children's Svc. Adv. Bd. Maxillofacial Defects; con. in field. Author: (with D. Hughes) Teacher Qualities, 1947; (test profiles) Personal Stress Balance Profile, 1982, Info. Processing Style, 1984, The Deep Screening Profile of Tongue Thrusting Activity, 1985, The Tongue Thrust Screening Test, 1986, Learning Style Profile, 1986; writer, contbr. guides, workbooks, studies and films in field. Fellow Northwest Acad. Speech Pathology (pres. 1978-82, 86—); mem. Internat. Assn. Oral Myology, Am. Speech and Hearing Assn., Wash. State Speech and Hearing Assn., Inland Empire Speech and Hearing Assn., Wash. Assn. Home Health Agys. (past v.p.), Am. Speech-Lang.-Hearing Assn. (pres. bd. Oakbridge U. 1989—). Home: 4708-64th Ave W Tacoma WA 98466 Office: 4113 Bridge Port Way W Ste B Tacoma WA 98466

VEBLEN, MARTHANNA ELVIDGE, retired librarian and retirement consultant; b. Seattle, Oct. 3, 1920; d. Ford Quint and Anita Emily (Miller) Elvidge; m. John Veblen, Oct. 24, 1942; children: John Elvidge, Christopher Ford. BA, U. Wash., 1942, MLS, 1959. Rsch. cons. Wash. State Gov.'s Coun. on Aging, Olympia, 1959-61; asst. librarian Seattle Pacific Coll., 1960-65, head librarian, 1965-66; regional supr. King County Library System, Seattle, 1969-72; coordinator book mobile ext. King County Library System, 1972-75, govt. documents librarian, 1975-82; retirement cons., pres. Creative Retirement Cons., Inc., Seattle, 1980-86. Author: Aging in the State of Washington, 1961, Giant Strides Since Andrew Carnegie, 1975, Aging-Where to Turn in Washington State, 1976; contbr. articles to profl. jours. Gov.'s appointee Wash. State Coun. on Aging, 1967-71; trustee Seattle-King County Coun. on Aging, 1968-80, chmn., 1973-76; mem. Wash. Adv. Com. Depository Standards, 1975-79; mem. library com. Found. for Preservation Gov.'s Mansion, Olympia, 1975-77; mem. health svcs. panel United Way King County, 1977-80; trustee Women's Heritage Ctr., Seattle, 1983-85. Mem. Northwest Coll. Assn. (chmn. 1964), Pacific Northwest Library Assn. (sec. Ednl. div. 1964-66), Washington Library Assn. (fed. relaions coordinator 1973-77), Women's Profl. Managerial Network, Internat. Soc. Pre-Retirement Planners, Univ. Wash. Grad. Sch. Sci. and Info., Kappa Kappa Gamma, Beta Phi Mu, Alpha Delta Kappa, City Club Seattle, Sunset Club, DAR, Nat. Soc. Colonial Daumes Am. in Wash., Daughters Soc. Calif. Pioneers, Women's U. Club. Home: 6720 Green Lake Way N Seattle WA 98103

VEGA, BENJAMIN URBIZO, retired judge; b. La Ceiba, Honduras, Jan. 18, 1916. AB, U. So. Calif., 1938, postgrad., 1939-40; LLB, Pacific Coast U. Law, 1941. Bar: Calif. 1947, U.S. Dist. Ct. (so. dist.) Calif. 1947, U.S. Supreme Ct. 1958. Assoc. Anderson, McPharlin & Connors, Los Angeles, 1947-48, Newman & Newman, Los Angeles, 1948-51; dep. dist. atty. County of Los Angeles, 1951-66; judge Los Angeles, County Mcpl. Ct., East Los Angeles Jud. Dist., 1966-86, retired, 1986; leader faculty seminar Calif. Jud. Coll. at Earl Warren Legal Inst., U. Calif-Berkeley, 1978. Mem. Calif. Gov.'s Adv. Com. on Children and Youth, 1968; del. Commn. of the Califs., 1978; bd. dirs. Los Angeles-Mexico City Sister City Com.; pres. Argentine Cultural Found., 1983. Recipient award for outstanding services from Mayor of Los Angeles, 1973, City of Commerce, City of Montebello, Calif. Assembly, Southwestern Sch. Law, Disting. Pub. Service award Dist. Atty. Los Angeles County. Mem. Conf. Calif. Judges, Mcpl. Ct. Judges' Assn. (award for Outstanding Services), Los Angeles County, Am. Judicature Soc., World Affairs Council, Pi Sigma Alpha. Home: 101 California Ave Apt 1207 Santa Monica CA 90403

VEGA, JOSE GUADALUPE, psychologist, clinical director; b. San Benito, Tex., June 4, 1953; s. Jose Guadalupe and Bertha (Saenz) V.; m. Beth Susan Brimmer, Aug. 20, 1979 (div. 1986); children: Lilian Anna, Jose Guadalupe III; m. Andrea M. Arnold, Mar. 23, 1988 (div. 1989). BA, Pan. Am. U., Edinburg, Tex., 1975; MA, U. Denver, 1976, PhD, 1979. Lic. psychologist, Colo., 1983; lic. profl. counselor, Tex., 1983; diplomate Am. Bd. Med. Psychotherapists. With Oasis of Chandala, Denver, 1978-79, Maytag-Emrick Clinic, Aurora, Colo., 1979; psychologist Spanish Peaks Mental Health Ctr., Pueblo, Colo., 1980-85; pvt. practice Assocs. for Psychotherapy and Edn., Inc., 1985-86; co-owner Affiliates in Counseling, Psychol. Assessment and Consultation, Inc., Pueblo, 1986—; psychologist Parkview Psychol. Testing Clinic, Pueblo, 1987—; mem. state grievance bd. Psychology Augment Panel, 1988—. Active Colo. Inst. Chicano Mental Health Community Youth Orgn., Boys Club Pueblo. Mem. Am. Psychol. Assn., Nat. Acad. Neuropsychologists, Am. Assn. for Counseling and Devel., Health and Human Services Com. City of Pueblo, Colo. Psychol. Assn., Nat. Hispanic Psychol. Assn., Phi Delta Kappa, Kappa Delta Pi. Democrat. Roman Catholic. Office: 56 Club Manor Dr Pueblo CO 81008

VEGA, MICHAEL ROBLES, podiatrist; b. Loma Linda, Calif., June 18, 1955; s. Trinidad and Emelia (Robles) V.; m. Julie Louise Haak, Apr. 29, 1978; children: Bianca Pilar, Michael Louis. BA, U. San Diego, 1977; D in Podiatric Medicine, Ohio Coll. Podiatric Medicine, 1982. Resident Hillside Hosp., San Diego, 1982-83; podiatrist Community Health Found., Los Angeles, 1983-86; pvt. practice podiatry Montebello, Calif., 1985—; clin. asst. prof. podiatric medicine Calif. Coll. Podiatric Medicine, 1987—. Contbr. articles to profl. jours. Fellow Am. Coll. Foot Surgeons; mem. Podiatry Soc. Los Angeles, Am. Podiatric Med. Assn., Am. Acad. Podiatric Sports Medicine, Am. Running and Fitness Assn., Am. Podiatric Med. Writers Assn., Pi Delta. Democrat. Roman Catholic. Home: 1577 Las Palomas Dr La Habra Heights CA 90631 Office: West Beverly Podiatry Group 433 N 4th St Ste 202 Montebello CA 90640

VEGLIA, EDWARD PATRICK, security consultant; b. Denver, May 13, 1950; s. Edward Leo and Anne Louise (Zarlengo) V. Student, Met. State Coll., Denver, 1968-70; grad., Columbia Sch. Broadcasting, 1970. Salesman Nat. Shirt Shops, Denver, 1968-69; news reporter Sta. KBTR, Denver, 1969-73; counselor Columbia Sch. Broadcasting, Denver, 1970-73; news announcer Sta. KDEN, Denver, 1973-74; dir. sales promoting Security Life Ins. Co., Denver, 1973-74; freelance promoter, photographer Denver, 1974-78; police officer Denver Police Dept., 1978-87; v.p. Risk Mgmt. Internat., Inc., Denver, 1987-88; safety security coord. Fiddlers Green Amphitheater, Denver, 1988. Contbr. articles to various publs. Mem. Am. Soc. Indsl. Security, Internat. Assn. Bomb Technicians & Investigators, Assn. Former Intelligence Officers, Acad. Polit. Sci., Hale Found., Club Aquarius. Republican. Roman Catholic.

VELA, CHARLES F., protective services official; b. L.A., May 22, 1936; s. L. Francisco and Julia Mary (Martinez) V.; m. Anna Joyce Loper, Aug. 13, 1955; children: Charles F. Jr., Anna Marie, Richard L., John P. AS, Riverside Community Coll., 1970; BS, Calif. State U., 1977. Cert. fire officer, Calif. Exam, patrolman Tex. Dept. of Pub. Safety, Houston, 1957-58; teller Bank of America, El Centro, Calif., 1958-60; armory supt. Calif. NG, El Centro, 1960-61; fire fighter City of El Centro, 1961-66; fire capt. City of Riverside, 1966—. Vice-pres. Riverside Colt League, Riverside, Calif., 1986-87, coach, mgr., bd. mem., 1976-84; coach mgr., bd. mem. Pony Baseball, Riverside Pony League, 1974-76, Little League, Riverside, 1969-74. Mem. Calif. State Firefighters Assn., Riverside Firefighters Assn., Nat. Intercollegiate Soccer Officials (pres. Inland, Calif. chpt. 1988—, referee 1983—), U.S. Soccer Fedn. (referee class 5, 1980—, cert. referee assessor, 1987), Active 20-30 Club (to v.p. 1962-66). Democrat. Baptist. Home: 6366 Barranca Dr Riverside CA 92506

VELDE, JOHN ERNEST, JR., business executive; b. Pekin, Ill., June 15, 1917; s. John Ernest and Alga (Anderson) V.; m. Shirley Margaret Walker, July 29, 1940 (dec. 1969); 1 dau., Drew; m. Gail Patrick, Sept. 28, 1974 (dec. July 1980); m. Gretchen Swanson Pullen, Nov. 7, 1981. A.B., U. Ill., 1938. Pres. Velde, Roelfs & Co., Pekin, 1955-60; dir. Herget Nat. Bank, 1948-75, Kroehler Mfg. Co., 1974-81; pres. Paisano Prodns., Inc., 1980—. Trustee Pekin Pub. Library, 1948-69, Pekin Meml. Hosp., 1950-69; chmn. Am. Library Trustee Assn. Found., 1976; trustee Am. Library Assn. Endowment, 1976-82, Everett McKinley Dirksen Research Center, 1965-74; chmn. trustees, bd. dirs. Center Ulcer Research and Edn. Found., 1977-82; mem. bd. councilors Brain Research Inst. UCLA, 1977-82; trustee Center for Am. Archeology, Evanston, 1978-83; mem. Nat. Commn. on Libraries and Info. Sci., 1970-79; mem. adv. bd. on White House Conf. on Libraries, 1976-80; trustee Joint Council on Econ. Edn., 1977-83; bd. dirs. U. Ill. Found., 1977-83, Omaha Pub. Library Found., 1985—; vice chmn. U. Ill. Pres.' Council, 1977-79, chmn., 1979-81, mem. fin. resources council steering com., 1976-78; mem. adv. council UCLA Grad. Sch. Library and Info. Sci., 1981-82; pres. Ill. Valley Library System, 1965-69; dir. Lakeview Center for Arts and Scis., Peoria, Ill., 1962-73; mem. Nat. Book Com., 1969-74. Served as lt. (j.g.) USNR, World War II. Mem. Am. Library Trustee Assn. (regional v.p. 1970-72, chmn. internat. relations com. 1973-76), Kappa Sigma. Clubs: Chgo. Yacht, Internat. (Chgo.); California (Los Angeles); Outrigger Canoe (Honolulu); Thunderbird Country (Rancho Mirage, Calif.); Chaine des Rotisseurs, Chevaliers du Tastevin; Circumnavigators (N.Y.C.); Omaha, Omaha Country; Old Baldy (Saratoga, Wyo.), Eldorado Country (Indian Wells, Calif.), Morningside (Rancho Mirage, Calif.). Home: 8405 Indian Hills Dr Omaha NE 68114 also: 40-231 Club View Dr Rancho Mirage CA 92270

VELEZ, RALPH JOHN, Spanish teacher; b. Bronx, N.Y., Jan. 31, 1934; s. Ralph Angel Velez and Melita Theresa Bingham; m. Nilda Rosaura Garcia, Dec. 25, 1955; children: Ralph, Steve, Jeff. BS, Pratt Inst., 1957; MS, Queens Coll., 1961. Cert. secondary sch. tchr., N.Y., Calif. Tchr. art, horticulture, Spanish East Meadow (N.Y.) Sch. Dist., 1957-61, Garden Grove (Calif.) Sch. Dist., 1961—; tchr. English as a second lang. Mem. Garden Grove Edn. Assn. (faculty rep. 1987-89), Palm Soc. So. Calif. (pres. 1974-77, 87-88). Democrat. Roman Catholic. Home: 15461 Devonshire Circle Westminster CA 92683

VELK, ROBERT JAMES, psychologist; b. Chgo., Feb. 27, 1938; s. Jerry E. and Sylvia B. (Wladar) Vlk; m. Vera A. Kraml, Nov. 25, 1961; children—Robert Frank, Cheryl Anne. B.B.A., Northwestern U., 1963, M.B.A., 1968; M.A., Rutgers U., 1980, Ph.D., 1983. Asst. mgr. product decorations Meyercord Co., Carol Stream, Ill., 1959-65, nat. account mgr., 1965-68; assoc. Kepner Tregoe, Inc., Princeton, N.J., 1968-70, Western region mgr., 1970-72, dir. mktg. N.Am. ops., 1972-73; pres. Creative Leadership Inc., Princeton, 1973-83; pres. Cognitive Sci. Corp., Ft. Collins, Colo., 1983—. Author: Information and Imagination, 1978; Thinking About Thinking, 1978. Mem. Am. Psychol. Assn., Am. Soc. Tng. and Devel., Nat. Soc. Performance and Instrn., Cognitive Sci. Soc. Clubs: Christian Businessmen's Com. of Central Jersey (chmn. 1974-75), Gideon's. Office: Cognitive Sci Corp PO Box 1487 Fort Collins CO 80522

VELLA, STEPHEN MICHAEL, radiation therapy technologist; b. San Francisco, June 21, 1958; s. Charles and Mary Louise (Sunseri) V.; m. Maria Palma Pellegrini, July 30, 1983; 1 child, Matthew Christopher. BA in Biol. Scis., U. of the Pacific, 1980. Cert. radiologic technologist. Staff technologist Santa Rosa (Calif.) Radiation Oncology Ctr., 1982—. Mem. Am. Soc. Radiologic Technologists, Calif. Soc. Radiologic Technologists, Northern Calif. Soc. Radiation Therapy Technologists (sec. 1987—). Democrat. Roman Catholic. Home: 1936 San Salvador Dr Santa Rosa CA 95403 Office: Santa Rosa Radiation Oncology Ctr 510 Doyle Park Dr Santa Rosa CA 95405

VELO, LUIS FERNANDEZ, operations and communications executive, consultant; b. Manila, Oct. 23, 1950; came to U.S., 1981; s. Antonio Celestino and Pacita (Fernandez) V.; m. Rosabella Mendoza, May 7, 1983. Liberal Arts in English Lit. and Philosophy, Maryhurst Sem., Baguio City, Philippines, 1966; MA in Philosophy, Maryhurst Sem., 1972. Reservation clk. Philippine Airlines, Manila, 1972-78, sr. programmer, 1978-80; mgr. Oriental Data Systems, Hong Kong, 1980-82, Jersey City, 1982-84; gen. mgr. Seapac Services, N.Y.C., 1984-86; mgr. proposal Electronic Data Systems, Morristown, N.J., 1986-87, tech. specialist, 1987; asst. gen. mgr. OOCL USA, Inc., Oakland, Calif., 1987—; designer in field. Roman Catholic. Home: 401 Picadilly Pl Unit #8 San Bruno CA 94066 Office: OOCL USA Inc 433 Hepenberger Rd Oakland CA 94621

VENCE, BRIAN SCOTT, dentist; b. Elgin, Ill., Mar. 9, 1959; s. José and Joanne Lee (Saunders) V. BS in Biology, U. Ill., 1981; BS in Dentistry, U. Ill., Chgo., 1983, DDS, 1985. Gen. practice resident VA Med. Ctr., Wadsworth, L.A., 1985-86; pvt. practice dentistry Manhattan Beach, Calif., 1986-87, Irvine, Calif., 1987—; cons. Am. Dental Examiners, Irvine, Calif., 1988—; med. staff, Hoag Hosp., Newport Beach, Calif., 1988—. Mem. ADA, Calif. Dental Assn., Am. Assn. Hosp. Dentists, Orange County Dental Soc., Acad. Gen. Dentistry. Democrat. Office: Irvine Dental Assocs 18124 Culver Dr Irvine CA 92715

VENDRELL, JOHN DONALD OROMI, accountant; b. Barcelona, Spain, Nov. 14, 1934; came to U.S., 1962; s. Juan Sarda and Agnes Capell (Oromi) V.; m. Donna Gene Barnsley, Nov. 13, 1961 (div. 1974); children: Michael John, Daniel Edward, Marina Gene; m. Ana Isabel Regazzoni Gonzalez, Oct. 3, 1978; children: John Charles, Andrew Peter. Degree in French, Instituto Inter, Barcelona, 1960, degree in English, 1961; BS in Acctg., Golden Gate U., 1967, MBA in Acctg., 1970. Final inspector Ultonix, San Mateo, Calif., 1962-63; treas. Arita Porcelian Co., Tokyo, 1969-70, Internat. Air Svc. Co., Ltd., Burlingame, Calif., 1964-70; chief postal accts. Post Office Dept., San Mateo, 1970-72; chief revenue U.S. Customs Dept., San Francisco, 1972-75, regulatory auditor, 1975-80, systems acct., 1980-81; asst. to commr. USN, Moffett Field, Calif., 1981—; pvt. practice acct., mgmt. cons. John D. & Ana I. Vendrell, Foster City, Calif., 1964—. Vice pres. Young Reps., Foster City, 1969-70. 2d lt. Spanish Army. Mem. Gov. Soc. Accts., Gov. Comptrollers Soc., N.Am. Catalonian Soc., Casal dels Catalans de Calif. Democrat. Roman Catholic. Home: 950 Edgewater Blvd Foster City CA 94404 Office: Comml Activities Office Bldg 23 Moffett Field CA 94035

VENEZIANO, PHILIP JOHN, architect; b. New Britain, Conn., Aug. 1, 1951; s. Angelo Salvator and Natalie Ann (Cianci) V.; m. Diane Leigh Morris, Sept. 11, 1982; children: Andrea Leigh, David Andrew. BArch., U. Ariz., 1983. Reg. profl. architect, Ariz. Job. capt. Wilson Hines & Assocs., Tucson, 1983-84, Kim Acorn & Assocs., Tucson, 1984-86; project mgr. Smith Peterson Assocs., Tucson, 1986, James Barg & Assocs., Tucson, 1986-88; architect Gromatzky Dupree & Assocs., Tucson, 1988—. Office: Gromatzky Dupree & Assocs 4811 E Grant Rd Tucson AZ 85712

VENTLING, THOMAS LEE, banker; b. Dodge City, Kans., Nov. 20, 1948; s. Doyle L. and Mary E. (Burkhart) V.; m. Jennifer L. Lacy, Aug. 28, 1976; children: Richard, John, Jason, Justin. BSBA, Calif. State U., L.A., 1978. Asst. v.p. Security Pacific, Pasadena, Calif., 1978-82; v.p. BT Comml. Corp. (Bankers Trust Co.), L.A., 1982—. With USN, 1970-73. Republican. Roman Catholic. Home: 3432 Monticello Ave Simi Valley CA 93063

VENTURA, MICHAEL JOE, engineer; b. Kansas City, Kans., Oct. 20, 1954; s. George Joseph and Patricia Mae (Nichell) V.; m. Ellen Ruth Runge, Aug. 2, 1980. BS in Civil Engring., U. Wyo., 1985. Engring. aide City of Lincoln, Nebr., 1972-77; engring. technician Arch Mineral Corp., Hanna, Wyo., 1977-81; plant engr. Tenneco Minerals Corp., Green River, Wyo., 1985—. Mem. AIME (sec.-treas. 1987-88, vice chmn. 1988—), Tau Beta Pi. Democrat. Office: Tenneco Minerals Corp PO Box 1167 Westvaco Rd Green River WY 82935

VERARDO, JENNIE, writer; b. Salinas, Calif., Apr. 14, 1948; d. Claude and Beatrice Dennis; m. Denzil Verardo, Aug. 21, 1971; 1 child, Mark. BA, U. Calif., 1970. Cert. non-profit mgr. Freelance writer Castroville, Calif., 1973—; freelance cons. Castroville, 1978—; pub. info. officer Gilroy Unified Sch. Dist., 1988—; trainer, cons. William Penn Mott Jr. Tng. Ctr., Pacific Grove, Calif., 1987-88; non-profit instr. Hartnell Community Coll., Salinas, Calif., 1988; speaker historical topics. Author: (books) Teachers Guide to California, 1986; (with Denzil Verardo) The Bale Grist Mill, 1984, Napa Valley, 1986, Santa Cruz County, 1987; contbr. articles to various jours. Pres. N. Monterey County Sch. Bd., Moss Landing, Calif., 1988; bd. dirs. Castroville Artichoke Festival, 1983—, Friday's Child, Carmel, Calif., 1986—, Waddell Creek Assn., Santa Cruz, Calif., 1986-87, Friends of the Castroville Library, 1984—; sponsor Sempervirens Fund, 1974—; mem. Monterey County Hist. Soc., 1986—, Calif. Sch. Bd. Assn., Am.-Japanese Pacific Environmental Forum, 1987—. Recipient commendation Calif. State Park Commn., Sacramento, 1984. Democrat. Roman Catholic. Home: 10899 Palm St Castroville CA 95012

VERBEKE, FRANK GIRARD, JR., mechanical engineer; b. Detroit, Dec. 11, 1934; s. Frank Girard and Elizabeth Aurelia (Winter) V.; children: Kerri Lynn, Frank Girard III. BSME, U. Mich., 1958. Registered profl. engr., Calif. Devel. engr. Continental Aviation and Engring., Detroit, 1958-59, Curtiss Wright Corp., Santa Barbara, Calif., 1959-60; devel. engr. solar div. Internat. Harvester Co., San Diego, 1960-68; v.p. King-Knight Co., Emeryville, Calif., 1968-70; pres. Alturdyne, Inc., Altur-Service, Altuair, Verbeke & Assocs., Engring. Reps. Co., Emeryville, 1970—. Mem. ASME, IEEE, Soc. Automotive Engrs., Exptl. Aircraft Assn., San Diego C. of C., Mission Bay Yacht Club. Republican. Episcopalian. Office: 8050 Armour St San Diego CA 92111

VERBISCAR, ANTHONY JAMES, chemist, research company executive; b. Chgo., Mar. 22, 1929; s. Anthony Michael and Anna (Ostronic) V.; m. Sheila M. Walsh, June 27, 1959; children: Stephen, Paul, Ann. Student, Benedictine Coll., 1947-49; BS, De Paul U., 1951; PhD in Organic Chemistry, U. Notre Dame, 1954; postgrad., U. Chgo., 1956-57, UCLA, 1964-65. Research chemist Hercules, Inc., Wilmington, Del., 1954; co-founder, v.p. research Regis Chemical Co., Chgo., 1957-63; pres. Anver Biosci. Design, Inc., Sierra Madre, Calif., 1965—; prin. investigator grants and contracts NIH, U.S. Army Med. Research and Devel. Command, FDA, Oak Ridge Nat. Lab., Nat. Sci. Found.; cons., researcher various govt. agys., cos. and colls. Contbr. numerous scientific articles to profl. publs.; patentee in field. Served as pvt., U.S. Army, 1954-56. Mem. Am. Chem. Soc., Am. Inst. Chemists (pres. Western sect. 1978-79, local com.), Am. Soc. Pharmacognosy, Oriental Healing Arts Inst. Roman Catholic. Home: 491 Crestvale Dr Sierra Madre CA 91024 Office: Anver Biosci Design 160 E Montecito Ave Sierra Madre CA 91024

VERDIOA, KENNETH LOUIS, broadcast journalist; b. San Francisco, Sept. 7, 1952; s. Mario Peter and Marjorie Jean (Hilton) V.; m. Carol Lynette Carpenter, Apr. 16, 1988. BA, San Jose State U., 1974; postgrad., U. Utah, 1983—, Cambridge (Eng.) U., 1985. Reporter KALL AM/FM, Salt Lake City, 1974-77; news bur. mgr. InterMountain Radio Network, Denver, 1977; reporter, news anchor KTVX TV, Salt Lake City, 1977-80; pres. Verdoia and Assocs., Salt Lake City, 1980—; sr. producer KUED TV, Salt Lake City, 1981—. Producer, dir. nat. documentaries Uncertain Harvest, 1983, 30 Years to Justice, 1985, Topaz, 1987. Bd. dirs. Utah Women's Adoption Ctr., Salt Lake City, 1985-86, Guadelupe Ctr., Salt Lake City, 1987. Recipient Blue Ribbon award Am. Film Festival, 1985, 88, Iris award Nat. Assn. TV Program Execs., 1986. Mem. Soc. Profl. Journalists, Investigative Reporters/Editors, Inc., Am. Polit. Sci. Assn. (congl. fellow 1983-84), Nat. Acad. TV Arts and Scis., Am. Film Inst. Office: Sta KUED-TV 101 Gardner Hall Salt Lake City UT 84112

VERHEY, JOSEPH WILLIAM, psychiatrist, educator; b. Oakland, Calif., Sept. 28, 1928; s. Joseph Bernard and Anne (Hanken) V.; BS summa cum laude, Seattle U., 1954; MD, U. Wash., 1958; m. Darlene Helen Seiler, July 21, 1956. Intern, King County Hosp., Seattle, 1958-59; resident Payne Whitney Psychiatric Clinic, N.Y. Hosp., Cornell Med. Center, N.Y.C., 1959-

62, U. Wash. Hosp., Seattle, 1962-63; pvt. practice, Seattle, 1963—; mem. staff U. Providence Hosp., Fairfax Hosp., VA Med. Center, Tacoma; clin. instr. psychiatry U. Wash. Med. Sch., 1963-68, clin. asst. prof. psychiatry, 1968-82, clin. assoc. prof., 1982—; cons. psychiatry U.S. Dept. Def., Wash. State Bur. Juvenile Rehab.; examiner Am. Bd. Psychiatry and Neurology. Diplomate Am. Bd. Psychiatry and Neurology. Fellow N. Pacific Soc. Psychiatry and Neurology, Am. Psychiat. Assn.; mem. AMA, Am. Fedn. Clin. Rsch., World Fedn. Mental Health, Soc. Mil. Surgeons of U.S., Wash. Athletic Club, Swedish Club (life). Home: 1100 University St Seattle WA 98101 Office: VA Med Ctr Tacoma WA 98493

VERIGAN, TERRENCE, small business owner, marketing and operations consultant; b. Seattle, May 18, 1948; s. Donald Calvin and Mary (Voigt) V.; m. Kathy Jeannette Higgins, Aug. 28, 1970. BA, U. New Orleans, 1971, postgrad., 1972-74; postgrad., Loyola U., New Orleans, 1980-82. Tchr., Jefferson Parish Schs., Metairie, La., 1971-75; sr. sales rep. Xerox Corp., Metairie, 1975-79; owner Terry Verigan Cons., Metairie, 1979-83; market analyst AT&T, Metairie, 1983-84, sales mgr., 1984-86; dir. mktg., SE Health Plan, Baton Rouge, 1986-87, Delta Health, New Orleans, 1987-88; br. mgr., Pleion Corp., Phoenix, 1988— owner, Mktg. Mgmt. Resources, 1987—; spl. lectr. Inst. Politics Loyola U., New Orleans, 1979, La. Close Up Found., 1983. Rep. Dist. 8 Jefferson Parish Pub. Sch. Bd., Metairie, 1977-82, chmn. exec. com., 1979, chmn. ins. com., 1980, v.p., 1981; mem. Jefferson Parish exec. com. Rep. Party of La., 1977-83. Recipient Community Leader of the Yr. award U. New Orleans, 1981; award of Excellence for Br. Leadership AT&T, 1983; Inst. Politics Loyola U., fellow, 1975. Mem. New Orleans C. of C., Plimsoll Club, Omicron Delta Kappa, Kappa Delta Pi (pres. 1969-70), Phi Delta Kappa. Roman Catholic. Home and Office: Mktg Mgmt Resources 7354 E San Miguel Scottsdale AZ 85253

VERKOZEN, TOMAS HENRY, realtor, columnist; b. San Francisco, May 5, 1946; s. Andrew J. and Margaret (Konijn) V.; m. Barbara Gorton, June 19, 1971; 1 child, Alexis Christine. BS, UCLA, 1968; grad., Realtor's Inst. Calif., 1985. Educator Prince William County Schs., Manassas, Va., 1974-76; fin. analyst U.S. Dept. Housing & Urban Devel. Office Indian Programs, San Francisco, 1976-79; columnist Marin Ind. Jour., San Rafael, Calif., 1982—; realtor Marin County Bd. Realtors, San Rafael, 1979—; bd. dirs., founder Pierce Point Learning Ctr., Point Reyes, Calif.; bd. dirs. Slide Ranch, Muir Beach, Calif., Dancing Coyote Beach, Inverness, Calif. Contbr. articles to newspaper Marin Real Estate, 1982—. Instr. Grief Counseling Svc., Coroners Office, Marin County, 1980-85; chmn. San Anselmo Fin. Com., 1985. With U.S. Army, 1968-71, Vietnam. Decorated Bronze Star, Soldiers medal. Mem. Marin County Bd. Realtors (chmn. edn. com. 1986-87). Republican. Unitarian. Office: FH Allen Realtors 1016 Irwin San Rafael CA 94912

VERMEER, RICHARD DOUGLAS, investment banking executive; b. Bronxville, N.Y., July 2, 1938; s. Albert Casey and Helen (Valentine Casey) V.; m. Grace Dorothy Ferguson, May 22, 1960; children—Carin Dawn, Catherine Jeanne, Robert Brooke. B.S., Fairleigh Dickinson U., 1960; M.B.A., Lehigh U., 1967; postgrad. Corp. Fin. Mgmt. Program, Harvard U., 1983. Dir. fin. systems TWA, N.Y.C., 1967-71; dir. MIS Kaufman & Broad, Los Angeles, 1971-74, group controller, 1974-76; from asst. to pres. to v.p., controller Global Marine Inc., Los Angeles, 1976-82; v.p. control and adminstrn. Global Marine Inc., Houston, 1982-84, sr. v.p., 1984-86; exec. v.p. Printon, Kane Corp., Short Hills, N.J., 1986-87; v.p., chief fin. officer, treas., sec. Stars To Go, Inc., Los Angeles, Calif., 1987—. Recipient award Am. Legion, 1956; award Am. Mktg. Assn., 1960. Mem. Fin. Exec. Inst. (com. Nat. Mgmt. Info. Systems), Jonathan Club (Los Angeles), Club at Falcon Point (Houston). Home: 11401 Bolas St Los Angeles CA 90049 Office: Stars To Go Inc 4751 Wilshire Blvd Los Angeles CA 90010

VERNIERO, JOAN EVANS, educator; b. Wilkes-Barre, Pa., Nov. 30, 1937; d. Raymond Roth and Cary Hazel (Casano) Evans; m. Daniel Eugene Verniero Jr., Jan. 7, 1956; children: Daniel Eugene III, Raymond Evans. BA, Kean Coll., 1971; MS in Edn. Adminstrn., Monmouth Coll., West Long Branch, N.J., 1974; postgrad., Calif. Coast U., 1986—. Cert. elem. sch. tchr.; cert. spl. edn. tchr.; cert. sch. adminstr., N.J., N.Mex., Colo. Tchr. Children's Psychiat. Ctr., Eatontown, N.J., 1965-69; tchr. Arthur Brisbane Child Treatment Ctr., Farmingdale, N.J., 1969-71, prin., 1971-75; prin. S.A. Wilson Ctr., Colorado Springs, Colo., 1976-82; tchr. pub. schs. Aurora, Colo., 1982—; edn. rep. Aurora Public Schs. Crew leader Black Forest (Colo.) Rescue Squad, 1979-85, treas., bd. dirs.fire protection dist., 1980-85. Mem. Phi Delta Kappa (chpt. del.). Republican. Presbyterian. Home: 12244 E 2d Dr Aurora CO 80011 Office: NE Alternative Ctr 1498 Laredo St Aurora CO 80011

VERNSTROM, ROY NELS, communication consultant, writer; b. Spokane, Wash., June 13, 1915; s. Nels and Ida (Petersson) V.; m. Ruth Marie Froude, Dec. 4, 1942 (div. 1977); children: Kristine Ruth, Jon Roy, Sten Gustaf, Marta Marie. BA in Journalism, U. Oreg., 1941; postgrad., Portland State U., 1968-69. News editor Rose City Herald, Portland, Oreg., 1933-34; editor U. Oreg. Alumni Mag., Eugene, 1940-41; account exec. Joseph R. Gerber Advt. Agy., Portland, Oreg., 1945-47; advt. mgr. Pacific Power and Light Co., Portland, Oreg., 1947-49, exec. asst. to pres., 1949-51, div. mgr., 1951-53, mgr. indsl. sales and area devel., 1953-57, asst. gen. mgr., 1957-60, cons. chmn. bd. dirs., 1960-62; owner Roy Nels Vernstrom Mktg./Communication Cons., Portland, Oreg., 1968-71, 1974—; pres. Oreg. Title Ins. Co., Portland, Oreg., 1965-68; regional adminstr. Gen. Svcs. Adminstrn., Auburn, Wash., 1971-74. Author: Western Water Shortage?, 1984 (Nat. Water Resources Assn. award). Editor: Hardboard/Particle Board Study, 1956 (WHO award 1957). Founding mem. Freedoms Found., Santa Maria, Calif., 1948-49; Oreg. chmn. nat. adv. com. Radio Free Europe, Portland, 1949-53; active Sci. and Tech. Com., Holden Village, Wash., 1973—; chmn. Hilton Hotel Debenture Campaign, Portland, 1956-58, various tax campaigns, 1968-69, Tri-County United Way, Portland, 1958-59 (pres. 1959-60), Oreg. Tech. Review Com., 1970-71; chmn., treas. recreation com. expn. Memorial Coliseum, Portland, 1962-71; bd. dirs. Oreg. Grad. Ctr., Portland, 1963-71, Oreg. Mus. Sci. and Industry, Am. Red Cross; chmn. bd. dirs. Portland Met. Future Unlimited, 1962-65, Fed. Exec. Bd., Seattle, 1972-73; trustee Multnomah Coll., Portland, 1950-68. Served with USMC, 1941-45. Recipient Distinguished Service award U.S. Jr. C. of C., 1951, NWRA award, 1984. Mem. Oreg. Advt. Fedn. (treas. 1947-48), Portland C. of C.(bd. dirs. 1960—), U. Oreg. Alumni Assn. (Portland chpt. chmn. 1953-54), Delta Tau Delta. Republican. Lutheran. Clubs: Arlington (bd. dirs. 1962—). Lodge: Rotary. Home: 1969 SW Park Ave Portland OR 97201

VERRONE, PATRIC MILLER, lawyer, writer; b. Glendale, N.Y.C., Sept. 29, 1959; s. Pat and Edna (Miller) V. BA, Harvard U., 1981; JD, Boston Coll., 1984. Bar: Fla. 1984, U.S. Dist. Ct. (mid. dist.) Fla. 1984, Calif. 1988. Assoc. Allen, Knudsen, Swartz, DeBoest, Rhoads & Edwards, Ft. Myers, Fla., 1984-86; writer The Tonight Show, Burbank, Calif., 1987—; counsel Fla. Motion Picture and TV Assn., Ft. Myers, 1985-86. Editor Harvard Lampoon, 1978-84, Boston Coll. Law Rev., 1983-84, editor Fla. Bar Jour., 1987-88; contbr. articles to profl. jours. Mem. ABA, Assn. Trial Lawyers Am., Fla. Bar, Writers Guild of Am. West (mem. acad. liaison com. 1988—), Harvard Club Lee County (v.p. 1985-86), Harvard Club So. Calif.. Republican. Roman Catholic. Home and Office: 6466 Odin St Hollywood CA 90068

VER STEEG, DONNA LORRAINE FRANK, nurse, sociologist, educator; b. Minot, N.D., Sept. 23, 1929; d. John Jonas and Pearl H. (Denlinger) Frank; B.S. in Nursing, Stanford, 1951; M.S. in Nursing, U. Calif. at San Francisco, 1967; M.A. in Sociology, UCLA, 1969, Ph.D. in Sociology, 1973; m. Richard W. Ver Steeg, Nov. 22, 1950; children—Juliana, Anne, Richard B. Clin. instr. U. N.D. Sch. Nursing, 1962-63; USPHS nurse research fellow U. Cal. Los Angeles, 1969-72; spl. cons., adv. com. on physicians' assts. and nurse practitioner programs Calif. State Bd. Med. Examiners, 1972-73; asst. prof. UCLA Sch. Nursing, 1973-79, assoc. prof., 1979—, asst. dean, 1981-83, chmn. primary ambulatory care, 1976-87, assoc. dean, 1983-86; co-prin. investigator PRIMEX Project, Family Nurse Practitioners, UCLA Extension, 1974-76; assoc. cons. Calif. Postsecondary Edn. Commn., 1975-76; spl. cons. Calif. Dept. Consumer Affairs, 1978; accredited visitor Western Assn. Schs. and Colls., 1985—; mem. Calif. State Legis. Health Policy Forum, 1980-81. Recipient Leadership award Calif. Area Health Edn. Ctr. System; named Outstanding Faculty Mem., UCLA Sch. Nursing, 1982. Fellow Am. Acad. Nursing; mem. AAAS, Am. Pub. Health Assn., Am. Soc. Law and Medicine, Gerontol. Soc. Am., Nat League Nursing, Calif. League Nursing, N.Am. Nursing Diadnosis Assn., Soc. Study Social Problems, Assn. Health Services Research, Am. Nurse Assn., Calif. Nurse Assn. (pres. 1979-81), Am. Sociol. Assn., Stanford Nurses Club, Sigma Theta Tau, Sigma Xi. Contbr. articles to profl. jours., chpts. to books. Home: 708 Swarthmore Ave Pacific Palisades CA 90272 Office: UCLA Sch Nursing 10833 LeConte Ave Los Angeles CA 90024-6919

VERTIKOFF, ALEXANDER PAUL, artist, photographer, educator; b. Tunis, Tunisia, Oct. 28, 1955; came to U.S., 1959; s. Nicolas Constantine and Irene (Metevsky) V. m. Nora Nixon, Dec. 24, 1984. BFA, Calif. Inst. Arts, 1983, MFA, 1985. Mem. faculty photograhpy dept. Otis Parsons Art Inst., L.A.; asst. supr. photog. lab. Calif. Inst. Arts., Valencia, Calif.; freelance audio engr., designer clients include Rolling Stones, Beach Boys, Willie Nelson, Kris Kristofferson, INXS, Booker T., Iannis Xanakis, Tri-Star Pictures, Altantic Releasing Corp.; guest lectr. U. N.Mex., Ohio State U., Calif. State U., Fullerton. Exhibited in group shows Wuhan Ea. Art Gallery, 1985, Gallery 200, Columbus, Ohio, 1985, 86, Photogenesis Gallery, Albuquerque, 1985, Tzavta Gallery, L.A., 1985, Los Angeles County Mus. Art, 1986, Shanghai Youth Palace, 1986, Susan Spiritus Gallery, Newport Beach, Calif., 1986, Ctr. Pacific Rim Studies, UCLA, 1986; exhibitor Calif Inst. Arts, Pierce Coll., Santa Monica Coll., Guangzhou Inst. Arts, Canton, Peoples Republic China, Zhongshan U., Canton, Wuhan Fine Arts Inst., Guanzhou Med. Coll.; traveling exhibit People's Republic China, 1987 (1st fgn. artist); multi-media engr., designer intercorp. media presentation La Wrence Deutsch Design, L.A.; mongraph cataloger retrospective conversion project UCLA Libr. Home: PO Box 10414 Marina Del Ray CA 90295

VERTS, LITA JEANNE, university administrator; b. Jonesboro, Ark., Apr. 13, 1935; d. William Gus and Lolita Josephine (Peeler) Nash; m. B. J. Verts, Aug. 29, 1954 (div. 1975); 1 child, William Trigg. BA, Oreg. State U., 1973; MA in Lingustics, U. Oreg., 1974; postgrad., U. Hawaii, 1977. Librarian Forest Research Lab., Corvallis, Oreg., 1966-69; instr. English Lang. Inst., Corvallis, 1974-80; dir. spl. svcs. Oreg. State U., Corvallis, 1980—. Editor ann. book: Trio Achievers, 1986, 87, 88; contbr. articles to profl. jours. Precinct com. Republican Party, Corvallis, 1977-80; adminstrv. bd. First United Meth. Ch., Corvallis, 1987—, mem. fin. com., 1987—, tchr. Bible, 1978—. Mem. N.W. Assn. Spl. Progs. (pres. 1985-86), Nat. Council Ednl. Opportunities Assns. (bd. dirs. 1984-87), Nat. Gardening Assn. Republican. Methodist. Home: 530 SE Mayberry Corvallis OR 97333 Office: Special Services Project Waldo 337 OSU Corvallis OR 97331

VESTAL, CHARLES SCOTT, management information systems executive; b. Springfield, Mass., Aug. 29, 1944; s. Marion Scott and Phyllis Ruth (Rugg) V.; m. Lucille Rowen, Jan. 30, 1971; 1 child, Lisa. BA in Anthropology, Mich. State U., 1966; MSLS, U. So. Calif., 1971. Librarian Long Beach (Calif.) Pub. Library, 1971-87; research dir. Calif. Pub. Workers, Long Beach, 1987—; owner Rivendell MIS Svcs., Long Beach, Calif., 1987--. Contbr. articles to newspapers. Lt. U.S. Army, 1966-68. Decorated Bronze Star medal. Mem. Spl. Libraries Assn., So. Calif. On-Line Users Group,, Los Angeles Newspaper Guild, Long Beach City Employees Assn. (pres. 1985, 87), Leather Craft Guild. Democrat. Unitarian Uiversalist. Home: 5261 E 27th St Long Beach CA 90815 Office: Rivendell MIS Svcs 5261 E 27th St Long Beach CA 90815

VETTEL, STEVEN LEE, lawyer; b. Bismarck, N.D., Aug. 26, 1955; s. Loren E. and Joyce C. (Worle) V. AB, Stanford U., 1977; JD, U. Calif., Berkeley, 1984. Bar: Calif. 1984. Adminstrv. asst. Coro Found., San Francisco, 1979-80; law clk. Feldman, Waldman & Kline, San Francisco, 1983-84; assoc. Feldman, Waldman & Kline, 1984-88, Morrison & Foerster, 1988—. Precinct ldr. Agnos for Mayor, San Francisco, 1987; fundraiser AIDS Inative Com., San Francisco, 1988. Mem. Bay Area Lawyers for Individual Freedom (dir. 1988—), Order of the Coif. Democrat. Home: 2245 Bush #5 San Francisco CA 94115 Office: Morrison & Foerster 345 California St San Francisco CA 94104-2105

VETTER, CONNIE, nurse; b. Spokane, Wash., Oct. 13, 1946; d. Milton Elmer and Vivian Magdelan (Klingenberg) V. BS in Nursing, U. Wash., 1969. RN, Wash. Mem. Am. Nurses Assn. (cert.). Home: 517 S Maple St Spokane WA 99204 Office: St Luke's Meml Hosp S 711 Cowley Spokane WA 99202

VETTER, JOYCE MARIE, singer, songwriter, producer; b. Winnemucca, Nev., Oct. 3, 1959; d. John Westly and Emma Lousie (Erquiaga) V. Lead guide Mid. Fork River Co., Sun Valley, Idaho, 1980—, Epic Expeditions, Sun Valley, Idaho, 1984—; prodn. asst. Group One, L.A., 1986—; yacht decor and refinishing specialist Swenson's Marine, Sausalito, Calif., 1986—; owner Wild Rose Records, Winnemucca, Nev. and Mill Valley, Calif., 1987—; songwriter, composer, pub. Broadcast Music Inc., 1986—. Author: Rosy's Pedals, 1985; producer rec. Walkin' on the Sunny Side, 1987; artist, producer rec. From the River and My Soul, 1988. Mem. Nat. Assn. Ind. Record Distbrs., 99's Women Flying Club (Marin chpt.). Office: Wildrose Records PO Box 1411 Mill Valley CA 94942

VETTERLI, DORIS ARLENE, construction company executive; b. Montrose, Colo., July 25, 1941; d. Thalmer Peter and Jina Elizabeth (Coker) Johnson; m. Peter Miles Standish, May 15, 1957 (div.); children: Mary Candace, Janine Sue, Steffani Arlene, Peter Miles Jr.; m. Byron Godfrey Vetterli, June 10, 1979. Cert., Bryman Schs., San Jose, Calif., 1975. Office mgr. Dr. Orhan Oral, Los Gatos, Calif., 1979-81, Dr. Henry Kung, Walnut Creek, Calif., 1981-83; owner, operator Contempo Exec. Computers, Bethel Island, Calif., 1980-84, Seville Enterprises, Palm Desert, Calif., 1978—, R&B Lathing & Plastering, Phoenix, 1983-85, Revelation Beauty Salon, Inc., Phoenix, 1983-85, Vetterli Constrn. Co., Palm Desert, 1985—, Vetterli Plastering Co., Palm Desert, 1985—. Mem. Nat. Assn. Women in Constrn. (sec. 1987—, bd. dirs. 1987—), Scaffold Industry Assn., Desert Contractors Assn., Western Lath, Plaster and Drywall Industries Assn. Republican. Office: Vetterli Plastering Inc PO Box 4540 Palm Desert CA 92261

VIANSON, PAOLO MARIO, engineer; b. Genoa, Italy, Sept. 20, 1959; s. Enrico Rinaldo Vianson and Elena Hardouin Di Gallese; m. Christie Lynn Hardwick, Aug. 31, 1985; 1 child, Matteo Enrico Vianson. M in Mech. Engring. magna cum laude, U. Milan Poly., 1983. Registered profl. engr., Italy. Researcher U. Milan Poly., 1980-83; project mgr. involved in switchgear design Square D Co., San Leandro, Calif., 1984—. Author: Research About the Periodical Irregularity of the Flow in Volumetric Pumps, 1983. Mem. Am. Soc. Metals, 1985—. Roman Catholic. Home: 48242 Purpleleaf St Fremont CA 94539 Office: Square D Co 1998 Republic Ave San Leandro CA 94577

VICE, CHARLES LOREN, mechanical engineer; b. LaVerne, Okla., Jan. 2, 1921; s. Cyrus Christopher and Ethel Segwitch (Hoy) V.; m. Katherine Margaret Maxwell, July 16, 1949; children: Katherine Lorene, Charles Clark, Ann Marie. Cert., Oreg. State U., 1944, BSME, 1947; postgrad., U. So. Calif., 1948-55. Registered profl. engr., Calif. Mgr. magnetic head div. Gen. Instrument Corp., Hawthorne, Calif., 1959-62; sr. staff engr. magnetic head div. Ampex Corp., Redwood City, Calif., 1962-66; chief mech. engr. Collins Radio Corp., Newport Beach, Calif., 1967-69; pres. FerraFlux Corp., Santa Ana, Calif., 1970-78; sr. staff engr. McDonnell Douglas Computer Systems Co., Irvine, Calif., 1979-89, Santa Ana, Calif., 1989—; cons. Teac Corp. Japan, 1974-78, Otari Corp. Japan, 1975-77, Univac Corp., Salt Lake City, 1975-76, Crown Radio Corp. Japan, 1979-80, Sabor Corp. Japan, 1982, Empire Corp., Tokyo, 1987—, DIGI SYS Corp., Fullerton, Calif., 1988—. Patentee in field. Served with U.S. Army Engrs., 1943-46. Decorated Bronze Star. Mem. NSPE. Republican. Club: Toastmasters. Home: 5902 E Bryce Ave Orange CA 92667 Office: McDonnell Douglas Corp 1801 E st and Rew Pl Santa Ana CA 92705

VICIAN, THOMAS ALLEN, SR., educator; b. Mason City, Iowa, Jan. 31, 1935; s. Stephen Roy and Blanche (Lucas) V.; AB, Luther Coll., 1957; BD, Luther Theol. Sem., 1961; postgrad. San Jose State Coll., 1963-64; PhD, Claremont Grad. Sch., 1971; m. Elizabeth Ann Overgaard, Aug. 11, 1957; 1 child, Thomas Allen, Jr. Ordained minister Luth. Ch., 1961; assoc. minister Gloria Dei Luth. Ch., Rochester, Minn., 1961-62, Grace Luth. Ch., Palo Alto, Calif., 1962-64; asst. prof. philosophy Calif. State Coll., Hayward, 1966-67, U. Nev., Reno, 1967-68; prof. philosophy De Anza Coll., Cupertino, Calif., 1968—, also chmn. dept.; philos.-religious cons., Palo Alto, Calif. Woodrow Wilson fellow, 1964-65, Nat. Endowment Humanities fellow, 1973. Mem. AAUP, Philosophy of Sci. Assn., Bay Area Ednl. TV Assn., World Future Soc., Sierra Club, Smithsonian Assos., Center Study Democratic Instns., Am. Philos. Assn. Home: 3718 Redwood Circle Palo Alto CA 94306 Office: De Anza Coll 21250 Stevens Creek Blvd Cupertino CA 95014

VICINSKY, RONALD ALLAN, video producer, computer company executive; b. Pitts., Apr. 12, 1952; s. John Anthony Vicinsky and Dorothy (Kosanovich) Fitzurka; m. Karen Carbonare, Oct. 3, 1973 (div.); m. Elsa Minerva Salinas, Oct. 11, 1981; 1 child, Danny Edgel. AS, Chaffey Coll., Alta Loma, Calif., 1981; BS, U. Md., 1975; MBA, Calif. State U., 1983. Employment mgr. Sunkist, Ontario, Calif., 1980-83; personnel mgr. Burroughs Corp./Unisys, Westlake, Calif., 1983-84; personnel rep. Rantec, Calabasas, Calif., 1984-85; simulation designer Unisys, Camarillo, Calif., 1985—; owner, videographer Love Memories Video Prodns., Camarillo, Calif., 1983—. With USAF, 1971-74. Republican. Roman Catholic. Home: 2346 Jeffrey Rd Camarillo CA 93010

VICKERMAN, SARA ELIZABETH, ecology organization executive; b. Aspen, Colo., Sept. 20, 1949; d. Harry Edwin and Sarah Elizabeth (Forbes) V.; m. Charles Polenick, Feb. 5, 1972 (div. Feb. 1982). AA, Fullerton (Calif.) Jr. Coll., 1969; BS in Anthropology, Calif. State U., Fullerton, 1972; MS in Biology Geography Edn., So. Oreg. State Coll., 1974. Tchr. Medford (Oreg.) Sch. Dist., 1974-78; NW field rep. Defenders of Wildlife, Salem, Oreg., 1978-82; legis. dir. Defenders of Wildlife, Washington, 1982-84; dir. regional program Defenders of Wildlife, Washington, Portland (Oreg.), 1984—; mem. adv. council Bur. Land Mgmt., Medford, 1978-80; chairperson adv. council Oreg. Dept. Fish and Wildlife. Bd. dirs. Oreg. League Conservation Voters. Mem. Wildlife Soc., Nat. Audubon Soc., The Nature Conservancy. Democrat. Club: Portland City. Office: Defenders of Wildlife 0434 SW Iowa St Portland OR 97201

VICKERY, BYRDEAN EYVONNE HUGHES (MRS. CHARLES EVERETT VICKERY, JR.), library services administrator; b. Belleview, Mo., Apr. 18, 1928; d. Roy Franklin and Margaret Cordelia (Wood) Hughes; m. Charles Everett Vickery, Jr., Nov. 5, 1948; 1 dau., Camille. Student Flat River (Mo.) Jr. Coll., 1946-48; B.S. in Edn., S.E. Mo. State Coll., 1954; M.L.S., U. Wash., 1964; postgrad. Wash. State U., 1969-70. Tchr., Ironton (Mo.) Pub. Schs., 1948-56; elem. tchr. Pasco (Wash.) Sch. Dist. 1, 1956-61, jr. high sch. librarian, 1961-68, coordinator libraries, 1968-69; asst. librarian Columbia Basin Community Coll., Pasco, 1969-70, head librarian, dir. Instructional Resources Center, 1970-78, dir. library services, 1979-87, assoc. dean library services, 1987—; chmn. S.E. Wash. Library Service Area, 1977-78, 88—. Bd. dirs. Pasco-Kennewick Community Concerts, 1977-88, pres., 1980-81, 87-88; bd. dirs. Mid-Columbia Symphony Orch., 1983—; trustee Wash. Commn. Humanities, 1982-85. Author, editor: Library and Research Skills Curriculum Guides for the Pasco School District, 1967; author (with Jean Thompson), also editor Learning Resources Handbook for Teachers, 1969. Recipient Woman of Achievement award Pasco Bus. and Profl. Women's Club, 1976. Mem. AAUW (2d v.p. 1966-68, corr. sec. 1969), Wash. Dept. Audio-Visual Instrn., ALA, Wash. Library Assn., Am., Wash. assns. higher edn., Wash. State Assn. Sch. Librarians (state conf. chmn. 1971-72), Tri-Cities Librarians Assn., Wash. Library Media Assn. (community coll. levels chmn. 1986-87), Am. Assn. Research Libraries, Soroptimist Internat. Assn. (rec. sec. Pasco-Kennewick chpt. 1971-72, treas. 1973-74, pres. 1978-80), Columbia Basin Coll. Adminstrs. Assn. (sec.-treas. 1973-74), Pacific N.W. Assn. Ch. Libraries, Women in Communications, Pasco Bus. and Profl. Women's Club, P.E.O. Beta Sigma Phi, Delta Kappa Gamma, Phi Delta Kappa (sec. 1981-82, Outstanding Educator award 1983). Home: 4016 W Park St Pasco WA 99301 Office: Columbia Basin Community Coll 2600 N 20th Ave Pasco WA 99301

VICKERY, MELBA, nurse, artist; b. Granite City, Ill., Jan. 28, 1925; d. George Abert and Eulah Edna (Hunt) Reis; m. Walter C. Kawelaske, Oct. 25, 1969 (dec. Mar. 1975); m. Earl Clark Vickery, June 13, 1979. Diploma summa cum laude, St. Elizabeth Hosp. Sch. Nursing, Granite City, 1949; BS in Nursing Edn. cum laude, St. Louis U., 1951; diploma summa cum laude, Barnes Hosp. Anesthesia Sch., 1958. RN., Mo., Ill.; cert. RN Anesthetist Am. Assn. Nurse Anesthetists. Dir. nursing edn., research and service St. Elizabeth Hosp., Granite City, 1951-55; instr. clin. anesthesia Barnes Hosp. Group, St. Louis, 1958, 65-68; anesthetist Greater St. Louis Hosps., 1965-79; cons. patient care Hope Clinic Women, Granite City, 1975—; writer, portait artist free lance, Sierra Vista, Ariz., 1983—; instr., lectr. Personal and Health Cons., St. Louis, 1959-79, Hypnosis in Nursing and Anesthesia, 1965-79. Author: Introducing Patients to Med. Procedures, 1950's; author hosp. cartoon book and poetry, 1950's; contbr. articles to profl. jours.; inventor in field. Vol. Reagan Campaign, St. Louis, 1970's, Civil Def. Nursing and Air-Raid Shelter set-ups, Granite City, 1940's. Republican. Home and Office: PO Box 872 Sierra Vista AZ 85636-0872

VICTORS, ALEXIS PETER, real estate executive; b. San Francisco, Sept. 13, 1937; s. Peter and Alexandra Victors; m. Joan Diane Whitham, June 12, 1960; children: Gregory, Mark, Charissa, Katherine. BS in Engring. and Physics, U. Calif., Berkeley, 1960; MSME, Stanford U., 1966. Lic. broker, Calif. Engring. trainee Boeing Co., Seattle, 1959; design engr. United Techs., Sunnyvale, Calif., 1962-66; design engring. project mgr. Gen. Motors Corp., Santa Barbara, Calif., 1966-72; from market mgr. to sr. v.p. Western Pacific R.R. Co., San Francisco, 1972-82; pres. Standard Realty and Devel. Co., 1973-82; from exec. v.p. to pres. Upland Industries Corp., Omaha, 1982-87; prin. Victors & Assocs., Tahoe City, Calif., 1987—; cons. in field. Contbr. articles to profl. jours. Served with USNR, 1960-62. Mem. Soc. Ind. Realtors, Nat. Assn. Indsl. and Office Parks, Urban Land Inst. (chmn. edn. com., trustee). Clubs: Bankers (San Francisco); Happy Hollow (Omaha). Office: 5 Applewood Ln Portola Valley CA 94025

VIDMAR, RICHARD ANTHONY, utility executive; b. Washington, Pa., July 26, 1947; s. John Anthony and Lena Helen (Beri) V.; m. Melissa Meriam Lewis, Sept. 26, 1980; children: Jennifer, Scott. BS in Acctg., Pa. State U., 1973; MBA, Temple U., 1977. Acct. analyst Commonwealth of Pa., Harrisburg, 1973-76; staff auditor Coopers & Lybrands, Phila., 1977-78; mgmt. cons. Sci. Mgmt. Corp., Moorestown, N.J., 1978-79; cons. Planmetrics, Chgo., 1979-80; utility planner Salt River Project, Phoenix, 1980—, ind. cons., 1983—; cons. in field. With USAF, 1965-69. Republican. Home: 2659 W Oak Grove Ln Chandler AZ 85224 Office: Salt River Project 1521 Project Dr Tempe AZ 85281

VIEGLAIS, NIKOLAJS, clergyman; b. Dundaga, Latvia, Mar. 31, 1907; s. Andrew P. and Eugenia (Jakobson) V.; grad. Theol. Sem., Latvia, 1928, Music Sch., 1932; baccalaureate Theol. Faculty, U. Latvia, 1940; m. Natalija Calders, Oct. 18, 1931; children: Natalija, Marina (Mrs. Alfredo Alva), Alexis, Olga (Mrs. J. Kuhlman), Tatjana (Mrs. C. Tressler); came to U.S., 1949, naturalized, 1955. Ch. choir dir., Cesis, Latvia, 1928-34; deacon cathedral, Riga, Latvia, 1934-37; ordained priest Eastern Orthodox Ch., Latvia, 1937; priest, Riga, 1937-44; priest refugee camps, Germany, 1944-49; apptd. priest Orthodox Ch. in Am., 1949; priest, Lykens, Pa., 1949-51, Berkeley, Calif., 1952—. Editor, pub. ch. books and music, Latvia, 1935-40, 41-44, Germany, 1946-49, U.S.A., 1950-79; dean No. Calif., Orthodox Ch. in Am., 1955-74, 75-76; sec. Exarchate for Baltic States, 1942-44; sec. San Francisco Diocese, 1960-72, mem. council, 1952-76; spiritual adviser local chpt. Federated Russian Orthodox Clubs, 1964-70, Pacific-Alaska Dist., 1967-68. Home: 1908 Essex St Berkeley CA 94703 Office: 1900 Essex St Berkeley CA 94703

VIERRA, BRIAN C., medical devices company executive; b. San Jose, Calif., Mar. 8, 1961; s. Edward J. and Marilyn D. (Orcutt) V. BSEE, Calif. Poly. Inst., 1985; MBA, U. LaVerne (Calif.), 1989. Assoc. engr. Cilco, Inc.,

Pomona, Calif., 1981-83; sr. elec. engr. Loral Electro Optical Systems, Pomona, 1984-86; product mgr. Staar Surgical Co., Monrovia, Calif., 1986—; pres. Puddle Jumper Restorations, Claremont, Calif., 1988—; cons. in field. Author various user manuals. Mem. IEEE, Red Baron Club. Republican.

VIG, BALDEV KRISHAN, genetics educator, researcher; b. Lyalpur, Punjab, India, Oct. 1, 1935; came to U.S., 1964; s. Behari Lal and Sheela Wanti (Watta) V.; m. Gargi Dilawari, Dec. 13, 1964; children: Anjana, Pamela. BS, Khalsa Coll., Amritsar, India, 1957; MS, Punjab U., 1961; PhD, Ohio State U., 1967. Diplomate Am. Bd. Med. Genetics. Cytogeneticist Children's Hosp., Columbus, Ohio, 1967-68; asst. prof. U. Nev., Reno, 1968-72, assoc. prof., 1972-78, prof. genetics, 1978—, chmn. biology dept., 1985-88; pvt. practice med. genetics Reno, 1982-87; Dir. genetics program State of Nev., Reno, 1975-81; panel mem. environ. biology EPA, Washington, 1983—; chmn. Somatic Cell Genetics, 1982, internat. conf. Aneuploidy, 1989. Recipient Outstanding Researcher award Grad. Sch U. Nev., 1979; D.F. Jones fellow, 1974-75, Alexander vonHumboldt Found. fellow, 1975, Deutscher Akademischer Austauschdienst fellow, 1985, German Cancer Research Ctr. fellow, 1987, 88, 89; named U. Nev. Found. Prof., Reno, 1986-89. Mem. Genetics Soc. Am., Am. Soc. Human Genetics, Genetics Soc. Can., Sigma Xi, Phi Kappa Phi. Democrat. Hindu. Office: U Nev Dept Biology Reno NV 89557

VIGAR, STEPHEN LAWRENCE, sales executive; b. New Albany, Ind., Feb. 10, 1951; s. Carl William Vigar and Betty Lou (Whitlock) Crosley; m. Kathryn Arlene DeSilva, Aug. 13, 1988. BA in Indsl. Edn., Ball State U., 1973; postgrad., U. Calif., Berkeley, 1989. cert. tchr. Ky. Tchr. swim coach Jefferson County Pub. Schs., Louisville, 1973-78; mktg. rep. Proctor & Gamble Distributing, Louisville, 1978-79; mktg. applications rep. Triad Systems, Louisville, 1979-80; sales rep. Triad Systems, Atlanta, 1980-83; applications & sales trainer Triad Systems, Sunnyvale, Calif., 1983-84; regional sales mgr. Triad Systems, Pleasanton, Calif., 1984-86; mgr. of customer edn. Triad Systems, Livermore, Calif., 1986-89; mgr. tng. Triad Systems, Livermore, 1989—. Recruiter Ball State U., 1983-84, 1987—. Ranked in top 10 U.S. swimmers, 1981, 83, 86, U.S. Swimming Assn. Mem. Am. Soc. for Tng. & Devel., U.S. Masters Swimming Assn. Republican. Office: Triad Systems Corp 3055 Triad Dr Livermore CA 94550

VIGIL-GIRON, REBECCA D., state official; b. Taos, N.Mex., Sept. 4, 1954. Grad., N. Mex. Highlands Univ. Formerly with Public Service Co. of N.Mex, elected sec. of state of N.Mex., Santa Fe, 1986. Mem. Young Democrats (pres. Bernalillo County); Dem. Party precinct official, N. Mex. Democrat. Office: Office of State Sec 400 State Capitol Santa Fe NM 87503

VIGLIONE, EUGENE LAWRENCE, automotive executive; b. Paterson, N.J., Nov. 23, 1931; s. Fred and Caroline (Cantilina) V.; m. Vera Yonkens, June 12, 1954 (div. June 1976), m. Evila (Billie) Larez Viglione, Sept. 19, 1976; children: Victoria, David, Valerie, Vanessa, Francine, Margaret, Robert. Student, Cooper Union, N.Y., 1950-51. Sales mgr. Village Ford, Ridgewood, N.J., 1953-66, Carlton Motors, Frankfurt, Germany, 1966-67, Jones Minto Ford, Burlingame, Calif., 1967-72, Terry Ford, Pompano Beach, Fla., 1974-75; gen. mgr. Kohlenberg Ford, Burlingame, 1975-76; v.p. Morris Landy Ford, Alameda, Calif., 1976-80, Burlingame Ford, 1980-85; chmn. bd. Valley Isle Motors, Wailuku, Hawaii, 1985—; pres. Maui Auto Dealers Assn., Wailuku, 1986-87. Del. Rep. State Conv., Honolulu, 1988; v.p. Rep. Party Precinct, Lahaina, Hawaii, 1988, trustee Rep. Presidl. Task Force, Washington, 1983-88. Sgt. USMC, 1950-52. Named Top 250 Exec. Hawaii Bus. Mag., 1986-88. Mem. Nat. Auto Dealers Assn., Internat. Auto Dealers Assn., Nat. Fed. of Ind. Bus., Maui Rotary, Lahaina Yacht Club, Maui Country Club, Gideons, Maui C. of C. Home: 2481 Kaanapali Pkwy Lahaina, Maui HI 96761 Office: Valley Isle Motors 2026 Main St Wailuku HI 96793

VIHSTADT, ROBERT FRANCIS, real estate broker; b. Rochester, Minn., Oct. 6, 1941; s. Francis A. and Catherine P. (Condon) V.; m. Kathleen A. McGuire, Sept. 14, 1963 (div. Oct. 1976); children: Maureen T., Michael R., Mark T.; m. Leslie P. Teutsch, Mar. 16, 1979 (div. Jan. 1988). BA, Mankato State Coll., 1962. Employment counselor Minn. Dept. Employment Security, St. Paul, 1963-64; mktg. adminstr. IBM Corp., St. Paul, 1964-65; dir. mktg. adminstrn. Control Data Corp., Albuquerque, Los Angeles, and Bloomington, Minn., 1965-70; mgr. Ackerman-Grant, Inc., Realtors, Albuquerque, 1970-74; pres. Key Realty, Albuquerque, 1974—; dir. mktg. Stewart Title Co., Albuquerque, 1984-86; exec. v.p. Am. Property Tax Co., 1988—. Active Ronald McDonald House, John Baker PTA, Mile-High Little League. Mem. Nat. Assn. Realtors, Realtors Assn. N. Mex., Albuquerque Bd. Realtors (bd. dirs., com. chmn.). Democratic. Roman Catholic. Lodge: Lions. Office: Key Realty PO Box 11771 Albuquerque NM 87192

VIJAYAKUMAR, RAJAGOPAL, environmental engineer; b. Madras, Tamil Nadu, India, Jan. 8, 1950; came to U.S., 1975; s. A.V. and Bhania (Rajan) Rajagopal; m. Sarojini Sockalingam, June 21, 1972; children: Vinod, Sayithri, Gayathri. BE, U. Madras, India, 1971; MS, U. Minn., 1977, PhD, 1982. Trainee mgmt. Easun Engring., Madras, India, 1971-73; engr. works Torrance and Sons, Madras, 1973-75; grad. asst. U. Minn., 1976-82; staff tech. EMSI, Camarillo, Calif., 1982-86; sr. scientist EMSI, Camarillo, 1986-89; dir. product and engring. devel. Cambridge Filters, Syracuse, 1989—. Contbr. articles to profl. jours. Mem. ASME (assoc., bd. dirs. 1982-84), Air Pollution Control Assn., Am. Assn. Aerosol Rsch., Madras Boat Club (capt. 1973-75). Hindu.

VILARDI, AGNES FRANCINE, real estate broker; b. Monson, Mass., Sept. 29, 1918; d. Paul and Adelina (Mastrioanni) Vetti; m. Frank S. Vilardi, Dec. 2, 1939; children: Valerie, Paul. Cert. of dental assisting Pasadena Jr. Coll., 1954. Lic. real estate broker. Real estate broker, owner Vilardi Realty, Yorba Linda, Calif., Placentia, Calif., Fullerton, Calif., 1968—; cons. in property mgmt. Mem. Am. Dental Asst. Assn., North Orange County Bd. Realtors (sec./treas. 1972), Yorba Linda Country Club, Desert Princess Club. Home and Office: 18982 Vila Terr Yorba Linda CA 92686

VILARINO, JOSEPH, small business owner; b. Inglewood, Calif., Mar. 14, 1926; s. John and Josephine (Cippresso) V.; divorced; children: Steven, Jeffery, Ronald. Student, Woodbury Bus. Coll., L.A., 1947. Owner Vilarino's, Redondo Beach, Calif., 1956—. Foundraiser Inglewood (Calif.) YMCA, 1952-55, Rivinia Village Community Park Fund Raising Com., 1970; Mem. 46th and 51st Assembly Dist. Cen. Com., 1966-78, L.A. County Rep. Cen. Com., 1966-78, Rep. State Cen. Com., 1966-74. With USN, 1944-46. Named Outstanding Man of the Year, 20/30 Internat. Club, 1955. Mem. Redondo Beach C. of C. (past. dir., v.p. 1958-81), Rotary (past pres.), Redondo Beach Round Table. Office: 1201 S Pacific Coast Hwy Redondo Beach CA 90277

VILKER, VINCENT LEE, chemical engineer educator; b. Beaver Dam, Wis., Jan. 17, 1943; s. Vincent Chester and Louise Marie (Frank) V.; m. Martha Rosmond Stone, Aug. 30, 1981; 1 child, Kirby. BSChemE, U. Wis., 1967; PhD, MIT, 1976. Research engr. Exxon Research and Engring. Co., Baton Rouge, 1967-70; asst. prof. UCLA, 1975-81, assoc. prof. chem. engring., 1981-86, prof. chem. engring., 1986—; mem. stringfellow sci. adv. panel Calif. State Senate, Sacramento, 1983—. Contbr. articles to profl. jours. and chpts. to books. Mem. Westside YMCA, Los Angeles. Recipient Fulbright Sr. Research award Netherlands Am. Commn., 1984-85; Sr. Research fellow The Agrl. U., 1984-85. Mem. AAAS, Am. Inst. Chem. Engrs., Am. Chem. Soc. Home: 247 N Bowling Green Way Los Angeles CA 90049 Office: UCLA 5531 Boelter Hall Los Angeles CA 90025

VINATIERI, MICHAEL TODD, environmental scientist; b. Vallejo, Calif., Jan. 4, 1944; s. Felix William and Jean Ann (Smith) V.; m. Dolores Jeanette Huffman, June 18, 1966 (div. Feb. 1973); m. Glady Barbara Maurice, May 18, 1974; children: Michael Dante, Sarah Dawn, Monica Renee, Ryan Mathew. AA, Vallejo Jr. Coll., 1964; BA, San Jose (Calif.) State U., 1966, MPh, 1977. Environtl. health sanitarian Santa Clara County Pub. Health, Calif., 1974-77; supervising sanitarian Sonoma County Pub. Health Dept., Santa Rosa, Calif., 1977-79; dir. environtl. health Sonoma County Pub. Health Dept., 1979—; sec. Well adv. com. Sonoma County, 1984—, Sonoma County Hazardous Materials Mgmt. Coun., 1986. Staff sgt. USAF, 1968-72. Mem. Calif. Conf. Dirs. of Environ. Health (pres. 1986-87, various offices), Calif. Conf. Local Health Officers, Am. Pub. Health Assn., Nat. Environ. Health Assn., Calif. Environ. Assn., Empire Sports Car Assn., Calif. Assn. Environ. Health Adminstrs., Valley CORSA (SAn Jose pres., founder 1975-77). Republican. Roman Catholic. Office: Sonoma County Pub Health Dept 3313 Chanate Rd Santa Rosa CA 95404

VINCENT, ALBERT VERNON, real estate executive; b. Rector, Ark., Sept. 4, 1921; s. Albert Wesley and Helen (Wilcher) V. student pub. schs. m. Kay Tokie Nagata, Sept. 4, 1960; children: Armond Vernon, Linda Carol, Sharon Lynn, Albert Vernon, Wendi Vernelle. Supr., Naval Supply Ctr., Pearl Harbor, 1942-48; div. mgr. Century Metalcraft Corp., 1948-54; gen. mgr. Saladmaster of Hawaii, 1954-56; realtor, 1957-60; pres. Tropic Shores Realty, Ltd., 1960-88. Named Hawaii Realtor of Yr. Mem. Nat. (dir., v.p. 1970), Hawaii (pres. 1978) assns. realtors, Nat. Inst. Real Estate Brokers (gov.), Honolulu Bd. Realtors (pres.), Inst. Real Estate Mgmt., Nat. Inst. Farm and Land Brokers, Internat. Real Estate Fedn., Calif. Real Estate Assn., Realtors Nat. Mktg. Inst. (gov.), Real Estate Securities and Syndication Inst. (gov. 1973), Am. Soc. Real Estate Counselors (gov.), Internat. Platform Assn., Honolulu Press Club. Clubs: Pacific, Plaza, Honolulu. Home: 1517 Makiki St #506 Honolulu HI 96822-4516 Office: 33 S King St Honolulu HI 96813

VINCENT, DAVID RIDGELY, information executive; b. Detroit, Aug. 9, 1941; s. Charles Ridgely and Charlotte Jane (McCarroll) V.; m. Margaret Helen Anderson, Aug. 25, 1962 (div. 1973); children—Sandra Lee, Cheryl Ann; m. Judith Ann Gomez, July 2, 1978; 1 child, Amber; stepsons—Michael Jr., Jesse Joseph Flores. B.S., B.A., Calif. State U.-Sacramento, 1964; M.B.A., Calif. State U.-Hayward, 1971. Sr. ops. analyst Aerojet Gen. Corp., Sacramento, 1960-66; controller Hexcel Corp., Dublin, Calif., 1966-70; mng. dir. Memorex, Austria, 1970-74; sales mgr. Ampex World Ops., Switzerland, 1974-76; dir. product mgmt. NCR, Sunnyvale, Calif., 1976-79; v.p. Boole & Babbage Inc., gen. mgr. Inst. Info. Mgmt., Sunnyvale, Calif., 1979-85; pres. The Info. Group, Inc., Santa Clara, Calif., 1985—. Trustee Republican Nat. Task Force; deacon Union Ch., Cupertino, Calif.; USSF/NCAA soccer referee. Author: Perspectives in Information Management, Information Economics, 1983, Handbook of Information Resource Management, 1987, The Information Based Corporation: Stakeholder Economics and the Technology Investment, 1989; contbr. monographs and papers to profl. jours. Home: 2803 Kalliam Dr Santa Clara CA 95051 Office: PO Box Q Santa Clara CA 95055-3756

VINCENT, RICHARD AINSLEY DIXON, marketing executive; b. Harrogate, Yorkshire, England, Feb. 4, 1945; came to U.S., 1988; s. Reginald Cecil and Florence Sybil (Reeder) V.; m. Helen Oi Keng Ng, May 13, 1978 (div. 1985); 1 child, Richmond Mark; m. Leeanne French, Apr. 25, 1987. M in Aerodyns., Cambridge/RAF Coll., U.K., 1966; chartered engr., RAF Coll., U.K., 1966. Engring officer, flight lt. RAF, Swanton Morley, U.K., 1962-70; acct. mgr. IBM (UK), London, 1970-73; European mgr. Tex. Instruments (UK), London, 1973; gen. mgr. ICL Singapore, Singapore, 1973-78; mktg. training mgr. IBM, Sydney, Australia, 1978-80; sales mgr. Data Gen. Australia, Melbourne, 1980-84; sales dir. Hewlett-Packard Australia, Sydney, 1984-86; gen. mgr. CO-CAM Computer Services, Sydney, 1986-88; v.p. mktg., internat. sales XA Systems Corp., Los Gatos, Calif., 1988—. Contbr. papers to publs. Pres. Seascape Meadows Home Owners Assn., Aptos, Calif., 1988—. Flight lt. RAF, 1962-70. Recipient Gold award, Duke of Edinburgh, London, 1962. Fellow Inst. of Dirs.; mem. Inst. Electronic and Radio Engrs. (cert.), "Old Crows" Electronic Warfare, Courtside Club, Los Gatos, RAF Club, London. Office: XA Systems Corp 983 University Ave Los Gatos CA 95030

VINCENT, SCOTT ANTHONY, architect, planning consultant; b. Fresno, Calif., Dec. 17, 1957; s. Tony Mrtin and Betty Sue (Sconyers) V.; m. Jamie K. Kobzefff, Nov. 15, 1986. BArch, Calif. Poly. U., 1981; M. City Planning, Calif. State U., Fresno, 1987. Registered architect, Calif. Project coordinator Oakley Kirusu Okimura, Inc., Fresno, 1981-83; project architect Schoenwald Norwood House Oba, Inc., Fresno, 1983-86; owner, prin. Vincent Co., Fresno, 1986—; cons. Fresno Zool. Soc., 1986—. Author: Housing in the Future, 1982. Mem. AIA (assoc. bd. dirs. Fresno 1983-84), Calif. Council Architects, Constrn. Specifications Inst., Bldg. Industry Assn., Fresno City and County C. of C. Democrat. Roman Catholic. Home: 9102 N Red Lion Dr Fresno CA 93710 Office: Vincent Co 1500 W Shae St Ste 301 Fresno CA 93711

VINCENTI, SHELDON ARNOLD, legal educator, lawyer; b. Ogden, Utah, Sept. 4, 1938; s. Arnold Joseph and Mae (Burch) V.; m. Elaine Cathryn Wacker, June 18, 1964; children—Matthew Lewis, Amanda Jo. A.B., Harvard U., 1960, J.D., 1963. Bar: Utah 1963. Sole practice law, Ogden, 1966-67; prtnr. Lowe and Vincenti, Ogden, 1968-70; legis. asst. to U.S. Rep. Gunn McKay, Washington, 1971-72, adminstrv. asst., 1973; prof., assoc. dean U. of Idaho Coll. of Law, Moscow, Idaho, 1973-83, dean, prof. law, 1983—. Home: 2480 W Twin Rd Moscow ID 83843 Office: U Idaho Coll Law Moscow ID 83843

VINDUM, JORGEN OLE, mechanical engineer; b. Copenhagen, May 25, 1945; came to U.S., 1960; s. Elidt and Anne Mary V.; m. Carolyn Doll, July 13, 1968; children: Christa, Ryan. BME, U. Calif.-Berkeley, 1967, MME, 1968. Registered profl. engr., Calif. Mech. engr. Jet Propulsion Lab., Pasadena, Calif., 1967; mech. engr. MB Assocs., San Ramon, Calif., 1968-71, project mgr., 1971-75; sr. project mgr. Acurex Co., Mountain View, Calif., 1975-78; bus. area mgr. Acurex Solar Corp., Mountain View, 1978-83; regional sales mgr. Am. Robot Corp., San Ramon, 1983-85; v.p. sales Litton Core Rsch., Mountain View, 1985-87, pres., 1987; pres. Vindum Engring., San Ramon, 1987—; bd. dirs. Sierra Electric Co., South Lake Tahoe, Calif. Patentee high temperature solar collector, high pressure valve. Mem. Soc. Petroleum Engrs., Soc. Core Analysis. Home: 1 Woodview Ct San Ramon CA 94583 Office: Vindum Engring 1 Woodview Ct San Ramon CA 94583

VINES, DOYLE RAY, municipal official; b. Anna, Ill., Sept. 16, 1947; s. William Raymond and Lova Maldetta (Karraker) V.; m. Patricia Ruthann Sprague, Aug. 22, 1987. BA, So. Ill. U., 1969. Underwriter USF&G, Chgo., 1969-70; reimbursement officer Maricopa Community Health Network, Phoenix, 1972-74; cons. various orgns. including Maricopa County Health Dept. Phoenix, 1974-75; owner, mgr. Desert Flower, Tempe, Ariz., 1976-80; mgr. Town of Jerome, Ariz., 1980-86; treas., city clk. City of Bisbee, Ariz., 1986—. Bd. dirs. Alcoholism Council Cochise County, Bisbee. Mem. Internat. Inst. of Mcpl. Clks., Govt. Fin. Officers' Assn., Ariz. City Mgmt. Assn., Ariz. Mcpl. Clks. Assn. Libertarian. Office: City of Bisbee 118 Arizona St Bisbee AZ 85603

VINES, JEANETTE LORIS, retail executive; b. Birmingham, Ala., Oct. 25, 1949; d. James H. and Clifford (Cash) V.; m. C.L. Byrd; 1 child, Byron David. BSBA, U. So. Calif., 1971. Asst. buyer May Co. Calif., Los Angeles, 1971-72, mgr. dept., 1972-74, buyer, 1974-80; buyer J.W. Robinson's, Los Angeles, 1980-84, group buyer, 1984-86, gen. store mgr., 1987—. Mem. Ebonics Support Group (U. So. Calif. chpt.).

VINEYARD, C L, lawyer; b. Hale County, Tex., Nov. 9, 1927; s. Clarence Calvin and Louella Ruby (Ray) V.; m. Nora Lee Crawford, July 15, 1978; children from previous marriage: John, Paul, Anne. AA, Valley Coll., San Bernardino, Calif., 1953; BA in Adminstrn. and Acctg., Claremont Men's Coll., 1955; JD, U. Calif., Los Angeles, 1959. Bar: Calif. 1960. Ptnr. King & Mussell, San Bernardino, Calif., 1960-71; sole practice San Bernardino, Calif., 1971-74; ptnr. Eckhardt, Youmans & Vineyard, San Bernardino, Calif., 1974-75; assoc. Sprague, Milligan & Beswick, San Bernardino, Calif., 1975-76, sole practice, 1976—; judge pro tem San Bernardino County Mcpl. Ct., 1975-81; arbitrator personal injury panel San Bernardino Superior Ct., commr. 1975—; prin. referee Calif. State Bar, Los Angeles, 1979—. Served with USN, 1944-48. Mem. ABA, Am. Arbitration Assn. (arbitrator for claims, comml., constrn. and med. malpractice), San Bernardino County Bar Assn., Internat. Assn. for Ins. Counsel, Am. Bd. Trial Advocates, Calif. Trial Lawyers Assn., Calif. State Bar (prin. referee state bar ct.), Phi Delta Phi. Republican. Lodges: Lions, Elks, Masons, Shriners. Home: 808 E Avery San Bernardino CA 92404 Office: Pacific Savs Plaza 330 N D St Ste 430 San Bernardino CA 92401

VINOPAL, TIMOTHY JOHN, aerospace engineer; b. Rice Lake, Wis., Mar. 15, 1959; s. Emanuel J. and Margaret R. (LePlant) V.; m. Evelyn Struck, June 6, 1987. BSME, Rensselaer Polytechnic Inst., 1981; postgrad. in astronautics, U. Wash., 1982-85. Registered profl. engr. Mechanism designer Digital Equipment Corp., Maynard, Mass., 1979; thermodynamicist Cons. Engrs., Mpls., 1980; flight performance analyst Swissair, Zurich, Switzerland, 1981; designer space sta. Boeing Aerospace, Seattle, 1981-82, dep. study mgr. manned planetary transp., 1982-83, study mgr. upper stage, 1983-85; lead designer space sta. lab. Boeing Aerospace, Huntsville, Ala., 1985-87; upper stages configurator Boeing Aerospace, Seattle, 1987-89, study mgr. upper stage, 1989—. Author: Aeroassist Orbital Transfer Technologies, 1985; editor: Closed Cycle Life Support Systems, 1983, 84; contbr. articles to profl. jours. Active Habitat for Humanity, Seattle, 1988—; Dem. precinct committeeman, 1988—. Fellow Space Studies Inst.; mem. Am. Inst. Aeronautics and Astronautics (pub. policy dir. 1988—, young mems. com. 1985—, space transp. com. 1989—); Am. Soc. Mech. Engrs., Nat. Space Soc. (local pres. 1980-82). Home: 4658 Eastern Ave N Seattle WA 98103 Office: Boeing Aerospace Seattle WA 98124

VINTON, ALICE HELEN, real estate company executive; b. McMinnville, Oreg., Jan. 10, 1942; d. Gale B. and Saima Helen (Pekkola) V. Student, Portland State Coll., Northwestern Sch. Commerce. Lic. realtor assoc., broker, Hawaii. Owner, prin. broker Vinton Realty, Honolulu, 1988—. Founder, bd. dirs. Kekuaanaui, Hawaii Big Sisters, 1972-76; former vol. Child and Family Svc., women's div. Halawa Prison; bd. dirs. Kindergarten and Children's Aid Assn., 1977-88, advisor, mem. long range planning com., 1988—; former mem. tuition aid com., chmn. nominating com. and capital improvements com. Laura Morgan Pre-Sch.; bd. dirs. Hawaii Theatre Ctr., 1985-86. Recipient proclamation Hawaii Ho. of Reps. Mem. Nat. Assn. Realtors, Hawaii Assn. Realtors, Honolulu Bd. Realtors, Honolulu Press Club (membership chmn. 1988—), Rainbow Girls (life). Republican. Episcopalian. Office: 1000 Bishop St Ste 504 Honolulu HI 96813

VIOLET, WOODROW WILSON, JR., retired chiropractor; b. Columbus, Ohio, Sept. 19, 1937; s. Woodrow Wilson and Alice Katherine (Woods) V.; student Ventura Coll., 1961-62; grad. L.A. Coll. Chiropractic, 1966; m. Judith Jane Thatcher, June 15, 1963; children: Woodina Lonize, Leslie Alice. Pvt. practice chiropractic medicine, Santa Barbara, Calif., 1966-73, London, 1973-74, Carpinteria, Calif., 1974-84; past mem. coun. roentgenology Am. Chiropractic Assn. Former mem. Parker Chiropractic Rsch. Found., Ft. Worth. Served with USAF, 1955-63. Recipient award merit Calif. Chiropractic Colls., Inc., 1975, cert. of appreciation Nat. Chiropractic Antitrust Com., 1977. Mem. Nat. Geog. Soc., L.A. Coll. Chiropractic Alumni Assn., Delta Sigma. Patentee surg. instrument.

VIRAY, GERALDINE FERNANDO, court reporter; b. Pampanga, Philippines, Oct. 1, 1964; d. Leandro D. Fernando and Gloria P. (Pabustan) Martinez. Cert., Ct. Reporter Tng. Ctr., San Francisco, 1986. Ct. reporter Mount Eden, Calif., 1986-88, L.A. County Superior Ct., L.A., 1988—. Mem. Nat. Shorthand Reporters Assn. Office: LA County Superior Ct 111 N Hill St Rm 216 Los Angeles CA 90012

VIRGO, MURIEL AGNES, swimming school owner; b. Liverpool, Cheshire, Eng., Apr. 3, 1924; d. Harold Thornhill and Susan Ann (Duff) Franks; m. John Virgo, Aug. 13, 1942; children: John Michael, Angele Victoria, Barbara Ann, Collin Anthony, Donna Marie. Grad. parochial schs. Co-owner Virgo Swim Sch., Garden Grove, Calif., 1967—. Mem. Ancient Mystical Order Rosae Crucis, Traditional Martinist Order. Republican. Roman Catholic. Home: 12751 Crestwood Circle Graden Grove CA 92641 Office: Virgo Swim Sch 12851 Brookhurst Way Garden Grove CA 92641

VIRTUE, JOYCE SWAIN, nutritionist; b. San Antonio, Apr. 13, 1936; d. Gladstone Benjamin and Delphine (Tafolla) Swain; m. Nick Virtue, Sept. 16, 1963; children: Eugene Michael, David Alexis, Paul Nicholas. Student, San Antonio Coll., 19652; BA, PhD, Internat. U. Nutrition Edn., 1979; postgrad., Internat. Coll. Applied Nutrit, 1981, Johns Hopkins U., 1984--. Cert. nutritional specialist Nat. Bd. Nutritional Examiners, 1986. Paralegal, adminstrv. sec. various attys. L.A., 1969-80; owner, operator beauty boutique Beverly Hills, Calif., 1976-80; nutritional supr. Optimum Health Labs., Encino, Calif., 1980; dir. nutrition and food sci. Ford-Kennedy Labs., Reseda, Calif., 1980-82; dir. nutritional therapeutics Nutritional Sci. Testing Labs., Sherman Oaks, Calif., 1982-85; adminstr., dir. nutritional therapeutics Silver Virtue Med. & Nutrition Group, L.A., 1985-87; health educator Med. Health Ctr., Indio, Calif., 1987—; cons. various physicians, med. ctrs. Author: (with Sally Struthers) The Natural Beauty Book, 1979, Your Appearance and Allergies, 1983, Pesticides, Insecticides and Allergens--Their Impact on the Human Body, 1987. Contbr. articles to profl. jours. Recipient Golden Eagle award Nosotros, 1980. Mem. Am. Coll. Nutrition (assoc.), Internat. Coll. Applied Nutrition, Internat. Acad. Med. Preventics, Am. Soc. for Parenteral and Enteral Nutrition. Roman Catholic. Office: Nat Health Cons 1087-A N Palm Canyon Dr Palm Springs CA 92262

VISBAL, JONATHAN RALPH, communications executive; b. Lima, Peru, Sept. 17, 1957; came in U.S., 1959; s. Ralph Albert and Elizabeth Victoria (Krystyniak) V. BA, U. Colo., 1979; MBA, Stanford U., 1984. Network mgr. AT&T Long Lines, San Francisco, 1980-81; ops. mgr. AT&T Long Lines, Gardena, Calif., 1981-82; mgr. market devel. Latin Am. Pacific Telesis Internat., San Francisco, 1984-85; dir. mktg. and sales Pacific Telesis Iberica, Madrid, 1986, mng. dir., 1986-87; internat. product mgr. Octel Communications Corp., Milpitas, Calif., 1987—; student lectr. Stanford U., 1984. Tchr. Jr. Achievement, Gardena, 1982. Named Outstanding Young Man of Am. U.S. Jaycees, 1983. Mem. Omicron Delta Upsilon. Roman Catholic. Home: 1553 Escondido Way Belmont CA 94002 Office: Octel Communications Corp 890 Tasman Dr Milpitas CA 95035

VISINTAINER, CARL LOUIS, insurance company executive; b. Parlett, Ohio, Dec. 7, 1939; s. Joseph L. and Louise E. (Salamon) V.; m. Linda M. Yott, Sept. 3, 1961; children: Eva, Michelle, Laurie, Lindy, Joseph. PhB, U. Detroit, 1962. CLU; CPCU. Agt. State Farm Ins. Cos., Allen Park, Mich., 1963-68; agy. mgr. State Farm Ins. Cos., Rochester, Mich., 1968-72, Albuquerque, 1980-84; agy. dir. State Farm Ins. Cos., Marshall, Mich., 1972-75; exec. asst. State Farm Ins. Cos., Bloomington, Ill., 1975-77, v.p. agy. svcs., 1977-80; agy. dir. State Farm Ins. Cos., Phoenix, 1984—. Mem. Nat. Republican Com., 1980-87. Mem. Soc. CLU, Soc. CPCU, ACLU, Coun. Dem. and Secular Humanism. Office: State Farm Ins Cos 1665 W Alameda Tempe AZ 85289

VITALE, JOHN VINCENT, advertising and graphics company executive; b. West Covina, Calif., June 19, 1958; s. Donald Eugene and Sarah Alice (Brengle) V.; m. Dana Claudia Lewis, Dec. 8, 1984; 1 stepchild, Rose, 1 child, Hannah. Student, Saddleback Community Coll., Mission Viejo, Calif., 1976-77, Advt. Ctr., Los Angeles, 1985-86. Prodn. asst. Charger Publs. Inc., Capistrano Beach, Calif., 1976, art dir. Bow & Arrow mag., 1976-77; art dir. Gun World mag. Gallant Pub., Inc., Capistrano Beach, Calif., 1977-84; freelance designer advt. graphics Laguna Niguel, Calif., 1979-86; prodn. mgr. Smith & Myers Advtg., Inc., Santa Ana, Calif., 1984, agy. art dir., 1985-86; prin. Rolling Bay Design Co., Bainbridge Island, Wash., 1986-88, Vitale Creative Svcs., Bainbridge Island, 1988—. Bd. dirs. Bainbridge Island Arts Coun., 1988—, chmn. mem. steering com., 1988-89. Mem. Sportsman's Club (Bainbridge Island). Democrat. Office: Vitale Creative Svcs PO Box 4688 Rollingbay WA 98061-0688

VITALE, VINCENT PAUL, lawyer; b. L.A., Oct. 14, 1947; s. Vincent and Alice Louise (Withrow) V.; divorced; 1 child from previous marriage, Catherine Starr Preece; children: Matthew, Christine; m. Judith M. Rick. BA in Govt., U. Calif., Santa Cruz, 1969; JD, U. Calif., Davis, 1972. Cert. civil trial specialist. Atty. Alaska Legal Svcs. Corp., Anchorage, 1972-73; asst. city atty. City of Anchorage, 1973-74; assoc. Johnson, Christensen & Shambers, Anchorage, 1974-75; sole practice Anchorage, 1975—. Chmn. Alaska Commn. on Jud. Conduct, Anchorage, 1987. Mem. ABA, Nat. Bd. Trial Advocacy, Chugcak-Eagle River C. of C. (pres. 1987-88). Home: 2830 E 88th Ave Anchorage AK 99507 Office: 725 Christensen Dr Anchorage AK 99501

VITALI, JAMES JOSEPH, medical association administrator; b. Chisholm, Minn., Aug. 31, 1932; s. Alexander Ernest and Ann Clara (Shuster) V.; m. Lois Johanna Salo, July 17, 1954; children: Corrine, Brian, Randall. BA, St. Thomas Coll., St. Paul, 1954. Office mgr. R. Maturi, Corp., Chisholm, 1954-64; adminstr. East Range Clinics, Virginia, Minn., 1964-76, San Luis Med. Clinics, Ltd., San Luis Obispo, Calif., 1976-80; chief exec. officer Thomas-Davis Med. Ctrs., Tucson, Green Valley, Ariz., 1980—; sec./treas. Intergroup of Ariz., Tucson, 1984—, TD Healthnet, Phoenix, 1987—; speaker in field of medical group administration. Bd. dirs. Chisholm Sch. Dist., 1958-64. Recipient Pvt. Enterprise award for Jaycees Minn. Power and Light, 1962. Mem. Am. Coll. Med. Group Adminstrs. (mgmt. achievement award 1988), Med. Group Mgmt. Assn. (pres. midwest sect. 1974-75, sec.-treas. western sect. 1986-87), Minn. Med. Group Mgmt. Assn. (pres. 1975-76), Ariz. Med. Group Mgmt. Assn. (pres. 1985-86), Exec. Assn. of Tucson (bd. dirs. 1983-85), Elks. Roman Catholic. Office: Thomas Davis Med Ctrs PC 630 N Alvernon Way Tucson AZ 85711

VITALIE, CARL LYNN, pharmacist; b. Clinton, Ind., Aug. 31, 1937; s. Paul Gilman and Martha Irrydell (Heidrick) V. D. Pharm., U. So. Calif., 1961, JD, 1965; postgrad., UCLA, 1977. Lic. pharmacist, Calif., Nev., Tex.; diplomate Am. Bd. Diplomates in Pharmacy. Community pharmacy practice various pharmacies, Southern Calif., 1961-65; staff atty. Am. Pharm. Assn., Washington, 1965-66; staff pharmacist Sav-On Drugs, Inc., Anaheim, Calif., 1966-69, asst. dir. indsl. and pub. rels., 1969-71, dir. pharmacies, 1971-74, v.p. pharmacy ops., 1974-85; v.p. pharmacy div. The Vons Cos., Inc., El Monte, Calif., 1985-88; asst. prof. sch. pharmacy U. of the Pacific, Stockton, 1988—; lectr. pharmacy law and ethics U. So. Calif., L.A., 1968-70; U.S. liaison sec. Internat. Pharm. Students Fedn., 1959-62; mem. Calif. Bd. Pharmacy, 1968-76; bd. dirs. Bloomfield Leasing Corp., Chgo., U. Pacific; researcher Earthwatch. Co-author: (with Nancy J. Wolff) Establishment and Maintenance of Membership Standards in Professional Societies of Pharmacists, 1967; mem. editorial adv. bd. Legal Aspects of Pharmacy Practice, 1978-80; also contbr. articles to profl. jours. Bd. dirs. Anderson YMCA. with USAF, 1961-62, Calif., W.Va. Air N.G., 1962-68. Mem. ABA, Va. State Bar Assn., State Bar Assn. Calif., Am. Mgmt. Assn., Soc. for Advancement of Mgmt., Am. Soc. Pharmacy Law, Am., Calif. Pharm. Assns., Nat. Assn. Bds. Pharmacy, Acad. Gen. Practice Pharmacy, Town Hall Calif., Delta Theta Phi, Phi Delta Chi, Masons. Home: 5061 Gadwall Circle Stockton CA 95207 Office: U Pacific Sch Pharmacy Stockton CA 95211

VITE, MARK STEVEN, educational administrator; b. Elkhart, Ind., Oct. 18, 1956; s. Frank Anthony and Barbara Ann (Decio) V. BS, Miami U., Oxford, Ohio, 1978. Educator Elkhart (Ind.) Commmunity Schs., 1979-81; asst. high sch. swim coach Elkhart Cen., 1980-81; educator Judson Sch., Scottsdale, Ariz., 1981-82; supr. Marriott's Mountain Shadows, Scottsdale, Ariz., 1982-83; educator Camelback Desert Sch., Scottsdale, Ariz., 1983-85; pres. Marc III Inc., Tempe, Ariz., 1985—. Water safety instr. ARC, Elkhart, 1973-81, Phoenix, 1981—; bd. dirs. United Food Bank, Mesa, Ariz., 1988—. Named Employee of Month Marriott's Mountain Shadows, 1982-83. Mem. Tempe C. of C. (ambassador's com.). Republican. Roman Catholic. Home: 1616 E Fremont Dr Tempe AZ 85282 Office: Marc III Inc 1985 E 5th St Ste 12 Tempe AZ 85281

VITEK, JAMES ALLEN, nuclear engineer; b. Youngstown, Ohio, Mar. 30, 1958; s. John Paul and Eleanor Merrie (Sinclear) V. BE in Chem. Engring., Youngstown State U., 1983; MS in Nuclear Engring., Bettis Atomic Lab Nat. Research Found., 1984. Nuclear plant engr. Westinghouse, Idaho Falls, Idaho, 1983—, engring. officer of the watch, 1984, from engring. duty officer, to nuclear plant engr. of tng. to nulcear plant engr. of ops., 1985, quality control engr., 1986, nuclear plant engr. of tng., 1986—, sr. tng. asst., 1986, naval reactors engr., 1987, shift supr., 1988. Assoc. staff mem. Campus Life, Youngstown Ohio, 1976-82. Mem. NSPE, Am. Nuclear Soc., Am. Inst. Chem. Engrs., Idaho Soc. Profl. Engrs. (Engring. Deans Council pres. 1982-83), Omega Chi Epsilon (v.p. 1982-83). Republican. Mem. United Ch. Christ. Home: 4970 Mohawk Pocatello ID 83204 Office: Westinghouse Electric NRF PO Box 2068 Idaho Falls ID 83401

VITOUSEK, PAIGE BOVEE, real estate educator, executive; b. Los Angeles, Dec. 30, 1936; d. Daniel Snyder and Doris (Hume) Bovee; m. Martin J. Vitousek, Mar. 12, 1965 (div.). BS, U. So. Calif., 1958; cert. real estate broker, Grad. Realtors Inst. Hawaii. Pres. Vitousek Real Estate Sch., Honolulu, 1970—; v.p. Vitousek & Dick, Inc., Honolulu, 1974. Co-author Principles and Practices of Hawaiian Real Estate, 1972, 11th rev. edit., Questions and Answers to Help You Pass the Real Estate Exam, 1980, 3d rev. edit. Mem. Mayor's Com. Status for Women, Honolulu, 1976. Mem. Hawaii Assn. Real Estate Schs. (pres. 1985-86), Hawaii Assn. Realtors, Real Estate Educators Assn. (designated real estate instr. 1985), Outrigger Canoe Club, The Honolulu Club, Oahu Country Club. Republican.

VIVIAN, LINDA BRADT, sales and public relations executive; b. Elmira, N.Y., Nov. 22, 1945; d. Lorenz Claude and Muriel (Dolan) Bradt; m. Robert W. Vivian, Apr. 5, 1968 (div. Sept. 1977). Student, Andrews U., 1966. Adminstrv. asst. Star-Gazette, Elmira, 1966-68; editor Guide, staff writer Palm Springs (Calif.) Life mag., 1970-75; dir. sales and pub. rels. Palm Springs Aerial Tramway, 1975—; sec. Hospitality and Bus. Industry Coun. Palm Springs Desert Resorts, 1989—. Mem. Hotel Sales and Mktg. Assn. (allied nominating chmn. Palm Springs 1986-88), Am. Soc. Assn. Execs., Travel Industry Am., Nat. Tour Assn., Calif. Travel Industry Assn., Palm Springs C. of C. (bd. dirs. 1984-85), Navy League. Republican. Office: Palm Springs Aerial Tramway One Tramway Rd Palm Springs CA 92262

VIVIO, JOSEPH ANDREW, electrical engineer; b. Pitts., Dec. 16, 1963; s. Edward John and Bernice Mae (Bergman) V.; m. Priscilla Jane Poulson, May 31, 1986. BSEE, Ariz. State U., 1986; postgrad., U. So. Calif., 1987—. Engineer Hughes Aircraft Radar Systems div. subs. Gen. Motors Corp., El Segundo, Calif., 1986—. Mem. IEEE, Tau Beta Pi, Eta Kappa Nu. Home: 2102 Summertime Ln Culver City CA 90230 Office: Hughes Radar Systems PO Box 92426 Los Angeles CA 90009-2426

VIZENOR, GERALD ROBERT, literature educator, writer; b. Mpls., Oct. 22, 1934; s. Clement William and LaVerne Lydia Vizenor; m. Judith Horns, Sept. 1960 (div. 1969); 1 child, Robert Thomas; m. Laura Jane Hall, May 1981. BA, U. Minn., 1960. Staff writer Mpls. Tribune, 1968-70; prof. Am. studies U. Minn., Mpls., 1980-83; prof. ethnic studies U. Calif., Berkeley, 1986; prof. lit. U. Calif., Santa Cruz, 1987—; chmn. Native Am. Lit. Prize Com., Santa Cruz. Author: Word Arrows: Indians and Whites in the New Fur Trade, 1976, The People Named the Chippewa: Narrative Histories, 1984, (novels) Darkness in Saint Louis Bearheart, 1978, Griever: An American Monkey King in China, 1987 (award Fiction Collective 1987, Am. Book award Before Columbus Found. 1988), The Trickster of Liberty, 1988. Fellow Porter Coll. Mem. PEN. Home: 236 Dicken Way Santa Cruz CA 95064 Office: U Calif Porter Coll Santa Cruz CA 95064

VLASAK, WALTER RAYMOND, state official, management development consultant; b. Hartsgrove, Ohio, Aug. 31, 1938; s. Raymond Frank and Ethel (Chilan) V.; m. Julia Andrews, Feb. 25, 1966; children: Marc Andrew, Tanya Ethel. BSBA, Kent State U., 1963; MA, U. Akron, 1975. Commd. 2d lt. U.S. Army, 1963; platoon leader, anti-tank platoon leader and battalion adjutant 82d Airborne Div., 1963-65; combat duty Viet Nam, 1965-66, 68-69; exec. officer, co. comdr. and hdqrs. commandant of the cadre and troops U.S. Army Sch. Europe, Oberammergau, Fed. Republic Germany, 1966-68; asst. prof. Mil. Sci. Kent (Ohio) State U., 1970-74; infantry battalion exec. officer 9th Infantry Div., Ft. Lewis, Wash., 1976-77, orgnl. effectiveness cons. to commanding gen., 1977-79, brigade exec. officer, 1980-82; orgnl. effectiveness cons. to commanding gen. 8th U.S. Army, U.S. Forces, Korea, 1979-80; advanced through ranks to lt. col. U.S. Army, 1980, ret., 1984; pres. Comsult, Inc., Tacoma, 1984—; mgr. employee devel. tng. dept. social and health svcs. State of Wash., Tacoma, 1985—. Decorated Legion of Merit, Bronze Star with V device and two oak leaf clusters, Air medal, Purple Heart, Vietnamese Cross of Gallantry with Silver Star. Mem. Am. Soc. for Tng. and Devel., Assn. U.S. Army (bd. dirs. Tacoma 1984—). Home: 10602 Hill Terr Dr SW Tacoma WA 98498 Office: State of Wash Dept Social and Health Svcs 8315 W 27th St Tacoma WA 98466

VO, HUU DINH, pediatrician, educator; b. Hue, Vietnam, Apr. 29, 1950; came to U.S., 1975; s. Chanh Dinh and Dong Thi (Pham) V.; m. Que Phuong Tonnu, Mar. 22, 1984; 1 child, Katherine Hoa-An. MD, U. Saigon, 1975. Diplomate Am. Bd. Pediatrics. Adminstr. bilingual vocat. tng. Community Care and Devel. Svc., L.A., 1976-77; resident in pediatrics Univ. Hosp., Jacksonville, Fla., 1977-80; physician, surgeon Lanterman Devel. Ctr., Pomona, Calif., 1980—, chief med. staff, 1984-88, coord. med. ancillary svc., 1988—; physician Pomona Valley Community Hosp., 1984—; asst. clin. prof. Loma Linda (Calif.) Med. Sch., 1985—; bd. dirs. Pomona Med. Clinic Inc. Pres. Vietnamese Community Pomona Valley, 1983-85, 87—; bd. dirs. YMCA, Pomona, 1988—, Sch.-Community Partnership, Pomona, 1988—. Mem. AMA (physician recognition award 1986), L.A. Pediatrics Soc., Vietnamese-Am. Physicians Assn. L.A. and Orange County (founding, sec. 1982-84, bd. dirs. 1987—). Republican. Buddhist. Home: 654 E Lennox Ct Brea CA 92651 Office: Lanterman Devel Ctr 3530 W Pomona Blvd Pomona CA 91767

VOAKE, RICHARD CHARLES, banker; b. Albuquerque, July 21, 1940; s. Charles Frederick and Irene Adelaide (Simms) V.; m. Karen Anderson, Sept. 24, 1966. AB in Econ., Stanford U., 1962; MBA in Fin., UCLA, 1965. With Security Pacific Nat. Bank, L.A., 1965-87, sr. v.p., 1984-87; sr. v.p. Security Pacific Corp., L.A., 1987—. Trustee U. LaVerne, Calif., 1988—. Mem. Assn. Calif. Inst. Tech., Jonathan Club. Republican. Lutheran. Office: Security Pacific Corp 333 S Beaudry Ave Ste W28-30 Los Angeles CA 90017

VOBEJDA, WILLIAM FRANK, aerospace engineer; b. Lodgepole, S.D., Dec. 5, 1918; s. Robert and Lydia (Stefek) V.; m. Virginia Parker, Oct. 24, 1942; children—William N., Margaret, Mary Joan, Barbara, Lori. B.C.E., S.D. Sch. Mines and Tech., 1942. Registered profl. engr., Colo. Stress analyst Curtiss Wright Corp., Columbus, Ohio, 1942-45; civil/hydraulic engr. Bur. Reclamation, Denver, 1945-54; mech. supr. Stearns Roger Corp., Denver, 1954-62; mgr. Martin Marietta Corp., Denver, 1962-86, mgr. engring. M-X Program, 1978-86; pres. BV Engring., Inc., Englewood, Colo., 1986—. Active Boy Scouts Am. Recipient Silver Beaver award. Mem. Englewood City Council 1984-87. Mem. AIAA. Democrat. Roman Catholic. Clubs: St. Louis Men's, K.C., Martin Marietta Chess, Lions (sec.).

VODA, ISADORE LEON, dentist; b. Clinton, Ind., Mar. 12, 1913; s. Harold and Tillie (Bass) V.; m. Tillie Balch, Dec. 28, 1939; children: Hal M., Lynne, Alan M. DDS, Washington U., St. Louis, 1937. Pvt. practice Las Vegas, N.Mex., 1937-83, Albuquerque, 1983—. V.p. N.Mex. unit Am. Cancer Soc., 1963-66, pres., 1966-68. 1st lt. U.S. Army, 1942-46. Recipient Disting. Alumnus award Sch. Dental Medicine Wash. U., 1976. Fellow Internat. Coll. Dentists (dep. regent 1987—, life), Am. Coll. Dentists (life), Acad. Gen. Dentistry; mem. ADA (life, del. N.Mex. chpt. 1952-63), N.Mex. Dental Assn. (life, v.p. 1959-60, pres.-elect 1960-61, pres. 1961-62, Disting. Service award 1984, 50-Yr. cert. 1987), N.Mex. Acad. Gen. Dentistry, Am. Soc. Geriatric Dentistry, Am. Assn. Pub. Health Dentists (life), Am. Prosthodontic Soc., Santa Fe Dist. Dental Soc. (life, v.p. 1953, pres. 1954). Office: 6800 K Montgomery NE Albuquerque NM 87109

VOEGELI, PAUL THOMAS, JR., podiatric physician, surgeon; b. Boise, Idaho, Nov. 18, 1953; s. Paul Thomas and Nancy C. (Charuhas) V. BS in Biology cum laude, Regis Coll., 1976; BS, Calif. Coll. Podiatric Medicine, 1981, D in Podiatric Medicine, 1983. Diplomate Nat. Bd. Podiatry Examiners. Resident in surgery U.S. VA Med. Ctr., Albuquerque, 1983-84; practice medicine specializing in podiatry Foothills Podiatry Ctr., Lakewood, Colo., 1985—; tech. advisor, cons. Sanmarco Internat., Aspen, Colo., 1983—; cons. podiatry U.S. Nat. Disabled Ski Team, Winter Park, Colo., 1983—. Contbr. articles to profl. jours. Vol. med. staff Regional Health Fairs, Denver; lectr. sr. citizens groups, Denver; podiatric med. cons. Colo. Prescription Drug Abuse Task Force, 1987—. Mem. Am. Podiatric Med. Assn., Colo. Podiatric Med. Assn., Am. Acad. Podiatric Sports Medicine. Greek Orthodox. Office: Foothills Podiatry Ctr 405 Urban St Ste 201 Lakewood CO 80228

VOELKER, ESTELLE ROSE, software engineer, educator; b. Bozeman, Mont., July 20, 1936; d. Stanley Walter and Dorothy May (Bennette) V.; m. LaVerne A. Neuharth, Oct. 6, 1956 (div. Nov. 1965); 1 child, Paul Stanley; m. Robert J. Grove, Apr. 5, 1975 (div. Oct. 1984). BS in Math., N.D. State U., 1964. Tchr. math. Crooston (Minn.) Pub. Sch., 1964-65; software engr. Gen. Dynamics, San Diego, 1967—. Democrat.

VOGEL, HOWARD MICHAEL, lawyer; b. Phila., June 8, 1947; s. Edward Nathan and Sara C. (Harris) V. BS summa cum laude, U. Fla., 1970; postgrad., Stanford U., 1973-74, U. Geneva, Switzerland, 1974-75; JD, U. Calif., Berkeley, 1975. Bar: Fla. 1977, D.C. 1980, U.S. Supreme Ct. 1980. Legal officer Internat. Commn. on Jurists, Geneva, 1974-75; assoc. Brobeck, Phleger & Harrison, San Francisco, 1975-76; gen. counsel, fin. advisor Nationwide Chems., Ft. Lauderdale, Fla., 1978-82; sole practice Miami, Fla., 1982—. Author: Racial Discrimination and Repression in Southern Rhodesia, 1975, Universal Human Rights: Do They Exist in Rhodesia?, 1975. Ford Found. fellow, DuPont fellow; United Nations scholar, Dinkelspiel legal scholar. Mem. ABA, Internat. Bar Assn., Assn. Trial Lawyers Am., Internat. and Comparative Law Soc. (chmn.), Phi Beta Kappa, Kappa Tau Alpha, Tau Delta Tau. Home: 536 Shasta Way Mill Valley CA 94941 Other: 2602 Nassau Bend #C-2 Coconut Creek FL 33066

VOGEL, ROGER ARLEN, electrical engineer; b. Kansas City, May 16, 1955; s. Robert Neil and Billie Jean (Kennedy) V.; m. Yilma Del Carmen De Leon, Jan. 7, 1984; 1 child, Ryan Michael. BSEE, U. Mo., 1984, MSEE, 1986. Mem. tech. staff Sandia Nat. Labs., Albuquerque, 1986—. Contbr. articles to profl. jours. With U.S. Army, 1975-79. Mem. IEEE. Home: 5415 Vista Del Cerro NE Albuquerque NM 87111 Office: Sandia Nat Labs-Div 2312 PO Box 5800 Albuquerque NM 87185

VOGLER, KEVIN PAUL, aerospace engineer; b. Detroit, Aug. 17, 1957; s. Roger James and Vera Mae (Streng) V.; m. Michelle Marie Bensch, May 5, 1984; 1 child, Brian William. BSChemE, Mich. Technol. U., 1980; MBA, U. Santa Clara, 1987. Registered profl. engr., Calif. Program mgr. nuclear power systems div. GE Co., San Jose, Calif., 1980-81, project engr. domestic projects dept., 1981-86; systems safety engr. space systems div. Lockheed Missiles and Space Co., Sunnyvale, Calif., 1986-88, sr. rsch. engr. space systems div., 1988—. Active Big Brothers/Sisters Santa Clara (Calif.), 1980-81; instr. econs. Jr. Achievement, Santa Clara, 1987. Mem. Calif. Soc. Profl. Engrs., Mensa, Beta Gamma Sigma, Sigma Tau Gamma. Republican. Roman Catholic. Home: 3065 Cedar Ridge Ct San Jose CA 95148 Office: Lockheed Missiles and Space Co 33-40 Bldg 107 1111 Lockheed Way PO Box 3504 Sunnyvale CA 94088-3504

VOGT, ROCHUS EUGEN, physicist, educator; b. Neckarelz, Germany, Dec. 21, 1929; came to U.S., 1953; s. Heinrich and Paula (Schaefer) V.; m. Micheline Alice Yvonne Bauduin, Sept. 6, 1958; children: Michele, Nicole. Student, U. Karlsruhe, Germany, 1950-52, U. Heidelberg, Germany, 1952-53; S.M., U. Chgo., 1957, Ph.D., 1961. Mem. faculty dept. physics Calif. Inst. Tech., Pasadena, 1962—, assoc. prof., 1965-70, prof., 1970-82, R. Stanton Avery Disting. Service prof., 1982—, chmn. faculty, 1975-77, chmn. div. physics, math. and astronomy, 1978-83, v.p. and provost, 1983-87, chief scientist Jet Propulsion Lab., 1977-78; acting dir. Owens Valley Radio Obs., 1980-81; vis. prof. physics, Mass. Inst. Tech., 1988—; dir. CALTECH/MIT Laser Interferometer Gravitational Wave Observatory Project, 1987—. Fellow Am. Phys. Soc.; mem. AAAS. Office: Calif Inst Tech 102-33 Pasadena CA 91125

VOKAC, PETER RUSSELL, electronics engineer; b. Rahway, N.J., Oct. 28, 1935; s. Roland N. and Helen (Russell) V.; m. Myra Hilborn, Dec. 15, 1962; 1 child, Heather Ann. BS with high honors, Pacific U., 1957; BS in Engring., U. Mich., 1962; postgrad., U. Ariz., 1965-72. Tchr. Tucson Unified Sch. Dist., 1963; engr., physicist Nat. Optical Astron. Observatory, Tucson, 1963-81; engr., designer, mgr. Digital TV Imagery, Tucson, 1981-88; pres. Third Domain, Inc., Tucson, 1983-86, Audel, Inc., Tucson, 1985-87; product designer, chief exec. officer DTI, Inc., Tucson, 1988—; owner, mgr. Monadics, Tucson, 1970-72; lectr. in field. Patentee in field. Pres. La Canada-Magee Neighborhood Assn., Tucson, 1978—; mem. ad hoc planning com. Riverside Terr., Pima County, Ariz., 1984. With U.S. Army, 1959-61. Republican. Home: 7835 N Ave de Carlotta Tucson AZ 85704

VOLAND, HOWARD MANLEY, newspaper publisher; b. East Chicago, Ind., May 27, 1949; s. Howard William and Mary Alice (Sharpe) V. BS, U.S. Mil. Acad., 1972. Lt. U.S. Army, Ft. Lewis, Wash., 1972-75; advanced through grades to capt. U.S. Army, 1976; editor Monroe (Wash.) Monitor, 1978-80; pub. Monroe Monitor and Sultan Valley News, 1980-82, pub., owner, 1982--; white water rafting guide Swiftwater, Seattle, 1985--. Bd. dirs. Arts Coun. of Snohomish County, Everett, Wash., 1980-84, Monroe Library Bd., 1985--; trustee Monroe Hist. Soc., 1985--, Friends of the Monroe Library, 1987--. Mem. Wash. Newspapers Pub. Assn. (trustee 1988--), Nat. Newspapers Assn., Monroe C. of C., Sigma Delta Chi. Democrat. Office: Monroe Monitor/Valley News 113 W Main PO Box 399 Monroe WA 98272

VOLCKMANN, MICHAEL H., data processing executive; b. Albuquerque, June 19, 1949; s. Willis H. and Patricia E. (Tompkins) V.; m. Catherine F. Yankovich, 1974. Student, Mesa Community Coll., 1969-72, U. Iowa, 1972-74. Proprietor Delicious Software, Phoenix; systems and applications programmer, tech. support specialist 1st Interstate Bank, Tempe, Ariz., 1980-86; SAS cons. Ariz. Pub. Svcs., Phoenix, 1986--. Bd. dirs. Roosevelt Action Assn., Phoenix, 1985-87, Neighborhood Coalition Greater Phoenix, treas., 1988. Mem. SAS Users Group Internat. Home: 545 W Portland Phoenix AZ 85003 Office: Delicious Software PO Box 2548 Phoenix AZ 85002

VOLCKMANN, PETER TERREL, investor; b. E. Orange, N.J., June 13, 1941; s. Herbert Richard and Solveig (Kolstad) V.; m. Rosemary Esther True, June 30, 1973. BS, U. N.H., 1968. Cert. emergency paramedic. Program adminstr. Sanders Assocs., Inc., Nashua, N.H., 1961-70; pres., chief exec. officer Troll House, Inc., Nashua, 1973-80; gen. ptnr. P. Volckmann & Assocs., Inc., Sedona, Ariz., 1981—; pres., dir. Foothills North Assocs., Sedona, 1982-88; dir., v.p. Am. Heart Assn., Sedona-Verde Valle, 1988—. Vice mayor City of Sedona, Ariz., 1988; bd. dirs. Bd. Adjustment & Appeal, Yavapai County, Ariz., 1988, Sedona Fire Dept. Pension Bd., 1982-89. Mem. Rotary, Masonic. Republican. Home and Office: 160 Camino del Caballo Sedona AZ 86336

VOLGY, THOMAS JOHN, mayor of Tucson, political science educator; b. Budapest, Hungary, Mar. 19, 1946; m. Susan Dubow, Feb. 1987. BA magna cum laude, Oakland U., 1967; MA, U. Minn., 1969, PhD, 1972. Assoc. prof. polit. sci. U. Ariz., Tucson; dir. Univ. Teaching Ctr.; mayor City of Tucson, 1987—; cons. high sch. curriculum project Ind. U. Editor: Exploring Relationships Between Mass Media and Political Culture: The Impact of Television and Music on American Society, 1976; contbr. numerous articles to profl. jours.; producer two TV documentaries for PBS affiliate. Mem. Nat. Women's Polit. Caucus Conv., 1983, U.S. Senate Fin. Com., 1985, U.S. Ho. of Reps. Telecommunications Com., 1988—, Polit. Sci. Adminstrn. Com., 1986, Gov.'s Task Force on Women and Poverty, 1986, United Way, 1985-87; bd. dirs. Honors Program, 1981—, U. Teaching Ctr., 1988—, Tucson Urban League, 1981, Ododo Theatre, 1984, So. Ariz. Mental Health Care Ctr., 1987, Nat. Fedn. Local Cable TV Programmers; chmn. Internat. Rels. Caucus, 1981, 86—, Transp. and Telecommunications Com. Nat. League Cities, 1986, 88. Recipient NDEA scholarship, 1964-76, NDEA fellowship, 1967-70, Oasis award for outstanding prodn. of local affairs TV programming; named Outstanding Young Am., 1981, Outstanding Naturalized Citizen of Yr., 1980; faculty research grantee U. Ariz., 1972-73, 73-74, 74-75, 77-78. Mem. Pima Assn. Govts., Nat. Fedn. Local Cable Programmers. Democrat. Jewish. Office: Mayor's Office 255 W Alameda Tucson AZ 85701

VOLPE, RICHARD GERARD, insurance accounts executive, consultant; b. Swickley, Pa., Apr. 10, 1950; s. Ralph Carl and Louise P. (Cosentino) V.; m. Janet Lynn Henne, May 10, 1986; 1 child, John Ralph. BA, Vanderbilt U., 1972. CPCU. Trainee, asst. mgr. Hartford (Conn.) Ins. Group, 1973-74; v.p. sales Roy E. Barker Co., Franklin, Tenn., 1975-80; asst. v.p., product mgr. comml. ins. Nat. Farmers Union Ins., Denver, 1980-82; prin. R.G. Volpe & Assocs, Denver, 1982-85; account exec. Millers Mut. Ins., Aurora, Colo., 1985-89; pres, chief exec. officer AccuSure, Inc., Bennett, Colo., 1989—; edn. chmn. Insurors Tenn., Nashville, 1978-79; new candidate chmn. Mid-Tenn. chpt. CPCU, Nashville, 1979-80, cons. Bennett Nat. Bank Colo., mktg. mgr., 1989—; cons. Plains Ins., Inc., 1987—. Contbr. articles to profl. jours. Dem. chmn. Williamson County, Tenn., 1979; campaign mgr. legis., Franklin, 1979. Named Hon. Col. Gov. Tenn., 1979. Mem. Soc. Property Casualty Underwriters, Aurora County C. of C. Roman Catholic. Home: 10908 Snowcloud Trail Littleton CO 80125 Office: Millers Mut Ins 791 Chambers Rd Ste 103 Aurora CO 80011

VOLPERT, RICHARD SIDNEY, lawyer; b. Cambridge, Mass., Feb. 16, 1935; s. Samuel Abbot and Julia (Fogel) V.; m. Marcia Flaster, June 11, 1958; children: Barry, Sandy, Linda, Nancy. B.A., Amherst Coll., 1956; LL.B. (Stone scholar), Columbia U., 1959. Bar: Calif. bar 1960. Atty. firm O'Melveny & Myers, Los Angeles, 1959-86; ptnr. O'Melveny & Myers, 1967-86, Skadden, Arps, Slate, Meagher & Flom, Los Angeles, 1986—; pub. Jewish Jour. of Los Angeles, 1985-87 . Editor, chmn.: Los Angeles Bar Jour, 1965, 66, 67, Calif. State Bar Jour, 1972-73. Chmn. community relations com. Jewish Fedn.-Council Los Angeles, 1977-80; bd. dirs. Jewish Fedn.-Council Greater Los Angeles, 1976—, v.p., 1978-81; pres. Los Angeles County Natural History Mus. Found., 1978-84, trustee, 1974—; chmn. bd. councilors U. So. Calif. Law Center, 1979-85; vice chmn. Nat. Jewish Community Relations Adv. Council, 1981-84, mem. exec. com., 1978-85; bd. dirs. U. Judaism, 1973-89, bd. govs., 1973-89; bd. dirs. Valley Beth Shalom, Encino, Calif., 1964-88; mem. capital program major gifts com. Amherst Coll., 1978-86; bd. dirs., mem. exec. com. Los Angeles Wholesale Produce Market Devel. Corp., 1978—, v.p., 1981—; mem. exec. bd. Los Angeles chpt. Am. Jewish Com., 1967—; vice-chmn. Los Angeles County Econ. Devel. Council, 1978-81; bd. dirs. Jewish Community Found., 1981—; mem. Pacific S.W. regional bd. Anti Defamation League B'nai B'rith, 1964—. Named Man of Year, 1978. Fellow Am. Bar Found.; mem. ABA, Am. Soc. Planning Ofcls., Urban Land Inst., Los Angeles County Bar Assn. (trustee 1968-70, chmn. real property sect. 1974-75), Los Angeles County Bar Found. (trustee 1977-80), Calif. Bar Assn. (com. on adminstrn. justice 1973-76), Am. Coll. Real Estate Lawyers. Jewish. Clubs: Amherst of So. Calif. (dir. 1968—, pres. 1972-73); University (Los Angeles). Home: 4001 Stansbury Ave Sherman Oaks CA 91423 Office: Skadden Arps Slate Meagher & Flom 300 S Grand Ave Los Angeles CA 90071

VOLZ, ARTHUR WILLIAM, clergyman; b. Washington, May 13, 1942; s. Frederick Emil and Mabel Grace (Fulk) V.; m. Arlene Catherine Grow, July 10, 1965; children: Jonathan Frederick, Julee Catherine. BCE, U. Wash., 1965; ThM, Dallas Sem., 1970. Ordained to ministry non-denominational community ch., 1970. Dir. edn. and youth Calvary Bible Ch., Wenatchee, Wash., 1970-74; dir. edn. and youth West Park Baptist Ch., Bakersfield, Calif., 1974-77; adminstr. Community Christian Acad., Cave Junction, Oreg., 1978-81; minister edn. Lacey (Wash.) Bapt. Chapel, 1981—; seminar instr. Walk Thru Bible Ministries, Atlanta, 1987--. Asst. athletic coach Evergreen Christian Sch., Olympia, Wash., 1981-82; mem. human relations coun. North Thurston High Sch., Olympia, 1988. Home: 7910 Shasta Ct SE Olympia WA 98503 Office: Lacey Bapt Chapel 6646 Pacific Ave SE Lacey WA 98503

VOMHOF, DANIEL WILLIAM, chemist; b. Grant, Nebr., Apr. 19, 1938; s. Milton W. and Viola H. (Louis) V.; m. Joan Elizabeth Lienemann, July 16, 1960 (div. 1975); children: Daniel William III, Tanya Sue, Lysia Ann. BS in Chem., Augsburg Coll., Mpls., 1962; MS, U. Ariz., 1966, PhD, 1967; BS, MS, Nat. U., 1986. Research assoc. corn industry rsch. found. Nat. Bur. Standards, Washington, 1967-69; dir. lab. div. U.S. Customs Service, Chgo., 1969-72; forensic scientist U.S. Customs Service, San Diego, 1972-74; pres. Expert Witness Services, Inc., La Mesa, Calif., 1974-88; mng. ptnr. 4NG XPRT Systems, La Mesa, 1988—; adj. prof. Nat. U., San Diego, 1984—; instr., chmn. dept. gen. edn. Coleman Coll., La Mesa, Calif., 1986—. Recipient Cert. Appreciation Evidence Photographers Internat. Council, U. So. Calif., 1984, Cert. Appreciation San Diego Trial Lawyers Assn., 1983. Fellow Am. Inst. Chemists; mem. Am. Soc. Testing and Materials, Am. Assn. Advancement Sci., Forensic Cons Assn. (founder, first pres.), Sigma Xi. Office: Expert Witness Svcs Inc 8387 University Ave La Mesa CA 92041

VON ARB, JOHN J., dentist; b. Davenport, Iowa, Oct. 15, 1952; s. Doris Ann Baehnk; m. Phyllis Helen Marshall, Aug. 20, 1976. AS, Palmer Jr. Coll., 1975; BS, U. Iowa, 1978, DDS, 1982. Resident in dentistry USA Dentac, Ft. Bragg, N.C., 1982-83; chief operative dentistry USA Dentac, Bremerhaven, Fed. Republic Germany, 1983-86; gen. dentistry USA Dentac, Ft. Carson, Colo., 1986-88; div. dental surgeon F Co 704 Support Bn. 4th Inf. Div., Ft. Carson, 1988—; chief operative dentistry Bremerhaven Dental Clinic, 1985-86; chief endodontics Larson Dental Clinic, Ft. Carson, 1987. Lutheran. Home: 1031 Paradise Valley Dr Woodland Park CO 80863 Office: F Co 704 Support Bn Fort Carson CO 80913

VONDERHEID, ARDA ELIZABETH, nursing administrator; b. Pitts., June 19, 1925; d. Louis Adolf and Hilda Barbara (Gerstacker) V.; diploma Allegheny Gen. Hosp. Sch. Nursing, 1946; B.S. in Nursing Edn., Coll. Holy Names, Oakland, Calif., 1956; M.S. in Nursing Adminstrn., UCLA, 1960. Head nurse Allegheny Gen. Hosp., Pitts., 1946-48; staff nurse Highland-Alameda County Hosp., Oakland, Calif., 1948-51, staff nurse poliomyelitis units, 1953-55; pvt. duty nurse Directory Registered Nurses Alameda County, Oakland, 1951-53; adminstrv. supervising nurse Poliomyelitis Respiratory and Rehab. Center, Fairmont, Alameda County Hosp., Oakland, 1955-58; night supr., relief asst. dir. nursing Peninsula Hosp., Burlingame, Calif., 1960, adminstrv. supr., 1961-62, inservice educator, 1963-69; staff nurse San Francisco Gen. Hosp., 1969, asst. dir. nurses, 1969-72; mem. faculty continuing edn. U. Calif., San Francisco, 1969-71; dir. nursing services Kaiser Permanente Med. Center, South San Francisco, 1973-1982, asst. adminstr. Med. Center Nursing Services, 1982-85; asst. adminstr. Kaiser Hosp., San Francisco, 1985-87; ret. 1987. Chmn. edn. com. San Mateo County (Calif.) Cancer Soc., 1962-69; bd. dirs. San Mateo County Heart Assn., 1968-71; mem., foreman pro tem San Mateo County Civil Grand Jury, 1982-83; mem. San Mateo County Health Council, 1982-85, vice chmn., 1984. Cert. advanced nursing adminstrn. Mem. San Mateo County (dir. 1964-69, pres. elect 1967-68, pres. 1968-70), Golden Gate (1st v.p. 1974-78, dir. 1974-78), Calif., Am. nurses assns., Nat. League Nursing, Soc. for Nursing Service Adminstrs., State Practice and Edn. Council, AAUW, San Mateo County Grand Jury Assn., Calif. Grand Jury Assn., Sigma Theta Tau. Republican. Lutheran. Club: Kai-Perm. Contbr. articles in field to profl. jours. Home: 1047 Aragon Ct Pacifica CA 94044

VON DER HEYDT, JAMES ARNOLD, lawyer, judge; b. Miles City, Mont., July 15, 1919; s. Harry Karl and Alice S. (Arnold) von der H.; m. Verna E. Johnson, May 21, 1952. A.B., Albion (Mich.) Coll., 1942; J.D., Northwestern, 1951. Bar: Alaska bar 1951. Pvt. law practice Nome, 1953-59; judge superior ct. Juneau, Alaska, 1959-66; U.S. dist. judge Alaska, 1966—; U.S. commr. Nome, Alaska, 1951—; U.S. atty. div. 2 Dist. Alaska, 1951-53; mem. Alaska Ho. of Reps., 1957-59. Pres. Anchorage Fine Arts Mus. Assn. Mem. Alaska Bar Assn. (mem. bd. govs. 1955-59, pres. 1959-60), Wilson Ornithologists Soc., Am. Judicature Soc., Sigma Nu, Phi Delta Phi. Club: Mason (32 deg.), Shriner. Office: US Dist Ct 222 W 7th Ave Box 40 Anchorage AK 99513

VON KALINOWSKI, JULIAN ONESIME, lawyer; b. St. Louis, May 19, 1916; s. Walter E. and Maybelle (Michaud) von K.; m. Penelope Jayne Dyer, June 29, 1981; children by previous marriage: Julian Onesime, Wendy Jean von Kalinowski. B.A., Miss. Coll., 1937; J.D. with honors, U. Va., 1940. Bar: Va. 1940, Calif. 1946. Assoc. Gibson, Dunn and Crutcher, Los Angeles, 1946-52, ptnr., 1953-62, mem. exec. com., 1962-82, adv. ptnr., 1982—; dir. W. M. Keck Found., mem. exec. com.; mem. faculty Practising Law Inst. programs, 1971, 76, 78, 79, 80; instr. Columbia Law Sch., N.Y.C., summer 1981; mem. lawyer dels. com. to 9th Circuit Jud. Conf., 1953-73; UN expert Mission to People's Republic of China, 1982. Contbr. articles to legal jours.; author: Antitrust Laws and Trade Regulation, 1969, desk edit., 1981; gen. editor: World Law of Competition, 1978, Antitrust Counseling and Litigation Techniques, 1984. With USN, 1941-46, capt. Res. ret. Fellow Am. Bar Found., Am. Coll. Trial Lawyers (chmn. complex litigation com. 1984-87); mem. ABA (ho. of dels. 1970, chmn. antitrust law sect. 1972-73), State Bar of Calif., Los Angeles Bar Assn., U. Va. Law Sch. Alumni Assn., Phi Kappa Psi, Phi Alpha Delta. Republican. Episcopalian. Clubs: Calif, Los Angeles Country; Bohemian, Pacific-Union (San Francisco); Los Jolla Beach and Tennis; N.Y. Athletic, The Sky (N.Y.C.). Home: 12320 Ridge Circle Los Angeles CA 90049 Office: Gibson Dunn & Crutcher 333 S Grand Ave Los Angeles CA 90071

VON KRENNER, WALTHER G., artist, writer, art consultant and appraiser; b. W. Ger., June 26, 1940; s. Frederick and Anna-Marie (von Wolfrath) von K.; m. Hana Renate Geue, 1960; children—Michael P., Karen P. Privately educated by Swiss and English tutors; student Asian studies, Japan, 1965-68; student of Southeast Asia studies, Buddhist U., Bankok, Thailand, Cambodia. Curator, v.p. Gallery Lahaina, Maui, Hawaii; pres. Internat. Valuation, Honolulu, 1974-84; researcher culture of Indians of No. Plains, Kalispell, Mont., 1980—; owner Al Hilal Arabians; instr. aikido, 1962—. Mem. Am. Soc. Appraisers (sr. mem.; pres., dir.). Author books on Oriental art. Home: PO Box 1338 Kalispell MT 59903

VON MINDEN, MILTON CHARLES, JR., internist; b. La Grange, Tex., Nov. 29, 1936; s. Milton and Lillian (Falke) Von M.; m. Catherine Brawner, July 5, 1963; children: Milton III, Susan, Mark. BS, Tex. A&M U., 1958; MD, Baylor Med. Schl, 1962. Diplomate Am. Bd. Internal Medicine. Intern Ben Taub Hosp., Houston, 1962-63; resident in internal medicine Baylor U. affiliated hosps., Houston, 1967-69, nephrology fellow, 1969-70; practice medicine specializing in internal medicine and nephrology Colorado Springs, Colo., 1970—. Mem. ACP, Am. Soc. Nephrology, Internat. Soc. Nephrology, AMA, Colo. Med. Soc., El Paso Med. Soc., Pikes Peak Nephrology Assn. (pres. 1977—). Office: 2130 E LaSalle Colorado Springs CO 80906

VON RHEINWALD, EVA, psychologist; b. Prague, Czechoslovakia, Nov. 17, 1932; came to U.S. 1968, naturalized, 1975; d. Frantisek and Ludmila (Stara) Von R.; m. Jaromir Otto Karel, July 17, 1956 (div.); 1 child, Michaela Karlova. BA in Psychology summa cum laude, UCLA, 1975; MA in Psychology, Pepperdine U., 1976; PhD in Profl. Psychology, U.S. Internat. U., 1979. Lic. marriage and family counselor, Nev.; lic. psychologist, Calif. Psychol. therapist trainee South Bay Therapeutic Clinic, Hawthorne, Calif., 1975-76; psychol. counselor trainee Clinic Pepperdine U., Malibu, Calif., 1975-76; psychol. counselor trainee therapist Manhattan Beach (Calif.) Free Clinic, 1975-76; psychol. asst. Anxiety Treatment Ctr., San Diego, 1976-78; movement therapist Alvarado Convalescent and Rehab. Hosp., San Diego, 1977-78; clin. intern Las Vegas (Nev.) Mental Health Ctr., 1978-79, psychologist V, 1979-82; pvt. practice psychotherapy, marriage and family counseling Las Vegas, 1979—; pvt. practice Ctr. for Hypnoanalysis and Psychotherapy, 1986; instr. U. Humanistic Studies, 1980—; condr. workshops in field; lectr. in field. Author musicals, lyrices, movie and TV scripts, short stories, translator, Prague, U.S., Can., 1952—; danced with Nat. Theatre, Kosice, Czechoslovakia, 1952-54, County Theatre, Pilsen, Czechoslovakia, 1954-61, Theatre of Prague, 1961-67; also TV apperances and European tours; contbr. articles to profl. jours. Vol. dance and movement therapist St. John's Hosp., Santa Monica, Calif., 1971-74; companion community psychology project Ocean Side Residential Setting, Santa Monica, 1974. Grantee UCLA, 1975; J. Hovorkas scholar Pepperdine U., 1976. Mem. AAUW, Am. Psychol. Assn., Calif. State Psychol. Assn., Soc. Clin. Hypnosis San Diego, Am. Dance Therapist Assn., Am.-Czechoslovak Art and Sci. Orgn., Acad. San Diego Psychologists, Assn. Humanistic Psychology, Nat. Speakers Assn., Press Women. Clubs: Ski, Las Vegas; Club Med. Office: 6306 Caminito Adreta San Diego CA 92111-7205

VON SAXE-COBURG, DEIRDRE ANNE, cat breeder; b. N.Y.C., Nov. 22, 1952; d. James Patrick and Marie (von Kiessling) Daly; m. Siegfried von Saxe-Coburg, Apr. 19, 1982 (dec. 1983). BA, Coll. Notre Dame Md., 1974. Gen. mgr. Thistledowne Farms, New Berlin, N.Y., 1974-84; ptnr. Stellamaris Ltd., Martinez, Calif., 1984--; cons. in field. Editor, contbr. Van-Ities newsletter, 1987--. Contbr., adviser Winn Found., Ocean, N.J., 1983--. . Mem. Japanese Bobtail Fanciers (pres. 1986--), Japanese Bobtail Breeders Soc. (treas. 1986--; Omoi Meml. award 1987), Internat. Turkish Van Fanciers (sec.-treas. 1987--; Suleiman award 1988), Japanese Bobtail Breed Council, Oriental Shorthair Breed Council, Golden Gate Cat Club, Coronado Cat Club (sec. 1985--). Home and Office: 312 Mill Rd Martinez CA 94553

VON STUDNITZ, GILBERT ALFRED, state official; b. Hamburg, Fed. Republic Germany, Nov. 24, 1950; came to U.S., 1954.; s. Helfrid and Rosemarie Sofie (Kreiten) von S.; m. Erica Lynn Hoot, Aug. 9, 1989. BA, Calif. State U., Los Angeles, 1972. Mgr. I Dept. Motor Vehicles, State Calif., Los Angeles, 1983-87; adminstrv. hearing officer State of Calif., Montebello, 1987—. Author: Aristocracy in America, 1989; editor publs. on German nobility in U.S., 1986—. Active Sierra Club, Los Angeles Conservancy, West Adams Heritage Assn. (dir. 1989—). Mem. Assn. German Nobility in N. Am. (pres. 1985—), Calif. State mgrs. Assn., MENSA, Phi Sigma Kappa (v.p. Calif. State L.A. chpt. 1978). Roman Catholic. Club: Intertel (Denver). Home: 1638 S Norton Ave Los Angeles CA 90019

VON WIESENBERGER, ARTHUR, beverage industry executive; b. N.Y.C., Sept. 13, 1953; s. Arthur and Frances Louise (Bayes) Von W.; m. Leslie Sinclair, May 13, 1988. Art and Lang. Studies, Aiglon Coll., Villars, Switzerland, 1968-73; BA, Brooks Inst. Photography, 1977. Assoc. producer Swiss Air, Zurich, Switzerland, 1972, Warriors of the Wind, Hamamatsu, Japan, 1977, Sta. NBC-TV, Burbank, Calif., 1978; producer Toursit Mktg. & Devel., Geneva, 1973, Aurora Films Worldwide, Switzerland, 1974; author Capra Press, Santa Barbara, Calif., 1978-81; chmn. bd. Internat. Source mgmt. Inc., Beverly Hills, Calif., 1982-87, Arthur Von Wiesenberger, Inc., Santa Barbara, Calif., 1987—; founder, dir. Festival Internat. de Film de Villars, Switzerland, 1976-77; cons. in field. Author: Oasis, 1978, H20, 1988; producer film Comro, 1975 (Best Travel Film award 1975), White on White, 1976; contbr. articles to profl. jours.; travel editor Celebrity-Soc. mag.; contbg. editor Entree. Bd. dirs. Westside Boys Club, Santa Barbara, 1987-89. Mem. Internat. Food, Wine and Travel Writer's Assn., Am. Inst. Wine and Food (bd. dirs), Coral Casino Club, Santa Barbara Polo and Racquet Club. Republican. Mem. Ch. of Eng. Office: PO Box 5658 Santa Barbara CA 93150

VOORHEES, DONALD SHIRLEY, judge; b. Leavenworth, Kans., July 30, 1916; s. Ephraim and Edna Mary (Oliphint) V.; m. Anne Elizabeth Spillers, June 21, 1946; children: Stephen Spillers, David Todd, John Lawrence, Diane Patricia, Richard Gordon. A.B., U. Kans., 1938; LL.B., Harvard U., 1946. Bar: Okla. 1947, Wash. State 1948. Practiced law Tulsa, 1946-47, Seattle, 1947-74; partner firm Riddell, Williams, Voorhees, Ivie, & Bullitt, Seattle, 1952-74; judge U.S. Dist. Ct., Western dist., Wash., 1974—; Bd. dirs. Fed. Jud. Center. Served with USN, 1942-46. Mem. Am., Washington State, Seattle-King County bar assns., Maritime Law Assn., Am. Judicature Soc., Phi Beta Kappa. Office: US Dist Ct 713 US Courthouse 1010 5th Ave Seattle WA 98104

VOOS, KENNETH AUGUST, environmental engineer; b. Hill AFB, Utah, Jan. 26, 1951; s. Arthur Agust and Virginia Anna (Brkhardt) V. Student, Stevens Inst. Tech., 1971; BS in Environ. Sci., Rutgers U., 1973; MS in Engring., Utah State U., 1978, PhD, 1981. Cons. in environ. engring. U.S. Fish and Wildlife Svc., Ft. Collins, Colo., 1980-82; rsch. analyst U. Alaska, Anchorage, 1982-84; project engr. Woodward-Clyde Cons., Oakland, Calif., 1984—. Author: Instream Water Temperature Model, 1984, Terrestrial Ecosystem Model, 1988. Mem. ASCE, Am. Water Resources Assn., Am. Fisheries Soc. Home: 1620 Armstrong Ct Concord CA 94521 Office: Woodward-Clyde Cons 500 12th St Ste 100 Oakland CA 94607

VORE, MARVIN ESLI, blood bank official; b. Dayton, Ohio, Oct. 15, 1945; s. John Benjamin and Josephine (Dils) Boxheimer Vore; m. Elizabeth Sta. Maria, June ll, 1970 (div.); children: Cris Manuel Crispin, Maria Cristina. Student applied sci., Air Force Community Coll. Enlisted USAF, 1965, advanced through grades to tech. sgt., 1980; assigned to Philippines, Republic China, Thailand, Japan, Vietnam, Fed. Republic of Germany, 1965-85; ret. 1985; bellman Sheraton Hotel, Boston, 1985-86; bagger Mather AFB Commissary, Rancho Cordova, Calif., 1986-88; systems specialist blood bank Sacramento Med. Found., 1988—. Novice 3d Order of St. Francis, Centerville, Ohio, 1965—; active Cub Scouts Am., Boy Scouts Am., 1960-65, Explorer Scouts, Waynesville, Ohio, 1980-82. Decorated Cross of Gallentry with device (Vietnam). Republican. Roman Catholic. Home: 3600 Data Dr Apt 536 Rancho Cordova CA 95670 Office: Sacramento Med Found 1625 Stockton Blvd Sacramento CA 95816-7089

VORHIES, CARL BRAD, dentist; b. Indpls., Jan. 21, 1949; s. Jack Mckim and Georgia Thelma (Reese) V.; m. Catherine Isabel, Aug. 30, 1975; children: Michael, Colin. BA, Ind. U., 1971, DDS, 1975. Practice dentistry Beaverton, Oreg., 1975—; team dentist Portland Winterhawks Hockey Team, 1979—. Vol. Dental Aid for Children, Washington County, Oreg. Paul Harris fellow, 1985. Fellow Internat. Coll. Dentists; mem. Washington County Dental Soc. (sec., treas. 1980-82), Oreg. Dental Assn. (sec., treas. 1986-87), Am. Dental Assn., Acad. Gen. Dentistry (pres. 1985-86, Master 1986, nat. bd. dirs. 1987—). Lodge: Rotary. Home: 5240 SW Humphrey Blvd Portland OR 97221 Office: 12755 SW 2nd St Beaverton OR 97005

VORIES, DENNIS LYNN, consulting electrical engineer; b. Walla Walla, Wash., July 5, 1952; s. Eldon Lynn and Barbara Lou (Merklin) V. BS in Elec. Engring., Walla Walla Coll., 1974. Registered profl. engr., Nev., Calif. Electronics engr. Naval Weapons Ctr., China Lake, Calif., 1974-79; pvt. practice cons. engr., Valley Ctr., Calif., 1979—. Author: Solar Savers, 1977; patentee in field. Mem. IEEE, Nat. Soc. Profl. Engrs., Calif. Soc. Profl. Engrs. Seventh-Day Adventist. Home and Office: 29142 Via Piedra Valley Center CA 92082

VORIS, WILLIAM, educational administrator; b. Neoga, Ill., Mar. 20, 1924; s. Louis K. and Faye (Hancock) V.; m. Mavis Marie Myre, Mar. 20, 1949; children: Charles William II, Michael K. BS, U. So. Calif., 1947, MBA, 1948; PhD, Ohio State U., 1951; LLD, Sung Kyun Kwan U. (Korea), 1972, Eastern Ill. U., 1976. Teaching asst. Ohio State U., Columbus, 1948-50; prof. mgmt. Wash. State U., Pullman, 1950-52; prof., head dept. mgmt. Los Angeles State Coll., 1952-58, 60-63; dean Coll. Bus. and Pub. Adminstrn., U. Ariz., Tucson, 1963-71; pres. Am. Grad. Sch. Internat. Mgmt., Glendale, Ariz., 1971—. Ford Found. research grantee Los Angeles State Coll., 1956; prof. U. Tehran (Iran), 1958-59; Ford Found. fellow Carnegie Inst. Tech., Pitts., 1961; prof. Am. U., Beirut, Lebanon, 1961, 62; cons. Hughes Aircraft Co., Los Angeles, Rheem Mfg. Co., Los Angeles, Northrop Aircraft Co., Palmdale, Calif., Harwood Co., Alhambra, Calif., ICA, Govt. Iran. Served with USNR, 1942-45. Fellow Acad. Mgmt.; mem. Ariz. Acad., Beta Gamma Sigma, Alpha Kappa Psi, Phi Delta Theta. Author: Production Control, Text and Cases, 1956, 3d edit., 1966; Management of Production, 1960. Research in indsl. future of Iran, mgmt. devel. in Middle East. Home: Thunderbird Campus Glendale AZ 85306

VORPAGEL, WILBUR CHARLES, historical consultant; b. Milw., Feb. 26, 1926; s. Arthur Fred and Emma (Hintz) V.; Betty J. Hoch, June 19, 1952; stepchildren: Jerry L., Sharon Belveal Sullenberger. Student Army specialized tng. program, U. Ill., 1943-44; BBA, U. Wis., 1949; MBA, U. Denver, 1953. Cert. tchr., Colo. Instr. Montezuma County High Sch., Cortez, Colo., 1949-51; coord. bus. edn. Pueblo (Colo.) Pub. Schs., 1951-56; pvt. practice bus. cons. Pueblo and Denver, 1956—; tchr. bus. edn. Emily Griffith Opportunity Sch., Denver, 1959-69; various positions with Denver & Rio Grande Western R.R. Co., Denver, 1959-88; cons. in field. Bd. dirs. Colo. Ret. Sch. Employees Assn., Denver, 1988—; rep. Custer Battlefield Hist. & Mus. Assn. Sgt. U.S. Army, 1944-46, ETO. Mem. Augustan Soc., St. John Vol. Corp., S.E. Colo. Geneal. Soc., Rio Grande Vets. Club (bd. dirs. Pueblo chpt.), Biblical Archaeol. Soc. (contbg. writer), Nat. Huguenot Soc., Colo. Huguenot Soc. (organizing pres. 1979-89), 70th Inf. Div. Assn., Shriners, Masons. Republican. Mem. Christian Ch. Home and Office: 335 Davis Ave Pueblo CO 81004

VOSBURGH, JAMES, financial executive; b. Denver, Nov. 21, 1955; s. James Monroe and Jane Kathryn (Finnegan) V. BA, We. State Coll., Gunnison, Colo., 1978. Reg. sales rep. R.J. Reynolds Tobacco Co., Denver, 1978-83; mgmt. trainee Capital Fed./Savs., Denver, 1983-84; fin. analyst Citicorp Retail Svcs., Denver, 1984-87; unit mgr. Citicorp Diners Club, Denver, 1987—; cons. PAR, Inc., Denver, 1987—. Inventor in field. Active various charitable orgns. Home: 4140 C S Evanston Cir Aurora CO 80014 Office: Citicorp Diners Club 183 Inverness Dr W Box 5462 Denver CO 80217

VOSHELL, MARY ELLEN, foreign exchange area coordinator; b. Boise, Idaho, Sept. 10, 1952; d. Daniel Carl and Carmelyn Jean (McMahon) Johnson; m. Stanley Lee Voshell, Dec. 27, 1976; children: Jennifer, Alex. BS in Edn., U. Idaho, 1973, MA in Teaching, 1979; postgrad., Boise State U., 1970—. Cert. tchr., Idaho. Tchr. Spanish and English Nampa Idaho Sch. Dist., 1974-76; tchr. Spanish Meridian (Idaho) Sch. Dist., 1976-81, tchr. lang., 1982-83; area coordinator Nacel Cultural Exchanges, Boise, Idaho, 1982—; tchr. Spanish Boise Sch. Dist., 1984-85, 88—. Placement advisor Jr. League of Boise, 1983-85 (newsletter editor 1982). Kappa Kappa Gamma Alumnae (pres. 1988-89). Roman Catholic. Clubs: Beaux Arts Societe, Morrison Ctr. Aux. (Boise). Home and Office: Nacel Cultural Exchs 6174 Winstead Pl Boise ID 83704

VOSSELER, HARRIET ELAINE, federal program recruiter; b. Columbus, Nebr., Aug. 19, 1928; d. Franz Wilhelm and Ruby Mabel (Koch) Luchsinger; m. Erwin Gene Vosseler, Oct. 10, 1948 (div. 1965); children: Linda Kay, David Gene, Cheryl Lynn, Judith Ann, Martin Paul. Student, Midland Luth. Coll., Fremont, Nebr., 1946-47, Fresno (Calif.) City Coll., 1972-73, Calif. State U., Fresno, 1973-78, UCLA, 1983. Missionary Luth. Ch. Am., Guyana, 1951-54; salesperson Liberty House div. AMFAC, Inc., Honolulu, 1962-63; clk. Fresno City Unified Sch. Dist., 1965-67; clerical asst. Calif. State U., 1967-78; mgr. Shortstop, Fresno, 1978-79; vol. Peace Corps, Jamaica, 1979-82; recruiter Peace Corps, Los Angeles, 1982-87, Ednl. Resource Devel. Trust, Los Angeles, 1988; with U.S. Com. for UNICEF, Los Angeles, 1988—; mem. So. Calif. Peace Corps Service Council, 1983—. Contbr. numerous articles to profl. jours. Mem. com. on missions 1st. United Meth. Ch., Santa Monica, Calif., 1984-85; active Nat. Alliance for Mentally Ill, Calif. Alliance for Mentally Ill, Nat. Com. Preserve Social Security and Medicare, Smithsonian Instn. Mem. NOW, Am. Assn. Retired Persons, Nat. Assn. Female Execs. Democrat. Home: 1074 Elkgrove Ave #1 Venice CA 90291

VOTH, ANDREW CHARLES, museum director; b. Akron, Ohio, Aug. 4, 1947; s. Roland L. and Dorothy (Fynn) V. BA, Ambassador Coll., 1970. Chmn. art Amb. Coll., Pasadena, Calif., 1976-78; dir. galleries and fine arts Amb. Coll., Pasadena, 1979; dir. Pasadena Festival of Art, 1980, Carnegie Art Mus., Oxnard, Calif., 1981—; cultural arts supr. City of Oxnard, 1981—; ptnr. Pacific Art Svcs., Santa Barbara, 1987—; reviewer Inst. Mus. Svcs., Washington, 1985—. Author: Working with Artists and Other Creative Souls, 1988, (catalog) Mcpl. Art Collection, 1984. Pres. Pasadena Inst. Arts, 1978-80; v.p. Pasadena Arts Coun., 1979-80; tech. adv. Ventura County Arts Commn., 1981—; treas. Patrons of Cultural Arts, 1985—. Recipient numerous awards for paintings, 1960—. Mem. Calif. Assn. Mus. (trustee 1987—), Am. Assn. Mus., L.A. County Mus. Art, Tower (com. mem.). Office: Carnegie Art Mus 424 South C St Oxnard CA 93030

VOULKOS, PETER, artist; b. Bozeman, Mont., Jan. 29, 1924. B.S., Mont. State U., hon. doctorate, 1968; M.F.A., Calif. Coll. Arts and Crafts, hon. doctorate, 1972; hon. doctorate, Otis Inst. of Parsons Sch. Design, 1980, San Francisco Art Inst., 1982. Tchr. Archie Bray Found., Helena, Mont., Black Mountain Coll., Los Angeles County Art Inst., Mont. State U., Greenwich House Pottery, N.Y.C., Columbia U. Tchrs. Coll., U. Calif.-Berkeley, ret. 1985. One man shows include Gump's Gallery, San Francisco, U. Fla., Hist. Soc. Mont., Felix Landau Gallery, Chgo. Art Inst., Bonniers, Inc., N.Y.C., Fresno State Coll., Scripps Coll., U. So. Calif., Pasadena Art Mus. (purchase prize), Scripps Coll., Nat. Ceramic Exhbn., U. Tenn., Brussels World's Fair, 1958, de Young Mus., Seattle World's Fair, 1962, Whitney Mus. Art, Denver Art Mus. (purchase prize), Smithsonian Instn. (purchase prize), Los Angeles County Mus. Art (purchase prize), Okun-Thomas Gallery, St. Louis, 1980, Morgan Gallery, Kansas City, Kans., 1980, Exhibit A, Chgo., 1976, 79, 81, Braunstein Gallery, N.Y.C., 1968, 75, 78, 82, 86, 87, Cowles Gallery, N.Y.C., 1981, 83, Thomas Segal Gallery, Boston, 1981, 88, Twining Gallery, N.Y.C., 1988, 89, Point View, Tokyo, 1983, travelling retrospective show, San Francisco Mus. Modern Art, 1978-79, Contemporary Arts Mus., Houston, Mus. Contemporary Craft, N.Y.C., Milw. Art Ctr.; exhibited in group shows, including Whitney Mus., N.Y.C., 1981, San Francisco Mus. Modern Art, 1981, Los Angeles County Mus. Art; represented in permanent collections Balt. Mus. Art, Denver Art Mus., Univs. Calif., Colo., Fla., Ill., Mich., Utah, Wis., Ind., Mont. State U., Ariz. State U., Bemidji State U., Fresno State U., Iowa State U., Tokyo Folk Art Mus., Los Angeles County Art Mus., Mus. Contemporary Crafts, N.Y.C., Oakland Art Mus., Pasadena Mus. Art, San Francisco Mus. Modern Art, Smithsonian Instn., Boston Mus. Fine Arts, Corcoran Gallery, Washington, Den Permanente, Copenhagen, Fed. Bldg., Honolulu, Everson Mus., Syracuse, N.Y., Long Beach (Calif.) Mus. Art, Milw. Art Mus., Minn. Mus. Art, Mus. Boymans van Beuningen, Netherlands, Mus. Modern Art, N.Y.C., Portland Art Mus., Whitney Mus., N.Y.C., Stedelijk Mus., Amsterdam and Eindhoven, Netherlands, Nelson Atkins Mus., Kansas City. Recipient first prize RAC, Nat. Decorative Art Show, Wichita, award N.W. Craft Show, award Pacific Coast Ceramic Show, purchase prize Cranbrook Art Mus., award Los Angeles County Fair, Ford. Found., Silver medal Internat. Ceramic Exhbn., Ostend, Belgium, 1954, Gold medal Cannes, France, award I Paris Biennial, 1959, Rodin Mus. prize in sculpture, citation for disting. contbns. to visual arts Nat. Assn. Schs. Art, 1980, award of honor San Francisco Art Commn., 1981, Creative Arts Awards medal for sculpture Brandeis U., 1982, Gold medal Am. Craft Council, 1986; Nat. Endowment for Arts sr. fellow, 1976 and grantee, 1986; Guggenheim fellow, 1984. Address: 951 62d St Oakland CA 94608

VOYLES, MARK CLYDE, management professional; b. Phoenix, Sept. 14, 1948; s. Kenneth Dale and Beverly Ann (Erhardt) V.; m. Camilla Sue Toalson; children: Daren, Patrick. BBA, Ariz. State U., 1978; postgrad., Ariz State U., 1979-80. Teller, collector Valley Nat. Bank, Phoenix, 1972-75; mgr. Space Designs, Tempe, Ariz., 1976-77, Spirits & Sports Restaurant, Tempe, Ariz., 1980; with Sun Packaging Prodn., Tempe, Ariz., 1980-81; mgr. adminstrn. Franzoy, Corey Engring. Co., Phoenix, 1981—. Author, editor: Project Management Manual, 1986, Contracting Manual, 1987. Coach Little League Baseball; mem. Phoenix Symphony. Recipient scholarship Sta. KPHO-TV. Mem. Chandler C. of C., Ariz. State Alumni Assn., Phoenix Metro C. of C., Phoenix 300, Sigma Iota Epsilon. Methodist. Home: 1809 W Marlboro Dr Chandler AZ 85224 Office: Franzoy Corey Engring Co 7776 Pointe Pkwy W #290 Phoenix AZ 85044

VOYLES, MARY VIRGINIA, mining company executive; b. Findlay, Ohio, Oct. 12, 1923; d. Harold Van Delore and Venus Mae (Boday) Hickerson; m. George D. Cook, July 5, 1940 (div. 1954); children: Delores Jean, Timothy George. Grad. pub. schs., Dubois, Wyo. Sec. Ariz. Western Mines, Inc., Tucson, 1969—, bd. dirs., 1970-88. Republican. Baptist. Office: Ariz Western Mines Inc PO Box 7001 Tucson AZ 85725

VOYLES, RICHARD MEREDITH, electrical engineer; b. Indpls., Feb. 21, 1962; s. Richard Meredith Sr. and Mabel (Livezey) V.; m. Kathleen Marie Lawless, Nov. 24, 1984; children: Caroline Halley, Sarah Allison. BSEE, Purdue U., 1983, postgrad., 1983-84; postgrad., Stanford U., 1987-89. Engr. Dart Controls, Zionsville, Ind., 1981-83; robotics intern artificial intelligence lab. MIT, Cambridge, Mass., 1983; mfg. engr. IBM Corp., Endicott, N.Y., 1984—; rsch. asst. Stanford Robotics Lab., Calif., 1987-89; sta. mgr. WRFL-FM, West Lafayette, Ind., 1982-83; instr. Broome Community Coll., Binghamton, N.Y., 1986. Editor Purdue Engr. Mag., West Lafayette, 1982-83; contbr. articles to profl. jours. Wrestling coach Tecumseh Jr. High Sch., Lafayette, Ind., 1982-83; wrestling asst. Union Endicott (N.Y.) High Sch., 1984-86. Recipient Fessenden-Trott Scholarship Purdue U., 1983, Purdue 500, 1981-82. Mem. Am. Soc. Engring. Edn., Am. Mensa, Planetary Soc., Eta Kappa Nu. Presbyterian. Home: 1787 Montecito Ave Mountain View CA 94043 Office: Stanford U Cedar Hall B8 Stanford CA 94305

VOYTKO, JAMES EMERY, electrical engineer; b. Windber, Pa., Jan. 30, 1933; s. Joseph and Mary (Adeline) V.; m. Mary Elizabeth Weis, June 4, 1955; children: Wayne Edward, David Allan, Karen Louise Turner. BEE, Johns Hopkins U., 1964; MS in Materials Scis., Lehigh U., 1966; postgrad., Ohio State U., 1966-68. Sr. engr. Western Electric Co., Columbus, Ohio, 1956-67; v.p. engring. Swift Ohio Corp., Kenton, 1967-69; sr. staff engr. Western Electric/AT&T, Atlanta, 1969-84, AT&T Techs., Omaha, 1984-86; mem. tech. staff Sandia Nat. Labs., Albuquerque, 1986—; cons. in electroplating and surface finishing. Inventor connector manufacture. Fellow Inst. of Metal Finishing; mem. Am. Electroplater and Surface Finisher Soc.

(pres. 1980-81, bd. dirs. 1973-78, cert. electroplater, finisher), Am. Soc. for Metals, Soc. Mfg. Engrs. Republican. Roman Catholic. Home: 14415 Soula Dr NE Albuquerque NM 87123-1947

VRADENBURG, BEATRICE WHITE, symphony orchestra executive; b. Manhattan, Kans., Nov. 1, 1922; d. Richard Peregrine and Marian (Tyler) White; m. George Albert Vradenburg, Jr., Sept. 10; 1 son, George Albert. Student Oberlin Coll., to 1944. Mgr. Colorado Springs (Colo.) Symphony Orch., 1954—. Active Colo. Council on the Arts, 1965-71; pres. Spring-spree. Recipient Gov.'s award for Excellence in the Arts, 1978, Mayor's award, Colorado Springs, 1979. Mem. Am. Symphony Orch. League (Louis Sudler award 1980), Nat. Endowment for the Arts (music panel 1979-82). Republican. Episcopalian. Clubs: El Paso, Garden of the Gods. Office: PO Box 1692 Colorado Springs CO 80901

VREDENBURGH, MARK DE, chemical engineer; b. Long Beach, Calif., Aug. 13, 1957; s. David Gowen and Gloria Jean (Knapp) V. BSChemE, Calif. Poly. U., Pomona, 1981. Refinery engr. Chevron U.S.A., El Segundo, Calif., 1981-83; project engr. M.C. Gill Corp., El Monte, Calif., 1984-85; chief engr. Space-Flex Co. div. M.C. Gill Corp., L.A., 1985—. Mem. Soc. for Advancement of Material and Process Engring., Belmont Shore Sailing Assn. (commodore 1988), Morgan Plus 4 Club (pres. 1988). Office: Space Flex Co 12902 S Broadway Los Angeles CA 90061

VREELAND, ROBERT WILDER, electronics engineer; b. Glen Ridge, N.J., Mar. 4, 1923; s. Frederick King and Elizabeth Lenora (Wilder) V.; m. Jean Gay Fullerton, Jan. 21, 1967; 1 son, Robert Wilder. BS, U. Calif., Berkeley, 1947. Electronics engr. Litton Industries, San Carlos, Calif., 1948-55; sr. devel. electronics engr. U. Calif. Med. Ctr., San Francisco, 1955-89; ret.; cons. electrical engring; speaker 8th Internat. Symposium Biotelemetry, Dubrovnik, Yugoslavia, 1984, RF Expo, Anaheim, Calif., 1985, 86, 87. Contbr. articles to profl. jours., also to internat. meetings and symposiums; patentee in field. Recipient Chancellor's award U. Calif., San Francisco, 1979; cert. appreciation for 25 years' service U. Calif., San Francisco, 1980. Mem. Nat. Bd. Examiners Clin. Engring. (cert. clin. engr.), IEEE, Assn. Advancement Med. Instrumentation (bd. examiner), Am. Radio Relay League (pub. service award 1962). Home: 45 Maywood Dr San Francisco CA 94127 Office: U Calif Med Ctr 4th and Parnassus Sts San Francisco CA 94143

VREELAND, SUSAN JOYCE, English educator; b. Racine, Wis., Jan. 20, 1946; d. W. Alex and Esther Alberta (Jancovius) Vreeland-Wilborn; m. Joseph Gray. BS in English, San Diego State U., 1968, MA in Edn., 1971, MA in English Lit., 1979. English tchr. San Diego Unified Sch. Dist., 1969—. Author: (biog. novel) What Love Sees, 1988, (guidebook) Skiing. Mem. U.S. Ski Writers Assn. (Lowell Thomas award 1988). Home: 6246 Caminito Araya San Diego CA 92122

VRYONIS, SPEROS, JR., historian, educator; b. Memphis, July 18, 1928; s. Speros Panayis, Sr., and Helen (Touliatou) V.; children—Speros Basil, Demetrios, Nikolas. B.A., Southwestern U., Memphis, 1950; M.A., Harvard U., 1952, Ph.D., 1956. Instr. history Harvard U., 1956-60; prof. history UCLA, 1960—, dir. G.E. von Grunebaum Ctr. of UCLA, 1972-75, 79-82; vis. prof. U. Chgo., 1966-67; fellow Dumbarton Oaks, Harvard U., 1979-84; chmn. medieval and modern history U. Athens, 1976-84. Recipient Kokkinos award Acad. Athens, 1974. Fellow Am. Mediaeval Acad. (Haskins medal); mem. Am. Philos. Soc., Am. Acad. Arts and Scis., Soc. Macedonian Studies. Author: Byzantium and Europe, 1967; Byzantium: Its Internal History and Relations with Muslim World, 1971; Decline of Medieval Hellenism in Asia Minor, Process of Islamization, 1971; Studies on Byzantium, Seljuks, Ottomans, 1981; Istoria ton valkanikon laon, 1979; Readings in Medieval Historiography, 1968; The Balkans: Continuity and Change, 1972; The Role of the "Past" in Medieval and Modern Greek Culture, 1978; editor: (with others Islam and Cultural Change in the Middle Ages, 1975; contbr. articles to profl. jours. Office: UCLA Dept History 405 Hilgard Ave Los Angeles CA 90024 *

VUCANOVICH, BARBARA FARRELL, congresswoman; b. Camp Dix, N.J., June 22, 1921; d. Thomas F. and Ynez (White) Farrell; m. Ken Dillon, Mar. 8, 1950 (div. 1964); children: Patty Dillon Cafferata, Mike, Ken, Tom, Susan Dillon Stoddard; m. George Vucanovich, June 19, 1965. Student, Manhattanville Coll. of Sacred Heart, 1938-39. Owner, operator Welcome Aboard Travel, Reno, 1968-74; Nev. rep. for Senator Paul Laxalt 1974-82; mem. 98th-101st Congresses from 2d Nev. dist., 1983—; mem. coms. interior and insular affairs, house adminstrn. Pres. Nev. Fedn. Republican Women, Reno, 1955-56; former pres. St. Mary's Hosp. Guild, Lawyer's Wives. Roman Catholic. Club: Hidden Valley Country (Reno). Office: US Ho of Reps 312 Cannon House Office Bldg Washington DC 20515 *

VUICH, ROSE ANN, state legislator; b. Cutler, Calif.; d. Obren and Stana V. Ed. Cen. Calif. Comml. Coll. Mem. Calif. Senate from 15th dist., 1976—. Mem. Nat. Soc. Pub. Accts., Beta Sigma Phi. Democrat. First woman elected to Calif. State Senate. Office: State Capitol #5066 Sacramento CA 95814

VUKASIN, JOHN PETER, JR., federal judge; b. Oakland, Calif., May 25, 1928; s. John P. and Natalie Vukasin; m. Sue D., July 1, 1956; children: John P. III, Kirk E., Alexander G., Kim J., Karen L. AB, U. Calif., 1950, JD, 1956. Bar: Calif. 1956. Commr. Calif. Pub. Utilities Commn., 1969-74, chmn., 1971, 72; mem. Calif. Conf. of Pub. Utility Council; judge Superior Ct. of Calif., 1974-83, U.S. Dist. Ct. (no. dist.) Calif., San Francisco, 1983—; mem. Adminstrv. Conf. of U.S., 1972-75, Conf. Calif. Judges. Contbr. articles to legal jours. Served with U.S. Army, 1951-53. Mem. ABA (chmn. pub. utility law sect. 1981-82). Republican.

VUKOVICH, MIKRO B., real estate executive; b. Tacna, Peru, Nov. 18, 1954; came to U.S., 1959; s. Borislav M. and Natalija (Ilitch) V.; m. Elizabeth Anne Driscoll, Feb. 17, 1 979; children: Mirko J., Nikolas M., Susan E., Jessica A. AA, Arapahoe Community Coll., Littleton, Colo., 1978; BS, Colo. State U., 1978. Lic. real estate broker, Colo. Carpenter Inter Continental Constrn. Co., Littleton, 1974-79; staff acct. Cambellick & Reynolds, CPA's, Englewood, Colo., 1979-80; gen. ptnr. various real estate cos. Littleton, 1981-88; controller, mgr. Colo. Real Estate and Investment Co., Littleton, 1980—; investment adviser SEC, Washington, 1985; securities broker Colo. Securities Div., Denver, 1988. Player, Colo. Amateur Soccer League, Littleton, 1973; deacon Foothills Fellowship Bapt. Ch., Littleton, 1984; referee Columbine Soccer Assn., Littleton, 1987--. Recipient 1st Place award in Photography, U.S. Soccer Fedn., 1987. Mem. Colo. Realtors Assn., Real Estate Syndication and Securities Inst., Colo. Manufactured Housing Assn., Nat. Fedn. Independent Bus. Republican. Home: 1 Desert Willow Ln Littleton CO 80127 Office: Colo Real Estate and Investment Co 6509 S Santa Fe Dr Littleton CO 80120

VYDEN, JOHN KEITH, cardiologist; b. Sydney, New South Wales, Australia, June 12, 1933; s. Keigh and Mona Mary (Caldwell) V.; m. Barbara A. Harmatuk, Jan. 5, 1979; children: Sarah, David, Christopher. MBBS, U. Sydney, 1963. Intern Prince Henry Hosp., Sydney, NSW, Australia, 1963-64; resident Royal Perth (Australia) Hosp., 1964-65; rsch. fellow in cardiology Am. Coll. Cardiology Cedars-Sinai Med. Ctr., L.A., 1966-68; med. dir. Vascular Diagnostic Lab. Cedars-Sinai Med. Ctr, Los Angeles, 1970-82, Nat. Inst. Health fellow in cardiology, 1968-70, med. dir. Cardiac Rehabilitation, 1974-82; asst. prof. medicine UCLA Sch. Medicine, 1974-77, assoc. prof. medicine, 1977-83, clin. assoc. prof., 1983—; specialist physician and cons. in cardiology Los Angeles, 1982—; chmn. bd. dirs. Cardiac Rehab. Corp., Beverly Hills, Calif., 1983—. Author: (books) Postmyocardian Infarction Management and Rehabilitation, 1983, How to Prevent Your Next Heart Attack, 1988. Post-doctoral fellow The Arthritis Found., 1971-74; recipient Gov.'s award Am. Coll. Cardiology, 1969. Fellow Am. Coll. Angiology, Am. Coll. Cardiology, Am. Heart Assn., Am. Fedn. for Clin. Research. Republican. Episcopalian. Office: 200 N Robertson Blvd Ste 205 Beverly Hills CA 90211

WACHBRIT, JILL BARRETT, accountant, bank holding company executive; b. Ventura, Calif., May 27, 1955; d. Preston Everett Barrett and Lois JoAnne (Fondersmith) Batchelder; m. Michael Ian Wachbrit, June 21, 1981; 1 child, Michelle. AA, Santa Monica City Coll., 1975; BS, Calif. State U., Northridge, 1979; M in Bus. Taxation, U. So. Calif., 1985. CPA. Supervising sr. tax acct. Peat, Marwick, Mitchell & Co., Century City, Calif., 1979-82; sr. tax analyst Avery Internat., Pasadena, Calif., 1982-83; tax mgr., asst. v.p. First Interstate Leasing, Pasedena, 1983-88, Gibraltar Savs., 1988, Security Pacific Corp., L.A., 1988—. Republican. Jewish.

WACHTELL, THOMAS, petroleum company executive, lawyer; b. Crestwood, N.Y., Mar. 27, 1928; s. Theodore and Carolyn (Satz) W.; grad. Choate Sch., 1946; B.S., Syracuse U., 1950; LL.B., Cornell U., 1958; m. Esther Carole Pickard, Jan. 27, 1957; children—Roger Bruce, Wendy Ann, Peter James. Bar: N.Y. 1958. Assoc. Livingston, Wachtell & Co., C.P.A.s, N.Y.C., 1958-60; pres. Allied Homeowners Assn., Inc., White Plains, N.Y., 1960-63, pres. Gen. Factoring Co., White Plains, N.Y., 1960-63; exec. asst. to pres. Occidental Petroleum Corp., Los Angeles, 1963-65, v.p., exec. asst., chmn. bd., 1965-72, exec. v.p., 1972-73, officer, dir. numerous subs.; pres. Hydrocarbon Resources Corp., 1973-81; chmn. Oriental Petroleum Corp., 1982—; exec. v.p. Frontier Oil and Refining Co., Denver, 1985-87, also bd. dirs.; chmn. bd. Frontier Oil Internat., 1985-87; pres., chief exec. officer, dir. NMR Ctrs., Inc., 1982-83; pres., dir. Cayman Petroleum Corp., 1974-75, Ridgecrest Energy Corp., 1979; dir. Tanglewood Consol. Resources, 1982-84. Panelist, lectr. Nat. Indsl. Conf. Bd.; bd. govs. The Los Angeles Music Center, 1973—; chmn., chief exec. officer, bd. dirs. Los Angeles Music Center Opera Assn., 1972—, chmn., chief exec. officer, 1981—; trustee Good Hope Med. Found., Los Angeles, 1974—. Served to lt. Office Naval Intelligence, USNR, 1952-56. Mem. Am. Mgmt. Assn., Los Angeles World Affairs Council, Choate Alumni Assn. So. Cal. (chmn. 1969—), Confrerie des Chevaliers du Tastevin, Beta Theta Pi, Phi Delta Phi.

WADA, OSAMU, computer company executive; b. Tokyo, Mar. 16, 1948; came to U.S., 1985; s. Hiroshi and Kinuko (Ono) W.; m. Moriko Iwamura, Apr. 3, 1978; children: Tomoko, Keiko, Kyouko, Aiko. BS, Keio U., 1970, MS, 1972. Sr. engr. Fujitsu Ltd., Kawasaki, Japan, 1972-85; dir. Fujitsu Am. Inc., San Jose, Calif., 1985—; cons. SuperMedia, Tokyo, 1983--. Patentee in computer field. Mem. Assn. for Computing Machinery, Japan Info. Processing Soc., Japan Office Automation Soc. (chief editorial staff). Home: 12186 Woodside Dr Saratoga CA 95070 Office: Fujitsu Am Inc 3055 Orchard Dr San Jose CA 95134

WADDINGTON, GARY L., physician; b. Grand Island, Nebr., Feb. 6, 1944; s. C. Earl and Edna E. (Baade) W.; m. Mary Jane Boden, Dec. 16, 1968; children: Erin Michael, Sara Nicole, Ryan Matthew. BS, U. Nebr., 1968, MD, 1972. Commd. 2d lt. U.S. Army, 1972, advanced through grades to lt. col., 1981; intern U.S. Army M. C., San Francisco, 1972-73; chief U.S. Army M. C., Buffalo, 1973-74; resident in tng. U.S. Army M. C., San Francisco, 1974-77; chief dept. medicine and dermatology U.S. Army M. C., Nuremberg, Fed. Republic of Germany, 1977-80; physician U.S. Army M. C., Colorado Springs, 1980-81; ret. U.S. Army M. C., 1981; ptnr. Allergy & Dermatology Specialists, Phoenix, 1981—; chief dermatology Maricopa County Med. Ctr., Phoenix, 1981-84, St. Joseph's Hosp. & Med. Ctr., Phoenix, 1984—; mem. adv. counsel Biltmore Nat. Bank, Phoenix, 1988—. Fellow Am. Acad. Dermatology. Republican. Lutheran. Office: Allergy & Dermatology 5040 N 15th Ave #301 Phoenix AZ 85015

WADDOUPS, CLARK, lawyer; b. Arco, Idaho, Apr. 21, 1946; s. Royal and Veta Lorene (Jones) W.; m. Vickie Lee Tibbitts, Dec. 16, 1967; children: Douglas Clark, Lorene, James Clark, Mary, Amy. Student, Ricks Coll., 1964-65; BA, Brigham Young U., 1970; JD, U. Utah, 1973. Bar: Calif. 1973, Utah 1982. Law clk. to presiding justice U.S. Ct. Appeals (9th cir.), San Diego, 1973-74; assoc. O'Melveny & Myers, L.A., 1974-81; ptnr. Kimball, Parr, Crockett & Waddoups, Salt Lake City, 1981—. Home: 29 Rollingwood Ln Sandy UT 84092

WADDY, LAWRENCE HEBER, religious writer; b. Sydney, Australia, Oct. 5, 1914; came to U.S., 1963; s. Percival Stacy and Etheldred (Spittal) W.; m. Laurie Hancock, July 10, 1972. BA, Oxford (Eng.) U., 1937, MA, 1945. Asst. master Winchester Coll. Eng., 1938-42; headmaster Tombridge Coll., Eng., 1949-62; edn. officer BBC, Eng., 1962-63; chaplain The Bishop's Sch., La Jolla, Calif., 1963-67; lectr. in Greek and Latin lit. U. Calif., San Diego, 1969-80; vicar Ch. of Good Samaritan, University City, Calif., 1970-74; hon. asst. St. James By The Sea Episcopal Ch., La Jolla, 1975—. Author: Pax Romana & World Peace, 1950, The Bible as Drama, 1975, Drama in Worship, 1978, Symphony, 1976, A Parish By the Sea, 1988. Chaplain Royal Navy of Eng., 1942-46. Recipient Drama 1st prize BBC, 1964. Republican. Home: 5910 Camino De La Costa La Jolla CA 92037

WADE, MICHAEL STEPHEN, management consultant; b. Mesa, Ariz., Sept. 13, 1948; s. William Conrad and Geraldine (Pomeroy) W.; m. Mary Ann Kraynick, Aug. 30, 1971; children: Jonathan, Hilary. BA, U. Ariz., 1970, JD, 1973. Command equal opportunity officer U.S. Army Criminal Investigation Command, Washington, 1974-76; EEO investigative specialist City of Phoenix, 1977-79, EEO adminstr., 1979-84; cons. Phoenix, 1984—; instr. Ariz. Govtl. Tng. Service. Author: The Bitter Issue: The Right to Work Law in Arizona, 1976. Active Phoenix Art Mus., Friends of Phoenix Library, Ariz. Rep. Caucus. Served with U.S. Army, 1974-76. Recipient Phoenix Mayor's Com. on Employment of Handicapped award, 1984, Cert. Appreciation award Phoenix Fire Dept. Mem. Nat. Assn. Pub. Sector EEO Officers (founding pres. 1984-85, Pres.'s award 1986), Ariz. Affirmative Action Assn. (bd. dirs. 1984-86), North Cen. Phoenix Homeowners Assn. Home: 7032 N 3rd Ave Phoenix AZ 85021 Office: PO Box 34598 Phoenix AZ 85067

WADE, PATRICIA LYNNE, operations manager; b. Phoenix, Oct. 24, 1950; d. Buster and Tomi Tiny (Kishiyama) Collins; m. Howard William Wade III, Aug. 15, 1970 (div. July 1971); 1 child, Nicole Michelle. AAS, Maricopa Tech. Community Coll., 1985. Asst. dir. edn. Camelback Hosps., Inc., Phoenix, 1973-80; systems mgr. Laventhol & Horwath, CPA's, Phoenix, 1981-83; v.p. adminstrn. Total Info. Systems, Inc., Phoenix, 1983-87; adminstrv. dir., info. systems mgr. Spector Devel. Corp., Scottsdale, Ariz., 1987-88; mgr. ops. PSI World Seminars, Phoenix, 1988—. Mem. Data Processing Mgmt. Assn. (edn. chair 1986-87), Nat. Computer Conf. (human resources com. 1984-85), JJP Booster Club (v.p. Tempe chpt. 1985-86, pres. 1987-88). Democrat.

WADE, PATRICK JOHN, neurosurgeon; b. Glendale, Calif., Dec. 27, 1941; s. William John and Yvonne Van (Phoenix) W.; m. Christina Theresa Gonzales, Apr. 30, 1966; children: Matthew Patrick, Theresa Anne, Thomas Edward. BS, Loyola U., 1963; MD, U. So. Calif., 1967. Intern L.A. U. So. Calif. Med. Ctr., 1967-68, resident, 1970-75; neurol. surgeon Glendale Neurosurgical Group, 1975—. Lt. cmdr. USN Med. Corp. Mem. Glendale C. of C., Jonathan Club, Verdugo Club. Republican. Roman Catholic. Office: Glendale Neurosurgical Group 655 N Central Ave Glendale CA 91203

WADE, ROBERT RICHARD, engineer; b. Nashville, Mar. 5, 1940; s. John and Emma Lake (Hutton) W.; m. Carol Louise Thompson, June 5, 1966 (div. June 1983); children: Angela C., Christopher R. AS in Engring., Allan Hancock Coll., 1970; BA in Math., LaVerne Coll., 1975; BS in Electronics Tech., Chapman Coll., 1980. Lic. radar endorsement 1st class, FCC. Aerospace engr. Titan missile system Martin Marietta Corp., Vandenberg AFB, Calif., 1971-78, sr. flight safety system ops. engr., 1978-82, info. systems adminstr., 1982—; data adminstr. FOW Investors, Lompoc, Calif., 1980—. Author: Introduction to Digital Troubleshooting, 1977. Served to sgt. USAF, 1959-63. Recipient Gold Medallion award Martin Marietta Corp., 1976. Home: PO Box 611 Lompoc CA 93438 Office: Martin Marietta Corp PO Box 1681 Vandenberg AFB CA 93437

WADE, RODGER GRANT, financial systems analyst; b. Littlefield, Tex., June 25, 1945; s. George and Jimmie Frank (Grant) W.; m. Karla Kay Morrison, Dec. 18, 1966 (div. 1974); children: Eric Shawn, Shannon Annelle, Shelby Elaine; m. Carol Ruth Manning, Mar. 28, 1981. BA in Sociology, Tex. Tech. U., 1971. Programmer First Nat. Bank, Lubbock, Tex., 1971-73, Nat. Sharedata Corp., Odessa, Tex., 1973; asst. dir. computing ctr. Odessa Community Coll., 1973-74; programmer/analyst Med. Sci. Ctr., Tex. Tech. U., Lubbock, 1974-76; sys. mgr. Hosp. Info. Sys., Addison, Tex., 1976-78; programmer, analyst Harris Corp., Grapevine, Tex., 1978-80, Joy Petroleum, Waxahachie, Tex., 1980-82; owner R&C Bus. Sys./Requerdos de Santa Fe, N.Mex., 1982-84; fin. sys. analyst Los Alamos (N.Mex.) Tech. Assocs., 1984—. Vol. programmer Los Alamos Arts Coun., 1987-88. Republican. Home: Rte 5 Box 271H Santa Fe NM 87501 Office: Los Alamos Tech Assocs 1650 Trinity Dr Los Alamos NM 87544

WADE, STEPHEN ERIC, biologist; b. Fairmont, W.Va., Feb. 21, 1953; s. A.J. and Marjorie A. (Layton) W.; m. Ann Louise Loughlin. BA, W.Va. U., 1975; PhD, Ind. U., 1983. Research asst. Inst. Psychiatric Research, Indpls., 1980-83; research assoc. U. Colo. Dept. Psychology, Boulder, 1984-86; pres., chief scientist Hammersmith Labs., Inc., Steamboat Springs, Colo., 1985—. Patentee in field; contbr. articles to profl. jours. Recipient research grantee, NIMH, 1986, 88. Mem. AAAS. Office: Hammersmith Labs Inc #9 W Acres Indsl Park Steamboat Springs CO 80477

WADE, WILLIAM CONRAD, health organization executive; b. Mesa, Ariz., June 17, 1943; s. William C. and Geraldine (Pomeroy) W.; m. Elizabeth A. Reynolds, June 13, 1964; children: William C. III, Leanne E. MA, No. Ariz. U., 1967, MPA, 1982. Exec. dir. No. Ariz. Council, Flagstaff, Ariz., 1970-78, No. Ariz. HSA, Flagstaff, 1978-82; pres. Health Mgmt. Assn., Cottonwood, Ariz., 1982—; instr. No. Ariz. U., Flagstaff, 1980-87. Mem. Aircraft Owners Pilots Assn., Sigma Chi. Democrat. Roman Catholic. Home: 1009 W Hazel Way Flagstaff AZ 86001 Office: Health Mgmt Assn PO Box 276 Cottonwood AZ 86326

WADE, WINSTON JAY, communications executive; b. Plainview, Nebr., Dec. 19, 1938; s. Jay Clump and Clara (Garling) W.; m. Linda Kathleen Jensen, May 3, 1969; 1 child, Karin. B.S.E.E., U. Nebr., 1962, M.B.A., 1965. Gen. mgr. Northwestern Bell, Omaha, 1978-79, asst. comptroller, 1980-81, asst. v.p., 1981-82; dir. ATT, N.J., 1982-83; v.p. Bell Tri-Co Network, Englewood, Colo., 1983-84; v.p. Mountain Bell Holdings, Inc., Denver, 1984-85; pres. advanced techs. div. US West, Englewood, 1985—; bd. dirs. Bellcore, Computer Tech. Assocs., Ameritas. Bd. dirs. U. Neb. Found. Mem. IEEE, Innocents Soc., Beta Gamma Sigma, Pi Mu Epsilon. Avocations: skiing, golfing. Home: 6883 S Chapparal Circle W Aurora CO 80016 Office: US West Advanced Techs 6200 S Quebec Ste 270 Englewood CO 80112

WADIA, MANECK SORABJI, management consultant; b. Bombay, Oct. 22, 1931; came to U.S., 1953.; s. Sorabji Rattanji and Manijeh M. (Pocha) W.; m. Harriet F. Schilit, Nov. 22, 1962; children: Sara Jean, Mark Sorab. MBA, Ind. U., 1958, PhD, 1957. Mem. faculty Ind. U., Bloomington, 1958-60; Ford Found. fellow U. Pitts., 1960-61; prof. Stanford U., Palo Alto, Calif., 1961-65; mgmt. and personal cons., pres. Wadia Assoc., Inc., Del Mar, Calif., 1965—; cons., lectr. presenter in field. Author: The Nature and Scope of Management, 1966, Management and the Behavioral Sciences, 1968, Cases in International Business, 1970; co-author: (with Harper W. Boyd, Jr.) Cases from Emerging Countries, 1966; contbr. articles to profl. publs. Fellow Soc. Applied Anthropology; mem. Soc. Advancement Mgmt., Acad. Mgmt., Ind. Acad. Sci. (pres. anthropology sect.), Sigma Xi (assoc.), Sigma Iota Epsilon. Home and Office: 1660 Luneta Dr Del Mar CA 92014

WADMAN, WILLIAM WOOD, III, health physicist, consulting company executive, consultant; b. Oakland, Calif., Nov. 13, 1936; s. William Wood, Jr., and Lula Fae (Raisner) W.; children—Roxanne Alyce Wadman Hubbing, Raymond Alan (dec.), Theresa Hope Wadman Foster; m. Barbara Jean Wadman; stepchildren: Denise Ellen Varine, Brian Ronald Varine. M.A., U. Calif., Irvine, 1978. Radiation safety specialist, accelerator health physicist U. Calif. Lawrence Berkeley Lab., 1957-68; campus radiation safety officer U. Calif., Irvine, 1968-79; dir. ops., radiation safety officer Radiation Sterilizers, Inc., Tustin, Calif., 1979-80; prin., pres. Wm. Wadman & Assocs. Inc., 1980—; pres. Intracoastal Marine Enterprises Ltd., Martinez, Calif.; mem. team No. 1, health physics appraisal program NRC, 1980-81; cons. health physicist to industry; lectr. dept. community and environ. medicine U. Calif., Irvine, 1979-80, Orange Coast Coll. Active Cub Scouts; chief umpire Mission Viejo Little League, 1973. Served with USNR, 1955-63. Recipient award for profl. achievement U. Calif. Alumni Assn., 1972, Outstanding Performance award U. Calif., Irvine, 1973. Mem. Health Physics Soc. (treas. 1979-81, editor proc. 11th symposium, pres. So. Calif. chpt. 1977, Professionalism award 1975), Internat. Radiation Protection Assn. (U.S. del. 4th Congress 1977), Am. Nuclear Soc., Am. Public Health Assn. (chmn. program 1978, chmn. radiol. health sect. 1979-80), Campus Radiation Safety Officers (chmn. 1975, editor proc. 5th conf. 1975), ASTM. Club: UCI Univ. (dir. 1976, sec. 1977, treas. 1978). Contbr. articles to tech. jours. Home: 3687 Red Cedar Way Lake Oswego OR 97035

WADSWORTH, KEVIN WARREN, banker; b. Fairmont, W.Va., May 22, 1948; s. Warren Wade and Gloria Jean (McClung) W. AA, Valencia Community Coll., 1969; BA in Communication, U. Central Fla., 1971; postgrad., Fla. A&M U., 1975. Chpt. svcs. dir. Tau Kappa Epsilon, Indpls., 1971; exec. asst. U.S. Senator Edward J. Gurney, Washington, 1972-74; adminstrv. asst. to mayor, coun. City of Orlando (Fla.), 1976-77; founder, dir. The Gallery Gloria Jean, San Francisco, 1977-80; dir. govt. affairs San Francisco C. of C., 1980; asst. v.p. purchasing Crocker Nat. Bank, San Francisco, 1981-86; v.p., chief fin. officer Pinnacle Courseware, Inc., San Jose, Calif., 1986-87; v.p., corp. adminstrv. svcs. First Nationwide Bank, San Francisco, 1987—. Author: Circuit Breakers, 1972, Thoughts ... and Other Transgressions, 1986. Pres. Concerned Reps. for Individual Rights, San Francisco, 1980; mem. employment com. Human Rights Commn., San Francisco, 1986—; mem. Rep. County Central Com., San Francisco, 1980, 86, Solano County, Calif., 1982. With USMC, 1966-67. Recipient Outstanding Vol. Svc. award Nat. Vols. Svc., 1983. Mem. DAV, Am. Legion., Coits. Home: 58 Martha Ave San Francisco CA 94131-2835 Office: First Nationwide Bank 495 Hickey Blvd Daly City CA 94015-2699

WAETJEN, HERMAN CHARLES, theologian, educator; b. Bremen, Germany, June 16, 1929; Arrived in U.S., Sept., 1931.; s. Henry and Anna (Ruschmeyer) W.; m. Mary Suzanne Struyk, July 15, 1960; children: Thomas (dec.), Thembisa, Lois, David. BA, Concordia Sem., St. Louis, 1950, BD, 1953; Dr. Theol., Tuebingen U., Fed. Republic Germany, 1958; postgrad., Hebrew U., Jerusalem, 1955. Instr. Concordia Sem., 1957; asst. prof. U. So. Calif., L.A., 1959-62; assoc. prof. San Francisco Theol. Sem., San Anselmo, Calif., 1962-70, prof., 1970-74, Robert S. Dollar prof. of new testament, 1974—; vis. prof. U. Nairobi, Kenya, 1973-74, Fed. Theol. Sem., Republic South Africa, 1979-80, U. Zimbabwe, 1986-87. Author: Origin and Destiny of Humanness, 1976, 78, A Reordering of Power, 1989. mem. Soc. Biblical Lit., Pacific Coast Theol. Soc., Pacific Coast Theol. Soc. Democrat. Presbyterian. Home: 83 Jordan Ave San Anselmo CA 94960 Office: San Francisco Theol Sem 2 Kensington Rd San Anselmo CA 94960

WAGATSUMA, BERT MAMORU, accountant; b. Hilo, Hawaii, Feb. 11, 1955; s. Shinichi and Kikue (Arai) W. BBA, U. Hawaii, 1977. CPA, Hawaii. Staff auditor U.S. Army Audit Agy., Ft. Lewis, Wash., 1978-79; mem. staff Thayer & Matsushita, Kahului, Maui, Hawaii, 1979-80; sr.-in-charge Lester Witte & Co., Honolulu, 1980-81; mgr. Thayer & Assocs., Kahului, 1981-83; controller Fuku Constrn., Wailuku, 1983, Build N Grow, Hilo, 1983; owner Bert M. Wagatsuma CPA, Hilo, 1983—. Advisor Jr. Achievement, 1988-89; mem. acctg. adv. com. Maui Community Coll., 1981-83; asst. treas. Dem. Party, 1984—; treas. Friends for Wayne Metcalf, Hilo, 1986—. Mem. AICPA, Hawaii Soc. CPAs, Hawaii Assn. Pub. Accts., Hawaii State Bd. Pub. Accountancy, Lehua Jaycees (exec. v.p. 1986-87, treas. 1985-86, pres. 1987-88), Univ. Hawaii Alumni Assn. (treas. 1986—), Hilo High Sch. Alumni Assn. (auditor 1986—, jr. achievement advisor 1988). Democrat. Home: PO Box 1676 Hilo HI 96721

WAGEMAKER, DAVID ISAAC, human resources developement executive; b. Grand Rapids, Mich., Feb. 10, 1949; s. Raymond Ogden and Inez Loraine W.; m. Sharon Williams, Jan. 30, 1977. BA in Philosophy, Grand Valley State U., 1971. Owner Edn. Ctr., Grand Rapids, 1970-72; apiarist Bee Haven Honey, Grand Rapids, 1970-72; cons. Am. Leadership Coll., Washington, 1972-78, Wagemaker Co., Honolulu, 1978-80; edn. cons. Batten, Batten, Hudson & Swab, Inc., San Diego, 1980-81, mgr., 1981; securities broker, ins. agt. The Equitable Assurance Co., San Diego, 1982; assoc. cons. Pacific S.W. Airlines, San Diego, 1982-83; organizational devel. adminstr. Hughes Aircraft Co., El Segundo, Calif., 1983—; v.p. Wagemaker, Inc.,

Grand Rapids, 1984—; sr. cons. Nat. Mgmt. Inst., Flower Mound, Tex., 1985—; mgmt. cons. Mgmt. Devel. Ctr., San Diego State U., 1980—; seminarist Penton Learning, Inc., N.Y.C., 1982—; pres. Par Golf Co., Redondo Beach, Calif., 1984—. Co-author: Build A Better You Starting Now, 1982; author: (cassette program) Effective Time Management, 1979, (with others) How to Organize Yourself to Win, 1988. Fellow Acad. Mgmt.; mem. Sigma Chi, Zeta Nu (pres. 1968-70), Hughes Golf Club (El Segundo). Republican. Congregationalist. Home: 2226 Bataan Rd Redondo Beach CA 90278

WAGENHALS, WALTER LINCOLN, lawyer; b. Dayton, Ohio, June 29, 1934; s. Howard Blaine and Frances (Durning) W.; m. Patricia Aura Garver, Apr. 24, 1959; 1 child, Ann. BA, U. Washington, 1956; LLB, U. Colo., 1962. Bar: Colo. 1962. Asst. city atty. City of Boulder, Colo., 1963-68, city atty., 1968-78; legal counsel Oxford Properties, Inc., Denver, 1978-81; assoc. atty. Bailey & Finegan, Lakewood, Colo., 1981—. Served to 1st lt. USMC, 1956-59. Mem. Colo. Bar Assn. (forms standardisation com. 1985-87). Republican. Office: Bailey & Finegan 165 S Union Blvd #700 Lakewood CO 80228

WAGER, JERRY WILLIAM, probation officer; b. Toledo, Ohio, Mar. 14, 1937; s. Montcalm Arnold and Elizabeth (Wagner) W.; married; children: Marc Anthony, Jerry Lance. BEd, U. Toledo, 1959; postgrad., U. Mich., Flint, 1961. Tchr., coach various schs., Ohio and Mich., 1959-61; west coast dir. Hickory Farms of Ohio, Las Vegas, Nev., 1961-63; dir. advt. and publicity Diamond Jim's Nev. Club, Las Vegas, 1963-66, adminstrv. asst., 1967-68; dir. advertising, publicity and entertainment El Dorado Club, Henderson, Nev., 1966-67; owner, dir. Promotion In Motion Advt. Agy., Las Vegas, 1968-70; supr. Clark County Road Dept., Las Vegas, 1970-80; probation officer Juvenile Ct., Clark County, Las Vegas, 1980—. Ofcl., coach, tour dir. Nat. Amateur Athletic Union, 1959—, U.S.A. Wrestling, 1984—, Jr. World Championships, 1977; head official World Police and Fire Games, 1979—, Nat. Law Enforcement Olympics, 1988—; coach Las Vegas YMCA, 1967-80; pres. So. Nev. Amateur Athletic Union, Las Vegas, 1977—. Coached 7 straight World Championship wrestling teams, 1975, 76, 77, 87. Mem. Fedn. Internat. Lutte Amateur (ofcl. 1962—, Gold medal 1977, Bronze medal 1988). Home: 1805 S 14h St Las Vegas NV 89104 Office: Clark County Juvenile Ct 3401 E Bonanza Rd Las Vegas NV 89110

WAGGENER, THERYN LEE, law enforcement professional; b. Cedar Rapids, Iowa, Sept. 7, 1941; s. Hollis Angisa (Fowler) Hogan; m. Zoetta Jean Hamilton, May 30, 1967; 1 child, Drugh Kincade. BBA, Nat. U., 1977, MBA, 1979. Traffic officer Calif. Hwy. Patrol, San Diego, 1966-72; owner, operator Am. Nat. Chem., San Diego, 1972-82; chief investigator N.Mex. Real Estate Commn., Albuquerque, 1983-86, Nev. Real Estate Div., Carson City, 1986—; prof., Sierra Nev. Coll., Incline Village, 1988—, Western Nev. Community Coll., Carson City, 1987—. Mem. Washoe County (Nev.) Rep. Cen. Com., 1989. With USN, 1960-65. Mem. Nat. Assn. Real Estate Lic. Law Ofcls. (enforcement and investigative com. 1987—), Toastmasters, Rotary, Lions, Masons, Nu Beta Epsilon.

WAGGONER, JAMES CLYDE, lawyer; b. Nashville, May 7, 1946; s. Charles Franklin and Alpha (Noah) W.; m. Diane Dusenbery, Aug. 17, 1968; children: Benjamin, Elizabeth. BA, Reed Coll., 1968; JD, U. Oreg., 1974. Bar: Oreg. 1974, U.S. Dist. Ct. Oreg. 1975, U.S. Ct. Appeals (9th cir.) 1980, U.S. Tax Ct. 1979, U.S. Supreme Ct. 1979. Clerk to presiding justice Oreg. Supreme Ct., Portland, 1974-75; assoc. Martin, Bischoff & Templeton, Salem, 1975-78; ptnr. Martin, Bischoff & Templeton, Portland, 1978-82, Waggoner, Farleigh, Wada, Georgeff & Witt, Portland, 1982—. Contbr. articles to profl. jours. Mem. ABA, Oreg. Bar Assn., Multnomah Bar Assn., Reed Coll. Alumni Assn. (v.p. 1988, bd. mgmt.), Order Coif, Phi Beta Kappa. Democrat. Office: Waggoner Farleigh Wada et al 121 SW Morrison Ste 1000 Portland OR 97204

WAGGONER, LAINE, public relations consultant; b. N.Y.C., Nov. 19, 1933; d. S. Balfour and Cathryn (Smith) Morais; m. Rex Robert Waggoner, Apr. 8, 1966. BA, Hunter Coll., N.Y.C., 1956; MA, NYU, 1957. Owner, dir. Waggoner Pub. Rels., L.A.,and Ventura County, Calif., 1967—; communications dir. CamaCal Corp., 1987—; dir. pub. rels. Dept. Adoptions, L.A., 1974-81; pub. affairs mgr. Calif. State U., L.A., 1981-84; pub. rels. cons., Camarillo, Calif., 1984—; exec. dir. Community Assns. Inst., 1985-89. Mem. Pub. Rels. Soc. Am. (accredited; Prisms award 1977), Nat. Assn. Pub. Info. Officers, Nat. Assn. Govt. Communicators (Excellence award 1979), Pub. Info. Radio & TV Edn. Soc. (Bucaneer award 1981, 82), Pub. Info. Communicators Assn., Camarillo C. of C., Phi Beta Kappa. Home and Office: 838 Piropo Ct Camarillo CA 93010

WAGNER, DAVID J., art center director; b. Fort Knox, Ky., Mar. 4, 1952; s. Walter W. and Elsie G. (Zillner) W.; m. Kaye M. Kronenburg, June 21, 1975. BMA, U. Wis., Stevens Point, 1974; MA, Ind. U., 1976; postgrad., U. Minn. Grad. asst. Univ. Mus., Bloomington, Ind., 1975-76; intern Children's Mus., Indpls., 1976; dir. Leigh Yawkey Woodson Art Mus., Wausau, Wis., 1977-87; exec. dir. Colorado Springs (Colo.) Fine Arts Ctr., 1987—; mem. adv. bd. Nat. Park Art Acad., Jackson Hale, Wyo., Nat. Art Mus. of Sport, Indpls.; bd. dirs. Arts Community Pikes Peak Region, Colorado Springs; mem. adv. com. U. Colo., Colorado Springs, 1987—. Contbr.: (exhbn. catalogs) Americans in Glass, 1984, Rembrandt's Etchings, 1985, Wildlife in Art, 1987; contbr. Wis. Acad. Rev., 1986, Arts for the Parks, 1988. Chmn. non-profit orgn. com. United Way, Wausau, 1981, 84; bd. dirs. Wis. Citizens for the Arts, Madison, 1984-86; negotiator Budapest Mus. Old Masters Am. Tour, 1986, Birds in China Art Exhbn. Tour, 1987; bd. dirs. Wis. Humanities Com., Madison, 1984-87; mem. adv. bd. Nat. Park Acad. of Arts, Jackson Hole, Wyo.; assoc. bd. Nat. Art Mus. of Sport, Indpls. Winterthur Summer Inst. scholar, 1979, Victorian Soc. scholar, 1981, Inst. European Studies scholar, 1982; U. Minn fellow, 1987. Mem. Am. Assn. Mus., Am. Studies Assn., Assn. Colls., Univs. & Community Arts Adminstrs., The Country Club of Colo. Office: Colo Springs Fine Arts Ctr 30 W Dale St Colorado Springs CO 80903

WAGNER, FRANCIS ROBERT, management educator, consultant; b. Santa Monica, Calif., Apr. 10, 1948; s. Francis Vincent and Virginia Mary (Heape) W.; m. Karen Yolanda Secchi, Sept. 13, 1969; children: James Francis, Jessica Monique. B in Commerce, Santa Clara U., 1969; MBA, UCLA, 1970, PhD, 1976, postdoctoral, 1976-78. Asst. prof. mgmt. Loyola Marymount U., Los Angeles, 1976-82; ptnr., dir. Keilty, Goldsmith & Boone, La Jolla, Calif., 1981-86; co-founder Prism Ltd., Santa Monica, 1986—; bd. advisors ACS, Concord, Calif., 1984—; cons. IBM, Coca-Cola, Dun & Bradstreet, IDS Fin. Services, Citibank, Warner Lambert, Apple Computer, Inc., Reebok Internat., Mai-Basic Four, Archdiocese Los Angeles. Contbr. articles to mgmt. and psychology jours. Co-leader CROP Hunger Walks, Pacific Palisades, Calif., 1980-81; cons. sec. gen. Can. Red Cross, 1985-86, Ont. div., 1988—. Served to 1st lt. U.S. Army, 1971-72. Named one of Outstanding Young Men in Am., 1979. Roman Catholic. Home: 832 Alma Real Dr Pacific Palisades CA 90272

WAGNER, JEFFREY HAROLD, real estate company executive; b. Pompton Plains, N.J., Sept. 29, 1959; s. James Robert and Jane Angela (Burton) W.; m. Debbie Sue Seaton, May 19, 1984; 1 child, Alysia Marie. BS in Bus., Miami U., Oxford, Ohio, 1981; MS in Taxation, Golden Gate U., 1988. CPA, Calif. Staff acct. Brunswick Corp., Anaheim, Calif., 1981-83; sr. acct. Lavine & Luxenberg, CPA's, Anaheim, 1983-85; tax supr. Coopers & Lybrand, CPA's, Newport Beach, Calif., 1985-87; dir. of taxation BCE Devel., Inc., Irvine, Calif., 1987—. Mem. Am. Inst. CPA's, Calif. Soc. CPA's, Miami U. Alumni Assn., Orange County C. of C. Republican. Methodist. Home: 11 Waynesboro Irvine CA 92720 Office: BCE Devel Inc Jamboree Ctr 1 Park Pla #1000 Irvine CA 92714

WAGNER, JOHN KYLE, corporate professional; b. Detroit; s. Robert Alexander Wagner and Gladys Riding; m. Janet Marie Juback, July 14, 1984; 1 child: Elizabeth Colleen. Postgrad., Regis Coll., 1988; BS, U. Fla., Gainesville, 1983. V.p. mktg and regional ops. Qual-Med, Inc., Colorado Sprgs; dir. mktg. Fairlane Health Svcs. Corp., Detroit, Mich.; nat. accounts rep. Gigna Healthplan, Tampa, Fla., account exec., account mgr. Mem. El Paso County Young Republicans, 1987. Mem. Am. Mktg. Assoc., Group Health Assn. Am. (voting del.). Republican. Catholic. Home: 121 Sunbird Cliffs Ln E Colorado Springs CO 80919

WAGNER, JUDITH BUCK, investment firm executive; b. Altoona, Pa. Sept. 25, 1943; d. Harry Bud and Mary Elizabeth (Rhodes) B.; m. Joseph E. Wagner, Mar. 15, 1980; 1 child, Elizabeth. BA in History, U. Wash., 1965; grad. N.Y. Inst. Fin., 1968. Chartered fin. analyst; registered Am. Stock Exchange; registered N.Y. Stock Exchange; registered investment advisor. Security analyst Morgan, Olmstead, Kennedy & Gardner, L.A., 1968-71; rsch. cons., St. Louis, 1971-72; security analyst Boettcher & Co., Denver, 1972-75; pres. Wagner Investment Counsel, 1975-84; chmn. Wagner & Hamil, Inc., Denver, 1983—; chmn., bd. dirs. The Women's Bank, N.A., Denver, 1977—, organizational group pres., 1975-77; chmn. Equitable Bankshares Colo., Inc., Denver, 1980—; bd. dirs. Equitable Bank of Littleton, 1983-88, pres., 1985; bd. dirs. Colo. Growth Capital, 1979-82; lectr. Denver U., Metro State, 1975-80. Author: Woman and Money series Colo. Woman Mag., 1976; moderator 'Catch 2' Sta. KWGN-TV, 1978-79. Pres. Big Sisters Colo., Denver, 1977-82, bd. dirs., 1973—; bd. fellows U. Denver, 1985—; bd. dirs. Red Cross, 1980, Assn. Children's Hosp., 1985, Colo. Health Facilities Authority, 1978-84, Jr. League Community Adv. Com., 1979—, Brother's Redevel., Inc., 1979-80; mem. Hist. Paramount Found., 1984, Denver Pub. Sch. Career Edn. Project, 1972; mem. investment com. YWCA, 1976-88; mem. adv. com. Girl Scouts U.s.; mem. agy. rels. com. Mile High United Way, 1978-81, chmn. United Way Venture Grant com., 1980-81; fin. chmn. Schoettler for State Treas., 1986; bd. dirs. Downtown Denver Inc., 1988—; bd. dirs., v.p., treas. The Women's Found. Colo., 1987—. Recipient Making It award Cosmopolitan Mag., 1977, Women on the Go award, Savvy mag., 1983, Minouri Yasoni award, 1986, Salute Spl. Honoree award, Big Sisters, 1987; named one of the Outstanding Young Women in Am., 1979; recipient Woman Who Makes A Difference award Internat. Women's Forum, 1987. Fellow Fin. Analysts Fedn.; mem. Women's Forum of Colo. (pres. 1979), Women's Found. Colo., Inc. (bd. dirs. 1986—), Denver Soc. Security Analysts (bd. dirs. 1976-83, v.p. 1980-81, pres. 1981-82), Leadership Denver (Outstanding Alumna award 1987), Pi Beta Phi (pres. U. Wash. chpt. 1964-65). Office: Wagner & Hamil Inc 410 17th St #840 Denver CO 80202

WAGNER, MICHAEL JOSEPH, electrical engineer; b. Havre, Mont., July 20, 1964; s. William Rodrick and Norma Louise (Chevallier) W. BSEE, Mont. State U., 1987. Data analyst Schlumberger Well Svc., Havre, 1981-84; bench technician Cherokee Internat. Inc., Irvine, Calif., 1986-87; engr. Space Systems div. Gen. Dynamics Co., San Diego, 1988—. Mem. IEEE, Convair Windsurfing Club (dockmaster 1988—). Democrat. Roman Catholic.

WAGNER, NORMAN ERNEST, energy company executive, formerly university president; b. Edenwold, Sask., Can., Mar. 29, 1935; s. Robert Eric and Gertrude Margaret (Brandt) W.; m. Catherine Hack, May 16, 1957; children—Marjorie Dianne, Richard Roger, Janet Marie. B.A., U. Sask., 1958, M.Div., 1958; M.A., U. Toronto, Ont., Can., 1960, Ph.D. in Near Eastern Studies, 1965; LL.D. (hon.), Wilfrid Laurier U., 1984. Asst. prof. Near Eastern studies Wilfrid Laurier U., Waterloo, Ont., 1962-65, assoc. prof., 1965-69, prof., 1970-78, dean grad. studies and research, 1974-78; pres. U. Calgary, Alta., Can., 1978-88; chmn. bd. Alta. Natural Gas Co., Ltd., 1988—; bd. dirs. Pacific Gas Transmission, Ltd., Angus Chem. Co., Ltd., CFCN Communications Ltd., Alta. and So. Gas Co. Ltd. Author: (with others) The Moyer Site: A Prehistoric Village in Waterloo County, 1974. Mem. Adv. Coun. on Adjustment, OCO '88, Alta. Heritage Found. for Med. Rsch.; nat. adv. bd. Sci. and Tech., Internat. Trade Adv. Com. Named Officer of the Order of Can., 1989; Can. Council grantee; recipient other grants. Mem. Can. Soc. Bibl. Studies. Lutheran. Home: Box 5 Site 33 RR 12, Calgary, AB Canada T3E 6W3 Office: Alta Natural Gas Co Ltd, 2400 425 First St SW, Calgary, AB Canada T2P 3L8

WAGNER, RICHARD, baseball club executive; b. Central City, Nebr., Oct. 19, 1927; s. John Howard and Esther Marie (Wolken) W.; m. Gloria Jean Larsen, May 10, 1950; children—Randolph G., Cynthia Kaye. Student, pub. schs., Central City. Gen. mgr. Lincoln Baseball Club, Nebr., 1955-58; mgr. Pershing Mcpl. Auditorium, Lincoln, 1958-61; exec. staff Ice Capades, Inc., Hollywood, Calif., 1961-63; gen. mgr. Sta. KSAL, Salina, Kans., 1963-65; dir. promotion and sales St. Louis Nat. Baseball Club, 1965-66; gen. mgr. Forum, Inglewood, Calif., 1966-67; asst. to exec. v.p. Cin. Reds, 1967-70, asst. to pres., 1970-74, v.p. adminstrn., 1975, exec. v.p., 1975-78, gen. mgr., 1977-83, pres., 1978-83; pres. Houston Astros Baseball Club, 1985-87; spl. asst. Office of Baseball Commr., 1988—; pres. RGW Enterprises, Inc., Phoenix, 1978—. Served with USNR, 1945-47, 50-52. Named Exec. of Yr., Minor League Baseball, Sporting News, 1958. Mem. Internat. Assn. Auditorium Mgrs. Republican. Methodist.

WAGNER, RICHARD ALLEN, marketing executive; b. Honolulu, Sept. 4, 1943; s. Wilbur Tilghman and Twila Kathryn (Longhofer) W.; m. Nancy Rae Yochim, July 9, 1965; children: David Scott, Erik Brandon, Sean Brant. BA, San Diego State U., 1972. Field service engr. Digital Systems, Covina, Calif., 1967-68; quality control inspector Teledyne/Ryan Aero., San Diego, 1968-72; stock broker E.F. Hutton & Co., La Jolla, Calif., 1972-75; acct. exec. Sta. KSON Radio AM/FM, San Diego, 1975, Storer Broadcasting Co., San Diego, 1975-77; gen. mgr. Mickey Finn Prodns., Las Vegas, Nev., 1978; owner, dir. Wagner Advt., Las Vegas, 1978—; dir. mktg. Klondike Inn Hotel and Casino, Las Vegas. Appeared in many TV network series including NBC TV movie Vegas Strip War, 1984. Sgt. USMC, 1964-67. Recipient award of Excellence Addy, 1987. Republican. Methodist. Office: Klondike Inn Hotel & Casino 5191 S Las Vegas Blvd Las Vegas NV 89014

WAGNER, RICHARD BRIAN, financial planner, consultant; b. San Diego, Calif., Mar. 1, 1949; s. John Robert Wagner and Ethel Louise (Wright) Smyres; m. P. Gail Pelsue, June 27, 1971; children: Jacob, Natalie. BA, Coll. Wooster, Ohio, 1971; JD, Lewis and Clark Coll., 1977. Bar: Colo. 1977, U.S. Ct. Appeals (9th cir.) 1978; cert. fin. planner. Adminstrv. aide City of Portland, Oreg., 1971-73; freelance pottery artist Portland, 1973-74; law clk. William T. Buckley, Lake Oswego, Oreg., 1975-77; lawyer Miller & Swearinger, Denver, 1979-81; fin. planner Fin. Architects, Aurora, Colo., 1982-84, Wagner/Howes Fin. Planners, Inc., Denver, 1984—; registered rep. T.L. Reed Securities, Inc., Denver, 1984-89. Contbr. articles to profl. publs. Elder, Montview Blvd. Presbyn. Ch., Denver, 1986—; packmaster Cub Scouts Am., Denver, 1987-88. Mem. Internat. Assn. Fin. Planners (pres. Rocky Mtn. chpt. 1986-87, chmn. bd. 1987-88), Colo. chpt. Inst. Cert. Fin. Planners, Aurora Bar Assn. (treas. 1984-85), Colo. Bar Assn., Masons. Republican. Home: 1149 Steele St Denver CO 80206 Office: Wagner/Howes Fin Inc 210 University #720 Denver CO 80206

WAGNER, RUTH JOOS, educator; b. L.A., June 1, 1933; d. Walter Joos and Ruth McKenzie (Edwards) J.; m. Gerald Dayton Wagner, Dec. 17, 1960; 1 child, Gregory Dayton. BA, UCLA, 1955, MA, 1976. Cert. primary Tchr., Calif. Kindergarten tchr. Inglewood (Calif.) Unified Sch. Dist., 1955-59, 63—, Coronado (Calif.) Unified Sch. Dist., 1959-62; pres. Rainbow West Assocs., L.A., 1986--. Ball chmn. League for Crippled Children, L.A., 1984, pres., 1988. Named Tchr. of Yr., Inglewood Sch. Dist., 1984. Mem. NEA, Calif. Tchrs. Assn, Inglewood Tchrs. Assn., Greater L.A. Zoo Assn., World Affairs Coun. Republican. Episcopalian. Home: 2117 Eric Dr Los Angeles CA 90049

WAGNER, SHELLEY ELIZABETH, marketing executive; b. Lewiston, Idaho, June 6, 1953; d. Shelton Brown Wagner and Mary Elizabeth (Oberlander) Aford; m. Harvey I. Mednick, Oct. 3, 1981. BA in Sociology, Colo. Women's Coll., 1975. Publicist HOH Rinehart Winston, N.Y.C., 1976-78; free-lance advt., publicity writer L.A., 1978-79; creativity asst. KABC Radio, L.A., 1979-86, dir. creative svcs., 1986-89; cons. mktg., creative svcs. L.A., 1989—. Mem. Advt. Industry Emergency Found.

WAGNER, STEVEN GEORGE, advertising executive; b. Mineola, N.Y., June 11, 1960; s. Alfred H. and Anneliese (Esch) W. BS, U. N.H., 1983. Acct. Veam, Litton Ind., Watertown, Conn., 1983-86; account exec. Patrick Outdoor Media, Inc., Hartford, Conn., 1985-86; sr. account exec. Patrick Outdoor Media, Inc., Hartford, 1986-87; area mgr. Patrick Media Group, Inc., San Diego, 1987-88, mktg. mgr., 1988—. Mem. San Diego Advt. Club, San Diego Advt. Golf Assn. Democrat. Roman Catholic. Office: Patrick Media Group Inc 2727 Camino Del Rio S #110 San Diego CA 92108

WAGNER, SUE ELLEN, state legislator; b. Portland, Maine, Jan. 6, 1940; d. Raymond A. and Kathryn (Hooper) Pooler; m. Peter B. Wagner, 1964; children—Kirk, Kristina. B.A. in Polit. Sci., U. Ariz., 1962; M.A. in History, Northwestern U., 1964. Asst. dean women Ohio State U., 1963-64; tchr. history and Am. govt. Catalina High Sch., Tucson, 1964-65; reporter Tucson Daily Citizen, 1965-68; mem. Nev. Assembly, 1975-83; now mem. Nev. Senate from 3d dist. Author: Diary of a Candidate, On People and Things, 1974. Mem. Reno Mayor's Adv. Com., 1973-84; chmn. Blue Ribbon Task Force on Housing, 1974-75; mem. Washoe County Republican Central Com., 1974-84, Nev. State Rep. Central Com., 1975-84; mem. Nev. Legis. Commn., 1976-77; del. social service com. Council State Govts.; v.p. Am. Field Service, 1973, family liaison, 1974, mem.-at-large, 1975. Kappa Alpha Theta Nat. Grad. scholar, also Phelps-Dodge postgrad. fellow, 1962; named Outstanding Legislator, Nev. Young Republicans, 1976, One of 10 Outstanding Young Women in Am. Mem. AAUW (legis. chmn. 1974), Bus. and Profl. Women, Kappa Alpha Theta. Episcopalian. Office: State Senate Carson City NV 89710 also: 845 Tamarack Dr Reno NV 89509

WAGNER, WILLIAM GERARD, university dean, physicist, consultant, information scientist; b. St. Cloud, Minn., Aug. 22, 1936; s. Gerard C. and Mary V. (Cloone) W.; m. Janet Agatha Rowe, Jan. 30, 1968 (div. 1978); children: Mary, Robert, David, Anne; m. Christiane LeGuen, Feb. 21, 1985. B.S., Calif. Inst. Tech., 1958, Ph.D. (NSF fellow, Howard Hughes fellow), 1962. Cons. Rand Corp., Santa Monica, Calif., 1960-65; sr. staff physicist Hughes Research Lab., Malibu, Calif., 1960-69; lectr. physics Calif. Inst. Tech., Pasadena, 1963-65; asst. prof. physics U. Calif. at Irvine, 1965-66; assoc. prof. physics and elec. engring. U. So. Calif., Los Angeles, 1966-69, prof. depts. physics and elec. engring., 1969—, dean div. natural scis. and math. Coll. Letters, Arts and Scis., 1973-87, dean interdisciplinary studies and developmental activities, 1987—, spl. asst. automated record services, 1975-81; founder Program in Neural, Informational and Behavioural Scis., Nat. Inst. Bldg. Scis. 1982—; chmn. bd. Malibu Securities Corp., Los Angeles, 1971—; cons. to Janus Mgmt. Corp., Los Angeles, 1970-71, Croesus Capital Corp., Los Angeles, 1971-74; allied mem. Pacific Stock Exchange, 1974-82; fin. and computer cons. Hollywood Reporter, 1979-81; mem. adv. council for emerging engring. techs., NSF, 1987—. Contbr. articles on physics to sci. publs. Richard Chase Tolman postdoctoral fellow, 1962-65. Mem. Am. Phys. Soc., Nat. Assn. Security Dealers, Sigma Xi. Home: 2828 Patricia Ave Los Angeles CA 90064-4425 Office: U So Calif 251 Allan Hancock Found Los Angeles CA 90089-0371

WAGONER, DAVID EVERETT, lawyer; b. Pottstown, Pa., May 16, 1928; s. Claude Brower and Mary Kathryn (Groff) W.; children—Paul R., Colin H., Elon D., Peter B. B.A., Yale U., 1950; LL.B., U. Pa., 1953. Bar: D.C. 1953, Pa. 1953, Wash. 1953. Law clk. U.S. Ct. Appeals (3d cir.), Pa., 1955-56; law clk. U.S. Supreme Ct., Washington, 1956-57; ptnr. Perkins & Coie, Seattle, 1957—. Mem. sch. com. Mcpl. League Seattle and King County, 1958—, chmn., 1962-65; mem. Seattle schs. citizens coms. on equal ednl. opportunity and adult vocat. edn., 1963-64; mem. Nat. Com. Support Pub. Schs.; mem. adv. com. on community colls., to 1965, legislature interim com. on edn., 1964-65; mem. community coll. adv. com. to state supt. pub. instrn., 1965; chmn. edn. com. Forward Thrust, 1968; mem. Univ. Congl. Ch. Council Seattle, 1968-70; bd. dirs. Met. YMCA Seattle, 1968; bd. dirs. Seattle Pub. Schs., 1965-73, v.p., 1966-67, 72-73, pres., 1968, 73; trustee Evergreen State Coll. Found., chmn. 1986-87, capitol campaign planning chmn.; trustee Pacific NW Ballet, v.p. 1986. Served to 1st lt. M.C., AUS, 1953-55. Fellow Am. Coll. Trial Lawyers; mem. English Speaking Union (v.p. Seattle 1961-62), ABA (chmn. appellate advocacy com.), Wash. State Bar Assn., Seattle-King County Bar Assn., Nat. Sch. Bds. Assn. (bd. dirs., chmn. Council Big City Bds. Edn. 1971-72), Chi Phi. Office: Perkins and Coie 1201 Third Ave 40th Fl Seattle WA 98101-3099

WAGONER, DOROTHY MILLIE VAN DONSELAAR, nurse; b. Grinnell, Iowa, July 7, 1927; d. Henry and Grace (Speas) Van Donselaar; m. Gerald Wagoner, Dec. 4, 1949 (div. may 1978); children: Diane, Paul, Susan, G. Ronald. Grad. nurse, St. Francis Hosp., Macomb, Ill., 1949; BS in Health Sci., Chapman coll., 1979, MA in Edn. Mgmt. Systems, 1982; credential in Health Service, Calif. State U., 1986. RN. Supr. med./surg. Mason Dist. Hosp., Havana, Ill., 1958-61; nurse pediatrics St. Joseph Hosp., Ft. Wayne, Ind., 1961-63; owner Town House Restaurant, Havana, 1963-64; nurse Balyki Sch. Dist., Bath, Ill., 1966-67, Strathroy Hosp., Can., 1967-68, Scenic Hosp., Modesto, Calif., 1971, Modesto Jr. Coll., 1972-75; dir. nurses Bel Air Convalesent Hosp., Turlock, Calif., 1975-78; supr. S. Meml. Hosp., Ceres, Calif., 1978-80; nurse Turlock Sch. Dist., 1981—; instr. nursing Modesto Jr. Coll., 1980-81; entrepeneur Van Dan Assocs. Patentee in field. Mem. Polit. Campaign Charles Percy, Ill., 1964-66; social chmn. PTA, Havana, 1966; sec. San Joaquin Epis. Mission, Ceres, 1975-81. Mem. Entrepreneur's Assn., Stanislaus Organist Guild, Modesto Civic Theater, Profl. Guild, Salvation Army. Republican. Club: Womens Community (Havana, chmn. pub. relations 1966-77). Office: Van Don Assocs 1620 River Rd Modesto CA 95351

WAHL, FLOYD MICHAEL, geologist; b. Hebron, Ind., July 7, 1931; s. Floyd Milford and Ann Pearl (DeCook) W.; m. Dorothy W. Daniel, July 4, 1953; children: Timothy, David, Jeffrey, Kathryn. A.B., DePauw U., 1953; M.S., U. Ill., 1957, Ph.D., 1958. Cert. profl. geologist. Prof. geology U. Fla., Gainesville, 1969-82, assoc. dean Grad. Sch., 1974-80, acting dean, 1980-81; exec. dir. Geol Soc Am., Boulder, Colo., 1982—. Contbr. articles to profl. jours. Served to cpl. U.S. Army, 1953-55. Recipient Outstanding Tchr. award U. Ill., 1967. Fellow Geol. Soc. Am.; mem. Mineral Soc. Am., Am. Inst. Profl. Geologists (chpt. pres.), Sigma Xi. Office: Geol Soc Am 3300 Penrose Pl Box 9140 Boulder CO 80301

WAHL, IVER WILLIAM, aerospace company executive; b. Denver, Aug. 26, 1923; s. Iver William and Pearl Geneva (Warriner) W.; student U. Wichita, 1941-43; BSME, U. Colo., 1949; m. Clayta Winifred Davis, June 23, 1945; children: Michael Dan, Eileen Annette. Registered profl. engr., Calif.; cert. profl. property mgr. Stores supr. Cessna Aircraft Co., Wichita, Kans., 1941-43; tool design engr. Maytag Co., Newton, Iowa, 1949-51; insp. supr. Heckethorn Mfg. Co., Littleton, Colo., 1951-57; acting chief quality planning Martin-Marietta, Denver, 1957-64; mgr. quality assurance, material, property and prodn. Ball Aerospace Systems Div., Boulder, 1964—; cons. quality, property mgmt. Bd. dirs. Littleton YMCA, 1952-55; mem. adv. council Met. State Coll., 1972-77. With USAAF, 1943-45. Recipient Skylab achievement award NASA. Fellow Am. Soc. Quality Control (officer, regional reliability counselor, testimonial award); mem. Nat. Security Industries Assn. (com. chmn., Outstanding Achievement award), Electronics Industries Assn., Nat. Property Mgmt. Assn. (v.p. for communications, membership, chpt. property Person-of-Yr. award 1983, 86, regional personal property Person of Yr. award 1986), DAV, Knife and Fork Club (regional dir. and v.p.), Elks. Presbyterian. Home: 1205 Eastridge Boulder CO 80303 Office: PO Box 1062 Boulder CO 80306

WAHL, JOAN CONSTANCE, technical writer, editor; b. Phila., Dec. 23, 1921; d. Frank L. and Sara E. (Timoney) O'Brien; B.A., Rosemont Coll., 1943; postgrad. U. Calif., Los Angeles, 1960-61; m. John Carl Wahl, Jr., Dec. 31, 1943 (div. 1959); children—John, Mark, David, Lawrence, Thomas, Jeanne, Madeleine Sophie, Eugene. Substitute tchr. Los Angeles City Bd. Edn., 1961; editor, proofreader Renner/Cal-Data Corp., Los Angeles, 1962-63; editor, tech. writer Volt Tech. Corp., 1964-66; sr. tech. editor, writer, project editor Aerospace Corp., El Segundo, Calif., 1966—. Sect. chmn. United Way, Los Angeles, 1963-64; mem. communications com. St. Paul the Apostle, Westwood, Calif., 1976-78. Recipient Outstanding Service award United Way, 1964. Mem. Soc. Tech. Communications (sr.), Aerospace Women's Com., Mental Health Assn. Los Angeles County, Kistler Honor Soc. Contbr. articles to profl. jours. Office: Aerospace Corp M3/377 2350 El Segundo Blvd El Segundo CA 90245

WAHL, RICHARD ALAN, physician, health organization administrator; b. N.Y.C., Mar. 24, 1952; s. Robert and Elaine (Arnow) W.; m. Margaret Wolf, May 28, 1978; 1 child, Rachel Lee. BA, U. Rochester, 1973; MD, George Washington U., 1978. Diplomate, Nat. Bd. Med. Examiners, Am. Bd. Pediatrics. Intern, then resident U. Mich., Ann Arbor, 1978-81; instr. U. Mich. Med. Ctr., Ann Arbor, 1978-81; med. officer U.S. Pub. Health Svc., Peekskill, N.Y., 1981-84; asst. prof. N.Y. Med. Coll., Valhalla, 1984-85; clin. lectr. U. Ariz. Med. Ctr., Tucson, 1985—; clinic chief staff CIGNA Health

Plan, Tucson, 1987—. Contbr. articles to profl. jours. Fellow Am. Acad. Pediatrics; mem. Pima County Pediatric Soc. Office: CIGNA Health Plan of Ariz 7901 E 22d St Tucson AZ 85710

WAHLGREN, ERIK, emeritus foreign language educator; b. Chgo., Nov. 2, 1911; s. Oscar G. and Marion I. (Wilkins) W.; m. Dorothy Sly, Nov. 9, 1939 (div. 1951); children: Nils, Arvid; m. Beverly Pont, Dec. 18, 1952 (div. 1969); children: Siri Wahlgren Grochowski, Thor; m. Helen Gilchrist-Wottring, July 2, 1971; 2 stepchildren. Ph.B., U. Chgo., 1933, Ph.D., 1938; M.A., U. Neb., 1936. Mem. faculty UCLA, 1938—, prof. Scandinavian langs., 1955-70, prof. Scandinavian and Germanic langs., 1970-77, prof. emeritus, 1977—, vice chmn. dept. Germanic langs., 1963-69; dir. U. Calif. study centers at Univs. Lund (Sweden) and Bergen (Norway), 1972-74; lectr. Uppsala U., also vis. prof. Stockholm Sch. Econs., 1947-48; exchange instr. U. B.C., summer 1940; vis. prof. Augustana Coll., summer 1946, U. Calif. at Berkeley, 1968, U. Wash., 1970, Portland State U., 1979-80; U.S. mem. Commn. Ednl. Exchange U.S.-Sweden, 1973-74; sr. fellow, cons. Monterey Inst. Fgn. Studies, 1977-78; adv. NEH, 1978—; advisor Oreg. Gov.'s Commn. on Fgn. Langs. and Internat. Study, 1981-83; German lang. dir. Army Specialized Tng. Program, 1943-44. Author: The Kensington Stone: A Mystery Solved, 1958, The Vikings and America, 1986; also several other books, translations and numerous articles on Scandinavian philology.; appeared various documentary films. Mem. Mayor's Community Adv. Com., 1964-73. Am.-Scandinavian Found. fellow Sweden, 1946-47, recipient Gold medal, 1975; grantee to Scandinavia Am. Philos. Soc., 1954-55; Guggenheim Meml. Found. fellow Scandinavia, 1961-62; recipient pub. citation Icelandic Community Los Angeles, 1964; decorated knight Royal Swedish Order of Polar Star, knight Order Lion of Finland, knight Icelandic Order of Falcon. Fellow Internat. Inst. Arts and Letters (life); mem. Swedish Cultural Soc. Am. (dir. 1940-48, pres. Los Angeles 1941-46), MLA So. Calif. (exec. bd. 1950-53), MLA Assn. Am. (chmn. Scandinavian sect. 1955, 67), Am.-Scandinavian Found. (pres. Los Angeles chpt. 1958-60), Soc. Advancement Scandinavian Study (assoc. editor 1947-57, 70-73, assoc. mng. editor 1957-69), Am. Assn. Tchrs. German (nat. exec. council 1957-59, 60-63), Finlandia Found., Medieval Acad. Am., Am. Swedish Hist. Mus., Swedish-Am. Hist. Soc. Calif., Nordic Heritage Mus. (Viking ship com.), World Affairs Council Oreg., Wash., Seattle Swedish Club, Oreg. Internat. Council, Tau Kappa Epsilon, Delta Sigma Rho, Delta Phi Alpha. Home and Office: 17722 Plaza Acosta San Diego CA 92128

WAHLQUIST, JANA SUE, small business owner; b. Ogden, Utah, Jan. 16, 1951; d. Clarence Edward and Rosella Afton (McMillan) W.;1 child, Dane Michael. BS, Brigham Young U., 1973; Elem. Cert., So. Utah State Coll., 1984. Owner Duck Ent., Redmond, Utah, 1982-88, Handcart Outfitters, Redmond, 1988—. Chmn. North Sevier Econ. Devel. Com., Salina, Utah, 1988; emergency med. technician Salina Ambulance Svcs., 1979-83. Mem. Nat. Assn. Female Execs. Mem. Ch. of Jesus Christ of Latter Day Saints. Home: 460 S 200 E Box 336 Redmond UT 84652

WAHLSTROM, HAROLD EUGENE, service executive; b. Chgo., Nov. 15, 1947; s. Winston Arthur Wahlstrom and Billie Louise (Cox) Day; m. Linda Marguerite Bezy, Apr. 20, 1968; children: Mary Ann, Rebecca Lynn, Veronica Sue, Von Christopher. Student, Phoenix Coll., 1966-67. Gen. mgr. Western World Foods, Inc., Phoenix, 1971-74, Sizzler, Phoenix, 1974-75; dist. mgr. Denny's Restaurants, Inc., Denver, 1975-80, Arlington, Tex., 1981-83, Phoenix, 1986—; pres. Net Line Living Assocs., Lubbock, 1979-81; v.p., gen. mgr. Lubbock's Big Apple Restaurants, 1980-81; div. mgr. Pizza Time Theatre, Inc., Euless, Tex., 1983-85; regional mgr. Sea Galley Stores East, Falls Church, Va., 1985-86; cons. LRG Internat., Inc., Scottsdale, Ariz., 1986, Showbiz Pizza, Irving, Tex., 1984. Bd. dirs. The Bridge Assn., Ft. Worth, Tex., 1982-83; officer Phoenix Police Dept. Res., 1968-69; dep. Coconino County Sheriff's Res., 1976-77. Mem. Ariz. Restaurant Assn., Nat. Restaurant Assn., Tau Omega (pres. 1966-67). Republican. Mem. Disciples of Christ. Home: 5244 W Cortez St Glendale AZ 85304 Office: Dennys Restaurants Inc 16700 Valley View La Mirada CA 90637

WAIBEL, CURTIS DU PONT, merchant banker; b. Passaic, N.J., Dec. 18, 1958; s. William Joseph and Cathleen duPont (Kirk) W. BA in Internat. Affairs, Bucknell U., 1981; MBA, U. Va., 1986. Mktg. rep. IBM Corp., Dallas, 1981-84; assoc. Bankers Trust Co., L.A., N.Y.C., London, 1985-89; v.p. Banque Paribas, L.A., 1989—. Charter mem. Big D Beat Am. Heart Assn., Dallas, 1982. Republican. Roman Catholic. Home: 136 S Roxbury Dr #4 Beverly Hills CA 90212 Office: Banque Paribas 2029 Century Pk E Los Angeles CA 90067

WAIDE, JACQUELINE ANN, aeronautical educator; b. Petersburg, Va., Sept. 18, 1938; d. William Edward and Elizabeth L. (Hunt) Tench; 1 child from previous marriage: Catherine Elizabeth; m. Jeffery William Hanson, Feb. 14, 1989. B of Aeronautics, Embry-Riddle, 1982-84; EdD, Calif. Coast U., 1983-85. Cert. tchr, airline transport pilot, FAA flight and ground instr, FAA flight examiner. Ground and flight instr. Nystrom Aviation, Palo Alto, Calif., 1966-68; instr. Ohlone Coll., Fremont, Calif., 1968—; cons. to adminstrn. FAA, Washington, 1963-70. Author: (with others) An Invitation to Fly Viewer Guide, 1985-86, 88-89. Recipient Unique Accomplishments in Am. Aviation, FAA, Washington, 1964, Outstanding Contribution to Transport Industry, Airport Execs., San Jose, Calif., 1974, Flight Instr. of the Year, FAA, Oakland, Calif., 1976. Mem. No. Calif. Examiner Assn. (pres.). Lodge: Order of Eastern Star. Office: Ohlone Coll 43600 Mission Blvd Fremont CA 94539

WAIHEE, JOHN DAVID, III, governor of Hawaii, lawyer; b. Honokaa, Hawaii, May 19, 1946; m. Lynne Kobashigawa; children: John David, Jennifer. B.A. in History and Bus., Andrews U., 1968; postgrad., Central Mich. U., 1973; J.D., U. Hawaii, 1976. Bar: Hawaii 1976. Community edn. coordinator Benton Harbor (Mich.) Area Schs., 1968-70, asst. dir. community edn., 1970-71; program evaluator, adminstrv. asst. to dirs., planner Honolulu Model Cities Program, 1971-73; sr. planner Office Human Resources City and County of Honolulu, 1973-74, program mgr. Office Human Resources, 1974-75; assoc. Shim, Sigal, Tam & Naito, Honolulu, 1975-79; ptnr. Waihee, Manuia, Yap, Pablo & Hoe, Honolulu, 1979-82; mem. Hawaiian Ho. of Reps., 1980-82; lt. gov. State of Hawaii, Honolulu, 1982-86, gov., 1986—. Del. 1978 Constnl. Conv.; del. Hawaii Dem. State Conv., 1972,74, 76, 78, 82; dir. and past pres. Kalihi-Palama Community Council; mem. steering com. Goals for Hawaii Orgn., past chmn. land use goals com., past co-chmn. outreach com.; past bd. dirs. Hawaii Sr. Citizens Travel Bd.; past mem. State Council on Housing and Constrn. Industry; mem. Kalihi-Palama Hawaiian Civic Club; past bd. dirs. Legal Aid Soc. of Hawaii, Alu Like. Mem. Hawaii Bar Assn. (chmn. unauthorized practice of law com. 1979, chmn. legis com. 1980), ABA, U. Hawaii Law Sch. Alumni, Filipino C. of C. Lodge: Kalakaua Lions. Office: Office of Gov State Capitol 5th Fl Honolulu HI 96813 *

WAIN, CHRISTOPHER HENRY, JR., marketing executive; b. L.A., Dec. 3, 1951; s. Christopher and Jeane (Thomas) W.; m. Katrina Sumner, Feb. 6, 1986. BA, Lafayette Coll., 1973; postgrad., Harvard U., 1973; MBA, UCLA, 1981. Cert. bus. communicator. Copywriter Prentice Hall, Englewood Cliffs, N.J., 1973-76; advt. prodn. mgr. Goodyear Pub., Santa Monica, Calif., 1976-80; advt. specialist Hewlett Packard, Corvallis, Oreg., 1981-83; channel support mgr. Hewlett Packard, Cupertino, Calif., 1983-84; communications mgr. Intel Corp., Hillsboro, Oreg., 1984—. Mem. Oreg. Direct Mktg. Assn., Bus. & Profl. Advt. Assn., Portland Advt. Fedn., Beta Gamma Sigma. Office: Intel Corp 5200 NE Elan Young Pkwy Hillsboro OR 97169

WAINER, STANLEY ALLEN, electronics industry executive; b. L.A., May 10, 1926; s. Calman and Katherine (Copeland) W.; m. Shirlene Joy Goldberg, Feb. 3, 1949; 1 child, William Edward. B.S. with honors, UCLA, 1950, postgrad., 1958. Acct. Price Waterhouse & Co., L.A., 1950-55; chief fin. and adminstrv. officer Paramount Pictures Corp., and subsidiaries, 1955-60; v.p., sec.-treas. Royal Industries, Pasadena, Calif., 1960-61; with Wyle Labs., El Segundo, Calif., 1962—; pres. Wyle Labs., 1970-85, chief exec. officer, 1979-88, chmn., 1984—, also dir., mem. exec. com.; dir. City Nat. Corp./City Nat. Bank; Pres., dir. UCLA Bus. Sch. Alumni Assn., 1968-69. Trustee, mem. exec. com. UCLA Found., 1972—; bd. visitors UCLA Grad. Sch. Mgmt., 1983—; bd. dirs. NCCJ, 1974-80, bd. govs., 1980—; bd. dirs. Los Angeles Urban League, 1978-80; regent U. Calif., 1980-82; trustee Orthopaedic Hosp., Los Angeles, 1974-81, adv. council, 1980—; bd. dirs. Coro Found., 1982—, El Segundo Ednl. Found., 1984—. Served with USNR, 1944-46. Named Man of Yr. City of Hope Aids, 1979; honoree NCCJ, 1981. Mem. Financial Execs. Inst., Technion Soc. (past dir.), Am. Inst. CPAs, C. of C. of U.S., Calif. C. of C. (dir.), L.A. C. of C. (dir. 1980—, chmn. fed. affairs com.), UCLA Alumni Assn. (dir. 1979—, pres. 1980-82), Soc. Order Blue Shield, Town Hall, Beta Gamma Sigma. Clubs: Regency, Riviera Tennis, Century West, Le Club de l'Ermitage, Hillcrest Country. Home: 1151 Hilary Ln Beverly Hills CA 90210 Office: Wyle Labs 128 Maryland St El Segundo CA 90245

WAINESS, MARCIA WATSON, legal administrator; b. Bklyn., Dec. 17, 1949; d. Stanley and Seena (Klein) Watson; m. Steven Richard Wainess, Aug. 7, 1975. Student, UCLA, 1967-71, 80-81, Grad. Sch. Mgmt. Exec. Program, 1987-88, grad. Grad. Sch. Mgmt. Exec. Program, 1988. Office mgr., paralegal Lewis, Marenstein & Kadar, L.A., 1977-81; office mgr. Rosenfeld, Meyer & Susman, Beverly Hills, Calif., 1981-83; adminstr. Rudin, Richman & Appel, Beverly Hills, 1983; dir. adminstrn. Kadison, Pfaelzer, L.A., 1983-87; exec. dir. Richards, Watson and Gershon, L.A., 1987—; faculty mem. UCLA Legal Mgmt. & Adminstrn. Program, 1983, U. So. Calif. Paralegal Program, L.A., 1985; mem. adv. bd. atty. asst. tng. program, UCLA, 1984-88. Mem. ABA (chmn. Displaywrite Users Group 1986, legal tech. adv. coun. litigation support working group 1986-87), State Bar Calif., L.A. County Bar Assn. (exec. com. law office mgmt. sect.), Assn. Profl. Law Firm Mgrs., Assn. Legal Adminstrs. (asst. regional v.p. Calif. 1987-88, regional v.p. 1988-89, pres. Beverly Hills chpt. 1985-86, membership chmn. 1984-85, chmn. new adminstrn. sect. 1982-84, others). Office: Richards Watson & Gershon 333 S Hope St 38th Fl Los Angeles CA 90071

WAINIO, MARK ERNEST, loss control specialist; b. Virginia, Minn., Apr. 18, 1953. BA, Gustavus Adolphus Coll., 1975. Cert. safety profl., assoc. loss control mgmt., assoc. risk mgmt., CPCU. Carpenter ABI Contracting Inc., Virginia, 1975-77; co-owner Mesabi Builders, Albuquerque and Eveleth, Minn., 1977-79; sr. engring. rep. Aetna Life & Casualty, Albuquerque, 1979-86; loss control specialist CNA Ins. Cos., Albuquerque, 1986—; owner M.E.W. Safety Assocs., 1989—. Mem. Am. Soc. Safety Engrs., CPCU. Home: 5525 Sonata Dr NE Albuquerque NM 87111 Office: CNA Ins Companies 8500 Menaul NE Albuquerque NM 87112

WAINWRIGHT, FRED EDWARD, JR., venture capital consultant; b. Bogota, Colombia, May 22, 1963; came to U.S., 1980 (parents Am. citizens); s. Fred Edward and Aura Sylvia (Murillo) W. BS in Petroleum Engring., Stanford U., 1984, BA in Quantitative Econs., 1987. Naval/drilling engr. Sedco-Schlumberger, Brazil, Atlantic Ocean, Gulf of Mex., Dallas, 1984-86; securities analyst Dean Witter Reynolds, Palo Alto, Calif., 1987; pres. Wainwright and Assoc., Palo Alto, 1987—; cons. Instl. Venture Ptnr., Menlo Park, Calif., 1987, McCown Deleeuw and Co., Menlo Park, 1988. Contbg. author Am. Poetry Anthology, 1987. Voter registrar Coll. Rep., Stanford, Calif., 1982; mem. Hunger Project; fundraiser Nathan Rosenberg for Congress, Calif., 1988; guest seminar leader and leadership course coord. Werner Erhard and Assoc., San Francisco, 1988—. Mem. World Future Soc., Am. Cons. League (cert. cons.), Am. Mgmt. Assn., Commonwealth Club, Masons. Roman Catholic. Office: 704 University Dr Menlo Park CA 94025

WAITMAN, B. A., investment banking company executive; b. Ft. Collins, Colo., May 17, 1946; d. Henry and Lydia (Frickel) Kerbel; 1 child, Craig A. Adminstrv. asst. Fleishcer & Co., Phoenix, 1970-78; legal adminstr. Shank, Irwin & Holmes, Denver, 1978-80; v.p. Franchise Fin. Corp. Am., Phoenix, 1980-86, sr. v.p., 1986—. Republican. Baptist. Office: Franchise Fin Corp Am 3443 N Central Ave 500 Financial Ctr Phoenix AZ 85012

WAITON, RUDOLPH O., physician; b. Monessen, Pa., June 11, 1922; s. Lawrence and Anna (Ostrander) W.; m. Marilyn Earle, Dec. 8, 1979; children: Richard, CorryAnn, Melanie, Thomas. BS, U. Pitts., 1949; MA, Stanford U., 1954, PhD, 1956; DO, Kirksville Coll., 1965; MD, U. Oreg., 1974. Diplomate Am. Bd. Osteo. Medicine. Intern Standring Meml. Hosp., Seattle, 1965-66; resident in rehab. medicine VA Hosp., Portland, Oreg., 1972-74; practice osteo. medicine and rehab. and phys. medicine Los Gatos, Calif., 1975—; mem. staff. Valley West Gen. Hosp.; pres., chmn. bd. dirs. Calif. Inst. Rehabilitative and Preventive Medicine; adj. prof. Coll. Osteo. Medicine of the Pacific. Served with USAAF, World War II, Korea. Decorated DFC with oak leaf cluster, Air medal with three oak leaf clusters, Purple Heart; recipient Nobel Peace Prize, 1985, diplomate Am. Osteo. Coll. Rehab. Medicine. Fellow Am. Acad. Med. Preventics, Internat. Coll. Gen. Practice (charter), Internat. Coll. Applied Nutrition; mem. AMA, Calif. Med. Assn., Am. Acad. Family Physicians, Am. Acad. Osteopathy, Santa Clara County Med. Assn., Osteo. Physicians and Surgeons Calif., Fed. Aviation Med. Assn., Am. Osteo. Assn., Am. Coll. Rehab. Medicine, Internat. Acad. Preventive Medicine, Orthomolecular Med. Soc., Union Concerned Scientists, Stanford chpt. Physicians for Social Responsibility Beyond War, Internat. Physicians for the Prevention of Nuclear War, Better World Soc., Plowshares, Inc., Sane. Lodges: Elks, Rotary, Masons. Office: 221 Almendra Ave Los Gatos CA 95030

WAKAI, WENDY ANN NAOMI, dentist; b. Honolulu, Dec. 8, 1958; d. Warren Teiji and Betty Yoshiko (Kuramoto) W.; m. Calvin Yoshito Shiroma, Aug. 23, 1986. BA, U. Hawaii, 1983; DMD, U. Portland, 1987. Dental hygienist instr. U. Hawaii, Honolulu, 1983; dental hygienist Drs. Yoshida, Uyehara, Honolulu, 1982-84; dental resident St. Francis Med. Ctr., Honolulu, 1987-88. Mem. ADA, Honolulu County Dental Soc., Am. Assn. Women Dentists, Acad. Gen. Dentistry, Am. Soc. Dentistry for Children, Southshore Study Club, Psi Omega. Democrat. Mem. Christian Ch.

WAKATSUKI, JAMES H., state supreme court associate justice; b. Honolulu, Aug. 17, 1929; m. Irene Natsuko Yoshimura; children—Janie, Stuart, Cora. Student, U. Hawaii, 1947, Bowling Green State U., 1949-51; LL.B., U. Wis., 1954. Mem. Hawaii Ho. of Reps., 1958-80, speaker, 1974-80; judge Circuit Ct., 1980-83; assoc. justice Hawaii Supreme Ct., Honolulu, 1983—. Served with U.S. Army, 1948-49; mem. Res. (ret.). Office: Hawaii Supreme Ct PO Box 2560 Honolulu HI 96804 also: Hawaii Supreme Ct Honolulu HI 96813

WAKE, DAVID BURTON, biology educator, researcher; b. Webster, S.D., June 8, 1936; s. Thomas B. and Ina H. (Solem) W.; m. Marvalee Hendricks, June 23, 1962; 1 child, Thomas Andrew. B.A., Pacific Luth. U., 1958; M.S., U. So. Calif., 1960, Ph.D., 1964. Instr. anatomy and biology U. Chgo., 1964-66, asst. prof. anatomy and biology, 1966-69; assoc. prof. zoology U. Calif., Berkeley, 1969-72, prof., 1972—; dir. Mus. Vertebrate Zoology U. Calif., Berkeley, 1971—. Author: Biology, 1979; co-editor: Functional Vertebrate Morphology, 1985, Complex Organismal functions: Integration and Evolution in the Vertebrates, 1989. Recipient Quantrell Teaching award U. Chgo., 1967, Outstanding Alumnus award Pacific Luth. U., 1979; grantee NSF, 1965—; Guggenheim fellow, 1982. Fellow AAAS, Calif. Acad. Scis., NAS/NRC Bd. Biology; mem. Soc. Study Evolution (pres. 1983, editor 1979-81), Am. Soc. Naturalists (pres. 1989), Soc. Systematic Zoology (pres. 1989, council 1980-84), Herpetologist's League (Disting. Herpetologist 1984), Am. Soc. Ichthyologist and Herpetologists (bd. govs.). Home: 999 Middlefield Rd Berkeley CA 94708

WAKE, MARVALEE HENDRICKS, zoology educator; b. Orange, Calif., July 31, 1939; d. Marvin Carlton and Velvalee (Borter) H.; m. David B. Wake, June 23, 1962; 1 child, Thomas A. BA, U. So. Calif., 1961, MS, 1964, PhD, 1968. Teaching asst./instr. U. Ill., Chgo., 1964-68, asst. prof., 1968-69; lectr. U. Calif., Berkeley, 1969-73, asst. prof., 1973-76, assoc. prof., 1976-80, prof. zoology, 1980—, chmn. dept. zoology, 1985—, assoc. dean Coll. Letters and Sci., 1975-78. Editor, co-author: Hyman's Comparative Vertical Anatomy, 1979; co-author: Biology, 1978; contbr. articles to profl. jours. NSF grantee, 1978—; Guggenheim fellow, 1988-89. Fellow AAAS, Calif. Acad. Scis.; mem. Am. Soc. Ichthyology and Herpetology (pres. 1984, bd. govs. 1978—), Internat. Union Biol. Scis. (U.S. Nat. Com. 1986-92). Home: 999 Middlefield Rd Berkeley CA 94708 Office: U Calif Dept Zoology Berkeley CA 94720

WAKEFIELD, HOWARD, medical representative; b. Chgo., Dec. 19, 1936; s. Howard and Thelma Elizabeth (Roach) W.; m. Laura Collier, Jan. 1, 1957 (div. June 1976); children: Kimberly, Howard III, Anthony. BA in Econs., U. Ariz., 1959. Sales rep. N.Y. Life, Tucson, 1959-63; sr. med. rep. Pfizer Pharm., Ventura County, Calif., 1963—. Fund raiser Am. Heart Assn., Ventura, Calif., 1983—; mgr. Pleasant Valley Boys Baseball, Camarillo, Calif., 1968-82. Mem. Ventura County Pharmacy Assn. Republican. Home: PO Box 626 Somis CA 93066 Office: Pfizer Pharm 16700 Red Hill Irvine CA 92714

WAKELAND, ROBIN GAY, graphic designer; b. Portsmouth, Va., June 29, 1948; d. William R. and Gloria (Suba) W.; children: Adrian Levin, James P. McCray II. BFA, U. N.C., Chapel Hill, 1972. Graphic designer Design Graphics, Santa Fe, 1979—; instr. Santa Fe Community Coll., 1989—, U. Los Alamos, 1988. Office: Design Graphics PO Box 15794 Santa Fe NM 87506

WALBA, DAVID MARK, chemistry educator; b. Oakland, Calif., June 29, 1949; s. Harold and Beatrice (Alpert) W.; m. Cassandra Geneson, Oct. 30, 1981; 1 child, Paul Geneson. BS, U. Calif., Berkeley, 1971; PhD, Calif. Inst. Tech., 1975; postdoctoral, UCLA, 1977. Asst. prof. chemistry U. Colo., Boulder, 1977-83, assoc. prof., 1983-87, prof., 1987—; cons. Displaytech Inc., Boulder, 1986—. Contbr. articles to profl. jours.; patentee in field. Sloan Found. fellow 1982-84; Dreyfus Tchr. scholar 1984-86. Mem. Am. Chem. Soc., Sigma Xi. Office: U Colo Dept Chemistry Box 215 Boulder CO 80309-0215

WALCHA, NANCY LA DONNA, flight attendant, stress consultant; b. Indpls., Feb. 12, 1947; d. Dennis L. and Eva Afton (Sitter) Stephens; m. Richard S. Walcha, Apr. 29, 1974 (div. Oct. 1986); 1 child, Rodney Alexander; m. Jeffery P. Mihalic, Oct. 14, 1989. Student, Ind. State U., 1965-66, Ind. U., 1966-68, Coll. San Mateo, Calif., 1975-80, George Meany Ctr., Washington, 1986. Dir. John Robert Powers Modeling Sch., Indpls., 1970-72; flight attendant United Airlines, San Francisco, 1972—, in-flight supr., 1977-80; owner, mgr. cons. Let's Talk Pacifica, Calif., 1987--; condr. tng. employee's assistance program United Airlines, San Francisco, 1986; staff instr. nat. employee assistance program George Meany Ctr., 1988. Vol. Suicide Prevention Crisis Ctr., San Mateo County, 1980-84; adv. Rape Crisis Svcs., San Mateo County, 1983-84; lectr. suicide to high schs. and clubs, San Mateo County, 1980-84. Nominee Commendation, Sta. KRON-TV, 1983. Mem. Assn. Flight Attendants (lectr., speaker, rep. to Pres.'s Coun. on Drug Abuse in Industry and Transp. 1987). Democrat. Office: Lets Talk PO Box 1032 Pacifica CA 94044

WALD, ROBERT GRAY, optical engineer; b. Kansas City, Mo., Nov. 9, 1963; s. Robert Irwin and Helen Jane (Gray) W. BS in Elec. Engring., Kans. State U., 1986; MS in Optical Engring., U. Colo., Boulder, 1987—. Power engring. intern Burns & McDonnel Engring., Kansas City, Mo., 1984; control engring. intern Black & Veatch Engring., Overland Park, Kans., 1985, Kansas City, 1986; artificial intelligence researcher Kans. State U., Manhattan, 1986-87; optical artificial intelligence computing researcher Dept. Elec. and Computer Engring. U. Colo., Boulder, 1987-88; laser power energy engr. Nat. Inst. of Stnadards and Technology, Boulder, 1988—. Contbr. articles to profl. jours. Mem. IEEE, Nat. Soc. Profl. Engr. (v.p. 1985-86), Computer Soc. of IEEE, Am. Assn. Artificial Intelligence, Soc. for Photo-Instrumentation Engr. Roman Catholic. Home: 513 University Ave Boulder CO 80302 Office: 325 Broadway Mailstop 724.02 Boulder CO 80303

WALDEN, JULIE MARIE, teacher; b. Chgo., Feb. 18, 1947; d. Clarence William and Elizabeth Grace (Kopnicky) Bayliff; m. Randy Dean Walden May 4, 1968 (div. Aug. 1981). BA, UCLA, 1968; MA, Sonoma State U., 1980. Reading specialist, elem. edn., gifted and talented credentials, Calif. Tchr. LA. Unified Sch. Dist., 1969-72, curriculum coord., 1972-73, tchr., 1973-74; reading resources tchr. Douglas Unified Sch. Dist., Douglas, Ariz., 1976-77; tchr. Strawberry Sch., Bennett Valley Unified Sch. Dist., Santa Rosa, Calif., 1977—; instr. Sonoma State U., Rohnert Park, Calif., 1984—; cons. Sonoma County, L.A., 1972-74, Santa Rosa, Calif., 1981—; part-time instr. Losa Jr. Coll. Supr. Safe Ride, Santa Rosa, 1988-89; educator team Beyond War, Santa Rosa, 1986—; mem. Nature Conservancy, Santa Rosa, N.Y.C., 1981—, Sister City, Santa Rosa, 1988-89. Mem. Sonoma County Math. Coun., Gateway Reading Coun., Bennett Valley Tchrs. Assn. (v.p. 1985-86, pres. 1986-87). Democrat. Office: Strawberry School 2311 Horseshoe Dr Santa Rosa CA 95405

WALDEN, OLIVER JOHN, data processing specialist; b. Greenville, Tex., Mar. 23, 1946; s. Oliver John and Kate (Beene) W.; m. Janice Leona Payne, Mar. 4, 1966; children: John Andrew, Jennifer Lynn. AA, Fullerton Jr. Coll., 1967; BA, Calif. State U., Fullerton, 1979. Computer operator Anaheim (Calif.) Union High Sch. Dist., 1970-76, programmer, 1976-79, systems analyst, 1979-81, asst. dir. data processing, 1981, dir., 1981—; mem. adv. com. Calif. State Dept. Edn., Sacramento, 1985—. Deacon 1st So. Bapt. Ch., Anaheim, 1971-81, Crescent Bapt. Ch., Anaheim, 1981—. Served with U.S. Army, 1968. Mem. Assn. Computing Machinery, Calif. Assn. Sch. Bus. Ofcls., Calif. Ednl. Data Processing Assn. Democrat. Home: 2775 E Verde Ave Anaheim CA 92806 Office: Anaheim Union High Sch Dist 501 Crescent Way Anaheim CA 92803-3520

WALDMAN, BARRY JEROME, aerospace company executive; b. Orlando, Fla., Oct. 29, 1940; s. George Robert and Mildred Freling W.; m. Phyllis Joan Biddelman, June 17, 1962 (div. 1984); children: Douglas, Adrianne; m. Marsha Grossman Greene, Dec. 21, 1984. BS in Aeronautics, Rensselaer U., 1962; MS in Aeronautics, U. So. Calif., 1965. Project engr. advanced propulsion Rockwell Internat. Rocketdyne, Canoga Park, Calif., 1965-71, mgr. laser mktg., 1972-76; chief engr. program lasers Rockwell Internat. Rocketdyne, Canoga Park, 1976-80; dir. laser programs Rockwell Internat. Rocketdyne, Canoga Park, Calif., 1980-86, v.p. advanced programs, 1986-88; v.p. Nat. Aero Space Plane Rockwell Internat. Rocketdyne, Canoga Park, 1988—; gen. mgr. Rockwell Power Systems Co., Albuquerque, N.M., 1987-89; also bd. dirs. Rockwell Power Systems Co., Albuquerque. Recipient Engring. 88 Merit award, San Fernando Valley Engrs. Coun., 1988, Disting. Sci. & Tech. Achievments award, Nat. Soc. Profl. Engrs., Calif. Soc. Profl. Engrs., 1988. Home: 7051 Shade Tree Ln Westhills CA 91307 Office: Rocketdyne Div Rockwell Internat 6633 Canoga Ave Canoga Park CA 91303

WALDO, BURTON CORLETT, lawyer; b. Seattle, Aug. 11, 1920; s. William Earl and Ruth Ernestine (Corlett) W.; m. Margaret Jane Hoar, Aug. 24, 1946; children: James Chandler, Bruce Corlett. BA, U. Wash., 1941, JD, 1948. Bar: Wash. 1949. Assoc. Vedova, Horswill & Yeomans, Seattle, 1949-50, Kahin, Carmody & Horswill, Seattle, 1950-54; ptnr. Keller Rohrback & predecessor firms, Seattle, 1954-86; mng. ptnr. Keller Rohrback & predecessor firms, 1978-83, sr. ptnr., 1983—. Mem. Seattle Bd. Theater Suprs., 1958-61, Mcpl. League of Seattle/King County, 1949—. Capt. U.S. Army, 1942-46; ETO. Mem. Seattle-Kikng County Bar Assn. (trustee 1965-68), ABA, Wash. Bar Assn., Wash. Def. Trial lawyers Assn., Fedn. of Ins. and Corporate Counsel, Internat. Assn. Def. Counsel, Rainier Club, Wash. Athletic, Delta Tau Delta, Phi Delta Phi, Alpha Kappa Psi.

WALDSCHMIDT, PAUL EDWARD, clergyman; b. Evansville, Ind., Jan. 7, 1920; s. Edward Benjamin and Olga Marie (Moers) W. B.A., U. Notre Dame, 1942; student, Holy Cross Coll., Washington, 1942-45; S.T.L., Laval U., Que., Can., 1947; S.T.D., Angelicum U., Rome, Italy, 1948. Ordained priest Roman Catholic Ch., 1946; prof. apologetics and dogmatic theology Holy Cross Coll., 1949-55; v.p. U. Portland, 1955-62, dean faculties, 1956-60, pres., 1962-78; aux. bishop of Portland, 1978—; mem. NCCB Com. on Doctrine; cons. Migration and Tourism. Mem. Cath. Theol. Soc. Am. (v.p. 1954-55), NEA, Delta Epsilon Sigma. Club: K.C. (4 deg.). Address: 5402 N Strong St Portland OR 97203

WALKER, BROOKS, JR., retired leasing company executive; b. Oakland, Calif., Apr. 28, 1928; s. Brooks and Marjory (Walker) W.; m. Margaret Myles Kirby, May 21, 1955 (dec. May 18, 1981); children: Kirby, Brooks III, Leslie; m. Danielle Musulin Carlisle, Jan. 4, 1985. B.A., U. Calif.-Berkeley, 1950; M.B.A. in Finance, Harvard U., 1957. Financial analyst Shasta Forest Corp., San Francisco, 1956; with U.S. Leasing Internat., Inc., San Francisco, 1957-87, asst. to treas., asst. to pres., treas., v.p. and treas., sr. v.p., dir., 1957-63, pres., 1963-69, chmn. bd., 1969-87; mng. gen. partner Ala

Moana Hawaii Properties; dir. The Gap Stores, Inc., Pope & Talbot, Inc., Di Giorgio Corp. Chmn. bd. San Francisco Mus. Modern Art; bd. dirs. San Francisco Opera Assn., Pacific Legal Found., Smith Kettlewell Eye Research Found.; trustee Santa Catalina Sch. Served to lt. (j.g.) USNR, 1951-55. Mem. Delta Kappa Epsilon.

WALKER, BURTON LEITH, engineering writer, psychotherapist; b. Mt. Morris Twp., Mich., Oct. 23, 1927; s. Dalton Hugh and Muriel Joyce (Black) W.; m. Norva Jean Trochman, June 28, 1949; children—Paul, Cynthia Halverson, Mark; m. 2d, Carol Jean DeAndrea, July 31, 1982. Cert. psychology. tchr., lic. psychotherapist, hypnotherapist, Calif. A.A., Allan Hancock Coll., 1971; B.A., Chapman Coll., 1974, M.A., 1975. Contract estimator Ryan Aeronaut., San Diego, 1949-59; logistics rep. GD/A, San Diego, 1960-62; systems engr., cons. fgn. service Ralph M. Parsons, Los Angeles, 1962-68; lead engring. writer, sr. analyst Fed. Electric, Vandenberg AFB, Calif., 1969-86 ; psychotherapist Access (formerly Employee Counseling Services), Vandenberg Village, Family Guidance Service, Santa Ynez, Calif., part time prof. Allan Hancock Coll., Santa Maria, Calif., small bus. owner 1974. Active Santa Ynez Valley Presbyn. Ch.; mem. Republican Nat. Com. Served with USN, 1946-48. Mem. Nat. Mgmt. Assn. (Outstanding Service award 1982), Am. Assn. Counseling and Devel., Calif. Assn. Marriage and Family Therapists, Solvang Bus. Assn., Assn. Advancement Ret. People. Republican. Home: 3149 Hwy 246 E Santa Ynez CA 93460

WALKER, CAROLYN LOUISE, nursing, researcher, educator; b. Ft. George, Wash., Apr. 4, 1947; d. Marvin John and Louise Olive (Billings) W.; m. Simon I. Zemel, Apr. 6, 1968 (div. 1981); children: Michelle, Brent Zemel. AA, Fullerton (Calif.) Coll., 1968; BSN, Calif. State U., Fullerton, 1976; MSN, Calif. State U., L.A., 1979; PhD in Nursing, U. Utah, 1986. RN, Calif., Utah. Staff nurse Children's Hosp. Orange (Calif.) County, 1969-71; instr. nursing Cypress (Calif.) Coll., 1978-81, 81-82, Saddleback Coll., Mission Viejo, Calif., 1979-80; nurse oncology Children's Hosp. Orange County, 1980-81; asst. prof. U. Utah, Salt Lake City, 1984-85, San Diego State U., 1986—. Mem. editorial rev. bd. Am. Jour. Continuing Edn. in Nursing, 1987—, Oncology Nursing Forum, 1988—. Mem. children's com. Am. Cancer Soc., Salt Lake City, 1984-86. Mem. Am. Nurse Assn., Assn. Pediatric Oncology Nurses Rsch. (chair 1983—), Oncology Nursing Soc. Democrat. Episcopalian. Office: San Diego State U Sch of Nursing San Diego CA 92182-0254

WALKER, DAVID EARL, military officer; b. Denton, Tex., June 12, 1958; s. Henry Leon and Katherine Jane (Andersen) W.; m. Takako Mochizuki, June 20, 1981; children: Christine, Cathleen, Frances, Anne. BS in Aerospace Engring., U. Tex., 1979, MS in Aerospace Engring., 1980; grad., USAF Test Pilot Sch., 1986. Commd. 2d lt. USAF, 1980, advanced through grades to maj., 1983; weapon systems officer 38th Tactical Reconnaissance Squadron, Zweibrucken AFB, Fed. Republic Germany, 1981-84, 16th Tactical Reconnaissance Squadron, Shaw AFB, S.C., 1984-85; flight test weapon system officer Edwards AFB, Calif., 1985—. Contbr. articles profl. jours. Recipient Raymond L. Jones USAF, 1986. Mem. AIAA, Soc. Flight Test Engrs., Air Force Assn. Republican. Home: 6806 Chamberlin Ave Edwards AFB CA 93523 Office: 6510 TW/TEVJ Edwards AFB CA 93523

WALKER, DEWARD EDGAR, JR., anthropologist, educator; b. Johnson City, Tenn., Aug. 3, 1935; s. Deward Edgar and Matilda Jane (Clark) W.; m. Candace A. Walker; children: Alice, Deward III, Mary Jane, Sarah, Daniel, Joseph Benjamin. Student, Eastern Oreg. Coll., 1953-54, 56-58, Mex. City Coll., 1958; BA in Anthropology with honors, U. Oreg., 1960-61, PhD in Anthropology, 1964; postgrad., Wash. State U., 1962. Asst. prof. anthropology George Washington U., Washington, 1964-65; asst. prof. anthropology Wash. State U., Pullman, 1965-67, research collaborator, 1967-69; assoc. prof., chmn. dept. sociology and anthropology, dir. lab. and anthropology U. Idaho, Moscow, 1967-69; prof. U. Colo., Boulder, 1969—, research assoc. in population processes program of inst. behavioral sci., 1969-73, assoc. dean Grad. Sch., 1973-76; affiliate faculty U. Idaho, 1971—. Co-editor Northwest Anthropol. Research Notes, 1966—, editor, Plateau Vol: Handbook of North American Indians, 1971—; contbr. articles to profl. jours. Served with U.S. Army, 1954-62. Fellow NSF, 1961, NDEA, 1961-64. Fellow Am. Anthropol. Assn. (assoc. editor Am. Anthropologist 1973-74), Soc. Applied Anthropology (life, exec. com. 1970-79, treas. 1976-79, chmn. High Plains Regional sect. 1980-82, cons., expert witness tribes of N.W., editor Human Orgn. 1970-76); mem. AAAS, Am. Acad. Polit. Social Scis., Northwest Anthropol. Conf. Home: PO Box 4147 Boulder CO 80306 Office: U Colo Dept Anthropology Box 233 Boulder CO 80309

WALKER, DUNCAN EDWARD, military officer; b. Washington, Aug. 2, 1942; s. Edward John and Katherine Edith (Duncan) W. BA in Indsl. Psychology, N.Mex. State U., 1965; MS in Systems Mgmt., U. So. Calif., 1978; MPA, Golden Gate U., 1980. Commd. 2d lt. USAF, 1965, advanced through grades to lt. col., 1981; grad. Squadron Officers Sch., 1973, Air Command and Staff Coll., 1974, Indsl. Coll. Armed Forces, 1977; chief devel. and deployment br. ICBM requirements SAC, Offutt AFB, Nebr., 1981-84; dep. for ICBM ops. and evaluation Air Force Operational Test and Evaluation Ctr., Vandenberg AFB, Calif., 1984-88; program engr. Fed. Electric Co., Western Space and Missile Ctr., Vandenberg AFB, Calif., 1988—. Decorated Bronze Star, Meritorious Service medal with two oak leaf cluster, Air Force Commendation medal with three oak leaf clusters. Mem. Internat. Test and Evaluation Assn., Air Force Assn., Mental Health Assn., Mil. Order of World Wars, Am. Legion. Republican. Methodist. Lodge: Elks. Home: 113 N Y St Lompoc CA 93436 Office: ITT/FEC-WTR Vandenberg AFB CA 93437

WALKER, ELJANA M. DU VALL, civic worker; b. France, Jan. 18, 1924; came to U.S., 1948; naturalized, 1954; student Med. Inst., U. Paris, 1942-47; m. John S. Walker, Jr., Dec. 31, 1947; children—John, Peter, Barbara. Pres., Loyola Sch. PTA, 1958-59; bd. dirs. Santa Claus shop, 1959-73; treas. Archdiocese Denver Catholic Women, 1962-64; rep. Cath. Parent-Tchr League, 1962-65; pres. Aux. Denver Gen. Hosp., 1966-69; precinct committeewoman Arapahoe County Republican Women's Com., 1973-74; mem. re-election com. Arapahoe County Rep. Party, 1973-78, Reagan election com., 1980; block worker Arapahoe County March of Dimes, Heart Assn., Hemophilia Drive, Muscular Dystrophy and Multiple Sclerosis Drive, 1978-81; cen. city asst. Guild Debutante Charities, Inc. Recipient Distinguished Service award Am.-by-choice, 1966; named to Honor Roll, ARC, 1971. Mem. Cherry Hills Symphony, Lyric Opera Guild, Alliance Franciase (life mem.), ARC, Civic Ballet Guild (life mem.), Needlework Guild Am. (v.p. 1980-82), Kidney Found. (life), Denver Art Mus., U. Denver Art and Conservation Assns. (chmn. 1980-82), U. Denver Women's Library Assn., Chancellors Soc, Passage Inc. Roman Catholic. Clubs: Union (Chgo.); Denver Athletic, 26 (Denver); Welcome to Colo. Internat. Address: 6185 S Columbine Way Littleton CO 80121

WALKER, FRANCIS JOSEPH, lawyer; b. Tacoma, Aug. 5, 1922; s. John McSweeney and Sarah Veronica (Meechan) W.; m. Julia Corinne O'Brien, Jan. 27, 1951; children—Vincent Paul, Monica Irene Hylton, Jill Marie Nudell, John Michael, Michael Joseph, Thomas More. B.A., St. Martin's Coll., 1947; J.D., U. Wash., 1950. Bar: Wash. Asst. atty. gen. State of Wash., 1950-51; sole practice, Olympia, Wash., 1951—; gen. counsel Wash. Cath. Conf., 1967-76. Served to lt. (j.g.) USNR, 1943-46; PTO. Home: 2723 Hillside Dr Olympia WA 98501 Office: 203 E 4th Ave Ste 301 Olympia WA 98501

WALKER, HENRY ALEXANDER, JR., diversified corporation executive; b. Honolulu, Mar. 5, 1922; s. H. Alexander and Una (Craig) W.; m. Nancy Johnston, Mar. 10, 1946; children: Henry Alexander III, Susan Walker Kowen. Student, Harvard U., 1940-42, Columbia U., 1946-47. With AMFAC, Inc., Honolulu, 1947—, v.p., ops., 1966, exec. v.p., 1966-67, pres., 1967-74, chief exec. officer, chmn. bd., 1974-78, chmn., chief exec. officer, pres., 1978-83, chmn., 1983—, chief exec. officer, 1987—; bd. dirs. Hawaiian Telephone Co., Gulf Westerns, Inc. Bd. dirs. Hawaii Maritime Ctr., Straub Found., East-West Ctr. Found., Aloha United Way; mem. adv. bd. U. Hawaii Coll. Bus. Adminstrn.; mem. dean's adv. bd. Chaminade U. Sch. Bus. Served with USNR, 1944-46. Mem. Hawaiian Sugar Planters Assn. Clubs: Pacific Union (San Francisco); Phoenix S.K, Massachusetts, Harvard (N.Y.C.); Pacific, Waialae Country, Oahu Country (Honolulu). Office: Amfac JMB Realty Corp 700 Bishop St Honolulu HI 96801 also: Amfac Inc 44 Montgomery St San Francisco CA 94104 *

WALKER, HENRY GILBERT, healthcare executive, consultant; b. Gowanda, N.Y., Feb. 16, 1947; s. Henry George and Grace Dayton (Moore) W.; m. Elaine Ruth Darbee, July 18, 1970 (div. Dec. 1979); 1 child, Matthew Case; m. Patricia Ann Andrade, May 14, 1983; children: Michael David, Christopher John. B.S. in Indsl. Engring., Cornell U., 1969; M.B.A., U. Chgo., 1975. Evening adminstr. Rush-Presbyn. St.-Luke's Med. Ctr., Chgo., 1973-75; mgmt. cons. Booz, Allen & Hamilton, Chgo., 1975-79; regional adminstr., v.p. S.W. Community Health Service, Albuquerque, 1979-83; adminstr., v.p. S.W. Community Health Service, 1983-86, v.p., 1986—; exec. v.p. Presbyn. Healthcare Services, Albuquerque, 1986—. Campaign mgr. United Fund, Newport, R.I., 1971, 72; bd. dirs. Park Dist., Elmhurst, Ill., 1978, 79; mem. Dist. III Community Action Com., Albuquerque, 1985; div. chmn. United Way of Albuquerque., 1985, 88. Recipient Hosp. Survey award U. Chgo., 1975, Bachmeyer award U. Chgo., 1975, Outstanding Midshipman award Cornell U., 1969; named one of Emerging Healthcare Leaders, Hosp. Forum Mag., 1985, 86, Healthcares Up and Comers, Modern Healthcare Mag., 1987. Mem. Am. Coll. Healthcare Execs.; Healthcare Fin. Mgmt. Assn., Am. Hosp. Assn., N.Mex. Hosp. Assn. (chmn. bd. dirs. 1983—), Healthcare Forum (bd. dirs.). Democrat. Presbyterian.

WALKER, JAMES DANIEL (DAN WALKER), academic adminstrator; b. Albuquerque, Feb. 15, 1940; s. Dennis Walker and Geneva Katherine (Whitehair) Walker Loy; m. Georgia Ellen May, Apr. 10, 1965; children: Danell Louise, Ryan Daniel. AA in Comml. Art, L.A. Trade Tech. Coll., 1960; BA in Fine Art, Calif. State U., 1962, MA in Design, 1966; MA in Counseling, San Jose State U., 1972, MA in Adminstrn., 1973; EdD, U. San Francisco, 1978. Tchr., asst. vice prin. Hollywood (Calif.) High Sch., 1962-65; dept. chairperson Lynbrook High Sch., Cupertino, Calif., 1965-70; instr. Milpitas (Calif.) High Sch., 1970; sales mgr. Will Ross Inc., San Jose, Calif., 1970-71; counselor Willow Glen High Sch., San Jose, Calif., 1971-75; dir. career planning, placement, contract edn. Foothill Coll., Los Altos, Calif., 1975-85; dir. The Los Rios Inst. for Bus., Govt. and Industry, Los Rios Community Coll. Dist., Sacramento, 1985—; asst. dir. Western Resource Ctr. for Coop. Edn., Atascadero, Calif., 1985—; cons. McDaniel Conf., Stanford U., Palo Alto, 1982—; cons. Master Trainers, Calif. Dept. Edn., 1975-80. Author student work book Plan Progress Grow, 1978; contbr. articles, presenter seminars in field. Founding mem. Sacramento Area Council for Total Quality, 1988—. Mem. ED-Net, Assn. Calif. Community Colls. Adminstrs., Calif. Community Coll. Adminstrs. of Occupational Edn., SAGES (cons. 1982—), Calif. Assn. Coop. Edn. (No. Calif. chair rep. 1987), Calif. Assn. Work Experience Educators, Comstock Club, West Sacramento C. of C., Sacramento Met. C. of C. Republican. Home: 6550 Countrywoods Ln Granite Bay CA 95661 Office: Los Rios Inst 1787 Tribute Rd Ste B Sacramento CA 95815

WALKER, JAMES GLENN, design engineer, entrepreneur; b. Klamath Falls, Oreg., Feb. 18, 1947; s. Glenn Leroy and Jeanie Lilian (Abraham) W.; m. Roseann Margret McClurg, Sept. 16, 1968; children: Gregory Scott, Brian Paul. A. Engring., Oreg. Inst. Tech., 1975. Cert. engring. tech. Engring. draftsman Weyerhaeuser Co., Klamath Falls, Oreg., 1972-77; tech. rep. Bonney, Bennet & Peters, Inc., Eugene, Oreg., 1977-80; design engr. Burley Industries, Coos Bay, Oreg., 1980-81; sr. design engr. Adel Med., Portland, Oreg., 1982-84; design engr., entrepreneur Omark Industries, Portland, 1984—; chief exec. officer Natural Velocity Sailcraft, Portland, 1982—; co. advisor for Oregon Bus. Week. Producer-dir. film: Old Friends, 1967; devel. labor-delivery beds for obstetric wards, air polution control systems for industry, one-design custom offshore yachts. Area dist. commr. Boy Scouts Am., Portland, 1987--. Served with U.S. Army, 1966-68. Mem. Soc. Mfg. Engrs. (sr.). Republican. Home: 18361 Willamette Dr West Linn OR 97068 Office: Omark Industries 4909 SE Internat Way Portland OR 97222

WALKER, JAMES LYNWOOD, seminary group executive. B.A., N.Carolina Central U., 1963; M.Div., Pacific Sch. Religion, 1967; Ph.D. Grad. Theol. Union/U. Calif.-Berkeley, 1970. Assoc. prof., asst. dean Grad. Theol. Union, 1970-73; exec. dir. Pastoral Inst. of Wash./Ida., 1973-78; pastor Magnolia Presbyn. Ch., Seattle, 1979-81; interim pastor Newport Presbyn. Ch., Bellevue, Wash., 1981-82; pres. Northwest Theol. Union, Seattle, 1984—; cons., therapist, 1982-84. Author: Body and Soul: Gestalt Therapy and Religious Experience, 1971; editor: Agendas for Black Churches, 1985. Office: Northwest Theol Union 914 E Jefferson St Seattle WA 98122 *

WALKER, JOHN SUMPTER, JR., lawyer; b. Richmond, Ark., Oct. 13, 1921; s. John Sumpter, Martha (Wilson) W.; m. Eljana M. duVall, Dec. 31, 1947; children—John Stephen, Barbara Monika Ann, Peter Mark Gregory. B.A., Tulane U., 1942; MS, U. Denver, 1955, JD, 1960; diploma Nat. Def. U., 1981. Bar: Colo. 1960, U.S. Dist. Ct. Colo. 1960, U.S. Supreme Ct., 1968, U.S. Ct. Appeals (10th cir.) 1960, U.S. Tax Ct., 1981. With Denver & Rio Grande Western R.R. Co., 1951-61, gen. solicitor, 1961-89 ; pres. Denver Union Terminal Ry. Co. With U.S. Army, 1942-46. Decorated Bronze Star. Mem. ABA, Colo. Bar Assn., Arapahoe County Bar Assn., Alliance Francaise (life), Order of St. Ives, U. Denver Chancellors' Soc., Cath. Lawyers Guild. Republican. Roman Catholic. Club: Denver Athletic.

WALKER, JOSEPH ROBERT, neurosurgeon; b. Atlantic City, N.J., Mar. 2, 1942; s. Joseph West and Helen (Mendte) W.; m. Mary Cynthia Long, Aug. 23, 1968; children: Joseph West II, Scott Robert, Heather Elizabeth. BS, St. Josephs Coll., 1964; MD, Creighton U., 1968. Diplomate Am. Bd. Neurol. Surgery. Intern Atlantic City (N.J.) Hosp., 1968-69; resident surgery Jefferson Med. Coll. Hosp., Phila, 1969-70; resident neurosurgery U. N.C., Chapel Hill, 1972-76, fellow, instr. neurosurgery, 1976-77; chief neurosurgery Washoe Med. Ctr., Reno, Nev., 1982, St. Mary's Hosp., Reno, 1982; vice-chief neurosurgery Washoe Med. Ctr., Reno, 1989, St. Mary's Hosp., Reno, 1989; asst. prof. U. Nev. Med. Sch., Reno, 1979—. Served as lt. comdr. USN, 1970-72. Office: 85 Kirman Reno NV 89502

WALKER, JUDITH RAE, medical company executive, physician; b. Pitts.; d. Raymond John and Marcella Elizabeth Wunderly; children: Evan Robert Adam, Valerie Lyn. BA, Pa. State U., 1964; BSc, U. Toronto, 1968, EdB, 1969; MD, McMaster U., 1976; postgrad., U. So. Calif., 1978. Instr. Jarvis Collegiate Inst., Toronto, Can., 1967-73; med. illustrator Toronto, Can., 1968-75; physician Los Angeles County-U. So. Calif. Med. Ctr., Los Angeles, 1976-79; pres., chief exec. officer Axiom Med. Inc., Los Angeles, 1979—. Illustrator: Disorders and Injuries of Musculo-Skeletal System, 1970, Small Animal Orthopaedica, 1973, Save Your Arteries, Save Your Life, 1987. Mem. Senatorial Inner Circle, 1987—, leader Girl Scouts U.S., Palos Verdes Penisula, Calif., 1986-87; v.p. Children's Charity League, Lynwood, Calif., 1988—. Mem. AMA, Nat. Assn. Female Execs., Nat. Assn. Women Bus. Owners, The Exec. Com., Am. Soc. Personnel Adminstrs. Republican. Clubs: St. Francis Hosp. Guild (Lynwood, Calif.); Women's Community (Rolling Hills, Calif.) (bd. dirs. 1986—). Office: Axiom Med Inc 7625 Rosecrans Ave Paramount CA 90723

WALKER, LELAND JASPER, civil engineer; b. Fallon, Nev., Apr. 18, 1923; s. Albert Willard and Grayce (Wilkinson) W.; m. Margaret Frances Noble, Jan. 21, 1946; children: Thomas, Margaret, Timothy. B.S. in Civil Engring, Iowa State U., 1944; D. Eng. (hon.), Mont. State U., 1983. Engr. with various govtl. depts. 1946-51, 53-55; v.p. Wenzel & Co. (cons. engrs.), Great Falls, Mont., 1955-58; pres., chmn. bd. No. Engring. and Testing, Inc., Great Falls, 1958-88; pres. Ind. Labs. Assurance Co., 1977-79; dir. Mont. Power Co., Sletten Constrn. Co., Entech Inc., Danforth Instruments Co., also vice-chmn. Pres., trustee Endowment and Research Found., Mont. State U., 1969-82, Mont. Deaconess Hosp., Great Falls, 1959-67; trustee, pres. Mont. Sch. for Deaf and Blind Found., 1984; trustee Rocky Mountain Coll., 1977-80, Dufresne Found., 1979-87; chmn., dir. Mont. Tech. Services Adv. Council; mem. Engring. Coll. adv. council Mont. State U.; bd. dirs. Mont. State Fair, Engring. Socs. Commn. on Energy, 1977-79, Mont. Bd. Sci. and Tech., 1983-88, Nat. Ctr. for Policy Analysis for Acid Rain, 1985-88. Served with USNR, 1943-46, 51-53. Fellow ASCE (pres. 1976-77), Cons. Engrs. Coun. (pres. Mont. 1971), AAAS, Accrediting Bd. Engring. and Tech. (v.p. 1978-79, pres. 1980-83); mem. Nat. Acad. Engring., Am. Council Ind. Labs. (hon., sec. 1973-76), Chi Epsilon (nat. hon.), Tau Beta Pi (hon.). Republican. Methodist. Clubs: Montana, Meadowlark Country, Black Eagle Country. Lodge: Kiwanis (pres. Great Falls 1970). Home: 2819 8th Ave S Great Falls MT 59405 Office: PO Box 7329 Great Falls MT 59405

WALKER, (EDNA) MARIE, nurse; b. Paterson, N.J., Mar. 6, 1934; d. James and Martha (Trione) Devino; m. George Walker Jr., Mar. 31, 1951; children: James Michael, George John. Diploma, Woodbridge (N.J.) Nursing Sch., 1962-63; AA, Maricopa Tech. Coll., Phoenix, 1970. RN, N.J., Ariz. Staff nurse Plainfield, N.J., 1963-64, Good Samaritan Hosp., Phoenix, 1964-70; coord. med. Maryvale Samaritan Hosp., Phoenix, 1970-80, coord. geriatrics, 1980-81, enterestomal nurse, 1981-82, coord. geriatric svcs. and enterostomal therapy, 1982-87; pvt. practice nursing Phoenix, 1987—; cons. Kimberly Nurses, Phoenix, Home Care Plus, Tempe, Ariz., Norell Nurses, Phoenix. Active in Valley Dem. Women, Phoenix, 1980—. Mem. Am. Nurses Assn., Am. Cancer Soc., United Ostomy Assn. (Volunteerism award 1987), Internat. Assn. Enterostomal Nurses, Internat. Urological Soc., Nat. Gerontological Nursing Assn., Am. Heart Assn., Nat. Conf. Gerontological Nurse Practitioners, Rocky Mountain Region Enterostomal Therapy Nurses, Phoenix Oncology Nurses Soc., Phoenix Urostomy/Ileostomy Chapt.(Outstanding Svc. award 1986, pres. 1988-89), Maricopa County Nurse Practitioners Counsel, Fairway Estates Garden Club (pres. 1986—). Roman Catholic.

WALKER, MOIRA KAYE, sales executive; b. Riverside, Calif., Aug. 2, 1940; d. Frank Leroy and Arline Rufina (Roach) Porter; m. Timothy P. Walker, Aug. 30, 1958 (div. 1964); children: Brian A., Benjamin D., Blair K., Beth E. Student, Riverside City Coll., 1973. With Bank of Am., Riverside, 1965-68, Abitibi Corp., Cucamonga, Calif., 1968-70, Lily div. Owens-Illinois, Riverside, 1970-73; salesperson Lily div. Owens-Illinois, Houston, 1973-77; salesperson Kent H. Landsberg div. Sunclipse, Montebello, Calif., 1977-83, sales mgr., 1983-85; v.p., sales mgr. Kent H. Landsberg div. Sunclipse, Riverside, 1985—. Mem. Nat. Assn. Female Execs., Women in Paper (treas. 1978-84). Lutheran. Office: Kent H Landsberg Div Sunclipse 1180 Spring St Riverside CA 92507

WALKER, NEAL THAYER, educator, business owner, accountant; b. Puunene, Hawaii, July 25, 1934; s. John Edgar and Hildreth Castle (Hitchcock) W.; m. Janet Thomson, Aug. 27, 1952 (div. 1985); m. Elizabeth Grinnell, Dec. 27, 1987; children: Neal Thayer Jr., Patrick John. BS, Stanford (Calif.) U., 1956, MBA, 1962. Fin. analyst FMC Corp., San Jose, Calif., 1962-65; treas. The Moses Co., Ltd., Hilo, Hawaii, 1965-70; pres., gen. mgr. MFC Corp., Hilo, 1970-75; co-owner Sailing Vessel Delivery, Hilo, 1975-76; prof. Orange Coast Coll., Costa Mesa, Calif., 1977—; co-owner Fairwinds Photography, Apple Valley, Calif., 1987—. Author: Sail By the Sun & Stars, 1979. Lt. USN, 1952-60, PTO. Home: 14101 Iroquois Rd Apple Valley CA 92307

WALKER, RAYMOND FRANCIS, business and financial consulting company executive; b. Medicine Lake, Mont., Nov. 9, 1914; s. Dennis Owen and Rose (Long) W.; m. Patricia K. Blakey, May 15, 1951; children: Richard A., Mark D., Maxie R. Forest, Victoria L. Le Huray, Suzanne J. Buhl, Tracy A. Grad. pub. schs.; student, Edison Vocat. Sch., 1935-39. Truck mgr. Pacific Food Products, Seattle, 1939-42; machinist Todd Shipyard, Seattle, 1943-45; owner Delbridge Auto Sales, Seattle, 1945-48; pres. Pacific Coast Acceptance Corp., 1949-60; v.p. West Coast Mortgage, Seattle, 1960-67, United Equities Corp., Seattle, 1965-69; pres. Income Mgmt. Corp., Seattle, 1970—; v.p. Internat. Mint and Foundry, Redmond, Wash., 1983—; cons. Life Ins. Co. Am., Bellevue, Wash., 1982-87, Consumer Loan Service, Lynwood Wash., 1980—; dir., cons., v.p. fin. Am. Campgrounds, Bellevue, 1971-74; cons., bd. dirs. Straits Forest Products, Inc., Port Angeles, Wash. Mem. Nat. Assn. Security Dealers. Methodist. Lodge: Elks. Home: 777 W Sequim Bay Rd Sequim WA 98382

WALKER, RICHARD ALLEN, data processing executive, consultant; b. Flushing, N.Y., Sept. 24, 1935; s. John Randall and Estella Viola (Stephanson) W.; m. Jauhree Ann Sparks, July 14, 1973. BA in Econs. and History, U.S. Internat. U., 1963, MS in Mgmt. Sci., 1968; PhD in Instructional Sci., Brigham Young U., 1978. Commd. ensign USN, 1958, advanced through grades to comdr., ret., 1976; sr. instructional psychologist Courseware, Inc., 1978-82, mgr. electronics pub. group, 1982-83; found., pres., acting v.p. instructional devel. Interactive Techs. Corp., 1983-86, chmn., 1986; pvt. practice 1986-87; dir. tng. svcs. WICAT Systems, Inc., 1987—. Mem. Eagle Boy Scouts Am. Mem. Soc. for Applied Learning Tech. (sr.), Am. Edn. Rsch. Assn., Assn. Aviation Psychologists, Arlberg Ski Club (silver), Crown Club (v.p. Coronado, Calif. chpt. 1985). Republican. Presbyterian. Home: 740 Olive Coronado CA 92118

WALKER, RUSSELL EDWARD, operations executive; b. Portsmouth, Ohio, Oct. 1, 1958; s. Harold Edward and Frances Marian (White) W.; m. Susan Ann Williamson, Feb. 6,1982. BS in Physics, Computers, Murray State U., 1980; MS in Applied Physics, Calif. Inst. Tech., 1982; postgrad., U. Colo., 1982-83. Tech. programmer Armco Inc., Ashland, Ky., 1979-80; assoc. systems analyst Hitco Inc., Gardena, Calif., 1981-82; tech. staff Hughes Aircraft, Denver, 1983-84; sect. mgr. Logicon, San Pedro, Calif., 1984-85; dir. engring, mfg. CompuMed Inc., Culver City, Calif., 1985-88; v.p. tech. ops. CompuMed Inc., Culver City, 1988--; instr. Aurora (Colo.) Community Coll., 1983-84; cons. pvt. practice, Denver, L.A., 1983--; mem. editorial bd. Computers in Biology & Med., 1987-88. Named grad. fellow Calif. Inst. Tech., IBM, Pasadena, 1980. Mem. Tanglefeet Square Dance Club (Whittier, Calif.) (v.p. 1988--). Office: CompuMed Inc 8549 Higuera St Culver City CA 90232

WALKER, SALLY C., fund raising executive. BA cum laude with honors, Stetson U., Deland, Fla., 1971; grad., Grantsmanship Ctr. Tng. Program, 1980, Mgmt. Fund Raisers Program, 1987. Cons. devel., dir. Direct Relief Found., Santa Barbara, Calif., 1977-82; prin., cons. Walker & Assocs., Santa Barbara, 1982—; endowment dir. planned giving United Way Santa Barbara, 1982—, devel. cons., 1982—; devel. cons., trainer United Way of Am., Alexandria, Va., 1984, 87; devel. cons. Santa Barbara Symphony, 1984-85, Child Abuse Listening Meditation, Santa Barbara, 1987-88, Easy Lift Transport., Inc., Goleta, Calif., 1988; mem. steering com., del. Nat. Conf. Planned Giving, 1987-88, Nat. Editorial Bur. chief, 1989; faculty mem. Nat. Acad. Voluntarism, Washington. Contbg. editor: The Endowment Builder. Co-founder, pres. Planned Giving Roundtable Santa Barbara County, Calif., 1986-88, v.p., 1984-86. Mem. Soc. Fund-Raising Execs., Santa Barbara Audobon Soc. (bd. dirs. 1989). Office: 1423 W Valerio St Santa Barbara CA 93101

WALKER, WALTER WYRICK, metallurgical engineer; b. Winslow, Ariz., Jan. 14, 1924; s. John Edward and Sadie Theresa (Moore) W.; m. Frances Ellen Sprawls, Jan. 16, 1952. BS, U. Ariz., 1950, MS (NDEA fellow 1959-62), 1962, PhD (NSF fellow 1966-67), 1968; PhD (hon.), U. Phys. Sci., 1958. Metall. engr., chemist in automotive, nuclear energy and aerospace field, 35 yrs.; group leader metall. tech. Hughes Aircraft Co., Tucson, 1978-82, staff engr., 1982-84, sr. staff engr., 1984-86, sr. scientist, 1986-89, ret. 1989; owner Andeco, Tucson, 1989—; mem. part-time and full-time faculty various univs. Mem. Pima County Pollution Control Hearing Bd., 1979—, Tucson Adv. Com. on Air Pollution, 1970-72, Tucson Citizens Transp. Adv. Com., 1989—. Served with USNR, World War II. Registered profl. engr., Ariz., Calif. Fellow Am. Inst. Chemists, AIME, Am. Soc. Metals, Nat. Soc. Profl. Engrs., AAAS, ASTM, Am. Geophys. Union, Am. Optical Soc., Nat. Assn. Corrosion Engrs., Ariz. Acad. Scis., N.Y. Acad. Scis., Brit. Inst. Metals, Mensa. German Shepherd Dog Club, So. Ariz. Rescue Assn., Sigma Xi. Democrat. Club: So. Ariz. Hiking. Author papers in field. Home: 5643 E 7th St Tucson AZ 85711

WALKWITZ, JON JEFFREY, lawyer; b. Kansas City, Mo., Nov. 11, 1949; s. Marvin Leroy and June Lavonne (Brown) W. BA, U. Colo., 1971, JD, 1978; MA, U. Colo., Denver, 1980; postgrad., Nat. Def. U., 1987. Bar: Colo. 1978. Atty. Towey and Zak, Westminster, Colo., 1979-80, Wagner and Waller, Denver, 1980-83, McNally and Bain, Boulder, 1983-84; law clerk to Judge D.P. Smith Colo. Ct. Appeals, Denver, 1978-79, dep. chief staff atty., 1984—. Mem. alumni adv. bd. U. Colo. Denver Coll. Liberal Arts and Scis., 1987—. Served to lt. (j.g.) USN, 1971-75; comdr. USNR, 1980—. Mem. Naval Res. Assn., U.S. Naval Inst., State Correspondent Seldon Soc., Colo. Bar Assn., Denver Bar Assn. Clubs: Army Navy (Washington),

Metropolitan (Denver), Mt. Vernon Country. Office: Colo State Jud Bldg 2 E 14th Ave Denver CO 80203

WALL, BRIAN RAYMOND, forest economist, policy analyst, consultant; b. Tacoma, Wash., Jan. 26, 1940; s. Raymond Perry and Mildred Beryl (Pickert) W.; m. Joan Marie Nero, Sept. 1, 1962; children: Torden Erik, Kirsten Noel. BS, U. Wash., 1962; MF, Yale U., 1964. Forestry asst. Weyerhaeuser Timber Co., Klamath Falls, Oreg., 1960; inventory forester West Tacoma Newsprint, 1961-62; timber sale compliance forester Dept. Nat. Resources, Kelso, Wash., 1963; rsch. forest economist Pacific N.W. Rsch. Sta., USDA Forest Svc., Portland, Oreg., 1964-88, cons. 1989—; co-founder, bd. dirs. Cordero Youth Care Ctr., 1970-81; owner Brian R. Wall Images and Communications; cons. to govt. agys., Congress univs., industry; freelance photographer. Co-author: An Analysis of the Timber Situation in the United States, 1982; contbr. articles, reports to profl. publs., newspapers. Interviewed and cited by nat. and regional news media. Recipient Cert. of Merit U.S. Dept. Agr. Forest Service, 1982. Mem. Soc. Am. Foresters (chmn. Portland chpt. 1973, Forester of Yr. 1975), Conf. of Western Forest Economists Inc. (founder, bd. dirs. 1988—, treas. 1982-87), Portland Photographic Forum, Zeta Psi. Home and Office: 7155 SW Alden St Portland OR 97223

WALL, HAROLD MARVIN, refrigeration company executive; b. Atlanta, July 9, 1922; s. Alva B. and Cora (Roper) W.; m. Stella Hoskins; children: Frank, Christine, James. Grad. high sch., San Deigo. Ptnr. Refrigeration Service Co., Denver, 1950-55; with Arctic Refrigeration Inc., Denver, 1955—, pres., owner, 1958—. Mem. Refrigeration and Air Conditioning Assn. (sec. 1973-76), Air Conditioning Contractors Am. Republican. Home: 1020 Sunset Ridge Greenwood Village CO 80121 Office: Arctic Refrigeration Inc 1175 S Cherokee St Denver CO 80223

WALL, LLOYD L., geological engineer; b. Jerome, Idaho, Feb. 2, 1936; s. Lloyd and Ola (Buck) W.; m. Myrna Bradshaw, Aug. 25, 1954; children: Jeffrey B., Julie, Neil S., Charlene, Gail, Matthew W., Suzzane, Michael L., Connie. AS, Coll. Eastern Utah, 1956; BS in Geology, Brigham Young U., 1958. Pres., owner Cons. Geologist, Salt Lake City and Brigham City, 1958—; plant mgr. Thiokol, Brigham City, Utah, 1958-66; mgr. ops. Sealcraft, Salt Lake City, 1966-68; mgr. programs Eaton-Kenway, Bountiful, Utah, 1968-76; pres., owner HydraPak, Inc., Salt Lake City, 1976—; pres. Kolt Mining Co., Salt Lake City, 1979—. Developer largest rocket motor vacuum casting system in free world, only high pressure water reclaimation system for solid propellant rocket motors in free world, only acceptable seal mfg. process for NASA Space Shuttle rocket motor. Vol. tchr. Alta Acad., Salt Lake City, 1983—. Served as sgt. N.G., 1954-62. Mem. Geol. Soc. Am., Utah Geol. Assn. Republican. Mormon. Home: 2180 East Clayborne Ave Salt Lake City UT 84109

WALL, MARK GEORGE, farmer, marketing consultant; b. Lawndale, Calif., Mar. 12, 1956; s. Samuel Garrett and Dorothy Lucille (Cerny) W. Grad., Calif. Scholastic Press Assn., Nat. Coop. Devel. Tng., USDA, Pierce Coll., 1976, El Camino Coll., 1978. Mgr. Gardena (Calif.) Cert. Farmers' Market, 1979-81; coordinator Southland Farmers' Market Assn., Los Angeles, 1981-88; owner Muscovy Grove Duck Farm, Oceanside, Calif.; Founder Calif. Direct Mktg. Assn., 1981—; organizer Nat. Dir. Mktg. Conf., Des Moines, 1986; dir. Summer Tasting of California Farms, 1987—. Author: Farmer's Guide, 1983; editor: Managing a Farmers' Market, 1981; contbr. articles to profl. jours. Anti-hunger grantee Kenny and Marianne Rogers Los Angeles County Fair, 1984; recipient mgr. award, Outstanding Exhibit, 1982. Mem. Calif. Assn. Family Farmers, Sustainable Agriculture Famers Adv. Bd. Univ. Calif. Coop. Extension. Home and Office: 5959 Las Tunas Dr Oceanside CA 92068

WALL, MICHAEL SAMUEL, truck rental company official; b. Ottawa, Ont., Can., Feb. 9, 1962; s. Michael Emmett and Pamela Anne (Tedesco) W. BS in Journalism, U. Colo., 1984. Rental rep. Saunders System, Inc., Commerce City, Colo., 1984-86; account mgr. Ryder Truck Rental, Inc., Denver, 1986--. Vol. Big Bros. Denver, 1986--. Home: PO Box 390473 Denver CO 80239

WALL, SONJA ELOISE, nurse; b. Santa Cruz, Calif., Mar. 28, 1938; d. Ray Theothornton and Reva Mattie (Wingo) W.; m. Edward Gleason Holmes, Aug. 1959 (div. Jan. 1968); children: Deborah Lynn, Lance Edward; m. John Aspesi, Sept. 1969 (div. 1977); children: Sabrina Jean, Daniel John; m. Kenneth Talbot LaBoube, Nov. 1, 1978; 1 child, Tiffany Amber. BA, San Jose Jr. Coll., 1959; BS, Madonna Coll., 1967; studnet, U. Mich., 1968-70. RN, Calif., Mich., Colo. Staff nurse Santa Clara Valley Med. Ctr., San Jose, Calif., 1959-67, U. Mich. Hosp., Ann Arbor, 1967-73, Porter and Swedish Med. hosp., Denver, 1973-77, Laurel Grove Hosp., Castro Valley, Calif., 1977-79, Advent Hosp., Ukiah, Calif., 1984-86; motel owner LaBoube Enterprises, Fairfield, Point Arena, Willits, Calif., 1979—; staff nurse Northridge Hosp., L.A., 1986-87, Folsom State Prison, Calif., 1987; co-owner, mgr. nursing registry Around the Clock Nursing Svc., Ukiah, 1985—; RN Kaiser Permanente Hosp., Sacramento, 1986—. Contbr. articles to various publs. Asst. leader Coloma 4-H, 1987, 88. Mem. Am. Heart Assn. (CPR trainer, recipient awards), Am. Assn. Critical Care Nurses, Calif. Bd. RNs, Calif. Nursing Rev., Calif. Critical Care Nurses, Am. Motel Assn. (beautification and remodeling award 1985), Am. Miniature Horse Assn. (winner nat. grand championship 1981, 82, 83), Cameron Park Country Club. Republican. Episcopalian. Home and Office: Around the Clock Nursing Svc PO Box 543 Coloma CA 95613

WALL, THOMAS ULRICH, real estate development executive; b. Washington, Nov. 20, 1944; s. Herbert and Doris (Hazel) W.; m. Elizabeth Ann Hallin, May 31, 1980. BA, Pa. State U., 1966; MA, U. Minn., 1977; MS, U. So. Calif., 1979; MBA with honors, Pepperdine U., 1985. Lic. real estate broker, Calif. Advanced through grades to lt. col. USMC, 1981, ret., 1986; dir. USN/USMC Helicopter Test Pilot Sch., 1970-71; asst. prof. naval sci. U. Minn., 1974-77; sr. instr. Dept. Def. Planning, Programming and Budgeting Sch., 1977-78; program mgr. USN, 1977-79; dir. facilities USMC Air Sta., Tustin, Calif., 1983-85; v.p. comml. devel. Polygon Group, 1986-87; pres., chief exec. officer Pacifica West Properties, Newport Beach, Calif., 1987-88; mgr. Transwestern Property Co., Newport Beach, 1988—; commd. 2nd lt. USMC, 1966. Commr. Orange County Airport Land Use Commn.; chmn. Irvine (Calif.) Scholar Athlete Program, Irvine Excellence in Teaching Program, Irvine Police Officer of Yr. Program; pres., bd. dirs. Turtle Rock Point Homeowners Assn.; 1st v.p., bd. govs. Irvine Valley Coll. Found. Decorated Purple Heart, 2 D.F.C. with bronze oak leaf cluster, 52 Air medals. Mem. Comml. Indsl. Devel. Assn. (1st v.p., bd. dirs. local chpt.), Irvine C. of C. (sr. vice chmn., chmn. bd. dirs.), Newport Beach C. of C., Exch. Club (Irvine). Republican. Office: Transwestern Property Co 5 Civic Pla Ste 380 Newport Beach CA 92660

WALL, WILLIAM E., utility executive; b. 1928. BS, U. Wash., 1951, LLB, 1954. Asst. atty. gen. State of Wash., 1956-59; chief examiner Pub. Svc. Commn., 1959; sec., house counsel Cascade Natural Gas Corp., 1959-64; pres. United Cities Gas Co., 1964-65; exec. v.p. Cascade Natural Gas Corp., 1965-67; spl. asst. to chmn. bd. Consol. Edison Co., N.Y.C., 1967-68, v.p., 1968-70, sr. v.p. gas ops., 1970-71, exec. v.p. div. ops., 1971-73; gen. mgr. pub. affairs Standard Oil Co., 1973-74; exec. v.p. Kans. Power and Light Co., Topeka, 1974-75, pres., 1975-85, chief exec. officer, 1976-88, chmn., 1979-88; of counsel Siderius, Lonergan & Crowley, Seattle, 1988—. Served with AUS, 1954-56. Office: Siderius Lonergan & Crowley 847 Logan Bldg Seattle WA 98101

WALLACE, DARRELL LOVELL, realtor, horseman; b. Long Beach, Calif., Oct. 27, 1946; s. Lovell Ray and Adele Eva (Mullins) W.; m. Elizabeth Sue Downard, Mar. 3, 1984; children: Molli Elizabeth, Ana Adele. AA, Ventura Coll, 1967. Livestock foreman Converse Ranch, Santa Paula, Calif., 1971-72; with USDA soil conservation service, Ventura County, Calif., 1973-74; freelance horse trainer Ventura and Kern Counties, Calif., 1974-77; agrl. realtor Franklin Realty, Ventura County, 1979—. Com. mem. Santa Barbara Fiesta Rodeo, Calif., 1982-87. With U.S. ARmy, 1967-69, Vietnam. Mem. Ventura Bd. Realty, Calif. Young Farmers. Democrat. Home: 80 Rio Via Oakview CA 93022

WALLACE, DOUGLAS ALAN, owner, accountant; b. Denver, Dec. 23, 1946; s. Maurice Emery and Helen Cora (Gould) W.; m. Riemerdina Poelman, Apr. 22, 1977; children: Ezra James, Alicia Marie, Nathaniel Alan, Karen E. BS in Acctg. summa cum laude, Met. State U., 1979; postgrad., U. Colo., 1985. Acct. Dave Cook Sporting Goods, Denver, 1979; sr. acct. Dresser Industries, Denver, 1979-86; controller Mat Glover Constrn., Arvada, Colo., 1987; owner Abacus Bus. Svcs., Arvada, 1987—; acct. Arvada C. of C., 1987—. De. county and state Rep. Convs., Colo., 1984-86; treas. Ward Rd. Bapt. Ch., Arvada, 1988. State of Colo. scholar, 1978; recipient Presdl. Sports award Nat. Coun. on Fitness, 1984. Mem. Colo. Soc. Pub. Accts. Home: 6273 Urban St Arvada CO 80004

WALLACE, GEORGE WASHINGTON, JR., infosystems specialist; b. Decatur, Ill., Nov. 24, 1930; s. George Washington Sr. and Sadie Alice (Strader) W.; m. Mary Katherine Glenn, Jan. 23, 1956; children: Elizabeth A. (dec.), Victoria L., Michael A., Kevin S. Student, U. Wyo., 1958-60, U. Ariz., 1973-76. Enlisted USAF, 1947, advanced through grades to 1st sgt., 1966, retired, 1970; asst. dir. transp. and communications Tucson Med. Ctr., 1970-72; supr. U. Ariz., Tucson, 1975-88, ret., 1988; cons. Western Interpretive Services, Sheridan, Wyo., 1972-74. Pres. Montezuma Council PTA, Tucson, 1971-73; mem. com. Precinct 113, Tucson, 1971-75; insp. Pima County and City of Tucson Election Bd., 1972—; bd. dirs. Pima Assn. Govt. Planning Commn., Tucson. Recipient Award of Merit, Italian War Graves Commn., 1959, commendation medal, USAF, 1962, 69, 70. Mem. U.S. Naval Inst. (life), Assn. Record Mgrs. and Adminstrs. (v.p. 1982-83), Smithsonian Inst., Alpha Kappa PSI Frat. Democrat. Episcopalian.

WALLACE, HELEN MARGARET, physician, educator; b. Hoosick Falls, N.Y., Feb. 18, 1913; d. Jonas and Ray (Schweizer) W. A.B., Wellesley Coll., 1933; M.D., Columbia U., 1937; M.P.H. cum laude, Harvard U., 1943. Diplomate: Am. Bd. Pediatrics, Am. Bd. Preventive Medicine. Intern Bellevue Hosp., N.Y.C., 1938-40; child hygiene physician Conn. Health Dept., 1941-42; successively jr. health officer, health officer, chief maternity and new born div., dir. bur. for handicapped children N.Y.C. Health Dept., 1943-55; prof., dir. dept. pub. health N.Y. Med. Coll., 1955-56; prof. maternal and child health U. Minn. Sch. Pub. Health, 1956-59; chief profl. tng. U.S. Children's Bur., 1959-60, chief child health studies, 1961-62; prof. maternal and child health U. Calif. Sch. Pub. Health, Berkeley, 1962-80; prof., head div. maternal and child health Sch. Pub. Health, San Diego State U., 1980—; Univ. Research lectr. San Diego State U., 1985—; cons. WHO, Uganda, 1961, Philippines, 1966, 68, 75, Turkey, 1968, India, Geneva, 1970, Iran, 1972, Burma, India, Thailand, Sri Lanka, 1975, East Africa, 1976, Australia, 1976, Burma, 1977, India, Indonesia, Thailand, Burma, 1978, 79, India, 1981, Burma, 1985, Peoples Republic of China, 1988; Cons. Ford Found., Colombia, 1971; Traveling fellow WHO, cons., 1989—; U.N. cons. to Health Bur., Beijing, China, 1987; WHO cons. to China, 1988; dir. Family Planning Project, Zimbabwe, 1984-87. Author 8 textbooks; contbr. numerous articles to profl. jours. Recipient Alumnae Achievement award Wellesley Coll., 1982, Outstanding Faculty award San Diego State U., 1983, Martha Eliot award Am. Pub. Health Assn., 1978, Job Smith award Am. Acad. Pediatrics, 1980, U. Minn. award, 1985, Ford Found. study grants 1986, 87, 88; Fulbright fellow, 1989—. Fellow Am. Acad. Pediatrics (Job Smith award 1980, award 1989), Am. Pub. Health Assn. (officer sect., Martha May Eliot award 1978); mem. AMA, Assn. Tchrs. Maternal and Child Health, Am. Acad. Cerebral Palsy, Ambulatory Pediatric Assn., Am. Sch. Preventive Medicine. Home: 850 State St San Diego CA 92101 Office: San Diego State U San Diego CA 92182

WALLACE, J. CLIFFORD, judge; b. San Diego, Dec. 11, 1928; s. John Franklin and Lillie Isabel (Overing) W.; m. Virginia Lee Schlosser, Apr. 8, 1957; children: Paige, Laurie, Teri, John. B.A., San Diego State U., 1952; LL.B., U. Calif., Berkeley, 1955. Bar: Calif. 1955. With firm Gray, Cary, Ames & Frye, San Diego, 1955-70; judge U.S. Dist. Ct. So. Dist. Calif., 1970-72, U.S. Ct. Appeals 9th Circuit, 1972—. Contrbr. articles to profl. jours. Served with USN, 1946-49. Mem. ABA, Am. Bd. Trial Advocates, Inst. Jud. Adminstrn. Mormon (stake pres. San Diego East 1962-67, regional rep. 1967-74, 77-79). Office: US Ct Appeals 940 Front St Rm 4N25 San Diego CA 92189

WALLACE, JAMES WENDELL, lawyer; b. Clinton, Tenn., July 13, 1930; s. John Nelson and Rose Ella (Carden) W.; m. Jeanne Mary Ellen Newlin; children: Karen Wallace Young, Michael James. Student, Syracuse U., 1952-53; BS, U. Tenn., Knoxville, 1959, JD, 1958. Bar: Calif. 1959, U.S. Dist. Ct. (cen. dist.) Calif. 1959, U.S. Ct. Appeals (9th cir.) 1977, U.S. Supreme Ct. 1964. Sec., legal counsel Guidance Tech., Inc., Santa Monica, Calif., 1958-65; sr. atty., asst. sec. Varian Assocs., Palo Alto, Calif., 1965-67; gen. counsel, asst. sec. Electronic Splty. Co., Pasadena, Calif., 1967-69; asst. gen. counsel, asst. sec. The Times Mirror Co., L.A., 1969-75, assoc. gen. counsel, asst. sec., 1976-85, assoc. gen. counsel, sec., 1985—. Mem. editorial bd. Tenn. Law Rev., 1956-58. Mem. Town Hall of Calif. World Affairs Coun., L.A. Served with USAF, 1951-55. Mem. ABA, Am. Soc. Corp. Secs. (bd. dirs. 1979-82), L.A. County Bar Assn., Am. Corp. Counsel Assn., Oakmont Country Club, Jonathan Club, Phi Delta Phi, Phi Kappa Phi. Home: 5822 Briartree Dr LaCanada Flintridge CA 91011 Office: The Times Mirror Co Times Mirror Sq Los Angeles CA 90053

WALLACE, JOEL KEITH, hospital chaplain; b. San Bernardino, Calif., Nov. 3, 1933; s. Perry A. and Margaret S. (McCuen) W.; m. Winifred Lynne Capps, June 17, 1961; children: David Mark, Susanne Lynne Wallace Trumble, Jason Glenn. BA, Bob Jones U., 1958; BD, Talbot Theol. Sem., 1961, MDiv, 1970; DMin, Luther Rice Sem., 1977. Commd. 2d lt. U.S. Army, 1962, advanced through grades to lt. col., chaplain, various locations including Vietnam, 1962-72; ret. USAR, 1986; pastor Amarillo (Tex.) Bible Ch., 1972-76; ins. agt. Prudential Ins. Co., Amarillo, 1976-80; intermittent chaplain VA Med. Ctr., Amarillo, 1975-80; staff chaplain VA Med. Ctr., Dayton, Ohio, 1980-87; chief chaplain svc. VA Med. Ctr., Boise, Idaho, 1987—; instr., Regional Med. Edn. Ctr., Salt Lake City, 1988—. Police dept. chaplain, City of West Carrollton, Ohio, 1986-87, mem. City Beautiful Commn., 1987. With USN, 1951-54, Korea. Decorated Bronze Star from Vietnam. Mem. Ind. Fundamental Churches Am., Idaho Assn. Pastoral Care, Coll. of Chaplains, Res. Officers Assn. (state chaplain Idaho), VFW (chaplain), Mil. Order World Wars , Mini Le Bois, Kiwanis, Dayton Miniature Soc. Democrat. Office: VA Med Ctr 500 W Fort St Boise ID 83702-4598

WALLACE, KENNETH ALAN, investor; b. Gallup, N.Mex., Feb. 23, 1938; s. Charles Garrett and Elizabeth Eleanor (Jones) W.; A.B. in Philosophy, Cornell U., 1960; postgrad. U. N.Mex., 1960-61; m. Rebecca Marie Odell, July 11, 1980; children—Andrew McMillan, Aaron Blue, Susanna Garrett, Megan Elizabeth. Comml. loan officer Bank of N.Mex., Albuquerque, 1961-64; asst. cashier Ariz. Bank, Phoenix, 1964-67; comml. loan officer Valley Nat. Bank, Phoenix, 1967-70; pres. WWW, Inc., Houston, 1970-72; v.p. fin. Hometels of Am., Phoenix, 1972-77, Precision Mech. Co., Inc., 1972-77; ptnr. Schroeder-Wallace, 1977—; mng. ptnr. Pala Partners, San Diego; pres. Blackhawk, Inc., Phoenix, 1977—; pres., dir. Kloron Corp., Johannesburg, South Africa, Blackhawk, Inc., Phoenix; dir. Schroeder Constrn. Co., Inc., Phoenix; v.p., dir. C.G. Wallace Co., Albuquerque ; ptnr. New Dynasty Mining Corp., Vancouver, FWS, Phoenix, Univ. Sq. Assocs., Flagstaff, Ariz., Banador, Mijas, Spain, Sunset Properties, Manzanillo, Mex.; bd. dirs. World Trading and Shipping, N.Y.C.; gen. ptnr. Wallco Enterprises, Ltd., Mobile, Ala.; mng. gen. ptnr. The Village at University Heights, Flagstaff. Loaned exec. Phoenix United Way, 1966, Tucson United Way, 1967; mem. Valley Big Bros., 1970—; bd. dirs. Phoenix Big Sisters, 1985-87; mem. Alhambra Village Planning Com.; fin. dir. Ret. Sr. Vol. Program, 1973-76; mem. Phoenix Men's Arts Council, 1968—, dir., 1974-75; mem. Phoenix Symphony Council. Campaign committeeman Republican gubernatorial race, N.Mex., 1964; treas. Phoenix Young Reps., 1966; bd. dirs. Devel. Authority for Tucson, 1967. Mem. Soaring Soc. Am. (Silver badge), Am. Rifle Assn. (life), Nat. Mktg. Assn. (Mktg. Performance of Year award 1966), Nat. Assn. Skin Diving Schs., Pima County Jr. C. of C. (dir. 1967), Phoenix Little Theatre, Phoenix Musical Theatre, S.W. Ensemble Theatre (dir.), Alpha Tau Omega. Mason (Shriner). Clubs: Univ., Plaza (Phoenix); Kona Kai (San Diego). Office: Schroeder-Wallace PO Box 7703 Phoenix AZ 85011

WALLACE, LEIGH ALLEN, JR., bishop; b. Norman, Okla., Feb. 5, 1927; s. Leigh Allen Sr. and Nellie Elizabeth (Whittemore) W.; m. Alvira Kinney, Sept. 2, 1949; children: Jenny Leigh, Richard Kinney, William Paul. BA, U. Mont., 1950; M in Divinity, Va. Theol. Sem., 1962, DD, 1979. Ordained priest Episcopal Ch.; vicar chs., Sheridan, Virginia City, Jeffers, Mont., 1962-65; rector St. Luke's Ch., Billings, Mont., 1965-71, Holy Spirit Parish, Missoula, Mont., 1971-78; bishop of Spokane, 1979—. Served with USNR, 1945-46. Address: 245 E 13th Ave Spokane WA 99202 *

WALLACE, MARC CHARLES, dentist; b. Portland, Oreg., Aug. 8, 1957; s. Francis Ronald and Donna Mae (Schulz) W. BS, U. Wash., 1979, DDS, 1983. Pvt. practice Woodinville, Wash., 1983-84, Beverly Hills, Calif., 1985-89, Bellevue, Wash., 1986-88, Costa Mesa, Calif., 1989—. Actor Poor Little Rich Girl Prodns., L.A., 1986, appeared in commls., L.A., 1986—. Mem. ADA, Acad. Gen. Dentistry, AFTRA, Screen Actors Guild, Loma Linda Implant Study Club. Republican. Roman Catholic. Home: 191 San Leon Irvine CA 92714 Office: 1503 S Coast Dr #201 Costa Mesa CA 92626

WALLACE, MARY ANN, development company executive; b. Reno County, Kans., Feb. 19, 1939; d. Ivan Lewis and Vina Sue (Smith) Newell; m. Alexander Wallace III, Feb. 17, 1968 (div. June 1982); 1 child, Alexander IV. BS, Wichita State U., 1961. Property mgr. 650 S. Grand Bldg. Co., Los Angeles, 1961-68; v.p. Milner Devel., Santa Monica, Calif., 1981-83; chief fin. officer Milner Devel., Los Angeles, 1983—; cons. Kitty Prodns., Los Angeles, 1978—; cons., v.p. Am. Mut. Prodns., Redlands, Calif., 1975—. V.p. Sister Servants of Mary Guild, Los Angeles, 1970-77; treas. Hosp. of Good Samaritan Aux., Los Angeles, 1969-75; press sec. Orphanage Guild Jrs., Los Angeles, 1974. Named Downtown Working Angel, Downtown Businessmen's Assn., Best Fund Raiser, Sister Servants of Mary Guild, 1974-76. Mem. Los Angeles World Affairs Council, Los Angeles Women in Bus., Nat. Art Assn. Republican. Roman Catholic. Club: Los Angeles Country (Beverly Hills, Calif.).

WALLACE, MATTHEW WALKER, entrepreneur; b. Salt Lake City, Jan. 7, 1924; s. John McChrystal and Glenn (Walker) W.; m. Constance Cone, June 22, 1954 (dec. May 1980); children—Matthew, Anne; m. Susan Struggles, July 11, 1981. B.A., Stanford U., 1947; M.C.P., MIT, 1950. Prin. planner Boston City Planning Bd., 1950-53; v.p. Nat. Planning and Research, Inc., Boston, 1953-55; pres. Wallace-McConaughy Corp., Salt Lake City, 1955-69; pres. Ariz. Ranch & Metals Co., Salt Lake City, 1969-84; chmn. Wallace Assocs., Inc., Salt Lake City, 1969—; dir. 1st Interstate Bank, Salt Lake City, 1956—, dir. Arnold Machinery Co., 1988—, dir. Roosevelt Hot Springs Corp., 1978—; mem. adv. bd. Mountain Bell Telephone Co., Salt Lake City, 1975-85. Pres., Downtown Planning Assn., Salt Lake City, 1970; chmn. Utah State Arts Council, Salt Lake City, 1977; mem. Humanities and Scis. Council, Stanford U., also mem. athletic bd.; mem. nat. adv. bd. Coll. Bus., U. Utah; chmn. endowment com. Utah Symphony Orch. Lt. (j.g.) USN, 1944-46; PTO. Recipient Contbn. award Downtown Planning Assn., 1977. Mem. Am. Inst. Cert. Planners (charter), Alta Club (dir.), Cottonwood Club (pres. 1959-63), Salt Lake Country Club (dir.) Club, Masons, Phi Kappa Phi. Home: 2510 Walker Ln Salt Lake City UT 84117 Office: Wallace Assocs Inc 165 S Main St Salt Lake City UT 84111

WALLACE, NANCY DIANE, industrial engineer; b. Artesia, Calif., Dec. 22, 1958; d. George and Juanita Reba (Gilliland) W.; 1 child, Toy Lynn. BS in Indsl. Engring., U. Okla., 1982. Indsl. engr. II Digital Equipment Corp., Phoenix, 1982-85, sr. indsl. engr., 1985-87, mgr. indsl. engring., 1987—. Chmn. Nat. Am. Week, Phoenix Indian Ctr., 1986. Mem. Inst. Indsl. Engrs., Am. Indian Sci. and Engring. Soc. (sec. bd. 1984-88), Nat. Assn. Minority Engring. Program Adminstrs. Democrat. Baptist. Office: Digital Equipment Corp 2500 W Union Hills Dr Phoenix AZ 85027

WALLACE, PAUL HARVEY, lawyer, educator; b. Fresno, Calif., Oct. 27, 1944; s. Samuel Dunn and Naomi (Hickman) W.; m. Randa Fay Steckler, Mar. 20, 1987; children: Tim, Laura, Christy. BS in Criminology, Calif. State U., Fresno, 1966; JD, U.S. Internat. U., 1974; postgrad. in pub. adminstrn., Golden Gate U., 1986—. Bar: Calif. 1974, U.S. Dist. Ct. (so. dist.) Calif. 1974, U.S. Dist. Ct. (no. dist.) Calif. 1982, U.S. Ct. Appeals (9th cir.) 1985. Dep. dist. atty. San Diego Dist. Atty.'s Office, 1975-79; assoc. Harrison and Watson, San Diego, 1979-81; dep. county counsel Butte County Counsel's Office, Oroville, Calif., 1981-85; county counsel Butte County Counsel's Office, Oroville, 1985-87; city atty. City of Freso, 1987—; adj. prof. Nat. U., Fresno, 1987—; lectr. Calif. State U., Fresno, 1988—. Asst. coord. San Diego County for U.S. Senator Alan Cranston, 1974. Lt. USMCR, 1967-70, lt. col. Res. Decorated Silver Star, Purple Heart with oak leaf cluster. Mem. State Bar Assn. Calif., Butte County Bar Assn., San Diego Dep. Dist. Attys. Assn. (sec.-treas. 1976-77, v.p. 1977-78, pres. 1978-79), Am. Legion, VFW, Masons, Shriners. Office: Office City Atty City Hall Fresno CA 93721

WALLACE, ROBERT EARL, geologist; b. N.Y.C., July 16, 1916; s. Clarence Earl and Harriet (Wheeler) W.; m. Gertrude Kivela, Mar. 19, 1945; 1 child: Alan R. BS, Northwestern U., 1938; MS, Calif. Inst. Tech., 1940, PhD, 1946. Registered geologist, Calif., engring. geologist, Calif. Geologist U.S. Geol. Survey, various locations, 1942—; regional geologist U.S. Geol. Survey, Menlo Park, Calif., 1970-74; chief scientist Office of Earthquakes, Volcanoes and Engring. U.S. Geol. Survey, Menlo Park, 1974-87; asst. and assoc. prof. Wash. State Coll., Pullman, 1946-51; mem. adv. panel Nat. Earthquake Prediction Evaluation Council, 1980—, Stanford U. Sch. Earth Sci., 1972-82; chmn. engring. criteria rev. bd. San Francisco Bay Conservation and Devel. Commn. Contbr. articles to profl. jours. Recipient Meritorious Service award U.S. Dept. Interior, 1978, Disting. Service award U.S. Dept. Interior, 1978; Japanese Indsl. Tech. Assn. fellow, 1984. Fellow AAAS, Geol. Soc. Am. (chair cordillidan sect. 1967-68), Earthquake Engring. Research Inst., mem. Seismol. Soc. Am. (medalist 1988). Office: US Geol Survey 345 Middlefield Rd Menlo Park CA 94025

WALLACE, ROBERT GEORGE, retired construction company executive, civil engineer; b. Flagstaff, Ariz., Apr. 30, 1928; s. William Robert Francis and Maeclaire (Wright) W.; m. Gloria Mae Reid, Oct. 29, 1960. B.S.C.E., U. Ariz., Tucson, 1953. Registered profl. civil engr. Pres. Wallace & Royden Equipment Co., Phoenix, 1956-67; v.p. Royden Constrn. Co., Phoenix, 1953-67; v.p. The Tanner Cos., Phoenix, 1967-81, exec. v.p., 1971-82, pres., 1982-88, also dir.; bd. dirs. Assn. Gen. Contractors, 1973-80, The Road Info. Program, 1978-82, The Beavers, 1982—, Western Force, 1972-78, Kasler Corp. Served with USN, 1946-48; PTO. Recipient award of Disting. Service Ariz. Assoc. Gen. Contractors, 1967; Disting. Citizen award U. Ariz. Engring. Coll., 1983. Mem. Rancho Santa Fe Country Club, Plaza Club (Phoenix), Masons (32nd degree). Republican. Episcopalian. Home: 17461 Avenida De Acacias PO Box 494 Rancho Santa Fe CA 92067

WALLAR, ROBERT EDWARD, economic development and Indian treaty consultant, author; b. St. Louis, Jan. 13, 1942; s. Robert E. and Anita E. (Krueger) W.; AA, Santa Barbara City Coll., 1967; BA, San Francisco State Coll., 1969; children: Jane Omunson, Lynn, Andrew. Assoc. planner City of Bellevue (Wash.), 1969-71, planning dir., 1971-73; v.p. Bert McNae, Inc., Bellevue, 1973-75; owner The Wallar Assocs., 1973-85, Bryant/Wallar Assocs., 1974-76; pres. Robert E. Wallar Real Estate, 1975-79, 83—; gen. mgr., chief exec. officer Puyallup Tribal Enterprises, Community Devel. & Port Authority, Tacoma, 1978-82; ptnr. Frolich-Wallar Assocs., 1984—; v.p. Red Tail Assocs., 1986—. Co-author: (with Judith O. Frolich) Modern Approach to Indian Jurisdiction, 1986. Mem. King County Agrl. Preservation Task Force, 1977-78, King County Growth Mgmt. Forum, 1978-80, Aquila Found., 1988—, Commencement Bay Environ. Impact Com., U.S.A.C.E., 1978-82. Served with AUS, 1962-65. Mem. Puyallup Tribal Bar, Washington State Hist. Soc., Mus. History and Industry, Puget Sound C. of C. (chmn. land use com. 1973-75), Kirkland C. of C., Seattle C. of C. (chmn. agrl. preservation com. 1977-78), Bellevue C. of C. (bd. dirs. 1973-76). Episcopalian. Home: 1356 Bellefield Ln Bellevue WA 98004 Office: 15 Brooks Bldg 611 Market St Kirkland WA 98083-2863

WALLEK, THOMAS ALLAN, construction company executive; b. Watertown, S.D., Jan. 28, 1950; m. Kathryn Elizabeth Pargeon, Sept. 28, 1973; children: Elizabeth, Kristine, Rebecca, Thomas Benjamin. Pres. Ducore, Inc., Reno, Nev., 1977--. Chmn. Reno-Sparks Crisis Pregnancy

Ctr., Reno, 1982-87. Served with Nev. N.G., 1970-77. Mem. Associated Gen. Contractors, Concrete Sawing and Drilling Assn., Reno Men's Golf. Republican. Office: Ducore Inc 2510 Tacchino St Reno NV 89512

WALLEN, JAMES MARSHALL, retail executive; b. Ft. Collins, Colo., Mar. 5, 1948; s. Henry Martenson and Ella Margret (Wehlitz) W.; m. Pamela Jean McGill, Mar. 21, 1969 (div. Feb. 1988); children: Jeremy James, Jennifer Jean. BA, Colo. State U., 1970. Secondary tchr. Wiley (Colo.) Consol. Schs., 1970-72; paint salesman, dealer Kohler McLister Paint Co., Denver, 1972-80; owner Jim's Paint & Paper, Inc., Longmont, Colo.; area mgr. Allen Paint Supply Co., Inc., Denver, 1983-86; ops. mgr., jobber sales MFC Allen Paint, Denver, 1987—. Office: MFC Allen Paint 141 S Broadway Denver CO 80209

WALLER, BRADLEY ALLAN, systems engineer; b. Panorama City, Calif., Nov. 17, 1963; s. Paul Siegfried and Joan (Coshever) W. BS, MIT, 1986. Engring. technician Litton Industries, Van Nuys, Calif., 1983-84; devel. engr. Tech. Assocs., Canoga Park, Calif., 1984-85; systems programmer IBM Instruments Inc., Cambridge, Mass., and Danbury, Conn., 1985-86; systems engr. Hughes Aircraft Co., El Segungo, Calif., 1986—. Democrat. Jewish. Home: 720 Ave D Redondo Beach CA 90277 Office: Hughes Aircraft EDSG PO Box 902 E51-A290 El Segundo CA 90245

WALLER, JAMES EARL, computer scientist; b. Woodburn, Oreg., May 29, 1945; s. Earl and Violet Marie (Seaton) W.; m. Jui-Lan Tang, Mar. 1, 1976; children: Julie, Jason. BS, Oreg. State U., 1975. Programmer Oreg. State U., Corvallis, 1975-79; analyst Control Data Corp., Monterey, Calif., 1979-81; software engr. Inlex Inc., Monterey, 1981--. With USAF, 1963-71. Office: Inlex Inc 1900 Garden Rd Ste 160 Monterey CA 93940

WALLER, JOHN JAMES, lawyer; b. Red Cloud, Nebr., May 14, 1924; s. James Emery and Gail Fern (Perry) W.; m. Norma Louise Kunz, June 19, 1949; children: Diane Leslie, John James Jr, William Scott. Student, Rhode Island State Coll., Kingston, 1943-44, Biarritz Am. U., France, 1945-46; BA magna cum laude, Harvard U., 1947, JD, 1950. Bar: Calif. 1951, U.S. Dist. (cen. dist.), 1951, U.S. Ct. Appeals (9th cir.) 1959, U.S. Tax Ct. 1959, U.S. Supreme Ct. 1976. Assoc. Gibson, Dunn & Crutcher, L.A., 1950-62, Flint & MacKay, L.A., 1962-67, Law Offices of Max Fink, Beverly Hills, Calif., 1968-73; pvt. practice Santa Ana, Tustin, Calif., 1973-83, Buena Park, Calif., 1984—; spl. counsel Fluor Corp., Irvine, Calif., 1983-84. Chmn. unification com. Buena Park Sch. Dist., 1969-70; pres., sec., dir. Bellehurst Community Assn., 1970; chmn., mem. City of Buena Park Airport Commn., 1969-74, City Buena Park Transp. Com., 1975-77; dist. vice chmn. Boy Scouts Am., 1970. Sgt. U.S. Army, 1943-46, ETO. Recipient Merit award Boy Scouts Am.. Mem. ABA, State Bar Calif., L.A. County Bar Assn., Orange County Bar Assn. (del. 1984), Am. Judicature Soc. Democrat. Office: 5591 Monticello Ave Buena Park CA 90621

WALLER, LARRY GENE, mortgage banking executive; b. Corpus Christi, Tex., Nov. 18, 1948; s. Paul Hobson and Marie (Armellini) W.; m. Mary Sandra Cupp, Dec. 27, 1969 (di v. 1987); children: Stacey Anna, Jaime Lynn; m. Sharon Elizabeth Falls, Jan. 28, 1988; 1 child, Lisa Suzanne Cantello. AA, Bakersfield Jr. Coll., 1970. Lic. real estate broker, Calif. Asst. v.p. Bank of Am., Stockton, Calif., 1970-78, Wells Fargo Realty Fin. Co., Sacramento, 1978-81; regional v.p. Weyerhaeuser Mortgage Co., Sacramento, 1981--. Mem. Com. to Help Attract Maj. Profl. Sports, Sacramento. Mem. Mortgage Bankers Assn. (income property com.), Calif. Mortgage Bankers Assn., Del Paso Country Club. Home: 180 Dawn River Way Folsom CA 95630 Office: Weyerhaeuser Mortgage Co 8950 Cal Center Dr Suite 300 Sacramento CA 95826

WALLER, PETER WILLIAM, public affairs executive; b. Kewanee, Ill., Oct. 1, 1926; s. Ellis Julian and Barodel (Gould) W.; m. Anne-Marie Appelius van Hoboken, Nov. 10, 1950; children: Catherine, Hans. BA with hons., Princeton U., 1949; MA with hons., San Jose State U., 1978. Bur. chief Fairchild Publs., San Francisco, 1953-55; freelance writer Mountain View, Calif., 1956-57; pub. relations coord. Lockheed Missiles and Space, Sunnyvale, Calif., 1957-64; pioneer info. mgr. for 1st mission to Jupiter, Saturn and beyond and 1st mapping and photo mission to Venus NASA Ames Rsch. Ctr., Mountain View, 1964-83, mgr. pub. info., 1983—; speechwriter for pres. Lockheed Missiles and Space, 1960-64. Producer (documentary) Jupiter Odyssey, 1974 (Golden Eagle, 1974); producer, writer NASA Aero. program, 1984; contbr. articles to profl. jours. Cons. concerning preservation of Lake Tahoe Calif. Resources Agy., Sacremento, 1984. With USN, 1944-45. Mem. No. Calif. Sci. Writers Assn., Sierra Club. Democrat. Congregationalist. Home: 3655 La Calle Ct Palo Alto CA 94306 Office: NASA Ames Rsch Ctr Moffett Field CA 94035

WALLER, ROBERT CARL, chiropractor; b. Chgo., Aug. 1, 1931; s. Morton Sam and Linea Matilda (Anderson) W.; children by previous marriage—Wendy, Jeff. B.S., U. Ill., 1957; D.Chiropractic, Los Angeles Coll. Chiropractic, 1979; postgrad. UCLA, 1968-74. Staff pharmacist Savon Drugs, Granada Hills, Calif., 1968-70; mgr. pharmacy Hy-Lo Drug Co., Sepulveda, Calif., 1970-79; practice chiropractic medicine, Santa Monica, Calif., 1980—. Served with USNR, 1949-50. Mem. Am. Pharm. Assn., Am. Chiropractic Assn., Calif. Chiropractic Assn., UCLA Alumni Assn., Mensa. Democrat. Home: 5870 Green Valley Circle #332 Culver City CA 90230 Office: 1530 Lincoln Blvd Ste C Santa Monica CA 90401

WALLERICH, PETER KENNETH, banker; b. Tacoma, Mar. 4, 1931; s. Clarence W. and Ellen (Hansen) W.; m. Marylu Ann Oakland, July 9, 1954; children—Karen, Kristen, Karla, Kaari. B.A.A., U. Wash., 1953. Investment officer N.Pacific Bank, Tacoma, 1956-59, exec. v.p., 1959-71, chmn. bd., 1971-73, pres., 1973—; gen. mgr. Soutn Tacoma Motor Co., 1959-68, pres., 1968-71; dir. North Pacific Bank, Western Fin. Co., Mountain View Devel. Co. Pres. Design for Progress, 1970-71; bd. dirs. Goodwill Industries, Wash. Research Council; trustee, treas. U. Puget Sound.; chmn. bd. trustees Mary Bridge Children's Hosp; trustee Lakewood Gen. Hosp.; bd. visitors Sch. Law U. Puget Soun.; gen. chmn. Tacoma Pierce County United Way, 1981. Mem. Wash. Bankers Assn. (dir., treas.), Am. Bankers Assn. (nat. exec. planning com.), C. of C. (dir.), Mensa, Beta Gamma Sigma (chpt. award 1980). Home: 12111 Gravelly Lake Dr SW Tacoma WA 98499 Office: N Pacific Bank 5448 S Tacoma Way Tacoma WA 98409 *

WALLERSTEIN, BRUCE LEE, psychologist; b. Boston, May 23, 1943; s. Michael and Mildred (Cohen) W. AB, Boston U., 1965; MS, PhD, U. Pa., 1968. Cons. Met. State Hosp., Norwalk, Calif., 1968-70; assoc. prof. U. So. Calif., L.A., 1970-72; pvt. practice Long Beach, Calif., 1969—. Author: A Place to Live Not to Die: A Practical Guide to Nursing Homes, 1975. Fellow Am. Orthopsychiat. Assn., Group Psychotherapy Assn. So. Calif. (pres. 1975-77), Calif. Assn. Health Facilities (assoc.), Long Beach Yacht Club, Naples Bus. Assn., Long Beach C. of C. Office: Naples Counseling Ctr 5855 E Naples Plaza Ste 308 Long Beach CA 90803

WALLERSTEIN, RALPH OLIVER, physician; b. Dusseldorf, Germany, Mar. 7, 1922; came to U.S., 1938, naturalized, 1944; s. Otto R. and Ilse (Hollander) W.; m. Betty Ane Christensen, June 21, 1952; children: Ralph Jr., Richard, Ann. A.B., U. Calif., Berkeley, 1943; M.D., U. Calif., San Francisco, 1945. Diplomate: Am. Bd. Internal Medicine. Intern San Francisco Hosp., 1945-46, resident, 1948-49; resident U. Calif. Hosp., San Francisco, 1949-50; research fellow Thorndike Meml. Lab., Boston City Hosp., 1950-52; chief clin. hematology San Francisco Gen. Hosp., 1953-87; faculty U. Calif., San Francisco, 1952—; clin. prof. medicine U. Calif., 1969—. Served to capt. M.C. AUS, 1946-48. Mem. AMA, Am. Soc. Hematology (pres. 1978), ACP (gov. 1977-81, chmn. bd. govs. 1980-81, regent 1981-87, pres., 1988-89), San Francisco Med. Soc., Am. Clin. and Climatol. Assn., Am. Fedn. Clin. Research, Am. Soc. Internal Medicine, Am. Bd. Internal Medicine (bd. govs. 1975-83, chmn. 1982-83), Am. Assn. Blood Banks, Inst. of Medicine, Calif. Acad. Medicine, Internat. Soc. Hematology, Western Soc. Clin. Research, Western Assn. Physicians. Republican. Home: 3447 Clay St San Francisco CA 94118 Office: 3838 California St Suite 707 San Francisco CA 94118

WALLERSTEIN, ROBERT SOLOMON, psychiatrist; b. Berlin, Germany, Jan. 28, 1921; s. Lazar and Sarah (Guensberg) W.; m. Judith Hannah Saretsky, Jan. 26, 1947; children—Michael Jonathan, Nina Beth, Amy Lisa. B.A., Columbia, 1941, M.D., 1944; postgrad., Topeka Inst. Psychoanalysis, 1951-58. Asso. dir., then dir. research Menninger Found., Topeka, 1954-66; chief psychiatry Mt. Zion Hosp., San Francisco, 1966-78; tng. and supervising analyst San Francisco Psychoanalytic Inst., 1966—; clin. prof. U. Calif. Sch. Medicine, Langley-Porter Neuropsychiat. Inst., 1967-75, prof., chmn. dept. psychiatry, also dir. inst., 1975-85, prof. dept. psychiatry, 1985—; vis. prof. psychiatry La. State U. Sch. Medicine, also New Orleans Psychoanalytic Inst., 1972-73, Pahlavi U., Shiraz, Iran, 1977, Fed. U. Rio Grande do Sul, Porto Alegre, Brasil, 1980; mem., chmn. research scientist career devel. com. NIMH, 1966-70; fellow Center Advanced Study Behavioral Scis., Stanford, Calif., 1964-65, 81-82. Author books and monographs; mem. editorial bd. 8 profl. jours.; contbr. articles to profl. jours. Served with AUS, 1946-48. Recipient Heinz Hartmann award N.Y. Psychoanalytic Inst., 1968, Distinguished Alumnus award Menninger Sch. Psychiatry, 1972, J. Elliott Royer award U. Calif. at San Francisco, 1973, Outstanding Achievement award No. Calif. Psychiat. Soc., 1987. Fellow Am. Psychiat. Assn., A.C.P., Am. Orthopsychiat. Assn.; mem. Am. Psychoanalytic Assn. (pres. 1971-72), Internat. Psychoanalytic Assn. (v.p. 1977-85, pres. 1985-89), Group Advancement Psychiatry, Phi Beta Kappa, Alpha Omega Alpha. Home: 290 Beach Rd Belvedere CA 94920 Office: Langley-Porter Neuropsychiat Inst 401 Parnassus St San Francisco CA 94143

WALLIN, SCOTT FREDERICK, communications executive; b. Milw., Dec. 31, 1951; s. E. Fred and Marilyn (Myrland) W.; m. Kathleen K. Bowman, Apr. 11, 1981; children: Jessica, Kimberly. BA, So. Ill. U., 1974; JD, Ariz. State U., 1979. Bar: Ariz. 1981, U.S. Dist. Ct. (11th dist.) 1981. Pvt. practice Tempe, Ariz., 1979-81; exec. producer Sta. KAET-TV, Tempe, 1981-84; v.p. Ripps Communications, Scottsdale, Ariz., 1984—; pres. Meridian Entertainment Corp., Scottsdale, 1986—; v.p. Total Fulfillment Inc., Scottsdale, 1989—; cons. Musical Theatre of Ariz., Tempe, 1988—; bd. dirs. Rip Com, Inc., Scottsdale, 1987—. Mem. Ariz. Bar Assn., Video Software Dealers Am., Direct Mktg. Assn. Democrat. Office: Meridian Entertainment Corp 2125 E Fifth St #106 Tempe AZ 85281

WALLING, CHEVES T., chemistry educator; b. Evanston, Ill., Feb. 28, 1916; s. Willoughby George and Frederika Christina (Haskell) W.; m. Jane Ann Wilson, Sept. 17, 1940; children—Hazel, Rosalind, Cheves, Janie, Barbara. A.B., Harvard, 1937; Ph.D., U. Chgo., 1939. Research chemist E. I. dePont de Nemours, 1939-43; research chemist U.S. Rubber Co., 1943-49; tech. aide Office Sci. Research, Washington, 1945; sr. research assoc. Lever Bros. Co., 1949-52; prof. chemistry Columbia U., N.Y.C., 1952-69; disting. prof. chemistry U. Utah, Salt Lake City, 1970—. Author: Free Radicals in Solution, 1957; also numerous articles. Fellow AAAS; mem. Nat. Acad. Scis., Am. Acad. Arts and Scis., Am. Chem. Soc. (editor jour. 1975-81, James Flack Norris award 1970, Lubrizol award 1984). Home: 2784 Blue Spruce Dr Holladay UT 84117 Office: U Utah Dept Chemistry Salt Lake City UT 84112

WALLING, DOUGLAS DEAN, air line pilot; b. Arcadia, Fla., Dec. 22, 1934; s. Curtis Eugene and Thelma Paulene (Johnson) W.; m. Shirley Anne Thomas, Sept. 7, 1956 (div. 1967); m. Anne Bernadete Lindberg, Feb. 5, 1980 (div. 1985). Student, U. Md., 1956-59, Coll. of Great Falls, Mont., 1960-62, Tex. Christian U., 1963-67. Commd. 2d lt. USAF, 1954, advanced through grades to lt. col., 1976, ret., 1967; from pilot to capt. Western Airlines, L.A., 1967-86, Delta Airlines, Atlanta, 1986—. Republican. Lutheran. Office: Delta Airlines Harts Field Atlanta Internat Airport Atlanta GA 30901

WALLIS, WAYNE JACK, physician; b. Seattle, Aug. 9, 1950; s. Vincent Rile and Olga Viola (Oylejar) W.; m. Dianne M. Glover, June 25, 1983; children: Spencer, Hanna. BS, Huxley Coll., 1972; MD, U. N.Mex., 1978. Diplomate Am. Bd. Internal Medicine, Am. Bd. Rheumatology. Intern U. Calif., San Diego, 1978-79, resident, 1979-81; fellow U. Wash., Seattle, 1981-83, instr., 1983-85; rheumatologist Group Health Cooperative of Puget Sound, Seattle, 1985; rheumatology sect. chief, Group Health Cooperative of Puget Sound, 1987—; clin. asst. prof., U. Wash., 1985—. Contbr. articles to profl. jours. Active Wash. chpt. Physicians for Social Responsibility, 1984—, West Wash. chpt. Arthritis Found., 1982—. Recipient teaching award U. Calif. San Diego Med. Sch., 1980-81. Fellow Am. Rheumatism Assn; mem. Am. Coll. Physicians, Am. Assn. Clin. Research, Am. Assn. Advancement Sci., Northwest Rheumatism Soc. Unitarian. Home: 1407 Bigelow Seattle WA 98109 Office: Group Health Coop F-215 15th E Seattle WA 98112

WALLMANN, JEFFREY MINER, author; b. Seattle, Dec. 5, 1941; s. George Rudolph and Elizabeth (Biggs) W.; B.S., Portland State U., 1962; m. Helga Reidun Eikefet, Dec. 1, 1974. Pvt. investigator Dale Systems, N.Y.C., 1962-63; asst. buyer, mgr. public money bidder Dohrmann Co., San Francisco, 1964-66; mfrs. rep. electronics industry, San Francisco, 1966-69; dir. public relations London Films, Cinelux-Universal and Trans-European Publs., 1970-75; editor-in-chief Riviera Life mag., 1975-77; cons. Marketeer, Eugene, Oreg., 1978—; books include: The Spiral Web, 1969, Judas Cross, 1974, Clean Sweep, 1976, Jamaica, 1977, Deathtrek, 1980, Blood and Passion, 1980; Brand of the Damned, 1981; The Manipulator, 1982; Return to Conta Lupe, 1983; The Celluloid Kid, 1984; Business Basic for Bunglers, 1984, Guide to Applications Basic, 1984; (under pseudonym Leon DaSilva) Green Hell, 1976, Breakout in Angola, 1977; (pseudonym Nick Carter) Hour of the Wolf, 1973, Ice Trap Terror, 1974; (pseudonym Peter Jensen) The Virgin Couple, 1970, Ravished, 1971; (pseudonmy Jackson Robard) Gang Initiation, 1971, Present for Teacher, 1972, Teacher's Lounge, 1972; (pseudonym Grant Roberts) The Reluctant Couple, 1969, Wayward Wives, 1970; (pseudonym Gregory St. Germain) Resistance #1: Night and Fog, 1982, Resistance #2: Maygar Massacre, 1983; (pseudonym Wesley Ellis) Lonestar on the Treachery Trail, 1982, numerous others in the Lonestar series; (pseudonym Tabor Evans) Longarm and the Lonestar Showdown, 1986; (psyeudonym Jon Sharpe) Trailsman 58: Slaughter Express, 1986, numerous others in Trailsman series; also many other pseudonyms and titles; contbr. articles and short stories to Argosy, Ellery Queen's Mystery Mag., Alfred Hitchcock's Mystery Mag., Mike Shayne's Mystery Mag., Zane Grey Western, Venture, Oui, TV Guide; also (under pseudonym William Jeffrey in collaboration with Bill Pronzini) Dual at Gold Buttes, 1980, Border Fever, 1982, Day of the Moon, 1983. Mem. Mystery Writers of Am., Sci. Fiction Writers Am., Western Writers Am., Crime Writers Assn., Eugene Bd. Realtors, Nat. Assn. Realtors.

WALLOP, MALCOLM, senator, rancher; b. N.Y.C., Feb. 27, 1933; s. Oliver M. and Jean (Moore) W.; m. French Carter, May 26, 1984; children: Malcolm, Amy, Paul, Matthew. B.A., Yale U., 1954. Owner, operator Canyon Ranch, Big Horn, Wyo.; mem. Wyo. Ho. of Reps., 1969-73, Wyo. Senate, 1973-77; mem. U.S. Senate from Wyo., 1976—, mem. coms. on energy and natural resources, armed svcs., small bus.; ofcl. observer from Senate on arms control negotiations; mem. Commn. on Security and Cooperation in Europe. Served to lt. U.S. Army, 1955-57. Mem. Wyo. Stockgrowers Assn., Am. Nat. Cattleman's Assn., Am. Legion. Republican. Episcopalian. Office: US Senate 237 Russell Senate Bldg Washington DC 20510

WALLSTRÖM, WESLEY DONALD, banker; b. Turlock, Calif., Oct. 4, 1929; s. Emil Reinhold and Edith Katherine (Lindberg) W.; student Modesto Jr. Coll., 1955-64; certificate Pacific Coast Banking Sch., U. Wash., 1974; m. Marilyn Irene Hallmark, May 12, 1951; children: Marc Gordon, Wendy Diane. Bookkeeper, teller First Nat. Bank, Turlock, 1947-50; v.p. Gordon Hallmark, Inc., Turlock, 1950-53; asst. cashier United Calif. Bank, Turlock, 1953-68, regional v.p., Fresno, 1968-72, v.p., mgr., Turlock, 1972-76; founding pres., dir. Golden Valley Bank, Turlock, 1976-84; pres. Wallström & Co., 1985—. Campaign chmn. United Crusade, Turlock, 1971; chmn., founding dir. Covenant Village, retirement home, Turlock, 1973—, treas. Covenant Retirement Communities West; founding pres. Turlock Regional Arts Coun., 1974, dir., 1975-76. Served with U.S. N.G., 1948-56. Mem. Nat. Soc. Accts. for Coops., Ind. Bankers No. Calif., Am. Bankers Assn., U.S. Yacht Racing Union, No. Calif. Golf Assn., Turlock C. of C. (dir. 1973-75), Stanislaus Sailing Soc. (commodore 1980-81), Turlock Golf and Country Club (pres. 1975-76, v.p., 1977, dir. 1977, 83), Masons, Rotary. Republican. Mem. Covenant Ch. Home: 1720 Hammond Dr Turlock CA 95380 Office: Wallstrom & Co 2925 Niagara Turlock CA 95380

WALRAD, CHARLENE CHUCK, computer system designer, consultant; b. Palm Beach, Fla., Feb. 21, 1946; d. Jack Maynard and Marian (Davenport) W.; m. Larry Starr, Oct. 1, 1972 (div. 1980). BA, Ariz. State U., 1967, MA, 1969; MA, U. Calif., San Diego, 1971. Linguist LATSEC, Inc., La Jolla, Calif., 1971-75, sr. linguist, 1975-84; v.p. World Translation Ctr., La Jolla, 1981-84; dir. mktg. Automated Lang. Processing Systems, Provo, Utah, 1984-85; dir. R & D, WICAT Systems, Orem, Utah, 1985-86; dir. quality mgmt. Relational Tech., Alameda, Calif., 1986-87; machine translation software cons. San Francisco, 1987—; cons. Xerox Corp., Webster, N.Y., 1983-84, Sci. Applications, Inc., La Jolla, 1984, Dept. Commerce, 1988, CIA, 1989, NAS, 1989; presenter in field. Co-author: Introduction to Luiseno, 1972. Bd. dirs. Shelter Ridge Assn., Mill Valley, Calif., 1988-89, v.p., 1989—. Mem. Ariz. State U. Alumni Assn. (pres. San Diego chpt. 1982-83, Utah chpt. 1985-86), Mensa. Home: 12 Brooke Circle Mill Valley CA 94941 Office: 21 Tamal Vista Blvd Ste 212 Corte Madera CA 94925

WALRATH, HARRY RIENZI, clergyman; b. Alameda, Calif., Mar. 7, 1926; s. Frank Rienzi and Cathren (Michlar) W.; A.A., City Coll. San Francisco, 1950; B.A., U. Calif. at Berkeley, 1952; M.Div., Ch. Div. Sch. of Pacific, 1959; m. Dorothy M. Baxter, June 24, 1961; 1 son, Gregory Rienzi. Dist. exec. San Mateo area council Boy Scouts Am., 1952-55; ordained deacon Episcopal Ch., 1959, priest, 1960; curate All Souls Parish, Berkeley, Calif., 1959-61; vicar St. Luke's, Atascadero, Calif., 1961-63, St. Andrew's, Garberville, Calif., 1963-64; asso. rector St. Luke's Ch., Los Gatos, 1964-65, Holy Spirit Parish, Missoula, Mont., 1965-67; vicar St. Peter's Ch., also headmaster St. Peter's Schs., Litchfield Park, Ariz., 1967-69; chaplain U. Mont., 1965-67; asst. rector Trinity Parish, Reno, 1969-72; coordinator counciling services Washoe County Council Alcoholism, Reno, 1972-74; adminstr. Cons. Assistance Services, Inc., Reno, 1974-76; pastoral counselor, contract chaplain Nev. Mental Health Inst., 1976-78; contract mental health chaplain VA Hosp., Reno, 1976-78; mental health chaplain VA Med. Ctr., 1978-83, staff chaplain, 1983-85, chief, chaplain service, 1985—, also triage coordinator for mental health; dir. youth Paso Robles Presbytery; chmn. Diocesan Commn. on Alcoholism; cons. teen-age problems Berkeley Presbytery; mem. clergy team Episcopal Marriage Encounter, 1979-85, also Episc. Engaged Encounter. Mem. at large Washoe dist. Nev. area council Boy Scouts Am., scoutmaster troop 73, 1976, troop 585, 1979-82, asst. scoutmaster troop 35, 1982—, assoc. adviser area 3 Western region, 1987-89, regional com. Western Region, 1989—; lodge adviser Tannu Lodge 346, Order of Arrow, 1982-87; South Humboldt County chmn. Am. Cancer Soc. Trustee Community Youth Ctr., Reno. Served with USNR, 1944-46. Decorated Pacific Theater medal with star, Am. Theater medal, Victory medal, Fleet Unit Commendation medal; recipient dist. award of merit Boy Scouts Am., St. George award Episc. Ch.-Boy Scouts Am., Silver Beaver award Boy Scouts Am., 1986, Founders' award Order of the Arrow, Boy Scouts Am., 1985; performance awards VA-VA Med. Ctr., 1983, 84; named Arrowman of Yr., Order of Arrow, Boy Scouts Am. Cert. substance abuse counselor, Nev. Mem. Ch. Hist. Soc., U. Calif. Alumni Assn., Nat. Model R.R. Assn. (life), Sierra Club Calif., Missoula Council Chs. (pres.), Alpha Phi Omega. Democrat. Club: Rotary. Home: 580 Huffaker Ln E Reno NV 89511 Office: VA Med Ctr 1000 Locust St Reno NV 89520

WALRAVEN, GARY DENNIS, management information systems specialist; b. Sioux City, Iowa, Feb. 5, 1941; s. Gerrit Arthur and Evelyn Marcela (Bjorkman) W.; m. Molly Torres, June 10, 1967; children: Lisa, John, Eric. BSBA and Indsl. Mgmt., San Jose State U., 1966; MBA, Golden Gate U., 1971. Prodn. supr. Ampex Co., Redwood City, Calif., 1966-69, supr. systems, systems analyst, 1970-74; prodn. planning mgr. Ampex Co., Colorado Springs, Colo., 1977-82, MIS project mgr., 1983--; systems planning mgr. Saga Corp., Menlo Park, Calif., 1975-76. Treas. St. Mary's High Sch. Parent-Tchr.-Student Orgn., Colorado Springs, 1986-87. Mem. Am. Prodn. and Inventory Control Soc., Am. Mgmt. Assn., Soc. for Advancement Mgmt. Republican. Roman Catholic. Office: Ampex Co 600 Wooten Rd Colorado Springs CO 80915

WALSH, BERNARD LAWRENCE, JR., physicist; b. Detroit, Jan. 11, 1932; s. Bernard Lawrence Sr. and Catherine Bridget (McCarthy) W.; m. Margaret Barbara Milko, Feb. 16, 1957; children: Bernard Lawrence III, Catherine Teresa. AB, U. Detroit, 1954. With Hughes Aircraft Co., L.A., 1954--, sr. scientist, 1968-75, chief scientist, 1975--. Contbr. articles to profl. jours.; patentee in field. Mem. IEEE, Am. Phys. Soc., ASM Internat., Profl. Group Electron Devices, Profl. Group Microwave Theory and Techniques. Home: 9609 Wystone Ave Northridge CA 91324 Office: Hughes Aircraft Co PO Box 92919 Los Angeles CA 90009

WALSH, DANIEL FRANCIS, bishop; b. San Francisco, Oct. 2, 1937. Grad., St. Joseph Sem., St. Patrick Sem., Catholic U. Am. Ordained priest, Roman Catholic Ch., 1963. Ordained titular bishop of Tigia, 1981; aux. bishop of San Francisco 1981-87, bishop of Reno-Las Vegas, 1987—. Office: 515 Court St Reno NV 89501

WALSH, EDWARD JOSEPH, toiletries and food company executive; b. Mt. Vernon, N.Y., Mar. 18, 1932; s. Edward Aloysius and Charlotte Cecilia (Borup) W.; m. Patricia Ann Farrell, Sept. 16, 1961; children: Edward Joseph, Megan, John, Robert. BBA, Iona Coll., 1953; MBA, NYU, 1958. Sales rep. M & R Dietetic Labs., Columbus, Ohio, 1955-60; with Armour & Co., 1961—; v.p. toiletries div. Armour Dial Co., Phoenix, 1973-76; exec. v.p. Armour Dial Co., 1976-77; former pres., now dir. Armour Internat. Co., Phoenix, 1978—; pres. The Dial Corp. (formerly Armour-Dial Co.), Phoenix, 1984—, chief exec. officer, 1986—; pres., chief exec. officer Purex Corp., from 1985; chmn., chief exec. officer The Sparta Group Ltd., Scottsdale, Ariz., 1988; bd. dirs. Phillips Ramsey Advt., San Diego, Phoenix, 1986, Guest Supply Inc., New Brunswick, N.J., 1985, WD-40 Co., San Diego, 1987; chief exec. officer Sparta Group Ltd., 1988. Pres. Mt. Vernon Fire Dept. Mems. Assn., 1960-61. Served with U.S. Army, 1953-55, Germany. Mem. Am. Mgmt. Assn., Nat. Meat Canner Assn. (pres. 1971-72), Cosmetic, Toiletries and Fragrance Assn. (bd. dirs. 1985—), Nat. Food Processors Assn. (bd. dirs.). Republican. Roman Catholic. Office: The Dial Corp 111 W Clarendon Phoenix AZ 85077

WALSH, JOHN, JR., museum director; b. Mason City, Wash., Dec. 9, 1937; s. John J. and Eleanor (Wilson) W.; m. Virginia Alys Galston, Feb. 17, 1961; children: Peter Wilson, Anne Galston, Frederick Matthiessen. B.A., Yale U., 1961; postgrad., U. Leyden, Netherlands, 1965-66; M.A., Columbia U., 1965, Ph.D., 1971. Lectr., rsch. asst. Frick Collection, N.Y.C., 1966-68; assoc. higher edn. Met. Mus. Art, N.Y.C., 1968-71; assoc. curator European paintings Met. Mus. Art, 1970-72, curator dept. European paintings, 1972-75, vice-chmn., 1974-75; adj. asso. prof. art history Columbia U., N.Y.C., 1969-72; adj. prof. Columbia U., 1972-75; prof. art history Barnard Coll., Columbia U., N.Y.C., 1975-77; Mrs. Russell W. Baker curator paintings Mus. Fine Arts, Boston, 1977-83; dir. J. Paul Getty Mus., Malibu, Calif., 1983—; vis. prof. fine arts Harvard U., 1979; mem. governing bd. Yale U. Art Gallery, 1975—; bd. Fellows Claremont U. Ctr. Grad. Sch., 1988—. Contbr. articles to profl. jours. Mem. county com. Democratic party, N.Y.C., 1968-71; mem. vis. com. Fogg Mus., Harvard U.; bd. fellows Claremont U. Ctr. and Grad. Sch., 1988—. With USNR, 1957-59. Fulbright grad. fellow The Netherlands, 1965-66. Mem. Coll. Art Assn., Am. Assn. Mus., Archaeol. Inst. Am., Am. Antiquarian Soc. Club: Century Assn. (N.Y.C.). Office: J Paul Getty Mus PO Box 2112 Santa Monica CA 90406

WALSH, MARY D. FLEMING, civic worker; b. Whitewright, Tex., Oct. 29, 1913; d. William Fleming and Anna Maud (Lewis) Fleming; B.A., So. Meth. U., 1934; LL.D. (hon.), Tex. Christian U., 1979; m. F. Howard Walsh, Mar. 13, 1937; children—Richard, Howard, D'Ann Walsh Bonnell, Maudi Walsh Roe, William Lloyd. Pres. Fleming Found.; v.p. Walsh Found.; partner Walsh Co.; mem. Lloyd Shaw Found., Colorado Springs, Big Bros. Tarrant County; guarantor Fort Worth Arts Council, Schola Cantorum, Fort Worth Opera, Fort Worth Ballet, Fort Worth Theatre, Tex. Boys Choir; hon. mem. bd. dirs. Van Cliburn Internat. Piano Competition; co-founder Am. Field Service in Ft. Worth; mem. Tex. Commn. for Arts and Humanities, 1968-72, mem. adv. council, 1972-84; bd. dirs. Wm. Edrington Scott Theatre, 1977-83, Colorado Springs Day Nursery, Colorado Springs Symphony, Ft. Worth Symphony, 1974-81; hon. chmn. Opera Ball, 1975, Opera Guild Internat. Conf., 1976; co-presenter (with husband) through Walsh Found., Tex. Boy's Choir and Dorothy Shaw Bell Choir ann. presentation of The Littlest

Wiseman to City of Ft. Worth; granter with husband land and bldgs. to Tex. Boy's Choir for permanent home, 1971, Walsh-Wurlitzer organ to Casa Manana, 1972. Sem. Recipient numerous awards, including Altrusa Civic award as 1st Lady of Ft. Worth, 1968; (with husband) Disting. Service award So. Bapt. Radio and Television Commn., 1972; Opera award Girl Scouts, 1977-79; award Streams and Valleys, 1976-80; named (with husband) Patron of Arts in Ft. Worth, 1970, Edna Gladney Internat. Grandparents of 1972, (with husband) Sr. Citizens of Yr, 1985; Mary D. and Howard Walsh Meml. Organ dedicated by Bapt. Radio and TV Commn., 1967, tng. ctr. named for the Walshes, 1976; Mary D. and Howard Walsh Med. Bldg., Southwestern Bapt. Theol. Sem.; library at Tarrant County Jr. Coll. N.W. Campus dedicated to her and husband, 1978; Brotherhood citation Tarrant County chpt. NCCJ, 1978; Spl. Recognition award Ft. Worth Ballet Assn.; Royal Purple award Tex. Christian U., 1979; Friends of Tex. Boys Choir award, 1981; appreciation award Southwestern Bapt. Theol. Sem., 1981, B. H. Carroll Founders award, 1982; numerous other award for civic activities. Mem. Ft. Worth Boys Club, Ft. Worth Children's Hosp., Jewel Charity Ball, Ft. Worth Pan Hellenic (pres. 1940), Opera Guild, Fine Arts Found. Guild of Tex. Christian U., Girl's Service League (hon. life, hon. chmn. Fine Arts Guild Spring Ballet, 1985), AAUW, Goodwill Industries Aux., Child Study Center, Tarrant County Aux. of Edna Gladney Home, YWCA (life), Ft. Worth Art Assn., Ft. Worth Ballet Assn., Tex. Boys Choir Aux., Friends of Tex. Boys Choir, Round Table, Colorado Springs Fine Art Center, Am. Automobile Assn., Nat. Assn. Cowbelles, Ft. Worth Arts Council (hon. bd. mem.), Am. Guild Organists (hon., Ft. Worth chpt.), Rae Reimers Bible Study Class (pres. 1968), Tex. League Composers (hon. life), Chi Omega (pres. 1935-36, hon. chmn. 1986), others. Baptist. Clubs: The Woman's (Club Fidelite), Colorado Springs Country, Garden of Gods, Colonial Country, Ridglea Country, Shady Oaks Country, Chi Omega Mothers, Chi Omega Carousel, TCU Woman's. Home: 2425 Stadium Dr Fort Worth TX 76109 also: 1801 Culebra Ave Colorado Springs CO 80907

WALSH, MICHAEL FRANCIS, marketing research executive; b. Bell Harbor, N.Y., Dec. 5, 1947; s. Michael Francis and Patricia (Bratz) W.; m. Julia Ann Finn, Apr. 17, 1983; 1 child, Kelly Michelle . Student, U. Tex., Arlington, 1966-67, Coll. San Mateo, 1967-69; BA in Psychology, U. Calif., Santa Barbara, 1971; MS in Psychology, U. Wis., 1976. Cert. instr. community colls., Calif. Instr. Berlitz Sprachenschule, Munich, 1971-72; research asst. U. Wis., Madison, 1972-75; project dir. Ednl. Testing Service, Berkeley, Calif., 1976-82, dir. representation of western states, 1980-82; founder, pres. Walsh and Assocs., El Sobrante, Calif., 1982—; mem. adv. bd. Internat. Trade Inst., Berkeley, 1983-88, chmn. funding com., 1986-88. Editor, contbg. author: Handbook for Proficiency Assessment, 1979; author: (state agy. reports) Evaluation of Artists in Social Institutions for California Arts Council, 1981, Evaluation of Creative Arts Computer Course, 1985, Humanists-in-Schools: Eight Years Later, 1986 (Joint Dissemination and Rev. Panel Nat. Dissemination Program award 1986). Commr. Richmond (Calif.) Arts Commn., 1988—. Pres.'s Research grantee U. Calif., 1970. Mem. Am. Mktg. Assn. (exec.), Am. Coun. Arts, Am. Ednl. Rsch. Assn., Am. Evaluation Assn., Nat. Coun. Measurement Edn. Democrat. Roman Catholic. Office: Walsh and Assocs 3817 San Pablo Dam Rd Ste 127 El Sobrante CA 94803

WALSH, WILLIAM, television broadcaster, former professional football coach; b. Los Angeles, Nov. 30, 1931. Student, San Mateo Jr. Coll.; BA, San Jose State U., 1954, MA in Edn., 1959. Asst. coach Monterey Peninsula Coll., 1955, San Jose State U., 1956; head coach Washington Union High Sch., Fremont, Calif., 1957-59; asst. coach U. Calif., Berkeley, 1960-62, Stanford U., 1963-65, Oakland Raiders, Am. Football League, 1966-67, Cin. Bengals, 1968-69, 70-75, San Diego Chargers, Nat. Football League, 1976; head coach Stanford U., 1977-78; head coach, gen. mgr. San Francisco 49ers, NFL, 1979-89, exec. v.p., 1989; broadcaster NBC Sports, 1989—. Named NFL Coach of Yr. Sporting News, 1981; coached Stanford U. winning team Sun Bowl, 1977, Bluebonnet Bowl, 1978; NFL Championship team, 1981, 84. Office: San Francisco 49ers 711 Nevada St Redwood City CA 94061 *

WALSMITH, CHARLES RODGER, psychologist, educator; b. Denver, May 19, 1926; s. Joseph Francis and Florence Ophelia (Brown-Smith) W.; children: Karen Frances, Cynthia Ann, Erik Konrad. BA (Chancellor's Ednl. scholar), U. Denver, 1956, MA, 1962; postgrad. U. Wash., 1968-76; PhD, Stanton U., 1976. Rsch. psychologist Personnel Tng. and Rsch. Ctr., Maintenance Lab., USAF Lowry AFB, Denver, 1956; rsch. asst. U. Colo. Med. Ctr., Denver, 1956-57, rsch. assoc., 1957-64; asst. prof. psychology North Park Coll., Chgo., 1965-66; sr. human engring. analyst, psychoacoustics Boeing Co., Seattle, 1965-68; instr. psychology dept. behavioral scis. Bellevue (Wash.) Community Coll., 1968-87, chmn. dept., 1968-75, 79-82, Phi Theta Kappa adviser, 1981-87, instr., chmn. dept. emeritus, 1987—. Resident trainer Gestalt Inst. of Can., Lake Cowichan, B.C., summers 1969-71, assoc., 1969—; dir. Gestalt Inst. of Wash., Bellevue, 1970—. Dem. precinct chmn., Renton, Wash., 1966-68; patron BCC Found. With USNR, 1944-46. Mem. Wash. State, Psychol. Assn., NEA, Wash. Edn. Assn., Phi Beta Kappa, Psi Chi. Home: Gestalt House 14909 SE 44th Pl Bellevue WA 98006

WALSTROM, THOMAS ARVID, business owner; b. Bellingham, Wash., June 3, 1933; s. Ernest Arvid and Winnifred Faye (Roberts) W.; m. Mary Lue Myrtle Henifin, Aug. 1, 1952; children: Kim F., Linda K., Richard A., Kevin T., Kristina J. Student, Olympic Jr. Coll., 1952-56. Supr. U.S. Dept. Energy Bonneville Power Adminstrn., Custer, Wash., 1966-88; owner, operator Win's Drive-In, Bellingham, 1978—. Freeholder Whatcom County, Bellingham, 1978. Mem. Nat. Restaurant Assn., Wash. State Restaurant Assn., Bellingham Yacht Club, Toastmasters (pres. 1976-77). Lutheran. Office: Wins Drive-In 1315 12th St Bellingham WA 98225

WALTER, BERT MATHEW, federal mediation commissioner; b. Devils Lake, N.D., July 11, 1915; s. Alois and Margaret (Bauer) W.; m. Phyllis Traynor, July 3, 1950. AA, U. Minn., 1936; BBA, U. Balt., 1938. Shop employee GE Co., Pittsfield, Mass., 1938-41; dir. indsl. relations Consol. Vultee Aircraft Co., Tucson, 1941-49, Bendix Aviation Corp., Kansas City, Mo., 1949-55; v.p. indsl. relations Clark Equipment Co., Buchanan, Mich., 1955-64, Chesebrough Pond's, N.Y.C., 1964-66; pres. Leasing Internat. Corp., Madrid, Spain, 1966-68; commr. Fed. Mediation and Conciliation Svc., L.A., 1968—; pres. Buchannan (Mich.) United Funds, 1956-57. Contbr. articles to profl. publs. Mem. Conseil Internat. Orgn. Scientifique (dir. 1967), Council Internat. Progress Mgmt. (dir. 1967), Nat. Metal Trades Assn. (pres. 1962-63), Am. Soc. Personnel Adminstrn. (founder, pres. 1958-59), Indsl. Relations Rsch. Assn., Soc. Profls. in Dispute Resolution, Rotary (pres. Niles, Mich. 1959-59), Elks. Republican. Roman Catholic. Home: 2598 N Ayala Dr Unit 92 Rialto CA 92376

WALTER, BRUCE ALEXANDER, physician; b. Seattle, Apr. 15, 1922; s. Ernest R. and Marion (Alexander) W.; BA, U. Wash., 1944, BS, 1948, MD, 1951; MPH, UCLA, 1962; m. Gloria Helen Parry, Feb. 4, 1956; children: Maia Marion, Wendy Diane, Shelley Kathleen, Allison Ann. Intern Los Angeles County Gen. Hosp., 1951-52; resident internal medicine Wadsworth Hosp., U. Calif., 1952-54; dir. grad. program hosp., health facilities adminstrn. UCLA, 1965-68; attending staff Salt Lake County Hosp., 1954-55; fellow medicine U. Utah, 1954-55; fellow medicine U. So. Calif., 1955-56, mem. faculty, 1956-65; attending staff Los Angeles County Hosp., 1956-65; physician internal medicine, Palm Springs, Calif., 1956-61; chief staff Desert Hosp., 1960-61; dir. med. care studies Calif. Dept. Pub. Health, Berkeley, 1962-65; dir. Med. Care Services, State of Utah, 1969-71, dep. dir. health, 1971-79, acting dir. health, 1979; cons. Newport Med. Group and Advanced Health Systems, Inc., Newport Beach, Calif., 1979-84; practice medicine specializing in internal medicine, Costa Mesa, Calif., 1984—; asst. prof. community and family medicine U. Utah Sch. Medicine, Salt Lake City, 1969-79; mem. Utah State Bd. Aging; bd. dirs. Blue Shield of Utah, Utah Profl. Standards Rev. Orgn. 1st lt. Signal Corps, AUS, 1943-46. Mem. Nat. Assn. Health Facility Licensing and Certification Dirs. (pres. 1975-76), Balboa Bay Club, Alpha Delta Phi, Alpha Kappa Kappa, Alpha Delta Sigma. Home: 2821 Blue Water Dr Corona del Mar CA 92625 Office: 275 Victoria St Costa Mesa CA 92627

WALTER, CAROL DANA, financial analyst; b. San Jose, Calif., Nov. 17, 1958; d. Robert Fredrick John and Cynthia Ellen (Cheney) Krieg; m. David Jerome Walter, June 1, 1957. AS in Bus., DeAnza Community Coll., Cupertino, Calif., 1978; BS in Bus. and Fin., San Jose State U., 1980. Prin., fin. analyst Motorola Computer Systems, Inc., Cupertino, 1981-88; fin. analyst Sun Microsystems, Inc., Mountain View, Calif., 1988—. Home: 4929 Augusta Way San Jose CA 95129 Office: Sun Microsystems Inc 2550 Garcia Ave Mountain View CA 94043

WALTER, FREDERICK JOHN, motel executive; b. East Orange, N.J., Jan. 26, 1944; s. Fred Gottlieb and Emily (Mast) W.; m. Jane Elizabeth Schackner, Aug. 20, 1966; children: Emily Jane, Meredith Waite. BA, N.C. State U., 1966; MBA, Ga. State U., 1968. Exec. Internat. Diversified Corp., Freeport, Bahamas, 1969-76; mng. ptnr. Best Western-Nellis Motor Inn, Las Vegas, Nev., 1977-87, Best Western-Lake Mead Motel, Henderson, Nev., 1984-87, Best Western-McCarran Inn, Las Vegas, 1986—; hotel-motel cons., sales rep. Helen Naugle & Assocs., Las Vegas, 1982—; regional gov. Best Western Internat., Inc., Phoenix, 1977—. Bd. dirs. Boys and Girls Clubs, Las Vegas, 1982—, Las Vegas Conv. and Visitors Authority, 1988—; mem. So. Nev. Civilian Mil. Coun., Las Vegas, 1983—. With USMC, 1963-65. Mem. Nev. Hotel and Motel Assn. (bd. dirs., v.p. 1981--), Greater Las Vegas C. of C., Am. Hotel and Motel Assn. (cert. hotel adminstr.), Air Force Assn., Rotary. Lutheran. Office: Best Western McCarran Inn 4970 Paradise Rd Las Vegas NV 89119

WALTER, MICHAEL CHARLES, lawyer; b. Oklahoma City, Nov. 25, 1956; s. Donald Wayne and Viola Helen (Heffelfinger) W. BA in Polit. Sci., BJ, U. Wash., 1980; JD, Univ. Puget Sound, 1983. Bar: Wash. 1985, U.S. Dist. Ct. (9th cir. 1985). Assoc. Keating, Bucklin & McCormack, Seattle, 1985—; instr. Bellevue (Wash.) Community Coll., 1983—. Mem. Internat. Assn. Bus. Communicators, Reporters Com. for Freedom of Press, ACLU, ABA, Wash. State Bar Assn., Seattle-King County Bar Assn., Wash. Assn. Def. Counsel, Seattle Claims Adjustors Assn., Wash. Assn. Mcpl. Attys. Home: 11552 3d Ave NW Seattle WA 98177 Office: Keating Bucklin & McCormack 4141 SeaFirst Fifth Ave Pla Seattle WA 98104

WALTER, RUSSELL EDWIN, electronics company executive; b. Buffalo, June 2, 1951; s. Edwin Arthur and June Shirley (Jerge) W.; m. Judith Carol Warren, Mar. 1, 1975; children: Elaine, Ellen, Warren, Lacey, Jessica. BEE, Mich. State U., 1973. Assoc. engr. Boeing Aerospace Corp., Seattle, 1973-74, engr., 1975-79, sr. engr., 1980-81, specialist engr., 1982-85; mgr. engring. support systems Boeing Electronic Corp., Seattle, 1985—. Republican. Home: 15040 Des Moines Meml Dr Seattle WA 98148 Office: Boeing Electronics M/S9F-50 1012 SW 41st St Renton WA 98055

WALTERS, ANNA LEE, writer, educational administrator; b. Pawnee, Okla., Sept. 9, 1946; d. Luther and Juanita Mae (Taylor) McGlaslin; BA Goddard Coll. children: Anthony, Daniel. Dir. Navajo Community Coll. Press, Tsaile (Navajo Nation), Ariz., 1982—; contbg. author: The Man to Send Rainclouds, 1974, Warriors of the Rainbow, 1975, Shantih, 1976, The Third Woman, 1979, The Remembered Earth, 1979, American Indians Today, Thought, Literature, Art, 1981; co-author textbook: The Sacred Ways of Knowledge, Sources of Life, 1977; author: The Otoe-Missiouria Tribe, Centennial Memoirs, 1881-1981, 1981; Earth Power Coming, 1983; The Sun is Not Merciful, 1985, Ghost Singer, 1988, The Spirit of Native America, 1989; contbr. articles to jours.; guest editor Frauen Offensive, 1978; also poet, feature writer. Recipient Am. Book award The Before Columbus Found., 1986, Virginia Scully McCormick Lit. award, 1986. Office: Navajo Community Coll Press Tsaile AZ 86556

WALTERS, JESSE RAYMOND, JR., judge; b. Rexburg, Idaho, Dec. 26, 1938; s. Jesse Raymond and Thelma Rachael (Hodgson) W.; m. Harriet Payne, May 11, 1959; children—Craig T., Robyn, J. Scott. Student Ricks Coll., 1957-58; B.A. in Polit. Sci., U. Idaho, 1961, J.D., 1963; postgrad. U. Washington, 1962. Bar: Idaho 1963, U.S. Dist. Ct. Idaho 1964, U.S. Ct. Appeals (9th cir.) 1970. Law clk. to chief justice Idaho Supreme Ct., 1963-64; sole practice, Boise, Idaho, 1964-77; atty. Idaho senate, Boise, 1965; dist. judge 4th Jud. Dist., Idaho, Boise, 1977-82, adminstrv. dist. judge, 1981-82; chief judge Idaho Ct. Appeals, Boise, 1982—; chmn. magistrate's commn. 4th jud. dist.; chmn. Supreme Ct. mem. services; mem. Civil Pattern Jury Instrn. Com; Republican committeeman, Boise, 1975-77; mem. Ada County Rep. Central Com., 1975-77. Mem. Idaho Bar Assn. (bankruptcy com.), Idaho Adminstrv. Judges Assn., ABA, Am. Judicature Soc., Assn. Trial Lawyers Am. Idaho Trial Lawyers Assn., Council Chief Judges Ct. Appeals, Boise Estate Planning Council, Jaycees (nat. dir. 1969-70, pres. Boise chpt. 1966-67). Mormon. Lodges: Lions, Elks, Eagles. Office: State Idaho Ct Appeals 537 W Bannock St Boise ID 83720

WALTERS, MARY COON, justice state supreme court; b. Baraga, Mich., Jan. 29, 1922; d. Marvin Leonard and Nancy Claire (Conway) Coon; m. Asa Lane Walters, July 9, 1952 (dec. June 1974); 1 child, Mark Richard. J.D., U. N.Mex., 1962. Bar: N.Mex. 1962, U.S. Supreme Ct., U.S. Ct. Appeals (4th and 10th cir.). Pvt. practice Albuquerque, 1962-71, 73-78; judge 2d Jud. Dist. N.Mex., Albuquerque, 1971-72; judge N.Mex. Ct. Appeals, Santa Fe, 1979-81, chief judge, 1981-83; justice N.Mex. Supreme Ct., Santa Fe, 1984-89; del. N.Mex. Constnl. Conv., 1969. Served with Women's Airforce Service Pilots, 1943-44, USAF, 1951-55. Named to N.Mex. Women's Hall of Fame, 1986. Mem. ABA, N.Mex. Bar Assn. (Disting. Jud. Svc. award 1988), Albuquerque Bar Assn., Santa Fe Bar Assn. Democrat. Roman Catholic.

WALTERS, STEPHEN GERARD, electrical engineer; b. Washington, Dec. 17, 1959; s. Richard Eugene and Elizabeth Ann (Fox) W. BEE, U. Md., 1982. Physical scientist Naval Surface Weapons Ctr., Silver Spring, Md., 1979-82; assoc. engr. Johns Hopkins U., Laurel, Md., 1982-86; tech. staff, elec. engring. Hughes Aircraft/Santa Barbara Research Ctr., Goleta, Calif., 1986—; design cons., Santa Barbara. Active Citizens Planning Assn., Santa Barbara, 1987-88. Recipient Group Achievement award NASA, 1985. Democrat. Roman Catholic. Home: 1321 Chino St Santa Barbara CA 93101 Office: Santa Barbara Rsch Ctr 75 Coromar Dr Goleta CA 93117

WALTON, CHRISANN VALERE, food research technician; b. Camden, N.J., Dec. 26, 1958; d. Edward F. and Valere H. (McCluskey) W. AA, Riverside City Coll., 1979; BA, Calif. State U., Fullerton, 1981, MA, 1983. Waitress John Wanamakers, Moorestown, N.J., 1975-77; cashier J.C. Penney Co., Riverside, Calif., 1977-79; mgr. women's sportswear Buffums, LaHabra, Calif., 1979-83; subs. tchr. Hebrew Acad., Westminster, Calif., 1983-85; counselor Social Vocat. Svcs., Alhambra, Calif., 1985-86; rsch. technician Beatrice/Hunt-Wesson, Fullerton, Calif., 1986—. Mem. DAR. Republican. Roman Catholic. Home: 2879 Standish Ave Anaheim CA 92806 Office: Beatrice/Hunt-Wesson 1701 W Valencia-MS 501 Fullerton CA 92806

WALTON, CRAIG, philosopher, educator; b. L.A., Dec. 6, 1934; s. Delvy Thomas and Florence (Higgins) W.; m. Nancy Young, June 6, 1965 (div. May 1977); children: Richard, Kerry; m. Vera Allerton, Aug. 30, 1980; children: Matthew, Ruth, Peter, Benjamin. BA, Pomona Coll., 1961; PhD, Claremont Grad. Sch., 1965. Asst. prof. U. So. Calif., L.A., 1964-68; asst. prof. No. Ill. U., DeKalb, 1968-71, assoc. prof., 1971-72; assoc. prof. U. Nev., Las Vegas, 1972-75, prof., 1975—, chair dept. philosophy, 1986-89, dir. Inst. for Ethics & Policy Studies, 1986—; mem. Admissions Selection com. Sch. Medicine U. Nev., 1983—; bd. dirs. Jour. of the History of Philosophy. Author: De la recherche du Bien, 1972, Philosophy & the Civilizing Arts, 1975, Hobbe's 'Science of Natural Justice', 1987; editorial bd. Studies in Early Modern Philosophy, 1986—; contbr. articles to profl. jours. V.p. Nev. Faculty Alliance, 1984-86; mem. Clark County Sch. Dist. Task Force on Ethics in schs., 1987. 1st lt. USAF, 1956-59. Recipient NDEA Title IV fellowship Claremont Grad. Sch, 1961-64, rsch. sabbaticals U. Nev., 1978, 85; named Barrick Disting. scholar U. Nev., 1988. Mem. AAUP (pres. Nev. chpt. 1983-84), Internat. Hume Soc.(exec. com. 1979-81), Am. Philos. Assn., Soc. for Study of History of Philosophy (exec. sec. 1974—), Internat. Hobbes Soc., Phi Beta Kappa. Democrat. Home: 6140 Eisner Ln Las Vegas NV 89131 Office: U Nev Dept Philosophy 4505 Maryland Pkwy Las Vegas NV 89154

WALTON, DEBORAH GAIL, advertising agency executive; b. L.A., June 22, 1950; d. Philip Hall and Virginia Mary (Schreiber) W.; m. Timothy Alan Schaible, Sept. 12, 1987; children: Adam, Melissa, Amanda, Jennifer. BA in English, Russell Sage Coll., 1972. Copywriter STA-Power Industries, San Rafael, Calif., 1972-73; asst. advt. mgr. Albany (N.Y.) Pub. Markets, 1973-75; dir. pub. relations Sta. WMHT-TV, Schenectady, N.Y., 1975-78; creative dir. LUYK Advt., Albany, 1978-81; freelance pub. relations cons. Albany, 1981-85; creative dir. H. Linn Cushing Co., Albany, 1985-87; pres. Genus Group, Inc., Santa Rosa, Calif., 1987—. Bd. dirs. Sonoma County Pvt. Industry Coun., 1988-89, Sonoma County World Affairs Coun., 1988-89. Recipient cert. excellence No. Calif. Addy awards, 1989. Mem. Am. Mktg. Assn., San Francisco Ad Club, Sonoma County Ad Club, Santa Rosa C. of C. Office: Genus Group Inc 1211 HN Dutton St Santa Rosa CA 95401

WALTON, JOHN ARTHUR, mechanical engineer, consultant; b. Chgo., Sept. 8, 1942; s. Charles F. and Constance B. (Pisek) W.; m. Carol Rice, May 1, 1965; 1 child, Thomas. BSME, Case Inst. Tech., 1965. Registered profl. engr., Ohio. Design engr. Rockwell Graphic Systems, Chgo., 1965-78, mgr. group tech., 1978-80, mgr. CAD-CAM tech., 1980-88; sr. applications engr. for image tech. Litton Ingegrated Automation, Alameda, Calif., 1988—. Contbr. articles to profl. jours. Mem. Unity Temple Concert Bd., Oak Park Ill., 1978-81, Oak Park Visitors Ctr., 1978-88, Oak Park Farmers' Market, 1979-87. Mem. ASME, Standards Engring. Soc. Office: Litton Integrated Auto 1301 Harbor Bay Pkwy Alameda CA 94501

WALTON, ROGER ALAN, public relations executive, writer; b. Denver, June 25, 1941; s. Lyle R. and Velda V. (Nicholson) W. Attended, U. Colo., 1960-63. Govt. rep. Continental Airlines, Denver, 1964-72; dir. pub. affairs Regional Transp. Dist., Denver, 1972-77; pub. affairs cons. Denver, 1977—. Author: Colorado--A Practical Guide to its Government and Politics, 1973, 5th rev. edit., 1985; columnist The Denver Post newspaper, 1983—, The Rocky Mountain Jour., 1977-81. Mem. U.S. Presdl. Electoral Coll., Washington, 1968; commr. U.S. Bicentennial Revolution Commn., Colo., 1972-76, U.S. Commn. on the Bicentennial of the U.S. Constitution, Denver, 1985—, pres.; trustee Arapahoe County (Colo.) Library Bd., 1982-86; chmn. lobbyist ethics com. Colo. Gen. Assembly. Republican. Home and Office: PO Box 10383 Denver CO 80210

WALTON, ROGER MICHAEL, marketing communications executive; b. Cirencester, Eng., July 9, 1943; came to U.S., 1954; s. Theodore Ronald and Judith Mary-Lees Walton; m. Rita Lois Bernstein, June 26, 1966; children: David George, Jonathan Mark. BA in Polit. Sci., U. Rochester, 1965; MBA in Fin., NYU, 1967. Analyst Singer Sewing Machine Co., London, 1967-69; contr. Europe Singer Info. Svcs. Co., London, 1970-73; contr. dept. product devel. Rank Xerox, London, 1974-78; dep. divisonal dir. small bus. Nat. Enterprise Bd., London, 1978-80; contr. Europe Intel Corp., Brussels, 1980-83; systems site contr. Intel Corp., Phoenix, 1983-85; prin. CFO Resources, Phoenix, 1985-88; pres. Internat. Solutions, Phoenix, 1988—; Southwest U.S. devel. dir. West Midlands Indsl. Devel. Assn., Birmingham, Eng., 1986—. Author newsletters. Pres. N.W. Surrey Synagogue, Weybridge, Eng., 1979-80, Ahavat Torah Congregation Synagogue, Scottsdale, Ariz., 1985-87; scoutmaster Boy Scouts Am., Phoenix, 1986-87; mentor Ariz. Dept. Commerce, Phoenix, 1986—; bd. dirs. Chaparral High Sch. Band, Scottsdale, 1988—. Mem. Ariz. Innovation Network (chmn. program com. 1986—, bd. dirs.), Ariz. Ctr. for Innovation (mem. curriculum com., workshop presenter 1988—), Planning Forum, Ariz. World Trade Assn., Enterprise Network, U. Rochester Alumni Club (Ariz. chpt.), Masons. Home: 6201 E Cactus Rd Scottsdale AZ 85254 Office: Internat Solutions Inc 8655 E Via de Ventura #G205 Scottsdale AZ 85254

WALTON, RONALD JOSEPH, government official, geologist; b. Loogootee, Ind., July 1, 1940; s. Talford James and Helen Louise (Smith) W.; m. Judith Ann Bethel, Dec. 28, 1963; children: Cynthia Lyn, Ronald Joseph Jr., Stephanie Marie. BS, Ind. U., Bloomington, 1961; MS, Am. U., Washington, 1973. Geological oceanographer USN Oceanographic Office, Washington, 1961-67; physical scientist U.S. Lake Survey, Detroit, 1967-70; computer system adminstr. U.S. Coastal Engring. Rsch. Ctr., Washington, 1970-75; computer mgr. U.S. Nat. Agrl. Library, Washington, 1975-79; computer geologist U.S. Geological Survey, Denver, 1979—. Contbr. articles to profl. jours. Chmn. social Young Republicans, Washington, 1962; chmn. Jr. C. of C., Plymouth, Mich., 1968, PTA, Tuckerman Elem. Sch., Potomac, Md., 1973. Mem. Am. Assn. Petroleum Geologists, Soc. Info. Mgmt., Assn. Computing Machinery (Outstanding New Mem. award 1976, chmn. 1977-78), Data Processing Mgmt. Assn., Geological Soc. Am., Marine Tech. Soc. (chmn. membership 1966-67), U.S./Can. Internat. Geological Soc. (chmn. Great Lakes study group 1968-69), Toastmasters Internat. Club (chmn. 1974), Jaycees, Wash. Ski Club. Republican. Baptist. Home: 24767 Giant Gulch Rd Evergreen CO 80439

WALTON, RONALD LINN, hospital administrator; b. Vallejo, Calif., Jan. 18, 1955; s. Frank J. and Joyce (Ellis) W.; m. Holly Ann Humpert, Apr. 29, 1978; children: Ronald Jr., Tyler, Janalee, Danielle. BS in Health Adminstrn., Idaho State U., 1982; MBA in Health Adminstrn., Golden Gate U., 1988. Adminstr. Care Enterprises, St. Helena, Calif., 1982-84, Casa Serena Nursing & Rehab. Hosp., Salinas, Calif., 1984—; preceptor Bd. Examiners of Nursing Home Adminstrs., Calif., 1985—. Patentee children's game. Eagle scout Boy Scouts Am., Napa Calif., 1971. Recipient medal of Merit Boy Scouts Am., 1970. Mem. Calif. Assn. Health Facilities (treas. 1986, v.p. 1987, pres. 1988-89). Republican. Mormon. Lodge: Elks. Home: 17527 Cross Rd Salinas CA 93907 Office: Casa Serena 720 E Romie Ln Salinas CA 93901

WALTON, WILLIAM VERNON, III, legal administrator; b. Columbus, Ohio, Aug. 26, 1941; s. William Vernon jr., and Gertrude Leona (James) W.; m. Julie Ann Froberg, Aug. 15, 1964 (div. Feb. 1972); m. Paula J. Seifert, Dec. 22, 1973; children: Matthew, Allison, Jeffrey, Laura. BA, Ohio State U., 1963, LLB, 1966, JD, 1966. Tax acct. Touche, Rosse and Co., Mpls., 1966-68; asst. tax mgr. U.S. Leasing Corp., San Francisco, 1966-72; v.p. adminstrn. Eldorado Electro Data Corp., Concord, Calif., 1972-73; exec. v.p. and chief fin. officer Inecon Agricorp., San Francisco, 1973-82; exec. dir. Fisher and Hurst, San Francisco, 1982—. County planning commr. Contra Costa Planning Commn., Martinez, Calif., 1975-80, chmn., 1980. Mem. ABA, Assn. Legal Adminstrs. (chmn. 1985, 86). Republican. Office: Fisher and Hurst 4 Embarcadero Ctr 25th Fl San Francisco CA 94111

WALTZ, MARCUS ERNEST, prosthodontist; b. Brownsville, Oreg., July 29, 1921; s. Roswell Starr and Eva Ione (Cherrington) W.; m. Constance Jean Elwood, May 31, 1952 (div. Nov. 1973); children: Melody Ann, Martha Louise, Kathryn Jean, Holly Jay, Joy Evalyn, Ross Elwood; m. Shelby Annette Schwab, June 10, 1975. AB, Willamette U., 1942; DMD, U. Oreg., 1945. Practice dentistry specializing in prosthodontics Forest Grove, Oreg., 1946-52, Reno, 1954—; councillor Pacific Coast Dental Conf.; pres. Pacific Coast Soc. of Prosthodontics, 1983. Served to lt. USN, 1945-46, 52-54, Korea. Decorated Combat Medics award, Battle Stars (oak leaf cluster). Fellow Internat. Coll. Dentistry, Acad. Dentistry Internat.; mem. ADA, Northern Nev. Dental Soc. (pres. 1959), Nev. Dental Assn., Nev. Acad. Gen. Dentistry (pres. 1974), Omicron Kappa Upsilon. Democrat. Methodist. Club: Reno Exec. (dir. 1960-66, pres. 1964-65). Lodges: Sigma Tau (pres. 1941-42), Masons (32 degree), Shriners. Home: 710 Mancor Dr Reno NV 89509

WALTZ, ROBERT READING, SR., lumberman; b. Seattle, Wash., Aug. 10, 1914; s. William Lee and Anna Belle (Reading) H.; m. Mary Francis Roberts, Sept. 21, 1938; children: Susan, Ann, Robert. BA in Econs. Bus., U. Wash., 1936. Underwriter Traveler's Ins. co., San Francisco, 1936-40; ptnr. Seattle Snohomish (Wash.) Mell Co., 1940-75; pres. Seattle Snohomish Mill Co., 1975-82, chmn. bd., 1982—. Mem. Snohomish Sch. Bd., 1942-60; Wash. State Sch. Bd., 1948-71. Republican. Home: 7603-129th Dr SE Snohomish WA 98290 Office: Seattle Snohomish 9925-99th Ave SE PO Box 949 Snohomish WA 98290

WAMBOLT, THOMAS EUGENE, financial consultant; b. Scottsbluff, Nebr., Aug. 9, 1938; s. Andrew, Jr. and Anne (Altergott) W.; B.S., Met. State Coll., Denver, 1976; m. Linda E. Shifflett, Oct. 31, 1967; 1 son, Richard Duane King. Pres. Universal Imports Co., Westminster, Colo., 1967-71; printer Rocky Mountain News, Denver, 1967-78; propr., accountant Thomas E. Wambolt Co., Arvada, Colo., 1974-77, fin. adviser, 1977—. Baptist. Address: 6035 Garrison St Arvada CO 80004

WAMPLER, W. NORMAN, small business owner; b. Morristown, Tenn., Feb. 27, 1907; s. W. Rieves and Lydia C. (Grizzle) W.; m. Lois E. Morse, Feb. 14, 1932 (dec. 1965); 1 child, Leland N.; m. Martha M. Maybury, June 30, 1967. BA, Rocky Mt. Coll., 1929; MA, U. Wash., 1933; PhD, U. So. Calif., 1947. Cert. sch. adminstr., Calif. Tchr. Mont. Pub. Schs., Hobson, Big Sandy, 1929-32; prin. Shelby (Mont.) Pub. Schs., 1932-33, supt., 1933-43; prin. Mt. Baldy Boys Sch., Los Angeles, 1943-46; supt. Bellflower (Calif.) Unified Sch. Dist., 1946-72; ednl. cons. Los Angeles County Schs., Downey, Calif., 1972-78; owner, operator Gem Roots Internat., Santa Monica, Calif., 1978—. Chmn. Bellflower Community Chest, 1958. Mem. Calif. Assn. Sch. Adminstrs. (pres. 1970-71), Los Angeles County Supts. Assn. (pres. 1956-58), NEA, Am. Assn. Sch. Adminstrs. Republican. Presbyterian. Lodge: Rotary (pres. Bellflower chpt. 1950-51). Home: 804 Princeton St Santa Monica CA 90403 Office: Gem Roots Internat 2210 Wilshire Blvd Suite 171 Santa Monica CA 90403

WAMSER, CARL CHRISTIAN, chemistry educator; b. N.Y.C., Aug. 10, 1944; s. Christian A. and Madeline G. (Miller) W.; m. Laurie A. Schmidt, Aug. 12, 1984; children: Scott C., Kimberly Joy. ScB, Brown U., 1966; PhD, Calif. Inst. Tech., 1970. Research fellow Harvard U., Cambridge, Mass., 1969-70; prof. chemistry Calif. State U.-Fullerton, 1970-83, Portland (Oreg.) State U., 1983--; vis. prof. U. So. Calif., 1975-76, U. Hawaii, 1981, Reed Coll., 1989-90; research assoc. U. Calif.-Berkeley, 1980; adj. prof. Oreg. Grad. Ctr., Beaverton, 1987--. Author: (with J.M. Harris) Fundamentals of Organic Reaction Mechanisms, 1976, (with G. W. Stacy) Organic Chemistry: A Background for the Life Sciences, 1985. Recipient Outstanding Prof. award, Calif. State U.-Fullerton, 1983, Alumni Disting. Faculty award, 1983. Mem. Am. Chem. Soc., Inter-Am. Photochem. Soc. Home: 19440 Wilderness Dr West Linn OR 97068 Office: Portland State U Dept Chemistry Portland OR 97207-0751

WAN, FREDERIC YUI-MING, applied mathematician; b. Shanghai, China, Jan. 7, 1936; s. Wai-Nam and Olga Pearl (Jung) W.; m. Julia Y.S. Chang, Sept. 10, 1960. SB, MIT, 1959, SM, 1963, PhD, 1965. Mem. staff MIT Lincoln Lab., Lexington, 1959-65; instr. math. MIT, Cambridge, 1965-67, asst. prof., 1967-69, assoc. prof., 1969-74; prof. math., dir. Inst. Applied Math. and Stats., U. B.C., Vancouver, 1974-83; prof. applied math. and math. U. Wash., Seattle, 1983—, chmn. Dept. Applied Math., 1984-88, assoc. dean scis. coll. arts and scis., 1988—; program dir. Div. Math. Sci. NSF, 1986-87; cons. indsl. firms and govt. agys. Mem. M.I.T. Ednl. Council for B.C. Area of Can. Contbr. articles to profl. jours. Sloan Found. fellow, 1973; Killam sr. fellow, 1979. Fellow ASME; mem. Am. Acad. Mechanics (sec. fellows 1985—), Soc. Indsl. and Applied Math., Can. Applied Math. Soc. (council 1980-83, pres. 1983-84), Am. Math. Soc., AAUP, Sigma Xi. Home: 11680 Sunrise Dr NE Bainbridge Island WA 98110 Office: U Wash Coll Arts & Scis GN-15 Dean's Office Seattle WA 98195

WANAGAS, JOHN DAVID, aerospace design engineer; b. Park Ridge, Ill., May 25, 1962; s. Bernard and Lena Mae (Mackey) W.; m. Cynthia Ann Schofield, May 30, 1981. BS in Aerospace/Aeronautical Engring., U. Ill., 1985. Design engr. Space Sta. Systems div. Rockwell Internat., Downey, Calif., 1985-88; project engr. Simula, Inc., Phoenix, 1988; design/project engr. Space Data Corp., Tempe, Ariz., 1988—. Inventor semi-automatic probe and drogue design, variably shaded liquid crystal window. Mem. AIAA.

WANDRO, MARK JOSEPH, nurse; b. San Mateo, Calif., June 28, 1948; s. Louis George and Louise Catherine (Sillers) W.; m. Joan Elizabeth Blank, June 2, 1973; children: Amika, Jamie Catherine Evans. BA in Humanities, St. Patrick's Coll., Mountain View, Calif., 1970; BS in Nursing, U. Calif., San Francisco, 1977. RN, Calif. With San Mateo County Health Dept., San Mateo, Calif., 1972-75, nurse ICU, 1978-80; nurse in recovery Waltham Hospital, Waltham, Mass., 1980-81; nurse in emergency Peninsula Hosp., Burlingame, Calif., 1980—. Co-author: My Daddy is a Nurse, 1981. Active Unitarian Ch. San Mateo, 1982—. Recipient Fund-raising award Am. Cancer Soc., 1986, Ann Benner Award Unitarian-Universalist Ch. of San Mateo, 1988. Mem. Am. Nurses Assn., Emergency Nurses Assn. (San Francisco pres. 1988, state sec. Calif. 1989). Democrat. Home: 1518 Burlingame Burlingame CA 94010

WANDS, JOHN MILLAR, department head, researcher, English professor; b. Buffalo, Jan. 18, 1946; s. John and Mildred Carmella (Denall) W.; m. Frances Terpak, June 22, 1974; 1 child, Ann. BA, Canisius Coll., 1968; MA, U. Chgo., 1970; PhD, Pa. State U., 1976. Instr. English Pa. State U., University Park, 1974; instr. English, European div. U. Md., Heidelberg, Fed. Republic of Germany, 1974-75; asst. prof. English Yale U., New Haven, 1976-78, Carnegie-Mellon U., Pitts., 1978-84; head English dept. Marlborough Sch., L.A., 1984—; fellow Calhoun Coll., Yale U., 1977-78; test cons. Ednl. Testing Svc., Princeton, N.J., 1979-80; reader Advanced Placement Ednl. Testing Svc., Princeton, 1987—. Contbr. articles to profl. jours. Mem. Friends of UCLA Library. NEH grantee, 1981, A. Whitney Griswold grantee Yale U., 1977-78, Falk Found. grantee, 1979, Elizabethan Club grantee, 1981; Exxon Found. fellow Newberry Library, 1982, Counc. Basic Edn./NEH fellow, 1987. Mem. Nat. Coun. Tchrs. of English, Modern Lang. Assn., Renaissance Soc. Am. Democrat. Home: 11817 Bellagio Rd Los Angeles CA 90049 Office: Marlborough Sch 250 S Rossmore Ave Los Angeles CA 90004

WANERUS, PRISCILLA JO, medical center official, consultant; b. Balt., Aug. 19, 1953; d. Philip Richard and Florence (Collins) W.; m. Eric Arthur Hughes, May 22, 1982; 1 child, Justin Nathaniel. BS/ Med. Record Adminstr., U. Ill., Chgo., 1975. Registered med. record adminstr. Asst. dir. med. records Swedish Covenant Hosp., Chgo., 1976-78; dir. med. records Belmont Community Hosp., Chgo., 1978-79; dir. med. records and patient care rev. Resurrection Health Care Corp., Chgo., 1979-82; dir. med. record info. svcs. Pacific Presbyn. Med. Ctr., San Francisco, 1982—; cons. Planned Parenthood, Chgo., 1980, Oakland (Calif.) Hosp., 1988—. Mem. Am. Med. Record Assn., Calif. Med. Record Assn. (chmn. edn. com. 1987-88), San Francisco Med. Record Assn. (pres.-elect 1988--). Democrat. Presbyterian. Office: Pacific Presbyn Med Ctr Clay and Buchanan Sts San Francisco CA 94115

WANG, CARL CHANG-TAO, research and development executive; b. Hankow, China, Dec. 2, 1935; came to U.S., 1955; s. Joseph Teh-Fong and Mona (Chen) W.; m. Linda Yuan-Hsui Chen, July 27, 1963; children: Paul, Andrew, David. Student, Taiwan Nat. U., 1953-54; BSEE, U. Ill., 1958, MSEE, 1959, PhDEE, 1964. With research staff Boeing Aircraft Co., Seattle, 1959-60; with research staff IBM Research Ctr., Yorktown Heights, N.Y., 1964-67; chief engr. Med. Instrument Lab., N.Y.C., 1967-69; dept. mgr. Micro-Bit Corp., Lexington, Mass., 1969-75; v.p. Berkeley Bio-Engring., San Leandro, Calif., 1975-79, Cooper Med. Devices, San Leandro, Calif., 1979-81; pres. Med. Instrument Devel. Lab., San Leandro, Calif., 1981-85; v.p. Alcon Surg. Instrumentation, San Leandro, Calif., 1985—; cons. Nat. Inst. Mental Health, Washington, 1968-77, Nat. Eye Inst., 1983-84, Jules Stein Eye Inst., L.A., 1982-86; bd. dirs. Internat. Tech. Service, Piedmont, Calif. Inventor 6 tech. patents; contbr. articles to profl. jours. Principal Chinese Language Sch., Lexington, Mass., 1972-75; coordinator (U.S.-China) World Eye Found., San Leandro, Calif., 1983—. Named grad. fellow U. Ill., Urbana, 1958-60; research grantee NSF, 1961-62, NIH, 1984-85. Mem. IEEE, Montclair Swim Club (Oakland, Calif.). Roman Catholic. Office: Alcon Surg Instrumentation 14450 Doolittle Dr San Leandro CA 94577

WANG, CHEN CHI, electronics company executive, real estate executive, finance company executive, food products executive; b. Taipei, Taiwan, China, Aug. 10, 1932; came to U.S., 1959, naturalized, 1970; s. Chin-Ting and Chen-Kim (Chen) W.; m. Victoria Rebisoff, Mar. 5, 1965; children: Katherine Kim, Gregory Chen, John Christopher, Michael Edward. B.A., Nat. Taiwan U., 1955; B.S.E.E., San Jose State U., 1965; M.B.A., U. Calif., Berkeley, 1961. With IBM Corp., San Jose, Calif., 1965-72; founder, chief exec. officer Electronics Internat. Co., Santa Clara, Calif., 1968-72, owner, gen. mgr., 1972-81, reorganized as EIC Group, 1982, now chmn. bd. and pres.; dir. Systek Electronics Corp., Santa Clara, 1970-73; founder, sr. partner Wang Enterprises, Santa Clara, 1974—; founder, sr. partner Hanson & Wang Devel. Co., Woodside, Calif., 1977-85; chmn. bd. Golden Alpha Enterprises, Foster City, Calif., 1979—; mng. ptnr. Woodside Acres-Las Pulgas Estate, Woodside, 1980-85; founder, sr. ptnr. DeVine & Wang, Oakland, Calif., 1977-83; Van Heal & Wang, West Village, Calif., 1981-82; founder, chmn. bd. EIC Fin. Corp., Redwood City, Calif., 1985—; chmn. bd. Maritek Corp., Corpus Christi, Tex., 1988-89. Served to 2d lt., Nationalist Chinese Army, 1955-56. Mem. Internat. Platform Assn., Tau Beta Pi. Mem. Christian Ch. Author: Monetary and Banking System of Taiwan, 1955; The Small Car Market in the U.S., 1961. Home: 195 Brookwood Rd Woodside CA 94062 Office: EIC Fin Corp 2055 Woodside Rd Ste 100 Redwood City CA 94061

WANG, GEORGE SHIH CHANG, marketing executive; b. Anking, People's Republic China, May 4, 1933; came to U.S., 1951; s. Chien-Shun and Ai-Lan (Kwong) W.; m. Ann Chen, Dec. 21, 1957; children: Julia, Gregory, Tracy. BS, U. Mich., 1958, MSCE, MS in Nuclear Engring., 1960; PhD in Engring., UCLA, 1970. Registered profl. engr., Calif. Research engr. Engring. Research Inst.-U. Mich., Ann Arbor, 1960-62; project engr. Bechtel Power Corp., Los Angeles, 1962-67, asst. chief nuclear engr., 1967-68, chief nuclear engr., 1968-72, engring. mgr., 1972-76, mgr. engring., 1977-80; v.p. Bechtel Nat., Inc., San Francisco, 1980-85, Bechtel N. Am. Power Corp., San Francisco, 1985-86, Bechtel Overseas Corp., San Francisco, 1985-86; gen. mgr. Helium Breeder Assocs., Newport Beach, Calif., 1976-77; v.p. strategic planning and market devel. Fluor Corp., Irvine, Calif., 1986-87; chmn., pres. World ComNet, Inc., Irvine, 1987—; dep. gen. mgr., gen. mgr. research and engring div. Bechtel Group, Inc., San Francisco, 1980-85, chief sci. officer, 1983-85, dirs. adv. group, 1974-75. Contbr. articles to profl. jours. Fellow NSF, 1960. Fellow ASCE; mem. Am. Nuclear Soc., Soc. Civil Engrs., Chi Epselon. Club: U. Mich. (Orange County) (pres. 1973-80). Office: World ComNet Inc 17310 Red Hill Ave Irvine CA 92714

WANG, I-TUNG, atmospheric scientist; b. Peking, People's Republic of China, Feb. 16, 1933; s. Shen and Wei-Yun (Wen) W.; m. Amy Hung Kong; children: Cynthia P., Clifford T. BS in Physics, Nat. Taiwan U., 1955; MA in Physics, U. Toronto, 1957; PhD in Physics, Columbia U., 1965. Rsch. physicist Carnegie-Mellon U., Pitts., 1965-67, asst. prof., 1967-70; environ. systems engr. Argonne (Ill.) Nat. Lab., 1970-76; mem. tech. staff Environ. Monitoring and Svcs. Ctr. Rockwell Internat., Creve Coeur, Mo., 1976-80, Newbury Park, Calif., 1980-84; sr. scientist, combustion engr. Environ. Monitoring and Svcs. Inc., Newbury Park, Camarillo, 1984-88; sr. scientist ENSR Corp (formerly ERT), 1988; pres. EMA Co., Thosand Oaks, Calif., 1989—; tech. advisor Bur. of Environ. Protection, Republic of China, 1985. Contbr. papers to profl jours. First violin Conejo Symphony Orch., Thousand Oaks, Calif., 1981-83. Grantee Bureau of Environ. Protection, Taiwan, 1985. Mem. N.Y. Acad. of Scis., Air Pollution Control Assn., Sigma Xi. Office: EMA Co 2219 E Thousand Oaks Blvd Ste 435 Thousand Oaks CA 91362

WANG, JAMES CHIA-FANG, political science educator; b. Nanling, China, Apr. 4, 1926; came to U.S., 1946, naturalized, 1962; s. Chien-Yu and Lilian W.; m. Sarah Cutter, May 7, 1960; children—Sarah, Eric. BA in Polit. Sci., Oberlin Coll., 1950; postgrad., N.Y. U., 1951; PhD in Polit. Sci, U. Hawaii, 1971. Rsch. asst., internat. study group Brookings Instn., 1951-53; adminstrv. and tng. officer UN Secretariat, N.Y.C., 1953-57; editor-in-charge UN Documents Edit., Readex Corp., N.Y.C., 1957-60; lectr. far eastern politics NYU, N.Y.C., 1957-60; instr. Asian history and econs. Punahou Sch., Honolulu, 1960-64; program officer Inst. Student Interchange, East-West Ctr., Honolulu, 1964-69, acting dir. participant svca., 1970, adminstrv. officer admissions, 1969-71; dir. freshmen integrated program Hilo (Hawaii) Coll., 1971-72; asst. prof. polit. sci. and internat. studies U. Hawaii, Hilo, 1971-72, assoc. prof., 1973-76, prof., 1976—; mem. U. Hawaii (Contemporary China Study Group), Hilo, 1971—, chmn. dept. polit. sci., 1973-75, 84—; profl. assoc. East-West Communications Inst., Honolulu, 1978, East-West Communications Inst. (Resource System Inst.), 1980-81; adviser to AAUW, Hawaii, 1978-79; cons. World Polit. Risk Forecast, Frost & Sullivan, Inc., N.Y.C., 1980-81. Author: The Cultural Revolution in China: An Annotated Bibliography, 1976, Contemporary Chinese Politics: An Introduction, 1980, 85, 89, Hawaii State and Local Politics, 1982, Study Guide for Power in Hawaii, 1982; contbr. articles to scholarly jours. Mem. Hawaii County Bicentennial Commn., 1975-76, Chinese Bicentennial Com., 1988-89; vice chmn. Democratic Party, County of Hawaii, 1972-76, chmn. 1982-84; mem. Dem. State Central Com., 1982-84; chmn. univ. adv. com. to Hawaii county council; mem. coordinating com. Hawaii Polit. Studies Assn., 1986—. U. Hawaii Rsch. Found. grantee, 1972-78. Mem. Assn. Asian Studies, Assn. Chinese Lang. Tchrs., Am. Polit. Sci. Assn., Internat. Studies Assn., Textbook Author Assn., Coun. Ocean Law. Home: PO Box 13 Hilo HI 96721-0013 Office: U Hawaii Dept Polit Sci Hilo HI 96720-4091

WANG, JAW-KAI, agricultural engineering educator; b. Nanjing, Jiangsu, Republic of China, Mar. 4, 1932; s. Shuling and Hsi-Ying (Lo) W.; m. Kwang Mei Chow, Sept. 7, 1957; children—Angela C.C., Dora C.C., Lawrence C.Y. BS, Nat. Taiwan U., 1953; MS in Agrl. Engring., Mich. State U., 1956, PhD, 1958. Registered profl. engr., Hawaii. Faculty agrl. engring. dept. U. Hawaii, Honolulu, 1959—; assoc. prof., chmn. dept. U. Hawaii, 1964-68, prof., 1968—, chmn. dept. agrl. engring., 1968-75; pres. Wang & Assocs., 1979—; spl. asst., Internat. Rsch. Dept., Office of Internat. Cooperation and Devel. U.S. Dept. Agr., 1988; co-dir. internat. sci. and ednl. coun. U.S. Dept. Agr.; vis. assoc. dir. internat. programs and studies office Nat. Assn. State Univs. and Land-Grant Colls., 1979; vis. prof. Nat. Taiwan U., 1965, U. Calif., Davis, 1980; cons. U.S. Army Civilian Adminstrn., Ryukus, Okinawa, 1966, Internat. Rice Rsch. Inst., Philippines, 1971, Pacific Concrete and Rock Co. Ltd., 1974, AID, 1974, Universe Tankships, Del., 1980-81, World Bank, 1981, 82, ABA Internat., 1981-85, Internat. Found. for Agrl. Devel./World Bank, 1981, Rockefeller Found., 1980, Orizaba, Inc., 1983, Agrisystems/FAO, 1983, Info. Processing Assocs., 1984, County of Maui, 1984, 85, Alexander and Baldwin, 1986; mem. expert panel on agrl. mechanization FAO/UN, 1984—; sr. fellow East-West Center Food Inst., 1973-74; dir. Info. Systems and Svcs. Internat., Inc., 1986—; mem. Am. Soc. Agrl. Cons. Internat. Dept. of State, 1985. Author: Irrigated Rice Production Systems, 1980; editor: Taro—A Review of Colocasia Esculenta and its Potentials, 1983; mem. editorial bd. Internat. Jour. Aquacultural Engring. Recipient Exemplary State Employee award State of Hawaii, 1986. Fellow Am. Soc. Agrl. Engrs. (chmn. Hawaii sect. 1962-63, chmn. grad. instrn. com. 1971-73, chmn. aquacultural engring. com. 1977-79, chmn. Pacific region 1975-76, emerging tech. task force, engr. of yr. 1976, Tech. Paper award 1978, assoc. editor aquac engring. com.); mem. Chinese Soc. Agrl. Engrs., Sigma Xi, Gamma Sigma Delta (pres. Hawaii chpt. 1974-75), Pi Mu Epsilon. Office: U Hawaii Dept of Agrl Engring 3050 Maile Way Honolulu HI 96822

WANG, JOSEPH Y., construction executive; b. Tainan, Taiwan, Republic of China, Apr. 27, 1950; came to U.S., 1979; s. Zei C. nd Chin O. (Lin) W.; m. Sonia D. Dzeng., Nov. 26, 1978; children: Eugene, Andrew. BCE, U. Taiwan, 1973; M in Constrn. Mgmt. and Engring., U. Mich., 1981. Assoc. engr. Taiwan Ry. Adminstrn., Taiwan, Republic of China, 1975-76; field supt. Prince Constrn. and Housing, Taiwan, Republic of China, 1976-79; assoc. cons. Wagner-Hohns-Inglis Inc., La Crescenta, Calif., 1981-84; estimator Badger Constrn. Co., Norwalk, Calif., 1984; chief estimator SBI Constrn. & Engring., Culver City, Calif., 1984-85; controller and ptnr. Milestone Contractors, Pasadena, Calif., 1985; prin. Milestone Constrn. Co., Pasadena, 1985-88; pres. Wang Milestone Constrn., Inc., Pasadena, 1989—. Editor, translator: 12 engring. books translated from English to Chinese, 1975-79. Served to lt. Army of Republic of China, 1973-75. Club: Holiday Spa, West Covina, Calif. Office: Wang Milestone Constrn Inc 260 S Los Robles Ave #114 Pasadena CA 91101

WANG, LIN, physicist, computer science educator, computer software consultant; b. Dandong, People's Republic China, June 11, 1929; came to U.S., 196l, naturalized, 197l; s. Lu-Ting and Shou-Jean (Sun) W.; m. Ling-Fen Tsow, July 8, 1961; children: W. Larry, Ben. BS in Physics, Taiwan U., 1956; MS in Physics, Okla. State U., 1965, PhD in Physics, 1972. Mem. physics faculty Cheng Kung U., Tainan, Republic of China, 1957-61; asst. prof. physics Southwestern Okla. State U., Weatherford, 1965-72; prof., chmn. physics dept. N.E. Coll. Arts and Sci., Maiduguri, Nigeria, 1973-75; mem. tech. staff Pacific Engring. Corp., Bellevue, Wash., 1976-78; sr. software engr., Far East cons. Electro-Sci. Industries, Inc., Portland, Oreg., 1979-82; mem. sr. computer sci. faculty South Seattle Community Coll., 1983—. Mem. Assn. for Computing Machinery, Am. Phys. Soc., AAUP. Home: 9322 l68th Pl NE Redmond WA 98052

WANG, TIM TZYY-SHIH, bank executive; b. Taipei, Taiwan, Republic China, Mar. 31, 1951; came to U.S., 1976; s. Shin-San and Hou-Jane (Chang) W.; m. Cathy Chi-Yu Chen, May 1, 1979; children: Brian, Allen. BS, Tamkang U., Tansui, Taiwan, 1974; MBA, Cen. Mo. State U., 1977. Systems analyst Richard D. Irwin Inc., Homewood, Ill., 1978-80; policy and procedure specialist Armak Co., Chgo., 1980-81; fin. data adminstr. Mattel Inc., Hawthorne, Calif., 1981-86; asst. v.p. 1st Interstate Bank Ltd., Los Angeles, 1986—. Office: 1st Interstate Bank Ltd 707 Wilshire Blvd #W11-7 Los Angeles CA 90017

WANG, TONY KAR-HUNG, automotive and aerospace company executive; b. Shanghai, People's Republic of China, Apr. 28, 1952; came to U.S., 1970; s. Kuo-Tung and Chien-Wen (Chu) W.; m. Vivian Wei-Pie, May 25, 1980; children: Stephen, Jason. BSEin Materials and Metall. Engring., U. Mich., 1973, MSE in Materials, 1975. Materials engr. Burroughs Corp., Detroit, 1976-78; sr. project engr. Gen. Motors Corp., Warren, Mich., 1978-85; staff engr. Hughes Aircraft Co., El Segundo, Calif., 1985; staff engr. Gen. Motors-Hughes Electronics Corp., El Segundo, 1986-87, mgr. program, staff engr., 1987—. Contbr. articles to profl. jours. Goodrich scholar, U. Mich., Ann Arbor, 1974. Mem. Soc. Advanced Materials and Process Engring. Republican. Office: GM Hughes Electronics Corp 2000 E El Segundo Blvd El Segundo CA 90245

WANG, TZYY-CHENG, engineer; b. Taipei, Taiwan, Rep. of China, Aug. 8, 1949; came to U.S., 1973; s. Shin-San and Hou-Jane (Chang) W.; m. Ye-Lian Liu, Sept. 6, 1974; children: Alice S., Emily L. BS, Taipei Inst. Tech., Taiwan, 1970; MSEE, U. Mo., 1975; doctoral program, U. Houston, 1975-77. Elec. engr. Motorola, Inc., Schaumburg, Ill., 1977-78; engr., scientist specialist Douglas Aircraft Co., Long Beach, Calif., 1978-85; engr. Rockwell Internat., Downey, Calif., 1988—. Contbr. articles and papers to profl. jours. City commr. Let Freedom Ring Commn., City of Cerritos (Calif.); prin. Chinese Sch., Cerritos, 1984. With USN 1970-72, Taiwan. Mem. IEEE, AIAA, L.A. S.E. Jaycees (v.p.), Chinese Culture Assn. of So. Calif. (pres. 1983). Republican. Office: Rockwell Internat 12214 Lakewood Blvd Downey CA 90701

WANG, WEN CHENG, physicist; b. Kaohsiung, Taiwan, Feb. 2, 1952; came to U.S. 1977; s. Shui Ou and NMoi Ji (Lu) W.; m. Suh Jing Chang, Aug. 13, 1977; children: Victor Yukai, Andrew Yuan. BS, Nat. Tsing Hua U., Taiwan, 1973, MS, 1977; PhD, U. So. Calif., 1982. Research assoc. U. So. Calif., L.A., 1982-83; research faculty San Diego State U., 1983-88; optical engr. Datagraphix Inc., San Diego, 1988--. Contbr. articles to profl. jours. Mem. Optical Soc. Am., N.Am. Taiwanese Prof. Assn. Home: 6440 Sommer Pl La Mesa CA 92042 Office: Datagraphix Inc 1895 Hancock St San Diego CA 92110

WANK, NEIL N., accountant, financial executive; b. N.Y.C., Sept. 9, 1944; s. Hyman and Mae (Perlberg) W.; m. Reneé Laddin, Nov. 1, 1969; children: Kenneth Bradley, Danielle Eden, Jeffrey Ross. BS in Acctg., CUNY, 1965. CPA, N.Y., Calif. Prin. Neil N. Wank & Co., N.Y.C., 1965-76; ptnr. Touche, Ross & Co., L.A., 1976-88; pres. Wank Fin. Group, L.A., 1989—. Mem. Jewish Fedn. Coun. Mem. AICPA, Calif. Soc. CPAs, N.Y. State Soc. CPAs, Calif. Soc. Real Estate Coms., Calif. Soc. Sports and Entertainment Coms., Variety Club. Republican. Home: 6244 Warner Dr Los Angeles CA 90048 Office: Legalstatt of LA 5900 Wilshire Blvd Los Angeles CA 90036

WARAPIUS, GLEN ROBERT, systems engineer; b. Oak Lawn, Ill., Feb. 17, 1953; s. Arthur Robert and Elizabeth Marie (Zalud) W.; m. Cynthia Louise Buck, Nov. 4, 1978; children: Todd, Jill. BSEE, U. Notre Dame, 1975. Programmer analyst Nixdor Computer, Chgo., 1975-78; systems analyst Hyatt Hotels Corp., Chgo., 1978-82; rsch. cons. Basic Software Svcs. Inc., Hayward, Calif., 1982-88; systems engr. Revenue Dynamics Corp., Hayward, Calif., 1988—. Republican. Roman Catholic. Home: 630 Forest Hills Dr Tracy CA 95376 Office: Revenue Dynamics Corp 3515 Breakwater Ave Hayward CA 94545

WARD, ALBERT EUGENE, research center executive, archeologist, ethnohistorian; b. Carlinville, Ill., Aug. 20, 1940; s. Albert Alan and Eileen (Boston) W.; m. Gladys Anena Lea, Apr. 26, 1961 (div. Apr. 4, 1974); children—Scott Bradley, Brian Todd; m. Stefanie Helen Tschaikowsky, Apr. 24, 1982. A.A., Bethany Luth. Jr. Coll., Mankato, Minn., 1961; B.S., No. Ariz. U., 1968; M.A., U. Ariz., 1972. Lab. asst., asst. archeologist Mus. No. Ariz., Flagstaff, 1965-67; research archeologist Desert Research Inst., U. Nev., Las Vegas, 1968; research archeologist Archeol. Survey, Prescott Coll., Ariz., 1969-71, research assoc., 1971-73; research archeologist Ariz. Archeol. Ctr., Nat. Park Service, Tucson, 1972-73, research collaborator Chaco Ctr., Albuquerque, 1975; founder, dir. archeol. research program Mus. Albuquerque, 1975-76; founder, dir., 1976-79l pres. bd. dirs. Ctr. Anthrop. Studies, Albuquerque, 1976—; lectr. U. N.Mex. Community Coll., 1974-77, others; contract archeol. salvage and research projects in N.Mex. and Ariz. Editorial adv. bd. Hist. Archeology, 1978-80; editor publs. Ctr. Anthrop. Studies, 1978—. Contbr. articles to scholarly jours. Grantee Mus. No. Ariz., 1972, S.W. Monuments Assn., 1973, CETA, 1975-79, Nat. Park Service, 1978-79. Mem. Soc. Am. Archeology, Soc. Hist. Archeology, No. Ariz. Soc. Sci. and Art, Ariz. Archeol. and Hist. Soc., Archeol. Soc. N.Mex., Albuquerque Archeol. Soc., Am. Anthrop. Assn., S.W. Mission Research Ctr., Am. Soc. Conservation Archeology, Soc. Archeol. Scis., Southwestern Anthrop. Assn., N.Mex. Archeol. Council, Living Hist. Farms and Agrl. Mus. Assn. Republican. Lutheran.

WARD, ANTHONY JOHN, lawyer; b. Los Angeles, Sept. 25, 1931; s. John P. and Helen C. (Harris) W.; A.B., U. So. Calif., 1953; LL.B., U. Calif. at Berkeley, 1956; m. Marianne Edle von Graeve, Feb. 20, 1960 (div. 1977); 1 son, Mark Joachim; m. 2d, Julia Norby Credell, Nov. 4, 1978. Admitted to Calif. bar, 1957; asso. firm Ives, Kirwan & Dibble, Los Angeles, 1958-61; partner firm Marapese and Ward, Hawthorne, Calif., 1961-69; individual practice law, Torrance, Calif., 1969-76; partner firm Ward, Gaunt & Raskin, 1976—. Served to 1st lt. USAF, 1956-58. Mem. ABA, Blue Key, Calif. Trial Lawyers Assn., Lambda Chi Alpha. Democrat. Home: 2136 Via Pacheco Palos Verdes Estates CA 90274 Office: Pavilion A 21525 Hawthorne Blvd Torrance CA 90503

WARD, BONNIE JEAN, interior designer; b. Jeffersonville, Ind., Mar. 31, 1947; d. Lloyd Russell and Wilma Jane (McKim) Hill; m. James Daniel Ware, Jan. 24, 1969 (div. 1984); m. Donald Devereux Ward, Nov. 16, 1985. BA, Purdue U., 1969. Sec., treas. Empire Designs Inc., Denver, 1969-74; pvt. practice interior design Denver, 1974-76; interior designer Victor Huff & Assoc., Denver, 1976-77; pres. ADR: The Design Group, Denver, 1977-88; co-owner Designward Inc., Orcas Island, Wash., 1988—. Mem. Am. Soc. Interior Designers (profl.) (bd. dirs. 1983-84), Inst. Bus. Designers (profl.). Home: Box 192 Orcas WA 98280 Office: Designward Inc Porter Sta Bldg PO Box 1267 Eastsound WA 98245

WARD, CARL EDWARD, research chemist; b. Albuquerque, Oct. 16, 1948; s. Joe E. and Loris E. (Wenk) W.; m. Bertha R. Schloer, June 9, 1970. BS in Chemistry, N.Mex. Inst. Mining and Tech., 1970; MS in Chemistry, Oreg. Grad. Ctr., 1972; PhD in Chemistry, Stanford U., 1977. Research chemist Union Carbide Corp., Charleston, W.Va., 1977-79, Dynapol Corp., Palo Alto, Calif., 1979-80; research chemist Chevron Chem. Co., Richmond, Calif., 1980-85, sr. research chemist, 1986-88; apptd. supr. chemical synthesis Chevron Chem. Co., Richmond, 1988—. Referee Jour. Organic Chemistry, 1983—; patentee in field; contbr. articles to profl. jours. Recipient NSF traineeship, Stanford U., 1972-73; Upjohn fellow, Stanford U., 1976-77. Mem. AAAS, Am. Chem. Soc., Plant Growth Regulatory Soc. Am., Stanford Alumni Assn, Planetary Soc., Calif. Acad. Sci. Democrat. Club: N.Mex. Inst. Mining and Tech. Pres.'s (Socorro). Home: 1355 Bagely Way San Jose CA 95122 Office: Chevron Chem Co Ortho Div PO Box 4010 C-326 Richmond CA 94804-0010

WARD, DIANE KOROSY, lawyer; b. Cleve., Oct. 17, 1939; d. Theodore Louis and Edith (Bogar) Korosy; m. S. Mortimer Ward IV, July 2, 1960 (div. 1978); children: Christopher LaBruce, Samantha Martha; m. R. Michael Walters, June 30, 1979. AB, Heidelberg Coll., 1961; JD, U. San Diego, 1975. Bar: Calif. 1977, U.S. Dist. Ct. (so. dist.) Calif. 1977. Ptnr. Ward & Howell, San Diego, 1978-79, Walters, Howell & Ward, A.P.C., San Diego,

1979-81; mng. ptnr. Walters & Ward, A.P.C., San Diego, 1981— ; dir., v.p. Oak Broadcasting Systems, Inc., 1982-83; dir. Elisabeth Kubler-Ross Ctr., Inc., 1983-85; sheriff Ranchos del Norte Corral of Westerners, 1985-87; trustee San Diego Community Defenders, Inc., 1986-88. Pres. bd. dirs. Green Valley Civic Assn., 1979-80; trustee Palomar-Pomerado Hosp. Found., chmn. Deferred Giving Found., 1985-89; v.p. Endowment Devel., 1989—; trustee Episc. Diocese of San Diego. Mem. ABA, Rancho Bernardo Bar Assn. (chmn. 1982-83), Lawyers Club San Diego, Profl. and Exec. Women of the Ranch (founder, pres. 1982—), San Diego Golden Eagle Club, Soroptimist Internat. (pres. chpt. 1979-80), Phi Delta Phi. Republican. Episcopalian. Home: 16503 Avenida Florencia Poway CA 92064 Office: Walters & Ward 11665 Avena Pl Ste 203 San Diego CA 92128

WARD, DOUGLAS MERRILL, energy consultant; b. Amarillo, Tex., Dec. 15, 1950; s. John Solomon and Frances (Hermon) W. BS, Colo. Sch. Mines, 1974. Engr. Conoco, Ventura, Calif., 1974-76, Tenneco, Denver, 1976-78; ops. mgr. Arapahoe Petroleum, Inc., Denver, 1978-81; v.p. Gerber Energy Corp., Denver, 1981-85; cons., pres. Starburt Energy, Denver, 1985—. Dir., Colo. Classic For Kids, Denver, 1987—; vol. Ronald McDonald House, 1986—; coach Little League Baseball. Mem. Soc. Petroleum Engrs., Independent Petroleum Engrs., Sigma Alpha Epsilon. Home: 543 S Devinney St Lakewood CO 80228

WARD, GORDON A(RTHUR), foundation adminstrator; b. Edgeley, N.D., May 22, 1926; s. Charles William and Eleanor Grace (Whitman) W.; B.S. in Edn., No. State Coll., 1950; M.A. in History, U. Wyo., 1958, Ph.D. in Higher Edn., 1969; postgrad. in econs. (Gen. Electrics fellow) Stanford U., 1961; m. Betty Lou Butler, Aug. 27, 1958; children—Cheryl Denise (dec.), Kimberly Ann. Adminstr. pub. schs., Casper, Wyo., N.D. and S.D., 1950-67; adminstrv. asst. to pres. Casper Coll., 1967; dean instrn. Central Wyo. Coll., 1968; pres. Sheridan Coll., 1973-88; chmn. Wyo. Pres.'s Council, 1982-84; pres. Wyo. Community Coll. Athletic Conf., 1977. Mem. Wyo. Ho. of Reps., 1964-66; sec. No. Wyo. Community Found., 1973—; chmn. Legis.-Exec. Commn. on Reorgn. State Govt. Wyo., 1974-76, mem., 1974-78; mem. Wyo. Gov.'s Task Force on Nondiscrimination on Basis of Handicap, 1976-77; v.p. Salvation Army Adv. Bd., Sheridan, 1977-78; mem. adv. bd. N.G., 1977-79; mem. adv. bd. Hugh O'Brian Found., 1981—; treas. Council Occupational Edn. Served with USN, 1944-45; PTO. Recipient Most Creative award Community Coll. Seminar, U. Wyo., 1967; Coe fellow, 1959. Mem. Am. Assn. Community and Jr. Colls., Mountain States Assn. Community Colls. (pres. 1982-83), Mountain Plains Adult Edn. Assn., Phi Delta Kappa, Delta Kappa Pi, Phi Theta Kappa. Presbyterian (elder). Home: 510 S Jefferson Sheridan WY 82801 Office: PO Box 1500 Sheridan WY 82801

WARD, JAMES ELLIS, architect; b. L.A., Feb. 21, 1932; s. Ellis Feltham and Julia Marie (Stark) W.; m. Lora Lee Barker, May 18, 1951 (div. 1983); children: Janet Lee Dooley, Richard, Robin, Michael, Jonathan. BS in Archtl. Engring., Calif. State Poly. U., 1958. Registered architect, Calif. Draftsman William Faulkner AIA, Santa Ana, Calif., 1958-59; sr. draftsman Regan & Teaubalt C.E., Santa Ana, Calif., 1959-60; ptnr. Blurock Partnership Architects & Planners, Newport Beach, Calif., 1961—. Chmn. Citizens Sch. Bonds, Santa Ana, 1970; councilman City of Santa Ana, 1973-81, mayor, 1979-81; bd. dirs. YMCA, Santa Ana, 1969-70; mem. SantaAna Unified Dists., 1983-87. With USCG, 1951-53. Mem. AIA (Design Merit award Orange County chpt. 1985). Home: 1110 Sharon Rd Santa Ana CA 92706 Office: Blurock Ptnrship Architects & Planners 2300 Newport Blvd Newport Beach CA 92663

WARD, JOHN J., bishop; b. Los Angeles, 1920. Student, St. John's Sem., Camarillo, Calif., Catholic U. Am. Ordained priest, Roman Catholic Ch., 1946. Ordained titular bishop of Bria, aux. bishop Diocese of Los Angels Roman Cath. Ch., 1963; now vicar gen. Roman Cath. Ch., Los Angeles. Office: 10425 W Pico Blvd Los Angeles CA 90064 *

WARD, KAREN GRAFF, public relations, marketing and advertising executive; b. Phoenix, Nov. 14, 1948; d. Charles Wesley and Doris Mae (Walker) Graff; m. Raymond Edward List, Sept. 2, 1972; m. Forrest Herndon Ward, Aug. 8, 1982 (div. July 1986). B.S., Ohio U., 1970; cert. in French, Italian, Internat. House, Rome, 1972; postgrad. U. Calif.-Berkeley, 1974, 78. Lic. ins. agent, Pa., 1975. Bilingual personnel agt. Kaiser Engrs. of Italy, Sardinia and Rome, 1970-74; agt. Lincoln Nat. Life Ins., Harrisburg, Pa., 1975-76; adminstrv. mgr. Peabody Office Furniture, Boston, 1976-78; mktg. dir., commd. sales Western Contract Furnishers, San Francisco, 1978-81; free lance cons. interior design and comml. Furnishings, San Francisco, 1981-82; dir. sales, mktg. Romex Sentinel Systems, Stockton, Calif., 1982-83; pres. owner Madison Ave. West div. Lexicon Corp., Stockton, 1983—; gen. mgr. Stockton Auto Ctr., Stockton, 1987-88; dir. pub. relations Stockton Women's Network, 1986—, Jr. Achievement San Joaquin, Stockton, 1986—, YMCA San Joaquin, 1984-88; bd. dirs. Women's Ctr. San Joaquin, 1984—; cons., lectr. in field. Planning Commr. City Stockton, 1985—. Recipient Disting. Leadership award Nat. Assn. Community Leadership Orgn., 1986, Disting. Grad. Achiever Jr. Achievement 1985; Woman of Achievement Bus. & Profl. Women, 1984, 85; named one of Outstanding Young Women in Am., 1981. Mem. Nat. Fedn. Bus. and Profl. Women, Am. Mktg. Assn., Stockton C. of C., Nat. Assn. Exec. Females, Am. Assn. Univ. Women, Leadership Stockton Alumni Assn. (bd. dirs. 1986-88), Chi Omega Alumnae. Republican. Presbyterian. Avocations: traveling, reading, cooking, boating. Office: Madison Ave West 242 N Sutter Suite 501 Stockton CA 95202

WARD, LESTER LOWE, JR., lawyer; b. Pueblo, Colo., Dec. 21, 1930; s. Lester Lowe and Alysmai (Pfeffer) W.; m. Rosalind H. Felps, Apr. 18, 1964; children: Ann Marie, Alison, Lester Lowe. AB cum laude, Harvard U., 1952, LLB, 1955. Bar: Colo. 1955. Pvt. practice Pueblo, 1957-89; ptnr. Predovich, Ward & Banner, Pueblo, 1974-89; pres., chief oper. officer Denver Ctr. for the Performing Arts, 1989—. Trustee, Thatcher Found., Frank I. Lamb Found., Helen G. Bonfils Found.; pres. bd. trustees Pueblo Pub. Library, 1960-66; trustee St. Mary-Corwin Hosp., 1972—, pres., 1979-80. Served with U.S. Army, 1955-57. Named Outstanding Young Man of Yr., Pueblo Jaycees, 1964. Fellow Am. Coll. Probate Counsel; mem. ABA (house of dels. 1986-88), Colo. Bar Assn. (bd. govs. 1977-79, 82-88, pres. 1983-84), Pueblo County Bar Assn. (Outstanding Young Lawyer award 1965, 67, pres. 1976-77), Harvard Law Sch. Assn. Colo. (pres. 1972), Kiwanis (pres. 1969). Democrat. Roman Catholic. Home: 1551 Larimer No 2601 Denver CO 80202 Office: 1050 13th St Denver CO 80204 also: Denver Ctr Performing Arts 1050 13th St Denver CO 80204

WARD, LOWELL SANFORD, state official; b. L.A., Nov. 21, 1949; s. Jimmy Lee and Artis Eleane (Nelson) W.;m. Victoria Vanderveer Connor, Feb. 8, 1985. AS, BA, U. Nev., Reno, 1974, postgrad., 1977-78; postgrad., U. Pacific, 1982-84, Portland State U., 1986. Detective organized crime City of Reno Police Dept., 1975-81; in-depth investigator State of Oreg. Liquor Control Commn., Portland, 1985-86; auto theft investigator Motor Vehicles div. State of Oreg., Medford, 1986-88; fraud investigator Dept. Justice State of Oreg., Salem, 1989—; Contbg. reporter Oreg. State Police Officer's Assn. Trooper News, 1987—. Contbg. reporter Oreg. State Police Officer's Assn. Trooper News, 1987—, Northwest Law Enforcement Jour., 1989—. Mem. Internat. Assn. Auto Theft Investigators, Western States Auto Theft Investigators. Republican. Methodist. Office: Dept Justice Fraud Sect Justice Bldg Salem OR 97310

WARD, MICHAEL GEORGE, mechanical engineering educator, consultant; b. San Francisco, Aug. 22, 1951; s. Peter Joseph and Lillian Hazel (Baker) W.; m. Teresa Marie Roche, Mar. 23, 1974; children: Eric John, Allan Jacob, Brian Thomas. BSME, U. Calif., Davis, 1973, MS in Mech. Engring., 1975; PhD in ME, Stanford U., 1983. Registered profl. engr., Calif. Engr. Gen. Electric Co., San Jose, 1975-78; sr. rsch. engr. Lockheed Missiles & Space Co., Sunnyvale, Calif., 1978-82; asst. prof. mech. engring. U. Pacific, Stockton, Calif., 1982-85, assoc. prof., 1985-88; assoc. prof. mech. engring. Calif. State U., Chico, 1988--. Mem. ASME, Am. Soc. for Engring. Edn., Soc. for Computer Simulation, Sigma Xi (Sci. Rsch. Soc.). Home: 1034 Sir William Ct Chico CA 95926 Office: Calif State U Dept Mech Engring Chico CA 95929-0930

WARD, ORVILLE ELVIN, insurance company executive; b. Topeka, May 6, 1926; s. John Edward and Sylvia (Anderson) W.; m. Dorothy Kathryn Brainard, Jan. 8, 1949; children: Claudia Ward McGrath, Virginia Ward Klevjer, Dona Ward Tindall, Jay. Student U. Wash., 1944-45. Ind. ins. agt., Seattle, 1955-62; field rep. SAFECO Life Ins. Co., Seattle, 1962-64, ins. educator, 1964-65, div. life mgr., 1965-69, v.p., dir. pensions, 1969-86, pres. Resource Planning Services Inc., 1986—; dir. Sound Bank, Federal Way, Wash.; chmn. bd. AeroFab, Inc.; lectr. in field. Bd. dirs. Seattle-King County ARC, St. Cabrini Hosp. Ethics Bd.; past chmn. Sr. Vol. Program King County. Served with USAF, 1944-45. Named Seattle Citizen of Day, 1985. Mem. Internat. Assn. Fin. Planners. CLU. Contbr. articles to profl. mags. Home: 35790 27th Ave S Federal Way WA 98003 Office: Resource Planning Svcs 2615 4th Ave Seattle WA 98121

WARD, PAUL HUTCHINS, otolaryngologist; b. Lawrence, Ind., Apr. 24, 1928; s. Howard Hutchins and Lillian (Anderson) W.; m. Suzanne Fowler, Feb. 7, 1976; children: Walter, Judith. AB, Anderson Coll., 1953; MD, John Hopkins U., 1957. Diplomate Am. Bd. Otolaryngology; licensed physician, Ill., Calif., Tenn., Md. Intern Henry Ford Hosp., Detroit, 1957-58; resident U. Chgo., Detroit, 1958-61; spl. fellow U. Chgo., 1962-64; asst. prof. surgery, chief head and neck service U. Chgo. Sch. Medicine, 1962-64; assoc. prof., chmn. div. otolaryngology Vanderbilt U. Sch. Medicine, Nashville, 1964-68; prof. surgery, chief div. head and neck surgery UCLA Sch. Medicine, 1968—; Cons. Wadsworth VA Hosp., Los Angeles, 1968—, U.S. Naval Hosp., 1969—; staff UCLA Hosps. and Clinic, 1968—, Los Angeles County-Harbor Gen. Hosp., Torrance, Calif., 1968—, Cedars-Sinai Med. Ctr., Los Angeles, 1977—, Los Angeles County-Olive View Hosp., Van Nuys, Calif., 1978—; lectr. in field. Contbr. over 265 articles to profl. jours. Bd. dirs., v.p. Hope for Hearing Found., 1969—, UCAL Hosp. Chpalaincy Service, 1975-82, pres. 1977-81; trustee Blalock Found., 1979—. Served as staff sgt. Med. Service Corps, U.S. Army, 1946-49. Mem. ACS (sr. advisor com. on med. motion pictures, 1984—, sr. advisor 1988—), Am. Acad. Ophthalmology and Otolaryngology (1st v.p. 1979-80, coord. continuing edn. 1983-89), NIH, Calif. Med. Assn., Am. Acad. Facial Plastic and Reconstructive Surgery (com. on rsch. 1973-80), Am. Coun. of Otolaryngology, Am. Laryngological Assn., Am. Soc. Head and Neck Surgery (pres. 1983-84), Triological Soc. (coun. mem. 1988—). Office: UCLA Sch Medicine 10833 Le Conte St Los Angeles CA 90024

WARD, ROBERT EDWARD, retired political science educator and university administrator; b. San Francisco, Jan. 29, 1916; s. Edward Butler and Claire Catherine (Unger) W.; m. Constance Regina Barnett, Oct. 31, 1942; children: Erica Anne, Katherine Elizabeth. B.A., Stanford U., 1936; M.A., U. Calif.-Berkeley, 1938, Ph.D., 1948. Instr. in polit. sci. U. Mich., 1948-50, asst. prof. polit. sci., 1950-54, assoc. prof., 1954-58, prof., 1958-73; prof. Stanford U., 1973-87, dir. Center for Research in Internat. Studies, 1973-87; cons. in field; advisor Center for Strategic and Internat. Studies, Washington, 1968-87. Author: Modern Political Systems: Asia, 1963, Political Modernization in Japan and Turkey, 1964. Mem. nat. council Nat. Endowment for Humanities, Washington, 1968-73; mem. Pres.'s Commn. on Fgn. Lang.-Internat. Studies, 1978-79; chmn. Japan-U.S. Friendship Commn., 1980-83; mem. Dept. Def. Univ. Forum, 1982-87. Served to lt. (j.g.) USN, 1942-45. Recipient Japan Found. award Tokyo, 1976; recipient Order of Sacred Treasure 2d class (Japan), 1983. Fellow Am. Acad. Arts and Scis.; mem. Am. Polit. Sci. Assn. (pres. 1972-73), Assn. Asian Studies (pres. 1972-73), Social Sci. Research Council (chmn. 1969-71), Am. Philos. Soc. Home: 1385 Westridge Dr Portola Valley CA 94025

WARD, ROBERTA CODIS, insurance agent; b. San Francisco, Jan. 8, 1937; d. Rene and Emolyn (Robert) Codis; m. Donald Peter Huber, Sept. 11, 1960 (div. May 1983); children: Rob A., Christie A.; m. James Martin Ward, Sept. 6, 1985. BS, U. Calif., San Francisco, 1959. RN, Calif. Staff nurse Tahoe Forest Hosp., Truckee, Calif., 1950-77, St. Mary's Hosp., Reno, 1982-83, Mono Gen. Hosp., Bridgeport, Calif., 1984-85; owner Huber Ins. Agy., Truckee, Calif., 1963-85, Ward Ins. Agy., Coleville, Calif., 1985—. Cofounder Woof Search Dog Unit, 1975-83; rep. cen. com. Dem. Party, Nevada County, Calif., 1972-75; bd. dirs. Truckee Recreation Dist., 1973-76, Truckee DonnerPub. Utility Dist., 1976-83. Recipient Life Saving award, Nat. Ski Patrol, 1983. Mem. Civil Service Employees Ins. Co. Agts. Assn., U. Calif. Alumni Assn., Sierra Club. Democrat. Office: Ward Ins Agy Walker Rt 1 Box 109A Coleville CA 96107

WARD, SEAN ALLEN, medical technologist; b. Montegomery, Ala., May 13, 1953; s. Randolph Allen and Patricia Ann (McCall) W.; m. Anita Elaine Bailey,. BS in Biology, New Mex. Inst. Mining & Tech., Socorro, 1975; Bs in Med. Technology, U. New Mex., 1977. Cert. MT, CHT, CHS, New Mex. Med. technologist, phlebotomist Presbyn. Hosp., Albuquerque, 1975-78; med. technologist, tech. specialist U. N.Mex. Hosp., Albuquerque, 1979—; mem. adv. bd. N.Mex. Donor Program, Albuquerque 1986—. Author: (with others) Histocompatibility Testing, 1988. Mem. Am. Soc. Clinical Pathologists, Am. Soc. for Meds. Technology, Am. Democrat. Methodist. Home: 1616 Cardenas NE Lomas NM 87110 Office: U NMex Hosp Blood Bank 2211 Lomas Albuquerque NM 87112

WARD, SIDNEY ALBERT, III, aerospace engineer; b. West Hartford, Conn., Jan. 6, 1959; s. Sidney Albert Jr., and Florence (Savinelli) W.; m. Paula Jean Smith, June 6, 1981; children: Kimberly Ann, Danielle Jesica. BS in Astronautics, U.S. Air Force Acad., 1981; MS in Systems Mgmt., U. So. Calif., 1985. Commd. lt. USAF, 1981, advanced through grades to capt., resigned, 1987; sub-task mgr., mem. tech. staff Gen. Rsch. Corp., El Segundo, Calif., 1987—. Mem. Nat. Physics Soc., AIAA, Nat. Honor Soc. Roman Catholic. Home: 22521 Meyer St Torrance CA 90502 Office: Gen Rsch Corp 240 N Nash St El Segundo CA 90245

WARD-STEINMAN, DAVID, composer, music educator; b. Alexandria, La., Nov. 6, 1936; s. Irving Steinman and Daisy Leila (Ward) W.-S.; m. Susan Diana Lucas, Dec. 28, 1956; children: Jenna, Matthew. B.Mus. cum laude, Fla. State U., 1957; Mus.M., U. Ill., 1958, D.M.A., 1961; studies with, Nadia Boulanger, Paris, 1958-59; postdoctoral vis. fellow, Princeton U., 1970. Grad. instr. U. Ill., 1957-58; mem. faculty San Diego State U., 1961—, prof. music, 1968—, dir. comprehensive musicianship program, 1972—, composer in residence, 1961—, univ. research lectr., 1986-87; mem. summer faculty Eastman Sch. Music Workshop, 1969; Ford Found. composer in residence Tampa Bay (Fla.) Area, 1970-72; acad. cons. U. North Sumatra (Indonesia), 1982; concert and lecture tour U.S. Info. Agy., Indonesia, 1982; mem. faculty Coll. Music Soc. Nat. Inst. for Music in Gen. Studies, U. Colo., 1983, 84, Calif. State Summer Sch. for the Arts, Loyola Marymount U., 1988; composer-in-residence Brevard Music Ctr., N.C., summer 1986. Composer: Symphony, 1959, Prelude & Toccata for orch., 1962, Concerto No. 2 for chamber orch., 1962, ballet Western Orpheus, 1964, Cello Concerto, 1966, These Three ballet, 1966, The Tale of Issoumbochi chamber opera, 1968, Rituals for Dancers and Musicians, 1971, Antares, 1971, Arcturus, 1972, The Tracker, 1976, Brancusi's Brass Beds, 1977; oratorio Song of Moses, 1964; Jazz Tangents, 1967, Childs Play, 1968; 3-act opera Tamar, 1977; Golden Apples, 1981; choral suite Of Wind and Water, 1982; Christmas cantata And In These Times, 1982; Moiré for piano and chamber ensemble, 1983, And Waken Green, song cycle on poems by Douglas Worth, 1983, Olympics Overture for orchestra, 1984, Children's Corner Revisited, song cycle, 1984, Summer Suite for oboe and piano, 1984, Quintessence for double quintet and percussion, 1985, Chroma concerto for multiple keyboards, percussion and chamber orch., 1985, Winging It for chamber orchestra, 1986, Elegy for Astronauts, for orchestra, 1986; recs. include Fragments from Sappho, 1969; Duo for cello and piano, 1974, Childs Play for bassoon and piano, 1974, The Tracker, 1981, Brancusi's Brass Beds, 1984, concert suite from Western Orpheus, 1987, Sonata for Piano Fortified, 1987, Moiré, 1987, 3 Songs for Clarinet and Piano, 1987; commd. by Chgo. Symphony, Joffrey Ballet, numerous others; author: (with Susan L. Ward-Steinman) Comparative Anthology of Musical Forms, 2 vols, 1976, Toward a Comparative Structural Theory of the Arts, 1989. Recipient Joseph H. Bearns Prize in Music Columbia U., 1961, SAI Am. Music award, 1962, Dohnanyi award, 1965, ann. BMI awards, 1970—, Broadcast Music prize, 1954, 55, 60, 61; named Outstanding Prof., Calif. State Univs. and Colls., 1968; sr. scholar Fulbright award Aus., 1989-90. Mem. Broadcast Music, Inc., Soc. Composers, Inc., Coll. Music Soc., Am. Music Center. Presbyterian. Club: Golden State Flying. Office: San Diego State U Dept Music San Diego CA 92182

WARE, JAMES EDMAN, utility executive; b. Nampa, Idaho, Jan. 19, 1937; s. Alden Edman and Ruby Lillian (Bachman) Ware.; m. Judith Lee Druxman, July 17, 1959; children: Bradford James, Heather Lee. BBA, U. Wash., 1959. Mgr. employee tng. Transamerican Ins. Co., Los Angeles, 1959-66; regional personnel mgr. Allstate Ins. Co., Pasadena, Calif., 1966-69, Salem, Oreg., 1969-70, Seattle, 1970-72; v.p. adminstrv. services Intermountain Gas Co., Boise, Idaho, 1972—. bd. dirs. Idaho St. Personnel Com., Boise, 1988, Boise City Civil Service Com., 1986-88, Ada County Civil Service Com., Boise, 1978-88. Named Profl. of the Year 1985, Human Resources Assn. of Treasure Valley, Boise, ID. Mem. Am. Soc. Personnel Adminstrn. Office: Intermountain Gas Co PO Box 7608 Boise ID 83702

WARE, WILLIS HOWARD, computer scientist; b. Atlantic City, Aug. 31, 1920; s. Willis and Ethel (Rosswork) W.; m. Floy Hoffer, Oct. 10, 1943; children—Deborah Susanne Ware Pinson, David Willis, Alison Floy Ware Manoli. B.S.E.E., U. Pa., 1941; M.S.E.E., MIT, 1942; Ph.D. in Elec. Engring, Princeton U., 1951. Research engr. Hazeltine Electronics Corp., Little Neck, N.Y., 1942-46; mem. research staff Inst. Advanced Study, Princeton, N.J., 1946-51, North Am. Aviation, Downey, Calif., 1951-52; mem. corp. research staff Rand Corp., Santa Monica, Calif., 1952—; adj. prof. UCLA Extension Service, 1955-68; first chmn. Am. Fedn. Info. Processing Socs., 1961, 62; chmn. HEW sec.'s Adv. Com. on Automated Personal Data Systems, 1971-73; mem. Privacy Protection Study Commn., 1975-77, vice chmn., 1975-77; mem. numerous other adv. groups, spl. coms. for fed. govt., 1959—. Author: Digital Computer Technology and Design, vols. I and II, 1963. Recipient Computer Scis. Man of Yr. award Data Processing Mgmt. Assn., 1975, Disting. Service award Am. Fedn. Info. Processing Socs. 1986, Exceptional Civilian Service medal USAF, 1979. Fellow IEEE (Centennial medal 1984); mem. Assn. Computing Machinery, AAAS, Nat. Acad. Engring., AIAA, Sigma Xi, Eta Kappa Nu, Pi Mu Epsilon, Tau Beta Pi. Office: The Rand Corp 1700 Main St Santa Monica CA 90406

WARFORD, STUART LEIGHTON, university official; b. Bakersfield, Calif., July 25, 1950; s. Earl Raymond and Susan (McGinty) W.; m. Colleen Dolton, Sept. 1971; children: Michael, Adam, Peter. BA, Pepperdine U., 1974, MBA, 1982. Asst. registrar Pepperdine U., Malibu, Calif., 1977-79, fin. systems analyst, 1979, coordinator decision support, 1979-85, dir. data adminstrn., 1985-86, dir. Info. Ctr., 1986--; tech. service coordinator IBM, Woodland Hills, Calif., 1986--. Deacon Conejo Valley Ch. of Christ, Thousand Oaks, Calif., 1985--. Recipient President's award Pepperdine U., 1985. Mem. Info Ctr. Mgmt. Assn. Republican. Office: Pepperdine U 24255 Pacific Coast Hwy Malibu CA 90245

WARMAN, KAF, theater director, theater educator, performer; b. N.Y.C., Oct. 27, 1949; d. Reginald and Jolanne Karen (Winston) W. BA, Goddard Coll., 1971, MA, 1973. Prof. Goddard Coll., Plainfield, Vt., 1972-77, U. R.I., Providence, 1977; artist-in-residence Arts in the Image of Man, Fair Oaks, Calif., 1981; prof. Calif. Inst. Arts, Valencia, 1981-82, U. Calif., Irvine, 1981-82, Dell'Arte Sch. Mime and Comedy, Blue Lake, Calif., 1983, Solstice Workshops in Arts, Sacramento, Calif., 1983-87; assoc. artistic dir. Island Theatre Workshop, Martha's Vineyard, Mass., 1987—; cons. Los Angeles Mask Theatre, 1979—, U. Hawaii D.O.E. Module, Honolulu, 1984; instr. Nathan Mayhew Sems., Martha's Vineyard, 1984-87; artist Very Spl. Art Festival, 1986—. Author: (handbook) Event, 1973. Vt. Council on Arts grantee, 1976. Home: 6154 Glen Alder Los Angeles CA 90068

WARNAS, JOSEPH JOHN, municipal official; b. Boston, Aug. 31, 1933; s. Augustas and Nellie (Pipiras) W.; m. Bernice Gearlene Sarver (dec. July 1983); children: Robert John, Kimberly Joanne; m. Ruth Ellen Haaker, Jan. 12, 1985. BS in Mgmt., Boston Coll., 1955; MBA in Mgmt., Ariz. State U., 1971. Adminstr. subcontract Gen. Motors, Oak Creek, Wis., 1958-65; mgr. purchasing Sperry Rand Corp., Phoenix, 1965-70; dir. material mgmt. dept. Maricopa County, Phoenix, 1970—; Mem. Joint Fed., State and local Govt. Adv. Bd GSA, Washington, 1974; mem. exptl. tech. adv. com. Nat. Inst. Govt. Purchasing & GSA, Washington, 1975; guest lectr. Ariz. State U., Tempe, Glendale Community Coll.; instr. seminars Nat. Inst. Govt. Purchasing, Washington. Assoc. editor Aljian's Purchasers Handbook, 4th rev. edit., 1982; contbr. articles to profl. jours. Mem. State Ariz. Purchasing Rev. Bd., Phoenix, 1980, Men's Zoo Aux., Phoenix, 1976—. Served as 1st lt. U.S. Army, 1956-58. Mem. Nat. Inst. Govtl. Purchasing (pres. 1971, bd. dirs. 1972—, sr. del. to Internat. Fedn. Purchasing and Mgmt. 1983), Ariz. State Capitol Chpt. Nat. Inst. Govtl. Purchasing Inc. (founder, pres. 1977), Purchasing Mgmt. Assn. Ariz. (pres. 1973), Sigma Iota Epsilon. Republican. Roman Catholic. Home: 12511 N 76th Pl Scottsdale AZ 85260-4839 Office: Maricopa County Material Mgmt Ctr 320 W Lincoln St Phoenix AZ 85003

WARNE, WILLIAM ELMO, irrigationist; b. nr. Seafield, Ind., Sept. 2, 1905; s. William Rufus and Nettie Jane (Williams) W.; m. Edith Margaret Peterson, July 9, 1929; children—Jane Ingrid (Mrs. David C. Beeder), William Robert, Margaret Edith (Mrs. John W. Monroe). A.B., U. Calif., 1927; D.Econs., Yonsei U., Seoul, 1959; LL.D., Seoul Nat. U., 1959. Reporter San Francisco Bull. and Oakland (Calif.) Post-Enquirer, 1925-27; news editor Brawley (Calif.) News, 1927, Calexico (Calif.) Chronicle, 1927-28; editor, night mgr. Los Angeles bur. A.P., 1928-31, corr. San Diego bur., 1931-33, Washington corr., 1933-35; editor, bur. reclamation Dept. Interior, 1935-37; on staff Third World Power Conf., 1936; assoc. to reviewing com. Nat. Resources Com. on preparation Drainage Basin Problems and Programs, 1936, mem. editorial com. for revision, 1937; chief of information Bur. Reclamation, 1937-42; co-dir. (with Harlan H. Barrows) Columbia Basin Joint Investigations, 1939-42; chief of staff, war prodn. drive WPB, 1942; asst. dir. div. power Dept. Interior, 1942-43, dept. dir. information, 1943; asst. commr. Bur. Reclamation, 1943-47; apptd. asst. sec. Dept. Interior, 1947, asst. sec. Water and Power Devel., 1950-51; U.S. minister charge tech. cooperation Iran, 1951-55, Brazil, 1955-56; U.S. minister and econ. coordinator for Korea, 1956-59; dir. Cal. Dept. Fish and Game, 1959-60, Dept. Agr., 1960-61, Dept. Water Resources, 1961-67; v.p. water resources Devel. and Resources Corp., 1967-69; resources cons. 1969—; pres. Warne & Blanton Pubs. Inc., 1985—, Warne Walnut Wrancho, Inc., 1979—; Disting. Practitioner in Residence Sch. Pub. Adminstrn., U. So. Calif. at Sacramento, 1976-78; adminstr. Resources Agy. of Calif., 1961-63; Chmn. Pres.'s Com. on San Diego Water Supply, 1944-46; chmn. Fed. Inter-Agy. River Basin Com., 1948, Fed. Com. on Alaskan Devel., 1948; pres. Group Health Assn., Inc., 1947-51; chmn. U.S. delegation 2d Inter-Am. Conf. Indian Life, Cuzco, Peru, 1949; U.S. del. 4th World Power Conf., London, Eng., 1950; mem. Calif. Water Pollution Control Bd., 1959-67; vice chmn. 1960-62; mem. water pollution control adv. bd. Dept. Health, Edn. and Welfare, 1962-65, cons., 1966-67; chmn. Calif. delegation Western States Water Council, 1965-67. Author: Mission for Peace—Point 4 in Iran, 1956, The Bureau of Reclamation, 1973, How the Colorado River Was Spent, 1975, The Need to Institutionalize Desalting, 1978; prin. author: The California Experience with Mass Transfers of Water over Long Distances, 1978; mng. editor Geothermal Report, 1985—. Served as 2d lt. O.R.C., 1927-37. Recipient Distinguished Service award Dept. Interior, 1951; Distinguished Pub. Service Honor award FOA, 1955; Order of Crown Shah of Iran, 1955; Outstanding Service citation UN Command, 1959. Fellow Nat. Acad. Pub. Adminstrn. (sr., chmn. standing com. on environ. and resources mgmt. 1971-78); mem. Nat. Water Supply Improvement Assn. (pres. 1978-80, Lifetime Achievement award 1984), Sigma Delta Chi, Lambda Chi Alpha. Clubs: Sutter (Sacramento); Nat. Press (Washington); Explorers (N.Y.C.). Home: 2090 8th Ave Sacramento CA 95818

WARNER, ANNE CLARY, association executive; b. Jesup, Ga., Mar. 22, 1948; d. William T. Jr. and Sarah (Riggins) Clary; m. Russell F. Warner, May 15, 1971. BA in Polit. Sci., U. Calif.-Santa Barbara, 1969, teaching credential, 1970; postgrad., U. Ariz., 1982—. Tutor Natal, Brazil, 1974-76; project asst. Ride Share Program Pima Assn. Govts., Tucson, 1977-82; program mgr. Pima Assn. Govts., 1982-88, work-study internship coordinator, 1980-82; prin., exec. ACW & Assocs., Tucson, 1989—. Mem. Am. Mktg. Assn., Assn. Commuter Transp., Downtown Transp. Mgmt. Assn. (working com.), Women's Transp. Seminar, Pi Alpha Alpha.

WARNER, DAVID GILL, wholesale food distributing company executive; b. Salt Lake City, 1928. Grad., U. Utah, 1954. Dir. store devel. Fleming Foods Co., 1963-65; with Associated Food Stores, Inc., Salt Lake City, 1965—, successively asst. gen. mgr., mgr. Salt Lake div., exec. v.p., gen mgr., pres., gen. mgr., 1972—; pres., bd. dirs. M & I Gen. Agy., Mcht., Inc.; bd. dirs. Rick-Warner Ford Co., Western Family Foods, Inc., Zions 1st Nat.

Bank. Office: Associated Food Stores Inc 1812 S Empire Rd Box 30430 Salt Lake City UT 84130 *

WARNER, ELLA LOUISE, management executive; b. Sacramento, Mar. 4, 1961; m. Gerhardt J. Geworsky, Dec. 21, 1985; 1 stepchild, Zach. Student, Western State Coll., 1979-80, Rocky Mountain Tech. Coll., 1983. Winder Sherwood Enterprises, Longmont, Colo., 1984-85; lead A.J. Electronics, Longmont, 1985-86; shipping clk. PMS Electro-Optics, Boulder, Colo., 1986-87; adminstrv. asst. PMS Electro-Optics, Boulder, 1987—. Democrat. Club: Future Bus. Leaders Am. (Broomfield, Colo.) (Historian 1977-78). Office: PMS Electro-Optics 1855 S 57th Ct Boulder CO 80301

WARNER, FRANK SHRAKE, lawyer; b. Ogden, Utah, Dec. 14, 1940; s. Frank D. and Emma (Sorensen) W.; m. Sherry Lynn Clary; 1 child, Sheri. JD U. Utah 1964. Bar: Utah 1964. Assoc. Young, Thatcher, Glasmann & Warner, and predecessor, Ogden, 1964-67, ptnr., 1967-72; chmn. Pub. Svc. Commn. Utah, Salt Lake City, 1972-76; ptnr. Warner & Wikstrom, Ogden, 1976-79, Warner, Marquardt & Hasenyager, Ogden, 1979-82; pvt. practice, Ogden, 1982—. Mem. Utah Gov.'s Com. on Exec. Reorgn., 1978-80. Mem. ABA, Utah Bar Assn. (ethics and discipline com. 1981—), Ogden Gun Club (pres.), Wolf Creek Country (Eden, Utah). Office: 543 25th St Ogden UT 84401

WARNER, ILA JUANITA HARRIS, educational administrator; b. Malvern, Ark., May 2, 1929; d. Sylvester and Lola Aquila (Tyree) H.; m. Jarriet Wallace Warner, Apr. 26, 1953 (div. 1982); children: Karen Antoinette Warner Patterson, Sylvet Phern. AA, Ark. Bap. Coll., 1951; BA, Lincoln U., 1953; MA, San Francisco State U., 1972. Elem. sch. tchr. Bell City (Mo.) Sch. Dist., 1951-55, East St. Louis (Ill.) Sch. Dist., 1955-59; supr. Richmond (Calif.) Parks and Recreation, 1960-62; elem. sch. tchr. Richmond Unified Sch. Dist., 1962-70, elem. sch. v.p., 1973-76; supr. student tchr. San Francisco State U., 1970-72; elem. sch. prin. Pittsburg (Calif.) Unified Sch. Dist., 1976—; facilitator Sci. Inservice for Tea. Lawrence Livermore (Calif.) Nat. Lab., 1983—; cons. Harcourt, Brace, and Javonovich, Inc., San Francisco, Calif. Facilitator Fine Arts Black Cultural Polit. League, Pittsburg, 1981—; mem. planning com. Sch. Desegregation-Integration, Richmond, 1965-70; active Richmond-Shimada Friendship Commn., 1968—; active Internat. Inst. of the East Bay, Oakland, Calif., 1980—; v.p. Coalition 100 Black Women, San Francisco; star panalist Lou Rawls Parade of Stars, Nat. United Negro Coll. Fund., 1986. Named Outstanding Educator, 1976, Model Tchr. Far West Lab. Edn. Research, 1971. Mem. Pittsburg Assn. Sch. Adminstrs. (chmn. com. 1976, Letter of Recognition 1976), Calif. Assn. Compensatory Edn. (local com. mem., Letter of Recognition), Lincoln U. Alumni Assn. (chairperson souvenir book com. San Francisco Bay area chpt. nat. conv. 1987), Black C. of C., Phi Delta Kappa (bd. dirs. 1982—), Delta Kappa Gamma, Beta Pi Sigma Sorority, Inc. (named Nat. Soror of Yr., 1977). Clubs: Bulah Cluster (Richmond) (pres. 1965, 75), Bowling League. Home: 3019 Barkley Dr Richmond CA 94806 Office: Village Sch 350 School St Pittsburg CA 94565

WARNER, JOHN GREER, dentist, classical music disc jockey; b. Hartford, Conn., Dec. 26, 1950; s. Julius Herbert and Suzanne (Greer) W.; m. Caralee Richey Lindeman, Aug. 12, 1972. BA, U. Colo., 1973, DDS cum luade, 1979. Pvt. practice gen. dentistry Breckenridge, Colo., 1980—; disc jockey Sta. KSMT, Breckenridge, Colo., 1982—. Vol. Summit County Rescue Group, Frisco, Colo., 1980—, med. dir., 1982-83, treas., 1983-84; campaign mgr. for Summit County clk. and recorcer, 1982; chmn. Blue River (Colo.) Bd. Zoning, 1983-89; precint capt. Summit County Democratic Com., 1985-86; mem. Brekenridge Mktg. Adv. Bd., 1986-87; pres. Breckenridge Music Inst., 1984-85, v.p., 1985-86. Named Citizen of Yr. Summit County Bar Assn., 1986, Breckenridge Resort Assn., 1987, Summit County Bd. Realtors, 1987. Mem. ADA, Colo. Dental Assn., Colo. Prosthodontic Soc., Met. Denver Dental Soc., Denver Dental Forum (sec.-treas. 1983-84, v.p. 1984-85, pres. 1985-86), Summit Huts and Trails Assn. (pres. 1987—). Methodist. Home: 288 Royal St Blue River CO 80424 Office: 100 S Ridge St Breckenridge CO 80424

WARNER, KERRI ALEXA, advertising and marketing executive; b. Sacramento, Mar. 23, 1961; d. Robert Abraham and Diana Carol (Lyons) Wyman; m. Stephen Thomas Warner, June 30, 1984; children: Samantha Jane, Amanda Elizabeth. BA, San Diego State U., 1982. Freelance artist Copy To Go, Sacramento, 1976-82; mktg. The Price Club, Sacramento, 1983; graphic artist Curran Hitomi & Assocs., Sacramento, 1983-84; owner The Wyman Group Design, Carmichael, Calif., 1984-87, Kerri Warner Antiques, Carmichael, 1987—; co-owner, office mgr. Warner Constrn., Carmichael, 1984—; v.p. The Wyman Group Inc., Sacramento, 1988—. Mem. Nat. Assn. Female Execs.

WARNER, PETER DERYK, psychotherapist, clinical director; b. Urmstom, Lancashire, Eng., Feb. 20, 1938; s. Hugh Francis and Belinda (Jones) W.; m. Susan Christine Halverson, Mar. 30, 1984; children—Andrew Peter, Sharon Ruth. Student Liverpool Sch. Architecture, 1954-56; D in Theology (hon.), Handsworth Coll., 1961; postgrad. Liverpool U. and U. West Indies, 1961-66; PhD Columbia Pacific U., 1987. Diplomate Am. Inst. Counseling and Psychotherapy. Mgr., Norman Hurst Hotel, Rhyl, Wales, 1954; draftsman Jim Porter & Co., Colwyn Bay, Wales, 1954-56; pastor, supt. schs. Jamaica, W.I., 1961-68; pastor Harrisburg Methodist Ch., Harrisburg, 1968-71; sr. pastor Park Rose Meth. Ch., Portland, Oreg., 1971-78; psychotherapist N.W. Counseling Assocs., Portland, 1971-78; gen. mgr. La. Pacific Corp., Portland, 1978-81; pvt. practice psychotherapy, Portland, Oreg., 1981-82, Vancouver, Wash., 1982-87; exec. dir. The Counseling Ctr.of Vancouver, Wash.; dir. East Portland Clinic, 1982-83; dir. N.W. Counseling Assn., 1975-83. Bd. dirs. Park Rose Sch. Dist., 1974-78, chmn. bd., 1977-78; Oreg. soccer commr., 1975-79; sec. Jamaica Council Chs., 1963-67; active Multnomah County Juvenile Services Commn., 1980-81; sr. pastor Rivercrest Ch., Portland, Oreg., 1987—. Served with Royal Air Force, 1956-58. Recipient NCCJ award, 1978. Fellow Am. Orthopsychiat. Assn.; mem. Am. Assn. Marriage and Family Therapy, Am. Mental Health Counselors Assn., Am. Bd. Med. Psychotherapists. Democrat. Office: 1112 Daniels St Vancouver WA 98660

WARNER, SHAWN DANIEL, manufacturing engineer, educator; b. Springfield, Mass., Mar. 5, 1961; s. Robert Oakley and Marna Faye (Perry) W. BA, Calif. State U., 1983, MA, 1989. Mechanic lite-duty Popoli Honda-Artic Cat, Westfield, Mass., 1977-78; asst. mgr. service Popoli Honda-Artic Cat, Westfield, 1978-81; asst. mgr. svc. Escondido (Calif.) Honda Motorcycles, 1981; home renovator E.R. Danoff Law Offices, Santa Ana, Calif., 1981-83; design draftsman Ameron Pipe Lining Div., Wilmington, Calif., 1983-84; illustrator tech. Aircraft Div. Northrop Corp., Hawthorne, Calif., 1984; engr. visual aids Aircraft Div. Northrop Corp., Hawthorne, 1984-85, engr. assoc. mfg., 1985-87, engr. composites mfg., 1988—; instr. Northrop Corp., 1984—, Calif. State U., Long Beach, 1985. Mem. Soc. Mfg. Engrs., Soc. Composites Mfg. Engrs., Soc. Aerospace Engrs., Soc. Materials and Process Engrs. Republican. Roman Catholic. Club: Sports Car Am. (crew 1986—). Home: 2514 Nelson Ave #1 Redondo Beach CA 90278

WARNER, WALTER DUKE, finance and management executive; b. Davenport, Iowa, Feb. 26, 1952; s. Robert Martin and Opal Louise (Gibbons) W.; m. Susan Dee Hafferkamp, Nov. 15, 1975 (div. 1982); 1 child, Natalie. Student, We. Ill. U., 1970-72; BS, Drake U., 1975. Ops. officer Iowa-Des Moines Nat. Bank, 1975-78; from asst. v.p. to v.p. ops., to v.p. corp. rsch. and devel., to v.p. and dir. mktg. and pub. rels. Cen. Savs. and Loan Assn., San Diego, Calif., 1978-84; pres. The Lomas Santa Fe Cos., Solana Beach, Calif., 1985—; bd. dirs. Torrey Pines Bank, Solana Beach, Lomas Group, Inc., Del Mar, Calif., Madison Valley Properties, Inc., La Jolla, Calif.; pres., bd. dirs. Regents Pk. Comml. Assn., La Jolla. Bd. dirs. Inst. of the Ams., La Jolla, 1986—, mem. internat. council, 1986—; chmn. bd. dirs., pres. San Diego chpt. Arthritis Found., 1985-87; dir., pres. Gildred Found., Solana Beach, 1986—. Mem. The Exec. Com., Soc. for Advancement of Mgmt., Iowa Club of San Diego (founding dir. 1984-85), Calif. League of Savs. and Loans (mem. mktg. and ops. com. 1982-84), Golden Eagle Club. Republican. Protestant. Home: 8652-1 Villa La Jolla Dr La Jolla CA 92037 Office: The Lomas Santa Fe Cos 462 Stevens Ave Ste 192 Solana Beach CA 92075

WARNER, WILSON KEITH, sociology educator; b. Heyburn, Idaho, Sept. 6, 1930; s. Wilson A. and Eva L. (Pratt) W.; m. Vila Jenks, Sept. 1, 1950; children—Karen, Janice, Randall, Neil. B.S., Utah State U., 1958, M.S., 1959; Ph.D., Cornell U., 1960. Asst. prof. rural sociology U. Wis.-Madison, 1960-66, assoc. prof., 1966-69, prof., 1969-71, vis. prof. dept. rural sociology, 1984; prof. sociology Brigham Young U., Provo, Utah, 1971—, assoc. dir. univ. honors program, 1978-79; Mem. steering com. for community progress program State of Utah, 1973. Served with U.S. Army, 1953-55. Named Outstanding Educator of Am., 1972, 1974-75. Mem. Am. Sociol. Assn., Rural Sociol. Soc. (pres. 1973-74, Disting. Rural Sociologist award 1985), Utah Acad. Scis., Arts and Letters, Sigma Xi. Contbr. articles to profl. jours.; editor Jour. Rural Sociology, 1968-69. Office: Brigham Young U Dept Sociology Provo UT 84602

WARNICK, CHARLES TERRY, research biochemist; b. Brigham City, Utah, Jan. 29, 1943; s. Charles W. and Blanche (Richards) W.; m. Sandra Hathaway, Sept. 2, 1970; children: Derek, Darren, Bryan, Amber, Ashlee. BS, Brigham Young U., 1965; PhD, U. Utah, 1971. Postdoctoral fellow U. Alta., Edmonton, Alta., Can., 1970-72; research assoc. U. Utah, Salt Lake City, 1972-74, research instr., 1974-79, asst. research prof., 1979-81; asst. prof. biochemistry Latter-day Saints Hosp. and U. Utah, Salt Lake City, 1981—, cons. clin. labs., 1985—, also dir. research lab. Contbr. articles to profl. jours. Fellow NASA, 1965, Nat. Cancer Inst. Can., 1970; grantee NIH, 1978, Utah Heart Assn., 1982. Mem. AAAS, Am. Chem. Soc., N.Y. Acad. Sci. Mormon. Office: Latter-day Saints Hosp Rsch Lab 325 8th Ave Salt Lake City UT 84143

WARNKE, ROGER ALLEN, pathology educator; b. Peoria, Ill., Feb. 22, 1945; s. Delmar Carl and Ruth Armanelle (Peard) W.; m. Joan Marie Gebhart, Nov. 18, 1972; children: Kirsten Marie, Lisa Marie. BS, U. Ill., 1967; MD, Washington U., St. Louis, 1971. Diplomate Am. Bd. Pathology. Intern in pathology Stanford (Calif.) U. Med. Sch., 1971-72, resident in pathology, 1972-73, postdoctoral fellow in pathology, 1973-75, postdoctoral fellow in immunology, 1975-76, asst. prof. pathology, 1976-82, assoc. prof., 1983—; cons. Becton Dickinson Monoclonal Ctr., Mountain View, Calif., 1982--, IDEC- Biotherapy Systems, Mountain View, 1985--; sci. advisor Immunodiagnostics, Inc., Tucson, 1986--. Contbr. over 150 articles to med. jours., chpts. to books. Recipient Benjamin Castleman award Mass. Gen. Hosp., 1981; Agnes Axtel Moule faculty scholar Stanford U., 1979-82; Nat. Cancer Inst. and NIH rsch. grantee, 1978—. Mem. So. Bay Pathology Soc., Calif. Soc. Pathologists, Internat. Acad. Path., Am. Assn. Pathologists, Soc. for Hematopathology, Histochem. Soc. Home: 845 Tolman Dr Stanford CA 94305

WARNKEN, VIRGINIA MURIEL THOMPSON, social worker; b. Anadarko, Okla., Aug. 13, 1927; d. Sam Monroe and Ruth L. (McAllister) Thompson; A.B., Okla. U., 1946; M.S.W., Washington U., 1949; m. Douglas Richard Warnken, Sept. 16, 1957; 1 son, William Monroe. Med. social cons. Crippled Children's Services, Little Rock, 1950-54; supr. VA Hosp., Little Rock, 1954-55; asst. prof. U. Tenn. Sch. Social Work, Nashville, 1955-57; dir. social services N.Y. State Rehab. Hosp., Rockland County, 1957-58; asst. prof. U. Chgo. Sch. Social Service Adminstrn., 1958-59; free lance editor, 1960—; instr. evening div. Coll. of Notre Dame, Belmont, Calif., 1967-68; asso. Mills Hosp., San Mateo, Calif., 1978—; med. aux. Community Hosp., Pacific Grove, Calif., 1980—. Com. mem. C. of C. Miss Belmont Pageant, 1971-84, co-chmn., 1975-78. U.S. Children's Bur. scholar, 1947-49. Mem. Assn. Crippled Children and Adults (dir. 1952-55), Assn. Mentally Retarded (dir. 1953-55), Am. Assn. Med. Social Workers (practice chmn. 1954-55), Nat. Assn. Social Workers (dir. 1962-66), Acad. Cert. Social Workers, Am. Assn. Med. Social Workers, Nat. Rehab. Assn., Am. Psychol. Assn., Am. Orthopsychiat. Assn., Council Social Work Edn. Democrat. Presbyterian. Clubs: Carmel Valley Golf and Country, Peninsula Golf and Country, Monterey Golf and Country (Palm Desert, Calif.). Author: Annotated Bibliography of Medical Information and Terminology, 1956. Address: 1399 Bel Aire Rd San Mateo CA 94402

WARNOCK, HAROLD CHARLES, lawyer; b. N.Y.C., Jan. 6, 1912; s. Harry Gustavus and Madge Olga (Leunig) W.; m. Mary Louise Phelps, Aug. 29, 1937; children: John Phelps, Martha Ann. LLB, U. Ariz., 1935. Bar: Ariz. 1935, U.S. Supreme Ct. 1952; cert. real estate specialist. Profl. baseball player 1935-36; spl. agt. U.S. Govt., various cities, 1936-38; atty., to pres. Bilby Shoenhair Warnock and Dolph, P.C., Tucson, 1938-88; sr. ptnr. Lesher and Borodkin, P.C., Tucson, 1988—. Contbr. articles to profl. jours. Active, Republican Party, 1938—; mem. Ariz. Commn. on Uniform Laws, 1955-61, Employment Security Commn., Ariz., 1970-76. Lt. commdr. USNR, 1942-46, Pacific. Fellow Am. Coll. Trial Lawyers, Am. Coll. Probate Counsel; mem. Am. Bd. Trial Advocates (pres. Tucson chpt. 1973), Nat. Assn. Railroad Trial Counsel (v.p. Pacific chpt. 1974), Tucson Country Club (dir. 1971-75), Old Pueblo Club (dir. 1976-79). Office: Lesher and Borodkin PC 3773 E Broadway Tucson AZ 85716

WARNOCK, PATRIC FRANCIS, comedy writer; b. Cin., May 5, 1951; s. Francis Michael and Ruth Jane (Benz) W.; m. Anna Elizabeth Vugrinecz, May 18, 1985. BA in Journalism and Math, Syracuse U., 1973, MLS, 1976; MBA, Pace U., 1986. Market researcher Find/SVP, N.Y.C., 1977-79, AT&T, Bedminister, N.J., 1979-86; market researcher Newton Evans Research Co., Redwood City, Calif., 1986-88, comedy writer, 1988—. Mem. Am. Mktg. Assn., Market Research Assn. Jewish.

WARREN, BACIL CHRISTOPHER, army officer; b. Tucson, July 24, 1948; s. Bacil Benjamin and Annelle (Griffin) W.; m. Gail Lynn Kearney, July 9, 1969; children: Bacil Donovan, Edward. Student, U. Ariz., 1966-69, George Mason Coll., 1968. Instrumentalist 75th U.S. Army Band, Ft. Belvior, Va., 1969-71; instrumentalist 8th U.S. Army Band, Seoul, Republic of Korea, 1971-72, bandmaster, 1983-85; sr. instrumentalist 36th U.S. Army Band, Ft. Huachuca, Ariz., 1972-74, bandmaster, 1983—; bandmaster 24th Inf. Div. Band, Ft. Stewart, Ga., 1975-83; lectr. in field. Composer: Grace Be Unto You, 1976, Shivaree! for band, 1988, Piano Variations, 1988. Mem. Music Educators Nat. Conf., Ariz. Music Educators Assn., Phi Mu Alpha. Democrat. Office: 36th US Army Band Fort Huachuca AZ 85613

WARREN, CAROL JOAN, senior administrator; b. Julesburg, Colo., Feb. 18, 1940; d. David and Thelma Fern (Krumm) Nein; m. Walter Graham Reuter, Jan. 24, 1960 (div. 1984); children: Brenda Sue, Helen Kay; m. 2d, Jesse Farley Warren, Oct. 13, 1984. Student, Barnes Bus. Sch., 1958, 60. Office mgr. Diebold Inc., Denver, 1961-64; exec. sec. Collins Radio Co., Newport Beach, Calif., 1961-64; office mgr. Manpower Inc., Idaho Falls, Idaho, 1975-76; sr. sec. Aeroject Nuclear, Idaho Falls, 1976-78; sr. sec. EG&G Idaho Inc., Idaho Falls, 1978-81, adminstrv. specialist, 1981-82, adminstr., 1982-84, sr. adminstr., 1984—. Republican. Lutheran. Home: 2718 Balboa Dr Idaho Falls ID 83404 Office: EG&G Idaho Inc PO Box 1625 Idaho Falls ID 83415

WARREN, CHARLES EARL, SR., astronautic company executive; b. Marietta, Ohio, Nov. 24, 1939; s. James Henry and Audrey Frances (Sprague) W.; m. Helen Marie Harshbarger, July 15, 1972; children: Audrey Frances, Charleen Sevim, Charles Earl Jr., David Lee, Michael John. Student, Syracuse U., 1958, N.Mex. State U., 1962-67, Weber State Coll., 1974-76. Missile devel. researcher Motorola Corp., Scottsdale, Ariz., 1965-66; aeromedical researcher Dynalectron Corp., Holloman AFB, N.Mex., 1966-67; nuclear researcher EG & G Inc., Kirkland AFB, N.Mex., 1967-68; with test range ops. Dynalectron Corp., 1968-69; flight test engr. Teledyne Ryan Aero., San Diego, 1969-77, Photosonics Inc., San Diego, 1977-78; sr. flight test engr. Gen. Dynamics-Convair Div., San Diego, 1978-80; test program mgr. Martin Marietta Astronautics, Denver, 1980—. Served to staff sgt. USAF, 1957-65. Recipient Excellence award Martin Marietta, Vandenberg AFB, Calif., 1983. Mem. Air Force Assn., Assn. for Unmanned Vehicle Systems, Nat. Mgmt. Assn. Republican. Lodge: Masons. Home: 3522 Winnebago Dr Sedalia CO 80135 Office: Martin Marietta PO Box 179 B1690 Denver CO 80201

WARREN, GERALD LEE, newspaper editor; b. Hastings, Nebr., Aug. 17, 1930; s. Hie Elias and Linnie (Williamson) W.; m. Euphemia Florence Brownell, Nov. 20, 1965 (div.); children: Gerald Benjamin, Euphemia Brownell; m. Viviane M. Pratt, Apr. 27, 1986. A.B., U. Nebr., 1952. Reporter Lincoln Star, Nebr., 1951-52; reporter, asst. city editor San Diego Union, 1956-61; bus. rep. Copley News Service, 1961-63; city editor San Diego Union, 1963-68, asst. mng. editor, 1968-69, editor, 1975—; dep. press. sec. to Pres. Richard M. Nixon, 1969-74, Pres. Gerald Ford, 1974-75. Served to lt. (j.g.) USNR, 1952-56. Mem. Am. Soc. Newspaper Editors, Sigma Delta Chi, Sigma Nu. Republican. Episcopalian. Office: Copley Press 350 Camino de la Reina San Diego CA 92108

WARREN, JAMES DAVID, JR., management consultant, musician; b. Ann Arbor, Mich., Jan. 1, 1951; s. James David and L. Eleanor (Newman) W. BSE in Indsl. and Ops. Engrng., U. Mich., 1974, BA in Music, 1974, MBA, 1976. Cert. mgmt. cons. Systems analyst, project leader, and fin. analyst The Gap Stores, Inc., San Bruno, Calif., 1976-79; sr. cons., mgr., and sr. mgr. Price Waterhouse, San Francisco, 1979-86; mgmt. dir. BDO/ Seidman, San Francisco, 1986-88, ptnr. in charge mgmt. cons., 1988—. Organist Park Blvd. Presbyn. Ch., Oakland, Calif., 1977—. Mem. Inst. Mgmt. Cons. v.p. San Francisco chpt. 1985-88), Bohemian Club (organist 1983—). Presbyterian. Home: 1770 Pacific Ave #303 San Francisco CA 94109 Office: BDO/Seidman 1 Sansome St Ste 1100 San Francisco CA 94104

WARREN, JEFFRY CLARY, clinical psychologist; b. Burbank, Calif., Nov. 1, 1949; s. Bernard W. and Florence S. W.; student Valley Coll., 1967-79; B.A., U. Calif.-Santa Barbara, 1971; Ph.D. in Clin. Psychology, Calif. Sch. of Profl. Psychology, 1976; 1 son, Adam Bernard. Registered psychologist Tech. Research, San Diego, 1976-78; developer, coordinator grad. tng. program Edwards Inst. for Advanced Studies, San Diego, 1980, dir. profl. and acad. tng., 1980; clin. psychologist TRI-Community Service Systems, San Diego, 1979-83; pvt. practice, La Jolla, Calif., 1983—; sr. v.p., dir. Grid Research Corp., 1982-83; cons. and educator in family therapy and child abuse. Developer task force on child abuse, San Diego, 1978-80. Mem. Am. Psychol. Assn., Nat. Register of Health Service Providers in Psychology, Calif. State Psychol. Assn., Acad. San Diego Psychologists, Western Psychol. Assn. Jewish. Contbr. papers to profl. assn. confs. Office: 7755 Fay St Ste I La Jolla CA 92037

WARREN, LARRY MICHAEL, clergyman; b. Bonne Terre, Mo., Nov. 25, 1946; s. Orson Wesley and Ruth Margaret (Stine) W.; m. Bonnie Jean Monk Chandler, Apr. 9, 1983; children: Samantha Chandler, John, Abigail Chandler, Anne, Meredith. BA cum laude, Lincoln U., 1969; MDiv with honors, St. Paul Sch. Theology, Kansas City, Mo., 1976; D of Ministry, San Francisco Theol. Sem., 1987. Ordained elder United Meth. Ch., 1978. Pastor Cainsville (Mo.) United Meth. Ch., 1975-76, Lakelands Parish, Rathdrum, Idaho, 1976-78; assoc. pastor Audubon Park United Meth. Ch., Spokane, Wash., 1978-83; pastor Faith United Meth. Ch., Everett, Wash., 1983—; adviser Kairos Prison Ministry Wash., Monroe, 1984—; conf. rep. grad. bd. St. Paul Sch. Theology, Kansas City, 1984. Contbr. to column Dialogue Everett Herald, 1984—. Adviser DeMolay, Spokane, 1979-81; team mem. Night-Walk, inner-city ministry, Spokane, 1979-82; coord. Ch. Relief Overseas Project Hunger Walk, Spokane and Everett, 1981, 85; vol. chaplain Gen. Hosp. Everett, 1983—; trustee Deaconess Children's Svcs., Everett, 1983-88. Recipient Legion of Honor DeMolay Internat., 1982. Mem. Fellowship of Reconciliation, North Snohomish County Assn. Chs. (v.p. 1985—), Pacific N.W. Ann. Conf. Bd. Global Ministries (sec. 1988—). Democrat. Home and Office: Faith United Meth Ch 125 112th St SW Everett WA 98204

WARREN, NICHOLAS WALTER, synergetics educator; b. Champaign, Ill., Apr. 12, 1941; s. William Joseph and Annette (Chemielewski) W.; m. Sally Lappen, Aug. 2, 1980; children: Adria, Caitrina, Kaitlin. BA in Physics, U. Calif., Berkeley, 1964; MA in Astronomy, Columbia U., 1966, PhD in Geophysics, 1971. Research geophysicist UCLA, 1971-80, assoc. research geophysicist, 1980-83; faculty Otis-Parsons Art Inst., Los Angeles, 1980—, Internat. Coll., Los Angeles, 1984-86; dean dept. natural sci. Sierra U., Santa Monica, Calif., 1986-87; cons. in art and sci., Santa Monica, 1984—. Editor IS Jour., 1989; contbr. articles to profl. jours. Mem. AAAS, Internat. Soc. for the Arts Scis and Technology, Nat. Sci. Tchrs. Assn., N.Y. Acad. Sci., Union Concerned Scientists, Wilderness Soc., Amnesty Internat., Sigma Xi. Home: 134 Hart Ave Santa Monica CA 90405 Office: Art/Sci Cons 134 Hart Ave Santa Monica CA 90405

WARREN, PETER, university dean; b. N.Y.C., Sept. 30, 1938. BA, U. Calif., Berkeley, 1950; MA with honors, U. Wis., 1965, PhD, 1970. Prof. math. and computer sci. U. Denver, 1970-78, dir. div. data processing, 1985-86, dean Univ. Coll., 1986—; dir. rsch. Colo. Energy Rsch. Inst., Denver, 1978-83; pvt. practice statistics cons., Denver, 1974-86. Contbr. over 40 articles to profl. jours. Pres., chmn. bd. Denver Internat. Film Festival, 1978-82; chmn. Urban Design Forum, Denver, 1983-85. Mem. Am. Assn. Computing Machinery, Am. Math. Soc. Democrat. Home: 936 Detroit St Denver CO 80206 Office: U Denver Denver CO 80208

WARREN, RICHARD WAYNE, obstetrician and gynecologist; b. Puxico, Mo., Nov. 26, 1935; s. Martin R. and Sarah E. (Crump) W.; B.A., U. Calif., Berkeley, 1957; M.D., Stanford, 1961; m. Rosalie J. Franzola, Aug. 16, 1959; children—Lani Marie, Richard W., Paul D. Intern, Oakland (Calif.) Naval Hosp., 1961-62; resident in ob-gyn Stanford Med. Center (Calif.), 1964-67; practice medicine specializing in ob-gyn, Mountain View, Calif., 1967—; mem. staff Stanford and El Camino hosps.; pres. Richard W. Warren M.D., Inc.; assoc. clin. prof. ob-gyn Stanford Sch. Medicine. Served with USN, 1961-64. Diplomate Am. Bd. Ob-Gyn. Fellow Am. Coll. Ob-Gyn; mem. AMA, Calif. Med. Assn., San Francisco Gynecol. Soc., Peninsula Gynecol. Soc., Am. Assn. Gynecologic Laparoscopists, Assn. Profs. Gynecology and Obstetrics, Royal Soc. Medicine. Contbr. articles to profl. jours. Home: 102 Atherton Ave Atherton CA 94025 Office: 2500 Hospital Dr Mountain View CA 94040

WARREN, RICK D., minister; b. San Jose, Calif., Jan. 28, 1954; s. James Russell and Dorothy Nell (Armstrong) W.; m. Elizabeth Kay Lewis, June 21, 1975; children: Amy Rebecca, Joshua James, Matthew David. BA, Calif. Bapt. Coll., 1977; MDiv, Southwestern Bapt. Theol. Sem., 1979; DMin, Fuller Theol. Sem., 1989. Youth evangelist Calif. So. Bapt. Convention, Fresno, 1970-74; assoc. pastor First Bapt. Ch., Norwalk, Calif., 1974-76; asst. to pres. Internat. Evangelism Assn., Fort Worth, 1977-79; founding pastor Saddleback Valley Community Ch., Mission Viejo, Calif., 1980—; lectr. How To Plan Church Seminars, 1982—. Author: Dynamic Bible Study Methods, 1981, Answers to Life's Difficult Questions, 1985. Named Outstanding Preacher of 1977, McGregor Found. Mem. No. Am. Soc. for Ch. Growth. Baptist. Office: Saddleback Valley Comm Ch 24194 Alicia Pkwy Ste M Mission Viejo CA 92691

WARREN, TORI JO, accountant; b. Palo Alto, Calif., Apr. 22, 1961; d. Raymond Gregory and Delphine Adeline (Peraldo) Betka; m. John Joseph Warren, Feb. 11, 1984; 1 child, Chase Logan. BS in Managerial Econs., U. Calif., Davis, 1983. Office mgr. Pediatric Office, Reno, Nev., 1984; pub. acct. Grant Thornton, Reno, 1985-88; pvt. practice, Seattle, 1988—. Mem. AAUW (auditor 1986-87), Am. Med. Aux. Democrat. Home and Office: 328 NE 162d St Seattle WA 98155

WARREN, WILLIAM DAVID, lawyer, educator; b. Mt. Vernon, Ill., Nov. 13, 1924; s. Arthur and Dorothy Davis (Phillips) W.; m. Susan C. Audren, Nov. 15, 1965; children: John David, Sarah Hartwell. A.B., U. Ill., 1948, J.D., 1950; J.S.D., Yale U., 1957. Asst. prof. law Vanderbilt U., 1951-53, Ohio State U., 1953-54; from asst. prof. to prof. U. Ill., Champaign, 1954-59; prof. UCLA, 1959-72, 75—, dean Sch. Law, 1975-82; William Benjamin Scott and Luna M. Scott prof. law Stanford, 1972-75; Cons. Fed. Res. Bd. (chmn. consumer adv. council 1979-80), Nat. Commn. on Consumer Fin., Calif. Legislature, Calif. Law Revision Commn., Nat. Conf. Commrs. Uniform State Laws, 1964-74, 85—. Co-author: California Commercial Law III, 1966, Attorney's Guide to Truth in Lending, 1968, Cases and Materials on Debtor Creditor Law, 2d edit, 1981, Commercial Law, 1983, Bankruptcy, 1985. Served with USAAF, 1943-45. Mem. ABA, Order of Coif, Phi Beta Kappa, Phi Kappa Phi, Phi Delta Phi. Office: U Calif Law Sch Los Angeles CA 90024

WARREN, WILLIAM HENRY, marketing executive; b. Sacramento, May 23, 1941; s. Lloyd William and Pauline Ann (McKenna) W.; m. Gretchen Green, June 15, 1963; children: Leslie, Mark. BA, Stamford U., 1963,

MBA, 1965. Sales rep. IBM Corp., San Francisco, 1967-69; product mgr. Memorex, Santa Clara, Calif., 1970-77; v.p. Computer Avionics, San Jose, Calif., 1978-79; pres. Fracture Tech., Palo Alto, Calif., 1980-81; mktg. mgr. Rolm Corp., Santa Clara, 1982-85; dir. ops. Nat. Svc. IBM/Rolm, Santa Clara, 1986-89; v.p. customer support Centigram, San Jose, 1989—. Lt. USN, 1963-65. Home: 14677 Saltarmontes Los Altos Hills CA 94022

WARTGOW, JEROME FREDRICK, college adminstrator; b. Milw., Aug. 20, 1942; s. Harold Fredrick and Doris Jane (Gaab) W.; m. Diane Carol Beirl, Aug. 15, 1964; children: Joel, Jeffrey. BS, U. Wis., 1964; MEd, U. Hawaii, 1967; PhD, U. Denver, 1972. Cert. sch. adminstr., Colo.; cert. secondary tchr., Wis., Calif., Colo. Dean of students Internat. Sch. of Bangkok, 1967-70; dir. research and evaluation Gov.'s State U., University Park, Ill., 1972-73; dep. exec. dir. Colo. Commn. on Higher Edn., Denver, 1973-78; exec. dir. Auraria Higher Edn. Ctr., Denver, 1978-86; pres. Colo. Community Coll. and Occupational Edn. System, Denver, 1986—. Contbr. articles to profl. jours. Mem. Gov.'s Job Tng. Coordinating Council, Gov.'s Econ. Devel. Action Council, Youth 2000 Task Force, Mayor's Platt Valley Devel. Com.; mem. community adv. com. Jr. League of Denver. Recipient Excellence in Govt. award Fed. Exec. Bd., 1982, East-West Ctr. fellowship, 1985; honored Jerome F. Wartgow Day Gov. of Colo., Oct. 15, 1986. Mem. Am. Assn. Community, Jr. Colls., Am. Assn. University Adminstrs., Colo. Inst. Pub. Adminstrs., Am. Vocat. Assn., Greater Metro Denver C. of C., Mensa, Mt. Vernon Country Club. Office: Colo Community Coll and Occupational Edn System 1391 Speer Blvd #600 Denver CO 80204

WASDEN, WINIFRED SAWAYA, English educator, freelance writer; b. Kemmerer, Wyo., Apr. 15, 1938; d. George Sabeh and Letta Louise (Gerken) Sawaya; m. John Frederic Wasden, Dec. 20, 1960; children: Frederic Keith, Carol Elizabeth. BA with honors, U. Wyo., 1960, MA, 1961. Emergency instr. U. Wyo., Laramie, 1960-61; tchr. English Worland (Wyo.) High Sch., 1963; from instr. to assoc. prof. English Northwest Community Coll., Powell, Wyo., 1964—. Contbr. articles to pubs.; author numerous poems. Mem. Powell Bd. Adjustments, 1974—; chmn., bd. dirs. Civic Orch. and Chorus, Powell, 1981-88; mem. Wyo. Council for the Humanities, 1978-79, coordinator Big Horn Basin Project, 1980-85. Mem. Wyo. Oral History and Folklore Assn. (v.p. 1984-85, bd. dirs. 1985-86), Wyo. Assn. Tchrs. English, N.W. Community Coll. Faculty Assn. (pres. 1977-78), AAAUW, Delta Kappa Gamma (pres. Powell chpt. 1978-80), Phi Rho Pi (hon.). Republican. Roman Catholic. Office: NW Community Coll Powell WY 82435

WASHBURN, FRANK MURRAY, management consultant; b. Portland, Oreg., Feb. 28, 1926; s. Fred Lucian and Dorothy (Murray) W.; m. Buena Stewart, Sept. 3, 1950; children: Bonnie Belle, Mary Ann, Terri Lee, Scott Stewart, Nancy Ellen. BA, Willamette U., 1950; MS, Springfield (Mass.) Coll., 1952. Camp dir. YMCA, Portland, 1950; youth work dir. YMCA, Salem, Oreg., 1952-57; adult program dir. YMCA, Seattle, 1957-59, asst. met. dir., 1959-63, assoc. met. dir., 1963-68; exec. dir. YMCA Blue Ridge Assembly, Black Mountain, N.C., 1968-85; pres. Frank M. Washburn and Assocs., Salem, 1985—. Contbr. articles to profl. jours. Active Nat. Repub. Com., Washington, 1989—; bd. dirs. Salem Family YMCA, 1989—; pres. Highland Farms Retirement Ctr., Black Mountain, 1980-82. Sgt. USAF, 1944-46. Named Jr. 1st Citizen Jaycees, Salem, 1956; recipient Distinguished Alumni award Willamette U., Salem, 1973. Mem. Am. Camping Assn. (pres. 1968-70, Disting. Service award 1974), Internat. Assn. Conf. Ctr. Adminstrs. (pres. 1976-80), North Am. Fellowship of YMCA Devel. Officers. Presbyterian. Home and Office: 398 Jerris Ave SE Salem OR 97302

WASHBURN, JACK BLENKIRON, finance and investment company executive; b. Los Angeles, Oct. 17, 1913; s. Harry Boardman Washburn and Esther Emma (Blenkiron) Louck; m. Cornelia Haskins, 1936 (div. 1951); children: Robert, Stephen, Scott, David; m. Lois Anne Scott, May 17, 1952. Degree in Bus., U. Denver, 1945. Clk. U.S. Treasury, Denver, 1936-41; chief statistician Remington Arms Co., Denver, 1941-44; office mgr. Continental Airlines, Denver, 1944-45; chief budget officer War Assets Adminstrn., Denver, 1945-48; loan examiner First Interstate Nat. Bank, Portland, Oreg., 1948-56; co-owner, pres. Bennett & Williams Assocs., Portland, 1956-63; sr. loan officer SBA, Portland, 1963-79; owner, pres. Life Enterprises Co., Portland, 1971—; owner Atlas Investment Co., Portland, 1956—, Atlas Realty, Portland, 1970—; pres. Denver chpt. Nat. Assn. Accts., 1944-50. Mem. Rep. Nat. Com. Mem. Portland C. of C. Republican. Methodist. Club: Multnomah Athletic. Lodges: Rotary, Masons. Home: 1009 SW Rivington Dr Portland OR 97201 Office: Atlas Realty 1009 SW Rivington Dr Portland OR 97201

WASHBURN, JAMES THOMAS, II, minister; b. Midland, Tex., Dec. 22, 1958; s. Almas Preston and Mary Wynola (Waters) W.; m. Julie Ellen Eakin, Dec. 27, 1983; 1 child, James Thomas III. BA in Bible, Lubbock Christian Coll., 1983. Ordained to ministry Ch. of Christ, 1979. Intern Broadway Ch. of Christ, Lubbock, Tex., 1979-82; youth minister Ft. Worth and Jax Ch. of Christ (now Fairmont Park Ch. of Christ), Midland, 1981-84, 3d and Kilgore Ch. of Christ, Portales, N.Mex., 1984—; adventure leader Adventures in Christian Living, 1985. Basketball official, 1984—, Football official, 1985—. Named one of Outstanding Young Men of Am., 1983. Mem. N.Mex. Activities Assn., N.Mex. Officials Assn. Republican. Home: 1708 S Globe Portales NM 88130 Office: 3d and Kilgore Ch of Christ Box 450 Portales NM 88130

WASHBURN, JERRY MARTIN, accountant, information systems company executive; b. Powell, Wyo., Dec. 31, 1943; s. Roland and Lavon (Martin) W.; divorced; children: Garth, Gavin, Kristina. BS in Acctg. Brigham Young U., 1969. CPA, Wash., Idaho, Oreg. Staff acct. Arthur Andersen & Co., Seattle, 1969-70, sr. auditor, Boise, Idaho, 1971-73, audit mgr., Boise and Portland, Oreg., 1976-79; v.p. controller Washburn Musicland, Inc., Phoenix, 1980-82; mgr., ptnr. Washburn Enterprises, Phoenix, 1977—; pres. Total Info. Systems, Inc., Phoenix, 1984—; founding dir. Internat. and Commerce Bank, Phoenix, 1985-86. Mem. Inst. Internal Auditors (pres. Boise chpt. 1974, bd. dirs. Boise and Portland chpts. 1975-77), Am. Mgmt. Soc., Am. Inst. CPAs, Wash. Soc. CPAs, Idaho Soc. CPAs. Republican. Office: Total Info Systems Inc 4201 N 24th St Ste 150 Phoenix AZ 85016

WASHBURN, PETER LLOYD, internist; b. Niagara Falls, N.Y., Mar. 3, 1943; s. Lloyd Jerome and Bonnie (Fenska) W. BA, U. Pa., 1965, MD, 1969. Diplomate Am. Bd. Internal Medicine. Lt. USN, 1971, advanced through grades to comdr., 1973; intern U. Conn., 1969-71; resident Portsmouth (Va.) Naval Hosp., 1973-75; chief alcohol rehab. svc. Naval Hosp., Newport, R.I., 1978-83; chief drug dependence treatment clinic VA, Boston, 1985; fellow in substance abuse VA, San Francisco, 1985-87; med. dir. Merritt Peralta Chem. Dependency Recovery Hosp., Oakland, Calif., 1987—. Mem. Am. Med. Soc. on Alcoholism and Other Drug Dependencies, Calif. Soc. for Treatment Alcoholism and Other Drug Dependencies. Office: Merritt Peralta Hosp 435 Hawthorne Ave Oakland CA 94609

WASHINGTON, CHARLES EDWARD, educator; b. Little Rock, Nov. 27, 1933; s. David D. and Hzel M. Washington; BA, Philander Smith Coll., Little Rock, 1958; MEd, U. Okla., 1962; postgrad. U. So. Calif., umpire Internat. Fedn. Amateur Softball Assn. Umpires, 1961-63; m. Ruby N. Jones, Sept. 4, 1956 (div. 1965); 1 dau., Toni Regail. Tchr. public schs., Ft. Smith, Ark., 1958-60, Oklahoma City, 1960-69, L.A., 1969—; registered rep. ITT Hamilton Mgmt. Corp., 1963-70; fin. counselor Fin. Congeneric Corp., 1971-74, Am. Inst. Property and Liability Underwriters; spl. agt. Welsh & Assos., Ins. Svcs., Walnut, Calif., 1979—; sales mgr. Sun Belt Ins. Svcs., Walnut, 1982—; gen. agt. Alvo Ins. and Fin. Svcs., 1984—. Mem. Crenshaw Christian Center. Served with USMC, 1951-54; Korea. Mem. NEA, Calif. Tchrs. Assn., United Tchrs. L.A., Ind. Ins. Assn. Calif., U. Okla. Alumni Assn. (class rep. 1964-67), Nat. Dunbar High Sch. Alumni Assn., Philander Smith Coll. Alumni Assn., Nat. Notary Assn. Omega Psi Phi. Democrat. Home and Office: 20023 Alvo Ave Carson CA 90745

WASHINGTON, DOLORES ELIZABETH, college instructor; b. Fresno, Calif., Nov. 3, 1936; d. John Earl and Claudine Elizabeth (Brandon) Abernathy; m. James Leon Boone, Sept. 13, 1960 (div. June 1965); 1 child, Marlene C.; m. Herman Doglas Washington (div. July 1984). AA, Reedley (Calif.) Coll., 1956; BE, Fresno State U., 1958; ME, Sacramento State U., 1978; postgrad., U. Jacksonville, 1986. Tchr. Corcoran (Calif.) Sch. Dist., 1958-61, Riverside (Calif.) Sch. Dist., 1961-62, Stockton (Calif) Unified Sch. Dist., 1962-69; food inspector U.S. Dept. Agr., Stockton, 1962-67; coll. instr. San Joaquin Delta Coll., Stockton, 1969—, cons. Stockton Seccuss Inst., 1988—; cons. in field; owner, founder DEW Ednl. Cons., Stockton, 1988—; speaker Stockton Speakers Bur., 1969—. Author: Introduction to Microwave Cooking, 1982, Personal Budgeting, 1989. Chmn. Foster Grandparent Stockton Hosp., 1973—; bd. dirs. Better Bus. Bur. Mid-Counties, Inc., 1989, Schs. Credit Union, 1981—. Mem. Calif. Tchrs. Assn., Delta Kappa Gamma (pres. 1984-88). Home: 2546 W Hammer Ln Stockton CA 95209 Office: San Joaquin Delta Coll 5151 Pacific Ave Stockton CA 95207 also: PO Box 691001 Stockton CA 95691

WASHINGTON, NAPOLEON, JR., insurance agent, clergyman; b. Ft. Baker, Calif., Apr. 12, 1948; s. Napoleon and Annie D. (Carter) W.; A.A., Merced Coll., 1976; student Stanislaus State Coll., 1976-77; grad. Billy Graham Sch. Evangelism, 1987; m. Nadine Reed, Nov. 6, 1968; children—Gregory D., Kimberlee N., Geoffrey N. Lic. Baptist minister. Agt., Met. Life Ins. Co., Merced, Calif., 1970-72, sr. sales rep., 1972-83; broker Gen. Ins. Brokers, Merced, 1973—; owner Washington Assocs. Fin. Services; tchr. salesmanship Merced Coll., 1979—. Chmn. bd. trustees St. Matthew Baptist Ch., 1978—, ordained deacon, lic. minister, assoc. minister, 1982—; vice-chmn. Merced County Pvt. Industries Council, 1981-83; mem. ins. adv. council City of Merced Schs.; vocat. mgr. New Hope Found., Dos Palos, Calif., 1984-85. Served with U.S. Army, 1968-70. Recipient Nat. Quality award Nat. Assn. Life Underwriters, 1979, Nat. Sales Achievement award, 1979, Health Ins. Quality award, 1977; mem. Million Dollar Round Table, 1973, 74, 75, 76, 77, 78; teaching cert. Calif. community colls. Mem. Nat. Assn. Life Underwriters, Calif. Assn. Life Underwriters (dir. 1975-76), Merced County Assn. Life Underwriters (pres. 1976-77), Merced County Estate Planning Council (dir.), Merced County Pvt. Industries Council, NAACP, Phi Beta Lambda. Democrat. Club: Rotary (dir. 1974-76). Home: 1960 Cedar Crest Dr Merced CA 95340 Office: 935 W 18th St Merced CA 95340

WASHINGTON, REGINALD LOUIS, pediatric cardiologist; b. Colorado Springs, Colo., Dec. 31, 1949; s. Lucius Louis and Brenette Y. (Wheeler) W.; m. Billye Faye Ned, Aug. 18, 1973; children: Danielle Larae, Reginald Quinn. BS in Zoology, Colo. State U., 1971; MD, U. Colo., 1975. Diplomate Nat. Bd. Med. Examiners, Am. Bd. Pediatrics, Pediatric Cardiology. Intern in pediatrics U. Colo. Med. Ctr., Denver, 1975-76, resident in pediatrics, 1976-78, chief resident, instr., 1978-79, fellow in pediatric cardiology, 1979-81, asst. prof. pediatrics, 1982-1988, assoc. prof. pediatrics, 1988—; staff cardiologist Children's Hosp., Denver, 1981—; mem. admissions com. U. Colo. Sch. Medicine, Denver, 1985-89; bd. dirs. Children's Health Care Assn., bd. dirs. treasRMS, Inc. Adv. bd. dirs. Equitable Bank of Littleton, Colo., 1984-86. Bd. dirs. Cen. City Opera, 1989—, Rocky Mountain Heart Fund for Children, 1984-89. Recipient Mosby award in Pediatrics, U. Colo. Med. Ctr., 1975. Fellow Am. Acad. Pediatrics (cardiology subsect.), Am. Coll. Cardiology, Am. Heart Assn. (council on cardiovascular disease in the young, exec. com. 1988—, vol. of yr. 1989, pres. 1989—, Torch of Hope 1987), editorial bd. Pediatric Exercise Sciences, 1988—, bd. dirs. Colo. chpt., exec. com. Colo. chpt. 1987—, grantee Colo. chpt. 1983-84), Soc. Critical Care Medicine; mem. Am. Acad. Pediatrics/Perinatology, N.Am. Soc. Pediatric Exercise Medicine (pres.). Democrat. Roman Catholic. Club: Denver Athletic. Home: 7423 Berkeley Circle Castle Rock CO 80104 Office: Dept Pediatric Cardiology 1056 E 19th Ave Denver CO 80218

WASHINGTON, VIRGINIA VAUGHN, office manager; b. Detroit, Mar. 20, 1930; d. Edward Milton Vaughn and Helen Geraldine (Osborne) Dailey; m. Lacy Karl Washington, Apr. 25, 1959; children: Krishna Henry, Craig. Student, Wayne State U., 1948-51. Office mgr. State of Ariz., Phoenix, 1968—. Pres. Phoenix Urban League Guild, 1971-74. Recipient Cert. Recognition, Phoenix Masjid, Inc., 1980. Mem. LWV, Consortium Black Orgns. for the Arts, Internat. Assn. Personnel Employment Security, Episcopal Commn. Black Ministries. Democrat. Episcopalian. Office: Dept Econ Security 4635 S Central Ave Phoenix AZ 85040

WASSERMAN, BRUCE ARLEN, dentist, mail order company executive; b. San Mateo, Calif., June 7, 1954; s. Albert and Dunia (Frydman) W.; m. Pamela Carole Ward, June 8, 1972; children:Rachael, Rebecca, Meir, Keren. BA in Mass Communications, Winona State U., 1981; DDS, U. Pacific, 1985. Blacksmith Walden Forge, Pine River, Minn., 1973-79; founding dir. Team Redeemed, San Mateo, 1984-; pvt. practice San Mateo, 1985-; pres. Manx USA, San Mateo, 1987-. Editor Good News, 1984—, The Mouthpiece, 1986-, No. Calif. Reporter, 1987—; assoc. editor Internat. Communicator, 1988. Cubmaster Boy Scouts Am., San Mateo, 1986-87; fund raiser Am. Lung Assn. San Mateo County, 1986-88; chmn. Bike Trek Am. Lung Assn., San Mateo County, 1989. Recipient Disting. Young Alumni award Winona State U., 1988; Mosby scholar Tau Kappa Omega, 1985. Fellow Acad. Dentistry Internat., Royal Soc. of Health; mem. ADA (cert. of recognition 1987), Calif. Dental Assn. (Disting. Svc. award 1987, 89), San Mateo County Dental Soc. (exec. bd. 1986—, editor 1986—, Bd. Dirs. award 1987), Pierre Fauchard Acad., Acad. Gen. Dentistry, Christian Classic Bikers Assn. (Calif. rep.), Order Ky. Col., Tau Kappa Omega. Office: 410 N San Mateo Dr San Mateo CA 94401

WASSERMAN, ISAAC MILES, vocational evaluator; b. Richmond, Va., Sept. 25, 1932; s. Joseph Benjamin and Eva W.; A.B.A., Nichols Jr. Coll., 1956; student in bus. adminstrn. Lynchburg Coll., 1953-55; B.S. in Edn., Boston U., 1958, M.Ed., 1959; 1 dau., Erica Jacqueline. Tutorial and remedial tchr. White Plains (N.Y.) Public Schs., 1959-60; tchr. English and geography Newton (Mass.) Public Schs., 1960; instr. psychology and public speaking Cambridge Jr. Coll., 1961-62; vocat. counselor Jewish Vocat. Service, Boston, 1962-63; guidance counselor jr. high schs. Winthrop (Mass.) Public Schs., 1963-68; elem. counselor, sch. psychologist Andover (Mass.) Public Schs., 1966-76; sch. psychologist, core team chmn. Greater Lowell (Mass.) Regional Vocat. Tech. Sch., 1976-77; sch. psychologist Lawrence (Mass.) pub. schs., 1977; vocat. evaluator/rehab. counselor Goodwill Industries, San Jose, Calif., 1977-81, vocat. evaluator, 1982—; vocat. evaluator Westcom Industries, Richmond Calif., 1981; psychol. cons. Lawrence Public Schs. Recipient Dr. Quincy Merrill award Nichols Jr. Coll., 1959 Mem. Am. Personnel and Guidance Assn., Nat. Vocat. Guidance Assn., Am. Sch. Counselors Assn. Club: Masons (Richmond, Va.). Home: 5545 Tilden Pl Fremont CA 94538 Office: Goodwill Industries 1080 N 7th St San Jose CA 95112

WASSERMAN, LEW R., film, recording, publishing company executive; b. Cleve., Mar. 15, 1913; m. Edith T. Beckerman, July 5, 1936; 1 dau., Lynne Kay. D (hon.), Brandeis U., NYU. Nat. dir. advt. and publicity Music Corp. Am., 1936-38, v.p., 1938-39, became v.p. charge motion picture div., 1940; now chmn., chief exec. officer, dir., mem. exec. com. MCA, Inc., also chmn. bd., chief exec. officer, dir. subsidiary corps.; dir. Am. Airlines; chmn. emeritus Assn. Motion Picture and TV Producers. Trustee John F. Kennedy Library, John F. Kennedy Center Performing Arts, Calif. Inst. Tech., Jules Stein Eye Inst., Carter Presdl. Ctr., Lyndon Baines Johnson Found.; pres. pres. Hollywood Canteen Found.; chmn. Research to Prevent Blindness Found.; hon. chmn. bd. Center Theatre Group Los Angeles Music Center; bd. dirs. Amateur Athletic Found. of Los Angeles (chmn. fin. com.), Los Angeles Music Ctr. Found.; bd. gov.'s Ronald Reagan Presdl. Found. Recipient Jean Hersholt Humanitarian award Acad. Motion Picture Arts and Scis., 1973. Democrat. Office: MCA Inc 100 Universal City Pla Universal City CA 91608 *

WASSERMAN, ROBERT, city official; b. Gary, Ind., Jan. 12, 1934; s. Morris K. and Alice W.; B.S., Calif. State U., 1963; M.P.A., U. So. Calif., 1975; m. Mary Linda Galantin, Sept. 13, 1958; children—Daniel Joseph, Jill Marie. Chief of police City of San Carlos (Calif.), 1969-72, City of Brea and Yorba Linda (Calif.), 1972-76, City of Fremont (Calif.), 1976—; chmn. adv. com. Calif. Commn. on Peace Officer Stds. and Tng., 1979-83; mem. Calif. Commn. on Peace Officer Standards and Tng.; mem. Pres.'s Adv. Com. Law Enforcement; cons. to police agys. Bd. mgrs. Fremont-Newark YMCA, 1978—. Served with U.S. Army, 1950-52. Mem. Calif. Peace Officers Assn. (pres. 1980), Internat. Assn. Chiefs of Police, Police Exec. Research Forum. Club: Rotary. Contbr. articles to profl. jours. Office: 39710 Civic Center Dr Fremont CA 94538

WASSMAN, DENNIS WAYNE, entrepreneur; b. Tacoma, Wash., Dec. 16, 1943; s. Harry Chester and Nancy (Martus) W.; m. Jacquelyn Joyce Zaspel, July 3, 1965; 3 children. BA, U. Washington, 1966. Mgmt. trainee Puget Sound Nat. Bank, Tacoma, 1966-70; asst. v.p. First Interstate Bank, Seattle, 1970-78; cons. Puyallup, Wash., 1978-79; pres., chmn. bd. dirs. Western Bldg. Devel., Inc., Mountlake Terr., Wash., 1978-79; exec. v.p., chief ops. officer Sea Galley Stores, Inc., Mountlake Terr., 1978-83; founder, v.p. Telecale, Inc., Bellevue, Wash., 1983—; also bd. dirs. Telecale, Inc.; chmn. Zao Med. Systems, INc., Kirkland, Wash., 1985—; pres., chmn. Zynex Capital Ltd., Puyallup, Wash., 1986—.

WASSON, BEVERLY FERNE, farmer; b. Healdsburg, Calif., Sept. 14, 1947; d. Fred Richard and Ruby Marjory (Osborn) W. BA, Humboldt State Coll., 1969. Tchr. Mt. Diablo Unified Sch. Dist., Concord, Calif., 1970-80; athletic dir. Mt. Diablo Unified Sch. Dist., Concord, 1974-79; vineyard mgr. Fred Wasson Vineyards, Geyserville, Calif., 1980-84; ptnr. Wasson Vineyards, Geyserville, Calif., 1984—. Basketball ofcl., No. Calif., 1966-85; coach Mt. Diablo Unified Sch. Dist., 1971-78; softball ofcl. Cloverdale (Calif.) Pony League, 1983-86. Named Outstanding Young Farmer Sonoma County Fair, Santa Rosa, Calif., 1986. Mem. Sonoma County Farm Bur. (1st v.p. 1987-88, pres. 1989—), Sonoma County Grape Growers Assn. (pres. 1986-87, dir. 1984-89), Calif. Wine Grape Growers Assn., Women's Recreation Assn., Spurs. Office: Wasson Vineyards 3674 Hwy 128 Geyserville CA 95441

WASSON, DAVID CARLISLE, catering company executive; b. Columbia, Mo., Oct. 3, 1952; s. John Marvin and Nataline Patricia (Dozier) W.; m. Pamela Sue Schlicting, Sept. 18, 1983; children: Julian Tremane, Desmond Paige. Student, Seattle Cen. Community Coll., 1981-83. Sous chef Pizza Haven, Pullman, Wash., 1974-76, Bellingham, Wash., 2976-78; sous chef Olympic Inn, Poulsbo, Wash., 1979-80, Contemporary Caterer, Seattle, 1981-83; les guillade Westin Towers-Palm Ct., Seattle, 1980-81; owner, chef, mgr. Am. Caterer, Seattle, 1983-; mem. tech. adv. com. Seattle Cen. Community Coll., 1983-. Mem. Seattle-King County Conv. Svcs. Bur., Palouse Jazz Soc. (founder, pres. 1979). Democrat. Buddhist. Home and Office: 333 NW 205th St Seattle WA 98177

WASSON, DAVID WESLEY, educational service agency director; b. Whitefish, Mont., Dec. 15, 1942; s. Lewis Henry and Betty F. (Bahm) Larter; m. Sue Caroll Gentry, Aug. 25, 1964; children: Wesley, Tammy, Bonnie, Kimberly. AA, York (Nebr.) Coll., 1962; BSE, Abilene (Tex.) Christian U., 1965; MA, No. Ariz. U., 1971. Cert. tchr. Ariz., Tex. (life), Calif. (life). Tchr., dept. head Needles (Calif.) High Sch., 1965-73; curriculum specialist Mohave County Career Edn., Kingman, Ariz., 1973-76; exec. dir. Mohave Ednl. Services, Kingman, Ariz., 1976—; res. instr. San Bernadino Valley Coll., Needles, 1966-73, Mohave County Community Coll., Kingman, 1973—, No. Ariz. U., Kingman, 1976—; cons. office career edn. U.S. Office Edn., Washington, 1978-80; bd. dirs. Harper & Wasson Pubs., Inc., Kingman, 1984—. Author, dir. (TV spl.) Sky-12 Visits Ariz., 1984; producer: (videotape) How to Speak Indian Sign Language, 1984, Wovoka and the Ghost Dance, 1985; author: The Silent Language of the Plains, 1986, Youth Awareness: A Drug Prevention Program, 1987, Teen Awareness: A Drug Awareness Program, 1987, Geography Basics, USA, 1988. Bd. dirs. Mohave Mus. History and Arts, Kingman, 1979-82; mem. exec. bd. Kingman Centennial Commn., Kingman, 1979-83, vocat. edn. task force Ariz. Dept. Edn., 1980-86. TIPS fellow U. Colo., 1971, COE fellow Pepperdine U., 1972. Mem. Ariz. Assn. Career Edn. Republican. Club: Toastmasters. Home: 2509 Valentine Ave Kingman AZ 86401 Office: Mohave Ednl Svcs 515 W Beale Kingman AZ 86401

WASSON, (ARNOLD) DOUGLAS, clergyman; b. Minot, N.D., Aug. 21, 1927; s. Robert Lawrence and Jenny Marguarite (Clark) W.; m. Mary Jo Peacock, June 2, 1958. BA, Case Western Res. U., 1950; M in Divinity, Oberlin (Ohio) Grad. Sch. of Theology, 1953; M in Edn., Auburn (Ala.) U., 1961. Ordained to ministry United Ch. of Christ, 1953. Adminstrv. asst. Pittman Community Ctr., Sevierville, Tenn., 1954-55; instr., pub. relations dir. So. Union Coll., Wadley, Ala., 1955-56, acting pres., 1956-58; asst. to pres. Snead Jr. Coll., Boaz, Ala., 1958-60; pastor First Congl. Ch., Rock Springs, Wyo., 1961-68, Colorado Springs, Colo., 1968-72; coordinator religious activities Woodmoor Corp., Monument, Colo., 1972-74; pastor The Ch. at Woodmoor, Monument, Colo., 1972—; moderator Wyo. Assn. United Ch. Christ, 1963, Southeast Assn. United Ch. Christ, 1970; mem. adv. bd. Franciscan Family Wellness Program, 1987—, Franciscan Ctr., Colorado Springs, 1988—. Chmn. Sweetwater County Outdoor Recreation Bd., Rock Springs, 1966-68; adv. mem. Wyo. Land and Water Conservation Com., Cheyenne, 1966-68. Recipient Citation for Service award Circle K Internat., 1979, Citation for Leadership award Heifer Project Internat., 1986, Citation for Fund Raising award Ch. World Svc., 1985; named Young Men of Yr. Rock Springs Jaycees, 1963. Mem. San Luis Valley Christian Community Services (Alamosa, Colo. bd. dirs. 1975—), Christian Ministry in Nat. Parks (nat. bd. dirs. 1965—), Kiwanis (pres. 1958, 61, lt. gov. 1963, gov. Rocky Mountain dist. 1968, internat. trustee 1974-78). Democrat. Mem. United Ch. of Christ. Home: 1677 Shrider Rd Colorado Springs CO 80920-3375

WASSON, JAMES WALTER, aircraft manufacturing company executive; b. Pitts., Dec. 9, 1951; s. George Fredrick and Dolores Helen (Weurl) W.; m. Evelyn Fay Gonzales, Dec. 28, 1974; children: Robert, Brian. AST, Pitts. Inst. Aeronautics, 1972; BSET, Northrop U., Inglewood, Calif., 1981; MBA, U. Phoenix, 1988. Avionics technician various cos., 1972-74; electronics prodn. mgr. Ostgaard Industries, Gardena, Calif., 1974-75; sr. avionics design engr. Airesearch Aviation Co., L.A., 1975-81; sr. tech. specialist Northrop Aircraft Div., Hawthorne, Calif., 1981-84; prog. mgr. McDonnell Douglas Helicopter Co., Mesa, Ariz., 1984-86; research mgr. McDonnell Douglas Helicopter Co., 1986—; cons. in field. Author: Avionics Technology, 1983; inventor in field; contbr. articles to profl. jours. Com. chmn. Northrop U. Industry Adv. Bd., 1981; organizer Boy Scouts Am., Mesa, 1988. Named Engr. of the Yr., Northrop U., 1980; Disting. Alumnus awad, Pitts. Inst. Aeronautics, 1981. Mem. Army Aviation Assn. (chpt. sr. v.p. 1988—), Am. Helicopter Soc., SAE, Nat. Soc. Profl. Engrs., IEEE. Republican. Roman Catholic. Home: 5213 E Fairfield Cir Mesa AZ 85205 Office: McDonnell Douglas 5000 E McDowell Rd 530/B338 Mesa AZ 85205

WAT, JAMES KAM-CHOI, retail executive; b. Hong Kong, Sept. 9, 1949; came to U.S., 1977; s. Biu Wat and Yuk (Ping) Tank; m. Miranda Kwa-Fong Leong, Oct. 6, 1974; children: Bryan, Vincent, Tiffany. Cert. edn., U. London, Hong Kong, 1969. Bus. mgr., asst. mgr., then sales mgr. Texwood Ltd., Hong Kong, 1970-77; gen. mgr. Texwood, Inc. (USA), N.Y.C., 1977-80, exec. v.p., dir., 1980-81; v.p. Jive Sportswear, Inc., N.Y.C., 1980-81; exec. v.p. Drager Industries, Inc., N.Y.C., 1980-81; pres. Am. Jeaneration Apparel, Inc., L.A., 1982-83; asst. import mgr. Millers Outpost Hub Distbg., Inc., Ontario, Calif., 1983-86; import mgr. Millers Outpost Hub Distbg., Inc., 1986-88, import dir. men's dept., 1988—. Office: Hub Distbg Inc 2501 E Guasti Rd Ontario CA 91761

WATANABE, COLIN KAZUO, stock brokerage executive; b. Lihue, Hawaii, Sept. 12, 1959; s. Herbert S. and Ellen (Tamura) W. BS, Ind. U., 1981. Therapeutic recreation specialist Rehab. Hosp. of Pacific, Honolulu, 1981-84; Shiatsu therapist, vice prin. Aisen Shiatsu Sch., Inc., Honolulu, 1983—; account exec. Pittock Fin. Corp., Honolulu, 1986-87; br. mgr., v.p. Fitzgerald, Talman, Inc., Honolulu, 1987—, Marshall Davis Inc, Honolulu, 1989—. Author, pub. newsletter Colin Watanabe Mo. Investment Perspective; contbg. edit or mag. col. The New You Mag. Recipient Black Belt, Japan Kendo Fedn., 1974. Democrat. Office: Marshall Davis Inc 1221 Kapiolani Blvd #810 Honolulu HI 96826

WATANABE, CORINNE KAORU AMEMIYA, lawyer, state official; b. Wahiawa, Hawaii, Aug. 1, 1950; d. Keiji and Setsuko (Matsumiya) Amemiya; m. Edwin Tsugio Watanabe, Mar. 8, 1975; children: Traciann Keiko, Brad Natsuo, Lance Yoneo. BA, U. Hawaii, 1971; JD, Baylor U., 1974. Bar: Hawaii 1974. Dep. atty. gen. State of Hawaii, Honolulu, 1974-84, 1st dep. atty. gen., 1984-85, 87—, atty. gen., 1985-87. Mem. ABA, Hawaii Bar Assn. Democrat. Office: Atty Gen 415 S Beretania St 405 State Capitol Honolulu HI 96813

WATANABE, JEFFREY NOBORU, lawyer; b. Wailuku, Hawaii, Jan. 30, 1943; s. Robert Wataru and Mildred Shizue (Shiramizu) W.; m. Lynn Shelley

Manildi, Dec. 28, 1969; children: Michael, Molly, Katherine, Robert. BA, U. Calif., 1965; JD, George Washington U., 1968. Dep. atty. gen. State of Hawaii, Honolulu, 1968-70; ptnr. Kobayashi, Watanabe, Sugita, Kawashima & Goda, Honolulu, 1970—; bd. dirs. Am. Savs. Bank, Grace Pacific Corp., Hawaiian Electric Industries. Vice-chmn. bd. trustees Children's TV Workshop, N.Y.C., 1982—; chmn. Blood Bank Hawaii, 1983—; trustee Bishop Mus., 1987—, The Nature Conservancy of Hawaii, 1988—; active U. Hawaii Found., 1985—. Mem. ABA, Hawaii State Bar Assn., Waialae Country Club, Pacific Club, Honolulu Club, Plaza Club. Democrat. Office: Kobayashi Watanabe Sugita el al 745 Fort St 8th Fl Honolulu HI 96813

WATANABE, LARRY GEO, biomaterials scientist; b. Fresno, Calif., May 7, 1950; s. George and Hanayo (Yokota) W.; m. Janice Elaine Lee, Nov. 1, 1980; 1 child, Lauren Elisabeth. AA, Fresno City Coll., 1970; BA in Indsl. Arts, Fresno State U., 1972; cert., San Francisco City Coll., 1974. Mgr. crown and bridge dept. McLaughlin Dental Lab., Oakland, Calif., 1975-76; sr. rsch. technician USPHS Hosp., San Francisco, 1976-83; coord. biomaterials rsch. testing, mgr. U. Calif., San Francisco, 1983—; presenter in field. Contbr. articles and abstracts to profl. jours. Bd. dirs. Wah Mei Presch. Mem. Internat. Assn. Dental Rsch., Am. Assn. Dental Rsch., ASTM, Acad. Dental Materials, San Francisco Amateur Golf Assn., U. Calif. Golf Sports Club, Epsilon Pi Tau. Buddhist. Home: 1963 12th Ave San Francisco CA 94116

WATERER, LOUIS PHILLIPP, aerospace engineer; b. Berger, Mo., Mar. 12, 1939; s. Frederick and Lillie Louise (Diederich) W.; m. Bonnie Clausing, June 18, 1961; children: Ryan, Reid. BS in Physics, Ohio State U., 1961; MS in Physics, San Jose State U., 1965; MBA, Santa Clara U., 1972. Test engr. Lockheed Missile and Space, Sunnyvale, Calif., 1961-67; design engr. Lockheed Missile and Space, Sunnyvale, 1967-73, system integration engr., 1973-85, group engr., 1985—. Council pres. Piedmont Sch., San Jose, Calif., 1984-85; com. chmn. troop 165 Boy Scouts Am., 1980-85. Mem. Internat. Interconnect Tech. Study Group. Republican. Methodist. Home: 3836 Suncrest Ave San Jose CA 95132

WATERMAN, HUGH E., aviation engineer; b. Elgin, Ill., Oct. 1, 1923; s. Roy Hawley and Mildred (Elfrink) W.; m. Doris R. McKinnon, Mar. 28, 1946 (div. Aug. 1978); children: Stephen J., Deane R., Laurie J.; m. Elva Jackson, Oct. 8, 1978; 1 adopted child, Larisa M. BS in Aerospace Engring., Purdue U., 1950. Engr. FAA, Ft. Worth, 1959-61; dist. office mgr. FAA, Atlanta, 1961-65; systems br. mgr. FAA, Washington, 1965-78; systems br. mgr., aircraft certification office FAA, Long Beach, Calif., 1978-83; mgr. aircraft certification office FAA, Seattle, 1983-86; pres. Aircraft Certification Inc., Huntington Beach, Calif., 1986—. Mem. AIAA, Sigma Alpha Epsilon (chmn. Warrenton, Penn. aircraft lighting com. 1976-82). Office: Aircraft Certification Inc 18362 Hartlund Ln Huntington Beach CA 92646

WATERMAN, LORI, artist; b. Eagle Lake, Tex., Mar. 3, 1914; d. Robert E. and Loretta (Dinkelspiel) Walker; m. Alan Tower Waterman Jr., Oct. 12, 1946; children: Linda Sloan, Donna Hickey, Alan Dane, Bruce Earl. AA, Foothill Coll., Los Altos, Calif., 1967; BA, San Jose (Calif.) State U., 1969. Cert. tchr., Calif. Tchr. Los Altos-Mountain View Sch. Dist., 1970-80; artist Stanford, Calif., 1980—. Represented in permanent collection Triton Mus., Monterey Peninsula Mus. Art, and numerous pvt. collections; one-woman shows include Triton Mus., Santa Clara, 1975, El Gatito Gallery, Los Gatos, Calif., 1976, 78, 80, Artists Coop. Gallery, San Francisco, 1979, 81, 83, 85, Rosicrucian Mus., Santa Clara, Calif., 1984, Spanish Town Gallery, Half Moon Bay, Calif., 1985. Active League Women Voters. Recipient numerous awards in juried shows. Mem. Artists' Coop. of San Francisco, Allied Artists West, Soc. Western Artists, San Francisco Women Artists, Artists Equity League, Nat. League Am. Pen Women. Home: 562 Gerona Rd Stanford CA 94305

WATERS, LESLIE ELLEN, family practice physician; b. Bay Shore, N.Y., June 13, 1954; d. Lester A. Jr. and Eleanor Mae (Harrigan) W.; m. John Martin Lake, Apr. 12, 1988. BS magna cum laude, Duke U., 1975; MD, U. N.C., 1980. Diplomate Am. Bd. Family Practice. Resident in family practice U. Mass. Med. Ctr., Worcester, 1980-84; staff physician Emergency Physicians Inc., East Longmeadow, Mass., 1984; vol. physician Aesculapius Internat. Medicine, Anuradhapura, Sri Lanka, 1984-85; pvt. practice Lawrence, Mass., 1986-88, Colville, Wash., 1988—. Co-author: Teaching Activities for Autistic Children, 1983. Mem. Planned Parenthood. Mem. Am. Acad. Family Practice, Am. Med. Women's Assn., Physicians for Social Responsibility, Internat. Physicians for Prevention Nuclear War, World Wildlife Fedn., Pax World Found. Office: Colville Med Group 1200 E Columbia Ave Colville WA 99114

WATERS, MARY EINSPAHR, nurse; b. Mpls., Nov. 13, 1946; d. John Emil and Irene Mavis (Williams) Einspahr; m. Earle Henry Waters Jr., Oct. 4, 1969; children: Cynthia Ann, Kristen Margaret, Gregory Earle. BS in Nursing, U. Iowa, 1968. RN. Nurse Langley Porter Neuro-Psychiat. Inst., San Francisco, 1968-69, Good Samaritan Hosp., Portland, Oreg., 1975-82; nurse specialist epilepsy Good Samaritan Hosp., Portland, 1982-87, co-facilitator epilepsy support group, 1987-88. Christian counselor Stephen Ministers at Our Savior's Luth. Ch., Lake Oswego, Oreg., 1988—; mem. choir Rolling Hills Community Ch. Mem. Am. Epilepsy Soc., Chi Omega. Democrat. Club: Multnomah Athletic. Office: Good Samaritan Hosp 1015 NW 22d Ave Ste 310 Portland OR 97210-5438

WATERS, MAXINE, state legislator; b. St. Louis, Aug. 15, 1938; d. Remus and Velma (Moore) Carr; m. Sidney Williams, July 23, 1977; children by previous marriage—Edward, Karen. Grad. in sociology Calif. State U., Los Angeles. Former tchr. Head Start; mem. Calif. Assembly from dist. 48, 1976—, Democratic caucus chair, 1984. Mem. Dem. Nat. Com.; del. Dem. Nat. Conv., 1980; mem. Nat. Adv. Com. for Women, 1978—. Office: Calif State Assembly State Capitol Sacramento CA 95814

WATKINS, DANE HANSEN, state senator, business executive; b. Idaho Falls, Idaho, Aug. 24, 1943; s. George W. and Hope C. (Hansen) W.; B.S., U. Utah, 1965; m. Sherry McNamara, Aug. 8, 1964; children—Tory, Tracey, Dane Hansen, Damond, Taryn, David, Tiffany. Ptnr. Watkins Enterprises, farming and investments, Idaho Falls, 1965—; mem. Idaho Senate, Idaho Falls, 1971—, chmn. local govt. and taxation com., 1980—, mem. agrl. affairs com., 1979-82, mem. fin. com., 1974-80, vice chmn. fin. com., 1982—. Pres. Idaho Employees Council, 1978-80; dir. Blue Cross Idaho, 1974-80; mem. Eastern Idaho Spl. Services Agy., 1981—, Bonneville County Home Health Agy., 1980-81; v.p. Teton Peaks Boy Scout Council, 1976-80; treas. Idaho Gasohol Commn., 1979—; mem. Nat. Gasohol Commn., 1978—; bd. dirs. Bonneville County United Way, 1968-74, YMCA, 1968-78, Eastern Idaho Regional Med. Ctr., 1983—; chmn. Bonneville County Rep. Cen. Com., 1968-71; Rep. candidate for congress, 1988; pres. Eastern Idaho Lincoln Day Assn., 1970-71, Idaho Citizens Against Pornography. Bishop Ch. of Jesus Christ of Latter-day Saints. Office: PO Box 781 Idaho Falls ID 83402

WATKINS, EDWARD A., electronics company executive; b. Fort Recovery, Ohio, Dec. 19, 1930; s. Edgar Arlington and Hazle May (Seewer) W.; m. Joan Elaine Carlson, Aug. 25, 1956; children: Todd Allen, Gregg Edward, Karl Richard, Kari Ann. BA, Miami U., Oxford, Ohio, 1952, MA, 1954. Dir. Sperry Corp. (Unisys), Blue Bell, Pa., 1956-86; asst. gen. mgr. comml. products Odetics Inc., Anaheim, Calif., 1987—. Mem. Computer Assn. of Minn. (pres. 1963-64), Acacia (pres. 1951-52). Democrat. Lutheran. Lodge: Masons. Home: 32902 Danapine Dana Point CA 92629 Office: Odetics Inc 1515 S Manchester Ave Anaheim CA 92802

WATKINS, EVAN PAUL, English educator; b. Wichita, Kans., Oct. 25, 1946; s. Evan Edward and Aileen Josephine (Elgin) W.; m. Diane Candace Logan, July 8, 1968; 1 child, Christopher Morgan. BA, U. Kans., 1968; PhD, U. Iowa, 1972. Asst. prof. English Mich. State U., 1972-77, assoc. prof. English, 1977-83; assoc. prof. English U. Wash., Seattle, 1983—; reader for numerous U. jours. and presses., 1972—. Author: The Critical Act, 1978, Work Time, 1989; contbr. essays on contemporary lit. and theory in profl jours. Recipient summer rsch. grant Mich. State U., 1973, '76, course devel. grant Mich. State U., 1977, U. Wash., 1986, Fulbright-Hays Rsch. grant, Rome, 1978-79. Mem. Modern Lang. Assn. Office: Dept of English GN-30 Univ Wash Seattle WA 98195

WATKINS, HAROLD WADE, computer analyst, real estate associate; b. Parkersburg, W.Va., Sept. 25, 1946; s. Harold Wade and Thelma K. (Rawls) W.; m. Dorinda Vaughn, June 17, 1967 (div. Jan. 1974); m. Antoinette Reyes, Mar. 9, 1979; children: Brian, Denyse, Kelly. BS, Regis Coll., 1986. Lic. real estate broker, Colo. Computer specialist Air Force Fin., Denver, 1970-73; computer scheduler City and County of Denver, 1973-76; real estate assoc. Crown Realty, Arvada, Colo., 1976-79, Hal Watkins Realty, Broomfield, Colo., 1979-88; computer analyst Amoco Corp., Denver, 1980—. Counselor, vol. probation dept. Denver Dept. Justice, 1974, 75. Served with USAF, 1966-69. Mem. Nat. Assn. Realtors, North Suburban Bd. Realtors, Colo. Assn. Realtors. Democrat. Roman Catholic. Office: Hal Watkins Realty PO Box 804 Broomfield CO 80020

WATKINS, JUDITH ANN, nurse; b. Chgo., Mar. 11, 1942; d. Russell and Louise Bernadine (Aloy) Keim; m. Thomas H. Watkins III, Dec. 24, 1961; children: Tamara Sue, Randall Scott. Cert. in Nursing, Knapp Coll. Nursing, Santa Barbara, Calif., 1963. RN, Calif.; Cert. CPR instr., vocat. edn. instr. Obstetrics supr. Bowling Green (Ky.) Warren County Hosp., 1963-67; clin. staff nurse Chula Vista (Calif.) Med. Clinic, 1967-69; nurse aide instr. Sawyers Coll., Ventura, Calif., 1972; ob-gyn. supr. Westlake (Calif.) Community Hosp., 1972-77; RN acute patient care Medical Personnel Pool, Bakersfield, Calif., 1984; med. asst. instr., dir. allied health San Joaquin Valley Coll., Bakersfield, 1984-88; dir. nurses Bakersfield Family Med. Ctr., 1988—. Mem. Kern County Assistance League, Bakersfield, 1989. Named Mother of Yr. Frazier Park (Calif.) Community Ch., 1979. Mem. Kern County RN Soc., Kern County Trade Club, Pine Mt. Golf Club (founder Liliac Festival 1982, Lady of Yr. 1983), Sundale Country Club. Home: 9513 Steinbeck Ln Bakersfield CA 93311 Office: Bakersfield Family Med Ctr 4580 California Ave Bakersfield CA 93309

WATKINS, KAY ORVILLE, college dean, chemistry educator; b. Nunn, Colo., Apr. 28, 1932; s. Paul Edmond and Freda May (Orndorff) W.; m. Janice Annette Rogers, June 24, 1961; children: Susan, Melissa, Laura. BA, Adams State Coll., 1955; PhD, Vanderbilt U., 1961. Prof. chemistry Adams State Coll., Alamosa, Colo., 1961—, dean Sch. Sci., 1977—; rsch. chemist Brandeis U., Waltham, Mass., 1961-62; vis. scientist Brookhaven Nat. Lab., Upton, N.Y., 1968, Argonne (Ill.) Nat. Lab., 1973, U. Utah, Salt Lake City, 1981; vis. prof. U. Hawaii, Honolulu, 1987. Contbr. articles to profl. jours. Advisor Colo. Minority Engring. Assn., San Luis Valley, 1983—; bd. dirs. San Luis Valley Regional Sci. Fair, Alamosa, 1975—. Named one of Outstanding Young Men Am., Alamosa Jaycees, 1967; grantee NSF, 1978, rsch. fellow, 1978. Mem. Am. Chem. Soc., Colo. Alliance for Sci., Sigma Xi. Republican. Home: 74 El Rio Alamosa CO 81101 Office: Adams State Coll Sch of Sci Math & Tech Office of the Dean Alamosa CO 81102

WATKINS, STEVEN DOUGLAS, agronomist, entomologist; b. Long Beach, Calif., Nov. 10, 1945; s. Fred C. and Margaret A. (Johnson) W.; children: Stephanie Lynn, Melissa Ann. BS, U. Ariz., 1967, MS, 1974. Entomologist Barkley Co. of Ariz., Somerton, 1968-79; tech. rep. ICI Ams., Inc., Yuma, Ariz., 1979-87, market devel. rep., 1987—. Mem. Am. Soc. Agronomy (cert. agronomist), Entomol. Soc. Am., Weed Sci. Soc. Am., Western Soc. Weed Sci., Am. Registry Cert. Profls. in Agronomy, Crops and Soils. Republican. Lutheran. Office: ICI Ams Inc 2210 Lorie Ln Yuma AZ 85365

WATKINSON, PATRICIA GRIEVE, museum director; b. Merton, Surrey, Eng., Mar. 28, 1946; came to U.S., 1972; d. Thomas Wardle and Kathleen (Bredl) Grieve. BA in Art History and Langs. with honors, Bristol U., Eng., 1968. Sec. Mayfair Fine Arts and The Mayfair Gallery, London, 1969-71; adminstr. Bernard Jacobson, Print Pub., London, 1971-73; freelance exhbn. work, writer Kilkenny Design Ctr., Davis Gallery, Irish Arts Council in Dublin, Ireland, 1975-76; curator of art Mus. Art, Wash. State U., Pullman, 1978-83, dir., 1984—; asst. prof. art history Wash. State U., Pullman, 1978. Co-author, co-editor: Gaylen Hansen: The Paintings of a Decade, 1985. Mem. Assn. Coll. & Univ. Museums and Galleries (western regional rep. 1986-88), Art. Mus. Assn. Am. (Wash. state rep. 1986-87), Internat. Council Museums (modern art com. 1986—), Wash. Mus. Assn. (bd. dirs. 1984-87), Am. Fedn. Arts (western freg. rep. 1987—). Office: Wash State U Mus Art Pullman WA 99164-7460

WATRING, WATSON GLENN, gynecologic oncologist, educator; b. St. Albans, W.Va., June 2, 1936; s. Neva J. Louise Bullington; m. Roberta Watring. BS, Washington & Lee U., 1958; MD, W.Va. U., 1962. Diplomate Am. Bd. Ob-Gyn, Am. Bd. Gynecol. Oncology. Intern The Toledo Hosp., 1963; resident in ob-gyn Ind. U., Indpls., 1964-66, Tripler Gen. Hosp., Honolulu, 1968-70; resident in gen. and oncologic surgery City of Hope Nat. Med. Ctr., Duarte, Calif., 1970-71, assoc. dir. gynecol. oncology, sr. surgeon, 1973-77; fellow in gynecol. oncology City of Hope Nat. Med. Ctr. and UCLA Med. Ctr., 1972-74; asst. prof. ob-gyn UCLA Med. Ctr., 1972-77; assoc. prof., sr. gynecologist, sr. surgeon Tufts New Eng. Med. Ctr. Hosp., Boston, 1977-80, asst. prof. radiation therapy, 1978-80; practice medicine specializing in ob-gyn Boston, 1980-82; assoc. prof. ob-gyn U. Mass., Worcester, 1982; regional dir. gynecol. oncology So. Calif. Permanente Med. Group, Los Angeles, 1982—, asst. dir. residency tng., 1985—; dir. gynecol. oncology St. Margarets Hosp. for Women, Dorchester, Mass., 1977-80; clin. prof. ob-gyn U. Calif., Irvine, 1982—. Contbr. articles to profl. jours. Mem. ch. council Luth. Ch. of the Foothills, 1973-75. Served to lt. col. M.C., U.S. Army, 1965-71. Fellow Am. Coll. Ob-Gyn, Los Angeles Obstet. and Gynecol. Soc.; mem. AAAS, ACS (Calif. and Mass. chpts.), Boston Surg. Soc., AMA, Mass. Med. Soc., Mass. Suffolk Dist. Med. Soc., Internat. Soc. Gynecol. Pathologists, Western Soc. Gynecologists and Obstetricians, Am. Soc. Clin. Oncology, Soc. Gynecol. Oncologists, Western Assn. Gynecol. Oncologists (sec.-treas. 1976-81, program chmn. 1984, pres. 1985—), New Eng. Assn. Gynecol. Oncologists (chmn. charter com.), New Eng. Obstet. and Gynecol. Soc., Obstet. Soc. Boston, Am. Radium Soc., Soc. Study Breast Disease, New Eng. Cancer Soc., Internat. Gynecol. Cancer Soc., Daniel Morton Soc., Sigma Xi. Republican. Office: So Calif Permanente Med Group 4950 Sunset Blvd Los Angeles CA 90027

WATSON, BARBARA K., publishing executive; b. Iowa Falls, Ia., May 2, 1943; d. Kenneth Scott and Ruth Frances (Beed) Titus; m. Eddie L. Watson, Dec. 27, 1962 (div. Mar. 1984); children: John Lee, Donna rae. Student, Amarillo Coll., 1960-62, Tex. Women's U., 1962-63. Sec. Phillips Petroleum Co., Amarillo, Tex., 1960-62; exec. sec. Am. Airmotive, Miami, Fla., 1963-64; sec. U.S. Army, Ft. Bragg, N.C., 1965-66, Ft. Sill, Okla., 1967; office mgr. Travel & Meeting Planners, Daytona Beach, Fla., 1971-72; owner, mgr. Creative Crafts, Enterprise, Ala., 1974-79; artist, pub. The Brushworks, Ontario, Calif., 1980—; judge Orange County (Calif.) Fair, 1985, 86, 87, 88; nationwide art seminar instr., 1979—; product cons. Binney and Smith, Easton, Pa., 1985-87, Blair Art Products, Twinsburg, Ohio, 1986-87. Artist, publ. (instrn. book) A Bit of Barb, Vol. I, 1980, Vol. II, 1982, The Color Book, 1986, Our World of Angels, Vol. I, 1986, Vol. II, 1987, (book) Its Really Acrylic, 1988; pub. Birds and Beasts Vol. I, 1983, Vol. II, 1984; contbr. articles to profl. jours. Leader Girl Scouts Am., Enterprise, Ala., 1973-74. Served with USNR, 1960-64. Recipient 2d Place award Coffee County Art Show, Elba, Ala., 1980, 1st Place award Piney Woods Art Festival, Enterprise, 1981. Mem. Nat. Soc. of Tole and Decorative Painters (judge cert. program, 1983, 84, 86, 88, edn. com. 1982-83, founder Barefoot Tolers chpt., 1978, recipient Master Decorative Artist award 1982). Republican. Club: Luncheon Pilot (pres. 1977-78) (Enterprise). Home: 5610 Howard Ave Ontario CA 91762 Office: The Brushworks PO Box 9311 Ontario CA 91762

WATSON, DAVID COLQUITT, electrical engineer, educator b. Linden, Tex., Feb. 9, 1936; s. Colvin Colquitt and Nelena Gertrude (Keasler) W.; m. Flora Janet Thayn, Nov. 10, 1959; children: Flora Janeen, Melanie Beth, Lorrie Gaylene, Cheralyn Gail, Nathan David, Amy Melissa, Brian Colvin. BSEE, U. Utah, 1964, PhD in Elec. Engring. (NASA fellow), 1968. Electronic technician Hercules Powder Co., Magna, Utah, 1961-62; research fellow U. Utah, 1964-65, research asst. microwave devices and phys. electronics lab., 1964-68; sr. mem. tech. staff ESL, Inc., Sunnyvale, Calif., 1968-78, head dept. Communications, 1969-70; sr. engring. specialist Probe Systems, Inc., Sunnyvale, 1978-79; sr. mem. tech. staff ARGO Systems, Inc., Sunnyvale, 1979—; mem. faculty U. Santa Clara, 1978-81, San Jose State U., 1981—. Contbr. articles to IEEE Transactions, 1965-78; co-inventor cyclotron-wave rectifier; inventor gradient descrambler. Served with USAF, 1956-60. Mem. IEEE, Phi Kappa Phi, Tau Beta Pi, Eta Kappa Nu. Mormon. Office: Argo Systems Inc 884 Hermosa Ct Sunnyvale CA 94086

WATSON, DAVID JOHN, investment executive; b. N.Y.C., Jan. 2, 1960; s. Arthur K. and Ann Carroll (Hemingway) W.; m. Michele Lorraine Carlino, Mar. 30, 1985; 1 child, Sarah Elizabeth. Lic. real estate broker. Pres. David J. Watson, Inc., Scottsdale, Ariz., 1979-84, Watcor, Inc., Scottsdale, 1984—. Bd. dirs. Scottsdale Prevention Inst. Mem. Scottsdale C. of C. Republican. Presbyterian. Lodge: Trunk and Tusk. Office: Watcor Inc 8757 E Via de Commercio Ste 200 Scottsdale AZ 85258

WATSON, HAROLD GEORGE, ordnance company executive, mechanical engineer; b. Phoenix, Oct. 19, 1931; s. Clarence Elmer and Eunice A. (Record) W.; m. Ruth May Thomas, Aug. 30, 1951; children—Patricia Ruth, Linda Darlene, Harold George. B.S., U. Ariz., 1954. Registered profl. engr. Engr., Shell Oil Co., L.A., 1954; project engr. Talco Engring. Co., Hamden Conn., 1956, area mgr., Mesa, Ariz., 1956-57, chief engr. Rocket Power, 1958-61, dir. engring., 1961-64; dir. engring. Space Ordnance Systems, El Segundo, Calif., 1964-68; dir. engring. Universal Propulsion Co., Riverside, Calif., 1968-70, gen. mgr., v.p. engring., Tempe, Ariz., 1970-76, v.p., mgr., 1976-77, pres., gen. mgr., Phoenix, 1977—. Patentee in field. 1st lt. USAR, 1954-56. Mem. Am. Ordnance Assn., SAFE Assn. (pres.), AIAA, Air Force Assn., Internat. Pyronetics Soc., Am. Def. Preparedness Assn. Office: Universal Propulsion Co Inc Box 1140 Black Canyon Stage Number 1 Phoenix AZ 85029

WATSON, HELEN RICHTER, educator, ceramic artist; b. Laredo, Tex., May 10, 1926; d. Horace Edward and Helen Mary (Richter) Watson. B.A., Scripps Coll., 1947; M.F.A., Claremont Grad. Sch. and U. Ctr., 1949; postgrad. Alfred U., 1966; Swedish Govt. fellow Konstfackskolan, Stockholm, 1952-53. Mem. faculty Chaffey Coll., Ontario, Calif., 1950-52; chmn. ceramics Mt. San Antonio Coll., Walnut, Calif., 1955-57; prof., chmn. ceramics dept. Otis Art Inst., Los Angeles, 1958-81; mem. faculty Otis-Parsons Sch. Design, 1983-88, ret. 1988 ; studio ceramic artist, Claremont, Calif. and Laredo, Tex., 1949—; design cons. Interpace, Glendale, Calif., 1963-64; artist-in-residence Clarement Men's Coll., 1977. Claremont Grad. Sch. fellow, 1948-49; Swedish Govt. grantee, 1952-53; recipient First Ann. Scripps Coll. Disting. Alumna award, Claremont, 1978. Mem. Artists Equity, Nat. Ceramic Soc., Am. Craftsmen's Council, Los Angeles County Mus. Art, Mus. Contemporary Art Los Angeles. Republican. Episcopalian. Address: 220 Brooks Ave Claremont CA 91711 also: 1906 Houston St Laredo TX 78040

WATSON, JEFFREY LYNN, airforce tech sargent; b. Furstenfeldbruck, Fed. Republic Germany, Sept. 3, 1956. Enlisted USAF, 1976, advanced through grades to tech. sargent; mem. Titan II ICBM launch crew 374 Strategic Missile Squadron, Little Rock, 1976-82; instr., technician Ground-Launched Cruise Missile at 501 Tactical Missile Wing, RAF Greenham Common, Eng., 1983-87, Ground-Launched Cruise Missile at 868 Tactical Missile Maintenance Squadron, Tucson, 1987—; guide, speaker Titan Missile Mus., Green Valley, Ariz., 1987—. Decorated Air medal with one oak leaf cluster. Mem. Air Force Assn., Air Force Sgts. Assn. Baptist. Club: Non-Commd. Officers. Home: 4880 E 29th St #8307 Tucson AZ 85711 Office: USAF 868 Tactical Missile Maintenance Squadron Davis-Monthan AFB AZ 85707

WATSON, KENNETH MARSHALL, physicist, educator; b. Des Moines, Sept. 7, 1921; s. Louis Erwin and Irene Nellie (Marshall) W.; m. Elaine Carol Miller, Mar. 30, 1946; children: Ronald M., Mark Louis. B.S., Iowa State U., 1943; Ph.D., U. Iowa, 1948; Sc.D. (hon.), U. Ind., 1976. Rsch. engr. Naval Rsch. Lab., Washington, 1943-46; mem. staff Inst. Advanced Study Princeton (N.J.) U., 1948-49; rsch. fellow Lawrence Berkeley (Calif.) Lab., 1949-52, mem. staff, 1957-81; asst. prof. physics U. Ind., Bloomington, 1952-54; asso. prof. physics U. Wis., Madison, 1954-57; prof. physics U. Calif., Berkeley, 1957-81; prof. oceanography, dir. marine physics lab. U. Calif., San Diego, 1981—; cons. Mitre Corp., Sci. Application Corp.; mem. U.S. Pres's. Sci. Adv. Com. Panels, 1962-71; adviser Nat. Security Coun., 1972-75; bd. dirs. Ctr. for Studies of Dynamics, 1979-88; mem. JASON Adv. Panel. Author: (with M.L. Goldberger) Collision Theory, 1964, (with J. Welch and J. Bond) Atomic Theory of Gas Dynamics, 1966, (with J. Nutall) Topics in Several Particle Dynamics, 1970, (with Flatté, Munk, Dashen) Sound Transmission Through a Fluctuating Ocean, 1979. Mem. Nat. Acad. Scis. Home: 2191 Caminito Circulo Norte La Jolla CA 92037 Office: U Calif Marine Physics Lab La Jolla CA 92093

WATSON, OLIVER LEE, III, aerospace engineering manager; b. Lubbock, Tex., Sept. 18, 1938; s. Oliver Lee Jr. and Sallie Gertrude (Hale) W.; m. Judith Valeria Horvath, June 13, 1964; 1 child, Clarke Stanford. BSEE, U. Tex., 1961; MSEE, Stanford U., 1963; MBA, Calif. State U., Fullerton, 1972; cert., U. So. Calif., 1980. Mgr. ballistic analysis Rockwell Internat. Autonetics Div., Anaheim, Calif., 1973-78, mgr. minuteman systems, 1978-83, mgr. preliminary engring., 1983-84, mgr. analysis group, 1984-85; mgr. aircraft systems Rockwell Internat. Autonetics Dept., Anaheim, Calif., 1985—; lectr. engring. Calif. State U., Fullerton, 1981—; ptnr. Hochman-Watson Pub., Orange, Calif., 1982—. Co-author Digital Computing Using Fortran IV, 1982; Fortran 77, A Complete Primer, 1986. Bd. dirs. Olive Little League, Orange, 1980; vol. Stanford U. Engring. Fund, Orange County, Calif., 1983, regional chmn., 1984-86, So. Calif. chmn. 1986—; mem. Stanford Assocs., 1988—. Named Div. Mgr. of Yr., Rockwell Autonetics Strategic Systems, Anaheim, 1983; Inst. Advancement Engring. fellow, Los Angeles, 1976; North Am. Aviation Sci.-Engring. fellow, Los Angeles, 1962, 63. Mem. IEEE (sr.; sect. v.p. 1974-75, sect. chmn. 1975-76), Am. Assn. Artificial Intelligence, Inst. Navigation (corp.), Jaycees (v.p. Orange chpt. 1973-74), Stanford Assocs., Beta Gamma Sigma. Republican. Club: Lido Sailing. Office: Rockwell Internat 3370 E Miraloma Ave OB23 Anaheim CA 92803

WATSON, SHARON GITIN, psychologist, administrator; b. N.Y.C., Oct. 21, 1943; d. Louis Leonard and Miriam (Myers) Gitin; m. Eric Watson, Oct. 31, 1969; 1 child, Carrie Dunbar. B.A. cum laude, Cornell U., 1965; M.A., U. Ill., 1968, Ph.D., 1971. Psychologist City N.Y. Prison Mental Health, Riker's Island, 1973-74; psychologist Youth Services Ctr., Los Angeles County Dept. Pub. Social Services, Los Angeles, 1975-77, dir. clin. services, 1978, dir. Youth Services Ctr., 1978-80; exec. dir. Crittenton Ctr. for Young Women and Infants, Los Angeles, 1980—. Contbr. articles to profl. jours. Pres. Calif. Assn. Services for Children, 1986-87, chmn. nominating com., 1987-88, chmn. program com. 1985-86, chmn. mgmt. info. services com., 1984-85, sec., treas., chmn. budget and fin. com., chmn. membership com., 1983-84; mem. community adv. com. Div. of Adolescent Medicine, Children's Hosp. of Los Angeles; bd. dirs. Los Angeles Children's Roundtable, Adolescent Pregnancy Child Watch; co-chair Los Angeles Children's Services Planning Council, 1986-88; pres. Assn. Children's Services Agys. So. Calif., 1984-85, sec., 1981-83; mem. steering com. western region Child Welfare League of Am., 1985-87; mem. Parents Council, Westridge Sch. for Girls. Mem. Am. Psychol. Assn., Am. Mgmt. Assn., Town Hall of Calif., Cornell Alumni Assn. of So. Calif., Nat. Conf. Social Welfare, So. Calif. Interclub Assn. (vice chmn.). Club: Pasadena (Calif.) Figure Skating (pres. 1985-87, bd. dirs.). Home: 4056 Camino Real Los Angeles CA 90065 Office: Crittenton Ctr for Young Women and Infants 234 E Avenue 33 Los Angeles CA 90031

WATSON, WESLEY WAYNE, engineering company executive, consultant; b. Delaware, Ohio, Sept. 2, 1943; s. Frank Wesley and Ivaloo (Smart) W.; m. Diana Lynn Burdette, June 20, 1965 (div. Nov. 1970); m. Marsha Ann Van Gundy, July 29, 1972; 1 child, Brian Wesley. Grad. high sch., Delaware. Tool and cutter grinder Dennison div. Abex Corp., Delaware, 1965-70; supr. Multicon Corp., Delaware, 1971-73; precision toolmaker Ranco, Inc., Delaware, 1973-80; mgr. tool rm. Gilbert Engring. Co., Glendale, Ariz., 1981—. Mem. Delaware County Coun. on Alcoholism, 1979. With USAR, 1964-70. Recipient proclamation City of Delaware, 1979. Mem. Internat. Assn. Machinists (steward Columbus, Ohio chpt. 1975-76), Soc. Mfg. Engrs., Am. Legion., Eagles. Lutheran. Office: Gilbert Engring Co 5310 W Camelback Rd Glendale AZ 85301

WATSON, WILLIAM ALFRED, III, minister; b. Banning, Calif., Apr. 14, 1960; s. William Alfred and Ruth (McGriff) W. BA in Polit. Sci., Howard U., 1982. Asst. dir. security/safety Suburban Investigations, Inc., Washington, 1979-84; uniformed police officer U.S. Secret Svc., Washington, 1984-85; spl. agt. U.S. Secret Svc., Phila., 1985-87; dep. dir. security Claremont Colls., Claremont, Calif., 1987—; security cons. Tri-STate YMCA, Phila., 1986, Budd Co., Phila., 1986. Mem. Tri-County Ministers Assn., L.A. County Police Officers Assn., Calif. Police Officers Assn., Internat. Assn. Campus Law Enforcement, Alpha Phi Alpha. Democrat. Baptist. Home: 1850 Club Dr Pomona CA 91768

WATSON, WILLIAM RANDY, marketing executive; b. Roswell, N.Mex., July 13, 1950; s. William Floyd and Billie Dean (Mathews) W.; m. Dorothy Elinor Connole, Feb. 28, 1987; children: Matthew Scott, Amy Suzanne, Chadd William; 1 stepdau., Nicole Maloney. AAS, N.Mex. Jr. Coll., 1970; BBA, Ea. N.Mex. U., 1972. Telecommunications specialist Electronic Data Systems, Dallas, 1973-78; regional product specialist Storage Tek, Dallas, 1978-82; hdqr. product specialist Storage Tek, Louisville, Colo., 1982-84, disk mktg. product mgr., 1984-85; dir. tech mktg. Aweida Systems, Boulder, Colo., 1985-86; owner, pres. Tech. Mktg. Cons., Boulder, 1986—. Election judge Boulder County, 1988. Home: 445 Poplar Ave Boulder CO 80304 Office: Tech Mktg Cons 445 Poplar Ave Boulder CO 80304

WATT, DIANA LYNN, social worker; b. Leon, Iowa, Mar. 21, 1956; d. Charles Edward and Nora Eunice (Dickerson) W. BSW, Graceland Coll., 1980; postgrad., U. Kans., 1981-83. Social work intern St. Michael's (Ariz.) Sch., 1979, Father Benedict Justice Sch. and Seton Ctr., Kansas City, Mo., 1980, Mattie Rhodes Ctr., Kansas City, Mo., 1982-83; child care worker Gillis Home for Boys, Kansas City, 1980-84; community work experience program worker Social and Rehab. Services State of Kans., Kansas City, 1983-84; contractual assignee Reorganized Ch. of Jesus Christ of Latter-day Saints, San Jose, Calif., 1984-87; counselor II summer youth NOVA/SYEP, 1987; tchr. ESL Overfelt Adult Edn. Ctr., Wilson Adult Edn. Ctr., 1987-88; Occupational Tng. Inst. JTPA Intake specialist for GAIN, JTPA, NOVA; instr. DTAC Serra Residential Ctr., Fremont, Calif. Counselor in tng. for camps and bible schs. Reorganized Ch. Jesus Christ Latter-day Saints, Iowa, 1969-73, counselor children's camp, San Jose, 1985, mem. ethnic community program com., East San Jose, 1984-87. Honored for Community Outreach in Ethnic Ministries, Reorganized Ch. Jesus Christ Latter-day Saints, 1985-87. Mem. Nat. Assn. Soc. Workers (cert.). Club: Intercultural (Lamoni, Iowa) (activity chmn. 1977-79).

WATTS, DENNIS LESTER, military officer; b. Rockford, Ill., Sept. 26, 1947; s. Lester George and Marjorie Doris (Kindell) W.; m. Betty Ann Homb, Oct. 9, 1970; 1 child, Kimberly. BS in Radiol. Tech., Midwestern State U., 1975; MS in Radiol., U. Colo., 1986. X-ray technician USAF, Wichita Falls, Tex., 1971-76, nuclear medicine technician, 1976-79; commed. capt. U.S. Army, San Antonio, 1979—; med. physics chief Brook Army Med. Ctr., Ft. Sam Houston, Tex.; radiation protection officer Reynolds Army Hosp., Ft. Sill, Okla. Author: (with others) Medical Physics, 1987. Mem. Am. Assn. Physicists in Medicine, Health Physics Soc.

WATTS, JACK KING, retired air force officer; b. Oklahoma City, June 11, 1927; s. Columbus David and Vera Mae (King) W.; children: Susan, Richard. BS, William Carey Coll., 1973; BS in Computing, Roosevelt U., Chgo., 1984. FCC lic. gen. radiotelephon operator, 1985. Commd. USAF, advanced through grades to lt. col., 1972. Inventor Calendarpad computer program. Mem. Hawaiian Astronomical Soc., Hawaiian Amateur Radio Club, Mensa.

WATTS, JAMES LAWRENCE, investment banker; b. Minot, N.D., June 3, 1949; s. Lawrence Robert and Deloris Marie (Anderson) W. BA in Econs., U. Wis., Green Bay, 1972; MA in Econs., Am. U., 1975, JD, 1981. Bar: D.C., U.S. Supreme Ct. Legis. asst. U.S. Ho. Reps., Washington, 1975-76; assoc. dir. Nat. Assn. Small Bus. Investment Cos., Washington, 1976-81; fin. cons. Leighton, Lemov, Jacobs & Buckley, Washington, 1981-85; ptnr. Venture Internat., Alexandria, Va., 1985-86; v.p. corp. fin. McKewon & Timmins, San Diego, 1986-87; sr. v.p. Cruttenden & Co., Newport Beach, Calif., 1987—. Chmn. fin. com. Canal Way Homeowners Assn., Alexandria, 1981-83. Recipient Presdl. cert. White Ho. Conf. on Small Bus., 1980, Cert. Achievement, Nat. Assn. Small Bus. Investment Cos., 1981. Mem. ABA, Nat. Rep. Club. Home: 3150 Manistee Dr Costa Mesa CA 92626 Office: Cruttenden & Co 4600 Campus Dr Newport Beach CA 92660

WATTS, JEFFREY ALAN, venture capitalist; b. Pontiac, Mich., Sept. 28, 1950; s. Harold Maurice and Jeanne Lucille (Helgeson) W.; m. Linda Ginsburg, Sept. 2, 1978; 1 child, Robert. BS in Cellular Biology, U. Mich., 1972, MBA in Fin. and Acctg., 1975. CPA, Calif., Ill., chartered fin. analyst. Acct., sr. cons. Arthur Andersen & Co., Chgo., 1975-78; loan officer No. Trust & Co., Chgo., 1978-82; sr. investment officer Union Venture Corp., Los Angeles, 1982-86, v.p., 1986-87, pres., 1987—; bd. dirs. Bipolar Integrated Tech., Portland, Oreg., Carlyle Systems, Emeryville, Calif. Mem. AICPA, Nat. Assn. Small Bus. Investment Cos. (bd. govs. 1986—, mem. exec. com. 1987-88), Western Regional Assn. Small Bus. Investment Cos. (pres. 1986), Fin. Analysts Fedn., Calif. Soc. CPA's, Ill. Assn. CPA's, Los Angeles Soc. Fin. Analysts. Avocations: skiing, scuba diving, swimming, golf. Office: Union Venture Corp 445 S Figueroa St Los Angeles CA 90071

WATTS, JIMMY DENIS, banker; b. Altadena, Calif., Mar. 18, 1949; s. James William and Ruby Helen (Mayfield) W.; m. Carole Anne Hamilton; children: Arielle Denise, Jameson Carl Hamilton. BS, Calif. State U., Long Beach, 1972; MBA, Calif. Poly., 1981. Loan officer World Savs. and Loan, Lynwood, Calif., 1974-77; exec. v.p. Mechanics Nat. Bank, Paramount, Calif., 1977—; instr. Mt. S.A.C. Community Coll., Walnut, Calif., 1977-78, Calif. Poly. U., Pomona, 1983—. Mem. Mortgage Banks Assn. Republican. Mormon. Home: PO Box 1049 Pomona CA 91769

WATTS, MARVIN LEE, minerals company executive, chemist, educator; b. Portales, N.Mex., Apr. 6, 1932; s. William Ellis and Jewel Reata (Holder) W.; m. Mary Myrtle Kiker, July 25, 1952; children: Marvin Lee, Mark Dwight, Wesley Lyle. BS in Chemistry and Math., Ea. N.Mex. U., 1959, MS in Chemistry, 1960; postgrad. U. Okla., 1966, U. Kans., 1967. Analytical chemist Dow Chem. Co., Midland, Mich., 1960-62; instr. chemistry N.Mex. Mil. Inst., Roswell, 1962-65, asst. prof., 1965-67; chief chemist AMAX Chem. Corp., Carlsbad, N.Mex., 1967-78, gen. surface supt., 1978-84; pres. N.Mex. Salt and Minerals Corp., 1984—; chem. cons. Western Soils Lab., Roswell, 1962-67; instr. chemistry N.Mex. State U., Carlsbad, 1967—; owner, operator cattle ranch, Carlsbad and Loving, N.Mex., 1969—; gen. mgr. Eddy Potash, Inc., 1987—; dir. Soil Conservation Service; mem. Roswell dist. adv. bd. Bur. Land Mgmt. Bd. dirs. Southeastern N.Mex. Regional Sci. Fair, 1966; mem. adv. bd. Roswell dist. Bur. Land Mgmt.; mem. Eddy County Fair Bd., 1976—, chmn., 1978, 82; bd. dirs. Carlsbad Regional Med. Center, 1976-78; pres. bd. Carlsbad Found., 1979-82; adv. bd. N.Mex. State U. at Carlsbad, 1976—; vice chmn. bd. Guadalupe Med. Center; bd. dirs. N.Mex. State U. Found.; state senator N.Mex. Legis., 1984-89. Mem. Republican State Exec. com., 1972—; Rep. chmn. Eddy County (N.Mex.), 1970-74, 78-82. dirs. Conquistador council Boy Scouts Am., Regional Environ. Ednl. Research and Improvement Orgn. Served with Mil. Police Corps, AUS, 1953-55; Germany. Recipient Albert K. Mitchell award as outstanding Rep. in N.Mex., 1976; hon. state farmer N.Mex. Future Farmers Am.; hon. mem. 4-H. Fellow N.Mex. Acad. Sci.; mem. Am. Chem. Soc. (chmn. subsect.), Carlsbad C. of C. (dir. 1979—), N.Mex. Mining Assn. (dir.), AIME (chmn. Carlsbad potash sect. 1975), Am. Angus Assn., Am. Quarter Horse Assn., N.Mex. Cattle Growers Assn. (bd. dirs. 1989—), Carlsbad Farm and Ranch Assn., Nat. Cattleman's Assn. Baptist. Kiwanis (Disting. lt. gov.), Elks. Home: PO Box 56 Carlsbad NM 88220 Office: PO Box 56 Carlsbad NM 88220

WATTS, OLIVER EDWARD, engineering consultancy company executive; b. Hayden, Colo., Sept. 22, 1939; s. Oliver Easton and Vera Irene (Hockett) W.; m. Charla Ann French, Aug. 12, 1962; children—Erik Sean, Oliver Eron, Sherilyn. B.S., Colo. State U., 1962. Registered prof. engr., Colo., Calif. Crew chief Colo. State U. Research Found., Ft. Collins, 1962; with Calif. Dept. Water Resources, Gustine and Castaic, 1964-70; land and water engr. CF&I Steel Corp., Pueblo, Colo., 1970-71; engring. dir. United Western Engrs., Colorado Springs., Colo., 1971-76; ptnr. United Planning and Engring Co., Colorado Springs., Colo., 1976-79; owner Oliver E. Watts, cons. engr., Colorado Springs., Colo., 1979—. Dir. edn. local Ch. of Christ, 1969-71, deacon, 1977-87, elder, 1987— . Served to 1st lt. C.E., AUS, 1962-64. Recipient Individual Achievement award Colo. State U. Coll. Engring., 1981. Fellow ASCE (v.p. Colorado Springs br. 1975, pres. 1978); mem. Nat. Soc. Profl. Engrs. (pres. Pikes Peak chpt. 1975, sec. Colo. sect. 1976, v.p. 1977, pres. 1978, 79, Young Engr. award 1976, Pres.'s award 1979), Cons. Engrs. Coun. Colo. (cert.; dir. 1981-83), Am. Cons. Engrs. Coun., Profl. Land Surveyors Colo., Colorado Springs Homebuilders Assn., Colo. Engrs. Council (del. 1980—), Colo. State U. Alumni Assn. (v.p., dir. Pike's Peak chpt. 1972-76), Lancers, Lambda Chi Alpha. Home: 7195 Dark Horse Pl Colorado Springs CO 80919 Office: Oliver E Watts Cons Engr 614 Elkton Dr Colorado Springs CO 80907

WATTS, PATSY JEANNE, management company executive; b. Portland, Oreg., Oct. 19, 1943; d. Eugene Estelle and Maxine (Muldoon) Nicks; m. James Lowell Watts, June 5, 1964 (div. Aug. 1974); 1 child, Douglas James. Hon. cert. in realty, Grossmont Coll., 1978; paralegal cert., U. San Diego, 1980. Realtor assoc. Schwab Realty, La Mesa, Calif., 1976-78; office mgr. Office of Dist. Atty., Fallon, Nev., 1978-81; cons., adminstr. Calif. and Fla., 1981-85; real estate and legal exec. adminstr. keegan Mgmt. Co., San Jose, Calif., 1985—. Co-Author: Real Estate Marketing, 1977. Fund-raiser Citizens for Pete Wilson, San Diego, William Cleator for San Diego City Coun., 1981-82; staff reporter Citizens vs. Pub. Funds for Pvt. Contracting of San Diego Conv. Ctr., 1983. Named Miss Water Festival City of Portland, 1961. Mem. Nat. Assn. Female Execs., San Francisco Assn. Legal Assts., Internat. Council Shopping Ctrs., Ams. For Legal Reform. Republican. Office: Keegan Mgmt Co 1798 Technology Dr San Jose CA 95110

WATUMULL, GULAB, clothing executive; b. Hyderabas, Pakistan, Apr. 27, 1924; came to U.S., 1953; s. Jhamandas Watumull and Radhibai Dharamdas; m. Indru Gobindram, Apr. 15, 1953; children: Jaidev, Chitra, Vikram, Jyoti. BS, U. Bombay, Karachi, 1945; BA, U. Bombay, Hyderabad Sind, 1947. Mgr. Leilani Gift Shop, Honolulu, 1953-55; exec. v.p. Watumull Bros. Ltd., Honolulu, 1955-86, pres., 1986—; pres. Happy Shirts, Inc., Honolulu, 1976—, Malihini Gifts, Inc., Honolulu, 1984—, Watumull Properties, Inc., Honolulu, 1986—; bd. dirs. Am. Fin. Svcs. of Hawaii, Inc., Honolulu, Bishop Trust Co. Ltd., Honolulu. Mem. Hawaii Visitors Bur., 1980, Waikiki Improvement Assn., 1981-84; pres. J. Watumull Fund, Honolulu, 1986—; bd. dirs. Hawaii Community Found., Honolulu, 1987—; bd. regents Chaminade U. Mem. Honolulu C. of C. (bd. dirs. 1982-85), Hawaii Hotel Assn., Rotary. Hindu. Home: 4131 Papu Circle Honolulu HI 96816 Office: Watumull Bros Ltd 1439 Kapiolani Blvd Honolulu HI 96814

WAUGH, RICHARD ROY, director, program or activities; b. Wichita, Kans., June 29, 1938; s. Victor Roy and Maxine (Wilson) W.; m. Patricia Mae Baker, Dec. 14, 1962; children: Ronald Roy, Kelleen Renee, Jeffery Scott. BS, Kans. State U., 1966. Mgr. systems programming N.Mex. State U., Las Cruces, 1971-80, mgr. internal services, 1980-84, asst. dir., 1984—. Mem. SHARE (sec. 1977-78). Office: NMex State U Box 30001 Dept 3AT Las Cruces NM 88003

WAX, RAY VAN, state agency administrator; b. Sterling, Okla., June 7, 1944; s. Sam Van Wax and Betty Louise (Lucas) Landers; m. Linda Ann Willcutt, Dec. 31, 1972; children: Cody, Tiffany. Student, Pierce Coll., 1972-74, U. Wash., 1974, U. Ala., 1976. Cert. safety profl., Wash. Safety inspector State Wash. Dept. Labor and Industry, Olympia, 1973-83; sr. safety inspector State Wash. Dept. Labor and Industry, Tacoma, 1983-84, mgr. safety regulations program, 1984—; cons. Wax Safety Services, Graham, Wash., 1980—. Editor numerous safety and health standards publs.; contbr. articles to profl. jours. Served with USN, 1962-68. Mem. Am. Soc. Safety Engrs., Am. Nat. Standards Insts. (coms.), World Safety Orgn., Nat. Safety Coun. Home: 24214 64th Ave E PO Box 590 Graham WA 98338 Office: Wash Dept Labor/Industries Div Indsl Safety/Health 805 Plum St SE Box 207 Olympia WA 98504

WAXMAN, HENRY ARNOLD, congressman; b. Los Angeles, Sept. 12, 1939; s. Louis and Esther (Silverman) W.; m. Janet Kessler, Oct. 17, 1971; children: Carol Lynn, Michael David. B.A. in Polit. Sci, UCLA, 1961, J.D., 1964. Bar: Calif. 1965. Mem. Calif. State Assembly, 1969-74, 94th-101st Congresses from 24th Calif. Dist., 1975—; chmn. com. on health Calif. State Assembly until 1974. Pres. Calif. Fedn. Young Democrats, 1965-67. Mem. Calif. Bar Assn., Guardians Jewish Home for Aged, Am. Jewish Congress, Sierra Club, Phi Sigma Alpha. Club: B'nai B'rith. Office: 2418 Rayburn House Office Bldg Washington DC 20515

WAXMAN, WILLIAM H., educator; b. Burbank, Calif., Aug. 23, 1950; s. Everett and Evelyn (Schutz) W.; m. Patricia Murphy, Dec. 21, 1974. BA, Calif. State U., Long Beach, 1972, MA, 1984. Cert. tchr., Calif. Tchr. Santa Barbara (Calif.) High Sch. Dist., 1973-81; instr. theater Calif. State U., Long Beach, 1981-83; tchr. Huntington Beach (Calif.) High Sch. Dist., 1983—; Author plays: The Most Famous Man in America, 1983, Timmons' Retreat, 1984; columnist, Santa Barbara New Press, 1974-79; reviewer, Santa Barbara News & Rev., 1977-79; contbg. columnist, The Baseball Hobby News, San Diego. Democrat. Office: Ocean View High Sch 17071 Gothard St Huntington Beach CA 92647

WAY, E(DWARD) LEONG, pharmacologist, toxicologist, educator; b. Watsonville, Calif., July 10, 1916; s. Leong Man and Lai Har (Shew) W.; m. Madeline Li, Aug. 11, 1944; children—Eric, Linette. B.S., U. Calif., Berkeley, 1938, M.S., 1940; Ph.D., U. Calif., San Francisco, 1942. Pharm. chemist Merck & Co., Rahway, N.J., 1942; instr. pharmacology George Washington U., 1943-46, asst. prof., 1946-48; asst. prof. pharmacology U. Calif., San Francisco, 1949-52; assoc. prof. U. Calif., 1952-57, prof., 1957-87, prof. emeritus, 1987—, chmn. dept. pharmacology, 1973-78; USPHS spl. rsch. fellow U. Berne, Switzerland, 1955-56; vis. prof. rsch. fellow U. Hong Kong, 1962-63, China Med. Bd.; Sterling Sullivan disting. vis. prof. Martin Luther King U., 1982; hon. prof. pharmacology and neurosci. Guangzhou Med. Coll., 1987; mem. sci. adv. com. Pharm. Mfrs. Assn. Found., 1968—; mem. coun. Am. Bur. for Med. Advancement in China, 1982—; bd. dirs. Li Found., pres., 1985—; vis. prof. med. sch. Gunma U., Maebashi, Japan, 1989—; researcher on drug metabolism, analgetics, devel. pharmacology, drug tolerance and dependence. Contbr. numerous articles and revs. to profl. publs.; editor: New Concepts in Pain, 1967, (with others) Fundamentals of Drug Metabolism and Drug Disposition, 1971, Endogenous and Exogenous Opiate Agonists and Antagonists, 1979; editorial bd. Clin. Pharmacology, Therapeutics, 1975-87, Drug, Alcohol Dependence, 1976-87, Progress in Neuro-psychopharmacology, 1977—, Research Communications in Chem. Pathology and Pharmacology, 1978—, Alcohol and Drug Dependence Research, 1986—. Recipient 1st Achievement award in Pharmacodynamics Am. Pharm. Assn. Found., 1962, Faculty Rsch. Lectr. award U. Calif., San Francisco, 1974, San Francisco Chinese Hosp. award, 1976; Cultural citation and Gold medal Ministry of Edn. Republic of China, 1978; Nathan B. Eddy award Com. on Problems in Drug Dependence, 1979; Chancellor's award for pub. svc. U. Calif., 1986. Fellow Am. Coll. Neuropsychopharmacology, AAAS, Am. Coll. Clin. Pharmacology (hon.); mem. Am. Soc. Pharmacology, Exptl. Therapeutics (bd. editors 1957-65, pres. 1976-77), Fedn. Am. Socs. Exptl. Biology (exec. bd. 1975-79, pres. 1977-78), Am. Pharm. Assn. (life, co-recipient Ebert prize certificate 1962), AMA (affiliate), Soc. Aid and Rehab. Drug Addicts (Hong Kong, life), Western Pharmacology Soc. (pres. 1963-64), Japanese Pharm. Soc. (hon.), Coun. Sci. Soc. Pres.' (exec. com. 1979-84, treas. 1980-84), Com. on Problems of Drug Dependence (bd. dirs. 1978—, chmn. 1978-82), Chinese Pharmacology Soc. (hon.), Academia Sinica, Sigma Xi. Office: U Calif Dept of Pharmacology San Francisco CA 94143

WAY, GREG, business owner, consultant, writer; b. Seattle, Oct. 7, 1950; s. George Dean and Josephine Catherine (De Matis) W. BA in Sociology, U. Wash., Seattle, 1973. Owner Way Enterprises, Seattle, 1962—; newsroom aide Seattle Times, 1968-76, AP, Seattle, 1978. Author: stage play How Does Your Father Dance?, 1979,, Kiss Me or Bless Me!, 1981, screenplay The Queets, 1989; contbr. numerous articles to profl. jours. Campaign vol. Dem. Party, Seattle, 1968-88, mem. precinct caucus, 1984, 88, chmn., 1984. Mem. Seattle Film Soc. (charter), Am. Cryonics Soc., Mensa. Office: Way Enterprises PO Box 1182 Seattle WA 98111-1182

WAYLAND, L. C. NEWTON, public health pediatrician; b. Plainview, Tex., May 4, 1909; s. Levi Clarence and Connie Onita (Newton) W.; student Wayland Coll., Plainview, 1925-26, West Tex. State Tchrs. Coll., 1926-30; A.B., Stanford U., 1932, M.D., 1936; postgrad. U. Calif. Med. Sch., Children's, Gen. hosps., Los Angeles; m. Helen Hart, June 18, 1938 (div. 1966); children—Newton, Elizabeth, Constance. Intern, San Francisco City and County Hosp., Stanford Service, 1936; house officer San Mateo County Hosp., 1937, Children's Hosp., Los Angeles, 1938; dir. child health Santa Barbara (Calif.) County Health Dept., 1938-44; dir. health Santa Barbara City Schs., 1944-74; dir. health Santa Barbara City Coll., 1946-74; pvt. practice medicine specializing in pediatrics, 1955-70; ret. mem. pediatric staffs Santa Barbara Gen., St. Francis, Cottage, Goleta Valley hosps.; ret. med. cons. Calif. State Dept. Rehab., 1974-78; emeritus mem. med. staff Calif. State Prison at Soledad. Past non-nurse dir. exec. com., sch. nursing sect. Nat. Orgn. Pub. Health Nurses; past mem. adv. com. Calif. Dept. Edn. on Pub. Sch. Health; mem. Pub. Citizen Inc. Past 1st bd. dirs. Get Oil Out!; mem. vol. staff. Santa Barbara Zool. Gardens; mem. Children's Advocacy Council, Calif., 1988—. Recipient award Calif. Sch. Nurses Orgn., 1965, 71. Fellow Am. Pub. Health Assn., Am. Sch. Health Assn. (past pres. Calif. div.); mem. NEA (ret.), Calif. Tchrs. Assn. (ret.), Calif. Med. Assn. (ret.), Santa Barbara County Med. Soc. (ret.), Am. Acad. Pediatrics, Los Angeles pediatric socs. (ret.), World Council Chs., Nat. Council Chs. (founding mem. laymen's commn.), No. Calif. Ecumenical Council, UN Assn. (past pres. Santa Barbara chpt.), Ams. for Democratic Action, NAACP, ACLU, Calif. Congress Parents and Tchrs. (hon. life), Scholastic Socs. South, Nat. Audubon Soc., Save the Redwoods League, Wilderness Soc., Isaac Walton League, Nat. Parks Assn., Sierra Club, So. Christian Leadership Conf., Cousteau Soc., Planned Parenthood Fedn. Am., Environ. Protective Assn., Fellowship Reconciliation, Inst. for Am. Democracy, Com. for Improvement Med. Care, SANE, Nat. Indian Youth Council, Nat. and Internat. Wildlife Assn., Common Cause, Episcopal Peace Fellowship, Fund for Peace, Nat. and Internat. Nature Conservancy, Friends of the Earth, Green Peace, Gray Panthers, Defenders of Wildlife, Internat. Physicians for Prevention of Nuclear War, Leadership Circle of Physicians for Social Responsibility, Nat. Urban League, Religious Coalition for Abortion Rights, Nat. Abortion Rights Action League, Freedom from Hunger Found., Alliance for Survival, Inst. Aerobic Research, Ctr. War/Peace Studies, Am. Farmland Trust, Rural Advancement Fund, NOW, ERA, So. Poverty Law Center, United World Federalists, Zero Population Growth, Negative Population Growth, Amnesty Internat., Council for Livable World, Clergymen and Laymen Concerned, Am. Fedn. Scientists, Planning and Conservation League Calif., Am. Indian Fund, Humane Soc. U.S., Assn. for Vol. Sterilization, Council on Econ. Priorities, N. Am. Congress on Latin Am., Coalition for a New Fgn. Policy, Met. Opera Assn., Nat. Council on Aging, The Africa Fund., Ams. United for Separation of Ch. and State, Am. Friends Service Com., Nat. Assn. for R.R. Passengers, Calif. Tax Reform Assn., Nat. Com. for Peace in Cen. Am., LWV, Santa Barbara Citizens Planning Assn., Internat. Ctr. for Devel. Policy, Simon Wiesenthal Ctr., Am.-Israeli Civil Liberties Coalition, Internat. Platform Assn., Ctr. for Def. Info., OXFAM, Children's Aid Internat., Ctr. for Law in Pub. Interest, World Wildlife Fund, WAND, Children of War, Solar Lobby, Rainforest Action Network, Educators for Social Responsibility, PAX Ams., Nat. Cathedral Assn., People for the Am. Way, Cath. for Free Choice, N.Y. Acad. of Scis., Nat. Assn. World Health, YMCA, mem. hon. steering com. Ron Dellum's Nat. Adv. Bd., numerous others. Democrat. Episcopalian. Contbr. articles to ednl. and other profl. jours. Home: 1807 Paterna Rd Santa Barbara CA 93103

WAYNE, KYRA PETROVSKAYA, author; b. Crimea, USSR, Dec. 31, 1918; came to U.S., 1948, naturalized, 1951; d. Prince Vasily Sergeyevich and Baroness Zinaida Fedorovna (Fon-Haffenberg) Obolensky; m. George J. Wayne, Apr. 21, 1961; 1 child, Ronald George. B.A., Leningrad Inst. Theatre Arts, 1939, M.A., 1940. Actress, concert singer, USSR, 1939-46; actress, U.S., 1948-51; enrichment lectr. Royal Viking Line cruises, Alaska-Can., Greek Islands-Black Sea, Russia/Europe, 1978-79, 81-82, 83-84, 86-87. Author: Kyra, 1959; Kyra's Secrets of Russian Cooking, 1960; The Quest for the Golden Fleece, 1962; Shurik, 1971; The Awakening, 1972; The Witches of Barguzin, 1975; Max, The Dog That Refused to Die, 1979 (Best Fiction award Dog Writers Assn. Am. 1980); Rekindle the Dreams, 1979, Quest for Empire, 1986. Founder, pres. Clean Air Program, Los Angeles County, 1971-72; mem. women's council KCET-Ednl. TV. Served to lt. Russian Army, 1941-43. Decorated Red Star, numerous other decorations USSR; recipient award Crusade for Freedom, 1955-56; award Los Angeles County, 1972. Mem. Soc. Children's Book Writers, Authors Guild, P.E.N., UCLA Med. Faculty Wives (pres. 1970-71, dir. 1971-75) UCLA Affiliates (life), Los Angeles Lung Assn. (life), Friends of the Lung Assn. (pres. 1988), Idyllwild Sch. Music, Art and Theatre Assn. (trustee 1987). Home: 10561 Hidden Mesa Pl Monterey CA 93940

WAYNE, MARVIN ALAN, emergency medicine physician; b. Detroit, Dec. 11, 1943; s. Jack I. and Marian M. (Berk) W.; m. Joan A. Tobin, Dec. 30, 1971; children: Michelle, Dana. MD, U. Mich., 1968. Diplomate Am. Bd. Emergency Medicine. Fellow St. Bartholomew's Hosp., London, 1968, Virginia Mason Hosp., Seattle, 1973-74; resident in surgery U. Colo. Med. Ctr., Denver, 1968-71; pvt. practice Bellingham, Wash., 1974—; staff emergency dept. St. Joseph's Hosp. (merger St. Joseph's Hosp. and St. Luke's Hosp.), Bellingham, Wash., 1974—, vice chmn. dept. emergency medicine, 1980-83, chmn., 1984-86; med. dir. Emergency Med. Svcs., Bellingham, Wash., 1975—; asst. clin. prof. health scis. U. Wash., Seattle, 1986—; vice chmn. emergency med. svcs. com. State of Wash., 1982-83, chmn., 1983-86; med. dir. Med-Flight Helicopter, 1980--, Inst. for Pre-Hosp. Medicine, 1980--; pres. Whatcom County Emergency Med. Svcs. Coun., 1979; med. advisor Mt. Baker Ski Patrol; speaker nat. and internat. edn. programs; founder, owner Dr. Cookie Inc., Bothell, Wash., 1985--. Contbr. articles to med. jours. Bd. dirs. YMCA, Bellingham, 1980-84. Maj. M.C., U.S. Army, 1971-73, Vietnam. Recipient Outstanding Achievement award Whatcom County Emergency Med. Svcs. Coun., 1980, Outstanding Ednl. Achievement award Abbott Labs., 1982, Outstanding Advanced Life Support System award State of Wash., 1983, Emergency Med. Svc. rsch. award Wash. Assn. Emergency Med. Technicians and Paramedics, 1983. Fellow Am. Coll. Emergency Physicians (bd. dirs. Wash. chpt. 1977-84, pres. 1978, sci. meetings com. 1984, Outstanding Ednl. Achievement award 1982), Royal Soc. Medicine (Eng.); mem. Wash. State Med. Soc. (emergency med. svc. adv. com. 1978--), Whatcom County Med. Soc., Univ. Assn. for Emergency Medicine, Soc. Critical Care Medicine, Am. Trauma Soc. (founding), Nat. Assn. Emergency Med. Svc. Physicians, Am. Soc. Automotive Medicine, Nat. Assn. Emergency Med. Technicians. Office: Emergency Med Svcs 1200 Dupont Ste 1A Bellingham WA 98225

WEATHERBEE, LINDA, insurance executive; b. Decatur, Ill., July 20, 1956; d. Carl and V. Lucile (Westwood) W. BA magna cum laude, James Millikin U., 1977; postgrad., Ill. State U., 1981-82. CLU, chartered fin. cons. Fin. analyst State Farm Life Ins., Bloomington, Ill., 1979-82; supr. State Farm Life Ins., Austin, Tex., 1982-86; asst. supt. State Farm Life Ins., Salem, Oreg., 1986—. Cellist Decatur Civic Orch., 1973-75; ch. pianist, 1975-77, youth advisor Cen. Ill, 1979-81; Rep. vol., Bloomington, 1982; tutor adult edn. program Chemeketa Community Coll., Salem, 1986, 87; tchr. high sch. religion course, Salem, 1987—. Fellow Life Mgmt. Inst.; mem. Adminstrv. Mgmt. Soc., Life Office mgmt. Assn., Williamette Soc. CLU and Chrtered Fin. Cons. (bd. dirs. 1987—), Am. Horse Show Assn., N.W. Horse Council (Oreg.), Am. Bus. Women's Assn. (Townlake chpter Austin, Tex. 1984-86), Nat. Assn. Female Execs., Phi Kappa Phi. Mem. LDS Church. Office: State Farm Ins 4600 25th Ave NE Salem OR 97313

WEATHERFORD, GARY DEAN, lawyer, consultant; b. Riverside, Calif., Sept. 30, 1936; s. Clarence Austin and Bertha Mae (Bobbitt) W.; m. Jane Ann Gharst, Dec. 20, 1959 (div.); 1 child, Theodore Austin; m. Suzanne Marie Gassner, Sept. 29, 1985. BA magna cum laude, U. Redlands, 1958; BD, Yale U., 1961, LLB, 1964. Bar: Calif. Asst. prof. of law U. Oreg., Eugene, 1966-68; v.p. Ferris, Weatherford and Brennan, San Diego, 1968-76; dep. sec. Resources Agy. State of Calif., Sacramento, 1976-77; dir. John Muir Inst., Napa, Calif., 1977-81; vis. prof. law U. Santa Clara, Calif., 1982-84; pres. Watershed West, Berkeley, Calif., 1984-85; of counsel Ferris, Brennan & Britton, San Diego, 1986-88; spl. counsel Payne, Thompson, Walker and Taaffe, San Francisco, 1988—; bd. dirs. Water Sci. and Tech. Bd. NRC, Washington, Western Network, Santa Fe, L'Enfant Trust, Washington;. Editor: Water and Agriculture in the Western U.S., 1982, Acquiring Water for Energy, 1982; co-editor: New Courses for the Colorado River, 1986; also articles. Mem. Calif. Bar Assn., AAAS, Am. Geophys. Union (policy scis. com. hydrology sect. 1984—), Am. Water Resources Assn., Internat. Water Resources Assn. Democrat.

WEATHERS, BRIAN THOMAS, travel agency owner; b. Salem, Oreg., Oct. 12, 1965; s. Carl Wilfred and Charlene Marie (Kerr) W. Vice-pres. Keizer Travel & Cuise Ctr., Salem, Oreg., 1983—; chmn. Centennial Internat. Airlines, Inc., Salem, 1983—. Mem. Soc. Travel Agts., KC. Republican. Roman Catholic. Home: 1722 Waconda Rd NE Gervais OR 97026 Office: Centennial Internat Airline 3700 River Rd N Ste 10 Salem OR 97303-5672

WEATHERWAX, MICHAEL DWAINE, accountant; b. Austin, Minn., June 3, 1945; s. Dwaine Laverne and Ruby Joan (Teff) W.; m. Linda Dianne Penn, Aug. 3, 1968; children: Kristin Laine, Justin Michael. BS with distinction, U. So. Colo., 1967; MSBA, U. Denver, 1974. CPA, Colo.; cert. fin. planner. Grad. teaching asst. U. Denver, 1967-68; tax staff, mgr. Arthur Young & Co., Denver, 1968-76; tax ptnr. Rhode, Scripter & Assocs., Boulder, Colo., 1977-82; pres. Weatherwax & Assocs., P.C., Boulder, 1982—; Dir. Denver Paralegal Inst., 1982—. Author: Real Estate Taxation and Planning, 1980-88, Passive Activity Taxation and Management, 1987-88. Pres. Community Action Devel. Corp., Boulder, 1985; trustee Boulder County United Way, 1985-88. Fellow Colo. Soc. CPAs (prs. 1989—, continuing edn. faculty 1973—, Golden Key award 1967); mem. Am. Inst. CPAs, Nat. Accreditation Bd. for CPA Specialities, Inc. (pres. 1986), Denver Tax Assn., Boulder C. of C. (chmn. bd. 1988), Rotary Club. Democrat. Roman Catholic. Home: 5161 Ellsworth Pl Boulder CO 80303-1209 Office: Weatherwax & Assocs PC 5350 Manhattan Circle Boulder CO 80303-4219

WEAVER, AMANDA LOUISE, consultant, real estate; b. Waco, Tex., May 1, 1948; d. Thomas Marshall and Nancy Louise (Rhea) W.; m. James E. Beard, July 7, 1973 (div. 1979). BA in Sociology, Southwestern U., 1970; MBA, Ariz. State U., 1978. Residential dir. Job Corps, McKinney, Tex., 1970-71; dist. dir. Camp Fire Girls, Dallas, 1971-73; cons. Camp Fire Girls, Denver, 1973-74; mktg. dir. Lincoln Property Co., Des Plaines, Ill., 1974-76; cons. Med. Bus. Cons., Phoenix, 1979-81; dir. practice mgmt. J. Prekup & Assoc., Phoenix, 1981-82; v.p. Physician Mgmt. Consultants, Phoenix, 1982-83, Devenney Assoc. Ltd., Phoenix, 1983-86; pres. Weaver Enterprises, Phoenix, 1987—. Contbr. articles profl. jours. Bd. dirs., Artes Belles, Phoenix, 1980-88, pres., 1984-86; bd. dirs. City of Phoenix Solicitations, 1981-85, chmn., 1986; bd. dirs. Phoenix chpt. Nat. Council on Alcoholism, 1988—. Named Outstanding Young Women in Am. Mem. Women in Comml. Real Estate, Presidents' Club, Phoenix City Club. Democrat. Office: Weaver Enterprises 1661 E Camelback Rd Ste 250 Phoenix AZ 85016

WEAVER, CHARLES RICHARD, household products company executive; b. Kingman, Ind., Sept. 16, 1928; s. Atha Lavern and Jennie Mildred (Best) W.; m. Phyllis Jane Plaster, Sept. 30, 1950 (div. 1982); children—Wendy, Cynthia, Daniel; m. Donna Lee Lambert, Nov. 21, 1982. B.S., Purdue U., 1950. Sales trainee Faultless Caster Co., Evansville, Ind., 1950-51; product mgr. Westinghouse Corp., Pitts., 1951-53; brand mgr. Procter & Gamble Corp., Cin., 1953-59; mgr. spl. products div. Procter & Gamble Corp., Italy, 1963-66; mktg. mgr. Clorox Co., Oakland, Calif., 1959-62, advt. mgr., 1966-69, v.p., 1969-81, advt. mgr., 1969-82, pres., chief operating officer, 1982-85, pres., chief exec. officer, 1985-86, chmn., chief exec. officer, 1986—. Served with USMC, 1946-47. Office: Clorox Co 1221 Broadway Oakland CA 94612

WEAVER, HOWARD CECIL, newspaper editor; b. Anchorage, Oct. 15, 1950; s. Howard Gilbert and Lurlene Eloise (Gamble) W.; m. Alice Laprele Gauchay, July 16, 1970 (div. 1974); m. Barbara Lynn Hodgin, Sept. 16, 1978. BA, Johns Hopkins U., 1972. Reporter, staff writer Anchorage Daily News, 1972-76, columnist, 1979-80, mng. editor, 1980-83, editor, 1983—; editor, owner Alaska Advocate, Anchorage, 1976-79. Recipient Pulitzer prize, 1976, 89; Pulitzer Prize juror, 1988, 89. Pub. Svc. award AP Mng. Editor's Assn., 1976; Headliner award Press Club of Atlantic City, 1976. Mem. Am. Soc. Newspaper Editors, Investigative Reporters and Editors, Sigma Delta Chi (Nat. award 1989), Alaska Press Club (bd. dirs. 1972-84), Upper Yukon River Press Club (pres. 1972). Avocations: ice hockey, foreign travel.

WEAVER, JERRY THOMAS, JR., city planner, consultant; b. Indpls., Apr. 26, 1948; s. Jerry Thomas and Virginia (Lee) W. AA, Riverside City Coll., 1973; BA in Polit. Sci., Calif. State Coll., San Bernardino, 1975. Lic. real estate salesman, Alaska, comml. pilot. Planning technician Municipality of Anchorage, 1975-77, assoc. planner, 1977-80, planning supr., 1980—. Mem. Anchorage Mayor's Land Use Task Force, 1984-85. Mem. Am. Planning Assn., Anchorage Mcpl. Employees Assn. (pres. 1979-80). With USAF, 1967-71. Democrat. Methodist. Home: 1010 Fairwood Dr Anchorage AK 99518 Office: Municipality of Anchorage 630 W 6th Ave Anchorage AK 99501

WEAVER, JOHN HOSCH, lawyer; b. Great Falls, Mont., Sept. 4, 1914; s. James Albert and Bertha Katherine (Hosch) W.; m. Kay Shryne, Feb. 25, 1945; 1 child, Kristine Kay. AB, BS, U. Mont., 1936; JD, Harvard U., 1939. Bar: Mont. 1939. Ptnr. Jardine, Stephenson, Blewett, Weaver, Great Falls. Chmn. Supreme Ct.'s Commn. on Practice, Helena, Mont., 1970-75. Capt. JAGC, U.S. Army, 1943-46. Mem. ABA, Mont. Bar Assn. (pres. 1965), Mont. Trial Lawyers Assn., Cascade County Bar Assn. (pres. 1962), Order of Barristers. Lodge: Rotary.

WEAVER, LOIS JEAN, physician, educator; b. Wheeling, W.Va., May 23, 1944; d. Lewis Everett and Ann (Novak) W.; m. James A. Burke, Apr. 14, 1985. BA, Oberlin Coll., 1966; MD, U. Chgo., 1970. Pulmonary fellow Northwestern U., Evanston, Ill., 1975-77; trauma fellow U. Wash. Harborview Hosp., Seattle, 1977-79, research assoc., instr. medicine, 1979-81, clin. asst. prof. medicine, 1983—; clin. research fellow Virginia Mason Med. Research Ctr., Seattle, 1981-82; mem. med. staff Swedish Hosp., Seattle, 1984—; pulmonary cons. Fred Hutchinson Cancer Research Inst., Seattle, 1984-86, disability quality br. Social Security, Seattle, 1985—. Contbr. sci. articles to profl. jours. La Verne Noyes scholar U. Chgo., 1966; Parker B. Francis fellow Northwestern U., 1975. Mem. AMA, Am. Thoracic Soc., Wash. State Med. Assn., Wash. Lung Assn., Sigma Xi. Home: 1221 Madison #918 Seattle WA 98104 Office: Seattle Pulmonary Assn 1221 Madison Ste 918 Seattle WA 98104

WEAVER, MAX KIMBALL, social worker, consultant; b. Price, Utah, Apr. 4, 1941; s. Max Dickson and Ruth (Kimball) W.; m. Janet Hofheins, Sept. 13, 1963; children: Kim, Cleve, Chris, Wendy, Michael, Amyanne, Heather. Student, So. Utah State Coll., 1959-60; BS, Brigham Young U., 1965; MSW, U. Utah, 1967. Lic. clin. social worker and marriage counselor, Utah. Cons. Utah State Tng. Sch., American Fork, 1966; dir. Dept. Pub. Welfare, Cedar City, Utah, 1967-70; social worker Latter Day St. Social Services, Cedar City, 1970-75; with Mental Retardation Devel. Disabled Adult Services Dept. Social Services, Cedar City, 1975—; cons. nursing homes, Utah, 1974—; tchr. So. Utah State Coll., Cedar City, 1972, 77. Contbr. articles to mags. Pres. Am. Little League Baseball, 1977-84, 86, Cedar High Booster Club, 1984—; chmn. Rep. Precinct #1, 1984; v.p. Big League Baseball, 1986—. Mem. Nat. Assn. Social Work (nominating com., licensing com.), Am. Pub. Welfare Assn., Utah Pub. Employees Assn. Mormon. Lodge: Rotary. Home: 116 N 200 E Cedar City UT 84720 Office: Dept Social Svcs 106 N 100 E Cedar City UT 84720

WEAVER, MICHAEL JAMES, lawyer; b. Bakersfield, Calif., Feb. 11, 1946; s. Kenneth James and Elsa Hope (Rogers) W.; m. Valerie Scott, Sept. 2, 1966; children: Christopher James, Brett Michael, Karen Ashley. AB, Calif. State U., Long Beach, 1968; JD magna cum laude, U. San Diego, 1973. Bar: Calif., 1973, U.S. Dist. Ct. (so. dist.) Calif. 1973, U.S. Ct. Appeals (9th cir.) 1975, U.S. Supreme Ct. 1977. Law clk. to chief judge U.S. Dist. Ct. (so. dist.) Calif., San Diego, 1973-75; assoc. Luce, Forward, Hamilton & Scripps, San Diego, 1975-80, ptnr., 1980-86; ptnr. Sheppard, Mullin, Richter & Hampton, San Diego, 1986—; judge pro tem San Diego Superoir Ct.; lectr. Inn of Ct., San Diego, 1981—, Continuing Edn. of Bar, Calif., 1983—. Editor: San Diego Law Rev., 1973; contbr. articles to profl. jours. Bd. dirs., pres. San Diego Kidney Found., 1985—; bd. dirs. San Diego Aerospace Mus., 1985—. Served to lt., USNR, 1968-74. Mem. San Diego Trial Lawyers Assn., Am. Arbitration Assn., Standing Com. on Discipline, Ninth Cir. Jud. Conf. (del. 1987—). Republican. Presbyterian. Office: Sheppard Mullin Richter & Hampton 701 B St Ste 1000 San Diego CA 92101

WEAVER, NORMAN LAZELLE, software engineer; b. Rockingham, Vt., Nov. 25, 1951; s. Frank Linn and Martha (Norris) W.; m. Lynette Darlene Norton, Aug. 5, 1975; children: Bryn, Lauren. BSME, U. Colo., 1975; MS, Stanford U., 1976. Registered profl. engr., Colo. Mem. energy ctr. staff SRI Internat., Menlo Park, Calif., 1976-77; rsch. asst. Colo. State U., Ft. Collins, 1977-80; staff engr. Regional Systems Svcs. Group, Denver, 1980-84; software engr. Solar Energy Rsch. Inst., Golden, Colo., 1984—. Mem. Am. Assn. for Artificial Intelligence, IEEE (computer soc.). Office: Solar Energy Rsch Inst 1617 Cole Blvd Golden CO 80401

WEAVER, ROBERT WILLIAM, small business owner; b. Phoenix, Dec. 10, 1962; s. William Howard and Doreen (Bosley) W. BA in Speech, U. Ariz., 1985. Warehouseman Zims Restaurant Supply, Phoenix, 1977-78, installer, constrn., 1978-81, salesman, 1981-85; v.p. Weaver Restaurant Supply, Phoenix, 1986--. Republican. Office: Weaver Restaurant Supply PO Box 5645 Phoenix AZ 85010

WEBB, DEAN LEROY, engineering executive, consultant, civil, forensic, structural and investigative engineer; b. Murray, Utah, Feb. 18, 1949; s. Dean B. and Lawana (Williams) W.; m. Marla LaRue Wood, Aug. 6, 1971; children: Chanin Therin, Lacey LaRue. BS, BEE, Utah State U., 1973. Registered profl. engr., Utah, Calif., Idaho, Wyo., Colo., Ariz., Mont., Nev. Structural engr. Coon, King & Knowlton, Salt Lake City, 1973-81, DMJM, Coon, King & Knowlton, Salt Lake City, 1981-84; pres. Dean L. Webb & Assocs., Salt Lake City, 1984—. Recipient 1983 Portland Concrete Assn. Award of Excellence. Mem. NSPE (pres. Utah chpt. 1986-87), Salt Lake Area C. of C., Constrn. Specifications Inst. (pres. Salt Lake chpt. 1982-83), Utah Soc. Profl. Engrs. (pres. Salt Lake City chpt. 1983-84), Utah Engrs. Council (chmn. 1987-88), Am. Cons. Engring. Council, Structural Engrs. Assn. Utah (founding mem.), Am. Concrete Inst. (award of excellence, 1983), Am. Inst. Steel Constrn., Nat. Forensic Ctr. Republican. Mormon. Office: 5330 S 900 E Salt Lake City UT 84117

WEBB, DEWEY, insurance company executive; b. Wenatchee, Wash., Aug. 6, 1931; s. Admiral Dewey and Bess Ethel (Fritts) W.; m. Bette Rae Woodward, Sept. 31, 1952; children: Susan Kim, Jeffrey Dewey, Steven Robert. Student, U. Wash., 1954-59; cert. CLU, Am. Coll. Life Underwriters, Bryn Mawr, Pa., 1967. CLU. Life underwriter Cen. Life of Iowa, Wenatchee, Wash., 1959-61; agy. mgr. Equitable of Iowa, Tacoma, Wash., 1961-84; regional sales dir. Northern Life, Tacoma, 1984-86; regional v.p. Western United Life, Tacoma, 1986—; pres. Northwest Gen. Agts. Conf., Wash., Oreg., B.C., 1975-76, Tacoma Gen. Agts. and Mgrs., 1980-81, Tacoma Estate Planning Coun., 1982-83. S/Sgt. USAF, 1951-54. Recipient Nat. Mgmt. award, Gen. Agts. and Mgmt. Conf., 1973-79. Mem. Am. Coll. Life Underwriters, Internat. Assn. Registered Fin. Planners, Inc., Tacoma Life Underwriters Assn., Masons, Shriners, Tacoma Country Club. Republican. Presbyterian. Home: 11502 Gravelly Lake Dr SW Tacoma WA 98499 Office: WEBCO 10510 Gravelly Lake Dr SW Lakes Profl Ctr Ste 202 Tacoma WA 98499

WEBB, MICHAEL DENNIS PUZEY, writer; b. London, July 12, 1937; came to U.S., 1969; s. John Puzey and Daisy Emily (Pocock) W.; m. B. J. Van Damme, May 20, 1972 (div. 1974). BSc in Econs., London Sch. Econs., 1959. Editorial asst. The Times, London, 1959-62; assoc. editor Country Life, London, 1962-65; programming mgr. British Film Inst., London, 1965-69; dir. nat. film programming Am. Film Inst., Washington, 1969-80; ind. writer, cons. L.A., 1980—; exec. producer feature film On the Line, 1981; writer, assoc. producer Smithsonian documentary The Movie Palaces, 1983; writer, co-producer KTLA Spl. The Greatest Story Ever Sold, 1985; curator Smithsonian traveling exhibitions, 1985-88. Author: Architecture in Britain Today, 1969, Magic of Neon, 1983, Hollywood: Legend and Reality, 1986, City Squares: People and Places, 1989; contbg. editor Arts and Architecture, 1983-85. Bd. dirs. L.A. Conservancy, 1981-82. Recipient Chevalier de L'ordre des Arts et des Lettres, French Govt., 1978; travel-rsch. grantee Graham Found., Chgo., 1988. Home: 11013 1/2 Strathmore Dr Los Angeles CA 90024

WEBB, RICHARD LEE, insurance company executive; b. OklahomaCity, July 11, 1931; s. Dee Ulyses and Isabel Elizabeth (Doerksen) W.; m. Margaret Arlene Covault. BSBA, U. Denver, 1955. Dept. mgr. Sears Roebuck, Denver, 1953-55; agt. State Farm Ins. Co., Denver, 1955—. Bd. dirs. Denver Exch. Club 1970; vice chmn. Colo. chpt. Nat. Multiple Sclerosis Soc. Colo., Denver 1984-86, chmn. 1986-88. With USAF, 1951-53. Mem. Nat. Assn. Life Underwriters (Outstanding Agt. of Yr. 1988), Lambda Chi Alpha, Rolling Hills C. of C. (past pres.). Home: 14325 Crabapple Rd Golden CO 80401 Office: State Farm Webb Ins Agy Inc 1600 Carr #1 Lakewood CO 80215

WEBB, ROMMIE FRED, manufacturing executive; b. Owensboro, Ky., June 26, 1938; s. Rommie A. and Jessie May (Simpson) W.; m. Linda Sue Huang, Nov. 23, 1947; children: Rommie Andrew, Brian Patrick, Kevin Eric, Robert Fred. Student, DeVry Inst. Tech., 1959-60; BS in Math., Brescia Coll., 1986. Mem. staff div. electronic components GE, 1960-61; engr. GE, Owensboro, Ky., 1960-68; sales engr. GE, Chgo. and Ft. Wayne, Ind., 1968-72; product mgr. semiconductors GE, Auburn and Syracuse, N.Y., 1972-74; regional mgr. S.E. GE, Greensboro, N.C., 1974-79; mgr. mktg. semiconductors Auburn, 1979-82; mgr. mktg. AMF Potter & Brumfield, Princeton, Ind., 1982-84; pres., chmn., chief exec. officer RF Electronics Inc., Çosta Mesa, Calif., 1984—. Served with USN, 1956-59. Republican. Presbyterian. Office: RF Electronics Inc 3303 Harbor Blvd G-5 Costa Mesa CA 92626

WEBBER, CHARLES FRANKLIN, manufacturing executive; b. Monterey Park, Calif., Dec. 13, 1935; s. Carl John and Adelaide Julia (Foster) W.; m. Bernice Irene Jacks, July 26, 1958; children: Michael John, Nancy Alene. AS in Sci. and Math., Porterville Coll., 1979, AA in Bus. Adminstrn., 1983. Inside salesman W.P. Fuller & Co., L.A., 1956-59, purchasing agt., 1959-61; area mgr. Ful-Trim, So. El Monte, Calif., 1962-63; ops. mgr. Ful-Trim, City of Industry, Calif., 1963-64; warehouse supt. Ful-Trim, City of Commerce, Calif., 1964-66; gen. mgr. Olson Mirrors, Inc., Strathmore, Calif., 1966-85; v.p. Sierra Mirror, Inc., Strathmore, 1985—. With USN, 1961-62. Mem. Am. Legion, Lions (pres. Lindsay club 1971), Porterville Camera Club (pres. 1987). Republican. Roman Catholic. Home: 346 N Ohio Circle Porterville CA 93257

WEBBER, EDITH JUDITH, interior designer, politician; b. Budapest, Hungary, Nov. 2, 1946; came to U.S., 1957; d. Bela Kaltenekker and Julia (Herenyi) W.; m. William H. MacFaden (div.); m. Douglas Glyn, May 28, 1982. BA, Calif. State U., Dominguez Hills, 1972, MA, 1975; postgrad., South Bay Law Sch., 1975-78, Koenig Design Sch., 1986-88. Translator Hughes Tool Co., L.A., 1968-71; owner Antiques and Fine Art Shop, El Segundo, Calif., 1978-81; councilwoman City of Hermosa Beach, Calif., 1980-84; polit. rep. to assemblyman City of Torrance, Calif., 1984—; interior designer ELBA Design, Hermosa Beach, 1988—; v.p. Maverick Electronics, Hermosa Beach, 1983—, also bd. dirs. Mem. L.A. Opera League, 1986—; chairwoman South Bay Republican Women; bd. dirs. Community Ctr. Found., Hermosa Beach, 1985-88. Recipient Merit award Hermosa Beach Police Dept., 1987. Mem. Women in Govt., Friends of the Arts, C. of C. (Woman of Yr. 1987-88), Am. Legion, Women's Club (v.p. 1987—). Roman Catholic. Office: care Assemblyman Gerald Felando 3838 Carson St St #S110 Torrance CA 90503

WEBER, ANN CARLSON, software company executive; b. Tulsa, Oct. 19, 1945; d. John Swink and Sara Ann (Mott) Carlson; m. Chester Herman Weber, Jr., May 1, 1965; children: Elizabeth Brockenbrough, Chester Herman III. Student, Wheaton (Mass.) Coll., 1963-65; BA, Dominican (Tex.) Coll., 1971. Assoc. mgr. Prudential Ins. Co., Houston, 1978-83; support tng. co. coord. Matrix Systems, Inc., Houston, 1984; v.p. Small System Design, Inc., Boulder, Colo., 1985—; sec., treas., bd. dirs. Small System Design, Inc., 1988—. Sustaining mem. Jr. League of Houston, 1980—. Republican. Episcopalian. Office: Small System Design Inc 2540 Frontier Ave Ste 104 Boulder CO 80301

WEBER, CHARLENE LYDIA, social worker; b. Phila., Mar. 2, 1943; d. Walter Gotlieb and Dorothy (Peart) W.; m. Billy Mack Carroll, Oct. 3, 1959 (div. Sept. 1974); children: Dorothy Patricia, Robert Walter, Lydia Baker, Billy Bob, Elizabeth Louise; m. John Edward Thomaston, Sept. 26, 1974 (div. July 1986). BSW with honors, Coll. Santa Fe, 1983; MSW, N.Mex. Highlands U., 1988. Client service agt. I Social Services div. Dept. Human Services, Albuquerque, 1975-78, client service agt. IV, 1978-83; social worker II Social Services div. Dept. Human Services, Bernalillo, N.Mex., 1983, social worker III, 1983—. Mem. Nat. Assn. Social Workers, N.Mex. Council on Crime and Deliquency, Albuquerque Retarded Assn., Child Welfare League. Democrat. Home: 72 Umber Ct Rio Rancho NM 87124 Office: Dept Human Svcs Div Social Svcs PO Box 820 Bernalillo NM 87004

WEBER, DENNIS PAUL, social studies educator; b. Longview, Wash., Jan. 21, 1952; s. John L. and Emelia E. (Klein) W.; m. Kristine A. McElroy-Weber, March 26, 1977; children: Kathryn, Sarah, Juliana. BA in Polit. Sci., U. Wash., 1974. Cert. tchr., Wash. Social studies tchr. R.A. Long High Sch., Longview, Wash., 1975-78, social studies tchr. and dept. chmn., 1984—; alternative edn. tchr. Natural High Sch., Longview, Wash., 1978-84; mayor City of Longview, 1984—. Planning commr. and chmn. Cowlitz County, Kelso, Wash., 1977-84; chmn. and bd. dirs. Community Urban Bus. Systems Bd., Longview-Kelso, 1980-86, SW Wash. Air Pollution Control Authority Bd., Vancouver, Wash., 1984-88, chmn., 1988—; council mem. Longview City Council, 1980—. Recipient Outstanding Young Men in Am. award N.J. C. of C., 1978; Am. Govt. and Politics fellow Taft Inst. for Teaching, 1988. Mem. NEA (nat. del. 1980-82), Longview Edn. Assn. (bd. dirs. 1978-84), Wash. Edn. Assn. (state del. 1979), Wash. State Council for Social Studies, Assn. Wash. Cities (leagis. and resolutions com.), Ams. Alumni Assn. (life, presdl. classroom), U. Wash. Alumni Assn. (life), Ripon Soc., Nation Conservancy. Republican. Lodge: Rotary (Paul Harris fellow 1987). Office: City of Longview PO Box 128 Longview WA 98632

WEBER, DOROTHY JO, convention and tradeshow consultant; b. Denver, Nov. 3, 1951; d. Herbert Eugene and Marian Rose (Walsh) F.; m. Paul L. Weber, Aug. 21, 1971 (div. Nov. 1978); 1 child, Dawn Michelle. BBA, U. Denver, 1985. Sec. Jet-X-Corp., Denver, 1969-71, State of Colo., Denver, 1971-76; with meetings dept. AWWA, Denver, 1977-78; pres. ACE Mgmt., Denver, 1988—; asst. dir. meeting services AORN, Denver, 1978-87; v.p. Price & Assocs., Denver, 1987-88. Contbr. articles to profl. jours. Mem. NAEM Rocky Mountain Assn. (v.p. 1981-82, pres. 1983), RMAMPI (bd. dirs. 1981-82, sec. 1982-83). Republican. Roman Catholic. Office: ACE Mgmt 133 S Van Gordon #200 Lakewood CO 80228

WEBER, FRED J., state supreme court justice; b. Deer Lodge, Mont., Oct. 6, 1919; s. Victor N. and Dorothy A. (Roberts) W.; m. Phyllis M. Schell, June 2, 1951; children: Anna Marie, Donald J., Mark W., Paul V. B.A., U. Mont., 1943, J.D., 1947. Bar: Mont. 1947. Atty. Kuhr & Weber, Havre, Mont., 1947-55, Weber, Bosch & Kuhr, and successors, 1956-80; justice Supreme Ct. Mont., Helena, 1981—. Served to capt. inf. U.S. Army, 1943-46. Fellow Am. Bar Found., Am. Coll. Probate Counsel; mem. ABA, Am. Judicature Soc. Office: Mont Supreme Ct 215 N Sanders St Justice Bldg Rm 323 Helena MT 59620

WEBER, GEORGE RICHARD, accountant, author; b. The Dalles, Oreg., Feb. 7, 1929; s. Richard Merle and Maud (Winchell) W.; B.S., Oreg. State U., 1950; M.B.A., U. Oreg., 1962; m. Nadine Hanson, Oct. 12, 1957; children—Elizabeth Ann Weber Katooli, Karen Louise Weber Zaro, Linda Marie. Sr. trainee U.S. Nat. Bank of Portland (Oreg.), 1950-51; jr. acct. Ben Musa, C.P.A., The Dalles, 1954; tax and audit asst. Price Waterhouse, Portland, 1955-59; sr. acct. Burton M. Smith, C.P.A., Portland, 1959-62; pvt. C.P.A. practice, Portland, 1962—; lectr. acctg. Portland State Coll.; expert witness fin. and tax matters. Sec.-treas. Mt. Hood Kiwanis Camp, Inc., 1965. Exec. counselor SBA; mem. fin. com., powerlifting team U.S. Powerlifting Fedn., 1984, ambassador People to People, China, 1987. Served with AUS, 1951-53. Decorated Bronze Star; C.P.A., Oreg. Mem. Am. Inst. C.P.A.s, Internat. Platform Assn. Portland (com. fgn. rels. 1985—). Oreg. City Traditional Jazz Soc., Order of the Holy Cross Jerusalem, Order St. Stephen the Martyr, Order St. Gregory the Illuminator, Knightly Assn. St. George the Martyr., Literary Acad., Portland C.S. Lewis Soc., Beta Alpha Psi, Pi Kappa Alpha. Republican. Lutheran. Clubs: Kiwanis, Portland Track, City (Portland); Multnomah Athletic; Sunrise Toastmasters. Author: Small Business Long-term Finance, 1962, A History of the Coroner and Medical Examiner Offices, 1963. Contbr. to profl. publs. and poetry jours. Home: 2603 NE 32d Ave Portland OR 97212 Office: 4380 SW Macadam Suite 400 Portland OR 97201

WEBER, JOSEPH JAMES, management consultant; b. Lorain, Ohio, Aug. 12, 1942; s. Joseph Sylvester and Loyola Ruth (Oberst) W.; m. Joanne Carol Kenagy, Oct. 18, 1975. BS, Bowling Green U., 1964, MA, 1966. Registered psychologist, Ill. Asst. supt. Ill. Dept. Corrections, Decatur, 1971-75, supt., chief officer, 1975-80; sr. assoc. Contact, Inc., Tucson, Ariz., 1981-84, regional dir., 1984-86; pres. J. Weber & Assocs., Tucson, 1986—. Mem. Wellness Coun. Tucson, 1987-89. 1st U.S. Army, 1966-68. Mem. Employee Assistance Soc. N.Am., Wellness Coun. Tucson. Office: J Weber & Assocs 7700 N Lundberg Dr Tucson AZ 85741

WEBER, WILLIAM ALFRED, botany educator; b. N.Y.C., Nov. 16, 1918; s. Henry Paul and Emilie Agnes (Rilke) W.; m. Selma Ruth Herrmann, Aug. 5, 1940; children: Linna Louise, Heather Dawn, Erica Marion. BS, Iowa State U., 1940; MS, Wash. State U., 1942, PhD, 1945. From instr. to assoc. prof. U. Colo., Boulder, 1946-62, prof. botany, 1962—; Herbarium curator U. Colo. Museum, Boulder, 1946—; cons. various orgns., 1946—. Author: Rocky Mountain Flora, 1976, T.D.A. Cockerell, 1976, Colorado Flora: Western Slope, 1987. Linnean Soc. fellow, 1985; recipient Robert L. Stearns award, 1986. Mem. Am. Inst. Bot. Scis., Am. Bryological and Lichenological Soc. (past sec. and pres.) Nordic Bot. Soc., Swedish Bot. Soc., Calif. Bot. Soc. Democrat. Congregationalist. Office: U Colo Mus Campus Box 350 Boulder CO 80304

WEBER-JAVERS, FLORENCE RUTH, nurse; b. Milw., Mar. 29, 1953; d. Frank A. and E. Mae (Brown) Weber; m. Lawrence P. Wittig, Aug. 17, 1974 (div. 1983); children: Drew E. Wittig, Jodi C. Weber Wittig; m. Russell L. Weber Javers, Sept. 9, 1983;l children: Andrea K. Javers Notaro, Jennifer L., John R. AS, RN, Milw. Area Tech. Coll., 1977; student, Washington U., St. Louis, 1980. Nurse, cert. orthopedic fitter Knueppel Health Care Ctr., Milw., 1971-84; nurse con. enterostomal therapy Stein Med., Milw., 1984-86; nurse PRN Home Health Care, Las Vegas, 1986-87; nurse enterostomal therapy, home health care Las Vegas, 1987—; staff nurse St. Michael's Hosp., Milw., 1978-80; nurse cons. enterostomal therapy Health Maint. Orgn., home health care agys., Las Vegas, 1987—. Author, editor newsletter Am. Ostomy Supply, 1984-86, 88—. 1st lt. USAR, 1984—. Grantee, Am. Cancer Soc., 1980. Mem. Internat. Assn. Enterostomal Therapy Nurses, Am. Cancer Soc. (vol.), Am. Ostomy Assn. (v.p. 1979), Nat. Assn. Retail Druggists.

WEBSTER, DAVID JOHN, industrial executive; b. Brainerd, Minn., July 10, 1938; s. LuVerne John and Mildred (Rausch) W.; m. Francis Lavinia Young, July 8, 1961 (div. May 1985); children: Scott Michael, Stephen David; m. Janice Louisa Lovvorn, Jan. 18, 1986. Student, MIT, 1955-58; BBA, U. Tex., 1960; postgrad., U. N.Mex., 1982-87. Dept. indsl. engr. Procter & Gamble Mfg. Co., Dallas, 1960-63; distbn. engr. Xerox Corp., Rochester, N.Y., 1964-66; chief indsl. engr. Pine Bluff (Ark.) Ops., The Leisure Group, 1966-68; mkgt. coordinator BDM Internat., Inc. (formerly The BDM Corp.), El Paso, Tex., 1968-71; adminstrv. mgr. BDM Internat., Inc. (formerly The BDM Corp.), Albuquerque, 1971-75, mgr., 1975-81, systems dir., 1981-84, dir. indsl. systems, 1984—. Scoutmaster Albuquerque Boy Scouts Am.,1975-79; Rep. ward chmn., 1973-79. Mem. Soc. Mfg. Engrs., Soc. Logistics Engrs., Inst. Indsl. Engrs., Albuquerque C. of C. (econ. planning council). Roman Catholic. Office: The BDM Corp 1801 Randolph Rd Albuquerque NM 87102 Office: BDM Internat Inc 1801 Randolph Rd SE Watervliet NY 12189

WEBSTER, DONALD JORDAN, communications company executive; b. Seattle, May 23, 1946; s. William Daniel and Opal Louise (Olebare) W.; m. Francis Kay Devore, Nov. 25, 1973 (div. 1980); 1 child, William Lloyd; m. Nancy Jean Lillagore, Sept. 25, 1982; children: Donna Marie, Sandra Eileen, Todd William, Dawn Maria. Student, Willamette U., 1964-66; AS, AA, SUNY, Albany, 1974; BS, Pacific Western U., 1982. Staff specialist Gen. Research Corp., Reston, Va., 1974-75; computer specialist USN, Washington, 1975-77; software mgr. RCA, Camden, N.J., 1977-78, program mgr., 1978-81, dir., gen. mgr., 1981-83; sr. v.p., gen. mgr. Tech. for Communications Internat., Fremont, Calif., 1983—. Author tng. materials; contbr. articles to profl. publs. Served with USN, 1966-74. Mem. IEEE, Armed Forces Communications Electronic Assn., Security Affairs Support Assn. (bd. dirs. 1983-85). Home: 2274 Niki Jo Ln Palm Beach Gardens FL 33410 Office: TCI 34175 Ardenwood Blvd Fremont CA 94555

WEBSTER, DOROTHY MARGARET, healthcare consultant; b. Anaconda, Mont., Feb. 20, 1920; d. Thomas Alexander and Blanche Amelia (Thompson) Boyd; m. Jack H. Webster, Apr. 21, 1940 (div. Apr. 1975); children: Lynda Webster Dayton, Albert Thomas. Grad. high sch., San Bernardino, Calif. Accredited record technician, health record analyst; cert. health record cons. Dir. med. records Atascadero (Calif.) Hosp., 1962-71, 77-78, French Hosp., San Luis Obispo, Calif., 1972-77; pvt. practice Atascadero, 1977—. Author: Confidentiality Manual for State Mental Health Hospitals, 1988. Mem. Am. Med. Records Assn. (cert.), Calif. Med. Records Assn., Order of Eastern Star. Republican. Home and Office: 9525 San Marcos Rd Atascadero CA 93422

WEBSTER, NANCY MULVIHILL, small business owner; b. Southampton, N.Y., May 17, 1953; d. William Patrick and Mary Jubert (Marceau) M., m. Alan Bruce Webster, June 8, 1974. BA, U. N.H., 1975. Rsch. asst. Nat. Ctr. for Atmospheric Rsch., Boulder, Colo., 1981-83; sales mgr. Frontier Airlines, Kansas City, Boulder, and Colorado Springs, Colo., 1983-86; dist. sales mgr. Costa Cruises, various states, 1986-88; owner, art. dir. Webster Galleries, Boulder, 1988—; owner Visionquest Arts, Boulder, 1987—. Pres. Shanahan Ridge 7 Homeowners Assn., Boulder, 1980-83; com. mem. Visualeyes Art Show, Boulder, 1986. Democrat. Home: 3445 Cripple Creek Sq Boulder CO 80303 Office: Webster Gallery 1412 Pearl St Boulder CO 80302

WEBSTER, RALPH TERRENCE, metallurgical engineer; b. Crookston, Minn., Nov. 24, 1922; s. Clifford and Elmika Kathleen (Johnson) W.; m. Eileen Mathilde Carrow, Aug. 9, 1947; children: Paul David, Kathleen Mary, Keith Clifford, Richard Terrence. BS, U. Nev., 1949. Registered profl. engr., Calif., Oreg. Metall. engr. U.S. Steel, Pitts., 1949-51; group leader U. Calif. Radiation Lab., Livermore, Calif., 1951-52; asst. chief metallurgist Rockwell Nordston Valve Co., Oakland, Calif., 1953-54; sr. engr. Westinghouse Atomic Power, Pitts., 1954-59; supr. engr. Aerojet Nucleonics, San Ramon, Calif., 1959-62; plant mgr. metals div. Stauffer Corp., Richmond, Calif., 1962-64; prin. metall. engr. Teledyne Wah Chang, Albany, Oreg., 1964—; part time tchr. Linn Benton Community Coll., Albany, 1964—. Contbr. articles to profl. pubis. Active Episcopal Ch., Lebanon, Oreg., 1975-85. 1st lt. USAF, 1949-64. Fellow ASTM (award of merit 1981, 1st vice chmn. 1979—); mem. Am. Soc. Metals (chmn. com.), Am. Welding Soc. (chmn. com.), Nat. Assn. Corrosion Engring., ASME (chmn. com.). Democrat. Office: Teledyne Wah Chang PO Box 460 Albany OR 97321

WEBSTER, THAD NATHAN, data processing executive; b. Manhattan, Kans., Sept. 2, 1949; s. Ronnie Gill Webster and Jeanette (Walker) Humphries; m. Suzanne Lynn Brault, Aug. 15, 1981; 1 child, Katherine Ann. BS in Computer Sci., Kans. State U., 1971. Programmer, analyst Shell Oil Co., Tulsa, 1971-73; sales rep., sales mgr. ISBD Gen. Electric Co., Tulsa, St. Louis and Kansas City (Mo.), 1973-77; sales rep. Hewlett-Packard Co., Dallas, 1977-78; mgr. sales devel. Boise (Idaho) div. 1978-82; mgr. European mktg. Boblingen, Fed. Republic Germany, 1982-83; mgr. software quality assurance Boise div. 1983-85, mgr. market program Boise div., 1985-86, mgr. product planning Boise div., 1986—. Office: Hewlett-Packard Co 11311 Chinden Blvd Boise ID 83704

WEBSTER, TOM, professional hockey coach. Formerly coach Windsor Spitfires, Ont. Hockey Leagu, coach, New York Rangers, NHL, 1986-87, coach, Los Angeles Kings, NHL, 1989—. Office: care LA Kings 3900 W Manchester Blvd PO Box 17013 Inglewood CA 90306 *

WEDDLE, JUDITH ANN, social services administrator; b. Burlington, Iowa, Aug. 28, 1944; d. Kenneth Ivan and Betty Ruth (Neiswanger) Shipley; 1 child, Brian Douglas. BA, Midland Coll., 1966. Social worker Dodge County Welfare Dept., Fremont, Nebr., 1967-68; social worker L.A. County Dept. Pub. Social Svcs., 1969-71, appeals hearing specialist, 1971-78; supr., appeals hearing specialist L.A. Welfare Dept., 1978-86; program specialist Los Angeles Welfare Dept., 1986—. Pres. Gardena (Calif.) Hotline, 1971-72, Gardena Swimteam Parents, 1978-79; elder Presbyn. Ch., Gardena, 1987—. Republican.

WEDEL, KRISTINE LYNN, nurse; b. Denver, Jan. 10, 1955; d. Glenn Jesse Zepp and Donna LaDyne (Larsen) Needens; m. Timothy Paul Wedel, Apr. 24, 1976; children: Leah Kristen, Matt Timothy. BS in Nursing, U. Colo., 1977, MS in Nursing, 1988. R.N., Colo. Pub. health nurse Mesa County Health Dept., Grand Junction, Colo., 1977-81; staff nurse pediatrics St. Mary's Hosp., Grand Junction, 1982, diabetes educator, 1985-88, coord. cardiac rehab., 1988—; home health nurse Hilltop Rehab. Hosp., Grand Junction, 1982-84, wellness coord., 1984-85; cons., speaker Roundhouse Conf. on Children with Devel. Diabetes, Grand Junction, 1983-87, Eli Lilly Co., Indpls., 1987-88; speaker in field. Co-author: Take Care: A Self Care Manual, 1980, Ageless: Wellness for Seniors, 1985, Strategies for Living with Diabetes, 1986, Heart Smart, 1987. Mem. adv. bd.d, Mesa Young Moms, Granmd Junction, Women's Resource Ctr., Grand Junction. Mem. Am. Diabetes Assn. (bd. dirs. Grand Valley chpt. 1986-88), Am. Heart Assn. (charter mem. Mesa County chpt.). Lutheran. Home: PO Box 472 Palisade CO 81526 Office: Saint Marys Hosp PO Box 1628 Grand Junction CO 81502

WEDEL, MILLIE REDMOND, teacher; b. Harrisburg, Pa., Aug. 18, 1939; d. Clair L. and Florence (Heiges) Aungst; BA, Alaska Meth. U., 1966; MEd, U. Alaska, Anchorage, 1972; postgrad. in communications Stanford U., 1975-76; m. T.S. Redmond, 1956 (div. 1967); 1 child, T.S. Redmond II; m. Frederick L. Wedel, Jr., 1974 (div. 1986). Profl. model Charming Models & Models Guild of Phila., 1954-61; public rels. staff Haverford (Pa.) Sch., 1959-61; asst. dir. devel. in charge public rels. Alaska Meth. U., Anchorage, 1966, part-time lectr., 1966-73; communications tchr. Anchorage Sch. Dist., 1967—; owner Wedel Prodns., Anchorage, 1976-86; pub. rels. staff Alaska Purchase Centennial Exhibit, U.S. Dept. Commerce, 1967; writer gubernatorial campaign, 1971; part-time instr. U. Alaska, Anchorage, 1976-79, 89—; cons. Cook Inlet Native Assn., 1978, No. Inst., 1979. Bd. dirs. Sta. KAKM, Alaska Pub. TV, membership chmn., 1978-80, elected nat. lay rep. to Pub. Broadcasting Svc. and Nat. Assn. Pub. TV Stas., 1979; bd. dirs. Ednl. Telecommunications Consortium for Alaska, 1979, Mid-Hillside Community Coun., Municipality of Anchorage, 1979-80, 83-88, Hillside East Community Coun., 1984-88, pres. 1984-85; rsch. writer, legal asst. Vinson & Elkins, Houston, 1981. Recipient awards for newspapers, lit. mags.; award Nat. Scholastic Press Assn., 1968, 74, 77, Am. Scholastic Press Assn., 1981, 82, 83, 84; Alaska Coun. Econs., 1982, Merits award Alaska Dept. Edn.; lic. third class broadcasting, FCC, legis. commendation State of Alaska. Mem. Assn. Pub. Broadcasting (charter mem., nat. lay del. 1980), Indsl. TV Assn. (San Francisco), Alaska Press Club (chmn. high sch. journalism workshops, 1968, 69, 73, awards for sch. newspapers, 1972, 74, 77), Alaska Fedn. Press Women (dir. 1978-86, youth projects dir., award for brochures, 1978), NEA, Am. Educators in Communications Tech., World Affairs Coun., Nat. Coun. Tchrs. English, Alaska Coun. Tchrs. of English, Houston Legal Assts. Assn., Chugach Electric (nomination com., bd. dirs. 1988-89), Assn. Curriculum Devel., Stanford Alumni Club (pres. 1982-84), Capt. Cook Athletic Club, Delta Kappa Gamma. Presbyterian. Office: PO Box 730 Girdwood AK 99587

WEDEMEYER, JOHN MILLS, JR., social worker, social service administrator, consultant, planner; b. Olympia, Wash., Aug. 4, 1945; s. John Mills, Sr. and Helen (Gullett) W.; m. Marianne Jensen Wedemeyer, June 28, 1969; 1 child, Anne Marie. BA in Polit. Sci., Univ. Calif.-Davis, 1967; MSW, San Diego State U., 1969. Social worker San Diego County Dept. Social Service, Calif., 1969-71; exec. dir. San Diego Youth and Community Services, 1970-76; exec. dir. Community Congress of San Diego, 1976-82; dir. Youth Services Santa Cruz Community Counseling Ctr., Calif., 1982-83, June Burnett Inst. for Children, Youth and Families, San Diego State U. Found., 1984—. Chmn. supervisory comn. Golden Hill Community Fed. Credit Union, San Diego, 1969-71; co-founder, exec. dir., chmn. planning com. The Bridge, 1970; treas., vice chmn. Community Congress Sandiego, 1972-75; vice-chmn. San Diego County Juvenile Justice Task Force, 1974-76; sec. Nat. Network Runaway and Youth Services, Washington, 1975-76, nat. chmn., 1976-78; chmn. Western States Youth Svcs. Network, 1975-76; nominating com. chmn. Health Systems Agy. of San Diego and Imperial Counties, 1976-78; mem. vestry, St. Luke's Episcopal Ch. Named Alumnus of Yr., San Diego State U. Sch. Social Work, 1976. Mem. San Diego County Foster Parent Assn. (founding, parliamentarian, newsletter editor 1969-71), Nat. Assn. Social Workers, Am. Soc. Pub. Adminstrn., Calif. Child Youth and Family Coalition. Episcopalian. Home: 1438 Dale St San Diego CA 92102 Office: June Burnett Inst for Children Youth & Families 6310 Alvarado Ct San Diego CA 92120

WEDGE, BARBARA LYNN, educational marketing professional; b. Livingston, Mont., Oct. 23, 1946; d. Ralph Henry and Mildred (Olund) George; children: Stephanie, Chelsey. BS in Speech Pathology, Mankato State Coll., 1969; MA in Speech Pathology, U. Kans., 1979. Speech pathologist Osseo (Minn.) Pub. Schs., 1969-72, Mankato (Minn.) and Shawnee Mission (Kans.) schs., 1972-80; Univ. rep. U. Phoenix, San Jose, Calif., 1980—; dir. mktg. U. Phoenix, San Jose and San Ramon, Calif., 1985—; dir. programs Lab. Sci. Interrogation, Falls Church, Va. and Pleasanton, Calif., 1985-86; rep. TelPlus Communications, Pleasanton, Calif., 1986—; cons. Corp. Speakers Tng. Bur., Pleasanton, 1985—, Mgmt. Action Programs, 1987—. Contbr. articles to Jour. Speech and Hearing Disorders. Mem. Am. Soc. Indsl. Security, Am. Speech-Lang.-Hearing Assn. (cert. clin. competence). Club: Lakeview (Oakland, Calif.).

WEEKS, CHARLES WALKER, audio engineer; b. Middletown, N.Y., July 5, 1941; s. James Riley and Jean Adams (Walker) W. BA, Occidental Coll., 1963; MFA, Stanford U., 1970. Teaching asst. Stanford (Calif.) U., 1968-70; instr. U. Mo., Kansas City, 1971-72; asst. tech. dir. N.C. Sch. Arts, Winston-Salem, 1972-74; audio engr. Hollywood (Calif.) Sound Systems, 1974-77, Filmways Audio Svcs., North Hollywood, Calif., 1977-80; freelance audio mixer, cons. L.A., 1981-82; audio mixer CBS-TV, L.A., 1982—. Contbg. author: Scene Design and Stage Lighting, 1989. Mem. Audio Engring. Soc. Democrat. Congregationalist. Home: 6558 Ben Ave North Hollywood CA 91606

WEEKS, THELMA EVANS, manufacturing executive; b. Portland, Oreg., Jan. 15, 1921; d. Harry Emmett and Clarissa Belle (Marshall) Evans; m. Robert L. Weeks, Jan. 7, 1940 (dec. Feb. 1981); children: Barbara Weeks Patton, John Robert. BA, San Diego, 1962; PhD, Stanford U., 1973. V.p. Weeks Rsch. Assocs., Palo Alto, Calif., 1970-82, Snoozy's Rm., Sunnyvale, Calif., 1982—. Author: Slow Speech Development of the Bright Child, 1974, Born to Talk, 1979. Bd. dirs. Inst. for Literacy Devel., Palo Alto, 1973-81. Fellow Am. Psychol. Assn.; mem. Soc. Children's Book Writers. Republican. Methodist. Home: 21035 Cory St Cupertino CA 95014 Office: Snoozys Rm 933 Exmoor Way Sunnyvale CA 94086

WEEKS, WILFORD FRANK, glaciologist, educator; b. Champaign, Ill., Jan. 8, 1929; married; 2 children. BS, U. Ill., 1951, MS, 1953; PhD in Geology, U. Chgo., 1956. Geologist mineral deposits br. U.S. Geol. Survey, 1952-55; glaciologist USAF Cambridge Research Ctr., 1955-57; asst. prof. Washington U., St. Louis, 1957-62; adj. prof. earth scis. Dartmouth Coll., Hanover, N.H., 1962-85; glaciologist Cold Regions Rsch. and Engring. Lab., Hanover, 1962-89; prof. geophysics, chief sci. Alaska Synthetic Aperture Radar Facility, Geophys. Inst. of U. Alaska, Fairbanks, 1986—; vis. prof. Inst. Low Temperature Sci. Hokkaido U., Sapporo, Japan, 1973; chmn. Arctic marine sci. USN Postgrad. Sch., Monterey, Calif., 1978-79; mem. earth system sci. com. NASA, Washington, 1984-87; advisor U.S. Arctic Rsch. Commn., div. polar programs NSF, Washington, 1987-88; chief scientist Alaska Synthetic Aperture Radar Facility, Fairbanks, 1986—; mem. steering com. Office of Interdisciplinary Rsch. Univ. Corp. Atmospheric Rsch., Boulder, Colo., 1986-88. Capt. USAF, 1955-57. Fellow Arctic Inst. N.Am., Am. Geophys. Union; mem. NAE, Internat. Glaciological Soc. (v.p. 1969-72, pres. 1973-75, Seligman Crystal award 1989). Office: U Alaska Geophys Inst Fairbanks AK 99775-0800

WEEMS, GLADYS MARIE, management executive; b. Drumright, Okla., Oct. 19, 1932; d. Vencil Lafayette and Rita Maye (Bloom) W. AA in Bus. Sci., San Bernardino Valley Coll., 1952. Sec. Walter Culver, Architect, San Bernardino, 1952-53; clk. disability ins. br. State Calif. Employment Devel. Dept., San Bernardino, 1953-77; sec., steno, unit supr., group supr., asst. mgr. office mgr. State Calif. EDO, D1 Div., San Bernardino, 1977-88; ptnr. D & W Assocs., San Bernardino, 1988—; bd. dirs. Teddy Bear Tymes, Child Care Ctr., San Bernardino. Mem. Soroptimist (pres., 1980-82, 89—, regional chmn., nominating com., conf. locati ons regional conf. chmn.), Beta Sigma Phi (state area pres. 1977-78, Woman of Yr., 1960, 72, 77), Job's Daus. Democrat.

WEGNER, JOHN WILLIAM, manufacturing executive; b. Berwyn, Ill., June 16, 1949; s. Charles A. and Ruth P. (Koth) W.; m. Cathy A. Brunsman, Mar. 2, 1974. Student, Coll. of DuPage, Glen Ellyn, Ill., 1967-68, U. Nebr., 1968-70, U. Houston, 1986-87. Mgr. gulf coast ops. Advance Valve Installations Inc., Deer Park, Tex., 1969-82; pres. Seven Tech., Inc., Deer Park, 1982-84; regional mgr. Koppl Indsl. Systems, Inc., Deer Park, 1984-88; v.p., gen. mgr. Koppl Co., Inc., Montebello, Calif., 1988—; cons. chemola div. Hi-Port Industries, Houston, 1988—, Koppl Indsl. Systems, Inc., Concord, Calif., 1984—. Inventor valve and system, flange system. Mem. ASME (sr.). Office: Koppl Co Inc 1228 Date St Montebello CA 90640

WEGNER, SAMUEL JOSEPH, historical society executive; b. Twin Falls, Idaho, Aug. 27, 1952; s. Albert Henry and Eleanor Esther (Wright) W.; m. Linda Louise Talley, May 27, 1972; children: Ethan, Elena. BA, U. Ariz., 1973; MA, U. Idaho, 1975. Curator Mansion Mus.-Oglebay Inst., Wheeling, W.Va., 1975-76; curator of edn. State Hist. Soc. Wis., Madison, 1976-78; asst. supt. Region I Mo. Dept. Nat. Resources, Brookfield, 1978-85; dir. ops. So. Oregon Hist. Soc., Jacksonville, Oreg., 1985-87; exec. dir. So. Oregon Hist. Soc., Jacksonville, 1987—. Adv. com. Medford (Oreg.) Visitor and Conv. Bur., 1988. Mem. Rotary. Home: 3196 Springbrook Rd Medford OR 97504 Office: So Oreg Hist Soc PO Box 480 Jacksonville OR 97530

WEH, ALLEN EDWARD, airline executive; b. Salem, Oreg., Nov. 17, 1942; s. Edward and Harriet Ann (Hicklin) W.; m. Rebecca Ann Roberton, July 5, 1968; children: Deborah Susan, Ashley Elizabeth, Brian Roberton. BS, U. N.Mex., 1966, MA, 1973. Asst. to chief adminstrv. officer Bank N.Mex., Albuquerque, 1973; pres., owner N.Mex. Airways, Inc., Albuquerque, 1974; dep. dir. N.Mex. Indochina Refugee Program, Santa Fe, 1975-76; dir. pub. affairs UNC Mining & Milling Co., Albuquerque, 1977-79; pres., chief exec. officer Charter Svcs., Inc., Albuquerque, 1979—, Falls Church, Va., 1984—. Mem. steering com. Colin McMillan for lt. gov., Albuquerque, 1982; bd. dirs. N.Mex. Symphony Orch., Albuquerque Conv. and Visitors Bur., 1982; mem. Albuquerque Police Adv. Bd., 1977-78; treas., bd. dirs. Polit. Action Com., Albuquerque, 1982. Capt. USMC, 1966-71, Vietnam, col. USMCR. Decorated Bronze Star, Purple Heart with gold star, Air medal. Mem. Marine Corps. Res. Officers Assn. (life, bd. dirs. 1973, 86), Res. Officers Assn. U.S. (life), SCV (life), Mil. Order Stars and Bars (life), N.Mex. Amigos, Albuquerque Futures Club. Republican. Episcopalian. Home: 6722 Rio Grande Blvd NW Albuquerque NM 87107 Office: Charter Svcs Inc 3700 Rio Grande Blvd NW Albuquerque NM 87107

WEHRLY, JOSEPH MALACHI, industrial relations executive b. County Armagh, Ireland, Oct. 2, 1915; s. Albert and Mary Josephine (Gribbon) W.; came to U.S., 1931, naturalized, 1938; student Los Angeles City Coll., evenings 1947-49; certificate indsl. relations U. Calif. at Berkeley Extension, 1957; m. Margaret Elizabeth Banks, July 3, 1946; children—Joseph Michael, Kathleen Margaret, Stephen Patrick. Mgr. interplant relations Goodyear Tire & Rubber Co., Los Angeles, 1935-42; dir. indsl. relations Whittaker Corp., Los Angeles, 1946-60, Meletron Corp., Los Angeles, 1960-61; asst. indsl. relations mgr. Pacific Airmotive Corp., Burbank, Calif., 1961-63; personnel mgr. Menasco Mfg. Co., Burbank, 1963-66; indsl. relations adminstr. Internat. Electronic Research, Burbank, 1966; dir. indsl. relations Adams Rite Industries, Inc., Glendale, Calif., 1966-75, cons., 1975-76; personnel mgr. TOTCO div. Baker Internat. Corp., Glendale, 1975-80; instr. indsl. relations and supervision Los Angeles Pierce Coll., 1949-76. Served with U.S. Army, 1942-46. Mem. Personnel and Indsl. Relations Assn., Mchts. and Mfrs. Assn. Republican. Roman Catholic. Home: 4925 Swinton Ave Encino CA 91436

WEIDA, GEORGE ALBERT F., human resources executive; b. Pangkatan, Sumatra, Indonesia, Aug. 16, 1936; came to U.S., 1940; s. Frederick Shepherd and Flora (Miller) W.; m. Marilee Horton, Oct. 31, 1963 (div. 1974); children: Frederick Edmund, David James, George Bradley, Craig Miller; m. Julie Ann McGrain, Oct. 4, 1974. AB in Psychology, Kenyon Coll., 1958. Personnel mgr. Kaiser Aluminum and Chem. Corp., Oakland, Calif., 1963-69; v.p. indsl. rels. Republic Corp., L.A., 1969-78; corp. dir. employee rels. AM Internat., Inc., L.A., 1978-81; prin. Employers' Labor Rels. Coun., L.A., 1981-83; v.p. human resources Loral Electro/Opitcal Systems, Pasadena, Calif., 1983, San Diego Gas & Electric Co., 1983—. Mem. corp. adv. bd., Chicano Fedn., San Diego, 1988—; bd. dirs., Police Athletic League, San Diego, 1988—; human resource exec. adv. com., San Diego Zool. Soc., 1988—. Mem. Calif. Employment Law Coun. (bd. dirs. 1985—), Math. Engring. Sci. Achievement Soc. (industry adv. com., bd. dirs.), Found. on Employment and Disability, Orgn. Resources Counselors. Episcopalian. Home: PO Box 61 Rancho Santa Fe CA 92067 Office: San Diego Gas & Electric Co 101 Ash St San Diego CA 92112

WEIDE, WILLIAM WOLFE, housing and recreational vehicles manufacturer; b. Toledo, Aug. 19, 1923; s. Samuel and Pearl Celia (Weide) W.; m. Beatrice Lieberman, June 4, 1950; children: Brian Samuel, Bruce Michael, Robert Benjamin. Student, U. Toledo, 1942, Marquette U., 1943-44; B.S., U. So. Calif., 1949. Asst. controller Eldon Mfg., 1950; mem. Calif. Franchise Tax Bd., 1951; controller Sutone Corp., 1951-53; treas. Descoware Corp., 1953-58; sr. v.p., dir. Fleetwood Enterprises, Inc., Riverside, Calif., 1958-73, pres., chief exec. officer, 1973-83, vice chmn., 1982—, dir.; treas. So. Eastern Manufactured Housing Inst., Atlanta. Mem. City of Riverside Housing Com.; mem. exec. com. of policy adv. bd. Joint Center for Urban Studies, Harvard-MIT, Cambridge; trustee City of Hope Hosp., Duarte, Calif.; Orange County chmn. United Jewish Welfare Fund, 1982-83; mem. Pres.'s Circle of U. So. Calif.; pres. Orange County Jewish Community Found., 1986-88. Served with USNR, 1942-46, PTO. Recipient Jack E. Wells Meml. award for service to manufactured housing industry, 1976; named to Recreational Vehicle/Manufactured Housing Industry Hall of Fame Elkhart, Ind., 1981; named Man of Yr., City of Hope, 1986. Mem. Nat. Assn. Accts. (past v.p., dir. Los Angeles and Orange County chpt.), Manufactured Housing Inst. (chmn., founding com. Calif. chpt. 1986), Western Manufactured Housing Inst. (vice-chmn.), Trailer Coach Assn., NAM (public affairs com.), Riverside C. of C. Office: Fleetwood Enterprises Inc 3125 Myers St Riverside CA 92523

WEIDLEIN, JAMES REA, publishing executive; b. Latrobe, Pa., Nov. 5, 1949; s. Edward Ray and Mary (Rea) W.; m. Barbra Ariel Wakshul, Sept. 23, 1984. BA, Franconia Coll., 1975. Pub. assoc. Well-Being mag., San Diego, 1975-77; owner Bisbee (Ariz.) Catalog, 1977-82, Allegro Communications, Boulder, Colo., 1979-83; chief info. officer Telemedia Internat., Denver, 1983-85; pres. Info. Design Group, Boulder, 1985—; pub. Getting Married Mag., Denver; cons. in field. Author: Networking Personal Computers in Organizations, 1986; mng. editor Winds of Change mag., 1988—; contbr. articles to profl. jours. Mem. City of Bisbee Design and Rev. Bd., 1978, Downtown Boulder, Inc., others. Dept. Energy solar energy edn. grantee, 1978. Mem. Internat. Assn. Bus. Communicators, Colo. Soc. Assn. Execs., Boulder C. of C. Mem. United Ch. Religious Sci. Home: PO Box 2277 Boulder CO 80306-2277 Office: Info Design Group 934 Pearl St Boulder CO 80302

WEIGAND, WILLIAM KEITH, bishop; b. Bend, Oreg., May 23, 1937. Ed., Mt. Angel Sem., St. Benedict, Oreg., St. Edward's Sem. and St. Thomas Sem., Kenmore, Wash. Ordained bishop of Salt Lake City 1980; Ordained priest Roman Cath. Ch., 1963. Office: Pastoral Ctr 27 C St Salt Lake City UT 84103

WEIGEND, GUIDO GUSTAV, geographer, educator; b. Zeltweg, Austria, Jan. 2, 1920; came to U.S., 1939, naturalized, 1943; s. Gustav F. and Paula (Sorgo) W.; m. Areta Kelble, June 26, 1947; children: Nina, Cynthia, Kenneth. B.S., U. Chgo., 1942, M.S., 1946, Ph.D., 1949. With OSS, 1943-45; with mil. intelligence U.S. War Dept., 1946; instr. geography U. Ill., Chgo., 1946-47; instr. then asst. prof. geography Beloit Coll., 1947-49; asst. prof. geography Rutgers U., 1949-51, assoc. prof., 1951-57, prof., 1957-76, acting dept. chmn., 1951-52, chmn. dept., 1953-67, assoc. dean, 1972-76; dean Coll. Liberal Arts, Prof. geography Ariz. State U., Tempe, 1976-83, prof. geography, 1976—; Fulbright lectr. U. Barcelona, 1960-61; vis. prof. geography Columbia U., 1963-67, NYU, 1967, U. Colo., summer 1968, U. Hawaii, summer 1969; liaison rep. Rutgers U. to UN, 1950-52; invited by Chinese Acad. Scis. to visit minority areas in Chinese Cent. Asia, 1988; mem. U.S. nat. com. Internat. Geog. Union, 1951-58, 61-65; chmn. Conf. on Polit. and Social Geography, 1968-69. Author articles, monographs, bulls. for profl. jours.; contbr.: (4th edit.) A Geography of Europe, 1977; geog. editor-in-chief: Odyssey World Atlas, 1966. Bd. adjustment, Franklin Twp., N.J., 1959; mem. Bd. Edn., Highland Park, N.J., 1973-75, v.p., 1975; mem. Ariz. Council on the Humanities and Pub. Policy, 1976-80, Phoenix Com. on Fgn. Relations (vice-chmn. 1976-79, chmn., 1979-81), exec. com. Fedn. Pub. Programs in Humanities, 1977-82; bd. dirs. Council Colls. Arts and Scis., 1980-83; mem. Commn. on Insts. of Higher Edn. of North Cen. Assn. of Colls. and Schs., 1980-83. Research fellow Office Naval Research, 1952-55, Rutgers Research Council, 1970-71; grantee Social Sci. Research Council, 1956, Ford Found., 1966, Am. Philos. Soc., 1970-71, German Acad. Exchange Service, 1984; Fulbright travel grantee Netherlands, 1970-71. Mem. Assn. Am. Geographers (chmn. N.Y. Met. div. 1955-56, editorial bd. 1955-59, mem. council 1965-66, chmn. N.Y.-N.J. div. 1965-66), Am. Geog. Soc., Assn. Pacific Coast Geographers, North Cen. Assn. Colls. and Schs. (commr. 1976-80), Am. Geog. Soc., German Studies Assn., Sigma Xi (pres. Ariz. State U. chpt. 1989—). Home: 2094 E Golf Ave Tempe AZ 85282 Office: Ariz State U Dept Geography Tempe AZ 85287-0104

WEIGHT, MELVIN E., small business owner; b. Salt Lake City, Jan. 14, 1942; s. Sheldon James and Florence (Brailsford) W.,; m. Diane K. Ellis, Mar. 19, 1962; children: Cheri Suzanne, Jeffrey Paul, Melissa Danielle. Student, Latter-day Saints Bus., Coll., 1964-65. With Mountain States Bindery, Salt Lake City, 1958-64; sales mgr. Nat. Sales, Inc., Salt Lake City, 1964-68; sales-mktg. mgr. Coast Book Cover Co., L.A., 1968-78; west regional sales mgr. Nat. Cover div. Ga. Pacific Corp., St. Louis and L.A., 1978-83; owner Di-Mel Assocs., Fountain Valley, Calif., 1978—. Chmn. 24th of July Breakfast, Salt Lake City, 1966. Recipient Outstanding Service award Binding Industries Am., 1975, 76, 77. Mem. Sales Cons./Reps. Loose-Leaf (charter), Advt. Specialty Inst., Specialty Advt. Assn. Internat. Republican. Mormon. Office: Di-Mel Assoc 17175 Brookhurst St Ste E Fountain Valley CA 92708

WEIGLE, WILLIAM OLIVER, immunologist, educator; b. Monaca, Pa., Apr. 28, 1927; s. Oliver James and Caroline Ellen (Alsing) W.; m. Kathryn May Lotz, Sept. 4, 1948 (div. 1980); children—William James, Cynthia Kay; m. Carole G. Romball, Sept. 24, 1983. B.S., U. Pitts., 1950, M.S., 1951, Ph.D., 1956. Research assoc. pathology U. Pitts., 1955-58, asst. prof. immunochemistry, 1959-61; assoc. div. exptl. pathology Scripps Clinic and Rsch. Found., LaJolla, Calif., 1961-62, assoc. mem. div., 1962-63; mem. dept. exptl. pathology Scripps Clinic and Rsch. Found., LaJolla, 1963-74, mem. dept. immunopathology, 1974-82, chmn. dept. immunopathology, 1980-82, mem., vice chmn. dept. immunology, 1982-85, mem. dept. immunology, 1982—, chmn. dept. immunology, 1985-87; adj. prof. biology U. Calif., San Diego; McLaughlin vis. prof. U. Tex., 1977; mem. adv. bd. Immunetech Pharms., San Diego, 1988—; cons. in field. Author: Natural and Acquired Immunologic Unresponsiveness, 1967; assoc. editor: Clin. and Exptl. Immunology, 1972-79; Jour. Exptl. Medicine, 1974-84; Immunochemistry 1964-71; Procs. Soc. Exptl. Biology and Medicine, 1967-72; Jour. Immunology, 1967-71; Infection and Immunity, 1969-86, Aging: Immunology and Infectious Disease, 1987—; sect. editor: Jour. Immunology,

1971-75; editorial bd.: Contemporary Topics in Immunobiology, 1971—; Cellular Immunology, 1984—; contbr. articles to profl. jours. Trustee Lovelace Med. Found., Albuquerque. With USNR, 1945-46. Pub. Health Research fellow, Nat. Inst. Neurol. Diseases and Blindness, 1956-59; NIH sr. research fellow, 1959-61, Research Career award, 1962. Mem. Am. Assn. Immunologists, Am. Soc. Exptl. Pathology (Parke Davis award 1967), Am. Soc. Microbiology, N.Y. Acad. Scis., Am. Acad. Allergy, Western Assn. Clin. Research, Am. Assn. Pathologists, Soc. Exptl. Biology and Medicine. Home: 688 Via de la Valle Solana Beach CA 92075 Office: Scripps Clinic and Rsch Found Dept Immunology IMM9 10666 N Torrey Pines Rd La Jolla CA 92037

WEIGNER, BRENT JAMES, educator; b. Pratt, Kans., Aug. 19, 1949; s. Doyle Dean and Elizabeth (Hanger) W.; m. Sue Ellen Webber Hume, Mar. 30, 1985; children: Russell John Hume, Scott William Hume. BA, U. No. Colo., 1972; MEd, U. Wyo., 1977, PhD, 1984. Counselor, coach Olympia Sport Village, Upson, Wyo., summer 1968; dir. youth sports F.E. Warren AFB, Cheyenne, summers 1973, 74; instr. geography Laramie County Community Coll., Cheyenne, 1974-75; tchr. social sci. McCormick Jr. High Sch., Cheyenne, 1975—, Laramie County Sch. Dist. 1, Cheyenne, 1975—; dept. head Laramie County Sch. Dist. 1, 1987—; instr. edn. methods U. Wyo., 1989—; nat. chmn. Jr. Olympic cross-country com. AAU, Indpls., 1980-81; pres. Wyo. Athletic Congress, 1981-87. Deacon 1st Christian Ch., Cheyenne, 1987—. Track scholar U. No. Colo., 1968-72; Fulbright grantee, Jerusalem, summer 1984; Taft Found. fellow, summer 1976, Earthwatch-Hearst fellow, Punta Allen, Mex., summer 1987. Mem. Nat. Coun. Social Studies, Assn. Supervision and Curriculum Devel., Nat. Coun. Geog. Edn., NEA, U. No. Colo. Alumni Assn., Cheyenne C. of C., Cheyenne Track Club (head coach 1976—, pres. 1980-88), Lions (bd. dirs. Cheyenne chpt. 1987-88). Home: 3204 Reed Ave Cheyenne WY 82001 Office: McCormick Jr High Sch 6000 Education Dr Cheyenne WY 82001

WEIHAUPT, JOHN GEORGE, university administrator, scientist; b. La Crosse, Wis., Mar. 5, 1930; s. John George and Gladys Mae (Ash) W.; m. Audrey Mae Reis, Jan. 28, 1961. Student, St. Norbert Coll., De Pere, Wis., 1948-49; B.S., U. Wis., 1952, M.S., 1953; M.S., U. Wis.-Milw., 1971; Ph.D., U. Wis., 1973. Exploration geologist Am. Smelting & Refining Co., Nfld., 1953, Anaconda Co., Chile, S.Am., 1956-57; seismologist United Geophys. Corp., 1958; geophysicist Arctic Inst. N. Am., Antarctica, 1958-60, Geophys. and Polar Research Center, U. Wis., Antarctica, 1960-63; dir. participating Coll. and Univ. program, chmn. dept. phys. and biol. sci. U.S. Armed Forces Inst., Dept. Def., 1963-73; assoc. dean for acad. affairs Sch. Sci., Ind. U.-Purdue U., Indpls., 1973-78; prof. geology Sch. Sci., Ind. U.-Purdue U., 1973-78; asst. dean (Grad. Sch., prof. geoscis. Purdue U.), 1975-78; prof. geology, assoc. acad. v.p., dean grad. studies and research, v.p. Univ. Research Found., San Jose (Calif.) State U., 1978-82; vice chancellor for acad. affairs U. Colo., Denver, 1982—; Sci. cons., mem. sci. adv. bd. Holt Reinhart and Winston, Inc., 1967—; sci. editor, cons. McGraw-Hill Co., 1966—; hon. lectr. U. Wis., 1963-73; geol. cons., 1968—; editorial cons. John Wiley & Sons, 1968; editorial adv. bd. Dushkin Pub. Group, 1971—. Author: Exploration of the Oceans: An Introduction to Oceanography; mem. editorial bd. Internat. Jour. Interdisciplinary Cycle Research, Leiden; co-discoverer USARP Mountain Range (Arctic Inst. Mountain Range), in Victoria Land, Antarctica, 1960; discoverer Wilkes Land Meteorite Crater, Antarctic. Mem. Capital Community Citizens Assn.; mem. Madison Transp. Study Com., Found. for Internat. Energy Research and Tng.; U.S. com. for UN Univ.; mem. sci. council Internat. Center for Interdisciplinary Cycle Research; mem. Internat. Awareness and Leadership Council; mem. governing bd. Moss Landing Marine Labs.; bd. dirs. San Jose State U. Found. Served as 1st lt. AUS, 1953-55, Korea. Mt. Weihaupt in Antarctica named for him, 1966; recipient Madisonian medal for outstanding community service, 1973; Outstanding Cote Meml. award, 1974; Antarctic medal, 1968. Fellow Geol. Soc. Am., Explorers Club; mem. Antarctican Soc., Nat. Sci. Tchrs. Assn., Am. Geophys. Union, Internat. Council Corr. Edu., Soc. Am. Mil. Engrs., Wis. Alumni Assn., Soc. Study Biol. Rhythms, Internat. Soc. for Chronobiology, Marine Tech. Soc., AAAS, Univ. Indsl. Adv. Council, Am. Council on Edn., Expdn. Polaire France (hon.), Found. for Study Cycles, Assn. Am. Geographers, Nat. Council Univ. Research Adminstrs., Soc. Research Adminstrs., Man-Environ. Communication Center, Internat. Union Geol. Scis., Internat. Geog. Union, Internat. Soc. Study Time, Community Council Pub. TV, Internat. Platform Assn., Ind., Midwest assns. grad. schs., Western Assn. Grad. Schs., Council Grad. Schs. in U.S., Wis. Alumni Assn. of San Francisco. Clubs: Carmel Racquet (Rinconada Racquet); Kiwanis. Home: 23906 Currant Dr Golden CO 80401 Office: U Colo 1200 Larimer Campus Box 172 Denver CO 80204

WEIL, JACK BAUM, clothing manufacturing company executive; b. Denver, Nov. 13, 1928; s. Jack Arnold and Beatrice (Baum) W.; m. Candace Helene Taylor, 1973 (div. 1983); children: Steven Eugene, Judith B. Weil Oksner. BA, Tulane U., 1952. Sales mgr. Rockmount Ranch Wear Mfg. Co., Denver, 1954—, designer, v.p., 1957—; designer western apparel. Head planning group Humboldt Island Hist. Dist., Denver; committeeman Denver Rep. Com., 1974—; del. Rep. county, dist. and state convs., 1974—; dir. Bill Griffith for Congress, 1988; bd. dirs. 1st Universalist Ch., Denver. 1st lt. U.S. Army, 1952-54. Mem. West Coast Western Mktg. Assn., Midwest Western Wear and Equipment Assn., N.W. Western Wear and Equipment Assn., Denver Western Wear and Equipment Assn., Hat Inst. Am. (del. 1974—), Town Club, Sporting Club, Lincoln Club, 3M Club, Kappa Delta Phi. Home: 1025 Humboldt St Denver CO 80218 Office: Rockmount Ranch Wear Mfg Co 1626 Wazee St Denver CO 80218

WEIL, STEVEN MARK, educator; b. Chgo., Feb. 28, 1949; s. Ronald Leo and Leona Ann (Fein) W.; m. Mary Arlene Bartelheim, Aug. 1970 (div. 1977); 1 child, Meredith; m. Mary Clare Klaus, May 11, 1979; children: Nethaniel, Rachael. Student, Chgo. City Coll.-Loop Coll., 1966-68, Chgo. State Coll., 1968-69; BS in Psychology and Physical Sci. Edn., Roosevelt U., 1980; MS in Secondary Edn. Sci., U. Nebr., 1984, postgrad., 1982-84. Tchr. DuSable High Sch., Chgo., 1980, Millard Pub. Schs., 1980-81, Fremont (Nebr.) Pub. Schs., 1981-86, Stockton (Calif.) Unified Sch. Dist., 1986—. Contbr. articles to profl. jours. Mem. dist. computer com. Stockton Unified Sch. Dist.; instr. CPR and first aid ARC, Fremont and Stockton, 1985-88; mem. mcpl. relations commn., Village of Wheeling, Ill., 1976-77; grant proposal reader NSF, 1987. Grantee Fremont Alternative Learning Ctr., 1982-83, grantee Stockton Enrichment Found., 1986. Mem. Am. Vocat. Assn. (ops./policy com. 1984-85), Fremont Edn. Assn. (rep. bldg. 1981-82, 84-86, negotiations team mem. 1985-86), Millard Edn. Assn. (rep. bldg. 1980-81, negotiations com. 1980-81), Mo. Valley Alternative Edn. Council (pres. 1983-85), Nat. Sci. Tchrs. Assn. (life, spl. edn. adv. bd. 1984-87, chmn. spl. edn. adv. bd. 1986-87), Nebr. Assn. Vocat. Spl. Needs Personnel (pres. 1983-84), Nebr. Vocat. Assn., Sci. Handicapped Assn., Stockton Tchrs. Assn., Phi Delta Kappa. Mem. Conservative Judaism. Home: 8416 Mason Dr Stockton CA 95209 Office: Franklin High Sch 300 N Gertrude Stockton CA 95205

WEILBACH, PETER M., electrical engineer; b. Denver, May 6, 1987; s. Rolf Ludwig and Ingrid Ute (Aeckerle) W.; m. Jennifer Ann Lewis, June 20, 1987. BSEE, U. Colo., 1988. Cert. product integrity engr. Security officer Martin Marietta Aerospace, Denver, 1984-85; engrs. aide Martin Marietta Astronautics, Denver, 1985-87, assoc. engr., 1988—. Eagle Scout and asst. scout master, Boy Scouts of Am., Troop 266, Denver, 1980. Sgt. in USAFR, 1983—. Named Honor Grad., USAF Basic Military Tng., 1983, 302 Tactical Airlift Wing non-commd. Officer of the Yr., Peterson AFB, Colo., 1985. Mem. IEEE, Order of the Engineer, Link 76, Eagle Scouts Assn. of Am. Lutheran. Home: 8965 E Florida Ave 10-205 Denver CO 80231 Office: Martin Marietta Astrons PO Box 179 Denver CO 80201

WEILER, DOROTHY ESSER, librarian; b. Hartford, Wis., Feb. 21, 1914; d. Henry Hugo and Agatha Christina (Dopp) Esser; A.B. in Fgn. Langs., Wash. State U., 1935; B.A.L., Grad. Library Sch., U. Wash., 1936; postgrad. U. Ariz., 1956-57, Ariz. State U., 1957-58, Grad. Sch. Librarianship, U. Denver, 1971; m. Henry C. Weiler, Aug. 30, 1937; children—Robert William, Kurt Walter. Tchr.-librarian Roosevelt Elem. Schs., Dist. #66, Phoenix, 1956-59; extension librarian Ariz. Dept. Library and Archives, Phoenix, 1959-67; library dir. City of Tempe (Ariz.), 1967-79; asso. prof., dept. library sci. Ariz. State U., 1968; vis. faculty Mesa Community Coll., 1980—. Mem. public relations com. United Fund; treas. Desert Samaritan Hosp. and Health Center Aux., 1981, v.p. community relations Hosp., 1982, vol. asst. chaplain, 1988—. Named Ariz. Librarian of Yr., 1971; recipient Silver Book award Library Binding Inst., 1963. Mem. Tempe Hist. Soc., Ariz. Pioneers Hist. Soc., Am. Radio Relay League, Am. Bus. Women's Assn., ALA, Southwestern Library Assn., Ariz. State Libr. Assn. (pres. 1973-74), Ariz. Libr. Pioneer. Roman Catholic. Clubs: Our Lady of Mt. Carmel Ladies' Sodality, Soroptimist Internat. Founder, editor Roadrunner, Tumbling Tumbleweed; author Ency. Americana article on Tempe. Home: PO Box 26018 Tempe AZ 85285-6018

WEILL, SAMUEL, JR., automobile company executive; b. Rochester, N.Y., Dec. 22, 1916; s. Samuel and Bertha (Stein) W.; student U. Buffalo, 1934-35; m. Mercedes Weil, May 20, 1939 (div. Aug. 1943); children: Rita and Eric (twins); m. Cléanthe Kimball Carr, Aug. 12, 1960 (div. 1982); m. Jacqueline Natalie Bateman, Jan. 5, 1983. Co-owner, Brayton Air Coll., St. Louis, 1937-42; assoc. editor, advt. mgr., bus. mgr. Road and Track Mag., Los Angeles, 1951-53; pres. Volkswagen Pacific, Inc., Culver City, Calif., 1953-73, Porsche Audi Pacific, Culver City, 1953-73; chmn. bd. Minto Internat., Inc., London; v.p. fin. Chieftain Oil Co., Ojai, Calif. Recipient Tom May award Jewish Hosp. and Research Center, 1971. Served with USAAF, 1943-45. Home: 305 Palomar Rd Ojai CA 93023 Office: Chieftain Oil Co 306 E Matilija St Ojai CA 93003

WEIMER, BRUCE JAMES, neurologist; b. Ft. Leavenworth, Kans., Oct. 28, 1952; s. Robert and Frances (James) W.; m. Cheryl Ann Scott, Nov. 3, 1984. BS, U. Pitts., 1974, MD, 1978. Lic. physician, Calif.; diplomate Nat. Bd. Psychiatry and Neurology, Nat. Bd. Med. Examiners. Clin. instr. dept. neurology U. Pitts., 1982-85; pvt. practice in neurology 1982-85; physician Assocs. in Neurology, Pitts., 1982-85, Van Nuys, Calif., 1985—; dir. Med. Experts, Van Nuys.; med. intern Presbyn. U. Hosp., Pitts, 1978-79; resident ;in neurology U. Health Ctr. Pitts., 1979-82. U. Pitts. Med. Alumni grantee, 1975, 76. Mem. Am. Acad. Neurology, Am. Assn. Electromyography and Electrodiagnosis, Am. Med. Electroencephalographic Assn., Am. Acad. Thermology. Office: Med Experts 14545 Victory Blvd Ste 406 Van Nuys CA 91411

WEIMERS, LEIGH ALBERT, newspaper columnist; b. Napa, Calif., Nov. 11, 1935; s. Leigh and Stella Marie (Heflin) W.; m. Geraldine Louise Stone, Aug. 25, 1962; children: Kristin Louise, Karin Leigh. BA in Journalism, San Jose State Coll., 1958. Sports editor Napa Jour., 1952-53, Napa Register, 1954-55; reporter San Jose Mercury News, 1960-62, asst. city editor, 1962-65, columnist, 1965—; pres. Edgecombe Corp., Los Gatos, Calif., 1984—. Author: Insider's Guide to Silicon Valley, 1986, (with Gael Douglass) The Ghosts of Sarah Winchester, 1987. Bd. dirs. Redwood Mut. Water Co., Redwood Estates, Calif., 1965-66, Ctr. Living with Dying, San Jose, 1979-82, San Jose Trolley Corp., 1988. Served with U.S. Army, 1958-60. Mem. Newspaper Guild, San Jose State Alumni Assn. (bd. dirs 1984—), Sigma Chi. Lodge: Rotary (bd. dirs. San Jose chpt. 1988). Home: 21661 Woolaroc Dr Los Gatos CA 95030 Office: San Jose Mercury News 750 Ridder Park Dr San Jose CA 95190

WEINBERG, IRA JAY, interior designer; b. Los Angeles, Apr. 18, 1959; s. Jack and Roz (Candler) W.; m. Wendy Gates, Aug. 10, 1985. BS, Art Ctr. Coll. of Design, Pasadena, Calif., 1982. Jr. staff Milton Swimmer Planning and Design, Beverly Hills, Calif., 1977-79; space planner, designer Swimmer Cole Martinez & Curtis, Marina Del Rey, Calif., 1982-84, sr. designer, 1985-87; space planner, designer Robinson Mills & Williams, San Francisco, 1984-85; prin. Weinberg Design, Santa Monica, Calif., 1987—. Office: 206 W Channel Rd Santa Monica CA 90402

WEINBERG, LAWRENCE, professional basketball team owner. Owner, formerly pres. Portland Trail Blazers, Nat. Basketball Assn., Oreg.; now chmn. emeritus Portland Trail Blazers. Office: care Portland Trail Blazers 700 NE Multnomah St Ste 950 Lloyd Bldg Portland OR 97232 *

WEINBERGER, LYNNE MARSHA, real estate executive; b. Santa Monica, Calif., May 4, 1955; d. Eugene Julius Weinberger and Helen (Nicholas) Devor. BA, UCLA, 1977; MBA, U. So. Calif., 1980. Real estate assoc. Continental Ill. Nat. Bank, Chgo., 1980-82; v.p. Union Bank, L.A., 1982-84; assoc. v.p. Zelman Devel. Co., L.A., 1984-87; pres. Touchstone Devel. Co., L.A., 1987—. Mem. Women in Comml. Real Estate, Internat. Coun. Shopping Ctrs. Democrat. Jewish. Home: 11919 Tennessee Pl Los Angeles CA 90064

WEINER, DORA B., medical humanities educator; b. Furth, Germany, 1924; d. Ernest and Emma (Metzger) Bierer; m. Herbert Weiner, 1953; children—Timothy, Richard, Antony. Baccalaureat, U. Paris, 1941; B.A. magna cum laude, Smith Coll., 1945; M.A., Columbia U., 1946, Ph.D., 1951. Lectr. gen. studies Columbia U., N.Y.C., 1949-50, instr., 1950-52, vis. lectr. Tchrs. Coll., 1962-63; instr. Barnard Coll., 1952-56; fellow in history of medicine Johns Hopkins U., Balt., 1956-57; mem. faculty dept. social sci. Sarah Lawrence Coll., 1958-62; asst. prof. history Manhattanville Coll., 1964-65, assoc. prof., 1966-78, prof., 1978-82; adj. prof. med. humanities UCLA Sch. Medicine, Los Angeles, 1982—, prof., 1987—; cons. and lectr. in field. Author: Raspail: Scientist and Reformer, 1968; The Clinical Training of Doctors: An Essay of 1793, 1980; co-editor: From Parnassus; Essays in Honor of Jacques Barzun, 1976; contbr. chpts. to books, articles to profl. jours. Grantee numerous profl. and ednl. instns. Mem. Am. Hist. Assn. (nominating com. 1979-82, Leo Gershoy award com. 1985-88), AAUP, Am. Assn. History Medicine (past mem. numerous coms.), Soc. 18th Century Studies, Soc. for French Hist. Studies (exec. com. 1978-81), History of Sci. Soc. Office: UCLA 12-138 Ctr Health Scis Los Angeles CA 90024

WEINER, SHARON ROSE, public relations executive. d. Mike and Elaine (Feinberg) W.; m. William H. Stryker. BA, Northwestern U., 1965; MBA, U. Hawaii, 1975. Sales rsch. asst. WBBM-TV, Chgo., 1965-66; acct. exec. Pub. Relations Bd., Chgo., 1966-67; pub. relations mgr. Levi Strauss & Co., San Francisco, 1967-73, C. Brewer Co., Honolulu, 1975-76; v.p. Fawcett McCermott Cavanagh Inc., Honolulu, 1976-79; pres., chief exec. officer Stryker Weiner Co., Honolulu, 1979—. Bd. dirs. Hawaii Vis. Bur., Honolulu; v.p. bd. dirs. Aloha coun. Boy Scouts Am. Aloha United Way, Honolulu, Honolulu Symphony. Mem. Pub. Relations Soc. Am. (Gregg W. Perry award 1988), Soc. Am. Travel Writers, Pacific Area Travel Assn., Oahu Country Club, Pacific Club. Home: 1455 Kalanikai Pl Honolulu HI 96821

WEINER, STEWART GEORGE, magazine editor, writer, book publisher; b. Cin., Sept. 11, 1945; s. Dr. Alfred Lawrence and Janet Katherine (Lackner) W.; m. Ellen Faye Lustbader, Feb. 14, 1987; 1 child, Maxwell Spencer. Bachelor of Journalism, U. Mo., 1967. Founder bailey/erskine/roberts, Cin., 1968-73; editor-in-chief Writer's Digest, Cin., 1973-75; in-house writer Rolling Stone mag., San Francisco, 1975; editor Provincetown mag., Cape Cod, Mass., 1976-77; sr. editor Playboy Enterprises, L.A., 1977-80; pub., owner The Galliard Press, L.A., 1983-84; editor-in-chief Caesars World's SEVEN mag., L.A., 1984-88, Alan Weston Communications, Burbank, Calif., 1988—. Pub.: Radio Eyes, 1984; author: GERI, 1984. Home: 4104 Farmdale Ave Studio City CA 91604

WEINER, VIRGINIA L. See WESTOVER, VIRGINIA L.

WEINSTEIN, ELEANOR HOLDRIDGE, educator; b. Huntington Park, Calif., Jan. 24, 1938; d. Wilfred Lee and Kathryn Eleanor (Scott) Holdridge; m. Stephen Theodore Weinstein, Dec. 17, 1961; children: Thomas Lee, Stanley William. BA, Calif. State U., Long Beach, 1960. Cert. elementary tchr. Elementary tchr. Los Angeles City Schs., South Gate, Calif., 1960-66; tng. tchr. Long Beach State Coll., South Gate, 1963-66; Watts, Calif., 1965; cooperating tchr. Calif. Poly. State U., San Luis Obispo, 1988; elementary tchr. San Luis Coastal Unified Sch. Dist., San Luis Obispo, 1984—ž; lang. arts demonstration tchr., South Gate, 1964, adv. aide, San Luis Obispo, 1971-78, chmn. secondary curriculum rev. com., 1979-80; tchr. gifted and talented in alternative sch., 1984-88. Unit dir. League Women Voters, San Luis Obispo, 1982; trustee bd. edn. San Luis Obispo, 1973-77 (pres. 1977). Mem. San Luis Obispo Reading Assn., PTA (hon. life), Calif. Poly. Women's Club, San Luis Obispo, (v.p. 1971-72). Home: 1222 San Carlos Dr San Luis Obispo CA 93401 Office: San Luis Coastal Unified Sch Dist 1499 San Luis Dr San Luis Obispo CA 93401

WEINSTEIN, JUDITH, artist, art producer; b. Chgo., Feb. 11, 1927; d. Julius and Charlotte (Brandau) Braun; m. Irwin Weinstein, Jan. 20, 1951; children: James, David. BS in Psychology, U. Wis., 1950. Tchr. N.Y. State Child Care Ctr., N.Y.C., 1950-52, U. Chgo., 1952-53; interior designer, color cons. Paul Bennett and Assocs., 1953-58; dir. Ethnic Arts Shop, Bookshop and George Page Mus. Shop, Los Angeles County Mus. Natural History; producer ethnic art shows and research asst. dept. anthropology Los Angeles County Mus. Natural History, 1971-77; dir., continuing edn. Artsreach program UCLA Extension, 1978-85; producer Judith Weinstein Prodns., 1985—; v.p. T.S.B. Prodns., 1986—, Humorx. Mem. polit. campaign coms. U.S. Senate, mayor L.A., 1958-63; bd. dirs. L.A. Mcpl. Art Gallery Assocs., 1980—, pres., 1987—; pres., bd. dirs. L.A. Mcpl. Art Gallery, 1987—; bd. dirs. L.A. Art Showcase, 1972-75, spl. advisor art U.S. sen. Alan Cranston; mem. planning com. Dem. Nat. Telethon, 1960; bd. dirs. Calif. Chamber Symphony, 1960-71, Alternative Living Aging, L.A., 1979—, Street Scene Festival, 1978-88, Israel Cancer Rsch. Fund, 1986—; v.p. Pacific chpt. UN Assn., 1963-69, adv. bd., 1969-71; organizer, developer, dir. UN Ctr., Westwood, Calif., 1963-71; del. 1st women's conf. Dem. Nat. Com., 1971; adv. com. L.A. Children's Mus., 1978; mem. com. Corp. Disabilities & Telecommunication, 1981—. Office: Los Angeles Mcpl Art Gallery 4804 Hollywood Blvd Los Angeles CA 90027

WEINSTOCK, GEORGE A., security alarm manufacturing company; b. Cleve., Oct. 4, 1937; s. Morris Fred and Anne (Orner) W.; m. Linda Jane Katz, Mar. 13, 1960; children: David, Jennifer, Amy. With Morse Signal Devices of Calif. Inc., Los Angeles, 1955-81, pres., dir., 1969-81; pres., dir. Morse Signal Devices, Oxnard, Calif., 1970-81, Morse Signal Devices of Ohio, Cleve., 1969-74; exec. v.p., dir. Morse Security Group, Sylmar, Calif., 1969—; ptnr. Ans-R-Tel Answering Service, San Diego, 1957-83; v.p., dir. Am. Home Security, Van Nuys, Calif., 1983-84, pres., chief exec. officer, 1984—; ptnr. Weinstock Co. I, 1967—, Weinstock Co. II, 1978—, The Grill Restaurant, Beverly Hills, Calif., 1983—; mem. Blue Ribbon com. Los Angeles Police Commn., 1969, liaison com. alarm industry and Law Enforcement Administrv. Agy., 1972-73; participant industry adv. conf. Burglary Protection Systems and Services of Underwriters' Labs., Inc., 1969-76; bd. dirs., mktg. com., audit com., mem. exec. com. Charter Nat. Bank. Bd. dirs., mem. budget/fin. com., planning com. Rancho Encino Hosp., 1985—, chmn. search com., 1986; bd. dirs. Temple Shir Chadash Bldg./Land Planning Corp., 1986-87, chmn. project coordinator com., 1988—; mem. Found. for the Jr. Blind, Jr. Diabetes Assn., The Guardians of the Jewish Home for the Aged. Served to sgt. USAF, 1958-63. Recipient Certifications of Appreciation Internat. Security Conf., 1967, Nat. Police Officers Assn., 1971; named Hon. Citizen City New Orleans, 1974. Mem. Nat. Burglar and Fire Alarm Assn. (chmn. industry regulations com. 1969-71, grievance com. 1971-72, govt. liaison com. 1974-75, nominating com. 1976-77, pres. 1973-74, Western v.p. 1971-72, executor Morris F. Weinstock Meml. Man-of-the-Yr. award 1970—, award of appreciation 1974), Western Burglar and Fire Alarm Assn. (chmn. pub. relations com. 1971-72, industry regulations com. 1972-73, by-lawd com. 1984—, dir. exec. com. 1978-84, mem. govt. leaison com. 1973-74, pres. 1976-77, v.p. so. region 1973-74, Disting. Services award 1977), Cen. Sta. Electrical Protection Assn. (chmn. city and state ordinance com. 1971-72, bd. dirs. 1972-73), Nat. Assn. Pvt. Security Vaults (bd. dirs. 1982-84), Am. Soc. Indsl. Security, Calif. Automatic Fire Alarm Assn., Nat. Safety Council, Hollywood C. of C., Stanford Alumni Assn., Brandeis Inst. Alumni Assn., Am. Philatelic Soc., Porsche Club Am., Sunrise Alejo Property Owners Assn. (bd. dirs. 1984-86). Office: Am Home Security 7650 Gloria Ave Van Nuys CA 91406

WEINTRAUB, LLOYD WAYNE, communications executive; b. Bklyn., June 30, 1952; s. Jerome and Tobie (Meyer) W.; m. Sherry Ruth Horwitz, Aug. 31, 1974; children: Ian Jacob, Mathew Ira. BA, CUNY, 1974, MFA, 1978. Talent agt. Fifi Oscard Assocs., Inc., N.Y.C., 1974-76; TV and theater agt. Hesseltine Baker & Assocs., N.Y.C., 1976-78; TV and motion picture agt. Agy. for the Performing Arts, L.A., 1978-80; v.p. creative affairs dept. Bud Astin Prodns./Universal TV, L.A., 1980-82; v.p. movies and mini-svc. MGM/UA TV, L.A., 1982-84; v.p. devel. Viacom Prodns., L.A., 1984-86; TV packaging agt. Triad Artists, Inc., L.A., 1986-88; exec. v.p. Rastar TV, L.A., 1988—. Mem. Hollywood (Calif.) Radio and TV Soc. Democrat. Jewish. Office: Rastar TV 10 Universal City Pla Universal City CA 91608

WEINY, GEORGE AZEM, physical education educator, consultant; b. Keokuk, Iowa, July 24, 1933; s. George Dunn and Emma Vivian (Kraushaar) W.; m. Jane Louise Eland, Sept. 29, 1956 (div. 1985); children: Tami L., Tomas A., Aaron A., Arden G.; m. Lori Arlene Rowe, Aug. 6, 1985; children: Austin George, Breck Philip. BA, Iowa Wesleyan Coll., 1957; MA, State U. Iowa, 1962; PhD, U. Beverly Hills, 1980. Phys. dir. YMCA, Keokuk, 1956-57; asst. dir. pub. relations Iowa Wesleyan Coll., Mt. Pleasant, Iowa, 1957-58; prin., tchr., coach Hillsboro (Iowa) High Sch., 1958-59; tchr., coach Burlington (Iowa) High Sch. and Jr. Coll., 1959-62, Pacific High Sch., San Bernardino, Calif., 1962-67; prof. phys. edn. Calif. State U., San Bernardino, 1967—; ednl. cons. Belau Modekngei Sch., West Caroline Islands, 1984-85; swim meet dir. Nat. Collegiate Athletic Assn., 1982-84, 86—; tng. dir. for ofcls. So. Calif. Aquatics Fedn., 1967-78; asst. swim coach Calif. State U., Chico, 1979, scuba tour guide Dive Maui Resort, Hawaii, 1982-83; salvage diver U.S. Trust Territories, 1973; coach YMCA swim team, San Bernardino, 1962-77, 84—. Editor: Swimming Rules and Case Studies, 1970-73; author: Snorkeling Fun for Everyone, 1982; contbr. articles to profl. jours. Mem. county water safety com. ARC, San Bernardino, 1968-80; bd. dirs. YMCA, San Bernardino, 1970-77; mem. Bicentennial Commn., San Bernardino, 1975-76. Served to sgt. U.S. Army, 1953-55, Iowa N.G., 1955-58. Recipient Outstanding Service award So. Calif. Aquatics Fedn., 1978. Mem. Profl. Assn. Diving Instrs. (cert.), Nat. Assn. Underwater Instrs. (cert.), Am. Assn. Health Phys. Edn. Recreation and Dance, Coll. Swim Coaches Assn. Am. (25-Yr. Service award 1987), Am. Swim Coaches Assn. (cert.), Nat. Interscholastic Swim Coaches Assn. (25-Yr. Service award 1985). Club: Sea Sons Dive (Rialto, Calif.) (pres. 1982-83, sec. 1983-88, Diver of Yr. award 1983, 87). Home: PO Box 30393 San Bernardino CA 92413 Office: Calif State U 5500 University Pkwy San Bernardino CA 92407

WEIR, ALEXANDER, JR., utility consultant; b. Crossett, Ark., Dec. 19, 1922; s. Alexander and Mary Eloise (Field) W.; m. Florence Forschner, Dec. 28, 1946; children—Alexander III, Carol Jean, Bruce Richard. B.S. in Chem. Engring., U. Ark., 1943; M.Ch.E., Poly Inst. Bklyn., 1946; Ph.D., U. Mich., 1954; cert., U. So. Calif. Grad. Sch. Bus. Adminstrn., 1968. Analyst, chemist Am. Cyanimid and Chem. Corp., summers 1941, 42; chem. engr. Am. Cyanimid Co., Stanford Research Labs., 1943-47; with U. Mich., 1948-58; rsch. assoc., project supr. Engring. Research Inst., U. Mich., 1948-57; lectr. chem. and metall. engring. dept. U. Mich., 1954-56, asst. prof., 1956-58; cons. Ramo-Wooldridge Corp., Los Angeles, 1956-57, mem. tech. staff, sect. head, asst. mgr., 1957-60, incharge Atlas Missile Captive test program, 1956-60; tech. adv. to pres. Northrop Corp., Beverly Hills, Calif., 1960-70; prin. scientist for air quality So. Calif. Edison Co., Los Angeles, 1970-76, mgr. chem. systems research and devel., 1976-86, chief research scientist, 1986-88; utility cons. Playa Del Rey, Calif., 1988—; rep. Am. Rocket Soc. to Detroit Nuclear Council, 1954-57; chmn. session on chem. reactions Nuclear Sci. and Engring. Congress, Cleve., 1955; U.S. del. AGARD (NATO) Combustion Colloquium, Liege, Belgium, 1955; Western U.S. rep. task force on environ. research and devel. goals Electric Research Council, 1971; electric utility advisor Electric Power Research Inst., 1974-78, 84-87; industry advisor Dept. Chemistry and Biochemistry Calif. State U., Los Angeles, 1981-88. Author: Two and Three Dimensional Flow of Air through Square-Edged Sonic Orifices, 1954; (with R.B. Morrison and T.C. Anderson) Notes on Combustion, 1955; also tech. papers. Inventer Weir power plant stack scrubber. Bd. govs., past pres. Civic Union Playa del Rey, chmn. sch., police and fire, nominating, civil def., army liaison coms; mem. Senate, Westchester YMCA, chmn. Dads sponsoring com., active fundraising; chmn. nominating com. Paseco del Rey Sch. PTA, 1961; mem. Los Angeles Mayors Community Adv. Com.; asst. chmn. advancement com., merit badge dean Cantinella dist. Los Angeles Area council Boy Scouts Am. Mem. Am. Geophys. Union, Navy League U.S. (v.p. Palos Verdes Peninsula council 1961-62), N.Y. Acad. Scis., Sci. Research Soc. Am., Am. Chem. Soc., Am. Inst. Chem. Engrs., AAAS, Combustion Inst., Air Pollution Control Assn., U.S. Power Squadron, Sigma Xi, Phi Kappa Phi, Phi Lambda Upsilon, Alpha Chi

Sigma, Lambda Chi Alpha. Club: Santa Monica Yacht. Office: 8229 Billowvista Dr Playa Del Rey CA 90293

WEIR, DONALD D., physician; b. Sussex, Wis., June 27, 1928; s. Donald E. and Mary E. W.; m. Donna Johnson, Aug. 22, 1948 (dec. Nov. 11, 1988); children: Shawnee, Shay, Janna. BA, Drake U., 1948; MD, State U. Iowa, 1953. Diplomate Am. Bd. Internal Medicine. From asst. prof. to assoc. prof. medicine and preventive medicine U. N.C., 1959-71, rehab. coord., 1959-68, dr. sect. allied edn. program, 1962-69, chmn. univ. commn. on allied health scis., 1967-69, dir. div. rehab., 1968-69; dir. rehab. St. Luke's Hosp., Cedar Rapids, Iowa, 1969-78; attending physician St. Luke's Meth. Hosp. and Mercy Hosp., Cedar Rapids, 1970-78; clin. assoc. prof. rehabilitative medicine State U. Iowa, 1970-78; attending physician phys. medicine and rehab. VA Hosp., Iowa City, 1972-78; med. dir. Americana Healthcare Ctr., Cedar Rapids, Iowa, 1973-78; cons. Rehab. Med. Monroe Devel. Ctr., Cedar Rapids, 1975-79; med. dir. Regional Rehab. Ctr. Pitt County Meml. Hosp., Greenville, N.C., 1978-82; chmn., prof. Dept. Rehab. Medicine E. Carolina U. Sch. Medicine, Greenville, 1978-82; chmn., Dept. Rehab. Medicine Pitt County Meml. Hosp., Greenville, 1978-82; med. dir. Casa Colina Comprehensive Back Services Program, Pomona, Calif., 1982—, Casa Colina Hosp. for Rehab. Medicine, Pomona, 1982—; cons. rehabilitative medicine Iowa Vet.'s Home, Marshalltown, 1972-78, Monroe Devel. Ctr., Cedar Rapids, 1975-78. Contbr. articles to profl. jours. With U.S. Army, 1946-48. Mem. AMA, Calif. Med. Assn., Am. Assn. for the Advancement of Science, Am. Rheumatism Assn., Am. Congress Rehab. Medicine. Office: Casa Colina Hosp 255 E Bonita Ave Pomona CA 91767

WEIR, JIM DALE, small business owner; b. Phoenix, Feb. 2, 1956; s. Jim Earl and Laverne Alice (Maman) W.; m. Myra Yvonne Anglin, July 19, 1980; children: Justin, Kevin, Amanda. Student, Phoenix Coll., 1978; BS, Grand Canyon Coll., 1980. Owner Quality S Mfg., Phoenix, 1980—. Vol. Tempe (Ariz.) Ch. of the Nazarene, 1987-89, Latin Am. Ch. of the Nazarene, Phoenix, 1988-89. Recipient Key ofCity award Phoenix, 1987, Fast Frowth award Inc. mag., 1988. Republican. Home: Box 23910 Phoenix AZ 85063

WEIR, MICHAEL R., pediatrician; b. Austin, Tex., Dec. 30, 1942. BA, Harvard U., 1965; MD, U. Tex., 1969. Lic. physician, Tex.; diplomate Am. Bd. Pediatrics, 1975, recert., 1981. Commnd. 2d lt. U.S. Army, 1970; intern Letterman Army Med. Ctr., San Francisco, 1970, resident in pediatrics, 1970-72; chief pediatrics U.S. Army Hosp., Vicenza, Italy, 1972-76, chief outpatient clinic, 1973-74, staff pediatric nephrologist, 1976-87; chief pediatric outpatient svc. William Beaumont Army Med. Ctr., El Paso, 1978-82, asst. chief dept. pediatrics, 1982-84, chief. dept. clin. investigation, 1984-87, dir. pediatric/medicine residency program, 1984-87; chief dept. pediatrics Madigan Army Med. Ctr., Tacoma, Wash., 1987—; affiliated asst. prof. U. Health Scis., 1980-86; assoc. clin. prof. U. Wash., 1987—, U. Health Scis., 1986—, U. N.Mex., 1980-87, Tex. Tech. U., 1976-77; adj. assoc. prof. biol. scis. U. Tex., El Paso, 1985-87; speaker, presenter in field. Contbr. numerous articles to profl. jours. Nephrology minifellow U. Tex., 1979; recipient Robert Skelton award, 1972. Fellow Am. Acad. Pediatrics; mem. Alpha Omega Alpha, Mu Delta, Sigma Xi.

WEISKOPF, WENDY LOUISE, commercial interior designer; b. Wheatrige, Colo., July 20, 1964; d. Henry J. and Carolyn M. (Tice) S. BS, Colo. State U., 1986. Designer Design Services for AIRCOA, Englewood, Colo., 1986-87; Designer RNL Design, Denver, 1987—. Mem. Am. Soc. Interior Designers. Democrat. Methodist. Office: RNL Design 1225 17th St #1700 Denver CO 80202

WEISMAN, MARTIN DWAIN, broadcasting executive; b. Santa Monica, Calif., Sept. 18, 1958; s. Jack and Anna Jean (Hawkins) W. Grad., Beverly Hills High Sch., Calif., 1976. With Embasey Pictures Corp., Hollywood, Calif., 1981-82; account exec. World Northal/WW Entertainment, L.A., 1982, Worldvision Ent., Inc., Beverly Hills, 1982-85, 87-88; programming exec. Worldvision Ent., Hollywood, 1988—; v.p. Evergreen Prog., Inc., Beverly Hills, 1985-87; lectr. in field. With USCG Aux., 1988. Mem. Nat. Assn. TV Programming Execs., Ind. TV Broadcasters Assn. Jewish. Home: 2372B S Beverly Glen Los Angeles CA 90064 Office: Worldvision/Spelling Ent 9465 Wilshire Blvd Beverly Hills CA 90212

WEISMAN, MARTIN JEROME, manufacturing company executive; b. N.Y.C., Aug. 22, 1930; s. Lewis E. and Estelle (Scherer) W.; m. Sherrie Cohen, Jan. 27, 1952; children: Jane Dory, Andrea Sue, Amy Ellen. B in Chem. Engring., N.Y.U., 1951. Sr. chem. engr. Ideal Toy Corp., Hollis, N.Y., 1951-57; research chemist Chesebrough-Ponds, Stamford, Conn., 1957-62; mgr. nail products lab. Max Factor and Co., Hollywood, Calif., 1962-81; v.p., tech. dir. Sher-Mar Cosmetics div. Weisman Industries, Inc., Canoga Park, Calif., 1981—. Patentee in field. Mem. Soc. Cosmetic Chemists, Los Angeles Soc. Coatings Tech., Am. Chem. Soc. Office: Sher-Mar Cosmetics 8755 Remmet Ave Canoga Park CA 91304

WEISMAN, ROBERT EVANS, caterer; b. N.Y.C., Feb. 11, 1950; s. Arnold and Selma (Leinow) W.; m. Margaret Lavin, July 3, 1983; 1 child, Sarah Miriam. BA, U. Wis., 1972. Gen. mgr. Medieval Manor, Boston, 1976-80, Ruppert's Restaurant, N.Y.C., 1980-82; owner Bowen Weisman, Los Angeles, 1983—. Office: Bowen Weisman 1105 S LaBrea Ave Los Angeles CA 90019

WEISMULLER, THOMAS PAUL, chemist; b. Pomona, Calif., Feb. 26, 1949; s. Oliver Thomas and Jean Katherine (Nolan) W.; m. Penny Christine Klein, Oct. 17, 1975; children: Nathan Thomas, Sarah Elizabeth. AA, Fullerton Coll., 1969; BA, Calif. State U., Fullerton, 1971, MS, 1977. Cert. secondary tchr. Analytical chemist Rockwell Internat., Anaheim, Calif., 1974-77, sr. staff scientist, 1980—; tech. staff scientist Hughes Aircraft Co., Fullerton, 1978-79; sr. mfg. devel. engr. Gen. Dynamics Corp., Pomona, 1979-80. Contbr. articles to profl. jours.; multiple patentee in field. Recipient Service award Rockwell Internat., 1984. Mem. Am. Chem. Soc., The Metall. Soc., U.S. Karate Assn. (cert. master instr.). Democrat. Mormon. Office: Rockwell Internat PO Box 4192 MZ BD 14 Anaheim CA 92803-4192

WEISS, CHARLES FREDERICK, holding company executive; b. Los Angeles, Nov. 9, 1939; s. Walter E. and Marie E. Weiss; m. Katherine Joyce Weiss, June 26, 1959; children: Bryan Scott, Michael Craig. B.S., Calif. State U., Los Angeles, 1963; M.B.A., U. So. Calif., 1965. Vice pres. Great Western Savs. & Loan Assn., Los Angeles, 1963-69; corp. dir. orgn. devel. Rep. Corp., Los Angeles, 1969-72; corp. v.p. Beverly Hills Bancorp, Calif., 1972-75, 20th Century Fox Film Corp., Los Angeles, 1975-82; acting chief exec. officer Sta. KCET-TV, Los Angeles, 1982-83; exec. Pacific Enterprises, Los Angeles, 1984—. Bd. dirs., exec. com. Calif. Found. on Employment and Disability; bd. dirs. Hollywood Presbyn. Hosp. Found. Clubs: Los Angeles Turf, Jonathan, Los Angeles, City Club on Bunker Hill. Home: 1542 Moreno Dr Glendale CA 91207 Office: Pacific Enterprises 801 S Grand Ave Los Angeles CA 90017

WEISS, DAVID JOHN, film and television producer, director, writer; b. Kansas City, Mo., Feb. 22, 1941; s. Ned and Rose (Bernstein) W.; m. Margaret Nikoloric, June 10, 1970 (div. 1975). BA, U. Mo., Kansas City, 1963; MA, U. Mo., 1966. Writer, producer Westinghouse Broadcasting, N.Y.C., 1967-68; producer, dir. Group W TV, San Francisco, 1968-69; free-lance writer San Francisco, Los Angeles, 1970-73; writer, producer KCET-TV, Los Angeles, 1973-75; free-lance writer, producer, dir. Los Angeles, 1978-79; news editor Apparel News Group, Los Angeles, 1981-82; exec. producer Redken Labs., Canoga Park, Calif., 1982-85; pres. Beachfront Prodns., Marina Del Rey, Calif., 1985—; cons. indsl., informational and mktg. communications. Writer, producer, dir. (TV special) Gene Autry: American Hero, 1980 (nominated for Emmy award); contbr. articles to profl. jours. Active Mus. Contemporary Art, Los Angeles. Pilot/planning grantee Nat. Endowment Humanities, Los Angeles, 1974. Mem. Assn. Free-lance Profls. (charter), Assn. Visual Communicators. Democrat. Jewish. Home and Office: 14 Outrigger St Marina Del Rey CA 90292

WEISS, HERBERT KLEMM, aeronautical engineer; b. Lawrence, Mass., June 22, 1917; s. Herbert Julius and Louise (Klemm) W.; m. Ethel Celesta Gitner, May 14, 1945; children—Janet Elaine, Jack Klemm (dec.). B.S., MIT, 1937, M.S., 1938. Engr. U.S. Army Arty. Bds., Ft. Monroe, Va, 1938-46; engr. U.S. Army Arty. Bds., Camp Davis, N.C., 1938-46, Ft. Bliss, Tex., 1938-46; chief WPN Systems Lab., Ballistic Research Labs., Aberdeen Proving Grounds, Md, 1946-53; chief WPN systems analysis dept. Northrop Aircraft Corp., 1953-58; mgr. advanced systems devel. mil. systems planning aeronutronic div. Ford Motor Co., Newport Beach, Calif., 1958-61; group dir., plans devel. and analysis Aerospace Corp., El Segundo, Calif., 1961-65; sr. scientist Litton Industries, Van Nuys, Calif., 1965-82; cons. mil. systems analysis 1982—; Mem. Sci. Adb. Bd. USAF, 1959-63, sci. adv. commn. Army Ball Research Labs., 1973-77; advisor Pres.'s Commn. Law Enforcement and Adminstrn. Justice, 1966; cons. Office Dir. Def., Research and Engring., 1954-64. Contbr. articles to profl. jours. Patentee in field. Recipient Commendation for meritorious civilian service USAF, 1964. Fellow AAAS, Am. Inst. Aeros. and Astronautics (assoc.); mem. Ops. Research Soc. Am., IEEE, Inst. Mgmt. Scis. Republican. Presbyterian. Club: Cosmos. Home: PO Box 2668 Palos Verdes Peninsula CA 90274

WEISS, IRA LEE, corporate financial officer, consultant; b. Apr. 1, 1957; s. Samuel H. and Thelma L. (Rosenthal) W.; m. Lisa A. Salaun, Sept. 26, 1987. Student, San Diego State U., 1975-79. Lab. mgr. Scripps Clinic and Rsch. Fedn., La Jolla, Calif., 1978-86; v.p. fin. Engreval Ltd., La Jolla, 1984-85, pres., chief exec. officer, 1985—. Repubican. Jewish. Office: Engreval Ltd PO Box 8413 La Jolla CA 92038

WEISS, LAWRENCE ROBERT, investment banking executive; b. Pasadena, Mar. 8, 1937; s. Joseph B. and Elsie (Shaw) W.; BS in Applied Physics, UCLA, 1959; MS in Mgmt. Sci., U. So. Calif., 1974; m. Elaine Saxon, June 23, 1963; children: Jeffrey Arthur, Jason Ashley. Electronic systems engr., N.Am. Aviation, Inc., L.A., 1960-62, Litton Systems, Inc., 1962-63; group head Hughes Aircraft Co., Culver City, Calif., 1963-67, group head, sales rep., br. sales mgr., 1967-70; with Sci. Data Systems, Systems Engring. Labs., Gen. Automation, Inc., Interdata Corp., Applied Digital Data Systems, Inc., 1973-80; co-founder, chmn., pres. Health-tronics Labs. Inc., Rochester, N.Y., 1970-72, Cal-trend Personality Systems, Inc., L.A., 1973-85; co-founder, chmn. bd., v.p. Evolution Computer Systems Corp., (name changed to Evolution Techs., Inc. 1981), Irvine, Calif., 1980-82; co-founder, chmn., pres. Capital Tech. Group Inc., Irvine, 1981-83; co-founder, pres. Tek-Net Funding Corp., Irvine, 1984-85; fin. cons. Shearson Lehman Bros., Inc., Orange, Calif., 1985-86; v.p. investments Drexel Burnham Lambert Inc., Newport Beach, Calif., 1986-87; chmn. Covest Holdings, Inc., 1987-88; v.p. Wedbush-Morgan Securities, Inc., Newport Beach, 1988-89; pres. Pub. Equities Planning Corp., 1989—. Mem. Planetary Soc., U.S. Naval Inst., Am. Def. Preparedness Assn., Mensa. Home: 22706 Islamare Ln El Toro CA 92630 Office: 18552 MacArthur Blvd Ste 410 Irvine CA 92715

WEISS, MARTIN HARVEY, neurosurgeon, educator; b. Newark, Feb. 2, 1939; s. Max and Rae W.; m. R. Debora Rosenthal, Aug. 20, 1961; children: Brad, Jessica, Elisabeth. A.B. magna cum laude, Dartmouth Coll., 1960, B.M.S., 1961; M.D., Cornell U., 1963. Diplomate Am. Bd. Neurol. Surgery (bd. dirs. 1983-89, vice chmn. 1987-88, chmn. 1988-89). Intern Univ. Hosps., Cleve., 1963-64; resident in neurosurgery Univ. Hosps., 1966-70; sr. instr. to asst. prof. neurosurgery Case Western Res. U., 1970-73; asso. prof. neurosurgery U. So. Calif., 1973-76, prof., 1976-78, prof., chmn. dept., 1978—; chmn. neurology B study sect. NIH; mem. Residency Rev. Com. for Neurosurgery, 1989—. Author: Pituitary Diseases, 1980; editorial bd.: Neurosurgery, 1979-84, Neurol. Research, 1980—; editor in chief: Clin. Neurosurgery, 1980-83; assoc. editor: Bull. Los Angeles Neurol. Socs, 1976-81, Jour. Clin. Neurosci., 1981—; mem. editorial bd. Jour. Neurosurgery, 1987—; contbr. articles sci. jours. Served to capt. USAR, 1964-66. Decorated; Army Commendation Medal; NIH spl. fellow in neurosurgery, 1969-70. Mem. Soc. Neurol. Surgeons, Am. Coll. Surgeons (adv. council neurosurgery 1985—), Neurosurg. Soc. Am., Am. Acad. Neurol. Surgery (exec. com. 1988-89), Research Soc. Neurol. Surgeons, Am. Assn. Neurol. Surgeons (bd. dirs. 1988—), Congress Neurol. Surgeons (v.p. 1982-83), Western Neurosurg. Soc., Neurosurg. Forum, So. Calif. Neurosurg. Soc. (pres. 1983-84), Phi Beta Kappa, Alpha Omega Alpha. Home: 357 Georgian Rd Flintridge CA 91011 Office: 1200 N State St Box 1931 Los Angeles CA 90033

WEISS, MAX TIBOR, aerospace company executive; b. Hajduananas, Hungary, Dec. 29, 1922; came to U.S., 1929, naturalized, 1936; s. Samuel and Anna (Hornstein) W.; m. Melitta Newman, June 28, 1953; children: Samuel Harvey, Herschel William, David Nathaniel, Deborah Beth. BEE, CCNY, 1943; MS, MIT, 1947, PhD, 1950. Rsch. assoc. MIT, 1946-50; mem. tech. staff Bell Tel. Labs., Holmdel, N.J., 1950-59; assoc. head applied physics lab. Hughes Aircraft Co., Culver City, Calif., 1959-60; dir. electronics rsch. lab. The Aerospace Corp., L.A., 1961-63; gen. mgr. labs. div. The Aerospace Corp., 1963-67, gen. mgr. electronics and optics div., 1968-78, v.p., gen. mgr. lab. ops., 1978-81, v.p. engring. group, 1981-86; v.p. tech. and electronic systen group Northrop Corp., L.A., 1986—; asst. mgr. engring. ops. TRW Systems, Redondo Beach, Calif., 1967-68. Contbr. articles to physics and electronics jours.; patentee in electronics and communications. With USNR, 1944-45. Fellow Am. Phys. Soc., IEEE, AIAA, AAAS; mem. Nat. Acad. Engring., Sigma Xi. Office: Northrop Corp 1840 Century Pk E Los Angeles CA 90067

WEISS, NORM A., minister of recreation and parks; b. Edmonton, Alta., Can., Dec. 23, 1935; m. Carol Weiss; 1 child, Jill. Grad. high sch., Edmonton. Zone mgr. for farm equipment manufacture, then market devel. oil and gas industry, then co-owner restaurant, real estate co., car wash-service station, sporting goods retail store; Minister of Parks and Recreation Province of Alta., Edmonton, 1986—; with Alta. Legislature, 1979—, bd. dirs. Northern Alta. Devel. Council, 1979-82, chmn., 1982-86. Past pres. Lac La Biche/Ft. McMurray Polit. Constituency Assn.; past v.p. Ft. McMurray Jaycees; former mem. Alberta Oil Sands Tech. and Research Authority; past adv. com. Northeastern Alberta Regional Commn.; bd. dirs. Edmonton Oil Barons Hockey Club, Alberta '85 Summer Games, Can.-Chinese Cultural Assn, Ft. McMurray Interpretive Centre, Keyano Coll. Found. Mem. Ft. McMurray Businessmen's Assn. (past bus. mgr.), Ft. McMurray C. of C., Kinsmen, Rotary (bd. dirs.), Muffaloose Trailblazers (hon.). Office: Alta Legislature, Legislature Bldg, Edmonton, AB Canada T5K 2B6

WEISS, PETER H., business consultant; b. N.Y.C., Oct. 12, 1956; s. Edward and Janis (Silbert) W. AB cum laude, Princeton U., 1979; MBA, Harvard U., 1984. Gen. mgr. Paprikas Weiss Importer, N.Y.C., 1979-80; fin. analyst Warburg Paribas Becker, N.Y.C., 1980-82; asst. to pres. Barnes Drill Co., Rockford, Ill., 1983-84; v.p. Trump Group, N.Y.C., 1984-86; pres. P. Weiss & Co., Inc., Seattle, 1986—, Call Carpet, Inc., Seattle, 1987—; bd. dirs. Gerbeaud, Inc., N.Y.C.; cons. Alatus Projects Corp., Vancouver, B.C., Can., 1987—. Mem. regional adv. bd. AntiDefamation League Pacific N.W. Office: P Weiss & Co 2917 1st Ave S Seattle WA 98134

WEISS, ROBERT CORYELL, investor; b. N.Y.C., Nov. 26, 1927; s. William I. Weiss and Rose Mary (Cone) Mearson; m. Gwynneth Faire Grobin, Oct. 24, 1954; 1 child, Sabrina. BA, NYU, 1949; LLB, Bklyn. Law Sch., 1951. Bar: N.Y. 1952. Investor. Home: 3111 Bel Air Dr #28A Las Vegas NV 89109

WEISS, ROBERT STEPHEN, medical manufacturing company financial executive; b. Honesdale, Pa., Oct. 25, 1946; s. Stephen John and Anna Blanche (Lescinski) W.; BS in Acctg. cum laude, U. Scranton, 1968; m. Marilyn Annette Chesick, Oct. 29, 1970; children: Christopher Robert, Kim Marie, Douglas Paul. CPA, N.Y. Supr., Peat, Marwick, Mitchell & Co., N.Y.C., 1971-76; asst. corp. controller Cooper Labs., Inc., Parsippany, N.J., 1977-78, v.p./corp. controller, Palo Alto, Calif., 1981-83; v.p., corp. controller The Cooper Cos., Inc. (formerly CooperVision, Inc.), Palo Alto, Calif., 1984— ; v.p. fin./controller CooperVision Pharms., Mountain View, Calif., 1979. Served with U.S. Army, 1969-70. Decorated Bronze Star with oak leaf cluster, Army Commendation medal. Mem. AICPA, N.Y. State Soc. CPAs. Home: 446 Arlington Ct Pleasanton CA 94566 Office: The Cooper Cos Inc 3145 Porter Dr Palo Alto CA 94304

WEISS, (PAUL) SHANDOR, naturopathic physician; b. Miami, Fla., Jan. 4, 1954; s. Arthur David and Gloria Gladys (Kronowitt) W.; m. Gaea L. Emaus, May 7, 1978; children: Danielle Madonia, Sophia Lhamo. BA, Hampshire Coll., Amherst, Mass., 1976; D of Naturopathy, Nat. Coll. Naturopathic Medicine, 1988; Cert. in Acupuncture, Oreg. Coll. Oriental Medicine, Portland, 1988. Adminstr. Berkeley (Calif.) Holistic Health Ctr., 1976-77; dir. Gathering Together Ctr. for Healing, Ashland, Oreg., 1977-80; intern Portland Naturopathic Clinic, 1986-88; dir. Arura Clinic of Natural Medicine, Ashland, 1989—. V.p. Yeshe Nyingpo Inc., Ashland, 1978-83. Mem. Oreg. Assn. Naturopathic Physicians, Oreg. Acupuncture Assn., Am. Assn. Naturopathic Physicians, Homeopathic Acad. Naturopathic Physicians. Democrat. Buddhist. Office: 238 E Main St Ste D Ashland OR 97520

WEISS, SIDNEY, musician. b. Chgo.; m. Jeanne Weiss. With Cleve. Orch.; concertmaster, Chgo. Symphony, 1968-72, Monte Carlo Philharm., 1973-79, Los Angeles Philharm. Orch., 1979. Office: Los Angeles Philharm Assn 135 N Grand Ave Los Angeles CA 90012 *

WEISS, STANLEY IRWIN, research and development executive; b. N.Y.C., Oct. 27, 1925; s. Maurice H. and Malvina (Toffler) W.; m. Catherine Jordan, Oct. 2, 1952; children: Ann, Audrey, Janet, Marion. B in Aero. Engring., Rensselaer Poly. Inst., 1945, MS, 1948; PhD, U. Ill., 1950; post-grad., Harvard Bus. Sch., 1969. Dynamicist, project engr. Goodyear Aerospace, Akron, Ohio, 1950-55; chief engr. Kawneer Corp., Niles, Mich., 1955-57; program mgr. mfg. and quality assurance mgmt., AGM-programs, v.p. engring., advanced programs and devel. space systems div. Lockheed Missiles and Space Co., Inc., Sunnyvale, Calif., 1957-78; dep. asst. sec. Dept. Energy, Washington, 1978-80; assoc. adminstrv. chief engr. NASA, Washington, 1980-83; corp. v.p. engring., v.p. rsch. and devel. Lockheed Corp., Burbank and Palo Alto, Calif., 1983—; lectr. Akron (Ohio) U., 1950-53; dir. Non-Ferrous Metals Rsch. Coun., Washington, 1973-78; exec. in residence U. Santa Clara (Calif.) Bus. Sch., 1976-78; chmn. engring. adv. bd. Rensselaer Poly. Inst., 1983—; mem. exec. com. adv. bd. Coll. Engring., U. Ill., Urbana, 1987—. Contbr. numerous articles to profl. jours. Lt. USN, 1943-47. Recipient Meritorius Exec. award Dept. Energy, Washington, 1980, D.S.M. NASA, 1983. Fellow AIAA; mem. World Affairs Coun., Commonwealth Club, Sigma Xi. Home: 13208 E Sunset Dr Los Altos Hills CA 94022 Office: Lockheed Missiles/Space Co R&D Div 3251 Hanover St Palo Alto CA 94304

WEISS, WILLIAM HANS, small business owner; b. Spokane, Wash., Feb. 25, 1952. BA in Human Svcs., Western Wash. U., 1977; MA in Psychology, Goddard Coll., 1980. Prin. Vocat. Mgmt. Resources, Redmond, Wash., 1980—; vocat. cons. various cities, Soc. Security Adminstrn. Roman Catholic. Office: Vocat Mgmt Resources PO Box 381 Redmond WA 98073

WEISSMAN, SUZANNE HEISLER, analytical chemist; b. The Dalles, Oreg., June 20, 1949; d. Donald Eugene and Roberta Myrth (Van Valkenburgh) Heisler; m. Steven Jay Weissman, May 29, 1976. BS, Oreg. State U., 1971; MS, U. Ill., 1973, PhD, 1975. Rsch. and teaching asst., then vis. asst. prof. U. Ill., Urbana, 1971-76; sr. scientist Lovelace ITRI, Albuquerque, 1976-80; mem. tech. staff Sandia Nat. Labs., Albuquerque, 1980-86, supr., 1986—. Mem. Soc. Applied Spectroscopy (chmn. 1983-84, 86-87), N.Mex. for Women in Sci. and Engring. (v.p. 1981-82), Am. Chem. Soc. Office: Div 1821 Sandia Nat Labs PO Box 5800 Albuquerque NM 87185

WEITZEL, ALBERT LEE, mechanical engineer; b. Long Beach, Calif., July 10, 1961; s. Edgar Richard Weitzel, Jr. and Della May (Morris) Clark. SB, MIT, 1984. Tech. supr. Hughes Aircraft Co., El Segundo, Calif., 1984-88; mech. engring cons. ISC Aerospace, Westlake Village, Calif., 1988; mech. project engr. ISC Aerospace, Westlake Village, 1989—. Mem. Campus Crusade for Christ, San Bernadino, Calif., 1983—, Prison Fellowship, L.A., 1988—. Recipient numerous grants and scholarships. Mem. AIAA. Republican. Presbyterian. Home: 909 Paseo Camarillo #788 Camarillo CA 93010

WEITZEL, JOHN QUINN, bishop; b. Chgo., May 10, 1928; s. Carl Joseph and Patricia (Quinn) W. BA, Maryknoll (N.Y.) Sem., 1951, M of Religious Edn., 1953; PMD, Harvard U. Ordained priest Roman Cath. Ch., 1955. With ednl. devel. Cath. Fgn. Mission Soc. of Am., Maryknoll, 1955-63, nat. dir. vocations for Maryknoll, dir. devel. dept. and info. services, 1963-72, mem. gen. council, 1972-78; asst. parish priest Cath. Ch., Western Samoa, 1979-81, pastor, vicar gen., 1981-86; consecrated bishop 1986; bishop Cath. Ch., Am. Samoa, 1986—. Office: Diocese of Samoa-Pago Pago Fatuoaiga PO Box 596 Pago Pago AS 96799 *

WELARATNA, SRI RAMYA, engineering company executive; b. Colombo, Sri Lanka, July 6, 1945; came to U.S., 1979; s. Dhanu Edimun and Lalitha (Rodrigo) W.; m. Usha Sripalee Bandaratilaka, June 19, 1971; children: Ruwan, Sumudu, Deepthi. BSc (with honors), U. Ceylon, Peradeniya, Sri Lanka, 1967; PhD, U. Bradford, Eng., 1975. Sr. applications engr. Hewlett Packard Co., Eng., 1976-79, Santa Clara, Calif., 1979-82; pres. Data Physics Corp., San Jose, Calif., 1984—; cons. signal processing, IBM, San Jose, 1982—. IEEE scholar, Bradford, Eng., 1973. Home: 767 Sunshine Dr Los Altos CA 94022 Office: Data Physics Corp 1210 S Bascom Ave #224 San Jose CA 95128

WELCH, BETTY LEONORA, accountant; b. Missoula, Mont., July 18, 1961; d. George Oliver and Betty June (Dolton) W. BBA, U. Mont., 1983. CPA, Mont. Staff acct. Ellis & Assocs., Boise, Idaho, 1984; acct. Glacier Electric Coop., Cut Bank, Mont., 1984-86, office mgr., 1986—; income tax cons. Mem. AICPA, Beta Gamma Sigma. Democrat. Roman Catholic. Avocations: skiing, sewing, reading, hunting. Office: Glacier Electric Coop Inc 410 E Main St Cut Bank MT 59427

WELCH, CLAUDE (RAYMOND), theology educator; b. Genoa City, Wis., Mar. 10, 1922; s. Virgil Cleon and Deone West (Grenelle) W.; m. Eloise Janette Turner, May 31, 1942 (div. 1970); children—Eric, Thomas, Claudia; m. Theodosia Montigel Blewett, Oct. 5, 1970 (dec. 1978); m. Joy Neuman, Oct. 30, 1982. BA summa cum laude, Upper Iowa U., 1942; postgrad., Garrett Theol. Sem., 1942-43; BD cum laude, Yale U., 1945, PhD, 1950; DD (hon.), Ch. Div. Sch. of Pacific, 1972, Jesuit Sch. Theology, 1982; LHD (hon.), U. Judaism, 1976. Ordained to ministry Meth. Ch., 1947. Instr. religion Princeton (N.J.) U., 1947-50, asst. prof., 1950-51, vis. prof., 1962; asst. prof. theology Yale U. Div. Sch., New Haven, 1951-54, assoc. prof., 1954-60; Berg prof. religious thought, chmn. dept. U. Pa., Phila., 1960-71, assoc. dean Coll. Arts and Scis., 1964-68, acting chmn. dept. philosophy, 1965-66; prof. hist. theology Grad. Theol. Union, Berkeley, Calif., 1971—, dean, 1971-87, pres., 1972-82; vis. prof. Garrett Theol. Sem., 1951, Pacific Sch. Religion, 1958, Hartford Sem. Found., 1958-59, Princeton Theol. Sem., 1962-63, U. Va., 1987; Fulbright sr. lectr. U. Mainz, Germany, 1968; Sprunt lectr. Union Theol. Sem., Richmond, Va., 1958; dir. study of grad. edn. in religion Am. Council Learned Socs., 1969-71; del. World Conf. on Faith and Order, 1963. Author: In This Name: the Doctrine of the Trinity in Contemporary Theology, 1952, (with John Dillenberger) Protestant Christianity, interpreted through its Development, 1954, 2d rev. edit., 1988, The Reality of the Church, 1958, Graduate Education in Religion: A Critical Appraisal, 1971, Religion in the Undergraduate Curriculum, 1972, Protestant Thought in the 19th Century, vol. 1, 1799-1870, 1972, vol. 2, 1870-1914, 1985; Editor, translator: God and Incarnation in Mid-19th Century German Theology (Thomasius, Dorner and Biedermann), 1965; Contbr. to publs. in field. Recipient decennial prize Bross Found., 1970; Guggenheim fellow, 1976; NEH research fellow, 1984, Fulbright research fellow, 1956-57. Mem. Am. Acad. Religion (pres. 1969-70), Council on Study of Religion (chmn. 1969-74, 1985—), Soc. for Values in Higher Edn. (pres. 1967-71), Am. Theol. Soc., Phi Beta Kappa. Home: 123 Fairlawn Dr Berkeley CA 94708

WELCH, FERN STEWART, magazine editor; b. Redford, Mo., Aug. 13, 1934; d. Elza L. and Ruby I. (Bounds) DeMente; m. John M. Stewart Jr., May 24, 1954; children—Joni Stewart Chanko, Susan Stewart Caldwell, John D.; m. 2d, Kenneth A. Welch, Apr. 25, 1981. A.A., Phoenix Coll., 1953; student Ariz. State U., 1954, Phoenix Coll., 1965, Bellevue Community Coll., 1967, Lake Washington Community Coll., 1968. Writer/reporter, columnist Sammamish Valley News, Redmond Wash., 1967-71; staff writer, asst. to pub. relations dir. First Nat. Bank Oreg., Portland, 1971-72; asst. pub. relations dir. The Ariz. Bank, Phoenix, 1972-73, pub. relations dir., 1973-77;

founder, prin. Fern Stewart and Assocs., Ltd., Phoenix, 1977-84; editorial dir. Metro Phoenix Mag., 1984; lectr. pub. relations. Bd. dirs. Central Ariz. chpt. ARC, 1976-82, mem. adv. bd., 1982-89; bd. dirs. Combined Met. Arts and Scis.; mem. Arizonans for Cultural Devel., Scottsdale Art Ctr. Assn., Valley Shakespeare Co. Recipient awards of merit and excellence Internat. Assn. Bus. Communicators, 1975-77. Mem. Ariz. Press Women, Women in Communications. Republican. Clubs: Phoenix Country, Plaza (Phoenix). Contbr. numerous articles to local and regional mags.

WELCH, GEORGE WALTER, III, corporate officer; b. Odgen, Utah, Mar. 29, 1958; s. George Walter and Marilyn (Carpenter) W.; m. Kelly June Fuller, Mar. 18, 1982; children: Nathan George, Elizabeth June. BS, U. Utah, 1982; MBA, DePaul U., 1986. Ski instr. Red Lodge (Mont.) Mountain, 1976-78; acct. exec. U.S. Ski Team, Park City, Utah, 1982-84; comml. loan analyst Exchange Nat. Bank of Chgo., 1985-86; corp. officer Valley Nat. Bank of Ariz., Phoenix, 1986—; assoc. Robert Morris Assocs. Mem. Toastmasters. Home: 8543 E Montecito Scottsdale AZ 85251 Office: Valley Nat Bank of Ariz 3636 N Central Ave Phoenix AZ 85012

WELCH, KEEFER D., hotelier; b. Topeka, Kans., Feb. 11, 1945; s. William Dee and Etta Marie (Heisler) W.; m. Elizabeth Louise Gustine, Aug. 5, 1973; (div. Aug., 1984); children: Charles, Michael; m. Patricia Ann Youngblood, Sept. 29, 1984. BS, U.S. Naval Acad., 1967. Commd. ensign USN, 1968, advanced through grades to lt. commdr., resigned, 1978, carrier based fighter pilot, 1968-78; sales mgr. Westin Hotels, L.A., 1978-80; dir. sales Westin Hotels, Washington, 1980-83; exec. v.p. and gen. mgr. Snowmass (Colo.) Resort Assn., 1983-86; gen. mgr., project devel. officer Grand Champion Resorts, Indian Wells, Calif., 1986-87; v.p. dir. mktg. Sheraton Corp., L.A., 1987—; instr. Navy Fighter Weapons Sch., San Diego, 1974-75; test controller ameval-aceval fighter weapons test, Las Vegas, 1977-78. Mem. Airport Adv. Bd., Aspen, Colo., 1984-86. Decorated Air Medals, U.S. Navy, 1970-74, Viet Nam, Legion of Merit U.S. Navy, 1978; named Sales Mgr. of the Year, Sales Mgmt. Execs., L.A., 1979; recipient Chmns. award, U.S. C. of C., Washington, 1984. Mem. Am. Soc. Assn. Execs. (chmn. exhibitor adv. coun. 1982), Profl. Conv. Mgmt. Assn., Rotary. Republican. Office: The Sheraton Corp 345 S Figueroa Los Angeles CA 90071

WELCH, LLOYD RICHARD, engineering educator, consultant; b. Detroit, Sept. 28, 1927; s. Richard C. and Helen (Felt) W.; m. Irene Althea Main, Sept. 12, 1953; children—Pamela Irene Welch Towery, Melinda Ann, Diana Lia Welch Worthington. B.S. in Math., U. Ill., 1951; Ph.D. in Math., Calif. Inst. Tech., 1958. Mathematician NASA-Jet Propulsion Lab., Pasadena, Calif., 1956-59; staff mathematician Inst. Def. Analyses, Princeton, N.J., 1959-65; prof. elec. engring. U. So. Calif., Los Angeles, 1965—; cons. in field. Contbr. articles to profl. jours. Served with USN, 1945-49, 51-52. Fellow IEEE; mem. Nat. Acad. Engring., Am. Math. Soc., Math. Assn. Am., Soc. for Indsl. and Applied Math., Phi Beta Kappa, Sigma Xi, Phi Kappa Phi, Pi Mu Epsilon, Eta Kappa Nu. Office: U So Calif Dept Elec Engring Powell Hall University Pk Los Angeles CA 90089

WELCH, LUCILLE, owner rental agency; b. Chgo., Feb. 7, 1925; d. David L. Cooper and Sarah (Bower) Polacek; m. Joseph Preston Welch, June 5, 1946; children: Crystal Diamond, Carol Cress, Gale, JoAnne. Clk. U.S. Govt., Chgo., 1943-46; bookkeeper Welch's Union Service Sta., Flagstaff, Ariz., 1946-58, Flagstaff Radio & T.V., 1958-61; sec. Ariz. State Hwy. Dept., Flagstaff, 1961-66; legal sec. John H. Grace, Atty., Flagstaff, 1966-67; steno sec. Fed. Govt. Navajo Army Dept., 1967-71; owner Welch Rentals, Flagstaff, 1969—. Jewish-Mormon. Home and Office: Welch Rentals 4200 Country Club Dr Flagstaff AZ 86004

WELCH, ROBERT GIBSON, steel industry consultant; b. Kewanee, Ill., July 9, 1915; s. Thomas John and Mabel Emily (Bunton) W.; m. Helen Taylor, Mar. 23, 1940; children—Sherry, Wendy, Taylor. A.B., Stanford, 1937. With Dun & Bradstreet, Inc., 1937-42; asst. to treas. Henry J. Kaiser Co., 1942-45; asst. to v.p., gen. mgr. Permanente Cement Co., 1945-46, Permanente Metals Corp., 1946; mgr. distbn. Kaiser Aluminum & Chem. Corp., 1947-54; exec. sec. Steel Service Center Inst. (formerly Am. Steel Warehouse Assn.), 1954-57, exec. v.p., 1957-62, pres., 1962-80, vice chmn., 1981, cons., 1981—; owner Welch Research Internat.; internat. mktg. cons.; lectr. indsl. distbn., trade assn. mgmt., econs. of steel industry; mem. various govt. adv. coms.; dir. Pitt-Des Moines Corp., Pitts. Author numerous articles. Bd. dirs. Distbn. Research Edn. Found.; trustee Freedom Found., Valley Forge, Pa. Mem. Am. Iron and Steel Inst., Am. Soc. Assn. Execs. (cert. assn. exec., past mem. exec. com., Key award 1970, internat. com.), Am. Soc. Assn. Execs. Found. (past chmn.), Nat. Assn. Wholesale Distbrs. (past mem. exec. com.), U.S. C. of C., Citizens Choice Tax Commn., Cleve. Mus. Art, Insts. Orgn. Mgmt. (former chmn. bd. regents, exec. com.), Cleve. Soc. Contemporary Art, Mus. Modern Art (N.Y.C.), Phi Gamma Delta. Clubs: Chicago (Chgo.); Mid Ocean (Bermuda); Metropolitan (N.Y.C.); Garden of Gods (Colorado Springs); Mayfield, Union (Cleve.); Duquesne (Pitts.); Metropolitan (Washington); LaQuinta Hotel Golf (Calif.). Home: PO Box 630 La Quinta CA 92253 also: 50057 Calle Oaxaca PO Box 630 La Quinta CA 92253

WELCH, WILLIAM FRANCIS, mining engr.; b. Monarch, Wyo., Mar. 12, 1909; s. Frank and Mary Ellen (Scullen) W.; student Regis Coll., Denver, 1928-29; Engring. degree in metallurgy Colo. Sch. Mines, 1933; m. Lorene Elizabeth Wondra, Dec. 31, 1952. Mining engr. Sheridan-Wyo. Coal Co., Monarch, 1933-40; ranching and pvt. engring. practice, Acme, Wyo., 1940-48; supt. Welch Coal Co., Sheridan, 1948—, dir., 1948—; pres. Tongue River Ditch Co., 1951—; bd. dirs. Rocky Mountain Fed. Savs. and Loan, Steel Creek Producers, Ranchester State Bank, Capital Savs.; v.p. Wymo Oil Co. Treas. Sch. Dist. 24, 1955-58; pres., 1958-65; treas. Tongue River Soil Conservation Dist., 1949-60. Bd. dirs. Whitney Benefits Ednl. Found., 1964-69; pres. bd. Tongue River Fire Dist., 1954-78; mem. pres.'s council Regis Coll., Denver, Colo. Sch. Mines, Golden; bd. dirs. Billings (Mont.) Deaconess Hosp. Found. Life mem. Nat. Cowboy Hall of Fame; Paul Harris fellow; William F. Welch Mining Ctr. at Sheridan Coll. named for him; Welch Regional Heart Ctr., Billings Deaconess Hosp. named for him. Mem. Wyo. Mining Assn., Wyo. Stockgrowers, Wyo. Sch. Trustees Assn. AIME, Wyo. Water Resources Assn., Rocky Mountain Coal Mining Inst., Soc. Mining Engrs., Alpha Tau Omega, Theta Tau. Clubs: Elks, Rotary. Roman Catholic. Address: 155 Scott Dr Sheridan WY 82801

WELD, GERTRUDE KATHERINE, sales executive; b. Somerville, Mass., Aug. 30, 1911; d. Joseph and Jessie (Gray) McElroy; m. Dillwyn Parrish, Oct. 3, 1927 (div. 1935); m. John Weld, Feb. 12, 1937. Student, Ecole Superieure de Jeunes Filles Vevey, Switzerland, 1926-27. Actress United Artists, Samuel Goldwyn, Columbia, MGM, Warners, Hollywood, Calif., 1932-36; newspaper mgr., co-pub. Laguna Beach (Calif.) Post, 1950-57; real estate salesperson Harbor Investment Co., Newport Beach, Calif., 1963, Good Real Estate, Laguna Beach, 1963-68; co-owner Adventure Travel, Laguna Beach, 1968-75; real estate salesperson Pauma Valley (Calif.) Realty, 1980—. Life mem. Aux./Silver and Gold Chpt. S. Coast Med. Ctr., So. Laguna, Calif., 1974. Named Hon. Col. Am. Legion, 1934, Hon. Col., Ky., 1934. Mem. Designing Woman Art Inst. of So. Calif., Pauma Valley Country Club (pres. Women's Assn.). Home: 23800 Hillhurst Dr Laguna Niguel CA 92677

WELD, ROGER BOWEN, clergyman; b. Greenfield, Mass., Dec. 1, 1953; s. Wayland Mauney and Luvycie (Bowen) W.; m. Patricia Ann Kaminski, June 7, 1978 (div. 1979). Student, U. Nev.-Reno, 1983-85. Ordained to ministry, Internat. Community of Christ Ch. of Second Advent, 1977. Adminstrv. staff Internat. Community of Christ Ch. of Second Advent, Reno, 1977—, exec. officer dept. canon law, 1985—, exec. officer advocates for religious rights and freedoms, 1985—, exec. officer speakers bur., 1985—, exec. officer office pub. info., 1986—, mgr. Jamilian Univ. Press, 1987—, dir. advt. prodns., 1988—. Author: Twelve Generations of the Family of Weld: Edmund to Wayland Mauney, 1986. Staff sgt. USAF, 1971-75. Mem. Andean Explorers Found. and Ocean Sailing Club (exec. sec. 1988—). Republican. Office: Internat Community Christ 643 Ralston St Reno NV 89503

WELDON, DORIS MAY, former computer programmer; b. Lincoln, Nebr., May 18, 1925; d. Marcus Dunlap and Pauline Mayham (Bancroft) W. BA, U. Nebr., 1947; MS in Mgmt., Am. U., 1978. Clk., typist, stenographer various cos., Lincoln and Denver, 1944-52; clk., typist, stenographer U.S. Army, Japan, 1952-54, London and Heidelberg, Fed. Republic Germany, 1954-59; sec., stenographer U.S. Army, Arlington, Va., 1966-70; computer programmer U.S. Pentagon, Arlington, Va., 1970-73; sec., stenographer, bilingual sec. Office of U.S. Army Attache, Am. Embassy, Australia and Republic of Panama, 1959-64; stenographer Conf. Am. Armies, 1964; computer programmer CSC, Washington, 1973-78, ret., 1978. Mem. AAUW (editor bull.), AARP, Nat. Assn. Ret. Fed. Employees, Sun City Geneal. Soc., Sun City Photo Club and Workshop (sec.), Spanish Club, French Club. Home: 10741 Wedgewood Dr Sun City AZ 85351

WELKER, JAROLD LAVERNE, publisher; b. Mesa, Ariz., June 17, 1952; s. LaVerne E. and Helen (McDaniel) W.; m. Theresa Anne Negrette, Jan. 2, 1981; children: Genevieve, Lindsey, Daniel. BA in History, Ariz. State U., 1976. Courier Plan Service of Ariz., Phoenix, 1971-74, printer, 1974-78; missionary LDS Ch., Tex. and Idaho, 1978-80; printer Constrn. Week, Phoenix, 1980-82, mng. editor, 1982-85; gen. mgr. Contrn. News West, Phoenix, 1985-88, pub., 1988—. Mem. Rep. Precinct Com., Phoenix, 1988. Home: 1922 N 45th St Phoenix AZ 85008 Office: Contrn News West 2050 E University Dr Phoenix AZ 85034

WELLER, GUNTER ERNST, geophysics educator; b. Haifa, June 14, 1934; came to U.S., 1968; s. Erich and Nella (Lange) W.; m. Sigrid Beilharz, Apr. 11, 1963; children: Yvette, Kara, Britta. BS, U. Melbourne, Australia, 1962, MS, 1964, PhD, 1968. Meteorologist Bur. Meteorology, Melbourne, 1959-61; glaciologist Australian Antarctic Exps., 1964-67; from asst. prof. to assoc. prof. geophysics Geophys. Inst., U. Alaska, Fairbanks, 1968-72, prof., 1973—, dep. dir., 1984-86; project mgr. NASA-UAF Alaska SAR Facility, Fairbanks, 1986—; program mgr. NSF, Washington, 1972-74; pres. Internat. Commn. Polar Meteorology, 1980-83; chmn. polar research bd. Nat. Acad. Scis., 1985—, Global Change Steering Com. Sci. Com. on Antarctic Rsch., 1988—. Contbr. numerous articles to profl. jours. Recipient Polar medal Govt. Australia, 1969; Mt. Weller named in his honor by Govt. Australia, Antarctica; Weller Bank named in his honor by U.S. Govt., Arctic. Fellow Arctic Inst. N.Am.; mem. Internat. Glaciological Soc., Am. Meteorol. Soc. (chmn. polar meteorology com. 1980-83), Am. Geophys. Union, AAAS. Home: Box 81024 Fairbanks AK 99708 Office: U Alaska Geophys Inst Fairbanks AK 99775-0800

WELLES, MELINDA FASSETT, artist, educator; b. Palo Alto, Calif., Jan. 4, 1943; d. George Edward and Barbara Helena (Todd) W.; m. Robert Joseph Sbordone, June 30, 1972 (div. Aug. 1977). Student fine arts San Francisco Inst. Art, 1959-60, U. Oreg., 1960-62; BA in Fine Arts, UCLA, 1964, MA in Spl. Edn., 1971, PhD in Ednl. Psychology, 1976; student fine arts and illustration Art Ctr. Coll. Design, 1977-80. Cert. ednl. psychologist, Calif. Asst. prof. Calif. State U., Northridge, 1979-82; Pepperdine U., L.A., 1979-82; assoc. prof. curriculum, teaching and spl. edn. U. So. Calif., L.A., 1980—; mem. acad. faculty Pasadena City Coll., 1973-79, Art Ctr. Coll. Design, 1978—, Otis Art Inst. of Parsons Sch. Design, L.A., 1986—, UCLA Extension, 1980-84, Coll. Devel. Studies, L.A., 1978-87, El Camino Community Coll., Redondo Beach, Calif., 1982-86; cons. spl. edn.; pub. adminstrn. analyst UCLA Spl. Edn. Rsch. Program, 1973-76; exec. dir. Atwater Park Ctr. Disabled Children, L.A., 1976-78; coord. Pacific Oaks Coll. in svc. programs for L.A. Unified Schs., Pasadena, 1978-81. Author: Calif. Dept. Edn. Tech. Reports, 1972-76; editor: Teaching Special Students in the Mainstream, 1981; group shows include: San Francisco Inst. Art, 1960, U. Hawaii, 1978, Barnsdall Gallery, Los Angeles, 1979, 80; represented in various pvt. collections. HEW fellow, 1971-72; grantee Calif. Dept. Edn., 1975-76, Calif. Dept. Health, 1978. Mem. Calif. Assn. Neurologically Handicapped Children, Am. Council Learning Disabilities, Clearing House for Info. on Learning Disabilities, Calif. Scholarship Fedn. (life), Alpha Chi Omega. Democrat. Office: 700 Levering Ave 1 Los Angeles CA 90024

WELLMAN, ROBIN ELIZABETH, nurse; b. Washington, July 21, 1945; d. Charles Newton and Margaret Jane (Seiple) Graham; m. Dana Richard Wellman, Jan. 6, 1968; children: Christopher, Jeffrey, Sarah. BS in Nursing, Duke U., 1967; MA in Psychology, Columbia Pacific U., 1986; Master of Nutripathy, Am. Coll. Nutripathy, Scottsdale, Ariz., 1988, postgrad., 1989-. RN. Staff nurse transplant team Colo. U. Hosp., Denver, 1968-70; staff nurse coronary intensive care St. Joseph's Hosp., Denver, 1971; staff nurse Ft. Logan Mental Health Ctr., Englewood, Colo., 1971-73; pvt. practice phychiatric-holistic nursing Longmont, Colo., 1973—; co-founder, Health Works Holistic Clinic Longmont, 1988, Counselling and Mediation Ctr., 1987. Bd. dirs. Longmont Acad. for Religious Studies, United Ch. of Christ. Mem. AAUW, Peoples Med. Soc., Union of Concerned Scientists, Colo. Nurses Assn., Am. Holistic Nurses Assn., Greenpeace. Democrat. Home: 1729 Danbury Dr Longmont CO 80501 Office: Healthworks Holistic Clinic 2350 17th Ave Longmont CA 80501

WELLS, CECIL HAROLD, JR., consulting engineer; b. San Mateo, Calif., Apr. 21, 1927; s. Cecil H. and Bertha (Teeter) W.; m. Elizabeth Anne O'Leary (dec.); children—Cecilia E. A., Timothy; m. Christina Maria Poelzl; children—Kristy-Sue, Jeff-Dean. Student, Menlo Coll., 1948, San Jose State Coll., 1948, U. Calif., 1949, 52; BCE, U. Santa Clara, 1951, U. Wis., 1980. Registered profl. engr., Calif., Alaska, Ariz., Colo., Mont., Nev., Oreg., Tex., Utah, Wash. Engr. Hall & Pregnoff, San Francisco, 1951-56; engr. Graham Hayes, San Francisco, 1956-58; cons. engr. on bldgs. and structures Cecil H. Wells, Jr. & Assocs., San Mateo, 1953—; pres. 20th Ave. Catering Corp., 1971-72, 2031 Pioneer Ct. Corp., 1958-70; tchr. engring. Menlo Coll., 1948-62; lectr. lateral design of bldgs. Stanford U., 1956-61. Author: Structural Engineering Design for Architects and Design of Buildings for Earthquakes and Wind. Mem. San Mateo County Regional Planning Bd., pres., 1964-65; mem. San Francisco, San Mateo, Santa Clara Tri County Planning Bd., pres., 1959-60; chmn. Elks Charity, 1964-65; mem. Calif. Bay Conservation and Devel. Commn., 1965-67; bd. dirs. Pvt. Fin. Service, Corp., 1988—; mem. Internat. Conf. World Planners, Mexico City, 1964; commr. San Mateo City Planning, 1956-67, chmn., 1958-59, 61-62, 64-67; mem. San Mateo City Govtl. Efficiency Commn., chmn. 1970-72; engr. San Mateo County Harbor Dist., 1969-83; active Boy Scouts Am., mem. exec. bd. county, 1969—, county v.p., exec. bd., 1972-75, chmn. Explorers, 1969-74; pres. Menlo Alumni Council, 1967-68; mem. men's adv. com. LWV, 1970-71, 73-74; trustee Drew Sch., 1972-73; bd. dirs. Purissima Mut. Water Dist., 1968-71, San Mateo County Devel. Assn., 1964—, San Mateo County Growth Policy Council, 1982—. Served with Submarine Service, USNR, World War II. Named Citizen of Day, Sta. KABL, 1970, 74; recipient 1st place award in apt. design City of Fremont Environ. Design Com., 1973, Silver Beaver award Boy Scouts Am., 1975; Paul Harris fellow Rotary Internat., 1980. Fellow ASCE; mem. ASTM, Structural Engring. Assn. Calif. (sec. 1954-58), Seismol. Soc. Am., Am. Concrete Inst., San Mateo C. of C. (bd. dirs. 1965—, pres. 1969-72), Nat. Soc. Profl. Engrs., Am. Soc. Mil. Engrs., Am. Inst. Timber Constrn., Prestressed Concrete Inst., Nat. Rifle Assn., San Mateo County Hist. Soc. Club: Peninsula Golf and Country. Lodges: Rotary (pres. 1972-73), Elks (exalted ruler 1966-67, trustee 1967-72, chmn. 1971-72). Office: 2031 Pioneer Ct Ste 12 San Mateo CA 94403

WELLS, DONNA FRANCES, distribution company executive; b. Lima, Ohio, Dec. 19, 1948; d. Arthur Robert and Frances Lucille (Knudtson) W.; m. Darrell Donald Erickson, Nov. 26, 1980. Cert., Parks Bus. Sch., 1972; student, Sheridan Coll., 1984—. Dir. purchasing Wolff Distbg., Gillette, Wyo., 1973—. Mem. Nat. Assn. Purchasing Mgmt., Nat. Assn. of Female Execs., Gillette Racing Assn. (aux. v.p. 1986—), VFW Aux., Am. Legion Aux. Home: 105 Sequoia Gillette WY 82716

WELLS, FRANK G., lawyer, film studio executive; b. Mar. 4, 1932. BA summa cum laude, Pomona Coll., 1953; MA in Law, Oxford (Eng.) U., 1955; LLB, Stanford U., 1959. Former vice chmn. Warner Bros. Inc.; ptnr. Gang Tyre & Brown, 1962-69; pres., chief operating officer Walt Disney Co., Burbank, Calif., 1984—. Co-author: Seven Summits. Bd. trustees Pomona Coll., Nat. History Mus., Sundance Inst.; bd. overseers for RAND/UCLA Ctr. Study of Soviet Behavior; mem. svcs. policy adv. com. U.S. Trade Regulation. 1st lt. U.S. Army, 1955-57. Rhodes scholar, 1955. Mem. ABA, State Bar Calif., L.A. County Bar Assn., Explorer's Club, Phi Beta Kappa. Office: The Walt Disney Co 500 S Buena Vista St Burbank CA 91521

WELLS, JOHN MARCUM, producer, writer; b. Alexandria, Va., May 28, 1956; s. Llewellyn Wallace Jr. and Marjorie Elizabeth (Risberg) W.; m. Belinda Casas, Dec. 30, 1978. BFA in Drama, Carnegie-Mellon U., 1979; MFA in Cinema, U. So. Calif., 1982. Founder, artistic dir. Pitts. New Playwrights Festival, 1978-79; asst. to v.p. mktg. Paramount Pictures Corp., 1981-82; theatrical producer various plays, Los Angeles, 1982-85; producer, writer Just In Time Warner Bros. TV, Los Angeles, 1987; producer, writer China Beach Warner Bros. TV, 1988; producer Nice Girls Don't Explode New World Pictures, Los Angeles, 1986-87; suprg. producer, creater Roughhouse, Los Angeles, 1988. Producer: (plays) Balm In Gilead, She Also Dances, Battery, Judgement, Ground Zero, Steaming, Femme Fatale, Tanzi. Assoc. producer nat. Dem. fundraising events, Los Angeles, 1984, Carnegie-Mellon U. Endowment Drive, Pitts., 1986. Recipient Los Angeles Drama Critics Circle award, 1982, Los Angeles Weekly award, Drama-Logue mag. award, 1985; grantee Triseme Corp., 1982. Mem. Writers Guild Am., Nat. Acad. TV Arts and Scis., Carnegie-Mellon U. West Coast Alumni Assn. (bd. dirs. 1982—, pres. 1986—). Democrat. Episcopalian. Office: Warner Bros Bldg 3-A 4000 Warners Blvd #2 Burbank CA 91522

WELLS, MERLE WILLIAM, historian, state archivist; b. Lethbridge, Alta., Can., Dec. 1, 1918; s. Norman Danby and Minnie Muir (Huckett) W.; student Boise Jr. Coll., 1937-39; A.B., Coll. Idaho, 1941, L.H.D. (hon.), 1981; M.A., U. Calif., 1947, Ph.D., 1950. Instr. history Coll. Idaho, Caldwell, 1942-46; assoc. prof. history Alliance Coll., Cambridge Springs, Pa., 1950-56, 58, dean students, 1955-56; cons. historian Idaho Hist. Soc., Boise, 1956-58, historian and archivist, 1959—; hist. preservation officer, archivist State of Idaho, Boise, 1968-86. Treas., So. Idaho Migrant Ministry, 1960-64, chmn., 1964-67, 70—; nat. migrant adv. com. Nat. Council Chs., 1964-67, gen. bd. Idaho council, 1967-75; bd. dirs. Idaho State Employees Credit Union, 1964-67, treas., 1966-67; mem. Idaho Commn. Arts and Humanities, 1966-67; mem. Idaho Lewis and Clark Trail Commn., 1968-70, 84-88; mem. Idaho Bicentennial Commn., 1971-76; bd. dirs. Sawtooth Interpretive Assn., 1972—, dept. history United Presbyn. Ch., 1978-84; v.p. Idaho Zool. Soc., 1982-84, bd. dirs., 1984—, treas., 1988—. State Hist. Preservation Officers (dir. 1976-81, chmn. Western states council on geog. names 1982-83), Am. Hist. Assn., Western History Assn. (council 1973-76), AAUP, Am. Assn. State and Local History (council 1973-77), Soc. Am. Archivists, others. Author: Anti-Mormonism in Idaho, 1978, Boise: An Illustrated History, 1982, Gold Camps and Silver Cities, 1984, Idaho: Gem of the Mountains, 1985. Office: Idaho Hist Soc 610 N Julia Davis Dr Boise ID 83702-7695

WELLS, PATRICIA BENNETT, business administration educator; b. Park River, N.D., Mar. 25, 1935; d. Benjamin Beekman Bennett and Alice Catherine (Peerboom) Bennett Breckinridge; A.A., Allan Hancock Coll., Santa Maria, Calif., 1964; B.S. magna cum laude, Coll. Great Falls, 1966; M.S., U. N.D., 1967, Ph.D., 1971; children—Bruce Bennett, Barbara Lea Ragland. Fiscal acct. USIA, Washington, 1954-56; public acct., Bremerton, Wash., 1956; statistician U.S. Navy, Bremerton, 1957-59; med. services accounts officer U.S. Air Force, Vandenberg AFB, Calif., 1962-64; instr. bus. adminstrn. Western New Eng. Coll., 1967-69; vis. prof. econs. Chapman Coll., 1970; vis. prof. U. So. Calif. systems Griffith AFB, N.Y., 1971-72; assoc. prof., dir. adminstrn. mgmt. program Va. State U., 1973-74; assoc. prof. bus. adminstrn. Oreg. State U., Corvallis, 1974-81, prof. mgmt., 1982—, univ. curriculum coordinator, 1984-86, dir. adminstrv. mgmt. program, 1974-81, pres. Faculty Senate, 1981; cons. process tech. devel. Digital Equipment Corp., 1982. Pres., chmn. bd. dirs. Adminstrv. Orgnl. Services, Inc., Corvallis, 1976-83, Dynamic Achievement, Inc., 1983—; bd. dirs. Oreg. State U. Bookstores, Inc., 1987—. Cert. adminstrv. mgr. Pres. TYEE Mobil Home Park, Inc. Fellow Assn. Bus. Communication (mem. internat. bd. 1980-83, v.p. Northwest 1981, 2d v.p. 1982-83, 1st v.p. 1983-84, pres. 1984-85); mem. Am. Bus. Women's Assn. (chpt. v.p. 1979, pres. 1980, named Top Businesswoman in Nation 1980, Bus. Assoc. Yr. 1986), Assn. Info. Systems Profls., Adminstrv. Mgmt. Soc., AAUP (chpt. sec. 1973, chpt. bd. dirs. 1982, 84-897, pres. Oreg. conf. 1983-85), Am. Vocat. Assn. (nominating com. 1976), Associated Oreg. Faculties, Nat. Bus. Edn. Assn., Nat. Assn. Tchr. Edn. for Bus. Office Edn. (pres. 1976-77, chmn. public relations com. 1978-81), Corvallis Area C. of C. (v.p. chamber devel. 1987-88, pres. 1988—, Pres.' award 1986), Sigma Kappa. Roman Catholic. Lodge: Rotary. Contbr. numerous articles to profl. jours. Office: Oreg State U Coll Bus 418C Bexell Corvallis OR 97331

WELLS, ROGER FREDERICK, mechanical engineer; b. Portsmouth, Eng., Jan. 6, 1945; s. Frederick Arthur and Edith Mary (Wort) W.; m. Carol Menthe; stepchildren: Lance R., Darrel C.; children from previous marriage: Nicholas R., Simon P., Geoffrey J. Student, Southampton Tech. Coll., Eng., 1961-63; Higher Nat. Diploma in Mech. Engring., Portsmouth Coll. Tech., 1966. Chartered Mech. Engr., U.K. Engr. apprentice Hawker Siddeley Aviation Ltd., Hamble, Eng., 1961-66; engr.-in-charge fuel systems dept. Royal Aircraft Establishment, Ministry of Tech., Farnborough, Eng., 1966-71; engring. facilities mgr. Mil. Vehicle Establishment, Ministry of Def., Chertsey, Eng., 1971-78; projects mgr. Autosense Equipment, Inc. div. United Techs., Oxford, Eng., 1978-81; chief engr. preliminary design Hamilton Test Systems div. United Techs., Tucson, 1981-86; mgr. sensors devel. Hamilton Standards Controls div. United Techs., Lexington, Ohio, 1986-87; mgr. automotive sensors Spectrol Electronics div. United Techs., City of Industry, Calif., 1987—; co-dir. Menthe-Wells Cons., Fullerton, Calif., 1985—. Contbr. articles to tech. jours.; patentee in field. Fellow Instn. Diagnostic Engrs. (founding); mem. Instn. Mech. Engrs., Soc. Automotive Engrs. Home: PO Box 3854 Fullerton CA 92634-3854 Office: United Techs Spectrol Electronics Div 17070 E Gale Ave City of Industry CA 91749

WELLS, TOMM, title insurance executive, real estate consultant; b. Lynwood, Calif., Oct. 24, 1948; s. Thomas Edward and Lee Ann (Marianella) W. BA, U. Calif., Northridge, 1970; MA in Multicultural Edn., Pepperdine U., 1976. Asst. vice prin. L.A. City Schs., 1971-72, elem. prin., 1972-78; sales mgr. Safeco Title Ins. Co., Panorama City, Calif., 1978-82; subdiv. sales mgr. Chicago Title Ins. Co., L.A., 1982-88; v.p., maj. account exec. Ticor Title Ins. Co., L.A., 1983—; real estate cons. Hallmark Fin., Van Nuys, Calif., 1983—. Sec. Nat. Forest Recreation Assn., L.A., 1987; mem. Sci. of Mind Ch. Mem. Cen. City Assn., Assn. Real Estate Attys., Nat. Assn. Corp. Real Estate Execs., Bldg. Industry Assn., Bus. and Profl. Assn. (treas. 1982-84). Republican. Home: 4155 Camellia Ave Studio City CA 91604 Office: Ticor Title Ins Co 300 S Grand Ave 7th Fl Los Angeles CA 90071

WELSCH, LAURA MARINO, business owner; b. Woodstock, Ill., May 10, 1961; d. Jacob Angelo and Karen Sue (Campbell) Marino; m. Richard Andrew Rosebrock, Apr. 5, 1980 (div. 1982); 1 child, Jessica Michele; m. David James Welsch, Aug. 23, 1986; children: Michael Richard, Debra Erin, Jessica Michele. Grad., Crystal Lake (Ill.) South, 1979. Owner/cons. LMR & Assocs., Garland, Tex., 1982-84; pres./cons. Task Mgmt. Sys., Inc., Garland, 1984-86; owner/cons. Welsch & Welsch, Huntington Beach, Calif., 1986—. Contbr. articles to profl. jours. Mem. Huntington Beach C. of C. (com. chmn. 1988—, ambassador 1986—), Nat. Assn. Female Execs., Orange Coast IBM PC Users Group, Huntington Beach/Fountain Valley Bd. Realtors, Lew Epstein Women's Club. Office: Welsch & Welsch 17610 Beach Blvd #26 Huntington Beach CA 92647

WELSCH, SUZANNE CAROL, mathematics educator; b. Chgo., Nov. 23, 1941; d. James Dumont Seiler and Lotta May Marjorie (Grayson) Langford; m. Ralph Kelley Ungermann, Mar. 31, 1962 (div. Mar. 1980); children: Annette Carol, Scott Kelley; m. John Henry Welsch, Jan. 2, 1981; children: James Henry, Lee William. AA in Math., Ventura Coll., 1962; BA in Stats., U. Calif., Berkeley, 1964; MA in Math., U. Calif., Irvine, 1972. Computer programmer N.Am. Space & Info. Systems, Downey, Calif., 1964-65; biostatistician U. Calif., Irvine, 1969-73; owner, mgr. Ungermann Assocs., developers Logcap software, Los Altos, 1972-80; prof. math., stats. and computers Sierra Nevada Coll., Incline Village, Nev., 1983—; chmn. sci.dept. Sierra Nevada Coll., Incline Village, 1989—; founder, owner, mgr. Zilog, Los Altos, Calif., 1974; cons. Long Beach Heart Assn., 1972-75. Contbr. articles to profl. jours. Neighborhood chmn., bd. dirs., coun. treas., leader Girl Scouts U.S.A., 1971—, treas., Reno, 1985-87. Recipient appreciation pin Sierra Nevada coun. Girl Scouts U.S.A., 1986, Outstanding Tchr. award Sierra Nev. Coll., 1987. Mem. Math. Assn. Am., Am. Statis. Assn., U. Calif. Alumni Assn., Soccer (pres. 1988), Gymnastics (treas. 1984-87)

(Incline Village). Republican. Home: 680 Saddlehorn Dr Incline Village NV 89451 Office: Sierra Nevada Coll 800 Coll Blvd Incline Village NV 89451

WELSH, LAWRENCE H., bishop; b. Winton, Wyo., Feb. 1, 1935. Ed., U. Wyo., St. John's Sem., Minn., Cath. U. Am. Ordained priest Roman Cath. Ch., 1962. Bishop Diocese of Spokane, Wash., 1978—. Office: Spokane Diocese 1023 W Riverside Ave PO Box 1453 Spokane WA 99210 *

WELSH, MARY MCANAW, educator, family mediator; b. Cameron, Mo., Dec. 7, 1920; d. Francis Louis and Mary Matilda (Moore) McA.; m. Alvin F. Welsh, Feb. 10, 1944; children: Mary Celia, Clinton F., M. Ann. AB, U. Kans., 1942; MA, Seton Hall U., 1960; EdD, Columbia U., 1971. Reporter, Hutchinson (Kans.) News Herald, 1942-43; house editor Worthington Pump & Machine Corp., Harrison, N.J., 1943-44; tchr., housemaster, coordinator Summit (N.J.) Pub. Schs., 1960-68; prof. family studies N.Mex. State U., Las Cruces, 1972-85; adj. faculty dept. family practice Tex. Tech. Regional Acad. Health Ctr., El Paso, 1978-82, Family Mediation Practice, Las Cruces, 1986—. Mem. AAUW (pres. N.Mex. 1981-83), AAUP, N.Mex. Council Women's Orgn. (founder, chmn. 1982-83), LWV, Nat. Council Family Relations, Am. Home Econs. Assn., Western Gerontol. Soc., Theta Sigma Phi, Delta Kappa Gamma, Kappa Alpha Theta. Democrat. Roman Catholic. Author: A Good Family is Hard to Found, 1972; Parent, Child and Sex, 1970; contbr. articles to profl. jours.; writer, presenter home econs. and family study series KRWG-TV, 1974; moderator TV series The Changing Family in N.Mex./LWV, 1976. Home and Office: PO Box 3483 University Park Las Cruces NM 88003

WELTER, THOMAS ALAN, marketing executive; b. Tiffin, Ohio, Jan. 3, 1951; s. Richard Eugene and Annabel (McClintock) W.; m. Kathleen McClelland, July 21, 1974; children: Kristine, Kelli Ann, Thomas Richard Jr. BA in Polit. Sci., Baldwin-Wallace Coll., 1973. Scout exec. Boy Scouts Am., Cleve., 1973; sales rep. Burroughs Corp. (UNISYS), Cleve., 1973-78, Gen. Electric Info. Svcs., Cleve., 1978-79, Sperry, Cleve., 1979-81, Prime Computer, Cleve., 1981-82; terr. mktg. mgr. Cimlinc, Inc., Cleve. and Seattle, 1984-89, mgr. computer integrated mfg., rep. major accounts, 1989—. Treas. election com. Don Glass for mayor, Sheffield Lake, Ohio, 1986; chmn. bd. of trustees Sheffield Lake United Ch. of Christ, 1986-87. Republican. Home: 33513 7th Pl SW Federal Way WA 98023 Office: Cimlinc Inc 16300 Christensen Ste 203 Seattle WA 98188

WELTON, CHARLES EPHRAIM, lawyer; b. Cloquet, Minn., June 23, 1947; s. Eugene Frances and Evelyn Esther (Koski) W.; m. Nancy Jean Sanda, July 19, 1969; children: Spencer Sanda, Marshall Eugene. BA, Macalester Coll., 1969; postgrad., U. Minn., 1969-70; JD, U. Denver, 1974. Bar: Colo. 1974, U.S. Dist. Ct. Colo. 1974, U.S. Supreme Ct. 1979, U.S. Ct. Appeals (10th cir.) 1980. Assoc. Davidovich & Assocs., and predecessor firm, Denver, 1974-77, Charles Welton and Assocs., Denver, 1978-80, 1984-88; ptnr. Davidovich & Welton, Denver, 1981-84, OSM Properties, Denver, 1982—; lectr. in field. Contbr. articles to profl. jours. Sch. pres. PTSA, Denver, 1983-84; coach Colo. Jr. Soccer League, 1980-85; coach Odessey of the Mind (formerly Olympics of the Mind), 1986—. Served alt. mil. duty Denver Gen. Hosp., 1970-72. Mem. Denver Bar Assn. (legal fee arbitration com.), Colo. Bar Assn. (legal fee arbitration com.), Assn. Trial Lawyers Am., Colo. Trial Lawyers Assn. (bd. dirs. 1985—, chmn. seminar com. 1986-88, exec. com. 1987-88, legis. com. 1988—), Americans Building a Lasting Earth (founder), Exec. Ventures Group of Am. Leadership Forum (adv. bd.). Democrat. Lutheran. Club: Midtown Athletic. Home: 5020 Montview Blvd Denver CO 80207 Office: Old Smith Mansion 1751 Gilpin St Denver CO 80218

WELTON, MICHAEL PETER, dentist; b. Milw., Apr. 19, 1957; s. Lloyd Peter and Allegra (Nimmer) W.; m. Etsuko Suehiro, Nov. 21, 1986. BS in Biology, Carroll Coll., 1979; DDS, U. Minn., 1983. Commd. lt. USN, 1983; resident Naval Hosp. Camp Pendleton, Oceanside, Calif., 1983-84; with periodontics dept. Naval Dental Clinic, Yokosuka, Japan, 1984-85; clinic dir. Negishi Dental Annex, Yokohama, Japan, 1985-87; gen. dentistry Br. Dental Clinic Mare Island Naval Sta., Vallejo, Calif., 1987—; legis. extern Am. Student Dental Assn., Washington, 1982; student rep. Minn. Dental Assn., Mpls., 1980. Active Rep. Presdl. Task Force, Washington, 1981—, Nat. Rep. Congl. Com., Washington, 1982—. Mem. ADA, Calif. Dental Assn., Napa-Solano Dental Soc., Acad. Gen. Dentistry, Assn. Mil. Surgeons, Bay Area Armed Forces Dental Study Group, Delta Sigma Delta (treas. Mpls. chpt. 1982-83, Outstanding Mem. award 1982-83), Commonwealth Club, Vallejo Golf Club, No. Calif. Golf Assn. Home: 480 Evelyn Circle Vallejo CA 94589 Office: Br Dental Clinic Naval Sta Mare Island Vallejo CA 94592

WENCK, FREDERICK, dentist; b. Evanston, Ill., July 8, 1939; s. Frederick Sr. and Virginia (Hart) W.; m. Karen Simonini, Sept. 17, 1966 (div. June 1981); children: Kelary Ann, Frederick Gilbert, Brennan Phillip, Brooke Elizabeth. BS, St. Bonaventure U., 1961; DDS, Northwestern U., Chgo., 1966. Pvt. practice South Lake Tahoe, Calif., 1970—; chief dental staff Barton Meml. Hosp., South Lake Tahoe, 1974, 78. Pres. bd. trustees Lake Tahoe Community Coll., South Lake Tahoe, 1984-85, 89; mentor Formation for Christian Ministry, South Lake Tahoe, 1980—; lector Eucharistic Minister St. Theresa's Parish, South Lake Tahoe, 1970—. Lt. comdr. USNR, 1966-70, capt., 1984. Mem. ADA, Naval Res. Assn., Assn. Mil. Surgeons U.S., Naval Enlisted Res. Assn., U.S. Naval Inst., Calif. Soc. Preventive Dentistry (pres. 1978), Calif. Dental Assn., Sacramento Dist. Dental Soc., Optimist (pres. South Lake Tahoe chpt. 1984). Home: 2201 Texas Ave PO Box 7648 South Lake Tahoe CA 95731

WENDEL, DOUGLAS JOHN, petroleum engineer; b. Salt Lake City, May 26, 1951; s. Allen Martin and Rose Eileen (Chabot) W.; m. Sylvia Keding, Aug. 20, 1975; children: Chantelle Ann, Jared Richard, Jason Allen, Angela. BSChemE, U. Utah, 1975, MSChemE, 1977. Research technician Flammability Research, Salt Lake City, 1974-78; research engr. Conoco, Inc., Ponca City, Okla., 1978-84; research and devel. mgr. Petroleum Testing Service, Santa Fe Springs, Calif., 1984—. Contbr. articles to profl. jours. Asst. scoutmaster Boy Scouts Am., Ponca City, 1980-84, Whittier, Calif., scoutmaster, 1984—. Internat. Isocyanate Inst. fellow, 1975-77; named Outstanding Young Man of Am., U.S. Jaycees, 1984. Fellow Am. Inst. Chemists; mem. Soc. Petroleum Engrs., Am. Inst. Chem. Engrs., Soc. Core Analysts. Mormon. Office: Petroleum Testing Svc 12051 Rivera Rd Santa Fe Springs CA 90670

WENDT, MICHAEL JAMES, production potter; b. Bemidji, Minn., Jan. 7, 1948; s. George Rudolph and Isabel Mary (Zimmermann) W.; m. Rosemary Ann Pittenger, Nov. 10, 1972; children: Natalie Kathleen, Elizabeth Mary. BA, U. Idaho, 1971. Cert. secondary edn. tchr. Idaho. Tchr. German, English Lewiston (Idaho) High Sch., 1971-73; tchr. art Culdesac (Idaho) Sch. Dist., 1974; research asst. U. Idaho, 1976; instr. Walla Walla Community Coll., Clarkston, Wash., 1979, Lewis Clark State Coll., Lewiston, 1985; owner Wendt Pottery, Lewiston, 1973—. Mem. Phi Beta Kappa, Phi Kappa Phi, Am. Field Service Club (pres. 1978), Computer Literacy Support Soc. Home: 1510 9th Ave Lewiston ID 83501 Office: Wendt Pottery 2729 Clearwater Ave Lewiston ID 83501

WENDT, STEVEN WILLIAM, business educator; b. Rockford, Ill., Sept. 18, 1948; s. Roy W. Wendt and Betty Lou (Phillips) Wendt Oser. AAS, Clark County Community Coll., North Las Vegas, Nev., 1982; BS, U. Nev., 1985, MBA, 1987. Cert. vocat. adult educator, Nev. Electronics tech. engr. Rockford Automation, Inc., 1972-74; owner, operator S.W. Ltd., Rockford, 1972-76, S.W. Enterprises, Henderson, Nev., 1977—; instr. electronics Nev. Gaming Sch., Las Vegas, 1977-83; gen. mgr., corp. sec. treas. Customs by Peter Schell, Las Vegas, 1977-83; field engr. Bell & Howell Mailmobile Ops. div., Zeeland, Mich., 1982—; instr. bus. U. Nev., Las Vegas, 1985—; bus. cons. Small Bus. Devel. Ctr., Las Vegas, 1985—; incorporator, sec. treas. ZyZx, Inc., Henderson, 1988—; fin. cons. Failsafe Techs. Corp., Las Vegas, 1987-88, sr. arbitrator Better Bus. Bur., Las Vegas, 1982—. Treas. U. Nev. Grad. Student Assn., 1986-87. Served with USN, 1967-71. Recipient Cert. Appreciation UNICEF, 1984. Mem. Strategic Gaming Soc., U. Nev. Alumni Assn., Am. Legion, Phi Lambda Alpha, Fin. Mgmt. Assn. (Nat. Honor Soc. 1985—). Home: 1325 Chestnut St Henderson NV 89015 Office: U Nev 4505 Maryland Pkwy Las Vegas NV 89154

WENTINK, MAUREEN ANN MCGUIRE, realtor, educator; b. Passaic, N.J., Nov. 2, 1929; d. John Edwin and Helene Rose (Davide) McGuire; m. Paul John Wentink Jr., Mar. 31, 1951; children: Paul John III, Maureen Ann, Michael Gerard, Mark Andrew, Helen Marie. Student, Calif. State U., Los Angeles, 1965, San Fernando Valley State U., 1966-67; AA, Seattle U., 1976, BEd cum laude, 1978; postgrad., Seattle Pacific U., 1986-87. Cert. secondary tchr., Wash. Personnel counselor The Skill Exchange, Mercer Island, Wash., 1978-79; sub. tchr. Bellevue, Snogualmie Valley, Wash., 1980-82; instr. Griffin Coll., Bellevue, 1982-85, 87-88; realtor ERA Sno Valley Realty, Fall City, Wash., 1987—. Sec., treas., bd. dirs. Spring Glen Assn., Fall City, 1985-88, bus. mgr., 1982-85; lay eucharistic minister Our Lady of Sorrow Ch., Snogualmie, 1979-88. Mem. Nat. Bd. Realtors, Alpha Sigma Nu, Kappa Delta Pi. Republican. Roman Catholic. Home: 36102 SE 49th St Fall City WA 98024 Office: ERA Sno Valley Realty PO Box 399 Fall City WA 98024

WENTWORTH, THEODORE SUMNER, lawyer; b. Bklyn., July 18, 1938; s. Theodore Sumner and Alice Ruth (Wortmann) W.; AA, Am. River Coll., 1958; JD, U. Calif., Hastings Coll. Law, 1962; m. Sharon Linelle Arkush, 1965 (dec. 1987); children: Christina Linn, Kathryn Allison. Admitted to Calif. bar, 1963; assoc. Adams, Hunt & Martin, Santa Ana, Calif., 1963-66; partner Hunt, Liljestrom & Wentworth, Santa Ana, 1967-77; pres. Solabs Corp.; chmn. bd., exec. v.p. Plant Warehouse, Inc., Hawaii, 1974-82; prin. Law Offices of Theodore S. Wentworth, specializing in personal injury, product liability and profl. malpractice litigation, Irvine, Calif.; judge pro tem Superior Ct. Attys. Panel, Harbor Mcpl. Ct. Pres., bd. dirs. Santa Ana-Tustin Community Chest, 1972; v.p., trustee South Orange County United Way, 1973-75; pres. Orange County Fedn. Funds, 1972-73; bd. dirs. Orange County Mental Health Assn.; v.p., sec. Haase Inst. Advanced Studies. Diplomate Nat. Bd. Trial Advocacy. Mem. State Bar Calif., ABA, Orange County Bar Assn. (dir. 1972-76), Am. Trial Lawyers Assn., Calif. Trial Lawyers Assn. (bd. govs. 1968-70), Orange County Trial Lawyers Assn. (pres. 1967-68), Lawyer-Pilots Bar Assn., Aircraft Owners and Pilots Assn., Bahia Corinthian Yacht Club, Balboa Bay Club, Lincoln Club, Corsair Yacht Club, Pacific Club, Newport. Research in vedic prins., natural law, metaphysics. Office: 2112 Business Center Dr Ste 220 Irvine CA 92715

WENZEL, CAROL MARION NAGLER, family therapist; b. Chgo., Nov. 17, 1936; d. Philip L. and Grace (Hindley) Nagler; m. Gene H. Wenzel, July 25, 1954; children: Scott, Jamie, Philip, Sue Ellen. BA in Communication and Social Scis., Marylhurst Coll., 1982; MSW, Portland State U., 1984. Registered clin. social worker. Family therapist Intensive Family Service, Inc., Portland, Oreg., 1984—; pvt. practice counseling Child Within, Oreg., 1986—; trainer alcoholic family systems, various agys., Portland, 1982-86. Mem. Nat. Assn. Social Workers (cert.), Acad. Clin. Social Workers. Democrat. Lutheran. Home: 8325 SE Carnation Milwaukie OR 97267 Office: Child Within 12608 SE Stark St Portland OR 97233

WERDERMAN, WILLIAM ROBERT, small business owner; b. Chgo., July 28, 1937; s. William Theodore and Margaret (Snyder) W.; m. Ree Parrish, Mar. 31, 1979; children: William S., Jody Lynn. BA, Drury Coll., 1962. V.p. Polrized Corp., Northridge, Calif., 1964-80; gen. mgr. U.S. Alarms, Tulare, Calif., 1980-84; area mgr. ADT Security, Daly City, Calif., 1984-87; owner Glass Works, Calistoga, Calif., 1985—; cons. in field. Patentee continuous process for panels. Sgt. U.S. Army, 1960-64. Fellow Illuminating Engr. Soc. Republican. Home: 901 Cape Cod Ct Napa CA 94558 Office: Glass Works 1458 Lincoln Ave Calistoga CA 94515

WERMERS, MARY ANN, nursing educator; b. St. Louis, Nov. 19, 1946; d. Anthony Gaylord and Cecilia Agnes (Tewes) Minnick; m. Joseph J. Wermers, July 11, 1970; children: Patricia, Alyssa, Aaron. BSN, St. Louis U., 1968, MSN, 1970. RN, Colo.; vocat. credential, Colo. Staff nurse, nurse aide John Cochran VA Hosp., St. Louis, 1967-69; staff nurse, head nurse Incranate Word Hosp., St. Louis, 1969-70; staff nurse Rush-Presbyn. Hosp., Chgo., summer 1970, St. Benedict's Hosp., Ogden, Utah, 1972-73; instr. nursing U. Ill., Chgo., 1970-72; asst. prof. nursing, coord. U. Nebr., Omaha, 1974-75; instr. nursing, coord. Pikes Peak Community Coll., Colorado Springs, Colo., 1976-82, mem. nursing adv. bd., 1987--; asst. prof. nursing, coord. instr. nursing, chmn. dept. Pueblo (Colo.) Community Coll., 1985—, mem. nursing adv. bd., 1987—; staff nurse Fantus Clinic, Cook County Hosp., Chgo., part-time 1971-72; workshop speaker; adminstrv. cons. Parkview Hosp., Pueblo, summer 1987. Mem. coun. Divine Redeemer Parish, Colorado Springs, 1983-85; participant Career Days, Pueblo, 1985--; mem. adv. bd. Divine Redeemer Sch., 1987--. Recipient Outstanding Women's award U. So. Colo., 1985, Nightingale award U. Colo., 1986; edn. grantee St. Louis U., 1964-65, President's honor scholar, 1968; Pueblo Community Coll. faculty grantee, 1987-88. Mem. NEA, Colo. Edn. Assn., Colo. Orgn. for Advancement Assoc. Degree Nursing (pres. 1987-88), Colo. Orgn. Practical Nurse Educators, Colo. Orgn. Assoc. Degree Educators, St. Mary's High Sch. Booster Club (Colorado Springs), Sigma Theta Tau. Republican. Roman Catholic. Office: Pueblo Community Coll 900 W Orman St Pueblo CO 81004

WERNER, OLIVER JAMES, law librarian; b. St. Louis, June 14, 1924; s. Oliver James and Ethel Claire (Lively) W.; m. Geraldine F. Childers (dec. Nov. 1959); children: Daniel (dec. Nov. 1959), Jonathan (dec. Nov. 1959); m. Nora Valentine Campbell, July 22, 1961. PhB, U. Chgo., 1948, JD, 1956; M in Law Libr., U. Washington, 1969. Trust officer Seattle First Nat. Bank, 1956-68; asst. libr., instr.Law Sch. U. Tex., Austin, 1969-71; dir., asst. prof. Coll. Law U. Okla., Norman, 1971-72; dir. San Diego County Law Libr., 1972-87; pvt. practice San Diego, 1987—; pres. San Diego Greater Metro Area Libr. Coun., 1979-80. Author: Manual for Prison Law Librs., 1973; editor State Ct. and County Law Librs. Newsletter, 1977-79; contbr. articles to profl. jours. With USCG, 1942-46. Mem. Am. Assn. of Law Librs. (exec. bd. 1983-84), So. Calif. Assn. Of Law Librs. (pres. 1979-80, svc. to legal edn.). Democrat. Home: 4247 5th Ave San Diego CA 92103

WERNER, ROGER HARRY, archaeologist; b. N.Y.C., Nov. 11, 1950; s. Harry Emile and Rena (Roode) W.; m. Kathleen Diane Engdahl, Feb. 20, 1982; children: Meryl Lauren, Sarah Melise, Jeremy Marshall; 1 stepchild, Amber Fawn. BA, Belknap Coll., 1973; MA, Sonoma State U., Rohnert Park, Calif., 1982. Curatorial aide Anthro. Lab. Sonoma State Coll., 1975-76, curatorial asst., 1976-77, staff archaeologist, 1977-80; staff archaeologist Planning Dept., Lake County, Calif., 1977; cir. riding archaeologist western region Nat. Park Service, Tucson, Ariz., 1978; prin. investigator Archaeol. Services, Inc., Stockton, Calif., 1979—; cons. Calif. Indian Legal Services, Ukiah, 1977, Geothermal Research Impact Projection Study, Lakeport, Calif., 1977; instr. Ya-Ka-Ama Indian Ednl. Ctr., Santa Rosa, Calif., 1978-79; lead archaeologist No. Calif., WESTEC Services, Inc., San Diego, 1979-81. Sec. Colonial Heights PTA, 1983-84, 2d v.p., 1985-86, historian, 1986-87, v.p., 1987—; cons., instr. Clovis Adult Sch., 1984-85; instr. U. Pacific Lifelong Learning Ctr., 1987—; bd. dirs. Valley Mountain Regional Ctr., 1987-88, treas., 1989—; active Spl. Olympics, Stockton, Calif., 1986—. Anthropology dept. research grantee, Sonoma State U., 1980. Mem. Great Basin Anthropol. Conf., Soc. for Am. Archaeologists, Soc. for Calif. Archaeology, Soc. Profl. Archaeologists, Assn. for Retarded Citizens, Kiwanis. Democrat. Lodge: Kiwanis (Stockton). Home: 1117 Aberdeen Ave Stockton CA 95209 Office: Archaeol Svcs Inc 1308 W Robin Hood Dr Stockton CA 95207

WERT, HARRY EMERSON, engineering company executive, engineer; b. Phila., Dec. 7, 1932; s. Mark Hopkins and Susan Elizabeth (Reed) W.; m. Mary Lou Cox, May 9, 1959; children: Kimberly Dawn, Joanna Reed Wert, Stephen Emerson. BS in Pre-Engring., Lebanon Valley Coll., 1959; B of Gen. Studies in Physics and Math., Rollins Coll., 1973. Elec. engr. Melpar, Inc., Falls Church, Va., 1958-60; sr. elec. engr. Nat. Sci. Labs., Washington, 1960-64; dept. mgr. Emerson Electric, Florissant, Mo., 1964-66; tech. dir. Martin Marietta Aerospace, Orlando, Fla., 1966-79; sr. v.p., chief operating officer Engineered Magnetics, Hawthorne, Calif., 1979—; pres. READ, Inc., Orlando, 1967-79. Inventee microwave amplifier multiplexer adapter. Staff sgt. USAF, 1952-56, ETO. Mem. IEEE. Republican. Home: PO Box 7000-625 Redondo Beach CA 90277 Office: Engineered Magnetics Inc 18435 Susana Rd Rancho Dominguez CA 90221

WERTHEIMER, THOMAS, film executive; b. N.Y.C., 1938. BA, Princeton U., 1960; LLB, Columbia U., 1963. V.p. bus. affairs subs. ABC, 1964-72; with MCA, Inc., Universal City, Calif., 1972—, v.p. Universal TV div., corp. v.p., 1974-83, exec. v.p., 1983—, also bd. dirs. Office: MCA Inc 100 Universal City Pla Universal City CA 91608

WESLEY, JANE CATHERINE, marketing executive, consultant; b. Washington, Dec. 15, 1953; d. George Herman and Jean Catherine (Cavanaugh) W.; m. Joseph Philip Cavalli, June 5, 1975 (div. Dec. 1982). BA, James Madison U., 1976; MS, U. Hawaii, 1979; MBA, Golden Gate U., 1988. Tchr. Hawaii Pub. Schs., Honolulu, 1976-80; libr. Lockheed Missiles & Space, Sunnyvale, Calif., 1980-83; cons. Wescom, San Jose, Calif., 1983—. Campaign worker Get On the Vote, San Jose, 1984. Mem. Exec. Women in Sales, Am. Bus. Womens Assn. Home and Office: 3014 Breen Ct San Jose CA 95121

WESLEY, PHILLIP, librarian; b. Los Angeles, June 3, 1930; s. George Gregor and Olive Vessie (Barnette) W.; A.A., Glendale, Coll., 1950; B.A., U. Calif. at Los Angeles, 1956; M.S., U. So. Calif., 1959. Sr. library asst. U. Calif. at Los Angeles Law Library, 1955-58; bindery clk., acquisitions librarian, cataloger Los Angeles County Law Library, 1958-59; ltd. loan and serials librarian Calif. State U. at Los Angeles Library, 1959-60; acquisitions librarian Los Angeles County Law Library, 1960-61, reference librarian, 1961-62, head catalog librarian, 1961-66; head catalog librarian Calif. State U., Northridge, 1966-67, chief tech. services, 1967-69, acting coll. librarian, 1969; dir. ednl. resources ctr. Calif. State U., Dominguez Hills, 1969-77, dean ednl. resources, 1977—. Mem. Am. Assn. Law Libraries, So. Calif. Assn. Law Libraries (pres. 1964-65), Spl. Libraries Assn. (chpt. treas. 1969-70), So. Calif. Tech. Processes Group (pres. 1972-74), Am., Calif. library assns. Home: 2287 Panorama Terr Los Angeles CA 90039 Office: 1000 E Victoria St Carson CA 90747

WESLEY, VIRGINIA ANNE, real estate property manager; b. Seattle, Apr. 29, 1951; d. Albert William and Mary Louise (Heusser) W. BA in Speech, U. Hawaii, Hilo, 1978. Cert. property mgr. Mgr. office, traffic Sta. KIPA-Radio, Hilo, 1972-74; reporter West Hawaii Today, Kailua-Kona, Hawaii, 1974; mgr. office U. Hawaii, Hilo, 1975-78; dir. property mgmt. First City Equities, Seattle, 1978-88, Winvest Devel. Corp., Seattle, 1988—; instr. Bellevue (Wash.) Community Coll., 1982-85. Bd. dirs. Mayor's Small Bus. Task Force, Seattle, 1981-83, First Hill Improvement Assn., Seattle, 1982—. Mem. Inst. Real Estate Mgmt., Internat. Coun. Shopping Ctrs., Comml. Real Estate Women, Women's Bus. Exch., Seattle-King County Bd. Realtors, Big Island Press Club, Phi Kappa Phi. Home: 4841 S Raymond St Seattle WA 98118

WESNICK, RICHARD JAMES, newspaper editor; b. Racine, Wis., Oct. 14, 1938; s. John and Julia (Kassa) W.; m. Elaine Apoline Smith, Sept. 30, 1967; children: Catherine Elaine, Julia Ann. BA, U. Houston, 1961. Reporter Jour. Times, Racine, 1965-76; mng. editor Ind. Record, Helena, Mont., 1976-80; editor Billings Gazette, Mont., 1980—. Editor: Death Sentences, 1984, Best of Bragg, 1985. Served with USMC, 1961-64. Mem. Mont. AP (chmn., bd. dirs. 1985-88, freedom of info. com., legis. rev. com.), Soc. Newspaper Designers, Am. Soc. Newspaper Editors. Roman Catholic. Lodges: Kiwanis, Rotary. Home: 2214 22d St W Billings MT 59102 Office: The Billings Gazette 401 N Broadway Billings MT 59101

WESOLOWSKI, DANIEL FRANCIS, reporter; b. Irvington, N.J., July 27, 1952; s. Frank Richard W.; m. Anna Portia Roberts, Jan. 1, 1983. BA in English, Notre Dame U., 1974; MA in English, U. Calif., Santa Barbara, 1978, teaching cert., 1979. Free-lance advertiser Am. Passage, Chgo., 1981—; surf reporter Surfer Mag., Dana Point, Calif., 1981—; freelance writer, 1974—; fitness trainer, 1984—; meteorologist, 1974—. Mem. Greenpeace, Nature Conservancy. Named Comeback Rider of Yr., Spenco Med. Corp., 1984; record holder Ultra-Marathon Cycling Assn., 1985, 87. Democrat. Roman Catholic. Home: 6587 Del Playa # 1 Santa Barbara CA 93117

WESSLER, MELVIN DEAN, farmer, rancher; b. Dodge City, Kan., Feb. 11, 1932; s. Oscar Lewis and Clara (Reiss) W.; grad. high sch.; m. Laura Ethel Arbuthnot, Aug. 23, 1951; children: Monty Dean, Charla Cay, Virgil Lewis. Farmer-rancher, Springfield, Colo., 1950—; dir., sec. bd. Springfield Co-op. Sales Co., 1964-80, pres. bd., 1980—. Pres., Arkansas Valley Co-op. Council, SE Colo. Area, 1965-87, Colo. Co-op. Council, 1969-72, v.p. 1974, sec. 1980-86; community com. chmn. Baca County, Agr. Stablzn. and Conservation Service, Springfield, 1961-73, 79—, vice chmn. Baca County Com., 1980—; mem. spl. com. on grain mktg. Far-Mar-Co.; mem. adv. bd. Denver Baptist Bible Coll., 1984—; chmn., bd. dirs. Springfield Cemetery Bd., 1985—; apptd. spl. com. Farmland Industries spl. project Tomorrow, 1987—. Mem. Colo. Cattlemen's Assn., Colo. Wheat Growers Assn., Southeast Farm Bus. Assn., Big Rock Grange (treas. 1964-76, master 1976-82). Baptist. Address: 18363 Colorado Rd PP Springfield CO 81073

WEST, BILLY GENE, public relations company executive; b. Richmond, Ind., Nov. 22, 1946; s. Billy D. and Jean C. (Cox) W.; AA, Cerritos Coll., 1966; BA, U. So. Calif., 1969; MA, U. Minn., 1971. Salesman, Marina Art Products, Los Angeles, 1967-73; v.p. Am. Telecon Network, Dallas, 1974-77; gen. mgr. Phoenix Publs., Houston, 1977-78; pres. San Dark, Inc., San Francisco, 1978-82; gen. ptnr. Billy West & Assocs., 1982—; pres. V.G. Prodns., 1983—; chief exec. officer Westmarking, 1989— ; exec. dir. Young Ams. for Freedom, Minn. and Wis., 1970-72; pres. S.F.P.A., San Francisco, 1982-83. Mem. Assn. MBA Execs. Mem. Am. Ref. Ch.

WEST, BRUCE ALAN, artist, museum curator; b. Anchorage, Jan. 4, 1948; s. Raymond Spires Westerman and Marcella Antoinette (Knight) Stein. Student, Heidelburg Sch. Art, 1958, Scottsdale Coll., 1974; BS, Ariz. State U., 1977; postgrad., Cen. Ariz. Coll., 1979; MSA, Pinal Art Inst., Florence, Ariz., 1980, PhD, 1983. Race car and motorcycle driver various locations Ariz., Calif., 1968-73; profl. welterweight boxer 1973-78; chauffeur TMS Records, Hollywood, Calif., 1979; curator, bd. dirs. Pinal County Art Gallery, Florence, Ariz., 1980--; creative cons. Aardvark Corps., 1980--, Dee Dot Fashions, 1984--; corrections officer Ariz. State Prison, Florence, 1983-84; pres., inventor, designer Bruce West Designs & Constrn., Florence, 1984--. Author, illustrator: Touch Me Gently, 1974; inventor pistolpainting. Libertarian. Office: 193 King St Florence AZ 85232-1228

WEST, CHRISTOPHER WAYNE, small business manager; b. Pueblo, Colo., June 11, 1961; s. Billy W. and Josie L. W. Grad. high sch., Delta, Colo. Salesman Gambles, Delta, 1978-80; office mgr. West's Home Ctr., Delta, 1982—; mil. advisor U.S. Army Res., Mid-States region, 1982—. Mem. Republican Nat. Com., 1986—. Served to 2d lt. U.S. Army, 1980-82. Mem. Am. Fedn. Police (cert. appreciation 1988), Council Inter-Am. Security, Delta Jaycees (officer 1988). Office: West's Home Ctr 327 Main St Delta CO 81416

WEST, CLELL ALBERT, protective services official; b. Searcy, Ark., Aug. 23, 1934; s. Albert and Della Mae (Lawson) W.; m. Stella Ruth Webb, Sept. 4, 1953; children: Michael, Sherry, Rick. AA, Phoenix Coll., 1972; BA, U. Phoenix, 1981. Capt. Phoenix Fire Dept., 1968-72, bn. chief, 1973-76, dep. chief, 1978-82, asst. chief, 1983-84; fire chief Las Vegas (Nev.) Fire Dept., 1984—. Mem. Nat. Fire Protection Assn. (bd. dirs. 1985—), Internat. Assn. Fire Chiefs, Ariz. Fire Chief's Assn. (pres. 1984-85), Internat. Fire Service Tng. Assn. (com. chmn. 1981-85), Nev. Fire Chiefs Assn. Democrat. Lodge: Lions (sec. Las Vegas club 1985, Lion of Yr. 1985). Home: 6208 Peppermill Dr Las Vegas NV 89102 Office: City of Las Vegas Fire Dept 500 N Casino Center Blvd Las Vegas NV 89101 *

WEST, DARBY LINDSEY, manufacturing company executive; b. Melrose, N.Mex., Jan. 13, 1938; s. Wayne Burton and Mildred Minnie (Lindsey) W.; grad. high sch.; m. Angelina Loomis, Feb. 9, 1980; children—Rebecca, Darby, Jr., Johnny Wayne. Well attendant El Paso Natural Gas Co., Farmington, N.Mex., 1957-65, instrument technician, 1965-67, dehydrator man, 1967-77; v.p., partner Natural Gas Prodn. Equipment P & A, Inc., Farmington, 1977—. Republican. Baptist. Home: PO Box 1187 Bloomfield NM 87413 Office: Natural Gas Prodn Equipment P & A Inc 768 US Hwy 64 Farmington NM 87401

WEST, EDWARD ALAN, graphics communications executive; b. Los Angeles, Dec. 25, 1928; s. Albert Reginald and Gladys Delia (White) W.; m. Sonya Lee Smith, Jan. 2, 1983; children: Troy A., Tamara L. A.A., Fullerton Coll., 1966; student, Cerritos Coll., 1957, UCLA, 1967. Circulation mgr. Huntington Park (Calif.) Signal Newspaper, 1946-52; newspaper web pressman Long Beach (Calif.) Press Telegram, 1955-62; gravure web pressman Gravure West, Los Angeles, 1966-67; sales engr. Halm Jet Press, Glen Head, N.Y., 1968-70; salesman Polychrome Corp., Glen Head, 1970-74; supr. reprographics Fluor Engring & Construction, Irvine, Calif., 1974-81; dir. reprographics Fluor Arabia, Dhahran, Saudi Arabia, 1981-85, Press Telegram, Long Beach, 1986—. Author: How to Paste up For Graphic Reproduction, 1967. Editor The Blue & Gold Legion of Honor unit El Bekal Temple, 1989—. Served as sgt. USMC, 1952-55. Decorated three battle stars, Korea. Mem. Newspaper Web Pressman's Union #285 (bd. dirs. 1966—), In-Plant Printing Assn. (cert. graphics communications mgr. 1977, editor newsletter 1977—, pres. Orange County chpt. 1979—; Internat. Mem. of Yr. 1980), VFW, Masons, Shriners (v.p. South coast club). Presbyterian. Lodges: Mason, Shriners (v.p. South Coast club). Home: 198 Monarch Bay South Laguna CA 92677 Office: 604 Pine Long Beach CA 90844

WEST, EDWARD FOULKE (TED WEST), publishing and marketing executive; b. Phila., Mar. 16, 1953; s. David Alexander and Susan (Quillen) W.; m. Anna Louchheim; children: David Louchheim, Jonathan William. AB with high honors, Princeton U., 1975; MBA, Harvard U., 1979. Policy analyst Delaware Valley Regional Planning Commn., Phila., 1975-76; legislative asst. U.S. Senator H.J. Heinz III, Washington, 1977; sr. assoc. cons. Cambridge (Mass.) Resch. Inst., 1979-82; sr. assoc., v.p. The Berwick Group, Boston, 1983-86; pres. West & Co., Inc., Lexington, Mass., 1986; v.p. mktg. and bus. devel. Pacific Bell Directory, San Francisco, 1986-88, v.p., gen. mgr. mktg. svcs., 1988—. Mem. Info. Industry Assn. Episcopalian. Home: 22 Venado Dr Tiburon CA 94920 Office: Pacific Bell Directory One Rincon Center 101 Spear St Suite 410 San Francisco CA 94105

WEST, HUGH STERLING, aircraft leasing company executive; b. Kansas City, Kans., Apr. 5, 1930; s. Gilbert Eugene and Dorothy (Johnson) W.; BS, U. Va., 1952; BS in Aero., U. Md., 1959; grad. U.S. Naval Test Pilot Sch., 1959; m. Willa Alden Reed, Jan. 16, 1954; children: Karen, Phillip, Susan. Commd. 2d lt. U.S. Marine Corps., 1948, advanced through grades to maj., 1961; exptl. flight test pilot, U.S. Naval Air Test Center, Patuxent River, Md.; resigned, 1961; program mgr. Boeing Aircraft Co., Seattle and Phila., 1961-66, dir. airworthiness, comml. airplane div., 1969-71; dir. aircraft sales Am. Airlines, Tulsa, 1971-76; v.p. equipment mgmt. GATX Leasing Corp., San Francisco, 1976-80; v.p. tech., partner Polaris Aircraft Leasing Corp., San Francisco, 1980-85; v.p., co-founder U.S. Airlease, Inc., 1986—; aircraft cons. Mem. Soc. Exptl. Test Pilots, Army Navy Country Club. Republican. Episcopalian. Home: 387 Darrell Rd Hillsborough CA 94010 Office: U S Airlease Inc 615 Battery St San Francisco CA 94111

WEST, JACK HENRY, petroleum geologist; b. Washington, Apr. 7, 1934; s. John Henry and Zola Faye (West) Pigg; m. Bonnie Lou Ruger, Apr. 1, 1961; children: Trent John, Todd Kenneth. BS in Geology, U. Oreg., 1957, MS, 1961. Cert. petroleum geologist. Geologist Texaco Inc., L.A and Bakersfield, Calif., 1961-72; asst. dir. devel. geologist Texaco Inc., L.A., 1972-78; geologist Oxy Petroleum Inc., Bakersfield, 1978-80, div. geologist, 1980-83; exploitation mgr. Oxy U.S.A. Inc./Cities Svc. Oil and Gas, Bakersfield, 1983—. Active Beyond War, Bakersfield, 1983—. Mem. Am. Assn. Petroleum Geologists (pres. Pacific sect. 1988-89), Soc. Petroleum Engrs., San Joaquin Well Logging Assn., San Joaquin Geol. Soc. (pres. 1984-85), Alfa Romeo Owners Club. Republican. Methodist.

WEST, JAMES DORITY, JR., financial consultant; b. Toledo, Oct. 22, 1938; s. James Dority and Betty (Boyd) W.; m. Martha Aaron Simoni, June 14, 1969 (div. 1977); 1 child, Wendy Ann. BA, BS in Edn., Bowling Green State U., 1964; MA, So. Meth. U., 1970; PhD, U. N.Mex., 1977. Grad. asst. U. N.Mex., Albuquerque, 1965-66, 75-77; tchr. Albuquerque Pub. Schs., 1966-69, developer alternative schs., fed. proposals and curriculum, 1970-75; dir. edn. N.Mex. Corrections Dept., Sante Fe, 1977-80; div. dir. N.Mex. Corrections Dept., Santa Fe, 1980-82; fin. cons. Merrill Lynch, Santa Fe, 1982—; cons. div. IV, U.S. Office Edn., Dallas, 1971-75, N.Mex. Dept. Edn., Sante Fe, 1972-75. Author: The School on Wheels, 1971. Mem. N.Mex. Adv. Coun. on Vocat. Edn., 1980-82; bd. dirs. Santa Fe Dessert Chorale, 1984-86; treas. Park Plazas Community Svcs. Assn., Santa Fe, 1988—; pres. bd. dirs. El Castillo, Santa Fe, 1988—. With USMC, 1957-60. Experienced Profl. Devel. Act scholar, 1969, Am. Assn. Sch. Adminstrs. scholar, 1975. Mem. Rotary (program chmn. Santa Fe, 1988—). Democrat. Presbyterian. Home: 3142 Plaza Blanca Santa Fe NM 87505

WEST, JERRY ALAN, professional basketball team executive; b. Chelyan, W.Va., May 28, 1938; s. Howard Stewart and Cecil Sue (Creasey) W.; m. Martha Jane Kane, May, 1960 (div. 1977); children: David, Michael, Mark; m. Karen Christine Bua, May 28, 1978; 1 son, Ryan. BS, W.Va. Coll.; LHD (hon.), W.Va. Wesleyan Coll. Mem. Los Angeles Lakers, Nat. Basketball Assn., 1960-74, coach, 1976-79, spl. cons., from 1979, gen. mgr., 1982—; mem. first team Nat. Basketball Assn. All-Star Team, 1962-67, 70-73, mem. second team, 1968, 69. Author: (with William Libby) Mr. Clutch: The Jerry West Story, 1969. Capt. U.S. Olympic Basketball Team, 1960; named Most Valuable Player NBA Playoff, 1969, Allstar Game Most Valuable Player, 1972; named to Naismith Meml. Basketball Hall of Fame, 1979, NBA Hall of Fame, 1980; mem. NBA 35th Anniversary All-Time Team, 1980. Office: LA Lakers 3900 W Manchester Blvd PO Box 10 Inglewood CA 90306 *

WEST, JOHN BURNARD, physiologist, educator; b. Adelaide, Australia, Dec. 27, 1928; came to U.S., 1969; s. Esmond Frank and Meta Pauline (Spehr) W.; m. Penelope Hall Banks, Oct. 28, 1967; children: Robert Burnard, Joanna Ruth. M.B.B.S., Adelaide U., 1952, M.D., 1958, D.Sc., 1980; Ph.D., London U., 1960; Dr. honoris causa, U. Barcelona, Spain, 1987. Resident Royal Adelaide Hosp., 1952, Hammersmith Hosp., London, 1953-55; physiologist Sir Edmund Hillary's Himalayan Expdn., 1960-61; dir. respiratory research group Postgrad. Med. Sch., London, 1962-67; reader medicine Postgrad. Med. Sch., 1968; prof. medicine and physiology U. Calif. at San Diego, 1969—; leader Am. Med. Research Expdn. to Mt. Everest, 1981; mem. life scis. adv. com. NASA, 1985-88, mem. task force sci. uses of space sta., 1984-87, chmn. sci. verification com. Spacelab SLS-1; mem. study sect. NIH, chmn., 1973-75; mem. U.S. nat. com. Internat. Union Physiol. Scis. Author: Ventilation/Blood Flow and Gas Exchange, 1965, Respiratory Physiology-The Essentials, 1974, Translations in Respiratory Physiology, 1975, Pulmonary Pathophysiology-The Essentials, 1977, Bioengineering Aspects of the Lung, 1977, Regional Differences in the Lung, 1977, Pulmonary Gas Exchange (2 vols.), 1980, High Altitude Physiology, 1981, High Altitude and Man, 1984, Everest-The Testing Place, 1985, Best and Taylor's Physiological Basis of Medical Practice, 1985, High Altitude Medicine and Physiology, 1989. Recipient Ernest Jung Prize for Medicine, Hamburg, 1977, Reynolds Prize for History, Am. Physiol. Soc., 1987. Fellow Royal Coll. Physicians (London), Royal Australasian Coll. Physicians, Royal Geog. Soc. (London), AAAS (med. sci. nominating com. 1987); mem. Nat. Acad. Scis. (com. space biology and medicine), Nat. Bd. Med. Examiners (physiology com. 1973-76), Am. Physiol. Soc. (pres. 1984-85, chmn. sect. on history of physiology 1984—), Am. Soc. Clin. Investigation, Brit. Physiol. Soc., Am., Brit. thoracic socs., Assn. Am. Physicians, Western Assn. Physicians, Explorers Club, Am. Alpine Club, Brit. Alpine Club, Fleischner Soc. (pres. 1985). Home: 9626 Blackgold Rd La Jolla CA 92037 Office: U Calif San Diego Sch Medicine M-023A Dept Medicine La Jolla CA 92037

WEST, JUDITH ANNE, librarian; b. Whittier, Calif., Mar. 14, 1940; d. Emile Roland and Florence Lucile (Binford) Crumly; m. Joseph West, Dec. 18, 1965; (div. 1974). BA, Whittier Coll., 1963; MLS, U. So. Calif., 1964. Librarian, Los Angeles County Library, 1965-69; city librarian Turlock Library, Calif., 1969-71; librarian Stanislaus County Free Library, Modesto, Calif., 1971-82, county librarian, 1982—. Mem. AIA, AAUW, Calif. Library Assn., Calif. County Librarians Assn. Democrat. Mem. Soc. of Friends. Lodge: Soroptimist. Office: Stanislaus County Libr 1500 I St Modesto CA 95354

WEST, LOUIS JOLYON, psychiatrist; b. N.Y.C., Oct. 6, 1924; s. Albert Jerome and Anna (Rosenberg) W.; m. Kathryn Louise Hopkirk, Apr. 29, 1944; children—Anne Kathryn, Mary Elizabeth, John Stuart. B.S., U. Minn., 1946, M.B., 1948, M.D., 1949. Diplomate: Nat. Bd. Med. Examiners, Am. Bd. Psychiatry and Neurology. Mem. faculty Cornell U., 1950-52; chief psychiatry service USAF Hosp., Lackland AFB, San Antonio, 1952-56; prof. psychiatry, head dept. psychiatry, neurology and behavioral scis. U. Okla. Sch. Medicine, 1954-69; chief mental health sect. Okla. Med. Research Found., 1956-69; cons. psychiatry Oklahoma City VA Hosp., Tinker AFB Hosp., 1956-69; fellow Center for Advanced Study in Behavioral Scis., Stanford U., 1966-67; prof., chmn. dept. psychiatry and biobehavioral sci. UCLA, 1969—; dir. Neuropsychiat. Inst. at UCLA Center for Health Scis., 1969—; psychiatrist-in-chief UCLA Med. Ctr., 1969—; nat. cons. psychiatry Surgeon Gen. USAF, 1957-62; cons. psychiatry Brentwood and Sepulveda VA hosps., 1969—; mem. nat. adv. coms. NIMH, USAF Office Sci. Research, USPHS, VA, HEW, Nat. Acad. Scis., NRC, Nat. Inst. Medicine, U.S. Army Med. Research and Devel. Panel, A.M.A., White House Conf. Civil Rights; mem. internat. adv. bd. Israeli Ctr. for Psychobiology, Jerusalem Mental Health Ctr. Author: Hallucinations, 1962; editor: Hallucinations: Behavior, Experience, and Theory, 1975, Treatment of Schizophrenia: Progress and Prospects, 1976, Research on Smoking Behavior, 1977, Critical Issues in Behavioral Medicine, 1982, Alcoholism and Related Problems: Issues for the American Public, 1984; mem. editorial bd. Directions in Psychiatry, Medical Update, Cultic Studies Jour., Violence, Aggression, Terrorism; contbr. articles to profl. jours., chpts. in books. Bd. dirs. Brain Research Inst., UCLA Found., Alcoholism Council Calif. Fellow AAAS, Am. Coll. Neuropsychopharmacology (founding), Am. Coll. Psychiatrists, Am. Psychiat. Assn. (life), Soc. Behavioral Medicine; mem. AMA, Am. Acad. Psychiatry and Law, Soc. Biol. Psychiatry, Am. Orthopsychiat. Assn., Acad. Psychoanalysis, Assn. Psychophysiol. Study Sleep, Am. Psychosomatic Soc., Am. Psychopath. Assn., Am. Psychol. Assn., Assn. Research in Nervous and Mental Disease, Assn. Am. Med. Colls., Nat. Acad. Religion and Mental Health (founding), Nat. Council on Alcoholism, Pavlovian Soc. (pres. 1975), Soc. Biol. Psychiatry, Soc. Psychophysiol. Research, So. Profs. Psychiatry (pres. 1963), Soc. Clin. and Exptl. Hypnosis, Alpha Omega Alpha, Sigma Xi. Office: UCLA Neuropsychiat Inst 760 Westwood Pla Los Angeles CA 90024

WEST, MICHAEL DENNIS, labor mediator; b. Los Angeles, Feb. 27, 1938; s. Gerald West and Marie Elizabeth (Redmond) Fink; m. Patsy Jolene Smith, Sept. 18, 1957 (div. 1982); children: Dennis Michael, Bradley Russell. AA with honors, San Jose City Coll., 1963; BS summa cum laude, San Jose State U., 1965. Adminstrv. asst. Santa Clara County Employees Assn., San Jose, Calif., 1965-66; gen. mgr. Santa Clara County Employees Assn., San Jose, 1966-71; coord. SEIU Counc. 40 AFL-CIO, Los Angeles, 1972; field rep. local 715 Service Employees Union, San Jose, 1972; rep. employee relations Santa Clara County, San Jose, 1973-76; mediator indsl. relations dept. State of Calif., San Jose, 1976—; arbitrator Arbitration West, Los Gatos, Calif., 1981—; treas. Pub. Employee Staff Orgn., Los Angeles, 1971-72. Author mediator tng manual, 1982. Chmn. parent adv. com. Los Gatos Elem. Sch. Dist., 1975; arbitrator City of San Jose, 1980—, City of Hayward, 1983-87, Santa Clara County Bar Assn., 1982—, Better Bus. Bur., 1982—; mem. pub. protection com. State Bar Calif., 1987-88. Mem. Am. Arbitration Assn., Soc. Profls. in Dispute Resolution, Indsl. Relations Research Assn., Jaycees, Alpha Gamma Sigma (Alpaha Al Sirat award). Democrat. Home: 20000 Old Santa Cruz Hwy Los Gatos CA 95030 Office: State of Calif Mediation Div 455 Golden Gate Ave San Francisco CA 94101

WEST, RICHARD PAUL, academic program administrator; b. Carlsbad, Calif., June 19, 1947; s. O. Kenneth and Mildred S. (Ponstler) W.; m. Catherine Held, June 28, 1969. BA in Econs., U. Calif., Santa Cruz, 1969; MBA, U. Calif., Berkeley, 1971. Sr. adminstrv. analyst U. Calif., Berkeley, 1969-72, coordinator student info. systems office of pres., 1972-75, mgr. student fin. aid, 1975-76, dir. info. mgmt., 1976-79, asst. v.p. info. systems and adminstrv. svcs., 1979-89, assoc. v.p. info. systems and adminstrv. svcs., 1989—; lectr. Sch. Bus., U. Calif., Berkeley, 1984—, corp. edn., 1988—. Contbr. articles to profl. jours. Republican. Home: 1600 Mountain Blvd Oakland CA 94611 Office: 300 Lakeside Dr Oakland CA 94612

WEST, RICHARD VINCENT, art museum official; b. Prague, Czechoslovakia, Nov. 26, 1934; came to U.S., 1938, naturalized, 1947; s. Jan Josef and Katherine Frieda (Mayer) Vysloužil; m. Emily Ann Pagenhart, June 26, 1961; 1 child, Jessica Katherine. Student, UCLA, 1952-55; B.A. with highest honors, U. Calif., Santa Barbara, 1961; postgrad., Akademie der Bildenden Kuenste, Vienna, 1961-62; M.A., U. Calif., Berkeley, 1965. Curatorial intern Cleve. Art Mus., 1965-66; curatorial intern Albright-Knox Art Gallery, Buffalo, 1966-67; curator Bowdoin Coll. Mus. Art, 1967-69, dir., 1969-72; dir. Crocker Art Mus., Sacramento, Calif., 1973-83, Santa Barbara Mus. Art, Calif., 1983—; mem. Joint Yugoslav-Am. Excavations at Sirmium, 1971; bd. dirs. Sacramento Regional Art Council, 1973-77. Author: Painters of the Section d'or, 1967, Language of the Print, 1968; The Walker Art Building Murals, 1972, An Enkindled Eye: The Paintings of Rockwell Kent, 1985; exhbn. catalogues, also various revs. and articles. Served with USN, 1956-57. Ford Found. fellow, 1965-67; Smithsonian fellow, 1971. Mem. Assn. Art Mus. Dirs., Am. Assn. Mus., Coll. Art Assn., Internat. Coun. Mus., Western Assn. Art Mus. (pres. 1975-78), Calif. Assn. Mus. (bd. dirs. 1980-82, v.p. 1986—), University Club, Rotary Internat. Office: Santa Barbara Mus Art 1130 State St Santa Barbara CA 93101

WEST, ROBERT SUMNER, surgeon; b. Bowman, N.D., Nov. 20, 1935; s. Elmer and Minnie (DeBode) W.; m. Martha W. Hopkins, Mar. 23, 1957; children: Stephen, Christopher, Anna Marie, Catherine, Sarah. BA, U. N.D., 1957, BS in Medicine, 1959; MD, Harvard U., 1961. Diplomate Am. Bd. Surgery. Intern U.S. Naval Hosp., Chelsea, Mass., 1961-62; resident in surgery U. Vt. Med. Ctr. Hosp., 1965-69; pvt. practice Coeur d'Alene, Idaho, 1969—; coroner Kootenai County, Coeur d'Alene, 1984—. Trustee, pres. Coeur d'Alene Sch. Dist. 271 Bd. Edn., 1973-77. Lt. M.C., USN, 1960-65. Fellow ACS (pres. Idaho 1985, chmn. com. on trauma); mem. Idaho Med. Assn. (pres. 1989—, trustee), Kiwanis. Republican. Lutheran. Office: 920 Ironwood Dr Coeur d'Alene ID 83814-2601

WEST, ROD ALLEN, radio syndication executive; b. Grand Rapids, Mich., July 4, 1952; s. Peter and Lenora V. (Hall) Westerling; m. Margo Millner, Dec. 31, 1984. Lic. broadcaster. Radio announcer Sta. WPJB-FM, Providence, 1975-80; radio announcer Sta. WPRO-AM FM, 1980-84, Sta. KZLA, L.A., 1984-85, Sta. KIIS-AM-FM, L.A., 1985-86, Transtar Radio Network, L.A., 1986-87; clearance mgr. Premier Radio Network, L.A., 1987; gen. mgr. ABC Watermark, L.A., 1987—; bd. dirs. Vital Options, Studio City, Calif. Mem. Am. Fedn. TV and Radio Artists. Office: ABC Watermark 3575 Cahuenga Blvd W 555 Los Angeles CA 90068

WEST, SANDI JEAN, financial administrator; b. San Francisco, Sept. 12, 1945; d. Lyle Hazen and Georgia Arlene (West) Reiswig. AA in Bus. Adminstrn., San Joaquin Delta Jr. Coll., 1977. Eligibility worker San Joaquin County Welfare Dept., Stockton, Calif., 1968-75; child support collections supr. San Joaquin County Dist. Atty.'s Office, Stockton, 1975-79; credit mgr. E.D. Wilkinson Grain Co., Stockton, 1979-80; agt., estates mgr. Calif. Dept. Devel. Svcs., Sacramento, 1980-85; trust officer Sonoma Devel. Ctr., Eldridge, Calif., 1985-88; chief counselor Coll. Assistance Program, Sonoma, 1988—. Vol. police officer Stockton Police Dept., 1968-74. Republican. Home: PO Box 1488 Eldridge CA 95431 Office: College Assistance Program 164 Vista Dr Sonoma CA 95476

WEST, SCOTT HARRISON, cardiologist; b. Salt Lake City, Dec. 12, 1954; s. Verneil LaVar and Sally Dianne (Harrison) W.; m. Theresa Anastasia Lemos, Nov. 27, 1982; 1 child, Alexander Harrison. BS, U. Utah, 1975, MD, 1979. Diplomate Am. Bd. Internal Medicine, Am. Bd. Cardiology. Intern, then resident U. Calif.-Davis Med. Ctr., Sacramento, 1979-82; cardiology fellow U. Utah Med. Ctr., Salt Lake City, 1982-84; pvt. practice Sacramento, 1984--; pres., med. dir. Sacramento Heart Inst., 1987--. Bishop, Mormon Ch., Sacramento, 1988. Fellow Am. Coll. Cardiology; mem. Phi Kappa Phi. Republican. Home: 451 45th St Sacramento CA 95819 Office: Med Clinic Sacramento 3160 FolsomBlvd Sacramento CA 95816

WEST, THOMAS MOORE, educator; b. Weston, W.Va., Nov. 10, 1940; s. Stanley Rymer and Dorothy (Moore) W.; m. Carmen Wessner West, Aug. 31, 1967. BS in Engring., U. Tenn., 1963, MS in Indsl. Engring., 1965; PhD, Oreg. State U., 1976. Registered profl. engr., Tenn., Oreg. Engrs. analyst Monsanto, Greeneville, S.C., 1964-66; instr. Ga. Inst. Tech., Atlanta, 1966-67; systems engr. IBM, Essex Junction, Vt., 1967; asst. prof. U. Tenn., Knoxville, 1l968-72; asst. prof. Oreg. State U., Corvallis, 1976-80, assoc. prof., 1980-88, head. dept., 1988--; engring. cons. Union Carbide, Oak Ridge, Tenn., 1975-76, U.S. govt. agys., Pacific Northwest, 1976-87. Co-author: Engineering in Economy, 1986, Essentials of Engineering, 1986; author: Review of 1986 Tax Act, 1988; author numerous articles in field. Mem. Inst. Indsl. Engring. (sr., v.p.), Soc. Mfg. Engrs., Am. Soc. Engring., Edn., Ops. Rsch. Soc. Am. Office: Oreg State U Indsl Engring Dept Corvallis OR 97331

WEST, VIKKI LYNN, employment agency executive; b. Oklahoma City, Dec. 16, 1948; d. Stanley Richard and Lynn (Shelton) Kaplan; m. John Michael Black, Aug, 31, 1967; children: Michael Scott Black, Christopher Lee Black, Jennifer Michelle Black; m. Kenneth William West, June 2, 1984. Student, U. Tex., 1966-67; student, N. Tex. State U., 1967-68, Rio Salado Coll., Phoenix, 1988-89. Bookkeeper, mktg. asst. Paradynamics, Inc., Scottsdale, Ariz., 1975-77; ins. agt. Lincoln Nat., Phoenix, 1977-78; sales mgr. Plymouth Tube Co., Chandler, Ariz., 1978-81; v.p. Robert Half Ariz., Inc., Phoenix, 1981—. Mem. Ariz. Assn. Temp. Svcs. (treas. 1987—), Phoenix Personnel Mgmt. Assn., Ariz. Small Bus. Assn., United Methodist Women. Republican. Office: Robert Half Ariz Inc 100 W Clarendon Ave Ste 1150 Phoenix AZ 85013

WEST, WILLIAM BRENT, circuit court judge; b. Salt Lake City, May 17, 1951; s. Richard William West and Beverly Jean (Woodhead) Monson; m. Judy Ann Hill, Mar. 18, 1971; children: Jennifer Lee, Jason William. BS, U. Utah, 1973; JD, Southern Meth. U., 1975. Bar: Utah, 1976. Pvt. practice Ogden, Utah, 1976-79; asst. corp. counsel City of Ogden, 1979-81, chief prosecutor, 1981-84; circuit court judge State of Utah, Ogden, 1984—; presiding judge 3rd Cir. Ct. Bd. Judges, 1985-88, 2nd Cir. Ct. Bd. Judges, 1988—; mem. Cir. Ct. Bd. Judges, 1986, 1988—. Bd. dirs. Children's Aid Soc. (treas. 1978-80, v.p. 1987-89), Ogden City Schs. Vols. Assn. (pres. 1980-86), Moweda, 1985-87; mem. Common Ct. Boundaries Com., 1987; Vice chmn. Warrants Task Force, 1987; mem. Utah Task Force on Gender and Justice 1986—; chmn. Uniform Bail Schedule Com., 1987—.; group leader Parents United 1986; mem. Weber, Morgan Counties Child Abuse Coordination Coun., 1988—. Mem. Utah Bar Assn., Weber County Bar Assn. (treas. 1977-79), Ogden Unit Contract Bridge League (dir. 1978-80,1987-89, pres. 1979-80, 1987-88, 1988-89). Office: 2549 Washington Blvd Ogden UT 84401

WESTBO, LEONARD ARCHIBALD, JR., electronics engineer; b. Tacoma, Wash., Dec. 4, 1931; s. Leonard Archibald and Agnes (Martinson) W.; B.A. in Gen. Studies, U. Wash., 1958. Electronics engr. FAA, Seattle Air Route Traffic Control Center, Auburn, Wash., 1961-72; asst. br. chief electronics engring. br. 13th Coast Guard Dist., Seattle, 1972-87. Served with USCG, 1951-54, 1958-61. Registered profl. engr., Wash. Mem. Aircraft Owners and Pilots Assn., IEEE, Am. Radio Relay League. Home: 10528 SE 323d St Auburn WA 98002 Office: 10528 SE 323d St Auburn WA 98002

WESTBROOK, KARLA RENEÉ, wholesale company executive; b. Hollywood, Fla., Nov. 26, 1964; d. William Fred and Maggie (Williams) W. BA in Fashion, Am. Coll. for Applied Arts, L.A., 1988; cert. merchandising, Bauder Fashion Coll., Atlanta, 1984. With retail sales Three Sisters, Ft. Lauderdale, Fla., 1981-82, Susie's Casuals, Hollywood, Fla., 1982-84; waitress numerous restaurants, Atlanta and Encino, 1985-88; v.p. asst., with sales Frank L. Robinson Co., L.A., 1988—. Home: 7425 Sepulveda Blvd Van Nuys CA 91405 Office: Frank L Robinson Co 1150 S Flower St Los Angeles CA 90015

WESTBROOK, KENNETH KIRK, hospital administrator; b. Long Beach, Calif., May 25, 1950; s. Woodrow Wilson and Phyllis E. (Kirk) W.; m. Linda Diane Kuhn, June 19, 1976; children: Bryan, Sandra, Rochelle. AA in Econs., Cerritos Coll., 1972; AS in Respiratory Therapy, Rio Hondo Coll., 1975; BBA, U. Redlands, 1982, MA in Mgmt., 1986, MBA, 1989. Asst. dir. pulmonary svcs. La Mirada (Calif.) Med. Ctr., 1974-75, Rio Hondo Hosp., Downey, Calif., 1975-80; dir. cardiopulmonary svcs. Los Altos Hosp., Long Beach, 1980-82, South Bay Hosp., Redondo Beach, Calif., 1982-84; adminstrv. dir. support svcs. Robert F. Kennedy Med. Ctr., Hawthorne, Calif., 1984-87; assoc. adminstr. Charter Suburban Hosp., Paramount, 1988—; educator El Camino Coll., Torrance, Calif., 1985-87. Editor: The Respiratory Practitioner, 1985—; contbr. articles to profl. jours. Named one of Outstanding Young Men in Am., 1985. Mem. Am. Coll. Health Care Execs., Health Care Execs. So. Calif., Calif. Soc. for Respiratory Care, Am. Assn. for Respiratory Care, Nat. Bd. for Respiratory Care. Lodge: Rotary. Office: Charter Med Corp 577 Mulberry St Macon GA 31201

WESTENBERG, ROBERT WILLIAM, writer; b. Chgo., Mar. 30, 1933; s. William F. and Catherine E. (Lackner) W.;m. Carol Godey, June 20, 1954 (div. July 1978); children: Bruce R., Mark A., Lynn C., Lawrence J.; m. Jeanne Hysell, Oct. 20, 1979. BA in Journalism/Advt., U. Ill., Champaign, 1953. Advt. mgr. All-Pets Mag., Fond du Lac, WI, 1957-60, Can-Pro Corp., Fond du Lac, 1960-63, David C. Cook Pub. Co., Elgin, Ill., 1963-73; pub. Ch. Mail Market, Elgin, 1973-86; pres. Robert W. Westenberg & Co., Inc., Sedona, Ariz., 1986—; cons. Trio Pub., Buffalo Grove, Ill., 1986-88, Hughes Communications, Rockford, Ill., 1987-88, Marketshare Pub., Overland Park, Kans., 1986-88. Author: Portfolio of Bank Letters, 1974; author monthly column Bookstore Jour. Mag., 1972-75. 1st lt. U.S. Army, 1955-75. Recipient Direct mail Leader award Direct Mail Mktg. Assn., 1967, 68, 70, 71, Cartnell Gold medal award Dartnell Assn., 1970. Republican. Office: Robert W Westenberg & Co 6018-F Hwy 179 Sedona AZ 86336

WESTENBORG, JACK ARTHUR, manufacturing company executive; b. Springfield, Ill., Aug. 6, 1942; s. Arthur John and Betty (Franke) W.; m. Marilyn McQuitty, July 17, 1965 (div. Oct. 22, 1982). BS in Fin., U. Ill., 1966. Officer USAF, 1966-73; v.p. Cen. Pipe and Supply Co., Tucson, 1973-78; exec. v.p. Old Tucson Corp., 1978-81; v.p. Krueger Mfg. Co., Tucson, 1981-85; pres. Krueger Mfg. Co., 1985; exec. v.p. Krueger Div. of Philips Industries, Tucson, 1985-87; pres. Westpar Corp., Phoenix, 1987—; v.p. Air Diffusion Counsel, Chgo., 1984-87; bd. dirs. Cadence Corp., Tucson, 1981--, Old Presidio Corp., Tucson, 1986--. Served to lt. col. USAFR, 1966--. Decorated Bronze Star. Mem. Skyline Club. Republican. Presbyterian. Office: Westpar Corp 48 N 56th St Phoenix AZ 85034

WESTENBURG, CHARLES EDWARD, construction company executive; b. Alamosa, Colo., Aug. 3, 1933; s. Peter and Jeanette (Bylsma) W.; m. Donna Lee Saenger, Feb. 15, 1952; children: Barbara, Victoria, Leah. Grad. high sch., Alamosa, 1951. Pres., owner Chuck Westenburg Inc., Tucson, 1958—. Recipient Gov.'s award Ariz. Wildlife Fedn., 1982. Mem. Associated Builders and Contractors, Am. Assn. Subcontractors (bd. dirs. 1986), Am. Soc. Profl. Estimators (bd. dirs. 1986—). Republican. Baptist. Clubs: Safari Internat., Tucson Rod and Gun. Office: Chuck Westenburg Inc 7025 E 21st St Tucson AZ 85710

WESTER, KEITH ALBERT, film and television recording engineer; b. Seattle, Feb. 21, 1940; s. Albert John and Evelyn Grace (Nettell) W., m. Judith Elizabeth Jones, 1968 (div. Mar. 1974); 1 child, Wendy Elizabeth. AA, Am. River Coll., Sacramento, 1959; BA, Calif. State U., L.A., 1962; MA, UCLA, 1965. Lic. multi-engine rated pilot. Prodn. asst. KCRA-TV, Sacramento, 1956; announcer KSFM, Sacramento, 1960; film editor, sound rec. technician Urie & Assocs., Hollywood, Calif., 1963-66; co-owner Steckler-Wester Film Prodns., Hollywood, 1966-70; owner Profl. Sound Recorders, Studio City, Calif., 1970—, Aerocharter, Studio City, 1974—. Mem. Acad. Motion Picture Arts Scis. (Sound Branch exec. bd.), Acad. of Television Arts & Scis. (Emmy award An Early Frost 1986, Emmy nominations: Further Adventures of Tom Sawyer and Huck Finn 1982, Gambler II 1984, Malice in Wonderland 1985, Amerika 1987), Cinema Audio Soc. (sec. 1985—, Sound award 1987), Soc. Motion Picture and TV Engrs., Internat. Sound Technicians, Local 695, Assn. Film Craftsmen (sec. 1967-73, treas. 1973-76), Screen Actors Guild, Aircraft Owners & Pilots Assn., Am. Radio Relay League. Home: 4146 Bellingham Ave Studio City CA 91604 Office: Profl Sound Recorders 22440 Clarendon Woodland Hills CA 91367

WESTERDAHL, JOHN BRIAN, nutritionist, health educator; b. Tucson, Dec. 3, 1954; s. Jay E. and Margaret (Meyer) W. AA, Orange Coast Coll., 1977; BS, Pacific Union Coll., 1979; MPH, Loma Linda U., 1981. Registered dietitian. Nutritionist, health educator Castle Med. Ctr., Kailua, Hawaii, 1981-84, health promotion coordinator, 1984-87, asst. dir. health promotion, 1987-88, dir. health promotion, 1988—; talk show host Nutrition and You, Sta. KGU-Radio, Honolulu, 1983—; nutrition com. mem. Hawaii Heart Assn., Honolulu, 1984—; mem. nutrition study group Govs. Conf. Health Promotion and Disease Prevention for Hawaii, 1985. Named One of Outstanding Young Men Am., 1984, One of 10 Outstanding Young Persons in Hawaii, 1988. Mem. AAAS, Am. Coll. Sports Medicine, Am. Dietetic Assn., Am. Pub. Health Assn., Hawaii Nutrition Council (v.p. 1983-86, pres. elect 1988-89, pres. 1989—), Hawaii Dietetic Assn., Seventh-day Adventist Dietetic Assn., Soc. for Nutrition Edn., Soc. Pub. Health Edn., Assn. for Fitness in Bus., Nat. Wellness Assn., N.Y. Acad. Scis., Am. Coll. Nutrition, Nutrition Today Soc. Republican. Seventh Day Adventist. Office: Castle Med Ctr 640 Ulukahiki St Kailua HI 96734

WESTERGREN, MARK WAYNE, military officer, laser engineer; b. McAllen, Tex., Mar. 21, 1962; s. Clifford Marshall and Dona Marlene (Doss) W. BS in Chem. Engring., Syracuse U., 1984; MBA in Fin., Webster U., 1989. Commd. 2nd lt. USAF, 1985, advanced through grades to capt., 1989; Solid state physicist Air Force Weapons Lab., Kirtland Air Force Base, N.Mex., 1985—. Mem. Smithsonian Inst., Nat. Geographic Soc. Republican. Mem. Christian and Missionary Alliance. Home: 200 Figueroa NE 82 Albuquerque NM 87123

WESTFALL, RICHARD MERRILL, chemist, research administrator; b. Denver, Dec. 17, 1956; s. Robert Raymond and Madelyn Evastine (Cornwell) W. Student, U. Colo., 1976-80. Mem. lab. staff NOAA, Boulder, Colo., 1978-79, Solar Energy Rsch. Inst., Golden, Colo., 1979-80; dir. rsch. Galactic Products, Denver, 1981-82; pres., dir. rsch. CEL Systems Corp., Arvada, Colo. and Schertz, Tex., 1982—; process chemist, optical detector fabrication engr. Tex. Med. Instruments, Schertz, 1986-87; dir. rsch., chief exec. officer Galactic Mining Industries, Denver, 1988-89; founder, exec. dir. Galactic Ednl. Devel. Inst., Denver, 1989—. Inventor electrolytic growth tin and other metals, and process, 1980-82; patentee in field. Mem. AIAA, Air Force Assn. Home: 4838 Stuart St Denver CO 80212

WESTLAKE, JUDE ANN, photographer; b. Chillicothe, Ohio, Apr. 12, 1952; d. Wendell Wayne and Betty Joanne (Shear) W. Student, Moore Coll. Art, 1970-72, Slade Sch. Fine Art, U. London, 1974-75; BFA, Pa. State U., 1975; MFA, La. State U., 1977. Supr. film Parkway Color Lab., Chgo., 1977-78; exec. dir. Doshi Ctr. Contemporary Art, Harrisburg, Pa., 1981-82; chmn. photography dept. Antonelli Inst. Art & Photography, York, Pa., 1981-84; dir. comml. photography Plaza 3 Acad., Phoenix, 1984-85; founder, pres. Visual Images West, Inc., Tempe, Ariz., 1985—; prof. art dept. Messiah Coll., Grantham, Pa., 1982; mem. exhibits adv. bd. City Govt. Ctr., Harrisburg, 1982; guest lectr. Gov.'s Sch. for Arts, Bucknell U., Lewisburg, Pa., 1982. Exhibited in group shows: Gov.'s Office, Wash., 1982, Elaine Horwitch Gallery, Scottsdale, Ariz., 1984; represented in permanent collection Cromer-Young Group, Harrisburg. Mem. Am. Soc. Mag. Photographers (bd. dirs. Ariz. chpt. 1983-84, 88—), Picture Agy. Coun. Am., Phoenix Soc. Communicating Arts, Women in Design (exhibits chmn. 1985), Phoenix City Club. Republican. Presbyterian. Office: Visual Images West Inc 600 E Baseline Rd Ste B6 Tempe AZ 85283

WESTLING, LOUISE HUTCHINGS, English educator; b. Jacksonville, Fla., Feb. 13, 1942; d. William Evelyn and Louise Dillon (Van Winkle) Hutchings; m. George Attout Wickes, Nov. 8, 1975. AB, Randolph-Macon Woman's Coll., 1964; MA, U. Iowa, 1965; PhD, U. Oreg., 1974. Instr. English Centre Coll., Danville, Ky., 1965-67; research assoc. N.W. Regional Ednl. Lab., Portland, Oreg., 1968-71; instr. English Oreg. State U., Corvallis, 1974-77; grad. teaching fellow U. Oreg., Eugene, 1971-74, asst. prof. Honors Coll., 1977-81, instr., 1981-85, asst. prof., 1985-88, assoc. prof., 1988. Author: Sacred Groves & Ravaged Gardens, 1985, Eudora Welty, 1989; editor He Included Me: The Autobiography of Sarah Rice, 1989. Mem. MLA , SAMLA, Philol. Assn. Pacific Coast (exec. dir. 1985—). Democrat. Office: U Oreg Dept English Eugene OR 97403

WESTON, DARVIN LEE, aircraft company executive; b. Kansas City, Mo., Apr. 13, 1942; s. Emanuel Albert and Velma Marie (Carter) W.; m. Susan Wu, Feb. 16, 1977; children: James Weijen, Kristie Lyn. BA in History, Govt., U. Mo., Kansas City, 1964; cert. Mandarin Chinese, Washington U., St. Louis, 1965, U. Kans., 1966; MA in Asian Studies, Claremont Grad. Sch., 1974. Commd. ensign USN, 1968, advanced through grades to comdr.; intelligence liaison officer Comdr. Naval Forces USN, Vietnam, 1968-69; agt. Naval Investigative Svc. USN, Honolulu, 1969-71; comdr. carrier div. USN, Vietnam, 1971-72; officer U.S. Taiwan Def. Command USN, Taipei, 1974-77; resigned USN, 1977; with USNR, 1977—, advanced through ranks to comdr., 1988; office mgr. Hughes Aircraft Systems, Internat., Taipei, 1977-79; head internat. adminstrv. svcs. Hughes Aircraft Co., L.A., 1979-84, asst. mgr. internat. govt. liaison, 1984—. Author: Newcomer's Guide to Taiwan, 1977. Vol. interpreter Chinese lang., police depts. in So. Calif., 1980—; scout leader, El Segundo PTA, 1989—. Decorated Bronze Star with V medal, 3 Air medals, others. Mem. Navy Res. Assn. (speaker), Internat. Narcotic Law Enforcement Officers Assn., U. Mo. Kansas City Alumni Club So. Calif. (founding mem. 1988), Masons, Shriners. Republican. Home: 224 W Maple Ave El Segundo CA 90245 Office: Hughes Aircraft Co Internat 7200 Hughes Terr Los Angeles CA 90045

WESTON, EDWARD, art dealer, consultant; b. N.Y.C., Feb. 25, 1925; s. Joseph and Mona (Gould) W.; m. Ann Jean Weston, May 4, 1974; children: Jon Marc, Cari Alyn Rene. News editor Sta. WMCA, N.Y.C., 1940-41; announcer news dept. Sta. WSAV, Savannah, Ga., 1941-43; newscaster, disc jockey Sta. WNOX, Knoxville, Tenn., 1943-45; program dir. Sta. WXLH, Okinawa, Japan, 1945-47; newscaster, announcer Sta. WAVZ, New Haven, 1947-48; program dir. Sta. WCCC, Hartford, Conn., 1948-49; asst. gen. mgr. Sta. WCPO AM-FM-TV, Cin., 1949-59; pres., gen. mgr. Sta. WZIP, Cin., 1959-61; pres. Weston Entertainment, Northridge, Calif., 1961—; chmn. bd. Fulton J. Sheen Communications; pres. Inspirational Programs, Inc., 1983—, Weston Editions, 1970—, Marilyn Monroe Editions, 1975—. Producer TV/video cassettes Life Is Worth Living; PBS TV series How to Paint with Elke Sommer, 1984. Founder Cin. Summer Playhouse, 1950. Served with U.S. Army, 1945-46. Recipient Outstanding News Coverage award Variety mag., 1949, Outstanding Sta. Ops. award Variety mag., 1950, Best Programming award Nat. Assn. Radio TV Broadcasters, 1951. Home: 10511 Andora Ave Chatsworth CA 91311 Office: Weston Entertainment 19355 Business Ctr Dr Northridge CA 91324

WESTON, PAUL T., data processing executive; b. Ft. Lewis, Wash., July 29, 1947; s. Paul J. and Anne Marie (Tighe) W.; m. Carol J. Thompson, Sept. 27, 1987. BS in Math., U. Wash., 1972; MS in Systems Engring., U. Petroleum & Mining, Dhahran, Saudi Arabia, 1974. Cert. data processor. V.p. Dynalogic, Seattle, 1979-81; pres. Software Extraordinaire, Seattle, 1981—. Mem. Puget Sound VS Users Group (bd. dirs. 1981—). Office: Software Extraordinaire 1419 8th Ave W Seattle WA 98119

WESTOVER, CAROLYN DOREEN, publisher; b. Knoxville, Apr. 21, 1944; d. Lloyd Paul and Margaret Elaine (Swindall) Smith; m. Robert Lee Westover, Oct. 13, 1963; children: Paul Dwight, Richard Lee. Student, Mesa Coll., 1980-88. Intermediate stenographer City of San Diego, 1973-75; sec. to pres. Continental Swiss, San Diego, 1975-76; branch mgr. Tri-City Blueprinting, San Diego, 1976-77; intermediate stenographer City of San Diego, 1977-79; security lighting coord. San Diego Gas & Electric, 1979-87; owner Data Pro's Network, San Diego, 1987—. Mem. Golden Triangle C. of C., San Diego, 1988; vol. Am. Heart Assn., San Diego, 1970—, Am. Lung Assn., San Diego, 1970—, Nat. Diabetes Found., San Diego, 1989, Nat. Asthma Found., San Diego, 1989; mem., vol. San Diego Railroad Mus., Campo, Calif., 1987-89. Mem. Assn. Office Support Profls. (program chmn. 1988-89, bylaws com. 1988-89, newsletter editor 1988-89), Am. Bus. Women's Assn., Nat. Assn. Profl. Organizers, Assn. Home-Based Businesses (newletter typesetting 1988-89), Ventura Users N. Am. Democrat. Presbyterian. Office: Data Pros Network 4951 Clairemont Sq Ste 243 San Diego CA 92117

WESTOVER, VIRGINIA L. (VIRGINIA L. WEINER), copywriter; b. Bay City, Mich., May 20, 1938; d. Edwin Frederick and Virginia Elizabeth (Snyder) Westover; m. Michael D. Ryan II, Apr. 23, 1960 (div. 1965); m. Joseph J. Weiner, Sept. 29, 1978. Student, Wheaton Coll., Norton, Mass., 1957-59; BA in English Lit., U. Mich., 1961. Pub. relations asst. Univ. Relations of U. Mich., Ann Arbor, 1961-62; reporter Ann Arbor News, 1962-66, Detroit News, 1966-67; reporter, writer San Francisco Chronicle, 1967-71, soc. editor, 1971-73; asst. dir. devel. San Francisco Opera, 1974-76; publicity dir. San Francisco Symphony, 1976-78; project dir. The Presence of the Past, 1980-82; freelance writer San Francisco, 1984—. Active San Francisco Art Inst. Council, 1978-86, Modern Art Council, San Francisco Mus. Modern Art., 1985—; trustee U. Art. Mus., U. Calif., Berkeley, 1985—. Democrat. Presbyterian. Club: Met. (San Francisco).

WETCH, JOSEPH RONALD, power engineer; b. Santa Rosa, Calif., July 27, 1928; s. Joseph Ralph and Anna Marie (Laufer) W.; m. Evelyn Jeanne Bennett, Jan. 27, 1951 (div. 1972); children: Stephen Bennet, Catherine Ann, Stanley Joseph; m. Debra Ann Haywood, Aug. 17, 1974; children: Heather Ann, Joanna Maria. BS in Chem. Engring., U. Calif., Berkeley, 1951; postgrad., U. So. Calif., L.A., 1952-54, UCLA, 1954-56. Registered profl. engr., Calif. Nuclear engr. Hanford Ops., GE, Hanford, Wash., 1951-52; nuclear engr. N. Am. Aviation, Downey, Calif., 1952-55; PE, PM dept. dir. N. Am. Aviation, Canoga Park, Calif., 1955-65; dir. advanced tech. mktg. N. Am.-Rockwell, Canoga Park, 1965-72; cons. Rockwell Internat., Canoga Park, 1972-73; plant mgr., v.p. Regal Racing Inc., Chatsworth, Calif., 1973-74; v.p. Victory Racing Plate Co., Balt., 1975-80; program mgr.nuclear waste mgmt. Rockwell Hanford, Richland, Wash., 1980-83; pres. Space Power, Inc., Sunnyvale, Calif., 1983-86; chief exec. officer, pres. Space Power, Inc., San Jose, Calif., 1987—; chmn. power source subcom., Nat. Security Industry Assn., Washington, 1962-64; sr. mem. power com. Am. Rocket Soc, Washington, 1960-64; adv. com. on nuclear processes NASA, Washington, 1960-62. Prin. inventor organic cooled ·& moderated reactors, homogeneous hydride moderated reactors, reflector controlled reactors; prin. innovator thermionic thermal reactor and the world's first nuclear power reactor in space. Pres. U.S. Navy League, San Fernando Valley, Calif., 1965-67; chmn. United Republicans Calif., San Fernando Valley, 1963-65. 2nd lt. U.S. Army. Office: Space Power Inc 621 River Oaks Pkwy San Jose CA 95134

WETHERILL, TOM OLIVER, construction engineer, building consultant; b. Sand Springs, Okla., July 11, 1930; s. Donald Shirley and Martha (Wetherill) Stewart; m. Nancy Caroline Duerlou, Nov. 4, 1956 (dec. Jan. 1966); children: Victoria Lee, Lynda Susan, Cara Ann, Megan Angela; m. Laurin Letitia Dilcher, Nov. 14, 1981; 1 child, Samantha Ann. BSME, Tulsa U., 1956. Tool designer Douglas Aircraft Co., Tulsa, 1950-56; bldg. designer, owner Alaska Bldg. Svc., Anchorage, 1960-68; comml. bldg. contractor, owner Wetherill Constrn. Co., Denver, 1968-77; comml. bldg. designer Modern Iron Works, Farmington, N.Mex., 1977-82; constrn. cons., owner Toweco, Inc., Farmington, 1982—. Author: (with Laurin L. Wetherill) Navajo Nation Trails, 1987; inventor non-rising stem valves. Lt. (j.g.) USN, 1956-60. Recipient svc. award Little League Baseball, Farmington, 1981, Girl Scouts U.S.A., Farmington, 1988; Douglas Aircraft Co. scholar, 1950-56. Mem. Masons (32d degree). Republican. Baptist. Home: 221 E Paso Dr Farmington NM 87401 Office: Toweco Inc PO Box 2057 Farmington NM 87499

WETMORE, RALPH FREDERICK, engineer and tool manufacturer; b. Meriden, Conn., Nov. 17, 1934; s. James Russell Wetmore and Genevieve Berniece (Modrejewczski) Myers; divorced; children: James Stephan, Judith Ann; m. Jennifer Louise Patterson, Nov. 22, 1969; children: Daniel Wilbur, Suzanne Elizabeth. Grad. high sch., Downey, Calif. Apprentice toolmaker Wetmore Tool & Engring. Co., Los Angeles, 1956-56, apprentice tool designer, 1957-60, tech. sales, 1960-62, v.p., 1962-76; pres. Wetmore Cutting Tools, Pico Rivera, Calif., 1976-. Cubmaster, Boy Scouts of Am., ElMonte, Calif., 1962-64; pres. La Mirada Little League, La Mirada, Calif., 1981, 1982. Served to s/sgt. in USAF, 1952-56, Korea. Mem. U.S. Cutting Tools Inst., Cutting Tool Mfrs. Assn. (dir., 1985-87), Soc. of Carbide Engrs. (chmn. 1969-70), Pico Rivera, C. of C., Masons, Scottish Rite Shriners, Elks, Peace Officers Shrine Club. Republican. Protestant. Home: 13015 San Jacinto St La Mirada CA 90638 Office: Wetmore Cutting Tools PO Box 68/9129 Perkins St Pico Rivera CA 90660

WETTERSCHNEIDER, LARRY KAY, securities company executive; b. Santa Monica, Calif., Aug. 31, 1947; s. Egon Wetterschneider and Sally (King) Brand; divorced; 1 child, Elan. BA with honors in Bus., Calif. State Coll., L.A., 1969; MA, Calif. State U., L.A., 1971. With mktg. dept. Syntex Labs., L.A., 1969-71; sales mgr. Searle Analytical Co., New Orleans, 1971-77, GE, Tucson, 1977-79; lst v.p., resident mgr. Rauscher, Pierce Refsnes, Inc., Tucson, 1979—. Mem. gov. relations com. United Way, Tucson, 1983-84; bd. dirs. Tucson Mus. Art, 1987—, pres., 1988—; mem. community relations com. Jewish Council, Tucson, 1983-85; bd. dirs. Jewish Community Ctr., 1983-84, Tucson Parks Found., 1988—. Mem. Tucson Leadership Alumni, La Paloma Country Club (bd. dirs. 1988—), Lions (pres. Tuscon chpt. 1980-85). Republican. Home: 7201 N Sunset Canyon Tucson AZ 85718 Office: Rauscher Pierce Refsnes Inc 3561 E Sunrise Dr Ste 125 Tucson AZ 85718

WETTHER, KAREN LEE, nurse, consultant; b. Atascadero, Calif., Sept. 2, 1948; d. Norman A. and Joyce E. (Reid) W. BSN, Biola Coll., 1971. RN, Ill., Calif. Staff nurse pediatric outpatient clinic U. Ill. Med. Ctr., Chgo., 1971-73; nurse Morrison Acad., Taichung, Taiwan, 1973-74; clin. nurse med.-surg. orthopedic unit Cen. DuPage Hosp., Winfield, Ill., 1974-76, discharge planning nurse, 1976-79; clin. nurse II newborn nursery U. Calif. Med. Ctr., San Diego, 1979-80; med. legal nurse cons. Wingert, Grebing, Anello & LaVoy, San Diego, 1981—; cons., speaker Med. Legal Resources, San Diego, 1987—. Vol. Make-A-Wish Found., San Diego, 1985—. Recipient Best Workshop award Arthritis Health Professions Assn., 1987. Mem. NAFE, Calif. Assn. Med. Legal Nurse Cons. (sec. 1987), San Diego Trial Lawyers Assn. (assoc.), Nat. Nurses in Bus. Assn., Calif. Nurses Assn. Democrat. Methodist. Office: Med Legal Resources 6065 Mission Gorge Rd #136 San Diego CA 92120

WEXLER, STEVEN MARK, minister; b. Los Angeles, Sept. 3, 1955; s. Allan Irving and Gloria (Gingold) W.; m. Lois Ann Krause, June 17, 1988; children: David Aaron, Daniel Adam. BA in Lit., Psychology, Azusa Pacific U., 1978, ministries diploma, 1978; MDiv., Western Evangelical Seminary, Portland, Oreg., 1984. Chaplain intern UCLA Med. Ctr., Los Angeles, 1976-77; asst. chaplain Inter-Community Hosp., West Covina, Calif., 1977-78; tchr., counselor Portland Christian Schs., 1980-84; pastor Portland Foursquare Ch., 1984-88; talk show host Sta. KPDQ Radio, Portland, 1987—; pvt. practice as counselor, Portland, 1987—. Tchr. ARC, Portland, 1980-85; active Heritage Christian Schs. Bd., Portland, 1984-88. Served as lt. USAF, 1982-84, chaplain USAFR, 1982—. Stamps Found. grantee, 1976-77. Mem. Am. Assn. Marriage and Family Therapists (assoc.), Greater Portland Assn. Evangelists. Republican. Office: KPDQ Radio Sta 5110 SE Stark St Portland OR 97215

WEY, ALBERT HORNG-YHI, communications company executive; b. I-Lan, Rep. of China, Feb. 6, 1944; s. Chieh-Chi and Lian (Chen) W.; m. Mei-Hwei Kang, June 28, 1975; children: Brian Dau-Yuen, Enrico Dau-Yang. PhD in Physics, U. Chgo., 1975; MBA, Ariz. State U., 1981. Sr. engr. Westinghouse Corp., Pitts., 1975-77; prin. engr. Beckman Instrument, Scottsdale, Ariz., 1977-78; prin. engr. Motorola Semicondr., Phoenix, 1983, mem. tech. staff, 1983; chmn. bd., pres. Advanced Fiberoptico Corp., Scottsdale, 1983—; advisor optoelectronic in industry Govt. of Rep. of China, 1985; mem. adv. bd. U.S. West Corp., Denver, 1987—; adv. bd. mem. on small bus. Govt. of Ariz., 1988—. Contbr. articles to profl. jours. Named Nat. Minority Mfr. of Yr. Dept. of Commerce, Washington, 1985. Mem. IEEE (sr.), Chinese-Am. Profl. Assn. of Ariz. (founding pres.). Home: 10305 N 78th Way Scottsdale AZ 85258

WEYERHAEUSER, GEORGE HUNT, forest products company executive; b. Seattle, July 8, 1926; s. John Philip and Helen (Walker) W.; m. Wendy Wagner, July 10, 1948; children: Virginia Lee, George Hunt, Susan W., Phyllis A., David M., Merrill W. BS with honors in Indsl. Engring., Yale U., 1949. With Weyerhaeuser Co., Tacoma, 1949—, successively mill foreman, br. mgr., 1949-56, v.p., 1957-62, exec. v.p., 1962-66, pres., 1966-88, chief exec. officer, from 1966, chmn., 1988—; bd. dirs. Boeing Co., SAFECO Corp., Chevron Copr.; mem. adv. bd. sch. of bus. adminstrn. U. Wash., the Bus. Council, Bus. Roundtable, Wash. State Bus. Roundtable. Office: Weyerhaeuser Co Office of Chmn Tacoma WA 98477

WEYGAND, LAWRENCE RAY, insurance company executive; b. South Haven, Mich., Jan. 5, 1940; s. Ray and Lorraine (Berkins) W.; B.A., Drake U., 1962, postgrad., 1962-63; m. Paula West, May 2, 1987; 1 son, Chad C. Comml. multi-peril ins. underwriter Aetna Casualty & Surety Co., Mpls., also Indpls., 1964-66, Safeco Ins. Co., Denver, 1966-69; pres., chmn. bd. Weygand & Co., ins. agts., brokers and consultants, Denver, 1969—; pres. Homeowners Ins. Agy., Inc., Scottsdale, Ariz., Homeowners Ins., Inc., Denver, Weygand & Co. of Ariz., Inc., Scottsdale, Transatlantic Underwriters, Inc.; owner U.S. Insurors, Inc., Ariz. Dealers Ins. Services, Inc., Colo. Dealers Ins. Services, Inc., Denver, Storage Pak Ins., Inc.; owner, pres. gen. agy. serving Colo., Ariz., Nev., Utah and N.Mex.; asst. to Gov. State of Iowa, 1961-62. Mem. bus. community adv. council Regis Coll., Denver, 1976—. Mem. Ind. Ins. Agts. Colo. (chmn. fair and ethical practice com.), Ind. Ins. Agts. Am., Profl. Ins. Agts. Colo., Profl. Ins. Agts. Am., Alpha Tau Omega. Republican. Congregationalist. Club: Denver Athletic. Office: 1250 S Parker Rd Denver CO 80231

WEYGAND, LEROY CHARLES, service executive; b. Webster Park, Ill., May 17, 1926; s. Xaver William and Marie Caroline (Hoffert) W.; BA in Sociology cum laude, U. Md., 1964; m. Helen V. Bishop, Aug. 28, 1977; children: Linda M. Weygand Vance (dec.), Leroy Charles, Cynthia R., Janine P. Enlisted in U.S. Army, 1944, commd. 2d lt., 1950, advanced through grades to lt. col., 1966; service in Korea, 1950; chief phys. security U.S. Army, 1965-70; ret., 1970; pres. Weygand Security Cons. Srvcs., Anaheim, Calif., 1970—, W & W Devel. Corp., 1979—; security dir. Jefferies Banknote Co., 1972-78; exec. dir Kern County Taxpayers Assn., 1986—; dir. Mind Psi-Biotics, Inc. Bd. dirs. Nat. Assn. Control Narcotics and Dangerous Drugs. Decorated Legion of Merit. Mem. Am. Soc. Indsl. Security. Contbr. articles profl. jours. Patentee office equipment locking device. Home: 19880 Comanche Pl PO Box 140 Tehachapi CA 93581 Office: Kern County Taxpayers Assn 1415 18th St Ste 407 Bakersfield CA 93301

WHALEN, ANNA HART, activist, secretary; b. Ames, Iowa, Aug. 25, 1947; d. Dwight Deforest and Grace (Mease) Hart; m. Leonard D. Whalen, Dec. 20, 1970; children: Christopher Benjamin, Elizabeth Anne. BS in Edn., Iowa State U., 1971, MS in Journalism, 1979. Cert. elem. tchr., Iowa. Instr. Daycare, Des Moines, 1971-74; substitute tchr. Des Moines Sch. System, 1974-75; instr. Pub. Sch. System, Urbandale, Iowa, 1975-77; intern pub. rels. Iowa Legislature, Urbandale, 1978-79; sec. Kelly Services, Renton, Wash., 1986—. Chmn. Kent (Wash.) area coun. PTA, 1987; publicity chmn. Renton Annual Art Show, 1988—. Mem. AAUW (pres. Renton chpt. 1984-85, sec. 1987—, scholarship com. 1988—), Kiwanis. Home: 16219 142d St Renton WA 98058

WHALEN, MARGARET CAVANAGH, teacher, municipal or county goverment official; b. Des Moines, Iowa, Mar. 9, 1913; d. Thomas J. and Ann Lenore (Paul) Cavanagh; m. George Hubert Whalen, Aug. 3, 1946; children: Michael T., Ann Whalen Carrillo, George Patrick (dec.), Cheryl. BS in Commerce, St. Teresa Coll., Winona, Minn., 1935. Head bus. dept. St. Augustine High Sch., Austin, Minn., 1935-36, Parochial High Sch., Caledonia, Minn., 1936-37; clk., typist U.S. Govt., Dept. Socicl Security, Des Moines, 1937-38; county investigator for old age asst., aid to blind Marion County, Knoxville, Iowa, 1938; hydro dept. U.S. Weather Bur. Regional Office, Iowa City, Kansas City, Mo., 1939-42; head bills/warrants dept. IRS, Des Moines, 1942-46; substitute tchr. Los Gatos High Sch., Calif., 1961-65, Saratoga High Sch., Calif., 1961-65. Vol. Girl Scouts U.S., Boy Scouts Am., Saratoga, 1957-62; poll insp. Santa Clara County Regional Voters, Saratoga; precinct insp. in Saratoga for Santa Clara County Registrar of Voters; organizer, vol. Saratoga Area Sr. Coordinate Council, 1979—; Eucharistic Minister, lector, commentator Sacred Heart Ch., Saratoga, 1986—; charter pres. Oz chpt. Children's Home Soc. Calif.; lectr., commentor, Saratoga. Recipient Papal Bronze Medal for Pub. Relations Nat. Council Cath. Women, Saratoga, 1958, Merit award Friends of Saratoga Libraries, 1975—, Merit award Saratoga Area Sr. Coordinating Council, 1980; fellow Los Gatos, 1981. Mem. Am. Assn. U. Women (corr. sec., chmn. social arts, bridge, hospitality Los Gatos Saratoga br.), Alumnae Assn., Montalvo Assn., Saratoga Foothill Club (Calif. 1978—). Democrat. Roman Catholic. Home: 14140 Victor Pl Saratoga CA 95070

WHAM, DOROTHY STONECIPHER, state legislator; b. Centralia, Ill., Jan. 5, 1925; d. ERnest Jospeh and Vera Thelma (Shafer) Stonecipher; m. Robert S. Wham, Jan. 26, 1947; children: Nancy S. Wham Mitchell, Jeanne Wham Ryan, Robert S. II. BA, MacMurray Coll., 1946; MA, U. Ill., 1949. Counsellor Student Counselling Bur. U. Ill., Urbana, 1946-49; state dir. ACTION program, Colo./Wyo. U.S. Govt., Denver, 1972-82; mem. Colo. Ho. of Reps., 1986-87; mem. Colo. Senate, 1987—, chair jud. com., 1988—, vice-chair capital devel. com., health, environ., welfare and instns. Mem. Civil Rights Commn. Denver, 1972-80; bd. dirs. Denver Com. on Mental Health, 1985—, Denver Symphony, 1985—. Mem. Am. Psychol. Assn., Colo. Mental Health Assn. (bd. dirs. 1986—), LWV. Republican. Methodist. Lodge: Civitan. Home: 2790 S High St Denver CO 80210 Office: State Capitol Rm 333 Denver CO 80203

WHARTON, TOM MICHAEL, newspaper editor; b. Salt Lake City, Nov. 9, 1950; s. John R. and Violet M. (Ruga) W.; m. Gayen Lee Bennett, June 17, 1972; children: Emma, Rawl, Jacob, Bryer. BS, U. Utah, 1973. Sports writer Deseret News, Salt Lake City, 1969-70; sports writer, outdoor editor Salt Lake Tribune, 1970—. Author: Utah! A Family Travel Guide, 1987. Bd. dirs. Utah Friendship Force, Salt Lake City, 1981. Recipient award Utah Football Coaches Assn., 1987, Media Support award Utah Div. Parks and Recreation, 1987, 1st ann. media award Utah Marine Dealers Assn., 1988. Mem. Outdoor Writers Assn. Am. (com. 1988), Utah N.G. Assn. (pub. affairs officer 1970—). Roman Catholic. Home: 1024 Ramona Ave Salt Lake City UT 84105 Office: Salt Lake Tribune 143 S Main St Salt Lake City UT 84110

WHEAT, JAMES DAVIDSON, JR., management professional; b. Flint, Mich., Dec. 18, 1957; s. James Davidson and Mabel Joyce (Eng) W.; m. Ruth Su, July 9, 1988. BBA with distinction, U. Mich., 1980; MBA, U. Pa., 1985. CPA, Calif.; lic. real estate broker, Calif.; cert. prodn. inventory mgr., Calif. Cost control acct. Honeywell, Inc., Mpls., corp. auditor, 1981-83; fin. analyst Spectra-Physics, Inc., San Jose, Calif.; corp. acctg. supr. Spectra-Physics, Inc., San Jose, 1985-88; mgr. bus. planning Core-Mark Internat., San Francisco, 1988—; instr. U. Pa. acctg. dept., San Jose State U. dept. of fin. ; cons. U. Pa. Wharton Small Bus. Devel. Ctr. and Wharton Entrepreneurial Ctr. Mem. Big Bros. Organ. U. Mich. scholar, 1976. Mem. Am. Inst. CPA's. Office: Core-Mark Internat 395 Oyster Point Blvd Ste 415 South San Francisco CA 94080

WHEATLEY, ERNEST HAROLD, newspaper executive; b. Calgary, Alta., Can., June 2, 1927; s. Ernest Harold and Kathleen May Ellen (Gregory) W.; m. Vera Isabelle Procter, Sept. 15, 1940; children: Christopher Mark, Patrick Scott. Student, U. Alta., 1945-46. Advt. salesman Calgary Herald, 1945-50, nat. advt. rep., 1958-60; nat. rep. Southam Newspaper, Toronto, Ont., Can., 1950-58; advt. dir. Edmonton Jour., (Alta.), 1960-68; mktg. dir. Edmonton Jour., (Alta.), 1968-70; asst. to pub., mktg. dir. Edmonton Jour., (Alta.), 1970-71; pub. Brantford Expositor, (Ont.), 1971-76, Windsor Star, (Ont.), 1976-77; v.p. Southam Inc., Toronto, 1976; pub. Winnepeg Tribune, Man., 1977-80; pres., gen. mgr. Pacific Press Ltd., Vancouver, 1980-83, pres., chief exec. officer, 1983-88, dep. chmn., chief exec. officer, 1988—; pub. Vancouver Sun. Mem. Can. Daily Newspaper Pubs. Assn. (bd. dirs.), Can. Press., Commonwealth Press Union, Inter-Am. Press Assn., Audit Bur. Circulations (dir.), C. of C. Presbyterian. Clubs: Arbutus, Vancouver Golf. Office: Pacific Press Ltd, 2250 Granville St, Vancouver, BC Canada V6H 3G2

WHEATLEY, JEFF R., lawyer; b. Lawton, Okla., July 14, 1927; s. J. Carl and Dennis Belle (Roper) W.; m. Garline J. Johnson, Aug. 2, 1949; children: Michael Jeff, Kayci Garline, Kelly Donald. BSEE, U. Okla., 1956; JD cum laude, Pepperdine U., 1970. Bar: Calif. 1971, U.S. Dist. Ct. (9th dist.) Calif. 1971. Sole practice, Long Beach, Calif., 1971-73, Placentia, Calif., 1973-77, Fullerton, Calif., 1977—; tchr. constrn. law 1981-82; mem. five atty. firm,

Fullerton. Publisher (newsletter) Contractors Advocate. Served with USN 1945-46. Recipient Charles R. Mower award Orange County Builders Assn., 1981. Mem. ABA (Constrn. Forum), Orange County Bar Assn., So. Calif. Builders Assn., USCG Aux. Producer audio tapes on constrn. law for Calif. contractors. Club: Dana Point Yacht. Office: 2600 E Nutwood Ave Ste 101 Fullerton CA 92631

WHEATLEY, ROBERT MACK, lawyer; b. San Mateo, Calif., Apr. 2, 1943; s. Robert Melvin and Arloene Lorena (Biernes) W.; m. Judith Gail Gilpin, June 25, 1966; 1 child, Andrew. BA, Stanford U., 1965; JD, U. Calif., Hastings, 1968. Bar: Calif. 1969. Pvt. practice law Sacramento, 1969; ptnr. Evans, Jackson & Kennedy, Sacramento, 1970-74, Jackson, Kennedy, Walters & Wheatley, Sacramento, 1974-75, Jackson & Wheatley, Sacramento, 1976-79, Memering and DeMers, Sacramento, 1979-81, Bullen, McKinley, Gay, Keitges & Pach, Sacramento, 1981-88, Laurie, Maloney & Wheatley, Folsom and Cameron Park, Calif., 1988—; judge pro tem, jud. arbitrator Sacramento Superior Ct. Mem. El Dorado Hills (Calif.) Planning Adv. Coun.; pres. El Dorado Hills Youth Soccer Club. Mem. ABA, Calif. State Bar Assn., El Dorado County Bar Assn., Sacramento County Bar Assn. (bd. dirs.), Sacramento County Young Lawyers Assn. (pres.). Office: Laurie Maloney & Wheatley 1004 River Rock Dr Folsom CA 95630

WHEATON, HARRY JAMES, corporate executive; b. Alliance, Ohio, May 11, 1947; s. Harry E. and Eila F. (Cowles) W.; m. Margo Ann Stubblefield, Oct. 2, 1985. BSBA, Franklin U., 1975. Salesman Texaco, Chgo., 1971-76, Firestone, Providence, 1976-77; sales mgr. United Foam, Bremen, Ind., 1978-80; v.p. of sales Creative Foam Corp., Flint, Mich., 1980-83; pres. Cantrick Corp., Lexington, Mich., 1983-85; v.p., gen. mgr., bd. dirs. Hartech USA Ltd., Scottsdale, Ariz., 1987—; bd. dirs. U.S. Tool, Chgo., Tarva Industries, Detroit. With USN, 1967-71, Vietnam. Democrat. Presbyterian. Home: 3442 E Campbell Phoenix AZ 85018 Office: Hartech USA Ltd 8341 E Evans #106 Scottsdale AZ 85260

WHEATON, JOHN SOUTHWORTH, distribution company executive; b. Balt., Dec. 26, 1928; s. Ezra Almon and Ruth Adelaide (Otis) W.; m. Joy Lorraine Thuressen, Dec. 16, 1950; children: Sandra, Jason, Christopher. B.A., Stanford U., 1951; M.B.A., Columbia U., 1953. Mgr. fin. TRW, Inc., Redondo Beach, Calif., 1956-60; v.p. ops. Bissett-Berman Corp., Santa Monica, Calif., 1960-71; v.p. ops. control Foremost-McKesson, Inc., San Francisco, 1971-74; v.p. planning and analysis McKesson Corp., San Francisco, 1974-86, exec. v.p. adminstrn., 1986—; bd. dirs. Armor All, Irvine, Calif., Pharm. Card Systems, Scottsdale, Ariz. Served to lt. USNR, 1953-56. Club: Olympic. Office: McKesson Corp One Post St San Francisco CA 94104

WHEELER, BENITA LOUISE, artist; b. St. Ignatius, Mont., Sept. 25, 1939; d. Thomas B. and Lucille (Brush) Williamson; m. Camille D. Bisson, Mar. 17, 1963 (div. Aug. 1970); m. Walter L. Wheeler; children: Daniel, James, Marshall (dec.). BA, Coll. Great Falls, 1976. Logging acct. Champion Internat., Polson, Mont., 1962-67; rep. patient accounts Columbus Hosp., Great Falls, Mont., 1970-73, Mont. Deaconess Med. Ctr., Great Falls, 1977-86; artist Great Falls, 1986—. Bd. dirs. Intermt. Planned Parenthood, Great Falls, 1988—. Recipient 1st place watercolor award, St. Fair, Great Falls, 1985, juried whow, West Side Meth. Ch., Great Falls, 1986. Mem. NOW, Great Falls Art Assn., Western Heritage Artists (v.p. 1987—, show chmn. 1988—), Bus. and Profl. Women (pres. 1985-86). Democrat. Unitarian. Home: 1804 16th Ave S Great Falls MT 59405

WHEELER, BRANDON WILLIAM, SR., mathematics educator; b. Washington, Aug. 28, 1936; s. Harvey William and Lora Jane (Goodman) W.; m. Barbara Frances Canty, June 20, 1964; children: Colleen Patricia, Brandon W. Jr., Erin Lisa. BA in Math., Calif. State U., Sacramento, 1958, MS in Applied Math., 1960. Prof. dept. math. Sacramento City Coll., 1962—; mem. math. diagnostic testing project U. Calif. and Calif. State U., 1968—; state sec. Calif. Math. Coun., 1977-79. Author: (with others) Introduction to Mathematical Ideas, 1969, Calculus for Business, Biology and the Social Sciences, 1972, Finite Mathematics, 1977. Mem. Nat. Council Tchrs. Math., Mathematical Assn. Am., Calif. Math. Council, Calif. Math. Council Community Colls., Calif. State U. Alumni Assn. (pres. 1982, bd. dirs. 1983—). Office: Sacramento City Coll Dept Math Sacramento CA 95822

WHEELER, DIANA ESTHER, biologist, educator; b. New Haven, Aug. 4, 1950; d. Walter Hall and Eula Virginia (Krueger) W. B.S., Duke U., 1972, Ph.D., 1982; M.S., U. Del., 1977. Postdoctoral fellow Smithsonian Instn., Washington, 1982-83; research fellow Harvard U., Cambridge, Mass., 1983-85; asst. prof. U. Southwestern La., 1985-87, U. Ariz., Tucson, 1987—. Contbr. articles to profl. jours. U. Del. E.I. DuPont fellow, 1975; Cocos Found. fellow, 1980-82. Mem. Entomol. Soc. Am., Internat. Union for Study of Social Insects, Kans. Entomol. Soc., Sigma Xi. Democrat.

WHEELER, GAY GIBSON, educator, medical clinic department supervisor; b. Tyler, Tex., Aug. 17, 1934; d. George Allen and Alice Rhoda (Sanders) Yeager; m. Douglas A. Thibodeaux, June 10, 1955 (div. Sept. 1979); children: Lane David, Lynn Alice, Lee Douglas; m. Jeffrey Joe, Sept. 21, 1982. BA in History and English, Lamar U., 1955. Cert. tchr., Tex., 1989. Tchr. Ball High Sch., Galveston, 1955-58; tutor high schs., Mich., La., Tex., 1958-71, 71-88, colls., Tex., 1971-77; receptionist Theatre Under the Stars, Houston, 1978; asst. mgr. (Beautiful) Heavenly Body Health Spa, Houston, 1979-80; salesperson Carbondale, Colo., 1980-82; dept. supr. Glenwood Med. Assoc., Glenwood Springs, Colo., 1983-88; tutor Colo. Mt. Coll., Glenwood Springs, 1988—; ladies mgr., aerobics instr. Tex. LAdy-Texan Spa, Houston, 1988-89; curriculum cons. St. Barnabas Ch., Glenwood Springs, 1983-85, St. Christopher's Pre-Sch., Houston, 1968-70; text book cons. Galveston schs., 1957. Author weekly coll. activity column, essays, poems; acted, directed and produced local dramas including Truman Capote's A Christmas Memory; acted in several movies and TV commls. Century Casting, 1978-81. Vol. St. Barnabas Ch. Thrift Gift Sale, 1983-85, St. Christopher's Thrift Shop, 1960-69; outreach chmn. St. Barnabas Ch. Vestry, 1983-86. Phi Kappa Phi. Episcopalian. Home: 10303 Kerr Conroe TX 77385

WHEELER, LARRY RICHARD, accountant; b. Greybull, Wyo., Nov. 30, 1940; s. Richard F. and Olive B. (Fredrickson) W.; m. Marjorie A. Frady, Dec. 20, 1961; m. Patricia C. Marturano, Dec. 3, 1977; children: Anthony, Richard, Teresa, Kara. BS, U. Wyo., 1965. CPA, Colo. Staff acct. H. Greger CPA, Ft. Collins, Colo., 1965-66, sr. acct. Lester Draney & Wickham, Colorado Springs, Colo., 1966-67; acct., controller/treas., J.D. Adams Co., Colorado Springs, 1967-74; ptnr. Wheeler Pierce & Hurd, Inc., Colorado Springs, 1974-80; gen. mgr., v.p. Schneebeck's, Inc., Colorado Springs, 1980-81; prin. L.R. Wheeler & Co., P.C., Colorado Springs, 1981—; dir. Schneebeck's Industries, Williams Printing, Inc. Mem. U.S. Taekwond Union; bd. dirs. Domestic Violence Prevention Ctr. Paul Stock Found. grantee, 1962. Mem. Internat. Assn. Fin. Planners, Am. Inst. CPA's, Nat. Contract Mgmt. Assn., Colo. Soc. CPA's, Colo. Litigation Support Group (map com.). Club: Colorado Springs Country. Office: 317 E San Rafael Colorado Springs CO 80903

WHEELER, TAMARA, nurse; b. East Chicago, Ind., Aug. 2, 1949; d. Benjamin A. and Helen L. (Jaskulski) Tamburo; m. Carl S. Wheeler, May 3, 1969; 1 child, Daniel. LPN, Purdue U., 1968; AA in Health Care Mgmt., Gateway Coll., Phoenix, 1989. Nurse St. Catherine Hosp., East Chicago, 1968-70; nurse, instr. H. Borstein MD MPH, Gary, Ind., 1970-71; obstet. nurse, instr. St. Anthony Med. Ctr., Crown Point, Ind., 1974-78; patient coordinator, adminstrv. nurse Crown Point Clinic, 1974-85; head nurse infectious disease dept. Scottsdale (Ariz.) Med. Specialists, 1985—; asst. adminstr. C.S. Wheeler & Assocs., Scottsdale; speaker, instr. AIDS various area high schs., Scottsdale. Co-author Our Family Favorites, 1985. Pres., dist. mgr. Jr. Achievement, East Chicago, 1964-67. Named Little Miss East Chicago, 1952. Mem. Ariz. Nurses Assn. Republican. Roman Catholic. Home: 8609 E Vista Dr Scottsdale AZ 85253 also: Scottsdale Med Specialists 3301 N Miller Rd #130 Scottsdale AZ 85251

WHEELER, THOMAS FRANCIS, data processing executive; b. Norristown, Pa., Jan. 27, 1937; s. Thomas Francis and Dorothy Marie (Kane) W.; m. Margaret Anne Raleigh, April 4, 1964; children: Thomas A., Michael T., Margaret T. BA, Villanova U., 1960; postgrad., Cath. U. Am., 1960-61. Physics, math. tchr. St. Pius X High Sch., Pottstown, Pa., 1962-63; computer programmer IBM Corp., Endicott, N.Y., 1963-68, mgr. programming, 1968-74; asst. to v.p. systems devel. IBM Corp., Poughkeepsie, N.Y., 1974-75; design mgr. communications and distributed systems IBM Corp., Kingston, N.Y., 1975-78; cons. for engring., programming, tech. IBM Corp., Armonk, N.Y., 1978-81; mgr. systems architecture IBM Corp., White Plains, N.Y., 1981-84; v.p. advanced systems Gen. Elec. Calma, San Diego, 1984-87; pres. Daplus Co., 1987-88; cons. Am. Express Co. Travel Related Services, Phoenix, 1988—; mem. steering com. for engring. mgmt. edn. San Diego State U., 1985—; lectr. Mfg. Tech. Inst., 1981-84, devel. mgmt. tng. 1981-84; frequent speaker; mem. adv. com. U. Calif. San Diego Sch. Engring., 1986—, engr. dean adv. bd., 1985—. Author: Computers and Engineering Management; contbg. author: Creative Innovators; editor Journal of Applications and Computers for Engineering; columnist San Diego Business Journal; contbr. articles to tech. jours. Various positions Boy Scouts Am., Binghamton, N.Y., Poughkeepsie, N.Y., White Plains N.Y., Dallas, 1961-84, San Diego, 1961-88; mem. fin. com. campaign Sen. James Buckley, N.Y., 1976. Recipient Silver Beaver award Boy Scouts Am., Poughkeepsie, 1978. Mem. IEEE (computer soc., Disting. Lectr. award 1985), AAAS, N.Y. Acad. Sci., World Future Soc., Assn. of Computing Machinery, San Diego C. of C., Am. Electronic Assn. (chmn. edn. com. 1987—, air space Am. protocol com.), Acad. Mgmt., Nat. Computer Graphics Assn. Republican. Roman Catholic. Lodge: Kiwanis. Office: Am Express Co Travel Related Svcs 1647 E Morten Ave Phoenix AZ 85020

WHEELON, ALBERT DEWELL, physicist; b. Moline, Ill., Jan. 18, 1929; s. Orville Albert and Alice Geltz (Dewell) W.; m. Nancy Helen Hermanson, Feb. 28, 1953 (dec. May 1980); children—Elizabeth Anne, Cynthia Helen; m. Cicely J. Evans, Feb. 4, 1984. B.Sc., Stanford U., 1949; Ph.D., Mass. Inst. Tech., 1952. Teaching fellow, then research assoc. physics MIT, Boston, 1949-52; with Douglas Aircraft Co., 1952-53, Ramo-Wooldridge Corp., 1953-62; dep. dir. sci. and tech. CIA, Los Angeles, 1962-66; with Hughes Aircraft Co., Los Angeles, 1966—, chmn., chief exec. officer, 1970-87; mem. Def. Sci. Bd., 1967-77, Pres.'s Fgn. Intelligence, 1983—, presdl. commn. on space shuttle Challenger accident, 1986; trustee Calif. inst. Tech. Author 30 papers on radiowave propagation and guidance systems. Fellow IEEE, AIAA (Von Karman medal 1986); mem. Nat. Acad. Engring., Am. Phys. Soc., Sigma Chi. Republican. Episcopalian. Office: Hughes Aircraft Co 7200 Hughes Terrace Los Angeles CA 90045-0066 *

WHELAN, ANN MARIE, hotel chain executive; b. Cleveland, Tenn., Mar. 20, 1957; d. William Wyman Whelan and Mabel (Sallis) Whelan-Godbout. AS in Archt. Tech., Cleve. State Community Coll., 1977; student, Auburn U., 1977-78; BS in Engring. Tech., Memphis State U., 1979. Coord. spl. projects Holiday Inns, Inc., Memphis, 1980-81, project engr., 1981-84, mgr. svc. devel., 1984-85; mgr. market planning Holiday Corp., Memphis, 1985-87; dir. devel. Holiday Corp., Denver, 1987—. Roman Catholic. Office: Holiday Inns Inc 1526 Cole Blvd Ste 260 Golden CO 80401

WHELAN, CRISTINA GARCIA, city clerk; b. Phoenix, Sept. 15, 1949; d. Eduardo H. and Virginia (Soto) G.; m. Charles E. Whelan Jr., Aug. 7, 1976; children: Alma Crystal, Tirza Aida. AA, Cochise Coll., 1969. Ward clk. Palo Verde Hosp., Tucson, 1972-74; utility clk. Valley Nat. Bank, Willcox, Ariz., 1974-79; city clk. City of Willcox, 1981—. Democrat. Roman Catholic. Office: City of Willcox 207 W Maley St Willcox AZ 85643

WHELAN, MARTIN, air force officer; b. Knoxville, Tenn., June 20, 1962; s. Paul Augustin and Patricia Lucelle (Welsh) W.; m. Susan Prather, July 14, 1984; children: Jared Michael, Daniel Patrick. BS in Aerospace Engring., Parks Coll., Cahokia, Ill., 1983; postgrad. systems mgmt., Golden Gate U., 1988—. Commd. 2d lt. USAF, 1983, advanced through grades to capt., 1987; space shuttle hyperbolic systems engr. 6595th Shuttle Test Group, Vandenberg AFB, Calif., 1984-86, space shuttle project engr., 1986-87; space systems field comdr. 4th Satellite Communications Squadron, Holloman AFB, N.Mex., 1987-89, space systems flight comdr., 1989—; chief standardization/evaluation 1989—. Coach, referee, bd. dirs. Am. Youth Soccer Orgn., Vandenberg AFB, 1985-86; instr. religion Base Cath. Parish, Vandenberg AFB, 1986-87, Holloman AFB, 1987-88. Mem. Cruces Apple Users Group (Las Cruces, N.Mex.). Republican. Home: 2729-A Socorro Loop Holloman AFB NM 88330 Office: 4th Satellite Communications Squadron Holloman AFB NM 88330

WHELCHEL, SANDRA JANE, writer; b. Denver, May 31, 1944; d. Ralph Earl and Janette Isabelle (March) Everitt; m. Andrew Jackson Whelchel, June 27, 1965; children: Andrew Jackson, Anita Earlyn. BA in Elem. Edn., U. No. Colo., 1966; postgrad. Pepperdine Coll., 1971, UCLA, 1971. Elem. tchr. Douglas County Schs., Castle Rock, Colo., 1966-68, El Monte (Calif.) schs., 1968-72; br. librarian Douglas County Libraries, Parker, Colo., 1973-78; zone writer Denver Post, 1979-81; reporter The Express newspapers, Castle Rock, 1979-81; history columnist Parker Trail newspapers, 1985—; columnist Authorship mag.; contbr. short stories and articles to various publs. including: Ancestry Newsletter, Empire mag., Calif. Horse Rev., Host mag., Jack and Jill, Child Life, Children's Digest; author (non-fiction books): Your Air Force Academy, 1982; (coloring books): A Day at the Cave, 1985, A Day in Blue, 1984, Pro Rodeo Hall of Champions and Museum of the American Cowboy, 1985, Pikes Peak Country, 1986, Mile High Denver, 1987; lectr. on writing. Mem. Internat. Platform Assn., Nat. Writers Club (treas. Denver Metro chpt. 1985-86, v.p. membership 1987), Parker Area Hist. Soc. (pres. 1987, 88, 89).

WHINNERY, JOHN ROY, electrical engineering educator; b. Read, Colo., July 26, 1916; s. Ralph V. and Edith Mable (Bent) W.; m. Patricia Barry, Sept. 17, 1944; children—Carol Joanne, Catherine, Barbara. B.S. in Elec. Engring, U. Calif. at Berkeley, 1937, Ph.D., 1948. With GE, 1937-46; part-time lectr. Union Coll., Schenectady, 1945-46; asso. prof. elec. engring. U. Calif.-Berkeley, 1946-52, prof., vice chmn. div. elec. engring., 1952-56, chmn., 1956-59; dean Coll. Engring. U. Calif-Berkeley, 1959-63, prof. elec. engring., 1963-80, Univ. prof. Coll. Engring., 1980—; vis. mem. tech. staff. Bell Telephone Labs., 1963-64; research sci. electron tubes Hughes Aircraft Co., Culver City, 1951-52. Author: (with Simon Ramo) Fields and Waves in Modern Radio, 1944, 2d edit. (with Ramo and Van Duzer), 1985, (with D. O. Pederson and J. J. Studer) Introduction to Electronic Systems, Circuits and Devices; also tech. articles. Chmn. Commn. Engring. Edn., 1966-68; mem. sci. and tech. com. Manned Space Flight, NASA, 1963-69; mem. Pres.'s Com. on Nat. Sci. Medal, 1970-73, 79-80; standing com. controlled thermonuclear research AEC, 1970-73. Recipient Edn. medal IEEE, 1967, Lamme medal Am. Soc. Engring. Edn., 1975; Microwave Career award IEEE Microwave Theory and Techniques Soc., 1977; Engring Alumni award U. Calif. at Berkeley, 1980; named to Hall of Fame Modesto High Sch. (Calif.), 1983; Guggenheim fellow, 1959. Fellow I.R.E. (dir. 1956-59), Optical Soc. Am., Am. Acad. Arts and Scis.; mem. Nat. Acad. Engring. (Founders award 1986), Nat. Acad. Scis., IEEE (life mem., dir. 1969-71, sec. 1971, Centennial medal 1984, Medal of Honor 1985), Phi Beta Kappa, Sigma Xi, Tau Beta Pi, Eta Kappa Nu. Congregationalist. Home: One Daphne Ct Orinda CA 94563 Office: U Calif Berkeley CA 94720

WHIPPLE, DAVID PEARLMAN, electronics design executive; b. Wilmington, Del., Jan. 4, 1951; s. George Henry and Joan (Pearlman) W.; m. Ritchie Keel, Aug. 12, 1972; children: Andrew D., Charles S. BSEE, Purdue U., 1972, MSEE, 1973. Prodn. engr. Hewlett-Packard Co., Palo Alto, Calif., 1973-76, prodn. engr. mgr., 1976-79; prodn. engr. mgr. Spokane, Wash., 1979-83; project mgr. Spokane, 1983—. Inventor in field. Mem. Am. Soc. Engring. Educators (chmn. Pacific N.W. 1987-88, governing bd. 1983—). Jewish. Office: Hewlett-Packard Co TAF C-34 Spokane WA 99220

WHIPPLE, GEORGE STEPHENSON, architect; b. Evanston, Ill., Sept. 21, 1950; s. Taggart and Katharine (Brewster) W.; m. Lydia Buckley, May 30, 1981; children: Katherine Elizabeth, John Taggart. B.A., Harvard U., 1974; student Boston Architectural Ctr., 1975-76. Vice-pres., Call Us Inc., Edgartown, Mass., 1970-74; pres. Cattle Creek Assocs., Carbondale, Colo., 1976—, Earthworks Constrn., Carbondale, 1978-87; pres., Whipple and Brewster Corp., Aspen, 1988—. Chmn., Redstone Hist. Preservation Commn., Colo. Mem. Pitkin County Planning and Zoning Commn., 1989—. Mem. Rocky Mountain Harvard Club. Office: 121 S Galena Ste 203 Aspen CO 81611

WHIPPLE, WALTER LEIGHTON, electrical engineer; b. Washington, June 23, 1940; s. Walter Jones and Marian Katharine (Leighton) W.; m. Jean Anne Ewer, Sept. 11, 1965; children: Kathryn Ann, Sara Marie. BS in Engring. Sci., Harvey Mudd Coll., 1962; MS in Computer, Info. and Control Engring., U. Mich., 1974, PhD in Computer, Info. and Control Engring., 1988. Registered profl. engr., Calif., Mich., Mass. Field svc. rep. ordnance dept. Grn. Electric Co., Pittsfield, Mass., 1962-65; insp. Welker & Assocs., Marietta, Ga., 1966-67; engr. space and info. systems div. Raytheon Co., Sudbury, Mass., 1967-69; sr. elec. engr. profl. svc. div. Control Data Corp., Waltham, Mass., 1969-73; sr. programmer-analyst Control Data Corp., Southfield, Mich., 1973-78; design specialist Gen. Dynamics Corp., Pomona, Calif., 1978-83; prin. engr. electro-magnetic systems div. Raytheon Co., Santa Barbara, Calif., 1983—. Contbr. articles to profl. publs. Loaned exec. Santa Barbara (Calif.) United Way, 1988—; bd. dirs. Tres Condados counl. Girl Scouts U.S., 1985-86. With USN, 1958-59. Gen. Electric Found. fellow, 1973. Fellow AIAA (assoc.); mem. IEEE (sr., editor newsletter Santa Barbara chpt. 1988—), Assn. Computing Machinery, Assn. Old Crows, AAUP. Office: Raytheon Co Software Design Engring Dept 9283 6380 Hollister Ave Goleta CA 93117

WHISLER, KIRK, publishing executive; b. Omaha, Calif., June 7, 1951; s. Donald Dee and Biddy Louise (Covert) W.; m. Magdalena Gonzalez, June 15, 1985; 1 child, Spencer Diego. Student, U. Calif., Santa Barbara, 1969-72, Escuela de Artes Plasticas, Guadalajara, Mex., 1972; BA in History and Politics, U. Calif., Riverside, 1973. Pub. Somos Mag., San Bernardino, Calif., 1977-79, Caminos Mag., Los Angeles, 1979-86; dir. mktg. Embassy Pictures-Gregorio Cortez, Los Angeles, 1983-84; pres. Am. Internat. Hispanic Communications, Los Angeles, 1983—; pres. Nat. Assn. Hispanic Publs., Los Angeles, 1984—. Editor: National Hispanic Conventioneer, 3d rev. edit., 1985, National Hispanic Media Directory, 1986; author: National Hispanic Readership Study, 1985, Familia Latina Hispanic Market Fact Book, 1984; pub. Nev. Mag., 1986—, Nev. Events, 1987—. Del. Commn. of the Califs., Sacramento and Mex., 1977—; mem. Los Angeles Organizing Com., 1981-84, San Bernardino (Calif.) City Community Devel. Commn., 1979-83, San Bernardino City Econ. Devel. Council, 1981-83. Recipient Golden Eagle award Nosotros, 1979, Leadership award San Bernardino Unified Sch. Dist. Bilingual Dist. Adv. Com., 1981, Contributor award Children's Mus., Los Angeles, 1985. Mem. U.S. Hispanic C. of C., Nat. Assn. Hispanic Journalists, Western Publs. Assn., San Bernardino County Mus. Assn. Democrat. Methodist. Office: Nev Mag 101 S Fall Carson City NV 89710

WHITACRE, ANNE FRANK, specification writer; b. Aberdeen, Wash., Sept. 30, 1953; d. Samuel Duane Whitacre and Jane Marie (Frank) Wise. BA, U. Wash., 1975. Cert. constrn. specifier. Researcher James Adkins AIA, Seattle, 1976-78; specification mgr. Wyatt Stapper Architect, Seattle, 1986-88, Meng Assocs., Seattle, 1988-89; specification writer NBBJ Group, Seattle, 1978-86; ptnr. Matson, Carlson, Whitacre, Seattle, 1989—; cons. various mfg. cos. and design firms, Wash., 1985--; instr. Seattle Community Coll., 1982, Seattle U., 1985. Contbr. column to Arcade Jour. Architecture in the Northwest, 1986--. Mem. AIA, Constrn. Specifications Inst. (pres. Puget Sound chpt., region chairperson certification com., 1987--, citation 1987, region citation 1988), Masterspec Review-Nat. Office: Matson Carlson Whitacre 209 1/2 1st Ave S #300 Seattle WA 98104

WHITACRE, WENDELL BRITT, plastic surgeon; b. Columbus, Ohio, Oct. 6, 1927; s. Asia Harold and Lena May (Sams) W.; m. Pierette Jeanine Pechmajou, Aug. 4, 1952 (div. 1982); children: Marc Michel, Eric Bruce, Anne Laura, Alice Lena; m. Sandy Marie Vigil, June 3, 1982. AB, Ohio U., 1951; MD, Ohio State U., 1955. Diplomate Am. Bd. Plastic and Reconstructive Surgery. Rotating intern Phila. Gen. Hosp., 1955-56; resident in gen. surgery Hosp. U. Pa., Phila., 1956-60, resident in plastic and reconstructive surgery, 1960-62; pvt. practice Tucson, 1962--; assoc. in plastic surgery Coll. Medicine, U. Ariz., 1974-87; clin. lectr. in surgery U. Ariz., 1987--. Contbr. articles to profl. jours. Bd. dirs. Found. for St. Joseph's Hosp., Tucson, 1976-86; mem. profl. com. BCBS of Ariz., 1979-88. Fellow ACS; mem. Am. Soc. Plastic and Reconstructive Surgeons, AMA, Phi Beta Kappa, Alpha Omega Alpha. Republican. Methodist. Home: 5133 E River Rd Tucson AZ 85718 Office: Rincon Plastic Surgery PC 310 N Wilmot Rd #104 Tucson AZ 85711

WHITAKER, BRUCE D., interior designer; b. Pocatello, Idaho, June 1, 1948; s. Donald C. Whitaker and Lois R. (Wilson) Wright; m. Juliana Stockman, Sept. 7, 1969; children: Jennifer Elizabeth, Laura Melissa. BA in Interior Design, Bus. Adminstrn., Wash. State U., 1971. Designer Lloyds Interiors, Portland, Oreg., 1971-73; prin. Bruce Whitaker Design Co., Portland, 1973-76, 77-78; sr. project designer Howard Hermanson & Assocs. Inc., Portland, 1976-77; v.p. for design Petter Moe & Assocs. Inc., Portland, 1978-87; prin. Whitaker Assocs., Portland, 1987—. Mem. Am. Soc. Interior Designers (various offices Portland chpt. 1973—, Presdl. citation 1979, 87, 88). Home: 3654 SW Patton Rd Portland OR 97221 Office: Whitaker Assocs 4247 SW Corbett Portland OR 97201

WHITAKER, CYNTHIA FRANCES, auditor; b. Ft. Wayne, Ind., Apr. 12, 1962; d. Ronald Edwin Gettel and Frances McGill (Waterfield) LeMay; m. Kim Duane Whitaker, Mar. 12, 1988. BS in Bus. Econs., Ind. U., Ft. Wayne, 1985; MBA in Fin., Ind. U., Bloomington, 1988. Loan specialist Waterfield Mortgage Co., Inc., Ft. Wayne, 1977-83; consumer lending rep. Union Fed. Savs. Bank, Indpls., 1987-88; sr. internal auditor Boise Cascade Corp., Boise, Idaho, 1988—; owner River Route Ranch, Emmett, Idaho, 1988—. Recipient Econs. award for scholastic achievement, Ind. U., Ft. Wayne, 1985, Outstanding Student Leadership award, Ind. U., Ft. Wayne, 1985. Republican. Baptist.

WHITAKER, DAN OSCAR, software company executive; b. Prineville, Oreg., Mar. 7, 1954; s. Harry Jackson and Dorothy (Brown) W.; m. Helen Patricia Owen, Aug. 10, 1973; children: Benjamin Owen, Kevin Jackson. BS, Oreg. State U., 1979. Owner, operator D.O.W. Painting, Anchorage, Alaska, 1973-75; v.p. Gen. Info. Systems, Inc., Corvallis, Oreg., 1979-82; pres., chief exec. officer Software Support Services, Inc., Corvallis, 1982—; bd. dirs. Bus. Incubator, Corvallis. Bd. advisors Oreg. State U. Coll. Bus. Mem. Am. Mgmt. Assn. (Pres.' Club). Clubs: Petersen Karate, Timberhill Athletic. Home: PO Box 1294 Corvallis OR 97339 Office: Software Support Svcs Inc 1965 SW Airport Rd Corvallis OR 97333

WHITBECK, LORI LEE, small business owner; b. North Hollywood, Calif., Sept. 11, 1960; d. Jack L. and Shirley Anne (Markham) W. A in Restaurant Mgmt., Coll. Canyons, 1978. Owner Rue Montmartre, Canyon Country, Calif., 1978-86, Fox Nutrition and Good Life, Los Angeles, 1987—, Fox Persian and Oriental Rugs, Los Angeles, 1987—. Contbr. Vote Yes, 1987. Organizer Santa Clarita (Calif.) Citizens for Animal Rights, 1987-88, Humane Farming Assn., 1988; fund raiser city formation com. Santa Clarita, 1987-88. Recipient Order of the Battered Boot March of Dimes, 1978. Mem. Polit. Women, SUPPRESS, Orton Soc. Dyslexia, Phi Theta Kappa. Liberterian. Jewish. Office: 1033 S Genesee Los Angeles CA 90019

WHITCOMB, BRUCE MAGILL, electro-optics scientist and educator; b. Manhattan, Kans., June 9, 1943; s. Stuart Estes and Katherine (Magill) W.; m. Trudi Lillian Carley, Aug. 5, 1967 (div. Aug. 1974); children: Tara Brandylane, Heathera Paige, Hans David. BA in Physics, Earlham Coll., 1965; MS in Physics, U. Mo. at Rolla, 1967; postgrad., Purdue U., 1967-72; PhD, U. Nev. at Reno, 1988. Asst. grad. tchr. Physics Dept., Univ. Mo. at Rolla, 1965-67, Phyics Dept., Purdue U., West Lafayette, Ind., 1967-69; research asst. Thermophys. Property Research Ctr., West Lafayette, Ind., 1969-71; asst. grad. tchr. Physics Dept, U. Nev. at Reno, 1974-77; research assoc. Desert Research Inst., U. Nev. at Reno, 1976-81; sect. head and elctro-optics scientist EG&G/ and Energy Measurements, Las Vegas, Nev., 1981—; instr. Physics Dept., U. Nev. at Las Vegas, 1985—. Author: (chpt. of book) Commercial Fiber Optic Components, 1987; contbr. articles to profl. jours. Mem. Optical Soc. Am., Soc. of Photo-Optical Instrumentation Engrs., Sigma Xi, Sigma Pi Sigma. Office: EG&G Energy Measurements P O Box 1912 M/S S-08 Las Vegas NV 89125

WHITE, ALICE JUNE, retired educator; b. Oasis, Wis., June 22, 1905; d. Alfred Leroy and Florence Edna (Wilson) Leavitt; m. Gabriel Otto Anderson, July 8, 1933 (dec. 1972); children: Adeline Daniels, Alice Wilhyde, Amy Biggins; m. John Orville White, Feb. 28, 1987. BA, U. Oreg., 1965, MA, 1972. Missions tchr. Liberia, 1929-32; tchr. B.I.A. Chemawa Indian Sch., Salem, Oreg., 1966-81. Contbr. articles to profl. publs.; author, composer poems, hymns and ballads, 1933—. Mem. Oreg. Fedn. Rep. Women, 1983—. Mem. Oreg. State Poets' Assn. (Salem chpt., treas., mem. editorial bd. quarterly publ. 1985). Home: 2285 Rogers Ln NW Salem OR 97304

WHITE, ARTHUR T., energy engineering consultant; b. Berlin, N.H., July 7, 1923; s. Ernest D. and Grace M. (Pinkham) W.; m. Wanda L. Bowman, Dec. 18, 1949; children: Susan, Thomas, Linda, Mary, Dean. BS in EE, U.S. Naval Acad., 1945; BS in Electronics, MIT, 1948, MS in Nuclear Engring., 1958. Registered profl. engr., Wash. Commd. ensign, advanced through grades to capt. U.S. Navy, 1945, line officer, 1945-51, engring. officer, 1951-74; ret.; mgr. quality assurance safety and nuclear matls. Atlantic Richfield Hanford Co., Richland, Wash., 1974-77; mgr. quality assurance and control Arco Med. Products (Ireland) Ltd., Dublin, 1977-78; mgr. quality assurance and regulatory affairs Arco Med. Products Co., Leechburg, Pa., 1978-81; mgr. major projects Arco Solar Inc., Chatsworth, Calif., 1981-84; energy engring. cons. Canoga Park, Calif., 1984--. Insp. voting poll L.A. Co., Canoga Park, 1985--. Mem. Assn. Energy Engrs., Assn. Energy Engrs. So. Calif., MIT Alumni Assn., U.S. Naval Acad. Alumni Assn., MIT Alumni Club So. Calif. (v.p. membership 1988-). Republican. Episcopalian. Address: 6411 Valley Circle Terr West Hills CA 91307

WHITE, BARBARA EMMALY, sales educator; b. Culver City, Calif., May 7, 1950; d. Byrl Elmer and Virginia Cora (Anderson) Robinson; m. Rush Tracy White, Apr. 6, 1974; children: Megan Robinson, Jared Robinson. BA, UCLA, 1973. Tchr. adult edn. L.A. Unified Sch. Dist., 1973-78; sta. sales rep. Mexicana Airlines, L.A., 1978-80, sales instr., 1981—. Mem., officer Taxco and Canoga Park (Calif.) Sister City Program, 1969-71, 85—. Mem. Am. Soc. for Tng. and Devel., Alpha Chi Omega (pres. L.A. chpt. 1979-81, treas. 1984—). Democrat. Lutheran. Home: 22619 Marlin Pl Canoga Park CA 91307 Office: Mexicana Airlines Tng Ctr 5757 W Century Blvd Ste 600 Los Angeles CA 90045

WHITE, BETTY ANN, nurse; b. Tuscola, Ill., July 12, 1959; d. Lawrence Fredrick and Agatha Christine (Hettinger) Koeberlein; m. Steven Wayne White, May 28, 1983; children: Christopher Adam, Matthew Alan. Assoc. in Nursing, Parkland Coll., 1980. RN, Nev. Staff nurse Carle Found. Hosp., Urbana, Ill., 1980-83, Humana Hosp., San Antonio, 1983-86; relief charge nurse Humana Hosp. Sunrise, Las Vegas, Nev., 1986—. Roman Catholic. Home: 6911 E Picccadily Dr Las Vegas NV 89115 Office: Humana Hosp Sunrise 3186 Maryland Pkwy Las Vegas NV 89109

WHITE, BRITTAN ROMEO, manufacturing company executive; b. N.Y.C., Feb. 13, 1936; s. Brittan R. and Matilda H. (Baumann) W.; m. Esther D. Friederich, Aug. 25, 1958 (dec. May 1981); children: Cynthia E., Brittan R. VII. BSChemE, Drexel U., 1958; MBA, Lehigh U., 1967; JD, Loyola U., Los Angeles, 1974; MA, Pepperdine U., 1985. Bar: Calif., U.S. Dist. Ct. Calif.; registered profl. engr., Calif. Process engr. Air Reduction Co., Bound Brook, N.J., 1958-64; area supr. J.T. Baker Chem. Co., Phillipsburg, N.J., 1964-66; asst. plant mgr. Gamma Chem. Co., Great Meadows, N.J., 1966-69; plant mgr. Maquite Corp., Elizabeth, N.J., 1969-70; purchasing mgr. Atlantic Richfield Co., Los Angeles, 1970-79; dir. mfg. Imperial Oil, Los Angeles, 1979-82; mgr. infosystems and spl. projects Hughes Aircraft Co., Los Angeles, 1982—; bd. dirs. Diversified Resource Devel. Inc., Los Angeles, 1979—; seminar moderator and speaker Energy Conservation Seminars, 1979-83. Editor Rottweiler Rev., 1979-81; chief award judge Chem. Processing mag., 1976, 78, 80; contbr. articles to profl. jours. Vice chmn. Bd. Zoning and Adjustment, Flemington, N.J., 1970-72; pres. bd. dirs. Homeowners Assn., Palm Springs, Calif., 1983—. Served to capt. C.E., U.S. Army, 1958-60, Res., 1960-68. Mem. ABA, Am. Inst. Chem. Engrs., Am. Chem. Soc., Mensa, Psi Chi. Republican. Lodge: Elks. Home: 3664 Vigilance Dr Rancho Palos Verdes CA 90274 Office: Hughes Aircraft Co 7200 Hughes Terr Los Angeles CA 90045

WHITE, CECIL RAY, librarian, consultant; b. Hammond, Ind., Oct. 15, 1937; s. Cecil Valentine and Vesta Ivern (Bradley) W.; m. Frances Ann Gee, Dec. 23, 1960 (div. 1987); children—Timothy Wayne, Stephen Patrick. B.S. in Edn., So. Ill. U., 1959; cert. in Czech., Syracuse, U., 1961; M. Div., Southwestern Bapt. Sem., 1969; M.L.S., N. Tex. State U., 1970, Ph.D., 1984. Librarian, Herrin High Sch. (Ill.), 1964-66; acting reference librarian Southwestern Sem., Ft. Worth, 1968-70, asst. librarian, 1970-80; head librarian Golden Gate Bapt. Sem., Mill Valley, Calif., 1980-88; head librarian West Oahu Coll., Pearl City, Hawaii, 1988-89; sir. spl. projects North State Coop. Library System, Yreka, Calif., 1989—; library cons. Hist. Commn., So. Bapt. Conv., Nashville, 1983-84, mem. Thesaurus Com., 1974-84. Bd. dirs. Hope and Help Ctr., 1986—, vice chmn. 1987—. Served with USAF, 1960-64. Lilly Found. grantee Am. Theol. Library Assn., 1969. Mem. Am. Theol. Library Assn. (coord. consultation svc. 1973-78, program planning com. 1985-88, chmn., 1986-88), Nat. Assn. Profs. Hebrew (archivist 1985—), ALA, Calif. Library Assn., Assn. Coll. and Rsch. Librarian, Phi Kappa Phi, Beta Phi Mu. Democrat. Baptist. Home: Box 1669 Yreka CA 96097 Office: Siskiyou County Libr 719 Fourth St Yreka CA 96097

WHITE, DANIEL JOSEPH, venture capital company executive; b. Memphis, Apr. 5, 1962; s. William C. and Patricia A. (Heiting) W.; m. Elizabeth A. Borkowski, June 21, 1986. BBA, U. San Diego, 1985. Acct. Coherent, Inc., Palo Alto, Calif., 1985-86; controller Venture Resources, Inc., San Jose, Calif., 1986-87; v.p. Venture Resources, Inc., Redwood Shores, Calif., 1987—, also bd. dirs.; bd. dirs. VRI Investments, Inc., Redwood Shores, VRI-Four, Calif., Ltd. Partnership, Redwood Shores. Home: 332 Yale Rd Menlo Park CA 94025 Office: Venture Resources Inc 100 Marine Pkwy Ste 325 Redwood Shores CA 94065

WHITE, DAUN ELOIS, association official; b. Winsted, Conn., Feb. 11, 1955; d. Robert Hamilton and Bessie Emma (Land) Daly; m. Stephen Scott White, Feb. 9, 1974; children: Stephen Scott Jr., Derik James. Student, Tri-Community Coll., Covina, Calif., 1974-76. Sec., bookkeeper Century 21 Comml., West Covina, Calif., 1978-80; sec. Century 21 Regional, West Covina, 1980-82; adminstrv. asst. Century 21 Real Estate, Covina, 1982-84, Covina Bd. Realtors, 1984-86; asst. to v.p. acquisitions Occidental Land Rsch., Diamond Bar, Calif., 1986-87; exhibit mgr. Soc. for Advancement Material and Process Engrs., Covina, 1987-89. Men. Nat. Assn. Expn. Mgrs., NAFE. Episcopalian. Home: 1055 W San Bernardino Upland CA 91786 Office: SAMPE 843 W Glentana Covina CA 91722

WHITE, DIANE EDRINE, nurse, poet; b. Long Beach, Calif., June 24, 1938; d. Lawrence M. (dec.) and Florence (Thompson-Patterson) M.; m. Arthur Lee White, June 25, 1961 (div. Feb. 1982); children: Donald L., Laura D. Diploma in nursing, Eastern N.Mex. U., 1979. Nurse Clovis (N.Mex.)-High Plains Hosp., 1973—. Author New American Poetry, 1987, World of Poetry, 1988. Recipient Golden Post award, 1988. Democrat. Roman Catholic. Home: 316 Axtell #3 Clovis NM 88101 Office: Clovis-High Plains Hosp 2100 N Thomas Clovis NM 88101

WHITE, DON WILLIAM, bank executive; b. Santa Rita, N.Mex., June 27, 1942; s. Thomas Melvin and Barbara (Smith) W.; m. Jacqueline Diane Bufkin, June 12, 1965; children: Don William Jr., David Wayne. BBA, Western N.Mex. U., 1974, MBA, 1977. Field acct. Stearns Roger Corp., Denver, 1967-70; controller, adminstrv. mgr. USNR Mining and Minerals Inc., Silver City, N.Mex., 1970-72; devel. specialist County of Grant, Silver City, 1973-77; divisional controller Molycorp. Inc., Taos, N.Mex., 1977-78; mgr. project adminstrn. Kennecott Minerals Co., Hurley, N.Mex., 1978-83; sr. v.p. Sunwest Bank Grant County, Silver City, N.Mex., 1983-84, exec. v.p., 1984-85, pres., chief exec. officer, 1985—. Bd. dirs. Silver City/Grant County Econ. Devel., 1983—; councilman Town Silver City, 1977; chmn. Dems. for Senator Pete Domenici, 1986. Named Outstanding Vol., Silver City/Grant County Econ. Devel., 1987, FFA, 1985. Mem. Am. Bankers Assn., N.Mex. Bankers Assn., Bank Adminstrn. Inst., Assn. Commerce and Industry, N.Mex. Mining Assn. (assoc.), Rotary. Office: Sunwest Bank Grant County 1203 N Hudson PO Box 1449 Silver City NM 88062

WHITE, DONALD HARVEY, physicist, educator; b. Berkeley, Calif., Apr. 30, 1931; s. Harvey Elliott and Adeline White; m. Beverly Evalina Jones, Aug. 8, 1953; children: Jeri M., Brett D., Holly G., Scott E., Erin N. AB, U. Calif., Berkeley, 1953; PhD, Cornell U., 1960. Rsch. physicist Lawrence Livermore (Calif.) Nat. Lab., 1960-71; prof. physics Western Oreg. State Coll., Monmouth, 1971—; cons. Lawrence Livermore Nat. Lab., 1971—. Author (with others): Physics, an Experimental Science, 1968, Physics and Music, 1980; contbr. numerous articles to profl. jours. Pres. Monmouth-Independence Community Arts, 1983; pres. E. Smith Fine Arts Program, Monmouth, 1987. DuPont Found. scholar, 1958; Minna-Heineman Found. fellow, Hannover, Fed. Republic Germany, 1977. Mem. Am. Phys. Soc., Am. Assn. Physics Tchrs. (pres. Oreg. sect. 1974-75), Oreg. Acad. Sci. (pres. 1979-80), Phi Kappa Phi. Democrat. Presbyterian. Home: 411 Walnut Dr Monmouth OR 97361-1948 Office: Western Oreg State Coll Dept Phys & Earth Scis Monmouth OR 97361

WHITE, DONALD HERBERT, aircraft company executive; b. Long Beach, Calif., Oct. 7, 1931; s. Orville Herbert and Mildred Florence (Spencer) W.; m. Janice Margaret Jacobs, Nov. 15, 1953; children: Marleigh Ellen, Spencer William. AB magna cum laude, Stanford U., 1953, MBA summa cum laude, 1958; SM, MIT, 1970. Sales trainee IBM, San Francisco, 1958-59; v.p., ast. gen. mgr. Northrop Archtl. Systems, City of Industry, Calif., 1959-67; v.p. fin. Northrop Corp. Aircraft Div., Hawthorne, Calif., 1967-74; sr. v.p., controller Hughes Aircraft Co., El Segundo, Calif., 1974-83, pres., chief operating officer, 1983—, also bd. dirs. Bd. govs. Music Ctr. Los Angeles County; bd. dirs. Nat. Action Council for Minorities in Engring., Inc. Served to lt. (j.g.) Signal Corps, USN, 1953-56, Japan. Mem. Nat. Contract Mgmt. Assn., Nat. Aero. Assn. (bd. dirs.), Am. Def. Preparedness Assn. (bd. dirs.), Calif. Bus. Roundtable. Republican. Clubs: Rolling Hills Country (Rolling Hills Estates, Calif.); Bel-Air Country (Los Angeles). Office: Hughes Aircraft Co 7200 Hughes Terr PO Box 45066 Los Angeles CA 90045 *

WHITE, ELIZABETH FLAD, financial executive; b. Kenosha, Wis., Oct. 22, 1954; d. Gilbert George and Laura Antoinette (Johnson) Flad; m. Daniel Christopher White, Nov. 23, 1979. BS, U. Wis., Oshkosh, 1977. Account exec. Kenosha Broadcasting, Wis., 1977-80; assoc. editor Bender Pubs., Dallas, 1980-83; sales rep. NCR Corp., Dallas, 1983-85; account mgr. NCR Corp., 1985-88; account exec. Fin. Info. Trust, L.A., 1988—; lectr. in field. Mem. AAUW. Roman Catholic. Office: Financial Info Trust 1801 Avenue of the Stars #640 Los Angeles CA 90067

WHITE, EUGENE R., computer manufacturing company executive. With Gen. Electric Co., Fairfield, Conn., 1958-70, Fairchild Camera & Instrument Corp., 1970-74; chmn., chief exec. officer Amdahl Corp., Sunnyvale, Calif., from 1974, now vice chmn., also bd. dirs. Office: Amdahl Corp 1250 E Arques Ave PO Box 3470 Sunnyvale CA 94088 *

WHITE, GAYLE CLAY, data processing executive; b. Wyandotte, Mich., Sept. 28, 1944; d. John Leonard and Irene Francis (Clay) W.; m. Sharon Wong, June 8, 1968; children: Lai Jean, Quinn Yee. BBA, Ea. Mich. U., 1967; MBA, Utah State U., 1971; MPA, Auburn U., 1976; postgrad., Nova U., 1985—. Computer system analyst USAF Logistics Command, Odgen, Utah, 1967-71, U.S.-Can. Mil. Officer Exec., Ottawa, Ont., 1971-73; mgr. software devel. USAF Data System Design Ctr., Montgomery, Ala., 1973-77; data base adminstr. Supreme Hdqrs. Allied Powers Europe, Casteau, Belgium, 1977-81; mgr. software configuration System Integration Office, Colorado Springs, Colo., 1981-83; mgr. computer ops. N.Am. Aerospace Def. Command, Colorado Springs, 1983-84; dir. ops. 6 Missile Warning Squadron, Space Command, Cape Cod, Mass., 1984-86, comdr., 1986-87; mgr. program devel. Rockwell Internat., Colorado Springs, 1987—; mem. faculty. computer sci. Regis Coll., Colorado Springs, 1981—. Trustee Christian Ctr. Ch., Colorado Springs, 1989—. Recipient Mil.-Civilian Rels. award Otis Civilian Adv. Coun., 1987. Mem. Am. Mgmt. Assn., Armed Forces Communications Electronics Assn., Internat. Test and Evaluation Assn., United Space Found., Nat. Security Indsl. Assn., Christian Businessmens Assn., Am. Amateur Racquetball Assn., The Point Racquet Club, Racquet Club, Toastmasters (pres. 1975-76), Alpha Kappa Psi. Republican. Home: PO Box 17184 Colorado Springs CO 80935 Office: Rockwell Internat 1250 Academy Park Loop Colorado Springs CO 80910

WHITE, GEORGE HARVEY, school superintendent; b. Durango, Colo., Feb. 5, 1939; s. Loyd Oscar and Sally Beatrice (Mullenix) W.; m. Janice Pope, Sept. 30, 1960. BA in History, U. Alaska, 1964; MEd in Adminstrn., Eastern Wash. State Coll., 1969. Supt., div. regional schs. Beltz Regional High Sch., Nome, Alaska, 1968-69; regional supt. N.W. Region Div. State Operated Schs., Nome, 1970-71; assoc. supt. Alaska State Operated Sch. System, Anchorage, 1971-75; supt. Alaska Unorganized Borough Sch. Dist., Anchorage, 1975-76; dist. supt. N.W. Arctic Sch. Dist., 1976-82; supt. Kake (Alaska) City Sch. Dist., 1982—; vice chmn. Alaska Profl. Teaching Practices Commn., 1977-80; chmn. Alaska Public Offices Commn., 1980-84; mem. adv. bd. Alaska Airlines, 1980-81. Ex-officio mem. U. Alaska adv. council Kotzebue Community Coll., 1976-82; instl. rep. Boy Scouts Am., 1968-69; mem. Juvenile Adv. Com. to Superior Ct., Nome, 1968-69; mem. exec. com. N.W. Alaska Regional Strategy Planning Council, 1977-82; mem. Cross-Cultural Edn. Program Consortium, to 1980; bd. dirs. S.E. Regional Resource Center. Mem. Am. Assn. Sch. Adminstrs., Alaska Assn. Sch. Adminstrs. (pres.-elect, mem. exec. bd.; sec.-treas. 1979-80). Cert. prin., tchr., supt., Alaska. Home: Box 317 Kake AK 99830 Office: Box 450 Kake AK 99830

WHITE, HOWARD ASHLEY, emeritus university president; b. Cloverdale, Ala., Sept. 28, 1913; s. John Parker and Mabel Clara (Hipp) W.; m. Maxcine Elliott Feltman, June 17, 1952; children—Ashley Feltman, Howard Elliott. Diploma, David Lipscomb Coll., 1932; B.A., Tulane U., 1946, M.A., 1950, Ph.D., 1956. Ordained to ministry Ch. of Christ, 1933; minister Carrollton Ave. Ch. of Christ, New Orleans, 1941-52; assoc. prof. history David Lipscomb Coll., Nashville, 1953-56; prof., chmn. dept. David Lipscomb Coll., 1956-58; chmn. social sci. dept. Pepperdine U., Malibu, Calif., 1958-65; dean grad. studies Pepperdine U., 1965-67, dean undergrad. studies, 1967-70, exec. v.p., 1970-78, pres., 1978-85, pres. emeritus, 1985—. Mem. Am. Hist. Assn., So. Hist. Assn., Orgn. Am. Historians, Phi Alpha Theta, Phi Delta Kappa. Clubs: Calif, Lincoln, Regency, Rotary. Home: 24440 Tiner Ct Malibu CA 90265 Office: Pepperdine U 24255 Pacific Coast Hwy Malibu CA 90265

WHITE, HUBERT WILLIAM, film producer, director; b. New Orleans, Nov. 23, 1944; s. Hubert William and Jule Marie (Bell) W.; m. Katherine Ann White, Feb. 11, 1967; children: Michelle, Juli. BA, U. Minn., 1966; MA, San Francisco State U., 1974; student, Am. Film Inst., 1976. Documentary filmmaker Sta. WCCO-TV, Mpls., 1973-74; dir., producer Chris Craft Video, Los Angeles, 1975-78, Bill White Prodns., Los Angeles, 1978—. Dir. films and commls.; contbr. articles to profl. jours. Served to capt. USAF, 1966-71. Honored Marin Film Festival, Calif., 1972, Atlanta Film Festival, 1974; Pacific Film Archive, Berkeley, Calif., 1973. Mem. Assn. Ind. Comml. Producers (bd. dirs. 1986), Dirs. Guild of Am., TV Acad. of Arts and Scis. Office: 5907 W Pico Blvd Los Angeles CA 90035

WHITE, JAMES DAVID, ceramist, corporate executive; b. Ft. Worth, Nov. 17, 1941. Grad. with honors, Noncommissioned Officer Acad., 1963; BA in Edn., Cen. State Coll., Edmond, Okla., 1968; grad., Denver Police Res. Acad., 1970, Sgt. Maj. Acad., 1989. Cert. secondary tchr., Okla., Colo. Tchr. Sch. Dist. No. 1, Denver, 1968-69; with Hartford Ins. Group, 1970, Merlyn Smith Ins. Agy., Colorado Springs, Colo., 1971, Morrison and Morrison Inc., Denver, 1971-73; mgr. ins. Western Mobile Homes, Denver, 1973-76; ptnr., pres. Wolds Classic Ceramics, Denver, 1976—; lectr.; presenter seminars in field; nat. bd. dirs. Bus. Edn. Seminars for Ceramic Arts. Columnist Ceramic Scope, 1986. With U.S. Army, 1960-63, command sgt. maj. Colo. Army N.G., 1973—. Recipient Ceramic Ind. award Ceramic Distbrs. for Svc. to Industry, 1987, Hero Next Door award NBC affiliate, Denver, 1987. Mem. Ceramic Arts Fedn. Internat. (dealer chmn. 1986-88), Colo. Columbine Ceramic Assn. (exec. dir. 1986), N.G. Assn. Colo. Republican. Seventh Day Adventist. Home: 9125 Rampart St Denver CO 80221 Office: Wolds Classic Ceramics 8860 Federal Denver CO 80221

WHITE, JAMES EDWARD, geophysicist; b. Cherokee, Tex., May 10, 1918; s. William Cleburne and Willie (Carter) W.; m. Courtenay Brumby, Feb. 1, 1941; children: Rebecca White Vanderslice, Peter McDuffie, Margaret Marie White Curren, Courtenay White Forte. B.A., U. Tex., 1941, M.A., 1946; Ph.D., MIT, 1949. Dir. Underwater Sound Lab., MIT, Cambridge, 1941-45; scientist Def. Research Lab., Austin, Tex., 1945-46; research assoc. MIT, 1946-49; group leader, field research lab. Mobil Oil Co., Dallas, 1949-55; mgr. physics dept. Denver Research Center, Marathon Oil Co., 1955-69; v.p. Globe Universal Scis., Midland, Tex., 1969-71; adj. prof. dept. geophysics Colo. Sch. Mines, Golden, 1972-73, C.H. Green prof., 1976-87, prof. emeritus, 1986—; L.A. Nelson prof. U. Tex., El Paso, 1973-76; Esso vis. prof. U. Sydney, Australia, 1975; vis. prof. MIT, 1982, U. Tex.-Austin, 1985, Macquarie U., Sydney, 1988; del. U.S.-USSR geophysics exchange Dept. State, 1965; mem. bd. Am. Geol. Inst., 1972; mem. space applications bd. Nat. Acad. Engring., 1972-77; exchange scientist Nat. Acad. Sci., 1973-74; del. conf. on oil exploration China Geophys. Soc.-Soc. Exploration Geophysicists, 1981; cons. world bank Chinese U. Devel. Project II, 1987. Author: Seismic Waves: Radiation, Transmission, Attenuation, 1965, Underground Sound: Application of Seismic Waves, 1983, (with R.L. Sengbush) Production Seismology, 1987; editor: Vertical Seismic Profiling (E.I. Galperin), 1974; contbr. articles to profl. jours.; patentee in field. Fellow Acoustical Soc. Am.; mem. Soc. Exploration Geophysicists (hon., Maurice Ewing medal 1986, Halliburton award 1987), Nat. Acad. Engring., Sigma Xi. Unitarian. Club: Cosmos. Office: Colo Sch Mines Dept Geophysics Golden CO 80401

WHITE, JANET LYNN, business consulting company executive; b. Yonkers, N.Y., July 14, 1949; m. Frank A. White, Aug. 7, 1967 (div. July 1986); 1 child, Shawn. BA in Acctg., Columbia Pacific U., 1984. Asst. gen. mgr. western facilities Greyhound Food Mgmt., 1967-70; asst. chief cost acct. United Bank Denver, 1970-74; controller, mgr. cost acctg. IT Corp., Martinez, Calif., 1978-80; mgr. cost acctg., budget dir., mgr. data processing, coordinator systems task force Membrana Inc., Pleasanton, Calif., 1980-1982; pres., prin. cons. JW Bus. Solutions, Walnut Creek, Calif., 1983—; cons. of referral Assoc. Builders and Contractors, 1986-87; chief fin. officer, bd. dirs. Gamma Graphics, Dublin, Calif., 1987-88; lectr., interviewer in field. Author: Cost Accounting Techniques and Applications for Layman Use, 1984; contbr. articles to bus. publs. Pres. Jayceettes, Denver, 1976. Mem. Nat. Assn. Accts. (bd. dirs. 1980-85, cert. of merit 1985, 88), Internat. Trade Assn., Entrepreneur Assn. Diablo Valley (mem. Contra Costa coun.), Bay Area Soc. Info. Ctrs., Walnut Creek C. of C. Home: 2121 N California Blvd Ste 1010 Walnut Creek CA 94596 Office: JW Bus Solutions 160 Cedar Pointe Loop Ste 303 San Ramon CA 94583

WHITE, JOAN MARIE, naturopathic physician; b. Seattle, Aug. 1, 1955; d. Edward James and Frances Marie (Ball) W. BS in Zoology, Howard U., 1976; BS in Human Biology, Kansas Newman Coll., 1979; D of Naturopathic Medicine, Nat. Coll. of Naturopathic Medicine, 1981. Research asst. U. Wash. Hosp., Seattle, 1976; research lab. technician NIH, Bethesda, Md., 1976-77; med. extern Portland (Oreg.) Clinic, 1979-81; mgr., sales assoc. Frederick & Nelson, Seattle, 1981-83; biologist The Seattle Aquarium, 1983-87, corp. mgmt. adv. com., 1983; program mgr. teen parents' transition to work program North Seattle Community Coll., Seattle, 1987—. Recipient Ebony Excellence award Portland Adv. Newspaper, 1981. Home: 4710 University Way NE #1238 Seattle WA 98105-4495 Office: N Seattle Community Coll Teen Parents Transition Work Program 9600 College Way N Seattle WA 98103

WHITE, JOHN ABIATHAR, pilot, consultant; b. Chgo., May 29, 1948; s. Abiathar Jr. and Gretchen Elizabeth (Zuber) W.; m. Therese Ann Denz, June 21, 1980; children: Kathryn Ann, Laura Ellen. Student, Art Ctr. Coll. of Design, 1969-70, Calif. Inst. Tech., 1966-67; BArch, U. Ill., 1972. Archtl. apprentice Farner Und Grunder Industriearchitekten, Zurich, Switzerland, 1972; archtl. draftsman Walter Carlson Assocs., Elk Grove, Ill., 1973; archtl. designer Unteed Assocs., Palatine, Ill., 1974-75; flight instr. Planemasters, Inc., West Chicago, Ill., 1976; pilot Aero Am. Aviation, West Chicago, 1977, Beckett Aviation, Cleve., 1978; pilot Am. Airlines, Chgo. and L.A., 1979—, capt., 1988—; archtl. cons. Nat. Accelerator Lab., Batavia, Ill., 1980, Constrn. Collaborative, Park Ridge, Ill., 1982, L.K. White Assocs., San Diego, 1988—. Nat. Coun. Tchrs. of English scholar, 1966. Mem. Nat. Assn. Flight Instrs., Planetary Soc. Unitarian. Home: 2610 El Aguila St Carlsbad CA 92009 Office: Am Airlines World Way Postal Ctr Los Angeles CA 90009

WHITE, LELIA CAYNE, librarian; b. Berkeley, Calif., Feb. 22, 1921; d. James Lloyd and Eulalia Fulton (Douglass) Cayne; children by previous marriage—Douglass Fulton, Cameron Jane. B.A., U. Calif., Berkeley, 1943, M.L.S., 1969. Bibliographer, lectr., asso. U. Calif. at Berkeley Sch. Library and Info. Studies, 1969-72; reference librarian Berkeley-Oakland (Calif.) Service Systems, 1970-76, supervising librarian, 1973-76; dir. Oakland Public Library, 1976—; mem. adv. com. U. Calif. Berkeley Sch. Library and Info. Studies. Contbr. to: Public Library User Education, 1981. Bd. dirs. Nat. Ednl. Film Festival, Oakland Youth Works; Vista Coll. adv. bd. Internat. Trade Inst.; adv. com. Mayor's Fgn. Investment Program; community services policy com. League of Calif. Cities. Mem. ALA, Calif. Library Assn., Public Library Assn., Calif. Inst. Libraries (pres.), Public Library Execs. Central Calif., LWV, Oakland Dalian (China) Friendship City Soc. (pres.). Office: Oakland Pub Libr 125 14th St Oakland CA 94612 *

WHITE, LESLIE BOYD, chiropractic orthopedist; b. San Diego, Dec. 17, 1944; s. Boyd Ethelbert and Evelene Adlaid (McCrory) W.; m. Karen Lynn Buck; children: Donna Marie, Gregory Donald, Richard Wayne, Sherri Lin. Dr. of Chiropractic, Palmer Coll. of Chiropractic, 1967. Diplomate in Chiropractic Orthopedics. Assoc. Sherwood Chiropractic Clinic, Seattle, 1967-68; owner Burien Chiropractic Ctr., Seattle, 1968—; mem. State of Wash. Chiropractic Disciplinary Bd., 1979—, chmn., 1983-88. Contbr. articles to profl. jours., 1976—. Fellow Internat. Coll. Chiropractors, 1986; mem. Am. Chiropractic Assn., Wash. Chiropractic Assn. (treas. 1975-77, 2d v.p. 1977-79, 1st v.p. 1979-80, pres. 1981-82, chmn. exec. bd. 1982-83, now bd. dirs. emeritus, chmn. peer rev. com. 1976-78, chmn. legis. com. 1981-82), Gold Ring Rd. Riders Assn. (Phoenix). Office: Burien Chiropractic Ctr 445 S 152d Seattle WA 98148

WHITE, MAHLON THATCHER, banker; b. Apr. 21, 1936; s. William Mathew and Helen (Thatcher) W.; m. Maylan Timberlake Wolverton, Dec. 19, 1942; children: Mahlon Thatcher II, Mathew Whitney, Mark Andrew. BA, U. Colo., 1959, bus. (hon.), 1980. With First Nat. Bank-Denver, 1959-60; asst. cashier to pres. First Nat. Bank-Durango, 1960; pres., chmn. bd. First Nat. Bank-Alamosa, 1966-83, First Nat. Bank-Salida, 1966-83, Bank of Aspen, Aspen, Colo., 1966-80; chmn. bd. Bank of Monte Vista, Monte Vista, Colo., 1980—, First Nat. Bank-Durango, 1980—, The Minnequa Bank, Pueblo, Colo., 1980—; pres. The Thatcher Found., Pueblo, 1983—; dir. Colo. Assn. Commerce and Industry, Pueblo, 1970—; pres. Shikar Safari Internat., 1989—. Trustee U. So. Colo. Found., Pueblo, 1970—, Ft. Lewis Coll. Found., Durango, 1966—. Republican. Office: The Minnequa Bank 401 W Northern Pueblo CO 81004

WHITE, MARGARET ALYSONE, teacher; b. Timmins, Ont., Can., Feb. 25, 1942; came to U.S., 1951; d. Francis Alan and Grace (Newton) Woodbury; m. Robert Newton White, Sept. 2, 1967; children: Nicole Denise, Heather Joyce. AA, San Antonio Coll., 1962; BA, Stephen F. Austin U., 1965; postgrad., U. Dayton, 1984-85, Wright State U. Cert. tchr., Tex. Tchr. Lufkin (Tex.) Ind. Schs., 1964-65, Northside Ind. Sch. Dist., San Antonio, 1965-69; tchr. Vandalia-Butler (Ohio) City Schs., 1985-87, reading and math. resource tchr., 1988—. Dir. choir Trinity Episc. Ch., Troy, Ohio, 1980-85, St. David's, Vandalia, 1976-80; vocalist Dayton, Ohio Philharm., 1985—; instr. guitar YMCA. Mem. Sister Cities Club, Ohio Mission Club.

WHITE, MATTHEW, family practice physician; b. Phila., May 21, 1941; s. Frank and Minerva (Shiffmann) W.; m. Kristina J. Johnson, Aug. 15, 1978. AB in Chemistry, Temple U., 1963; MD, Jefferson Med. Coll., 1967. Diplomate Am. Bd. Family Practice. Commd. lt. USN, 1967, advanced through grades to comdr., 1975; intern U.S. Naval Hosp., Newport, R.I., 1967-68; resident U.S. Naval Hosp., Jacksonville, Fla., 1968-70; family practice medicine USN, Japan, 1970-73, Bremerton, Wash., 1973-77; family practice medicine Sand Pt. Naval Air Sta., Seattle, 1977-78; resigned USN,

1978; family practice medicine Tacoma, 1978—; mem. active staff, mem. bd. dirs., mem. exec. com. Lakewood Gen Hosp.; mem. courtesy staff Humana Hosp., Multicare Hosp., St. Joseph's Hosp.; pres. med. staff Lakewood Hosp., 1989—. Mem. utilization com. Sherwood Terr. Nursing Home, Georgian House Nursing Home, and Meadow Park Nursing Home. Fellow Am. Acad. Family Practice; mem. AMA, Nat. Assn. Family Practice, Wash. State Assn. Family Practice, Wash. State Med. Assn., Tacoma Med. Assn., Tacoma Assn. Family Practice. Republican. Jewish. Office: 7424 Bridgeport Way W Tacoma WA 98467

WHITE, MORGAN WILSON, investment executive; b. L.A., May 10, 1945; s. Robert Jenkins and Lorraine (Keck) W.; m. Nancy Macdonald, June 22, 1969 (div. Dec. 1981); children: Marshall Garrett, Stephanie Lynn; m. Joyce Donovan Nash, Feb. 6, 1983. BSEE, Stanford U., 1967, MSEE, 1968, MBA, 1974. V.p. Bailard, Biehl & Kaiser, Inc., San Mateo, Calif., 1974-79, The Portola Group, Inc., Menlo Park., Calif., 1979-87; pres. Woodside Asset Mgmt., Inc., Menlo Park, 1987—. Bd. dirs. The Catalyst Found., Palo Alto, Calif., 1987—. Lt. USNR, 1969-71. Mem. Security Analysts of San Francisco. Republican. Home: 55 Skywood Way Woodside CA 94062 Office: Woodside Asset Mgmt Inc 3000 Sand Hill Rd 3/160 Menlo Park CA 94025

WHITE, NANCY JOANNE, librarian, administrator; b. Sharon, Pa., Oct. 1, 1953; d. William Roy and Lorraine Irene (Taylor) Aggers; 1 dau., Samantha Rae. B.A. in Latin, Oberlin Coll., 1975; M.L.S., U. Calif.-Berkeley, 1980. Library asst. Case Western Res. U., Cleve., 1976; clk. treas. Cleve. Area Met. Library System, 1976-78; med. library asst. Letterman Army Med. Ctr., San Francisco, 1978-79; research asst. Sta. KRON-TV, San Francisco, 1980; reference librarian Standard Oil Co. of Calif., San Francisco, 1980; library asst. Pacific Gas and Electric Co., San Francisco, 1980-81, info. specialist, 1981, dir. corp. library, 1981-83, administrv. asst. rate dept., 1983-84, cost acctg. supr., 1984-85, project mgr. fuel filings, 1985-86, forecasting supr., 1986-87, dir. revenue requests, 1988—, corp. planning, 1989—. Pres. alumni bd. dirs. Grad. Sch. of Library and Info. Sci., U. Calif.-Berkeley. C-lub: Commonwealth (San Francisco). Office: Pacific Gas & Electric Co 77 Beale St Ste 2949 San Francisco CA 94106

WHITE, PRESTON CHARLES, city official; b. Norfolk, Va., July 28, 1933; s. Charles and Luvenia (Simmons) W.; m. Mabel Mercedes Aitcheson, Aug. 31, 1963; children: John, Robert, Mark, Brian, Gail. MPA, U. Denver, 1981. Enlisted USAF, 1956; logistic plan technician USAF, Syracuse, N.Y., 1956-59, Newburgh, N.Y., 1960-61; exec. support officer USAF, Greece, 1962-63; logistics plans mgr. USAF, Colorado Springs, Colo. and Vietnam, 1963-71; pers. mgr. USAF, Colorado Springs, 1972-77, adminstr., housing officer, 1977-78, ret., 1978; human rels. specialist City of Colorado Springs, 1979—. Chmn. Colo. Gov.'s Adv. Bd. for Sickle Cell Anemia, 1980-87; pres. Colo. Assn. for Retarded Citizens, 1986—; mem. exec. com. 5th Congl. Com. for Bush, Colorado Springs, 1987-88. Recipient Dedicated Svc. award Colorado Springs Sch. Dist 11, 1983-87, Colo. Gov.'s Adv. Com. on Sickle Cell Anemia, 1984-87, Outstanding Svc. award Harrison Sch. Dist. 2, Colorado Springs, 1987. Mem. Am. Mgmt. Assn., Colorado Springs C. of C., Civitan (lt. gov. Colo. chpt. 1978-79). Home: 3204 Squaw Valley Dr Colorado Springs CO 80918 Office: City of Colorado Springs 545 E Pikes Peak Ste 101 Colorado Springs CO 80903

WHITE, RICHARD, computer consulting company executive; b. N.Y.C., Aug. 14, 1951; s. Richard A. and Agnes (Coleman) W. BS, MIT, 1972; MA, U. Wis., 1979. Programmer Honeywell Inc., Waltham, Mass., 1973; system analyst Infonex, Arlington, Mass., 1974; dep. press sec. U.S. Senator John Durkin, Manchester, N.H., 1975; asst. press sec. Mass. Gov. Michael Dukakis, Boston, 1974-75; exec. asst. Assembly Speaker, Madison, Wis., 1976-84; pres. Info. Edge Inc., Avon, Colo.; bd. dirs. Iris Inc., N.Y.C. Mem. Dane County Library Bd., Madison, 1985-87, South Cen. Library Bd., Madison, 1986-87, Middleton Zoning Bd. Appeals, Wis., 1986-87. Mem. IEEE, Assn. Computing Machinery. Democrat. Home: PO Box 2427 Avon CO 81620 Office: Info Edge Inc PO Box 1756 Vail CO 81658

WHITE, RICHARD H., fund raising professional; b. Chgo., June 1, 1950; s. Herman S. and Luvenia (Young) W.; m. Valencia Peters, June 12, 1950. BA, Cath. U., 1973; MA, Howard U., 1978. Cert. fund raising exec. Mem. staff Howard U. Hosp., Washington, 1975-80; dir. clin. social devel. ARC, Atlanta, 1980-85; devel. dir. Civitan Internat., Birmingham, Ala., 1985-88; found. dir. Riverside (Calif.) Community Coll. Found., 1989—. V.p. Ala. Sickle Cell Found., Birmingham, 1987; bd. dirs. Ga. Joint Bd. Family Practice, Atlanta, 1983, Ala. Children's Trust Fund, Montgomery, 1986. Named Outstanding Atlantan, Mayor of Atlanta, 1983, one of Outstanding Young Men of Am., U.S. Jaycees, 1983, 85; recipient Disting. Leadership award UN Children's Fund, 1984. Mem. Nat. Soc. Fund Raising Execs. Home: 11673 Canvasback Circle Moreno Valley CA 92387 Office: Riverside Community Coll 4800 Magnolia Ave Riverside CA 92506

WHITE, ROBERT LEE, electrical engineer, educator; b. Plainfield, N.J., Feb. 14, 1927; s. Claude and Ruby Hemsworth Emerson (Levick) W.; m. Phyllis Lillian Arlt, June 14, 1952; children: Lauren A., Kimberly A., Christopher L., Matthew P. B.A. in Physics, Columbia U., 1949, M.A., 1951, Ph.D., 1954. Assoc. head atomic physics dept. Hughes Rsch. Labs., Malibu, Calif., 1954-61; head magnetics dept. Gen. Tel. and Electronics Rsch. Lab., Palo Alto, Calif., 1961-63; prof. elec. engring. Stanford U., Palo Alto, 1963-89, chmn. elec. engring. dept., 1981-86; William E. Ayer prof. elec. engring. Stanford U., 1985-88; exec. dir. The Exploratorium, San Francisco, 1987—; dir. Inst. for Electronics in Medicine, 1973-87; bd. dirs. Analog Design Tools Inc.; initial ltd. partner Mayfield Fund, Mayfield, II and Alpha II Fund, Rainbow Co-Investment Ptnrs., Halo Ptnrs.; cons. in field. Author: (with K.A. Wickersheim) Magnetism and Magnetic Materials, 1965, Basic Quantum Mechanics, 1967; Contbr. numerous articles to profl. jours. With USN, 1945-46. Fellow Guggenheim, Oxford U., 1969-70, Kantonsspital Zurich, 1977-78, Christensen fellow Oxford, 1986. Fellow Am. Phys. Soc., IEEE; mem. Sigma Xi, Phi Beta Kappa. Home: 450 El Escarpado Way Stanford CA 94305 Office: The Exploratorium 3601 Lyon St San Francisco CA 94123

WHITE, ROBERT LOUIS, pharmacist; b. Los Angeles, Sept. 23, 1952; s. Robert Lawrence and Maxine Edith (Wolf) W. BS, Oreg. State U., 1976. Registered pharmacist, Oreg. Mgr. nursing home services M&M Stores Inc., Portland, Oreg., 1976-84; owner, dir., chief exec. officer White, Mack & Wart, Inc., Portland, Oreg., 1984—; preceptor Oreg. Bd. Pharmacy, 1976—, nursing home subcom., 1988; adj. faculty Oreg. State U., Corvallis, 1978—, clin. edn. com., Portland, 1988—; cons. Good Samaritan Hosp. and Med. Ctr., Portland, 1987—. Vol. Oreg. Council on Alcoholism and Drug Addiction, Portland, 1987. Fellow Am. Soc. Cons. Pharmacists; mem. Oreg. State Pharm. Assn., Oreg. Soc. Cons. Pharmacists (nominating com. 1988), Oreg. Health Care Assn., Rho Chi, Phi Sigma, Phi Kappa Phi. Republican. Baptist. Office: White Mack & Wart 10570 SW Washington Ste 204 Portland OR 97216

WHITE, ROBERT M., personnel executive; b. Ravenswood, W.Va., Aug. 30, 1942; s. Thomas Michael and Margaret (Blazier) W.; m. Geraldine White (div. 1969); children: Thomas, Gary, Greg; m. Henrietta Katherine White (div. 1988); 1 child, Robert; m. Dianna Lynn, July 1, 1988; children: Levi, Megan, Alicia. Diploma, East High Sch., Green Bay, Wis., 1960. Br. mgr. Local Loan Co., Milw., 1962-69; owner, pres. Marketmasters, Milw., 1967-69; sr. cons. Sales Dynamics Inst., N.Y.C., 1969-71; pres. Mind Dynamics, inc., San Rafael, Calif., 1971-73; chmn., chief exec. officer Arc Internat., Ltd., Tokyo and Denver, 1974—. Author: One World One People, 1984. Chmn. Republicans Abroad, Tokyo, 1983-86, Internat. Eagles, Washington, 1984-86; bd. dirs. Windstar Found., Aspen, Colo., 1988—; advisor, underwriter New Dimensions Radio, San Francisco, 1986—. Baden Powell fellow, 1985. Mem. Pacific Basin Econ. Coun. (vice chmn. 1986—), Am. C. of C.-Japan (gov. 1984-86), Am. Soc. Tng. and Devel., Am. Mgmt. Assn., Met. Club, Instructional Systems Assn. (v.p. 1989—). Republican. Home: PO Box 12396 Aspen CO 81672 Office: Arc Internat 5445 DTC Pkwy Denver CO 80111

WHITE, ROBERT MILTON, lawyer; b. Tachikawa AFB, Japan, Oct. 10, 1948; came to U.S., 1948; s. Triggs Reeves and Josephine (Fowler) W. BA, U. N.Mex., 1970; JD, U. Houston, 1973. Bar: N.Mex. 1973, U.S. Dist. Ct. 1973. Ptnr. Levy, White, Ferguson and Grady, Albuquerque, N.Mex., 1973-80, Lastrapes and White, Albuquerque, 1980-83; deputy dir. Dept. of Corrections City of Albuquerque, 1983-86; asst. city atty. City of Albuquerque, 1986—; bd. dirs. Quote-Unquote, Inc., Hogares, Inc; mem. Med. Review Commn. State Bar of N.Mex., 1987—. Mem. Albuquerque City Coun., 1979-83, pres. 1983, Nat. League of Cities, Wilmington, Del. (steering com. on transp. and communications), 1981-83, Arthritis Found. 1983-85. Mem. State Bar N.Mex., Order of Barons, Phi Delta Phi. Democrat. Home: 8414 San Juan NE Albuquerque NM 87108 Office: Legal Dept City of Albuquerque PO Box 1293 Albuquerque NM 87103

WHITE, ROBERT STEPHEN, physics educator; b. Ellsworth, Kans., Dec. 28, 1920; s. Byron F. and Sebina (Leighty) W.; m. Freda Marie Bridgewater, Aug. 30, 1942; children: Nancy Lynn, Margaret Diane, John Stephen, David Bruce. AB, Southwestern Coll., 1942, DSc hon., 1971; MS, U. Ill., 1943; PhD, U. Calif., Berkeley, 1951. Physicist Lawrence Radiation Lab., Berkeley, Livermore, Calif., 1948-61; head dept. particles and fields Space Physics Lab. Aerospace Corp., El Segundo, Calif., 1962-67; physics prof. U. Calif., Riverside, 1967—, dir. Inst. Geophysics and Planetary Physics, 1967, chmn. dept. physics, 1970-73; lectr. U. Calif., Berkeley, 1953-54, 57-59. Author: Space Physics, 1970; contbr. articles to profl. jours. Sr. Postdoctoral fellow NSF, 1961-62; grantee NASA, NSF, USAF, numerous others. Fellow Am. Phys. Soc. (exec. com. 1972-74); mem. AAAS, AAUP, Am. Geophys. Union, Am. Astron. Soc. Republican. Methodist. Home: 2535 Horace St Riverside CA 92506 Office: U Calif Inst Geophysics & Planetary Physics Riverside CA 92521

WHITE, ROBIN SHEPARD, geologist; b. Oak Ridge, Tenn., July 30, 1950; s. George Shepard and Maida Linn (Robinson) W. BA, Alfred U., 1972; MS, U. Ariz., 1976. Lic. geologist, N.C.; cert. geologist, Ind. Geologist Century Geophys. Corp., Tulsa, 1977-79; supr. Century Geophys. Corp., Grants, N.Mex., 1979-80; area mgr. Century Geophys. Corp., Moab (Utah) and Kenedy (Tex.), 1980-81; phys. sci. technician U.S. Dept. Army, Yuma, Ariz., 1983-84; trainee geologist Soil Conservation Service, USDA, Davis, Calif., 1984-85; state geologist Soil Conservation Service, USDA, Speedway, Ind., 1985-87; watershed planning and river basin staff geologist Soil Conservation Service, USDA, Davis, 1987-88; river basin staff geologist Soil Conservation Service, USDA, 1988—. Copyright electronic spreadsheet template computer program on sediment routing. Mem. Computer-Oriented Geol. Soc., Am. Assn. Individual Investors, Soc. Mining Engrs. (assoc.), Assn. Engring. Geologists (jr.), Health Physics Soc. (plenary). Office: USDA Soil Conservation Svc 2121-C 2d St Ste 102 Davis CA 95616

WHITE, RUSSELL LYNN, fashion designer; b. Omaha, May 8, 1950; s. Russell Alfred White and Jo Ann (Steepy) Blotti. AA, Modesto Jr. Coll., 1970; BA in Art, Calif. State U., San Francisco, 1971; student, Coll. of Alameda, 1971-72, Laney Coll., 1976-78, Pierce Coll., 1981-82, Otis Art Inst. of Parsons Sch. Design, 1984-85. Designer Levi Strauss & Co., San Francisco, 1976-79, Jantzen Inc., L.A., 1979-80; head designer Keepers Industries, Woodland Hills, Calif., 1981-83; merchandiser, designer Domino/Victory Mens Wear, L.A., 1983-85; merchandiser, designer Joel/Cal-Made, Ltd., L.A., 1985-86, mdse. mgr., 1986; dir. design Balboa Sportswear Co., L.A., 1986—; prin. BRW & Assocs., L.A., 1986-89, Catalina Swimwear, L.A., 1989—; tchr. fashion design Learning Tree U., L.A., 1989—. Music dir. Holy Trinity Community Ch., L.A., 1981-85, v.p., sec., 1981-83, social dir., 1984-85, treas. 1987—; buddy vol. AIDS project, L.A., 1987—; facilitator Being Alive Support Group, L.A., 1989—. Frank S. Ione Mancini scholar 1968. Mem. Am. Designer Guild (treas. Los Angeles steering com. 1987), Textile Assn. Los Angeles. Republican. Club: Mcpl. Election Com. of Los Angeles (election com. 1982, mem. adv. council) Lodge: Masons (De Molay of Yr. 1968, chevalier 1971). Home and Office: 20300 Valerio St Canoga Park CA 91306

WHITE, STANLEY ARCHIBALD, research electrical engineer; b. Providence, R.I., Sept. 25, 1931; s. Clarence Archibald White and Lou Ella (Givens) Arford; m. Edda María Castaño-Benítez, June 6, 1956; children: Dianne, Stanley Jr., Paul, John. BSEE, Purdue U., 1957, MSEE, 1959, PhD, 1965. Registered profl. engr., Ind., Calif. Engr. Rockwell Internat., Anaheim, Calif., 1959-68, mgr., 1968-84, sr. scientist, 1984—; adj. prof. elec. engring. U. Calif., 1984—; cons. and lectr. in field; bd. dirs. Asilomar Signals Systems, Computer Corp. Publisher, composer music; contbr. chpts. to books; articles to profl. jours.; patentee in field. Bd. dirs., mem. exec. com. SSC Conf. Corp., Dayle McIntosh Ctr. for Ind. Living. Fellow N.Am. Aviation Sci. Engring, 1963-65; recipient Disting. Lectr. award Nat. Electronics Conf., Chgo., 1973, Engr. of Yr. award Orange County (Calif.) Engring. Council, 1984, Engr. of Yr. award Rockwell Internat., 1985, Leonardo Da Vinci Medallion, 1986, Sci. Achievement award, 1987, Disting. Engring. Alumnus award Purdue U., 1988, Meritorious Inventor's award Rockwell Internat. Corp. 1989. Fellow AAAS, IEEE (founding chmn. Orange County chpt. of Acoustics, Speech and Signal Processing Soc., vice chmn. internat. symposium on circuits and systems 1983, 1989—, gen. chmn. internat. conf. on acoustics, speech, and signal process, 1984, Centennial medal 1984, gen. chmn. Internat. Symposium on Cirs. and Systems, 1982), Inst. Advancement Engring., N.Y. Acad. Scis.; mem. Audio Engring. Soc., Sigma Xi (pres. Autonetics club), Eta Kappa U. (internat. dir. emeritus), Tau Beta Pi. Home: 433 E Ave Cordoba San Clemente CA 92672 Office: Rockwell Internat Corp 3370 Miraloma Ave Anaheim CA 92803-3170

WHITE, VICTORIA LEE, physical therapist; b. Charleston, W.Va., Mar. 26, 1950; d. John Clark and Mary Nelson (Freels) W.; m. J. Marc Carpenter, Feb. 8, 1985; children: Kristen, Kelly. BA, Vanderbilt U., 1972; MA, Stanford U., 1976. Staff therapist Presbyn. Med. Ctr., Denver, 1976-77, Luth. Med. Ctr., Wheatridge, Colo., 1977-79, SCOR, Denver, 1979; co-owner Back and Conditioning Clinic, Lakewood, Colo., 1979—, Southwest Phys. Therapy, Littleton, Colo., 1982—; 1982— Golden (Colo.) Phys. Therapy, 1983—. Mem. Am. Phys. Therapy Orgn., Colo. Orthopedic Study Group (pres. 1979-80), Preferred Independent Phys. Therapy Orgn. (treas. 1984—, bd. dirs. 1984—). Office: Back & Conditioning Clinic 2020 Wesdsworth #18 Lakewood CO 80215

WHITE, VIRGINIA MATHIAS, sales executive; b. Riverside, N.J., Nov. 17, 1949; d. William Herbert and Helen Marie (Olsen) Mathias; m. Eliot Carter White, 1978 (div.). BA, Syracuse U., 1971; MBA, San Jose State U., 1976. Advt. saleswoman Valley Jour., Sunnyvale, Calif., 1972-73; with profl. resources dept. GE, San Jose, Calif., 1974-77, mgr. mfg. engring., 1977-79, mgr. mech. prodn. scheduling, 1979-82; mgr. corp. sales program Calma Corp., Santa Clara, Calif., 1982-84; mgr. internat. hdqrs. ops. Calma Corp., Milpitas, Calif., 1984-86; dir. internat. ops. Ridge Computers, Santa Clara, 1986-88; dir. European ops. Arix Corp., San Jose, 1988—. Mem. Beta Gamma Sigma, Delta Gamma. Republican. Moravian. Office: Arix Corp 821 Fox Ln San Jose CA 95131

WHITE-DANIELS, SANDRA, company executive; b. Columbus, Ga., Nov. 21, 1956; d. Otis and Rose Helen (Lamb) White; m. Otis Daniels, Apr. 14, 1979 (div. Jan. 1985); 1 child, Brandi Nicole. BS in Community Planning, Columbus Coll., 1978. City planner technician Columbus Consol. Govt., 1978; office mgr. Dr. Hugh E. Ogletreee, Phenix City, Ala., 1979-85; acctg. asst. Trust Co. Bank, Atlanta, 1985-86; pres./chief exec. officer S&B Creative Concepts, L. A., 1986—; cons. rep. Syntrom Legal Svc., L.A., 1987—, Primerica, L.A., 1988—, Fund Am., L.A., 1988—. Sec. Ira Aldridge Inner Cultural Ctr., L.A., 1988—, 100 Black Men L.A., Inc. 1988—. Fellow: Grant's Young Women Missionary. Democrat. Methodist. Office: S&B Creative Concepts 4249 W Imperial Hwy Ste 226 Inglewood CA 90304

WHITE-HUNT, KEITH, industrial development executive; b. Rowlands Gill, Eng., Sept. 6, 1950; s. Thomas William and Louisa (Robson) W-H.; m. Brenda Liddle, Jan. 1, 1970; children: Keith Brendan, John Roland, Daniel Thomas, Brooke Arran, Edward James. BA in Econ. Studies with honors, U. Exeter, United Kingdom, 1973; MS in Indsl. Mgmt., U. Bradford, Eng., 1975; cert. in edn., U. Leeds, 1976; DSc in Bus. Econs., U. Lodz, Poland, 1982; postgrad., Cornell U., 1986, Stanford U., 1987. Registered cons. in info. tech., registered cons. in export sales. Asst. prof. U. Bradford, 1973-77; assoc. prof. U. Sokoto, Nigeria, 1977-78, U. Stirling, Scotland, 1978-80; v.p. corp. devel. Lithgows Ltd., Scotland, 1980-83; deputy chief exec.. & pres. N. Am. Yorkshire & Humberside Deve. Assn., Eng., 1983—; vis. prof. U. R.I., 1980—, Tech. U. of Lodz, 1980—, U. of Lodz, 1985—; bd. dirs. White-Hunt Industries Ltd., Eng. contbr. numerous articles to profl. jours. Recipient David Forsyth award U. Leeds, 1976, Amicus Poloniae award for Contbn. to Coop. Acad. Research in Poland, 1981. Fellow British Inst. Mgmt., Inst. Sales and Mktg. Mgmt., Inst. Petroleum, Internat. Inst. Social Econs., Chartered Inst. Mktg.; mem. Inst. Info. Scientists, Inst. of Wastes Mgmt. Lodge: Rotary. Home: 141 Pepper Ct Los Altos CA 94022 also: 102 Valley Dr, Ben Rhydding, Ilkley, West Yorkshire LS29 8PA, England Office: Yorkshire & Humberside Devel 435 Tasso St Ste 140 Palo Alto CA 94301 also: Yorkshire & Humberside, Westgate House, 100 Wellington St, Leeds, West Yorkshire LS1 4LT, England

WHITEHURST, DEBORAH ANNE, government commissioner; b. Alton, Ill., Mar. 7, 1951; d. Robert Wayne and Esther A. (Merritt) Hardesty; m. Michael Whitehurst, June 13, 1970. BA, Ariz. State U., 1974, postgrad. Asst. Univ. Art Mus., Ariz. State U., Tempe, 1976-78; mus. coordinator Ariz. Commn. on Arts, Phoenix, 1978-82, spl. projects coordinator, 1982-84, dep. dir., 1984-86; exec. dir. Phoenix Arts Commn., 1986—; Mem. adv. panel Nat. Endowment Arts, Washington, 1987. Author: Ariz. Mus. Dir., 1982; editor: Staging a Comeback, 1983; contbr. to book: Boosters, Streetcars and Bungalows, 1985. Nat. Endowment Arts fellow, 1980. Mem. Nat. Assembly Local Arts Agys., U.S. Urban Arts Fedn. Office: Phoenix Arts Commn 2 N Central Ave Ste 125 Phoenix AZ 85004

WHITEHURST, HARRY BERNARD, chemistry educator; b. Dallas, Sept. 13, 1922; s. Clement Monroe and Grace Annette (Walton) W.; m. Audry Lucile Hale, June 12, 1948; children: Jonathan Monroe, Katherine Annette Whitehurst Hilburn. BA, Rice U., 1944, MA, 1948, PhD, 1950. Rsch. chemist Manhattan Project, Oak Ridge, Tenn., 1944-46, U.S. Naval Radiol. Def. Lab., San Francisco, 1959; postdoctoral fellow U. Minn., Mpls., 1950-51; rsch. chemist Owens-Corning Fiberglas Corp., Newark, Ohio, 1951-55, rsch. dept. head, 1955-59; assoc. prof. chemistry Ariz. State U., Tempe, 1959-70, prof., 1970—. Contbr. articles on oxides to profl. jours.; patentee glass fibers field. With C.E., AUS, 1944-46. Fellow Am. Inst. Chemists, AAAS, Ariz. Acad. Sci. (pres. 1960-61); mem. Am. Chem. Soc., Phi Lambda Upsilon. Democrat. Baptist. Home: 630 E Concorda Dr Tempe AZ 85282 Office: Ariz State U Chemistry Dept Tempe AZ 85287-1604

WHITELEY, BENJAMIN ROBERT, insurance company executive; b. Des Moines, July 13, 1929; s. Hiram Everett and Martha Jane (Walker) W.; m. Elaine Marie Yunker, June 14, 1953; children: Stephen R., Benjamin W. BS, Oregon State U., 1951; MS, U. Mich, 1952. Actuarial clk. Standard Ins. Co., Portland, Oreg., 1956-59; dept. head Group Actuarial Standard Ins. Co., Portland, 1959-61, asst. actuary, 1961-63, asst. v.p., asst. actuary, 1963-64, assoc. actuary, 1964-70, v.p. Group Ins. Adminstrn., 1970-72, v.p. Group Ins., 1972-80, exec. v.p. Group Ins., 1980-83, pres., chief exec. officer, 1983—, also bd. dirs.; bd. dirs. Gunderson Inc., U.S. Nat. Bank of Oreg., Standard Mgmt., Inc., Portland. Trustee Pacific U., Forest Grove, Oreg., 1981—, chmn. 1986—; bd. dirs. Oreg. Independent Colls. Found.; pres. Columbia Pacific Coun. Boy Scouts Am., 1984-86; trustee Oreg. State U. Found., St. Vincent Med. Found. 1st lt. U.S. Air Force, 1952-55. Recipient Silver Beaver award, Boy Scouts Am., Portland, Oreg., 1983. Fellow Soc. of Actuaries; mem. Am. Acad. Actuaries (bd. dirs. 1983-86), Actuarial Club of the Pacific States (v.p. 1969, pres. 1970), Oregon Bus. Coun., Portland C. of C., Am. Coun. Life Ins. (bd. dirs.), Arlington Club (bd. dirs. 1987—), Waverly Country Club, Multnomah Athletic Club. Office: Standard Ins Co PO Box 711 Portland OR 97207

WHITESIDE, CAROL GORDON, mayor; b. Chgo., Dec. 15, 1942; d. Paul George and Helen Louise (Barre) G.; m. John Gregory Whiteside, Aug. 15, 1964; children: Brian Paul, Derek James. BA, U. Calif., Davis, 1964. Pers. mgr. Emporium Capwell Co., Santa Rosa, 1964-67; pers. asst. Levi Strauss & Co., San Francisco, 1967-69; project leader Interdatum, San Francisco, 1983—; with City Coun. Modesto, 1982-87; mayor City of Modesto, 1987—. Trustee Modesto City Schs., 1979-83. Named Outstanding Woman of Yr. Women's Commn., Stanislaus County, Calif., 1988. Republican. Lutheran. Office: City of Modesto PO Box 642 Modesto CA 95353

WHITE-VONDRAN, MARY ELLEN, retired stockbroker; b. East Cleveland, Ohio, Aug. 21, 1938; d. Thomas Patrick and Rita Ellen (Langdon) White; m. Gary L. Vondran, Nov. 25, 1961; children: Patrick Michael, Gary Lee Jr. BA, Notre Dame Coll., South Euclid, Ohio, 1960; postgrad., John Carroll U., 1960, U. Mass., 1961, U. S.C., 1969, San Jose State U., 1971-75, U. Santa Clara, Calif., 1972, Stanford U., 1989. Cert. life secondary tchr., Calif. Tchr. Cleve. Sch. Dist., 1960-61, East Hartford (Conn.) Sch. Dist., 1961-62, San Francisco Bay Area Sch. Dist., 1970-75; life and disability agt. Travelers Ins. Co. and BMA Ins. Co., San Jose, Calif., 1975-77; stockbroker Reynolds, Bache, Shearson, Palo Alto, Calif., 1977-78, Schwab & Co., San Francisco, 1980; adminstr. pension and profit Crocker Nat. Bank, San Francisco, 1980-82; stockbroker Calif. Fed./Invest Co., San Francisco, 1982-83; head trader, br. mgr. Rose & Co., San Francisco, 1983-84, ret., 1984; tchr. citizenship for fgn. born adult community edn. Fremont Union High Sch. Dist., Sunnyvale, Calif., 1988—; tchr. lively arts Stanford U. Author: Jo Mura-Renaissance Man, 1973, Visit of Imperial Russian Navy to San Francisco, 1974, John Franklin Miller, 1974, 1905 Quail Meadow Road. Sec. Quota Internat., Los Altos, Calif., 1987; constn. chair LWV, Los Altos, 1985—, lectr. speakers bur., 1987; precinct capt. 1988 Elections, Los Altos; apptd. Santa Clara County Ad Hoc. Com. for Transp. Mobility Impaired, 1988; active Peninsula Dem. Coalition, Calif. History Ctr., Cupertino, Calif., Palo Alto Neighbors Abroad; vol. tchr. English in Action. Recipient Valley Cable Recognition award, 1988. Mem. Women in West Hist. Assn., Los Altos Women in Bus., The Great War Soc., AAUW, NOW, World Affairs Forum, Commonwealth Club, Kenna Club. Democrat. Roman Catholic.

WHITING, ALLEN SUESS, political science educator, writer, consultant; b. Perth Amboy, N.J., Oct. 27, 1926; s. Leo Robert and Viola Allen (Suess) W.; m. Alice Marie Conroy, May 29, 1950; children: Deborah Jean, David Neal, Jeffrey Michael, Jennifer Hollister. B.A., Cornell U., 1948; M.A., Columbia U., 1950, cert. Russian Inst., 1950, Ph.D., 1952. Instr. polit. sci. Northwestern U., 1951-53; asst. prof. Mich. State U., East Lansing, 1955-57; social scientist The Rand Corp., Santa Monica, Calif., 1957-61; dir. Office Research and Analysis Far East U.S. Dept. State, Washington, 1962-66; dep. consul gen. Am. Consulate Gen., Hong Kong, 1966-68; prof. polit. sci. U. Mich., Ann Arbor, 1968-82; prof. U. Ariz., Tucson, 1982—, dir. Ctr. for East Asian Studies, 1982—; cons. U.S. Dept. State, 1968—; dir. Nat. Com. on U.S.-China Relations, N.Y.C., 1977—; assoc. The China Council, 1978—; pres. Ariz. China Council, Tucson, 1983—. Author: Soviet Policies in China: 1917-1924, 1954, China Crosses the Yalu, 1968, Chinese Calculus of Deterrence, 1975, Siberian Development and East Asia, 1981, China Eyes Japan, 1989, others; contbr. articles to profl. jours.; spl. commentator McNeill-Lehrer Program; CBS and NBC Spls. on China. Served with U.S. Army, 1945. Social Sci. Research Council fellow, 1950, 74-75; Ford Found. fellow, 1953-55; Rockefeller Found. fellow, 1978. Mem. Assn. Asian Studies, Council Fgn. Relations. Home: 125 Canyon View Dr Tucson AZ 85704 Office: U Ariz Dept Polit Sci Tucson AZ 85721

WHITING, ARTHUR MILTON, diversified company executive; b. St. Johns, Ariz., 1928. With Kaibab Industries, chmn., chief exec. officer, also dir., formerly pres.; dir. Western Savs. & Loan, Western Fin. Corp. Office: Kaibab Industries PO Box 52111 Phoenix AZ 85072 *

WHITING, LUCILLE DRAKE, educational consultant; b. San Diego, Dec. 17, 1929; d. Robert Emmett and Helen Anglim; m. V. Edward Drake (div.); m. Erle Francis Whiting, Mar. 27, 1982; 1 cvhild, Cecilie Anne. BA, U. Calif.-Santa Barbara, 1951; MEd, LaVerne (Calif.) U., 1975. Cert. Miller-Unruh reading specialist. Owner, dir. Little Buckaroo Nursery Sch., Santa Barbara, Calif., 1956-65; tchr. various sch. dists. Calif., 1951-72; Title I resource tchr. Oxnard (Calif.) Sch. Dist., 1972-73, reading specialist, 1973-86; extension instr. Calif. Luth. Coll., Thousand Oaks, 1978-84, U. Calif.-Santa Barbara, 1976-82; ind. ednl. cons. Ventura, Calif., 1976-86, Cromberg, Calif., 1986-. Active, Plumas County Arts Commn., Quincy, Calif., 1987—, bd. dirs. 1989—; mem.Quincy Main St. USA. Mem. Calif. Reading Assn. (ex-officio 1978-81; exemplary service award 1982), Ventura County Reading Assn. (pres. 1979-80), Reading Specialists of Calif., AAUW,Calif. Assn. Neurologically Handicapped Children (v.p. Ventura County chpt. 1976-78), Ventura County Panhellenic Assn. (v.p. 1970-72). Republican.

WHITLEY, GAIL ANN, retail executive; b. Shamokin, Pa., Aug. 18, 1951; d. William Thomas and Jane Blodwyn (Yeager) Whitley; m. Russell Joseph Abbott, Apr. 26, 1981; children: Michael Cole Abbott-Whitley, Julian Carey Abbott-Whitley, Danielle Lynn Abbott-Whitley. BA, Pa. State U., 1974. Tchr. Durham (N.C.) pub. schs., 1974-76; Denver Sch. Dist., 1975-76; vol. Peace Corps, St. Lucia, W.I., 1976-77; computer systems analyst Calif. State U. & Colls., Los Angeles, 1978-83; owner Retail Svc. Bus., Northridge, Calif., 1983—. Mem. Nat. Assn. Self-Employed. Home: 19832 Labrador St Chatsworth CA 91311 Office: Mail & Photo 18533 Roscoe Blvd Northridge CA 91311

WHITMAN, KENNETH JAY, advertising executive; b. N.Y.C., May 4, 1947; s. Howard Jay and Suzanne Marcia (Desberg) W.; m. Linda Loy Meisnest, Nov. 25, 1968; 1 child, Tyler Ondine. Student, Berklee Sch. Mus., 1965-66, Hubbard Acad., 1968-70. Nat. dep. dir. Pub. Relations Bur., Los Angeles, 1970-75; pres. Creative Cons., Los Angeles, 1975-82; pres., creative dir. Whitman & Green Advt., Toluca Lake, Calif., 1982-86, Whitman-Olson, Toluca Lake, 1986—. Co-author: Strategic Advertising, 1986; editor Freedom news jour., 1971-79; contbr. newspaper column Shape of Things, 1971-79. Pres. Los Angeles Citizens Commn. Human Rights, 1971-75. Recipient Cert. of Design Excellence Print Regional Design Ann., 1985, 87, Award of Excellence Consolidated Papers, 1985, Award of Excellence Print Mag., 1985, 87, 1st place award Sunny Creative Radio, 2 Telly awards, 1988, Belding award Advt. Club Los Angeles, Excellence award Bus. and Profl. Advt. Assn., 1987. Mem. Art Dirs. Club of Los Angeles, VSC (pres. 1964-65). Office: Whitman-Olson 10200 Riverside Dr Toluca Lake CA 91602

WHITMILL, LONN ROLAND, food company executive; b. Idaho Falls, Idaho, July 28, 1952; s. Don Roland Whitmill and Mary Alice (Salisbury) Heffington; m. Dianne Kay Klaversma, June 16, 1972; children: Angela Dianne, Nicole Lee, Jennifer Lynn, Amanda Marie. Salesman Carnation Co., Scottsbluff, Nebr., 1977-80; group mgr. Carnation Co., Denver, 1980-82; dist. sales mgr. Coca Cola Foods, Denver, 1982—. Mem. Denver Assn. Mfrs. Reps. Republican. Mormon.

WHITNEY, CHARLES RALPH, ophthalmologist; b. Fullerton, Calif., Feb. 23, 1943; s. Harry Gilles and Dorothy (Abbott) W.; m. Darlene Jean Lutosky, June 29, 1968; 1 child, Kendall Abbott. AB, U. Calif., Riverside, 1964; MD, Stanford U., 1969. Diplomate Am. Bd. Ophthalmology. Intern U. Oreg., Portland, 1969-70; resident ophthalmology Stanford (Calif.) U., 1970-74; pvt. practice Los Altos, Calif., 1974—; chmn. div. ophthalmology El Camino Hosp., Mountain View, Calif., 1984-85. Capt. Calif. Army Nat. Guard, 1970-76. Fellow Am. Acad. Ophthalmology; mem. Am. Soc. Cataract and Refractive Surgeons, Contact Lens Assn. Ophthalmologists, Calif. Med. Soc., Santa Clara County Med. Soc. Republican. Presbyterian. Office: 762 Altos Oaks Dr Los Altos CA 94022

WHITNEY, CONSTANCE CLEIN, psychologist, educator, organizational consultant; b. Seattle; BA, Stanford U.; MA; PhD, Washington U., St. Louis; children: Mark, Caroline. Instr. U. Mo., St. Louis, 1976-78; rsch. assoc., Wash. U. Med. Sch., St. Louis, 1977-78; dir. Motivation Rsch. Inst. U. Wash., St. Louis., 1979-83; post doctoral fellow Grad. Sch. Bus. and Pub. Adminstrn. Wash. U., St. Louis, 1983-86; assoc. prof. Mt. St. Mary's Coll., 1987—; dir., exec. edn. Town Hall Calif., 1989—. Bd. dirs. UCLA Arts Coun. Stanford Alumni So. Calif., Nat. Commn. for UN Conv. to eliminate discrimination. Mem. Pres.' Circle Los Angeles County Mus. Art; Club 100, Music Ctr; Edn. Commn. L.A. C. of C.; Robinson Gardens Friends of French Art, Bus. Profl. Women, Am. Psychol. Assn., Calif. Psychol. Assn., AAUP, ASTD, Acad. Mgmt., Orgn. Behavior and Tchrg. Soc. Author, producer, dir.: (film) Women and Money: Myths and Realities. Home: 10601 Wilshire Blvd Los Angeles CA 90024

WHITNEY, DAVID CLAY, educator, consultant, writer; b. Astoria, Oreg., May 30, 1937; s. Rolla Vernon and Barbara (Clay) W.; m. Kathleen Donnelley, 1956 (div. 1963); children: David Jr., Gordon, Sara; m. Zelda Gifford, 1967 (div. 1973). BS in Chemistry, San Diego State U., 1959; PhD in Chemistry, U. Calif., Berkeley, 1963. Cert. data processor, cert. data educator. Acting asst. prof. U. Calif., Davis, 1962-63; chemist, mathematician Shell Devel. Corp., Emeryville, Calif., 1963-72; dir. computer services Systems Applications, Inc., San Rafael, Calif., 1973-77; prof. San Francisco State U. Sch. Bus., 1977—; info. systems cons. numerous cos., 1977—; textbook reviewer numerous pubs., 1979—. Author: Instructors' Guides to Understanding Fortran 77, 1983, 87, Understanding Fortran, 1984, Basic, 1988. Mem. Assn. Computing Machinery, Data Processing Mgmt. Assn., Soc. Data Educators, Mensa. Home: 982 Shoal Dr San Mateo CA 94404 Office: San Francisco State U Sch of Bus San Francisco CA 94132

WHITNEY, GINA MARIE, chemical engineer; b. Berea, Ohio, Sept. 3, 1958; d. Warren John and Rose Mildred (Litrenta) W. BS in Chem. Engring., Case Western Res. U., 1980; PhD in Chem. Engring., U. Calif., Berkeley, 1987. Adv. chem. engr. IBM Corp., San Jose, Calif., 1987—. Contbr. tech. articles to various publs. NSF fellow, 1980-83; teaching fellow, Exxon Edn. Found., Berkeley, 1982-85. Mem. Electrochem. Soc., Am. Soc. Chem. Engrs., Am. Electroplaters and Surface Finishers Soc. Democrat. Office: IBM Corp 5600 Cottle Rd San Jose CA 95193

WHITSEL, RICHARD HARRY, biologist; b. Denver, Feb. 23, 1931; s. Richard Elstun and Edith Muriel (Harry) W.; B.A., U. Calif., Berkeley, 1954; M.A., San Jose State Coll., 1962; m. Joanne Elissa Cox, June 26, 1982; 1 son, Russell David; children by previous marriage: Robert Alan, Michael Dale, Steven Deane. Sr. research biologist San Mateo County Mosquito Abatement Dist., Burlingame, Calif., 1959-72; environ. program mgr., chief of planning Calif. Regional Water Quality Control Bd., Oakland, 1972—; mem. grad. faculty water resource mgmt. U. San Francisco, 1987-89. Served with Med. Service Corps, U.S. Army, 1954-56. Mem. Entomol. Soc. Am., Entomol. Soc. Wash., Am. Mosquito Control Assn., Calif. Alumni Assn., Sierra Club. Democrat. Episcopalian. Contbr. articles to profl. jours. Home: 4331 Blenheim Way Concord CA 94521 Office: Calif Regional Water Quality Control Bd 1111 Jackson St Oakland CA 94607

WHITSITT, ROBERT JAMES, professional sports executive; b. Madison, Wis., Jan. 10, 1956; s. Raymond Earl and Dolores June (Smith) W.; m. Jan Leslie Sundberg; children: Lillian Ashley, Sean James. BS, U. Wis., Stevens Point, 1977; MA, Ohio State U., 1978. Intern Indiana Pacers, Inpls., 1978, bus. tickets mgr., 1979, dir. bus. affairs and promotions, 1980, asst. gen. mgr., 1981-82; v.p. mktg. Kansas City (Mo.) Kings, 1982-84, v.p., asst. gen. mgr., 1984-85; v.p., asst. gen. mgr. Sacramento Kings, 1985-86; pres. Seattle Supersonics, 1986—. Mem. Nat. Basketball Assn. (alternate gov., mem. competition and rules com.). Republican. Lutheran. Lodge: Rotary. Office: Seattle Supersonics 190 Queens Anne Ave N Seattle WA 98109

WHITT-HELM, SHARON LYNN, credit union insurance professional; b. Richlands, Va., Mar. 5, 1949; d. Buford Nathaniel Street and Doris Fay (Hall) Hooker; m. Ronnie Edwin Whitt, Mar. 30, 1969 (div. 1978); children: Wendy Renee, Eric Shane; m. John Russell Helm, Nov. 28, 1986. Student sch. nursing, Johnston Meml. Hosp., 1969; student, Ins. Inst. Am., 1987-89. Underwriter GEICO, Washington, 1969-74; underwriting supr. GEICO, Macon, Ga., 1974-81; mktg. mgr. Pacific Internat. Ins. Co., Tucson, 1981-82; office mgr. C. Lamb Ins. Agy., Tucson, 1982-85; account rep. John Burnham & Co., San Diego, 1985-86, mgr. Internat. C. U. Svcs. Group, 1986-88, v.p. Internat. C. U. Svcs. Group, 1988—. Office: Internat C U Svcs Group Ste 1508 610 W Ash St San Diego CA 92101

WHITTINGSLOW, MICHAELA, marketing executive; b. Bucarest, Romania, July 30, 1938; d. Pietro and Lucia (Daciu) Moccia; m. Robert B. Holmes, 1960 (div. 1969); 1 child, Peter Morgan; m. Peter Durst von Schatzberg, 1970 (div. 1984); m. Thomas Edward Whittingslow, Feb. 14, 1985. Scientific Lyceum, Righi U., Rome, 1956; Humanities, U. Rome, 1959. Sec., chief exec. officer Alitalia Airlines, N.Y.C., 1964-66; co-owner, mng. ptnr. The Gryphon, Locust Valley, N.Y., 1967-70; asst. mgr. Valentino Retail Wear and Apparel Div., Rome, 1971-73; gen. mgr. Mila Schön Due Retail Wear, Milan, 1973-76; asst. to owner Martha Inc., N.Y.C., 1977-80; gen. mgr. retail div. Roberta di Camerino, N.Y.C.; gen. mgr. Yves St. Laurent Rive Gauche, Scottsdale, Ariz., 1980-82; mktg. cons. The Borgata, Scottsdale, 1980-82; agt. mktg., pub. relations and leasing The Courtyard, Palm Springs, Calif., 1982-84; gen. mgr. Yves St. Laurent Rive Gauche, Palm Springs, 1982-84; ptnr. Whittingslow & von Schatzberg, Grass Valley, Calif., 1984—. Bd. dirs. Women's Prison Assn., N.Y.C., 1968, Opera Dames, 1981-82; chmn. Fad Auction, Northwood Inst., Palm Springs, 1984. Mem. Italian Fifth Ave Retailers Assn. (bd. dirs. 1977-78). Home and Office: Whittingslow & von Schatzberg 303 Pleasant St Grass Valley CA 95945

WHOOLEY, KATHLEEN A., physical therapist; b. Medford, Mass., May 13, 1954; d. William and Agnes (Kelly) Whooley; m. Jay Jacoby, Sept. 20, 1986. BS in Phys. Therapy, Boston U., 1976; MBA, Pepperdine U., 1982; Cert. Manual Therapy, Inst. Grad. Health, Atlanta, 1987; Cert. of Neurodevel., Bobath Ctr., London, 1982. Staff phys. therapist William Moore Ctr., Manchester, N.H., 1976-77, Vis. Nurse Assn., Wakefield, Mass., 1977-78; parttime lectr. Mt. St. Mary's, L.A., 1983-86; dir. S.W. Phys. Therapy, L.A., 1978-85; pres. owner Larchmont Phys. Therapy, L.A., 1985—. Mem. Nat. Assn. Female Execs., Am. Phys. Therapy Assn., Kiwanis (dir. 1988—). Office: Larchmont Phys Therapy 321 N Larchmont Blvd Ste 921 Los Angeles CA 90004

WHORF, CHRISTOPHER TROY, graphic artist, designer; b. N.Y.C., Oct. 29, 1940; s. Richard Baker and Margaret (Smith) W.; m. Betsy Jones, Aug. 23, 1978; 1 child, Margaret Elizabeth. BA, Stanford U., 1962; BArch, U. So. Calif., 1967. Sr. v.p. Casablanca Record & Filmworks, Los Angeles, 1978-80; v.p. Gribbitt, Inc., Los Angeles, 1976-80; pres. Art Hotel, Inc., Los Angeles, 1980—. Recipient Grammy award, for Mason Proffit record cover, Nat. Assn. Recording Artists, 1972 and Gold Medal, N.Y. Art Dirs., 1970, also numerous other awards, Los Angeles Art Dirs., Belding awards, Los Angeles Advtg. Club, 1970. Mem. Am. Inst. Graphic Arts. Home: 9834 San Circle Dr Beverly Hills CA 90210 Office: Art Hotel 6609 Santa Monica Blvd Los Angeles CA 90038.

WHYTE, HELENA MARY, chemist, educator; b. Albuquerque, Dec. 19, 1948; d. Alexander Peter and Helen (Mriz) M.; m. Kent Neil Whyte, July 6, 1973; children: Stacey Helene, Kurt Neil. BS in Chemistry with honors, N.Mex. Inst. Mining Tech., 1970; MA in Sci. Teaching, U. N.Mex., 1971. Lab. asst. N.Mex. Bur. Mines, Socorro, 1966-70; research asst. Los Alamos (N.Mex.) Sci. Lab., 1970-71; chemistry tchr. Los Alamos High Sch., 1971-79; chemistry instr. U. N.Mex., Los Alamos, 1981-84; staff mem. Los Alamos Nat. Lab., 1979—; appointed to women's com. Los Alamos Nat. Lab., 1986-88, sect. leader, 1988. Mem. manuscript rev. panel for Sci. Tchr. mag., 1987-89; contbr. articles to profl. publs. Fellow Am. Inst. Chemists (cert.); mem. AAUW (liaison legal advocacy fund 1988-89), Am. Chem. Soc., Nat. Sci. Tchrs. Assn., Women in Sci., Alpha Delta Kappa (local pres. 1979-80). Democrat. Roman Catholic. Office: Los Alamos Nat Lab M589 HRD3 Los Alamos NM 87545

WIBORG, JAMES HOOKER, chemicals distribution company executive; b. Seattle, Aug. 26, 1924; s. John R. and Hazel (Hooker) W.; m. Ann Rogers, July 1948; children: Katherine Ann, Mary Ellen, Caroline Joan, John Stewart. B.A., U. Wash., 1946. Owner, Wiborg Mfg. Co., Tacoma, 1946-50; securities analyst Pacific N.W. Co., Seattle, 1950-53; founder Western Plastics Corp., Tacoma, 1953; pres. Western Plastics Corp., 1953-55, chmn. bd., dir., ret.; exec. v.p. Wash. Steel Products Co., Tacoma, 1955-58; mgmt. cons. Tacoma, 1958-60; v.p. United Pacific Corp., Seattle, 1960; pres. Pacific Small Bus. Investment Corp., Seattle, 1961-63; sr. v.p. indsl. div. United Pacific Corp., Seattle, 1963-65; pres., chief exec. officer, dir. United Pacific Corp., 1965; past pres., chief exec. officer, dir. Univar Corp. (formerly VWR United Corp.), Seattle, from 1966; chmn., chief exec. officer Univar Corp. (formerly VWR United Corp.), 1983-86, chmn., chief strategist, 1986—; dir., chmn., chief strategist VWR Corp., 1986—; dir. Seattle, Seafirst Corp., PACCAR Inc., Seattle-First Nat. Bank, Gensco Inc., Tacoma, Penwest Ltd. Trustee U. Puget Sound. Clubs: Tacoma Country and Golf, Tacoma, Tacoma Yacht; Rainier (Seattle), Harbor (Seattle). Office: Univar Corp 1600 Norton Bldg Seattle WA 98104

WICK, ALBERT MARION, anesthesiologist; b. Watford City, N.D., June 21, 1929; s. Thedore Albert and Annie Martha (Jacobson) W.; m. Donnis Esther Krietzky Wick, Sept. 5, 1948; children: Sharon, Joan, Kenneth, Dennis. BS, Union Coll., Lincoln, Nebr., 1954; MD, Loma Linda U., 1958. Diplomate Am. Bd. Anesthesiology. Intern Porter Meml. Hosp., Denver, 1958-59; resident White Meml. Hosp., Denver, 1959-61; anesthesiologist South Denver Anesthesiologists, P.C., 1961-88. Inventor Kelly-Wick Tunneler. Fellow Am. coll. Anesthesiologists; mem. Colo. Med. Soc., Colo. Soc. Anesthesiologist. Republican. Seventh-Day Adventist. Home: 745 Front Range Rd Littleton CO 80120 Office: South Denver Anesthesiologists 850 E Harvard Ave Denver CO 80210

WICK, RAYMOND VICTOR, physicist, laser optics scientist; b. Pitts., Mar. 17, 1940; s. Charles Victor and Sara Ruby (Calhoun) W.; m. Kathy Greenfield, Aug. 15, 1942; children: David Victor, Michael Wesley, Matthew James. BA in Physics, Thiel Coll., 1962; MS in Physics, Pa. State U., 1964, PhD in Physics, 1966. Project officer effects br. Air Force Weapons Lab., Kirtland AFB, N.Mex., 1966-72, sci. advisor tech. br., 1972-74; tech. advisor optics br. Air Force Weapons Lab., Kirtland AFB, 1974-76, laser div., 1976-84, program office, 1984-88, laser optics div., 1988—; chmn. laser and optics com. Inst. for Def. Analysis, Washington, 1982—; chmn. directed energy com. Office of Under Sec. of Def./Analysis, Washington, 1984—; dept. def. tech. rep. to coord. com. NATO, Paris, 1982—; Air Force Systems Command tech. rep. to Internat. Cooperation Program, Paris, 1987—; cons. Inst. for Def. Analyses, Washington, 1984-88. Contbr. articles on lasers and optics to profl. jours.; patentee in field. NASA fellow, 1964-66, NRC fellow, 1966-67. Mem. Optical Soc. Am., Soc. Photog. Instrumentation Engrs. (conf. chmn. 1978-89), Am. Inst. Physics, ASTM, Internat. Sci. Soc., Coronado Club. Home: 10421 Karen NE Albuquerque NM 87111 Office: Air Force Weapons Lab ARO Kirkland AFB Albuquerque NM 87117

WICKIZER, CHARLES ROBERT, data processing executive; b. Springfield, Mo., Dec. 9, 1951; s. Wilbur Francis and Catherine Edith (Moon) W.; m. Martha G. Sallwasser, Aug. 13, 1971 (div. June 1975); m. Joan T. Speckhals, May 17, 1980; children: Rebecca, Laura. BS in Physics, U. Mo., 1972; MA in Physics, Washington U., St. Louis, 1975. Staff scientist Artronix Inc., St. Louis, 1976-78; assoc. prof. radiology U. Mo. Med. Sch., Columbia, 1978-79; pres. Mid-Continent Computer Svcs. Inc., Columbia, Mo., 1979-83; gen. mgr. Adac Labs., Sunnyvale, Calif., 1983-84; sr. sales rep. SDK Healthcare Info. Systems, Boston, 1984-86; dir. healthcare and office automation products Inteck Inc., San Jose, Calif., 1986—; cons. Indsl. Engring., St. Louis, 1973-74, U. Mo. Vet. Coll., Columbia, 1985-87; guest lectr. U. Chgo., 1980, Boston U., 1985. Author: Analysis of Beam Hardening, 1977. Mem. IEEE, MUMPS Users Group (nat. chmn. 1980), Sierra Club (nat. chmn. 1980). Episcopalian. Office: PO Box 20788 San Jose CA 95160

WICKIZER, CINDY LOUISE, teacher; b. Pitts., Dec. 12, 1946; d. Charles Sr. and Gloria Geraldine (Cassidy) Zimmerman; m. Leon Leonard Wickizer, Mar. 21, 1971; 1 child, Charlyn Michelle. BS, Oreg. State U., 1968. Tchr. Enumclaw (Wash.) Sch. Dist., 1968—. Mem. NEA, Wash. Edn. Assn., Enumclaw Edn. Assn., Enumclaw Ednl. Council, Buckley Ednl. Agrl. Council, Buckley C. of C., Washington Contract Loggers Assn., Enumclaw Bus. and Profl. Women, Am. Rabbit Breeders Assn. (pres. 1988—, judge, chmn. scholarship found. 1986-87, chmn. youth com. 1983-87, Disting. Service award 1987), Wash. State Rabbit Breeders Assn. (life, Pres.'s award 1983), Vancouver Island Rabbit Breeders Assn. (life), Fla. White Rabbit Breeders Assn. (pres. 1984-88), Wash. State Evergreen Rabbit (sec., v.p., pres.), Alpha Gamma Delta. Home: 26513 112th St E Buckley WA 98321

WICKMAN, PAUL EVERETT, public relations executive; b. Bisbee, Ariz., Aug. 21, 1912; s. Julius and Hilda Wilhelmina (Soderholm) W.; m. Evelyn Gorman, Nov. 22, 1969; children by previous marriage: Robert Bruce, Bette Jane, Marilyn Faye. Student, La Sierra Coll., Arlington, Calif., 1928-30, Pacific Union Coll., Angwin, Cal., 1931-32; spl. student, Am. U., 1946. Internat. traveler, lectr., writer 1937-44; assoc. sec Internat. Religious Liberty Assn., 1944-46; travel lectr. Nat. Lecture Bur., 1944-55; exec. sec., dir. internat. radio and TV prodns. Voice of Prophecy Corp., Faith for Today Corp., 1946-53; v.p. Western Advt. Agy., Los Angeles, 1953-55; dir. devel. Nat. Soc. Crippled Children and Adults, Inc., Chgo., 1955-56; exec. dir. Pub. Relations Soc. Am., Inc., N.Y.C., 1956-57; dir. corp. pub. relations Schering Corps., Bloomfield, N.J., 1957-58; pres. Wickman Pharm. Co., Inc., Calif., 1959-83, Paul Wickman Co., 1984—. Mem. Newport Beach CSC, mem. Orange County Children's Hosp. Fund. Mem. Newcomen Soc., Pub. Relations Soc. Am. (accredited), Internat. Platform Assn. Clubs: Swedish (Los Angeles) (past pres.); Newport Beach (Calif.) Country; Vikings, 552 Hoag Hospital. Lodges: Elks, Masons, Shriners, Royal Order Jesters, Kiwanis (past pres. Newport Beach club, lt. gov. local div. 1990—). Home and Office: 28 Point Loma Dr Corona Del Mar CA 92625

WICKS, PATRICK HEATH, chemical engineering consultant; b. Albany, Calif., Mar. 17, 1943; s. Alansen Heath and Lois Mariam (Thompson) W.; m. Patricia Anne Shafer, Apr. 8, 1967; 1 child, Tereia Shannon. BSChemE, U. Idaho, 1966. Registered profl. engr., Oreg. Engr. Shell Oil Co., Wilmington (Calif.), N.Y.C. and Houston, 1965-72; sect. supr. Dept. Environ. Quality, Portland, Oreg., 1972-76; mgr., pres. Chem-Security Systems, Bellevue, Wash., 1976-82; dir. Chem-Nuclear Systems, Bellevue, 1982-83; prin. Hazardous Waste Cons., Redmond, Wash., 1983-86; pres. ERM-Northwest, Redmond, 1986-88; owner Environ. Engring. & Cons., Bothell, Wash., 1989—. Author: Hazardous Waste Management Planning; contbr. articles to profl. jours. Mem. Hazardous Waste Task Force, Olympia, Wash., 1983—, Ad Hoc Com. Hazardous Wash., State of Wash., 1977-78; speaker numerous community and indsl. groups hazardous waste, 1973—. Mem. Am. Inst. Chem. Engring., Am. Chem. Soc., NSPE, Wash. Soc. Profl. Engrs., Redmond C. of C. (chmn. environ. com. 1984), Alpha Tau Omega, Sigma Tau, Phi Kappa Phi. Republican. Home: 19708 182d Ave NE Woodinville WA 98072

WICKSTRAND, ALAN KEITH, service executive; b. Portland, Oreg., Nov. 3, 1953; s. Arthur Theodore and Eleanor Florence (Tucker) W.; m. Georgene Mae Cowles, June 12, 1976; children: Philip Arthur, Emily Anne, Laura Jayne. Student, Mt. Hood Coll., 1972-74. Janitor, supr. Mchts. Bldg. Maintenance, Portland, 1973-77; br. mgr. Mchts. Bldg. Maintenance, Eugene, Oreg., 1973-77; v.p. ops. Mchts. Bldg. Maintenance, Portland, 1978-79; owner, mgr. New Life Cleaning Systems, Portland, 1979—. Mem. Bldg. Maintenance Assn. Am. (bd. dirs. 1985-89), Nat. Fedn. Ind. Bus., Portland Metro C. of C. Republican. Baptist. Office: New Life Cleaning Systems 1985 SW 6th Ave Portland OR 97201

WICKWIRE, PATRICIA JOANNE NELLOR, psychologist, educator; b. Sioux City, Iowa; d. William McKinley and Clara Rose (Pautsch) Nellor; BA cum laude, U. No. Iowa, 1951; MA, U. Iowa, 1959; PhD, U. Tex., Austin, 1971; postgrad. U. So. Calif., UCLA, Calif. State U., Long Beach, 1951-66; m. Robert James Wickwire, Sept. 7, 1957; 1 son, William James. Tchr., Ricketts Ind. Schs., Iowa, 1946-48; tchr., counselor Waverly-Shell Rock Ind. Schs., Iowa, 1951-55; reading cons., head dormitory counselor U. Iowa, Iowa City, 1955-57; tchr., sch. psychologist, adminstr. S. Bay Union High Sch. Dist., Redondo Beach, Calif., 1962—, dir. student svcs. and spl. edn.; cons. mgmt. and edn.; mem. Calif. Interagency Mental Health Council, exec. bd., 1968-72; chmn. Friends of Dominguez Hills (Calif.), 1981-85; mem. exec. bd. Beach Cities Symphony Assn., 1970-82. Lic. ednl. psychologist, marriage, family and child counselor, Calif. Mem. AAUW (exec. bd., chpt. pres. 1962-72), L.A. County Dirs. Pupil Svcs. (chmn. 1974-79), L.A. County Personnel and Guidance Assn. (pres. 1977-78), Assn. Calif. Sch. Adminstrs. (dir. 1977-81), L.A. County SW Bd. Dist. Adminstrs. for Spl. Edn. (chmn. 1976-81), Calif. Assn. Sch. Psychologist (dir. 1981—), Am. Psychol. Assn., Am. Assn. Sch. Adminstrs., Calif. Assn. for Measurement and Evaluation in Guidance (dir. 1981, pres. 1984-85), Am. Assn. Counseling and Devel., Assn. Measurement and Eval. in Guidance (Western regional editor 1987—, conv. chair 1986), Calif. Assn. Counseling and Devel. (exec. bd. 1984—, pres. 1988—), Internat. Career Assn. Network (chair 1985—), Pi Lambda Theta, Alpha Phi Gamma, Psi Chi, Kappa Delta Pi, Sigma Alpha Iota. Contbr. articles in field to profl. jours. Home and Office: 2900 Amby Pl Hermosa Beach CA 90254

WIDDICOMBE, ROLAND MARC, food products executive; b. Winnipeg, Manitoba, Canada, Dec. 4, 1950; came to U.S., 1951; s. Roland and Aimee Eugine (Weir) W. BS, Chapman Coll., 1973. V.p., treas. Widdicombe Enterprises Inc., Garden Grove, Calif., 1973—. Bd. trustees Orange County Ronald McDonald House; adv. bd. Garden Grove Symphony, Pediatric Cancer Research Found. of Orange County; bd. dirs. So. Calif. Children's Cancer Svcs.; El Capitan Fin. Chmn. Boy Scouts Am., 1984-86, El Capitan Dist. Chmn., 1986-87, El Capitan Co-Dist. Chmn., 1987-88. Recipient Ronald McDonald award McDonald's Corp., 1987. Mem. McDonald's Operators Assn. of So. Calif. (bd. dirs. 1978-80, 86—), Garden Grove C. of C. (bd. dirs. 1976-79, 85—), Rotary Club (bd. dirs. 1989—). Office: Widdicombe Enterprises Inc 9845 Chapman Ave Garden Grove CA 92641

WIDENOJA, PATRICIA DIANE, nurse; b. Bend, Oreg., July 14, 1955; d. Jess Fancler and Roberta Louise (Buick) Miles; m. Roger Jay Widenoja, Sept. 12, 1976; children: Benjamin Jay, Raya Dawn. BS in Nursing, U. Oreg., 1978. Staff nurse North Lake County Br. Lake County Health Dept., Lakeview, Oreg., 1979-88, Cen. Oreg. Dist. Hosp., Redmond, Oreg., 1988--; supr. night shift Lake Dist. Skilled Care Facility, Lakeview, 1981-83. Organizer, supporter North Lake County Healthcare Ctr., Christmas Valley, Oreg., 1982. Recipient Emergency Med. Technician of Yr. award Cen. Oreg. Emergency Med. Svcs., 1985, Instr. of Yr. award Cen. Oreg. Community Coll., 1988. Mem. Internat. Childbirth Educators Assn. (instr. 1979-86), U.S. Dept. Mine Safety & Health Adminstrs. (instr. 1982--), Cen Oreg. Emergency Med. Technician Assn. (instr. first response 1981--), Am. Holistic Nurses Assn., Am. Heart Assn. (BLS instr. 1982--). Home: VanhaVio HC61 Box 9604 Silver Lake OR 97638

WIDMAN, JOSEPH JAMES, magazine editor; b. Washington, Dec. 6, 1952; s. Joseph William and Marguerite Marie (Phelan) W.; m. Caryn Louise Leschen, June 9, 1985. BA in Anthropology, Brown U., 1974. Sr. editor Oceans, San Francisco, 1983-85, Calif. Waterfront Age, Oakland, 1985-86; assoc. editor Publish, San Francisco, 1986—. Editor: Public Beaches, 1987, The Whales of Hawaii, 1988. Democrat. Office: Publish Mag 501 2d St San Francisco CA 94107

WIEBE, JACQUELINE CATHERINE, chemical research associate, musician; b. Neustadt an der Weinstrasse, Pfalz, West Germany, Mar. 24, 1957; came to U.S., 1958; d. Franklin Edward and Frieda (Minder) W. BA in Music, San Jose State U., 1980. Music dir. San Jose City Coll. Shakespeare Festival, 1976-77; guest conductor San Jose State U. Faculty Artist Series, 1978-79; music dir. San Jose Civic Light Opera, 1981; asst. conductor San Jose Symphony Orch., 1978-86; staff conductor San Jose Symphony/Opera, 1979-84; clin. data specialist Syntex Rsch., Palo Alto, Calif., 1981-83; bioanalyst Syntex Rsch., Palo Alto, 1983-88, clin. rsch. assoc., 1988—; violist, Willow String Quartet, No. Calif., 1985—. Mem. Assocs. Clin. Pharmacology, No. Calif. Pharm. Discussion Group, Am. Fedn. Musicians. Democrat. Office: Syntex Rsch 3401 Hillview Ave Palo Alto CA 94304

WIEBE, LEONARD IRVING, radiopharmacist, educator; b. Swift Current, Sask., Can., Oct. 14, 1941; s. Cornelius C. and Margaret (Teichroeb) W.; m. Grace E. McIntyre, Sept. 5, 1964; children—Glenis, Kirsten, Megan. BSP, U. Sask., 1963, MS, 1966; PhD, U. Sydney, Australia, 1970. Pharmacist Swift Current Union Hosp., 1963-64; sessional lectr. U. Sask., Can., 1965-66; asst. prof. U. Alta., Can., 1970-73, assoc. prof., 1973-78, prof., 1978—, dir. Slowpoke Reactor Facility, 1975—, asst. dean research, 1984-87; sessional lectr. U. Sydney, Australia, 1973; sec. Internat. Bionucleonics Cons. Lts., 1975—; rsch. assoc. Cross Cancer Inst., Edmonton, Can., 1978—, Med. Rsch. Council of Can.; vis. prof. Royal P.A. Hosp., Sydney, 1983-84, Searle vis. prof., 1986, vis. prof., Toronto, 1987, PMAC, 1988; radiopharmacy cons. Australian Atomic Energy Commn., Sydney, 1983-84. Editor: Liquid Scintillation: Science and Technology, 1976; Advances in Scintillation Counting, 1983; guest editor Jour. of Radioanalytical Chemistry, 1981; editor Internat. Jour. Applied Radiation Instruction Sect. A, 1988—. Commonwealth Univs. Exchange grantee, 1966; Alexander von Humboldt fellow, 1976-79, 82. Mem. Pharm. Bd. of New South Wales, Sask. Pharm. Assn., Soc. Nuclear Medicine, Assn. Faculties of Pharmacy of Can. (McNeil Rsch. award 1988), Can. Radiation Protection Assn., Can. Assn. Radiopharm. Scientists, Am. Pharm. Assn., Am. Assn. Pharm. Sci. Mem. Mennonite Ch. Club: University (Edmonton) (pres. 1985-86). Home: 11739 38A Ave, Edmonton, AB Canada T6J 0L8 Office: U Alta, Edmonton, AB Canada T6G 2N8

WIEBE, MICHAEL EUGENE, microbiologist, cell biologist; b. Newton, Kans., Oct. 1, 1942; s. Austin Roy and Ruth Fern (Stucky) W.; m. Rebecca Ann Doak, June 12, 1965; 1 child, Brandon Clark. BS, Sterling Coll., 1965; PhD, U. Kansas, 1971. Rsch. assoc. Duke U. Med. Ctr., Durham, N.C., 1971-73; asst. prof. Cornell U. Med. Coll., N.Y.C., 1973-81, assoc. prof., 1981-85; assoc. dir. rsch. and devel. N.Y. Blood Ctr., N.Y.C., 1980-83, dir. Leukocyte products, 1983-84; sr. scientist Genentech Inc., South San Francisco, Calif., 1984-88, assoc. dir. cell banking and characterization, 1988—. Contbr. articles to profl. jours. Postdoctoral fellow NIH, 1971-73. Mem. AAAS, Am. Soc. for Microbiology, Am. Soc. Virology, Am. Soc. Tropical Medicine and Hygiene, Soc. of Exptl. Biology and Medicine, Tissue Culture Assn., N.Y Acad. Sci. Presbyterian. Home: 44 Woodhill Dr Redwood City CA 94061 Office: Genentech Inc 460 Point San Bruno Blvd South San Francisco CA 94080

WIEBELHAUS, PAMELA SUE, educator; b. Stanley, Wis., May 28, 1952; d. Wilbur Leroy and Marjorie Jean (Bernse) Thorne; m. Mark Robert Wiebelhaus, Apr. 27, 1985. AS in Nursing, No. Ariz. U., 1973, BS in Gen. Home Econs., 1974. R.N. Ariz., Colo; cert. post secondary vocat. tchr., Colo. Nurse Flagstaff (Ariz.) Community Hosp., 1973-75, Children's Hosp., Denver, 1975, St. Joseph's Hosp., Denver, 1980; office nurse, surg. asst. OB-Gyn Assocs., P.C., Aurora, Colo., 1975-78; nursing coordinator perinatal services Smaritan Health, Phoenix, 1978-79; nurse, mem. personnel pool Good Samaritan Hosp., Phoenix, 1979-80, J. Bains, MD, Phoenix, 1979-80; file clk. Pharm. Card Systems, Inc., Phoenix, 1979-80; office nurse S. Eisenbaum, MD, Aurora, Colo., 1980; tchr. coordinator T.H. Pickens Tech. Ctr., Aurora Pub. Schs., Aurora, Colo., 1980-; med. supr. healthfair sites, Denver, 1982-85; mem. adv. com. Emily Griffith Opportunity Sch., Denver, 1984; mem. survey team North Central Bd. Edn. 1985, Colo. Bd. Edn., Denver, 1987. Acad. scholar No. Ariz. U., 1970, nat. def. grantee, 1970-74; PTA and Elks Club scholar, 1970. Mem. Am. Assn. Med. Assts. (cert.; membership chmn. Capitol chpt. Colo. Soc. 1981). Lutheran. Home: 3020 S Roslyn St Denver CO 80231 Office: Aurora Pub Schs TH Pickens Tech Ctr 500 Buckley Rd Aurora CO 80011

WIEDERHOLT, WIGBERT C., neurologist, educator; b. Germany, Apr. 22, 1931; came to U.S., 1956, naturalized, 1966; m. Carl and Anna-Maria (Hoffmann) W.; student (Med. Sch. scholar), U. Berlin, 1952-53; M.D., U. Freiburg, 1955; M.S., U. Minn., 1965; children—Sven, Karen, Kristin. Intern in Ob-Gyn, Schleswig (W. Ger.) City Hosp., 1955-56; rotating intern Sacred Heart Hosp., Spokane, Wash., 1956-57; resident in medicine Cleve. Clinic, 1957-58, 60-62, U.S. Army Hosp., Frankfurt, W. Ger., 1958-59; resident in neurology Mayo Clinic, Rochester, Minn., 1962-65; assoc. prof. medicine, dir. clin. neurophysiology Ohio State U. Med. Sch., Columbus, 1966-72; prof. neuroscis. U. Calif. Med. Sch., San Diego, 1972—, neurologist-in-chief, 1973-83, chmn. dept. and group in neuroscis. 1978-83; chief neurology VA Hosp., San Diego, 1972-79. Fulbright scholar, 1956-58. Diplomate Am. Bd. Psychiatry and Neurology. Fellow Am. Acad. Neurology (S. Weir Mitchell award 1956); mem. Internat. Brain Research Orgn., Am. Assn. EEG and Electrodiagnosis (sec.-treas. 1971-76, pres. 1977-78), AAAS, Soc. for Neurosci., Am. Neurol. Assn., Am. EGG Soc., Western EEG Soc., Calif. Neurol. Soc., San Diego Neurol. Soc., N.Y. Acad. Scis., AMA, Calif. Med. Assn., San Diego County Med. Soc. Club: La Jolla Tennis. Contbr. numerous articles to med. jours. Home: 6683 La Jolla Scenic Dr La Jolla CA 92037 Office: Univ Calif at San Diego Dept Neuroscis M-024 La Jolla CA 92093

WIEDERSPAHN, ALVIN LEE, senator, lawyer; b. Cheyenne, Wyo., Jan. 18, 1949; s. John Arling and Edvina (Fahrenbruch) W.; m. Cynthia Marie Lummis, May 30, 1983; 1 child, Annaliese. BS, U. Wyo., 1971; JD, U. Denver, 1976. Bar: Wyo. 1978, U.S. Dist. Ct. Wyo. 1978, U.S. Ct. Appeals (10th cir.) 1985. Assoc. Guy, Williams & White, Cheyenne, 1977-79, Kline & Swainson, Cheyenne, 1979-81, Holland & Hart, Cheyenne, 1981-85; pvt. practice law Cheyenne, 1985—; senator State of Wyo., Cheyenne, 1984-88; pres. Rocky Mountain Fed. Savs. and Loan Assn., Cheyenne, 1988—, chmn. bd. Rep. Wyo. Legis., Cheyenne, 1978-84; chmn. Devel. Disabilities Protection and Advocacy System, Cheyenne, 1978-83, Downtown Devel. Authority, Cheyenne, 1984—, Southeast Wyo. Mental Health Ctrs., Cheyenne, 1982-85, Gov.'s Task Force on Chronically Mentally Ill., Cheyenne, 1984—, Wyo. Energy Conservation Office, Cheyenne, 1980-83; pres. Assn. for Retarded Citizens, Cheyenne, 1979-81; bd. dirs. Symphoney and Choral Soc., Cheyenne, 1984-86, Rocky Mountain Fed. Savs. and Loan Assn., Wyoming Taxpayers Assn. Named Outstanding Vol., Youth Alternatives, 1982, one of Outstanding Young Men of Am., 1980, 81, 83; recipient Disting. Service award Rocky Mountain Conf. Community Mental Health Ctrs., Outstanding Service award Assn. for Retarded Citizens, 1986. Mem. ABA (pub. utility sect.), Wyo. State Bar. Democrat. Congregationalist. Club: Cheyenne Athletic. Home: 3905 Bent Ave Cheyenne WY 82001 Office: 2020 Carey Ave Cheyenne WY 82001

WIEDHOLZ, LAURIE SUSAN, sales company executive; b. Milw., May 27, 1963; d. James Francis and Mary Lou (Maurer) W. BBA, U. Wis., 1985. Sales rep. Wallace Computer Svcs., Madison, Wis., 1986-87; sales rep. Wallace Computer Svcs., Phoenix, 1987-88, healthcare sales rep., 1988—. Republican. Roman Catholic. Home: 5640 E Bell #1058 Scottsdale AZ 85254 Office: 3101 W Peoria St #B301 Phoenix AZ 85029

WIEDMANN, TIEN-WEN TAO, medical scientist; b. Shanghai, China, Jan. 12, 1938; came to U.S., 1955; d. Pai-chuan and Su-chuin (Chang) T.; m. Walter Wiedmann, June 20, 1966; children: Christian, Ulrich. Student, Nat. Taiwan U., Republic of China, 1953-55; BS, U. Okla., 1957; MS, Harvard U., 1958, PhD, 1963. Research assoc. Harvard U., Boston, 1965-69; scientist Basel (Switzerland) Inst. for Immunology, 1970-74, Bioctr., Basel, 1975-80; sr. research assoc. Stanford (Calif.) U., 1980-84, assoc. prof. biology, 1984—; vis. assoc. prof. Nat. Taiwan U., 1969. Contbr. articles to profl. jours. Home: 50 Peter Cts Stanford CA 94305 Office: Stanford U Med Ctr Dept Nuclear Medicine Stanford CA 94305

WIEMANN, JOHN M., educator; b. New Orleans, July 11, 1947; s. John M. and Mockie (Oosthuizen) W.; m. Mary Eileen O'Loghlin, June 7, 1969; children: Molly E., John M. BA, Loyola U., New Orleans, 1969; postgrad., NYU, 1970-71; MS, Purdue U., 1973, PhD, 1975. With employee communications dept. IBM, East Fishkill, N.Y., 1969-71; asst. prof. Rutgers U., New Brunswick, N.J., 1975-77; prof. U. Calif., Santa Barbara, 1977—. Editor: Nonverbal Interaction, 1983, Advancing Communications Science, 1988; series editor Sage Ann. Rev. Communication Research, 1988—. Bd. dirs. Goleta Youth Basketball Assn., 1987-89; mem. sch. site council Foothill Elem. Sch., 1987-88, budget advt. com. Goleta Union Sch. Dist., 1982-84. David Ross fellow Purdue U., 1975; Fulbright-Hayes sr. research scholar U. Bristol, U.K., 1985, W.K. Kellogg Found., 1980-83. Mem. Internat. Communication Assn. (bd. dirs. 1988—), Speech Communication Assn. (bd. dirs. 1984-86), Am. Psychol. Assn., Western Speech Communication Assn., Sigma Xi, Phi Kappa Phi. Democrat. Roman Catholic. Office: U Calif Communication Studies Program Santa Barbara CA 93106

WIEMER, ROBERT ERNEST, film and television producer; b. Highland Park, Mich., Jan. 30, 1938; s. Carl Ernest and Marion (Israelian) W.; m. Rhea Dale McGeath, June 14, 1958; children: Robert Marshall, Rhea Whitney. BA, Ohio Wesleyan U., 1959. Ind. producer 1956-60; dir. documentary ops. WCBS-TV, N.Y.C., 1964-67; ind. producer of television, theatrical and bus. films N.Y.C., 1967-72; exec. producer motion pictures and TV, ITT, N.Y.C., 1973-84; pres. subs. Blue Marble Co., Inc., Telemontage, Inc., Alphaventure Music, Inc., Betaventure Music, Inc. ITT, 1973-84; founder, chmn., chief exec. officer Tigerfilm, Inc., 1984—; chmn., bd. dirs. Golden Tiger Pictures, Hollywood, Calif., 1988—; bd. dirs. Princeton-Am. Communications, Inc., 1986-87; exec. producer Emmy and Peabody award winning children's television show Big Blue Marble; writer, producer, dir. feature films: My Seventeenth Summer, Witch's Sister, Do Me a Favor, Anna to the Infinite Power, Somewhere, Tomorrow, Night Train to Kathmandu. Child actor, Jam Handy Orgn., Detroit, 1946-48. Deacon Dutch Reform Ch. in Am. Served to capt. USAF, 1960-64. Recipient CINE award, 1974, 76, 77, 79, 81. Mem. Nat. Acad. TV Arts and Scis., Info. Film Producers Assn. (Outstanding Producer award), Nat. Assn. TV Programming Execs., Am. Women in Radio and TV, N.J. Broadcasters Assn. Office: Golden Tiger Pictures 6565 Sunset Blvd Hollywood CA 90028

WIENER, JON, history educator; b. St. Paul, May 16, 1944; s. Daniel N. and Gladys (Aronsohn) Spratt. B.A., Princeton U., 1966; Ph.D., Harvard U., 1971. Vis. prof. U. Calif.-Santa Cruz, 1973; acting asst. prof. UCLA, 1973-74; asst. prof. history U. Calif.-Irvine, 1974-83, prof., 1984—; plaintiff Freedom of Info. Lawsuit against FBI for John Lennon Files, 1983—. Author: Social Origins of the New South, 1979; Come Together: John Lennon in his Time, 1984. Contbr. articles to profl. jours. including The Nation, The New Republic and New York Times Book Review. Rockefeller Found. fellow, 1979; Am. Council Learned Socs.-Ford Found. fellow, 1985. Mem. Am. Hist. Assn., Nat. Book Critics Circle, Orgn. Am. Historians, Nat. Writers' Union, The Authors' Guild, So. Hist. Assn. Office: U Calif Dept History Irvine CA 92717

WIENER, SYDNEY PAUL, mortgage broker; b. N.Y.C., Aug. 18, 1918; s. Nathan and Lillian (Fortunoff) W.; m. Charlotte Rosen, Jan. 28, 1945; children: Laura Jane Mills, Barbara Hanawalt. DMD, U. Louisville, 1943. Gen. practice dentistry Flushing, N.Y., 1947-68; pvt. investor El Cajon, Calif., 1968—; mortgage sales rep. El Cajon, 1972—; dentist Booth Meml. Hosp., Flushing, 1963-68; researcher Anti-Coronary Club N.Y.C. Dept. Health, 1962-67. Contbr. articles on coronary disease, remedial edn. to profl. jours. Bd. dirs. Calif. Community and Jr. Colls., Calif. Community Coll. Trustees, Sacramento, 1975-87; chmn. bd. trustees Grossmont-Cuyamaca Community Coll. Dist., El Cajon, 1973—; dep. sheriff San Diego Sheriff Aero-squadron, 1971-82; pres. El Cajon San Diego County civic Ctr. Authority, 1973-77. Served to capt. U.S. Army, 1941-47. Recipient Commendation, Sheriff Maricopa County, Phoenix, 1981, Commendation, Sheriff San Diego County, 1981; award, City El Cajon, 1973-74, award Associated Students Grossmont Coll., El Cajon, 1975, Grossmont Coll. Learning Skills award, 1983, Calif. Community Coll. Trustees award, 1987. Democrat. Jewish.

WIENER, VALERIE, public relations executive; b. Las Vegas, Oct. 30, 1948; d. Louis Isaac and Tui Ava (Knight) W. BJ, U. Mo., 1971, MA, 1972; MA, Sangamon State U., 1974; postgrad., McGeorge Sch. Law, 1976-79. Producer TV show "Checkpoint" Sta. KOMU-TV, Columbia, Mo., 1972-73; v.p., owner Broadcast Assocs., Inc., Las Vegas, 1972-86; pub. affairs dir. First Ill. Cable TV, Springfield, 1973-74; editor Ill. State Register, Springfield, 1973-74; producer and talent Nev. Realities Sta. KLVX-TV, Las Vegas, 1974-75; account exec. Sta. KBMI (now KFMS), Las Vegas, 1975-79; nat. traffic dir. six radio stas., Las Vegas, Albuquerque and El Paso, Tex., 1979-80; exec. v.p., gen. mgr. Stas. KXKS and KKJY, Albuquerque, 1980-81; exec. adminstr. Stas. KSET AM/FM, KVEG, KFMS and KKJY, 1981-83; press sec. U.S. Congressman Harry Reid, Washington, 1983-86; adminstrv. asst Friends for Harry Reid, Nev., 1986; press sec. U.S. Senator Harry Reid, Washington, 1987-88. Sponsor Futures for Children, Las Vegas, Albuquerque and El Paso, 1979-83; mem. Exec. Women's Coun., El Paso, 1981-83, VIP bd. Easter Seals, El Paso, 1982; appointee Gov.'s Coun. Small Bus.; mem. Nev. Devel. Authority, Clark Coun. Sch. Dist/Bus. Community PAYBAC Speakers Program, Mt. Charleston vol. Assn. Bd. Named one of Outstanding Young Women of Am., 1982, Outstanding Vol. United Way, El Paso, 1983. Mem. Nat. Mgmt. Assn., Dem. Press Secs. Assn., El Paso Assn. Radio Stas., NAFE, U.S. Senate Staff Club, Las Vegas C. of C., Nev. State Press Assn., Allied Arts Coun., Am. Bus. Women's Assn., N. Las Vegas C. of C., Friends of Gov.'s Mansion Com., Sigma Delta Chi. Democrat. Christian Scientist.

WIERZBA, HEIDEMARIE B., information management specialist; b. Heinrichswalde, Fed. Republic of Germany, Sept. 26, 1944; came to U.S., 1967; d. Heinz Hugo and Kaethe Liselotte (Trutnau) Krink; m. Leonard Bernard Wierzba, May 14, 1969 (div. 1980). Buchhandel, Dt. Buchh. Schule, Kiel, Republic of Germany, 1965; profl. cert., Coll. of Further Edn., Oxford, Eng., 1966; BA, Calif. State U., Fullerton, 1979. Library asst. Allergan, Inc., Irvine, Calif., 1975-76; info. analyst Allergan Pharms., Irvine, Calif., 1976-79, library supr., 1979-81, mgr. corp. info. ctr., 1982—; cons. in field, Tustin, Calif., 1975-77; translator Unitran, Fullerton, Calif., 1980—; mem. adv. bd. CB&S Career Cons., Orange, Calif., 1987—. Editor sci. articles. Bd. dirs. Nat. Woman's Polit. Caucus, Irvine, 1984-85. Mem. Indsl. Tech. Info. Mgmt. Group (steering com. mem. 1984—, acting pres. 1986) Cooperative Library Agy. for Systems and Services (com. mem.), Am. Soc. Info. Sci., Spl. Library Assn., Med. Libraries of O.C. (pres. 1978), Pharm. Mfg. Assn. (com. mem. info. mgmt. sect. 1985—). Democrat. Home: 634 Colonial Circle Fullerton CA 92635 Office: Allergan Inc 2525 Dupont Dr Irvine CA 92715

WIESE, FREDERICK WILLIAM, JR., technological company manager; b. Balt., Apr. 22, 1948; d. Frederick William and Julia (Davis) W.; m. Miriam Guadalupe Aldana, Aug. 27, 1970; children: Ann Marie, Monica J., Michelle G. BS in Chemistry, St. Louis U., 1970; MS ChemE, U. Mo., Rolla, 1972. Mfg. engr. Proctor & Gamble, Cin., 1973-77, Tex. Instruments, Lubbock, 1977-84; ops. and tech. mgr. Johnson Matthey, San Diego, 1984—. Contbr. articles on silver glass die attachment to popular mags; inventor low temperature silver glass. Mem. Hispanic Advocacy Com., San Diego, 1987-88. Fellow Soc. Mfg. Engring.; mem. Internat. Electronic Packaging Soc., Internat. Soc. Hybrid Mfg. Office: Johnson Matthey 10080 Willow Creek Rd San Diego CA 92131

WIESE, KEVIN GLEN, entrepreneur; b. Ogden, Utah, Mar. 19, 1960; s. Glen James and Kay Jon (Mildon) W. BS in Fin. and Mktg., U. Utah, 1982; MBA, Golden State U., 1987; PhD in Internat. Bus., Columbia Pacific U., 1987. Fin. advisor Silverstein Fin., L.A., 1983-85; fin. cons. Christopher Weil & Co., Inc., L.A., 1985-87; chief exec. officer, pres. Internat. Venture Enterprises, L.A., 1988—, Internat. Venture Rsch., L.A., 1988—, Internat. Leadership Performance Advisors, L.A., 1988—, Internat. Wealth Group, Ltd., L.A., 1988—; adj. prof. Loyola Marymount U., Los Angeles, 1986-87, Coll. for Fin. Planning Denver, 1986-87; cons. OneCard Internat., Inc., L.A., 1988—, United Industries, L.A., 1987-88, Rouse Fin. Network, Phoenix, 1989—; researcher Harvard U., Boston, 1987—, Oxford U., Eng., 1987—, Stanford U., Palo Alto, Calif., 1987—, Cambridge U., Eng., 1987—. Bus. liason Mega-Cities Project L.A. Sect., 1988—; vol. Hugh O'Brian Youth Found., L.A., 1986-88. Mem. Internat. Assn., for Fin. Planning (bd. dirs. L.A. chpt. 1985-86, sec., treas. 1984-85), Inst. Cert. Fin. Planning, Nat. Speakers Assn., Toastmasters. Republican. Office: Internat Wealth Group Ltd 12400 Wilshire Blvd Ste 650 Los Angeles CA 90025

WIESENFELD, IRVING HAROLD, otolaryngologist; b. San Francisco, June 14, 1912; s. Louis and Ann (Berke) W.; A.B., U. Calif., 1934, M.D., 1938, C.P.H. (Calif. State fellow), 1939, M.S., 1941, Dr.P.H., 1947; m. Betsey Ramsay Straub, May 11, 1939; children—Stephen Lee, Ramsay. Intern, U. Calif. Hosp., San Francisco, 1937-38; chief bur. maternal and child health Calif. Dept. Health, San Francisco, 1939-41; resident in otolaryngology Los Angeles County Hosp. on U. So. Calif. Service, 1941-42; chief otolaryngology service Kaiser Found. Hosp., Oakland, Calif., 1942-46; practice medicine specializing in otolaryngology, Oakland, 1946—; mem. staffs Herrick Meml. Hosp. (name now Alta Bates-Herrick Hosps.), Berkeley, Calif., Providence Hosp., Oakland, Children's Hosp., Oakland, Cowell Hosp., Berkeley; med. dir. Oakland Unified Sch. Dist., 1949—. Diplomate Am. Bd. Otolaryngology, Internat. Bd. Surgery. Fellow ACS, Internat. Coll. Surgeons; mem. AMA, Calif., Alameda-Contra Costa med. assns., Am. Med. Tennis Assn., Phi Beta Kappa, Sigma Xi, Alpha Omega Alpha. Republican. Jewish. Club: Oakland Athletic. Home: 120 Monte Av: Piedmont CA 94611 Office: 400 30th St Ste 403 Oakland CA 94609

WIESENTHAL, ANDREW MICHAEL, pediatrician; b. N.Y.C., Mar. 5, 1950; s. Jerome Mitchell and Gladys (Heilig) W.; m. Billie Gunkel, July 1, 1978. BA, Yale U., 1971; MD, SUNY, Bklyn., 1975. Diplomate, Am. bd. Pediatrics. Intern U. Colo. Health Scis. Ctr., Denver, 1975-76; resident in pediatrics U. Colo. Health Scis. Ctr., 1976-78, fellow in pediatric infectious disease, 1980-83, instr. pediatrics, 1982-84, clin. asst. prof. pediatrics, 1984—; epidemic intelligence svc. officer Ctrs. Disease Control/USPHS, Atlanta, 1978-80; pediatrician Colo. Permanente Med. Group, Denver, 1983—, chief pediatrics, 1987—, dir. quality assurance, 1988—; clin. assoc., dept. pediatrics, So. Ill. U., Springfield, 1979-80. Contbr. numerous articles to profl. jours. Mem. Am. Acad. Pediatrics, Epidemic Intelligence Svc. Alumni Assn., Denver Med. Soc. Jewish. Home: 6003 Montview Blvd Denver CO 80207 Office: Colo Permanente Med Group 2045 Franklin St Denver CO 80205-5494

WIGGINS, CHARLES EDWARD, federal judge; b. El Monte, Calif., Dec. 3, 1927; s. Louis J. and Margaret E. (Fanning) W.; m. Yvonne L. Boots, Dec. 30, 1946 (dec. Sept. 1971); children: Steven L., Scott D.; m. Betty J. Koontz, July 12, 1972. B.S., U. So. Calif., 1953, LL.B., 1956; LL.B. (hon.) Ohio Wesleyan, 1975, Han Yang. U., Seoul, Korea, 1976. Bar: Calif. 1957, D.C. 1978. Lawyer, Woods & Wiggins, El Monte, Calif., 1956-66, Musick, Peeler & Garrett, Los Angeles, 1979-81, Pierson, Ball & Dowd, Washington, 1982-84, Pillsbury, Madison & Sutro, San Francisco, 1984; mem. 90-95th congresses from 25th and 39th Calif. Dists.; judge U.S. Ct. Appeals 9th Circuit, 1984—. Mayor City of El Monte, Calif., 1964-66; mem. Planning Commn. City of El Monte, 1956-60; mem. Commn. on Bicentennial of U.S. Constitution, 1985—, mem. standing com. on rules of practice and procedure, 1987—. Served to 1st lt. U.S. Army, 1945-48, 50-52, Korea. Mem. ABA, State Bar Calif., D.C. Bar Assn. Republican. Lodge: Lions. Office: US Ct Appeals 50 W Liberty St #950 Reno NV 89501

WIGGINS, WALTON WRAY, publisher; b. Roswell, N.Mex., May 13, 1924; s. Miles Burgess and Mona Cecil (Brown) W.; grad. Motion Picture Cameraman Sch., Astoria, N.Y., 1945; m. Roynel Fitzgerald, Apr. 30, 1963; children—Walton Wray, Kimberly Douglas, Lisa Renee. Free-lance photojournalist for nat. mags., 1948-60; dir. public relations Ruidoso Racing Assn., Ruidoso Downs, N.Mex., 1960-69, v.p., 1967-68; founder, pub. Speedhorse Publs., Roswell, N.Mex. and Norman, Okla., 1969-78; owner/operator Wiggins Galleries Fine Art, 1978—; pres. Quarter Racing World, 1970-78, Am. Horse Publs., Washington, 1978; del. leader People to People, Internat. Served with U.S. Army, 1943-46. Recipient Detroit Art Dirs. award, 1955, Greatest Contbr. award Quarter Racing Owners Am., 1974. Mem. Overseas Press Club, Am. Soc. Mag. Photographers, Am. Horse Publs. Republican. Author: The Great American Speedhorse, 1978; Cockleburs and Cowchips, 1975; Alfred Morang-A Neglected Master, 1979; Ernest Berke-Paintings and Sculptures of the Old West, 1980; Juan Dell-The First Lady of Western Bronze, 1981; Go Man Go-The Legendary Speedhorse, 1982; The Transcendental Art of Emil Bisttram, 1988. Office: 526 Canyon Rd Santa Fe NM 87501

WIGGS, P. DAVID, real estate executive; b. Alva, Okla., Dec. 6, 1942; s. Conrad Lee and Wanda B. (Kreie) W.; B.S., Ariz. State U., 1964, 77; postgrad. Chapman Coll., 1967; M.B.A., Ariz. State U., 1974; grad. Realtors Inst.; m. Saundre Eugenia Young, June 6, 1964. Cashier, A.J. Bayless Markets, Phoenix, 1960-64; staff accountant Peat, Marwick, Mitchell & Co., C.P.A.'s, Dallas, 1964-66, sr. auditor, Phoenix, 1970-72; commd. 2d lt. USAF, 1967, advanced through grades to capt., 1970; Officer Tng. Sch., 1966-67, logistics officer Vandenberg AFB, Cal., 1967-68, dir. logistics plans, 1968-70; staff accountant Diehl, Evans & Co., C.P.A.'s Santa Maria, Calif., 1967-70; gen. partner Satellite Investment Co., Ltd., Tempe Ariz., 1968—, DPI Assos., Tempe, 1977-85, Homevest Assos., Tempe, 1978—; controller Valley Enterprises, Inc., Phoenix, 1972-73, Diversified Properties, Inc., Tempe, 1973-76, v.p., treas., 1976-88; treas. Freeway Lumber and Materials, Inc., Phoenix, 1972-73; Realtor, 1980—; pres. Wiggs Co., Tempe, Ariz., 1980—; div. controller Pulte Home Corp., Tempe, 1981-82; v.p., treas. Hunsinger Homes, Inc., Tempe, 1982-83; controller Val Vista Lakes, 1983-88; contr. Osselaer Co., Phoenix, 1988—. Sec., supervisory com. Vandenberg Fed. Employees Credit Union, Vandenberg AFB, Calif., 1969-70. Bd. dirs., treas. Lakes Community Assn., Tempe, 1974-77, treas. Val Vista Lakes Community Assn., Gilbert, Ariz., 1985-88. CPA, Tex., Ariz. Mem. AICPA, Ariz. Soc. CPA's, Tex. Soc. CPA's, Nat. Assn. Realtors, Beta Gamma Sigma, Beta Alpha Psi, Delta Sigma Pi. Republican. Baptist (deacon). Home: 1902 E Julie Dr Tempe AZ 85283 Office: 49 E Thomas Rd Phoenix AZ 85012

WIGH, STEVEN CLARENCE, insurance agency executive; b. Kingsburg, Calif., June 18, 1954; s. Clarence Samuel and Evelyn Cecilia (Carlson) W. AA, Reedley (Calif.) Jr. Coll., 1974; BS, Calif. State U., Fresno, 1976, MBA, 1978. Underwriter Travelers Ins. Co., San Jose, Calif., 1978-79; acct. exec. Van Beurden & Assocs., Kingsburg, 1979-83, asst. v.p., 1983-85, v.p., 1985-87, sr. v.p., 1987—. Councilman, City of Kingsburg, 1980-84; trustee, chmn. bd. dirs. Evangelical Covenant Ch., Kingsburg, 1986-87; chmn. Kingsburg Bus. and Profl. Com., 1988—. Mem. Profl. Ins. Agts. Am., Beta Gamma Sigma, Phi Kappa Phi, Kings River Golf and Country Club (Kingsburg). Office: Van Beurden & Assoc 1615 Draper Kingsburg CA 93631

WIGHT, RANDY LEE, military officer; b. Seattle, Sept. 8, 1951; s. Guy Eugene and Jeraline Mae (Green) W.; m. Linda Ann Ruark, June 8, 1973; chidren: Kathryn Ann, David Michael. BS, U.S. Naval Acad., 1973; student, Naval Aviation Schs. Command, Pensacola, Fla., 1973-74, Naval Postgrad. Sch., Monterey, Calif., 1988--. Commd. ensign USN, 1973; advanced through grades to comdr. 1988; VAQ-129 Naval Air Sta , Whidby Island, Oak Harbor, Wash., 1974-75; from legal to div. officer Naval Air Sta , Whidby Island, Oak Harbor, 1975-78, flight instr., 1978-81, asst. maintenance and tng. officer, 1981-83, flight instr., 1983-85, maintenance officer, 1985-88; comdg. officer golden intruder squadron U.S. Naval Sea Cadet Corps., Oak Harbor, 1979-81. Mem. U.S. Naval Acad. Alumni Assn., U.S. Naval Inst. Roman Catholic.

WIGINTON, MORRIS S., III, data processing executive; b. Austin, Tex., June 13, 1950; s. Morris S. Wiginton Jr. and Bernice (Moreland) Lilley; m. Deborah Joyce, Aug. 8, 1978 (dec. Aug. 1984); m. Gerry, Feb. 7, 1987. U. Houston, 1972. Mgr. transit dept. 1st City Bank, Houston, 1973-76; br. mgr. Univ. Computer Svcs., San Antonio, 1976-80; v.p. systems and procedures The Benson Cos., San Antonio, 1980-81; gen. mgr. Universal Computer Forms, Inc., Houston, 1982-87; regional mgr., Western U.S. Universal Computer Systems, Houston, 1983-87, v.p. tng. and installations, 1982-87, v.p. mktg., 1984-87; dealer trainer Penske Cos., L.A., 1988—; cons. Hitchcock Cos., La Puente, Calif., 1988, Universal Computer Systems, Houston, 1989—. Creator Car Connectors Database, 1989. With USMC, 1969-71. Mem. Mensa, Rocky Mt. Elk Found. Republican. Home: 7215 Northampton Way Houston TX 77055

WIGNALL, FRANK STEPHEN, physician, naval officer; b. Jackson, Miss., Jan. 13, 1948; s. Frank and Amy Southern (Cooper) W. BA in Biology, Loyola U., New Orleans, 1971; MD, St. Louis U., 1975. Diplomate Nat. Bd. Medical Examiners, Am. Bd. Family Practice. Commd. ens. USN, 1975, advanced through grades to capt., 1989; intern Naval Hosp., Jacksonville, Fla., 1975-76, resident in family practice, 1976-78; fellow infectious disease Naval Hosp., San Diego, 1980-82; officer in charge U.S. Naval Med. Rsch. Inst. Detachment, Lima, Peru, 1986-88, Navy Environ. and Preventive Medicine Unit #6, Pearl Harbor, Hawaii, 1988—; lectr., instr. Panama Canal Coll. Sch. Med. Tech., 1982-83; dir. edn. programs Gorgas Meml. Lab., Republic of Panama, 1982-86; officer in charge Gorgas Meml. Lab., 1982-86; clin. asst. prof. La. State U. Sch. Medicine, New Orleans, 1982-86; cons. in field. Contbr. articles to profl. publs. Recipient Order of Chammori award Gov. of Guam, 1980. Fellow Am. Acad. Family Practice; mem. AMA, Am. Venereal Disease Assn., Am. Soc. Microbiology, Sierra Club, Nature Conservancy, Phi Beta Kappa, Beta Beta Beta, Alpha Omega Alpha. Roman Catholic. Office: Navy Environ and Preventive Medicine Unit 6 Box 112 Pearl Harbor HI 96860-5040

WIKTOROWICZ, ANDREW CHARLES, engineering company executive; b. Valevade, India, Nov. 25, 1945; came to U.S., 1951; s. Janusz Stanislaus and Kristina (Dziedzic) W.; m. Annajean Kessel, Sept. 7, 1968; children: Tanya, Daniel, Dustin. BS in Physics, Ill. Inst. Tech., 1967. Instrument physicist CPC Internat., Argo, Ill., 1967-70; project engr. Fluor Corp., Irvine, Calif., 1970-73; engring. group leader Bechtel Power Corp., Norwalk, Calif., 1973-74; engr. chief controls Ameron Process Systems Div., Santa Ana, Calif., 1974-76; v.p. J.P.W. Industries, Orange, Calif., 1976-78; pres. Automated Dynamics Corp., Laguna Hills, Calif., 1978-85; v.p. Nova Power, Inc., Santa Ana, 1985-89; west regional mgr. ATS, Inc., Santa Ana, 1989—; bd. dirs. Unigen, Mission Viejo, Calif., 1987—; prof. engring. Calif. Dept. Consumer Affairs, Sacramento, 1975, 78. Co-author: Instrument Engineers' Handbook-Programmable Controllers, 1985; contbr. articles to profl. jours. Expert examiner control systems Calif. Dept. Consumer Affairs-Bd. Profl. Engring., Sacramento, 1976—; trustee welfare fund Internat. Brotherhood of Electrical Workers, Orange, 1976-80. Undergrad. research grantee NSF, Washington, 1966. Mem. Instrument Soc. Am. Internat. (v.p. 1981-83, bd. dirs. 1981-83, fin. com. 1983—, dir. publs. 1983—, long-range planning com. 1988—), Orange County Instrument Soc. Am., Western Council Constrn.

Consumers (program com. 1987—). Republican. Roman Catholic. Home: 22611 La Quinta Mission Viejo CA 92691 Office: ATS Inc 2110 E First St Ste 109 Santa Ana CA 92691

WILBUR, GLENN ARTHUR, service executive; b. Wichita, Kans., Dec. 18, 1954; s. Horace Wesley and Genevieve Nadine (Greer) W. Student, Wichita State U., 1973-78; student, Kans. State U., 1979, Kans. Newman Coll., 1983. Hotel mgr. The Phoenix, San Francisco, 1984—. Republican. Home: 825 Geary St Apt 701 San Francisco CA 94109 Office: The Phoenix 601 Eddy St San Francisco CA 94109

WILBUR, LESLIE EUGENE, education educator; b. Modesto, Calif., Jan. 11, 1924; s. Horace Gilbert and Grace (King) W.; m. Norma June Lash, June 14, 1946; children: Stuart Alan, Lesley Lynn. AA, Modesto Jr. Coll., 1943; BA, U. Ill., 1948; MA, U. Calif., Berkeley, 1951; PhD, U. So. Calif., 1962. Instr. Bakersfield (Calif.) Coll, 1950-60, assoc. dean, 1960-62; pres. Barstow (Calif.) Coll., 1962-65; prof. edn. U. So. Calif., L.A., 1965—, chmn. higher edn. dept., 1969-81, pres. faculty senate, 1972-73; cons. L.A. County Office Schs., 1966-79; dir. Pullias Lecture Programs, L.A., 1978—; v.p. So. Calif. Consortium, Orange, 1979—. Co-author: Improving College English, 1960, Teaching in the Community College, 1972, Principles and Values for College and University Administrators, 1984. With AUS, 1943-46, ETO. Recipient We Honor Ours award Calif. Tchrs. Assn., 1972. Mem. Am. Assn. for Higher Edn., Assn. for Study Higher Edn., Community Coll. Rsch. Assn. (bd. dirs. 1975—), Calif. Coll. and Univ. Faculty Assn. (pres. U. So. Calif. chpt. 1965-68). Democrat. Mem. United Ch. of Christ. Home: PO Box 2669 Rolling Hills CA 90274 Office: U So Calif WPH 701 Los Angeles CA 90089-0031

WILBUR-COULTER, JULIE KAYE, director surgical technologists program; b. Warren, Minn., Jan. 22, 1960; d. Neil Byron and Deloris Marlene (Johnson) Coulter; m. Gerald Malcolm Wilbur, Sept. 4, 1987. Cert., Area Vocat. Tech. Inst., 1982. Cert. basic life support instr. Asst. clin. dir. adminstrv. asst. N.D. Found. for Women's Health, U. N.D., Grand Forks, 1982-84; surg. technologist Phoenix Gen. Hosp., 1984-86; clin. dir., asst. ops. mgr. Scottsdale (Ariz.) Ob.-Gyn., 1986-87; coord. surgery inventory control Phoenix Gen. Healthcare System, 1987-88; instr. Tempe Tech. Inst./Southwestern Med. Acad., Phoenix, 1988-89—, dir. surg. technologists program, 1989—; dir. materials mgmt. Tempe Tech. Inst./Dulaney Eye Inst., Sun City, Ariz., 1989—; liaison EatingDisorders Group, Grand Forks, 1983-84; orientator new techs. Phoenix Gen. Hosp., 1984-86. Mem. Asn. Surg. Technologists, NAFE, Women's Found., Jaycees (dist. dir. Warren, Minn. chpt. 1979-81). Home: 4548 W Lane Ave Glendale AZ 58301 Office: Tempe Tech Inst Dulaney Eye Inst 9425 W Bell Rd Sun City AZ 85351

WILBURN, RONALD PAUL, controller; b. East St. Louis, Ill., Aug. 10, 1937; s. Frank Cecil and Virginia Catherine (Shephard) W. m. Frances Rose Sever, Nov. 6, 1965 (div. Nov. 1985); children: Rhonda Lynn, Landon Aron, Amanda Lynette. BBA, So. Ill. U., 1960; student, U. Paris-Sorbonne, 1963; BA in Acctg., Pacific Western Coll., 1968, MBA in Fin., 1970. Pres., fin. cons. Fin. Systems, Inc., Bellevue, Wash., 1970-80; pres., fin. cons. Questron Fin. Svcs., Inc., Bellevue, 1981, founder, chief exec. officer, 1981—; controller Mon Arc Electric Corp., Redmond, Wash., 1979, Synetix Industries, Inc., Redmond, Wash., 1980-82; tchr. acctg. City Coll. Seattle; chief fin. officer Precision Engine Specialists, Inc., Seattle, 1985-87, Craftech Pressworks, Inc., Bellevue, Washington, 1987-89, Butcher Boy Sausage Co. Inc., Seattle and Naches, Wash., 1987-88. Rep. precinct committeeman, 1976-85; active budget bldg. com. Issaquah (Wash.) Sch. Dist.; founder, past pres. Issaquah Commn. Edn. Served with USMC, 1960-66. Decorated Purple Heart, Bronze Star. Mem. Internat. Assn. Fin. Planners, Nat. Assn. Accts., Internat. Platform Assn., Masons, Shriners, Order of Eastern Star. Mormon. Home: 6406 143d SW Edmonds WA 98020 Office: 320-108th Ave NE Bellevue WA 98004

WILBURN, STEVE, energy executive, consultant; b. Chgo., Dec. 19, 1948; s. Melvin Wren and Joan June (Evans) W.; m. Cherri Lynn Renner; children: Stephanie, Nathan. BCE, Washington U., St. Louis, 1972. Research asst. Monsanto Corp., St. Louis, 1973-77; dir. tech. mktg. Gundlach Machine Co., St. Louis, 1977-79; pres. Steve Wilburn & Assocs., Tucson, 1980-87; v.p. bus. devel. GWF Power div. Allied-Signal Corp., Irvine, Calif., 1987—. Served as cpl. USMC, 1967-69, Vietnam. Decorated Purple Heart. Mem. Internat. Cogeneration Soc. (chmn. midwest region 1983), Assn. Energy Engrs. Republican. Roman Catholic. Club: Engineers (St. Louis). Lodge: Optimists (v.p. 1981-82). Home and Office: 91 W Yale Loop Irvine CA 92714

WILCOX, DANIEL EDWARD, III, state employee; b. Bryn Mawr, Pa., Dec. 27, 1946; s. Daniel Edward and Laura Elsie (Church) W.; m. Anita Leah Warwick, July 7, 1949; children: Crystal, Heather, Daniel. BS in Occupational Edn., So. Ill. U., 1982. Enlisted USAF, 1966; adminstrv. technician, McChord AFB, Tacoma, Wash., 1966-71; edn./tng. supt. Fairchild AFB, Spokane, Wash., 1971-82; dep. dir. personnel Travis AFB, Calif., 1982-86, ret., 1986; trades name specialist dept. licensing Wash. State Bus. License Service, Olympia, 1986-88; master bus. lic. application verifier Bus. Lic. Svcs., 1986-88; licensing supr. corp. div. Office Sec. of State, 1989—. Decorated Meritorious Service medal with two oak leaf clusters, Air Force Commendation medal with two oak leaf clusters. Mem. Am. Vocat. Assn., Noncommd. Officer Acad. Grad. Assn., Air Force Assn., Nat. Thespian Soc. Democrat. Methodist. Office: Sec of State Corp Div 505 E Union 2d Fl Olympia WA 98504

WILCOX, EVLYN, businesswoman, former city official. children: Wayne, Moire, Marlene. Owner, pres. Manpower, Inc., San Bernardino, Riverside, Upland, San Gabriel Valley and Corona, Calif.; former mayor City of San Bernardino. Pres. Arrowhead United Way, 1983, campaign chmn., 1981; pres. Community Arts Prodns.; treas., bd. dirs. Nat. Orange Show; bd. dirs. YMCA; bd. councillors Calif. State U., San Bernardino. Named Citizen of Yr. Inland Empire mag., 1979. Mem. Exec. Women Internat. (pres Inland Empire chpt. 1975), Uptown Bus. and Profl. Women, Bus. and Profl. Women USA (pres. San Orco dist.), San Bernardino Area C. of C. (pres. Athena award 1986). Lodge: Zonta Internat. Office: City of San Bernardino 300 North D St San Bernardino CA 92418 *

WILCOX, HAROLD EDGAR, procurement management executive; b. Washington, Feb. 15, 1940; s. Harold Edgar and Glenna Maude (Austin) W.; m. Catherine E. Kruger, June 25, 1971. BSBA, Miami U., 1961; MBA, George Washington U., 1972. Commd. ensign USN, 1961, advanced through grade to capt., 1982, supt. purchasing Phila. Naval Shipyard, 1967-69, dep. dir. Aircraft Weapon Systems Purchasing div., 1972-76; with Naval Air Systems Command Hdqrs. USN, Washington, 1972-76; comptroller USN, dir. Regional Contracting Dept.; dir. Naval Supply Ctr. USN, Pearl Harbor, Hawaii, 1976-79; dir. purchasing Navy Aviation Supply Office USN, Phila., 1979-82; dir. acquisition Joint Cruise Missiles Project USN, Washington, 1982-84; ret. USN, 1984; dir. contracts for aerospace and logistics Cubic Corp., San Diego, 1985-88. Decorated Def. Superior Svc. medal, Merit svc. medal with gold star recipient Recognition award U.S. Dept. Commerce, 1978, Vietnam Svc. medal with silver and bronze stars. Mem. U.S. Naval Inst., Nat. Contracts Mgmt. Assn. (cert. conract mgr. 1976), Denver Sporting Club. Republican. Methodist. Office: AIRCOA Hospitality Svcs 4600 S Ulster St Ste 1200 Denver CO 80237

WILCOX, J. KEVIN, airline pilot; b. Livermore, Calif., July 20, 1956; s. Allison J. and Donna Irene (Humbert) W.; m. Lorraine Carole Scanlon, Dec. 20, 1980; 1 child, J. Kevin Jr. AS in Aeronautics, Grossmont Coll., 1979; BSBA, U. Phoenix, 1988. Lic. airlin pilot. Freelance flight instr. El Cajon, Calif., 1974-80; capt. Dorado Wings, Puerto Rico, 1980; free lance pilot, instr. El Cajon, Calif., 1980-81; aerobatic instr. Amelia Reid Aviation, San Jose, Calif., 1981-83; courier Fed. Express Corp., San Jose, Calif., 1981-84; pres. Wilcox & Harding, Inc., San Jose, Calif., 1981-84; capt., check airman Air Cortex Internat., Denver, 1984-86; 1st officer Aspen Airways, Denver, 1986—; aviation cons. J. Thompson Photographic, Aurora, Colo., 1985—. Mem. Fairbank family in Am. Inc. Mem. Air Line Pilots Assn., Aircraft Owners & Pilots Assn. Republican. Office: Aspen Airways 3860 Quebec St Denver CO 80107

WILCOX, RHODA DAVIS, teacher; b. Boyero, Colo., Nov. 4, 1918; d. Harold Francis and Louise Wilhelmina (Wilfert) Davis; m. Kenneth Edward Wilcox, Nov. 1945 (div. 1952); 1 child, Michele Ann. BA in Elem. Edn., U. No. Colo., 1941; postgrad., Colo. Coll., 1955-65. Cert. tchr., Colo. Elem. tchr. Fruita (Colo.) Pub. Sch., 1938-40, Boise, Idaho, 1940-42; sec. civil service USAF, Ogden, Utah, 1942-43, Colorado Springs, Colo., 1943-44; sec. civil service hdqtrs. command USAF, Panama Canal Zone; elem. tchr. Colorado Springs Sch. Dist. 11, 1952-82, mem. curriculum devel. com., 1968-69; lectr. civic, profl. and edn. groups, Colo. author: Man on the Iron Horse, 1959, Colorado Slim and His Spectacklers, 1964, (with Joan Pierpoint) Changing Colorado, 1968-69, The Bells of Manitou, 1973. Mem. Hist. Adv. Bd. State Colo., Denver, 1976; mem. Garden of the Gods Master Plan Rev. Com. City of Colorado Springs, 1987—; mem. cemetery adv. bd. City Colorado Springs, 1988—, mem. adv. bd. centennial com., 1971; mem. steering com. Spirit of Palmer Festival, 1986; judge Nat. Hist. Day U. Colo., Colorado Springs; hon. trustee Palmer Found., 1986—. Mem. AAUW (Woman of Yr. 1987), Colo. Ret. Tchrs. Assn., Colorado Springs Ret. Tchrs. Assn., Helen Hunt Jackson Commemorative Coun. Congregationalist. Home: 1620 E Cache La Poudre Colorado Springs CO 80909

WILCOX, WINTON WILFRED, JR., computer specialist, consultant; b. Independence, Mo., Aug. 24, 1945; s. Winton Wilfred Wilcox Sr. and LaPreal (Adams) Craig; m. Janette Moss, Oct. 9, 1965 (div. 1989); 1 child, Steven Michael. BS, U. Nev., 1973. Nat. product dir. Am. Photography Corp., N.Y.C., 1974-77; gen. mgr. Golden Valley (Minn.) Coffee, 1977-80; div. mgr. Cable Data, Sacramento, 1981-84; v.p., chief operating officer Cultch Enterprises, Inc., Sacramento, 1980-86; v.p. mktg. div. Parallex, Winston-Salem, N.C., 1985-88; Western regional mgr. Datamatic Processing, Inc., San Ramon, Calif., 1988—; cons. Lyons Security, Sacramento, 1985—, Camilia City Landscape Mgmt., Sacramento, 1988—. Author: How to Create Computer Entertainment, 1985; contbg. author: Apple Fun & Games, 1986. With USAF, 1966-70. Mem. Cable TV Adminstrn and Mktg. (pay view com. Washington chpt. 1985-87, SE chpt. formation com. Tampa, Fla. chpt. 1986-87), Crown Rm., Red Carpet. Republican. Home: 9435 Roseburg Ct Sacramento CA 95826 Office: IK & Cons 782 Park Ave Ste #4 San Jose CA 95126

WILDE, NEVA MAXINE, educator, artist; b. Sacramento, Calif., May 31, 1916; d. William Henry and Hazel Helen (Houck) Pimentel; m. Thomas Ernest Wilde Jr., Dec. 5, 1937; children: Suzanne Sharon Bushnell (dec.), Stephanie Dianne Valle. AA, Sacramento (Calif.) City Coll., 1936; BA, San Jose (Calif.) State U., 1943; MFA, U. Calif., Sacramento, 1955, MEd, 1955. Cert. tchr., Calif., cert. sch. administr. Tchr. various Sacramento Area Elem. Schs., 1945-60; prin. John Morse Elem. Sch., Sacramento, 1960-76. Columnist: bi-monthly bridge advice and events column. Vol. driver, bridge tchr. and ptnr. Am. Cancer Soc.; vol. bridge tchr. and ptnr., cons., lectr. Sr. Citizens Groups; on-call juror; vol. campaigner Repub. Party; founder day care ctrs. various Air Force bases, 1940-44. Recipient Honorary Air Force Wives' award, 1944, Sr. Citizen Faithful Service award, 1982-88, Certs. of Appreciation Superior Ct. of Sacramento County, 1988. Mem. AAUW, Duplicate Am. Contract Bridge League (dir. 1944—), Grant Union High Sch. Alumni Assn. (cons.), Am. Contract Bridge League (chartered mem., host regional and section games, life master gold group, performs opening Invocation), Master Tchr. Soc. (participant child study seminars, master bridge instr. for duplicate bridge), Pres. Assn., Principal's Assn. (pres., sec.-treas.), McCellan Field Women's Officers Club, Pan Hellenic Soc. (past pres.), Pi Epsilon Pi, Delta Pi Delta, Sigma Phi Kappa (past pres.).

WILDE, TERUKO, artist; b. Nagoya, Mie, Japan, Apr. 20, 1945; d. Sadao and Moto (Minami) Takeuchi; m. Davis S. Wilde, June 27, 1970 (div. Feb. 26, 1987); 1 child, Emily. Student, U. Cin., 1962-64, Columbus Coll. Arts & Design, 1967-69. Graphic artsit Nationwide Ins. Co., Columbus, Ohio, 1968-70; owner Teruko's Studio Gallery, Willard, Ohio, 1971-80; co-pub., mktg. dir. Prisum Mag., Willard, 1980-82, Willard Junction, Willard, 1982-85; artist self-employed, Taos, N.Mex., 1986—. Founder Prism, 1980-82, Willard Junction, 1982-85. Bd. dirs. Willard Fine Arts, Inc., 1981-85, City Mgrs. Adv. Com., Willard, 1984-86; tchr. First United Meth. Ch., Willard, 1976-80; art tchr. Sandusky (Ohio) Cultural Ctr., 1973-74. Named Best in Painting Mansfield Art Ctr., 1979, Best of Show Columbia Art Show, 1976. Mem. N.Y. Artists Equity Assn. Inc., Taos Art Assn., Mansfield Art Ctr., Ohio Water Color Soc., Bay Crafters, Research Club. Home: PO Box 2060 Taos NM 87571 Office: Total Arts Gallery Kit Carson Rd Taos NM 87571

WILDEMAN, ALBERT SMOKEY, communications company executive; b. Waupun, Wis., Oct. 9, 1946; s. Albert and Marie (Griffeon) W.; m. Judy L. Rosol, July 1, 1967; children: Pamela, Albert, Jodi. Grad. high sch., Waupun. Police officer Waupun, 1970-78; gen. mgr. Grocery Super Market, Buffalo, Wyo., 1979-83; salesperson Sta. KLGT-Radio, Buffalo, Wyo., 1983, gen. mgr., 1983—; also ptnr. Communication System III-KLGT, Buffalo, 1988—. Mem. Buffalo C. of C. (v.p. 1987, pres. 1988, Spl. Recognition award 1986), Lions. Home and Office: 1221 Fort St Buffalo WY 82834

WILDER, JAMES D., geology and mining administrator; b. Wheelersburg, Ohio, June 25, 1935; s. Theodore Roosevelt and Gladys (Crabtree) W.; children: Jaymie Deanna, Julie Lynne. Graduated high sch., Wheelersburg. Lic. real estate agt. Portsmouth, Ohio; mgr. comml. pilots, fixed base operator Scioto County Airport, Ohio; mgr. and part owner sporting goods store, Portsmouth; cons. geologist Paradise, Calif., 1973-81; pres. Mining Consultants, Inc., Paradise, 1981-84; dir. Geology and Devel. Para-Butte Mining, Inc., Paradise, 1984-88, pres., 1988—. Served with U.S. Army, 1956-57. Home and Office: Para-Butte Mining Inc 1737 Drayer Dr Paradise CA 95969

WILDRICK, CRAIG DOUGLAS, financial company executive; b. Ft. Sill, Okla., Oct. 11, 1951; s. Richard Minter and Ruth Joan (Stroud) W.; m. Susan Edith Mapother Brown, June 12, 1989; children: Brian Richard, Kevin Michael, Daniel Joseph, Heather. BS, U.S. Mil. Acad., 1973; M.Pub. Policy, Harvard U., 1979. Asst. prof. econs. U.S. Mil. Acad., West Point, 1983-86; dir. quality assurance and svc. process Citicorp Diners Club, Englewood, Colo., 1987-88; ops. mgr. corp. client relations Citicorp Diners Club, 1988, v.p. corp. customer svc., 1988—. Contbr. articles to profl. jours. Maj. U.S. Army, 1973-87. Mem. Denver Bicycle Touring Club, Phi Kappa Phi. Office: Citicorp Diners Club 183 Inverness Dr Englewood CO 80112

WILEY, DAVID OWEN, public relations executive; b. Philipsburg, Pa., Jan. 26, 1935; s. Franklin Williams and Mary (Owens) W.; divorced; children: Bethalee Dawn Jones, Jeffrey Brian. Student, Mich. State U., 1959-62. Editor Ford Motor Co., Dearborn, Mich., 1966-70; pubs. specialist Goodyr. Tire and Rubber Co., Akron, Ohio, 1970-74; mgr. communication services Wean United Inc., Warren, Ohio, 1974-78; dir. pub. relations The Patton Agy., Phoenix, 1978-79; pres. Petroglyph Communications, Inc., Phoenix, 1979-86; prin. Cook, Riggs & Wiley, Inc., Phoenix, 1986-87, David C. Wiley Assocs. Inc., Phoenix, 1987—. Mem. speakers bur. New Detroit Inc., 1969; bd. dirs. West Side Neighborhood Inc., Akron, 1971-72, Phoenix City Club, 1987—, Valley Citizens League, 1988—; chmn. state pub. info. Ariz. Chpt. Nat. Cancer Soc., Phoenix, 1980. Served as sgt. USMC, 1955-59. Mem. Pub. Relations Soc. Am. (bd. dirs. Phoenix chpt. 1979—, pres. 1988), Internat. Assn. Bus. Communicators (pres. Phoenix chpt. 1979-80, dist. v.p., bd. dirs. 1975-77, Gold Quill award 1973). Democrat. Episcopalian. Club: Phoenix City. Office: David O Wiley Assocs Inc 2700 N Central Ave #600 Phoenix AZ 85004

WILEY, DONOVON LINN, banker; b. Oregon City, Oreg., Oct. 20, 1938; s. Donovan Jean and Thelma Maxine (Linn) W.; m. Nancy Leigh White, Aug. 22, 1964; children: Jeffrey Richard, Kristen Linn. B.A. in Econs, U. Calif.-Davis, 1964; M.B.A., Calif. State U.-Long Beach, 1971; grad., Grad. Sch. Credit and Financial Mgmt., Harvard U., 1972, Grad. Sch. Sales Mgmt. and Mktg., Syracuse U., 1978. With First Western Bank & Trust Co., 1964-72; mgr. Santa Ana corp. office, 1969-72; sr. v.p., dir. Kans. State Bank & Trust Co., Wichita, 1972-73; pres. Ahmanson Bank & Trust Co., Beverly Hills, Calif., 1973-74; v.p. corp. banking div. Lloyds Bank Calif., 1974-75, sr. v.p., dir. mktg., dir. planning, 1975-77; regional v.p. Lloyds Bank Calif., No. Calif., 1977-81; exec. v.p. Banking div. Lloyds Bank Calif., Los Angeles, 1981-83; pres., chief exec. officer Am. Nat. Bank, Bakersfield, Calif., 1983—. Chmn. 3d Ann. Wichitennial; bd. dirs. Orange County Heart Assn., Orange County Lung Assn., 1970-72, Calif. Pediatric Center, 1974-78, Los Angeles Central City Assn., 1976-77, mem. com. for new dimensions Calif. Luth. Coll., 1975—; bd. dirs. Bridgemont Found., 1981, Golden Gate Energy Center., Calif. Hosp., 1983, Am. Cancer Soc. Kern County, 1983—. Served with USMC, 1956-60. Named Boss of Year Orange County chpt. Am. Inst. Bankers, 1969-70; Mgr. of Year First Western Bank and Trust Co., 1971. Mem. Robert Morris Assos. Republican. Roman Catholic. Clubs: Rotary, The Family. Office: Am Nat Bank 5016 California Ave Bakersfield CA 93309 *

WILEY, KEITH, physician; b. Springfield, Ohio, Mar. 3, 1949; s. Carl Atwood and Jean Wiley. BS in Biology, U. Calif., Davis, 1971, MA in Biology, 1973; MD, U. Calif., San Francisco, 1977; cert. in internal medicine, SUNY, Syracuse, 1980. Intern SUNY, Syracuse, 1978, resident, 1979-80; practice medicine specializing in emergency medicine R.K. Davies Hosp., San Francisco, 1980-83; practice medicine specializing in internal medicine San Jose, Calif., 1983-85; gen. practice medicine, owner Mariner Med. Ctr., San Mateo, Calif., 1985—. Mem. ACP, Am. Coll. Emergency Physicians, Lions Club. Home: 1247 Moonsail Ln Foster City CA 94404 Office: Mariner Med Ctr 1900 A Arthur Hansen Wy San Mateo CA 94404

WILEY, MARIA ELENA (NENA WILEY), writer; b. Mexico City, June 2, 1947; came to U.S., 1965; d. Mario Hector and Martha Joy Gottfried; m. Michael Bolin Wiley, Dec. 19, 1967; children: Michael, Marta Elena, Cristiana Joy, Samuel. Student, U. Ariz., 1965-67, U. Americas, Mexico City, 1967, Stanford U., 1967; BFA in Graphics, Ariz. State U., 1969; postgrad., No. Calif. State U., Stanislau, 1972-73. Pres. Canapes, SA, Mexico City, 1975-76, Little Eden, SA, Mexico City, 1976-79, Edens Design, Miami, 1983-85; mktg. dir. South Fla. Aviation News, Miami, 1985; owner, v.p. Fla. Aviation News, Miami, 1985-87, editor, owner, 1987. Author mil. novels, 1989—; free-lance photojournalist to major aviation publs.; contbr. aviation news articles on air def. to profl. jours. Bd. dirs. Jr. League, Mexico City, 1972-79, Jr. Women's Club, Miami, 1980-86; active Coral Gables Jr. Women's Club, Miami, 1980-86. PAO/mission pilot Civil Air Patrol USAF, Miami and Phoenix, 1986-88. Mem. Nat. Aero. Assn., Aircraft Owners and Pilots Assn., Air Force Assn., Ariz. Author's Assn., Freedom Coalition of Ariz., Challenger Ctr., Assn. Naval Aviation, Air & Space Assn. Republican. Home and Office: 940 Castillo Dr Litchfield Park AZ 85340

WILEY, MARTHA BURTON, environmental consultant; b. New Haven, Nov. 4, 1953; d. Douglas Walker and Louise Lile (Hickerson) W.; m. Karl Thies, Mar. 13, 1976; children: Mary Ellyson, Elizabeth Stuart. BA in Geography, U. Del., 1975; MA in Geography, San Diego State U., 1978. Environ analyst Westec Svcs., San Diego, 1979-82; mgr. environ. projects Nasland Engring., San Diego, 1982-87; prin. Martha B. Wiley Environ. Cons., San Diego, 1987-89; sr. project mgr. Michael Brandman Assocs., San Diego, 1989—. Contbr. numerous environ. studies to profl. publs. Mem. Assn. Environ. Profls. (cert. of appreciation San Diego chpt. 1987), Am. Planning Assn., San Diego Master Chorale. Methodist. Office: 4918 N Harbor Dr Ste 205 San Diego CA 92106

WILEY, MICHAEL DAVID, chemistry educator; b. Long Beach, Calif., Nov. 28, 1939; s. David Michael and Elsie Louise (Magnuson) W.; m. Mary Alice Kuehne, Dec. 16, 1961 (div. July 1986); children—David Michael, Heather Jane; m. Joan Lilian Battersby, Aug. 23, 1986. B.S. in Chemistry, U. So. Calif., 1961; Ph.D. in Organic Chemistry, U. Wash., 1969. Asst. prof. chemistry Calif. Luth. U., Thousand Oaks, 1968-74, assoc. prof., 1974-84, prof., 1984—; research assoc. U. Liverpool, Eng., 1981. NSF fellow, 1963-64; State of Calif. scholar, 1957-61. Mem. Am. Chem. Soc., Royal Soc. Chemistry, AAUP. Democrat. Lutheran. Office: Calif Luth U 60 Olsen Rd Thousand Oaks CA 91360

WILEY, WILLIAM RODNEY, microbiologist, administrator; b. Oxford, Miss., Sept. 5, 1931; s. William Russell and Edna Alberta (Threlkeld) W.; m. Myrtle Louise Smith, Nov. 10, 1952; 1 child: Johari. B.S., Tougaloo Coll., Miss., 1954; M.S., U. Ill., Urbana, 1960; Ph.D., Wash. State U., Pullman, 1965. Instr. electronics and radar repair Keesler AFB-U.S. Air Force, 1956-58; Rockefeller Found. fellow U. Ill., 1958-59; research assoc. Wash. State U., Pullman, 1960-65; research scientist dept. biology Battelle-Pacific N.W. Labs., 1965-69, mgr. cellular and molecular biology sect. dept. biology, 1969-72, inst. coordinator, life scis. program, assoc. mgr. dept. biology, 1972-74, mgr. dept. biology, 1974-79, dir. research, 1979-84; dir. Pacific N.W. div. Battelle Meml. Inst., Richland, Wash., 1984—; adj. assoc. prof. microbiology Wash. State U., Pullman, 1968—; cons. and lectr. in field. Contbr. chpts. to books, articles to profl. jours. Co-author book in microbiology. Mem. Wash. Tech. Ctr., 1984-88, sci. adv. panel Wash. Tech. Ctr., 1984—; mem. adv. com. U. Wash. Sch. Medicine, 1976-79; trustee Gonzaga U., 1981-89; bd. dirs. MESA program U. Wash., Seattle, 1984—, United Way of Benton & Franklin Counties, Wash., 1984—, Tri-City Indsl. Devel. Council, 1984—; mem. Wash. Council Tech. Advancement, 1984-85 ; bd. dirs. Econ. Devel. Partnership for Wash., 1984—, N.W. Coll. and Univ. Assn. for Sci., 1985—; mem. Tri-City Univ. Ctr. Citizens Adv. Council, 1985—; apptd. Wash. State Higher Edn. Coordinating Bd., 1986-89, Wash. State Found., 1986—; mem. Wash. State U. bd. Regents, 1989—; bd. dirs. Washington Roundtable. Served with U.S. Army, 1954-56. Mem. Am. Soc. Biol. Chemists, Am. Soc. Microbiology, AAAS, Soc. Exptl. Biology and Medicine, Sigma Xi. Office: Battelle Meml Inst Pacific NW Div Battelle Blvd Richland WA 99352

WILHELM, ROBERT OSCAR, lawyer, civil engineer; b. Balt., July 7, 1918; s. Clarence Oscar and Agnes Virginia (Grimm) W.; m. Grace L. Sanborn Luckie, Apr. 4, 1919. B.S. in Civil Engring., Ga. Tech. Inst., 1947, M.S.I.M., 1948; J.D., Stanford U., 1951. Bar: Calif. 1952, U.S. Sup. Ct. Mem. Wilhelm, Thompson, Wentholt and Gibbs, Redwood City, Calif., 1952—; gen. counsel Bay Counties Gen. Contractors; pvt. practice civil engring., Redwood City, 1952—; pres. Bay Counties Builders Escrow, Inc., 1972—. Served with C.E., AUS, 1942-46. Mem. Bay Counties Civil Engrs. (pres. 1957), Peninsula Builders Exchange (pres. 1958-71, dir.), Calif. State Builders Exchange (tres. 1971). Clubs: Mason, Odd Fellows, Eagle, Elks. Author: The Manual of Procedures for the Construction Industry, 1971, Manual of Procedures and Form Book for Construction Industry, 1987; columnist Law and You in Daily Pacific Builder, 1955—; author: Construction Law for Contractors, Architects and Engineers. Home: 463 Raymondo Dr Woodside CA 94062 Office: 600 Allerton Redwood City CA 94063

WILHITE, RICHARD JAMES, media company executive; b. Boston, June 5, 1938; s. Richard Dodge and Mary Mildred (Crum) W.; m. Patricia Norris Ahern, Sept. 7, 1971; 1 child, Jennifer Jamie. AA, Worcester Jr. Coll., 1958; BS, Boston U., 1960; postgrad., U. So. Calif., 1960-62. Dir. community relations Orange & Rockland Utilities, Spring Valley, N.Y., 1964-69; comptroller Video Systems, L.A., 1969-71; pres. Wilhite Prodns., Inc., Malibu, Calif., 1971—. Produced Sorry No Vacancy, 1972. With USCG Aux., 1988-89. Mem. Acad. TV Arts and Scis. Republican. Home and Office: 3742 Seahorn Dr Malibu CA 90265

WILHOIT, JOSEPH WILLIAM, fuel company executive; b. Wickenburg, Ariz., Dec. 2, 1931; s. Francis A. and Christine (Montgomery) W.; m. Theresa Ann Moynahan, June 6, 1953; children: Katherine C., William F. BS in Bus., Ariz. State U., 1953. Pres. Phoenix Fuel Co., Inc., 1946—. Mem. Ariz. Motor Transport Assn. (pres. 1963), Western Oil Marketers Assn. (pres. 1981), Exec. Assn. of Greater Phoenix (dir. 1986). Republican. Office: Phoenix Fuel Co Inc PO Box 6176 Phoenix AZ 85005

WILKENING, JANE SHEPARD, secondary school teacher; b. Jacksonville, N.C., Jan. 24, 1943; d. Percil Henry and Margaret Susan (King) S.; m. Peter Kohler Wilkening, Feb. 12, 1970; children: Brent Colin, Derek Stefan. BA, Atlantic Christian Coll., 1965. Cert. English, mental retarded educator, learning handicapped educator, resource specialist. English tchr. Perry High Sch., Pitts., 1965-67, Northwoods Park Jr. High, Jacksonville, N.C., 1967-68; tchr. of the educable retarded Sun Valley Jr. High, Los Angeles Unified Sch. Dist., 1968-73, reading coordinator, 1973-80; tchr. of educable retarded Sun Valley Jr. High, Los Angeles, 1980—; lectr. ednl. colloquium LAUSD, Calif., 1984, spl. edn. fall conf., LAUSD, Calif., 1985; leader staff devel. programs: needs assessment for spl. edn., Sun Valley, Calif., 1983-85. Contbr. articles to profl. jours. Sec. Laurel Hall Day Sch. Com., North Hollywood, Calif., 1984-87; mem. ch. council Emmanuel Lutheran Ch., 1984-87. Mem. Spl. Educator's Resource Network, Downs Syndrome Parent's Group, Council for Exceptional Children, Computer

Using Educators, NEA, United Tchrs. Los Angeles. Home: 14032 Hartsook St Sherman Oaks CA 91423 Office: Sun Valley Jr High Sch 7330 Bakman Ave Sun Valley CA 91352

WILKENING, LAUREL LYNN, university official, planetary scientist; b. Richland, Wash., Nov. 23, 1944; d. Marvin Hubert and Ruby Alma (Barks) W.; m. Godfrey Theodore Sill, May 18, 1974. BA, Reed Coll., 1966; PhD, U. Calif.-San Diego, 1970. Asst. prof., assoc. prof. U. Ariz., Tucson, 1973-80, dir. Lunar and Planetary Lab., head planetary scis., 1981-83, vice provost, prof. planetary scis., 1983-85, v.p. rsch., dean Grad. Coll., 1985-88; div. scientist NASA Hdqrs., Washington, 1980; prof. geol scis., provost U. Washington, Seattle, 1988—; vice chmn. Nat. Commn. on Space, Washington, 1984-86; co-chmn. primitive bodies mission study team NASA/European Space Agy., 1984-85; chmn. com. rendezvous sci. working group NASA, 1983-85; mem. panel on internat. cooperation and competition in space Congl. Office Tech. Assessment, 1982-83. Author: (monograph) Particle Track Studies and the Origin of Gas-Rich Meteorites, 1971; editor: Comets, 1982. Mem. Ariz. Gov.'s Adv. Com., 1984-86. U. Calif. Regents fellow, 1966-67; NASA trainee, 1967-70. Fellow Meteoritical Soc. (councilor 1976-80), AAUW; mem. Am. Astron. Soc. (chmn. div. planetary scis. 1984-85), Am. Geophys. Union, AAAS, Internat. Astron. Union (orgn. com. 1979-82), Phi Beta Kappa. Democrat. Office: U Wash Office of Provost Seattle WA 98195

WILKES, CHARLES FRED, corporate professional; b. Ripley, Tenn., July 19, 1926; s. Charles Ophir and Isabel Rebecca (Abbott) W.; children: Chas A., Tina W. Gaafary, Carol W. Henn. BS, Memphis State U., 1950. Chief acct. Richmond (Calif.) Schs., 1955-65; mgr. IBM Corp., San Jose, Calif., 1965—; bd. dirs. of various employment credit unions, Calif, Md. Home Owners Assn., San Jose. Author: Japanese Chess, 1952, Chinese Chess, 1955. Sgt. USAF, 1944-46. Fellow Augustan Soc. (awarded 1968). Home: 101 Morrow Ct San Jose CA 95139 Office: IBM Corp 650 Harry Rd San Jose CA 95120

WILKES, DONALD FANCHER, mechanical engineer; b. Portland, Oreg., July 20, 1931; s. Gordon Buell and Catherine Amey (Fancher) W.; m. Joan Adell Petersen, June 27, 1954; children: Martin Carey, Norma Jean, Roger Allen. BSME, Wash. State U., 1954; MSME, U. N.Mex., 1962. Staff rsch. mech. engr. Sandia Corp., Albuquerque, 1954-67; sr. v.p., inventor, engr., dir. rsch. & devel. Foothill Lab Foothill Group, Inc. and predecessor Rolamite, Inc., Albuquerque, 1968-78; mgr., prin. tech. staff mem. Arco Solar Industries subs. Atlantic Richfield, Albuquerque, 1978-81; inventor, mech. engr., owner Albuquerque Mech. Lab, 1982—. Patentee in field. Bd. dirs. Albuquerque Rehab. Ctr., 1986—. With U.S. Army, 1954-56. Recipient Alumni Achievement award Wash. State U., 1987. Mem. ASME, Phi Kappa Phi, Tau Beta Pi, Alpha Phi Omega, Phi Tau Sigma. Republican. Presbyterian. Home: 937 Bobcat Blvd NE Albuquerque NM 87122 Office: Albuquerque Mech Lab 3768 Hawkins NE Albuquerque NM 87109

WILKES, JENNIFER R., interior designer, artist; b. St. Louis, Oct. 13, 1960; d. Philip Henry and Sheila Marlene (Meyer) Ilten; m. Evan T. Wilkes, Sept. 7, 1985. BA cum laude, U. Calif., San Diego, 1983. Designer, sr. ptnr. Wilkes Ltd., L.A., 1985—. Exhbn. design asst. San Diego Mus. Art, 1983. Mem. L.A. County Mus. Art, 1985—. Mem. Palisades Art Assn., Palisades Jr. Women's Club. Democrat. Lutheran. Home: 1594 Palisades Dr Pacific Palisades CA 90272

WILKES, JOHN EDMUND, airline pilot; b. Santa Monica, Calif., Mar. 4, 1949; s. Edmund and Frances (Johnson) W.; m. Linda Dodson, June 8, 1974; 1 child, Ryan Christopher. BA in Geography, UCLA, 1972. Lic. airline transport pilot. Clk. McDonnell Douglas Co., Long Beach, Calif., 1968; agt. Mercury Svc., L.A., 1969-71, Air Cal., Newport, 1973-74; painter Hardin Constrn. Co., Dallas, 1972; pilot Nat. Jet, Newport Beach, Calif., 1980-81, Transco Energy Co., Houston, 1981-84, Orion Air, Raleigh, N.C., 1984-85, N.W. Airlines, Mpls., 1985—. Coach Mission Viejo (Calif.) Little League, 1988. Capt. USMC, 1975-80. Mem. Beta Theta Pi. Republican. Presbyterian. Home: 22321 Oropel St Mission Viejo CA 92691 Office: NW Airlines Inc Mpls/St Paul Internat Airport Saint Paul MN 55111

WILKES, PENNY FERANCE, writer; b. Pasadena, Calif., Aug. 8, 1946; d. Wesley Innis and Margaret (Lewis) Dumm; m. Michael B. Wilkes, June 29, 1968. BA in Anthropology, U. So. Calif., L.A., 1968. Dir. publs. The Bishop's Sch., La Jolla, Calif., 1973-78; editorial coord. Am. Jour. Orthodontics, La Jolla, 1978-84; writer, cons., owner Creative Communications, La Jolla, 1984—. Contbr. to numerous publs. Mem. Calif. Press Women, San Diego Writers and Editors Guild, Nat. League Am. Pen Women (publicist La Jolla chpt. 1988-89, v.p. 1989—), Nat. Carousel Assn. (archivist 1986—). Home and Office: PO Box 2201 La Jolla CA 92038-2201

WILKIE, AL, conservation/recreation organization executive; b. Dallas, Feb. 8, 1938. Student, U. Tex., Arlington, So. Meth. U. Real estate cons. Dallas, 1966—; pres. Dallas Fly Fishers, 1982-83; v.p. membership Fedn. Fly Fishers, Dallas, 1980, pres. So. Council, 1984-87; pres. Fedn. Fly Fishers, West Yellowstone, Mont., 1987—. Bd. dirs. Dallas Civic Opera, 1968-72; past mem. Big Bros. With USAF, 1960-66. Mem. Dal-Tex. Bassett Hound Club (past pres.). Office: Fedn Fly Fishers PO Box 1088 West Yellowstone MT 59758

WILKIE, DONALD WALTER, biologist, aquarium museum director; b. Vancouver, B.C., Can., June 20, 1931; s. Otway James and Jessie Margaret (McLeod) W.; m. Patricia Ann Archer, May 18, 1980; children: Linda, Douglas, Susanne. B.A., U. B.C., 1960, M.Sc., 1966. Curator Vancouver Pub. Aquarium, 1961-63, Phila. Aquarama, 1963-65; dir. aquarium-mus. Scripps Instn. Oceanography, La Jolla, Calif., 1965—; aquatic cons. Author books on aquaria; contbr. numerous articles to profl. jours. Fellow San Diego Mus. Natural History.; mem. Am. Assn. Zoo Parks and Aquariums, Internat. Assn. Aquatic Animal Medicine, Nat. Marine Edn. Assn., Am. Assn. Mus., Am. Soc. Ichthyologists and Herpetologists, San Diego Zool. Soc. (animal health and conservation com.). Club: Miramar Gun (bd. dirs.). Home: 4548 Cather Ave San Diego CA 92122 Office: Scripps Aquarium-Mus Scripps Instn Oceanography 8602 La Jolla Shores Dr La Jolla CA 92093 Mailing: U Calif at San Diego La Jolla CA 92093

WILKIE, MARGERY MICHELLE, banker; b. Longview, Wash., Mar. 15, 1958; d. Alan B. and Marilyn E. (Carlstrom) W.; m. James P. Miller, Aug. 3, 1985; 1 child, Lucas Alan Miller. BS in Econs., Whitman Coll., 1979. Lic. assoc. fin. planner. Nat. bank examiner U.S. Treasury Dept., Great Falls, Mont., 1979-83; loan rev. officer 1st Interstate Bank, Great Falls, 1983-84; asst. v.p., mktg. officer 1st Interstate Bank, 1984-85; asst. v.p., comml. loan officer 1st Interstate Bank, Casper, Wyo., 1985-87; v.p., mktg. mgr. 1st Interstate Bank, 1987—. Founder Leadership Casper, 1987; Casper Image Com., 1987-88; head pub. relations and promotions United Way, Casper, 1988, bd. dirs. 1989—. Named Young Career Woman of Yr., Casper Bus. and Profl. Women's Club, 1988. Democrat. Presbyterian.

WILKIN, SUSAN MARGARET, architect; b. Topeka, Nov. 25, 1955; d. Donald Keith and Ruth Margaret (Warren) W.; William Michael Racek, Apr. 18, 1987. BArch., Kans. State U., 1979. Architect Davis Partnership, Denver, 1979-85; pvt. practice architecture Telluride, Colo., 1985—; cons. SSC Architects, Telluride, 1987—. Mem. Nat. Trust for Hist. Preservation. Democrat.

WILKINS, KAY H., lawyer; b. Eagar, Ariz., June 4, 1940; d. Milford A. and Genevieve (Udall) Hall; m. Phelps W. Wilkins, Sept. 9, 1960; children: Wallace P., Kent. BA, Brigham Young U., 1962; JD, Ariz. State U., 1976. Bar: Ariz. 1976. Corp. counsel Johnson Stewart Johnson, Mesa, Ariz., 1976-81; assoc. Law Offices of Edward Doney, Phoenix, 1981-86; owner Kay H. Wilkins, atty., Mesa, 1986-81; ptnr. Wilkins & Tidd, Mesa, 1986—. Democrat. Office: Wilkins & Tidd 644 E Southern Ave Mesa AZ 85204

WILKINSON, DANIEL FRANCIS, investment counselor; b. Charleston, Ill., Aug. 28, 1940; s. Leonard Quay and Grace Eloise (Whitlock) W.; m. Candace Lee Hughes, Sept. 21, 1971; children: Scott Lee, Todd Curtis, Kyle Cushing, Melissa Bowquay. BS, U. Indpls., 1963; postgrad., N.Y. Inst. Fin., 1981. Cert. fin. planner. Supt. sales Coll./Univ. Corp., Indpls., 1963-70; dir. equity sales Hamilton Funding Corp., Farmington, Mich., 1970-73; v.p. Pioneer Group, Boston, 1973—; pres. Wilkinson Fin. Corp., Phoenix, 1981—; guest lectr. Ariz. State U., Tempe, 1981—; mem. adv. com. Ariz. Securities Div., Phoenix, 1984—. With U.S. Army, 1965-67. Named to Internat. Assocs., Fin. Svc. Corp., Atlanta, 1981, 82, 83, 84. Mem. Inst. Cert. Fin. Planners (regional chmn. 1987-88), Internat. Assn. Fin. Planning (pres. 1980, Mem. of Yr. 1980, registry fin. planning practitioners), Ariz. State Assn. Cert. Fin. Planners (chmn. 1989). Republican. Unitarian. Home: 5539 E Sanna St Paradise Valley AZ 85253 Office: Wilkinson Fin Corp 6991 E Camelback Rd #D 212 Scottsdale AZ 85251

WILKINSON, DAVID LAWRENCE, lawyer; b. Washington, Dec. 6, 1936; s. Ernest LeRoy and Alice Valera (Ludlow) W.; m. Patricia Anne Thomas, Dec. 30, 1976; children: David Andrew, Samuel Thomas, Margaret Alice, Katherine Anne. B.A. cum laude in History, Brigham Young U., 1961; B.A. in Jurisprudence, Oxford U., Eng., 1964, M.A., 1969; J.D., U. Calif.-Berkeley, 1966. Bar: Calif. 1966, Utah 1972. Assoc. Lawler, Felix & Hall, Los Angeles, 1966-71; ptnr. Cook & Wilkinson, Los Angeles, 1971-72; asst. atty. gen. State of Utah, Salt Lake City, 1972-76, 77-79; chief dep. to Salt Lake County Atty., 1979-80; atty. gen. State of Utah, Salt Lake City, 1981-89; spl. instr. Brigham Young U. Sch. Law, 1976-77, bd. visitors Sch. of Law, 1983-85; panelist Robert A. Taft Inst. Of Govt., Salt Lake City, 1974-76, 83-84; founder, mgr. Utah Bar. Rev. Course, 1973-76. Mem. Utah Council Criminal Justice Adminstrn., 1974-76, 77, Council Criminal and Juvenile Justice, 1984-89. Served with U.S. Army, 1961-62. Rhodes scholar, 1961-64. Mem. Utah Bar Assn. (chmn. eminent domain sect. 1979-80). Republican. Mormon.

WILKINSON, JOHN TAYLOR, dentist; b. N.Y.C., May 16, 1955; s. Herbert and Dorothy W.; m. Donna Risa Maxwell, Apr. 26, 1980; children: Ashley Alaina, Lindsay Michelle. BS, Brigham Young U., 1980; DDS, UCLA, 1984; MS in Dentistry, U. Wash., 1986. Pvt. practice, San Jose, Calif., 1986—. Mem. ADA, Calif. Soc. Orthodontists, Pacific Coast Soc. Orthodontists, Santa Clara County Dental Soc. (asst. editor), Calif. Dental Assn., Am. Assn. Orthodontist, San Jose City Coll. Dental Assisting Program (adv. bd.). Office: 3535 Ross Ave #305 San Jose CA 95124

WILKINSON, TEDD ROBERT, accountant; b. Salem, Apr. 2, 1956; s. Eugene Foster and Jeanette (Brown) W.; m. Linda Lee Corbin, Mar. 18, 1978; children: Eric Robert, Kelly Marie. BS in Biology, Oreg. Coll. Edn., 1978; M in Mgmt., Willamette U., 1983. Mem. systems engring. devel. program Electronic Data Systems Corp., Detroit, 1984, fin. analyst, 1984-86, sr. fin. analyst, 1985-87; acct. Litton Guidance and Control Systems div. Litton Industries, Grants Pass, Oreg., 1988—, quality circle leader, 1988-89. Ch. sch. tchr. Newman United Meth. Ch., Grants Pass, 1988—; mem. Grants Pass PTA, 1988—. Mem. Litton Mgmt. Club. Republican. Home: 1340 Ojai Ave Grants Pass OR 97527 Office: Litton Guidance & Control Controllers Office 1001 Redwood Hwy Spur Grants Pass OR 97526

WILL, TIMOTHY JOSEPH, military officer; b. Poughkeepsie, N.Y., July 18, 1960; s. Joseph John and Patricia Ann (Smith) W.; m. Kelly Kathleen Cooper, June 9, 1989. BS in Biology, USAF Acad., 1982. Commd. lt. USAF, 1982, advanced through grades to capt., 1986; biologist Bird/Aircraft Strike Hazard Team, Panama City, Fla., 1982-86; orbital analyst Space Surveillance Ctr., Cheyenne Mountain Complex, Colorado Springs, Colo., 1986-87; orbital analyst instr. Air Force Space Command, 1013th Combat Crew Tng. Squadron, Colorado Springs, 1987—. Republican. Lutheran. Office: 1013th Combat Crew Tng Squadron Peterson AFB CO 80914

WILLARD, H(ARRISON) ROBERT, electrical engineer; b. Seattle, May 31, 1933; s. Harrison Eugene and Florence Linea (Chelquist) W.; B.S.E.E., U. Wash., 1955, M.S.E.E., 1957, Ph.D., 1971. Staff asso. Boeing Sci. Research Labs., Seattle, 1959-64; research asso. U. Wash., 1968-72, sr. engr. and research prof. applied physics lab., 1972-81; sr. engr. Boeing Aerospace Co., Seattle, 1981-84; dir. instrumentation and engring. MetriCor Inc. (previously Tech. Dynamics, Inc.), 1984—. Served with AUS, 1957-59. Lic. profl. engr., Wash. Mem. IEEE, Am. Geophys. Union, Phi Beta Kappa, Sigma Xi, Tau Beta Pi. Contbr. articles to tech. jours. Patentee in field. Office: 18800 142d Ave NE Ste 4 Woodinville WA 98072

WILLARD, JAMES DOUGLAS, healthcare administrator; b. St. Edward, Nebr., Aug. 13, 1945; s. Merrell and Eloise Vanell (Andreasen) W.; m. Sylvia Lawrence, Jan. 2, 1970; children: James Christopher, Elizabeth. B.S., Colo. State U., 1967; M.H.A., U. Minn., 1972. Asst. adminstr. People to People Health Found (HOPE), Washington, 1968-70; assoc. dir. Comprehensive Health Plan Agy., Worcester, Mass., 1973-74; v.p., adminstr. Luth. Med. Ctr., Wheat Ridge, Colo., 1974-80, exec. v.p., 1980-82, pres., 1982—, chief exec. officer, 1984—, also dir.; dir. Hosp. Shared Services, Denver, 1981-85; dir., treas. InterHealth, 1985—, dir. Lutheran Hosp. Assn. Am., 1986—; clin. faculty mem. U. Minn. Health Service Adminstrn. Mem. Met. Denver Hosp. Council, past pres.; bd. dirs. Met. Denver Provider Network Medically Indigent, MetroNet. Mem. Am. Hosp. Assn. (del. region 8 policy bd. 1988—, met. sect. council 1988—, council mem. sect. for met. hosps. governing bd.), Colo. Hosp. Assn. (bd. dirs. 1986—, med. indigent com.), Denver C. of C. (leadership roundtable). Mem. United Ch. of Christ. Club: Rotary of Denver. Home: 10888 W 30th Pl Lakewood CO 80215 Office: Luth Med Ctr 8300 W 38th Ave Wheat Ridge CO 80033

WILLARD, RUTH HENDRICKS, public historian, writer; b. Portland, Oreg., May 13, 1921; d. Leland Laumann and Lillian May (Harrison-Anderson) Hendricks; m. Orris Wilson Willand, Dec. 11, 1942; children: Patricia Lee Hendricks Leicher, Gayle Joan Willard Higaki. Jr. cert., Oreg. State U., 1942; BA in History and Mus. Studies summa cum laude, San Francisco State U., 1981. Asst. buyer, buyer I Magnin & Co., San Francisco, 1944-49; exhbn. cons. Macys Calif., San Francisco, 1979-80; intern Calif. Council for Humanities, San Francisco, 1981; resource specialist Sta. KPBS-TV, San Diego, 1981-85; reseach assoc. Oral History Assocs., San Francisco, 1983; editor, mem. coordinating com. Women in Hist. Profession, Manhattan, Kans., 1985—; writer Windsor Press, Northridge, Calif., 1986—; cataloger Nat. Maritime Mus. Library, 1979; community cons., guest lectr. classical archaeology, history and humanities depts. San Francisco State U., 1980—, also exhbn. curator art gallery; exhbn. curator Temple Emanu-El, San Francisco, Grad. Theol. Union, Berkeley, Calif., Kaiser Ctr., Oakland, Calif.; lectr. San Francisco Hist. Assn., various service clubs, 1985—. Author: The White House: Treasury of Our Heritage, 1980; co-author: Sacred Places of San Francisco, 1985; contbr. articles and book revs. to various publs. Troop and camp leader San Francisco council Girl Scouts U.S.A., 1956-62; health career tour leader Mt. Zion Hosp., San Francisco, 1962-67; vol. hostess driver San Francisco Internat. Hospitality Ctr., 1960-70. Recipient award San Diego chpt. Nat. Acad. TV Arts and Scis., 1985; United Calif. Bank grantee, 1980, L.J. Skaggs. and Mary C. Skaggs. Found. grantee, 1986. Mem. Coordinating Com. on Women in Hist. Profession (editor newsletter 1985—), Inst. for Hist. Study (workshop participant), Authors Guild, Western Assn. Women Historians (conf. participant), Coalition for Western Women's History (conf. participant), Am. Hist. Assn., Orgn. Am. Historians, Calif. Humanities Assn. Republican. Presbyterian. Home: PO Box 27565 San Francisco CA 94127

WILLBANKS, ROGER PAUL, publishing and book distributing company executive; b. Denver, Nov. 25, 1934; s. Edward James and Ada Gladys (Davis) W.; m. Beverly Rae Masters, June 16, 1957; children—Wendy Lee, Roger Craig. B.S., U. Denver, 1957, M.B.A., 1965. Economist, bus. writer, bus. forecaster Mountain States Telephone Co., Denver, 1959-66; dir. pub. relations Denver Bd. Water Commrs., 1967-70; pres. Royal Publs. Inc., Denver, 1971—, Nutri-Books Corp., Denver, 1971—, Inter-Sports Book and Video, 1986—. Editor Denver Water News, 1967-70, Mountain States Bus., 1962-66. Mem. Gov. of Colo.'s Revenue Forecasting Com., 1963-66. Served with U.S. Army, 1957-58. Recipient pub. relations award Am. Water Works Assn., 1970. Mem. Am. Booksellers Assn., Nat. Nutritional Foods Assn., Pub. Relations Soc. Am. (charter mem. health sect.), Denver C. of C., SAR. Republican. Lutheran. Clubs: Columbine Country, Denver Press, Auburn Cord Duesenberg, Rolls Royce Owners, Classic Car of Am., Denver U. Century (Denver). Address: Royal Publs Inc PO Box 5793 Denver CO 80217

WILLEMS, ARNOLD LEE, curriculum and instruction educator; b. Millersburg, Ohio, Sept. 16, 1942; s. Abraham Lincoln and Ruth (Miller) W; m. Wanda Lucille Mast, June 5, 1964; children: Emily Marie, David Arnold. BA, Goshen Coll., 1964; MA, Western Mich. U., 1968; EdD, Ind. U., 1971. Elem. tchr. Goshen (Ind.) Community Schs., 1964-69; from. asst. prof. to prof. curriculum and instruction U. Wyo., Laramie, 1971—, head dept. curriculum and instruction, 1983-85, asst. dean Coll. Edn., 1984-87; cons. pub. schs. and profl. orgns. Co-author textbook Living Wyoming's Past, 1983; editor (books) Elementary Music Theory: Curriculum Ideas and Guides for Teachers, 1978, Peopling the High Plains-Wyoming's European Heritage: Curriculum Ideas and Guides for Teachers, 1977, India Seminar: Primary Curriculum Unit, 1974, India Seminar: Intermediate Curriculum Unit, 1974. Recipient Merit award for edn. leadership Project Innovation, Chula Vista, Calif., 1985; Sch. Edn. fellow Ind. U., 1970-71. Mem. Assn. for Supervision and Curriculum Devel., Assn. Tchr. Educators, Internat. Reading Assn., Nat. Coun. Tchrs. of English, Phi Delta Kappa (rsch. dir. 1986-88, Rsch. award 1986), Kappa Delta Pi. Democrat. Presbyterian. Home: 5517 Bill Nye Laramie WY 82070 Office: U Wyo McWhinnie Hall Rm 316 Laramie WY 82071

WILLENS, SHERWIN, bank executive; b. Chgo., Aug. 25, 1925; s. Harry and Sarah (Leibovitz) W.; m. Merle Levitt; children: Jill Rachel, Debra Sue, Eric Alan. BS, Roosevelt U., 1948; JD, Northwestern U., 1951. Bar: Ill. 1951. Ptnr. Hoellen & Willens, Chgo., 1954-69; sole practice Chgo., 1969-74; chmn., pres., chief exec. officer North Community Bank, Chgo., 1974-79, Edens State Bank, Wilmette, Ill., 1978-83, Bank of the North Shore, Northbrook, Ill., 1981-87, Columbia Bank, Avondale, Ariz., 1987—. Mem. Rep. Com., Niles Twp., Ill., 1962-66; pres. Niles Twp. Jewish Congregation, Skokie, Ill., 1967-68. Served as cpl. USAF, 1943-46. Office: Columbia Bank 11 W Van Buren Avondale AZ 85323

WILLEY, CHRISTOPHER STEPHEN, lazer graphics specialist; b. Phoenix, June 13, 1969; s. Earl Charles and DeLois (Rea) W. V.p. Willey Enterprises, Inc., Phoenix, 1986-87; publisher, editor-in-chief AmiTak Magazine, Phoenix, 1986-87; mgr., electronic publishing dept. Health Econs. Corp., Dallas, 1987-88; cons. Shank, Irwin, Conant, Lipshy and Casterline, Dallas, 1988; mgr. lazer graphics dept. Alphagraphics Printshop of the Future, Phoenix, 1988—. Home: 4502 E Paradise Village Pkwy Apt #1025 Phoenix AZ 85032 Office: Alphagraphics Printshop of the Future 4657 E Cactus Rd Phoenix AZ 85032

WILLI, JIM HENRY, television news director; b. Green Bay, Wis., Mar. 30, 1948; s. John Hubert and Jane (Peters) W.; m. Sherylin Anne Kath, Oct. 10, 1970; children: Zachary James, Joshua James. BS, U. Wis., River Falls, 1970. News/program dir. Sta. WEVR-AM-FM, River Falls, 1968-70; news dir. Sta. WXCO-AM, Wausau, Wis., 1970-71, Sta. WDUZ-AM-FM, Green Bay, Wis., 1971-75; reporter, producer Sta. WLUK-TV, Green Bay, 1975-78, asst. news dir., 1978-80; news dirs. Sta. WGR-TV, Buffalo, 1980-83; news dirs. Sta. KPNX-TV, Phoenix, 1983-87, v.p. news, 1988-89; sr. account exec. Audience Rsch. and Devel., Dallas, 1989—; instr. journalism SUNY, Buffalo, 1982. Mem. Medaille Coll. Adv. Bd., Buffalo, 1981-83, Maricopa Couty Law/Media Com., Phoenix, 1986—. Recipient 2 Emmy awards NATAS Rocky Mountain chpt., Phoenix, 1986. Mem. Radio-TV News Dirs. Assn. (Edward R. Murrow award 1988), Ariz. Press Club, Sigma Delta Chi Soc. Profl. Journalists (mem. exec. bd. 1987—). Roman Catholic. Home: 5334 W Paradise Ln Glendale AZ 85306

WILLIAMS, ALBERT PAINE, economist; b. Elgin, Tex., Mar. 5, 1935; s. Albert Paine and Mary Dempes (Hudler) W.; m. Elizabeth Ann Whitaker, June 22, 1957; children: Albert, Robert, John. B.S., U.S. Naval Acad., 1957; M.A., Fletcher Sch., Tufts U., 1963; M.A.L.D., Tufts U., 1964, Ph.D., 1967. Budget examiner, internat. economist Bur. Budget, Washington, 1965-67; adv. on fgn. assistance strategy and econ. policy White House Staff, Washington, 1967-68; economist RAND Corp., Santa Monica, Calif., 1968-72, sr. economist, 1972—, dir. health scis. program, 1976—; dir. RAND/UCLA Ctr. for Health Policy Study, 1982—; prof. RAND Grad. Inst., 1971—, mem. adv. bd., 1975—. Scoutmaster Great Western coun. Boy Scouts Am., 1971-78, 82-88. With USN, 1957-62. Recipient Profl. Achievement award Exec. Office of Pres., 1967. Mem. AAAS, Am. Econ. Assn., Assn. Pub. Policy Analysis and Mgmt., Assn. for Health Svcs. Rsch., Sierra Club. Unitarian. Home: 508 12th St Santa Monica CA 90402 Office: 1700 Main St Santa Monica CA 90406

WILLIAMS, ALLIE FAYE, teacher; b. Lisbon, La., Nov. 27, 1944; d. Marvin and Adell (Mack) Reed; 1 child, Edyth V. BS in Speech, Drama and Social Studies, Grambling U., 1968; MA, U. Colo., 1976. Tchr. Denver Pub. Schs., 1968-75, library media specialist, 1976—; tchr. Shakespeare Festival, Denver, 1987-88; judge Odyssey of the Mind, Denver and Aurora, Colo., 1987-88. Presenter Nat. Mid. Sch. Assn. 15th Ann. Conf., 1988. Mem. Denver Classroom Tchrs. Assn., Denver Tchrs. Club. Democrat. Roman Catholic. Club: BPW. Home: 17976 E Berry Ave Aurora CO 80015 Office: Denver Pub Schs 4050 E 14th Denver CO 80022

WILLIAMS, ANGELA ANDERSON, health care administrator; b. Columbus, Ga., Aug. 12, 1956; d. Homer C. and Bernice Willene (Davis) Anderson; m. Charles Arthur Williams, June 3, 1978; children: Kimberly Faith, Angela Renee. AA in Nursing, Columbus Coll., Ga., 1977, BS in Health Sci., 1978; MS in Health Sci. Adminstrn., Jersey City State Coll., Ga., 1986; postgrad., SUNY-Albany, Ga., 1986—. RN. Nursing supr. Stewart Webster Hosp., Richland, Ga., 1978; therapist St. Peters' Hosp., Olympia, Wash., 1979-80; anesthesia asst. St. Peter's Hosp., Olympia, Wash., 1980-82; head nurse Nutri-System Weight Loss Clinic, Columbus, Ga., 1980-82; staff nurse Vet.'s Med. Ctr., East Orange, N.J., 1984-85; asst. adminstr. North Jersey Community Union Health Ctr., Newark, N.J., 1985-86; program dir. Optifast Program, Charter North Hosp., Anchorage, Alaska, 1987-88; asst. adminstr. Charter Winds Hosp., Athens, Ga., 1988—. Tchr. Sunday Sch., Army Chapel, Bayonne, 1985-86. Mem. Am. Pub. Health Assn., Nat. Assn. Female Execs., Officer's Wives Club, ARC, N.J. Pub. Health Assn. Lodges: Internat Order Rainbow (Columbus), Order Eastern Star. Home: 145 Avalon Dr Athens GA 30606

WILLIAMS, ANTHONY LEROY, computer aided design engineer; b. Frankfurt, Fed. Republic Germany, May 1, 1963; (parents Am. citizens); s. Finis Thomas and Shirley Elizabeth (Nelson) W.; m. Valynne Falicia Boyd, June 25, 1988. BA in Indsl. Tech., San Francisco State U., 1986. Draftsman Kaiser Electronics Co., San Jose, Calif., 1986-87; CAD designer Fairchild Weston Systems Inc., Milpitas, Calif., 1987—. Mem. Epsilon Pi Tau. Democrat. Office: Fairchild Weston Systems 1801 McCarthy Blvd Milpitas CA 95035

WILLIAMS, ARTHUR CHAVIS, mechanical engineer; b. Ottawa, Ont., Can., June 13, 1930; came to U.S., 1936; s. Ernest Richie and Jane Gladys (Smallwood) W.; m. Patricia Ann Backus, Aug. 25, 1956 (div. July 1976); children: Colleen D., Michael A., Allison M., Jennifer K.; m. Eula Chavis, Aug. 19, 1979. BME, U. Santa Clara, 1958; MEng, U. Calif., Berkeley, 1969. Registered profl. engr., Calif. Mech. engr. Lawrence Radiation Lab., Lawrence Livermore (Calif.) Lab., 1958-70; mech. engr. energy systems div. EG&G, Inc., Sam Ramon, Calif., 1970-78; mgr. mech. engring. dept. EG&G, Inc., Morgantown, W.Va., 1978-83; mech. engr., project mgr. Lawrence Livermore Nat. Lab., 1983—; owner, mgr. DEFT engring. cons., Tracy, Calif., 1984—; acting chief engr. DBI, product rsch., San Leandro, Calif., 1987—, trustee 1988—. With USN, 1950-54. Republican. Home: 75 Yosemite Dr Tracy CA 95376 Office: Lawrence Livermore Nat Lab PO Box 5508 Livermore CA 94550

WILLIAMS, BEN ALBERT, state official; b. San Diego, Dec. 14, 1946; s. Ben Albert and Frances Elizabeth (Arnold) W.; m. Gloria Jean Dieken, Sept. 25, 1976; children: Megan Ann, Alec Benjamin. BSBA, San Diego State U., 1969; MPA, Calif. State U., 1977. Budget and econ. analyst Calif. Dept. Indsl. Rels., San Francisco, 1973-76; administrv. officer Calif. Coastal Commn., San Francisco, 1976-79; dep. dir. adminstrn. Calif. Gov.'s Office Planning and Rsch., Sacramento, 1979—, interim dir., 1988—; mem. Calif. Commn. on State Mandates, 1988. Contr. articles to profl. publs. Mem. adv. com. office automation project Lincoln Tng. Ctr.-CETA, Sacramento, Calif. 1986. With U.S. Army, 1969-71, Vietnam. Mem. Am. Soc. for Pub. Administrn. (treas. Sacramento chpt. 1984-86, coun., 1987-88, pres. 1988—), Calif. Forum on Info. Tech. (exec. com. 1986-88). Presbyterian. Office: Govs Office Planning and Rsch 1400 10th St Sacramento CA 95814

WILLIAMS, BEVERLY BEATRICE, elementary school teacher; b. El Nido, Calif., Mar. 30, 1932; d. James and Beatrice Idaho (Haskins) Buchholz; m. Harvey Donald Williams, Dec. 5, 1953; children: Eileen Celeste, Corinne Beth, Kevin Keoki. BS, U. Calif., 1953. Tchr. TIVY Union Elem. Sch., Sanger, Calif., 1959-61, Armona (Calif.) Union Elem. Sch., 1963-64, Trust Ter. of The Pacific, Tinian and Saipan, 1964-66, Hawaii Dept. of Edn., Wailuka, Paia and Kula, 1966—; grade level chmn. Iao Sch., 1970-71, 1973-74, 1978-79, 1985-87; chmn. lang. arts dept., 1980-81. Precinct vice chmn. Dem. Party, Kahului, Hawaii, 1986-88; state conv. del. Dem. party, Kahului, 1982, 84, 86; mem. PTA, PTSA, Wailuku, 1977-78, 1985—. Mem. Hawaii State Tchrs. Assn. (faculty rep. 1987-88), Hawaii Fedn. Bus. and Profl. Women, Inc. (state pres. 1985-86). Home: 605 S Oahu Kahului HI 96732 Office: Iao Intermediate Sch 1910 Kaohu Wailuku HI 96793

WILLIAMS, C. BASIL, cardiologist; b. Salt Lake City, Mar. 29, 1931; s. Carroll B. and Gurtha (Petersen) W.; m. Stephanie Rich, Aug. 24, 1954; children—Deborah, Barton, Megan, Raquel, Rebecca, Melissa. B.S., U. Utah, 1953, M.D., 1956. Fellow in cardiology, resident in medicine U. Utah, 1956-58, 59-61, Boston City Hosp., 1958-59; cardiologist Ogden Clinic, Utah, 1961—. Fellow ACP, Am. Coll. Cardiology; mem. Utah Heart Assn. (pres. 1968), Utah Soc. Internal Medicine (pres. 1969), Phi Beta Kappa, Alpha Omega Alpha. Mormon. Office: Ogden Clinic 4650 Harrison Ogden UT 84403

WILLIAMS, DAVID L., title insurance company executive; b. Prineville, Oreg., Apr. 5, 1950; s. John Lawrence and Dorothy (Payton) W.; m. Cherie L. Ballou, Nov. 7, 1986; 1 child, K. Eric. BS in Psychology, Oreg. Coll. Edn., 1973, postgrad., 1973-75. Mgr., asst. sec. Transamerica Title Ins. Co., Dallas, Oreg., 1973-77; home bldr., real estate sales Salem, Oreg., 1977-80; v.p., mgr. Willamette Valley Title Ins. Co., Coos Bay, Oreg., 1980—; lectr. in field. Councilor City of Coos Bay City Council, 1988—; chmn. Waterfront Devel. Com., Empire Community Assn., Coos Bay, 1988. Mem. Bay Area C. of C., Am. Land Title Assn., Oreg. Land Title Assn., Coos County Bd. Realtors, Music Enrichment Assn., Southwestern Oreg. Youth Assn., Coos Country Club. Republican. Home: 1135 Lakewood Ln Coos Bay OR 97420 Office: Willamette Valley Title 454 Commercial St Coos Bay OR 97420

WILLIAMS, DAVID WELFORD, U.S. district judge; b. Atlanta, Mar. 20, 1910; s. William W. and Maude (Lee) W.; m. Ouida Maie White, June 11, 1939; children: David Welford, Vaughn Charles. A.A., Los Angeles Jr. Coll., 1932; A.B., UCLA, 1934; LL.B., U. So. Calif., 1937. Bar: Calif. 1937. Practiced in Los Angeles, 1937-55; judge Mcpl. Ct., Los Angeles, 1956-62, Superior Ct., Los Angeles, 1962-69, U.S. Dist. Ct., Central Dist. Calif., Los Angeles, 1969—; now sr. judge U.S. Dist. Ct., Central Dist. Calif.; judge Los Angeles County Grand Jury, 1965. Recipient Russwurm award Nat. Assn. Newspapers, 1958; Profl. Achievement award UCLA Alumni Assn., 1966. Mem. ABA, Los Angeles Bar Assn., Am. Judicature Soc. Office: US Dist Ct 312 N Spring St Los Angeles CA 90012

WILLIAMS, DEREK WILLIAM, JR., surgical counselor; b. Ft. Rucker, Ala., June 25, 1958; s. Derek W. and Carol (Kaufman) W. BA in Psychology, U. Colo., 1984, postgrad., 1988—; MA in Psychology, U. Nev., 1986. Mktg. asst. Feyline Presents, Inc., Denver, 1979-81; surg. asst. St. Luke's Hosp., Denver, 1981-83; asst. mgr. Sparks Lodge Hotel/Casino, Reno, 1983-85; rsch. asst., then asst. counselor U. Nev., Reno, 1984-86; surg. counselor St. Luke's Hosp., Denver, 1987—; cons., AMI Health Care Rocky Mountain, Denver, 1987—. Contbr. articles to profl. publs. Vol., Dumb Friends League animal shelter, Denver, 1982—, Rep. campaigns, Denver, 1984—. Mem. NRA, MBA Execs., Am. Psychol. Assn., U.S. Naval Inst., Ducks Unlimited. Home: 3150 A Tamarac Dr Denver CO 80231

WILLIAMS, DIANE RENEE, marketing executive; b. Mpls., Mar. 19, 1950; d. Andrew Albert Habedank and Lucille Eileen (Minette) Olsen; m. Charles William Williams, Oct. 9, 1976. BA, DePaul U., 1981. With promotion dept. Star Publs., Chicago Heights, Ill., 1978-79, mgr. coop. advt., 1979-81; dir. mktg. Star Pubs., Chicago Heights, Ill., 1981-86, bd. dirs.; pres., owner C.A.S. Interiors Inc., Indian Wells, Calif., 1989—. Bd. dirs. Ill. Philharm., Park Forest, Ill., 1986—, Bethel Community Facility, Chicago Heights, 1985—, Chicago Heights Salvation Army, 1984-86. Recipient Humanitarian award Gavin Found., 1986. Mem. Internat. Newspaper Promotion Assn., Am. Mktg. Assn., Suburban Newspapers Am. (bd. dirs. 1986—), Oak Forest C. of C. (pres. 1985-86). Republican.

WILLIAMS, DONALD SPENCER, scientist; b. Pasadena, Calif., May 28, 1939; s. Charles Gardner and Delia Ruth (Spencer) W. BS, Harvey Mudd Coll., 1961; MS, Carnegie Inst. Tech., 1962; PhD, Carnegie-Mellon U., 1969. Asst. project dir. Learning Rsch. & Devel. Ctr., Pitts., 1965-67; cons. system design, Pitts., 1967-69; mem. tech. staff RCA Corp., Palo Alto, Calif., 1969-72; prin. investigator robot vision Jet Propulsion Lab., Calif. Inst. Tech., Pasadena, 1972-80; chief oper. engr. TRW, Inc., Redondo Beach, 1980—; cons. system design, 1984—. Japan Econ. Found. grantee, 1981. Mem. AAAS, Assn. Computing Machinery, Audio Engring. Soc., Nat. Fire Protection Assn., IEEE, Soc. Motion Picture & TV Engrs., Town Hall Calif. Contbr. articles to profl. jours. Home: 1210 N Allen Ave Pasadena CA 91104 Office: 1 Space Park Rd Redondo Beach CA 90278

WILLIAMS, DOUGLAS, management consultant; b. Newburgh, N.Y., Oct. 13, 1912; s. Everett Frank and Marjorie Tuthill W.; m. Esther Grant, Sept. 23, 1939; children: Penelope Williams Winters, Grant. AB, Cornell U., 1934; MBA, Harvard U., 1936. With Air Reduction Co., 1936-37, Am. Inst. Pub. Opinion, 1938, Elmo Roper Co., 1939-40; assoc. dir. Nat. Opinion Research Ctr., U. Denver, 1940-42; pres. Douglas Williams Assos., Carefree, Ariz. and N.Y.C., 1948—. Pres. Community Chest, Larchmont, N.Y., 1959; bd. mgrs. West Side YMCA, N.Y.C., 1957-60; mem. nat. adv. bd. Heard Mus.; mem. Ariz. State U. Council of 100, Ariz. State U. Council of Emeritus Advisers, Foothills Com. Adv. Council. Served to lt. col. U.S. Army, 1942-45. Republican. Episcopalian. Clubs: Larchmont Yacht, Desert Mountain, Garden of the Gods, Harvard, Union League, Cornell, Winged Foot Golf, Desert Forest Golf, Ariz. Home: 7612 E Horizon Dr PO Box 941 Carefree AZ 85377 Office: Exec Ctr PO Box 941 Carefree AZ 85377

WILLIAMS, DOUGLAS ALLAN, household products company executive; b. Elgin, Ill., Dec. 17, 1938; s. Robert Orren and Margaret (Perry) W.; m. Barbara Annette Brown,. BA, Beloit Coll., 1960. Mgr. tech. suppport CNA Ins., Chgo., 1969-75; regional mgr. computer audit Coopers & Lybrand, San Francisco, 1976-82; audit mgr. Sohio Petroleum, San Francisco, 1982-83; mgr. fin. systems The Clorox Co., Oakland, Calif., 1983—; cons. in field. Bd. dirs. Berkeley Schs. Computer adv. Council, 1981—. Mem. EDP Auditors Assn. (pres. 1984-85), Assn. for Systems Mgmt. Episcopalian. Home: 174 Glorietta Blvd Orinda CA 94563 Office: The Clorox Co 1221 Broadway Oakland CA 94612

WILLIAMS, EARL DUANE, accounting executive; b. Hiwasse, Ark., Mar. 2, 1929; s. James Martin and Goldie Faye (Reeves) W.; m. Dorothy Jean Rasner, May 3, 1952; children: Earl Duane, Ronald Lee. BS, San Jose State U.; LLB, U. Chgo.; MBA, U. Calif. Acctg. mgr. Philco Ford, Palo Alto, Calif., 1966-69; instr. acctg. Foothill and Deanza Coll., Cupertino, Calif., 1967-69; controller, treas. Bekins Maintenance, Los Angeles, 1969-70; chief acct. Title Ins. & Trust Co., Los Angeles, 1970-72; controller Continental Devel. Co., El Segundo, Calif., 1972-76; v.p. fin. Computer Infomatrix, Inc., Los Angeles, 1976-77; pres. Nationwide Acctg. Svc., Woodland Hills, Calif., 1977—; instr. acctg. Calif. Credential C.P.A.'s. Chmn. Liaison League Rehab. Group, 1973—; co-chmn. Re-election of Judge Sanches;com. mem. to re-elect Sen. Ed Davis; mem. com. re-election of Los Angeles County Sheriff; mem. West Hills Property Owners Assn. (bd. dirs.); mem. Los Angeles Philanthropic Found. Served with USAF, 1951-55. Recipient Cert. of Appreciation Vikings of Scandia, 1975, 76, 77, 78-87, Boy Scouts. Am., 1967. Mem. Nat. Assn. Accts., Controllers Assn., Internat. Footprint Assn. , Internat. Chili Soc., Nat. Soc. Pub. Accts., Calif. Assn. Ind. Accts., Nat. Soc. Tax Profls., Nat. Tax. Certificatio Bd., Navy League (life), Gold Pennant Gourmet (pres.), Woodland Hills C. of C., Masons (32nd degree), Elks, Friars, L.A. Club, Hollywood Press Club, Greater L.A. Press Club, Vikings of Scandia Club (chief 1984), Silver Dollar Club, Masquers Club, Town Hall Club, Shriners, Am. Legion, VFW. Republican. Home: 23427 Strathern St West Hills CA 91304

WILLIAMS, EILEEN NAOMI, teacher; b. Maui, Hawaii, June 8, 1944; d. Katsumi and Alice Sadame (Hongo) Sakata; m. Mark Doraign Williams, Jan 17, 1943; children: James, Tammy. BS, Western Oreg. State Coll., 1966, MEd, 1969. Cert. tchr., Oreg. Tchr. elem. grades Salem (Oreg.) Pub. Schs., 1965-66, Silverton (Oreg.) Pub. Schs., 1968—, Cen. Sch. Dist., Monmouth, Oreg., 1970-75; rsch. instr. Oreg. State System Higher Edn., Monmouth, 1966-68. Mem. NEA, Oreg. Edn. Assn., Silverton Edn. Assn., Silverton Hosp. Aux., Silverton Hist. Soc., Beta Sigma Pi. Democrat. Lutheran. Office: Eugene Field Sch 421 N Water St Silverton OR 97381

WILLIAMS, FELTON CARL, college administrator; b. L.A., Mar. 30, 1946; s. Abraham and Lula Mae (Johnson) W.; m. Maryetta Baldwin, july 3, 1966; children: Sonia Yvette, Felton Jr. AA, L.A. Harbor Coll., Wilmington, Calif., 1970; BA, Calif. State U., Long Beach, 1972, MBA, 1975; PhD, Claremont Grad. Sch., 1985. Jr. staff analyst Calif. State U., Long Beach, 1972-73, adminstrv. asst., 1973-74, supr., 1974-79; coord. Calif. State U. Dominguez Hills, Carson, Calif., 1979-84; asst. to pres. Calif. State U. Dominguez Hills, Carson, 1984-85, acting dir. learning assistance ctr., 1985—; cons. U. So. Calif. Physician's Asst., L.A., 1983—, physician's asst. program Drew Med. Sch. Martin Luther King Hosp., Calif., 1981—; bd. dirs. Employee Readiness Support Svcs., Carson. Pres. San Pedro/Wilmington NAACP, San Pedro, Calif., 1974—, So. Area Cons. NAACP, L.A., 1979-80; chmn. region I, NAACP, San Francisco, 1979-80. With U.S. Army, 1966-68. Named Outstanding Young Man Am., U.S. Jaycees, 1977, in resolution-community contributions Calif. State Assembly, 1980; recipient cert. appreciation women's div. San Pedro C. of C., 1980. Mem. Western Coll. Reading/Learning Assn., Nat. Assn. for Devel. Edn., Am. Mgmt. Assn., Pi Lambda Theta. Home: 2126 Daisy Ave Long Beach CA 90806 Office: Calif State U Dominguez Hills 1000 E Victoria St Carson CA 90747

WILLIAMS, FRANCIS LEON, retired engineering executive, consultant; b. McGill, Nev., Sept. 19, 1918; s. Leon Alfred and Mazie Arabella (Blanchard) W.; m. Ailsa Bailey, Oct. 1944 (div.); children: Rhonda, Graham, Alison; m. Marita I. Fury, Feb. 23, 1974. Student, Calif. Inst. Tech., 1940-41, UCLA, 1946-47, Am. TV Labs., 1948; BME, Sydney U., Australia, 1952; postgrad., San Jose State Coll., 1958-60, Foothill Coll., 1961, Regional Vocat. Ctr., San Jose, Calif., 1962, Alexander Hamilton Inst., 1971-72, Lane Community Coll., 1978-85. Project engr., prodn. supr. Crompton, Parkinson, Australia Pty., Ltd., Sydney, 1949-50; field and sales engr. Perkins Australia Pty., Ltd., Sydney, 1951-54; chief mech. engr. Vicon Corp., San Carlos, Calif., 1955-60; design engr., group leader Lockheed Missiles and Space Co., Sunnyvale, Calif., 1960-70; prin. Astro-Tech Cons. Co., Los Altos, Calif., 1971-72; mech. designer Morvue and Morden Machines, Portland, Oreg., 1973-74; sr. mech. design engr. Chip-N-Saw div. Can-Car of Can., Eugene, Oreg., 1974-75; sales mgr. Indsl. Constrn. Co., Eugene, 1975-76, gen. mgr., 1977-78; ops. mgr. Steel Structures, Eugene, 1976-77; mech. design and project engr. Carothers Co., Eugene, 1978-80; chief engr. Bio Solar and Woodex Corps., Eugene and Brownsville, Oreg., 1980-83; cons. and design engr. Am. Fabricators, Woodburn, Oreg., 1983-84; design engr., draftsman Peterson Pacific Corp., Pleasant Hill, Oreg., 1984-85, Jensen Drilling Co., Glenwood, Oreg., 1985; design engr. Judco & Ball Flight Dryers, Inc., Harbor City, Calif., 1985-86; sr. v.p. The Richelsen Co., also cons.; advisor solid waste recovery County Bd. Commr.'s Office, Eugene, 1984-85. Contbr. articles to profl. jours.; patentee in field. Chmn. bldg. and grounds Westminster Presbyn. Ch., Eugene, 1984-86. Served with USAF, 1941-45. Democrat. Lodge: Elks. Home: 2324 Lillian St Eugene OR 97401

WILLIAMS, FRANK BELLOWS, manufacturing company executive; b. Dallas, Jan. 31, 1942; s. W. Nicholas and Elizabeth (Bellows) W.; m. Parmele Dunn, Aug. 10, 1968. BS in Engring., Stanford U., 1963; MBA, Harvard U., 1966. Sucessively mgr. divisional pers., mgr. SE Asia pers., mgr. corp. pers. Hewlett-Packard Co., Palo Alto, Calif., 1966-86; v.p. human resources Finnigan Corp., San Jose, Calif., 1986—; founding chmn. Vis. Nurse Assn., Inc., San Jose, 1984; pres. bd. dirs. Dependable Health Care Inc., San Jose, 1986-89; bd. dirs., past pres. VNA Home Health Care, Inc., San Jose, 1981-82. Bd. dirs. Stanford coun. Boy Scouts Am., Palo Alto, 1988. Office: Finnigan Corp 355 River Oaks Pkwy San Jose CA 95134

WILLIAMS, GENE BARTON, author, literary consultant; b. Salt Lake City, Jan. 31, 1950; s. Gorden Barton and Edith Mary (Gragert) W.; m. Cynthia Lynn, May 22, 1972; 1 child, Daniel Gorden. Student, U. Minn., 1968-71. Fiction editor, photo editor E. Go Enterprise Mag. Group, Reseda, Calif., 1974-80; assoc. editor Jalart House Mag. Group, Phoenix, 1976-82; asst. headmaster The Trivium, Mesa, Ariz., 1977-84; freelance writer, cons. Queen Creek, Ariz., 1984—. Author: (9 book series) Chilton's Guide to ..., 1984-87, Nuclear War - Nuclear Winter, 1987, Ella Petrovna, 1988, The New Father's Panic Book, 1988, The Homeowner's Pest Extermination Handbook, 1989, How To Be Your Own Architect, 1989. Mem. Superstition Amateur Radio Club, Apache Junction, 1983, Amateur Radio Relay League, 1986; sponsor Save the Children, N.Y., 1987, Mecham Recall, Phoenix, 1987-88. Recipient Svc. award Mpls. Pub. Schs., 1968, Orkin, Mesa, 1973, 74, Anchor award Terminex, Phoenix, 1975. Office: PO Box 547 Queen Creek AZ 85242

WILLIAMS, GEORGE JOSEPH, III, author, publisher; b. Springfield, Mass., Mar. 3, 1949; s. George Joseph Jr. and Millie (Dalton) W.; m. Edie Karen Godfrey, Sept. 18, 1976; children: Sarah, Michael. Student Riverside (Calif.) City Coll., 1967-69; BA in Music Composition, Calif State U.-Fullerton, 1971; BA in English, U. Calif.-Riverside, 1974. Owner, operator recording studio, Riverside, Calif., 1976-84; owner, pub. Tree by the River Pub. Co., Riverside, 1980—. Author: Rosa May: The Search for a Mining Camp Legend, 1980; The Guide to Bodie, 1981; The Murders at Convict Lake, 1984; The Songwriter's Demo Manual and Success Guide, 1984; The Redlight Ladies of Virginia City, Nevada, 1984; Mark Twain: His Adventures at Aurora and Mono Lake, 1986; Mark Twain: His Life in Virginia City, Nevada, 1986; Hot Springs of Eastern Sierra, 1988; Mark Twain: Jackass Hill and the Jumping Frog, 1989; On the Road with Mark Twain in California and Nevada, 1989. Recipient John Stone award Riverside City Coll., 1969; nominated for Nobel Prize in Lit., 1984, Pulitzer prize, 1986. Mem. Publishers Assn. So. Calif. Office: Box 935 Dayton NV 89403

WILLIAMS, HARRIETTE FLOWERS, educational administrator; b. Los Angeles, July 18, 1930; d. Orlando and Virginia (Carter) Flowers; BS, UCLA, 1952, EdD, (HEW fellow), 1973; MA, Calif. State U., Los Angeles, 1956; m. Irvin F. Williams, Apr. 9, 1960; children: Lorin Finley, Lori Virginia. Tchr., Los Angeles Unified Sch. Dist., 1952-59, counselor, 1954-59; psychometrist, 1958-62, faculty chmn., 1956-57, student activities coordinator, 1955-59, leader insts. and workshops, 1952-76, dir. counseling, 1960-65, supr. Title I programs Elem. Secondary Edn. Act, 1965-68, asst. prin., 1968-76, prin., 1976-82, dir. instrn. sr. high sch. div., 1982-85, adminstr. ops., 1985—; asst. dir. HEW project for high sch. adminstrn. UCLA, 1971-72; adj. prof. in Masters in Sch. Adminstrn. program Pepperdine U., Los Angeles, 1974-78. Recipient Sojourner Truth award Nat. Assn. Negro Bus. and Profl. Women's Clubs, Los Angeles, 1968; Life Membership Service award Los Angeles PTA, 1972-75; Los Angeles Mayor's Golden Apple award for ednl. excellence. Mem. Los Angeles Assn. Secondary Sch. Adminstrs., Assn. Calif. Sch. Adminstrs. (state chmn. urban affairs com. 1985-88, region pres.), Nat. Assn. Secondary Sch. Prins., Sr. High Sch. Asst. Prins. Assn. of Los Angeles (dir. 1974-76, sponsor 1985—), Sr. High Sch. Prins. Orgn., Nat. Council of Negro Women (life mem.), Lullaby Guild of Children's Home Soc. Los Angeles (pres. 1987-89), UCLA Gold Shield, Los Angeles PTA, NAACP, Urban League, Inglewood-Pacific cpt. Links Inc. (sec. 1984-86, treas. 1987), Jack and Jill of Am., Inc., UCLA Alumni Assn. (dir.), Delta Sigma Theta (pres. Los Angeles chpt. 1964-66, regional dir. 1968-72, nat. committeewoman 1966—), Pi Lambda Theta, Kappa Delta Pi, Delta Kappa Gamma. Baptist. Adr. Los Angeles Unified Sch Dist,644 W 17th St, Los Angeles, CA 90015. 213-742-7504. Office: 644 W 17th St Los Angeles CA 90015

WILLIAMS, HARRY EDWARD, manufacturing company executive, consultant; b. Oak Park, Ill., July 20, 1925; s. Harry E. and Mary W.; m. Jean Horner; l child, Jeanne. Student, West Coast U., Los Angeles, 1958-60; BS, Calif. Coast Coll., Santa Ana, 1975; MA, Calif. Coast Coll., 1975; PhD, Golden State U., Los Angeles, 1981. Registered profl. engr., Calif. Mgr. Parker Aircraft Co., Los Angeles, 1958-60, Leach Corp., Los Angeles, 1968-69, Litton, Data Systems, Van Nuys, Calif., 1969-72; dir. Electronic Memories, Hawthorne, Calif., 1972-78, Magnavox Co., Torrance, Calif., 1978-80; v.p. Stacoswitch Inc., Costa Mesa, Calif., 1981-87; mgmt. cons. Seal Beach, Calif., 1987--; cons. in field. Contbr. articles to profl. jours. With USAF, 1943-46. Named Mgr. of the Yr., Soc. Advancement of Mgmt., 1984; recipient Phil Carrol award, 1985. Fellow Internat. Acad. Edn., Am. Soc. Quality Control; mem. Soc. for Advancement Mgmt. Republican. Methodist. Home: 13451 Saint Andrews 124F Seal Beach CA 90740 Office: PO Box 2015 Seal Beach CA 90740

WILLIAMS, HENRY STRATTON, radiologist; b. N.Y.C., Aug. 26, 1929; m. Frances S. Williams; children: Mark I, Paul S., Bart H. BS, CCNY, 1950; MD, Howard U., 1955. Diplomate Nat. Bd. Med. Examiners. Intern Brooke Army Hosp., San Antonio, 1956; resident in radiology Letterman Army Hosp., San Francisco, 1957-60; pvt. practice radiology Los Angeles, 1963—; assoc. clin. prof. radiology Charles R. Drew Med. Sch., Los Angeles; chmn. bd. Charles Drew U. Medicine and Sci. Found. Mem. ad hoc adv. com. Joint Commn. Accreditation Hosps. Served to maj. U.S. Army, 1960-63. Fellow Am. Coll. Radiology; mem. Calif. Physicians Service (bd. dirs. 1971-77), Calif. Med. Assn. (counselor, mem. appeals bd., del., chmn. urban health com.), AMA, Los Angeles County Med. Assn. Office: 3756 Santa Rosalia Dr Los Angeles CA 90008

WILLIAMS, HENRY WILTON, brokerage firm executive; b. San Diego, July 14, 1937; s. Henry Wilton and Edyth (Johnstone) W.; m. Jan F. Ray, Sept. 5, 1959; children: Ken, Clint, Corey. BS in Agrl. Bus. Mgmt., Calif. State Polytechnic Coll., 1960. Mgr. J. W. Williams Co., San Diego, 1959-63; pres. Williams Brokerage Co., Inc., San Diego, 1963-83; v.p. Pacific States Truck Brokerage Inc., San Diego, 1977-85; pres. Williams Agrl. Commodities Brokerage Inc., San Diego, 1983--; bd. advisor, Westlands Bank, San Diego, 1980-82. Mem. San Diego Wholesale Fresh Fruit and Vegetable Assn. (dir. of planning, 1980--, pres. 1974-80), Safari Club Internat. (treas. San Diego chpt. 1985-87, 1st v.p. 1976-87, pres. 1987-88), Singing Hills Tennis Club. Home: 1780 Lisbon Ln El Cajon CA 92020 Office: Williams Agrl Commodities 808 J St San Diego CA 92101

WILLIAMS, HOWARD VERNON, physician; b. N.Y.C., Dec. 23, 1951; s. Sylvester Francis and Faye Marie (Smock) W.; m. Kathy Browder, May 7, 1983. BA, Cornell Coll., 1973; MD, U. So. Calif., Los Angeles, 1982. Diplomate Am. Bd. Internal Medicine. Chief resident internal medicine U. Calif. San Francisco-Fresno Med. Edn. Program, Fresno, Calif., 1985-86; chmn. dept. internal medicine Smith-Hanna Med. Group, San Diego, 1986-88; pvt. practice internal medicine San Diego, 1989—. Mem. Sierra Club. Office: 4060 Fourth Ave Suite 420 San Diego CA 92103

WILLIAMS, HOWARD WALTER, aerospace engineer; b. Evansville, Ind., Oct. 18, 1937; s. Walter Charles and Marie Louise (Bollinger) W.; m. Phyllis Ann Scofield, May 4, 1956 (div. Sept. 1970); m. Marilee Sharon Mulvane, Oct. 30, 1970; children: Deborah, Steven, Kevin, Glenn, Lori, Michele. AA, Pasadena City Coll., 1956; BSME, Calif. State U., Los Angeles, 1967; BSBA, U. San Francisco, 1978. Turbojet, rocket engr. Aerojet-Gen. Corp., Azusa, Calif., 1956-59, infrared sensor engr., 1959-60, rocket, torpedo engr., 1960-66; power, propulsion mgr. Aerojet-Gen. Corp., Sacramento, 1967-73, high speed ship systems mgr., 1974-78, combustion, power mgr., rocket engine mktg. mgr., 1979—. Author: (with others) Heat Exchangers, 1980, Industrial Heat Exchangers, 1985; co-inventor Closed Cycle Power System, 1969. Recipient Energy Innovations award U.S. Dept. Energy, 1985. Mem. AIAA (sr.; Best Paper 1966), Am. Soc. Metals (organizing dir. indsl. heat exchange confs. 1985—). Office: Aerojet TechSystems Co Aerojet Rd & Folsom Blvd Rancho Cordova CA 95670

WILLIAMS, JACK LLOYD, real estate executive; b. Hanford, Calif., Oct. 13, 1946; s. Robert D. and Evelyn Elisabeth (Whitman) W.; m. Janet Louise Johnson, Dec. 2, 1966; children: Thomas Gregory, David Michael. BA, Fresno State U., 1969; postgrad., 1970. With United Airlines, Fresno, Calif., 1968-76; owner United Travel Svc., Fresno, Selma (Calif), Hanford, 1976-82; salesperson Charles Tingey Comml. Real Estate, Fresno, 1983-85; salesperson Grubb & Ellis Comml. Real Estate, Fresno, 1985—, sr. mktg. cons., 1988—. Mem. Lions (pres. 1969-70). Democrat. Home: 116 E Audubon Fresno CA 93710 Office: Grubb and Ellis Co 5250 N Palm Ste 120 Fresno CA 93704

WILLIAMS, JAMES DELANO, international and business management educator; b. Yakima, Wash., July 24, 1947; s. James Doddison and Kathryn (Turner) W.; m. Chrys Ford (div. May 1979). AA, Portland (Oreg.) Community Coll., 1970; BS, San Jose (Calif.) State U., 1975; MS, Purdue U., 1976; D in Bus. Adminstrn. magna cum lauda, U.S. Internat. U., 1988. Cert. tchr., Calif. Mktg. rep. IBM Corp., San Francisco, 1977-80; instr. Coll.of Marin, Corte Madera, Calif., 1980-81; account exec. Chase Bank Info. Services, San Francisco, 1981-84; instr. Pacific Coast Coll., Los Angeles, 1985; asst. instr. U.S. Internat. U., San Diego, 1987; instr. San Diego Community Coll. Dist., 1986—; chmn. Bus. Adminstrn. div. U. V.I.; market planning cons. V.I. Govt., Internat. bus. cons. Ea. Caribbean Ctr., Caribbean Rsch. Inst. Served to cpl. USMC, 1966-68, Vietnam. Purdue U. grantee, 1975. Mem. World Trade Assn., Black MBA Soc., MBA's Assn., Acad. Internat. Bus., Jr. C. of C. Democrat. Home: 8979 Capcano Rd San Diego CA 92126 Office: U Virgin Islands, Bus Adminstrn Div, RR2 Box 10000 Kingshill, Saint Croix USVI 00580

WILLIAMS, JAMES E., food products manufacturing company executive. married. With Golden State foods Corp., 1961—; pres., chief exec. officer Golden State foods Corp., Pasadena, Calif., 1978—. Office: Golden State Foods Corp 234 E Colorado Blvd Pasadena CA 91101 *

WILLIAMS, JAMES FRANK, controller, financial planning consultant; b. Chgo., Jan. 25, 1940; s. James and Anna R. (Casto) W.; m. Mary Ann Shibovich, Sept. 29, 1962; children: Marilyn Kay, James P. BS in Commerce, De Paul U., 1962. Cert. fin. planner. Sr. auditor Peat, Marwick, Mitchell & Co., Chgo., 1962-67; asst. controller ABA, Chgo., 1967-72; controller The Nat. Jud. Coll., Reno, Nev., 1972—; registered rep. Fin. Network Investment Corp., Sacramento, Calif., 1987—. Coach, league pres. Babe Ruth Baseball, Reno, Nev., 1980-85; pres. Our Lady of the Snows Sch. Bd., Reno, 1977. Mem. Inst. Cert. Fin. Planners, Internat. Assn. Fin. Planning, Inc., Serra Club (treas. Reno chpt. 1987—). Republican. Roman Catholic. Home: 229 Bonnie Briar Pl Reno NV 89509 Office: The Nat Jud Coll Jud Coll Bldg/U Nev Reno NV 89557

WILLIAMS, JEANNETTE J., educator, artist; b. Modesto, Calif., Aug. 1, 1945; d. Herbert V. and Gladys (Rafter) Johnston; m. Robert A. Williams (div. 1974). AA, Modesto Community Coll., Calif., 1965; BA, Calif. State U., San Jose, 1968; MA, U. N.Mex.; postgrad., N.Mex. State U. Teaching asst. Modesto Community Coll., Calif., 1965; layout artist Sunnyvale Dailey Std. News, Calif., 1966; tchr. White Sands Missile Range Elem. Sch., N.Mex., 1968-69, Albuquerque Pub. Schs., 1969—; faculty U. N.Mex., Albuquerque Tech. Voc. Inst., Albuquerque Mus. of Art, others part-time to date. exhibited in group shows Albuquerque Conv. Ctr., 1972, El Paso Internat. Designer Craftsmen Show (2nd award jewelry), 1973, San Antonio Arts and Crafts Fair, 1973, Internat. Print Salon, N.Mex. State Fair, 1974, New West Gallery, Albuquerque, 1975, Santa Fe Biennial Show, N.Mex., 1978, Downtown Ctr. for Arts, Albuquerque, 1979, Merdian Gallery, Albuquerque, 1981, Stables Gallery, N.Mex., 1982, Downtown Ctr. for Arts, Albuquerque, 1983, 84; represented in group collections El Paso Mus. Art. Mem. Santa Fe Ctr. for Photography, Albuquerque United Arts. Home: 1928 La Veta Dr NE Albuquerque NM 87110

WILLIAMS, JEFFREY THOMAS, economist; b. Duluth, Minn., Sept. 30, 1952; s. Bruce Foch Pershing and Kathleen (Griffee) W.; m. Theresa Ann Moore, May 29, 1987; 1 child, Spencer Thomas. BS in Finance, U. Utah, 1975, BS in Econs., 1975, MS in Econs., 1981. Research fellow Utah Ctr. for Pub. Affairs, U. Utah, Salt Lake City, 1981; economist Utah Energy Office, State of Utah Dept. of Nat. Resources, Salt Lake City, 1981-85; sr. economist Com. of Consumer Svcs., State of Utah Dept. Commerce, Salt Lake City, 1985—; mem. Salt Lake Community Coll. Computer Tech. Adv. Com., Salt Lake City, 1985-89; expert witness, Utah Power and Light Co., Pacificorp merger case, 1988, fuel procurement cases, 1986. Co-author: State Review of the Bonneville Unit Central Utah Project, 1984; author, editor:

Study of a Conceptual Nuclear Energy Center at Green River, 1982 and others. Vol. Nat. Ski Patrol System #6925, Park City, Utah, 1980-89. Recipient Disting. Svc. award, Com. of Consumer Svcs., State of Utah, 1989. Mem. Internat. Assn. Energy Economists. Episcopalian. Home: 1510 Blaine Ave Salt Lake City UT 84105 Office: Committee Consumer Svcs 160 East 300 South Rm 408 Salt Lake City UT 84111

WILLIAMS, JOHN CHARLES, II, data processing executive; b. Dayton, Ohio, Jan. 29, 1955; s. John Charles and Frances Jerline (McKean) W.; m. Diane Catherine Busch, Feb. 11, 1978; 1 child, Tabitha Anne. Licensed mfr. low explosive devices. Programmer Kino Starr, Tucson, 1977-78, City of Boise (Idaho), 1978; data processing mgr. Nat. Assn. Ind. Businesses, Inc., Boise, 1978-79; chief exec. officer Williams Research Assoc., Boise, 1979-80, MRW Data Systems, Inc., Tucson, 1981-82, Computer Security, Tucson, 1983-86, Modern Magic, Tucson, 1986-88; tech. support dir. Program Sources, Inc., Tucson, 1988--; chief exec. officer Cactus Explosives Corp., 1989—. Area coordinator Kolbe For Congress Campaign, Tucson, 1984; Ariz. Rep. State Committeeman, 1986--; mem. Ariz. Sonora Desert Mus., Tucson, 1983--. Mem. Tucson Radio Control Club, Barnstormers (asst. mgr. 1987). Republican. Home: 450 S Jerrie Ave Tucson AZ 85711

WILLIAMS, JOHN JAMES, JR., architect; b. Denver, July 13, 1949; s. John James and Virginia Lee (Thompson) W.; m. Mary Serene Morck, July 29, 1972. BArch, U. Colo., 1974. Registered architect, Colo. Project architect Gensler Assoc. Architects, Denver, 1976, Heinzman Assoc. Architects, Boulder, Colo., 1977, EZTH Architects, Boulder, 1978-79; prin. Knudson/Williams PC, Boulder, 1980-82, Faber, Williams & Brown, Boulder, 1982-86, John Williams & Assocs., Boulder, 1986—; panel chmn. U. Colo. World Affairs Conf.; vis. faculty U. Colo. Sch. Architecture and Planning, Coll. Environtl. Design. Author (with others) State of Colorado architect licensing law, 1986. Commr. Downtown Boulder Mall Commn., 1985-88; bd. dirs. U. Colo. Fairway Club, 1986-88. Recipient Teaching Honorarium, U. Colo. Coll. Architecture and Planning, 1977, 78, 79, 80, 88, Excellence in Design and Planning award City of Boulder, 1981, 82, Citation for Excellence, WOOD Inc., 1982, Disting. Profl. Service award Coll. Environ. Design U. Colo., 1988. Mem. Nat. Council Architect Registration Bd., AIA, (sec., bd. dirs. Colo. North chpt. 1985-86, 88, sec. 1987, 88, ednl. fund Fisher I traveling scholar 1988), Architects and Planners of Boulder (v.p. 1982), Nat. Golf Found. (sponsor), Am. Philatelic Soc., Kappa Sigma (chpt. pres. 1970). Home: 3345 16th ST Boulder CO 80302 Office: John Williams & Assocs 1137 Pearl St Suite 206 Boulder CO 80302

WILLIAMS, JOHN MARK, aerospace engineer, consultant; b. Mpls., Oct. 12, 1961; s. Clifford Gus Sr. and Mildred Lucille (Christianson) W. BS in Areospace Engrng., U. Minn., 1983. Engr. Boeing Mil. Airplane Co. div. The Boeing Co., Seattle, 1984-88, sr. engr. Boeing Advanced Systems div., 1988—. Contbr. Seattle Children's Shelter, 1987, 88. Mem. AIAA. Democrat. Lutheran. Office: The Boeing Co Boeing Advanced Systems 1730 Pacific Hwy S PO Box 3999 Seattle WA 98188

WILLIAMS, JOHN PERSHING, consultant, retired mining company executive; b. Bluefield, W.Va., July 25, 1919; s. Deck Christopher and Zeora Monte (Brocklehurst) W.; m. Ruth Elizabeth Jones, July 10, 1947; 1 child, Jeanne Lynn. BS, U. Mich., 1951. Mem. indsl. rels. staff King-Seeley Thermos Co., Ann Arbor, Mich., 1950-63; personnel mgr., then indsl. rels. mgr. Butler Mfg. Co., Kansas City, Mo., 1963-66; dir. indsl. rels. Mueller Brass Co., Ft. Huron, Mich., 1966-69; v.p. indsl. rels. Mueller Brass Co., Port Huron, 1969-78; dir. indsl. rels. U.S. Smelting, Refining & Mining, N.Y.C., 1966-69; indsl. rels. cons. UV Industries, N.Y.C., 1969-78; dir. indsl. rels. Fed. Pacific Electric Co., Newark, 1970-76; dir. labor rels. Anamax Mining Co., Sahuarita, Ariz., 1978-85; pres. Alert Consulting Corp., Tucson, 1985—. Co-author: Collective Bargaining, 1985, Strike Planning, 1985. Pres., Perry Nursery Sch., Ann Arbor, Mich., 1957; rd. commr., Scio Twp., Ann Arbor, 1961; del. State Rep. Conv., Detroit, 1961; mem. parents coun., Adrian (Mich.) Coll., 1973-74; bd. dirs., Blue Cross-Blue Shield Mich., Detroit, 1971-77. Mem. Masons. Methodist. Home and Office: Alert Consulting Corp 775 W Samalayuca Dr Tucson AZ 85704

WILLIAMS, JUDY CAROL, teacher; b. Ft. Worth, Jan. 4, 1946; d. Wells Wallis and Hazel (Nunn) W. BEd, Tex. Christian U., 1968; cert. English as 2d Lang., Tex. Western U., 1985; postgrad., U. Calif., Irvine, 1985-87, Calif. State U., Long Beach, 1987, Chapman Coll., 1989. Tchr. Dallas Ind. Sch. Dist., 1968-85, Calif. Elem. Sch., Orange, 1987—. Named Tchr. of Yr. at Lakewood Sch., Dallas Ind. Sch. Dist., 1984-85. Mem. Internat. Reading Assn., NEA, Classroom Tchrs. Dallas, Calif. Tchrs. Orange, Unified Tchrs. Home: 3405 S Plaza Dr Apt D Santa Ana CA 92704 Office: Calif Elem Sch 1080 N California St Orange CA 92667

WILLIAMS, KEN MICHAEL, logistics engineer; b. Charleston, W. Va., Mar. 7, 1944; s. R. Don and Ruth Norma (Berg) W.; m. Khanh Thi Tran, July 26, 1973; children: Xali Khanh, Donn Christopher. BA, Ohio State U., 1968; MA, Mich. State U., 1977; AA, Cerritos Coll., 1987. Cert. bus. and indsl. mgmt. tchr., Calif. Commd. U.S. Army, 1968, resigned, 1984; logistics specialist McDonnell Douglas, Long Beach, Calif., 1985; asst. material mgmt. officer Fed. Agy., Long Beach, 1986—; bd. dirs. TFW Scis., Long Beach; pres. Wms. Scis., Westminster, Calif., 1984-89; cons. Success Strategy Tng., Orange, Calif., 1985-88; logistics instr. Cerritos Coll., Norwalk, Calif., 1985—. Bd. dirs. Site Council Clegg Sch., Westminster, 1985—. Recipient Community Service award Camp Zama, 1978; numerous awards U.S. Army, 1968-84. Mem. Soc. Logistics Engrs. (chmn. 1987-88, vice-chmn. ops. 1986-87, newsletter editor 1985-86, chpt. chmn. 1987-88, Award of Excellence 1986, 87, Internat. Logistics award 1987, Internat. Newsletter award 1987, Pres.' Honor Roll 1986, 87, Soc. Commendation 1987), Am. Prodn. Inventory Control Soc., Retired Officers Assn., VFW. Republican. Methodist. Lodges: Masons, Shriners. Home: 13801-A Cherry St Westminster CA 92683 Office: Div Material Mgmt Office 3700 Spring St Long Beach CA 90822

WILLIAMS, KENNETH JAMES, retired county official; b. Eureka, Calif., Apr. 28, 1924; s. E. J. and Thelma (Hall) W.; student Humboldt State Coll., 1942-43; B.S., U. Oreg., 1949, M.Ed., 1952; m. Mary Patricia Warring, Sept. 3, 1949; children—James Clayton, Susan May, Christopher Kenneth. Engaged as mountain triangulation observer with U.S. Coast and Geodetic Survey, 1942; instr. bus. and geography Boise (Idaho) Jr. Coll., 1949-51; tchr. Prospect High Sch., 1952-54; prin. Oakland (Oreg.) High Sch., 1954-58; supt. prin. Coburg Public Schs., 1958-64; supt. Yoncalla (Oreg.) Public Schs., 1964-66, Amity (Oreg.) Public Schs., 1966-72; adminstr. Yamhill County, McMinnville, Oreg., 1974-85; cons., 1985—; county liaison officer Land and Water Conservation Fund, 1977-85. Dist. lay leader Oreg.-Idaho ann. conf. United Methodist Ch., 1968-80, bd. dirs. western dist. Ch. Extension Soc., 1976; mem. Mid-Willamette Manpower Council, 1974-85; bd. dirs. Lafayette Noble Homes, 1970-72; mem. adv. com. local budget law sect. State of Oreg. Served with AUS, 1943-46. Recipient Purple Heart, Good Conduct medal, battle stars. Mem. NEA, Oreg. Edn. Assn., Oreg. Assn. Secondary Prins., Nat. Assn. Secondary Prins., AAUP, Oreg., Am. assns. sch. adminstrs., Assn. Supervision and Curriculum Devel., Nat. Sch. Pub. Relations Assn., Phi Delta Kappa. Mason (Shriner), Lion. Home: 21801 SE Webfoot Rd Dayton OR 97114

WILLIAMS, KIMBERLY DICKEY, nurse; b. Mich., Sept. 17, 1960; d. James Fulton and Alice (Nowak) Dickey; m. James Park Williams Jr., May 12, 1984. BS in Nursing, Mich. State U., 1983. RN, Mich. Nurse Wyandotte (Mich.) Gen. Hosp., 1983-84, E.W. Sparrow Hosp., Lansing, Mich., 1984-85; dir. nursing Quality Care, Inc., Lansing, 1985-87; nurse St. Joseph's Hosp. & Med. Ctr., Phoenix, 1987—. Vol. Spl. Olympics, Phoenix, 1988; ann. donor United Way; mem. Am. Heart Assn. Mem. Mich. State U. Coll. of Nursing, Mich. State U. Alumni Assn. (bd. dirs. 1987-88), Ariz. Pub. Health Assn. Roman Catholic. Home: 9022 E Corrine Dr Scottsdale AZ 85260 Office: St Josephs Hosp & Med Ctr Home Health 350 W Catalina Dr Ste 3C34 Phoenix AZ 85013

WILLIAMS, KNOX, water conditioning company executive; b. Grandfield, Okla., Aug. 9, 1928; s. Knox B. and Clara Mae (Butler) W.; m. Juanita June Wood, Sept. 9, 1951; children—Jodi Ann and Jeri Ruth (twins), Drue Knox. B.A., UCLA, 1951. With Wilson-McMahan Furniture Stores, Santa Barbara, Calif., 1951-61; prin., pres. Rayne of North San Diego County, Vista, Calif., 1961—, Aqua Fresh Drinking Water Systems, Inc., San Diego, 1980—. Mem. bd. counsellors UCLA. Served with USNR, 1947-48. Mem. Carlsbad C. of C., Pacific Water Quality Assn. (pres. 1975-76), Water Quality Assn. (bd. dirs. 1980-83). Republican. Presbyterian. Clubs: El Camino Rotary (Oceanside, Calif.), Masons (Santa Barbara). Office: Rayne of North San Diego County 2011 W Vista Way Vista CA 92083 also: Aqua Fresh Drinking Water Systems 7370 Opportunity Rd Ste I San Diego CA 92111

WILLIAMS, LARRY RICHARD, commodities trader; b. Miles City, Mont., Oct. 6, 1942; s. Richard Sigwart and Sylva (Brurs) W.; m. Carla Williams, Jan. 19, 1976; children: Kelley, Jason, Sarah, Shelley, Paige. BS, U. Oreg., 1964. Prin. Larry Williams, Commodity Trading Adviser, Solana Beach, Calif., 1967—. Author: The Secret of Selecting Stock, 1970, How I Made Million Dollars Trading Commodities, 1973, How Seasonal Factors Influence Commodity Prices, 1976, How to Prosper in the Coming Good Years, 1982, The Definitive Guide to Futures Trading, vols. I and II, 1988. Republican. Office: Po Box 8162 Rancho Santa Fe CA 92067

WILLIAMS, LEONA RAE, small business owner; b. Fairfield, Nebr., July 1, 1928; d. Melton M. and Helga D. (Sorensen) Brown; m. Eugene F. Williams, June 6, 1946; 1 child, Dennis D. Grad. high sch., Fairfield. Owner Intimate Apparel, Tucson, 1953—. Sponsor Distributive Edn. Program, 1978-82; coord. fashion shows Am. Cancer Soc., Tucson, 1987, 88, 89. Mem. Exec. Women's Internat. Assn., Merchants Assn. (pres., 1987—), Soroptimists. Republican. Baptist. Office: Alice Rae Intimate Apparel 2914 N Campbell Ave Tucson AZ 85719

WILLIAMS, LEONARD TODD, JR., hotel sales and marketing executive; b. Portchester, N.Y., Jan. 9, 1947; s. Leonard Todd and Elsie Pauline (Brasa) W.; m. Barbara Ellen Warsh, Jan. 20, 1982; 1 child, Stephanie. BS, U. Nev., Las Vegas, 1979. Asst. gen. mgr. Holiday Inn Fin. Ctr., San Francisco, 1978-79; resident gen. mgr. Holiday Inn Center Strip, Las Vegas, 1979-80; gen. mgr. Holiday Inn South, Las Vegas, 1980-81; dir. lodging and beverages Holiday Inn, Holiday Casino, Las Vegas, 1981-86, dir. sales promotion mktg., 1985-86; dir. tourist mktg. Tropicanna Hotel, Las Vegas, 1986-87; regional dir. sales and mktg. Summitt Hotel Mgmt. Corp., Phoenix, 1987—; adj. prof. Golden Gate U., San Francisco, 1978-79, U. Nev., Las Vegas, 1979-84. Bd. dirs. Easter Seals Soc. Nev., 1976-83, Sands Branch Boys and Girls Club, Phoenix; area exec. coord. United Way So. Nev., 1982-83; mem. exec. coun. Phoenix Boys and Girls Club. Recipient Exec. of Yr. award Profl. Secs. Assn., Las Vegas, 1985, also appreciation awards Easter Seals, Muscular Dystrophy Assn., Boys Club. Mem. Hotel Sales and Mktg. Assn., Fedn. Hoteliers (pres. Las Vegas 1978-79), Kiwanis (pres. Las Vegas 1978-79). Democrat. Lutheran. Home: 8791 E Lupine St Scottsdale AZ 85260 Office: Summit Hotel Mgmt Corp 3600 N 2d Ave Phoenix AZ 85213

WILLIAMS, LEWIS ISAAC, IV, investment banker; b. Los Angeles, Aug. 4, 1949; s. Lewis Isaac III and Elizabeth Virginia (Hayes) W.; m. Anne Boyle Archibald, Jan. 21, 1984; children: Alexandrea Hayes, Jessica McCarthy. AB in Econs., Stanford U., 1972; MS in Mgmt., MIT, 1976; MA in Econs., Acctg. and Info. Systems, Northwestern U., 1980. Adminstr., dir. Chase Comml. Corp., Los Angeles, 1980-82; asst. nat. mgr. credit, adminstr. Chase Comml. Corp., 1983-84; project mgr., corp. fin. Bank of Boston, 1984-87; v.p., sr. underwriter Heller Internat., Glendale, Calif., 1987-88; project cons., chief operating officer Arch-Will Enterprises, Los Angeles, 1988—; asst. football coach Northwestern U., 1976-77. Council for Opportunity in Grad. Mgmt. Edn. fellow, 1974-76. Libertarian. Roman Catholic.

WILLIAMS, LINDA JO, art consultant; b. Wichita Falls, Tex., Jan. 17, 1942; d. Cleburne Milton and Jonell (Acuff) Maier; m. James Legrand Williams, June 7, 1963 (div. 1987); children: Brent Legrand, Kent Milton. BA in English, U. Tex., 1964. Tchr. English, Speech Spring Branch (Tex.) Ind. Sch. Dist., 1963-65; prin. Designs by Linda, Houston, 1978-81; pres. Linda Williams--By Design Inc., Houston, 1981-87; art cons. Simic Art Galleries, Carmel, Calif., 1987-88, Coast Gallery, Pebble Beach, Calif., 1988—. Mem. Am. Soc. Interior Design. Methodist. Home and Office: PO Box 4505 Carmel CA 93921

WILLIAMS, LINDA TURNER, foundation administrator; b. St. Louis, Oct. 28, 1941; d. Lucius Don IV and Louise Patton (Richardson) Turner; m. John Howard Williams, Aug. 17, 1963; children: Don Sheldon, John Rolland. AB, U. Ill., 1963; MA, Santa Clara U., 1976. Lic. marriage, family and child counselor, Calif. Tchr. Community Sch. Music and Art, Mountain View, Calif., 1972-77; therapist intern North County Mental Health, Palo Alto, Calif., 1975-77; dir. social svcs. Palo Alto chpt. ARC, 1977-80, exec. dir., 1982—; project dir. Bus. Info. Analysis Corp., Haverford, Pa., 1980-82, mgmt. cons. Western chpts., 1987—; chmn. strategic planning Pvt. Industry Coun., Sunnyvale, Calif., 1987—; bd. dirs. Vol. Exch., San Jose, Calif., Woodside (Calif.) Consulting Group. Vol. Santa Clara (Calif.) United Way, 1983—. Mem. Nat. Soc. Fund-Raising Execs. (v.p. 1985-86), Assn. United Way Agys. (mem. exec. com., past pres. Santa Clara chpt.), Palo Alto C. of C., Neighbors Abroad, Rotary, Phi Beta Kappa, Kappa Kappa Gamma. Republican. Office: ARC 400 Mitchell Ln Palo Alto CA 94301

WILLIAMS, MARLON ARRINGTON, lawyer; b. Raleigh, N.C., May 22, 1960; s. Ella (Arrington) Williams-Vinson. BA in Econs., U. Notre Dame, 1982; JD, U. N.C., 1985. Bar: Calif. 1987. Loan specialist Small Bus. Adminstrn., L.A., 1986-87; legal asst. Lillick, McHose, L.A., 1987—. Contbr. poems to mags. and books. Recipient Editor's Choice award Nat. Libr. Poetry, 1989, Poet of Merit award APA, 1989. Mem. Calif. Bar Assn. Democrat. Roman Catholic. Home: 209 21st Pl Manhattan Beach CA 90266

WILLIAMS, MARSHALL MACKENZIE, utility company executive; b. Londonderry, N.S., Can., Dec. 11, 1923; s. Millard Filmore and Gladys Christine (MacKenzie) W.; m. Joan Atlee Ross, Sept. 6, 1952; children: Peter, Alex, Stephen, Margot. Student, Acadia U., 1942-45; B of Engring., Tech. U. N.S., Halifax, 1947, M of Engring., 1949, D of Engring. (hon.), 1978. Exec. v.p. TransAlta Utilities Corp., Calgary, Alta., Can., 1968-73, pres., 1973-85, chief exec. officer, 1980—, chmn., 1984—, also bd. dirs.; bd. dirs. Royal Trustco Ltd., Toronto, Ont., Can., Can. Energy Rsch. Inst., AEC Power, Ltd., Can. N.W. Energy, Ltd., Stelco, Inc., TransAlta Utilities Corp., TransAlta Resources Corp., Fortis, Inc., St. John's, Can., Sun Life Assurance Co., Toronto; chmn. Ind. Cons. Group, Royal Trust Energy Corp. Bd. govs. The Banff Ctr., Jr. Achievement Can.; chmn. western regional com. C.D. Howe Inst., v.p., trustee Manning Awards Found. Mem. Assn. Profl. Engrs., Geologists and Geophysicists Alta., Can. Elec. Assn. (past pres.), N.W. Electric Light and Power Assn. (past pres.), Calgary Jaycees. Club: Ranchmen's (Calgary, Alta., Can.). Office: TransAlta Utilities Corp, 110 12th Ave SW, Calgary, AB Canada T2P 2M1

WILLIAMS, MARY D(ENNEN), psychologist; b. Cin.; d. Frank Eugene and Katharine Powell (Wiley) D.; children from previous marriage: John Wiley Hartung, Katharine D. Hartung, Denny Hartung. AB, Radcliffe Coll., 1943; MS, U. Vt., 1948; MPA in Pub. Health, U. R.I., 1965; PhD, U. Oreg., 1982. Lic. psychologist, Oreg. Instr. zoology U. R.I., Kingston, 1950-51, asst. prof. zoology in Pub. Health, 1957-59; grad. teaching fellow U. Oreg., Eugene, 1978-80; resident psychologist Portland, Oreg., 1982-85; pvt. practice psychologist Portland, 1985—. Mem. Am. Psychological Assn., Oreg. Psychological Assn., Portland Psychological Assn., Oreg. Acad. Sci., Am. Assn. Sci, Sigma Xi, Pi Sigma Alpha, Phi Kappa Phi. Office: 1618 SW First Ave Ste P2 Portland OR 97201

WILLIAMS, MICHAEL JAMES, health care services administrator; b. Royal Oak, Mich., Sept. 23, 1951; s. Robert Burgett and Elizabeth (McGuire) W.; m. Karyn Leigitt, July 28, 1978. BA in Police Adminstrn., Wayne State U., 1974, BS in Psychology, 1974; M in Pub. Adminstrn., Calif. State U., Fullerton, 1978. Asst. mgr. Suburban Ambulance Co., Royal Oak, 1970-74; dir. Emergency Med. Services Imperial County, El Centro, Calif., 1974-76, Orange County, Santa Ana, Calif., 1976-80; pres. EMS Systems Design, Irvine, Calif., 1980—; instr., trainer advanced cardiac life support, Am. Heart Assn., 1978-80, CPR, 1971-80. Contbr. numerous articles to profl. jours. Recipient Recognition award Orange County Emergency Care Commn., 1980, Appreciation award UCI Med. Ctr., Orange, Calif., 1980, Orange County Fire Chiefs Assn., 1980. Mem. Am. Trauma Soc., Am. Soc. Health and Law, Am. Heart Assn. (bd. dirs. Orange County chpt., 1976-82), So. Calif. Health Care Execs., Orange County Trauma Soc. (bd. dirs. 1981—, program achievement award, 1987). Democrat. Office: EMS Systems Design 14451 Chambers St Ste 230 Tustin CA 92680

WILLIAMS, NANCY ELLEN-WEBB, social services administrator; b. Quincy, Ill., Aug. 1; d. Charles and Garnet Naomi (Davis) Webb; m. Jesse B. Williams, Apr. 11, 1959; children: Cynthia L. Williams Clay, Troy Andrea Williams Redic, Bernard Peter. BA, Quincy Coll., 1957; postgrad., Tenn. A&I U., 1961; M Pub. Adminstrn., U. Nev., Las Vegas, 1977; LHD (hon.), U. Humanistic Studies, 1986. Cert. peace officer, Nev. (chmn. Standards and Tng. Com., 1978-81); cert. social worker. Tchr. Shelby County Tng. Sch., Memphis, 1957-61; dep. probation officer Clark County Juvenile Ct., Las Vegas, 1961-66, supervising probation officer, 1966-74, dir. probation services, 1974-80, dir. intake admissions, 1980-81, dir. Child Haven, 1981—; mem. Nev. Crime Commn., 1970-81. Author: When We Were Colored, 1986, Dinah's Pain and Other Poems of the Black Life Experience, 1988, Them Gospel Songs, 1989; contbr. poetry to various mags. Mem. exec. com. Clark County Econ. Opportunity Bd., Las Vegas, 1963-71; chmn. So. Nev. Task Force on Corrections, 1974-81; mem. Gov.'s Com. on Justice Standards and Goals, 1979-81; bd. dirs. U. Humanistic Studies, Las Vegas, 1984—. Recipient Friend of the Golden Gloves award Golden Gloves Regional Bd., 1981, Tribute to Black Women award U. Nev., Las Vegas, 1984. Fellow Am. Acad. Neurol. and Orthopedic Surgeons (assoc.); mem. AAUW, Nat. Council Juvenile Ct. Judges, Nat. Writers Assn. Democrat. Office: Child Haven 3401 E Bonanza Rd Las Vegas NV 89101

WILLIAMS, PAT, congressman; b. Helena, Mont., Oct. 30, 1937; m. Carol Griffith, 1965; children: Griff, Erin, Whitney. Student, U. Mont., 1956-57, William Jewell U.; BA, U. Denver, 1961; postgrad., Western Mont. Coll.; LLD, Carroll Coll., Montana Coll. of Mineral Sci. and Tech. Mem. Mont. Ho. of Reps., 1967, 69; exec. dir. Hubert Humphrey Presdl. campaign, Mont., 1968; exec. asst. to U.S. Rep. John Melcher, 1969-71; mem. Gov.'s Employment and Tng. Council, 1972-78, Mont. Legis. Reapportionment Commn., 1973; co-chmn. Jimmy Carter Presdl. campaign, Mont., 1976; mem. 96th-101st Congresses from 1st Mont. dist. Coordinator Mont. Family Edn. Program, 1971-78. Served with U.S. Army, 1960-61; Served with Army N.G., 1962-69. Mem. Mont. Fedn. Tchrs. Democrat. Lodge: Elks. Office: 2457 Rayburn House Office Bldg Washington DC 20515

WILLIAMS, PHILIP F. C., Chinese literature educator; b. Little Rock, Apr. 5, 1956; s. Franklin Springer and Elizabeth Corbett (Bassett) W.; m. Ruo Hao Zhu, Mar. 19, 1984 (div. Feb. 1987). BA, U. Ark., 1978; postgrad., Cornell U., 1978-79; MA, UCLA, 1981, PhD, 1985. Rsch. grantee Com. for Scholarly Communication with People's Republic China Nat. Acad. Scis., Beijing, 1982-83; lectr. Occidental Coll., L.A., 1984; vis. asst. prof. UCLA, 1986; asst. prof. Ariz. State U., Tempe, 1986—; escort interpreter U.S. Dept. State, Washington, 1986—; lectr. student affairs com. Ctr. Asian Studies, Ariz. State U., 1987, chair library com., 1988—. Mem. editorial bd. Ctr. Asian Studies, monograph series, Ariz. State U., 1986—, Jour. Asian Culture, 1979-81, 84-86. NDEA fellow Cornell U., UCLA, 1978, 80, 81, 83, 84; faculty grantee-in-aid Ariz. State U., 1988, rsch. grantee NEH, summer 1989. Mem. Assn. Asian Studies, Chinese Lang. Tchrs. Assn., Am. Comparative Lit. Assn., UCLA Alumni Assn. (acad. achievement award 1981), Phi Beta Kappa. Democrat. Unitarian. Office: Ariz State U Dept Fgn Langs Tempe AZ 50697

WILLIAMS, RANDALL JAMES, construction company executive, accountant; b. Eugene, Oreg., Sept. 9, 1951; s. Frank James and Florence Lucille (Crowell) W.; m. Darlean Marguerite Harris, June 3, 1978; children: Tyler James, Anthony Scott, Kara Sydney. BS in acctg., U. Oreg., 1976. CPA, Oreg. Staff acct Kohnen Larson & Co., CPA's, Eugene, 1976-79; asst. controller Eugene Sand & Gravel Co., Inc., 1979-80; chief fin. officer Pierce Corp., Eugene, 1980-86; audit sr. Aldrich Kilbrides & Tatone, CPA's, Salem, Oreg., 1986-87; v.p. fin. R & H Constrn. Co., Portland, Oreg., 1987—. Mem. Am. Inst. CPA's, Oreg. Soc. CPA's, Constrn. Fin. Mgrs. Assn. Republican. Home: 5 Offenbach Pl Lake Oswego OR 97035 Office: R & H Constrn Co 338 NW 5th Ave Portland OR 97208

WILLIAMS, RICHARD DUDLEY, management executive; b. Mpls., Aug. 23, 1946; s. Raymond Warren and Donna June (Thibodo) W.; m. Janet Louise Anderson, July 8, 1972; children: Sean Richard, Patrick Loran, Shannon Rae. BS in Polit. Sci., San Diego State U., 1970; postgrad., Western States U., 1970-71. Sales mgr. J. Kudsy & Co., Inc., L.A., 1971-74, Derentz & Co., Inc., Van Nuys, Calif., 1974-76, Intra-World Imports, Chatsworth, Calif., 1976-79; gen. mgr. Internat. Parts Import & Export Co., North Hollywood, Calif., 1979-81; dist. mgr. Walker Mfg. Co., Seattle, 1981-87; regional mgr. Bowman Distbg. Co., Seattle, 1987—. Pres. bd. dirs. Green Valley County Water Dist., Calif., 1977-81, Maple Valley (Wash.) Pony Baseball, 1988; bd. dirs. Winterwood Estates Homeowners Assn., Kent Wash., 1988. With USN, 1964-71, Vietnam. Mem. Am. Mgmt. Assn., Masons. Republican. Home: 28604 181st Ave SE Kent WA 98042 Office: Bowman Distbg Co 7640 S 196th St Kent WA 98032

WILLIAMS, RICHARD HIRSCHFELD, professional baseball manager; b. St. Louis, May 7, 1929; s. Harvey Grote and Kathryn Louise (Rhode) W.; m. Norma Marie Mussato, Oct. 23, 1954; children: Kathi, Richard Anthony, Marc Edmund. Student, Pasadena City Coll., 1946-47. Profl. baseball player 1947-64; mem. Bklyn. Dodgers, 1951-56, Balt. Orioles, 1956-58, 61-62, Cleve. Indians, 1957, Kansas City Athletics, 1959-60, Boston Red Sox, 1963-64; baseball mgr. Toronto Maple Leafs, 1965-66, Boston Red Sox, 1967-69, Oakland A's, 1971-73, Calif. Angels, 1974-76, Montreal Expos, 1977-81, San Diego Padres, 1982-86; mgr. Seattle Mariners, 1986-88. Served with U.S. Army, 1951. Named All Star Mgr., 1968, 73-74, 85; Am. Mgr. of Yr., 1967; Nat. League Mgr. of Yr. AP, 1979, played in World Series, 1952-53; managed teams in World Series, 1967, 72-73, 84. Mem. Baseball Players Assn. Am. Roman Catholic. Home: 98 Union Apt 507 Seattle WA 98101

WILLIAMS, ROBERT C., engineering psychologist; b. Berkeley, Calif., Sept. 21, 1954; m. Anne-Marie E. Marz. AA, Macon Jr. Coll., 1982; BS, Gerogia Coll., 1984, MS, 1986. Enlisted USAF, 1972, advanced through grades to staff sgt.; telecommunications operator USAF, Travis AFB, Calif., 1972-74; telecommunications supr. USAF, RAF Greenham Common, Eng., 1974-78; assoc. dir. Pain Evaluation and Treatment Ctr., Macon, Ga., 1986-87; engrng. psychologist U.S. Army, White Sands Missile Range, N.M., 1987—; assoc. dir. dept. psychology Project Life Changes, Milledgville, Ga., 1984-87. Mem. Am. Psychol. Assn., Southeastern Psychol. Assn., Am. Pain Soc., Soc. for Behavioral Medicine, Gamma Beta Phi, Phi Beta Kappa. Office: Attn: ATOR-WHE US Army Tradoc Analysis Command White Sands Missile Range NM 88802-5502

WILLIAMS, ROBERT STONE, protective services official; b. Mathews, Va., Jan. 22, 1952; s. Charles H. and Anne (Stone) W.; m. Danielle Williams, July 1987. A.A.S., Rowan Tech. Inst., 1972; B.S. in Fire Protection and Safety Engring., Okla. State U., 1975, M.B.A., 1976. Adminstrv. specialist Oklahoma City Fire Dept., 1977-79; dep. fire chief Clovis Fire Dept., N.Mex., 1979-82; fire chief Billings Fire Dept., Mont., 1982-88; fire chief City of Spokane, Wash., 1988— . Bd. dirs. Salvation Army, Billings, 1984-85, Am. Heart Assn., Clovis, N.Mex., 1980-82. Named Fireperson Yr. Billings Downtown Exchange Club, 1988. Mem. Western Fire Chiefs Assn. (1st v.p. 1984-85, pres. 1985-86), Internat. Assn. Fire Chiefs, Nat. Fire Protection Assn., Curry County Jaycees (v.p. 1981-82, Jaycee of Yr. 1982), Billings Jaycees (bd. dirs. 1983-87, v.p. community devel. 1985, Outstanding Jaycee 1983, Disting. Service award 1985), Mont. Jaycees (treas. 1986-87, speak-up program mgr. 1986-87, Outstanding Young Montanan award 1985-86). Methodist. Office: Spokane Fire Dept W 44 Riverside Spokane WA 99201

WILLIAMS, ROBERT WAYLAND, motion picture television producer; b. Ottumwa, Iowa, Sept. 21, 1922; s. Henry Herbert and Bertha Emily (Barnett) W.; m. Joan Roberta, July 18, 1952; children: Angela, Robin, Robert. Student, Tuskegee Inst., 1943, Temple U., 1947, UCLA, 1947-49. Advt. salesman Ebony Mag. subs. Johnson Publ. Co., Chgo., 1949-50; salesman Bohemian Distbg. Co., L.A., 1951-55, Rheingold Brewing Co., L.A., 1955-56; pub. rels. rep. Falstaff Brewing Co., L.A., 1957-65; dist. mgr. Somerset Importers, Inc., L.A., 1965-74; account exec. Norton Simon

Communications, L.A., 1974-75; corp. community rels. Hunt Wesson Foods, Inc., L.A., 1975-85; pres. True Image Prodns., Inc., Pasadena, Calif., 1985—. Writer, producer, actor, author: Images and Attitudes, 1965. Co-founder Men of Tomorrow; pres. Devel. Bd. Calif.; bd. dirs. Pasadena Neighborhood Housing Svc.; exec. bd. mem. NAACP; found. bd. Calif. State U., L.A., pres. adv. bd.; bd. dirs. five acres faculty for abused children. Capt. USAAF, 1943-47. Mem. Screen Actors Guild, Kappa Alpha Psi. Democrat. Methodist. Club: J.A.N.S. Home and Office: 1220 N Arroyo Blvd Pasadena CA 91103

WILLIAMS, RONALD DAVID, electronics materials executive; b. Marshall, Ark., Mar. 15, 1944; s. Noble Kentucky and Elizabeth (Karns) W.; m. Beth L. Williams, Nov. 1977; children: Stephanie Noble, Keith Michael. BA, Columbia U., 1966, BS, 1967, MBA, 1973. Process engr. DuPont, Deepwater, N.J., 1966; design engr. Combustion Engring. Co., Hartford, 1971; cons. Arthur Andersen & Co., N.Y.C., 1973-76; corp. planner Amax Inc., Greenwich, Conn., 1976-77, group planning adminstr., 1978-80, mgr. corp. planning and analysis, 1980-84, dir. fin. analysis, 1984-86; project mgr. Olin Corp., Stamford, Conn., 1977-78; mgr. ops planning, analysis Savin Corp., Stamford, 1986-88; dir. fin., Bandgap Tech. Corp., Broomfield, Colo., 1988—. Served with USN, 1967-70: Vietnam. NASA traineeship, 1971; S.W. Mudd scholar, 1971. Mem. AAAS, Am. Chem. Soc., Fgn. Policy Assn., Am. Mgmt. Assn. Democrat. Club: Appalachian Mountain, Stamford Running, Boulder Road Runners. Home: 7361 S Meadow Ct Boulder CO 80301 Office: Bandgap Tech Corp 891 A Interlocken Pkwy Broomfield CO 80020

WILLIAMS, RONALD OSCAR, systems engineer; b. Denver, May 10, 1940; s. Oscar H. and Evelyn (Johnson) W. BS in Applied Math., U. Colo. Coll. Engring., 1964, postgrad. U. Colo., U. Denver, George Washington U. Computer programmer Apollo Systems dept., missile and space div. Gen. Electric Co., Kennedy Space Ctr., Fla., 1965-67, Manned Spacecraft Ctr., Houston, 1967-68; computer programmer U. Colo., Boulder, 1968-73; computer programmer analyst def. systems div. System Devel. Corp. for NORAD, Colorado Springs, 1974-75; engr. def. systems and command-and-info. systems Martin Marietta Aerospace, Denver, 1976-80; systems engr. space and communications group, def. info. systems div. Hughes Aircraft Co., Aurora, Colo., 1980—. Vol. fireman Clear Lake City (Tex.) Fire Dept., 1968; officer Boulder Emergency Squad, 1969-76, rescue squadman, 1969-76, liaison to cadets, 1971, personnel officer, 1971-76, exec. bd., 1971-76, award of merit, 1971, 72, emergency med. technician 1973—; spl. police officer Boulder Police Dept., 1970-75; spl. dep. sheriff Boulder County Sheriff's Dept., 1970-71; nat. adv. bd. Am. Security Coun., 1979—, Coalition of Peace through Strength, 1979—; mem. Rep. Nat. Com., Nat. Rep. Senatorial Com. Served with USMCR, 1958-66. Decorated Organized Res. medal; recipient Cost Improvement Program award Hughes Aircraft Co., 1982, Systems Improvement award, 1982, Top Cost Improvement Program award, 1983. Mem. AAAS, Math. Assn. Am., Am. Math. Soc., Soc. Indsl. and Applied Math., AIAA, Armed Forces Communications and Electronics Assn., Assn. Old Crows, Am. Def. Preparedness Assn., Marine Corps Assn., Air Force Assn., Nat. Geog. Soc., Smithsonian Instn. (assoc.), Met. Opera Guild, Colo. Hist. Soc., Hist. Denver, Inc., Historic Boulder, Inc., Denver Art Mus., Denver Botanic Gardens, Denver Mus. Natural History, Denver Zool. Found., Inc., Am. Mensa Ltd., Denver Mile Hi Mensa, Hour of Power Eagles Club. Lutheran. Home: 7504 W Quarto Ave Littleton CO 80123-4332 Office: Hughes Aircraft Co Bldg S-75 MS CHL 16800 E Centretech Pkwy Aurora CO 80011

WILLIAMS, RUTH LEE, clinical social worker; b. Dallas, June 24, 1944; d. Carl Woodley and Nancy Ruth (Gardner) W. BA, So. Meth. U., 1966; M Sci.in Social Work, U. Tex., Austin, 1969. Milieu coordinator Starr Commonwealth, Albion, Mich., 1969-73; clin. social worker Katherine Hamilton Mental Health Care, Terre Haute, Ind., 1973-74; clin. social worker, supr. Pikes Peak Mental Health Ctr., Colorado Springs, Colo., 1974-78; pvt. practice social work Colorado Springs, 1978—; pres. Hearthstone Inn, Inc., Colorado Springs, 1978—; practitioner Jin Shin Jyutsu, Colorado Springs, 1978—; pres., bd. dirs. Premier Care (formerly Colorado Springs Mental Health Care Providers Inc.), 1986-87, chmn. quality assurance com., 1987—. Author, editor: From the Kitchen of The Hearthstone Inn, 1981, 2d rev. edit., 1986. Mem. Nat. Registry Health Care Providers in Clin. Social Work (charter mem.), Colo. Soc. Clin. Social Work (editor 1976), Nat. Assn. Soc. Workers (diplomate), Nat. Bd. Social Work Examiners (cert.), Nat. Assn. Ind. Innkeepers, So. Meth. U. Alumni Assn. (life). Home: 11555 Howell Rd Colorado Springs CO 80908 Office: 536 E Uintah Colorado Springs CO 80903

WILLIAMS, SPENCER M., judge; b. Reading, Mass., Feb. 24, 1922; s. Theodore Ryder and Anabel (Hutchison) W.; m. Kathryn Bramlage, Aug. 20, 1943; children: Carol Marcia (Mrs. James B. Garvey), Peter, Spencer, Clark, Janice, Diane. A.B., U. Calif. at Los Angeles, 1943; postgrad., Hastings Coll. Law, 1946; J.D., U. Calif. at Berkeley, 1948. Bar: Calif. bar 1949, U.S. Supreme Ct. bar 1952. Assoc. Beresford & Adams, San Jose, Calif., 1949, Rankin, O'Neal, Center, Luckhardt, Bonney, Marlais & Lund, San Jose, Evans, Jackson & Kennedy, Sacramento; county counsel Santa Clara County, 1955-67; adminstr. Calif. Health and Welfare Agy., Sacramento, 1967-69; judge U.S. Dist. Ct. (no. dist.) Calif., San Francisco, from 1971, now sr. judge; County exec. pro tem, Santa Clara County; adminstr. Calif. Youth and Adult Corrections Agy., Sacramento; sec. Calif. Human Relations Agy., Sacramento, 1967-70. Chmn. San Jose Christmas Seals Drive, 1953, San Jose Muscular Dystrophy Drive, 1953, 54; team capt. fund raising drive San Jose YMCA, 1960; co-chmn. indsl. sect. fund raising drive Alexian Bros. Hosp., San Jose, 1964; team capt. fund raising drive San Jose Hosp.; mem. com. on youth and govt. YMCA, 1967-68; Candidate for Calif. Assembly, 1954, Calif. Atty. Gen., 1966, 70; Bd. dirs. San Jose Better Bus. Bur., 1955-66, Boys City Boys' Club, San Jose, 1965-67; pres. trustees Santa Clara County Law Library, 1955-66. Served with USNR, 1943-46; to lt. comdr. JAG Corps USNR, 1950-52, PTO. Named San Jose Man of Year, 1954. Mem. ABA, Calif. Bar Assn. (vice chmn. com. on publicly employed attys. 1962-63), Santa Clara County Bar Assn., Sacramento Bar Assn., Calif. Dist. Attys. Assn. (pres. 1963-64), Nat. Assn. County Civil Attys. (pres. 1963-64), Ninth Circuit Dist. Judges Assn. (pres. 1981-83), Fed. Judges Assn. (pres. 1982—), Theta Delta Chi. Club: Kiwanian. Office: US Dist Ct 280 S 1st St San Jose CA 95113

WILLIAMS, STANLEY CLARK, medical entomologist, educator; b. Long Beach, Calif., Aug. 24, 1939; s. Thomas and Sadie Elenore (Anderson) W.; m. Charlene E. Fernald; children: Lisa M., Thomas S.; m. Roxanna Berlin, Aug. 30, 1981; 1 child, Erin B. AB, San Diego State Coll., 1961, MA, 1963; postgrad., U. Kans., 1963-64; PhD, Ariz. State U., 1968. Cert. secondary tchr., Calif. Instr. San Diego Mus. Nat. History, 1957-59, asst. curator herpetology, 1957-61; park naturalist U.S. Nat. Park Svc., San Diego, 1960-62; instr. Grossmont (Calif.) High Sch. Dist., 1962-63, Ariz. State U., Tempe, 1964-66; prof. biology San Francisco State U., 1967—; bd. dirs. West Point Acad. Sci., Calif.; mem. adv. bd. San Francisco Insect Zoo. Contbr. over 60 articles to profl. jours. Grantee NSF, 1968-72; recipient Travel grant T.P. Hearne Co. Fellow Calif. Acad. Sci.; mem. Am. Arachnological Soc., Ecol. Soc. Am., San Francisco Beekeepers Assn. (pres. 1984-85), Pacific Coast Entomol. Soc. (pres. elect 1986, pres. 1987), Assn. Biologists for Computing (pres. 1986-88), Soc. Vector Ecologists (edit. bd. 1986—), Western Apicultural Soc. (v.p. 1987-88, pres. 1988-89), Soc. Systems Biologists, Willi Hennig Soc., Brit. An. Soc., Sigma Xi. Office: San Francisco State U Dept Biology San Francisco CA 94132

WILLIAMS, THEODORE E., state health services executive; b. Kansas City, Kans., Nov. 13, 1943; s. Walter H. Williams and Marjorie L. (McCord) Spearman; m. Myra Smith, May 17, 1986; 1 child, Malcom S.; children from previous marriage: Shawnna, Bryce. BS in Engring., Ariz. State U., 1979, JD, 1984. Switchman N.Y. Telephone Co., N.Y.C., 1965-69; systems engr. IBM, Phoenix, 1969-75; spl. asst. Office of Gov. of Ariz., Phoenix, 1975-76; dep. dir. Ariz. Dept. Health Svcs., Phoenix, 1976-80, dir., 1987—; dep. dir. Ariz. Dept. Transp., Phoenix, 1980-81; cons. Ariz. State Legis., Phoenix, 1982-83; exec. v.p. Bapt. Hosps. and Health Systems, Phoenix, 1984-86; v.p. ops. Valley View Community Hosp. Bapt. Hosps. and Health Systems, Youngtown, Ariz., 1986-87; mem. faculty Coll. Medicine U. Ariz., 1987—. Bd. dirs. Ariz. Acad., Phoenix, 1987—. Mem. Assn. State & Territorial Health Officers, Ariz. Med. Assn. (exec. com. 1987—). Office: Ariz Dept Health Svcs 1740 W Adams Phoenix AZ 85007

WILLIAMS, TYRELL CLAY, computer science and math educator, small business owner; b. St. Helena, Calif., Mar. 16, 1949; s. William Ollie and Lois Irene (Gribble) W.; m. Patricia Kathlene McDonald, May 1, 1970; children: Robin Tracy, Courtney Elizabeth. AA, Cabrillo Coll., Aptos, Calif., 1968; BA, U. Calif., San Cruz, 1970. Cert. secondary tchr., Calif. Tchr. jr. high sch. math. North Monterey County Unified Sch. Dist., Moss Landing, Calif., 1970-83; tchr. computer sci. North Monterey County Unified Sch. Dist., Castroville, Calif., 1983—; owner Dataphile, Watsonville, 1983—; seasonal ranger Dept. of Parks and Recreation State of Calif., Felton, 1967-70. Mem. Calif. Fedn. Tchrs. Democrat. Club: F.I.A.S.C.O. (Watsonville) (sgt.-at-arms 1987—). Home: 215 Ponderosa Ave Watsonville CA 95076

WILLIAMS, VALENA MARIE, public human resource administrator; b. Cleve., Dec. 22, 1948; d. John Bentley and Valena (Minor) W.; 1 child, Mosi Adesina Morrison. BS, San Jose State U., 1972; MS, Ill. State U., 1978. Cert. techr. Sr. tng. writer Allstate Ins. Co., Northbrook, Ill., 1978-82; pres. RIZULTS, 1979—, Chgo. Organ. Devel. Assn., 1980-82; program mgr. Bank Adminstrn. Inst., Schaumburg, Ill., 1982-83; corp. tng. projects supr. Motorola, Inc., Schaumburg, 1984-85; dir. tng. and edn. corp. offices Merritt Peralta Med. Ctr., Oakland, Calif., 1985-86; project analyst, personnel specialist County of San Mateo, Belmont, Calif., 1986-89; sr. employee devel. specialist, systems engring. div. Bank of Am., Oakland, 1989—; speaker, guest lectr. various assns., univs. and radios stas. Bd. dirs. Cen. Pl., Oakland, 1985—, YMCA, Oakland, 1986—. Mem. Am. Soc. Tng. and Devel., Bay Area Orgn. Deve. Network, No. Calif. Human Resource Coun., Oakland Athletic Club. Home: 6505 Lucas ave Oakland CA 94611

WILLIAMS, VERLE ALVIN, consulting engineer; b. New Virginia, Iowa, Apr. 8, 1933; s. Donald Oliver and Josephine Emily (Read) W.; A.A., Pueblo Jr. Coll., 1957; B.S. in M.E., B.S. in Bus., Colo. U., 1960; m. Mary Sue Earley, June 2, 1957; children—Steven Lee, Randall Joe, LeAnne Sue. Sales engr. Johnson Controls, Inc., Portland, Oreg., 1960-67, Los Angeles, 1967-68, San Diego, 1968-69, br. mgr., 1970-79; assoc. in charge of energy conservation systems dept. Dunn, Lee, Smith, Klein & Assos., National City, Calif., 1979-81; owner Verle A. Williams & Assos., Inc., profl. energy and control cons., San Diego, 1981—; lectr. in field. Founding mem. Rancho Bernardo Bapt. Ch., chmn., treas., 1970—. Served with U.S. Army, 1953-55. Registered profl. engr., Calif.; cert. energy auditor, Calif. Fellow ASHRAE (chmn. energy mgmt. com. 1979-81, past pres., v.p., bd. govs.); mem. Am. Mgmt. Assn., Soc. Level Tech. Com. on Automatic Control Systems, Assn. Energy Engrs. (cert. energy mgr.; founding pres. San Diego chpt. 1981; Engr. of Yr. 1982, Regional Engr. of Yr. 1983, Internat. Energy Engr. of Yr. 1984, v.p. Region V 1984-86), Soc. Energy Mgmt. (vice chmn. energy mgmt. 1985—), Energy Monitoring and Control Soc. Clubs: Rancho Bernardo Bowleros (pres. 1969-71). Home: 12394 Fairway Pointe Row San Diego CA 92128 Office: Williams Engring Ctr 7047 Carroll Rd San Diego CA 92121

WILLIAMS, WALTER BAKER, mortgage banker; b. Seattle, May 12, 1921; s. William Walter and Anna Leland (Baker) W.; m. Marie Davis Wilson, July 6, 1945; children: Kathryn Williams-Mullins, Marcia Frances Williams Swanson, Bruce Wilson, Wendy Susan. BA, U. Wash., 1943; JD, Harvard U., 1948. With Bogle & Gates, Seattle, 1948-63, ptnr., 1960-63; pres. Continental Inc., Seattle, 1963—; bd. dirs. United Graphics Inc., Seattle, 1973-86, Fed. Nat. Mortgage Assn., 1976-77. Rep. Wash. State Ho. of Reps., Olympia, 1961-63; sen. Wash. State Senate, Olympia, 1963-71; chmn. Econ. Devel. Council of Puget Sound, Seattle, 1981-82; pres. Japan-Am. Soc. of Seattle, 1971-72; chmn. Woodland Park Zoo Commn., Seattle, 1984-85. Served to capt. USMC, 1942-46, PTO. Recipient Brotherhood Citation, NCCJ, Seattle, 1980. Mem. Mortgage Bankers Assn. of Am. (pres. 1973-74), Wash. Mortgage Bankers Assn., Fed. Home Loan Mortgage Corp. Adv. Com., Wash. Savs. League (bd. dirs.). Republican. Congregationalist. Club: Rainier (pres. 1987-88) (Seattle). Lodge: Rotary (pres. local club 1984-85).

WILLIAMS, WARREN LLOYD, entrepreneur; b. Denver, Feb. 13, 1947; s. Robert Lloyd and Isabelle Virginia (Andersen) W.; m. Yvonne G. Shockley, July 5, 1970; children: Tammara, Rebecca, Deborah. BS, U. Colo., 1970, MBA, 1987. Pres. Williams/Ladd Enterprises, Inc., Boulder, Colo., 1970-77; pub. works dir. City of Lafayette, 1977-84; pres. Aaron Assoc. Affiliates, Inc., Lafayette, Colo., 1984-88; broker assoc. Re/Max Northwest, Westminster, Colo., 1988—; v.p. Scapeze Mfg. Tech. Inc., Boulder, 1988—, Transpn. Systems Engring. Inc., 1987-88; cons. in field. Author ednl. materials. Pres. Birthright of Boulder, 1976—; elder Foursquare Ch., Bulder, 1974; lay leader Vinyard Christian Fellowship, Denver, 1985; city adminstr. City of Lafayette, 1981; precinct chmn. Boulder County Rep. Party, 1978, 84. Named Coach of Yr., Lafayette Youth Recreation Club, 1980; recipient Outstanding Svc. award Centaurus High Sch., 1981, Outstanding Young Men Am. award, 1982. Mem. N. Suburban Bd. Realtors, Lions (bd. dirs. local chpt. 1985), Exec. Club. Home: 940 Cedwick Dr Lafayette CO 80026

WILLIAMS, WILHO EDWARD, engineering consultancy company executive; b. Spokane, Wash., Mar. 7, 1922; s. Emil Wilho and Lulu May (Johnson) W.; m. Virginia May Knudsen, June 26, 1954; children: Craig Wilho, Kim Ann, Kevin Jon. BSCE, Wash. State U., 1944; MSCE, U. Ill., 1947. Registered profl. engr., Wash., Idaho, Oreg., N.Mex.; registered profl. land surveyor, Idaho. Ptnr. Culler, Gale, Martell, Ericson and Norrie, Spokane, 1958-73; assoc. Bovay Engrs., Inc., Spokane, 1973-85; v.p. Bovay Northwest, Inc., Spokane, 1985—; mem. State of Wash. Bd. Registration for Profl. Engrs. and Land Surveyors, 1978-83, 85—. Mem. City of Spokane Bldg. Commn., 1980-83. Served to capt. USNR, 1942-75, Korea. Fellow ASCE (Engr. of Merit 1986); mem. Wash. Soc. Profl. Engrs. (pres. 1979-80), Structural Engrs. Assn. of Wash. (pres. 1975, Engr. of Yr. 1976), Am. Concrete Inst., Tau Beta Pi, Sigma Tau. Republican. Lutheran. Home: E 2331 34th Ave Spokane WA 99223 Office: Bovay NW Inc E 808 Sprague Ave Spokane WA 99202

WILLIAMS, WILLIAM COREY, professor of Old Testament, consultant; b. Wilkes-Barre, Pa., July 12, 1937; s. Edward Douglas and Elizabeth Irene (Schooley) W.; m. Alma Simmenroth Williams, June 27, 1959; 1 child, Linda. Diploma in Ministerial Studies, NE Bible Inst., 1962; BA in Bibl. Studies, Cen. Bible Coll., 1963, MA in Religion, 1964; MA in Hebrew and Near Ea. Studies, NYU, 1966, PhD in Hebrew Lang. and Near Ea. Studies, 1975. Ref. libr. Hebraic section Libr. of Congress, Washington, 1967-69; adj. prof. Old Testament Melodyland Sch. Theology, Anaheim, Caif., 1975-77; vis. prof. Old Testament Fuller Theol. Sem., Pasadena, Caif., 1978-81, 84, Asian Theol. Ctr. for Evangelism and Missions, Singapore and Sabah, E. Malaysia, 1985, Continental Bible Coll., Saint Pieters-Leeuw, Belgium, 1985, Mattersey Bible Coll., Eng., 1985, Inst. Holy Land Studies, Jerusalem, 1986; prof. Old Testament So. Calif. Coll., Costa Mesa, 1969—; transl. cons. and reviser New Am. Standard Bible, 1969—; transl. cons. The New Internat. Version; transl. cons. and editor Internat. Children's Version, 1985-86. Author: (book, tapes) Hebrew I: A Study Guide, 1986, Hebrew II: A Study Guide, 1986; contbr. articles to profl. jours. Nat. Def. Foreign Lang. fellow NYU, 1964-67; Alummi scholar N.E. Bible Inst., 1960-61. Mem. Soc. Bibl. Lit., Am. Oriental Soc., Evang. Theol. Soc. (exec. office 1974-77), Am. Acad. Religion, Nat. Assn. Profs. of Hebrew, Inst. Bibl. Rsch., The Lockman Found. (editorial bd. 1974—). Home: 617 W Aurora Santa Ana CA 92707 Office: So Calif Coll 55 Fair Dr Costa Mesa CA 92626

WILLIAMS, WILLIAM JERRY, real estate developer; b. Las Vegas, May 5, 1933; s. Doby and Mary Alice (Breen) W.; m. Barbara Helen Dickie, June 6, 1952; children: James, Leah, Shaun, Kimberly. Grad. high sch., Prescott, Ariz. Apprentice Local 359, Prescott, 1953-57, journeyman, 1957-63; comml. and indsl. contractor, foreman Glau Gas & Equipment Co., Prescott, 1963-89; project developer J-B Williams & Assocs., Prescott, 1979—. Mem. founding bd. Prescott Town Hall, 1979—, Prescott Charities, 1980—; pres. Prescott Bd. Edn., 1977-79; bd. dirs. Ariz. Sch. Bd. Assn., 1977-79, Prescott Indsl. Devel. Authority, 1987—, Prescott Area Econ. Devel., 1988-89. Named Man of Yr., Salvation Army, Prescott, 1988. Mem. Ariz. Assn. Indsl. Developers (bd. dirs. 1986-88), Urban Land Inst., Ariz. Acad., Lions (pres. Prescott 1976), Masons, Rotary (sgt. at arms Prescott 1986). Republican. Office: 1021 Commerce Dr Prescott AZ 86301

WILLIAMSON, BARBARA DIANE, lawyer; b. Riverside, N.J., July 24, 1950; d. Frederick Raymond and Dorothy (Jessup) Ott; m. Luis Williamson, May 4, 1973. BFA, William Paterson Coll., 1972; lic. vocat. nurse, Yakima Valley Community Coll., 1981; BS in Nursing with honors, Seattle U., 1983; MS in Community Health Nursing with honors, U. Wash., 1984; JD, U. Puget Sound, 1988. Bar: N.J. 1988; cert. hazardous control mgr. Art tchr. Delran (N.J.) Twp. Schs., 1972-78; recreational coord. Delran (N.J.) Twp. Summer Schs., 1973-76; nurse Yakima (Wash.) Valley Meml. Hosp., 1980-85; occupational health cons., researcher Evergreen Legal Svcs., Granger, Wash., 1986; environ. analyst Westinghouse Hanford Co., Richland, Wash., 1987; atty. Westinghouse Co., Richland, 1988—; cons. Occupational and Envirn. Cons. Svcs., 1988; occupational health and safety mgmt. researcher U. Hosp., Seattle, 1983-84; pesticide educator Evergreen Legal Svcs., Granger, Wash., 1986; smoking policy cons. U. Puget Sound Law Sch., Tacoma, 1986-87; researcher, legal assoc. Dept. of Ecology Wash. State Atty. Gen., Lacey, 1987. Grantee U. Puget Sound, 1986, Alaskan-Northwest Synod of Presbyn. Chs., 1986. Mem. ABA, Wash. Assn. Occupational Health Nurses, Wash. State Pub. Health Assn. (legis. com. 1984), N.W. Occupational Health Nurses Assn. (mem. nominating com. 1984), Am. Pub. Health Assn., Am. Assn. of Occupational Health Nurses, Phi Delta Phi, Alpha Sigma Nu, Sigma Theta Tau. Home: 1900 Stevens Dr Box 626 Richland WA 99352 Office: Westinghouse Hanford Co B3-06 1100 Jadwin Ave Richland WA 99352

WILLIAMSON, HARWOOD DANFORD, utility company executive; b. Waimea, Kauai, Hawaii, 1932. Grad., Stanford U., 1956. Pres., chief operating officer Hawaiian Electric Co., Inc., also bd. dirs.; v.p., bd. dirs. Hawaiian Electric Industries, Inc.; chmn. Hawaii Electric Light Co., Inc., Maui Electric Co., Ltd. Office: Hawaiian Electric Co Inc 900 Richards St PO Box 2750 Honolulu HI 96813 *

WILLIAMSON, JACK (JOHN STEWART WILLIAMSON), writer; b. Bisbee, Ariz., Apr. 29, 1908; s. Asa Lee and Lucy Betty (Hunt) W.; m. Blanche Slaten Harp, Aug. 15, 1947 (dec. Jan. 1985); stepchildren: Keign Harp (dec.), Adele Harp Lovorn. BA, MA, Eastern N.Mex. U., 1957, LHD (hon.), 1981; PhD, U. Colo., 1964. Prof. English Eastern N.Mex. U., Portales, 1960-77. Author numerous sci. fiction books including The Legion of Space, 1947, Darker Than You Think, 1948, The Humanoids, 1949, The Green Girl, 1950, The Cometeers, 1950, One Against the Legion, 1950, Seetee Shock, 1950, Seetee Ship, 1950, Dragon's Island, 1951, The Legion of Time, 1952, Dome Around America, 1955, The Trial of Terra, 1962, Golden Blood, 1964, The Reign of Wizardry, 1965, Bright New Universe, 1967, Trapped in Space, 1968, The Pandora Effect, 1969, People Machines, 1971, The Moon Children, 1972, H.G. Wells: Critic of Progress, 1973, Teaching SF, 1975, The Early Williamson, 1975, The Power of Blackness, 1976, The Best of Jack Williamson, 1978 Brother to Demons, Brother to Gods, 1979, Teaching Science Fiction: Education for Tomorrow, 1980, The Alien Intelligence, 1980, The Humanoid Touch, 1980, Manseed, 1982, The Queen of a Legion, 1983, Wonder's Child: My Life in Science Fiction, 1984 (Hugo award 1985), Lifeburst, 1984, Firechild, 1986; (with Frederik Pohl) Undersea Quest, 1954, Undersea Fleet, 1955, Undersea City, 1956, The Reefs of Space, 1964, Starchild, 1965, Rogue Star, 1969, The Farthest Star, 1975, Wall Around a Star, 1983, Land's End, 1988; (with James Gunn) Star Bridge, 1955; (with Miles J. Breuer) The Birth of an New Republic, 1981. Served as staff sgt. USAAF, 1942-45. Mem. Sci. Fiction Writers Am. (pres. 1978-80, Grand Master Nebula award 1976), Sci. Fiction Research Assn. (Pilgrim award 1968), World Sci. Fiction, Planetary Soc. Home: PO Box 761 Portales NM 88130 Office: Ea NMex U Golden Libr Portales NM 88130

WILLIAMSON, JERRY DEAN, radio station executive; b. Appleton City, Mo., Mar. 14, 1934; s. Charles Murry and Eunice Lee (Davis) W.; m. Joan Hawkes, Apr. 22, 1955; children: Kirk Dean, Vicky Lynn, Kimberly Dawn, Gregory Alan, Robert Todd. Student, Idaho State U., 1952-56, Ea. Wash. U., 1956-57. Radio announcer Sta. KOSI, Denver, 1957-61; sales mgr. Sta. KLAK-AM-FM, Denver, 1961-76; account exec. Sta. KIRO, Seattle, 1976-78; gen. mgr. Stas. KIDO, KIDQ, Boise, Idaho, 1978-80, Sta. KART/KFMA, Twin Falls, Idaho, 1980-82; gen. sales mgr. Sta. KUTV-TV, Salt Lake City, 1982-85; nat. sales mgr. Stas. KLTQ, KUTR, Salt Lake City, 1985; sta. mgr. Sta. KGHL/KIDX, Billings, Mont., 1985—; sales cons. Sta. KART/KFMA, Twin Falls, 1982—. Mem. Mont. Broadcasters Assn., Billings Advt. Club., Rotary. Republican. Mormon. Home: 931 Silverbell Circle Billings MT 59105 Office: Sta KGHL 2070 Overland Ave Ste 103 Billings MT 59102

WILLIAMSON, JOHN R., mechanical engineer; b. Michigan City, Ind., Jan. 13, 1924; s. J. Russell and Blanche (Kaser) W.; m. Mary Anne Baird, Mar. 1, 1948; children: Susan, Doug, Nanci. BME, Purdue U., 1951. Project engr. prodn. div. Bendix Corp., South Bend, Ind., 1951-65; staff engr. Garrett Engine Co., Phoenix, 1965--. Patentee aerospace devices. Sgt. U.S. Army, 1942-46, ETO. Home: 6326 E Joshua Tree Ln Paradise Valley AZ 85253

WILLIAMSON, LOWELL JAMES, oil industry executive; b. Canton, Ohio, July 19, 1923; s. Daryl and Catherine (Hayes) W.; m. Dorothy McGuire, Dec. 6, 1958; children: Eric Dean, Rhonda Lynn, Rex Edward, David James. BA, Anderson U., 1950; postgrad, Ind. U., 1950-52; LLD (hon.), Warner Pacific Coll., 1973. Pres., chief exec. officer Williamson Oil & Gas Ltd., Denver and Russell, Kans., 1952-57, Calgary, Alta., Can., 1955-74; pres., chief exec. officer Glenex Petroleum, Ltd., Calgary, 1963-88, MGF Mgmt., Inc., Calgary, 1964-73, Glenex Petroleum, Inc., Scottsdale, Ariz., 1974—, Williamson Group, Inc., Scottsdale, 1984—. Served as tech. sgt. USAAF, 1943-45, prisoner of war, ETO. Decorated Purple Heart, Air medal with three oak leaf clusters, Ex-Prisoner of War medal. CLubs: Paradise Valley Country, Calgary Golf and Country. Home: 6721 E Caballo Dr Paradise Valley AZ 85253 Office: The Williamson Group 7573 N Scottsdale Rd Ste 145C Scottsdale AZ 85253

WILLIAMSON, MELISSA SUE, nurse; b. Colorado Springs, Colo., Mar. 14, 1956; d. William Frederick and Laura Jean (Buck) Short; m. Charles Clyde Williamson II, Aug. 10, 1979; 1 child, Genevieve Catlyn. Student, U. So. Calif., 1974-77; BS in Nursing, Tex. Christian U., 1981. Cert. oncology nurse. Staff nurse Med. Plaza Hosp., Ft. Worth, 1981-85; asst. head nurse Med. Pla. Hosp., Ft. Worth, 1985-87; staff nurse oncology unit Redding (Calif.) Med. Ctr., 1987-89; staff nurse neurology surg. ICU Enloe Hosp., Chico, Calif., 1989—; guest speaker Am. Cancer Soc., Ft. Worth, 1980—; asst. chmn. Am. Cancer Conf. for Nurses, Ft. Worth, 1985. Vol. Mayfest, Ft. Worth, 1983. Mem. Oncology Nursing Soc., Delta Gamma. Episcopalian.

WILLIAMSON, NEIL ROBERT, psychiatrist; b. LaGrande, Oreg., Oct. 14, 1940; s. Robert Elton and Lorene Adeline (Johnson) W. BS, U. Oreg., Eugene, 1962; MD, U. Oreg., Portland, 1967; postgrad. in Advanced Studies Social Welfare, Heller Sch., Brandeis U., 1973-77. Intern Balt. City Hosps., 1967-68; fellow in medicine Johns Hopkins U. Hosps., Balt., 1967-68; staff physician Hall Health U. Wash., Seattle, 1970-72; resident in psychiatry Worcester (Mass.) State Hosp., 1973-77; instr. U. Mass. Med. Sch., Worcester, 1978-82; cons. Josephine County Mental Health Program, Grants Pass, Oreg., 1982-88; pvt. practice in psychiatry Grants Pass, Oreg., 1982—; med. dir. Southern Oreg. Adolescent Study and Treatment Ctr., Grants Pass, Oreg., 1986—. Donor Ashland Shakespearean Festival. Served to capt. U.S. Army, 1968-70. Mem. Oreg. Med. Assn., Josephine County Med. Soc., Grants Pass C. of C. Democrat. Office: Williamson MD PC 243 Northeast C St Grants Pass OR 97526

WILLIAMSON, NEIL SEYMOUR, III, aircraft company executive, retired Army officer; b. Dumont, N.J., Jan. 5, 1935; s. Neil Seymour and Mary Louise (Bittenbender) W.; m. Sue Carrole Cooper, Dec. 15, 1985; children: Deborah D., Leisa L., Neil S. IV, Dirk A., Wendy L. BS, U.S. Mil. Acad., 1958; MSME, U. Mich., 1963. Commd. 2d lt. U.S. Army, 1958, advanced through grades to col.; assoc. prof. dept. earth, space and graphic scis. U.S. Mil. Acad., West Point, N.Y., 1965-68; chief edn. sect. U.S. Army, Ft. McNair, D.C., 1970-71; analyst armor infantry systems group Pentagon U.S. Army, Washington, 1972-73, systems analyst requirements office Pentagon, 1974-75, program analyst, 1975-76; chief advanced systems concept office U.S. Army, Redstone Arsenal, Ala., 1976-77; comdr., dir. fire control & small caliber weapon systems lab. U.S. Army, Dover, N.J., 1977-78; project mgr. TOW U.S. Army, Redstone Arsenal, 1978-81; ret. U.S. Army, 1981; program mgr. Hughes Aircraft Co., El Segundo, Calif., 1981—. Decorated

Bronze Star with one oak leaf cluster, Legion of Merit with one oak leaf cluster, Air medal with seven oak leaf clusters, Purple Heart. Mem. Soc. Automotive Engrs., Am. Def. Preparedness Assn., Army Aviation Assn. (pres. Tenn. Valley chpt. 1980), Am. Helicopter Soc., U.S. Armor Assn., Disabled Am. Vets. Office: Hughes Aircraft Co PO Box 902 El Segundo CA 90245

WILLIAMSON, STEPHEN VICTOR, state official; b. Tulare, Calif., May 20, 1950; s. Grady Edgar and June Bernice (Gragg) W. BA, U. Calif.-Davis, 1971. Sr. coordinator U. Calif. Statewide Student Body Presidents Council-Student Lobby, 1971-73; cons. budget div. Calif. Dept. Fin., 1973-74, Systems Research Inc., Los Angeles, 1974-76, Calif. Research, Sacramento, Calif., 1976-78; dir. Calif. State Clearinghouse, Gov.'s. Office Planning and Research, Sacramento, 1978-82; exec. com. State EDP Policy, 1983-84; mgr. info. systems Calif. Housing Fin. Agy., Sacramento, 1983-84; sr. mgr., cons. info. tech. Price Waterhouse, 1984—. Mem. Assn. Environ. Profls. (Achievement of Yr. award 1982), Assn. for Computing Machinery, Data Processing Mgmt. Assn., Assn. Systems Mgmt., Am. Soc. Pub. Adminstrs. (Sacramento chpt. exec. bd.), Chi Phi. Office: Price Waterhouse 455 Capitol Mall Sacramento CA 95814

WILLIE, ELVIN, JR., Indian tribal executive; b. Schurz, Nev., Sept. 15, 1953; s. Elvin and Rosalie Irene (McKay) W.; m. Georgina A. Willie; children: James X. II, Everett Z. B.A., U. Calif.-Berkeley, 1976; postgrad., 1988—. Media coordinator native Am. studies U. Calif.-Berkeley, 1973-76; curriculum devel. coordinator tribal edn. program Walker River Paiute Tribe, Schurz, Nev., 1976-77, tribal chmn., 1979—; smokeshop mgr. Walker River Tribal Enterprise, 1977-79. Election bd. chmn. precinct 11, Mineral County, Nev., 1980-83. Mem. Western Nev. Dirt Track Racing Assn.

WILLIG, KARL VICTOR, computer firm executive; b. Idaho Falls, Idaho, June 4, 1944; s. Louis Victor and Ethel (McCarty) W.; m. Julianne Erickson, June 10, 1972; 1 son, Ray. BA magna cum laude, Coll. of Idaho, 1968; MBA (Dean Donald Kirk David fellow), Harvard U., 1970. Pres. Ariz. Beef, Inc., Phoenix, 1971-73; group v.p. Ariz.-Colo. Land & Cattle Co., Phoenix, 1973-76; v.p. Rufenacht, Bromagen & Hertz, Inc., Chgo., 1976-77; pres. Sambo's Restaurants, Inc., Santa Barbara, Calif., 1977-79; ptnr. Santa Barbara Capital, 1979-85; pres. EURUSA Equities Corp., 1985-86; pres., chief exec. officer InfoGenesis, 1986—; trustee Am. Bapt. Sem. of West, 1977-85. Named one of Outstanding Young Men of Am., 1972; recipient Assn. of U.S. Army award, 1964.

WILLING, JAMES RICHARD, computer technician; b. Portland, Oreg., Apr. 1, 1958; s. James Albert and Venita Faye (Fishburn) W.; m. Carole Marguerite Babbitt, Feb. 10, 1979; 1 child, Robert James. Grad. Beaverton High Sch., Oreg. Shop technician Byte N.W. Inc., Beaverton, 1976-79; field service technician N.W. Computer Support, Beaverton, 1979-81; systems programmer Johnson-Laird Inc., Portland, 1982; project dir. CB CBBS/NW, Beaverton, 1979—; lead technician Computerland, Tigard, Oreg., 1982-86; field engr., tech. Compu-Shop, 1986-88, Portland Computer Arts Resource Ctr., 1986-88; field svc. rep. Sears Computer and Peripheral Svc., Tigard, Oreg., 1988—; mem. steering com. Portland Computer Arts Resource Ctr., 1986—. Mem. computer edn. task force Oreg. Mus. Sci. and Industry, Portland, 1984. Mem. Control Program for Microcomputers User's Group NW (founder 1979), pres. 1979-82). Republican. Methodist. Home: 14120 SW 20th Beaverton OR 97005-4971 Office: Sears Computer & Peripheral Svc 11844 SW Pacific Hwy Tigard OR 97223

WILLIS, DAVID WILLIAM, pediatrician; b. Salisbury, Md., Mar. 6, 1950; s. William Every and Beatrice Alice (Adkins) W.; m. Margaret A. Fratto, Mar. 21, 1980; children: Adam Matthew, Andrew Martin. BA, DD (hon.), U. Del., 1972; MD, Thomas Jefferson U., 1976. Intern Oreg. Health Sci. U., Portland, 1976-77; resident in pediatrics Oreg. Health Sci. U., 1977-78, fellow in child devel., crippled children div., 1978-80; practice medicine specializing in pediatrics McMinnville, Oreg., 1980-85; practice medicine specializing in behavioral pediatrics Portland, 1985—; clin. dirs. Behavioral Pediatric Clinic, Oreg. Health Sci. U., 1980—. Fellow Am. Acad. Pediatrics (com. psychosocial aspects child family health 1983—); mem. AMA, Am. Psychiat. Assn., Oreg. Psychiat. Assn., Oreg. Med. Assn. Democrat. Roman Catholic. Home: 4103 SW 48th Pl Portland OR 97221 Office: 2801 N Gantenbein Ave Portland OR 97227

WILLIS, HAROLD WENDT, SR., real estate developer; b. Marion, Ala., Oct. 7, 1927; s. Robert James and Della (Wendt) W.; student Loma Linda U., 1960, various courses San Bernardino Valley Coll.; m. Patsy Gay Bacon, Aug. 2, 1947 (div. Jan. 1975); children: Harold Wendt II, Timothy Gay, April Ann, Brian Tad, Suzanne Gail; m. Vernette Jacobson Osborne, Mar. 30, 1980 (div. 1984); m. Ofelia Alvarez, Sept. 23, 1984; children: Ryran Robert, Samantha Ofelia. Ptnr., Victoria Guernsey, San Bernardino, Calif., 1950-63, co-pres., 1963-74, pres., 1974—; owner Quik-Save, 1966—, K-Mart Shopping Ctr., San Bernardino, 1969—; pres. Energy Delivery Systems, Food and Fuel, Inc. San Bernardino City water commr., 1965—. Bd. councillors Loma Linda (Calif.) U., 1968-85, pres., 1971-74. Served as officer U.S. Mcht. Marine, 1945-46. Recipient Silver medal in 3000 meter steeplechase Sr. Olympics, U. So. Calif., 1979, 81, 82, 83; lic. pvt. pilot. Mem. Calif. Dairy Industries Assn. (pres. 1963, 64), Liga Internat. (2d v.p. 1978, pres. 1982, 83). Seventh-day Adventist (deacon 1950-67). Office: PO Box 5607 San Bernardino CA 92412

WILLIS, JIMMY ROY, accountant; b. Hunsville, Ala., July 21, 1941; s. Roy P and Estelle E. (Callas) W.; m. Linda Elizabeth Shoemaker, June. BS, Pepperdine U., 1964; MBA, Oregon State U., 1970. CPA. Job acct. Swinerton & Walberg Co., Honolulu, 1964; acctg. supr. Coopers & Lybrand, Eugene, Oreg., 1970-76; acctg. mgr. Lee, Coleman & Allen, Eugene, Oreg., 1977-78; CPA, ptnr. Young, Willis & Co., Eugene, Oreg., 1978-80; CPA ptnr. Molatore Gerbert, Eugene, Oreg., 1981-88, Isler & Co., Eugene, Oreg., 1988—; Instr. Lane Community Coll., Eugene, 1976-81, Ore. State U., 1984; cons. treas. SW Ore. Mus. of Sci. & Industry, Eugene, 1974, Lane Regional Arts. Recipient: 3rd place, Nat. Masters, Eugene, 1985. mem. Nat Assn. Accts. (pres., 1980-81), Oregon Soc. of CPAs (pres.,. Republican. Home: 2172 Elysium Eugene OR 97401 Office: Isler and Co 1976 Garden Ave Eugene OR 97403

WILLISON, BRUCE GRAY, banker; b. Riverside, Calif., Oct. 16, 1948; s. Walter G. and Dorothy (Phillips) W.; m. Gretchen A. Illig; children: Patrick, Bruce G., Kristen, Jeffery, Geoffrey, Lea. B.A. in econs., UCLA, 1970; M.B.A., U. So. Calif., 1973. With Bank of Am., Los Angeles, 1973-79; dir. mktg. First Interstate Bancorp, Los Angeles, 1982-83; exec. v.p. world banking group First Interstate Bank, Los Angeles, 1983-85; pres., chief exec. officer First Interstate Bank, 1985-86; chmn., chief exec. officer First Interstate Bank Oreg., Portland, 1986—. Served to lt. USN, 1970-72. Home: Portland OR Office: First Interstate Bank Oreg 1300 SW 5th Ave Portland OR 97201

WILLMS, RICHARD SCOTT, chemical engineer; b. San Bernadino, Calif., Feb. 26, 1957; s. Richard Kenneth and Wilda Jane (Foushee) W.; m. Mary Patricia Hurstell, Aug. 5, 1983; 1 child, Richard Benjamin. BS, La. State U., 1980, MS, 1983, PhD, 1985. With Los Alamos (N.Mex.) Nat. Lab., 1985—. Mem. Am. Inst. Chem. Engrs., Am. Chem. Soc. Republican. Mem. Evangelical Free Ch. Office: Los Alamos Nat Lab Mail Stop C-348 Los Alamos NM 87545

WILLOUGHBY, JAMES RUSSELL, artist; b. Toronto, Ohio, Apr. 22, 1928; s. Russell Lee and Edna Gertrude (McKeown) W.; m. Dorothy M. Ponder, Sept. 12, 1952 (div. 1958); children: Jim Jr., David; m. Susan N. Boettjer, Nov. 28, 1980. AFA, Pasadena City Coll., 1951; postgrad., Art Ctr. Sch. Mem. staff Chrysler Corp., Maywood, Calif., 1951-57; adminstrv. asst., tech. artist Ramo-Woolridge Corp., El Segundo, Calif., 1957-59; adminstr. asst. Space Tech. Labs., El Segundo, 1959-61; intelligence analyst Aerospace Corp., El Segundo, 1961-65; freelancer Calif., 1965-72, Filmation Studios, Reseda, Calif., 1972-82, various orgns., 1982—. Illustrator Cowboy Country Cartoons, 1988. Mem. Nat. Cartoonist Soc. Home: 1407 Sierra Vista Dr Prescott AZ 86303

WILLS, JOHN CLARENCE, marketing and training consultant; b. Chgo., July 16, 1942; s. Clarence Wills and Dorothy Wanita (Penman) Nanartowich; m. Nancy E. Driver, June 18, 1964 (div. 1975); children: Steven, Craig, Christine. BSBA, San Diego State U., 1965; postgrad., Wayne State U., 1970-73. Internal auditor Del Mar (Calif.) Turf Club, 1963-65; dir. edn. Burroughs Corp., Detroit, 1969-75; v.p. devel. and mktg. Tratec, Inc., L.A., 1975-79; gen. mgr. Tratec-McGraw Hill, L.A., 1979-80; pres. FLI, Inc., L.A., 1980—; also dir. FLI, Inc. Editor tng. programs; contbr. articles to profl. publs. Mem. computer adv. com., L.A. City Schs., 1986. Capt. USAF, 1965-69. Mem. Nat. Soc. Performance and Instrn. (chmn. leadership devel. com. 1980—, past pres. L.A. chpt.), Data Processing Mgmt. Assn. (CDP), Sports Connection. Home: 6634 Orion Ave Van Nuys CA 91406 Office: FLI Inc Ste 205 3500 S Figueroa St Los Angeles CA 90007-4385

WILLSON, LAURA FAULK, education consultant; b. San Antonio, Aug. 20, 1937; d. David Reynolds and Alma Laura (Reveley) Faulk; m. Robert Edward Willson, May 31, 1958 (div. 1983); children: Ryan Faulk, Brannan Faulk. BBA, U. Tex., Austin, 1958; MBA in Mktg., U. Houston, 1963; PhD in Psychology, U. Calif., Berkeley, 1973. Cert. tchr., adminstr., Tex. Tchr. San Antonio Ind. Sch. Dist., 1958-60; rsch. assoc. to pvt. practice consulting economist Houston, 1960-61; market analyst Cleco Tools, Houston, 1961-62; instr. San Jacinto Coll., Houston, 1962-63; teaching fellow U. Houston, 1964-65; assoc. dir. rsch. D'Arcy Advt. Agy., San Francisco, 1965-66; v.p., dean, prof. Marin Community Colls., Kentfield, Calif., 1966-86; vice chancellor academic affairs Calif. Community Colls., Sacramento, 1986-87; ind. cons. higher edn. Belvedere, Calif., 1974—; team mem., chair accrediting commn., Western Assn. Schs. and Colls., 1976-87. Treas., bd. dirs. Planned Parenthood of Marin, San Rafael, Calif., 1985; vol. Reach to Recovery, Marin County, 1987—; mem. Redwood High Parents Assn., Larkspur, Calif., 1987—. Mem. Assn. Calif. Community Coll. Adminstrs., Beta Gamma Sigma, Omicron Delta Epsilon. Office: 107 Blackfield Dr Tiburon CA 94920

WILSON, ALLAN CHARLES, biochemistry educator; b. Ngaruawahia, New Zealand, Oct. 18, 1934; came to U.S., 1955; s. Charles and Eunice Boyce (Wood) W.; m. Leona Greenbaum, Sept. 13, 1958; children: Ruth, David. BS, U. Otago, New Zealand, 1955, DSc (hon.), 1989; MS, Wash. State U., 1957; PhD, U. Calif., Berkeley, 1961. Postdoctoral fellow Brandeis U., Waltham, Mass., 1961-64; asst. prof. U. Calif., Berkeley, 1964-68, assoc. prof., 1968-72, prof. biochemistry, 1972—. Contbr. numerous articles to profl. jours. and books. Fellow Guggenheim Meml. Found., 1972-73, 79-80, Am. Acad. Arts and Scis., 1983, Royal Soc., 1986, MacArthur Found., 1986—. Mem. Am. Soc. Biol. Chemists. Office: U Calif 401 Barker Hall Berkeley CA 94720

WILSON, ALMON CHAPMAN, physician, retired naval officer; b. Hudson Falls, N.Y., July 13, 1924; s. Almon Chapman and Edith May (Truesdale) W.; m. Sofia M. Bogdons, Jan. 24, 1945; 1 child, Geoffrey Peter. B.A., Union Coll., Schenectady, 1946; M.D., Albany Med. Coll., 1952; M.S., George Washington U., 1969; student, Naval War Coll., Newport, R.I., 1968-69. Diplomate: Am. Bd. Surgery. Served as enlisted man and officer U.S. Navy, 1943-46, lt. j.g., M.C., 1952, advanced through grades to rear adm., 1976; intern U.S. Naval Hosp., Bremerton, Wash., 1952-53; resident VA Hosp., Salt Lake City, 1954-58; chief of surgery Sta. Hosp. Naval Sta., Subic Bay, Philippines, 1959-61; staff surgeon Naval Hosp., San Diego, 1961-64; asst. chief surgery Naval Hosp., Chelsea, Mass., 1964-65; comdg. officer 3d Med. Bn., 3d Marine Div. Fleet Marine Force, Pacific, Vietnam, 1965-66; chief surgery Naval Hosp., Yososuka, Japan, 1966-68; assigned Naval War Coll., 1968-69; fleet med. officer, comdr. in chief U.S. Naval Forces, Europe and; sr. med. officer Naval Activities London, 1969-71; dep. dir. planning div. Bur. Medicine and Surgery Navy Dept., Washington, 1971-72; dir. div. Navy Dept., 1972-74; with additional duty as med. adv. to dep. chief naval ops. (logistics) and personal physician to chmn. Joint Chiefs of Staff, 1972-74; comdg. officer Naval Hosp., Gt. Lakes, Ill., 1974-76; asst. chief for material resources Bur. Medicine and Surgery Navy Dept., Washington, 1976-79; comdg. officer (Navy Health Scis. Edn. and Tng. Command), 1979-80; the med. officer U.S. Marine Corps., 1980-81, project mgr. Fleet Hosp. Programs, 1981-82; dir. Resources Div. 1982-83; dep. dir. naval medicine, dep. surgeon gen. Dept. Navy, 1983-84; ret. 1984; mem. grad. med. edn. adv. com. Dept. Def. Decorated Legion of Merit with gold V (3 stars), Meritorious Service medal, Joint Service Commendation medal Gold Star. Fellow ACS (gov.); mem. Assn. Mil. Surgeons U.S.

WILSON, ANN, singer, recording artist; b. 1950; d. John and Lou Wilson. Ed., Cornish Allied Inst. Fine Arts, Seattle. Lead singer rock group Heart, 1975—. Albums include: Dreamboat Annie, 1975, Magazine, 1975, Little Queen, 1977, Dog and Butterfly, 1978, Bebe le Strange, 1980, Heart Live-Gr, Private Audition, 1982, Passionworks, 1983, Heart, 1985, Bad Animals, 1987; single recs. include: Magic Man, 1976, Barracuda, 1977, Crazy on You, 1976, Straight On, 1978, Even It Up, 1980, Sweet Darlin', 1980, Tell It Like It Is, 1981, Unchained Melody, 1981, This Man is Mine, 1982, City's Burning, 1982, Bright Light Girl, 1982, How Can I Refuse, 1983, Sleep Alone, 1983, Almost Paradise, 1984, The Heat, 1984, What About Love, 1985, Never, 1985, These Dreams, 1986, Nothin' at All, 1986, Alone, 1987, Who Will Run to You, 1987, There's The Girl, 1987, I Want You So Bad, 1988, Surrender to Me, 1988. Office: 219 1st Ave N Ste 333 Seattle WA 98109

WILSON, A(RNOLD) J(ESSE), city manager, consultant, communications executive; b. St. Louis, Oct. 18, 1941; s. Arnold Jesse and Eleanor (Zinn) W.; m. Patricia Ann Wilson, Mar., 7, 1961 (div. Aug. 1970); children: Mark, Mary Beth; m. Sara Roscoe, Aug. 29, 1970; children: Kristin, Jesse. AA, S.W. Bapt. Coll., 1961; BA in Psychology, William Jewell Coll., 1963; BD, Yale U., 1966, ThM, 1967. Assoc. minister, community cons. United Ch. on the Green, New Haven, 1964-67; salesperson Clark Deeper Co., St. Louis, 1967-68; dir. human resources City of University City, Mo., 1968-69; exec. dir. St. Louis County Mcpl. League, Clayton, Mo., 1969-70; exec. asst. to mayor City of St. Louis, 1971-76; mgr. City of Portland, Maine, 1976-80, City of Santa Ana, Calif., 1980-83, City of Kansas City, Mo., 1983-85; pres. Wilson Communications, Kansas City and Fallbrook, Calif., 1985-88; city adminstr. City of Pomona, Calif., 1988—; cons. U.S. Dept. HUD, Washington, 1975-76, U.S. Dept. HHS, Washington, 1978, 1st Nat. Bank of Boston, 1979-80, Nat. League of Cities, Washington, 1988—. Contbr. articles to profl. jours. Mem. human devel. com. Nat. League of Cities, Washington, 1978-84, 88; mem. resolutions com. Mo. Mcpl. League, 1978-79; mem. com. on revenue and fin. Calif. League of Cities, 1980-83; chmn. exec. adv. com. St. Louis Regional Coun., 1975. Recipient Golden City award City of Santa Ana, 1983, Community Svc. award Orange County (Calif.) Bd. of Suprs., 1983, Life Svc. award S.W. Bapt. Coll., 1984. Mem. Internat. City Mgmt. Assn., Am. Soc. Pub. Adminstrn., Govt. Fin. Officers Assn., Internat. Assn. Human Rights Orgn., Nat. Assn. Housing Redevel. Officers, Calif. Community Renewal Assn., Women and Minorities in Mgmt., City Mgrs. Assn. (social action com. 1987—). Home: 1523 Green Canyon Rd Fall Brook CA 92028 Office: City of Pomona City Hall Pomona CA 91766

WILSON, BARBARA LOUISE, communications executive; b. Bremerton, Wash., Aug. 3, 1952; d. Algernon Frances and Dorothy Virginia (Martin) W.; m. Ashby A. Riley III, Feb. 7, 1979 (div. Dec. 1983). BA in Fin. and Econs., U. Puget Sound, 1974; MBA, U. Wash., Seattle, 1975. With Pacific N.W. Bell, 1974-86; dir. pub. communications Pacific N.W. Bell, Seattle, 1983-85, dir. number svcs. mktg., 1985-86; v.p. implementation planning US West, Inc., Englewood, Colo., 1986-87; pres. US West Info. Systems, Englewood, 1987-89; v.p. bus. div. US West Communications, Englewood, 1989—; bd. dirs. U.S. West New Vector Group, Bellevue, Wash. Bd. dirs., exec. com. Wash. Cun. for Econ. Edn., Seattle, 1985-86; team capt. major gifts com. Boys and Girls Club, Seattle, 1986; chairperson co. campaign United Way, Seattle, 1985. Republican. Roman Catholic. Office: US West 6200 S Quebec St Ste 310 Englewood CO 80111

WILSON, CARL ARTHUR, real estate broker; b. Manhasset, N.Y., Sept. 29, 1947; s. Archie and Florence (Hefner) W.; m. Mary Elizabeth Coppes; children: Melissa Starr, Clay Alan. Student UCLA, 1966-68, 70-71. Tournament bridge dir. North Hollywood (Calif.) Bridge Club, 1967-68, 70-71; computer operator IBM, L.A., 1967-68, 70-71; bus. devel. mgr. Walker & Lee Real Estate, Anaheim, Calif., 1972-76; v.p. sales and mktg. The Estes Co., Phoenix, 1976-82, Continental Homes Inc., 1982-84; pres. Roadrunner Homes Corp., Phoenix, 1984-86, Lexington Homes, Inc., 1986, Barrington Homes, 1986—; adv. dir. Liberty Bank. Mem. Glendale (Ariz.) Citizens Bond Coun., 1986-87, Ariz. Housing Study Commn., 1988, Valley Leadership, 1988—; pres.'s coun. Am. Grad. Sch. Internat. Mgmt., 1985—; vice-chmn. Glendale Planning and Zoning Commn., 1986—, chmn., 1987—; mem. bd. trustees Valley of Sun United Way, 1987—, chmn. com. Community Problem Solving and Fund Distbn., 1988—. Mem. Nat. Assn. Homebuilders (bd. dirs. 1985—), Cen. Ariz. Homebuilders Assn. (adv. com. 1979-82, treas. 1986, sec. 1987, v.p. 1987-89, pres. 1989—, bd. dirs. 1985—); mem. bd. adjustments City of Glendale, 1976-81, chmn., 1980-81, mem. bond coun., 1981—; planning and zoning commr. City of Glendale, 1981—; mem. real estate edn. adv. coun. State Bd. Community Coll., 1981—; precinct committeeman, dep. registrar, 1980-81. With U.S. Army, 1968-70. Mem. Glendale C. of C. (dir. 1980-83), Sales and Mktg. Coun. (chmn. edn. com. 1980, chmn. coun. 1981—, Mame grand award 1981). Home: PO Box 10141 Phoenix AZ 85064

WILSON, CARLOS EUGENE, symphony director; b. Kansas City, Kans., Dec. 17, 1935; s. Alva Curtis and Jessie Arline (Grace) W.; m. Mary Jane Anderson, Nov. 1, 1963. Grad. U. Denver. Gen. mgr. Kalamazoo Symphony, 1968-71, Fresno Philharm., Calif., 1971-73; gen. mgr., asst. gen. mgr. Houston Symphony, 1973-77; exec. dir. Denver Symphony, 1977-82; mng. dir. San Antonio Symphony, 1982-86, Oreg. Symphony, 1986—. Served with U.S. Army, 1953-57. Office: Oreg Symphony 711 SW Alder Ste 200 Portland OR 97205

WILSON, CHARLES ZACHARY, JR., newspaper publisher; b. Greenwood, Miss., Apr. 21, 1929; s. Charles Zachary and Ora Lee (Means) W.; m. Doris J. Wilson, Aug. 18, 1951 (dec. Nov. 1974); children: Charles III, Joyce Lynne, Joanne Catherine, Gary Thomas, Jonathan Keith; m. Kelly Freeman, Apr. 21, 1986; 1 child Amanda Fox. BS in Econs., U. Ill., 1952, PhD in Econs. and Stats., 1956. Asst. to v.p. Commonwealth Edison Co., Chgo., 1956-59; asst. prof. econs. De Paul U., Chgo., 1959-61; assoc. prof. bus. SUNY, Binghamton, 1961-67, prof. econs. and bus., 1967-68; prof. mgmt. and edn. UCLA, 1968-84, vice chancellor acad. programs, 1969-84; pub./pres. Cen. News-Wave Publs., Los Angeles, 1985-87, chmn., bd. dirs., publisher, 1987—; mem. adv. council Fed. Res. Bank, San Francisco, 1986—, 2001 com. Office of Mayor of Los Angeles, 1986—. Author: Organizational Decision-Making, 1967; contbr. articles on bus. to jours. Bd. dirs. Los Angeles County Mus. Art, 1972-84; com. on Los Angeles City Revenue, 1975-76, United Nations Assn. panel for advancement of U. and Japan Relations, N.Y.C. 1972-74; chmn. Mayor's task force on Africa, 1979-82. Fellow John Hay Whitney, U. Ill., 1955-56, Ford Found., 1960-61, 81-82, 84, Am. Council of Edn., UCLA, 1967-68, Aspen Inst. for Human Studies; named one of Young Men of Yr., Jaycees, 1965. Mem. AAAS, Am. Econ. Assn., Nat. Newspaper Pub. Assn., Am. Mgmt. Assn., Alpha Phi Alpha (pres., pledgemaster 1952-54), Phi Kappa Phi, Order of Artus (pres.). Home: 1053 Tellem Dr Pacific Palisades CA 90272 Office: Cen Newspaper Publs 2621 W 54th St Los Angeles CA 90043

WILSON, DARRELL STEVEN, aerospace engineer; b. L.A., July 20, 1964; s. Ronald F. and Maria J. (Mendez) W. BME, Stanford U., 1986. Registered engr., Calif. Structural design engr. McDonnell Douglas Corp., Long Beach, Calif., 1986-88; prodn. devel. engr. McDonnell Douglas Corp., Long Beach, 1988—. Mem. ASME. Home: 257 Ximeno Long Beach CA 90803

WILSON, DAVID LEE, clinical psychologist; b. Mooresville, N.C., July 5, 1941; s. William John Mack and Joyce Evelyn (Evans) W.; m. Barbara Ann Klepfer, Apr. 22, 1960 (div. Jan. 1982); children: Cheryl, Lisa, David; m. Cheryl Jean Andersen, May 22, 1983; stepchildren: Jennifer Dalrymple, Richard Dalrymple. Student, Auburn U., 1959-60; AB in Psychology, Davidson Coll., 1963; PhD in Clin. Psychology, U. N.C., 1967. Diplomate Am. Bd. Med. Psychotherapists. Teaching fellow U. N.C., Chapel Hill, 1964; psychology intern Letterman Hosp., San Francisco, 1966-67, supr., 1967-70; sr. psychologist Kaiser Hosp., Hayward, Calif., 1970-72; pvt. practice Psychology Ctr. for Growth, San Francisco, 1970-72; mem. staff Far No. Regional Ctr., Redding, Calif., 1970-74; dir. Redding Psychotherapy Group, 1974—, Vietnam Vets. Readjustment Program, Shasta and Tehama, 1984—; cons. in field. Author: play The Moon Cannot Be Stolen, 1985. Chmn. Shasta Dam P.U.D. Com., Shasta County, 1981-82, Shasta County Headstart Bd., 1982-85, Criminal Justice Adv. Bd. Shasta County, 1982-87, Youth and Family Counseling Ctr., Shasta County, 1986—. Capt. U.S. Army, 1965-70. Recipient Danforth award Danforth Found., 1963; Woodrow Wilson Found. fellow, 1963; Smith Fund grantee, 1966. Fellow Am. Bd. Med. Psychotherapy; mem. Am. Psychol. Assn., Calif. State Psychol. Assn. Democrat. Office: Redding Psychotherapy Group 1824 Mistletoe Redding CA 96002

WILSON, DONTE, corporate executive, software developer, producer; b. L.A., May 18, 1949; s. LeRoy Delano and Leola W. Grad. in computer design, Cleve. Inst., 1974. Title officer Title Ins. and Trust Co., L.A., 1969-70; v.p. Farrington-Hart Music Co., Encino, Calif., 1970-74; pres. Optimum II Corp., San Francisco, 1974-77, Arion II, Gardena, Calif., 1977-88, Telncom, Carson, Calif., 1988—; cons. Andromeda subs. Arion II, Inglewood, Calif., 1977—. Author: (software) Account Pac, Sched. I. Mem. The Computer User's Group. Democrat. Roman Catholic. Home and Office: Arion II 41369 154th St Lancaster CA 93535 Office (regional): Arion II Arifaxx Systems Div 22232 S Vermont Ave Bldg #104 Torrance CA 90502 also: Telncom 17819 S Lysander Dr Carson CA 90746-1623

WILSON, DOUGLAS EDWIN, lawyer; b. Sacramento, Apr. 23, 1917; s. Richard Matthew and Ruth (O'Brien) W.; A.B., U. of Pacific, 1940; J.D., U. Calif. at San Francisco, 1948; m. Helen Marie Lewis, Apr. 5, 1942; children—Sandra Jane (Mrs. Kenneth Arthur Olds), Kent Lewis, Jay Douglas. Admitted to Calif. bar, 1949; partner Forslund & Wilson, Stockton, 1949-83, Wilson & Wison, 1983—; U.S. magistrate Stockton, Eastern Dist. of Calif., 1962-76. Mem. San Joaquin County Retirement Bd., 1952-72. Served to capt. AUS, 1941-46. Recipient Silver Beaver award Boy Scouts, 1955, Distinguished Eagle Scout award, 1971. Mem. San Joaquin County, Calif. State bars, Am. Legion. Republican. Methodist. Mason (Shriner, K.T.), Elk, Rotary (Paul Harris fellow). Club: Commonwealth (San Francisco). Home: 2134 Gardena Ave Stockton CA 95204 Office: 11 S San Joaquin Stockton CA 95202

WILSON, EMILY MARIE, manufacturing company sales executive; b. Aberdeen, Wash., Mar. 24, 1951; d. Charles Robert and Alice Adele (Robinson) W.; m. Michael A. Rich, July 1, 1976. Student, U. Puget Sound, 1969-71, Austro-Am. Inst., Vienna, 1971; BA in Polit. Sci., U. Wash., 1973. Tour counselor, documents and receipts, air reservationist Princess Cruises and Tours, Seattle, 1973-75; with Clairol, Inc., Seattle, 1975-81, sales rep. N.W. Wash., drug-mass mdse. div., 1975-77, sales rep. Met. Seattle, 1977-78, dist. mgr. sales western Wash., 1978-81; trainer territorial sales reps., mgr. dist. dollar sales, and dist. sales mgr. of Wash., Oreg., Idaho and Mont., Clorox, Inc., Seattle, 1981-82, assoc. regional mgr. Western div. spl. markets, 1982-83; regional mgr. Olympic Stain Co., Bellevue, Wash., 1983-86; dir. sales Inscape Products The Weyerhauser Co., Tacoma, 1986-88; dir. ops. Wildland Journeys, Seattle, 1988—. Mem. Transcendental Meditation Soc., Oreg. Hist. Soc., Sons and Daus. of Oreg. Pioneers, Pioneer Assn. Wash., Seattle Hist. Soc., Sidha of the Age of Enlightenment World Govt. Assn., Grad. Sci. of Creative Intelligence, Women's Profl. Managerial Network (bd. dirs. Seattle chpt.). Club: Zonta (Seattle). Office: 4417 54th Ave NE Seattle WA 98105

WILSON, F(RANK) DOUGLAS, geneticist; b. Salt Lake City, Dec. 17, 1928; s. Frank LeRoy and Nellie Mae (Roach) W.; m. Beverly Ann Urry, Nov. 27, 1950; children: Kerry, Leslie, Eileen, John, Greg, Cynthia, Angela, David. BS, U. Utah, 1950, MS, 1953; PhD, Wash. State U., 1957. Rsch. geneticist agrl. rsch. svcs. U.S. Dept. Agr., Belle Glade, Fla., 1957-65; geneticist agrl. rsch. svcs. U.S. Dept. Agr., College Station, Tex., 1965-71, Phoenix, 1971—. Bd. dirs., tng. chmn. Boy Scouts Am., Phoenix, 1977—. Recipient Silver Beaver award Boy Scouts Am., 1984. Mem. Agronomy Soc. Am. (assoc. editor 1978-80), AAAS, Ariz-Nev. Acad. Sci. Mormon. Office: Western Cotton Rsch USDA 4135 E Broadway Phoenix AZ 85040

WILSON, GAIL TOLLKUEHN, foundation adminstrator, consultant. d. Harold Frank and Lucille Margaret (Jacobsen) Tollkuehn; m. James Alan Wilson, Mar. 29, 1969. BS, Wittenberg U., 1965; postgrad., U. Colo., 1986-88. Tchr. El Paso Sch. Dist. 8, Fountain, Colo., 1972-86; dir. and founder Pikes Peak Child Care Resource, Inc., Colorado Springs, 1987—; cons. Pikes Peak Child Care Resource, Colorado Springs, 1987-88; founding mem. State Resource and Referral Network, Denver, 1988—. Mem. Gov's. Task Force on Children, Colo., 1987, Dist. Attys. Task Force on Child Abuse, El Paso, Colo., 1987; mem. steering com. County Coalition on Teen Pregnancy, El Paso, 1987-88. Mem. Nat. Assn. Educating Young Children, Pikes Peak Assn. Educating Young children (bd. dirs. 1988—), AAUW (state bd. dirs. 1985—), Plaza Club, Colorado Springs Tennis Club. Democrat. Mem. Christian Ch. Home: 3008 San Luis Dr Colorado Springs CO 80909 Office: Pikes Peak Child Care Inc 12 N Meade Colorado Springs CO 80909

WILSON, GERALD ALAN, retail executive; b. Portland, Oreg., Jan. 30, 1951; s. Robert Watts and Marjorie Jane (Scobert) W.; m. Francee Lee Davies, Aug. 21, 1972 (div. Nov. 1980); 1 child, Joel Alan. BS in Biology, U. Oreg., 1973, MS in Curriculum and Instrn., 1975. Cert. tchr., Oreg. Tchr. biology Molalla (Oreg.) Union High Sch., 1974-75; instr. biology Lane Community Coll., Eugene, Oreg., 1975; with sci. curriculum, design and implementation dept. Oaklea Mid. Sch., Junction City, Oreg., 1975-78; ptnr. Wilson Music House, Eugene, 1978-83, prin., 1983—; adviser small bus. mgmt. com. Lane Community Coll., Eugene, 1983—. Mem. budget com. City of Eugene, 1978-80; chairperson Westside Neighborhood Orgn., 1977-78; mem. bachelor auction Lane County March of Dimes, 1987—. Mem. U. Oreg. Alumni Assn. (dir. Lane County chpt. 1987—). Republican. Methodist. Club: Downtown Athletic (Eugene) (charter). Office: Wilson Music House 806 Charnelton St Eugene OR 97401

WILSON, HERSCHEL MANUEL (PETE WILSON), journalism educator; b. Candler, N.C., July 17, 1930; s. Shuford Arnold and Ida Camilla (Landreth) W.; m. Ruby Jean Herring, Aug. 10, 1952. AB in Journalism, San Diego State U., 1956; MS in Journalism, Ohio U., Athens, 1959; postgrad., U. So. Calif., 1966-70. Reporter, copy editor, picture editor The San Diego Union, 1955-58; reporter, wire editor Long Beach (Calif.) Ind., 1959-65; prof. journalism Calif. State U., Northridge, 1965-71; fgn. desk copy editor L.A. Times, 1966-71; prof. and former chmn. journalism Humboldt State U., Arcata, Calif., 1971—; cons. KVIQ-TV News Dept., Eureka, Calif., 1985-87. Contbr. articles to profl. jours. Publicity dir. Simi Valley (Calif.) Fair Housing Coun., 1967; bd. dirs., publicity dir. NAACP, Eureka, Calif., 1978-80. With USN, 1948-52, Korea. Named Nat. Outstanding Advisor, Theta Sigma Phi, 1970. Mem. Soc. Profl. Journalists. (named Disting. Campus Advisor 1982), San Fernando Valley Press Club (v.p. 1969-70), Beau Pre Men's Golf Club (McKinleyville, Calif., pub. rels. dir., treas. 1978). Democrat. Methodist. Home: Rte 1 Box 71 Trinidad CA 95570 Office: Humboldt State U Journalism Dept Bret Harte House Arcata CA 95521

WILSON, IRA LEE, middle school teacher; b. Taylor, La., Dec. 20, 1927; d. Henry and Sadie Mae (Milbon) Parker; m. Odie D. Wilson, Jr., May 11, 1946; children: Ervin Charles, Annie Jo, Carrido Michelle. BS, Grambling State U., 1954; postgrad., Pepperdine U., 1974, Pepperdine U., 1976; MEd, La Verne Coll., 1976. Tchr. Willowbrook Sch. Dist., Los Angeles, 1955-68, Compton (Calif.) Unified Sch. Dist., 1968—; grade level chairperson Roosevelt Middle Sch. P.T.A., Compton, 1988—; correspondence sec. Roosevelt Middle Sch. P.T.A., Compton, 1988—; asst. activity chairperson Grambling Alumni Assn., Los Angeles, 1987—. Asst. sec. Los Angeles Police Dept. Sweethearts Area Club, Los Angeles, 1988—. Recipient Perfect Attendance award Compton Unified Sch. Dist., 1987-88, S.W. Area Sweethearts for Outstanding Svcs. Los Angeles Police Dept., 1988, Disting. Svc. award Compton Edn. Assn., 1987-88, 83, Cert. of Achievement Roosevelt Jr. High Sch., 1984-85, Perfect Attendance award Roosevelt Middle Sch., 1984, Cert. of Achievement Mayo Elem. Sch., 1973-74, Roosevelt Mid. Sch., 1989. Mem. NEA, Block Club. Democrat. Baptist. Home: 828 W 126 St Los Angeles CA 90044

WILSON, J. ROBERT, utility company executive, lawyer; b. Meade, Kans., Dec. 3, 1927; s. Robert J. and Bess O. (Osborne) W.; m. Marguerite Jean Reiter, Nov. 27, 1960; 1 son, John Ramsey. B.A., Kans. U., 1950, LL.B., 1953. Bar: Kans. 1953, Nebr. 1961, Colo. 1981. Practiced in Meade, 1954-57; county atty. Meade County, Kans., 1954, 56; city atty. Meade, 1954-57; asst. gen. counsel Kans. Corp. Commn., 1957-59, gen. counsel, 1959-61, mem., 1961; atty. KN Energy, Inc., 1961-75, personnel dir., 1964-67, v.p., treas., 1968-75, exec. v.p., 1975-78, pres., chief operating officer, 1978-82, pres., chief exec. officer, 1982-85, chmn., pres., chief exec. officer, 1985-88, chmn., 1988-89. With USNR, 1945-46. Mem. Phi Kappa Sigma. Democrat. Home: 1725 Foothills Dr S Golden CO 80401 Office: KN Energy Inc 165 S Union Blvd Ste 718 Lakewood CO 80228

WILSON, JAMES ERNEST, petroleum consultant, writer; b. McKinney, Tex., Apr. 19, 1915; s. James Ernest and Agnes (Neill) W.; m. Elloie Barkely, Apr. 4, 1940; children: Judith Wilson Grant, Elizabeth Wilson. BS, Tex. A&M U., 1937. Surface geologist Shell Oil Co., Tex., 1938-41, various positions, 1945-59, v.p., Houston, New Orleans and Denver, 1959-73; cons., Denver, 1973—. Trustee and chmn. Am. Assn. Petroleum Geologists Found., 1975—; trustee Children's Hosp. Denver, 1970-83, Denver Symphony, 1968-82, Inst. Internat. Edn., Denver, 1968-82. Served to maj. U.S. Army, 1941-45; ETO. Fellow Geol. Soc. Am., Soc. Petroleum Engrs., Am. Assn. Petroleum Geologists (hon.). Republican. Methodist. Clubs: Cherry Hill Country (Denver); Confrerie des Chevaliers du Tastevin (pres. 1983). Home: 4248 S Hudson Pkwy Englewood CO 80110

WILSON, JAMES NEWMAN, laboratory executive; b. San Diego, Aug. 28, 1927; s. Jack Alexander and Irene (Newman) W.; m. Alice Ann Gorcie, Sept. 19, 1954 (div. July 1979); children: Patricia Ann Brugman, Martin James. BS, U. Calif., Berkeley, 1951; SM, MIT, 1952. With Calif. Inst. Tech. Jet Propulsion Lab., Pasadena, 1952—, asst. spacecraft system mgr., 1969-74, with Mariner Venus Mercury program, 1973, project mgr., 1985—. Author: An Arm and a Leg or Two, 1989. Ednl. officer U.S. Power Squadron, Pasadena, 1982-84. With U.S. Army, 1945-46. Recipient Exceptional Svc. medal NASA, 1974, Presidential award Gerald R. Ford, 1974. Mem. Los Angeles Yacht Club. Home: 260 Malcolm Dr Pasadena CA 91105 Office: Jet Propulsion Lab 4800 Oak Grove Dr Pasadena CA 91109

WILSON, JEFFREY LEIGH, exploration geologist; b. Santa Monica, Calif., May 1, 1948; s. Billy George and Gladys Jean (Phillips) W.; m. Maria Elvira Correa, Aug. 18, 1973; children: Jon Phillip, Ryan Jeffrey. AA, L.A. Pierce Coll., 1971; BS, Calif. State U., Northridge, 1973; MS, U. So. Calif., 1976. Geol. cons. Tenneco Mining Inc., Death Valley, Calif., 1973-75; geol. supr. Tenneco Oil Co., Minerals Dept., Tucson, 1976-80; staff geologist Houston Internat. Minerals Corp., Denver, 1981-83; exploration mgr. we. U.S. Tenneco Minerals Co., Carson City, Nev., 1984-86; dir. exploration western U.S. Echo Bay Exploration, Inc., Reno, Nev., 1987—. Contbr. articles to profl. jours. Asst. ldr. Boy Scouts Am., Carson City, 1987-88. With U.S. Army, 1968-70, Vietnam. Decorated Silver Star, Bronze Star. Mem. Geol. Soc. Nev., Soc. Econ. Geologists, Soc. Mining Engrs. Republican. Methodist. Home: 325 Tahoe Dr Carson City NV 89703 Office: Echo Bay Exploration Inc 5250 Neil Rd #300 Reno NV 89502

WILSON, JOHN JAMES, judge; b. Boston, Dec. 23, 1927; s. John J. and Margaret (Thomas) W.; m. Joan Ellen Bostwick, Sept. 1, 1951 (div. Sept. 1975); children: Jeffrey, John, Julie; m. Elizabeth Brower, Dec. 4, 1975; 1 child, Stephane. AB, Tufts U., 1951; LLB, Stanford U., 1954. Bar: Calif. 1954, Mass. 1954, Oreg. 1982, U.S. Dist. Ct. (no., cen., ea. and so. dists.) Calif., U.S. Dist. Ct. Oreg. Asst. U.S. atty. U.S. Dept. of Justice, L.A., 1958-60; ptnr. Hill, Farrer & Burrill, L.A., 1960-85; bankruptcy judge U.S. Dist. Ct. Calif., San Bernardino, 1985-87, Santa Ana, Calif., 1989—. Lt. (j.g.) USN, 1945-50. Seventh Day Adventist. Office: US Bankruptcy Ct 506 Federal Bldg 34 Civic Center Pla PO Box 12600 Santa Ana CA 92712

WILSON, JOHN LEWIS, academic administrator; b. Columbus, Ohio, Mar. 18, 1943; s. John Robert and Betty Marie (Barker) W.; m. Linda Patricia Kiernan, Apr. 23, 1966; 1 child, Heidi Annette. BA in Internat. Relations, Am. U., 1963, MA in Econs., 1973, PhD, 1977. Staff asst. Congressman Paul N. McCloskey, Washington, 1968-72; sr. assoc. Govt. Affairs Inst., Washington, 1973-77; pres. Experience Devel., Inc., Tucson, 1978-85; asst. dean U. Ariz., Tucson, 1985—, acting asst. to sr. v.p. adminstrn. & finance, 1988—; instr. U. Phoenix, Tucson, 1980-83; asst. sr. v.p. U. Ariz., Tucson, 1988. Author: (with others) Managing Planned Agricultural Development, 1976. 1st lt. U.S. Army, Vietnam, 1964-68. Decorated Bronze Star with oak leaf cluster. Mem. Am. Econ. Assn., Tucson Met. C. of C., Sabino Vita Recreation Assn. (pres. 1981-82), Am. Soc. Tng. and Devel. (pres. 1984), Toastmasters (v.p. edn. 1987-88, pres. 1988-89). Democrat. Home: 8030 E Garland Rd Tucson AZ 85715 Office: U Ariz Gould-Simpson 1025 Tucson AZ 85721

WILSON, JOHN PASLEY, law educator; b. Newark, Apr. 7, 1933; s. Richard Henry and Susan Agnes (Pasley) W.; m. Elizabeth Ann Reed, Sept 10, 1955; children—David Cables, John, Jr., Cicely Reed. A.B., Princeton U., 1955; LL.B., Harvard U., 1962. Bar: N.J. 1963, U.S. Dist. Ct. N.J. 1963, Mass. 1963, U.S. Dist. Ct. Mass. 1963. Budget examiner Exec. Office of Pres., Bur. of Budget, Washington, 1955-56; assoc. Riker, Danzig, Scherer & Brown, Newark, 1962-63; asst. dean Harvard U. Law Sch., Cambridge, Mass., 1963-67; assoc. dean Boston U. Law Sch., 1968-82; dean Golden Gate U. Sch. Law, San Francisco, 1982-88, prof., 1988—; vis. prof. dept. health policy and mgmt. Harvard U., 1988; cons. Nat. Commn. for the Protection of Human Subjects of Biomed. and Behavioral Research; mem. Mass. Gov's. Commn. on Civil and Legal Rights of Developmentally Disabled; mem. adv. com. Ctr for Community Legal Edn., San Francisco. Author: The Rights of Adolescents in the Mental Health System. Contbr. chpts. to books, articles to profl. jours. Bd. dirs. Greater Boston Legal Services, Chewonki Found., Concord Home Owning Corp.; mem. Health Facilities Appeals Bd., Commonwealth of Mass.; mem. Concord Moderate Income Housing Com.; assoc. mem. Democratic Town Com., Concord; chmn. Bd. Assessors, Concord; bd. overseers Boston Hosp. for Women, past chmn. med. affairs com. Served to lt. (j.g.) USNR, 1956-59. NIMH grantee, 1973. Mem. Am. Arbitration Assn., Alameda/Contra Costa Med. Assn. (bioethics com.). Office: Golden Gate U Sch Law 536 Mission St San Francisco CA 94105

WILSON, KIRK G., service executive; b. Great Falls, Mont., Apr. 1, 1951; s. Floyd Daniel and Lorna (Stark) W.; m. Monica Jane Moline, Aug. 17, 1975; 1 child, Bret Michael. BABS, Concordia Coll., Moorhead, Minn., 1972; MA in Hosp. Adminstrn., U. Iowa, 1975. Adminstrv. asst. Columbus Hosp., Great Falls, 1975-78, asst. adminstr., 1978-80; asst. adminstr., profl. services St. Anthony Hosp., Oklahoma City, Okla., 1981-83, St. Vincent Med. Ctr., Portland, Oreg., 1983-86; adminstr. Meml. Women's/Childrens Hosp., Meml. Med. Ctr., Long Beach, Calif., 1987-88; pres., chief exec. officer Mont. Deaconess Med. Ctr., Great Falls, 1988—; bd. dirs. Red Cross Blood Svcs., Great Falls, Mountain States Regional Bd., Denver, Voluntary Hosps. Am. Co-author: (monograph) Mental Health Care Systems, 1975. Bd. dirs. Symphony Assn. Bd., Great Falls, 1988—, United Way, Great Falls, 1988—; regional bd. dirs. Boy Scouts Am.; mem. pres.'s coun. Coll. Great of Falls. Recipient Leadership award, Great Falls C. of C., 1981. Fellow Am. Coll. Healthcare Execs., Mont. Hosp. Assn. (bd. dirs. Dist. II), Rotary. Republican. Lutheran. Home: 520 Fox Ct Great Falls MT 59404 Office: Montana Deaconess Med Ct 1101 26th St South Great Falls MT 59405

WILSON, LENA RUTH, educational administrator; b. Ganado, Ariz., Nov. 21, 1934; d. Roger and Grace (Segar) Davis; divorced; children: Thomas Raymond, Louis, Roger Descheenie, Barbara Grace. B Music Edn., Coll. of Emporia, 1958; MEd in Adminstrn., No. Ariz. U., 1988. Cert. tchr., tchr. supr., Ariz. Tchr. music Whiteriver (Ariz.) Pub. Sch., 1958-59; chief clk. cts. Navajo Tribe, Window Rock, Ariz.zz, 1959-66; tchr. Window Rock Pub. Schs., Ft. Defiance, Ariz.zz, 1966-68; tchr. Bur. Indian Affairs, Toyei, Ariz.zz, 1968-71, 76-81, Many Farms, Ariz.zz, 1971-73, Wide Ruins, Ariz.zz, 1981-83; prin. Pine Springs Boarding Sch. Bur. Indian Affairs, Houck, Ariz.zz, 1983—. Bd. dirs. Boy Scouts Am., Many Farms, 1971-73, Navajo Nation Family Planning, 1971-73; cons. youth groups Navajo Tribe, 1978; orgn. Presbyn. Ch., Ganado, 1976-83, Ft. Defiance, 1983-89, elder, Ft. Defiance, 1973-76, deacon, 1976—. Mem. Bur. Indian Affairs Prins. Orgn. Republican. Home: Box 593 Window Rock AZ 86515 Office: Pine Springs Boarding Sch Box 198 Houck AZ 86506

WILSON, LIONEL J., mayor of Oakland, California; b. New Orleans, 1915; m. Dorothy P.; children: Robin and Lionel (twins), Stephen. A.B., U. Calif., 1939, J.D., 1949. Judge Superior Ct. Calif., to 1977; mayor of Oakland, 1977—. Recipient numerous awards including West Coast Merit award NAACP; Outstanding Profl. Service award Calif. Med., Dental, and Pharm. Assn.; Judge for all Seasons award Oak Center Inc.; Man of Yr. award Oakland Lodge, B'nai B'rith, 1978; Leadership award Chinese Am. Citizens Alliance, 1979; award Marcus Foster Inst.; Outstanding Alumnus award Oakland Public Schs., 1979. Mem. Calif. League Cities (bd. dirs.), U.S. Conf. Mayors (various coms.), Nat. League Cities (various coms.). Democrat. Office: City Hall 1 City Hall Pla Rm 302 Oakland CA 94612 *

WILSON, LOIS MAYFIELD, English language educator; b. Berea, Ky., Jan. 28, 1924; d. Samuel Martin and Flora Terrill (Sweeney) Mayfield; m. Graham Cunningham Wilson, July 9, 1948; 1 child, Erin Cressida. BS, Bowling Green State U., 1943; MA, U. Mich., 1944; PhD, Stanford U., 1954. Reporter Toledo Morning Times, summer 1944; instr. English, U. Ill., Urbana, 1944-46, Stanford (Calif.) U., 1946-48; from instr. to prof. San Francisco State U., 1949—; research fellow U. Chile, Santiago, 1947; Fulbright prof. linguistics U. Rome, 1956-57. Co-author: Inglese Parlato, 1958. Mem. selection com. for Fulbright scholars, Inst. Internat. Edn., Washington, 1979; Transpacific orientation dir. & lectr. Inst. Internat. Edn./Asia Found., 1956, 61. Mem. Tchrs. English to Speakers of Other Langs., Calif. Assn. Tchrs. English to Speakers of Other Langs., Nat. Assn. Fgn. Student Advisors. Democrat. Unitarian. Office: San Francisco State U Dept English 1600 Holloway Ave San Francisco CA 94132

WILSON, MAURICE LEE, merchant; b. Hutchinson, Kans., Dec. 5, 1939; s. Clarke Edgar and Leota May (Wright) W.; m. JoAnne Graves, June, 1958 (div. June, 1962); children: Michelle Fitzgerald, Lorie Bramble; m. Beverly Jean Klein, Dec. 22, 1963; children: Kelly Annette, Jill Joyce. Grad., high sch., Wichita, Kans. Salesman Pacific Mutual Life Ins. Co., Wichita, 1962-64, Motors, Inc., Santa Fe Springs, Calif., 1965-71; counterman, salesman Jay Auto Parts, Los Angeles, 1964-65; ptnr. S & W Ltd., Santa Ana, Calif., 1971-76; pres. Auto Parts San Marcos Inc., San Marcos and Vista, Calif., 1976--. With USN, 1960-62. Mem. Optimists (v.p. San Marcos 1986-88). Republican. Methodist. Home: 788 Virginia Pl San Marcos CA 92069

WILSON, MORRIS LEE, musician; b. Easton, Md., Jan. 21, 1951; s. Lewis Albert and Ada (Favors) W. Student, Chesapeake Coll., 1972; student, U. Pa., 1974. Intelligence officer Berlin Police Dept., Berlin, Md., 1975-78; intelligence officer Fed. Corrections Inst., Terminal Island, Calif., 1978-86; exec. producer Muse Studios, Northridge, Calif., 1980—; owner, operator Wilson's Exec. Protection Svc., Canoga Park, Calif., 1986—. Songwriter (record) Special Lady (Songwriter award 1986). Mem. NAACP, Phila. 1974, ARC, Long Beach, Calif; Boy Scout master asst. Boy Scouts Am., Trappe, Md., 1969-71; lt. Civil Air Patrol, Easton, Md., 1972-74; VISTA vol. U.S. govt., L.A., 1986-87. Mem. Fed. Order Police, Olympic Yacht Club. Democrat. Methodist. Office: Wilsons Music Co PO Box 702 Van Nuys CA 91408

WILSON, MYRON ROBERT, JR., pyschiatrist; b. Helena, Mont., Sept. 21, 1932; s. Myron Robert Sr. and Constance Ernestine (Bultman) W. BA, Stanford U., 1954, MD, 1957. Diplomate Am. Bd. Psychiatry and Neurology. Dir. adolescent psychiatry Mayo Clinic, Rochester, Minn., 1965-71; pres. and psychiatrist in chief Wilson Ctr., Faribault, Minn., 1971-86; chmn. Wilson Ctr., 1986—; assoc. clin. prof. psychiatry UCLA, 1985—. Contbr. articles to profl. jours. chmn. Wilson Found., Los Angeles, 1986—; mem. bd. dirs. Pasadena Symphony Orchestra Assn., Calif., 1987. Served to lt. comdr., 1958-60. Fellow Mayo Grad. Sch. Medicine, Rochester, 1960-65. Fellow Am. Psychiatric Assn., Am. Society for Adolescent Psychiatry; mem. Internat. Soc. for Adolescent Psychiatry (founder, treas. 1985), Soc. Sigma Xi (Mayo Found. chpt.). Episcopalian. Home: 2565 Zorada Dr Los Angeles CA 90046 Office: Wilson Found 8981 Sunset Blvd Ste 311 Los Angeles CA 90069

WILSON, PETE, senator; b. Lake Forest, Ill., Aug. 23, 1933; s. James Boone and Margaret (Callaghan) W.; m. Betty Robertson (div.); m. Gayle Edlund, May 29, 1983. B.A. in English Lit., Yale U., 1955; J.D., U. Calif., Berkeley, 1962; LL.D., Grove City Coll., 1983, U. Calif., San Diego, 1983, U. San Diego, 1984. Bar: Calif. 1962. Mem. Calif. Legislature, Sacramento, 1966-71; mayor City of San Diego, 1971-83; U.S. Senator from Calif. 1983—. Trustee Conservation Found.; mem. exec. bd. San Diego County council Boy Scouts Am.; hon. trustee So. Calif. Council Soviet Jews; adv. mem. Urban Land Inst., 1985-86; founding dir. Retinitis Pigmentosa Internat.; hon. dir. Alzheimer's Family Ctr., Inc., 1985; hon. bd. dirs. Shakespeare-San Francisco, 1985. Recipient Golden Bulldog award, 1984, 85, 86, Guardian of Small Bus. award, 1984; ROTC scholar Yale U., 1951-55; named Legislator of Yr., League Calif. Cities, 1985; Man of Yr. award Nat. Guard Assn. Calif., 1986, Man of Yr. citation U. Calif. Boalt Hall, 1986. Mem. Nat. Mil. Family Assn. (adv. bd.), Phi Delta Phi, Zeta Psi. Republican. Episcopalian. Office: US Senate 720 Hart Senate Bldg Washington DC 20510 *

WILSON, RICHARD EDWARD, JR., service executive; b. Boston, Oct. 20, 1956; s. Richard Edward and Lilian Anita (Wonstolen) W.; m. Joanne Louise Liesegang, Sept. 12, 1987. BA in Internat. Relations, U. Mass., 1981. Store mgr. Kay Jewelers Corp., Sunnyvale, Calif., 1981-82, San Mateo, Calif., 1982-83, San Diego, Calif., 1983-85; asst. to pres. Century Parking Inc., L.A., 1986-87, exec. v.p., 1987—. Mem. adv. bd. Found. of the Peoples' of South Pacific. Mem. Calif. Parking Assn. (chmn. ethics com. 1987), L.A. Athletic Club. Democrt. Roman Catholic. Office: Century Parking Inc 3200 Wilshire Blvd Los Angeles CA 90010

WILSON, ROBERT BALLOU, savings and loan executive; b. Salem, Mass., Mar. 17, 1954; s. Everett Stuart and Joan (Eastty) W.; m. Melissa Woodburn Moore, Sept. 3, 1977; children: Victoria Woodburn, Andrew Moore, Reynolds Everett. BA, Williams Coll., 1976; MBA, UCLA, 1979. Salesman Armstrong World Indsutries, Toronto, Ont., Can., 1976-77; auditor Price Waterhouse Co., L.A., 1979-80; adminstrv. asst. Weyerhaeuser Mortgage Co., L.A., 1980-81, v.p., 1981-84, sr. v.p., 1984-85; exec. v.p., chief operating officer Republic Fed. Savs. & Loan, L.A., 1985-87, pres., 1987—. V.p. fin. Western L.A. council Boy Scouts Am., 1988—. Mem. U.S. Savs. League, Calif. League Savs. (secondary mktg. com. 1985—), Mortgage Bankers Assn. Office: Republic Fed Savs & Loan 6320 Canoga Ave Woodland Hills CA 91367

WILSON, ROBERT DANA, insurance executive; b. Phoenix, June 10, 1954; s. Robert Gene and Wanda (Joyce) W. BBA, Ariz. State U., 1977. Hotel mgr. Marriott Corp., Lahaina, Hawaii, 1981-85; real estate broker AmeraWest Investments, Phoenix, 1985-88; mgr. market sales Allstate Ins. Co., Phoenix, 1988—. Mem. Valley Big Brothers, Phoenix, 1985—. Mem. Scottsdale Bd. Realtors. Home: 8330 N 19th Ave #3087 Phoenix AZ 85021

WILSON, ROBIN SCOTT, university president, writer; b. Columbus, Ohio, Sept. 19, 1928; s. John Harold and Helen Louise (Walker) W.; m. Patricia Ann Van Kirk, Jan. 20, 1951; children: Kelpie, Leslie, Kari, Andrew. B.A., Ohio State U., 1950; M.A., U. Ill., 1951, Ph.D., 1959. Fgn. intelligence officer CIA, Washington, 1959-67; prof. English Clarion State Coll., (Pa.), 1967-70; assoc. dir. Com. Instnl. Cooperation, Evanston, Ill., 1970-77; assoc. provost instrn. Ohio State U., Columbus, 1977-80; pres. Calif. State U., Chico, 1980—. Author: Those Who Can, 1973; short stories, criticism, articles on edn. Served to lt. USN, 1953-57. Mem. AAAS, Phi Kappa Phi. Democrat. Office: Calif State U 105 Kendall Hall Chico CA 95929

WILSON, ROGER DUANE, athletic director; b. Thief River Fall, Minn., Oct. 8, 1938; s. Morris Arnold and Ruth Orbetina (Mostrom) W.; m. Glynn Delores Stein. BA, Cen. Wash. U., 1961; postgrad., Seattle U., 1966-69. Tchr., coach Issaquah (Wash.) High Sch., 1961-62, 1962-87; athletic dir. Issaquah Sch., 1987—; cons. expert witness, various legal firms. Seattle and Tacoma. Contbr. articles to profl. jours. Mem. Wash. Edn. Assn., Wash. State Athletic Asminstr. Assn., Nat. High. Home: 23134 SE 58th St Issaquah WA 98027 Office: Issaquah High Sch 565 NW Holly Issaquah WA 98027

WILSON, RONALD JAMES, engineering journal editor; b. Portland, Oreg., Jan. 3, 1950; s. James Daniel Wilson and Ruby Alma (Hall) Hicks; m. Laurel Victoria Uffelman, Mar. 3, 1973 (div. 1981). BS in Applied Sci., Portland State U., 1971. Design engr. Tektronix Inc., Beaverton, Oreg., 1973-76, instr., 1976-80, mkgt. specialist, product mkgt. mgr., 1980-85; dir. product mkgt. Microfield Graphics, Beaverton, Oreg., 1985-87; sr. editor Computer Design Mag., Portland, 1987—. Author trng. materials McGraw-Hill, 1984; contbr. articles to Klien Computer Graphics Rev., 1987-88; patentee computer graphics. Democrat. Home: 1111 SW Gaines #8 Portland OR 97201

WILSON, SONJA MARY, business educator; b. Lake Charles, La., Mar. 28, 1938; d. Albert Ronald and Annelia (DeVille) Molless; m. Willie McKinley Williams, Apr. 28, 1956 (div. May 1969); children: William P. Williams, Dwayne L. Williams, Rachelle A. Smith, Devon A. Williams, Lisa M. Lewis, Ricardo Soto Williams; m. Howard Brooks Wilson, Nov. 12, 1982; stepchildren: Howard N. Wilson, Yvonne Wilson. Student, Mt. St. Jacinto Jr. Coll., 1976-87, U. Calif., San Bernardino, 1983, Calif. State Poly. U., 1986, Laverne U., 1984-85, So. Ill. U., 1985-86. Cert. tchr. Prin.'s sec. Elsinore (Calif.) High Sch., 1974-83, tchr. adult vocat. edn., 1979-84, notary pub., 1981-85, coord. vocat. edn., 1983-84, tchr. bus. and vocat. edn., class adviser, 1983-88. Pres. Lake Elsinore (Calif.) Unified Elem. Sch. Bd.; v.p. Lake Elsinore Elem. Sch. Bd.; adviser Black Student Union/Future Leaders of Am.; leader Girl Scouts U.S.A.; den mother Boy Scouts Am. Tribute in her honor Black Student Union/Future Leaders of Am., 1989; recipient plaque City of Lake Elsinore, 1988. Mem. Calif. Sch. Bds. Assn. (mem. conf. planning com., legis. com., media com., dir. region 18), Calif. Bus. Edn. Assn., Calif. Elected Women Ofcls. Assn., Calif. Sch. Employees Assn. (pres., treas., regional rep. asst., mem. state negotiation com., del. to conf.), Sojourner Truth Media Network (plaque), NAACP (Lake Elsinore chpt., plaque), Hilltop Community Club (plaque), Eta Phi Beta (Gamma Alpha chpt., plaque). Democrat. Home: 21330 Waite St Lake Elsinore CA 92330

WILSON, STEPHEN EDWARD, military officer, consultant, free lance writer; b. Ellensburg, Wash., May 12, 1945; s. Edward and Marjorie Louise (Tucker) W.; m. Mary Lynne Halwas, Aug. 28, 1966; children: Troy, Aubree-Anna. BA in English, Cen. Wash. State Coll., 1967; MA in Guidance Counseling, Wayne State U., 1973. Commd. USAF, 1967, advanced through grades to lt. col., 1983; chief intelligence career mgmt. USAF Mil. Personnel Ctr. USAF, Randolph AFB, Tex., 1976-80; br. chief Intelligence Ctr. Pacific, USAF, Camp Smith, Hawaii, 1980-81; Commdr. in Chief Pacific Staff USAF, Camp Smith, 1981-83; dir. Alert Ctr. Hdqrs. Electronic Security Command USAF, Kelly AFB, Tex., 1983-84, dir. tng., 1984-85; commdr. 6981 Electronic Security Squadron USAF, Elmendorf AFB, Alaska, 1985-88; cons. Betac Corp., San Antonio, 1989—; free lance writer Psycholog. Corp., San Antonio, 1989—; mem. USAF Intelligence Career Field Study Group, Washington, 1978-84, Dept. Def. Intelligence Career Devel. Panel, Washington, 1976-80; chmn. Computer Intelligence Officer Study Group, Washington, 1979-80, Pacific Target Actions Group, Honolulu, 1981-83. Author: North Vietnamese Use of Inland Waterways, 1970, Petroleum Pipelines in the Laotian Panhandle, 1971. Founding mem. San Antonio Council of Adoptable Children, 1976-80; charter mem. Hosanna! Luth. Ch., San Antonio, 1983-85; mem. Friends of Luth. Social Services Tex., San Antonio, 1976-80. Decorated Bronze Star. Mem. Air Force Assn., Assn. Old Crows. Home: PO Box 691586 San Antonio TX 78269 Office: 7323 Highway 90 W Ste 510 San Antonio TX 78227

WILSON, STEPHEN JOEL, lawyer; b. Martin, Tenn., Oct. 8, 1950; s. Aubrey Lorain and Dora Margaret (Hurt) W. BA, SE Mo. State U., 1972; JD, U. Mo., 1976. Bar: Mo. 1976, U.S. Dist. Ct. (we. dist.) Mo. 1976, U.S. Supreme Ct. 1980, Oreg. 1980, U.S. Dist. Ct. Oreg. 1981, U.S. Ct. Appeals (9th cir.) 1982. Asst. atty. gen. Office of Atty. Gen. of Mo., Jefferson City, 1976-80; ptnr. Bullivant, Houser, Bailey, Portland, Oreg., 1980—. Mem. ABA, Def. Rsch. Inst., Oreg. Assn. Def. Counsel, Oreg. Bar Assn., Mo. Bar Assn. Democrat. Office: Bullivant Houser Bailey 1211 SW 5th Ave Ste 1400 Portland OR 97204

WILSON, STEPHEN RIP, communications company executive; b. Twin Falls, ID, Apr. 26, 1948; s. Jerome P. and Epsy Jane (Griggs) W.; m. Judith

Ann Newcomb, June 2, 1972 (dec. Nov. 16, 1977); children: Paul, Sloan; m. Misdee Chauncey Wrigley, Aug. 1, 1987. BA, Columbia U., 1970. Editor Sta. KABC TV, Los Angeles, 1970-72; owner, mgr. Oro Verde Farms, Hagerman, ID, 1972-77; new dir. Sta. KAET TV, Phoenix, 1978-83; adminstrv. aide U.S. Senator Dennis DeConcini, Phoenix, 1983-89; chief exec. officer Flatt & Assocs., Mesa, Ariz., 1989—; trustee Ariz. Edn. Found., Phoenix, 1982—. Commnr. Gov.'s Council Physical Fitness, Phoenix, 1986—; bd. dirs. Crime victim Found., Phoenix, 1984, Make-A-Wish Found., Phoenix, 1983—; mem. Jefferson Forum. Mem. Nucleus Club, Com. on Fgn. Relations. Democrat. Home: 1055 W Baseline Apt 2090 Mesa AZ 85210

WILSON, SYD ROBERT, physicist; b. Brownwood, Tex., Nov. 6, 1951; s. Darrell Key and Madeline Burke (Healer) W.; m. Carol Perkins, Aug. 27, 1972; children: Leia Carol, Daryl Kaye. BA in Physics, North Tex. State U., 1974, MS in Physics, 1976, PhD, 1979. Engr. Semicondr. R & D Labs., Motorola Co., Phoenix, 1979-80, sr. engr., 1980-83, prin. engr., 1983-86, mem. tech. staff, 1986-87; mem. tech. staff Bipolar Tech. Ctr. Motorola Co., Mesa, Ariz., 1987—; session chmn. Conf. on Applications of Accelerators, Denton, Tex., 1980, 82, 84, Electronic Materials Conf., 1981; speaker sci. confs., 1974-88; speaker Oxford (Eng.) Conf. on Electron Microscopy, 1987. Editor: Rapid Thermal Processing of Electronic Materials, 1987; contbr. numerous articles to profl. jours.; patentee in field. Mem. Sun Angel Found., Phoenix, 1986-88. Oak Ridge Assoc. Univs. fellow, 1978-79. Mem. Am. Phys. Soc., Electrochem. Soc., Materials Rsch. Soc. (symposium chmn. 1987). Republican. Baptist. Home: 14215 N 43d Place Phoenix AZ 85032 Office: Bipolar Tech Ctr 2200 W Broadway Rd Mesa AZ 85202

WILSON, THEODORE HENRY, electronics company executive, aerospace engineer; b. Eufaula, Okla., Apr. 23, 1940; s. Theodore V. and Maggie E. (Buie) W.; m. Barbara Ann Tassara, May 16, 1958 (div. 1982); children: Debbie Marie, Nita Leigh Wilson Axten, Pamela Ann, Brenda Louise, Theodore Henry II; m. Colleen Fagan, Jan. 1, 1983 (div. 1987); m. Karen L. Lerohl, Sept. 26, 1987. BSME, U. Calif., Berkeley, 1962; MSME, U. So. Calif., 1964, MBA, 1970, MSBA, 1971. Sr. rsch. engr. N.Am. Aviation Co. div. Rockwell Internat., Downey, Calif., 1962-65; propulsion analyst, supr. div. applied tech. TRW, Redondo Beach, Calif., 1965-67, mem. devel. staff systems group, 1967-71; sr. fin. analyst worldwide automotive dept. TRW, Cleve., 1971-72; contr. systems and energy group TRW, Redondo Beach, 1972-79; dir. fin. control equipment group TRW, Cleve., 1979-82, v.p. fin. control indsl. and energy group, 1982-85; mem. space and def. group TRW, Redondo Beach, 1985—; lectr., mem. com. acctg. curriculum UCLA Extension, 1974-79. Mem. Fin. Execs. Inst. (com. govt. bus.), Machinery and Allied Products Inst. (govt. contracts coun.), Nat. Contract Mgmt. Assn. (bd. advisors), Aerospace Industries Assn. (procurement and fin. coun.), UCLA Chancellors Assocs., Tau Beta Pi, Beta Gamma Sigma, Pi Tau Sigma. Republican. Home: 3617 Via La Selva Palos Verdes Estates CA 90274 Office: TRW Space and Def Group E2/11091 1 Space Park Redondo Beach CA 90278

WILSON, THOMAS RAYBURN, III, urban planner, consultant; b. Midland, Tex., Sept. 5, 1946; s. Thomas Rayburn Jr. and Bennie Lee (Harlow) W.; m. Melody Harp, Oct. 28, 1967. BA in Geography, Tex. Tech U., 1972. Asst. planner City of Lubbock, Tex., 1973-74, assoc. planner, 1974-78; prin. planner City of Odessa, Tex., 1978-85; pvt. practice planning cons. Santa Fe, 1985—; dir. Office Land Use, Santa Fe County, 1986—. Co-author: Land Use Report, 1974, Community Facilities Report, 1974, Urban Image Analysis, 1974, Rural Land Use Study, 1976, Santa Fe Comprehensive Extraterritorial Plan, 1988. Served with U.S. Army, 1969-72, Vietnam. Mem. Am. Inst. Cert. Planners, Am. Soc. Photogrammetry and Remote Sensing, Am. Planning Assn. (N.Mex. chpt.). Republican. Presbyterian. Home and Office: 144 Verano Loop Santa Fe NM 87505

WILSON, WARREN BINGHAM, artist, art educator; b. Farmington, Utah, Nov. 4, 1920; s. Alma L. and Pearl E. (Bingham) W.; B.S. in Edn., Utah State U., 1943; M.F.A., Iowa State U., 1949; m. Donna Myrle VanWagenen, Dec. 22, 1948; children—Vaughn Warren, Michael Alma, Annette, Pauline, Douglas George, Craig Aaron, Robert Kevin. Asst. prof. art Utah State U., Logan, 1949-54; vis. instr. Salt Lake Art Center, Utah, 1952-53; prof. art and edn. Brigham Young U., Provo, Utah, 1954-83; ret., 1983 vis. lectr. ceramics U. Calif., Davis, 1968; fellow in residence Huntington Hartford Found., Pacific Palisades, Calif., 1960-61; vis. instr. Pioneer Crafthouse, Salt Lake City, 1969-70; one-man shows of paintings and/or sculpture include: Salt Lake Art Center, 1951, Yakima Valley Coll., 1962, UCLA, 1962, Mont. State U., Bozeman, 1963, Stanford U., 1963, Wash. State U., Pullman, 1964, Central Wash. State Coll., Ellensburg, 1964, Nev. So. U., Las Vegas, 1967, Ricks Coll., Rexburg, Idaho, 1976, 80, Brigham Young U., Provo, Utah, 1970, 75, 79, 82, retrospective retirement exhbn. of sculpture, ceramics and paintings, 1983; group shows include: Denver Art Mus., 1951, Colorado Springs (Colo.) Fine Arts Center, 1951, Santa Fe Art Mus., 1953, Madison Sq. Gardens, N.Y.C., 1958, Wichita Art Center, 1960, Ceramic Conjunction Invitational, Glendale, Calif., 1973; represented in permanent collections: Utah State Inst. Fine Arts Salt Lake City, Utah State U., Logan, Utah State Fair Assn., Utah Dixie Coll., St. George, Coll. So. Utah, Cedar City, Brigham Young U., also numerous pvt. collections. Asst. dist. commr. Boy Scouts Am., 1975-80; counselor in Ward Bishopric, Ch. of Jesus Christ of Latter-day Saints, 1981-83. Served with USAAF, 1943-46. Recipient Am. Craftsman Council merit award, 1964; Silver Beaver award Boy Scouts Am. Mem. Nat. Council for Edn. in Ceramic Arts. Republican. Home: 1000 Briar Ave Provo UT 84604

WILSON, WILLIAM ALBERT, former ambassador to Vatican, financial consultant; b. Los Angeles, Nov. 3, 1914; s. William Webster and Adamarian (Smith) W.; m. Elizabeth Ann Johnson, Feb. 5, 1938; children—Anne Marie Solomone, Marcia Lou Hobbs. Student Harvard Sch., 1925-32, U. Mex., 1932; A.B., Stanford U., 1937; LL.D., Barry U., 1984, Pepperdine U., 1985. Draftsman, engr. Web Wilson Oil Tools, Huntington Park, Calif., 1937-42; pres. Web Wilson Oil Tools, Inc., Gardena, Calif., 1945-60; v.p. Baash-Ross, Compton, Calif., 1960, Smith Dynamics, Gardena, 1960; pres. San Vicente Investments, Inc., Los Angeles, 1964—; engring. cons. EB Wiggins Oil Tool, Los Angeles, 1937-42; regent U. Calif., 1972—; U.S. Ambassador to Vatican City State, 1981-86; fin. cons. Shearson-Lehman-Hutton ; bd. dirs. Pennzoil, Houston, Earle Jorgensen Steel. Republican del., 1968, 72, 76, 80; bd. dirs. St. John's Hosp., Santa Monica, Calif., 1976—. Served as capt. U.S. Army, 1942-45. Recipient Theodore Roosevelt Meml. award Navy League, 1982, Gold medal Italian Red Cross, Rome, 1983; Brotherhood award NCCJ, 1983. Republican. Roman Catholic. Lodge: Knights of Malta. Clubs: Los Angeles Country, Los Angeles Athletic. Avocations: hunting, horseback riding.

WILSON, WILLIAM FREDERICK, data processing executive; b. Seattle, Dec. 9, 1949; s. John Charles and Frances Jean (Fairweather) W.; m. Catherine Mary Chaffey, Dec. 13, 1975; children: Christopher John, Stephen Chaffey. Student, U. Wash., 1973-75, U. Wash., 1986-88. Ops. analyst Rainier Nat. Bank, Seattle, 1973-79; sr. systems analyst Chase Manhattan Bank, N.Y.C., 1979-80; sr. mem. tech. staff TTI/Citicorp, Santa Monica, Calif., 1980-81; v.p., mgr. Union Bank Computer, L.A., 1981—; cons. Coast Composition Equipment, Redmond, Wash., 1988-89, McKinsey & Co., L.A., 1989. Bd. mem. YMCA, Montebello, Calif., 1988-89; pres. PTO, L.A., 1986-87; block capt. Neighborhood Watch, L.A., 1985-88. Recipient Citation, YMCA, Montebello, 1988. Mem. Long Beach Jr. C. of C. (bd. mem. 1982-84). Republican. Episcopalian. Home: 9241 SE 60th St Mercer Island WA 98040 Office: Union Bank Computer 1980 Saturn St Monterey Park CA 91754

WILSON, WILLIE CLYDE, air force officer; b. Ala., Apr. 7, 1934; s. Willie Clyde and Meridian (Traywick) W; m. Marie M. Nickelson (div. 1979); children: Tina M., Toni L., Traci A. BS, U. Md., 1964; MBA, N.Mex. Highlands U., 1980. Enlisted USAF, 1951, advanced through grades to maj., 1966; commdr. hdqrs. squadron USAF, Lowry AFB, Colo., 1965-66; staff officer Combat Support Group, Viet Nam, 1969-70; chief of base plans McClellan AFB, Sacramento, 1970-71, ret., 1971; biomedical engr. VA, Albuquerque, 1977-87. Recipient Vietnam Combat medal, Rep. S. Vietnan, 1970, Air Force Commendation medal, USAF, 1971. Home: 2700 Vista Grande Dr NW Unit 3 Albuquerque NM 87120

WILTSE, CHLORYCE JERENE, home economics and computer science educator, electronics executive; b. Arnolds Park, Iowa, Nov. 25, 1933; d. Carl J. and Leila L. (Gibbs) Ode; m. Gary L. Wiltse, June 9, 1957; children—Mark, Lynn Wiltse Braswell. B.S., U. Nebr., 1955; postgrad. Iowa State, 1982, Mont. State U., 1968-81, U. Mont., 1967-72, Eastern Mont. Coll., 1965. Tchr. home econs. Osceola (Nebr.) High Sch., 1955-57; rural tchr. Billup Sch., Powder River County, Mont., 1957-58; tchr. home econs., computer sci. Powder River High Sch., Broadus, Mont., 1964-83; lectr. computers in home econs. edn., rural family fin. mgmt. Named Mont. Home Econs. Tchr. of Yr., Mont. Home Econs. Assn. and Family Circle mag., 1976. Mem. Am. Home Econs. Assn., Mont. Home Econs. Assn. (named Mont. Outstanding Home Economist 1989), Assn. for Devel. Co. Instrnl. Systems, Internat. Council for Computers in Edn., NW Council for Computer Edn., Mont. Council Computers in Edn., Mortar Bd., Delta Kappa Gamma, Phi Upsilon Omicron, Omicron Nu, Gamma Alpha Chi, Alpha Lambda Delta, Phi Sigma Chi, Kappa Delta, Women in Farm Econs. Republican. Lutheran. Order of Eastern Star. Author publs. in field. Home: Box 72 Volborg MT 59351

WIMMER, JOHN CHARLES, construction company executive; b. Albany, Calif., May 25, 1944; s. Herbert Fredrick and Cornelia Marie (Rothove) W. BBA with distinction, San Jose State U., 1974; MBA, Stanford U., 1977. Real estate salesman Security Pacific Real Estate Co., Walnut Creek, Calif., 1971-73; adminstrv. asst. to pres. Anthony Sch. of Santa Clara Valley, Inc., 1973-75, v.p., dir., 1977-81; pres. Lifestyle Homes Inc., Santa Clara, Calif., 1977-81; v.p. constrn. The Meads Group, Santa Clara, 1981-82, Heflin Corp., Palo Alto, Calif., 1982-84; project mgr. First S.W. Constrn. Co., Temple, Tex., 1984-85, Lincoln Properties, Foster City, Calif., 1985-86; sr. project mgr. Oxford Constrn. Svcs., Inc., Encino, Calif., 1986-87, Altamont Enterprises, LTD, Pleasanton, Calif., 1987-88; owner J.C. Wimmer Constrn., Walnut Creek, 1988—. Home and Office: 1142 Roxie Ln Walnut Creek CA 94596

WINARSKI, DANIEL JAMES, mechanical engineer; b. Toledo, Dec. 16, 1948; s. Daniel Edward and Marguerite (Pietersien) W.; BS in Engring., U. Mich., 1970, PhD (NSF fellow), 1976; MS, U. Colo., 1973; m. Donna Ilene Robinson, Oct. 10, 1970; 1 son, Tyson York. Mech. engr. Libbey Owens Ford Co., Toledo, summers 1968, 69, 72; petroleum engr. Exxon Production Research, Houston, 1976-77; staff engr. mech. engring. sect. IBM, Tucson, 1977-84, adv. engr., 1984-86, systems engr., performance evaluator, 1986—; assoc. prof. dept. mechanics U.S. Mil. Acad., 1980—; instr. minority computer edn. No. Ariz. U., 1983-85. Served to 1st lt. U.S. Army, 1970-72; maj. Res., 1984. Recipient IBM Invention Achievement award, 1981, 82, 83, 88, IBM Mfg. award, 1986; registered profl. engr., Ariz., Colo. Mem. ASME (pub. chmn. U. Mich. 1974), Phi Eta Sigma, Pi Tau Sigma, Tau Beta Pi. Republican. Methodist. Designer adjustable artificial leg; patentee tape reel hub, tape loose-wrap check, tape reel sizing, tape reel-cartridge. Office: IBM Corp 67E/060-1 Tucson AZ 85744

WINCHELL, ROBERT ALLEN, government agency administrator, accountant; b. Ft. Monmouth, N.J., Oct. 28, 1945; s. Robert Winslow Winchell; B.A., U. Calif., Santa Barbara, 1967; M.B.A., U. Pa., 1969. CPA, Calif. Air Force Audit Agy., El Segundo, Calif., 1972-73; accountant Scholefield, Bellanca & Co., W. Los Angeles, 1974-75, So. Calif. Gas Co., Los Angeles, 1975-76; auditor Def. Contract Audit Agy., Dept. Def., Los Angeles, 1976-86, supervisory auditor, 1986—. Served with AUS, 1969-71; Vietnam. Decorated Bronze Star. Mem. Assn. Govt. Accountants, Am. Inst. C.P.A.'s, Alpha Kappa Psi. Republican. Presbyterian. Club: Los Angeles Country. Home: 2008 California Ave Santa Monica CA 90403

WINCOR, MICHAEL Z., psychopharmacology educator; b. Chgo., Feb. 9, 1946; s. Emanuel and Rose (Kershner) W.; m. Emily E.M. Smythe, Sept. 14, 1980; children: Meghan Heather, Katherine Rose. SB in Zoology, U. Chgo., 1966; PharmD, U. So. Calif., 1978. Research project specialist U. Chgo. Sleep Lab., 1968-75; psychiat. pharmacist Brotman Med. Ctr., Culver City, Calif., 1979-83; asst. prof. U. So. Calif., Los Angeles, 1983—; cons. Fed. Bur. Prisons Drug Abuse Program, Terminal Island, Calif., 1978-81, Nat. Inst. Drug Abuse, Bethesda, Md., 1981, The Upjohn Co., Kalamazoo, Mich., 1982-87, Area XXIV Profl. Standards Rev. Orgn., Los Angeles, 1983, Brotman Med. Ctr., Culver City, Calif., 1983-88. Contbr. articles to jours. and chpts. to books, reviewer. Mem. adv. coun. Franklin Ave. Sch. Recipient Cert. Appreciation, Mayor of Los Angeles, 1981, Bristol Labs Award, 1978; Faculty scholar U. So. Calif. Sch. Pharmacy, 1978. Mem. Am. Coll. Clin. Pharmacy, Am. Assn. Colls. of Pharmacy, Am. Soc. Hosp. Pharmacists, Am. Pharm. Assn., Sleep Rsch. Soc., Am. Sleep Disorders Assn., Rho Chi. Office: U So Calif 1985 Zonal Ave Los Angeles CA 90033

WINDER, DAVID KENT, district judge; b. Salt Lake City, June 8, 1932; s. Edwin Kent and Alma Eliza (Cannon) W.; m. Pamela Martin, June 24, 1955; children: Ann, Kay, James. BA, U. Utah, 1955; LLB, Stanford U., 1958. Bar: Utah 1958, Calif. 1958. Assoc. firm Clyde, Mecham & Pratt Salt Lake City, 1958-66; law clk. to chief justice Utah Supreme Ct., 1958-59; dep. county atty. Salt Lake County, 1959-63; chief dep. dist. atty. 1965-66; asst. U.S. atty. Salt Lake City, 1963-65; partner firm Strong & Hanni, Salt Lake City, 1966-77; judge U.S. Dist. Ct., Dist. Utah, Salt Lake City, 1979—; examiner Utah Bar Examiners, 1975-79, chmn., 1977-79. Served with USAF, 1951-52. Mem. Am. Bd. Trial Advocates, Utah State Bar (Judge of Yr. award 1978), Salt Lake County Bar Assn., Calif. State Bar. Democrat. Office: US Dist Ct 235 US Courthouse 350 S Main St Salt Lake City UT 84101 *

WINDHAM, EDWARD JAMES, bank executive, leasing company executive; b. Salt Lake City, Dec. 13, 1950; s. James Rudolph and Margaret Ann (Griffith) W.; m. Marilyn Ann Kenyon, Mar. 27, 1973; children: Ian James, Kendra Ann. Student, U. Calif., San Diego, 1969-70, 72-74, U. Calif., Santa Barbara, 1970-72. Cert. mortgage credit examiner HUD. Emergency med. technician Hartson's Mobile Intensive Care Unit, San Diego, 1973-76; salesman Bonanza Properties, Tustin, Calif., 1976; loan officer Medallion Mortgage, Santa Cruz, Calif., 1976-80; sr. loan officer Cen. Pacific Mortgage, Santa Cruz, 1980-83, v.p., 1983-86; ptnr. Winn Leasing Co., Santa Cruz, 1983—; v.p. Community West Mortgage, 1986—; cons. Contour Inc., San Jose, Calif., 1983-85. Pres. Evergreen Estates Homeowners Assn., Soquel, Calif., 1983-85. Recipient Best Havana Brown award S.W. region Cat Fanciers Assn., 1976,77. Mem. Nat. Assn. Rev. Appraisers and Rev. Underwriters (sr., cert.), Mortgage Bankers Assn., Calif. Mortgage Bankers Assn., Mensa, Intertel. Republican. Lodge: Masons (master Santa Cruz 1987). Home: 3907 Adar Ln Soquel CA 95073 Office: Community West Mortgage PO Box 939 Capitola CA 95010-0939

WINDUS, ROBERT LEON, utility executive; b. Kansas City, Mo., July 6, 1945; s. Harry Leon and Helen Edith (Schaupmeyer) W.; m. Kathleen Carol O'Connell, Dec. 28, 1966 (div. Aug. 1976); children: Robbin Kathleen, John Robert. BBA, Western Wash. U., Bellingham, 1967; MPA, Golden Gate U., 1974. Commd. 2d lt. U.S. Army, 1968, advanced through grades to capt., 1970; 2d lt. U.S. Army, Ft. Eustis, Va., 1968, Oakland Army Base, Calif., 1968-69; 1st lt. U.S. Army, Republic of Vietnam, 1969-70; capt. U.S. Army, Oakland Army Base, 1970-74; mgmt. analyst Bonneville Power Adminstrn., Dept. Interior, Portland, Oreg., 1975-78; asst. security mgr. Bonneville Power Adminstrn., Dept. Energy, Portland, 1978-85, security mgr., 1985—; advisor Govt. of Western Samoa and U.S. Embassy, 1989, Govt. of Papua New Guinea and U.S. Embassy, 1988, Fed. Emergency Mgmt. Agy., Seattle, 1980—. Vol. Salvation Army, Portland, 1982-88, Loaves and Fishes, Meals on Wheels, Portland, 1982-86, Project Linkage, Home Security for the Elderly, Portland, 1982-85. Decorated Bronze Star. Mem. Res. Officers Assn. (pres. 1987-88), Civil Affairs Assn., Assn. U.S. Army, Rotary (chmn. 1986-87). Episcopalian. Home: 3607 SE 167th Ct Camas WA 98607 Office: Bonneville Power Adminstrn 905 NE 11th St Portland OR 97232

WING, JANET ELEANOR SWEEDYK BENDT, nuclear scientist; b. Detroit, Oct. 12, 1925; d. Jack and Florence C. (Springman) Sweedyk; m. Philip J. Bendt, Sept. 4, 1948 (div. Jan. 1972); children: Karen Ann Bendt Sox, Paul Philip, Barbara Jean Bendt Medlin, Linda Sue; m. G. Milton Wing, Aug. 26, 1972 (div. Jan. 1987). BSEE with distinction, Wayne State U., 1947; MA in Physics, Columbia U., 1950; postgrad., U. Oreg., 1966-67, U. N.Mex., 1968-71. Research engr. Gen. Motors Corp., Detroit, 1944-48; physicist, mathematician Manhattan Project Columbia U., N.Y.C., 1950-51; mem. research staff Los Alamos (N.Mex.) Nat. Lab, 1951-57, 68—, project leader, 1976-81, asst. group leader, 1980-84, assoc. group leader, 1985—. Bd. dirs., treas. Esperanza Shelter, Santa Fe, N. Mex., 1984—. Mem. Am. Nuclear Soc., AAAS, Women in Sci. and Engring., Los Alamos Women in Sci., Sigma Xi, Tau Beta Pi. Office: Los Alamos Nat Lab Los Alamos NM 87545

WING, ROGER, management consultant; b. N.Y.C., May 26, 1945; s. John A. and Norma M. (LeBlanc) W.; m. Judith A., June 7, 1963 (div. 1980); m. Peggy J. McFall, Aug. 27, 1983; children: Roger, Karin, Nicole. BBA, Cleve. State U., 1972, MBA, 1975. Supr. Am. Greetings Co., Brooklyn, Ohio, 1969-74; dir. Revco D.S. Inc., Twinsburg, Ohio, 1974-78; mgr. Hughes Aircraft Co., Los Angeles, 1978-79; sr. dir. Continental Airlines, Los Angeles, 1979-81; dir. Coopers & LyBrand, Los Angeles, 1981-83; pres. Huntington Cons. Group, Huntington Beach, Calif., 1983—; prof. Cleve. State U., 1977-78. Named Systems Man of Yr., Assn. Systems Mgmt., 1978. Office: The Huntington Cons Group 8531 Topside Circle Huntington Beach CA 92646

WING, WILLIAM HINSHAW, research physicist, educator; b. Ann Arbor, Mich., Jan. 11, 1939; s. Leonard William and Anne Marie (Hinshaw) W.; m. Jennifer Patai, June 10, 1967 (div. Aug. 18, 1979); children: Benjamin Patai, Jessica Grace. BA, Yale U., 1960; MS, Rutgers U., 1962; PhD, U. Mich., 1968. Research assoc., research staff physicist Yale U., New Haven, 1968-72, asst. prof. physics, 1972-74; assoc. prof. U. Ariz., Tucson, 1974-78, prof., 1978—; vis. prof. U. Colo., Boulder, 1979-80; prof. associé École Normale Supérieure, Paris, 1981; chmn. atomic and molecular div. Ariz. Research Labs. of U. Ariz., Tucson, 1983-86; chmn. com. on fundamental constants Nat. Acad. Scis./Nat. Research Council, 1983-87; founder, pres. Odyssey in Tech., Inc., Tucson, 1986—. Named U.S. Sr. Scientist Alexander Von Humboldt Stiftung, Fed. Republic of Germany, 1981; fellow John Simon Guggenheim Meml. found., 1980-81; vis. fellow Joint Inst. Lab. Astrophysics, Boulder, 1979-80. Fellow Am. Phys. Soc. (exec. com. div. atomic, molecular and optical physics, 1984-87, chmn. founding com. topical group on fundamental constants and precise tests of phys. laws, 1983-88), Optical Soc. Am.; mem. IEEE, N.Y. Acad. Scis., Am. Chem. Soc., Sigma Xi. Office: U Ariz Dept Physics Tucson AZ 85721

WINGO, ROBERT DEAN, JR., motion picture set decorator; b. Phila., Aug. 19, 1949; s. Robert Dean Wingo Sr. and Philomena (Ciardelli) Chaffin. BS in Interior Design summa cum laude, Woodbury U., 1978. Art dir. No. Communications, Los Angeles, 1976; set decorator Universal City (Calif.) Studios, 1978—. Nominated Emmy award Acad. TV Arts and Scis., Burbank, 1984, 85, 86. Mem. Acad. TV. Arts and Scis., Am. Film Inst., Internat. Alliance Theatrical and Stage Employees, Amnesty Internat. Democrat. Office: Universal City Studios 100 Universal City Pla Universal City CA 91608

WINIARSKI, WARREN PAUL, winemaker, winery executive; b. Chgo., Oct. 22, 1928; s. Stephen and Lottie (Lacki) W.; m. Barbara Ann Dvorak, Mar. 28, 1958; children: Catherine, Stephen, Julia. BA, St. John's Coll., Annapolis, Md., 1952; MA, U. Chgo., 1963. Lectr. U. Chgo., 1954-64; cellarman Souverain Winery, Napa, Calif., 1964-66; asst. winemaker Robert Mondavi Winery, Napa, 1966-68; founder, owner, mgr. Stag's Leap Vineyards, Napa, 1970—, Stag's Leap Wine Cellars, Napa, 1972—; owner, mgr. Fay Vineyard, Napa, 1986—. Contbg. author: History of Political Philosophy, 1963; contbr. to trade publs. Mem. Congl. recognition selection com. Claremont (Calif.) Colls., 1987, 89. Mem. Soc. Enologists (profl.), Napa Valley Vintners Assn. (chmn. com. for sub-appelations 1981—, bd. dirs. 1987—), Wine Inst. (rules and regulations com. 1980—), Brotherhood of Knights of Vine (Supreme Knight 1986—). Republican. Episcopalian. Office: Stag's Leap Wine Cellars 5766 Silverado Trail Napa CA 94558

WINKLER, AGNIESZKA M., advertising agency executive; b. Rome, Italy, Feb. 22, 1946; came to U.S., 1953, naturalized, 1959; d. Wojciech A. and Halina Z. (Owsiany) W.; m. M.T. Sworakowski, 1966 (div. 1981); children: Renata G., Dana C.; m. Arthur K. Lund. BA, Coll. Holy Name, 1967; MA, San Jose State U., 1972; MBA, U. Santa Clara, 1981. Teaching asst., San Jose State U., 1968-70; in-house sales rep. Sci. Products, Menlo Pk., Calif., 1971; account exec. Graphic Assocs., Palo Alto, Calif., 1972; founder, pres. Commart Advt., Santa Clara, Calif., 1973-84, Winkler McManus Inc., Santa Clara, 1984—; dir. Lefcourt Group, Inc.; bd. dirs. Skopos Corp., 1983-85; cons. Ea. European Bus. Adv. bd. U. Santa Clara Sch. Bus., 1984—; bd. regents, Holy Names Coll., 1987—; bd. trustees, O'Connor Found., 1987—. Recipient CLIO Advt. award, 1980, B/PAA Best in West award, 1980; Lester Tinneman award, 1966; Named One of "100 Best and Brightest Women in Mktg. and Advt. Ad Age; Coll. Holy Names President's scholar., 1964-66; Bill Raskob Found. grantee, 1965. Bd. dirs., Living Bus. Press. Mem. Polish Am. Congress, Women in Advt., San Jose Advt. Club, Women's Network, Bus./Profl. Assn, Am. Assn. Advtg. Agys., Bus. Profl. Advtg. Assn., Charge de Presse (exec. com. 1987). Office: Winkler McManus 150 Spear St16th Fl San Francisco CA 94105 also: 4701 Patrick Henry Dr Bldg F Santa Clara CA 95054 also: 1901 Avenue of the Stars Ste 1774 Los Angeles CA 90067

WINKLER, HENRIETTA IRENE, travel agency executive; b. N.Y.C., Dec. 15, 1919; d. George and Miriam (Beckerman) Israel; m. Sidney Kartin, June 25, 1950 (div. June 1961): m. Ervin Winkler, July 5, 1976. AA, L.A. City Coll., 1941; BA, UCLA; master's cert., North Orange Community Coll., 1975. Cert. competence in Spanish, Calif.; life diploma Kindergarten-primary, gen. edn., Calif. Tchr. L.A. City Schs., 1943-44, Bklyn. Pub. Schs., 1945-46, Alhambra (Calif.) City Schs., 1947-50, Bellflower (Calif.) City Schs., 1950-53, Norwalk (Calif.)-La Mirada Unified Schs., 1953-83; social worker L.A. County, 1944-45; travel counselor Travel Ctr., Pico Rivera, Calif., 1977-88, Gt. Western Travel Svc., Downey, Calif., 1988—. Mem. Pico Rivera Bicentennial Commn., 1975-76, Pico Rivera 25th Anniversary Commn., 1983; pres. Pico Rivera Sister City Commn., 1976-78, youth adviser, 1983-87; treas. So. Calif. chpt. Sister Cities Internat., 1976-85, rep. for Calif., 1986—; pres. B'nai B'rith Women, Huntington Park, Calif., 1954-55, Temple Ner Tamid Sisterhood, 1988—; life mem. Moffitt Sch. PTA. Recipient commendation L.A. County Bd. Suprs., 1988, Woman of Yr. award Women's Conf., Ea. Region Jewish Fedn. Council Greater L.A., 1988. Life mem. Phi Delta Kappa. Democrat. Home: 8327 Fernadel Ave Pico Rivera CA 90660 Office: Gt Western Travel Svc 11002 S Downey Ave Downey CA 90241

WINKLER, IRWIN, motion picture producer; b. N.Y.C., May 28, 1931; s. Sol and Anna Winkler. BA, NYU, 1955. Mailroom messenger William Morris Agy., N.Y.C., 1955-62; motion picture producer, owner Winkler Films, Culver City, Calif. Producer: Rocky, 1976 (10 Acad. award nominations, winner 3 including Best Picture, Los Angeles Film Critics award for best picture), They Shoot Horses Don't They, 1969 (9 Acad. award nominations), Nickelodeon, 1976, The Gambler, 1974, Up the Sandbox, 1972, The New Centurions, 1972, Point Blank, 1967, Double Trouble, 1967, Leo the Last (Best Dir. award Cannes Film Festival 1970, Belgrade Film Festival 1970), The Strawberry Statement (Jury prize Cannes Film Festival 1970), The Split, 1968, Breakout, 1975, Believe in Me, 1971, The Gang That Couldn't Shoot Straight, 1971, The Mechanic, 1972, Busting, 1974, S.P.Y.S, 1974, Peeper, 1975, New York, New York, 1977, Valentino, 1977, Uncle Joe Shannon, 1978, Comes A Horseman, 1978, Rocky II, 1979, Raging Bull, 1980 (8 Acad. award nominations, winner 2 Los Angeles Film Critics award for best picture), Rocky III, 1981, True Confessions, 1981, Author, Author, 1982, The Right Stuff, 1983 (8 Acad. award nominations), Rocky IV, 1984, Revolution, 1985, 'Round Midnight, 1986 (2 Acad. award nomiations, Acad. award Best Original Score), Betrayed, 1988, Music Box, 1989. Served with U.S. Army, 1951-53. Named Commander d'Artes et de Lettres, French Govt. Minister of Culture, 1985. Office: Winkler Films 10125 W Washington Blvd Culver City CA 90230

WINKLER, JUDY J., nurse; b. Charleston, Ill., Oct. 1, 1962; d. John Jay and Rebecca Jane (Bartimus) W. BS in Nursing, Millikin U., 1984. RN, Colo. Nurse S.W. Meml. Hosp., Cortez, Colo., 1986-87, Porter Meml. Hosp., Denver, 1988—. Home: 7777 E Yale Ave #D302 Denver CO 80321

WINKLER, KAREN STAPLETON, medical planning consultant; b. Milw., Mar. 21, 1939; d. Thomas John and Olive Patrea (Thorbjornsen) Stapleton; m. Max Kurt Winkler, Dec. 18, 1965 (dec. June 1976). BS in Nursing, U. Mich., 1961; MBA, U. Nev., 1974. Project nurse Langley Porter N.P.I., San

Francisco, 1962-64; asst. dir. nursing Milw. County Mental Health Ctr., 1964-66; instr. Fond du Lac (Wis.) Sch. Dist., 1966-67; sch. nurse Inglewood (Calif.) Sch. Dist., 1968-69; instr. nursing U. Nev., Reno, 1969-74; health planner manpower State of Nev. Comp B. Agy., Carson City, 1974-75; sr. system analyst U. Calif., San Francisco, 1976-79; planning analyst St. Mary's Hosp., Reno, 1974-76; med. planning cons. Stone Marraccini & Patterson, San Francisco, 1979—; staff nurse VA Hosp., Milw., 1961-62. Mem. citizen's adv. group City of Richmond, Calif., 1987-88. Mountain State Regional Planning Commn. grantee, 1973-74. Home: 1308 Mallard Dr Point Richmond CA 94801 Office: Stone Marraccini et al One Markert Pla San Francisco CA 94133

WINN, GEORGE MICHAEL, electrical equipment company executive. Student U. Wash., 1968. Pres., chief exec. officer, John Fluke Mfg. Co., Everett, Wash., 1988— Office: John Fluke Mfg Co Inc PO Box C9090 6920 Seaway Blvd Everett WA 98206 *

WINN, ROBERT CHARLES, military officer, aeronautical engineer; b. Chgo., Sept. 4, 1945; s. Bart James and Dorothy Eleanor (Smith) W.; m. Kathleen Nowak, Aug. 3, 1968; children: Eric Michael, Kara Michelle. BSME, U. Ill., 1968, MSME, 1969; PhD in Mech. Engring., Colo. State U., 1982. Registered profl. engr., Colo. Enlisted USAF, 1969, advanced through grades to lt. col., 1988; instr. pilot 14 student squad USAF, Columbus AFB, Mo., 1970-74; instr. pilot 61 Tactical Airlift Squad USAF, Little Rock AFB, 1974-76; asst. prof. dept. aeornatuics USAF Acad., Colorado Springs, Colo., 1976-79, assoc. prof., 1982—. Contbr. articles to profl. jours. Fellow AIAA (assoc. vice chmn. Rocky Mountain sect. 1985, sec. 1984, Terrestrial Energy Systems Nat. Tech. Com. 1984—); mem. Am. Soc. Engring. Edn., Air Force Assn. Roman Catholic. Office: USAF Acad Dept Aeronautics Colorado Springs CO 80840

WINOGRAD, TERRY ALLEN, computer science educator; b. Takoma Park, Md., Feb. 24, 1946; m. Carol Hutner; children: Shoshana, Avra. BA in Math., Colo. Coll., 1966, DSc (hon.), 1986; postgrad., U. Coll., London, 1967; PhD in Applied Math., MIT, 1970. Instr. math. MIT, 1970-71, asst. prof. elec. engring, 1971-74; vis. asst. prof. computer sci. and linguistics Stanford (Calif.) U., 1973-74, from asst. prof. to assoc. prof., 1974-86, assoc. prof. computer sci., 1986—; cons. Xerox Palo Alto (Calif.) Rsch. Ctr., 1972-85, Hermenet Inc., San Francisco, 1981-83, Action Techs., 1983—, Logonet Inc., San Francisco, 1986—; lectr. in field; mem. adv. bd. Ctr. for Teaching and Learning Stanford U., 1979-83, mem. acad. council com. on info. tech., 1981-83, mem. undergrad. council Sch. Engring., 1985—; adviser State of Calif., 1983. Bd. dirs. Live Oak Inst., Berkeley, Calif., 1980—, pres., 1984—. Grantee Advanced Research Project Agys., 1969-75, NSF, 1975-77, 82-85, Xerox, 1975-80, System Devel. Found., 1982-83; Hon. Woodrow Wilson fellow, 1966, Hon. NSF fellow, 1966, Fulbright fellow, 1966-67, Danforth fellow, 1966-70, Mellon Jr. Faculty fellow, 1977. Mem. Computer Profls. for Social Responsibility (mem. nat. exec. com. 1983—, mem. nat. bd. dirs. 1984—, pres. 1987—), Assn. Computational Linguistics (mem. editorial bd. jour. 1974-77), Am. Assn. Artificial Intelligence, Union of Concerned Scientists, Assn. for Computing Machinery. Home: 746 Esplanada Way Stanford CA 94305 Office: Stanford U Dept Computer Sci Stanford CA 94305-2140

WINSLOW, NORMAN ELDON, business executive; b. Oakland, Calif., Apr. 4, 1938; s. Merton Conrad and Roberta Eilene (Drennen) W.; m. Betty June Cady, Jan. 14, 1962 (div. Aug. 1971); 1 child, Todd Kenelm; m. Ilene Ruth Jackson, Feb. 3, 1979. BS, Fresno (Calif.) State U., 1959. Asst. mgr. Proctors Jewelers, Fresno, 1959-62; from agt. to dist. mgr. Allstate Ins. Co., Fresno, 1962-69; ins. agt. Fidelity Union Life Ins., Dallas, 1969-71; dist. and zone mgr. The Southland Corp., Dallas, 1971-78; owner Ser-Vis-Etc., Goleta, Calif., 1978—. Contbr. numerous articles to profl. jours. With USAFNG, 1961-67. Mem. Nat. Coalition of Assn. of 7-Eleven Franchises (affiliate, mem. adv. bd. Glendale, Calif. chpt. 1984—), Sigma Chi. Republican. Methodist. Home: 1179 N Patterson Goleta CA 93117 Office: Ser-Vis-Etc PO Box 2276 Goleta CA 93118

WINSLOW, PAUL GEORGE, interior designer, artist; b. Gunnison, Colo., Aug. 23, 1931; s. Frank William and Georgia (Hawkyard) W.; m. Dana Bartleson Winslow, July 18. 1960 (div. 1978); children: Scott, Lisa, Stuart. BA, Western State Coll., Gunnison, 1953, MA, 1954; postgrad., U. Calif. Santa Barbara, 1956, UCLA, 1957. Cert. tchr., Calif. Tchr. Santa Maria High Sch., Calif., 1960-79, Allan Hancock coll., Santa Maria, 1961-78, U. Calif. Santa Barbara, 1988—; designer Design Source, Santa Maria, 1978-88; designer Santa Barbara County Fair, 1963-74, 76-83, 86-87; coordinator design seminars Calif. Poly. Tech., San Luis Obispo, 1986-87, U. Calif. Santa Barbara, 1988. V.P. Santa Maria Arts Council, 1966; pres. Santa Maria Arts Council, 1967; bd. dirs. YMCA, Santa Maria. Served as pfc US Army, 1954-56. Mem. Am Soc. Interior Designers. Democrat. Home: 1223 Lela Ln Santa Maria CA 93454 Office: Design Source 705 E Main St Santa Maria CA 93454

WINSLOW, PHILIP CHARLES, agriculturist, marketing consultant; b. Carthage, Ind., Jan. 13, 1924; s. William Howard and Ione (Morris) W.; m. Arlis Brown, Oct. 6, 1951; children: Mark, Jay, Julie. BS, Purdue U., 1948. Successively dist. mgr., regional product mgr., asst. div. sales mgr., div. sales mgr., nat. product mgr., nat. mktg. mgr. Ralston Purina Co., 1950-1970; v.p. mktg. Namolco, Inc., Willow Grove, Pa., 1971-84; dir. mktg. molasses div. Cargill, Inc., Willow Grove, 1984-85; nat. mktg. cons. Cargill, Inc., Mpls., 1986-88; v.p. Walt Montgomery Assoc., 1989—; pres., dir. Winslow Farms, Inc., Carthage, 1982—. Sgt. U.S. Army, 1948-50. Mem. Am. Feed Industry Assn. (com. chmn. 1975-76, com. sec. 1982-83), Big 10 Club Phila. (pres. 1981), Shadowridge Golf Club, Purdue Club Phila. (v.p. 1982-83, pres. 1983-86), Masons. Republican. Lutheran. Home: 1305 La Salle Court Vista CA 92083

WINSOR, DAVID JOHN, cost consultant; b. Duluth, Minn., May 27, 1947; s. Alphonse Joseph and Sylvia Mae (Petrich) W.; m. Linda Kay Sanders, /dec. 22, 1968 (div. Mar. 1974). BA in Bus., U. Puget Sound, 1978; M of Mech. Engring., Pacific Western U., 1979. Jr. engr. J.P. Head Mech., Inc., Richland, Wash., 1965-67; estimator, project engr. Subs. of Howard S. Wright Co., Seattle, 1972-75; sr. estimator Massart Co., Seattle, 1975-76; project mgr. Univ. Mechanical, Portland, Oreg., 1976; cons. Kent, Wash., 1976-79; owner Leasair, Federal Way, Wash., 1978-83; pres., owner Expertise Engring. & Cons., Inc., Bellevue, Wash., 1979-82; cons. Winsor & Co., Walnut Creek, Calif., 1983—; cons. Nasa, Mountain View, Calif., 1986, Lockheed Missile & space, Sunnyvale, Calif., 1984-87, The Boeing Co., Seattle, 1979-82, travel agt. Accent on Travel, Pleasant Hill, Calif., 1986—. Author: (with others) Current Construction Costs, 1987, 88, 89, Construction Materials Inventory Systems, 1973, 74, Construction Inflation Trends, 1975, 76, 77, 78, 79, 80, 81, Construction Claims and Prevention, 1981, 82. Served to sgt. USAF, 1967-71. Mem. Jaycees (state dir. 1972-73, state chmn. 1973-74). Republican. Roman Catholic. Office: Winsor & Co PO Box 6788 Concord CA 94524

WINSOR, TRAVIS WALTER, cardiologist, educator; b. San Francisco, Dec. 1, 1914; s. Samuel Wiley and Mabel Edna (Mc Carthy) W.; BA, Stanford U., 1937, MD, 1941; m. Elizabeth Adams, Sept. 1, 1939; children—David Wiley, Susan Elizabeth. Intern, Alameda County Hosp., Oakland, Calif., 1940-41; asso. fellow and instr. in medicine and cardiology Tulane U. Sch. Medicine, New Orleans, 1941-45; practice medicine specializing in cardiovascular disease; mem. staff L.A. County Hosp., Hosp. of Good Samaritan (hon.), St. Vincent's Med. Ctr., L.A.; clin. instr. in medicine U. So. Calif., L.A., 1945-47, asst. clin. prof. medicine, 1947-61, asso. clin. prof. medicine, 1961-75, clin. prof. medicine, 1975—; dir. Meml. Heart Rsch. Found., Inc., L.A., 1957—. Diplomate Am. Bd. Internal Medicine. Fellow ACP, Am. Coll. Cardiology, Am. Coll. Chest Physicians, Internat. Coll. Angiology, Am. Coll. Angiology (pres. 1982-83), AMA, Am. Heart Assn.; mem. Calif. Med. Assn., L.A. County Med. Assn., L.A. Soc. Internal Medicine, Am. Coll. Thermology (pres. 1968-69), Royal Soc. Medicine London, Calif. Heart Assn., Internat. Cardiovascular Soc., Sigma Xi. Club: L.A. Author: (with George E. Burch) A Primer of Electrocardiography, 1944; (with C. Hyman) A Primer of Peripheral Vascular Diseases, 1965; A Primer of Vectorcardiography, 1972; (with A. Kappert) Diagnosis of Peripheral Vascular Diseases, 1972, Peripheral Vascular Diseases on Objective Approach, 1958; contbr. articles on cardiovascular diseases to profl. jours. Home: 541 S Lorraine Blvd Los Angeles CA 90020 Office: 4041 Wilshire Blvd Los Angeles CA 90010

WINSTON, ROBERT LAWRENCE, investment executive; b. Boston, May 27, 1938; s. Lawrence James and Mary Jane (Usick) W.; m. Judith Teehan Winston, Aug. 14, 1965; children: Robert W., Maribeth. AB, Boston Coll., 1960; MBA, U. Pitts., 1964. Cert. fin. planner, Colo. Mgr. Safeco Ins., L.A., 1965-68; account exec. Shearson Hammill, Beverly Hills, Calif., 2968-70; sr. v.p. Am. Funds Distbrs., L.A., 1970--. Pres. coun. Boston Coll., Chestnut Hills, Calif., 1988, Regis Coll., Denver, 1988; advisor Boy Scouts Am., Westlake Village, Calif., 1988. Capt. U.S. Army, 1960-62. Mem. Am. Mgmt. Assn., Internat. Assn. Fin. Planners, L.A. Athletic, Westlake Village Racquet, Toastmasters (pres. 1968-70). Home: 1238 Willowgreen Ct Westlake Village CA 91361 Office: Am Funds Distbrs Inc 333 S Hope St Los Angeles CA 90071

WINTER, BEVERLY PETTIBONE, nurse; b. Denver, Mar. 26, 1953; d. Mahlon Arthur and Mary Virginia (Brown) Pettibone; m. Monty Dale Winter, 1975. BSN, U. Wyo., 1975, MSN, 1987. RN, Calif.; cert. family nurse practitioner. Surg. staff nurse St. Luke's Hosp., Denver, 1975; staff nurse, in-svc. dir., supr. Ivinson Meml. Hosp., Laramie, Wyo., 1976-79; emergency nurse Ivinson Meml. Hosp., Laramie, 1985-87; nurse provider Comprehensive Nursing Svcs., St. Louis, 1979-80; pvt. practice nutritional and personal counseling Rawlins, Wyo., 1980-85; nurse provider Ramona Profl. Staffing, Hemet, Calif., 1987—; emergency nurse Hemet Valley Hosp., 1988—; nurse faculty Mt. San Jacinto Coll., 1988-89; family nurse practitioner Riverside/San Bernadino County/Indian Health, 1989—; rsch. presentor Primary Care Nurse Practitioner Conv., Keystone, Colo., 1987. Named Young Career Woman of Yr., Bus. and Profl. Women, 1980. Mem. Am. Nurses Assn., Wyo. Coun. Primary Care Nurse Practitioners, Sigma Theta Tau, Phi Kappa Phi, Beta Sigma Phi, Delta Delta Delta, Soroptomist. Home: 42159 Mayberry Ave Hemet CA 92344

WINTER, DAVID KENNETH, college president; b. L.A., Sept. 15, 1930; s. Hugo H. and Hazel C. (Patterson) W.; m. Laura Fischer, July 9, 1960 (div. 1985); m. Helene Eaton, July 16, 1988; children: Laura, Ruth, Bruce. BA, UCLA, 1953, MA, 1956; PhD, Mich. State U., 1968. Instr. Wheaton (Ill.) Coll. 1959-62; asst. prof. Mich. State U., East Lansing, 1965-68, assoc. prof., 1968-70; acad. v.p. Whitworth Coll., Spokane, Wash., 1970-74, exec. v.p., 1974-76; pres. Westmont Coll., Santa Barbara, Calif., 1976—. Vice chmn. bd. dirs. Cottage Hosp., Santa Barbara, 1986—; campaign chmn. United Way, Santa Barbara, 1988-89. Lt. (j.g.) USNR, 1955-59. Mem. Am. Assn. Pres. Ind. Colls. and Univs. (bd. dirs. 1986—), Christian Coll. Coalition (chmn., bd. dirs. 1980—), Christian Coll. Consortium (chmn., bd. dirs. 1976—), Assn. Ind. Colls. So. Calif. (pres., bd. dirs. 1976—), Assn. Ind. Calif. Colls. and Univs. (chmn. exec. com. 1982—), Coun. Ind. Colls. (bd. dirs. 1980-84), Western Assn. Schs. and Colls. (commr. 1989—), Santa Barbara Ind. Edn. Coun. (chmn., bd. dirs. 1980—), Santa Barbara Club, Rotary. Republican. Presbyterian. Office: Westmont College 955 La Paz Rd Santa Barbara CA 93108

WINTER, HUBERT, JR. (HERB WINTER), employment services executive; b. Henryetta, Okla., June 22, 1944; s. Hubert and Hattie Adeline (Sallee) W.; m. Susan Lynn Bankus, July 15, 1970 (div. 1978); 1 child, Justin M.; m. Gayle Gwen Gunnerson, Jan. 26, 1980; 1 child, Erin Snider. AA, Modesto (Calif.) Jr. Coll., 1971; BA, Calif. State U., Turlock, 1973. Cert. employment specialist. Dist. mgr. Southland Corp. dba 7-Eleven, San Jose, Calif., 1973-75; owner Mifax-Cen. Valley, Modesto, 1983-85; owner, gen. mgr. Acclaimed Personnel Svc., Modesto, 1984-86, Health Care Profls. Personnel Svc., Modesto, 1984-86; pres., chief fin. officer ConTemporary, Inc. dba Able 2 Staff, Modesto, 1986--, ConTemporary, Inc. dba Able 2 Staff Temp Svc, Turlock, Calif., 1987--. Mem. Modesto C. of C., Turlock C. of C. Office: Able 2 Staff Temp Svc 1367 Standiford Ave Ste C Modesto CA 95350

WINTER, IRWIN FLOYD, radiologist; b. Parkston, S.D., June 12, 1914; s. John G. and Aline Louise (Jaton) W.; m. Leona LaVon Luchsinger, June 23, 1939; children: Kathleen Dee, Brian Irwin, Kent Louis. BA, Huron (S.D.) Coll., 1935; BS, U. S.D., 1937; MD, Rush Med. Sch., Chgo., 1939; MS in Radiology, U. Minn., 1945. Intern Washington Blvd. Hosp., Chgo., 1939-40; resident St. Mary's and Pima County Hosps., Tucson, 1940-41; fellow in radiology Mayo Clinic, Rochester, Minn., 1941-44, jr. staff dept. radiology, 1944-46; practice medicine specializing in radiology Seattle, 1946-48; radiologist Swedish Hosp., Seattle, 1946-48, Salt Lake Clinic, Salt Lake City, 1948-51; instr. radiology U. Utah, 1948-50; practice medicine specializing in radiology Salt Lake City, 1948—. Mem. Utah Med. Soc., Salt Lake County Med. Soc., Am. Coll. Radiology, Utah Radiol. Soc. Lodge: Masons. Home: 900 Donner Way Apt #508 Salt Lake City UT 84108 Office: 508 E S Temple St Salt Lake City UT 84102

WINTER, MICHAEL WAYNE, radiologic technologist; b. Oceanside, Calif., Oct. 23, 1956; s. Ronald Wayne and Mary (Teresa) W.; m. Suzanne Denise Oliver (div. Dec. 1985); children: Kendra Dawn; m. Karen Lee Sterling, May 10, 1987. AS, Portland (Oreg.) Community Coll., 1983. Registered radiologic technologist. Furniture assembly Barker Mfg., Portland, 1977-78; shipping clk. Cascade Electronics, Portland, 1978-79; parts distribution clk. Diversified Distbg., Portland, 1979; grocery clk. Coll. Dairy Store, College Place, Wash., 1979-81; transp. aide Portland Adventist Med. Ctr., 1981-83; delivery driver J.C. Penney Co., Portland, 1981-82; radiologic tech. Gresham (Oreg.) Community Hosp., 1983-84; x-ray camera operator East Portland X-Ray Services, 1982-84; radiologic tech. Bedside X-Ray Services, Portland, 1984—. Mem. Oreg. Soc. Radiologic Techs. Seventh Day Adventist. Club: Portland Atari. Home: 1425 SE 89th Portland OR 97216 Office: Bedside X-Ray Svcs 183 NE 102d St Portland OR 97230

WINTERBOTTOM, MICHAEL CHARLES, software analyst; b. Fountaine Bleau, France, June 6, 1959; came to U.S., 1961; s. Matthew Charles Winterbottom and Norma Jean (Bednar) Nichols. BA in Math. Valedictorian, Colgate U., 1981; postgrad., U. Colo., 1983. Technician Par Tech. Corp., Rome, N.Y., 1978-81; software analyst Par Govt. Systems Corp., New Hartford, N.Y., 1981, Colorado Springs, 1982-89; software analyst SofTech Corp., Colorado Springs, 1989—; cons. Artisan Software, Colorado Springs, 1986—. Software programmer: BlackBook, 1986, Conference Planner, 1989. War Meml. scholar Colgate U., 1978-81, Dana scholar Colgate U., 1978-81. Mem. Math. Assn. of Am., Apple Programmer/Developers Assn., Phi Beta Kappa. Roman Catholic. Home: 2325 Stepping Stones Way Colorado Springs CO 80904 Office: SofTech Corp 1670 N Newport Rd Colorado Springs CO 80918

WINTERS, TERENCE EDWIN, venture capitalist; b. Exeter, Devon, U.K., Apr. 26, 1942; came to U.S., 1967; s. Horace Edwin and Minnie Lily Emily (Moule) W.; m. Eileen Young, Jan. 1, 1981. BS in Chemistry, U. Wales, 1964, PhD in Chemistry, 1967. Post doctoral fellow UCLA, 1967-68; sr. research chemist, project mgr. Goodyear Tire and Rubber Co., Akron, Ohio, 1968-77; mgr. Diamond Shamrock Corp., Cleve., 1977-80; v.p. DS Ventures Cleve., 1981-83; gen. ptnr. Columbine Venture Fund Ltd., Denver, 1983--; bd. dirs. Microgenics Corp., Concord, Calif., 1984--, Evans Biocontrol Inc., Boulder, Colo., 1985--, Maxell Hybrids Inc., Montgomery, Ala., 1985--, Iatromed Inc., Phoenix, 1987--. Patentee in field; contbr. articles to profl. jours. Mem. Am. Chem. Soc., Nat. Venture Capital Assn., Soc. for Corp. Growth, Metropolitan (Denver), The Country Club (Castle Pines, Colo.). Home: 18776 E Briarwood Dr Aurora CO 80016 Office: Columbine Ventures 5613 DTC Pkwy #510 Englewood CO 80111

WINTHROP, JOHN, real estate executive, lawyer; b. Salt Lake City, Apr. 20, 1947; m. Marilyn MacDonald, May 17, 1975; children: Grant Gordon, Clayton Hanford. AB cum laude, Yale U., 1969; JD magna cum laude, U. Tex., 1972. Bar: Calif. 1972. Law clk. U.S. Ct. of Appeals, L.A., 1972-73; conseil juridique Coudert Freres, Paris, 1973-75; v.p. gen. counsel MacDonald Group, Ltd., L.A., 1976-82; pres., chief exec. officer MacDonald Mgmt. Corp. and MacDonald Group Ltd., L.A., 1982-86, MacDonald Corp. (gen. contractors), L.A., 1982-86; chmn., chief exec. officer Comstock Mgmt. Co., L.A., 1986—; pres., chief exec. officer Winthrop Investment Properties, Los Angeles, 1986—; bd. dirs. Plus Prods., Tiger's Milk Prods., Irvine, Calif., 1977-80. Bd. dirs. L.A. Sheriff's Dept. Found. Mem. Calif. Bus. Properties Assn. (bd. advisors 1981-87), Internat. Council Shopping Ctrs., French-Am. C. of C. (bd. dirs. 1982-87), Urban Land Inst., Nat. Realty Bd., Regency Club, Yale of N.Y., Calif. Club, The Beach Club. Republican. Episcopalian. Office: Comstock Mgmt Co 445 S Figueroa St Ste 2600 Los Angeles CA 90071

WINTHROP, KENNETH RAY, insurance executive; b. N.Y.C., Dec. 29, 1950; s. Ralph and Lore (Bruck) W.; m. Sharon Swinnich, 1976 (div. 1978); m. Diane Louise Denney, June 27, 1981; children: Alyssa Louise, Matthew Lawrence. BA in English, SUNY, Buffalo, 1972. Agt. Northwestern Mut. Life Ins., Woodland Hills, Calif., 1975-78, Nat. Life of Vermont, L.A., 1978—. Mem. Nat. Life of Vt. Pres. Club, Million Dollar Round Table. Democrat. Home: 7609 W 83d St Playa Del Rey CA 90293 Office: 1900 Avenue of the Stars #2701 Los Angeles CA 90067

WIPRUD, VIRGINIA MILLER, respiratory therapist, educator; b. Tuscola, Ill.; d. George Bernard and Edith Mae (Baker) Miller; m. Glenn C. Wiprud, Dec. 16, 1955 (div. 1974); children: Barbara C., Valerie L. BS in Journalism, So. Ill. U., 1953; Cert. Respiratory Therapy, UCLA, 1973; MPH, Calif. State U., Northridge; 1983. Registered respiratory therapist, Calif. Women's editor Hollywood (Calif.) Citizen News, 1953-54; news writer L.A. Times-Mirror Co., 1954-56; promotion assoc. KOMO-TV, Seattle, 1956-57; promotions, pub. rels. writer L.A. Times, 1957-63; respiratory therapist UCLA Med. Ctr., 1973-76; respiratory care educator L.A. Valley Coll., Van Nuys, Calif., 1976—; vice chairperson Calif. Respiratory Care Examining Com., Sacramento. Author curriculum guide, editor syllabus. Instr. CPR, L.A. chpt. Am. Heart Assn.; com. mem. Long Beach (Calif.) chpt. Am. Lung Assn. Grantee, L.A. Community Coll. Dist., 1988-90. Mem. Calif. Soc. Respiratory Care (pres. chpt. 4 L.A. 1986-87, state com. chair 1986—), Am. Assn. Respiratory Care, Phi Kappa Phi, Pi Delta Epsilon, Sigma Sigma Sigma. Office: LA Valley Coll Dept Health Sci 5800 Fulton Ave Van Nuys CA 91401

WIRT, MICHAEL JAMES, library director; b. Sault Ste. Marie, Mich., May 21, 1947; s. Arthur James and Blanche Marian (Carruth) W.; m. Barbara Ann Hallesy, Aug. 12, 1972; 1 child, Brendan. BA, Mich. State U., 1969; MLS, U. Mich., 1971. Cert. librarian, Wash. Acting librarian Univ. Mich., Ctr. for Research on Econ. Devel., Ann Arbor, 1971-72; instnl. services librarian Spokane County Library Dist., Wash., 1972-76, asst. dir., 1976-79, acting dir., 1979, dir., 1980—. Mem. Adv. com. Partnership for Rural Improvement, Spokane, 1982-85, Wash. State Library Planning and Devel. Com., 1984-85, Ea. Wash. U. Young Writers Project Adv. Bd., 1988—. Mem. Wash. Library Assn. (2d v.p. 1984-86, Merit award 1984, v.p., treas. State Users Group, 1986-87), Wash. Library Network (rep. Computer Service Council 1983-86), Spokane Valley C. of C., Spokane Area C. of C. (local govt. com. 1987—).

WIRTH, TIMOTHY ENDICOTT, senator; b. Santa Fe, Sept. 22, 1939; s. Cecil and Virginia Maude (Davis) W.; m. Wren Winslow, Nov. 26, 1965; children: Christopher, Kelsey. B.A., Harvard U., 1961, M.Ed., 1964; Ph.D., Stanford U., 1973. White House fellow, spl. asst. to sec. HEW, Washington, 1967; asst. to chmn. Nat. Urban Coalition, Washington, 1968; dep. asst. sec. for edn. HEW, Washington, 1969; v.p. Great Western United Corp., Denver, 1970; mgr. Rocky Mountain office Arthur D. Little, Inc. (cons. firm), Denver, 1971-73; mem. 94th-99th Congresses from 2d Colo. Dist., 1975-87, mem. energy and commerce com., sci. and tech. com., budget com., chmn. subcom. telecommunications, fin. and consumer protection; U.S. senator from Colo. 1987—, mem. armed services com., energy and natural resources com., budget com., banking com., housing and urban affairs com. Mem. Gov.'s Task Force on Returned Vietnam Vets., 1970-73; mem. bd. visitors U.S. Air Force Acad., 1978—; advisor Pres.'s Commn. on the 80's, 1979-80; trustee Planned Parenthood, Denver Head Start. Recipient Disting. Service award HEW, 1969; Ford Found. fellow, 1964-66. Mem. White House Fellows Assn. (pres. 1968-69), Denver Council Fgn. Relations (exec. com. 1974-75). Office: US Senate Office Senate Members Washington DC 20510 *

WISCOMBE, JOHN PAUL, travel agency owner; b. Norman, Okla., Nov. 17, 1945; s. Raymond and June (Rose) W.; m. Joy Ferrin, May 18, 1972; children: Wendy, Alexandra, Taylor, Luke, Hillary, Katie, Peter. BA, U. Utah, 1970. Dir. Internat. Exchange Sch., Salt Lake City, 1970-72; pres., dir. Study Guild Internat., Salt Lake City, 1972-74; dir. Internat. Inst., Phoenix, 1974-75; pres., owner The Journey Assocs., Mesa, Ariz., 1975—. Author: (travel/study manual) Introduction to Europe, 1985. Recipient Nat. Group Mktg. award Nat. Tour Assn., 1988, Am. Bicentennial Parade award City of Paris, 1988. Mem. Am. Soc. Travel Agts. Republican. Mormon. Lodge: Rotary. Office: The Journey Assocs 1030 W Southern Ave Mesa AZ 85210

WISDOM, SHIRLEEN LOUISE, finance company executive; b. Eugene, Oreg., Feb. 11, 1948; d. Shirley Leroy Wisdom and Louise Marguerite (Wilken) Finnigan; m. William Louise Grouell, Nov. 28, 1968 (div. 1979); children: Heidi Lynn, Dane Leigh; m. Charles Emerson Helfrick Jr., Feb. 18, 1989. Br. mgr. Morris Plan Co., Hayward, Calif., 1978-87; fin. supr. Sears Consumer Finance, Cupertino, Calif., 1987-88; with comml. loan dept. Imperial Thrift & Loan, Pleasanton, Calif., 1988—; br. mgr. Imperial Thrift & Loan, Stockton, Calif., 1989—. Republican. Lutheran. Home: 7 Rainbow Circle Danville CA 94526

WISE, DAVID EDWARD, transportation executive; b. Sarnia, Ont., Can., Oct. 12, 1947; came to U.S., 1975; s. Donald Eric and Barbara Elaine (Jennings) W.; m. Patricia Helene Branaghan, July 14, 1970; children: David, Sarah, Leslie. BBA, Ohio U., 1970; MBA, U. Colo., Denver, 1989. Underwriting supr. Allstate Ins. Co., Toronto, Ont., Can., 1970-74, regional salesman, 1974; dist. mgr. Saunders System, Inc., various, 1975-82; area v.p. Saunders System, Inc., Milw., 1982-84; v.p. field mktg. Saunders System, Inc., Birmingham, Ala., 1984-86; exec. dist. mgr. Ryder Truck Rental, Denver, 1987—. Home: 5773 S Kittredge St Aurora CO 80015 Office: Ryder Truck Rental 4150 Holly St Denver CO 80216

WISE, JANET ANN, university program administrator; b. Detroit, Aug. 8, 1953; d. Donald Price and Phyllis (Licht) W.; m. Peter Anthony Eisenklam, Oct. 16, 1976 (div. Aug. 1982); m. Edward Henry Moreno, Mar. 31, 1984; 1 child, Talia. Student, U. N.Mex., 1971-73; BA in English, Coll. Santa Fe, 1989. Editorial asst., writer The New Mexican, Santa Fe, 1975-77; press asst., press sec. Office of Gov. N.Mex., Santa Fe, 1979-82; dir. pub. relations City of Santa Fe, 1983-84, Coll. Santa Fe, 1984—. Bd. dirs. Santa Fe Bus. Bur., 1984-87, Santa Fe Girl's Club, 1986—. Recipient Exemplary Performance award Office of N.Mex., Santa Fe, 1981, Outstanding Service award United Way of Santa Fe, 1982. Mem. Pub. Relations Soc. Am., N.Mex. Press Women. Democrat. Unitarian. Home: 104 Lugar de Oro Santa Fe NM 87501 Office: Coll Santa Fe La Salle Hall St Michael's Dr Santa Fe NM 87501

WISE, ROGER LEE, transportation executive; b. San Jose, Calif., June 26, 1959; s. George Cleve and Aileen Hope (Ryan) W.; m. Emily Mata, May 31, 1980; 1 child, Amy Nicole. BA with honors, No. Calif. Bible Coll., 1981. Account exec. Graebel Movers, San Jose, 1981-83; sales devel. mgr. N.Am. Van Lines, Ft. Wayne, Ind., 1983-84; mgr. sales and mktg. Nevill/N.Am. Van Lines, San Jose, 1984-86; sr. v.p., gen. mgr. Campbell Moving/N.Am. Van Lines, San Jose, 1986—. Mem. Calif. Scholarship Fedn. Presbyterian. Office: Campbell Moving Co Inc 660 N King Rd San Jose CA 95133

WISE, WOODROW WILSON, JR., small business owner; b. Alexandria, Va., Mar. 9, 1938; s. Woodrow Wilson Sr. and Helen (Peverill) W.; m. Barbara Jean Hatton, Oct. 6, 1956 (div. 1975); m. Sandra Kay Habitz, Dec. 17, 1983; children: Anthony P., Laura J. Gen. mgr. Alexandria (Va.) Amusement Corp., 1956-73; curator Harold Lloyd Estate, Beverly Hills, Calif., 1973-75; pres. Discount Video Tapes, Inc., Burbank, Calif., 1975—. Office: Discount Video Tapes Inc PO Box 7122 833 "A" N Hollywood Way Burbank CA 91510

WISEMAN, JAY DONALD, photographer, heating contractor; b. Salt Lake City, Dec. 23, 1952; s. Donald Thomas and Reva (Stewart) W.; m. Barbara Helen Taylor, June 25, 1977; children: Jill Reva, Steve Jay. Ed. Utah State U., Logan, U. Utah. Cert. profl. photographer. Pvt. practice photography; owner, pres. JB&W Corp. Recipient Grand prize Utah State Fair, 1986,

Kodak Crystal for Photographic Excellence, 1986, 87, Master of Photography award, 1989; cover photo, 1988; numerous photos requested for inclusion in Internat. Photographic Hall of Fame, 1989; photo named one of World's Greatest, Kodak, 1987-88; 2 photos named among World's Best, Walt Disney World and Profl. Phototgraphers Assn, 1988. Mem. Profl. Photographers Assn. Am. (one of top 10 scores internat. photo contest), Rocky Mountain Profl. Photographers (Best of Show, highest score ever 1987), Toronto Camera Club, Inter-Mountain Profl. Photographers Assn. (Master's Trophy Best of Show 1982, 86, 88, Photographer of Yr. award 1986), Photographers Soc. Am (Best of Show award Utah chpt. 1986). Mormon. One man shows include Busath's 701 Gallery, Salt Lake City; represented in Salt Lake City Internat. Airport permanent photo exhibit, various traveling loan collections, U.S. and Europe, 1988, loan collection Epcot Ctr., 1988; photographs published profl. jours.

WISNIEWSKI, WIT TADEUSZ, electrical engineer; b. Krakow, Poland, Apr. 22, 1962; came to U.S., 1969; s. Wieslaw Zygmunt and Maria Elzbieta (Jaworek) W. BSEE, U. Ariz., 1985, postgrad., 1988—. Registered profl. engr., Ariz.; cert. flight instr. FAA. Cons. engr. Wit T. Wisniewski, Tucson, 1985-87; design engr. Interactive Concepts, Tucson, 1987—. Mem. Soaring Soc. Am., So. Ariz. Hiking Club, Tucson Soaring Club (flight instr. 1985—). Home: 1421 N Sarnoff Dr Tucson AZ 85715 Office: Interactive Concepts 40 N Swan Rd Ste 207 Tucson AZ 85711

WISOTSKY, JERRY JOSEPH, graphic arts company executive; b. N.Y.C., Oct. 22, 1928; s. Abraham I. and Anna P. (Slipoy) W.; student CCNY, 1946-48; m. Helen E. Lerner, Nov. 12, 1949; children: Pearle Eve Wisotsky Marr, Ronald Ian. Apprentice, Triplex Lithographic Corp., N.Y.C., 1949-51; pres. Kwik Offset Plate Inc., N.Y.C., 1952-59; chmn. bd. Imperial Litho/Graphics Inc., Phoenix, 1959—; ptnr. M.J. Enterprises, Phoenix, 1959—. Mem. bd. appeals, Phoenix, 1974-76; pres. Ariz. Found. for Handicapped, 1976—; campaign chmn. corp. div. United Way, 1975, gen. campaign chmn., 1977; trustee St. Luke's Hosp. Med. Center; pres. Phoenix Jewish Community Center, 1970-71; v.p. bd. dirs. United Way; pres. United Way Phoenix-Scottsdale, 1981; chmn. Valley of Sun United Way, 1981; chmn. Ariz. bd. dirs. Anti-Defamation League, also nat. commr.; bd. dirs. NCCJ; charter pres. Metro-Phoenix Citizens Council, 1986-87; pres. Boys'& Girls' Clubs Met. Phoenix, 1989— ; bd. dirs. Ariz.-Weizmann Inst., 1984, Ariz. Mus. Sci. and Tech., 1984, Golden Gate Settlement Devel. Council, Phoenix Community Alliance, 1984; pres. Dean's Council of 100 Coll. Bus. Ariz. State U., 1989; chmn. Combined Health Resources, 1984; mem. 1986 Nat. UN Day Program, state exec. bd. U.S. West Communications, 1984; hon. bd. dirs. Valley of the Sun United Way; past chmn. bd. dirs. St. Luke's Hosp., Phoenix; bd. dirs. Combined Health Resources, 1982-83. Recipient Disting. Service award Rotary Internat., Phoenix, 1985, Humanitarian award Nat. Asthma Ctr. Nat. Jewish Hosp., Torch of Liberty award Anti-Defamation League, 1977, 12 Who Care Hon Kachina award, 1980, Tom Chauncey award, 1984, Volunteerism award Valley of the Sun United Way, Gates of Jerusalem award State of israel Bonds, 1987, Human Rels. award Na; named Phoenix Man of Yr., 1985. Mem. Am. Greyhound Found. (bd. dirs.), NCCJ, 1989. Immunology & Respiratory Medicine, Met. C. of C. (intercity com.), Ariz. Jewish Hist. Soc. (bd. dirs. 1984), Valley Forward Assn., Econ. Club Phoenix (founding bd. dirs. 1984), Phoenix 40 Club. Home: 7520 N 1st St Phoenix AZ 85020 Office: 210 S 4th Ave Phoenix AZ 85003

WISSINGER, ROBERT ALAN, biomedical engineer; b. Painesville, Ohio, Sept. 16, 1950; s. Robert Ralph and Opal (Hacker) W.; m. Barbara Ellen Paul, June 7, 1974; children: John Robert, Lisa Ann. BS in Pharmacy, U. Cin., 1974; MS in Biomed. Sci., Ohio State U., 1978. Registered pharmacist, Calif., Ohio. Pharmacist, asst. mgr. Gray Drug Stores, Columbus, Ohio, 1975; pharmacist Riverside Meth. Hosp., Columbus, 1976; programmer analyst Ohio State U., Columbus, 1976-77; systems coordinator M.D. Anderson Hosp. and Tumor Inst., Houston, 1977-80; dir. pharmacy systems U. Calif. Med. Ctr., San Diego, 1980-86; cons. Meml. Sloan Kettering Cancer Ctr. Pharmacy, N.Y.C., 1985-86, VA Med. Ctr. Pharmacy, San Diego, 1984-86. Contbr. articles to profl. jours. Mem. Am. Soc. Hosp. Pharmacists (chmn. working group on computer systems 1980-81), ASTM (com. mem. 1982—), Electron Computing Health Oriented Assn., Rho Chi. Republican. Home: 8501 E Turquoise Scottsdale AZ 85258 Office: Emtek Health Care Systems 2929 S Fair Ln Tempe AZ 85282

WISSLER, JON RODNEY, accountant; b. Portland, Oreg., Aug. 15, 1957; s. Rodney Lynn and Charlotte Jane (Bohle) W.; m. Susan Lorraine Timm, Mar. 29, 1981; children: Paula, Scott. BS, Oreg. State U., 1979. Charter revenue supr. Evergreen Internat. Airlines, McMinville, Oreg., 1979, gen. ledger supr., 1979-80, revenue acctg. mgr., 1980-81; staff acct. Portland Gen. Electric, 1985-88, budget analyst, 1988—. Mem. City of Fairview (Oreg.) Planning Community, 1987—; advisor Jr. Achievement, McMinville, 1980-81. Mem. Interlachen Assn. (sec., bd. dirs. 1986-88). Republican. Lutheran. Home: 21245 NE Interlachen Troutdale OR 97060 Office: Portland Gen Electric 121 SW Salmon Portland OR 97204

WISSLER, STANLEY GEBHART, geologist, consultant; b. N.Y.C., Mar. 31, 1900; s. Clark and Viola (Gebhart) W.; BS, Earlham Coll., 1922; MA, Columbia U., 1923; m. Agnes Elizabeth Meerhoff, Oct. 26, 1926; children: Ann Elizabeth Wissler Malcolm, Clark William, John Benjamin. Grad. asst. in geology and paleontology Columbia U., 1923-25; various positions oil and gas exploration and rsch. and adminstrn., Alaska, contiguous U.S., Can., Mex., Costa Rica, Philippines, Indonesia, Malaysia, Thailand, Burma, Pakistan, Ecuador, Union Oil Co. Calif., 1925-65; oil and gas cons., 1965-68; cons. Internat. Resources Co., S.E. Asia, 1969-70; ptnr. Hazzard, Morris & Assos., L.A., 1970-73; cons. geologist, Long Beach, Calif., 1973—. Registered geologist, Calif. Fellow Geol. Soc. Am., AAAS; mem. Am. Assn. Petroleum Geologists (cert. petroleum geologist, hon. life mem. Pacific sect.), Soc. Econ. Paleontologists and Mineralgists (hon. life mem. pres. 1937, pres. Pacific sect., 1928), Am. Inst. Profl. Geologists (cert.), Geol. Soc. Malaysia, Am. Security Council, Sigma Xi, Petroleum of L.A., Retired Oil Man's Club. Republican. Congregationalist. Contbr. sci. papers to profl. publs. in field. Home: 4245 Chestnut Ave Long Beach CA 90807

WISTAR, STEPHEN MOYLAN, chemical company executive; b. Phila., Apr. 7, 1954; s. C. Cresson and Ailsa Fox (Freeman) W. Diploma, U. St. Andrews, Scotland, 1975-76; BA, Antioch Coll., Yellow Springs, Ohio, 1977. Pres. Wistar Chem. Co., Denver, 1980—, Ferrous Am. Co., Denver, 1986—. Author: Cocaine Bodyguard Screenplay, 1959, Linde's Sament, 1988; editor: Colo. Bus. & Tech. Update Newsletter, 1984. Del. Col. Dem. Party, Boulder, 1988; active Vols. for Outdoor Colo., 1986—, Kairos Prison Ministries, 1988, St. Francis Ctr., 1984—, Fellowship Cos. Christ. Named Andrew Mutch scholar, St. Andrews Soc., Phila., 1975. Episcopalian. Club: Colo. Mountain. Home: 1230 Logan St Denver CO 80203 Office: Wistar Chem Co 1350 17th St Ste 350 Denver CO 80202

WITCHER, JOHN EDGAR, manufacturing company executive; b. Indpls., May 11, 1938; s. Edgar and Grace L. (Shrum) W.; m. Marilyn Jean Minor, Mar. 26, 1942; children—John M., Mark A. B.S., Ind. U.-Bloomington, 1961; LL.B. Blackstone Sch. Law, 1969. Quality engr. Cummins Engine Co., Inc., Columbus, Ind. and divs., 1961-70, materials dir., 1969-70; ops. mgr., v.p. ops. Remcom Systems, Inc., Garland, Tex., 1970-72; v.p., pres. Transtronics Corp., Garland, 1972-74; dir. purchasing, dir. materials Mitsubishi Aircraft Internat., Inc., San Angelo, Tex., 1975-80; dir. material Weber Aircraft div. Kidde, Inc., Burbank, Calif., 1980-82; dir. ops. control, 1982—. Mem. Am. Statis. Assn., Soc. Mfg. Engrs. Club: Masons. Office: Weber Aircraft Div 2820 Ontario St Burbank CA 91510

WITHERS, GREGORY PORTEE, research chemist; b. Chgo., June 14, 1950; s. John Lovelle and Daisy (Portee) W.; m. Carol Winette Jones, Oct. 12, 1985. BS, MIT, 1972; postgrad., U. Pitts., 1977-78; PhD, Rutgers U., 1978. Devel. research chemist Am.Cyanamid Co., Princeton, N.J., 1978-85; process devel. chemist Syntex Pharms., Inc., Freeport, Bahamas, 1985-87; devel. chemist. Syntex Chems., Inc., Boulder, Colo., 1987--. Patentee in organic chemistry, process development. Mem. Am. Chem. Soc. Home: 4806 EdisonAve Boulder CO 80301 Office: Syntex Chems Inc 2075 N 55th St Boulder CO 80301

WITHERS, MARK FRED, actor; b. Binghamton, N.Y., June 25, 1947; s. Donald Robert Withers and Norma Doris (Gibson) Lenzu; m. Patricia Ann Kelly, Aug. 19, 1968 (div. 1973); m. Phyllis Jean Hyre, 1974 (div. 1976); 1 child, Torran Isa; m. Brenda Faye Washington, Mar. 4, 1982; 1 child, Jessie Leith Norma May Withers. Student, Pa. State U., 1965-67, U. Upsalla, Sweden, 1967, UCLA, 1974-75, 89—; studies with Laura Rose, L.A., studies with Ed Couppee. participant Rick Walter's Theatercraft Wkshp., L.A., Film Actor's Wkshp., L.A., Pasadena (Calif.) Playhouse; creator, conductor acting seminar, L.A., 1988—. TV appearences include L.A. Law, Hill St. Blues, Dallas, Remington Steele, Gen. Hosp., and numerous others, 1977-89; recurring roles include Days of Our Lives, Santa Barbara, Dynasty, others; TV movies of the week include Something About Amelia, Alex, The Life of a Child, The Dorothy Stratton Story; theater appearences include The Owl and The Pussycat, The Crucible, You Can't Take it With You, and others. Mem. Screen Actors' Guild, AFTRA, Actors' Equity Assn., AGVA, Masquers Club, Reiki Alliance (2d degree), Southern Calif. Triumph. Republican. Methodist. Office: Alisha Tamburri Mgmt 10625 Magnolia Blvd North Hollywood CA 91601

WITHERSPOON, GREGORY JAY, financial services company executive; b. Quantico, Va., Sept. 30, 1946; s. Thomas Sydenham and Dorothy M. (Jordan) W.; m. Judith A. Klein, Feb. 11, 1966 (dec. Oct. 1984); children: Lisa Marie, Michelle, Rene. BS, Calif. State U., Long Beach, 1970. CPA, Calif. Sr. acct. Peat, Marwick & Main, L.A., 1969-72; sr. mgr. Touche Ross & Co., L.A., 1972-79; v.p. fin. Nanco Enterprises, Santa Barbara, Calif., 1979-84; pres. Pea Soup Andersen's, Buellton, Calif., 1984-86, VWB & P Cons., Santa Barbara, 1986-87; sr. v.p. fin. and adminstrn. Aames Fin. Svcs., L.A., 1987—; owner, founder Witherspoon Properties Ltd., L.A., 1976—; owner, mgr. Witherspoon Leasing, L.A., 1976—. Mem. Calif. Rep. Com., 1978—, Nat. Rep. Com., 1978—. Mem. AICPA, Calif. Inst. CPA's, Tennis Club, Ski Clubs. Office: Aames Fin Svcs 43ll Wilshire Blvd Los Angeles CA 90010

WITT, NEIL ORAND, educator, management consultant; b. Milw., Oct. 30, 1941; s. Orand A. and Ruth E. W.; A.S., Clark County Community Coll., 1974; B.S., U. Nev., 1976; M.B.A., Golden Gate U., 1980; student Nev. So. U., 1965. Radiol. tech. So. Nev. Meml. Hosp., Las Vegas, 1965-79; adj. prof. in mgmt. Clark County Community Coll., North Las Vegas, 1976—, instr. CETA program, 1979-80, advisor intermurals, promotions and spl. events, student activities Clark County Community Coll., 1986-88; adj. prof. psychology and human behavior Nat. U., 1985—; tech. cons. Lincoln County Hosp., Caliente, Nev., 1974; mgmt. cons., pres., chief exec. officer M.C.S. Assos., 1979—; coord. bus. lab. Clark County Community Coll.; adj. prof. bus. mgmt. Nev. State Prison, 1980—; instr. psychology & human behavior, Nat. U., N. Las Vegas, Nev.; promotions and fundraising, Radio Sta. KFM-Radio, Las Vegas, 1979—, pub. rels., promotions and community svc., 1980-82; owner Neil O. Witt & Assocs., Mgmt. and Tng. Cons.; bd. dirs., exec. com. Goodwill Industries So. Nev., Inc., 1988—. Mem. Nat. Bus. Edn. Assn., AAUP, Am. Registry Radiologic Techs., Am. Soc. Radiologic Techs. (speakers bur.), Am. Mgmt. Assn. Home: 5809 Granada Ave Las Vegas NV 89107

WITT, RICHARD FRANKLIN, physician; b. Oklahoma City, May 29, 1941; s. Paul Everett and Sarah Ellen (Stark) W.; m. Toni Ann Tregear, May 17, 1977 (div. 1982); 1 child, Richael Lynn Witt Michels. BA in Chemistry, U. Mo., Kansas City, 1971; MD, U. Kans., 1975. Diplomate Am. Bd. Family Practice. Resident in family practice So. Colo. Family Medicine U. Colo., Pueblo, 1975-78; pvt. practice Pueblo, Colo., 1978-85; med. dir. Community Health Care Delivery System, Tacoma, 1986-88, family physician, 1989—. Fellow Am. Acad. Family Practice. Home: 1301 Aqua Vista Dr NW Gig Harbor WA 98335-1539 Office: Community Health Care 1702 Tacoma Ave S Tacoma WA 98405

WITTBERGER, RUSSELL GLENN, advertising executive; b. Milw., July 7, 1933; s. Anton George and Libbie Elizabeth (Kresnicka) W.; m. Patricia Elizabeth Bradley, June 26, 1971; children: Steven, Robert, Elizabeth, Gary, Scott, Jennifer. BS in Journalism, Marquette U., 1955. Pres. Rand Broadcasting Corp., Miami, Fla., 1970-73; v.p., gen. mgr. KCBQ Inc., San Diego, 1973-78; pres. Charter Broadcasting Co., San Diego, 1978-83; exec. v.p. Cantor Advt. Corp., San Diego, 1983-85; v.p., gen. mgr. Boyd and Farmer Advt., San Diego, 1985-86; v.p., gen. mgr., prin. KLZZ-FM, San Luis Obispo, Calif., 1987—. Bd. dirs. Project Concern Internat., 1975-78; vice chmn. Food Bank San Luis Obispo County, 1989. Mem. Bldg. Industry Assn., San Diego Broadcasters (pres. 1973-75). Republican. Home: 263 Canyon Way Arroyo Grande CA 93420 Office: KLZZ-FM 321 Madonna Rd Ste 23 San Luis Obispo CA 93401

WITTIG, LAURENCE ROBERT, teacher; b. Bisbee, Ariz., Oct. 12, 1937; s. Edward Earl and Lillian Jane (Carlson) W.; m. Connie Phyllis Abbott, Feb. 6, 1959; children: Laurence Randall Wittig, Tami Rene Wittig O'Connell. BS in Edn., No. Ariz. U., 1959; MA in Edn., Ariz. State U., 1964. Cert. secondary tchr., Ariz. Choral music tchr. Paradise Valley Schs., Phoenix, 1959—; condr. Orpheus Male Chorus of Phoenix, 1980—; owner L.R.W. Piano Tuning. Composer various choral arrangements. Registrar of voters Rep. party, 1978-79. Recipient Condr. of Music award Presbyn. Nat. Assembly, 1985; bicentennial award (choir) U.S. Office of Edn./Canyon Press, 1976; Western Div. Performance Music Educators Nat. Conf., 1971, 73; Western Div. Performance Am. Choral Dirs. Assn., 1974, 78, 80. Mem. Paradise Valley Edn. Assn. (pres. 1965); Music Educators Nat. Conf. (Ariz. v.p. 1971), Am. Choral Dirs. Assn. (pres. 1978-80), Ariz. Edn. Assn., Nat. Edn. Assn. Republican. Lutheran. Office: Paradise Valley High Sch 3950 E Bell Rd Phoenix AZ 85032

WITTROCK, MERLIN CARL, educational psychologist; b. Twin Falls, Idaho, Jan. 3, 1931; s. Herman C. and Mary Ellen (Baumann) W.; m. Nancy McNulty, Apr. 3, 1953; children: Steven, Catherine, Rebecca. BS in Biology, U. Mo., Columbia, 1953, MS in Ednl. Psychology, 1956; PhD in Ednl. Psychology, U. Ill., Urbana, 1960. Prof. grad. sch. edn. UCLA, 1960—, founder Ctr. Study Evaluation, 1966, chmn. div. ednl. psychology; fellow Ctr. for Advanced Study in Behavioral Scis., 1967-68; vis. prof. U. Wis., U. Ill., Ind. U., Monash U., Australia. Author or editor: The Evaluation of Instruction, 1970, Changing Education, 1973, Learning and Instruction, 1977, The Human Brain, 1977, Danish transl., 1980, Spanish transl., 1982, The Brain and Psychology, 1980, Instructional Psychology: Education and Cognitive Processes of the Brain, Neuropsychological and Cognitive Processes of Reading, 1981, Handbook of Research on Teaching, 3d edit., 1986, The Future of Educational Psychology, 1989; editor-in-chief: Readings in Educational Research, 7 vols, 1977; assoc. editor: Ednl. Psychologist; contbr. articles to profl. jours. Capt. USAF. Ford Found. grantee; recipient Thorndike award for outstanding psychol. rsch., 1987. Fellow Am. Psychol. Assn. (mem. assn. coun. 1987—), AAAS; mem. Am. Ednl. Rsch. Assn. (chmn. ann. conv., chmn. publs. 1980-83, assn. coun. 1986-89, bd. dirs. 1987-89, award for outstanding rsch. 1986), Phi Delta Kappa. Office: UCLA 321 Moore Hall Los Angeles CA 90024

WIZARD, BRIAN RUSSELL, publisher, author; b. Newburyport, Mass., June 24, 1949; s. Russell and Ruth (Hidden) Willard. BA, Sonoma (Calif.) State U., 1976. Pvt. practice jeweler, sculptor, craftsman Sebastopol, Calif., 1974-79; prin. The Starquill Pub., Port Douglas, Queensland, Australia, 1981--; pub., movie producer, dir. Starquill Internat., Santa Rosa, Calif., 1986--; singer, songwriter 1988-. Author: Permission to Kill, 1985, Tropical Pair, 1986, Shindara, 1987, Metempsychosis, 1988; movie producer video documentary Thunderbanks, 1986; songwriter, producer cassette Brian Wizard Sings for His Supper, 1989. Served with U.S. Army, 1967-70. Decorated Air medals (26). Mem. Vietnam Helicopter Crewmember Assn., 145th Combat Aviation Bn. Assn., Vietnam Combat Vets. Assn., Vietnam Vets. Am., Vietnam Vets. Australia Assn. Office: 1579 Farmers Ln #66 Santa Rosa CA 95405

WODELL, GEOFFREY ROBERT, retail company executive; b. Madison, Wis., June 15, 1949; s. Robert Holland and Juanita Jacqueline (Francisco) W.; m. Lynn Johnson, Aug. 2, 1975; 1 child, Haaland Johnson. BA, U. Wis., 1971; postgrad., Metropolitan State U., 1987, U. Oslo, Norway, 1987, Loretto Heights U., 1987-88. Mgr. Contact Electronics, Madison, 1972-74; buyer, mgr. Cecil's Boot Ranch, Madison, 1974-76; salesman Miller Stockman div. Miller Internat., Denver, 1976-77, asst. mgr., 1977-78; mgr. Miller Internat., Inc., Denver, 1978-79; buyer Miller Internat., Inc., 1979-80, real estate exec., 1980—. Mem. Internat. Transactional Analysis Assn., Sons of Norway (mgmt. trainer 1980—, pres. 6th dist. 1988—, internat. dir. 1988), Nordmanns Forbundet, Eagles Soccer Club, Kicker Sports, Masons (Order of Chevalier 1974). Lutheran. Home: 3935 Garland St Wheat Ridge CO 80033 Office: Miller Internat Inc 8500 Zuni St Denver CO 80221

WOELFEL, MARY TERESA, real estate appraiser; b. Wichita Falls, Tex., Aug. 23, 1941; d. Patrick Cornelius and Bulah Faye (Hansard) McNamara; m. Justin George Woelfel, Nov. 28, 1959; children: Justin Jr., Jacqueline, Joani, James. Student, Tex. Western Coll., 1960-62, U. Colo., 1978. Sales agr. Wagner Co. Real Estate, El Paso, Tex., 1973-76, Holder Real Estate, El Paso, 1976-78; broker, owner Six Oaks Real Estate Brokerage, El Paso, 1978—, Santa Teresa (N.Mex.) Real Estate, 1984-85; property mgr. Cromo Bldg., Don Reilly Investments, El Paso, 1981-85; owner Cromo Secretarial Service, El Paso, 1981-84; staff appraiser City of El Paso, 1983—; sec., treas. Artcraft Tile Co., Inc., El Paso, 1981-88, Paso del Norte Marble & Tile, El Paso, 1988—. Pres., Mark Condominium Owners Assn., Ruidoso, N.Mex., 1982-84; bd. dirs. Jr. Woman's club, El Paso, 1965-66; leader, camp cons. Rio Grande council Girl Scout's U.S. Am., 1970-73; sec., v.p. Gadsen High Sch. Parent Council, Anthony, N.Mex., 1981-83; mem. El Paso Parents Awareness for Drugs, 1981-83. Mem. El Paso Bd. Realtors (com. mem. 1981-83), Tex. Assn. Realtors (profl. standards com. 1981-83), N.Mex. Realtors Assn. (legis. com. 1981-83), Nat. Assn. Realtors, Ind. Fee Appraisers. Republican.

WOESSNER, FREDERICK T., composer, pianist; b. Teaneck, N.J., July 23, 1935; s. Fred and Bertha W.; m. Lise Woessner, Feb. 14, 1960 (div. 1973); children: Betty, Allison. Student, Peabody Conservatory of Music, Balt., 1960-61; MBA, NYU, 1968; MA, Calif. State U., Los Angeles, 1975; pvt. study with, David Diamond, Charles Haubiel, Albert Harris. Pres., chmn. Music and the Arts Found. of Am., Inc., Los Angeles, 1971—; owner Al-Fre-Bett Music, Los Angeles, 1980—. Composer (for orch.) Nursery Song, Variations on an Irish Air, Reflections for Strings, Fanfare for Winds, String Quartet, Concerto for piano improvisations and orch., (music for films) Sky Bandits, Pale Horse, Pale Rider, The Curb Your Appetite Diet, Centerfold, (title music for TV) Actors Forum, (for stage) From Berlin to Broadway, Oh Atlantis, Kurt, Lil Nell (Sugar Babies II), Another Town; composer and pianist Sonic Arts, album-film/video, In My Forest Cathedral; rec. artist Sonic Arts Records. Founding dir., sec. Aids Crusades, Inc., L.A.; v.p., bd. dirs. U. of Hollywood. Served with U.S. Army, 1960-61. Mem. ASCAP, Soc. Composers and Lyricists, Am. Fedn. Musicians, Am. Soc. Music Arrangers (treas. 1978—), Composers and Arrangers Found. Am. (sec.). Democrat. Office: Al-Fre-Bett Music PO Box 45 Hollywood CA 90078

WOESTENDIEK, WILLIAM JOHN, university director; b. Newark, Mar. 14, 1924; s. William Anton and Alice Catherine (Mundy) W.; m. Mary Josephine Pugh, June 12, 1947 (div. 1966); children: Mary Kathryn, William John Jr., Theodore Joseph; m. Bonnie Jeanine Prock Stahl; children: Maurita Thomas, Lauri Olsen. BA in Journalism, U. N.C., 1947; MS in Journalism, Columbia U., 1948; postgrad., Harvard U., 1954-55. Sundary editor Winston-Salem (N.C.) Jour., 1948-56; editorial dir. Newsday, L.I., N.Y., 1956-64; mng. edior Houston Post, 1964-69; editor Think IBM Corp., Armonk, N.Y., 1969; editor This Week mag., N.Y.C., 1969; anchorman newsroom Sta. WETA-TV, Washington, 1970; editor, pub. Colorado Springs (Colo.) Sun, 1971-76; exec. editor Ariz. Daily Star, Tucson, 1976-81, The Plain Dealer, Cleve., 1981-87; dir. Sch. of Journalism U. So. Calif., L.A., 1988—. Mem. Gov.'s Prison Com., Phoenix, 1978-79; bd. dirs. Literacy Coalition Cleve., 1985-87; pres. City Club of Cleve., 1985. 1st lt. U.S. Army, 1943-46, 51-52, Korean. Recipient Pulitizer Prize, Houston Post, 1965, Pulitzer Prize, Ariz. Star, 1980; named Nat. Column of Yr., Am. Newspaper Assn., 1973; Nieman fellow. Mem. Assn. Sch. of Journalism and Mass Edn., New Directions for News (bd. dirs. Columbia, Mo. 1986—), Am. Soc. Newspapers Editors (bull. editor 1959-62, chair edn. com. 1977-78), Sigma Chi (Significant Sigma in 1984), Phi Beta Kappa. Methodist. Home: 6404 Ridgebyrne Ct Rancho Palos Verdes CA 90275 Office: U So Calif Sch Journalism University Pk GFS 315 Los Angeles CA 90089-1695

WOHL, ARMAND JEFFREY, cardiologist; b. Phila., Dec. 11, 1946; s. Herman Lewis and Selma (Paul) W.; m. Marylouise Katherine Giangrossi, Sept. 4, 1977; children: Michael Adam, Todd David. Student, Temple U., 1967; MD, Hahnemann U., 1971. Intern Bexar County Hosp., San Antonio, 1971-72; residency Parkland Hosp., Dallas, 1972-74; fellow U. Tex. Southwestern Med. Ctr., Dallas, 1974-76; chief cardiologist USAF Hosp. Elmendorf, Anchorage, 1976-78, Riverside (Calif.) Med. Clin., 1978-79; cardiologist Grossmont Cardiology Med. Group, La Mesa, Calif., 1980-84; pvt. practice, La Mesa, 1985—; chief of cardiology Grossmont Hosp., La Mesa, 1988—. Contbr. articles to profl. jours. Bd. dirs. San Diego County chpt. Am. Heart Assn., 1981-87. Maj. USAF, 1976-78. Fellow Am. Coll. Cardiology, Am. Coll. Physicians, Coun. on Clin. Cardiology. Office: 5565 Grossmont Center Dr #126 La Mesa CA 92042

WOHLETZ, KENNETH HAROLD, volcanologist; b. Chico, Calif., Jan. 19, 1952; s. Norbert Harold and Martha Deborah (Fochi) W.; m. Ann Grayson. BA, U. Calif., 1974; MS, Ariz. State U., 1976, PhD, 1980. Grad. rsch. asst. Ariz. State U., Tempe, 1974-79; vis. staff mem. Los Alamos (New Mex.) Nat. Lab., 1975-80; vis. scientist Consiglio Nationale della Ricerche, Pisa, Italy, 1980; postdoctoral rsch. asst. Ariz. State U., Tempe, 1980-81; instr. U. New Mex., Los Alamos, 1982-83; postdoctoral fellow Los Alamos Nat. Lab., 1981-83, staff mem., 1983—; Ariz. coord. Internat. Kimberlite Conf., Tempe, 1977-78. Author: Explosive Volcanism, 1984, Volcanic Ash, 1985 (award of excellence 1986); contbr. articles to profl. jours. Mem. Internat. Assn. Volcanology and Chemistry of the Earth's Interior, Am. Geophys. Union. Roman Catholic. Home: 4 Karen Circle Los Alamos NM 87544 Office: Los Alamos Nat Lab ESS-1 MS D462 Los Alamos NM 87545

WOHLGEMUTH, BARRY LEE, dentist; b. Mt. Vernon, N.Y., Aug. 11, 1948; s. Arthur and Rose (Schlomowitz) W.; m. Anita Susan Condiotte, Sept. 5, 1970; 1 child, Bret Lane. BA, SUNY, Stony Brook, 1970; DDS, NYU, 1976. Pvt. gen. dentistry Aurora, Colo., 1980—; chmn. exam rev. com. Cen. Regional Gen. Testing Service, Topeka, 1986-88, treas. 1989—. Mem. com. Martha Ezzard for Congress, Englewood, Colo., 1988—. Capt. USAF, 1976-78; liaison Colo. Dental Assocs., 1989. Mem. ADA, Met. Denver Dental Soc., Am. Assn. Dental Examiners (editor 1988—), Colo. Bd. Dental Bd. Examiners (v.p. 1984, sec., treas. 1986, chmn. task force 1987—, pres. 1987). Jewish. Home: 5891 S Geneva St Englewood CO 80111 Office: 1450 S Havana #200 Aurora CO 80012

WOHLGENANT, RICHARD GLEN, lawyer; b. Porterville, Calif., Dec. 2, 1930; s. Carl Frederick and Sara Alice (Moore) W.; m. Teresa Joan Bristow, Dec. 27, 1959; children—Mark Thomas, Tracy Patrice, Timothy James. B.A., U. Mont., Missoula, 1952; LL.B., Harvard U., Cambridge, Mass., 1957. Bar: Colo. 1957, U.S. Dist. Ct. Colo. 1957. Assoc. Holme Roberts & Owen, Denver, 1957-62, ptnr., 1962—; Dir. United Bank Cherry Creek, Denver, 1985—. Active City Club, Denver, 1970—; dir. Adopt-A-Sch., Denver, 1976-80. Mem. Am. Coll. Real Estate Lawyers, ABA, Colo. Bar Assn., Denver Bar Assn. Republican. Roman Catholic. Clubs: Univ., Law. Home: 300 Ivy St Denver CO 80220 Office: Holme Roberts & Owen 1700 Lincoln Denver CO 80203

WOHLSTETTER, ALBERT JAMES, defense research executive; b. N.Y.C., Dec. 19, 1913; s. Philip and Nellie (Friedman) W.; m. Roberta Morgan, June 7, 1939. BA in Mathematical Logic, Columbia U., MA, 1938. Vis. prof. UCLA and U. Calif. Berkeley, 1962-64; asst. to pres. Rand Corp., 1950-64; prof. U. Chgo., 1964-80; pres., dir. rsch. PAN Heuristics Svcs. Inc., L.A., 1979—; v.p. Security Conf. on Asia and Pacific, 1980—; mem. Pres.' Fgn. Intelligence Adv. Bd., 1985-88, Def. Policy Bd.; advisor to under sec. def. for policy and chief naal ops.; former advisor to asst. to Pres. for nat. secutiy, dir. ACDA, Dept. State; advisor Geneva Conf. on Surprise Attack, 1958. Author and co-author of several books; contbr. numerous articles to profl. publs. Recipient Disting. Pub. Svc. medal Dept. Def., 1965, 76, Presdl. Medal of Freedom, 1985; fellow All Souls Coll., Oxford U.; sr. fellow Hoover Instn., Stanford U. Fellow AAAS; mem. European Am. Inst. for Security Rsch. (pres. 1975—).

WOJTASZEK, MARIA HAYDEE, transportation executive; b. Havana, Cuba, Aug. 24, 1958; d. Eugene and Haydee (Marino) W. BA, UCLA, 1981. Traffic coord. U.S. Army, 1982-86; mgr. mktg/sales Mobility Sys. &

Equip. Co., L.A., 1986—; traffic operator Proficient Food Co., Irvine, Calif., 1986-87; supr. traffic claims Continental Foodsvc., L.A., 1987-88; logis. S.E. Rykoff & Co., —, 1988—. Mem. NAFE, Delta Nu Alpha (cons. traffic of transp. related programs). Republican Catholic. Home: 1815 E Merced Ave West Covina CA 91791

WOLD, JOHN SCHILLER, geologist, former congressman; b. East Orange, N.J., Aug. 31, 1916; s. Peter Irving and Mary (Helff) W.; m. Jane Adele Pearson, Sept. 28, 1946; children: Peter Irving, Priscilla Adele, John Pearson. A.B., St. Andrews U., Scotland and Union Coll., Schenectady, 1938; M.S., Cornell U., 1939. Dir. Fedn. Rocky Mountain States, 1966-68; v.p. Rocky Mountain Oil and Gas Assn., 1967, 68; mem. Wyo. Ho. of Reps., 1957-59; Republican candidate for U.S. Senate, 1964, 70; mem. 91st Congress at large from, Wyo.; pres. BTU, Inc., J & P Corp., Wold Nuclear Co., Wold Mineral Exploration Co., Casper, Wyo.; founding pres. Wyo. Heritage Found., Central Wyo. Ski Corp.; chmn. Wyo. Nat. Gas Pipeline Authority, 1987—; bd. dirs. Plains Petroleum Co., Coca Mines, Inc. Contbr. articles to profl. jours. Chmn. Wyo. Rep. Com., 1960-64, Western State Rep. Chmns. Assn., 1963-64; mem. exec. com. Rep. Nat. Com., 1962-64; chmn. Wyo. Rep. State Fin. Com.; Active Little League Baseball, Boy Scouts Am., United Fund, YMCA, Boys Clubs Am.; pres. Wyo. Heritage Soc.; former pres. bd. trustees Casper Coll.; trustee Union Coll. Served to lt. USNR, World War II. Named Wyo. Man of Yr. AP-UPI, 1968; Wyo. Mineral Man of Yr., 1979. Mem. Wyo. Geol. Assn. (hon. life, pres. 1956), Am. Assn. Petroleum Geologists, Ind. Petroleum Assn. Am., AAAS, Wyo. Mining Assn., Sigma Xi, Alpha Delta Phi. Espicopalian (past vestryman, warden). Home: 1231 W 30th Casper WY 82604 Office: Mineral Resource Ctr Ste 200 Casper WY 82604

WOLD, NANA BEHA, social services administrator; b. N.Y.C., Nov. 4, 1943; d. William John and Margaret (Robinson) Beha. BA, Tex. Women's U., 1965; M in Social Welfare, U. Calif., Berkeley, 1967. Lic. clin. social worker. Psychiat. social worker Mendocino State Hosp., Talmage, Calif., 1967-70, Calif. State Dept. Mental Health, San Diego, 1972-74; supervising psychiat. social worker Calif. State Dept. Health, San Diego, 1974-81; assoc. chief, case mgmt. services San Diego Regional Ctr. Devel. Disabled, 1981—; instr. social work Chapman Coll., San Diego, 1972; mem. adv. com. Community Living Project, San Diego, 1973-76, Sr. Citizens Day Care Ctr., San Diego, 1976-77; mem. Assembly Woman Bentley adv. com. on devel. disabilities, San Diego, 1984—; co-chair Com. Community Care for Devel. Disabled, San Diego, 1978—. Co-author: Sex Education for the Mentally Retarded, 1975, (pamphlet) Happiness is a Good Home, 1977. Vol. Army Community Services, Ft. Wolters, Tex., 1968-69. Mem. Nat. Assn. Social Workers (diplomate in clin. social work), Am. Assn. Mental Deficiency. Republican. Roman Catholic. Office: San Diego Regional Ctr Devel Disabled 4355 Ruffin Rd #306 San Diego CA 92123

WOLF, ARON S., psychiatrist; b. Newark, Aug. 25, 1937; B.A., Dartmouth Coll., 1959; M.D., U. Md., 1963; married; children—Jon, Lisa, Laurie. Intern, U. Md. Hosp., Balt., 1963-64; resident in psychiatry Psychiat. Inst., U. Md. Hosp., Balt., 1964-67, chief resident, 1966-67; practice medicine specializing in psychiatry, Anchorage, 1967—; dir. Springfield Hosp. Alcoholic Clinic, Balt., 1966-67; psychiat. cons. Levindale Hebrew Home and Infirmary, Balt., 1966-67, McLaughlin Yough Center, Anchorage, 1969-72; mem. staff Providence Hosp., chief psychiatry sect., 1977-81; mem. staff Humana Hosp., Alaska, Kodiak Island Hosp., Palmer Valley Hosp., Valdez Community Hosp., Bethel Community Hosp., Cordova Alaska Hosp.; mem. staff Charter North Hosp., exec. com., 1984-86; staff psychiatrist Langdon Psychiat. Clinic, 1970-71; partner Langdon Clinic, Anchorage, 1971—, clinic pres., 1981; med. dir. Cordova Community Mental Health Center, 1976-80, 84—; cons. Alaska Native Med. Center, 1975-77, Woman's Resource Center, Anchorage, 1977-81; instr. dept. psychology U. Alaska, Anchorage, 1968-75; assoc. clin. prof. psychiatry U. Alaska, Fairbanks, 1974-85, clin. prof., 1985—; assoc. clin. prof. U. Wash., 1974-85, clin. prof., 1985—, adj. prof.psychiatry Sch. Medicine U. N.Mex.; participant weekly mental health TV talk show, Anchorage, 1970—; guest lectr. to various profl. and civic groups, 1967—. Vice pres. Greater Anchorage Area Borough Sch. Bd., 1971-72, pres., 1973-74; pres. Chugach Optional Sch. Parent Adv. Bd., 1976-77; mem. med. adv. com. Alaska Kidney Found., 1977-82; mem. Alaska Gov.'s Mental Health Adv. Bd., 1976-84, chmn., 1983; mem. Gov's. Task Force on Criminally Committed Patients, 1980—; bd. dirs. Greater Anchorage Drug Mgmt. Group, 1972-73. Served with M.C., USAF, 1967-70. Recipient Wendell-Muncie award Md. Med. Soc., 1967; diplomate Am. Bd. Psychiatry and Neurology, Am. Bd. Forensic Psychiatry. Fellow Am. Psychiat. Assn. (pres. Alaska dist. br. 1975, sec. Alaska br. 1984-85, del. assembly 1975-81, 86, area III chmn. assembly procedures com. 1982—, nat. planning com. 1981, nat. membership com. 1981-86, chmn. confidentiality com., 1986—, recorder of assembly 1984-85, chmn. 1988, Alaska del., 1986—); mem. Am. Acad. Psychiatry and Law (mem. ethics com., 1987) , Am. Soc. Law and Medicine, Soc. Air Force Psychiatrists, ACLU, AMA (chmn. mental health com. 1971-75, medicine and law com. 1980-81), Alaska Med. Assn., N.Y. Acad. Scis. Contbr. articles on psychiatry to profl. jours. Home: 8133 Sundi Dr Anchorage AK 99502 Office: 4001 Dale St Anchorage AK 99508

WOLF, CHARLES, JR., economist, educator; b. N.Y.C., Aug. 1, 1924; s. Charles and Rosalie W.; m. Theresa van de Wint, Mar. 1, 1947; children: Charles Theodore, Timothy van de Wint. B.S., Harvard U., 1943, M.P.A., 1948, Ph.D. in Econs., 1949. Economist, fgn. service officer U.S. Dept. State, 1945-47, 49-53; mem. faculty Cornell U., 1953-54, U. Calif., Berkeley, 1954-55; sr. economist The Rand Corp., Santa Monica, Calif., 1955-67; head econs. dept. The Rand Corp., 1967-81; dean The Rand Grad. Sch., 1970—, dir. internat. econ. policy program, 1981—; dir. Fundamental Investors Fund, Found. for 21st Century, Capital Income Builder Fund; co-chmn., mem. exec. com. Calif. Seminar on Internat. Security and Fgn. Policy; mem. exec. com. Rand-UCLA Health Policy Ctr.; bd. visitors Duke U. Inst. Policy Scis.; mem. adv. com. UCLA Clin. Scholars Program; lectr. econs. UCLA, 1960-72; mem. exec. com. Rand-UCLA Ctr. for Study of Soviet Internat. Behavior. Author: United States Policy and the Third World: Problems and Analysis, 1967, Rebellion and Authority: An Analytic Essay on Insurgent Conflicts, 1970, The Costs and Benefits of the Soviet Empire, 1986, Markets or Governments; Choosing Between Imperfect Alternatives, 1988, Developing Cooperative Forces in the Third World, 1987, (with others) The Future of the Soviet Empire, 1987; contbr. articles to profl. jours. Mem. Assn. for Public Policy Analysis and Mgmt. (pres. 1980-81, policy council), Am. Econs. Assn., Econometric Soc., Council Fgn. Relations, Internat. Inst. Strategic Studies London. Clubs: Cosmos (Washington); Riviera Tennis (Los Angeles); Harvard (N.Y.). Office: The Rand Grad Sch 1700 Main St Santa Monica CA 90406

WOLF, CYNTHIA TRIBELHORN, library educator; b. Denver, Dec. 12, 1945; d. John Baltazar and Margaret (Kern) Tribelhorn; m. H.Y. Rassam, Mar. 2l, 1969 (div. Jan. 1988); children: Najma C., Yousuf J. BA, Colo. State U., 1970; MLS, U. Denver, 1985. Cert. permanent profl. librarian, N.Mex. Elem. tchr. Sacred Heart Sch., Farmington, N.Mex., 1973-78; asst. prof. library assn. U. N.Mex., Albuquerque, 1985—; fine arts resource person for gifted edn. Farmington Pub. Schs., 1979-83. Mem. Farmington Planning and Zoning Commn., 1980-8l; bd. dirs. Farmington Mus. Assn., 1983-84; pres. Farmington Symphony League, 1978. Mem. ALA, N.Mex. Library Assn., Greater Albuquerque Library Assn., LWV (bd. dirs. Farmington, 1972-74, 75, pres.). Roman Catholic. Office: U NMex Dept Ednl Found Library Sci Div Albuquerque NM 87131

WOLF, DOUGLAS JEFFREY, lawyer; b. Merced, Calif., June 19, 1953; s. Stanley William and Phyllis (Donner) W.; m. Vicki Lynn Fields, July 8, 1979; children: Joshua Michael, Carly Suzanne. AB, U. Calif., Davis, 1974; JD, Southwestern U., Los Angeles, 1977. Bar: U.S. Dist. Ct. (cen. dist.), U.S. Ct. of Appeals (9th cir.). Criminal justice planner San Mateo County Criminal Justice Council, Burlingame, Calif., 1972-74; law clk. Friedman and Cone, Los Angeles, 1974-79; pvt. practice Los Angeles, 1979-82, Woodland Hills, Calif., 1982—; pres. The Cheryl Fields Found. for Victims, Los Angeles, 1984—; pres.-elect, bd. dirs. Adam Walsh Child Resource Ctr., Orange, Calif., 1986—; advisor Visiting Nurses Assn, Van Nuys, Calif. Mem. Calif. State Bar, San Fernando Valley Bar Assn., Los Angeles County Bar Assn., Woodland Hills C. of C. Democrat. Jewish. Home: 23651 Gerrad Way West Hills CA 91307 Office: 6355 Topanga Canyon Blvd Ste 326 Woodland Hills CA 91367-2102

WOLF, FREDERICK GEORGE, environmentalist; b. Paterson, N.J., Aug. 30, 1952; s. Frederick George and Doris (Miller) W. BS, U. S.C., 1974; postgrad. Clemson U., 1976-77; MS, East Tenn. State U., 1978. Cert. profl. geologist, Alaska. Phys. scientist U.S. Army Environ. Hygiene Agy., Edgewood, Md., 1974-75; environ. engr. S.C. Dept. Health and Environ. Control, Columbia, 1977-78; hydrogeologist EPA, Atlanta, 1978-79, hydrologist, Boston, 1979-81, regional hydrogeologist, Seattle, 1981-86; mgr. hazardous waste sect. Parametrix Inc., Bellevue, Wash., 1986-88, mgr. environ. affairs Pennwalt Corp., Tacoma, 1988—. Lt. USNR, 1974-87. Recipient Spl. Svc. award EPA, 1982; decorated Bronze medal, 1983. Mem. Am. Inst. Profl. Geologists (cert. profl. geol. scientist), Acad. of Hazardous Materials Mgmt. (cert. hazardous materials mgr. master level), Soaring Soc. Am., Sigma Xi, Epsilon Nu Eta. Home: 4225 67th Ave NW Gig Harbor WA 98335 Office: Pennwalt Corp 2901 Taylor Way Tacoma WA 98421

WOLF, KENNETH ERWIN, audiologist; b. Los Angeles, Dec. 24, 1948; s. Max B. and Sarah (Segal) W.; m. Laurel Adrianne Weinstein, June 20, 1970; children: Allison, Wendy. BA, U. Calif., 1970, MA, 1972; PhD, U. Wis., 1977. Asst. dir. Cin. Ctr. Developmental Disorders, 1977-78; dir. audiology Pulec Ear Clinic, Los Angeles, 1978-79; chief communicative sci. & disorders, asst. prof. otoloaryngology King/Drew Med. Ctr., Los Angeles, 1980—; adj. prof. Calif. State U., Northridge, 1985—. Contbr. articles to profl. jours. Bd. dirs. Inst. Human Services, Van Nuys, Calif., 1987, Van Gogh St. Sch., Granada Hills, Calif., 1974-87; mem. profl. adv. bd. TRIPOD, Los Angeles, 1988. Fellow Soc. Ear, Nose & Throat Advances Children: mem. Am. Speech-Lang.-Hearing Assn. (cert. 1979, councilor 1988—), Calif. Speech-Lang.-Hearing Assn. (commn. legis. 1985—), Am. Auditory Soc., Am. Acad. Otolaryngology. Democrat. Jewish. Office: King/Drew Med Ctr 12021 S Wilmington Los Angeles CA 90059

WOLF, MONICA THERESIA, procedures analyst; b. Germany, Apr. 26, 1943; came to U.S., 1953, naturalized, 1959; d. Otto and Hildegard Maria (Heim) Bellemann; children: Clinton, Danielle. BBA, U. Albuquerque, 1986. Developer Word Processing Ctr., Pub. Service of N.Mex., Albuquerque, 1971-74, word processing supr., 1974-78, budget coordinator, 1978-80, lead procedures analyst, 1980—; mem. adv. bd., student trainer APS Career Enrichment Ctr. Instr. firearm safety and pistol marksmanship. Mem. Internat. Word Processing Assn. (founder N.Mex. chpt.), Nat. Assn. Female Execs., Nat. Rifle Assn., N.Mex. Shooting Sports Assn. Democrat. Club: Sandia Gun (adv. bd., coach). Home: 305 Alamosa Rd NW Albuquerque NM 87107 Office: 414 Silver Ave SW Albuquerque NM 87103

WOLF, NORMAN ANDERSON, personnel executive; b. Jefferson City, Mo., July 6, 1925; s. Simon Anderson and Bessie Mae (Wilson) W.; m. Nancy Ellyn Petty, June 24, 1945 (div. 1956); children: James Norman, Debra Sue; m. Karoline Marguerite Hildreth, Sept. 20, 1963; 1 child, Lori Jean; stepchildren: Susan Richards Schuck, Karin Lucille Richards Park. Student, Fullerton Jr. Coll., Calif., 1963-64, West Valley Jr. Coll., Campbell, Calif., 1965-67. Stockroom clk. Mo. Div. Employment Security, Jefferson City, 1948-50; with Dept. of Army, Ft. Leonardwood, Mo., 1950-56; warehouse supr. Hallamore Electronics Co., Anaheim, Calif., 1956-58; identification analyst Hughes Aircraft Co., Fullerton, Calif., 1958-64; identification analyst FMC Corp., San Jose, Calif., 1964-67, programmer, 1967-70; data processing mgr. Babbitt Bros. Trading Co., Flagstaff, Ariz., 1970-85, personnel mgr., 1985--. Mem. Am. Soc. Personnel Adminstrs., No. Ariz. Personnel Assn. Democrat. Christian Ch. Office: Babbitt Bros Trading Co PO Box 1328 Flagstaff AZ 86002

WOLF, STEVEN RAYMOND, clinical psychologist; b. N.Y.C., Sept. 8, 1945; s. Leo and Miriam W. BA, Queens Coll., 1966; MA, Conn. Coll., 1968; PhD, Saybrook Inst., 1986. Dir. Riker's Island Prison Therapeutic Community and Prog. Rehab., N.Y.C., 1971-73; pvt. practice L.A., 1980—; clin. dir., bd. dirs. Crime Prevention Substance Abuse Treatment, L.A., 1986-88; trainer Adult and Couple Devel. Workshop, L.A., 1984—; cons. Stress Mgmt., L.A., 1986—. Dir., vol. Acupuncture Detox Program, L.A., 1986-88. Mem. Am. Psychol. Assn., Calif. State Psychol. Assn. Jewish.

WOLFE, BRIAN AUGUSTUS, sales executive, small business owner; b. Mexico City, Nov. 23, 1946; came to U.S., 1947; s. Steward Augustus and Vivia Idalene (Fouts) W.; m. Holly Joyce Gilhart, Dec. 29, 1981; 1 child, Derek Augustus. BSME, Tex. A&M U., 1968. Project engr. Tex. Power & Light Co., Dallas, 1968-72; service engr. Babcock & Wilcox, Chgo., 1972-74; sales engr., New Eng. dist. Babcock & Wilcox, Boston, 1974-79; area mgr., Far East, internat. bus. Babcock & Wilcox, Barberton, Ohio, 1979-81; dist. sales mgr. Babcock & Wilcox, Lakewood, Colo., 1981—; pres., bd. dirs. Rocky Mountain Beer Co., Denver, 1987-88. Mem. Assn. Brewers, Rocky Mountain Elec. League (bd. dirs. 1988—). Home: 7285 W Vassar Ave Lakewood CO 80227 Office: Babcock & Wilcox 7401 W Mansfield Suite 410 Lakewood CO 80235

WOLFE, CLIFFORD EUGENE, architect, author; b. Harrington, Wash., Mar. 26, 1906; s. Delwin Lindsley and Luella Grace (Cox) W.; m. Frances Lillian Parkes, Sept. 12, 1936 (dec.); children—Gretchen Yvonne Wolfe Mason, Eric Von; m. Mary Theye Worthen. A.B. in Architecture, U. Calif.-Berkeley, 1933. Registered architect, Calif. Assoc. architect John Knox Ballantine, Architect, San Francisco, 1933-42; supervising architect, prodn. engr. G.W. Williams Co. Contractors, Burlingame, Calif., 1942-44; state-wide coordinator med. schs. and health ctrs. U. Calif.-Berkeley, San Francisco and Los Angeles, 1944-52; sec. council on hosp. planning Am. Hosp. Assn., Chgo., 1952-59; dir. planning dept. Office of York & Sawyer, Architects, N.Y.C., 1959-74; prin. Clifford E. Wolfe, AIA-E, Oakland, Calif., 1974—; assoc. designer State of Calif. Commn. for Golden Gate Internat. Exposition, San Francisco, 1938-39; cons. Fed. Hosp. Council, Washington, 1954-60; mem. Pres.'s Conf. on Occupational Safety, Washington, 1955; research architect Hosp Research and Ednl. Trust, Chgo., 1957-59; instr. hosp. planning Columbia U., N.Y.C., 1961-73. Author, editor manuals on hosp. planning, engring. and safety, 1954-58. Author: Ballad of Humphrey The Humpback Whale, 1985; contbr. poetry to Tecolote Anthology, 1983, The Ina Coolbrith Circle, 1985, 1987 (Grand prize Ina Coolbrith award 1986), Islandia, 1986. Hosp. planning research grantee USPHS, 1956. Mem. AIA (chmn. honor awards com. Chgo. chpt. 1958-59, chmn. activities com. N.Y. chpt. 1972-74, mem. emeritus East Bay chpt. 1974—). Address: 3900 Harrison St Apt 306 Oakland CA 94611

WOLFE, EDWARD WILLIAM II, music educator, composer; b. Albuquerque, Sept. 24, 1946; s. Edward William and Mary Ellen (Gabriele) W.; m. Nancy Jean Brown, Aug. 16, 1980. B in Music Edn., U. N.Mex., 1968, MA, 1973. Cert. elem., secondary tchr., N.Mex., Calif. Tchr. Grant Jr. High Sch., Albuquerque, 1970-75, Manzano High Sch., Albuquerque, 1974-75, Hoover Mid. Sch., Albuquerque, 1975-77, San Dimas (Calif.) High Sch., 1977-85; instr. music Calif. Poly. State U., Pomona, Calif., 1984; tchr. Bonita High Sch., LaVerne, Calif., 1985—; tchr. Hummingbird Music Camp, Jemez, N.Mex., 1970-76; cons. BUSD, San Dimas, 1980—. Author: The Language of Music, 1974; composer Quartet for Horns, 1967, Oboe Sonata, 1967, Trio for Flute, Violin and Horn, 1968, Caverna, 1972, numerous compositions and jazz arrangements, 1972—. Recipient award Juvenile Justice Commn. City of San Dimas, 1984. Mem. Music Educators Nat. Conf. (adjudicator 1969-77, 80—, v.p. dist. 7 1972, pres. 1975-76), Nat. Assn. Jazz Educators (adjudicator 1980—, treas. N.Mex. chpt. 1972), Calif. Tchrs. Assn., So. Calif. Sch. Band and Orch. Assn., Bonita Unified Teaching Assn., Phi Mu Alpha Sinfonia. Home: 817 Dumaine San Dimas CA 91773

WOLFE, LAWRENCE IRVING, internist; b. Duluth, Minn., Mar. 31, 1924; s. Joseph and Edith (Kremen) W.; B.S., U. Minn., 1944, M.B., 1946, M.D., 1947; m. Charlotte Ione Avrick, Dec. 16, 1945; children—Jonathan, Douglas, Lori Allison. Intern, Ancker Hosp., St. Paul, 1947; postgrad. U. Minn. Hosp., Mpls., 1947-48; resident So. Pacific Gen. Hosp., San Francisco, 1948-50, Permanente Hosp., Oakland, Calif., 1950-51; pvt. practice specializing in internal medicine, San Carlos, Calif., 1951—; mem. staff Sequoia, San Mateo County Gen., Stanford-Palo Alto, Belmont Hills hosps.; faculty dept. medicine Stanford U., 1958—, now clin. asso. prof. Served with USNR, 1943-45, 1953-55. Diplomate Am. Bd. Internal Medicine, Pan Am. Med. Assn. Mem. Am., Calif. med. assns., San Mateo County Med. Soc., Am. Geriatrics Soc., Royal Soc. Medicine, A.C.P., Am., Calif. socs. internal medicine, Am. Heart Assn. Clubs: Stanford Faculty, Menlo Circus. Home: 180 Elena Ave Atherton CA 94025 Office: 1100 Laurel St San Carlos CA 94070

WOLFE, STEVEN JON, motion picture producer; b. L.A.; s. Elliott Sidney and Phillene (Lehrman) W. Student, Calif. State U., Northridge, 1978-82, UCLA, 1988. Projectionist United Artists Theatre, L.A., 1976-78; mgr. Frozen Assets, Inc., Laguna Hills, Calif., 1978-80; various positions with motion picture cos., 1980—; ind. producer Sneak Preview Prodns., L.A., 1986—. Writer (teleplay) Seven Minutes in Heaven, 198l, (screenplay) One Night To Live, 1988; producer: (films) My Mom's a Werewolf, Hunk. Mem. Am. Film Inst., Ind. Feature Project-West, L.A. Conservancy, L.A. Historic Theatre Found. Republican. Jewish. Office: Sneak Preview Prodns 13906 Ventura Blvd Ste l02 Sherman Oaks CA 91423

WOLFE, WILLIAM DOWNING, state agency administrator; b. Zanesville, Ohio, Nov. 14, 1947; s. William Jr. and Wava Benetta (Downing) W.; m. Laura Olivia Soza, July 29, 1972; children: Lisa Anne, Erin Nicole. BBA, U. Ariz., 1969. Instr. RTV Internat., N.Y.C., 1969-70; mgr. prodn. Sta. KUAT-TV/AM/FM, Tucson, 1969-76; lectr. U. Ariz., Tucson, 1970-78; mgr. prodn. Sta. KGUN-TV, Tucson, 1976-79; exec. producer Sta. KTVK-TV, Phoenix, 1979-82; writer, producer Ariz. Pub. Svc. Co., Phoenix, 1982-83, supr. pub. info., 1983-86; coord. emergency planning Ariz. Nuclear Power Project, Phoenix, 1986—; cons. Nat. Student Films, Hollywood, Calif., 1975, Warner for Gov., Phoenix, 1986, various advt. agys., Tucson, Phoenix, various U.S. locations, 1974-83. writer, producer, dir. over 800 TV and multi-media programming and comml. advertisements for PM Mag., Wide World Sports, Good Morning Am., local, others, 1969—. Advisor Jr. Achievement, Tucson, 1976; chmn. com. Ariz. Citizens for Edn., Phoenix, 1988—; mem. budget adv. com. Deer Valley Sch. Dist.; bd. dirs. So. Ariz. chpt. Muscular Dystrophy Assn., 1976-79. Grantee Ford Found., 1969; recipient Golden Sch. Bell award Ariz. Dept. Edn., 1974-79, Emmy nomination Nat. Acad. TV Arts and Scis., 1979, Bronze Anvil nat. award Pub. Rels. Soc. Am., 1983, award Excellance Inster. Assn. Bus. Communicators. Mem. Nat. Emergency Mgmt. Assn. Democrat. Roman Catholic. Office: Palo Verde Nuclear Generating Sta PO Box 52034 Phoenix AZ 85072-2034

WOLFE, WILLIAM LOUIS, optics educator; b. Yonkers, N.Y., Apr. 5, 1931; s. William Louis and Louise Helene (Becker) W.; m. Mary Lou Bongort; children: Carol, Barbara, Douglas. BS in Physics, Bucknell U., 1953; MS in Physics, U. Mich., 1956, MSEE, 1966. Research engr., lectr. U. Mich., Ann Arbor, 1953-66; dept. mgr., chief engr. Honeywell Radiation Ctr., 1966-69; prof. Optical Sci. Ctr., U. Ariz., Tucson, 1969—. Author (with others) Fundamentals of Infrared Technology, 1962; (with George J. Zissis) The Infrared Handbook, 1979; series editor: Optical Physics and Engineering; editor: Handbook of Military Infrared Technology; Am. editor Infrared Physics; contbr. numerous articles to profl. jours. Fellow Optical Soc. Am. (many bds. and coms.), Soc. Photo-optical Instrumentation Engrs. (pres., bd. govs., chmn. symposia, exec. com.); mem. IEEE (sr. mem.), Nat. Acad. Sci. (many coms.), Infrared Info. Symposia, Naval Intelligence Adv. Bd. (sci. adv. bd.), Air Force Ad Hoc Electro-Optics Com., Army Research Office Adv. Com., Army Scientific Adv. Bd., Am. Men of Sci., Leaders in Am. Sci., Phi Beta Kappa, Sigma Xi, Omicron Delta Kappa, Pi Mu Epsilon, Sigma Pi Sigma, Phi Eta Sigma. Office: U Ariz Tucson AZ 85721

WOLFENBARGER, ANNE GAIL, cosmetics company executive; b. Independence, Mo., Apr. 8, 1953; d. Marshall Edward and Rose Marie (Myers) W. Grad. high sch., Lakewood, Colo. V.p. Givens Glass, Inc., Denver, 1984-89; pres. Colo. Shower Door, Inc., Denver, 1989—. Active animal rights issues. Mem. Home Builders Assn. Denver, Rocky Mountain Glass Assn. Office: Colo Shower Door Inc 1185 S Cherokee St Denver CO 80223

WOLFF, GARY JOE, engineering consulting company executive; b. Bryan, Tex., Nov. 18, 1952; s. Walter Fred and Nora Jean (Zapalac) W.; m. Debby Lynn Sayre, June 7, 1980; children: Melissa, Bridget, Heather, Brian. BS in Civil Engring., U. Tex., 1975; MS in Civil Engring., U. Tex., Arlington, 1981. Registered profl. civil engr., Ariz., Tex. Project engr. Wilbur Smith & Assocs., Denver, 1976-78; area traffic engr. Gov.'s Office of Traffic Safety, Nacogdoches, Tex., 1978-79; project mgr. Rady & Assocs., Ft. Worth, 1979-80; transp. engr. City of Ft. Worth, 1980-83; nat. sales dir. SMI Internat., Waco, Tex., 1983-85; traffic engr. Tex. Dept. Highways, Waco, 1985-87; dir. traffic engring. Dunaway Assocs., Ft. Worth, 1987-88; regional v.p. Kimley-Horn & Assocs., Phoenix, 1988—; cert. instr. defensive driving course Nat. Safety Coun., Ft. Worth, 1978-83; transit planning com. Regional Pub. Transp. Authority, Phoenix, 1988—. Contbr. articles to ITE Jour., 1986-88, ASCE Transp. Engring. Jour., 1982. Project chmn. Phoenix Jaycees, 1988—; mem. Phoenix Futures Forum, 1988—; capt. Neighborhood Block Watch, Waco, 1985-86. Mem. Inst. Transp. Engrs. (regional coord. 1982-83, newsletter com. 1988—), ASCE (transp. com. chmn. 1981-83), NSPE, Toastmasters (competent toastmaster Waco chpt. 1979-85), Texzonis Club, High Points Club, Tau Beta Pi, Chi Epsilon. Republican. Lutheran. Home: 5005 W Torrey Pines Circle Glendale AZ 85308 Office: Kimley Horn and Assocs 9630 N 25th Ave Ste 311 Phoenix AZ 85021

WOLFF, HOWARD KEITH, educator, consultant; b. Los Angeles, Mar. 28, 1948; s. Fred and Yvonne (Primock) W.; m. Anna Bornino, Dec. 6, 1966 (div. June 1971); 1 child, Francesca; m. Cindy Brattan, June 4, 1981. BA, Calif. State U., Dominguez Hill, 1969; MPA, U. So. Calif., 1971; PhD, 1973. Prin. investigator U. Simon Fraser, Vancouver, B.C., Can., 1970-71; prof. U. So. Calif., Los Angeles, 1971-73, Tribhuan (Nepal) U., 1974-75, Calif. State U., Chico, 1976-85, 87—, Colo. State U., Ft. Collins, 1985-87; evaluation cons. Nat. Planning Commn., Kathmandu, Nepal, 1973-75; statis. cons. Nat. Population Commn., Kathmandu, 1983-87; cons. Butte Canyon Research Assocs., Chico, Calif., 1979-87. Author: Social Science and Thesis Handbook, 1974; contbr. articles to profl. jours. Research grantee Can. Govt., Vancouver, 1970. Mem. Am. Computing Machinery, Am. Soc. Pub. Adminstrn., Soc. Computer Simulations. Democrat. Club: Gears (Chico). Office: Calif State U Dept Computer Sci Chico CA 95929

WOLFF, LOUIS ARTHUR, computer information systems educator; b. Altamont, Ill., Nov. 26, 1933; s. Louis August and Eileen Alice (Koberlein) W.; m. Norma Jean Weaver, June 21, 1952; children: Larry Alan, Cathy Ann Wolff Gustafson, Susan Eileen Wolff Beck. BS in Bus. Mgmt., U. La Verne, 1984, MS in Bus. Orgnl. Mgmt., 1986. Field engr. IBM, Madison, Wis., 1957-59; computer instr. IBM, Kingston, N.Y., 1959-63, program analyst, 1963-65; program rev. analyst IBM, Huntsville, Ala., 1965-71; program control mgr. IBM, Westlake Village, Calif., 1971-78, program adminstr., 1978-82; instr. computer software Moorpark (Calif.) Coll., 1974-82, prof. computer info. systems, 1982—; cons. The Other Office, Thousand Oaks, Calif., 1982—. Co-author: Fundamentals of Structured COBOL Programming, 1988. With USN, 1952-56. Mem. Assn. for Computing Machinery, Data Processing Mgmt. Assn. Democrat. Mem. Christian Ch. Home: 1443 Warwick Ave Thousand Oaks CA 91360 Office: Moorpark Coll 7075 Campus Rd Moorpark CA 93021

WOLFF, SCOTT EARL, forest seed certifier, consultant; b. Great Falls, Mont., Apr. 26, 1947; s. Eugene Earl and Ruth (Perrine) W.; m. Donna M. Wagner (div. Mar. 1974); 1 child, Jeffrey Michael; m. Susan Johnson, Aug. 3, 1974; children: Katherine Christine, Scott Eugene. BS in Crop Sci., Oreg. State U., 1977, MS in Forest Sci., 1984. Cert. project leader Forest reproductive material, Oreg. State U., Corvallis, 1978—; tech. rep. OECD, Paris, 1987; cons. Wash. Crop Improvement, Yakima, 1978—, Calif. Crop Improvement Assn., Davis, 1978—, Idaho Crop Improvement Assn., Boise, 1978—. Author: (with others) User's Guide for Seeds of Western Trees and Shrubs, 1986. Co-chair Garfield Sch. Parent Tchr. Group, Corvallis, 1982; active in local Boy Scouts Am., 1983-87; coach soccer AYSO, Corvallis, 1987; asst. baseball Am. Legion, 1983-84; asst. coach Boys and Girls Club Baseball, 1988; mem. Corvallis Parents for Extended Edn., 1982-85. Served with USN, 1965-69. Mem. Northwest Forest and Range Seed Council (chmn. subcom. Olympia, Wash. chpt. 1981—), Northwest Forest Tree Seed Certifiers Assn. (chmn. 1978), Assn. Ofcl. Seed Certifying Agys., Western Forest Genetics Assn., Intermountain Nurseryman's Assn., Western Forest Nursery Council. Office: Oreg State U Seed Cert 31A Crop Sci Bldg Corvallis OR 97331-3003

WOLFF, SIDNEY CARNE, astronomer, observatory administrator; b. Sioux City, Iowa, June 6, 1941; d. George Albert and Ethel (Smith) Carne;

m. Richard J. Wolff, Aug. 29, 1962. BA, Carleton Coll., 1962, DSc (hon.), 1985; PhD, U. Calif., Berkeley, 1966. Postgrad. research fellow Lick Obs, Santa Cruz, Calif., 1969; asst. astronomer U. Hawaii, Honolulu, 1967-71, assoc. astronomer, 1971-76; astronomer, assoc. dir. Inst. Astronomy, Honolulu, 1976-83, acting dir., 1983-84; dir. Kitt Peak Nat. Obs., Tucson, 1984-87, Nat. Optical Atronomy Observatories, 1987—. Author: The A-Type Stars—Problems and Perspectives, 1983; (with others) Exploration of the Universe, 1987, Realm of the Universe, 1988; contbr. articles to profl. jours. Research fellow Lick Obs. Santa Cruz, Calif., 1967. Mem. Astron. Soc. Pacific (pres. 1984-86, bd. dirs. 1979-85), Am. Astron. Soc. (council 1983-86), Internat. Astron. Union. Office: Kitt Peak Nat Obs 950 N Cherry Ave PO Box 26732 Tucson AZ 85726

WOLFINGER, BARBARA KAYE, film company executive; b. N.Y.C., Sept. 3, 1929; d. Louis and Margaret (Goodman) Klatzkie; m. Raymond E. Wolfinger, Aug. 7, 1960; 1 child, Nicholas Holm. AB, U. Mich., 1951. Dir., design researcher McCann-Erickson Advt., N.Y.C., 1954-58; research assoc. Calif. Dept. Pub. Health, Berkeley, 1961-64, Stanford (Calif.) U., 1968-70, Inst. Research in Social Behavior, Berkeley, 1971-73; producer Berkeley Stage Co., 1973-78; pres. Berkeley Prodns., Inc., 1978—. Producer: (educational films) Black Girl, Sister of the Bride, Poetry Playhome, Chile Pequin, Nine Months, Almost Home, Your Move, 1980-87. Dir. Planned Parenthood, San Francisco, 1985—. Recipient Noble Hancock Found. award, 1973, NEH award, 1975, Golden Eagle award Coun. Internat. Nontheatrical Events, 1978, Creative Excellence award U.S. Industry Film Festival, 1979, ESSA award U.S. Dept. Edn., 1979, 80, 81, 82, red ribbon Am. Film Festival, 1983, Learning award Nat. Coun. Human Rels., 1983, 84. Democrat. Jewish. Home: 715 The Alameda Berkeley CA 94707 Office: Berkeley Prodns 2288 Fulton Berkeley CA 94704

WOLFLEY, VERN ALVIN, dentist; b. Etna, Wyo., Aug. 4, 1912; s. Rudolf E. and Eliza (Neuenschwander) W.; m. Bernice Michaelson, June 12, 1936; children: Norda Beth Wolfley Brimley, Vern A. Jr., Paul R., Carol Jo Wolfley Bennett. BS, U. Wyo., 1934; BS in Dentistry and DDS, U. Nebr., 1947. Pvt. practice, Phoenix, 1947—. Pres. Ariz. Children's Soc., Phoenix, 1960-61. 1st lt. USAF, 1954. Mem. ADA (life), Ariz. Dental Assn. (life), Idaho Falls Dental Soc. (pres. 1949-50), Upper Snake River Dental Soc. (pres. 1955-56), Am. Soc. Dentistry for Children, Acad. Gen. Dentistry, Internat. Assn. Orthodontics, Am. Assn. Functional Orthodontists, Federation Dentaire Internat., Cent. Ariz. Dist. Soc., Lions (v.p. 1956), Omicron Kappa Upsilon. Republican. Mormon. Office: 2837 W Northern Ave Phoenix AZ 85051

WOLFRUM, WILLIAM HARVEY, bishop; b. Warrensburg, Mo., Jan. 16, 1926; s. Oscar William and Lucille Bales (Insley) W.; m. Beverly Ann Gunn, Nov. 30, 1947; 3 children. BS, Cen. Mo. State Coll., 1949; MS, Cornell U., 1953; BD, Episcopal. Theol. Sem. of S.W., 1959, DD, 1981. Ordained deacon, Episcopal. Ch., 1959, priest, 1960. Deacon-in-charge St. Paul Ch., Artesia, N.Mex., 1959-60, rector, 1960-62; rector Trinity-on-the-Hill Ch., Los Alamos, N.Mex., 1962-68; chaplain, chmn. dept. religious studies St. Stephen's Sch., Austin, 1968-71; rector St. Alban's Ch., Worland, Wyo., 1971-81; suffragan bishop Diocese of Colo., Denver, 1981—. Office: Box 18-M Capitol Hill Sta 1300 Washington Denver CO 80218 *

WOLFSEN, LAURA ANN, electronics company manager; b. L.A., Aug. 13, 1954; d. Herbert Christian Jr. and Elaine (Hiebert) W. BBA, Pacific Union Coll., 1977; MBA, U. Phoenix, 1982. Sec. nuclear energy div. GE, San Jose, Calif., 1976-79, logistics coord. nuclear energy div., 1979-81, logistics specialist nuclear energy div., 1981-84, customer svc. rep., 1984-87, team leader, 1987—. Mem. NAFE. Home: 191 E El Camino Real #168A Mountain View CA 94040

WOLFSON, ROBERT PRED, aerospace engineer; b. Miami, Fla., May 29, 1926; s. O. Philip and Nora Jacqueline (Pred) W.; m. Helene Clare Abrahm, Nov. 12, 1949; children: Philip Michael, Robert P. BE, Tulane U., 1948; postgrad., Pa. State U., 1962-64, Poly. Inst. Bklyn., 1965. Air conditioning engr. Equitable Equipment Co., New Orleans, 1948-49, Wood-Leppard Air Conditioning Co., Houston, 1949, Conditioned Air Corp., Miami, 1949-50, Lewco Co., Miami, 1950-54, Hill-York Corp., Miami, 1954-55; thermoelectric energy research engr. The Franklin Inst Labs. Research and Devel., Phila., 1955-59; thermoelectric research and devel. mgr. Tenn. Products & Chem. Corp., Nashville, 1959-61; photovoltaic power systems devel. engr., planetary quarantine mgr. Gen. Electric Co., Phila., 1961-71; sci. contamination specialist for Viking spacecraft Bionetics Corp., Hampton, Va., 1972; planetary quarantine project mgr., Mars/Earth back contamination research mgr., dir. energy programs Exotech. Inc., Gaithersburg, Md., 1972-80; project engr. The Aerospace Corp., El Segundo, Calif., 1980—. Contbr. articles to profl. jours. Served with USNR, 1944-46. Mem. IEEE, Wash. Acad. Scis. Home: 19 Laguna Ct Manhattan Beach CA 90266

WOLLENBERG, DAVID ARTHUR, real estate developer; b. Longview, Wash., Aug. 6, 1947; s. Richard Peter and Leone (Bonney) W.; m. Katrina Moulton, Aug. 30, 1975; children: Andrew Richard, Blake Endicott. BA, Brown U., 1969; MBA, Stanford U., 1973. Front office mgr. Caneel Bay Plantation, St. John, V.I., 1969-71; adminstrn. asst. AMFAC Communities-Hawaii, Honolulu, 1973-77; exec. v.p. The Cortana Corp., Palo Alto, Calif., 1977-83, pres., 1983—; dir. Longview Fibre Co., Wash. 1979—. Dir. Peninsula Ctr. for the Blind, Palo Alto Calif., 1984—. Mem. Outrigger Canoe Club Honolulu, Menlo Circus Club. Republican. Office: The Cortana Corp Palo Alto CA 94303

WOLLENBERG, RICHARD PETER, paper manufacturing company executive; b. Juneau, Alaska, Aug. 1, 1915; s. Harry L. and Gertrude (Arnstein) W.; m. Leone Bonney, Dec. 22, 1940; children: Kenneth Roger, David Arthur, Keith Kermit, Richard Harry, Carol Lynne. BS in Mech. Engring, U. Calif.-Berkeley, 1936; MBA, Harvard U., 1938; grad., Army Indsl. Coll., 1941; D in Pub. Affairs (hon.), U. Puget Sound, 1977. Prodn. control Bethlehem Ship, Quincy, Mass., 1938-39; with Longview (Wash.) Fibre Co., 1939—, safety engr., asst. chief engr., chief engr., mgr. container operations, 1951-57, v.p., 1953-57, v.p. ops., 1957-60, exec. v.p., 1960-69, pres., 1969-78, pres., chief exec. officer, 1978-85, pres., chief exec. officer, chmn. bd., 1985—, also bd. dirs.; mem. Wash. State Council for Postsecondary Edn., 1969-79, chmn., 1970-73; mem. western adv. bd. Allendale Ins. Bassoonist SW Washington Symphony. Chmn. bd. trustees Reed Coll., Portland. Served to lt. col. USAAF, 1941-45. Mem. NAM (bd. dirs. 1981-86), Pacific Assn. Pulp and Paper Mfrs. (pres. 1982—), Inst. Paper Chemistry (trustee), Wash. State Roundtable. Home: 1632 Kessler Blvd Longview WA 98632 Office: Longview Fibre Co PO Box 606 Longview WA 98632

WOLLERT, GERALD DALE, food company executive; b. LaPorte, Ind., Jan. 21, 1935; s. Delmar Everette and Esther Mae W.; m. Carol Jean Burchby, Jan. 26, 1957; children—Karen Lynn, Edwin Del. B.S., Purdue U., 1957. With Gen. Foods Corp., 1959—; dir. consumer affairs Gen. Foods Corp., White Plains, N.Y., 1973-74; mng. dir. Cottee Foods div. Gen. Foods Corp., Sydney, Australia, 1974-76; gen. mgr. Mexico div. Gen. Foods Corp., Mexico City, 1978-79; pres. Asia/Pacific ops. Gen. Foods Corp., Honolulu, corp. v.p. worldwide coffee and internat. div., 1979—; dir. Gen. Foods cos., Japan, Peoples Republic China, Korea, India, Taiwan, Singapore, Philippines. Webelos leader Boy Scouts Am., Mexico City, 1978-79; co. gen. chmn. United Fund campaign, Battle Creek, Mich., 1964-65, White Plains, N.Y., 1972-73. Served with U.S. Army, 1958. Mem. Asian-U.S. Bus. Council. Club: Oahu (Hawaii) Country. Office: Gen Foods Corp 615 Piikoi St Honolulu HI 96814

WOLTERS, GALE LEON, forestry professional; b. Portis, Kans., Apr. 25, 1939; s. Lester Orin and Dalice Marie (Smith) W.; m. Justine Louise Beatty, May 29, 1960; children: Ty, Amy. BS, Ft. Hays State U., 1961, MS, 1962; PhD, N.D. State U., 1968. Instr. N.D. State U., Fargo, 1965-66; range scientist Southern Forest Experiment Sta. USDA, Alexandria, La., 1966-75; project leader Pacific Southwest Forest and Range Experiment Sta. USDA, Fresno, Calif., 1975-80; range rsch. br. chief U.S. Forest Svc., Washington, 1980-87; range scientist Rocky Mountain Forest and Range Experiment Sta., Albuquerque, 1987—; del., Internat. Rangeland Congress, Adelaide, Australia, 1984, Agr. Goodwill Tour, People-to-People program, People's Republic China, 1986. Contbr. to Jour. Range Mgmt. Mem. Soc. Range Mgmt. (pres. regional sects., 1972, 82), Wildlife Soc., Soc. Am. Foresters, Sigma Xi, Beta Beta Beta. Home: 801 Navarra Way SE Albuquerque NM 87123 Office: Rocky Mountain Exptl Sta 2205 Columbia St SE Albuquerque NM 87106

WOLTING, ROBERT ROY, city official; b. Faulkton, S.D., Dec. 29, 1928; s. George and Minnie (Meeter) W.; m. Nancy Catherine O'Brien, Nov. 26, 1953; children: Robert Roy, Linda Marie. Acct. Wolting Implement and Motor Co., Wessington Springs, S.D., 1954-60; city auditor City of Wessington Springs, 1960-64, City of Brookings, S.D., 1964-68; dir. fin. City of Fairbanks, Alaska, 1968-78, city mgr., 1978-79, dir. fin., treas., 1984—; city adminstr., clk. City of Union Springs, Ala. Mem. S.D. Retirement Bd., 1966-68. Sgt. USAF, 1950-54. Mem. Mcpl. Fin. Officers Assn. (pres. S.D. chpt. 1965-67, sec. Fairbanks chpt. 1976-78, bd. dirs. 1985—). Democrat. Methodist. Home: 431 Le Ann Dr Fairbanks AK 99701 Office: City of Fairbanks 410 Cushman St Fairbanks AK 99701

WOLVERTON, MONTE K., art director, illustrator; b. Vancouver, Wash., Sept. 25, 1948; s. Basil and Honor (Lovette) W.; m. Kayte Youngblood, June 28, 1970; 1 child, Monika. BA in Liberal Arts, Ambassador Coll., Pasadena, Calif., 1970. Prodn. artist Ambassador Coll. Press, 1970-71; asst. art dir. The Plain Truth mag., Pasadena, 1971-77, art dir., 1985—; freelance art dir., illustrator Seattle, 1977-79, Vancouver, 1979-85; art dir. Business mag., Vancouver, 1983-85. Mem. Columbia River Econ. Devel. Council, Vancouver, 1983-85. Office: The Plain Truth 300 W Green Pasadena CA 91123

WOMACK, THOMAS HOUSTON, manufacturing company executive; b. Gallatin, Tenn., June 22, 1940; s. Thomas Houston and Jessie (Eckel) W.; Linda Walker Womack, July 20, 1963; children: Britton Ryan, Kelley Elizabeth. BSME, Tenn. Tech. U., Cookeville, 1963. Project engr. U.S. Gypsum Co., Jacksonville, Fla., 1963-65; project mgr. Maxwell House Div. Gen. Foods Corp., Jacksonville, 1965-68; mfg. mgr. Maxwell House Div. Gen. Foods Corp., Hoboken, N.J., 1968-71, div. ops. planning mgr., 1971-73; industry sales mgr. J.R. Schneider Co., Tiburon, Calif., 1973-79; pres. Womack Internat., Inc., Novato, Calif., 1979—. Mem. Soc. Tribologists and Lubrication Engrs., Am. Filtration Soc., Soc. Mfg. Engrs., Am. Soc. Chem. Engrs. Office: Womack Internat Inc One Digital Dr Novato CA 94949

WONDERS, WILLIAM CLARE, geography educator; b. Toronto, Ont., Can., Apr. 22, 1924; s. George Clarence and Ann Mary (Bell) W.; m. Lillian Paradise Johnson, June 2, 1951; children—Karen Elizabeth, Jennifer Anne, Glen William. B.A. with honors, Victoria Coll., U. Toronto, 1946; M.A., Syracuse U., 1948; Ph.D., U. Toronto, 1951; Fil. Dr. h.c., Uppsala U., 1981. Teaching asst. dept. geography Syracuse U., 1946-48; lectr. dept. geography U. Toronto, 1948-53; asst. prof. geography dept. polit. economy U. Alta., 1953-55, assoc. prof. geography, 1955-57, prof., head dept. geography, 1957-67, prof. dept. geography, 1967-87, emeritus, 1987—, Univ. prof., 1983—; vis. prof. geography U. B.C., 1954; U. Okla., 1965-66, St. Mary's U., 1977; guest prof. Inst. Geography, Uppsala (Sweden) U., 1962-63; research fellow in geography U. Aberdeen, Scotland, 1970-71, 78; vis. fellow in Can. Studies, U. Edinburgh, Scotland, 1987. Author: Looking at Maps, 1960; co-author: (with T. Drinkwater et al.) Atlas of Alberta, 1969, (with J. C. Muller et al.) Junior Atlas of Alberta, 1979; Contbr., editor: Canada's Changing North, 1971, The North, 1972, The Arctic Circle, 1976, Knowing the North, 1988; Contbr. articles to jours., encys., chpts. to books. Mem. Nat. Adv. Com. on Geog. Research, 1965-69; mem. Canadian Permanent Com. on Geog. Names, 1981—, Alta. Historic Sites Bd., 1978-83; mem. policy bd. Canadian Plains Research Centre, U. Regina (Sask.), 1975-86; mem. adv. bd. Tyrrell Mus. Paleontology, 1984—; bd. dirs. The Muttart Found., 1986—. NSF sr. fgn. scientist fellow, 1965-66; Canada Council leave fellow, 1969-70, 77-78; Nuffield Found. fellow, 1970-71. Fellow Arctic Inst. N. Am., Royal Soc. Can.; mem. Canadian Assn. Geographers (past pres.), Assn. Am. Geographers, Royal Scottish Geog. Soc., Canadian Assn. Scottish Studies (councillor 1974-77), Am.-Scandinavian Found., Canadian Scandinavian Found., Royal Canadian Geog. Soc., Champlain Soc. (councillor 1981-86), Sigma Xi, Gamma Theta Upsilon. Office: U Alta, Dept Geography, Edmonton, AB Canada T6G 2H4

WONG, ALFRED MUN KONG, lawyer; b. Honolulu, Sept. 12, 1930; s. Inn and Mew Kung (Choy) W.; m. Laureen Hong, Nov. 20, 1965; children—Peter Marn On, Julie Li Sharn. Student U. Hawaii, 1948-50; B.S., Marquette U., 1953; J.D., U. Calif., 1964. Bar: Hawaii 1964. With Thomas Lee, C.P.A., 1961-62, firm Scott and Balacco, San Francisco, 1962-64; contract atty. Honolulu Redevel. Agy., 1968-71; mng. dir. Okumura, Takushi, Funaki & Wee, Attys. at Law, A Law Corp., Honolulu, 1964—; adj. prof. U. Hawaii Law Sch., 1980-82; mem. bd. bar examiners State of Hawaii, 1968-79; mem. Hawaii Jud. Selection Commn., 1979-85, chmn., 1983-85. Bd. dirs. Pacific council Girl Scouts U.S.A., 1973-78 (Outstanding Service award 1978); pres. Niu Valley Community Assn., 1975, bd. dirs., 1974, 76, 77. Served to capt. C.E., U.S. Army, 1953-61. Recipient Chicago Tribune medal, 1952, 53. Mem. ABA, Hawaii Bar Assn. (dir., chmn. unauthorized practice of law com., nominating com.), Hastings Coll. Law Alumni Assn. (bd. govs., Disting. Service award 1987), Am. Judicature Soc., Friends of U. Hawaii Law Sch. (bd. dirs.), Am. Soc. Engrs. Clubs: Waialae Country (Honolulu), Honolulu (founding dir.), Beverly Hills Country. Office: Okumura Takushi Funaki Wee 733 Bishop St Honolulu HI 96813

WONG, ASTRIA WOR, cosmetic business consultant; b. Hong Kong, Oct. 23, 1949; came to U.S., 1970; B in Vocat. Edn., Calif. State U., Long Beach, 1976. Cert. coll. tchr. (life), Calif. West coast sales trainer Revlon Inc., N.Y.C, 1975-82; nat. tng. dir. diReniel Internat., Palm Springs, Calif., 1982; dir. Beauty Cons. Service Agy., Long Beach, Calif., 1983—. Author: The Art of Femininity, 1971; editor (newsletter) So. Calif. Cosmetic, 1983-86. Named Salesperson of Yr., Revlon, Inc., N.Y.C., 1978. Mem. So. Calif. Cosmetic Assn. (correspondence sec. 1982—), Women's Council, Cosmetologist Tchr. Assn., Bus. and Profl. Women. Republican. Office: Beauty Cons Service Agy 7121 1st Ave Scottsdale AZ 85251

WONG, BENJAMIN YAU-CHEUNG, medicine care delivery executive; b. Hong Kong, July 15, 1943; s. Hung and Ku (Yip) W.; came to U.S., 1964, naturalized, 1979; BCE, Hong Kong Bapt. Coll., 1964; postgrad in Math., Baylor U., 1965; PhD, Vanderbilt U., 1968; m. Beatrice Loh, Nov. 15, 1969; children: Carolyn, Jeffrey. Sr. structural engr. Smith, Hinchman & Grylls Assocs., Inc., 1968-72; rsch. fellow computer based tech. transfer Carnegie Mellon U., 1972-74; mgr. bldg. systems and computer applications devel. Architecture/Engring. Svcs., Kaiser Permanente Med. Care Program, Kaiser Found. Hosps., Inc., Oakland, Calif., 1974—. Recipient Scholastic award Hong Kong Bapt. Coll., 1964. Mem. Nat., Calif. (v.p. East Bay chpt., Achievement award) socs. profl. engrs., AAUP, ASCE, Am. Soc. Engring. Edn., Earthquake Engring. Rsch. Inst., Structural Engring Assn. No. Calif., Med. Entities Mgmt. Assn., Tau Beta Pi. Contbr. articles on engring., bldg. systems, computer application, tech. transfer and health care delivery systems to profl. jours. Office: Kaiser Permanente Med Care Program Box 12916 Oakland CA 94604

WONG, BONNIE LEE, systems analyst; b. L.A., Nov. 30, 1957; d. Robert Lee and Betty Rose (Woo) W. Student, Cambridge (Eng.) U., 1979; BS, U. So. Calif., L.A., 1979, MPA, 1981. Resident, adminstrv. asst. Olive View Med. Ctr., Sylmar, Calif., 1980-81; quality assurance coord. Lincoln Hosp. Med. Ctr., L.A., 1982; cons. Ernst & Whinney, L.A., 1983-85; systems coord., analyst, then cons. Am. Med. Internat., L.A., 1985-87; client svcs. rep. McDonnell Douglas Health Systems, L.A., 1987-89; mktg. support rep. Sci. Dynamics Corp., Torrance, Calif., 1989—. Mem. Healthcare Fin. Mgmt. Assn. (mem. roster com. 1985, info. systems com. 1988), U. So. Calif. Healthcare Alumni. Office: Science Dynamics Corp 2140 W 190th St Torrance CA 90504-6199

WONG, GERARD CHI-NG, state official; b. Kwongtung, People's Republic China, Sept. 22, 1939; came to U.S., 1959; s. Tin-Kuen and Yuet-Yung (Lau) W.; m. Viviana Jocca Yao, Nov. 19, 1971. BA, Calif. State U., San Jose, 1963; PhD, U. Calif., Davis, 1971. Health physicist Calif. Dept. Health, Sacramento, 1975-79; sr. health physicist Calif. Dept. Health Svcs., Sacramento, 1979-84, chief radiation mgmt., 1984-87, chief radiation material control, 1987—; rsch. assoc. Brookhaven Nat. Lab., Upton, N.Y., 1971-73, U. Calif., San Francisco, 1974; lectr. San Francisco City Coll., 1973-74; advisor on food irradiation, 1984; coord. Statewide Nuclear Emergency Svcs., 1985—; guest speaker Oceania Congress Nuclear Medicine, Taipei, Republic of China, 1988. Author: Nuclear Medicine Update, 1988. U. Calif. scholar, 1960; NIH fellow, 1966-71, 71-73. Mem. Health Physics Soc., Conf. Radiation Control Dirs. Democrat. Office: Calif Dept Health Svcs 714 P St Sacramento CA 95814

WONG, HARRY CHOW, anesthesiologist, educator; b. Beloit, Wis., June 26, 1933; s. Charles T. and Yee S. W.; m. Jean A. Nagahiro, June 21, 1958; children: Jeffrey, Stacey, Daphne, Steven. BS, U. Wis., 1955, MD, 1958. Diplomate, Am. Bd. Anesthesiology. Intern Providence Hosp., Portland, Oreg., 1958-59; resident in anesthesiology U. Wis., Madison, 1959-61; pvt. practice Salt Lake City, 1961—; chmn. dept. anesthesiology, Latter-day Saints Hosp., 1966-67, 74-76, chmn. ICU com., 1971-75; pres. med. staff, Salt Lake Surg. Ctr., 1976-88; mem. Joint Commn. Accreditation Health Orgns., 1983—, cons. surveyor, 1985—; prof. anesthesiology, U. Utah, Salt Lake City, 1988—. Mem. AMA, Am. Soc. Anesthesiologists, Internat. Anesthesia Rsch. Soc., Am. Heart Assn., Federated Ambulatory Surg. Assn. (bd. dirs. 1976—), Soc. Ambulatory Anesthesia (bd. dirs. 1985—), Utah Med. Ins. Assn. (bd. govs. 1980—), Utah State Soc. Anesthesiologists (pres. 1966). Home: 1060 Oak Hills Way Salt Lake City UT 84108 Office: Dept Anesthesiology 50 N Medical Dr Salt Lake City UT 84132

WONG, HENRY LI-NAN, banker, economist; b. Rangoon, Burma, Nov. 3, 1940; s. Chew King and Jenny (Yu) W.; came to U.S., 1946. m. Laurie Yap, Apr. 11, 1968; children: Rachael S.Y., Remle S.M. BS, Waynesburg Coll., 1965; MS, U. Hawaii, 1968, PhD, 1969. Economist, Econ. Research Service U.S. Dept. Agr., Washington, 1969-70; economist Hawaii Dept. Budget and Fin., Honolulu, 1970-73; dir. Hawaii film office Hawaii Dept. Planning and Econ. Devel., Honolulu, 1973-84; exec. adminstr., sr. v.p. for office of chmn. City Bank, Honolulu, 1984—. V.p. bd. dirs. Friends of East West Ctr., Honolulu, 1983-84. NDEA fellow, 1965-69. Mem. Assn. Film Commrs. (pres. 1980), Am. Econ. Assn., Am. Agrl. Econs. Assn., Hawaii Internat. Film Festival, Chinese C. of C., Hawaii Soc. Corp. Planners, Lanakila Crafts (trustee), Alpha Kappa Psi, Theta Chi. Democrat. Presbyterian. Lodges: Elks, Masons (trustee), Shriners. Office: City Bank City Fin Tower 201 Merchant St Honolulu HI 96813

WONG, JAMES BOK, economist, engineer, technologist; b. Canton, China, Dec. 9, 1922; came to U.S., 1938, naturalized, 1962; s. Gen Ham and Chen (Yee) W.; m. Wai Ping Lim, Aug. 3, 1946; children: John, Jane Doris, Julia Ann. BS in Agr., U. Md., 1949, BS in Chem. Engring., 1950; MS, U. Ill., 1951, PhD, 1954. Research asst. U. Ill., Champaign-Urbana, 1950-53; chem. engr. Standard Oil of Ind., Whiting, 1953-55; process design engr., research engr. Shell Devel. Co., Emeryville, Calif., 1955-61; sr. planning engr., prin. planning engr. Chem. Plastics Group, Dart Industries, Inc. (formerly Rexall Drug & Chem. Co.), Los Angeles, 1961-66, supr. planning and econs., 1966-67, mgr. long range planning and econs., 1967, chief economist, 1967-72, dir. econs. and ops. analysis, 1972-78, dir. internat. techs., 1978-81; pres. James B. Wong Assocs., Los Angeles, 1981—; chmn. bd. dirs. United Pacific Bank, 1988—; tech. cons. various corps. Contbr. articles to profl. jours. Bd. dirs., pres. Chinese Am. Citizens Alliance Found.; mem. Asian Am. Edn. Commn., 1971-81. Served with USAAF, 1943-46. Recipient Los Angeles Outstanding Vol. Service award, 1977. Mem. Am. Inst. Chem. Engrs., Am. Chem. Soc., VFW (vice comdr. 1959), Commodores (named to exec. order 1982), Sigma Xi, Tau Beta Pi, Phi Kappa Phi, Pi Mu Epsilon, Phi Lambda Upsilon, Phi Eta Sigma. Home: 2460 Venus Dr Los Angeles CA 90046

WONG, JOHN WING-CHUNG, psychiatrist; b. Canton, China, Aug. 12, 1934; came to U.S., 1962; s. Min Sam and Yee Fern (Lau) W.; m. Lily Jent-Ju Chen, May 4, 1962; children: Diana, John Wing-Chung Jr., Gloria, Angela. MD, Queen's U., Kingston, Ont., Can., 1959. Diplomate Am. Bd. Psychiatry and Neurology. Resident physician in psychiatry Ohio State U. Hosp., Columbus, 1963-65; intern St. Michael's Hosp., Toronto, 1959-60; resident internal medicine univ. med. unit Queen Mary Hosp., Hong Kong, 1960-61; practice medicine specializing in psychiatry L.A., 1969—; dir. Pacific Clinic, Pasadena, Calif., 1987—; bd. dirs. Ea. Savs. Bank, Alhambra, Calif.; staff psychiatrist Dammasch State Hosp., Wilsonville, Oreg., 1966-67; dir. day treatment program Resthaven Community Mental Health Ctr., L.A., 1967-69; dir. area XXIV Profl. Standard Rev. Orgn., L.A., 1980-83; chmn. dept. psychiatry St. Vincent Hosp., 1978-79; mem. staff Hosp. of the Good Samaritan, L.A., St. Vincent Hosp., L.A., Calif. Hosp. Med. Ctr., L.A., Las Encinas Hosp., Pasadena. Bd. dirs. San Marino (Calif.) Community Chest, 1986-88, pres. 1987-88. Mem. AMA, Am. Psychiat. Assn., So. Calif. Psychiat. Soc., L.A. County Med. Assn., Assocs. of Calif. Inst. Tech. Office: 1127 Wilshire Blvd Suite 500 Los Angeles CA 90017

WONG, KENNETH LEE, software engineer, consultant; b. L.A., Aug. 15, 1947; s. George Yut and Yue Sam (Lee) W.; m. Betty (Louie) Wong, June 29, 1975; children: Bradford Keith, Karen Beth. BS in Engring., UCLA, 1969, MS in Engring., 1972, postgrad., 1972-73, 76-78. Cert. community coll. instr., Calif. Mem. tech. staff Hughes Aircraft Co., various cities, Calif., 1976-78, 79-81, TRW Def. and Space Systems Group, Redondo Beach, Calif., 1975-76, 78-79; engring. specialist Northrop Corp., Hawthorne, Calif., 1981-84; mem. tech. staff Jet Propulsion Lab., Pasadena, Calif., 1984-87; software cons. EG&G Spl. Projects, Las Vegas, Nev., 1987, AT&T Bell Labs., Warren, N.J., 1987-88, Westinghouse Electric Corp., Linthicom, Md., 1988, E Systems, Inc., Greenville, Tex., 1988-89; prin. Wong Soft Works, L.A., 1989—; engring. aide, Singer Librascope, Glendale, Calif., 1972-73; computer system design engr., Air Force Avionics Lab., Wright-Patterson AFB, Ohio, 1973-75. Author tech. reports. Coach, Tigers Youth Club, L.A. 1st lt. USAF, 1973-75. Mem. AIAA, IEEE, Assn. Computing Machinery, Upsilon Pi Epsilon. Republican. Home and Office: Wong Soft Works 3385 McLaughlin Ave Los Angeles CA 90066

WONG, KEVIN BRUCE, control systems engineer; b. Oakland, Calif., Jan. 1, 1955; s. Douglas S. and Mary (Kau) W.; m. Julianna Lin Chow, May 21, 1978; children: Bruce Matthew, Janine Marie, Emily Aileen. BSCE, U. Calif., Berkeley, 1977. Registered profl. engr., Calif. Chem. engring. and control systems Alta Plating Co., Oakland, Calif., 1977-78; process engr., chems. div. Union Oil Co., Rodeo, Calif., 1978-80; sr. engr. Kaiser Engrs., Oakland, 1980-84; applications engr. Bellofe Co., Engrs., Oakland, 1984-85; process control engr. Descon Engring. Co., Walnut Creek, Calif., 1985-86; assoc. elec. engr. East Bay Mcpl. Utility Dist., Oakland, 1986—; prin. KBW Design Svcs., Alameda, Calif., 1987—; guest lectr. chem. engring. San Jose State U., San Francisco State U. Mem. Instrument Soc. Am. (chmn. roster com. 1987-88). Democrat. Baptist. Office: East Bay Mcpl Utility Dist 2127 Adeline St Oakland CA 94607

WONG, KIN-PING, university dean, biotechnology researcher, educator, science administrator; b. Guangzhou, China, Aug. 14, 1941; s. Kwok-Keung and Yuan-Kwan (Loo) W.; m. Anna S.K. Koo, Sept. 16, 1968; children: Voon-Chung Wong, Ming-Chung Wong. BS, U. Calif., Berkeley, 1964; PhD, Purdue U., 1968. Postdoctoral fellow Duke U., Durham, N.C., 1968-70; asst. and assoc. prof. chemistry U. South Fla., Tampa, 1970-75; vis. scientist Max Planck Inst. Molecular Genetics, Berlin, 1972; vis. prof. U. Uppsala, Sweden, 1975; assoc. and prof. biochemistry U. Kans., Kansas City, 1975-83, dean grad. studies, 1980-83; vis. prof. biochemistry U. Tokyo, 1979; program dir. of biophysics NSF, Washington, 1981-83; sci. dean, prof. Calif. State U., Fresno, 1983—; vis. prof. biochemistry Stanford U. Med. Ctr., summer 1985; adj. prof. medicine U. Calif. San Francisco Med. Sch., 1986—; adj. prof. biochemistry and biophysics, U. Calif., San Francisco, 1987—; hon. prof. Shantou U. Med. Coll., People's Republic China; mem. U.S. Govt. Interagency Com. on Radiation, Washington, 1982-83; gov. Moss Landing (Calif.) Marine Labs., 1983—; cons. HHS, Washington, 1985—; trustee U. Calif., San Francisco, Fresno, Med. Found.; mem. rev. panel NSF; mem. expert panel Calif. Commn. Tchr. Credentialing. Contbr. over 50 research articles to prof. jours.; 32 pub. research abstracts; author various keynote speeches, convocation lectures. Chmn. sci. com. Fresno Met. Mus., 1983-85; bd. dirs. Fresno Chinese Assn., 1986-88; chmn. planning com. Cen. Calif. Biomed. Rsch. Inst., Fresno, 1987—; co-chmn. multicultural coun. Clovis Unified Sch. Dist. Recipient cancer research grants and awards, Damon Runyan Fund, Milheim Found., Am. Cancer Soc., Eli Lilly Corp., Research Corps., Am. Heart Assn., 1970-86; grantee HHS, 1986-89, Nat. Inst. Heart Lung and Blood, 1972-87, Nat. Inst. Gen. Med. Scis., 1972-80; research career devel. awardee NIH, 1972-75; sr. research fellow European Molecular Biology Orgn., 1975; summer research professorship NSF, 1985;

Laval Research award in innovation scis. and tech., Calif. State U., Fresno, 1985; scholarship Pepperdine U. presdl. and key exec. program, 1986-88; Calif. Sea grant Dept. Commerce, 1987-90. Fellow Am. Inst. Chemists, Royal Soc. Chemistry; mem. Am. Soc. Biol. Chemistry (membership com. 1983-86), AAAS, Biophys. Soc., Am. Chem. Soc., Sigma Xi. Office: Calif State U Sch of Natural Sci Fresno CA 93740-0090

WONG, MEL, dance educator; b. Oakland, Calif.; s. Tom and Louise (Lee) W.; m. Betty Jean Erickson (div.); m. Constance Kreemer, Aug. 14, 1984. BA, San Francisco State U., 1965; postgrad., UCLA, 1967-68; MFA, Mills Coll., Oakland, Calif., 1967. Dance tchr. Profl. Dance Classes, N.Y.C., 1975-87; tchr. Am. Dance Festival, New London, Conn., 1975-77 summers; dancer Merce Cunningham Dance Co., N.Y.C., 1968-72; lectr. Cornell U., Ithaca, N.Y., 1972-74; artistic dir. The Mel Wong Dance Co., N.Y.C., 1975—; asst. prof., lectr. SUNY, Purchase, 1974-87; artistic dir. U. Colo., Boulder, 1988—; guest artist Ariz. State U., Tempe, 1985-86, Hong Kong Acad. Performing Arts, 1987-88; dance panelist Asian Pacific Dance Alliance, Hong Kong, 1988; choreographer for TV, Centro Assocs., Hong Kong, 1988; keynote panelist Congress on Research in Dance, Hartford, 1984. Choreographer dances, Blue Mesa, 1987, Buddha Meets Einstein, 1985, Future Antiquities, 1984, Scenario on a Bridge, 1983. With USN, 1958-60. Guggenheim Found. choreographic fellow, 1983-84; N.Y. State Council on Arts dance co. grantee, 1986-87; Nat. Endowment for Arts choreographic fellow 1981-82, 86-87. Mem. Dance Theatre Workshop. Democrat. Office: Univ Colo Dance Dept Campus Box 261 201 Univ The Boulder CO 80309

WONG, OTTO, epidemiologist; b. Canton, China, Nov. 14, 1947; came to U.S., 1967, naturalized, 1976; s. Kui and Foon (Chow) W.; m. Betty Yeung, Feb. 14, 1970; children: Elaine, Jonathan. BS, U. Ariz., 1970; MS, Carnegie Mellon U., 1972; MS, U. Pitts., 1973, ScD, 1975. Cert. epidemiologist, Am. Coll. Epidemiology, 1982. USPHS fellow U. Pitts., 1972-75; asst. prof. epidemiology Georgetown U. Med. Sch., 1975-78; mgr. epidemiology Equitable Environ. Health Inc., Rockville, Md., 1977-78; dir. epidemiology Tabershaw Occupational Med. Assocs., Rockville, 1978-80; dir. occupational rsch. Biometric Rsch. Inst., Washington, 1980-81; exec. v.p., chief epidemiologist, ENSR Health Scis., Alameda, Calif., 1981—. cons. Nat. Cancer Inst., Nat. Inst. Occupational Safety and Health, Occupational Safety and Health Adminstrn., Nat. Heart, Lung and Blood Inst., Ford Motors Co., Gen. Electric, Mobil, Chevron, Union Carbide, Fairfax Hosp., Va. U. Ariz. scholar, 1967-68. Fellow Am. Coll. Epidemiology, Human Biology Council; mem. Am. Pub. Health Assn., Biometric Soc., Soc. Epidemiologic Rsch., Phi Beta Kappa, Pi Mu Epsilon. Republican. Contbr. articles to profl. jours. Office: ENSR Health Scis 1320 Harbor Bay Pkwy Alameda CA 94501

WONG, PENELOPE LYNN, marketing consultant, writer; b. Salinas, Calif., May 22, 1945; d. Gung Jue and Nellie Sue (Lee) W.; m. Stephen Timothy Kochis. AB in English, U. Calif., Berkeley, 1967. Editor Stolen Paper Edits., San Francisco, 1967-71; co-founder The Innerspace Project, Mill Valley, Calif., 1969-72; publ. dir. Interaction Assocs., San Francisco, 1971-74; pres. Penelope Wong & Assocs., Berkeley, Calif., 1974-78; copy chief The Franklin Mint, Wawa, Pa., 1978-79; mng. dir. Jennifer Wong Ltd., N.Y.C., 1979-81; sr. v.p. Ogilvy & mather Direct, San Francisco, 1981-87; pres. Penelope Wong & Assocs., San Francisco, 1987—; lectr. in field. Author: Lift for Life, 1978; contbg. editor AsiAm mag. Bd. dirs. Oakland (Calif.) East Bay Symphony, 1989. Recipient Echo Silver award Direct Mktg. Assn., 1986, Pioneer Awards Direct Mktg. Creative Guild, 1983-87. Mem. Direct Mktg. Creative Guild, The City Club. Democrat. Roman Catholic. Home: 7245 Skyline Blvd Oakland CA 94611 Office: 333 Broadway San Francisco CA 94133

WONG, ROBERTA JEAN, pharmacist, educator; b. Cleve., Nov. 23, 1957; d. Robert Y. and Ellen J. (Woo) W. Student, U. Calif., Davis, 1976-79; PharmD, U. Calif., San Francisco, 1983, cert., 1984. Lic. pharmacist, Calif. Pharmacist intern Good Samaritan Hosp., San Jose, Calif., 1980-82, Kaiser Found. Hosp., South San Fancisco, Calif., 1982-83; pharmacist Kaiser Found. Hosp., South San Fancisco, 1983-87; clin. pharmacist AIDS activities div. San Francisco Gen. Hosp., 1984-89; asst. clin. prof. pharmacy div. clin. pharmacy U. Calif., San Francisco, 1985—; numerous lectures, presentations in field; reviewer Am. Hosp. Formulary Svc., Bethesda, Md., 1987—; mem. Asian AIDS Task Force, 1987—; cons. Quality Planning Corp., Oakland, Calif., 1988—. Contbr. articles to profl. jours. Mem. Am. Soc. Hosp. Pharmacists, Calif. Soc. Hosp. Pharmacists (Ho. of dels. 1985-86), Golden Gate Soc. Hosp. Pharmacists (chmn. programs 1986-87), Am. Pharm. Assn., N.Y. Acad. Scis. Office: UCLA Med Ctr Drug Info A4-190 CHS 10833 Le Conte Ave Los Angeles CA 90024

WONG, RONALD JAMES, pediatric dental surgeon; b. Fresno, Calif., Dec. 21, 1931; s. Raymond Arthur and Ruth (Moe) W.; B.S., U. So. Calif., 1954, D.D.S., 1956; m. Edith Mok, June 21, 1962 (div. 1986); children: Gary Hunter, Julie, Christy, Carina, Lara, Sabrina. Intern, P.T.A. Clinic, Los Angeles Sch. Dist., 1956-57; resident Greenpark Sch. dental clinic, Chofu, Japan, 1958-59; practice dentistry specializing in pediatric dental surgery, Hollywood, Calif., 1959—; mem. staff Hollywood Presbyn. Hosp.; asst. clin. prof. pedodontics U. So. Calif., Los Angeles, 1959-68; cons. Children's Hosp. Los Angeles, 1960-73, head dental div., 1973-78. Coordinator Lang. Services Archery Venue XXIII Olympics, Los Angeles. Served to capt. USAF, 1957-59. Nat. Flight Archery Champion U.S.A., 1984; First place winner 25 KG class U.S. Nat. Archery Flight Championship, 1982, Silver Wescott medal No. 2 amateur flight archer in U.S., 1983. Mem. Hollywood, Los Angeles dental socs., Hollywood Acad. Medicine, Am. Stomatological Soc. Japan, Am. Analgesia Soc., Am. Acad. Pedodontics, Am., So. Calif. (pres. 1968-69) socs. dentistry for children, So. Calif., Am. dental assns., Calif. Pedodontic Research Group, Western Pedodontic and Odontic Soc., Am. Endodontic Soc., Am. Hypnodontic Soc., Acad. of Dentistry for the Handicapped, Chinese Am. Citizen's Alliance, Delta Sigma Delta, Alpha Tau Omega. Rotarian. Author: Pedodontic Dental Preparations, 1961. Home: 3372 Rowena Ave #1 Los Feliz CA 90027 Office: 1616 Hillhurst Ave Hollywood CA 90027

WONG, STEPHANIE LAM, columnist, educator, entrepreneur; b. San Francisco, July 16, 1949; d. Franklin Mager and Suey Quon (Wong) Lam; m. Darryl Eugene Wong, July 29, 1978 (div. 1989); children: Jessica Marie, Marshall. AA in Gen. Edn., Coll. of Marin Jr. Coll., 1969; B in Spanish, U. Calif., Santa Barbara, 1972; M in Spl. Edn., U. Santa Clara, 1983. Cert. spl. edn. and health credential, community coll. instr. credential. Tchr. East Side Union, San Jose, Calif., 1976-86; program dir. San Jose Community Coll., 1982-83, spl. projects coordinator, 1983—; syndicated columnist Tribune Media, Orlando, Fla., 1983-85; columnist Chronicle, San Francisco, 1986—; spl. projects coord. and adv. com. mem. Emergency Med. Tech. Program, San Jose, 1983-89; instr. dept. health scis. San Jose City Coll. Photographer: La Cumbre, 1972 (spl. judges award for black and white photography, intercollegiate press award 1972). Office: 1844 Calistoga Dr San Jose CA 95124

WONG, STEVEN WYMANN, management executive, educator; ; b. Honolulu, Oct. 24, 1946; s. Gerald Y.K. and Amy (Gwendolyn (Chun) W.; BA, Claremont McKenna Coll., 1968; MA, San Diego State U., 1969; MBA, So. Ill. U., Edwardsville, 1976. Exec. asst. to exec. dept. Pacific Fruit Express div. So. Pacific Industries, San Francisco, 1970; actuarial analyst Judson Br. Rsch. Ctr. div. Allstate Ins. Co. subs. Sears & Roebuck, Inc., Menlo Park, Calif., 1971; econ. devel./manpower coord. Oakland (Calif.) Model Cities Program, 1972-73; econ. cons. Marshall Kaplan, Gans & Kahn, San Francisco, 1973; econ. devel. dir. Econ. and Social Opportunities, Inc., San Jose, Calif., 1974-76; cons. to bus. and social svcs. on fin. and mgmt., 1976—; prof. accountancy Merritt Coll., Oakland, Calif., 1983-88; mem. faculty U. San Francisco, 1976-81, Vista Coll., Berkeley, Calif., 1979-83, Chapman Coll., Orange, Calif., 1980-88, Columbia Coll., 1983-88; chmn. bus. div. San Joaquin Delta Coll., Stockton, Calif., 1988—. Home: 1714 Timberlake Circle Lodi CA 95242-4283 Office: San Joaquin Delta Coll Bus Div 5151 Pacific Ave Stockton CA 95207

WONG, WALTER FOO, county official; b. San Francisco, Apr. 11, 1930; s. Harry Yee and Grace (Won) W. AA, Hartnell Coll., 1952; BS, U. Calif., Berkeley, 1955; MPH, U. Hawaii, 1968. Registered sanitarian, Calif. Sanitarian Stanislaus County Health Dept., Modesto, Calif., 1955-56; sanitarian Monterey County Health Dept., Salinas, Calif., 1956-67, sr. sanitarian, 1968-69, supervising sanitarian, 1969-70, dir. environ. health, 1971--; sec. Monterey County Solid Waste Mgmt. Com., 1976--, Monterey County Hazardous Waste Mgmt. Com., 1987--; coord. Monterey County Genetic Engring. Rev. Com., 1987--; mem. Monterey County Hazardous Materials Response Task Force, 1988--. Chmn. Salinas Bicentennial Internat. Day Celebration, 1974. Mem. Calif. Conf. Dirs. Environ. Health (pres. 1982-83), Calif. Assn. Environ. Health Adminstrs. (pres. 1982-83), Salinas C. of C. (Mem. of Yr. award 1971), U. Calif.-Berkeley Alumni Assn., U. Hawaii Alumni Assn. Republican. Presbyterian. Home: 234 Cherry St Salinas CA 93901 Office: Monterey County Health Dept 1270 Natividad Rd Rm 301 Salinas CA 93906

WONG-DIAZ, FRANCISCO RAIMUNDO, lawyer; b. Havana, Cuba, Oct. 29, 1944; came to U.S., Nov. 1961; s. Juan and Teresa (Diaz de Villegas) Wong; 1 child, Richard Alan. BA with honors, No. Mich. U., 1963; MA with highest honors, U. Detroit, 1967; PhD, MA, U. Mich., 1973; JD, U. Calif.-Berkeley, 1976. Bar: Calif. 1980, U.S. Dist. Ct. (no. dist.) Calif. 1985, Fla. 1987. Asst. prof. San Francisco State U., 1977; vis. scholar U. Calif. Berkeley Sch. Bus., Berkeley, 1983-84; prof. City Coll. San Francisco, 1975—, dept. chmn., 1978-85; rsch. atty. Marin Superior Ct., 1980-81; ct. arbitrator Marin Mcpl. Ct., 1985; sole practice, Kentfield, Calif., 1980—; assoc. dean Miami-Dade Coll., 1986; dir. Cutcliffe Consulting, Inc., Hawthorne, LaFamila Ctr., Inc., San Rafael, Calif., 1980-85, Small Bus. Inst., Kentfield, 1982-86. Bd. editors Indsl. Relations Law Jour., 1975-76; lector St. Sebastian's Ch., 1984—. Diplomat-scholar U.S. Dept. State, Washington, 1976; Horace C. Rackham fellow U. Mich., 1970; NEH fellow, summer 1981. Mem. ABA, Am. Polit. Sci. Assn., Cuban Am. Nat. Council, World Affairs Council (seminar leader San Francisco 1980). Roman Catholic. Club: Commonwealth.

WOO, DEXTER JU-WEI, chemist; b. Hong Kong, Mar. 28, 1952; s. Wei Yen and Lucie (Feng) W.; m. Helen Mar, Aug. 26, 1984. AB, U. Calif., Berkeley, 1976; MS, U. Bridgeport, 1989. Jr. chemist Colgate-Palmolive Co., Berkeley, 1976-79; research chemist Stanford U., Palo Alto, Calif., 1979-81; applications chemist Chromatics, Sunnyvale, Calif., 1981-82, Interaction Chems., Mountain View, Calif., 1982-88; sr. rsch. chemist Bio-Rad Labs., Richmond, Calif., 1988—. Contbr. articles to profl. jours. Mem. AAAS, Inst. Food Technologists (profl.), Am. Chem. Soc., Assn. Ofcl. Analytical Chemists. Home: 313 Klamath Rd Milpitas CA 95035 Office: Bio-Rad Labs 1414 Harbour Way S Richmond CA 94804

WOO, SAVIO LAU-YUEN, bioengineering educator; b. Shanghai, Peoples Republic of China, June 3, 1942; s. Kwok CHong and Fung Sing (Yu) W.; m. Patricia Tak-kit Cheong, Sept. 6, 1969; children: Kirstin Wei-Chi, Jonathan I-Huei. BSME, Chico State U., 1965; MS, U. Wash., 1966, PhD, 1971. Research assoc. U. Wash., Seattle, 1968-70; asst. research prof. U. Calif.-San Diego, La Jolla, 1970-74, assoc. research prof., 1974-75, assoc. prof., 1975-80, prof. surgery and bioengring., 1980—; prin. investigator VA Med. Ctr., San Diego, 1972—; cons. bioengr. Childrens Hosp., San Diego, 1973-80; cons. med. implant co., 1978-85; vis. prof. biomechanics Kobe, Japan U., 1981-82; dir., chief exec. officer M&D Coutts Inst. for Joint Reconstrn. and Research, 1984—. Assoc. editor: Jour. Biochem. Engring., 1979-87, Jour. Biomechanics, 1978—, Jour. Orthopedic Research, 1983—; contbr. articles to profl. jours. Recipient Elizabeth Winston Lanier Kappa Delta Award, 1983, 85, award for excellence in basic sci. research Am. Orthopaedic Soc. Sports Medicine, 1983, 86, Wartenweiler Meml. Lectureship Internat. Soc. Biomechs., 1987; Citation award Am. Coll. Sports Medicine, 1988; Japan Soc. of Promotion of Sci. fellow, 1981; Research Career Devel. award NIH, 1977-82. Mem. ASME (sec., chmn. biomechanics com., chmn. honors com. bioengring. div., mem. exec. com., 1983-88, sec. 1985-86, chmn. 1986-87), Western Orthopaedic Assn., Biomed. Engring. Soc. (bd. dirs. 1984-86), Am. Acad. Orthopedic Surgeons, Orthopaedic Research Soc. (exec. com. 1983-88, chmn. program com. 1985-86, pres. 1986-87), Am. Soc. Biomechs. (pres. 1985-86, exec. com. 1977-80, 84-87), Internat. Soc. Fractures Repair (bd. dirs. 1984—, v.p. 1987—). Home: 4455 Heritage Glen Ln San Diego CA 92310 Office: U Calif San Diego Div Orthopaedic Surgery M-030 La Jolla CA 92093

WOO, VERNON YING-TSAI, lawyer, real estate developer; b. Honolulu, Aug. 7, 1942; s. William Shu-Bin and Hilda Woo; m. Arlene Gay Ischar, Feb. 14, 1971; children: Christopher Shu-Bin, Lia Gay. BA, U. Hawaii, 1964, MA, 1966; JD, Harvard U., 1969. Pres. Woo Kessner Duca & Maki, Honolulu, 1972-87; pvt. practice law Honolulu, 1987—; judge per diem Honolulu Dist. Ct., 1978-84. Bd. dirs. Boys and Girls Club of Honolulu, 1985—, pres. 1989; counsel Hawaii Med. Assn., 1988—. Mem. ABA, Hawaii Bar Assn., Honolulu Bd. Realtors, Waikiki Yacht Club (judge advocate 1987—), Pacific Club. Home: 2070 Kalawahine Pl Honolulu HI 96822 Office: 1019 Waimanu St Ste 205 Honolulu HI 96814

WOOD, CHARLES CRESSON, information systems security consultant, educator; b. Phila., Feb. 22, 1955; s. Charles Wistar and Margaret Davis (Ansley) W. B.S.E. with honors in Acctg., U. Pa., 1976, M.S.E. in Computer and Info. Sci., 1979, M.B.A. in Fin., 1979. C.P.A., Calif. Teaching fellow computer sci. U. Pa., Phila., 1976-79; system performance engr. Booz-Allen & Hamilton, Washington, 1976; systems designer Am. Mgmt. Systems, Washington, 1977; acct. Richard Eisner & Co., N.Y.C., 1978; security cons., analyst specializing in fin. info. systems, computer security and privacy, cryptography; cons. in computer systems security Stanford Research Inst., Menlo Park, Calif., 1979-83; sr. info. security cons. Bank of Am., San Francisco, 1984-85; mem. faculty Golden Gate U., 1984-88; founder, prin. cons. Info. Integrity Investments, 1984—. Contbg. editor: Computers and Security mag., 1983—. Author 2 books on computer security; co-author 2 computer security software packages; contbr. 45 tech. articles on info. security to profl. jours. Founder and former pres. Found. for Alternative Research; past bd. dirs. Mid-Peninsula Peace Ctr. EDP Auditors' Assn., World Future Soc., Info. Systems Security Assn. Quaker. Office: PO Box 1219 Sausalito CA 94966

WOOD, DANIEL CARTER, investment executive; b. Hartford, Conn., Mar. 2, 1955; s. Glenn Max and Eleanor Marie (Murray) W. BA in Polit. Sci., Tufts U., 1977; MBA in Fin., U. Conn., 1979. Cert. fin. planner. Investment exec. Paine Webber, San Diego, 1978-80; v.p. Wagenseller & Durst, San Diego, 1980-81; account exec. E.F. Hutton, San Diego, 1981-85; pres. The Sorrento Corp., San Diego, 1985—. Editor, pub. Sorrento Valley Area Bus. Directory, 1986—, (newsletter) Sorrento Valley Area Bus. News, 1987—. Mem. Sorrento Bus. Assn. (exec. bd. 1987—, pres.), LeTip Internat. (exec. bd. Sorrento Mesa chpt. 1988—). Office: The Sorrento Corp 5871 Oberlin Dr San Diego CA 92121

WOOD, DAVID JAMES, academic administrator, educator; b. Lima, Ohio, Mar. 21, 1948; s. Floyd Arley and Erma Vondale (Briggs) W.; m. Linda Louise Tropf, Aug. 18, 1973; children: Joann, Sara. BA, Ohio State U., 1970; MEd, St. Francis Coll., 1975; PhD, U. Toledo, 1978; postgrad., Bowling Green U., Ind. U., Ohio No. U., Wright State U. Tchr. Lima City Schs., 1970-75; supr. student tchrs., adminstrv. asst. to dean U. Toledo Coll. Edn., 1975-77; asst. dir. N.W. Ind. Spl. Edn. Coop., Crown Point, 1977-85; exec. dir. spl. edn. Aurora (Colo.) Pub. Schs., 1985—; asst. prof. edn. Bluffton (Ohio) Coll., 1975-77; adj. asst. prof. Purdue U., Hammond, Ind., 1977-80, Ind. U., Gary, 1979-85; edn. cons. The Cedars, 1979-82; activity therapy dir. N.W. Community Mental Health Clinic and St. Rita's Hosp. Psychiat. Wards, Lima, 1972-74. Coordinator coop. programs Lucas County Schs. and Med. Coll. Ohio, Toledo, 1976-77; mem. Ind. U. Field Experiences Adv. Com., 1978-83; mem. Ind. Task Force on Emotional Disturbance, 1980-88; mem. Ind. Dept. Edn. and Dept. Mental Health Com. task force on Interagy. Planning and Programming, 1983-88—; coordinator Lake County Tchr. Inst. on Tchr. Burnout, Merrillville, Ind., 1980; bd. dirs. Southlake Ctr. for Mental Health, 1978-82, Aurora Community Mental Health Ctr., 1986—, Leadership Aurora Coun., 1988—. Edn. Policy fellow, Washingotn, 1988-89. Mem. Am. Assn. Sch. Adminstrs., Assn. Supervision and Curriculum Devel., Nat. Orgn. Legal Problems in Edn., Coun. for Exceptional Children, Council for Adminstrn. of Spl. Edn., Council for Adminstrn. of Spl. Edn. in Colo. (pres. 1986), Phi Delta Kappa (editor 1985-86, pres. 1989—). Home: 13906 E Hamilton Dr Aurora CO 80014 Office: Aurora Pub Schs 11023 E 5th Ave Aurora CO 80010

WOOD, DAVID MILES, biochemist; b. Schenectady, N.Y., June 4, 1950; s. Robert Gordon and Mary Louise (Chedzoy) W. BS, Cornell U., 1972; PhD, St. Louis U., 1980. Postdoctoral fellow Population Coun. Ctr. for Biomed. Rsch., N.Y.C., 1980-82; postdoctoral fellow dept. human genetics and devel. Coll. Physicians and Surgeons, Columbia U., 1982-83; rsch. asst. Cardiovascular Rsch. Inst. Calif., San Francisco, 1983; postdoctoral fellow, immunologist Lab. Immunogenetics and Transplantation, San Francisco, 1984-86; rsch. scientist dept. immunology XOMA Corp., Berkeley, Calif., 1987—; mem. faculty clin. methods in flow cytometry Hershey Med. Ctr., Pa. State U., HErshey, 1986. Contbr. articles to profl. jours. Named Eagle Scout BoyScouts Am., Scotia, N.Y., 1962-68. Mem. Audubon Soc., Am. Soc. for Microbiology, AAAS, Defenders of Wildlife, Nature Conservancy, Golden Gate Raptor Observatory, Sierra Club. Home: 76 Woodside Dr San Anselmo CA 94960 Office: XOMA Corp 2910 7th St Berkeley CA 94710

WOOD, DENNIS PATRICK, clinical psychologist, educator; b. Oakland, Calif., Aug. 5, 1949; s. Donald James and Helen Winfred (Reimann) W.; m. Joan Anne Treinen, Feb. 14, 1971; children—Ross, Trevor, Megan. B.A., St. Mary's Coll., Moraga, Calif., 1971; M.A. (Univ. scholar 1972-73), U. Nebr., 1973; Ph.D., Calif. Sch. Profl. Psychology, 1976. Lic. psychologist, Nev., Calif. Psychology intern In-Between Youth Ctr., San Diego, 1973-74, Golden State Community Mental Health Ctr. (now Hope Community Mental Health Ctr.), Lakeview Terrace, Calif., 1974-75, Alcohol Rehab. Ctr., Naval Sta., San Diego; postdoctoral intern dept. psychiatry Balboa Navy Hosp., San Diego, 1976-77; staff psychologist dept. psychiatry, 1976-80; co-dir. La Jolla (Calif.) Profl. Workshops, 1977-84; pvt. practice clin. and health psychology, San Diego and Las Vegas, Nev., 1980—; clin. instr. Sch. Medicine, U. Calif.-San Diego, 1979—; cons. to bus. and med. facilities. Vice pres. Donald James Wood Found., Oakland, Calif., 1971-77, trustee, 1977—. Served to lt. comdr. USNR, 1976—. Recipient Outstanding Service cert. Commandant of 11th Naval Dist., 1975. Mem. Am. Psychol. Assn., Med. Psychology Network (program coordinator Western U.S.), Calif. Psychology Assn., Navy League, Res. Officers Assn., Naval Res. Assn., Am. Soc. Clin. Hypnosis. Democrat. Roman Catholic. Co-author: Clinical Hypnosis Primer, 1984, Updated & Expanded, 1988. Contbr. articles on psychology, hypnosis, disaster interventions and alcoholism to profl. jours. Office: 2225 E Flamingo #200 Las Vegas NV 89119 also: 550 Washington St #215 San Diego CA 92103

WOOD, DONALD FRANK, transportation educator, consultant; b. Waukesha, Wis., Feb. 22, 1935; s. Frank Blaine and Uilah (Mathson) W.; m. Doreen Johnson, July 5, 1968; children: Frank, Tamara. BA, U. Wis., 1957, MA, 1958; PhD, Harvard U., 1970. Transp. planner State of Wis., Madison, 1960-70; prof. San Francisco State U., 1970—. Author: El Camino, 1982, Keeping on Trucking, 1989; author: (with others) Contemporary Physical Distribution, 1986, Contemporary Transportation, 1989, Fire Apparatus of the West, 1989. 2d lt. U.S. Army, 1958. Mem. Coun. of Logistics Mgmt. (chpt. pres. 1975-76), Transp. Rsch. Forum (chpt. pres. 1974), Am. Truck Hist. Soc. Presbyterian. Home: 321 Riviera Cir Larkspur CA 94939 Office: San Francisco State Sch Bus San Francisco CA 94132

WOOD, DONALD JAMES, newspaper publishing executive, educator, author; b. Modesto, Calif., Apr. 7, 1922; s. Ezra Benjamin and Maude Emma (Gardenhire) W.; m. Helen Winifred Reimann, Oct. 26, 1946; children: James, Dennis, Kathleen, Matthew. BS in Econs., St. Mary's Coll. of Calif., Moraga, 1946; MBA, Armstrong U., 1954; MJ, U. Calif., Berkeley, 1956; MA in Theology, Grad. Theol. Union, 1983; PhD in Edn., Walden U., 1972. Circulation supr. The Oakland (Calif.) Tribune, 1941-52; asst. to publ. San Francisco Call-Bulletin, San Francisco, 1952-59; mgr. circulation and promotion Berkeley Gazette, 1959-65; gen. mgr. Voice, Oakland, 1965—; pres. Am Cal Printing and Mailing Co., 1972—; prof. Oakland City Coll., 1956-62, Armstrong Coll., Berkeley, 1956-77; adj. prof. Dominican Sch. Philosophy and Theology, 1984; founder, cons. Wood Found., 1972. Author: Newspaper Circulation Management; William Randolph Hearst-His First Years in Journalism; Needed - A Media Doctor; co-author (with Helen Winifred Wood) Men: Ideas, Issues (4 vols.); contbr. articles to newspapers and mags. Served with USN, 1943-44. Recipient Circulation Promotion award Editor and Publ., 1956, Newspaper Publicity award Calif. Circulation Mgrs. Assn., 1964, Sales Promotion award Internat. Circulation Mgrs. Assn., 1965, Advt. award Cath. Press Assn., 1972. Democrat. Roman Catholic.

WOOD, FERGUS JAMES, geophysicist, consultant; b. London, Ont., Can., May 13, 1917; came to U.S., 1924, naturalized, 1932; s. Louis Aubrey and Dora Isabel (Elson) W.; student U. Oreg., 1934-36; AB, U. Calif., Berkeley, 1938, postgrad., 1938-39; postgrad. U. Chgo., 1939-40, U. Mich., 1940-42, Calif. Inst. Tech., 1946; m. Doris M. Hack, Sept. 14, 1946; children: Kathryn Celeste Wood Madden, Bonnie Patricia Wood Ward. Teaching asst. U. Mich., 1940-42; instr. in physics and astronomy Pasadena City Coll., 1946-48, John Muir Coll., 1948-49; asst. prof. physics U. Md., 1949-50; assoc. physicist Johns Hopkins U. Applied Physics Lab., 1950-55; sci. editor Ency. Americana, N.Y.C., 1955-60; aero. and space rsch. scientist, sci. asst. to dir. Office Space Flight Programs, Hdqrs., NASA, Washington, 1960-61; program dir. fgn. sci. info. NSF, Washington, 1961-62; phys. scientist, chief sci. and tech. info. staff U.S. Coast and Geodetic Survey (now Nat. Ocean Service), Rockville, Md., 1962-66, phys. scientist Office of Dir., 1967-73, rsch. assoc. Office of Dir., 1973-77; cons. tidal dynamics, Bonita, Calif., 1978—. Capt. USAAF, 1942-46. Recipient Spl. Achievement award Dept. Commerce, NOAA, 1970, 74, 76, 77. Mem. Sigma Pi Sigma, Pi Mu Epsilon, Delta Phi Alpha. Democrat. Presbyterian. Author: The Strategic Role of Perigean Spring Tides in Nautical History and North American Coastal Flooding, 1635-1976, 1978; Tidal Dynamics; Coastal Flooding and Cycles of Gravitational Force, 1986; contbr. numerous articles to encys., reference sources, profl. jours.; writer, tech. dir. documentary film: Pathfinders from the Stars, 1967; editor-in-chief: The Prince William Sound, Alaska, Earthquake of 1964 and Aftershocks, vols. 1-2A and sci. coordinator vols. 2B, 2C and 3, 1966-69. Home: 3103 Casa Bonita Dr Bonita CA 92002

WOOD, FLOYD WILLIAM, insurance company executive; b. Inglewood, Calif., Aug. 6, 1929; s. William Henry Harrison and Evelyn Jean (Robson) W.; m. Barbara Ann Yates, Apr. 7, 1951; children: Donna Joyce Wood Bongirno, Karen Sue Wood Fuller, Gerald Patrick, John Barry. Student, El Camino Coll., 1947-48, 75. Cert. comml. agt.; lic. in securities. Dept. head J.C. Penney Co., Inglewood and L.A., 1947-53; agt., staff mgr. Nat. Life Ins. Co., Inglewood, 1953-61; sr. account agt. Allstate Ins. Co., L.A., 1961--. Elder, mem. sch. bd., fin. sec. Lockhaven Christian Ch., Inglewood, 1960-80; active various charities, L.A., 1983--. Mem. Lax C. of C. (bd. dirs. 1970-81, 87--). Republican. Office: Allstate Ins Co 8930 S Sepulveda Blvd Ste 101 Los Angeles CA 90045

WOOD, GARY LEE, repair service specialist; b. Orange, Calif., May 12, 1944; s. Robert Melvin and Pearl (Holding) W.; divorced; 1 child, Jada Renee. Student, U. Wash., Long Beach City Coll., Foley-Belsaw Inst., Kansas City, 1988. Asst. engr. KBM Prodn., Seattle, 1965-66; engr. aid Aircraft Manufacturing, Burbank, Calif., 1966-67; owner Small Engine Repair Svcs., San Luis Obispo, Calif., 1989—. Recipient Am. Police Hall of Fame citation, 1986. Mem. Am. Fedn. of Police. Republican. Presbyterian. Home and Office: Complete Small Engine Repair Svc 1730 Santa Rosa San Luis Obispo CA 93401

WOOD, GERALD LLOYD, management consultant, industrial designer; b. Seminole, Okla., Feb. 6, 1938; s. Delmer Lloyd and Neva Irene (Dillon) W.; m. Linda Lee Taylor, May 9, 1964; children: David Taylor, Brian Bennett, Jonathan Britton. BFA, U. Okla., 1960, MPA, 1971; postgrad., U. Ariz., 1988—. Designer Hallmark Cards Inc., Kansas City, Mo., 1960-64, sr. package designer, 1964-67, mdse. display mgr., 1967-73, adminstrv. asst. to pres. retail plans and mgmt., 1973-74; fixture control, budget mgr. Hallmark Cards Inc., Kansas City, 1974-75, operational analysis mgr., 1975-77, nat. store ops. mgr., 1977-79, cons., 1979—; pres., chief exec. officer G.L.W., Inc., Tucson, 1979—; assoc. faculty Pima Community Coll., Tucson, 1988—, applied design adv. com., 1987-88; rsch. cons. U. Ariz., Tucson, 1989—. Design engr. Card Cartridge System, 1985; indsl. engr. Disposable Display Rack, 1968, Mdse. Display Unit, 1970; package designer Mdse. Container, 1966; author operating manuals. V.p. Dist. 229 Sch. Bd., Southeast Johnson County, Kans., 1977-79; alt. del. Rep. Nat. Conv., Kansas City, 1976, precinct committeeman, Aubrey Twp., Kans., 1974; gen. chmn. Eleven County Kaw-Rama Scout Show, Kansas City, 1974; founder Heart of Am.

Council Boy Scouts Am., 1975; gen. chmn. United Way Campaign, 1969. With USNG, 1955-63. Recipient Outstanding Merchandising Achievemnt awards (4) Point-Of-Purchse an dAdvt. Inst., 1968, 70, 72, Gold award Fibre Box Assn., 1974, Excellence award Kansas City Art Dirs. Club, 1965. Mem. Indsl. Designers Soc. Am., Higher Edn. Student Orgn. (v.p. 1989—), Delta Phi Delta. Methodist. Home and Office: GLW Inc 5252 E Hawthorne Pl Tucson AZ 85711

WOOD, GLADYS BLANCHE, retired educator and journalist; b. Sanborn, N.D., Aug. 12, 1921; d. Charles Kershaw and Mina Blanche (Kee) Crowther; m. Newell Edwin Wood, June 13, 1943; children: Terry N., Lani, Brian R., Kevin C. BA in Journalism, U. Minn., 1943; MS in Mass Communication, San Jose State U., 1972. Cert. secondary tchr., Calif. Reporter St. Paul Pioneer-Dispatch, 1943-45; editor J.C. Penney Co., N.Y.C., 1945-46; tchr. English and journalism Willow Glen High Sch., San Jose, Calif., 1968-87; freelance writer, photographer, 1947—; cons. in field. Named Secondary Journalism Tchr. of Yr. Calif. Newpaper Pubs. Assn., 1977. Mem. AAUW, Soc. Profl. Journalists, Journalism Edn. Assn., Calif. Tchrs. English, Calif. Ret. Tchrs. Assn., Women in Communications, Montalvo Assn., LWV, Delta Kappa Gamma. Republican. Methodist. Home: 14161 Douglass Ln Saratoga CA 95070

WOOD, HARRY GEORGE, packaging engineering and electrostatic discharge control consultant; b. Orchard Park, N.Y., Jan. 22, 1915; s. William A. and Marie E. (Schmidt) W.; m. Ruth Farber, Oct. 20, 1939; children—Keith F., Eugene F. B.S. in Edn., SUNY-Buffalo, 1936. Planning supr. Morrison Steel Products, Buffalo, 1944-51; sr. methods engr., materials handling supr. Schlage Lock Co., San Francisco, 1953-57; prodn. mgr. M. Greenberg's Sons Foundry & Machine Shop, San Francisco, 1957-58; packaging mgr. Hewlett-Packard Co., Santa Clara, Calif., 1959-83, established electrostatic discharge control program, 1981-83; cons. on packaging engring. and electrostatic discharge. H.G. Wood & Assocs., Palo Alto, 1983—; instr. factory planning and plant layout Foothill Jr. Coll., Los Altos, 1959-60; mem. nat. packaging industry adv. council U. Calif.-Davis, 1971-73; chmn. Internat. Air Cargo Forum, 1968-71; designed and built Ruth Wood Nursery Sch., 1962, ptnr. and bus. mgr., 1962—. Contbr. articles to profl. jours. Patentee in field. Recipient Grayson Lynn award for package design Lockheed Missile and Space Div., 1964, Ann. Achievement award Nat. Inst. Packaging Handling and Logistics Engrs., 1974. Fellow Soc. Packaging and Handling Engrs. (hon. life mem., cert. profl. in packaging, 5 Nat. Design awards, exec. v.p., program chmn. Golden Gate chpt. 1955, 63, pres. chpt. of yr. 1964-65, chmn. bd. dirs. 1966), Internat. Materials Mgmt. Soc. (nat. bd. dirs. 1956-57, pres. No. Calif. chpt. 1956-57); mem. Internat. Platform Assn. Home and Office: 849 Mesa Ave Palo Alto CA 94306

WOOD, HELEN LUCILLE, civic volunteer; b. Cook, Nebr., July 22, 1912; d. Lewis and Lucy Ann (Ellam) Richards; m. Harry Harold Richards Himes, June 1931 (div. 1940); m. Leroy Eugene Richards Wood, Nov. 10, 1941; children: Edwin Kirk, Donald David (dec.). Sec. Pacific Gas & Electric Co., Oakdale, Calif., 1930-35; with clerical div. Real Estate & Ins., Oakdale, 1937-47; soc. editor Oakdale Leader, 1960-61; planning commn. mem. City of Oakdale, 1973-82, city council mem., 1982-86. Hon. Chmn. Stanislaus County Cerebral Palsy Telethon, Modesto, Calif., 1988; mem. Stanislaus County Solid Waste Com., Modesto, 1982-86; mem. Solid Waste Adv. Bd. State of Calif.; appointee planning commn. Stanislaus County, Calif., 1989—. Mem. Oakdale Women's Club, Oakdale C. of C. (dir. 1987-89), Oakdale Town Criers-Toastmasters. Republican. Methodist. Home: 532 W "F" St Oakdale CA 95361

WOOD, JOHN DENISON, utility company executive; b. Calgary, Alta., Can., Sept. 28, 1931; s. Ernest William and Ellen Gartshore (Pender) W.; m. Christena Isabel; 1 dau., Donna M. BSCE, U. B.C., 1953; MSCE, Stanford U., 1954, PhDCE and Engring. Mechs., 1956. Research asst. in civil engring. and engring. mechs. Stanford U., Palo Alto, Calif., 1953-56; assoc. mgr. dynamics dept. Engring. Mechs. Lab. Space Tech. Labs., Inc., Redondo Beach, Calif., 1956-63; pres., dir. Mechs. Research, Inc., El Segundo, Calif., 1963-66; sr. v.p. engring. and research ATCO Ind., Ltd., Calgary, Alta., 1966-68, sr. v.p. eastern region, 1968-75, sr. v.p. planning, 1975-77; pres., chief exec. officer ATCO Industries N.A., Ltd., Calgary, Alta., 1977-82, ATCOR Resources Ltd., Calgary, 1982-84; pres., chief operating officer Can. Utilities, Ltd., Edmonton, Alta., 1984-88, pres., chief exec. officer, 1988—, also bd. dirs.; bd. dirs. ATCO Ltd., Can. Utilities, Ltd., ATCOR Ltd., ATCO Enterprises Ltd., Frontec Logistics Corp., BioTechnica Internat., Inc., Vencap Equities Alta. Ltd.; chmn. bd., chief exec. officer Can. Western Nat. Gas Co. Ltd., Northwestern Utilities Ltd., Alta. Power Ltd., Northland Utilities Enterprises Ltd. Co-author: Ballistic Missile and Space Vehicle Systems, 1961. Mem. pres.'s club adv. com. U Alta; mem. Jr. Achievement of Can. Athlone fellow. Mem. Engring. Inst. of Can., Sci. Research Soc. Am., Assn. Profl. Engrs. Alta., Sigma Xi, Tau Beta Pi. Baptist. Clubs: Glencoe, Earl Grey, Calgary Petroleum, Mayfair Golf and Country. Office: Can Utilities Ltd, 10035 105th St, Edmonton, AB Canada T5J 2V6 also: Can Western Natural Gas Co Ltd, 909-11 Ave S W, Calgary, AB Canada T2R 1L8

WOOD, LARRY (MARY LAIRD), journalist, author, university educator, public relations executive; b. Sandpoint, Idaho; d. Edward Hayes and Alice (McNeel) Small; children: Mary, Marcia, Barry. BA magna cum laude, U. Wash., 1938, MA with highest honors, 1940; postgrad., Stanford U., 1941-42, U. Calif., Berkeley, 1946-47; cert. in photography, U. Calif., Berkeley, 1971; postgrad. journalism, U. Wis., 1971-72, U. Minn., 1971-72, U. Ga., 1972-73; postgrad. in art, architecture and marine biology, U. Calif., Santa Cruz, 1974-76, Stanford Hopkins Marine Sta., Santa Cruz, 1977-80. Feature writer and columnist 1939—; prof. pub. relations, journalism and investigative reporting, San Diego State U., 1974, 75; disting. vis. prof. journalism San Jose State U., 1976; assoc. prof. journalism Calif. State U., Hayward, 1978; prof. sci. and environ. journalism U. Calif. Berkeley Extension grad. div., 1979—; press del. Am. Geophysical Union Internat. Conf., 1987, 88, 89, Nat. Conf. for Advancement of Sci., 1989; expert witness on edn., affirmative action, pub. rels., journalism and copyright. Contbr. over 5,000 articles on real estate, architecture, edn., oceanography, science, environ., health, medicine, sports, recreation, bus. and travel for newspapers, nat. mags., popular sci. mags., nat. and internat. newspaper syndicates, inflight mags., city mags., travel and architecture mags. including Oakland Tribune, Seattle Times, San Francisco Chronicle, Parade, San Jose Mercury News, Christian Sci. Monitor, MonitoRadio, Sports Illus., Mechanix Illus., Popular Mechanics, Parents, House Beautiful, Oceans, Sea Frontiers, PSA Mag., AAA Westways, AAA Motorland, Hawaiian Airlines in Paradise, Linguapress, Travel & Leisure, Family Handyman, Chevron USA, others. Significant works include home and garden columnist and editor, 5-part series Pacific Coast Ports, 5-part series Railroads of the West, San Francisco Cultural Scene, Endangered Species, Megamouth New Species of Shark, Columbia Alaska's Receding Glacier (selected as top sci. article in U.S., 1987), Calif. Underwater Parks, Ebey's Landing Nat. Hist. Preserve, Los Angeles Youth Gangs, Hist. Carousels; author: Wonderful U.S.A.: A State-by-state Guide to Its Natural Resources, 1989; co-author over 20 books including: McGraw-Hill English for Social Living, 1944, Fawcett Boating Books, 1956-66, Fodor's San Francisco, Fodor's California, 1989, Charles Merrill Focus on Life Science, Focus on Physical Science, 1983, 87; 8 works selected for use by Wolters-Nordoff-Longman English Language Texts, 1988; reviewer for Charles Merrill texts, 1983-84; book reviewer for Professional Communicator, 1987—; selected writings in permanent collections Oakland Pub. Libr., U. Wash. Main Libr. Nat. chmn. travel writing contest for U.S. univ. journalism students Assn. for Edn. in Journalism/Soc. Am. Travel Writers, 1979-83; judge writing contest for Nat. Assn. Real Estate Editors, 1982—. Numerous awards, honors, citations, speaking engagements including induction into Broadway Hall of Fame U. Wash., Seattle, 1984, citations for environ. writing from Nat. Park Service, U.S. Forest Service, Bur. Land Mgmt., Oakland Mus. Assn., Oakland C. of C.; co-recipient Nat. Headliner award for Best Sunday Newspaper Mag.; co-recipient citation Oakland Mus. for archtl. features, 1983. Mem. Pub. Relations Soc. Am. (charter mem. travel, tourism and edn. div.), Nat. Sch. Pub. Relations Assn., Environ. Cons. N.Am., Assn. Edn. in Journalism (exec. bd. nat. mag. div. 1978, panel chmn. 1979, 80), Women in Communications (nat. bd. officer 1975-77), Soc. Profl. Journalists (nat. bd. for hist. sites 1980—), Nat. Press Photographers Assn., Bay Area Advt. and Mktg. Assn., Nat. Assn. Sci. Writers, Calif. Writers Club (officer 1967, 72), Am. Assn. Med. Writers, Internat. Assn. Bus. Communicators, Am. Film Inst., Am. Heritage Found. (citation 1986, 87, 88), Soc. Am. Travel Writers, Internat. Oceanographic Found., Oceanic Soc., Calif. Acad. Environ. News Writers, Seattle Advd Sales Club (former officer), Seattle Jr. Advt. Club (charter), U. Wash. Alumni (life, charter mem. ocean scis. alumni, Disting. Alumni 1987), U. Calif., Berkeley Alumni (life), Stanford Alumni (life), Mortar Board Alumnae Assn., Phi Beta Kappa, Theta Sigma Phi. Home: 6161 Castle Dr Oakland CA 94611

WOOD, LINDA MAY, librarian; b. Fort Dodge, Iowa, Nov. 6, 1942; d. John Albert and Beth Ida (Riggs) Wiley; m. C. James Wood, Sept. 15, 1964 (div. 1984). BA, Portland State U., 1964; MLibrarianship, U. Wash., 1965. Reference librarian Library Assn. Portland (Oreg.), 1965-67, br. librarian, 1967-72, adminstrv. asst. to the librarian, 1972-73, asst. librarian, 1973-77; asst. city librarian L.A. Pub. Library, 1977-80; library dir. Riverside (Calif.) City and County Pub. Library, 1980—. Chmn. bd. dirs. Inland Library System, 1983-84; League of Calif. Cities Community Svcs. Com., 1985-89. Mem. AAUW, ALA, Pub. Library Assn., Library Adminstrn. and Mgmt. Assn., Calif. Library Assn. (pres. 1985), Calif. County Librarians Assn., LWV, OCLC Users Coun. Democrat. Office: Riverside City & County Pub Libr 3851 7th St PO Box 468 Riverside CA 92502-0468 *

WOOD, MICHAEL NEALL, surgeon; b. Temple, Tex., Feb. 15, 1956; s. Harold Lee and Betty Jane (Bottomley) W.; m. Sandra jean Quinn, Aug. 6, 1988. BA in Chemistry, Southern Coll., 1977; Dr.med., Loma Linda U., 1981. Diplomate Am. Bd. Surgery. Resident Med. Ctr. Loma Linda (Calif.) U., 1981-86, cardiothoracic resident Med. Ctr., 1986—, cardiothoracic surgeon Med. Ctr., 1989—, instr. surgery Med. Sch., 1985—. Mem. Calif. Med. Assn., Am. Coll. Cardiology, Am. Coll. Chest Physicians. Republican. Office: Loma Linda U Med Ctr Surgery Dept 11234 Anderson St Loma Linda CA 92354

WOOD, ROBERT WARREN, lawyer; b. Des Moines, July 5, 1955; s. Merle Warren and Cecily Ann (Sherk) W.; m. Beatrice Wood, Aug. 4, 1979; 1 child, Bryce Mercedes. Student, U. Sheffield, Eng., 1975-76; AB, Humboldt State U., 1976; JD, U. Chgo., 1979. Bar: Ariz. 1979, Calif. 1980, U.S. Tax Ct. 1980, N.Y. 1989. Assoc. Jennings, Strouss, Phoenix, 1979-80, McCutchen, Doyle, San Francisco, 1980-82, Broad, Khourie, San Francisco, 1982-85; assoc. Steefel, Levitt & Weiss, San Francisco, 1985-87, ptnr., 1987—; instr. in law U. Calif. San Francisco, 1981-82. Author: Taxation of Corporate Liquidations: A Complete Planning Guide, 1987, The Executive's Complete Guide to Business Taxes, 1989; author: (with others) California Closely Held Corporations: Tax Planning and Practice Guide, 1987; mem. editorial bd. Corporate Taxation, Taxation for Lawyers, Jour. Real Estate Taxation, Jour. Bank Taxation, Journal of Taxation of S Corporations, S Corporations: The Journal of Tax, Legal and Business Strategies; contbr. BusinessWeek newsletter; contbr. articles to profl. jours. Mem. Calif. Bd. Legal Specialization (cert. specialist taxation), Internat. Platform Assn., Bohemian Club. Republican. Office: Steefel Levitt & Weiss One Embarcadero Ctr 29th Fl San Francisco CA 94111

WOOD, SUSAN MARIE, visual artist; b. Monterey, Calif., Dec. 29, 1962; d. Rex Stewart and Naomi (Matsuda) W. BA in Art, U. Calif., Santa Cruz, 1985. Freelance artist, graphic and visual arts San Francisco Bay Area, 1977—; engring. svcs. coord. Daisy Systems Corp., Mountain View, Calif., 1986—. Mem. NAFE. Office: 10330 N Foothill Blvd #A22 Cupertino CA 95014

WOOD, WILLIS BOWNE, JR., utility holding company executive; b. Kansas City, Mo., Sept. 15, 1934; s. Willis Bowne Sr. and Mina (Henderson) W.; m. Dixie Gravel, Aug. 31, 1955; children: Bradley, William, Josh. BS in Petroleum Engring., U. Tulsa, 1957; grad. advanced mgmt. program, Harvard U., 1983. Various positions So. Calif. Gas Co., Los Angeles, 1960-74, v.p. then sr. v.p., 1975-80, exec. v.p., 1983-84; pres., chief exec. officer Pacific Lighting Gas Supply Co., Los Angeles, 1981-83, exec. v.p., 1984—. Trustee Harvey Mudd Coll., Claremont, Calif., Calif. Med. Ctr., Los Angeles, S.W. Mus. Los Angeles. Mem. Soc. Petroleum Engrs., Am. Gas Assn., Pacific Coast Gas Assn., Pacific Energy Assn. Republican. Presbyterian. Clubs: Center (Orange County); L.A., City Club on Bunker Hill. Office: Pacific Enterprises 810 S Grand Ave Los Angeles CA 90017

WOODALL, PHILLIP SCOTT, educator, therapist; b. Lexington, Ky., July 26, 1947; s. James William and Anna Sue (Scott) W.; m. JoAnne Schabacker, Mar. 20, 1971; children: Kristin Ann, Erin Amanda. BS, Ea. Ky. U., 1969; MA, U. Ky., 1972. Marriage and family therapist The Luth. Ch. Mo. Synod, Santa Rosa, Calif., 1976-80; lay pastor Peace Luth. Ch., Flagstaff, Ariz., 1980-83; counselor Flagstaff Pub. Schs., 1980—; adminstrv. asst. Flagstaff Pub. Schs., Flagstaff, 1987—; therapist Ariz. Prfl. Counseling, Flagstaff, 1986—; project dir. Flagstaff Pub. Schs., 1987—. Ct. appointed spl. child advocate Coconino County Superior Ct., 1988; moderator Flagstaff Town Hall, 1988; bd. dirs. Flagstaff Big Bros., 1976; Ariz. Supreme Ct. Rev. Bd., Phoenix, 1988, Family Life Line, Parents Anonymous, Flagtaff, 1988. Mem. Ariz. Sch. Administrs., Phi Delta Kappa. Republican. Lodge: Kiwanis (bd. dirs. 1988). Home: 2330 N Kramer St Flagstaff AZ 86001

WOODARD, ALVA ABE, business consultant; b. Roy, N.Mex., June 28, 1928; s. Joseph Benjamin and Emma Lorraine (Watkins) W.; m. Esther Josepha Kaufmann, Apr. 5, 1947; children: Nannette, Gregory, Loreen, Arne, Mark, Kevin, Steven, Curtis, Marlee, Julie, Michelle. Student, Kinman Bus. U., 1948-49, Whitworth Coll., 1956, Wash. State U., 1953-54. Sec.-treas., dir. Green Top Dairy Farms, Inc., Clarkston, Wash., 1948-52; v.p., treas., sec., dir. ASC Industries, Inc., Spokane, Wash., 1953-75; dir. Guenther Irrigation, Inc., Pasco, Wash., 1966-71; mng. dir. Irrigation Rental, Inc., Pasco, 1968-75, Rain Chief Irrigation Co., Grand Island, Nebr., 1968-75; sec., dir. Keeling Supply Co., Little Rock, 1969-72; pres., dir. Renters, Inc., Salt Lake City, 1971-75, Woodard Western Corp., Spokane, 1976-86, Woodard Industries, Inc., Auburn, Wash., 1987—; cons., Woodard Assocs., Spokane, 1985—. Newman Lake (Wash.) Rep. precinct committeeman, 1964-80; Spokane County del. Wash. Rep. Conv., 1968-80. Mem. Adminstrv. Mgmt. Soc. (bd. dirs. 1966-68), Optimists. Home: E 1714 Rockwell St Spokane WA 99207

WOODARD, CLINTON EARL (BUD WOODARD), construction executive; b. Kadaka, S.D., Aug. 6, 1918; s. Hiram Jay and Iona I. (Kelling) W.; m. Catherine Caye Arnold, Apr. 22, 1940; children: Arnold Jon, Frederick Henry, Catherine Joy. Student, Seattle Coll., 1947-48; student, Anchorage Community Coll., Anchorage, Alaska, 1975-76. Prin. C.E. Woodard Constrn. Co., Wash., Alaska, 1952-78; pres. Woodard Constrn.Co., Alaska, 1978--. Bd. dirs. Wallingford Boys Club, Seattle, 1956-57. With USCG, 1938-47. Named Boss of the Year by Anchorage chpt. Nat. Assn. Women in Constrn., 1975. Mem. Associated Gen. Contractors of Am. (bd. dirs. Alaska chpt.), Airplane Owners and Pilots Assn., Am. Arbitration Assn., Izaak Walton League, Am. Legion, Nat. Rifle Assn., Elks. Home: 1381 Hillcrest Dr #301 Anchorage AK 99503 Office: Woodard Constrn Co 511 W 54th Anchorage AK 99518

WOODARD, DOROTHY MARIE, insurance broker; b. Houston, Feb. 7, 1932; d. Gerald Edgar and Bessie Katherine (Crain) Floeck; student N.Mex. State U., 1950; m. Jack W. Woodard; June 19, 1950 (dec.); m. Norman W. Libby, July 19, 1982. Partner, Western Oil Co., Tucumcari, N.Mex., 1950—; owner, mgr. Woodard & Co., Las Cruces, N.Mex., 1959-67; agt., dist. mgr. United Nations Ins. Co., Denver, 1968-74; agt. Western Nat. Life Ins. Co., Amarillo, Tex., 1976—. Exec. dir. Tucumcari Indsl. Commn., 1979—; dir. Bravo Dome Study Com., 1979—; owner Libby Cattle Co., Libby Ranch Co.; regional bd. dirs. N.Mex., Eastern Plains Council Govts., 1979—. Mem. Tucumcari C. of C. Club: Mesa Country. Home: PO Box 823 Tucumcari NM 88401

WOODARD, DUANE, attorney general of Colorado; b. Kansas City, Mo., Jan. 12, 1938; s. Duane and Maxine (Reed) W.; m. Thelma Hanser, Apr. 11, 1964; children—Elizabeth, Mary. B.A., U. Wyo., 1963; J.D., U. Okla., 1967. Bar: Okla. 1967, Colo. 1968, U.S. Dist. Ct. Colo. 1968, U.S. Supreme Ct. 1972, U.S. Ct. Appeals (10th cir.) 1986. Practice law Fort Collins, Colo., 1967—, dep. dist. atty., 1970-72; mem. Colo. State Senate Denver, 1977-80; pub. utility commr. State of Colo., 1980-82, atty. gen., 1982—. Mem. Fort Collins Planning and Zoning Commn., 1974-76. Lodge: Rotary. Home: 1749 Grape St Denver CO 80220 Office: Office of Colo Atty Gen 1525 Sherman St Denver CO 80203 *

WOODARD, LARRY L., federal bureau executive; b. Lebanon, Oreg., Apr. 16, 1936; s. Hugh Frank and Ima Ellen (Bilyeu) W.; m. Bette Jeanette Brown, Aug. 10, 1956; children: Perry, Craig, Stacy. BS in Forestry, Oreg. State U., 1957. Forester Bur. of Land Mgmt., Oreg., 1957-69, Washington, 1969-72; dist. mgr. Bur. of Land Mgmt., Coeur d'Alene, Idaho, 1972-76; assoc. state dir. Bur. of Land Mgmt., Boise, Idaho, 1976-78, Santa Fe, 1978-82, Boise, 1982-86; state dir. Bur. of Land Mgmt., Santa Fe, 1987—. Author: A to Z, The Biography of Arthur Zimmerman, 1988. Bd. dirs. Boise Bible Coll., 1977—; trustee N.Mex. Nature Conservancy, 1987—. Republican. Home: 2172 Candelero St Santa Fe NM 87505 Office: Bur of Land Mgmt PO Box 1449 Santa Fe NM 87501

WOODHALL, WILLIAM FULTON, minister, religious organization administrator; b. Peoria, Ill., Jan. 27, 1944; s. William Rozell and Elsie Lucille (Fulton) W.; m. Gayle Marie Phillips, May 11, 1964; children: Heather Suzanne Dominguez, Matthew Charles, Blake Jarrod. BA, Sacramento Bapt. Coll., 1972; ThB, Sacramento Bapt. Theol. Sem., 1973, MA, 1973, MDiv, 1977, ThM, 1979; BA, Bapt. Christian Coll., 1984; PhD, Bapt. Christian U., 1981, ThD, 1983; DD (hon.), Calif. Christian Coll., 1973; LLD (hon.), John Wesley Coll., 1980. Lic. minister, 1968; ordained to ministry, 1970. Pastor E. Belmont Community Bible Ch., Fresno, Calif., 1970-71, Sierra Hills Bapt. Ch., Auberry, Calif., 1972-74; sr. pastor Fountain Ave. Bapt. Ch., Hollywood, Calif., 1975-76, Mountain View Presbyn., Grand Terrace, Calif., 1976-85; pvt. practice as ch. cons. Eugene, Oreg., 1986; pres. Bible Analysis Cons., Inc., Grand Terrace, 1987—; vis. lectr. Calif. Christian Coll., Fresno, 1973-74; prof. Bible Thomas Road Bible Inst., Fresno, 1973-74; chaplain, reserve officer Los Angeles Police Dept. Hollywood div., 1975-76; prof. hermeneutics San Bernardino (Calif.) Bible Coll., 1979. Mem. Pacific Presbytery-Presbyn. Ch. Am. (stated clk. 1977-82), Fellowship Christian Peace Officers (assoc.), Christian Edn. Fellowship (hon.), Christian Legal Soc. Ctr. Law and Religious Studies (assoc.). Republican. Home: 12168 Mount Vernon Ave #67 Grand Terrace CA 92324 Office: Bible Analysis Cons Inc 22797 Barton Rd Ste 171 Grand Terrace CA 92324-5207

WOODHOUSE, FRED NYE, sporting goods distribution executive; b. Buffalo, Apr. 1, 1943; s. Fred Nye and Esther E. (Putt) W.; m. Linda Lee Ryon, Sept. 18, 1966; children: Fred Nye, Tara Lynn. BS, U. Nebr., 1966. Supr. A.C. Neilsen Co., Lincoln, Nebr., 1968-72, Neodata Inc., Boulder, Colo., 1972-73; supr. dealer sales Head Sports, Inc., Boulder, 1973-74, warehouse supr., 1974-76, mgr. prodn. control, 1976-80, mgr. prodn. control/purchasing, 1980-84, materials mgr., 1984-88, dir. distbn., 1988—; instr. AT&T Denver Wks., 1984-87. Mem. Am. prodn. and Inventory Control Soc. (cert.; pres. 1980-82), Purchasing Mgrs. Assn., Optimists (pres. Boulder 1986-87, lt. gov. 1987-88). Home: 1449 Adams Pl Louisville CO 80027 Office: Head Sports Inc 4801 N 63d St Boulder CO 80301

WOODLE, ALAN STUART, podiatrist, foot and ankle surgeon; b. Vancouver, Wash., July 31, 1953; s. Malcolm Stuart and Lorraine Marie (Evans) W.; m. Roslyn Louise Knodel. BS (2), U. Wash., 1975, 76; D in Podiatric Medicine, Calif. Coll. Podiatric Medicine, 1979. Cert. Am. Bd. Foot and Ankle Surgery. Resident in surgery Valley West Gen. Hosp., Los Gatos, Calif., 1981; practice medicine specializing in foot and ankle surgery, also sports medicine Seattle, 1980—; clin. asst. prof. foot and ankle surgery VA Med. Ctr. Seattle, 1984—; lectr. U. Wash. Med Sch.; exec. com. Waldo Gen. Hosp., Seattle, 1985—, Northwest Hosp., 1986—; mem. med. adv. com. Blue Cross of Wash., Alaska, 1987—; podiatrist Pacific N.W. Ballet, U.S. Biathlon Team. Contbr. chpts. to textbooks, articles to profl. jours. Bd. dirs. Wash. State div. U.S. Olympic Com., Seattle, 1984, Home Health Care, Okanogan County, Wash., 1984, Multiple Sclerosis Assn., King County, Wash., 1986, also v.p., 1988, Arthritis Found., 1986—. Fellow Am. Acad. Podiatric Sports Medicine, Am. Coll. Foot Surgeons; mem. Am. Coll. Sports Medicine, Wash. State Podiatric Med. Assn. (trustee 1986—, sec. 1987—, v.p. 1989—). Presbyterian. Office: 9730 3d NE Ste 208 Seattle WA 98115

WOODRUM, DONALD, advertising company executive; b. N.Y.C., Aug. 6, 1917; s. Donald and Gertrude (Conn) W.; m. Mary Harvey, Mar. 18, 1944 (div. 1956); 1 child, Mary Lynn; m. Dorothea Enzor, Nov. 27, 1957. AB, U. Calif., Berkeley, 1937. Pres. Woodrum & Staff Ltd., Honolulu, 1946—; chmn. bd. DiCarlo & Woodrum Advt., Honolulu, 1988—. Author: This is Hawaii, 1974. Served with USNR, 1941-45, 50-53; now comdr. ret. Mem. Honolulu Advt. Fedn. (founding pres., awards of distinction 1977, 84, Ad Man of Yr. award 1986), Honolulu C. of C., Advt. Assn. West (lt. gov. 1965-67), Advt. Agy. Assn. Hawaii (past pres.), Bishop Mus. Assn., Alpha Sigma Phi. Republican. Club: Outrigger Canoe (Honolulu). Home: 207 Kawaikui Pl Honolulu HI 96821 Office: DiCarlo & Woodrum Advt 720 Kapiolani Blvd Honolulu HI 96813

WOODS, BOBBY JOE (BOB WOODS), transportation executive; b. Frederick, Okla., June 20, 1935; s. Vivin Richard and Mattie Marie (Malone) W.; m. O. Dell Smith, July 21, 1957; children: Donald B., Kathryn M., David R., Lynda J. Student, U. Calif., Berkeley, 1955-56; AA, Phoenix Coll., 1955; student, Glendale (Ariz.) Coll., 1968, 75. Credit mgr. Sam Boren Tire Co., Albuquerque, 1966-67; office mgr. Menke Transp., Albuquerque, 1967-68; dist. exec. Boy Scouts Am., Phoenix, 1968-76; pres. Southwest Prorate Inc., Phoenix, 1976—; owner S.W. Vehicle Title Svc., Phoenix, 1985—. Commr. Boy Scouts Am., Ariz., N.Mex. Mem. Profl. Trucking Svcs. Assn. (2d vice pres.). Republican. Lodge: Lions (zone chmn. South Phoenix 1983-84, dep. dist. gov. 1984-85, dist. sight and hearing chmn. 1985-89, Sight and Hearing Found. state hearing chmn. 1987-89). Home: 918 W Cochise Phoenix AZ 85021 Office: SW Prorate Inc 8611 N Black Canyon Hwy Ste 108 Phoenix AZ 85021

WOODS, DONALD PETER, real estate executive, marketing professional; b. Seneca Falls, N.Y., Oct. 14, 1911; s. James Henry and Isabell Teresa (McDonald) W.; m. June 17, 1935; children: Donald Peter Jr., Richard, Terrence, Lynn, Thomas. PhB, Niagara U., Niagara Falls, N.Y., 1933; postgrad., Bklyn. Law Sch., 1933-36. Law clk. N.Y. State Ins. Dept., N.Y.C., 1933-36; title examiner Abstract Title and Mortgage, Rochester, N.Y., 1936-38; title officer Monroe Abstract & Title, Rochester, 1938-43; pres., chief exec. officer D.P. Woods, Inc., Rochester, 1945-54, Don Woods Realty, Phoenix, 1954-82; assoc. v.p. Iliff Thorn & Co., Phoenix, 1982—. Lt. USN, 1943-45, PTO. Mem. Cert. Real Estate Appraisal, Internat. Coun. of Shopping Ctrs., Ariz. Club, Camelback Racquet Club (pres. Phoenix chpt. 1959—), Phi Delta Phi. Republican. Roman Catholic. Home: 5301 E Palomino Rd Phoenix AZ 85018 Office: Iliff Thorn & Co 3636 N Central Ste 600 Phoenix AZ 85012

WOODS, JAMES HOWARD, actor; b. Vernal, Utah, Apr. 18, 1947. Student, MIT, 1965-69. Actor Broadway prodns. including Borstal Boy, Saved (Obie award, Clarence Derwent award), Trial of the Catonsville 9, Finishing Touches, Moonchildren (Theatre World award), films include The Gambler, 1974, Night Moves, 1975, Alex & the Gypsy, 1976, The Choirboys, 1977, The Onion Field, 1979 (Golden Globe nomination), The Black Marble, 1980, Eyewitness, 1981, Split Image, 1982, Fast-Walking, 1982, Videodrome, 1983, Against All Odds, 1984, Once Upon a Time in America, 1984, Cat's Eye, 1985, Joshua Then and Now, 1985, Salvador, 1986 (Acad. award nomination, 1987), Best Seller, 1987, Cop, 1988, The Boost, 1988, True Believer, 1989; appeared in TV miniseries Holocaust, 1978; in TV movies All the Way Home, 1971, Footsteps, 1972, A Great American Tragedy, 1972, The Disappearance of Aimee, 1976, Raid on Entebbe, 1977, The Gift of Love, 1978, And Your Name is Jonah, 1979, Badge of the Assassin, 1985, Promise, 1986 (Emmy award, Golden Apple award, Golden Globe award), In Love and War, 1987 (Emmy award nomination, Golden Globe award nomination). Office: care Creative Artists Agy Inc/Ste 1400 1888 Century Park E Los Angeles CA 90067

WOODS, JOE ELDON, general contractor; b. Hammon, Okla., Apr. 24, 1933; s. Joseph W. and Gertrude E. (Martin) W.; student Ariz. State U., 1955-61; O.P.M. Program Harvard U., 1984-87; m. Nina Jo Shackelford, July 5, 1952; 1 son, Joel Grant. Vice-pres. Kitchell Corp., Phoenix, 1965-71; v.p. devel. Doubletree, Inc., Phoenix, 1969-78; pres., owner Joe E. Woods, Inc., Mesa, Ariz., 1977—; ptnr. Price-Woods Premier Homes, Mesa, 1985—;

chmn., bd. dirs. Joe Woods Devel., Mesa, 1986—. Bd. dirs. Mesa United Way, 1983-84; v.p., bd. dirs. East Valley Partnership, Mesa, 1985—. With U.S. Army, 1953-55, Korea. Mem. Associated Gen. Contractors, Mesa C. of C. (bd. dirs. 1983-85, chmn. 1985-86, v.p. 1984-85, pres. 1985-86). Republican. Presbyterian. Clubs: Mesa Country, White Mountain Country (Pinetop, Ariz.). Lodge: Rotary. Avocations: golf, fishing, skiing. Office: Joe E Woods Inc 145 N Centennial Way Ste 416 Mesa AZ 85201

WOODS, JOHN THOMAS, JR., broadcast station manager; b. Durham, N.C., Feb. 1, 1947; s. John Thomas Sr. and Eleanor Maye (Whitt); m. Henri Jean Gibson, Oct 28, 1970, (div. May 1980); m. Jessie Lynn Rich, June 8, 1980; children: John Thomas III, Joseph Michael. Grad. high sch., Durham, 1967. Lic. broadcaster. Air personality Sta. WTMA, Charleston, S.C., 1967, Sta. WKIX, Raleigh, N.C., 1968, Sta. WWOK, Miami, Fla., 1969, Sta. KWIZ, L.A., 1970; dir. prodn. Sta. KLOK, San Jose, Calif., 1971-79; announcer, producer Sta. KNTV-TV, San Jose, 1971-75, Sta. KICU-TV, San Jose, 1976-82; pres. J.Thomas Woods Advt., San Jose, Lake Tahoe, 1981-85; adminstrv. asst. Sta KVIP, Redding, Calif., 1985-88, mgr., 1989—; cons. Community Access TV, Redding, 1988—. Author curriculum on TV producing, 1988. Govt. chair Shasta County Grand Jury, Calif., 1988—; mem., del. Atty. Gen.'s Commn. on Drugs, Shasta County, 1986; mem. mayor's adv. bd. City of San Jose, 1976; bd. mem. Shasta Bible Coll., Redding, 1989. With U.S. Army, 1967-68. Mem. Nat. Assn. Broadcasters, Nat. Religious Broadcasters. Republican. Home: 1288 Dusty Ln Redding CA 96002 Office: Pacific Cascade Communicaitons 1139 Hartnell Ave Redding CA 96049-2727

WOODS, LESLIE VICTOR, optometrist; b. L.A., Dec. 26, 1925; s. Kenneth Campbell and Ada Lucille (Meyers) W.; student U. B.C., 1944-46; BS, Pacific U., 1948, OD, 1949; m. Noreen Ellen Barry, Nov. 23, 1950; children—Deirdre Ann, Megan Louise. Individual practice optometry, Sedro Wooley, Wash., 1949, Spokane, 1950, 65—, Chelan, Wash., 1951-65; optometrist dept. ophthalmology Pacific Med. Ctr.; mem. faculty Columbia-Pacific U., advisor to faculty Coll. Optometry; mem. optometric faculty Spokane Community Coll., 1975-78. Chmn. optometric affairs State and County CD, 1958-65; dir. Chelan CD, 1951; mem. Wash. Welfare Med. Care Com., 1958-66; councilman, Chelan, 1952; trustee Fort Wright Coll. of the Holy Names, Spokane; vice-chmn. bd. trustees Ft. Wright Coll., 1978-79; mem. adv. bd. Pacific U. Coll. Optometry, Forest Grove, Oreg., 1989. Coauthor Intra-ocular Lenses, 1989. Mem. Wash. Optometric Assn. (pres. Inland soc. 1975-77), North Cen. Wash. Optometric Soc. (pres. 1954-56, 63-64, state trustee 1954-56, 63-64), Calif. Optometric Assn., Am. Optometric Assn., Omega Delta, Delta Upsilon. Democrat. Roman Catholic. Club: Lions (dir. N. Spokane 1975-76, v.p. 1976, pres. 1977-78). Home: 1979 Clay St San Francisco CA 94109 Office: 2340 Clay St Rm 635 San Francisco CA 94115

WOODS, MELANIE ANN, sales professional; b. Oakley, Kans., Oct. 24, 1957; d. Richard L. and Myrle E. (Arie) Stanfield; m. George K. Woods Jr., Oct. 16, 1982. BSBA, Kans. State U., 1979. Sales rep. George A. Hormel & Co., Kansas City, Mo., 1980-82; sales rep. Hershey Chocolate USA, Phoenix, 1985-86, key account rep., 1987-88, dist. account supr., 1988—. Mem. Los Hospederos, Kans. State U. Alumni Assn., Kappa Kappa Gamma Alumni Assn. Republican. Home: 3838 E Mountain Sky Ave Phoenix AZ 85044

WOODS, NORMAN JAMES, academic administrator; b. Springfield, Mo., Mar. 5, 1934; s. Norman O. and Doris Ena (Noblitt) W.; m. Phyllis Darlene Foster, Aug. 16, 1959; children: Michael J., Julie L. Woods Scott. BA, Union Coll., Lincoln, Nebr., 1960; MEd, Cen. Wash. U., 1966; PhD, U. Oreg., 1969. Tchr., asst. dean men Auburn (Wash.) Acad., 1960-61; Tchr., asst. dean men Auburn Acad., Wash., 1960-61; asst., then assoc. and dean men Walla Walla Coll., College Place, Wash., 1961-66; dean students Loma Linda U., Calif., 1966-67, asst. then assoc. dean admissions and student affairs, 1969-74, v.p. acad. adminstrn., 1974-84, pres., 1984—. With U.S. Army, 1956-58. Mem. Am. Assn. Pres. Ind. Colls. and Univs. (bd. dirs. 1985—). Seventh-day Adventist. Office: Loma Linda U Office of Pres Loma Linda CA 92350

WOODS, ROBERT DOUGLAS MURPHY, lawyer, priest; b. Wimbledon Park, Eng., July 31, 1946; came to U.S., 1950; s. Eric Robert and Dorothea Elizabeth (Armstrong) W.; m. Joan Frances Shoop, Apr., 1970 (div. 1974); m. Alexis Jean Perry, May 23, 1975; children: David S. M.; stepchildren: Heidi J. Kone, James J. Kone Jr., Yvette M. Kone. BA in Polit. Sci., U. San Diego, 1968, JD, 1973; Sem. diploma, Claremont (Calif.) Coll., 1986; Cert., Georgetown U., 1988. Bar: Calif. 1973, U.S. Ct. Appeals (9th cir.) 1973, U.S. Supreme Ct. 1980; ordained to priest Episcopal Ch., 1988. Assoc. Higgs, Fletcher & Mack, San Diego, 1970-77; ptnr. Schall, Boudreau & Gore, Inc., San Diego, 1978-86; chief litigation sect. Kern County, Bakersfield, Calif., 1986—; deacon St. Paul's Ch., Bakersfield, 1986; interim deacon and priest St. Andrew's Ch., Taft, Calif., 1986-88; assisting priest St. Luke's Ch., Bakersfield, 1988—; adj. prof. Thomas Jefferson Extension Paralegal Sch., Bakersfield, 1989—. Author: chpt. Marine P&I Policy Annotations, 1980. Mem. Dem. Profl. Club, San Diego, 1973-79; pledge drive worker United Way, Bakersfield, 1987-88; chieftan San Diego Scottish Highland Games, Inc., San Diego, 1973; charter dir. San Diego Edinburgh Sister City Soc., 1978. With U.S. Army, 1969-70. Fellow Kegley Inst. of Ethics Calif. State U., 1988—. Mem. Kern County Bar Assn. (lawyer referral com. 1986-88, chair superior ct. com. 1989—), Calif. State Bar Assn. (lectr., contbr. continuing edn. of the bar com. 1979-86, Pro Bono Svc. award 1985), Kern Scottish Soc. Democrat. Office: Kern County 1415 Truxtun Ave Ste 500 Bakersfield CA 93301

WOODS, ROBERT LAWRENCE, insurance company executive, consultant; b. Los Angeles, May 17, 1911; s. Walter A. and Alice (Strang) W.; A.B., U. Calif. at Los Angeles, 1933; C.L.U., Am. Coll. Life Underwriters, 1937; m. Dorothy Welbourn, Oct. 10, 1942; children—Robert Lawrence, Susan Welbourn Woods Barker. With Los Angeles agy. of Mass. Mut. Life Ins. Co., 1934—, asst. gen. agt., 1938-46, assoc. gen. agt., 1946-49, gen. agt. in partnership, 1949-57, sole gen. agt., 1957-73. Fund raising chmn. Los Angeles chpt. ARC, 1961, dir., 1960-63. Trustee Am. Coll., 1958-61, 71-79. Served to lt. col., inf., AUS, 1941-46. Recipient John Newton Russell award Nat. Assn. Life Underwriters, 1971, Will G. Farrell award Los Angeles Life Ins. Assns., 1974; named to Mgmt. Hall of Fame, Nat. Gen. Agts. and Mgrs. Conf., 1974. Mem. Am. Soc. C.L.U.'s (pres. Los Angeles 1953-54, nat. pres. 1959-60), Mass. Mut. Gen. Agts. Assn. (pres. 1959-60), Gen. Agts. and Mgrs. Assn. (pres. Los Angeles 1957-58, nat. pres. 1967-68), Phi Gamma Delta. Home: 720 N Oakhurst Dr Beverly Hills CA 90210 Office: 4401 Wilshire Blvd Los Angeles CA 90010

WOOD-TROST, LUCILLE MARIE, psychotherapist, educator; b. Candor, N.Y., Nov. 4, 1938; d. Stiles and Alice E. (Keim) Wood; m. Charles Trost, June 18, 1960 (div. 1981); 1 child, Scott. BS in Zoology, Pa. State U., 1960; MS in Biology, U. Fla., 1964; PhD in Human Behavior, Union Grad. Sch., Cin., 1975. Writer 1960-75, 82-84; asst. prof. Westminster Coll., Salt Lake City, 1975-80; therapist, writer Garden of Peace Healing Ctr., Stanwell Tops, NSW, Australia, 1980-81; pvt. practice psychotherapy Bellingham, Wash., 1982-84; assoc. prof. human behavior Northwest Indian Coll. (formerly Lummi Community Coll.), Bellingham, 1984—; dir. Tamarack Learning Coop., Pocatello, Idaho, 1969-74. Author: Lives and Deaths in a Meadow, 1973 (award, Am. Assn. Sci. Tchrs.-Children's Book Coun. 1976), others. Mem. Sigma Xi, Phi Sigma. Mem. Science of Mind Church. Home: 2636 MacKenzie Rd Bellingham WA 98226 Office: Northwest Indian Coll 2522 Kwina Rd Bellingham WA 98226

WOODWARD, JOHN RUSSELL, motion picture production executive; b. San Diego, July 10, 1951; s. Melvin C. and Dora M. (Rorabaugh) W. BA in Visual Arts, U. Calif., San Diego, 1973; MA in Cinema Prodn., U. So. Calif., 1978. V.p. prodn. World Wide Motion Pictures Corp., 1982—. Prodn. asst. various commls., 1977; asst. producer The Manitou, 1977; 1st asst. dir. Mortuary, 1981, They're Playing With Fire, 1983, Prime Risk, 1984, Winners Take All, 1986, Kidnapped, 1986, Slam Dance, 1986, Honor Betrayed, 1986, Hidden, 1987, New Monkees, 1987, Bad Dreams, 1987, Night Angel, 1988; location mgr. Star Chamber, 1982, To Be or Not To Be, 1983, Flashdance, 1983, Two of a Kind, 1983, Touch and Go, 1984, Explorers, 1984, Sweet Dreams, 1985, The Long Shot, 1985, The Running Man, 1985, A Different Affair, 1985, Bobo, 1986, Disorganized Crime, 1988, UHF, 1988, The Horror Show, 1988, Fear, 1989.

WOODWARD, JOHN STEELE, engineer; b. Berkeley, Calif., May 2, 1942; s. John Wesley and Marjorie Steele (Jackson) W.; m. Betty Lynn Calloway. BS, U. Calif., 1965; MS, Stanford U., 1966. Field engr. Gen. Electric Co., San Jose, Calif., 1966-68; civil engr. Ralph M. Parsons Co., 1968-74; mgr. constrn. Kinetics Technol. Internat., Vancouver, Wash., 1974-78; chief field engr. Ralph M. Parsons, Iran and Saudi Arabia, 1979-80; mgr. constrn. Kinetics Technol., Monrovia, Calif., 1980—. Home: 2211 Highland Vista Dr Arcadia CA 91006 Office: Kinetics Technol Internat Monrovia CA 91016

WOODWARD, STEPHEN RICHARD, newspaper editor; b. Fukuoka City, Japan, July 27, 1953; came to U.S., 1954; s. Leonard Edwin and Etsuko (Okumura) W.; m. Sandra Elizabeth Richardson, Dec. 31, 1979; children: Daniel Joseph, Elizabeth Etsuko. BA in English, Wright State U., 1975; MA in Journalism, U. Mo., 1979. Advt. coordinator Wright State U., Dayton, Ohio, 1976-77; reporter Kansas City (Mo.) Star, 1979-82; assoc. editor then editor Kansas City Bus. Jour., 1982-83; editor then gen. mgr. Portland (Oreg.) Bus. Jour., 1984-86; exec. bus. editor The Hartford (Conn.) Courant, 1986-87; editor San Francisco Bus. Times, 1987-88; bus. editor The Oregonian, Portland, 1989—. Recipient 1st Place Investigative Reporting award Assn. Area Bus. Publs., 1983, 1st Place Column Writing award Assn. Area Bus. Publs., 1985. Mem. Investigative Reporters and Editors Inc. Home: 3309 NE Irving St Portland OR 97232 Office: The Oregonian 1320 SW Broadway Portland OR 97201

WOODWARD, WILLIAM HERBERT, industrial engineer; b. Springfield, Mass., July 31, 1941; s. Herbert William and Catherine Louise (Carney) W.; m. Mary Martha Schukoske, July 4, 1964; children: Brian William, Mitchell Todd. BS in mgmt. engring., Rensselaer Polytechnic Inst., 1964; MS in indsl. adminstrn., Union Coll., 1972. Indsl. engr. IBM, East Fishkill, N.Y., 1967-77; prodn. control mgr. IBM, East Fishkill, 1977-79; indsl. engring. mgr. IBM, Tucson, 1979-81, project mgr., 1981-85, adv. engr., 1985—. Firearms instr. NRA, 1985—. Lt. USNR, 1964-67, Vietnam. Mem. Inst. Indsl. Engrs. (pres. chpt. 1986-87, 1st chpt. achievement award 1987, chpt. dir. 1982—), U.S. Naval Inst., Rensselaer Alumni Assn. (so. Ariz. dir. Alumni recruiting 1985—, alumni scholarship chairperson), Chatham Yacht Club (race patrol mem.). Republican. Roman Catholic. Home: 6452 E Calle De Amigos Tucson AZ 85715 Office: IBM 9000 S Rita Rd Tucson AZ 85744

WOODWORTH, HARRY EADES, III, brokerage house executive; b. Honolulu, Sept. 26, 1941; s. Harry Eades Woodworth Jr. and Catherine Rose (Maier) Williams. AA, Hartnell Coll., 1966; BSBA, Armstrong Coll., 1968. Stockbroker Dean Witter, Anchorage, 1973-76; sr. v.p. Dean Witter Reynolds (formerly Dean Witter), Anchorage, 1981—; stockbroker Merrill Lynch, Anchorage, 1976-81; Prin. Eagle Land Assocs, Anchorage, 1983—, prin. Eagle Investments, Anchorage, 1983; bd. dirs. L. Nebel and Assocs. Landscape Architects, Anchorage, 1983—, bd. dirs. Eagle Broadcasting, Inc., Anchorage, 1983-85, bd. dirs. Pacific Rim Broadcasting, Inc., Anchorage, 1985—. Recipient Pacesetters award Dean Witter Reynolds, Inc., 1983-85. Mem. N.Y. Stock Exchange (registered rep.), Nat. Assn. Security Dealers (registered rep.), N.Y. Commodities Exchange (registered rep.), Chgo. Commodities Exchange (registered rep.), Chgo Bd. Options Exchange (registered rep.), Ducks Unltd.,Nat. Rifle Assn., Ferrari Owners Club, Mercedes Owners Club. Republican. Roman Catholic. Club: U.S. Boat, Ducks Unltd. Lodge: Elks. Home: 13900 Jarvi Dr Anchorage AK 99515 Office: Dean Witter Reynolds Inc 3601 C St Anchorage AK 99503

WOODWORTH, JAMES VICKERS, internist; b. Dover, N.H., Aug. 27, 1921; s. Hazlett A. Vickers and Sarah Louise (Nelson) Woodworth; m. Cara Elisabeth Davis, Sept. 22, 1945; children: Gail L. Woodworth, Vicki S. Terhorst, Linda C. Becker. AB, Whitman Coll., 1943; MD, U. Oreg., 1946. Diplomate Am. Bd. Internal Medicine; lic. MD in Oreg., Calif., Washington, Alaska. Intern French Hosp., San Francisco, 1946-47; resident USPHS, San Francisco, 1947-52; pvt. practice in internal medicine Portland, Oreg., 1952-76; founder Suburban Med. Clinic, Portland, 1956; instr. medicine Sch. Dentistry Oreg. Health Scis. U., Portland, 1952—, clin. assoc. medicine, 1953-76, assoc. prof., chmn. dept. medicine, 1976-79, prof., chmn. dept. medicine, 1979-82; affiliate faculty advanced cardiac life support Am. Heart Assn., Portland, 1983-88; cons. indsl. medicine So. Pacific Transpn. Co. and Burlington No. RR, Portland, 1977—; cons. indsl medicine Portland, 1982—; cons. Cardiac Resuscitator Corp., Portland, 1983-87; active staff Providence Med. Ctr., Portland, 1952-77, Portland Adventist Hosp., 1952-76. Contbr. articles to profl. jours. Fellow Am. Coll. Physicians; mem. Am. Soc. Internal Medicine, AMA, Oreg. State Med. Assn. (bd. trustees, house dels.), Multnomah County Med. Soc., Oreg. Heart Assn. (chmn. life support procedures com. 1978-80), Am. Occupational Med. Assn. Republican. Presbyterian. Home: 999 NE 169th Dr Portland OR 97230

WOODWORTH, STEPHEN DAVIS, business and financial consultant, investment banker; b. Stillwater, Okla., Nov. 4, 1945; s. Stanley Davis and Elizabeth (Webb) W.; m. Elizabeth Roberts, Apr. 15, 1968; children: Lisa Alexander, Ashley Ives. BA, Claremont McKenna Coll., 1967; MBA, Calif. Lutheran U., 1975. Div. mgr. Security Pacific Bank, L.A., 1970-86; mgr. policy inst. U. So. Calif., L.A., 1981-88; pres. Cen. Coast Equities, Ltd., Oxnard, Calif., 1988-89; prin. Woodworth Assocs., Westlake Village, Calif., 1987—; advisor to bd. Pacific InterTrade Corp., Westlake Village, Calif., 1987-89, Hanson Lab Furniture Ind. Inc., Newbury Park, Calif., 1988-89; trustee Calif. Lutheran Edn. Found., Thousand Oaks, Calif., 1983-89; fin. chmn. Cen. Coast MIT Enterprise Forum, Santa Barbara, Calif., 1988-89; instr. fin. and banking Calif. Lutheran U., 1978-79. Contbr. articles to profl. jours. Chmn. Alliance for the Arts, Thousand Oaks, Calif., 1982-89; vice chmn. Conejo Symphony Orchestra, Thousand Oaks, 1986-89. 1st Lt. U.S. Army, 1968-70, Korea. Recipient Outstanding Alumnus Calif. Lutheran U., 1986. Mem. Res. Officers Assn. of the U.S., Ventura County Economic Devel. Assn., Am. Mgmt. Assn., Conejo Future Found., Marine Meml. Club, Tower Club. Democrat. Roman Catholic. Home: 1993 Channelford Westlake Village CA 91361 Office: Woodworth Assocs 2899 Agoura Rd #262 Westlake Village CA 91361

WOODY, PHILLIP LESLIE, small business owner; b. Portland, Oreg., July 31, 1933; s. Lacey Emanual and Jessie Corrine (Bragg) W.; widowed; 1 child, Jennifer Marie; m. Marjorie A. Doran, Oct. 15, 1989. BBA, U. Oreg., 1958. Chief purser States Steamship Corp., San Francisco, 1960-79; mgr. real estate Seattle, 1980—; owner Herfy's Drive-In, Seattle, 1985—. Served with U.S. Army, 1955-57, Korea. Mem. Washington Restaurant Assn., Tau Kappa Epsilon. Baptist. Home: 17220 40th Ave S Seattle WA 98188

WOOLF-SCOTT, HELENE LYDA, real estate developer; b. N.Y.C., Apr. 2, 1938; d. Harry and Eleanor (Wolfson) Burke; m. William Woolf, Aug. 17, 1958 (div. 1982); 1 child, Gina Karen; m. Walter Scott Jr., May 1, 1987. BA, NYU, 1959. Lic. real estate agt. Calif. Realtor Wright & Co., Los Altos, Calif., 1974-80; v.p. Munsey Devel. Corp., Los Altos, Calif., 1978—; v.p. McKeon, Scott, Woolf & Assocs., 1982-84; pres. GKW Enterprises, Inc. 1978—, Scott, Woolf & Assocs., 1984— ; bd. dirs. Mulford Moreland & Assocs., Inc., San Jose, Calif. Mem. Los Altos Bd. Realtors, Nat. Assn. Realtors, Calif. Assn. Realtors, Am. Mgmt. Assn. Democrat. Home: 564 Santa Rita Palo Alto CA 94301 Office: Scott Woolf & Assocs 701 Welch Rd Ste 1119 Palo Alto CA 94304

WOOLLEY, GEOFFREY TANNER, venture capitalist; b. San Francisco, Apr. 5, 1959; s. Jack Boyd and Norma Rae (Tanner) W. BS inFin., Brigham Young U., 1980; MBA, U. Utah, 1983. Dir. Equatec Fin. Group, Inc., Oakland, Calif., 1983-85; chmn., chief exec. officer Dominion Ventures Inc., San Francisco, 1985—; bd. dir. EasTek Corp. Fin. officer Names Project, AIDS Rsch., San Francisco, 1987—. Mem. Western Venture Capital Assn. Mormon. Office: Dominion Ventures Inc 300 Montgomery St 600 San Francisco CA 94104

WOOLSEY, ROY BLAKENEY, electronics company executive; b. Norfolk, Va., June 12, 1945; s. Roy B. and Louise Stookey (Jones) W.; m. Patricia Bernadine Elkins, Apr. 17, 1988. Student, Calif. Inst. Tech., 1962-64; BS with distinction, Stanford U., 1966, MS, 1967, PhD, 1970. Sr. physicist Tech. for Communications Internat., Mountain View, Calif., 1970-75; mgr. radio direction finding systems Tech. for Communications Internat., Mountain View, 1975-80, program mgr., 1980-83, dir. strategic systems, 1983-88, dir. research and devel., 1988—. Contbr. articles to profl. jours. Active YMCA, Palo Alto, Calif. Fellow NSF, 1966-70. Mem. Sigma Xi, Phi Beta Kappa. Republican. Presbyterian. Home: 26649 Snell Ln Los Altos Hills CA 94022 Office: Tech for Communications Internat 34175 Ardenwood Blvd Fremont CA 94536

WOOSLEY, LINDA DIANE SAIA, industrial engineer; b. Woodbury, N.J., Jan. 19, 1957; d. Joseph Jack and Joyce Ellen (Lyon) Saia; m. Steven Lee Woosley, July 19, 1986. BS in Mech. Engring., U. Tex., 1979; MS in Indsl. Engring., Lamar U., 1986. Registered profl. engr., Tex. Pvt. practice in computer consulting Austin, Tex., 1980-82; co-owner Linco Handyman, Beaumont, Tex., 1982-86; monitor computer lab. Lamar U., Beaumont, 1984-86, instr., 1983-87; simulator engr. Wash. Pub. Power Supply System, Richland, Wash., 1987—. Teaching fellow Lamar U., 1985-87. Mem. Inst. Indsl. Engrs., ASME, IEEE (computer soc. chpt.), AAAS. Home: 235 N 58th Pl West Richland WA 99352 Office: Wash Pub Power Supply System 3000 George Washington Way Md 1034 Richland WA 99352

WOOSLEY, PATRICK GLENN, bank executive; b. Dallas, Nov. 12, 1938; s. Pat and Florrie (Smith) W.; m. Valerie White, Oct. 19, 1974 (div. 1980); children: Trina, Jeff; m. Kazuko Ando, Dec. 29, 1984; children: Christine, Katherine. BBA, N. Tex. State U., 1960; MBA, So. Meth. U., 1965, JD, 1968; LLM in Tax, NYU, 1969. Bar: Tex. 1968, Calif. 1973. Tax mgr. Latin Am. Gulf Oil Co., London and Miami, Fla., 1969-73; assoc. Lawler, Felix and Hall, L.A., 1973-75; 1st v.p., sr. tax counsel Security Pacific Nat. Bank, L.A., 1983-84; v.p. tax Parsons Corp., Pasadena, Calif., 1975-83, 84—. Mem. Tax Execs. Inst., Tex. Bar Assn., Calif. Bar Assn., Nation Constrn. Assn. (chmn. tax com. 1980-82, 86-87).

WOOTON, SUZANNE K, vitamin stores owner; b. Point Townsend, Wash., Mar. 22, 1943; d. Gordon R. Bader and Constance (Johnson) Childers; m. Gary Ellsworth Wooton, Mar. 26, 1966. BA, teaching credential, Wash. State U., 1965; MA in Art, Long Beach State U., 1974; MS, Donsbauch U., 1982. Educator Garden Grove Unified Schs., Garden Grove, Calif., 1965-80; co-owner, operator Great Earth Vitamin Stores, San Anselmo and Santa Rosa, Calif., 1980—. Contbr. articles to profl. jours. Chairperson Dance for Heart, Am. Heart Assn., 1984-88; pub. rels. dir. Sonoma County Dance for Heart, 1989; mem. Northern Calif. Franchise assn. Great Earth Vitamin Stores, 1984-89; sec., bd. dirs. Red Hill Shopping Ctr., San Anselmo, Calif., 1983-87. Recipient Continuing Excellence award Great Earth Internat., 1983, Founder's award, 1987, cert. apreciation Los Rosas (Calif.) Bus. and Profl. Women, 1985, outstanding service award Las Rosas Bus. & Profl. Women's Luncheon Club, 1984. Mem. Nat. Assn. Profl. Saleswomen, Soroptimist Internat. (bd. dirs. Ways and Means, West Santa Rosa, Calif., chpt. 1986-89). Office: Great Earth Vitamin Stores PO Box 9291 Santa Rosa CA 95405

WORDEN, DAVID EUGENE, marine insurance company executive; b. Albany, N.Y., Jan. 28, 1943; s. Reese Edwards and Mary Catherine (Bailey) W.; m. Barbara Ann Green, June 27, 1970; children: Brandon David, Rebecca Lynn. AA, Fullerton Coll., 1963; BA, Calif. State U., 1966. Underwriter Safeco Ins. Co., Panorama City, Calif., 1970-74; underwriting mgr. Aetna Ins. Co., L.A., 1974-81; regional v.p. Ahmanson Ins. Co., Lakewood, Calif., 1981-84; sr. v.p. Crump E-S, Huntington Harbor, Calif., 1984—. Editor Pawprints, 1960-61, Hornet, 1962-63 (State Best Sports award 1963), Innerviews, 1975-81. Mem. Holy Family Adoptive Parents, L.A., 1980—, pres., 1983-84; v.p. Colinas de Capistrano Assn., Laguna Niguel, Calif., 1987-88. Sgt. USAF, 1966-70, Vietnam. Mem. So. Calif. Marine Assn. Republican. Roman Catholic. Home: 28762 Mira Vista Laguna Niguel CA 92677 Office: Crump E S 15922 Pacific Coast Hwy 209 Huntington Harbor CA 92649

WORK, STEPHEN WALTER, engineer; b. Pueblo, Colo., Sept. 19, 1944; s. Walter Douglas and Frances (McInnes) W.; m. Carol R. Gaskill, Oct. 6, 1969; children: Jeanne F., Lori K. BSCE, U. Colo., 1968, MSCE, 1969. Asst. hydraulic engr. Denver Water Dept., 1968-70, reclamation engr., 1973-76; mgr. treated water planning and control Denver Water Dept., Denver, 1977-80, mgr. quality control, 1981-83, coordinator spl. projects, 1984-87, chief of water quality and research, 1988—; mgr. two forks EIS Denver Water Dept., 1981—, potable water reuse project, 1976-81, Metro Water Study State Legislature, 1974-75. Contbr. articles to profl. jours. Bd. dirs. Littleton (Colo.) United Meth. Ch., 1985—. Served to lt. USNR, 1969-73. Mem. Am. Water Works Assn. (chmn. Rocky Mountain sect. 1984-85, Fuller award 1986). Office: Denver Water Dept Denver CO 80254

WORKIEWYCZ, DANUSIA, publishing executive; b. Regensberg, Fed. Republic of Germany, Nov. 1, 1946; s. Walter I. and Albina (Gruszcecka) W. AAS, Pima Coll., 1978; BS, U. Ariz., 1980. Editorial asst. Trinity Ch., N.Y.C., 1965-70; graphic designer M.J.H. Advt. Agy., N.Y.C., 1970-75, Home Fed. Savs. & Loan, N.Y.C., 1975-78; chief fiscal officer Tombstone (Ariz.) City Gov., 1981-82; adminstv. asst. Pima County Gov., Tucson, 1982-84; adminstrv. asst. U. Med. Ctr., Tucson, 1984-85; ednl. svcs. coord. Tucson Newspapers Inc., 1985—; sub com. chmn. Ariz. Gov. Taskforce on Adult Literacy, 1985-86; mem. Drop-Out Prevention Collaborative, Tucson Unified Sch. Dist. Contbr. articles to profl. jours. Bd. dirs. Houghton Rd. Neighborhood Assn., Tucson; judge Ariz. Dept. Mem. T.A.R.C., A.R.C., I.R.A., Working Women-Female Execs., Am. Bus. Women Assn. Democrat. Roman Catholic. Home: 801 S Calle Escondido Tucson AZ 85748

WORKMAN, LAURAL ANN, retail association executive; b. Monrovia, Calif., Feb. 13, 1960; d. Albert Robert and Laura Louise (Benton) W. BMus, U. Oreg., 1983. Acctg. clk. Renfield Importers, N.Y.C., 1981-82; adminstrv. asst. Internat. Council Shopping Ctrs., N.Y.C., 1983-84, meetings mgr., 1984-85, western meetings dir., San Francisco, 1986—. Co-author: Guide to ICSC Idea Exchanges, 1985. Mem. NOW, Nat. Assn. Female Execs., Phi Beta (pres. 1981-82). Democrat. Avocations: classical musician, tennis, travel, swimming. Home: 5401 Diamond Heights Blvd Apt 4 San Francisco CA 94131 Office: Internat Coun Shopping Ctrs 353 Sacramento St Ste 400 San Francisco CA 94111

WORONOFF, DAVID SMULYAN, lawyer; b. Balt., June 20, 1937; s. Samuel Murray and Ella Sarah (Smulyan) W.; m. Karen Gail Scholz, Apr. 18, 1978; children—Jamie, Keith, Robin; children by previous marriage—Stefan, Bonnie. B.S. in Elec. Engring., M.I.T., 1959; J.D. (scholar), Boston Coll., 1962; postgrad. Utica Coll., 1965-66, Rutgers U., 1968-69. Bar: Conn. 1962 U.S. Dist. Ct. Conn. 1963, U.S. Patent Office 1965, N.J. 1972, U.S. Dist. Ct. N.J. 1972, R.I. 1979, U.S. Dist Ct. R.I. 1979. U.S. Ct. Customs and Patent Appeals 1980, U.S. Ct. Appeals (Fed. cir.) 1981, Colo. 1988, U.S. Dist. Ct. Colo. 1988, U.S. Ct. Appeals (3d cir.) 1989. Mem. patent dept. Western Electric Co., Washington, 1961-62; law clk. Conn. Supreme Ct., 1962-63; sole practice, Bridgeport, Conn., 1972-75; patent atty. Bendix Corp., 1964-66; patent counsel Vitramon, Inc., 1966-68; line, staff mgmt. positions Singer Co., 1968-70, Xerox Corp., 1970-72; exec. v.p. Servco Leasing Corp., N.Y.C., 1972-74; sole practice, Bridgewater, N.J., 1972-77, Ormond Beach, Fla., Windsor, Colo., 1977—; ptnr. Colo. land devel.; cons. to industry on tech. devel.; lectr., tchr. profl. seminars various schs., univs., and govt. agys. Vol., United Jewish Appeal, 1974-76 M.I.T. Alumni Assn., 1975-78, Am. Cancer Soc., 1978-82; dir. No. Colo. Med. Ctr. Found., Inc., No. Colo. Found.; mem. accountability com. RE-4 Sch. Dist., 1987, Wels County Bd. Adjustment. Mem. ABA (litigation, patent sects., ethics com. patent sect.), Colo. Bar Assn., N.J. Bar Assn., R.I. Bar Assn., Weld County Bar Assn., Rotary (officer local club, bd. dirs.). Editor: Boston Coll. Bus. and Comml. Law Rev., 1961-62.

WORRELL, EDWARD DOUGLAS, health facility administrator, educator; b. Missoula, Mont., Aug. 10, 1953; s. Edward Marshall Worrell and Patricia Marie (Mulloy) Dira; m. Bonnie Lee Hahka, July 13, 1979; children: Cassandra Ann, Edward Marshall. Student, U. Mont., 1972-73, Missoula Vocat.-Tech. Ctr., 1973-74. Programmer Sch. Dist. #1, Butte, Mont., 1974-79; tchr. Sch. Dist. #1, Great Falls, Mont., 1977—; programmer Bank of Mont. System, Great Falls, 1979-84; programmer, analyst Mt. Deaconess Med. Ctr., Great Falls, 1984-87, ops. supr., 1987—. Home: 601 6th Ave N Great

Falls MT 59401 Office: Mt Deaconess Med Ctr 1101 26th St S Great Falls MT 59405

WORRELL, RICHARD VERNON, orthopedic surgeon, college dean; b. Bklyn., June 4, 1931; s. John Elmer and Elaine (Callender) W.; B.A., NYU, 1952; M.D., Meharry Med. Coll., 1958; m. Audrey Frances Martiny, June 14, 1958; children—Philip Vernon, Amy Elizabeth. Intern Meharry Med. Coll., Nashville, 1958-59; resident gen. surgery Mercy-Douglass Hosp., Phila., 1960-61; resident orthopaedic surgery State U. N.Y. Buffalo Sch. Medicine Affiliated Hosps., 1961-64; resident in orthopaedic pathology Temple U. Med. Center, Phila., 1966-67; pvt. practice orthopaedic surgery, Phila., 1964-68; asst. prof. acting head div. orthopaedic surgery U. Conn. Sch. Medicine 1968-70; attending orthopaedic surgeon E.J. Meyer Meml. Hosp., Buffalo, Millard Fillmore Hosp., Buffalo, VA Hosp., Buffalo, Buffalo State Hosp.; clin. instr. orthopaedic surgery SUNY, Buffalo, 1970-74; chief orthopedic surgery VA Hosp., Newington, Conn., 1974-80; asst. prof. surgery (orthopaedics) U. Conn. Sch. Medicine, 1974-77, assoc. prof., 1977-83, asst. dean student affairs, 1980-83; prof. clin. surgery SUNY Downstate Med. Ctr., Bklyn., 1983—; dir. orthopedic surgery Brookdale Hosp. Med. Ctr., Bklyn., 1983-86; prof. of orthopaedics U. N.Mex. Sch. of Medicine, 1986—; dir. orthopaedic oncology U. N.Mex. Med. Ctr., 1987—; mem. med. staff U. N.Mex. Cancer Ctr., 1987—; chief orthopaedic surgery VA Med. Ctr., Albuquerque, 1987—; cons. in orthopaedic surgery Newington (Conn.) Children's Hosp., 1968-70; mem. sickle cell disease adv. com. NIH, 1982-86. Bd. dirs. Big Bros. Greater Hartford. Served to capt. M.C., U.S. Army Res., 1962-69. Diplomate Am. Bd. Orthopaedic Surgery, Nat. Bd. Med. Examiners. Fellow ACS, Am. Acad. Orthopaedic Surgeons; mem. Orthopaedic Research Soc., Internat. Soc. Orthopaedic Surgery and Traumatology, AMA, Royal Med Soc. (affiliate), Alpha Omega Alpha.

WORRILOW, RICHARD CHARLES, small business owner; b. L.A., Feb. 28, 1944; s. Richard Morris and Helen Elizabeth (Charleston) W.; m. Janice Joanne Ludwick, Mar. 9, 1944 (div. Dec. 1977); 1 child, Lisa Anne. BA in Polit. Sci., Calif. State U., Northridge, 1971; MS in Recreation Mgmt., Calif. State U., L.A., 1978. Profl. model L'Image/Robert Black Agys., L.A., Scottsdale, Ariz., 1958—; sr. account rep. Travelers Ins. Co., L.A., Hartford, Conn., 1971-85; owner Villa Maria Pasta Products, Mesa, Ariz., 1987-88; ptnr. Rickman Assocs., Scottsdale, 1987-88; owner Gourmet Imports, Phoenix, 1982—, Scottsdale Cookie Co., 1985-89, Vis a'Vis, Phoenix, 1984—. Pres. Men's League of Scottsdale, 1986-87. With U.S. Army, 1966-69, Vietnam. Mem. Scottsdale C. of C., Phoenix C. of C. Republican. Home: 128 E Wood Dr Phoenix AZ 85022 Office: Gourmet Imports 128 E Wood Dr Phoenix AZ 85022

WORTHEN, DAVID SCOTT, insurance company executive; b. Salt Lake City, Utah, Apr. 25, 1948; s. Paul Warren and Billie Elaine (Winkleman) W.; m. Kristine K. Weaver, June 9, 1973 (div. 1980); m. Sharla R. Schmidt, Jan. 1, 1982; children: Michael Lynn, Terri Ranae, Mark Douglas. BS in Bus. and Econ., U. Mont., 1975. Producer Piper Jaffray Hopwood, Boise, Idaho, 1976-78; ptnr. Capital Ins. Corp., Boise, Idaho, 1978-82; pres. Worthen Craig Agys., Boise, Idaho, 1982—. Mem. Idaho Safety Mgmt. Council, Boise, 1985—. Mem. Profl. Ins. Agts. Assn., Idaho Motor Trans. Assn. (adv.), Boise C. of C., Am. Trucking Assn. (assoc.), Delta Nu Alpha. Republican. Mormon. Office: Worthen Craig Agys 7440 Lemhi Box 7873 Boise ID 83709

WORTHEY, CAROL, composer; b. Worcester, Mass., Mar. 1, 1943; d. Bernard Krieger and Edith Lilian (Cramer) Symonds; m. Eugene Worthey III, June 1969 (div. 1980); 1 child, Megan; m. Raymond Edward Korns, Sept. 21, 1980. BA in Music Composition, Columbia U., 1965; grad., Dick Grove Sch. Music., L.A., 1979; grad. filmscoring prog., UCLA, 1978; music studies with Darius Milhaud, Walter Piston, Elliot Carter, Vincent Persichetti, Grant Beglarian, Karl Korte, Otto Luening, Eddy Lawrence Manson, Dick Grove. Sr. composer, arranger Celebrity Ctr. Internat. Choir, Hollywood, Calif., 1985—. Composer, arranger The Hollywood Chorale; composer ballets Athena, 1963, The Barren, 1965; composer, lyricist, librettist full-length musical The Envelope Please, 1988; composer piano works performed in France, Italy, Germany, Can., U.S. and Eng. by Mario Feninger, 1982; compositions performed at Aspen Music Festival, 1963, Carnegie Hall, 1954, Dorothy Chandler Pavilion, 1986-88; appeared as singer-songwriter on L.A. Songwriter's Showcase, 1977; arranger Merv Griffin Show, 1981, The Night Before Christmas, L.A. Children's Theatre, 1988. Vol. performer various childcare ctrs., old folks homes, etc. Recipient Silver Poet award World of Poetry, 1987. Mem. Broadcast Music Inc., Nat. Acad. Songwriters, Songwriters and Composers Assn. Jewish.

WORTHY, JAMES, professional basketball player; b. Gastonia, N.C., Feb. 27, 1961; m. Angela Worthy. Grad., U. N.C., 1985. Forward Los Angeles Lakers, 1982—; player NBA All-Star Game 1986-88, mem. NBA championship team, 1985, 87, 88. Named MVP, NBA playoffs, 1988. Office: LA Lakers PO Box 10 Inglewood CA 90306 *

WORTHY, JOHN THOMAS, communications technician; b. Long Beach, Calif., Apr. 17, 1959. Cert. tech., Palomar Jr. Coll., San Marcos, Calif., 1983. Technician Show Biz Pizza, Escondido, Calif., 1983-84, Coded Communications Co., San Marcos, 1983-84, Northern Telecom Co., San Diego, 1984.

WOSKOW, ROBERT MARSHALL, management consultant; b. N.Y.C., Aug. 1, 1951; s. Martin and Marion (Kloder) W.; m. Gail Berrin, Apr. 1, 1979; children: Belle Ilysa, Benjamin Hale. BSEE, UCLA, 1973; MSEE, Calif. State U., Northridge, 1976; MBA, Pepperdine U., 1982. Elec. engr. various orgns., L.A., 1973-84; engring. dir. Arts and Sci. Tech., L.A., 1984-85; programs mgr. Pacesetter Systems, Sylmar, Calif., 1985-87; chief exec. officer Robert Marshall and Assocs., Encino, Calif., 1982—. Patentee in field. Home and Office: Robert Marshall and Assocs 16801 Severo Pl Encino CA 91436

WOTT, JOHN ARTHUR, horticulture educator; b. Fremont, Ohio, Apr. 10, 1939; s. Arthur Otto Louis and Esther Wilhelmina (Werth) W.; children: Christopher, Timothy, Holly. BS, Ohio State U., 1961; MS, Cornell U., 1966, PhD, 1968. Mem. staff Ohio State Coop. Extension Svc., Bowling Green, 1961-64; rsch. asst. Cornell U., Ithaca, N.Y., 1964-68; prof. Purdue U., West Lafayette, Ind., 1968-81; prof. Ctr. Urban Horticulture U. Wash., Seattle, 1981—. Contbr. numerous papers to profl. jours. Mem. Am. Soc. Horticultural Sci. (com. chmn. 1967—), Am. Assn. Botanic Gardens and Arboreta, Internat. Plant Propagators Soc. (pres. 1984), Internat. Security (treas. 1985—). Office: U Wash Ctr Urban Horticulture 3501 NE 41st St Seattle WA 98195

WOUDENBERG, PAUL RICHARD, chaplain; b. Highland Park, Ill., Sept. 1, 1927; s. John Anton and Rosina Wilhelmina (Maechtle) W.; m. Emily Wiltse, June 5, 1967; children: Mary C., Elizabeth L. BA, Occidental Coll., 1949; MDiv, Boston U., 1952, PhD, 1959. Ordained to ministry Meth. Ch., 1952. Minister Echo Park United Meth. Ch., L.A., 1954-61, Calif. Heights United Meth. Ch., L.A., 1961-67, 1st United Meth. Ch., Santa Monica, Calif., 1968-76, Ch. of the Wayfarer, Carmel, Calif., 1975-86; chaplain Robert Louis Stevenson Sch., Pebble Beach, Calif., 1986—. Author: Ford in the Thirties, 1976, Lincoln--The Post War Years, 1980, Buyes Guide to Rolls Royce, 1984, Buyers Guide to Aston Martin, 1986, Buyers Guide to Fords, 1987. Served with USN, 1945-46. Republican. Home: PO Box 1583 Pebble Beach CA 93953

WOZNIAK, JOYCE MARIE, sales executive; b. Detroit, Aug. 3, 1955; d. Edmund Frank and Bernice (Liske) W. BA, Mich. State U., 1976; MA, Nat. U., San Diego, 1988. Probation officer San Diego County Probation, 1979-81; prodn. engr. Tuesday Prodns., Inc., San Diego, 1981-85; nat. sales mgr. Advance Rec. Products, San Diego, 1986-88; owner Joyce Enterprises, San Diego, 1986—; sales exec. Audio-Video Supply Inc., San Diego, 1988—. Producer (video) Loving Yourself, 1987, southwest cable access program, 1986—, Registered Marriage, Family, and Child Counselor-Intern, California, 1989. Active Zool. Soc. San Diego. Mem. Art Glass Assn. So. Calif., Calif. Assn. Marriage and Family Therapists, Internat. Television Assn. Home: PO Box 3532 Rancho Santa Fe CA 92067 Office: Audio-Video Supply Inc 4674 Cardin St Ste D San Diego CA 92111

WRALSTAD, PHILLIP EVANS, electronic engineer; b. Grand Forks, N.D., Nov. 11, 1932; s. Carl Manvil and Ellen Amanda (Evens) W.; m. Mickie L. Thornton; children: Mark Evans, Beth Ellen Wralstad Voltmann, Laurie Ann. BSEE, U. N.D., 1956; postgrad., U. Denver, 1961, U. Ariz., 1964-65; MPA, U. Okla., 1974. Chief engr. test div. U.S. Army Security Agy. Test and Evaluation Ctr., Ft. Huachuca, Ariz., 1967-77, U.S. Army Electronic Proving Ground, Ft. Huachuca, Ariz., 1977-78; tech. dir. U.S. Army Intelligence and Security Bd., Ft. Huachuca, Ariz., 1978--. Mem. Sierra Vista (Ariz.) Sch. Bd., 1972-76, clk., 1974, pres., 1975. Capt. U.S. Army, 1957-63. Mem. IEEE (sr., sect. pres. 1970), Armed Forces Communications and Electronics Assn., Assn. Old Crows (bd. dirs. 1980-83, 88--), Tau Kappa Epsilon, Huachucans Club, Rotary Internat. (pres. Sierra Vista chpt. 1971, v.p. 1972). Republican. Lutheran. Home: 1264 Yucca Dr Sierra Vista AZ 85635 Office: US Army Intelligence and Security Bd Fort Huachuca AZ 85613

WRAY, KARL, newspaper broker, former newspaper owner and publisher; b. Bishop, Tex., June 8, 1913; s. Ernest Paul and Gertrude (Garvin) W.; m. Flora-Lee Koepp, Aug. 11, 1951; children: Diana, Mark, Kenneth, Norman, Thomas. A.B., Columbia U., 1935. Auditor U.S. Dept. Agr., Washington, also Little Rock, 1935-37; salesman O'Mara & Ormsbee, Inc., N.Y.C., 1937-42; advt. mgr. Lompoc (Calif.) Record, 1947-54; owner, pub. San Clemente (Calif.) Daily Sun-Post, 1954-67, Coastline Dispatch, San Juan Capistrano, Calif., 1956-67, Dana Point (Calif.) Lamplighter, 1966-67; cons. Lear Siegler, Inc., Washington, 1967-68; pub. Daily Star-Progress, La Habra, Calif., 1969-74, Anaheim (Calif.) Bulletin, 1974-86. Mem. Calif. State Park Commn., 1960-64, vice chmn., 1961-62; mem. exec. bd. Orange County council Boy Scouts Am., 1961-64, 76-87; mem. citizens adv. com. Orange Coast Coll., 1963-66; bd. dirs. Calif. Newspaper Youth Found., 1978-84; pres. Freedom Bowl, Inc., Anaheim, Calif., 1981-84, chmn. bd., 1984-86, bd. dirs., 1986— . Served to capt. USMC, 1942-46. Mem. Calif. Newspaper Advt. Execs. Assn. (pres. 1952-53), Calif. Newspaper Pubs. Assn. (dir. 1960-64), Am. Theatre Critics Assn., Baseball Writers Assn. Am., Football Writers Assn. Am., Calif. Press Assn., San Juan Capistrano C. of C. (pres. 1966), San Clemente C. of C. (pres. 1956-57), La Habra C. of C. (dir. 1970-74), Anaheim C. of C. (dir. 1974-86). Presbyterian (elder). Address: 2420 S Ola Vista San Clemente CA 92672-4360

WRIGHT, BERNARD, artist; b. Pitts., Feb. 23, 1938; s. Garfield and Emma (Jefferson) W.; m. Corrine Westley, Mar. 7, 1964; 1 son, Jeffrey. Student Otis Art Inst., Los Angeles, 1969-70, Los Angeles Trade Tech. Coll., 1971-73. Exhibited traveling art show Moscow, Baku, Leningrad, Alma Alta, USSR, European capitals, 1966, Los Angeles City Hall Rotunda Gallery, 1967, Calif. Lutheran Coll., Thousand Oaks, 1967, Alley Gallery, Beverly Hills, 1968, Florenz Art Gallery, Los Angeles, 1969, San Diego Mus., 1969, Phillip E. Freed Gallery of Fine Arts, Chgo., 1969, Art West Gallery, Los Angeles, 1973, N.J. State Mus., Trenton, Detroit Inst. Arts, Mich., 1974, U. So. Calif., Calif. Mus. Sci. and Industry, 1974, City Art Mus., St. Louis, 1976, N.Y.C. Pub. Library, 1977, Pitts. City Hall Rotunda, 1982, The Mus. of African Am. Art, Los Angeles, 1982, Main Bridge Art Gallery, Los Angeles City Hall, 1983; represented in pvt. and pub. collections including Howard U., Library of Congress. collections past pres. co-founder Wright's & Westley Prodns., furniture and garment designers. Cited by U.S. Rep. Cardiss Collins, Ill., 1978, state senator Bill Greene, Calif, 1981, Mayor Richard S. Callguiri, Pitts., 1981, Mayor Coleman A. Young, Detroit, 1981, Mayor Tom Bradley, Los Angeles. bd. supr. Kenneth Hahn, Los Angeles, 1981; active community involvement Sta. KHJ-TV, 1982. Mem. Art West Assn. (bd. dirs.). Contbr. articles to profl. jours. Home: PO Box 8990 Los Angeles CA 90008

WRIGHT, BRUCE ALAN, aerospace engineer; b. Syracuse, N.Y., Jan. 5, 1945; s. Alfred Sidney Wright and Lorna Mae (Camp) Dilley; m. Patricia Proo, Apr. 8, 1989; 1 child, Jennifer Ann. BS in Engring., U.S. Naval Acad., 1967. Registered profl. engr., Calif. Commd. ensign USN, 1967, ret., 1973; engr. Burroughs Corp., Rancho Bernardo, Calif., 1973-75; agt. Century-21, Del Mar, Calif., 1975-79; owner The Brokerage, Encinitas, Calif., 1979-81, Albatross Restaurant, Delmar, 1980-81; engr., analyst Mathetics Corp., San Diego, 1981-82; prin. design engr. Northrop B-2 Div., Pico Rivera, Calif., 1982—. Coach Youth Soccer League, Del Mar, 1977-80; pres. Little League, Del Mar, 1977-80, Condominium Assn., Downey, Calif., 1987. Commdr. USNR, 1989—. Mem. AIAA, Naval Res. Assn., Northrop Mgmt. Club, Masons (Master), Shriner. Republican. Home: 2237 Calle Margarita San Dimas CA 91773 Office: Northrop B2 Div 8900 E Washington E541/3E Pico Rivera CA 90660

WRIGHT, CAROLE YVONNE, chiropractor; b. Long Beach, Calif., July 12, 1932; d. Paul Burt and Mary Leoan (Staley) Fickes; 1 dau., Morgan Michelle. D. Chiropractic, Palmer Coll., Davenport, Iowa, 1975. Instr. Palmer Coll., 1975-76; dir., owner Wright Chiropractic Clinic, Rocklin, Calif., 1978—, Woodland, Calif., 1980-81; co-owner Ft. Sutter Chiropractic Clinic, Sacramento, 1985-89; owner Weight Chiropractic Health Ctr., Sacramento, 1989—; cons. in field; lectr., speaker on radio programs, at seminars. Contbr. articles to profl. jours. Co-chmn. Harold Michaels for Congress campaign, Alameda, Calif., 1972; dist. dir. 14th Congl. Dist., 1983—. Mem. Internat. Chiropractic Assn. Calif. (bd. dirs. 1978-81, pres. 1983-85), Palmer Coll. Alumni Assn. (Calif. state pres. 1981-83), Rocklin C. of C. (bd. dirs. 1979-81), Rocklin-Loomis Bus. and Profl. Women. Republican. Avocations: reading; travel. Home: 4270 Cavitt Stallman Rd Roseville CA 95661 Office: Ft Sutter Chiropractic 2720 Capitol Ave #102 Sacramento CA 95816

WRIGHT, CHARLES LEE, information systems consultant; b. Dalton, Ga., Dec. 18, 1949; s. Charlie William and Catherine Christine (Quarles) W.; m. Lora Langford, May 11, 1968; children: Charles Lee, Christina. AA in Bus., Dalton Jr. Coll., 1971; BS in Bus., U. Tenn., Chattanooga, 1977; also numerous IBM classes on various machines and systems;. Trainee Ludlow Carpets, Dalton, 1971, EDP supr., 1971-73, EDP mgr., 1973-77; ops. mgr. Walter Carpet Mills, Industry, Calif., 1977-80; ptnr., cons. TCT Systems, San Dimas, Calif., 1978-81; ptnr., chief exec. officer Williams, Wright and Assocs., Upland, Calif., 1981—; profl. svcs. mgr. Southern Calif. Williams Wright and Assocs. (subs. Internat. Customer Solutions), Upland, 1988—. Served as sgt. U.S. Army, 1969-71; Vietnam, Cambodia. Decorated Bronze Star, Army Commendation medal with oak leaf and oak leaf cluster, Air medal. Mem. Data Processing Mgmt. Assn., Am. Mgmt. Assn., Small Systems User Group, COMMON. Home: 2410 Sandpiper Pl Ontario CA 91761 Office: 400 N Mountain Ave Upland CA 91786

WRIGHT, CURTIS LYNN, advertising agency executive; b. Beloit, Wis., Sept. 16, 1944; s. Kenneth Archie and Lorraine Millicent (Hanamann) W.; student Purdue U., 1963-66; m. JoAnn Margaret Korn, Apr. 16, 1966; children: Christopher Michael, Bryan Edward. Advt. prodn. mgr. L.S. Ayres & Co., Indpls., 1962-66; advt. mgr. John Bean div. FMC Corp., Tipton, Ind., 1966-67, mktg. asst. Riverside (Calif.) div., 1967-68, asst. advt. mgr. ordnance div., San Jose, Calif., 1968-69; pres. Battenberg, Fillhardt & Wright, Inc., San Jose, 1969—. Bd. dirs. San Jose Symphony, 1971-72, Santa Clara (Calif.) County Performing Arts League, 1972, San Jose Community Theater, 1972, Santa Clara County Jr. Achievement, 1973—, Better Bus. Bur., 1977-78, Live Oaks Found., 1982—; elected councilman City of Morgan Hill, Calif., 1986—; elected mayor, 1988—. Recipient Ad Man of Yr. award Am. Advt. Fedn., 1973, Andy award Advt. Club N.Y.C., 1973, 74, 75, 77, 79, 80, 81, 82, 84, 87, 1st pl. awards (23) San Francisco Soc. Communicating Arts, 1973, 75, 76, 77, 78, 79, 80, 81, 82, 83, 84, 86, 87, Western Art Dirs. competition award, 1973, 75, 76, 77, 78, 79, 80, 81, 82, 86, 87, Communication Arts competition award, 1974, 77, 79, 81, 86, 87, others. Mem. Am. Assn. Advt. Agys. (gov. No. Calif. council 1974-75), San Jose C. of C. (chmn. communications com. 1974-76), No. Calif. Assn. Indsl. Advertisers (dir. 1973-74), Santa Clara Valley Assn. Advt. Agys. (bd. dirs. 1982—), San Jose Advt. Club (pres. 1974-76). Home: 18540 Castle Hill Dr Morgan Hill CA 95037 Office: 70 N Second St San Jose CA 95113

WRIGHT, DAVID LEE, special events producer, design consultant; b. Peoria, Ill., Nov. 8, 1946; s. Lowell Grandon Wright and Helen Joann (Snyder) Hohstadt; m. Barbara Jane Wick, 1971 (div. 1974); 1 child, Rachael Elizabeth; m. Kathleen Elaine Workman, Oct. 24, 1987. BA in English, Ill. State U., 1975; MA in English, U. Ill., 1977. Mgr. Studio Instrument Rentals, Chgo., 1980-81; prodn. mgr. Chip Monck Industries, Redondo Beach, Calif., 1981-83; ops. mgr. Greek Theatre, L.A., 1983-84; exec. producer Simas & Assocs., Ventura, 1984—; prodn. mgr. Del Mar (Calif.) Fair, 1983—; pres. Stage Wright Prodns., Inc., Rancho La Costa, Calif., 1980—; prodn. mgr. 22d Dist. Agrl. Assn., Del Mar, 1984—, Southland Concerts, San Diego, 1985-87; dept. supr. Del Mar Satellite Wagering, 1987—; tech. dir. Western Fairs Assn., Sacramento, 1988—; prodn. cons. Hard Rock Cafe, San Diego, 1988—. Campaign worker Hunter S. Thompson, Aspen, Colo., 1980; event coord. Missing Children's Found., San Diego, 1988. With U.S. Army, 1966-68. Mem. Am. Mus. Natural History, Nat. Geographic Soc., San Diego Mus. Fine Art, Audubon Soc., Smithsonian Instn. Home: 2564 Navarra Apt 108 Rancho La Costa CA 92009 Office: Del Mar Fair 2260 Jimmy Durante Blvd Del Mar CA 92014

WRIGHT, DEAN ROBERT, physician; b. Oberlin, Ohio, June 19, 1949; s. C. Robert and Leatrice Pearl (Barr) W.; m. Marizabel Estrada, Dec. 20, 1975; children: Kevin, Kelly, Kristen. BS in Biology, Oberlin College, 1971; MD in Medicine and Surgery, U. Autonoma de Guadalajora, Guadalajura, Jalisco, Mex., 1975; postgrad., New Jersey Coll. of Medicine, Dentistry, 1976. Diplomate Am. Bd. of Family Practice. Resident family practice Mercy Hosp., Toledo, 1976-79; staff physician El Rio Neighborhood Health Clinic, Tucson, 1979-81; physician Thomas Davis Clinic, Tucson, 1981—; chmn. family practice dept. El Dorado Hosp., Tucson, 1984—; preceptor family practice dept. Ariz. Coll. Medicine, Tucson, 1979—. Mem. Pima County Med. Soc., Ariz. Med. Soc., Am. Med. Soc. Republican. Presbyterian. Office: Thomas Davis Clinic 9302 E 22d St Tucson AZ 85710

WRIGHT, EUGENE ALLEN, federal judge; b. Seattle, Feb. 23, 1913; s. Elias Allen and Mary (Bailey) W.; m. Esther Ruth Ladley, Mar. 19, 1938; children: Gerald Allen, Meredith Ann Wright Morton. AB, U. Wash., 1935, JD, 1937; LLD, U. Puget Sound, 1984. Bar: Wash. 1937. Assoc. Wright & Wright, Seattle, 1937-54; judge Superior Ct. King County, Wash., 1954-66; v.p., sr. trust officer Pacific Nat. Bank Seattle, 1966-69; judge U.S. Ct. of Appeals 9th Circuit, Seattle, 1969—; acting municipal judge, Seattle, 1948-52; mem. faculty Nat. Jud. Coll., 1964-72; lectr. Sch. Communications, U. Wash., 1965-66, U. Wash. Law Sch., 1952-74; lectr. appellate judges' seminars, 1973-76, Nat. Law Clks. Inst., La. State U., 1973; chmn. Wash. State Com. on Law and Justice, 1968-69; mem. com. on appellate rules Jud. Conf., 1978-85, mem. com. on courtroom photography, 1983-85, com. jud. ethics, 1984—, com. Bicentennial of Constn., 1985-87. Author: (with others) The State Trial Judges Book, 1966; also articles; editor: Trial Judges Jour., 1963-66; contbr. articles to profl. jours. Chmn. bd. visitors U. Puget Sound Sch. Law, 1979-84; bd. dirs. Met. YMCA, Seattle, 1955-72; lay reader Episc. ch. Served to lt. col. AUS, 1941-46; col. Res.; ret. Decorated Bronze Star, Combat Inf. badge; recipient Army Commendation medal, Disting. Service award U.S. Jr. C. of C., 1948, Disting. Service medal Am. Legion. Fellow Am. Bar Found.; mem. ABA (council div. jud. adminstrn. 1971-76), Fed. Bar Assn. (Disting. Jud. Service award 1984), Wash. Bar Assn. (award of merit 1983), Seattle-King County Bar Assn. (Spl. Disting. Service award 1984), Appellate Judges Conf., Ret. Officers Assn., Order of Coif, Delta Upsilon (Disting. Alumni Achievement award 1989), Phi Delta Phi. Clubs: Nat. Lawyers, Wash. Athletic, Rainier. Lodges: Masons (33 degree), Shriners. Office: US Ct Appeals 902 US Courthouse 1010 5th Ave Seattle WA 98104

WRIGHT, FRANCES JANE, educational psychologist; b. Los Angeles, Dec. 22, 1943; d. step-father John David and Evelyn Jane (Dale) Brinegar. BA, Long Beach State U., 1965, secondary tchr. cert., 1966; MA, Brigham Young U., 1968, EdD, 1980; postgrad. U. Nev., 1970, U. Utah, 1972-73; postdoctoral Utah State U., 1985-86. Cert. tchr., adminstr. Utah. Asst. dir. Teenpost Project, San Pedro, Calif., 1966; caseworker Los Angeles County, 1966-67; self-care inservice dir. Utah State Tng. Sch., American Fork, Utah, 1968, vocat. project designer, 1968; tchr. mentally handicapped Santa Ana Unified Schs., Calif., 1968-69; state specialist intellectually handicapped State Office Edn., Salt Lake City, 1969-70; vocat. counselor Manpower, Salt Lake City, 1970-71; tchr. severely handicapped Davis County Schs., Farmington, Utah, 1971-73, diagnostician, 1973-74, resource elem. tchr., 1974-78; instr. Brigham Young U., Salt Lake City, 1976-83; resource tchr. jr. high Davis County Schs., Farmington, 1978—; ednl. cons., Murray, Utah, 1973—; cons. and lectr. in field. Author curriculums in spl. edn.; contbr. articles to profl. jours. Named Profl. of Yr., Utah Assn. for Children with Learning Disabilities, 1985. Mem. Assn. Children/Adults with Learning Disabilities (del. 1979-85, 87, nat. nominating com. 1985-86, nat. bd. dirs. 1988—), NEA, Nat. Assn. Female Execs., Utah Assn. Children/Adults with Learning Disabilities (exec. bd. 1978-84, profl. adv. bd. 1985—), Council Exceptional Children (div. learning disabilities, ednl. diagnostics, behavioral disorders), Utah Ednl. Assn., Davis County Edn. Assn., Council Learning Disabilities, Windstar Found., Smithsonian Found., Nat. Hist. Preservation Found., Cousteau Soc., Am. Biographical Inst. (life, hon. advisor rsch. bd. advisors nat. div.), Nat. Assn. Sch. Adminstrs. Democrat. Mormon. Lodge: Job's Daughters. Avocations: geneology research, horseback riding, sketching, crafts, reading. Home: 5212 Gravenstein Park Murray UT 84123 Office: Kaysville Jr High Sch Kaysville UT 84037

WRIGHT, FREDERICK HERMAN GREENE, II, computer systems engineer; b. Quincy, Mass., Feb. 23, 1952; s. Frederick Herman Greene and Dorothy Louise (Harrold) W. Student, MIT, 1968-69. Test and measurement technician The Foxboro (Mass.) Co., 1968; hardware and software designer MIT Project MAC, Cambridge, Mass., 1969, Info. Internat., Brookline, Mass., 1969, Stanford Artificial Intelligence Lab, Palo Alto, Calif., 1971-73, Systems Concepts, San Francisco, 1973-74, 1970, 73-74, 76—; hardware and software designer, then pres. Resource One, San Francisco, 1974-76; computer cons. Langley-Porter Neuropsychiatric Inst., San Francisco, 1976. membership chmn. Pacific Soaring Council, San Francisco, 1983-85, bd. dirs., 1984-85. Recipient Gold Soaring Badge Fed. Aeronautique Internat., 1983. Mem. Digital Equipment Corp. Users Soc., Bay Area Soaring Assn. Republican. Home: 251 C St San Rafael CA 94901-4916 Office: Systems Concepts 55 Francisco St San Francisco CA 94133

WRIGHT, GORDON BROOKS, musician, conductor, educator; b. Bklyn., Dec. 31, 1934; s. Harry Wesley and Helen Philomena (Brooks) W.; m. Inga-Lisa Myrin Wright, June 13, 1958 (div. 1979); children: Karin-Ellen Blindenbacher, Charles-Eric, Daniel Brooks. MusB, Coll. Wooster, 1957; MA, U. Wis., 1961; postgrad., Salzburg Mozarteum, 1972, Loma Linda U., 1979. Founder, music dir. Wis. Chamber Orch. (formerly Madison Summer Symphony), 1960-69; music dir. Fairbanks (Alaska) Symphony Orch., 1969—; prof. music Univ. Alaska, Fairbanks, 1969-89, prof. emeritus, 1989—; founder, music dir. Arctic Chamber Orch., Fairbanks, 1970-89; exec. dir. The Reznick Soc., Fairbanks, 1982—. Guest condr. Philarmonia Hungarica, Philomusica London, Siegerland Orch. Westfalia, Anchorage Symphony Orch.; composer: Suite of Netherlands Dances, 1965, Six Alaskan Tone Poems, 1974, Symphony in Ursa Major, 1979 (Legis. award 1979), 1984 Overture, Scott Joplin Suite, 1987; columnist Alaska Advocate, Fairbanks Daily News-Miner. Founder, bd. dirs. No. Alaska Environ. Ctr., Fairbanks, 1971-78. Served as pvt. AUS, 1957-59. Mem. Am. Musicol. Soc., Internat. Musicol. Soc., Am. Symphony Orch. League, Galpin Soc., Condr's. Guild, Dolmetsch Found., Arturo Toscanini Soc., Alaska Assn. Arts, Am. Fedn. Musicians, Royal Mus. Assn., Sierra Club (chmn. Fairbanks Group 1969-71), Friends of Earth-Alaska (bd. dirs. 1978—), Wilderness Soc., Audubon Soc., Alaska Conservation Soc. (editor Rev. 1971-78), China Poot Bay Soc. (bd. dirs. 1982—). Home: PO Box 80051 Fairbanks AK 99708 Office: Fairbanks Symphony Orch PO Box 82104 Fairbanks AK 99708

WRIGHT, HELENE SEGAL, editor; b. L.A., Jan. 31, 1955; d. Alan and Lila E. (Hambro) Segal; m. David Scott Wright, May 6, 1979. Student, Calif. State U., Fullerton, 1973-75; BA in English, U. Calif., Santa Barbara, 1978. Library asst. ABC-CLIO, Santa Barbara, 1979-80, editorial asst., 1980-81, asst. editor, 1981-83, mng. editor, 1983—. Mem. Am. Polit. Sci. Assn., Current World Leaders (adv. bd. 1989—). Home: 142 La Vista Grande Santa Barbara CA 93103 Office: ABC-CLIO 130 Cremona Dr Santa Barbara CA 93117

WRIGHT, JAMES BRYAN, lawyer; b. Olympia, Wash., Apr. 12, 1955; s. James Carol and Charlotte Elizabeth (Guffey) W. BA in Philosophy with honors, U. Puget Sound, 1978; JD, Coll. William and Mary in Va., 1982. Bar: Alaska 1983. Law clk. Third Judicial Dist. State of Alaska, Anchorage, 1982-83; assoc. Lynch, Crosby and Sisson, Anchorage, 1983-89, ptnr., 1989—. Mem. ABA (litigation sect., tort and ins. practice sect.), Alaska Bar Assn., Def. Research Inst. (com. ins. law), Def. Counsel Alaska, Phi Delta Phi. Presbyterian. Home: 646 W 21st Ave Anchorage AK 99503 Office: Lynch Crosby & Sisson 550 W 7th Ave 11th Fl Anchorage AK 99501

WRIGHT, JANET SCRITSMIER, investment consultant; b. Pomona, Calif., May 21, 1960; d. Jerome Lorenzo and Mildred Joan (Lloyd) Scritsmier; m. James Calvin Wright, Mar. 26, 1983; children—Justin Michael, Corey Gray. Student Calif. State Poly. U., 1978-79. Vice pres. sales E.L.A. Co., Industry, Calif., 1979-84; investment cons. Cameron Properties Inc., Covina, Calif., 1980—. Asst. instr. Dale Carnegie Sales Course, 1981-82, Human Relations, 1983. Republican. Mormon. Avocation: snow skiing. Home: 2454 N Cameron Ave Covina CA 91724

WRIGHT, JOHN H., winery executive. Chmn., pres., chief exec. officer Domaine Chandon, Yountville, Calif. Office: Domaine Chandon PO Box 2470 Yountville CA 94599 *

WRIGHT, JOHN ROBERT, electronics executive; b. Ft. Walton Beach, Fla., May 14, 1953; s. Robert Kenneth and Patricia Ruth (Schachtili) W.; m. Jo Ann Mistich, Dec. 8, 1973 (div. June 1982); children: Cassandra Nicole, Michele Elizabeth; m. Joyce Elena Cohen, Aug. 31, 1984. AS in Electronics, Goldenwest Jr. Coll., 1976; BS in Electronic Tech., So. Ill. U., 1978; postgrad., Webster U., 1986-88. With computer hardware maintenance dept. Computer Consoles Inc., Denver, 1979-81; with computer hardware maintenance dept. Mountain Bell Telephone, Denver, 1981-87, asst. supr., electronic data base technician, 1987—; owner P.C.'s By Design, Denver, 1988—. Vestry mem. Intercession Episc. Ch., Northglenn, Colo., 1986-87; ptarmigian dist. postleader Explorer, Denver, 1987—; leader Boy Scouts Am., Altus, Okla., 1975-79. Served with USAF, 1975-79. Mem. Nat. Rifle Assn. Republican. Episcopalian. Home: 6568 W 84th Ave Arvada CO 80003

WRIGHT, KATHLEEN JEAN, nurse; b. Butte, Mont., May 15, 1955; d. Kiernan Joseph and Edna (Husnik) Minehan; m. Steve Dell Wright, Oct. 13, 1978; children: Christopher, Annie, Michael. BSN, Mont. State U., 1977. RN, Mont. Nurse Pondera County Hosp., Conrad, Mont., 1977, Riverview Meml. Hosp., St. Paul, 1977-78, St. James Community Hosp., Butte, 1979-80, 88—; nurse, substitute tchr. Butte Vo-Tech program, 1987. Catechism tchr. St. Anne's Cath. Ch., Butte, 1984-87; den leader Butte council Boy Scouts Am. Mem. Mont. Nurses Assn. Democrat. Roman Catholic. Home: 112 Rocky Mountain Ln Butte MT 59701

WRIGHT, KENNETH JAMES, chemistry and environmental science educator; b. Pitts., Aug. 26, 1939; s. William Orville and Laura Louise (Husted) W.; m. Virginia Louise Brodin, Jan. 1, 1966; children: Kody James, Clark William. Student, Harvey Mudd Coll., 1957-59; BS in Chemistry, Portland State U., 1962; postgrad., Oreg. State U., 1962-63; PhD in Chemistry, U. Idaho, 1971. Analytical and rsch. chemist Harvey Aluminum Corp., The Dalles, Oreg., 1963-66; prof. chemistry and environ. sci. N. Idaho Coll., Coeur d'Alene, 1971—, chmn. div. sci., 1972-77, chmn. faculty, 1982-83; rsch. trainee NSF, U. Idaho, 1967; ednl. cons. The Bunker-Hill Co., Kellogg, Idaho, 1977. Contbr. articles to profl. jours. Founder Hanford Edn. Action League, Spokane, Wash, 1985; appointee Hazardous Waste Cm., Coeur d'Alene, 1986, chmn., 1987; appointee Recycling Adv. Com. of Kootenai County, Idaho, 1988. Fellow NDEA, U. Idaho, 1968-70. Mem. Am. Chem. Soc. (sect./treas. Inland Empire sect. 1979, vice-chmn. 1980, chmn. 1981, div. of chem. edn.), Idaho Conservation League, Sierra Club (chmn. Idaho-Mont. chpt. 1976, NW regional conservation com. 1977-79), Nat. Ry. Hist. Soc., Better World Soc., Zero Population Growth, Sigma Xi. Office: N Idaho Coll 1000 W Garden Ave Coeur d'Alene ID 83814

WRIGHT, KENNETH LYLE, psychologist; b. American Falls, Idaho, Sept. 11, 1926; s. Jesse Joshua and Martha Sophia (Dickenson) W. children—Anne Collins, Corrella Carmelette Brown, Sandra Lynne Sutherland. B.A., U. Wash., 1941; M.A., U. So. Calif., 1957; Ph.D., San Gabriel Coll., 1958. Coach State Tng. Sch. for Boys, Chehalis, Wash., 1941; dep. probation officer, Los Angeles County, Calif., 1954-56; vis. lectr. Whittier Coll. (Calif.), 1955-56; dist. sch. psychologist Anaheim Union High Sch. Dist. (Calif.); guidance counselor, vice prin. Orleans Am. High Sch., Dept. Army (France), also psychol. services and spl. edn. coordinator Dependent Edn. Group Hdqrs., Karlsruhe, W.Ger., 1959-62; edn. specialist U.S. Navy, San Diego, 1962-63; pvt. practice psychology, San Diego, 1963-64, 69—; psychol. cons. Clin. Bd. Speech Therapy, Children's Hosp., San Diego, 1963-64; vis. prof. U. Western Ont., lectr., sch. psychologist London Bd. Edn. (Ont., Can.), 1964-66; dir. psychol. services Niagara Falls Dist. Bd. Edn. (N.Y.), 1966-69; lectr. Syracuse U., 1968. Pres. Whittier Coordinating Council; a founder Can. Sch. Vol. Program; founder Niagara Inst. Human Devel., founder San Diego Forensic Soc., 1988 European Assns. Am. Personnel and Guidance and Speech and Hearing in Dependent Schs., chmn. Instl. Research Bd., 1987-88. Served with USNR, 1941-46. Recipient outstanding award San Diego County Assn. Retarded Children, 3 awards Bio-Med. Rsch. Inst. Am. Fellow San Diego Biomed. Research Inst. (past pres.); mem. Assn. Children with Learning Disabilities, Council Exceptional Children (past pres. Niagara Falls chpt.), Royal Soc. Medicine, Am. Psychol. Assn., Calif. Psychol. Assn., San Diego County Psychol. Assn., Am. Soc. Clin. Hypnosis, Calif. Soc. Clin. Hypnosis (sec.), San Diego County Soc. Clin Hypnosis (pres. 1975-76), San Diego Assn. Clin. Psychologists (past pres.), Instl. Research Bd. (chmn.), Mensa (10-yr. cert. as proctor). Club: Koha Kai. Lodge: Masons. Author: My Name Is Kim; The American Symbol; The Fantastic Journey with Visualization and Imagery; The Psychological Effects of Allergy; Allergy and Learning Disabilities in Children. Home: 751 Amiford Dr San Diego CA 92107 Office: 4070 Goldfinch San Diego CA 92103

WRIGHT, LIN M., theater educator; b. Mpls., Jan. 19, 1933; d. Nathanial F. and Mary F. (Hargarten) Sommers; m. James L. Wright, Aug. 5, 1963; 1 child, Miriam Sommers. BS, U. Minn., 1954, MA, 1960, PhD, 1973. Cert. secondary tchr., Minn. Tchr. Gilbert (Minn.) High Sch., 1954-55, Mounds View High Sch., New Brighton, Minn., 1957-63; instr. theatre U. Minn., Mpls., 1965-72, asst. prof., 1972-73; prof. theatre Ariz. State U., Tempe, 1973-84, chmn. theatre dept., 1984—; bd. dirs. Ariz. Theatre Co., Nat. Arts Edn. Rsch. Ctr. Bd. dirs. Ariz. Theatre Co., 1986. Recipient Outstanding Contbns. award So. Calif. Edn. Theatre Assn., 1984. Mem. Am. Assn. Theatre for Youth (chair, founding bd. dirs., rsch. citation 1986), Children's Theatre Assn. Am. (pres. 1981-83, v.p. rsch. 1977-79, Human Awareness award 1976), East Valley Art Assn. (Outstanding Tchr. award 1988). Office: Ariz State U Dept Theater Tempe AZ 85287

WRIGHT, LORIN RODERICK, physical therapist; b. Billings, Mont., May 17, 1948; s. Roderick Roy and Bessie Helen (Steele) W.; m. Barbara Ann Keiser, Jan 13, 1973; children: Danielle, Heather. BA in Phys. Edn., U. Mont., 1971; cert. phys. therapy, U. Pa., 1972. Phys. therapist Gottsche Rehab. Ctr., Thermopolis, Wyo., 1972-73, 74-76, St. Vincent's Hosp., Billings, 1973-74; outreach phys. therapist Mont. Ctr. for Handicapped Children, Ea. Mont. Coll., Billings, 1976-80; founding ptnr., v.p. Phys. Therapy Clinic of Billings, 1979—; cons. Eastmont Human Svcs. Ctr., Glendive, Mont., 1976—; chmn. bd. of physical therapist examiners, Helena, Mont., 1986—; faculty affiliate U. Mont. Physical Therapy Sch., 1980—. Author: (with others, book tape series) Stress & Burnout Reasons & Remedies, 1988. Bd. dirs. Spl. Tgn. for Exceptional People, Billings, Mont., 1978-81; pres. elect Messiah Luth. Ch., Red Lodge, Mont. Mem. Am. Phys. Therapy Assn. (v.p. Mont. chpt., lectr. combined sect. meeting 1987), Mont. Assn. Pvt. Practice Phys. Therapists (chmn. 1986-88), Bd. Phys. Therapy Examiners (chmn. bd. 1988—), Rotary Club (pres. 1987-88) Inquiry Club (program dir 1987-88). Office: Phys Therapy Clinic 1 S Oaks PO Box 430 Red Lodge MT 59068

WRIGHT, MICHAEL TERRILL, electrical engineer; b. Vallejo, Calif., Mar. 27, 1951; s. John Newton and Marion Lorene (Terrill) W.; m. Mary Elizabeth Holguin, Apr. 28, 1979. BEE, Ariz. State U., 1973; MEE, &, 1980. Elect. engr. Motorola Govt. Electronics Group, Scottsdale, Ariz., 1974—. Mem. Eta Kappa Nu, Tau Beta Pi. Republican. Home: 4214 E Weldon Ave Phoenix AZ 85018 Office: Motorola Govt Electronics Group 8201 E McDowell Rd Scottsdale AZ 85252

WRIGHT, NADINE ANOHIN, data processing executive; b. Harbin, Hailongjiang, Peoples Rep. China, Sept. 30, 1945; came to U.S., 1960; d. Feofan Firsovitch and Tamara Viacheslavovna (Firsova) Anohin; m. Harry Franklin Wright, Nov. 22, 1978; children: Adrian Christopher, Devon Brhett. AA, City Coll. San Francisco, 1966; diplomas in French and internat. econs., U. Strasbourg, France, 1967, 69; BA, San Francisco State U., 1972, MBA, 1976. Programmer, auditor electronic and data processing Bechtel Corp., San Francisco, 1973-76; specialist electronic data processing Levi Strauss and Co., Frankfurt, Brussels, 1976-78; chief analyst/tech. advisor Calif. State Automobile Assn., San Francisco, 1978-79; supr. electronic data processing audit Crocker Bank, San Francisco, 1979-80, Ampex Corp., Redwood City, Calif., 1980-81; sr. staff analyst, sr. electronic data processing auditor Safeway Stores Corp., Oakland, Calif., 1981-86; cons. Breuners Inc., San Ramon, Calif., 1987—, Bay Area Remodeling and Construction, San Francisco, 1987—; systems engr. IBM Corp., San Francisco 1972-73. Chmn. Community Chest VFW, San Francisco, 1965. Mem. Inst. Internal Auditors (bd. dirs. 1987—, chmn. electronic data processing audit 1983-84), Nat. Assn. Accts. (scholarship com. 1982-83), Electronic Data Processing Auditor Assn. Democrat.

WRIGHT, ROSALIE MULLER, newspaper and magazine editor; b. Newark, June 20, 1942; d. Charles and Angela (Fortunata) Muller; m. Lynn Wright, Jan. 13, 1962; children: James Anthony Meador, Geoffrey Shepard. B.A. in English, Temple U., 1965. Mng. editor Suburban Life mag., Orange, N.J., 1960-62; assoc. editor Phila. mag., 1962-64, mng. editor, 1969-73; founding editor Womensports mag., San Mateo, Calif., 1973-75; editor scene sect. San Francisco Examiner, 1975-77; exec. editor New West mag., San Francisco and Beverly Hills, Calif., 1977-81; features and Sunday editor San Francisco Chronicle, 1981-87, asst. mng. editor features, 1987—; tchr. mag. writing U. Calif.-Berkeley, 1975-76; participant pub. procedure's course Stanford U., 1977-79; chmn. mag. judges Council Advancement and Support Edn. Conf., 1980, judge, 1984. Contbr. numerous mag. articles, critiques, revs., Compton's Ency. Mem. Am. Assn. Sunday and Feature Editors (treas. 1984, sec. 1985, 1st v.p. 1986, pres. 1987), Am. Soc. Newspaper Editors (mem. minority task force com. 1988). Office: Chronicle Pub Co 901 Mission St San Francisco CA 94119

WRIGHT, SHERMAN S., information and records executive, consultant; b. Honolulu, May 12, 1953; s. Walter Alden and Natalie Mary (Freitas) W.; m. Tamara Reneé, May 19, 1973; children: Jeremy Brooks, Amanda Lynnette. Student, DeAnza Jr. Coll., Cupertino, Calif., 1971-73, Foothill Jr. Coll., Los Altos, Calif., 1975-77. Records supr. Fairchild Camera & Instrument Corp., Mountain View, Calif., 1972-79; records administrator Blue Shield of Calif., San Francisco, 1979-81; adminstrv. mgr. Synertek Corp., Santa Clara, Calif., 1981-83; adminstrv. coordinator Syva Co., Palo Alto, Calif., 1983-88; records mgr. L.S.I. Logic Corp., Milpitas, Calif., 1988—; cons. Memorex Corp., Santa Clara, 1977-78, Xydex Corp. Santa Clara, 1987-88. Mem. Assn. Records Mgrs. and Adminstrs. (bd. dirs. 1984-86). Democrat. Roman Catholic. Home: 230 Douglas Ave Boulder Creek CA 95006

WRIGHT, TIM EUGENE, packaging development executive; b. Weed, N.Mex., Oct. 13, 1943; s. Clyde Everett and Juanita Delores (Barrett) W.; m. Nancy Ann Ausenbaugh, Oct. 2, 1965 (div. 1975); 1 child, Ramsey Jordan. Diploma, Dayton Art Inst., 1967, M.F.A., U. Idaho, 1969. Designer, Lawson Mfg. Co., Troy, Idaho, 1968-70, Boise Cascade, Burley, Idaho, 1970-72; project coordinator Boise Cascade, Golden, Colo., 1972-76, product devel. mgr., Wallula, Wash., 1976-84; mng. ptnr. Matrix Applications Co., Pasco, Wash., 1984—. Patentee folding carton. Recipient Silver award for packaging, 1978. Mem. Soc. Packaging and Handling Engrs., Western Packaging Assn., TAPPI. Office: Matrix Applications Co PO Box 1407 Pasco WA 99301

WRIGHT, WADELL, engineer; b. Greenville, S.C., Aug. 29, 1944; s. Thomas C. and Marie (Tate) W.; m. Ines Rosario Teran, Sept. 1, 1977; children: Andre Tyrone, Anthony Wadell, Fionna Michelle, Aljonn Jerome. Diploma, Control Data Inst., Burlington, Mass., 1970. With RCA, Marlboro, Mass., 1971, Honeywell Info. Systems, Waltham, Mass., 1971-74, Bendix Field Engring. Corp., Columbia, Md., 1975-79, Ford Aerospace & Communications Corp., Palo Alto, Calif., 1979-80, Kentron Internat., Pasadena, Calif., 1980-82, Rockwell Internat., Anaheim, Calif., 1983-84; sr. computer engr. Al-Johi Internat., Dhahran, Saudi Arabia, 1984-85; sr. test engr. Gen. Dynamics, San Diego, 1985-87; sr. standards lab. engr. Gen. Dynamics, Rancho Cucamonga, Calif., 1987-88; owner, mgr. WRIGHT Vending Svc., Colton, Calif., 1988—; performed work related duties Ascension Island, Atlantic Ocean, Quito, Ecuador, S.Am., Kauai, Hawaii, Seychelles Island, Indian Ocean, Dharan, Saudi Arabia. Author: Its Up to You in America, 1987-88; inventor in field. With U.S. Army, 1962-65. Home: 1397 N Topsail Ave Colton CA 92324 Office: WRIGHT Vending Svc PO Box 1107 Colton CA 92324

WRIGLEY, ELIZABETH SPRINGER (MRS. OLIVER K. WRIGLEY), foundation executive; b. Pitts., Oct. 4, 1915; d. Charles Woodward and Sarah Maria (Roberts) Springer; BA U. Pitts., 1935; BS, Carnegie Inst. Tech., 1936; m. Oliver Kenneth Wrigley, June 16, 1936 (dec. July 1978). Procedure analyst U.S. Steel Corp., Pitts., 1941-43; rsch. asst. The Francis Bacon Found., Inc., Los Angeles, 1944, exec., 1945-50, trustee, 1950—, dir. rsch., 1951-53, pres., 1954—, dir. Francis Bacon Libr.; mem. adv. coun. Royal Skakespeare Authorship Roundtable, Santa Monica, Calif.; mem. regional Fine Arts adv. coun. Calif. State Poly. U., Pomona. Mem. ALA, Calif. Libr. Assn., Renaissance Soc. Am., Modern Humanities Rsch. Assn., Cryptogram Assn., Alpha Delta Pi. Presbyn. Mem. Order Eastern Star, Damascus Shrine. Editor: The Skeleton Text of the Shakespeare Folio L.A. (by W.C. Arensberg), 1952. Compiler: Short Title Catalogue Numbers in the Library of the Francis Bacon Foundation, 1958; Wing Numbers in the Library of the Francis Bacon Foundation, 1959; Supplement To Francis Bacon Library Holdings in the STC of English Books, 1967; (with David W. Davies) A Concordance to the Essays of Francis Bacon, 1973. Home: 4805 N Pal Mal Ave Temple City CA 91780 Office: Francis Bacon Libr 655 N Dartmouth Ave Claremont CA 91711

WU, HOFU, architecture educator; b. Taipei, Taiwan, Mar. 28, 1949; came to U.S., 1973; s. Yung-Hwa and Chin-Chau W.; m. Meina Lin, July 30, 1983; children: Annie, Michelle, Tiffany. BArch, Tamkang U., Taipei, 1971; MArch, U. Ill., 1975; ArchD, U. Mich., 1988. Registered architect, Ill., Mich., Ariz. Project architect Kenyon & Assocs., Peoria, Ill., 1975-77, Herrman, Holman & Assocs., Inc., Ann Arbor, Mich., 1977-80; from lectr. to asst. prof. architecture U. Mich., 1980-83; asst. prof., dir. environ. test lab. Coll. Architectue & Environ. Design, Ariz. State U., 1984—. Contbr. articles to profl. jours. U.S. Dept. Energy rsch. grantee, 1985—. Mem. AIA, ASHRAE, Internat. Solar Energy Soc., Rotary. Presbyterian. Office: Ariz State U Coll Architecture & Environ Design Tempe AZ 85287

WU, OSCAR KANG, real estate developer; b. Chefu, Shantung, Republic of China, Jan. 15, 1946; came to U.S., 1969; s. Kai Chu and Chin (Lo) W.; m. Tessie Kuang Chu, Sept. 10, 1970; children: Alexander, Carolyn. BArch, Chinese Culture U., Taipei, Taiwan, 1968; MArch, U. Va., 1971. Lic. gen. contractor, Calif., real estate agt., Calif., Tex. Planner City of Beaumont, Tex., 1971-77; pres. O.K. Wu and Assocs., Inc., Alamo, Calif., 1977—. Mem. Chinese Assn. Polit. Action, Contra Costa County, Calif., 1986; vol. various local, state and nat. elections. Recipient Honorable Recognition award Beaumont C. of C. and HUD, 1984. Office: OK Wu & Assocs 2975 Roundhill Rd Alamo CA 94507

WU, PO-SHUN, biochemical researcher; b. Taipei, Republic of China, July 26, 1947; came to U.S., 1969; s. Ann-Pan and Zuei-Mei (Lee) W.; m. Susan H.W. Chen, Apr. 1, 1981; 1 child, Martin Jason. BS, Nat. Taiwan U., Taipei, 1969; MS, U. Akron, 1972; PhD, Georgetown U., 1977. Research fellow Albert Einstein Coll. Medicine, Bronx, N.Y., 1977-79, Calif. Inst. Tech., Pasadena, 1980-82; asst. prof. Calif. State U., Los Angeles, 1982; research scientist Pacific Med. Ctr., San Francisco, 1982-84; mgr. quality control Xoma Corp., Berkeley, Calif., 1984-85; mgr. tech. ops. Gene Labs Inc., San Carlos, Calif., 1985—. Contbr. articles to profl. jours. and chpts. to books. Mem. AAAS, Am. Chem. Soc., N.Y. Acad. Scis. Home: 1366 28th Ave San Francisco CA 94122 Office: Gene Labs Inc 505 Penobscot Dr Redwood City CA 94063

WULF, ROBERT FINDLEY, financial consultant; b. Phila., Mar. 6, 1937; s. Robert Fischer and Pauline (Findley) W.; m. Evelyn Nelson, July 23, 1983. AB in Econs., Stanford U., 1959; MBA, Columbia U., 1964. Chartered fin. analyst. V.p., security analyst Smith Barney & Co., N.Y.C., 1964-74; fin. analyst, mgr. Potlatch Corp., San Francisco, 1974-78, treas., 1978-84; pvt. practice fin. cons., Salem, 1984—; chmn., pres., chief exec. officer Am. Fed. Savs. & Loan, Salem, Oreg., 1986-87; chmn. Am. Home Savs. Fed. Savs. Bank, Salem, 1987-88. Elder 1st Presbyn. Ch., 1986-88; bd. dirs. Edgewood Children's Home, San Francisco, 1979-84, Pacific Med. Found., San Francisco, 1980-83; trustee Salem Hosp., 1987—. Served to 1st lt. USAF, 1959-62. Mem. Beta Gamma Sigma. Republican.

WUNDER, BRUCE ARNOLD, zoologist, educator; b. Monterey Park, Calif., Feb. 10, 1942; s. Edwin Claude and Phyllis Viviene (Lehman) W.; m. Gayle Virginia Anderson, June 16, 1963; children—Michael Brent, Kristin Kathleen. B.A., Whittier Coll., 1963; Ph.D., UCLA, 1968. Teaching asst. in zoology UCLA, 1963-65, assoc. in zoology, 1965-66, USPHS trainee in cardiovascular zoophysiology, 1966-68; postdoctoral fellow NIH, 1968-69; asst. prof. zoology Colo. State U., Ft. Collins, 1969-76, assoc. prof. zoology and entomology, 1976-84, prof., 1984—, asst. chmn. zoology and entomology, 1978-79, 83-84, interim chmn. zoology, 1984-85, chmn., 1985-87, interim chmn. biology, 1987-88, chmn. 1988—; small mammal and physiol. ecologist Ecology Cons., Inc., Biol. Research Assocs., Inc., Fort Collins, Thorne Ecol. Inst., Boulder, U.S. Army C.E., U.S. Fish and Wildlife Service; vis. investigator at biotron U. Wis., Madison, 1971; summer faculty Nat. Wildlife Fedn. Conservation Summit, Estes Park, Colo., 1972-77; summer faculty U. Mich. Biol. Sta., Douglas Lake, 1976, 78; Alexander von Humboldt Research fellow J.W. Goethe U., Frankfort, W.Ger., 1979-80; vis. prof. zoology U. Mont. Biol. Sta., Flathead Lake, 1981, 83, 85, vis. prof. biology, Rocky Mtn. Lab., Gothic, Colo., 1987. Mem. AAAS, Am. Soc. Zoologists, Am. Soc. Mammalogists, Ecol. Soc. Am., Sigma Xi, Omicron Delta Kappa. Contbr. numerous articles to profl. jours. Home: 505 Canadian Pkwy Fort Collins CO 80524 Office: Colo State U Dept Zoology Fort Collins CO 80523

WUNSCH, DAVID E., electronic engineer; b. La Junta, Colo., Feb. 4, 1932; s. Aleck H. and Kathryn (Hardy) W.; m. Rosemarie Korajczyk, Dec. 29, 1956; children: Grant C., Larry D. BSEE, U. Houston, 1955; MSEE, So. Meth. U., 1960. Devel. engr. Collins Radio Co., Dallas, 1955-67; section head Collins Radio Co., Richardson, Tex., 1967-70; staff engr. Martin Marietta Corp, Orlando, Fla., 1970-74; dept. head Aydin Corp. Microwave Div., Palo Alto, Calif., 1974-76, Calif. Microwave Inc., Sunnyvale, 1976-81; v.p., chief engr. REL Inc., Boynton Beach, Fla., 1981-84, Aydin Corp. Microwave Div., San Jose, Calif., 1986-88; sr. engr. Mirage Systems, Inc., Sunnyvale, 1988—. Mem. IEEE Microwave Theory and Techniques Soc. Republican. Home: 6235 Prospect Rd San Jose CA 95129 Office: Mirage Systems Inc 537 Lakeside Dr Sunnyvale CA 94086

WURTS, WILLIAM WHITNEY, financial consulting company executive; b. Paterson, N.J., Apr. 14, 1937; s. John Halsey and LaVonne (Whitney) W.; m. Oct. 12, 1962; children: Anne, Patricia, John, Elizabeth. BA, Yale U., 1959. Mgmt. trainee Wells Fargo Bank, San Francisco, 1961-62; from acct. exec. to sr. v.p. Merrill Lynch Capital Markets, Seattle, 1962-85; founder Wurts, Johnson & Co. Investment & Performance Cons., 1986—. Mem. precinct com. Bellevue, Wash. Reps., 1964-66. Served with U.S. Army, 1960-62. Mem. Western Pension Conf. (pres. 1976-77), Seattle C. of C., Yale Alumni Assn. Western Wash. (pres. 1970-71). Republican. Episcopalian. Clubs: Broadmore Golf, Wash. Athletic (Seattle). Lodge: Rotary. Office: Wurts Johnson & Co 111 Third Ave Ste 1200 Seattle WA 98101

WUTHNOW, ALAN WAYNE, sales executive; b. Herington, Kans., July 26, 1939; s. Edwin Willard and Helen (Robbins) W.; m. Sondra Sue Ewald, June 15, 1963; children: Todd Alan, Erica Sue. BS, U. Kans., 1961, MBA, 1963. Mgmt. trainee Eastman Kodak Co., Rochester, N.Y., 1963-64, mkt. rsch. analyst, 1964-68, coord. mkt. rsch., 1968-72; asst. regional mgr. Eastman Kodak Co., San Francisco, 1972-80; gen. mgr., v.p. Alpha Photo Products Inc., Oakland, Calif., 1980-82; pres., chief exec. officer Alpha Photo Products Inc., Oakland, 1982—. Bd. dirs. County Svc. Area #14, Marin County, Calif., 1984—, Homestead Valley Land Trust, 1987—. Mem. Nat. Graphic Arts Dealer Assn. (mem. vendor com. 1985, Front Line award 1985), Coun. of Photographic Suppliers (bd. dirs. 1983—), Photo Mktg. Assn., Soc. Indsl. Photography, Am. Craftsmens Club, Profl. Photographers Am., Oakland C. of C., Rotary Club, Mill Valley (Calif.) Soccer Club (treas. 1985). Methodist. Office: Alpha Photo Products Inc 985 Third St PO Box 23955 Oakland CA 94623

WYANT, JAMES CLAIR, engineering company executive, educator; b. Morenci, Mich., July 31, 1943; s. Clair William and Idah May (Burroughs) W.; m. Louise Doherty, Nov. 20, 1971; 1 child, Clair Frederick. BS, Case Western Reserve, 1965; MS, U. Rochester, 1967, PhD, 1968. Engr. Itek Corp., Lexington, Mass., 1968-74; instr. Lowell (Mass.) Tech. Inst., 1969-74; prof. U. Ariz., Tucson, 1974—; vis. prof. U. Rochester, N.Y., 1983; pres. WYKO Corp., Tucson, 1984—; chmn. Gordon Conf. on Holography Plymouth (N.H.) State Coll., 1984. Editor: Applied Optics and Optical Engineering, vols. VII-X, 1979, 80, 83, 87. Mem. Optical Soc. Am. (bd. dirs. 1979-81), Soc. Photo-Optical Instrumentation Engring. (pres. 1986). Home: 1881 King St Tucson AZ 85749 Office: U Ariz Optical Scis Ctr Tucson AZ 85721

WYATT, FARICITA HALL, social services employment coordinator, consultant; b. Bakersfield, Calif., Oct. 29, 1912; d. William Mason Hall and Susie Sylindia Pinkney; m. Thomas Edward Wyatt, Oct. 20, 1953 (dec. 1954). BA in Speech, San Jose State U., 1935. Cert. tchr. (life). Employment officer State of Calif., Berkeley, 1946-58; exec. sec. Congressman Jeffrey Cohelan, Washington, 1959-61; tchr. English Skyline High Sch., Oakland, Calif., 1962-68; tchr., chmn. English dept. Skyline High Sch., Oakland, 1969-75; employment officer U. Calif., Berkeley, 1968-69; employment rep. retirees' employment program U. Calif., San Francisco, 1979—; founder, dir. Impact Assocs., San Francisco, 1976—; conductor workshops, consultant in field. Author (poetry) The River Must Flow, 1965, By The Banks of the River, 1974, TRIAD-ICAR, 1986—. Bd. suprs. Internat. Soc. Pre-retirement Planners, San Francisco, 1987; bd. dirs. Am. Soc. Aging, San Francisco, 1983—, Ret. Sr. Vol. Program, San Francisco, 1984—, San Francisco Sr. Ctr., 1984—. Capt. WAC, 1943-46. Mem. Internat. Interactive Communictions Soc. (San Francisco Bay Area chpt. 1988—). Democrat. Club: Commonwealth (San Francisco). Home: 1200 Lakeshore Ave Apt 6C Oakland CA 94606 Office: U Calif 1350 7th Ave San Francisco CA 94143

WYATT, JOSEPH LUCIAN, JR., lawyer, educator; b. Chgo., Feb. 21, 1924; s. Joseph Lucian and Cecile Gertrude (Zadico) W.; m. Marjorie Kathryn Simmons, Apr. 9, 1954; children: Daniel, Linn, Jonathan. AB in English Lit. with honors, Northwestern U., 1947; LLB, Harvard U., 1949. Bar: Calif. 1950, U.S. Dist. Ct. (cen. dist.) Calif. 1950, U.S. Ct. Appeals (9th cir.) 1950, U.S. Tax Ct., U.S. Supreme Ct. 1965. Assoc. firm Brady, Nossaman & Walker, Los Angeles, 1950-58; ptnr. Brady, Nossaman & Walker, L.A., 1958-61; pvt. practice L.A., 1961-71; sr. mem. Cooper, Wyatt, Tepper & Plant, P.C., L.A., 1971-79; of counsel Beardsley, Hufstedler & Kemble, L.A., 1979-81; ptnr. Hufstedler, Miller, Kaus & Beardsley, L.A., 1981—; mem. faculty Pacific Coast Banking Sch., Seattle, 1963—, Southwestern Grad. Sch. Banking, 1988—. Author: Trust Administration and Taxation, 4 vols., 1964—; editor: Trusts and Estates, 1962-74. Lectr. continuing legal edn. programs, Calif. and Tex.; trustee Pacific Oaks Coll. and Children's Sch., 1969—; counsel, parliamentarian Calif. Democratic party and presdl.

conv. dels., 1971—; mem. Calif. State Personnel Bd., 1961-71, v.p., 1963-65, pres., 1965-67; bd dirs. Calif. Pub. Employees Retirement System, 1963-71. Served with USAAF, 1943-45. Fellow Am. Coll. Probate Counsel; mem. ABA, Am. Law Inst., L.A. Bar Assn. (trustee 1956), Internat. Acad. Estate and Trust Law, Calif. State Bar Assn. (del. state bar conf. 1956, 62-67). Democrat. Christian Scientist. Home: 1119 Armada Dr Pasadena CA 91103 Office: Hufstedler Miller Kaus & Beardsley 355 S Grand Ave 45th Fl Los Angeles CA 90071-3107

WYCKOFF, MARGO GAIL, pyshologist; b. Omaha, Jan. 30, 1941; d. Winfield Jenning and Gail Claudia (Leach) Hartland; m. Thomas Lawrence Wyckoff, Mar. 17, 1971; children: Ted, Elizabeth. BA, U. Wash., 1973, MSW, 1975; PhD, Union Grad. Sch., Seattle, 1978; cer. Licensed psychologist. Clin. lectr. U. Wash. Med. Sch., Seattle, 1976-78, asst. prof. univ. Pain Ctr., 1980-87; assoc. dir. pain ctr. Swedish Med. Ctr., Seattle, 1979-83, dir. behavioral svcs., 1979-83; pvt. practice Seattle, 1983—; psychology cons. Providence Med. Ctr., Seattle, 1979-87. Contbr. articles to jours., chpts. to books. Mem. Wash. Psychol. Assn. (bd. dirs. 1986-87), Nat. Orgn. Soc. Workers, Internat. Assn. for the Study of Pain, Psychoanalytic Assn. (bd. dirs. 1982-84), Wash. Environ. Council. Democrat. Office: Springbrook Psychol Group 4540 Sand Point Way NE Seattle WA 98105

WYCKOFF, SUSAN, astronomy researcher; b. Santa Cruz, Calif., Mar. 18, 1941; d. Stephen and Jean (Taft) W.; m. Peter Augustus Wehinger, July 29, 1967. BA in Astronomy, Mount Holyoke, 1962; postgrad., Swarthmore Coll., 1962-63; PhD in Astronomy, Case Inst. Technology, 1967. Postdoctoral fellow U. Mich., Ann Arbor, 1967-68; asst. prof. Albion (Mich.) Coll., 1968-70; rsch. assoc. U. Kans., Lawrence, 1970-72; sr. lectr. Tel-Aviv U., Israel, 1972-75; prin. rsch. fellow Royal Greenwich Observatory, Sussex, Eng., 1975-78; vis. prof. Ohio State U., Columbus, 1978-79; assoc. prof. Ariz. State U., Tempe, 1979-82, prof., 1982—; adj. prof. Sussex U., 1975-77, U. Heidelberg Theoretical Astrophysics Inst., 1980, U. Ariz., Tucson, 1984—; vis. astronomer Royal Grennwich Observatory, Sussex, Eng., 1983, Mt. Stromlo Observatory, Australian Nat. U., Canberra, 1987, Smith Coll., 1985; NSF Shapley lectr., 1985-86; vis. com. Aura, Inc., Tucson, 1985-88; mem. Internat. Astron. Union Working Group High Resolution Spectra Comets, 1982—, space telescope working group key projects Extragalactic Astronomy, 1984-85. Contbr. articles profl. jours. Mem. Gov.'s Disease Control Commn., Phoenix, 1985-87. Named Woman of Achievement Yr. Phoenix Jr. League, 1983. Fellow Royal Astronomical Soc. (Eng.); mem. NSF adv. com. 1983—, Nat. Acad. Sci. space sci. bd. 1984—, Ariz. State U. Faculty Women's Assn. (pres. 1983-84, exec. bd. 1983—), Am. Astron. Soc. Coun. (A.J. Cannon award comm. 1982-87), Internat. Astron. Union, Mt. Graham Internat. Observatory (citizen's coun.), Am. Astronomical Soc. (mem. coun. 1985-88), Sigma Xi. Home: 2135 E Loma Vista Dr Tempe AZ 85282 Office: Ariz State U Physics/Astronomy Dept Tempe AZ 85287-1504

WYCOFF, CHARLES COLEMAN, retired anesthesiologist; b. Glazier, Tex., Sept. 2, 1918; s. James Garfield and Ada Sharpe (Braden) W.; m. Gene Marie Henry, May 16, 1942; children: Michelle, Geoffrey, Brian, Roger, Daniel, Norman, Irene, Teresa. AB, U. Calif., Berkeley, 1941; MD, U. Calif., San Francisco, 1943. Diplomate Am. Bd. Anesthesiology. Founder The Wycoff Group of Anesthesiology, San Francisco, 1947-53; chief of anesthesia St. Joseph's Hosp., San Francisco, 1947-52, San Francisco County Hosp., 1953-54; asst. prof. anesthesiology Columbia U., N.Y.C., 1955-63; creator residency tng. program in anesthesiology St. Joseph's Hosp., San Francisco, 1950, San Francisco County Hosp., 1954; practice anesthesiology, tchr. Presbyn. Med. Ctr., N.Y.C., 1955-63; clin. practice anesthesiology St. Francis Meml. Hosp., 1963-84; councilor at large Alumni Faculty Assn. Sch. Medicine U. Calif., San Francisco, 1979-80. Producer, dir. films on regional anesthesia; contbr. articles to sci. jours. Scoutmaster Boy Scouts Am., San Francisco, 1953-55. Capt. M.C., U.S. Army, 1945-47. Republican. Home: 870 Joost Ave San Francisco CA 94127

WYCOFF, ROBERT E., petroleum company executive; b. Tulsa, 1930; married. B.S.M.E., Stanford U., 1952, M.S.M.E., 1953. With Atlantic Richfield Co., Los Angeles, 1953—, various engrng. and mgmt. positions, 1957-70, mgr. western region Internat. div., 1971-73, v.p., resident mgr. Alaska region N.Am. Producing div., 1973-74, corp. planning v.p., 1974-77, sr. v.p. planning and fin., 1977-80, exec. v.p., 1980-84, chief corp. officer, 1984, vice chmn., 1985, pres., chief operating officer, 1986—, also dir. Mem. ASME, Am. Petroleum Inst. Office: Atlantic Richfield Co 515 S Flower St Los Angeles CA 90071

WYDEN, RONALD LEE, congressman; b. Wichita, Kans., May 3, 1949; s. Peter and Edith W.; m. Laurie Oseran, Sept. 5, 1978; 1 child, Adam David. Student, U. Santa Barbara, 1967-69; A.B. with distinction, Stanford U., 1971; J.D., U. Oreg., 1974. Campaign aide Senator Wayne Morse, 1972, 74; co-founder, co-dir. Oreg. Gray Panthers, 1974-80; dir. Oreg. Legal Services for Elderly, 1977-79; instr. gerontology U. Oreg., 1976, U. Portland, 1980, Portland State U., 1979; mem. 97th-101st congresses from 3d Oreg. Dist. Recipient Service to Oreg. Consumers award Oreg. Consumers League, 1978, Citizen of Yr. award Oreg. Assn. Social Workers, 1979, Significant Service award Multnomah County Area Agy. on Aging, 1980; named Young Man of Yr. Oreg. Jr. C. of C., 1980. Mem. Am. Bar Assn., Iowa Bar Assn. Democrat. Jewish. Office: 2542 Rayburn Bldg Washington DC 20515 *

WYETH, HENRIETTE, artist; b. Wilmington, Del., Oct. 22, 1907; d. Newell Convers and Caroline (Bockius) W.; m. Peter Hurd, June 28, 1929; children—Peter Wyeth, Ann Carol, Michael. Student Pa. Acad. Fine Arts, 1922-25; pvt. study with N.C. Wyeth. One-man shows: Phila., 1932, Washington, 1934, Wilmington, Del., 1938, N.Y.C., 1942, Brandywine Mus., Chadds Ford, Pa., 1980, Santa Fe, 1982; exhibited in numerous group shows; represented in pvt. and pub. collections, Albuquerque Mus., Roswell, N.Mex. Mus. Collection; commd. work includes portrait Mrs. Richard Nixon, White House, 1979, Andrew Wyeth, 1986. Address: Sentinel Ranch San Patricio NM 88348

WYLAND, STEWART WAYNE, military officer; b. Coral Gables, Fla., June 9, 1950; s. Robert Wayne and Joan Alden (Stewart) W.; m. Debra Lynn Deville, July 5, 1985; 1 child, Carol Sue. BS in Bus., U. Nev., 1973; MA in Mgmt., Webster U., 1987. Commd. 2d lt. U.S. Army, 1973—, advanced through grades to maj., 1988; scout helicopter pilot 7/17 Cavalry Attack Squadron, Ft. Hood, Tex., 1974-76; attack helicopter pilot leader 7/17 Cavalry Attack Squadron, Hanau, Fed. Republic of Germany, 1977-78; helicopter platoon leader 503d Combat Aviation Bn., Hanau, 1977-78; combat support co. comdr. 2/32 Armor Bn., Kirchgoens, Fed. Republic of Germany, 1979-80; utility helicopter instr. pilot Lowe Army Heliport, Ft. Rucker, Ala., 1980-83; aviation advisor 1st Republic of Korea Army, Wonju, 1983-84; insp. gen. III Corps and Ft. Hood, 1984-86; exec. officer 1-9 Attack Helicopter Bn., Ft. Lewis, Wash., 1988-89; cmmdr. A-Co. 2-58 Aviation Bn. (ATC), Ft. Lewis, 1989—. Mem. Army Aviation Assn. Am., Assn. U.S. Army, U.S. Golf. Assn. (assoc.), Smithsonian Air and Space Assn. (chartered). Republican. Episcopalian. Home: 3003 31st Ave SE Puyallup WA 98374

WYLE, EWART HERBERT, clergyman; b. London, Eng., Sept. 12, 1904; s. Edwin and Alice Louise (Durman) W.; B.A., U. Louisville, 1930; B.D., Lexington Theol. Sem., 1933; postgrad. Louisville Presbyn. Theol. Sem., Temple U., 1933-35; D.D., Tex. Christian U., 1953; m. Prudence Harper, June 12, 1959; 1 son, Ewart Herbert. Ordained to ministry Christian Ch., 1935; pastor First Ch., Palestine, Tex., 1935-37, First Ch., Birmingham, Ala., 1937-41, First Ch., Tyler, Tex., 1944-54, Country Club Ch., Kansas City, Mo., 1954-59; minister Torrey Pines Ch., La Jolla, Calif., 1959-79, minister emeritus, 1979—. Bd. dirs. Scripps Meml. Hosp., pres., 1980-81. Served as chaplain, maj., AUS, 1941-44. Mem. Mil. Order World Wars, Am. Legion, Tau Kappa Epsilon, Pi Kappa Delta. Clubs: Masons (32 deg.), Shriners, Rotary, LaJolla Beach and Tennis. Home: 8850 LaJolla Scenic Dr N La Jolla CA 92037

WYLIE, STEVEN WARE, city official; b. Glendale, Calif., Apr. 4, 1952; s. John Ware and Lola Mae (Owen) W.; m. Laura Magelnicki, Sept. 25, 1983. BA, U. Calif., Irvine, 1974; MA, Harvard U., 1975. Adminstrv. analyst City of Burbank (Calif.), 1976-83; asst. to city mgr. City of West Covina (Calif.), 1983—. Charles Warren fellow Harvard U., 1975. Mem. Mcpl. Mgmt. Assts. So. Calif. (regional chmn. 1987), Calif. Assn. Pub. Info. Ofcls., 2100 Club, Lions, Phi Beta Kappa. Home: 710 Fairmount Rd Burbank CA 91501 Office: City of West Covina 1444 W Garvey Ave West Covina CA 91791

WYMAN, HERBERT JACK, marketing executive; b. San Francisco, Aug. 27, 1921; s. Herbert Wayne and Ruth B. (Jacobs) Wyman; m. Barbara Rose Voorsanger, Apr. 28, 1951 (div. Nov. 1979); children: Gareth, John, Joann; m. Elaine Johnson Snay, Jan. 3. 1980. Student, San Mateo City Coll., 1939-40; AA, San Francisco City Coll., 1941; student, San Francisco State Coll., 1942-43. Account exec., prodn. mgr. Kirschner & Co., San Francisco, 1946-50; pres., founder Wyman Co., San Francisco, 1950-83; pres., founder Wyman Communications Inc., Scottsdale, Ariz., 1988-89, Larkspur, Calif., 1989—. Contbr. articles to religious and bus. jours. Bd. trustees Ross (Calif.) Sch. Dist., 1969-71. Served with U.S. Navy, 1943-46, Atlantic. Mem. Am. Assn. Advt. Agencies (chmn. No. Calif. Coun. 1965). Republican.

WYMAN, JOAN ANN, government official; b. Canton, Ohio, Oct. 25, 1943; d. James Henry and Ruth Elizabeth (Prickman) Blankenship; m. Rae Eugene Wyman, Nov.1, 1966 (div. May 1983); children: Kirby, Kimberly, Kaysie-Rae. AA, Coll. of Desert, 1977; BA in Sociology, Calif. State U., Chico, 1985. Accredited record technician. Asst. adminstr. Indio (Calif.) Community Hosp., 1966-74; tng. technician U.S. Postal Svc., Palm Springs, Calif., 1974-79; tour supr. of mails U.S. Postal Svc., Redding, Calif., 1980-84; account rep. U.S. Postal Svc., Redding, 1984-88, dir. mktg. and communications, 1988—. Mem. Redding C. of C., Bus. and Profl. Women, Sweet Adelines, Psi Chi. Home: PO Box 611 Redding CA 96099-0611

WYMAN, RICHARD VAUGHN, engineering educator, exploration company executive; b. Painesville, Ohio, Feb. 22, 1927; s. Vaughn Ely and Melinda (Ward) W.; m. Anne Fenton, Dec. 27, 1947; 1 son, William Fenton. B.S., Case Western Res. U., 1948; M.S., U. Mich., 1949; Ph.D., U. Ariz., 1974. Diplomate: registered profl. engr., Nev.; lic. water right surveyor, Nev.; registered geologist, Ariz., Calif. Geologist N.J. Zinc Co., 1949, 52-53, Cerro de Pasco Corp., 1950-52; chief geologist Western Gold & Uranium, Inc., St. George, Utah, 1953-55, gen. supt., 1955-57, v.p., 1957-59; pres. Intermountain Exploration Co., Boulder City, Nev., 1959—; tunnel supt. Reynolds Electric & Engring. Co., 1961-63, mining engr., 1965-67; asst. mgr. ops. Reynolds Electric and & Engring. Co., 1967-69; constrn. supt. engr. Sunshine Mining Co., 1963-65; lectr. U. Nev.-Las Vegas, 1969-73, assoc. prof., 1973-80, dept. chmn., 1976-80, prof., 1980—, chmn. dept. civil and mech. engring., 1984—; mineral rep. Ariz. Strip Adv. Bd., 1976-80; chmn. Pacific S.W. Minerals Conf., 1972; peer rev. com. Nuclear Waste Site, Dept. of Energy, Las Vegas, 1978-82; pres. Ariz. Juno Resources, Boulder City, 1980-83, Wyman Engring. Cons., 1987—; cons. Corp. Andina de Fomento, Caracas, Venezuela, 1977-78; v.p. Comstock Gold, Inc., 1984—. Contbr. articles to profl. jours. Sec. Washington County Republican Party, Utah, 1958-60; del. Utah Rep. Conv., 1958-60; scoutmaster Boy Scouts Am., 1959-69. Served with USN, 1944-46. Mem. AIME (chmn. So. Nev. sect. 1971-72, dir. 1968—, sec.-treas. 1974—, gen. chmn. nat. conv. 1980, Disting. Mem. award 1989), Assn. Engring. Geologists, Soc. Econ. Geologists (life), ASCE, Nev. Mining Assn. (assoc.), Ariz. Small Mine Operators Assn., Arctic Inst. N.Am. (life), Internat. Glaciol. Soc., Geol. Soc. Am., ASEE, Sigma Xi (pres. Las Vegas sect. 1986—), Phi Kappa Phi (pres. U. Nev. Las Vegas chpt. 100, 1982-83), Sigma Gamma Epsilon. Congregationalist. Home: 610 Bryant Ct Boulder City NV 89005 Office: U Nevada Dept Civil and Mech Engring 4505 Maryland Pkwy Las Vegas NV 89154

WYNN, ROBERT RAYMOND, engineer; b. Omaha, Mar. 4, 1929; s. Horace Oscar and Yvonne Cecil (Witters) W.; m. Joann Elizabeth Swicegood, June 28, 1974; children: Kay, William, Frederick, Andrew, Emma, Lawrence, Robert. Diploma in Nuclear Engring., Capitol Radio Engring. Inst., 1964; BSEE, Pacific Internat. Coll. Arts and Scis., 1964; AA in Bus. Adminstrn., Allen Hancock Coll., 1969; MSEE, Pacific Internat. Coll. Arts and Scis., 1971; MSMS, West Coast U., 1975, ASCS, 1985; BSCS, U. State of N.Y., 1985. Registered profl. engr., Calif. Meteorologist United Air Lines, Calif., 1949-53; engring. planner Aircraft Tools Inc., Inglewood, Calif., 1953-55; field service engr. N. Am. Aviation, Inglewood, Calif., 1955-59; R and D engr. Carstedt Research Inc., N. Long Beach, Calif., 1959-60; test engr. Martin Marrietta Corp., Vandenburg AFB, Calif., 1960-64; project engr. Fed. Electric Corp., Vandenburg AFB, Calif., 1965-69; systems engr. Aeronutronic Ford Corp., Pasadena, Calif., 1970-75; MTS Jet Propulsion Lab., Pasadena, Calif., 1975-83; engring. mgr. Space Com., Redondo Beach, Calif., 1983-84; engring. specialist Boeing Service Inc., Pasadena, 1984-86; cons., MTS Jet Propulsion Lab., Pasadena, 1986—; instr. computer sci. and CAD, Jet Propulsion Lab., 1980-82. With USAAF, 1946. Mem. Calif. Soc. Profl. Engrs., Exptl. Aircraft Assn. (pres. Lompoc chpt. 1968), W. Coast U. Alumni Assn. Democrat. Home: 3328 Prospect Ave LaCrescenta CA 91214 Office: Jet Propulsion Lab 4800 Oak Grove Dr Pasadena CA 91103

WYNN, STEPHEN A., hotel, entertainment facility executive; b. 1941; married. Pres., chief exec. officer Best Brands, Inc., 1969-72; pres., chmn. bd. dirs. Golden Nugget, Inc., 1973—, now also chief exec. officer, bd. dirs. Office: Golden Nugget Inc 129 E Fremont St Las Vegas NV 89101 *

WYRICK, WEY NEVADA, high school counselor; b. Hollister, Calif., Dec. 9, 1945; d. George Weyman and Vera Nevada (Friis) Thomas; m. Steve Allen Wyrick, Dec. 27, 1970; 1 child, Travis Justin. BA, U. Calif., Santa Barbara, 1968; MEd, Calif. State Poly U., 1970. Cert. tchr., Calif. Counselor Lemoore (Calif.) High Sch., 1970—; cons. Ednl. Fin. Svcs., Visalia, Calif., 1987--. Mem. Kings Tulare Guidance Assn., Am. Fedn. Tchrs., Calif. Assn. Fin. Aid Advisors. Republican. Presbyterian. Home: 2306 Woodland Dr Visalia CA 93277 Office: Lemoore High Sch 101 E Bush St Lemoore CA 93245

WYSE, WILLIAM WALKER, lawyer; b. Spokane, Wash., July 20, 1919; s. James and Hattie (Walker) W.; m. Janet E. Oswalt, Jan. 30, 1944; children: Wendy L., Scott E., Duncan C. A.B., U. Wash., 1941; LL.B., Harvard U., 1948. Bar: Oreg. 1948. Since practiced in Portland; ptnr. Stoel, Rives, Boley, Jones & Gray, 1953—; pres. Wyse Investment Services, 1988—; dir. Treasureland Savs. and Loan Assn.; past trustee, sec. Pacific Realty Trust; trustee Holladay Park Plaza. Bd. dirs. Community Child Guidance Clinic, 1951-57, pres., 1956-57; chmn. cen. budget com. United Fund, 1958-60; 1st v.p. United Good Neighbors; chmn. dir. Portland Sch. Bd., 1959-66; pres. Oreg. Symphony Soc., Tri-County Community Council, 1971-73; bd. dirs. Portland Mental Health Assn.; bd. dirs., sec. Oreg. Parks Found. Served to lt. USNR, 1942-46. Mem. ABA, Oreg. Bar Assn., Multnomah County Bar Assns., Am. Coll. Real Estate Lawyers, Delta Upsilon. Republican. Presbyterian (trustee 1955-58, chmn. 1958). Clubs: University (Portland), Arlington (Portland), City (Portland) (sec. 1957). Home: 3332 S W Fairmount Ln Portland OR 97204 Office: 900 S W 5th Ave Portland OR 97201

YABUTANI, KOICHI MOLE, aerospace exec.; b. Brawley, Calif., Jan. 21, 1931; s. Shunzo K. and Toyoko (Kondo) Y.; BS, U. Utah, 1958; Master in Engring., U. Calif. at Los Angeles, 1975; m. Pauline T. Tanabe, Oct. 8, 1960. Equipment engr. RCA, Riverton, N.J., 1959-62; engr. Northrop Corp., Hawthorne, Calif., 1962-63; mem. tech. staff Hughes Aircraft Co., Culver City, 1958-59, group head, 1965-67, staff engr., 1967-68, sr. system engr., 1968-70, section head, 1970-72, asst. dept. mgr., 1972-79, asso. lab. mgr., 1979-82, lab. mgr., 1982-88, asst. lab. mgr., 1988—. With USAF, 1950-54. Mem. IEEE, Eta Kappa Nu, Tau Beta Pi, Phi Kappa Phi. Home: 4665 Guava St Seal Beach CA 90740 Office: Hughes Aircraft Co MX 1014 Bldg R7 PO Box 92426 Los Angeles CA 90009

YADON, VERNAL LEE, museum director, artist; b. Exeter, Calif., Feb. 18, 1930; s. Jacob Nelson and Hazel Winifred (Miller) Y. B.S., Oreg. State U., 1952, M.S., 1954. Dir. Pacific Grove (Calif.) Mus. Natural History, 1957—. Active Calif. Native Plant Soc., Audubon Soc.; former chmn. Ventura Chpt. Sierra Club. Served with U.S. Army, 1954-56. Mem. Am. Assn. Mus. (sr. counselor accreditation commn.; former pres. Western Regional Mus. Conf.), AAAS.

YAGER, EDWIN GEORGE HARLAND, management education consultant; b. Detroit, July 13, 1938; s. William Edwin and Myrtle Veronica (Harland) Y.; student U. Detroit, 1956-57, Brigham Young U., 1958-60; MBA, Mich. State U., 1966; m. Judith Mae Hartmann, June 14, 1960; children—Juline Lambert, Lori Cawley, Jon, Suzanne, Carol, Karen. With J. L. Hudson Co., Detroit, 1960-68; corp. staff Ford Motor Co., Dearborn, Mich., 1968-73, dir. mgmt. devel., 1971-73; pres. Cons. Assocs., Inc., Novi, Mich., 1973-81; pres. Yager Assocs., 1981—; lectr. Brigham Young U., U. Pitts., U. Colo., U. Mich., Eastern Mich. U., Wayne State U. Cons. to urban groups through Profl. Skills Alliance, Detroit, 1967-73; active numerous civic coms., election campaigns, others. Mem. Am. Soc. Tng. Devel., Coll. Placement Coun., Internat. Assn. Quality Circles, Orgn. Devel. Network. Bishop Mormon ch. Club: Mich. Mormon Concert Choir (condr. 1975-80). Author: Making The Training Process Work, 1979; Organization Development for Managers, 1981; Is There Life After Assessment, The Game of Work Instructional Systems; contbr. 200 articles on human resource devel. to profl. publs. Home and Office: 55 Matterhorn Park City UT 84060

YAGJIAN, ANITA PALEOLOGOS, lawyer; b. Fresno, Calif., Apr. 5, 1954; d. Maria (Konstantopoulos) Paleologos. BA in Philosophy, Stanford U., 1976, MA in Philosophy, 1977; JD, U. Santa Clara, 1980. Bar: Calif. 1980, U.S. Dist. Ct. (cen. dist.) Calif. 1983, U.S. Tax Ct. 1983. Atty. Sanford, Harmssen & Wilson, San Jose, Calif., 1980-82; assoc. Deering, Walther & Sands, Santa Monica, Calif., 1982-86; assoc. counsel Autoclub of So. Calif., Los Angeles, 1986—. Commr. Santa Monica Fair Election Practice Commn., 1985; appointed by Gov. Deukmejian to Santa Monica Mountains Conservancy Adv. Com., 1986—; mem. Los Angeles Opera League; bd. dirs. Santa Monica Rep. Club, 1984-85. Assoc. editor Santa Clara Law Review, 1979-80. Mem. ABA, Calif. Bar Assn., Santa Monica Bar Assn., Westside Women Lawyers, Los Angeles Profl. Rep. Women (v.p., treas. 1984-85), Stanford Profl. Women.

YAKATAN, STAN, executive; b. Phila., Sept. 2, 1942; m. Harriet Schwartz, Oct. 28, 1968; children: Seth, Blake. Student, U. Pa., 1965. Sales rep. Sandoz Pharm., Hanover, N.J., 1965-68; sales mgr., mktg. mgr., biotech planning mgr. NEN div. E.I. Dupont, Boston, 1968-82; dir. mktg. ICN BioMedicals, Irvine, Calif., 1982-85; pres. Biosearch, San Rafael, Calif., 1986-88; exec. v.p. New Brunswick Scietific, Edison, N.J., 1985—; bd. dirs. BioMed Mgmt. Corp., England, NBS UK, England, BU GmBH, Netherlands, Fed. Republic of Germany, NGS SARL, Paris, France, NBS GMBH, Fed. Republic of Germany, NBS B.U. Netherlands, NBS Denmark, Copenhagen. With U.S. Army, 1964-66. Mem. AAAS, Inst. Dirs. U.K., Tustin Hills Racquet Club. Jewish. Home: 10521 Newport Blvd Santa Ana CA 92705 Office: 12341 Newport Blvd Ste 200 A Santa Ana CA 92705

YAKICH, DAVID ELI, sales executive; b. Denver, May 31, 1957; s. Eli and Josephine (Goodnough) Y. Jr.; m. Carrie Elizabeth. BS, Colo. State U., 1979; postgrad., U. Minn., 1980-82; BA, U. Colo., 1984. Geophys. tech. Amoco Prodn. Corp., Denver, 1980-81; cons. geophysicist Lear Petroleum, Denver, 1982-84; computer svc. mgr. Daniel Geophys., Denver, 1984-87; nat. sales mgr. Graphics Info. Inc., Denver, 1987—; computer cons. Daniel Geophysical, Denver, 1983. Mem. Soc. Exploration Geophysics, Denver C. of C. Republican. Roman Catholic. Office: Graphics Info Inc 600 17th St Ste 2020 Denver CO 80202

YAM, JOHN IVAN, pediatrician; b. Canton, Kwangtung, China, Oct. 11, 1944; m. Elena Yam, June 14, 1970; children: Garrett, Kevin, Clarie. MB, BS, U. Hong Kong, 1968. Diplomate Am. Bd. Pediatrics, Am. Bd. Family Practice. Intern Ellis Hosp., Schenectady, N.Y., 1969-70; resident SUNY Upstate Med. Ctr., Syracuse, 1970-72; fellow U. Brit. Columbia, Vancouver, Can., 1972-73; pres. Walk-In Clinic, Bellevue, Wash., 1985-87; staff Interlake Med. Ctr., Redmond, Wash., 1974—, Overlake Hosp. Med. Ctr., Bellevue, Evergreen Hosp. Med. Ctr., Kirkland, Children's Orthopedic Hosp. Med. Ctr., Seattle. Fellow Am. Acad. Pediatrics, Am. Acad. Family Practice; mem. Wash. State Chinese Med. Soc. (pres. 1985-87), King County Med. Soc., Wash. Med. Assn. Office: Interlake Med Ctr 2103 152nd Ave NE Redmond WA 98052

YAMADA, OSAMU, banker. Chmn. bd., pres., chief exec. officer Bank of Calif., San Francisco. Office: Bank of California Office of the Pres PO Box 45000 San Francisco CA 94145 *

YAMAKAWA, DAVID KIYOSHI, JR., lawyer; b. San Francisco, Jan. 25, 1936; s. David Kiyoshi and Shizu (Negishi) Y. BS, U. Calif.-Berkeley, 1958, JD, 1963. Bar: Calif. 1964, U.S. Supreme Ct. 1970. Prin. Law Offices of David K. Yamakawa Jr., San Francisco, 1964—; bd. dirs. Mt. Zion Ventures Inc. Dep. dir. Community Action Agy., San Francisco, 1968-69; dir. City Demonstration Agy., San Francisco, 1969-70; mem. adv. coun. Calif. Senate Subcom. on the Disabled, 1982-83; chmn. community residential treatment system adv. com. Calif. Dept. Mental Health, 1980-85, San Francisco Human Rights Commn., 1977-80; pres. Legal Assistance to the Elderly, 1981-83 ; 2d v.p. Nat. Conf. Social Welfare, 1983—; v.p. Region IX, Nat. Mental Health Assn., 1981-83; vice-chmn. Mt. Zion Hosp. and Med. Ctr., 1986-88 ; bd. dirs. United Neighborhood Ctrs. of Am., 1977-83, ARC Bay Area, 1988—; chmn. bd. trustees United Way Bay Area, 1983-85; chief fin. officer Assisi Nature Coun./USA, 1987—; v.p. Friends of Legal Assistance to the Elderly, 1984—; vice chmn. Friends of the San Francisco Human Rights Commn., 1985—; bd. dirs. Ind. Sector, 1986—, Keep Librs. Alive, 1986—, La Madre de los Pobres, 1982—, Nat. Concilio Am., 1987—, Friends of the Arts, 1987—; pres. Coun. Internat. Programs, San Francisco, 1987—. Recipient John S. Williams Outstanding Planning and Agy. Rels. vol. award United Way of the Bay Area, 1980, Mortimer Fleishhacker Jr. Outstanding Vol. award United Way, 1985, Spl. Recognition award Legal Assistance to the Elderly, 1983, Commendation award Bd. Suprs. City and County of San Francisco, 1983, cert. Honor, 1985, San Francisco Found. award, 1985; David Yamakawa Day proclaimed in San Francisco, 1985. Mem. ABA (Liberty Bell award 1986), Internat. Inst. San Francisco (bd. dirs. 1989—). Office: 582 Market St Ste 410 San Francisco CA 94104

YAMAMOTO, CHRISTOPHER SEIICHI, tourist industry, executive property manager.; b. Tokyo, May 1, 1949; came to U.S., 1974; s. Yoshiyuki and Kineko (Oguchi) Y. LLB in Internat. Law, St. Paul U., Tokyo. Sales staff Tokyu Tourist Corp., 1971-74; v.p. Aloha Pacific Tours, Inc., Honolulu, 1974-80, North Pak Hawaii, Inc., Honolulu, 1981-87, Jetset Hawaii Corp., Honolulu, 1981—, Ocean Express Tours, Inc., Los Angeles, 1982—; pres. Hawaii Tour System, Honolulu, 1987—; cons. New Life System, Inc., Tokyo, 1987—. Club: Plaza (Honolulu). Office: Hawaii Tour System Inc 738 Kaheka St Ste 206 Honolulu HI 96814

YAMAOKA, SEIGEN H., church official. Bishop Buddhist Ch. Am., San Francisco. Office: Hdqrs Buddhist Chs Am 1710 Octavia St San Francisco CA 94109 *

YAMARONE, CHARLES ANTHONY, JR., aerospace engineer, consultant; b. Bronxville, N.Y., Oct. 30, 1936; s. Charles Anthony and Mildred (La Manna) Y.; m. Catherine MacMullan, May 31, 1957; children: Charles Anthony III, Thomas, Stephen, Mark, James. BSEE, Manhattan Coll., 1958. Design engr. Gen. Precision Inc., Pleasantville, N.Y., 1958-62; engr. supr. Jet Propulsion Lab., Calif. Inst. Tech., Pasadena, 1962-69, sect. mgr., 1969-76, data processing mgr., 1976-80, project mgr., 1980--. Mem. Am. Geophys. Union, Am. Inst. for Advancement of Science. Office: Jet Propulsion Lab Topex Project Office 4800 Oak Grove Dr Pasadena CA 91109

YAMASAWA, MASAO, manufacturer executive; b. Niigata, Japan, Jan. 22, 1946; came to U.S., 1985; s. Shyo Saku and Fumy Y.; m. Akiko Sasaki, May 18, 1980; children: Miyuki, Sophia Aya. BE, Tokyo Inst. of Technology, 1964, ME, 1968, PhD, 1973. Mgr. Transmission Network Div. Fujitsu Ltd., Kawasaki, Japan, 1973-84; dir. Transmission Devel. Div. Fujitsu Am. Inc., San Jose, Calif., 1985-87; v.p. Transmission Devel. Div. Fujitsu Am. Inc., San Jose, 1988—. Author: Telecom Engineering Handbook; patentee in field. Mem. IEEE, Network Mgmt. Forum. Office: Fujitsu Am Inc 3055 Orchard Dr San Jose CA 95134

YAMASHIRO, JANE MIEKO, college administrator; b. Volcano, Hawaii, Mar. 29, 1939; d. Jay Jiro and Misayo (Goya) Y.; divorced; children:

Michael, Kenneth Bates. BA, U. Wash., 1960; MA, U. Alaska, 1973. Cert. sch. adminstr. Dir. North Pacific Rim, Anchorage, Alaska, 1972-74; sr. assoc. Ctr. Equality of Opportunity in Schooling, Anchorage, 1974-78; research assoc. U. Alaska Inst. Social and Econ. Research, Anchorage, 1978-80; dir. Upward Bound U. Hawaii, Hilo, 1980-82; coordinator programs U. Hawaii Ctr. Continuing Edn. and Community Service, Hilo, 1982-86; program analyst U. Hawaii Community Coll., Honolulu, 1986-88, coord. community and student affairs Office of the Chancellor, 1988—. Sec., organizer Hawaii Agrl. Leadership Found., Honolulu, 1980—; commr. Equal Rights Commn., Anchorage, 1976-80; chmn. Commn. on Status of Women, Anchorage, 1977-80; organizer Kona Coffee Council, Kealakekua, Hawaii, 1984-85. Recipient Nat. Alumni award 4-H Clubs, 1985. Mem. Am. Assn. Women of Community and Jr. Colls., Big Island Ocean Recreation Tourism Assn. (organizer, sec. 1982-84). Democrat. Buddhist. Club: Hui Laulima (Honolulu). Home: 1455 Hunakai St Apt #2 Honolulu HI 96816

YANG, ANTHONY TSU-MING, architect; b. Chung-King, Szechuan, Republic of China, Apr. 28, 1944; came to U.S., 1973; s. Chih-Chuan and Hui-Wen (Kwei) Y.; m. Grace Li-Hwa Chu, 1968; children: Angela, Cecil. BA, U. Chinese Culture, Taipei, Republic of China, 1968. Registered profl. architect, Calif. Draftsman Vincent Kevin Kelly & Assoc., Santa Monica, Calif., 1973-74, Facility Concept Inc., Encino, Calif., 1974; designer/draftsman S&T Western Inc., Long Beach, Calif., 1974-75; designer Denny's Archtl. Svcs., La Mirada, Calif., 1976; designer/assoc. David E. Harper & Assocs., Downey, Calif., 1976-79; project mgr. Sam Chang Architect & Assocs., West Los Angeles, Calif., 1979-80; pres./architect Chi Pao Devel. Inc., Alhambra, Calif., 1981—. Works include: Hsi Lai Temple and Buddhist Monastery, Hacienda Heights, Calif., Buddhist Tng. Acad. and Temple, Talmage, Calif. 2nd lt. Chinese Army Engring. Corp., 1968-69. Mem. AIA (Pasadena and Foothill chpt.), Calif. Chinese Assn. Constrn. Profls., Calif. Lincoln Club, Lions (dir. L.A. Chinatown 1982-83). Republican. Buddhist. Avocations: basketball, golf, photography. Home: 1594 Arriba Dr Monterey Park CA 91754 Office: Chi Pao Devel Inc 1041 S Garfield Ave #207 Alhambra CA 91801

YANG, LINDA TSAO, financial executive; b. Shanghai, China, Sept. 5, 1926; came to U.S., 1946; d. Ying Yung and Yu-shun (Ng) Tsao; m. An Tzu Yang, June 20, 1953; children—Yeulin T., Eton Y. B.A., St. John's U., Shanghai, 1945; M.S., Grad. Sch. Bus., Columbia U., 1948, M.Phil. in Econs., 1975. Instr. econs. and fin. Rutgers U., Newark, 1952-54; econ. analyst Am. Overseas Fin. Corp., N.Y.C., 1955-58; founder, dir. Mother Lode Savs., Sacramento, 1977-80; savs. and loan commr. State of Calif., San Francisco and Los Angeles, 1980-82; prin. Linda Tsao Yang & Assocs., Davis, Calif., 1983—; bd. dirs., mem. budget and fin. com. Blue Cross Of Calif.; vice chmn. investment com., v.p. bd. adminstrn. Pub. Employees Retirement System, State of Calif., 1977-80; invited expert on restructuring fin. instrn. Senate Banking Com., Senate Fin. Com., Washington, 1981-82. Author article in field. Mem. policy adv. com. Coll. Agrl. and Environ. Scis., U. Calif.-Davis, 1979-85; mem. policy adv. com. Ctr. for Real Estate and Urban Econs., Grad. Sch. Bus., U. Calif.-Berkeley, 1980-82; mem. fairness commn. Dem. Nat. Com., 1984-85, compliance assistance commn., 1986-88; commr. Calif. Commn. on Teaching Profession, 1984-863. Recipient award Am. Savs. and Loan League, 1980, Achievement award Los Angeles YWCA, 1982, Outstanding Service award United Chinese-Am. League, 1982. Mem. Nat. Assn. Bus. Economists, Am. Econ. Assn., Acad. Polit. Sci., Orgn. Chinese-Ams., Trusteeship for Betterment of Women, Los Angeles, Asian-Pacific Women's Network Calif., Nat. Assn. State Savs. and Loan Suprs. (bd. dirs., nat. legis. com. 1980-82), Nat. Economists (Washington), Downtown Economists Luncheon Group (N.Y.C.). Office: 1619 Holly Ln Davis CA 95616

YANG, SUSAN SU-LUNE, realtor; b. Kau-Shung, Republic of China, Dec. 25, 1958; came to U.S., 1983; d. Thomas C.A. and Victoria S.I. (Ku) Meng; m. Sung Chung Yang, June 19, 1982; children: David, Gilbert. BA, Nat. Taiwan Normal U., Taipei, 1980. Tchr. Chen-Der Jr. High Sch., Hsinchu, Taiwan, 1980-83; realty agt. Century 21-Beachside Realtors, Upland, Calif., 1987—; chief editor Jr. High Sch. Tchr. Assn. Hsinchu, 1982-83. V.p. The Brave New World mag., Upland, 1988; treas. Pomona (Calif.) Valley Chinese Assn., 1987-88. Mem. Inland Empire West Bd. Realtors. Office: Century 21 Beachside Realtors 400 N Mountain Ste 121 Upland CA 91786

YANG, YENTING, environmentalist; b. Shanghai, Republic of China, Dec. 5, 1933; came to U.S., 1964; s. Peishen and Quen (Chu) Y.; m. Yu-Hsiw Joy Huang, Dec. 25, 1970. BS, Nat. Taiwan U., 1959; MA, U. Calif., Davis, 1967, PhD, 1973. Teaching asst. Nat. Taiwan U., Taipei, 1959-60, 62-64; mgr. Oceanographic Rsch. Inst., Taipei, 1962-64; sci. researcher U. Calif., Davis, 1965-72; environ. specialist State of Calif., L.A., 1973-78; pres. Yang Internat. Co., Arcadia, Calif., 1978—; cons. Puerto Rican Govt., 1974-76. Author: Lake Productivity, 1973, Statistics, 1989. 2d Lt. Republic of China Army, 1960-62.

YANISH, MICHAEL JOHN, gastroenterologist; b. Yonkers, N.Y., Apr. 14, 1953; s. Casimir V. and Ruth T. (Joyce) Y. BS, U. Pa., 1975; MD, Hahneman U., Phila., 1980. Diplomate Am. Bd. Gastroenterologist. Intern Emory U., Atlanta, 1980-81, resident in internal medicine, 1980-83, res. assoc., 1983-84; fellow in gastroenterology Southwestern Med. Sch., Dallas, 1985-87; pvt. practice Phoenix, 1987—. Mem. Am. Gastroenterological Assn. Office: Ariz Digestive Liver Cons 6036 N 19th Ave Ste 309 Phoenix AZ 85015

YANNONE, MARK JOSEPH, investigating agency executive, consultant; b. Hornell, N.Y., Sept. 1, 1949; s. Phillip Michael and Marguerite Joan (Chislett) Y.; m. Toni Cansdale, Jan. 1971 (div. May 1976). BS in Mgmt., Ariz. State U., 1985. Owner, mgr. Auto Svc. Ctr., 1968-76; foreman various constn. projects middle east 1976-82; owner, founder, mgr. Better Way Systems, Phoenix, 1982—, Prose Perfect, Glendale, Ariz., 1987—; pres., founder Cert. Credentials, Inc., Glendale, 1985—; microcomputer consultant, Phoenix, 1982—. Author, editor: Directory of U.S. Courts; contbr. numerous articles to mags. Editor Ariz. Libertarian Party, 1988. Scholar, 1967, 82. Mem. Golden Key, Beta Gamma Sigma, Phi Kappa Phi, Sigma Iota Epsilon, Phi Theta Kappa. Home and Office: 2015 W Cactus Rd Ste 215 Phoenix AZ 85029

YANO, LOVELLE MISUZU, small business owner; b. San Francisco, Jan. 23, 1962; d. Yoshizo Okada and Ayako (Yoshinari) Yano. BA, San Francisco State U., 1985, postgrad. Asst. mgr. Double Rainbow Gourmet Ice Creams, Inc., San Francisco, 1976-79; cosmetician Walgreens, San Francisco, 1979-85; staff rsch. assoc. Univ. Calif., San Francisco, 1985—; proprietor, owner Double Rainbow Franchise, Oakland, Calif., 1986—; tchr.'s asst. San Francisco State U., 1988-89. Contbr. articles to profl. jours. Office: VAMC 4150 Clement St 116T San Francisco CA 94121

YANUCK, GILBERT A., industrial executive, engineer; b. Bklyn., July 27, 1940; s. Joseph Pierce and Roslyn Ann (Wishner) Y.; m. Annette Giattuso, May 19, 1982; children: Michael, Jeffrey, Angela. BSMe, U. Ala., 1963; MBA, Calif. State U., 1971. Engr. Ford Motor Co., Livonia, Mich., 1962, Ford Aeronutronic Div., Newport Beach, Calif., 1963; project engr. controls div. Leach Corp., Azusa, Calif., 1964-66; chief engr. Monogram Industries, N. Hollywood, Calif., 1966-70; engring. supr. Monogram Industries, Venice, Calif., 1971-72; gen. mgr. Monogram Industries, Compton, Calif., 1978—; chief engr. Infonics, Santa Monica, Calif., 1970-71; plant mgr. Advance Industries, L.A., 1972-73, Keysor Century Corp., Saugus, Calif., 1973-78. Neighborhood commr. Boy Scouts Am., Costa Mesa, Calif., 1963. Mem. Nat. Realtors Assn., Calif. Rifle and Pistol Assn., Pi Tau Sigma, Theta Tau. Home: 21209 Vintage St Chatsworth CA 91311 Office: Monogram Industries 800 W Artesia Blvd Compton CA 90224

YAO, LILY KING, banker; b. Shanghai, Republic of China, July 14, 1943; came to U.S., 1966; d. J.L. and Y.Z. (Lok) King; m. James Yao, June 29, 1966. BBA, U. Hawaii, 1977. Teller-cashier Hwa-Nan Comml. Bank, Taipei, Republic of China, 1958-62; flight attendant Civil Air Transport, Taipei, 1962-66; teller Crocker Nat. Bank, San Francisco, 1967; from teller to exec. v.p. Pioneer Fed. Savs. Bank, Honolulu, 1968-84, pres., chief exec. officer, 1984 , also bd. dirs.; chmn., pres., chief exec. officer Pioneer Properties, Inc., Honolulu, 1985—, Pioneer Insurance, Inc., Honolulu, 1985—, Pioneer Real Estate, Honolulu, 1985—; chmn. Hawaii League of Savs. Instns., Honolulu, 1985-86; nat. dir. Inst. Fin. Edn., Chgo., 1987-88. Mem. Gov.'s Congress on Hawaii's Internat. Role, 1988; bd. govs. Center for Internat. Comml. Dispute Resolution, Honolulu, 1987—; 2d vice-chmn. ARC, Honolulu, 1987—; bd. dirs. Aloha United Way, 1988, Oahu Pvt. Industry Council, 1986-89. Recipient Outstanding Achievement in Bus. award Honolulu YWCA, 1985, Cert. Appreciation ARC, 1988, Gov. Hawaii, 1985, Lt. Gov. Hawaii, 1984. Mem. U.S. League Savs. Instns. (nat. bd. dirs. 1987-88), Chinese C. of C. (bd. dirs. 1982—), Hawaii C. of C. (bd. dirs. 1987—), Grad. Sch. of Savs. and Loan Alumni Assn. (nat. pres. 1987-88), Pioneer Plaza Club. Office: Pioneer Fed Savs Bank 900 Fort Street Mall Honolulu HI 96813

YARANOFF, CHRISTO DIMITER, advertising agency executive, graphic designer, photographer; b. Berlin, Germany, June 2, 1943; came to U.S., 1967; s. Dimiter A. and Vera C. (Vavov) Y.; m. Karen E. Jacobson, Feb. 18, 1968 (div. May 1976); children—Christo D. Jr., Victoria E. Diploma artist, Art Inst., Sofia, Bulgaria, 1964; M.A., Beaux Arts, Paris, 1967; M.A. (hon.), Profl. Graphic Inst., Chgo., 1969. Art dir. Swingline Corp., Chgo., 1968-71; design dir. Alphatype Corp., Chgo., 1971-72; mem. faculty Ariz. State U., Tempe, 1972-75; pres. Yaranoff & Assocs. Advt. Inc., Phoenix, 1975—. Served with Bulgarian Army, 1960-63. Recipient numerous awards including: Merit award Art Dirs. Club N.Y., Clio award, Phoenix Art Dirs. Club awards. Mem. Am. Assn. Advt. Agys., Am. Mktg. Assn., Phoenix Art Dirs. Club, Phoenix C. of C., Pub. Relations Soc. Am. Republican. Eastern Orthodox. Club: University (Phoenix). Home: 2323 N Central Ave Phoenix AZ 85004 Office: Yaranoff & Assocs Advt Inc 2035 N Central Ave Phoenix AZ 85004

YARYMOVYCH, MICHAEL IHOR, manufacturing company executive; b. Bialystok, Poland, Oct. 13, 1933; came to U.S., 1951, naturalized, 1956; s. Nicholas Joseph and Olga (Kruczowy) Y.; m. Roxolana Abramiuk, Nov. 21, 1951; children—Tatiana, Nicholas. B.Aero. Engring., NYU, 1955; M.S. in Engring. Mechanics, Columbia U., 1956, D. Engring. Sci., 1969. Dep. asst. sec. research and devel. U.S. Air Force, Washington, 1967-70; dir. AGARD, NATO, Paris, 1970-73; chief scientist U.S. Air Force, 1973-75; asst. adminstr. field ops. ERDA, 1975-77; v.p. engring. N.Am. aerospace ops. Rockwell Internat. Corp., El Segundo, Calif., 1977-81, v.p. advanced systems devel., 1981-86, v.p., assoc. dir. Strategic Defense Ctr., 1986—; cons. in field. Author papers in field. Translator Russian books and periodicals. Recipient Exceptional Civilian Service award Dept. Air Force, 1968, 73, 75, Disting. Service award ERDA, 1977; Guggenheim fellow, 1956-58. Fellow AIAA (dir., pres., gen. chmn. ann. meeting 1978); mem. Air Force Assn., Nat. Mgmt. Assn., Nat. Security Industries Assn., AAAS, Am. Astronautical Soc., Aerospace Industry Assn., Internat. Acad. Astronautics (v.p. sci. programs). Office: Rockwell Internat Corp 2230 E Imperial Hwy El Segundo CA 90245

YAS, KENNETH MARK, film director; b. Newton, Mass., Sept. 17, 1949; s. Julius and Anna (Lubich) Y.; m. Sherry Anne Kearney, Sept. 21, 1975; children: Jessica Anne, Alyssa Lyn. BA, Boston Coll., 1971; postgrad., Am. Film Inst., 1979. Film and video producer Stone & Webster, Inc., Boston, 1973-76; video producer AMI, Inc., Beverly Hills, Calif., 1976-78; field producer Arco, Inc., L.A., 1980-82; video cons. The Sony Corp., Hollywood, Calif., 1982-84; product mgr. Lucasfilm, Ltd., San Rafael, Calif., 1984-89; dir. film unit The Post Group, Hollywood, 1986—; freelance news cameraman, Boston, 1973-77; lectr. Soc. Motion Picture and TV Engrs., L.A., 1986—, UCLA Extension Sch., 1984—. Contbr. articles to profl. jours. Mem. AFTRA. Jewish.

YASNYI, ALLAN DAVID, television production company executive; b. New Orleans, June 22, 1942; s. Ben Z. and Bertha R. (Michalove) Y.; BBA, Tulane U., 1964; children: Benjamin Charles, Evelyn Judith. Free-lance exec. producer, producer, writer, actor and designer for TV, motion picture and theatre, 1961-73; producer, performer The Second City; dir. fin. and adminstrn. Quinn Martin Prodns., Hollywood, Calif., 1973-76, v.p. fin., 1976-77, exec. v.p. fin. and corp. planning, 1977; vice chmn., chief exec. officer QM Prodns., Beverly Hills, Calif., 1977-78, chmn. bd., chief exec. officer, 1978-80; pres., chief exec. officer The Synapse Communications Group, Inc., 1981—; chmn. bd. dirs. Found. of Global Broadcasting. Trustee Hollywood Arts Coun.; exec. v.p., trustee Hollywood Hist. Trust; bd. dirs. Internat. Ctr. for Intergative Studies. Served with U.S. Army, 1964-66. Mem. Acad. TV Arts and Scis., Am. Advt. Fedn., Am. Mgmt. Assn., Hollywood Radio and TV Soc., Hollywood C. of C. (dir., vice-chmn.), Screen Actors Guild. Office: 3343 Laurel Canyon Blvd Studio City CA 91604

YASUDA, MAC, import/export executive; b. Nishinomiya, Hyogo, Japan, Jan. 29, 1949; came to U.S, 1984; s. Osamu and Tamako (Yoshida) Y.; m. Kimiyo Kojima, Dec. 5, 1975; children: Ken, Sotaro. BS, Himeji (Japan) Inst. Tech., 1972; student, Mich. Tech. U., 1970-71. Registered profl. engr., Japan. Asst. mgr. W.T. Grant Co., Osaka, Japan, 1973-76; pres. Macs Internat. Corp., Kobe, Japan, 1976-84, Princeton Acad., Ashiya, Japan, 1979-84; v.p. Yudachi U.S.A. Inc., Torrance, Calif., 1984-85, exec. v.p., 1985-86; pres. Yudachi U.S.A. Inc., Newport Beach, Calif., 1986-88, Tsumura Art & Apparel of the World, Newport Beach, 1988—; pres. Corp. 85, Newport Beach, 1985—. Author: Vintage Guitar Vol. I, 1984, Vintage Guitar Vol. II, 1989. Home: 1429 Keel Dr Corona Del Mar CA 92625 Office: Tsumara Art & Apparel of World 1550 Bristol St N Newport Beach CA 92660

YATES, ABBY HARRIS, oil and gas exploration company executive; b. Roswell, N.Mex., June 5, 1952; d. Lawrence C. and Marion V. (Sandrs) Harris; m. George M. Yates, June 12, 1975; children: Lauren S., Lindsey A. BA in Psychology, Okla. State U., 1973. Ptnr. Abby Corp., Roswell, N.Mex., 1973-80; pres. Laurelind Corp., Roswell, 1983—; bd. dirs. Abby Corp. Vice pres., chmn. ann. giving com. Ea. N.Mex. Med. Ctr. Found., Roswell, 1985—; membership drive chmn. YMCA, Roswell, 1980-86; elder, steward First Presbyn. Ch., 1985-87; mem. fin. com. Keep Am. Beautiful, 1987—, Chaves County Rep. Party, 1987—; bd. dirs. United Way, 1987—; pres. Mil. Hts. PTA, 1988-89; v.p. Ea. N.Mex. Med. Ctr. Found., 1988-89, pres., 1989—. Mem. Ind. Petroleum Assn. Am., Ind. Petroleum Assn. Mt. States, Ind. Petroleum Assn. N.Mex., N.Mex. Landmans Assn., Roswell Econ. Forum, Roswell C. of C., Shakespeare Club, PEO. Republican. Presbyterian. Office: Laurelind Corp 500 N Main Box 2143 Roswell NM 88202

YATES, GEORGE MARTIN, oil and gas executive; b. Artesia, N.Mex., Aug. 26, 1946; s. Harvey E. and Louise (Davidson) Y.; m. Abby Harris, June 12, 1975; children: Lauren, Lindsey. BBA, U. Tex., 1969. V.p. Harvey E. Yates Co., Roswell, N.Mex., 1969-80; pres. Harvey E. Yates Co., Roswell, 1981—. Mem. Petroleum Assn. N. Mex. (pres. 1985-86), Mountain States Legal Found. (dir. 1982-88), Ind. Petroleum Assn. Am. (dir. or v.p. 1976-88). Republican. Presbyterian. Office: Harvey E Yates Co 500 N Main #1 Sunwest Ctr Roswell NM 88201

YATES, KEITH LAMAR, manufacturing executive; b. Bozeman, Mont., Oct. 29, 1927; s. Thomas Bryan and Altha (Norris) Y.; m. Dolores Hensel, Aug. 30, 1948; children: Thomas A., Molly Yates McIntosh, Richard A., Nancy Yates Sands, Penny Dannielle Yates Clark, Pamela Yates Beeler. BA, Eastern Wash. State U., 1953. Salesman Ancient Order United Workmen, Spokane, Wash., 1952-53, sales mgr., 1953-56, corp. sec., 1956-73; corp. sec. Neighbors of Woodcraft, Portland, Oreg., 1973—. Author: Life of Willie Willey, The Fogarty Years, History of The Woodcraft Home. Pres. Wash. State Christian Mens Fellowship, Seattle, 1965-67; pres. Met. Area Assn. Christian Chs., 1981-83. Command sgt.-maj., ret., 1987; served with USN, USAF, USANG, 1946-87. Mem. Wash. State Frat. Cong., (cert. Commendation 1969, sec. 1957-68, pres., mem. exec. bd., chmn. conv. program advt. com. 1960-73), Oreg. State Frat. Cong. (Outstanding Frat. 1975-76, Spl. Appreciation award 1984, Frat. Family of Yr. 1986, sec. 1975-87, pres., mem. exec. bd. 1974—), Nat. Fraternal Congress Am. (conv. arrangement com. 1964, publicity com. 1964, 65, 68, credentials com. 1970, 77, 78, pres. press & pub. rels. sec. 1971-72, pub. rels. com. 1971-73, chmn. 1972, co-chmn. press and pub. rels. frat. seminar 1972, frat. monitor com. 1974-75, mem. com. 1975-76, family life com. 1978-80, constitution com. 1980, pres. state frat. congs. sec. 1981-82, historian 1987—, Washington County's Disting. Patriot, 1988), Portland Ins. Acctg. and Statis. Soc. Assn. Records Mgrs. and Adminstrs. (Oreg. chpt.), Portland C. of C., Wash. Ins. Coun., Wash. Claims Assn., Seattle Underwriting Assn. Home: Rte 4 Box 482 Hillsboro OR 97123 Office: Neighbors of Woodcraft 1410 SW Morrison St Portland OR 97205

YATES, MARGARET MARLENE, educational psychologist; b. Sheridan, Wyo., Feb. 1, 1942; d. James H. and Dorothy H. (Weeks) Guy; m. Alan R. Yates, June 20, 1965 (div. 1978); stpchildren: Elizabeth, Samuel, LaDonna, Susan, Sally. AA, Sheridan Jr. Coll., 1962; BA, U. Wyo, 1964, PhD, 1974; EdS, MA, U. No. Colo., 1968. Lic. clin. psychologist, Wyo.; cert. nat. sch. psychologist, Calif. Caseworker, adminstrv. asst. Wyo. Dept. Health and Social Svcs., Cheyenne, 1964-68; counselor, pschometrist Gradenville Diagnostic Ctr., St. Louis, 1968-70; counselor, instr. Laramie County Community Coll., Cheyenne, 1970-74; psychol. cons. div. mental health Wyo. Bd. Coop. Ednl. Svcs., Rock Springs, 1974-79; guidance counselor Colegio Karl C. Parrish, Barrangvilla, Colombia, 1979-80; sch. psychologist Marin County Office Edn., San Rafael, Calif., 1981—; cons. in field. Founder, pres., Sweetwater County Task Force on Sexual Abuse, Rock Springs, 1974-76; mem. adv. com. Open Day Care Ctr.,Rock Springs, 1974-76, Spl. Edn. Task Force, San Rafael, 1985-87; judge academic decathlon, Marin County Office Edn., 1984-87; mem. adult edn. com., Community Congl. Ch., Tiburon, Calif., 1988—. Mem. Nat. Assn. Sch. Psychologists, Am. Orthopsychiatric Assn., Commonwealth Club San Francisco, Phi Kappa Phi. Republican. Home: 269 Scenic Rd Fairfax CA 94930 Office: Marin County Office Edn 1111 Las Callinas St San Rafael CA 94913

YATES, RAEBURN PAUL, credit services executive; b. Livermore Falls, Maine, Aug. 30, 1939; s. Harold Raybourne and Alice Maud (Bird) Y.; m. Phyllis Rae Wheeler Dumay, Dec. 9, 1961 (div. Nov. 1981); children: Raeburn Paul Jr., Darrick Wheeler; m. Lindseyann Paine, Nov. 27, 1982. BS, Boston U., 1961. Sales audit supr. Jordan Marsh Co., Boston, 1961-62, asst. mgr. sales audit, 1962-64, mgr. sales audit, 1964-71, gen. mgr. accounts receivable, 1971-73, asst. gen. mgr., 1973-80, asst. controller, 1980-81; v.p. credit services Emporium Capwell, Oakland, Calif., 1981—; advisor Focus Group Trans Union Credit Bur., Chgo., 1988—. Bd. dirs. Internat. Credit Council-East Bay, Oakland, 1983-84; adv. council TRW Credit Bur., Los Angeles, 1986-87. Mem. Calif. Retail Assn. (retail credit mgrs. com., 1982—), Internat. Credit Council Assn., Nat. Retail Mchts. Assn., Credit Mgmt. Div. (bd. dirs. 1988—). Republican. Methodist. Home: 707 Center Ave Martinez CA 94553 Office: Emporium Capwell 20th & Broadway Oakland CA 94612

YATES, TEDDY LEE, investment banker, real estate consultant; b. Newport News, Va., Dec. 4, 1952; s. Gilbert Earl and Mary Francis (Mitchell) Y.; m. Diana Marie Cipov, Feb. 26, 1972; 1 child, Jacqulyn. BS, Calif. State Polytechnic U., 1976. Sr. appraiser Bank Am., Los Angeles, 1976-80; asst. v.p. Wells Fargo Realty Advisors, Marina Del Rey, Calif., 1980-83; v.p., chief appraiser Lloyds Bank Calif., Los Angeles, 1983-85; v.p. Merrill Lynch Capital Markets, Los Angeles, 1985—; bd. dirs. Waverly Ptnrs., Los Angeles. Served in U.S. Army, 1971-73. Mem. Am. Inst. Real Estate Appraisers (cert., admissions and ethics coms.), Am. Soc. Appraisers (cert.). Democrat. Baptist. Home: 728 Rocking Horse Rd Walnut CA 91789 Office: Merrill Lynch Capital Markets 400 S Hope St #19 Los Angeles CA 90071

YATES, THOMAS EUGENE, broadcasting executive; b. L.A., Dec. 3, 1942; s. William W. and Mary Jane (McCauley) Y.; m. Vicky Sheldon Watts, Dec. 1, 1987. BA in Communications, U. Nebr., 1963. Program dir. KMPX, San Francisco, 1967-71, KLOS, ABC, L.A., 1971-78; talent dir. ABC-FM, L.A., N.Y.C., 1975-78; owner, cons. Nova Broadcast Svcs., L.A., San Francisco, 1978-81; editor, cons. Goodphone Weekly Communications, L.A., San Francisco, 1978-84; program mgr. KSAN Metromedia, San Francisco, 1980; owner Hiatus Prodns., L.A., San Francisco, 1981-86; creator, programmer KKCY, City Broadcasting, San Francisco, 1985-86; program mgr. KLSX, Greater Media Inc., L.A., 1986—; bd. mem. Bay Area Music Archives, San Francisco, 1980-86; bd. dirs. L.A. Free Clinic, 1972-78; event coordinator Goodphone Symposiums, L.A., 1979, 80. Bd. dirs. Mus. of Rock, San Francisco, 1985-86. Named Radio Sta. of Yr., Billboard Mag., 1975, Program Dir. of Yr., 1974, 76. Democrat. Office: Greater LA Radio KLSX 3580 Wilshire Los Angeles CA 90010

YAW, CHARLES EDWARD, quality control manager; b. Battle Creek, Mich., Nov. 12, 1938; s. Victor Lenard and Brittie (Parker) Y.; m. Phyllis Thayer, Apr. 16, 1961 (div. Oct. 1965); children: Shelly, Cyntha; m. Audrey M. Howell, May 12, 1967; children: Chalres E. II, Debra A., Robert J. BS in Quality Control Engring., Kellogg Community Coll., 1960. Quality control leader Tex. Aluminum, Mojave, Calif., 1967-72; shift supr. Cadillac Plastics, Kalamazoo, 1972-73; shift foreman Swanson Pipe Co., Phoenix, 1973-76; electrician's asst. Thermoliac Systems, Phoenix, 1976-77; mgr. quality control Ariz. Aluminum Co., Phoenix, 1977—; bd. dirs. 47 Place, Phoenix, Almex, Phoenix. Mem. ASTM, Am. Soc. Quality Control (cert.). Democrat. Roman Catholic. Home: 5137 W Vogel Glendale AZ 85302 Office: Easco Aluminum 249 S 51 Ave PO Box 6736 Phoenix AZ 85005

YAZHE, HERBERT, superintendent of national monument; b. Naschitti, N.Mex., Feb. 8, 1938; m. Helena Yazhe, May 26, 1959; children: Lucinda, Herman. Student, Colo. State U., 1966-69. Navajo ranger Navajo Nation, Window Rock, Ariz., 1959-64, asst. chief ranger, 1964-66, asst. dept. head, 1969-72, asst. dir., 1982-85; tng. coordinator Nat. Park Service, Grand Canyon, Ariz., 1972-74; chief interpreter Canyon de Chelly Nat. Monument, Chinle, Ariz., 1974-78, asst. supt., 1985-86, supt., 1986—; program officer Bur. Indian Affairs, Chinle, Ariz., 1978-82. Active Chinle Planning Bd., 1985—, Joint Mgmt. Plan, Chinle, 1985—, Navajo Studies Conf., Tsaile, Ariz., 1987—. Mem. Rotary (spl. recognition, 1973). Democrat. Roman Catholic. Home: PO Box 2191 Chinle AZ 86503 Office: Canyon de Chelly Nat Monument Box 588 Chinle AZ 86503

YEAGER, CHARLES FLOYD, gaming executive; b. Canon City, Colo., May 5, 1944; s. Churchill Farris and Verna Arlene (Mitchell) Y.; m. Pamela Rae Burns, Feb. 29, 1964; children: Timothy Michael, Tory Ann. Student, Coalinga Coll., 1962-63, U. Nev., 1964-66. Exec. trainee lst Nat. Bank, Reno, 1964-65, lic. key employee; asst. gen. mgr., shift mgr., cashier mgr., cashier, cashier shift supr., internal cons., asst. to pres. Harrah's Hotel-Casino, Reno, 1965-86; v.p. ops. Harold's Club-Hughes Corp., Reno, 1987-88; owner, mgr. P.D.Q. Alterations, Reno, 1987—, Sparks, Nev., 1988—; v.p., gen. mgr. Eddie's Fabulous 50's, Reno, 1988—. Mem. Nev. and Calif. Check Investigations Assn., Reno Downtown Redevel. Assn., Reno C. of C., Western Nev. Peace Officers Assn., Elks, Alpha Tau Omega. Democrat. Presbyterian. Home: 4115 Underwood Pl Reno NV 89509 Office: Eddie's Fabulous 50's 45 W 2d St Reno NV 89501

YEAGER, FREDERICK JOHN, stock broker; b. Davenport, Iowa, June 22, 1941; s. John Aufderheide and Roselyn Mae (Chapman) Y.; m. Melanie Jane Grant, Aug. 15, 1964; children: John Frederick, Paul Monroe, James Abraham, Penelope Jane. BS in Engring. Scis., U.S. Naval Acad., 1963; MBA, U. Santa Clara, 1976. Acct. exec. Reynolds Securities, San Mateo, Calif., 1969-74; sr. v.p. Dean Witter Reynolds, San Mateo, 1974—; mem. Dean Wittier Pres.'s Club. Ruling elder Burlingame (Calif.) Presbyn. Ch., 1971—; dir. San Mateo Arboretum, 1981-82; mem. Nat Eagle Sout Assn.; pres. Burterian Found., 1987—. Served to capt. U.S. Army, 1963-68, Vietnam. Mem. Naval Acad. Alumni Assn., Stanford Alumni Assn., Kiwanis (distinguished pres. 1983), Commonwealth Club, Beta Gamma Sigma. Republican. Home: 200 Occidental Ave Burlingame CA 94010 Office: Dean Witter Reynolds 181 E 2d Ave San Mateo CA 94401

YEAGER, JACQUES S., construction company executive; b. Riverside, Calif., Oct. 26, 1921; s. Ernest Louis and Emma (Leah) Y.; m. Mary Barbara Gibbs, July 1, 1948; 5 children. BSCE, U. Calif., Berkeley, 1947. With E.L. Yeager Constrn. Co. Inc., Riverside, 1947-56, pres., 1956—; bd. dirs. Security Pacific Nat. Bank, Inland, Security Pacific Nat. Bank, Los Angeles, First Am. Title Ins. Co., Ri. Bd. dirs. Riverside Community Hosp., 1960-70, chmn. bd. dirs. 1959-60, mem. exec. com. 1979—, nominating com., 1979—, spl. contributions com., 1979-80, Founder's Club, (charter), 1974—, Monday Morning Group, 1960—, pres. Monday Morning Group, 1974-75; bd. dirs.

Riverside Community Hosp. found. Ventures Corp., 1985—; bd. dirs. United Fund Riverside, 1966-74, chmn. 1975-76, mem. 1965—; active U. Calif. Riverside, 1969—; mem. Riverside County Energy Task Force, 1974-75, Riverside and San Bernardino Counties Transp. Support Group, 1974—, chmn. Riverside Civic Ctr. Art Fund Raising Com., 1974-76; bd. dirs. Riverside Internat. Raceway, 1975-78; com. mem. Inland Empire Cultural Found., 1980—; mem. Loma Linda (Calif.) U. Community Adv. Com., 1981-84; dir. at large Calif. Water Resources Assn., 1983—; hon. com. mem. ARC, 1984—; mem. needs assessment steering com. Riverside County Local Streets and Hwys., 1984—; chmn. Riverside Transp. Com., 1984—; bd. dirs. Regional Inst. So. Calif., 1985—. Served with USN, WWII. Mem. Greater Riverside C. of C. (2% Club, 1982—, co-chmn. Keep Riverside Ahead, 1983—, named Citizen of Yr. 1984), U. Calif. Berkeley Alumni Assn. (steering com. Coll. Engring., 1979—, Inland Colls. chpt. Alumni Associates, 1979—), Calif. C. of C. (statewide indsl.safety and health com. 1984—). Club: Exchange (Riverside) (recipient The Book Golden Deeds 1984) Lodge: Kiwanis. Office: E L Yeager Constrn Co Inc PO Box 87 Riverside CA 92502 *

YEARSLEY, DEWAINE, computer engineer; b. Safford, Ariz., Sept. 24, 1943; s. Karl Gibbs and Netta (Hancock) Y.; m. Carol Sue Delhagen, Apr. 5, 1969; children: Dawn Sharlet, Beth Alison, Kent Edward. BA in Physics, Brigham Young U., 1972, postgrad., 1972-74; postgrad., Pacific Luth. U., 1975-76, Wash. State U., 1978-79. Software engr. Boeing Aerospace, Kent, Wash., 1974-76; software devel. mgr. Azurdata, Richland, Wash., 1976-78; sr. engr. Westinghouse Hanford Co., Richland, Wash., 1978-80; supr. cen. area ARAMCO, Dhahran, Saudi Arabia, 1980-82; chief ILMF Martin Marietta of Denver, Vandenberg AFB, Calif., 1982-83; specialist lead engr. Northrop-Ventura, Newbury Park, Calif., 1984-86; software lead Delco Systems Orgn., Goleta, Calif., 1986—; tchr. Carden Conejo Sch., Westlake Village, Calif., 1985—; cons. in field. Co-editor lab. manual Physics of Photography, 1967; inventor food dehydrator kit, 1976. Troop leader Boy Scouts Am., Alaska and Wash., 1970-80; Rep. precinct rep., Richland, 1980. Served with U.S. Army, 1967-70. Mem. Am. Orchid Soc. Mormon. Office: Delco Systems Orgn 6767 Hollister Goleta CA 93117

YEATS, ROBERT SHEPPARD, geologist, educator; b. Miami, Fla., Mar. 30, 1931; s. Robert Sheppard and Carolyn Elizabeth (Rountree) Y.; m. Lillian Eugenia Bowie, Dec. 30, 1952; children: Robert Bowie, David Claude, Stephen Paul, Kenneth James, Sara Elizabeth. B.A., U. Fla., 1952; M.S., U. Wash., 1956, Ph.D., 1958. Registered geologist, Oreg., Calif. Geologist, petroleum exploration and prodn. Shell Oil Co., Ventura and Los Angeles, Calif., 1958-67; Shell Devel. Co., Houston, 1967; assoc. prof. geology Ohio U., Athens, 1967-70; prof. Ohio U., 1970-77; prof. geology Oreg. State U., Corvallis, 1977—; chmn. dept. Oreg. State U., 1977-85; geologist U.S. Geol. Survey, 1968, 69, 75; Glomar Challenger scientist 1971, co-chief scientist, 1973-74, 78; mem. Oreg. Bd. Geologist Examiners, 1981-83; vis. scientist N.Z. Geol. Survey, 1983-84; chmn. Working Group 1 Internat. Lithosphere Program, 1987—; chmn. Subcom. on Himalayan Active Faults Internat. Geol. Correlation Program, Project 206, 1984—; researcher on Cenozoic tectonics of So. Calif., Oreg., N.Z. and Pakistan, active faults of Calif. Transverse Ranges, deep-sea drilling in Eastern Pacific. Mem. Ojai (Calif.) City Planning Commn., 1961-62, Ojai City Council, 1962-65. Served to 1st lt. U.S. Army, 1952-54. Ohio U. research fellow, 1973-74; grantee NSF; grantee U.S. Geol. Survey. Fellow Geol. Soc. Am. (chmn. structural geology and tectonics div.1984-85, chmn. Cordilleran Sect. 1988-89, assoc. editor bull. 1987—); mem. Am. Assn. Petroleum Geologists, Am. Geophys. Union, Seismol. Soc. Am., AAAS, Oreg. Acad. Sci. Home: 1654 NW Crest Pl Corvallis OR 97330 Office: Oreg State U Dept Geology Corvallis OR 97331

YECKLEY, ROBERT QUENTIN, insurance company executive; b. Pitts., Aug. 11, 1952; s. Quentin Joseph and Kathleen Mary (Moran) Y. BA cum laude, Slippery Rock State Coll., 1974. Claims coord. GE Supply Co., Pitts., 1974-76; claims coord. GE, Sharonville, Ohio, 1976; credit specialist GE, 1976-78, Oakbrook, Ill., 1978-79; supr. cash app. GE, Bridgeport, Conn., 1979-80; corp. auditor GE, Schenectady, N.Y., 1980-84; mgr. mfg. & engring. Carboloy System Bus. Dept., Detroit, 1984-85; v.p. GE Mortgage Ins., Anaheim, Calif., 1985-89; regional v.p. GE Mortgage Ins., Concord, Calif., 1989—; treas. GECC Area Mktg. Coun., Anaheim, 1987-88, vice chmn., 1989. Mem. 65 Roises Club (Cystic Fibrosis), Anaheim, 1985-89; vol. United Way Orange County, Anaheim, 1986-87. Mem. Calif. Mortgage Bankers Assn. (speaker 1985—), Nat. Assn. Review Appraisers & Underwriters (speaker 1986—). Republican. Roman Catholic. Office: GE Mortgage Ins Co 1320 Willow Pass Rd Concord CA 94520

YEDLICKA, WILLIAM GEORGE, sales professional; b. Apollo, Pa., Dec. 25, 1922; s. Joseph Frank and Katie (Cadena) Y.; m. Theresa Rosamond Unger, July 17, 1970; 1 child, Monte. BS, U. Pitts., 1949, M Letters, 1957. Asst. sales mgr. Bowers Battery & Spark Plug Co. div. Gen. Battery Co., Reading, Pa., 1965-66; regional sales mgr. Gen. Battery Co., Atlanta, 1966-67; spl. products mgr. East Pa. Mfg. Co., Inc., Lyon Station, 1967-74, sales mgr. R.R. and mining, 1974-79, v.p. sales, indsl., R.R. and mining, 1979—; bd. dirs., Molds Corp., Kansas City, Mo. Author tech. papers, procedural manuals. Lt. col. USAF, 1942-46. Decorated, DFC, Air medal with 4 clusters. Mem. Material Handling Inst., Material Handling Equipment Dealers Assn., Nat. Elec. Mfrs. Assn., Ind. Battery Mfrs. Assn., Battery Coun. Internat. (chmn. indsl. battery com.), Indsl. Truck Assn., Indsl. Battery Soc., Pinehurst Country Club, Shriners, Elks. Republican. Presbyterian. Home: 14122 White Rock Dr Sun City West AZ 85375

YEE, JAMES BAIR, computer engineer; b. Kittanning, Pa., June 19, 1952; s. James Seafong and Sin Soon (Fong) Y.; m. Wendy Eng King, Dec. 14, 1980; children: Angela, Byron. BS in Biophysics, U. Pitts., 1974; MBA, Nat. U., Vista, Calif., 1986. Chemist Cutter Lab., Covina, Calif., 1974-76; nuclear engr. GE, San Jose, Calif., 1981; nuclear engr. So. Calif. Edison, San Clemente, Calif., 1982-86, computer engr., 1986—. Lt. USN, 1976-81. Republican. Presbyterian. Home: 26571 Sierra Vista Mission Viejo CA 92692 Office: So Calif Edison Co PO Box 128 San Clemente CA 92672

YEE, ROY JENSON, electrical sales and service company executive; b. Honolulu, Sept. 29, 1943; s. Ken and Nancy (Wong) Yee; m. Andre Yvonne McIntosh, Dec. 18, 1975; children: Traci, Allison, Todd. BSEE, Oreg. State U., 1967. Registered profl. engr., Hawaii. Field engr. Gen. Electric, San Francisco, Honolulu, N.Y.C., Boston, 1967-69; v.p. KEMS Inc., Honolulu, 1969—; v.p. Honolulu Shipyard Inc., 1986-88, pres., 1988—. Chmn. Homeport Hawaii Task Force, Honolulu, 1983-85, project mgr., 1984; mem. Kaneohe Neighborhood Bd., 1983-84; vice chmn. Mil. Affairs Council, Honolulu, 1985—. Mem. IEEE (sr., chmn. regional mem. devel. com.), NSPE, Soc. Naval Architects and Marine Engrs., Hawaii C. of C. (bd. dirs. 1986—). Office: Honolulu Shipyard Inc PO Box 30989 Honolulu HI 96820

YEE, STEVE, artist; b. Sacramento, Jan. 22, 1953; s. J. Bok Yee. Art dir. Photo Design Studios, Sacramento, 1974-76, Griswold Advt., Sacramento, 1976-79, Hubbard Advt., Sacramento, 1979-82, Corcoran Co., Sacramento, 1982-84; artist State of Calif., Sacramento, 1984-88; tchr. Argonaunt Ctr., Sacramento, 1976. Author: The World Alters as We Walk in it, 1976, Art in the Third Century, 1976. Active Religious Community for Peace, Sacramento, Am. Soc. for Aesthetics, N.Y.C. Named Selected Artist Palais Des Congres, Paris, 1975, Centro De Arte y Commicacion, Buenos Aires, 1979, Bradford Mus., Yorkshire, Eng., 1982, U. Man., Winnipeg, 1984. Democrat. Baptist. Home: PO Box 8145 Sacramento CA 95818

YEGGE, ROBERT BERNARD, lawyer, educator; b. Denver, June 17, 1934; s. Ronald Van Kirk and Fairy (Hill) Y. A.B. magna cum laude, Princeton U., 1956; M.A. in Sociology, U. Denver, 1958, J.D., 1959. Bar: Colo. 1959, D.C. 1978. Partner firm Yegge, Hall and Evans, Denver, 1959-78; with Nelson & Harding, 1979—; prof. U. Denver Coll. Law, 1965—, dean, 1965-77, dean emeritus, 1977—; asst. to pres. Denver Post, 1971-75. Author: Colorado Negotiable Instruments Law, 1960, Some Goals; Some Tasks, 1965, The American Lawyer: 1976, 1966, New Careers in Law, 1969, The Law Graduate, 1972, Tomorrow's Lawyer: A Shortage and Challenge, 1974, Declaration of Independence for Legal Education, 1976. Mng. trustee Denver Center for Performing Arts, 1972-75; chmn. Colo. Council Arts and Humanities, 1968-80, chmn. emeritus, 1980—; mem. scholar selection com. Henry Luce Found., 1975—; Active nat. and local A.R.C., chmn. Denver region, 1985—; Trustee Denver Symphony Soc., Inst. of Ct. Mgmt.; trustee, vice chmn. Nat. Assembly State Arts Agys.; vice chmn. Mexican-Am. Legal Edn. and Def. Fund, 1970-76. Recipient Disting. Service award Denver Jr. C. of C., 1965; Harrison Tweed award Am. Assn. Continuing Edn. Adminstrs., 1985. Mem. Law and Soc. Assn. (life, pres. 1965-70), ABA (chmn. lawyers conf. 1987—, chmn. accreditation commn. for legal assistant programs 1987—), Colo. Bar Assn. (bd. govs. 1965-77), Denver Bar Assn., D.C. Bar Assn., Am. Law Inst., Am. Judicature Soc. (bd. dirs. 1968-72, 75—, Herbert Harley award 1985), Am. Acad. Polit. and Social Sci., Am. Sociol. Soc., Assn. Am. Law Schs., Order St. Ives, Phi Beta Kappa, Beta Theta Pi, Phi Delta Phi, Alpha Kappa Delta, Omicron Delta Kappa. Home: 4209 W 38th Ave Denver CO 80212 Office: Nelson and Harding 717 17th St Denver CO 80202 *

YEN, CHEN-WAN LIU, aerospace engineer; b. Tainan, Taiwan, China, Jan. 26, 1932; came to U.S. 1956.; d. Mau-Yun and Mei (Chen) Liu; m. I-Kuen Yen, Feb. 4, 1958; children: Fred, Albert. BS, Nat. Taiwan U., 1954; PhD, MIT, 1964. With tech. staff Jet Propulsion Lab., Pasadena, 1972--. Contbr. articles to profl. jours. Mem. AIAA. Office: Jet Propulsion Lab 4800 Oak Grove Dr Pasadena CA 91109

YEN, SAMUEL S(HOW)-C(HIH), obstetrics-gynecology educator; b. Beijing, Feb. 22, 1927; s. K.Y. and E.K. Yen; children: Carol Amanda, Dolores Amelia, Margaret Rae. BS, Cheeloo U., China, 1949; MD, U. Hong Kong, 1954, DSc, 1980. Diplomate Am. Bd. Ob-Gyn (bd. examiners 1973-78), Am. Bd. Reproductive Endocrinology (bd. examiners 1976-82). Intern Queen Mary Hosp., Hong Kong, 1954-55; resident Johns Hopkins U., Balt., 1956-60; assoc. prof. reproductive biology Case Western Res. U., Cleve., 1970—; prof. ob-gyn U. Calif., San Diego, 1972-83, chmn. dept. reproductive medicine, 1972-83, prof. reproductive medicine, 1983—; dir. reproductive endocrinology U. Calif. Med. Ctr., San Diego, 1983—, W.R. Persons chair, 1987; assoc. dir. obstetrics Univ. Hosp., Cleve., 1968-70; cons. FDA, Calif. 1979—; Howard and Georgianna Jones lectr. Johns Hopkins Med. Ctr., Balt., 1984. Editor: Reproductive Endocrinology—Physiology, Pathophysiology and Clinical Management, 1978, 2d rev. edit., 1986; editorial cons. Current Ob-Gyn Techniques, 1975—; mem. editorial bd. Endocrine Revs., 1984—. Oglebay fellow 1968-69; recipient Axel Munthe award Govt. Italy, 1982. Mem. Am. Gynecol. Soc. (fellowship com. 1978-81), Inst. Medicine-the Nat. Acad. Sci. Office: U Calif-San Diego Reproductive Medicine T-002 La Jolla CA 92093

YEN, TEH FU, civil engineering and environmental educator; b. Kun-Ming, China, Jan. 9, 1927; came to U.S., 1949; s. Kwang Pu and Ren (Liu) Y.; m. Shiao-Ping Siao, May 30, 1959. B.S., Cen. China U., 1947; M.S., W.Va. U., 1953; Ph.D., Va. Poly. Inst. and State U., 1956; hon. doctoral degree, Pepperdine U., 1982. Sr. research chemist Good Yr. Tire & Rubber Co., Akron, 1955-59; fellow Mellon Inst., Pitts., 1959-65; sr. fellow Carnegie-Mellon U., Pitts., 1965-68; assoc. prof. Calif. State U., Los Angeles, 1968-69; assoc. prof. U. So. Calif., 1969-80, prof. civil engring. and environ. engring., 1980—; cons. Universal Oil Products, 1968-76, Chevron Oil Field Research Co., 1968-75, Finnigan Corp., 1976-77, Gen. Electric Co., 1977-80, United Techs., 1978-79, TRW Inc., 1982-83, Exxon, 1981-82, DuPont, 1985—, Ministry of Petroleum, Bejing, Peoples Republic China. Author over ten tech. books; contbr. articles to profl. jours. Recipient Disting. Service award Tau Beta Pi, 1974; Imperial Crown Gold medal, Iran, 1976; Achievement award, Chinese Engring. and Sci. Assocs. of So. Calif., 1977; award Phi Kappa Phi, 1982; outstanding contbn. honor Pi Epsilon Tau, 1984; hon. professorship East China U., 1986, U. of Petroleum, Beijing, 1987. Fellow Royal Chem. Soc., Inst. Petroleum, Am. Inst. Chemists; mem. Am Chem. Soc. (chmn. geochemistry div. 1979-81). Home: 2378 N Morslay Rd Altadena CA 91001 Office: U So Calif University Park BHE 213A Los Angeles CA 90089

YEN, WILLIAM KUANG-HAN, real estate developer, architect; b. Taipei, Taiwan, Sept. 8, 1952; came to U.S., 1979; s. King-Kwun and Mei-King (Wang) Y.; m. Ruth Hsiao-Lan Wang Yen, Oct. 23, 1980; children: Wilson W.I., Jonathan W.J. BArch, Tunghai U., Taichung, Taiwan, 1976; MArch, U. Pa., 1980; MS, Carnegie-Mellon U., 1981. Registered architect, Tex. Constrn. coordinator Chinese Marine Corp., Kaoshung, Taiwan, 1976-78; project coordinator/teaching asst. Tunghai U., Taichung, Taiwan, 1978-79; studio teaching asst. Carnegie-Mellon U., Pitts., 1980; researcher Inst. of Bldg. Sci., Pitts., 1981; design architect Skidmore, Owing & Merrill, Houston, 1982; project architect Henry Milton Roberts Inc., Houston, 1982-87; prin. William Yen Architects, AIA, Houston, 1987—; pres. Yenco Internat., Inc., Houston, 1987—, L & Y Interests Inc., San Diego, 1987—; investment cons. Stoa Internat., Inc., Houston. Author: (journal) The Image of a Village, 1975; editor (photo exhibition) Taiwan Today, 1986. Mem. Assn. of Am-Chinese Profls. (exec. dir. 1986-87, editor preceding pubn., 1986), AIA (urban design com. 1986-87), Tex. Soc. of Architects, Urban Land Inst. Office: L&Y Interests Inc 12270 High Bluff Dr Ste 370 San Diego CA 92130

YENOWINE, WADE CURTIS, educator; b. Cin., Sept. 23, 1946; s. Wade Curtis and Bette Yenowine; m. Susan Lorraine Rhodes, Mar. 3, 1984. BA Sociology-Psychology, Morehead State U., 1969; MA in Ednl. Psychology, U. Cin., 1976. Cert. tchr. Tchr. Campbell County High Sch., Alexandrea, Ky., 1969-71, Finneytown (Ohio) Jr. High Sch., 1971-79; supr. spl. edn. S.E. Met. Bd. Coop. Svcs., Englewood, Colo., tchr., 1984—; speaker Internat. Reading Assn., Bangkok, Thailand, 1987, Brisbane, Australia, 1988. County del. Park County Democrats, Fairfax, Colo., 1988; treas. Park County Artists Guild, Bailey, Colo., 1987-89. Mem. Internat. Reading Assn., Head Injury Found. Office: Craig Hosp 3425 S Clarkson Englewood CO 80110

YEO, RONALD FREDERICK, librarian; b. Woodstock, Ont., Can., Nov. 13, 1923; s. Frederick Thomas and Jugertha Aleda (Vansickle) Y.; m. Margaret Elizabeth Horsley, Oct. 12, 1953; children: Joanne, Peter. B.A., U. Toronto, 1948, B.L.S., 1966. Mgr. book dept. Am. News Co., Toronto, 1948-53; sales mgr., dir. Brit. Book Service, Toronto, 1953-63; mgr. trade div. Collier-Macmillan Can., Ltd., Toronto, 1963-65; pub. services coordinator North York (Ont.) Pub. Library, 1971; chief librarian Regina (Sask.) Pub. Library, 1971-88; mem. Nat. Library Adv. Bd., 1982-87, chmn., 1986-87. Served with RCAF, 1942-45. Recipient Silver Jubilee medal, 1977. Mem. Can. Library Assn. (pres. 1978-79), Can. Assn. Pub. Libraries (chmn. 1975-76), Sask. Library Assn., Adminstrs. of Large Pub. Libraries (chmn. 1973-74). Club: Regina Kiwanis. Office: Regina Pub Libr, 2311 12th Ave, PO Box 2311, Regina, SK Canada S4P 3Z5

YEOMANS, DONALD KEITH, astronomer; b. Rochester, N.Y., May 3, 1942; s. George E. and Jessie (Sutherland) Y.; m. Laurie Robyn Ernst, June 20, 1976; children: Sarah, Keith. BA, Middlebury (Vt.) Coll., 1964; MS, U. Md., 1967, PhD, 1970. Supr. Computer Scis. Corp., Silver Spring, Md., 1973-76; rsch. astronomer Jet Propulsion Lab., Pasadena, Calif., 1976—; discipline specialist Internat. Halley WAtch, 1982—; prin. investigator NASA Comet Mission, 1987. Author: Comet Halley: Once in a Lifetine. Recipient Space Achievement award AIAA, 1985, Exceptional Svc. medal NASA, 1986, Achievement award Middlebury Coll. Alumni, 1987. Mem. Internat. Astron. Union, Am. Astron. Soc., Astron. Soc. Pacific. Democrat. Presbyterian. Office: Jet Propulsion Lab 4800 Oak Grove Dr Pasadena CA 91109

YEUNG, PAT HOK-KWONG, import and export company executive; b. Hong Kong, Hong Kong, Feb. 2, 1965; came to U.S., 1983; s. Miu-Hon and Yook-Ling (Shum) Y. BS, San Francisco State U., 1988. Cons. mgr. Lam Co., San Jose, Calif., 1986-88; gen. mgr. Far East Internat. Corp., San Francisco, 1988-89; mng. dir. Far East Internat. Corp., San Jose, Calif., 1989—.

YFANTIS, SHIRLEY CHAO, thermodynamics engineer; b. Salt Lake City, July 12, 1954; d. Fu-chuan and Lydia (Chui Lai-Yuk) Chao; m. John A. Yfantis, July 6, 1986; 1 child, Crystalia Lydia. BSChemE, U. Calif., Berkeley, 1976. Registered engr.-in-tng., Calif. Sr. engr. thermodynamics Lockheed Missiles & Space Co., Sunnyvale, Calif., 1978—. Mem. Tau Beta Pi. Office: Lockheed Missiles & Space Co 1111 Lockheed Way Sunnyvale CA 94088-3504

YGUADO, ALEX ROCCO, economics educator; b. Lackawanna, N.Y., Jan. 17, 1939; s. Manuel and Rose (Barrillio) Y.; m. Patricia Ann Rieker; children: Gary Alexander, Melissa Rose, Charissa Ann. BA, San Fernando State Coll., Northridge, 1968; MA, Calif. State U., Northridge, 1970; MS, U. So. Calif., 1972. Contractor Los Angeles, 1962-69; instr. Calif. Poly. State U., San Luis Obispo, 1969-70, U. So. Calif., Los Angeles, 1970-74; prof. econs. Mission Coll., San Fernando, Calif., 1975—; cons. Community Service Orgn., Los Angeles, 1969-71. Author: Principles of Economics, 1978; contbr. chpts. to books. Served with U.S. Army, 1957-60. Recipient: Blue Ribbon landscape design City of Albuquerque, 1962, Cert. Appreciation Los Angeles Mission Coll., 1978; Fulbright scholar, 1986-87. Mem. Calif. Small Bus. Assn. Democrat. Roman Catholic. Clubs: Newman (Los Angeles), Sierra Retreat (Malibu) (sponsor). Home: 30960 N Romero Cyn Castaic CA 91384 Office: LA Mission Coll 1212 San Fernando Rd San Fernando CA 91340

YIN, GERALD ZHEYAO, process research and development manager; b. Beijing, Jan. 29, 1944; came to U.S., 1980; s. Huaixing and Halumi Yin; m. Junling June Yen, Feb. 28, 1971; 1 child, John Changjiang. BS in Chemistry, U. Sci. & Tech. China, Beijing, 1967; postgrad., Beijing U., 1978-80; PhD in Chemistry, UCLA, 1984. Process engr. Lanzhou Oil Refinery, Lanzhou, People's Republic of China, 1968-73; mgr. research staff Chinese Acad. Sciences, Lanzhou, 1973-78; sr. process engr. Intel Corp. Santa Clara TD, Santa Clara, Calif., 1984-86; mgr., staff engr. Lam Research Corp., Research & Devel., Fremont, Calif., 1986—. Author: Introducing Orthogonal Design to Semiconductor Industry, 1985; maj. inventor multistep power reduction plasma etching, rainbow oxide plasma etcher. Recipient Nat. Acad. award People's Republic of China, 1979, Nat. Acad. Invention award, People's Republic of China, 1980. Mem. Electrochemical Soc., Am. Chem. Soc., Am. Vacuum Soc., Chinese Engr. Club (pres. Silicon Valley chpt.). Home: 10132 Bilich Pl Cupertino CA 95014 Office: Lam Rsch Corp 4650 Cushing Pkwy Fremont CA 94538

YINGLING, DOUGLAS RICHARD, food product executive; b. Tiffin, Ohio, Feb. 28, 1958; s. Richard Martin and Margie Ann (Tucker) Y.; m. Elizabeth Diane Reese, May, 1988. BS in Gen. Bus., S.W. Mo. State U., 1981. PMT mem. Anheuser-Busch, Inc., Dallas, 1982-83; PMT supr. Anheuser-Busch, Inc., San Antonio, Tex., 1983-85; div. rep. Anheuser-Busch, Inc., Denver, 1985; dist. mgr. Anheuser-Busch, Inc., Cheyenne, Wyo., 1985-86; v.p. sales and mktg. Ace Beverage Co., L.A., 1986—. Republican. Methodist. Office: Ace Beverage Co 401 S Anderson St Los Angeles CA 90033

YINGLING, ROBERT GRANVILLE, JR., accountant; b. Lakewood, Ohio, Nov. 8, 1940; s. Robert Granville and Natalie (Phillips) Y.; m. Linda Kay Patterson, Mar. 30, 1968; 1 child, Michael Philip. AB in Polit. Sci., U. Mo., 1963; postgrad., U. Ariz., 1966-67, Portland State U., 1971-73. CPA, Oreg. Mgmt. trainee Mich. Nat. Bank, Flint, 1963-65; comml. note teller First Nat. Bank Ariz., Tucson, 1965-67; spl. asst. Travelers Ins. Cos., Phoenix, then Portland, Oreg., 1967-70; chief acct. Am. Guaranty Life Ins. Co., Portland, 1970-73; supr. Peat, Marwick, Mitchell & Co., Portland, 1973-79; ptnr. Dietrich, Bye, Griffin & Youel, Portland, 1979-84; prin. Isler, Collins & McAdams, Portland, 1984-85; owner, acct. R.G. Yingling Jr., CPA, Portland, 1985—; adj. asst. prof., U. Portland, 1988. Treas., Portland Amateur Hockey Assn., 1977-78; mem. exec. bd. Columbia Pacific coun. Boy Scouts Am., 1980-85. Recipient Silver Beaver award, Boy Scouts Am., 1986. Mem. AICPA, Oreg. Soc. CPAs, Nat. Assn. Accts. (nat. dir. 1985-87), Assn. Govt. Accts. (nat. v.p. 1983), Nat. Conf. CPA Practitioners, City Club Portland, Rotary. Office: RG Yingling Jr CPA 11409 SE Ash Ct Portland OR 97216

YIP, EDMUND Y.K., restaurateur, photographer; b. Canton, Republic of China, Jan. 16, 1933; s. Fox and Mui (Vong) Y.; m. Vicky H.F. Chiu, Dec. 9, 1966; children: Colleen H.Y., William W.L. Mgr. House of Dragon Chop Suey, Pearl City, Hawaii, 1970-82; pres. Pearlridge Chinese Restaurant, Aiea, Hawaii, 1982—; pres. 6&6 Corp., Pearlridge, 1982—, Bagdad Investment Co., Pearl City, 1981—. Recipient Gold trophy Am. Chinese Photgraphic Exhbn., 1972, Gold medal 2d NCPA Internat. Salon Photography, 1974, 3d Internat. Salon Photography China, 1965; Silver medal 5th Thai Internat. Salon of Pictorial Photography, 1972; Bronze medal 11th Internat. Salon Photography China, 1965; and numerous others. Fellow Photographic Soc. China, N.Y. (excellent exhibitor 1989); mem. Royal Photographic Soc. Great Britain, 1972 (assoc.). Home: 98-1371-C Nola St Pearl City HI 96782 Office: PO Box 222 Pearl City HI 96782

YIRDAW, AREGA, aerospace engineering executive; b. Gondar, Ethiopia, Sept. 27, 1942; came to U.S., 1981; s. Yirdaw Hailu and Eteanchi Teshome; m. Alemtshay Tenga, Jan. 10, 1964; children: Seblework, Mesfin, Yeshak, Tsion, Eyob, Berhanayehu, Addisalem, Bezayenesh, Bizuayehu. BSMechE, Haile Selassie I Univ., Ethiopia, 1970; MS in Aeronautical Engring., Cranfield Inst. Tech, Eng., 1980. Assoc. engr. to supr. engring. Ethiopian Airlines, Addis Ababa, 1970-81; design engr., sr. engr., project engr., sr. project engr. then mgr. project engring. BW/IP Internat. Inc. (formerly Borg Warner), Van Nuys, Calif., 1982—; researcher in pneumatic/hydraulic actuation systems/components. Mem. AIAA, Brit. Royal Aero. Soc. Office: BW/IP Internat Fluid Controls Div 7500 Tyrone Ave Van Nuys CA 91409

YNDA, MARY LOU, artist, educator; b. Los Angeles, Apr. 4, 1936; d. Ernest Pastor Ynda and Mary Estella (Ruiz) Zapotocky, m. Gary Lynn Coleman, Sept. 1, 1956 (div. Feb. 1983); children: Debra Lynn, Lisa Annette, David Gary. Student, Immaculate Heart Coll., Los Angeles, 1973-79; AA in Fine Arts, Los Angeles City Coll., 1976; student, Calif. State U., Los Angeles, 1977-79. instr. Fashion Inst. Design, Los Angeles, 1980-81. Group shows include Double Rocking G Gallery, Los Angeles, 1983, Improv Theater West, West Hollywood, Calif., 1983, Exposition Gallery Calif. State U., Los Angeles, 1983, L.A. Art Core Gallery, 1985, Poly. Sch., Pasadena, Calif., 1986, Bad Bye Gallery, Los Angeles, 1987, Art in the Hall VI West Hollywood City Hall, 1989; contbg. author poetry Spoken Word Voices of the Angels, 1982. Mem. Artists for Survival, Los Angeles, 1983, Sane/Freeze, Los Angeles, 1988. Mem. Women's Caucus for Art, Los Angeles Artcore. Democrat. Office: 2118 7th Pl Los Angeles CA 90021

YOB, DAVID J., business owner, consultant; b. Missoula, Mont., Mar. 15, 1952; s. ParryC. and Flora E. (Curren) Y. BS, Mont. State U., 1974. Engr. Texasgulf, Granger, Wyo., 1974-78; engr. ventilation div. United Nuclear, Gullup, N.Mex., 1978-82; systems analyst, program analyst Data Mgmt. Associated, Colorado Springs, Colo., 1983-86; system analyst El Paso County, Colorado Springs, 1986-87; owner YSoft, Colorado Springs, 1987—. Inventee flow simulation, appraisal programs. Mem. BFA.

YOCAM, DELBERT WAYNE, computer company executive; b. Long Beach, Calif., Dec. 24, 1943; s. Royal Delbert and Mary Rose (Gross) Y.; m. Janet McVeigh, June 13, 1965; children—Eric Wayne, Christian Jeremy, Elizabeth Janelle. B.A. in Bus. Adminstrn., Calif. State U.-Fullerton, 1966; M.B.A., Calif. State U., Long Beach, 1971. Mktg.-supply changeover coordinator Automotive Assembly div. Ford Motor Co., Dearborn, Mich., 1966-72; prodn. control mgr. Control Data Corp., Hawthorne, Calif., 1972-74; prodn. and material control mgr. Bourns Inc., Riverside, Calif., 1974-76; corp. material mgr. Computer Automation Inc., Irvine, Calif., 1976-78; prodn. planning mgr. central staff Cannon Electric div. ITT, World hdqrs., Santa Ana, Calif., 1978-79; exec. v.p., chief operating officer Apple Computer Inc., Cupertino, Calif., 1979—; mem. faculty Cypress Coll., Calif., 1972-79. Active Los Angeles County Heart Assn., 1966. Mem. Control Data Corp. Mgmt. Assn. (co-founder 1974). Republican. Methodist. Office: Apple Computer Inc 20525 Mariana Ave Cupertino CA 95014

YOCHELSON, SAUL B., electrical engineer; b. Cleve., Dec. 1, 1925; s. Julius and Etta (Lesser) Y.; m. Barbara Baturin, Dec. 7, 1952; children: Alan Scott, Karen Ann. BEE, Ohio State U., 1948; MSEE, U. Ill., 1950. Registered profl. engr., Ohio. Aero. research scientist NACA, Cleve., 1948-51; sr. engring. specialist Goodyear Aircraft, Akron, Ohio, 1951-61; staff engr. Librascope, Glendale, Calif., 1961-62, Lockheed Missile and Space Co., Van Nuys, Calif., 1962-64; chief scientist Hughes Aircraft Co., El Segundo, Calif., 1964—. Patentee in field; contbr. articles to profl. jours. Served with Merchant Marine, 1944-46. Mem. IEEE. Home: 10010 Lasaine Ave Northridge CA 91325 Office: Hughes Aircraft Co PO Box 92426 MS R11/11044 Los Angeles CA 90009

YOCHEM, BARBARA JUNE, sales executive, shooting coach, lecturer; b. Knox, Ind., Aug. 22, 1945; d. Harley Albert and Rosie (King) Runyan; m. Donald A. Yochem (div. 1979); 1 child, Morgan Lee; m. Don Heard, Dec. 12, 1987. Grad. high school, Knox, Ind., 1963. Sales rep. Hunter Woodworks, Carson, Calif., 1979-84, sales mgr., 1984-87; sales rep. Comml. Lumber and Pallet, Industry, Calif., 1987—; owner By By Prodns., Glendora, Calif., 1976—. Contbr. articles to profl. jours. Recipient U.S. Bronze medal U.S. Olympic Com., 1976, World Bronze Medal U.S. Olympic Com., 1980. Home: 600 Hunters Trail #40 Glendora CA 91740 Office: By By Prodns PO Box 1676 Glendora CA 91740

YOCKSTICK, MERLIN L., communications executive; b. Waverly, Iowa, Sept. 18, 1947; m. Elizabeth A. Lyons (div.). BE, U. No. Iowa, 1970. Tchr. Cedar Falls (Iowa) Community Sch., 1971-72; ednl. sales rep. Am. Geographic Co., Fenton, Mich., 1972-73; pres., founder Continental Geographic Co., Des Moines, 1974-75; pres. Continental Geographic Co., Boulder, Colo., 1975-78; pres., founder Graphic Learning Internat., Tallahassee, Fla., 1978-88, Boulder, 1987—; frequent speaker. Mem. Sierra Club. Methodist. Home: 1999 Beacon Ct Boulder CO 80302 Office: Graphic Learning Internat 1123 Spruce St Boulder CO 80302

YODER, AMOS, political science educator; b. Falls City, Nebr., Mar. 2, 1921; s. Amos Howard and Mildred Ann (Johnson) Y.; m. Janet Lee Tatman, June 15, 1946; children: James Amos, Barbara Ann Yoder Gorga, Sally Irene Yoder Ramseyer. B.A., Ohio Wesleyan U., 1942; Ph.D., U. Chgo., 1949. Jr. econs. editor Bd. of Econ. Warfare, Washington, 1942-43; fgn. service officer Dept. of State, Washington, 1949-74; Borah Disting. prof. polit. sci. U. Idaho, Moscow, 1974—; vis. lectr. U. Calif.-Davis, 1964-65. Author: International Politics and Policymakers Ideas, 1982, The Conduct of American Foreign Policy Since World War II, 1986, World Politics and the Causes of War Since 1914, 1986, The Evolution of the United Nations, 1989; guest editor: Terrorism-An Internat. Jour., summer 1983; contbr. articles to profl. jours. Served to sgt. USAF, 1943-46. Recipient commendation ribbon War Dept., 1946; recipient merit honor award Dept. of State, 1967, meritorious civilian service award USAF, 1972; Fulbright prof. Fgn. Affairs Coll., Beijing, People's Republic of China, 1986-87. Mem. Internat. Studies Assn., Am. Polit. Sci. Assn., Idaho Polit. Sci. Assn. (v.p., pres. 1980-81), Amnesty Internat. Democrat. Presbyterian. Lodge: Kiwanis (Moscow, Idaho) (pres. 1981-82). Home: 1433 Sunnyside Ave Moscow ID 83843 Office: U Idaho Moscow ID 83843

YODER, FRANKLIN DUANE, medical educator; b. Cheyenne, Wyo., July 25, 1913; m. Catherine Will; children: Diane Janson, Jean Willemin, Mary F. BS, Northwestern U., 1935, MD, 1939; MPH, U. Calif., Berkeley, 1948. Intern Mercy Hosp., Chgo., 1938-39, resident in ob.-gyn., 1939-40; chief of staff Laramie County Meml. Hosp., Cheyenne, 1940-47; dir. Wyo. Dept. Health, Cheyenne, 1948-59, Ill. Dept. Pub. Health, Chgo. and Springfield, 1961-73, Weld County Health Dept., Greeley, Colo., 1973-79; pvt. cons. 1979—; affiliate prof. U. No. Colo. Sch. Nursing, 1976—; pvt. cons. Preventive Med. and Environ. Health, Greeley, Colo., 1979—; lectr. Northwest U., prof. pub. health; sr. mem. Ill. Ctr. Zoonoses Rsch., U. Ill.; prof., Ill. Sch. Pub. Health, 1972; clin. assoc., So. Ill. U., 1971—; clin. assoc. prof., U. Colo., 1974—; clin. prof. preventive med., U. Wyo., 1985—; lectr. U. Ill. Sch. Pub. Health, 1972—; mem. Nat. Com. Accreditation Coun. for Continuing Med. Edn. Chmn. Ohio River Valley Sanitation commn., 1968—. Served as flight surgeon with USAAF, 1942-45. Recipient Alumni Merit award Northwestern U., 1965. Mem. AMA (exec. staff, dir. environ. med. 1959-61, chmn. residency rev. com. for preventive medicine 1977), Am. Assn. Pub. Health Physicians (pres. 1963-64, Disting. Svc. award 1967), Assn. State and Territorial Health Ofcls. (sec., treas. 1954-56, pres. 1957), State and Provincial Health Auths. of N.Am. (conf. participant, hon. life pres. 1968-69), Am. Pub. Health Assn. (governing council 1969-70, 73-77, 79-80, vice-chmn. health adminstrn. sect. 1971-73, chmn. 1973-74), Colo. Med. Soc. (mem. jud. coun. 1988, mem. com. for rev. and recognition, coun. on profl. edn. 1988—). Home: 1011 48th Ave Greeley CO 80634 Office: PO Box 298 Greeley CO 80632

YOKLEY, RICHARD CLARENCE, fire marshal; b. San Diego, Dec. 29, 1942; s. Clarence Ralph and Dorothy Junese (Sackman) Y.; m. Jean Elizabeth Liddle, July 25, 1964; children: Richard Clarence II, Karin Denise. Student, San Diego City Coll., 1967; AS, Miramar Coll., 1975. Cert. fire officer, Calif. Disc jockey Sta. KSDS-FM, San Diego, 1966-67; bldg. engr. Consolidated Systems, Inc., San Diego, 1968-72; with Bonita-Sunnyside Fire Dept., Calif., 1972—; capt. Bonita-Sunnyside Fire Dept., 1981—; med. technician Hartson Ambulance, San Diego, 1978-80, Bay Gen. Hosp., Chula Vista, Calif., 1980-83; chmn. South Bay County Emergency Med. Svc., 1988. Contbr. articles to jours., newspapers and mags. Asst. curator Firehouse Mus., San Diego, 1972—; scoutmaster Boyscout Troop #874, Bonita, Calif., 1978-79. With USAF, 1962-66. Recipient Heroism & Community Svc. award Firehouse Mag., N.Y.C., 1987, Golden Svc., San Diego County Credit Union, 1988. Mem. San Diego County Fire Prevention Officers (pres. 1985), San Diego County Fire and Arson Investigators, Calif. Conf. Arson Investigators, Soc. Fire Prevention Engrs., Bonita Bus. and Profl. Assn. (Historian award 1987), South Bay Communications, Bonita Hist. Mus. (co-founder 1986), Masons. Republican. Methodist. Office: Bonita-Sunnyside Fire Dept 4035 Bonita Rd Bonita CA 92002-1327

YOKOM, DIANE ELAINE, design consultant, video producer, writer; b. Detroit, Aug. 11, 1949; d. Robert William and Dorothy Mae (Leddick) Y.; m. John Richard Houghtaling, June 29, 1985. BS in Interior Design, Mich. State U., 1971. Designer Yokom Design, Boston, The Architects Collaborative, Cambridge, Mass.; retail design cons. The Rouse Co., Columbia, Md., Durango, Colo.; lectr. The Rouse Co., 1983—, Melvin Simon and Assocs.; photographer workshops, seminars, shops and developers, 1985—; mfr. Sugarplum Stockings, Durango, 1986. Author: Retail Design Idea Book, 1985; (instrnl. videotape) Visual Merchandising-10 Steps to Success, The ABC's of Pushcart and Kiosk Display Faculty; designer The Chocolate Rule, 1980— (Silver medal 1980); contbg. editor Visual Merchandising and Store Design Mag. Recipient Merit award Communication Arts, 1980, Merit award Art Dirs. Club Boston, 1978, 80. Mem. Nat. Trust for Hist. Preservation, Save the Children Found. Office: 375 Broadway #105 Laguna Beach CA 92651

YON, JOSEPH LAUGHAM, gynecologist, oncologist; b. Charlotesville, Va., Feb. 9, 1936; s. Joseph Laugham and Sallie Pugh (Haden) Y.; m. Dagmar Camilla Hallusgyi, June 27, 1959 (div. 1979); children: Joseph III, Steven A., Laura C.; m. Edith Jane Maffeo, Nov. 26, 1979. BA in Biology, V.M.I., 1957; MD, U. Va., 1961. Diplomate Am. Bd. Ob-Gyn. With med. corps USN, Jacksonville, Fla., 1961-62; med. officer U.S.S. Yellowstone, Jacksonville, 1962-63; resident OB-Gyn USN, Portmouth, Va., 1962-66; staff OB-Gyn USN, Quantiro, Va., 1967-69, Oakland, Calif., 1970-72; fellow Gyn-Oncology Jackson Meml. Hosp., Miami, 1972-74; staff Gyn-Oncology USN, San Diego, 1974-80; head OB-Gyn and OB-Oncology Va. Mason Clinic, Seattle, 1983—; clin. prof. U. Wash. Sch. Medicine, Seattle, 1983—. Contbr. articles to profl. jours. Fellow Am. Coll. Obstetrics and Gynecology (vice-chair 1971-80, bd. cert. Ob-Gyn), Am. Coll. Surgery, Soc. of Gyn Oncologists (bd. cert. Gyn-Oncology), Am. Soc. Clin. Oncologists. Republican. Office: Virginia Mason Clinic 1100 9th Ave Seattle WA 98111

YON, STANLEY RAYMOND, real estate consulting company executive; b. Sacramento, Apr. 28, 1949; s. Elmer R. and Helen E. (Malone) Y.; m. Rose Mary Thompson, Apr. 28, 1979; children: Christopher Thompson, Jeremy Francis. AB in Socioecons., U. Pacific, 1971; AM in Econs., U. So. Calif., 1973, MA in Planning and Rsch., 1973. Urban planner, economist VTN Consol., Inc., Irvine, Calif., 1973-76; sr. economist Williams-Kuebelbeck & Assoc., Marina del Rey, Calif., 1976-79; gen. ptnr. Lawndale Villas Condos, Redondo Beach, Calif., 1974-81; sr. real estate analyst Coldwell Banker, L.A., 1981, asst. v.p., 1985-88; cons. harbor planning and econ. analysis Port of L.A., 1081-83; sr. assoc. Robert Charles Lesser & Co., Beverly Hills, Calif., 1983-85; pres. Thompson-Yon Planning and Econs., Inc., L.A., 1988—. Mem. Urban Land Inst., Am. Planning Assn., Urban Regional Info. Systems Assn. Methodist. Office: Thompson-Yon Planning and Econs Inc PO Box 13066 Los Angeles CA 90013-0006

YONEDA, MICHAEL NAOKI, university administrator; b. Aiea, Hawaii, Nov. 12, 1948; s. Naoto and Kinuko (Yoshida) Y.; m. Codie Chiemi Kaneshiro, May 1, 1983; children: Kristel Rie, Alyssa Mari Kiilani. B-MechE, U. Hawaii, 1970. Asst. divisional engr., chief engr. Sheraton Hotels in Hawaii, Honolulu, 1970-76; chief engr. Hyatt Regency Waikiki Hotel, Honolulu, 1976-78, Queen's Med. Ctr., Honolulu, 1978-84; acting dir. bldg. and grounds mgmt. office U. Hawaii at Manoa, Honolulu, 1984-87, dir. facilities planning and mgmt. office, 1984—. Mem. ASHRAE, ASME, Assn. Phys. Plant Adminstrs., Soc. Coll. and Univ. Planners. Office: U Hawaii 2002 E West Rd Honolulu HI 96822

YONEMURA, EARL TSUNEKI, real estate developer; b. Honolulu, Sept. 1, 1939; s. Stanley Masao Yonemura and Alice Sonoko Onishi; children by previous marriage: children: Evie Ann T., Ellyse Ann T.; Betty Kan Man Pang, Oct. 2, 1985. BBA, U. Hawaii, 1972. V.p. treas. G. H. Onishi Gen. Contracting, Honolulu, 1963-69; office mgr. Oahu Amusement, Inc., Honolulu, 1966-67; pres., gen. mgr. Bowling City, Honolulu, 1967-69; treas., dir. bus. affairs Cannon's Bus. Coll., Honolulu, 1971-73; owner Honolulu Bowling Pro Shop, Honolulu, 1973-80; pres., gen. mgr. Pacific Bowling Ctr., Inc., Honolulu, 1980-82; mng. dir. Niten Ichiryu Group, Honolulu, 1982—; instr. U. Hawaii, 1972-78. Served with USAF, 1959-63. Named Hawaii Bowler Yr., 1979-80. Buddhist. Home: 2233 Nuna St Honolulu HI 96821 Office: Niten Ichiryu Group PO Box 831 Honolulu HI 96808

YONG, DAVID CHO TAT, public health laboratory director; b. Kaula Lipis, Pahang, Malaysia, Feb. 9, 1943; s. Ban Yien and Shin Yin (Ngaw) Y.; m. Lily Goik Lian Loh, Dec. 21, 1968; children: Celina Mei, Charles Tat. BSc with honors, U. Manitoba, Can., 1968; MSc in Virology, U. Manitoba, 1970, PhD in Med. Microbiology, 1973, postdoc. studies, 1974. Cert. pub. health and clin. microbiologist, Calif. Microbiologist, scientist Pub. Health Lab. Ontario Ministry of Health, Windsor, Ontario, 1975-85; pub. health lab. dir. Sonoma County Health Dept., Santa Rosa, Calif., 1986—; sessional lectr. Sonoma State U., Rohnert Park, Calif., 1986-87; adj. asst. prof. U. Windsor, Ontario, 1983-84; sessional instr. St. Clair Coll., Windsor, 1976-84. Contbr. articles profl. jours. Pres. Chinese United Methodist Ch. Fellowship, San Francisco, 1989. Recipient Master of Photographic Arts award, Profl. Photographers of Can., 1986, Craftsman of Photographics Arts award, 1984; Dr. Stanley Reitman Meml. award for Outstanding Achievement in Teaching, Internat. Soc. Clin. Lab. Tech. and Am. Assn. Bioanalysts, 1988. Mem. Am. Soc. Microbiology, Calif. Assn. Pub. Health Lab. Dirs. (exec. com. mem. 1988-89). Methodist. Office: Sonoma County Pub Health 3313 Chanate Rd Santa Rosa CA 95404

YONG, SUZANNE MAYLEEN, financial analyst; b. Coronado, Calif., Dec. 3, 1961; d. Chung Lim and Sonia (Goon) Y. BS, Ariz. State U., 1984; cert. in Chinese Language, Nat. Taiwan Normal U., Taipei, 1983. Savs. rep. First Federal Savs. and Loan, Phoenix, 1980-82; technical writer Multitech, Taipei, Taiwan, 1982-83; sales assoc. Joske's, Phoenix, 1983-85; acceptance tester Prudential Ins. Co., Phoenix, 1986-87; programmer AVCO Fin. Svcs., Irvine, Calif., 1988; assoc. programmer, analyst AVCO Fin. Svcs., Irvine, 1988—. Recipient Farrington Acad. Scholarship, Ariz. State U., Tempe, 1980-82, Ariz. Bd. Regents Scholarship, Ariz. State U., Tempe, 1981-82, Phoenix Sister Cities Scholarship, Phoenix Sister Cities Commn., Inc., Phoenix, 1982-83. Mem. Assn. for Systems Mgmt., Alpha Mu Gamma (sec., treas. 1981-82). Office: AVCO Fin Svcs 3349 Michelson Dr Irvine CA 92713

YORGASON, PHILLIP A., interior designer; b. Worland, Wyo., July 14, 1963; s. Merrill E. and Maxine (Anderson) Y. AA, N.W. Community Coll., Powell, Wyo., 1984; BFA, Acad. of Art Coll., San Francisco, 1987. Freelance design cons. San Francisco Bay Area, 1985-87; interior designer Pleasanton, Calif., 1987—; lectr., cons. in field. sec. elders quorum Tri-Valley Ward, Ch. of Jesus Christ of Latter Day Saints, athletic dir., family home evening group leader. Republican. Home: 4475 Shearwater Ct Pleasanton CA 94566

YORK, EARL DANA, oil company executive, engineering consultant; b. Gary, Ind., July 28, 1928; s. Emil and Irene (Fink) Y.; m. Feb. 12, 1961 (div. June 1988); 1 child, Earl D. II. BS in Chem. Engring., Purdue U., 1950; postgrad., Poly. Inst. Bklyn., 1950-51, U. Tenn., 1951-52, Purdue U.-Calumet, Hammond, Ind., 1959-62. Engr. Otto H. York Co., Inc., East Orange, N.J., 1950-52; devel. engr. Oak Ridge (Tenn.) Nat. Lab., 1952-53; various positions Amoco Oil Co., Whiting, Ind., 1953-64; dir. rsch. assocs. R & D dept. Amoco Oil Co., Naperville, Ill., 1975-79; various positions Amoco Internat., N.Y.C. and Chgo., 1964-69; mgr. tech. svcs. Amoco U.K. Ltd., London and Milford Haven, Wales, 1969-74; spl. engring. assignment Kharg Chem. Co., Tehran, Iran, 1974-75; v.p. Rio Blanco Oil Shale Co. div. Amoco Corp., Denver, 1976-79; rsch. assoc., dir. Amoco Oil R&N, Naperville, Ill., 1976-79; pres. Rio Blanco Oil Shale Co. div. Amoco Corp., Denver, 1986—. Patentee in field. With U.S. Army, 1954-56. Mem. Am. Chem. Soc., Am. Inst. Chem. Engrs., AAAS. Lutheran. Home: 8330 E Quincy Ave Apt H-2ll Denver CO 80237 Office: Rio Blanco Oil Shale Co 4380 S Syracuse St Ste 500 Denver CO 80237

YORK, HARRY LAWRENCE, chamber of commerce executive; b. Grants Pass, Oreg., Aug. 8, 1944; s. Evans H. and Clara A. (Zumstien) Y.; m. Patricia M. Wolfe, Feb. 21, 1964 (div. Oct. 1977); children: John F., David A.; m. Sharon Kay Grisham, Dec. 26, 1977; 1 child, Christina Kay. Student, Diablo Valley Coll.; grad., Inst. Organizational Mgmt.; BA in Mgmt., St. Mary's Coll., 1989. Mgr. Silver Dollar Garden Ctr., Concord, Calif., 1960-72; adminstrv. asst. Calif. Legis., Concord, 1972-80; exec. v.p. Concord C. of C., 1980—; pres. York & Assocs., Concord, 1978-81. Mem. park and recreation commn., Concord, 1970-73, planning commn., Concord, 1970-79, chmn. 1973, 76; mem. Mt. Diablo Sch. Dist. Bd., Concord, 1979-83, pres. 1982. Mem. Am. Assn. Chamber Execs., Calif. Assn. Chamber Execs. (bd. dirs. 1982-84), Rotary. Democrat. Roman Catholic. Home: 36 Kirkwood Ct Concord CA 94521 Office: Concord C of C 2151 Salvio St Ste A Concord CA 94520

YORK, HERBERT FRANK, physics educator, government official; b. Rochester, N.Y., Nov. 24, 1921; s. Herbert Frank and Nellie Elizabeth (Lang) Y.; m. Sybil Dunford, Sept. 28, 1947; children: David Winters, Rachel, Cynthia. A.B., U. Rochester, 1942, M.S., 1943; Ph.D., U. Calif.-Berkeley, 1949; D.Sc. (hon.), Case Inst. Tech., 1960; LL.D., U. San Diego, 1964, Claremont Grad. Sch., 1974. Physicst Radiation Lab., U. Calif., Berkeley, 1943-58; assoc. dir. Radiation Lab., U. Calif., 1954-58; asst. prof. physics dept. U. Calif., 1951-54, assoc. prof., 1954-59, prof., 1959—; dir. Lawrence Radiation Lab., Livermore, 1952-58; chief scientist Advanced Research Project Agy., Dept. Def., 1958; dir. advanced research projects div. Inst. for Def. Analyses, 1958; dir. def. research and engring. Office Sec. Def., 1958-61; chancellor U. Calif.-San Diego, 1961-64, 70-72, prof. physics, 1964—, chmn. dept. physics, 1968-69, dean grad. studies, 1969-70, dir. program on sci., tech. and pub. affairs, 1972-88; dir. Inst. Global Conflict and Cooperation, 1983-88; amb. Comprehensive Test Ban Negotiations, 1979-81; trustee Aerospace Corp., Inglewood, Calif., 1961-87; mem. Pres.'s Sci. Adv. Com., 1957-58, 64-68, vice chmn., 1965-67; trustee Inst. Def. Analysis, 1963—; gen. adv. com. ACDA, 1962-69; mem. Def. Sci. Bd., 1977-81; spl. rep. of sec. def. at space arms control talks, 1978-79; cons. Stockholm Internat. Peace Research Inst.; researcher in application atomic energy to nat. def., problems of arms control and disarmament, elementary particles. Author: Race to Oblivion, 1970, Arms Control, 1973, The Advisors, 1976, Making Weapons, Talking Peace, 1987, Does Strategic Defense Breed Offense?, 1987, (with S. Lakoff) A Shield in the Sky, 1989; also numerous articles on arms or disarmament.; bd. dirs. Bull Atomic Scientists. Trustee Bishop's Sch., La Jolla, Calif., 1963-65. Recipient E.O. Lawrence award AEC, 1962; Guggenheim fellow, 1972. Fellow Am. Phys. Soc. (Forum on Physics and Society award 1976), Am. Acad. Arts and Scis.; mem. Internat. Acad. Astronautics, Fedn. Am. Scientists (chmn. 1970-71, mem. exec. com. 1969-76), Phi Beta Kappa, Sigma Xi. Home: 6110 Camino de la Costa La Jolla CA 92037 Office: U Calif-San Diego Mail Code Q-068 La Jolla CA 92093

YORK, JESSE LOUIS, chemical engineering and consultant; b. Plains, Tex., May 1, 1918; s. Jesse Lewis and Alma Terrell (Sealy) Y.; m. Eva Jean Woods, Dec. 15, 1945 (div. Sept. 1975); children: Terrell Mae, Kathleen Lenore; m. Ruth Roberta Robinson, Sept. 17, 1975. BS in Engring., U. N.Mex., 1938; MS, U. Mich., 1940, PhD in Chem. Engring., 1950. Registered profl. engr., Mich., Colo., N. Mex. From instr. to prof. dept. chem. and metall. engring. U. Mich., Ann Arbor, 1941-70; chief environ. scientist Stearns-Roger Engring. Corp., Denver, 1970-83; v.p. Sr. Mgmt. Cons., Denver, 1984—; engring. cons., Denver, 1983—. Author: Unit Operations, 1950; contbr. articles to tech. mags.; patentee in field. Chmn. planning bd. Scio Twp., Washtenaw County, Dexter, Mich., 1963-70; bd. dirs. Colo. Sch. Mines Found., Golden, 1973—, Denver Symphony Orch., 1982—; mem. nat. adv. bd. Santa Fe Opera, 1985—. Mem. Am. Inst. Chem. Engrs., Nat. Soc. Profl. Engrs., ASME, Am. Chem. Soc., Am. Acad. Environ. Engrs. (diplomate). Republican. Home and Office: 3557 S Ivanhoe St Denver CO 80237

YOSHIDA, JENNY KAZUE, internist; b. L.A., Oct. 9, 1956; d. Nobuo Roy and Tomoko (Shiramatsu) Y.; m. Tyrone Wesley Klingensmith, May 6, 1988. BA, Calif. State U., Carson, 1979; MD, Am. U., Montserrat, B.W.I., 1983. Intern D.C. Gen. Hosp., 1983-84; resident Georgetown U., Washington, 1984-86; occupational med. physician Nev. Test Site, Mercury, 1986; med. dir. Crook County Meml. Hosp., Sundance, Wyo., 1986-87; staff physician Group Health Plan, St. Louis, 1987-88, U. N.Mex., Albuquerque, 1988—; dep. dir. Bernalillo Community Detention Ctr., Albuquerque, 1988—; physician emergency rm. Medicus, Inc., 1988—; staff physician Lovelace Urgent Care Clin., 1988. Mem. AMA, Am. Heart Assn. Office: U N Mex 2211 Lomas Blvd NE Albuquerque NM 87106

YOSHIDA, MARK MASAYOSHI, bank executive; b. Honolulu, Jan. 14, 1951; s. Wilfred Toyoki and Dorothy Kazuko (Kodama) Y.; m. Kathryn Michiko Takishita, July 31, 1976; children: Landon Makoto, Logan Masashi. BBA, U. Hawaii, 1973; postgrad., U. Wis., 1986. Mgmt. trainee 1st Hawaiian Bank, Honolulu, 1973-74, asst. ops. supr., 1974-76, ops. supr., 1976-77, asst. br. mgr., 1977-78, br. mgr., system devel. officer, 1978, br. ops. mgr., 1978-81, trust ops. officer, 1981—; asst. auditor 1st Hawaiian Inc., Tokyo, 1978; chmn. Trustware Users Group, 1976-78. bd. dirs. Heights at Wailuna Condominium Assn., Pearl City, Hawaii, 1987—. Democrat. Buddhist. Home: 98-1810-V Kaahumanu Pearl City HI 96782 Office: 1st Hawaiian Bank 161 S King St Honolulu HI 96813

YOSHIOKA, GRACE KEIKO, teacher; b. Wailuku, Hawaii, Dec. 5, 1930; d. Thomas Kumataro and Haru (Higeukon) Y. BMus, MacMurray Coll., 1952. Cert. secondary tchr. music and English, Hawaii. Tchr. music, pub. schs., Olaa, Hawaii, 1954-56; tchr. music pub. schs., Honolulu, 1956-62, tchr. English, 1962-78. Mem. First United Meth. Ch., 1962—.

YOSHIZUMI, DONALD TETSURO, dentist; b. Honolulu, Feb. 18, 1930; s. Richard Kiyoshi and Hatsue (Tanouye) Y.; BS, U. Hawaii, 1952; DDS, U. Mo., 1960, MS, 1963; m. Barbara Fujiko Iwashita, June 25, 1955; children: Beth Ann E., Cara Leigh S., Erin Yuri. Clin. instr. U. Mo. Sch. Dentistry, Kansas City, 1960-63; pvt. practice, Santa Clara, Calif., 1963-70, San Jose, Calif., 1970—. With USAF, 1952-56. Mem. Am. Dental Assn., Calif. Dental Assn., Santa Clara County Dental Soc., Omicron Kappa Upsilon, Delta Sigma Delta. Contbr. articles to profl. jours. Home: 5054 Parkfield Ave San Jose CA 95129 Office: 2011 Forest Ave San Jose CA 95128

YOST, BERNICE, special agent Internal Revenue Service; b. Houston, Oct. 7, 1936; d. Kenneth Wayne and Georgia (Sampson) Cox; m. Matthew Yost, July 10, 1956. Student, Los Angeles Trade Tech, 1968-70, Compton Coll., 1974-76, Ariz. State U., 1983-85. Staff acct. Moultrie, Liggens, Terrel CPA's, Los Angeles, 1969-72; spl. agt. IRS, Los Angeles, 1972-79; supervisory spl. agt. IRS, Phoenix, 1979—. Mem. Nat. Orgn. of Black Law Enforcement Execs. Democrat. Baptist. Home: 4901 Calle Los Cerros Tempe AZ 85282 Office: Internal Revenue Svc 2120 N Central Phoenix AZ 85004

YOUMANS, CLAIRE, lawyer; b. Seattle; d. Lynn and Margaret (Kingsley) Y.; 1 child, Tracie Ann Dates. BA, U. Wash., 1971; JD, U. Oreg., 1975. Bar: Wash. 1975. Pvt. practice Seattle, 1975-82, 84—; assoc. gen. counsel IFG Leasing Co., Redmond, Wash., 1982-83. Contbr. articles to profl. jours. Mem. Wash. State Bar Assn., Seattle-King County Bar Assn. (speakers bur. 1976—, chmn. 1981-82, mem. exec. com. 1977), Wash. Women Lawyers Assn., Seattle Tennis, Wash. Athletic. Home and Office: 410 10th Ave E Seattle WA 98102

YOUMANS, JULIAN RAY, neurosurgeon, educator; b. Baxley, Ga., Jan. 2, 1928; s. John Edward and Jennie Lou (Milton) Y.; children—Reed Nesbit, John Edward, Julian Milton. B.S., Emory U., 1949, M.D., 1952; M.S., U. Mich., 1955, Ph.D., 1957. Diplomate: Am. Bd. Neurol. Surgery. Intern U. Mich. Hosp., Ann Arbor, 1952-53; resident in neurol. surgery U. Mich. Hosp., 1953-55, 56-58; fellow in neurology U. London, 1955-56; asst. prof. neurosurgery U. Miss., 1959-62, asso. prof., 1962-63; asso. prof. Med. U. S.C., 1963-65, prof., 1965-67, chief div. neurosurgery, 1963-67; prof. U. Calif., Davis, 1967—; chmn. dept. neurosurgery U. Calif., 1967-82; cons. USAF, U.S. VA, NRC. Editor: Neurological Surgery, 1973, 2d edit., 1981; contbr. articles in field to profl. jours. No. vice chmn. Republican State Central Com. of Calif., 1979-81. Served with U.S. Navy, 1944-46. Mem. U.S. C. of C., ACS (bd. govs. 1972-78), Congress of Neurol. Surgeons (exec. com. 1967-70), Am. Acad. Neurology, Am. Assn. Neurol. Surgeons, Am. Assn. Surgery of Trauma, Pan-Pacific Surg. Assn., Western Neurosurg. Soc., Neurosurg. Soc. Am., Soc. Neurol. Surgeons, Soc. Univ. Neurosurgeons, N. Pacific Soc. Neurology and Psychiatry, Royal Soc. Medicine, Am. Trauma Soc. Republican. Episcopalian. Clubs: Bohemian (San Francisco); Rotary (Sacramento); Sutter (San Francisco), Sacramento Yacht. Office: 4301 X St Sacramento CA 95817

YOUNG, ALAN KEITH, aerospace company executive; b. Lodi, Calif., Sept. 25, 1950; s. Herbert J. and Valeta M. (Joyner) Y.; divorced; children: Brett A., Carrie E. BS in Computer Sci., Calif. State U., Sacramento, 1981. Software project engr. Lockheed Missiles & Space Co., Sunnyvale, Calif., 1981-84, mgr. program software quality engring., 1984—. With USAF, 1971-76. Democrat. Home: 1830 S Hutchins #210 Lodi CA 95240

YOUNG, AMIE RUTH, financial planner; b. N.Y.C, Aug. 22, 1960; d. Robert Norman and Irene Olson A.; m. Jonathan Griffith Young, May 5; children: Brandon, Justin. BA in Sociology, U. Calif., Goleta, 1982. Sec. State Farm Ins., San Diego, 1984-85; mktg. rep. John Hancock Fin. Svcs., San Diego, 1985-88; fin. planner S.G. Zimmerman & Assocs., San Diego, 1988; founder, dir. Women Investors' Club, San Diego, 1987—; coord. Women Investors' Club, Carlsbad, Calif., 1987—; coord. Leads Club, San Diego, 1988—. Mem. Internat. Assn. Fin. Planners. Republican. Office: Women Investors' Club 800 Grand Ave AG-8-180 Carlsbad CA 92008

YOUNG, BERT B., infosystems specialist; b. Provo, Utah, Apr. 11, 1954; s. Robert B. and Gladys (Andersen) Y.; m. Jennifer Barney, Dec. 15, 1978; children: Becca, Emily, Tyler, Jessie. BS in Acctg., Utah State U., 1981. Contr., treas. Horizon Airlines, Seattle, 1981-84; contr. Elkhorn Resort, Sun Valley, Idaho, 1984-85; project contr. Waste Mgmt., Inc., Southfield, Mich., 1985-86, PC project mgr., 1986-87; chief info. officer Waste Mgmt., Inc., Irvine, Calif., 1987—. Vol. community Drug Counseling Ctr., Livonia, Mich., 1974; bd. dirs. Sun Valley Airport Commn., Sun Valley, 1985. Republican. Mormons. Home: 24652 Creekview Laguna Hills CA 92653 Office: Waste Mgmt Inc 18500 Von Karman #900 Irvine CA 92715

YOUNG, C. CLIFTON, state supreme court justice; b. Nov. 7, 1922, Lovelock, Nev.; m. Jane Young. BA, U. Nev., 1943; LLB, Harvard U., 1949. Justice Nev. Supreme Ct., Carson City, 1985—, chief justice, 1989—. Office: Nev Supreme Ct 100 N Carson St Carson City NV 89710 *

YOUNG, CHARLES EDWARD, university chancellor; b. San Bernardino, Calif., Dec. 30, 1931; s. Clayton Charles and Eula May (Walters) Y. A.A., San Bernardino Coll., 1954; A.B., U. Calif.-Riverside, 1955; M.A., U. Calif.-Riverside, Los Angeles, 1957, Ph.D., 1960; D.H.L. (hon.), U. Judaism, Los Angeles, 1969. Congl. fellow Washington, 1958-59; adminstrv. analyst Office of the Pres., U. Calif., Berkeley, 1959-60; asst. prof. polit. sci. U. Calif., Davis, 1960; asst. prof. polit. sci. UCLA, 1960-66, assoc. prof., 1966-69, prof., 1969—, asst. to chancellor, 1960-62, asst. chancellor, 1962-63, vice chancellor, adminstrn., 1963-68, now chancellor.; dir. UMF Systems, Inc., Intel Corp., Maxicare Health Plans, Inc.; Cons. Peace Corps., 1961-62, to Ford Found. on Latin Am. Activities, 1964-66. Mem. NCAA Pres.'s Commn., Coun. for Govt.-Univ.-Industry Rsch. Roundtable and the Nat. Rsch. Coun. Adv. Bd.-Issues in Sci. and Tech., Nat. Com. on U.S.-China

Rels.; mem. chancellor's assos. UCLA; past chair. Assn. Am. Univs.; mem. adminstrv. bd. Internat. Assn. Univs.; bd. govs. Found. Internat. Exchange Sci. and Cultural Info. by Telecommunications, The Theatre Group Inc.; v.p. Young Musicians Found.; bd. dirs. Los Angeles Internat. Visitors Council, Greater Los Angeles Energy Coalition, Los Angeles World Affairs Coun.; trustee UCLA Found. Served with USAF, 1951-52. Named Young Man of Year Westwood Jr. C. of C., 1962. Office: UCLA Office Chancellor 405 Hilgard Ave Los Angeles CA 90024

YOUNG, DONALD ALLEN, writer, consultant; b. Columbus, Ohio, June 11, 1931; s. Clyde Allen and Helen Edith (Johnston) Y.; m. Rosemary Buchholz, Feb. 26, 1955 (div. Nov. 1976); children: Kent Allen, Kelly Ann; m. Marjorie Claire Shapiro, Aug. 20, 1977; stepchildren: Jo Alene, Andrea Lynn, Beth Ellen. Student, Ohio State U., 1949-51, Columbia Coll., 1952, North Cen. Coll., Naperville, Ill., 1956, Coll. DuPage, 1978. Editor various newspapers, mags., Detroit, Chgo., Columbus, 1946-63, 1973-74, 1978-79; v.p. Frydenlund Assocs., Chgo., 1963; pub. relations mgr. info. systems div. Gen. Electric Co., Phoenix, 1963-70; publs. dir. Data Processing Mgmt. Assn., Park Ridge, Ill., 1970-72; pub. relations mgr. Addressograph-Multigraph Corp., Arlington Heights, Ill., 1975-76; acct. exec. John Ripley & Assocs., Glenview, Ill., 1977-78; editorial dir. Radiology/Nuclear Medicine mag., Des Plaines, Ill., 1979-81; pres. Young Byrum Inc., Hinsdale, Ill., 1982-83; writer, consultant Tucson, 1983—; cons. various companies, 1973—; sports reporter, Copley newspapers, 1975-83; mem. adv. council Oakton Community Coll., 1970-75. Author: Principles of Automatic Data Processing, 1965, Data Processing, 1967, Rate Yourself As a Manager, 1985, Nobody Gets Rich Working for Somebody Else, 1987, Rate Your Executive Potential, 1988, If They Can...You Can, 1989. Bd. dirs. Glen Ellyn (Ill.) Jaycees (SPOKE award 1959, Outstanding Jaycee 1960); v.p. Young Republicans Club, 1960; arbitrator Better Bus. Bur., Tucson, 1987—. Recipient Jesse Neal award Indsl. Mktg. Mag., 1959, 61, Silver Anvil awards Pub. Relations Soc. Am., 1976. Mem. Publicity Club of Chgo. (pres. 1978-79). Home: 4866 N Territory Loop Tucson AZ 85715

YOUNG, DONALD E., congressman; b. Meridian, Calif., June 9, 1933; m. Lula Fredson; children—Joni, Dawn. Grad., Chico (Calif.) State Coll. Former educator, river boat capt.; mem. Fort Yukon City Council, 6 years, mayor, 4 years; mem. Alaska Ho. of Reps., 1966-70, Alaska Senate, 1970-73, 93d-101st Congresses from Alaska. Republican. Office: US Ho of Reps 2331 Rayburn House Office Bldg Washington DC 20515

YOUNG, GEORGE ANDREW, JR., editor, publisher; b. San Francisco, Sept. 11, 1935; s. George Andrew and Mary Edna (Floegel) Y.; m. Diana Lynn Williams, Dec. 23, 1961; children: Mollie Kathryn Young Moreno, Melinda Ann Young Garcia. BA in Internat. Rels., San Francisco State U., 1965. Various mktg. and editorial positions pub. cos., 1957-69; editor-in-chief Ballantine Books, Inc., N.Y.C., 1969-74; gen. mgr., v.p. Celestial Arts Pub. Co., Millbrae, Calif., 1975-77; v.p., editor-in-chief Ten Speed Press, Berkeley, Calif., 1978—; pub., pres. Comstock Edits., Inc., Sausalito, Calif., 1986—. Mem. Western Book Pubs. Assn. (pres. 1978-80). Home: 568 Arballo Dr San Francisco CA 94132 Office: Comstock Editions Inc 3030 Bridgeway Sausalito CA 94965

YOUNG, GERALD LEONARD, SR., farm equipment manufacturing executive; b. Billings, Mont., June 18, 1937; s. Leonard V. and Gladys (Laughery) Y.; m. Georgia M. Hartman, Mar. 5, 1982; children: Gerald L. Jr., Robert C. Student, Eastern Mont. Coll.; BA, Mont. State U., 1962. Territory mgr. Cert. Labs., Dallas, 1968-72, Midland Implement, Billings, 1972-75; ops. mgr. Renn U.S. div. Anthes Industries, Billings, 1975-80; gen. mgr. Renn U.S. div. Anthes Industries, Ft. Benton, Mont., 1980-84; dir. mktg. Renn div. Anthes Industries, Edmonton, Alta., Can., 1984-85, gen. mgr., 1985-87; v.p., gen. mgr. Renn-Verter, Edmonton, Alberta, Can., 1987—; corp. officer Anthes Industries, Mississauga, Ont., Can., 1985-86, Strathcond Resource, Edmonton, 1986—. Served with USN, 1954-58, Korea. Republican. Lodge: Elks. Home: 1101 S 97th Pl Mesa AZ 85208 Office: Renn-Vertec Inc 464 Foote St Billings MT 59101

YOUNG, J. LOWELL, soil chemist, biologist; b. Perry, Utah, Dec. 13, 1925; s. I.A. and Elzada (Nelson) Y.; m. Ruth Ann Jones, Sept. 15, 1950; children: Gordon, LoAnn, Colene, Kathryn. BS, Brigham Young U., 1953; PhD, Ohio State U., 1956. Rsch. asst. Ohio Agrl. Expt. Sta., Columbus, 1953-56, postdoctoral fellow, 1956-57; chemist Agrl. Research Service USDA, Corvallis, Oreg., 1957-64, research chemist, 1964-78; asst. prof. Oreg. State U., Corvallis, 1957-63, assoc. prof., 1963-78, prof. soil sci., 1978—; research chemist Horticultural Crops Research Unit U.S. Dept. Agrl., Corvallis, 1978—. Contbr. articles to profl jours. Served with USAAF, 1944-46. Mem. Internat. Soil Sci. Soc., Internat. Humic Substances Soc., Soil Soc. of Am. (officer 1972-75, assoc. editor jour. 1975-80), Am. Soc. Agronomy (officer western 1966-72), AAAS, Western Soc. Soil Sci. (officer 1966-71), Inst. for Alternative Agrl. Office: Oreg State U Soil Sci Dept Corvallis OR 97331

YOUNG, JAMES DUANE, sales executive; b. Spokane, Wash., Nov. 23, 1959; s. Dale Walter and Pauline (Huff) Y.; m. Lynette Diane Young, May 18, 1980 (div. 1986); 1 child, Shannon Kristine. Student, Spokane Falls Coll., 1980, 86—. Asst. mgr. Safeway Stores, Inc., Spokane, 1978-87; reg. sales rep. Commtron Corp., Kent, Wash., 1987—. Exec. bd. Spokane County Rep. Orgn., 1988—, dist. ldr., 1988—, precinct chmn. 1988—;/ organizer Morning Star Boys Ranch, Spokane, 1979—; bd. dirs. Trinity Cath. Sch., Spokane, 1985-87. Recipient Community Pride award, Safeway Stores, 1986. Mem. Toastmasters (exec. v.p. 1986—). Republican. Roman Catholic. Home: N 3821 E St Spokane WA 99205 Office: Commtron 6411 S 216th Bldg F Kent WA 98032

YOUNG, JOHN ALAN, electronics company executive; b. Nampa, Idaho, Apr. 24, 1932; s. Lloyd Arthur and Karen Eliza (Miller) Y.; m. Rosemary Murray, Aug. 1, 1954; children: Gregory, Peter, Diana. B.S. in Elec. Engring, Oreg. State U., 1953; M.B.A., Stanford U., 1958. Various mktg. and finance positions Hewlett Packard Co. Inc., Palo Alto, Calif., 1958-63, gen. mgr. microwave div., 1963-68, v.p. electronic products group, 1968-74, exec. v.p., 1974-77, chief oper. officer, 1977-84, pres., 1977—, chief exec. officer, 1978—, also bd. dirs.; bd. dirs. Wells Fargo Bank, Wells Fargo Co., Chevron Corp. Chmn. ann. fund Stanford, 1966-73, nat. chmn. corp. gifts, 1973-77; Bd. dirs. Mid-Peninsula Urban Coal., 1971-80, co-chmn., 1975-80; mem. adv. council Grad. Sch. Bus., Stanford U., 1967-73, 75-80, univ. trustee, 1977-87, chmn. Pres.'s Commn. Indsl. Competitiveness, 1983-85; chmn. Nat. Jr. Achievement, 1983—. Served with USAF, 1954-56. Mem. Am. Electronics Assn. (founder, chmn. council on competitiveness, 1986), Policy Com. Bus. Roundtable, Bus. Council, Pacific Union Club, Palo Alto Club.

YOUNG, JON NATHAN, archeologist; b. Hibbing, Minn., May 30, 1938; s. Robert Nathan Young and Mary Elizabeth (Barrows) Roy; m. Karen Sue Johnson, June 5, 1961 (div. May 1980); children: Shawn Nathan, Kevin Leigh; m. Tucker Heitman, June 18, 1988. BA magna cum laude, U. Ariz., 1960, PhD, 1967; MA, U. Ky., 1962. Archeologist Nat. Park Svc. Southwest Archeol. Ctr., Globe and Tucson, Ariz., 1967-76; exec., camp dir. YMCA of Metro. Tucson, 1976-78; asst. dir. Kit Carson Meml. Found., Taos, N.Mex., 1978-79; co-dir. Las Palomas de Taos, 1979-80; archeologist Nat. Forest Svc., Carson Nat. Forest, Taos, 1980—; exec. order cons. U.S. Sec. Interior, 1973-76. Author: The Salado Culture in Southwestern Prehistory, 1967; co-author: Excavation of Mound 7, 1981. Grantee NEH, 1977; Ariz. Wilson Found, NSF, Ky. Rsch. Found. fellow, 1960-66; Baird Found., Bausch and Lomb, Elks; recipient cert. merit USDA, 1987. Fellow AAAS, Am. Anthrop. Assn., Explorers Club, Royal Anthrop. Inst.; mem. Current Anthropology (assoc.), Ariz. Archaeol. and Hist. Soc., Ariz. Hist. Soc., Colonial N.Mex. Hist. Found., Coun. on Am's. Mil. Past., Soc. Hist. Archaeology , Soc. Am. Archaeology, Harwood Found., Millicent Rogers Mus., Wheelwright Mus. Am. Indian, Taos Archaeol. Soc., Sigma Xi, Phi Beta Kappa, Alpha Kappa Delta, Phi Kappa Phi, Delta Chi. Home: Box 2207 Taos NM 87571 Office: Nat Forest Svc Suprs Office Box 558 208112 Cruz Alta Rd Taos NM 87571

YOUNG, JOYCE HENRY, educator, consultant; b. Oak Park, Ill., July 3, 1930; d. Jesse Martin and Adelina Patti (Gillander) H.; m. James Edward Young, Apr. 26, 1958; children: Richard Allen, Patti Ann. BA, Calif. State U., Fresno, 1951; MA, Northwestern U., 1952; EdD, U. So. Calif., 1986. Tchr. Glencoe (Ill.) Pub. Schs., 1952-53, Hayward (Calif.) Schs., 1953-59, Honolulu Dept. Edn., 1969-83, Kamehameha Schs., Honolulu, 1987; instr. Hawaii Pacific Coll., Honolulu, 1987, Honolulu Community Coll., 1988; cons. Computer Lab., Honolulu, 1988. Mem. AAUW, Am. Ednl. Research Assn., Educom, Delta Epsilon, Kappa Delta Pi, Pi Lamda Theta. Democrat. Presbyterian.

YOUNG, KENNETH ROGER, teacher; b. L.A., Aug. 25, 1936; s. John Richardson and Jency Florence (Lehman) Y.; m. Lavonne Kurowski, Mar. 17, 1963 (div. June, 1970); m. Suzanne Cecelia Murray, June 20, 1970; children: Christina, Steven, Joseph. AA, Sacramento City Coll., 1956; BA, Sacramento State U., 1958, MA, 1968. Cert. secondary tchr., Calif. Tchr. Roseville (Calif.) High Sch., 1960-65, Oakmont High Sch., Roseville, 1965-70; tchr., resource specialist San Carlos (Calif.) High Sch., 1970-73, tchr., dept. chmn., 1973-82; tchr. Britton Middle sch., Morgan Hill, Calif., 1982-85, Live Oak High Sch., Morgan Hill, 1985—; performer Living Artists' Theater, Calif., 1980—; cons. art history workshop, San Juan Sch. Dist., Sacramento, 1986-87. Performer San Jose Fine Art Mus., 1983-84, Festival of the Arts Week, 1986-88, Fresno Art Mus., 1987. Served with Calif. N.G., 1959-65. Recipient Golden Bell award Calif. Sch. Bds. Assn., 1987. Mem. Am. Fedn. Tchrs., Young Audiences San Jose (bd. dirs. 1985-88), Calif. Art Edn. Assn. (no. area sec. rep. 1988—). Democrat. Roman Catholic. Home: 1137-A Reed Ave Sunnyvale CA 94086 Office: Live Oak High Sch PO Box 927 Morgan Hill CA 95037

YOUNG, LAURENCE BYRON, investment analyst; b. Highland Park, Mich., Jan. 13, 1932; s. Victor Peter and Evangeline (Murphy) Y.; m. Barrie Bruce, Jan. 25, 1964 (div. Sept. 1971); 1 child, Brian Bruce. AB, Stanford (Calif.) U., 1953; MBA, Harvard U., 1960. V.p. Kidder, Peabody and Co., N.Y.C., 1960-64, Capital Research Co., Los Angeles, 1964-72, Scudder, Stevens and Clark, Los Angeles, 1972-74, First Interstate Bancorp, Los Angeles, 1977-88, CMB Investment Counselors, Los Angeles, 1988—. Contbr. chpts. to book. Active Town Hall of So. Calif., Los Angeles, 1966—. Served to cpl. U.S. Army, 1953-55. Mem. Nat. Investor Relations Inst. So. Calif. (bd. dirs. 1987—), Los Angeles Soc. Fin. Analysts, N.Y. Soc. Security Analysts, Inst. Chartered Fin. Analysts. Republican. Clubs: Harvard (N.Y.C.); Univ. (Los Angeles). Home: 101 Ocean Ave Santa Monica CA 90402 Office: CMB Investment Counselors 1880 Century Park E Los Angeles CA 90067

YOUNG, LESTER REX, engineer; b. Marion, Ind., Aug. 26, 1946; s. Harold Leroy and Willow Marie (May) Y.; m. Bonnie Darline Denison, Sept. 5, 1965; children: Tamara Lynn, Kelby Gene. BSEE, Kans. State U., 1969; MBA, Wichita State U., 1979. Reg. engr. Colo., Kans., Ohio, Mont., Utah, La. Plant engr. Beech Aircraft Corp., Wichita, Kans., 1973-75; asst. to v.p. mfg. Beech Aircraft Corp., Wichita, 1975-77; sr. project mgr. Smith & Boucher, Inc., Overland Park, Kans., 1977-80; dir. engring. R.M. Henning, Inc., New Philadelphia, Ohio, 1980-82; mgr. indsl. engring. Williams Internat., Ogden, Utah, 1982-84; mgr. plant engring. Sundstrand Corp., Denver, 1984-86; pres. ECS Engrs. Inc., Arvada, Colo., 1986—; cons. Compliance Recycling Industries, Denver, 1984-87. Author: (reference manuals) Selection of Reverse Osmosis for Boiler Applications, 1987, Applications for Enzyme Activated Carbon, 1989. Capt. U.S. Army, 1969-73, Europe. Republican. Nazarene. Office: ECS Engrs PO Box 5190 Arvada CO 80005

YOUNG, MICHAEL ANTHONY, educator; b. Trieste, Italy, Dec. 30, 1948; came to U.S., 1951; s. Edward Anthony and Josephine Antoinette (Verderosa) Y.; m. Jeanette Burton, Apr. 11, 1976 (div. Jan. 1979); m. Eileen Karen Hughes, June 26, 1988. BA in Psychology, U. Maine, 1975; MEd, San Francisco State U., 1978; postgrad., U. Oreg., 1986-87. Cons. Anchorage, 1978—; tchr. Anchorage Sch. Dist., 1978-81, 88—, vocational coordinator, 1981-86, project dir., 1987-88; script writer Anchorage, 1987—; adj. lectr., Anchorage Community Coll., 1980-82; adv. council Anchorage Community Coll.; bd. dirs. State Infant Learning Program, Anchorage; task force mem. Spl. Edn. Svcs. Agy., Anchorage, 1988—. Author, editor: (video) Educating Alaska, 1989 (Pub. Rels. Soc. Am. Alaska chpt. award 1989), (slide productions) Hunger Projects, 1987, Willamete Science Museum, 1987, (photo exhibit) Anchorage Public Library. Task force mem. various coms., Anchorage, 1985-86; organizer first chartered youth group ending hunger in Am.; active Hunger Project and Food First Inst. Mem. Anchorage Orienteering Club (pres. 1985-86), Camber Club. Democrat. Home: 14401 Buffalo Rd Anchorage AK 99516 Office: Anchorage Sch Dist 4600 Debarr Rd Anchorage AK 99503

YOUNG, PATRICIA JANEAN, speech pathologist; b. San Diego, Nov. 30, 1953; d. Bernarr Elbert and Janean Elizabeth (Romig) Y. AA, Palomar Community coll., 1974; BA, Calif. State U., Chico, 1976; MA, Calif. State U., Long Beach, 1981. Mgmt. trainee J.W. Robinson's Dept. Store, Los Angeles, 1977-78; screening coordinator Riverview Hearing, Speech and Lang. Ctr., Long Beach, 1978-81, speech pathologist, 1981-84; speech pathologist, dir. Speech Pathology Services, Carlsbad, Calif., 1984—; mem. Senator Ellis' assemblywoman Bentley's adv. com. for Developmentally Disabled, San Diego, 1985—; coordinator for Pub. Service Announcement for Disabilities Awareness Week, ABC TV, 1986, "Inside San Diego", for Disabilities Awareness Week, ABC, 1988. Producer (cable TV series), Communicative Disorders, 1983. Recipient Outstanding Young Women award, 1983. Mem. Am. Speech Lang. and Hearing Assn. (cert.), Calif. Speech Lang. and Hearing Assn. (div. rep. 1985-88, Outstanding Achievement award 1987), Calif. Speech Pathologist Audiologists in Pvt. Practice, Nat. Assn. for Hearing and Speech Action (chmn. Disney benefit 1983-84), Assn. for Retarded Citizens, Calif. Scholastic Fedn., Zeta Tau Alpha, Phi Delta Gamma (sec. 1982-83, v.p. 1983-84). Republican. Home: 2880 Andover Ave Carlsbad CA 92008 Office: Speech Pathology Svcs PO Box 4355 Carlsbad CA 92008

YOUNG, PAUL HOWARD, engineering and computers educator; b. Chgo., Sept. 26, 1940; s. Theodore Howard and Dorothy Emma (Davis) Y.; m. Beryl Elaine Cole, July 6, 1981; children: John, James, Sara. BSEE, Calif. State U., San Diego, 1965; MSEE, Calif. State U., San Jose, 1981. Cert. secondary and community coll. tchr., Calif.; registered profl. engr., Calif. Electronic engr. Cubic Corp., San Diego, 1964-70, sr. engr., 1970-74; engring. cons. San Diego, 1974-76; instr. engring. City Coll. San Francisco, 1976-81; assoc. prof. Ariz. State U., Tempe, 1981—; cons. Hewlett-Packard Corp., Rolm Corp., Motorola, Scottsdale, Ariz., 1985. Author: (text) Electronic Communication Techniques, 1985; contbr. tech. articles, papers to profl. jours. With USNR, 1960-62. NASA fellow, 1983-84, 86, 87. Mem. NSPE, Am. Soc. for Engring. Edn., Nat. Assn. Telecom Engrs. (master cert.), IEEE (sr.), Sierra Club. Home: 6926 E Willetta Scottsdale AZ 85257 Office: Ariz State U Dept Electronics-Computer Tech Tempe AZ 85287

YOUNG, PETER EDMUND, real estate developer; b. Manchester, N.H., July 20, 1948; s. Edmund O. and Helen E. (Apostolos) Y. BA, U. Neb., 1969; MA, SUNY, Buff, 1974, JD, 1977. Staff counsel Sansone & Sansone, Lockport, N.Y., 1972-74; founder, pres. Niagara Bus. Svcs., Buff, 1974-81; pres. 1st Consol. Cos., Carson City, Nev., 1981—; lectr. SUNY Law Sch., Buff, 1979-81. Author (book): The Upside, 1984. Served to capt. USMC, 1969-72, Vietnam. Decorated Purple Heart. Roman Catholic. Home: PO Box 941 Anderson CA 96007 Office: First Consol Co 1000 E Williams Ste 100 Carson City NV 89701

YOUNG, PETER THOMAS, real estate appraisal company executive; b. Honolulu, Jan. 28, 1952; s. Kenneth Marr and Lydia Bingham (Sutherland) Y. Student, U. Denver, 1970-73; BBA, U. Hawaii, 1974. Lic. real estate salesman and broker, Hawaii. Sales mgr. Kanaloa Realty, Kailua-Kona, Hawaii, 1977-80; pres. Real Estate Works Hawaii Inc., Kailua-Kona, 1980-86, Real Estate Svcs., Inc., Kamuela, Hawaii, 1986--; instr. real estate U. Hawaii, Manoa, 1977--; expert witness Fed. Bankruptcy Ct.; appraiser U.S. Dist. Ct. for Hawaii; mem. tenant hearing rev. bd. Hawaii Housing Authority, 1984-88; mem. Hawaii County Bd. Appeals, 1985-87; dir. Big Island Community Mediation Ctr., 1987-88. Weekly columnist Today's Real Estate, 1978-80. Bd. dirs. Hawaii Island chpt. Hawaii Visitors Bur., 1984-86; del. Hawaii Gov.'s Tourism Congress, 1984; pres. Waimea-Kawaihae Community Assn., 1987--; chmn. Community Orgn. for Edn. Devel., 1985-86; mem. chancellor's adv. coun. U. Hawaii, Hilo, 1986-88; del. Big Island Bus. Coun., 1982-88, v.p., 1984-85, 86-87; Hawaii chmn. agrl. adv. coun. Nat. Republican Com.; West Hawaii rep. Hawaii Com. for Humanities, 1979-85; former mem. Kona Community Planning Group, West Hawaii Community Forum; chmn. adv. coun. W. Hawaii Svc. Ctr., ARC and bd. dirs. Hawaii State chpt. Mem. Nat. Assn. Realtors (cert. real estate brokerage mgr.), Hawaii Assn. Realtors (v.p., exec. com. 1986), Kona Bd. Realtors (pres. 1986), Nat. Assn. Rev. Appraisers and Mortgage Underwriters (sr., registered mortgage underwriter, cert. rev. appraiser), Am. Real Estate and Urban Econs. Assn., Internat. Real Estate Inst. (sr., sr. cert. valuer, past chpt. pres.), Appraisal Inst., Nat. Assn. Real Estate Appraisers (sr., cert. real estate appraiser), Kona-Kohala C. of C. (pres.-elect 1988--). *. Republican. Home: PO Box 2665 Kamuela HI 96743 Office: Real Estate Svcs Inc PO Box 2665 Kamuela HI 96743

YOUNG, PHILIP DONALD, anthropology educator; b. Ottawa, Ill., Oct. 18, 1936; s. Donald Everett and Jean Magdeline (Ftacek) Y.; m. Cendrina Magaly Angeles, 1957 (div. 1976); children: Andrew Philip, Juanita Maria, Tanya Desiree; m. Barbara Ann Sellers, July 20, 1981. BA, U. Ill., 1961, PhD, 1968. From asst. prof. to assoc. prof. anthrop. U. Oreg., Eugene, 1966-81, prof., 1982—, chmn. dept. anthrop., 1985—; dir. field projects Inter-Am. Devel. Inst., Washington, 1976-78; curriculum devel. specialist, tech. adviser Devel Alternatives Inc., Washington, 1981-82. Author: Ngawbe: Tradition and Change Among the Western Guaymi of Panama, 1971 (Choice award 1971); editor: Ritual and Symbol in Native Central America, 1976; contbr. articles to profl. jours. With U.S. Army, 1955-58. Fellow Am. Anthrop. Assn., Soc. Applied Anthropology, Royal Anthrop. Inst. Democrat. Office: U Oreg Dept Anthropology Eugene OR 97403

YOUNG, ROBERT EDWARD, finance company executive; b. L.A., Nov. 28, 1943; s. David and Sue (Wise) Y.; m. Sharon Johnson, Dec. 8, 1967. Student, E. Los Angeles Coll., 1973, Santa Monica Coll., 1975; BA, UCLA, 1978. Cert. securities analyst N.Y. Inst. Fin., 1972. Computer operator Rocketdyne Corp., Canoga Park, Calif., 1963-65; computer ops. supr. Hughes Aircraft Corp., El Segundo, Calif., 1965-67; with investment securities dept. Smith, Tilton & Co., Inc., Santa Ana, Calif., 1967-70, Morton Seidel & Co., Inc., L.A., 1970-78; sales mgr. of comml. interior constrn. NICO Constrn. Co., Inc., L.A., 1978-80; sales mgr. Strauss Constrn. Co., Inc., L.A., 1981-82; v.p., instl. investment officer FCA Asset Mgmt./Am. Savs., Los Angeles, 1982-87; pres., chief exec. officer Avalon Fin. Group, Inc., Los Angeles, 1988—; bd. dirs. RESA Prodns. 1973-80, Edu Care, L.A., 1981—, ASC Edn. Svcs. Inc., L.A., chmn. fin. com.; mktg. cons. Shehata Enterprises, L.A., 1978-79; sales tng. cons. Versailles Gallery, L.A., Schwartz Constrn., L.A., 1982. Photographer: prin. works include Man at Work or Play UN, Geneva, 1976, Cat of Yr. photo, 1977, Photomontage U. So. Calif. Early Childhood Edn. Ctr., 1977; producer weekly pub. affairs program for family fin. planning sta. KPOL Radio, 1974, Stocks and bonds show KWHY-TV, 1975-78. Fin. cons. Hofheinz Fund, Houston, 1988. Served with USCGR, 1964-70. Mem. AIA, Cosmopolitan Internat. (pres. 1967-68), Soc. Archtl. Historians, L.A. Conservancy, West Los Angeles Constitution Observance Day (chmn. 1970), Archtl. Hist. Soc. (life mem. So. Calif. chpt.), Valley MacIntosh User Group, Downtown High Twelve Club (past pres.), Masons, Toastmasters (Outstanding Toastmaster 1973-74, 76). Home: 945 Hauser Blvd Los Angeles CA 90036 Office: Avalon Fin Group Inc 8306 Wilshire Blvd Ste 499 Beverly Hills CA 90211

YOUNG, ROBERT EMMETT, informations systems management executive; b. Bronxville, N.Y., May 2, 1952; s. William L. and Christine Winifred Young; m. Karlin Graham, Feb. 5, 1984; children: Sean, Travis, Braiden. BS, U. Denver, 1974. Computer scheduler Credit Card div. Diners Club, Denver, 1974, programmer analyst, 1975-76, sr. user analyst, 1977, mgr. credit rsch.-risk mgmt., 1978-82; dir. info. systems Keystone (Colo.) Resort Mgmt. Inc., 1983—. Mem. Soc. Info. Mgmt., IBM User Group, Common Club, Toastmasters (v.p. edn. 1988-). Republican. Office: Keystone Resorts Mgmt Inc 22010 Hwy 6 Keystone CO 80435

YOUNG, ROGER CARL, computer company executive; b. Clayton, Mo., Mar. 21, 1932; s. Gerald Lee Young and Bertha Augusta (Schlottach) McCulloh; m. Nadine Fay Basch, Apr. 27, 1952; children: Julia Allyn, David Ford. Student, Washington U., St. Louis, 1956-57, U. Calif., Berkeley, 1957-60, Contra Costa Coll., 1970. V.p. and div. mgr. Crocker Nat. Bank, San Francisco, 1967-75; nat. accts. mgr. Wang Labs., San Francisco, 1975-78; industry cons. Fortune 500, 1978-81; pres. ComTrak, Richmond, Calif., 1981-83; dir. mktg. Delphi Systems, Inc., Westlake Village, Calif., 1983-89. Served with USAF, 1951-55. Mem. Data Processing Mgmt. Assn. (cert., dir., sec. San Francisco chpt. 1965-67), Am. Contract Bridge League (life master 1959). Republican. Club: Concord (Calif.) Mens Golf. Home and Office: 779 Arbor Oaks Dr Vacaville CA 95687

YOUNG, ROY ALTON, university administrator, educator; b. McAlister, N.Mex., Mar. 1, 1921; s. John Arthur and Etta Julia (Sprinkle) Y.; m. Marilyn Ruth Sandman, May 22, 1950; children: Janet Elizabeth, Randall Owen. BS, N.Mex. A&M Coll., 1941; MS, Iowa State U., 1942, PhD, 1948; LLD (hon.), N.Mex. State U., 1978. Teaching fellow Iowa State U., 1941-42, instr., 1946-47, Indsl. fellow, 1947-48; asst. prof. Oreg. State U., 1948-50, assoc. prof., 1950-53, prof., 1953—, head dept. botany and plant pathology, 1958-66, dean research, 1966-70, acting pres., 1969-70, v.p. for research and grad. studies, 1970-76, dir. Office for Natural Resources Policy, 1986—; chancellor U. Nebr., Lincoln, 1976-80; mng. dir., pres. Boyce Thompson Inst. Plant Research, Cornell U., Ithaca, N.Y., 1980-86; bd. dirs. Pacific Power and Light, PacifiCorp; mem. Commn. on Undergrad. Edn. in Biol. Scis., 1963-68, Gov.'s Sci. Council, 1987—; cons. State Expt. Stas. div. USDA; chmn. subcom. plant pathogens, agriculture bd. Nat. Acad. Scis.-NRC, 1965-68, mem. exec. com. study on problems of pest control, 1972-75; mem. exec. com. Nat. Govs.' Council on Sci. and Tech., 1970-74; mem. U.S. com. man and biosphere UNESCO, 1973-82; mem. com. to rev. U.S. component Internat. Biol. Program, Nat. Acad. Scis., 1974-76; mem. adv. panel on post-doctoral fellowships in environ. sci. Rockefeller Found., 1974-78; bd. dirs. Boyce Thompson Inst. for Plant Research, 1975—; mem. adv. com. Directorate for Engring. and Applied Sci., NSF, 1977-81, mem. sea grant adv. panel, 1978-80; mem. policy adv. com. Office of Grants, USDA, 1985-86. Bd. dirs. Boyce Thompson Southwestern Arboretum, 1981—, Am. Phytopath. Soc. Found., 1986—, Oreg. Grad. Ctr., 1987—; trustee Ithaca Coll., 1982—. Served to lt. USNR, 1943-46. Fellow AAAS (exec. com. Pacific div. 1963-67, pres. div. 1971), Am. Phytopath. Soc. (pres. Pacific div. 1957, chmn. spl. com. to develop plans for endowment 1984-86); mem. Oreg. Acad. Sci., Nat. Assn. State Univs. and Land Grant Colls. (chmn. council for research policy and adminstrn. 1970, chmn. standing com. on environment and energy 1974-82, chmn. com. on environment 1984-86), Sigma Xi, Phi Kappa Phi, Phi Sigma, Sigma Alpha Epsilon. Home: 3605 NW Van Buren St Corvallis OR 97330 Office: Oreg State U Natural Resources Policy Snell Hall Corvallis OR 97331-1651

YOUNG, RUSSEL RAY, insurance company executive; b. Portland, Oreg., Dec. 14, 1934; s. Walton Meyers and Charlotte Francis (Bottemiller) Y.; m. Barbara Jean Koonce, Mar. 24, 1956; children: Russel Ray, Cheryl Lynne. BS in Mgmt., Golden Gate U., 1974; MS in Safety, U. So. Calif., 1984. Cert. safety profl. Bd. Cert. Safety Profls. Commd. officer U.S. Air Force, 1954, advanced through grades to maj., 1966; transport pilot U.S. and Orient, 1955-61; acad. instr. aircraft maintenance, 1961-63; aircraft instrument pilot instr., 1963-65; aircraft comdr., Vietnam, 1965-66; chief command post European Hdqrs. Command and Control Ctr., 1966-70; chief flight safety br. Mather AFB, Calif., 1970-74, ret., 1974; loss control rep. Continental Ins. Co., Sacramento, Calif., 1974-76, loss control mgr., 1976-79; loss control mgr. Mission Ins. Co., Sacramento, 1979-86; mgr. systems safety, Sacramento Regional Transit dist., 1986-88; loss control mgr. Hanover Ins. Co., Sacramento, 1988—. Decorated Bronze Star, D.F.C., Air medal with 8 clusters, Air Force Commendation medal with cluster, Meritorious Service medal, Air Force Expeditionary medal, Republic of Vietnam Service medal. Mem. Am. Soc. Safety Engrs. (chpt. v.p.), Exptl. Aircraft Assn. Office: 1400 29th St Sacramento CA 95816

YOUNG, STEPHEN BERTON, insurance company executive; b. Denver, July 6, 1947; s. William Robert and Margaret Jayne (Kuni) Y.; m. Susan Christy Kowal, Feb. 17, 1968; children: William Arnold, Jennifer Holly, Theodore John. BA, Hamline U., 1969. CLU, CPCU. Underwriting asst. State Farm Ins., St. Paul, Minn., 1968-69; mgmt. trainee State Farm Ins., Greeley, Colo., 1969, underwriter, 1969-70, sr. underwriter, 1970-72, comml. accts. underwriter, 1972-74, field underwriter, 1974-78, underwriting supr., 1978-79; underwriting supt. State Farm Ins., Salem, Oreg., 1979-83; fire claims supt. State Farm Ins., Tacoma, Wash., 1983-87; mgr. edn. & tng. State Farm Ins., Greeley, Colo., 1987—. Mem. Soc. Chartered Property and Casualty Underwriters (Oregon chpt. officer 1980-84, pub. relations com. 1986-89, nat. commnity mem.), Soc. for Preservation and Encouragement of Barbershop Quartet Singing in Am. Episcopalian. Office: State Farm Cos 3001 8th Ave Greeley CO 80631

YOUNG, STEPHEN JEROME, lawyer; b. Berkeley, Calif., Oct. 20, 1956; s. William Jordan and Marina Solveig (Amdahl) Y.; m. Amy Marie Seminario, Feb. 21, 1987. BA, U. Pa., 1978; MBA, U. Calif., Berkeley, 1983; JD, U. Calif., 1983. Bar: Calif. 1983, Mass. 1986. V.p. E.F. Hutton & Co., Inc., San Francisco, 1982-85; assoc. Csaplar & Bok, Boston and San Francisco, 1986—. Mem. ABA, Phi Beta Kappa. Office: Csaplar & Bok 655 Montgomery St San Francisco CA 94111

YOUNG, SUZANNE MARYE, chamber of commerce executive; b. Kansas City, Mo., Nov. 1, 1946; d. Charles S. and Anne M. (Ceccone) Y. BA, U. Mich., 1968; postgrad., Pepperdine U., 1987-89. Comml. coordinator Sta. WXYZ-TV, Southfield, Mich., 1968; prodn. mgr. Daystar Multi-Media, Ann Arbor, Mich., 1969-74; dir. major events U. Mich., Ann Arbor, 1974-78, dir. spl. programs, 1978-80; exec. dir. Mich. Union, Ann Arbor, 1979-80; adminstr. Tourism Promotion Bur., Jackson Hole, Wyo., 1983-85; exec. dir. Jackson Hole C. of C., 1985—. Chmn. tourism task force Wyo. Futures Project, 1986-87; mem. Wyo. Tourism Policy Council, 1985-87; bd. dirs. Old West Trail Found., 1988—. Named Promoter of Yr., Billboard mag., 1975, 77, Disting. Service award Jackson Hole C. of C., 1986. Mem. Yellowstone-Teton Travel Assn. (v.p. 1986-88), Orgn. Devel. Network, Wyo. C. of C. Execs. (bd. dirs. 1987-88). Home: PO Box 3351 Jackson WY 83001 Office: Jackson Hole Area C of C PO Box E Jackson WY 83001

YOUNG, THOMAS HARLAN, lawyer; b. Bethlehem, Pa., Dec. 13, 1946; s. Harlan A. and Dorothy E. (Kelchner) Y.; m. Karen L. Rogers, Oct. 30, 1987. BS in Chem. Engring., U. Pa., 1968; JD, Georgetown U., 1972. Bar: Va. 1972, Ill. 1973, Colo. 1980. Examiner U.S. Patent Office, Washington, 1968-70; law clk. U.S. Dept. Interior, Washington, 1970-72, U.S. Dist. Ct. Del., Wilmington, 1972-73; ptnr. Kirkland & Ellis, Chgo., 1973-79, Rothgerber, Appel, Powers & Johnson, Denver, 1980—; cons., Solar Energy Rsch. Inst., Lakewood, Colo., 1979-80. Contbr. to profl. publs. Mem. ABA, Va. Bar Assn., Ill. Bar Assn., Colo. Bar Assn. (ethics com.), Petroleum Club Denver. Democrat. Mem. United Ch. of Christ. Home: 540 S Forest St Denver CO 80222 Office: Rothgerber Appel et al 1200 17th St Denver CO 80202

YOUNG, WALTER KWAI WHUN, otolaryngologist; b. Honolulu, Sept. 24, 1934; s. Leon Quan and Mildred (Chang) Y.; m. Joan Audrey Nichols, Mar. 30, 1963; children: Walter Leong, Adriene Lianne, Curt Yen Pui. Student, U. Hawaii, 1952-54; BA, Gerrysburg Coll., 1956; MD, Jefferson Med. Coll., 1960. Diplomate Am. Bd. Otolaryngology. Intern, then resident in gen. surgery St. Luke's Hosp., Bethlehem, Pa., 1960-62; resident in otolaryngology Grad. Hosp., Phila., 1962-63, Upstate Med. Ctr., Syracuse, N.Y., 1963-65; pvt. practice Honolulu, 1968—; assoc. prof. John A. Burns Sch. Medicine U. Hawaii, past chief of surgery Children's Hosp.; chief of pediatric surgery Kapiolani Med. Ctr. Women and Children. Capt. USAF, 1965-67. Fellow Am. Acad. Otolaryngology and Head and Neck Surgery, ACS; mem. AMA, Hawaii Med. Assn., Honolulu County Med. Soc., Am. Coll. Surgeons, Pacific Coast Opthlmology and Otolaryngology Assn., State Bd. Hearing Aid Dealers and Fitters. Presbyterian. Office: 1380 Lusitana St Ste 615 Honolulu HI 96813-2421

YOUNG, WILLIAM CHARLES, media production company executive; b. Fond du Lac, Wis., Oct. 5, 1936; s. Warner Roy and Hannah Elizabeth (Nixon) Y.; children: Donovan Charles, Jamison William. BA, Mich. State U., 1958. Reporter, producer Sta. WKZO-TV, Kalamazoo, Mich., 1958-60; writer, producer W.B. Doner Advt. Co., Chgo., 1960-63, Gardner Advt. Co., St. Louis, 1963-68; pres., creative dir. Creative Coalition, Chgo. and Los Angeles, 1968-85; pres., owner Eventures, Beverly Hills, Calif., 1985—; bd. dirs. M.P.I.C., Irvine, Calif. Writer, producer film: Good to See You, Alice Cooper, 1974, play: Let's Party, Suzann, 1988, TV special: Summit Too, 1988. Bd. dirs. Friendship Fund, Los Angeles, 1988, Friends of Calif. Mus. of Ancient Arts, Musicians for Musicians, Young Reps., 1958-64; pres. Kalamazoo County Young Reps., 1958-60; founding dir. Bellini Found., Huntington Beach, Calif., 1988. Recipient Clio award, 1967. Mem. Alliance of Motion Picture and TV Producers. Republican. Office: Eventures 9903 Santa Monica Blvd Beverly Hills CA 90212

YOUNGBLOOD, RICK DWAYNE, corporate executive; b. Boise, Idaho, Aug. 20, 1954; s. C.D. Wayne and M. Shirley (Alspaugh) Y.; m. C. Arlene Stoneman, Nov. 25, 1972; children: Chandra D., Richard H. Student, N. Idaho Coll., 1972-73, Wash. State U., 1982-84. From loan officer to br. mgr. First Interstate Bank Idaho, Boise, 1976-80; asst. v.p. First Interstate Bank Idaho, Caldwell, 1984-88, v.p. comml. banking, 1987-88; asst. v.p., br. mgr. Treasure Valley Bank, Caldwell, 1980-84; v.p., ops. mgr. AIM Internat., Inc., Nampa, Idaho, 1988—; bd. dirs. SBA Cert. Devel. Co., Boise. V.p. allocations United Way Canyon County, Caldwell, 1986. Recipient Vol. Leadership award United Way, 1984; named Nat. Oldtime Fiddling Champion Weiser Nat. Oldtime Fiddle Assn., 1979. Mem. Caldwell C. of C. (pres. 1985), Rotary (pres. Caldwell chpt. 1988). Republican. Mem. Ch. of Nazarene. Home: 2503 High St Nampa ID 83651 Office: AIM Intrenat Inc 3904 E Flamingo Nampa ID 83687

YOUNGBLOOD, SCOT ALAN, small business manager; b. Lubbock, Tex., June 15, 1962; s. Oley William and Frances Lee (Ham) Y.; m. Patricia June Lavelett, Aug. 7, 1982; children: Scot Aric, Nathaniel Martin. Assocs., N.Mex. Jr. Coll., 1987. V.p. O&S Quik Change Oil, Inc., Hobbs, N.Mex., 1986—; owner Premier Pick-up & Offroad, Hobbs, 1987—. Mem. Hobbs Bowling Assn. Republican. Baptist. Home: 1510 W Millen Hobbs NM 88240 Office: O&S Quik Change Oil Inc 520 W Bender Hobbs NM 88240

YOUNGER, JOHN PATRICK, JR., employee benefits director; b. Johnson AFB, Japan, Jan. 29, 1949; came to U.S., 1949; s. John Patrick and Helen Martha (Doka) Y.; m. Karen Lynn Ruse, July 20, 1985; 1 child, Shannon Marie. BA in Econs., Claremont (Calif) Men's Coll., 1971. Asst. group underwriter Occidental Life Ins., Los Angeles, 1972-74; sr. cons. Peat Marwick, Mitchell & Co., Los Angeles, 1974-80; mgr. employee benefits TRW- Space & Def., Redondo Beach, Calif., 1980-86, mgr. Benefits planning & fin. mgmt., 1986-88; dir. employee benefits Pacific Enterprises, Los Angeles, 1988—; bd. dirs. U.S. Corp. Athletic Assn., Los Angeles, So. Calif. Corp. Athletic Assn, Los Angeles. Mem. Am. Compensation Assn., Nat. Assn. Realtors, Calif. Assn. Realtors, Profl. Coast Bowlers. Republican. Office: Pacific Enterprises 801 S Grand Ave Los Angeles CA 90017

YOUNGER, VIVIAN MAXINE, rehabilitation counselor; b. Ruston, La., Nov. 13, 1952; d. Huey P. and Willie Mae (Frazier) Y. BA, San Jose State U., 1976, teaching credential, 1977, MPA, 1986. Cert. specialist civil rights for disabled, Calif. Music dir. for visually ltd. Found. for Jr. Blind, L.A., 1973-75, 78-79; elem. tchr. San Jose (Calif.) Unified Sch. Dist., 1977-79; program dir. disabled youth tng. program Econ. and Social Opportunities, Inc., San Jose, 1980-81; substitute tchr. San Jose Unified Sch. Dist. and Oakgrove Sch. Dist., 1981; rehab. counselor for disabled adults Calif. Dept. Rehab., San Jose, 1981—; mem. Santa Clara County Com. for Employment of Disabled, 1980—, Santa Clara County Adv. Commn. on Devel. Disabled, 1980-81; mem. disability adv. com. City of San Jose, 1987; program dir. for ednl., recreational social program for visually ltd. children K-12 Assistance League Santa Clara County, Los Altos, Calif., 1977-87. Mem. faculty student instrn. com. for disabled students San Jose State U., 1973-75; bd. dirs. Santa Clara Valley Blind Ctr., 1977-78, Adult Independence Devel. Ctr., 1980-83; mem. Calif. Gov.'s Adv. Com. for Developing Master Plan for Children and Youth in Calif., 1980-81, Santa Clara County Commn. on Status of Women, 1983-86. Recipient Woman of Achievement award Santa Clara County Commn. on Status of Women, 1981. Mem. Phi Kappa Phi (life). Democrat. Office: Calif Dept Rehab 100 Paseo San Antonio 324 San Jose CA 95113

YOUNGREN, DAVID ROBERT, insurance company executive; b. Bessmer, Mich., Aug. 14, 1937; s. Sigmund and Jean (Mitchell) Y.; m. Carole Faye Kopitzke, Dec. 25, 1958. Grad. high sch., Iron River, Mich. Ins. agt. Beneficial Std. Life, Fresno, Calif., 1959-69; supr. Beneficial Standard Life, Fresno, Calif., 1969-74; gen. agt., supr. Res. Life Ins. Co., Fresno, 1974-76; co-owner, pres. Compare Ins. Agy., Inc., Clovis, Calif., 1976-88. With USAF, 1955-59. Mem. Life Underwriters Assn. Republican. Methodist. Office: Compare Ins Agy Inc 180 Clovis Ave Clovis CA 93612

YOUNGS, JACK MARVIN, cost engineer; b. Bklyn., May 2, 1941; s. Jack William and Virginia May (Clark) Y.; BEngring., CCNY, 1964; MBA, San Diego State U., 1973; m. Alexandra Marie Robertson, Oct. 31, 1964; 1 child, Christine Marie. Mass properties engr. Gen. Dynamics Corp., San Diego, 1964-68, rsch. engr., 1968-69, sr. rsch. engr., 1969-80, sr. cost devel. engr., 1980-81, cost devel. engring. specialist, 1981—. Dist. dir. Scripps Ranch Civic Assn., 1976-79; pres. Scripps Ranch Swim Team, 1980-82; dir., 1986-87; judge Greater San Diego Sci. and Engring. Fair, 1981-88. Mem. Princeton U. Parents Assn. Recipient 5th place award World Body Surfing Championships, 1987, 6th place award, 1988. Mem. AIAA, Inst. Cost Analysis (cert., charter mem., treas. Greater San Diego chpt. 1986), Internat. Soc. Parametric Analysts (bd. dirs. San Diego chpt. 1987-88), Nat. Mgmt. Assn. (space systems div. charter mem. 1985, award of honor Covair chpt. 1975), Assn. MBA Execs., San Diego State U. Bus. Alumni Assn. (charter mem. 1986), Scripps Ranch Swim and Racquet Club (dir. 1977-80, treas. 1978-789, pres. 1979-80), Beta Gamma Sigma, Chi Epsilon, Sigma Iota Epsilon. Lutheran. Research in life cycle costing and econ. analysis. Home: 11461 Tribuna Ave San Diego CA 92131 Office: PO Box 85990 San Diego CA 92138

YOUNGS, JAMES MURRAY, freelance writer, photographer; b. Abilene, Tex., Apr. 15, 1947; s. William Murray and Mary Nell (Brown) Y.; m. Carolyn Sue Allen, Aug. 14, 1971; children: James Murray Jr., Monica Sue. BA in Journalism, Pepperdine U., 1972. Adminstrv. asst. Los Angeles County Bd. Suprs., 1966-67; photogrpahy coordinator Pepperdine U., Malibu, Calif., 1971-72; phtographer, draftsman Brehler Legal Photos, Los Angeles, 1973; pub. relations, advt. mgr. Griswolds Restuarants, Inc., Claremont, Calif., 1973-74; gen. mgr. Cinemodule, Hollywood, Calif., 1974-77; editor-in-chief Trailer Boats Mag., Carson, Calif., 1977-88; freelance writer Englewood, Colo., 1988—. Contbg. editor Trailer Boats Mag., Boat Mag., Boating Mag., Lakeland Boating, Water Ski, The Western Boatman; writer Boat Owners Corner, 1988-89. With USN, 1966-70. Mem. Boating Writers Internat. (dir. 1987—), Nat. Marine Mfg. Assn., Sigma Delta Chi. Republican. Church of Christ. Home and Office: 34 Sedgwick Dr Englewood CO 80110

YOUNKIN, ROBERT RAY, physician; b. Brush, Colo., Apr. 4, 1947; s. Clarence Ellis and Dorothy Lucille (Devore) Y.; m. Constance Ann Neal, June 21, 1969; children: Hilary, Rebecca, Sarah, Rachel. Student, U. Colo., 1968, MD, 1972. Diplomate Am. Bd. Family Practice. Intern U.S. Naval Hosp., Boston, 1972-73; resident U.S. Naval Hosp., Jacksonville, Fla., 1973-75; physician U.S. Naval Hosp., Annapolis, Md., 1975-78, Silver Lake Family Med. Ctr., Everett, Wash., 1978-88; pvt. practice Everett, Wash., 1988—. Mem. Snohomish City Acad. Family Physicians (pres. 1984-88), Snohomish City Med. Soc. (bd. dirs. 1985-87), Rotary. Democrat. Episcopalian. Home: 2225 101st Pl St Everett WA 98208 Office: 9505 19th Ave SE Everett WA 98208

YOUNT, DAVID EUGENE, physicist, university official; b. Prescott, Ariz., June 5, 1935; s. Robert Ephram and Jeannette Francis (Judson) Y.; m. Christel Marlene Notz, Feb. 22, 1975; children—Laura Christine, Gregory Gordon, Steffen Jurgen Robert, Sonja Kate Jeannette. B.S. in Physics, Calif. Inst. Tech., 1957; M.S. in Physics, Stanford U., 1959, Ph.D. in Physics, 1963. Instr. Princeton U., 1962-63, asst. prof. physics, 1963-64, Minn. Mining and Mfg. fellow, 1963; NSF postdoctoral fellow U. Paris, Orsay, France, 1964-65; rsch. assoc. Stanford Linear Accelerator Ctr. Stanford U., 1965-69; assoc. prof. U. Hawaii, 1969-73, prof., 1973—, chmn. dept. physics and astronomy, 1979-85, acting asst. v.p. for acad. affairs, 1985-86, v.p. rsch. and grad. edn., 1986—. Mem. Am. Phys. Soc., Undersea and Hyperbaric Med. Soc., Am. Chem. Soc., U.S. Tennis Assn., Sigma Xi. Republican. Lutheran. Home: 5468 Opihi St Honolulu HI 96821 Office: U Hawaii 2505 Correa Rd Honolulu HI 96822

YOUNT, GEORGE STUART, paper company executive; b. Los Angeles, Mar. 4, 1949; s. Stanley George and Agnes (Pratt) Y.; m. Geraldine Marie Silvio, July 18, 1970; children: Trisha Marie, Christopher George. Grad. student, Harvard U., 1983-86. Mgmt. trainee Fortifiber Corp., L.A., 1969-71, asst. to v.p. ops., 1971-75, adminstrv. v.p., treas., sec., 1975-85, exec. v.p., sec., chief fin. officer, 1985—; treas., bd. dirs. Stanwall Corp., L.A.; past pres. Hollister Ranch Cattle Coop., Gaviota, Calif.; bd. dirs. Consol. Media Corp., Pasadena, Calif. Team leader L.A. United Way, 1981-86; mem. Drug Abuse Resistance Edn. Com., 1986—; bd. dirs. Big Bros. of Greater Los Angeles, 1984-87. Mem. Am. Paper Inst., Nat. Assn. Corp. Dirs., Harvard Bus. Club So. Calif. Clubs: Jonathan (Los Angeles); San Marino City (Calif.); Harvard Bus. Sch. So. Calif. Lodge: Rotary. Home: 684 Winston Ave San Marino CA 91108 Office: Fortifiber Corp 4489 Bandini Los Angeles CA 90023-4777

YRASTORZA, JAIME ALONSO, oral surgeon; b. Cebu, The Philippines, Dec. 23, 1930; came to U.S., 1950; s. Gregorio C. and Adelina R. (Alonso) Y.; m. Patricia A. Laverty, June 19, 1957; children: Teresa, David, Timothy, Laura, Anne. BA in Psychology, U. Minn., 1953; DMD, Washington U., St. Louis, 1957; MS in Surgery, Georgetown U., 1961. Diplomate Am. Bd. Oral and Maxillofacial Surgery. Staff oral surgeon VA Hosp., Wadsworth, Kans., 1961-63; chief oral and maxillofacial surgery Luth. Med. Ctr., Wheat Ridge, Colo., 1964—; clin. assoc. prof. U. Colo., Denver, 1974-78; pres. Wheat Ridge Oral Surgery, 1963—. Contbr. articles to profl. jours. NIH grantee, 1960. Fellow Am. Coll. Dentist, Am. Assn. Oral and Maxillofacial Surgeons, Internat. Assn. Oral and Maxillofacial Surgeons; mem. Am. Dental Assn., Rocky Mountain Dental Study Club. Office: Wheat Ridge Oral Surgery 4485 Wadsworth Blvd Wheat Ridge CO 80033

YU, KITSON SZEWAI, computer science educator; b. Toishan, Kwangtung, China, Apr. 4, 1950; came to U.S., 1969; s. Ho Yee and Yin Sang (Chan) Y.; m. Mabel Griseldis Wong, July 15, 1972; 1 child, Roberta Emily. BS, Troy State U., 1974, MS, 1977, BS, 1980. Cert. systems profl., data processing educator, Oreg. V.p. Troy (Ala.) Computer Ctr., 1976-81; computer instr. Tory State U., 1980-81, Linn Benton Community Coll., Albany, Oreg., 1981—; dir. real estate program Linn Benton Community Coll., 1985—; mng. broker Kitson Realty, Albany, 1975—. Vice-pres. econ. devel. Daleville C. of C., Ala., 1976. With AUS, 1972-74. Mem. Data Processing Mgmt. Assn. (dir. at large 1982—, v.p. 1984-85, pres. 1985-86), Greater Albany Rotary (treas. 1985—), Gamma Beta Phi. Home: 2621 NW Lupine Pl Corvallis OR 97330 Office: Linn Benton Community Coll 6500 SW Pacific Blvd Albany OR 97321

YU, KUO CHING CASEY, chemist, researcher; b. Kai-Fon, China, Oct. 10, 1945; came to U.S., 1970; s. Rong-Chern and Chu-Ru (Chen) Y.; m. Christine Ruey Jong Shen, Aug. 5, 1972; children: Anthony, Alexander. BS, Tamkang U., Taiwan, 1968; MS, U. Miss., 1972. Cert. Hazardous Material Mgmt. U. Calif., Irvine. Research chemist U. Miss., Oxford, 1970-72; analytical analyst U.S. Dept. Agrl., Oxford, Miss., 1972-74; mgr. lab. Intex Plastics, Gardena, Calif., 1978-79; supr. quality control McKesson Chem., Santa Fe Springs, Calif., 1980-86; Chief chemist, lab. dir. Rho Chem Corp., Ingelwood, Calif., 1986—. Teaching and research fellowship U. Miss., 1970. Mem. Am. Chem. Soc., Am. Mass Spectroscopy Soc., Alumni Assn. U. Miss. Republican. Roman Catholic. Home: 424 S Archer St Anaheim CA 92804 Office: Rho Chem Corp 425 Isis Ave Inglewood CA 90301

YUAN, SIDNEY WEI KWUN, cryogenic engineer, consultant; b. Hong Kong, July 30, 1957; came to U.S., 1975; s. Chia Chi and Tso Tak (Wong) Y.; m. Katherine K.Y. Dai, Sept. 8, 1981; children: Jacquelyn Kate, Chrystal Sidney. BSc, UCLA, 1980, MSc, 1981, PhD, 1985. Research asst. UCLA, 1980-81, research engr., 1981-85, teaching asst., 1984-85; rsch. sci. Lockheed Missiles & Space Co., Palo Alto, Calif., 1985—. Contbr. articles on low-temperature physics, storage and transfer of cryogenic fluids in space to profl. jours. Recipient Nat. Excellence Recognition award Space Found., 1985. Mem. Am. Inst. Chem. Engrs., Am. Inst. Aeronautics and Astronautics, Sigma Xi, Tau Beta Pi. Republican. Home: 3571 Brookdale Dr Santa Clara CA 95051 Office: Lockheed Missiles & Space Co 3251 Hanover St 92-40 Bldg 205 Palo Alto CA 94304

YUEN, ANDY TAK SING, electronics executive; b. Wanchai, Hong Kong, Aug. 26, 1952; came to U.S., 1984; s. Yan Chong and Chi Oi (Tse) Y.; m. Kathy Man Kwan Chan, Jan. 29, 1983; children Lambert Hann Shi, Robin Hann Lang. Cert. in Elec. Engring., Hong Kong Poly., 1975; Diploma in Bus. Mgmt., Hong Kong Bapt. Coll., 1976; Diploma in Exec. Devel., Chinese U., Hong Kong, 1981; MBA, Chui Hai Coll., Hong Kong, 1981; PhD in Bus. Mgmt., Calif. Coast U., 1987. Supervising engr. Teledyne Semiconductor Ltd., Kowloon, Hong Kong, 1976-79; ops. mgr. Microsemi (Hong Kong) Ltd., Kowloon, 1979-81, gen. mgr., 1981-84; corp. mgr. Microsemi Corp., Santa Ana, Calif., 1984-89, corp. v.p., 1989—; corp. dir. Semcon Electronics Pvt. Ltd., Bombay, 1984—. Author (books): Can Quality Circles Bring the Breakthrough to Hong Kong Industrial Management, 1982, Harnessing Japanese Quality Circles in Hong Kong, 1987. Fellow Inst. Sales and Mktg. Mgmt., Brit. Inst. Mgmt., Inst. Elec. and Electronics Inc. Engrs. Office: Microsemi Corp 2830 S Fairview St Santa Ana CA 92704

YUHNKE, PAM, sales executive; b. Enid, Okla., Jan. 21, 1951; d. Clarence and Leola (Kilian) Krittenbrink; m. Dick Yuhnke, Mar. 5, 1977; 1 child, Ryan Jeffrey. BSBA, Okla. State U., 1973, postgrad., 1974. Flight attendant Am. Airlines, L.A. and N.Y.C., 1973-84, dir. flight svc., 1977; rep. flight svc. recruitment Am. Airlines, L.A., 1975-81; sales rep. Fabricut, City of Commerce, Calif., 1986—. Chmn. Octoberfest Raffle and Auction, Yorba Linda, Calif., 1986—. Mem. Drapery Mfrs. Am. (v.p. 1987—). Democrat. Roman Catholic. Home: 17430 Olive Tree Cir Yorba Linda CA 92686 Office: Fabricut 17430 Olive Tree Cir Yolba Linda CA 92686

YUKELSON, RONALD ALAN, public relations executive, writer; b. Culver City, Calif., Aug. 30, 1956; s. Joseph N. and Faye (Grossman) Y. AA in Journalism, Los Angeles Valley Coll., 1976; BA in Journalism, San Diego State U., 1978; postgrad., U. So. Calif. Sports editor Madera (Calif.) Tribune, 1978-79; sports writer/columnist Desert Sun, Palm Springs, Calif., 1979-80; dir. sports info. Calif. State U., Northridge, 1980-85; assoc. dir. pub. relations U. So. Calif. Sch. Bus. Adminstrn., Los Angeles, 1985-86; mgr. pub. relations Centinela Hosp. Med. Ctr., Inglewood, Calif., 1987-88; dir. pub. relations and mktg. communications Meml. Med. Ctr. of Long Beach, Calif., 1988—; venue press chief/boxing Los Angeles Olympic Organizing Com., 1984. Writer in sports field. Cons. pub. relations/mktg. Santa Monica (Calif.) Family YMCA, 1985—, also recording sec. physical edn. com., 1985—; bd. dirs. Cheviot Hills Basebal League, Los Angeles, 1984-85. Recipient of numerous awards in sports writing field; named Outstanding Young Man Am., Nat. Jaycees, 1977, 78, 82, 83. Mem. Healthcare Pub. Relations Mktg. Assn., AP Sports Editors, Sigma Delta Chi. Club: Publicity Los Angeles.

YUKL, RICHARD LESTER, surgeon; b. Marshalltown, Iowa, Sept. 2, 1945; s. Lester and Vera (Svetlik) Y.; m. Joylin May Campbell, Dec. 16, 1972. BA, Andrews U., 1967; MD, Loma Linda U., 1971. Diplomate Am. Bd. Surgery. Resident in surgery Mayo Clinic, Rochester, Minn., 1974-78; practice medicine specializing in surgery Denver, 1978—; pres. Harvard Park Gen. Surgery, Denver, 1980—, The Cookie Jar, 1986; mem. adv. bd. on cancer Colo. Dept. Health, 1985. With USPHS, 1972-74. Fellow ACS. Adventist. Home: 3230 S Monroe St Denver CO 80210 Office: Harvard Park Gen Surgery 950 E Harvard St Denver CO 80210

YUREK, GEORGE, real estate associate, investor; b. Thompson #2, Pa., Apr. 9, 1934; s. Charles and Anna (Beshia) Y.; m. Betty L. Heminsky, Sept. 6, 1956; 1 child, Maria. Student, Wabash Coll., 1953-54. With sales dept. Hallcraft Homes, Inc., Phoenix, 1971-77; br. mgr. Design Master Homes, Phoenix, 1977-83; pres. Yurek Enterprises, Inc., Scottsdale, Ariz., 1983—; v.p. Butler & Yurek Securities, Inc., Mesa, Ariz., 1987—. Avocations: travel, business. Home: 9426 Calle De Valle Scottsdale AZ 85255 Office: Butler & Yurek Securities Inc 1455 S Stapley Dr Ste 28 Mesa AZ 85204

YURICICH, MATTHEW JOHN, matte artist; b. Lorain, Ohio, Jan. 19, 1923; s. Antone and Anna (Plesivac) Y.; children: Mark, LIsanne, Dirk, Dana, Tanya. BFA, Miami U., Oxford, Ohio, 1949. Asst. matte artist 20th Century Fox, L.A., 1950-54; matte artist MGM Studios, Culver City, Calif., 1954-76, EEG, Culver City, 1977-84, Boss Films, Marina Del Rey, Calif., 1984—. Recipient Acad. award, Motion Picture Acad. Arts. and Scis., 1976. Home and Office: 23133 Gainford St Woodland Hills CA 91364

YURIST, SVETLAN JOSEPH, mechanical engineer; b. Kharkov, USSR, Nov. 20, 1931; came to U.S., 1979, naturalized, 1985; s. Joseph A. and Rosalia S. (Zoilman) Y.; m. Imma Lea Erlikh, Oct. 11, 1960; 1 child, Eugene. M.S. in Mech. Engring. with honors, Poly. Inst., Odessa, USSR, 1954. Engr. designer Welding Equipment Plant, Novaya Utka, USSR, 1954-56; sr. tech. engr. Heavy Duty Automotive Crane Plant, Odessa, 1956-60, asst. chief matallugist, 1971-78; supr. research lab. Inst. Spl. Methods in Foundry Industry, Odessa, 1960-66, project engr. sci. research, 1966-71; engr. designer Teledyne Cast Product, Pomona, Calif., 1979-81; sr. mech. engr. Walt Elliot Disney Enterprises, Glendale, Calif., 1981-83; foundry liaison engr. Pacific Pumps div. Dresser Industries, Inc., Huntington Park, Calif., 1984-86; casting engr. Superior Industries Internat., Inc., Van Nuys, Calif., 1986—. Recipient award for design of automatic lines for casting electric motor parts USSR Ministry Machine Bldg. and Handtools Mfr., 1966, for equipment for permanent mold casting All Union Exhbn. of Nat. Econ. Achievements, 1966-70. Mem. Am. Foundrymen's Soc. Contbr. reports, articles to collections All Union Confs. Spl. Methods in Foundry, USSR; USSR patentee permanent mold casting. Home: 184 W Armstrong Dr Claremont CA 91711 Office: Superior Industries Internat Inc 7800 Woodley Ave Van Nuys CA 91406-1788

YUROVICH, DOUGLAS PAUL, marine officer; b. Lorain, Ohio, May 16, 1957; s. Richard Michael and Doris Katherine (Matos) Y.; m. Donna Marie Mortimer, Apr. 5, 1986; l child, Deanna Marie. BS in Math. and Edn., Ohio State U., 1979. Designated naval aviator, 1981. Forward air controller USMC, Camp LeJeune, N.C., 1980; schedules officer USMC, Cherry Point, N.C., 1982; ground safety officer USMC, Yuma, Ariz., 1982-83; asst. logistics officer USMC, Beaufort, S.C., 1983-84, pilot tng. officer, 1984-85, weapons & tactics instr., 1985, asst. ops. officer, 1985, ops. officer, 1985-86; F-18 Hornet instr. USMC, Lemoore, Calif., 1986—; low altitude tactics mgr. U.S. Navy/U.S. Marine Corps., Lemoore, 1987—; advisor F18D Night Attack Aircraft U.S. Marine Corps., Lemoore, 1986—. Editor: Low Altitude Tactics, 1987 (instr. the quarter award 1988). Charter mem. Rep. Presdl. Task Force, Washington, 1985. Mem. DAV (comdr.'s club), Ohio State Alumni Assn. (life), Commander's Club, The Army and Navy Club, Air and Space Smithsonian (charter), Smithsonian Assocs. (nat. contbg. mem.), Tailhook Assn., Wilson Assocs., Assn. Naval Aviation. Republican. Roman Catholic. Home: 66 W Deodar Ln Lemoore CA 93245

ZABACK, MARK ALLEN, banker; b. Minot, N.D., May 9, 1955; s. Robert Casper and Ardyce (Bean) S.; m. Karen Kay Smith, June 3, 1978; children: Katie, Andrew, Robert, Maggie. BSBA, U. Nebr., 1977. Mgmt. trainee 1st Nat. Bank, Lincoln, Nebr., 1973-78, corr. loan officer, 1978-82; comml. loan officer, v.p. Wyo. Nat. Bank, Casper, 1982-83; v.p., br. mgr. United Savs. Bank Wyo., Casper, 1983-86, exec. v.p., 1986, pres., chmn., chief exec. officer, 1987—. Bd. dirs., treas. Casper Day Care & Child Devel., 1984-86; mem. 1st Presbyn. Ch., deacon, 1985-86. Republican. Club: Cheyenne Country. Lodge: Rotary (Outstanding Sr. Hastings, Nebr. chpt. 1973). Home: 936 Apache Cheyenne WY 82003 Office: United Savs Bank Wyo 2121 Capital Ave Cheyenne WY 82003

ZABRISKIE, STEWART CLARK, bishop; b. White Plains, N.Y., Nov. 7, 1936; s. Cornelius and Florence I. (Caffrey) Z.; m. Sarah Kriby Miller, Sept. 14, 1963; children: Joanna Ellen, Michael Stewart. BA, Yale U., 1958; STB, Gen. Theol. Sem., N.Y.C., 1963, DD (hon.), 1986. Ordained to ministry Episcopal Ch., 1963. Asst. to rector Ch. of Incarnation, N.Y.C., 1963-65; rector St. Mary's, Scarborough, N.Y., 1966-69; asst. to rector St. John's, Pleasantville, N.Y., 1969-73; rector St. Andrew's and Christ Ch., Cloquet and Proctor, Minn., 1973-77, Ch. of the Epiphany, Plymouth, Minn., 1977-86; consecrated bishop Diocese of Nev., Reno, 1986—; trustee Ch. Div. Sch.

of Pacific, Berkeley, Calif., 1987—. Mem. adv. com. Sex Edn., Washoe County, Nev., 1987—. Office: Diocese of Nev Box 6357 Reno NV 89513-6357 *

ZACCARI, FRANK ANTHONY, JR., marketing professional; b. Dunkirk, N.Y., June 1, 1953; s. Frank A. Sr. and Carmela (Mancuso) Z.; m. Diana Andem, Aug. 2, 1985. BS in Fin., Calif. State U., Sacramento, 1979. Exec. acct. mgr. NCR, Sacramento, 1979-82; century analysts NCR, Pacheco, Calif., 1982-86; product mgr. NCR, Columbia, S.C., 1986-88; dist. sales mgr.State Govt. Calif. NCR, West Sacramento, 1988—; speaker EDP related meetings and seminars, 1983—. Served as sgt. USAF, 1973-77. Mem. NCR Sierra User Group (sec. 1985), Data Processing Mgmt. Assn. Republican. Roman Catholic. Office: NCR 1515 Harbor Blvd West Sacramento CA 95691

ZACHMAN, JOHN ARTHUR, information planning consultant; b. Toledo, Dec. 16, 1934; s. Arthur S. and Margaret M. (Morrow) Z.; m. Constance L. DeVito, May 14, 1972; children: Sherri L., Zachman Christian, John P. BA, Northwestern U., 1957. Commd. ensign USN, 1957, advanced through grades to lt. comdr., 1964, ret. 1964; food broker Stoler Brokerage Co., South Bend, Ind., 1965; mktg. rep. IBM Corp., Chgo., 1965-70; account mgr. IBM Corp., N.Y.C., 1970-74; cons. IBM Corp., L.A., 1974—; bd. councillors Sch. Library and Info. Mgmt., U. So. Calif., L.A., 1982-86; bd. advisers info. mgmt. Seattle Pacific U., 1986—; owner Cristiano's Restaurant, Santa Monica, Calif., 1986—; bd. dirs. Worship Seminars Internat. Mem. elder council First Foursquare Ch., Van Nuys, Calif., 1978—; bd. dirs. Marriage Plus Ministries, 1985—. Mem. Data Adminstrn. Mgmt. Assn. Internat. (bd. advisors), N.Y.C. Data Adminstrn. Mgmt. Assn. (named Man of the Year 1988). Home: 1635 Virden Dr Glendale CA 91208 Office: IBM Corp 355 S Grand Ave Los Angeles CA 90071

ZACK, JAMES G(ORDON), JR., construction manager, consultant; b. Springfield, Mass., Sept. 6, 1946; s. James Gordon Sr. and Marione Mildred (Langevin) Z.; m. Yvonne Eileen Beezley, Oct. 26, 1970; children: Jennifer Yvonne, Stacy Rebecca, James William. AB in Polit. Sci., Assumption Coll., 1968; MPA, U. S.C., 1975. Dir. budgets and grants adminstrn. S.C. Dept. Health and Environ. Control, Columbia, 1972-78; mgr. constrn. contracts group CH2M Hill, INc., Milw., 1978-85; mgr. scheduling and claims dept. CH2M Hill, INc., L.A., 1986—; cons. U.S. EPA, 1977-88; reviewer Engring. Mgmt. Jour., 1987—. Contbr. articles to profl. jours. Dep. dist. commr. Pacifica Dist. Boy Scouts Am., 1987—; mem. Calif. Compact Com., Huntington Beach, Calif., 1988—. Capt. U.S. Army, 1968-72, Vietnam. Mem. Am. Assn. Cost Engrs., ASCE, Project Mgmt. Inst. Methodist. Home: 9531 Netherway Dr Huntington Beach CA 92646 Office: CH2M Hill Inc 2510 Red Hill Ave Santa Ana CA 92705

ZADROZNY, STEFAN PAWEL, design engineer; b. London, Feb. 17, 1953; came to U.S., 1967; s. Zbigniew Pawel and Mefys Bronwen (Edwards) Z. BS in Math. and Stats., U. Calif., Irvine, 1988. Research and devel. methods engr. Garrett Corp., Torrance, Calif., 1973-78; process engr. Rex Precision Products, Gardena, Calif., 1978-79; product devel. engr. Precision Founders Inc., San Leandro, Calif., 1979; design engr. LeFiell Mfg., Santa Fe Springs, Calif., 1980-82; sr. design engr. Smith Tool, Irvine, Calif., 1982-85; project mgr. Aluminum Forge Co., Santa Ana, Calif., 1985-89; tech. specialist, mfg. systems engr. Douglas Aircraft Co., Long Beach, Calif., 1989—; tooling design cons. Swiss Pattern, Costa Mesa, Calif., 1986-87; tech. seminar speaker U.S. Air Force Indsl. Modernization Incentives Program, Wesley Chapel, Fla., 1987. Mem. Soc. Mfg. Engrs. (sr.), Computer and Automated Systems Assn., Am. Mgmt. Assn. Republican. Office: Douglas Aircraft Co IMC 52-90 3855 Lakewood Blvd Long Beach CA 90846

ZAFREN, KEN, physician; b. Cin., Oct. 12, 1953; s. Herbert Cecil and Miriam (Koenigsberg) Z.; m. Christina Tower, June 29, 1984. BA in Math., New Coll., Sarasota, Fla., 1975; MD, U. Wash., 1984. Diplomate Nat. Bd. Med. Examiners. Transitional intern Presbyn.-St. Luke's Med. Ctr., Denver, 1985-86; pvt. practice Anchorage, 1986—. Mem. Rocky Mountain Rescue Group, Boulder, 1976-80, Mountain Rescue Council, Seattle, 1979-83. NIH tng. grantee, 1979-83; grand prize winner 1988 MD Magazine photo contest. Mem. Am. Alpine Club, Mountaineering Club Alaska. Home: 10181 Curvi St Anchorage AK 99516

ZAGORSKI, FRANK JOHN, educator; b. Meriden, Conn., Dec. 21, 1925; s. Jacob and Elizabeth (Dobrzanski) Z.; m. Marianne Ashley Rice, aug. 11, 1951; children: Rebecca Zagorski Silver, James P., Elizabeth M. BS, U.S. Mil. Acad., 1950; M in Pub. and Internat. Affairs, U. Pitts., 1960; MA, Webster U., 1982. Commd. 2d lt. USAF, 1950, advanced through grades to col., 1971; pilot USAF, various locations, 1950-59; grad. student U. Pitts., 1959-60; tenure assoc. prof. USAF Acad., Colorado Springs, Colo., 1960-70; dep. dir. of tng. USAF Adv. Group, Saigon, 1970-71; dep. commdt. Def. Intelligence Sch., Washington, 1971-79; proram dir. Webster U., Colorado Springs, 1980—. Decorated Bronze Star, Legion of Merit, Meritorious Service medal. Mem. Data Processing Mgmt. Assn., Purchasing Mgmt. Assn., Air Force Assn., The Retired Officers' Assn., Better Bus. Bur., Colorado Springs C. of C. Republican. Roman Catholic. Home: 2540 Bricker Rd Monument CO 80132 Office: Webster U 6165 Lehman Dr Ste 103 Colorado Springs CO 80918

ZAHARIA, ERIC STAFFORD, developmental disabilities program administrator; b. Pomona, Calif., Aug. 24, 1948; s. Edgar A. and Dorothy (Stafford) Z.; m. Caryle Koentz, Dec. 23, 1967; children: Tye W., Tieg A. BA, Pomona Coll., 1970; MEd, U. Ariz.-Tucson, 1973; PhD, George Peabody Coll., 1978; postgrad., Govt. Execs. Inst. U. N.C., Chapel Hill, 1981. Mental retardation worker Ariz. Tng. Program, Tucson, 1970-71, unit dir., 1971-73; dir. residential svcs. Willmar State Hosp., (Minn.), 1973-76; rsch. asst. Inst. on Mental Retardation and Intellectual Devel., Nashville, 1976-78; dir. mental retardation program svcs. Dept. Mental Health/Mental Retardation, State of Tenn., Nashville, 1978-79; dir. Caswell Ctr., Kinston, N.C., 1979-86; program adminstr. Colo. Div. of Devel. Disabilities, Denver, 1986—; mem. adj. faculty East Carolina U., Greenville, 1979-86; bd. dirs. Neuse Enterprises Inc., Kinston. Guest reviewer: Mental Retardation, Jour. Community Psychology. Chmn. Big Bros./Sisters Kinston Inc., 1980-83; mem. N.C. Coalition for Community Svc., 1982-85. Mem. Am. Assn. Mental Retardation, Nat. Assn. Supts. Pub. Residential Facilities, Assn. Retarded Citizens, Kinston C. of C. (dir. 1983-86), Rotary. Home: 7362 S Downing Circle Littleton CO 80122 Office: 3824 W Princeton Circle Denver CO 80236

ZAHNISER, RICHARD ALLEN, software engineer; b. Pitts., Sept. 16, 1935; s. Richard Bayard and Mary M. (Kirk) Z.; m. JoAnn Jolley; children: Timothy Scott, Tricia Jolley; m. Charlotte Lenore Thorne, July 11, 1981. BA in Psychology, U. Ariz., 1964; MBA, U. Colo., 1983. Field rep. Kellogg Communications Systems div. ITT, Chgo., 1961-63; systems engr. data processing div. IBM, L.A., Denver, 1964-71; sr. systems analyst, project leader Cibar, Inc., Colorado Springs, 1972-74, 77; computer systems specialist, mgr. system support System Devel. Corp., Colorado Springs, 1974-77; exec. dir. Cibar Systems Inst., Colorado Springs, 1977-81; pres. RIX Software Engring., Colorado Springs, 1981—; founder, exec. dir. CASELab, Colorado Springs, 1989—; founder, v.p. ops. Colo. Software Solutions, Colorado Springs, 1982-84; course author, instr. Integrated Computer Systems, Culver City, Calif., 1981—; mgr. productivity project IBM Users Group, Share, 1978-80; hon. prof. U. Colo., Colorado Springs, 1979. Author, editor software sect. Engring, Computing Applications Newsletter, 1981-83; contbr. articles to profl. jours. Cubmaster, scoutmaster Boy Scouts Am., Denver and Colorado Springs, 1968-74. With U.S. Army, 1953-55. Recipient Outstanding Svc. award Colo. Country Music Assn., 1969. Mem. IEEE, Assn. Computing Machinery (chmn. Pike's Peak chpt. 1975-77), Data Processing Mgmt. Assn. (pres. local chpt. 1984-85), Am. Fedn. Musicians, Tuesday Afternoons Rest and Aspiration Club (sec. 1987—), Delta Sigma Phi. Republican. Presbyterian.

ZAIDI, IFTAKHAR HAIDER, consulting engineer; b. Allahabad, India, Dec. 1, 1933; came to U.S., 1957; s. Mujtaba Husain and Kaniz (Fatmah) Z.; m. Bilquis Iftakhar Zaidi, July 17, 1965; children: Ali I., Aliya I. BSCE, N.E.D. Univ., 1955; MSCE, U. Minn., 1959. Registered profl. and civil engr., Minn., Calif. Registered structural engr., Minn. Constrn. supr. Karachi and MacDonald Layton Ltd., 1955-56; engr. exec. Transeast Dist. U.S. Army Corps of Engrs., Karachi, Pakistan, 1956-57; with structural dept. Ellerbe and Co., St. Paul, 1959-60, Pfeifer and Schultz, Mpls., 1960-61, Kaiser Engrs., Oakland, 1962; cons. I.Z. Assocs., Karachi, Pakistan, 1963-79, Hacienda Heights, Calif., 1979—. Mem. Internat. Conf. Bldg. Officials (Los Angeles and Orange Empire chpts.), Structural Engrs. Assn. Calif. Moslem. Home and Office: 3249 Gotera Dr Hacienda Heights CA 91745

ZAIKINE, VICTOR EUGENE (ZAK ZAIKINE), sculptor; b. Queens, N.Y., Sept. 7, 1941; s. Eugene and Valentina (Rodinoff) Z. Student Pratt Inst., 1959-64, Woodstock Sch. Art, 1981-82. Owner, Vick's Kustom Auto Body Shop, Jamaica, N.Y., 1963-69; one-man shows: Work of Art Galleries, Sangerties, N.Y., 1983—, Cultural Ctr. for Arts, Kingston, N.Y., 1984, Woodstock Artist Assn. (N.Y.), 1985, J. Noblett Gallery, Sonoma, Calif., 1986, Jessica Darraby Gallery, Los Angeles, 1986, Calvin R. Vanderwoude Gallery, Palm Springs, Calif., 1988, Calif. Mus. Art, 1988, others; exhibited in group shows: Schenectady Mus. (N.Y.), 1983, Silvermine Guild Ctr. for Arts, 1983, Sculptors Galleries, N.Y.C., 1984, Kleinert Art Ctr., Woodstock, N.Y., 1984, 85, Jamie Szoke Gallery, N.Y.C., Clark Whitney Gallery, Lenox, Mass., 1984, 85, 86, 88, SUNY Art Gallery, Albany, 1985 (award of distinction), Pittsfield (Mass.) Atrs Ctr., 1988, Calif. Mus. Art, Santa Rosa, 1988, Norman S. Rice Gallery The Albany Inst. History and Art, 1987, Craft & Folk Art Mus., Laguana Art Mus.; pub. installations: Mill Valley Arts Festival, 1979, Woodstock Guild of Craftsmen, 1981, Woodstock Arts Assn., 1983; curator first mems. exhibition Woodstock Guild Kleinart Art Ctr., Renselaer County Council for the Arts, Troy, N.Y., 1985, Clark Whitney Gallery. Mem. gallery com. Sonoma Arts Council, Santa Rosa, Calif., 1976-78; organizer art exhibits Queens Council for the Arts, 1965-68. Recipient N.Y.C. Ceramic award, 1959; 1st place sculpture award Pan Am. World Airways, 1964; 1st place award Fiesta De Artes, Los Gatoes Calif., 1976, 1st place and Best of show awards La Quinta Arts Found., 1986, numerous others. Mem. Woodstock Artists Assn., Woodstock Guild Craftsmen, Cooperstown Art Assn. Home: 1589 Westside Rd PO Box 1342 Heraldsburg CA 95448

ZAISER, SALLY SOLEMMA VANN, retail book company executive; b. Birmingham, Ala., Jan. 18, 1917; d. Carl Waldo and Einnan (Herndon) Vann; student Birmingham-So. Coll., 1933-36, Akron Coll. Bus., 1937; m. Foster E. Zaiser, Nov. 11, 1939. Acct., A. Simionato, San Francisco, 1958-65; head acctg. dept. Richard T. Clarke Co., San Francisco, 1966; acct. John Howell-Books, San Francisco, 1967-72, sec., treas., 1972-83, 84-85, dir., 1982-85; sec. Great Eastern Mines, Inc., Albuquerque, 1969-81, dir., 1980-85. Braille transcriber for ARC, Kansas City, Mo. 1941-45; vol. worker ARC Hosp. Program, São Paulo, Brazil, 1952. Mem. Book Club Calif., Calif. Hist. Soc., Soc. Lit. and Arts, Gleeson Library Assocs. (dir. 1984-87, editor GLA newsletter 1984-87), Nat. Notary Assn., Capital Hill Club, Theta Upsilon. Republican. Episcopalian. Home: 355 Serrano Dr Apt 4-C San Francisco CA 94132

ZAJAC, JOHN, semiconductor equipment company executive; b. N.Y.C., July 21, 1946; s. John Andrew and Catherine (Canepa) Z.; m. Vera Barbagallo, Jan. 13, 1973; children: Jennifer, Michelle. AAS, NYU, 1966; BEE, U. Ky., 1968. Project engr. B.C.D. Computing, N.Y.C., 1968-70; v.p. Beacon Systems, Commack, N.Y., 1970-73, E.T. Systems, Santa Clara, Calif., 1973-77; v.p. research and devel. Eaton Corp., Sunnyvale, Calif., 1977-81; pres. Semitech/Gen. Signal, Los Gatos, Calif., 1981-83; mgr. advanced product div. Tegal/Motorola Inc., Novato, Calif., 1983-86; v.p. research and devel. U.S.A. Inc., San Jose, Calif., 1986—. Author: Delecate Balance, 1988; patentee in field. Office: PO Box 21237 San Jose CA 95121

ZAK, MICHELE WENDER, university administrator, consultant; b. Beckley, W.Va., Apr. 3, 1940; d. Max Harris and Freda (Lewis) Wender; m. Laurence Michael Zak, Aug. 31, 1963; children: Peter Andrew, Colin Mark. BA in English, Ohio State U., 1962, MA, 1966, PhD in English, 1973. Lectr. Dept. of English Ohio State U., 1968-71, grad. teaching assoc. Dept. of English, 1971-73; exec. dir. Women's Resource and Policy Devel. Ctr., 1974-76; dir. Office of Human Resource Utilization Kent (Ohio) State U., 1976-82; spl. asst. to the v.p. U. Calif., 1982-83, dir. faculty devel. and affirmative action, 1983—; asst. equal employment opportunity coordinator State of Ohio, 1974-75, chief Office of Women's Affairs, 1974-75; coord. Women's Studies Cert. Program, Coll. of Arts and Scis. Kent State U., 1977-82, asst. prof. Dept. of English, 1976-82; pres. Michaels Assocs. Personnel Cons., Oakland, 1979—, The Michaels Agy. Profl. Staff Assignments, 1979—; speaker in field. Author: (with Longman) Women and the Politics of Culture, 1983; contbr. articles to profl. jours. and publs. Edn. com. mem. Ohio Task Force on the Implementation of the Equal Rights Amendment, 1972-73; mem. Govs. Com. on Women in Ohio, 1973-74, Nat. Coalition for Women, 1975-77; bd. of trustees Women's Resource ad Policy Devel. Ctr., 1975—. Mem. Modern Language Assn. of Am., Nat. Women's Studies Assn., Coun. of Grad. Schs. of the U.S., Nat. Assn. Interdisciplinary Ethnic Studies, Assn. of Graduate Schs, Oakland C. of C. Office: Michaels Assocs 420 40th St Oakland CA 94609

ZAK, RAYMOND EUGENE, cleaning service company executive; b. Inglewood, Calif., Mar. 24, 1967; s. Eugene Paul and Patricia Ann (Mullaly) Z.; m. Peggy Volz, 1984; children: Shawn David, Sarah Nicole. Sales mgr. Valley Furniture, Yocca Valley, Calif., 1985-86, May Co., Palm Desert, Calif., 1986-87; pres. mgr. Sun Cleaning Svc., Palm Springs, Calif., 1986—. Mem. Carpet Cleaners Inst., Blue Skies Country Club. Republican. Roman Catholic. Home: 7848 Mariposa Dr Yocca Valley CA 92284 Office: Sun Cleaning Svc 653 Comml Rd #10 Palm Springs CA 92262

ZALESKI, JAMES VINCENT, electronics executive; b. Kenosha, Wis., Oct. 8, 1943; s. Louis Edward and Lena Louise (Bellotti) Zalewski; m. Beverly Rae Neumann, Nov. 8, 1969. BBA, U. Wis., 1966, BSME, 1966, MS, 1967. Project engr. AC Electronics div. Gen. Motors Corp., Milw., 1968-73; ops. mgr. Applied Computer Sci., Inc., Milw., 1970-72; sect. mgr. Delco Electronics div. Gen. Motors Corp., Santa Barbara, Calif., 1973-84, dept. mgr., 1984-85, chief engr., 1985-87; pres., chief exec. officer Vetronix Corp., Santa Barbara, Calif., 1984—. Contbr. articles to profl. jours.; patentee in field. Mem. Soc. Automotive Engrs., Evans Scholars Assn., Mensa. Club: South Shore Yacht (Milw.). Home: 2785 E Valley Rd Montecito CA 93108 Office: Vetronix Corp 1421 State St Santa Barbara CA 93101

ZALLE, PAUL MARTIN, financial services company executive; b. L.A., Aug. 13, 1945; s. Morris D. and Esther M. (Kahn) Z.; m. Judith Ann Willen, Mar. 31, 1968; children: Melissa Elise, Michael Brandon. BSBA, Calif. State U., Northridge, 1968; postgrad. in acctg., Calif. State U., L.A., 1969-71. Cert. internal auditor, info. systems auditor. Sr. acct. Cohen & Cohen, CPA's, L.A., 1968-72; mgr. auditing Carte Blanche Corp., L.A., 1973-77; regional audit mgr. Avco. Corp., Newport Beach, Calif., 1978-82; regional dir. auditing Textron Corp., Irvine, Calif., 1983-86; v.p. auditing Avco Fin. Svcs., Inc., Irvine, 1987--; cons. to pres. Bus. Spltys., Inc., Santa Ana, Calif., 1986--; cons. to chmn. Imperial Thrift & Loan Assn., Burbank, Calif., 1987--. Contbr. articles to profl. publs. Family advisor prosthetic program for handicapped UCLA, 1975--. Mem. Am. Fin. Svcs. Assn. (nat. audit com. 1985--), Inst. Internal Auditors (editor, advisor 1980--, hon. svc. award 1983), EDP Auditors Assn., Orange County P vt. Investment Club. Democrat. Jewish. Home: 20072 Midland Ln Huntington Beach CA 92646 Office: Avco Fin Svcs Inc 3349 Michelson Dr Irvine CA 92715

ZALLEN, DENNIS MICHAEL, combustion and environmental engineer; b. East Chicago, Ill., Dec. 6, 1943; s. Stanley George and Ann (Kloac) Z.; m. Sallie-White Harvey, May 14, 1977. BSME, Purdue U., 1965, MSME, 1967; postgrad., So. Meth. U., 1968-79; PhD, Purdue U., 1973. Registered profl. engr. Calif. Research engr. Gen. Dynamics Corp., Ft. Worth, 1967-70; asst. project engr. Pratt & Whitney Aircraft, East Hartford, Conn., 1973-75; asst. prof. N.M. State U., Las Cruces, 1975-76; group leader Inst. Mining and Minerals Research Ky. Ctr. Energy Research, Lexington, 1977-78; mgr. energy systems devel. Ultrasystems, Inc. and Energy and Environ. Research Corp., Santa Ana, Calif., 1978-80; sr. engr. analyst, mgr. N.Mex. Engring. Research Inst. U. N.Mex., Alberquerque, 1980—; cons. environ, instrumentation Dept. of Energy; tracked vehicle fire survivability Army Safety Ctr. Contbr. articles to profl. jours.; patentee low emissions burner system, automatic fire extinguisher with notification. David Ross fellow Purdue U., 1973. Mem. Combustion Inst., Air Pollution Control Assn., ASME, Am. Phys. Soc., AIAA, Sigma Pi Sigma, Pi Tau Sigma. Home: 14216 Turner Ct NE Albuquerque NM 87123 Office: NMex Engring Rsch Inst PO Box 25 Albuquerque NM 87131

ZALTA, EDWARD, otorhinolaryngologist; b. Houston, Mar. 2, 1930; s. Nouri Louis and Marie Zahde (Lizmi) Z.; m. Carolyn Mary Gordon, Oct. 8, 1971; 1 child, Ryan David; children by previous marriage: Nouri Allan, Lori Ann, Barry Thomas, Marci Louise. BS, Tulane U., 1952, MD, 1956. Diplomate Am. Bd. Quality Assurance and Utilization Rev. Physicians. Intern Brooke Army Hosp., San Antonio, 1956-57; resident in otolaryngology U.S. Army Hosp., Ft. Campbell, Ky., 1957-60; practice medicine specializing in otolaryngology Glendora, West Covina and San Dimas, Calif., 1960-82; ENT cons. City of Hope Med. Ctr., 1961-76; mem. staff Foothill Presbyn.; past pres. Los Angeles Found. Community Service, Los Angeles Poison Info. Ctr., So. Calif. Physicians Council, Inc.; founder pres., chmn. bd. CAPP CARE, INC.; chmn. bd. MDM; founder Inter-Hosp. Council Continuing Med. Edn. Author: (with others) Medicine and Your Money; contbr. articles to profl. jours. Pres. bd. govs. Glendora Unified Sch. Dist., 1965-71; mem. Calif. Cancer Adv. Council, 1967-71, Commn. of Californias, Los Angeles County Commn. on Economy and Efficiency. Served to capt. M.C. AUS, 1957-60. Recipient Award of Merit Order St. Lazarus, 1981. Mem. AMA, Calif. Med. Assn., Los Angeles County Med. Assn. (past pres.), Am. Acad. Otolaryngology, Am. Council Otolaryngology, Am. Assn. Preferred Provider Orgns. (past pres.), Am. Coll. Utilization Rev. Physicians, Kappa Nu, Phi Delta Epsilon. Republican. Jewish. Clubs: Glendora Country, Centurion, Sea Bluff Beach and Racquet; Center (Costa Mesa, Calif.); Pacific Golf (San Juan Capistrano, Calif.). Home: Three Morning Dove Dr Laguna Niguel CA 92677 Office: 17390 Brookhurst Ave Fountain Valley CA 92708

ZALUTSKY, MORTON HERMAN, lawyer; b. Schenectady, Mar. 8, 1935; s. Albert and Gertrude (Daffner) Z.; m. Audrey Englebardt, June 16, 1957; children—Jane, Diane, Samuel. B.A., Yale U., 1957; J.D., U. Chgo., 1960. Bar: Oreg. 1961. Law clk. Oreg. Supreme Ct., 1960-61; assoc. Hart, Davidson, Veazie & Hanlon, 1961-63, Veatch & Lovett, 1963-64, Morrison, Bailey, Dunn, Cohen & Miller, 1964-69; prin. Morton H. Zalutsky, P.C., 1970-76; ptnr. Dahl, Zalutsky, Nichols & Hinson, 1977-79, Zalutsky & Klarquist, P.C., Portland, Oreg., 1980-85, Zalutsky, Klarquist & Johnson, P.C., Portland, 1985—; instr. Portland State U., 1961-64, Northwestern Sch. Law, 1969-70; assoc. prof. U. Miami Law Sch.; lectr. Practicing Law Inst., 1971—, Oreg. State Bar Continuing Legal Edn. Program, 1970, Am. Law Inst.-ABA Continuing Legal Edn. Program, 1973—, 34th, 37th NYU ann. insts. fed. taxation, So. Fed. Tax Inst., U. Miami Inst. Estate Planning, Southwestern Legal Found., Internat. Found. Employee Benefit Plans, numerous other profl. orgns. Author: (with others) The Professional Corporation in Oregon, 1970, 82; contbg. author: The Dentist and the Law, 3d edit.; contbr. to numerous publs. in field. Mem. vis. com. U. Chgo. Law Sch., 1985-88. Mem. ABA (vice chairperson profl. services 1987—, mem. council tax sect. 1985-87, spl. coordinator 1980-85, vice chmn. profl. services 1987—), Am. Bar Retirement Assn. (bd. dirs.), Multnomah County Bar Assn., Oreg. State Bar Assn., Oreg. Estate Planning Council. Jewish. Home: 3118 SW Fairmount Blvd Portland OR 97201 Office: 215 SW Washington St 3d Fl Portland OR 97204

ZAMBETTI, DENIS EGAN, sales executive; b. Riverdale, N.Y., Oct. 18, 1953; s. Emil John and Teresa Veronica (McSherry) Z. BS, U.S. Mil. Acad., 1977; MBA, Golden Gate U., 1985. Commd. 2d lt. U.S. Army, 1977, advanced through ranks to capt., 1977-81, resigned, 1985; platoon leader B Co. 2d/22d Inf., Wiesbaden, Fed. Republic Germany, 1977-78, mortar platoon leader, 1978-79, exec. officer, 1979-80; communications and electronics officer HHC Co. 2d/22d Inf., Wiesbaden, 1980-81; morale support fund custodian U.S. Mil. Command Activity Group, Bad Kreuznach, Fed. Republic Germany, 1981-82; equal opportunity staff officer HQ Presidio of San Francisco, 1982-83, chief reserve pay, 1983-85; peninsula area mgr. Beringer Wines/Wineworld, San Francisco, 1985-87; nat. accts. mgr. SW region Beringer Wines/Wineworld, Mission Viejo, Calif., 1987—; field sales rep. Anthem Electronics, San Jose, Calif., 1988—. Named One of Outstanding Young Men of Am. Jaycees, 1983. Mem. Knights of the Vine. Democrat. Roman Catholic. Clubs: West Point Soc. of Bay Area (bd. govs. 1982-85), West Point Soc. Orange County (admissions rep. 1987—). Home: 6530H Cotton Wood Circle Dublin CA 94568

ZANDER, CARL MATHEW, controller; b. Sacramento, Aug. 24, 1940; s. Carl Edward and Lorraine (Brown) Z.; m. Rosalie E. Zander (div. 1978); children: Stephen, Theresa. BA in Adminstrn./Acctg., Fresno (Calif.) State Coll., 1962. Office mgr. Rainbo Bakery, Sacramento, Fresno and Visalia, Calif., 1960-68; mgr. data processing Sperry New Holland, Fresno, 1968-78; owner, operator Western Flame Restaurant, Fresno, 1978-80; office mgr. Waco Heating & Air Conditioning, Albuquerque, 1980-85; controller Slade Enterprises, Albuquerque, 1986-87, Bueno Foods, Albuquerque, 1987—. Mem. city council City of Rio Rancho, N.Mex., 1986—, mayor pro tem, 1988; bd. dirs. Urban Transp. Policy & Planning Bd., Albuquerque, 1988—. Republican. Home: 283 Vancouver Rd Rio Rancho NM 87124 Office: Bueno Foods 2001 4th St SW Albuquerque NM 87103

ZANE, GLENN ALAN, forester, consultant; b. Modesto, Calif., Sept. 21, 1939; s. Alan Mortimer Zane and Lois Olive (Leach) Leydecker; m. Cora Charlotte Sanders; children: Elaina C., Eric A., Tobe G., Nancy M., Diana R., Betsey E. BS, Humboldt State U., 1965. Profl. forester, Calif. Forester Hollow Tree Lumber Co., Ukiah, Calif., 1965-66; resources mgr. Walker Forest/Paul Bunyan Lumber Co., Anderson, Calif., 1966-74; cons. forester Mason, Bruce and Girard Inc., Portland, Oreg., 1974—. Rep. precinct organizer, Redding, Calif., 1978—. Mem. Soc. Am. Foresters (chpt. chair 1970—). Nazarene. Office: Mason Bruce and Girard PO Box 218 Redding CA 96099

ZANETTI, JOSEPH MAURICE, JR., corporate executive; b. San Francisco, Aug. 3, 1928; s. Joseph Maurice and Lillian Mary (Solari) Z.; m. Marilyn Ruth Parker, Aug. 11, 1956; children: Pamela, Gregory, Geoffrey, Regina. BA, Saint Mary's Coll., 1950; postgrad., U. Calif., Berkeley, 1950-51, 53-55, 56-57; postgrad. in Edn., San Francisco State Coll., 1955-56. Cert. elem. tchr., Calif. Tchr. Piedmont (Calif.) High Sch., 1956-57, Pleasant Hill (Calif.) High Sch., 1957-58; supr. Sandia Labs., Albuquerque, 1958-64; mktg. dir. Ednl. Research Assocs., Albuquerque, 1964-66; exec. asst. Sandia Labs., Albuquerque, 1966-73; pres. U. of Albuquerque, Albuquerque, 1973-75; dir. area devel. Pub. Svc. Co. of N.Mex., Albuquerque, 1975-86; pres., chmn. bd. dirs. Rio Grande Trading Co. Inc., Albuquerque, 1986-88; pres. Foresight, Inc., Albuquerque, 1988—; cons. Pub. Service Co. N.Mex., Albuquerque, 1986—; bd. dirs. N.Mex. Industry Devel. Corp., Albuquerque, 1980—; pres. N.Mex. Internat. Trade and Investment Council Inc., Albuquerque, 1984—; chmn. Adv. Bd. Coll. and U. Partnership Program, Memphis, 1984—. bd. dirs. N.Nex. Hispanic Cultural Found., Albuquerque, 1985—; vice chmn., bd. govs. Albuquerque Tech. Vocat. Inst., 1971-77. Capt. USNR, 1948-83. Mem. Res. Officers Assn. (life), Naval Intelligence Profls., Navy League of U.S., Resource Devel. Com., Albuquerque Pub. Schs. (chmn.). Republican. Roman Catholic. Home: 1722 Dietz Loop NW Albuquerque NM 87107 Office: Foresight Inc 4255 Baloon Park Rd NE Albuquerque NM 87107

ZANIN, MARGARET ELIZABETH, nonprofit foundation executive; b. Plainfield, N.J., Mar. 16, 1933; d. Edward Henderson and Margaret Catherine (Ryan) Turner; m. John C. Malinowski, Oct. 17, 1953 (div. 1982); children: Diane, John, David; m. Stelvio J. Zanin, Jan. 1982 (dec.); stepchildren: Blair, Ian. AA, N.Y. State Regents External, 1976; BS in Psychology, L.I. U., 1978, MPS, 1981. With Sagamore Children's Ctr., Melville, N.Y., 1976-81; psychologist Dutchess Community Svc., Milbrook, N.Y., 1981-83; exec. dir. Dr. Rosa Minoka Hill Fund, Boulder, Colo., 1984-89; dir. profl. devel. and membership Am. Indian Sci. and Engring. Soc., Boulder, 1984-89. Vol. adv. network Regents External Deg. Prog., Albany, 1978—. Recipient Cert. of Appreciation LaLeche League of N.Y. State, 1980, Cert. of Recognition for outstanding contbn. Alumni Assn. of Haskell Indian Jr. Coll., 1984, Outstanding Svc. award Am. Indian Sci. and Engring. Soc., 1987. Mem. NAFE, Mensa. Home: 2423 N 119th St Lafayette CO 80026

ZANOTTI, GINA, association administrator; b. Charles City, Iowa, Sept. 21, 1953; d. Artage and Mary Ann (Kautman) Z. Student, Iowa State U., 1971-73; BS in Journalism, U. Iowa, Iowa City, 1979; student, San Diego State U., 1977-78. Editor Emergency Product News, Carlsbad, Calif., 1976-

78; mgr., recruiter Mgmt. Recruiters, San Diego, 1978-80; recruiter Dunhill Agy., San Diego, 1980-83; congresl. aide Congressman Bill Lowery, San Diego, 1983-86; owner Schuman & Zanotti, San Diego, 1986-88; v.p., dir. San Diego C. of C., 1988—; chmn. Golden Triangle Mktg. Consortium, San Diego, 1988—; treas. North City TMA Bd. Officer bd. Girl Scouts Am., San Diego chpt., 1983-88, Alzheimer's Disease Soc., 1983-88; chmn. Multiple Sclerosis Soc., 1988—, bd. dirs. 1983—. Recipient Outstanding Young Citizen award Jr. C. of C., San DIego, 1985-86; named one of Outstanding Young Women in Am., 1986, 88. Mem. Rotary (bd. dirs. 1987—). Republican. Methodist. Office: San Diego C of C 4275 Executive Sq #920 La Jolla CA 92037

ZAPATA, RICHARD ARTHUR, aerospace engineer; b. San Antonio, Dec. 11, 1959; s. Fernando Arturo and Irma Esther (Fernandez) Z. BS in Aerospace Engring., Tex. A&M, 1981, MS in Aerospace Engring., 1982; postgrad., Pepperdine U. Registered profl. engr., Tex. Structures engr. LTV Aerospace Co., Dallas, 1983-85; sr. liaison engr. B-2 div. Northrop Corp., Pico Rivera, Calif., 1986—. Mem. AIAA, Tex. Soc. Registered Profl. Engrs., Toastmasters (exec. v.p. Irving, Tex. chpt. 1984-85). Office: Northrop Corp B-2 Div 8900 E Washington Blvd Pico Rivera CA 90660 also: PO Box 6686 Pico Rivera CA 90661

ZAPEL, EDWIN JOSEPH, aerospace engineer; b. Chgo., May 31, 1923; s. Edwin John and Katherine Helen (Friss) Z.; m. Betty Jean Adams, Mar. 7, 1947; children: Kathleen, Edwin, David, John. BS, Gonzaga U., 1952, MS, 1952; MS, U. Wash., 1962. Registered profl. engr., Wash. Engring. aide U.S. Bur. Reclamation, Ephrata, Wash., 1947, GE, Richland, Wash., 1948; instrumentman U.S. Dept. Pub. Rds., Fairbanks, Alaska, 1949; sales engr. Layrite Concrete Products, Spokane, Wash., 1951; engr. Lockheed Aircraft Corp., Burbank, Calif., 1952-54; program specialist Boeing Co., Seattle, 1954—. Patentee in field. Webelos leader Boy Scouts Am., Maple Valley, Wash., 1972-78; chmn. bd. dirs. Maple Valley Christian Sch., 1972-78; mem. Tahoma Raven Heights Planning Com., Maple Valley, 1978-80; mem. Greater Maple Valley Community Coun., 1977-80. Staff sgt. USAF, 1943-46, ETO. Republican. Lutheran. Home: PO Box 82 Hobart WA 98025

ZAPOR, JOHN RANDOLPH, trade association executive; b. Latrobe, Pa., June 26, 1944; s. John Stanley and Esther Mae (Ragan) Z.; m. Rose Mary Barnes, July 11, 1980; children: Miranda Rhea, Jessica Pauline. BA, Elizabethtown Coll., 1981. Claims examiner I Pa. Dept. Labor and Industry, Indiana, 1970-81; mgr. Wewoka (Okla.) C. of C., 1981-84; exec. v.p. Northland C. of C., Kansas City, Mo., 1984-86; mng. dir. Mountain States Hardware and Implement Assn., Lakewood, Colo., 1986--. Contbr. articles to trade publs., book revs. to newspapers; playwright, plays produced in Fed. Republic of Germany, New Eng. Served with U.S. Army, 1963-67. Recipient Citations, Pa. Senate and Ho. of Reps., 1979. Mem. Am. Soc. Assn. Execs., Colo. Soc. Assn. Execs. Republican. Home: 6630 W 30th St Wheatridge CO 80214 Office: Mountain States Hardware and Implement Assn 1380 Carr St Lakewood CO 80214

ZAPPIA, CHARLES ANTHONY, history educator; b. DuBois, Pa., Feb. 26, 1947; s. Joseph Carl and Orpha Hortense (Mancuso) Z.; m. Mary Jane Sara Regan, Aug. 15, 198l; l child, Angela. BA, U. Pitts., 1969; postgrad., U. Oreg., 1970-72, San Jose State U., 1974; MA, U. Calif., Berkeley, 1982. Community coll. teaching credential, Calif. Instr. West Valley Coll., Saratoga, Calif., 1976-78, Canada Coll., Redwood City, Calif., 1976-8l, City Coll. San Francisco, 1980-85, Chabot Coll., Hayward, Calif., 1981-85, Coll. of San Mateo (Calif.), 1984-86; assoc. prof. history San Diego Mesa Coll., l986—; acting instr. U. Calif., Berkeley, 198l-86; lectr. San Francisco State U., 1983-86, San Diego State U., 1986—; reviewer, cons. Houghton Mifflin Pub. Co., Boston, 1987, Prentice-Hall Pub. Co., Englewood Cliffs, N.J., 1988. Mem. Com. for Better Colls., San Diego, 1986—. McCormack fellow, 198l. Mem. Am. Hist. Assn. (conf. presenter 1986), Orgn. Am. Historians, Am. Italian Hist. Assn., Immigration History Soc., S.W. Labor Studies Assn., Am. Fedn. Tchrs. (negotiator San Diego Community Coll. Guild, 1987—, editor Excellence newsletter 1988—). Democrat. Roman Catholic. Home: 4804 34th St San Diego CA 92116 Office: Mesa Coll History Dept 7250 Mesa College Dr San Diego CA 92111

ZARE, RICHARD NEIL, chemistry educator; b. Cleve., Nov. 19, 1939; s. Milton and Dorothy (Amdur) Z.; m. Susan Leigh Shively, Apr. 20, 1963; children—Bethany Jean, Bonnie Sue, Rachel Amdur. B.A., Harvard, 1961; postgrad., U. Calif. at Berkeley, 1961-63; Ph.D. (NSF predoctoral fellow), Harvard, 1964. Postdoctoral fellow Harvard, 1964; postdoctoral research asso. Joint Inst. for Lab. Astrophysics, 1964-65; asst. prof. chemistry Mass. Inst. Tech., 1965-66; asst. prof. dept. physics and astrophysics U. Colo., 1966-68, assoc. prof. physics and astrophysics, asso. prof. chemistry, 1968-69; prof. chemistry Columbia, 1969-77, Higgins prof. natural sci., 1975-77; prof. Stanford U., 1977—, Shell Disting. prof. chemistry, 1980-85, Marguerite Blake Wilbur prof. chemistry, 1987—; cons. Aeronomy Lab., NOAA, 1966-77, radio standards physics div. Nat. Bur. Standards, 1968-77, Lawrence Livermore Lab., U. Calif., 1974—, Stanford Research Inst., 1974—, Los Alamos Sci. Lab., U. Calif., 1975—; fellow adjoint, Joint Inst. Lab. Astrophysics, U. Colo.; mem. IBM Sci. Advisory Com., 1977—; researcher and author publs. on laser chemistry and chem. physics. editor Chem. Physics Letters, 1982-85. Recipient Fresenius award Phi Lambda Upsilon, 1974; Michael Polanyi medal, 1979; Nat. Medal Sci., 1985 award Spectroscopy Soc. Pitts., 1983, Michelson-Morley award, Case Inst. Tech./ Case Western Res. U., 1986; nonresident fellow Joint Inst. for Lab. Astrophysics, 1970—; Alfred P. Sloan fellow, 1967-69; Christensen fellow St. Catherine's Coll., Oxford U., 1982; Stanford U. fellow, 1984-86. Fellow AAAS; mem. Nat. Acad. Sci., Am. Acad. Arts and Scis., Am. Phys. Soc. (Earle K. Plyler prize 1981, Irving Langmuir prize 1985), Am. Chem. Soc. (Harrison Howe award Rochester sect. 1985, Remsen award Md. sect. 1985, Kirkwood award, Yale U., New Haven sect. 1986), Chem. Soc. London, Phi Beta Kappa. Office: Stanford U Dept Chemistry Stanford CA 94305

ZARUTSKIE, PAUL WALTER, reproductive endocrinologist, obstetrician/ gynecologist; b. Darby, Pa., May 4, 1951; s. Michael Andrew and Nita (Tatusko) Z. BS, Duke U., 1972; MD, Hahnemann Med. Coll., 1976. Diplomate Am. Bd. Obstetrics and Gynecology, Reproductive Endocrinology. Resident Duke U. Med. Ctr., Durham, N.C., 1976-79, chief resident, 1979-80; clin. fellow reproductive endocrinology Brigham and Women's Hosp., Boston, 1980-82; instr. ob-gyn Harvard U., Boston, 1980; asst. prof. U. Pitts., 1982-84; asst. prof. U. Wash., Seattle, 1984-89, assoc. prof., 1989—, clin. dir. in vitro fertilization program, 1984-88; co-dir. Andrology Lab., 1987—; dir. Spl. Fertility Programs, 1988—. Contbr. articles to profl. jours. Med. adv., bd. trustees Resolve Puget Sound. Fellow Am. Coll. Ob-gyn; mem. Am. Fertility Soc., Am. Andrology Soc., Bayard Carter Soc., Alpha Omega Alpha, Sigma Xi. Office: U Wash Dept Ob-Gyn RH-20 1959 NE Pacific St Seattle WA 98195

ZASTROW, JOHN THURMAN, judge; b. Wausau, Wis., Dec. 2, 1937; s. Raymond Henry and Helen Octavie (Sanche) Z.; m. Christel Schulz, Nov. 21, 1964; 1 child, Stephen Alexander. AB in Polit. Sci., UCLA, 1961, M of Pub. Adminstrn., 1964; JD, Ariz. State U., 1971. Bar: Ariz. 1971, U.S. Dist. Ct. Ariz. 1971, U.S. Ct. Appeals (9th cir.) 1972, U.S. Supreme Ct., 1975. Asst. dir. League of Ariz. Cities and Towns, Phoenix, 1964-68; assoc. Perry and Head, Phoenix, 1971-73; asst. city atty. City of Scottsdale, Ariz., 1973-76; judge City of Phoenix, 1976-83; judge pro tem Superior Ct. Maricopa County, Phoenix, 1982; immigration judge U.S. Dept. Justice, Phoenix, 1983—; faculty assoc. Ariz. State U., Tempe, 1965; faculty advisor Nat. Jud. Coll., Reno, 1980; pres. Ariz. City Atty.'s Assn., Phoenix, 1974-75. Contbr. numerous articles to profl. jours. Dem. candidate for Ariz. Ho. Reps., 1970. Served to 1st lt. U.S. Army, 1961-67. Recipient Award for Service, Valley Big Bros., 1970. Mem. ABA, Ariz. Bar Assn. (ct. improvement com.), Maricopa County Bar Assn., Ariz. State U. Law Alumni Assn. (Merit award 1981), Am. Legion, SAR (mem. nat. soc.). Episcopalian. Office: US Dept Justice EOIR Office Immigration Judge 230 N 1st Ave PO Box 0090 Room 3114 Phoenix AZ 85025

ZATZKIS, MARK ASHER, cardiologist; b. Newark, Jan. 9, 1954; s. Henry and Natalie (Serlin) Z.; m. Melissa Harris, Aug. 25, 1984; 1 child, Elliot David. AB, Harvard U., 1975; MD, Columbia U., 1979. Dimplomate Am. Bd. Internal Medicine, 1982, Am. Bd. Cardiology, 1985. Fellow in cardiology U. Calif., San Francisco, 1983-85; sr. fellow in angioplasty San Francisco Heart Inst., 1985-86; clin. faculty memb. cardiology UCLA Hosp., 1986—; cons. in coronary angioplasty, Calif. Fellow Am. Coll. Cardiology; mem. Am. Heart Assn., Alpha Omega Alpha. Office: 2001 Santa Monica Blvd Ste 1250 W Santa Monica CA 90404

ZAUPER, ROBERT, military officer; b. Wilkinsburg, Pa., May 21, 1955; s. Alfred Robert and Eileen Marguerite (Ringbloom) Z. BS in Math., Pa. State U., 1978, BS in Physics, 1978. Commd. ensign USN, 1979, advanced through grades to lt. comdr., 1988; div. officer USS Bremerton, Groton, Conn., 1980-82, USS La Jolla, San Diego, 1982-84; dir. engring. dept. Naval Submarine Tng. Ctr. Pacific, Pearl Harbor, Hawaii, 1984—; instr. chemistry and radiological controls Naval Submarine Tng. Ctr. Pacific, Pearl Harbor, 1986—. Mem. Phi Beta Kappa, Phi Kappa Phi, Pi Mu Epsilon. Home: 3775 Third Ave Apt #1 Dan Diego CA 92103-4141

ZAVADA, LINDA, cardiovascular technologist; b. Kileen, Tex., Oct. 8, 1956; d. Leonard Miller and Monique (Perrault) Benarrosh; m. Stephen Joseph Zavada III, July 4, 1984. BA, San Diego State U., 1979; Cert., Grossmont Coll., 1986. Vascular technologist intern AMI Diagnostics Inc., San Diego, 1986-87; vascular technologist Health Assessment Systems, Tustin, Calif., 1987-88; peripheral vascular technologist East Co. Cardiovascular Med., San Diego, 1987-88, Kaiser Permenante Med. Group, San Diego, 1988—; instr. Grossmont Coll., El Cajon, Calif., 1987—. Mem. Soc. Non-invasive Vascular Technologists, Soc. Diganostic Med. Sonographers. Democrat. Jewish. Home: 8844 Gardena Way Lakeside CA 92040

ZAVALA, ALBERT, research psychologist; b. Chgo., Mar. 10, 1930; s. Edward and Maria Soledad (Herrejon) Z.; div.; children—Camille, Sally, Elena, Jenifer, Alexis. B.A., Willamette U., Salem, Oreg., 1959; M.A. Mich. State U., 1961; Ph.D., Kans. State U., 1966. Prof., head life scis. Calspan, Buffalo, 1967-73; prof. SUNY Coll. at Buffalo, 1968-78; exec. dir. Corp. IV, Cheektowaga, N.Y., 1973-77; dir. projects Inpsych, Cupertino, Calif., 1978-80; sr. research psychologist SRI Internat., Menlo Park, Calif., 1980-85; staff human factors engr., Lockheed Missiles and Space Co., Sunnyvale, Calif., 1985—. Mem. Erie County (N.Y.) sheriff's sci. staff, 1972-78. Served with U.S. Army, 1955-57. Dunlap fellow, 1964; Greater Kans. City Mental Health Found. fellow, 1962-63. Mem. Am. Psychol. Assn., Human Factors Soc., Sigma Xi, Psi Chi, Phi Kappa Phi. Author: (with J.J. Paley) Personal Appearance Identification, 1972. Contbr. numerous articles to profl. jours. Office: 1111 Lockheed Way Sunnyvale CA 94089-3504

ZAX, STANLEY R., insurance company executive. Pres., chmn. bd. Zenith Nat. Ins. Corp., Woodland Hills, Calif. Office: Zenith Nat Ins Corp 21255 Califa St Woodland Hills CA 91367 *

ZDARSKY, IVO JOSEF, manufacturing executive; b. Hradec Kralove, Czechoslovakia; came to U.S., 1984; s. Josef Zdarsky and Zdenka (Jiraskova) Zdarska. Student, Czechoslovak Tech U., Prague, Czechoslovakia, 1979-84. Pres. Ivoprop Corp., Long Beach, Calif., 1986—. Home and Office: Ivoprop Corp 8724 Artesia Blvd Bell Flower CA 90706

ZEBROSKI, EDWIN LEOPOLD, nuclear engineer; b. Chgo., Apr. 1, 1921; s. Peter Paul and Sophie (Rydz) Z.; m. Gisela Karin Rudolph, Sept. 6, 1969; children: Lars, Zoe, Susan, Peggy. BS, U. Chgo., 1941; PhD, U. Calif., Berkeley, 1947. Registered prof. engr., Calif. Project engr. Gen. Electric Co., Schenectady, N.Y., 1947-53; mgr. devel. engring. Gen. Electric Co., San Jose, Calif., 1958-73; mgr. engring. SRI Internat., Menlo Park, Calif., 1954-58, dir. systems and materials dept., 1974-79; dir. nuclear safety analysis ctr. EPRI, Palo Alto, Calif., 1979-81; chief nuclear scientist EPRI, 1983-87; v.p. engring. INPO, Atlanta, 1981-83; prin. engr. APTECH Engring. Svcs., Sunnyvale, Calif., 1988—; vis. prof. Purdue U., West Lafayette, Ind., 1977-78; cons. OTA, Washington, 1980, 82-83, Dept. Energy, Washington, 1985—, Dept. Interior, Washington, 1987—; mem. commn. engring. edn. NRC, Washington, 1970-73. Contbr. chpts. to books, numerous articles to profl. jours.; patentee in field. Pres. bd. Unitarian Ch., Palo Alto, 1965-68. Recipient Charles A. Coffin award Gen. Electric Co., Schenectady, 1954. Fellow AAAS, Am. Nuclear Soc. (bd. exec. com. 1970), Am. Inst. Chemists; mem. Am. Phys. Soc., Nat. Acad. Engring. (chmn. peer com. 1984-86, chmn. mem. com. 1986-87), Soc. for Risk Analysis. Office: APTECH Engring Svcs 1257 Elko Dr Sunnyvale CA 94089

ZEHNER, RICHARD NORMAN, diagnostic imaging company executive; b. Pottsville, Pa., Feb. 26, 1953; s. Norman Benjamin and Ada Mildred (Bennsinger) Z.; m. Barbara Louise Haddad, Feb. 23, 1974; children: Matthew, Michelle. AS in Radiol. Tech., Long Beach City Coll., 1974; BS in Health Adminstrn., U. Phoenix, 1981. Cert. radiol. tech., Calif. Mgr. dept. radiology Doctor's Hosp., Lakewood, Calif., 1974-79; dir. Curacare div. Nat. Med. Enterprises, L.A., 1980-84; pres., chief operating officer Alliance Imaging, Inc., La Palma, Calif., 1983-88, chmn., chief exec. officer, 1988—; bd. dirs. G&H Leasing Corp., Long Beach; tech. advisor Long Beach Community Coll., 1989. Mem. Am. Hosp. Radiology Adminstrs., Am. Imaging Assn. Republican. Home: 9881 Orchard Ln Villa Park CA 92667 Office: Alliance Imaging Inc 1 Center Pointe Dr Ste 310 La Palma CA 90623

ZEHR, NORMAN ROBERT, association administrator; b. Niagara Falls, N.Y., May 19, 1930; s. George Andrew and Ina Kate (Morrell) Z.; Engr. of Mines, Colo. Sch. Mines, 1952, M.S., 1956; m. Janet Hutchinson, Apr. 24, 1976; children—Jeannette Ann, Leslie. Sales trainee Ingersoll-Rand Co., N.Y.C., 1955-56, sales engr., Lima, Peru, 1956-64, regional mgr. mining and constrn. sales, Lima, Peru and N.Y.C., 1964-68, gen. sales mgr. Latin Am., N.Y.C., 1968-69, gen. mgr. Latin Am. ops., N.Y.C., 1969-71, v.p. Ingersoll Rand Internat., Woodcliff Lake, N.J., 1971-72, pres., 1972-83, , v.p. Ingersoll-Rand Co., 1975-83; exec. dir. Colo. Sch. Mines Alumni Assn., 1984—. Served with AUS, 1952-54. Recipient Colo. Sch. Mines Disting. Achievement medal, 1977. Mem. AIME, Scabbard and Blade, Nat. Soc. Pershing Rifles, Mining and Metall. Soc. Am., Sigma Nu. Club: Mining. Office: Colo Sch Mines Twin Towers Golden CO 80401

ZEHREN, JOHN VERNON, architect; b. Moorhead, Minn., July 22, 1944; s. Vernon F. and Bernice V. (Erickson) Z.; children: Heather, Kristen, Stephanie. BS in Engring., U.S. Mil. Acad., 1966; MArch, U. Minn., 1973. Architect Hall & Goodhue Design Group, San Francisco, 1973-75; architect, planner The Design Team HBE Corp., Eagle, Colo., 1975-78; dir. architecture and planning Vail Assocs., Inc., Vail, Colo., 1978-81; pres. Zehren and Assocs., Inc., Vail, Scottsdale, Ariz., 1982--. Author: (with others) Personal Rapid Transit, 1973. Chmn. Beaver Creek (Colo.) Design Review Bd., 1979--; active Telluride (Colo.) Mountain Village Design Review Bd., 1986, Phoenix City Club, 1987--. Capt. U.S. Army, 1966-70, Vietnam. Decorated Bronze Star; Ford Found. fellow U. Minn., 1970-73. Mem. AIA, NCARB, Scottsdale C. of C., Peruvian Horse Club (pres. Colo. chpt. 1979-83, v.p. Ariz. chpt. 1987--). Office: Zehren and Assocs Inc 7373 N Scottsdale Rd Ste 200D Scottsdale AZ 85253

ZEIG, JEFFREY KENNETH, psychologist; b. N.Y.C., Nov. 6, 1947; s. Martin Joel and Ruth (Epstein) Z.; divorced; 1 child, Nicole Rachel. BS in Zoology, Mich. State U., 1969; MS in Clin. Psychology, San Francisco State U., 1973; PhD, Ga. State U., 1977. Cert. psychologist, Ariz.; lic. marriage, family and child counselor, Calif. Psychologist Ariz. State Hosp., Phoenix, 1978-79; dir. Milton H. Erickson Found., Phoenix, 1979—; lectr. in field. Author: Experiencing Erickson, 1985; editor: The Evolution of Psychotherapy, 19 87, Developing Ericksonian Psychotherapy, 1988, also 8 books and monographs translated into 6 langs. Recipient Milton H. Erickson award Netherlands Soc. Clin. Hypnosis, 1980. Fellow Am. Soc. Clin. Hypnosis (Milton H. Erickson award 1981); mem. Am. Psychol. Assn. Office: Milton H Erickson Found 3606 N 24th St Phoenix AZ 85016

ZEIGER, STEPHEN ALLEN, management consultant; b. Joliet, Ill., Mar. 29, 1951; s. Jack and Doris (Barkin) Z.; m. Robin Sellin, Oct. 21, 1978; children: Alexis Barkin, Joshua Edward. BS in Psychology, Loyola U., Chgo., 1972; MS in Edn., No. Ill. U., 1973. Mgr. counseling Jewish Vocat. Service, Los Angeles, 1972-75; mgr. contract placement Mainstream Engring., Inc., Encino, Calif., 1975-76; dir., exec. recruitment Purcell Employment Service, Inc., Los Angeles, 1976-79, Creative Employment Agy., Inc., Tarzana, Calif., 1979-80; pres., chief exec. officer Zeiger Tech. Careers, Inc., Tarzana, 1980—; mem., cons. Fordice Letters, St. Louis, 1982—. Contbr. articles to profl. jours. Mem. IEEE, Calif. Assn. Personnel Cons., Calif. Bur. Employment Agys., Bena Brigh. Office: Zeiger Tech Careers Inc 18455 Burbank Blvd Ste 310 Tarzana CA 91356

ZEITLER, BILL LORENZ, aviation engineer; b. Columbus, Ohio, July 14, 1920; s. Walter Andrew and Naomi Lee (Limes) Z.; BSCE, Calif. State U., Long Beach, 1965; m. Betty Eileen Thomas, Nov. 8, 1942; children: Eddie, Naomi Parker. Loftsman, Curtiss Wright Corp., Columbus, 1941-43, 44-46; linesman Lockheed Corp., Burbank, Calif., 1943-44; linesman N.Am. Rockwell (and predecessor firms), Inglewood, Calif., 1946-50, airframe designer, 1950-62, supr. engring. coll. unit, 1962-65, project engr. life scis., health care delivery systems, 1965-68, project dir. health care delivery systems;, Princeton, W.Va., 1968-69, mem. tech. staff, Downey, Calif., 1956-85; ret. 1985. project engr. space shuttle design, 1971-75, shuttle alignment and mating, 1975-77, space shuttle design support extra vehicular stowage and testing, 1978-85; mem. Space Shuttle Speakers Bur. Cert. vocat. tchr., Calif. Mem. AIAA, Nat. Space Inst., Nat. Geog. Soc., Smith Instn. Assocs., Rockwell Mgmt. Club, Toastmasters. Office: 12241 Lakewood Blvd AE47 Downey CA 92041

ZEITLER, EDDIE LORENZ, information systems executive; b. Hollywood, Calif., Aug. 24, 1943; s. Bill Lorenz and Betty Eileen (Thomas) Z.; m. Victoria Lee Duncan, Sept. 21, 1968 (div. Apr. 1984); children: Viena Lee, Erin Lynne. BS in Math., U. Ariz., 1968, MS in Systems Engring., 1970; postgrad., U. Alta., Can., 1971-73. Radar systems analyst ITT Gilfillan, Van Nuys, Calif., 1970-71; computer performance analyst Rockwell Internat., Downey, Calif., 1973-75; mgr. computer capacity mgmt. Transam. Info. Systems, L.A., 1975-76; dir. tech. svcs. Federated Dept. Stores, Cin., 1976-78, dir. computer ops., 1978-79; v.p. info. systems security Security Pacific Nat. Bank, Glendale, Calif., 1979—; mem. FMS security adv. panel U.S. Dept. Treas., Washington, 1985; mem. interoperability subcom. E.F.T. task force U.S. Dept. Treas. Author: Information Retrieval Systems, 1970. Mem. Los Angeles County Computer Crime task force, 1984-86; vol. guide Los Angeles Zoo Assn. Served with USAF, 1963-67. Mem. IEEE, Assn. Computing Machinery, Am. Nat. Standards Inst. (mem. subcom. fin. industry), Security Pacific Nat. Bank Securiteam, Am. Bankers Assn. (mem. data security com.), Nat. Bur. Standards (mem. computer system security and privacy adv. bd.), Theta Tau, Alpha Sigma Phi. Baptist. Club: Beachcraft Flying (Van Nuys). Home: 520 S 6th St Apt R Burbank CA 91501 Office: Security Pacific Nat Bank 611 N Brand Blvd G12-01 Glendale CA 91203

ZEITLIN, GERALD MARK, electrical engineer; b. Phila., May 7, 1937; s. David Edward and Charlotte (Freedman) Z.; m. Frances Loretta Scherr, May 17, 1983 (div. 1988). BEE, Cornell U., 1960; MSEE, U. Colo., 1969. Electronic engr. Nat. Security Agy., Ft. Meade, Md., 1962-64, Westinghouse Georesearch Lab., Boulder, Colo., 1966-69; owner Sunrise Books, Estes Park, Colo., 1969-71; asst. research computer sci. U. Calif., San Francisco, 1972-78; assoc. devel. engr. U. Calif., Berkeley, 1978-82; sr. systems engr. EEG Systems Lab., San Francisco, 1982-86; computer cons., expert systems design Pacific Bell, San Francisco, 1986-87; systems analyst Pacific Bell, San Ramon, Calif., 1987—. Contbr. articles to profl. jours. Served to 1st lt. U.S. Army, 1960-62. Summer Faculty fellow NASA-Am. Soc. Engring. Edn., Ames Research Ctr., 1981. Mem. IEEE, Computer Soc. IEEE, Assn. Computing Machinery, Info. Systems Security Assn., Computer Security Inst. Democrat. Jewish. Home: 196 Caldecott Ln #212 Oakland CA 94618 Office: Pacific Bell 2600 Camino Ramon Rm 3CS90 San Ramon CA 94583

ZEITLIN, MAURICE, sociology educator, author; b. Detroit, Feb. 24, 1935; s. Albert J. and Rose (Goldberg) Z.; m. Marilyn Geller, Mar. 1, 1959; children: Michelle, Carla, Erica. BA cum laude, Wayne State U., 1957; MA, U. Calif.-Berkeley, 1960, PhD, 1964. Instr. anthropology and sociology Princeton (N.J.) U., 1961-64, research assoc. Ctr. Internat. Studies, 1962-64; asst. prof. sociology U. Wis.-Madison, 1964-67, assoc. prof., 1967-70, prof., 1970-77, dir. Ctr. Social Orgn., 1974-76; prof. sociology UCLA, 1977—, also research assoc. Inst. Indsl. Relations; vis. prof. polit. sci. and sociology Hebrew U., Jerusalem, 1971-72. Author: (with R. Scheer) Cuba: An American Tragedy, 1963, 1964, Revolutionary Politics and the Cuban Working Class, 1967, 1970, The Civil Wars in Chile, 1984, Landlords and Capitalists, 1988; Latin Am. editor Ramparts mag., 1967-73; editor-in-chief: Political Power and Social Theory, 1980—; editor: (with J. Petras) Latin America: Reform or Revolution?, 1968, American Society, Inc., 1970, 1977, Father Camilo Torres: Revolutionary Writings, 1972, Classes, Class Conflict, and the State, 1980, How Mighty a Force?, 1983, Insurgent Workers: The Origins of Industrial Unionism, 1987. Chmn. Madison Citizens for a Vote on Vietnam, 1967-68; chmn. Am. Com. for Chile, 1973-75; mem. exec. bd. U.S. Com. for Justice to Latin Am. Polit. Prisoners, 1977-84; mem. exec. com. Calif. Campaign for Econ. Democracy, 1983-86. Ford Found. fellow, 1965-67, 70-71; Guggenheim fellow, 1981-82; NSF grantee, 1981, 82; recipient Project Censored award Top Censored Story, 1981; named to Ten Best Censored list, 1978. Mem. Am. Sociol. Assn. (governing council 1977-80), Internat. Sociol. Assn. (editorial bd. 1977-81), Latin Am. Studies Assn., Orgn. Am. Historians. Democrat. Jewish. Office: UCLA Haines 237 405 Hilgard Ave Los Angeles CA 90024

ZEKMAN, TERRI MARGARET, graphic designer; b. Chgo., Sept. 13, 1950; d. Theodore Nathan and Lois (Bernstein) Z.; m. Alan Daniels, Apr. 12, 1980; 1 child, Jesse Logan. BFA, Washington U., St. Louis, 1971; postgrad, Art Inst. Chgo., 1974-75. Graphic designer (on retainer) greeting cards and related products Recycled Paper Products Co., Chgo., 1970—; apprenticed graphic designer Helmuth, Obata & Kassabaum, St. Louis, 1970-71; graphic designer Container Corp., Chgo., 1971; graphic designer, art dir., photographer Cuerden Advt. Design, Denver, 1971-74; art dir. D'Arcy, McManus & Masius Advt., Chgo., 1975-76; freelance graphic designer Chgo., 1976-77; art dir. Garfield Linn Advt., Chgo., 1977-78; graphic designer Keiser Design Group, Van Noy & Co., Los Angeles, 1978-79; owner and operator graphic design studio Los Angeles, 1979—. Recipient cert. of merit St. Louis Outdoor Poster Contest, 1970, Denver Art Dirs. Club, 1973.

ZELDES, DAVID MARK, lawyer; b. Detroit, Jan. 15, 1950; s. Norman Irving and Zelda (Rogovein) Z.; m. Janice Michelle Noble, Aug. 12, 1973. BA, Wayne State U., 1971, JD, 1974. Bar: Mich. 1975, Ariz. 1977, U.S. Dist. Ct. Ariz. 1977, U.S. Ct. Appeals (9th cir.) 1977. Assoc. Henry, Kimerer and LaVelle, Phoenix, 1978-81; atty. Samaritan Health Svc., Phoenix, 1981-82; legal counsel Valley Acceptance Corp., Phoenix, 1982-86; assoc. counsel DynaCor, Phoenix, 1986-87, gen. counsel, 1987—. Pres. Ariz. Community Service Legal Assistance Found., Phoenix, 1988—. Mem. Ariz. State Bar Assn., Maricopa County Bar Assn. (pres. corp. counsel sect. 1985-86, golf tournament chmn. 1987—, vol. of month 1987), ABA, Nat. Health Lawyers Assn., Grand Canyon B'nai B'rith (pres. 1987-89). Democrat. Jewish.

ZELDIN, C. ARTHUR, management consultant; b. N.Y.C., Dec. 18, 1918; s. Isidore and Dorothy (Kaufman) Z.; m. Helen Hoffman, Aug. 18, 1940;. BS, Mass. Inst. Technol., Cambridge, 1939; AMP Program, Harvard Bus. Sch., Cambridge, Mass., 1962. Registered profl. metall. engr. Plant metallurgist Kennecott Corp. - Utah Refinery, Magna, 1950-56; project devel. engr. Kennecott Corp. - Research Ctr., S.L.C., 1956-59; supt. ops. Kennecott Corp. - Utah Refinery, Magna, 1959-60, plant mgr., 1960-63; gen. mgr. Kennecott Refining Corp., Balt., 1963-69; smelting & refining mgr. Kennecott Corp. - Utah Copper Division, S.L.C., 1969-75, spl. project mgr., 1975-79; v.p. Kennecott Minerals Co., S.L.C., 1979-82; cons. C.A. Zeldin, S.L.C., 1982--; pres. Utah Chap. Am. Soc. for Metals, S.L.C. 1960-61; bd. dirs. Union Trust Co. of Md. Co-Author: Patent, Continuous Casting 1967. V.P. So. Balt. Gn. Hosp., 1964-469, Anne Arundel County Trade Council; chmn. Utah Water Pollution Control Com., 1985-89. Mem. The Minerals, Metals & Materials Soc. (Chmn. Tech. Com. 1963-64),AIME (pres. Utah chpt. 1981-82). Club: Ft. Douglas-Hidden Valley Country. Home and Office: 1024 Oak Hills Way Salt Lake City UT 84108

ZELEZNY, WILLIAM FRANCIS, retired physical chemist; b. Rollins, Mont., Sept. 5, 1918; s. Joseph Matthew and Birdie Estelle (Loder) Z.; m. Virginia Lee Scarcliff, Sept. 14, 1949. BS in Chemistry, Mont. State Coll., 1940; MS in Metallurgy, Mont. Sch. Mines, 1941; PhD in Phys. Chemistry,

State U. Iowa, 1951. Scientist NACA, Cleve., 1951-54; metallurgist div. indsl. research Wash. State Coll., Pullman, 1954-57; scientist atomic energy div. Phillips Petroleum Co., Idaho Falls, Id., 1957-66, Idaho Nuclear Corp., Idaho Falls, 1966-70; mem. staff Los Alamos (N.Mex.) Sci. Lab., 1970-80; instr. metallurgy State U. Iowa, Iowa City, 1948-49; asst. prof. metallurgy Wash. State Coll., 1956-57; instr. U. Idaho, Idaho Falls, 1960-68; bd. dirs. U. Mont. Biol. Sta. Contbr. articles to profl. jours.; patentee in field. Served with AUS, 1944-46. Mem. Am. Chem. Soc. (sec. N.Mex. sect. 1978-79), Microbeam Analysis Soc., Am. Soc. Metals, Am. Inst. Mining Metall. and Petroleum Engrs., Sigma Xi, Alpha Chi Sigma. Democrat. Methodist. Home: PO Box 37 Rollins MT 59931

ZEMER, JACK DAVID, engineer; b. Veiden, Fed. Republic Germany, Apr. 19, 1947; came to U.S., 1974; s. Arie and Shoshana Zemer; children: Ori, Tal. Student, U. Santa Clara; BS, Israel Inst. Tech., Haifa, Israel, 1973, BA. Engr. Gen. Electric, San Jose, Calif., 1974-79; pres. Al-Or Internat. Ltd., Los Angeles, 1980—. Mem. Am. Gem Trade Assn. (charter), 24 Kt. Club. Office: Al-Or Internat Ltd 19400 Bus Ctr Dr Northridge CA 91324

ZENAHLIK, THOMAS PERCY, sales and marketing executive; b. Grandhaven, Mich., Dec. 25, 1946; s. James Joseph and Juanita (Stanley) Z.; m. Ginger Thelma Giannotti, Aug. 1969 (div. July 1975); m. Carolyn Hughes, Oct. 16, 1976; children: Thomas Jason, Marcus John, Anthony Michael, Kael Adam. AA, Foothill Community Coll., Los Altos Hills, Calif., 1966; BA, San Jose State Coll., 1969; postgrad. in teaching, U. Calif., Berkeley, 1971; mktg. cert., Seneca Coll., Toronto, Ont., Can., 1985. Police officer City of San Jose (Calif.), 1967-77; sales mgr. Recreational Sports, Idaho Falls, Idaho, 1977-81, Bombardier Corp., Valcourt, Que., Can., 1981-86; nat. sales mgr. Calkins Boat Trailers, Spokane, Wash., 1986-88; nat. sales and mtkg. dir. E.Z. Loader Boat Trailers, Spokane, 1988—. Chmn. Hayden Lake (Idaho) Recreational Water Dist., 1978-81. Republican. Mem. Nat. Marine Mfrs. Assn., Hayden Lake Country Club. Republican. Home: 1291 Circle Dr Hayden Lake ID 83835 Office: EZ Loader Boat Trailers Inc PO Box 3263 Spokane WA 99220

ZENGER, JOHN HANCOCK, company executive; b. Salt Lake City, Nov. 13, 1931; s. John H. and L. (Hancock) Z.; m. Dixie Robison, June 1, 1955 (div. 1978); children: Mark R., Robin, Todd R., Blake R., Mitchell R., Drew R.; m. Holly Olsen, June 29, 1979; stepchildren: Roger, Kirk, Lori, Michael. BS, Brigham Young U., 1955; MBA, UCLA, 1957; D in Bus. Adminstrn., U. So. Calif., Los Angeles, 1963. Asst. prof. Grad Sch. Bus. U. So. Calif., L.A., 1966-67; exec. v.p. Blanfield-Smith and Co., Pasadena, Calif., 1965-67; v.p. human resources Syntex Corp., Palo Alto, Calif., 1967-77; pres. Zenger-Miller Inc., Cupertino, Calif., 1977—; v.p. Instl. Systems Assn., 1987-88. Chmn. Palo Alto Human Rels. Coun., 1961-66. Ford Found. fellow, 1962-63; recipient Disting. Svc. award Brigham Young U., 1983. Mem. Am. Soc. Tng. and Devel., Brigham Young U. Alumni Assn. (pres. 1981). Republican. Mormon. Home: 27300 Altamont Rd Los Altos Hills CA 94022 Office: 1735 Techology Dr San Jose CA 95110

ZENZ, BARBARA ELIZABETH, advertising executive; b. Stockton, Calif., Jan. 24, 1956; d. Robert Lee and Patricia Frances (Lowdon) Zenz; m. Kim K. Yamaguchi Sept. 29, 1979. A.A., Sacramento City Coll., 1976; B.A., San Jose State U., 1979; postgrad. U. Santa Clara, 1979-80. Ops. mgr. Hotel Ste. Clair, San Jose, Calif., 1976-78; pub. relations specialist Santa Clara County Housing Authority, 1978-80; pres. The Stephenz Group, Inc., Campbell, Calif., 1980—; advt./mktg. communications cons. Mem. Project Area Com. for Redevel. of Downtown Campbell, 1983—. Republican. Roman Catholic. Club: Campbell Culture, Western Art Dirs. Address: 300 Orchard City Dr Ste 133 Campbell CA 95008

ZEPEDA, SUSAN GHOZEIL, health care agency executive; b. N.Y.C., Aug. 8, 1946; d. Harry S. and Anne (Golden) Kantor; m. Isaac Ghozeil, Jan. 29, 1967 (div. Oct. 1979); children: Daniel Jacob, Adam Leo; m. Fernando Zepeda, Jan. 2, 1983; children: Paloma Andrea, Sofia Elisa. BA, Brown U., 1967; MA, U. Ariz., 1971, postgrad., 1971-75; PhD, Internat. Coll., 1985. Rsch. assoc. div. bus. and econ. rsch. U. Ariz., Tucson, 1971-73, rsch. assoc. Coll. Medicine, 1975-76; assoc. dir. Pima Alcoholism Consortium, Tucson, 1976-79, exec. dir., 1979-80; dep. dir. pub. health Orange County Health Care Agy., Santa Ana, Calif., 1980—; cons. Tucson Sch. Dist. No. 1, 1973-75, U.S. Dept. Labor, Washington, 1976-79, Indian Health Svc., Rockville, Md., 1984-85; ptnr. Zepeda Assocs., Fullerton, Calif., 1987—; presenter confs. Mem. Fullerton Planning Commn., 1984—; mem. Calif. Task Force on Comparable Worth, 1984-85, Calif. Dist. Appeal Bd. No. 510., L.A., 1986—. Recipient Woman of Achievement award Orange County Bd. Suprs., 1988, Disting. Achievement awards Nat. Assn. Counties, 1985, 86, 87. Mem. Am. Pub. Health Assn., Internat. Council on Alcohol and Addictions, U.S. Mex. Border Health Assn., County Alcohol Program Adminstrs. Assn. Calif. (v.p. 1983, pres. 1984-85), Santiago Club (Santa Ana). Home: 1508 Moon Beam Pl Fullerton CA 92633 Office: Orange County Health Care Agy 515 N Sycamore St Santa Ana CA 92701

ZERELLA, JOSEPH T., pediatric surgeon; b. Youngstown, Ohio, Mar. 7, 1941; s. Atilio and Ann (Capuzello) Z.; m. Diana Isabelle Talbot, Aug. 5, 1967; children—Ann, Michael, Mark. B.S., Northwestern U., 1962, M.D., 1966. Diplomate Am. Bd. Surgery, Am. Bd. Pediatric Surgery. Intern Med. Coll. Wis., Milw., 1966-67, resident in surgery, 1967-68, 70-73; tng. fellow in pediatric surgery Children's Hosp. Med. Ctr., Cin., 1973-75; staff pediatric surgeon Phoenix Children's Hosp., 1975—, chmn. dept. surgery 1987—; staff Ariz. Children's Hosp., Phoenix, 1975—; pvt. practice medicine specializing in pediatric surgery, Phoenix, 1975—; mem. staff Good Samaritan Hosp., Phoenix, 1975—, sect. chief pediatric surgery, 1979—; mem. staff St. Joseph's Hosp., Phoenix, 1975—, sect. chief pediatric surgery, 1980—; Contbr. articles to profl. jours. Served as capt. U.S. Army, 1968-70. Fellow ACS, Am. Acad. Pediatrics, Am. Pediatric Surg. Assn., Pacific Assn. Pediatric Surgeons. Roman Catholic. Office: Associated Pediatric Surgeons 1010 E McDowell Rd LL4 Phoenix AZ 85006

ZERLAUT, GENE ARLIS, chemist; b. Bailey, Mich., June 23, 1930; s. George David and Glenna Mae (Palm) Z.; student Western Mich. U., 1948-49; B.S., U. Mich., 1956; m. Cecelia Gail McGukin, Mar. 4, 1961; children—Scott Michael, Christopher Robert. Chemist, U.S. Army Ballistic Missle Agy., Huntsville, Ala., 1958-60; aerospace technologist, chemist NASA, Huntsville, 1960-62; sr. chemist, mgr. polymer chemistry research Ill. Inst. Tech. Research Inst., Chgo., 1962-73; pres., tech. dir. DSET Labs., Inc., Phoenix, 1973—. Coach, Little League Baseball, 1974-76; bd. dirs., vice chmn. bd. Solar Energy Research and Edn. Found., 1978-79; commr. Ariz. Solar Commn., 1979-83. Served with U.S. Army, 1956-58. Recipient Invention awards NASA, 1968, Innovation award, 1973. Mem. Solar Energy Industries Assn. (bd. govs. 1976, v.p. 1978-79, exec. com. 1979-81, bd. dirs. 1981-86), Am. Inst. Chemists (dir. 1975), ASTM (nat. chmn. solar energy conversion com. 1978-83, award of merit 1987), Am. Council Ind. Labs., Am. Inst. Aeros. and Astronautics, Am. Nat. Standards Inst. (mem. solar energy standards coordinating com. 1979-83, tech. adv. group on plastics, 1974—,), Internat. Solar Energy Soc., Internat. Standards Orgn. (chmn. U.S. tech. adv. com. on solar energy), Soc. Plastics Engrs., Fedn. Paint Socs. Patentee in field. Contbr. articles to profl. jours. Research in spectral solar radiometry and accelerated environ. testing. Home: 346 W Pine Valley Dr Phoenix AZ 85023 Office: Box 1850 Black Canyon Stage I Phoenix AZ 85029

ZERNOW, LOUIS, physicist; b. N.Y.C., Dec. 27, 1916; s. Meyer and Lena (Fradkin) Z.; m. Edith Hazel Weinstein, Nov. 2, 1940; children: Lenore R., Elaine, Melvin R., Richard H. BChemE, Cooper Union Inst. Tech., 1938; PhD in Physics, Johns Hopkins U., 1953. Chief detonation physics br. Ballistic Rsch. Lab., Aberdeen Proving Ground, Md., 1940-55; mgr. ordnance rsch. div. Aerojet Gen. Corp., Downey, Calif., 1955-63; pres. Shock Hydrodynamics Inc., Sherman Oaks, Calif., 1963-67, Shock Hydrodynamics div. Whittaker Corp., N. Hollywood, Calif., 1967-81, Zernow Tech. Svcs. Inc., San Dimas, Calif., 1981—. Contbr. over 125 tech. reports to Dept. of Def. agys.; holder 6 patents. Recipient Meritorious Civilian Svc. award U.S. Army Ballistic Rsch. Lab., 1945. Mem. AIME, Am. Phys. Soc., Accoustical Soc. Am., Am. Soc. for Metals, Am. Def. Preparedness Assn. (exec. bd. ballistics and vulnerability div. 1973—, Outstanding Leadership award 1987). Home: 1103 E Mountain View Glendora CA 91740 Office: Zernow Tech Svcs Inc 425 W Bonita Ave San Dimas CA 91773

ZERZAN, CHARLES JOSEPH, JR., gastroenterologist; b. Portland, Oreg., Dec. 1, 1921; s. Charles Joseph and Margaret Cecelia (Mahony) Z.; BA, Wilamette U., 1948; MD, Marquette U., 1951; m. Joan Margaret Kathan, Feb. 7, 1948; children: Charles Joseph, Michael, Kathryn, Paul, Joan, Margaret, Terrance, Phillip, Thomas, Rose, Kevin, Gregory. Commd. 2d. lt., U.S. Army, 1940, advanced through grades to capt., 1945, ret., 1946, re-enlisted, 1951, advanced through grades to lt. col., M.C., 1965; intern Madigan Gen. Hosp., Ft. Lewis, Wash., 1951-52; resident in internal medicine Letterman Gen. Hosp., San Francisco, 1953-56, Walter Reed Gen. Hosp., Washington, 1960-61; chief of medicine Rodriquez Army Hosp., 1957-60, U.S. Army Hosp., Fort Gordon, Calif., 1962-65; chief gastroenterology Fitzsimmons Gen. Hosp., Denver, 1965-66; chief profl. services U.S. Army Hosp., Ft. Carson, Colo., 1967-68; dir. continuing med. edn. U. Oreg., Portland, 1968-73; partner Permanente Clinic, Portland, 1973—; assoc. clin. prof. medicine U. Oreg., 1973—; individual practice medicine, specializing in gastroenterology, Portland, 1968—; staff Northwest Permanente, P.C.; dir., 1980-83. Mem. Portland Com. Fgn. Rels., 1986—. Decorated Legion of Merit, Army Commendation medal with oak leaf cluster. Diplomate Am. Bd. Internal Medicine. Fellow A.C.P.; mem. Am. Gastroenterol. Assn., Oreg. Med. Assn. (del. Clackamas County), Ret. Officers Assn. Republican. Roman Catholic. Home: 6364 SE McNary Rd Milwaukie OR 97267 Office: 10200 SE Sunnyside Rd Clackamas OR 97015

ZEVGOLIS, SUSAN STELLA, professional association administrator; b. Washington, Mar. 24, 1955; d. George Paul and Beba (Hangelia) Z. BA, U. Md., 1977. Counter mgr. Bloomingdale's, Tysons Corner, Va., 1978-79; with tng. and edn. dept. Am. Pub. Power Assn., Washington, 1980-82; pvt. practice cons. to various cosmetics firms San Francisco, 1982-85; ter. mgr. Ben Rickert, Inc., San Francisco, 1985-87, Charles of the Ritz, San Francisco, 1987-88; dist. mgr. Nat. Assn. Mfrs., San Francisco, 1988—; dir. womens' affairs U. Md., College Park, 1976-77. Democrat. Greek Orthodox. Home: PO Box 14243 San Francisco CA 94114 Office: Nat Assn of Mfrs 22300 Foothill Blvd Ste 510 Hayward CA 94541

ZEZZA, MYRNA MAZZOLA, human development trainer; b. Boston, May 28, 1938; d. Michael John and Mary Theresa (Costra) Mazzola; m. Ralph Michael Zezza, June 14, 1958 (div. Aug. 1975); m. William Gerald Chung, Apr. 16, 1988. Student, Tufts U., 1956; BA, U. Hawaii, 1960. Trainee Sun Press Newspapers, Honolulu, 1961-62; asst. buyer, sales mgr. Liberty House, Honolulu, 1962-66; pres., U.S. rep. House of Nora Noh, Inc., Honolulu, 1966-68; customer svc. rep. Paul Revere Cos., San Francisco, 1969-71; v.p., gen. mgr. Wedding Shoppe, Inc., Honoluluu, 1972-83; human devel. trainer Gt. Lovers of World, Honolulu, 1983—; cons., trainer Wåxthuset, Våddo, Sweden, 1987—. Author: How To Be a Great Lover, 1989. Vol. San Francisco Sch. Dept., 1971, Friends of Carol Fukunaga, Honolulu, 1986, 88. Mem. Am. Soc. for Tng. and Devel., Nat. Speakers Assn., Hawaii Speaking Assocs. (v.p. 1986-87), Powerful Women Hawaii (founding com. 1985-86, v.p. 1987-88), Toastmasters Club. Office: Gt Lovers of World PO Box 1103 Aiea HI 96701

ZHELUTKA, MARA, music programmer; b. Whittier, Calif., Sept. 15, 1949; d. Walter Eugene and Wanda Marie (Grimes) Ferrell; m. Ty E. Allison, July 19, 1987. Student, Humboldt State U., Arcata, Calif., 1973. Radio programmer KHSU, Arcata, 1973-75; promotions dir. KCRW, Santa Monica, Calif., 1978-79; radio programmer KCRW, 1977-85; artist, resource cons. specializing in medieavel, Renaissance and Baroque music ROM Records, L.A., 1987—; radio programmer KCRW, Santa Monica, 1985—. Voice over/narration Long Beach (Calif.)Mus.of Art Video series, 1984. Mem. RadioWest (treas. 1984-87). Office: KCRW 1900 Pico Blvd Santa Monica CA 90405

ZIEGENBUSCH, TED WAYNE, radio-television personality, actor; b. Lima, Ohio, Mar. 10, 1951; s. Charles Paul and Esther Colleen (Newman) Z.; m. Anne Pearl Cordell, Aug. 21, 1970 (div. Sept. 1977); 1 child, Jeffrey; m. April Ann Lorenz, Dec. 10, 1977; 1 child, Ryan. AA, San Bernardino Valley Coll., 1971. Music dir., radio personality KMEN Radio, San Bernardino, Calif., 1968-73, KCAL Radio, San Bernardino, 1973-80; program dir., radio personality The Mighty 690, San Diego, 1980-81; radio personality KGB Radio, San Diego, 1981, KIFM Radio, San Diego, 1981-82, KOST Radio, Los Angeles, 1982—; actor motion pictures, tv commercials, various, 1982—; cons. KOLA Radio, San Bernardino, 1980-87. Named Best Actor, Nat. Thespian Soc., 1969. Mem. Screen Actors Guild, Am. Fedn. TV and Radio Artists. Republican. Protestant. Office: COX Broadcasting 610 S Ardmore Los Angeles CA 90005

ZIEGLER, DAROLD E., financial executive; b. Denver, Aug. 29, 1951; s. Stanley and Betty Ann (Whitman) Z.; m. Theresa Ann Palmer, Sept. 5, 1971; children: Kimberly Palmer, Jamie Kendall. BBA, U. Denver, 1974. V.p. Profl. Services Corp., Denver, 1973-77; owner, operator Pasta King Restaurant, Denver, 1977-78; pvt. practice as mgmt., fin. cons. Denver, 1978-80; mgmt., fin. analyst Farmbank Services, Englewood, Colo., 1980-81, asst. treas. fin. analysis, 1981-84, dir. fin. ops., analysis, 1984-86; fin. officer Farm Credit Corp. of Am., Englewood, 1986—; pvt. practice as cons., Golden, Colo., 1980—. Republican. Lutheran. Office: Farm Credit Corp Am 5500 S Quebec Englewood CO 80111

ZIEMKOWSKI, JAMES ANTHONY, corporate executive officer; b. Lewistown, Mont., Feb. 15, 1936; s. Isadore John and Gertrude (Broad) Z.; m. Betty Lou Hawkins, Sept. 5, 1955; children: Debi, Randy Alan, Diana, Ronald Jerry, Donna Lynn. Stockboy A.J. Bayless, Phoenix, 1954-55, Fry's Food Stores, Phoenix, 1959; mgr. Fry's Food Stores, 1959-63, grocery merchandiser, 1964-65; corp. exec. officer Fairway Foods and Fashions, Clarkdale, Ariz., 1965, Fairway Food, Ariz., Calif., 1965—, Foxbrier Apparel and Fashions, Ariz., 1965—; v.p. Seedling Nursery and Florist, Camp Verde, Ariz., 1982—; bd. dirs. Assoc. Grocer's, Ariz., 1983-85. Mem. Cath. Bishop's Com. for the Youth of Ariz., Phoenix, 1980, Bishop's Pastorial Council for No. Ariz., Flagstaff, 1988—; chmn. Dollars for Scholars Fundraising, Cottonwood, Ariz., 1978, Businessmen for New Hwys. in Ariz., 1977. With USAF, 1956-58. Mem. Retail Grocer's of Ariz. Assn. (bd. dirs. 1967—, named grocer of the yr. 1986), Kiwanis (pres. 1970-71). Roman Catholic. Office: Fairway Foods PO Box 310 Camp Verde AZ 86322

ZIERNICKI, RICHARD MIECZYSLAW, engineering firm executive; b. Krakow, Poland, Feb. 3, 1950; came to U.S., 1981; m. Mila Kristine Czarnecka, Apr. 1, 1952; children: Maciek, Daniel. BS in Mech. Design, U. Mining and Metallurgy, Krakow, 1973, MS in Mech. Engring., 1975, PhD in Tech. Sci. cum laude, 1979. Registered profl. engr., Colo., Calif., Tex. and Wyo. Asst. prof. engring. Inst. Vibrations and Acoustics, Krakow, 1975-80; mgr. rsch. and devel. Inst. Tech., Krakow, 1980-81; mgr. mech. engring. Over-Lowe Co., Denver, 1981-84; sr. cons., pres. Knott Lab., Denver, 1984—; invited speaker Denver U. Dept. Engring. Contbr. articles to profl. jours.; patentee in field. Mem. ASME, NSPE, Soc. Automotive Engrs., Soc. for Exptl. Stress Analysis, Robotic Internat. Soc. Mfg. Engrs., Profl. Engrs. Colo., Nat. Assn. Profl. Accident Reconstruction Specialists, Nat. Forensic Ctr., Nat. Acad. Forensic Engrs. Home: 8809 S Blue Mountain Pl Highlands Ranch CO 80126 Office: Knott Lab Inc 2727 W 2d Ave Denver CO 80219

ZIGLER, GILBERT LENK, electrical engineer; b. Rio de Janeiro, Mar. 19, 1945; s. Daniel Gilbert and Maria (Lenk) Z.; m. Patricia Lyn Bolton, Aug. 19, 1969; children: Bryan, Andrea. BSEE, U. N.M., 1967; MS in Nuclear Engring., Air Force Inst. Tech., Dayton, Ohio, 1969. Nuclear research officer USAF, Albuquerque, 1967-73; reactor diagnostic engr. Babcock and Wilcox Co., Lynchburg, Va., 1973-77; scientist Sci. Applications Inc., Oak Ridge, Tenn., 1977-84; sr. scientist/engr. Sci. and Engring. Assocs. Inc., Albuquerque, 1984—. Contbr. articles to profl. jours. Capt. USAF, 1967-73. Mem. ASME (charter mem. Vibration Monitoring com. 1976—, Loose Parts Monitoring Subgroup 1984—). Office: Sci and Engring Assocs Inc PO Box 3722 Albuquerque NM 87190

ZIGMAN, PAUL EDMOND, environmental consultant executive; b. Los Angeles, Mar. 10, 1924; s. Fernand and Rose (Orligan) Z.; children: Andrea, Eric. BS in Chemistry, UCLA, 1948. Supr., applied research U.S. Naval Radiol. Def. Lab., San Francisco, 1949-59, head tech. mgmt. office, 1961-69; supr., analytical chemistry Atomics Internat., Canoga Park, Calif., 1960-61; pres. Environ. Sci. Assocs., San Francisco, 1969—. Contbr. articles to profl. jours. Served as pvt. U.S. Army, 1943. Recipient USN Meritorious Civilian Service award, 1968. Mem. Am. Chem. Soc., Nat. Assn. Environ. Profls. (v.p. 1977), Assn. Environ. Profls. (pres. 1974-76) (Outstanding Service award 1977, Cert. Appreciation 1984). Office: Environ Sci Assocs 760 Harrison San Francisco CA 94107

ZIKMUND, BARBARA BROWN, minister, educator; b. Ann Arbor, Mich., Oct. 16, 1939; d. Henry Daniels and Helen (Langworthy) Brown; m. Joseph Zikmund II, Aug. 26, 1961; 1 child, Brian Joseph. BA, Beloit Coll., 1961; BDiv, Duke U., 1964, PhD, 1969; D in Div (hon.), Doane Coll., 1984, Chgo. Theol. Sem., 1985. Ordained to ministry United Ch. of Christ, 1964. Instr. Albright Coll., Reading, Pa., 1966-67, Temple U., Phila., 1967-68, Ursinus Coll., Collegeville, Pa., 1968-69; asst. prof. religion studies Albion Coll., Mich., 1970-75; asst. prof. ch. history, dir. studies Chgo. Theol. Sem., 1975-80; dean and assoc. prof. ch. history Pacific Sch. Religion, Berkeley, Calif., 1981-85, dean and prof. ch. history, 1985—; chmn. United Ch. of Christ Hist. Coun., 1983-85, mem. coun. for ecumenism, 1983—; mem. Nat. Coun. Chs. Commn. on Faith and Order, 1979-87, World Coun. of Chs. Programme Theol. Edn., 1984—. Author: Discovering the Church, 1983. Editor: Hidden Histories in the UCC, 1984, vol. 2, 1987; (with Manschreck) American Religious Experiment, 1976; editorial bd. Jour. Ecumenical Studies, 1987—; contbr. articles to profl. jours. Mem. City Coun., Albion, Mich., 1972-75. Woodrow Wilson fellow, 1964-66; NEH grantee, 1974-75. Mem. Assn. Theol. Schs. (v.p. 1984-86, pres. 1986-88, issues implementation grantee 1983-84), Am. Soc. Ch. History (council 1983-85), Internat. Assn. Women Ministers (v.p. 1977-79), AAUW (v.p. 1973-75). Democrat. Home: 1281 Peachwood Ct San Bruno CA 94066 Office: Pacific Sch Religion 1798 Scenic Ave Berkeley CA 94709

ZILBERBERG, NAHUM NORBERT, publishing and communications executive; b. Manheim, Germany, Feb. 13, 1925; s. Mendel Max and Pasia Paula (Morgenstern) Z.; came to U.S., 1957, naturalized, 1961; grad. Sem. for Art Tchrs., Tel Aviv, 1952; BFA, Yale U., 1960, MFA, 1961; m. Rita Orechovsky, 1946 (div.); children: Oded, Doron; m. Barbara Cahn, 1968 (div.); children: Jedediah, Noah. Print shop apprentice, 1936; master of trade, lectr. on printing, 1940; prof. Sem. for Art Tchrs., Tel Aviv, also tchr. arts and crafts in elementary and high sch., 1952-57; teaching fellow Yale U., New Haven, 1958-61; designer Macmillan Pub. Co., Inc., 1963; asst. designer, Harcourt Brace & World (name changed to Harcourt Brace Jovanovich, Inc.), 1964-72, v.p. Center for Study of Instrn. div., San Francisco, 1972-73, pres. Harcourt Brace Jovanovich Films div., San Francisco, 1973-80; founder, pres. NZ Videodisc Prodns., Mill Valley, Calif., 1980—; founder, pres., chmn. bd. Silver Mountain Pubs., Mill Valley, 1986—; founder You're Publishing, Inc., Mill Valley, 1987—; adj. prof. edn. tech. San Francisco State U. Served with Israel Def. Forces, 1948-5. Recipient film and audio-visual awards including: Grand award Internat. Film and TV Festival N.Y., 1976, 80, Gold awards 1977, 78, 79, 80; Cindy award Info. Film Producers Am., 1976, Gold Camera award U.S. Indsl. Film Festival, 1977, Gold Camera award for videodisc U.S. Indsl. Film Festival, 1979, Gold Hugo award Chgo. Internat. Film Festival, 1980, Gold awards, 1977, 78; Gold award 10th Ann. Festival of Ams., 1977; Disting. Tech. Service awards Soc. Tech. Communication, 1979; Gold award Houston Internat. Film Festival, 1979; grand award Film Council Greater Columbus, 1981. Mem. Bookbuilders West, Am. Inst. Graphic Arts, Calif. Humanities Assn., Assn. Ednl. Communications and Tech. (study com. on videodisc). Address: 412 Corte Madera Town Ctr Corte Madera CA 94925

ZIMKAS, CHARLES PATRICK, JR., space foundation director; b. Scranton, Pa., Sept. 8, 1940; s. Charles Zimkas Sr. and Margaret (Bakunas) Sullick; m. Ursula Frediel Marten; children: Robert L., Uwe F., Michael P., Brian David. Enlisted USAF, advanced through grades to chief master sgt. 1958; dep. chief of staff, personnel adminstrv. div. Aerospace Def. Command, Colorado Springs, Colo., 1971-74; exec. to dep. chief of staff personnel Aerospace Def. Command, Colorado Springs, 1975-80; chief of adminstrn. Air Forces Iceland, Keflavik, 1974-75; first sr. enlisted advisor USAF Space Command, Colorado Springs, 1980-84; ret. 1984; dir. regional devel. Noncommissioned Officers Assn., San Antonio, 1984-86; dir. ops. U.S. Space Found., Colorado Springs, 1986—. Named Air Force Outstanding Airman of Yr., 1978; recipient Air Force Legion Merit. Mem. Noncommissioned Officers Assn. (bd. dirs. 1978-84, chmn. bd. dirs. 1982-84, Excalibur award 1979, Order of Sword 1978). Home: 729 Drew Dr Colorado Springs CO 80911 Office: US Space Found PO Box 1838 Colorado Springs CO 80901

ZIMMER, CHERYL POIRIER, city recreation facility official; b. Montreal, Que., Can., May 7, 1958; came to U.S., 1968; d. Gordon Frederick and Margaret Beverley (Green) Poirier; m. John Patrick Zimmer, Sept. 13, 1986; 1 child, Jared Michael. BS in Physical Edn., Springfield Coll., Springfield, Mass., 1980. Asst. dir. physical edn. Downey Family YMCA, Downey, Calif., 1980-81; pre-sch. tchr. Creative Beginnings Sch., Downey, 1981-82; recreation leader City of Cerritos, Calif., 1982-84; swim coach Cerritos Aquatic Club, 1982-84; pool mgr. Armed Forces Reserve Ctr., Los Alamitos, Calif., 1984; swim coach Arroyo Grande (Calif.) Swim Club, 1984-85, Santa Maria (Calif.) Swim Club, 1985-87; recreation program coord. City of Santa Maria, 1985-88, recreation facility mgr., 1988—; swim coach Santa Maria High SCh., 1985-86; all-star swim coach Cen. Coast Swimming, L.A., 1986. Active athlete svcs. Spl. Olympics, Santa Maria, 1985—. Recipient Kay Fromer meml. award New England Women's Intercollegiate Swimming & Diving Assn., 1980; named All-Am. Swimmer, AAUW, 1977-80. Mem. Delta Kappa Phi (sec. Santa Maria chpt. 1988—), Beta Sigma Phi (sec. Santa Maria chpt. 1988—). Episcopalian. Office: City of Santa Maria 110 E Cook Santa Maria CA 93454

ZIMMER, ELIZABETH BAILEY RICHTER, critic; b. N.Y.C., Jan. 26, 1945; d. Frank Nelson and Beatrice (Yannet) Richter; m. Peter G. Zimmer, July 12, 1969 (div. 1979). BA in Lit., Bennington Coll., 1966; MA in English, SUNY, Stony Brook, 1974. Tchr. English Nova Scotia Coll. of Art and Design, Halifax, Can., 1969-72; tchr., counselor Bd. of Trade Youth Project, Halifax, 1972-74; freelance journalist Can. Broadcasting Corp., 1971-78; tchr., communications Capilano Community Coll., North Vancouver, B.C., Can., 1975-78; exec. dir. Am. Dance Guild, N.Y.C., 1979-80; freelance journalist numerous dance magazines, N.Y.C., 1978—; dir. spl. projects Arts Connection, N.Y.C., 1980-88; dir. Bates Coll. Dance Festival, Lewiston, Maine, 1985-87; dance critic L.A. Herald Examiner, 1988—; cons. N.Y. State Coun. on the Arts, 1978-88, N.Y. Found. for the Arts, N.Y.C., 1983-88. Author: Presenting the Performing Arts, 1988, Class Acts, 1988, Dance: A Social Study, 1989, Body Against Body, 1989. Can. Coun. Nat. Endowment fellow Am. Dance Festival, New London, 1976. Mem. Dance Critics Assn. (bd. mem. 1979-82). Office: LA Herald Examiner 1111 S Broadway Los Angeles CA 90015

ZIMMER, MARK VANCE, architect; b. Pitts., June 14, 1960; s. Arnold Arthur and Thelma (Vance) Z. BS in Archtl. Engring., U. Kans., 1983, B in Environ. Design, 1983. Registered architect. Mgr. design dept. Vavrus Assocs., Joliet, Ill., 1983-86; project architect, cadd mgr. Krommenhoek McKeown Assocs., San Diego, 1986—. Club: So. Calif. Sigma Users Group (rep. 1986—). Office: Krommenhoek McKeown Assocs 1515 Morena Blvd San Diego CA 92110

ZIMMER, MARKUS B., court administrator; b. Basel, Switzerland, Oct. 10, 1946; naturalized U.S. citizen; s. Max Bernhard and Elisabeth (Sulzmann) A.; m. Shelley Elaine Melcomian; children: Jessica Elaine, Christopher Montana. BA cum laude, U. Utah, 1971, MA in Philosophy, 1975; EdM, Harvard U., 1977, EdD, 1980. Rsch. asst., teaching fellow law and ethics Harvard Law Sch., Cambridge, Mass., 1977-78; ednl. specialist div. continuing edn. and tng. Fed. Jud. Ctr., Washington, 1978-79, spl. asst. to dir. div. continuing edn. and tng., 1979-81, asst. dir. div. continuing edn. and tng., 1981-83, acting chief legal svcs. tng. br., 1983-84, chief mgmt. tng. br., div. continuing edn. and tng., 1984-87; clk. of ct., ct. adminstr. U.S. Dist. Ct. Utah, Salt Lake City, 1987—; adj. lectr. mgmt., U. Md., College Park, 1986-87. Contbr. articles to topical publs. With U.S. Army Res., 1964-70. Fulbright fellow, U. Zurich, Switzerland, 1972-73; recipient Swiss-Am. Alumni Assn award, 1972. Mem. Am. Soc. Tng. and Devel. (dir. justice systems trainers 1984-86), Harvard Club Washington (exec. bd. Utah combined fed. campaign). Office: US Dist Ct Utah 350 S Main St Salt Lake City UT 84101-2180

ZIMMERMAN, ADAM HARTLEY, mining, forest industries company executive; b. Toronto, Ont., Can., Feb. 19, 1927; s. Adam Hartley and Mary Ethelwyn (Ballantyne) Z.; m. Janet Lewis, May, 1951; children: Thomas, Barbara, Mary, Kate. Attended, Upper Can. Coll., Toronto, Ridley Coll., St. Catharines, Ont., Royal Can. Naval Coll., U. Toronto; postgrad. in philosophy, 1951. Chartered acct., Ont. With sales dept. Procter & Gamble, 1950; with Clarkson, Gordon & Co., Toronto, 1950-58; asst. comptroller Noranda Mines Group of Cos., beginning 1958; comptroller Noranda Mines Ltd., Toronto, 1961, v.p., 1966-74, exec. v.p., 1974-82, pres., chief operating officer, 1982—; pres. Northwood Pulp and Timber Ltd.; chmn. MacLaren Power & Paint, Noranda Aluminum, Noranda Metal Industries; vice chmn. Can. Wire and Cable, MacMillan Bloedel Ltd., 1981, Fraser, Inc.; bd. dirs. Algona Steel Corp., Brunswick Mining & Smelting Corp., Can. Packers Inc., Econ. Investment Trust Ltd., Placer Devel. Ltd., Royal Ins. Co. Can., Toronto-Dominion Bank, Southam Inc. Chmn. Can.-Am. Com.; trustee Hosp. for Sick Children.; mem. adv. bd. Faculty of Commerce and Bus. Adminstrn. U. B.C. Served to lt. Royal Can. Navy Res., 1946-52. Fellow Ont. Inst. Chartered Accts.; mem. Zeta Psi. Clubs: The York, Toronto Golf, Univ, Mt. Royal, Madawaska, Craigleigh Ski. Office: Noranda Inc, Commerce Ct W PO Box 45, Toronto, ON Canada M5L 1B6 also: MacMillan Bloedel Ltd, 1075 W Georgia St, Vancouver, BC Canada V6E 3R9 *

ZIMMERMAN, ARNOLD I., recruiting company executive; b. N.Y.C., Apr. 5, 1946; s. Sydney Harry and Gladys (Chitkin) Z.; m. Jianulla Chapralis, Oct. 20, 1978; children: Kevin, Timothy, Paula, Brian. BS in Chem. Engring., CCNY, 1968; MBA, Iona Coll., 1972. Chem. engr. Gen. Foods, Inc., White Plains, N.Y., 1969-73; group leader Hunt-Wesson, Inc., Fullerton, Calif., 1973-78; exec. search cons. Paul Norsell and Assoc., L.A., 1978-79; pres. Horizon/Afjan Assoc., Redondo Beach, Calif., 1979—. Vice pres. South Bay L.A. Pvt. Industry Council, Inglewood, Calif., 1986—; chmn. Beyond War, Torrance, Calif., 1987—. Mem. Inst. Food Technologists, Nat. Assn. Exec. Recruiters (recruitment chmn. 1985—). Democrat. Jewish. Home: 322 S Broadway Redondo Beach CA 90277 Office: Arjan/Horizon Assoc 322 S Broadway Redondo Beach CA 90277

ZIMMERMAN, CAROLYN ANN, nurse; b. Van Nuys, Calif., Jan. 25, 1944; d. Jack and Alice (Plummer) Mason; m. Mike Zimmerman; children: Annika, Josh, Kelli, Jessica. RN, U. Ky., 1974. RN, Calif. Nurse Community Hosp., Chico, Calif., 1975-79, Feather River Hosp., Paradise, Calif., 1980—; tchr. vocat. edn. Butle County Schs., Paradise, 1983—. Home: 2360 Stearns Rd Paradise CA 95969

ZIMMERMAN, HAROLD SAMUEL, newspaper executive, state senator, state administrator; b. Valley City, N.D., June 1, 1923; s. Samuel Alwin and Lulu (Wylie) Z.; m. Julianne Williams, Sept. 12, 1946; children—Karen, Steven, Judi Jean (dec.). B.A., U. Wash., 1947. News editor Sedro-Woolley (Wash.) Courier-Times, 1947-50; editor, pub. Advocate, Castle Rock, Wash., 1950-57; pub. Post-Record, Camas, Wash., 1957-80; assoc. pub., columnist, 1980; assoc. pub., columnist, dir. Eagle Publs., Camas, 1980-88. Mem. Wash. Ho. of Reps., 1967-80; mem. Wash. Senate, 1981-88, Wash. State Environ. Hearings Bd., Lacey, 1988—. Served with USAAF, 1943-46. Mem. Grange, Sigma Delta Chi, Sigma Chi. Republican. United Methodist. Clubs: Lions, Kiwanis.

ZIMMERMAN, LINDA FRAN, periodical publisher; b. Chgo., Sept. 30, 1946; d. Louis Joseph and Sydell Muriel (Lakowitz) Z. Student, Roosevelt U., 1963-65, Santa Monica Coll., 1981-83. Production asst. films, asst. video editor various features, 1970-81; freelance photographer 1979-86, freelance writer, 1983—; editor, pub. The Food Yellow Pages, Los Angeles, 1987—; creative svcs. dir. El Cholo Restaurants, L.A.; instr. food journalism UCLA and various colls.; speaker radio and TV; specialist food and restaurants L.A. Author various mag., newspaper articles. Mem. Women's Culinary Alliance (bd. dirs. 1988—), So. Calif. Culinary Guild (bd. dirs.). Home: 135 S Harper Ave Los Angeles CA 90048 Office: The Food Yellow Pages PO Box 461449 Los Angeles CA 90046

ZIMMERMAN, MICHAEL DAVID, judge; b. Chgo., Oct. 21, 1943; m. Lynne Mariani; children: Evangeline Albright, Alessandra Mariani, Morgan Elisabeth. BS, U. Utah, 1966, JD, 1969. Bar: Calif. 1971, Utah 1978. Law clk. to Chief Justice Warren E. Burger U.S. Supreme Ct., Washington, 1969-70; assoc. O'Melveny & Myers, L.A., 1970-76; assoc. prof. law U. Utah, 1976-78, adj. prof. law, 1978-84; of counsel Kruse, Landa, Zimmerman & Maycock, Salt Lake City, 1978-80; staff Gov. of Utah, Salt Lake City, 1978-80, spl. counsel, 1980-84; ptnr. Watkiss & Campbell, Salt Lake City, 1980-84; justice Supreme Ct. of Utah, Salt Lake City, 1984—. Editor: Utah Law Rev., 1968-69; contbr. numerous articles to legal pubs. Named Utah State Bar Appellate Ct. Judge of Yr., 1988; recipient fellowship Justice and Soc. Program of Aspen Inst. for Humanistic Studies, 1988. Mem. ABA, Jud. Conf. of U.S. (adv. com. civil rules 1986—), Utah Jud. Coun. (supreme ct. rep., 1986—), Utah State Bar, Utah Constl. Revision Commn., Salt Lake County Bar Assn., Order of Coif, Phi Kappa Phi. Office: Utah Supreme Ct 332 State Capitol Bldg Salt Lake City UT 84114

ZIMMERMAN, NATALIE MARIE, film, commercials and video producer, actress; b. St. Louis, Dec. 23, 1960; d. Thomas Alfred and Nancy Marie (Russo) Z. Student, Fontbonne Coll., 1978-79. Model Zoli, N.Y.C., 1978-81, Nina Blanchard, Los Angeles, 1981-83; ind. producer commls. and videos Los Angeles, 1983--. Producer movie Helmet Newton's Sleepless Nights, 1988; star Hero of Our Time, 1986; guest role film Lethal Weapon, 1987. Democrat. Roman Catholic. Home and Office: 8360 Hollywood Blvd Hollywood CA 90069

ZIMMERMAN, ROBERT DALE, systems engineer; b. Madison, Wis., Nov. 26, 1946; s. Ernest Leroy and Helene (Swanson)ú Z. BS in Chem. Engring., U. Wis., 1968; MS in Chem. Engring., U. Calif., Berkeley, 1971. Summer engr. Proctor and Gamble, Cin., 1967; engr. Rohm and Haas, Phila., 1968-69; sr. engr. Gen. Atomic Co., San Diego, 1971-72, mgr. pilot plant devel., 1973-80, mktg. mgr., 1980-81, sr. bus. planner, 1982-83, sr. staff engr., 1984-85; systems engr., asst. div. mgr. Sci. Applications Internat. Corp., Las Vegas, Nev., 1986--; ptnr. real estate devel., gen. partnerships, San Diego, 1972--. Served with U.S. Army Res., 1969. Mem. Am. Inst. Chem. Engring. (program chmn. 1987, dir. nuclear engring. div. 1988-89), Am. Nuclear Soc., Torrey Pines Sailing, Sierra. Democrat. Lutheran. Home: 820 Avocado Ln Carlsbad CA 92008 Office: Sci Application Internat Corp Ste 860 101 Convention Ctr Dr Las Vegas NV 89109

ZIMMERMAN, WAYNE EDWARD, protective services official; b. Merced, Calif., Mar. 4, 1949; s. Thukman Hershel and Josephine Mary (Crocker) Z.; m. Gayle J. Hollenbeck, May 29, 1970; children: Stephen Wayne, Brian Edward. Grad. high sch., Merced; Cert. Emergency Med. Tech., Merced Coll., 1969. Fire dispatcher Moraga (Calif.) Fire Dept., 1973-75; firefighter Kensington (Calif.) Fire Dept., 1975—; owner Hobby Depot, Antioch, Calif., 1980—, Hood's Handicrafts, Richmond, Calif., 1988—. Bd. dirs. Downtown Merchant Group, Antioch, 1988. Served to HT2, USN, 1969-73. Mem. Antioch C. of C., Hobby Industry Am. Republican. Baptist. Club: Driftwood Yacht. Office: Hood's Handicrafts 12260 San Pablo Ave Richmond CA 94805

ZIMMERMANN, STEPHAN FRITZ-PETER, investment management company executive; b. Leipzig, Sachsen, Germany, Nov. 28, 1945; came to U.S., 1956; s. Andreas and Senta Agnes Klara (Bergmann) Z.; m. Pamela Clare Dawson, Mar. 29, 1980 (div. Aug. 1984); 1 child, Helen Jennifer. BA, U. Calif., Berkeley, 1971; cert. in econs., Cambridge U., 1975; MA, Monterey Inst. Internat. Studies, 1976. Underwriter Home Ins. Co., San Francisco, 1968-70; stockbroker Dean Witter Reynolds, Berkeley, Calif., 1971-73; analyst Bartle Wells Assocs., San Francisco, 1973-74; pres. Zimmermann, Wilson & Co. Inc., Carmel, Calif., 1976-88. Producer record albums Pat DuVal-Old Monterey, 1985, Heartsounds, 1986; columnist Zimmermann Notes, 1971-88; author (book) Be Your Own Boss, 1988. Bd. dirs. Monterey County Rep. Cen. Com., Salinas, Calif., 1976. Served with USAF, 1966-67. Recipient Dow Jones award in Econs., 1976. Home: PO Box 22-2218 Carmel CA 93922

ZINGALE, DONALD PAUL, health and human services educator; b. Bklyn., Aug. 3, 1946; s. Charles and Helen (Puglisi) Z. BS in Health, Phys. Edn., Bklyn. Coll., 1967; MS in Phys. Edn., U. Mass., 1969; PhD in Phys. Edn., Ohio State U., 1973; MSW, Calif. State U., Sacramento, 1974. Lic. clin. Social worker, Calif.; lic. marriage and family counselor, Calif.; cert. health and phys. edn. instr. secondary schs., N.Y.C. and N.Y.; cert. Alpine Ski Instr. Teaching asst. Sch. Phys Edn. U. Mass., Amherst, 1967-69; instr. health, phys. edn. NYU, 1969-70; teaching assoc. Sch. Health, Phys. Edn. and Recreation Ohio State U., 1970-72; clin. social work intern Napa County Mental Health Ctr., 1982-83; mental health counselor Sacramento Mental Health Ctr., 1985-86; clin. social work intern U. Calif., Davis, 1983-85; clin. social worker III U. Calif., 1987-88, clin. instr. in psychiatry, 1988—; prof., assoc. dean health, human svcs. and phys. edn. Calif. State U., Sacramento, 1973—; clin. social worker Calif. State U., 1984-85; dir. skiing, Calif. State U., Sacramento, 1973—; ski instr. and educator various orgns., 1967—; pvt. practice psychotherapy, Sacramento, 1985—; lectr. CUNY,1969-70, Bklyn. Coll., 1969-70, Baruch Coll., 1969-70; exec. dir. R.S.V.P., Columbus, 1972-73. Contbr. articles to profl. jours. and publs. Mem. NEA, AAUP, Nat. Assn. Social Workers, Am. Alliance Health Phys. Edn. Recreation and Dance, Congress Faculty Assns., Calif. Assn. Health Phys. Edn. Recreation and Dance (northern dist. pres. 1976-77), Profl. Ski Instrs. of Am. Roman Catholic. Office: Calif State U Sch Health Human Svcs 6000 J Street Sacramento CA 95819

ZINGEROV, ANNA, insurance agent; b. Kishinev, Moldavia, U.S.S.R., Jan. 9, 1948; d. Volf Shteinberg and Sofia (Zilberman) S.; m. Alexander Zingerov, Dec. 4, 1970; 1 child, Vladimir. BA, Music Sch., Kishinev, 1968; MA, Inst. Art Sch., 1972. Music educator Music Sch., Kiev, U.S.S.R., 1972-81; tchr. Temple Israel Hollywood, L.A., 1981-83; ins. agt., registered rep. Prudential Ins., L.A., 1983—. Home: 11426 Yolanda Ave Northridge CA 91326 Office: Prudential Ins Co 1246 S La Cienega Blvd #200 Los Angeles CA 90035

ZINSER, ELISABETH A., university president. Formerly v. chancellor acad. affairs U. N.C. at Greensboro; pres. U. Idaho, Moscow 1989—. Office: U Idaho Office of Pres Moscow ID 83843 *

ZIPPER, STUART CHARLES, journalist; b. Bklyn., Mar. 24, 1946; s. Alfred and Annette (Garn) Z.; m. Orah Tovah Friedland, Oct. 12, 1968; children: Michal, Ari, Natan, Avital, Nechama. BA, Queens Coll., 1967; postgrad., U. Miami, Coral Gables, Fla., 1970-72. Staff writer various newspapers N.Y. and Fla., 1967-74; corr. Electronic News, Miami, Fla., 1975-77, Dallas, 1981-84; corr. Electronic News, Denver, 1984-88, regional mgr., 1988—; corr. Fairchild News Svc., Jerusalem, 1977-81; copy sub-editor Jerusalem Post, 1977-81; writing, research and photography cons. Sec. Hillel Acad., Denver, 1985-87; asst. scoutmaster Boy Scouts Am., 1988—. With U.S. Army, 1968-70, Vietnam. Decorated. Democrat. Jewish. Home: 351 S Glencoe Denver CO 80222 Office: Electronic News 300 S Jackson Denver CO 80209

ZIRATO, BRUNO, marketing consultant; b. Buffalo, Oct. 6, 1922; s. Bruno and Nina (Morgana) Z.; m. Barbara Keefe, Sept. 18, 1949 (dec. Nov. 1978); children: Nina Elizabeth, John Bruno; m. Gail Kohler, Apr. 3, 1982. BA, Duke U., 1943; MA, Columbia U., 1944. Asst. dir. CBS, N.Y.C., 1945-48, dir., 1948-52, producer, dir., 1952-62; exec. producer Goodson-Todman Ltd., N.Y.C., 1962-78; dir. mktg. DeHaven Mgmt., Phoenix, 1978; exec. producer Sandy Frank Prodns., Hollywood, Calif., 1979; dir. mktg. Texcon Corp., Nicoli Internat., Phoenix, 1980-83, People & Places Travel, Phoenix, 1984-86; with Lyon Engring. Inc., Phoenix, 1986-87; dir. mktg. Tomaso's Restaurants, Inc., Phoenix, 1987-89. Contbr. articles to porfl. jours. Mem. Les Amis Du Vin, Brotherhood of the Knights of the Vine (master councillor 1979—), Phi Beta Kappa. Democrat. Home: 1027 E Desert Cove Phoenix AZ 85020

ZIRKLE, LEWIS GREER, physician, executive; b. Pittsfield, Mass., July 23, 1940; s. Lewis Greer and Vivian (Shaw) Z.; m. Sara K. Zirkle, Aug. 24, 1963; children: Elizabeth, Molly, Julie. BS, Davidson Coll., 1962; MD, Duke U., 1966. Intern Duke U. Hosp.; resident Duke U. Hosp., U.S. Army, SHriner's Hosp.; pvt. practice Richland, Wash., 1973—; bd. dirs. Keytronic Corp., 1983—, Orthopedics Overseas, 1985—. Contbr. articles to profl. jours. Bd. dirs. Whitworth Coll., Spokane, Wash., 1986—, Duke U. Sch. Forestry, 1986—. Maj. U.S. Army, 1968-73, Vietnam. Presbyterian. Home: 2548 Harris Richland WA 99352 Office: Northwest Orthopedics 875 Swift Richland WA 99352

ZITTER, DONALD STANLEY, university official; b. Bklyn., Aug. 1, 1945; s. Herbert L. and Frances B. Zitter; m. Trudy E. Mumm, Aug. 21, 1981. BS, Cooper Union, 1966; MS, Northwestern U., 1967; PhD, Boston Coll., 1986. Internal cons. Western Electric Corp., N.Y.C., 1968-69; cons. N.Y.C., 1969-72; systems mgr. Permutit Corp., Paramus, N.J., 1972-75; mgr. internat. systems devel. Schering Plough Corp., Kenilworth, N.J., 1975-78; dir. mgmt. info. services Somerset County Coll., Somerset, N.J., 1978-81; dir. computing services Boston Coll., 1981-85, asst. prof., 1985-86; dir. info. services State of Wash., Olympia, 1986-88; exec. dir. computing services U. Nev. System, Reno, 1988—. Contbr. articles to profl. jours. Mem. Assn. for Computing Machinery. Office: U Nev System PO Box 9060 Reno NV 89507

ZIVE, WILLIAM, chemist; b. Chgo., July 20, 1929; s. Jacob and Anna (Goodman) Z.; m. Patricia Carolyn Burns, Feb. 25, 1950; children: Martha June, Robert David, Paul Jacob, Richard Simon. BS in Chemistry, Northwestern U., 1956. Chemist Armour & Co., Chgo., 1952-53; asst. chief chemist Studebaker Aircraft, Chgo., 1953-54; assoc. engr. Crane Co., Chgo., 1954-56; rsch. chemist and prodn. planning mgr., materials mgr. U.S. Borax & Chem. Corp., L.A., 1956-62, 74—; tech. svc. rep. U.S. Borax & Chem. Corp., Atlanta, 1962-64; tech. svc. mgr. U.S. Borax & Chem. Corp., N.Y.C., 1964-74; mgr. prodn. planning U.S. Borax & Chem. Corp., L.A., 1974-77, mgr. distbn. and prodn. planning, 1978-82, materials mgr., 1982—. Author: The World of Ubiquitous Borates, 1974; patentee in field. Leader Boy Scouts Am., Peekskill, N.Y., 1965-70. Mem. Nat. Ind. Traffic League, Nat. Freight Transp. Assn., Sunset Hills Club. Democrat. Jewish. Home: 1455 Calle Colina Thousand Oaks CA 91360 Office: US Borax & Chem Corp 3075 Wilshire Blvd Los Angeles CA 90010

ZOBELL, KARL, lawyer; b. La Jolla, Calif., Jan. 9, 1932; s. Claude E. and Margaret (Harding) ZoB.; m. Barbara Arth, Nov. 22, 1968; children: Bonnie, Elizabeth, Karen, Claude, Mary. Student, Utah State U., 1949-51, Columbia U., 1951-52; AB, Columbia U., 1953, student of law, 1952-54; JD, Stanford U., 1958. Bar: Calif., 1959. Assoc., lawyer Gray, Cary, Ames and Frye, San Diego, 1959-64, ptnr., lawyer, 1964—; bd. dirs., founder La Jolla (Calif.) Bank and Trust Co. Trustee La Jolla Town Coun., 1962-87, chmn. bd. trustees, 1967-68, pres. 1976-77, 80-81, v.p., 1986-87; trustee La Jollans Inc., 1964-80, founder, 1964, pres. 1965-68, 73-76, 78-79; mem. charter rev. com. City San Diego, 1968, 73; chmn. City of San Diego Planning Commn., 1988—; trustee La Jolla Mus. Art, 1964-72, pres. 1967-70, bd. dirs Scripps Meml. Hosp. Found., 1980-84, bd. overseers, Stanford Law Sch., 1977-80, U. Calif., San Diego, 1974-76. Served to lt. USCG, 1954-57. Fellow Am. Coll. Probate Counsel; mem. ABA, Calif. Bar, San Diego Planning Commn., La Jolla Beach and Volleyball Club (pres. 1982—), La Jolla Beach and Tennis Club. Republican. Home: 1555 Coast Walk PO Box 1 La Jolla CA 92037 Office: Gray Cary Ames & Frye 1200 Prospect St Ste 575 La Jolla CA 92037

ZOCK, RICHARD, finance educator, consultant; b. Paterson, N.J., Dec. 28, 1934; s. Cornelis Marinus and Neeltje (Snoek), Z.; m. Jacqueline Charles Zock, Dec. 22, 1958; children: Derek Charles, Diana Katya. BA, Dartmouth Coll., 1956; MBA, Amos Tuck Sch. Bus. Adminstrn., 1957; DBA, U. Colo., 1971. Asst. prof. USAF Acad., Colorado Spring, Colo., 1963-67; asst. prof. fin. U. Houston, 1977-84; prof. fin. Calif. State U., Hayward, 1984—; cons. Prudence, Inc., Spring, Tex., 1982—. Contbr. articles to prof. jours. Mem. City of Hayward Investment Com., Calif., 1985—. Served to lt. col. USAF, 1957-77. Mem. Fin. Mgmt. Assn. Republican. Methodist. Club: Praesidio Army Golf (San Francisco). Office: Calif State U Sch Bus and Econ Dept Mgmt and Fin Hayward CA 94542

ZOELLNER, ROBERT WILLIAM, chemistry educator; b. Marshfield, Wis., May 30, 1956; s. Willard Rudolph and Marie Martha (Prihoda) Z.; m. Barbara Moore, Feb. 5, 1983; 1 child, Joan Moore. BS, St. Norbert Coll., De Pere, Wis., 1978; PhD, Kans. State U., 1983. Postdoctoral assoc. Cornell U., Ithaca, N.Y., 1983-84; vis. scientist U. Aix-Marseille (France) III, 1984-85; asst. prof. No. Ariz. U., Flagstaff, 1986—. Mem. AAAS, Am. Chem. Soc., N.Y. Acad. Sci., N.D. Acad. Sci., Wis. Acad. Sci., Arts and Letters, Sigma Xi, Alpha Chi Sigma, Phi Lambda Upsilon. Office: No Ariz U Dept Chemistry PO Box 5698 Flagstaff AZ 86011-5698

ZOGRAFOS, GEORGE ARISTIOIS, industrial designer; b. Volos, Thesalia, Greece, July 27, 1930; came to U.S., 1959; s. Aristidis G. and Gleni (Anastasio) Z.; m. Wilma Horvath, Jan. 17, 1959; children: Ecy Louize Eleni, Jacqueline. Student indsl. design, Nat. Tech. Sch., L.A., 1965. Tool and die maker Echlin Mfg. Co., Brandford, Conn., 1959-64; plastic technologist Bullard Tech. Co., Bridgeport, Conn., 1960-6l; sr. tool maker Master Spltys. Co., Costa Mesa, Calif., 1966-69, Babcock Electronics Co., Costa Mesa, 1970-72; tool and die designer Orange Coast Coll., Costa Mesa, 1967; supr. Korry Electronics Co., Seattle, 1983-85; sr. tech. jig and fixtures builder Northrop Corp., L.A., 1985—; owner, mgr. Appolo Rsch. Co., Santa Ana, Calif., 1971-74, Atlas Tool Co., Santa Ana, 1975-77, Polymetric Tool Co., Santa Ana, 1977-83; owner R & D Mfg. Inventor electronic connectors. With Greek Air Force, 1950-53. Mem. Pacific Asia Bus. Coun., Order of Ahepa. Democrat. Greek Orthodox. Home: 11381 Bluebell Ave Fountain Valley CA 92708

ZOHOURY, BAHRAM ROBERT, tile company executive; b. Tehran, Iran, Sept. 9, 1960; came to U.S., 1969; s. James and Gitty (Mohtadi) Z. AA, Valley Coll., L.A., 198l; BSCE, UCLA, 1984. Registered profl. engr., Calif. Owner, mgr. Royal Exchange, L.A., 1980-81, Tile Emporium Internat., Santa Monica, Calif., 1984—; real estate salesman Fred Sands, L.A., 1981-84; owner, mgr. Sunset Colonial Apts., L.A., 198l-84. Active L.A. Republican Com., 1984—, Iranian Rep. Party, P.A., , 1988—. Mem. Marina City Club, Pips Club. Mem Baha'i Faith. Home: 9816 Millboro Pl Beverly Hills CA 90210 Office: Tile Emporium Internat 1432 Lincoln Blvd Santa Monica CA 90401

ZOLBER, KATHLEEN KEEN, nutrition educator; b. Walla Walla, Wash., Dec. 9, 1916; d. Wildie H. and Alice (Johnson) Keen; m. Melvin L. Zolber, Sept. 19, 1937. BS in Foods and Nutrition, Walla Walla Coll., 1941; MA, Wash. State U., 1961; PhD, U. Wis., 1968. Registered dietitian. Dir. food service Walla Walla Coll., 1941-50, mgr. coll. store, 1951-59, asst. prof. food and nutrition, 1959-62, assoc. prof., 1962-64; assoc. prof. nutrition Loma Linda (Calif.) U., 1964-72, prof. nutrition, 1973—, dir. dietetic edn., 1967-84, dir. dietetics Med. Ctr., 1972-84, dir. nutrition program, 1984—. Mead Johnson grantee, 1965-67; recipient Alumna of Yr. award Walla Walla Coll., 1977; Delores Nyhus award Calif. Dietetic Assn., 1978. Mem. Am. Dietetic Assn. (pres. 1982—), Am. Pub. Health Assn., Am. Home Econs. Assn., Am. Mgmt. Assn., AAUP, Soc. Food Service Research, Soc. Personnel Adminstrn., Omicron Nu, Delta Omega. Office: Loma Linda U Sch Pub Health Dept Nutrition Loma Linda CA 93354

ZOLEZZI, SAMUEL MAURICE, airline pilot; b. San Diego, Oct. 5, 1949; s. Albert and Jo Noveline (Williams) Z.; m. Victoria Brooke Strickler, Mar. 22, 1980. AB in Theater and TV, San Diego State U., 1971. Lic. airline transport pilot; lic. instrument flight instr. Commd. 2d lt. USAF, 1971, advance through grades to capt., 1978; pilot active duty USAF, Southeast Asia, 1971-74; res. pilot USAF, San Bernardino, Calif., 1974-80; resigned USAF, 1980; first officer New World Airways, Chula Vista, Calif., 1974-75; asst. chief pilot 21st Century Aviation, Chula Vista, 1975-76; first officer World Airways, Oakland, Calif., 1978-86, Pacific S.W. Airlines (bought by US Air), San Diego, 1986—. Home: 3012 Colina Verde Ln Jamul CA 92035-9677

ZOLIN, FRANK STANLEY, county administrator; b. Chgo., Nov. 18, 1932; s. Eugene H. Zwolinski and Genevieve (Blazak) Lin; m. Beverley M. Vaughn, 1957 (div. 1977); m. Carole Lynn Ervin, Oct. 2, 1978 (div. 1987). AA, L.A. City Coll., 1956; BA, Calif. State U., L.A., 1958; postgrad., Calif. State U., 1958-59. Chief analyst Chief Adminstrv. Office County of L.A., 1962-68, adminstrv. dep. Chief Aministrv. Office, 1968-69, county clk., exec. officer, jury commr. Superior Ct., 1969—. Bd. dirs. Constl. Rights Found., L.A., 1987-88, Guiding Eyes, Sylmar, Calif., 1988-89; mem. Town Hall, L.A. Recipient Herbert Lincoln Harley award Am. Judicature Soc., 1983. Mem. Superior Ct. Adminstrs. Assn. (pres. 1981-82), L.A. County Mgmt. Council (pres. 1976), Nat. Assn. for Ct. Mgmt. (past regional dir.), Rotary, Phi Alpha Delta. Office: LA Superior Ct 111 N Hill St Rm 204 Los Angeles CA 90012

ZONGOLOWICZ, HELEN MICHAELINE, school principal; b. Kenosha, Wis., July 22, 1936; d. Edmund S. and Helen (Ostrowski) Z.; Ed.B., Dominican Coll., 1966; M.A., Cardinal Stritch Coll., 1973; Ed.D., U. No. Colo., 1977. Tchr. elem. schs. Kenosha, 1956-58, Center Line, Mich., 1958-59, Taft, Calif., 1960-61, Lake Wales, Fla., 1962-63, Albuquerque, 1963-65; tchr., asst. prin. St. Mary's Sch., Taft, 1965-69; asst. sch. supt. Diocese of Fresno, Calif., 1969-70; tchr. primary grades Greasewood Boarding Sch., Ganado, Ariz., 1970-72, coordinator spl. projects, 1972-75, liaison to parent adv. council, 1972-75, tchr. supr., 1972-76; ednl. specialist Ft. Defiance Agy., Navajo Area, Ariz., 1974-75, ednl. diagnostician, 1979-80; vis. asst. prof. U. Colo., 1976; asst. prof. Auburn (Ala.) U., 1977-79, U. N.Mex.-Gallup, 1981—; prin. Chuska Sch., 1980—. Recipient Spl. Achievement award U.S. Dept. Interior, 1971, 73, Superior Performance award, 1982. Mem. Am. Assn. Mental Deficiency, Assn. for Supervision and Curriculum Devel., Council for Exceptional Children, Council for Basic Edn., Am. Ednl. Research Assn., Nat. Assn. Female Execs., Internat. Reading Assn., Assn. for Children with Learning Disabilities Nat. Council Tchrs. of English. Navajo Nation North Cen. Assn. (chmn.), Kappa Delta Pi, Phi Delta Kappa. Address: Chuska Sch Box 321 Tohatchi NM 87325

ZOOK, JOHN EDWIN, physician, surgeon, missionary; b. Tabor, Iowa, Oct. 3, 1924; s. Abram Eyster Zook and Eunice (Francis) Brenneman; m. Jeanne Pierson, Sept. 7, 1952; children—Rebecca Clair, Daniel John, Paul Michael. B.A., Lewis and Clark Coll., 1950; M.D., U. Oreg., 1954; cert. tropical medicine Antwerp Sch. Tropical Medicine, Belgium, 1956. Diplomate Am. Bd. Surgery. Intern Emanuel Hosp., Portland, Oreg., 1954-55; resident in surgery Good Samaritan Hosp., Portland, 1965-69; ednl. missionary Unevangelized Tribes Mission, Congo, 1943-46; med. missionary Congo Inland Mission, 1955-65; dir. med. activities Africa Intermennonite Mission, Zaire, 1961-65, surgeon, 1969-77; practice medicine specializing in gen. surgery, Portland, 1977—; chief staff Mt. Hood Med. Ctr., 1982, Woodland Park Hosp., 1989; mem. bd. dirs., 1988-91; exchange physician China Ednl. Exchange Program, Chungquin Med. Coll., 1984—. V.p. Mennonite Men of Gen. Conf., Mennonite Ch., 1982—. Fellow ACS, Internat. Coll. Surgeons (Oreg. regent 1980-84, v.p. 1985), Portland Surg. Soc. Republican. Office: E Portland Surg Clinic 169 NE 102nd St Portland OR 97220

ZORN, GLENN ALLEN, biological research director; b. Rockville Center, N.Y., Apr. 6, 1950; s. Leroy Paul and Bernice Christine (Horkey) Z.; m. Marie Elizabeth Ciano, Sept. 7, 1969; children: Amy Marie, Julie Anne, Douglas Michael. Wyatt Matthew. BS, SUNY, Stony Brook, 1972, PhD in Biology, 1977. Postdoctoral fellow Brookhaven (N.Y.) Nat. Lab., 1978-80; asst. research cell biologist Children's Hosp., Oakland, Calif., 1980-82; in vitro lab. dir. John Muir Meml. Hosp., Walnut Creek, Calif., 1983—; cons. human in vitro fertilization Hanna Media, Inc., Berkeley, Calif., 1984; pres. Ygnacio Andrology Services, Walnut Creek, 1986—; supervisor 2d frozen embryo pregnancy in U.S.; dir. one of largest test tube baby programs in N.W. U.S., with over 150 live births. Contbr. articles to profl. jours. N.Y. State Regents scholar., 1968-72, N.Y. State Predoctoral grantee, 1975-77, NIH postdoctoral fellow. Mem. Soc. Exptl. Biology and Medicine, Am. Fertility Soc., Am. Soc. Cell Biology, Tissue Culture Assn., AAAS. Republican. Home: 1202 Chesterton Ct Walnut Creek CA 94596 Office: John Muir Med Ctr 1601 Ygnacio Valley Rd Walnut Creek CA 94598

ZORZ, RAYMOND BARRY, law office automation consultant; b. N.Y.C., Jan. 15, 1955; s. Edward and Marion Arlene (Ferro) Z.; m. Pauline Mary Bertucci; 1 child, Kyle Ryan. BBA, SUNY, Fredonia, 1977. Technician, support analyst Micor, Inc., Phoenix, 1978-81; support analyst, mgr. Informatics Legal Systems, Phoenix, 1981-87; pres. Griffin & Zorz, Inc., Phoenix, 1987—. Home: 3951 E Waltann Ln Phoenix AZ 85032 Office: Griffin & Zorz Inc 3951 E Waltann Ln Phoenix AZ 85032

ZUBRIN, ROBERT MAYNARD, nuclear engineer, educator; b. Bklyn., Apr. 9, 1952; s. Charles and Roslyn (Fallenberg) Z. BA in Math., U. Rochester, 1974; MS in Nuclear Engring., U. Washington, 1984, MS in Aero. and Astronautics, 1986. Cert. math. and sci. tchr., N.Y., N.J., Wash. Tchr. various pub. schs., N.Y., 1974-83; grad. research assoc. Los Alamos (N.Mex.) Nat. Lab., 1985; recording sec. magnetic fusion adv. com. U.S. Dept. of Energy, Washington, 1986-88; health physicist Wash. State Office of Radiation Protection, Seattle, 1987-88; sr. engr. Martin Marietta Astronautics, Denver, 1988—. Inventor Three Player Chess Game, 1972; author play Benedict Arnold, 1983; contbr. articles to profl. jours. Mem. AIAA, AAAS, Am. Nuclear Soc. (v.p. U. Wash. chpt., pub. speaker 1986-88) Am. Phys. Soc., Planetary Soc., Moutaineers Club, Wash. Yacht Club, Tau Beta Pi, Alpha Nu Sigma. Home: 1801 E Girord Pl #222 Englewood CO 80110

ZUCKER, ALFRED JOHN, educator, school adminstrator; b. Hartford, Sept. 25, 1940; s. Samuel and Rose (Zucker) Z.; A.A., Los Angeles Valley Coll., 1960; B.A., U. Calif. at Los Angeles, 1962, M.A., 1963, Ph.D., 1966; m. Sallie Lea Friedheim, Dec. 25, 1966; children—Mary Anne, John James, James Patrick, Patrick Jonathan, Anne-Marie Kathleen, Kathleen Mary. Lectr. English, Los Angeles City Coll., 1963-68; prof. English, philosophy, chmn. div. humanities Los Angeles Southwest Coll., 1968-72, chmn. English dept., 1972-74, asst. dean instruction, 1974—; prof. English El Camino Coll., 1985—. Mem. Los Angeles Jr. Coll. Dist. Senate, 1969—. Mem. Los Angeles Coll. Tchrs. Assn. (dir.), Calif. Jr. Coll. Assn., Calif. Tchrs. Assn., AAUP, Phi Beta Kappa, Phi Delta Kappa (pres. U. Calif. at Los Angeles chpt. 1966-67, v.p. 1967-68). Lodge: KC. Contbr. articles to profl. jours. Office: 1600 W Imperial Hwy Los Angeles CA 90047

ZUCKER, BLANCHE MYRA, civic worker; b. Schenectady, N.Y., July 27, 1925; d. Cassius Alexander and Winifred Estelle (Davis) Millington; m. Nelson Marsh, July 7, 1947 (div. July 1967); children: Kay Patricia, Gary Nelson; m. Reuben Zucker, July 22, 1967 (dec. June 1987). Grad., Meth. Hosp. Sch. Nursing, Bklyn., 1946; BS in Nursing Edn., Columbia U., 1962; MEd, U. Nev., 1975. RN, N.Y. Night shift head nurse Meth. Hosp., Bklyn., 1947; floor nurse Carle Meml. Hosp.Clinic, Urbana, Ill., 1947; med. librarian So. Nev. Meml. Hosp. (now Univ. Med. Ctr.), Las Vegas, 1963-66; librarian St. Viator Sch., Las Vegas, 1966-74; del. Nev. Gov.'s Conf. on Library and Info. Services, 1978, publicity dir., 1978-79; alt. Nev. del. White House Conf. on Library and Info. Services, 1979. Mem. Univ. Med. Ctr. So. Nev. Aux., 1980—; trustee Univ. Library Soc., Las Vegas, 1985—; pres. We Can, 1985-86; mem. Com. for Protection Children, 1985—, vice chmn., 1987—; mem. Citizens Com. Victim Rights, 1986—. Recipient service award St. Viator Sch., 1975, Adminstrn. for Children, Youth and Families award HHS, 1985, Book of Golden Deeds award Las Vegas Exchange Club, 1986, Humanitarian award Las Vegas Women, 1986; appreciation award We Can, Inc., 1987, Citizens Com. Victim Rights, 1987; named Vol. of Yr., Citizens Com. Victim Rights, 1989. Mem. ALA, Nev. Library Assn. (publicity dir. 1979, appreciation award 1979), Friends So. Nev. Libraries, Clark County Med. Soc. Aux. (pres. 1971-72), Gen. Fedn. Women's Clubs (chmn. Nev. chpt. child abuse project 1984—, mem. Past. Pres.'s Club, pres. Mesquite Club 1980-81, nat. 1st place Today's Women-the Vol. award 1986). Democrat. Home: 1501 Birch St Las Vegas NV 89102

ZUCKER, ROBERT STEPHEN, neurophysiologist, physiology educator; b. Phila., Apr. 18, 1945; s. Irving Aaron and Dorothy Ruth (Pittenturf) Z.; m. Glenda Anita Teal, Sept. 1, 1968 (div. Apr. 1982); 1 child, David Aaron; m. Susan Henrietta Schwartz, Jan. 3, 1983; children: Mark Daniel Isaac, Ariel Dana. SB in Physics, MIT, 1966; PhD in Neurol. Sci., Stanford U., 1971. Asst. prof. physiology U. Calif., Berkeley, 1974-80, assoc. prof., 1980-85, prof., 1985—; vis. investigator Univ. Coll. London, 1971-73, Ctr. Nat. de la Recherche Sci., Gif-sur-Yvette, France, 1973-74; corp. mem. Marine Biology Lab., Woods Hole, Mass., 1981—; mem. bd. sci. counselors Nat. Inst. Neurol. And Communicative Disorders and Stroke, Washington, 1982; mem. study sects. NIH, 1983-84. Mem. editorial bd. Jour. Neurobiology, 1982-86, Jour. Neurosci., 1988—; contbr. articles to profl. jours. Fellow Helen Hay Whitney Found., NIH, NSF, NATO, Alfred P. Sloan Found.; grantee NIH, NSF, 1976—; recipient Jacob Javits award, 1987—. Mem. AAAS, AAUP, Soc. Neurosci., Biophys. Sci., Fedn. Am. Scientists, Union Concerned Scientists, Common Cause, ACLU, Sierra Club, Sigma Xi. Democrat. Jewish. Home: 1236 Oxford St Berkeley CA 94709 Office: U Calif Dept Physiology-Anatomy Berkeley CA 94720

ZUCKERKANDL, EMILE, molecular evolutionary biologist, scientific institute executive; b. Vienna, Austria, July 4, 1922; came to U.S., 1975; s. Frederic and Gertrude (Stekel) Z.; m. Jane Gammon Metz, June 2, 1950. M.S., U. Ill., 1947; Ph.D., Sorbonne, Paris, 1959. Postdoctoral research fellow Calif. Inst. Tech., Pasadena, 1959-64; research dir. CNRS, Montpellier, France, 1967-80, dir. Ctr. Macromolecular Biochemistry, 1965-75; pres. Linus Pauling Inst., Palo Alto, Calif., 1980—; cons. in genetics Stanford U., 1963, vis. prof., 1964; vis. prof. U. Del., 1976. Contbg. author: Evolving Genes and Proteins, 1965; co-author: Genetique des Populations, 1976; editor Jour. Molecular Evolution, 1971—. Decorated Order of Merit (France). Fellow AAAS; mem. Societe de Chimie Biologique, N.Y. Acad. Scis., Internat. Soc. Study Origin of Life. Home: 565 Arastradero Rd Palo Alto CA 94306 Office: Linus Pauling Inst Sci & Medicine 440 Page Mill Rd Palo Alto CA 94306

ZUK, JOHN, aerospace engineer; b. Westhampton, N.Y.; s. George and Anna (Stachnik) Z.; m. Maureen Elizabeth Kelly. BSME, Ohio State U., 1961; MS in Aerospace Engring., U. Rochester, 1965; PhD in Engring., Case Western Reserve U., 1972. Registered profl. engr., Ohio. Research engr. NASA Lewis Reseach Ctr., Cleve.; program mgr. NASA Hdqrs., Washington; branch chief NASA Ames Research Ctr., Moffett Field, Calif.; div. chief NASA Ames Research Ctr.; study contributor Ctr. for Strategic & Internat. Studies, Washington, 1984-88, Nat. Research Coun.'s Transp. Research Bd., Washington, 1986-88, Office Sci. & Tech. Policy, Washington, 1981-84, Nat. Acad. Engring., Washington, 1983-84. Author: Fundamentals of Fluid Sealing, 1976. Named for contribution to aviation FAA, 1988; recipient Collier Trophy (Teammember) Nat. Aeronautic Assn., 1987. Home: 2707 Mignon Dr San Jose CA 95132 Office: NASA Ames Rsch Ctr MS 237-11 Moffett Field CA 94035

ZULUETA, LEOPOLDO PASTELERO, real estate company executive; b. Morong, Bataan, Philippines, Dec. 23, 1945; came to U.S., 1966; s. Godofredo and Maria Marcelino (Pastelero) Z.; m. Elvira del Rosario Santamaria, June 9, 1973; children: John Paul, Anna Lisa. BBA magna cum laude, Nat. U., San Diego, 1985. Enlisted U.S. Navy, 1966-87, ret., 1987; owner, broker Ideal Homes and Properties, National City, Calif., 1987—. Mem. Nat. Mgmt. Assn., Nat. Assn. Realtors, Filipino Am. C. of C., Morong Assn. U.S.A. (co-founder, 1st pres., 1988). Republican. Roman Catholic. Home: 1427 Canyon Ct Bonita CA 92002 Office: Ideal Homes & Properties 1631 E 8th St National City CA 92050

ZUMBERGE, JAMES HERBERT, university president, geologist; b. Mpls., Dec. 27, 1923; s. Herbert Samuel and Helen (Reich) Z.; m. Marilyn Edwards, June 21, 1947; children: John Edward, JoEllen, James Frederick, Mark Andrew. Student, Duke, 1943-44; BA, U. Minn., 1946, PhD, 1950; LLD, Grand Valley State Coll., 1970, Kwansei Gakuin U., Japan, 1979; LHD, Nebr. Wesleyan U., 1972, Hebrew Union Coll.-Jewish Inst. Religion, 1987; DSc, Chapman Coll., 1982. Instr. Duke U., 1946-47; mem. faculty U. Mich., 1950-62, prof. geology, 1960-62; pres. Grand Valley State Coll., Allendale, Mich., 1962-68; prof. geology, dean U. Ariz. Coll. Earth Sci., Tucson, 1968-72; chancellor U. Nebr. at Lincoln, 1972-75; pres. So. Meth. U., Dallas, 1975-80, U. So. Calif., Los Angeles, 1980—; cons. geologist ground water and non-metallic minerals, 1950-62; chief glaciologist Ross Ice Shelf Project, IGY, 1957-58; dir. Litton Industries, Pacific Enterprises, Security Pacific Nat. Bank; U.S. del., 1970-86; pres. Sci. Com. on Antarctic Research, 1982-86; chmn. Ross Ice Shelf Project NSF, 1970-73, also mem. steering group Greenland Ice Sheet Program, 1971-82; del. numerous internat. confs. on polar rsch., Moscow, 1958, Chamonix, 1958, Helsinki, 1960, Obergurgl, Austria, 1962, Poland, 1967, Oslo, 1970, Sydney, Australia, 1972, Mendoza, Argentina, 1976, Warsaw, 1978, New Zealand, 1980; mem. Nat. Sci. Bd., 1974-80. Author: The Lakes of Minnesota, 1952, Laboratory Manual for Physical Geology, 1951, 7th edit., 1988, Elements of Geology, 1963, 72, Elements of Physical Geology, 1976; numerous jour. articles and papers. Bd. overseers Hoover Instn. on War, Revolution and Peace, 1978-84; chmn. U.S. Arctic Research Commn., 1984-87. Recipient Antarctic Service medal, 1966; Distinguished Alumni award U. Minn., 1972; James H. Zumberge Library, Grand Valley State Coll., named, 1968; Cape Zumberge, Antarctica named, 1960; Zumberge Coast, Antarctica, named 1986. Mem. Geol. Soc. Am., Am. Geophys. Union, Soc. Econ. Geologists, Internat. Glaciological Soc., AAAS, Mich. Acad. Scis. (pres. 1967); Conf. Bd.; Mem. Sigma Xi (nat. lectr. 1978-80). Clubs: Cosmos (Washington); Calif; University (N.Y.C.), Explorers (N.Y.C.); Bohemian (Los Angeles), One Hundred (Los Angeles). Office: U So Calif Office Pres Univversity Park Los Angeles CA 90089-0012

ZUMWALT, GLEN ALLEN, oil company executive; b. Garden City, Kans., Nov. 23, 1940; s. Paul Lawrence and Lila Ann (Birky) Z.; m. Judith Ann Troxell, Jan. 27, 1963; 1 child, Karen Ann. BS in Civil Engring., U. Ill., Urbana, 1963. Surveyor U.S. Corps of Army Engrs., Peoria, Ill., 1958-62; assoc. engr. The Boeing Co., Seattle and Ogden, 1963-66; from mine engr. to mine ops. supt. Stauffer Chem. Co., Green River, Wyo., 1966-77; v.p., gen. mgr. So. Utah Fuel Co., Salina, Utah, 1977-81, Utah Fuel Co., Scofield, 1981—; mine foreman, examiner Utah and Wyo., 1978-84; shotfire and surface blaster, Utah, 1987; mem. Diesel Adv. Com., U.S. Dept. Labor, 1988, Wyo. Bd. Mines, 1975-77. Inventor dust collection head system; contbr. articles profl. publs. Chmn. Castle Rock Spl. Hosp. Dist. Bd., 1973-77; mem. Sevier Valley Hosp. Governing Bd., 1979-81; fin. chmn. Sanpete Dist., Boy Scouts Am., Utah, 1983-89. Recipient Silver Beaver award, Boy Scouts Am., Utah, 1985. Mem. Mine Safety and Health Administrn. (adv. com.), AIME, Utah Mining Assn. (bd. dirs.), Lions (bd. dirs. Fountain Green chpt.), Jaycees (Disting. Svc. award). Home: PO Box 158 Fountain Green UT 84632 Office: Utah Fuel Co PO Box 719 Helper UT 84526

ZUNKER, RICHARD, insurance company executive; b. 1938. BS, U. Wis., 1964. With Employers Ins. Wausau, Wis., 1964-69, Northwestern Nat. Investors Life, 1969-75; with Safeco Life Ins. Co., Seattle, 1975—, pres., also bd. dirs. With U.S. Army, 1956-58. Office: Safeco Life Ins Co Safeco Pla Seattle WA 98185 *

ZUSSY, NANCY LOUISE, librarian; b. Tampa, Fla., Mar. 4, 1947; d. John David and Patsy Ruth (Stone) Roche; m. R. Mark Allen, Dec. 20, 1986. BA in Edn., U. Fla., 1969; MLS, U. So. Fla., 1977, MS in Pub. Mgmt., 1980. Cert. librarian, Wash. Ednl. evaluator State of Ga., Atlanta, 1969-70; media specialist DeKalb County Schs., Decatur, Ga., 1970-71; researcher Ga. State Libr., Atlanta, 1971; asst. to dir. reference Clearwater (Fla.) Pub. Libr., 1972-78, dir. librs., 1978-81; dep. state libr. Wash. State Libr., Olympia, 1981-86; state libr. Wash. State Library, Olympia, 1986—; chmn. Consortium Automated Librs., Olympia, 1982—; cons. various pub. librs., Wash., 1981—; exec. officer Wash. Libr. Network, 1986—. Contbr. articles to profl. jours. Treas. Thurston-Mason Community Mental Health Bd., Olympia, 1983-85, bd. dir., 1982-85; mem. race com. Seafair Hydroplane Race, Seattle, 1986—. Mem. ALA (Assn. Specialized and Coop. Libr. Agys. legis. com. 1983-86, chmn. legis. com. 1985-87, vice chmn. state libr. agys. sect. 1985-86, chmn. state ibr. agys. sect. 1986-87, chmn. govt. affairs com. Libr. Adminstrn. and Mgmt. Assn. 1986-87), Freedom to Read Found. (bd. dirs. 1987—), Chief Officers of State Libr. Agys. (bd. dir.-at-large 1986—), Wash. Libr. Assn. (co-founder legis. planning com. 1982—, fed. rels. coord. 1984—), Fla. Libr. Assn. (legis. and planning com. 1978-81), Pacific N.W. Libr. Assn., Phi Kappa Phi, Phi Beta Mu. Home: 904 E Bay Dr #B-404 Olympia WA 98506 Office: Wash State Libr AJ-11 Olympia WA 98504-0111

ZWAAF, DAVID, restaurant corporation executive; b. N.Y.C., Sept. 28, 1951; s. Emanuel and Paulette Rose (Groensteen) Z.; m. Rosa Maria Lopez, July 27, 1974; children: David Emanuel, Christopher Robin. Student, Washington U., St. Louis, 1970-71, NYU, 1971-73. Supr. The Saloon, Beverly Hills, Calif., 1973-74; comptroller Mr. Chow, Beverly Hills, 1974; pres. Rangoon Racquet Club, Beverly Hills, 1974—. Mem. Beverly Hills Restaurant Assn. (polit. action com. 1986-88, v.p. 1986—), Calif. Restaurant Assn., Beverly Hills C. of C. Republican. Jewish. Home: 18647 Keswick St Resedo CA 91335 Office: Rangoon Racquet Club 9474 Santa Monica Blvd Beverly Hills CA 90210

ZWAHLEN, FRED CASPER JR., journalism educator; b. Portland, Oreg., Nov. 11, 1924; s. Fred and Katherine (Meyer) Z.; m. Grace Eleanor DeMoss, June 24, 1959; children: Molly, Skip. BA, Oreg. State U., 1949; MA, Stanford U., 1952. Reporter San Francisco News, 1949-50; acting editor Stanford Alumni Rev., Palo Alto, Calif., 1950; successively instr. journalism, news bur. asst., prof. journalism, chmn. journalism dept. Oreg. State U., Corvallis, 1950—; corres. Portland Oregonian, 1950-67. Author: (with others) Handbook of Photography, 1984. Coord. E.E. Wilson Scholarship Fund, 1964—; active budget com. Corvallis Sch. Dist., 1979. Mem. Assn. for Edn. in Journalism and Mass Communications (conv. chmn. 1983, pres.' award 1988), Oreg. Newspaper Pubs. Assn. (bd. dirs. 1980-85, student loan fund named in his honor 1988), Soc. Profl. Journalists (nat. svc. citation 1988), Corvallis Country Club, Shriners, Masons, Elks, Moose, Eagles, Delta Tau Delta. Republican. Presbyterian. Home: 240 SW Seventh Corvallis OR 97333 Office: Oreg State U Dept Journalism Corvallis OR 97331

ZWASCHKA, KENNETH GEORGE, business owner; b. Salem, Oreg., Jan. 25, 1949; m. Carolyn Kay Mowe, Dec. 27, 1969; children: James Edward, John Eugene. BA, Linfield Coll., 1971. Mgr. Marriott Corp., Washington, 1971-74; div. mgr. The Bon Matche, Seattle, 1974-76; owner Coffee Corral Restaurant, Seattle, 1976-78; dist. mgr. Denny's Inc., La Mirada, Calif., 1978-79, recruiting & tng. mgr., 1978-80; sr. recruiter Murphy, Symonds & Sowell, Portland, Oreg., 1980-87; prin. Ken Zwaschka & Assocs., Portland, 1987—. Mem. Oreg. chpt. Cert. Personnel Cons. (bd. dirs. Oreg. chpt. 1989—), City Club, Inst. Food Technologists. Office: 618 NW Glisan Ste 407 PO Box 2226 Portland OR 97208-2226

ZWEIFEL, DONALD EDWIN, automobile dealer, civic affairs volunteer; b. L.A., Nov. 30, 1940; s. Robert Fredrick and Eugenia Bedford (White) Z.; m. Donna Jean Croslin; 1 child, Phillip Matthew. Student, Orange Coast Coll., 1963-67, U. Calif., Irvine, 1968-70, Western State U. Coll. Law, 1973, Irvine U. Coll. Law, 1974-75, Rancho Santiago Jr. Coll., 1988, Chapman Coll., 1989—. Cert. Student Pilot, 1989. Devel. tech. Hughes Aircraft, Newport Beach, Calif., 1963-64; station mgr., co-founder Sta. KUCI-FM, Irvine, Calif., 1 yr.; owner, mgr. Zweifel Jaguar Car Sales and Svc., Santa Ana, Calif., 1975; pres. Zweifel & Assocs. Inc., Santa Ana, 1977, Zweifel South Coast Exotic Cars, Inc., Orange, Calif., 1987—. Vol. emergency coordinator emergency mgmt. div. Orange County Fire Dept., 1985-87. Cadet CAP, USAF auxiliary, Long Beach, Calif., 1953-60, 62-64. With Army N.G., 1958-59. Recipient Cert. of Achievement Fed. Emergency Mgmt. Agy., 1989. Mem. Air Force Assn. (life mem., vice-chmn. civilian recruitment Calif. state membership com. 1988-89, v.p. membership, Gen. Doolittle chpt. bd. dirs. 1987-89, Exceptional Svc. award Gen. Jimmy Doolittle chpt. 1988, Calif. Meritorious Svc. award 1988), Marine Corps Hist. Found. (life), Aerospace Edn. Found. (life mem., Gen. Jimmy Doolittle fellow 1988, Pres.'s award 1988), U.S. Naval Inst., AIAA (Cert. of Appreciation 1989, L.A. chpt. hist. com. 1989), Marine Corps Assn. (assoc.), Navy League, Vietnam Vet. Hist. Assn. (cons., co-founder, trustee 1983—), John Birch Soc., Am. Def. Preparedness Assn., Assn. of Old Crows, U.S. Marine Corps Combat Correspondents Assn. (affiliate), Confederate Air Force (col. 1989, adj. 1st Composite Group detachment 1989), Aircraft Owners and Pilots Assn. Office: Vietnam Vets Hist Assn 773 N Cypress Ave Orange CA 92667

ZWEIG, ALAN EDWARD, dentist; b. N.Y.C., May 7, 1951; s. Charles and Bernice (Feltenstein) Z.; m. Judith Ruth Weiss, Sept. 6, 1981; children: Jonathan Noah, Michael Joseph. BA, Washington U., St. Louis, 1973; DMD, Washington U., 1976; cert. in prosthodontics, U. So. Calif., 1980. Pvt. practice dentistry St. Louis, 1977-78; assoc. Cherokee Dental Group, St. Louis, 1978; instr. fixed prosthodontics Washington U., 1976-78; clin. asst. prof. U. So. Calif. Sch. Dentistry, L.A., 1980—; pvt. practice Beverly Hills, Calif., 1981—. Fellow Acad. Gen. Dentistry; mem. Am. Dental Assn., Calif. Dental Assn., L.A. Dental Soc., Am. Coll. Prostohodontics, Alpha Omega. Office: 433 N Camden Dr #1133 Beverly Hills CA 90210

ZWERLING, DARRELL, actor, optometrist; b. Pitts.. OD, No. Ill. Coll. Optometry, Chgo., 1949; student, H.B. Studio, N.Y.C., 1963-64. Pvt. practice Pitts., 1950-63; actor theater, films and TV N.Y.C. and Los Angeles, 1963—. Appeared in theater prodns. including Room Service New York Revival, 1970; films include Chinatown, Doc Savage, Grease, And Justice for All, Ultimate Warrior; TV series include Kojak; also TV commls. With U.S. Army, 1951-53.

ZWICK, BARRY STANLEY, newspaper editor, speechwriter; b. Cleve., July 21, 1942; s. Alvin Albert and Selma Davidovna (Makofsky) Z.; m. Roberta Joan Yaffe, Mar. 11, 1972; children: Natasha Yvette, Alexander Anatol. BA in Journalism, Ohio State U., 1963; MS in Journalism, Columbia U., 1965. Copy ediotr Phila. Inquirer, 1964; night news editor Detroit Free Press, 1965-67; West Coast editor L.A. Times/Washington Post News Svc, 1967-77; makeup editor L.A. Times, 1978—; adj. prof. U. So. Calif., L.A., 1975-77. Author: Hollywood Tanning Secrets, 1980. NEH profl. journalism fellow Stanford U., 1977-78. Jewish. Office: LA Times Times Mirror Sq Los Angeles CA 90053

ZWICK, THOMAS THEODORE, geology educator, geological consultant; b. Appleton, Wis., Apr. 30, 1937; s. John Theodore and Lydia Bertha (Kunze) Z.; m. Marion Agness Kersten, Aug. 20, 1962 (div. 1983); children: Renee, Annette, Michelle; m. Yvonne Louise De Mars, Aug. 14, 1984. BS, Wis. State Coll., 1962; MA, Colo. Coll., 1965; EdD, U. No. Colo., 1977. Geologist Wis. State Geological Survey, Madison, 1962-63; earth sci. tchr. Preble High Sch., Green Bay, Wis., 1963-69; geology instr. El Paso Community Coll., Colo. Springs, Colo., 1970-72; earth sci. tchr. Colo. Springs Public Schs., 1969-72; prof. of geology Eastern Mont. Coll., Billings, 1972—; geological cons., 1962—; geological researcher Eastern Mont. Coll., 1972—. Contbr. articles to profl. jours. Chmn. sch. bd. Ind. Sch. Dist., Billings, 1975-86; bd. mem. Hardin (Mont.) Public Sch. System, 1987-88. Served with USMC, 1955-58. Recipient award Fed. Mineralogical Soc. Am., 1978. Mem. Nat. Assn. Geology Tchrs. (north cen. div. pres. 1980-84), Am. Geological Inst., Mont. Acad. Scis. (sec. 1978-80, bd. dirs. 1986—). Democrat. Episcopalian. Lodge: Elks. Home: 820 N Crow Hardin MT 59034 Office: Ea Mont Coll 1500 N 30th Dept Phys Sci Billings MT 59101

ZWIEBEL, IMRE, chemical, biological and materials engineering educator; b. Budapest, Hungary, June 13, 1932; came to U.S., 1948, naturalized, 1954; s. Herman and Bella (Schonberg) Z.; m. Barbara E. Copeland, Dec. 23, 1962; children: Karen, Jeffrey, Kenneth, Hannah. B.S., U. Mich., 1954; M.S., Yale U., 1959, Ph.D., 1961. Registered profl. engr., Mass. Devel. engr. E. I. DuPont Co., Wilmington, Del., 1954-57; research engr. Exxon (Esso) Research Co., Linden, N.J., 1960-64; prof. Worcester Poly. Inst., (Mass.), 1964-79; prof. Ariz. State U., Tempe, 1979—, chmn., 1979-88. Served with U.S. Army, 1956-57. Mem. Am. Inst. Chem. Engrs., Am. Chem. Soc., Am. Soc. for Engring. Edn., AAAS, Sigma Xi, Phi Lambda Upsilon. Jewish. Home: 642 W Linger Ln Phoenix AZ 85021 Office: Ariz State U COB-B210 Tempe AZ 85287

ZWOYER, EUGENE MILTON, consulting engineer; b. Plainfield, N.J., Sept. 8, 1926; s. Paul Ellsworth and Marie Susan (Britt) Z.; m. Dorothy Lucille Seward, Feb. 23, 1946; children: Gregory, Jeffrey, Douglas. .Student, U. Notre Dame, 1944, Mo. Valley Coll., 1944-45; BS, U. N.Mex., 1947; MS, Ill. Inst. Tech., 1949; PhD, U. Ill., 1953. Mem. faculty U. N.Mex., Albuquerque, 1948-71, prof. civil engring., dir. Eric Wang Civil Engring. Research Facility, 1961-70; research assoc. U. Ill., Urbana, 1951-53; owner, cons. engr. Eugene Zwoyer & Assocs., Albuquerque, 1954-72; exec. dir., sec. ASCE, N.Y.C., 1972-82; pres. Am. Assn. Engring. Socs., N.Y.C., 1982-84; exec. v.p. T.Y. Lin Internat., San Francisco, 1984-86, pres., 1986—. Trustee Small Bus. Research Corp., 1976-80; trustee Engring. Info., Inc., 1981-84; internat. trustee People-to-People Internat. 1974-86; v.p. World Fedn. Engring. Orgns., 1982-85. Served to lt. (j.g.) USN, 1944-46. Named Outstanding Engr. of Yr. Albuquerque chpt. N.Mex Soc. Profl. Engrs., 1969, One Who Served the Best Interests of the Constrn. Industry, Engring. News Record, 1980; recipient Disting. Alumnus award the Civil Engring. Alumni Assn. at U. Ill., 1979, Disting. Alumnus award Engring. Coll. Alumni Assn., U. N.Mex., 1982, Can.-Am. Civil Engring. Amity award Am. Soc. Civil Engrs., 1988, Award for Outstanding Profl. Contbns. and Leadership Coll. Engring. U. N.Mex., 1989. Mem. ASCE (dist. dir. 1968-71), NSPE, Am. Concrete Inst., Am. Soc. Engring Edn., AAAS, Nat. Acad. Code Adminstrn. (trustee, mem. exec. com. 1973-79), Engrs. Joint Council (dir. 1978-79), Engring. Soc. Commn. on Energy (dir. 1977-82), Sigma Xi, Sigma Tau, Chi Epsilon. Home: 6363 Christie Ave Apt 1326 Emeryville CA 94608 Office: T Y Lin Internat 315 Bay Street San Francisco CA 94133

ZYLSTRA, KENNETH JAMES, principal; b. Kalamazoo, Mich., Apr. 8, 1941; s. Cornelius and Hendrena Johanna (VanWesep) Z.; m. Karen Sue Nienoord, Sept. 1, 1973; children: Kendall, Kevin, Michael, Kirsten, Keri. BA, Calvin Coll., Grand Rapids, Mich., 1963; MA, U. No. Colo., 1972; EdS, Fla. Atlantic U., 1979. Cert. life supt. S.D. Tchr., prin. Arcadia (Calif.) Christian Sch., 1963-69, 73-75; tchr. Timothy Christian Jr. High Sch., Elmhurst, Ill., 1969-73; guidance dir. Ft. Lauderdale (Fla.) Christian Sch., 1975-79; prin. Ripon (Calif.) Christian High Sch., 1979-82; prin., supt. Sioux Falls (S.D.) Christian High Sch., 1982-85; agt. Washington Nat. Ins. Co., Sioux Falls, 1985-87; prin. Phoenix Christian Grade Sch., 1987—; mem. long range planning com. Sioux Falls Calvin Christian Sch., 1984-85. Bd. dirs. Scottsdale Christian Retirement Home, 1987—. Recipient Meritorious Svc. award Sioux Falls M-2 Program, 1987. Mem. Assn. Christian Sch. Adminstrs., Ariz. Coun. Academic Pvt. Edn. (pres.-elect 1988—), Kiwanis (dir. 1983-86). Republican. Christian Reformed Ch. Home: 1830 N 37th Pl Phoenix AZ 85008 Office: Phoenix Christian Grade Sch 2425 N 26th St Phoenix AZ 85108

ZYLSTRA, STEVEN GLENN, engineering research executive; b. Grand Rapids, Mich., Mar. 11, 1954; s. Gerrit Glen and Bonnie Marie (Luyk) Z. BS in Automotive Engring., Western Mich. U., 1978. Design engr. Ford Motor Co., Dearborn, Mich., 1978-80, Ford Aerospace & Communications Corp., Newport Beach, Calif., 1980-81; tech. mgr. Bendix Guidance Systems Div., Teterboro, N.J., 1981-82; dir. engring. Gen. Pneumatics Corp., Orange, N.J., 1982-84; gen. mgr. research Gen. Pneumatics Corp., Scottsdale, Ariz., 1984—; v.p., bd. dirs. Botanical Designs Inc.; pres., chmn. Ariz. Innovation Network, Scottsdale, 1986—; spokesman Ariz. Focus on Tech., Scottsdale, 1986—; mem. Cen. Ariz. Entrepreneurial Strategic Planning Team, Phoenix, 1988—. Mem. Soc. Automotive Engrs. (assoc.), Ariz. Small Bus. Fedn. (organizer). Republican. Office: Gen Pneumatics Corp Western Rsch Ctr 7662 E Gray Rd Ste 107 Scottsdale AZ 85260

ZYWICKI, KATHLEEN MCDONNELL, consulting firm executive; b. Chgo., Apr. 24, 1957; d. Edward Joseph and Judith Ann (Prendergast) McDonnell; m. Jeffrey Thomas Zywicki, Nov. 28, 1987. BA, Ariz. State U., 1979. Account coord. D'Arcy-MacManus & Masius, Chgo., 1979-82; asst. to chmn. Del. E. Webb Corp., Phoenix, 1983-87; asst. sec., dir. investor rels. Tri-City Properties, Inc., Phoenix, 1984-88; asst. to chmn. RKS, Inc., Phoenix, 1987—. Bd. dirs., sec. Camp Fire Coun. Greater Phoenix, 1986—; bd. dirs. N. Community Behavioral Health Ctr., Phoenix, 1985-87. Bd. Regents scholar Ariz. State U., 1975-79. Democrat. Roman Catholic. Office: RKS Inc 3003 N Central Ave Ste 1800 Phoenix AZ 85012